THE WRITERS DIRECTORY

THIRTIETH EDITION

THE WRITERS DIRECTORY

THIRTIETH EDITION
VOLUME 1: A-C

Editor
Lisa Kumar

ST. JAMES PRESS
A part of Gale, Cengage Learning

GALE
CENGAGE Learning

Detroit • New York • San Francisco • New Haven, Conn • Waterville, Maine • London

GALE
CENGAGE Learning

Writers Directory, 30th Edition

Project Editor: Lisa Kumar

Editorial Support Services: Natasha Mikheyeva

Manufacturing: Rita Wimberley

Gale
27500 Drake Rd.
Farmington Hills, MI, 48331-3535

ISBN-13: 978-1-4144-8712-0 (set)
ISBN-13: 978-1-4144-8713-7 (vol. 1)
ISBN-13: 978-1-4144-8714-4 (vol. 2)
ISBN-13: 978-1-4144-9901-7 (vol. 3)
ISBN-13: 978-1-4144-9902-4 (vol. 4)
ISBN-13: 978-1-4144-9903-1 (vol. 5)
ISBN-13: 978-1-4144-9904-8 (vol. 6)

ISBN-10: 1-4144-8712-6 (set)
ISBN-10: 1-4144-8713-4 (vol. 1)
ISBN-10: 1-4144-8714-2 (vol. 2)
ISBN-10: 1-4144-9901-9 (vol. 3)
ISBN-10: 1-4144-9902-7 (vol. 4)
ISBN-10: 1-4144-9903-5 (vol. 5)
ISBN-10: 1-4144-9904-3 (vol. 6)

ISSN 0084-2699

Printed in the United States of America
1 2 3 4 5 16 15 14 13 12

FD156

Contents

Preface

The Writers Directory is the newly revised and expanded thirtieth edition of this acclaimed reference work. It lists 26,615 writers—writing under 29,776 names—from all countries of the world who have had at least one work published in English.

The Directory is published in 6 individual volumes, with content divided as follows:

Volume 1: Lists entries from A-C
Volume 2: Lists entries from D-G
Volume 3: Lists entries from H-L
Volume 4: Lists entries from M-Q
Volume 5: Lists entries from R-U
Volume 6: Lists entries from V-Z, Obituaries, Index to Writing Categories, and Country of Citizenship Index

The *Directory* lists approximately 26,526 living writers of fiction and non-fiction who have published at least one full-length work in English. Listees run the gamut from the best-known, best selling authors of fiction and the most prominent non-fiction writers to those writers just embarking on their literary careers. The thirtieth edition includes nearly 1,000 writers whose listings have not appeared in a previous edition of *The Writers Directory.*

The **Obituaries** Section contains the entries for approximately 89 writers whose listings have appeared in previous editions of *The Writers Directory* and whose passing was made known to us in preparing this edition.

Compilation Methods

Selection of writers to appear in *The Writers Directory* is based primarily on reference value. Biographical and career information is researched for each writer, then a copy of the entry is sent to the writer for his or her approval and updates. By this process, the editors can assure comprehensive, current information. At the same time, entries in the previous edition were rigorously reviewed with an eye toward their current research value. As a result, some writers' entries have been retired to make way for those of new writers.

How to Read a Citation

Entries in *The Writers Directory* contain some or all of the following elements (please note that this is a sample entry-for demonstration purposes only):

▮ 1 ▮ WILLIAMS, Mae. ▮ 2 ▮ (Allison May Williams) ▮ 3 ▮ Also writes as William Allison. ▮ 4 ▮ American (born Malta), ▮ 5 ▮ b. 1945. ▮ 6 ▮ **Genres:** Novels, Biography. ▮ 7 ▮ **Career:** Freelance writer. ▮ 8 ▮ **Publications:** Paris, L'amour, 1972; (ed.) Running through the Weeds, 1982; (as William Allison) Louis, My Love (biography), 1987; The Waves at My Back, 1997. ▮ 9 ▮ **Address:** 27500 Drake Rd., Farmington Hills, MI 48331U.S.A. ▮ 10 ▮ **Online address:** maewil@aol.com ▮ 11 ▮ Died 1997.

▮ 1 ▮ Name of writer with fuller name information in parentheses

▮ 2 ▮ Full name of writer if different from writing name or pseudonyms but not used for writing

▮ 3 ▮ Pseudonym information

▮ 4 ▮ Nationality—if birthplace is different from nationality, it will follow the nationality in parentheses

▮ 5 ▮ Birth year

▮ 6 ▮ Genres—corresponds to **Index to Writing Categories**

▮ 7 ▮ Brief career information

▮ 8 ▮ Publications: title, year of publication, pseudonym if used, special awards

▮ 9 ▮ Address

▮ 10 ▮ Online address and/or web site

▮ 11 ▮ Death notation and year (in **Obituaries** Section only)

Cross references appear in the following form:

To main entry in main section: **ALLISON, William**. See **WILLIAMS, Mae.**

From main section to main entry in **Obituaries** section: **WILLIAMS, Mae.** See Obituaries.

From pseudonym in main section to main entry in **Obituaries** section: **ALLISON, William**. See **WILLIAMS, Mae** in the Obituaries.

Writers (and cross references) are listed alphabetically by surname which are sorted letter-by-letter. In cases where surnames are identical, writers are listed first by surname, then by given and middle names, and finally by suffixes such as Jr., Sr., II, or III. Surnames beginning with a prefix (such as Du, Mac, or Van), however spaced, are listed alphabetically under the first letter of the prefix and treated as if there were no space. Other compound surnames, hyphenated names, and names with apostrophes are alphabetized as if there were no space or punctuation. Surnames beginning with Saint or St. appear after names beginning with Sains and before names beginning with Sainu.

Entries in the **Obituaries** Section follow the same style as those in the main entries with the addition of the notation *Died* and the death year (if known) at the end of the entry.

Features

The Writers Directory contains many features to enhance its usefulness:

Boldface Rubrics allow quick and easy scanning for specifics on genre, career, publication, and mailing and online addresses.

The Obituaries Section lists the entries for those writers whose listing appeared in previous editions of The Writers Directory and whose passing was made known to us in preparing this edition. Cross references have been provided in the main body of the Directory to those deceased writers.

Indexing

The Writers Directory includes two indexes. In the **Index to Writing Categories**, one can locate writers by the type of works they write. New categories are added to The Writers Directory as needed to reflect new topics of interest and to define a writer's body of work more accurately. The **Country of Citizenship Index** lists writers by their country of citizenship as provided by the writer. Users are advised that one writer with multiple citizenship may appear under one country grouping (e.g., Canada-England) while another with the same citizenships may appear under a different grouping (e.g., England-Canada) depending on how the writer submitted the information.

The **Index to Writing Categories and Country of Citizenship Index** can be found in Volume 6 of the Directory following the **Obituaries** Section.

Also Available in Electronic Formats

Licensing. *The Writers Directory* is available for licensing. The complete database is provided in a fielded format and is deliverable on such media as disk or CD-ROM. For more information, contact Gale's Business Development Group at 1-800-877-GALE, or visit us on our web site at gale. cengage. com.

Online. *The Writers Directory* is accessible as part of Gale's Biography in Context database, as well as through the Gale Biographies database (File GALBIO) through Lexis-Nexis. For more information on Biography in Context, visit us on our web site at gale.cengage.com. For more information on Gale Biographies, contact LexisNexis, P.O. Box 933, Dayton, OH 45401-0933; phone (937) 865-6800; toll- free: 800-227-4908.

Suggestions Welcome

Comments and suggestions from users of *The Writers Directory* on any aspect of the product as well as suggestions for writers to be included in a future edition are cordially invited. Please write:

The Editor

The Writers Directory

St. James Press

Gale, a part of Cengage Learning

27500 Drake Rd.

Farmington Hills, Michigan 48331-3535.

Entry in *The Writers Directory* is at the discretion of the editor.

Abbreviations Used In The Writers Directory

A

AB	Alberta
ABC	American Broadcasting Company
ACT	Australian Capital Territory
AK	Alaska
AL	Alabama
Apt.	Apartment
AR	Arkansas
Assn.	Association
Assoc.	Associate
Asst.	Assistant
Ave.	Avenue
AZ	Arizona

B

b.	born
BBC	British Broadcasting Corporation
BC	British Columbia
Beds.	Bedfordshire
Berks.	Berkshire
Bldg.	Building
Blvd.	Boulevard
Brig.	Brigadier
Bros.	Brothers
Bucks.	Buckinghamshire

C

CA	California
Cambs.	Cambridgeshire
Can.	Canada
Capt.	Captain
CBC	Canadian Broadcasting Company
CBS	Columbia Broadcasting System (US)
CIA	Central Intelligence Agency (US)
CO; co.	Colorado; Company; County
Co-ed.	Co-editor
Co-trans.	Co-translator
Col.	Colonel
Contrib.	Contributor; Contributing
Corp.	Corporation
CPA	Certified Public Accountant
Cres.	Crescent
CT; Ct.	Connecticut; Court

D

DC	District of Columbia
DE	Delaware
Dept.	Department
Derbys.	Derbyshire
Dir.	Director
Div.	Division
Dr.	Doctor; Drive

E

E.	East
Ed.	Editor; Edition
Exec.	Executive

F

FBI	Federal Bureau of Investigation (US)
FL	Florida
Ft.	Fort

G

GA	Georgia
Gen.	General
Glam.	Glamorgan
Glos.	Glouchestershire
Gov.	Governor
Govt.	Government

H

Hants.	Hampshire
HE	His Eminence; His/Her Excellency
Herts.	Hertfordshire
HI	Hawaii
HM	His/Her Majesty
HMS	His/Her Majesty's Ship; His/Her Majesty's Service
Hon.	Honorable; Honorary

I

IA	Iowa
ID	Idaho
IL	Illinois
IN	Indiana
Inc.	Incorporated
Inst.	Institute
Intl.	International

J

Jr.	Junior

K

KS	Kansas
KY	Kentucky

L

LA	Louisiana
Lab.	Laboratory
Lancs.	Lancashire
Leics.	Leicestershire
LI	Long Island
Lincs.	Lincolnshire
Lt.	Lieutenant
Ltd.	Limited

M

MA	Massachusetts
Mag.	Magazine
Maj.	Major
MB	Manitoba
MD	Maryland
ME	Maine
Mgr.	Manager
MI	Michigan
Middx.	Middlesex
MN	Minnesota
MO	Missouri
MP	Member of Parliament
MT; Mt.	Montana; Mount, Mountain

N

N.	North
NASA	National Aeronautics and Space Administration
NATO	North Atlantic Treaty Organization
NB	New Brunswick
NBC	National Broadcasting System (US)
NC	North Carolina
NE	North East
NF	Newfoundland
NH	New Hampshire
NJ	New Jersey
NL	Newfoundland and Labrador
NM	New Mexico
No.	Number

Northants.	Northamptonshire
Notts.	Nottinghamshire
nr.	Near
NS	Nova Scotia
NSW	New South Wales
NT	Northern Territory (Australia); Northwest Territories (Canada)
NU	Nunavut
NV	Nevada
NW	North West
NWT	Northwest Territories
NY	New York
NYC	New York City

O

OH	Ohio
OK	Oklahoma
ON	Ontario
OR	Oregon
Orch.	Orchestra
Org.	Organization
Oxon.	Oxfordshire

P

PA	Pennsylvania
PE, PEI	Prince Edward Island
PEN	Poets, Playwrights, Essayists, Editors, Novelists
Pl.	Place
PO	Post Office
Pres.	President
Prof.	Professor
Prog.	Program
Publrs.	Publishers
Publs.	Publications

Q

QC	Quebec
QLD	Queensland

R

Rd.	Road
Rep.	Representative
Rev. ed.	Revised edition
RI	Rhode Island
RR	Rural Route
Rte.	Route

S

S.	South
SA	South Australia
Salop.	Shropshire
SC	South Carolina
Sch.	School
SD	South Dakota
SE	South East
Sec	Secretary
SK	Saskatchewan
Soc.	Society
Sq.	Square
Sr.	Senior
St.	Saint; Street
Staffs.	Staffordshire
Ste.	Suite
Supt.	Superintendent
SW	South West

T

Tas.	Tasmania
Terr.	Terrace
TN	Tennessee
Trans.	Translator; Translation
Treas.	Treasurer
TX	Texas

U

UK	United Kingdom
UN	United Nations
Unesco	United Nations Educational, Scientific and Cultural Organization
Unicef	United Nations Children's Emergency Fund
Univ.	University
US;	USA United States, United States of America
USS	United States Ship; United States Service
USSR	Union of Soviet Socialist Republics
UT	Utah

V

VA	Virginia
VIC	Victoria
Vol(s).	Volume(s)
VT	Vermont

W

W.	West
WA	Washington; Western Australia
Warks.	Warwicks; Warwickshire
WHO	World Health Organization
WI	Wisconsin
Wilts.	Wiltshire
Worcs.	Worcestershire
WV	West Virginia
WY	Wyoming

Y

YM-YWHA	Young Men's-Young Women's Hebrew Association
YMCA	Young Men's Christian Association
Yorks.	Yorkshire
YWCA	Young Women's Christian Association
YT	Yukon Territory

A

AAKER, Everett. American/British (born England), b. 1954. **Genres:** Communications/Media, Biography, Autobiography/Memoirs, Film, Mystery/Crime/Suspense, Reference, Art/Art History, History, Music. **Career:** London Academy of Music and Dramatic Art, associate, 1977. Writer. **Publications:** Television Western Players of the Fifties: A Biographical Encyclopedia of All Regular Cast Members in Western Series, 1949-1959, 1997; Television Crimebusters of the Fifties, 2005; Encyclopedia of Early Television Crime Fighters: All Regular Cast Members in American Crime and Mystery Series, 1948-1959, 2006. Contributor to magazines. **Address:** c/o McFarland & Co., Hwy. 88, PO Box 611, Jefferson, NC 28640, U.S.A.

AALAND, Mikkel. American (born United States), b. 1952?. **Genres:** Information Science/Computers, Technology. **Career:** FOTO Magazine, West Coast editor; American Photographer, columnist; Stanford University, lecturer, instructor; Drexel University, lecturer, instructor; University of California, lecturer, instructor. **Publications:** NONFICTION: Sweat: The Illustrated History and Description of the Finnish Sauna, Russian Bania, Islamic Hammam, Japanese Mushi-buro, Mexican Temescal, and American Indian & Eskimo Sweat Lodge, 1978; County Fair: Portraits, 1981; The Sword of Heaven: A Five Continent Odyssey to Save the World, 1999. PHOTOGRAPHY INSTRUCTION: (with R. Burger) Digital Photography, 1992; Still Images in Multimedia, 1996; Photoshop for the Web, 1998, 2nd ed., 1999; Photoshop Elements Solutions: The Art of Digital Photography, 2001; Photoshop Elements 2 Solutions: The Art of Digital Photography, 2002; Shooting Digital: Pro Tips for Taking Great Pictures with Your Digital Camera, 2003, 2nd ed., 2007; Photoshop Elements 3 Solutions: The Art of Digital Photography, 2005; Photoshop Elements 4 Solutions: The Art of Digital Photography, 2005; Photoshop CS2 RAW: Using Adobe Camera Raw, Bridge, and Photoshop to Get the Most Out of Your Digital Camera, 2006 as Photoshop CS3 RAW: Transform Your RAW Images into Works of Art, 2008; Photoshop Lightroom Adventure: Mastering Adobe's Next-Generation Tool for Digital Photographers, 2007; Photoshop Lightroom 2 Adventure: Mastering Adobe's Next-Generation Tool for Digital Photographers, 2009. Contributor of articles to periodicals. **Address:** O'Reilly Media Inc., 1005 Gravenstein Hwy. N, Sebastopol, CA 95472, U.S.A. **Online address:** maaland@mikkelaaland.com

AALTONEN, Sirkku. Finnish (born Finland), b. 1952. **Genres:** Theatre, Translations, Literary Criticism And History. **Career:** University of Vaasa, Department of English Studies, lecturer and head, 1982-, professor and head of discipline. Writer. **Publications:** Acculturation of the Other: Irish Milieux in Finnish Drama Translation (monograph), 1996; (ed.) Käännetyt illuusiot (monograph), 1998; Time-Sharing on Stage, 2000. Contributor to books and journals. **Address:** Department of English Studies, University of Vaasa, Yliopistonranta 10, PO Box 700, Vaasa, 65200, Finland. **Online address:** sirkku.aaltonen@uwasa.fi

AAMODT, Donald. American (born United States), b. 1935?. **Genres:** Science Fiction/Fantasy, Young Adult Fiction. **Career:** Writer. **Publications:** ZARATHANDRA SERIES: A Name to Conjure With, 1989; A Troubling Along the Border, 1991. **Address:** Avon Books, 1350 Ave. of the Americas, New York, NY 10019, U.S.A.

AAMODT, Michael G. American (born United States), b. 1957. **Genres:** Psychology, Medicine/Health. **Career:** University of Arkansas, Department of Psychology, research assistant, 1978-80; Radford University, professor of psychology, 1983-2008, professor emeritus, 2008-; Journal of Police and Criminal Psychology, associate editor, 1985-; Applied H.R.M. Research, editor, 1990, 1993, 1999-, associate editor, 1994-98; Assessment Council News, associate editor, 1995-; Journal of Business and Psychology, associate editor; DCI Consulting Group, principal consultant. **Publications:** Applied Industrial/Organizational Psychology, 1991, 7th ed., 2011; I/O Psychology in Action (workbook), 1996; (with B.L. Raynes) Human Relations in Business: Developing Interpersonal and Leadership Skills, 2001; Industrial/Organizational Psychology; An Applied Approach, 2007, 6th ed., 2010. Contributors to books and periodicals. **Address:** DCI Consulting Group Inc., 1920 I St. NW, Washington, DC 20006, U.S.A. **Online address:** maamodt@dciconsult.com

AARON, Chester. American (born United States), b. 1923. **Genres:** Novels, Novellas/Short Stories, Agriculture/Forestry, Children's Fiction, Autobiography/Memoirs. **Career:** Alta Bates Hospital, chief X-Ray technician, 1958-71; MKI Engineering, technical writer, 1971-72; St. Mary's College, professor of English, 1972-97, professor emeritus, 1997-. Writer. **Publications:** About Us (novel), 1967; Better Than Laughter (children's fiction), 1972; An American Ghost, 1973; Hello to Bodega, 1976; Spill, 1977; Catch Calico!, 1979; Gideon, 1982; Duchess, 1982; Out of Sight, Out of Mind, 1985; Lackawanna, 1986; Alex, Who Won His War, 1991; Garlic is Life: A Memoir with Recipes, 1996; The Great Garlic Book: A Guide With Recipes, 1997; Garlic Kisses: Human Struggles With Garlic Connections, 2001; Black and Blue Jew (novel), 2002; Home to the Sea (young adult novel), 2004; Whispers (novel), 2004; Symptoms of Terminal Passion, 2006; Willa's Poppy, 2007; Garlic Kisses and Tasty Hugs, 2008; Murder by Metaphor, 2009. Contributor to periodicals. **Address:** PO Box 388, Occidental, CA 95465, U.S.A. **Online address:** chgarlic@comcast.net

AARON, David. Israeli (born Israel), b. 1957?. **Genres:** Theology/Religion, Cultural/Ethnic Topics. **Career:** Isralight, founder and dean, 1986-. Writer. **Publications:** Endless Light: The Ancient Path of the Kabbalah to Love, Spiritual Growth, and Personal Power, 1997; Seeing God: Ten Life-Changing Lessons of the Kabbalah, 2001; The Secret Life of God: Discovering the Divine within You, 2004; Inviting God In: Celebrating the Soul-Meaning of the Jewish Holy Days, 2006; Living a Joyous Life: The True Spirit of Jewish Practice, 2007; God-powered Life: Awakening to Your Divine Purpose, 2009. **Address:** Isralight, 25 Misgav Ladach, Old City, Jerusalem, 97500, Israel. **Online address:** david.aaron@isralight.org

AARON, James E. American (born United States), b. 1927. **Genres:** Education, Transportation. **Career:** High school teacher, 1950-56; New York University, teacher of driver education, 1956-57; Southern Illinois University, assistant professor of driver and safety education, 1957-88, coordinator of safety center, 1960-; Office of Superintendent of Public Instruction, consultant, 1960-; Transportation Research Board, staff, 1975-; Safety and Health Hall of Fame, chairman, 1986-89. Writer. **Publications:** (With A.J. Shafter) The Police Officer and Alcoholism, 1963; (with M.K. Strasser) Driver and Traffic Safety Education: Content, Methods, and Organization, 1966, 2nd ed., 1977; First Aid and Emergency Care: Prevention and Protection of Injuries, 1972, 2nd ed., 1979; Driving Task Instruction: Dual-Control, Simulation, and

Multiple-Car, 1974; 2nd ed., 1977; (with M.K. Strasser and R.C. Bohn) Fundamentals of Safety Education, 3rd ed., 1981; (contrib.) Responsible Driving: AAA, 1993; How to Drive: AAA, 1993. **Address:** PO Box 1404, Sagamore Beach, MA 02562, U.S.A.

AARON, Relentless. *See* **GILMORE, Dewitt.**

AARONOVITCH, David. British (born England), b. 1954. **Genres:** Theology/Religion, History. **Career:** Guardian, reporter; Independent, reporter; Independent on Sunday, reporter; New Statesman, reporter; Observer, reporter; Times Comment, reporter; Times, commentator. Journalist, broadcaster and commentator. **Publications:** Paddling to Jerusalem: An Aquatic Tour of Our Small Island, 2000; (contrib.) The Hutton Inquiry and Its Impact (essays), 2004; Voodoo Histories: The Role of the Conspiracy Theory in Shaping Modern History, 2009. Contributor of articles to periodicals. **Address:** England. **Online address:** aaronovitchwatch@gmail.com

ABAJIAN, Kathryn J. American (born United States), b. 1944. **Genres:** Novels, Autobiography/Memoirs, Biography, History. **Career:** Diablo Valley College, San Ramon Valley Campus, instructor in English. Writer. **Publications:** First Sight of the Desert: Discovering the Art of Ella Peacock, 2005. **Address:** Diablo Valley College, 1690 Watermill Rd., San Ramon, CA 94582, U.S.A. **Online address:** kathryn@kathrynabajian.com

ABANI, Chris. (Christopher Abani). American/Nigerian (born Nigeria), b. 1966. **Genres:** Novels. **Career:** Antioch University, instructor, associate professor of creative writing, 2001-; University of California, visiting assistant professor of creative writing, 2003-04, associate professor, professor of creative writing. Writer. **Publications:** Masters of the Board, 1985; Sirocco, 1987; Kalakuta Republic, 2000; Daphne's Lot, 2002; Grace Land, 2004; Dog Woman, 2004; Becoming Abigail, 2006; Hands Washing Water, 2006; The Virgin of Flames, 2007; Song for Night, 2007; (ed.) Abstraction und einfuhlung, 2008; There are No Names of Red, 2009; (ed.) The Lesser Tragedy of Death, 2010; Sanctificum, 2010. **Address:** The Department of Creative Writing, University of California, 900 University Ave., 4153 INTS, Riverside, CA 92521, U.S.A. **Online address:** abani@chrisabani.com

ABANI, Christopher. *See* **ABANI, Chris.**

ABATE, Carmine. Italian (born Italy), b. 1954. **Genres:** Novels. **Career:** Writer. **Publications:** Nel labirinto della vita (poetry), 1977; (with others) Annaherungen, 1982; Den Koffer und weg! (short stories), 1984; (ed.) Die Germanesi, 1984; (ed.) Giuseppe Fiorenza Dill'Elba, Un freddo estraneo: Memorie di un emigrato in svizzera, 1991; Il ballo tondo (novel), 1991; Terre di andata (poetry), 1996; La moto di Scanderbeg (novel), 1999; Tra due mari: Romanzo (novel), 2002; (contrib.) Raccontare la legalita: 34 scrittori interrogano una parola, 2004; La festa del ritorno (novel), 2004; Il mosaico del tempo grande: Romanzo, 2006. **Address:** Trentino, Italy. **Online address:** carmine.abate@tin.it

ABBAS. French/Iranian (born Iran), b. 1944?. **Genres:** Picture/Board Books, Adult Non-fiction. **Career:** Al Chaab (newspaper), reporter and photographer, 1962-63; Olympic Games, photographer, 1968-69; Jeune Afrique (magazine), freelance photographer, 1970-71; Magnum Photos, photographer, 1981-. **Publications:** Le Zaire Aujourd'hui, 1977; Gamma: Le Secret des Grandes Photos, 1978; Iran: La Révolution Confisquée, 1980; Retornos a Oapan, Fondo de Cultura Economica 1986; Return to Mexico: Journeys Beyond the Mask, 1992; Allah O Akbar: A Journey Through Militant Islam, 1994; (with I.B. Prayogo and R. Wahyuhadi) Upacara baayun mulud di Banua Halat, Kabupaten Tapin, 1994; (with I.B. Prayogo) Kesenian wayang gong di Kalimantan Selatan, 1996; Voyage En chrétienté, 2000; (contrib.) Iran Diary, 1971-2002, 2002; (contrib.) Sur la Route Des Esprits, 2005; Iran Diaro: 1971-2005, 2005; Abbas, I Grandi Fotografi Di Magnum, 2005; The Children of Abraham, 2007; In Whose Name?: The Islamic World after 9/11, 2009. **Address:** Magnum Photos, 19 Rue Hegesippe Moreau, Paris, 75018, France.

ABBAS, Jailan. Egyptian (born Egypt), b. 1952. **Genres:** Mythology/Folklore, Children's Fiction, Children's Non-fiction, Science Fiction/Fantasy, Theology/Religion. **Career:** Helwan University, School of Tourism and Hotel Management, professor of guiding methodology, 1979-93; Cairo American College, teacher of Egyptian culture, 1981-, head of department. Writer. **Publications:** Metals and Jewelry of Islamic Egypt, 1987; The Monuments of Ancient Egypt as Seen by Middle Ages Travelers, 1992; The Festivals of Egypt, 1994. FORTHCOMING: The Palm Tree in the Egyptian Culture; Egypt: Land and People; Athar Misr Al-Islameyyah Fi Kitabat Al-Rahalah; Feasts and Festivals of Egypt and Their Historical Origins. **Address:** Cairo American College, 1 Midan Digla, PO Box 39, Maadi, Cairo, 11431, Egypt. **Online address:** jabbas@cacegypt.org

ABBOT, Sara. *See* **ZOLOTOW, Charlotte.**

ABBOTSON, Susan C.W. British/American (born United States), b. 1961. **Genres:** Literary Criticism And History, Theatre, Biography, Plays/Screenplays, Reference. **Career:** King Edward VI Boys School, staff, 1985-90; Highbury Little Theater, actress and stage designer, 1986-90; University of Connecticut, teaching assistant, 1990-97; Johnson and Wales University, adjunct professor of English, 1998-99; Rhode Island College, adjunct professor of English, 1999-2005, assistant professor of English, 2005-09, associate professor of English, 2009-. Writer. **Publications:** (With B. Murphy) Understanding Death of a Salesman, 1999; Student Companion to Arthur Miller, 2000; Thematic Guide to Modern Drama, 2003; Masterpieces of Twentieth Century American Drama, 2005; A Critical Companion to Arthur Miller, 2007; (ed.) The Crucible, 2010. **Address:** Department of English, Rhode Island College, 600 Mount Pleasant Ave., Providence, RI 02908, U.S.A. **Online address:** sabbotson@ric.edu

ABBOTT, Ainsley. *See* **MCMAHON, Maureen M.**

ABBOTT, Elizabeth. (Elizabeth Louise Abbott). Canadian (born Canada), b. 1946?. **Genres:** History, Psychology, Social Sciences, Technology. **Career:** Centre d'Etude du Québec, Concordia University, research director, 1966-84; Dawson College, professor of history, 1972-84; Reuters, Haiti correspondent, 1986-88; Chronicle Publications, editor-in-chief, 1989-91; Urban Pet Magazine, editor-in-chief, 1991-93; University of Toronto, Trinity College, dean of women, 1991-2004, St. Hilda's College, dean, Trinity College-Mount Sinai Hospital Pet Therapy Programme, coordinator, 1995-2007, research associate, 2008-, senior research associate. Writer. **Publications:** (Comp.) Bibliographie pour Servir à L'Etude de l'Histoiredu Canada Français, 1966; (ed.) Racism or Responsible Government?: The French Canadian Dilemma of the 1840s, 1967; L'inventaire de la Collection Louis-Hippolyte La Fontaine, 1968; (ed.) Debates of the Legislative Assembly of United Canada, 1841-1854, 19 vol., 1970; Tropical Obsession: A Universal Tragedy in Four Acts (play), 1986; Haiti: The Duvaliers and Their Legacy, 1988, rev. ed., 1991; (as Elizabeth Louise Abbott) The Reluctant P.M.: Notes on the Life of Sir John Abbott, Canada's Third Prime Minister, 1997; All Heart: Notes on the Life of Dr. Maude Elizabeth Abbott, M.D., Pioneer Woman Doctor and Cardiologist, 1997; A History of Celibacy: Experiments through the Ages, 1999 as A History of Celibacy: From Athena to Elizabeth I, Leonardo da Vinci, Florence Nightingale, Gandhi, and Cher, 2000; A History of Mistresses, 2003; Sugar: A Bittersweet History, 2008; Marriage: Where We've Been and Where We're Heading, 2010; A History of Marriage, 2011; Haiti: A Shattered Nation, 2011. **Address:** Trinity College, University of Toronto, 6 Hoskin Ave., Toronto, ON M5S 1H8, Canada. **Online address:** info@elizabethabbott.ca

ABBOTT, Elizabeth Louise. *See* **ABBOTT, Elizabeth.**

ABBOTT, Hailey. American (born United States) **Genres:** Novels, Romance/Historical, Young Adult Fiction. **Career:** Writer. **Publications:** SUMMER BOYS SERIES: Summer Boys, 2004; Next Summer, 2005; After Summer, 2006; Last Summer 2007. NOVELS: The Bridesmaid, 2005; Getting Lost with Boys, 2006; The Secrets of Boys, 2006; The Perfect Boy, 2007; Waking Up to Boys, 2007; Forbidden Boy, 2008; The Other Boy, 2008; Girls in Love: A Summer Girls Novel, 2010. OTHERS: (co-author) Mistletoe, 2006; Summer Girls, 2009; Flirting With Boys, 2009; Boy Crazy, 2009. **Address:** Scholastic Inc., 557 Broadway, New York, NY 10012, U.S.A.

ABBOTT, Jax. *See* **HOLLIDAY, Alesia.**

ABBOTT, John Jamison. *See* **ABBOTT, John Patrick.**

ABBOTT, John Patrick. (John Jamison Abbott). British (born England), b. 1930. **Genres:** Air/Space Topics, Genealogy/Heraldry. **Career:** St. Paul's V.C.J.M., School, headmaster, 1970-89. Writer. **Publications:** Family Patterns, 1971; Airship The Story of R.34, 1973, rev. ed., 1994; The British Airship at War, 1914-1918, 1989; Airships, 1991; British Airships in Pictures, 1998. **Address:** 30 Vibart Rd., Yardley, Birmingham, B26 2AD, England.

ABBOTT, Karen. American (born United States), b. 1973. **Genres:** Ethics, Novels, History. **Career:** Journalist. **Publications:** Sin in the Second City: Madams, Ministers, Playboys, and the Battle for America's Soul, 2007; American Rose: A Nation Laid Bare: The Life and Times of Gypsy Rose Lee, 2010. Contributor to periodicals. **Address:** c/o Simon Lipskar, Writers House, 21 W 26th St., New York, NY 10010-1003, U.S.A. **Online address:** karen@karenabbott.net

ABBOTT, Lynn. (Rob Walker). American (born United States), b. 1946. **Genres:** Biography. **Career:** Bruce Daigrepont's Cajun Band, drummer, 1987-2000; Tulane University, William Ransom Hogan Archive of New Orleans Jazz, assistant curator, 2002-. Writer. **Publications:** (With D. Seroff) Out of Sight: The Rise of African American Popular Music, 1889-1895, 2002; (with D. Seroff) Ragged but Right: Black Traveling Shows, Coon Songs and the Dark Pathway to Blues and Jazz, 2007; I Got Two Wings: Incidents and Anecdotes of the Two-winged Preacher and Electric Guitar Evangelist Elder Utah Smith 2009. Contributor to periodicals. **Address:** Hogan Jazz Archive, Tulane University Libraries, Jones Hall, New Orleans, LA 70118, U.S.A. **Online address:** labbott1@tulane.edu

ABBOTT, Pamela. Scottish/British (born England), b. 1947. **Genres:** Medicine/Health, Social Sciences, Sociology, Women's Studies And Issues. **Career:** School teacher, 1972-74; Northwest Kent College of Technology, lecturer, 1975-80; Open University, research assistant and consultant, 1982-84; Brighton Polytechnic, lecturer in sociology, 1984-85; Plymouth Polytechnic, lecturer, 1987-90, senior lecturer in sociology and social policy, 1992; Polytechnic South West, principal lecturer in sociology and social policy, 1990-93; University of Derby, professor of sociology and assistant dean, 1993-96; University of Teesside, School of Social Sciences, professor and director, 1996-99; Glasgow Caledonian University, pro vice chancellor and vice principal, 2000-03, professor of social policy; Glasgow Caledonia University, Center for Equality and Diversity, director and director of graduate centre, 2003-05; Kigali Institute of Science, vice rector academic, 2005-06; Kigali Institute of Education, vice rector, academic, 2006-07; University of Aberdeen, honorary professor school of social sciences, 2008-; Glasgow Caledonian University, professor emeritus, 2009-. Writer. **Publications:** (With R.J. Sapsford) Community Care for Mentally Handicapped Children, 1987; (with Sapsford) Women and Social Class, 1987, 2nd ed., 1996; (with C. Wallace) An Introduction to Sociology: Feminist Perspectives, 1990, (with C. Wallace and M. Tyler) 3rd ed., 2005; (with C. Wallace) The New Right and the Family, 1992; (with R. Sapsford and contrib.) Research Methods for Nurses and the Caring Professionals, 1992; (with Ackers) Social Policy for Nurses and the Caring Professionals, 1996; (with L. Ackers) Social Policy for Nurses and the Caring Professions, 1996; (contrib.) Quelle citoyenneté pour les femmes?, 1996. EDITOR: (with C. Wallace and contrib.) The Sociology of the Caring Professions, 1990; (with G. Payne and contrib.) Women and Mobility, 1990; (with G. Payne and contrib.) New Directions in the Sociology of Health, 1990; (with G. Payne) The Social Mobility of Women, 1990; (with C. Wallace) Gender, Power and Sexuality, 1991; (with R. Sapsford) Research into Practice, 1992; (with R. McSherry and M. Simmons) Evidence-Informed Nursing: A Guide for Clinical Nurses, 2001. Works appear in anthologies. **Address:** Department of Sociology, School of Social Sciences, University of Aberdeen, Edward Wright Bldg., Aberden, AB24 3QY, Scotland. **Online address:** p.abbott@abdn.ac.uk

ABBOTT, Tony. American (born United States), b. 1952. **Genres:** Autobiography/Memoirs, Literary Criticism And History, Writing/Journalism, Children's Fiction, Essays. **Career:** Writer. **Publications:** Danger Guys, 1994; Danger Guys Blast Off, 1994; Danger Guys: Hollywood Halloween, 1994; Danger Guys Hit the Beach, 1995; Danger Guys on Ice, 1995; Danger Guys and the Golden Lizard, 1996; Space Bingo, 1996; Orbit Wipeout, 1996; Mondo Meltdown, 1996; Zombie Surf Commandos from Mars, 1996; The Incredible Shrinking Kid, 1996; The Beast from beneath the Cafeteria, 1996; Attack of the Alien Mole Invaders, 1996; Into the Zonk Zone, 1996; Splash Crash, 1997; Zero Hour, 1997; Shock Wave, 1997; Doom Star, 1997; The Brain That Wouldn't Obey, 1997; Gigantopus from Planet X, 1997; Cosmic Boy versus Mezmo Head, 1997; Revenge of the Tiki Men, 1997; Sitcom School, 1999; The Fake Teacher, 1999; The Hidden Stairs and the Magic Carpet, 1999; Journey to the Volcano Palace, 1999; The Mysterious Island, 1999; City in the Clouds, 1999; The Great Ice Battle, 1999; The Sleeping Giant of Goll, 2000; Into the Land of the Lost, 2000; The Golden Wasp, 2000; The Tower of the Elf King, 2000; Quest for the Queen, 2000; The Hawk Bandits of Tarkoom, 2001; Under the Serpent Sea, 2001; The Mask of Maliban, 2001; Trapped in Transylvania: Dracula, 2002; Mississippi River Blues: The Adventures of Tom Sawyer, 2002; What a Trip!: Around the World in Eighty Days, 2002; Humbug Holiday: A Christmas Carol, 2002; X Marks the Spot: Treasure Island, 2002; Voyage of the Jaffa Wind, 2002; The Moon Scroll, 2002; The Knights of Silversnow, 2002; The Magic Escapes, 2002; Crushing on a Capulet: Romeo and Juliet, 2003; Dream Thief, 2003; Search for the Dragon Ship, 2003; The Coiled Viper, 2003; In the Ice Caves of Krog, 2003; Flight of the Genie, 2004; Wizard or Witch?, 2004; Isle of the Mists, 2004; The Fortress of the Treasure Queen, 2004; The Race to Doobesh, 2005; The Riddle of Zorfendorf Castle, 2005; Voyagers of the Silver Sand, 2005; Kringle, 2005; The Moon Dragon, 2006; Fire Girl, 2006; The Chariot of Queen Zara, 2006; In the Shadow of Goll, 2006; Sorcerer, 2006; Pirates of the Purple Dawn, 2007; Escape from Jabar-Loo, 2007; Treasure of the Orkins, 2008; The Postcard, 2008; Moon Magic, 2008; Mondo Meltdown, 2008; Into the Zonk Zone!, 2008; Flight of the Blue Serpent, 2009; In the City of Dreams, 2009; Crown of Wizards, 2009; Knights of the Ruby Wand, 2010; The Genie King, 2010; The Final Quest, 2010; Lunch-Box Dream, 2011; Underworlds: The Battle Begins, 2011; Underworlds: When Monsters Escape, 2012; Goofballs, 2012. **Address:** George Nicholson, Sterling Lord Literistic Inc., 65 Bleecker St., New York, NY 10012, U.S.A. **Online address:** tonyabbott@sbcglobal.net

ABDEL-MAGID, Islām Muḥammad. (Islām Muḥammad Abd al-Mājid). Saudi (born Saudi Arabia), b. 1952. **Genres:** Environmental Sciences/Ecology, Engineering, Industrial Relations. **Career:** General Corporation for Irrigation and Drainage, civil engineer, 1977; University of Khartoum, assistant professor, 1982-87, associate professor of civil engineering, 1987-88; University of the United Arab Emirates, assistant professor of civil engineering, 1988-91; Sultan Qaboos University, assistant professor of engineering, 1991-96; Sudan University for Science and Technology, professor of water resources and environmental engineering, 1996-; Omdurman Islamic University, professor of water resources and environmental engineering, 1996-97; Juba University, principal and professor of water resources and environmental engineering, 1997-98; Sudanese Engineering Council, consultant engineer; Scientific Research and Foreign Affairs Center, director, 1998-2002, dean, 2001-02; Ministry of Science and Technology, Industrial Research and Consultancy Center, general manager, 2002-05; Sudan Academy for Sciences, president, 2005-07; King Faisal University, professor. Writer. **Publications:** (Ed. with D.A. Al-Turabi and H.A.E.H. Ismail) Proceedings of the First National Conference on the Science and Technology of Buildings, 1985; (with B.M. Al-ḥasan as Islām Muḥammad Abd al-Mājid) Ṣinā'ah wa-al-bī'ah, 1986; Selected Problems in Water Supply, 1986; Selected Problems in Wastewater Engineering, 1987; (with D.R. Rowe) Handbook of Wastewater Reclamation and Reuse, 1995; (with D.R. Rowe and A.M. Hago) Modeling Methods for Environmental Engineers, 1997; (as Islām Muḥammad Abd al-Mājid) Buḥūth Nadwat al-Ta'hīl wa-al-Tadrīb bi-al-Jāmi'ā, 1998. IN ARABIC: (with B.M. El-Hassan and M.E. Siddig) Guidelines for the Operation and Maintenance of Slow Sand Filters in Rural Sudan, 1983; Water Treatment and Sanitary Engineering, 1986; (with El-Hassan) Water Supply in the Sudan, 1986; (with El-Hassan) Industry and the Environment: The Treatment of Industrial Wastes, 1986; Environmental Engineering, 1995; Pollution: Hazards and Control, 1995; Pollution: Problems and Solutions, 1996; (with T.M. Dirdeery) Water, 1999, 2nd ed., 2001; Wastewater, 2000; Fluids, 2001; Guide to Scientific Research Preparation, 2001. **Address:** College of Engineering, King Faisal University, 10 Bldg., PO Box 407, Dammam, 31413, Saudi Arabia. **Online address:** isammohamed@sustech.edu

ABEGUNRIN, Olayiwola. American/Nigerian (born Nigeria), b. 1946. **Genres:** Economics, Politics/Government, Social Sciences. **Career:** Obafemi Awolowo University, senior lecturer in international relations and department chair, 1980-90; University of North Carolina, visiting professor, 1989-91; Howard University, College of Arts and Sciences, Department of Political Science, professor of international relations, 1997-. Writer and consultant. **Publications:** (Ed. with R.I. Onwuka and D.N. Ghista) African Development: The OAU/ECA Lagos Plan of Action and Beyond, 1985; (with H.E. Newsum) United States Foreign Policy towards Southern Africa: Andrew Young and Beyond, 1987; Economic Dependence and Regional Cooperation in Southern Africa: SADCC and South Africa in Confrontation, 1990; Nigeria and the Struggle for the Liberation of Zimbabwe: A Study of Foreign Policy Decision Making of an Emerging Nation, 1992; (ed. with F. Vivekananda) The Political Economy of South-South Cooperation: Towards a New International Economic Order, 1998; Nigerian Foreign Policy under Military Rule, 1966-1999, 2003; (ed. with O. Akomolafe) Nigeria in Global Politics: Twentieth Century and Beyond: Essays in Honor of Professor Olajide Aluko, 2006; Africa in

Global Politics in the Twenty-First Century: Challenges and Opportunities, 2007; Africa in Global Politics in the Twenty-first Century: A Pan-African Perspective, 2009. **Address:** Department of Political Science, College of Arts & Sciences, Howard University, Rm. 530, Howard Ctr., Douglass Hall, Washington, DC 20059, U.S.A. **Online address:** oabegunrin@howard.edu

ABEL, Emily K. American (born United States), b. 1942?. **Genres:** Education, Women's Studies And Issues, Medicine/Health. **Career:** University of California, School of Public Health, adjunct associate professor, Department of Health Services, professor, now professor emeritus of health services and womens studies. Writer, historian and educator. **Publications:** (Ed. with E. Abel) The Signs Reader: Women, Gender, & Scholarship, 1983; Terminal Degrees: The Job Crisis in Higher Education, 1984; Love Is Not Enough: Family Care of the Frail Elderly, 1987; (ed. with M.L. Pearson) Across Cultures: The Spectrum of Women's Lives, 1989; (ed. with M.K. Nelson) Circles of Care: Work and Identity in Women's Lives, 1990; Who Cares for the Elderly?: Public Policy and the Experiences of Adult Daughters, 1991; Hearts of Wisdom: American Women Caring for Kin, 1850-1940, 2000; Suffering in the Land of Sunshine: A Los Angeles Illness Narrative, 2006; Tuberculosis and the Politics of Exclusion: A History of Public Health and Migration to Los Angeles, 2007; (with S. Subramanian) After the Cure: The Untold Stories of Breast Cancer Survivors, 2008. **Address:** School of Public Health, University of California, 10833 Le Conte Ave., PO Box 951772, Los Angeles, CA 90095-1772, U.S.A. **Online address:** eabel@ucla.edu

ABEL, Kenneth. *See* **LOBANOV-Rostovsky, Sergei.**

ABELA, Deborah Anne. Australian (born Australia), b. 1966. **Genres:** Children's Fiction, Novels, Art/Art History, Music. **Career:** Network TEN, Cheez TV, assistant producer, 1996-2001; writer, 1999-. **Publications:** MAX REMY, SPY FORCE SERIES: In Search of the Time and Space Machine, 2002; Spy Force Revealed, 2002; The Nightmare Vortex, 2003 as Mission: The Nightmare Vortex, 2005; The Hollywood Mission, 2003 as Mission: Hollywood, Simon 2006; The Amazon Experiment, 2004; Blue's Revenge, 2004; The Venice Job, 2005; Mission in Malta, 2006; The French Code, 2007; The Final Curtain, 2008. NOVELS: The Remarkable Secret of Aurelie Bonhoffen, 2009; Grimsdon, 2010; The Ghosts of Gribblesea Pier, 2011. JASPER ZAMMIT SERIES WITH JOHNNY WARREN: The Game of Life, 2005; The Striker, 2005; The Finals, 2006. **Address:** c/o Rick Raftos, Rick Raftos Management, PO Box 445, Paddington, NW 2021, Australia. **Online address:** max@maxremy.com.au

ABERAVON, Howe of. *See* **HOWE, (Richard Edward) Geoffrey.**

ABERBACH, David. Canadian/British (born England), b. 1953. **Genres:** Literary Criticism And History, Social Sciences, Theology/Religion. **Career:** Tavistock Clinic, nurse, 1980-82; Oxford University, faculty, 1982-83; Cambridge University, faculty, 1982-83; Leo Baeck College, faculty, 1984; Cornell University, faculty, 1985; McGill University, Department of Jewish studies and comparative literature, assistant professor, 1986-87, associate professor, professor, 1987-; University College, visiting professor, 1992-. Writer. **Publications:** Shoot From a Severed Bough and Other Poems, 1977; At the Handles of the Lord: Themes in the Fiction of S.J. Agnon, 1984; Bialik, 1988; Surviving Trauma: Loss, Literature and Psychoanalysis, 1989; Realism, Caricature and Bias: The Fiction of Mendele Mocher Sefarim, 1993; Imperialism and Biblical Prophecy, 750-500 B.C.E., 1993; Charisma in Politics, Religion and the Media: Private Trauma, Public Ideals, 1996; Revolutionary Hebrew, Empire and Crisis: Four Peaks in Hebrew Literature and Jewish Survival, 1998; (with M. Aberbach) The Roman-Jewish Wars and Hebrew Cultural Nationalism, 2000; Major Turning Points in Jewish Intellectual History, 2003; (ed. and trans.) C.N. Bialik: Selected Poems, 2004; Jewish Cultural Nationalism: Origins and Influences, 2008; (ed. and trans.) Jewish Education and History: Continuity, Crisis and Change, 2009. **Address:** Department of Jewish Studies, McGill University, Rm. 300, 3438 McTavish St., Montreal, QC H3A 1A9, Canada. **Online address:** david.aberbach@mcgill.ca

ABERCROMBIE, Joe. British (born England), b. 1974. **Genres:** Novels, Young Adult Fiction. **Career:** Writer. **Publications:** FIRST LAW SERIES: The Blade Itself, 2007; Before They Are Hanged, 2007; Last Argument of Kings, 2008; Best Served Cold, 2009; The Heroes, 2011. **Address:** c/o Robert Kirby, United Agents, 12-26 Lexington St., London, GL W1F 0LE, England. **Online address:** joe@joeabercrombie.com

ABERJHANI. American (born United States), b. 1957. **Genres:** Novels, Poetry, History, Humanities, inspirational/Motivational Literature, Intellectual History, Literary Criticism And History, Local History/Rural Topics, Mythology/Folklore, Paranormal, Philosophy, Popular Culture, Race Relations, Travel/Exploration, Writing/Journalism, Autobiography/Memoirs, Civil Liberties/Human Rights, Cultural/Ethnic Topics. **Career:** Black Heritage Festival, spoken-word artist, 1998; editorial consultant, freelance journalist and independent author, 2000-; Underwriters Report, publishing manager; U.S. Air Force, journalist and editor; Waldenbooks Bookstore, manager; Books-a-Million, manager; Media Play, manager. **Publications:** I Made My Boy out of Poetry, 1997; Encyclopedia of the Harlem Renaissance, 2003; The Wisdom of W.E.B. Du Bois, 2003; Visions of a Skylark Dressed in Black, 2005; The Bridge of Silver Wings, 2007; Christmas When Music Almost Killed the World, 2007; The American Poet Who Went Home Again, 2008; Elemental, The Power of Illuminated Love, 2008; The River of Winged Dreams, 2010; The American Poet Who Returned to Savannah, 2011. **Address:** Bright Skylark Literary Productions, PO Box 3781, Savannah, GA 31414, U.S.A. **Online address:** danceofangels777@hotmail.com

ABIDI, Azhar. Australian/Pakistani (born Pakistan), b. 1968. **Genres:** Novels, Young Adult Fiction. **Career:** Cipher Literary Magazine, co-founder and editor, 1993-94. **Publications:** Passarola Rising, 2006; Twilight, 2008; The House of Bilqis, 2009. Contributor to periodicals. **Address:** c/o Author Mail, Penguin Group, Viking Publicity, 375 Hudson St., New York, NY 10014, U.S.A. **Online address:** azhar.abidi@gmail.com

ABI-EZZI, Nathalie. British/Lebanese (born Lebanon), b. 1972. **Genres:** Young Adult Non-fiction, Novels. **Career:** Writer. **Publications:** The Double in the Fiction of R.L. Stevenson, Wilkie Collins, and Daphne Du Maurier (nonfiction), 2003; A Girl Made of Dust (novel), 2008. **Address:** c/o Isobel Dixon, Blake Friedmann Agency, 122 Arlington Rd., London, GL NW1 7HP, England.

ABILDSKOV, Marilyn. American (born United States), b. 1961?. **Genres:** Autobiography/Memoirs. **Career:** St. Mary's College of California, School of Liberal Arts, associate professor of English, professor. Writer. **Publications:** The Men in My Country, 2004. Contributor to periodicals. **Address:** MFA Program in Creative Writing, St. Marys College of California, 322 Dante Hall, PO Box 4730, Moraga, CA 94575-4686, U.S.A. **Online address:** mabildsk@stmarys-ca.edu

ABINADER, Elmaz. American (born United States) **Genres:** Autobiography/Memoirs, Poetry, Cultural/Ethnic Topics. **Career:** University of Nebraska, writing instructor, 1981-85; City University of New York, John Jay College, associate professor of writing, 1987-91; Mills College, professor of creative writing, 1993-, The Place for Writers, faculty director, 1994-, Frederick Rice chair of English and department head, 2004-06; Helwan University, visiting professor, 1998-99. Writer, artist, speaker and broadcaster. **Publications:** Children of the Roojme: A Family's Journey (memoir), 1991; Children of the Roojme: A Family's Journey from Lebanon, 1997; Poetry Everyday, 1993; In the Country of My Dreams: Poetry by Elmaz Abinader, 1999; Women from the Occupied Territories, 1999; The Water Cycle, 2010; Torture Quartet and Other Acts of Poetry, forthcoming; Arabic Music, forthcoming. Contributor to journals and periodicals. **Address:** English Faculty, Mills College, 313 Mills Hall, 5000 MacArthur Blvd., Oakland, CA 94613, U.S.A. **Online address:** elmaz@earthlink.net

ABISH, Walter. American/Austrian (born Austria), b. 1931. **Genres:** Novels, Novellas/Short Stories, Poetry, Essays, Young Adult Fiction, Young Adult Non-fiction. **Career:** State University of New York, Empire State College, adjunct professor, 1975; Columbia University, lecturer in English and comparative literature, 1979-88; Conjunctions Magazine, contributing editor, 1981-; Yale University, visiting professor, 1985; Brown University, visiting professor, 1986; DAAD-Deutscher Akademischer Austauschdienst, visiting professor, 1987; Cooper Union, staff. Writer. **Publications:** Duel Site (poetry), 1970. NOVELS: Alphabetical Africa, 1974; How German is It, 1980; Eclipse Fever, 1993. SHORT FICTION: Minds Meet, 1975; In the Future Perfect, 1977; 99: The New Meaning, 1990. NON FICTION: (with J. Ashbery) Contemporary American Fiction, 1983; Double Vision: A Self-Portrait, 2004. **Address:** Donadio & Olson Inc., 121 W 27th St., Ste. 704, New York, NY 10001-6207, U.S.A.

ABLARD, Jonathan D. American (born United States), b. 1966. **Genres:**

Psychology, Medicine/Health, History. **Career:** University of West Georgia, assistant professor, 2000-05; Ithaca College, assistant professor, 2005-. Writer. **Publications:** (Co-author) Instituciones y formas de control social en America Latina, 1840-1940: Una revision, 2005; (ed. with A.S. MacKinnon) (Un)healthy Interiors: Contestations at the Intersection of Public Health and Private Space, 2005; Madness in Buenos Aires: Patients, Psychiatrists, and the Argentine State, 1880-1983, 2008. **Address:** Department of History, Ithaca College, Muller 403, Ithaca, NY 14850, U.S.A. **Online address:** jablard@ithaca.edu

ABLEMAN, Michael. Canadian/American (born United States), b. 1954. **Genres:** Agriculture/Forestry, Environmental Sciences/Ecology. **Career:** Fairview Gardens, farm manager, 1981-2001, Center for Urban Agriculture, founder 1981-, executive director, 1981-2001, executive director emeritus, 2001-. Writer. **Publications:** SELF-ILLUSTRATED: From the Good Earth: A Celebration of Growing Food Around the World, 1993; Fields of Plenty: A Farmer's Journey in Search of Real Food and the People Who Grow It, 2005. OTHER: On Good Land: The Autobiography of an Urban Farm, 1998. Contributor of articles to periodicals. **Address:** Chronicle Books, 680 Second St., San Francisco, CA 94107, U.S.A. **Online address:** m.ableman@fieldsofplenty.com

ABLOW, Keith Russell. American (born United States), b. 1961. **Genres:** Novels, Medicine/Health, Psychiatry. **Career:** Tri-City Mental Health Center, medical director and psychiatrist, 1992-94; Heritage Hospital, associate medical director and psychiatrist, 1993-94; Boston Regional Medical Center, psychiatrist, 1996-; Fox News, columnist; Good Housekeeping Magazine, contributing editor; Men's Fitness, contributing editor; New York Post, columnist. Writer. **Publications:** Medical School: Getting in and Staying Human, 1987, rev. ed., 1990; (with R.J. DePaulo) How to Cope with Depression: A Complete Guide for You and Your Family, 1989; To Wrestle with Demons: A Psychiatrist Struggles to Understand His Patients and Himself, 1992; Anatomy of a Psychiatric Illness: Healing the Mind and the Brain, 1993; The Strange Case of Dr. Kappler: The Doctor Who Became a Killer, 1994; Denial: A Novel, 1997; Projection: A Novel of Terror and Redemption, 1999; Compulsion, 2002; Psychopath, 2003; Murder Suicide, 2004; Inside the Mind of Scott Peterson, 2005; Architect, 2005; Living the Truth: Transform Your Life Through the Power of Insight and Honesty, 2007; (with G. Beck) The 7: Seven Wonders That Will Change Your Life, 2011. **Address:** 12 49th St., Newbury, MA 01951-1412, U.S.A. **Online address:** info@keithablow.com

ABOUZEID, Leila. (Laylá Abū Zayd). Moroccan (born Morocco), b. 1950. **Genres:** Area Studies, Women's Studies And Issues, Economics, Novellas/Short Stories. **Career:** Television anchor person, 1972-73; Office of the Moroccan Prime Minister, minister of information, minister of equipment, 1974, press secretary, 1974, 1990-92; writer, 1983-. **Publications:** (As Layla Abu Zayd) ām-al-fil, 1983; A Moroccan Woman's Journey Toward Independence, and Other Stories, 1989; Year of the Elephant: A Moroccan Woman's Journey Toward Independence and Other Stories, 1989, rev. ed., 2009; (as Layla Abu Zayd) Amrīkā: Al-WajhAl-ākhar, 1991; (trans. with H.L. Taylor) Return to Childhood: The Memoir of a Modern Moroccan Woman, 1998; Al-Fasl al-akhīr, 2000; The Last Chapter: A Novel, 2000, 2nd ed., 2003; Al-Ghareeb, Qassas Mina emaghrib, 2003; Director and Other Stories from Morocco, 2005; Al-Mudir, wa-qiṣ aṣ ukhr min al-Maghrib, 2008. **Address:** 420 5th Ave., 3rd Fl., New York, NY 10018-2729, U.S.A. **Online address:** abouzeid@iam.net.ma

ABRAHAM, A(ntoine) J. American (born United States), b. 1942. **Genres:** Area Studies, History, Humanities. **Career:** New York Institute of Technology, associate professor, 1975-92; City University of New York, John Jay College of Criminal Justice, associate professor, professor, 1992, adjunct professor. Consultant and writer. **Publications:** Lebanon at Mid-Century: Maronite-Druze Relations in Lebanon, 1840-1860: A Prelude to Arab Nationalism, 1981; Lebanon: A State of Siege, 1975-1984, 1984; Islam and Christianity: Crossroads in Faith, 1987; Khoumani & Islamic Fundamentalism: Contributions of Islamic Sciences to Modern Civilization, 1989, 2nd ed. as Khoumani, Islamic Fundamentalism and The Warriors of God: An Islamic Reader, 1999; (with G. Haddad) The Warriors of God: Jihad (Holy War) and the Fundamentalists of Islam, 1990; The Awakening of Persia: The Reign of Nasr al-Din Shah, 1848-1896, 1993; The Lebanon War, 1996; The Cross and the Crescent: An Ecumenical Perspective, 2001; Islamic Fundamentalism and The Doctrine of Jihad, 2002; Lebanon in Modern Times, 2009. Contributor to periodicals. **Address:** John Jay College of Criminal Justice, City University of New York, Rm. 4309N, 445 W 59th St., New York, NY 10019, U.S.A. **Online address:** aabraham@jjay.cuny.edu

ABRAHAM, Henry J. (Henry Julian Abraham). American/German (born Germany), b. 1921. **Genres:** Civil Liberties/Human Rights, Law, Politics/Government. **Career:** May, Stern & Co., assistant service manager, 1939-41; Charles Berman Co., office manager, 1941-43; University of Pennsylvania, instructor, 1949-53, assistant professor, 1953-57, associate professor, 1957-62, professor of political science, 1962-73; Swarthmore College, visiting lecturer, 1955, 1956, 1961, 1962; University of Colorado, visiting professor, 1964; European University, visiting professor, 1965, 1966, 1967, 1969, 1971; City University, City College, visiting professor, 1967, 1968; Columbia University, visiting professor, 1969; University of Virginia, Henry L. and Grace Doherty Memorial Foundation professor of government and foreign affairs, 1972-78, James Hart professor of government and foreign affairs, 1978-97, professor emeritus, 1997-. Writer. **Publications:** Compulsory Voting, 1955; Government as Entrepreneur and Social Servant, 1956; (with J.A. Corry) Elements of Democratic Government, 1958, 4th ed., 1964; Courts and Judges: An Introduction to the Judicial Process, 1959; The Judicial Process: An Introductory Analysis of the Courts of the United States, England and France, 1962, 7th ed., 1998; The Judiciary: The Supreme Court in the Governmental Process, 1965, 10th ed., 1996; Freedom and the Court: Civil Rights and Liberties in the United States, 1967, 8th ed., 2003; (with J.C. Phillips) Essentials of American National Government, 3rd ed., 1971; Justices and Presidents: A Political History of Appointments to the Supreme Court, 1974, 3rd ed., 1992; (with W.E. Keefe) American Democracy, 1983, 7th ed., 1998; To Secure These Rights: The Declaration of Independence and Constitutional Interpretation, 1996; Justices, Presidents and Senators: A History of the U.S. Supreme Court Appointments from Washington to Clinton, 1999. **Address:** Department of Government and Foreign Affairs, University of Virginia, S187 Gibson Hall, 1540 Jefferson Park Ave., PO Box 400787, Charlottesville, VA 22904, U.S.A.

ABRAHAM, Henry Julian. *See* **ABRAHAM, Henry J.**

ABRAHAM, Spencer. American (born United States), b. 1952. **Genres:** International Relations/Current Affairs, Politics/Government. **Career:** Thomas M. Cooley Law School, assistant professor, 1981-83; Denfield, Timmer & Taylor, consultant, 1981-83; Michigan Republican Party, chair, 1983-94; Office of Vice President Dan Quayle, deputy chief-of-staff, 1990-91; Miller, Canfield, Paddock & Stone, counsel, 1993-94; U.S. Senate, State of Michigan, senator, 1995-2001; United States secretary of energy, 2001-05; Occidental Petroleum Corp., staff, 2005; Abraham Group L.L.C., chair and chief executive officer, 2005-; Areva Inc., non-executive chair, 2006-; Harvard Journal of Law and Public Policy, founder and acting president. Writer. **Publications:** National Transmission Grid Study, 2003; (co-author) Immigration and America's Future: A New Chapter: Report of the Independent Task Force on Immigration and America's Future, 2006; (with W. Tucker) Lights Out! Ten Myths about and Real Solutions to America's Energy Crisis, 2010. **Address:** Abraham Group L.L.C., 600 14th St. NW, Ste. 500, Washington, DC 20005, U.S.A.

ABRAHAM, Thomas. Hong Kong (born Hong Kong), b. 1956. **Genres:** Adult Non-fiction, Medicine/Health, Sports/Fitness. **Career:** The Hindu (newspaper in India), foreign correspondent; British Broadcasting Corp., World Service Television, commentator; South China Morning Post (newspaper in Hong Kong), editor; University of Hong Kong, Journalism and Media Studies Centre, Public Health Media Programme, director and assistant professor. **Publications:** Twenty-first Century Plague: The Story of SARS, 2005. **Address:** Journalism and Media Studies Centre, University of Hong Kong, Eliot Hall, Pokfulam Rd., Hong Kong, 1, Hong Kong. **Online address:** thomas@hku.hk

ABRAHAMS, Peter. Jamaican/South African (born South Africa), b. 1919. **Genres:** Novels, Novellas/Short Stories, Autobiography/Memoirs, Documentaries/Reportage, Animals/Pets, Songs/Lyrics And Libretti, Poetry. **Career:** Daily Worker, contributor, 1941-52; The Observer, correspondent, 1952-54; New York Herald Tribune, correspondent, 1952-54; Radio Jamaica, radio journalist, 1957-; West Indian Economist, editor, 1958-62; West Indian News Program, radio commentator and controller, 1958-62; Holiday Magazine, staff writer; writer, 1964-. **Publications:** Here, Friend: Poems, 1941; A Blackman Speaks of Freedom (poetry), 1941; Dark Testament (short stories), 1942; Song of the City, 1945; Mine Boy, 1946; The Path of Thunder, 1948;

Wild Conquest, 1950; Cierny zlatokop, 1950; Return to Goli (autobiography), 1953; Tell Freedom: Memories of Africa, 1954; A Wreath for Udomo, 1956; Jamaica: An Island Mosaic (travel), 1957; (ed.) Souvenir Pictorial Review of the West Indies Federation, 1947-57, 1958; (co-author) The World of Mankind, 1962; (co-author) History of the Pan-African Congress, 1963; A Night of Their Own, 1965; This Island Now, 1966, rev. ed., 1985; The View from Coyaba, 1985; The Black Experience in the 20th Century: An Autobiography and Meditation, 2000; The Coyaba Chronicles: Reflections on the Black Experience in the 20th Century, 2001. Contributor to periodicals. **Address:** Faber & Faber Ltd., 74-77 Great Russell St., London, GL WC1B 3DA, England. **Online address:** pa@cape.com

ABRAHAMS, Peter. American (born United States), b. 1947. **Genres:** Mystery/Crime/Suspense, Young Adult Fiction, Criminology/True Crime, Biography. **Career:** Canadian Broadcasting Co., producer. Writer. **Publications:** NOVELS: The Fury of Rachel Monette, 1980; Tongues of Fire, 1982; Red Message, 1986; Hard Rain, 1988; Pressure Drop, 1989; Turning the Tide, 1991; Revolution No. 9, 1992; Lights Out, 1994; The Fan, 1995; A Perfect Crime, 1998; Crying Wolf, 2000; Last of the Dixie Heroes, 2001; The Tutor, 2002; Their Wildest Dreams, 2003; Oblivion, 2005; Down the Rabbit Hole, 2005; End of Story, 2006; Behind the Curtain, 2006; Nerve Damage, 2007; Delusion, 2008; Up All Night, 2008; Into the Dark, 2008; Reality Check, 2009; Bullet Point, 2010; Quacky Baseball, 2011; Robbie Forester and the Outlaws of Sherwood Street, 2012. Contributor to periodicals. **Address:** The Friedrich Agency, 136 E 57th St., 19th Fl., New York, NY 10022, U.S.A. **Online address:** pa@cape.com

ABRAMO, J(oe) L. American (born United States), b. 1947. **Genres:** Mystery/Crime/Suspense, Young Adult Fiction. **Career:** Educator, writer and director. **Publications:** MYSTERIES: Catching Water in a Net, 2001; Clutching at Straws, 2003; A Second Helping of Murder, 2003; Counting to Infinity, 2004; Circling the Runway, forthcoming; Chasing Charlie Chan, forthcoming; Gravesend, forthcoming. **Address:** c/o Author Mail, St. Martin's Press/Minotaur Books, 175 5th Ave., New York, NY 10010, U.S.A. **Online address:** jakediamond@att.net

ABRAMS, Douglas Carl. American (born United States), b. 1950. **Genres:** History, Social Sciences, Theology/Religion. **Career:** Bob Jones University, professor of history, 1974-, Africa Mission Team, director, 1991-2005, Department of Social Studies Education, chair, 1992-. Writer. **Publications:** Conservative Constraints: North Carolina and the New Deal, 1992; Selling the Old-Time Religion: American Fundamentalists and Mass Culture, 1920-1940, 2001. Contributor to history journals. **Address:** Department of Social Studies Education, Bob Jones University, PO Box 34627, Greenville, SC 29614, U.S.A. **Online address:** cabrams@bju.edu

ABRAMS, Douglas Carlton. American (born United States), b. 1967?. **Genres:** Marine Sciences/Oceanography, Novels. **Career:** University of California Press, editor; Harper San Francisco, editor; Just Give.org, vice president and editorial director; Idea Architects, co-founder, 2000, chief executive officer. **Publications:** The Lost Diary of Don Juan: An Account of the True Arts of Passion and the Perilous Adventure of Love, 2007; (with D. Tutu) God's Dream, 2008; Eye of the Whale, 2009; (ed.) Made for Goodness: And Why this Makes all the Difference, 2010. Contributor to books. **Address:** Idea Architects, 106 Corinne Ave., Santa Cruz, CA 95065, U.S.A. **Online address:** doug@douglascarltonabrams.com

ABRAMS, Jeanne E. (Jeanne Esther Abrams). American/Swedish (born Sweden), b. 1951. **Genres:** Theology/Religion, History. **Career:** AMC Cancer Research Center and Hospital, history consultant, 1981; University of Denver, Rocky Mountain Jewish Historical Society, director, 1982-, Beck Archives, director, 1982-, Penrose Library, assistant professor, 1997-99, associate professor, 1999-2006, professor, 2006-, Center for Judaic Studies, acting academic director, 1999-2000; Rocky Mountain Society of Archivists, staff, 1982-2006, vice president for programming, 1998-99, preservation officer, 2004-05; Colorado Preservation Alliance, staff, 1982-2004, president, 2002-04; Local Jewish Historical Society News, editor, 1987-91; Jewish Women's League of Denver, vice president, 1988-; Yeshiva Toras Chaim High School Parent Teacher Association, president, 1989-91; Rocky Mountain Jewish Historical Notes, editor, 1999-; Jewish Consumptives' Relief Society (JCRS) Isaac Solomon Historic Preservation Foundation, history consultant. Historian and archivist. **Publications:** Historic Jewish Denver, 1982; (with N. Hitch and A. Wenner) Colorado Jewish History: A Guide for Teachers, 1983; Blazing the Tuberculosis Trail: The Religio-ethnic Role of Four Sanatoria in Early Denver, 1990; (with M.A. Fitzharris) A Place to Heal: The History of National Jewish Medical and Research Center: Global Leader in Lung, Allergic and Immune Diseases, 1997; (with A. Wenner) A Curriculum Guide: An Early History of the Jews of Colorado, 1998; Jewish Women Pioneering the Frontier Trail: A History in the American West, 2006; Jewish Denver: 1859-1940, 2007; Dr. Charles David Spivak: A Jewish Immigrant and the American Tuberculosis Movement, 2009. Contributor of articles to journals. **Address:** University of Denver, 2000 E Asbury Ave., Denver, CO 80210-4323, U.S.A.

ABRAMS, Jeanne Esther. *See* **ABRAMS, Jeanne E.**

ABRAMS, Judith Z. American (born United States) **Genres:** Theology/Religion, Women's Studies And Issues. **Career:** Congregation Emanu El, assistant rabbi, 1985-88; Congregation Ner Shalom, rabbi, 1988-91; Congregation Beth El, rabbi, 1991-95; National Jewish Center for Learning and Leadership, associate, 1994-; Maqom (school for adult Talmud study), founder and director, 1995-; University of Houston, Law Center, adjunct faculty, 1997; Aleph Rabbinical Ordination (Smichah) Program, faculty, 2001-; State of Texas, senior religious advisor, 2000; Siegal College of Jewish Studies, adjunct faculty, 2002-05. Writer. **Publications:** Hesed V'Emet, AIDS: Our Responsibility as Jews, 1989; The Talmud for Beginners, 1991; (with S.A. Abrams) Jewish Parenting: Rabbinic Insights, 1994; Learn Talmud: How to Use the Talmud-Steinsaltz, 1995; The Women of the Talmud, 1995; Bright Lights in Dark Times, 1995; Talmud for Beginners III: Living in a Non-Jewish World, 1997; Judaism and Disability: Portrayals in Ancient Texts from the Tanach through the Bavli, 1998; A Beginner's Guide to the Steinsaltz Talmud, 1999; (ed. with D.L. Freeman) Illness and Health in the Jewish Tradition: Writings from the Bible to Today, 1999; Guided Meditations for Torah Portions, Holidays, and Healing, 2001; Jewish Texts: The Owner's Manual, 2001; The Babylonian Talmud: A Topical Guide, 2002; Secret World of Kabbalah, 2006; Torah & Company: The Weekly Portion of the Torah, Accompanied by Generous Helpings of Mishnah and Gemara, Served Up with Discussion Questions to Spice Up Your Sabbath Table, 2006; (ed. with W.C. Gaventa) Jewish Perspectives on Theology and the Human Experience of Disability, 2006; (ed. with M.L. Raphael) What is Jewish about America's Favorite Pastime?: Essays and Sermons on Jews, Judaism, and Baseball, 2006; Talmud Tale, 2009. FOR CHILDREN: Yom Kippur: A Family Service, 1990; Selichot: A Family Service, 1990; Rosh Hashana: A Family Service, 1990; Shabbat: A Family Service, 1991; Sukkot: A Family Seder, 1993; Simchat Torah: A Family Celebration, 1995; (ed. with P.L. Citrin) Gates of Repentance for Young People, 2002. **Address:** Maqom, PO Box 31900-323, Houston, TX 77231, U.S.A. **Online address:** maqom@compassnet.com

ABRAMS, Linsey. American (born United States), b. 1951. **Genres:** Novels, History, Young Adult Fiction. **Career:** City University of New York, Queens College, adjunct lecturer in English, 1978-80; Sarah Lawrence College, teacher of fiction writing, 1980-; City College of New York, writer-in-residence, 1986-, MA Program in English, acting director, M.F.A. Creative Writing Program, director and professor; Global City Review, founding editor; Global City Press, founding editor. **Publications:** Charting by the Stars, 1979; Double Vision, 1984; Our History in New York, 1994. **Address:** Department of English, City College of New York, 6/219 North Academic Bldg., 160 Convent Ave., New York, NY 10031, U.S.A. **Online address:** gradenglish@ccny.cuny.edu

ABRAMS, M(eyer) H(oward). (M. Howard Abrams). American (born United States), b. 1912. **Genres:** Literary Criticism And History. **Career:** Harvard University, instructor, 1938-42, Psycho-Acoustic Laboratory, research associate, 1942-45; Cornell University, assistant professor, 1945-47, associate professor, 1947-53, professor, 1953-60, Frederic J. Whiton professor, 1960-63, Class of 1916 professor of English emeritus, 1963-; Royal University of Malta, Fulbright lecturer, 1953; Cambridge University, Fulbright lecturer, 1953; W.W. Norton and Company Inc., advisory editor, 1961-; University of Indiana, Roache lecturer, 1963; University of Toronto, Alexander lecturer, 1964; University of California, Ewing lecturer, 1974. **Publications:** Il mestiere di poeta, 1965; Fuori storia, 1967; La moglie del tiranno, 1969; Il quinto stato, 1970; La vita eterna, 1972; Liberare l'animale, 1973; Mestiere di scrittore, 1973; Letteratura e classi subalterne, 1974; Occidente, 1975; Avanti popolo, 1977; Un altare per la madre, 1978, trans. as Memorial, 1996; La chiamata uomo, 1981, trans. as The Sickness Called Man, 1992; Mestiere di poeta, 1982; Storia di Sirio: parabola per la muova generazione, 1984, trans. as, The Story of Sirio: A Parable, 1985; La donna dei fili, 1986; Autoritratto di Primo Levi, 1987; I miei personaggi mi scrivono, 1987; Romanzi della pianura, 1988; Alberto Moravia: Io e il mio tempo: conversazioni critiche con Ferdinando Camon, 1988; Il canto delle balene, 1989; Il Super-Baby, 1991; Il santo assassino: dichiarazioni apocrife, 1991; Mai visti sole e luna, 1994; La terra é di tutti, 1996; Dal silenzio delle campagne: tori mucche diavoli contadini drogati mercanti di donne e serial-killer: scene e raccontini in versi, 1998; La cavallina la ragazza e il diavolo: racconto campestre, 2004; Tenebre su tenebre, 2006; Figli perduti, la droga discussa con i ragazzi, 2009; La mia stirpe, 2011. **Address:** 378 Savage Farm Dr., Ithaca, NY 14850, U.S.A. **Online address:** mha5@cornell.edu

ABRAMS, M. Howard. *See* **ABRAMS, M(eyer) H(oward).**

ABRAMS, Nita. American (born United States), b. 1953?. **Genres:** Romance/Historical. **Career:** Writer and educator. **Publications:** COURIERS SERIES: HISTORICAL ROMANCES: A Question of Honor, 2002; The Exiles, 2002; The Spy's Bride, 2003; The Spy's Kiss, 2005; Spy's Reward, 2006. **Address:** 1730 New Brighton Blvd., Ste. 104-313, Minneapolis, MN 55413-1248, U.S.A. **Online address:** nkabrams@comcast.net

ABRAMS, Ovid (S. McL.). American/Ghanaian (born Ghana), b. 1939. **Genres:** Area Studies, Business/Trade/Industry, Poetry. **Career:** CNS News (wire service), city editor, 1972-75; Fairchild Publications, news editor, 1976-78; Publishers Weekly, assistant news editor, 1978-80; E.F. Hutton, vice-president and research analyst, 1980-89; McGraw-Hill Book Co., senior editor, 1989-; Baruch College, faculty. **Publications:** Guyana Metegee, 1970; How to Find the Job of Your Dreams: A Do-It-Yourself Manual, 1993; Let God Answer Your Prayers, 1994; Metegee: The History and Culture of Guyana, 1997; (co-author) The Columbia University Guide to Business Journalism; 760 Degrees of Love (poetry), 2002; The Mystery of Christ Jesus, 2004. **Address:** 113-27 210th St., Queens Village, NY 11429-2216, U.S.A. **Online address:** ovidabrams@baruch.cuny.edu

ABRAMSKY, Sasha. American/British (born England), b. 1972. **Genres:** Adult Non-fiction, Politics/Government. **Career:** University of California, University Writing Program, lecturer; Demos, senior fellow. Freelance journalist. **Publications:** Hard Time Blues: How Politics Built a Prison Nation, 2002; Ill-Equipped: U.S. Prisons and Offenders with Mental Illness, 2003; Conned: How Millions Went to Prison, Lost the Vote, and Helped Send George W. Bush to the White House, 2006; American Furies: Crime, Punishment, and Vengeance in the Age of Mass Imprisonment, 2007; Breadline USA: The Hidden Scandal of American Hunger and How to Fix It, 2009; Inside Obama's Brain, 2009. Contributor to periodicals. **Address:** University Writing Program, University of California, 350 Voorhies Hall, 1 Shields Ave., Davis, CA 95616-8581, U.S.A. **Online address:** sabramsky@ucdavis.edu

ABRAMSON, Bruce. (Bruce D. Abramson). American (born United States), b. 1963. **Genres:** Economics, Information Science/Computers, Politics/Government. **Career:** University of Southern California, assistant professor, 1987-93; Informationism Inc. (formerly Gordian Solutions Inc. and BDA Consulting), president, 1988-; Information Extraction and Transport Inc., principal scientist, 1993-94; Cambridge Research Associates Inc., director of economic and policy analysis, 1994-96; Carnegie Mellon University, adjunct associate professor, 1994-99, adjunct professor, 1999-2003; CRA Intl. (formerly Charles River Associates), consultant, 1998-2000, principal, 2000-03, senior consultant, 2004-; U.S. Court of Appeals for the Federal Circuit, law clerk, 2003-04; World Bank Group, consultant, 2006-; Rimon Law Group P.C., partner, 2011-. Writer. **Publications:** The Expected-Outcome Model of Two-Player Games, 1991; Digital Phoenix: Why the Information Economy Collapsed and How It Will Rise Again, 2005; (as Bruce D. Abramson) The Secret Circuit: The Little-Known Court Where the Rules of the Information Age Unfold, 2007; Article 2: The Right of Non-Discrimination, 2008. **Address:** CRA Intl., John Hancock Tower, 200 Clarendon St., T-33, Boston, MA 02116-5092, U.S.A. **Online address:** bdabramson@gmail.com

ABRAMSON, Bruce D. *See* **ABRAMSON, Bruce.**

ABRAMSON, Edward A. British/American (born United States), b. 1944. **Genres:** Area Studies, Literary Criticism And History, Young Adult Fiction. **Career:** East Carolina University, instructor, 1966-69; University of Hull, Department of American Studies, lecturer, 1971-, senior lecturer, professor, now professor emeritus; College of William and Mary, visiting professor, 1986-87. Writer. **Publications:** The Immigrant Experience in American Literature (pamphlet), 1982; Chaim Potok (monograph), 1986; Bernard Malamud Revisited (monograph), 1993. **Address:** Department of American Studies, University of Hull, Cottingham Rd., Hull, HB HU6 7RX, England. **Online address:** e.a.a.bramson@amstuds.hall.ac.uk

ABRAMSON, Leslie W. American (born United States) **Genres:** Law, Criminology/True Crime. **Career:** University of Louisville, D. Brandeis School of Law, assistant professor of law, 1973-76, associate professor of law, 1976-79, professor of law, 1979-, acting assistant university provost, 1984, associate dean, 1991-93, Frost Brown Todd professor of law. Writer. **Publications:** (Ed.) Basic Bankruptcy: Alternatives, Proceedings and Discharges (edited transcript of seminar proceedings), 1971; Criminal Detainers, 1979; Judicial Disqualification under Canon 3C of the Code of Judicial Conduct, 1986, 2nd ed., 1991; Criminal Practice and Procedure, 1987, 5th ed., 2010; (with C.D. Edwards) Questions and Answers: Criminal Law, 1988; Substantive Criminal Law, 1990, 3rd ed., 2010; (with J.R. Cox) Civil Procedure Forms, 1994, 2nd ed., 2006; (with R. Flaste) The Defense is Ready: Life in the Trenches of Criminal Law, 1997; A Century in Celebration: The United States District Court for the Western District of Kentucky 1901-2001, 2001; Commentary to Proposed Kentucky Penal Code Revision, 2003; (with J.D. Grano) Problems in Criminal Procedure, 2004; (with J.T. Cross and E.E. Deason) Civil Procedure: Cases, Problems, Exercises, 2006, 3rd ed., 2011; Acing Criminal Procedure: A Checklist Approach to Solving Procedural Problems, 2007, 2nd ed., 2010; Acing Professional Responsibility: A Checklist Approach to Professional Responsibility Problems, 2009. **Address:** Louis D. Brandeis School of Law, University of Louisville, Rm. 260, 2301 S 3rd St., Louisville, KY 40208, U.S.A. **Online address:** les.abramson@louisville.edu

ABRESCH, Peter E. American (born United States), b. 1931. **Genres:** Mystery/Crime/Suspense, Writing/Journalism, Poetry, Autobiography/Memoirs, Novellas/Short Stories, Theology/Religion, Plays/Screenplays, Literary Criticism And History, Literary Criticism And History. **Career:** Smithsonian Institute, teacher of fiction writing. Writer. **Publications:** MYSTERY NOVELS: Bloody Bonsai, 1998; Killing Thyme, 1998; Tip-a-Canoe, 2001; Painted Lady, 2003; Sheep in Wolf's Clothing (novella), 2003; If They Ask for a Hand, Only Give Them a Finger, 2008; Name Games: A James P. Dandy Elderhostel Mystery, 2008; The Faltese Malcom: The Real Story about the Second Bird from Malta, 2009; Capitol Coven, 2010. NONFICTION: Easy Reading Writing: Easy Reading about Writing Easy Reading, 2001; Deadly Morsels, 2003. Contributor to magazines. **Address:** PO Box 548, Prince Frederick, MD 20678-0548, U.S.A. **Online address:** peter@sidewalkbooks.com

ABSE, Dannie. British/Welsh (born Wales), b. 1923. **Genres:** Novels, Plays/Screenplays, Poetry, Autobiography/Memoirs. **Career:** Poverty magazine, editor, 1949-54; Central London Medical Establishment, specialist in charge of chest clinic, 1954-89; Princeton University, senior fellow and visiting writer-in-residence, 1973-74; Poetry Society, president, 1978-92; Royal Society of Literature, fellow, 1983; Welsh Academy of Letters, president, 1995; Cardiff University, College of Medicine, honorary fellow, 1997; University of Wales College of Medicine, honorary fellow, 1999. Writer. **Publications:** After Every Green Thing, 1948; Walking under Water, 1952; Ash on a Young Man's Sleeve (novel), 1954; Some Corner of an English Field (novel), 1956; Fire in Heaven (play), 1956; Tenants of the House, 1957; The Eccentric (play), 1961; Poems, Golders Green, 1962; Dannie Abse: A Selection, 1963; Medicine on Trial, 1967; Three Questor Plays, 1967; A Small Desperation: Poems, 1968; Demo, 1969; O. Jones, O. Jones (novel), 1970; Selected Poems, 1970; Funland and Other Poems, 1973; The Dogs of Pavlov (play), 1973; A Poet in the Family (autobiography), 1974; (with D.J. Enright and M. Langley) Penguin Modern Poets No. 26, 1975; Poetry Dimension Annual 4, 1977; Poetry Dimension Annual 5, 1977; Collected Poems 1948-1976, 1977; More Words, 1977; My Medical School, 1978; Pythagoras, 1979; Way Out in the Centre (poems), 1981; Miscellany One, 1981; A Strong Dose of Myself, 1983; One-Legged on Ice: Poems, 1983; Ask the Bloody Horse (poems), 1986; Journals from the Ant-Heap, 1986; White Coat, Purple Coat: Collected Poems 1948-88, 1989; Remembrance of Crimes Past (poetry), 1990; The View from Row G (plays), 1990; There Was a Young Man from Cardiff, 1991; Intermittent Journals, 1994; On the Evening Road (Poetry), 1994; Welsh Retrospective, 1997; Arcadia, One Mile, 1998; Be Seated, Thou: Poems, 1989-1998, 2000; Goodbye Twentieth Century (autobiography), 2001; The Strange Case of Dr. Simmonds and Dr. Glas (novel), 2002; New and Collected Poems, 2003; The Yellow Bird, 2004; Running Late, 2006; Presence, 2007. EDITOR: (with H. Sergeant) Mavericks, 1957; Modern European Verse, 1964; Thirteen Poets, 1972; Poetry Dimension 2, 1974; Poetry Dimension Annual 3, 1975; (intro.)

Wales in Verse, 1983; (with J. Abse) Voices in the Gallery, 1986; (with J. Abse) The Music Lover's Literary Companion, 1988; The Hutchinson Book of Post-War British Poetry, 1989; (with A. Stevenson) The Gregory Anthology, 1991-1993, 1994; Twentieth Century Anglo-Welsh Poetry, 1997; New Selected Poems, 2009; Two for Joy: Scenes from Married Life, 2010. Contributor to periodicals. **Address:** Drury House, 34-43 Russell St., London, GL WC2B 5HA, England.

ABSHIRE, David Manker. American (born United States), b. 1926. **Genres:** International Relations/Current Affairs, Politics/Government. **Career:** American Enterprise Institute for Public Policy Research, director of special projects, 1961-62; Georgetown University, Center for Strategic and International Studies, co-founder, 1962, executive director, 1962-70, chairman, 1973-82, chief executive, School of Foreign Service, adjunct professor; U.S. Department of State, assistant secretary of State for congressional relations, 1970-73; Center for Strategic and International Studies, founder, chairman, 1973-83, president, 1987-, chief executive officer, vice chairman of board of trustees; U.S. Board for International Broadcasting, chairman, 1974-77; National Security Group, Transition Office of President-Elect Reagan, director, 1980-81; U.S. Permanent Representative on NATO, ambassador, 1983-87; Ogden Corp., director; Procter & Gamble, director, 1987-96; Center for the Study of the Presidency, president, 2002-, chief executive officer; Richard Lounsbery Foundation, president, 2002-; Infantry School, Ft. Benning, instructor; Edmund A. Walsh School of Foreign Service, adjunct professor. Writer. **Publications:** EDITOR: (with R.V. Allen) National Security: Political, Military and Economic Strategies in the Decade Ahead, 1963; (M.A. Samuels) Portuguese Africa: A Handbook, 1969; (with G.D. Gayle) Research Resources for the Seventies: Proceedings, 1971; (with R.D. Nurnberger) The Growing Power of Congress, 1981; Triumphs and Tragedies of the Modern Presidency: Seventy-Six Case Studies in Presidential Leadership, 2001. OTHERS: (contrib.) Détente, 1965; The South Rejects a Prophet: The Life of Senator D.M. Key, 1824-1900, 1967; Conference on the Plans and Needs for International Strategic Studies, 1969; International Broadcasting: A New Dimension of Western Diplomacy, 1976; Egypt and Israel: Prospects for a New Era, 1979; Foreign Policy Makers: President vs. Congress, 1979; (contrib.) International News: Freedom Under Attack, 1979; (co-author) Parlamentarische Zusammenarbeit in der Allianz: Die Zukunft der Nordatlantischen Versammlung: Bericht der Arbeitsgruppe des Atlantic Council of the United States über die Nordatlantische Versammlung, 1983; Preventing World War III: A Realistic Grand Strategy, 1988; (co-author) Defense Economics for the 1990's: Resources, Strategies and Options: A Report, 1989; (with R.R. Burt and R.J. Woolsey) Atlantic Alliance Transformed, 1992; (contrib.) The New Promise of American Life, 1995; (with B. Brower) Putting America's House in Order: The Nation as a Family, 1996; Saving the Reagan Presidency: Trust is the Coin of the Realm, 2005; A Call to Greatness: Challenging Our Next President, 2008. Contributor to books. **Address:** Center for Strategic and International Studies, 1800 K St. NW, Washington, DC 20006, U.S.A. **Online address:** email@thepresidency.org

ABT, Jeffrey. American (born United States), b. 1949. **Genres:** Art/Art History, Institutions/Organizations, Intellectual History. **Career:** Des Moines Public Schools, instructor, 1973-77; Wichita Art Museum, curator of collections, 1977-78; Billy Hork Galleries Ltd., general manager, 1978-80; University of Chicago, exhibitions co-ordinator at university library, 1980-86, resident head, 1982-87, assistant director, 1986-87, David and Alfred Smart Museum of Art, acting director, 1987-89; Wayne State University, associate professor of art and art history, 1989-, chairman, 1989-94, interim assistant dean, 2007-08. Writer, artist and sculptor. **Publications:** The Printer's Craft: An Exhibition Selected from the R.R. Donnelley and Sons Company Collection, 1982; The Book Made Art: A Selection of Contemporary Artists' Books, 1986; Water: Sheba's Story (poetry), 1997; A Museum on the Verge: A Socioeconomic History of the Detroit Institute of Arts, 1882-2002, 2001; (ed.) Up from the Streets: Detroit Art from the Duffy Warehouse Collection, 2001; American Egyptologist: The Life of James Henry Breasted and the Creation of His Oriental Institute, 2011; Series of Paintings Exploring the Poetics of Display, Transience and Abandonment, forthcoming; Abstraction and Assimilation: The Jewish Museum of New York and Its Avant-Garde Exhibitions, 1957-1971, forthcoming. Contributor of articles to periodicals. **Address:** Department of Art and Art History, Wayne State University, 150 Art Bldg., Detroit, MI 48202, U.S.A. **Online address:** ad5565@wayne.edu

ABU EL-HAJ, Nadia. American (born United States), b. 1962?. **Genres:** Archaeology/Antiquities, History, Adult Non-fiction. **Career:** University of Chicago, anthropology faculty, 1997-2002; Columbia University, Barnard College, assistant professor of anthropology, 2002, associate professor of anthropology, director of graduate studies, 2008-09. Writer. **Publications:** Facts on the Ground: Archaeological Practice and Territorial Self-Fashioning in Israeli Society, 2001. **Address:** Department of Anthropology, Columbia University, Rm. 452, Schermerhorn Ext., 1200 Amsterdam Ave. W 119th St., New York, NY 10027-7054, U.S.A. **Online address:** ne2008@columbia.edu

ABU-JABER, Diana. American (born United States), b. 1959. **Genres:** Novels, Autobiography/Memoirs. **Career:** Iowa State University, visiting assistant professor of English, 1990; University of Oregon, assistant professor of English, 1990-95; Portland State University, Department of English, writer-in-residence and associate professor of English, 1996-. Writer. **Publications:** NOVELS: Arabian Jazz, 1993; Crescent, 2003; Origin, 2007; Birds of Paradise, 2011. NON-FICTION: The Language of Baklava (memoir), 2005. Contributor to books and periodicals. **Address:** Department of English, Portland State University, M403 Neuberger Hall, 724 SW Harrison St., PO Box 751, Portland, OR 97201-3295, U.S.A. **Online address:** abujaber@aol.com

ABUKHALIL, As'ad. American (born United States), b. 1960. **Genres:** International Relations/Current Affairs, Politics/Government. **Career:** Tufts University, instructor; Georgetown University, instructor; George Washington University, instructor; Public Broadcasting Service, middle east analyst; Cable News Network, Middle East analyst; National Broadcasting Co., Middle East analyst; ABC News, Middle East analyst; Al Jazeera, Middle East analyst; University of California, visiting professor; Colorado College, faculty; Randolph-Macon Woman's College, faculty; Cal State Stanislaus, professor of politics and comparative government, 1993-. Writer. **Publications:** (Contrib.) Amal and The Palestinians: Understanding The Battle of The Camps: Viewpoints, 1985; Historical Dictionary of Lebanon, 1998; Bin Laden, Islam, and America's New War on Terrorism, 2002; The Battle for Saudi Arabia: Royalty, Fundamentalism, and Global Power, 2004. Contributor of articles to journals and periodicals. **Address:** Department of Politics & Public Administration, California State University, Rm. 126A, Bizzini Hall, 1 University Cir., Turlock, CA 95382-0299, U.S.A. **Online address:** aabukhalil@csustan.edu

ABU-LUGHOD, Lila. American (born United States), b. 1952. **Genres:** Literary Criticism And History, Women's Studies And Issues, History, Humanities. **Career:** Williams College, assistant professor of anthropology, 1983-87; University of Pennsylvania, Mellon fellow, 1988-89; Princeton University, assistant professor of religion, 1990-91; New York University, associate professor and professor of anthropology and Middle East studies, 1991-99; Columbia University, professor of anthropology and women's studies, 2000-, Joseph L. Buttenwieser professor of social science. Writer. **Publications:** Veiled Sentiments: Honor and Poetry in a Bedouin Society, 1986, rev. ed., 1999; (ed. with C.A. Lutz) Language and the Politics of Emotion, 1990; Writing Women's Worlds: Bedouin Stories, 1993; (ed. and contrib.) Remaking Women: Feminism and Modernity in the Middle East, 1998; (ed. with F.D. Ginsburg and B. Larkin) Media Worlds: Anthropology On New Terrain, 2002; Dramas of Nationhood: The Politics of Television in Egypt, 2005; (ed. with A.H. Sa'di) Nakba: Palestine, 1948 and the Claims Of Memory, 2007. Contributor of articles to journals. **Address:** Department of Anthropology, Columbia University, Rm. 756, Schermerhorn Ext., 1200 Amsterdam Ave. & W 119th St., New York, NY 10027-7003, U.S.A. **Online address:** la310@columbia.edu

ABUSHARAF, Rogaia Mustafa. American/Egyptian/Nepalese (born Nepal), b. 1961. **Genres:** Trivia/Facts, Women's Studies And Issues. **Career:** Wellesley College, visiting assistant professor; Tufts University, Department of Sociology and Anthropology, lecturer; Brown University, Pembroke Center for Teaching and Research on Women, senior research associate; Harvard Divinity School, fellow, 2003-05; Georgetown University, visiting associate professor of anthropology. Writer. **Publications:** Wanderings: Sudanese Migrants and Exiles in North America, 2002; (ed.) Female Circumcision: Multicultural Perspectives, 2006; Transforming Displaced Women in Sudan: Politics And The Body in a Squatter Settlement, 2009. Contributor to periodicals. **Address:** Department of Anthropology, Georgetown University, Rm. 0D55, Georgetown Bldg., PO Box 23689, Doha, 1, Bahrain. **Online address:** arogaia@hotmail.com

ABZUG, Robert Henry. American (born United States), b. 1945. **Genres:** History, Humanities, Intellectual History, Psychology. **Career:** University of California-Berkeley, instructor in history, 1976-77; University of California-Los Angeles, lecturer in history, 1977-78; University of Texas, assistant professor of history, 1978-84, associate professor of history, 1984-90, professor of history and American studies, 1990-96, Religious Studies Program, director, 1989-90, Department of American Studies, chair and director, 1990-96, Oliver H. Radkey Regents professor of history, 2002-, Liberal Arts Plan I Honors Programs, director, 1996-2002, Schusterman Center for Jewish Studies, director, 2007-; Carver Museum of Black History, trustee, 1981-83; University of Munich, Eric Voegelin visiting professor, 1990-91. Writer. **Publications:** Passionate Liberator: Theodore Dwight Weld and the Dilemma of Reform, 1980; Inside the Vicious Heart: Americans and the Liberation of Nazi Concentration Camps, 1985; (ed. with S. Maizlish) New Perspectives on Race and Slavery in America: Essays in Honor of Kenneth M. Stampp, 1986; (intro.) Liberation of the Nazi Concentration Camps 1945: Eyewitness Accounts of the Liberators, 1987; Cosmos Crumbling: American Reform and the Religious Imagination, 1994; America Views the Holocaust, 1933-1945: A Brief Documentary History, 1999; William James, The Varieties of Religious Experience, forthcoming; Rollo May and the Modern Search for Self, forthcoming. **Address:** Department of History, University of Texas, 1 University Sta., PO Box B7000, Austin, TX 78712-0220, U.S.A. **Online address:** zug@mail.utexas.edu

ACCAD, Evelyne. American/Lebanese (born Lebanon), b. 1943. **Genres:** Novels, Literary Criticism And History, Third World, Women's Studies And Issues, Autobiography/Memoirs. **Career:** Anderson College, teaching assistant in French language, grammar and literature, 1965-67, part-time instructor in French, 1967-68; International College, teacher of French and English language, grammar and literature, 1968-70; Indiana University, teaching assistant in comparative literature, 1971-73; University of Illinois at Urbana-Champaign, assistant professor in French, 1974-79, associate professor in French, 1979-88, professor of French comparative literature and core faculty at African center, Women's Studies Center and Center for Asian Studies, 1988-2004, professor emeritus, 2004-; Beirut University College, teacher, 1978, 1984; Northwestern University, visiting professor in French, 1991. Writer. **Publications:** Veil of Shame: The Role of Women in the Modern Fiction of North Africa and the Arab World, 1978; (contrib.) Women in the Moslem World, 1978; (trans. and intro.) N. Aba, Montjoie Palestine!; Or, Last Year in Jerusalem (poem), 1980; (contrib.) Arabic Literature in North Africa, 1982; L'Excisee (novel), 1982, trans. as The Excised, 1989, 2nd ed., 1994; (contrib.) The Image of the Prostitute in Modern Literature, 1984; (with R. Ghurayyib) Contemporary Arab Women Writers and Poets, 1985; Coquelicot du massacre (novel), 1988; Sexuality and War: Literary Masks of the Middle East, 1990; (contrib.) Third World Women and the Politics of Feminism, 1991; Des femmes, des hommes et la guerre: Fiction et realite au Proche-Orient, 1993; Blessures des Mots: Journal de Tunisie (novel), 1993, trans. as Wounding Words: A Woman's Journal in Tunisia, 1996; (contrib.) Arab Women: Old Boundaries, New Frontiers, 1993; (contrib.) Emotions, 1994; Les filles de Tahar Haddad (play), 1995; (contrib.) Radically Speaking: Feminism Reclaimed, 1996; Voyages en Cancer, 2000, trans. as The Wounded Breast: Intimate Journeys through Cancer, 2001; (ed. and contrib.) Routledge International Encyclopedia of Women: Global Women's Issues and Knowledge, 2001. Contributor to books and periodicals. **Address:** Department of French, University of Illinois, 2090 Foreign Languages Bldg., 707 S Mathews Ave., Urbana, IL 61801, U.S.A. **Online address:** e-accad@uiuc.edu

ACCATTOLI, Luigi. Italian (born Italy), b. 1943. **Genres:** Adult Non-fiction, Photography. **Career:** Corriere della sera (newspaper), correspondent, 1988-; La Repubblica, journalist; Catholic University of FUCI, co-director of research. **Publications:** (Co-author) Da Paolo VI a Giovanni Paolo II, 1979; (ed.) Chiesa Galassia E L'ultimo Cocordato, 1987; (with D.D. Rio) Wojtyla: Il Nuovo Mosé, 1988; Quando il Papa chiedeperdono, 1998; Karol Wojtyla: L'uomo Di Fine Millenio, 1998; Life in the Vatican with John Paul II, 1999; Chiamatemi Karol: 365 motti di Papa Wojtya, 1999; Man of the Millennium: John Paul II, 2000; La Santitaà, 2001; John Paul II: A Pope for the People, 2004; Giovanni Paolo: La Primabiografia Completa, 2006. Contributor to periodicals. **Address:** c/o Author Mail, Abrams Books, 100 5th Ave., New York, NY 10011, U.S.A.

ACCAWI, Anwar F. American (born United States), b. 1943. **Genres:** Young Adult Non-fiction. **Career:** University of Tennessee, English Language Institute, full-time instructor, ESL professor, 1979-; National Evangelical Institute, Sidon High School, teacher; American University of Beirut, instructor. Writer. **Publications:** (Contrib.) The Camera in Homeworks, 1996; The Boy from the Tower of the Moon, 1999; The Telephone in The Best American Essays, 1998; Unbreakable Wonder in Harper's, 2005. Works appear in anthologies. Contributor to periodicals. **Address:** English Language Institute, University of Tennessee, 907 Mountcastle St., Knoxville, TN 37996, U.S.A. **Online address:** aaccawi@utk.edu

ACCINELLI, Robert. Canadian/American (born United States), b. 1939. **Genres:** Education, History, Politics/Government, International Relations/Current Affairs. **Career:** University of Toronto, Department of History, professor of history and modern American foreign relations, 1966-, now professor emeritus. Writer. **Publications:** Crisis and Commitment: United States Policy toward Taiwan, 1950-1955, 1996. **Address:** Depatment of History, University of Toronto, Rm. 2074, Sidney Smith Hall, 100 St George St., Toronto, ON M5S 3G3, Canada. **Online address:** accinell@chass.utoronto.ca

ACHEBE, (Albert) Chinụ a(lụ mọgụ). *See* **ACHEBE, Chinua.**

ACHEBE, Chinua. ((Albert) Chinụ a(lụ mọgụ) Achebe). Nigerian/American (born United States), b. 1930. **Genres:** Novels, Novellas/Short Stories, Children's Fiction, Poetry, Essays, Young Adult Fiction, Literary Criticism And History. **Career:** Nigerian Broadcasting Corp., talk show producer, 1954-57, Eastern Region in Enugu, controller, 1958-61, Voice of Nigeria, founder and director, 1961-66; Citadel Books Ltd., chair, 1967; University of Nigeria, senior research fellow, 1967-72, professor of English, 1976-81, professor emeritus, 1985-; Heinemann Educational Books Ltd., director, 1970-; Nwamife Publishers Ltd., director, 1970-; African Commentary Magazine, chair and publisher, 1970-; University of Massachusetts, visiting professor of English, 1972-75, professor, 1987-88; University of Connecticut, Afro-American Studies Department, visiting professor, 1975-76; University of California, Regents lecturer, 1984; Anambra State University of Technology, pro-chancellor and chair, 1986-88; Bard College, Charles P. Stevenson professor of languages and literature, 1990-2009; Cambridge University, Clare Hall, visiting fellow and Ashby lecturer, 1993; Brown University, David and Marianna Fisher university professor and professor of Africana studies, 2009- . Writer. **Publications:** Things Fall Apart, 1958; No Longer at Ease, 1961; The Sacrificial Egg and Other Stories, 1962; Arrow of God, 1964; Mapolet ba-umuofyah, 1965; A Man of the People, 1966; Chike and the River, 1966; (co-author) The Insider; Stories of War and Peace from Nigeria, 1971; Beware, Soul-Brother, and Other Poems, 1971, rev. ed., 1972; Girls at War and Other Stories, 1972, 2nd ed., 1988; (co-author) How the Leopard Got His Claws, 1972; Christmas in Biafra and Other Poems, 1973; Morning Yet on Creation Day (essays), 1975; Winds of Change: Modern Stories from Black Africa, 1977; The Flute, 1978; The Drum, 1978; (co-ed.) Don't Let Him Die: An Anthology of Memorial Poems for Christopher Okigbo, 1978; (co-ed.) Aka Weta: Egwu Aguluagu Egwuedeluede, 1982; The Trouble with Nigeria (essays), 1983; (ed. with C.L. Innes) African Short Stories, 1985; The World of the Ogbanje, 1986; Hopes and Impediments: Selected Essays 1965-1987, 1988; The University and the Leadership Factor in Nigerian Politics, 1988; The African Trilogy (fiction), 1988; Anthills of the Savannah, 1988; An Image of Africa: Racism in Conrad's Heart of Darkness, 1988; A Tribute to James Baldwin, 1989; (co-ed.) Beyond Hunger in Africa: Conventional Wisdom and an African Vision, 1990; (ed. with C.L. Innes) The Heinemann Book of Contemporary African Short Stories, 1992; The Voter, 1994; (co-author) The South Wind and the Sun, 1996; Eagle on Iroko, 1996; Conversations with Chinua Achebe, 1997; Another Africa, 1997; (co-author) Order and Chaos, 1997; Echi Di Ime, 1999; Home and Exile, 2000; (contrib.) The Short Century: Independence and Liberation Movements in Africa, 1945-1994, 2001; Collected Poems, 2004; Africa: A Short History, 2004; Eagle in Ascendance, 2005; The Education of a British-protected Child: Essays, 2009; (co-author) The Steve Biko Memorial Lecture, 2009; (co-author) Steve Biko Memorial Lectures: 2000-2008, 2009; First Festival on Igbo Civilization, 2009; Chike and the River, 2011; (with J. Iroaganachi) How the Leopard Got His Claws, 2011; There was a Country, 2012. **Address:** Department of Africana Studies, Brown University, 155 Angell St., PO Box 1904, Providence, RI 02912, U.S.A. **Online address:** chinua_achebe@brown.edu

ACHENBACH, Joel. (Joel Leroy Achenbach). American (born United States), b. 1960. **Genres:** Classics, Adult Non-fiction, Local History/Rural Topics. **Career:** Miami Herald, staff writer, 1982-90; Washington Post, Rough Draft Column, staff writer, 1990-, reporter, Washington Post.com, columnist; National Enterprise, writer, 2007-; National Geographic Magazine, columnist; National Public Radio, commentator. Journalist. **Publications:** Why Things Are, vol. I: Answers to Every Essential Question in Life, 1991, vol. II: The Big Picture, 1993; Why Things Are and Why Things Aren't, 1996; Captured by Aliens: The Search for Life and Truth in a Very Large Universe,

1999; It Looks like a President Only Smaller: Trailing Campaign 2000, 2001; The Grand Idea: George Washington's Potomac and the Race to the West, 2004; Hole at the Bottom of the Sea: The Race to Kill the BP Oil Gusher, 2011. **Address:** Washington Post, 1150 15th St. NW, Washington, DC 20071-0001, U.S.A. **Online address:** achenbachj@washpost.com

ACHENBACH, Joel Leroy. *See* **ACHENBACH, Joel.**

ACHESON, David C(ampion). American (born United States), b. 1921. **Genres:** Autobiography/Memoirs, History. **Career:** Atomic Energy Commission, Office of the General Counsel, attorney, 1948-49; Covington and Burling, attorney, 1950-61; District of Columbia, U.S. attorney, 1961-65; U.S. Secretary of the Treasury, special assistant, 1965-67; Communications Satellite Corp., general counsel, 1967-74, vice-president, 1967-69, senior vice-president, 1969-74; Jones, Day, Reavis and Pogue, partner, 1974-78; Drinker Biddle and Reath, partner, 1978-83; Atlantic Council of the United States, president, 1993-99. Writer. **Publications:** (Ed.) This Vast External Realm, 1973; (ed. with D.S. McLellan) Among Friends: The Personal Letters of Dean Acheson, 1980; Acheson Country, A Memoir, 1993; (ed. with R. Geselbracht) Affection and Trust: The Personal Correspondence of Harry S. Truman and Dean Acheson, 1953-1971, 2010. Contributor to books. **Address:** 2700 Calvert St. NW, Apt. 414, Washington, DC 20008, U.S.A. **Online address:** dcampach@aol.com

ACHINSTEIN, Sharon. British/American (born United States), b. 1963. **Genres:** History, Literary Criticism And History, Politics/Government. **Career:** Northwestern University, assistant professor, 1989-95, associate professor of English literature, 1995; University of Maryland, associate professor of English; Oxford University, tutor in English, reader, lecturer, professor of renaissance literature. Writer. **Publications:** Milton and the Revolutionary Reader, 1994; Gender, Literature and the English Revolution, 1995; Literature and Dissent in Milton's England, 2003; (ed. with E. Sauer) Milton and Toleration, 2007; (ed.) Complete Works of John Milton, forthcoming. **Address:** Oxford University, St. Edmund Hall, St. Cross Bldg., Oxford, OX OX1 3UQ, England. **Online address:** sharon.achinstein@seh.ox.ac.uk

ACKELSBERG, Martha A. American (born United States), b. 1946. **Genres:** Politics/Government, Urban Studies, Women's Studies And Issues, Philosophy. **Career:** Smith College, lecturer, 1972-76, assistant professor, 1976-80, associate professor, 1980-87, professor of government, 1987-, professor of women's studies, 1995-, Five College Fortieth Anniversary professor, 2006-07, William R. Kenan, Jr. professor, 2007-, Programa de Estudios Hispanicos-Cordoba, resident director, 2010-11; University of Sussex, visiting lecturer, 1977; Radcliffe College, Bunting Institute, fellow, 1983-84; Harvard University, Center for European Studies, faculty associate, 1983-84; University of Massachusetts, visiting professor, 1989, 2007; Rutgers University, Walt Whitman Center for the Culture and Politics of Democracy, visiting fellow, 1992-93. Writer. **Publications:** (Ed. with R. Bartlett and R. Buchele) Women, Welfare and Higher Education: Toward Comprehensive Policies, 1988; Free Women of Spain: Anarchism and the Struggle for the Emancipation of Women, 1991; Mujeres Libres: El anarquismo y la lucha por la emancipacion de las mujeres, 1999; Mujeres Libres: L'attualita della lotta delle donne anarchiche nella rivoluzione spagnola, 2005; Resisting Citizenship: Feminist Essays on Politics, Community, and Democrary, 2009; La vie sera mille fois plus belle: Les Mujeres Libres espagnoles et l'emancipation des femmes, 2010. Contributor to periodicals. **Address:** Department of Government, Smith College, Rm. 104, 10 Prospect St., Northampton, MA 01063, U.S.A. **Online address:** mackelsb@smith.edu

ACKER, James R. American (born United States), b. 1951. **Genres:** Law, Social Sciences. **Career:** Loflin, Loflin & Acker, attorney-at-law, 1976-80; State University of New York, University at Albany, School of Criminal Justice, lecturer, 1983-88, assistant professor, 1988-94, associate dean, 1991-95, 2004-06, associate professor, 1994-99, professor, 1999-2004, interim dean, 2000-02, distinguished teaching professor, 2004-, Department of Biological Sciences, faculty, Capital Punishment Research Initiative, co-director. Writer. **Publications:** NONFICTION: (with R. Irving) Basic Legal Research for Criminal Justice and the Social Sciences, 1998; (ed. with R.M. Bohm and C.S. Lanier) America's Experiment with Capital Punishment: Reflections on the Past, Present, and Future of the Ultimate Penal Sanction, 1998; (with D.C. Brody) Criminal Procedure: A Contemporary Perspective, 1999, 2nd ed., 2004; (with D.C. Brody and W.A. Logan) Criminal Law, 2001, 2nd ed., 2010; (with E.B. Acker) Two Voices on the Legal Rights of America's Youth, 2004; (ed. with D.R. Karp and J.B. Warshaw) Wounds That Do Not Bind: Victim-Based Perspectives on the Death Penalty, 2006; Criminal Law, 2008; Scottsboro and Its Legacy: The Cases That Challenged American Legal and Social Justice, 2008; (ed. with C.S. Lanier and W.J. Bowers) The Future of America's Death Penalty: An Agenda for the Next Generation of Capital Punishment Research, 2009; (with D.C. Brody and W.A. Logan) Criminal Law, 2009; (with A.D. Redlich) Wrongful Conviction: Law, Science, and Policy, 2011. Contributor to books and journals. **Address:** School of Criminal Justice, University at Albany, State University of New York, 221B Draper Hall, 135 Western Ave., Albany, NY 12222, U.S.A. **Online address:** acker@albany.edu

ACKERLY, Brooke A. (Brooke Ann Ackerly). American (born United States), b. 1966?. **Genres:** Social Sciences, Women's Studies And Issues. **Career:** University of California, Department of political science, visiting assistant professor, 1997-2000; University of Southern California, Center for International Studies, post-doctoral research fellow, 2000-01; Vanderbilt University, Women's and Gender Studies Program, faculty, Department of Political Science, assistant professor, 2001-07, associate professor of philosophy, 2007-. Writer. **Publications:** Political Theory and Feminist Social Criticism, 2000; (ed. with M. Stern and J. True) Feminist Methodologies for International Relations, 2006; Universal Human Rights in a World of Difference, 2008; (with J. True) Doing Feminist Research in Political and Social Science, 2010; Dangerous Dissections, forthcoming. **Address:** Department of Political Science, Vanderbilt University, PO Box 1817, Sta. B, Nashville, TN 37235-1817, U.S.A. **Online address:** brooke.ackerly@vanderbilt.edu

ACKERLY, Brooke Ann. *See* **ACKERLY, Brooke A.**

ACKERMAN, Diane. American (born United States), b. 1948. **Genres:** Poetry, Adult Non-fiction, Children's Non-fiction. **Career:** College of William and Mary, writer-in-residence, 1982-83; Washington University, Writer's Program, director, 1984-86; Cornell University, Society for the Humanities, professor, 1999-, visiting writer; University of Richmond, National Endowment for the Humanities distinguished professor of English, 2001; Duke University, poet-in-residence, 2006; Columbia University, visiting writer; University of Pittsburgh, visiting writer. **Publications:** POETRY: The Planets: A Cosmic Pastoral, 1976; Wife of Light, 1978; Lady Faustus, 1983; Reverse Thunder, 1988; Jaguar of Sweet Laughter: New and Selected Poems, 1991; I Praise My Destroyer, 1998; Origami Bridges: Poems of Psychoanalysis and Fire, 2002; Animal Sense (for children), 2003. OTHERS: Twilight of the Tenderfoot: A Western Memoir, 1980; On Extended Wings, 1985; A Natural History of the Senses, 1990; The Moon by Whale Light, 1992; A Natural History of Love, 1994; Monk Seal Hideaway (children's nonfiction), 1995; The Rarest of the Rare, 1995; A Slender Thread, 1997; Bats: Shadows in the Night, 1997; (ed. with J. Mackin) The Book of Love, 1998; Deep Play, 1999; The Senses Of Animals:Poems, 2000; Cultivating Delight, 2001; Alchemy of Mind, 2004; Within the Stone: Photography, 2004; The Zookeeper's Wife, 2007; Dawn Light: Dancing with Cranes and Other Ways to Start the Day, 2009; One Hundred Names for Love: A Stroke, a Marriage and the Language of Healing, 2011. Works appear in anthologies. Contributor to journals. **Address:** William Morris Endeavor Entertainment, 1325 Ave. of the Americas, New York, NY 10019, U.S.A. **Online address:** inkdream@hotmail.com

ACKERMAN, James D. American (born United States), b. 1950. **Genres:** Horticulture, Botany. **Career:** University of Puerto Rico, Department of Biology, professor, 1981-. Writer. **Publications:** The Orchids of Puerto Rico and the Virgin Islands, 1992; An Orchid Flora of Puerto Rico and the Virgin Islands, 1995; (intro.) The Orchids of Cuba, 2005. Contributor of articles to journals. **Address:** Department of Biology, University of Puerto Rico, FB-233, PO Box 23360, San Juan, PR 00931-3360, U.S.A. **Online address:** jdackerman@uprrp.edu

ACKERMAN, James S(loss). American (born United States), b. 1919. **Genres:** Architecture, Art/Art History. **Career:** Yale University, part-time instructor, 1946-48; American Academy in Rome, research fellow, 1949-52; University of California, assistant professor, 1952-, professor, through 1960; Art Bulletin, editor-in-chief, 1956-60; Harvard University, professor, 1960-90, chairman, 1963-68, 1982-84, Arthur Kingsley Porter professor of fine arts, 1982-90, emeritus, 1990-; Cambridge University, Slade professor of fine arts and fellow, 1969-70; Columbia University, Meyer Shapiro professor, 1989-90; New York University, adjunct professor, 1992. **Publications:** The Cortile del Belvedere, 1964; The Architecture of Michelangelo, 1961, 2nd ed., 1986;

(with R. Carpenter) Art and Archaeology, 1963; Palladio, 1967, 3rd ed., 2008; Palladio's Villas, 1967; The Villa: Form and Ideology of Country Houses, 1990; Distance Points: Essays in Theory and Renaissance Art and Architecture, 1991; Origins, Imitation, Conventions, 2002. **Address:** Harvard University, 12 Coolidge Hill Rd., Cambridge, MA 02138, U.S.A. **Online address:** jsackerm@fas.harvard.edu

ACKERMAN, Jennifer G. American (born United States), b. 1959?. **Genres:** Natural History, Travel/Exploration. **Career:** National Geographic Society, staff writer and researcher, 1982-89; writer, 1989-; The Curious Naturalist, editor-in-chief, 1991; University of Virginia Press, editorial board, 1998-2002. **Publications:** The Curious Naturalist, 1991; Notes from the Shore, 1995; Chance in the House of Fate: A Natural History of Heredity, 2001; Sex Sleep Eat Drink Dream: A Day in the Life of Your Body, 2007; (with M.E. Nelson) Strong Women's Guide to Total Health, 2010; Ah-Choo! The Uncommon Life of Your Common Cold, 2010. Works appear in anthologies. **Address:** Melanie Jackson Agency, 41 W 72nd St., Apt. 3F, New York, NY 10023, U.S.A. **Online address:** inquiries@jenniferackerman.net

ACKERMAN, Lowell J. American/Canadian (born Canada), b. 1956. **Genres:** Animals/Pets, Adult Non-fiction, Crafts, Sciences. **Career:** Dermvet Inc., president, 1985-; PHI Inc., staff, 1990-; Mesa Veterinary Hospital Ltd., Department of Clinical Resources, director, 1998-; Bizvet Inc., team leader. Veterinarian and writer. **Publications:** Practical Canine Dermatology, 1989; Practical Equine Dermatology, 1989; Practical Feline Dermatology, 1989; Healthy Dog, 1993; Guide to Skin and Haircoat Problems in Dogs, 1994; Dr. Ackerman's Book of Boxers, 1996; Dr. Ackerman's Book of Cocker Spaniels, 1996; Dr. Ackerman's Book of Collies, 1996; Dr. Ackerman's Book of Dachshunds, 1996; Dr. Ackerman's Book of Dalmatians, 1996; Dr. Ackerman's Book of Doberman Pinscher, 1996; Dr. Ackerman's Book of Great Danes, 1996; Dr. Ackerman's Book of Poodles, 1996; Dr. Ackerman's Book of Shar-Pei, 1996; Dr. Ackerman's Book of ShihTzu, 1996; Dr. Ackerman's Book of the German Shepherd, 1996; Dr. Ackerman's Book of the Golden Retriever, 1996; Dr. Ackerman's Book of the Labrador Retriever, 1996; Dr. Ackerman's Book of the Rottweiler, 1996; Dr. Ackerman's Book of the Yorkshire Terrier, 1996; (with G.M. Landsberge and W. Hunthausen) Handbook of Behaviour Problems of the Dog and Cat, 1997, 2nd ed., 2003; (with G.H. Nesbitt) Canine and Feline Dermatology: Diagnosis and Treatment, 1998; (Medical advisor) Dogs: The Ultimate Care Guide: Good Health, Loving Care, Maximum Longevity, 1998; Canine Nutrition: What Every Owner, Breeder and Trainer Should Know, 1999; The Genetic Connection: A Guide to Health Problems in Purebred Dogs, 1999, 2nd ed., 2011; (with A. Moore) The Guilt-free Guide for on-the-Go Dog Lovers, 2002; (with A. Moore) Happy Dog: How Busy People Care for Their Dogs: A Stress-free Guide for All Dog Owners, 2003; (with G. Landsberg and W. Hunthausen) Handbook of Behavior Problems of the Dog and Cat, 2003. EDITOR AND COMPILER: Skin and Coat Care for Your Dog, 1995; (with G. Landsberg and W. Hunthausen) Dog Behavior and Training: Veterinary Advice for Owners, 1996; Skin and Coat Care for Your Cat, 1996; (with G. Landsberg and W. Hunthausen) Cat Behavior and Training: Veterinary Advice for Owners, 1996; The Biology, Husbandry and Health Care of Reptiles, 1997. EDITOR: Owner's Guide to Cat Health, 1996; Cat Health Encyclopedia, 1998; Blackwell's Five-Minute Veterinary Practice Management Consult, 2007. Contributor of articles to journals. **Address:** Mesa Veterinary Hospital, 858 N Country Club Dr., Mesa, AZ 85201, U.S.A.

ACKERMAN, Michael J. American (born United States), b. 1946. **Genres:** History, Sciences. **Career:** Naval Medical Research Institute, Hyperbaric Medicine and Physiology Department, research physiologist, Biomedical Engineering and Computing Branch, division head, 1979-87; National Library of Medicine, branch chief, 1987-92, division chief, 1992-94, assistant director for high performance computing and communications, 1994-; George Washington University, adjunct associate professor, 1987-; Uniformed Services University of the Health Sciences, assistant professor, 2000-. Writer and educator. **Publications:** (with B.A. Rifkin and J. Folkenberg) Human Anatomy: From the Renaissance to the Digital Age, 2006. **Address:** National Library of Medicine, Rm. B1N-30, Bldg. 38A, 8600 Rockville Pke., Bethesda, MD 20894-0001, U.S.A. **Online address:** ackerman@nlm.nih.gov

ACKERMAN, Susan Yoder. American (born United States), b. 1945. **Genres:** Children's Fiction, Children's Non-fiction, inspirational/Motivational Literature, Local History/Rural Topics, Autobiography/Memoirs. **Career:** Teacher, 1966-67, 1969-72, 1979-80, 1984-86, 1989-96; Newport News, director, 1989-90; Island Institute, resident fellow, 2000; principal, 2000-; Warwick River Christian School, principal. Writer. **Publications:** Copper Moons, 1990; The Flying Pie and Other Stories, 1996; See This Wonderful Thing, 1998. Contributor to periodicals. **Address:** 524 Marlin Dr., Newport News, VA 23602, U.S.A. **Online address:** susan@ackerman.net

ACKLAND, Len. American (born United States), b. 1944. **Genres:** History. **Career:** AND Corp., researcher, 1967-69; Brookings Institute, research assistant, 1969-71; reporter and editor, 1971-73; Cervi's Journal, reporter, 1973-75; Des Moines Register, reporter, 1975-78; Chicago Tribune, reporter, 1978-84; Bulletin of the Atomic Scientists, editor, 1984-91; University of Colorado, School of Journalism and Mass Communication, associate professor, 1991-, Center for Environmental Journalism, director, 1992-, co-director. **Publications:** (Ed. with S. Brown) Why Are We Still in Vietnam?, 1970. HISTORY: Credibility Gap: A Digest of the Pentagon Papers, 1972; (ed. with S. McGuire) Assessing The Nuclear Age: Selections From The Bulletin of the Atomic Scientists, 1986; Making a Real Killing: Rocky Flats and the Nuclear West, 1999. **Address:** School of Journalism & Mass Communication, University of Colorado, 1511 University Ave., Armory 213B, 478 UCB, Boulder, CO 80309, U.S.A. **Online address:** ackland@spot.colorado.edu

ACKMANN, Martha (A.). American (born United States), b. 1951. **Genres:** Air/Space Topics, Women's Studies And Issues. **Career:** Mount Holyoke College, Department of Gender Studies, lecturer in women's studies, 1987-, senior lecturer in gender studies, Weissman Center for Leadership, Community-Based Learning Program, director; University of Nebraska Press, Legacy: A Journal of American Women Writers, founding editor. Journalist. **Publications:** The Mercury 13: The Untold Story of Thirteen American Women and the Dream of Space Flight, 2003; Curveball: The Remarkable Story of Toni Stone, the First Woman to Play Professional Baseball in the Negro League, 2010. Contributor to periodicals. **Address:** c/o Ellen Geiger, The Francis Goldin Agency, 57 E 11th St., Ste. 5B, New York, NY 10003-4605, U.S.A. **Online address:** martha@marthaackmann.com

ACKROYD, Peter. British (born England), b. 1949. **Genres:** Novels, Poetry, Literary Criticism And History, Biography, Young Adult Non-fiction, History. **Career:** Spectator, literary editor, 1973-77, managing editor, 1977-81; Times, television critic, 1977-81; The Times, chief book reviewer and regular broadcaster for radio, 1986-. **Publications:** POETRY: Ouch, 1971; London Lickpenny, 1973; Country Life, 1978; The Diversions of Purley and Other Poems, 1987. NOVELS: The Great Fire of London: A Novel, 1982; The Last Testament of Oscar Wilde, 1983; Hawksmoor, 1985, 2nd ed., 1986; Chatterton, 1988; First Light, 1989; English Music, 1992; The House of Doctor Dee, 1993, 2nd ed., 1994; Dan Leno and the Limehouse Golem, 1994 in US as The Trial of Elizabeth Cree: A Novel of the Limehouse Murders, 1995; Milton in America, 1997; The Plato Papers, 2000; The Clerkenwell Tales, 2003; Kingdom of the Dead, 2004; The Mystery of Edwin Drood, 2004; The Lambs of London: A Novel, 2006; The Fall of Troy: A Novel, 2007. NONFICTION: Notes for a New Culture: An Essay on Modernism, 1976; Dressing Up: Transvestism and Drag: The History of an Obsession, 1979; Ezra Pound and His World, 1981; T.S. Eliot: A Life, 1984; (ed.) P.E.N. New Fiction I, 1984; (intro.) Dickens' London: An Imaginative Vision, 1987; Dickens, 1992; Introduction to Dickens, 1992; (intro.) Recent Works, 1994; Blake, 1995; (ed.) The Picture of Dorian Gray, 1995; The Life of Thomas More, 1998; London: The Biography, 2000; The Collection, 2001; Dickens: Public Life and Private Passion, 2002; Albion: The Origins of the English Imagination, 2003; Cities of Blood, 2004; Chaucer, 2005; Ancient Greece, 2005; Ancient Rome, 2005; Shakespeare: The Biography, 2005; Isaac Newton, 2006; J.M.W. Turner, 2006; Foundation: The History of England, vol. I, 2011; Wilkie Collins, 2012. OTHERS: The Mystery of Charles Dickens (play), 2002; Escape from Earth (juvenile fiction), 2003; The Beginning (juvenile fiction), 2003; (intro.) A Christmas Dinner by Charles Dickens, 2007; Thames: The Biography, 2007; Poe: A Life Cut Short, 2008; Casebook of Victor Frankenstein, 2009; Venice: Pure City, 2009; (intro.) Brief Guide to William Shakespeare, 2010; The English Ghost, 2010; London Under: The Secret History Beneath the Streets, 2011. Contributor to periodicals. **Address:** Anthony Sheil Associates Ltd., 43 Doughty St., London, GL WC1N 2LF, England.

ACOSTA, Carlos. Cuban (born Cuba), b. 1973. **Genres:** Dance/Ballet. **Career:** English National Ballet, principal dancer, 1991-92; National Ballet of Cuba, principal dancer, 1992-93; Houston Ballet, principal dancer, 1993-98; Royal Ballet of England, principal dancer, 1998-. Writer, ballet dancer and choreographer. **Publications:** No Way Home: A Cuban Dancer's Tale, 2007 in US as No Way Home: A Dancer's Journey from the Streets of Havana to the

Stages of the World, 2008. **Address:** Valid Worldwide Ltd., Aviation House, 1-7 Sussex Rd., Haywards Heath, WS RH16 4DZ, England. **Online address:** info@carlosacosta.com

ACUFF, Jerry. American (born United States), b. 1949?. **Genres:** Business/Trade/Industry. **Career:** Hoechst-Roussel Pharmaceuticals, salesman, vice president, general manager; JBI Associates (healthcare consulting firm), founder, 1995-2001; Delta Point Inc., founder and principal, president; Dartmouth College, Amos Tuck School of Business, executive-in-residence; Virginia Military Institute, Athletic Foundation, board governor. Writer. **Publications:** (With W. Wood) The Relationship Edge in Business: Connecting with Customers and Colleagues When It Counts 2004, 3rd ed. as The Relationship Edge: The Key to Strategic Influence and Selling Succes 2011; (with W. Wood) Stop Acting like a Seller and Start Thinking like a Buyer: Improve Sales Effectiveness by Helping Customers Buy, 2007. Contributor to periodicals. **Address:** Delta Point Inc., 12196 E Sand Hills Rd., Scottsdale, AZ 85255, U.S.A. **Online address:** jacuff@gottochange.com

ACZEL, Amir. *See* **ACZEL, Amir D.**

ACZEL, Amir D. (Amir Aczel). American/Israeli (born Israel), b. 1950. **Genres:** Mathematics/Statistics, Adult Non-fiction, Sciences, Physics. **Career:** University of Alaska, associate professor of mathematics, 1982-88; Bentley College, associate professor, professor of mathematics, 1988-2006; John Simon Guggenheim Memorial Foundation, fellow; Boston University, research fellow. Writer. **Publications:** (With J. Sounderpandian) Complete Business Statistics, 1989, 7th ed., 2009; How to Beat the IRS: Strategies to Avoid and Survive an Audit, 1994, 2nd rev. ed. as How to Beat the IRS at Its Own Game: Strategies to Avoid and Fight an Audit, 1995; Statistics: Concepts and Applications, 1995; Fermats Last Theorem, 1996; Probability 1: Why There Must Be Intelligent Life in the Universe, 1998; Gods Equation: Einstein, Relativity and the Expanding Universe, 1999; Mystery of the Aleph: Mathematics, the Kabbalah, and the Search for Infinity, 2000; The Riddle of the Compass: The Invention that Changed the World, 2001; Entanglement: The Greatest Mystery in Physics, 2002; Pendulum: Leon Foucault and the Triumph of Science, 2003; Chance: A Guide to Gambling, Love, the Stock Market, and Just About Everything Else, 2004; Descartes Secret Notebook: A True Tale of Mathematics, Mysticism and the Quest to Understand the Universe, 2005; The Artist and the Mathematician: The Story of Nicolas Bourbaki, the Genius Mathematician Who Never Existed, 2006; The Jesuit and the Skull: Teilhard de Chardin, Evolution and the Search for Peking Man, 2007; Cave and the Cathedral: How a Real-life Indiana Jones and a Renegade Scholar Decoded the Ancient Art of Man, 2009; Uranium Wars: The Scientific Rivalry that Created the Nuclear Age, 2009; Present at the Creation: The Story of CERN and the Large Hadron Collider, 2010. Contributor to periodicals. **Address:** Department of Mathematics, Bentley College, 175 Forest St, Waltham, MA 02452, U.S.A. **Online address:** aaczel@bentley.edu

ADAIR, Aaron J. American (born United States), b. 1980. **Genres:** Autobiography/Memoirs, Biography. **Career:** Writer. **Publications:** You Don't Know Where I've Been (autobiography), 2003. **Address:** 1111 Oak Tree St., Apt. 215D, Norman, OK 73072-8071, U.S.A. **Online address:** changing_lives_forever@aaronadair.com

ADAIR, Cherry. American/South African (born South Africa), b. 1951. **Genres:** Novels, Young Adult Fiction, inspirational/Motivational Literature. **Career:** Romance novelist. **Publications:** The Mercenary, 1994; Kiss and Tell, 2000; Seducing Mr. Right, 2001; Hide and Seek, 2001; In Too Deep, 2002; Take Me, 2002; Out of Sight, 2003; (with A. Stuart and M. Jensen) Date with a Devil, 2004; On Thin Ice, 2005; (with J. Shalvis and J.E. Leto) Dare Me, 2005; (L. Banks, P. Britton and K. Roberts) Red Hot Santa, 2005; Hot Ice: A Novel, 2005; White Heat: A Novel, 2007; (with L. Leigh and C. Gerard) Rescue Me, 2008; Night Shadow, 2008; Night Fall, 2008; Night Secrets, 2008; Black Magic, 2010; Tropical Heat, 2010; Dangerous Magic, 2010; (with L. O'Clare and G. Showalter) The Bodyguard, 2010; Chemeleon, 2011; Playing for Keeps, 2011; Undertow, 2011; Hush, 2011; Riptide, 2011; Vortex, 2012; Afterglow, 2012. **Address:** PO Box 8591, Covington, WA 98042, U.S.A. **Online address:** cherry@cherryadair.com

ADAIR, Christy. British (born England), b. 1949. **Genres:** Cultural/Ethnic Topics, Dance/Ballet, Women's Studies And Issues. **Career:** Teacher, 1971-; University of Leeds, faculty; Northern School of Contemporary Dance, faculty; University of Hull, faculty; York St. John University, professor of dance studies; Research in Dance Education Journal, Dancelines, editor. **Publications:** Women and Dance: Sylphs and Sirens, 1992; Dancing the Black Question: The Phoenix Dance Company Phenomenon, 2007. Contributor of articles to periodicals. **Address:** York St. John University, Lord Mayor's Walk, York, NY YO31 7EX, England. **Online address:** c.adair@yorksj.ac.uk

ADAIR, Daryl John. Australian (born Australia), b. 1960. **Genres:** Young Adult Non-fiction. **Career:** University of Technology Sydney, UTS: Business, Sports Management, associate professor, 2007-; Flinders University, De Montfort University, faculty; University of Queensland, faculty; University of Canberra, faculty; Australian Centre for Olympic Studies, associate director. Writer. **Publications:** NONFICTION: (with W. Vamplew) Sport in Australian History, 1997; (with M. Cronin) The Wearing of the Green: A History of St. Patrick's Day, 2002; (ed. with B.W. Ritchie) Sport Tourism: Interrelationships, Impacts and Issues, 2004; (ed. with B. Coe and N. Gouth) Beyond the Torch: The Olympics and Australian Culture, 2005; (ed.) Sport, Race, and Ethnicity: Narratives of Difference and Diversity, 2011. Contributor to books. **Address:** Cosmopolitan Civil Societies Research Centre, UTS Business, Rm. KG01.06.76, PO Box 222, Lindfield, NW 2070, Australia. **Online address:** daryl.adair@uts.edu.au

ADAIR, Jack. *See* **PAVEY, Don.**

ADAIR, Vivyan Campbell. American (born United States), b. 1953. **Genres:** Novels, Social Commentary, Women's Studies And Issues, Genealogy/Heraldry, Gay And Lesbian Issues, Education. **Career:** University of Washington, Department of English, lecturer and teaching associate, 1991-99, Department of Women's Studies, lecturer and teaching associate, 1991-99; North Seattle College, instructor, 1998; Hamilton College, Center for Bilingual and Multicultural Studies, instructor, 1993, assistant professor, 1998-2003, ACCESS Project, founder and director, 2000-, associate professor, 2004-, Elihu Root endowed chair in women's studies, 2002-09. Writer. **Publications:** From Good Ma to Welfare Queen: A Genealogy of the Poor Woman in American Literature, Photography and Culture, 2000; (ed. with S.L. Dahlberg) Reclaiming Class: Women, Poverty and the Promise of Higher Education in America, 2003. Contributor to books. **Address:** Womens Studies Program, Hamilton College, 198 College Hill Rd., Clinton, NY 13323, U.S.A. **Online address:** vadair@hamilton.edu

ADAM, David. British (born England), b. 1936. **Genres:** inspirational/Motivational Literature, Theology/Religion, Cultural/Ethnic Topics, Music. **Career:** National Coal Board, coal miner, 1951-54, chaplain. Writer and educator. **Publications:** The Cry of the Deer: Meditations on the Hymn of St. Patrick, 1987; The Edge of Glory: Prayers in the Celtic Tradition, 1988; Tides and Seasons: Modern Prayers in the Celtic Tradition, 1989; The Eye of the Eagle: Meditations on the Hymn Be Thou My Vision, 1990; (with J. Douglas) Visions of Glory for Voices (music), 1990; Border Lands: The Best of David Adam's Celtic Vision, 1991; Power Lines: Celtic Prayers about Work, 1992; Fire of the North: The Illustrated Life of St. Cuthbert, 1993; The Open Gate: Celtic Prayers for Growing Spiritually, 1994; The Rhythm of Life: Celtic Christian Prayer, 1996 in US as The Rhythm of Life: Celtic Daily Prayer, 1997; (comp. and intro.) The Wisdom of the Celts: A Compilation, 1996; A Celtic Daily Prayer Book: A Compilation, 1997 in US as A Celtic Book of Prayer, 1997; Flame in My Heart: St. Aidan for Today, 1998; Clouds and Glory: Prayers for the Church Year; Year A, 1998; On Eagles' Wings: The Life and Spirit of St. Chad, 1999; Traces of Glory: Prayers for the Church Year; Year B, 1999; Forward to Freedom: A Journey into God, 1999 in US as Forward to Freedom: From Exodus to Easter, 2001; A Desert in the Ocean: God's Call to Adventurous Living in US as A Desert in the Ocean: The Spiritual Journey according to St. Brendan the Navigator, 2000; Glimpses of Glory: Prayers for the Church Year, 2000; (comp.) A Celtic Psaltery: Psalms from the Celtic Tradition, 2001; Island of Light: An Illustrated Collection of Prayers, 2002; Walking the Edges: Celtic Saints along the Roman Wall, 2003; The Road of Life: Reflections on Searching and Longing, 2004; (contrib.) You are My God, 2006; Rhythm of Life: Celtic Daily Prayer, 2007; Living in Two Kingdoms, 2009. **Address:** The Vicarage, Holy Island, Berwick-upon-Tweed, TD15 2RX, England.

ADAM, Paul. Australian/British (born England), b. 1951. **Genres:** Environmental Sciences/Ecology. **Career:** Cambridge University, Emmanuel College, research fellow, 1975-78; University of New South Wales, lecturer, 1978-83, senior lecturer, 1983-90, associate professor of biology, 1991-. Writer. **Publications:** Coastal Wetlands of New South Wales, 1985; New South

Wales Rainforests, 1987; Saltmarsh Ecology, 1990; Australian Rainforests, 1992. **Address:** School of Biological, Earth & Environmental Sci., University of New South Wales, Sydney, NW 2052, Australia. **Online address:** p.adam@unsw.edu.au

ADAMCHAK, Raoul W. American (born United States), b. 1953. **Genres:** Agriculture/Forestry. **Career:** IPM Practitioners, co-editor; University of California, IBM Manual Group, senior writer, Agriculture Sustainability Institute, Student Farm, market garden, CSA, coordinator; Full Belly Farm, partner. **Publications:** (With P.C. Ronald) Tomorrow's Table: Organic Farming, Genetics and the Future of Food, 2008. **Address:** Agriculture Sustainability Institute, University of California, 1 Shields Ave., Davis, CA 95616, U.S.A. **Online address:** rwadamchak@ucdavis.edu

ADAMEC, Christine. American (born United States), b. 1949. **Genres:** Adult Non-fiction, How-to Books, Human Relations/Parenting, Ghost Writer. **Career:** State of New Hampshire, Division of Welfare, training officer, 1974-77; freelance writer, 1981-. **Publications:** There are Babies to Adopt: A Resource Guide for Prospective Parents, 1987, 2nd ed., 1996; (with W.L. Pierce) The Encyclopedia of Adoption, 1991, 3rd ed., 2007; (ed.) How to Adopt Your Baby Privately: The Nationwide Directory of Adoption Attorneys, 1992-1993, 1992; Start and Run a Profitable Freelance Writing Business: Your Step-by-Step Business Plan, 1994; How to Live with a Mentally Ill Person: A Handbook of Day-To-Day Strategies, 1996; (with J.L. Thomas) Do You Have Attention Deficit Disorder?, 1996; When Your Pet Dies, 1996, rev. ed. as When Your Pet Dies: Dealing with Your Grief and Helping Your Children Cope, 2000; Is Adoption for You?: The Information You Need to Make the Right Choice, 1998; Complete Idiot's Guide to Adoption, 1998, 2nd ed., 2004; Unofficial Guide to Eldercare, 1999; Adoption Option Complete Handbook, 2000-2001, 1999; Moms with ADD: A Self-Help Manual, 2000; Writing Freelance, 2000; (with R.E. Clark and J.F. Clark) Encyclopedia of Child Abuse, 2001, 3rd ed., 2007; (with A. Minocha) How to Stop Heartburn: Simple Ways to Heal Heartburn and Acid Reflux, 2001; (with W.A. Petit Jr.) Encyclopedia of Diabetes, 2002, 2nd ed., 2011; (with R. Staud) Fibromyalgia for Dummies, 2002, 2nd ed., 2007; (with J. Kandel) Encyclopedia of Senior Health and Well-Being, 2003; (with P.H. Lange) Prostate Cancer for Dummies, 2003; (with A. Adesman) Parenting Your Adopted Child: A Positive Approach to Building a Strong Family, 2004; (with A. Minocha) The Encyclopedia of the Digestive System and Digestive Disorders, 2004, (with A. Minocha) 2nd ed., 2011; (with W.A. Petit) Encyclopedia of Endocrine Diseases and Disorders, 2005; (with E. Gwinnell) Encyclopedia of Addictions and Addictive Behaviors, 2006; The Encyclopedia of Phobias, Fears and Anxieties, 3rd ed., (with R.M. Doctor and A.P. Kahn), 2008; (with E. Gwinnell) The Encyclopedia of Drug Abuse, 2008; Impulse Control Disorders, 2008; (with J. Kandel) Encyclopedia of Elder Care, 2009; (with M.S. Gold) Encyclopedia of Alcoholism and Alcohol Abuse, 2010; Pathological Gambling, 2010; (with I.D. Weiner) The Encyclopedia of Kidney Diseases and Disorders, 2011; Amphetamines and Methamphetamine, 2011; Pneumonia, 2011; Barbiturates and other Depressants, 2011. Contributor to periodicals. **Address:** 1921 Ohio St., Ste. 2 NE, Palm Bay, FL 32907, U.S.A. **Online address:** adamec@aol.com

ADAMEC, Ludwig W. American/Austrian (born Austria), b. 1924. **Genres:** Geography, History, International Relations/Current Affairs. **Career:** University of Arizona, professor, 1967-, now professor emeritus, Near Eastern Center, director, 1975-85; Afghanistan Journal, editor, 1973-75; Voice of America, Afghanistan Branch, chief, 1986-87. **Publications:** Afghanistan 1900-1923: A Diplomatic History, 1967; (with G. Grassmuck) Afghanistan: Some New Approaches, 1969; Tarikh-e Ravabet-e Siya-si-ye Afghanistan az Zaman-e Amir Abdur Rahman ta Isteqlal, 1970; Afghanistan's Foreign Affairs to the 20th Century: Relations with the U.S.S.R., Germany and Britain, 1974; Political and Historical Gazetteer of Afghanistan, 6 vols., 1972-85; Historical Gazetteer of Iran, 4 vols., 1976-88; Who is Who of Afghanistan, 1974; Biographical Dictionary of Contemporary Afghanistan, 1987; Historical Dictionary of Afghanistan, 1991, 3rd ed., 2003; Dictionary of Afghan Wars, Revolutions and Insurgencies, 1996, 2nd ed., 2005; Historical Dictionary of Islam, 2000, 2nd ed., 2009; The A to Z of Islam, 2002; (with F.A. Clements) Conflict in Afghanistan: An Encyclopedia, 2003. **Address:** Department of Near Eastern Studies, University of Arizona, Tucson, AZ 85721, U.S.A. **Online address:** adamec@u.arizona.edu

ADAMS, Abby. American (born United States), b. 1939. **Genres:** Horticulture, Homes/Gardens, Horror, Sciences. **Career:** Writer. **Publications:** An Uncommon Scold, 1989; The Gardener's Gripe Book: Musings, Advice and Comfort for Anyone Who Has Ever Suffered the Loss of a Petunia, 1995. **Address:** 681 Rte. 7, Ancram, NY 12502, U.S.A. **Online address:** abbywest@taconic.net

ADAMS, Carol J. American (born United States), b. 1951. **Genres:** Animals/Pets, Environmental Sciences/Ecology, Social Commentary, Theology/Religion, Women's Studies And Issues, How-to Books, Human Relations/Parenting, Literary Criticism And History, Social Commentary. **Career:** Women's Theological Coalition of the Boston Theological Institute, staff, 1974-75; Goddard College, Goddard-Cambridge Graduate Program in Social Change, Feminist Studies Program, field faculty, 1975-76; Chautauqua County Rural Ministry Inc., executive director, 1977-81, 1983-87; Chautauqua Institution, lecturer, 1977-85; State University of New York College, part-time lecturer, 1980-84; Perkins School of Theology, Southern Methodist University, visiting lecturer, 1989, 1991, 1993, 1999, 2001. Writer. **Publications:** The Sexual Politics of Meat: A Feminist-Vegetarian Critical Theory, 1990; Woman-Battering, 1994; Neither Man nor Beast: Feminism and the Defense of Animals, 1994; (with M.M. Fortune) Violence Against Women and Children: A Christian Theological Sourcebook, 1995; The Inner Art of Vegetarianism: Spiritual Practices for Body and Soul, 2000; Meditations on the Inner Art of Vegetarianism: Spiritual Practices for Body and Soul, 2001; (with B. Buchanan and S. Allison) Journey to Game land: How to Make a Board Game from Your Favorite Children's Book, 2001; Living Among Meat Eaters: The Vegetarian's Survival Handbook, 2001, 2nd ed., 2009; (intro.) Ethics of Diet: A Catena of Authorities Deprecatory of the Practice of Flesh-Eating, 2003; The Pornography of Meat, 2003; Help! My Child Stopped Eating Meat!: An A-Z Guide to Surviving a Conflict in Diets, 2004; Prayers for Animals, 2004; God Listens When You're Sad: Prayers When Your Animal Friend is Sick or Dies, 2005; God Listens to Your Love: Prayers for Living with Animal Friends, 2005; God Listens to Your Care: Prayers for all the Animals of the World, 2006; God Listens When You're Afraid: Prayers for When Animals Scare You, 2006; (with D. Buchanan and K. Gesch) The Bedside, Bathtub & Armchair Companion to Frankenstein, 2007; (with P. Breitman) How to Eat Like a Vegetarian Even If You Never Want to Be One, 2008; (with D. Buchanan and K. Gesch) The Bedside, Bathtub and Armchair Guide to Jane Austen, 2008. EDITOR: Ecofeminism and the Sacred, 1993; (with J. Donovan) Animals and Women: Feminist Theoretical Explorations, 1995; (with J. Donovan) Beyond Animal Rights: A Feminist Caring Ethic for the Treatment of Animals, 1996; (with J. Donovan) The Feminist Care Tradition in Animal Ethics: A Reader, 2007. Contributor of articles to books, journals and periodicals. **Address:** 814 Grinnell Dr., Richardson, TX 75081, U.S.A. **Online address:** cja@caroljadams.com

ADAMS, Cat. *See* **CLAMP, Cathy.**

ADAMS, Charles. American/Canadian (born Canada), b. 1930. **Genres:** Economics, History, Law, Money/Finance, Photography. **Career:** Attorney, 1957-71; Cayman Islands International College, professor of history, 1971-75; Ludwig von Mises Institute, speaker. Writer. **Publications:** Fight, Flight, Fraud: The Story of Taxation, 1982; For Good and Evil: The Impact of Taxes on the Course of Civilization, 1993, 2nd ed., 1999; Those Dirty Rotten Taxes, 1998; When in the Course of Human Events: Arguing the Case for Southern Secession, 2000; Slavery, Secession, and Civil War: Views from the United Kingdom and Europe, 1856-1865, 2007. Contributor to periodicals. **Address:** Ludwig von Mises Institute, 518 W Magnolia Ave., Auburn, AL 36832-4501, U.S.A. **Online address:** cwadams@nexicom.net

ADAMS, Charles J. American (born United States), b. 1947. **Genres:** Mythology/Folklore, Travel/Exploration, Sports/Fitness, Theology/Religion, Ghost Writer, Mystery/Crime/Suspense. **Career:** U.S. Navy, journalist, 1966-68; Berks County Record, editor, 1968-76; WEEU-Radio, broadcaster, 1978-; Exeter House Books, founder, 1982; Reading Eagle-Times, chief travel correspondent, 1985-; Reading Public Library, president, 1992-94. **Publications:** (Ed.) A reader's Guide to the Great Religions, 1965, 2nd ed., 1977; (ed.) Iranian Civilization and Culture: Essays in Honour of the 2, 500th Anniversary of the Founding of the Persian Empire, 1972; (J.K. O'Dea and T.F. O'Dea) Judaism, Christianity and Islam, 1972; Ghost Stories of Berks County, 1982; Ghost Stories of Berks County, Book Two, 1984; (with D.J. Seibold) Legends of Long Beach Island, 1985; (with D.J. Seibold) Shipwrecks Off Ocean City, 1986; (co-ed.) The Encyclopedia of Religion, 1987, 2nd ed., 2005; (with D.J. Seibold) Shipwrecks and Legends 'round Cape May, 1987; (with G.S. Clothier) Book Three, 1988; Cape May Ghost Stories, 1988; Ghost Stories of Berks County, Book Three, 1988; (with D.J. Seibold) Shipwrecks, Sea Stories and

Legends of the Delaware Coast, 1989; (with D.J. Seibold) Ghost Stories of the Delaware Coast, 1990; (with D.J. Seibold) Pocono Ghosts, Legends and Lore, 1991; Great Train Wrecks of Eastern Pennsylvania, 1992; (with D.J. Seibold) Ghost Stories of the Lehigh Valley, 1993; Pennsylvania Dutch Country Ghosts, Legends and Lore, 1994; (with B.E. Trapani) Ghost Stories of Pittsburgh and Allegheny County, 1994; (with D.J. Seibold) Shipwrecks near Barnegat Inlet, 2nd ed., 1995; Berks the Bizarre, 1995; A Day Away in Sovereign Country (travel book), 1995; Curtains (audience-participation murder mystery), 1995; Mysterious Cape May, 1996; New York City Ghost Stories, 1996; Philadelphia Ghost Stories, 1998; Bucks County Ghost Stories, 1999; Montgomery County Ghost Stories, 2000; Reading, 2000; Reading in Vintage Postcards, 2000; Ghost Stories of Chester County and the Brandywine Valley, 2001; Reading, Pa.: A Postcard History, 2001; Baseball in Reading, Arcadia, 2003; Ghost Stories of Delaware County, 2005; Tales from Baseballtown, 2006. **Address:** Exeter House Books, PO Box 6411, Wyomissing, PA 19610, U.S.A. **Online address:** gohaunting@aol.com

ADAMS, Colin C. American (born United States), b. 1956. **Genres:** Novellas/Short Stories, Adult Non-fiction, Mathematics/Statistics, Sciences. **Career:** Oregon State University, professor of mathematics, 1983-85; Williams College, professor of mathematics, 1985-; University of California-Santa Barbara, professor, 1988-89; University of California-Davis, professor, 1991-92. Writer. **Publications:** The Knot Book, 1994; (with J. Hass and A. Thompson) How to Ace Calculus: The Streetwise Guide, 1998; (ed.) Knot Theory and its Applications: Expository Articles on Current Research, 1998; (with J. Hass and A. Thompson) How to Ace the Rest of Calculus: The Streetwise Guide, 2001; Why Knot?, 2004; (with R. Franzosa) Introduction to Topology: Pure and Applied, 2007; Riot at the Calc Exam and Other Mathematically Bent Stories, 2009. **Address:** Department of Mathematics, Williams College, BSC 209, Bronfman Science Ctr., Williamstown, MA 01267, U.S.A. **Online address:** colin.adams@williams.edu

ADAMS, C. T. American (born United States) **Genres:** Novels, E-books, Science Fiction/Fantasy, Horror, Novellas/Short Stories, Romance/Historical. **Career:** Writer. **Publications:** (With C.L. Clamp) Road to Riches: The Great Railroad Race to Aspen, 2003; The Abyss: Dark Romance Anthology, 2003; Secrets, Fact or Fiction?, 2005; Magic's Design, 2009. TALES OF THE SAZI SERIES: (with C. Clamp): Hunter's Moon, 2004; Moon's Web, 2005; Captive Moon, 2006; Howling Moon, 2007; Moon's Fury, 2007; (with C. Clamp) Timeless Moon, 2008; Cold Moon Rising, 2009; Serpent Moon, 2010. THRALL SERIES: (with C. Clamp): Touch of Evil, 2006; Weirdly: A Collection of Strange Tales, 2007; Touch of Madness, 2007; Touch of Darkness, 2008; BLOOD SINGER SERIES: (with C. Clamp): Blood Song, 2010; Siren Song, 2010; Demon Song, 2011. **Address:** c/o Lucienne Diver, The Knight Agency, 570 East Ave., Madison, GA 30650, U.S.A. **Online address:** catadamsfans@gmail.com

ADAMS, Deborah. American (born United States), b. 1956. **Genres:** Mystery/Crime/Suspense, Young Adult Fiction. **Career:** Writer and lawyer. **Publications:** JESUS CREEK: All the Great Pretenders, 1992; All the Crazy Winters, 1992; All the Dark Disguises, 1993; All the Hungry Mothers, 1994; All the Deadly Beloved, 1995; All the Blood Relations, 1997; All the Dirty Cowards: A Jesus Creek Mystery, 2000; Kudzu and Corpses, 2010; Mystic Grits, 2010. **Address:** Oconee Spirit Press L.L.C., 714 Harrison Dr., Evans, GA 30809, U.S.A. **Online address:** dksadams@yahoo.com

ADAMS, E. C. *See* **ADAMS, Ernest Charles.**

ADAMS, Ernest Charles. (E. C. Adams). British (born England), b. 1926?. **Genres:** Technology, Architecture, Sciences, Engineering. **Career:** George Wimpey and Company Ltd., materials testing and concrete engineer, 1953-59; Crawley College of Further Education, lecturer, 1959-71; Leeds Polytechnic, lecturer, senior lecturer, 1971-84. Writer. **Publications:** Science in Building, 1964; Fundamentals of Building Science, 1980. **Address:** 10 Kenworthy Vale, Holt Pk., Adel, Leeds, WY LS16 7QG, England.

ADAMS, Eve. *See* **COONTS, Stephen (Paul).**

ADAMS, Gerald R. (Gerald Robert Adams). American (born United States), b. 1946. **Genres:** Sociology, Psychology, Education. **Career:** Utah State University, assistant professor of family and human development, 1975-78, associate professor of family and human development, 1978-81, professor of family and human development, 1982-90, Department of Family and Human Development, head, 1980-82, Cooperative Ph.D. Program in Developmental Psychology, chair, 1983-85, Laboratory for Research on Adolescence, research director, 1986-89, professor of family and human development and psychology, 1984-90; University of Guelph, Department of Family Studies, professor and chair, 1990-92, professor of family relations and human development, 1992-; West Virginia University, Division of Family Resources, visiting professor, 1994-95. Writer. **Publications:** (With T.P. Gullotta) Adolescent Life Experiences, 1983, 3rd ed., 1994; Understanding Research Method, 1985, 2nd ed., 1991; (with T.P. Gullotta and S. Alexander) Today's Marriages and Families: A Wellness Approach, 1986; (with T.P. Gullotta) Adolescent Life Experiences, 1989, (with T.P. Gullotta and C.M. Adams) 3rd ed., 1994; (with R. Montemayor and T.P. Gullotta) Psychosocial Development during Adolescence, 1996; (with J. Cote and S. Marshall) Parent/Adolescent Relationships and Identity Development: A Literature Review and Policy Statement, 2001. EDITOR: (with T.P. Gullotta and R. Montemayor) The Biology of Adolescent Behavior and Development, 1989; From Childhood to Adolescence, 1990; Developing Social Competency in Adolescence, 1990; Adolescent Identity Formation, 1992; Adolescent Sexuality, 1993; Adolescent Drug Misuse, 1994; Adolescent Development: The Essential Readings, 2000; (with T.P. Gullotta and C.A. Markstorm) Adolescent Experience, 2000; (with R. Montemayor and T.P. Gullotta) Adolescent Diversity in Ethnic, Economic and Cultural Contexts, 2000; (with M.D. Berzonsky) Blackwell Handbook of Adolescence, 2003; (with T.P. Gullotta) Handbook of Adolescent Behavioral Problems: Evidence-based Approaches to Prevention and Treatment, 2005; (with G. Cameron and N. Coady) Moving toward Positive Systems of Child and Family Welfare: Current Issues and Future Directions, 2007. **Address:** Department of Family Relations, University of Guelph, Guelph, ON N1G 2W1, Canada. **Online address:** gadams@uoguelph.ca

ADAMS, Gerald Robert. *See* **ADAMS, Gerald R.**

ADAMS, Gerry. Irish (born Ireland), b. 1948. **Genres:** Autobiography/Memoirs, Young Adult Non-fiction. **Career:** Sinn Fein Political Party, vice president, 1979-83, president, 1983-. Writer and politician. **Publications:** The Street and Other Stories (fiction), 1992. NON-FICTION: Falls Memories (autobiography), 1982 in US as Falls Memories: A Belfast Life, 1994; The Politics of Irish Freedom, 1986 in US as Free Ireland: Towards a Lasting Peace, 1994, rev. ed., 1995; A Pathway to Peace, 1988; Cage Eleven (autobiography), 1990; Who Fears to Speak-? The Story of Belfast and the 1916 Rising, 1991, rev. ed., 2001; Selected Writings, 1994; Before the Dawn: An Autobiography, 1997; An Irish Voice: The Quest for Peace, 1997; An Irish Journal, 2001; A Farther Shore: Ireland's Long Road to Peace in UK as Hope and History: Making Peace in Ireland, 2003; The New Ireland: A Vision for the Future, 2005; An Irish Eye, 2007. **Address:** Sinn Féin, 44 Parnell Sq., Dublin, 1, Ireland. **Online address:** paul.macmanus@sinn-fein.ie

ADAMS, Hazard. American (born United States), b. 1926. **Genres:** Novels, Poetry, Literary Criticism And History. **Career:** Cornell University, instructor to assistant professor, 1952-56; University of Texas, assistant professor, 1956-59; Washington University, visiting professor, 1959; Michigan State University, associate professor, professor, 1959-64; Trinity College, lecturer, 1962-63; University of California, professor, 1964-74, Department of English, chairman, 1964-69, School of Humanities, dean, 1970-72, vice-chancellor for academic affairs, 1972-74, Department of English, founding chair; University of Washington, professor of English, Lockwood professor of humanities in comparative literature, 1977-97, Byron W. and Alice L. Lockwood professor emeritus of humanities, comparative literature, 1997-, Center for the Humanities, director. Writer. **Publications:** Blake and Yeats, 1955; William Blake: A Reading of the Shorter Poems, 1963; The Contexts of Poetry, 1963; The Horses of Instruction (novel), 1968; The Interests of Criticism, 1969; The Truth about Dragons (novel), 1971; Lady Gregory, 1973; The Academic Tribes, 1976, 2nd ed., 1988; Philosophy of the Literary Symbolic, 1983; Joyce Cary's Trilogies: Pursuit of the Particular Real, 1983; The Book of Yeats's Poems, 1990; Antithetical Essays in Literary Criticism and Liberal Education, 1990; The Book of Yeat's Vision, 1995; Farm at Richwood and Other Poems, 1997; Many Pretty Toys: A Novel, 1999; Four Lectures on the History of Criticism in the West, 2000; Home: A Novel, 2001; Offense of Poetry, 2007; Academic Child: A Memoir, 2008; Blake's Margins: An Interpretive Study of the Annotations, 2009; William Blake on His Poetry and Painting: A Study of A Descriptive Catalogue, Other Prose Writings, and Jerusalem, 2011. EDITOR: Poems by R.S. Adams, 1952; Poetry: An Introductory Anthology, 1968; Fiction as Process, 1968; (intro.) Jerusalem, Selected Poems and Prose, 1970; William Blake, 1970; Critical Theory since Plato, 1971, 3rd ed., 2004; Critical Theory since 1965, 1986; Critical Essays on William Blake, 1991. Contributor of journals to periodicals. **Address:** 3930 NE 157th Pl., Seattle, WA 98155-6730, U.S.A. **Online address:** hadams3048@aol.com

ADAMS, Hunter Doherty. *See* **ADAMS, Patch.**

ADAMS, Jad. British (born England), b. 1954. **Genres:** Biography, History, Novels. **Career:** Writer and television producer, 1982-; Nightwatch, chair, 1992-; University of London, associate research fellow. **Publications:** AIDS: The HIV Myth, 1989; Tony Benn: A Biography, 1992; Double Indemnity: Murder for Insurance, 1994; The Dynasty: The Nehru-Gandhi Story, 1997; Madder Music, Stronger Wine: The Life of Ernest Dowson, 2000; Pankhurst: A Biography, 2003; Hideous Absinthe: A History of the Devil in a Bottle, 2004; Kipling, 2005; Gandhi: Naked Ambition, 2010. FICTION: Choice of Darkness, forthcoming. Contributor to periodicals. **Address:** MBA Literary Agents, 62 Grafton Way, London, GL W1T 5DW, England. **Online address:** jadadams@btinternet.com

ADAMS, James F(rederick). American/Korean (born Korea (South)), b. 1927. **Genres:** Psychology, Sociology. **Career:** Temple University, Department of Psychology, staff of testing bureau, 1951-52, assistant professor, 1959-62, associate professor, 1962-66, professor of psychology, 1966-80, chairman of counselor education and director of counseling psychology, 1969-72, chairman of department of counseling psychology, 1973-80, Division of Educational Psychology, coordinator, 1974-80; Whitworth College, assistant professor of psychology, 1952-55; Washington State University, instructor, 1955-57; Miami University, Experimental Study in Instructional Procedures, research associate, 1957-59; University of Puerto Rico, faculty, 1963-64; Catholic University of Puerto Rico, faculty, 1971-72; University of Nevada, professor of psychology and dean of graduate school, 1980-85; Longwood College, senior vice president (academic), 1985-86. Writer. **Publications:** A Workbook to Occupations, 1953; Adams Self-Analysis Inventory, 1954; (with C.L. Davis) The Use of the VuGraph as an Instructional Aid, 1960; (with R.B. Hackman) Adams-Hackman Test of Occupational Information, 1961; Problems in Counseling, 1962. EDITOR: Counseling and Guidance: A Summary View, 1965; Understanding Adolescence: Current Developments in Adolescent Psychology, 1968, 4th ed. 1980; Instructors Manual for Understanding Adolescence, 1969; (intro.) The Philosophy of Human Nature, 1970; Human Behavior in a Changing Society, 1973. Contributor to journals. **Address:** 130 Palacio Rd., Corrales, NM 87048, U.S.A.

ADAMS, James (Macgregor David). American/British (born England), b. 1951. **Genres:** Novels, Plays/Screenplays, Military/Defense/Arms Control, Politics/Government, Literary Criticism And History, Young Adult Fiction. **Career:** Evening Chronicle, staff, 1972-75; freelance writer, 1975-78; Eight Days Magazine, reporter, head reporter and news editor, 1978-81; Sunday Times, foreign manager, 1981-82, special assistant, 1982-84, defense correspondent, 1984-91, managing editor, 1989-91, Washington Bureau Chief, 1991; United Press Intl., chief executive officer, 1995-96; iDEFENSE, founder, chairman, chief executive officer, 1996-2001; Ashland Institute for Strategic Studies, founder, chief executive officer, 2001-04; Vortx, chairman, 2004-07; BeeAudio, founder and chief executive officer, 2009-; ADRevolution, chairman; Adams Strategy Group, chief executive officer. **Publications:** (With P. Frischer) The Artist in the Marketplace: Making Your Living in the Fine Arts, 1980; The Unnatural Alliance, 1984; The Financing of Terror: Behind the PLO, IRA, Red Brigades, and M-19 Stand the Paymasters: How the Groups that are Terrorizing the World Get the Money to Do It, 1986; Secret Armies: Inside the American, Soviet, and European Special Forces, 1988 in UK as Secret Armies: The Full Story of S.A.S., Delta Force, and Spetsnaz, 1988; (with R. Morgan and T. Bambridge) Ambush: The War between the SAS and the IRA, 1988; Engines of War: Merchants of Death and the New Arms Race, 1990; Trading in Death: Weapons, Warfare, and the New Arms Race, 1990; Bull's Eye: The Assassination and Life of Supergun Inventor Gerald Bull, 1992; The New Spies: Exploring the Frontiers of Espionage, 1995; Sellout: Aldrich Ames and the Corruption of the CIA, 1995; The Next World War: Computers are the Weapons and the Front Line is Everywhere, 1998. FICTION: The Final Terror, 1991; Taking the Tunnel, 1993; Hard Target, 1995; Crucible, 1997. **Address:** Janklow & Nesbit Associates, 445 Park Ave., New York, NY 10022-2606, U.S.A. **Online address:** james.adams.press@adrevolution.com

ADAMS, Jerome R(obertson). American (born United States), b. 1938. **Genres:** Area Studies, Biography, Politics/Government, Social Sciences, History. **Career:** Writer. **Publications:** Liberators and Patriots of Latin America: Biographies of Twenty-three Leaders from Dona Marina (1505-1530) to Bishop Romero (1917-1980), 1991, 2nd ed., 2010; Notable Latin American Women: Liberators, Rebels, Poets, Battlers and Spies, 1500-1900, 1995; Greasers and Gringos: The Historical Roots of Anglo-Hispanic Prejudice, 2006. **Address:** 20 Banner Ave., Winston-Salem, NC 27127, U.S.A.

ADAMS, Jessica. British/Australian (born Australia), b. 1964. **Genres:** Young Adult Non-fiction, Novels. **Career:** The Daily Telegraph, staff; New Woman, staff; Elle, staff. Astrologer and writer. **Publications:** MIND BODY SPIRIT SERIES; NONFICTION: Astrology for Women, 1997; The New Astrology for Women, 1998; Handbag Horoscopes: Aquarius, 2000; Handbag Horoscopes: Aries, 2000; Handbag Horoscopes: Cancer, 2000; Handbag Horoscopes: Capricorn, 2000; Handbag Horoscopes: Gemini, 2000; Handbag Horoscopes: Leo, 2000; Handbag Horoscopes: Libra, 2000; Handbag Horoscopes: Pisces, 2000; Handbag Horoscopes: Sagittarius, 2000; Handbag Horoscopes: Scorpio, 2000; Handbag Horoscopes: Taurus, 2000; Handbag Horoscopes: Virgo, 2000; Fantasy Futures: The Amazing New Way to Predict Your Future... and Make It Happen, 2002; (with J. Glisic and A. Paul) 21st Century Goddess: The Modern Girl's Guide to the Universe, 2002; (ed.) Just Below South: Inter cultural Performance in the Caribbean and the U.S. South, 2006; (co-author) Revolutionary Freedoms: A History of Survival, Strength and Imagination in Haiti, 2006; Essential Astrology for Women, 2006; Wounds of Returning: Race, Memory and Property on the Postslavery Plantation Wounds of Returning: Race, Memory and Property on the Post Slavery Plantation, 2007; (co-author) How We Met: True Confessions of Love, Lust and that Fateful First Meeting, 2007; Astro Love, 2008. NOVELS: Single White E Mail, 1998; Tom, Dick and Debbie Harry, 2002; Cool for Cats, 2003; I'm a Believer, 2004; The Summer Psychic, 2005; (intro.) Drums at Dusk, 2009; Should I Stay or Should I Go, 2009; 20 20 Vision, 2009. EDITOR; "NIGHT" SHORT STORY COLLECTIONS: (with C. Manby and F. Walker) Girls' Night In, 2000; (with C. Manby and F. Walker) Girls' Night In: Gentlemen by Invitation, 2001, also published as Girls' Night Out/ Boys' Night In, 2001; (co-ed.) Big Night Out, 2002; (with J. Partridge and N. Earls) Kids' Night In: A Midnight Feast, 2003; (with C. Manby and F. Walker) Girls' Night In 4, 2005; (with M. Alderson, I. Edwards-Jones and C. Manby) Ladies' Night, 2005; Kids' Night In 2: A Feast of Stories, 2005; Astrobloke, 2005; Astrobabe, 2007; (co-ed.) In Bed With, 2009. AMAZING YOU! SERIES FOR YOUNG ADULTS: Psychic Power, 2004; Astrology, 2004. **Address:** c/o Eileen Cope, Trident Media Group, 41 Madison Ave., New York, NY 10010, U.S.A.

ADAMS, John. (John Coolidge Adams). American (born United States), b. 1947. **Genres:** Autobiography/Memoirs, Music. **Career:** Marlboro Festival, composer-in-residence, 1970; New Music Ensemble, director, 1972-81; San Francisco Conservatory, faculty, 1972-83; San Francisco Symphony Orchestra, composer, conductor and artistic advisor, 1978-85, composer-in-residence, 1982-85; St. Paul Chamber Orchestra, creative chair, 1988; Carnegie Hall, Richard and Barbara Debs Composer, 2003-07. Writer. **Publications:** Available Light, 1983; Nixon in China: An Opera in Two Acts, 1987; Nixon in China: Opera in Three Acts, 1988; I Was Looking at the Ceiling and Then I Saw the Sky: Earthquake/Romance, 1995; Hallelujah Junction: Composing an American Life (autobiography), 2008. **Address:** Elektra/Nonesuch, 75 Rockefeller Plz., New York, NY 10019-6908, U.S.A.

ADAMS, John A. American (born United States), b. 1951. **Genres:** Adult Non-fiction, Military/Defense/Arms Control. **Career:** National Bank of Texas, vice president and manager; Enterprise Florida Inc., president and chief executive officer, 2005-11; Texas A&M University, adjunct professor; GATT Negotiations, delegate; World Trade Organization, advisor. Writer and historian. **Publications:** We Are the Aggies: The Texas A&M University Association of Former Students, 1979; Damming the Colorado: The Rise of the Lower Colorado River Authority, 1933-1939, 1990; Softly Call the Muster: The Evolution of a Texas Aggie Tradition, 1994; Mexican Banking and Investment in Transition, 1997; Keepers of the Spirit: The Corps of Cadets at Texas A&M University, 1876-2001, 2001; Bordering the Future: The Impact of Mexico on the United States, 2006; (with H.C. Dethloff) Texas Aggies Go to War: In Service of Their Country, 2006; If Mahan Ran the Great Pacific War: An Analysis of World War II Naval Strategy, 2008; Conflict and Commerce on the Rio Grande, 2008. **Address:** Indiana University Press, 601 N Morton St., Bloomington, IN 47404-3797, U.S.A.

ADAMS, John Coolidge. *See* **ADAMS, John.**

ADAMS, John Coolidge. American (born United States), b. 1947. **Genres:** Music, Autobiography/Memoirs. **Career:** New Music Ensemble, director, 1972-82; San Francisco Conservatory, head of composition department, 1971-81, faculty, 1972-83; San Francisco Symphony Orchestra, composer, conductor and artistic advisor, 1978-85, composer-in-residence, 1982-85; St. Paul Chamber Orchestra, creative chair, 1988. Writer. **Publications:** Available Light, 1983; Nixon in China: An Opera in Two Acts, 1987; Nixon in China: Opera in Three Acts, 1988; I Was Looking at the Ceiling and Then I Saw the Sky: Earthquake/Romance, 1995; Hallelujah Junction: Composing an American Life (autobiography), 2008. **Address:** Elektra/Nonesuch, 75 Rockefeller Plz., New York, NY 10019, U.S.A.

ADAMS, Kathleen M(arie). American (born United States), b. 1957. **Genres:** Anthropology/Ethnology, Social Sciences, Business/Trade/Industry. **Career:** Women's Jail Study Group, research assistant, 1979-80; Thomas Burke Memorial Washington State Museum, assistant curator of ethnology, 1981-82; Hasanuddin University, visiting researcher, 1984-85; Beloit College, assistant professor of anthropology, 1988-93, Mouat assistant professor of international studies, 1990-93; Logan Museum, research associate in Asian ethnology, 1988-93; Northern Illinois University, adjunct faculty, 1990-96; Loyola University Chicago, assistant professor, 1993-98, associate professor of anthropology, 1998, Center for Ethics, faculty fellow, 1998; University of Pittsburgh, assistant professor, 1996; Field Museum of Natural History, Department of Anthropology, adjunct curator, 1998-; Soka University of America, professor and coordinator of social and behavioral science concentration, 2000-01. Writer. **Publications:** (Ed. with S. Dickey) Home and Hegemony: Domestic Service and Identity Politics in South and Southeast Asia, 2000; Art as Politics: Re-crafting Identities, Tourism and Power in Tana Toraja, 2006; (ed. with K. Gillogly) Everyday Life in Southeast Asia, 2011. Contributor of articles to periodicals. **Address:** Department of Anthropology, Loyola University of Chicago, 6430 N Kenmore, Chicago, IL 60660, U.S.A. **Online address:** kadams@luc.edu

ADAMS, Lorraine. American (born United States), b. 1960?. **Genres:** Novels, Travel/Exploration. **Career:** Concord Monitor, reporter, 1983-84; Dallas Morning News, reporter, 1984-92; Washington Post, reporter, 1992-2003; Columbia University, graduate fellow. **Publications:** (Comp. with T. Handiseni) A Tourist Guide to Rock Art Sites in Northern Zimbabwe, 1991; (contrib.) The Dark Wilderness of Time, 2002; Harbor, 2004; Room and The Chair: A Novel, 2010. Contributor to periodicals. **Address:** c/o Author Mail, Knopf Publishers, 1745 Broadway, New York, NY 10019-4368, U.S.A.

ADAMS, Marie. Canadian (born Canada), b. 1945. **Genres:** Psychology, How-to Books, inspirational/Motivational Literature, Sociology, Human Relations/Parenting. **Career:** Centennial College, professor, 1982-, General Arts and Science Program, coordinator, 1988-95, acting chair, 1992; Parents for Youth, group psychotherapist, 1993-98. Writer. **Publications:** Our Son, a Stranger: Adoption Breakdown and Its Effects on Parents, 2002. **Address:** Centennial College, PO Box 631, Sta. A, Toronto, ON M1K 5E9, Canada. **Online address:** m.adams@aci.on.ca

ADAMS, Marilyn Jager. American (born United States), b. 1948. **Genres:** Psychology, Education, Young Adult Fiction. **Career:** Planning Research Corp., programmer and research assistant, 1967; General Electric Information Systems Division, systems programmer and student intern, 1969-70; Bolt, Beranek and Newman Inc., cognitive and developmental psychologist, 1975-; Brown University, senior research scientist, 1989-, visiting professor, 1994-95, Department of Cognitive and Linguistic Sciences, visiting professor; Soliloquy Learning, chief scientist; Public Broadcasting Service, senior advisor; University of Illinois at Urbana-Champaign, Center for the Study of Reading, senior staff. Writer. **Publications:** (Ed. and contrib.) Odyssey: A Curriculum for Thinking, vol. I: Foundations of Reasoning, vol. II: Understanding Language, vol. III: Problem Solving, vol. IV: Decision Making, vol. V: Inventive Thinking, 1986; Beginning to Read: Thinking and Learning about Print, 1990; (with Y.J. Tenney, R.W. Pew) Strategic Workload and the Cognitive Management of Advanced Multitask Systems, 1991; (co-author) Collections for Young Scholars, K-2, 1995; (co-author) Pickled Peppers, 1995; Market, 1995; (co-author) Phonemic Awareness in Young Children, 1998. Work appears in anthologies. **Address:** Bolt, Beranek and Newman Inc., 10 Moulton St., Cambridge, MA 02138, U.S.A.

ADAMS, Marilyn McCord. American (born United States), b. 1943. **Genres:** Theology/Religion, Philosophy, History. **Career:** State University of New York, instructor, 1967-68; University of Michigan, visiting lecturer and assistant professor of philosophy, 1968-72; University of California, associate professor of philosophy, 1968-72, professor, 1978-93, chair of philosophy, 1985-87; Yale University, Department of Religious Studies, professor of historical theology, 1993-2003, Horace Tracy Pitkin chair of historical theology, 1998-2003, Divinity School, professor of historical theology, 1993-2003; Oxford University, Regius professor of divinity, 2004-09; University of North Carolina, College of Arts and Sciences, Department of Philosophy, distinguished research professor, 2009-. Writer. **Publications:** (Trans. and intro.) Predestination, God's Foreknowledge, and Future Contingents, 1969, 2nd ed., 1983; (trans. and intro.) Pauli Veneti Logica Magna, 1978; William Ockham, 1987; (ed. with R.M. Adams) The Problem of Evil, 1990; (ed. with A.B. Wolter) The Philosophical Theology of John Duns Scotus, 1990; What Sort of Human Nature?: Medieval Philosophy and the Systematics of Christology, 1999; Horrendous Evils and the Goodness of God, 1999; Wrestling for Blessing, 2005; Christ and Horrors: The Coherence of Christology, 2006; Opening to God: Childlike Prayers for Adults, 2008; Some Later Medieval Theories of the Eucharist, 2010; (co-author) Christian Holiness and Human Sexuality, 2011. Contributor of articles to books and journals. **Address:** Department of Philosophy, College of Arts and Sciences, University of North Carolina, 202-A Caldwell Hall, 240 E Cameron, Chapel Hill, NC 27599-3125, U.S.A. **Online address:** marilyna@email.unc.edu

ADAMS, Mark. American (born United States), b. 1967?. **Genres:** Biography. **Career:** National Geographic Adventure, contributing editor. **Publications:** Mister America: How Muscular Millionaire Bernarr Macfadden Transformed the Nation through Sex, Salad, and the Ultimate Starvation Diet, 2009. Contributor to magazines. **Address:** U.S.A. **Online address:** bernarrmacfadden@gmail.com

ADAMS, Mike S. American (born United States), b. 1964. **Genres:** Criminology/True Crime, Education. **Career:** University of North Carolina, associate professor of criminology, 1993-, professor. Writer. **Publications:** Welcome to the Ivory Tower of Babel: Confessions of a Conservative College Professor, 2004; Feminists Say the Darndest Things: A Politically Incorrect Professor Confronts womyn on Campus, 2007. Contributor to periodicals. **Address:** College of Arts & Science, University of North Carolina, 601 S College Rd., Wrightsville Beach, NC 28480, U.S.A. **Online address:** adamsm@uncw.edu

ADAMS, Nicholas. *See* **MACDONALD, James D.**

ADAMS, Nicholas. *See* **SMITH, Sherwood.**

ADAMS, Nicholas. *See* **PINE, Nicholas.**

ADAMS, Nicholas. *See* **DOYLE, Debra.**

ADAMS, Patch. (Hunter Doherty Adams). American (born United States), b. 1945. **Genres:** Medicine/Health, Novels. **Career:** Gesundheit! Institute, founder and president, 1971-, director, lecturer. Writer. **Publications:** (With M. Mylander) Gesundheit!: Bringing Good Health to You, the Medical System, and Society through Physician Service, Complementary Therapies, Humor and Joy, 1992; House Calls: How We Can All Heal the World One Visit at a Time, 1998; (foreword) It's Up to Us, 1999; (foreword) J. Graham-Pole, Illness and the Art of Creative Self-Expression: Stories and Exercises from the Arts for Those with Chronic Illness, 2000. Contributor to books. **Address:** Gesundheit Institute, PO Box 307, Urbana, IL 61803, U.S.A.

ADAMS, Richard (George). British (born England), b. 1920. **Genres:** Novels, Novellas/Short Stories, Children's Fiction, Poetry, Autobiography/Memoirs, Romance/Historical. **Career:** British Home Higher Civil Service, Department of Environment, staff, assistant secretary of department, 1968-74; full-time writer, 1974-; University of Florida, writer-in-residence, 1975; Hollins College, writer-in-residence, 1976; Royal Society for the Prevention of Cruelty to Animals, president, 1980-82. **Publications:** NOVELS: Watership Down, 1972; Shardik, 1974; The Plague Dogs, 1977; The Girl in a Swing, 1980; Maia, 1985; Traveller, 1988; The Outlandish Knight, 2000; Daniel, 2006. POETRY: The Tyger Voyage(narrative), 1976; The Ship's Cat (narrative), 1977; The Adventures & Brave Deeds of the Ship's Cat on the Spanish Maine: Together with the Most Lamentable Losse of the Alcestis and Triumphant Firing of the Port of Chagres, 1977; The Legend of Te Tuna (narrative), 1982; (ed. and contrib.) Occasional Poets: An Anthology, 1986. OTHERS: (with M. Hooper) Nature through the Seasons, 1975; (with M. Hooper) Nature Day and Night, 1978; The Watership Down Film Picture Book: With Linking Text, 1978; (intro.) Georgi Vladimov, Faithful Ruslan, 1979; The Iron Wolf and Other Stories, 1980; (ed.) The Birds and Other Stories, 1980; The Unbroken Web: Stories and Fables, 1980; (ed.) Grimm's Fairy Tales, 1981; (ed.) Richard Adams's Favourite Animal Stories, 1981; (ed.) The Best of Ernest Thompson Seton, 1982; (with R. Lockley) Voyage through the Antarctic, 1982; The Bureaucats, 1985; A Nature Diary, 1985; The Day Gone By (autobiography), 1990; Antarctica: Voices from the Silent Continent, 1990; Tales from Watership Down, 1996. Contributor to books and periodicals. **Address:** David Higham Associates, 5-8 Lower John St., Golden Sq., London, GL W1F 9HA, England.

ADAMS, Robert Merrihew. American (born United States), b. 1937. **Genres:** Philosophy. **Career:** Montauk Community Church, pastor, 1962-65; University of Michigan, lecturer, 1968, assistant professor of philosophy, 1969-72; University of California, associate professor, 1972-76, professor of philosophy, 1976-94, professor emeritus, 1994-; Yale University, professor of philosophy, 1993-2003, Clark professor of moral philosophy and metaphysics, 1995-2003, emeritus, 2004-, chairperson of department, professor of religious studies and faculty; Yale Divinity School, visiting professor, 1988-; University of Oxford, visiting professor of philosophy, 2004-09; Mansfield College, senior research fellow, 2004-; University of North Carolina, Chapel Hill, distinguished research professor of philosophy, 2009-. Writer. **Publications:** The Virtue of Faith and Other Essays in Philosophical Theology, 1987; (ed. with G.M. Logan) Utopia, 1989; (ed. with M.M. Adams) The Problem of Evil, 1990; Leibniz: Determinist, Theist, Idealist, 1994; (ed. with I. Shapiro and intro.) Integrity and Conscience, 1998; A Finite and Infinite Goods: A Framework for Ethics, 1999; A Theory of Virtue: Excellence in Being for the Good, 2006. Contributor to periodicals and journals. **Address:** Department of Philosophy, University of North Carolina, PO Box 3125, Chapel Hill, NC 27599-3125, U.S.A. **Online address:** adamro@email.unc.edu

ADAMS, Roy J(oseph). Canadian/American (born United States), b. 1940. **Genres:** Administration/Management, Business/Trade/Industry, Civil Liberties/Human Rights, Economics, Ethics, Industrial Relations, Organized Labor. **Career:** Chase Manhattan Bank, industrial relations specialist, 1967-68; McMaster University, assistant professor, 1973-78, Human Resources and Labour Relations Area, head, 1976-78, associate professor, 1978-83, professor of industrial relations, 1984-97, Theme School on International Justice and Human Rights, director, 1996-97, professor emeritus, 1997-, McMaster and Ariel F. Sallows chair of human rights, 2009-10; Rutgers University, Labor Education Center, visiting professor, 1980; Institute for International Studies and Training-Japan, visiting professor, 1985; Beijing University, Iron and Steel Technology, visiting professor, 1985; European Institute of Business Administration-France, visiting professor, 1987; Case Western Reserve University, Dallas M. Young distinguished lecturer, 1989; University of Science and Technology-China, visiting professor, 1989; University of Toronto, Centre for Industrial Relations, distinguished visiting professor, 1990, Canadian Pacific distinguished visiting professor, 1990; Comparative Industrial Relations Newsletter, editor and publisher, 1990-99; Institute for Labour Research-Budapest Hungary, visiting professor, 1991; Victoria University of Wellington, International Labour Office, visiting fellow, 1992; International Industrial Relations Association, senior list manager, 1993-98; Antioch University, adjunct professor of labor studies, 1994-99; University of Bologna, SINNEA Summer School in Comparative Industrial Relations, visiting professor, 1994; Industrial Relations Research Association, president, 1996; Society for the Promotion of Human Rights in Employment, co-founder, 1997-2002; University of Western Australia, distinguished visiting professor, 1996; Hamilton Spectator, columnist, 1997-2002; rabble.ca, columnist, 2001-; Hamilton Civic Coalition, convenor and executive director, 2003-07; Straight Goods, columnist, 2006-; University of Saskatchewan, Ariel F. Sallows chair of human rights, 2009-10; International Employee Relations Network, developer; Comparative Industrial Relations Research and Teaching Society, founder. Consultant. **Publications:** The Growth of White-Collar Unionism in Britain and Sweden, 1975; Industrial Relations under Liberal Democracy, 1995; (with G. Betcherman and B. Bilson) Good Jobs, Bad Jobs, No Jobs: Tough Choices for Canadian Labour Law, 1995; Labour Left Out, 2006. EDITOR: Comparative Industrial Relations, 1991; (with N.M. Meltz and contrib.) Industrial Relations Theory, 1993. Contributor to books and articles. **Address:** DeGroote School of Business, McMaster University, DSB-234, DeGroote Bldg., 1280 Main St. W, Hamilton, ON L8S 4M4, Canada. **Online address:** adamsr@mcmaster.ca

ADAMS, Scott. American (born United States), b. 1957. **Genres:** Cartoons. **Career:** Crocker National Bank, bank teller, computer programmer, financial analyst, product manager and commercial lender, 1979-86; Pacific Bell, staff, 1986-95; Scott Adams Foods Inc., chief executive officer; Stacey's Café, co-owner. Writer. **Publications:** HUMOR: The Dilbert Principle: A Cubicle-Eye View of Bosses, Meetings, Management Fads and Other Workplace Afflictions, 1996; Dogbert's Top Secret Management Handbook, 1996; The Dilbert Future: Thriving on Stupidity in the 21st Century, 1997; The Joy of Work, 1998. DILBERT COMIC STRIP COLLECTIONS: Dogbert's Clues for the Clueless: All-New Original Cartoons Featuring Dogbert from the Nationally Syndicated Dilbert Strip, 1993; Always Postpone Meetings with Time-Wasting Morons, 1994; Build a Better Life by Stealing Office Supplies, 1994; Shave the Whales, 1994; It's Obvious You Won't Survive by Your Wits Alone, 1995; Bring Me the Head of Willie the Mailboy, 1995; Conversations with Dogbert, 1996; You Don't Need Experience If You've Got Attitude, 1996; Access Denied: Dilbert's Quest for Love in the Nineties, 1996; Fugitive from the Cubicle Police, 1996; Still Pumped from Using the Mouse, 1996; Casual Day Has Gone Too Far, 1997; The Boss: Nameless, Blameless and Shameless, 1997; The Dilbert Bunch, 1997; Work Is a Contact Sport, 1997; Please Don't Feed the Egos, 1997; No-You'd Better Watch Out, 1997; Seven Years of Highly Defective People: The Origins and Evolutions of Dilbert, 1997; I'm Not Anti-Business, I'm Anti-Idiot, 1998; Dilbert Gives You the Business, 1998; Dilbert 2.0: 20 Years of Dilbert, 2008; Freedom's Just Another Word for People Finding Out You're Useless, 2009; I'm Tempted to Stop Acting Randomly, 2010; Problem Identified: And You're Probably Not Part of the Solution, 2010; Your Accomplishments Are Suspiciously Hard to Verify, 2011; How's That Underling Thing Working Out for You?, 2011. OTHER: (foreword) G. Kawasaki, How to Drive Your Competition Crazy: Creating Disruption for Fun and Profit, 1996; Telling It Like It Isn't: A Tiptoe Approach to Communications-A Dilbert Little Book, 1996; Dilbert Postcard Book, 1997; You Can't Schedule Stupidity, 1998; Random Acts of Catness, 1998; Joy of Work: Dilbert's Guide to Finding Happiness at the Expense of Your Co-Workers, 1998; Journey to Cubeville, 1998; Work-the Wally Way, 1999; Don't Step in the Leadership, 1999; Alice in Blunderland, 1999; Random Acts of Management, 2000; Dilbert, A Treasury of Sunday Strips, Version 00, 2000; When Did Ignorance Become a Point of View?, 2001; God's Debris: A Thought Experiment, 2001; Excuse Me while I Wag, 2001; What do You Call a Sociopath in a Cubicle?, 2002; Dilbert and the Way of the Weasel, 2002; Another Day in Cubicle Paradise, 2002; Words You Don't Want to Hear during Your Annual Performance Review, 2003; When Body Language Goes Bad, 2003; Religion War, 2004; It's not Funny if I have to Explain It, 2004; Don't Stand where the Comet is Assumed to Strike Oil, 2004; Thriving on Vague Objectives, 2005; Fluorescent Light Glistens Off Your Head, 2005; What would Wally Do?, 2006; Try Rebooting Yourself, 2006; Stick to Drawing Comics, Monkey Brain!: Cartoonist Ignores Helpful Advice, 2007; Positive Attitude, 2007; Dilbert's Guide to the Rest of Your Life: Dispatches from Cubicleland, 2007; This is the Part where You Pretend to Add Value, 2008; 14 Years of Loyal Service in a Fabric-Covered Box: A Dilbert Book, 2009. Contributor to periodicals. **Address:** United Media, 200 Madison Ave., New York, NY 10016-3905, U.S.A. **Online address:** scottadams@aol.com

ADAMS, Sheila Kay. American (born United States), b. 1953. **Genres:** Novels, Literary Criticism And History. **Career:** Madison County Board of Education, teacher, 1975-92. Writer. **Publications:** NOVELS: Come Go Home with Me, 1995; My Old True Love, 2004. Contributor to periodicals. **Address:** PO Box 1188, Mars Hill, NC 28754, U.S.A. **Online address:** sheila@jimandsheila.com

ADAMS, Susan S. *See* **KISSEL, Susan S.**

ADAMS, Timothy Dow. American (born United States), b. 1943. **Genres:** Literary Criticism And History, Autobiography/Memoirs, Biography. **Career:** Northern Virginia Community College, lecturer in English, 1971-72; Old Dominion University, instructor in English, 1972-75; Christian Brothers College, adjunct assistant professor of English, 1978-79; University of Arkansas, assistant professor of English, 1979-81; McMurry College, assistant professor of English, 1981-82; West Virginia University, assistant professor, 1982-86, associate professor of English, 1986-91, professor, 1991-, chair of English, 2000-; A/B: Auto/Biography Studies, associate editor. **Publications:** Telling Lies in Modern American Autobiography, 1990; Light Writing and Life Writing: Photography in Autobiography, 2000. Contributor to periodicals. **Address:** Department of English, West Virginia University, 100 Colson

Hall, 1503 University Ave., PO Box 6296, 467 Sta., Morgantown, WV 26506-6296, U.S.A. **Online address:** tadams@wvu.edu

ADAMS, Will. (William Petre). British (born England), b. 1963. **Genres:** Novels. **Career:** Writer and consultant. **Publications:** (As William Petre with B. Goldstein) Navigating the Century: A Personal Account of Alter Company's First Hundred Years, 1998; The Alexander Cipher, 2007; The Exodus Quest, 2008; The Lost Labyrinth, 2009. **Address:** c/o Luigi Bonomi, Luigi Bonomi Associates, 91 Great Russell St., London, GL WC1B 3PS, England.

ADAMS, William James. American (born United States), b. 1947. **Genres:** History, Economics. **Career:** Harvard University, Department of Economics, teaching fellow, 1969-73, assistant head tutor, 1971-73, visiting assistant professor, 1973-74, senior research fellow, 1987-88; University of Michigan, assistant professor of economics and public policy, 1973-78, associate professor of economics, 1978-88, professor of economics, associate professor of law, 1979-83, adjunct professor of law, 1989-93, associate dean of academic affairs, 2000-02, Arthur F. Thurnau professor; Quarterly Journal of Economics, associate editor, 1973-74; University of Aix-Marseille, visiting professor, 1980-81; L'Industria-Rivista Di Economia E Politica Industriale, associate editor, 1981-; Brookings Institution, Foreign Policy Studies, staff, 1983-; The University of Paris XIII, Program in Industrial Economics, board director, 1985-90; University of Paris I, visiting professor of economics, 1989, 1997; Chicago Council on Foreign Relations, project director on europe after 1992, 1989-92; Fondation Jean Monnet pour l'Europe, board director, 1990; Review of Industrial Organization, associate editor, 1990-2002; The Atlantic Council, academic associate, 1992-; European University Institute, Academy of European Law, visiting professor, 1993; The University of Basel, Europa Institute, visiting professor, 1996. **Publications:** (Ed. with Stoffaës) French Industrial Policy, 1986; Restructuring the French Economy, 1989; (ed.) Singular Europe, 1992. **Address:** Department of Economics, University of Michigan, 611 Tappan St., Ann Arbor, MI 48109, U.S.A. **Online address:** jimadams@umich.edu

ADAMS, Zach. *See* **BUNGERT, D. Edward.**

ADAMSON, Donald. British (born England), b. 1939. **Genres:** Novellas/Short Stories, History, Literary Criticism And History, Philosophy, Biography, Translations, Autobiography/Memoirs. **Career:** Manchester Grammar School, assistant master, 1962-64; J. Walter Thompson Company Ltd., executive, 1965-67; St. George's School, head of modern languages, 1968; Goldsmiths' College, lecturer, 1969-70, senior lecturer, 1970-77, principal lecturer in French, 1977-89; University of London, faculty of arts, 1971-89; Wolfson College, visiting fellow, 1989-90. Writer. **Publications:** The Genesis of Le Cousin Pons, 1966; Dusty Heritage: A National Policy for Museums and Libraries, 1971; (with P. Dewar) The House of Nell Gwyn: The Fortunes of the Beauclerk Family, 1670-1974, 1974; A Rescue Policy for Museums, 1980; Balzac: Illusions perdues, 1981; Les Romantiques francais devant la peinture espagnole, 1988; Blaise Pascal: Mathematician, Physicist, and Thinker about God, 1995; The Curriers' Company: A Modern History, 2000; Balzac and the Tradition of the European Novel, 2001; Pascal's Views on Mathematics and the Divine, 2005; Oskar Kokoschka at Polperro, 2009; William Golding Remembered, 2010; St John in Cornwall, 2011. EDITOR: T.S. Eliot: A Memoir, 1971; Rides Round Britain, the Travel Journals of John Byng, 5th Viscount Torrington, 1996. TRANSLATOR: Balzac, The Black Sheep, 1970; Balzac, Ursule Mirouet, 1976; Maupassant, Bed 29 and Other Stories, 1993. **Address:** 171 Cliffords Inn, Fetter Ln., London, GL EC4A 1BY, England. **Online address:** aimsworthy@tesco.net

ADAMSON, Gil. Canadian (born Canada), b. 1961. **Genres:** Novels, Poetry, Novellas/Short Stories. **Career:** Coach House Press, publicist and editorial assistant, 1985-87; Canadian Broadcasting Corp., Radio Guide, publishing assistant, 1987-. **Publications:** Primitive (poetry), 1991; Help Me, Jacques Cousteau (short stories), 1995; (with D. Connolly) Mulder, It's Me, 1997; Ashland (poetry), 2003; The Outlander (novel), 2007, 1st ed., 2008. Contributor to journals and periodicals. **Address:** ECW Press, 2120 Queen St. E, Ste. 200, Toronto, ON M4E 1E2, Canada. **Online address:** gadamson@interlog.com

ADAMSON, M(ary) J(o). (Yvonne Adamson). American (born United States), b. 1935. **Genres:** Mystery/Crime/Suspense, Novels, Young Adult Fiction, Romance/Historical. **Career:** High School English teacher, 1956-57; Humboldt State College (now Humboldt State University), instructor in English, 1967-68; University of Denver, Department of Mass Communications, internship director and lecturer, 1979-83. Writer. **Publications:** Not till a Hot January, 1987; A February Face, 1987; Remember March, 1987; April When They Woo, 1989; May's Newfangled Mirth, 1989; Bridey's Mountain, 1993; The Blazing Tree: A Michael Merrick Mystery, 2000; The Elusive Voice: A Michael Merrick Mystery, 2001. Contributor to periodicals. Works appear in anthologies. **Address:** John Farquharson Ltd., 250 W 57th St., New York, NY 10107, U.S.A.

ADAMSON, Robin. Australian (born Australia), b. 1938. **Genres:** Language/Linguistics. **Career:** University of Western Australia, tutor in French, 1965-67, honorary research fellow, 2001-; University of Dundee, lecturer in French, senior lecturer in French, 1968-99, Centre for Applied Language Studies, director, 1967-2001; Scottish Universities French Language Project, founding member, 1973-99; University of Stirling, Scottish Centre for Language Teaching, consultant and research fellow, 1999-2001; Panel on Advanced Higher Examination, HM Chief Inspector for Modern Languages, consultant and advisor, 1999-2000; Università Bocconi, visiting professor, 2000. Writer. **Publications:** La Poésie Résistante: Lexis, Semantics and Syntax in the War Poetry of Paul Eduard, 1983; (with S. Taylor) Communicative Competence in French at Final Honours Level, 1988; En fin de compte Livre de l'enseignant, 1988; French Grammar, 1998; Le Francais en faculté, 3rd ed., 1999; The Defence of French: A Language in Crisis?, 2007. **Address:** Department of European Languages and Studies, University of Western Australia, Rm. G01, 73 Fairway, Nedlands, 35 Stirling Hwy., Crawley, WA 6009, Australia. **Online address:** robin.adamson@uwa.edu.au

ADAMSON, Yvonne. *See* **ADAMSON, M(ary) J(o).**

ADAMZ-BOGUS, S. Diane. Also writes as Diane Adams Bogus, S. Diane Bogus. American (born United States), b. 1946. **Genres:** Poetry, Education, Gay And Lesbian Issues, inspirational/Motivational Literature, Women's Studies And Issues, Autobiography/Memoirs, Theology/Religion. **Career:** WIM Publications, writer, 1971-, founder, 1979-, publisher; Northwestern University, M.A. Teaching Program, student teaching supervisor, 1972; Los Angeles Southwest Community College, English instructor, 1976-81, 1985-86; Compton Unified School District, English Department, chair, 1979-80; Woman in the Moon Publications, founder and owner, 1979-99; Miami University, instructor, 1981-84, Walser Fellow, 1983; City College, English instructor, 1985-86; California State University, professor of American literature, 1986-90, visiting lecturer, 1987-89; DeAnza College, instructor, 1990, professor of composition and literature, 1990-2001. Writer. **Publications:** Sapphire's Sampler, 1982; (ed. with J. Sebastian) Intro to Finé, 1985; Dyke Hands and Sutras Erotic Lyric, 1988; The Chant of the Women of Magdalena and the Magdalena Poems, 1988; For the Love of Men, 1991; Spirit in the Dark (autobiography), 1994; The Studenthood New Age Reader, 1994; I'm Off to See the Goddamn Wizard, Alright!, 1995; Woman in the Moon, 1995; Buddhism in the Classroom, 1995; The New Age Reader, 1998; Education by Metaphor, 1998; Bearstories, 2000; Spirit in the Dark (essays), 2001; Greatest Hits Collection, 2001. Works appear in anthologies. Contributor of articles to journals. **Address:** New Age Book Publisher, PO Box 2087, Cupertino, CA 95015-2087, U.S.A. **Online address:** sdianeadamzbogus@yahoo.com

ADCOCK, Fleur. British/New Zealander (born New Zealand), b. 1934. **Genres:** Poetry. **Career:** University of Otago, assistant lecturer in classics, 1958, assistant librarian, 1959-61; Alexander Turnbull Library, assistant librarian, 1962; Foreign and Commonwealth Office, assistant librarian, 1963-79; University of East Anglia, writing fellow; freelance writer, 1980-. **Publications:** The Eye of The Hurricane, 1964; Tigers, 1967; High Tide In The Garden, 1971; The Scenic Route, 1974; The Inner Harbour, 1979; Below Loughrigg, 1979; (ed.) The Oxford Book of Contemporary New Zealand Poetry Selected Poems, 1983; The Virgin and the Nightingale: Medieval Latin Poems, 1983; The Incident Book, 1986; 4-Pack, One: Four from Northern Women, 1986; (trans.) G. Tartler, Orient Express, 1989; (with A. Brownjohn and J. Silkin) Trei poeti englezi contemporani, 1989; (trans.) D. Crasnaru, Letters from Darkness, 1991; Time Zones, 1991; (contrib.) Poet's Voice and Craft, 1994; Looking Back, 1997; Poems 1960-2000, 2000; Dragon Talk, 2010. EDITOR: The Oxford Book of Contemporary New Zealand Poetry, 1982; The Faber Book of 20th Century Women's Poetry, 1987; (trans.) Hugh Primas and the Arch poet, 1994; (with J. Simms) The Oxford Book of Creatures, 1995. Contributor to periodicals. **Address:** 14 Lincoln Rd., London, GL N2 9DL, England.

ADDAE, Akili. *See* **OBIKA, Akili Addae.**

ADDERSON, Caroline. (Caroline Louise Adderson). Canadian (born Canada), b. 1963. **Genres:** Novels, Novellas/Short Stories, Plays/Screenplays. **Career:** Banff School of Fine Arts, resident, 1987, 1991; Tyrone Guthrie Centre for Artists, resident, 1989, 1992; Leighton Artist Colony, resident, 1993; Westwood Creative Artists, affiliate; University of British Columbia, instructor in creative writing, 2000-01; Simon Fraser University, instructor in writing and publishing, 2002-; Vancouver Community College, instructor. Writer. **Publications:** SHORT STORIES: Bad Imaginings, 1993; Tokyo Cowboy, 1993; Pleased to Meet You, 2006. NOVELS: A History of Forgetting, 1999; Sitting Practice, 2003. NOVELLAS: Mr. Justice, 2005; CHILDREN'S FICTION: Very Serious Children, 2007; I, Bruno, 2007; Bruno for Real, 2008; OTHER: The Sky is Falling, 2010. Contributor to periodicals. Works appear in anthologies. **Address:** Simon Fraser University, 8888 University Dr., Burnaby, BC V5A 1S6, Canada.

ADDERSON, Caroline Louise. *See* **ADDERSON, Caroline.**

ADDINALL, Peter. British (born England), b. 1932. **Genres:** Theology/Religion, Philosophy, Young Adult Non-fiction. **Career:** Teacher, 1954-58, 1968-83; Methodist Missionary Society, teacher, 1959-68. Writer. **Publications:** Philosophy and Biblical Interpretation: A Study in Nineteenth-Century Conflict, 1991. Contributor to periodicals. **Address:** Myrtle Grove, Carperby, Leyburn, NY DL8 4DA, England.

ADDINGTON, Arthur Charles. British (born England), b. 1939. **Genres:** Genealogy/Heraldry, Adult Non-fiction, History, Reference. **Career:** Writer. **Publications:** Royal House of Stuart: The Descendants of King James VI of Scotland, James I of England, vol. I, 1969, vol. II, 1971, vol. III, 1975; (ed.) The Lineage and Ancestry of H.R.H. Prince Charles, Prince of Wales, 2 vols., 1977; (with Z. Burke) Origine et Famille de Felix Nicolaievitch Elston, Comte Soumarokov-Elston, 1983. Contributor to journals. **Address:** 6 Fairfield Close, Harpenden, HF AL5 2SX, England.

ADDINGTON, Larry Holbrook. American (born United States), b. 1932. **Genres:** History, Military/Defense/Arms Control. **Career:** San Jose State College, assistant professor of history, 1962-64; The Citadel, The Military College of South Carolina, Department of History, assistant professor of history, 1964-66, associate professor, 1966-70, professor, 1970-94, chair, 1989-94, professor emeritus, 1994-; U.S. Army War College, Institute of Advanced Studies, consultant, 1968-69. Writer. **Publications:** From Moltke to Hitler: The Evolution of German Military Doctrine, 1865-1939, 1966; The Blitzkrieg Era and the German General Staff, 1865-1941, 1971; (co-ed.) Selected Papers from the Citadel Conference on War and Diplomacy, 1978, 1979; The Patterns of War since the Eighteenth Century, 1984, 2nd ed., 1994; America's War in Vietnam: A Short Narrative History, 2000. Contributor to journals. **Address:** Department of History, The Citadel, Military College of South Carolina, 430 Capers Hall, 171 Moultrie St., Charleston, SC 29409-0001, U.S.A. **Online address:** larrya103@aol.com

ADDISCOTT, T. M. (Tom M. Addiscott). British (born England) **Genres:** Young Adult Non-fiction. **Career:** United Nations Association International Service, volunteer; Lawes Chemical Co., advisory chemist, 1965-66; Rothamsted Experimental Station, research scientist, 1966-2002. Writer. **Publications:** NONFICTION: Farming, Fertilizers and the Nitrate Problem, 1991; Nitrate, Agriculture and the Environment, 2005. Contributor to journals. **Address:** Rothamsted Research, Harpenden, HF AL5 5LU, England. **Online address:** tom.addiscott@ukf.net

ADDISCOTT, Tom M. *See* **ADDISCOTT, T. M.**

ADDISON, Linda D. American (born United States), b. 1952. **Genres:** Science Fiction/Fantasy, Horror. **Career:** Bristol Myers Squibb, senior system analyst, 1991-99; AXA Financial Solutions, senior system analyst, 1999-2006; Applimation, business analyst, 2006-07; Logical Apps, senior business analyst, 2007-; Space and Time Magazine, editor; Circles In The Hair (CITH), Writing Group, founding member. Poet. **Publications:** SCIENCE FICTION: Animated Objects, 1997; Consumed, Reduced to Beautiful Grey Ashes, 2001; Being Full of Light, Insubstantial, 2007. Works appear in anthologies. Contributor to periodicals. **Address:** 3444 Cannon Pl., Bronx, NY 10463, U.S.A. **Online address:** nytebird45@aol.com

ADDISON, Paul S. British/Scottish (born Scotland), b. 1966. **Genres:** Mathematics/Statistics, Sciences. **Career:** Napier University, lecturer, 1992-, professor in fluid mechanics; Cardiodigital Ltd., co-founder, chief executive officer, director. Writer. **Publications:** Fractals and Chaos: An Illustrated Course, 1997; The Illustrated Wavelet Transform, 2002. **Address:** CardioDigital Ltd., Elvingston Science Ctr., East Lothian, EH33 1EH, England. **Online address:** p.addison@napier.ac.uk

ADDLETON, Jonathan S. (J. S. Addleton). Jordanian/Pakistani (born Pakistan), b. 1957. **Genres:** Area Studies. **Career:** U.S. Agency for International Development, Counselor, program director, 1985-, mission director, 2001-; Mongolia, Ambassador; World Bank, faculty; Carnegie Endowment for International Peace, faculty; Macon Telegraph, faculty. Writer. **Publications:** (With M. Geijbels as J.S. Addleton) The Rise and Development of Urdu and the Importance of Regional Languages in Pakistan, 1980; Undermining the Center: The Gulf Migration and Pakistan, 1992; Some Far and Distant Place (memoir), 1997. Contributor to periodicals. **Address:** US Agency for International Development, Ste. 70206, PO Box 6, Amman, 09892-0206, Jordan. **Online address:** jaddleton@usaid.gov

ADDLETON, J. S. *See* **ADDLETON, Jonathan S.**

ADDONIA, Sulaiman S. M. Y. British (born England), b. 1974?. **Genres:** Novels. **Career:** SOAS Centre for Development, Policy and Research, researcher, 2001-03. Writer. **Publications:** The Consequences of Love: A Novel, 2009. **Address:** Tibor Jones & Associates, Piano House, 9 Brighton Terr., Ste. 12b, London, GL SW9 8DJ, England.

ADDONIZIO, Kim (Theresa). American (born United States), b. 1954. **Genres:** Novels, Poetry, Literary Criticism And History, Sex, Women's Studies And Issues, Writing/Journalism. **Career:** Writer, 1986-. **Publications:** NOVELS: Crimes of Passion, 1984; In the Box Called Pleasure: Stories, 1999; Little Beauties, 2005; Ordinary Genius: A Guide for the Poet Within, 2009; Lucifer at the Starlite: Poems, 2009. POETRY: (with L. Duesing and D. Laux) Three West Coast Women, 1987; The Philosopher's Club, 1994; Jimmy & Rita: Poems (verse novel), 1997; Tell Me, 2000; What Is This Thing Called Love, 2004. OTHERS: (with D. Laux) The Poet's Companion: A Guide to the Pleasures of Writing Poetry, 1997; (ed. with C. Dumesnil) Dorothy Parker's Elbow: Tattoos on Writers, Writers on Tattoos, 2002; My Dreams Out in the Street, 2007. Works appear in anthologies. Contributor to periodicals. **Address:** Lippincott Massie McQuilkin Literary Agency, 27 W 20th St., Ste. 305, New York, NY 10011, U.S.A. **Online address:** kimaddonizio@comcast.net

ADELBERG, Doris. *See* **ORGEL, Doris.**

ADELL, Sandra. American (born United States), b. 1946. **Genres:** Adult Non-fiction, Autobiography/Memoirs. **Career:** University of Wisconsin, associate professor of Afro-American studies, 1989-2003, professor of literature, 2003-. Writer. **Publications:** Double-Consciousness/Double Bind: Theoretical Issues in Twentieth-Century Black Literature, 1994; (co-ed.) African American Culture, 1996; Toni Morrison, 2002; Confessions of a Slot Machine Queen: A Memoir, 2010. **Address:** Department of Afro-American Studies, University of Wisconsin, Rm. 4115, Helen C. White Hall, 600 N Park St., Madison, WI 53706, U.S.A. **Online address:** saadell@wisc.edu

ADELMAN, Clifford. American (born United States), b. 1942. **Genres:** Politics/Government, Social Commentary, Education. **Career:** City College of New York, instructor and lecturer, 1968-71; Roosevelt University, faculty; Yale University, visiting lecturer, 1972-73; William Paterson (State) College of New Jersey, associate dean for academic development and research and associate professor of communications, 1974-79; U.S. Department of Education, Office of Research, senior associate, 1979-; Institute for Higher Education Policy, senior associate, 2006-. Writer. **Publications:** Generations: A Collage on Youth Cult, 1972; No Loaves, No Parables: American Politics and the English Language, 1974; Starting with Students, 1983; The Standardized Test Scores of College Graduates, 1985; Performance and Judgment, 1988; A College Course Map, 1990, 2nd ed. as The New College Course Map, 1999; Light and Shadows on College Athletes, 1990; Women at Thirty Something: Paradoxes of Attainment, 1991; The Way We Are: The Community College as American Thermometer, 1992; Tourists in Our Own Land: Cultural Literacies and the College Curriculum, 1992; Lessons of a Generation: Education and Work in the Lives of the High School Class of 1972, 1994; Leading, Concurrent or Lagging: The Knowledge Content of Computer Science in Higher Education and the Labor Market, 1997; Women and Men of the Engineering Path, 1998; Answers in the Tool Box, 1999; The New College Course

Map and Transcript Files, 2nd ed., 1999; A Parallel Post Secondary Universe, 2000; (co-author) Nuevas miradas sobre la Universidad, 2002; (with B. Daniel and I. Berkovits) Postsecondary Attainment, Attendance, Curriculum, and Performance, 2003; Empirical Curriculum: Changes in Post Secondary Course-Taking, 1972-2000, 2004; Moving into Town-and Moving On: The Community College in the Lives of Traditional-Age Students, 2005; Toolbox Revisited: Paths to Degree Completion from High School through College, 2006. EDITOR: Assessment in American Higher Education, 1986; Signs and Tracers: Indicators of College Student Learning, 1989. **Address:** The Institute for Higher Education Policy, 1320 19th St. NW, Ste. 400, Washington, DC 20036, U.S.A. **Online address:** cadelman@ihep.org

ADELMAN, Deborah. American (born United States), b. 1958. **Genres:** Novellas/Short Stories, Literary Criticism And History, Essays, Translations. **Career:** New York University, instructor of English, 1986-90; Loyola University, instructor of English, 1991-92; Oakton Community College, instructor of English, 1991-92; College of DuPage, assistant professor of English, professor of English, 1992-. Writer. **Publications:** The Children of Perestroika: Moscow Teenagers Talk About Their Lives and the Future, 1992; The Children of Perestroika Come of Age: Young People of Moscow Talk About Life in the New Russia, 1994. **Address:** Department of English, College of DuPage, Rm. IC 2059F, 425 Fawell Blvd., Glen Ellyn, IL 60137-6599, U.S.A. **Online address:** adelman@cdnet.cod.edu

ADELSON, Alan. (Alan Merrill Adelson). American (born United States), b. 1943. **Genres:** History, Bibliography. **Career:** Wall Street Journal, feature writer; Jewish Heritage Project, executive director, 1983-. Journalist. **Publications:** SDS, 1972; (ed. with R. Lapides) Lódz Ghetto: Inside a Community under Siege, 1989; (ed. and cont.) The Diary of David Sierakowiak: Five Notebooks from the Lódpz Ghetto, 1996. **Address:** Jewish Heritage Project, 150 Franklin St., Ste. 1W, New York, NY 10013, U.S.A. **Online address:** aadelson@jps.net

ADELSON, Alan Merrill. *See* **ADELSON, Alan.**

ADELSON, Roger. American (born United States), b. 1942. **Genres:** History, Biography, Essays. **Career:** Oxford University, Alistair Horne Research Fellow; Harvard University, faculty, through 1974; Arizona State University, College of Liberal Arts and Sciences, assistant professor, 1974-77, associate professor, 1977-96, professor of history, 1996-2010, dean, professor emeritus of history, 2010-; The Historian, editor, 1990-95, consulting editor, 1996-2001; Washington University, lecturer; American Graduate School of International Management, lecturer; University of Arizona, lecturer. **Publications:** Mark Sykes: Portrait of an Amateur (biography), 1975; London and the Invention of the Middle East: Money, Power, and War, 1902-1922, 1995; (ed.) Speaking of History: Conversations with Historians, 1990-1995, 1997. **Address:** Department of History, Arizona State University, Coor 4578, Tempe, AZ 85287-4302, U.S.A. **Online address:** roger.adelson@asu.edu

ADEPOJU, Aderanti. Nigerian (born Nigeria), b. 1945. **Genres:** Area Studies, Demography, Economics, Social Sciences, Local History/Rural Topics. **Career:** University of Ife, lecturer, 1964-80, Department of Demography and Social Statistics, professor and head, 1980-84, research professor, 1984-; University of Lagos, Research and Advisory Services Unit, research professor and head, professor and dean, 1984-90, Business Administration, faculty, dean, 1988, Human Resources Development Center, chief executive; African Institute for Economic Development and Planning, training coordinator for United Nations Fund for Population Activities, 1988-; Population, Human Resources and Development, training coordinator, 1988-98; Population and Labour Policy, pioneer regional advisor; University of Swaziland, chief technical advisor; USA National Academy of Sciences, staff; Network on Migration Research in Africa, scientific coordinator. Writer. **Publications:** Population Growth in Nigeria and Its Impact on the Labour Force, 1976; Medium-sized Towns in Nigeria, 1982; Redistributing Population: Challenges and Prospects, 1984; Demography of Swaziland, 1991; Introduction to Demography, 1991; Introduction to Population Studies, 1991; The African Family in the Development Process, 1996; Population, Poverty, Structural Adjustment Programmes, and Quality Of Life in Sub-Saharan Africa, 1996; African Families in the Twenty-First Century: Prospects and Challenges, 2005; Adolescent Sexual And Reproductive Health In Nigeria: Behavioural Patterns and Needs, 2006; Migration in Sub-Saharan Africa, 2008. EDITOR: (with O. Adejuyigbe and L. Dare) Creation of States in Nigeria: A Review of Rationale, Demands and Problems up to 1980, 1982; Technical and Political Aspects of Population Enumeration in Nigeria, 1983; Swaziland: Population, Economy, Society, 1991; The Impact of Structural Adjustment on the Population of Africa, 1993; (with J. Currey) The Impact of Structural Adjustment on the Population of Africa: The Implications for Education, Health, and Employment, 1993; (with C. Oppong) Gender, Work & Population in Sub-Saharan Africa, 1994; (with T. Hammar) International Migration In And From Africa: Dimensions, Challenges, and Prospects, 1996; Family, Population, and Development in Africa, 1997; (with T.V. Naerssen and A. Zoomers) International Migration and National Development in Sub-Saharan Africa: Viewpoints and Policy Initiatives in the Countries of Origin, 2008; International Migration Within To and From Africa in A Globalised World, 2010. **Address:** UN Fund for Population Activities Project, African Inst for Economic Development & Planning, PO Box 3186, Dakar, SEN, Senegal. **Online address:** aadepoju@infoweb.abs.net

ADES, Dawn. British (born England), b. 1943?. **Genres:** Art/Art History, Photography. **Career:** University of Essex, Department of Art, university lecturer, 1968-, professor, 1989-. Writer. **Publications:** Dada and Surrealism, 1974; Photomontage, 1976, 1986; Dada and Surrealism Reviewed, 1978; Experimental Photography, 1980; Salvador Dali, 1982; The 20th-Century Poster: Design of the Avant-Garde, 1984, 2nd ed., 1990; (with A. Forge) Francis Bacon, 1985; Art in Latin America, 1989; André Masson, 1994; Siron Franco: figuras e semelhanças, pinturas de 1968 a 1995, 1995; Surrealist Art: The Lindy and Edwin Bergman Collection at the Art Institute of Chicago, 1997; (with N. Cox and D. Hopkins) Marcel Duchamp, 1999; (ed.) Dali's Optical Illusions, 2000; (with P. Blake and N. Rudd) Peter Blake: About Collage, 2000; (ed. with J. Mundy) Surrealism: Desire Unbound, 2001; (co-author) José Clemente Orozco in the United States, 1927-1934, 2002; Herchcovitch, Alexandre, 2002; Dalí, un creador disidente, 2004; (ed.) Dada Reader: A Critical Anthology, 2006; (ed. with S. Baker) Undercover Surrealism: Georges Bataille and Documents, 2006; (with A. McClean) Revolution on Paper: Mexican Prints 1910-1960, 2009; In Wonderland, 2012. **Address:** Department of Art, University of Essex, Rm. 6.130, Wivenhoe Pk., Colchester, EX CO4 3SQ, England. **Online address:** ades@essex.ac.uk

ADICHIE, Amanda N. *See* **ADICHIE, Chimamanda Ngozi.**

ADICHIE, Chimamanda Ngozi. (Amanda N. Adichie). Nigerian (born Nigeria), b. 1977. **Genres:** Novels. **Career:** Princeton University, Hodder Fellow, 2005-06; Wesleyan University, visiting writer, 2008; Johns Hopkins University, instructor. Writer. **Publications:** AS AMANDA N. ADICHIE: Decisions, 1998; For Love of Biafra, 1998. NOVELS: Purple Hibiscus, 2003; Half of a Yellow Sun, 2006; The Thing Around Your Neck, 2009. Contributor to journals and periodicals. **Address:** c/o Author Mail, Algonquin Books of Chapel Hill, 127 Kingston Dr., Ste. 105, PO Box 2225, Chapel Hill, NC 27514-1650, U.S.A. **Online address:** chimamanda@halfofayellowsun.com

ADICKES, Sandra. (Sandra Elaine Adickes). American (born United States), b. 1933. **Genres:** Literary Criticism And History, Novels. **Career:** City University of New York, faculty; WBAI-FM Radio, producer of the weekly series Urban Education, 1971-73; Winona State University, associate professor of English, 1988-, now professor emeritus of English; College of New Jersey, Women's and Gender Studies Program, adjunct professor. Writer. **Publications:** The Social Quest: The Expanded Vision of Four Women Travellers in the Era of the French Revolution, 1991; Legends of Good Women (novel), 1992; To Be Young Was Very Heaven: Women in New York before the First World War, 1997; (as Sandra E. Adickes) The Legacy of a Freedom School, 2005. Contributor to magazines and journals. **Address:** Department of English, Winona State University, Rm. 302, Minne Hall, 175 W Mark St., PO Box 5838, Winona, MN 55987, U.S.A. **Online address:** sadickes@optonline.net

ADICKES, Sandra Elaine. *See* **ADICKES, Sandra.**

ADIELE, Faith. (Jane Harvard). American (born United States), b. 1963?. **Genres:** Travel/Exploration, Autobiography/Memoirs, Adult Non-fiction, Documentaries/Reportage. **Career:** Massachusetts Immigrant and Refugee Advocacy Coalition, program assistant, 1987-89; Radcliffe College, Education for Action and Special Programs, coordinator, 1990-96; Framingham State College, visiting professor and Christa McAuliffe chair, 1996-98; University Honors College Field Studies Program In South Africa, lead instructor; University of Iowa, teaching assistant, 2000, Division of Sponsored Programs, research assistant, 2001-02; University of Pittsburgh, assistant professor of creative nonfiction 2002-. Writer. **Publications:** (As Jane Harvard) The Student Body, 1998; Time for Kids Reader: A Village Celebration, 2002;

Time for Kids Reader: Life in the City, 2002; Meeting Faith: The Forest Journals of a Black Buddhist Nun, 2004; (ed. with M. Frosch) Coming of Age Around the World: A Multicultural Anthology, 2007. Contributor to periodicals. **Address:** Department of English, University of Pittsburgh, CL 526, 4200 5th Ave., Pittsburgh, PA 15260, U.S.A. **Online address:** faith@adiele.com

ADJIBOLOSOO, Senyo B. S. K. American/Canadian/Ghanaian (born Ghana), b. 1953. **Genres:** Business/Trade/Industry, Economics. **Career:** Trinity Western University, professor of business and economics, 1988-2000; Wattlekainum Cooperative, board director, 1991-93; International Institute for Human Factor Development, founder and executive director, 1992-; Smile Africa Intl., board director, 1993-; African Enterprises, board director, 1995-98; African Leadership Development Institute, teacher, 1997; Point Loma Nazarene University, professor of economics, 2000-; Center for Justice and Reconciliation, board director, 2002-; Human Factor Leadership Academy, founder and president, 2006-. Writer. **Publications:** The Human Factor in Developing Africa, 1995; Global Development the Human Factor Way, 1998; Rethinking Development Theory and Policy: A Human Factor Critique, 1999; Developing Civil Society: Social Order and the Human Factor, 2006. EDITOR AND CONTRIBUTOR: (with F. EzealaHarrison) Perspectives on Economic Development in Africa, 1994; The Significance of the Human Factor in African Economic Development, 1995; Human Factor Engineering and the Political Economy of African Development, 1996; International Perspectives on the Human Factor in Economic Development, 1998; (with B. Ofori-Amoah) Addressing Misconceptions about Africa's Development: Seeing beyond the Veil, 1998; Human Factor in Shaping the Course of History and Development, 2000; Portraits of Human Behavior and Performance: The Human Factor in Action, 2001; (with E.O.K. Prempeh and J. Mensah) Globalization and the Human Factor: Critical Insights, 2004. FORTHCOMING: 1.The Millennium Development Goals: A Critical Human Factor Assessment; 1.The Agony of Human Factor Decay: Human Spheres Throbbing in Firestorms of Corruption; Magnifying the Imprint of Virtue: Brightening the Light Within. Contributor to books. Contributor of articles to journals. **Address:** Fermanian School of Business, Point Loma Nazarene University, 3900 Lomaland Dr., San Diego, CA 92106, U.S.A. **Online address:** senyoadjibolosoo@pointloma.edu

ADKIN, Mark. British (born England), b. 1936. **Genres:** International Relations/Current Affairs, Military/Defense/Arms Control, Politics/Government, History. **Career:** Overseas Civil Service, Solomon Islands and the Gilbert and Ellice Islands, district officer and administrative officer, 1968-81; military historian and writer, 1987-. **Publications:** Urgent Fury: The Battle for Grenada, 1989; The Last Eleven?: The Story of the Post-war VCs, 1991; Goose Green: A Battle is Fought to be Won, 1992; (with M. Yousaf) The Bear Trap: Afghanistan's Untold Story, 1992; (with J. Simpson) The Quiet Operator: Special Forces Signaller Extraordinary: The Story of Major L.R.D. Willmott, 1993; (with G. Wright-North) Prisoner of the Tunipheads: The Fall of Hong Kong and the Imprisonment by the Japanese, 1994; The Charge: The Real Reason Why the Light Brigade Was Lost, 1996; The Sharpe Companion, 1998; (with G. Wright-Nooth) Prisoner of the Turnip Heads: The Fall of Hong Kong and the Imprisonment by the Japanese, 1999; The Waterloo Companion: The Complete Guide to History's Most Famous Land Battle, 2001; (with M. Yousaf) Afghanistan-the Bear Trap: The Defeat of a Superpower, 2001; The Sharpe Companion: The Early Years, 2003; The Trafalgar Companion: A Guide to History's Most Famous Sea Battle and the Life of Admiral Lord Nelson, 2005; The Daily Telegraph Guide to Britain's Military Heritage 2005; (with M. Yousaf) Battle for Afghanistan: The Soviets Versus the Mujahideen during the 1980s, 2007; The Gettysburg Companion 2008. Contributor to periodicals. **Address:** 34 Putnoe Ln., Bedford, MK41 9AB, England. **Online address:** mark.adkin@ntlworld.com

ADKINS, Lesley. British (born England), b. 1955. **Genres:** History, Archaeology/Antiquities, Young Adult Non-fiction, Social Sciences. **Career:** Milton Keynes Development Corp., archaeological assistant, 1976; Museum of London, senior archaeologist, 1983-87; Devon Engineering, archaeological consultant, 1987; historian and archaeologist. Writer. **Publications:** Empires of the Plain, 2003. WITH R.A. ADKINS: A Thesaurus of British Archaeology, 1982; The Handbook of British Archaeology, 1983; Under the Sludge, Beddington Roman Villa, 1986; Archaeological Illustration, 1989; An Introduction to Archaeology, 1989; Talking Archaeology, 1990; Abandoned Places, 1990; Introduction to the Romans, 1991; A Field Guide to Somerset Archaeology, 1992; Handbook to Life in Ancient Rome, 1994; Dictionary of Roman Religion, 1996; Handbook to Life in Ancient Greece, 1997; The Keys of Egypt, 2000; The Little Book of Egyptian Hieroglyphs, 2001; The War for All the Oceans, 2006; Jack Tar, Life in Nelson's Navy, 2008. **Address:** AM Heath, 6 Warwick Ct., Whitestone, London, GL WC1R 5DJ, England. **Online address:** adkinshistory@btinternet.com

ADKINS, Roy A(rthur). British (born England), b. 1951. **Genres:** Archaeology/Antiquities, History, Military/Defense/Arms Control, Mythology/Folklore, Reference. **Career:** Milton Keynes (Eng.) Development Corp., assistant archaeologist, 1974-78; writer, 1977-; Surrey Archaeological Society, field officer, 1978-83; Museum of London, senior archaeologist, 1983-87, consultant, 1987. **Publications:** (With R. Jackson) Neolithic Stone and Flint Axes from the River Thames: An Illustrated Corpus, 1978; Trafalgar: The Biography of a Battle, 2004; Nelson's Trafalgar: The Battle that Changed the World, 2005. WITH L. ADKINS: A Thesaurus of British Archaeology, 1982 as The Handbook of British Archaeology, 1983; Under the Sludge: Beddington Roman Villa: Excavations at Beddington Sewage Works 1981-1983, 1986; Archaeological Illustration, 1989; An Introduction to Archaeology, 1989; Abandoned Places, 1990; Talking Archaeology: A Handbook for Lecturers and Organizers, 1990; Introduction to the Romans, 1991; A Field Guide to Somerset Archaeology, 1992; Handbook to Life in Ancient Rome, 1994, rev. ed., 2005; Dictionary of Roman Religion, 1996; Handbook to Life in Ancient Greece, 1997, rev. ed., 2005; The Keys of Egypt: The Obsession to Decipher Egyptian Hieroglyphs, 2000 as The Keys of Egypt: The Race to Read the Hieroglyphs, 2000 as The Keys of Egypt: The Race to Crack the Hieroglyph Code, 2001; The Little Book of Egyptian Hieroglyphs, 2001; The War for All the Oceans: From Nelson at the Nile to Napoleon at Waterloo, 2007; Jack Tar: Life in Nelson's Navy, 2008. Contributor to journals. **Address:** Little, Brown Book Group, 100 Victoria Embankment, London, GL EC4Y 0DY, England. **Online address:** mail@adkinshistory.com

ADLARD, Mark. British (born England), b. 1932. **Genres:** Novels, Science Fiction/Fantasy, Children's Fiction. **Career:** Teacher of economics, 1985-92. Writer. **Publications:** Interface, 1971; Volteface, 1972; Multiface, 1975; The Greenlander, 1978. **Address:** John Farquharson Ltd., 15 Red Lion Sq., London, GL WC1R 4QW, England.

ADLER, David A. American (born United States), b. 1947. **Genres:** Children's Fiction, Children's Non-fiction, Biography, Humor/Satire, Picture/Board Books, Mystery/Crime/Suspense, Money/Finance, History, Young Adult Non-fiction, Sports/Fitness, Children's Non-fiction, Civil Liberties/Human Rights. **Career:** New York City Board of Education, teacher, 1968-77; editor, 1978-90. **Publications:** PICTURE BOOKS: A Little at a Time, 1976; The House on the Roof: A Sukkot Story, 1976; The Children of Chelm, 1979; You Think It's Fun to Be a Clown!, 1980; My Dog and the Key Mystery, 1982; Bunny Rabbit Rebus, 1983; A Picture Book: Israel, 1984; My Dog and the Knock Knock Mystery, 1985; My Dog and the Green Sock Mystery, 1986; My Dog and the Birthday Mystery, 1987; I Know I'm a Witch, 1988; Happy Hanukkah Rebus, 1989; Malke's Secret Recipe: A Chanukah Story, 1989; Happy Thanksgiving Rebus, 1991; One Yellow Daffodil: A Hanukkah Story, 1995; Chanukkah in Chelm, 1997; The Babe and I, 1999; Mama Played Baseball, 2003; It's Time to Sleep, It's Time to Dream, 2008. RIDDLE BOOKS: The Carsick Zebra and Other Animal Riddles, 1983; The Twisted Witch And Other Spooky Riddles, 1985; The Purple Turkey and Other Thanksgiving Riddles, 1986; Remember Betsy Floss: And Other Colonial American Riddles, 1987; Wild Pill Hickok and Other Old West Riddles, 1988; The Dinosaur Princess And Other Prehistoric Riddles, 1988; A Teacher On Roller Skates, and Other School Riddles, 1989; Calculator Riddles, 1995. BIOGRAPHIES: Our Golda: The Story of Golda Meir, 1984; Martin Luther King Jr.: Free at Last, 1986; Thomas Jefferson: Father of Our Democracy, 1987; George Washington: Father of Our Country, 1988; Jackie Robinson: He Was the First, 1989; Thomas Alva Edison: Great Inventor, 1990; Christopher Columbus: Great Explorer, 1991; Benjamin Franklin: Printer, Inventor, Statesman, 1992; Lou Gehrig: The Luckiest Man, 1997; America's Champion Swimmer: Gertrude Ederle, 2000; B. Franklin, Printer, 2001; A Hero and The Holocaust: The Story of Janusz Korczak and His Children, 2002; Heroes of the Revolution, 2003; Enemies of Slavery, 2004; Joe Louis: America's Fighter, 2005; President George Washington, 2005; Campy: The Story of Roy Campanella, 2007; Heroes for Civil Rights, 2007; Satchel Paige: Don't Look Back, 2007. PICTURE BOOK BIOGRAPHY SERIES: A Picture Book of Martin Luther King, Jr., 1989; A Picture Book of Abraham Lincoln, 1989; A Picture Book of George Washington, 1989; A Picture Book of Benjamin Franklin, 1990; A Picture Book of Thomas Jefferson, 1990; A Picture Book of Helen Keller, 1990; A Picture Book of Christopher Columbus, 1991; A Picture Book of

John F. Kennedy, 1991; A Picture Book of Eleanor Roosevelt, 1991; A Picture Book of Simón Bolívar, 1992; A Picture Book of Florence Nightingale, 1992; A Picture Book of Jesse Owens, 1992; A Picture Book of Harriet Tubman, 1992; A Picture Book of Frederick Douglass, 1993; A Picture Book of Anne Frank, 1993; A Picture Book of Rosa Parks, 1993; A Picture Book of Sitting Bull, 1993; A Picture Book of Robert E. Lee, 1994; A Picture Book of Jackie Robinson, 1994; A Picture Book of Sojourner Truth, 1994; A Picture Book of Patrick Henry, 1995; A Picture Book of Paul Revere, 1995; A Picture Book of Davy Crockett, 1996; A Picture Book of Thomas Alva Edison, 1996; A Picture Book of Louis Braille, 1997; A Picture Book of Thurgood Marshall, 1997; A Picture Book of Amelia Earhart, 1998; A Picture Book of George Washington Carver, 1999; A Picture Book of Sacagawea, 2000; A Picture Book of Dwight David A Picture Book of Eisenhower, 2002; A Picture Book of Lewis and Clark, 2003; A Picture Book of Harriet Beecher Stowe, 2003; (with M.S. Adler) Samuel Adams, 2005; (with M.S. Adler) A Picture Book of John and Abigail Adams, 2007; (with M.S. Adler) A Picture Book of John Hancock, 2007; (with M.S. Adler) A Picture Book of Dolley and James Madison, 2009. CAM JANSEN MYSTERY SERIES: Cam Jansen Mystery: The Stolen Diamonds, 1980; Cam Jansen and the Mystery of the U.F.O., 1980; Cam Jansen Mystery: The Dinosaur Bones, 1981; Cam Jansen Mystery: The Television Dog, 1981; Cam Jansen Mystery: The Babe Ruth Baseball, 1982; Cam Jansen Mystery: The Gold Coins, 1982; Cam Jansen Mystery: The Circus Clown, 1983; Cam Jansen Mystery: The Carnival Prize, 1984; Cam Jansen Mystery: The Monster Movie, 1984; Cam Jansen and the Mystery at the Monkey House, 1985; Cam Jansen Mystery: The Stolen Corn Popper, 1986; Cam Jansen Mystery: Flight Fifty-Four, 1989; Cam Jansen and the Mystery at the Haunted House, 1992; Cam Jansen and the Chocolate Fudge Mystery, 1993; Cam Jansen and the Triceratops Pops Mystery, 1995; Cam Jansen and the Scary Snake Mystery, 1997; Cam Jansen and the Catnapping Mystery, 1998; Cam Jansen and the Barking Treasure Mystery, 1999; Cam Jansen and the Birthday Mystery, 2000; Cam Jansen and the School Play Mystery, 2001; Cam Jansen and the First Day of School Mystery, 2002; Cam Jansen and the Tennis Trophy Mystery, 2003; Cam Jansen and the Snowy Day Mystery, 2004; Cam Jansen and the Valentine Baby Mystery, 2005; Cam Jansen, the Ghostly Mystery, 2005; Cam Jansen and the Secret Service Mystery, 2006; Cam Jansen and the Mystery Writer Mystery, 2007; Cam Jansen and the Summer Camp Mysteries: A Super Special, 2007; Cam Jansen and the Green School Mystery, 2008; Cam Jansen and the Wedding Cake Mystery, 2010. YOUNG CAM JANSEN MYSTERY SERIES: Young Cam Jansen and the Dinosaur Game, 1996; Young Cam Jansen and the Missing Cookie, 1996; Young Cam Jansen and the Lost Tooth, 1997; Young Cam Jansen and the Ice Skate Mystery, 1998; Young Cam Jansen and the Baseball Mystery, 1999; Young Cam Jansen and the Pizza Shop Mystery, 2000; Young Cam Jansen and the Library Mystery, 2001; Young Cam Jansen and the Double Beach Mystery, 2002; Young Cam Jansen and the Zoo Note Mystery, 2003; Young Cam Jansen and the New Girl Mystery, 2004; Young Cam Jansen and the Substitute Mystery, 2005; Young Cam Jansen and the Spotted Cat Mystery, 2006; Young Cam Jansen and the Lions' Lunch Mystery, 2007; Young Cam Jansen and the Molly Shoe Mystery, 2008. JEFFREY'S GHOST ADVENTURE SERIES: Jeffrey's Ghost and the Leftover Baseball Team, 1984; Jeffrey's Ghost and the Fifth-grade Dragon, 1985; Jeffrey's Ghost and the Ziffel Fair Mystery, 1987. FOURTH FLOOR TWINS ADVENTURE SERIES: The Fourth Floor Twins and the Fortune Cookie Chase, 1985; The Fourth Floor Twins and the Fish Snitch Mystery, 1985; The Fourth Floor Twins and the Disappearing Parrot Trick, 1986; The Fourth Floor Twins and the Silver Ghost Express, 1986; The Fourth Floor Twins and the Skyscraper Parade, 1987; The Fourth Floor Twins and the Sand Castle Contest, 1988. T.F. BENSON MYSTERY SERIES: T.F. Benson and the Dinosaur Madness Mystery, 1992; T.F. Benson and the Funny-money Mystery, 1992; T.F. Benson and the Jewelry Spy Mystery, 1992; T.F. Benson and the Detective Dog Mystery, 1993. HOUDINI CLUB MAGIC MYSTERY SERIES: Onion Sundaes, 1994; Wacky Jacks, 1994; Lucky Stars, 1996; Magic Money, 1997. ANDY RUSSELL SERIES: The Many Troubles of Andy Russell, 1998; Andy and Tamika, 1999; School Trouble for Andy Russell, 1999; Parachuting Hamsters and Andy Russell, 2000; Andy Russell, NOT Wanted by the Police, 2001; It's a Baby, Andy Russell, 2006. JEFFREY BONES BEGINNING-READER MYSTERY SERIES: Bones and the Big Yellow Mystery, 2004; Bones and the Dog Gone Mystery, 2004; Bones and the Cupcake Mystery, 2005; Bones and the Dinosaur Mystery, 2005; Bones and the Birthday Mystery, 2007; Bones and the Math Test Mystery, 2008; Bones and the Roller Coaster Mystery, 2010. NON-FICTION: Base Five, 1975; 3D, 2D, 1D, 1975; Roman Numerals, 1977; Redwoods are the Tallest Trees in the World, 1978; 3-2-1 Number Fun, 1981; A Picture Book of Jewish Holidays, 1981; A Picture Book of Passover, 1982; A Picture Book of Hanukkah, 1982; Calculator Fun Book, 1982; Hyperspace! Facts and Fun from All over the Universe, 1982; Our Amazing Ocean, 1983; All about the Moon, 1983; World of Weather, 1983; Wonders of Energy, 1983; Amazing Magnets, 1983; All Kinds of Money, 1984; Prices Go Up, Prices Go Down: The Laws of Supply and Demand, 1984; Inflation: When Prices Go Up, Up, Up, 1985; Banks: Where the Money Is, 1985; The Number on My Grandfather's Arm, 1987; The Children's Book of Jewish Holidays, 1987; We Remember the Holocaust, 1989; You Breathe In, You Breathe Out: All about Your Lungs, 1991; Hilde and Eli: Children of the Holocaust, 1994; Child of the Warsaw Ghetto, 1995; Fractions Fun, 1996; Easy Math Puzzles, 1997; Hiding from the Nazis, 1997; Shape Up: All about Triangles and Other Polygons, 1998; How Tall, How Short, How Far Away, 1999; You Can, Toucan, Math: Word Problem-Solving Fun, 2006; Working with Fractions, 2007. OTHERS: Hanukkah Fun Book: Puzzles, Riddles, Magic, and More, 1976; Passover Fun Book: Puzzles, Riddles, Magic, and More, 1978; Hanukkah Game Book: Games, Puzzles, Riddles, and More, 1978; The Bible Fun Book: Puzzles, Riddles, Magic, and More, 1979; Finger Spelling Fun, 1980; A Children's Treasure of Chassidic Tales, 1983; Eaton Stanley and the Mind Control Experiment, 1985; Benny, Benny, Baseball Nut, 1987; Jewish Holiday Fun, 1987; Rabbit Trouble and the Green Magician, 1987; Brothers in Egypt, 1998; My Writingday, 1999; The Kid's Catalog of Hanukkah, 2004; The Day I Lost My Hampster: And Other True School Stories, 2006; Money Madness, 2007; Don't Talk To Me About the War, 2008; Fun With Roman Numerals, 2008; Honest Abe Lincoln: Easy-To-Read Stories About Abraham Lincoln, 2008; Frederick Douglass: Noble Life, 2010; Time Zones, 2010; Bones and the Clown Mix-up Mystery, 2010; Mystery Math, 2011; Young Cam Jansen and the Circus Mystery, 2011; Cam Jansen and the Graduation Day Mystery, 2011; The Story of Hanukkah, 2011; The Speedy Car Mystery, 2011; Perimeter, Area, and Volume, 2012; (with D.S. Adler) Picture Book of Sam Houston, 2012; Bones and the Football Mystery, 2012; Cam Jansen and the Millionaire Mystery, 2012; Millions, Billions, and Trillions, 2012; Young Cam Jansen and the Magic Bird Mystery, 2012. Works appear in anthologies. Contributor to periodicals. **Address:** PO Box 66, Hewlett, NY 11557, U.S.A. **Online address:** camj563@aol.com

ADLER, Elizabeth. Irish/British (born England) **Genres:** Novels, Romance/Historical. **Career:** Writer. **Publications:** Leonie, 1985; Private Desires, 1985; Peach, 1986; (as Ariana Scott) Fleeting Images, 1987; The Rich Shall Inherit, 1989; The Property of a Lady, 1991; Fortune Is a Woman, 1992; Legacy of Secrets, 1993; The Secret of the Villa Mimosa, 1995; Now or Never, 1997; Sooner or Later, 1998; All or Nothing, 1999; In a Heartbeat, 2001; Last Time I Saw Paris, 2001; Summer in Tuscany, 2002; The Hotel Riviera, 2003; Invitation to Provence, 2004; The House in Amalfi, 2005; Sailing to Capri, 2006; One of Those Malibu Nights, 2008; Meet Me in Venice, 2008; There's Something About St. Tropez, 2009; It All Began in Monte Carlo, 2010; From Barcelona, With Love, 2011. Contributor to periodicals. **Address:** c/o Anne Sibbald, Janklow & Nesbit Associates, 598 Madison Ave., New York, NY 10022, U.S.A.

ADLER, Jeffrey S(cott). American (born United States), b. 1957. **Genres:** History, Race Relations, Politics/Government, Humanities, Social Sciences, Criminology/True Crime. **Career:** Wellesley College, assistant professor, 1986-87; University of Florida, assistant professor, 1987-92, associate professor, 1992-, professor of history and criminology. Writer. **Publications:** Yankee Merchants and the Making of the Urban West: The Rise and Fall of Antebellum St. Louis, 1991; (ed. with D.R. Colburn) African-American Mayors: Race, Politics, and the American City, 2001; First in Violence, Deepest in Dirt: Homicide in Chicago, 1875-1920, 2006. **Address:** Department of History, University of Florida, 211 Keene-Flint Hall, W University Ave., PO Box 117320, Gainesville, FL 32611-7320, U.S.A. **Online address:** jadler@history.ufl.edu

ADLER, Laure. French (born France), b. 1950. **Genres:** History, Translations. **Career:** France Culture Radio, secretary, 1974, director, 1999-2005; Francois Mitterand, cultural advisor, 1989; Journalist, broadcaster, historian and writer. **Publications:** A l'aube du féminisme: le premières journalistes, 1830-1850, 1979; Misérable et glorieuse la femme du XIXe siècle, 1980; Secrets d'alcôve: histoire du couple de 1830 a 1930, 1983; L'amour à l'arsenic: histoire de Marie Lafarge, 1985; Amour á l'arsenic: histoire de Marie Lafarge, 1985; (with A. Veinstein) Avignon: 40 ans de festival, 1987; La vie quotidienne dans les maisons closes: 1830-1930, 1990; Les femmes politiques, 1993; L'année des adieux, 1995; Marguerite Duras, 1998; A ce soir (memoir), 2001; (contrib.) Avant que la nuit ne vienne: entretiens avec Laure Adler,

2002; (co-author) Paris aux noms des femmes, 2005; Dans les pas de Hannah Arendt (title means: 'In the Steps of Hannah Arendt'), 2005; Les femmes qui lisent sont dangereuses, 2006; L'insoumise: récit, 2008; Les femmes qui aiment sont dangereuses, 2009; Dangerous Women: The Perils of Muses and Femmes Fatales, 2009; (with R. Dumas) Entretiens, 2010; (intro.) Beauté des nuits du monde, 2010; Françoise, 2011. Contributor to periodicals. **Address:** c/o Author Mail, Editions Gallimard 5, rue Sebastien-Bottin, Paris, 75328, France.

ADLER, Niclas. Swedish (born Sweden), b. 1971. **Genres:** Business/Trade/Industry, Economics. **Career:** Institute for Management of Innovation and Technology, research fellow and project leader, 1993-; Stockholm School of Entrepreneurship, co-founder, 1996, executive director, 1999-2000; Stockholm School of Economics, co-founder, 1997-2000, FENIX Center for Research on Knowledge and Business Creation, associate director, 1997-2000, director, 2000-, associate professor, 2002-, FENIX Centre for Innovations in Management, co-founder; Chalmers University of Technology, research fellow and project director, 1997; University of Gothenburg, research fellow and project director, 1997; Global Executive Master in Business Creation, project leader, 2000-02; Research Leader Academy, program director, 2002-; Competitive Advantage, Regulation, and Environment (research program), program director, 2002-; Cambridge University, Judge Institute for Management, Centre for International Business and Management, associate faculty, 2003-; Linköping University, lecturer; Chinese University of Hong Kong, lecturer; Jönköping University, Jönköping International Business School, chief executive officer, dean and professor; Immune Therapy Holdings, president; United Kingdom's National School of Government, The Sunningdale Institute, fellow. Writer. **Publications:** (With B. Frössevi) Identifikation av organisatorisk kompetens-nyekelntill framgang?, 1995; Managing Complexity in Product Development: Three Approaches, 1999; (ed. with A. Styhre and A.B. Shani) Collaborative Research in Organizations: Foundations for Learning, Change, and Theoretical Development, 2004. **Address:** Jönköping International Business School, Jönköping University, Rm. B7028, PO Box 1026, JönKöping, SE-551 11, Sweden. **Online address:** niclas.adler@ihh.hj.se

ADLER, Patricia A. American (born United States), b. 1951. **Genres:** Social Sciences, Business/Trade/Industry, Economics, Criminology/True Crime, Sociology. **Career:** University of California, teaching assistant, 1976-78; Tulsa Junior College, instructor, 1981-84; University of Tulsa, visiting assistant professor, 1984-85; Oklahoma State University, assistant professor, 1985-86; Washington University, visiting assistant professor, 1986-87; University of Colorado, Department of Sociology, assistant professor, 1987-93, associate professor, 1993-99, professor of sociology, 1999-; University of Hawaii, visiting associate professor, 1996-99, adjunct professor, 1999-2007; University of Odense, distinguished Lego lecturer, 1996. Writer. **Publications:** (Co-author) Introduction to the Sociologies of Everyday Life, 1980; (ed. with P. Adler) The Social Dynamics of Financial Markets, 1984; Wheeling and Dealing: An Ethnography of an Upper-Level Drug Dealing and Smuggling Community, 1985, 2nd ed., 1993; (with P. Adler) Membership Roles in Field Research, 1987; (with P. Adler) Backboards & Blackboards: College Athletes and Role Engulfment, 1991; (ed. with P. Adler) Constructions of Deviance: Social Power, Context and Interaction, 1994, 6th ed., 2009; (with P. Adler) Peer Power: Preadolescent Culture and Identity, 1998; (ed. with P. Adler and H.J. Corzine) Encyclopedia of Criminology and Deviant Behavior, 2001; (ed. with P. Adler) Sociological Odyssey; Contemporary Readings in Sociology, 2001, 4th ed., 2012; (with P. Adler) Paradise Laborers: Hotel Work in the Global Economy, 2004; (with P. Adler) Tender Cut, 2011; (with P. Adler and P. Adler) Drugs and the American Dream, 2011. **Address:** Department of Sociology, University of Colorado, 217 Ketchum Hall, 1440 15th St., Boulder, CO 80302, U.S.A. **Online address:** adler@colorado.edu

ADLER, Peter. American (born United States), b. 1952. **Genres:** Sociology, Cultural/Ethnic Topics. **Career:** University of California, teaching assistant, 1976-78, faculty associate, 1979-80; University of Tulsa, assistant professor, 1980-86; Washington University, visiting associate professor, 1986-87; University of Hawaii, visiting professor, 1986-2008; University of Denver, Department of Sociology and Criminology, associate professor of sociology, department chair and director of graduate studies, 1987-93, professor of sociology, 1993-, Department of Urban Studies, professor of urban studies, 1993-, distinguished university lecturer, 1997-98. Writer. **Publications:** (Co-author) Introduction to the Sociologies of Everyday Life, 1980; Momentum: A Theory of Social Action, 1981. WITH P.A. ADLER: (ed.) The Social Dynamics of Financial Markets, 1984; Membership Roles in Field Research, 1987; Backboards & Blackboards: College Athletes and Role Engulfment, 1991; (ed.) Constructions of Deviance: Social Power, Context, and Interaction, 1994, 7th ed., 2012; Peer Power: Preadolescent Culture and Identity, 1998; (ed.) Sociological Odyssey: Contemporary Readings in Sociology, 2001, 3rd ed. as Sociological Odyssey: Contemporary Readings in Introductory Sociology, 2010; Paradise Laborers: Hotel Work in the Global Economy, 2004; The Tender Cut, 2011; (ed. with P.K. O'Brien) Drugs and the American Dream, 2012. Contributor to books. **Address:** Department of Sociology and Criminology, University of Denver, 425 Sturm Hall, 2000 E Asbury Ave., PO Box 0942, Denver, CO 80208-0942, U.S.A. **Online address:** padler@du.edu

ADLER, Rich. *See* **ADLER, Richard.**

ADLER, Richard. (Rich Adler). American (born United States), b. 1948. **Genres:** Sports/Fitness, Regional/Urban Planning. **Career:** University of Michigan, Department of Natural Science, associate professor of biology and microbiology. Writer. **Publications:** (As Rich Adler) Baseball at the University of Michigan, 2004; (with R. Adler) Jewish Ann Arbor, 2006; Mack, McGraw, and the 1913 Baseball Season, 2008. Contributor of articles to books and periodicals. **Address:** Department of Natural Sciences, University of Michigan, 115 E SB, 125 Science Bldg., 4901 Evergreen Rd., Dearborn, MI 48128, U.S.A. **Online address:** radler@umd.umich.edu

ADLER, Stephen J. American (born United States), b. 1956?. **Genres:** Biography, Law. **Career:** American Lawyer, newspaper group editor and editorial director, 1983-88; Wall Street Journal, legal editor, 1988-94, special projects editor, 1994-97, deputy page-one editor, 1997-99, assistant managing editor, 1998, deputy managing editor and editorial director of online edition, 1999-2004; Business Week, editor-in-chief, 2005-07; Tampa Times, reporter; Tallahassee Democrat, reporter; Goddard-Riverside Community Center, board of directors; Thomson Reuters, senior vice president, Professional Division, editorial director. **Publications:** The Jury: Trial and Error in the American Courtroom, 1994; (ed. with L. Grunwald) Letters of the Century: America, 1900-1999, 1999; (ed. with L. Grunwald) Women's Letters: America from the Revolutionary War to the Present, 2005. Contributor to periodicals. **Address:** Thomson Reuters, 1 N Dearborn St., Ste. 650, Chicago, IL 60602, U.S.A.

ADLERMAN, Danny. (Kin Eagle). American (born United States), b. 1963. **Genres:** Children's Fiction, Animals/Pets, Picture/Board Books. **Career:** Macmillan Publishing Co., production manager. Writer and consultant. **Publications:** Africa Calling: Nighttime Falling, 1996; (comp. with K. Adlerman) Songs for America's Children, 2002; Rock-a-Bye Baby, 2004; How Much Wood Could A Woodchuck Chuck?, 2006; Oh No, Domino!, 2007; (with K. Alderman) Mommy's Having a Watermelon, 2009. WITH K. ADLERMAN AS KIN EAGLE: It's Raining, It's Pouring, 1994; Hey, Diddle Diddle, 1997; (reteller) Rub a Dub Dub, 1999; (reteller) Humpty Dumpty, 1999. **Address:** Kids at Our House, 47 Stoneham Pl., Metuchen, NJ 08840, U.S.A. **Online address:** info@dannyandkim.com

ADLERMAN, Kimberly M. (Kin Eagle). American (born United States), b. 1964. **Genres:** Children's Fiction, Poetry, Cartoons. **Career:** Macmillan Publishing Co., senior designer, 1990-94; Kids at Our House, owner and creative director, 1994-. Writer, graphic designer, art director, game inventor and illustrator. **Publications:** Africa Calling, 1996; Songs for America's Children, 2002; Rock-a-Bye Baby, 2004; (As Kim Adlerman) Oh No, Domino!, 2007; How Much Wood Could a Woodchuck Chuck?, 2007; (with D. Adlerman) Mommy's Having a Watermelon, 2009. AS KIN EAGLE: It's Raining, It's Pouring, 1994; Hey, Diddle Diddle, 1997; Rub a Dub Dub, 1998; Humpty Dumpty, 1999. **Address:** Kids at Our House, 47 Stoneham Pl., Metuchen, NJ 08840, U.S.A. **Online address:** kim@dannyandkim.com

ADNAN, Etel. American/Lebanese (born Lebanon), b. 1925. **Genres:** Novels, Novellas/Short Stories, Plays/Screenplays, Poetry, Biography. **Career:** Bureau de la Presse, 1941-45; Al-Ahliya School for Girls, teacher of French literature, 1947-49; Dominican College, professor of philosophy, 1958-72; al-SAFA and L'Orient-Le Jour (French-language newspapers), literary editor, 1972-75; Radius of Arab-American Writers Inc., president. **Publications:** POETRY: Moonshots, 1966; Five Senses for One Death, 1971; Jebu/L'Express Beyrouth-Enfer, 1973; L'Apocalypse Arabe, 1980; From A to Z, 1982; Pablo Neruda Is a Banana Tree, 1982; The Indian Never Had a Horse, and Other Poems, 1985; The Arab Apocalypse, 1989, 3rd ed., 2006; The Spring Flowers Own and The Manifestations of the Voyage, 1990; Kitab Al Bahr (title means: 'The Book of the Sea'), 1994; There: In the Light and the Darkness of the

Self and of the Other (prose poem), 1997; In/somnia, 2002. OTHER: Sitt Marie Rose (novel), 1982; Maroc: l'artisanat créateur, 1983; Journey to Mount Tamalpais (essay), 1986; (contrib.) Russell Chatham, 1987; Paris, When It's Naked (essay), 1993; Of Cities and Women (Letters to Fawwaz), 1993; In the Heart of the Heart of Another Country, 2005; Seasons, 2008; Master of the Eclipse: And other Stories, 2009. Works appear in anthologies. **Address:** 35 Marie St., Sausalito, CA 94965, U.S.A.

ADOFF, Arnold. American (born United States), b. 1935. **Genres:** Poetry, Novellas/Short Stories, Children's Fiction, Essays, Young Adult Fiction, Adult Non-fiction, Autobiography/Memoirs, History, History. **Career:** Teacher, 1957-69; Arnold Adoff Agency, literary agent, 1977-; Queens College, visiting professor, 1986-87; New York University, instructor; Connecticut College, instructor. Writer. **Publications:** POETRY: Make a Circle, Keep Us In: Poems for a Good Day, 1975; Big Sister Tells Me That I'm Black, 1976; Tornado! Poems, 1977; Under the Early Morning Trees, 1978; Where Wild Willie, 1978; Eats, 1979; I Am the Running Girl, 1979; Friend Dog, 1980; Today We Are Brother and Sister, 1981; Outside Inside Poems, 1981; Birds, 1982; All the Colors of the Race, 1982; The Cabbages Are Chasing the Rabbits, 1985; Sports Pages, 1986; Greens, 1988; Chocolate Dreams, 1989; In for Winter, Out for Spring, 1991; Street Music: City Poems, 1995; Slow Dance Heart Break Blues, vol. I, 1995; Touch the Poem, 1996; Touch Stone, 1997; Love Letters, 1997; The Basket Counts, 2000; Touch the Poem, 2000; Daring Dog and Captain Cat, 2001; Black is Brown is Tan, 2002. EDITOR: I Am the Darker Brother: An Anthology of Modern Poems by Negro Americans, 1968; City in All Directions: An Anthology of Modern Poems, 1969; Black Out Loud: An Anthology of Modern Poems by Black Americans, 1970; Malcolm X, 1970; It Is the Poem Singing into Your Eyes: An Anthology of New Young Poets, 1971; The Poetry of Black America: An Anthology of the 20th Century, 1973; My Black Me: A Beginning Book of Black Poetry, 1974; (ed.) Celebrations: A New Anthology of Black American Poetry, 1977; (with K. Cook) Virginia Hamilton: Speeches, Essays and Conversations, 2010. FICTION: Mandala, 1971; Black Is Brown Is Tan, 1973; Flamboyan, 1988; Hard to Be Six, 1991; The Return of Rex and Ethel, 2000; Daring Dog and Captain Cat, 2001; Roots and Blues: A Celebration, 2010. NONFICTION: Black on Black, 1968, rev. ed., 1997; Brothers and Sisters: Modern Stories by Black Americans, 1970. Contributor of articles to periodicals. Works appear in anthologies. **Address:** Arnold Adoff Agency Inc., PO Box 293, Yellow Springs, OH 45387, U.S.A. **Online address:** arnoldadoff@aol.com

ADOFF, Jaime. American (born United States), b. 1967?. **Genres:** Children's Fiction, Songs/Lyrics And Libretti, Picture/Board Books. **Career:** Writer, 1998-. **Publications:** The Song Shoots out of My Mouth: A Celebration of Music, 2002; Names Will Never Hurt Me, 2004; Jimi and Me, 2005; The Death of Jayson Porter, 2008; Small Fry, 2008. **Address:** c/o Arnold Adoff, 750 Union St., Yellow Springs, OH 45387, U.S.A. **Online address:** jaime@jaimeadoff.com

ADOLPHSON, Mikael S. Swedish (born Sweden), b. 1961. **Genres:** History. **Career:** University of Oklahoma, assistant professor, 1995-99; Harvard University, assistant professor, 1999-2003, associate professor, 2003-. Writer and historian. **Publications:** The Gates of Power: Monks, Courtiers, and Warriors in Premodern Japan, 2000; (co-author) Treasures of the Yenching: Seventy-Fifth Anniversary of the Harvard-Yenching Library: Exhibition Catalogue, 2003; (ed. with S. Matsumoto) Heian Japan, Centers and Peripheries, 2007; The Teeth and Claws of the Buddha: Monastic Warriors and Sohei in Japanese History, 2007. **Address:** Department of East Asian Languages and, Civilizations, Harvard University, 2 Divinity Ave., Cambridge, MA 02138, U.S.A.

ADSHEAD, S(amuel) A(drian) M(iles). New Zealander (born New Zealand) **Genres:** History, Civil Liberties/Human Rights, Theology/Religion. **Career:** University of Canterbury, professor in history, through 1997, professor emeritus in history, 1997-. Writer. **Publications:** Debate on China, 1969; The Modernization of the Chinese Salt Administration, 1900-1920, 1970; The End of the Chinese Empire, 1973; Province and Politics in Late Imperial China: Viceregal Government in Szechwan, 1898-1911, 1984; China in World History, 1988, 3rd ed., 2000; Salt and Civilization, 1992; Central Asia in World History, 1993; Material Culture in Europe and China, 1400-1800: The Rise of Consumerism, 1997; Philosophy of Religion in Nineteenth-Century England and beyond, 2000; T'ang China: The Rise of the East in World History, 2004. **Address:** Department of History, University of Canterbury, PO Box 4800, Christchurch, 8020, New Zealand.

AFARY, Janet. American/Iranian (born Iran) **Genres:** Adult Non-fiction, Social Commentary, Social Sciences. **Career:** University of Michigan, lecturer, 1984-85; University of Chicago, research associate, 1985-91; Columbia University, assistant professor of history, 1991-92; Purdue University, assistant professor of history, 1992-95, associate professor of history and women's studies, 1997-, professor of history; University of California-Santa Barbara, professor of religious studies and feminist studies, Mellichamp chair in global religion and modernity, Duncan and Suzanne Mellichamp professor of global religion and modernity; University of California-Los Angels, Keddie-Balzan fellow, 2009; Coordinating Council for Women in History, president, 2001-03; Association for Middle East Women's Studies, president, 2004-05; International Society for Iranian Studies, president, 2004-06. Writer. **Publications:** (Ed. with H. Javadi, M. Marashi and S. Shekarloo) Disciplining of Women and Vices of Men, 1992; The Iranian Constitutional Revolution, 1906-1911: Grassroots Democracy, Social Democracy and the Origins of Feminism, rev. ed. as The Iranian Constitutional Revolution, 1996; (ed.) The Semi-Secret Councils of Women in the Iranian Constitutional Revolution, 1998; (ed. with M. Alibakhshian and M. Fatoorehchi) A Look at Women and Gender in the Iranian Constitutional Revolution, 2000; (with K.B. Anderson) Foucault and the Iranian Revolution: Gender and the Seductions of Islamism, 2005; Sexual Politics in Modern Iran, 2009. Contributor to books. **Address:** Department of Feminist Studies, University of California, 4631 South Hall, Santa Barbara, CA 93106-7110, U.S.A. **Online address:** afary@purdue.edu

AFFRON, Charles. American (born United States), b. 1935. **Genres:** Film, Music. **Career:** University of Brandeis, instructor, assistant professor of romance languages; New York University, assistant professor, 1965-68, professor of French, 1968-, now emeritus. Writer. **Publications:** Patterns of Failure in La Comédie Humaine, 1966; A Stage for Poets: Studies in the Theatre of Hugo and Musset, 1971; Star Acting: Gish, Garbo, Davis, 1977; Cinema and Sentiment, 1982; Divine Garbo, 1985; Fellini's 8 1/2, 1987; (with M.J. Affron) Sets In Motion: Art Direction and Film Narrative, 1995; Lillian Gish: Her Legend, Her Life, 2001; (with M.J. Affron) Best Years: Going to the Movies, 1945-1946, 2009. **Address:** Department of French, New York University, 5 Washington Sq. N, 1st Fl., New York, NY 10003-6667, U.S.A. **Online address:** charles.affron@nyu.edu

AFKHAMI, Mahnaz. American/Iranian (born Iran), b. 1941. **Genres:** Area Studies, Women's Studies And Issues. **Career:** Abstracts of English Studies, assistant editor, 1965-66; University of Colorado, lecturer, 1966-67; National University of Iran (also known as Melli University), Department of English, assistant professor, 1967-68, department head, 1968-70; Women's Organization of Iran, secretary general, 1970-79, School of Social Work, chair of board of trustees, 1973-79; consultant on women and development, 1979-81; Government of Iran, minister for women's affairs, 1976-78; Foundation for Iranian Studies, founder and executive director, 1981-; Iran Nameh, publisher, 1981-; Oral History of Iran Archives, founder, 1982, director, 1982-; Sisterhood Is Global Institute, vice-president, 1989-96, executive director, 1992-96, president, 1996-99; Women's Learning Partnership for Rights, Development and Peace, founder and president, 2000-. Writer. **Publications:** (With C. Albright) Iran: A Pre-Collegiate Handbook, 1992; Women in Exile, 1994; (ed. with E. Friedl) In the Eye of the Storm: Women in Post-revolutionary Iran, 1994; (ed. and intro.) Women and the Law in Iran, 1967-1978, 1994; (ed. with G. Emami) Readings in Feminist Theory: An Anthology (in Persian), 1995; (ed.) Faith and Freedom: Women's Human Rights in the Muslim World, 1995; (with H. Vaziri) Claiming Our Rights: A Manual for Women's Human Rights Education in Muslim Societies, 1996; (contrib.) Radically Speaking: Feminism Reclaimed, 1996; (ed. with E. Friedl) Muslim Women and the Politics of Participation: Implementing the Beijing Platform in Muslim Societies, 1997; (with M. Afkhami, G.H. Nemiroff and H. Vaziri) Safe and Secure: Eliminating Violence Against Women and Girls in Muslim Societies, 1998; (contrib.) In Our Own Words: A Guide for Human Rights Education Facilitators, 1999; (contrib.) A Map of Hope, 1999; (contrib.) Religious Fundamentalisms and the Human Rights of Women, 1999; al-Qiyādah ila-ittikhāal-qarārāt dalī litarīb al-nisā alāal-Qiyādah 2001; (co-author) Leading to Choices: A Leadership Training Handbook for Women, 2001; (ed.) Toward a Compassionate Society, 2002; (co-author) Abhirucī paricāla, 2002; (co-author) Tawaṣ ṣ ul ilá al-khayrāt, al-qiyādah al-mafahim, al-māharāt wa-al-khibrāt, 2002; (co-author) Tanlovga etaklab, 2003; Apāmbā khañjabā, 2003; Jāmiah, dawlat va junbish-i zanān-i īrān, 1357-1342, 2003; Jāmiah, dawlat va junbish-I zanān-I īrān, 1357-1342: muṣ āḥibah bā Mahnāz Afkhmī 2003; (co-author) Memimpin menuju pilihan: buku panduan latihan kepimpinan wanita, 2005. Works appear in anthologies. Contributor to periodicals. **Address:** c/o Edite Kroll, Edite Kroll Literary Agency, 12 Grayhurst Pk., Portland, ME 04102, U.S.A.

AFONG, Milo S. American (born United States) **Genres:** Novellas/Short Stories, Military/Defense/Arms Control, Biography. **Career:** Writer. **Publications:** HOGs in the Shadows: Combat Stories from Marine Snipers in Iraq, 2007; Hunters: U.S. Snipers in the War on Terror, 2010. **Address:** Penguin Group Inc., 375 Hudson St., New York, NY 10014, U.S.A. **Online address:** msa8541@yahoo.com

AFZAL, Omar. American/Indian (born India), b. 1939. **Genres:** Cultural/Ethnic Topics, Biography. **Career:** Gauhati University, teacher of English literature, 1965-68; American Institute of Indian Studies, teacher of Urdu and Hindi, 1970-72; Delhi University, teacher of English language and literature, 1972-73; Cornell University, Southeast Asia assistant, 1973-, Center for Research and Communication, chairperson, now retired. Writer. **Publications:** The Life of Muhammad (biography), 1971; Aap ki uljhane, 1972; Issues in the Lunar Calendar, 1988; Calculating Prayer Times, 1993; (ed. with N.H. Barazangi and M.R. Zaman) Islamic Identity and the Struggle for Justice, 1996. Contributor of stories to magazines. **Address:** 180 Kroch Library, Cornell University, Day Hall Lobby, Ithaca, NY 14853, U.S.A. **Online address:** omarafzal1@yahoo.com

AGARD, John. British/Guyanese (born Guyana), b. 1949. **Genres:** Children's Fiction, Poetry, Novellas/Short Stories, Young Adult Fiction. **Career:** Commonwealth Institute, touring lecturer, 1977, faculty, 1978-85; South Bank Centre, writer-in-residence, 1993; British Broadcasting Corp., poet-in-residence, Windrush Project, writer-in-residence; Sunday Chronicle, sub-editor and feature writer; National Maritime Museum, poet-in-residence. **Publications:** POETRY FOR ADULTS: Shoot Me with Flowers (poetry), 1974; Man to Pan: A Cycle of Poems to Be Performed with Drums and Steel Pans, 1982; Limbo Dancer in the Dark, 1983; Limbo Dancer in Dark Glasses, 1983; Livingroom, 1983; Mangoes & Bullets: Selected and New Poems, 1972-84, 1985; Lovelines for a Goat-born Lady, 1990; A Stone's Throw from Embankment: The South Bank Collection, 1993; Weblines, 2000; (with G. Nichols) From Mouth to Mouth, 2004; Baby Poems, 2005; Half-Caste, 2005; (with B. Cattell) Butter-Finger, 2006; (with J. Bent) Wriggle Piggy Toes, 2006; We Brits, 2006; (with B. Cattell) Shine On, Butter-Finger, 2007; The Young Inferno, 2008; (with G. Nicholls) Tiger Dead! Tiger Dead!: Stories from the Caribbean, 2008; Clever Backbone, 2009. CHILDREN'S FICTION: Letters for Lettie and Other Stories, 1979; Dig away Two-Hole Tim, 1981; Lend Me Your Wings, 1987; The Emperor's Dan-Dan, 1992; Oriki and the Monster Who Hated Balloons, 1994; The Monster Who Loved Telephones, 1994; The Monster Who Loved Cameras, 1994; The Monster Who Loved Toothbrushes, 1994; (with K. Paul) Brer Rabbit, the Great Tug-o-War, 1998. JUVENILE AND YOUNG ADULT POETRY: I Din Do Nuttin and Other Poems, 1983; Say It Again, Granny! Twenty Poems from Caribbean Proverbs, 1986; The Calypso Alphabet, 1989; Go Noah, Go!, 1990; Laughter is an Egg, 1990; (with G. Nichols) No Hickory, No Dickory, No Dock: A Collection of Caribbean Nursery Rhymes, 1991 as No Hickory, No Dickory, No Dock: Caribbean Nursery Rhymes, 1994; Grandfather's Old Bruk-a-down Car, 1994; (co-author) Another Day on Your Foot and I Would Have Died, 1996; We Animals Would Like a Word with You, 1996; Get Back, Pimple!, 1996; From the Devil's Pulpit, 1997; Hello New! New Poems for a New Century, 2000; Points of View with Professor Peekaboo, 2000; Come Back to Me, My Boomerang, 2001; Einstein, the Girl Who Hated Maths, 2002; (co-author) Number Parade, 2002; Hello H2O, 2004; Alternative Anthem: Selected Poems, 2009. OTHERS: Life Doesn't Frighten Me at All: Poems, 1990; The Great Snakeskin (children's play), 1993; (ed. with G. Nichols) A Caribbean Dozen: Poems from Caribbean Poets, 1994; A Child's Year of Stories and Poems, 2000; (ed.) Under the Moon & Over the Sea, 2002. **Address:** Jubilee Books, Eltham Green School Complex, Middle Park Ave., London, GL SE9 5EQ, England. **Online address:** enquiries@jubileebooks.co.uk

AGARWAL, Shilpa. American/Indian (born India), b. 1971. **Genres:** Novels, Human Relations/Parenting, Novellas/Short Stories. **Career:** University of California-Los Angeles, instructor; University of California-Santa Barbara, instructor; South Asian Artists' Collective, co-founder. Writer. **Publications:** Haunting Bombay, 2009. **Address:** InkWell Management, 521 5th Ave., 26th Fl., New York, NY 10175, U.S.A. **Online address:** shilpa@shilpaagarwal.com

AGASSI, Andre Kirk. American (born United States), b. 1970. **Genres:** Autobiography/Memoirs. **Career:** Professional tennis player, 1986-2006; Andre Agassi Charitable Foundation, founder, 1995-. Writer. **Publications:** (With J.R. Moehringer) Open: An Autobiography, 2009. **Address:** Andre Agassi Foundation, 3883 Howard Hughes Pkwy., 8th Fl., Las Vegas, NV 89169, U.S.A. **Online address:** info@agassi.net

AGEE, Chris. Irish/American (born United States), b. 1956. **Genres:** Poetry. **Career:** Poetry Ireland Review, editor; Belfast Institute of Further and Higher Education, lecturer in literacy, 1979; Queen's University, School of Education, lecturer, 1985-90; University of Massachusetts, William Joiner Center for the Study of War and Social Consequences, international writing fellow, 2003; The Open University in Northern Ireland, tutor; University of East London, adult education advisor; Irish Pages, editor. **Publications:** POETRY: In the New Hampshire Woods, 1992; (ed.) Scar on the Stone: Contemporary Poetry from Bosnia, 1998; The Sierra de Zacatecas, 1998; First Light, 2003; (ed.) The New North: Contemporary Poetry from Northern Ireland, 2008; Next to Nothing, 2008. **Address:** The Daedalus Press, 13 Moyclare Rd., Baldoyle, Dublin, DU 13, Ireland.

AGEE, Jonis. American (born United States), b. 1943. **Genres:** Novels, Novellas/Short Stories, Poetry, Autobiography/Memoirs, Essays. **Career:** College of St. Catherine, professor of English, director of the creative writing program, 1975-95; Walker Arts Center, Performing Arts Program, literary consultant, 1978-84; Macalester College, adjunct teacher, 1980-88; Literary Post Program for Senior Citizen Writers (COMPAS), teacher and editor, 1986-89; University of Michigan, teacher in creative writing and English, 1995-98; University of Nebraska, Department of English, professor in creative writing and English, 2000-, Adele Hall professor of English. Writer. **Publications:** POETRY: Houses, 1976; Mercury, 1981; Two Poems, 1982. EDITOR: Border Crossings, 1984; Stiller's Pond, 1988, rev. ed., 1991. STORIES: Bend This Heart, 1989; Pretend We've Never Met, 1989; A .38 Special and a Broken Heart, 1995; Taking the Wall (stories), 1999; Acts of Love on Indigo Road: New and Selected Stories, 2003. NOVELS: Sweet Eyes, 1991; Strange Angels, 1993; Salvation Sister, 1994; South of Resurrection, 1997; The Weight of Dreams, 1999; The River Wife, 2007. Works appear in anthologies. Contributor to periodicals. **Address:** Department of English, University of Nebraska, 215 Andrews Hall, PO Box 880333, Lincoln, NE 68588-0333, U.S.A. **Online address:** jagee@unl.edu

AGELL, Charlotte. American/Swedish (born Sweden), b. 1959. **Genres:** Children's Fiction, Illustrations, Novels, Picture/Board Books. **Career:** Author and illustrator. **Publications:** SELF-ILLUSTRATED: The Sailor's Book, 1991; Mud Makes Me Dance in the Spring, 1994; I Wear Long Green Hair in the Summer, 1994; Wind Spins Me Around in the Fall, 1994; I Slide into the White of Winter, 1994; Dancing Feet, 1994; I Swam with a Seal, 1995; I Love the Seasons, 1995; We Kiss Monsters, 1996; To the Island, 1998; Up the Mountain, 2000; Welcome Home or Someplace Like It (young adult novel), 2003; Shift, 2008; The Accidental Adventures of India McAllister, 2010. **Address:** c/o Edite Kroll, Edite Kroll Literary Agency Inc., 20 Cross St., Saco, ME 04072, U.S.A. **Online address:** cagell@comcast.net

AGGARWAL, Ravina. American (born United States), b. 1965. **Genres:** Humanities, International Relations/Current Affairs, Politics/Government. **Career:** Smith College, Department of Anthropology, assistant professor, associate professor. Anthropologist and writer. **Publications:** (Trans. and ed.) Abdul Ghani Sheikh, Forsaking Paradise: Stories from Ladakh, 2001; (ed.) Into the High Ranges, 2002; Beyond Lines of Control: Performance and Politics on the Disputed Borders of Ladakh, India, 2004. Contributor to journals. **Address:** Department of Anthropology, Smith College, Wright Hall 214, Northampton, MA 01063, U.S.A. **Online address:** raggarwa@smith.edu

AGHA-JAFFAR, Tamara. American/Iraqi (born Iraq), b. 1952. **Genres:** Novels, Literary Criticism And History, Politics/Government. **Career:** University of North Carolina, adjunct instructor in English, 1980-83; Johnson County Community College, adjunct instructor in English, 1984-87; Kansas Community College, faculty, 1987-, coordinator of women's studies, 1995-2003, Department of English, coordinator, 1999-2001, professor of English, Department of Humanities and Fine Arts, dean, acting associate provost for academic affairs, provost for academic affairs, chief academic officer. Writer. **Publications:** Demeter and Persephone: Lessons from a Myth, 2002; (ed.) Women and Goddesses in Myth and Sacred Text: An Anthology, 2005. Contributor to periodicals. **Address:** Kansas Community College, 7250 State Ave., Kansas City, KS 66112, U.S.A. **Online address:** taghajaf@kckcc.edu

AGICH, George J. American (born United States), b. 1947. **Genres:** Ethics, Medicine/Health, Philosophy. **Career:** University of Texas, teaching assistant, 1969-73, Medical Branch, research fellow, 1975-76; Southern Illinois University, assistant professor, 1976-81, associate professor, 1981-88, professor of medical humanities and psychiatry, 1988-97, Ethics and Philosophy of Medicine Program, director, 1976-86, Medical Ethics Program, director, 1990-97; University of Illinois, adjunct professor, 1978-97; Sangamon State University, adjunct professor of philosophy, 1978-; Cambridge University, director; Wayne State University, Paul E. Ruble memorial lecturer, 1987; Memorial Medical Center, staff, Ethics Consultation Service, director, 1991-; Cleveland Clinic Foundation, Department of Bioethics, F.J. O'Neill chair in clinical bioethics, 1997-2005, Transplantation Center, staff, 1998-; Ohio State University, School of Medicine, Department of Internal Medicine, professor of clinical medicine, 1999-; University of Basel, Freiwillige Akademische Gesellschaft visiting professor, 2003-04; Cleveland Clinic Lerner College of Medicine of Case Western Reserve University, Department of Medicine, professor, 2003-05; Bowling Green State University, Department of Philosophy, adjunct professor, 1997-2005, professor, 2005-, BGeXperience Program, director, Social Philosophy and Policy Center, senior research fellow, 2006-; Planned Parenthood, consultant. Writer. **Publications:** Autonomy and Long-Term Care, 1993; Dependence and Autonomy in Old Age: An Ethical Framework for Long-term Care, 2nd rev. ed., 2003. EDITOR AND CONTRIBUTOR: Responsibility in Health Care, 1982; (with C.E. Begley) The Price of Health, 1986. Works appear in anthologies. Contributor of articles to journals. **Address:** BGeXperience Program, Bowling Green State University, 122 Conklin N, Bowling Green, OH 43403, U.S.A. **Online address:** agichg@ccf.org

AGINS, Teri. American (born United States), b. 1953. **Genres:** Marketing, Fash Ion/Costume, Art/Art History, Photography. **Career:** Fairchild Publications, staff, 1977-; Wall Street Journal, reporter, 1984-88, fashion reporter, 1988-, senior writer, columnist, now retired. Educator. **Publications:** The End of Fashion: The Mass Marketing of the Clothing Business, 1999; The End of Fashion: How Marketing Changed the Clothing Business Forever, 2000. Contributor to periodicals. **Address:** Quill/William Morrow, 10 E 53rd St., New York, NY 10022-5244, U.S.A.

AGNEW, Eleanor. American (born United States), b. 1948. **Genres:** Adult Non-fiction. **Career:** Berkshire Sampler, feature writer, columnist and reporter, 1970-75; Worcester Telegram, feature writer, columnist, and reporter, 1970-75; Gazette, feature writer, columnist, and reporter, 1970-75; Francis Marion University, instructor, 1986-89; Georgia Southern University, associate professor of writing, 1989-, associate professor emeritus. Writer. **Publications:** (With S. Robideaux) My Mama's Waltz, 1998; Back from the Land: How Young Americans Went to Nature in the 1970s, and Why They Came Back, 2004; Final Notice, forthcoming. Contributor to books and periodicals. **Address:** Georgia Southern University, PO Box 8026, Statesboro, GA 30460, U.S.A. **Online address:** eagnew@gsvms2.cc.gasou.edu

AGONITO, Rosemary. (Rosemary Giambattista Agonito). American (born United States), b. 1937. **Genres:** Novels, Business/Trade/Industry, Self Help, Women's Studies And Issues, History, Social Sciences. **Career:** Maria Regina College, instructor in philosophy, 1966-68; Syracuse University, instructor in philosophy, 1968-73; Colgate University, assistant professor of philosophy, 1973-75; Rochester Institute of Technology, Eisenhower College, associate professor of philosophy and humanities, 1976-83, director of women's studies, 1980-83; New Futures Enterprises, president, 1983-; Wells College, lecturer in philosophy, 1984-; Task Force on Employment/Economics for Women, chairman, 1986-. Writer. **Publications:** (Ed.) History of Ideas on Woman: A Source Book, 1977; Promoting Self Esteem in Young Women: A Teacher's Manual, 1988; No More Nice Girl: Power, Sexuality and Success in the Workplace, 1993; Your Dream Made Easy: How to Start a Successful Business, 1999; Dirty Little Secrets: Sex in the Workplace: What Have We Learned and Where Do We Go from Here, 2000; A Good Day to Die (novel), 2005; (with J. Agonito) Buffalo Calf Road Woman: The Story of a Warrior of the Little Bighorn, 2006. **Address:** New Futures Enterprises, 4502 Broad Rd., Syracuse, NY 13215, U.S.A. **Online address:** info@agonito.com

AGONITO, Rosemary Giambattista. *See* **AGONITO, Rosemary.**

AGRAN, Edward G. (Edward Gale Agran). American (born United States), b. 1949. **Genres:** History, Biography, Autobiography/Memoirs. **Career:** Centre College, assistant professor of American history, 1985-91; Wilmington College, associate professor of American history, 1993-, professor of history. Writer. **Publications:** (As Edward Gale Agran) Too Good a Town: William Allen White, Community, and the Emerging Rhetoric of Middle America, 1998. Contributor to journals. **Address:** Department of History, Wilmington College, 1870 Quaker Way, Wilmington, OH 45177-2473, U.S.A. **Online address:** eagran@wilmington.edu

AGRAN, Edward Gale. *See* **AGRAN, Edward G.**

AGRAWAL, Arun. American (born United States), b. 1962. **Genres:** Politics/Government, Administration/Management, Technology, Economics. **Career:** University of Florida, assistant professor, 1993-97; Yale University, Department of Political Science, assistant professor, 1997-2000, associate professor, 2000-02; McGill University, McGill School of Environment, Department of Political Science, associate professor, 2002-03; University of Michigan, School of Natural Resources and Environment, associate professor, 2003-08, professor, 2008-, research associate dean, 2009-; International Forestry Resources and Institutions Program, coordinator, 2006-. Writer. **Publications:** The Grass is Greener on the Other Side: A Study of Raikas, Migrant Pastoralists of Rajasthan, 1992; (with C. Britt and K. Kanel) Decentralization in Nepal: A Comparative Analysis: A Report on the Participatory District Development Program, 1999; Greener Pastures: Politics, Markets, and Community among a Migrant Pastoral People, 1999; (with J.C. Ribot) Analyzing Decentralization: A Framework with South Asian and West African Environmental Cases, 2000; (ed. with K. Sivaramakrishnan) Agrarian Environments: Resources, Representations, and Rule in India, 2000; (ed. and intro. with C.C. Gibson) Communities and the Environment: Ethnicity, Gender, and the State in Community-Based Conservation, 2001; (ed. with K. Sivaramakrishnan) Regional Modernities: The Cultural Politics of Development in India, 2003; Environmentality: Technologies of Government and the Making of Subjects, 2005. Contributor of articles to journals. **Address:** School of Natural Resources and Environment, University of Michigan, 3502 Dana Bldg., 440 Church St., Ann Arbor, MI 48109-1041, U.S.A. **Online address:** arunagra@umich.edu

AGRAWAL, Govind P. American/Indian (born India), b. 1951. **Genres:** Engineering, Physics. **Career:** Eole Polytechnique, research associate, 1974-76; City University of New York, research associate, 1977-80; Quantel S.A., staff scientist, 1980-81; AT&T Bell Laboratories, technical staff, 1982-88; University of Rochester, professor of optics, 1989-, Department of Physics and Astronomy, professor, Laboratory for Laser Energetics, senior scientist; Journal of the Optical Society of America, topical editor, 1993-98, Optics Express, associate editor, 2001-04; Academic Press, editor, 1998-2008; South China Normal University, honorary professor, 1999; Shanghai Institute of Optics and Mechanics, honorary professor, 2005; Friedrich-Schiller University, Carl-Zeiss visiting professor, 2006. **Publications:** Long-Wavelength Semiconductor Lasers, 1986; Nonlinear Fiber Optics, 1989, 4th ed., 2007; Fiber-Optic Communication Systems, 1992, 4th ed. as Fiber-Optic Communication Systems with Cd, 2010; (ed. with R.W. Boyd) Contemporary Nonlinear Optics, 1992; (with N.K. Dutta) Semiconductor Lasers, 2nd ed., 1993; (ed.) Semiconductor Lasers: Past, Present and Future, 1995; Applications of Nonlinear Fiber Optics, 2001, 2nd ed., 2008; (with Y.S. Kivshar) Optical Solitons: From Fibers to Photonic Crystals, 2003; Lightwave Technology: Components and Devices, 2004; (ed. with C. Headley) Raman Amplification in Fiber Optical Communication Systems, 2005; Lightwave Technology: Telecommunication Systems, 2005; (with M. Premaratne) Light Propagation in Gain Media, 2011. **Address:** Department of Physics and Astronomy, University of Rochester, 515 Goergen Hall, 500 Wilson Blvd., PO Box 270171, Rochester, NY 14627, U.S.A. **Online address:** gpa@optics.rochester.edu

AGUILAR, Rosario. *See* **FIALLOS, Rosario.**

AGUIRRE, Forrest. American (born United States), b. 1969. **Genres:** Sociology, Horror, Novellas/Short Stories. **Career:** Writer. **Publications:** The Butterfly Artist (chapbook; stories), 2002; (ed. with J. VanderMeer) Leviathan 3: Libri Quosdam ad Scientiam, Alios ad Insaniam Deduxere, 2002; (ed.) Leviathan 4: Cities, 2004; (ed. with D. Layne) The Nine Muses, 2005; Fugue XXIX, 2005; (with H. Duncan and R. Parks) Paper Cities: An Anthology of Urban Fantasy, 2007; Swans Over the Moon, 2007. Contributor of articles to journals. **Address:** c/o Author Mail, Raw Dog Screaming Press, 5103 72nd Pl., Hyattsville, MD 20784, U.S.A.

AGUOLU, Christian Chukwunedu. Nigerian (born Nigeria), b. 1940.

Genres: Information Science/Computers, Librarianship, Bibliography, Social Sciences, Humanities. **Career:** Anglican Grammar School, teacher and head of department of French and Latin, 1965-66; University of California, reference librarian and bibliographer, 1968-72; University of Maiduguri, senior lecturer, 1977-79, dean of education, 1979-82, 1984-86, associate professor/reader, 1979-82, professor of library science, 1982-, University Press, acting director, 1988-, chairman, 1996-. Writer. **Publications:** Ghana in the Humanities and Social Sciences, 1900-1971: A Bibliography, 1973; Nigerian Civil War, 1967-70: An Annotated Bibliography, 1973; Nigeria: A Comprehensive Bibliography in the Humanities and Social Sciences, 1900-1971, 1973; Selecting Materials for School Libraries in a Developing Society, 1982; Library Development in Borno State, 1984; Selecting Materials for School Libraries in a Developing Society, 1982; Libraries, Knowledge and National Development: Inaugural Lecture Delivered on 29th March, 1989; What's Wrong With Your English?, 1994, 2nd ed., 1999; Libraries and Information Management in Nigeria, 2002. Contributor to journals. **Address:** Department of Library Science, University of Maiduguri, Bama Rd., PO Box 1069, Maiduguri, BR 45341, Nigeria. **Online address:** aguoluci@unimaid.edu.ng

AGUTTER, Paul S. Dutch (born Netherlands), b. 1946. **Genres:** Biology, Medicine/Health. **Career:** The Theoretical Medicine and Biology Group, Theoretical Biology and Medical Modelling, editor-in-chief. Biologist. **Publications:** Between Nucleus and Cytoplasm, 1991; (with P.L. Taylor) The Meaning of Nucleocytoplasmic Transport, 1996; (with D.N. Wheatley) About Life: Concepts in Modern Biology, 2007; (with P.C. Malone) Aetiology of Deep Venous Thrombosis: A Critical, Historical and Epistemological Survey, 2008. **Address:** The Theoretical Medicine and Biology Group, 26 Castle Hill, Glossop, DB SK13 7RR, England. **Online address:** psa@tmedbiol.com

AGYEMAN, Opoku. Ghanaian (born Ghana), b. 1942. **Genres:** Politics/Government, Third World. **Career:** University of Ghana, Ghana National Students Association, secretary, 1965-66; University of the West Indies, lecturer, 1975-76; University of Dar-es-Salaam, lecturer, 1976-77; University of California, lecturer, 1977-79; Cornell University, assistant professor, 1979-82; Bard College, visiting professor, 1982; Montclair State University, associate professor, 1982-, professor of political science, Native African Students Organization, faculty advisor, 2001-; Drew University, visiting professor, 1989; Fairleigh Dickinson University, adjunct professor, 1994-95. Writer. **Publications:** The Pan-Africanist Worldview, 1985; Requisite Values for Political and Economic Development in Africa, 1990; Pan-Africanist Federalism, 1991; Nkrumah's Ghana and East Africa, 1992; Panafricanism and Its Detractors: A Response to Harvard's Race-Effacing Univeralists, 1997; Africa's Persistent Vulnerable Link to Global Politics, 2001; The Failure of Grassroots Pan-Africanism: The Case of the All-African Trade Union Federation, 2003. **Address:** Department of Political Science, Montclair State University, Rm. 208, Dickson Hall, Upper Montclair, NJ 07043, U.S.A. **Online address:** agyemano@mail.montclair.edu

AHEARN, (Edward) Allen. American (born United States), b. 1937. **Genres:** Librarianship, Bibliography, Economics. **Career:** U.S. Department of the Navy, contracting officer, 1960-73; Office of the U.S. Secretary of Defense, advisor on major systems acquisitions, 1973-80; Quill and Brush (antiquarian book store), partner, 1976-, senior appraiser; defense procurement consultant, 1980-84. Writer. **Publications:** The Book of First Books, 1975, 4th ed., 1986; (with P. Ahearn) Author Price Guides, 1986; (with P. Ahearn) Book Collecting: A Comprehensive Guide, 1989; (with P. Ahearn) Collected Books: The Guide to Value, 1991; Book Collecting 2000: A Comprehensive Guide, 2000. **Address:** Quill and Brush, 1137 Sugarloaf Mountain Rd., Dickerson, MD 20842-8754, U.S.A. **Online address:** allen@qbbooks.com

AHEARN, Patricia. American (born United States), b. 1937. **Genres:** Librarianship, Bibliography. **Career:** Quill and Brush (antiquarian book store and art gallery), partner, 1976-. Writer. **Publications:** (With A. Ahearn) Author Price Guides, 1986; (with A. Ahearn) Book Collecting: A Comprehensive Guide, 1989, rev. ed., 2000; (with A. Ahearn) Collected Books: The Guide to Value, 1991, rev. ed., 2002. **Address:** Quill & Brush, 1137 Sugarloaf Mountain Rd., Dickerson, MD 20842, U.S.A. **Online address:** firsts@qbbooks.com

AHLGREN, Gillian T. W. American (born United States), b. 1964. **Genres:** Theology/Religion, History, Social Sciences, Psychology. **Career:** Xavier University, associate professor of theology, 1990-, professor of theology, Faculty Programs, Honors Programs, director, Theology Graduate Program, professor. Writer. **Publications:** (Contrib.) Dear Sister: The Letters of Medieval Women, 1993; Teresa of Avila and the Politics of Sanctity, 1996; (ed.) The Human Person and the Church, 1999; (ed. and trans.) The Inquisition of Francisca: A Sixteenth-Century Visionary on Trial, 2005; Entering Teresa of Avila's Interior Castle: A Reader's Companion, 2005. Contributor of articles to books and periodicals. **Address:** Department of Theology, Xavier University, 327 Hinkle Hall, 3800 Victory Pkwy., PO Box 4442, Cincinnati, OH 45207-4442, U.S.A. **Online address:** ahlgren@xavier.edu

AHLQUIST, Dale. American (born United States) **Genres:** Autobiography/Memoirs, Biography. **Career:** American Chesterton Society, president and co-founder; Gilbert Magazine, publisher and editor; Eternal Word Television Network (EWTN), show host; Gilbert Magazine, publisher; Oklahoma Wesleyan Worldview Institute, fellow. Writer. **Publications:** (Ed.) The Gift of Wonder: The Many Sides of G.K. Chesterton, 2001; G.K. Chesterton: The Apostle of Common Sense, 2003; (ed.) Lepanto, 2004; Common Sense 101: Lessons from G.K. Chesterton, 2006; (ed.) Universe According to G.K. Chesterton: A Dictionary of the Mad, Mundane, and Metaphysical. Contributor of articles to magazines. **Address:** American Chesterton Society, 4117 Pebblebrook Cir., Minneapolis, MN 55437, U.S.A. **Online address:** info@chesterton.org

AHMAD, Imran. British/Pakistani (born Pakistan), b. 1962. **Genres:** Biography. **Career:** Unilever, staff; Oracle Systems, staff; Ernst & Young Management Consulting, staff; Whittman-Hart, staff; General Electric, staff, 2000-. Writer. **Publications:** Unimagined: A Muslim Boy Meets the West, 2007; The Perfect Gentleman: A Muslim Boy Meets The West, 2012. **Address:** Center Street Publishing, New York, NY 10014, U.S.A. **Online address:** author@unimagined.co.uk

AHMED, Akbar S(alahudin). American/Indian (born India), b. 1943. **Genres:** International Relations/Current Affairs, Sociology, Theology/Religion. **Career:** Civil Service of Pakistan, assistant commissioner in Frontier Province and Punjab, 1966-71, deputy secretary, 1971-76, political agent, 1976-77, 1978-80, additional secretary, 1977; London University, Ford Foundation fellow, 1977-78; General of the National Center for Rural Development-Islamabad, founder, director-general, 1982-88; Centre of Social Sciences, director; Harvard University, Department of Anthropology, visiting professor, 1981-82; Washington University, visiting professor, Department of Anthropology, affiliate professor, 1982-2000; Cambridge University, faculty, Selwyn College, fellow, 1988-99, Iqbal Fellow, 1988-93, visiting professor, 2000-01; Princeton University, Department of Anthropology, visiting professor and fellow, 2000-01; American University, professor of international relations and Ibn Khaldun Chair of Islamic Studies, 2001-; U.S. Naval Academy, Middle East/Islamic Studies, distinguished chair, 2008-; The Brooking's Institution, senior fellow. Writer. **Publications:** Mansehra: A Journey, 1973; A Strategy for Cooperation: A Study of the North-West Frontier Province, 1973; (trans.) Mataloona: Pukhto Proverbs, 1973, rev. ed., 1975; Millennium and Charisma among Pathans, 1976; Social and Economic Change in the Tribal Areas, 1972-1976, 1977; Pieces of Green: The Sociology of Change in Pakistan, 1964-1974, 1977; A Bibliography of the North-West Frontier Province, 1979; More Lines (poems), 1980; Pukhtun Economy and Society, 1980; Religion and Politics in Muslim Society, 1983; Pakistan Society, 1986; Toward Islamic Anthropology, 1987; Discovering Islam, 1988, rev. ed., 2002; Resistance and Control in Pakistan, 1991, rev. ed., 2004; Postmodernism and Islam, 1992, rev. ed., 2004; Living Islam, 1993; Jinnah, Pakistan and Islamic Identity, 1997; (contrib.) The Conceit of Innocence, 1997; Islam Today, 1999; Islam under Siege, 2003; Journey into Islam: The Crisis of Globalization, 2007; Journey into America: The Challenge of Islam, 2010. EDITOR: (with D.M. Hart) Islam in Tribal Societies: From the Atlas to the Indus, 1984; Pakistan: The Social Sciences' Perspective, 1990; (with H. Donnan) Islam, Globalization and Postmodernity, 1994; (with C. Shore) The Future of Anthropology, 1995; (with T. Sonn) The SAGE Handbook of Islamic Studies, 2010. Contributor to journals. **Address:** School of International Service, American University, 200G SIS, 4400 Massachusetts Ave. NW, Washington, DC 20016-8071, U.S.A. **Online address:** akbar@american.edu

AHMED, Syed Naeem. Canadian (born Canada), b. 1965?. **Genres:** Physics, Sciences, Engineering. **Career:** Radbound University, researcher and teacher; Max-Planck Institute for Physics, researcher; Fermi National Accelerator Laboratory, researcher; Sudbury Neutrino Observatory, researcher; Laurentian University, adjunct professor, senior research scientist and physics teacher; Penguin Automated Systems, staff. Writer. **Publications:** Physics and Engineering of Radiation Detection, 2007. **Address:** Department of Physics,

Laurentian University, Science II Bldg., 935 Ramsey Lake Rd., Sudbury, ON P3E 2O6, Canada. **Online address:** sahmed@laurentian.ca

AHRONS, Constance (Ruth). American (born United States), b. 1937. **Genres:** Human Relations/Parenting. **Career:** University of Wisconsin, School of Social Work, clinical instructor, 1969-71, part-time instructor, 1971-73, assistant professor, 1974-81, associate professor, 1981-84; Mental Health Associates, associate, 1972-79; Wisconsin Family Studies Institute, co-founder and therapist, 1979-84; University of Southern California, School of Social Work, associate professor, 1984-86, Human Relations Center, associate director, 1986, professor of sociology, 1987-2001, professor emeritus, 2001-, Human Relations Center, Marriage and Family Therapy Training Program, director, 1996-2001; Radcliffe Institute for Advanced Study at Harvard, fellow, 2000-01; Divorce and Remarriage Consultation Services, director, 2001-. Writer. **Publications:** (With R.H. Rodgers) Divorced Families: A Multidisciplinary Developmental View, 1987; The Good Divorce: Keeping Your Family Together When Your Marriage Comes Apart, 1994; We're Still Family: What Grown Children Have to Say about Their Parents' Divorce, 2004. **Address:** Department of Sociology, University of Southern California, 3620 S Vermont Ave., Los Angeles, CA 90089-2539, U.S.A. **Online address:** ca@constanceahrons.com

AHUJA, Sunil. American (born United States), b. 1965. **Genres:** History. **Career:** University of Louisiana, assistant professor, 1995-98; Seton Hall University, assistant professor, 1998-2002; Youngstown State University, assistant professor, 2002-05, associate professor of political science, 2005-. Writer. **Publications:** Government at Work: Issue Evolution, Passage, Implementation, and Feedback, 1998; (ed. with R.E. Dewhirst) The Roads to Congress 2000, 2001; (ed. with R.E. Dewhirst) The Roads to Congress 2002, 2003; (ed. with R.E. Dewhirst) Congress Responds to the Twentieth Century, 2003; (ed. with R.E. Dewhirst) The Road to Congress 2004, 2005; (ed. with R.E. Dewhirst) The Roads to Congress 2006, 2007; Congress Behaving Badly: The Rise of Partisanship and Incivility and the Death of Public Trust, 2008. **Address:** Department of Political Science, Youngstown State University, 1 University Plz., Youngstown, OH 44555, U.S.A. **Online address:** sahuja@ysu.edu

AIDELLS, Bruce. American (born United States), b. 1944. **Genres:** Food And Wine, Cultural/Ethnic Topics, Reference. **Career:** Imperial Cancer Research Fund, research fellow, 1974-77; National Institute of Health, research fellow, 1977-78; Poulet Deli, founder and chef, 1979-83; Aidells Sausage Co., owner, 1983-, chef, 1983-2002; Bon Appetit, 1985-; ABC TV Station, cooking segment host, 2006-; KCBS-Radio, host. Restaurant consultant, new business adviser and writer. **Publications:** Great Meals in Minutes: Salads, 1985; (co-author) Regional American Classics, 1987; (with R. Clark) Barbecuing, Grilling and Smoking, 1988; (with D. Kelly) Hot Links and Country Flavors: Sausages in American Regional Cooking, 1990; (with D. Kelly) Real Beer and Good Eats: The Rebirth of America's Beer and Food Traditions, 1992; (co-author) Classic American Cooking from the Academy, 1993; (co-author) Barbecuing, Grilling & Smoking at the Academy, 1994; (with D. Kelly and B. Aidells) Flying Sausages: Simple, Savory Recipes for Creating and Cooking With Chicken and Turkey Sausages, 1995; (with D. Kelly) The Complete Meat Cookbook: Juicy and Authoritative Guide to Selecting, Seasoning and Cooking Today's Beef, Pork, Lamb and Veal, 1998; (with D. Kelly) Bruce Aidells' Complete Sausage Book, 2000; (with L. Weiss) Bruce Aidells' Complete Book of Pork: A Guide to Buying, Storing and Cooking the World's Favorite Meat, 2004. Contributor to periodicals and books. **Address:** c/o Martha Casselman, PO Box 342, Calistoga, CA 94515, U.S.A. **Online address:** bruce@aidells.com

AIDINOFF, Elsie V. American (born United States), b. 1931?. **Genres:** Novels, Young Adult Fiction, Romance/Historical. **Career:** New York City School Volunteer Program, junior high school tutor, 1965-80; Children's Storefront School, teacher, administrator, trustee and president of board, 1980-. Writer. **Publications:** The Garden, 2004. Contributor to periodicals. **Address:** c/o Author Mail, HarperCollins Publishers, 10 E 53rd St., New York, NY 10022, U.S.A.

AINSWORTH, Patricia. (Patricia Nina Bigg). Australian (born Australia), b. 1932. **Genres:** Romance/Historical, Language/Linguistics, Medicine/Health, Psychology. **Career:** Commonwealth Trading Bank, secretary, 1948-51; G. & R. Wills & Company Ltd., secretary, 1952-55; writer, 1967-. **Publications:** The Flickering Candle, 1968; The Candle Rekindled, 1969; Steady Burns the Candle, 1970; The Devil's Hole, 1971; Portrait in Gold, 1971; A String of Silver Beads, 1972; The Bridal Lamp, 1975; The Enchanted Cup, 1980; Understanding Depression, 2000; (with P.C. Baker) Understanding Mental Retardation, 2004. **Address:** 3/2 Lorraine Ave., Mitcham, SA 5062, Australia.

AIRA, César. Argentine (born Argentina), b. 1949. **Genres:** Novels, Essays, Novellas/Short Stories, Young Adult Fiction. **Career:** University of Buenos Aires, translator and lecturer; University of Rosary, translator and lecturer. Writer. **Publications:** Ema, la Cautiva, 1981; La Luz Argentina, 1983; Canto Castrato, 1984; Los Fantasmas: Novela, 1990; El Bautismo: Novela, 1991; Copi, 1991; La Liebre, 1991; Embalse, 1992; El Llanto, 1992; La Prueba, 1992; El Volante, 1992; Cómo Me Hice Monja, 1993; Diario De La Hepatitis, 1993; La Guerra De Los Gimnasios, 1993; Madre e hijo, 1993; (comp.) Tadeys, 1994; La costurera y el viento, 1994; Losmisterios de Rosario, 1994; Argentina: The Great Estancias, 1995; Los dospayasos, 1995; La fuente, 1995; La abeja, 1996; El mensajero, 1996; Dante y reina, 1997; La serpiente, 1997; Taxol: precedido de Duchamp en Mexico y la Broma, 1997; Alejandra Pizarnik, 1998; Las curas milagrosas del doctor Aira, 1998; La mendiga, 1998; El sueno, 1998; Latrompeta de Mimbre, 1998; El Congreso De Literatura, 1999; Un Episodio En La Vida Del Pintor Viajero, 2000; El juego de los mundos: novela deciencia ficcion, 2000; Diccionario De Autores Latinoamericanos, 2001; Un Sueño Realizado, 2001; Las tres fechas, 2001; La Villa, 2001; El Mago, 2002; Fragmentos De Un Diario En Los Alpes, 2002; Varamo, 2002; (co-author) Argentina, un País desperdiciado, 2003; El Tilo, 2003; Princesa Primavera, 2003; Yo Era Una Chica Moderna, 2004; Edward Lear, 2004; Noches De Flores, 2004; Pequeño Monje Budista, 2005; Yo era una niña de siete años, 2005; Novela China, 2005; Cómo Me Reí, 2005; Parménides, 2006; Cena, 2006; Vida Nueva, 2007; Conversaciones, 2007; Aventuras De Barbaverde, 2008; Confesión, 2009; Divorcio, 2010; Yo era una mujer casada, 2010; (co-author) Ciudad, espacio público y cultura urbana: 25 conferencias de la Cátedra Permanente de Imágenes Urbanas, 2010; El Error, 2010; Cecil Taylor, 2011. **Address:** c/o Author Mail, Interzona, Lavalle 750 Piso 19B, Buenos Aires, 1047, Argentina.

AIRD, Catherine. (Kinn Hamilton McIntosh). British (born England), b. 1930. **Genres:** Mystery/Crime/Suspense, Local History/Rural Topics, Novels, Young Adult Fiction, Adult Non-fiction. **Career:** Crime Writers' Association, chair, 1990-91. Writer. **Publications:** The Religious Body, 1966; A Most Contagious Game, 1967; Henrietta Who?, 1968; The Complete Steel, 1969 as The Stately Home Murder, 1970; A Late Phoenix, 1971; His Burial Too, 1973; Slight Mourning, 1975; Parting Breath, 1977; Some Die Eloquent, 1980; Passing Strange, 1981; Last Respects, 1982; Harm's Way, 1984; A Dead Liberty, 1987; The Body Politic, 1990; Mystery Voices: Interviews with British Crime Writers, 1991; A Going Concern, 1993; The Catherine Aird Collection, 1993; The Second Catherine Aird Collection, 1994; Injury Time, 1995; After Effects, 1996; The Third Catherine Aird Collection, 1997; Stiff News, 1999; The Oxford Companion to Crime and Mystery Writing, 1999; Little Knell, 2001; Amendment of Life, 2003; Chapter and Hearse, 2004; A Hole in One, 2005; Losing Ground, 2008; Past Tense, 2010. **Address:** Invergordon, 1 Sturry Hill, Sturry, Canterbury, KT CT2 0NG, England.

AITCHISON, Ian J(ohnston) R(hind). British (born England), b. 1936?. **Genres:** Physics. **Career:** Brookhaven National Laboratory, research associate, 1961-63; Cavendish Laboratory, research associate, 1964-66; Oxford University, lecturer in theoretical physics, 1966-96, professor of Physics, 1996-, now emeritus. Writer. **Publications:** Relativistic Quantum Mechanics, 1972; (ed. with J.E. Paton) Rudolf Peierls and Theoretical Physics, 1977; (with A.J.G. Hey) Gauge Theories in Particle Physics, 1982, 3rd ed., 2002; Informal Introduction to Gauge Field Theories, 1982; (ed. with C.H.L. Smith and J.E. Paton) Plots, Quarks and Strange Particles, 1991; Supersymmetry in Particle Physics, 2007. **Address:** Rudolf Peierls Center for Theoretical Physics, Oxford University, 1 Keble Rd., Oxford, OX OX1 3NP, England. **Online address:** i.aitchison1@physics.ox.ac.uk

AITCHISON, James. Scottish (born Scotland), b. 1938. **Genres:** Poetry, Education, Writing/Journalism, Young Adult Fiction. **Career:** Freelance writer, 1968-; Napier University, Department of Print Media, Publishing and Communication, senior lecturer. **Publications:** POETRY: Sounds before Sleep, 1971; Spheres, 1975; Second Nature, 1990; Brain Scans, 1998; Bird-Score, 2002; Foraging: New and Selected Poems, 2009. OTHERS: (ed. with A. Scott) New Writing Scotland, vol. I, 1983, vol. II, 1984, vol. III, 1985; Writing for the Press: An Introduction, 1988; The Golden Harvester: The Vision of Edwin Muir, 1988; The Cassell Guide to Written English, 1994; (co-ed.)

Collaborate or Compete?: Educational Partnerships in a Market Economy, 1995; Dictionary of English Grammar, 1996; (with J. Gordon) Shamp of the City-Solo, 1998. **Address:** 10 Royal Gardens, Hillcourt Rd., Stirling, FK8 2RJ, Scotland.

AITKEN, Rosemary. (Rosemary Rowe). British (born England), b. 1942. **Genres:** Mystery/Crime/Suspense, Romance/Historical, Education, Novellas/Short Stories. **Career:** Secondary teacher, 1964-67; teacher-trainer and lecturer in higher education, 1967-72, senior lecturer, 1972-87, ESOL program, tutor in charge, 1978-87; Quillen Postal Writing Course, tutor-in-charge, 1990-2000; Trinity College, examiner and moderator, 1990-2009. Writer. **Publications:** CORNISH SAGA SERIES: The Girl from Penvarris, 1995; The Tinner's Daughter, 1996; Cornish Harvest, 1999; Stormy Waters, 2000; The Silent Shore, 2001; The Granite Cliffs, 2002; A Cornish Maid, 2009. NOVELS: Against the Tide, 2004; The Tregenza Girls, 2006; From Penvarris with Love, 2008. MYSTERY NOVELS. LIBERTUS SERIES AS ROSEMARY ROWE: The Germanicus Mosaic, 1999; A Pattern of Blood, 2000; Murder in the Forum, 2001; The Chariots of Calyx, 2002; The Legatus Mystery, 2003; The Ghosts of Glevum, 2004; Enemies of the Empire, 2005; A Roman Ransom, 2006; A Coin for the Ferryman, 2007; Death at Pompeia's Wedding, 2008; Requiem For A Slave, 2010. OTHERS: Make Up Your Mind, 1979; Teaching Tenses, 1992; Writing a Novel: A Practical Guide, 2003. Works appear in anthologies. Contributor to books and periodicals. **Address:** Dorian Literary Agency, Upper Thornehill, 27 Church Rd., St. Mary Church, Torquay, Devon, DN TQ1 4QY, England. **Online address:** raitken@wyenet.co.uk

AIZLEY, Harlyn. American (born United States) **Genres:** Sex, Gay And Lesbian Issues, Adult Non-fiction. **Career:** Writer. **Publications:** Buying Dad: One Woman's Search for the Perfect Sperm Donor, 2003; (ed.) Confessions of the Other Mother: Nonbiological Lesbian Moms Tell All, 2006. Contributor of articles to magazines and journals. Works appear in anthologies. **Address:** c/o Author Mail, Liberation Publications Inc., 6922 Hollywood Blvd., Ste. 1000, Los Angeles, CA 90028, U.S.A. **Online address:** buyingdad@aol.com

AJAMI, Fouad. American/Lebanese (born Lebanon), b. 1945. **Genres:** Cultural/Ethnic Topics, Politics/Government, Theology/Religion. **Career:** Lehrhman Institute, research fellow; Princeton University, Department of Politics and Center of International Studies, staff, 1973-, faculty, through 1980, Princeton's Center of International Studies, fellow; Johns Hopkins University, Paul H. Nitze School of Advanced International Studies, associate professor and director of Middle East studies, Majid Khadduri professor of Islamic studies, 1980-2011; U.S. News and World Report, contributing editor; CBS News, consultant; Stanford University, Hoover Institution, senior fellow, Herbert and Jane Dwight Working Group, co-chair. **Publications:** The Global Populists: Tthird-World Nations and World-Order Crises, 1974; Human Rights and World Order Politics, 1978; The Arab Predicament: Arab Political Thought and Practice Since 1967, 1981, rev. ed., 1992; The Vanished Imam: Musa al Sadr and the Shia of Lebanon, 1986; Beirut: City of Regrets, 1988; The Dream Palace of the Arabs: A Generation's Odyssey, 1998; The Foreigner's Gift: The Americans, the Arabs and the Iraqis in Iraq, 2006; Crosswinds: The Way of Saudi Arabia, 2010. **Address:** Paul H. Nitze School of Advanced, International Studies, Johns Hopkins University, Rm. 504, Nitze Bldg., 1740 Massachusetts Ave. NW, Washington, DC 20036, U.S.A. **Online address:** lrizzo2@jhu.edu

AKAMATSU, Ken. (Awa Mizuno). Japanese (born Japan), b. 1968. **Genres:** Novels, Graphic Novels, Humor/Satire, Young Adult Fiction. **Career:** Writer and artist. **Publications:** GRAPHIC NOVELS: A. I. Love You, 1994; Love Hina, 1999; Negima!: Magister Negi Magi, 2004; Love Hina: Perfect Collection, 2002; Mao-Chan, 2003. **Address:** c/o Author Mail, Del Rey, 1745 Broadway, New York, NY 10019-4368, U.S.A.

AKARLI, Engin Deniz. American (born United States), b. 1945. **Genres:** History, Area Studies, Politics/Government. **Career:** Turkish Glass and Bottle Manufacturing Corp., research expert, 1967; University of Wisconsin, head research assistant, 1969, research assistant, 1969-70; Middle East Technical University, head research assistant, 1969; Princeton University, Department of Near Eastern Studies, teaching assistant and research assistant, 1971-73, lecturer, 1975-76; Bosphorus University, Department of History, assistant professor, 1976-83, associate professor of history, 1982-; Yurt Publications, consultant, 1982-83; Yarmouk University, Department of History, associate professor, 1983-85, 1986-89, senior associate professor, 1988-; Institute for Advanced Study-Berlin, research fellow, 1985-86; Washington University, Department of History, associate professor, through 1995, professor, 1989-96; Institute for Advanced Study, NEH fellow, 2003-04; Harvard University, Law School, Islamic Legal Studies Program, research fellow, 2005-06; Brown University, Department of History, Joukowsky Family distinguished professor of modern Middle East history, 1996-, professor of history, 1996-. Writer. **Publications:** (Ed. with G. Ben-Dor) Political Participation in Turkey: Historical Background and Present Problems, 1975; Political Testaments of Ali and Fuad (in Turkish), 1977; The Long Peace: Ottoman Lebanon, 1861-1920, 1993; (co-author) Osmanli Devleti'nde Din ve Vicdan hürriyeti, 2000. Contributor to periodicals. **Address:** Department of History, Brown University, 79 Brown St., PO Box N, Providence, RI 02912, U.S.A. **Online address:** engin_akarli@brown.edu

AKBAR, Said Hyder. American/Afghani (born Afghanistan), b. 1984?. **Genres:** Autobiography/Memoirs, Biography, History, Travel/Exploration. **Career:** Wadan Afghanistan (rebuilds Afghan schools and roads), founder and co-director. Writer. **Publications:** (With S. Burton) Come Back to Afghanistan: A California Teenager's Story, 2005. Contributor to periodicals. **Address:** c/o Author Mail, Bloomsbury Publishing, 175 5th Ave., New York, NY 10010-7703, U.S.A.

AKERA, Atsushi. American (born United States) **Genres:** Sciences, History, Business/Trade/Industry, Botany. **Career:** Massachusetts Institute of Technology, intern, 1984, 1985; George Mason University, research associate, 1986-87; Microelectronics and Computer Technology Corp., technology analyst, 1988-91; University of Pennsylvania Libraries, associate curator, 1995-96, historical consultant, 1994-96, instructor, 1994, 1999; Rensselaer Polytechnic Institute, lecturer, 1999-2002, assistant professor, 2002-, associate professor. Writer and teacher. **Publications:** (Ed. with F. Nebeker) From 0 to 1: An Authoritative History of Modern Computing, 2002; Calculating a Natural World: Scientists, Engineers and Computers during the Rise of U.S. Cold War Research, 2007. **Address:** Science and Technology Studies Department, Rensselaer Polytechnic Institute, 5206 Sage Bldg., 110 8th St., Troy, NY 12180-3590, U.S.A. **Online address:** akeraa@rpi.edu

AKERLOF, George A. American (born United States), b. 1940. **Genres:** Economics. **Career:** University of California, assistant professor, 1966-70, associate professor, 1970-77, professor, 1977-78, 1980-, Koshland professor of economics; London School of Economics, Cassell professor of money and banking, 1978-80; Brookings Institution, senior fellow, 1994. Writer and economist. **Publications:** An Economic Theorist's Book of Tales: Essays That Entertain the Consequences of New Assumptions in Economic Theory, 1984; (with J.L. Yellen) Efficiency Wage Models of the Labor Market, 1986; Explorations in Pragmatic Economics: Selected Papers of George A. Akerlof, 2005; (with R.J. Shiller) Animal Spirits: How Human Psychology Drives the Economy, and Why It Matters for Global Capitalism, 2009, rev. ed., 2010; (with R.E. Kranton) Identity Economics: How Our Identities Shape Our Work, Wages, and Well-Being, 2010. Contributor to books and journals. **Address:** Department of Economics, University of California, 549 Evans Hall Ste. 3880, Berkeley, CA 94720-3880, U.S.A. **Online address:** akerlof@econ.berkeley.edu

ÅKERMAN, Susanna (Kristina). Swedish (born Sweden), b. 1959. **Genres:** Intellectual History, Adult Non-fiction. **Career:** Uppsala Universitet, History of Ideas Department, research fellow, 1989-92; Stockholm University, research fellow, 1992-97. Writer. **Publications:** Queen Christina of Sweden and Her Circle: The Transformation of a Seventeenth-Century Philosophical Libertine, 1991; Rose Cross Over the Baltic: The Spread of Rosicrucianism in Northern Europe, 1998. **Address:** Artillerig 57 III, Stockholm, 11445, Sweden. **Online address:** susanna.akerman@zeta.telenordia.se

AKINS, Ellen. American (born United States) **Genres:** Novels, Novellas/Short Stories, Literary Criticism And History. **Career:** Johns Hopkins University, teaching fellow, 1982-83; University of Notre Dame Press, advertising director, 1983-85; University of Chicago Press, promotions manager, 1985-88. Writer. **Publications:** NOVELS: Home Movie, 1988; Little Woman, 1990; Public Life, 1993; Hometown Brew, 1998. COLLECTION: World Like a Knife, 1991. Contributor to periodicals. **Address:** Charlotte Sheedy Literary Agency, 65 Bleecker St., Ste. 12, New York, NY 10012-2420, U.S.A.

AKINSHA, Konstantin. American/Ukranian (born Ukraine), b. 1960.

Genres: Art/Art History, Photography. **Career:** ArtNews, moscow correspondent and contributing editor, 1990-93; Kunstverein Bremen, research fellow, 1993-95; Germanisches National Museum, research fellow, 1995-96; Art and Cultural Property of the Presidential Advisory Commission, deputy research director, 1999-2000. **Publications:** (Co-author) Dialog mit Kiew: Acht Ukrainische Künstler in München: Ein Album, 1993; (with G. Kozlov) Stolen Treasure, 1995; (with Kozlov and S. Hochfield) Beautiful Loot: Russia's Treasure Troves of Stolen Art from World War II, 1995; (with Kozlow and C. Toussaint) Operation Beutekunst, 1995; (with N.H. Yeide and A.L. Walsh) The AAM Guide to Provenance Research, 2001; (co-author) Rukopisi i arkhivnye dokumenty Evreiskoi obshchiny goroda Veny v rossiiskikh sobraniiakh: katalog, 2006; (with G. Kozlov and S. Hochfield) The Holy Place: Architecture, Ideology, and History in Russia, 2007. **Address:** Andrew Nurnberg, 45-47 Clerkenwell Green, London, GL EC1R 0HT, England.

AKSIN, Sina. Turkish (born Turkey), b. 1937?. **Genres:** History. **Career:** University of Ankara, professor. Writer. **Publications:** (With P. Dumont and J. Bacqué- Grammont) La Turquie et la France L'époque d'Atatürk: études, 1981; Jön Türkler ve Itihat ve Terakki, 1987; (co-author) Ankara Nereye?, 1997; Türkiye'nin önünde üc Model, 1997; Ankara Anlasmasinin 75. Yldönümünde Birinci Dünya Savasindan Günümüze Türk-Fransiz Iliskileri, 1999; Essays in Ottoman-Turkish Political History, 2000; Atatürkccü Partiyi Kurmanin Sirasi Geldi, 2002; Yakin Tarihimizi Sorgulamak, 2006; Turkey from Empire to Revolutionary Republic: The Emergence of the Turkish Nation from 1789 to the Present, 2007. **Address:** 838 Broadway, 3rd Fl., New York, NY 10003-4812, U.S.A. **Online address:** saksin@politics.ankara.edu.tr

AKST, Daniel. American (born United States), b. 1956?. **Genres:** Novels, Bibliography, Politics/Government. **Career:** Paterson News, Statehouse reporter, 1979-80; New York Times, stringer, 1980-81; Record, reporter, 1981-84; Los Angeles Times, reporter, editor and columnist, 1985-96; Wall Street Journal, reporter, 1987-88; University of California-Berkeley, Graduate School of Journalism, Koret teaching fellow, 2000. Writer. **Publications:** Wonder Boy: Barry Minkow, The Kid Who Swindled Wall Street (nonfiction), 1990; Saint Burl's Obituary: A Novel, 1996; The Webster Chronicle, 2001; We Have Met the Enemy: Self-control in an Age of Excess, 2011. Contributor to periodicals. **Address:** c/o Sloan Harris, International Creative Management, 825 8th Ave., New York, NY 10019, U.S.A. **Online address:** dan@akst.com

AKYEAMPONG, Emmanuel K(waku). Ghanaian (born Ghana), b. 1962. **Genres:** History. **Career:** University of Virginia, instructor in history, 1992; Harvard University, assistant professor, 1993-97, associate professor of history, 1997-2000, professor, 2000-. Writer. **Publications:** Drink, Power, and Cultural Change: A Social History of Alcohol in Ghana, c. 1800 to Recent Times, 1996; Between the Sea and the Lagoon: An Eco-social History of the Anlo of Southeastern Ghana, c. 1850 to Recent Times, 2001; (ed.) Yaa Asantewaa and the Asante-British War of 1900-1, 2003; (ed.) Themes in West Africa's History, 2006; Race, Political Identity, and Citizenship in Ghana: The Example of the Lebanese, 2006; Dictionary of African Biography, 2012. Contributor of articles to books and periodicals. **Address:** Department of History, Harvard University, Rm. S433, 1730 Cambridge St., Cambridge, MA 02138, U.S.A. **Online address:** akyeamp@fas.harvard.edu

ALAGOA, Ebiegberi Joe. Nigerian (born Nigeria), b. 1933. **Genres:** Area Studies, History, Music, Cultural/Ethnic Topics. **Career:** National Archives of Nigeria, senior archivist, 1959-62; University of Lagos, lecturer in African history, 1965-67; University of Ibadan, Institute of African Studies, senior research fellow, 1967-72; University of Lagos, Centre of Cultural Studies, professor of history and director, 1972-77; University of Port Harcourt, School of Humanities, dean, 1977-82, deputy vice chancellor, 1980-81, acting vice chancellor, 1982, School of Graduate Studies, dean, 1982-83, 1985-87, School of Humanities, dean, 1987-92, Niger Delta Research Group, chair of faculty of humanities, 1990-98, now professor emeritus; Order of the Niger, officer, 2000; Historical Society of Nigeria, fellow and president, 1981-83, 1991-94; Nigerian Association for Oral History and Tradition, president, 1985-94; Niger Delta University, pro-chancellor, 2001; Nigerian Academy of Letters, fellow. Writer. **Publications:** The Akassa Raid 1895, 1960; The Small Brave City-State, 1964; Kien abibionde fa pugu, 1967; Jaja of Opobo (juvenile nonfiction), 1970; (with A. Fombo) A Chronicle of Grand Bonny, 1972; A History of the Niger Delta, 1972; War Canoe Drums and Topical Songs from Nembe, Rivers State, 1974; King Boy of Brass (juvenile nonfiction), 1975; (with N. Nzewunwa) The History of Ogbakiri, 1980; The Python's Eye: The Past in the Living Present, 1981; Sagbe Obasi, 1986; People of the Fish and Eagle, 1996; The Ijaw Nation in the New Millennium, 1999; Beke you mi: Nembe against the British Empire, 2001; Creation of the Niger Delta West Diocese: The Challenges, 2001; Okpu: Ancestral Houses in Nembe and European Antiquitieson the Brass and Nun Rivers of the Niger Delta, 2001; (with A.A. Derefaka) The Land and People of Rivers State: Eastern Niger Delta, 2002; Uses of Hindsight as Foresight: Reflections on Niger Delta and Nigerian History, 2004; Practice of History in Africa: A History of African Historiography, 2006; Festac Remembered: Cultural Intolerance in the Nigerian Nation, 2007. EDITOR: (with B. Awe and contrib.) Nigerian Antiquities, 1972; (with T.N. Tamuno) Eminent Nigerians of the Rivers State, 1980; (with K. Williamson) Ancestral Voices, 1981; The Teaching of History in African Universities, 1981; More Days, More Wisdom: Nembe Proverbs, 1983; Oral Historical Traditions in Africa, 1987; (with F. Anozie and N. Nzewunwa) The Early History of the Niger Delta, 1988; (with T. Tamuno) Land and People of Nigeria, 1989; Oral Tradition and Oral History in Africa and the Diaspora, 1990; Dike Remembered, 1998; A History of the University of Port Harcourt 1977-1998, 1999; The Land and People of Bayelsa State, 1999; Harold Dappa-Biriye: His Cotributions to Politics in Nigeria, 2003. Contributor to books. **Address:** School of Humanities, University of Port Harcourt, PO Box 125, Port Harcourt, RV 00176, Nigeria. **Online address:** kala_joe@yahoo.com

ALAI. Chinese (born China), b. 1959?. **Genres:** Science Fiction/Fantasy. **Career:** Science Fiction Journal, president and editor-in-chief. **Publications:** (With T. Dawa and Sebo) An den Lederriemen geknotete Seele: Erzähleraus Tibet, 1997; Chen ai luo ding, 1998; Yue guang xia de yin jiang, 1999; Da di de jie ti, 2000; Red Poppies, 2002; Jiu zhe yang ri yi feng ying, 2002; Sources Lointaines, 2003; Chen ai fei yang/Chen ai fei yang, 2005; Yao yuan de wen quan, 2005; Nie yuan, 2005; Kong shan: Ji cun chuan shuo, 2005; Aoda de ma dui, 2005; Bao dao, 2009; (with Z.B.Z. Yuefeng) Sichuang hui da shih jie, 2011. **Address:** Science Fiction World, 11, Section 4, S People's Rd., Chengdu, Sichuan, 610041, China. **Online address:** alai@sfw-cd.com

AL-ALI, Nadje Sadig. British (born England), b. 1966. **Genres:** Military/Defense/Arms Control, History, Novels, Women's Studies And Issues, Social Sciences. **Career:** University of Exeter, Institute of Arab and Islamic Studies, senior lecturer; University of London, School of Oriental and African Studies, lecturer, reader in gender studies, Centre for Gender Studies, chair; Act Together: Women's Action for Iraq, founder. Writer. **Publications:** Gender Writing/ Writing Gender: The Representation of Women in a Selection of Modern Egyptian Literature, 1994; Secularism, Gender, and the State in the Middle East: The Egyptian Women's Movement, 2000; (ed. with K. Koser) New Approaches to Migration? Transnational Communities and the Transformation of Home, 2002; The Women's Movement in Egypt, with Selected References to Turkey, 2002; Iraqi Women: Untold Stories from 1948 to the Present, 2007; (afterword) Zubaida's Window: A Novel of Iraqi Exile, 2008; (with N. Pratt) What Kind of Liberation? Women and the Occupation of Iraq, 2009; (ed. with N. Pratt) Women and War in the Middle East: Transnational Perspectives, 2009. Contributor to books and periodicals. **Address:** School of Oriental and African Studies, University of London, Thornhaugh St., Russell Sq., London, GL WC1H 0XG, England. **Online address:** n.s.al-ali@soas.ac.uk

ALAMA, Pauline J. American (born United States), b. 1964. **Genres:** Science Fiction/Fantasy, Young Adult Fiction. **Career:** Helen Keller Intl., public relations assistant, 1986-88; New York Mission Society, information officer, 1988-89; New York University, employee development senior project analyst, 1989-91; University of Rochester, instructor in English, 1991-99; Rochester Institute of Technology, instructor in English, 1991-99; Teach for America, development associate, 1999-2000; New York Foundling, associate director of development, 2000-; Elizabeth Seton Pediatric Center, associate director of development. Writer. **Publications:** The Eye of the Night, 2002; The Ghost-Bearers, forthcoming. Contributor to periodicals. **Address:** 71 Chestnut St., Rutherford, NJ 07070-1705, U.S.A. **Online address:** paulinejalama@verizon.net

ALAMEDDINE, Rabih. American/Lebanese (born Lebanon), b. 1959?. **Genres:** Novels, Young Adult Fiction, Medicine/Health. **Career:** Engineer, painter and novelist, 1998-. **Publications:** Koolaids: The Art of War, 1998; The Perv: Stories, 1999; I, the Divine: A Novel in First Chapters, 2001; The Hakawati, 2008. Contributor to periodicals. **Address:** c/o Kate Runde, Random House Inc., 745 Broadway, New York, NY 10019, U.S.A.

ALAN, Theresa. American (born United States), b. 1972. **Genres:** Young

Adult Non-fiction, Novellas/Short Stories, Romance/Historical, inspirational/Motivational Literature, Literary Criticism And History. **Career:** Writer. **Publications:** ROMANCE FICTION: Who You Know, 1993; Spur of the Moment, 1994; (with F. Michaels and L.L. Miller) Jingle all the Way, 1994; (with C. Alexander and H. Chamberlain) Sex and the Single Witch, 2005; The Girls' Global Guide to Guys, 2005; Girls Who Gossip, 2005; (co-author) I Shaved My Legs For This?!, 2006; The Dangers of Mistletoe, 2006; Getting Married, 2007; Spa Vacation, 2007. **Address:** Alison Picard, PO Box 2000, Cotuit, MA 02635, U.S.A. **Online address:** theresa@theresaalan.com

ALARCON, Daniel. American (born United States), b. 1977?. **Genres:** Novels, Young Adult Non-fiction. **Career:** Mills College, distinguished visiting writer, 2005-07; Etiqueta Negra, associate editor; Granta, contributing editor. Educator. **Publications:** War by Candlelight, 2005; Lost City Radio, 2007; (ed.) Secret Miracle: The Novelist's Handbook, 2010; Ciudad de Payasos, 2010. Contributor to periodicals. **Address:** HarperCollins Publishers Inc., 10 E 53rd St., 7th Fl., New York, NY 10022-5244, U.S.A.

ALARCON, Francisco X. American (born United States), b. 1954. **Genres:** Poetry, Language/Linguistics. **Career:** California State University, research assistant in Mexican-American studies, 1976-77; Milagro Books, program director, 1981-82; Computer Curriculum Corp., translator, 1984; Golden Gate National Recreation Area, park ranger, 1984; University of California-Santa Cruz, lecturer, 1985-92; Monterey Institute of International Studies, lecturer, 1988; University of California-Davis, Spanish for Native Speakers, program director, 1992-; Children's Book Press, board director, 1998-. Writer. **Publications:** POETRY: Tattoos, 1985; (with R. Reyes and J.P. Gutierrez) Ya vas, Carnal, 1985; Quake Poems, 1989; Body in Flames/Cuerpo en llamas, 1990; Loma Prieta, 1990; Of Dark Love/De amor oscuro, 1991; Snake Poems: An Aztec Invocation, 1992; No Golden Gate for Us, 1993; Sonnets to Madness and Other Misfortunes, 2001; From the Other Side of Night/Del otro lado de la noche: New and Selected Poems, 2002; Ce/Uno/One: Poems for the New Sun, 2010. POETRY FOR CHILDREN: Laughing Tomatoes and Other Spring Poems, 1997; From the Bellybutton of the Moon and Other Summer Poems, 1998; Angels Ride Bikes and Other Fall Poems, 1999; Iguanas in the Snow and Other Winter Poems, 2001; Poems to Dream Together, 2005; Animal Poems of the Iguazú, 2008. OTHERS: Mundo 21, 1995; Dime! Pasaporte al Mundo 21, 1995; Tu Mundo, Nuestro Mundo, 2000. Works appear in anthologies. Contributor to periodicals. **Address:** Department of Spanish & Portuguese, University of California, 604 Sproul Hall, 1 Shields Ave., Davis, CA 95616, U.S.A. **Online address:** fjalarcon@ucdavis.edu

ALAYA, Flavia. American (born United States), b. 1935. **Genres:** Cultural/Ethnic Topics, History, Literary Criticism And History, Urban Studies, Women's Studies And Issues, Autobiography/Memoirs, Biography, Art/Art History, Art/Art History. **Career:** University of North Carolina, instructor in English, 1959-60; Barnard College, lecturer and assistant in English, 1960-62; Hunter College of the City University of New York, lecturer, 1962-66; New York University, instructor, 1966-67, assistant professor of English, 1967-71; Ramapo College of New Jersey, associate professor and director of school of intercultural studies, 1971-73, professor of literature and cultural history, 1971-, now professor emeritus, School of Social Science and Human Services, professor of English and comparative literature; City of Paterson Historic Preservation Commission, Commissioner, 1989-98, chair, 1990-98; National Trust for Historic Preservation, advisor, 1991-2000; Center for Historic American Building Arts, founding director. Writer. **Publications:** William Sharp-Fiona Macleod 1855-1905, 1970; The Imagination Is a Square Wheel, 1977; Gaetano Federici: The Artist as Historian, 1980; Silk and Sandstone, 1984; Signifying Paterson, 1989; (with D.V. Rensalier) Bridge Street to Freedom: Landmarking a Station on the Underground Railroad, 1998; Under the Rose: A Confession, 1999. Contributor to periodicals. **Address:** Ramapo College of New Jersey, School of Social Science, 505 Ramapo Valley Rd., Mahwah, NJ 07430, U.S.A. **Online address:** flavia@bigplanet.com

AL-AZM, Sadik J. Syrian (born Syrian Arab Republic), b. 1934. **Genres:** International Relations/Current Affairs, Philosophy. **Career:** Yale University, Department of Philosophy, assistant in instruction, 1960-61; Hunter College, instructor in philosophy, 1961-62; University of Damascus, lecturer in philosophy, 1962-63, professor of philosophy, 1977-99, Department of Philosophy and Sociology, chairman, 1998-, now emeritus professor of modern European philosophy; American University, assistant professor of philosophy, 1963-68, Cultural Studies Program, assistant professor, 1967-68; Beirut University College, lecturer in philosophy, 1965-68; University of Jordan, assistant professor of philosophy, 1968-69; Arab Studies Review, editor, 1969-73; University of Hamburg, visiting professor, 1998; Princeton University, Department of Near Eastern Studies, visiting professor, through, 2007; Harvard University, visiting professor. **Publications:** Studies in Modern Western Philosophy, 1966; Dirāsāt fī al-falsafah al-gharbīyah, 1966; Kant's Theory of Time, 1967; Fī al-ḥubb wa-al-ḥubb al-udhrī, 1968; Naqd al-dhātī bada al-hazīmah, 1968; Of Love and Arabic Courtly Love, 1968; Self-Criticism after the Defeat, 1968; Naqd al-fikr al-dīnī, 1969; Dirāsāt yasārīyah ḥawla al-qadīyah al-Filasṭīnīyah, 1970; Critique of Religious Thought, 1970; The Origins of Kant's Arguments in the Antinomies, 1972; A Critical Study of the Palestinian Resistance Movement, 1973; Dirāsah naqdīyah li-fikr al-muqāwamah al-Filasṭīnīyah, 1975; Sihyūnīyah wa-al-ṣ irā al-ṭabaqī, 1975; Siyāsat Kārtir wa-munaẓẓirū al-ḥiqbah al-Saūdīyah, 1977; Ziyārat al-Sādāt wa-bon's al-salām al-ādil, 1978; Thalāth muḥāwarāt falsafīyah difāan an al-māddīyah wa-al-tārīkh: mudākhalah naqdiyah muqārabah fī tārīkh al-falsafah al-ḥadīthah wa-al-mu āṣ irah, 1990; Materialism and History: A Defense, 1990; (with M. al-Tawātī and M. Aḥmūdah) Athar al-thawrah al-Faransīyah fī fikr al-nahḍ ah, 1991; Dhihnīyat al-taḥrīm: Salmān Rushdī wa-ḥaqīqat al-adab, 1992; Salman Rushdie and the Truth of Literature, 1992, 2nd ed., 1994; Unbehagen in Der Moderne: Aufkärung im Islam, 1993; Reading the Satanic Verses: A Reply to Critics, 1997; Mābada Dhihnīyat al-taḥrīm: qirā'at al-āyāt al-Shayṭānīyah: radd wa-taqīb, 1997; Al-Almānīyah wa-al-mujtama al-madanī, 1998; (with H. ḥanafī) Mā al-awlamah?, 1999; The Satanic Verses Post Festum, 2000; L'illuminismo Islamico, 2001, 2nd ed., 2002; (contrib.) Il Mediterraneo, 2004; Islam und säkularer Humanismus, 2005.Contributor to periodicals. **Address:** Department of Philosophy and Sociology, Damascus University, PO Box 11574, Damascus, 22743, Syrian Arab Republic. **Online address:** s_j_azmzade@postmaster.co.uk

ALAZRAKI, Jaime. American/Argentine (born Argentina), b. 1934. **Genres:** Literary Criticism And History, Essays, Education. **Career:** Columbia University, instructor in Spanish, 1964-67, professor of Spanish and Portuguese, 1987-; University of California, assistant professor, 1967-68, associate professor, 1968-71, professor of Spanish, 1971-77, head of Spanish section of the department of literature, 1970-74; University of Wisconsin-Madison, visiting professor, 1972; University of California, visiting professor, 1975-76; Harvard University, professor of romance languages, 1977-87, head tutor of Spanish section, 1979-82; Universidad Autonoma de Barcelona, visiting faculty, 1985-86. Writer. **Publications:** Poética y poeśa de Pablo Neruda, 1965; La Prosa Narrativa de JorgeLuis Borges: temas, estilo, 1968, rev. ed., 1974; Jorge Luis Borges, 1971, 2nd ed., 1976; El Escritor y la critica: Borges, 1976; Versiones, Iversiones, Reversiones: El espejo como modelo estructural del relato enlos cuentos de Borges, 1977; Antologia de la novela latino americana, 2 vols., 1982; En busca del unicornio: les cuentos de Julio Cortázar: Elementos para una poética de lo neofantástico, 1983; Isla Final: Julio Cortázar, 1983; Critical Essays on Jorge Luis Borges, 1987; Borges and the Kabbalah: And Other Essays on His Fiction and Poetry, 1988; Voluntad de humanismo: Homenaje a Juan Marichal, 1990; España en Borges, 1990; Hacia Cortázar: aproximaciones a suobra, 1994; Teorías de lo fantástico, 2001; Cortzar: Ann¨herungen an sein Werk, 2009. CONTRIBUTOR: El ensayoy la critica literaria en Iberoamerica, 1970; Homenaje a Joaquin Casalduero, 1972; El cuento hispanoamericano ante la crítica, 1973; Estudios sobre los cuentos de Julio Cortazar, 1975; Jane Austen: Bicentennial Essays, 1975; Actas: Simposio Pablo Neruda, 1976; Surrealismo/surrealismos, 1977; Narrativa y crítica de nuestraAmérica, 1978; Rayuela, 1980; The Analysis of Literary Texts: Current Trends in Methodology, 1980; Octavio Paz: Homage to the Poet, 1980; The Academic American Encyclopedia, 1980; Carlos Fuentes: A Collection of Critical Essays, 1982; Simply a Man of Letters, 1982; Borges at Eighty: Conversations, 1982; A Critical View: Carlos Fuentes, 1982; Homenaje aLuis Alberto Sanchez, 1983; De los romances-villancico a la poesia de Claudio Rodriguez, 1984; Actas del Symposium on the Hispanic Essay, 1984. EDITOR: (with R. Grass and R. Salmon) Homenaje a Andres Iduarte, 1976; (with J. Jvask and contrib.) The Final Island: The Fiction of Julio Cortázar, 1978; (with J. Cortázar) Obra Crítica, 1994; (with J. Cotázar) Final del juego, 1995; Critical Essays on Julio Cortázar, 1999. **Address:** Department of Spanish and Portuguese, Columbia University, 612 W 116th St., New York, NY 10027, U.S.A.

ALBAHARI, David. Canadian/Yugoslav (born Canada), b. 1948. **Genres:** Novels, Novellas/Short Stories, Essays, Adult Non-fiction, Children's Fiction, Children's Non-fiction, Literary Criticism And History. **Career:** Pismo, editor-in-chief. **Publications:** NOVELS: Sudija Dimitrijevic, 1978; Cink, 1988; Kratka knjiga, 1993; Snezni covek, 1996; Mamac, 1996; Tsing, 1997.

SHORT STORIES: Porodicno vreme, 1973; Obicne price, 1978; Opis smrti: pripovetke, 1982; Fras u supi, 1984; Jednostavnost: Price, 1988; Pelerina, 1993; Izabrane price, 1994; Words Are Something Else: Writings from an Unbound Europe, 1996; Neobicne price, 1999; Drugi jezik, 2003. ESSAYS: Prepisivanjesveta, 1996; Teret: eseji, 2004; Pijavice, 2005; Marke, 2006; Ludvig, 2007; Senke, 2007; Svake noći u drugom gradu, 2008; Dijaspora i druge stvari, 2008; Ema I Jez Koji Nestaje, 2008; Brat, 2008; Nema pesma, 2009. NON-FICTION: (co-author) Drugom stranom: Almanah novog talasa u SFRJ, 1983; (intro.) Seacanja, 1995. OTHERS: Te ur shel mavòet, 1986; Beschreibung des Todes: Erzählungen, 1993; (with M. Pantić, V. Pavković) Nisam tu, aliradim na tome: Izbor najboljih prica sa VII konkursa za kratkuprîu na jednoj stranici, 1994; Ha-Sefer ha-katsar, 1995; Sećanja, 1995; Mrak, 1997; Pelerina i nove price, 1997; Antologija Jevrejskih Pripovedaca, 1998; Gec i Majer, 1998; Svetski Putnik (fiction), 2001; Drugi Jezik (fiction), 2003; Kako pisci pisu, 2006; ćerka, 2010; Pamtivek, 2010. EDITOR: Savremenasvetska prica, 1982; (with M. Pantic) Najbolje price 1989; Savremenaamericka knjizevnost, 1989; Uhvati ritam: Rok i knjizevnost, 1990; Najkraće price na svetu, 1993; Antologija jevrejskih pripovedaca, 1998. Contributor to periodicals. **Address:** Liepman AG Literary Agency, Englischviertelstrasse 59, Zurich, 8032, Switzerland. **Online address:** albahard@telus.net

ALBAN, Andrea. *See* **GOSLINE, Andrea Alban.**

ALBANESE, Laurie Lico. American (born United States), b. 1959?. **Genres:** Novels, Autobiography/Memoirs, Literary Criticism And History. **Career:** Wagner College, literature and writing instructor, 2004-08; Montclair Times, reporter. **Publications:** (With E. Winters) Calligraphy in Ten Easy Lessons, 1984, rev. ed., 2002; Resumes for Successful Women, 1985; Lynelle by the Sea: A Novel, 2000; Blue Suburbia: Almost a Memoir, 2004; (with L. Morowitz) The Miracles of Prato, 2009. Works appear in anthologies. Contributor to periodicals. **Address:** c/o Author Mail, HarperCollins Publishers, 10 E 53rd St., 7th Fl., New York, NY 10022-5244, U.S.A.

ALBANY, James. *See* **RAE, Hugh C(rawford).**

ALBARELLA, Joan K. American (born United States), b. 1944?. **Genres:** Novels, Poetry. **Career:** Alpha Press Publishing, founder, owner and publisher, 1973-; Western New York Catholic, writer and photographer, 1983-86; State University of New York, Educational Opportunity Center, professor, professor emerita of writing, 1986-2006; Melody Fair Theater, director, performer and playwright; Front Row Theater, director, performer and playwright; Lancaster Opera House, director, performer and playwright. **Publications:** POETRY: Mirror Me, 1973; Poems for the Asking, 1975; Women, Flowers, Fantasy, 1987; Spirit and Joy, 1993. NOVELS: Agenda for Murder, 1999; Called to Kill, 2000; Close to You, 2003; Sister Amnesia 2009. Contributor of articles to magazines and newspapers. **Address:** Alpha Press, 337 Summit Ave., Buffalo, NY 14224, U.S.A. **Online address:** joanalbarella@aol.com

ALBARN, Keith. British (born England), b. 1939. **Genres:** Art/Art History, Design. **Career:** Freelance artist and designer, 1961-63; Keith Albarn and Partners Ltd. (design consultants), founder, 1964-, managing director, 1964-71; North East London Polytechnic, course leader in fine art, 1973, principal lecturer in fine art, 1974-89; Colchester Institute, School of Art and Design, head, 1981-97; Minories Gallery, director/instigator; Cuckoo Farm Studios, director/instigator; Colchester District Visual Arts Trust, chair. Writer. **Publications:** (With J. Miall-Smith and S. Fraser-Steele) The Language of Pattern, 1974; (with J. Miall-Smith) Diagram: Instrument of Thought, 1977. **Address:** Academy Apartments, Flat 46, Institute Pl., London, GL E8 1JZ, England. **Online address:** keith.albarn@btinternet.com

ALBER, Charles J. American (born United States) **Genres:** Language/Linguistics, Literary Criticism And History, Social Sciences, Biography. **Career:** University of South Carolina, Chinese program, director, Department of Germanic, Slavic and East Asian Languages and Literatures, professor of Chinese language and literature, now retired. Writer. **Publications:** (Trans. and ed.) V.I. Semanov, Lu Sin'i ego predshestvenniki (title means: 'Lu Hsuñ and His Predecessors'), 1980; Enduring the Revolution: Ding Ling and the Politics of Literature in Guomindang China, 2002; Embracing the Lie: Ding Ling and the Politics of Literature in the People's Republic of China, 2004. Contributor to periodicals. **Address:** Department of Germanic, Slavic & East Asian, Languages & Literatures, College of Arts & Science, University of South Carolina, 1620 College St., Columbia, SC 29208, U.S.A. **Online address:** alber@sc.edu

ALBERT, Bill. American/British (born England), b. 1942. **Genres:** Novels, History, Transportation, Business/Trade/Industry, Economics. **Career:** University of East Anglia, reader in economic history, 1968-92. Writer. **Publications:** NOVELS: Et Rodriguez alors?, 1990; Desert Blues, 1994; Castle Garden, 1996. OTHERS: Turnpike Road System in England, 1663-1840, 1972; (contrib.) Portsmouth and Sheet Turnpike Commissioners' Minute Book 1711-1754, 1973; An Essay on the Peruvian Sugar Industry, 1880-1922, 1976; (co-author) Transport in the Industrial Revolution, 1983; South America and the World Economy from Independence to 1930, 1983; (ed.) Crisis and Change in the International Sugar Economy, 1860-1914, 1984; (ed. with A. Graves) The World Sugar Economy in War and Depression, 1914-40, 1988; (with P. Henderson) South America and the First World War: The Impact of the War on Brazil, Argentina, Peru, and Chile, 1988. **Address:** The White House, Marionville Rd., St. Clements Hill, Norwich, NF NR3 4DD, England. **Online address:** w.albert@uea.ac.uk

ALBERT, Hans. German (born Germany), b. 1921. **Genres:** Sociology, Philosophy, Theology/Religion, Social Sciences. **Career:** University of Cologne, assistant professor, 1952-58, dozent, 1958-63; University of Mannheim, professor and chair of philosophy of science and sociology, 1963-89, professor emeritus, 1989-. Writer. **Publications:** ökonomische Ideologie und politische Theorie: Das ökonomische Argument in der ordnungspolitischen Debatte, 1954, 2nd ed., 1972; Marktsoziologie und Entscheidungslogik: öekonomische Probleme insoziologischer Perspektive, 1967; Theoretische und institutionelle Grundlagen der Wirtschaftspolitik, 1967; Traktat über kritische Vernunft, 1968, 4th ed., 1980, trans. as Treatise on Critical Reason, 1985; Plädoyer fuer kritischen Rationalismus, 1971; Konstruktion undKritik: Aufsätze zur Philosophie des kritischen Rationalismus, 1972; Theorie und Realität. Ausgew. Aufsätze zur Wissenschaftslehre der Sozialwissenschaften, 1972; Theologische Holzwege: Gerhard Ebeling und derrechte Gebrauch der Vernunft, 1973; Transzendentale Träumerien: Karl-Otto Apels Sprachspiele u. sein hermeneut. Gott, 1975; The Positivist Dispute in German Sociology, 1976; Rationaliteitin wetenschap en Samenleving, 1976; Aufklärung und Steuerung: Aufsätze zur Sozialphilosophie und zur Wissenschaftslehre der Sozialwissenschaft, 1976; Kritische Vernunft und menschliche Praxis: Mite. autobiogr. Einl, 1977; Traktat ueber rationale Praxis, 1978; ökonometrische Modelle und sozialwissenschaftliche Erkenntnisprogramme: Beitr. zu e. Symposium anlässl. d. 90. Geburtstages von W.G. Waffenschmidt, 1978; ética y metaética: eldilema de la filosofia moral analítica, 1978; Das Elend derTheologie: Kritische Auseinandersetzung mit Hans Küng, 1979; DieWissenshaft und die Fehlbarkeit der Vernunft, 1982; Treatise on Critical Reason, 1985; Freiheit und Ordnung: Zwei Abhandlungen zum Problem einer offenen Gesellschaft, 1986; Kritik derreinen Erkenntnislehre: Das Erkenntnisproblem in realistischer Perspektive, 1987; Kritik der Reinen Hermeneutik: Der Antirealismus unddas Problem des Verstehens, 1994; Ordine, conflitto e libertà neigrandi mutamenti del nostro tempo: Certosa di Pontignano (Siena), 10-12 dicembre 1992, 1995; Rationalität und Kritik, 1996; Between Social Science, Religion and Politics. Essays on Critical Rationalism, 1999; (co-author) Renaissance der Gesellschaftskritik?, 1999; No Latitude for Fools, 2000; Kritischer Rationalismus: Vier Kapitel zur Kritik illusionären Denkens, 2000; (with D. Antiseri) Epistemologia, ermeneutica e scienzesociali, 2002; (with K.R. Popper) Briefwechsel 1958-1994, 2004. EDITOR: (with F. Karrenberg) ozialwissenschaft und Gesellschaftsgestaltung, 1963; Theorie und Realität: ählte Aufsätze zur Wissenschaftslehreder Sozialwissenschaften, 1964; Sozialtheorie und soziale Praxis: Eduard Baumgarten zum 70, 1971; (with E. Topitsch) Werturteilsstreit, 1971, 2nd ed., 1979; Rechtstheorie als Grundlagenwissenschaft der Rechtswissenschaft, 1972; (with H. Keuth) Kritik der Kritischen Psychologie, 1973; (co-author) Forschungslogik der Sozialwissenschaften, 1974; (with K.H. Stapf) Theorie und Erfahrung: Beitr. zur Grundlagenproblematik d. Sozialwiss, 1979; ökonomisches Denken undsoziale Ordnung: Festschrift für Erik Boettcher, 1984; (with K. Salamun) Mensch und Gesellschaft: aus der Sicht des kritischen Rationalismus, 1993; Soziologie in und aus Wien, 2004; (with K.R. Popper) Briefwechsel 1958-1994, 2005; In Kontroversen verstrickt: vom Kulturpessimismus zum kritischen Rationalismus, 2007; Joseph Ratzingers Rettung des Christentums: Beschrankungen des Vernunftgebrauchs im Dienste des Glaubens, 2008; ökonomische Theorie als politische Ideologie: das ökonomische Argument in der ordnungspolitischen Debatte, 2009. **Address:** University of Mannheim, 68 Mannheim, Schloss, 68161, Germany.

ALBERT, Michael. American (born United States), b. 1966. **Genres:** Art/Art History, Young Adult Non-fiction. **Career:** Gold Coast Enterprises, cofounder, 1988-91; Tri-State Natural Food Products, founder, 1991-2000; Sir

Real (organic fruit juices), founder, 1994-. Writer. **Publications:** An Artist's America, 2008. **Address:** White Plains, NY , U.S.A. **Online address:** info@michaelalbert.com

ALBERT, Michael. American (born United States), b. 1947. **Genres:** Administration/Management, Economics, Politics/Government, Writing/Journalism, Essays. **Career:** South End Press, founder, 1977-; Z Magazine, co-editor, cofounder, editorial writer, columnist, 1988-; ZNet, co-editor. **Publications:** What Is to Be Undone: A Modern Revolutionary Discussion of Classical Left Ideologies, 1974; (with R. Hahnel) Unorthodox Marxism: An Essay on Capitalism, Socialism, and Revolution, 1978; (with R. Hahnel) Socialism Today and Tomorrow, 1981; (with R. Hahnel) Marxism and Socialist Theory, 1981; (ed. and contrib. with D. Dellinger) Beyond Survival: New Directions for the Disarmament Movement, 1983; (co-author) Liberating Theory, 1986; (with R. Hahnel) Quiet Revolution in Welfare Economics, 1990; (with R. Hahnel) Looking Forward: Participatory Economics for the Twenty-first Century, 1991; (with R. Hahnel) The Political Economy of Participatory Economics, 1991; Stop the Killing Train: Radical Visions for Radical Change, 1994; Moving Forward: Programme for a Participatory Economy, 2000; The Trajectory of Change: Activist Strategies for Social Transformation, 2002; Parecon: Life after Capitalism, 2003; Thought Dreams: Radical Theory for the Twenty-First Century, 2004; Realizing Hope: Life Beyond Capitalism, 2006; Remembering Tomorrow: From SDS to Life After Capitalism, 2006. Contributor of articles to periodicals and magazines. **Address:** Z Magazine, 18 Millfield St., Woods Hole, MA 02543, U.S.A. **Online address:** michael.albert@zmag.org

ALBERT, Neil. American (born United States), b. 1950. **Genres:** Mystery/Crime/Suspense, Young Adult Fiction, Horror. **Career:** Attorney, 1976-. Writer. **Publications:** MYSTERIES: The January Corpse, 1991; The February Trouble, 1992; Burning March: A Dave Garrett Mystery, 1994; Cruel April: A Dave Garrett Mystery, 1995; Appointment in May: A Dave Garrett Mystery, 1996; Tangled June: A Dave Garrett Mystery, 1997. **Address:** 22 S Duke St., Lancaster, PA 17602-3508, U.S.A. **Online address:** nalbert@epix.net

ALBERT, Steve. American (born United States), b. 1950. **Genres:** Documentaries/Reportage, Politics/Government, Law, Adult Non-fiction. **Career:** Miami Review, reporter, 1985-90; Recorder, associate editor, 1990-95. Freelance journalist, 1995-. **Publications:** The Case against the General: Manuel Noriega and the Politics of American Justice, 1993. Contributor to books. **Address:** Scribner, Barnes & Noble, 396 Ave. of the Americas, New York, NY 10011, U.S.A.

ALBERT, Susan Wittig. (Robin Paige). American (born United States), b. 1940. **Genres:** Mystery/Crime/Suspense, Young Adult Fiction, Literary Criticism And History, Writing/Journalism, Novels, Adult Non-fiction, Translations. **Career:** University of San Francisco, instructor, 1969-71; University of Texas, assistant professor, 1972-77, associate professor, 1977-79, associate dean of graduate school, 1977-79; Sophie Newcomb College, dean, 1979-81; Southwest Texas State University, graduate dean, 1981-82, vice president for academic affairs, 1982-86, university professor of English, 1981-85; writer, 1985-; Story Circle Network Inc., founder and president, 1997-; Story Circle Book Reviews, editor; Story Circle Journal, editor, 1997-. **Publications:** NONFICTION: (co-trans. and ed.) The Poetics of Composition, 1973; Steps to Structure (textbook), 1975; (ed.) Structuralism, 1976; Stylistic and Narrative Structures in the Middle English Verse Romances, 1977; (co-author) The Participating Reader (textbook), 1979; Work of Her Own: How Women Create Success and Fulfillment off the Traditional Career Track, 1992 as Work of Her Own: A Woman's Guide to Success off the Career Track, 1994; Writing from Life, 1997; An Unthymely Death and Other Garden Mysteries, 2003. CHINA BAYLES MYSTERY NOVELS SERIES: Thyme of Death, 1992; Witches' Bane, 1993; Hangman's Root, 1994; Rosemary Remembered, 1995; Rueful Death, 1996; Love Lies Bleeding, 1997; Chile Death, 1998; Lavender and Lies, 1999; Mistletoe Man, 2000; Bloodroot, 2001; Indigo Dying, 2003; A Dilly of a Death, 2004; Dead Man's Bones, 2005; Bleeding Hearts, 2006; China Bayles' Book of Days, 2006; Spanish Dagger, 2007; Nightshade, 2008; Wormwood, 2009. COTTAGE TALES OF BEATRIX POTTER SERIES: The Tale of Hill Top Farm, 2004; The Tale of Cuckoo Brow Wood, 2005; The Tale of Holly How, 2005; The Tale of Hawthorn House, 2007; The Tale of Briar Bank, 2008. AS ROBIN PAIGE: KATE AND CHARLES MYSTERY NOVELS (with B. Albert): Death at Bishop's Keep, 1994; Death at Gallows Green, 1995; Death at Daisy's Folly, 1997; Death at Devil's Bridge, 1998; Death at Rottingdean, 1999; Death at Whitechapel, 2000; Death at Epsom Downs, 2001; Death at Dartmoor, 2002; Death at Glamis Castle, 2003; Death in Hyde Park, 2004; Death at Blenheim Palace, 2005; Death on the Lizard, 2006; Together, alone, 2009; The Tale of Oat Cake Crag, 2010; An Extraordinary Year of Ordinary Days, 2010; The Tale of Applebeck Orchard, 2010; The Darling Dahlias and the Cucumber Tree, 2010; Mourning Gloria, 2011; Holly Blues, 2011. OTHERS: Lavender Lies, 1999; (ed. and intro., with D. Finet) With Courage and Common Sense, 2003; (co-ed.) What Wildness is this, 2007; The Tale of Castle Cottage, 2011; The Darling Dahlias and the Naked Ladies, 2011; Cat's Claw, 2012. **Address:** PO Box 1616, Bertram, TX 78605-1616, U.S.A. **Online address:** salbert@tstar.net

ALBERTI, Fay Bound. British (born England), b. 1971. **Genres:** Medicine/Health. **Career:** Queen Mary University of London, senior research fellow in history; Lancaster University, faculty; University of Manchester, faculty; University of London, faculty; Open University, faculty. Writer and cultural historian. **Publications:** (Ed.) Medicine, Emotion and Disease, 1700-1950, 2006; Matters of the Heart: History, Medicine, and Emotion, 2010. Contributor of articles to journals. **Address:** Department of History, Queen Mary University of London, Mile End Rd., London, GL E1 4NS, England. **Online address:** f.boundalberti@qmul.ac.uk

ALBERTS, Laurie. American (born United States), b. 1953?. **Genres:** Novels, Literary Criticism And History, Biography, Autobiography/Memoirs, Young Adult Fiction, inspirational/Motivational Literature, Crafts. **Career:** Writer and teacher. **Publications:** Tempting Fate, 1987; Goodnight Silky Sullivan, 1995; The Price of Land in Shelby, 1996; Lost Daughters, 1999; Fault Line, 2004; Between Revolutions: An American Romance with Russia, 2005; Showing & Telling: Learn How to Show & When to Tell for Powerful & Balanced Writing, 2010. **Address:** c/o Author Mail, University of Nebraska Press, 233 N 8th St., Lincoln, NE 68588-0255, U.S.A. **Online address:** albertslaurie@yahoo.com

ALBIACH, Anne-Marie. French (born France), b. 1937. **Genres:** Poetry, Translations. **Career:** Siécle à Mains (journal), founding editor. Poet and translator. **Publications:** Flammigère: poème, 1967; (trans.) Louis Zukofsy, A-9 (première partie), 1970; état, 1971; H II: linéaires, 1974; Césure: le corps, avec des collages originaux de Raquel, 1975; Objet, 1976; Anawratha, 1984; Mezza voce, 1984; Vocative Figure, 1985, rev. ed., 1992; Le chemin de l'ermitage, 1986; Travail vertical et blanc, 1989; A Geometry, 1998; A Discursive, Space: Interviews with Jean Daive, 1999; Figured Image, 2006. Contributor to books. **Address:** c/o Author Mail, The Post-Apollo Press, 35 Marie St., Sausalito, CA 94965, U.S.A.

ALBOM, Mitch. American (born United States), b. 1958. **Genres:** Sports/Fitness, Biography. **Career:** Queens Tribune, editor, 1981-82; Philadelphia Inquirer, contributing writer, 1982-83; GEO, contributing editor, 1982-83; Fort Lauderdale News, sports columnist, 1983-85; Sun Sentinel, sports columnist, 1983-85; Detroit Free Press, sports columnist, 1985-; WLLZ-Radio, sports director, 1985-, Sunday Sports Albom, co-host, 1988-99; WDIV-TV, broadcaster and commentator, 1987-; Dream Team, founder, 1989; The Mitch Albom Show, host, 1995-; Monday Sports Albom, host, 1999-. **Publications:** The Live Albom: The Best of Detroit Free Press Sports Columnist Mitch Albom, 1988; (with B. Schembechler) Bo: The Bo Schembechler Story, 1989; The Live Albom II, 1990; The Live Albom III, 1992; The Fab Five: Basketball, Trash Talk, the American Dream, 1993; Live Albom IV, 1995; Tuesdays with Morrie: An Old Man, a Young Man, and Life's Greatest Lesson, 1997; The Five People You Meet in Heaven, 2003; For One More Day, 2006; And the Winner Is, 2008; Duck Hunter Shoots Angel, 2008; (with J. Hatcher) Mitch Albom's Tuesdays with Morrie, 2008; Have a Little Faith, 2009. Contributor to periodicals. **Address:** Detroit Free Press, 615 W Lafayette, Detroit, MI 48226, U.S.A. **Online address:** mitch@mitchalbom.com

ALBOROUGH, Jez. British (born England), b. 1959. **Genres:** Children's Fiction, Poetry, Illustrations. **Career:** A&C Black Publishers, editor. Illustrator. **Publications:** FOR CHILDREN: SELF-ILLUSTRATED: Bare Bear, 1984; Running Bear, 1985; Willoughby Wallaby, 1986; The Grass Is Greener in US as The Grass Is Always Greener, 1987; Esther's Trunk, 1988; The Tale of Hillary Hiccup, 1988; Cupboard Bear, 1989; Beaky, 1990 in UK as Hello, Beaky, 1998; Archibald, 1991; Shake before Opening (poems), 1991; Where's My Teddy, 1992; Cuddly Dudley, 1993; Washing Line, 1993 in US as Clothesline, 1993; Hide and Seek!, 1994; There's Something at the Letterbox, 1994 in US as There's Something at the Mail Slot, 1995; It's the Bear!, 1994; Can You Jump Like a Kangaroo?, 1996; Can You Peck Like a Hen?, 1996; Watch Out! Big Bro's Coming, 1997; Ice Cream Bear, 1997, 2nd ed.,

1999; My Friend Bear, 1998; Balloon, 1998; Whose Socks Are Those?, 1999; Hug, 2000; The Latest Craze, 2002; Some Dogs Do, 2003; Tall, 2005; Duck's Key, Where Can It Be?, 2005; Yes, 2006; Hit the Ball Duck, 2006; Gobble Gobble Moo Tractor Book, 2010. FEATHER BY HOUSE FABLES SERIES: The Candle's Story, 1988; The Clock's Story, 1988; The Mirror's Story, 1988; The Umbrella's Story, 1988. DUCK SERIES: Duck in the Truck, 2000; Fix-It Duck, 2002; Captain Duck, 2003. OTHERS: Super Duck, 2009; Duck's Day Out, 2012; Duck to the Rescue, 2012. Illustrator of books by others. Contributor to periodicals. **Address:** Walker Books, 87 Vauxhall Walk, London, GL SE11 5HJ, England.

ALBRECHT, Ernest (Jacob). American (born United States), b. 1937. **Genres:** Cultural/Ethnic Topics, Recreation, Biography. **Career:** East Brunswick High School, teacher, 1960-65; Middlesex Community College, assistant professor of English, 1967-; Spectacle Magazine, editor and publisher, 1997-. **Publications:** A Ringling by Any Other Name: The Story of John Ringling North and his Circus, 1989; The New American Circus, 1995; Contemporary Circus: Art of the Spectacular, 2006. **Address:** Spectacle Magazine, PO Box 1420, Edison, NJ 08818-1420, U.S.A. **Online address:** circusplus@aol.com

ALBRECHT, Gary L(ouis). American (born United States), b. 1937. **Genres:** Medicine/Health, Sociology. **Career:** National Training Laboratories' Southern Community Leadership, faculty, 1966; Emory University, Department of Psychiatry, Sociology Division, associate, 1968-69, assistant professor, 1969-72, Department of Psychology, assistant professor, 1969-72; Northwestern University, Rehabilitation Institute of Chicago, Sociological Research Unit, director, 1972-75, Department of Sociology, assistant professor, 1972-75, associate professor, 1975-79, Department of Rehabilitation Medicine, assistant professor, 1972-75, Center for Health Services and Policy Research, associate, 1975-79, Kellogg School of Management, Department of Sociology, associate professor, 1975-79; University of Illinois, School of Public Health, associate professor, 1979-80, professor of health policy and administration, 1981-2006, acting director of health policy and administration, 1985-89, 1995, 1998, professor emeritus, 2006-, College of Applied Health Sciences, Department of Disability and Human Development, professor of disability and human development, 1981-2006, professor emeritus, 2006-, Institute of Government and Public Affairs, faculty affiliate, 1992-2006; Royal Belgian Academy of Arts and Sciences, fellow, 2006-. Writer. **Publications:** (Contrib.) Alcoholism, 1973; (contrib.) Life-span Developmental Psychology, Normative Life Crises, 1975; The Disability Business: Rehabilitation in America, 1992. EDITOR: Sociology of Physical Disability and Rehabilitation, 1976; (with P.C. Higgins) Health, Illness, and Medicine, 1979; Cross National Rehabilitation Policies, 1981; (with J. Levy) Advances in Medical Sociology, vol. II: Chronic Disease across the Life Course, 1992; (with R. Fitzpatrick and S.C. Scrimshaw) Handbook of Social Studies in Health and Medicine, 2000; (with K.D. Seelman and M. Bury) The Handbook of Disability Studies, 2001; Encyclopedia of Disability, 2006. **Address:** School of Public Health, University of Illinois, 1603 W Taylor St., Chicago, IL 60612-4394, U.S.A. **Online address:** garya@uic.edu

ALBRECHT, Gloria H. American (born United States) **Genres:** Ethics. **Career:** Teacher, 1963-66; Social Security Administration, policy specialist, 1966-69; Box Project (nonprofit organization), board director, 1974-80; Presbyterian Church, ordained minister, 1983, associate pastor, 1983-91, detroit, 1992-; Saint Mary's Seminary and University, Ecumenical Institute, lecturer, 1985-92; Maryland Religious Coalition for Abortion Rights, chair of policy council, 1989-91; Temple University, adjunct faculty, 1991-92; University of Detroit Mercy, Women Studies program, director, associate professor of religion and ethics, 1992-; Johns Hopkins University, lecturer; Towson State University, lecturer; University of Maryland, lecturer. Writer. **Publications:** The Character of Our Communities: Toward a Liberative Ethic for the Church, 1995; Hitting Home: Feminist Ethics, Women's Work, and the Betrayal of Family Values, 2002. Contributor to books. **Address:** Department of Religious Studies, University of Detroit Mercy, Briggs 333 B, PO Box 19900, Detroit, MI 48219-0900, U.S.A. **Online address:** albrecgh@udmercy.edu

ALBRECHT, Steve. American (born United States), b. 1963. **Genres:** Business/Trade/Industry, Law. **Career:** Albrecht Training and Development, writer and seminar leader, 1985-, managing partner, 1987-2001; San Diego Police Reserve, police officer, 1984-85, reserve officer, 1985-94, reserve training officer, 1987-89, reserve sergeant, 1994-99, retired, 1999; Central Texas College, adjunct faculty, 1996-97; National University, adjunct faculty, 1996-2000; American Society for Industrial Security, adjunct faculty, 1998-99; Grossmont College, adjunct faculty, 2000-; Baron Center Inc., president, 2000-02, senior consultant, 2002-04; California State University, adjunct faculty, 2003-; Association of Threat Assessment Professionals, national secretary, 2003-05; University of Southern California, Delinquency Control Institute, adjunct faculty, 2004-; San Diego State University, College of Extended Studies, adjunct faculty, 2007-. **Publications:** (With K. Albrecht) The Creative Corporation, 1987; (with J. Morrison) Contact and Cover: Two-Officer Suspect Control, 1992; Street Work: The Way to Police Officer Safety and Survival, 1992; One-Strike Stopping Power, 1992; The Paralegal's Desk Reference, 1993; (with Albrecht) Added Value Negotiating, 1993; (with M. Mantell) Ticking Bombs: Defusing Violence in the Workplace, 1994; Service, Service, Service!, 1994; (with J. Clemens) Timeless Leaders, 1995; Corporate Self-Defense, 1995; Fear and Violence on the Job: Prevention Solutions for the Dangerous Workplace, 1997; Surviving Street Patrol: The Officer's Guide to Safe and Effective Policing, 2001; Tough Training Topics: A Presenter's Survival Guide, 2006. **Address:** Albrecht Training & Development, 9528 Miramar Rd., Ste. 270, San Diego, CA 92126, U.S.A. **Online address:** drsteve@drstevealbrecht.com

ALBRITTON, Robert. Canadian/American (born United States), b. 1941. **Genres:** Politics/Government, History. **Career:** University of California, teaching assistant, 1966-69; York University, Department of Political Science, lecturer, 1969-72, associate professor, 1972-2001, professor, 2001-05, professor emeritus, 2005-. Writer. **Publications:** A Japanese Reconstruction of Marxist Theory, 1986; (ed. with V. Gray and H. Jacob) Politics in the American States: A Comparative Analysis, 5th ed., 1990; A Japanese Approach to Stages of Capitalist Development, 1991; (ed. with T.T. Sekine) A Japanese Approach to Political Economy: Unoist Variations, 1995; Dialectics and Deconstruction in Political Economy, 1999; (co-ed.) Phases of Capitalist Development, 2001; (ed. with J. Simoulidis) New Dialectics and Political Economy, 2003; (co-ed.) New Socialisms: Futures beyond Globalization, 2004; (ed. with R. Jessop and R. Westra) Political Economy and Global Capitalism: The 21st Century, Present and Future, 2007; Economics Transformed: Discovering the Brilliance of Marx, 2007; Let Them Eat Junk: How Capitalism Creates Hunger and Obesity, 2009. **Address:** Department of Political Sciences, York University, S663 Ross Bldg., 4700 Keele St., Toronto, ON M3J 1P3, Canada. **Online address:** ralbritt@yorku.ca

ALCALDE, Miguel. *See* **REGINALD, Robert.**

ALCHON, Suzanne Austin. (Suzanne Austin). American (born United States), b. 1952. **Genres:** History, Medicine/Health. **Career:** University of Delaware, professor. Writer, educator and historian. **Publications:** Native Society and Disease in Colonial Ecuador, 1991; A Pest in the Land: New World Epidemics in a Global Perspective, 2003. **Address:** Department of History, University of Delaware, 236 John Munroe Hall, 46 W Delaware Ave., Newark, DE 19716-2547, U.S.A. **Online address:** salchon@udel.edu

ALCOSSER, Sandra (B.). American (born United States), b. 1944. **Genres:** Poetry. **Career:** Mademoiselle, associate editor, 1966-69; writer-in-residence and workshop director, 1973-85; Poets-in-the-Park, director, 1975-77; Louisiana State University, instructor, 1982-85, assistant professor of English, 1985-87; San Diego State University, associate professor of English, 1986-89, Master of Fine Arts Program in Creative Writing, director, 1988-91, founder, professor of English; University of Michigan, professor of English, 1990-, visiting professor of creative writing, 1994, writer-in-residence; University of Montana, visiting professor of creative writing; Central Park Zoo, poet-in-residence, writer-in-residence; Poets House New York, poet-in-residence; The Wildlife Conservation Society, poet-in-residence; National University of Ireland, writer-in-residence; Pacific University, faculty. **Publications:** POETRY: Each Bone a Prayer, 1982; A Fish to Feed All Hunger, 1986; Sleeping inside the Glacier, 1997; Except by Nature, 1998; Glyphs, 2001. Works appear in anthologies. Contributor to books and periodicals. **Address:** Department of English and Comparative Literature, San Diego State University, 5500 Campanile Dr., PO Box 6020, San Diego, CA 92182-6020, U.S.A. **Online address:** alcosser@mail.sdsu.edu

ALDCROFT, Derek Howard. British/Welsh (born Wales), b. 1936. **Genres:** Economics, History, Transportation, Bibliography, Business/Trade/Industry. **Career:** University of Glasgow, assistant lecturer in economic history, 1960-62, lecturer in economic history, 1964-67; University of Leicester, assistant lecturer, 1962-63, senior lecturer, 1967-70, reader, 1970-73, professor of economic history and head of department, 1976-94, Department of Economic and Social History, university fellow, 2002-; University of Sydney, professor of economic history and head of department, 1973-76; Anglia Polytechnic University, visiting professor, 1993-99; Manchester Metropolitan University, research professor in economic history, 1994-2001, visiting professor, 2001-. Writer. **Publications:** British Railways in Transition, 1968; (with H.W. Richardson) Building in the British Economy between the Wars, 1968; (with H.W. Richardson) The British Economy, 1969; (with H.J. Dyos) British Transport, 1969; (with H.W. Richardson) The British Economy, 1870-1939, 1969; The Inter-War Economy, Britain 1919-1939, 1970; Finanz und Wirtschaftspolitische Fragender Zwischenkriegszeit, 1973; Studies in British Transport History 1879-1970, 1974; British Transport since 1914, 1975; From Versailles to Wall Street, 1977; The East Midlands Economy, 1979; The European Economy, 1914-80, 1980; Rail Transport (bound with Sea Transport by Derrick Mort), 1981; The British Economy between the Wars, 1983; Full Employment: The Elucive Goal, 1984; (with M.J. Freeman) The Atlas of British Railway History, 1985; The British Economy: vol. I, Years of Turmoil, 1920-1951, 1986; Education, Training and Economic Performance 1944-1990, 1992; The European Economy, 1914-1990, 1993; Bibliography of European Economic and Social History 1750-1939, 1993; Economic Change in Eastern Europe since 1918, 1995; Studies in the Interwar European Economy, 1997; (with M.J. Oliver) Exchange Rate Regimes in the Twentieth Century, 1998; (with M. Oliver) Trade Unions and the Economy, 2000; The European Economy 1914-2000, 2001; Europe's Third World: The European Periphery in the Interwar Years, 2006. EDITOR: The Development of British Industry and Foreign Competition 1875-1914, 1968; (with P. Fearon) Economic Growth in Twentieth Century Britain, 1969; (intro. and ed. with P. Fearon) British Economic Fluctuations 1790-1939, 1972; (with N.K. Burton) British Industry between the Wars: Instability and Industrial Development, 1919-1939, 1979; (with P.L. Cottrell) Shipping, Trade and Commerce, 1981; (with A. Slaven) Business, Banking, and Urban History, 1982; (with M.J. Freeman) Transport in the Industrial Revolution, 1983; (with R. Rodger) Bibliography of European Economic and Social History, 1984; (with M.J. Freeman) Transport in Victorian Britain, 1988; (contrib.) Atlas of the World Economy, 1991; (with S.P. Ville) The European Economy, 1750-1914: A Thematic Approach, 1994; (with A. Slaven) Enterprise and Management: Essays in Honour of Peter L. Payne, 1995; (with R.E. Catterall) Rich Nations, Poor Nations: The Long-Run Perspective, 1996; (with A. Sutcliffe) Europe in the International Economy, 1500 to 2000, 1999; (with M.J. Oliver) Trade Unions and the Economy: 1870-2000, 2000; (ed. with R.E. Catterall) Exchange Rate Regimes and Economic Policy in the 20th Century, 2004; (ed. with M.J. Oliver) Economic Disasters of the Twentieth Century, 2008. **Address:** The School of Historical Studies, The University of Leicester, University Rd., Leicester, LE LE1 7RH, England.

ALDEN, Chris. British (born England), b. 1959. **Genres:** History, Politics/Government. **Career:** University of London, London School of Economics and Political Science, Department of International Relations, senior lecturer in international relations, reader. Writer. **Publications:** Apartheid's Last Stand: The Rise and Fall of the South African Security State, 1995; (contrib.) War and Peace in Mozambique, 1998; (contrib.) Pays Lusophones D'Afrique: Sources D'Information Pour Le Développement: Angola, Cap-Vert, Guinée-Bissau, Mozambique, São Tomé E Príncipe, 2000; Mozambique and the Construction of the New African State: From Negotiations to Nation Building, 2001; (with K. Hirano) Japan and South Africa in a Globalising World: Distant Mirror, 2002; (with G.L. Pere) South Africa's Post-Apartheid Foreign Policy: From Reconciliation to Revival?, 2003; China in Africa, 2007; From Soldiers to Citizens: The Social, Economic and Political Reintegration of Unita Ex-Combatants in US (with J.G. Porto and I. Parsons) as From Soldiers to Citizens: Demilitarization of Conflict and Society, 2007; Foreign Policy Analysis: Understanding the Diplomacy of War, Profit and Justice, 2008; (with W. Anseeuw) Land, Liberation and Compromise in Southern Africa, 2009; (with S. Morphet and M.A. Vieira) South in World Politics, 2010; (with M. Thakur and M. Arnold) Militias and the Challenges of Post-conflict Peace, 2011; (with A. Aran) Foreign Policy Analysis: New Approaches, 2011. EDITOR: (with J. Daloz) Paris, Pretoria, and the African Continent: The International Relations of States and Societies in Transition, 1996; (with G. Martin) France and South Africa: Towards a New Engagement with Africa, 2003; (with D. Large and R.S.D. Oliveira) China Returns to Africa: A Rising Power and a Continent Embrace in US as China Returns to Africa: A Superpower and a Continent Embrace, 2008; (with W. Anseeuw) Struggle over Land in Africa, 2010. Contributor to periodicals and journals. **Address:** London School of Economics and Political Science, University of London, Houghton St., London, GL WC2A 2AE, England. **Online address:** j.c.alden@lse.ac.uk

ALDEN, Edward H. American (born United States), b. 1961. **Genres:** History, Young Adult Non-fiction, Politics/Government. **Career:** Inside U.S. Trade, managing editor; Vancouver Sun, senior reporter; Financial Times, Washington bureau chief; Council on Foreign Relations, Bernard L. Schwartz Senior Fellow. Writer. **Publications:** Why We Need Ideologies in American Foreign Policy: Democratic Politics and World Order, 1990; The Closing of the American Border: Terrorism, Immigration and Security since 9/11, 2008. **Address:** U.S.A. **Online address:** ealden@cfr.org

ALDEN, Pat. *See* **FRANCIS, Dorothy Brenner.**

ALDEN, Patricia. American (born United States), b. 1945?. **Genres:** Literary Criticism And History, Education, Young Adult Fiction, Social Sciences. **Career:** St. Lawrence University, instructor, 1976-78, assistant professor, 1978-84, associate professor, 1985-92, professor of English, 1993-, associate dean for international and intercultural studies. Writer. **Publications:** Social Mobility in the English Bildungsroman: Gissing, Hardy, Bennett, and Lawrence, 1986; (ed. with D.T. Lloyd and A.I. Samatar) African Studies and the Undergraduate Curriculum, 1994; (with L. Tremaine) Nuruddin Farah, 1999. Contributor to books and periodicals. **Address:** Department of English, St. Lawrence University, Carnegie Hall, 23 Romoda Dr., Canton, NY 13617, U.S.A. **Online address:** palden@stlawu.edu

ALDEN, Sue. *See* **FRANCIS, Dorothy Brenner.**

ALDER, Ken(neth L.). American (born United States), b. 1959. **Genres:** History, Novels, Young Adult Fiction, Adult Non-fiction. **Career:** Northwestern University, assistant professor, 1991-97, Science in Human Culture Program, founding director, 1994-2010, associate professor of history, 1997-2003, Harold and Virginia Anderson outstanding teaching professor, 1999-2003, professor of history, 2003-, Milton H. Wilson professor in the humanities, 2003-. Writer. **Publications:** The White Bus (novel), 1987; Engineering the Revolution: Arms and Enlightenment in France, 1763-1815 (nonfiction), 1997; The Measure of All Things: The Seven-year Odyssey and Hidden Error that Transformed the World, 2002; The Measure of the World, 2003; The Lie Detectors: The History of an American Obsession, 2007. Contributor to periodicals. **Address:** Department of History, Northwestern University, Rm. 309, Harris Hall, 1881 Sheridan Rd., Evanston, IL 60208-2220, U.S.A. **Online address:** mail@kenalder.com

ALDERMAN, Ellen. American (born United States), b. 1957?. **Genres:** Law, Young Adult Non-fiction, Politics/Government, Social Sciences. **Career:** Attorney and writer. **Publications:** (With C. Kennedy) In Our Defense: The Bill of Rights in Action (nonfiction), 1991; (with C. Kennedy) The Right to Privacy (nonfiction), 1995. Contributor of articles to journals. **Address:** Alfred A. Knopf Inc., 201 E 50th St., New York, NY 10022, U.S.A.

ALDERSEY-WILLIAMS, Hugh. American/British (born England), b. 1959. **Genres:** Design, Architecture, Business/Trade/Industry, Sciences, Chemistry. **Career:** Butterworth Scientific, science journal editor, 1980-84; freelance writer, 1986-; Design Business Association. project consultant. **Publications:** New American Design, 1988; Hollington Industrial Design, 1990; King and Miranda: The Poetry of the Machine, 1991; World Design: Nationalism and Globalism in Design, 1992; The Most Beautiful Molecule: The Discovery of the Buckyball, 1995; Zoomorphic, 2003; Findings: Hidden Stories in First-Hand Accounts of Scientific Discovery, 2005; (with S. Briscoe) Panicology, 2009; British Design, 2010; Periodic Tales, 2011. Contributor to magazines. **Address:** c/o Robert I. Ducas, 350 Hudson St., New York, NY 10014, U.S.A. **Online address:** hugh@hughalderseywilliams.com

ALDERSON, Sue Ann. Canadian/American (born United States), b. 1940. **Genres:** Young Adult Fiction, Children's Fiction, History. **Career:** Simon Fraser University, instructor in English, 1967-71; Capilano College, instructor in English, 1972-80; University of British Columbia, Department of Creative Writing, assistant professor, 1980-84, associate professor, 1984-92, professor, through 1992, now professor emeritus. Writer. **Publications:** Shaftesbury and the Deist Manifesto, 1951; Benjamin Franklin and His French Contemporaries, 1957; Man of Reason: The Life of Thomas Paine, 1959; (contrib.) The Unforgettable Americans, 1960; Essai sur lespersonnages des Liaisons Dangereuses en tant que types litteraires, 1960; (contrib.) Early Dickinsonia, 1961; (contrib.) Utopia et institutions auXVIII e siecle: Le Pragmatisme de

Lumieres, 1963; Jonathan Edwards, 1964, 2nd ed., 1966; Benjamin Franklin: Philosopher and Man, 1965; Benjamin Franklin and Nature's God, 1967; (contrib.) Essays on American Literature in Honor of Jay B. Hubbell, 1967; Bonnie McSmithers You're Driving Me Dithers, 1974; Voltaire and the Century of Light, 1975; Hurry Up, Bonnie!, 1976; The Adventures of Prince Paul, 1977; The Finding Princess, 1977; Bonnie McSmithers Is at It Again!, 1979; Comparative Literature East-West, 1979; Early American Literature: A Comparatist Approach, 1982; Comet's Tale, 1983; The Not Impossible Summer, 1983; Thomas Paine's American Ideology, 1984; The Something in Thurlo Darby's House, 1985; Fiction in Japan and the West, 1985; The Reemergence of World Literature: A Study of Asia and the West, 1986; Ida and the Wool Smugglers, 1988; Maybe You Had to Be There, by Duncan, 1989; Chapter One, 1990; Sure As Strawberries, 1992; A Ride for Martha, 1993; The Dragon and the Eagle: The Presence of China in the American Enlightenment, 1993; Ten Mondays for Lots of Boxes, 1995; Pond Seasons, 1996; Wherever Bears Be: A Story for Two Voices, 1999; Eco-Diary of Kiran Singer, 2007. EDITOR: Comparative Literature: Matter and Method, 1969; The Ibero-American Enlightenment, 1970; Explorations 1, 1986; Explorations 2, 1987. **Address:** 4004 W 32nd Ave., Vancouver, BC V6S 1Z6, Canada. **Online address:** salderso@interchange.ubc.ca

ALDHOUSE-GREEN, Miranda Jane. British (born England), b. 1947. **Genres:** Archaeology/Antiquities, Mythology/Folklore, History. **Career:** Open University, administrator, 1982-88, assistant staff tutor, 1989-; University of Wales-Newport, University College, lecturer in Celtic studies, Gwent College of Higher Education, senior lecturer in archaeology, 1991-94, visiting lecturer, professor of archaeology, SCARAB Research Centre, director; Cardiff University, Cardiff School of History, Archaeology and Religion, professor of archaeology, 1998-. Writer. **Publications:** (Co-author) Bradwell Roman Villa: First Interim Report, 1975; Corpus of Religious Material from the Civilian Areas of Roman Britain, 1976; Guide Catalogue to the Prehistoric Archaeological Collections in the Peterborough City Museum, 1977; Corpus of Small Cult-Objects from the Military Areas of Roman Britain, 1978; Gods of Roman Britain, 1983; Wheel as a Cult-Symbol in the Romano-Celtic World: With Special Reference to Gaul and Britain, 1984; The Gods of the Celts, 1986; Symbol and Image in Celtic Religious Art, 1989; The Sun Gods of Ancient Europe, 1991; Dictionary of Celtic Myth and Legend, 1992; Animals in Celtic Life and Myth, 1992; Celtic Myths, 1993; (ed.) Celtic World, 1995; Celtic Goddesses: Warriors, Virgins, and Mothers, 1996; Celtic Art: Reading the Messages, 1996; (ed. with S. Billington) Concept of the Goddess, 1996; Celtic Art: Symbols & Imagery, 1997; World of the Druids, 1997; Pilgrims in Stone: Stone Images from the Gallo-Roman Sanctuary of Fontes Sequanae, 1999; Celtic Wales, 2000; Dying for the Gods, 2001; (ed. with P. Webster) Artefacts and Archaeology: Aspects of the Celtic and Roman World, 2002; An Archaeology of Images: Iconology and Cosmology in Iron Age and Roman Europe, 2004; (ed. with R.A. Griffiths) Gwent County History, 2004; (with S. Aldhouse-Green) Quest for the Shaman: Shape-shifters, Sorcerers, and Spirit-healers of Ancient Europe, 2005; Boudica Britannia: Rebel, War-Leader and Queen, 2006; Caesar's Druids, 2010. **Address:** Cardiff School of History, Archaeology & Religion, Cardiff University, Rm. 3.17, Humanities Bldg., Colum Dr., Cardiff, CF10 3EU, Wales. **Online address:** aldhouse-greenmj@cardiff.ac.uk

ALDING, Peter. *See* **JEFFRIES, Roderic.**

ALDISS, Brian (Wilson). Also writes as C. C. Shackleton, Jael Cracken. British (born England), b. 1925. **Genres:** Young Adult Non-fiction, Novellas/Short Stories, Science Fiction/Fantasy, Poetry, Autobiography/Memoirs, Adult Non-fiction. **Career:** Oxford Mail, literary editor, 1958-70; Penguin Science Fiction, editor, 1961-64; Guardian, art correspondent, 1971-78; World SF, president, 1982-84; Avernus Publishing, managing director, 1988-; West Buckland School, vice-president, 1990-; H.G. Wells Society, vice president; Birmingham Science Fiction Group, co-president. **Publications:** NOVELS: The Brightfount Diaries, 1955; Non-Stop in US as Starship, 1958; Equator, 1958 in US as Vanguard from Alpha, 1959; Bow Down to Nul, 1960 in US as The Interpreter, 1961; The Male Response, 1961; The Primal Urge, 1961; Long Afternoon of Earth in UK as Hothouse, 1962; Greybeard, 1963; The Dark Light Years: A Science Fiction Novel, 1964; Earthworks: A Science Fiction Novel, 1965; (as C.C. Shackleton) Two Modern Myths, 1967; An Age, 1967 in US as Cryptozoic!, 1968; Report on Probability A, 1968; A Brian Aldiss Omnibus, 1969; Barefoot in the Head: A European Fantasia, 1969; The Hand-Reared Boy, 1970; A Soldier Erect, 1971 in UK as A Soldier Erect or Further Adventures: The Hand-Reared Boy, 1971; Brian Aldiss Omnibus (2), 1971; The Eighty-Minute Hour: A Space Opera, 1974; The Malacia Tapestry, 1976; Brothers of the Head: And Where The Lines Converge, 1977; A Rude Awakening, 1978; Enemies of the System: A Tale of Homo Uniformis, 1978; Life in the West: A Novel, 1980; Moreau's Other Island, 1980 in US as An Island Called Moreau, 1981; Farewell To A Child, 1982; Helliconia Spring, 1982; Helliconia Summer, 1983; Helliconia Winter, 1985; The Helliconia Trilogy, 1985; The Horatio Stubbs Saga, 1985; (as Jael Cracken) The Year Before Yesterday: A Novel in Three Acts, 1987; Ruins, 1987; Forgotten Life, 1989; Dracula Unbound, 1991; Remembrance Day, 1993; Somewhere East of Life: Another European Fantasia, 1994; White Mars or The Mind Set Free: A 21st Century Utopia, 2000; The Cretan Teat, 2002; Super-State: A Novel of a Future Europe, 2002; (intro.) Around the World in Eighty Days, 2004; Affairs at Hampden Ferrers, 2004; Jocasta, 2005; Sanity and the Lady, 2005; Harm, 2007. NON-FICTION: Cities and Stones: A Traveller's Jugoslavia, 1966; The Shape of Further Things: Speculations On Change, 1970; Billion Year Spree: The History of Science Fiction, 1973; Science Fiction Art, 1975; Science Fiction As Science Fiction, 1978; This World and Nearer Ones: Essays Exploring the Familiar, 1979; Pile: Petals from St. Klaed's Computer, 1979; The Pale Shadow of Science, 1985; And the Lurid Glare of the Comet, 1986; Trillion Year Spree: The History of Science Fiction, 1986; Bury My Heart at W.H. Smith's: A Writing Life, 1990; The Detached Retina: Aspects of SF and Fantasy, 1995; Songs from the Steppes of Central Asia: The Collected Poems of Makhtumkuli: Eighteenth Century Poet-Hero of Turkmenistan, 1996; The Twinkling of an Eye or My Life as an Englishman, 1998; When the Feast Is Finished, 1999; Art After Apogee, 2000; Plutonian Monologue On His Wife's Death, 2000; The Starry Messenger: Visions of the Universe, 2006. STORY COLLECTIONS: Space Time and Nathaniel, 1957; The Canopy of Time, 1959; No Time Like Tomorrow, 1959; Galaxies Like Grains of Sand, 1960; The Airs of Earth: Science Fiction Stories, 1963; Stars Warm, 1964; Best Science Fiction Stories of Brian W. Aldiss, 1965 in US as Who Can Replace a Man?, 1966; The Saliva Tree and Other Strange Growths, 1966; The Future Makers: A Selection of Science Fiction from Brian Aldiss, 1968; Intangibles Inc. And Other Stories: Five Novellas, 1969; (contrib.) The Inner Landscape, 1969; The Moment of Eclipse, 1970; Neanderthal Planet, 1970; The Book of Brian Aldiss, 1972, rev. ed. as The Comic Inferno, 1972; Last Orders and Other Stories, 1977; New Arrivals, Old Encounters: Twelve Stories, 1979; Foreign Bodies: Stories, 1981; Seasons in Flight, 1984; The Magic of the Past, 1987; Best Short Stories of Brian Aldiss, 1988 in US as Man in His Time: The Best Science Fiction Stories of Brian W. Aldiss, 1989; Science Fiction Blues: The Show that Brian Aldiss Took on the Road, 1988; A Romance of the Equator: Best Fantasy Stories, 1989; (contrib.) Pulp House Science-Fiction Short Stories, 1991; A Tupolev Too Far: And Other Stories, 1994; The Secret of This Book: 20 Odd Stories, 1995; Common Clay: 20 Odd Stories, 1996; Supertoys Last All Summer Long: And Other Stories: Future Time, 2001; The Dark Sun Rises, 2002; Cultural Breaks, 2005; An Prehistory of Mind, 2008. EDITOR: Penguin Science Fiction, 1961; More Penguin Science Fiction, 1962; Best Fantasy Stories, 1962; Science Fiction Horizons, Numbers 1-2, 1964-65; Yet More Penguin Science Fiction, 1964; Introducing Science Fiction: A Science Fiction Anthology, 1964; (with H. Harrison) Nebula Award Stories II, 1967; (with H. Harrison) All about Venus: A Revelation of the Planet Venus in Fact and Fiction, 1968 in UK as Farewell Fantastic Venus! A History of the Planet Venus in Fact and Fiction, 1968; (with H. Harrison) The Astounding-Analog Reader, vol. I, 1972, vol. II, 1973; Penguin Science Fiction Omnibus, 1973; Space Opera: An Anthology: Way-Back-When Futures, 1974; (with H. Harrison) Hell's Cartographers: Some Personal Histories of Science Fiction Writers, 1975; Space Odysseys, 1975; Evil Earths, 1975; Galactic Empires, 1976; (with H. Harrison) Decade: The 1940s, 1977; (with H. Harrison) Decade: The 1950s, 1977; (with H. Harrison) Decade: The 1960s, 1977; Perilous Planets, 1978; Mary Shelley: The Last Man, 1985; (as C.C. Shackleton) The Greatest Saga of All Times, 1985; The Penguin World Omnibus: Science Fiction: An Anthology, 1986; My Madness: The Selected Writings of Anna Kavan, 1990; The Island of Doctor Moreau, 1993; Mini Sagas from the Daily Telegraph Competition, 1997; Mini Sagas 1999, 1999; (ed.) Science Fiction Omnibus, 2007. OTHERS: Science Fiction Quiz, 1983; Crackenat Critical: A Novel in Three Acts, 1989; Bodily Functions, 1991; Home Life with Cats, 1992; At the Caligua Hotel and Other Poems, 1995; The Squire Quartet, 1999; Soft as Steel: The Art of Julie Bell, 1999; The Land That Time Forgot, 2002; The Coming Race, 2002; (intro.) The War of the Worlds, 2005; (intro.) Dirty Limericks, 2008; Walcot, 2009; Mortal Morning, 2011; (foreword) The Mythic Fantasy of Robert Holdstock, 2011. **Address:** c/o Michael Shaw, Curtis Brown, Haymarket House, 28/29 Haymarket, London, GL SW1Y 4SP, England. **Online address:** aldiss@dial.pipex.com

ALDOUS, Richard. American (born United States), b. 1967. **Genres:** History. **Career:** University College of Dublin, professor, 1995-, School of History and Archives, chair, 2006-09; Irish Times, contributor, book reviewer and commentator; British Broadcasting Corp., commentator; Bard College, Eugene Meyer professor of British history and literature. Writer. **Publications:** Harold Macmillan and the Search for a Summit with the U.S.S.R., 1958-60, 1993; (ed. with S. Lee) Harold Macmillan and Britain's World Role, 1996; (ed. with S. Lee) Harold Macmillan: Aspects of a Political Life, 1999; Tunes of Glory: The Life of Malcolm Sargent, 2001; Macmillan, Eisenhower and the Cold War, 2005; The Lion and the Unicorn: Gladstone vs Disraeli, 2007; Great Irish Speeches, 2007; (with N. Puirseil) We Declare: Landmark Documents in Ireland's History, 2008; Reagan and Thatcher: The Difficult Relationship, 2012. **Address:** Bard College, PO Box 5000, Annandale-On-Hudson, NY 12504-5000, U.S.A. **Online address:** raldous@bard.edu

ALDRETE, Gregory S. American (born United States), b. 1966?. **Genres:** History. **Career:** University of Wisconsin, assistant professor, 1995-99, associate professor, 2000-04, professor of humanistic studies and history, 2005-, Wisconsin teaching fellow, 1997-98; Phaeton Group Science and Media, ancient historian. Writer. **Publications:** Gestures and Acclamations in Ancient Rome, 1999; Daily Life in the Roman City: Rome, Pompeii, and Ostia, 2004; (ed. with J.E. Salisbury) The Greenwood Encyclopedia of Daily Life, vol. I: The Ancient World, 2004; Floods of the Tiber in Ancient Rome, 2007; (with J. Popiel) After the Fact: Western Civilization, forthcoming; (with A. Aldrete) What Have the Greeks and Romans Done For Us?: Surprising and Essential Ways the Ancient World has Shaped the Modern, forthcoming; (with S. Bartell) Reconstructing and Testing Ancient Laminated Linen Body Armor, forthcoming; (with S. Bartell and A. Aldrete) Unraveling the Linothorax Mystery: Ancient Linen Armor Reconstructed and Tested, forthcoming. Contributor to periodicals. **Address:** Department of Humanistic Studies, University of Wisconsin, Theatre Hall 331, 2420 Nicolet Dr., Green Bay, WI 54311, U.S.A. **Online address:** aldreteg@uwgb.edu

ALDRICH, Ann. *See* **MEAKER, Marijane (Agnes).**

ALDRICH, Mark. American (born United States), b. 1941. **Genres:** Economics, Business/Trade/Industry, Technology, Air/Space Topics. **Career:** Smith College, assistant professor, associate professor, 1968-94, professor, 1995-, Marilyn Carlson Nelson Professor of Economics, now professor emeritus of economics; Occupational Safety and Health Administration, senior economist. Writer, academic and economist. **Publications:** (with R. Buchele) The Economics of Comparable Worth, 1986; Safety First: Technology, Labor, and Business in the Building of American Work Safety, 1870- 1939, 1997; Death Rode the Rails: American Railroad Accidents and Safety, 1828-1965, 2006; (with K. Pescador) San Diego's North Island, 19111941, 2007; (with K. Pescador) Consolidated Aircraft Corporation, 2008. Contributor to journals. **Address:** Department of Economics, Smith College, 12 Wright Hall, Northampton, MA 01063, U.S.A. **Online address:** maldrich@email.smith.edu

ALDRIDGE, Delores P(atricia). American (born United States), b. 1941. **Genres:** Sociology, Cultural/Ethnic Topics, Race Relations. **Career:** Tampa Urban League, associate director, 1966; Greater Lafayette Community Centers, director of community development, 1969-70, executive director, 1969-71; Emory University, Department of Afro-American and African studies, founding director, 1971-90, assistant professor, associate professor, 1971-88, professor of sociology, 1988-, Grace Towns Hamilton professor of sociology, 1990-, director of American and African studies, project director, 1997-, distinguished chair of African American studies; Spelman College, adjunct associate professor of sociology, 1971-75; Shaw University, adjunct associate professor of sociology, 1971-75; Southern Regulatory Council, consultant, 1972-78; Southern Association of College and Schools, consultant, 1973-; Center for the Study of Black Family Life, consultant, 1975-. Writer. **Publications:** A Statement on Racial Ethnic, 1987; (ed.) Black Male-Female Relationships: A Resource Book of Selected Materials, 1989; Focusing: Black Male-Female Relationships, 1991; (ed. with C. Young) Out of the Revolution: The Development of Africana Studies, 2000; (ed. with E.L. James) Africana Studies: Philosophical Perspectives and Theoretical Paradigms, 2007; Imagine a World, 2008; Our Last Hope: Black Male-female Relationships in Change, 2008. **Address:** Department of Sociology, Emory University, 228 Tarbutton Hall, 1555 Dickey Dr., Atlanta, GA 30322, U.S.A. **Online address:** daldri2@emory.edu

ALDRIDGE, (Harold Edward) James. British/Australian (born Australia), b. 1918. **Genres:** Novels, Children's Fiction, Plays/Screenplays, Travel/Exploration, Novellas/Short Stories, Biography. **Career:** Sun, reporter, 1937-38; Herald, reporter, 1937-38; Daily Sketch and Sunday Dispatch, feature writer, 1939. Freelance writer. **Publications:** NOVELS: Signed with Their Honour, 1942; Firmado Con Su Honor, 1943; The Sea Eagle, 1944; Of Many Men, 1946; The Diplomat: Roman, 1949, rev. ed., 1955; The Hunter, 1951; Heroes of the Empty View, 1954; I Wish He Would Not Die, 1957; The Last Exile, 1961; A Captive in the Land, 1962; The Statesman's Game, 1966; My Brother Tom in US as My Brother Tom: A Love Story, 1966; A Sporting Proposition, 1973 in US as Ride a Wild Pony, 1976; Mockery in Arms, 1974; The Untouchable Juli, 1975; One Last Glimpse, 1977; Goodbye Un-America, 1979. SHORT STORIES: Gold and Sand, 1960. PLAYS: The 49th State, 1946; One Last Glimpse, 1981. FOR CHILDREN: The Flying 19, 1966, rev. ed., 1979; The Marvelous Mongolian, 1974; The Lion's Cavalcade, 1980; The Broken Saddle, 1982; The True Story of Lilli Stubeck, 1984; The True Story of Spit MacPhee, 1986; The True Story of Lola Mackellar, 1992. OTHERS: Parolad'onore, Romanzo, 1946; Delo Chesti, 1947; Underwater Hunting for the Inexperienced Englishman, 1955; Poslednīl diūim, 1959; (with P. Stand) Living Egypt, 1969; Cairo: Biography of a City, 1969; Girl From the Sea, 2002; The Wings of Kitty St Clair, 2006. **Address:** Curtis Brown Ltd., 28/29 Haymarket, London, GL SW1Y 4SP, England.

ALESHIRE, Peter. American (born United States), b. 1952. **Genres:** History, Biography, Young Adult Non-fiction, Animals/Pets. **Career:** Arizona State University West, Department of American Studies, professor, 1992-2002, senior lecturer of writing, 1993-; Phoenix Magazine, associate editor; Arizona Republic, journalist; Oakland Tribune, journalist; Contra Costa Times, journalist; Indio Daily News, journalist; Palm Springs Desert Sun, journalist. Freelance writer. **Publications:** Reaping the Whirlwind: The Apache Wars, 1998; The Fox and the Whirlwind: Gen. George Crook and Geronimo: A Paired Biography, 2000; Cochise: The Life and Times of the Great Apache Chief, 2001; Warrior Woman: The Story of Lozen, Apache Warrior and Shaman, 2001; Eye of the Viper: The Making of an F-16 Pilot, 2004; Desert Rivers: (contrib.) From Lush Headwaters to Sonoran Sands, 2006; Ocean Ridges and Trenches, 2007; Deserts, 2008; Mountains, 2008; Bats, 2011. Contributor to periodicals. **Address:** Department of American Studies, Arizona State University West, FAB N217, 4701 W Thunderbird Rd., PO Box 37100, Phoenix, AZ 85069-7100, U.S.A. **Online address:** peter.aleshire@asu.edu

ALESSANDRA, Tony. American (born United States), b. 1947. **Genres:** Psychology, Human Relations/Parenting, Industrial Relations, inspirational/Motivational Literature, Marketing, Self Help, E-books, Administration/Management, Business/Trade/Industry. **Career:** Alessandra & Associates Inc., partner; Assessment Business Center, president; The Cyrano Group, founding partner; Platinum Rule Group, founding partner. Writer. **Publications:** (With P.S. Wexler and J.D. Deen) Non-Manipulative Selling, 1979, (with P.S. Wexler and R. Barrera) 2nd ed., 1987; (with P.L. Hunsaker) The Art of Managing People, 1980; (with J. Cathcart) The Business of Selling, 1984; (with J. Cathcart and P.S. Wexler) Selling by Objectives, 1988; (with J. Cathcart and J. Monoky) Be Your Own Sales Manager, 1990; (with M.J. O'Connor) People Smart, 1990; (with G. Schaeffer) Publish and Flourish, 1992; (with R. Barrera) Collaborative Selling, 1993; (with P.L. Hunsaker) Communicating at Work, 1993; (with M.J. O'Connor) People Smarts, 1994; (with J. Monoky) The Sales Manager's Idea-a-Day Guide, 1996; (with G. Baron and J. Cathcart) The Sales Professional's Idea-a-Day Guide, 1996; (with M.J. O'Connor) The Platinum Rule, 1996; Charisma, 1998; (with F. Sarr and P.L. Truax) Performance Counts and Accountability Pays, 2001; (with S. Zimmerman) The Platinum Rule for Sales Mastery, 2006; (with M.J. O'Connor) People Smart with Family, Friends and Significant Others, 2006; (with M.J. O'Connor) People Smart in Business, 2006; (with R. Finkelstein and S. Zimmerman) The Platinum Rule for Small Business Mastery, 2007; (with S. Underation and S. Zimmerman) The Platinum Rule for Trade Show Mastery, 2007; (with P.L. Hunsaker) The New Art of Managing People, 2008; (with D. Hutson and S. Zimmerman) Selling with Style, 2009; (with J.V. Teplitz) Switched On Selling, 2010; (with S.M. Johnson and J.D. Moody) and Game Changing Life Strategies, 2011; (with S. Zimmerman) The Platinum Rule for DISC Sales Mastery, 2011. **Address:** Alessandra & Associates Inc., 5927 Balfour Court, Ste. 103, Carlsbad, CA 92008, U.S.A. **Online address:** ta@alessandra.com

ALEXANDER, Adele Logan. American (born United States), b. 1938. **Genres:** History, Race Relations, Women's Studies And Issues. **Career:** University of Maryland, instructor, 1989-92; Howard University, instructor, 1991; Trinity College, instructor, 1993; George Washington University, associate professor of history, adjunct professor of history, professor, Writer and consultant. **Publications:** Ambiguous Lives: Free Women of Color in Rural Georgia, 1789-1879, 1991; Homelands and Waterways: The American Journey of the Bond Family, 1846-1926, 1999; Parallel Worlds: The Remarkable Gibbs-Hunts and the Enduring (in) Significance of Melanin, 2010. Contributor of articles to periodicals. **Address:** Department of History, The George Washington University, 801 22nd St. NW, Ste. 303, Washington, DC 20052-0058, U.S.A. **Online address:** alalex@gwu.edu

ALEXANDER, Ann Field. American (born United States), b. 1946?. **Genres:** Biography, History, Autobiography/Memoirs, Cultural/Ethnic Topics. **Career:** Mary Baldwin College, professor of history, Adult Degree Program, faculty, 1989-, Roanoke Center, director, 1989-. Writer. **Publications:** Race Man: The Rise and Fall of the Fighting Editor John Mitchell Jr., 2002. **Address:** Mary Baldwin College, 108 N Jefferson St., Ste. 816, Roanoke, VA 24016, U.S.A. **Online address:** aalexand@mbc.edu

ALEXANDER, Carly. *See* **BAILEY, Roz.**

ALEXANDER, Caroline. American (born United States), b. 1956. **Genres:** Travel/Exploration, History, Young Adult Fiction. **Career:** University of Malawi, Chancellor College, lecturer in classics, 1982-85. Writer. **Publications:** One Dry Season: In the Footsteps of Mary Kingsley, 1990; The Way to Xanadu, 1994; Battle's End: A Seminole Football Team Revisited, 1995; Mrs. Chippy's Last Expedition: The Remarkable Journal of Shackleton's Polar-Bound Cat, 1997; Endurance: Shackleton's Legendary Antarctic Expedition, 1998; Bounty: The True Story of the Mutiny on the Bounty, 2003; (intro.) The Worst Journey in the World, 2005; The War that Killed Achilles: The True Story of Homer's Iliad and the Trojan War, 2009. **Address:** c/o Anthony Sheil, 43 Doughty St., London, GL WC1N 2LF, England.

ALEXANDER, Elizabeth. American (born United States), b. 1962. **Genres:** Poetry, inspirational/Motivational Literature, Essays. **Career:** Washington Post, reporter, 1984-85; University of Pennsylvania, instructor, 1985-89; University of Chicago, assistant professor of English, 1991-97; Smith College, Grace Hazard Conkling poet-in-residence, 1997-99; Yale University, lecturer in African American studies and English, Thomas E. Donnelley professor of African American studies and professor American studies and English; Cave Canem Poetry Workshop, instructor, chair poet and writer. **Publications:** POEMS: The Venus Hottentot, 1990; Body of Life, 1996; Antebellum Dream Book, 2001; American Sublime, 2005. OTHER: (co-author) Workings of the Spirit: The Poetics of Afro-American Women's Writing, 1991; Diva Studies (verse play), 1996; The Black Interior (essays), 2004; (ed. with G. Brooks) Gwendolyn Brooks, 2005; Power and Possibility: Essays, Reviews and Interviews, 2007; (with M. Nelson) Miss Crandall's School for Young Ladies and Little Misses of Color: Poems, 2007; (with L.V. Stefanon) Poems in Conversation and a Conversation, 2008; Canto de Alabanza para el Día, 2009; Praise Song for the Day, 2009; Crave Radiance: New and Selected Poems, 1990-2010, 2010; (contrib.) Harlem: A Century in Images, 2010. **Address:** Department of African American Studies, Yale University, 81 Wall 304, PO Box 203388, New Haven, CT 06520, U.S.A. **Online address:** elizabeth.alexander@yale.edu

ALEXANDER, Floyce. American (born United States), b. 1938. **Genres:** Poetry, Literary Criticism And History. **Career:** Washington State University Press, editorial assistant, 1963-70, teaching assistant in English, 1970-71; University of Massachusetts, teaching assistant in rhetoric, 1972-74; Tacoma-Pierce County Civic Arts Commission, artist-in-residence, 1977-78; University of New Mexico, teaching assistant in English, 1978-81, lecturer in film, 1987-89, freelance editor, 1983-. **Publications:** POETRY: Ravines, 1971; Machete, 1972; Bottom Falling out of the Dream, 1976; Red Deer, 1982; Memory of the Future, 1998; The Ice House, 2006. OTHERS: (contrib.) Forty Poems Touching on Recent American History, 1970; (ed.) Risking a Somersault in the Air: Conversations with Nicaraguan Writers, 1984; Succor, 2002; American Fires, 2003. Contributor of articles to periodicals. **Address:** Red Dragonfly Press, 307 Oxford St., Northfield, MN 55057, U.S.A. **Online address:** fmklalex@charter.net

ALEXANDER, Gary. American (born United States), b. 1941. **Genres:** Mystery/Crime/Suspense, Novels, Novellas/Short Stories. **Career:** Writer. **Publications:** Pigeon Blood (novel), 1988; Unfunny Money (novel), 1989; Kiet and the Golden Peacock (novel), 1989; Kiet and the Opium War (novel), 1990; Deadly Drought (novel), 1991; Kiet Goes West, 1992; Blood Sacrifice: A Mystery of the Yucatán, 1993; Dead Dinosaurs: A Luis Balam Mystery of the Yucatán, 1994; Disappeared: A Buster Hightower Mystery, 2010; Zillionaire, 2011. Contributor to periodicals. **Address:** 122 SW 104th St., Seattle, WA 98146, U.S.A. **Online address:** alexagr61@hotmail.com

ALEXANDER, Greg. American (born United States), b. 1970. **Genres:** Business/Trade/Industry. **Career:** Recall Corp., vice president; EMC Corp., staff; Sales Benchmark Index, chief executive officer. Writer. **Publications:** (With A. Bartles and M. Drapeau) Making the Number: How to Use Sales Benchmarking to Drive Performance, 2008; (with B.D. Smart) Topgrading for Sales: World-class Methods to Interview, Hire, and Coach Top Sales Representatives, 2008. Contributor of articles to journals. **Address:** Sales Benchmark Index, 2451 Cumberland Pkwy., Ste. 3481, Atlanta, GA 30339, U.S.A.

ALEXANDER, Harriet Semmes. American (born United States), b. 1949. **Genres:** Literary Criticism And History, Young Adult Fiction. **Career:** Oklahoma State University, assistant reference librarian, 1974-77; University of Memphis, reference librarian, 1977-, assistant professor; Tennessee Library, editor, 1996-. Writer. **Publications:** (Comp.) American and British Poetry: A Guide to the Criticism, 1925-1978, 1984; (comp.) English Language Criticism on the Foreign Novel, 1989; American and British Poetry: A Guide to the Criticism, 1979-1990, 1995. **Address:** University of Memphis Libraries, PO Box 526500, Memphis, TN 38152, U.S.A. **Online address:** halexndr@cc.memphis.edu

ALEXANDER, Jeff. American (born United States), b. 1962. **Genres:** History. **Career:** Muskegon Chronicle, staff. Writer. **Publications:** The Muskegon: The Majesty and Tragedy of Michigan's Rarest River, 2006; Pandora's Locks: The Opening of the Great Lakes-St. Lawrence Seaway, 2009. Contributor to periodicals. **Address:** Grand Haven, MI , U.S.A. **Online address:** jalexander8288@gmail.com

ALEXANDER, Jeffrey C(harles). American (born United States), b. 1947. **Genres:** Sociology, Anthropology/Ethnology. **Career:** University of California-Berkeley, lecturer, 1974-76; University of California-Los Angeles, assistant professor, 1976-81, professor, 1981-2001, professor emeritus, 2001-, Department of Sociology, Graduate Studies, vice chair and director, 1987-89, chair, 1989-92, Undergraduate Social Science Collegium, director and founder, 1992-97; Institute for Advanced Studies, School of Social Science, fellow, 1985-86; Nankai University, visiting professor, 1989; Swedish Collegium for Advanced Study in the Social Sciences, fellow, 1992, 1996; Hebrew University, visiting professor, 1993; Ecole des Hautes Etudes des Sciences Politiques, visiting professor, 1993; University of Bordeaux, visiting professor, 1994; Ecole des Hautes Etudes en Sciences Sociales, visiting professor, 1994, 2001; Center for Advanced Study in the Behavioral Sciences, fellow, 1998-99; Yale University, Department of Sociology, professor of sociology, 2001-04, Graduate Studies, director, 2001-02, chair, 2002-05, Lillian Chavenson Saden professor of sociology, 2004-, Center for Cultural Sociology, co-director; Konstanz University, visiting professor, 2002; The London School of Economics, Centre for the Study of Global Governance, visiting fellow, 2005; University of London, Goldsmiths College, visiting fellow, 2005, senior research professor, 2007-08. Writer. **Publications:** Theoretical Logic in Sociology, 1982; Twenty Lectures: Sociological Theory since World War II, 1987; Action and Its Environments: Toward a New Synthesis, 1988; Structure and Meaning: Relinking Classical Sociology, 1989; Fin de Siècle Social Theory: Relativism, Reduction, and the Problem of Reason, 1995; (contrib.) Emile Durkheim, contributi ad una rilettura critica, 2002; The Meanings of Social Life: A Cultural Sociology, 2003; (co-author) Cultural Trauma and Collective Identity, 2004; The Civil Sphere, 2006; Object Lessons, 2007; (with K. Thompson) A Contemporary Introduction to Sociology: Culture and Society in Transition, 2008, (with K. Thompson and L.D. Edles) 2nd ed., 2011; Remembering the Holocaust: A Debate, 2009; The Performance of Politics: Obama's Victory and the Democratic Struggle for Power, 2010. EDITOR: Neofunctionalism, 1985; The Micro-Macro Link, 1987; Durkheimian Sociology: Cultural Studies, 1988; (with S. Seidman) Culture and Society: Contemporary Debates, 1990; (with P. Colomy) Differentiation Theory and Social Change: Comparative and Historical Perspectives, 1990; (with P. Sztompka) Rethinking Progress: Movements, Forces, and Ideas at the End of the 20th Century, 1990; (with R. Boudon and M. Cherkaoui) The Classical Tradition in Sociology: The American Tradition, 1997; Neofunctionalism and After, 1998; Real Civil Societies: Dilemmas of Institutionalization, 1998; (with N.J. Smelser) Diversity and Its Discontents: Cultural Conflict and Common Ground in Contemporary American Society, 1999; Mainstream and Critical

Social Theory: Classical, Modern, and Contemporary, 2001; (and intro. with S. Seidman) The New Social Theory Reader, 2001, 2nd ed., 2008; (G.T. Marx and C.L. Williams) Self, Social Structure, and Beliefs, 2004; (with P. Smith) The Cambridge Companion to Durkheim, 2005; (with D. Zhenglai) Guo jia yu shi min she hui, 2006; (with B. Giesen and J. Mast) Social Performance: Symbolic Action, Cultural Pragmatics and Ritual, 2006; (co-ed.) Culture, Society, and Democracy, 2007; (with I. Reed) Meaning and Method: The Cultural Approach to Sociology, 2009; (with P. Smith and R. Jacobs) The Oxford Handbook of Cultural Sociology, 2011; (with D. Bartmanski and B. Giesen) Iconic Power, 2011; (with R. Eyerman and E.B. Breese) Narrating Trauma, 2011. Contributor to books. **Address:** Department of Sociology, Yale University, Rm. 203, 493 College St., PO Box 208265, New Haven, CT 06511-8933, U.S.A. **Online address:** jeffrey.alexander@yale.edu

ALEXANDER, Jennifer Karns. American (born United States), b. 1963?. **Genres:** Social Sciences, Business/Trade/Industry, History. **Career:** University of Minnesota, associate professor. Writer and historian. **Publications:** The Mantra of Efficiency: From Waterwheel to Social Control, 2008. Contributor of articles to journals. **Address:** U.S.A. **Online address:** jalexand@me.umn.edu

ALEXANDER, John Thorndike. American (born United States), b. 1940. **Genres:** History, Biography, Translations. **Career:** University of Kansas, Department of History, assistant professor, 1966-70, associate professor, 1970-74, professor of history and Russian and East European studies, 1974-, now professor emeritus. Writer. **Publications:** Autocratic Politics in a National Crisis: The Imperial Russian Government and Pugachev's Revolt, 1773-1775, 1969; Emperor of the Cossacks: Pugachev and the Frontier Jacquerie of 1773-1775, 1973; Bubonic Plague in Early Modern Russia: Public Health and Urban Disaster, 1980; Catherine the Great: Life and Legend, 1989. TRANSLATOR: (and ed. with S.F. Platonov) The Time of Troubles, 1970; (ed. with E.V. Anisimov) The Reforms of Peter the Great, 1993; (ed. and intro.) E.V. Anisimov, Empress Elizabeth: Her Reign and Her Russia, 1741-1761, 1995. Contributor to books and journals. **Address:** Department of History, University of Kansas, 3650 Wescoe Hall, 1445 Jayhawk Blvd., Lawrence, KS 66045-7594, U.S.A. **Online address:** jatalex@ku.edu

ALEXANDER, Joseph H(ammond). American (born United States), b. 1938. **Genres:** Military/Defense/Arms Control, History, Plays/Screenplays, Documentaries/Reportage. **Career:** United States Marine Corps, career officer, 1960-88, Third Marine Division, chief of staff, Marine Corps Research and Development Center, director, colonel, now retired; historian and writer, 1989-; Habitat for Humanity, board director, 1990-95; Buncombe Shelter Inc., director, 1992-93; Smithsonian Magazine, consultant, 1993; National Geographic Television, consultant, 1995; United Defense Limited Partnership, consultant, 1995. **Publications:** MONOGRAPHS: Across the Reef: The Marine Assault of Tarawa, 1993; Closing In: Marines in the Seizure of Iwo Jima, 1994; Final Campaign: Marines in the Victory on Okinawa, 1996; 20th Century Marines: Three Touchstone Battles, 1997; (with D. Horan and N.C. Stahl) A Fellowship of Valor: Battle History of the United States Marines, 1997; (with D. Horan and N.C. Stahl) The Battle History of the U.S. Marines: A Fellowship of Valor, 1999; Battle of the Barricades: U.S. Marines in the Recapture of Seoul, 2000; Edson's Raiders: The 1st Marine Raider Battalion in World War II, 2000; Fleet Operations in a Mobile War: September 1950-June 1951, 2000. NONFICTION: (with M.L. Bartlett) Sea Soldiers in the Cold War: Amphibious Warfare, 1945-1991, 1994; Utmost Savagery: The Three Days of Tarawa, 1995; Storm Landings, 1997; (with E.H. Simmons) Through the Wheat: The U.S. Marines in World War I, 2008. Contributor of articles to books and journals. **Address:** 18 Sunset Summit, Asheville, NC 28804-3730, U.S.A. **Online address:** tractorrat@aol.com

ALEXANDER, Meena. American/Indian (born India), b. 1951. **Genres:** Poetry, Autobiography/Memoirs, Literary Criticism And History, Novels, Autobiography/Memoirs. **Career:** University of Khartoum, tutor in English, 1969; University of Delhi, lecturer in English, 1974; Central Institute of English and Foreign Languages, lecturer in English, 1975-77; University of Hyderabad, lecturer, 1977-79, reader in English, 1979; Fordham University, assistant professor of English, 1980-87; Hunter College, City University of New York, assistant professor, 1987-89, associate professor, 1989-91, professor of English, 1992-, professor of creative writing, 1993-, distinguished professor of English, 1999-, MFA program, teacher; Columbia University, Center for American Culture Studies, writer-in-residence, 1988, lecturer in writing program, 1990, lecturer in poetry, 1991-; American College, poet-in-residence, 1994; Arts Council of England, international writer-in-residence, 1995; Asian American Renaissance, Lila Wallace writer-in-residence, 1995; National University of Singapore, poet-in-residence, 1999; Sorbonne (Paris IV), visiting fellow; Brown University, Frances Wayland Collegium lecturer; Kerala University, University Grants Commission fellow; Indian Institute of Advanced Study, visiting professor. Writer. **Publications:** POETRY: The Bird's Bright Ring, 1976; I Root My Name, 1977; Without Place, 1978; Stone Roots, 1980; House of a Thousand Doors: Poems and Prose Pieces, 1988; The Storm, (chapbook) 1989; Night-Scene, The Garden, (chapbook) 1992; River and Bridge, 1995; The Shock of Arrival (and essays), 1996; Poetics of Dislocation, 2009. OTHER: In the Middle Earth (play), 1977; The Poetic Self: Towards a Phenomenology of Romanticism, 1980; Women in Romanticism: Mary Wollstonecraft, Dorothy Wordsworth and Mary Shelley, 1989; Nampally Road (novel), 1991; Fault Lines (memoir), 1993, rev. ed., 2003; Manhattan Music (novel), 1997; Illiterate Heart, 2002; Raw Silk, 2004; (ed.) Indian Love Poems, 2005; Quickly Changing River, 2008; Passage to Manhattan, 2009. **Address:** Department of English, Hunter College, City University of New York, 695 Park Ave., New York, NY 10065, U.S.A. **Online address:** malexander@gc.cuny.edu

ALEXANDER, M(ichael) J(oseph). British (born England), b. 1941. **Genres:** Poetry, Literary Criticism And History, Translations. **Career:** University of California, lecturer, 1966-67; Andre Deutsch, editor, 1967-68; University of East Anglia, lecturer in English, 1968-69; University of Stirling, lecturer in English, 1969-85, lecturer, 1969-77, senior lecturer, 1977-85, reader in English studies, 1985; University of St. Andrews, School of English, Berry professor of English literature, 1985-2003, honorary professor, now professor emeritus. Writer. **Publications:** TRANSLATOR: (intro.) The Earliest English Poems, 1966, 3rd ed., 1991; Beowulf: A Verse Translation, 1973, rev. ed., 2003; Old English Riddles from the Exeter Book, 1980, 3rd ed., 1984; Ruin: An Elegy, 1980; Beowulf and Grendel, 1995. OTHERS: Twelve Poems, 1978; The Poetic Achievement of Ezra Pound, 1979, 2nd ed., 1998; The Prologue to the Canterbury Tales, 1980, 2nd ed., 1999; Ruin: For Double Eight-Part Chorus and Solo Horn, 1980; The Knight's Tale, 1981; A History of Old English Literature, 1983; The Miller's Tale, 1986; Macmillan Anthologies of English Literature, 5 vols., 1989; (ed. with A.N. Jeffares) St. Martin's Anthologies of English Literature, 1990; (ed.) Beowulf: A Glossed Text, 1995; Sons of Ezra, 1995; (ed.) The Canterbury Tales: The First Fragment, 1996; (ed.) The Canterbury Tales: Illustrated Prologue, 1996; The Merchant of Venice, 1998; A History of English Literature, 2000, 2nd ed., 2007; Medievalism: The Middle Ages in Modern England, 2007. **Address:** School of English, University of St. Andrews, Castle House, St. Andrews, OK KY16 9AL, Scotland. **Online address:** michael.alexander@mbzonline.net

ALEXANDER, Peter F. Australian/South African (born South Africa), b. 1949. **Genres:** Literary Criticism And History, Biography, Autobiography/Memoirs. **Career:** University of New South Wales, School of the Arts and Media, lecturer, 1978-83, senior lecturer, 1983-88, associate professor of English, 1989-95, professor of English, 1996-, now professor emeritus; Cambridge University, Clare Hall, visiting fellow, 1990-91; Duke University, visiting professor, 1996; Princeton University, visiting fellow, 1996. Writer. **Publications:** Roy Campbell: A Critical Biography, 1982; William Plomer (biography), 1989; Leonard and Virginia Woolf: A Literary Partnership, 1992; Alan Paton: A Biography, 1994; Les Murray: A Life in Progress, 2000; Liberal Response, forthcoming. EDITOR: The Selected Poems of Roy Campbell, 1982; (with M. Chapman and M. Leveson) The Collected Works, vol. I, 1985, vol. II, 1987, vol. III, 1988, vol. IV, 1989; (with R. Hutchison and D. Schreuder) Africa Today: A Multi-Disciplinary Snapshot of the Continent in 1995, 1996; The Diary of Iris Vaughan, Sydney, 2004; (and intro.) Alan Paton: Selected Letters, 2009. Contributor of articles to periodicals and journals. **Address:** School of the Arts and Media, University of New South Wales, Gate 9, High St., Kensington, NW 2052, Australia. **Online address:** p.alexander@unsw.edu.au

ALEXANDER, (Robert) McNeill. British/Irish (born Ireland), b. 1934. **Genres:** Zoology, Animals/Pets, Sciences. **Career:** University College of North Wales, assistant lecturer, 1958-61, lecturer, 1961-68, senior lecturer, 1968-69; University of Leeds, professor of zoology, 1969-99, professor emeritus, 1999-. Writer. **Publications:** Functional Design in Fishes, 1967; Animal Mechanics, 1968; Size and Shape, 1971; The Chordates, 1975, 2nd ed., 1981; Biomechanics, 1975; (ed. with G. Goldspink) Mechanics and Energetics of Animal Locomotion, 1977; The Invertebrates, 1979; Locomotion of Animals, 1982; Optima for Animals, 1982, rev. ed., 1996; (ed.) The Encyclopedia of

Animal Biology, 1987; Elastic Mechanisms in Animal Movement, 1988; The Dynamics of Dinosaurs and Other Extinct Giants, 1989; Animals, 1990; Exploring Biomechanics: Animals in Motion, 1992; The Human Machine, 1992; Bones: The Unity of Form and Function, 1994; Energy for Animal Life, 1999; Principles of Animal Locomotion, 2003; Human Bones: A Scientific and Pictorial Investigation, 2005; (contrib.) The Post-Medieval Farm and Vicarage Sites, 2010. **Address:** Institute for Integrative and Comparative Biology, University of Leeds, Manton 6.91, Leeds, WY LS2 9JT, England. **Online address:** r.m.alexander@leeds.ac.uk

ALEXANDER, Ruth M. American (born United States), b. 1954. **Genres:** Women's Studies And Issues, History, Essays, Sex. **Career:** Colorado State University, Department of History, assistant professor, 1988-93, associate professor of history, 1993-99, professor and chair, 1999-, American Studies Program, acting director, 1993-94. Writer. **Publications:** The Girl Problem: Female Sexual Delinquency in New York, 1900-1930, 1995; (ed. with M.B. Norton) Major Problems in American Women's History: Documents and Essays, 1996, 4th ed., 2007. Contributor to books and periodicals. **Address:** Department of History, Colorado State University, B-363 Clark Hall, PO Box 1776, Fort Collins, CO 80523-2941, U.S.A. **Online address:** ruth.alexander@colostate.edu

ALEXANDER, Sally Hobart. (Sarah Alexander). American (born United States), b. 1943. **Genres:** Children's Fiction, Autobiography/Memoirs, Young Adult Non-fiction, Travel/Exploration, Biography. **Career:** Teacher, 1965-69; Guild for the Blind, teacher, 1969-70; St. Francis Hospital, child therapist, 1973-76; Western Pennsylvania School for Blind Children, consultant, 1976-77; Chatham College, teacher; Chatham University, College for Continuing and Professional Studies, MFA Program, adjunct faculty. Writer. **Publications:** Mom Can't See Me, 1990; Sarah's Surprise, 1990; Mom's Best Friend, 1992; Maggie's Whopper, 1992; Taking Hold: My Journey into Blindness (nonfiction), 1994; On My Own: The Journey Continues, 1997; Do You Remember the Color Blue?: And Other Questions Kids Ask about Blindness, 2000; (with R. Alexander) She Touched the World: Laura Bridgman, Deaf-blind Pioneer, 2008. Contributor of articles to books. **Address:** College for Continuing and Professional Studies, Chatham University, Woodland Rd., Pittsburgh, PA 15232-2814, U.S.A. **Online address:** salexander@chatham.edu

ALEXANDER, Sarah. *See* **ALEXANDER, Sally Hobart.**

ALEXANDER, Tori. *See* **ALEXANDER, Victoria N.**

ALEXANDER, Vanessa. *See* **DOHERTY, P(aul) C.**

ALEXANDER, Victoria N. (Tori Alexander). American (born United States), b. 1965. **Genres:** Novels. **Career:** Hunter College, adjunct instructor and tutor, 1988-94; Dactyl Foundation for the Arts and Humanities, co-founder and director, 1996-; City University, New York Graduate School, faculty of English, 2002. Writer. **Publications:** Smoking Hopes, 1996; The Bird Girl, 1997; (co-author) The Cat's Meow, 1998; Naked Singularity, 2002; The Pursuit of Marriage, 2004; Trixie, Mad Pixie, 2009; (as Tori Alexander) Trixie, 2010; The Biologist's Mistress: Rethinking Self-Organization in Art, Literature, and Nature, 2011. Nabokov's Bugs, Ghosts & Artists, forthcoming. Contributor to periodicals. **Address:** Dactyl Foundation, 64 Grand St., New York, NY 10013, U.S.A. **Online address:** alexander@dactyl.org

ALEXIE, Sherman (Joseph). American (born United States), b. 1966. **Genres:** Novels, Novellas/Short Stories, Adult Non-fiction, Poetry. **Career:** Longhouse Media, founding member, 2005-; University of Washington, artist-in-residence; Falls Apart Productions Inc., owner. Playwright. **Publications:** POETRY: The Business of Fancydancing, 1991; I Would Steal Horses, 1992; First Indian on the Moon, 1992; Old Shirts and New Skins, 1993; Water Flowing Home, 1994; Seven Mourning Songs for the Cedar Flute I Have Yet to Learn to Play, 1994; The Summer of Black Widows, 1996; The Man Who Loves Salmon, 1998; One Stick Song, 2000; Face, 2009. NOVELS: Reservation Blues, 1995; Indian Killer, 1996, Flight, 2007; The Absolutely True Diary of a Part-Time Indian, 2007; Radioactive Love Song, 2009; War Dances, 2009. SHORT STORIES: The Lone Ranger and Tonto Fistfight in Heaven, 1993; The Toughest Indian in the World, 2000; Ten Little Indians, 2003. PLAY: Smoke Signals, 1998. **Address:** Falls Apart Productions Inc., 10002 Aurora Ave. N, Ste. 36, PO Box 2294, Seattle, WA 98133-9334, U.S.A. **Online address:** fallsapartproductions@gmail.com

ALEXIS, Andre. Canadian/Trinidadian (born Trinidad and Tobago), b. 1957. **Genres:** Novels, Novellas/Short Stories, Plays/Screenplays, Literary Criticism And History. **Career:** Writer. **Publications:** Despair and Other Stories of Ottawa, 1994 in US as Despair and Other Stories, 1999; Childhood: A Novel, 1998; Lambton Kent: A Play, 1999; Night Piece, 1999; Ingrid and the Wolf, 2005; Enfance: Roman, 2006; Asylum, 2008. **Address:** McClelland & Stewart Inc., 481 University Ave., Toronto, ON M5G 2E9, Canada.

ALEXSEEV, Mikhail A. Ukranian (born Ukraine), b. 1963. **Genres:** Politics/Government, Sciences. **Career:** Radio Kiev, news editor, producer, 1984-87, senior correspondent, 1987-90; University of Washington, graduate teaching assistant, 1991-96, adjunct master professor of international relations, 1997-, post-doctoral research fellow, 1997-98; Appalachian State University, assistant professor, 1998-2000; San Diego State University, Department of Political Science, assistant professor, 2000-02, associate professor, 2002-, professor, International Security and Conflict Resolution, faculty. **Publications:** Without Warning: Threat Assessment, Intelligence and Global Struggle, 1997; (ed.) Center-Periphery Conflict in Post-Soviet Russia: A Federation Imperiled, 1999; Instrumental Internationalism: Regional Foreign and Security Policy Interests in Primorskii Krai, 2002; Immigration Phobia and the Security Dilemma: Russia, Europe and the United States, 2006. Contributor of articles to books and periodicals. **Address:** Department of Political Science, San Diego State University, 5500 Campanile Dr., 105 Nasatir Hall, San Diego, CA 92182-4427, U.S.A. **Online address:** alexseev@mail.sdsu.edu

AL-FAQĪH, Ahmad Ibrāhīm. *See* **FAQIH, Ahmed.**

ALFEYEVA, Valeria. Russian (born Russia) **Genres:** Autobiography/Memoirs. **Career:** Journalist and writer. **Publications:** Tsvetnye sny, 1978; Pilgrimage to Dzhvari: A Woman's Journey of Spiritual Awakening, 1989; Palomnichestvo na Sinai, 1998. **Address:** c/o Bell Tower, Harmony Books, 201 E 50th St., New York, NY 10022, U.S.A.

ALFINO, Mark (R.). American (born United States), b. 1959. **Genres:** Philosophy, Information Science/Computers, Librarianship, Essays. **Career:** University of Kentucky, instructor in philosophy, 1984-86; Loyola University of Chicago, lecturer, 1985; University of Texas, instructor in philosophy, 1987-88; Blinn College, instructor in philosophy, 1988; St. University of Toronto, lecturer, 1989; Edward's University, instructor in philosophy, 1989; Gonzaga University, Department of Philosophy, assistant professor, 1989-95, associate professor of philosophy, 1995-2001, professor, 2001-; Evergreen State College, lecturer, 1991, University of California, lecturer, 1992; Ohio State University, lecturer, 1997. Writer. **Publications:** (With L. Pierce) Information Ethics for Librarians, 1997; (ed. with R. Wynyard and J.S. Caputo and contrib.) McDonaldization Revisited: Critical Essays in Consumer Culture, 1998. Contributor to periodicals. **Address:** Department of Philosophy, Gonzaga University, 203 Rebman, 502 E Boone Ave., PO Box 49, Spokane, WA 99258, U.S.A. **Online address:** alfino@gonzaga.edu

ALFORD, Bernard William Ernest. (B. W. E. Alford). British (born England), b. 1937. **Genres:** Economics, History. **Career:** University of London, London School of Economics and Political Science, assistant lecturer in economic history, 1961-62; University of Bristol, assistant lecturer, 1962-64, lecturer, 1964-73, senior lecturer, 1973-76, reader, 1976-82, professor of economic and social history, 1982-, now emeritus, School of History, chairman, 1990-. Writer. **Publications:** (With T.C. Barker) A History of the Carpenters Company, 1968; Depression and Recovery? British Economic Growth 1918-1939, 1972; W.D. and H.O. Wills and the Development of the U.K. Tobacco Industry 1786-1965, 1973; British Economic Performance, 1945-75, 1988; (with R. Lowe and N. Rollings) Economic Planning in Britain, 1943-1951, 1992; (contrib.) Wege nach Europa: Wirtschaft Und Aussenpolitik Grossbritanniens Im 20. Jahrhundert, 1992; Britain in the World Economy since 1880, 1995. Contributor of articles to journals. **Address:** Department of Economic & Social History, University of Bristol, Bristol, BS8 1UL, England. **Online address:** b.alford@bristol.ac.uk

ALFORD, Brenda. *See* **ALFORD, Edna.**

ALFORD, B. W. E. *See* **ALFORD, Bernard William Ernest.**

ALFORD, Edna. (Brenda Alford). Canadian (born Canada), b. 1947. **Genres:** Novellas/Short Stories, Women's Studies And Issues, Poetry, Literary Criticism And History, Young Adult Fiction. **Career:** Dandelion (literary magazine), co-founder and co-editor, 1974-80; Regina Public Library, writer-in-residence, 1985-86; Grain Magazine, fiction editor, 1985-90; Saskatchewan Summer School of the Arts, teacher of creative writing; Sage Hill Writing Experience, teacher of creative writing; Mount Royal College, teacher of creative writing; Lakeland College, teacher of creative writing; Okanagan Summer School of the Arts, teacher of creative writing; University of Alberta, Extension Department, women and words, teacher of creative writing; Banff Centre, Writing and Publishing Program, faculty, 1992-, Writing with Style Program, director, Writing Studio, associate director of fiction; Banff Centre Press, contributor; Joan Clark of Dandelion Magazine, co-founder and co-editor; psychotherapist. **Publications:** A Sleep Full of Dreams (short stories), 1981; The Garden of Eloise Loon (short stories), 1986; (ed. with C. Harris) Kitchen Talk: Contemporary Women's Prose and Poetry, 1992; (ed.) Meltwater, 1998; (ed.) Rig Rap, 1999; (ed. with R. Tregebov) Intersections: Fiction and Poetry from The Banff Centre for the Arts, 2000. Contributor of stories to anthologies and journals. **Address:** The Banff Centre, PO Box 1020, Banff, AB T1L 1H5, Canada.

ALFORD, Jeffrey. Canadian/American (born United States), b. 1947?. **Genres:** Food And Wine, Travel/Exploration. **Career:** Writer. **Publications:** WITH N. DUGUID: Flatbreads and Flavors: A Baker's Atlas, 1995; Seductions of Rice, 1998; Hot, Sour, Salty, Sweet: A Culinary Journey through Southeast Asia, 2000; Home Baking: The Artful Mix of Flour and Tradition around the World, 2003; Mangoes & Curry Leaves: Culinary Travels through the Great Subcontinent, 2005; Beyond the Great Wall: Recipes and Travels in the Other China, 2008. Contributor to periodicals. **Address:** Asia Access, 64 Henry St., Toronto, ON M5T 1X2, Canada. **Online address:** asiaaccess@sympatico.ca

ALFORD, Kenneth D. American (born United States), b. 1939. **Genres:** Military/Defense/Arms Control. **Career:** Signet Bank, staff, 1958-94. Author. **Publications:** The Spoils of World War II: The American Military's Role in Stealing Europe's Treasures, 1994; Great Treasure Stories of World War II, 2000; Nazi Plunder: Great Treasure Stories of World War II, 2001; Historias de Grandes Tesoros de la II Guerra Mundial, 2001; (with T.P. Savas) Nazi Millionaires: The Allied Search for Hidden SS Gold, 2002; Civil War Museum Treasures: Outstanding Artifacts and the Stories Behind Them, 2008; Allied Looting in World War II: Thefts of Art, Manuscripts, Stamps and Jewelry in Europe, 2011. Contributor to periodicals. **Address:** 8711 Huguenot Rd., Richmond, VA 23235, U.S.A.

ALGAZE, Guillermo. American/Cuban (born Cuba), b. 1954. **Genres:** History. **Career:** University of California, Department of Anthropology. assistant professor, 1990-92, associate professor, 1992-98, professor, 1998-, chair, 2000-04; Titris Höyük Excavation, project director, 1991-. Writer, archaeologist and anthropologist. **Publications:** (Ed. and contrib.) Town and Country in Southeastern Anatolia, 2 vols., 1990; The Uruk World System: The Dynamics of Expansion of Early Mesopotamian Civilization, 1993, 2nd ed., 2005; Ancient Mesopotamia at the Dawn of Civilization: The Evolution of an Urban Landscape, 2008. Contributor of articles to books and journals. **Address:** Department of Anthropology, University of California, 9500 Gilman Dr., La Jolla, CA 92093-0532, U.S.A. **Online address:** galgaze@ucsd.edu

ALGEO, John. American (born United States), b. 1930. **Genres:** Language/Linguistics, Intellectual History, Theology/Religion. **Career:** Florida State University, instructor, 1959-61; University of Florida, assistant professor, 1961-66, associate professor, 1966-70, professor of English, 1970-71, Graduate School, assistant dean, 1969-71; University of Georgia, faculty, 1971-94, head of the department, 1975-79, Alumni Foundation Distinguished Professor of English, through 1994, professor emeritus, 1994-; American Speech Magazine, editor, 1971-81; University of Erlangen-Nuremberg, visiting professor, 1985; University of London, Fulbright research fellow and Guggenheim Fellow, 1986-87; Quest Magazine, editor, 1993-2002. **Publications:** Problems in the Origins and Development of the English Language, 1966, 7th ed., 2012; (with T. Pyles) English: An Introduction to Language, 1970; (co-author) Spelling: Sound to Letter, 1971; On Defining the Proper Name, 1973; Exercises in Contemporary English, 1974; (with T. Pyles) Origins and Development of the English Language, 1982, 7th ed., 2012; Reincarnation Explored, 1988; (co-author) Elements of Literature, 1989, rev. ed. 1997; (with S.J. Nicholson) The Power of Thought: A Twenty-first Century Adaptation of Annie Besant's Classic Work, Thought Power, 2001; Unlocking the Door: Studies in The Key to Theosophy: H.P. Blavatsky's Introduction to Theosophy and the Theosophical Society, 2001; British or American English? A Handbook of Word and Grammar Patterns, 2006. EDITOR: Thomas Pyles: Selected Essays on English Usage, 1979; (with A.S. Algeo) Fifty Years among the New Words: A Dictionary of Neologisms, 1941-1991, 1991; (co-ed.) The Oxford Companion to the English Language, 1992; Cambridge History of the English Language, vol. VI: English in North America, 2001; The Letters of H.P. Blavatsky, vol. I, 2003; Echoes from the Gnosis, 2006; The Light Of The Russian Soul: A Personal Memoir of Early Russian Theosophy, 2008. **Address:** 1800 Westen St., Ste. 1308, Bowling Green, KY 42104, U.S.A. **Online address:** jalgeo@jalgeo.com

ALI, Ayaan Hirsi. Somali/Dutch (born Netherlands), b. 1969. **Genres:** Social Sciences, Politics/Government, Biography, Autobiography/Memoirs, Women's Studies And Issues, Essays. **Career:** Dutch Parliament, 2003-06; American Enterprise Institute, fellow, 2006; AHA Foundation, founder, 2007-. Writer. **Publications:** De Zoontjesfabriek: Over Vrouwen, Islam en Integratie, 2003; De Maagdenkooi, 2004; Insoumise, 2005; Ayaan Verzameld: Essays En Toespraken, 2006; The Caged Virgin: An Emancipation Proclamation for Women and Islam (essays and other writings), 2006; Infidel (memoir), 2007; Caged Virgin: An Emancipation Proclamation for Women and Islam, 2008; Nomad: From Islam to America--A Personal Journey Through The Clash of Civilizations, 2010. **Address:** The American Enterprise Institute, for Public Policy Research, 1150 17th St. NW, Washington, DC 20036, U.S.A. **Online address:** ayaan.hirsiali@aei.org

ALI, Kazim. American/British (born England), b. 1971. **Genres:** Poetry, Autobiography/Memoirs. **Career:** Cocoon Theatre Modern Dance Co., dancer; Shippensburg University, assistant professor; Culinary Institute of America, assistant professor; Oberlin College, assistant professor; University of Southern Maine, instructor; Nightboat Books, publisher, 2004-07, founding editor. **Publications:** The Far Mosque, 2005; Quinn's Passage, 2005; The Fortieth Day: Poems, 2008; Bright Felon: Autobiography and Cities, 2009; Disappearance of Seth, 2009; Orange Alert: Essays on Poetry, Art, and the Architecture of Silence, 2010; Fasting for Ramadan: Notes from a Spiritual Practice, 2011. Contributor of articles to periodicals. **Address:** Creative Writing Program, Oberlin College, 13 Rice Hall, 10 N Professor St., Oberlin, OH 44074-1095, U.S.A. **Online address:** info@kazimali.com

ALI, Saleem H. American (born United States), b. 1973. **Genres:** Education. **Career:** Institute for Global Communication, network writer, 1990-92; Smithsonian Institution, Museum of Natural History, research training associate, 1992; British Parliament (House of Commons), parliamentary intern, 1993; Tufts University, Fletcher School of Law and Diplomacy, Global Development and Environment Institute, research assistant, 1994; Yale University, School of Forestry and Environmental Studies, teaching fellow, 1994-96; General Electric Co., Corporate Environmental Programs, international environmental management intern, 1996, Plastics Division, technical leadership program associate and environmental engineer, 1996-97; Massachusetts Institute of Technology, teaching fellow and instructor, 1997-2000; Harvard Business School, Baker Foundation research fellow, 1998; ENSR Corp., environmental consultant, 1998-99; Industrial Economics Inc., environmental associate, 2000-02; Brown University, adjunct faculty, 2000-; University of Vermont, assistant professor, 2002-06, associate professor of environmental planning and conflict resolution, 2006-10, associate dean for graduate education, 2006-08, Institute for Environmental Diplomacy and Security, director, professor of environmental studies, 2010-. **Publications:** Mining, the Environment, and Indigenous Development Conflicts, 2003; (ed.) Peace Parks: Conservation and Conflict Resolution, 2007; (ed. with C. O'Faircheallaigh) Earth Matters: Indigenous Peoples, the Extractive Industries and Corporate Social Responsibility, 2008; Treasures of the Earth: Need, Greed, and a Sustainable Future, 2009; Islam and Education: Conflict and Conformity in Pakistan's Madrassahs, 2009; Pakistan's Daily Times, columnist. Contributor to periodicals. **Address:** Watson Institute for International Studies, Brown University, PO Box 1970, Providence, RI 02912, U.S.A. **Online address:** saleem@alum.mit.edu

ALI, Samina. American/Indian (born India), b. 1969?. **Genres:** Novels, Young Adult Fiction, Literary Criticism And History. **Career:** Writer. **Publications:** Madras on Rainy Days, 2004 in Spain as Madrás Bajo La Lluvia, 2005. Contributor to periodicals. **Address:** c/o Eric Simonoff, Janklow Nesbit Associates, 445 Park Ave., New York, NY 10022-2606, U.S.A.

ALI, Shahrazad. American (born United States), b. 1947. **Genres:** Human

Relations/Parenting, Self Help, Social Sciences, Young Adult Non-fiction. **Career:** Cincinnati Enquirer, contributing editor, 1965-67; Cincinnati Call, news and feature editor, 1966-67; Cincinnati Post, news and feature editor, 1966-67; Cincinnati Herald, editor, 1966-67, medical transcriptionist, 1977-83; Clark College, assistant, 1983-85; Civilized Publications, founder, 1985; Ali's Unlimited Accessories, executive assistant, 1986-89; Temple University, PASCEP Program for Independent Publishing, teacher, 1987. Writer. **Publications:** How Not to Eat Pork: Or Life Without the Pig, 1985; The Blackman's Guide to Understanding the Blackwoman, 1990; The Blackwoman's Guide to Understanding the Blackman, 1992; Are You Still a Slave?, 1994; Day by Day, 1996; Things Your Parents Should Have Told You, 1998; Urban Survival for the Year 2000, 1999; How to Tell if Your Man Is Gay or Bisexual, 2003. Contributor to periodicals. **Address:** Civilized Publications, 2023 S 7th St., Philadelphia, PA 19148-2439, U.S.A.

ALIBER, Robert Z(elwin). American (born United States), b. 1930. **Genres:** Money/Finance. **Career:** Commission on Money and Credit, staff economist, 1959-61; Committee for Economic Development, staff economist, 1961-64; University of Chicago, Graduate School of Business, Center for Studies in International Finance, associate professor, 1964-, professor of international economics and finance, director, now professor emeritus; U.S. Department of State, Agency for International Development, senior economic adviser, 1964-65. Writer. **Publications:** Management of the Dollar in International Finance, 1964; Future of the Dollar as an International Currency, 1966; (ed. with G.P. Shultz) Guidelines, Informal Controls and the Market Place; Policy Choices in a Full Employment Economy, 1966; Choices for the Dollar; Costs and Benefits of Possible Approaches to the Balance-of-Payments Problem, 1969; (ed.) International Market for Foreign Exchange, 1969; International Money Game, 1973, 7th ed. as The New International Money Game, 2009; National Preferences and the Scope for International Monetary Reform, 1973; Monetary Reform and World Inflation, 1973; (and ed.) National Monetary Policies and the International Financial System, 1974; Policies Toward the OPEC Oil and Wealth, 1975; (ed.) The Political Economy of Monetary Reform, 1977; Exchange Risk and Corporate International Finance, 1978; (with T. Mayer and J.S. Duesenberry) Money, Banking and the Economy, 1981, 6th ed., 1996; Your Money and Your Life, 1982; (ed.) Reconstruction of International Monetary Arrangements, 1987; Handbook of International Financial Management, 1989; (ed. with B.R. Bruce) Global Portfolios: Quantitative Strategies for Maximum Performance, 1991; Readings in International Business: A Decision Approach, 1993; The Multinational Paradigm, 1993; Liberalización e innovación financiera en los paises desarrollados y América Latina, 1995; (ed.) International Finance, 2000; (with C.P. Kindleberger) Manias, Panics and Crashes: A History of Financial Crises, 2005, 6th ed., 2011; Your Money and Your Life: A Lifetime Approach to Money Management, 2010; (ed. with G. Zoega) Preludes to the Icelandic Financial Crisis, 2011. **Address:** Graduate School of Business, University of Chicago, 5807 S Woodlawn Ave., Chicago, IL 60637, U.S.A.

ALIKI. British/American (born United States), b. 1929. **Genres:** Children's Fiction, Children's Non-fiction, Illustrations, Art/Art History, Novellas/Short Stories. **Career:** Muralist and artist, 1951-56, 1957-60; artist, writer and illustrator, 1960-; J.C. Penney Co., Display Department, staff. **Publications:** SELF ILLUSTRATED: The Wish Workers, 1962; The Story of Johnny Appleseed, 1963; The Story of William Penn, 1964; A Weed Is a Flower: The Life of George Washington Carver, 1965; Three Gold Pieces, 1967; New Year's Day, 1967; Diogenes: The Story of the Greek Philosopher, 1968; The Eggs: A Greek Folk Tale, 1969; The Long Lost Coelacanth and Other Living Fossils, 1973; Green Grass and White Milk, 1974; At Mary Bloom's, 1976; Corn Is Maize: The Gift of the Indians, 1976; The Many Lives of Benjamin Franklin, 1977; Wild and Woolly Mammoths, 1977, rev. ed., 1996; The Twelve Months: A Greek Folktale, 1978; Mummies Made in Egypt, 1979; The Two of Them, 1979; A Medieval Feast, 1983; (co-author) The Big Book for Our Planet, 1993; Gods and Goddesses of Olympus, 1994; William Shakespeare and the Globe, 1999; All by Myself!, 2000; Ah, Music!, 2003; A Play's the Thing, 2005; Quiet in the Garden, 2009. OTHERS: The Story of William Tell, 1961; My Five Senses, 1962, rev. ed., 1989; My Hands, 1962, rev. ed., 1990; George and the Cherry Tree, 1964; Keep Your Mouth Closed, Dear, 1966; My Visit to the Dinosaurs, 1969, rev. ed., 1985; Fossils Tell of Long Ago, 1972, rev. ed., 1990; June 7!, 1972; Dipsa gi' aera, leuteria, 1980; Digging Up Dinosaurs, 1981, rev. ed., 1988; We Are Best Friends, 1982; Use Your Head, Dear, 1983; Feelings, 1984; Dinosaurs Are Different, 1985; Jack and Jake, 1986; How a Book is Made, 1986; Overnight at Mary Bloom's, 1987; Welcome Little Baby, 1987; Dinosaur Bones, 1988; King's Day: Louis XIV of France, 1989; My Feet, 1990; Manners, 1990; Christmas Tree Memories, 1991; I'm Growing!, 1992; Milk From Cow to Carton, 1992; Aliki's Dinosaur Dig: A Book and Card Game, 1992; Communication, 1993; My Visit to the Aquarium, 1993; Tabby: A Story in Pictures, 1995; Best Friends Together Again, 1995; Hello! Good-bye!, 1996; Those Summers, 1996; My Visit to the Zoo, 1997; Marianthe's Story: Painted Words and Spoken Memories, 1998; One Little Spoonful, 2001; Push Button, 2010. Contributor to books and periodicals. Illustrator of books by others. **Address:** 17 Regent's Park Terr., London, GL NW1 7ED, England.

ALINDER, Mary Street. American (born United States), b. 1946. **Genres:** Photography, Biography, Art/Art History, Autobiography/Memoirs. **Career:** The Weston Gallery, manager, 1978-79; Ansel Adams Publishing Rights Trust, executive editor and business manager, 1984-87; Alinder Gallery, co-owner, 1990-; Coast Magazine, staff, 1993-98; Biz Travel.com, staff, 1997-98. Writer. **Publications:** Ansel Adams: The Eightieth Birthday Retrospective, 1982; (with A. Adams) Ansel Adams: An Autobiography, 1985; (ed. with A.G. Stillman) Ansel Adams: Letters and Images, 1916-1984, 1988; (contrib.) Seeing Straight: F64 Revolution in Photography, 1992; Ansel Adams: A Biography, 1996. Contributor to books. **Address:** The Alinder Gallery, 39140 S Hwy. 1, PO Box 449, Gualala, CA 95445, U.S.A. **Online address:** alinders@mcn.org

ALKALI, Zaynab. Nigerian (born Nigeria), b. 1950. **Genres:** Novels, Novellas/Short Stories, Literary Criticism And History, History. **Career:** University of Maiduguri, lecturer; National Primary Health Care Agency, Head of Resource Centre, deputy director, 2000-03; Nasarawa State University, Faculty of Arts, dean, 2004-05, DVC administration, 2005-09, acting vice chancellor, through 2006, associate professor, professor, Post Graduate School, dean. Writer. **Publications:** NOVELS: The Stillborn, 1984; The Virtuous Woman, 1987. OTHERS: (ed. with A. Imfeld) Vultures in the Air: Voices from Northern Nigeria (stories), 1995; Cobwebs & Other Stories, 1997; The Descendants, 2005; The Initiates, 2007. Contributor to periodicals. **Address:** Department of English, Nasarawa State University, PO Box 1022, Nasarawa State, 00234, Nigeria.

ALKEBULAN, Paul. American (born United States), b. 1948. **Genres:** History. **Career:** Virginia State University, associate professor of history. Writer and historian. **Publications:** Survival Pending Revolution: The History of the Black Panther Party, 2007. Contributor to books and periodicals. **Address:** Department of History and Philosophy, Virginia State University, 101G Colson Hall, 1 Hayden Dr., PO Box 9070, Petersburg, VA 23806, U.S.A. **Online address:** palkebul@vsu.edu

ALKIRE, Sabina. British (born England) **Genres:** Young Adult Non-fiction. **Career:** Oxford University, Oxford Policy and Human Development Initiative, director; Harvard University, Global Equity Initiative, research associate. Writer. **Publications:** NONFICTION: Valuing Freedoms: Sen's Capability Approach and Poverty Reduction, 2002; (with E. Newell) What Can One Person Do? Faith to Heal a Broken World, 2005; (ed. with F. Comim and M. Qizilbash) The Capability Approach: Concepts, Measures and Applications, 2008. Contributor to books and journals. **Address:** Department of International Development, Oxford Poverty & Human Development Initiative, University of Oxford, Queen Elizabeth House, Mansfield Rd., Oxford, OX OX1 3TB, England. **Online address:** sabina.alkire@qeh.ox.ac.uk

ALKIVIADES, Alkis. (Luke Sharp). British/Cypriot (born Cyprus), b. 1953. **Genres:** Science Fiction/Fantasy, Information Science/Computers, Sports/Fitness, History, Children's Non-fiction. **Career:** Civil Service Commission, executive officer, 1977-79; Kilburn Skills College, lecturer, 1979-85; London Software Studio, graphic designer, 1985-87; MicroProse Software Ltd., copywriter, 1991-92, communications manager, 1992-95, product information manager, 1995-99; The Write Stuff, managing director, 1999-; Freelance writer, 1999-. **Publications:** The Sports Game, 1985; Star Strider, 1986; Daggers of Darkness, 1988; Dotto and the Pharaoh's Mask: An Interactive Connect-the-Dots Adventure, 1997; Dotto and the Minotaur's Maze: An Interactive Connect-the-Dots Adventure, 1998; Passatempo, forthcoming. AS LUKE SHARP: (co-author) Steve Jackson and Ian Livingstone Present: Chasms of Malice, 1987; Steve Jackson and Ian Livingstone Present Fangs of Fury, 1989. **Address:** Anchor Cottage, Brownshill, Stroud, GC GL6 8AG, England. **Online address:** aalkivia@aol.com

ALKON, Paul K. American (born United States), b. 1935. **Genres:** Literary Criticism And History, Education, Reference. **Career:** University of

California, instructor, assistant professor of English, 1962-70; University of Maryland, associate professor of English, 1970-71; University of Minnesota, associate professor, 1971-73, professor of English, 1973-80; Ben Gurion University, visiting professor, 1977-78; University of Southern California, Leo S. Bing professor of English and American literature, 1980-. Writer. **Publications:** Samuel Johnson and Moral Discipline, 1967; Defoe and Fictional Time, 1979; Samuel Johnson: Pictures and Words: Papers Presented at a Clark Library Seminar 23 October, 1982, 1984; Origins of Futuristic Fiction, 1987; Science Fiction before 1900: Imagination Discovers Technology, 1994; (ed. with G. Slusser, R. Gaillard and D. Chatelain) Transformations of Utopia: Changing Views of the Perfect Society, 1999; Winston Churchill's Imagination, 2006. Contributor of articles to journals and books. **Address:** Department of English, University of Southern California, 404 Taper Hall of Humanities, 3501 Trousdale Pkwy., Los Angeles, CA 90089-0354, U.S.A. **Online address:** alkon@usc.edu

ALLABY, (John) Michael. Scottish/British (born England), b. 1933. **Genres:** Environmental Sciences/Ecology, Meteorology/Atmospheric Sciences, Earth Sciences, Air/Space Topics. **Career:** Drama student, actor, 1954-64; Soil Association, Editorial Department, editor, 1964-72; Span Magazine, editor, 1967-72; Ecosystems Ltd., board director; Ecologist Magazine, associate editor, 1970-72, managing editor, 1972-73. Writer, 1973-. **Publications:** The Eco-Activists, 1971; Who Will Eat, 1972; (with F. Allen) Robots behind the Plow, 1974; Ecology, 1975; (co-author) The Survival Handbook, 1975; Inventing Tomorrow, 1975; (with C. Tudge) Home Farm, 1977; World Food Resources, Actual and Potential, 1977; Wildlife of North America, 1979; Animals That Hunt, 1979; Making and Managing a Smallholding, 1979; (with D. Baldock and C. Blythe) Food Policy and Self Sufficiency, 1979; (with P. Bunyard) The Politics of Self Sufficiency, 1980; A Year in the Life of a Field, 1980; (with P. Crawford) The Curious Cat, 1982; Animal Artisans, 1982; (with J. Lovelock) The Great Extinction, 1983; (with J. Lovelock) The Greening of Mars, 1984; The Food Chain, 1984; 2040, 1985; (with J. Burton) Nine Lives: A Year in the Life of a Cat Family, 1985; The Woodland Trust Book of British Woodlands, 1986; Ecology Facts, 1986, 2nd ed. as Green Facts, 1989; (with J. Burton) Dog's Life, 1986; The Ordnance Survey Outdoor Handbook, 1987; (with J. Burton) A Pony's Tale: A Year in the Life of a Foal, 1987; Conservation at Home, 1988; Guide to Gaia, 1989; Thinking Green, 1989; Living in the Greenhouse, 1990; Into Harmony with the Planet, 1990; The Concise Oxford Dictionary of Botany, 1992; How the Weather Works, 1995; Facing the Future, 1995; (with N. Curtis) Planet Earth, 1995; How It Works: The Environment, 1996; (with M. Kent) Collins Pocket Reference Biology, 1996; Basics of Environmental Science, 1996; Dangerous Weather, 6 vols., 1997-98; Temperate Forests, 1999, rev. ed., 2008; DK Guide to Weather, 2000; Biomes of the World, 9 vols., 2000; Plants and Plant Life, 5 vols., 2000; Deserts, 2001, rev. ed, 2008; Encyclopedia of Weather and Climate, 2002, rev. ed., 2007; How It Works: The Worlds Weather, 2002; Facts on File Weather and Climate Handbook, 2002; (with R. Anderson and I. Crofton) Deserts and Semi Deserts, 2002; India, 2005; (with J.O.E. Clark and A. Beer) Timelines of Science and Technology, 2006; Tropical Forests, 2006; Grasslands, 2006; Visual Encyclopedia of Earth, 2008; Oceans: A Scientific History of Oceans and Marine Life, 2009; (co-author) Everything on Earth, 2009; Earth Science: A Scientific History of the Solid Earth, 2009; Atmosphere: A Scientific History of Air, Weather and Climate, 2009; Animals: From Mythology to Zoology, 2010; Plants: Food, Medicine, and the Green Earth, 2010; Ecology: Plants, Animals, and the Environment, 2010; Exploration: New Lands, New Worlds, 2010. ELEMENTS SERIES: Air, 1992; Water, 1992; Earth, 1993; Fire, 1993. DANGEROUS WEATHER SERIES: Hurricanes, 1997, 2nd ed., 2003; Blizzards, 1997, 2nd ed., 2004; Droughts, 1998, 2nd ed., 2003; Tornadoes, 1997, 2nd ed., 2004; Floods, 1998, 2nd ed., 2003; A Chronology of Weather, 1998, 2nd ed., 2004; Fog, Smoke and Poisoned Rain, 2003; A Change in the Weather, 2004. EDITOR: A Dictionary of the Environment, 1977, 4th ed. as Macmillan Dictionary of the Environment, 1994; The Oxford Dictionary of Natural History, 1986; (with A. Allaby) The Concise Oxford Dictionary of Earth Sciences, 1990, 3rd ed., 2008; The Concise Oxford Dictionary of Zoology, 1991, 3rd ed., 2009; The Concise Oxford Dictionary of Botany, 1992, 2nd ed., 1998; The Concise Oxford Dictionary of Ecology, 1994, 4th ed., 2010; A Dictionary of Plant Sciences, 2nd, ed., 1998, rev. ed., 2006. **Address:** Braehead Cottage, Tighnabruaich, Argyll, PA21 2ED, Scotland. **Online address:** mike_allaby@compuserve.com

ALLAHAR, Anton L. Canadian/Trinidadian (born Trinidad and Tobago), b. 1949. **Genres:** History, Local History/Rural Topics. **Career:** University of Toronto, assistant professor, 1981-84; University of Western Ontario, assistant professor of sociology, 1994-89, associate professor of sociology, 1989-95, professor of sociology, 1996-; Saint Petersburg State University (formerly University of Leningrad), visiting professor; Caribbean Studies Association, president, 2007-08. Writer. **Publications:** Agriculture and the Peasantry in Cuba, 1980; The Sugar Planters of Colonial Cuba, 1982; Merchants, Planters and Merchants-Become-Planters: Cuba, 1820-1868, 1983; Sociology and the Periphery: Theories and Issues, 1989, rev. ed., 1995; Class, Politics and Sugar in Colonial Cuba, 1990; (with J.E. Cote) Generation on Hold: Coming of Age in Advanced Industrial Society, 1994; (with J.E. Cote) Richer and Poorer: The Structure of Inequality in Canada, 1998; (with J.E. Cote) Ivory Tower Blues: A University system in Crisis, 2007; (with J. Cote) Lowering Higher Education: The Rise of Corporate Universities and the Fall of Liberal Education, 2011. EDITOR: (with R.G. Cecil) Is There Life after Debt?, 1993; Caribbean Charisma: Reflections on Leadership, Legitimacy and Populist Politics, 2001; Ethnicity, Class and Nationalism: Caribbean and Extra-Caribbean Dimensions, 2005. Contributor to books and journals. **Address:** Department of Sociology, Social Science Center, University of Western Ontario, 5206 SSC, London, ON N6A 5C2, Canada. **Online address:** allahar@uwo.ca

ALLAN, Adrian R. British (born England) **Genres:** Librarianship, History. **Career:** University of Liverpool, Department of Archives and Special Collections, assistant archivist, university archivist, retired, 2008. Writer. **Publications:** (Ed. with M. Cook) Records Management, 1977; University Bodies: A Survey of Inter- and Supra-University Bodies and Their Records, 1990; (ed. and intro. with A.L. Mackenzie) Redbrick University Revisited: The Autobiography of Bruce Truscot, 1996. Contributor to periodicals. **Address:** Liverpool University Press, 4 Cambridge St., Liverpool, MS L69 7ZU, England.

ALLAN, Barbara. *See* **COLLINS, Barbara.**

ALLAN, David. British (born England), b. 1964. **Genres:** History. **Career:** University of Lancaster, administrator, 1990-95, lecturer in history and independent studies, 1995-; Pendle College, vice principal, 1994-. Writer. **Publications:** (Ed.) Pulp & Paper Pricebook, 1984; Virtue, Learning, and the Scottish Enlightenment: Ideas of Scholarship in Early Modern History, 1993; Philosophy and Politics in Later Stuart Scotland: Neo-Stoicism, Culture, and Ideology in an Age of Crisis, 1540-1690, 2000; Ireland for Dummies, 2002; Selfish Young Man: An Honest Look at Christ and Christianity Plus Other Selected Essays, 2005; Making British Culture: English Readers and the Scottish Enlightenment, 2008; Commonplace Books and Reading in Georgian England, 2010. **Address:** Department of History, University of Lancaster, Bailrigg, LA1 4YG, England.

ALLAN, Keith. British/Australian (born Australia), b. 1943. **Genres:** Language/Linguistics. **Career:** Monash University, professor of linguistics, 1978-, now professor emeritus; Australian Journal of Linguistics, editor. **Publications:** Linguistic Meaning, 1986; (with K. Burridge) Euphemism and Dysphemism: Language Used as Shield and Weapon, 1991; Natural Language Semantics, 2001; (with K. Burridge) Forbidden Words: Taboo and the Censoring of Language, 2006; Western Classical Tradition in Linguistics, 2007, 2nd ed., 2009; Concise Dictionary of Semantics, 2009; (co-author) English Language and Linguistics Companion, 2010; (ed. with K. Jaszczolt) Cambridge Handbook of Pragmatics, 2012; (ed.) Oxford Handbook of the History of Linguistics, 2012; (ed. with K. Jaszczolt) Salience and Defaults in Utterance Processing, 2012. Contributor to journals. **Address:** Linguistics Program, School of Languages, Cultures and Linguistics, Monash University, Bldg. 11, Clayton, VI 3800, Australia. **Online address:** keith.allan@arts.monash.edu.au

ALLAN, Robin. British/Malawian (born Malawi), b. 1934. **Genres:** Children's Fiction, Film, Education. **Career:** Eyre and Spottiswoode Ltd. (publisher), typographical designer, 1957-60; British Council, lecturer in English, 1961-65, television officer, 1965-70; International Theatre of Teheran, president, 1969-70; Educational Aids Department, assistant director, 1970-71; Basingstoke Technical College, lecturer in drama, 1972-73; College of Adult Education, lecturer in drama and film, 1973-; Green Room Theatre, chairman, 1975-77. Writer. **Publications:** Come Into My Castle, 1964; Beyond the Blue Mountains, 1979; The Luck of Katania, 1980; Walt Disney and Europe: European Influences on the Animated Feature Films of Walt Disney, 1999. Contributor to books. **Address:** Hilles House, 101 Mellor Rd., New Mills, Stockport, NY SK12 4DX, England. **Online address:** robinallan@intertheatre.ndo.co.uk

ALLAN, Von. (Eric Allan Julien). Canadian (born Canada), b. 1974. **Genres:** Graphic Novels, Illustrations. **Career:** Comic book writer and illustrator. **Publications:** SELF-ILLUSTRATED: Li'l Kids: Road to God Knows... Adventures!, 2008; The Road to God Knows...: A Graphic Novel, 2009; Stargazer, vol. I, 2010. **Address:** 390 Rideau St., PO Box 20520, Ottawa, ON K1N 1A3, Canada. **Online address:** von@vonallan.com

ALLASON, Rupert (William Simon). (Nigel West). British (born England), b. 1951. **Genres:** Criminology/True Crime, History, International Relations/Current Affairs, Reference, Young Adult Fiction, Adult Non-fiction. **Career:** British Broadcasting Corp., journalist, 1978-82; Intelligence Quarterly, European editor, 1985-; The St Ermin's Press, editorial director; Torbay, member of parliament, 1987-97; Centre for Counterintelligence and Security Studies, staff; Westintel Research Ltd., Owner. **Publications:** NONFICTION AS NIGEL WEST: (with R. Deacon) Spy!, 1980; MI5: British Security Service Operations 1909-1945, 1981; A Matter of Trust: MI5 1945-1972, 1982; MI6: British Secret Intelligence Service Operations 1909-1945, 1983; The Circus: MI5 Operations 1945-1972, 1983; Unreliable Witness: Espionage Myths of the Second World War, 1984 as A Thread of Deceit: Espionage Myths of World War II, 1985; (with J. Pujol) Garbo, 1985; (with J. Pujol) Operation Garbo: The Personal Story of the Most Successful Double Agent of World War II, 1985; GCHQ: The Secret Wireless War, 1900-1986, 1987; Molehunt: The Full Story of the Soviet Mole in MI5, 1987 in US as Molehunt: Searching for Soviet Spies in MI5, 1987; The Friends: Britain's Postwar Secret Intelligence Operations, 1988; The SIGINT Secrets: The Signals Intelligence War, 1900 to Today: Including the Persecution of Gordon Welchman, 1988; Games of Intelligence: The Classified Conflict of International Espionage, 1989; Cuban Bluff, 1991; Seven Spies Who Changed the World, 1991; Secret War: The Story of SOE, Britain's Wartime Sabotage Organisation, 1992; The Illegals, 1993; (foreword) A Spy's London, 1993; The Secret War for the Falklands: The SAS, MI6 and the War Whitehall Nearly Lost, 1997; Counterfeit Spies, 1998; (with O. Tsarev) The Crown Jewels: The British Secrets at the Heart of the KGB Archives, 1998; Venona: The Greatest Secret of the Cold War, 1998; The Third Secret, 1999; (with O. Tsàrev) KGB v Anglii 1999; Historical Dictionary of British Intelligence, 2005; MASK: MI5's Penetration of the Communist Party of Great Britain, 2005; Historical Dictionary of International Intelligence, 2006; At Her Majesty's Secret Service: The Chiefs of Britain's Intelligence Agency, M16, 2006; Historical Dictionary of Cold War Counterintelligence, 2007; Historical Dictionary of World War II Intelligence, 2008; Historical Dictionary of Ian Fleming's World of Intelligence: Facts and Fiction, 2009; Historical Dictionary of Sexspionage, 2009; Historical Dictionary of Naval Intelligence, 2010. NONFICTION: (as Allason Rupert) The Branch: A History of the Metropolitan Police Special Branch, 1883-1983, 1983. FICTION: The Blue List, 1989; Murder in the Commons, 1992; Murder in the Lords, 1994; Murder in the Cabinet, 1998. EDITOR: The Faber Book of Espionage, 1993; The Faber Book of Treachery, 1995; (ed.) The Guy Liddell Diaries: MI5's Director of Counter-Espionage in World War II, vol. I, 2005; (with O. Tsarev) TRIPLEX: More Secrets From The Cambridge Spies, 2009. AUTHOR OF INTRODUCTION: John Moe: Double Cross System of the War of 1939-45, 1995; British Security Coordination, 1998; False Flag, 1999; Fortitude, 2000. OTHER: (with I. C. Smith) Historical Dictionary of Chinese Intelligence, 2012. Contributor to periodicals. **Address:** Westintel Research Ltd., 6 Burton Mews, London, GL SW1W 9EP, England. **Online address:** nigel@westintel.co.uk

ALLCORN, Seth. American (born United States), b. 1946. **Genres:** Business/Trade/Industry, Medicine/Health, Economics. **Career:** University of Missouri, internal auditor, 1972-75, Department of Medicine, administrative manager, 1975-87, Center For the Study of Organizational Change, associate; University of Rochester, program administrator for medicine service and administrator of medicine department, 1987-90, manager; Loyola University of Chicago, Stritch School of Medicine, associate dean for fiscal affairs, 1990-95; DYAD Management and Organizational Consulting Co., principal, 1995-; University of New England in Biddeford, vice-president for business and finance; Texas Tech School of Medicine, assistant dean; International Society for the Psychoanalytic Study of Organizations, founding member. Writer and consultant. **Publications:** Internal Auditing for Hospitals, 1979; Workplace Superstars in Resistant Organizations, 1991; Codependency in the Workplace: A Guide for Employee Assistance and Human Resource Professionals, 1992; (with T. S. Wirth) Creating New Hospital-Physician Collaboration, 1993; Anger in the Workplace: Understanding the Causes of Aggression and Violence, 1994; Working Together: Building Integrated Healthcare Organizations through Improved Executive/Physician Collaboration, 1995; (co-author) The Human Cost of a Management Failure: Organizational Downsizing at General Hospital, 1996; (with M.A. Diamond) Managing People during Stressful Times: The Psychologically Defensive Workplace, 1997; Death of the Spirit in the American Workplace, 2002; The Dynamic Workplace: Present Structure and Future Redesign, 2003; Organizational Dynamics and Intervention: Tools for Changing the Workplace, 2005; (with M.A. Diamond) Private Selves in Public Organizations: The Psychodynamics of Organizational Diagnosis and Change, 2009. CONTRIBUTOR: Psychoanalysis and Management, 1994; Organizations in Depth: The Psychoanalysis of Organizations, 1999. Works appear in anthologies. Contributor of articles to periodicals. **Address:** Center For the Study of Organizational Change, Truman School of Public Affairs, University of Missouri, 101 Middlebush Hall, Columbia, MO 65211, U.S.A. **Online address:** sallcorn@csoc.missouri.edu

ALLEGRETTO, Michael. American (born United States), b. 1944?. **Genres:** Mystery/Crime/Suspense, Novels, Horror, Literary Criticism And History. **Career:** Writer. **Publications:** JACOB LOMAX MYSTERY NOVELS: Death on the Rocks, 1987; Blood Stone, 1988; The Dead of Winter, 1989; Blood Relative, 1992; Grave Doubt, 1995. OTHER THRILLER/MYSTERY NOVELS: Night of Reunion, 1990; The Watchmen, 1991; The Suitor, 1993; Shadow House, 1994. Contributor to periodicals. **Address:** Dominick Abel Literary Agency Inc., 146 W 82nd St., Apt. 1B, New York, NY 10024-5530, U.S.A.

ALLEN, Ann Taylor. American (born United States), b. 1944. **Genres:** Literary Criticism And History, Social Sciences. **Career:** University of Louisville, faculty, 1971-86, professor, 1986-. University of Bielefeld, lecturer; Humboldt University, lecturer. Writer. **Publications:** Satire and Society in Wilhelmine Germany: Kladderadatsch & Simplicissimus, 1890-1914, 1984; Feminism and Motherhood in Germany, 1800-1914, 1991; (co-author) Malwida Von Meysenbug-Durch Lauter Zaubergärten Der Armida: Ergebnisse Neuer Forschungen, 2005; Feminism and Motherhood in Western Europe, 1890-1970: The Maternal Dilemma, 2005; Women in Twentieth- Century Europe, 2008. Contributor to books and periodicals. **Address:** Department of History, University of Louisville, Louisville, KY 40292, U.S.A. **Online address:** ann.allen@louisville.edu

ALLEN, Barry. American/Canadian (born Canada), b. 1957. **Genres:** Philosophy. **Career:** University of Chicago, postdoctoral fellow, 1984-86, lecturer in philosophy, 1984-86; McMaster University, professor of philosophy, 1986-; Common Knowledge, associate editor, 1993-; Hebrew University of Jerusalem, Lady Davis Trust visiting professor, 2000-01; Dalhousie University, visiting professor, 2003. Writer. **Publications:** Truth in Philosophy, 1993; Knowledge and Civilization, 2003; Artifice & Design: Art & Technology in Human Experience, 2008. **Address:** Department of Philosophy, McMaster University, 301 University Hall, 1280 Main St. W, Hamilton, ON L8S 4K1, Canada. **Online address:** bgallen@mcmaster.ca

ALLEN, Craig M(itchell). American (born United States), b. 1954. **Genres:** Communications/Media, History, Sociology, Social Sciences, Art/Art History. **Career:** Oregon Journal, copy editor, reporter and writer, 1971-74; Statesman Journal, correspondent, 1972-74; Linfield College, sports information director, 1974-76; KPNW AM-FM, reporter and news editor, 1976-77; Station KPTV, reporter and anchor, 1976-78; KAPP-TV, executive producer, News director, 1978-81; KRDO-TV, news director, 1981-82; KMGH-TV, assistant news operations manager, news manager, 1982-84; KHQ TV-AM-FM, News assignment editor and operations manager, 1983-85; Whitworth College, instructor, 1984-86; Ohio University, E.W. Scripps School of Journalism, teaching assistant, 1986-89; University of Alabama, assistant professor of communications and broadcast news coordinator, 1989-91; Arizona State University, Walter Cronkite School of Journalism and Mass Communication, assistant professor, associate professor, 1991-; Arizona Summer Broadcast Institute, director, 1997-; U.S. Department of the Interior, media relations consultant. Writer. **Publications:** Women and Men Who Sexually Abuse Children: A Comparative Analysis, 1991; Eisenhower and the Mass Media: Peace, Prosperity, and Prime-Time TV, 1993; Eating out in Barcelona and Catalunya: A Personal Guide to Over 75 Local Restaurants, 1994; The Global Media Revolution, 2001; News is People: The Rise of Local TV News and The Fall of News From New York, 2001. Contributor to journals. **Address:** School of Journalism and Mass Communication, Arizona State University, Rm. 388, 555 N Central Ave., Phoenix, AZ 85004, U.S.A. **Online address:** craig.allen@asu.edu

ALLEN, Dean. American (born United States), b. 1950. **Genres:** Economics, Money/Finance, Business/Trade/Industry. **Career:** Interamerican Management Group, president and chief executive officer, 1974-99; Better Business Bureau Inc., national arbitrator; Restore Our American Republic Inc. (ROAR), founder and national executive director. Writer. **Publications:** Freedom 2000: How to Survive, Thrive & Prosper Financially during the New Millennium, 1999. **Address:** PO Box 1732, Forest City, NC 28043-1732, U.S.A. **Online address:** dean@deanallen.com

ALLEN, Dick. American (born United States), b. 1939. **Genres:** Poetry, Literary Criticism And History, Popular Culture. **Career:** Syracuse University, manager of community relations, 1961; Brown University, teaching associate, 1962-64; Wright State University, instructor in creative writing and American literature, 1964-68; University of Bridgeport, Department of English, assistant professor, 1968-71, associate professor, 1971-75, director of creative writing, 1972-2001, professor, 1976-2001, Dana Professor of English, 1979-2001, Charles A. Dana professor of English, now Charles A. Dana professor emeritus of English. Writer. **Publications:** POETRY: West Is Up, 1961; Anon, and Various Time Machine Poems, 1971; Regions with No Proper Names, 1975; Overnight in the Guest House of the Mystic: Poems, 1984; Flight and Pursuit: Poems, 1987; Ode to the Cold War: Poems New and Selected, 1997; The Day Before: New Poems, 2003; Present Vanishing: Poems, 2008. EDITOR: Science Fiction: The Future, 1971, 2nd ed., 1983; (with D. Chacko) Detective Fiction: Crime and Compromise, 1974; (with L. Allen) Looking Ahead: The Vision of Science Fiction, 1975; Expansive Poetry: The New Formalism and the New Narrative, 1989. Works appear in anthologies. Contributor of articles to periodicals. **Address:** University of Bridgeport, 126 Park Ave., Bridgeport, CT 06604, U.S.A. **Online address:** rallen285@earthlink.net

ALLEN, Diogenes. American (born United States), b. 1932. **Genres:** Philosophy, Theology/Religion. **Career:** Windham Presbyterian Church, minister, 1958-61; York University, Department of Philosophy, assistant professor, 1964-66, associate professor, 1966-67; Princeton Theological Seminary, associate professor, 1967-74, professor, 1974-81, Stuart professor of philosophy, 1981-2002, Stuart professor emeritus of philosophy, 2002-; All Saints' Episcopal Church, priest associate. Writer. **Publications:** (Ed. and intro.) Theodicy, 1966; The Reasonableness of Faith, 1968; Finding Our Father, 1974; Between Two Worlds, 1977; Traces of God in a Frequently Hostile World, 1981; Three Outsiders: Pascal, Kierkegaard, Simone Weil, 1983; Mechanical Explanations and the Ultimate Origins of the Universe According to Leibniz, 1983; Philosophy for Understanding Theology, 1985, (with E.O. Springsted) 2nd ed., 2007; Temptation, 1986; Love: Christian Romance, Marriage, Friendship, 1987; (co-author) Postmodern Theology, 1989; Christian Belief in a Postmodern World: The Full Wealth of Conviction, 1989; Quest: The Search for Meaning through Christ, 1990, 2nd ed., 2000; The Path of Perfect Love, 1992; (ed. with E.O. Springsted) Primary Readings in Philosophy for Understanding Theology, 1992; (with E.O. Springsted) Spirit, Nature, and Community: Issues in the Thought of Simone Weil, 1994; (with E. Maurer) Philosophie für das Theologiestudium, 1995; Spiritual Theology: The Theology of Yesterday for Spiritual Help Today, 1997; Steps along the Way: A Spiritual Autobiography, 2002; Theology for a Troubled Believer: An Introduction to the Christian Faith, 2010. **Address:** Princeton Theological Seminary, 64 Mercer St., PO Box 821, Princeton, NJ 08542-0803, U.S.A.

ALLEN, Ed. *See* **ALLEN, Edward (Hathaway).**

ALLEN, Edward (Hathaway). (Ed Allen). American (born United States), b. 1948. **Genres:** Novels, Poetry. **Career:** Suffern High School, substitute teacher, 1980-81; Ohio University, teaching assistant, 1984-89; Rhodes College, assistant professor, 1989-91; freelance writer, 1989-; San Jose State University, faculty, 1995-96; University of South Dakota, associate professor of English, 1996-; University of Central Oklahoma, senior Fulbright fellow; Jagiellonian University, senior Fulbright fellow. **Publications:** NOVELS: Straight Through the Night, 1989; Mustang Sally, 1992; Ate It Anyway, 2003; 67 Mixed Messages: Poems, 2006. Contributor to journals. **Address:** Department of English, The University of South Dakota, UDD DakotaDome 218, 414 E Clark St., Vermillion, SD 57069, U.S.A. **Online address:** ed.allen@usd.edu

ALLEN, E. John B. American/British (born England), b. 1933. **Genres:** History, Sports/Fitness, Adult Non-fiction. **Career:** Plymouth State College (now Plymouth State University), assistant professor, professor of history, 1968-, now professor emeritus of history; Public Broadcasting System, consultant, 1984; Spirit of the Mountains, consultant, 1993. Writer. **Publications:** Post and Courier Service in the Diplomacy of Early Modern Europe, 1973; Reflections of Berlin, 1984; Teaching and Technique: A History of Professional Ski Instruction, 1987; From Skisport to Skiing: One Hundred Years of an American Sport, 1840-1940, 1993; New Hampshire on Skis, 2002; (ed.) International Ski History Congress: Selected Papers, 2002; Le Ski en France 1840-1940, 2003; New England Skiing, 1870-1940, 2004; (with C. Conniff) Skiing in Massachusetts, 2006; The Culture and Sport of Skiing: From Antiquity to World War II, 2007; Historical Dictionary of Skiing, 2012. Contributor of articles to periodicals. **Address:** Plymouth State University, 17 High St., Plymouth, NH 03264-1595, U.S.A. **Online address:** jallen@mail.plymouth.edu

ALLEN, Fergus. British (born England), b. 1921. **Genres:** Poetry, Animals/Pets, Literary Criticism And History. **Career:** Hydraulics Research Station, director, 1958-65; Cabinet Office, chief scientific officer, 1965-69; Civil Service Commission, civil service commissioner, 1969-74, first civil service commissioner, 1974-81; Boyden International Ltd., consultant, 1982-86. Writer. **Publications:** POETRY: The Brown Parrots of Providencia, 1993; Who Goes There?, 1996; Mrs. Power Looks over the Bay, 1999; Gas Light & Coke, 2006. Contributor of articles to magazines. **Address:** Dundrum, Wantage Rd., Streatley, Reading, BR RG8 9LB, England.

ALLEN, Jane. Australian (born Australia), b. 1941. **Genres:** Biography, History, Art/Art History. **Career:** Barry Stern Art Gallery, assistant, 1969-72; Watters Gallery, assistant, 1984-88; University of Sydney, associate lecturer in psychology, 1994-97; Breast Cancer Support Group, convenor, 2001-. Writer. **Publications:** Pier Angeli: A Fragile Life, 2002; A Walk through Blue Poppies: The Letters of Eric Shipton to Margaret Bradshaw, 1934-1974, 2004; Teeny Tiny Tess stories for children, 2006, La Paolina, opera libretto, 2008. **Address:** 22 Hopewood Rd., Bowral, NW 2576, Australia. **Online address:** fjallen@ozemail.com.au

ALLEN, Jeffner. American (born United States), b. 1947. **Genres:** Gay And Lesbian Issues, Philosophy, Social Sciences, Poetry. **Career:** State University of New York, Binghamton University, professor of philosophy and women's studies, 1987-. Writer. **Publications:** Lesbian Philosophy: Explorations, 1986; (ed. with I.M. Young) Thinking Muse: Feminism and Modern French Philosophy, 1989; (ed.) Lesbian Philosophies and Cultures, 1990; Reverberations: Across the Shimmering Cascadas, 1994; Sinuosities: Lesbian Poetic Politics, 1996. **Address:** Department of Philosophy, Binghamton University, State University of New York, LT 1304, 4400 Vestal Parkway E, PO Box 6000, Binghamton, NY 13902-6000, U.S.A. **Online address:** jeffn@binghamton.edu

ALLEN, John Edward. *See* **ALLEN, John Jay.**

ALLEN, John E(lliston). (Paul M. Danforth). British (born England), b. 1921. **Genres:** Air/Space Topics, Children's Non-fiction, Design, Sciences, Education, Institutions/Organizations, Intellectual History, Local History/Rural Topics, Military/Defense/Arms Control, Technology, Transportation. **Career:** Royal Aircraft Establishment, scientific officer, 1941-44; Marine Aircraft Experimental Establishment, senior scientific officer, 1944-50; Royal Aircraft Establishment, principal scientific officer, 1950-54; A.V. Roe and Company Ltd., Weapons Research Division, Projects and Assessment Department, head of aerodynamics, 1954-63; Hawker Siddeley Aviation, Advanced Projects Group, deputy chief engineer, 1963-69, British Aerospace, chief future projects engineer, 1969-83; Kingston University, visiting professor, 1999-. Writer. **Publications:** Aerodynamics, A Space-Age Survey, 1963; (as Paul M. Danforth) Transport Control, 1970; (as Paul M. Danforth) Transportation: Managing Man on the Move, 1970; (ed. with J. Bruce) The Future of Aeronautics, 1970; (co-author) Energy and Humanity; Aeronautics in a Finite World, 1974; (as Paul M. Danforth) The Channel Tunnel, 1974; Early Aircraft, 1976; Have Energy, Will Travel, 1977; Modern Aircraft, 1978; Aerodynamics, The Science of Air in Motion, 1982; Chambers Air and Space Dictionary, 1990; Chambers Bibliographic Dictionary, 1990; The Future of Aircraft Propulsion, 1992; The Motor Car in 2065 AD, 1993; Global Energy Issues Affecting Aeronautics Progress in Aerospace Sciences, 1999; (with E.M. Goodger) Transport Fuels Technology, 2000; Quest for a Novel Force: A Revolution in Aerospace, 2003. Contributor to professional journals. **Address:** The Gabriels, Angel Ln., Blythburgh, SU IP19 9LU, England.

ALLEN, John Jay. (John Edward Allen). American (born United States), b. 1932. **Genres:** Novels, Novellas/Short Stories, Literary Criticism And History. **Career:** University of Florida, assistant professor, 1960-65, associate professor, 1966-68, professor of Spanish, 1969-83; University of Kentucky, professor, 1983, now professor emeritus. Writer. **Publications:** Don Quixote: Hero or Fool?, 1969, vol.II, 1979; (ed.) Don Quijote de LaMancha, 1977, 7th ed., 1985; The Reconstruction of a Spanish Golden Age Playhouse: El Corral del Principe 1583-1744, 1983; Los teatros comerciales del siglo XVII y la escenificacion de la comedia, 1994; (ed. with D. Ynduran) El gran teatro delmundo/Pedro Calderon de la Barca, 1997; (with P.S. Finch) Don Quijote en el arte y pensamiento de occidente, 2004; Don Quixote: Hero or Fool?: Remixed, 2008. Contributor to periodicals. **Address:** Department of Spanish and Italian, University of Kentucky, Lexington, KY 40506, U.S.A.

ALLEN, John L. Italian/American (born United States), b. 1965?. **Genres:** History, Biography, Theology/Religion, Adult Non-fiction, Sociology. **Career:** National Catholic Reporter, opinion editor, 1997-2000, Rome correspondent, 2000-, online columnist, 2001-, senior correspondent. Journalist. **Publications:** Cardinal Ratzinger: The Vatican's Enforcer of the Faith, 2000, rev. ed. as Pope Benedict XVI: A Biography of Joseph Ratzinger, rev. ed. as Benedict XVI: Labourer in the Vineyard, 2005; Conclave: The Politics, Personalities, and Process of the Next Papal Election, 2002, rev. ed., 2004; All the Pope's Men: The Inside Story of How the Vatican Really Thinks, 2004; Common Ground in a Global Key: International Lessons in Catholic Dialogue, 2004; The Rise of Benedict XVI: The Inside Story of How the Pope Was Elected and Where He Will Take the Catholic Church, 2005; Opus Dei: An Objective Look behind the Myths and Reality of the Most Controversial Force in the Catholic Church, 2005; Díez cosas que el papa Benedicto XVI quíere que sepas, 2007; The Future Church: How Ten Trends are Revolutionizing the Catholic Church, 2009; (with T.M. Dolan) Archbishop Timothy Dolan on Faith, Hope, and the Future of the Catholic Church, 2011; A People of Hope: Archbishop Timothy Dolan in Conversation with John L. Allen Jr., 2012. **Address:** National Catholic Reporter Publishing Co., 115 E Armour Blvd., Kansas City, MO 64111-1203, U.S.A. **Online address:** jallen@natcath.org

ALLEN, Jonathan B(urgess). British (born England), b. 1957. **Genres:** Children's Fiction, Illustrations, Young Adult Fiction, Reference. **Career:** Children's book illustrator and writer. **Publications:** Pocketbook of Painful Puns and Poems, 1983; I Am a Dog, 2002; (co-ed.) Piedad romántica: sentimiento y religioìn en la estampa yel grabado del siglo XIX, 2004; Banana!, 2006; I'm not Cute!, 2006; I'm not Scared!, 2007; I'm not Santa!, 2008. SELF-ILLUSTRATED FOR CHILDREN: Guthrie Comes Clean, 1984; My Cat, 1986; My Dog, 1989; Mucky Moose, 1990; Who's at the Door?, 1993; Keep Fit Canaries, 1993; Two by Two by Two, 1995; Sweetie, 1994; Chicken Licken, 1996, 2nd ed., 1999; Fowl Play, 1996; Wake Up, Sleeping Beauty!, 1997; Wolf Academy, 1997; Jonathan Allen Picture Book, 1997; Flying Squad, 1998; Don't Wake the Baby!: An Interactive Book with Sounds, 2000; I'm Not Sleepy!, 2010. POETRY: A Bad Case of Animal Nonsense, 1981; A Pocketful of Painful Puns and Poems, 1983. JONATHAN ALLEN BOARD BOOKS SERIES: Purple Sock, Pink Sock, 1992; Big Owl, Little Towel, 1992; One with a Bun, 1992; Up the Steps, Down the Slide, 1992. WIZARD GRIMWEED SERIES: B.I.G. Trouble, 1993; Potion Commotion, 1993; The Funniest Man in the World, 1994; Nose Grows, 1994; The Witch Who Couldn't Spell, 1996; Dragon Dramatics, 1996. FRED CAT BOARD BOOKS SERIES: Dressing Up, 1997; My Noisy Toys, 1997; Weather and Me, 1997; What My Friends Say, 1997. Illustrator of books by others. **Address:** Acorn Cottage, South St., Litlington Royston, HF SG8 0QR, England.

ALLEN, Justin. American (born United States), b. 1974. **Genres:** History. **Career:** Dances Patrelle, administrative director. Writer. **Publications:** Slaves of the Shinar, 2007; Year of the Horse, 2009; Tomorrow Land: A Novel of Time, forthcoming. Contributor to periodicals. **Address:** Curtis Brown Ltd., 10 Astor Pl., New York, NY 10003-6935, U.S.A. **Online address:** kf@cbltd.com

ALLEN, Kieran. Irish (born Ireland), b. 1954?. **Genres:** Sociology. **Career:** Teacher, 1979-88; University College Dublin, lecturer, 1996-2002, senior lecturer in sociology, 2002-. Writer. **Publications:** The Politics of James Connolly, 1990; Fianna Fáil and Irish Labour, 1997; The Celtic Tiger: The Myth of Social Partnership in Ireland, 2000; (with C. Coulter) The Irish Republic, the United States, and the Iraq War: A Critical Appraisal, 2003; Max Weber: A Critical Introduction, 2004; The Corporate Takeover of Ireland, 2007; Ireland's Economic Crash: A Radical Agenda for Change, 2009; Marx and the Alternative to Capitalism, 2011. Contributor to periodicals. **Address:** University College Dublin, John Henry Newman Bldg., Rm. D205, University College, Belfield, DU 4, Ireland. **Online address:** kieran.allen@ucd.ie

ALLEN, Laura Jean. American (born United States) **Genres:** Children's Fiction, Illustrations, Animals/Pets. **Career:** Writer. **Publications:** SELF-ILLUSTRATED FOR CHILDREN: A Fresh Look at Flowers, 1963; Mr. Jolly's Sidewalk Market: A Story Told in Pictures, 1963; Ottie and the Star, 1979; Rollo and Tweedy and the Case of the Missing Cheese, 1983; Where is Freddy?, 1986; Rollo and Tweedy and the Ghost at Dougal Castle, 1992; The Witches Secret; The Secret Snow Country. Illustrator of books by others. **Address:** 51-02 39th Ave., Woodside, NY 11377, U.S.A.

ALLEN, Michael Patrick. American (born United States), b. 1945. **Genres:** Sociology, Mathematics/Statistics, Psychology, Business/Trade/Industry, Economics. **Career:** Washington State University, Department of Sociology, assistant professor, 1972-79, associate professor, 1979-89, director of graduate studies, 1987-88, professor, 1989-; University of Newcastle, professor of sociology. Writer. **Publications:** The Founding Fortunes: A New Anatomy of the Super-Rich Families in America, 1987; Understanding Regression Analysis, 1997. **Address:** Department of Sociology, Washington State University, Wilson-Short Hall 250, Pullman, WA 99164-4020, U.S.A. **Online address:** allenm@wsu.edu

ALLEN, Myron B. American (born United States), b. 1954. **Genres:** Mathematics/Statistics, Adult Non-fiction, Sciences. **Career:** University of Wyoming, Department of Mathematics, professor, 1983-, head, associate vice president of academic affairs, 1999-, provost and vice president for academic affairs. Writer. **Publications:** Collocation Techniques for Modeling Compositional Flows in Oil Reservoirs, 1984; (with G.A. Behie and J.A. Trangenstein) Multiphase Flow in Porous Media: Mechanics, Mathematics and Numerics, 1988; (with I. Herrera and G.F. Pinder) Numerical Modeling in Science and Engineering, 1988; (with E.L. Isaacson) Numerical Analysis for Applied Science, 1998. Contributor to journals. **Address:** Office of Academic Affairs, University of Wyoming, Dept. 3302, 312 Old Main, Laramie, WY 82071, U.S.A. **Online address:** allen@uwyo.edu

ALLEN, Nancy. American (born United States), b. 1938. **Genres:** Adult Non-fiction, Biography. **Career:** North Kingstown School Department, teacher, 1964-69; Pine School, teacher, 1971-73; journalist, 1973-78. **Publications:** Fair Seafarer: A Honeymoon Adventure with the Merchant Marine, 1997. Contributor to periodicals. **Address:** 1641 Binney Dr., Ft. Pierce, FL 34949-3190, U.S.A. **Online address:** seafarer30@hotmail.com

ALLEN, Nancy Kelly. American (born United States), b. 1949. **Genres:** Children's Non-fiction, Young Adult Non-fiction, Children's Fiction. **Career:** Social worker, 1971-76; Walkertown Primary School, library media specialist, 1977-. Writer. **Publications:** Once upon a Dime: A Math Adventure, 1999; On the Banks of the Amazon, 2004; Daniel Boone: Trailblazer, 2005; Whose Food Is This? A Look at What Animals Eat-Seeds, Bugs, and Nuts, 2005; Whose Sound Is This? A Look at Animal Noises-Chirps, Clicks, and Hoots, 2005; Whose Work Is This? A Look at Things Animals Make-Pearls, Milk, and Honey, 2005; The Munched-Up Flower Garden, 2006; Slate and Other Metamorphic Rocks, 2009; Granite and Other Igneous Rocks, 2009; Earth's Rock Cycle, 2009; Identifying Rocks, 2009; Minerals and Rocks, 2009; Limestone and Other Sedimentary Rocks, 2009; Happy Birthday: The Story of the World's Most Popular Song, 2010; Trouble in Troublesome Creek: A Troublesome Creek Kids Story, 2010; What is an Attribute?, 2010; Truth About Princesses, 2010; Is It Symmetrical?, 2011; What Sea Creature is This?, 2012. **Address:** Karen Mendez Smith, 2685 Spurr Rd., Lexington, KY 40511, U.S.A. **Online address:** nkallen@nancykellyallen.com

ALLEN, Pamela (Kay). New Zealander (born New Zealand), b. 1934. **Genres:** Children's Fiction, Illustrations. **Career:** Pio Pio District High School, art teacher, 1956; Rangitoto College, art teacher, 1957-58, 1960-64; Birkenhead Play Centre, education officer and assistant supervisor, 1969-74; writer and illustrator, 1979-. **Publications:** SELF-ILLUSTRATED FOR CHILDREN: Mr. Archimedes' Bath, 1980; Who Sank the Boat?, 1982; Bertie and the Bear, 1984; A Lion in the Night, 1985; Simon Said, 1985; Herbert and Harry, 1986; Hidden Treasure, 1987; Mr. McGee, 1987; Fancy That!, 1988; Simon Did, 1988; Watch Me Now, 1988; I Wish I Had a Pirate Suit, 1990; My Cat Maisie, 1990; Black Dog, 1991; Belinda, 1992; Mr. McGee Goes to Sea, 1992; Alexander's Outing, 1993; Mr. McGee and the Blackberry Jam, 1993; Clippity Clop, 1994; Waddle Giggle Gargle!, 1996; The Bear's Lunch, 1997; Mr. McGee and the Biting Flea, 1998; The Pear in the Pear Tree, 1999; Mr

McGee and the Perfect Nest, 2000; Inside Mary Elizabeth's House, 2000; Can You Keep a Secret?, 2001; Brown Bread and Honey, 2001; The Potato People, 2002; Daisy All-Sorts, 2002; Grandpa and Thomas and the Green Umbrella, 2006; Resources for Learning Mentors: Practical Activities for Group Sessions, 2007; Shhh! Little Mouse, 2007; Where's the Gold?, 2010. Illustrator of books by others. Contributor to periodicals. **Address:** Curtis Brown Pty Ltd., 27 Union St., PO Box 19, Paddington, Sydney, NW 2021, Australia. **Online address:** jo@pamelaallenbooks.co.nz

ALLEN, Patricia. American (born United States), b. 1954. **Genres:** Agriculture/Forestry, Environmental Sciences/Ecology, Social Sciences, Economics. **Career:** University of California, Agroecology, Applied Behavioral Sciences, research associate, 1980-81, Small Farm Center, coordinator, 1981-84, Agroecology Program, senior analyst, Center for Agroecology and Sustainable Food Systems, analyst, 1984-89, specialist and associate director, 1996-2006, director, 2007-, Environmental Studies, adjunct professor, 2008-. **Publications:** (Ed. with D. Van Dusen) Global Perspectives on Agroecology and Sustainable Agricultural Systems: Proceedings of the Sixth International Scientific Conference of the International Federation of Organic Agriculture Movements, 1988; (ed.) Food for the Future: Conditions and Contradictions of Sustainability, 1993; Together at the Table: Sustainability and Sustenance in the American Agrifood System, 2004. **Address:** Center for Agroecology and Sustainable Food System, University of California, 1156 High St., Santa Cruz, CA 95064, U.S.A. **Online address:** rats@ucsc.edu

ALLEN, Philip M(ark). American (born United States), b. 1932. **Genres:** Travel/Exploration, Third World, Area Studies. **Career:** U.S. Department of State, foreign service officer, 1956-66; African-American Institute, regional representative, Training and Program Development, director, 1966-70; University of Vermont, associate professor of African studies, 1970-71; Haiti Ministry of Agriculture, Management Training Seminar, director, 1977-78; Johnson State College, associate professor of social science, through 1978, Humanities Division, chairperson, 1978-81, professor of humanities, 1986-87; University of Dakar, senior Fulbright lecturer, 1981-82; University of Constantine, senior Fulbright lecturer, 1985-86; Frostburg State University, dean of arts and humanities, 1987-99, distinguished university professor, 1999-2005; University of Antananarivo, senior Fulbright lecturer, 1999-2000; consultant on international political cultures, 2005-; Arundel on the Bay newsletter, editor, 2007-. **Publications:** Self-Determination in the Western Indian Ocean, 1966; (with A. Segal) The Traveler's Africa, 1973; (ed. and intro.) Vermont and the Year 2000, 1976; (with J.M. Ostheimer) Africa and the Islands of the Western Indian Ocean, 1976; Security and Nationalism in the Indian Ocean: Lessons from the Latin Quarter Islands, 1987; Madagascar: Conflicts of Authority, 1995; (ed.) Reciprocal Cultures: Ireland and the USA, 1998; Historical Dictionary of Madagascar, 1995, 2nd ed. 2005. Contributor of articles to books and periodicals. **Address:** 3463 Rockway Ave., Annapolis, MD 21403-4849, U.S.A. **Online address:** pallen@frostburg.edu

ALLEN, Preston L. American (born United States), b. 1964?. **Genres:** Novels, Novellas/Short Stories. **Career:** Writer and educator. **Publications:** Hoochie Mama (novel), 2001; Bounce (novel), 2003; Churchboys & Other Sinners (short story collection), 2003; Come with Me, Sheba (novel), 2004; All or Nothing (novel), 2007; Jesus Boy, 2010. Contributor to periodicals. Works appear in anthologies. **Address:** Carolina Wren Press, 120 Morris St., Durham, NC 27701, U.S.A. **Online address:** pallensky@webtv.net

ALLEN, Richard William. American (born United States), b. 1959. **Genres:** Young Adult Non-fiction, Essays. **Career:** New York University, Tisch School of the Arts, associate professor of cinema studies, department chair. Film historian and writer. **Publications:** Projecting Illusion: Film Spectatorship and the Impression of Reality, 1995; Hitchcock's Romantic Irony, 2007; (with I. Bhaskar) Islamicate Cultures of Bombay Cinema, 2009. EDITOR: (with M. Smith) Film Theory and Philosophy, 1997; (with S. Ishii-Gonzales) Alfred Hitchcock: Centenary Essays, 1999; (with M. Turvey) Wittgenstein, Theory and the Arts, 2001; (with M. Turvey) Camera Obscura, Camera Lucida: Essays in Honor of Annette Michelson, 2003; (with S. Ishii-Gonzales) Hitchcock: Past and Future, 2004; (with S. Gottlieb) Hitchcock Annual Anthology: Selected Essays from Volumes 10-15, 2009. **Address:** Tisch School of the Arts, 721 Broadway, New York, NY 10003, U.S.A. **Online address:** ra4@nyu.edu

ALLEN, Roberta. American (born United States), b. 1945. **Genres:** Novels, Novellas/Short Stories, How-to Books, Information Science/Computers, Self Help, Third World, Travel/Exploration, Women's Studies And Issues, Writing/Journalism, Autobiography/Memoirs, Young Adult Fiction, Young Adult Non-fiction. **Career:** Corcoran School of Art, lecturer, 1975; Kutztown University, lecturer, 1979; C.W. Post Center of Long Island University, C.W. Post College, lecturer, 1979; Parsons School of Design, adjunct instructor in creative writing, 1986; Art Gallery of Western Australia, artist-in-residence, 1989; The Writer's Voice, adjunct instructor, instructor, 1991-97; New York University, The New School, adjunct assistant professor of the writing program, 1992-2010, New School for Social Research, Department of Continuing Education, adjunct instructor, 1993-2001, Eugene Lang College, adjunct instructor; Columbia University, School of the Arts, adjunct assistant professor, 1998-99; University of the South, Tennessee Williams fellow, 1998, creative writing fellow, 1998. Writer. **Publications:** Partially Trapped Lines, 1975; Pointless Arrows, 1976; Pointless Acts, 1977; Everything in the World There is to Know is Known by Somebody, But Not by the Same Knower, 1981; The Daughter (novella in stories), 1992; Certain People and Other Stories, 1997; The Dreaming Girl: A Novel, 2000; Traveling Woman: A Novel, 2000. NON-FICTION: Amazon Dream (travel memoir), 1993; Fast Fiction: Creating Fiction in Five Minutes, 1997; The Playful Way to Serious Writing: An Anything-Can-Happen Workbook to Inspire and Delight, 2002; The Playful Way to Knowing Yourself, 2003. Works appear in anthologies. Contributor to periodicals. **Address:** c/o DeAnna Heindel, Gerorges Borchardt Inc., 136 E 57th St., New York, NY 10021, U.S.A. **Online address:** robertaallen1@me.com

ALLEN, Roland. *See* **AYCKBOURN, Alan.**

ALLEN, Ronald J. American (born United States), b. 1948. **Genres:** Law. **Career:** University of Nebraska, visiting professor of law, 1973-74; State University of New York, assistant professor, 1974-77, associate professor of law, 1977-79; University of Iowa, visiting professor, 1978-79, professor of law, 1979-84, University Faculty Senate, vice-president, 1980-81, president, 1981-82; Northwestern University, School of Law, professor, 1984-, Stanford Clinton Jr. research professor, 1990-91, John Henry Wigmore professor of law, 1992-, Journal of Criminal Law & Criminology, adviser, 1985-93, 2002-, Center for the Humanities, fellow, 1994-95; Federal Judicial Center, lecturer, 1987; Marshall University, distinguished lecturer, 1991. Writer. **Publications:** (With R.B. Kuhns) Constitutional Criminal Procedure: An Examination of the Fourth, Fifth and Sixth Amendments and Related Areas, 1985, 3rd ed. (with R.B. Kuhns and W.J. Stuntz), 1995; (with R.B. Kuhns) An Analytical Approach to Evidence: Text, Problems and Cases, 1989, 4th ed., 2006; (ed. with R.B. Kuhns) Federal Rules of Evidence with Legislative History and Case Supplement, 1989, 2nd ed. (with R.B. Kuhns and E. Swift), 1996; (with V.A. Brander and S.D. Stulberg) Arthritis of the Hip and Knee: The Active Person's Guide to Taking Charge, 1998; (co-author) Comprehensive Criminal Procedure, 2001, 3rd ed., 2011; (co-author) Criminal Procedure: Investigation and Right to Counsel, 2005, 2nd ed., 2011; Criminal Procedure: Adjudication and Right to Counsel, 2011; The Nature of Juridical Proof, forthcoming. Contributor of articals to books and journals. **Address:** School of Law, Northwestern University, 357 E Chicago Ave., Chicago, IL 60611, U.S.A. **Online address:** rjallen@law.northwestern.edu

ALLEN, Samuel W. (Paul Vesey). American (born United States), b. 1917. **Genres:** Poetry. **Career:** New York City, deputy assistant district attorney, 1946-47; U.S. Armed Forces, civilian attorney, 1951-55; Texas Southern University, faculty, 1958-60; U.S. Information Agency, assistant general counsel, 1961-64; Community Relations Service, chief counsel, 1965-68; Tuskegee Institute, Avalon professor of humanities, 1968-70; Wesleyan University, faculty, 1970-71; Tuskegee University, writer-in-residence; Rutgers University, writer-in-residence; Boston University, professor of English, 1971-81; New England Poetry Club, board director. Writer. **Publications:** Ivory Tusks, 1956; (co-ed.) Pan-Africanism Reconsidered, 1962; Ivory Tusks and Other Poems, 1968; (ed.) Poems From Africa, 1973; Paul Vesey's Ledger, 1975; Every Round and Other Poems, 1987. Contributor to periodicals. **Address:** 145 Cliff Ave., Winthrop, MA 02152, U.S.A.

ALLEN, Sarah Addison. (Katie Gallagher). American (born United States) **Genres:** Novels, Romance/Historical. **Career:** Antique appraiser's assistant and writer. **Publications:** (As Katie Gallagher) Tried and True, 2003; Garden Spells, 2007; The Sugar Queen, 2008; The Girl Who Chased the Moon, 2010; The Peach Keeper, 2011. Works appear in anthologies. **Address:** c/o Andrea Cirillo, Jane Rotrosen Agency, 318 E 51st St., New York, NY 10022, U.S.A. **Online address:** sarah@sarahaddisonallen.com

ALLEN, Thomas M. Canadian (born Canada), b. 1967?. **Genres:** History. **Career:** University of Ottawa, associate professor of English. Writer. **Publications:** A Republic in Time: Temporality and Social Imagination in Nineteenth-Century America, 2008. Contributor to journals. **Address:** Department of English, University of Ottawa, Rm. 338, Arts Hall, 70 Laurier Ave. E, Ottawa, ON K1N 6N5, Canada. **Online address:** tallen@uottawa.ca

ALLEN, William Sheridan. American (born United States), b. 1932. **Genres:** History. **Career:** Bay City Junior College, instructor in history, 1958-59; Massachusetts Institute of Technology, instructor in humanities, 1960-61; University of Missouri, assistant professor, 1961-67; Wayne State University, associate professor, 1967-70; State University of New York, Department of History, professor of history, 1970-, chairman, 1987-90, now professor emeritus. Writer. **Publications:** The Nazi Seizure of Power: The Experience of a Single German Town, 1930-1935, 1965, rev. ed. as Nazi Seizure of Power: The Experience of a Single German Town, 1922-1945, 1984; Das haben wir nicht gewollt Die national-sozialistische Machtergreifung in einer Kleinstadt 1930-1935, 1966; (ed. and trans.) The Infancy of Nazism: The Memoirs of Ex-Gauleiter Albert Krebs, 1923-1933, 1976. **Address:** Department of History, State University of New York, 546 Park Hall, Buffalo, NY 14214, U.S.A. **Online address:** allentrawler@adelphia.net

ALLEN, Woody. (Allan Stewart Konigsberg). American (born United States), b. 1935. **Genres:** Film, Plays/Screenplays, Young Adult Fiction, Humor/Satire, Mystery/Crime/Suspense, Poetry. **Career:** National Broadcasting Corp., staff writer, 1952-; The New School, faculty. **Publications:** PUBLISHED PLAYS: Don't Drink the Water, 1967; Play It Again, Sam, 1969; Death: A Comedy in One Act, 1975; God: A Comedy in One Act, 1975; The Floating Light Bulb, 1982; Death Defying Acts: 3 One-Act Comedies, 1995; Three One-Act Plays, 2003. OTHERS: Getting Even, 1971; Without Feathers, 1975; Non-Being and Somethingness, 1978; Side Effects, 1980; Four Films of Woody Allen, 1982; The Lunatic's Tale, 1986; Three Films of Woody Allen, 1987; Mere Anarchy, 2007; The Insanity Defense: The Complete Prose, 2007. **Address:** c/o Jack Rollins, Rollins & Joffe, 130 W 57th St., New York, NY 10019-3303, U.S.A.

ALLENDE, Isabel. American/Chilean (born Chile), b. 1942. **Genres:** Novels, Children's Fiction, Autobiography/Memoirs, Literary Criticism And History. **Career:** United Nations Food and Agricultural Organization, secretary, 1959-65; Paula magazine, journalist, editor and advice columnist, 1967-74; Mampato magazine, journalist, 1969-74; Canal 13/Canal 7, television interviewer, 1970-75; El Nacional, journalist, 1974-75, columnist, 1976-83; Colegio Marroco, administrator, 1979-82; Barnard College, Gildersleeve lecturer, 1988-; University of California, teacher of creative writing, 1989-. **Publications:** Civilice a su troglodita: Los impertinentes de Isabel Allende (humor), 1974; La casa de los espiritus, 1982, trans. as The House of the Spirits, 1985; La gorda de porcelana (juvenile) (title means: 'The Fat Porcelain Lady'), 1984; De amor y de sombra, 1984, trans. as Of Love and Shadows, 1987; (co-author) Los Libros tienen sus propiosespíritus: Estudios sobre Isabel Allende, 1986; Eva Luna, 1987; Cuentos de EvaLuna, 1990, trans. as The Stories of Eva Luna, 1991; (co-author) El Amor, 1991; El Plan infinito, trans. as The Infinite Plan, 1993; Paula (autobiography), 1994; (co-author) Salidas de madre, 1996; Afrodita: cuentos, recetas y otros afrodisíacos, 1997, trans. as Aphrodite: A Memoir of the Senses, 1998; Hija de la fortuna, trans. as Daughter of Fortune, 1999; (intro.) Conversations with Isabel Allende, 1999, rev. ed., 2004; Retrato en sepia, 2001; Periodismo en primera persona, 2001; La Ciudad de las bestias trans. as City of the Beasts, 2002; Mi país inventado: un paseo nostálgicopor Chile, 2003 trans. as My Invented Country: A Nostalgic Journey through Chile, 2003; El Reino del dragon de oro, 2003 trans. as Kingdom of the Golden Dragon, 2004; El bosque de los Pigmeos, 2004 trans. as Forest of the Pygmies, 2005; William Morris: Mazorca: Objects of Common Ceremony, 2004; Zorro: A Novel, 2005 trans. as Zorro: una novella, 2005; El Zorro: comienza la leyenda, 2005; Forest of the Pygmies, 2005; Young Zorro: The Iron Brand, 2006; Inés delalma mía, 2006 trans. as Inés of My Soul, 2006; La suma de losdías, 2007 trans. as The Sum of Our Days, 2007; Isla bajo el mar, 2009; Island Beneath the Sea: A Novel, 2010. Contributor to periodicals. **Address:** c/o Carmen Balcells, Diagonal 580, Barcelona, 08021, Spain. **Online address:** assistant@isabelallende.com

ALLERT, Tilman. German (born Germany), b. 1947?. **Genres:** Education, History. **Career:** University of Frankfurt, professor of sociology and social psychology. Writer and academic. **Publications:** Interpretationen einer Bildungsgeschichte, 1980; (co-author) Familie, Milieu und Sozialpädagogische Intervention, 1994; Professionen im Wandel der Arbeitswelt, 1998; Die Familie: Fallstudien Zur Unverwüstlichkeit einer Lebensform, 1998; Mutter, Kind Vater, 2000; (contrib.) Dein Wille Geschehe: Das Bild des Vaters in Zeitgenössischer Kunst und Wissenschaft: Eine Initiative des Siemens Kulturprogramms, 2000; Der Deutsche Gruss: Geschichte Einer Unheilvollen Geste, 2005; Der Keimling: Die Familiengeschichte eines Autistischen Mädchens: Eine Soziologische Theorie des Autismus, 2006. **Address:** University of Frankfurt, Soziologie u. Sozialpsychologie m. d. Schwerp., Bildungssoziologie, Robert-Mayer-Str. 5, Frankfurt, 60054, Germany. **Online address:** alert@soz.uni-frankfurt.de

ALLEYNE, Mervyn C. Jamaican/Puerto Rican/Trinidadian (born Trinidad and Tobago), b. 1933. **Genres:** Anthropology/Ethnology, Language/Linguistics, History. **Career:** University of West Indies, professor of sociolinguistics, 1959-98, professor emeritus, 1998-; University of Puerto Rico, Department of English, professor, 2003-, visiting professor; Yale University, visiting professor; State University of New York, visiting professor; Indiana University, visiting professor; University of Kansas, visiting professor; University of Amsterdam, visiting professor. Writer. **Publications:** Les Noms des Vents en Gallo-Roman, 1962; Krio Language Training Manual, 1965; Acculturation and the Cultural Matrix of Creolization, 1971; Comparative Afro-American: An Historical-Comparative Study of English-Based Afro-American Dialects of the New World, 1980; Theoretical Issues in Caribbean Linguistics, 1982; Studies in Saramaccan Language Structure, 1987; The Roots of Jamaican Culture, 1988; (contrib.) Language and the Social Construction of Identity in Creole Situations, 1994; Syntaxe Historique Créole, 1996; The Construction and Representation of Race and Ethnicity in the Caribbean and the World, 2002; The Folk Medicine of Jamaica, 2004; Indigenous Languages of the Caribbean, 2004. **Address:** Department of English, College of Humanities, University of Puerto Rico, 8 Pedreira Bldg., PO Box 23356, San Juan, 00931-3356, Puerto Rico. **Online address:** mervynalleyne@yahoo.com

ALLFREY, Anthony. Portuguese/British (born England), b. 1930. **Genres:** History, Biography, Military/Defense/Arms Control, Young Adult Fiction. **Career:** Historian and writer. **Publications:** Man of Arms: The Life and Legend of Sir Basil Zaharoff, 1989; Edward VII and His Jewish Court, 1991. **Address:** Santo Antonio, Casal Meirames, Varzea de Sintra, 2710, Portugal.

ALLGOOD, Myralyn F(rizzelle). American (born United States), b. 1939. **Genres:** Biography, Translations, Literary Criticism And History, Autobiography/Memoirs. **Career:** Samford University, instructor, 1963-68, Department of World Languages and Cultures, assistant professor, 1968-86, associate professor, 1986-89, professor, 1989-, chair of department, 1982-2007, director, U.S.D.E. Foreign Language and International Studies, administrator. Writer. **Publications:** (Ed. and trans.) Another Way to Be: Selected Works of Rosario Castellanos, 1990; (ed., intro. and trans.) Remembering Rosario, Scripta Humanistica, 1990. **Address:** Department of World Languages and Cultures, Samford University, CHAPM 134, 800 Lakeshore Dr., Birmingham, AL 35229-2298, U.S.A. **Online address:** mfallgoo@samford.edu

ALLIE, Scott. American (born United States) **Genres:** Adult Non-fiction, Mystery/Crime/Suspense, Ghost Writer, Graphic Novels. **Career:** Glimmer Train Stories (magazine), writer, editor; Dark Horse Comics, editor, writer, publisher, 1994-. Theater technical director. **Publications:** Tilazeus Meets the Messiah, 1996; Planet of the Apes, 2001; Hellboy: Odder Jobs, 2004; Shinobi: The Rise of Hotsuma, 2002; (with R. Benjamin and B. Horton) Star Wars El Imperio, 2006; The Dark Horse Book of Monsters, 2006; Solomon Kane, 2008; Exurbia, 2009; (with M.E. Russell) Sacred to the Memory, forthcoming. EDITOR: Buffy the Vampire Slayer: Creatures of Habit, 2002; Reveal, 2002; Hellboy: Weird Tales, 2003; The Dark Horse Book of Hauntings: Eight Uncanny Tales of Spirit Manifestations, Apparitions, and Other worldly Horrors-Told in Words and Pictures, 2003; The Devil's Footprints, vol. I, 2003, vol. II, 2005; Hellboy Junior, 2004; The Dark Horse Book of Witchcraft: Eight Weird Mysteries of Powerful Women and Supernatural Skill Told in Words and Pictures: Also, High Priestess Phyllis Currott Reveals the Wisdom of Witchcraft: Tales Of Magic and Splendor, 2004; B.P.R.D.: The Soul of Venice and Other Stories, 2004; Dark Horse Book of the Dead, 2005; Star Wars Omnibus: At War With the Eempire, 2011; Star Wars, Jedi, vol. I: The Dark Side, 2012. **Address:** Dark Horse Comics, 10956 SE Main St., Milwaukie, OR 97222, U.S.A. **Online address:** scott@scottallie.com

ALLIGOOD, Kathleen T. American (born United States) **Genres:** Mathematics/Statistics, Sciences. **Career:** George Mason University, Department of

Mathematical Sciences, professor of mathematics. Writer and mathematician. **Publications:** (Co-author) Chaos and Fractals: The Mathematics Behind the Computer Graphics, 1989; (with T.D. Sauer and J.A. Yorke) Chaos: An Introduction to Dynamical Systems, 1997. Contributor to books and journals. **Address:** Department of Mathematical Sciences, George Mason University, Rm. 304, Enterprise Hall, MS: 3F2, 4400 University Dr., Fairfax, VA 22030-4422, U.S.A. **Online address:** alligood@gmu.edu

ALLIN, Lou. Canadian (born Canada), b. 1945. **Genres:** Mystery/Crime/Suspense. **Career:** Ohio State University, lecturer in English, 1968-71; Cambrian College, professor of English, 1977-2005, now retired. Writer. **Publications:** Northern Winters Are Murder, 2000; Blackflies Are Murder, 2002; Bush Poodles Are Murder, 2003; A Little Learning Is a Murderous Thing, 2005; Murder, Eh?, 2006; Memories Are Murder, 2007; And On the Surface Die, 2008; Man Corn Murders, 2009; 2. She Felt No Pain, 2010; That Dog Won't Hunt, 2010. Works appears in anthologies. **Address:** 1903 W Bay Rd., Garson, ON P3L 1V3, Canada. **Online address:** louallin@shaw.ca

ALLINGTON, Maynard. American (born United States), b. 1931. **Genres:** Novels, Writing/Journalism, Essays. **Career:** Novelist, 1976-. **Publications:** The Grey Wolf, 1986; The Fox in the Field: A WWII Novel of India, 1994; The Court of Blue Shadows, 1995. Contributor to periodicals. Works appear in anthologies. **Address:** 336 Lake Victoria Cir., Melbourne, FL 32940-1870, U.S.A. **Online address:** mallington@earthlink.net

ALLISON, Amy. American (born United States), b. 1956. **Genres:** Children's Non-fiction, Writing/Journalism, Young Adult Fiction, Social Sciences, Biography. **Career:** Teacher and Writer. **Publications:** Shakespeare's Globe, 1999; Antonio Banderas, 2000; Life in Ancient China, 2000; Roger Williams: Founder of Rhode Island, 2001; John Leguizamo, 2001; Germany, 2001; Edwin Stanton: Secretary of War, 2001; Gargoyles on Guard, 2002; Machu Picchu, 2003; Luis Alvarez and the Development of the Bubble Chamber, 2002. Contributor of articles to journals. **Address:** Mitchell Lane Publishers Inc., 20 Shea Way, Newark, DE 19713-3447, U.S.A. **Online address:** editourist@yahoo.com

ALLISON, Dale C. American (born United States), b. 1955. **Genres:** Theology/Religion. **Career:** Texas Christian University, resident associate, 1982-86; Friends University, resident fellow, 1989-97; Pittsburgh Theological Seminary, associate professor, professor, 1997-. Writer. **Publications:** JESUS: The End of the Ages Has Come: An Early Interpretation of the Passion and Resurrection of Jesus, 1985; Jesus of Nazareth: Millenarian Prophet, 1998; (co-ed.) The Apocalyptic Jesus: A Debate, 2001; Resurrecting Jesus: The Earliest Christian Tradition and Its Interpreters, 2005; The Historical Christ and the Theological Jesus, 2009; Constructing Jesus: Memory, Imagination, and History, 2010. EXEGESIS OF THE GOSPEL OF MATTHEW: (with W.D. Davies) Matthew: vol. I: 1-7, 1988, vol. II: 8-18, 1991, vol. III: 19-28, 1997. COMMENTARY ON MATTHEW: The New Moses: A Matthean Typology, 1993; (with W.D. Davies) A Critical and Exegetical Commentary on the Gospel according to Saint Matthew, 2004; (ed.) Matthew: A Shorter Commentary, 2004; Studies in Matthew: Interpretation Past and Present, 2005. OTHERS: The Silence of Angels, 1995; The Jesus Tradition in Q, 1997; The Sermon on the Mount: Inspiring the Moral Imagination, 1999; The Intertextual Jesus: Scripture in Q, 2000; Scriptural Allusions in the New Testament: Light from the Dead Sea Scrolls, 2000; Testament of Abraham, 2003; The Luminous Dusk: Finding God in the Deep, Still Places, 2006; The Love There That's Sleeping: The Art and Spirituality of George Harrison, 2006. EDITOR: (with A. Levine and J.D. Crossan) Documenting Jesus: A Reader, 2006; (with A. Levine and J.D. Crossan) The Historical Jesus in Context, 2006; (with P. Law) Testament: From the Text of the Revised English Bible, 2006. **Address:** Pittsburgh Theological Seminary, 616 N Highland Ave., Pittsburgh, PA 15206, U.S.A. **Online address:** dallison@pts.edu

ALLISON, Henry E(dward). American (born United States), b. 1937. **Genres:** Philosophy, Humanities. **Career:** State University of New York College, assistant professor of philosophy, 1964-65; Pennsylvania State University, assistant professor of philosophy, 1965-68; University of Florida, Department of Philosophy, associate professor, 1968-72, professor of philosophy, 1972-73; University of California, Department of Philosophy, professor of philosophy, 1973-94, chair, 1978-82, research professor, 1995-97, professor emeritus, 1997-; Boston University, Department of Philosophy, faculty, 1996-2004, professor emeritus, 2004-. Writer. **Publications:** Lessing and the Enlightenment: His Philosophy of Religion and Its Relation to Eighteenth-Century Thought, 1966; (ed.) The Kant-Eberhard Controversy, 1973; Benedict de Spinoza, 1975, rev. ed. as Benedict de Spinoza: An Introduction, 1987; Kant's Transcendental Idealism: An Interpretation and Defense, 1983, rev. ed., 2004; Kant's Theory of Freedom, 1990; (foreword) Kant: De La Crítica a la Filosofía de la Religión: En el Bicentenario de la Religión En Los Límites de la Mera Razón, 1994; Idealism and Freedom, 1996; Kant's Theory of Taste, 2001; (ed. with P. Heath) Theoretical Philosophy after 1781, 2002; Custom and Reason in Hume: A Kantian Reading of the First Book of the Treatise, 2008; Kant's Groundwork for the Metaphysics of Morals: A Commentary, 2011. Contributor to journals. **Address:** Department of Philosophy, University of California, 9500 Gilman Dr., Ste. 0119, La Jolla, CA 92093-0119, U.S.A. **Online address:** hea@surewest.net

ALLISON, Jennifer. American (born United States) **Genres:** Novels, Children's Fiction. **Career:** Educator and news reporter. **Publications:** Gilda Joyce: Psychic Investigator, 2005; Gilda Joyce: The Ladies of the Lake, 2006; Gilda Joyce: The Ghost Sonata, 2007; Gilda Joyce: The Dead Letter Drop, 2009; Gilda Joyce: The Bones of the Holy, 2011. **Address:** c/o Author Mail, Penguin Young Readers Group, 345 Hudson St., New York, NY 10014, U.S.A. **Online address:** jennifer@gildajoyce.com

ALLISON, Robert J. (Robert James Allison). American (born United States), b. 1957. **Genres:** Politics/Government, History, Theology/Religion. **Career:** Suffolk University, Department of History, professor and chair. Writer and educator. **Publications:** Creating the Empire of Reason: Massachusetts Ratifies the United States Constitution: An Exhibition of Materials from the Houghton Library, Widener Library Rotunda, Harvard University, September 7- October 12, 1988, 1988; (ed. and intro.) The Interesting Narrative of the Life of Olaudah Equiano, 1995; The Crescent Obscured: The United States and the Muslim World, 1776-1815, 1995; American Eras: The Development of a Nation, 1783-1815 (part of the "American Eras" series), 1997; A Short History of Boston, 2004; Revolutionary Sites of Greater Boston, 2005; Stephen Decatur: American Naval Hero, 1779-1820, 2005; The Boston Massacre, 2006; The Boston Tea Party, 2007; (ed.) Narratives of Barbary Captivity: Recollections of James Leander Cathcart, Jonathan Cowdery, and William Ray, 2007. **Address:** U.S.A. **Online address:** ballison@suffolk.edu

ALLISON, Robert James. *See* **ALLISON, Robert J.**

ALLISON, Will. American (born United States) **Genres:** Novels, Writing/Journalism. **Career:** Writer and educator. **Publications:** What You Have Left (novel), 2007; Long Drive Home (novel), 2011. **Address:** c/o Julie Barer, Barer Literary L.L.C., 270 Lafayette St., Ste. 1504, New York, NY 10012, U.S.A. **Online address:** will@willallison.com

ALLMAND, Christopher. *See* **ALLMAND, C. T.**

ALLMAND, C. T. (Christopher Allmand). British (born England) **Genres:** History, Biography. **Career:** Liverpool University, professor of medieval history, now professor emeritus. Writer. **Publications:** Henry V (pamphlet), 1968, rev. ed., 1997; Lancastrian Normandy, 1415-1450: The History of a Medieval Occupation, 1983; The Hundred Years War: England and France at War, c. 1300-c. 1450, 1988; Henry V, 1992. EDITOR: Society at War: The Experience of England and France during the Hundred Years War, 1973; War, Literature, and Politics in the Late Middle Ages: Essays in Honour of G.W. Coopland, 1976; (with C.A.J. Armstrong) English Suits before the Parlement of Paris 1420-1436, 1982; Power, Culture and Religion in France, c. 1350-c. 1550, 1989; War, Government and Power in Late Medieval France, 2000. **Address:** Department of History, University of Liverpool, 9 Abercromby Sq., PO Box 147, Liverpool, L69 7WZ, England.

ALLRED, Alexandra Powe. (Alexandra Powe-Allred). German (born Germany), b. 1965. **Genres:** Sports/Fitness, Recreation, Animals/Pets, Education. **Career:** U.S. Women's Bobsled Team, staff, 1994-98; U.S. Men's Olympic Bobsled Team, crew staff, 2002. Writer. **Publications:** AS ALEXANDRA POWE-ALLRED: (with M. Powe) The Quiet Storm: A Celebration of Women in Sport, 1997; Entering the Mother Zone: Balancing Self, Health and Family, 2000; Passion Rules! Inspiring Women in Business, 2001; Teaching Basic Obedience: Train the Owner, Train the Dog, 2001; Hummer, the Bee Who Couldn't Buzz, 2002; Your Outta Control Puppy, 2002; Atticus Weaver and His Triumphant Leap from Outcast to Hero and Back Again, 2002; The Code, Perfection Learning, 2002; (with M. Powe and K. Powe)

Atta Girl! A Celebration of Women in Sport, 2003; Retold Middle Eastern Myths: Folktales for Children, 2003; Crossing the Line, 2003; Dogs' Most Wanted: The Top 10 Book of Historic Hounds, Professional Pooches and Canine Oddities, 2004; Cats' Most Wanted: The Top 10 Book of Mysterious Mousers, Talented Tabbies and Feline Oddities, 2005; (with P. Britz) Athletic Scholarships for Dummies, 2006; Swingman, 2010. Contributor to periodicals. **Address:** World Audience, Inc., 303 Park Ave. S, Ste. 1440, New York, NY 10010-3657, U.S.A. **Online address:** redburn4@gmail.com

ALLSOBROOK, David Ian. Welsh (born Wales), b. 1940. **Genres:** Education, Music. **Career:** Teacher, 1963-70; Loughborough University, lecturer in education, 1970-72; Cardiff University, lecturer in history of education, 1972-. Writer. **Publications:** Schools for the Shires: The Reform of Middle-Class Education in Mid-Victorian England, 1986; Liszt: My Travelling Circus Life, 1991; Music for Wales: Walford Davies and the National Council of Music, 1918-1941, 1992; (with B.B. James) First in the World: The Story of the National Youth Orchestra of Wales, 1995. **Address:** Southern Illinois University Press, 1915 University Press Dr., PO Box 6806, Carbondale, IL 62966, U.S.A.

ALLSTON, Aaron. American (born United States), b. 1960. **Genres:** Science Fiction/Fantasy, Novels, Horror. **Career:** Space Gamer Magazine, circulation manager, assistant editor, editor, 1980-83; freelance computer games scripter and designer of role playing game supplements, 1983-; Science fiction and fantasy writer. **Publications:** Web of Danger, 1988; Dungeons and Dragons Rules Cyclopedia, 1991; Wrath of the Immortals, 1992; Poor Wizard's Almanac and Book of Facts, 1992; Galatea in 2-D, 1993; Double Jeopardy, 1994; Doc Sidhe, 1995; (with H. Lisle) Thunder of the Captains, 1996; (with H. Lisle) Wrath of the Princes, 1997; Wraith Squadron, 1998; Iron Fist, 1998; Sidhe Devil, 2001; Rebel Stand, 2002; Rebel Dream, 2002; Terminator 3: Terminator Dreams: A Novel, 2003; Terminator Hunt, 2004; Star Wars: Legacy of the Force: Betrayal, 2006; Star Wars: Legacy of the Force: Fury, 2007; Star Wars: Legacy of the Force: Exile, 2007; Outcast, 2009; Backlash, 2010; Conviction, 2011. **Address:** c/o Russ Galen, Scovil Chichak Galen Literary Agency Inc., 381 Park Ave. S, Ste. 1020, New York, NY 10016, U.S.A. **Online address:** allston@aaronallston.com

ALLYN, Doug. American (born United States), b. 1942. **Genres:** Mystery/Crime/Suspense, Novels, Young Adult Fiction, Novellas/Short Stories. **Career:** Devils Triangle (rock music group), musician, singer, and songwriter, 1975-. Author. **Publications:** LUPE GARCIA SERIES: The Cheerio Killings, 1989; Motown Underground, 1993. MITCH MITCHEL SERIES: Icewater Mansions, 1995; Black Water, 1996; A Dance in Deep Water, 1997. OTHERS: (contrib.) Cat Crimes Through Time, 1998; St. Margaret's Kitten, 1999; All Creatures Dark and Dangerous, 1999; Welcome to Wolf Country, 2001; The Hard Luck Klub, 2002; The Burning of Rachel Hayes, 2004. Contributor to magazines. Works appear in anthologies. **Address:** Macmillan Publishers, 175 5th Ave., New York, NY 10010, U.S.A.

ALLYN, Pam. American (born United States), b. 1963. **Genres:** Education. **Career:** Teachers College Reading and Writing Project, staff developer and director of funded projects; LitLife, founder and executive director; LitWorld, founder and executive director; Books for Boys, founding director. Writer and motivational speaker. **Publications:** NONFICTION: The Complete 4 for Literacy: How to Teach Reading and Writing through Daily Lessons, Monthly Units and Yearlong Calendars, 2007; (with J. Margolies) The Complete Year in Reading and Writing: Daily Lessons, Monthly Units, Yearlong Calendar. Grade 1, 2008; (with K. McNally) The Complete Year in Reading and Writing. K: Daily Lessons, Monthly Units, Yearlong Calendar, 2008; (with L. Pastore) The Complete Year in Reading and Writing. Grade 4: Daily Lessons, Monthly Units, Yearlong Calendar, 2008; (with P. Vitale-Reilly) The Complete Year in Reading and Writing. 2: Daily Lessons, Monthly Units, Yearlong Calendar, 2008; (with L. Pastore) The Complete Year in Reading and Writing. 5: Daily Lessons, Monthly Units, Yearlong Calendar, 2008; (with A. Gotthelf) The Complete Year in Reading and Writing. 5: Daily Lessons, Monthly Units, Yearlong Calendar, 2008; What to Read When: The Books and Stories to Read with Your Child and All the Best Times to Read Them, 2009; The Great Eight: Management Strategies for the Reading and Writing Classroom, 2010; Pam Allyn's Best Books for Boys: How to Engage Boys in Reading in Ways That Will Change Their Lives, 2011; Your Child's Writing Life: How to Inspire Confidence, Creativity, and Skill at Every Age, 2011; (contrib.) Writing above Standard: Engaging Workshop Lessons That Take Standards to New Heights and Help Kids Become Skilled, Inspired Writers, 2009. **Address:** LitLife Inc., PO Box 450, Hastings on Hudson, NY 10706, U.S.A. **Online address:** pamallyn@litworld.org

ALMA, Ann. Canadian/Dutch (born Netherlands), b. 1946?. **Genres:** History, Education. **Career:** Teacher, through 1992. Writer. **Publications:** Camping with Children: A How-to Guide for Teachers, 1991; Skateway to Freedom, 1993; Under Emily's Sky, 1997; Something to Tell, 1998; Summer of Changes, 2001; Summer of Adventures, 2002; Brave Deeds: How One Family Saved Many from the Nazis, 2008. **Address:** S8 C5, RR 1, South Slocan, BC V0G 2G0, Canada. **Online address:** annalma@shaw.ca

AL-MĀJID, Islām Muḥammad Abd. *See* **ABDEL-MAGID, Islām Muḥammad.**

ALMAND, James. *See* **HAYNES, Jim.**

AL-MARAYATI, Abid A(min). American/Iraqi (born Iraq), b. 1931. **Genres:** International Relations/Current Affairs, Politics/Government. **Career:** University of Toledo, Department of Political Science, Center for International Studies, intern, 1954, professor and director, 1968-90, professor emeritus, 1990-, chair, teacher, 1981-82; United Nations General Assembly, Delegation of Iraq, secretary, 1955, Delegation of Yemen, secretary, 1956-60; University of Massachusetts, Department of Government, instructor, 1960; International Atomic Energy Agency, Division of Economic and Technical Assistance, technical assistance officer, 1960-62; State University College of New York, associate professor of political science, 1962-64; Harvard University, research fellow, 1964-65; Arizona State University, associate professor, 1965-68, Foreign Service, advisor, International Relations Club, advisor, Center for Latin American Studies, faculty consultant; American Institute for Foreign Trade, lecturer and international education consultant, 1965-68; The University of Kuwait, visiting professor, 1982-83; The Institute for Public Administration, visiting professor, 1985-86; Group for the Advancement of Psychiatry, Committee on International Relations, consultant. Writer. **Publications:** A Diplomatic History of Modern Iraq, 1961; (comp.) Middle Eastern Constitutions and Electoral Laws, 1968; (contrib.) The Middle East: Its Government and Politics, 1972; (ed.) International Relations of the Middle East and North Africa, 1984; United Nations Enforcement Action: The Case of Iraq, A Comparative Study, forthcoming. Contributor of articles to journals. **Address:** University of Toledo, 2801 W Bancroft St., Toledo, OH 43606-3390, U.S.A. **Online address:** a_almarayati@yahoo.com

ALMOG, Ruth. (Almog Etinger). Israeli (born Israel), b. 1936?. **Genres:** Novels, Novellas/Short Stories, Children's Fiction. **Career:** Ha'aretz newspaper, deputy editor; Tel Aviv University, faculty; Hebrew University of Jerusalem, writer-in-residence; journalist. **Publications:** Hasade ha-lailah shel Margaretah, 1969; Be-erets gezerah, 1971; Aḥare ṭ u bi-Sheṿaṭ: shishah sipurim, 1979; Yamim shel etmol, 1981; Nashim (title means: 'Women'), 1986; Raḳefet, ahavati ha-rishonah (title means: ' Rakefet, My First Love'), 1992; Tiḳun omanuti (title means: 'Artistic Emendation'), 1993; Ha-Agam ha-penimi, 2000; Od ḥibuḳ eḥad, 2003; Kol ha-osher ha-mufraz ha-zeh: sipurim 1967-1997, 2003; Be-ahavah, Naṭalyah, 2005; Meil ḳaṭon, 2008; Zarah be-gan Eden, 2008. NOVELS: Be-erets gezerah (title means: 'Don't Hurry the Journey'), 1971; Et ha-zar yeha-oyev: duaḥ al ḥasimah, 1980; Mạvet ba-gashem: Roman, 1982 (title means: 'Death in the Rain: A Novel'), 1993; Shorshe ạvir (title means: ' Dangling Roots'), 1987; Six Israeli Novellas, 1999; The Inner Lake, 2001. CO-WRITER AS ALMOG ETINGER: A Perfect Lover; Eshtelina My Love. JUVENILE: Nafi, nesikh ha-ḳarnapim, 1979; Tso 'anim ba-pardes (title means: 'Gypsies in the Orchard'), 1986; Gilgil, 1986; Kadur ha-kesef, 1986; My Journey with Alex, 2000. Contributor to newspapers. **Address:** David R. Godine Publisher, 9 Hamilton Pl., Boston, MA 02108, U.S.A.

AL-MOHAIMEED, Yousef. Saudi (born Saudi Arabia), b. 1964. **Genres:** Novels, Translations. **Career:** Al- Jeel magazine, cultural page editor; Al-Jeel Al-Jadeed, children's magazine, founder; Al- Yamamah magazine, cultural editor. **Publications:** Rajfat athwabihim al beed, 1993; La budda anna ahadan harraka al kurrasa, 1996; Fikhakh al ra'iha, 2003; (trans.) Yousef al-Mohaimeed, Laghat mawta (title means: "The Dead's Gossip"), 2003; (trans.) Yousef al-Mohaimeed, Al nakhil wa al qirmid: Mushahadat min al Basra ila Norwich (title means "Palms & Brick: From Basra to Norwich"), 2004; (trans.) Yousef al-Mohaimeed, Al qarura (title means "The Bottle"), 2004; (trans.) Yousef al-Mohaimeed, Akhi yufattishuan 'an Rimbaud (title means "My Brother Is Looking for Rimbaud"), 2005; (trans.) Yousef al-Mohaimeed, Nozhat ad dolphin (title means "The Dolphin's Excursion"), 2006.

Address: PO Box 90521, Riyadh, 11623, Saudi Arabia. **Online address:** yalmohimeed@hotmail.com

ALMON, Russell. *See* **DOWNING, David A(lmon).**

ALMOND, Brenda. British (born England), b. 1937. **Genres:** Education, Ethics, Medicine/Health, Philosophy. **Career:** University of Connecticut, visiting lecturer, 1969-70; University of Surrey, lecturer to reader in philosophy, 1974-86; University of Hull, reader in philosophy and education, 1986-92, professor of moral and social philosophy, 1992-, now professor emeritus; Belle van Zuylen chair of philosophy, Utrecht University, visiting professor, 2003; Philosophical Society of England, president, Society for Applied Philosophy, vice president. Writer. **Publications:** Educational Thought: An Introduction, 1969; Education and the Individual, 1981; Means and Ends in Education, 1982; Moral Concerns, 1987; The Philosophical Quest, 1988, 2nd ed. as Exploring Philosophy, 1995; Exploring Ethics: A Traveller's Tale, 1998; The Fragmenting Family, 2006. EDITOR: (with B. Wilson) Values: A Symposium, 1988; (with G. Enderle and A. Argandona) People in Corporations: Ethical Responsibilities and Corporate Effectiveness, 1990; AIDS, a Moral Issue: The Ethical, Legal, and Social Aspects, 1990, 2nd ed., 1996; (with D. Hill) Applied Philosophy: Morals and Metaphysics in Contemporary Debate, 1991; Introducing Applied Ethics, 1995; (with M. Parker) Ethical Issues in the New Genetics, 2002. Contributor to journals. **Address:** Department of Philosophy, University of Hull, Cottingham Rd., Hull, SY HU6 7RX, England. **Online address:** brenda.almond@freedom255.co.uk

ALOFF, Mindy. American (born United States), b. 1947. **Genres:** Poetry, Dance/Ballet, Humanities, Literary Criticism And History, Writing/Journalism, Essays. **Career:** University of Portland, instructor in English, 1973-75; freelance writer and editor, 1975-80, 1988-89; Dance, national staff correspondent, 1976-80, associate critic, 1979-80, senior critic, 1980-91; Vassar Quarterly, editor, 1980-88; Nation, dance critic, 1983-93; New Yorker, weekly writer, 1987-93; New Republic, dance critic, 1993-2001; Princeton University, visiting lecturer, 1996; Portland State University, lecturer, 1976, 1977, 1979; Barnard College, adjunct professor, 1999-2000, adjunct associate professor, 2000-, assistant professor of professional practice, 2002-03, assistant professor dance, 2003-, lecturer in first-year seminar program, 2003-; Sarah Lawrence College, visiting lecturer, 2004; DCM, New York Philharmonic, telefundraiser, 2008-; Dance Critics Association, president, editor of newsletter, 2003-06, 2009-; Woodrow Wilson Foundation, fellow. **Publications:** Night Lights, 1979; Dance Anecdotes: Stories from the Worlds of Ballet, Broadway, The Ballroom and Modern Dance, 2006; (ed. and foreword) The Unpicturelikeness of Pollock, Soutine and Others: Selected Writings and Talks, 2008; Hippo in a Tutu: Dancing in Disney Animation, 2008; (ed.) Leaps in the Dark: Art and the World by Agnes de Mille, 2011. Contributor to periodicals. **Address:** Department of Dance, Barnard College, 3009 Broadway, New York, NY 10027-6598, U.S.A. **Online address:** mindyaloff@aol.com

ALOFSIN, Anthony. American (born United States), b. 1949. **Genres:** Novellas/Short Stories, Architecture, Art/Art History, Biography. **Career:** Columbia University, Graduate School of Architecture, Planning and Preservation, Division of Historic Preservation, associate chairman, 1983-84; University of Texas, associate professor of architecture, 1987-, adjunct professor of art and art history, 1988-, Center for American Architecture and Design, director, 1990-93, Kermacy professor, 1999-2000, Roland Gommel Roessner centennial professor in architecture, 2000-, professor of art and art history; National Gallery of Art, Center for Advanced Studies in the Visual Arts, Ailsa Mellon Bruce Senior Fellow, 2003-04; Internationales Forschungszentrum Kulturwissenschaften, fellow; Academy of Fine Arts Vienna, Fullbright professor. Writer. **Publications:** (With J.P. Conron) Socorro, a Historic Survey, 1980; (ed. and intro.) Frank Lloyd Wright: An Index to the Taliesin Correspondence, 1988; Frank Lloyd Wright: The Lost Years, 1910-1922, 1993; (foreword) Studies and Executed Buildings by Frank Lloyd Wright, 1998; (ed.) Frank Lloyd Wright: Europe and Beyond (essays), 1999; The Struggle for Modernism: Architecture, Landscape Architecture and City Planning at Harvard, 2002; (ed.) Prairie Skyscraper: Frank Lloyd Wright's Price Tower, 2005; When Buildings Speak: Architecture as Language in the Habsburg Empire and its Aftermath, 1867-1933, 2006; (ed.) Modernist Museum in Perspective: The East Building, National Gallery of Art, 2009; Frank Lloyd Wright, Art Collector: Secessionist Prints from the Turn of the Century, 2012. Contributor of articles to books and journals. **Address:** School of Architecture, University of Texas, WMB 4 102B, 1 University Sta. B7500, Austin, TX 78712, U.S.A. **Online address:** alofsin@mail.utexas.edu

ALON, Ilan. American/Israeli (born Israel), b. 1971. **Genres:** History, Economics, Business/Trade/Industry. **Career:** Kent State University, instructor of marketing and economics, 1994-98; State University of New York, assistant professor of international business, 1998-2002; Marketing Education Review, senior editor, 2000-; Rollins College, associate professor of international business, 2002-07, professor of international business, 2007-, Rollins China Center, executive director, director, 2005-, Jennifer J. Petters chair of international business, 2005-09, George D. and Harriet W. Cornell chair of international business, 2009-; Harvard University, China Goes Global, chair, 2008. **Publications:** The Internationalization of U.S. Franchising Systems, 1999; (ed. with D.H.B. Welsh) International Franchising in Emerging Markets: China, India and Other Asian Countries, 2001; (ed. with D.H.B. Welsh) International Franchising in Emerging Markets: Central and Eastern Europe and Latin America, 2001; International Franchising in Industrial Markets: North America Pacific Rim and Other Developed Countries, 2002; (ed.) Chinese Culture Organizational Behavior and International Business Management, 2002; (ed.) Chinese Economic Transition and International Marketing Strategy, 2003; (ed. with D.H.B. Welsh) International Franchising in Industrial Markets: Western and Northern Europe, 2003; (ed. with J.R. McIntyre) Business Education and Emerging Market Economies: Perspectives and Best Practices, 2004; (ed. with J.R. McIntyre) Business and Management Education in China: Transition, Pedagogy and Training, 2005; (ed. with J.R. McIntyre) Business and Management Education in Transitioning and Developing Countries: A Handbook, 2005; Business and Management Education in China, 2005; Service Franchising: An International Perspective, 2005; (ed. with J.R. McIntyre) Globalization of Chinese enterprises, 2008; (ed. with W. Zhang) Biographical Dictionary of New Chinese Entrepreneurs and Business Leaders: Zhongguo jing ji feng yun ren wu, 2009; (ed.) China Rules: Globalization and Political Transformation, 2009; Franchising Globally: Innovation, Learning and Imitation, 2010; (ed. with W. Zhang) Guide to the Top 100 Companies in China, 2010. Contributor of articles to books and periodicals. **Address:** Crummer Graduate School of Business, Rollins College, 100 Holt Ave., Ste. 2722, Winter Park, FL 32789-4499, U.S.A. **Online address:** ialon@rollins.edu

ALONSO, Eric Frattini. Spanish (born Spain), b. 1963?. **Genres:** Novels, Young Adult Fiction. **Career:** Writer. **Publications:** (With Y. Colias) Tiburones de la comunicación: grandes lideres de los grupos multimedia, 1996; Mafia, S.A.: 100 años de la cosa nostra, 2002; Secretos Vaticanos, 2003; La Santa Alianza, 2004; ONU: historia de la corrupción, 2005; El quinto mandamiento, 2007; CIA, Joyas de Familia, 2008; El laberinto de agua, 2009; Mossad, La ira de Israel, 2009; El oro de Mefisto, 2010; Los Papas y el Sexo, 2010. **Address:** St. Martin's Press, 175 5th Ave., New York, NY 10010, U.S.A. **Online address:** autor@ericfrattini.com

ALPERT, Mark. American (born United States), b. 1961. **Genres:** Novels, Sciences, Mystery/Crime/Suspense. **Career:** Claremont Eagle Times, reporter, 1984-85; Montgomery Advertiser, reporter, 1985-87; Fortune, writer, 1987-92; Popular Mechanics, freelance writer, 1992-97; Cable News Network, Moneyline, freelance writer, 1996-97; Scientific American, editor, 1998-. **Publications:** Final Theory: A Novel, 2008; Armageddon Theory: A Novel, 2011; Omega Theory: A Novel, 2011. Contributor of articles to newspapers and magazines. **Address:** Simon & Schuster Inc., 1230 Ave. of the Americas, New York, NY 10020, U.S.A. **Online address:** info@markalpert.com

ALPHIN, Elaine Marie. American (born United States), b. 1955. **Genres:** Children's Fiction, Young Adult Fiction, Children's Non-fiction, How-to Books, Young Adult Non-fiction, Novels. **Career:** Rice Thresher, writer and department editor, 1974-76; Houston (magazine), feature editor and writer, 1978-79; freelance writer, 1978-; A-Square Co., advertising manager and technical service manager, 1982-93; Hieroglyphics UnLtd., owner and cross-stitch designer, 1986-; Institute of Children's Literature, instructor, 1992-. **Publications:** The Ghost Cadet, 1991; The Proving Ground, 1992; 101 Bible Puzzles, 1993; Tournament of Time, 1994; Rainy Day/Sunny Day/Any Day Activities, 1994; A Bear for Miguel, 1996; Counterfeit Son, 2000; Creating Characters Kids Will Love, 2000; Ghost Soldier, 2001; Simon Says, 2002; Germ Hunter: A Story about Louis Pasteur, 2003; Davy Crockett, 2003; Dinosaur Hunter, 2003; Picture Perfect, 2003; I Have not Yet Begun to Fight: A Story about John Paul Jones, 2004; Dwight Eisenhower, 2004; The Perfect Shot, 2005; Unspeakable Crime: The Prosecution and Persecution of Leo Frank, 2009. HOUSEHOLD HISTORY SERIES: Vacuum Cleaners, 1997; Irons, 1998; Toasters, 1998; Telephones, 2000. Works appear in anthologies. Contributor of articles to periodicals. **Address:** PO Box 11423, Bozeman, MT 59719, U.S.A. **Online address:** elainemalphin@aol.com

ALPHONSO-KARKALA, John B. *See* **KARKALA, John A.**

AL-QAZWINI, Hasan. *See* **QAZWINI, Hassan.**

AL-RASHEED, Madawi. British/French (born France), b. 1962. **Genres:** Young Adult Non-fiction, Politics/Government, Theology/Religion. **Career:** University of London, Goldsmiths College, researcher, 1989-90, tutor, 1990-91, lecturer, 1990-91, King's College, London, lecturer, 1995-2001, senior lecturer, 2001-04, professor, 2004-; University of Oxford, Nuffield College, research fellow, 1991-94, university lecturer, 1994-95. Writer. **Publications:** NONFICTION: Politics in an Arabian Oasis: The Rashidi Tribal Dynasty, 1991; Iraqi Assyrian Christians in London: The Construction of Ethnicity, 1998; A History of Saudi Arabia, 2002, 2nd ed., 2010; Al-saudiyyah Wa Mazaq al-Islah Fi al-Qam al-Hadi Wa al-Ishrin, 2005; Contesting the Saudi State: Islamic Voices from a New Generation, 2007. EDITOR: (with R. Vitalis) Counter-Narratives: History, Contemporary Society and Politics in Saudi Arabia and Yemen, 2004; Transnational Connections and the Arab Gulf, 2005; Kingdom without Borders: Saudi Political, Religious and Media Frontiers, 2008; (with M. Shterin) Dying for Faith: Religiously Motivated Violence in the Contemporary World, 2009. Contributor of articles to journals. **Address:** Department of Theology and Religious Studies, King's College, University of London, London, GL WC2R 2LS, England. **Online address:** madawi.al-rasheed@kcl.ac.uk

ALS, Hilton. American (born United States), b. 1961?. **Genres:** Women's Studies And Issues, Art/Art History, Music, Biography. **Career:** Village Voice, staff writer; New Yorker, staff writer, 1994-2002, contributor, 1989-96, theatre critic, 2002; Vibe, editor-at-large; Grand Street, advisory editor; Backstage, dance critic; Ballet Review, dance critic. **Publications:** (Contrib.) Jane Wilson: October 12 through November 11, 1995, 1995; The Women (nonfiction), 1996; (contrib.) Our Town: Images and Stories from the Museum of the City of New York, 1997; (intro.) Leigh Bowery, 1998; David Salle, 1999; (with J. Lewis and L. Litwack) Without Sanctuary: Lynching Photography in America, 2000; (foreword) Strange Fruit: Billie Holiday, Cafe Society, and an Early Cry for Civil Rights, 2000; (with D. Margolick) Strange Fruit: The Biography of a Song, 2001; Drawing Us In: How We Experience Visual Art, 2001; (ed. with D.A. Turner) White Noise: The Group, 2001; The Eminem Collection, 2003; (contrib.with K. Schampers) Dana Lixenberg: Homeless in Jeffersonville, Indiana: Portraits and Landscapes Between 1997 and 2004, 2005; (contrib.) Lorna Simpson, 2006; (contrib.) Glenn Ligon: America, 2011. Contributor to periodicals. **Address:** 20 W 43rd St., New York, NY 10036, U.S.A.

ALSAMARI, Lewis. (Sarmed Al-Samarrai). British (born England), b. 1976?. **Genres:** Autobiography/Memoirs, Biography. **Career:** Writer, actor, producer and human rights activist. **Publications:** Escape from Saddam: The Incredible True Story of One Man's Journey to Freedom (autobiography), 2007; Out of Iraq, 2007. Contributor to periodicals. **Address:** c/o Barbara Levy, 64 Greenhill, Hampstead High St., London, GL NW3 5TZ, England.

AL-SAMARRAI, Sarmed. *See* **ALSAMARI, Lewis.**

AL-SAMMAN, Ghadah. Lebanese (born Lebanon), b. 1942?. **Genres:** Novels, Poetry, History. **Career:** Manshurat Ghadah al-Samman, founder and publisher; Damascus University, teacher; Syrian University, president. Novelist. **Publications:** Layl al-ghuraba', 1966; Hubb, 1973; Bayrut '75, 1974; Aynaka qadari, 1975; La bahr fi Bayrut, 1975; A'lantu 'alayka al-hubb, 1976; Kawabis Bayrut, 1977; Al-A'mal ghayr al-kamilah, 1978; Ghurbah tahta al-sifr, 1986; Laylat al-milyar, 1986; Al-A'maq al-muhtallah, 1987; Raheel al-Marafi' al-Kadima, 1992; Al-Qamar al-murabba': Qisas ghara'ibiyah, 1994; 'Ashiqah fi mihbarah, 1995; Shahwat al-ajnihah, 1995; Rasa'il al-hanin ila al-yasam, 1996; Al-Riwayah al-mustahilah: fusayfasa? Dimashqiyah, 1997; Al-Qalb nawras wahid, 1998; Al-Abadiyah lahzat hubb, 1999; Sahrah tanakkuriyah lil-mawta, 2003; Al-Raqs ma'a al-bum, 2003; Ra'shat al-hurriyah, 2003; Muhakamat Hubb, 2004; Al Habeeb al Iftiradi, 2005; Imra ah 'Arabiyah-wa-hurrah, 2006. **Address:** Manshurat Ghada Samman, PO Box 111813, Beirut, 416, Lebanon.

ALSCHULER, William R. American (born United States) **Genres:** Science Fiction/Fantasy, Astronomy. **Career:** Future Museums, founder and principal; California Institute of Arts, professor of science; Harvard University, faculty; Massachusetts Institute of Technology, faculty; Boston Architectural Center, staff; University of California, Science Center, consultant; Getty Education Institute, consultant; California College of the Arts, senior adjunct professor of critical studies. Writer. **Publications:** (Ed. with B. Preiss) The Microverse, 1989; (ed. with B. Preiss, H. Zimmerman and B. Bova) First Contact: The Search for Extraterrestrial Intelligence, 1990; UFOs and Aliens: What Would You Do If You Met an Alien?, 1991; The Science of UFOs: An Astronomer Examines the Technology of Alien Spacecraft, How They Travel, and the Aliens Who Pilot Them, 2001. **Address:** c/o Author Mail, St. Martin's Press, 175 5th Ave., New York, NY 10010-7703, U.S.A. **Online address:** alschulr@calarts.edu

ALSDORF, Debbie. American (born United States), b. 1955?. **Genres:** Theology/Religion. **Career:** Cornerstone Fellowship, pastor and director of women's ministries; Design4Living Conferences, founder and director, 2000-. Writer and biblical lay-counselor. **Publications:** Steadfast Love, 2000; Living Love, 2000; Restoring Love, 2001; My New Relationships in Christ, 2003; Deeper: Living in the Reality of God's Love, 2008; A Different Kind of Wild: Is Your Faith Too Tame?, 2009; Faith Dare: 30 Days to Live your Life to the Fullest, 2010; (with R. Alsdorf) Beyond the Brady Bunch: Hope and Help for Blended Families, 2010; Woman who Trusts God: Finding the Peace You Long For, 2011. **Address:** c/o Les Stobbe, Leslie H. Stobbe Agency, 300 Doubleday Rd., Tryon, NC 28782-2982, U.S.A. **Online address:** debbie@design4living.org

ALSENAS, Linas. Swedish/American (born United States), b. 1979. **Genres:** Children's Fiction, Young Adult Non-fiction, Picture/Board Books. **Career:** Harry N. Abrams Inc., editor. Illustrator and writer. **Publications:** SELF ILLUSTRATED: Mrs. Claus Takes a Vacation, 2006; Peanut, 2007; Gay America: Struggle for Equality, 2008; Hello, My Name is Bob, 2009. Contributor to periodicals. **Address:** Scholastic Inc., 557 Broadway, New York, NY 10012-3999, U.S.A. **Online address:** linas@alsenas.com

ALSHAWI, Hiyan. American/Iraqi (born Iraq), b. 1957. **Genres:** Language/Linguistics, Technology, Information Science/Computers, Humanities. **Career:** Cambridge University, postdoctoral research fellow, 1984-85; SRI Intl., senior computer scientist, 1986-92; American Telephone and Telegraph Bell Laboratories, staff, 1993-. Writer. **Publications:** Memory and Context for Language Interpretation, 1987; (ed.) The Core Language Engine, 1992. **Address:** American Telephone and Telegraph Bell Laboratories, 2C-548C, 600 Mountain Ave., Murray Hill, NJ 07974-2070, U.S.A. **Online address:** hiyan@research.att.com

ALSON, Peter (H.). American (born United States), b. 1955. **Genres:** Autobiography/Memoirs, Sports/Fitness, Biography. **Career:** Writer. **Publications:** Confessions of an Ivy League Bookie, 1996; (with N. Dalla) One of a Kind: The Rise and Fall of Stuey the Kid Ungar, the World's Greatest Poker Player, 2005; Take Me to the River: A Wayward and Perilous Journey to the World Series of Poker, 2006; (with N. Dalla) One of a Kind: The Rise and Fall of Stuey 'The Kid' Ungar, the World's Greatest Poker Player, 2006; (with T. Atlas) Atlas: From the Street to the Ring: A Son's Struggle, 2007. Contributor of articles to periodicals. Work appears in anthologies. **Address:** c/o Elizabeth Shinkman, Elaine Markson Literary Agency, 44 Greenwich Ave., New York, NY 10011, U.S.A. **Online address:** peteralson@aol.com

ALT, Betty L. *See* **ALT, Betty Sowers.**

ALT, Betty Sowers. (Betty L. Alt). American (born United States), b. 1931. **Genres:** History, Sociology, Social Sciences. **Career:** University of Colorado, instructor in sociology, 1989-95; Colorado State University, instructor in sociology, 1991-. Free-ance writer; Hawaii Pacific College, lecturer; Christopher Newport College, lecturer; University of Maryland, lecturer; Auburn University, lecturer. **Publications:** (With B.D. Stone) Uncle Sam's Brides, 1990; (with Stone) Campfollowing: A History of the Military Wife, 1991; (with S. Folts) Weeping Violins: The Gypsy Tragedy in Europe, 1996; (with W.K. Patterson) Slaughter in Cell House 3, 1997; (with S. Wells) Wicked Women, 2000; (with W. Alt) Black Soldiers-White Wars, 2002; (with W.K. Patterson) Keeper of the Keys: A Warden's Notebook, 2003; (with S. Wells) Fleecing Grandma and Grandpa, 2004; (with S.K. Wells) Police Women: Life With the Badge, 2005; Following the Flag: Marriage and the Modern Military, 2006; (with S. Wells)When Caregivers Kill, 2010. **Address:** The Seymour Agency, 475 Miner Street Rd., Canton, NY 13617-9614, U.S.A. **Online address:** balt@aol.com

ALTEMEYER, Bob. (Robert Altemeyer). Canadian/American (born United

States), b. 1940. **Genres:** Psychology, Theology/Religion, Social Sciences, Adult Non-fiction. **Career:** University of Manitoba, associate professor of psychology, 1968-, professor, now retired. Writer. **Publications:** Right-Wing Authoritarianism, 1981; Enemies of Freedom: Understanding Right-Wing Authoritarianism, 1988; The Authoritarian Specter, 1996; (with B. Hunsberger) Amazing Conversions: Why Some Turn to Faith and Others Abandon Religion, 1997; (with B.E. Hunsberger) Atheists: A Groundbreaking Study of America's Nonbelievers, 2006; The Authoritarians, 2006; Sex and Youth, 2009. **Address:** Department of Psychology, University of Manitoba, P404 Duff Roblin Bldg., 190 Dysart Rd., Winnipeg, MB R3T 2N2, Canada. **Online address:** altemey@cc.umanitoba.ca

ALTEMEYER, Robert. *See* **ALTEMEYER, Bob.**

ALTEN, Steve. American (born United States), b. 1959. **Genres:** Novels. **Career:** Writer. **Publications:** MEG SERIES: Meg: A Novel of Deep Terror (horror-thriller novel), 1997; The Trench, 1999; Meg: Primal Waters, 2004; Hell's Aquarium, 2009. DOMAIN SERIES: Domain, 2001; Resurrection, 2004; Phobos: Mayan Fear, 2011. NOVELS: Goliath, 2002; The Loch, 2005; The Shell Game, 2007; Grim Reaper: End of Days, 2010. **Address:** Alten Entertainment, 9447 Coventry Lake Ct., 2nd Fl., West Palm Beach, FL 33411, U.S.A. **Online address:** meg82159@aol.com

ALTENBURG, Matthias. (Jan Seghers). German (born Germany), b. 1958?. **Genres:** Novels, Novellas/Short Stories. **Career:** Ein kleiner Abend Glück, creator and performer; Frankfurt publishing house of the authors, lecturer, 1987-96; Freelance writer. **Publications:** Fremde Mütter, fremde Väter, fremdes Land: Gespräche mit Franz Josef Degenhardt, Gisela Elsner, Gerd Fuchs, Josef Haslinger, Hermann Peter Piwitt, E.A. Rauter, Michael Schneider, Guntram Vesper, 1985; Die Liebe der Menschenfresser: Roman, 1992; Die Toten von Laroque: Novelle, 1994; Alles wird gut, 1997; Landschaft mit Wölfen, 1997; Zwei Entwürfe zum Holocaust-Denkmal in Berlin, 2001; Partisanen der Schönheit, 2002; Irgendwie alles Sex, 2002; Ein allzu schönes Mädchen, 2004; (as Jan Seghers) Die Braut im Schnee, 2005; (as Jan Seghers) Partitur des Todes, 2008. Contributor to periodicals. **Address:** c/o Author Mail, Verlag Kiepenheuer und Witsch, Rondorfer Str. 5, Cologne, 50968, Germany.

ALTER, Judith MacBain. *See* **ALTER, Judy.**

ALTER, Judy. (Judith MacBain Alter). American (born United States), b. 1938. **Genres:** Novels, Children's Fiction, Children's Non-fiction, Local History/Rural Topics, Biography, Food And Wine. **Career:** Chicago Osteopathic Center, typist and secretary, 1954-61; Roundup Magazine, columnist; Kirksville College of Osteopathic Medicine, writer and editor in public relations, 1962-64; Texas College of Osteopathic Medicine, writer and editor in public relations, 1962-64, director of publications, 1972, acting director of public information, 1977-78, associate director of news and information, 1978-80; Fort Worth Osteopathic Hospital, secretary, 1965-66, editor of employee publication, 1965-73, public relations consultant, 1971-73; freelance writer, 1973-75; Ft. Worth Star Telegram, columnist, 1974-75; Texas Christian University, instructor of English, 1975-76, Texas Christian University Press, editor, 1982-87, director, 1987-2009, retired, 2009; Western Writers of America, president; Texas Institute of Letters, secretary-treasurer. **Publications:** (With P. Russell) The Quack Doctor, 1974; Stewart Edward White, 1975; After Pa was Shot, 1978; (with S. Pearson) Single Again, 1978; Dorothy Johnson, 1980; The Texas ABC Book, 1981; (ed. with J. Roach) Texas and Christmas: A Collection of Traditions, Memories & Folklore, 1983; Luke and the Van Zandt County War: A Novel, 1984; Thistle Hill: The History and the House, 1988; Mattie, 1988; Elmer Kelton and West Texas: A Literary Relationship, 1989; Maggie and a Horse Named Devildust, 1989; Maggie and the Search for Devildust, 1989; Women of the Old West, 1989; Growing Up in the Old West, 1989; Maggie and Devildust Ridin' High, 1990; Eli Whitney, 1990; American Osteopathic College of Radiology: A Fifty-year History, 1990; Texas College of Osteopathic Medicine: The First 20 Years, 1990; Jeanne Williams, 1991; Katie and the Recluse, 1991; A Ballad for Sallie, 1992; Libbie, 1994; (ed. with A.T. Row) Unbridled Spirits: Short Fiction about Women in the Old West, 1994; Comanches, 1994; Jessie: A Novel Based on the Life of Jessie Benton Fremont, 1995; Cherokee Rose: A Novel of America's First Cowgirl, 1996; Callie Shaw, Stableboy, 1996; (as Judith Alter) Rodeos: The Greatest Show on Dirt, 1996; Beauty Pageants: Tiaras, Roses and Runways, 1997; Wild West Shows: Rough Riders and Sure Shots, 1997; Meet Me at the Fair: County, State and World's Fairs and Expositions, 1997; Amusement Parks: Rollercoasters, Ferris Wheels and Cotton Candy, 1997; Sam Houston: A Leader for Texas, 1998; Cissie Palmer, 1998; The Santa Fe Trail, 1998; Extraordinary Woman of the American West, 1999; Christopher Reeve: Triumph Over Tragedy, 2000; Exploring and Mapping the American West, 2001; Great Women of the Old West, 2001; Extraordinary Explorers and Adventurers, 2001; Sundance, Butch and Me, 2002; Ulysses S. Grant, 2002; Texas, 2002; (ed. with J.W. Lee) Literary Fort Worth, 2002; Harry S. Truman, 2002; Indian Wars, 2002; New Mexico, 2002; Abraham Lincoln, 2002; Andrew Johnson: A MyReportLinks.com Book, 2002; Williamsburg, 2003; Washington, D.C., 2003; Christopher Columbus: Explorer, 2003; Sam Houston is My Hero, 2003; Samuel F.B. Morse: Inventor and Code Creator, 2003; Daniel Boone: Frontiersman, 2003; Illinois, 2003; Mexican Americans, 2003; Missouri, 2003; Montana, 2003; North Carolina, 2003; Sacagawea: Native American Interpreter, 2003; Native Americans, 2003; Discovering Australia's Land, People and Wildlife, 2004; The North Carolina Colony, 2004; Laura Ingalls Wilder: Pioneer and Author, 2004; Discovering North America's Land, People and Wildlife, 2004; (with P. Messersmith) Mirabeau B. Lamar: Second President of Texas, 2005; (with P. Messersmith) Henrietta King: Rancher and Philanthropist, 2005; Miriam Ma Ferguson: First Woman Governor of Texas, 2006; (co-ed.) Noah's Ride: A Collaborative Western Novel, 2006; Sue Ellen Learns to Dance: And Other Stories, 2006; (with P. Messersmith) Martín de Léon: Tejano Empresario, 2007; John Barclay Armstrong, Texas Ranger, 2007; Audie Murphy: War Hero and Movie Star, 2007; (contrib.) The Oscar E. Monnig Meteorite Gallery at TCU, 2007; Women's Rights, 2008; Extraordinary Texas Women, 2008; (as Judith Alter) Oprah Winfrey, 2008; Great Texas Chefs (cookbook), 2008; Vaccines, 2008; Surgery, 2008; Passenger ships, 2009; Cooking My Way Through Life with Kids and Books (cookbook), 2009; (ed. with K. Sherrod) Grace & Gumption: The Cookbook, 2010; (ed. with J.W. Lee) Elmer Kelton: Essays and Memories, 2011; Skeleton in a Dead Space, forthcoming. **Address:** Texas Christian University Press, 3000 Sandage, PO Box 298300, Fort Worth, TX 76109-1768, U.S.A. **Online address:** judy@judyalter.com

ALTER, Robert B. American (born United States), b. 1935. **Genres:** Literary Criticism And History, Theology/Religion, Biography. **Career:** Columbia University, instructor, 1962-64, assistant professor of English, 1964-66; University of California-Berkeley, associate professor, 1967-69, professor of Hebrew and comparative literature, 1969-89, chair of comparative literature department, 1970-72, 1988-89, professor, 1989-, Class of 1937 Professor of Hebrew and Comparative Literature, Jewish Studies, director. Writer. **Publications:** Rogue's Progress: Studies in the Picaresque Novel, 1964; Fielding and the Nature of the Novel, 1968; After the Tradition: Essays on Modern Jewish Writing, 1969; America and Israel, Literary and Intellectual Trends: Based on Lectures by Robert Alter, 1970; Partial Magic: The Novel as a Self-Conscious Genre, 1975; (ed. and intro.) Modern Hebrew Literature, 1975; Exchange of Letters between Robert Alter and Shlomo Avineri, 1975; Defenses of the Imagination: Jewish Writers and Modern Historical Crisis, 1977; (with C. Cosman) A Lion for Love: A Critical Biography of Stendhal, 1979, rev. ed., 1986; The Art of Biblical Narrative, 1981, rev. ed., 2011; Motives for Fiction, 1984; The Art of Biblical Poetry, 1985, rev. ed., 2011; (ed. with F. Kermode) The Literary Guide to the Bible, 1987; Invention of Hebrew Prose: Modern Fiction and the Language of Realism, 1988; The Pleasures of Reading in an Ideological Age, 1989; Necessary Angels: Tradition and Modernity in Kafka, Benjamin and Scholem, 1991; The World of Biblical Literature, 1992; Hebrew and Modernity, 1994; Genesis: Translation and Commentary, 1996; (trans.) Genesis, 1996; The David Story: A Translation with Commentary of 1 and 2 Samuel, 1999; Canon and Creativity: Modern Writing and the Authority of Scripture, 2000; On Biblical Narrative, 2000; Five Books of Moses: A Translation with Commentary, 2004; (ed. and intro.) Pleasure and Change: The Aesthetics of Canon, 2004; Imagined Cities: Urban Experience and the Language of the Novel, 2005; Gates of Bronze, 2005; The Book of Psalms: A Translation with Commentary, 2007; Pen of Iron: American Prose and the King James Bible, 2010; The Wisdom Books: Job, Proverbs and Ecclesiastes, 2010. **Address:** Department of Comparative Literature, University of California, 4315 Dwinelle Hall, Berkeley, CA 94720-2510, U.S.A. **Online address:** altcos@berkeley.edu

ALTERMAN, Eric (Ross). American (born United States), b. 1960. **Genres:** Politics/Government, History, Social Sciences. **Career:** Business Executives for National Security, associate for public policy, 1983-84; World Policy Institute, senior fellow, 1985-; Center for American Progress, senior fellow; The Nation, columnist, 1977-95; The Forward Magazine, columnist; The Daily Beast Magazine, columnist; Rolling Stone Magazine, columnist; Elle Magazine, contributing editor; London Sunday Express Magazine, columnist; The

Liberal Media Magazine, columnist; Worth Magazine, columnist; Stanford University, peace studies fellow, 1992; World Policy Journal, critic-at-large, 1992-; Mother Jones Magazine, columnist, 1992-; Microsoft/National Broadcasting Co., commentator, 1996; City University of New York, Brooklyn College, distinguished professor of English, 2007, Graduate School of Journalism, professor of journalism; New York University, adjunct professor of Journalism; Columbia University, adjunct professor of Journalism; Nation Institute, fellow; Media Matters for America, senior fellow, 2006. **Publications:** Sound and Fury: the Washington Punditocracy and the Collapse of American Politics, 1992; Sound and Fury: The Making of the Punditocracy, 1993, 2nd ed., 2000; Who Speaks for America? Why Democracy Matters in Foreign Policy, 1998; It Ain't No Sin to Be Glad You're Alive, 1999; What Liberal Media? The Truth About Bias and the News, 2003; (with M. Green) The Book on Bush, 2004; When Presidents Lie: A History of Official Deception and its Consequences, 2004; Why We're Liberals: A Political Handbook to Post-Bush America, 2008; Kabuki Democracy: The System vs. Barack Obama, 2011. Contributor to periodicals. **Address:** The Nation, 33 Irving Pl., 8th Fl., New York, NY 10003, U.S.A. **Online address:** alterman.eric@gmail.com

ALTERMAN, Glenn. American (born United States), b. 1946. **Genres:** Self Help, Art/Art History, Film, Photography, Humanities. **Career:** Old Dominion University, staff. Journalist and consultant. **Publications:** Street Talk: Character Monologues for Actors, 1991; Uptown: Original Monologues, 1992; Two Minutes and Under: Original Character Monologues for Actors, 1993; (ed.) What to Give Your Agent for Christmas: An 100 Other Suggestions for the Working Actor, 1995; Beginnings: Monologues of the Stars, 1996; Promoting Your Acting Career, 1998; Two-Minute Monologs: Original Audition Scenes for Professional Actors, 1998; Creating Your Own Monologue, 1999, rev. ed., 2005; An Actor's Guide: Making It in New York, 2002; More Two Minutes and Under: Character Monologues for Actors, 2002; The Perfect Audition Monologue, 2003; Promoting Your Acting Career: A Step-by-Step Guide to Opening the Right Doors, 2004; 60 Seconds to Shine, vol. III: 101 One-Minute Monologues, 2006; Glenn Alterman's Secrets to Successful Cold Readings, 2007; Actor's Guide-Making it in New York City, 2011. Works appear in anthologies. **Address:** The Glenn Alterman Studio, 400 W 43rd St., Ste. 7-9, New York, NY 10036-6304, U.S.A. **Online address:** glenn@glennalterman.com

ALTHEIDE, David L. American (born United States) **Genres:** Sociology, Popular Culture, Social Sciences, Social Commentary, Communications/Media, Cultural/Ethnic Topics. **Career:** Southern Colorado State College, instructor, 1968-70, assistant professor, 1970-71, acting department chair, 1971; University of California, teaching assistant, 1971-72; Grossmont College, part-time instructor, 1971-72; Chapman College, part-time instructor, 1972-73; San Diego State University, part-time instructor, 1972; Arizona State University, visiting assistant professor, 1974-75, assistant professor, 1975-79, associate professor of sociology, 1979-92, Center for the Study of Justice, associate professor, 1982-83, School of Justice Studies, professor, 1983-90, regents' professor, 1990-, now professor emeritus, interim director, 2000-01; Lincoln Center for Applied Ethics, teaching fellow, 2002; Evergreen State College, faculty, 2008-09. Writer. **Publications:** Creating Reality: How TV News Distorts Events, 1976; (with R.P. Snow) Media Logic, 1979; (with J.M. Johnson) Bureaucratic Propaganda, 1980; Media Power, 1985; (with R.P. Snow) Media Worlds in the Postjournalism Era, 1991; An Ecology of Communication: Cultural Formats of Control, 1995; Qualitative Media Analysis, 1996; Creating Fear: News and the Construction of Crisis, 2002; Terrorism and the Politics of Fear, 2006; Terror Post 9/11 and the Media, 2009. **Address:** School of Justice and Social Inquiry, Arizona State University, 50 Wilson Hall, 1711 S Rural Rd., Ste. 125, 240 E Orange Mall, PO Box 874902, Tempe, AZ 85287-4902, U.S.A. **Online address:** david.altheide@asu.edu

ALTHER, Lisa. American (born United States), b. 1944. **Genres:** Novels, Novellas/Short Stories, Writing/Journalism, Human Relations/Parenting. **Career:** Atheneum Publishers, secretary and editorial assistant, 1967; freelance writer, 1967-; Garden Way Inc., writer, 1970-; St. Michael's College, fiction instructor, 1980; East Tennessee State University, Basler Chair, 1999, instructor. **Publications:** NOVELS: Kinflicks, 1975; Original Sins, 1981; Other Women, 1984; Bedrock, 1990; Birdman and the Dancer, 1993; Five Minutes in Heaven, 1995; Kinfolks: Falling Off The Family Tree: The Search for My Melungeon Ancestors, 2007; Washed in the Blood, 2011. OTHERS: (intro.) A Good Man Is Hard to Find, 1980. Contributor of articles to magazines. **Address:** c/o Martha Kaplan, Martha Kaplan Agency, 115 W 29th St., Ste. 3, New York, NY 10001-5080, U.S.A. **Online address:** lisaalther@lisaalther.com

ALTMAN, Dennis. Australian (born Australia), b. 1943. **Genres:** Sex, Social Commentary, Gay And Lesbian Issues, Politics/Government. **Career:** Monash University, lecturer in politics, 1966-68; University of Sydney, lecturer, 1969-75, senior lecturer, 1975-80; University of California, regents lecturer, 1983; La Trobe University, reader and lecturer, 1986-94, professor, 1994-, Institute for Human Security, director, faculty of humanities and social sciences; AIDS Society of Asia and the Pacific, president, 2001-05; Harvard University, visiting professor of Australian studies, 2005; Writer. **Publications:** Homosexual: Oppression and Liberation, 1971, rev. ed., 1992; Coming Out in the Seventies, 1979; Rehearsals for Change, 1980, 2nd ed., 2004; Coming-Out in the Seventies, 1981; The Homosexualization of America, 1982; AIDS and the New Puritanism, 1986; AIDS in the Mind of America, 1986; Paper Ambassadors: The Politics of Stamps, 1991; The Comfort of Men, 1993; Power and Community, 1994; Defying Gravity, 1997; Global Sex, 2001; Rehersals for Change, 2004; 51st State, 2006. **Address:** Politics and international Relations Program, La Trobe University, Rm. Social Sciences 328, Bundoora, VI 3086, Australia. **Online address:** d.altman@latrobe.edu.au

ALTMAN, Mara. American (born United States), b. 1981. **Genres:** Autobiography/Memoirs, Biography. **Career:** International Herald Tribune, writer, 2005-06; Village Voice, staff writer, 2006-07; New York Times, journalist; Columbia University, Journalism School, adjunct faculty. **Publications:** Thanks for Coming: One Young Woman's Quest for an Orgasm, 2009. **Address:** c/o Chris Parris-Lamb, Gernert Co., 136 E 57th St., New York, NY 10022, U.S.A. **Online address:** maraaltman@yahoo.com

ALTMAN, Suzanne. *See* **ORGEL, Doris.**

ALTMANN, Simon L(eonardo). British/Argentine (born Argentina), b. 1924. **Genres:** Poetry, Philosophy, Physics, Sciences. **Career:** University of Buenos Aires, demonstrator, 1952, professor of chemical physics, 1957-58; Oxford University, Mathematical Institute, research assistant, 1953-57, lecturer in theory of metals, 1959-91, Brasenose College, fellow and lecturer in mathematical physics, 1964-91, vice-principal, 1990-91; University of Rome, lecturer, 1963, 1965, 1967, 1970, visiting professor, 1972, 1985; Shell Research Laboratories, lecturer, 1963; United Kingdom Atomic Energy Authority, lecturer, 1966; University of Darmstadt, lecturer, 1972; University of Stockholm, visiting professor, 1972; Technische Hochschule, visiting professor, 1975; Technion-Israel Institute of Technology, visiting professor, 1978; University of Texas, distinguished lecturer, 1979; University of Zaragoza, visiting professor, 1979, visiting lecturer, 1991; University of Perugia, lecturer, 1982; Johns Hopkins University, visiting professor, 1986; Catholic University of Louvain, Vlaamse Leergangen professor, 1989-90; University of Vienna, visiting professor, 1992. Writer. **Publications:** Band Theory of Metals: The Elements, 1970; Induced Representations in Crystals and Molecules: Point, Space and Nonrigid Molecule Groups, 1977; Rotations, Quaternions and Double Groups, 1986; Band Theory of Solids, 1991; Icons and Symmetries, 1992; (with P. Herzig) Point-Group Theory Tables, 1994; Is Nature Supernatural?, 2002; (ed. with E.L. Ortiz) Mathematics and Social Utopias in France: Olinde Rodrigues and his Times, 2005. Contributor to books and journals. **Address:** Brasenose College, Oxford University, Oxford, OX OX1 4AJ, England. **Online address:** simon.altmann@bnc.ox.ac.uk

ALTOFF, Gerard T(homas). American (born United States), b. 1949. **Genres:** History, Military/Defense/Arms Control, inspirational/Motivational Literature, Humanities. **Career:** U.S. Forest Service, Ashley National Forest, forest aide, 1972; National Park Service, Zion National Park, park technician, 1972-75; Theodore Roosevelt National Park, district naturalist, 1975-79; Perry's Victory and International Peace Memorial, chief ranger, 1979-2004, historian. Writer. **Publications:** The Great Lake Erie, 1987; War on the Great Lakes, 1991; Deep Water Sailors-Shallow Water Soldiers: Manning the United States Fleet on Lake Erie, 1813, 1993; Amongst My Best Men: African-Americans and the War of1812, 1996; Ohio: The Perry Group, 1996; (with D.C. Skaggs) A Signal Victory: The Lake Erie Campaign, 1812-1813, 1997; Oliver Hazard Perry and the Battle of Lake Erie, 1999. Contributor to books and periodicals. **Address:** The Perry Group, PO Box 484, Put in Bay, OH 43456, U.S.A. **Online address:** gerryaltoff@nps.gov

ALTSCHULER, Glenn C. American (born United States), b. 1950?. **Genres:** Music, History, Young Adult Non-fiction, Military/Defense/Arms Control, Humanities. **Career:** Cornell University, faculty, 1981-, Thomas and Dorothy Litwin professor of American studies, School of Continuing

Education and Summer Sessions, dean, 1991, Weiss Presidential fellow, University Relations, vice president. Writer. **Publications:** Andrew D. White: Educator, Historian, Diplomat, 1979; Race, Ethnicity and Class in American Social Thought, 1865-1919, 1982; (with J.M. Saltzgaber) Revivalism, Social Conscience and Community in the Burned-over District: The Trial of Rhoda Bement, 1983; Better Than Second Best: Love and Work in the Life of Helen Magill, 1990; (with D.I. Grossvogel) Changing Channels: America in TV Guide, 1992; (with S.M. Blumin) Rude Republic: Americans and Their Politics in the Nineteenth Century, 2000; All Shook Up: How Rock n Roll Changed America, 2003. (with I. Kramnick and R.L. Moore) The 100 Most Notable Cornellians, 2003; (with S.M. Blumin) GI Bill: A New Deal for Veterans, 2009. Contributor of articles to journals. **Address:** School of Continuing Education and Summer Sessions, Cornell University, B20 Day Hall, Ithaca, NY 14853, U.S.A. **Online address:** gca1@cornell.edu

ALTUN, Selcuk. Turkish (born Turkey), b. 1950?. **Genres:** Criminology/True Crime, Young Adult Fiction. **Career:** Writer. **Publications:** Songs My Mother Never Taught Me, 2008; Many and Many a Year Ago, 2009. **Address:** Istanbul, Turkey. **Online address:** saltun@superonline.com

ALVARADO, Lisa. American (born United States), b. 1956. **Genres:** Young Adult Fiction, Poetry, Novellas/Short Stories. **Career:** La Onda Negra Press, founder and publisher, 1995-; Chicago Public Library, artist teacher, 1995; R.E.A.C.H. Institute, artist instructor, 1996; General Woods Boys & Girls Club, artist instructor, 1996; WBEZ Radio, assistant producer, 1996; Gallery 37, lead artist, 1997; North Park University, adjunct faculty of English, 2008; Columbia College, adjunct professor of English, 2008-09. Novelist and literary critic. **Publications:** The Housekeeper's Diary, 2001; (with A.H. Cardinal and J.A. Coralin) Sister Chicas, 2006; Raw Silk Suture (poetry), 2008. **Address:** La Onda Negra Press, 2503 W Winnemac Ave., Chicago, IL 60625-2643, U.S.A. **Online address:** lisa@lisaalvarado.net

ALVAREZ, A(lfred). British (born England), b. 1929. **Genres:** Novels, Poetry, Literary Criticism And History, Autobiography/Memoirs, Education, Humanities. **Career:** Oxford University, Corpus Christi College, tutor in English, 1954-55; Princeton University, Observer, poetry editor and critic, 1956-66; freelance writer, 1956; Journal of Education, poetry critic and editor, 1957; Brandeis University, visiting professor, 1960-61; Penguin Modern European Poets in Translation, advisory editor, 1965-75; State University of New York, visiting professor, 1966; Channel 4 Television, Voices Program, presenter, 1982. **Publications:** NOVELS: Hers, 1974; Hunt, 1978; Day of Atonement, 1991. POETRY: A. Alvarez, 1952; The End of It, 1958; Twelve Poems, 1968; Lost, 1968; (with R. Fuller and A. Thwaite) Penguin Modern Poets 18, 1970; Apparition, 1971; The Legacy, 1972; Autumn to Autumn and Selected Poems 1953-1976, 1978; New and Selected Poems, 2002. OTHERS: The Shaping Spirit: Studies in Modern English and American Poets in US as Stewards of Excellence: Studies in Modern English and American Poets, 1958; The School of Donne, 1961; (ed. and intro.) The New Poetry: An Anthology, 1962, rev. ed. 1968; Under Pressure: The Writer in Society: Eastern Europe and the USA, 1965; Beyond All This Fiddle: Essays, 1955-67, 1968; The Savage God: A Study of Suicide, 1971; Samuel Beckett, 1973; (ed. with David Skilton) Thomas Hardy, 1978; Life after Marriage: Scenes from Divorce in US as Life after Marriage: Love in an Age of Divorce, 1982; The Biggest Game in Town, 1983; Offshore: A North Sea Journey, 1986; Feeding the Rat: Profile of a Climber, 1988; (with C. Blackman) Rainforest, 1988; Night: An Exploration of Night Life, Night Language, Sleep and Dreams, 1995; Where Did It All Go Right? (autobiography), 1999; Poker: Bets, Bluffs and Bad Beats, 2001; Feeding the Rat: A Climber's Life on the Edge, 2001; The Writer's Voice, 2005; Risky Business: People, Pastimes, Poker and Books, 2008. EDITOR: The New Poetry: An Anthology, 1962; The Faber Book of Modern European Poetry, 1992. **Address:** Gillon Aitken Associates Ltd., 29 Fernshaw Rd., London, GL SW10 0TG, England. **Online address:** aalvarez@compuserve.com

ALVAREZ, Julia. American (born United States), b. 1950. **Genres:** Novels, Young Adult Fiction, Poetry, Essays, Theology/Religion. **Career:** Kentucky Arts Commission, writer-in-residence; poet-in-schools, 1975-78; Phillips Andover Academy, instructor in English, 1979-81; The Artists Foundation, research consultant, 1980-81; University of Vermont, visiting assistant professor of creative writing, 1981-83; Middlebury College, thesis reader, 1982-84, associate professor of English, professor, 1988-97, writer-in-residence, 1997-; George Washington University, Jenny McKean Moore visiting writer, 1984-85; University of Illinois, assistant professor of English, 1985-88; American Library Association, honorary co-chair, 2009-. **Publications:** POETRY: (ed.) Old Age Ain't for Sissies, 1979; The Housekeeping Book, 1984; Homecoming: New and Selected Poems, 1984, rev. ed., 1996; The Other Side/El Otro Lado, 1995; Seven Trees, 1998; The Woman I Kept to Myself, 2004. NOVELS: How the Garcia Girls Lost Their Accents, 1991; In the Time of Butterflies, 1994; Yo!, 1997; In the Name of Salomé, 2000; Finding Miracles, 2004; Saving the World, 2006. OTHERS: My English, 1971; Something to Declare (nonfiction), 1998; Poetas en New York, 1998; The Secret Footprints (children's book), 2000; How Tia Lola came to Stay (young adult), 2001; A Cafecito Story, 2001 as A Cafecito Story/El cuento del cafecito, 2002; Before We Were Free (young adult), 2002; A Gift of Gracias: The Legend of Altagracia, 2005; Once Upon a Quinceañera, 2007; De cómo las muchachas Garciá perdieron el acento, 2007; Return to Sender, 2009; Devolver al Remitente, 2010; How Tiá Lola Learned to Teach, 2010; How Tiá Lola Saved the Summer, 2011. Contributor to periodicals. **Address:** Susan Bergholz Literary Services, 17 W 10th St., Ste. 5B, New York, NY 10011-8746, U.S.A. **Online address:** susan@susanbergholz.com

ALVAREZ, Rafael. American (born United States), b. 1958. **Genres:** History, Novellas/Short Stories, Music. **Career:** Baltimore Sun, truck dispatcher, 1977-78, sports desk, 1978-81, city desk, 1981-2001; Baltimore Examiner, columnist, 2008. Writer. **Publications:** Hometown Boy: The Hoodle Patrol and Other Curiosities of Baltimore, 2001; Storyteller, 2001; The Wire: Truth Be Told, 2004; Out of Tune: Stories about Music, 2006; First and Forever: The Archdiocese of Baltimore: A People's History, 2006. STORIES: The Fountain of Highlandtown: Stories, 1997; Orlo and Leini: Stories, 2000; (with T. Nugent and J.M. Rudolph) Crabtown Stories, 2003. Works appear in anthologies. Contributor to magazines. **Address:** 501 N Calvert St., Baltimore, MD 21278, U.S.A. **Online address:** crabtown@alvarezfiction.com

ALVAREZ, Walter. American (born United States), b. 1940. **Genres:** Geography, History, Essays. **Career:** American Overseas Petroleum Ltd., geologist, 1967-68, 1968-70; Columbia University, Lamont-Doherty Geological Observatory, faculty, 1971-77; University of California, professor of geology and geophysics, 1977, Miller research professor, 1986-87, 2001-02, Chancellor's professor, 1998-2002. National Academy of Sciences, fellow. Writer. **Publications:** (Ed. with K.H.A. Gohrbandt) Geology and History of Sicily: Petroleum Exploration Society of Libya, Tripoli, 1970; T. Rex and the Crater of Doom, 1997; The Idea of a Community of Scholars: Essays Honoring the Centennial of the Faculty Club of the University of California at Berkeley, March 15, 2002, 2003; The Mountains of Saint Francis: Discovering the Geologic Events That Shaped Our Earth, 2009. Contributor of articles to books, periodicals and journals. **Address:** Department of Geography, University of California, 317 McCone Hall, Berkeley, CA 94720-4740, U.S.A. **Online address:** platetec@berkeley.edu

ALVI, Moniza. British/Pakistani (born Pakistan), b. 1954. **Genres:** Poetry. **Career:** Scott Lidgett School, teacher, 1978-80; Aylwin School, teacher, 1980-, Department of English, head, 1989-; The Open College of the Arts, tutor. Writer. **Publications:** (With P. Daniels) Peacock Luggage, 1992; The Country at My Shoulder, 1993; A Bowl of Warm Air, 1996; Carrying My Wife, 2000; Souls, 2002; How the Stone Found Its Voice, 2005; Split World: Poems, 1990-2005, 2008; Europa, 2008; Homesick for the Earth, 2011. **Address:** Oxford University Press, Walton St., Oxford, OX OX2 6DP, England. **Online address:** contact@moniza.co.uk

ALVIS, Robert E. American (born United States) **Genres:** Young Adult Non-fiction. **Career:** Saint Meinrad School of Theology, assistant professor of church history. Writer. **Publications:** Religion and the Rise of Nationalism: A Profile of an East-Central European City (nonfiction), 2005. Contributor to journals. **Address:** St. Meinrad Archabbey, 200 Hill Drive, St. Meinrad, IN 47577, U.S.A.

ALVTEGEN, Karin. Swedish (born Sweden), b. 1965. **Genres:** Novels. **Career:** Writer. **Publications:** NOVELS: Skuld, 1998; Saknad, 2000; Svek, 2003; Missing, 2003; Skam, 2006; Shadow, 2009; Betrayal, 2009. **Address:** Brombergs Bokförlag, PO Box 12886, Stockholm, 112 98, Sweden.

AMABILE, George. (George A-mah-be-lay). Canadian/American (born United States), b. 1936. **Genres:** Novels, Novellas/Short Stories, Mystery/Crime/Suspense, Plays/Screenplays, Poetry, Songs/Lyrics And Libretti, Essays, Biography, Biography. **Career:** University of Manitoba, instructor, 1963-65, assistant professor, 1966-68, 1969-71, associate professor of English and creative writing, 1971-, professor of English, through 1997; University of British Columbia, writer-in-residence, 1968-69; Winnipeg Centennial Library, writer-in-residence, 2000-01. **Publications:** Blood Ties, 1972; Open Country, 1976; Flower and Song, 1977; Ideas of Shelter, 1981; The Presence of Fire, 1982; (ed. with K. Dales) No Feather, No Ink, 1985; Four of a Kind, 1994; Rumours of Paradise/Rumours of War, 1995; Tasting the Dark, 2001; (ed.) Snow Formations, 2002; (ed.) That Singing You Hear at the Edges, 2003; (ed.) Alterations, 2004; (ed.) Satie's Sad Piano: A Long poem, 2005; Arthur Adamson: A Celebration, 2006; (ed.) Iliarjuk: An Inuit Memoir, 2008; (ed.) Paper Oranges, 2008. **Address:** Department of English, University of Manitoba, 625 Fletcher Argue Bldg., Winnipeg, MB R3T 5V5, Canada. **Online address:** gamabile@home.com

AMADI, Elechi. Nigerian (born Nigeria), b. 1934. **Genres:** Novels, Plays/Screenplays, Ethics, Autobiography/Memoirs, Adult Non-fiction, Essays, Poetry. **Career:** Enugu Nigeria, surveyor, 1959-60; Nigerian schools, science teacher, 1960-63, headmaster, 1966-67; Asa Grammar School, principal, 1967-68; Government of Rivers State of Nigeria, government divisional officer, 1968-69, senior administrative officer, 1969-83, secretary, 1973-83, commissioner of education, 1987-89, commissioner of lands and housing, 1989-90; Rivers State College of Education, writer-in-residence, dean of arts, and director of general studies, 1984-87, head of department of literature, 1991-. **Publications:** The Concubine, 1966; The Great Ponds, 1969; Okpukpe (prayerbook in Ikwerre), 1969; (with O. Wali and G. Enyinda) Okwukwo Eri, 1969; Sunset in Biafra, 1973; Isiburu; A Play, 1973; Peppersoup; And, The Road to Ibadan, 1977; Dancer of Johannesburg, 1978; The Slave, 1977; Ethics in Nigerian Culture, 1982; Estrangement (novel), 1986; The Woman of Calabar, 2002; Speaking and Singing (essays and poems), 2003. Contributor to periodicals. **Address:** Heinemann Educational Books Inc., Hanover St., Portsmouth, NH 03802-3959, U.S.A. **Online address:** amadielechi@yahoo.com

A-MAH-BE-LAY, George. *See* **AMABILE, George.**

AMAKI, Amalia K. American (born United States), b. 1949. **Genres:** Art/Art History, Film, History, Photography, Women's Studies And Issues, Biography, Cultural/Ethnic Topics. **Career:** Spelman College, instructor, 1987-89, 1992-93, lecturer, 1994-98, assistant professor, 1999-2000; Morehouse College, instructor, 1989-91; Atlanta College of Art, adjunct instructor, 1990, 1994; Kennesaw State University, adjunct instructor, 1993; North Georgia College and State University, assistant professor, 1998-99; University of Delaware, assistant professor of art history 2000-05, professor of art history, 2005-06, Paul R. Jones Collection, curator, 2000-06; University of Alabama, professor of art history, 2007-. Writer, artist and film critic. **Publications:** (Ed.) A Century of African American Art: The Paul R. Jones Collection, 2004; (with A.B. Brownlee) Hale Woodruff, Nancy Elizabeth Prophet, and the Academy, 2007. Works appear in anthologies. Contributor to periodicals. **Address:** AA Studios, PO Box 42292, Atlanta, GA 30311-0292, U.S.A. **Online address:** amaliaamaki@gmail.com

AMANN, Janet. American (born United States), b. 1951. **Genres:** Education, Children's Fiction, Art/Art History. **Career:** Art teacher, 1973-86; elementary librarian and art teacher, 1986-91; North Woods Elementary School, library and media director, 1992-2006; University of Wisconsin-La Crosse, faculty of instructional technology, 1999-2004; University of Wisconsin-Eau Claire, Department of Education Studies, assistant professor; Viterbo University, faculty. Writer. **Publications:** The T-206 Honus Wagner Caper, 1991; Theme Teaching with Great Visual Resources, 1993. Contributor to magazines. **Address:** Department of Education Studies, University of Wisconsin, 286 Brewer Hall, Eau Claire, WI 54702-4004, U.S.A. **Online address:** amannjl@uwec.edu

AMAR, Akhil Reed. American (born United States), b. 1958. **Genres:** Law, Politics/Government. **Career:** The Yale Law Journal, editor, 1984; Judge Stephen Breyer, U.S. Court of Appeals, 1st Circuit, law clerk, 1984-85; Yale University, Law School, assistant professor, associate professor of law, 1985-90, professor of law, 1990-93, Southmayd professor of law, 1993-, Sterling professor of law and political science, 2008, Yale College, faculty; University of Colorado, Thirty-Sixth Annual Coen lecturer, 1992; Columbia Law School, Samuel Rubin visiting professor of law, 1993, B.R. Ambedkar professor of Indian constitutional law, 2010; University of Virginia, Hardy Cross Dillard lecturer, 1994; Cleveland-Marshall College, Fifty-Seventh Cleveland-Marshall lecturer, 1994; University of California-Davis, Seventh Annual Edward L. Barrett Jr. lecturer, 1994; Cumberland School of Law, Cumberland distinguished lecturer, 1995; Rutgers Camden School of Law, Eighth Annual State Constitutional Law lecturer, 1996; McGeorge School of Law, McGeorge distinguished lecturer, 1996; Washington University, William R. Orthwein professor, 1997; University of Cincinnati, William Howard Taft lecturer, 1999; American Academy of Arts and Sciences, fellow, 2007; Harvard Law School, visiting professor of law, 2008-; The West Wing, consultant. **Publications:** The Constitution and Criminal Procedure: First Principles, 1997; (with A. Hirsch) For the People: What the Constitution Really Says about Your Rights, 1998; The Bill of Rights: Creation and Reconstruction, 1998; (co-ed.) Processes of Constitutional Decisionmaking, 2000; America's Constitution: A Biography, 2005. Contributor to journals. **Address:** Department of Political Science, Yale University, Rm. M45, Sterling Law Bldg., 115 Prospect St., PO Box 208215, New Haven, CT 06520, U.S.A. **Online address:** akhil.amar@yale.edu

AMATO, Carol A. American (born United States), b. 1942. **Genres:** Children's Fiction, Children's Non-fiction, Animals/Pets. **Career:** Language-learning specialist, 1965-. Nature science educator and nature writer. **Publications:** YOUNG READERS SERIES: The Truth about Sharks, 1995; Captain Jim and the Killer Whales, 1995; To be a Wolf: A Learning Story about the Gray Wolf, 1995; Raising Ursa, 1996; Adios, Chi Chi: The Adventures of a Tarantula, 1996; The Bald Eagle: Free Again!, 1996; Penguins of the Galapagos, 1996; On the Trail of the Grizzly, 1997; Chessie, the Meandering Manatee, 1997; The Giant Panda, Hope for Tomorrow, 2000; Backyard Pets-Activities for Exploring Wildlife Close to Home, 2002; The Fourth of July: An Independence Day Feast of Fun, Facts, and Activities, 2007. OTHER: (with E. Ladizinsky) Fifty Nifty Science Fair Projects, 1993; Super Science Fair Projects, 1994; (with D.H.E. Forbes) The Earth, 1995; Backyard Pets: Activities for Exploring Wildlife Close to Home, 2002. **Address:** c/o Author Mail, John Wiley and Sons, 111 River St., Hoboken, NJ 07030-5774, U.S.A. **Online address:** jbreview@wiley.com

AMATO, Mary. American (born United States), b. 1961. **Genres:** Children's Fiction, Young Adult Fiction, Novels, Picture/Board Books. **Career:** Firefly Shadow Theater, co-founder; Charter Theatre, artistic associate, 2007-. Writer and educator. **Publications:** The Word Eater, 2000; Snarf Attack, Underfoodle, and the Secret of Life: The Riot Brothers Tell All, 2004; Naked Mole-Rat Letters, 2005; Drooling and Dangerous: The Riot Brothers Return!, 2006; Please Write in This Book, 2006; Stinky and Successful: The Riot Brothers Never Stop, 2007; The Chicken of the Family, 2008; Invisible Lines, 2009; Take the Mummy and Run: The Riot Brothers Are On a Roll, 2009; Edgar Allan's Official Crime Investigation Notebook, 2010; Guitar Notes, 2012. Contributor to periodicals. **Address:** c/o Author Mail, Holiday House Inc., 425 Madison Ave., New York, NY 10017-1110, U.S.A. **Online address:** info@maryamato.com

AMATO, Theresa Ann. American (born United States), b. 1964. **Genres:** Adult Non-fiction. **Career:** U.S. District Court, law clerk, 1989-90; Public Citizen Litigation Group, staff attorney and director of freedom of information clearinghouse, 1991-93; Citizen Advocacy Center, founder and executive director, 1993-2000; Citizen Works, 2001-03, executive director, 2009-; Oak Park-River Forest Community Foundation, executive director, 2006-07. Writer and attorney. **Publications:** NONFICTION: A Childhood Abducted: Children Cutting Sugar Cane in the Dominican Republic, 1991; Grand Illusion: The Myth of Voter Choice in a Two-Party Tyranny, 2009. Contributor to journals. **Address:** Citizen Works, PO Box 18478, Washington, DC 20036, U.S.A. **Online address:** theresa@amatomain.com

AMBARAS, David Richard. American (born United States), b. 1962. **Genres:** Politics/Government, History. **Career:** North Carolina State University, professor. Writer and educator. **Publications:** Bad Youth: Juvenile Delinquency and the Politics of Everyday Life in Modern Japan, 2006. Contributor of articles to journals. **Address:** Department of History, North Carolina State University, 350 Withers Hall, PO Box 8108, Raleigh, NC 27695-8108, U.S.A. **Online address:** david_ambaras@ncsu.edu

AMBERT, Anne Marie. Canadian (born Canada), b. 1940. **Genres:** Human Relations/Parenting, Sociology, Social Sciences. **Career:** University of Texas, Rehabilitation Research and Training Center in Mental Retardation, research associate, 1969-70, director of the center, 1970-71, assistant professor of social work, 1969-71; York University, assistant professor, 1971-74, associate professor of sociology, 1974, now associate professor emeritus, university professor, now university professor emeritus. Writer. **Publica-**

tions: Forgotten Ones: A Sociological Study of Anglo and Chicano Retardates, 1972; (with R.L. Henshel) Perspectives on Social Problems, 1973, 2nd ed., 1983; Sex Structure, 1973, 2nd ed., 1976; Divorce in Canada, 1980; Ex-Spouses and New Spouses: A Study of Relationships, 1989; The Effects of Children on Parents, 1992, 2nd ed., 2001; (ed. with D.H. Demo) Parents and Adolescents in Changing Families, 1995; Parents, Children and Adolescents: Interactive Relationships and Development in Context, 1997; The Web of Poverty: Psychosocial Perspectives, 1998; Families in the New Millennium, 2001; Same-Sex Couples and Same-Sex Parent Families: Relationships, Parenting and Issues of Marriage, 2003; Changing Families: Relationships in Context, 2006, 2nd ed., 2011. Contributor to journals. **Address:** Department of Sociology, York University, 2060 Vari Hall, 4700 Keele St., Toronto, ON M3J 1P3, Canada. **Online address:** ambert@yorku.ca

AMBLER, Scott W. Canadian (born Canada), b. 1966. **Genres:** Information Science/Computers. **Career:** Ambysoft Inc., founder; IBM Corp., chief methodologist for agile and lean, IBM Academy of Technology (AOT), co-chair. Writer, mentor and consultant. **Publications:** The Object Primer: The Application Developer's Guide to Object-Orientation, 1995, 3rd ed. as The Object Primer: Agile Model-Driven Development with UML 2.0, 2004; Building Object Applications That Work: Your Step-by-Step Handbook for Developing Robust Systems with Object Technology, 1997; Process Patterns: Building Large-Scale Systems Using Object Technology, 1998; More Process Patterns: Delivering Large-Scale Systems Using Object Technology, 1998; (ed. with L.L. Constantine) The Unified Process Construction Phase: Best Practices for Completing the Unified Process, 2000; (ed.) The Unified Process Elaboration Phase: Best Practices in Implementing the UP, 2000; The (comp. with L.L. Constantine)Unified Process Inception Phase: Best Practices for Implementing the UP, 2000; (ed. with L.L. Constantine) The Unified Process Transition and Production Phase: Best Practices in Implementing the UP, 2002; (with E. Roman and T. Jewell) Mastering Enterprise Javabeans, 2002; Agile Modeling, 2002; Agile Database Techniques, 2003; The Elements of UML Style, 2003; The Elements of UML 2.0 Style, 2005; (with J. Nalbone and M.J. Vizdos) The Enterprise Unified Process: Extending the Rational Unified Process, 2005; (with P.J. Sadalage) Refactoring Databases: Evolutionary Database Design, 2006. Contributor to periodicals. **Address:** Cambridge University Press, 40 W 20th St., New York, NY 10011, U.S.A. **Online address:** scott_ambler@ca.ibm.com

AMBROSE, Bonnie Holt. American (born United States), b. 1943. **Genres:** Fash Ion/Costume, Art/Art History. **Career:** Performing Arts Supply Co., owner, president, 1970-, head costume designer; seminar lecturer on costume construction; Costume Workshop, owner. Writer. **Publications:** The Little Hatmaking Book: A Workbook on Turn-of-the-Century Hats, vol. I, 1994; The Little Bodice Construction Book: A Workbook on Period Bodices, 1995; The Little Corset Construction Book: A Workbook on Period Underwear, 1997; Introduction to Costuming, 1997; Costume Crew, 2004; The Costume Workshop, forthcoming. **Address:** Performing Arts Supply Co., 11421-B Todd St., Houston, TX 77055, U.S.A. **Online address:** bhambrose@netscape.net

AMBROSINI, Richard. Italian (born Italy), b. 1955. **Genres:** Literary Criticism And History, Translations, Biography. **Career:** University of Rome, English language assistant, 1986-94, professor of English and researcher, 1994-; University of Milan, associate professor, 1998-2002. Writer. **Publications:** Conrad's Fiction as Critical Discourse, 1991; Introduzione a Conrad, 1991; Ulisse: Archeologia dell'uomo moderno, 1998; R. L. Stevenson: la poeticadel romanzo, 2001; The U.K.: Learning the Language, Studying the Culture, 2005; Robert Louis Stevenson: Writer of Boundaries, 2006; European Stevenson, 2009; (trans.) Joseph Conrad's An Outcast of the Islands and The Secret Agent, Robert Louis Stevenson's Treasure Island. Contributor to periodicals. **Address:** Department of English, University of Rome, Via Carlo Fea, Rome, 2-00161, Italy. **Online address:** ambrosin@uniroma3.it

AMBURN, Ellis. (Edward Douglas). American (born United States), b. 1933. **Genres:** Biography, Autobiography/Memoirs, Art/Art History. **Career:** Coward McCann, executive editor, 1960-71; Delacorte Press, editor-in-chief, 1971-78; William Morrow and Company Inc., senior editor, 1978-80, editor-in-chief; G.P. Putnam's Sons, editorial director, 1980-85; freelance writer, 1985-; Newsweek, reporter, researcher. **Publications:** (With T. Sanchez) Up and Down with the Rolling Stones, 1979; (with S. Winters) Shelley, Also Known as Shirley, 1980; (with P. Presley) Elvis and Me, 1985; (with M. Edwards) Priscilla, Elvis and Me, 1988; (with S. Winters) Shelley II, 1989; Dark Star: The Tragic Story of Roy Orbison, 1990; Pearl: The Obsessions and Passions of Janis Joplin, 1992; Buddy Holly: The Real Story, 1995; Subterranean Kerouac: The Hidden Life of Jack Kerouac, 1998; The Most Beautiful Woman in the World: The Obsessions, Passions and Courage of Elizabeth Taylor, 2000; The Sexiest Man Alive: A Biography of Warren Beatty, 2002; (as Edward Douglas) Jack: The Great Seducer-The Live and Many Loves of Jack Nicolson, 2004. **Address:** c/o Elaine Markson, Elaine Markson Literary Agency, 44 Greenwich Ave., New York, NY 10011, U.S.A.

AMEISEN, Olivier. French (born France), b. 1953. **Genres:** Medicine/Health, Autobiography/Memoirs. **Career:** New York-Presbyterian Hospital, attending physician, 1986; Cornell University Medical College, associate professor; State University of New York Downstate Medical Center, visiting professor. Writer. **Publications:** The End of My Addiction, 2009; (with H. Hinzmann) Heal Thyself: A Doctor at the Peak of His Medical Career, Destroyed by Alcohol and the Personal Miracle That Brought Him Back, 2010. Contributor of articles to periodicals and journals. **Address:** DOWNSTATE MEDICAL CENTER, State University of New York, 450 Clarkson Ave., Brooklyn, NY 11203, U.S.A. **Online address:** oa@olivierameisen.com

AMEND, Allison. American (born United States), b. 1974. **Genres:** Novellas/Short Stories, Children's Fiction. **Career:** Writer and educator. **Publications:** Cracking the SAT Literature Subject Test, 2007; Things That Pass for Love (stories), 2008; Asian-American Writers, 2010; Hispanic-American Writers, 2010; Stations West: A Novel, 2010. Contributor of articles to periodicals. **Address:** Chelsea House Publishers, 132 W 31st St., 17th Fl., New York, NY 10001, U.S.A. **Online address:** allison@allisonamend.com

AMERY, Colin. British (born England), b. 1944?. **Genres:** Novels, Young Adult Fiction, Architecture, Social Sciences. **Career:** Financial Times, architectural correspondent; World Monuments Fund, director; Lutyens Trust, founding trustee and chair, 1984-. Writer and architectural consultant. **Publications:** (Ed. with R. Reid) Nicholson's Guide to Great Britain, 1974; (ed.) Period Houses and Their Details, 1974; (with D. Cruickshank) The Rape of Britain, 1975; New Atlantis: The Secret of the Sphinx, 1976; (ed.) The National Theatre: The Architectural Review Guide, 1977; (ed.) Three Centuries of Architectural Craftsmanship, 1977; (with G. Stamp) Victorian Buildings of London, 1837-1887: An Illustrated Guide, 1980; (comp. with M. Richardson and G. Stamp) Lutyens, the Work of the English Architect Sir Edwin Lutyens (1869-1944): Hayward Gallery London SE1, 18 November 1981-31 January 1982, 1981; Four London Architects, 1985-1988: Chipperfield, Mather, Parry, Stanton Williams, 1987; Wren's London, 1988; A Celebration of Art and Architecture: The National Gallery Sainsbury Wing, 1991; (intro.) Pioneers of Modern Furniture: An Exhibition at Fischer Fine Art, London, 24 April-31 May 1991, 1991; Architecture, Industry, and Innovation: The Early Work of Nicholas Grimshaw and Partners, 1995; (co-ed.) The Pritzker Architecture Prize: The First Twenty Years, 1999; (with B. Curran) Vanishing Histories: 100 Endangered Sites from the World Monuments Watch, 2001; (with B. Curran, Jr.) The Lost World of Pompeii, 2002; (ed. with D. Ken) Sites Insight: Exploring the U.K.'s Buildings and Landscapes Through the Eyes of Public Figures, in Celebration of the Architectural Heritage Fund's 30th Anniversary, 2006. Contributor to periodicals. **Address:** The Lutyens Trust, Goddards, Abinger Common, Dorking, SR RH5 6JH, England.

AMERY, Francis. *See* **STABLEFORD, Brian M(ichael).**

AMES, Christopher. American (born United States), b. 1956. **Genres:** Literary Criticism And History, Film. **Career:** Stanford University, teaching administrator, 1983-84, lecturer in English; Thacher School, instructor in English and department head, 1984-86; Agnes Scott College, associate professor of English and department head, 1986-2001, Charles A. Dana professor of English; Oglethorpe University, provost and senior vice president, 2001-06; Washington College, professor of English, provost and dean of colleges, 2006-. Writer. **Publications:** The Life of the Party: Festive Vision in Modern Fiction, 1991; Movies about the Movies: Hollywood Reflected, 1997. Contributor of articles to journals. **Address:** Office of the Provost and Dean, Washington College, Bunting Hall, 1st Fl., 300 Washington Ave., Chestertown, MD 21620, U.S.A. **Online address:** cames2@washcoll.edu

AMES, Greg. American (born United States), b. 1971?. **Genres:** Novels. **Career:** City University of New York, Brooklyn College, instructor; Binghamton University, instructor. Writer. **Publications:** Buffalo Lockjaw (novel), 2009. Contributor of stories to literary journals. Work appears in anthology. **Address:** c/o Scott Moyers, Wylie Agency, 250 W 57th St., Ste. 2114, New York, NY 10107, U.S.A. **Online address:** amesinbrooklyn@gmail.com

AMES, Jonathan. American (born United States), b. 1964. **Genres:** Novels. **Career:** Columbia University, visiting faculty; Iowa Writers Workshop, visiting faculty; The New School, visiting faculty; New York Press, columnist. Boxer and writer. **Publications:** I Pass like Night (novel), 1989; The Extra Man (novel), 1998; Oedipussy, (one-man show), 1999; What's Not to Love?: The Adventures of a Mildly Perverted Young Writer, 2000; My Less than Secret Life: A Diary, Fiction, Essays, 2002; Wake Up, Sir, 2004; (ed.) Sexual Metamorphosis: an Anthology of Transsexual Memoirs, 2005; I Love You More Than You know, 2006; The Alcoholic, 2008; Double Life is Twice as Good, 2009. **Address:** c/o Rosalie Siegel, International Literary Agent Inc., 1 Abey Dr., Pennington, NJ 08534, U.S.A. **Online address:** jonathanames3@aol.com

AMES, Kenneth L. American (born United States), b. 1942. **Genres:** Antiques/Furnishings, History, Bibliography. **Career:** Franklin & Marshall College, assistant professor of art history, 1967-73, Department of Art, acting chair, 1971-72; University of Delaware, adjunct assistant professor, 1974-76, adjunct associate professor, 1976-88, adjunct professor, 1988-90; H. F. du Pont Winterthur Museum, Winterthur Summer Institute, director 1975-82, Office of Advanced Studies, chair, 1978-88, professor of early American culture, 1989-90; Delaware Humanities Council, chair, 1981-82; New York State Museum, chief of historical and anthropological surveys, head; Bard Graduate Center, American Decorative Arts and Material Culture of the 18th and 19th-centuries, professor, 1996-; Decorative Arts Society, founder. Writer and consultant. **Publications:** Beyond Necessity: Art in the Folk Tradition, 1977; Material Culture: A Research Guide, 1985; Death in the Dining Room and Other Tales of Victorian Culture, 1992; On Bishop Street: Avenue of Hawai'i Pioneers, 1996; (contrib.) Theatre of the Fraternity, 1996. EDITOR: Victorian Furniture, 1982; (with G.W.R. Ward) Decorative Arts & Household Furnishings in America, 1650-1920: An Annotated Bibliography, 1989; (with B. Franco and T. Frye) Ideas and Images: Developing Interpretive History Exhibits, 1992; (with K. Martinez) The Material Culture of Gender, the Gender of Material Culture, 1997; American Christmas Cards, 1900-1960, 2011. Works appear in anthologies. Contributor of articles to journals. **Address:** Bard Graduate Ctr., 38 W 86th St., New York, NY 10024, U.S.A. **Online address:** kenneth_ames@bgc.bard.edu

AMICK, Steve. American (born United States), b. 1964. **Genres:** Novels, Young Adult Fiction. **Career:** Freelance advertising copywriter, 1995-2004. Educator. **Publications:** Your Mother/Dead Horse, 1999; Jazz Genius, 2001; Mr. Smarty-Pants, 2002; We Were Soldiers, 2002; Theres Always Pie, 2005; Lake, the River & the Other Lake, 2005; Nothing But a Smile, 2009. Contributor to periodicals. **Address:** Artists Literary Group, 27 W 20th St., 10th Fl., New York, NY 10011, U.S.A.

AMIRREZVANI, Anita. American/Iranian (born Iran), b. 1961. **Genres:** Novellas/Short Stories, Novels. **Career:** Telelerning Inc., editor, 1983-84; PC World Magazine, senior associate editor, 1989-96; Contra Costa Times, assistant entertainment editor, 1994-95, staff writer, 1995-2005; San Jose Mercury News, dance critic, 2000-05; Hedgebrook Foundation for Women Writers, writer-in-residence; California College of the Arts, MFA Program in Writing, adjunct professor, Department of Writing and Literature, adjunct professor. Journalist. **Publications:** The Blood of Flowers: A Novel, 2007. Contributor to journals. **Address:** c/o Author Mail, Little, Brown & Co., 237 Park Ave., New York, NY 10017-3140, U.S.A. **Online address:** aa@bloodofflowers.com

AMIRY, Suad. Palestinian (born Palestine), b. 1951. **Genres:** Autobiography/Memoirs. **Career:** Birzeit University, instructor, 1981-91; Palestinian Government, deputy minister of culture, 1989-; RIWAQ Center for Architectural Conservation, founder and director, 1991-. Writer. **Publications:** (With V. Tamari) The Palestinian Village Home, 1989; Traditional Floor Tiles in Palestine, 2000; (co-author) Imarat Qura Al-Karasi: Min Tarikh Al-Iqta Fi Rif Filastin Fi Al-Qarnayn Al-Thamin Ashar wa-Al Tasi Ashar (title means: 'Throne Village Architecture'), 2003; (ed. with M. Hadid) Earthquake in-April, 2003; (with F. Rahhal) Manatir: Qusur Al-mazari Fi Rif Filastin (title means: 'Manatir: Agricultural Farmhouses in Rural Palestine'), 2003; Kaputsino be-Ramallah: Reshimot Min Ha-seger (title means: 'Cappucino in Ramallah: War Diaries'), 2003; Sharon and My Mother-in Law: Ramallah Diaries (memoir), 2004; No Sex in the City, 2007; Murad, Murad, 2009; Menopausal Palestine: Women At The Edge, 2010. **Address:** PO Box 212, Al Sharafeh, Ramallah, 2119, Israel. **Online address:** suad@riwaq.org

AMIS, Martin (Louis). British (born England), b. 1949. **Genres:** Novels, Novellas/Short Stories. **Career:** Times Literary Supplement, editorial assistant, 1972-75, fiction and poetry editor, 1974; New Statesman, assistant literary editor, 1975-77, literary editor, 1977-79; writer, 1980-; Observer Newspaper, special writer, 1980-; University of Manchester, Centre for New Writing, professor of creative writing, 2007. **Publications:** The Rachel Papers, 1973; Dead Babies, 1976 as Dark Secrets, 1977; Success, 1978; Other People: A Mystery Story, 1981; Invasion of the Space Invaders, 1982; Money: A Suicide Note, 1984; The Moronic Inferno and Other Visits to America, 1986; Einstein's Monsters (short stories), 1987; London Fields, 1989; Time's Arrow, or, The Nature of the Offence, 1991; Visiting Mrs. Nabokov and Other Excursions, 1993; The Information, 1995; Night Train, 1997; Heavy Water and Other Stories, 1998; Experience: A Memoir, 2000; War Against Cliché: Essays and Reviews, 1971-2000, 2001; Koba the Dread: Laughter and the Twenty Million, 2002; Yellow Dog, 2003; (contrib.) Pornoland, 2004; Vintage Amis, 2004; House of Meetings, 2006; The Second Plane: September 11: 2001-2007, 2008; The Pregnant Widow, 2010. Works appear in anthologies. Contributor of articles and short stories to periodicals. **Address:** The Wylie Agency (UK) Ltd., 17 Bedford Sq., London, GL WC1B 3JA, England.

AMMER, Christine (Parker). American/Austrian (born Austria), b. 1931. **Genres:** Business/Trade/Industry, Economics, Language/Linguistics, Medicine/Health, Music, Reference. **Career:** Physicians Publications and Parents Magazine Press, editor with national lexicographic board, 1953-62; freelance editor, 1962-66; Harvard University Press, editor, 1966-68; freelance writer, 1968-; Hospital Purchasing Institute in Boston, editor and publisher, 1976-79. **Publications:** Riches of the Animal World, 1967; Musician's Handbook of Foreign Terms, 1971; Harper's Dictionary of Music, 1972, 3rd ed., 1995; (with D.S. Ammer) Dictionary of Business and Economics, 1977, rev. ed., 1986; Unsung: A History of Women in American Music, 1980; The A to Z of Women's Health: A Concise Encyclopaedia, 1982, 4th ed., 2000; (with N.T. Sidley) A Common Sense Guide to Mental Health Care, 1982; The Harper Dictionary of Music, 1986; The A to Z of Investing, 1986; It's Raining Cats and Dogs and Other Beastly Expressions, 1989; The New A to Z of Women's Health, 1989, 4th ed., 2000; Fighting Words: From War, Rebellion and Other Combative Capers, 1989; The A to Z of Foreign Musical Terms, 1989; Getting Help: A Consumer's Guide to Therapy, 1991; Harper Collins Dictionary of Music, 1991, 3rd ed., 1995; Have A Nice Day-No Problem!: A Dictionary of Clichés, 1992; Seeing Red or Tickled Pink: Color Terms in Everyday Language, 1992; Southpaws & Sunday Punches: And Other Sporting Expressions, 1993; Fruitcakes & Couch Potatoes and Other Delicious Expressions, 1995; American Heritage Dictionary of Idioms, 1997; Cool Cats, Top Dogs and Other Beastly Expressions, 1999; American Heritage ESL Idioms Dictionary, 2000; Facts on File Dictionary of Clichés, 2001, 3rd ed., 2011; The Facts on File Dictionary of Music, 4th ed., 2004; The Encyclopedia of Women's Health, 2005, 6th ed., 2009. **Address:** 6 Filer Ln., Lexington, MA 02420-1231, U.S.A.

AMMERMAN, Nancy T(atom). American (born United States), b. 1950. **Genres:** Theology/Religion, Sociology. **Career:** Emory University, teacher of religion, 1984-95, Candler School of theology, assistant professor, 1984-90, associate professor of sociology of religion, 1990-95, Center for Religious Research, director, 1985-95, director of Baptist studies program, 1991-95; Georgia State University, fellow in gerontology and theological education, 1986-87; Samford University, Dotson M. Nelson lecturer, 1990; Carson Newman College, Carlyle Marney lecturer, 1991; University of Michigan, visiting lecturer; Loyola University of Chicago, visiting lecturer; Swarthmore College, visiting lecturer; Arizona State University, visiting lecturer; Shorter College, Staley lecturer, 1995; Hartford Seminary, Center for Social and Religious Research, professor of sociology of religion, 1995-2003; Mississippi College, N.W. Carpenter lecturer, 1995; Boston University, School of Theology, professor of religion, 2003-, chair. Writer. **Publications:** (Contrib.) Barbara W. Hargrove, Religion and the Sociology of Knowledge, 1984; Bible Believers: Fundamentalists in the Modern World, 1987; (contrib.) Pushing the Faith, 1988; Baptist Battles: Social Change and Religious Conflict in the Southern Baptist Convention, 1990; (ed. and contrib.) Southern Baptists Observed: Multiple Perspectives on a Changing Denomination, 1993; (contrib.) Accounting for Fundamentalisms, 1994; (ed. with W.C. Roof) Work, Family, and Religion in Contemporary Society, 1995; (with A.E. Farnsley II and T. Adams) Congregation and Community, 1997; (contrib.) Baptists in the Balance: The Tension between Freedom and Responsibility, 1997; (contrib.) Lived Religion in America, 1997; (co-ed.) Studying Congregations, 1998: (with C.S. Dudley) Congregations in Transition: A Guide for Analyzing,

Assessing, and Adapting in Changing Communities, 2002; Pillars of Faith: American Congregations and Their Partners, 2005; (ed.) Everyday Religion: Observing Modern Religious Live, 2007. Contributor of articles to periodicals. **Address:** School of Theology, Boston University, 260B, 745 Commonwealth Ave., Boston, MA 02215, U.S.A. **Online address:** nta@bu.edu

AMOIA, Alba della Fazia. Italian/American (born United States), b. 1928. **Genres:** Theatre, Literary Criticism And History, Biography. **Career:** United Nations Language Training, teacher of French and English, 1949-64; Columbia University, lecturer, 1950-54; Barnard College, instructor in French, 1951-59; City University of New York, Hunter College, associate professor of French, 1960-75, associate professor emeritus of romance language. Writer. **Publications:** Jean Anouilh, 1969; The Italian Theatre Today, 1977; Edmond Rostand, 1978; Albert Camus, 1989; Thomas Mann's Fiorenza, 1990; Women on the Italian Literary Scene: A Panorama, 1992; Feodor Dostoevsky, 1993; Twentieth-Century Italian Women Writers, 1996; (with E. Bruschini) Stendhal's Rome: Then and Now, 1997; No Mothers We!: Italian Women Writers and Their Revolt against Maternity, 2000. EDITOR: (with B.L. Knapp and N. Dormoy-Savage) An Anthology of Modern Belgian Theatre, 1982; (with B.L. Knapp) Multicultural Writer from Antiquity to 1945, 2002; (with B.L. Knapp) Multicultural Writers Since 1945: An A-to-Z Guide, 2004; (with B.L. Knapp) Great Women Travel Writers: From 1750 to the Present, 2005. Contributor of articles and reviews to periodicals. **Address:** Casella Postale 230, Roma-Centro, 00100, Italy.

AMOS, James H. American (born United States), b. 1946. **Genres:** Novels, Business/Trade/Industry. **Career:** Brice Foods, director of franchising, director of marketing and sales, national director of consultant training, vice-president, chief executive officer, I Can't Believe It's Yogurt, vice-president, executive director; Mail Boxes Etc Inc., president and chief executive officer, 1996-2002, chairman emeritus; UPS Store, chairman emeritus; Eagle Alliance Partners, managing partner, 2002, chairman emeritus, 2002-; Sona Med Spa International Inc., chairman and chief executive officer; Brice Group, chief executive officer; Tasti D-Lite L.L.C., chairman and chief executive officer; Insty-Prints Inc, consultant; Arby's Inc, consultant; Citizen's Choice, consultant; Snow Phipps, operating partner. Writer. **Publications:** NOVELS: The Memorial, 1989; Focus or Failure: America at the Crossroads, 1998; The Complete Idiot's Guide to Franchising, 2005. Contributor to journals. **Address:** Tasti D-Lite L.L.C., 222 E 86th St., New York, NY 10028, U.S.A.

AMOS, William (David). British (born England), b. 1933. **Genres:** Local History/Rural Topics, Young Adult Fiction, Novellas/Short Stories. **Career:** Liverpool Daily Post, daily columnist, 1963-70; Lancashire Life, editor, 1970-86; Whitethorn Press, director, 1974-85, editor-in-chief, 1982-86; Hotel Publishing Intl., editor-in-chief, 1986-89; Warwickshire & Worcestershire Life, editor, 1989-91; freelance editor, 1991-. **Publications:** Literary Liverpool, 1971; (ed.) Just Sithabod: Dialect Verse from Lancashire Life, 1975; (ed.) Steam-up in Lancashire: Railwayana from Lancashire Life, 1976; (ed.) Cheyp at T'Price: Dialect Verse from Lancashire Life, 1978; The Originals: Who's Really Who in Fiction in US as The Originals: An A-Z of Fiction's Real-Life Characters, 1985; Derbyshire, 1995; Tales of Old Lancashire, 1996. **Address:** Hacket Forge, Little Langdale, Ambleside, CM LA22 9NU, England.

AMRITANANDAMAYI, Mataji. (Sudhamani Idamannel). Indian (born India), b. 1953. **Genres:** inspirational/Motivational Literature. **Career:** Mata Amritanandamayi Center, founder and Hindu spiritual teacher. Writer. **Publications:** Bhajanāmrātamò, 2nd ed., 1985; For My Children: Spiritual Teachings of Mata Amritanandamayi, 1986; Amritanandamayi Sambhashanangal, 2 vols., 1990, 3rd ed., 1992; Awaken, Children: Dialogues with Sri Sri Mata Amritanandamayi, 1990, 3rd ed., 1992; Eternal Wisdom: Upadeshamritam, 1999; (ed. with J. Canan) Messages From Amma: In the Language of the Heart, 2004; Amma Makkalōṭa, 2009. **Address:** c/o Author Mail, Mata Amritanandamayi Center, PO Box 613, San Ramon, CA 94583, U.S.A. **Online address:** mam@amritapuri.org

AMSDEN, David. American (born United States), b. 1980?. **Genres:** Adult Non-fiction. **Career:** New Yorker Magazine, staff; New York Magazine, contributing writer. **Publications:** Important Things That Don't Matter, 2003. Contributor to magazines and periodicals. **Address:** c/o Author Mail, William Morrow/HarperCollins, 10 E 53rd St., 7th Fl., New York, NY 10022, U.S.A.

AMSTER-BURTON, Matthew. American (born United States), b. 1975?. **Genres:** Food And Wine, Human Relations/Parenting. **Career:** Writer. **Publications:** Hungry Monkey: A Food-Loving Father's Quest to Raise an Adventurous Eater, 2009. **Address:** Seattle, WA , U.S.A. **Online address:** rootsandgrubs@gmail.com

AMUSSEN, Susan Dwyer. American (born United States), b. 1954. **Genres:** History. **Career:** Connecticut College, assistant professor, 1984-91; Union Institute and University, professor, 1990-2008; University of California, School of Social Sciences, Humanities and Arts, professor, 2008-. Writer and historian. **Publications:** An Ordered Society: Gender and Class in Early Modern England, 1988; (ed. with M.A. Kishlansky) Political Culture and Cultural Politics in Early Modern England: Essays Presented to David Underdown, 1995; (ed. with A. Seeff) Attending to Early Modern Women, 1998; Caribbean Exchanges: Slavery and the Transformation of English Society, 1640-1700, 2007. Contributor of articles to books and journals. **Address:** School of Social Sciences, Humanities and Arts, University of California, PO Box 2039, Merced, CA 95344, U.S.A. **Online address:** samussen@ucmerced.edu

AMY, Lori E. American/German (born Germany), b. 1963. **Genres:** Social Sciences, Human Relations/Parenting. **Career:** Cleveland State University, visiting assistant professor, 1997-99; Georgia Southern University, assistant professor, 1999-2002, associate professor, 2005-, director of women's and gender studies, 2002-09; Albania-America Educational Networks, coordinator, 2009-. Writer. **Publications:** The Wars We Inherit: Military Life, Gender Violence, and Memory, 2010. Contributor to books and periodicals. **Address:** Georgia Southern University, 1201 Forest Dr., PO Box 8026, Statesboro, GA 30460, U.S.A. **Online address:** lamy@georgiasouthern.edu

AMYX, Jennifer A. American (born United States), b. 1970. **Genres:** History, Politics/Government, Business/Trade/Industry. **Career:** Australian National University, Australian Capital Territory, postdoctoral fellow, 1998-99, research fellow, 2000-01; University of Pennsylvania, assistant professor of political science, 2002-. Writer. **Publications:** (Ed. with P. Drysdale) Japanese Governance: Beyond Japan Inc., 2003; (ed. with T. Toya) Japan's Financial Crisis: Institutional Rigidity and Reluctant Change, 2004; (foreword) The Political Economy of the Japanese Financial Big Bang, 2006; (ed. with J. Oi and B. Kook Kim) System Restructuring in East Asia, forthcoming. CONTRIBUTOR: The Asian Financial Crisis and the Architecture of Global Finance, 2002; Ryudo-kino nihon seiji: "ushinawareta jyu-nen" no seijigakuteki kensho (title means: 'The Volatile Period of Japanese Politics: A Political Analysis of The Lost Decade'), 2002; Challenges for Japan: Political Leadership, U.S.-China-Japan Triangle, Financial Reform and Gender Issues, 2003; Beyond Bilateralism: U.S.-Japan Relations in the New Asia-Pacific Standard, 2003. Contributor to periodicals and journals. **Address:** Department of Political Science, University of Pennsylvania, Rm. 217, 208 S 37th. St., Philadelphia, PA 19104-6215, U.S.A. **Online address:** jamyx@sas.upenn.edu

AN, Na. American/Korean (born Korea (South)), b. 1972. **Genres:** Young Adult Fiction, Psychology, Novels, Romance/Historical. **Career:** Educator and writer. **Publications:** A Step from Heaven, 2001; Wait for Me, 2006; The Fold, 2008. Contributor to periodicals. **Address:** c/o Merrilee Heifetz, Writers House, 21 W 26th St., New York, NY 10010, U.S.A. **Online address:** anna@anwriting.com

ANAM, Tahmima. British/Bangladeshi (born Bangladesh), b. 1975?. **Genres:** Novels, Young Adult Fiction, Literary Criticism And History. **Career:** Writer. **Publications:** A Golden Age, 2007. Contributor to periodicals. **Address:** The Wylie Agency, 17 Bedford Sq., London, GL WC1B 3JA, England.

ANANIA, Michael (Angelo). American (born United States), b. 1939. **Genres:** Novels, Poetry, Essays, Literary Criticism And History, Young Adult Fiction. **Career:** State University of New York at Buffalo, bibliographer, 1963-64; State University of New York at Fredonia, instructor in English, 1964-65; Northwestern University, instructor in English, 1965-68; University of Illinois, instructor, 1968-70, professor of English, 1970-, now professor emeritus; Swallow Press, literary editor, 1968-74. **Publications:** (Ed.) New Poetry Anthology I, 1969; The Color of Dust, 1970; Set/Sorts, 1974; The Fall, 1977; Aesthetique du Rale, 1977; Riversongs, 1978; The Red Menace: A Fiction, 1984; Constructions/Variations: Poems, 1985; The Sky at Ashland; On the Conditions of Place: Two Poems, 1985 as Sky at Ashland, 1986; In Plain Sight: Obsessions, Morals and Domestic Laughter, 1991; Selected Poems, 1994; In Natural Light, 1999; Heat Lines, 2006. EDITOR: New Poetry Anthology I, 1969; Gardening the Skies: The Missouri Writer's Biennial

Anthology, 1988. **Address:** Department of English, University of Illinois, 2027 University Hall, Chicago, IL 60607-7120, U.S.A. **Online address:** anania@uic.edu

ANASTAS, Benjamin. American (born United States), b. 1971?. **Genres:** Essays, Novels, Literary Criticism And History. **Career:** Iowa Review, fiction editor; Grand Street, editor. **Publications:** An Underachiever's Diary, 1998; The Faithful Narrative of a Pastor's Disappearance, 2001; Am Fua des Gebirgs, 2007. Contributor to periodicals. **Address:** Dial Press, 1540 Broadway, New York, NY 10036, U.S.A.

ANATI, Emmanuel. Italian (born Italy), b. 1930. **Genres:** Anthropology/Ethnology, Archaeology/Antiquities, Art/Art History, History. **Career:** University of Tel Aviv, professor of prehistory, 1968-78; University of Lecce, professor ordinarius of palaeo-ethnology, 1980-99, now retired; Centro Camuno di Studi Preistorici, founder, executive director and editor-in-chief, 1964-; International Association for the Study of Prehistoric and Primitive Religions, general secretary, 1982-91; Institut des Arts Prehistoriques et Ethnographiques, president, 1992-. **Publications:** La Grande Roche de Naquane, 1959; La Civilisation du Val Camonica, 1960; Palestine before the Hebrews: A History, From The Earliest Arrival Of Man To The Conquest Of Canaan, 1963; (with F. Roiter and C. Roy) Naquane: Decouverte d'un Pays et d'une Civilisation, 1966; Arte Prehistorica in Valtellina: Presentazione di Renzo Sertoli Salis, 1967; Origini della Civilta Camuna, 1968; Arte Rupestre nelle regioni Occidentali della Penisola Iberica, 1968; Rock Art in Central Arabia, 4 vols., 1972-75; Le Statue stele della'Italia Settentrionale, 1972; Pugnalinell'arte Rupestre e Nelle Statue-Stele dell'Italia Settentrionale, 1972; Arte preistorica in Anatolia, 1972; (with M. Avnimelech, N. Haas and E. Meyerhof) Hazorea I, 1973; Capo di Ponte, 1975; Evoluzione e Stilenell'arte Rupestre Camuna, 1975; Evolution and Style in Camunian Rock Art, 1976; Valcamonica Rock Art: A Selection of Prints from the Original Tracings, 1977; Methods of Recording and Analysing Rock Engravings, 1977; L'art Rupestre: Negev et Sinai, 1979; Valcamonica: 10000 Anni di Storia, 1980; Le Statue Stele delle Lunigiana: I Testimoni dell'ultima Rivoluzione Culturale della Preistoria, 1981; Luine, Collina Sacra, 1982; I Camunialle Radici della Civiltà Europea, 1982; Il Caso Valcamonica: Rapporto Uomo-Territorio Nella Dinamica Della Storia, 1982; Gli Elementi Fondamentali della Cultura, 1983; I Sardi: La Sardegna dal Paleoliticoall'età Romana, 1984; Har Karkom, Montagna Sacra nel Desertodell' Esodo, 1984; La Lombardia e le sue Grandi Stagioni, 1985; La Prehistoire des Alpes, 1986; The Mountain of God, 1988; Origini dell'artee della concettualita, 1988; Les Origines de l'Art, 1989; 10, 00 Anni di Storia in Valcamonica, 1990; Le Origini e il Problema dell'homo Religious, 1990; Felsbilder Wiege der Kunst und des Geistes, 1991; Le Radici della Cultura, 1992; Har Karkom in the Light of New Discoveries, 1993; World Rock Art, The Primordial Language, 1993, 4th ed., 2010; Spedizione Sinai: Nuove Scopertead Har Karkom, 1994; Arte Rupestre: Il Linguaggio Dei Primordi, 1994; IlLinguaggio delle pietre: Valcamonica: Una Storia per l'Europa, 1994; Valcamonica Rock Art: A New History for Europe, 1994; La religione delleorigini, 1995; La racines de la culture, 1995; Brescia preistorica: 300 Mila Anni di Presenza Umana nel Territorio Bresciano, 1995; Il museoimmaginario della preistorica, 1995; I Segni della storia, 1997; Esodo tramito e storia: Archeologia, Esegesi e Geografia Storica, 1997; L'artrupestre dans le monde, 1997; Tapa Tapa: Stoffe di Corteccia d'albero Macerata e Battuta di Papua Nuova Guinea e Dintorni, 1997; Höhlenmalerei: die Bilderwelt der Prähistorischen Felskunst, 1997; La religion des origines, 1999; Har Karkom: 20 Anni di Ricerche Archeologiche, 1999; Les mysteres du mont Sinai, 2000; (ed.) 40, 00 anni di arte contemporanea: Materiali per una esposizione sull'artepreistorica d' Europa, 2000; (contrib.) Figure dello spazio, 2000; The Riddle of Mount Sinai, Archaeological Discoveries at Har Karkom, 2001; Gobustan, Azerbaijan, 2001; La Struttura Elementare dell'arte, 2002; Lo Stile Come Fattore Diagnostico nell'arte Preistorica, 2002; Arte Preistorica: Una Rassegna Regionale, 2003; Introduzione all'arte Preistorica e Tribale, 2003; Aux Origines de l'art, 2003; (contrib.) Mysteries of the Bible, 2004; La Civiltà delle Pietre: Valcamonica una storia per l'Europa, vol. XVI, 2004; L'art du Tapa: étoffe pour les Dieus, étoffe pour les Hommes, 2005; Har Karkom: A Guide to Major Sites, 2006; L'odyssée des premiers hommes en Europe, 2007; Capire l'arte rupestre, 2007; (ed.) Prehistoric Art and Ideology, 2008; The Civiliszation of Rocks: Valcamonica, a History for Europe, 2008. **Address:** Centro Camuno di Studi Preistorici, 4 Via Guglielmo Marconi, Capo di Ponte, 25044, Italy. **Online address:** emmanuel.anati@gmail.com

ANAYA, Rudolfo A(lfonso). American (born United States), b. 1937. **Genres:** Novels, Novellas/Short Stories, Children's Fiction, Plays/Screenplays, Young Adult Non-fiction. **Career:** Teacher, 1963-70; University of Albuquerque, director of counseling, 1971-73, associate professor, 1974-88, professor of English, 1988-93, professor emeritus, 1993-; Universidad Anahuac, lecturer, 1974; New Mexico Writers Workshop, teacher, 1977-79; University of New Mexico, Department of English Language and Literature, associate professor, 1974-88, professor, 1988-93, professor emeritus, 1993-. Writer. **Publications:** NOVELS: Bless Me, Ultima, 1972; Heart of Aztlan, 1976; Oral Interpretations, 5th ed., 1977; (contrib.) New Voices 4in Literature, Language and Composition, 1978; (intro.) Mi Abuela Fumaba Puros, 1978; Tortuga, 1979; (contrib.) Anuario De Letras Chicanas, 1979; The Season of La Llorona, 1979; (contrib.) Grito Delsol, 1979; The Legend of La Llorona, 1984; Lord of the Dawn: The Legend of Quetzalcóatl, 1987; (contrib.) Flow of the River, 1988; Alburquerque, 1992; Zia Sammer, 1995; gfThe Anaya Reader, 1995; Rio Grande Fall, 1996; Jalamanta: Message From the Desert, 1996; Jemez Spring, 2005; The Man Who Could Fly and Other Stories, 2006; Curse of the ChupaCabra, 2006; The First Tortilla: A Bilingual Story, 2007; ChupaCabra and the Roswell UFO, 2008; Randy Lopez goes Home, 2011. FOR CHILDREN: The Farolitos of Christmas, 1995; Maya's Children: The Story of La Llorona, 1996; Farolito's for Abuelo, 1998; My Land Sings: Stories from the Rio Grande, 1999; Roadrunner's Dance, 2000; Juan and the Jackalope: A Children's Book in Verse, 2009. OTHERS: The Silence of the Llano (short stories), 1982; The Adventures of Juan Chicaspatas (poetry), 1985; A Chicano in China, 1986; Aztlán: Essays on the Chicano Homeland, 1989; Incredible Elfego Baca, 1993; Growing Up Chicana/o, 1993; Man on Fire: Luis Jimenez: El Hombre en Llamas, 1994; Zia Summer, 1995; Descansos, 1995; Writing the Southwest, 1995; (foreword) Dictionary of Hispanic Biography, 1996; Keep Blessing Us, Ultima: A Teaching Guide for Bless Me, 1997; Farolitos for Abuelo, 1998; (co-author) The Floating Borderlands: Twenty-five Years of U.S. Hispanic Literature, 1999; (co-author) Saints and Sinners: The American Catholic Experience through Stories, Memoirs, Essays, and Commentary, 1999; Shaman Winter, 1999; An Elegy on the Death of César Chávez, 2000; Serafina's Stories (folktales), 2004; The Santero's Miracle: A Bilingual Story, 2004; Essays, 2009; Billy the Kid and other Plays, 2011. EDITOR: (with J. Fisher) Voices from the Rio Grande, 1976; (with A. Marquez) Cuentos Chicanos, 1980; (with J. Griego) Tales from the Hispanic Southwest (bilingual folk tales), 1980; (with S.J. Ortiz) A Ceremony of Brotherhood, 1680-1980, 1981; Voces: An Anthology of Nuevo Mexicano Writers, 1987; Aztlán: Essays on the Chicano Homeland, 1989; Tierra: Contemporary Fiction of New Mexico 1989; Blue Mesa Review, vol. VIII: Approaching the Millennium, 1996. **Address:** Department of English Language and Literature, University of New Mexico, 1 University of New Mexico, PO Box 03 2170, Albuquerque, NM 87131-0001, U.S.A.

ANCELET, Barry Jean. (Jean Arceneaux). American (born United States), b. 1951. **Genres:** Cultural/Ethnic Topics, Poetry, Songs/Lyrics And Libretti, Music, Adult Non-fiction. **Career:** Indiana University, associate instructor in French, 1974-76; University of Southwestern Louisiana (now the University of Louisiana-Lafayette), Center for Acadian and Creole Folklore, director, 1977-80, Center for Louisiana Studies, folklorist, 1980-85, research fellow, Festival de Musique Acadienne, director, 1980-, assistant professor of French, 1985-, professor and Granger and Debaillon endowed professor in francophone studies; Louisiana Folklife Commission, chairman, 1984-90; Festival de Musique Acadienne/Cajun Music Festival, president, 1980-. Writer. **Publications:** Anthologie, litteirature francaise de la Louisiane, 1981; The Makers of Cajun Music: Musiciens cadiens et creoles, 1984; (with M. Allain) History on the Table: An Annotated Cookbook of Cajun and Creole Cuisine, 1984; Cajun Music: Origins and Development, 1989; (contrib.) Capitaine, Voyage ton Flag: The Traditional Cajun Country Mardi Gras, 1989; (with J. Edwards and G. Pitre) Cajun Country, 1991; (comp.) Cajun and Creole Folktales: The French Oral Tradition of South Louisiana, 1994; (contrib.) Cajun and Creole Music Makers: Musiciens Cadiens et Créoles, 1999; (with P. Gould, B. Graeff and D. Simpson) One Generation at a Time: Biography of a Cajun and Creole Music Festival, 2007. EDITOR: Jean l'Ours et la fille du roi, 1979; Acadie Tropicale, 1983; (with K. James) Vivre pour manger: Cajun and Acadian Cooking, 1983; (intro.) Tout Bec Doux: The Complete Cajun Comics of Ken Meaux and Earl Comeaux, 2011. POETRY AS JEAN ARCENEAUX: (co-author) Cris sur le bayou: Naissance d'une poésie acadienne en Louisiane, 1980; Je suis Cadien (I Am Cajun), 1994; Suite duLoup, 1999. EDITOR AND CONTRIBUTOR AS JEAN ARCENEAUX: (with M. Allain) Anthologie de la litterature francaise de Louisiane (Anthology of Louisiana French Literature), 1981; The Cajuns: Essays on Their History and Culture, 3rd ed., 1983; Louisiana Tapestry: Ethnicity in Saint Landry Parish, 1983. Contributor of articles to journals. **Address:** Department of Modern Languages, University of Louisiana, Rm. 453, Griffin Hall, PO Box 43331, Lafayette, LA 70504, U.S.A. **Online address:** ancelet@louisana.edu

ANCONA, George. American (born United States), b. 1929. **Genres:** Children's Fiction, Children's Non-fiction, Travel/Exploration. **Career:** New York Times, Promotion Department, graphic designer, 1950-51; Esquire magazine, art director, 1951-53; Seventeen magazine, Promotion Department, art director, 1953-54; Grey Advertising, art director, 1954-57; Daniel & Charles, art director, 1957-59; W.B. Doner & Co., art director, 1959-61; freelance photographer, children's book author and lecturer, 1961-. **Publications:** Monsters on Wheels, 1974; (with R. Charlip and M. Beth) Handtalk: An ABC of Finger Spelling and Sign Language, 1974; And What Do You Do?, 1975; I Feel: A Picture Book on Emotions, 1977; Growing Older, 1977; It's a Baby!, 1979; Dancing Is, 1981; Bananas, 1982; Monster Movers, 1983; Teamwork: A Picture Essay about Crews and Teams at Work, 1983; Freighters: Cargo Ships and the People Who Work Them, 1985; Sheepdog, 1985; Helping Out, 1985; (with R. Charlip and M. Beth) Handtalk Birthday: A Number and Story Book in Sign Language, 1987; Turtle Watch, 1987; The American Family Farm: A Photo Essay, 1989; (with J. Anderson) Handtalk Zoo, 1989; Riverkeeper, 1990; (with M.B. Miller) Handtalk School, 1991; The Aquarium, 1991; Man and Mustang, 1992; My Camera, 1992; Powwow, 1992; Ser Util, 1993; Pablo Remembers: The Fiesta of the Day of the Dead, 1993; The Piñata Maker/El piñatero, 1994; The Golden Lion Tamarin Comes Home, 1994; Ricardo's Day/El Dia de Ricardo, 1995; Fiesta U.S.A., 1995; Cutters, Carvers and the Cathedral, 1995; Earth Daughter: Alicia of Acoma Pueblo, 1995; In City Gardens, 1996; Mayeros: A Yucatec Maya Family, 1997; Fiesta Fireworks, 1997; Let's Dance!, 1998; Barrio: José's Neighborhood, 1998; Charro: The Mexican Cowboy, 1999; Carnaval, 1999; Our Adobe House, 1999; Cuban Kids, 2000; Harvest, 2001; Murals, Walls That Sing, 2003; Self Portrait, 2006; Capoeira: Game! Dance! Martial Art!, 2007. VIVA MEXICO! SERIES: The Fiestas, 2002; The People, 2002; The Food, 2002; The Folk Arts, 2002; The Past, 2002. BILINGUAL SERIES WITH A.F. ADA AND F.I. CAMPOY: Mi barrio/My Neighborhood, 2004; Mi casa/My House, 2004; Mi escuela/My School, 2004; Mi familia/My Family, 2004; Mis amigos/My Friends, 2004; Mis bailes/My Dances, 2004; Mi musica/My Music, 2005; Mis abuelos/My Grandparents, 2005; Mis comidas/My Foods, 2005; Mis fiestas/My Celebrations, 2005; Mis juegos/My Games, 2005; Mis quehaceres/My Chores, 2005. OTHERS: Olé Flamenco!, 2010; Gio and His Family, 2010; Come and Eat, 2011; It's Our Garden, 2012. Illustrator of books for children by others. **Address:** Charlesbridge, 85 Main St., Watertown, MA 02472, U.S.A. **Online address:** geoancona@cybermesa.com

ANDAYA, Barbara Watson. American/Australian (born Australia), b. 1943?. **Genres:** History, Women's Studies And Issues, Translations. **Career:** University of Hawaii, professor of Asian studies, Center for Southeast Asian Studies, director, 2003-; National University of Singapore, Raffles chair in history, 2007-08; International Institute for Asian Studies, fellow, 2008; University of Auckland, senior lecturer in history; Australian National University, Institute of Advanced Studies, resident fellow. Writer. **Publications:** Perak, the Abode of Grace: A Study of an Eighteenth-Century Malay State, 1979; (trans. with V. Matheson) R.A. al-Haji, The Precious Gift, 1982; (with L.Y. Andaya) A History of Malaysia, 1982, 2nd ed., 2001; To Live as Brothers: Southeast Sumatra in the Seventeenth and Eighteenth Centuries, 1993; (ed.) Other Pasts: Women, Gender, and History in Early Modern Southeast Asia, 2000; The Flaming Womb: Repositioning Women in Early Modern Southeast Asia, 2006. Contributor to books, periodicals and journals. **Address:** Center for Southeast Asian Studies, University of Hawaii, 406 Moore Hall, 1890 E West Rd., Honolulu, HI 96822-2318, U.S.A. **Online address:** bandaya@hawaii.edu

ANDE, Jan Lee. American (born United States), b. 1948. **Genres:** Poetry. **Career:** Immune Response Corp., assistant and HIV/AIDS director, 1990-92; Union Institute & University, instructor of poetry, poetics, and history of religions, 1993-. Writer. **Publications:** Instructions for Walking on Water, 2001; Reliquary, 2003. Contributor to periodicals. **Address:** Union Institute & University, 440 E McMillan St., Cincinnati, OH 45206-1925, U.S.A. **Online address:** ande@poetrywriter.com

ANDEREGG, David. American (born United States), b. 1953. **Genres:** Psychology. **Career:** Cambridge School of Ballet, rehearsal and performance pianist; Walnut Hill School, rehearsal and performance pianist; Concert Dance Co., rehearsal and performance pianist; Boston Conservatory, rehearsal and performance pianist; Harvard University, Graduate School of Education, research assistant, Harvard Medical School, instructor; Research Institute for Educational Problems, research assistant; Smith College School for Social Work, instructor; Bennington College, instructor, 1999-. Writer and psychologist. **Publications:** Worried All the Time: Overparenting in an Age of Anxiety and How to Stop It, 2003; Nerds: Who They Are and Why We Need More of Them, 2007. Contributor of articles to books, periodicals and journals. **Address:** Bennington College, 1 College Dr., Bennington, VT 05201, U.S.A. **Online address:** danderegg@bennington.edu

ANDERS, Charlie. (Charlie Jane Anders). American (born United States) **Genres:** Sciences, Young Adult Fiction, Psychology, Social Sciences. **Career:** Writers with Drinks, organizer, 2001-; Other Magazine, publisher, 2002. Writer. **Publications:** The Lazy Crossdresser, 2002; Choir Boy, 2005; (ed. with A.Newitz) She's Such a Geek! Women Write about Science, Technology, & Other Nerdy Stuff, 2006. works appear in anthologies. Contributor to periodicals. **Address:** 584 Castro St., Ste. 674, San Francisco, CA 94114, U.S.A. **Online address:** charlieanders2@gmail.com

ANDERS, Charlie Jane. *See* **ANDERS, Charlie.**

ANDERS, C. J. *See* **BENNETT, Cherie.**

ANDERS, Isabel. American (born United States), b. 1946. **Genres:** Theology/Religion, inspirational/Motivational Literature, Biography, Young Adult Fiction. **Career:** David C. Cook Publishing Co., religion editor, 1969-76; Tyndale House Publishers, book editor, 1976-83; Synthesis Publications, managing editor, 1990-, contributing writer; Eggman Publishing, consultant, 1995-. **Publications:** Awaiting the Child: An Advent Journal, 1987; (with R.H. Calkin) Letters to Kristi (juvenile), 1990; The Lord's Prayer: Peace and Self-Acceptance for Those in Recovery, 1991; The Faces of Friendship, 1992; The Lord's Blessings: Hope and Peace for Those in Recovery, 1992; Walking with the Shepherd (devotional), 1994; Standing on High Places: The Story of Hannah Hurnard and Hinds' Feet on High Places (biography), 1994; A Book of Blessings for Working Mothers, 1994; (comp.) The Wisdom of Little Women, 1995; Sand and Shells, Carousels, Silver Bells: A Child's Seasons of Prayer, 1996; Simple Blessings for Sacred Moments, 1998; The Real Night before Christmas, Luke 2: 8-20, 1999; Easter ABCs: Matthew 28: 1-28; Mark 16: 1-8; Luke 24: 1-12; John 20: 1-18 (juvenile), 1999; Soul Moments: Times When Heaven Touches Earth, 2000; Jesus' Spiritual Laws, 2000; The Lord's Prayer for a New Millennium, 2001; Seasons for the Soul: 366 Days to Let the Light of God Shine Through, 2008; (ed.) 40-day Journey with Madeleine L' Engle, 2009; Blessings and Prayers for Married Couples: A Faith Full Love, 2011. **Address:** Systhesis, PO Box 328, Boyds, MD 20841-0328, U.S.A. **Online address:** isabel@isabelanders.com

ANDERS, Leslie. American (born United States), b. 1922. **Genres:** History, Politics/Government, Education. **Career:** Central Missouri State University, assistant professor, 1955-58, associate professor, 1958-63, professor, 1963-87, professor emeritus of history, 1987-. Writer and historian. **Publications:** The Ledo Road: General Joseph W. Stilwell's Highway to China, 1965; The Eighteenth Missouri, 1968; Education for Service: Centennial History of Central Missouri State College, 1971; The Twenty-First Missouri: From Home Guard to Union Regiment, 1975; Gentle Knight: The Life and Times of Major General Edwin F. Harding, 1985; (ed. and comp.) Confederate Roll of Honor: Missouri, 1989; The Test of Time, 1998; Twenty-first Missouri Volunteer Infantry, 1861-65, forthcoming. **Address:** Department of History, Central Missouri State University, PO Box 800, Warrensburg, MO 64093, U.S.A.

ANDERSEN, Kurt Byars. American (born United States), b. 1954. **Genres:** Novels, Plays/Screenplays. **Career:** National Broadcasting Co., NBC-TV, executive producer and head writer, 1976-80; Time Magazine, writer, 1981-83, associate editor, 1983-86, architecture critic, 1984-93, columnist, 1993-94; Spy Magazine, co-founder and co-editor, 1986-93; New York Magazine, editor-in-chief, 1994-96, contributing editor, 2004-, writer and columnist, 2004-08; New Yorker, columnist and staff writer, 1996-99; Inside.com, co-founder, 1999-2001; Public Radio International & WNYC, radio show host, 1999-; novelist, 1999-; Powerful Media, founder, 2000; USA Television, consulting executive producer, 2000-03; Colors Magazine, editorial director, 2003-05; Vanity Fair, contributing editor, 2007-; Random House, editor-at-large, 2007-. **Publications:** The Real Thing, 1980; (with M. O'Donnell and R. Parloff) Tools of Power, 1980; (intro.) Laughing Matters: A Celebration of American Humor, 1987; (with J. Malanowski and L. Birnbach) Loose Lips, 1995; Turn of the Century (novel), 1999; (contrib.) Pleasure, 2002; (ed. and intro. with G. Carter) Spy: The Funny Years, 2006; Heyday (novel), 2007; Reset: How this Crisis Can Restore Our Values and Renew America, 2009; (intro.) The Lost Honor of Katharina Blum, 2009; (intro.) The Photographs of John Vachon, 2010; (foreword) Spark, 2011. Contributor to books, magazines and newspapers. **Address:** c/o Suzanne Gluck, William Morris Agency, 1325 Ave. of the Americas, New York, NY 10019, U.S.A. **Online address:** emailandersen@aol.com

ANDERSEN, Martin Edwin. American (born United States), b. 1954?. **Genres:** Military/Defense/Arms Control, History. **Career:** New York Times, news assistant, 1980-81; freelance reporter, 1981-82; Newsweek, special correspondent, 1982-87; Washington Post, special correspondent, 1982-87; National Democratic Institute for International Affairs, director, 1987-90; U.S. Senate, office of Majority Whip, legislative assistant for defense and foreign policy, 1990-91; Noticias, special correspondent, 1993-94; City University of New York, John Jay College of Criminal Justice, international human rights lecturer, 1993-94; Center for Democracy, senior consultant, 1993-94; U.S. Department of Justice, International Criminal Investigation Training Assistant Program (ICITAP), consultant and program evaluator, 1993-95, Criminal Division, senior advisor for policy planning, Haitian Police Development Project, assistant project manager, 1995; International Foundation for Election Systems, consultant, 1998-99; Inter-American Development Bank, international consultant, 1997-2000; Government Accountability Project, media director, 2001-. Writer. **Publications:** (Ed.) Hacia una nueva relación: El papel de las fuerzas armadas en ungobierno democrático, 1990; Dossier Secreto: Argentina's Desaparecidos and the Myth of the Dirty War, 1993; La policía: Pasado, presente y propuestas para el futuro, 2002; Peoples of the Earth: Ethnonationalism, Democracy, and the Indigenous Challenge in Latin America, 2010. Contributor to periodicals. **Address:** Government Accountability Project, 1612 K St. NW, Ste. 1100, Washington, DC 20006, U.S.A. **Online address:** anacasti@aol.com

ANDERSON, Allan. British (born England), b. 1949?. **Genres:** Theology/Religion. **Career:** Minister in South Africa, 1973-95; Tshwane Theological College, founder and principal, 1988-95; University of South Africa, Pentecostalism Project of the Research Institute for Theology and Religions, part-time researcher, 1989-95; Centre for New Religious Movements, director, 1995; University of Birmingham, lecturer, 1995, professor of global pentecostal studies, Centre for Pentecostal and Charismatic Studies, director, 1995-, chair, 2005-, Graduate Institute of Theology and Religion, director, 2006-; Steering Group of the European Research Network on Global Pentecostalism, founding member. Writer. **Publications:** Moya: The Holy Spirit in an African Context, 1991; Bazalwane: African Pentecostals in South Africa, 1992; Tumelo: The Faith of African Pentecostals in South Africa, 1993; (ed. with W.J. Hollenweger) Pentecostals after a Century, 1999; Zion and Pentecost: The Spirituality and Experience of Pentecostal and Zionist/Apostolic Churches in South Africa, 2000; African Reformation: African Initiated Christianity in the 20th Century, 2001; An Introduction to Pentecostalism: Global Charismatic Christianity, 2004; (ed. with E. Tang) Asian and Pentecostal: The Charismatic Face of Christianity in Asia, 2005; Spreading Fires: The Missionary Nature of Early Pentecostalism, 2007; (co-ed.) Studying Global Pentecostalism: Theories and Methods, 2010. **Address:** Graduate Institute for Theology & Religion, University of Birmingham, Elmfield House, 996 Bristol Rd., Birmingham, WM B29 6LG, England. **Online address:** a.h.anderson@bham.ac.uk

ANDERSON, Alun M. British/Welsh (born Wales), b. 1948. **Genres:** Natural History, Sciences, Technology. **Career:** Nature, editor, 1980-83, Tokyo bureau chief, 1983-86, Washington bureau chief, 1986-90; Science, international editor, 1991-92; New Scientist, editor, 1992-99, editor-in-chief and publishing director, 1999-2005, senior consultant, 2005-; Xconomy.com, director, 2007-. Science journalist. **Publications:** Science and Technology in Japan, 1984, 3rd ed., 1995; Reisengo no Sekai to Nihon: Sekai no Chomei Janarisuto ga Chokugensuru, 1990; (ed. with M. O'Hare) Bizarre Tales from New Scientist, 1998; (ed. with M. O'Hare) Daughter of Bizarre Tales from New Scientist, 1999; After the Ice: Life, Death, and Geopolitics in the New Arctic, 2009. **Address:** New Scientist, Lacon House, 84 Theobald's Rd., London, GL WC1X 8NS, England.

ANDERSON, Amanda. American (born United States), b. 1960?. **Genres:** Young Adult Non-fiction, Cultural/Ethnic Topics, History. **Career:** University of Illinois, assistant professor, 1989-95, associate professor, 1995-99; Johns Hopkins University, professor, 1999-2002, Caroline Donovan Professor of English Literature, 2002-, department chair, 2003-, director of graduate studies, 2001-02; Cornell University (Summer Institute), School of Criticism and Theory, director, 2008-. Writer. **Publications:** NONFICTION: Tainted Souls and Painted Faces: The Rhetoric of Fallenness in Victorian Culture, 1993; The Powers of Distance: Cosmopolitanism and the Cultivation of Detachment, 2001; (ed. with J. Valente) Disciplinarity at the Fin De Siècle, 2002; The Way We Argue Now: A Study in the Cultures of Theory, 2006. **Address:** Department of English, Johns Hopkins University, 1102A Dell House, 3400 N Charles St., Baltimore, MD 21218-2608, U.S.A. **Online address:** aanderson@jhu.edu

ANDERSON, Annelise Graebner. American (born United States), b. 1938. **Genres:** Criminology/True Crime. **Career:** California State University, assistant professor, associate professor of business administration, 1975-80; U.S. Office of Management and Budget, associate director for economics and government, 1981-83; Federal Home Loan Bank of San Francisco, director, 1983-85; Stanford University, Hoover Institution, senior research fellow, 1984-; Financial Corporation of America, director, 1984-88. Writer. **Publications:** NONFICTION: The Business of Organized Crime: A Cosa Nostra Family, 1979; Illegal Aliens and Employer Sanctions: Solving the Wrong Problem, 1986; (ed. with D.L. Bark) Thinking about America: The United States in the 1990s, 1988. (co-author) Privatization: Toward More Effective Government: Report of the President's Commission on Privatization, 1988; The Ruble Problem: A Competitive Solution, 1992; Political Money: The New Prohibition, 1997; (ed.) Political Money: Deregulating American Politics: Selected Writings on Campaign Finance Reform, 2000; (ed. with K.K. Skinner and M. Anderson) Reagan, in His Own Hand, 2001; (ed. with K.K. Skinner and M. Anderson) Stories in His Own Hand: The Everyday Wisdom of Ronald Reagan, 2001; FreeBSD: An Open-Source Operating System for Your Personal Computer, 2001, 2nd ed., 2001; (ed. and intro. with K.K. Skinner and M. Anderson) Reagan: A Life in Letters, 2003; (ed. with K.K. Skinner and M. Anderson) Reagan's Path to Victory: The Shaping of Ronald Reagan's Vision: Selected Writings, 2004; (with M. Anderson) Reagan's Secret War: The Untold Story of His Fight to Save the World from Nuclear Disaster, 2009. Contributor to books and periodicals. **Address:** Hoover Institution, Stanford University, 434 Galvez Mall, Stanford, CA 94305-6010, U.S.A. **Online address:** andrsn@hoover.stanford.edu

ANDERSON, Barth. American (born United States) **Genres:** Novels, Young Adult Fiction, Mystery/Crime/Suspense. **Career:** Writer. **Publications:** The Patron Saint of Plagues, 2006; The Magician and the Fool, 2008. Works appear in anthologies. Contributor of articles to periodicals. **Address:** Scribe Agency L.L.C, 5508 Joylynne Dr, Madison, WI 53716, U.S.A. **Online address:** barthanderson@earthlink.net

ANDERSON, Brian C. American (born United States), b. 1961. **Genres:** Politics/Government, Adult Non-fiction. **Career:** American Enterprise Institute, research associate in social and political studies; Manhattan Institute, City Journal, editor, senior editor; Crisis, literary editor. **Publications:** The Pope in America, 1996; Raymond Aron: The Recovery of the Political, 1997; On Cultivating Liberty, 1999; South Park Conservatives: The Revolt against Liberal Media Bias, 2005; Democratic Capitalism and Its Discontents, 2007; (with A.D. Thierer) A Manifesto for Media Freedom, 2008. **Address:** Manhattan Institute, City Journal, 52 Vanderbilt Ave., New York, NY 10017, U.S.A.

ANDERSON, Burton. Italian/American (born United States), b. 1938. **Genres:** Food And Wine. **Career:** Rome Daily American, reporter, 1962-63, news editor, 1965-67; Tehran Journal, reporter, 1963; Minneapolis Tribune, reporter, 1964-65; Honolulu Advertiser, reporter, 1965; International Herald Tribune, news editor, 1968-77. **Publications:** Vino: The Wines and Winemakers of Italy, 1980; Burton Anderson's Guide to Italian Wines, 1982, rev. ed. as The Simon & Schuster Guide to the Wines of Italy, 1992; Simon & Schuster Pocket Guide to Italian Wines, 1982, 2nd ed., 1987; Burton Anderson's Guide to Italian Wines, 1984; The Wine Atlas of Italy, 1990; Treasures of the Italian Table: Italy's Celebrated Foods And The Artisans Who Make Them, 1994 in UK as Pleasures of the Italian Table, 1994; Wines of Italy, 2000, rev. ed., 2004; We Claim the Title: Korean War Marines, 2000; California Rodeo Salinas: 100 Years of History: A History Project by the California Rodeo Salinas, 2002; Boccadoro the Honorary Pirate, 2007. Contributor to periodicals. **Address:** Doe Coover Agency, PO Box 668, Winchester, MA 01890, U.S.A.

ANDERSON, Christy. (Christy Jo Anderson). Canadian (born Canada), b. 1959. **Genres:** History, Education, Architecture. **Career:** University of Toronto, associate professor of art history. Writer. **Publications:** National Register Sites and Historical Markers in South Carolina Associated with Education, 2001; (ed. with K. Koehler) The Built Surface, vol. I: Architecture and the Pictorial Arts from Antiquity to the Enlightenment, vol. II: Architecture and the Visual, 2002; Inigo Jones and the Classical Tradition, 2007. Contributor of articles to books, periodicals and journals. **Address:** Department of Art, University of Toronto, Sidney Smith Hall, 100 St. George St., Ste. 6036, Toronto, ON M5S 3G3, Canada. **Online address:** christy_anderson@utoronto.ca

ANDERSON, Christy Jo. *See* **ANDERSON, Christy.**

ANDERSON, David. American (born United States), b. 1952. **Genres:** Literary Criticism And History, Business/Trade/Industry, Young Adult Fiction, Poetry. **Career:** University of Rome, lecturer, 1979-80; University of Pennsylvania, assistant professor, 1980-87; American Academy in Rome, Mellon fellow, 1988-89; Universitat Tubingen, wissenschaftlicher assistant, 1990-95; Empire Valuation Consultants, associate, 1997-2000; EisnerAmper, Litigation Services Group, senior manager; American Society of Appraisers, chapter president. Writer. **Publications:** Pound's Cavalcanti: An Edition of the Translations, Notes and Essays, 1983; (ed.) Sixty Bokes Olde and Newe, 1986; Before the Knight's Tale: Imitation of Classical Epic in Boccaccio's Teseida, 1988; Boccaccio's Glosses on Statius, 1994. **Address:** Eisner-Amper LLP, 750 3rd Ave., New York, NY 10017, U.S.A. **Online address:** david.anderson@eisneramper.com

ANDERSON, David Daniel. American (born United States), b. 1924. **Genres:** Novels, Literary Criticism And History, Biography, Essays. **Career:** University of Karachi, Fulbright professor, 1963-64; Michigan State University, Department of American Thought and Language, instructor, 1956-, professor of American literature, university distinguished professor, now distinguished professor emeritus in American literature; Society for the Study of Midwestern Literature Inc, co-founder and executive director, 1971-. Writer. **Publications:** Louis Bromfield, 1964; (contrib.) Critical Studies in American Literature, 1964; Sherwood Anderson, 1967; Sherwood Anderson's Winesburg, Ohio, 1967; Barron's Simplified Approach to Winesburg, Ohio: Sherwood Anderson, 1967; Brand Whitlock, 1968; Abraham Lincoln, 1970; Robert Ingersoll, 1972; Woodrow Wilson, 1978; Ignatius Donnelly, 1980; William Jennings Bryan, 1981; Michigan: A State Anthology, 1982; Route 2, Titus, Ohio, 1993; The Path in the Shadow, 1998; Command Performances, 2003; Ohio in Myth, Memory, and Imagination, 2004. EDITOR: The Black Experience, 1969; (and intro.) The Literary Works of Abraham Lincoln, 1970; (with R.L. Wright) The Dark and Tangled Path, 1971; Sunshine and Smoke, 1971; Mid-America I-XXVII, 1974-2001; Sherwood Anderson: Dimensions of His Literary Art (essays), 1976; (with J. Salzman and K. Ohashi) Sherwood Anderson: The Writer at His Craft, 1979; Critical Essays on Sherwood Anderson, 1981; Michigan, a State Anthology: Writings about the Great Lake State, 1641-1981, 1983; The Durability of Raintree County, 1998; Lieutenant William E. Sleight and the 102nd Regiment, U.S. Colored Infantry, in the Civil War, 2003. **Address:** Department of Writing, Rhetoric, & American, Cultures, Michigan State University, 235 Bessey Hall, East Lansing, MI 48824-1033, U.S.A.

ANDERSON, Donna K. American (born United States), b. 1935. **Genres:** Music, Bibliography, Biography, Young Adult Fiction. **Career:** MacPhail School of Music, piano teacher, 1956-59; Summit School, piano teacher, 1959-61; Neighborhood Music School, piano teacher, 1965-66; New York Public Library for the Performing Arts, Music Division, research assistant, 1966-67; State University of New York College, assistant professor, 1967-70, associate professor, 1970-78, professor of music, 1978-, head of department, 1985-92, professor emeritus of music, 1997-. Writer. **Publications:** Charles T. Griffes: An Annotated Bibliography-Discography, 1977; The Works of Charles T. Griffes: A Descriptive Catalogue, 1983; Charles T. Griffes: A Life in Music, 1993. EDITOR: Three Preludes, 1967; Four Impressions, 1970; (trans.) Four German Songs, 1970; De Profundis, 1977; Song of the Dagger, 1983; Nachtlied, 1983; Rhapsody in B Minor, 1984; Seven English Songs, 1986; (trans.) Seven German Songs, 1986; The Pleasure Dome of Kubla-Khan, 1993; Charles T. Griffes: A Winter Landscape, 1997; Barcarolle, 2000. Contributor of articles to journals. **Address:** 4079 Highland Rd., Cortland, NY 13045, U.S.A. **Online address:** andersond@snycorva.cortland.edu

ANDERSON, Doug Douglas. (Keith Douglas Anderson). American (born United States), b. 1943. **Genres:** Poetry. **Career:** Mount Wachusett Community College, instructor; University of Connecticut, instructor; University of Massachusetts, William Joiner Center for the Study of War and Its Social Consequences, teacher; Smith College, faculty; Hampshire College, faculty; Claremont College, faculty; Pacific University of Oregon, MFA Program, faculty, 2010. Writer. **Publications:** Bamboo Bridge: Poems, 1991; Blues for Unemployed Secret Police: Poems, 2000; Keep Your Head Down: Vietnam, the Sixties, and a Journey of Self-Discovery (memoir), 2009. Contributor to periodicals. **Address:** Hartford, CT , U.S.A. **Online address:** doug.anderson1943@gmail.com

ANDERSON, Douglas A(llen). American (born United States), b. 1959. **Genres:** Literary Criticism And History, Bibliography. **Career:** Writer, 1994-. **Publications:** (Afterword) The Chalchiuhite Dragon: A Tale of Toltec Times, 1992; (with W.G. Hammond) J.R.R. Tolkien: A Descriptive Bibliography, 1993. EDITOR: (with C. Tolkien and intro.) The Lord of the Rings, 1987, rev. ed., 2002; The Annotated Hobbit, 1988, rev. ed., 2002; The Lady of Frozen Death, and Other Weird Tales, 1992; The Dragon Path: Collected Tales of Kenneth Morris, 1995; The Scarecrow and Other Tales, 2001; The Hobbit, 2001; (with S.T. Joshi and D.E. Schultz) Eyes of the God: The Weird Fiction and Poetry of R.H. Barlow, 2002; Tales before Tolkien: The Roots of Modern Fantasy, 2003; Seekers of Dreams, 2005; Adrift on the Haunted Seas: The Best Stories of William Hope Hodgson, 2005; Tales before Narnia: The Roots of Modern Fantasy and Science Fiction, 2008; (with V. Flieger) Tolkien On Fairy-stories, 2008; Devil's Drums, 2011; J.R.R. Tolkien: Interviews, Reminiscences, and Other Essays, forthcoming. CO-EDITOR: (with M.D.C. Drout and V. Flieger) Tolkien Studies: An Annual Scholarly Review, 8 vols., 2004-11. **Address:** PO Box 493, Marcellus, MI 49067, U.S.A. **Online address:** nodens100@hotmail.com

ANDERSON, Duane. American (born United States), b. 1943. **Genres:** Anthropology/Ethnology, Environmental Sciences/Ecology. **Career:** Sanford Museum and Planetarium, director, 1966-75; Iowa State Preserves Board, chairperson, 1975-86; University of Iowa, state archaeologist, 1975-86, teacher, Museum of Natural History, teacher; Dayton Museum of Natural History, executive director, 1986-92; School of American Research (now School of Advanced Research), vice president, 1992-, Indian Arts Research Center, vice president and director, 1992-99, research associate, 1999-; Indian Arts Research Center, director; New Mexico Museum of Natural History Foundation, director, 1994-97; Museum of Indian Arts and Culture/Laboratory of Anthropology, director, 2000-05, now retired. Writer. **Publications:** Brewster Site (13CK15): Lithic Analysis; 1973; Western Iowa Prehistory, 1975; (ed. with H.A. Semken, Jr.) The Cherokee Excavations: Holocene Ecology and Human Adaptations in Northwestern Iowa, 1980; Eastern Iowa Prehistory, 1981; Mill Creek Ceramics: The Complex from the Brewster Site, 1981; Stone, Glass, and Metal Artifacts from the Milford Site (13DK1): An Early 18th Century Oneota Component in Northwest Iowa, 1994; All That Glitters: The Emergence of Native American Micaceous Art Pottery in Northern New Mexico, 1999; (ed.) Legacy: Southwest Indian Art at the School of American Research, 1999; When Rain Gods Reigned: From Curios to Art at Tesuque Pueblo, 2002; (with F.H. Harlow and D.P. Lanmon) Pottery of Santa Ana Pueblo, 2005; (contrib.) Ten Kate Collection 1882-1888: American Indian Material Culture, 2010. **Address:** School for Advanced Research, School of American Research Press, 660 Garcia St., PO Box 2188, Santa Fe, NM 87505, U.S.A.

ANDERSON, Elijah. American (born United States), b. 1943?. **Genres:** Sociology, Human Relations/Parenting, Social Commentary, Social Sciences. **Career:** Swarthmore College, assistant professor of sociology, 1973-78; University of Pennsylvania, Department of Sociology, assistant professor, 1975-82, undergraduate chairman, 1976-77, associate professor, 1982-88, acting director of the Afro-American studies program, 1983-84, professor of sociology, 1988-2005, Max and Heidi Berry, term chair in the social sciences, 1989, Charles and William, day chair of the social sciences, 1991, Charles and William L. Day distinguished professor in social sciences, 2001; Yale University, William K. Lanman, Jr. professor of sociology, 2007-; Qualitative Sociology, associate editor, 1988; American Journal of Sociology, consulting editor, 1988-90; Ethnography, associate editor, 1999. Writer. **Publications:** A Place on the Corner: A Study of Black Street Corner Men, 1978, rev. ed., 2003; Streetwise: Race, Class and Change in an Urban Community, 1990; (intro.) The Philadelphia Negro: A Social Study, 1995; The Code of the Street: Decency, Violence and the Moral Life of the Inner City, 1999; (ed. with D.S. Massey) Problem of the Century: Racial Stratification in the United States, 2001; A Place on the Corner: A Study of the Black Street Corner Men, 2004; Being Here and Being There, 2004; (ed.) Against the Wall: Poor, Young, Black and Male, 2008; Cosmopolitan Canopy: Race and Civility in Everyday

Life, 2011. Contributor to periodicals. **Address:** Department of Sociology, Yale University, 140 Prospect St., PO Box 208265, New Haven, CT 06520-8265, U.S.A. **Online address:** elijah.anderson@yale.edu

ANDERSON, Elizabeth (S.). American (born United States), b. 1959. **Genres:** Ethics, Philosophy, Women's Studies And Issues, Law, Politics/Government. **Career:** Swarthmore College, visiting instructor in philosophy, 1985-86; University of Michigan, assistant professor of philosophy, 1987-93, associate professor of philosophy and women's studies, 1987-99, Arthur F. Thurnau professor, 1994, professor of philosophy and women's studies, 1999-, John Rawls collegiate professor of philosophy and women's studies, 2005-. Writer. **Publications:** Value in Ethics and Economics, 1993; The Imperative of Integration, 2010. Contributor of articles to books and journals. **Address:** Department of Philosophy, University of Michigan, 2239 Angell Hall, 435 S State St., Ann Arbor, MI 48109-1003, U.S.A. **Online address:** eandersn@umich.edu

ANDERSON, Fil. American (born United States), b. 1951. **Genres:** Young Adult Non-fiction, Theology/Religion, Self Help. **Career:** Young Life, area and regional director and national director of training, 1974-99; Journey Resources, founder, executive director, 2000-. Writer. **Publications:** Running on Empty: Contemplative Spirituality for Overachievers, 2004; Breaking the Rules: Trading Performance for Intimacy with God, 2010. Contributor to books. **Address:** Journey Resources, PO Box 9801, Greensboro, NC 27429, U.S.A. **Online address:** filanderson@triad.rr.com

ANDERSON, Gary L. American (born United States), b. 1948. **Genres:** Education, Young Adult Non-fiction, Administration/Management. **Career:** Teacher of English and Spanish, 1971-74; Higher Education Development Fund-Harlem Center, teacher director and coordinator of bilingual programs, 1974-81; State University of New York, Equal Opportunity Center, lecturer, 1981-82; American School of Puebla, high school principal, 1982-84; Ohio State University, instructor and field supervisor, 1984-87; Western Maryland College, adjunct faculty, 1987-88; University of New Mexico, assistant professor, 1988-94, associate professor of education, 1994-, director of Latin American programs in education, 1991-93, Language, Literacy and Socio-Cultural Studies Division, coordinator, 1993-94; New York University, Steinhardt School of Education, professor of educational administration. Writer. **Publications:** (With K. Herr and A. Nihlen) Studying Your Own School: An Educator's Guide to Qualitative, Practitioner Research, 1994, 2nd ed., 2007; (with J. Blase and S. Dungan) Democratic Principals in Action: Eight Pioneers, 1995; (with J. Blase) The Micropolitics of Educational Leadership: From Control to Empowerment, 1995; (ed. and trans. with M.M. Sieburth) Educational Qualitative Research in Latin America: The Struggle for a New Paradigm, 1998; (with K. Herr) Action Research Dissertation: A Guide for Students and Faculty, 2005; (ed. with K.G. Herr) Encyclopedia of Activism and Social Justice, 2007; Advocacy Leadership: Toward a Post-Reform Agenda in Education, 2009. Contributor to books. **Address:** Culture, Education, and Human Development, Steinhardt School, New York University, 82 Washington Sq. E, New York, NY 10003, U.S.A. **Online address:** gary.anderson@nyu.edu

ANDERSON, Henry L(ee Norman). (Henry L. N. Anderson). American (born United States), b. 1934. **Genres:** Education, Gay And Lesbian Issues, Human Relations/Parenting, Medicine/Health, Race Relations, Novels, Social Sciences. **Career:** Los Angeles County Schools, teacher, 1961-66; Los Angeles Unified Schools District, instructor, administrator, 1967-68; University of California, Department of Special Education Programs, associate director, 1968-69; Loyola University, Graduate School of Education, supervisor of student teachers, 1972-73; California State University, supervisor of student teachers, 1972-73; Windsor University, vice-president, 1973-75; City University, founding chancellor, 1974-, now chancellor emeritus; Evaluations and Management International Inc., director, 1971; Organic Wellness Crusade, founder and creator. Writer and radio and television host. **Publications:** You and Race: A Christian Reflects, 1960; No Use Cryin' (novel), 1961; Revolutionary Urban Teaching, 1973; (as Henry L.N Anderson) Helping Hand: Eight-Day Diet Programs for People Who Care about Wellness, 1986; Ihre gesundheit liegt in ihrerhand, 1992; (as Henry L.N Anderson) Organic Wellness Fasting Technique, 1992; (as Henry L.N Anderson) African: Born in America, 1993; The Nature and Purpose of Disease: Definitive Guide for Peoples with Melanin, 2001. Contributor to journals. **Address:** City University, PO Box 45227, Los Angeles, CA 90045-0221, U.S.A. **Online address:** dr.anderson@cula.edu

ANDERSON, Henry L. N. *See* **ANDERSON, Henry L(ee Norman).**

ANDERSON, H(ugh) George. American (born United States), b. 1932. **Genres:** Theology/Religion, Technology, Marketing, Social Sciences, Humanities. **Career:** Lutheran Theological Southern Seminary, faculty, 1970-82, president, 1970-82; Luther College, president, 1982-96; Minnesota Public Radio, director, 1984-90; Evangelical Lutheran Church in America, presiding bishop, 1995-2001. Writer. **Publications:** Lutheranism in the Southeastern States, 1860-1886: A Social History, 1969; A Good Time to Be the Church: A Conversation with Bishop H. George Anderson, 1997; (with H.W. Chilstrom and M.S. Hanson) Living Together as Lutherans: Unity Within Diversity, 2008. EDITOR: (with T.A. Murphy and J.A. Burgess) Justification by Faith, 1985; (with J.R. Crumley, Jr.) Promoting Unity: Themes in Lutheran-Catholic Dialogue, 1989; (with J.F. Stafford and J.A. Burgess) The One Mediator, The Saints, and Mary, 1992. **Address:** Evangelical Lutheran Church in America, 8765 W Higgins Rd., Chicago, IL 60631, U.S.A. **Online address:** hgeorgea@earthlink.net

ANDERSON, James G. Canadian (born Canada), b. 1967. **Genres:** Novels, Science Fiction/Fantasy. **Career:** St. Therese Institute of Faith and Mission, staff. Writer, musician and educator. **Publications:** (With M. Sebanc) The Stoneholding (fantasy novel), 2009; (with M. Sebanc) Darkling Fields of Arvon (fantasy novel), 2010. **Address:** Saskatoon, SK , Canada. **Online address:** contact@stoneharp.com

ANDERSON, James G. American (born United States), b. 1936. **Genres:** Education, Information Science/Computers, Medicine/Health, Sociology. **Career:** Loyola High School, teacher, 1959-62; Hamstead Hill Junior High School, teacher, 1961; Mount St. Agnes College, instructor in mathematics, 1962-64; Johns Hopkins University, Evening College, administrative assistant, 1964-65, Division of Engineering, director, 1965-66; New Mexico State University, research professor of educational administration, 1966-70; Purdue University, Schools of Engineering, Center for Large Scale Systems, faculty, 1970-73, Department of sociology and industrial engineering, associate professor, 1970-74, professor, 1974-, Department of Sociology and Anthropology, Health Service Research and Training Program, associate director, 1971-76, School of Humanities, Social Science, and Education, assistant dean for analytical studies, 1975-78, AIDS Research Center, assistant director, 1991-, Social Research Institute, director, 1995-98, professor of communication, 2004-; Methodist Hospital of Indiana, Department of Academic Affairs, visiting research professor of medical sociology, 1981-82, Graduate Medical Education Program, adjunct professor of medical sociology, 1991-; Indiana University and Purdue University, Rural Center for AIDS/STD Prevention, co-director 1994-. Writer and consultant. **Publications:** Bureaucracy in Education, 1968; (with J. Sullivan) Simulation in Health Care, 1991; Medical Sciences Simulation Conference, 1998; (co-author) Simulation in the Health and Medical Sciences, 2001; In Sickness and Health: Health Care in the U.S. and Great Britain, forthcoming; (intro.) Structural Equation Models in the Social Sciences, forthcoming. EDITOR: (with S.J. Jay) Use and Impact of Computers in Clinical Medicine, 1987; Simulation in Health Care and Social Services, 1992; (with M. Katzper) Simulation in the Health Sciences and Services, 1993; (with C. Aydin and S. Jay) Evaluating Health Care Information Systems, 1994; (with M. Katzper) Simulation in the Health Sciences, 1994; (with M. Katzper) Health Sciences, Physiological and Pharmacological Simulation Studies, 1995; (with M. Katzper) Simulation in the Medical Sciences, 1996; (with M. Katzper) Health Sciences Simulation, 1999, rev. ed., 2005; (with K.W. Goodman) Ethics and Information Technology: A Case-Based Approach to a Health Care System in Transition, 2002; (ed. with C. Aydin) Evaluating the Organizational Impact of Health Care Information Systems, 2005. **Address:** Department of Sociology and Anthropology, Purdue University, 353 Stone Hall, 700 W State St., West Lafayette, IN 47907-2059, U.S.A. **Online address:** andersonj@sri.soc.purdue.edu

ANDERSON, Jeffrey E. (Jeffrey Elton Anderson). American (born United States), b. 1974. **Genres:** Literary Criticism And History, Mythology/Folklore. **Career:** Middle Georgia College, faculty, 2003-07; University of Louisiana, assistant professor, professor. Writer. **Publications:** Conjure in African American Society, 2005; Hoodoo, Voodoo, and Conjure: A Handbook, 2008. **Address:** Department of History, University of Louisiana, Brown Hall 228, 700 University Ave., Monroe, LA 71203-3708, U.S.A. **Online address:** jeanderson@ulm.edu

ANDERSON, Jeffrey Elton. *See* **ANDERSON, Jeffrey E.**

ANDERSON, Joanne M. American (born United States), b. 1949. **Genres:** Food And Wine, Travel/Exploration, History, Animals/Pets. **Career:** Clay Corner Inn, owner and innkeeper, 1994-. Writer. **Publications:** Small-Town Restaurants in Virginia, 1998, 2nd ed., 2004; Solomon Says: Observations of an Innkeeper Dog, 2001. Contributor to magazines and newspapers. **Address:** John F. Blair Publisher, 1406 Plaza Dr., Winston-Salem, NC 27103, U.S.A. **Online address:** jmawriter@aol.com

ANDERSON, John B(ayard). American (born United States), b. 1922. **Genres:** Politics/Government, Economics. **Career:** Illinois Bar, lawyer, 1946; Northeastern University, instructor in law, 1947-49; private law practice, 1949-52; U.S. Department of State, foreign service officer assigned to East Berlin, 1952-55; National Unity Party, chairman; private law practice, 1955-56; Stanford University, visiting professor, 1981; University of Illinois College of Law, visiting professor, 1981; Brandeis University, visiting professor, 1985; Bryn Mawr College, visiting professor, 1985; Oregon State University, visiting professor, 1986; University of Massachusetts, visiting professor, 1986; Nova University, visiting professor, 1987, distinguished visiting professor of law. Writer. **Publications:** (Contrib.) We Propose: A Modern Congress, 1966; (contrib.) Republican Papers, 1968; Between Two Worlds: A Congressman's Choice, 1970; (ed. and contrib.) Congress and Conscience, 1970; Money, Interest Groups, and Politics: Realistic Reform and the Crisis of Confidence, 1975; Vision and Betrayal in America, 1976; Regulation of Political Campaigns: How Successful?, 1977; (ed.) Party Coalitions in the 1980s, 1981; The American Economy We Need-And Won't Get from the Republicans or the Democrats, 1984; A Proper Institution, 1988; Every Vote Equal: A State-based Plan for Electing the President by National Popular Vote, 2011. Contributor to journals. **Address:** 3917 Massachusetts Ave. NW, Washington, DC 20016, U.S.A. **Online address:** bauco@aol.com

ANDERSON, Jon Lee. British/American (born United States), b. 1957. **Genres:** Military/Defense/Arms Control, History. **Career:** New Yorker Magazine, contributor, 1998-, staff writer, 1999-. **Publications:** (With S. Anderson) Inside the League: The Shocking Expose of How Terrorists, Nazis, and Latin American Death Squads Have Infiltrated the World Anti-Communist League, 1986; (comp. with S. Anderson) War Zones: Voices from the World's Killing Zones, 1988; Guerrillas: The Men and Women Fighting Today's Wars, 1992; Che Guevara: A Revolutionary Life, 1997, rev. ed., 2010; The Lion's Grave: Dispatches from Afghanistan, 2002; (contrib.) Taliban, 2003; Guerrillas: Stories from the Insurgent World, 2003; The Fall of Baghdad, 2004; Guerrillas: Journeys in the Insurgent World, 2004; (contrib.) Baghdad: Truth Lies Within, 2004; (contrib.) Katrina: An Unnatural Disaster, 2006. **Address:** Grove/Atlantic Inc., 841 Broadway, 4th Fl., New York, NY 10003-4704, U.S.A.

ANDERSON, Judith. *See* **HENEGHAN, Judith.**

ANDERSON, Judy. American (born United States), b. 1943. **Genres:** Human Relations/Parenting, Business/Trade/Industry, Sports/Fitness. **Career:** Gateway Technical Institute, assistant registrar and adjunct instructor, 1971-79; Long Island University, associate registrar, 1979-85; American Express Financial Services, financial planner, 1985-86; Dime Savings Bank of New York, trainer and counselor, 1986-93; Business Golf Unlimited, golf, business coach and professional speaker, 1991-. Writer. **Publications:** (Intro.) Teeing Off to the Green: Using Golf as a Business Tool, 1995. **Address:** Business Golf Unlimited, 42253 Parkside Cir., Ste. 105, Sterling Heights, MI 48314, U.S.A. **Online address:** judy@bizgolf.com

ANDERSON, Katharine. Canadian (born Canada), b. 1965?. **Genres:** Education, History, Psychology, Physics. **Career:** York University, Department of Humanities, associate professor in the science and society program. Writer. **Publications:** (Contrib.) Nineteenth Century Psychological Thought: The Transition from Philosophy to Science, 2001; (contrib.) Culture and Science in the Nineteenth Century Media, 2004; Predicting the Weather: Victorians and the Science of Meteorology, 2005. Contributor to journals. **Address:** Department of Humanities, York University, 303 Bethune College, 4700 Keele St., Toronto, ON M3J 1P3, Canada. **Online address:** kateya@yorku.ca

ANDERSON, Kay. (K. J. Anderson). Australian (born Australia), b. 1958. **Genres:** Cultural/Ethnic Topics, Geography, History. **Career:** Durham University, professor of geography, Cultural Geography, chair, through 2003; University of Western Sydney, Centre for Cultural Research, part-time professor of cultural research, professor; Academy of Learned Societies for the Social Sciences, academician, 2004; Academy of the Social Sciences in Australia, fellow, 2007; Institute of Australian Geographers, fellow. Writer. **Publications:** Vancouver's Chinatown: Racial Discourse in Canada, 1875-1980, 1991, 5th ed., forthcoming; Race and the Crisis of Humanism, 2006; (co-author) Géographies Anglo-Saxonnes, 2001; Encyclopedia of Human Geography, forthcoming. EDITOR: (with F. Gale) Inventing Places: Studies in Cultural Geography, 1992; (with F. Gale) Cultural Geographies, 1999; (with M. Domosh, S. Pile and N. Thrift) Handbook of Cultural Geography, 2002; (ed. with B. Braun) Environment: Critical Essays in Human Geography, 2008; (with B. Braun) Essays on Environment, 2008. Contributor of articles to book and periodicals. **Address:** Center for Cultural Research, University of Western Sydney, EM.G.35 Parramatta Campus, PO Box 1797, Penrith South DC, NW 1797, Australia. **Online address:** k.anderson@uws.edu.au

ANDERSON, Keith Douglas. *See* **ANDERSON, Doug Douglas.**

ANDERSON, Kent. American (born United States), b. 1945?. **Genres:** Adult Non-fiction, Mystery/Crime/Suspense, Photography. **Career:** Writer. **Publications:** Television Fraud: The History and Implications of the Quiz Show Scandals, 1978; Sympathy for the Devil, 1987; Night Dogs, 1996; Liquor, Guns and Ammo, 1998. Contributor to periodicals. **Address:** Bantam Dell Publishing Group, 1540 Broadway, New York, NY 10036, U.S.A.

ANDERSON, Kevin J(ames). Also writes as Gabriel Mesta, Gabriel Mesta. American (born United States), b. 1962. **Genres:** Science Fiction/Fantasy, Young Adult Fiction, Novels. **Career:** Lawrence Livermore National Laboratory, technical writer and editor, 1983-95; Materials Research Society, columnist, 1988-94; International Society for Respiratory Protection, copy editor, 1989-95. **Publications:** WITH D. BEASON: Lifeline, 1991; The Trinity Paradox, 1991; Nanospac, 1992; Assemblers of Infinity, 1993; Ill Wind, 1995; Virtual Destruction, 1996; Ignition, 1997; Fallout, 1997; Lethal Exposure, 1998. WITH K.K. RUSCH: Afterimage, 1992; Aftershock, 1998. THE X-FILES SERIES: Ground Zero, 1995; Ruins, 1996; Antibodies, 1997. SCIENCE FICTION: Resurrection Inc., 1988; Climbing Olympus, 1994; Blindfold, 1995; (ed.) War of the Worlds: Global Dispatches (anthology), 1996; (as K.J. Anderson) Captain Nemo, 2002; Hopscotch, 2002. DUNE SERIES (with B. Herbert): Dune: House Atreides, 1999; House Harkonnen, 2000; House Corrino, 2001; The Butlerian Jihad, 2002; The Machine Crusade, 2003; The Battle of Corrin, 2004; The Road to Dune, 2005; Hunters of Dune, 2006; Sandworms of Dune, 2007; Paul of Dune, 2008; Winds of Dune, 2009. SAGA OF THE SEVEN SUNS SERIES: Hidden Empire, 2002; A Forest of Stars, 2003; Horizon Storms, 2004; Scattered Suns, 2005; Of Fire and Night, 2006; Metal Swarm, 2007; The Ashes of Worlds, 2008. GAMEARTH SERIES: Gamearth, 1989; Gameplay, 1989; Game's End, 1990. FOR YOUNG ADULTS: (with J.G. Betancourt) Born of Elven Blood, 1995; Darksaber, 1995. STAR WARS: JEDI ACADEMY TRILOGY: Jedi Search, 1994; Dark Apprentice, 1994; Champions of the Force, 1994. STAR WARS, YOUNG JEDI KNIGHTS SERIES WITH R. MOESTA: The Lost Ones, 1995; Shadow Academy, 1995; Heirs of the Force, 1995; Darkest Knight, 1996; Lightsabers, 1996; Jedi under Siege, 1996; Shards of Alderaan, 1997; Delusions of Grandeur, 1997; Diversity Alliance, 1997; The Emperor's Plague, 1997; Jedi Bounty, 1997; Crisis at Crystal Reef, 1998; Return to Ord Mantell, 1998; Trouble on Cloud City, 1998; Crisis on Crystal Reef, 1998; Titan A.E.: Cale's Story, 2000; Titan A.E.: Akima's Story, 2000; Supernova, 2000. EDITOR, STAR WARS ANTHOLOGIES SERIES: Star Wars: Tales from the Mos Eisley Cantina, 1995; Tales from Jabba's Palace, 1995; Tales of the Bounty Hunters, 1996. STAR WARS: TALES OF THE JEDI SERIES: Dark Lords of the Sith, 1996; Golden Age of the Sith, 1997; The Fall of the Sith Empire, 1998; Redemption, 2000. WITH R. MOESTA AS GABRIEL MESTA: Shadow of the Xel'Naga, 2001; Crystal Doors, 2006; Ocean Realm, 2007; Sky Realm, 2008. OTHERS: The Illustrated Star Wars Universe, 1995; (with R. Moesta) Star Wars: The Mos Eisley Cantina Pop-Up Book, 1995; The Outer Limits: Armageddon Dreams, 2000; Leviathan, 2000; Fantastic Voyage, 2001; Dogged Persistence, 2001; Artifact, 2003; The League of Extraordinary Gentlemen, 2003; The Saga of Seven Suns: Veiled Alliances, 2004; Sky Captain and the World of Tomorrow, 2004; (contrib. with D. Wallace) Star Wars: The New Essential Chronology, 2005; (with A.E.V. Vogt) Slan Hunter, 2007; (contrib.) Destiny's Drum, 2007; (contrib.) Hurtling Wings, 2007; The Last Days of Krypton, 2007; (contrib.) Cargo of Coffins, 2008; (contrib.) Brass Keys to Murder, 2008; (ed.) The Horror Writers Association Presents Blood Lite: An Anthology of Humorous Horror Stories, 2008; (with D. Koontz) Dean Koontz's Frankenstein, 2008; (contrib.) The Trail of the Red Diamonds, 2008; (with D. Koontz) Dean Koontz's Frankenstein: Prodigal Son, 2008; (contrib.) When Shadows Fall, 2008; Terra

Incognita, 2009; (with A. Bows and P. Upham) Aviation and Climate Change: Lessons for European Policy, 2009; Enemies & Allies, 2009; Edge of the World, 2009; Map of all Things, 2010; (contrib.) Timeshares, 2010; JSA: Strange Adventures, 2010; (with B. Herbert) Hellhole, 2011; The Key to Creation, 2011; (ed.) The Nebula Awards Showcase 2011, 2011; (with B. Herbert) The Sisterhood of Dune, 2011. Works appear in anthologies. Contributor to periodicals. **Address:** c/o John Silbersack, Trident Media Group L.L.C., 41 Madison Ave., Fl. 36, New York, NY 10010-2257, U.S.A.

ANDERSON, K. J. *See* **ANDERSON, Kay.**

ANDERSON, Lars. American (born United States) **Genres:** Sports/Fitness, Recreation, History. **Career:** Lincoln Journal Star, general assignment reporter; Sports Illustrated Magazine, staff writer, 1994-. **Publications:** (With C. Millman) Pickup Artists: Street Basketball in America, 1998; The Proving Ground: A Season on the Fringe in NFL Europe, 2001; The All Americans, 2004; Carlisle versus Army: Jim Thorpe, Dwight Eisenhower, Pop Warner, and the Forgotten story of Footballs Greatest Battle, 2007; The First Star: Red Grange and the Barnstorming Tour that Launched the NFL, 2009. **Address:** Sports Illustrated, 2 Embarcadero Ctr., San Francisco, CA 94111, U.S.A.

ANDERSON, Lauri (Arvid). American (born United States), b. 1942. **Genres:** Novellas/Short Stories, Poetry, Young Adult Fiction. **Career:** High school English teacher, 1967-69; University of the Pacific, lecturer, 1969-71; Mizpah Mission School, English teacher, department chair and dean of boys, 1971-72; American Collegiate Institute, English teacher and department chair, 1972-76; Finlandia University, professor, English Language and Literature Department, chair, 1976-, director of humanities program and rural studies coordinator; Indiana University, teacher of technical writing, 1983-84, professor of English; Phillips Academy (private secondary school), teacher of English, 1995, 1997; FinnFest, lecturer, 1996-97. Writer. **Publications:** Snow White and Others (poetry), 1971; Small Winter Wars (short fiction), 1983; Hunting Hemingway's Trout (short fiction), 1990; Heikki Heikkinen and Other Stories of Upper Peninsula Finns, 1995; Children of the Kalevala (short fiction): Contemporary American Finns Relive the Timeless Tales of the Kalevala, 1997; Misery Bay (short fiction): And Other Stories from Michigan's Upper Peninsula, 2002; Impressions of Arvo Laurila, 2005; Back to Misery Bay, 2007. Works appear in anthologies. Contributor of poetry to periodicals. **Address:** Department of Language and Literature, Finlandia University, Mannerheim 401, 601 Quincy St., Hancock, MI 49930, U.S.A. **Online address:** lauri.anderson@finlandia.edu

ANDERSON, Malcolm. British/Scottish (born Scotland), b. 1934. **Genres:** History, Politics/Government, Translations. **Career:** University of Manchester, lecturer in government, 1960-64; Fondation Nationale des Sciences Politiques, research fellow, 1964-65; University of Warwick, senior lecturer, 1965-73, professor of politics, 1973-79; University of British Columbia, visiting professor, 1989; University of Edinburgh, professor of politics, 1979-98, professor emeritus, 1998-, head, dean of social sciences, provost of law and social sciences, Centre of European Governmental Studies, director, International Social Sciences Institute, director; Centre for European Policy Studies, senior fellow, 1999-2002; New Mexico State University, visiting faculty. Writer. **Publications:** (Co-author) The Right in France, 1890-1919, 1962; (trans.) An Introduction to the Social Sciences: With Special Reference to Their Methods, by Maurice Duverger, 1964; Government in France, 1970; Conservative Politics in France, 1974; (ed.) Frontier Regions in Western Europe, 1983; (ed. with M. Buckley) Women, Equality, and Europe, 1988; Policing the World: Interpol and the Politics of International Police Cooperation, 1989; (ed. with M. den Boer) Policing across National Boundaries, 1994; (co-author) Policing the European Union, 1995; Frontiers: Territory and State Formation in the Modern World, 1997; (ed. with E. Bort) Frontiers of Europe, 1998; (ed. with E. Bort) Irish Border: History, Politics, Culture, 1999; States and Nationalism in Europe Since 1945, 2000; (with E. Bort) Frontiers of the European Union, 2001; (ed. with J. Apap) Police and Justice Cooperation and the New European Borders, 2002. Contributor to journals. **Address:** School of Social & Political Studies, University of Edinburgh, Chrystal Macmillan Bldg., 15A George Sq., Edinburgh, EH8 9LD, Scotland. **Online address:** malcolma@orange.fr

ANDERSON, Margaret Jean. American (born United States), b. 1931. **Genres:** Young Adult Fiction, Young Adult Non-fiction. **Career:** East Malling Research Station, statistician, 1953-55; Canada Department of Agriculture, entomologist, 1955-56; Oregon State University, statistician, 1956-57. Writer. **Publications:** FOR CHILDREN AND YOUNG ADULTS. FICTION: To Nowhere and Back, 1975; In the Keep of Time, 1977; Searching for Shona, 1978; In the Circle of Time, 1979; The Journey of the Shadow Bairns, 1980; The Brain on Quartz Mountain, 1982; Light in the Mountain, 1982; The Mists of Time, 1984; The Druid's Gift, 1989; The Ghost Inside the Monitor, 1990. NON-FICTION: Exploring the Insect World, 1974; Exploring City Trees, and the Need for Urban Forests, 1976; Food Chains: The Unending Cycle, 1991; Charles Darwin, Naturalist, 1994; (with N. Field and K. Stephenson) Ancient Forests: Discovering Nature, 1995; Bizarre Insects, 1996; Isaac Newton: The Greatest Scientist of All Time, 1996; Carl Linnaeus, Prince of Botany/Father of Classification, 1997; Children of Summer: Henri Fabre's Insects, 1997; (with N. Field and K. Stephenson) Leapfrogging through Wetlands, 1998; (with K. Stephenson) Scientists of the Ancient World, 1999; (with R.G. Vivian) Chaco Canyon, 2002; (with K. Stephenson) Aristotle, Philosopher and Scientist, 2004; (with Pamela J. Cressey) Alexandria, Virginia, 2006; Olla-Piska, Tales of David Douglas, 2006; (with N. Field and K. Stephenson) Discovering Black Bears, 2007; Charles Darwin, Naturalist, rev. ed., 2008; Isaac Newton, The Greatest Scientist of All Time, rev. ed., 2008; Carl Linnaeus, Father of Classification, rev. ed. 2009; Bugged-out Insects, 2011. **Address:** 3325 NW 60th St., Corvallis, OR 97330, U.S.A. **Online address:** mja@peak.org

ANDERSON, Marilyn D. American (born United States), b. 1943. **Genres:** Children's Fiction, Social Sciences, History. **Career:** Writer, 1983-; Institute of Children's Literature, instructor. Music teacher. **Publications:** The Horse Lover's Handbook (nonfiction), 1983; All for a Horse, 1983 as The Wild Arabian, 1987; The Horse That Came to Breakfast, 1983; No Home for Shannon, 1984; Hot Fudge Pickles, 1984; But Maggie Wanted a Pony, 1984 as Maggie's Wish, 1987; Barkley, Come Home, 1985 as Come Home Barkley, 1996; A Horse Named Bandit, 1985; The Bridesmaid Wears Trackshoes, 1985; Hungry as a Lion (picture book), 1985; Marshmallow Pickles, 1986; I Don't Want a New Horse, 1986; We Have to Get Rid of These Puppies, 1986; The Bubble Gum Monster, 1987; The Bubble Gum Monster Strikes Again, 1989; Nobody Wants Barkley, 1990; The Revenge of the Bubble Gum Monster, 1992; Bring Back Barkley, 1998; (with J. Chaitin and S.S. Estabrook) The Fourth Wise Man (play), 1998; Chris Farley (biography), 2001; The Vice Presidency (nonfiction), 2001; Sarah Michelle Gellar (biography), 2002; Will Smith (biography), 2003; Arab Americans, 2007; Benjamin Banneker (biography) 2006; Mules (nonfiction) 2008; Chicago's Burning (easy reader) 2008; A Girl and Her Horse Book, vol. I: Commodore & Sparkler, 2010, vol. II: Bandit & Count, 2010. **Address:** 10957 US Hwy. 50 W, Bedford, IN 47421, U.S.A. **Online address:** mandka2@gmail.com

ANDERSON, Mark M. American (born United States), b. 1955. **Genres:** Literary Criticism And History, Language/Linguistics, Young Adult Fiction, History, Young Adult Non-fiction. **Career:** Columbia University, assistant professor, 1985-90, associate professor of German and comparative literature, 1991-, director of deutsches haus, 1986-90, Department of Germanic Languages, chairman, 1993-, professor, fellow, 2001-02. Writer. **Publications:** Kafka's Clothes: Ornament and Aestheticism in the Habsburg Fin de Siecle, 1992; (contrib.) Bilder-Denken: Bildlichkeit und Argumentation, 2004. EDITOR: (intro. and trans.) I. Bachmann, In the Storm of Roses: Selected Poems, 1986; Reading Kafka: Prague, Politics, and the Fin de Siecle, 1989; (intro.) Franz Kafka, The Sons, 1989; (intro.) Three Paths to the Lake, 1989; Bachmann, Malina, 1990; Hitler's Exiles: Personal Stories of the Flight from Nazi Germany to America, 1998. Contributor to periodicals. **Address:** Department of Germanic Languages & Literatures, Columbia University, 405 Hamilton Hall, PO Box 2818, New York, NY 10027, U.S.A. **Online address:** mma2@columbia.edu

ANDERSON, Matthew Tobin. *See* **ANDERSON, M. T(obin).**

ANDERSON, Maureen. American (born United States), b. 1958. **Genres:** Self Help, Biography, Medicine/Health, Sports/Fitness. **Career:** Speaker and writer. **Publications:** (With D. Beardsley) Staying the Course: A Runner's Toughest Race, 2002; Northumberland, 2002; (with J. Hovde) Left for Dead: A Second Life after Vietnam, 2005; The Career Clinic: Eight Simple Rules for Finding Work You Love, 2009. Contributor of articles to periodicals and professional journals. **Address:** American Management Association, 1601 Broadway, Ste. 7, New York, NY 10036, U.S.A. **Online address:** maureen@thecareerclinic.com

ANDERSON, Molly D(elCarmen). American (born United States), b. 1955. **Genres:** Agriculture/Forestry. **Career:** Tufts University, research assistant professor, assistant professor of nutrition, 1991-, adjunct associate professor, co-founder and director of degree program in agriculture, food and the environment, 1994-, University College of Citizenship and Public Service, fellow, 2002-04, national food and society policy fellow, 2002-04, administrator, Institute of the Environment, director; Oxfam America, senior program officer, interim director, 2002-05; Henry A. Wallace Center, project manager, consultant; Wallace Center, Wallace Senior fellow, 2007-. Writer and research coordinator. **Publications:** (With W. Lockertz) Agricultural Research Alternatives, 1993. **Address:** Gerald J. and Dorothy R. Friedman School of, Nutrition Science and Policy, Tufts University, 150 Harrison Ave., Boston, MA 02111, U.S.A. **Online address:** manderson@earthlink.net

ANDERSON, M. T(obin). (Matthew Tobin Anderson). American (born United States), b. 1968. **Genres:** Novels, Mystery/Crime/Suspense, Horror, Science Fiction/Fantasy, Children's Fiction, Young Adult Fiction, Music, Biography, Picture/Board Books. **Career:** Candlewick Press, editorial assistant, 1993-96; Boston Review, intern; WCUW-Radio, disc jockey; Union Institute and University, Vermont College, MFA Program in Writing for Children, faculty, 2001-06, chair, 2003-06, trustee, 2009-; 3rd Bed (literary journal), fiction editor. **Publications:** Thirsty (horror novel), 1997; Burger Wuss, 1999; Handel, Who Knew What He Liked (picture book), 2001; Feed, 2002; Strange Mr. Satie, 2003; The Game of Sunken Places, 2004; The Serpent came to Gloucester, 2005; Whales on Stilts, 2005; Me, All Alone, at the End of the World, 2005; The Clue of the Linoleum Lederhosen, 2006; The Astonishing Life of Octavian Nothing, Traitor to the Nation, vol. I, The Pox Party, 2006, vol. II, The Kingdom on the Waves, 2008; (ed.) The Restless Dead: Ten Original Stories of the Supernatural, 2007; Jasper Dash and the Flame-Pits of Delaware, 2007; Agent Q, or the Smell of Danger!, 2010; The Suburb Beyond the Stars, 2010; Empire of Gut and Bone, 2011; Zombie Mommy, 2011. **Address:** c/o Tracy Miracle, Candlewick Press, 99 Dover St., Somerville, MA 02144, U.S.A. **Online address:** mta@mt-anderson.com

ANDERSON, Olive Ruth. British/Scottish (born Scotland), b. 1926. **Genres:** History, Psychology, Military/Defense/Arms Control. **Career:** University of London, assistant lecturer, 1949-57, lecturer, 1958-69, reader, 1969-86, professor and department head, 1986-89; Queen Mary and Westfield College, professor and department head, 1989-91, professor emeritus, 1991-, fellow, 1994-; Royal Historical Society, vice-president, 2001-. Writer. **Publications:** A Liberal State at War: English Politics and Economics During the Crimean War, 1967; Suicide in Victorian and Edwardian England, 1987. **Address:** Westfield College, University of London, London, GL NW3 7ST, England.

ANDERSON, Patricia J. Canadian (born Canada), b. 1950. **Genres:** Literary Criticism And History, Social Commentary. **Career:** University of British Columbia, Killam predoctoral fellow, 1978-89; freelance writer, 1980-91, 1993-; Simon Fraser University, postdoctoral fellow, 1991-93; historian, 1993-; Helping You Get Published, literary consultant, 1999-. **Publications:** The Printed Image and the Transformation of Popular Culture, 1790-1860, 1991; When Passion Reigned: Sex and the Victorians, 1995; Passion Lost: Public Sex, Private Desire in the Twentieth Century, 2001. EDITOR WITH J. ROSE: Dictionary of Literary Biography, vol. I: CVI: British Literary Publishing Houses, 1820-1880, 1991, vol. II: CXII: British Literary Publishing Houses, 1881-1965, 1991. Contributor to books and periodicals. Works appear in anthologies. **Address:** 1489 Marine Dr., Ste. 515, West Vancouver, BC V7T 1B8, Canada. **Online address:** patriciaanderson@helpingyougetpublished.com

ANDERSON, Rachel. (Rachel Bradby). British (born England), b. 1943. **Genres:** Novels, Children's Fiction, Plays/Screenplays, Literary Criticism And History. **Career:** Chatto & Windus Ltd., publicity assistant, 1963-64; Women's Mirror, editor, 1964; British Broadcasting Corp. (BBC), broadcaster. Writer. **Publications:** Pineapple, 1965; The Purple Heart Throbs, 1974; Moffatt's Road, 1978; Dream Lovers, 1978; Fairy Snow and the Disability Box (play for children), 1981; The Poacher's Son, 1982; Winston's Wonderful Weekend, 1983; Little Angel Comes to Stay, 1984; The War Orphan, 1986; Tim Walks, 1986; Little Angel, Bonjour, 1987; Jessy Runs Away, 1988; French Lessons, 1988; Little Angel, Bonjour, 1988; Best Friends, 1989; The Bus People, 1989; The Boy Who Laughed, 1989; For the Love of Sang, 1990; Happy Christmas Little Angel, 1990; Tough as Old Boots, 1991; When Mum Went to Work, 1992; The Working Class, 1993; Jessy & the Long-Short Dress, 1993; Paper Faces, 1993; Princess Jazz & the Angels, 1994; Black Water, 1994; The Dolls' House, 1995; Letters from Heaven, 1995; Julie and the Queen of Tonga, 1996; Carly's Luck, 1997; Ollie and the Trainers, 1997; The Scavenger's Tale, 1998; Big Ben, 1998; Grandmother's Footsteps, 1999; Bloom of Youth, 1999; War Lands, 2000; Joe's Story, 2001; Stronger Than Mountains, 2001; Hello Peanut, 2003; Hugo and the Long Red Arm, 2004; Red Moon, 2006. TRANSLATOR: The Cat's Tale, 1985; (with D. Bradby) Renard the Fox, 1986; Wild Goose Chase, 1986; Little Lost Fox, 1992. Contributor to periodicals. **Address:** c/o Author Mail, Oxford University Press, Walton St., Oxford, OX OX4 6DP, England.

ANDERSON, Richard Lloyd. American (born United States), b. 1926. **Genres:** History, Theology/Religion, Biography, Autobiography/Memoirs, Literary Criticism And History, Humanities. **Career:** Brigham Young University, instructor, 1955-56, assistant professor of religion, 1956-58, associate professor, 1961-62, professor, 1962-96, professor emeritus of ancient scripture, 1996-; University of California, lecturer in classical and medieval rhetoric, 1960-61. Writer. **Publications:** Joseph Smith's New England Heritage: Influences of Grandfathers Solomon Mack and Asael Smith, 1971, rev. ed., 2003; (contrib.) Hugh Nibley and Others, To the Glory of God, 1972; Investigating the Book of Mormon Witnesses, 1981; Understanding Paul, 1983, rev. ed., 2007. **Address:** Maxwell Institute for Religious Scholarship, Brigham Young University, 200 WAIH, Provo, UT 84602, U.S.A.

ANDERSON, Robert (David). British/Indian (born India), b. 1927. **Genres:** Archaeology/Antiquities, Art/Art History, Music, History, Social Sciences. **Career:** Record News, assistant editor, 1954-56; Gordonstoun School, assistant master and director of music, 1956-62; Moray Choral Union, conductor, 1958-62; Spoleto Festival, assistant conductor, 1962; St. Bartholomew's Hospital Choral Society, conductor, 1965-90; University of London, extramural lecturer on Egyptology, 1966-77; Musical Times, critic and associate editor, 1967-85; Egypt Exploration Society, Excavations at Qasr Ibrim, administrative director, 1977-79. Writer. **Publications:** Catalogue of Egyptian Antiquities in the British Museum, III, Musical Instruments, 1976; Wagner: A Biography, with a Survey of Books, Editions and Recordings, 1980; (ed. with I. Fawzy) Egypt Revealed: Scenes from Napoleon's Description de l'Egypte, 1987; (ed.) Chamber Music, 1988; Elgar in Manuscript, 1990; Elgar, 1993; Elgar and Chivalry, 2002; Crown of India, 2004. **Address:** 54 Hornton St., London, GL W8 4NT, England.

ANDERSON, Sarah. British (born England), b. 1947. **Genres:** Travel/Exploration. **Career:** Travel Bookshop, founder and owner, 1979-2004; City University, teacher of travel writing, 2005-06. Writer. **Publications:** Anderson's Travel Companion, 1995, rev. ed. as Sarah Anderson's Travel Companion, 2004; (ed.) The Virago Book of Spirituality, 1996 in US as Heaven's Face Thinly Veiled, 1998; (with J. Kelsey) Plants, 1999; (with M. Davies) Inside Notting Hill, 2001; Halfway to Venus, 2007. Contributor to books and periodicals. **Address:** c/o Clare Alexander, Aitken Alexander Associates Ltd., 18-21 Cavaye Pl., London, GL SW10 9PT, England. **Online address:** sarah@umbrellabooks.com

ANDERSON, Sheila E. American (born United States), b. 1957. **Genres:** Music. **Career:** Newark Museum, manager of public programs; National Association for the Advancement of Colored People, president, board director, 1977-81; WBGO, radio host, 1995-; Bookbinders' Guild of New York, staff, 1995-97; Oceana Magazine, staff writer. **Publications:** (Comp.) The Quotable Musician: From Bach to Tupac, 2003; How to Grow as a Musician: What All Musicians Must Know to Succeed, 2005. **Address:** Newark Public Radio Inc., 54 Park Pl., Newark, NJ 07102, U.S.A. **Online address:** sheila.anderson@gmail.com

ANDERSON, Sheryl J. American (born United States), b. 1958?. **Genres:** Novels, Mystery/Crime/Suspense. **Career:** Grant Tinkers GTG Entertainment, development executive; Act One (an instructional program for Christian screenwriters), teacher. Writer. **Publications:** Message in a Minute: Lighthearted Minidramas for Churches, 1992; Message in a Minute: More Lighthearted Minidramas for Churches, 1998; The Twelve Plays of Christmas: Original Christian Dramas, 1999; Killer Heels, 2004; Killer Cocktail, 2005; Killer Deal, 2006; Killer Riff, 2007. **Address:** c/o Author Mail, St. Martins Minotaur, 175 5th Ave., New York, NY 10010, U.S.A. **Online address:** sheryl@sheryljanderson.com

ANDERSON, Terry (A.). American (born United States), b. 1949. **Genres:** Autobiography/Memoirs, Biography. **Career:** Associated Press, reporter, 1974-85, chief middle east correspondent and bureau chief in Beirut, 1983-85; New York Renaissance, founder; University Of Kentucky, School of Journalism, faculty, 2009-, visiting lecturer. **Publications:** Den of Lions: Memoirs of Seven Years, 1993. Contributor of articles to periodicals. **Address:** School of Journalism & Telecommunications, University of Kentucky, 107 Grehan Bldg., Lexington, KY 40506-0042, U.S.A.

ANDERSON, Trevor A(ndrew). Australian (born Australia), b. 1959. **Genres:** Biology, Food And Wine, Technology. **Career:** University of Newcastle, research assistant in medicine, 1981; New South Wales Institute of Technology, tutor in physiology, 1985; Nepean College, tutor in physiology, 1986-87; Department of Primary Industries and Energy, Bureau of Rural Research, scientist, 1988; Deakin University, senior tutor, 1988-90, lecturer in aquaculture, 1990-93; James Cook University, School of Marine Biology and Aquaculture, adjunct senior lecturer, senior lecturer in aquaculture, 1994-. Writer. **Publications:** (With S.S. De Silva) Fish Nutrition in Aquaculture, 1995. Contributor of articles to journals. **Address:** School of Marine Biology and Aquaculture, James Cook University, 101 Angus Smith Dr., Townsville, QL 4811, Australia. **Online address:** trevor.anderson@jcu.edu.au

ANDERSON, Virginia DeJohn. American (born United States), b. 1954. **Genres:** History, Humanities. **Career:** University of Colorado, assistant professor, 1985-92, associate professor of U.S. history, 1992-2005, professor of U.S. history, 2005-, director of graduate studies. Writer. **Publications:** New England's Generation: The Great Migration and the Formation of Society and Culture in the Seventeenth Century, 1991; Creatures of Empire: How Domestic Animals Transformed Early America, 2004; (co-author) The American Journey: A History of the United States, 2007. Contributor of articles. **Address:** Department of History, University of Colorado, Rm. 204, 234UCB, Hellems, Boulder, CO 80309-0234, U.S.A. **Online address:** virginia.anderson@colorado.edu

ANDERSON, Wilda (Christine). American (born United States), b. 1951. **Genres:** Chemistry, History, Literary Criticism And History, Adult Nonfiction, Politics/Government. **Career:** Johns Hopkins University, assistant professor, 1978-84, associate professor, 1984-89, professor of French, 1989-; Emory University, visiting professor, 1989; Ecole Pratique des Hautes Etudes, visiting professor, 1994. **Publications:** Between The Library And The Laboratory: The Language of Chemistry in Eighteenth-Century France, 1984; Diderot's Dream, 1990. Contributor to books. **Address:** Department of Romance Languages and Literatures, Johns Hopkins University, Gilman Hall 330, 3400 N Charles St., Homewood Campus, Baltimore, MD 21218, U.S.A. **Online address:** wilda@wilda.org

ANDERSON, William Louis. American (born United States), b. 1941. **Genres:** History, Anthropology/Ethnology. **Career:** Western Carolina University, assistant professor, associate professor, 1969-86, professor of history, 1986-, now professor emeritus of history; Journal of Cherokee Studies, editor; Sesame Street, consultant; National Geographic, consultant; Discovery Channel, consultant. Writer. **Publications:** (With J.A. Lewis) Guide to Cherokee Documents in Foreign Archives, 1983; (with N. Anderson) Southern Treasures, 1987; (ed.) Cherokee Removal: Before and After, 1991; (with N. Anderson) Heritage of Healing: A Medical History of Haywood County, 1994; (ed. with J.L. Brown and A.F. Rogers) The Payne-Butrick Papers, 2010. **Address:** Department of History, Western Carolina University, 225 McKee Bldg., Cullowhee, NC 28723, U.S.A. **Online address:** anderson@wcu.edu

ANDES, Karen. American (born United States), b. 1956. **Genres:** Sports/Fitness, Women's Studies And Issues, Sports/Fitness. **Career:** Andes Productions, owner and producer of written, audio and visual materials, 1988-; World Dance Fitness, co-owner. Writer. **Publications:** A Woman's Book of Strength, 1995; A Woman's Book of Power: Dancing the Divine Feminine, 1998; A Woman's Book of Balance: Finding Your Physical, Spiritual, and Emotional Center with Yoga, Strength Training, and Dance, 1999; (co-ed.) The Complete Book of Fitness: Mind, Body, Spirit, 1999; A Woman's Book of Balance: Finding Your Physical, Spiritual, and Emotional Center with Yoga, Strength Training, and Dance, 1999; The Complete Book of Stretching, 2000; (co-ed.) Fitness Stretching, 2000. **Address:** World Dance Fitness, 40 Greenfield Ave., San Anselmo, CA 94960, U.S.A. **Online address:** kandes@worlddancer.com

ANDOE, Joe. American (born United States), b. 1955?. **Genres:** Novels, Autobiography/Memoirs. **Career:** Artist, 1981-. Writer. **Publications:** Jubilee City: A Memoir at Full Speed, 2007. Contributor to periodicals. **Address:** 113 W 27th St., 4th Fl., New York, NY 10011, U.S.A. **Online address:** info@andoedesign.com

ANDRE, Judith. American (born United States), b. 1941. **Genres:** Philosophy, Ethics. **Career:** Mercy College of Detroit, adjunct professor of philosophy, 1973-76; Wayne County Community College, adjunct professor of philosophy, 1973-76; Bowling Green State University, adjunct instructor, 1976-77; Washburn University of Topeka, visiting instructor, 1977-78; Loyola Marymount University, visiting instructor and adjunct instructor, 1978-80; Old Dominion University, assistant professor, 1980-85, associate professor of philosophy, 1986-91, associate professor of women's studies, 1990-91, Institute of Applied Ethics, director, 1985-88; Michigan State University, Center for Ethics and Humanities in the Life Science, Department of philosophy, associate professor, 1991-95, professor, 1995-2006, professor emeritus, 2006-. Writer. **Publications:** EDITOR: (with W. Brenner and contrib.) Essays in Introduction to Philosophy, 1985; (with D. James) Rethinking College Athletics, 1991. OTHERS: Bioethics as Practice, 2002; Cosmopolitan Virtue: On Becoming Citizens of the World, forthcoming. Work appears in anthologies. Contributed to journals. **Address:** Center for Ethics & Humanities, Michigan State University, C-208 E Fee Hall, East Lansing, MI 48824-1316, U.S.A. **Online address:** andre@msu.edu

ANDRE, Michael. (Laura LeNail). Canadian/American (born United States), b. 1946. **Genres:** Poetry, Young Adult Fiction, Adult Non-fiction. **Career:** City University, City College, adjunct lecturer, 1970-72; Bernard M. Baruch College, adjunct lecturer, 1970-72; Magazine Co-op, director, 1976-. Writer. **Publications:** My Regrets, 1977; Studying the Ground for Holes, 1978; Letters Home, 1979; (ed.) The Poets' Encyclopedia, 1979; It as It, 1980; Like a Few Things, 1981; Jabbing the Asshole Is High Comedy, 1981; Experiments in Banal Living, 1998. Works appear in anthologies. Contributor to magazines. **Address:** Unmuzzled Ox Press, 105 Hudson St., Ste. 311, New York, NY 10013, U.S.A. **Online address:** mandreox@aol.com

ANDREAS, Peter. American (born United States), b. 1965. **Genres:** History, Adult Non-fiction. **Career:** Brookings Institution, Brookings research fellow, 1995-96; Reed College, assistant professor of political science, 2000-01; Brown University, assistant professor of political science and international studies, 2001-06, associate professor of political science and international studies, 2006-10, professor of political science and international studies, 2010-, International Relations Program, director. Writer. **Publications:** NONFICTION: (with E. Bertram, M. Blachman and K. Sharpe) Drug War Politics: The Price of Denial, 1996; (ed. with H.R. Friman) The Illicit Global Economy and State Power, 1999; Border Games: Policing the U.S.-Mexico Divide, 2000, 2nd ed., 2009; (ed. with T. Snyder) The Wall around the West: State Borders and Immigration Controls in North America and Europe, 2000; (ed. with T.J. Biersteker) The Rebordering of North America: Integration and Exclusion in a New Security Context, 2003; (with E. Nadelmann) Policing the Globe: Criminalization and Crime Control in International Relations, 2006; Blue Helmets and Black Markets: The Business of Survival in the Siege of Sarajevo, 2008; Sex, Drugs and Body Counts: The Politics of Numbers in Global Crime and Conflict, 2010. Contributor to books. **Address:** Watson Institute, Brown University, PO Box 1970, Providence, RI 02912-1970, U.S.A. **Online address:** peter_andreas@brown.edu

ANDREJEVIC, Mark. American (born United States), b. 1964. **Genres:** Communications/Media. **Career:** Times Herald, reporter, 1992-94; Lansing State Journal, reporter, 1994-96; Fairfield University, assistant professor, 2001-03; University of Iowa, assistant professor, 2003-07, associate professor, 2007-; University of Queensland, postdoctoral researcher. Journalist. **Publications:** Reality TV: The Work of Being Watched, 2004; iSpy: Surveillance and Power in the Interactive Era, 2007. Contributor to books and journals. **Address:** Department of Communication Studies, University of Iowa, 105 Becker Communication Studies Bldg., Iowa City, IA 52242, U.S.A. **Online address:** mark-andrejevic@uiowa.edu

ANDRESS, David. British (born England), b. 1969. **Genres:** History, Social Sciences, Military/Defense/Arms Control. **Career:** University of Portsmouth, School of Social, Historical and Literary Studies, lecturer, 1994-99, senior lecturer, 1999-2002, principal lecturer in modern European history, 2002-, associate dean of research and professor of modern history. Writer. **Publications:** French Society in Revolution, 1789-1799, 1999; Massacre at the Champ de Mars: Popular Dissent and Political Culture in the French Revolution, 2000; The French Revolution and the People, 2004; The Terror: Civil War in the French Revolution, 2005 in US as The Terror: The Merciless War for Freedom in Revolutionary France, 2006; 1789: The Threshold of the Modern Age, 2009; Conquering Napoleon: How a Generation of Warfare

Transformed Britain, forthcoming. Works appear in anthologies. Contributor to periodicals. **Address:** School of Social, Historical and Literary Studies, University of Portsmouth, Burnaby Rd., Milldam, Portsmouth, HM PO1 3AS, England. **Online address:** david.andress@port.ac.uk

ANDREW, Edward. (Edward G. Andrew). Canadian (born Canada), b. 1941?. **Genres:** Philosophy, Politics/Government, History. **Career:** University of Toronto, Division of Social Sciences, professor, now professor emeritus. Writer. **Publications:** Closing the Iron Cage, 1981; Shylock's Rights: A Grammar of Lockean Claims, 1988; The Genealogy of Values: The Aesthetic Economy of Nietzsche and Proust, 1995; Conscience and Its Critics: Protestant Conscience, Enlightenment, Reason and Modern Subjectivity, 2001; Patrons of Enlightenment, 2006; Imperial Republics: Revolution, War, and Territorial Expansion from the English Civil War to the French Revolution, 2011. **Address:** Division of Social Sciences, University of Toronto, R5235, 1265 Military Trl., Scarborough, ON M1C 1A4, Canada. **Online address:** eandrew@chass.utronto.ca

ANDREW, Edward G. *See* **ANDREW, Edward.**

ANDREW, Joseph J(erald). American (born United States), b. 1960. **Genres:** Mystery/Crime/Suspense, Business/Trade/Industry. **Career:** United States Court of Appeals, Seventh Circuit, law clerk, 1985-86; Baker and Daniels, attorney, 1987-88; State of Indiana, deputy secretary of State, 1989; Bingham, Summers, Welsh & Spilman (law firm), attorney, 1991, partner, 1992-95; Indiana Democratic Party, chairman, 1995-99; Democratic National Convention, chairman, 2004; Sonnenschein Nath & Rosenthal L.L.P., partner and chairman, 2004-; New Democrat Network, chairman. Writer. **Publications:** The Disciples (spy thriller), 1993; (with D.F. Adamson) Blue Way: How to Profit by Investing in a Better World, 2007. **Address:** Sonnenschein Nath & Rosenthal L.L.P., 1301 K St. NW, Ste. 600, E Twr., Washington, DC 20005-3364, U.S.A. **Online address:** jandrew@sonnenschein.com

ANDREW, Sheila M. Canadian/British (born England), b. 1938. **Genres:** History, Local History/Rural Topics. **Career:** Saint Thomas University, Department of History, associate professor, 1988-, chair, 1995-98, tenured associate professor, 1996-, professor of history, now professor emeritus; Orienteering New Brunswick, president. Writer. **Publications:** The Development of Elites in Acadian New Brunswick, 1861-1881, 1996. **Address:** Department of History, St. Thomas University, Rm. 328, Edmund Casey Hall, 51 Dineen Dr., Fredericton, NB E3B 5G3, Canada. **Online address:** sandrew@stu.ca

ANDREWS, Andy. *See* **ANDREWS, Kenneth T.**

ANDREWS, Andy. American (born United States), b. 1959. **Genres:** Communications/Media, Novellas/Short Stories, Children's Fiction. **Career:** Writer. **Publications:** Storms of Perfection, vol. I: In Their Own Words, 1991, vol. II: Letters from the Heart, 1994, vol. III: A Pathway to Personal Achievement, 1996, vol. IV: Letters from the Past, 1997; Andy Andrews' Tales from Sawyerton Springs, 1995; The Traveler's Gift: Seven Decisions That Determine Personal Success, 2002; Go For It: Letters from American Heroes, 2002; Go For It: Letters from Celebrity Heroes, 2002; Go For It: Letters from Inspirational Heroes, 2002; Go For It: Letters from Sports Heroes; 2002; The Lost Choice: A Legend of Personal Discovery, 2004; (with A. Parker) Young Traveler's Gift, 2004; Island of Saints: A Story of the One Principle That Frees the Human Spirit, 2005; Socks for Christmas, 2005; Mastering the Seven Decisions That Determine Personal Success: An Owner's Manual to the New York Times Bestseller, The Traveler's Gift, 2008; Noticer: Sometimes, All a Person Needs is a Little Perspective, 2009; Heart Mender: A Story of Second Chances, 2010; Boy Who Changed the World, 2010; Final Summit: A Quest to Find the One Principle that will Save Humanity, 2010. Contributor to periodicals. **Address:** c/o Author Mail, Thomas Nelson Inc., PO Box 141000, Nashville, TN 37214, U.S.A. **Online address:** wecare@andyandrews.com

ANDREWS, Colin. *See* **WILSON, F(rancis) Paul.**

ANDREWS, Colin. American/British (born England), b. 1946. **Genres:** Paranormal, Food And Wine. **Career:** A.M.F. Legg, electrician, 1963-73; Brinklow Ltd., electrical technician, 1973-74; Test Valley Borough Council, supervisor, 1974-76, superintendent, 1976-78, coordinator, 1978-84, senior technical support services officer, 1984-; Circles Phenomenon Research Intl., founder. Writer. **Publications:** Shepherd of the Downs: The Life and Songs of Michael Blann of Upper Beeding, 1979; (with P. Delgado) Circular Evidence: A Detailed Investigation of the Flattened Swirled Crops Phenomenon, 1989; (with P. Delgado) Crop Circles: The Latest Evidence, 1990; (with S.J. Spignesi) Crop Circles: Signs of Contact, 2003; (with S. Andrews) The Complete Idiots Guide to 2012, 2008; Government Circles, 2009; (with S. Andrews) Complete Idiot's Guide to the Akashic Record, 2010. Contributor to magazines. **Address:** Circles Phenomenon Research Intl., 111 Great Hill Rd., Guilford, CT 06437, U.S.A. **Online address:** cprandrews@comcast.net

ANDREWS, Edgar Harold. British (born England), b. 1932. **Genres:** Chemistry, Physics, Sciences, Theology/Religion. **Career:** Imperial Chemical Industries Ltd., technical officer, 1953-55; Rubber Producer's Research Association, senior physicist, 1955-63; University of London, Queen Mary College, Department of Materials, founder, 1967-, head, reader, 1963-68, professor of materials, 1968-98, professor emeritus, 1998-, dean of engineering; Clarendon School Trust, chairman, 1975-81; Evangelical Press, director; Evangelical Times Newspaper, editor; QMC-Industrial Research Ltd., director; Dow Chemical Co., consultant. **Publications:** Fracture in Polymers, 1968; Is Evolution Scientific?, 1977; From Nothing to Nature: A Young People's Guide to Evolution and Creation, 1978; (ed.) Developments in Polymer Fracture, 1979; God, Science, and Evolution, 1980; The Promise of the Spirit, 1982; (co-ed.) Creation and Evolution, 1985; Christ and the Cosmos, 1986; Free in Christ, 1996; Preaching Christ, 2005; Who Made God? Searching for a Theory of Everything, 2009. CONTRIBUTOR: Physics and Chemistry of Rubber like Solids, 1963; Physical Basis of Yield and Fracture, 1966; Fracture 1969, 1969; Testing of Polymers IV, 1969; Shock Tube Research, 1971; Polymer Science: A Materials Science Handbook, 1972; MTP International Review of Science, 1972; Physics of Glassy Polymers, 1973; Polymer Surfaces, 1978; The Mechanical Properties of Biological Materials, 1980. Contributor to journals. **Address:** Department of Materials, Queen Mary College, University of London, Mile End Rd., London, GL E1 4NS, England. **Online address:** info@whomadegod.org

ANDREWS, Elmer. (Elmer Kennedy-Andrews). Irish (born Ireland), b. 1948. **Genres:** Plays/Screenplays, Literary Criticism And History. **Career:** Mohammed V University, lecturer in English, 1976-79; University of Ulster, lecturer in English, 1980-, professor of English. Writer. **Publications:** AS ELMER KENNEDY-ANDREWS: (ed.) Nathaniel Hawthorne The Scarlet Letter, 2000; (ed.) Poetry of Derek Mahon, 2002; Fiction and the Northern Ireland Troubles Since 1969: (De-) Constructing the North, 2003; (ed.) Irish Fiction Since the 1960s: A Collection of Critical Essays, 2006; (ed.) Paul Muldoon Poetry, Prose, Drama, 2006; Writing Home: Poetry and Place in Northern Ireland, 1968-2008, 2008; Ciaran Carson: Critical Essays, 2009. OTHERS: The Poetry of Seamus Heaney: All the Realms of Whisper, 1988; The Art of Brian Friel: Neither Reality Nor Dreams, 1995. EDITOR: Contemporary Irish Poetry: A Collection of Critical Essays, 1990; Seamus Heaney: A Collection of Critical Essays, 1992; Poetry of Seamus Heaney, 1998. Contributor to books, journals and magazines. **Address:** Department of English, University of Ulster, Rm. B035B, Cromore Rd., Coleraine, BT52 1SA, Northern Ireland. **Online address:** e.andrews@ulster.ac.uk

ANDREWS, George Reid. American (born United States), b. 1951. **Genres:** History, Area Studies, Race Relations, Cultural/Ethnic Topics. **Career:** Social Science Research Council, staff associate, 1978-81; University of Pittsburgh, Department of History, assistant professor, 1981-83, associate professor, 1983-91, professor, 1991-2008, chair, 1998-2001, 2006-07, distinguished professor of history, 2008-. Writer. **Publications:** The Afro-Argentines of Buenos Aires, 1800-1900, 1980; Blacks and Whites in São Paulo, Brazil, 1888-1988, 1991; (ed. with H. Chapman) Social Construction of Democracy, 1870-1990, 1995; Afro-Latin America, 1800-2000, 2004; Blackness in the White Nation: A History of Afro-Uruguay, 2010. Works appear in anthologies. Contributor to journals. **Address:** Department of History, University of Pittsburgh, 3527 Posvar Hall, Pittsburgh, PA 15260, U.S.A. **Online address:** reid1@pitt.edu

ANDREWS, Helena. American (born United States), b. 1980. **Genres:** Autobiography/Memoirs. **Career:** O, intern, 2002; Politico.com, staff writer, 2006; Seventeen Magazine, staff; Domino Magazine, staff; Rap Up Magazine, staff. Journalist and pop-culture critic. **Publications:** Bitch Is the New Black: A Memoir, 2010. Contributor to magazines. **Address:** Washington, DC , U.S.A.

ANDREWS, J(ames) S(ydney). (Jim Andrews). British/Irish (born Ireland), b. 1934. **Genres:** Medicine/Health, Children's Fiction, Adult Non-fiction,

Novels. **Career:** Isaac Andrews & Sons Ltd., director. Writer. **Publications:** The Bell of Nendrum (young adult novel), 1969 in US as The Green Hill of Nendrum, 1970; The Man from the Sea (young adult novel), 1970; Cargo for a King (young adult novel), 1972; (contrib. with T. Wilson) Ziggy's Gift, 1982; Andrews: Samuel George Andrews and Family, 2003. FOR ADULTS AS JIM ANDREWS: Catamarans for Cruising, 1974; Simple Sailing, 1975; (with J. Andrews) Food for Arthritics, Based on Dr. Dong's Diet, 1982; Twelve Ships A-Sailing: Thirty-Five Years of Home-Water Cruising, 1986. Contributor to journals. **Address:** Dove Wood, Storrs Pk., Windermere, CM LA23 3LB, England.

ANDREWS, Jim. *See* **ANDREWS, J(ames) S(ydney).**

ANDREWS, John (Malcolm). (John Malcolm). British (born England), b. 1936. **Genres:** Novels, Mystery/Crime/Suspense, Antiques/Furnishings. **Career:** Consultant, 1970-76; Antique Collecting Magazine, managing editor, 2003. **Publications:** NON-FICTION: The Price Guide to Antique Furniture, 1968, rev. ed., 1978; The Price Guide to Victorian Furniture, 1970; The Price Guide to Victorian, Edwardian and 1920s Furniture, 1980; British Antique Furniture, 1989; Victorian and Edwardian Furniture, 1992; Antique Furniture, 1997; Arts and Crafts Furniture, 2005. NOVELS AS JOHN MALCOLM: A Back Room in Somers Town, 1984; The Godwin Sideboard, 1984; The Gwen John Sculpture, 1985; Whistler in the Dark, 1986; Gothic Pursuit, 1987; Mortal Ruin, 1988; The Wrong Impression, 1990; Sheep, Goats and Soap, 1991; A Deceptive Appearance, 1992; The Burning Ground, 1993; Hung Over, 1994; Into the Vortex, 1996; Simpson's Homer, 2001; Circles & Squares, 2002; Mortal Instruments, 2003; Rogues' Gallery, 2005; The Chippendale Factor, 2008. OTHER: British Victorian and Edwardian Furniture: Price Guide and Reasons for Value, 1992. Contributor to periodicals. **Address:** Teresa Chris, 43 Musard Rd., London, GL W6 8NR, England. **Online address:** jma2274@aol.com

ANDREWS, Keith William. *See* **KEITH, William H(enry).**

ANDREWS, Kenneth T. (Andy Andrews). American (born United States) **Genres:** Civil Liberties/Human Rights, History. **Career:** Millsaps College, instructor, 1994-96; Harvard University, assistant professor, 1997-2001, associate professor, 2001-02, John L. Loeb associate professor of social sciences, 2002-03; University of North Carolina, assistant professor, 2003-07, associate professor, 2007-, Undergraduate Studies and Honors, Sociology, director, 2006-, coordinator; Writer. **Publications:** Freedom Is a Constant Struggle: The Mississippi Civil Rights Movement and Its Legacy, 2004. Contributor to journals. **Address:** Department of Sociology, University of North Carolina, CB 3210, 209 Hamilton Hall, Chapel Hill, NC 27599-3210, U.S.A. **Online address:** kta@unc.edu

ANDREWS, Molly. British (born England), b. 1959. **Genres:** Politics/Government, Psychology, History. **Career:** University of Cambridge, affiliated lecturer, 1989-90, postdoctoral research fellow, 1992; Colorado College, assistant professor, 1990-93; Max Planck Institute, associate research fellow, 1993-94; Temple University, assistant professor of sociology, 1994-96; University of East London, School of Social Sciences, Media, and Cultural Studies, reader in sociology and co-director of Center for Narrative Research, 2000-; University of Cambridge, instructor, 2004; Dartmouth College, visiting fellow, 2004. Writer, translator and administrator. **Publications:** Lifetimes of Commitment: Aging, Politics, Psychology, 1991; (ed.) Lines of Narrative: Psychosocial Perspectives, 2000; (ed. with M. Bamberg) Considering Counter Narratives: Narrating, Resisting, Making Sense, 2004; Shaping History: Narratives of Political Change, 2007; (ed. with C. Squire and M. Tamboukou) Doing Narrative Research, 2008. Contributor to books, periodicals and journals. **Address:** School of Soc Sci, Media, & Cultural Studies, University of East London, Docklands Campus, University Way, London, GL E16 2RD, England. **Online address:** m.andrews@uel.ac.uk

ANDREWS, Nin. American (born United States), b. 1958. **Genres:** Poetry, Literary Criticism And History. **Career:** Writer. **Publications:** POETRY: The Book of Orgasms, 1994, 2nd ed., 2000; Spontaneous Breasts, 1998; Why They Grow Wings, 2001; Any Kind of Excuse, 2003; (ed.) Someone Wants to Steal My Name: And Other Poems, 2003; Midlife Crisis with Dick and Jane, 2005; Sleeping with Houdini: Poems, 2007; Dear Professor: Do You Live in a Vacuum?, 2008; Southern Comfort, 2009. Works appear in anthologies. Contributor to periodicals. **Address:** CavanKerry Press Ltd., 6 Horizon Rd., Ste. 2901, Fort Lee, NJ 07024, U.S.A. **Online address:** nin.andrews@gmail.com

ANDREWS, Russell. *See* **HANDLER, David.**

ANDREWS, Sam S. American (born United States), b. 1942. **Genres:** Medicine/Health, Food And Wine, Human Relations/Parenting. **Career:** Mahorner Clinic, president, 1990; Mercy-Baptist Hospital, vice-president, 1995; Ochsner Medical Center, staff physician, 2006-. Writer. **Publications:** Sugar Busters!, 1998; (co-author) The New Sugar Busters! Cut Sugar to Trim Fat, 1998, rev. ed., 2003; (with M.C. Bethea and L.A. Balart) Sugar Busters!: Quick & Easy Cookbook, 1999; (co-author) Sugar Busters! For Kids, 2001. **Address:** Ochsner Medical Center, 1514 Jefferson Hwy., Fl. 9, New Orleans, LA 70121, U.S.A. **Online address:** drssa@aol.com

ANDREWS, Sarah. American (born United States), b. 1949. **Genres:** Novels. **Career:** U.S. Geological Survey, field geologist and research geologist, 1974-80; Colorado State University, Department of Earth Resources, research assistant, 1979-80; Amoco Oil Co., geologist, 1980-83; Angus Petroleum, geologist, 1983-86; Trans Tech Consultants, project geologist, 1989-92; consultant geologist, 1990-; Jacobs Engineering Group, task manager, 1993; Sonoma State University, Department of Geology, instructor in geology, 1997-. Writer. **Publications:** NOVELS: Tensleep, 1994; A Fall in Denver, 1995; (co-author) Medieval Art in America: Patterns of Collecting, 1800-1940, 1996; (contrib.) Beech House Inquiry: Report of the Internal Inquiry Relating to the Mistreatment of Patients Residing at Beech House, St Pancras Hospital During the Period March 1993 - April 1996, 1996; Mother Nature, 1997; Only Flesh and Bones, 1998; Bone Hunter, 1999; Eye For Gold, 2000; Fault Line, 2002; Killer Dust, 2003; Earth Colors, 2004; Dead Dry, 2005; In Cold Pursuit, 2007; Rock Bottom, 2011. Contributor to periodicals. **Address:** Department of Geology, Sonoma State University, 1801 E Cotati Ave., Rohnert Park, CA 94928, U.S.A. **Online address:** sarah@sarahandrews.com

ANDREWS, Thomas G. American (born United States), b. 1972. **Genres:** Social Sciences. **Career:** University of Colorado, historian and professor of history. Writer. **Publications:** Killing for Coal: America's Deadliest Labor War, 2008. **Address:** Department of History, College of Liberal Arts & Sciences, University of Colorado, PO Box 173364, Denver, CO 80217-3364, U.S.A.

ANDREWS, Walter G. American (born United States), b. 1939. **Genres:** Poetry, Translations, Essays. **Career:** University of Washington, Department of Near Eastern Languages and Civilization, acting assistant professor, 1968-70, assistant professor, 1970-76, associate professor, 1976-85, professor, 1985-91, affiliate professor, 1992-2001, research professor, 2001-, Ottoman Texts Archive Project, director, 1991-; NEH Arabic Script Publications Project, associate investigator, 1972-73; Edebiyat, co-founder and co-editor, 1976-91, staff, 1993-2001; MESA Bulletin, literature review editor, 1978-82, editor, 1979-80; IJMES, staff, 1979-84; American Research Institute in Turkey, delegate-at-large, 1981-82; Yeni Yaklasimlar, staff. **Publications:** An Introduction to Ottoman Poetry, 1976; Poetry's Voice, Society's Song: Ottoman Lyric Poetry, 1985; (ed. and trans. with N. Black and M. Kalpakli) Ottoman Lyric Poetry: An Anthology, 1997; (ed.) Intersections in Turkish Literature: Essays in Honor of James Stewart-Robinson, 2001; (with M. Kalpakli) The Age of Beloveds: Love and the Beloved in Early-Modern Ottoman and European Culture and Society, 2005; (with Ö. Felek) Victoria R. Holbrook'a armağan, 2006; (ed. and trans.) H. Yavuz, Seasons of the Word: Selected Poems, 2007; (trans.) A. Behramoğlu, I've Learned Some Things: Selected Poems, 2008. Contributor to books and periodicals. **Address:** Department of Near Eastern Languages and, Civilization, University of Washington, 229 Denny Hall, PO Box 353120, Seattle, WA 98195-3120, U.S.A. **Online address:** walter@uw.edu

ANDREWS, Wendy. *See* **SHARMAT, Marjorie Weinman.**

ANDREWS, William L(eake). American (born United States), b. 1946. **Genres:** Literary Criticism And History, Novellas/Short Stories, Biography. **Career:** Texas Tech University, assistant professor of English, 1973-77; University of Wisconsin, assistant professor, 1977-78, associate professor, 1978-84, professor of English, 1984-88, E. Maynard Adams professor of English, 1996-, College of Arts and Sciences, senior associate dean for the fine arts and humanities, University Press, editor, 1988-; University of Geissen, visiting professor, 1984; University of Kansas, Joyce and Elizabeth Hall professor of American literature, 1989-96; University of North Carolina, Department of English, E. Maynard Adams distinguished professor of English, 1997-, chair of department, 1997-2001, director of development, 2002-05, coordinator, 2003-04, Fine Arts and Humanities, senior associate dean, 2005-; Oxford University Press, editor, 1999-2004; NEH Institute for High School Teachers, National Humanities Center, co-director, 1999, 2006. **Publications:** The Literary Career of Charles W. Chesnutt, 1980; To Tell a Free Story: The First Century of Afro-American Autobiography, 1760-1865, 1986; (intro.) Quest of the Silver Fleece, 2007. EDITOR: Literary Romanticism in America, 1981; Critical Essays on W.E.B. DuBois, 1985; (and intro.) Sisters of the Spirit: Three Black Women's Autobiographies of the Nineteenth Century, 1986; (and intro.) My Bondage and My Freedom, 1987; Six Women's Slave Narratives, 1988; James Weldon Johnson, The Autobiography of an Ex-Colored Man, 1990; Journeys in New Worlds: Early American Women's Narratives, 1990; (and intro.) Three Classic African-American Novels, 1990; Bursting Bonds, 1991; Critical Essays on Frederick Douglass, 1991; Bursting Bonds: Enlarged Edition of The Heir of Slaves: The Autobiography of a New Negro, 1991; (and intro.) Two Biographies by African-American Women, 1991; Collected Stories of Charles W. Chesnutt, 1992; (and intro.) Classic American Autobiographies, 1992; (and intro.) The African-American Novel in the Age of Reaction: Three Classics, 1992; African American Autobiography: A Collection of Critical Essays, 1993; (and intro.) From Fugitive Slave to Free Man: The Autobiographies of William Wells Brown, 1993; Classic Fiction of the Harlem Renaissance, 1994; (and intro.) Up from Slavery, 1995; (and intro.) The Oxford Frederick Douglass Reader, 1996; (with W.S. McFeely) Narrative of the Life of Frederick Douglass: Authoritative Text, Contexts, Criticism, 1996; (with F.S. Foster and T. Harris) Oxford Companion to African American Literature, 1997; (with H.L. Gates, Jr.) Pioneers of the Black Atlantic: Five Slave Narratives from the Enlightenment, 1772-1815, 1998; (with N.Y. McKay) Toni Morrison's Beloved: A Casebook, 1999; (with H.L. Gates, Jr.) Civitas Anthology of African American Slave Narratives, 1999; (and intro.) Conjure Tales and Stories of the Color Line, 2000; (with S. Foster and T. Harris) The Concise Oxford Companion to African American Literature, 2001; North Carolina Slave Narratives: The Lives of Moses Roper, Lunsford Lane, Moses Grandy and Thomas H. Jones, 2003; (with D.Taylor) Richard Wright's Black Boy, 2003; Classic African American Women's Narratives, 2003; (intro. and contrib.) Behind the Scenes, or, Thirty Years a Slave and Four Years in the White House, 2005; North Carolina Roots of African American Literature: An Anthology, 2006; (with M. Kachun) Curse of Caste, or, The Slave Bride: A Rediscovered African American Novel, 2006; (with R.E. Mason) Life of William Grimes, the Runaway Slave, 2008; (and intro.) Portable Charles W. Chesnutt, 2008; (and intro.) The Life of John Thompson, a Fugitive Slave, 2011; Slave Narratives after Slavery, 2011. CO-EDITOR: African-American Literature, 1991; Norton Anthology of African American Literature, 1997; Literature of the American South: A Norton Anthology, 1997. **Address:** Department of English, University of North Carolina, Greenlaw Hall, PO Box 3520, Chapel Hill, NC 27599, U.S.A. **Online address:** wandrews@email.unc.edu

ANDRUS, Hyrum Leslie. American (born United States), b. 1924. **Genres:** Theology/Religion, History, Social Sciences. **Career:** Brigham Young University, Ricks College, director of religious studies, 1955-56, assistant professor, 1957-60, associate professor, 1960-64, professor of religion and social science, 1964-, professor of church history and doctrine, now professor emeritus. Writer. **Publications:** Joseph Smith and World Government, 1958; Joseph Smith, the Man and the Seer, 1960; Liberalism, Conservatism, Mormonism, 1965; Foundations of the Millennial Kingdom of Christ, 1968; (comp. with H.M. Andrus) They Knew the Prophet, 1974; (comp. and ed. with R.E. Bennett) Mormon Manuscripts to 1846: A Guide to the Holdings of the Harold B. Lee Library, 1977; Doctrinal Commentary on the Pearl of Great Price, 2003; (comp. with H.M. Andrus) Personal Glimpses of the Prophet Joseph Smith, 2009. Contributor of articles to journals. **Address:** Brigham Young University, 1 N University Ave., Provo, UT 84601-4429, U.S.A.

ANDRUS, Jeff. American (born United States), b. 1947. **Genres:** Novels, Mystery/Crime/Suspense, Young Adult Fiction, History. **Career:** Television writer, 1972-; University of California, Extension Program, instructor of screenwriting, 1991-92; The Writing Co., owner, editor, writing coach. **Publications:** NOVELS: Tracer Inc.: A Mystery Introducing the Tracer Family, 1994; Neighborhood Watch: A Tracer Family Mystery, 1996. **Address:** The Writing Co., 13908 Fiji Way, Ste. 162, Marina del Rey, CA 90292, U.S.A.

ANDRYSZEWSKI, Tricia. Also writes as Tricia Shapiro. American (born United States), b. 1956. **Genres:** Children's Non-fiction, Young Adult Non-fiction, Adult Non-fiction, History, Biography, Sociology. **Career:** Girard College, teacher, 1978-79; Human Service and Behavioral Science Consultants, administrator and proposal writer, 1979-80; Warner Books, staff, 1980-81; freelance editor, writer and researcher, 1981-; Twenty-Six-Acre Farm, owner and manager, 1987-91; Scholarly Resources, project editor, 1988-89; researcher/manager for Elizabeth Drew (writer), 1992-93. **Publications:** The Dust Bowl: Disaster on the Plains, 1993; Marjory Stoneman Douglas: Friend of the Everglades, 1994; Immigration: Newcomers and Their Impact on the U.S., 1995; The Seminoles: People of the Southeast, 1995; The Environment and the Economy, 1995; What to Do about Nuclear Waste, 1995; The Amazing Life of Moe Berg, 1995; Abortion Rights, Options, and Choices, 1996; 1963: Gathering to Be Heard, the March on Washington, 1963: Gathering to Be Heard, 1996; The Militia Movement in America, 1997; School Prayer, 1997; Communities of the Faithful, 1997; Step by Step along the Appalachian Trail, 1998; Step by Step along the Pacific Crest Trail, 1998; Kosovo: The Splintering of Yugoslavia, 1999; Bill Bradley, 1999; The Reform Party, 1999; Gay Rights, 1999; Terrorism in America, 2002; Walking the Earth: Human Migration and Population from Prehistory to the Present, 2006; Walking the Earth: The History of Human Migration, 2007; Same-Sex Marriage: Moral Wrong or Civil Right?, 2008; Mass Extinction: Examining the Current Crisis, 2008; Spirit Awakening, forthcoming; End of the Rainbow, forthcoming. **Address:** PO Box 153, West Cornwall, CT 06796, U.S.A. **Online address:** andryszews@aol.com

ANEES, Munawar Ahmad. American/Pakistani (born Pakistan), b. 1948. **Genres:** Cultural/Ethnic Topics, Literary Criticism And History, Medicine/Health, Sciences, Theology/Religion, Third World. **Career:** Zahra Publications, president, 1984; Indiana University, International Journal of Islamic and Arabic Studies, founding editor, 1984-; Asas Inc., director, 1984-85; East-West University, director of research and development, 1986-; Knowledge Management Systems, president and executive director, 1989-; John Templeton Foundation, consultant; Center for Theology and the Natural Sciences, Stars Program, consultant; Los Angeles Times Syndicate, Global Viewpoint, contributing correspondent, 1998-. **Publications:** Hadith and Sira Literature in Western Languages: A Bibliographic Study, 1980; (ed.) Health Sciences in Early Islam: Collected Papers, 1983; (with A.N. Athar) Guide to Sira and Hadith Literature in Western Languages, 1986; Issues in Islamic Science, 1988; (with Z. Sardar) Key Books of Islamic Resurgence, 1988; Islam and Biological Futures: Ethics, Gender, and Technology, 1989; (ed.) The Kiss of Judas: Affairs of a Brown Sahib, 1989; Computers Don't Byte, 1990; Communication and Information: Ethical Perspectives, 1991; Periodica Islamica, 1991; Christian-Muslim Relations: Yesterday, Today, Tomorrow, 1991. **Address:** 925 N 11th Ave., Tucson, AZ 85705-7627, U.S.A. **Online address:** dranees@att.net

ANELLI, Melissa. American (born United States), b. 1979. **Genres:** Literary Criticism And History. **Career:** MTV Networks, editorial assistant; Staten Island Advance, reporter. **Publications:** Harry, a History: The True Story of a Boy Wizard, His Fans, and Life Inside the Harry Potter Phenomenon, 2008. **Address:** Brooklyn, NY , U.S.A. **Online address:** melissa@penbitten.com

ANGEL, Ann. (Ann Marie Angel). American (born United States), b. 1952?. **Genres:** Young Adult Non-fiction. **Career:** Milwaukee Sentinel, reporter; Mount Mary College, assistant professor of English, 1989-. Writer. **Publications:** FICTION: Real for Sure Sister, 1988; (ed.) Such a Pretty Face: Short Stories about Beauty, 2007; NONFICTION: John Glenn: Space Pioneer, 1990; Lech Walesa: Champion of Freedom for Poland, 1992; Louis Pasteur: Leading the Way to a Healthier World, 1992; (ed.) America in the Twentieth Century: 1900-1909, 1995; (ed.) America in the Twentieth Century: 1910-1919, 1995; Milwaukee: City Smart Guidebooks, 1997; Robert Cormier: Author of "The Chocolate War," 2008; Amy Tan: Weaver of Asian-American Tales, 2009. **Address:** Mount Mary College, 2900 N Menomonee River Pkwy., Milwaukee, WI 53222-4597, U.S.A. **Online address:** aangel@aol.com

ANGEL, Ann Marie. *See* **ANGEL, Ann.**

ANGEL, Heather. British (born England), b. 1941. **Genres:** Natural History, Photography. **Career:** National Institute of Oceanography, assistant biologist, 1966-67; Royal Photographic Society, president, 1984-86; Nottingham University, Department of Life Science, visiting professor, 1994-; British Institute of Professional Photography, fellow; Nature in Art Trust, vice president. Photographer and writer. **Publications:** Your Book of Fishes, 1972; Nature Photography: Its Art and Techniques, 1972; The World of an Estuary, 1974;

(with M. Angel) Ocean Life, 1975; Photographing Nature: Trees, Seashore, Insects, Flowers, Fungi, 5 vols., 1975; Seashore Life on Rocky Shores, 1975; Seashore Life on Sandy Beaches, 1975; The World of a Stream, 1976; Sea Shells of the Seashore, 1976; Wild Animals in the Garden, 1976; Life on the Seashore, 1976; Life in the Oceans, 1976; Life in Our Rivers, 1977; Life in Our Estuaries, 1977; British Wild Orchids, 1977; The Countryside of the New Forest, 1977; Seaweeds of the Seashore, 1977; The Countryside of South Wales, 1977; Lichens, 1980; Mosses and Ferns, 1980; The Country Side of Devon, 1980; The Guinness Book of Seashore Life, 1981; The Book of Nature Photography, 1982; (with P. Wolseley) Water Naturalist, 1982; (with P. Wolseley) Family Water Naturalist, 1982; The Book of Close-Up Photography, 1983; Heather Angel's Countryside, 1983; A Camera in the Garden, 1984; A View from a Window, 1988; Nature in Focus, 1988; Landscape Photography, 1989; Living Pond, 1990; Animal Photography, 1991; Kew: A World of Plants in US as The World of Plants: Treasures from the Royal Botanic Gardens, Kew, 1993; Photographing the Natural World, 1994; Outdoor Photography: 101 Tips and Hints, 1998; How to Photograph Flowers, 1998; Pandas, 1998; How to Photograph Water, 1999; Natural Visions, 2000; Giant Pandas, 2005; Succeed in Wildlife Photography, 2007; Digital Outdoor Photography: 101 Top Tips, 2011. **Address:** Natural Visions, 6 Vicarage Hill, Farnham, SR GU9 8HG, England. **Online address:** heather@naturalvisions.co.uk

ANGELA, Alberto. Italian/French (born France), b. 1962. **Genres:** Zoology, Sciences, Animals/Pets. **Career:** Institute of Marine Zoology, staff, 1979. Paleontologist and writer. **Publications:** Musei e mostre a misura d'Uomo, 1988; (with P. Angela) La straordinaria Storia dell'Uomo, 1989; (with P. Angela) La straordinaria Storia della vita sulla Terra, 1992; (with P. Angela) Il pianeta dei Dinosauri, 1993; (with P. Angela and A.L. Recchi) Sharks!: Predators of the Sea, 1997; (with A. Angela and A.L. Recchi) Squali, 1997; (with P. Angela and G. Pederiali) Paesaggio cheverrà, 2000; Giornata Nell'antica Roma: Vita Quotidiana, Segreti E Curiosità, 2007; Impero, 2010. Contributor to periodicals. **Address:** Via Pieve di Cadore, Rome, 30-00135, Italy.

ANGELL, Roger. American (born United States), b. 1920. **Genres:** Social Commentary, Documentaries/Reportage, Essays, Humor/Satire, Sports/Fitness. **Career:** The New Yorker, general contributor, 1944-, fiction editor, 1956-, senior editor and staff writer; Magazine X, editor and writer, 1946-47; Holiday, senior editor, 1947-56. **Publications:** (Co-author) Holiday Magazine Book of the World's Fine Food; A Treasury of Adventures in Gastronomy, 1960; The Stone Arbor and Other Stories, 1960; A Day in the Life of Roger Angell, 1970, rev. ed. as A Day in the Life of Roger Angell: Parodies and Other Pleasures, 1990; The Summer Game, 1972; Five Seasons: A Baseball Companion, 1977; Late Innings: A Baseball Companion, 1982; Season Ticket: A Baseball Companion, 1988; Once More Around the Park: A Baseball Reader, 1991; (contrib.) The Yankees Reader, 1991; (ed.) Nothing But You, Love Stories from the New Yorker, 1997; (ed. and intro.) Here is New York, 1999; A Pitcher's Story: Innings with Davie Cone, 2001: (intro.) The Perfect Game: America Looks at Baseball, 2003; Game Time: A Baseball Companion, 2003; Let Me Finish, 2006; Ancient Mariner, 2009. Works appear in anthologies. **Address:** The New Yorker, 25 W 43rd St., New York, NY 10036-7406, U.S.A.

ANGELOU, Maya. (Marguerite Annie Johnson). American (born United States), b. 1928. **Genres:** Novels, Plays/Screenplays, Poetry, Picture/Board Books, Biography, Autobiography/Memoirs, Food And Wine, Social Sciences, Social Sciences. **Career:** Arab Observer, associate editor, 1961-62, editor; Ghanaian Times, writer, 1963-65; Ghanaian Broadcasting Corp., writer, 1963-65; University of Ghana, School of Music and Drama, Institute of African Studies, assistant administration, 1963-66; Ghanaian Broadcasting Corp., freelance writer, 1963-65; African Review, feature editor, 1964-66; University of California, lecturer, 1966; University of Kansas, writer-in-residence, 1970; California State University, distinguished visiting professor, 1974; Wichita State University, distinguished visiting professor, 1974; Wake Forest University, distinguished visiting professor, 1974, Reynolds professor of American studies, 1981-; Hallmark Greeting Card Co., writer, 2002-; XM Radio, host, 2006-. **Publications:** Getting' up Stayed on My Mind, 1967; I Know Why the Caged Bird Sings, 1970; Just Give Me a Cool Drink of Water 'Fore I Die, 1971; Gather Together in My Name, 1974; Oh Pray My Wings Are Gonna Fit Me Well, 1975; Singin' and Swingin' and Gettin' Merry Like Christmas, 1976; And Still I Rise, 1978; The Heart of a Woman, 1981; Shaker, Why Don't You Sing?, 1983; All God's Children Need Traveling Shoes, 1986; Mrs. Flowers: A Moment of Friendship, 1986; Now Sheba Sings the Song, 1987; Conversations with Maya Angelou, 1989; Poems, 1989; I Shall not Be Moved, 1990; Wouldn't Take Nothing for My Journey Now, 1993; Lessons in Living, 1993; On the Pulse of Morning, 1993; Life Doesn't Frighten Me, 1993; (contrib.) Soul Looks Back in Wonder, 1993; (foreword) African Americans: A Portrait, 1993; My Painted House, My Friendly Chicken and Me, 1994; The Complete Collected Poems of Maya Angelou, 1994; Phenomenal Woman: Four Poems Celebrating Women, 1994; A Brave and Startling Truth, 1995; Kofi and His Magic, 1996; Even the Stars Look Lonesome, 1997; A Song Flung Up to Heaven, 2002; I Know why the Caged Bird Sings, 2002; Music, Deep Rivers in My Soul, 2003; Hallelujah! The Welcome Table, 2004; Angelina of Italy, 2004; Izak of Lapland, 2004; Renée Marie of France, 2004; Mikale of Hawaii, 2004; The Collected Autobiographies of Maya Angelou, 2004; Amazing Peace: A Christmas Poem, 2005; Celebrations: Rituals Of Peace And Prayer, 2006; Mother: A Cradle To Hold Me, 2006; Maya Angelou, 2007; Poetry for Young People, 2007; Letter to My Daughter, 2008; Great Food, All Day Long: Cook Splendidly, Eat Smart, 2010; Touched by an Angel, 2011. **Address:** Lordly & Dame Inc., 1344 Main St., Waltham, MA 02451, U.S.A. **Online address:** mayaangelou@lordly.com

ANGELOV, Dimiter. British (born England), b. 1972. **Genres:** History. **Career:** Western Michigan University, assistant professor, 2002-05; University of Birmingham, research fellow, 2006-. Writer. **Publications:** Imperial Ideology and Political Thought in Byzantium, 1204-1330, 2007; (ed.) Church and Society in Late Byzantium, 2009. **Address:** Institute of Archaeology & Antiquity, University of Birmingham, Edgbaston, Birmingham, WM B15 2TT, England. **Online address:** d.angelov@bham.ac.uk

ANGLE, Kurt. American (born United States), b. 1968. **Genres:** Autobiography/Memoirs, Biography. **Career:** Writer and professional wrestler. **Publications:** (With J. Harper) It's True! It's True!, 2002. Contributor to periodicals. **Address:** c/o WWF Titan Tower, 1241 Main St., PO Box 3857, Stamford, CT 06902, U.S.A.

ANGLESEY. Welsh/British (born England), b. 1922. **Genres:** Military/Defense/Arms Control, Biography, History, Autobiography/Memoirs, Engineering. **Career:** County councillor for Anglesey, 1951; justice of the peace for Anglesey, 1959; Welsh National Opera Co., director, 1959-; deputy lord lieutenant of the Isle of Anglesey, 1960; National Museum of Wales, staff, 1960, president, 1962-67; UCW (Bangor), honorary professor, 1986. Writer. **Publications:** The Capel Letters, 1814-1817, 1955; One-Leg: The Life and Letters of Henry William Paget, First Marquess of Anglesey, K.G., 1768-1854, 1961; (ed.) Sergeant Pearman's Memoirs, 1969; (ed.) Little Hodge, 1971; A History of the British Cavalry, 1816 to 1919, 1973; (foreword) The Servant's Hall: A Domestic History of Erddig, 1980; (foreword) The Servant's Hall: A Downstairs History of a British Country House, 1980; (foreword) A National Trust Old Postcard Album, 1993; Western Front 1915-18 and Epilogue 1919-29, 1997. Contributor of articles to books, journals and newspapers. **Address:** Plas Newydd, Llanfairpwll, Anglesey, LL61 6DQ, Wales.

ANGLIM, Christopher Thomas. American/Irish (born Ireland), b. 1957. **Genres:** Librarianship, Bibliography, Law, Business/Trade/Industry, Economics, History. **Career:** South Texas College of Law, government documents librarian and archivist, 1990-98; University of St. Thomas, law librarian, 1998-2000; St. Mary's University, Law Library, professor, government documents librarian and archivist, 1998-2002; Prairie View A&M University, collection development and government documents librarian, 2002-06; University of the District of Columbia, professor, archivist and librarian, 2006-. Writer. **Publications:** Special Collections Policies, Procedures, and Guidelines: A Model Plan for Special Collections, 1993; Special Collections at South Texas College of Law: An Annotated Catalog, 1994; Labor, Employment, and the Law: A Dictionary, 1997; Religion and the Law, 1999; Survey on Emergency Preparedness Planning, 2000; USA Patriot Act, 2002; Iraq War, 2003; Joined in Common Enterprise, 2005; Encyclopedia of Religion and the Law in America, 2009. Contributor to periodicals. **Address:** Learning Resources Division, University of the District of Columbia, Rm. 41-102, 4200 Connecticut Ave. NW, Washington, DC 20008, U.S.A. **Online address:** canglim@udc.edu

ANGLIN, Douglas G(eorge). Canadian (born Canada), b. 1923. **Genres:** International Relations/Current Affairs, Politics/Government. **Career:** University of Manitoba, assistant professor, 1951-57, associate professor of political science and international relations, 1957-58; Carleton University, associate professor, 1958-65, professor of political science, 1965-93, professor emeritus, 1993-; University of Zambia, vice-chancellor, 1965-69. Writer. **Publica-**

tions: Africa: The Political Pattern, 1961; The St. Pierre and Miquelon Affaire of 1941, 1966; (ed. with T.M. Shaw and C.G. Widstrand) Conflict and Change in Southern Africa, 1978; (ed. with T.M. Shaw and C.G. Widstrand.) Canada, Scandinavia, and Southern Africa, 1978; (with T.M. Shaw) Zambia's Foreign Policy: Studies in Diplomacy and Dependence, 1979; (with T.M. Shaw) Alternative Sources of Event Data on Zambian Foreign Policy, 1981; (ed.) Canada and South Africa: Challenge and Response, 1986; Zambian Crisis Behaviour: Confronting Rhodesia's Unilateral Declaration Of Independence, 1965-1966, 1994; Conflict in Sub-Saharan Africa, 1997-1998, 1998; Confronting Rwandan Genocide: The Military Options: What Could and Should the International Community Have Done?, 2002. Contributor to books and journals. **Address:** Department of Political Science, Carleton University, Rm. B640, Loeb Bldg., 1125 Colonel By Dr., Ottawa, ON K1S 5B6, Canada. **Online address:** d_anglin@carleton.ca

ANGLIN, Patty. American (born United States), b. 1954?. **Genres:** Humanities. **Career:** Adopt America Network, consultant; Acres of Hope, co-founder and executive director. Writer. **Publications:** (With J. Musser) Acres of Hope: The Miraculous Story of One Family's Gift of Love to Children Without Hope, 1999. Contributor to periodicals. **Address:** Acres of Hope Inc., 29525 Four Corners Store Rd., Mason, WI 54836, U.S.A.

ANGUS, Christopher (K.). American (born United States), b. 1950. **Genres:** Adult Non-fiction, Autobiography/Memoirs, Biography. **Career:** Adirondac Magazine, editor; Environmental advocate, 1982-. Freelance writer. **Publications:** Reflections from Canoe Country: Paddling the Waters of the Adirondacks and Canada, 1997; Images of America: St. Lawrence County, 2001; The Extraordinary Adirondack Journey of Clarence Petty: Wilderness Guide, Pilot, and Conservationist, 2002; (ed.) Oswegatchie: A North Country River, 2006. **Address:** c/o Author Mail, Syracuse University Press, 621 Skytop Rd., Ste. 110, Syracuse, NY 13244-5290, U.S.A.

ANNE, Kelleher. *See* **BUSH, Anne Kelleher.**

ANNEAR, Robyn. Australian (born Australia), b. 1960?. **Genres:** Adult Non-fiction, History, Children's Fiction. **Career:** State Library of Victoria's, Naked Democracy: Governing Victoria 1856-2006, curator, 2006-; Friends of the Castlemaine Library, president. Historian and writer. **Publications:** Names for Your Baby, 1992; Bearbrass: Imagining Early Melbourne, 1995, rev. ed., 2005; (with R. Ballinger) There Are Not Many Votes in Books: A History of the Castlemaine Library, 1855-1996, 1996; Nothing but Gold: The Diggers of 1852, 1999; The Man Who Lost Himself: The Unbelievable Story of the Tichborne Claimant, 2002; Fly a Rebel Flag: The Battle at Eureka, 2004; A City Lost & Found: Whelan the Wrecker's Melbourne, 2005; (with J. Hirst) Naked Democracy: Governing Victoria 1856-2006, 2006. **Address:** State Library of Victoria, 328 Swanston St., Melbourne, VI 3000, Australia.

ANNERINO, John. American (born United States) **Genres:** Adult Non-fiction, History, Natural History, Photography, Race Relations, Social Commentary, Travel/Exploration, Sciences, Sports/Fitness. **Career:** Gamma-Liaison Picture Agency, freelance photojournalist, 1983-96; Liaison Intl., contract photographer, 1996-2000; TimePix, contract photographer, 2001-03; Landov L.L.C., contract photographer, 2003-. Writer. **Publications:** Hiking the Grand Canyon, 1986, 3rd ed., 2006; Outdoors in Arizona, 1987; Adventuring in Arizona, 1991, 3rd ed., 2003; Running Wild: Through the Grand Canyon, 1992; Running Wild: An Extraordinary Adventure of the Human Spirit, 1998; Canyoneering, 1999; Dead in Their Tracks: Crossing America's Desert Borderlands, 1999, rev. ed., 2003; Desert Survivor, 2001; Desert Light: A Photographer's Journey through America's Desert Southwest, 2006; Photographer's Guide to Canyon Country, 2006; Indian Country: Sacred Ground, Native Peoples, 2007; Vanishing Borderlands: The Fragile Landscape of the U.S.-Mexico Border, 2008; Arizona: A Photographic Tribute, 2011; New Mexico: A Photographic Tribute, 2011. PHOTO ESSAYS: High Risk Photography, 1991; Canyons of the Southwest, 1993; The Wild Country of Mexico/ La Tierra Salvaje de Mexico, 1994; People of Legend, 1996; Apache: The Sacred Path to Womanhood, 1999; Roughstock: The Toughest Events in Rodeo, 2000; Grand Canyon Wild, 2004; Canyon Country, 2005. **Address:** 2325 W Wagon Wheels Dr., Tucson, AZ 85745, U.S.A. **Online address:** john@johnannerino.com

ANNIS, Barbara. American (born United States), b. 1954. **Genres:** Business/Trade/Industry. **Career:** Barbara Annis & Associates Inc., chief executive officer; World Business Academy, co-chair; Department of Justice, Social Context and Gender Equality Initiative, subject matter expert; Canadian Women Entrepreneurs, president; Harvard University Kennedy School of Government, Women's Leadership Board, chair. Writer. **Publications:** Same Words Different Language: How Men and Women Misunderstand Each Other at Work and What to Do about It, 2003; (with M. Gurian) Leadership and the Sexes: Using Gender Science to Create Success in Business, 2008. **Address:** Barbara Annis & Associates Inc., New York, NY 10167-0002, U.S.A.

ANSA, Tina McElroy. American (born United States), b. 1949. **Genres:** Novels, History. **Career:** Atlanta Constitution, copy editor, 1971, makeup editor, layout editor, entertainment writer, editor, feature writer and news reporter; freelance journalist, 1982-; Good Lil' School Girl, founder, 2001; Sea Island Writers Retreats, founder, 2004-; DownSouth Press, founder, 2007; Charlotte Observer, copy editor, editor, feature writer and news reporter; Clark College, instructor on mass media; Spelman College, writing workshop supervisor, writing workshop instructor; Brunswick College, writing workshop instructor; Emory University, writing workshop instructor; Paine College, writing workshop instructor; Perimeter College, writing workshop instructor. **Publications:** Not Soon Forgotten: Cotton Planters and Plantations of the Golden Isles of Georgia, 1987. NOVELS: Baby of the Family, 1989; Ugly Ways, 1993; The Hand I Fan With, 1996; You Know Better, 2002; Taking After Mudear, 2007. Contributor to newspapers. **Address:** PO Box 20602, St. Simons Island, GA 31522, U.S.A.

ANSARY, Mir Tamim. American/Afghani (born Afghanistan), b. 1948. **Genres:** Children's Non-fiction, Education, Children's Fiction, History. **Career:** Portland Scribe, staff writer, 1972-76; The Asia Foundation, Asian Student, assistant editor, 1976-78, editor of development publications, 1979- ; Harcourt Brace Jovanovich, school department editor, 1980-89. freelance writer, educational consultant and columnist, 1990-. **Publications:** Afghanistan: Fighting for Freedom, 1991; Matter: Solids, Liquids, and Gases, 1997; Score Booster Handbook: For Reading and Language Arts, 2000; West of Kabul, East of New York: An Afghan American Story (memoir), 2002; (with F. Ahmedi) The Story of My Life: An Afghan Girl on the Other Side of the Sky, 2005; (with F. Ahmedi) Other Side of the Sky, 2008; Destiny Disrupted, 2009; The Widow's Husband, 2009. CAUGHT READING SERIES: Carmen's Card, 1995; The Sea House, 1995; Spiders from Outer Space, 1995; The Lost Boy, 1995. COOL COLLECTIONS SERIES: Model Cars, 1997; Stamps, 1997; Dolls, 1997; Natural Objects, 1997; Insects, 1997. SUPER READERS SERIES; Mysterious Places, 1997; Creepy Creatures, 1997; Unbelievable Beasts, 1998; Baffling Disappearances, 1998; Great Crime Busters, 1998. HOLIDAY HISTORIES SERIES: Veterans Day, 1999, new ed., 2006; Labor Day, 1999, 2nd ed., 2006, trans. as El Día del Trabajo, 2008; Martin Luther King, Jr. Day, 1999, 2nd ed., 2006, trans. as Día de Martin Luther King, Jr., 2008; Memorial Day, 1999, 2nd ed., 2006, trans. as El Día de los Caídos, 2008; Columbus Day, 1999, 2nd ed., 2006; Presidents' Day, 1999, 2nd ed., 2006, trans. as Día de los Presidentes, 2009; Thanksgiving Day, 2001, 2nd ed., 2006; Earth Day, 2002, new ed., 2006; Election Day, 2002, 2nd ed., 2006; Independence Day, 2002, 2nd ed., 2006, trans. as. Día de la Independencia, 2008; Flag Day, 2002, 2nd ed., 2006; Arbor Day, 2002, new ed., 2006. ADVENTURES PLUS SERIES (educational comic books): Alien Alert, 2000; Treasure Hunt, 2000; Lost in Time, 2000; Runaway Spaceship, 2000; That's Some Dog, 2000; Case of the Missing Maillie, 2000. NATIVE AMERICANS SERIES: Plains Indians, 2000; California Indians, 2000; Eastern Woodlands Indians, 2000; Southwest Indians, 2000; Northwest Coast Indians, 2000; Great Basin Indians, 2000; Arctic Peoples, 2000; Plateau Indians, 2000; Southeast Indians, 2000; Subarctic Indians, 2000. STATE STUDIES: CALIFORNIA SERIES: California History, 2003; All around California: Regions and Resources, 2003; People of California, 2003; (with S. Feinstein) Uniquely California, 2003; (with S. Feinstein) California Plants and Animals, 2003; (with S. Feinstein) California Native Peoples, 2003. Works appear in anthologies. Contributor to books and periodicals. **Address:** c/o Author Mail, Carol Mann Agency, 55 5th Ave., New York, NY 10003-4301, U.S.A.

ANSAY, A. Manette. American (born United States), b. 1962?. **Genres:** Novels, Novellas/Short Stories. **Career:** Cornell University, lecturer in English, 1991-92; Phillips Exeter Academy, George Bennett Fellow, writer-inresidence, 1992-93; Vanderbilt University, assistant professor of English, 1993-97; writer, 1997-; University of Miami, associate professor of English, professor of English; Warren Wilson College, visiting writer, instructor, University of the South, instructor; Marquette University, instructor, women's chair in humanistic studies. **Publications:** Vinegar Hill (novel), 1994; Read This and Tell Me What It Says (short stories), 1995; Sister (novel), 1996;

River Angel, 1998; Midnight Champagne, 1999; Limbo: A Memoir, 2001; Blue Water, 2006; Good Things I Wish You: A Novel, 2009. Works appear in anthologies. Contributor to periodicals. **Address:** c/o Deborah Schneider, Gelfman Schneider Literary Agents Inc., 250 W 57th St., New York, NY 10107, U.S.A. **Online address:** a.ansay@miami.edu

ANSBERRY, Clare. American (born United States), b. 1957. **Genres:** Local History/Rural Topics, Women's Studies And Issues, Theology/Religion. **Career:** Journalist, 1979-84; Wall Street Journal, Pittsburgh bureau chief, 1984-. **Publications:** The Women of Troy Hill: The Back-Fence Virtues of Faith and Friendship, 2000; (with D.W. Meston) Comes the Peace: My Journey to Forgiveness, 2007. **Address:** c/o Laurie Liss, Sterling Lord Literistic Inc., 65 Bleecker St., New York, NY 10012, U.S.A. **Online address:** clare.ansberry@wsj.com

ANSCOMBE, Roderick. American/British (born England), b. 1947. **Genres:** Novels, Psychiatry, Young Adult Fiction, Mystery/Crime/Suspense. **Career:** Beth Israel Hospital, resident in psychiatry, chief resident, 1976-80, associate in psychiatry, 1990-; Bridgewater State Hospital, staff psychiatrist, 1989-91, 1998-; Harvard Medical School, assistant clinical professor, 1992-; Tewksbury Hospital, staff psychiatrist, 1993-98. Writer. **Publications:** The Secret Life of Laszlo, Count Dracula (novel), 1994; Shank (novel), 1996; Interview Room, 2005; Virgin Lies, 2007. Contributor of articles to journals. **Address:** c/o Courtney Fischer, St. Martin's Press, 175 5th Ave., New York, NY 10010, U.S.A. **Online address:** author@roderickanscombe.com

ANSEL, Talvikki. American (born United States), b. 1962?. **Genres:** Poetry, Young Adult Fiction. **Career:** Lynchburg College, Richard H. Thornton Writer-in-residence, 1997; University of Rhode Island, College of Arts and Sciences, Department of English, instructor. Writer. **Publications:** My Shining Archipelago (poems), 1997; Jetty & Other Poems, 2003. Contributor to periodicals. **Address:** Department of English, University of Rhode Island, Rm. 208D, 114 Swan Hall, 60 Upper College Rd., Kingston, RI 02881-2000, U.S.A. **Online address:** tansel@mail.uri.edu

ANSHAW, Carol. American (born United States), b. 1946. **Genres:** Novels. **Career:** Norwich University, Vermont College, faculty member, 1994-99; School of the Art Institute of Chicago, adjunct associate professor, 1996-; National Endowment for the Arts, fellow. Writer. **Publications:** NOVELS: Aquamarine, 1992; Seven Moves, 1996; Lucky in the Corner, 2002. Work appear in anthologies. Contributor to periodicals. **Address:** c/o Author Mail, Houghton Mifflin, 215 Park Ave. S, New York, NY 10003, U.S.A. **Online address:** carolanshaw@gmail.com

ANTAL, Dan. British/Romanian (born Romania), b. 1954. **Genres:** Novels, Novellas/Short Stories, Autobiography/Memoirs, Biography. **Career:** Teacher, 1978-83, 1992-; West Heath College, French teacher, 1991-94; consultant, 1992-. Writer. **Publications:** Out of Romania (autobiography), 1995; The Penguin (novel), forthcoming; Maria (short stories), forthcoming; Behind the Curtains, forthcoming. **Address:** 17 Mortimer Cres., London, GL NW6 5NP, England.

ANTHES, Richard A. American (born United States), b. 1944. **Genres:** Meteorology/Atmospheric Sciences. **Career:** University of Wisconsin, NSF fellow, 1966-68; National Hurricane Research Laboratory, research meteorologist, 1968-71; Pennsylvania State University, assistant professor, associate professor, 1971-78, professor of meteorology, 1978-81; Naval Postgraduate School, research professor, 1977-78; National Center for Atmospheric Research, Atmospheric Analysis and Prediction Division, director, 1981-86; Journal of the Atmospheric Sciences, associate editor, 1983-86; National Center for Atmospheric Research, director, 1986-88, University Corporation for Atmospheric Research, president, 1988-2012, president emeritus, 2012-. **Publications:** (With A. Miller) Meteorology, 1967, 7th ed., 1997; (with J.J. Cahir, A.B. Fraser and H.A. Panofsky) The Atmosphere, 1975, 3rd ed., 1981; Weather Around Us, 1976; Tropical Cyclones: Their Evolution, Structure and Effects, 1982; (with W. Cotton) Storm and Cloud Dynamics, 1989; Toward a New National Weather Service: An Assessment of the Advanced Weather Interactive Processing System: Operational Test and Evaluation of the First System Build, 1997; (co-ed.) Hurricane!: Coping with Disaster: Progress and Challenges since Galveston, 1900, 2003. **Address:** University Corporation for Atmospheric Research, PO Box 3000, Boulder, CO 80307-3000, U.S.A. **Online address:** president@ucar.edu

ANTHONY, Crystal McCrary. American (born United States) **Genres:** Novels, Women's Studies And Issues, Social Commentary, Young Adult Fiction, Romance/Historical. **Career:** Writer. **Publications:** (With R. Ewing) Homecourt Advantage, 1998; (with T.L. Lee) Gotham Diaries, 2004; Inspiration: Profiles Of Black Women Changing Our World, 2012. Contributor to periodicals. **Address:** Hyperion Editorial Department, Hyperion Books, 114 5th Ave., New York, NY 10011, U.S.A. **Online address:** crystal@crystalmccraryanthony.com

ANTHONY, Evelyn. (Evelyn Bridget Patricia Stephens Ward-Thomas). British (born England), b. 1928. **Genres:** Mystery/Crime/Suspense, Romance/Historical, Novels, Young Adult Fiction. **Career:** Writer, 1949-. **Publications:** Imperial Highness, 1953 in US as Rebel Princess, 1953; Curse Not the King, 1954 in US as Royal Intrigue, 1954; Far Flies the Eagle, 1955; Anne Boleyn, 1957; Victoria and Albert: A Novel, 1958; All the Queen's Men, 1960; Charles the King, 1961; Clandara, 1963; The Heiress, 1964 in US as The French Bride, 1964; Valentina, 1966; The Rendezvous, 1967; Anne of Austria, 1968 in US as The Cardinal and the Queen, 1968; The Legend, 1969; The Assassin, 1970; The Tamarind Seed: A Novel, 1971; The Poellenberg Inheritance, 1972; The Occupying Power, 1973 in US as Stranger at the Gates 1973; The Malaspiga Exit, 1974 in US as Mission to Malaspiga, 1974; The Persian Ransom, 1975 in US as The Persian Price, 1975; The Silver Falcon, 1977; The Return, 1978; The Grave of Truth, 1979 in US as The Janus Imperative, 1980; The Defector, 1981; The Avenue of the Dead, 1981; Albatross, 1982; The Company of Saints, 1983; Voices on the Wind, 1985; No Enemy But Time, 1987 in US as A Place to Hide, 1987; The House of Vandekar, 1988; The Scarlet Thread, 1990; The Relic, 1991; The Doll's House, 1992; Exposure, 1994; Blood Stones, 1994; The Legacy, 1997; A Dubious Legacy, 2002; Sleeping with the Enemy, 2003; Codeword Janus, 2003; Betrayal, 2004; No Resistance, 2004; Mind Games, 2005. **Address:** Horham Hall, Thaxted, EX CM6 2NN, England.

ANTHONY, Joseph Patrick. American (born United States), b. 1964. **Genres:** Children's Fiction, Young Adult Fiction, Science Fiction/Fantasy. **Career:** Carpenter and writer. **Publications:** FOR CHILDREN: The Dandelion Seed, 1997; In a Nutshell, 1999. YOUNG ADULT FICTION: Innerworld: A Novel, 2002. **Address:** Dawn Publications, 12402 Bitney Springs Rd., Nevada City, CA 95959, U.S.A. **Online address:** joseph@moonstar.com

ANTHONY, Lawrence. South African (born South Africa), b. 1950. **Genres:** Military/Defense/Arms Control, History. **Career:** Thula Thula Game Reserve, owner and head of conservation; The Earth Organization, founder, 2003-. Writer. **Publications:** (With G. Spence) Babylon's Ark: The Incredible Wartime Rescue of the Baghdad Zoo, 2007; (with G. Spence) The Elephant Whisperer: My Life With the Herd in the African Wild in UK as Elephant Whisperer: Learning about Life, Loyalty and Freedom from a Remarkable Herd of Elephants, 2009. **Address:** The Earth Organization, PO Box 935, Westville, Durban, 3630, South Africa. **Online address:** la@thulathula.com

ANTHONY, Michael. Trinidadian (born Trinidad and Tobago), b. 1930. **Genres:** Novels, Novellas/Short Stories, History, Travel/Exploration. **Career:** Reuters News Agency, sub-editor 1964-68; Texas Star, assistant editor, 1970-72; Ministry of Culture, researcher, 1972-88; University of Richmond, teacher of creative writing, 1992. Writer. **Publications:** The Games Were Coming (novel), 1963; The Year in San Fernando (novel), 1965; Green Days by the River (novel), 1967; Cricket in the Road (short stories), 1973; Sandra Street and Other Stories, 1973; Glimpses of Trinidad and Tobago: With a Glance at the West Indies, 1974; (ed. with A. Carr) David Frost Introduces Trinidad and Tobago, 1975; Profile Trinidad: A Historical Survey from the Discovery to 1900, 1975; Streets of Conflict (novel), 1976; Folk Tales and Fantasies (short stories), 1976; The Making of Port of Spain: 1757-1939, 1978; All That Glitters (novel), 1981; Bright Road to El Dorado (novel), 1982; Port of Spain in a World at War, 1984; First in Trinidad, 1985, 2nd ed., 2003; Heroes of the People of Trinidad and Tobago, 1986, 2nd ed., 2005; The History of Aviation in Trinidad & Tobago, 1913-1962, 1987; A Better and Brighter Day, 1987, 3rd ed., 2004; Towns and Villages of Trinidad and Tobago, 1988; Parade of the Carnivals of Trinidad, 1839-1989, 1989; The Becket Factor, 1990, The Golden Quest-The Four Voyages of Christopher Columbia (history), 1992; The Chieftain's Carnival and Other Stories, 1993; In the Heat of the Day, 1996; Historical Dictionary of Trinadad & Tobogo, 1997; Green Days by the River, 2000; Anaparima: The History of San Fernando and its Environs(the Naparimas), 2001; High Tide of Intrigue, 2001. **Address:** 99 Long Circular Rd., St. James, Port of Spain, 00109-7000, Trinidad and Tobago.

ANTHONY, Patricia. American (born United States), b. 1947. **Genres:** Novels, Novellas/Short Stories, Science Fiction/Fantasy, Plays/Screenplays, Mystery/Crime/Suspense. **Career:** University of Lisbon, visiting professor of English literature; Universidade Federal de Santa Catarina, associate professor of English; Southern Methodist University, adjunct professor of creative writing. Writer. **Publications:** Cold Allies, 1993; Brother Termite, 1993; Conscience of the Beagle, 1993; Happy Policeman, 1994; Cradle of Splendor, 1996; God's Fires, 1997; Eating Memories, 1997; Flanders, 1998. Contributor to magazines. **Address:** c/o Donald Maass, Donald Maass Literary Agency, 121 W 27th St., Ste. 801, New York, NY 10001, U.S.A. **Online address:** patanthony@mindspring.com

ANTHONY, Piers. (Piers Anthony Dillingham Jacob). American/British (born England), b. 1934. **Genres:** Novels, Romance/Historical, Science Fiction/Fantasy, Westerns/Adventure, Young Adult Fiction, Autobiography/Memoirs, E-books. **Career:** Electronic Communications Inc., technical writer, 1959-62; freelance writer, 1962-63, 1966-; Admiral Farragut Academy, teacher of English, 1965-66. **Publications:** SCIENCE FICTION: (with R.E. Margroff) The Ring, 1968; Macroscope, 1969; (with R.E. Margroff) The E.S.P. Worm, 1970; Prostho Plus, 1971; Race against Time, 1973; Rings of Ice, 1974; Triple Detente, 1974; (with R. Coulson) But What of Earth?, 1976, rev. ed., 1989; (with F. Hall) The Pretender, 1979; Mute, 1981; Ghost, 1986; Shade of the Tree, 1986; (ed. with B.N. Malzberg, M.H. Greenberg and C.G. Waugh) Uncollected Stars, 1986; Total Recall, 1989; Balook, 1990; Hard Sell, 1990; (with R. Fuentes) Dead Morn, 1990; Mer-Cycle, 1991; (with P.J. Farmer) Caterpillar's Question, 1992; Killobyte, 1993; (with A. Tella) The Willing Spirit, 1996; Volk Internet 1996, 1997; (with C.A. Pickover) Spider Legs, 1998; (with J.R. Goolsby and A. Riggs) Quest for the Fallen Star, 1998; (with J. Brady) Dream a Little Dream, 1999; Realty Check, 1999; (with J.A. Taeusch) The Secret of Spring, 2000; (with R. Leming) The Gutbucket Quest, 2000. ATON SERIES: Chthon, 1967; Phthor, 1975. OMNIVORE SERIES: Omnivore, 1968; Orn, 1971; Ox, 1976. BATTLE CIRCLE SERIES: Sos the Rope, 1968; Var the Stick, 1972; Neq the Sword, 1975; Battle Circle, 1978. CLUSTER SERIES: Cluster, 1977, rev. ed. in UK as Vicinity Cluster, 1979; Chaining the Lady, 1978; Kirlian Quest, 1978; Thousandstar, 1980; Viscous Circle, 1982. TAROT: God of Tarot, 1979; Vision of Tarot, 1980; Faith of Tarot, 1980; Tarot, 1987. BIO OF A SPACE TYRANT SERIES: Refugee, 1983; Mercenary, 1984; Politician, 1985; Executive, 1985; Statesman, 1986; The Iron Maiden, 2002. FANTASY NOVELS: Hasan, 1977; (with R. Kornwise) Through the Ice, 1989; (with M. Lackey) If I Pay Thee Not in Gold, 1993. MAGIC OF XANTH SERIES: A Spell for Chameleon, 1977; The Source of Magic, 1978; Castle Roogna, 1979; The Magic of Xanth, 1981, rev. ed. as Piers Anthony: Three Complete Xanth Novels, 1994; Centaur Aisle, 1982; Ogre, Ogre, 1982; Night Mare, 1982; Dragon on a Pedestal, 1983; Crewel Lye: A Caustic Yarn, 1984; Golem in the Gears, 1985; Vale of the Vole, 1987; Heaven Cent, 1988; Man from Mundania, 1989; (with J.L. Nye) Piers Anthony's Visual Guide to Xanth, 1989; Isle of View, 1990; Question Quest, 1991; The Color of Her Panties, 1992; Demons Don't Dream, 1993; Harpy Thyme, 1994; Geis of the Gargoyle, 1995; Roc and a Hard Place, 1995; Yon Ill Wind, 1996; Faun and Games, 1997; Zombie Lover, 1998; Xone of Contention, 1999; The Dastard, 2000; Swell Foop, 2001; Up in a Heaval, 2001; Cube Route, 2003; Currant Events, 2004; Pet Peeve, 2005; Stork Naked, 2006; Air Apparent, 2007; Two to the Fifth, 2008; Jumper Cable, 2009; Knot Gneiss, 2010; Well-Tempered Clavicle 2011. INCARNATIONS OF IMMORTALITY SERIES: On a Pale Horse, 1983; Bearing an Hourglass, 1984; With a Tangled Skein, 1985; Wielding a Red Sword, 1986; Being a Green Mother, 1987; For Love of Evil, 1988; And Eternity, 1990; Under a Velvet Cloak, 2007. DRAGON GOLD SERIES WITH R.E. MARGOFF: Dragon's Gold, 1987; Serpent's Silver, 1988; Chimaera's Copper, 1990; Orc's Opal, 1990; Mouvar's Magic, 1992. APPRENTICE ADEPT SERIES: Split Infinity, 1980; Blue Adept, 1981; Juxtaposition, 1982; Double Exposure, 1982; Out of Phaze, 1987; Robot Adept, 1988; Unicorn Point, 1989; Phaze Doubt, 1990. MODE SERIES: Virtual Mode, 1991; Fractal Mode, 1992; Chaos Mode, 1993; Do Oon Mode, 2001. JASON STRIKER SERIES WITH R. FUENTES: Kiai!, 1974; Mistress of Death, 1974; The Bamboo Bloodbath, 1974; Ninja's Revenge, 1975; Amazon Slaughter, 1976. GEODYSSY SERIES: Isle of Woman, 1993; Shame of Man, 1994; Hope of Earth, 1997; Muse of Art, 1999; Climate of Change, 2010. CHROMAGIC SERIES: Key to Havoc, 2003; Key to Chroma, 2003; Key to Destiny, 2004; Key to Liberty, 2007; Key to Survival, 2007. OTHERS: Steppe, 1976; Anthonology (short stories), 1985; Bio of an Ogre: The Autobiography of Piers Anthony to Age Fifty, 1988; Pornucopia (erotic fantasy), 1989; Firefly, 1990; Tatham Mound (historical fiction), 1991; Alien Plot (short stories), 1992; Letters to Jenny (nonfiction), 1993; (ed. with R. Gilliam) Tales from the Great Turtle, 1994; How Precious was that While: An Autobiography, 2001; The Magic Fart (erotica), 2003; Tortoise Reform, 2006; Relationships, 2006; Relationships I, 2007; Alfred, A Biography, 2007; Relationships II, 2008; Relationships III, 2009; Xanth by Two, 2010; Relationships 4, 2011; Eroma (erotic romance), 2011; Pandora Park, 2011; The Sopaths, 2011; (with J.R. Rain) Aladdin Relighted, 2011; Aladdin Sins Bad, 2011; Trail Mix: Amoeba 2011; Trail Mix: Beetel Juice 2011. **Address:** Intellectual Property Group, 9200 Sunset Blvd., Ste. 820, Los Angeles, CA 90069-3605, U.S.A. **Online address:** piersanthony@hipiers.com

ANTHONY, Ted. American (born United States), b. 1968. **Genres:** Music, Poetry. **Career:** Patriot-News, staff, 1990-92; Associated Press, staff, 1992-96; International News Desk, national writer, 1996-2002, news editor, 2002-04, interim news editor, 2003, 2005. **Publications:** Chasing the Rising Sun: The Journey of an American Song, 2007. **Address:** Associated Press Headquarters, 450 W 33rd St., New York, NY 10001-2603, U.S.A.

ANTIEAU, Kim. American (born United States), b. 1955?. **Genres:** Novellas/Short Stories, Mystery/Crime/Suspense. **Career:** Daughters of Nyx: A Magazine of Goddess Stories, Mythmaking and Fairy Tales, editor, 1994-96. **Publications:** Blossoms, 1991; Trudging to Eden: A Collection of Short Stories, 1994; The Jigsaw Woman, 1996; The Gaia Websters, 1997; Coyote Cowgirl, 2003; Counting on Wildflowers: An Entanglement, 2005; Mercy, Unbound, 2006; Broken Moon, 2007; Ruby's Imagine, 2008; Church of the Old Mermaids. 2008; The Salmon Mysteries, 2010; Deathmark, 2011. **Address:** c/o Author Mail, Forge Books, 175 5th Ave., New York, NY 10010, U.S.A. **Online address:** kim@kimantieau.com

ANTLER, Joyce. American (born United States), b. 1942. **Genres:** Politics/Government, History. **Career:** Brandeis University, Samuel B. Lane Professor of American Jewish History and Culture and Women's and Gender Studies. Writer. **Publications:** (With E. Fuchs) Year One of the Empire: A Play of American Politics, War and Protest Taken from the Historical Record, 1973; The Educated Woman and Professionalization: The Struggle for a New Feminine Identity, 1890-1920, 1987; Lucy Sprague Mitchell: The Making of a Modern Woman, 1987; (ed. with S.K. Biklen) Changing Education: Women as Radicals and Conservators, 1990; (ed. and intro.) America and I: Short Stories by American Jewish Women Writers, 1990; (co-ed.) The Challenge of Feminist Biography: Writing the Lives of Modern American Women, 1992; The Journey Home: Jewish Women and the American Century, 1997; (ed.) Talking Back: Images of Jewish Women in American Popular Culture, 1998; (with N. Gabler and F. Rich) Television's Changing Image of American Jews, 2000; You Never Call! You Never Write! A History of the Jewish Mother, 2007. **Address:** Brandeis University, 415 South St., Waltham, MA 02453, U.S.A. **Online address:** antler@brandeis.edu

ANTOGNAZZA, Maria Rosa. British/Italian (born Italy), b. 1964?. **Genres:** Biography. **Career:** University of Aberdeen, lecturer and senior lecturer in philosophy; King's College London, reader, professor, 2003-. Writer. **Publications:** (Ed. and intro.) Alsted and Leibniz: On God, the Magistrate, and the Millennium, 1999; Trinita e Incarnazione: il rapporto tra filosofia e teologia rivelata nel pensiero di Leibniz, 1999; Leibniz: An Intellectual Biography, 2009. Contributor of articles to journals and books. **Address:** Department of Philosophy, King's College London, Strand, Westminster, GL WC2R 2LS, England. **Online address:** maria.rosa.antognazza@kcl.ac.uk

ANTOL, Marie Nadine. (Nikki Antol). American (born United States), b. 1930. **Genres:** Biography, Medicine/Health, Ghost Writer, Food And Wine. **Career:** Freelance writer, 1985-. **Publications:** (With N. Johnson) A Dud at Seventy-A Stud at Eighty! An Autobiography, 1982; Healing Teas: A Practical Guide to the Medicinal Teas of the World, 1996; The Incredible Secrets of Mustard: The Quintessential Guide to the History, Lore, Varieties, and Benefits, 1999; Incredible Secrets of Vinegar, 2000; Confessions of a Coffee Bean: The Complete Guide to Coffee Cuisine, 2002; Sophisticated-Olive: The Complete Guide to Olive Cuisine, 2004. Contributor to periodicals. **Address:** Avery Publishing Group, Penguin Putnam Inc., 375 Hudson St., New York, NY 10014, U.S.A.

ANTOL, Nikki. *See* **ANTOL, Marie Nadine.**

ANTON, Maggie. American (born United States) **Genres:** Novels, Young Adult Fiction. **Career:** Kaiser Permanente's Biochemical Genetics Laboratory, clinical chemist, through 2006, retired, 2006; full-time writer, 2006-.

Publications: RASHI'S DAUGHTERS SERIES: Joheved, 2005; Miriam, 2007; Secret Scholar, 2008; Rachel, 2009. **Address:** c/o Susanna Einstein, LJK Literary Management L.L.C., 133 W 25th St., Ste. 8W, New York, NY 10001, U.S.A. **Online address:** author@rashisdaughters.com

ANTON, Ted. American (born United States), b. 1957. **Genres:** Documentaries/Reportage, Sciences, Young Adult Non-fiction. **Career:** Great Books Foundation, National Training Instructor, 1985-87; DePaul University, lecturer, 1987-88, assistant professor, 1989-95, Internship Program, director, 1991-, associate professor of English, 1995-2001, Graduate Program in Writing, director, 1997-99, professor of English, 2001-, Humanities Center, fellow, 2005-06, associate chair, 2008-; Loyola University, instructor, 1988-89. Writer. **Publications:** (Ed. with R. McCourt) The New Science Journalists, 1995; Eros, Magic, and the Murder of Professor Culianu (non-fiction), 1996; Bold Science: Seven Scientists Who are Changing Our World, 2000. Works appear in anthologies. Contributor to periodicals. **Address:** Department of English, DePaul University, McGaw 230, 802 W Belden Ave., Chicago, IL 60614-3214, U.S.A. **Online address:** tanton@depaul.edu

ANTONETTA, Susanne. (Suzanne Paola). American (born United States), b. 1956?. **Genres:** Adult Non-fiction, Poetry, Psychology, Environmental Sciences/Ecology, Autobiography/Memoirs. **Career:** Writer. **Publications:** Body Toxic: An Environmental Memoir, 2001; A Mind Apart: Travels in a Neurodiverse World, 2005. AS SUZANNE PAOLA: Lives of the Saints, 2002; (with B. Miller) Tell it Slant: Writing and Shaping Creative Nonfiction, 2004, 2nd ed., 2012. POETRY AS SUZANNE PAOLA: Bardo, 1998. **Address:** c/o Jill Grinberg, Jill Grinberg Literary Management L.L.C., 16 Court St., Ste. 3306, Brooklyn, NY 11241, U.S.A.

ANTONETTE, Leslie. American (born United States), b. 1958. **Genres:** Literary Criticism And History, Adult Non-fiction. **Career:** East Stroudsburg University of Pennsylvania, assistant professor of English, 1996-, professor; Frederick Douglass Institute for Intercultural Studies, co-director, professor of English. Writer. **Publications:** The Rhetoric of Diversity and the Traditions of American Literary Study: Critical Multiculturalism in English, 1998. **Address:** Department of English, East Stroudsburg University, Rm. 309, Stroud Hall, 200 Prospect St., East Stroudsburg, PA 18301, U.S.A. **Online address:** lantonette@po-box.esu.edu

ANTONI, Brian. American (born United States), b. 1958. **Genres:** Novels. **Career:** Attorney, 1995-. Writer. **Publications:** Paradise Overdose: A Novel, 1994; (co-author) Naked Came the Manatee, 1996; South Beach: The Novel, 2008. Contributor to periodicals. **Address:** 451 Broome St., Ste. 9W, New York, NY 10013, U.S.A.

ANTONI, Robert (William). American/Trinidadian (born Trinidad and Tobago), b. 1958. **Genres:** Novels, Novellas/Short Stories, Young Adult Nonfiction. **Career:** Johns Hopkins University, assistant professor of creative writing, 1981-82; University of Iowa, assistant professor of creative writing and literature, 1985-90; Caribbean Writers Summer Institute, associate director; University of Miami, associate professor of creative writing and literature, 1992-2001; Columbia University, Barnard College, faculty, 2004-05; The New School, faculty; Paris Review, contributing editor; Conjunctions, senior editor; BOMB Magazine, contributing editor. **Publications:** NOVELS: Divina Trace, 1991; Blessed is the Fruit, 1997; My Grandmother's Erotic Folktales, 2000; Carnival, 2005. Works appear in anthologies. Contributor to periodicals. **Address:** c/o Kim Witherspoon, Inkwell Management, 521 5th Ave., 26th Fl., New York, NY 10175, U.S.A. **Online address:** robertantoni@earthlink.net

ANTONUCCI, Francesco. American/Italian (born Italy), b. 1956. **Genres:** Food And Wine. **Career:** Alo Alo Restaurant, executive chef, through 1987; Remi Restaurants Inc., New York, co-owner and chef, 1987-; Remi Restaurants, Santa Monica, co-owner, 1990-; Remi Restaurants, Mexico, co-owner, 1993-; Remi Restaurants, Tel Aviv, Israel, 1994-; El Toula, chef; Valentino Restaurant, sous chef; DDL Bistro, chef. Writer. **Publications:** (With F. Fabricant) Venetian Taste, 1994; (with M. Pulini and G. Salvaterra) Il Sapore della Memoria, trans. as The Art of Italian Regional Cooking, 1995. **Address:** Remi Restaurant Inc., 145 W 53rd St., New York, NY 10019-6005, U.S.A. **Online address:** remirestaurant@earthlink.net

ANTONY, Peter. *See* **SHAFFER, Peter (Levin).**

ANTOON, Sinan. American/Iraqi (born Iraq), b. 1967?. **Genres:** Novels. **Career:** New York University, assistant professor; documentary filmmaker; Dartmouth College, Arabic and Arab literature, teacher. Writer. **Publications:** (Trans. with M. Akash, C. Forche and A. El-Zein) Mahmoud Darwish, Unfortunately, It was Paradise: Selected Poems, 2003; Mawshur mubalalal bil-Hurub (novel), 2003; I'jaam: An Iraqi Rhapsody, 2007; Layl wāḥid fi kull al-mudun: shir, 2010. (trans.) M. Darwish, In the Presence of Absence, 2011. Contributor to periodicals. Work appears in anthology. **Address:** Office of Gallatin Graduate Admissions, New York University, 1 Wash Pl., Rm. 510, New York, NY 10003, U.S.A. **Online address:** sinan.antoon@gmail.edu

ANTRIM, Donald. American (born United States), b. 1958. **Genres:** Novels, Autobiography/Memoirs, Biography. **Career:** Columbia University, School of the Arts, associate professor. Novelist. **Publications:** NOVELS: Elect Mr. Robinson for a Better World, 1993; The Hundred Brothers, 1997; The Verificationist, 2000. OTHERS: The Afterlife, 2006; (intro.) All the Days and Nights, 2009. Contributor to journals and periodicals. **Address:** School of the Arts, Columbia University, 415 Dodge Hall, 2960 Broadway, PO Box 1808, New York, NY 10027-2342, U.S.A.

ANTRIM, Taylor. American (born United States), b. 1974?. **Genres:** Novels. **Career:** ForbesLife Magazine, editor; New York University, Gallatin School of Individualized Study, part-time faculty; The Daily Beast, fiction critic; Architectural Digest Magazine, senior editor. **Publications:** The Headmaster Ritual (novel), 2007. Contributor to periodicals. **Address:** c/o Emer Flounders, Houghton Mifflin Harcourt, 215 Park Ave. S, New York, NY 10003-1603, U.S.A. **Online address:** ltantrim@hotmail.com

ANUNOBI, Fredoline O. American (born United States), b. 1956. **Genres:** Economics, Politics/Government, Business/Trade/Industry. **Career:** Alabama A&M University, instructor in economics, 1984-85; Morris Brown College, teaching assistant in economics, 1987-88; Selma University, assistant professor of political science, head of Division of Business Administration and Social Sciences and director of Third World studies, 1988-92; Xavier University, Department of political science, assistant professor, 1992-, associate professor; Georgia Perimeter College, associate professor and chair of business. Writer. **Publications:** The Implications of Conditionality: The International Monetary Fund and Africa, 1992; International Dimensions of African Political Economy: Trends, Challenges and Realities, 1994; Challenge of African Development: From Neoclassical Liberalism to Structural Adjustment, 2008. Contributor to journals. Works appear in anthologies. **Address:** Department of Business, Georgia Perimeter College, 3251 Panthersville Rd., Decatur, GA 30034, U.S.A. **Online address:** fanunobi@gpc.edu

AOYAMA, Gosho. (Aoyama Yoshimasa). Japanese (born Japan), b. 1963. **Genres:** Novels. **Career:** Writer. **Publications:** MANGA: Yaiba, vol. 1-24, 1988-93; Magic Kaito, vol. 1-4, Shogakukan, 1988-2007; 3rd Baseman Number 4, 1993; Tell Me a Lie, 2007; DETECTIVE CONAN OR CASE CLOSED MANGA SERIES: Detective Conan, 61 vols., 2008. Contributor to periodicals.

APEL, Dora. American (born United States), b. 1952. **Genres:** Art/Art History. **Career:** Wayne State University, James Pearson Duffy Department of Art and Art History, adjunct professor, 1987-88, 1994-99, assistant professor, W. Hawkins Ferry endowed chair in modern and contemporary art history, 1999-, associate professor; Lawrence Technological University, lecturer in humanities, 1997-99. Writer. **Publications:** Memory Effects: The Holocaust and the Art of Secondary Witnessing, 2002; Imagery of Lynching: Black Men, White Women, and the Mob, 2004; (with S.M. Smith) Lynching Photographs, 2007; War Culture and the Contest of Images, 2012; You Can't Measure the Sky, forthcoming; War Culture: Art, Media and Contemporary War, forthcoming; The War of Images, forthcoming. Contributor to periodicals. **Address:** James Pearson Duffy Department of Art and Art, History, Wayne State University, 2160 Faculty/Administration Bldg., Detroit, MI 48202, U.S.A. **Online address:** dora.apel@wayne.edu

APOLLONIO, Carol. *See* **FLATH, Carol (Apollonio).**

APONTE, Harry J. American (born United States), b. 1935. **Genres:** Psychiatry, Social Work, Science Fiction/Fantasy. **Career:** Catholic Charities Family Service, staff, 1959-60; Menninger Clinic, staff member, 1961-68; Philadelphia Child Guidance Clinic, staff, 1968-69, administrator, coordinator of clinical services, 1969-74, director of outpatient department, 1974-75, director of the clinic, 1975-79; private practice of family therapy, 1979-; Family Therapy Training Program of Philadelphia, director, 1982-; Drexel University, clinical associate professor, 1983-; Menninger Foundation, administrator; Family Institute of Virginia, consultant. Writer. **Publications:** Bread and Spirit: Therapy with the New Poor, 1994. Contributor to books. **Address:** 1401 Walnut St., Ste. 32D, Philadelphia, PA 19102, U.S.A.

APOSTOLOU, Anna. *See* **DOHERTY, P(aul) C.**

APPACH, Anjana. (Anjana Appachana). Indian (born India), b. 1956. **Genres:** Novellas/Short Stories, Young Adult Fiction. **Career:** D.C.M. Data Products, officer, 1981-84; Pennsylvania State University, State College, teaching assistant, 1985-88; Arizona State University, faculty associate, 1989, visiting professor, 1998-99. Writer. **Publications:** Incantations & Other Stories, 1992; Listening Now, 1998. Contributor to periodicals. **Address:** c/o Victoria Gould Pryor, Arcadia, 31 Lake Pl. N, Danbury, CT 06810, U.S.A. **Online address:** mercara1@yahoo.com

APPACHANA, Anjana. *See* **APPACH, Anjana.**

APPELL, Scott D. American (born United States), b. 1954. **Genres:** Horticulture, Natural History, Botany. **Career:** Brooklyn Botanic Garden, part-time assistant to orchidologist, 1969-71, assistant to taxonomist, 1974-77; Ohio Nurserymen's Association, certified nurseryman, 1987; WCMH-TV, The Garden Spot (weekly gardening program), host, 1989; York Wildlife Conservancy, Bronx Zoo, horticulturist and gardener, 1994; Ken Druse Studio, staff horticulturist, 1994-95; The Green Man Inc., horticultural consultant, 1994-; Smith and Hawken, senior horticulturist, 1994-96; New Hort-in-Site Ltd. (Internet Web site), co-editor and staff horticulturist, 1994-98; Horticultural Society of New York, director of education, 1996-; Central Park Zoo, horticulturist, 1996; chef. **Publications:** (Intro.) Pansies, 1999; (intro.) Tulips, 1999; (intro.) Lilies, 2000; (with B.B. Garden) Landscaping Indoors, 2000; (intro.) Orchids, 2000; (ed.) Annuals for Every Garden, 2003. Contributor to books and periodicals. **Address:** Horticultural Society of New York, 128 W 58th St., New York, NY 10019-2103, U.S.A.

APPELT, Kathi. American (born United States), b. 1954. **Genres:** Children's Fiction, Young Adult Fiction, Children's Non-fiction, Autobiography/Memoirs. **Career:** Brazos Pre-natal Clinic, secretary, 1985-87; Texas A&M University, instructor in continuing education, 1992, assistant lecturer, 2002-; Jacques' Toys and Books, children's books buyer, 1992-94, 1994-95; Rice University, instructor in continuing education, 1996-2000; Vermont College, faculty, 2003-. Writer. **Publications:** Elephants Aloft, 1993; Bayou Lullaby, 1995; Bat Jamboree, 1996; The Thunderherd, 1996; Watermelon Day, 1996; A Red Wagon Year, 1996; I See the Moon, 1997; Just People and Paper/Pen/Poem, 1997; Bats on Parade, 1999; Cowboy Dreams, 1999; Someone's Come to Our House, 1999; The Toddler Two-Step, 2000; Bats around the Clock, 2000; Hushabye, Baby Blue, 2000; Kissing Tennessee and Other Stories from the Stardust Dance, 2000; Oh My Baby, Little One, 2000; Down Cut Shin Creek: The Pack Horse Librarians of Kentucky, 2001; Rain Dance, 2001; Bubbles, Bubbles, 2001; Poems from Homeroom: A Writer's Place to Start by Kathi Appelt, 2002; Bubba and Beau: Best Friends, 2002; The Alley Cat's Meow, 2002; Incredible Me!, 2002; Where, Where Is Swamp Bear, 2002; Poems from Home Room: A Writer's Place to Start, 2002; Best Kind of Gift, 2003; Piggies in a Polka, 2003; Bubba and Beau Go Night-Night, 2003; My Father's Summers: A Daughter's Memoir, 2004; Bubba and Beau Meet the Relatives, 2004; Merry Christmas, Merry Crow, 2005; Miss Lady Bird's Wildflowers: How a First Lady Changed America, 2005; My Father's House, 2007; Underneath, 2008; Brand-New Baby Blues, 2010; Keeper, 2010. **Address:** Pippin Properties Inc., 155 E 38th St., Ste. 2H, New York, NY 10016, U.S.A. **Online address:** k-author@kathiappelt.com

APPIAH, (K.) Anthony. American/British (born England), b. 1954. **Genres:** Philosophy, Cultural/Ethnic Topics, Novels. **Career:** University of Ghana, teaching assistant, 1975-76; Yale University, visiting fellow, 1979, assistant professor, 1981-85, associate professor of philosophy, 1985-86, Center for Research in Education, director, 1985-86; Cambridge University, Clare College, visiting fellow, 1983-84; Cornell University, visiting associate professor, 1986-89, associate professor, 1989, professor of philosophy, 1989; Duke University, professor of philosophy and literature, 1990-91; Harvard University, professor of Afro-American studies and philosophy, 1991-99, Charles H. Carswell professor of Afro-American studies and philosophy, 1999-2002, head tutor, 1991-2001, Black Fiction Project, associate director, 1991-96, Walter Channing Cabot fellow, 1998-99, director of graduate studies, 2001-02; Princeton University, Laurance S. Rockefeller university professor of philosophy, 2002-. Writer. **Publications:** Assertion and Conditionals, 1985; For Truth in Semantics, 1986; Necessary Questions: An Introduction to Philosophy, 1989; Avenging Angel, 1991; In My Father's House: Africa in the Philosophy of Culture, 1992; Nobody Likes Lehtia, 1993; Another Death in Venice, 1995; (with A. Gutmann) Color Conscious: The Political Morality of Race, 1996; (with H.L. Gates, Jr.) A Dictionary of Global Culture, 1996; Bu me be: Akan Proverbs, 2001; (co-author) Prejudicial Appearances: The Logic of American Antidiscrimination Law, 2001; Thinking it Through: An Introduction to Contemporary Philosophy, 2003; Ethics of Identity, 2005; Cosmopolitanism: Ethics in a World of Strangers, 2006; Experiments in Ethics, 2008; Politics of Culture, the Politics of Identity, 2008; (contrib.) Lyle Ashton Harris, 2008; Honor Code, 2010. EDITOR: (intro.) Early African-American Classics, 1990; (with H.L. Gates) Alice Walker: Critical Perspectives Past and Present, 1993; (with H.L. Gates) Gloria Naylor: Critical Perspectives Past and Present, 1993; (with H.L. Gates) Richard Wright: Critical Perspectives Past and Present, 1993; (with H.L. Gates, Jr.) Toni Morrison: Critical Perspectives Past and Present, 1993; (with H.L. Gates, Jr.) Zora Neale Hurston: Critical Perspectives Past and Present, 1993; (with H.L. Gates, Jr.) Langston Hughes: Critical Perspectives Past and Present, 1993; (with H.L. Gates, Jr.) Identities, 1995; (with H.L. Gates, Jr.) Dictionary of Global Culture, 1997; (with H.L. Gates, Jr.) Africana: The Encyclopedia of the African and African American Experience, 2003, 2nd ed., 2005; (with M. Bunzl) Buying Freedom, 2007; (with H.L. Gates, Jr.) Encyclopedia of Africa, 2010. Contributor to periodicals. **Address:** c/o Lynn Nesbit, Janklow & Nesbit Associates, 445 Park Ave., New York, NY 10022, U.S.A. **Online address:** kappiah@princeton.edu

APPLE, Hope. American (born United States), b. 1942. **Genres:** Adult Non-fiction, Language/Linguistics, Reference. **Career:** Skokie Public Library, part-time reference librarian, 1971-; Jackson House, owner, 1993-; freelance researcher and writer. **Publications:** (With M.L. Jacob) To Be Continued, 1995, 2nd ed., 2000. **Address:** 1614 Main St., Ste. B, Evanston, IL 60202, U.S.A.

APPLE, Max (Isaac). American (born United States), b. 1941. **Genres:** Novels, Novellas/Short Stories, Plays/Screenplays, Autobiography/Memoirs, Biography. **Career:** Reed College, assistant professor of literature and humanities, 1970-71; Rice University, assistant professor, 1972-76, associate professor, 1976-80, professor of English, 1980-2001, Gladys Louise Fox professor emeritus of English, 2001-; University of Pennsylvania, faculty. Writer. **Publications:** (Co-author) Studies in English, 1975; (co-author) Mom, the Flag and Apple Pie: Great American Writers on Great American Things, 1976; The Oranging of America and Other Stories, 1976; Zip: A Novel of the Left and the Right, 1978; (ed.) Southwest Fiction, 1980; Free Agents, 1984; The Propheteers: A Novel, 1987; Roommates: My Grandfather's Story, 1994; I Love Gootie: My Grandmother's Story, 1998; Jew of Home Depot and Other Stories, 2007. **Address:** Rice University, 6100 Main, Houston, TX 77005-1827, U.S.A.

APPLE, Rima D. American (born United States), b. 1944. **Genres:** Medicine/Health, Women's Studies And Issues, Bibliography. **Career:** State University of New York, lecturer in community and preventive medicine, 1981-83; University of Melbourne, visiting research fellow in history and philosophy of science, 1983, lecturer, 1984; University of Wisconsin-Madison, fellow in history of medicine, 1985-92, adjunct assistant professor, 1986-90, assistant professor, 1992, associate professor, 1992-94, professor of consumer science and women's studies, 1994-, visiting professor, 2001, Vilas life cycle professor, 2005-06, professor emeritus; University of Auckland, visiting lecturer, 1990; University of Trondheim, visiting researcher, 1992-94. Writer. **Publications:** (Comp.) Illustrated Catalogue of the Slide Archive of Historical Medical Photographs at Stony Brook, 1984; Mothers and Medicine: A Social History of Infant Feeding, 1890-1950, 1987; (co-ed.) The History of Women and Science, Health and Technology: A Bibliographic Guide to the Professions and the Disciplines, 1988, 2nd ed. (co-ed.) 1993; (ed. and contrib.) Women, Health and Medicine in America: A Historical Handbook, 1990; Vitamania: Vitamins in American Culture, 1996; (ed. with J. Golden) Mothers and Motherhood: Readings in American History, 1997; Perfect Motherhood: Science and Childrearing in America, 2006; (edited with G. J. Downey and S. L. Vaughn) Science in Print: Essays on the History of Science and the Culture of Print, 2012. Contributor of articles to books and journals. **Address:** Department of Consumer Science, School of Human Ecology, University of Wisconsin - Madison, 336 Human Ecology Bldg., 1300 Linden Dr., Madison, WI 53706, U.S.A. **Online address:** rdapple@wisc.edu

APPLE, Sam. American (born United States) **Genres:** Novels. **Career:** Jewish Student Press Service, director; New Voices Magazine, editor; The Faster Times, editor-in-chief and publisher; Nerve.com, director of interactive media; University of Pennsylvania, faculty; Rutgers-Camden, faculty. **Publications:** Schlepping Through the Alps: My Search for Austria's Jewish Past with its Last Wandering Shepherd, 2005; American Parent: My Strange and Surprising Adventures in Modern Babyland, 2009; In Search of My Foreskin, forthcoming. Contributor to magazines. **Address:** c/o Author Mail, Ballantine Books, 1745 Broadway, New York, NY 10019, U.S.A. **Online address:** samapple@gmail.com

APPLEBAUM, Anne. American/British (born England), b. 1964. **Genres:** International Relations/Current Affairs. **Career:** The Independent, correspondent, 1988-90; The Economist, writer and editor, correspondent, 1988-91; The Spectator, foreign editor, 1993-, deputy editor, 1994-; The Daily Telegraph, weekly columnist, 1994-; Sunday Telegraphs, columnist; Evening Standard, political editor; Washington Post, columnist; Slate Magazine, columnist. **Publications:** Between East and West: Across the Borderlands of Europe, 1994; Gulag: A History, 2003; (ed.) Gulag Voices: An Anthology, 2011. Contributor of articles to periodicals. **Address:** The Washington Post Co., 1150 15th St. NW, Washington, DC 20071, U.S.A. **Online address:** applebaumanne@washpost.com

APPLEBOME, Peter. American (born United States), b. 1949. **Genres:** Sociology, Politics/Government, Cultural/Ethnic Topics. **Career:** The Corpus Christi Caller, reporter, 1976, 1977; Dallas Morning News, writer, editor and columnist, 1978-82; Texas Monthly Magazine, writer, editor, columnist, 1982-86; New York Times, national correspondent, Houston Bureau, bureau chief, 1987-89, Atlanta Bureau, bureau chief, 1989-94, chief education correspondent, 1994-98, Culture Desk, correspondent, assistant metropolitan editor, 1999-, deputy metropolitan editor, editor and reporter. Journalist. **Publications:** Dixie Rising: How the South Is Shaping American Values, Politics and Culture, 1996; (with G.R. Sheets, L.D. Wilder and C.R. Wilson) The Grand Review: The Civil War Continues to Shape America, 2000; Scout's Honor: A Father's Unlikely Foray Into the Woods, 2003. Contributor to periodicals and journals. **Address:** c/o Author Mail, Harcourt Inc., 15 E 26th St., New York, NY 10003-4793, U.S.A. **Online address:** peappl@nytimes.com

APPLEBY, Louis. British (born England), b. 1955. **Genres:** Medicine/Health. **Career:** Victoria University of Manchester, senior lecturer in psychiatry, 1991-; consultant psychiatrist, 1991-; University of Manchester, professor of psychiatry, 1996-; government's health czar, Manchester Mental Health Partnership, honorary consultant psychiatrist; Department of Health, National Institute for Mental Health, national director for mental health, 2000-10, national clinical director for health and criminal justice, 2010-. Writer. **Publications:** (Ed. with D.M. Forshaw) Postgraduate Psychiatry: Clinical and Scientific Foundations, 1990, (co-author) 2nd ed., 2001; A Medical Tour through the Whole Island of Great Britain, 1995; (ed. with D. Tantam and A. Duncan) Psychiatry for the Developing World, 1996. **Address:** Department of Health, Area 217, Wellington House, 133-155 Waterloo Rd., London, GL SE1 8UG, England. **Online address:** mental-health-czar@doh.gsi.gov.uk

APPLEGATE, K. A. *See* **APPLEGATE, Katherine (Alice).**

APPLEGATE, Katherine (Alice). Also writes as L. E. Blair, K. A. Applegate. American (born United States), b. 1956. **Genres:** Children's Fiction, Young Adult Fiction, Children's Non-fiction, Young Adult Non-fiction, Novels, Picture/Board Books. **Career:** Writer. **Publications:** FOR JUVENILES: The Story of Two American Generals: Benjamin O. Davis Jr., and Colin L. Powell (nonfiction), 1992; Zoey Fools Around (novel), 1994; Jake Finds Out, 1994; Nina Won't Tell, 1994; Ben's in Love, 1994; Aisha Goes Wild, 1994; What Zoey Saw, 1994; Claire Gets Caught, 1994; Sharing Sam (novel), 1995; Zoey Plays Games, 1996; Don't Tell Zoey, 1996; Zoey Speaks Out, 1996; Two-Timing Aisha, 1996; Claire Can't Lose, 1996; Lara Gets Even, 1996; Aaron Lets Go, 1996; Ben Takes a Chance, 1996; Nina Shapes Up, 1996; Kate Finds Love, 1997; Always Loving Zoey, 1997; Lara Gets Lucky, 1997; Now Zoey's Alone, 1997; Trouble with Aaron, 1997; Never Trust Lara, 1997; Escape (picture book), 1998; Falling for Claire, 1998; Zoey's Broken Heart, 1998; Don't Forget Lara, 1998; Lucas Gets Hurt, 1998; Zoey Comes Home, 1998; Who Loves Kate?, 1999; Entertain the End, 2001; The Buffalo Storm, 2007; Home of the Brave, 2007; Beach Blondes, 2008; Tan Lines, 2008; Spring Break, 2010; The One and Only Ivan, 2012. ROSCOE RILEY RULES SERIES: Never Glue Your Friends to Chairs, 2008; Never Swipe a Bully's Bear, 2008; Don't Swap Your Sweater for a Dog, 2008; Never Swim in Applesauce, 2008; Don't Tap-dance on your Teacher, 2009; Never Walk in Shoes that Talk, 2009; Never Race a Runaway Pumpkin, 2009. SUMMER SERIES: June Dreams, 1995; July's Promise, 1995; August Magic, 1995; Sand, Surf and Secrets, 1996; Rays, Romance and Rivalry, 1996; Beaches, Boys and Betrayal, 1996; Spring Break Reunion, 1996; Sun-Kissed Christmas, 2010. REMNANTS SERIES: The Mayflower Project, 2001; Destination Unknown, 2001; Them, 2001; Nowhere Land, 2001; Mutation, 2002; Breakdown, 2002; Isolation, 2002; Mother, May I?, 2002; No Place Like Home, 2002; Lost and Found, 2003; Dream Storm, 2003; Aftermath, 2003; Survival, 2003; Begin Again, 2003. OCEAN CITY SERIES: Ocean City, 1993; Love Shack, 1993; Fireworks, 1993; Boardwalk, 1993; Heat Wave, 1994; Swept Away, 1995; Shipwrecked, 1995; Forever, 1995. ANIMORPHS SERIES FOR JUVENILES AS K.A. APPLEGATE: The Invasion, 1996; The Visitor, 1996; The Message, 1996; The Encounter, 1996; The Predator, 1996; The Capture, 1997; The Stranger, 1997; The Alien, 1997; The Secret, 1997; The Android, 1997; The Forgotten, 1997; The Reaction, 1997; The Change, 1997; The Unknown, 1998; The Warning, 1998; The Underground, 1998; The Escape, 1998; The Decision, 1998; The Departure, 1998; The Discovery, 1998; The Threat, 1998; The Solution, 1998; The Pretender, 1998; The Suspicion, 1998; The Extreme, 1999; The Attack, 1999; The Exposed, 1999; The Experiment, 1999; The Sickness, 1999; The Reunion, 1999; The Illusion, 1999; The Conspiracy, 1999; The Separation, 1999; The Proposal, 1999; The Prophecy, 1999; The Mutation, 1999; The Arrival, 2000; The Deception, 2000; The Diversion, 2000; The Familiar, 2000; The Ultimate, 2000; The Hidden, 2000; The Journey, 2000; The Other, 2000; The Resistance, 2000; The Return, 2000; The Revelation, 2000; The Test, 2000; The Unexpected, 2000; The Weakness, 2000; The Absolute, 2001; The Answer, 2001; The Beginning, 2001; The Sacrifice, 2001. ANIMORPHS MEGAMORPHS JUVENILE SERIES: The Andalite's Gift, 1997; In the Time of Dinosaurs, 1998; Elfangor's Secret, 1999; Back to Before, 2000. EVERWORLD YOUNG ADULT SERIES AS K.A. APPLEGATE: Search for Senna, 1999; Land of Loss, 1999; Enter the Enchanted, 1999; Realm of the Reaper, 1999; Discover the Destroyer, 1999; Brave the Betrayal, 1999; Fear the Fantastic, 2000; Inside the Illusion, 2000; Understand the Unknown, 2000; Entertain the End, 2001. MAKING WAVES SERIES: Secret, 1997; Tease, 2001; Heat, 2001; Sweet, 2001; Attitude, 2001; Burn, 2001; Wild, 2001; Chill, 2001. ANIMORPHS, ALTERNAMORPHS SERIES: The First Journey, 1999; The Next Passage, 2000. PRE-ANIMORPHS SERIES: The Andalite Chronicles, 1997; The Hork-Bajir Chronicles, 1999; The Ellimist Chronicles, 2000. OTHERS: The Boyfriend Mix-up, 1994; Disney's Christmas with All the Trimmings: Original Stories and Crafts from Mickey Mouse and Friends, 1994; Visser (companion book to The Hork-Bajir Chronicles), 1999; (with K. Lasky and E. Rodda) Fantastic Tales for Boys, 2006; (with G. Korman and R.L. Stine) Tales of Suspense for Boys, 2006. GIRL TALK SERIES AS L.E. BLAIR: Welcome To Junior High!, 1990; Face-off!, 1990; The New You, 1990; Rebel Rebel, 1990; It's All in the Stars, 1990; The Ghost of Eagle Mountain, 1990; Odd Couple, 1990; Stealing the Show, 1990; Peer Pressure, 1990; Falling in Like, 1990; Mixed Feelings, 1991; Drummer Girl, 1991; The Winning Team, 1991; Earth Alert!, 1991; On the Air, 1991; Here Comes the Bride, 1991; Star Quality, 1991; Keeping the Beat, 1991; Family Affair, 1991; Rockin' Class Trip, 1992; Baby Talk, 1992; Problem Dad, 1992; House Party, 1992; Cousins, 1992; Horse Fever, 1992; Beauty Queens, 1992; Perfect Match, 1992; Center Stage, 1992; Family Rules, 1992; The Bookshop Mystery, 1992; It's a Scream, 1992; Katie's Close Call, 1992; Randy and the Perfect Boy, 1992; Allison, Shape Up!, 1992; Katie and Sabrina's Big Competition, 1992; Sabrina and the Calf-raising Disaster, 1992; Randy's Big Dream, 1992; Allison To The Rescue, 1992; Katie and the Impossible Cousins, 1992; Sabrina Wins Big!, 1992; Randy and the Great Canoe Race, 1992; Allison's Baby-sitting Adventure, 1992; Katie's Beverly Hills Friend, 1992; Randy's Big Chance, 1992; Sabrina and Too Many Boys, 1992. **Address:** Scholastic Inc., 555 Broadway, New York, NY 10012-3919, U.S.A. **Online address:** kaapplegate@scholastic.com

APPLEMAN, Philip (Dean). American (born United States), b. 1926. **Genres:** Novels, Poetry, Anthropology/Ethnology, Biology, Demography. **Career:** Indiana University, instructor, 1955-58, assistant professor, 1958-63, associate professor, 1963-67, professor of English, 1967-82, distinguished professor, 1982-86, distinguished professor emeritus, 1986-; International School of America, instructor in world literature and philosophy, 1960-61, instructor and field director, 1962-63; visiting professor, State University of New York, 1973. Writer. **Publications:** POETRY: Kites on a Windy Day, 1967; Summer Love and Surf, 1968; Open Doorways: Poems, 1976; Darwin's Ark, 1984; Darwin's Bestiary, 1986; Let There Be Light, 1991; New and Selected

Poems, 1956-1996, 1996. NOVELS: In the Twelfth Year of the War, 1970; Shame the Devil: A Novel, 1981; Apes and Angels, 1989. OTHER: The Silent Explosion, 1965; Karma, Dharma, Pudding & Pie, 2009; Perfidious Proverbs and Other Poems, 2011. EDITOR: (with W.A. Madden and M. Wolff) 1859: Entering an Age of Crisis, 1959; Darwin, 1970, 3rd ed., 2001; The Origin of Species, 1975, rev. ed., 2002; Malthus: An Essay on the Principle of Population: Text, Sources and Background, Criticism, 1976, 2nd ed., 2004. **Address:** Department of English, Indiana University, 1020 E Kirkwood Ave., Bloomington, IN 47405-7103, U.S.A. **Online address:** phil.appleman@gmail.com

APPLETON, Sheldon Lee. American (born United States), b. 1933. **Genres:** International Relations/Current Affairs, Politics/Government. **Career:** New York University, faculty tuition fellow, 1954-55; U.S. AID, Public Reports Office, staff, 1955-56; U.S. Government, foreign service officer, 1956-57; Oakland University, assistant professor, 1960-64, associate professor of political science, 1964-69, Carter College, academic coordinator, 1965-66, professor, 1969-2002, associate dean, 1979-87, associate provost, 1987-93, distinguished professor of political science, 2002-05, distinguished professor emeritus of political science, 2005-; University of Hawaii, visiting professor of political science, 1969-70. Writer. **Publications:** The Eternal Triangle? Communist China, the United States and the United Nations, 1961; United States Foreign Policy, 1968. Contributor of articles. **Address:** Department of Political Science, Oakland University, 418 Varner Hall, Rochester, MI 48309-4488, U.S.A. **Online address:** slappleton@sbcglobal.net

APPLETON, Victor. *See* **DOYLE, Debra.**

APPLETON, Victor. *See* **MACDONALD, James D.**

APPLEWHITE, James. American (born United States), b. 1935. **Genres:** Poetry, Literary Criticism And History. **Career:** University of North Carolina, instructor, 1960-63, assistant professor, 1966-71; Duke University, Department of English instructor, 1966-67, visiting assistant professor, 1971-72, assistant professor, 1971-75, associate professor, 1975-96, professor, 1988-2008, Institute of the Arts, director, 1982-85, professor emeritus. Writer. **Publications:** POETRY: War Summer: Poems, 1972; Statues of the Grass, 1975; Following Gravity, 1980; Foreseeing the Journey, 1983; Ode to the Chinaberry Tree and Other Poems, 1986; River Writing: An Eno Journal, 1988; Lessons in Soaring, 1989; A History of the River: Poems, 1993; Daytime and Starlight, 1997; Quartet for Three Voices, 2002; Selected Poems, 2005; Diary of Altered Light, 2006. OTHER: Seas and Inland Journeys: Landscape and Consciousness from Wordsworth to Roethke, 1985; Inheriting the Homeplace, forthcoming. **Address:** Department of English, Duke University, 207 Allen Bldg., PO Box 90001, Durham, NC 27708-0001, U.S.A. **Online address:** jwa@duke.edu

APPLEYARD, Bryan (Edward). British (born England), b. 1951. **Genres:** Biography, Philosophy, Novels, Sciences, Theology/Religion, Social Sciences, Art/Art History. **Career:** United Newspapers, journalist, 1977-78; Times, assistant financial editor, 1978-81, deputy arts editor, 1981-84; Sunday Times, contributor and columnist, 1984-91; Independent, contributor, 1989, special features writer, 1993-; Sunday Times Magazine, special features writer, 1994-. **Publications:** The Culture Club: Crisis in the Arts, 1984; Richard Rogers: A Biography, 1986; The Pleasures of Peace: Art and Imagination in Postwar Britain, 1989; Understanding the Present: Science and the Soul of Modern Man, 1992; The First Church of the New Millennium: A Novel, 1994; Brave New Worlds: Genetics and the Human Experience, 1998; Understanding the Present: An Alternative History of Science, 2004; Aliens: Why They Are Here, 2005; How to Live Forever or Die Trying, 2007; The Brain is Wider than the Sky: Why Simple Solutions Don't Work in a Complex World, 2011. **Address:** c/o Giles Gordon, Sheil Land Associates Ltd., 43 Doughty St., London, GL WC1N 2LF, England. **Online address:** bryan@bryanappleyard.com

APPY, Christian G. American (born United States), b. 1955. **Genres:** History. **Career:** Massachusetts Institute of Technology, associate professor of history; University of Massachusetts, professor of history. Writer. **Publications:** (With T.V. DiBacco and L.C. Mason) History of the United States, 1991; Working-Class War: American Combat Soldiers and Vietnam, 1993; (ed.) Cold War Constructions: The Political Culture of United States Imperialism, 2000; Patriots: The Vietnam War Remembered from All Sides, 2003. **Address:** Department of History, University of Massachusetts, Herter Hall, 161 Presidents Dr., Amherst, MA 01004, U.S.A. **Online address:** appy@history.umass.edu

APTER, Andrew. American (born United States), b. 1957. **Genres:** Social Sciences, Anthropology/Ethnology, Cultural/Ethnic Topics, Adult Nonfiction. **Career:** Social Science Research Council, director of black atlantic studies; University of California, Department of Anthropology, professor of anthropology, Department of History, professor, African Studies Center, director, International Institute, chair. Writer. **Publications:** Black Critics & Kings: The Hermeneutics of Power in Yoruba Society, 1992; (contrib.) Civil Society and the Political Imagination in Africa, 1999; (contrib.) The Study of State Formation after the Cultural Turn, 1999; The Pan-African Nation: Oil and the Spectacle of Culture in Nigeria, 2005; Beyond Words: Discourse and Critical Agency in Africa, 2007; (ed. with L. Derby) Activating the Past: History and Memory in the Black Atlantic World, 2010. Contributor to periodicals and journals. **Address:** Department of History, University of California, 5369 Bunche Hall, PO Box 954173, Los Angeles, CA 90095-1473, U.S.A. **Online address:** aapter@history.ucla.edu

APTER, Emily (S.). American (born United States), b. 1954. **Genres:** Language/Linguistics, Literary Criticism And History, Psychology, Social Sciences, Theology/Religion. **Career:** Williams College, assistant professor, 1983-88, associate professor of romance languages, 1988-90; University of California, Davis, associate professor of French and Italian, 1990-93; University of California, Los Angels, Department of Comparative Literature, professor of French and comparative literature, 1993-97, 2000-, chair, 2000-; University of Pennsylvania, visiting professor, 1993; Cornell University, professor of comparative literature, 1997-2000; New York University, professor of French, comparative literature, 2002-; Harvard University, lecturer; Princeton University, lecturer, Princeton University Press, editor; University of New Hampshire, lecturer; Brown University, lecturer; State University of New York at Stonybrook, lecturer; University of Oklahoma, lecturer. **Publications:** André Gide and the Codes of Homotextuality, 1987; Feminizing the Fetish: Psychoanalysis and Narrative Obsession in Turn-of-the-Century France, 1991; (ed. with W. Pietz) Fetishism as Cultural Discourse, 1993; Continental Drift: From National Characters to Virtual Subjects, 1999; The Translation Zone: A New Comparative Literature, 2006. Contributor of articles to journals. **Address:** Department of Comparative Literature, New York University, 13 University Pl., 610, New York, NY 10003, U.S.A. **Online address:** emily.apter@nyu.edu

APTER, Michael John. British/American (born United States), b. 1939. **Genres:** Information Science/Computers, Psychiatry, Psychology, Medicine/Health. **Career:** Teaching Programmes Ltd., staff, 1964-67; University of Wales, University College Cardiff, lecturer, 1967-73, senior lecturer, 1973-84, reader in psychology, 1984-88; University of British Columbia, visiting professor, 1974, 1975; Purdue University, visiting professor, 1988-90; Northwestern University, visiting professor, 1990-93; University of Chicago, visiting professor, 1991-93; Yale University, visiting professor, 1994; Georgetown University, visiting professor, 1996-97; Apter Intl., non-executive development director, 1998-; University of Toulouse, visiting professor, 2000, 2002, 2003. Writer. **Publications:** Cybernetics and Development, 1966; An Introduction to Psychology, 1967; The New Technology of Education, 1968; The Computer Simulation of Behaviour, 1970; (ed. with G. Westby) The Computer in Psychology, 1973; (with K.C.P. Smith) A Theory of Psychological Reversals, 1975; (ed. with C. Rushton) Reversal Theory and Personality, 1981; The Experience of Motivation: The Theory of Psychological Reversals, 1982; (ed. with D. Fontana and S. Murgatroyd) Reversal Theory: Applications and Developments, 1985; (ed. with J.H. Kerr and M.P. Cowles) Progress in Reversal Theory, 1988; Reversal Theory: Motivation, Emotion, and Personality, 1989, 2nd. ed., 2007; (ed. with J.H. Kerr) Adult Play: A Reversal Theory Approach, 1991; The Dangerous Edge: The Psychology of Excitement, 1992; (ed. with J.H. Kerr and and S. Murgatroyd) Advances in Reversal Theory, 1993; (ed. with S. Svebak) Stress and Health: A Reversal Theory Perspective, 1997; (ed.) Motivational Styles in Everyday Life: A Guide to Reversal Theory, 2001; Personality Dynamics, 2005; Danger: Our Quest for Excitement, 2007. **Address:** Apter Intl., 35-37 High St., Barrow-Upon-Soar, Loughborough, LE LE12 8PY, England. **Online address:** mjapter@aol.com

APTER, T(erri) E. British/American (born United States), b. 1949. **Genres:** Literary Criticism And History, Psychology. **Career:** Cambridge University, English and American literature teacher, Betty Behvens research fellow; Newnham College, senior tutor. Writer and psychologist. **Publications:** Silken Lines and Silver Hooks, 1976; Adonis Garden, 1977; Thomas Mann: The

Devil's Disciple, 1978; Virginia Woolf: A Study of Her Novels, 1979; Fantasy Literature: An Approach to Reality, 1982; Why Women Don't Have Wives: Professional Success and Motherhood, 1985; Loose Relations: Your In-Laws and You, 1986; Altered Loves: Mothers and Daughters During Adolescence, 1990; Working Women Don't Have Wives: Professional Success in the 1990s, 1994; Secret Paths: Women in the New Midlife, 1995; The Confident Child: Raising Children to Believe in Themselves, 1997; (with R. Josselson) Best Friends: The Pleasures and Perils of Girls and Women's Friendships, 1998; The Myth of Maturity: What Teenagers Need from Parents to Become Adults, 2001; You Don't Really Know Me!: Why Mothers and Teenage Daughters Argue, 2004; Sister Knot: Why We Fight, Why We're Jealous, and Why We'll Love Each Other No Matter What, 2007; What Do You Want from Me?: Learning to Get Along with In-Laws, 2009. Contributor to periodicals. **Address:** c/o Michael Thomas, A.M. Heath & Comapny Ltd., 79 St. Martin's Ln., London, GL WC1N 4DD, England. **Online address:** tea20@cam.ac.uk

APTHEKER, Bettina. American (born United States), b. 1944. **Genres:** Education, Gay And Lesbian Issues, Race Relations, Women's Studies And Issues, Autobiography/Memoirs, Bibliography. **Career:** Freelance writer and lecturer, 1968-; People's World, editor and writer, 1969-; San Jose State University, lecturer in women's studies program, 1976-; University of California, Department of Feminist Studies, distinguished professor, professor. **Publications:** (With R. Kaufman and M.B. Folsom) FSM (Free Speech Movement), 1965; Big Business and the American University, 1966; Higher Education and the Student Rebellion in the United States 1960-69 (bibliography), 1969, rev. ed., 1972; (with H. Aptheker) Racism and Reaction in the United States: Two Marxian Studies, 1971; (with A.Y. Davis) If They Come in the Morning: Voices of Resistance, 1971; The Academic Rebellion in the United States: A Marxist Appraisal, 1972; The Morning Breaks: The Trial of Angela Davis, 1975, 2nd ed., 1999; Mary Church Terrell and Ida B. Wells: A Comparative Rhetoric/Historical Analysis, 1976; (ed. and intro.) Lynching and Rape: An Exchange of Views, 1977; (ed.) The Unfolding Drama: Studies in U.S. History, 1979; Woman's Legacy: Essays on Race, Sex and Class in American History, 1982; Tapestries of Life: Women's Work, Women's Consciousness, and the Meaning of Daily Experience, 1989; Intimate Politics: How I Grew Up Red, Fought for Free Speech and Became A Feminist Rebel, 2006. Contributor to books. **Address:** Department of Feminist Studies, University of California, Rm. 340, Humanities 1, 1156 High St., Santa Cruz, CA 95064-1077, U.S.A. **Online address:** bettinaf@ucsc.edu

ARAI, Masami. Japanese (born Japan), b. 1953. **Genres:** Romance/Historical, Area Studies, History. **Career:** Osaka City University, instructor, 1984-86, assistant professor, 1986-88, Faculty of Letters, associate professor, 1988-92; Osaka University, lecturer, 1991-92; Tokai University, associate professor in faculty of letters, 1992-95; Tokyo University of Foreign Studies, professor of Turkish studies, 1995-. Writer. **Publications:** Turkish Nationalism in the Young Turk Era, 1992; (ed. with J. Watkins) Proceedings of the SOAS/TUFS Postgraduate Symposium, London 20-21 February 2006, 2006. **Address:** Tokyo University of Foreign Studies, 3-11-1, Asahi-cho, Fuchu-shi, Tokyo, 183-8534, Japan.

ARAKAWA, Yoichi. American/Mexican (born Mexico), b. 1962. **Genres:** Music, Literary Criticism And History, Art/Art History. **Career:** Musician and author. **Publications:** Best of Red Hot Chili Peppers, 1993; Best of Black Crowes, 1993; Top Hits of the Country Superstars, 1993; You Too Can Play Soft Rock Guitar, 1993; Best of Count Basie, 1993; Best of Miles Davis, 1993; You Too Can Play Jazz Guitar, 1993; You too can Play Soft Rock Guitar, 1993; Jim Croce-The Greatest Hits, 1995; A Fingerstyle Christmas: 19 Beloved Contemporary and Standard Seasonal Favorites Arranged for Solo Fingerstyle Guitar (guitar solo), 1995; Jazz Riffs: For Guitar, 1995; Guitar Chords and Accompaniment, 1998, 2nd ed., 2001; 101 Basic Reading for Guitar, 1999; 101 Basic Blues Scales for Guitar, 1999; 101 Basic Major Pentatonic Scales for Guitar, 1999; 101 Basic Minor Pentatonic Scales for Guitar, 1999; 101 Basic Guitar Chords, 1999; More Guitar Chords and Accompaniment, 1999; More Jazz Guitar Chords and Accompaniment, 2002; Country Guitar Chords and Accompaniment, 2003; Rock Guitar Chords and Accompaniment, 2003; Blues Guitar Chords and Accompaniment, 2003; Plays and Teaches Music, forthcoming. WITH JOHN STIX: Minor Pentatonic Scales for Guitar, 1995; Basic Blues for Rock Guitar, 1995; Acoustic Rock for Guitar, 1995; Modes for Rock and Blues Guitar, 1995; Warm-up Exercises for Guitar, 1996; Rock Riffs for Guitar, 1996. **Address:** Six Strings Music Publishing, PO Box 7718-157, Torrance, CA 90504-9118, U.S.A. **Online address:** contact@sixstringsmusicpub.com

ARATON, Harvey. American (born United States), b. 1952. **Genres:** Sports/Fitness, Novels. **Career:** Staten Island Advance, sports reporter, night sports editor, city side reporter, copyboy, 1970-77; New York Post, sports reporter, 1977-83; New York Daily News, sports reporter and columnist, 1983-91; New York University, instructor, 1987; New York Times, sports reporter and national basketball columnist, 1991-, Sports of the Times, columnist, 1994-. **Publications:** (With F. Bondy) The Selling of the Green: The Financial Rise and Moral Decline of the Boston Celtics, 1992; (with A. Keteyian and M.F. Dardis) Money Players: Days and Nights inside the New NBA, 1997; Alive and Kicking: When Soccer Moms Take the Field and Change Their Lives Forever, 2001; Crashing the Borders: How Basketball Won the World and Lost Its Soul at Home, 2005; When the Garden was Eden, 2011. Contributor to periodicals. **Address:** c/o Author Mail, Free Press, 1230 Ave. of the Americas, New York, NY 10020, U.S.A.

ARBUTHNOTT, Gill. British/Scottish (born Scotland), b. 1958?. **Genres:** Novels, Young Adult Non-fiction, Science Fiction/Fantasy, Young Adult Fiction. **Career:** Writer, 2003-; biomedical researcher. **Publications:** NOVELS: The Chaos Clock, 2003; The Chaos Quest, 2004; Winterbringers, 2005; The Keepers' Daughter, 2009; The Keepers' Tattoo, 2010. NONFICTION: (with S. Grant) Crazy Creatures, 2007; (with M. Phillips) Mad Scientists, 2008. OTHERS: Lost at the Zoo, 2012. **Address:** Fraser Ross Associates, 6 Wellington Pl., Edinburgh, EH6 7EQ, Scotland. **Online address:** gilltomer@hotmail.com

ARCENEAUX, Jean. *See* **ANCELET, Barry Jean.**

ARCHER, Chalmers. American (born United States), b. 1938. **Genres:** Cultural/Ethnic Topics, History, Military/Defense/Arms Control. **Career:** Saints Junior College, assistant, 1968-70; Tuskegee Institute, career and placement counselor and coordinator of cooperative program, 1972-74, assistant dean for admissions and records, 1974-76, assistant, 1976-79, associate dean for admissions and records and assistant professor of educational administration and counseling, 1979-83; Northern Virginia Community College, Annandale Campus, coordinator of admissions and records, 1983-85, director of financial aid at Alexandria Campus, 1985-, administrator, professor, now retired; Cambridge University, lecturer, 1988-89; U.S. Department of Education, consultant. Writer. **Publications:** Growing up Black in Rural Mississippi: Memories of a Family, Heritage of a Place, 1992; An Invisible Hand at Work in the Community: Black Courage and Family Wisdom, 1995; Green Berets in the Vanguard: Inside Special Forces, 2001. **Address:** 4522 Commons Dr., Ste. 40, Annandale, VA 22003-4959, U.S.A.

ARCHER, Colleen Rutherford. Canadian (born Canada), b. 1949. **Genres:** Novels, Children's Fiction. **Career:** Illustrator and writer. **Publications:** Foxy and the Missing Mask, 1986; Riding High, 1986; If I Had a Camel, 1988; Stocking Stuffer Stories, 1990; The Horse Dealer, 2000; Brandys Story, 2001; The Touch of Something Wild, 2003; Collie Rescue, 2004; Accentuating the Positive: Trick Training Your Horse at Home, 2005; Galloping Goldrush: The Journey Begins, 2005; Raising Kane, the Guide Dog Pup, 2009. **Address:** Penumbra Press, PO Box 940, Manotick, ON K4M 1A8, Canada. **Online address:** archerc_a@sympatico.ca

ARCHER, Ian W. British (born England), b. 1960. **Genres:** History. **Career:** Cambridge University, Girton College, research fellow, 1986-89, Downing College, fellow and director of studies in history, 1989-91; Oxford University, Keble College, fellow and tutor in modern history, 1991-, sub-warden; Royal Historical Society Bibliography, general editor, 1999-2010; Institute of Historical Research, research associate, 2000-; Bibliography of British and Irish History, academic editor. **Publications:** (Ed. with C.M. Barron and V. Harding) Hugh Alley's Caveat: The Markets of London in 1598: Folger Ms V.a. 318, 1988; The Pursuit of Stability: Social Relations in Elizabethan London, 1991; The History of the Haberdashers Company, 1991; (ed. with S. Adams) Religion, Politics, and Society in Sixteenth-Century England, 2003; (ed. with A. Cameron) Keble Past and Present, 2008. Contributor periodicals. **Address:** Keble College, Oxford University, Oxford, OX OX1 3PG, England. **Online address:** ian.archer@keble.ox.ac.uk

ARCHER, Jeffrey (Howard). British (born England), b. 1940. **Genres:** Novels, Novellas/Short Stories, Children's Fiction, Plays/Screenplays, Young Adult Non-fiction. **Career:** British Parliament, member, 1969-74; Conservative Party, deputy chairman, 1985-86. Writer. **Publications:** Not a Penny More, Not a Penny Less, 1976; Shall We Tell the President?, 1977; Kane

& Abel, 1979; The Prodigal Daughter, 1982; First Among Equals, 1984; A Matter of Honour, 1986; (contrib.) Gemma Levine's Faces of the 80's, 1987; (ed. and intro. with S. Bainbridge) Fools, Knaves and Heroes, 1989; As the Crow Files, 1991; Honor Among Thieves, 1993; The Fourth Estate, 1996; The Eleventh Commandment, 1998; A Prison Diary, vol. I: Hell, 2003, vol. II: Purgatory, 2004, vol. III: Heaven, 2005; Belmarsh, Hell, 2003; Sons of Fortune, 2003; False Impression, 2006; (with F.J. Moloney) The Gospel According to Judas, 2007; A Prisoner of Birth, 2008; Paths of Glory, 2009; Only Time will Tell, 2011. SHORT STORIES: A Quiver Full of Arrows, 1980; A Twist in the Tale, 1988; Twelve Red Herrings, 1994; Collected Short Stories, 1997; To Cut a Long Story Short, 2000; Cat O'Nine Tales, 2007; And Thereby Hangs A Tale, 2010. CHILDREN'S FICTION: The First Miracle, 1980; Willy and the Killer Kipper, 1981; Willy Visits the Square World, 1982. PLAYS: Beyond Reasonable Doubt, 1987; The Accused, 2000. **Address:** St. Martins Press, 175 5th Ave., New York, NY 10010, U.S.A. **Online address:** info@jeffreyarcher.co.uk

ARCHER, Keith (Allan). Canadian (born Canada), b. 1955. **Genres:** Politics/Government, History. **Career:** Duke University, R. Taylor Cole Instructor, 1983-84; University of Calgary, Department of Political Science, assistant professor, 1984-88, associate professor, 1988-95, professor, 1995-, associate dean of social sciences, 1995-98, associate vice-president research, 1999-2000, Alberta Gaming Research Institute, chair, 1999-2002, interim vice-president, 2000-02, The Banff Centre, director of research, 2005-08, Canadian Society for the Study of Higher Education, president; Calgary Waldorf School, president, 1988-90, 1992-94; University of Prince Edward Island, Department of Political Science, visiting professor, 1990-91; Pollstar Research Inc., founding partner, 1992-95; Institute of Health Economics, vice-chair, 2000-02; University of Queensland, visiting fellow, 2002-03. Writer. **Publications:** Political Choices and Electoral Consequences, 1990; (ed. with R. Gibbins and S. Drabek) Canadian Political Life: An Alberta Perspective, 1990; (with A. Whitehorn) Canadian Trade Unions and the New Democratic Party, 1993; (with R. Gibbins, R. Knopff and L. Pal) Parameters of Power, 3rd ed., 2002; (with A. Whitehorn) Political Activists: The NDP in Convention, 1997; (with R. Gibbons and L. Youngman) Explorations: A Navagator's Guide to Quantitive Research in Canadian Political Science, 1998; (with D.K. Stewart) Quasi-Democracy? Parties and Leadership Selection in Alberta, 2000; (ed. with L. Young) Regionalism and Party Politics in Canada, 2002. Contributor to periodicals. **Address:** Department of Political Science, University of Calgary, 2500 University Dr. NW, Calgary, AB T2N 1N4, Canada. **Online address:** kaarcher@ucalgary.ca

ARCHER, Margaret Scotford. British (born England), b. 1943. **Genres:** Sociology, Cultural/Ethnic Topics. **Career:** Cambridge University, Christ's College, supervisor, 1964-66; London School of Economics, graduate tutor, 1965-66; University of Reading, lecturer, 1966-73; University of Warwick, reader, 1973-79, professor, 1979-. Writer and researcher. **Publications:** NONFICTION: (with M. Vaughan) Social Conflict and Educational Change in England and France, 1789-1848, 1971; Social Origins of Educational Systems, 1979; The University Edition of Social Origins of Educational Systems, 1984; Culture and Agency: The Place of Culture in Social Theory, 1988, 2nd ed., 1996; Realist Social Theory: The Morphogenetic Approach, 1995; Being Human: The Problem of Agency, 2000; (with J.Q. Tritter) Rational Choice Theory: Resisting Colonization, 2000; Structure, Agency, and the Internal Conversation, 2003; Making Our Way through the World: Human Reflexivity and Social Mobility, 2007. EDITOR: (with S. Giner) Contemporary Europe: Class, Status and Power, 1971; Students, University and Society: A Comparative Sociological Review, 1972; Current Research in Sociology: Published on the Occasion of the VIIIth World Congress of Sociology, Toronto, Canada, August 18-24, 1974, 1974; Problems of Current Sociological Research: The Work of the International Sociological Association's Research Committees, 1977; (with S. Giner) Contemporary Europe: Social Structures and Cultural Patterns, 1978; The Sociology of Educational Expansion: Take-Off, Growth, and Inflation in Educational Systems, 1982; (co-ed.) Critical Realism: Essential Readings, 1998; (with E. Malinvaud) Work & Human Fulfillment, 2003; (with W. Outhwaite) Defending Objectivity: Essays in Honour of Andrew Collier, 2004; Conversations about Reflexivity, 2010. Contributor of articles to books and journals. Works appear in anthologies. **Address:** Department of Sociology, University of Warwick, Coventry, WM CV4 7AL, England. **Online address:** m.s.archer@warwick.ac.uk

ARCHER, Peter. *See* **ARCHER of Sandwell.**

ARCHER, Peter Kingsley. *See* **ARCHER of Sandwell.**

ARCHER OF SANDWELL. Also writes as Peter Archer, Peter Kingsley Archer. British (born England), b. 1926. **Genres:** Civil Liberties/Human Rights, Law, Politics/Government, Theology/Religion, Social Sciences, Essays. **Career:** Parliamentary private secretary to the attorney general, 1967-70; solicitor general for England and Wales, 1974-79; private councilor, 1978-; State for Northern Ireland, shadow secretary, 1983-87; All-Party Group for World Governance, vice chair. Writer. **Publications:** The Queen's Courts, 1956, 2nd ed. 1963; (ed.) Social Welfare and the Citizen, 1957; Communism and the Law, 1963; (with L. Reay) Freedom at Stake, 1966; Human Rights, 1969; (co-author) Purpose in Socialism, 1973; The Universal Declaration of Human Rights, 1973; The Role of the Law Officers, 1978; (ed. with A. Martin) More Law Reform Now: A Collection of Essays on Law Reform, 1984. Contributor to periodicals. **Address:** House of Lords, London, GL SW1A 0PW, England.

ARCHERY, Helen. *See* **ARGERS, Helen.**

ARD, William. *See* **JAKES, John.**

ARDEN, J. E. M. *See* **CONQUEST, (George) Robert (Acworth).**

ARDEN, John. British (born England), b. 1930. **Genres:** Novels, Plays/Screenplays, Literary Criticism And History, Novellas/Short Stories, Horror, Young Adult Fiction, Humanities. **Career:** Playwright, 1957-; writer, 1958-; University of Bristol, fellow in playwriting, 1959-60; New York University, visiting lecturer in politics and drama, 1967; Corrandulla Arts and Entertainment, co-founder, 1971-; University of California, regents lecturer, 1973; University of New England, writer-in-residence and playwright-in-residence, 1975; Theatre Writers' Union, founding member, 1975; Galway Theater Workshop, co-founder, 1975-; Peace News, Pacifist Weekly, chair. **Publications:** Serjeant Musgrave's Dance, an Unhistorical Parable, 1960; (with M. D'Arcy) The Business of Good Government: A Christmas Play, 1963; The Workhouse Donkey, a Vulgar Melo-drama, 1964; Three Plays: The Waters of Babylon, Live Like Pigs, The Happy Haven, 1964; Ironhand, 1965; Armstrong's Last Goodnight, an Exercise in Diplomacy, 1965; Ars Longa, Vita Brevis, 1965; Left-Handed Liberty: A Play About Magna Carta, 1965; (with M. D'Arcy) The Royal Pardon, or The Soldier Who Became an Actor, 1967; Soldier, Soldier and Other Plays, 1967; (with M. D'Arcy) The Hero Rises Up: A Romantic Melodrama, 1969; Two Autobiographical Plays: The True History of Squire Jonathan and His Unfortunate Treasure and the Bagman, 1971; (with M. D'Arcy) The Island of the Mighty: A Play on a Traditional British Theme in Three Parts, 1974; (with M. D'Arcy) The Non-Stop Connolly Show: A Dramatic Cycle of Continuous Struggle in Six Parts, 5 vols., 1977-78; (intro.) Plays, 1977; (with M. D'Arcy) To Present the Pretence (essays), 1977; Pearl: A Play About a Play Within the Play: Written for Radio, 1979; (with M. D'Arcy) Vandaleur's Folly: An Anglo-Irish Melodrama: The Hazard of Experiment in an Irish Co-Operative, Ralahine, 1831, 1981; (with M. D'Arcy) The Little Gray Home in the West: An Anglo-Irish Melodrama, 1982; Silence among the Weapons: Some Events at the Time of the Failure of a Republic (novel) in US as Vox Pop: Last Days of the Roman Republic, 1982; (with M. D'Arcy) Whose is the Kingdom?, 1988; Books of Bale: A Fiction of History, 1988; (with M. D'Arcy) Awkward Corners, 1988; Cogs Tyrannic: Four Stories, 1991; Jack Juggler and the Emperor's Whore: Seven Tall Tales Linked Together for an Indecorous Toy Theater (novel), 1995; The Stealing Steps: Nine Stories, 2003; Gallows: And Other Tales of Suspicion and Obsession, 2009. Works appear in anthologies. Contributor to books and periodicals. **Address:** Casarotto Ramsay & Associates Ltd., Waverley House, 7-12 Noel St., London, GL W1F 8GQ, England.

ARDEN, Judith. *See* **TURNER, Judith.**

ARELLANO, Gustavo. American (born United States), b. 1979. **Genres:** History, Humor/Satire, Biography. **Career:** OC Weekly newspaper, reporter, 2003; Los Angeles Times, contributing editor. **Publications:** Ask a Mexican!, 2007; Orange County: A Personal History, 2008. **Address:** OC Weekly, 2975 Red Hill Ave., Ste. 150, Costa Mesa, CA 92626, U.S.A. **Online address:** themexican@askamexican.net

ARELLANO, Juan Estevan. American (born United States), b. 1947. **Genres:** Documentaries/Reportage, Sciences, Translations. **Career:** Academia de la Nueva Raza, co-founder, 1970. Writer. **Publications:** (Ed.) Entre verde y seco, 1972; Inocencio: ni pica ni escarda, pero siempre se come el mejor elote, 1992; Cuentos de café y tortilla, 1997; Low 'n Slow: Lowriding in New Mexico, 1999; (comp.) Ancient Agriculture: Roots and Application of Sustainable Farming, 2006; (trans. with E.R. Lamadrid) Juan the Bear and the Water of Life, 2008. Work appears in anthologies. Contributor to periodicals. **Address:** Taos News, 226 Albright St., PO Box 3737, Taos, NM 87571, U.S.A.

ARENA, Felice. Australian (born Australia), b. 1968. **Genres:** Children's Fiction, Sports/Fitness, Illustrations. **Career:** Children's author and illustrator. **Publications:** Dolphin Boy Blue, 1996; Mission Buffalo, 1997; Wish, 1999; Bravo, Billy!, 2000; Breakaway John, 2001; Hey Cat!, 2008; Whippersnapper, 2011. FARTICUS MAXIMUS SERIES: Farticus Maximus, 2008; Farticus Maximus: Stink-off Battle of the Century, 2009; Farticus Maximus: Bottomus Burps of Britannia, 2010. SPECKY MAGEE SERIES: WITH GARRY LYON: Specky Magee, 2002; Specky Magee and the Great Footy Contest, 2003; Specky Magee and the Season of Champions, 2004; Specky Magee and the Boots of Glory, 2005; Specky Magee and A Legend in the Making, 2006; Specky Magee and the Spirit of the Game, 2007; Specky Magee and the Battle of Young Guns, 2009. BOYZ RULE! SERIES: WITH P. KETTLE: Yabby Hunt, 2003 in US as Crawfish Hunt, 2004; Golf Legends, 2003; Test Cricket, 2003; Bull Riding, 2003; Basketball Buddies, 2003; Bike Daredevils, 2003; Skateboard Dudes, 2003; Camping Out, 2003; Water Rats, 2003; Secret Agent Heroes, 2004; Tree House, 2004; Tennis Ace, 2004; Wet World, 2004; Battle of the Games, 2004; Gone Fishing, 2004; Rock Star, 2004; Park Soccer, 2004; Olympic Champions, 2004; On the Farm, 2004; Pirate Attack in US as Pirate Ship, 2004; Hit the Beach, 2004; Halloween Gotcha!, 2004; Race Car Dreamers, 2004; Rotten School Day, 2004. STICK DUDES SERIES: Stick Dudes: Water Fight Frenzy, 2010; Stick Dudes: The Secret Four-ce, 2010; Stick Dudes: Champions of the World, 2010. SELF-ILLUSTRATED: Sally and Dave-A Slug Story, 2007. **Address:** Booked Out Speakers Agency, PO Box 580, Prahran, VI 3141, Australia.

ARENDS, Carolyn. Canadian (born Canada), b. 1968. **Genres:** Philosophy, Human Relations/Parenting, inspirational/Motivational Literature, Medicine/Health, Music, Biography. **Career:** Benson Music Publishing, songwriter; Christianity Today, columnist and film reviewer; musician. **Publications:** Living the Questions: Making Sense of the Mess and Mystery of Life, 2000; We've Been Waiting for You, 2002; Wrestling with Angels, 2007. Contributor to periodicals. **Address:** Running Arends Music, PO Box 74018, Surrey, BC V4N 5H9, Canada. **Online address:** carolyn@carolynarends.com

ARENS, Katherine (Marie). American (born United States), b. 1953. **Genres:** Intellectual History, Literary Criticism And History, Language/Linguistics, Adult Non-fiction, Dance/Ballet, Education. **Career:** Stanford University, teaching fellow, 1976-80; University of Texas, Department of Germanic Studies, assistant professor, 1980-86, associate professor, 1986-93, research professor, 1993-, Center for European Studies, affiliate, 2005-. Writer. **Publications:** Functionalism and Fin de siècle: Fritz Mauthner's Critique of Language, 1984; Structures of Knowing: Psychologies of the Nineteenth Century, 1989; (with J. Swaffar and H. Byrnes) Reading for Meaning: An Integrated Approach to Language Learning, 1991; (ed. with J.B. Johns) Elfriede Jelinek: Framed by Language, 1994; Austria and Other Margins: Reading Culture, 1996; Empire in Decline: Fritz Mauthner's Critique of Wilhelminian Germany, 2001; (with J. Swaffar) Remapping the Foreign Language Curriculum: An Approach Through Multiple Literacies, 2005. **Address:** Department of Germanic Studies, University of Texas, 3.102 E. P. Schoch, 1 University Sta. C3300, Austin, TX 78712-0304, U.S.A. **Online address:** k.arens@mail.utexas.edu

ARESTIS, Philip. British/Cypriot (born Cyprus), b. 1941. **Genres:** Economics, Essays. **Career:** Kingston Polytechnic, part-time lecturer in economics, 1968-69; Thames Polytechnic, lecturer in economics, 1969-71, senior lecturer, 1971-77, principal lecturer in economics and head of economics division, 1977-88, Division of Economics, director of studies, 1978-87; University of Surrey, part-time lecturer, 1969-80; University of Cambridge, part-time lecturer, 1971-80, professor, Cambridge Centre for Economic and Public Policy, director of research, Department of Land Economy, honorary departmental senior fellow; Copthall School, parent governor, 1988-92; University of East London, Department of Applied Economics, head and professor of economics, 1988-97, research professor, 1997-2000; Macmillan Publishing Ltd., academic consultant, 1997-2002; University of North London, visiting research fellow, 1998-2000; Bard College, Levy Economics Institute, senior research fellow, 1998-2002, research professor of economics, 2002; South Bank University, Business School, director of research and professor of economics, 2000-02; Wolfson College, senior research fellow, 2004-, now emeritus fellow; L'Université Paris 13, visiting professor of economics, 2004-05; University of Utah, distinguished adjunct professor of economics, 2005; University of London, Centre for Globalization Research, visiting fellow, 2007; Universidad del País Vasco, Department of Applied Economics V, professor of economics, 2009-; Central Bank of Cyprus, academic consultant; Centre of Economic Research, academic consultant; Macroeconomics, Money and Finance (MMF) Research Group, vice chairman; Manchester Metropolitan University, Department of Economics, head; Luton University, Department of Business Strategy, Ethics and Economics, head; Universite de Nice Antipolis, Department of Economics, research staff. Writer and editor. **Publications:** (With G. Hadjimatheou) Introducing Macroeconomic Modelling, 1982; The Post-Keynesian Approach to Economics, 1992; Money, Pricing, Distribution, and Economic Integration, 1997; (with A. Brown and M.C. Sawyer) The Euro: Evolution and Prospects, 2001; (with M.C. Sawyer) Re-Examining Monetary and Fiscal Policy for the 21st Century, 2004; (with E. Karakitsos) Post-bubble U.S. Economy: Implications for Financial Markets and the Economy, 2004; (with E. Karakitsos) The Post Great Recession U.S. Economy: Implications for Financial Markets and the Economy, 2010; (with R. Sobreira and J.L. Oreiro) The Recent Financial Crisis, Financial Regulation and Global Impact, vol. I: The Financial Crisis: Origins and Implications, vol. II: An Assessment of the Global Impact of the Financial Crisis, forthcoming. EDITOR: (with T. Skouras) Post Keynesian Economic Theory, 1985; Post-Keynesian Monetary Economics, 1988; Contemporary Issues in Money and Banking: Essays in Honour of Stephen Frowen, 1988; (with Y. Kitromilides) Theory and Policy in Political Economy (essays), 1990; (with V. Chick) Recent Developments in Post-Keynesian Economics, 1992; (with M. Sawyer) A Biographical Dictionary of Dissenting Economists, 1992, 2nd ed., 2000; Money and Banking: Issues for the Twenty-first Century: Essays in Honour of Stephen F. Frowen, 1993; (with M. Sawyer) The Elgar Companion to Radical Political Economy, 1994; (with V. Chick) Finance, Development, and Structural Change, 1995; (with M. Marshall) The Political Economy of Full Employment, 1995; Keynes, Money, and the Open Economy, 1996; Employment, Economic Growth, and the Tyranny of the Market, 1996; (with M. Sawyer and G. Palma) Capital Controversy, Post-Keynesian Economics and the History of Economic Thought, 1997; (with M. Sawyer) The Relevance of Keynesian Economic Policies Today, 1997; (with G. Palma and M. Sawyer) Markets, Unemployment, and Economic Policy, 1997; (with M. Sawyer) The Political Economy of Economic Policies, 1998; (with S. Daniel and J. Grahl) Money and Macroeconomic Policy, 1998; (with M.C. Sawyer) The Political Economy of Central Banking, 1998; Method, Theory, and Policy in Keynes: Essays in Honour of Paul Davidson, 1998; Money and Macroeconomic Policies: Essays in Macroeconomics in Honour of Bernard Corry and Maurice Peston, vol. I, 1999; (with S. Daniel and J. Grahl) The History and Practice of Economics: Essays in Honour of Bernard Corry and Maurice Peston, vol. II, 1999; (with S. Daniel and J. Grahl) Regulation Strategies and Economic Policies: Essays in Honour of Bernard Corry and Maurice Peston, vol. III, 1999; (with M. Baddeley and J. McCombie) What Global Economic Crisis?, 2001; (with M.C. Sawyer) Money, Finance and Capitalist Development, 2001; (with M. Sawyer) Economics of the Third Way, 2001; Money, Macroeconomics and Keynes: Essays in Honour of Victoria Chick, vol. I, 2002; Methodology, Microeconomics and Keynes: Essays in Honour of Victoria Chick, vol. II, 2002; (with L.F. De Paula) Monetary Union in South America, 2003; (with M. Baddeley and J. McCombie) Globalisation, Regionalism and Economic Activity, 2003; (with M. Sawyer) The Rise of the Market: Critical Essays on the Political Economy of Neo-Liberalism, 2004; (with M. Sawyer) Neo-Liberal Economic Policy: Critical Essays, 2004; (with M. Baddeley and J. McCombie) New Monetary Policy: Implications and Relevance, 2005; (with M. Sawyer) Financial Liberalization: Beyond Orthodox Concerns, 2005; (with M. Sawyer) Handbook of Alternative Monetary Economics, 2006; (with J. McCombie and R. Vickerman) Growth and Economic Development: Essays in Honour of A.P. Thirlwall, 2006; (with J. Ferreiro and F. Serrano) Financial Developments in National and International Markets, 2006; (G. Zezza) Advances in Monetary Policy and Macroeconomics, 2007; (with E.L. Heron and E. Hein) Aspects of Modern Monetary and Macroeconomic Policies, 2007; (with M. Baddeley and S.L. McCombie) Economic Growth: New Directions in Theory and Policy, 2007; Is There a New Consensus in Macroeconomics?, 2007; (with A. Saad-Filho) Political Economy of Brazil: Recent Economic

Performance, 2007; (with L.F. de Paula) Financial Liberalization and Economic Performance in Emerging Countries, 2008; (with J. Eatwell) Issues in Economic Development and Globalization: Essays in Honour of Ajit Singh, 2008; (with J. Eatwell) Issues in Finance and Industry: Essays in Honour of Ajit Singh, 2008; (with J. McCombie) Missing Links in the Unemployment Relationship, 2008; (with M. Sawyer) Critical Essays on the Privatization Experience, 2009; (with P. Mooslechner and K. Wagner) Housing Market Challenges in Europe and the United States, 2010; (with R. Sobreira and J.L. Oreiro) The Financial Crisis: Origins and Implications, 2010; (with M. Sawyer) 21st Century Keynesian Economics, 2010; (with R. Sobreira and J.L. Oreiro) An Assessment of the Global Impact of the Financial Crisis, 2011; (with M. Sawyer) New Economics as Mainstream Economics, 2011; Microeconomics, Macroeconomics and Economic Policy: Essays in Honour of Malcolm Sawyer, 2011. Contributor of articles to journals and periodicals. **Address:** Department of Land Economy, University of Cambridge, 19 Silver St., Cambridge, CB CB3 9EP, England. **Online address:** pa267@cam.ac.uk

ARGERS, Helen. (Helen Archery). American (born United States) **Genres:** Novels, Novellas/Short Stories, Romance/Historical, Plays/Screenplays, Music, Race Relations, Theatre, Writing/Journalism, Humor/Satire. **Career:** Freelance writer, 1982-. **Publications:** NOVELS: A Lady of Independence, 1982; A Scandalous Lady, 1991; A Captain's Lady, 1991; An Unlikely Lady, 1992; Noblesse Oblige, 1994; The Gilded Lily, 1998. AS HELEN ARCHERY: The Age of Elegance, 1992; The Season of Loving, 1992; Lady Adventuress, 1994; Duel of Hearts, 1994. **Address:** c/o Author Mail, St. Martin's Press, 175 5th Ave., New York, NY 10010-7703, U.S.A.

ARGIRI, Laura. American (born United States), b. 1958. **Genres:** Novels, Gay And Lesbian Issues. **Career:** Novelist. **Publications:** The God in Flight, 1994. **Address:** c/o Endeavor Agency, 9701 Wilshire Blvd., 10th Fl., Beverly Hills, CA 90212-2020, U.S.A.

ARGYROU, Vassos. Cypriot (born Cyprus), b. 1955. **Genres:** Anthropology/Ethnology. **Career:** University of Hull, professor. Writer and educator. **Publications:** Tradition and Modernity in the Mediterranean: The Wedding as Symbolic Struggle, 1996; Anthropology and the Will to Meaning: A Postcolonial Critique, 2002; The Logic of Environmentalism: Anthropology, Ecology and Postcoloniality, 2005. Contributor of articles to journals and books. **Address:** University of Hull, Cottingham Rd., Hull, HU6 7RX, England. **Online address:** v.argyrou@hull.ac.uk

ARICO, Santo L. American (born United States), b. 1938. **Genres:** Literary Criticism And History, Biography, Autobiography/Memoirs, History, Young Adult Fiction. **Career:** University of Mississippi, professor of French and Italian; teacher, 1960-. Writer. **Publications:** (Ed.) Contemporary Women Writers in Italy: A Modern Renaissance, 1990; The Art of Persuasion in Rousseau's La Nouvelle Héloïse, 1994; Oriana Fallaci: The Woman and the Myth, 1998. **Address:** 200 Sivley St., Oxford, MS 38655, U.S.A.

ARIDJIS, Chloe. British/American (born United States), b. 1971. **Genres:** Novels. **Career:** Writer, translator and photographer. **Publications:** Magic and the Literary Fantastique in Nineteenth-Century France (doctoral dissertation), 2002; Book of Clouds (novel), 2009. Contributor of articles to journals. **Address:** c/o Anna Stein, Irene Skolnick Agency, 22 W 23rd St., 5th Fl., New York, NY 10010, U.S.A.

ARIELY, Dan. American (born United States) **Genres:** Psychology, Education. **Career:** Massachusetts Institute of Technology, Sloan School of Management, Alfred P. Sloan professor of behavioral economics and principal investigator, 1998-2008, Media Laboratory, staff, 2000-10, Center for Advanced Hindsight and Rationality Research Group, director; University of California, instructor, 2001-02; Princeton University, Institute for Advanced Study, faculty, 2005-07; Duke University, Kenan Institute for Ethics, senior fellow, 2008-, Fuqua School of Business, James B. Duke professor of behavioral economics, 2008-, Center for Cognitive Neuroscience, faculty, 2008-, School of Medicine, faculty, 2008-. Writer. **Publications:** (With C. Hughes and D. Eckerman) The Joy of Experimental Psychology, 1998; Predictably Irrational: The Hidden Forces That Shape Our Decisions, 2008; Upside of Irrationality: The Unexpected Benefits of Defying Logic at Work and at Home, 2010. Contributor of articles to journals. **Address:** Fuqua School of Business, Duke University, 100 Fuqua Dr., Durham, NC 27708, U.S.A. **Online address:** dan.ariely@duke.edu

ARIFF, Mohamed. Australian (born Australia), b. 1942. **Genres:** Money/Finance, Economics, Adult Non-fiction, Marketing. **Career:** Monash University, staff, 1997-, head of finance faculty; Bond University, professor of finance. Writer. **Publications:** (Ed. with F.C. Onn and R. Thillainathan) ASEAN Cooperation in Industrial Projects: Papers and Proceedings of a Symposium, 11-12 April 1977, Kuala Lumpur, 1977; Malaysia and ASEAN Economic Cooperation, 1980; (with C.P. Lim and D. Lee) Export Incentives, Manufactured Exports and Employment: Malaysia, 1984; (with H. Hill) Export-Oriented Industrialisation: The ASEAN Experience, 1985; (ed. with T. Loong-Hoe) ASEAN Trade Policy Options: The Uruguay Round, 1988; Stock Pricing in Singapore, 1990; Công nghiêp hóa huõng vê xuât khâu: kinhnghiêm cua ASEAN/Export-Oriented Industrialization: The ASEAN Experience, 1992; The Role of ASEAN in the Uruguay Round: Opportunities and Constraints, 1993; (co-author) AFTA in the Changing International Economy, 1996; (with S. Mohamad and A.M. Nassir) Stock Pricing in Malaysia: Corporate Financial & Investment Management, 1998; (ed.) APEC Development Cooperation, 1998; (with A.M. Khalid) Liberalization, Growth and the Asian Financial Crisis: Lessons for Developing and Transitional Economies in Asia, 2000; (with J. Pope) Taxation and Compliance Costs in Asia Pacific Economies, 2002; (ed.) Global Financial Markets: Issues and Strategies, 2004; (with A.M. Khalid) Liberalization and Growth in Asia: 21st Century Challenges, 2005; (co-author) Capital Markets in Malaysia: Corporate Finance, Investment Management, Banking and Corporate Governance, 2008; (with C.F. Fah and N.V. Heng) Bond Markets in Malaysia and Singapore, 2009; Foundation of Islamic Banking: Theory, Practice and Education, 2010. **Address:** Department of Finance, Bond University, Rm. 411, Gold Coast, QL 4229, Australia. **Online address:** mohamed_ariff@bond.edu.au

ARIKHA, Noga. American/French (born France) **Genres:** Intellectual History, History, Biography, Medicine/Health, Sciences, Art/Art History, Essays, Social Sciences, Social Sciences, Food And Wine. **Career:** Columbia University, Italian Academy for Advanced Studies, fellow; Institut Jean-Nicod, visiting fellow; Bard College, faculty, Bard Graduate Center, faculty and visiting assistant professor in the humanities. Writer. **Publications:** Passions and Tempers: A History of the Humours, 2007; (with M. Simonetta) Napoleon and the Rebel: A Story of Brotherhood, Passion, and Power, 2011. **Address:** c/o Elizabeth Sheinkman, Curtis Brown Group Ltd., Haymarket House, 28-29 Haymarket, London, GL SW1Y 4SP, England. **Online address:** info@nogaarikha.com

ARINZE, Francis. (Francis A. Arinze). Italian/Nigerian (born Nigeria), b. 1932. **Genres:** Theology/Religion. **Career:** Bigard Memorial Seminary, lecturer in philosophy, professor, 1961-62; Archbishop of Onitsha, 1967-85; Pontifical Council for Inter-religious Dialogue, president, 1984-; Congregation for Divine Worship and the Discipline of the Sacraments, emeritus, 2008-. Ordained Roman Catholic priest and writer. **Publications:** Il Concilio Vaticano II: Carisma e profezia, 1997; Bishop and his Ministry, 1998; Christian-Muslim Relations in the Twenty-First Century, 1998; Meeting Other Believers, 1998; Brucken Bauen, 2000; A dieci anni dall'enciclica Redemptoris missio, 2001; Holy Eucharist: Christ's Inestimable Gift, 2001; Religions for Peace, 2002; God's Invisible Hand, 2003; (contrib.) Globalization & African Self-Determination, 2004. AS FRANCIS A. ARINZE: Sacrifice in Ibo Religion, 1970; Christian and Politics, 1982; Answering God's Call, 1982; Living Our Faith, 1983; Alone with God, 1986. AS CARDINAL ARINZE: Progress in Christian-Muslim Relations Worldwide, 1988. AS FRANCIS CARDINAL ARINZE: Spreading the Faith, 1990; Gospel to Society, 1990; Africans and Christianity, 1990; Motherhood and Family Life, the Blessed Virgin Mary, Christian in Christ, 1990; Church in Dialogue: Walking with Other Religions, 1990; Work and Pray for Perfection, 1990; Meeting Other Believers: The Risks and Rewards of Interreligious Dialogue, 1998; Religions for Peace: A Call for Solidarity to the Religions of the World, 2002; Celebrating the Holy Eucharist, 2006; God's Invisible Hand: The Life and Work of Francis Cardinal Arinze, 2006; Meeting Jesus and Following Him: A Retreat Given to Pope Benedict XVI and the Papal Household, 2010. **Address:** Largo del Colonnato 3, Rome, 00193, Italy.

ARINZE, Francis A. *See* **ARINZE, Francis.**

ARKIN, Marcus. South African (born South Africa), b. 1926. **Genres:** Economics, History, Theology/Religion, Reference, Business/Trade/Industry, Social Sciences. **Career:** Dictionary of South African Biography, contributor and consultant editor; University of Cape Town, lecturer, 1949-62, senior lecturer in economics, 1963-66; Rhodes University, professor of economics and head of department of economics and economic history, 1967-73, Faculty of Social Science, dean, 1970-73; South African Zionist Federation, director-general, 1973-; University of Durban-Westville, Department of Economics, faculty, now retired. **Publications:** John Company at the Cape, 1962; Supplies for Napoleon's Gaolers, 1964; Agency and Island, 1965; South African Economic Development: An Outline Survey, 1966; Economists and Economic Historians, 1968; Introducing Economics: The Science of Scarcity, 1971; The Economist at the Breakfast Table, 1971; Storm in a Teacup: The Cape Colonists and the English East India Company, 1973; Aspects of Jewish Economic History, 1975; The Zionist Idea: A History and Evaluation, 1977; (ed.) South African Jewry, 1984; One People, One Destiny: Some Explorations in Jewish Affairs, 1989. **Address:** Glenashley, PO Box 22179, KwaZulu-Natal, 4022, South Africa. **Online address:** arkin@iafrica.com

ARKIN, William M. American (born United States), b. 1956. **Genres:** Military/Defense/Arms Control, Young Adult Non-fiction, History. **Career:** National Resources Defense Council, consultant, 1980; Center for Defense Information, senior staff analyst, 1980-81; Institute for Policy Studies, director of national security program and arms race and nuclear weapons research project, 1981-89; Stern (magazine), military analyst, 1981-88; Greenpeace Intl., consultant, 1987-89; Greenpeace International/Greenpeace USA, director of nuclear information unit and director of military research, 1989-94; Greenpeace USA, political director, 1989-90; Federation of American Scientists, consultant, 1994-95, 1998; Human Rights Watch Arms Division, consultant, 1994; National Institute, investigative reporter, 1995-96; Air Force Judge Advocate General's School, lecturer and news analyst, 1995-96; Johns Hopkins University, Center for Strategic Education, consultant, 1997-98; MSNBC, military analyst, 1998; Washington Post, military analyst, 1998; NBC Nightly News, military analyst, 1998; Air War College, lecturer and news analyst; Naval War College, lecturer and news analyst. Writer. **Publications:** NONFICTION: Research Guide to Current Military and Strategic Affairs, 1981; (with P. Pringle) SIOP, the Secret U.S. Plan for Nuclear War, 1983; (with T.B. Cochran and M.M. Hoenig) Nuclear Weapons Databook, 5 vols., 1984; (with R.W. Fieldhouse) Nuclear Battlefields: Global Links in the Arms Race, 1985; (with J. Handler) Naval Accidents, 1945-1988, 1989; (co-author) Encyclopedia of the U.S. Military, 1990; (with J. Handler and A. Wickenheiser) Naval Safety, 1989: The Year of the Accident, 1990; (with J. Handler) Nuclear Warships and Naval Nuclear Weapons, 1990: A Complete Inventory, 1990; The U.S. Military Online: A Directory for Internet Access to the Department of Defense, 1997, 2nd ed., 1998; Code Names: Deciphering U.S. Military Plans, Programs, and Operations in the 9/11 World, 2005; Divining Victory: Airpower in the 2006 Israel-Hezbollah War, 2007; (with D. Priest) Top Secret America: The Rise of the New American Security State, 2011. **Address:** Little, Brown and Co., 237 Park Ave., New York, NY 10017, U.S.A. **Online address:** william.arkin@apni.com

ARKSEY, Neil. British (born England) **Genres:** Children's Fiction, Young Adult Fiction, Plays/Screenplays, Novellas/Short Stories. **Career:** Shakespeare's Globe Theatre, story editor, script editor and head writer. Producer and screenwriter. **Publications:** Brooksie, 1998; Result!, 1999; MacB, 1999; Playing on the Edge, 2000; Flint, 2000; Sudden Death, 2001; As Good as Dead in Downtown, 2004. **Address:** London, GL , England. **Online address:** author@neilarksey.com

ARKUSH, Michael. American (born United States), b. 1958. **Genres:** Sports/Fitness, Biography, Autobiography/Memoirs. **Career:** Golf World Magazine, associate editor; Los Angeles Times, reporter, 1988-; Washington Post, reporter; New York Times, staff writer. **Publications:** (With S. Springer) 60 Years of USC-UCLA Football, 1991; Rush!: An Up-Close Look at Rush Limbaugh, 1993; Tim Allen Laid Bare: Unauthorized, 1995; Fairways and Dreams: Twenty-Five of the World's Greatest Golfers and the Fathers Who Inspired Them, 1998; I Remember Payne Stewart: Personal Memories of Golf's Most Dapper Champion by the People Who Knew Him Best, 2000; (comp. with R. Cherney) My Greatest Shot: The Top Players Share their Defining Golf Moments, 2004; (with K. Venturi) Getting Up & Down: My 60 Years in Golf, 2004; (with P. Jackson) The Last Season: A Team in Search of Its Soul, 2005; Fight of the Century: Ali vs. Frazier March 8, 1971, 2008; (with S.R. Leonard) The Big Fight: My Life In and Out of the Ring, 2011. Contributor to periodicals. **Address:** New York Times, 270 W 43rd St., New York, NY 10036-3912, U.S.A.

ARLUKE, Arnold. American (born United States), b. 1947. **Genres:** Animals/Pets, Sociology, Social Sciences. **Career:** Yale University, Law School, visiting fellow, 1974; Harvard University, research associate of center for community health and medical care, 1977-78, postdoctoral fellow, 1977; Northeastern University, Department of Sociology and Anthropology, assistant professor, 1978-83, associate professor, 1984-91, professor of sociology, 1992-; Tufts University, senior fellow of center for animals, 1990-; Massachusetts Society for the Prevention of Cruelty to Animals, consultant. Writer. **Publications:** (With G. Gritzer) The Making of Rehabilitation: A Political Economy of Medical Specialization, 1989-1980, 1985; (with J. Levin) Gossip: The Inside Scoop, 1987; (with J. Levin) Sociology: Snapshots and Portraits of Society, 1996; (with C.R. Sanders) Regarding Animals, 1996; Great Apes and Humans, 2001; Brute Force: Animal Police and the Challenge of Cruelty, 2004; Just a Dog: Understanding Animal Cruelty and Ourselves, 2006; (with L. Birke and M. Michael) The Sacrifice: How Scientific Experiments Transform Animals and People, 2006; (with C. Killeen) Inside Animal Hoarding: The Case of Barbara Erickson and Her 552 Dogs, 2009; Between The Species: Readings in Human-Animal Relations, 2009; (with R. Bogdan) Beauty and the Beast: Human-Animal Relations as Revealed in Real Photo Postcards, 1905-1935, 2010. **Address:** Department of Sociology, Northeastern University, 519 Holmes Hall, 360 Huntington Ave., Boston, MA 02115, U.S.A. **Online address:** a.arluke@neu.edu

ARMAH, Ayi Kwei. Ghanaian (born Ghana), b. 1939. **Genres:** Novels, Theology/Religion, Poetry, History, Young Adult Non-fiction. **Career:** Revolution Africaine Magazine, translator, 1964, scriptwriter; Jeune Afrique, editor and translator, 1967-68; writer, 1968-; Teacher's College, visiting professor; Dar es Salaam University, visiting professor; University of Massachusetts, visiting professor; Amherst University, visiting professor; University of Lesotho, faculty and visiting professor; University of Wisconsin-Madison, visiting professor; College of National Education, faculty; Navrongo School, English teacher. **Publications:** The Beautyful Ones Are Not Yet Born, 1968; Fragments, 1970; Messages: Poems from Ghana, 1970; Why Are We So Blest?, 1971; The Two Thousand Seasons, 1973; The Healers: An Historical Novel, 1978; Osiris Rising: A Novel of Africa Past, Present and Future, 1995; KMT: In the House of Life: An Epistemic Novel, 2002. Contributor to magazines. Works appear in anthologies. **Address:** Per Ankh Publishers, Per Ankh Bldg., PO Box 2, Popenguine Village, 00000, Senegal.

ARMANTROUT, (Mary) Rae. American (born United States), b. 1947. **Genres:** Poetry, Autobiography/Memoirs, Biography. **Career:** California State University-San Francisco, teaching assistant, 1972-73; California State University-San Diego, lecturer, 1980-2004, professor, 2004-, New Writing Poetry Reading Series, director, 1989-2002, Department of Literature, professor of writing, poetry and poetics section head; California College of Arts and Crafts, poet-in-residence, 2000-01; Naropa University, Summer Program, poetry workshop instructor, 2000-. **Publications:** POETRY: Extremities, 1978; The Invention of Hunger, 1979; Precedence, 1985; Necromance, 1991; Made to Seem, 1995; Writing the Plot about Sets, 1998; Memoir: True, 1998; A Wild Salience, 1999; The Pretext, 2001; Veil: New and Selected Poems, 2001; Up to Speed, 2004; Next Life, 2007; Versed, 2009; Money Shot, 2011. OTHERS: The Oxford Book of American Poetry, 2006; American Hybrid, 2009; Poems of the Women's Movement, 2009. Works appear in anthologies. Contributor to periodicals and journals. **Address:** Department of Literature, University of California, LIT 350, 9500 Gilman Dr., Ste. 0410, La Jolla, CA 92093-0410, U.S.A. **Online address:** rarmantrout@ucsd.edu

ARMBRUSTER, Ann. American (born United States) **Genres:** Children's Fiction, Children's Non-fiction, History, Travel/Exploration, Sciences, Natural History, Environmental Sciences/Ecology, Geography, Geography. **Career:** Children's writer and urban designer. **Publications:** FOR CHILDREN: (with E.A. Taylor) Tornadoes, 1989; (with E.A. Taylor) Astronaut Training, 1990; The American Flag, 1991; The United Nations, 1995; The Life and Times of Miami Beach, 1995; Lake Erie, 1996; Lake Huron, 1996; Lake Michigan, 1996; Lake Ontario, 1996; Lake Superior, 1996; St. Lawrence Seaway, 1996; Floods, 1996; Wildfires, 1996. Contributor to periodicals. **Address:** c/o Author Mail, Franklin Watts/Children's Press, 555 Broadway, New York, NY 10012, U.S.A.

ARMISTEAD, John. American (born United States), b. 1941. **Genres:** Mystery/Crime/Suspense, Children's Fiction, Novels. **Career:** Waimea Baptist Church, pastor, 1975-77; Kailua Baptist Church, pastor, 1977-79; Calvary Baptist Church, pastor, 1979-94; Northeast Mississippi Daily Journal, religion editor, 1995-. Journalist. **Publications:** SHERIFF BRAMLETT MYSTERY SERIES: Legacy of Vengeance, 1994; Homecoming for Murder,

1995; Cruel as the Grave, 1996. NOVELS: The 66 Dollar Summer, 2000; The Return of Gabriel, 2002. OTHER: Bramlett's Return, 2006. **Address:** Evelyn Singer Literary Agency Inc., PO Box 594, White Plains, NY 10602-0593, U.S.A. **Online address:** johnarmistead@yahoo.com

ARMITAGE, David. British/New Zealander (born New Zealand), b. 1943?. **Genres:** Children's Fiction, Picture/Board Books, Fash Ion/Costume, Illustrations, Young Adult Fiction. **Career:** Author and illustrator. **Publications:** WITH R. ARMITAGE: The Lighthouse Keeper's Lunch, 1977; The Trouble with Mr. Harris, 1978; Don't Forget, Matilda!, 1979; The Bossing of Josie, 1980 as The Birthday Spell, 1981; Ice Creams for Rosie, 1981; One Moonlit Night, 1983; Grandma Goes Shopping, 1984; The Lighthouse Keeper's Catastrophe, 1986; The Lighthouse Keeper's Rescue, 1989; Watch the Baby, Daisy, 1991; When Dad Did the Washing, 1992; Looking after Chocolates, 1992; A Quarrel of Koalas, 1992 as Harry Hates Shopping!, 1992; The Lighthouse Keeper's Picnic, 1993; The Lighthouse Keeper's Cat, 1995. FOR CHILDREN: Portland Bill's Treasure Trove (activity book), 1987; Giant Stories, 1988; Jasper Who Jumps, 1990. OTHERS: Conservation in Museums and Galleries, 1974; (with B.Edwards) My Brother Sammy, 1999. Illustrator of books by others. **Address:** Old Tiles Cottage, Church Ln., Hellingly, ES BN27 4HA, England.

ARMITAGE, Ronda (Jacqueline). British/New Zealander (born New Zealand), b. 1943. **Genres:** Children's Fiction, Politics/Government. **Career:** Teacher, 1964-66, 1968-69; Dorothy Butler Ltd., adviser on children's books, 1970-71; Lewes Priory Comprehensive School, assistant librarian, 1976-77; East Sussex County Council, teaching staff, 1978-. Writer. **Publications:** WITH D. ARMITAGE: The Lighthouse Keeper's Lunch, 1977; The Trouble with Mr. Harris, 1978; Don't Forget, Matilda!, 1979; The Bossing of Josie, 1980 in US as The Birthday Spell, 1981; Ice Creams for Rosie, 1981; Let's Talk About Drinking, 1982; One Moonlight Night, 1983; Grandma Goes Shopping, 1984; The Lighthouse Keeper's Catastrophe, 1986; The Lighthouse Keeper's Rescue, 1989; When Dad Did the Washing, 1990; Watch the Baby, Daisy, 1991; Looking After Chocolates, 1992; A Quarrel of Koalas, 1992; Harry Hates Shopping!, 1992; The Light Housekeeper's Picnic, 1993; The Lighthouse Keeper's Cat, 1995; The Light Housekeeper's Favorite Stories, 1999; Queen of the Night, 1999; The Light Housekeeper's Breakfast, 2000; The Lighthouse Keeper's Tea, 2001; The Lighthouse Keeper's Christmas, 2002; A New Home for a Pirate, 2007; A Very Strange Creature, 2009; The Lighthouse Keeper's Surprise, 2009. OTHERS: New Zealand, 1988; Family Violence, 2000; Violence in Society: The Impact on Our Lives, 2004; Small Knight and George, 2007; (with E. Eaves) The Bungle Jungle Bedtime Kiss, 2008. **Address:** c/o Nancy Miles, Miles Stott Children's Literary Agency, E Hook Farm, Lower Quay Rd., Hook, Haverfordwest, DY SA62 4LR, Wales. **Online address:** rondaarmitage@hotmail.co.uk

ARMSTEAD, Joseph. American (born United States), b. 1956. **Genres:** Mystery/Crime/Suspense, Horror. **Career:** Writer and computer technologist. **Publications:** Painmaker: The First Tale in the Book of Dark Memory, 2000; Red Benediction: A Tale from the Book of Dark Memory, 2006; Nightflesh, 2006. MOON-CHOSEN SERIES: Nocturnes and Neon: A Novel of the Vampiric, 2001; Bleeding Twilight: A Tale of Quinn and the Moon-Chosen, 2001; Darkness Fears: A Tale of The Moon-Chosen and Le Grymmeuere, 2002; Endless Nocturnes: A Tale of Quinn and the Moon-Chosen, 2007; Krymsin Nocturnes, 2010. **Address:** Oakland, CA , U.S.A. **Online address:** vonarmstadt@hotmail.com

ARMSTRONG, Adam. (Jeff Gulvin). British (born England), b. 1962?. **Genres:** Novels, Novellas/Short Stories, Young Adult Fiction. **Career:** Writer, 1997-. **Publications:** AS JEFF GULVIN: Sleep No More, 1996; Sorted, 1996; Close Quarters, 1997; Storm Crow, 1998; Nom de Guerre, 1999; The Covenant, 2000; The Procession, 2000; The List, 2003; (C. Boorman) By Any Means, 2008; Long Way Down, 2008; (with E. McGregor) Long Way Down, 2009; (with C. Boorman) Right to the Edge, 2010. OTHERS: Cry of the Panther, 2000; Song of the Sound, 2001; Het Zandpaard, 2001; De vrouwen van Fossil Nash, 2004; The River Beneath, 2005. **Address:** Random House, 1745 Broadway, New York, NY 10019, U.S.A.

ARMSTRONG, Alan. American (born United States), b. 1950?. **Genres:** History, Military/Defense/Arms Control, Politics/Government. **Career:** Lawyer-Pilots Bar Association Journal, contributing editor; National Transportation Safety Board Bar Association, newsletter editor. **Publications:** Preemptive Strike: The Secret Plan That Would Have Prevented the Attack on Pearl Harbor, 2006. Contributor of articles to journals. **Address:** Park Ridge, Bldg. 5, 85 Office Pk., 2900 Chamblee-Tucker Rd., Atlanta, GA 30341-4100, U.S.A. **Online address:** alan@alanarmstronglaw.com

ARMSTRONG, Alan. (Alan W. Armstrong). American (born United States), b. 1939. **Genres:** Novels, Children's Fiction, Animals/Pets. **Career:** Writer and attorney. **Publications:** Regards, Rodeo: The Mariner Dog of Cassis, 1999; (ed. and intro. as Alan W. Armstrong) Forget Not Mee & My Garden...: Selected Letters, 1725-1768, of Peter Collinson, F.R.S., 2002; Whittington, 2005; Raleigh's Page, 2007; Looking for Marco, 2009. **Address:** c/o Author Mail, Random House, 1745 Broadway, New York, NY 10019, U.S.A.

ARMSTRONG, Alan W. *See* **ARMSTRONG, Alan.**

ARMSTRONG, Alexandra. American (born United States), b. 1939. **Genres:** Money/Finance, Business/Trade/Industry. **Career:** Ferris & Co., executive secretary, 1961-66, registered representative, 1966-77; New York Stock Exchange, registered representative, 1966-; Julia Walsh & Sons, senior vice president, 1977-83; Alexandra Armstrong Advisors Inc., president, 1983-91; Kennedy Center, National Council of the Friends, vice-chair, 1987-91; Deferred Giving, vice president, 1988-; Armstrong, Welch & MacIntyre Inc. (financial planning and investment firm), partner, 1991-, now chair. Writer. **Publications:** (With M.R. Donahue) On Your Own: A Widow's Passage to Emotional and Financial Well-Being, 1993, 4th ed., 2006. **Address:** Armstrong, MacIntyre & Severns Inc., 1155 Connecticut Ave. NW, Ste. 250, Washington, DC 20036-4314, U.S.A.

ARMSTRONG, Bob. American (born United States), b. 1942?. **Genres:** Autobiography/Memoirs, Criminology/True Crime. **Career:** Zen Escort Service, founder. Writer. **Publications:** Vanilla Slim: An Improbable Pimp in the Empire of Lust, 2005. **Address:** c/o Author Mail, Carroll & Graf, 245 W 17th St., 11th Fl., New York, NY 10011-5300, U.S.A.

ARMSTRONG, David. Welsh/British (born England), b. 1946?. **Genres:** Art/Art History, Mystery/Crime/Suspense, Novels, Young Adult Fiction. **Career:** Writer. **Publications:** Maitre Jacques: the Jacques Anquetil Story, 1970; Eternal Second, 1971; Emperor; the Rik van Looy Story, 1971; Outline of Sociology as Applied to Medicine, 1983; Night's Black Agents (novel), 1993; Less than Kind (novel), 1994; Until Dawn Tomorrow (novel), 1995; Thought for the Day (novel), 1997; Small Vices (novel), 2001; How NOT to Write a Novel (nonfiction), 2003; A Kind of Acquaintance, 2007; Written Out, 2009; A Pact of Silence, 2010. Contributor to periodicals. **Address:** c/o Author Mail, Bon Marche Centre, 241-251 Ferndale Rd., London, GL SW9 8BJ, England.

ARMSTRONG, David Malet. Australian (born Australia), b. 1926. **Genres:** Philosophy, Natural History, Physics, Essays, Sciences. **Career:** University of London, Birkbeck College, assistant lecturer in philosophy, 1954-55; University of Melbourne, lecturer and senior lecturer in philosophy, 1956-63; Yale University, visiting assistant professor, 1962; Sydney University, Challis professor of philosophy, 1964-91, emeritus professor of philosophy, 1992-; Stanford University, visiting professor, 1965, 1968; University of Texas, visiting professor, 1980, 1989; University of Wisconsin, 1985; University of California at Irvine, distinguished visiting professor, 1992; University of Graz, visiting professor, 1995; University of Notre Dame, visiting professor, 1997; Yale University, visiting professor, 1998; University of Connecticut, visiting professor, 1999; Davidson College, Kemp distinguished professor, 2002. Writer. **Publications:** Berkeley's Theory of Vision, 1960; Perception and the Physical World, 1961; Bodily Sensations, 1962; A Materialist Theory of the Mind, 1968, rev. ed., 1993; (contrib.) The Mind-Brain Identity Theory: A Collection of Papers, 1970; Belief, Truth and Knowledge, 1973; Universals and Scientific Realism, 1978; The Nature of Mind and Other Essays, 1980; What Is a Law of Nature?, 1983; (with N. Malcolm) Consciousness and Causality, 1984; A Combinatorial Theory of Possibility, 1989; Universals: An Opinionated Introduction, 1989; Ontology, Causality and Mind: Essays in Honor of D.M. Armstrong, 1993; (with C.B. Martin and U.T. Place) Dispositions: A Debate, 1996; A World of States of Affairs, 1997; The Mind-Body Problem, 1999; Truth and Truthmakers, 2004; Sketch for a Systematic Metaphysics, 2010. EDITOR: (and intro.) Berkeley's Philosophical Writings, 1965; (with C.B. Martin) Locke and Berkeley, 1968; (with C.B. Martin) Berkeley: A Collection of Critical Essays, 1988. **Address:** Department of Philosophy, Sydney University, Rm. N275, Institute Bldg. Annexe, Sydney, NW 2006, Australia. **Online address:** david.armstrong@arts.usyd.edu.au

ARMSTRONG, Diane (Julie). Australian/Polish (born Poland), b. 1939. **Genres:** Novels, History, Librarianship, Biography, Autobiography/Memoirs. **Career:** Freelance travel journalist, 1977-. **Publications:** Mosaic: A Chronicle of Five Generations, 1998; The Voyage of Their Life: The Story of the SS Derna and Its Passengers, 2001; Winter Journey (novel), 2005; Nocturne, 2008. Contributor to periodicals. **Address:** 181 Military Rd., Dover Heights, Sydney, NW 2030, Australia.

ARMSTRONG, Heather B. American (born United States), b. 1975. **Genres:** Autobiography/Memoirs, Sports/Fitness, Human Relations/Parenting. **Career:** Writer. **Publications:** (Ed.) Things I Learned about My Dad in Therapy: Essays, 2008; It Sucked and Then I Cried: How I Had a Baby, a Breakdown and a Much Needed Margarita, 2009; Dear Daughter: The Best of the Dear Leta Letters, 2012. **Address:** Blurbodoocery, 1338 Foothill Dr., Ste. 230, Salt Lake City, UT 84108, U.S.A. **Online address:** dooce@dooce.com

ARMSTRONG, Jeannette C. Canadian (born Canada), b. 1948?. **Genres:** Novels, Children's Fiction, Mythology/Folklore, Poetry. **Career:** En'owkin Centre, staff, 1978-, director, 1985-, executive director; University of Victoria, En'owkin School of International Writing, co-founder and director, 1989- ; University of St. Thomas, faculty. Writer. **Publications:** Enwhisteetkwa: Walk on Water (juvenile fiction), 1982; Neekna and Chemai (juvenile fiction), 1984; Slash (novel), 1985, rev. ed., 1988; (ed.) Looking at the Words of Our People: First Nations Analysis of Literature, 1993; The Native Creative Process: A Collaborative Discourse (non-fiction), 1991; Breathtracks (poetry), 1991; Whispering in Shadows (novel), 2000; (ed. with L. Grauer) Native Poetry in Canada: A Contemporary Anthology, 2001. Contributor of articles to periodicals. Works appear in anthologies. **Address:** En'owkin Centre, Lot 45, Green Mountain Rd., RR Ste. 2, Site-50, Comp. 8, Penticton, BC V2A 6J7, Canada. **Online address:** theytusbooks@vip.net

ARMSTRONG, Jennifer. (Julia Winfield). American (born United States), b. 1961. **Genres:** Novels, Children's Fiction, Young Adult Fiction, Children's Non-fiction, Young Adult Non-fiction, Picture/Board Books. **Career:** Cloverdale Press, assistant editor, 1983-85; freelance writer, 1985-; Smith College, recruiter, 1990-; Literacy Volunteers of Saratoga, board president, 1991-93; Writers Voice, writer-in-residence. **Publications:** Steal Away (novel), 1992; Wan Hu is in the Stars, 1995; King Crow, 1995; Spirit of Endurance, 2000; Becoming Mary Mehan: Two Novels, 2002; Photo by Brady: A Picture of the Civil War, 2005; Once Upon a Banana, 2006; The American Story: 100 True Tales from American History, 2006. PICTURE BOOKS: Hugh Can Do, 1992; Chin Yu Min and the Ginger Cat, 1993; That Terrible Baby, 1994; Little Salt Lick and the Sun King, 1995; The Whittler's Tale, 1995; Shipwreck at the Bottom of the World: The Extraordinary True Story of Shackleton and the Endurance, 1998; Pockets, 1998; The Century for Young People, 1999; Pierre's Dream, 1999; Spirit of Endurance, 2000; Audubon: Painter of Birds in the Wild Frontier, 2003; Magnus at the Fire, 2005; Once Upon a Banana, 2006. MIDDLE GRADE NOVELS: The Puppy Project, 1990; Too Many Pets, 1990; Hillary to the Rescue, 1990; That Champion Chimp, 1990; Theodore Roosevelt: Letters from a Young Coal Miner, 2000; Thomas Jefferson: Letters from a Philadelphia Bookworm, 2000. YOUNG ADULT FICTION: The Dreams of Mairhe Mehan, 1996; Mary Mehan Awake, 1997; The Kindling, 2003; The Keepers of the Flame, 2002; The Kiln, 2003. WILD ROSE INN SERIES: Bridie of the Wild Rose Inn, 1994; Ann of the Wild Rose Inn, 1994; Emily of the Wild Rose Inn, 1994; Laura of the Wild Rose Inn, 1994; Claire of the Wild Rose Inn, 1995; Grace of the Wild Rose Inn, 1995. JUVENILE NOVELS: Black-Eyed Susan: A Novel, 1995; The Snowball, 1996; Sunshine, Moonshine, 1997. JUVENILE NON-FICTION: A Three-Minute Speech: Lincoln's Remarks at Gettysburg, 2003. CHAPTER BOOKS: Patrick Doyle Is Full of Blarney, 1996; Foolish Gretel, 1997; Lili the Brave, 1997. ANTHOLOGIES: Shattered: Stories of Children and War, 2002; What a Song Can Do: 12 Riffs on the Power of Music, 2004. YOUNG ADULT NON-FICTION: In My Hands: Memories of a Holocaust Rescuer, 1999. YOUNG ADULT FICTION AS JULIA WINFIELD: Only Make-Believe, 1987; Private Eyes, 1989; Partners in Crime, 1989; Tug of Hearts, 1989; On Dangerous Ground, 1989. Contributor to periodicals. **Address:** PO Box 335, Saratoga Springs, NY 12866, U.S.A. **Online address:** mail@jennifer-armstrong.com

ARMSTRONG, John. Scottish (born Scotland), b. 1966?. **Genres:** Art/Art History, Philosophy, Biography, Social Sciences. **Career:** University of London, director of aesthetics program; Monash University, director of Center for Public Philosophy; University of Melbourne, senior research fellow in philosophy, associate professor, philosopher-in-residence, senior advisor. Art dealer and writer. **Publications:** Looking at Pictures: An Introduction to the Appreciation of Art, 1996; Move Closer: An Intimate Philosophy of Art, 2000; Conditions of Love: The Philosophy of Intimacy, 2003; Secret Power of Beauty, 2004; Love, Life, Goethe: How to be Happy in an Imperfect World, 2006; Love, Life, Goethe: Lessons of the Imagination from the Great German Poet, 2007; In Search Of Civilization: Remaking A Tarnished Idea, 2009. Contributor to periodicals. **Address:** Department of Philosophy, University of Melbourne, Rm. 117, Old Quad, Parkville, VI 3010, Australia. **Online address:** jarms@unimelb.edu.au

ARMSTRONG, Judith (Mary). Australian (born Australia), b. 1935. **Genres:** Novels, Literary Criticism And History, Biography, Essays, Translations. **Career:** University of Melbourne, lecturer, 1974-79, senior lecturer, 1974-79, reader in Russian, 1980-96. Writer. **Publications:** The Novel of Adultery, 1976; (ed. with R. Slonek) Essays to Honour Nina Christesen: Founder of Russian Studies in Australia, 1977; (trans.) O. Commetant, In the Land of Kangaroos and Goldmines, 1980; The Unsaid Anna Karenina, 1988; The Christesen Romance, 1996; Anya, Countess of Adelaide, 1998; The Experience of Democratization in Eastern Europe: Selected Papers from the Fifth World Congress of Central and East European Studies, Warsaw, 1995, 1999; The Cook and the Maestro, 2001; The French Tutor, 2003; The Case of Perowne v Dorme, 2005; The Maestro's Table, 2006; War & Peace and Sonya, 2011. **Address:** 5/157 Newry St., North Carlton, VI 3054, Australia. **Online address:** j.armstrong@unimelb.edu.au

ARMSTRONG, Karen (Anderson). British (born England), b. 1944. **Genres:** Theology/Religion, Autobiography/Memoirs, Biography, History, Women's Studies And Issues. **Career:** The First Christian, writer and presenter, 1984; Leo Baeck College for the Study of Judaism, teacher. **Publications:** Through the Narrow Gate (autobiography), 1981, rev. ed., 1995; The First Christian: Saint Paul's Impact on Christianity, 1983; Beginning the World (autobiography), 1983; The Gospel According to Woman: Christianity's Creation of the Sex War in the West, 1986; Holy War, 1988 as Holy War: The Crusades and Their Impact on Today's World, 1991; (co-author) Feminist Theology: A Reader, 1990; Muhammad: A Biography of the Prophet, 1992; The End of Silence: Women and the Priesthood, 1993; A History of God: The 4000-Year Quest of Judaism, Christianity and Islam, 1993; Visions of God: Four Medieval Mystics and Their Writings, 1994; Jerusalem: One City, Three Faiths, 1996; In the Beginning: A New Interpretation of Genesis, 1996; The Battle for God, 2000; Islam: A Short History, 2000, rev. ed., 2002; (co-author) Changing Face of God, 2000; Buddha, 2001; (co-author) Once & Future Faith, 2001; The Spiral Staircase: My Climb Out of Darkness, 2004; A Short History of Myth, 2005; Muhammad: A Prophet for Our Time, 2006; The Great Transformation: The Beginning of Our Religious Traditions, 2006; The Bible: A Biography, 2007; Case for God, 2009; Twelve Steps to a Compassionate Life, 2010; (contrib.) ālam-i Islām par mustashriqīn kī fikrī yalghār, 2010. EDITOR: (intro. and ed.) Tongues of Fire: An Anthology of Religious and Poetic Experience, 1985; (trans. and intro.) The English Mystics of the Fourteenth Century, 1991. **Address:** Curtis Brown Agency, 10 Astor Pl., New York, NY 10003, U.S.A.

ARMSTRONG, Kelley L. Canadian (born Canada), b. 1968. **Genres:** Novels, Paranormal, Young Adult Fiction, Criminology/True Crime. **Career:** Computer programmer and writer. **Publications:** Bitten, 2001; Stolen, 2003; Industrial Magic, 2004; Dime Store Magic, 2004; Haunted, 2005; (co-author) Dates from Hell, 2006; Broken, 2006; No Humans Involved, 2007; Exit Strategy, 2007; Living with the Dead, 2008; Personal Demon, 2008; The Summoning, 2008; Men of the Otherworld, 2009; Made to be Broken, 2009; Awakening, 2009; Frostbitten, 2009; Angelic, 2009; Waking the Witch, 2010; Counterfeit Magic, 2010; Tales of the Otherworld, 2010; Reckoning, 2010; Gathering, 2011; Spellbound, 2011; Becoming, 2011; Enthralled: Paranormal Diversions, 2011; Hidden, 2011; The Calling, 2012. Contributor to periodicals. **Address:** The Helen Heller Agency, 253 Eglinton Ave. W, Ste. 202, Toronto, ON M4R 1B1, Canada. **Online address:** kelley@kelleyarmstrong.com

ARMSTRONG, Kevin D. Canadian (born Canada), b. 1973. **Genres:** Novellas/Short Stories, Young Adult Fiction. **Career:** Writer. **Publications:** Night Watch, 2002; A Good Photo: A Novel, forthcoming. Contributor to books and periodicals. **Address:** Denise Bukowski, The Bukowski Agency, 14 Prince Arthur Ave., Ste. 202, Toronto, ON M5R 1A9, Canada. **Online address:** kevarm@telus.net

ARMSTRONG, Lori G. American (born United States), b. 1965. **Genres:**

Mystery/Crime/Suspense. **Career:** Writer. **Publications:** JULIE COLLINS MYSTERY SERIES: Blood Ties, 2005; Hallowed Ground, 2006; Shallow Grave, 2007; Snow Blind, 2008. MERCY GUNDERSON MYSTERY SERIES: Mercy Kill, 2010; No Mercy, 2010. **Address:** Rapid City, SD , U.S.A. **Online address:** info@loriarmstrong.com

ARMSTRONG, Luanne (A.). Canadian (born Canada), b. 1949. **Genres:** Novels, Adult Non-fiction, Autobiography/Memoirs, Children's Fiction. **Career:** Kamloops Women's Resource Centre, executive director, 1988-89; Nicola Valley Institute of Technology, instructor in English, 1989-92; Kootenay Lake Environmental Information Project, research coordinator, 1993; Eco-Sounder (environmental magazine), consultant, 1994; British Columbia Library Trustees Association, publicity and newsletter coordinator, 1998-2000; Berton House, writer-in-residence, 2000; College of the Rockies, teacher of creative writing. **Publications:** Castle Mountain, 1981; From the Interior: A Kootenay Women's Anthology, 1984; Annie, 1995; Bordering, 1995; The Woman in the Garden, 1996; Arly and Spike, 1997; The Colour of Water, 1998; Maggie and Shine, 1999; Jeannie and the Gentle Giants, 2002; The Bone House, 2002; Into the Sun, 2002; Breathing the Mountain, 2003; Blue Valley: An Ecological Memoir, 2007; Pete's Gold, 2008; (ed. with Zoë Landale) Slice Me Some Ttruth: An Anthology of Canadian Creative Non-Fiction, 2011; The Subtle Sea, forthcoming. **Address:** Wolsak and Wynn Publishers Ltd., 102-69 Hughson St. N, Hamilton, ON L8R 1G5, Canada. **Online address:** luannea@telus.net

ARMSTRONG, Mary (Elizabeth) Willems. American (born United States), b. 1957. **Genres:** Film, Art/Art History. **Career:** Friends of the Hardin County Public Libraries, publicity coordinator, 1984-86; WQXE-FM Radio, film critic, 1988-89; writer, 1989-; speech-language pathologist, 1993-. **Publications:** (With R.B. Armstrong) The Movie List Book: A Reference Guide to Film Themes, Settings, and Series, 1990, 2nd ed. as The Movie List Book: Hundreds of Fun and Fascinating Lists of Films by Their Settings and Major Themes, 1994; (with R.B. Armstrong) Encyclopedia of Film Themes, Settings, and Series, 2001. **Address:** Betterway Books, 4700 E Galbraith Rd., Cincinnati, OH 45236-2726, U.S.A.

ARMSTRONG, Richard. American (born United States), b. 1952. **Genres:** Novels, Politics/Government, Humor/Satire, Westerns/Adventure. **Career:** Copywriter and author. **Publications:** (With D. Armstrong) Leaving the Nest: The Complete Guide to Living on Your Own, 1986; The Next Hurrah: The Communications Revolution in American Politics, 1988; God Doesn't Shoot Craps: A Divine Comedy, 2006. Contributor to periodicals. **Address:** Sourcebooks Inc., 1935 Brookdale Rd., Ste. 139, Naperville, IL 60563-2773, U.S.A. **Online address:** richard@goddoesntshootcraps.com

ARMSTRONG, Richard B(yron). American (born United States), b. 1956. **Genres:** Film, Art/Art History, Photography. **Career:** WXII-TV, intern in writing and production, 1977-78; News-Enterprise, film critic, 1982-89; U.S. Army Armor School, instructional developer, 1982-. Writer. **Publications:** WITH M.W. ARMSTRONG: The Movie List Book: A Reference Guide to Film Themes, Settings, and Series, 1990; The Movie List Book: Hundreds of Fun and Fascinating Lists of Films by their Settings and Major Themes, 1994; Encyclopedia of Film Themes, Settings and Series, 2001; (co-author) Rough Guide to Film, 2007. **Address:** McFarland & Company Inc., PO Box 611, Jefferson, NC 28640, U.S.A.

ARMSTRONG, Robert Laurence. American (born United States), b. 1926. **Genres:** Philosophy, Translations, Politics/Government. **Career:** University of Nevada, instructor, 1962-64, assistant professor of philosophy, 1964-67; University of West Florida, Department of Philosophy and Religious Studies, associate professor, 1967-69, chairman, 1967-93, professor, 1969-93, professor emeritus, 1993-. Writer. **Publications:** Metaphysics and British Empiricism, 1970; (trans. with D.J. Herman) T.D. Thao, Investigations into the Origin of Language and Consciousness, 1984. Contributor to journals. **Address:** Department of Philosophy and Religious Studies, University of West Florida, Rm. 228, Bldg. 50, 11000 University Pkwy., Pensacola, FL 32514-5732, U.S.A.

ARMSTRONG, Thomas Leigh. American (born United States), b. 1951. **Genres:** Education. **Career:** Montreal Catholic School, special education instructor, 1976-78; Mt. Diablo School District, special education instructor, 1979-81; Armstrong Creative Training Services, staff, 1981; John F. Kennedy University, instructor, adjunct professor, 1981-87; Rosebridge Graduate School, instructor, 1985-86; California Institute of Transpersonal Psychology, instructor, 1985-86; California Institute of Integral Studies, instructor, 1985-88; Antioch University, instructor, 1988. Writer. **Publications:** Creating Classroom Structure: A Practical Guide for the Special Educator, 1984; In Their Own Way: Discovering and Encouraging Your Child's Personal Learning Style, 1985 as In Their Own Way: Discovering and Encouraging Your Child's Multiple Intelligences, 2000; The Radiant Child, 1985; Awakening Your Child's Natural Genius: Enhancing Curiosity, Creativity, and Learning Ability, 1991; Seven Kinds of Smart: Identifying and Developing Your Many Intelligences, 1993, rev. ed., 1999; Multiple Intelligences in the Classroom, 1994; The Myth of the A.D.D. Child: Fifty Ways to Improve Your Child's Behavior and Attention Span without Drugs, Labels, or Coercion, 1995; Awakening Genius in the Classroom, 1998; ADD/ADHD Alternatives in the Classroom, 1999; The Multiple Intelligences of Reading and Writing: Making the Words Come Alive, 2003; You're Smarter Than You Think: A Kid's Guide to Multiple Intelligences, 2003; The Best Schools: How Human Development Research Should Inform Educational Practice, 2006; The Human Odyssey: Navigating the Twelve Stages of Life, 2007; Neurodiversity: Discovering the Extraordinary Gifts of Autism, ADHD, Dyslexia, and Other Brain Differences, 2010. Contributor to books, periodicals and journals. **Address:** Armstrong Creative Training Services, PO Box 548, Cloverdale, CA 95425-0548, U.S.A. **Online address:** thomas@thomasarmstrong.com

ARNAUD, Claude. French (born France), b. 1955. **Genres:** Novels, Plays/Screenplays, Biography, Autobiography/Memoirs. **Career:** Printer, 1973-74; Cinematographe (cinema review magazine), journalist, 1977-83; freelance writer, 1984-. **Publications:** (With B. Minoret) Les Salons (play), 1985; Chamfort: biographie, suivie desoixante-dix maximes, anecdotes, mots et dialogues inédits, ou jamaisréédités, 1988; Chamfort, A Biography, 1992; Le Cameleon: Roman, 1994; La Chasse aux Tigres (title means: 'The Tiger Hunt'), 1994; Babel, 1994; Le Jeu des Quatre Coins, 1998; (co-author) Contre Offensive, 2002; Jean Cocteau (biography), 2003; Qui dit je en nous: une histoire subjective de l'identité, 2006; (co-author) Paris Portraits, 2007; Qu'as-tu fait de tes frères?: Roman, 2010; (contrib.) Picasso: The Mediterranean Years 1945-1962, 2010; Les chemins creux, 2011. Contributor to periodicals. Works appear in anthologies. **Address:** 13 rue de Verneuil, Paris, 75007, France. **Online address:** cl_arns_@club-internet.fr

ARNESON, Erik. American (born United States), b. 1965. **Genres:** Sports/Fitness. **Career:** Northeast Business Today, columnist; Florida Today, reporter; USA Today, design editor and motor sports reporter, 1991-99; Sfx/Cotter Group, public relations account manager, 1999-2002; CMI/Cotter Group, account manager, 1999-2002; SPEEDChannel, director of public relations, 2002-; Mototbooks/Bull Publishing, author, 2003-08. **Publications:** Darrell Gwynn: At Full Throttle-Triumphs and Tragedies from a Life Lived at Speed, 2003; John Force: The Straight Story of Drag Racing's 300-Mph Superstar, 2006, new ed. 2009; Mickey Thompson: The Fast Life and Tragic Death of a Racing Legend, 2008. **Address:** Bull Publishing Company, PO Box 1377, Boulder, CO 80306, U.S.A. **Online address:** earneson@speedtv.com

ARNETT, Peter (Gregg). American/New Zealander (born New Zealand), b. 1934. **Genres:** Autobiography/Memoirs, History. **Career:** Southland Times, reporter, 1951-54; Standard, reporter, 1955-56; Sun, Sydney, reporter, 1957; Bangkok World, associate editor, 1958-60; Vientiane World, editor, 1960; Associated Press, correspondent, 1961-81; Cable News Network (CNN-TV), international correspondent, 1981-; Daily Mirror, reporter, 2003-; National Geographic Magazine, staff. **Publications:** Exporting the First Amendment to the World, 1992; Live from the Battlefield: From Vietnam to Baghdad: Thirty Five Years in the World's War Zones, 1994; The media and the Gulf War: An Eyewitness Account, 1997. **Address:** Daily Mirror, 1 Canada Sq., Canary Wharf, London, GL E14 5AP, England.

ARNETT, Ronald C. American (born United States), b. 1952. **Genres:** Communications/Media, Ethics, Philosophy. **Career:** St. Cloud State University, assistant professor of speech communication, 1977-84; National Communication Association's Commission, founder, 1984; Marquette University, chair of communication and rhetorical studies, 1984-87; Manchester College, professor of communications, dean and vice president, 1987-93; Journal of Communication and Religion, editor, 1987-91; Duquesne University, Department of Communication and Rhetorical Studies, chair, 1993-, professor of communication; Encyclopedia of Identity, associate editor, 2007-09; Review of Communication, editor, 2008-09, 2010-12. **Publications:** Dwell in Peace:

Applying Nonviolence to Everyday Relationships, 1980; Communication and Community: Implications of Martin Buber's Dialogue, 1986; Dialogic Education: Conversation about Ideas and between Persons, 1992; (contrib.) The Dilemma of Anabaptist Piety: Strengthening or Straining the Bonds of Community?, 1997; (with P. Arneson) Dialogic Civility in a Cynical Age: Community, Hope, and Interpersonal Relationships, 1999; Dialogic Confession: Bonhoeffer's Rhetoric of Responsibility, 2005; (with J.M.H. Fritz and L.M. Bell) Communication Ethics Literacy: Dialogue and Difference, 2009. EDITOR: (with R. Anderson and K.N. Cissna) The Reach of Dialogue: Confirmation, Voice, and Community, 1994; (with J.M. Makau) Communication Ethics in an Age of Diversity, 1997; (with K.G. Roberts) Communication Ethics: Between Cosmopolitanism and Provinciality, 2008. Contributor to journals. **Address:** Department of Communication and Rhetorical Studies, Duquesne University, 340 College Hall, 600 Forbes Ave., Pittsburgh, PA 15282, U.S.A. **Online address:** arnett@duq.edu

ARNEY, James. *See* **RUSSELL, Martin (James).**

ARNOLD, A(lbert) James. American (born United States), b. 1939. **Genres:** Language/Linguistics, Translations, Law. **Career:** Hamilton College, instructor in romance languages, 1961-62; University of Virginia, assistant professor, 1966-, professor of French, through 2008; Professional translator, consultant, 2008-. Writer. **Publications:** Paul Valery and His Critics, 1970; (with J.P. Piriou) Genese et critiqued'une autobiographie: Les Mots de Jean-Paul Sartre, 1973; Modernism and Negritude: The Poetry and Poetics of Aime Cesaire, 1981. EDITOR: Albert Camus, Caligola: Testo inedito del 1941, 1983; Caligula, Version de 1941, 1984; A History of Literature in the Caribbean, 3 vols., 1994-2001; (trans. with C. Eshleman) Solar Throat Slashed by Aime Cesaire, 2011. **Address:** Arnold French Expert, 310 E Beverley St., Staunton, VA 24401, U.S.A. **Online address:** aja@virginia.edu

ARNOLD, Arnold F. British (born England), b. 1929?. **Genres:** Ethics, Crafts, Education, Mathematics/Statistics, Picture/Board Books. **Career:** Workshop School, director, 1949-52; Arnold Arnold Design Inc., president, 1960-66; Manuscript Press Inc., president, 1963-66; Arnold Arnold Collection of Culture of Childhood, collector and owner. Writer. **Publications:** SELF-ILLUSTRATED: How to Play with Your Child, 1955; The Arnold Arnold Book of Toy Soldiers, 1963; Big Book of Tongue Twisters & Double Talk, 1964; The Yes and No Book, 1970; The World Book of Children's Games, 1972. OTHERS: Look and Do Books Series, 1964; Games, 4 vols., 1965; Your Child's Play: How to Help Your Child Reap the Full Benefits of Creative Play, 1968; Violence and Your Child, 1969; Pictures and Stories from Forgotten Children's Books, 1969; Your Child and You, 1970; Career Choices for the '70s, 1971; Teaching Your Child to Learn from Birth to School Age, 1971; (ed.) Antique Paper Dolls, 1915-1920, 1975; Crowell Book of Arts and Crafts for Children, 1975; The World Book of Arts and Crafts for Children, 1976; Winners and Other Losers in War and Peace, 1989; The Corrupted Sciences, 1992. **Address:** c/o Tina Betts, Andrew Mann Ltd., 1 Old Compton St., London, GL W1D 5JA, England.

ARNOLD, David. British (born England), b. 1946. **Genres:** Politics/Government, Biography, Autobiography/Memoirs, History, Essays. **Career:** University of Warwick, professor of Asian and global history, 2006-; University of London, School of Oriental and African Studies, professor in history, 2006-; Flinders University of South Australia, social science research fellow. Writer. **Publications:** The Congress in Tamilnad: Nationalist Politics in South India, 1919-1937, 1977; The Age of Discovery, 1400-1600, 1983, 2nd ed., 2002; Police Power and Colonial Rule, Madras, 1859-1947, 1986; Imperial Medicine and Indigenous Societies, 1988; Famine: Social Crisis and Historical Change, 1988; (ed. with P. Robb) Institutions and Ideologies: A SOAS South Asia Reader, 1993; Colonizing the Body: State Medicine and Epidemic Disease in Nineteenth-Century India, 1993; (ed. with D. Hardiman) Subaltern Studies 8, 1994; (ed. with R. Guha) Nature, Culture, Imperialism: Essays on the Environmental History of South Asia, 1995; (ed.) Warm Climates and Western Medicine: The Emergence of Tropical Medicine, 1500-1900, 1996; The Problem of Nature: Environment, Culture, and European Expansion, 1996; Science, Technology, and Medicine in Colonial India, 2000; Gandhi, 2001; (ed. with C. Shackle) SOAS since the Sixties, 2003; (ed. with S. Blackburn) Telling Lives in India: Biography, Autobiography, and Life History, 2004; The Tropics and the Traveling Gaze: India, Landscape, and Science, 1800-1856, 2005; History of India, 2010. Contributor to periodicals and journals. **Address:** University of Warwick, Rm. H3.11, Humanities Bldg., Coventry, WM CV4 7AL, England. **Online address:** d.arnold@warwick.ac.uk

ARNOLD, Eleanor. American (born United States), b. 1929. **Genres:** Local History/Rural Topics, Women's Studies And Issues, History, Biography, Autobiography/Memoirs, Technology, Engineering, Sociology, Sociology. **Career:** Writer. **Publications:** EDITOR: Rush County Sesquicentennial History, privately printed, 1973; Memories of Hoosier Homemakers, 1983; Feeding Our Families, 1983; Party Lines, Pumps and Privies, 1984; Buggies and Bad Times, 1985; Voices of American Homemakers, 1985; Girlhood Days, 1987; Going to Club, 1988; Living Rich Lives, 1990; (co-author) Rich Lives (play), 1986; (co-author) Hoosier Rich Lives (play), 1988; Index of Memories of Hoosier Homemakers, 1993. **Address:** Rush County Historian, 1744 N County Rd. 450 E, PO Box 48, Rushville, IN 46173, U.S.A.

ARNOLD, Elizabeth. American (born United States), b. 1958. **Genres:** Poetry. **Career:** University of Chicago, faculty, 1985-88; University of Montana, Department of English, visiting assistant professor, 1989-90; University of North Florida, Department of English, adjunct professor, 1992-93; Fine Arts Work Center, poetry fellow, 1997-98; Warren Wilson College, Department of English, Joan Beebe graduate teaching fellow, 1998-99; Radcliffe Center for Advanced Study, Bunting Institute, fellow in poetry, 1999-2000, 2001-; University of Maryland, Department of English, assistant professor, associate professor; Bellagio Study and Conference Center, fellow, 2007. Writer. **Publications:** (Ed.) Insel, 1991; The Reef (poetry), 1999; Civilization (poetry), 2006; Effacement (poetry), 2010. **Address:** Department of English, University of Maryland, 3101 Tawes Hall, College Park, MD 20742, U.S.A. **Online address:** earnold3@umd.edu

ARNOLD, Elizabeth. British (born England), b. 1944?. **Genres:** Novels, Horror. **Career:** Science technician and quality control manager. Writer. **Publications:** The Parsley Parcel, 1995; Gold and Silver Water, 1997; A Riot of Red Ribbons, 1998; Scraggy Flies High, 1998; Spin of the Sunwheel, 1999; Thief in the Garden, 1999; The Triple Trouble Gang, 2000; The Gold Spectre, 2003. Contributor to periodicals. **Address:** David Higham Associates, 5-8 Lower John St., Golden Sq., London, GL W1F 9HA, England.

ARNOLD, Guy. (Stephen Fleming). British (born England), b. 1932. **Genres:** History, Industrial Relations, International Relations/Current Affairs, Politics/Government, Third World, Travel/Exploration. **Career:** Freelance writer, educator and traveler, 1955-58, 1960-61; teacher of English, 1958-60; Ryerson Institute, lecturer in political geography, 1961-63; Government of Northern Rhodesia, adviser on youth problems, 1963-64; Overseas Development Institute, researcher, 1965-66; Africa Bureau, director, 1968-72. Writer. **Publications:** Longhouse and Jungle, 1959; Towards Peace and a Multiracial Commonwealth, 1964; Economic Cooperation in the Commonwealth, 1967; Kenyatta and the Politics of Kenya, 1974; The Last Bunker: A Report on White South Africa Today, 1976; Modern Nigeria, 1977; (with R. Weiss) Strategic Highways of Africa, 1977; (with I. Maclean) Statistical Guide to the Nigerian Market, 1978; Britain's Oil, 1978; Aid in Africa, 1979; Held Fast for England: G.A. Henty, Imperialist Boys' Writer, 1980; The Unions, 1981; Modern Kenya, 1981; Datelines of World History, 1983; Aid and the Third World: The North/South Divide, 1985; Gas, 1985; Coal, 1985; Third World Handbook, 1988; Down the Danube: From the Black Forest to the Black Sea, 1989; Britain since 1945: Choice, Conflict, and Change, 1989; Book of Dates: A Chronology of World History, 1989; Journey round Turkey, 1989; Facts on Water, Wind, and Solar Power, 1990; Facts on Nuclear Energy, 1990; Wars in the Third World since 1945, 1991; (contrib.) The World Trade System, 1991; (contrib.) Revolutionary and Dissident Movements: an International Guide, 3rd ed., 1991; South Africa: Crossing the Rubicon, 1992; Brain Wash, 1992; The End of the Third World, 1993; Political and Economic Encyclopaedia of Africa, 1993; Historical Dictionary of Aid and Development Organizations, 1996; The Maverick State Gaddafi and The New World Order, 1996; World Government by Stealth: The Future of the United Nations, 1997; The Resources of the Third World, 1997; Historical Dictionary of Civil Wars in Africa, 1999, 2nd ed., 2008; Mercenaries: The Scourge of the Third World, 1999; World Strategic Highways, 2000; The New South Africa, 2000; A Guide to African Political & Economic Development, 2001; Historical Dictionary of the Crimean War, 2002; International Drugs Trade, 2004; Historical Dictionary of the Non-Aligned Movement and Third World, 2006; In the Footsteps of George Borrow: A Journey through Spain and Portugal, 2007; New Scramble for Africa, 2009. **Address:** c/o Michael Shaw, Curtis Brown Ltd., 162-168 Regent St., London, GL W1R 5TB, England.

ARNOLD, Jennifer. American (born United States), b. 1963?. **Genres:**

Animals/Pets. **Career:** Canine Assistants, founder and executive director, 1991-. Writer. **Publications:** Through a Dog's Eyes, 2010. **Address:** Canine Assistants, 3160 Francis Rd., Milton, GA 30004, U.S.A. **Online address:** info@canineassistants.org

ARNOLD, Kenneth L. American (born United States), b. 1957. **Genres:** Information Science/Computers, Technology, Engineering, Economics. **Career:** Tulsa Equipment Manufacturing, co-owner and president, 1993-. Writer. **Publications:** The Manager's Guide to ISO 9000, 1994; (with M. Holler) Quality Assurance: Philosophies, Methods and Technologies, 1994; (with M. Holler) Quality Assurance: Methods and Technologies, 1995. **Address:** 4045 N Garnett Rd., Tulsa, OK 74116-5206, U.S.A.

ARNOLD, Oliver. American (born United States), b. 1962?. **Genres:** History, Art/Art History, Young Adult Fiction. **Career:** Princeton University, associate professor of English, through 2010; University of California, Department of English, associate professor, 2010-. Writer. **Publications:** The Third Citizen: Shakespeare's Theater and the Early Modern House of Commons, 2007; (ed.) Julius Caesar, 2010. Contributor to books, periodicals and journals. **Address:** Department of English, University of California, 410 Wheeler Hall, Berkeley, CA 94720-1030, U.S.A. **Online address:** oarnold@berkeley.edu

ARNOLD, Peter. American (born United States), b. 1943. **Genres:** Criminology/True Crime, How-to Books, Medicine/Health, Travel/Exploration, Novellas/Short Stories, Plays/Screenplays, Advertising/Public Relations, Ghost Writer, Ghost Writer. **Career:** Universal Studios, writer and producer, 1967-68; freelance film writer, 1968-73; freelance nonfiction book writer, 1969-77; California Institute of Technology, Development Office, head of writing staff, 1973-74; Occidental College, director of special projects, 1974-76; Hugh O'Brian Youth Foundation, director, 1976-77; Peter Arnold Associates, president, 1977, chief executive officer, 1987-2010. Communications consultant, 2010-. **Publications:** (Ed. with J. Lewis) The Total Filmmaker, 1971; Burgler-Proof Your Home and Car, 1971; Off the Beaten Track in Copenhagen: A Nash Travel Guide, 1972; Lady Beware (crime prevention), 1974; Check List for Emergencies (health), 1974; Crime and Youth: A Practical Guide to Crime Prevention, 1976; How to Protect Your Child against Crime, 1977; (with E.L. Pendagast, Jr.) Emergency Handbook: A First-Aid Manual for Home and Travel, 1980; (with R. Germann) Bernard Haldane Associates Job and Career Building, 1980; (with R. Germann and D. Blumenson) Working and Liking It, 1984; (with E.J. Wallach) Job Search Companion: The Organizer for Job Seekers, 1984; (with B.A. Percelay) Packaging Your House for Profit, 1985. **Address:** 15850 N Thompson Peak Pkwy., Ste. 2031, Scottsdale, AZ 85260, U.S.A. **Online address:** parnold@parnold.com

ARNOLD, Tedd. American (born United States), b. 1949. **Genres:** Children's Fiction, Translations, Illustrations. **Career:** Cycles USA, advertising art director, 1981-84; Workman Publishing, book designer, 1984-85; freelance author and illustrator, 1986-. **Publications:** FOR CHILDREN: My First Drawing Book, 1986; No Jumping on the Bed, 1987 trans. as No se salta en la cama!, 1997; My First Play House, 1987; My First Play Town, 1987; Ollie Forgot, 1988; Mother Goose's Words of Wit and Wisdom: A Book of Months, 1990; Cross-Stitch Patterns for Mother Goose's Words of Wit and Wisdom: Samplers to Stitch, 1990; The Signmaker's Assistant, 1992; The Simple People, 1992; Green Wilma, 1993; No More Water in the Tub, 1995; Five Ugly Monsters, 1995; Bialosky's Bedside Books, 1996; Bialosky's Big Mess: An Alphabet Book, 1996; Bialosky's Bedtime: An Opposites Book, 1996; Bialosky's Bumblebees: A Counting Book, 1996; Bialosky's House: A Color Book, 1996; Parts, 1997; Huggly Gets Dressed, 1997; Huggly Takes a Bath, 1998; Huggly and the Toy Monster, 1998; Huggly's Pizza, 2000; Huggly Goes to School, 2000; More Parts, 2001; Huggly's Big Mess, 2001; Huggly's Christmas, 2001; Huggly's Snow Day, 2002; Huggly's Trip to the Beach, 2002; Huggly's Halloween, 2002; Huggly's Thanksgiving Parade, 2002; Huggly's Valentines, 2003; Huggly Goes Camping, 2003; Even More Parts: Idioms from Head to Toe, 2004; Catalina Magdalena Hoopensteiner Wallendiner Hogan Logan Bogan was her Name, 2004; Hi! Fly Guy, 2005; Super Fly Guy, 2006; Shoo, Fly Guy!, 2006; Rat Life, 2007; There was an Old Lady Who Swallowed Fly Guy, 2007; The Twin Princes, 2007; Fly High, Fly Guy!, 2008; Hooray for Fly Guy!, 2008; I Spy Fly Guy, 2009; Green Wilma, Frog in Space, 2009; Fly Guy Meets Fly Girl, 2010; Fly Guy and Buzz Boy, 2010; Buzz Boy and Fly Guy, 2010; Fly Guy vs. the Fly Swatter, 2011. OTHERS: Manners Mash-up: A Goofy Guide to Good Behavior, 2010; Detective Blue, 2011; There's a Fly Guy in My Soup, 2012; Ride, Fly Guy, Ride!, 2012. Illustrator of books by others. **Address:** Dial Books for Young Readers, 375 Hudson St., New York, NY 10014, U.S.A.

ARNOTT, Peter. Scottish (born Scotland), b. 1962. **Genres:** Plays/Screenplays, Theatre, Art/Art History, Music. **Career:** Writer, 1983-. **Publications:** Century's End, 1990; Salvation, 1990; (trans.) B. Brecht, Mr. Puntila and His Man Matti, 1997; Cyprus, 2007; The Breathing House, 2007; Losing Alec, 2007. Contributor to periodicals. **Address:** Tron Theatre Ltd., 63 Trongate, Glasgow, G1 5HB, Scotland. **Online address:** pfarnott@aol.com

ARNOUT, Susan. *See* **SMITH, Susan Arnout.**

ARNZEN, Michael A. American (born United States), b. 1967. **Genres:** Novels, Novellas/Short Stories, Horror, Film, Poetry, Young Adult Fiction, Children's Fiction. **Career:** Freelance writer, 1987-; University of Idaho, instructional assistant, 1992-94; University of Oregon, graduate teaching fellow, 1994-99; Paradoxa: Studies in World Literary Genres, editorial board, 1998-; Seton Hill University, associate professor, 1999-, full professor of English, tenured professor of English, Humanities Division, chair, 2009-. **Publications:** POETRY: Chew and Other Ruminations, 1991; Writhing in Darkness, vol. I-II, 1997; Paratabloids, 1999; Dying, 2003; Gorelets: Unpleasant Poems, 2003; Freakcidents, 2004; Rigormarole: Zombie Poems, 2005. OTHERS: Anthology of Psychological Horror in Verse, 1992; Grave Markings (novel), 1994; (ed.) The Return of the Uncanny, 1997; (ed.) Psychos: An (ed.) Pitchblende, 2004; Play Dead, 2005; Licker, 2006; The Bitchfight, 2008; Skull Fragments, 2009; The Popular Uncanny, 2009; (ed. with H.R. Miller) Many Genres, One Craft: Lessons in Writing Popular Fiction, 2011. SHORT STORIES: Needles and Sins, 1993; Fluid Mosaic, 2001; 100 Jolts, 2004; Proverbs for Monsters, 2007. Contributor to journals and periodicals. **Address:** Department of English, Seton Hill University, 1 Seton Hill Dr., PO Box 991, Greensburg, PA 15601, U.S.A. **Online address:** arnzen@gorelets.com

AROM, Simha. French/Israeli/German (born Germany), b. 1930. **Genres:** Anthropology/Ethnology, Cultural/Ethnic Topics, Music. **Career:** National Museum Barthelemy Boganda, founder and director, 1963-67; Centre National de la Recherche Scientifique, ethnomusicologist and researcher, 1967-, director of research, 1978-, now director of research emeritus; Hebrew University of Jerusalem, Jewish Music Research Centre, musicologist; Israel Broadcasting Corp., Music Division, head, 1980-82. Writer. **Publications:** Conte et chantefables ngbaka-ma'bo: Republique Centrafricaine, 1970; (with J.M.C. Thomas) Les mimbo: genies du piegeage et le monde surnaturel desNgbaka-Ma'bo: Republique Centrafricaine, 1975; Polyphonies et Polyrythmies instrumentales d'Afrique Centrale: Structure et methodologie, 2 vols., 1985; La boîte à outils d'un ethnomusicologue, 2007; (with F. Alvarez-Pereyre) Précis d'ethnomusicologie, 2007; La fanfare de Bangui, 2009; (co-ed.) Parole et musique, 2009. **Address:** 12 rue Ernest Psichari, Paris, 75007, France. **Online address:** arom@vjf.cnrs.fr

ARON, Michael. American (born United States), b. 1946. **Genres:** Politics/Government, Biography, Adult Non-fiction, Social Sciences. **Career:** Seattle Magazine, journalist, 1970-; West Magazine, staff; Harper's, associate editor, 1975-76; Rolling Stone, associate editor, 1977; New Jersey Monthly, editor, 1978-82; New Jersey Network, senior political correspondent, 1982-, interim director of NJN News and Public Affairs, 2008-; New Jersey Reporter, media columnist, 1991. **Publications:** Governor's Race: A TV Reporter's Chronicle of the 1993 Florio/Whitman Campaign, 1994. **Address:** NJN News, New Jersey Network, 25 S Stockton St., PO Box 777, Trenton, NJ 08608, U.S.A.

ARONIE, Nancy S(lonim). American (born United States), b. 1941?. **Genres:** Writing/Journalism, Medicine/Health. **Career:** Chilmark Writing Workshop, founder, 1986-; National Public Radio, commentator; Trinity College, writer-in-residence; Gardner Museum, artist-in-residence. **Publications:** Writing from the Heart: Tapping the Power of Your Inner Voice, 1998. Contributor of essays to magazines. **Address:** 1 W Meadow, Chilmark, MA 02535, U.S.A.

ARONOFF, Craig E(llis). American (born United States), b. 1951. **Genres:** Business/Trade/Industry, Human Relations/Parenting. **Career:** Georgia State University, assistant professor, 1975-79, associate professor of management, 1979-83; Kennesaw State University, professor of management and Dinos distinguished professor of private enterprise, 1983-2005, department head, 1984-86, professor emeritus, 2005-, Cox Family Enterprise Center, director, founder; Business Owner Resources, managing partner, 1989-; Southeastern Legal Foundation, board director, 1990-; Family Business Advisor, executive editor, 1991-; Family Business Consulting Group Inc., principal and co-founder, 1994-; Family Business Institute Inc., partner; Family Business Communications Inc., president; Nation's Business, columnist and contributing editor. Consultant. **Publications:** (With O.W. Baskin) Interpersonal Communication in Organizations, 1980; (co-author) Getting Your Message Across: A Practical Guide to Business Communication, 1981; (with O.W. Baskin) Public Relations: The Profession and the Practice, 1983, 3rd ed., 1992, (with D. Lattimore) 4th ed., 1997; (with M.B. Cauley) A Century of Service: A History of Cobb and Its Bank, 1987; (co-author) The Family Business Leadership Series, 15 vols., 1991; (with J. Pearl) Winning: The NSI Story, 1997; (with J.L. Ward) Family Business Ownership: How to be an Effective Shareholder, 2001; (co-author) Making Sibling Teams Work, 2011; (with F.M. de Visscher and J.L. Ward) Financing Transitions, 2nd ed., 2011; (with J.L. Ward) Family Business Governance, 2011; (with J.L. Ward) How to Choose & Use Advisors, 2011; (with J.L. Ward and J.H. Astrachan) Developing Family Business Policies, 2011; (with J.L. Ward) Preparing Your Family Business for Strategic Change, 2011; (with J.L. Ward) Family Business Values, 2011; (with O.W. Baskin) Effective Leadership in the Family Business, 2011; (with J.L. Ward) Family Meetings, 2011; (with J.L. Ward) Preparing Successors for Leadership, 2011; (with J.L. Ward and M. Whiteside) How Families Work Together, 2011; (with J.L. Ward) More than Family, 2011; (with J.L. Ward and S.L. McClure) Family Business Compensation, 2011; (with J.L. Ward and S.L. McClure) Family Business Succession; Make Change your Family Business Tradition, 2011; (with J.L. Ward) From Siblings to Cousins, 2011; Letting Go, 2011; (with J.L. Ward) How to Choose and use Advisors, 2011. EDITOR: Business and the Media, 1979; (with J.L. Ward) The Future of Private Enterprise, 3 vols., 1984-86; (with J. Ward) Initial Public Offerings Annual: 1989, 1990; (with J.L. Ward) Family Business Sourcebook, 1991, (with J. Astrachon) 3rd ed., 2003; (with J.L. Ward) Contemporary Entrepreneurs, 1992. **Address:** Cox Family Enterprise Center, Coles College of Business, Kennesaw State University, 1000 Chastain Rd., Ste. 0408, Kennesaw, GA 30144-5591, U.S.A.

ARONOWITZ, Stanley. American (born United States), b. 1933. **Genres:** Cultural/Ethnic Topics, Education, History, Politics/Government. **Career:** Driver-Harris Corp., staff, 1955-60; Amalgamated Clothing Workers, field director, 1960-64; Organizing of Northeast Region, Oil, Chemical and Atomic Workers, director, 1964-67; Mobilization for Youth Organization, associate director, 1968-70; Park East High School, director, 1970-72; City University of New York, College of Staten Island, associate professor, 1972-76, Youth and Community Studies, director, 1973-76, City College, visiting professor, 1982-83, Graduate Center, professor of sociology, 1983-, distinguished professor of sociology and urban education, 1983-, Center for Worker Education, faculty, 1983-87, Center for the Study of Culture, Technology and Work, director, 1987-, Faculty Committee New Visions in Undergraduate Education, chair, 1993-; University of California, visiting professor, 1976-77, School of Social Sciences, Graduate Studies, director, 1977-79, professor of social science and comparative literature, 1977-82; Columbia University, visiting professor, 1979-81; Metropolitan College of New York, consultant, 2001-04; Social Text, founding editor. **Publications:** Honor America: The Nature of Fascism, Historic Struggles Against It, and a Strategy for Today, 1971; False Promises: The Shaping of American Working Class Consciousness, 1973; Food, Shelter, and the American Dream, 1974; The Crisis in Historical Materialism: Class, Politics, and Culture in Marxist Theory, 1981; Working Class Hero: Evolution of the American Labor Movement, 1983; Science as Power, 1989; Post Modern Education, 1991; Politics of Identity, 1992; Roll over Beethoven, 1993; (with W. DiFazio) The Jobless Future, 1994, 2nd ed., 2010; Death and Rebirth of American Radicalism, 1996; From the Ashes of the Old, 1998; The Knowledge Factory, 2000; The Last Good Job in America: Work and Education in the New Global Technoculture, 2001; How Class Works: Power and Social Movement, 2003; (contrib.) Debating Empire, 2003; Just around the Corner: The Paradox of the Jobless Recovery, 2005; Left Turn: Forging a New Political Future, 2006; Against Schooling: Toward an Education that Matters, 2008. EDITOR: The Sixties without Apology: An Anthology, 1984; (co-ed.) Technoscience and Cyberculture, 1996; (ed. with J. Cutler) Post-work: The Wages of Cybernation, 1998; (co-ed.) Bangladesh: A Land of Beautiful Traditions & Culture, 2002; (with P. Bratsis) Paradigm Lost: State Theory Reconsidered, 2002; (with H. Gautney) Implicating Empire: Globalization and Resistance in the 21st Century World Order, 2003; C. Wright Mills, 2004. **Address:** Graduate Center, City University of New York, 365 5th Ave., New York, NY 10016-4309, U.S.A. **Online address:** saronowitz@igc.org

ARONSON, I(rwin) Michael. Israeli/American (born United States), b. 1942. **Genres:** History, Area Studies, Social Sciences. **Career:** Kendall College, instructor, 1968; Roosevelt University, instructor, 1968-70; Lawrence University of Wisconsin, instructor, 1970-71; Haifa University, lecturer, 1972-80; State of Israel, researcher and translator for Ministry of Foreign Affairs, 1981-. Writer and translator. **Publications:** Troubled Waters: The Origins of the 1881 Anti-Jewish Pogroms in Russia, 1990. Works appear in anthologies. Contributor to journals. **Address:** Rechov Borochov 23A, Raanana, 43434, Israel.

ARONSON, Sarah. American (born United States) **Genres:** Novels. **Career:** Jewish Lights Publishing, sales representative. Author. **Publications:** The Princess and the Pea: A Pop-Up Book, 2002; Head Case, 2007. **Address:** Barry Goldblatt Literary, 320 7th Ave., Ste. 266, Brooklyn, NY 11215, U.S.A. **Online address:** saraharonson@verizon.net

ARRINGTON, Stephen L(ee). American (born United States), b. 1948. **Genres:** Recreation, Autobiography/Memoirs, Westerns/Adventure. **Career:** College of Oceaneering, air diving supervisor, 1985-87; Cousteau Society, expedition leader and chief diver, 1987-93; motivational and drug education speaker and writer, 1993-; American Red Cross, instructor and cardiopulmonary resuscitation; Dream Machine Foundation, founder, president, chief executive officer. Educator. **Publications:** Journey into Darkness: Nowhere to Land (memoir), 1992; Expedition and Diving Operations Handbook, 1994; High on Adventure: Stories of Good, Clean, Spine-Tingling Fun, 1995; High on Adventure II: Dreams Becoming Reality, 1996; High on Adventure III: Building the Adventure Machine, 1997; Extreme, 2007. **Address:** Dream Machine Foundation, PO Box 3234, Paradise, CA 95967, U.S.A. **Online address:** steve@drugsbite.com

ARROW, Kenneth (Joseph). American (born United States), b. 1921. **Genres:** Economics, Mathematics/Statistics, Essays. **Career:** University of Chicago, Cowles Commission for Research in Economics, research associate, 1947-49, assistant professor of economics, 1948-49; Rand Corp., consultant, 1948-; Stanford University, acting assistant professor of economics and statistics, 1949-50, associate professor, 1950-53, professor of economics, statistics and operations research, 1953-68, Department of Economics, executive head, 1953-56, Joan Kenney professor of economics and professor of operations research, 1979-91, emeritus professor, 1991-; Center for Advanced Study in the Behavioral Sciences, fellow, 1956-57; U.S. Government, Council of Economic Advisors, economist, 1962; Churchill College, fellow, 1963, 1964, 1970, 1973; Harvard University, professor of economics, 1968-74, James Bryant Conant University professor, 1974-79. Economist. **Publications:** Social Choice and Individual Values, 1951, 2nd ed., 1963; (with L. Hurwicz and H. Uzawa) Studies in Linear and Non-Linear Programming, 1958; (with S. Karlin and H. Scarf) Studies in the Mathematical Theory of Inventory and Production, 1958; (with W.M. Capron) Dynamic Shortages and Price Rises, 1958; (with M. Hoffenberg) A Time Series Analysis of Interindustry Demands, 1959; (with A.C. Enthoven) Quasi-Concave Programming, 1959; Economic Welfare and the Allocation of Resources for Invention, 1960; The Economic Implications of Learning by Doing, 1962; (with M. Nerlove) Optimal Advertising Policy under Dynamic Conditions, 1962; Uncertainty and the Welfare Economics of Medical Care, 1963; Control in Large Organizations, 1963; Optimal Capital Policy with Irreversible Investment, 1968; (with D. Levhari) Uniqueness of the Internal Rate of Return with Variable Life of Investment, 1969; Essays in the Theory of Risk-Bearing, 1971; (with F.H. Hahn) General Competitive Analysis, 1971; Models of Job Discrimination, 1972; Gifts and Exchanges, 1972; Coinsurance Rates, 1973; The Limits of Organization, 1974; Two Notes on Inferring Long Run Behavior from Social Experiments, 1975; (co-author) Energy, the Next 20 Years, 1979; (with J.P. Kalt) Petroleum Price Regulation: Should We Decontrol?, 1979; (with S. Chang) Optimal Pricing, Use, and Exploration of Uncertain Resource Stocks, 1980; Optimal and Voluntary Income Redistribution, 1981; (co-author) On Partitioning a Sample with Binary-Type Questions in Lieu of Collecting Observations, 1981; Collected Papers, 6 vols., 1983-85; Innovation in Large and Small Firms, 1983; General Equilibrium, 1983; Social Choice and Justice, 1983; Economics of Information, 1984; Individual Choice Under Certainty and Uncertainty, 1984; Applied Economics, 1985; Production and Capital, 1985; Uncertainty, Information, and Communication, 1986; Social Choice and Public Decision Making, 1986; Equilibrium Analysis, 1986; (with H. Raynaud) Social Choice and Multi-criterion Decision-Making, 1986; The Demand for Information and the Distribution of Income, 1987; Informational Equivalence of Signals, 1992; Information and the Organization of Industry, 1994; (co-author) Benefit-cost Analysis in Environmental, Health, and Safety

Regulation: A Statement of Principles, 1996; Innovation and Increasing Returns to Scale, 1998; Discounting, Morality, and Gaming, 1999; Markets, Information, and Uncertainty: Essays in Economic Theory in Honor of Kenneth J. Arrow, 1999; Economic Transitions: Speed and Scope, 2000; Uncertainty and Discounting in Models of Economic Growth, 2009; Intergenerational Resource Transfers with Random Offspring Numbers, 2009; Conspicuous Consumption and Inconspicuous Leisure, 2009. EDITOR: (with L. Hurwicz) Studies in Resource Allocation Processes, 1977; (with C.C. Abt and S.J. Fitzsimmons) Applied Research for Social Policy: The United States and the Federal Republic of Germany, 1979; (with M.D. Intriligator) Handbook of Mathematical Economics, 1981; (with S. Honkapohja) Frontiers of Economics, 1985; The Balance between Industry and Agriculture in Economic Development: Proceedings of the Eighth World Congress of the International Economic Association, Delhi, India, 1986, vol. I: Basic Issues, 1988; (with M.J. Boskin) The Economics of Public Debt: Proceedings of a Conference Held by the International Economic Association at Stanford, California, 1988; Barriers to Conflict Resolution, 1995; Education in a Research University, 1996; Social Choice Re-examined: Proceedings of the I.E.A. Conference Held at Schloss Hernstein, Berndorf, Near Vienna, Austria, 1996; (co-ed.) The Rational Foundations of Economic Behaviour: Proceedings of the IEA Conference held in Turin, Italy, 1996; Increasing Returns and Economic Analysis, 1997; (with S. Bowles and S. Durlauf) Meritocracy and Economic Inequality, 2000; (with A.K. Sen and K. Suzumura) Handbook of Social Choice and Welfare, 2002; (with H. Gelband and C. Panosian) Saving Lives, Buying Time: Economics of Malaria Drugs in an Age of Resistance, 2004. Contributor of articles to journals. **Address:** Department of Economics, Stanford University, Landau 342, 579 Serra Mall, Stanford, CA 94305-6072, U.S.A. **Online address:** arrow@stanford.edu

ARRUDA, Marliss Melton. *See* **MELTON, Marliss.**

ARRUDA, Suzanne M. (Suzanne Middendorf Arruda). American (born United States), b. 1954?. **Genres:** Animals/Pets, Theology/Religion. **Career:** Kansas State University, lab technician, research assistant, biology instructor; Kansas Department of Wildlife and Parks, museum worker; Pittsburg State University, biology instructor, faculty, 2001, 2003-06; Joplin Writer's Guild, president and secretary. Writer. **Publications:** A Stocking for Jesus, 2005; Mark of the Lion, 2006; Stalking Ivory, 2007; Serpent's Daughter, 2008; Leopard's Prey, 2009; Treasure of the Golden Cheetah, 2009; Crocodile's Last Embrace, 2010. AS SUZANNE MIDDENDORF ARRUDA: From Kansas to Cannibals: The Story of Osa Johnson, 2001; Freedom's Martyr: The Story of Jose Rizal, 2003; The Girl He Left Behind: The Life and Times of Libbie Custer, 2004. Contributor to periodicals. **Address:** c/o Author Mail, Avisson Press Inc., 3007 Taliaferro Rd., Greensboro, NC 27408-2628, U.S.A. **Online address:** sarruda@pittstate.edu

ARRUDA, Suzanne Middendorf. *See* **ARRUDA, Suzanne M.**

ARSENAULT, Raymond. American (born United States), b. 1948. **Genres:** Politics/Government, Social Sciences. **Career:** University of South Florida, faculty member, 1980-, John Hope Franklin professor of southern history & co-director of the Florida Studies Program; University of Minnesota, Fulbright Commission's Summer Institute on American Studies, co-director, 1980-87; Universite d'Angers, Fulbright Lecturer, 1984-85; University of Minnesota, faculty; Brandeis University, faculty; National Park Service, consultant; National Civil Rights Museum, consultant; Rosa Parks Museum, consultant; United States Information Agency, consultant. Writer. **Publications:** The Wild Ass of the Ozarks: Jeff Davis and the Social Bases of Southern Politics, 1984; St. Petersburg and the Florida Dream, 1888-1950, 1988; (ed.) Crucible of Liberty: 200 Years of the Bill of Rights, 1991; (ed. with R.P. Clark and intro.) The Changing South of Gene Patterson: Journalism and Civil Rights, 1960-1968, 2002; (ed. with J.E. Davis) Paradise Lost? The Environmental History of Florida, 2005; Freedom Riders: 1961 and the Struggle for Racial Justice, 2006. Contributor to periodicals. **Address:** College of Arts & Sciences, Florida Studies Program, University of South Florida, SNL 200, 140 7th Ave. S, St. Petersburg, FL 33701, U.S.A. **Online address:** rarsenau@stpt.usf.edu

ARTELL, Mike. American (born United States), b. 1948. **Genres:** Children's Fiction, Children's Non-fiction, How-to Books, Trivia/Facts, Cartoons, Humor/Satire, Picture/Board Books, Young Adult Non-fiction, Young Adult Non-fiction. **Career:** Ford Motor Credit, automobile collection and repossession agent, 1971-73; Panatec, sales and marketing manager, 1976-79; Tano, sales and marketing manager, 1979-82; Digicourse, sales and marketing manager, 1983-85; Teknowledge, sales manager, 1985-87; WWL-TV, cartooning show host, 1989-91. Writer, illustrator and musician. **Publications:** The Wackiest Ecology Riddles on Earth, 1992; (with B. Armstrong) Fun with Expressions, 1992; Big Long Animal Song, 1992; The Wackiest Nature Riddles on Earth, 1992; How to Create Picture Books, 1993; Who Said Moo?, 1994; (with P. Schiller) The Earth and Me, 1994; Hidden Pictures, 1994; Weather Whys: Questions, Facts, and Riddles about Weather, 1995, 2nd ed., 2005; Writing Start-Ups, 1996; Write Fast-Write Funny, 1996; Legs: A Who's-under-the-Flap Book, 1996; (with P. Schiller) Parties Kids Love, 1996; (with P. Schiller) Rainy Day Recess, 1996; Classroom Cartooning for the Artistically Challenged, 1996; Starry Skies, 1997; Awesome Alphabets, 1999; (with J. Rosenbloom) The Little Giant Book of Tongue Twisters, 1999; Backyard Bloodsuckers, 2000; Petite Rouge: A Cajun Red Riding Hood, 2001; I See Some Squares, 2001; Where Are the Triangles?, 2001; My Pet, 2001; I See Circles, 2001; When I Say, 2001; Cartooning for Kids, 2001; Oodles of Doodles, 2003; Three Little Cajun Pigs, 2003; (with J. Rosenbloom) Zany Tongue-twisters, 2003; 2001 Knock-knocks & Tongue Twisters, 2004; Reaching the Reluctant Writer: Fast, Fun, Informational Writing Ideas, 2005; Ten-second Tongue Twisters, 2006; Laugh Your Head Off: Great Jokes and Giggles, 2006; Funny Cartooning for Kids, 2006; Jacques and De Beanstalk, 2010, Okey-Dokey Ding-a-Ling, 2010; Peyton Manning, 2012; Drew Brees, 2012. Illustrator of books by others. **Address:** PO Box 3997, Covington, LA 70434, U.S.A. **Online address:** mike@mikeartell.com

ARTER, David. Scottish/American (born United States) **Genres:** Politics/Government, Social Commentary, Young Adult Non-fiction. **Career:** University of Stockholm, visiting research fellow, 1981; Economics and Social Research Council, evaluator in politics, 1994; University of Helsinki, professor of politics; University of Jyväskylä, lecturer; Leeds Metropolitan University, professor of European integration; University of Aberdeen, School of Social Science, Department of Politics and International Relations, professor of Nordic politics, chair of politics, now professor emeritus. Writer. **Publications:** On the Emergence of a Strong Peasant Party in Finland: A Classification of Leaders and Conceptual Analysis of Support for the Nascent Agrarian Party, 1977; Bumpkin against Bigwig: The Emergence of a Green Movement in Finnish Politics, 1978; (with N. Elder and A.H. Thomas) The Consensual Democracies?: The Government and Politics of the Scandinavian States, 1982, rev. ed., 1988; The Nordic Parliaments: A Comparative Analysis, 1984; Politics and Policy-Making in Finland, 1987; One 'Ting' Too Many: The Shift to Unicameralism in Denmark, 1991; The Politics of European Integration in the Twentieth Century, 1993; Parties and Democracy in the Post-Soviet Republics: The Case of Estonia, 1996; Scandinavian Politics Today, 1999; (ed.) From Farmyard to City Square?: The Electoral Adaptation of the Nordic Agrarian Parties, 2001; The Scottish Parliament: A Scandinavian-Style Assembly?, 2004; Democracy in Scandinavia: Consensual, Majoritarian or Mixed?, 2006; (ed.) Comparing and Classifying Legislatures, 2007. Contributor to books and periodicals. **Address:** Department of Politics and International Relations, School of Social Science, University of Aberdeen, Edward Wright Bldg., Dunbar St., Aberdeen, BR AB24 3QY, Scotland. **Online address:** d.arter@abdn.ac.uk

ARTERBURN, Stephen. (Stephen Forrest Arterburn). American (born United States), b. 1953. **Genres:** How-to Books, Human Relations/Parenting, Autobiography/Memoirs, Theology/Religion. **Career:** Comprehensive Care Corp., nurse's aide, vice president of operations, 1977-86; Westworld Community Healthcare, chair, 1986-88; Minirth Meier New Life Clinics (now New Life Clinics), co-founder and chair, 1988-; New Life Ministries, co-founder and chairman; New Life Live! (daily national radio program), co-host; Heartland Church, teaching pastor. Writer. **Publications:** (With T. Timmons) Hooked on Life: From Stuck to Starting Over, 1985; Growing Up Addicted, 1987; (with J. Arterburn) How Will I Tell My Mother?, 1988; (with D. Stoop) When Someone You Love is Someone You Hate, 1988; (with J. Burns) Drug-Proof Your Kids, 1989; (with T. Timmons) Hooked on Life: How to Totally Recover from Addictions & Codependency, 1989; (with J. Felton) Toxic Faith: Understanding and Overcoming Religious Addiction, 1991 as Faith That Hurts, Faith That Heals, 1992; Addicted to Love, 1991; (with C. Dreizler) Fifty-Two Simple Ways to Say I Love You, 1991; (ed. with D. Stoop) The Life Recovery Bible, 1992; (with D. Stoop) The Twelve-Step Life Recovery Devotional, 1992; (with M. Ehemann and V. Lamphear) Gentle Eating, 1993; Hand-Me-Down Genes and Second-Hand Emotions, 1993; (with J. Burns) When Love is Not Enough, 1993; Winning at Work without Losing at Love, 1994; (comp.) Power Book: Spiritual Insights for Achieving

Excellence: A Daily Companion, 1996; (with P. Meier and F. Minirith) Safe Places: Finding Security in the Passages of Your Life, 1997; Surprised by God: Experiencing Grace from the God of Second Chances, 1997; (with D. Stoop) Seven Keys to Spiritual Renewal, 1998; 5 Minute New Testament: With Tools for Daily Reflection, 1999; (with J. Felton) More Jesus, Less Religion: Moving from Rules to Relationship, 2000; (with F. Stoeker and M. Yorkey) Every Man's Battle: Winning the War on Sexual Temptation: One Victory at a Time, 2000; (with M.J. Rinck) Avoiding Mr. Wrong (and What to Do if You Didn't): Ten Men Who Will Ruin Your Life, 2000; (with F. Minirth and P. Meier) The Spiritual Life Guide: Biblically Based, Medically Sound Solutions to All of Life's Challenges and Passages-Physical, Emotional, Spiritual, 2001; (with M.J. Rinck) Finding Mr. Right (And How To Know When You Have), 2001; Flashpoints, 2001; (with F. Stoeker and M. Yorkey) Every Woman's Desire: Every Man's Guide to Winning the Heart of a Woman, 2001; (with D. Stoop) 130 Questions Children Ask about War and Terrorists, 2002; (with F. Stoeker and M. Yorkey) Every Young Man's Battle: Strategies for Victory in the Real World of Sexual Temptation, 2002; (with P. Meier and R.L. Wise) Fear Less for Life: Break Free to Living with Hope and Confidence, 2002; (with A. Hunt) Flashpoints: Igniting the Hidden Passions of Your Soul, 2002; God of Second Chances: Experiencing His Grace for the Rest of Your Life, 2002; (with F. Stoeker and M. Yorkey) Every Woman's Desire Workbook: How To Win Your Wife's Heart-Again And Forever: A Guide For Personal or Group Study, 2003; (with F. Stoeker and M. Yorkey) Preparing Your Son for Every Man's Battle: Honest Conversations about Sexual Integrity, 2003; (with F. Stoeker and M. Yorkey) Every Young Man's Battle Guide, 2003; (with F. Stoeker and M. Yorkey) Every Young Man's Battle Workbook: Practical Help in the Fight for Sexual Purity: A Guide For Personal or Group Study, 2003; (with F. Stoeker and M. Yorkey) Battle: Honest Conversations About Sexual Integrity, 2003; (with F. Stoeker and M. Yorkey) Every Man's Battle Guide: Weapons for the War against Sexual Temptation, 2003; (with J. Florea) Young Believer 365: Devotions To Help You Stand Strong 24/7, 2003; (with C. Wilde and G. Wilde) Young Believer Case Files, 2003; (with K. Luck and M. Yorkey) Every Man, God's Man Workbook: Pursuing Courageous Faith and Daily Integrity, 2003; (co-author) Being God's Man-As A Satisfied Single: Real Men, Real Life, Powerful Truth, 2003; (with K. Luck and T. Wendorff) Being God's Man-In the Face of Temptation: Real Men, Real Life, Powerful Truth, 2003; (with K. Luck and T. Wendorff) Being God's Man-In Tough Times: Real Men, Real Life, Powerful Truth, 2003; (with K. Luck and T. Wendorff) Being God's Man-In the Search for Success, 2003; (with K. Luck and T. Wendorff) Being God's man-In Leading a Family: Real Men, Real Life, Powerful Truth, 2003; (with K. Luck and T. Wendorff) Being God's Man-By Pursuing Friendships: Real Men, Real Life, Powerful Truth, 2003; (with K. Luck and T. Wendorff) Being God's Man-By Resisting the World, 2003; (with K. Luck and M. Yorkey) Every Man, God's Man: Every Man's Guide To-Courageous Faith and Daily Integrity, 2003; (with K. Luck and T. Wendorff) Being God's Man-By Standing Firm under Pressure, 2003; (with L. Mintle) Lose it For Life: The Total Solution-Spiritual, Emotional, Physical-For Permanent Weight Loss, 2004; (with A. Hunt) Noah, 2004; (with B. Farrel) One Year Book of Devotions For Men on the Go, 2004; (with P. Farrel) One Year Book of Devotions For Women on the Go, 2004; (with A. Hunt) Paige. 2004; (with A. Hunt) Shane, 2004; (with A. Hunt) Taz, 2004; When You Love Too Much, 2004; (with S. Ethridge) Every Young Woman's Battle: Guarding Your Mind, Heart, and Body In a Sex-Saturated World, 2004; (with S. Ethridge) Every Young Woman's Battle Workbook: How To Pursue Purity in a Sex-Saturated World, 2004; Addicted to Love: Understanding Dependencies of the Heart: Romance, Relationships, and Sex, 2004; (F. Stoeker, B. Stoeker and M. Yorkey) Every Heart Restored: A Wife's Guide to Healing in the Wake of a Husband's Sexual Sin, 2004; (with F. Stoeker, B. Stoeker and M. Yorkey) Every Heart Restored Workbook: A Wife's Guide to Healing in the Wake of Every Man's Battle, 2004; (K. Luck and T. Wendorff) Being God's Man: By Claiming Your Freedom, 2004; (with K. Luck and T. Wendorff) Being God's Man: By Walking a New Path, 2004; (with K. Luck and T. Wendorff) Being God's Man: By Understanding a Woman's Heart, 2004; (with F. Stoeker and M. Yorkey) Every Man's Challenge: How Far Are You Willing to go for God?, 2004; (with D. Cherry) Feeding Your Appetites: Take Control of What's Controlling You, 2004; (with A. Hunt) Josiah, 2004; (with A. Hunt) Liane, 2004; (with J. Puff and M. Conaway) Lose It For Life, Day By Day: Devotions For Every Day of the Year, 2004; (with G. Garrett) Lose It For Life For Teens: The Spiritual, Emotional, and Physical Solution, 2004; (with F. Stoeker, K. Luck and M. Yorkey) Every Day For Every Man: 365 Readings For Those Engaged In the Battle, 2005; (with F. Stoeker and M. Yorkey) Every Single Man's Battle: Staying on the Path of Sexual Purity, 2005; (with K. Luck and M. Yorkey) Every Young Man, God's Man: Confident, Courageous, and Completely His, 2005; Healing is A Choice: Ten Decisions That Will Transform Your Life & Ten Lies That Can Prevent You From Making Them, 2005; (with M. Arterburn) One Year New Testament for Busy Dads: Arranged In 365 Daily Readings With Tools for Daily Reflection, 2006; (with M. Arterburn) One Year New Testament for Busy Moms: Arranged In 365 Daily Readings With Tools for Daily Reflection, 2006; (with D. Stoop) Boiling Point: Understanding Men and Anger, 2006; (with M. Moscoe) Forsaken: An Every Man Novel, 2006; Secrets Men Keep: How Men Make Life and Love Tougher Than It Has To Be, 2006; (with A. Hunt) Soul on Fire: Discover Your Life's Passion and Purpose, 2006; (with J. Burns) How to Talk to Your Kids about Drugs, 2007; (with R. Marsh) Internet Protect Your Kids: Keep Your Children Safe from the Dark Side of Technology, 2007; Reframe Your Life: Transforming Your Pain Into Purpose, 2007; (with N. Rue) Healing Stones, 2007; What Have You Got to Lose?: Experience a Richer Life by Letting Go of the Things That Confuse, Clutter and Contaminate, 2007; (with D. Stoop, L. Werbil and J. Puff) Life Recovery Workbook: A Biblical Guide through the 12 Steps, 2007; (with J. Shore) Being Christian: Exploring Where You, God, and Life Connect, 2008; (with J. Shore) Midlife Manual For Men: Finding Significance in the Second Half, 2008; (with S. Gallucci) Road Warrior: How To Keep Your Faith, Relationships, and Integrity When Away From Home, 2008; Secrets Men Keep, 2008; (with N. Rue) Healing Waters, 2008; (with J. Shore) Regret-free Living: Hope for Past Mistakes and Freedom from Unhealthy Patterns, 2009; (afterword) Her Choice to Heal: Finding Spiritual and Emotional Peace after Abortion, 2009; (with N. Rue) Healing Sands, 2009; (with D. Stoop) Life Recovery Devotional: Thirty Meditations from Scripture for Each Step in Recovery, 2009; (with F. Stoeker and M. Yorkey) Every Man's Marriage: An Every Man's Guide to Winning the Heart of a Woman, 2010; 10 Dates before I Do: Dating to Decide if This is the One, 2011. Contributor to periodicals. **Address:** New Life Ministries, PO Box 1018, Laguna Beach, CA 92652-1018, U.S.A.

ARTERBURN, Stephen Forrest. *See* **ARTERBURN, Stephen.**

ARTHUR, Chris. (Christopher John Arthur). Scottish/Irish (born Ireland), b. 1955?. **Genres:** Theology/Religion, Communications/Media. **Career:** University of Wales, senior lecturer in religious studies, 1989-; University of Edinburgh, faculty; University of St. Andrews, faculty. Writer. **Publications:** (As C.J. Arthur) In the Hall of Mirrors: Some Problems of Commitment in a Religiously Plural World, 1986; Biting the Bullet-Some Personal Reflections on Religious Education, 1990; (ed.) Religion and the Media: An Introductory Reader, 1993; Globalization of Communications: Some Religious Implications, 1998; Irish Nocturnes, 1999; Religious Pluralism: A Metaphorical Approach, 2000; Irish Willow, 2002; (co-author) Poetry Introductions 1, 2004; Irish Haiku, 2005; Irish Elegies, 2009; Words of the Grey Wind: Family and Epiphany in Ulster, 2009; On the Shoreline of Knowledge: Irish Wanderings, 2012. Contributor to books and periodicals. **Address:** University of Iowa Press, 100 Kuhl House, 119 W Park Rd., Iowa City, IA 52242-1000, U.S.A.

ARTHUR, Christopher John. *See* **ARTHUR, Chris.**

ARTHUR, Keri. Australian (born Australia) **Genres:** Novels, Romance/Historical. **Career:** Bureau of Meteorology, clerk; New York Times, author. **Publications:** Eryn, 2007. NIKKI AND MICHAEL SERIES: Dancing with the Devil, 2001; Hearts in Darkness, 2001; Chasing the Shadows, 2002; Kiss the Night Goodbye, 2004. DAMASK CIRCLE: Circle of Fire, 2001; Circle of Death, 2002; Circle of Desire, 2004. RIPPLE CREEK: Beneath a Rising Moon, 2003; Beneath a Darkening Moon, 2005. SPOOK SQUAD: Generation 18, 2004; Memory Zero, 2004; Penumbra, 2005. RILEY JENSON GUARDIAN: Full Moon Rising, 2006; Kissing Sin, 2007; Tempting Evil, 2007; Dangerous Games, 2007; Embraced by Darkness, 2007; The Darkest Kiss, 2008; Deadly Desire, 2009; Bound to Shadows, 2009; Moon Sworn, 2010. MYTH AND MAGIC: Destiny Kills, 2008; Mercy Burns, 2010; Darkness Unbound: A Dark Angels Novel, 2011. **Address:** c/o Author Mail, Bantam Publicity, 1745 Broadway, New York, NY 10019, U.S.A. **Online address:** kez@keriarthur.com

ARTHUR, W. Brian. American (born United States), b. 1945?. **Genres:** Adult Non-fiction. **Career:** Stanford University, Dean and Virginia Morrison professor of population studies and economics and professor of human biology, 1983-96; Santa Fe Institute, director of economics program, 1987-90, 1994-95; PARC Intelligent Systems Lab, visiting researcher. Consultant and writer. **Publications:** NONFICTION: Population Poicy under an Arbitrary Welfare Criterion: Theory and Issues, 1972; (with G. McNicoll) Optimal Population Policy, 1972; (co-ed.) Population, Food and Rural Development, 1988; (ed. with R.D. Lee and G. Rodgers) Economics of Changing Age Distributions in Developed Countries, 1988; Increasing Returns and Path Dependence in the Economy, 1994; (ed. with S.N. Durlauf and D.A. Lane) The Economy as an Evolving Complex System II, 1997; How Growth Builds upon Growth in High-Technology, 2002; The Nature of Technology: What It Is and How It Evolves, 2009. Contributor to journals. **Address:** Santa Fe Institute, 1399 Hyde Park Rd., Santa Fe, NM 87501, U.S.A. **Online address:** wbarthur@parc.com

ARURI, Naseer H. (Naseer Hasan Aruri). American (born United States), b. 1934. **Genres:** Area Studies, International Relations/Current Affairs, Politics/Government, Poetry, Cultural/Ethnic Topics. **Career:** Texas Tech University, instructor in political science, 1962-63; Greenfield Community College, instructor in political science, 1964-65; University of Massachusetts-Dartmouth, instructor, 1965-66, assistant professor, 1966-68, associate professor, 1968-73, professor, 1973-96, Chancellor professor emeritus of political science, 1996-; University of Kuwait, visiting professor, 1973-74; Trans-Arab Research Institute, president, chair; National Task Force on Cultural Diversification, co-chair, 1986. Writer and lecturer. **Publications:** (Ed.) The Palestine Resistance to Israel's Occupation, 1970; (with E. Ghareeb) Enemy of the Sun: Poems of Palestinian Resistance, 1970; Jordan: A Study in Political Development, 1921-1965, 1972; (with A. Tarabein) V. Brodine and M. Seldon, Open Secret: The Nixon-Kissinger Doctrine in Asia, 1974; (contrib.) The Middle East in World Politics: A Study in Contemporary International Relations, 1974; (ed.) Middle East Crucible: The Arab-Israeli Confrontation of October, 1973, 1975; (co-ed. and contrib.) Lebanon: A Challenge to the Arab World, 1977; (with F. Moughrabi and J. Strok) Regan and the Middle East, 1983; (ed.) Occupation: Israel over Palestine, 1983, 2nd ed., 1989; The Obstruction of Peace: The U.S., Israel and the Palestinians, 1995; (ed. with M.A. Shuraydi) Revising Culture, Reinventing Peace: The Influence of Edward W. Said, 2000; Palestinian Refugees: The Right of Return, 2001; (ed. with M.A. Shuraydi) Revising Culture, Reinventing Peace, 2001; Dishonest Broker: The U.S. Role in Israel and Palestine, 2003; Palestine and the Palestinians, 2nd ed., 2006. Contributor to books and journals. **Address:** Department of Political Science, University of Massachusetts at Dartmouth, 285 Old Westport Rd., North Dartmouth, MA 02747, U.S.A. **Online address:** naruri@aol.com

ARURI, Naseer Hasan. *See* **ARURI, Naseer H.**

ARVEY, Michael. American (born United States), b. 1948. **Genres:** Poetry, Paranormal, Psychology, Young Adult Non-fiction. **Career:** University of Colorado, Independent Learning and Correspondence Study Division, creative writing instructor, 1986-2011. Writer. **Publications:** OPPOSING VIEWPOINTS SERIES: ESP, 1988; Reincarnation, 1989; UFOs: Opposing Viewpoints, 1990; Miracles, 1991; End of the World, 1992. **Address:** 637B S Broadway, PO Box 220, Boulder, CO 80301, U.S.A. **Online address:** spiritmed@rocketmail.com

ARVIGO, Rosita. American (born United States), b. 1941. **Genres:** Medicine/Health, Theology/Religion, Horticulture. **Career:** Rainforest Remedies Co., owner and director; The Traditional Healers Foundation of Belize, founder, director and president; Rainforest Medicine Trail, founder; Ix Chel Tropical Research Foundation, director; The Arvigo Institute L.L.C., director; The Shangri-la Institute of Natural Hygiene, assistant health director, health director. Writer. **Publications:** Panti Maya Medicine Trail Field Guide, 1992; (with M. Balick) Rainforest Remedies: 100 Healing Herbs of Belize, 1993; (with N. Epstein and M. Yaquinto) Sastun: My Apprenticeship with a Maya Healer, 1994; (with N. Epstein) Rainforest Home Remedies: The Maya Way to Heal Your Body and Replenish Your Soul, 2001; (with N. Epstein) Spiritual Bathing: Healing Rituals and Traditions from around the World, 2003; Messages from the Gods: Ethnobotanical Wealth of Belize, forthcoming. **Address:** c/o Al Zimmerman, Writers House, 21 W 26th St., New York, NY 10010-1003, U.S.A. **Online address:** contactarvigo@yahoo.com

ARVIN, Reed. American (born United States) **Genres:** Novels. **Career:** Writer, record producer, musician and consultant. **Publications:** NOVELS: The Wind in the Wheat, 1994; The Will, 2000; The Last Goodbye, 2004; Blood of Angels, 2005. OTHER: (ed.) The Inside Track to Getting Started in Christian Music, 2000. **Address:** c/o Jane Dystel, Dystel & Goderich Literary Management, 1 Union Sq. W, Ste. 904, New York, NY 10003-3313, U.S.A. **Online address:** reed@reedarvin.com

ASADI, Houshang. French/Iranian (born Iran), b. 1950?. **Genres:** Biography, Autobiography/Memoirs. **Career:** Kayhan (newspaper), deputy editor, 1970-78; Aftab magazine, chief editor and founder, 1979; GozareshFILM (film magazine), editor-in-chief, 1988-2002; Rooz Online (Persian-language news site), founder, editor, 2005-09. **Publications:** Letters to My Torturer: Love, Revolution, and Imprisonment in Iran, 2010. Contributor to periodicals. **Address:** Paris, France. **Online address:** hooasadh@yahoo.fr

ASANTE, M. K. (Molefi Kete Asante). American/Zimbabwean (born Zimbabwe), b. 1982. **Genres:** Poetry, Music. **Career:** Morgan State University, Department of English and Language Arts, professor of creative writing and film. Writer. **Publications:** (As Molefi K. Asante, Jr.) Like Water Running off My Back: Poems, 2002; Time, 2002; Beautiful and Ugly Too: Poems, 2005; It's Bigger Than Hip- Hop: The Rise of the Post-Hip-Hop Generation, 2008; Buck, 2012. Contributor of articles to periodicals. **Address:** c/o Manie Barron, Menza Barron Literary Agency, 1170 Broadway, Ste. 807, New York, NY 10001, U.S.A. **Online address:** mk@mkasante.com

ASANTE, Molefi K. (Arthur L. Smith). American (born United States), b. 1942. **Genres:** Novels, Poetry, Cultural/Ethnic Topics, Speech/Rhetoric, History. **Career:** California State Polytechnic College, instructor, 1966-67; San Fernando Valley State College, instructor, 1967; Purdue University, assistant professor of communication, 1968-69; University of California, assistant professor, 1969-70, associate professor of speech, 1969-73, Center for Afro-American Studies, director, 1969-73; Trans-Cultural Education/Communication Foundation, president, 1971-81; Florida State University, visiting professor, 1972; State University of New York, Department of Communications, professor and chair, 1973-82, Department of African Studies, professor and chair, 1977-79; Howard University, visiting professor, 1979-80, 1995; Zimbabwe Institute of Mass Communication, Fulbright professor, 1981-82; Temple University, professor of African-American studies, 1984-, chair of department, 1984-96; National Council of Black Studies, vice-president, 1988-90; National Afrocentric Institute, founder and president, 1988-90; Afrocentric Infusion, Peoples Publishing Group, Asante Imprint Books, developer, 1993-2000; African Writers Endowment Foundation, president, 2000-; African Writers Endowment, president and chair, 2000-; Zhejiang University, visiting professor, 2007-; Molefi Kete Asante Institute, director; Textbook and Academic Authors Foundation, president, 2008-10; University of South Africa, professor extraordinarius, 2010-; Institute for the Study of Intercultural Communication, director. Writer and host. **Publications:** AS MOLEFI K. ASANTE: African and Afro-American Communication Continuities, 1975; (with E. Newmark) Intercultural Communication: Theory into Practice, 1976; (with J.K. Frye) Contemporary Public Communication, 1976; (ed. with M.B. Cassata) The Social Uses of Mass Communication, 1977; (with J.K. Frye) Contemporary Public Communication: Applications, 1977; Epic in Search of African Kings, 1978; (with M.B. Cassata) Mass Communication: Principles and Practices, 1979; (with K. Welsh) A Guide to African and African-American Art and Antiquities, 1979; (ed. with E. Newmark and C.A. Blake and contrib.) Handbook of Intercultural Communication, 1979; Afrocentricity: The Theory of Social Change, 1980; (ed. with A.S. Vandi and contrib.) Contemporary Black Thought: Alternative Analyses in Social and Behavioral Science, 1980; Research in Mass Communication: Guide to Practice, 1982; African Myths: New Frames of Reference, 1982; (co-author) Media Training Needs in Zimbabwe, 1982; Mfecane (novel), 1984; (ed. with K.W. Asante and contrib.) African Culture: The Rhythms of Unity, 1985; The Afrocentric Idea, 1987, rev. ed., 1998; Umfundalai: Afrocentric Rite of Passage, 1989; (ed. with W.B. Gudykunst and E. Newmark) Handbook of Intercultural and International Communication, 1989; Kemet, Afrocentricity, and Knowledge, 1990; (with M. Mattson) Historical and Cultural Atlas of African Americans, 1991, rev. ed. as The African-American Atlas: Black History and Culture, 1998; The Book of African Names, 1991; (with D. Ziegler) Thunder and Silence: The Mass Media in Africa, 1991; Classical Africa (high school textbook), 1993; Malcolm X As Cultural Hero, and Other Afrocentric Essays, 1993; Fury in the Wilderness, 1994; (ed. with A. Abarry) The Sources of the African Tradition, 1994; African American History: A Journey of Liberation, 1995, 2nd ed., 2001; (ed. with A.S. Abarry) African Intellectual Heritage: A Book of Sources, 1996; (with A. Mann) Activity Book for African American History, 1997; (co-ed.) Teacher's Guide for African American History, 1997, 2nd ed., 2001; (with R. Muntaqim) The African-American Book of Names and Their Meanings, 1999; The Painful Demise of Eurocentrism: An Afrocentric Response to Critics, 1999; The Egyptian Philosophers: Ancient African Voices from Imhotep to Akhenaten, 2000; (ed. with E.J. Min) Socio-Cultural Conflict between African American and Korean American, 2000; (co-ed.) Worktext for African

American History, 2nd ed., 2001; (with J. Mitchell) Discovery Essays for Teachers, 2001; (ed. with V.H. Milhouse and P.O. Nwosu) Transcultural Realities: Interdisciplinary Perspectives on Cross-cultural Relations, 2001; One Hundred Greatest African Americans: A Biographical Encyclopedia, 2002; Culture and Customs of Egypt, 2002; Scattered to the Wind (fiction), 2002; Customs and Culture of Modern Egypt, 2002; (ed. with A. Mazama) Egypt vs. Greece, and the American Academy, 2002; Erasing Racism: The Survival of the American Nation, 2003, 2nd ed., 2009; (ed. with A. Mazama) Encyclopedia of Black Studies, 2005; Race, Rhetoric, and Identity: The Architecton of Soul, 2005; (ed. with M. Karenga) Handbook of Black Studies, 2006; History of Africa: The Quest for Eternal Harmony, 2007; (with E. Nwadiora) Spear Masters: Introduction to African Religion, 2007; Cheikh Anta Diop: An Intellectual Portrait, 2007; (ed. with Y. Miike and J. Yin) The Global Intercultural Communication Reader, 2008; The Afrocentric Manifesto: Toward an African Renaissance, 2008; (ed. with A. Mazama) Encyclopedia of African Religion, 2009; (with R.E. Hall) Rooming in the Master's House: Power and Privilege in the Rise of Black Conservatism, 2010. AS ARTHUR L. SMITH: The Break of Dawn (poetry), 1964; The Rhetoric of Black Revolution, 1969; (with A. Rich) Rhetoric of Revolution: Samuel Adams, Emma Goldman, Malcolm X, 1970; Toward Transracial Communication, 1970; (ed. with S. Robb) The Voice of Black Rhetoric, 1971; (with A. Allen and D. Hernandez) How to Talk with People of Other Races, Ethnic Groups, and Cultures, 1971; Language, Communication, and Rhetoric in Black America, 1972; Transracial Communication, 1973. AS MOLEFI KETE ASANTE: Love Dance, 1996; Scream of Blood: Desettlerism in Southern Africa, 1999; 100 Greatest African Americans, 2002; Maulana Karenga: An Intellectual Portrait, 2009; Global African American History, 2010; (with J. Morgan) Resolve: Communication and Conflict Management, 2010; (with A. Mazama) Afrocentric Infusion for Urban Schools, 2010; Speaking My Mother's Tongue: Introduction to African American Language, 2010; As I Run Toward Africa, 2011; African American People: A Global History, 2012. **Address:** Department of African American Studies, Temple University, 615 Gladfelter Hall, 1115 W Berks St., Philadelphia, PA 19122, U.S.A. **Online address:** masante@temple.edu

ASANTE, **Molefi Kete.** *See* **ASANTE**, **M. K.**

ASCHAN, **Ulf.** Kenyan/Swedish (born Sweden), b. 1937. **Genres:** Novels, Travel/Exploration, Biography, Autobiography/Memoirs. **Career:** Ulf Aschan Safaris, owner, 1970-; Africa Air Rescue Health Services, director. Writer. **Publications:** Baron Blixen: ett porträtt av baron Bror von Blixen-Finecke, 1986; The Man Whom Women Loved: The Life of Bror Blixen, 1987. **Address:** Helen Brann Agency Inc., 94 Curtis Rd., Bridgewater, CT 06752, U.S.A. **Online address:** ulf.kiwayu@swiftkenya.com

ASCHER, **Barbara Lazear.** American (born United States), b. 1946. **Genres:** Adult Non-fiction, Essays, Autobiography/Memoirs, Romance/Historical, Psychology. **Career:** New York Times, columnist; Delphinium Books, editorial director; Elle Magazine, ethics columnist; Self Magazine, contributing editor; Webster and Sheffield (law firm), attorney, 1979-81; The University of Chicago, Graham School of General Studies, instructor; Bennington College M.F.A Program, faculty. **Publications:** Playing after Dark (essays), 1986; The Habit of Loving (essays), 1989; Landscape without Gravity: A Memoir of Grief, 1994; Dancing in the Dark: Romance, Yearning and the Search for the Sublime, 1999. Contributor to books and periodicals. **Address:** c/o Virginia Barber, The Writers Shop, 101 5th Ave., New York, NY 10003, U.S.A.

ASCHER, **Marcia.** American (born United States), b. 1935. **Genres:** Novels, Mathematics/Statistics, Sciences. **Career:** Ithaca College, School of Humanities and Sciences, Department of Mathematics, assistant professor, professor, 1961-95, professor emeritus, 1995-, Dana research fellow. Writer. **Publications:** (With R. Ascher) Code of the Quipu: A Study in Media, Mathematics, and Culture, 1981; Ethnomathematics: A Multicultural View of Mathematical Ideas, 1991; (with R. Ascher) Mathematics of the Incas: Code of the Quipu, 1997; Mathematics Elsewhere: An Exploration of Ideas Across Cultures, 2002. Contributor to periodicals. **Address:** Department of Mathematics, School of Humanities and Sciences, Ithaca College, 212B Williams Hall, 201 Muller Ctr., 953 Danby Rd., Ithaca, NY 14850, U.S.A. **Online address:** mascher@ithaca.edu

ASCHERSON, **(Charles) Neal.** British/Scottish (born Scotland), b. 1932. **Genres:** History, International Relations/Current Affairs. **Career:** East African Institute of Social Research, researcher, 1955-56; Guardian, journalist, 1956-58; Scotsman, commonwealth correspondent, 1958-59, journalist, 1959-60, Scottish politics correspondent, 1975-79; The Observer, journalist, 1960-75, columnist, 1979-89, associate editor, 1985-90; The Independent on Sunday, assistant editor, 1990-98; Institute of Archaeology, lecturer, 1998-, visiting professor, 2008; Public Archaeology, editor. **Publications:** The King Incorporated, 1963; (intro. and ed.) The French Revolution: Extracts from The Times, 1789-1794, 1975; The Polish August: The Self-Limiting Revolution, 1982; The Book of Lech Walesa, 1982; (with M. Linklater and I. Hilton) The Fourth Reich: Klaus Barbie and the Neo-Fascist Connection, 1984 in US as The Nazi Legacy: Klaus Barbie and the International Fascist Connection, 1985; The Struggles for Poland, 1987; Games with Shadows, 1988; Black Sea, 1995; (foreword) In the Land of Nod, 1996; Yes Road: A Reflection on Two Devolution Campaigns, 1999; Berlin: A Century of Change/Die Gesichter des Jahrhunderts, 2000, rev. ed., 2008; (contrib.) National Heritage, National Canon, 2001; Stone Voices: The Search for Scotland, 2002. **Address:** Institute of Archaeology, University College London, 31-34 Gordon Sq., London, GL WC1H 0PY, England. **Online address:** n.ascherson@ucl.ac.uk

ASCOLI, **Peter Max.** American (born United States), b. 1942?. **Genres:** Education, Social Sciences. **Career:** Utah State University, assistant professor, 1971-78; Chicago Opera Theater, director of development; Steppenwolf Theater Co., director of development; Spertus Institute of Jewish Studies, instructor. Writer and historian. **Publications:** (With F. Cromé) Dialogue d'entre le Maheustre et le Manant, 1977; Julius Rosenwald: The Man Who Built Sears, Roebuck and Advanced the Cause of Black Education in the American South, 2006. Contributor to periodicals. **Address:** Spertus Institute, 610 S Michigan Ave., Chicago, IL 60605, U.S.A.

ASH, **Constance (Lee).** American (born United States), b. 1950?. **Genres:** Science Fiction/Fantasy, Young Adult Fiction, Children's Fiction, Novellas/Short Stories, Literary Criticism And History. **Career:** Writer. **Publications:** FANTASY NOVELS: The Horsegirl, 1988; The Stalking Horse: An Evening-Length Opera Ballet in Five Acts, 1990; The Stallion Queen, 1992; (ed.) Not of Woman Born, 1999. SHORT FICTION: Made by Hand, 1994; Mrs. Langdon's Diary, 1996; Flower Kiss, 1998; The Leopard's Garden, 1999. Works appear in anthologies. **Address:** Ace Books, 375 Hudson St., New York, NY 10014-3657, U.S.A. **Online address:** c.ash1@genie.com

ASH, **Jennifer.** American (born United States), b. 1964. **Genres:** Documentaries/Reportage, Human Relations/Parenting. **Career:** Women's Wear Daily, associate editor, 1986-87; Town & Country, contributing editor, 1992-; Frick Museum, fellow. **Publications:** Private Palm Beach: Tropical Style, 1992; (with A.A. Brott) The Expectant Father: Facts, Tips, and Advice for Dads-to-Be, 1995, 3rd ed., 2010. **Address:** c/o Pam Bernstein, Pam Bernstein Inc., 790 Madison Ave., New York, NY 10021, U.S.A.

ASH, **Stephen V.** American (born United States), b. 1948. **Genres:** History. **Career:** University of Tennessee-Knoxville, teaching assistant, 1975-78, independent historian, 1983-95, instructor in american history, 1989-96, visiting assistant professor, 1990, 1994, 1995, assistant professor of American history, 1995-98, associate professor, 1998-2003, professor, 2003-; University of Tennessee-Chattanooga, Department of History, adjunct instructor, 1994. Writer. **Publications:** Middle Tennessee Society Transformed, 1860-1870: War and Peace in the Upper South, 1988; Messages of the Governors of Tennessee, vols. IX, X, 1990; When the Yankees Came: Conflict and Chaos in the Occupied South, 1861-1865, 1995; Secessionists and Other Scoundrels: Selections from Parson Brownlow's Book, 1999; Tennesseans and Their History, 1999; A Year in the South: Four Lives in 1865, 2002; Nineteenth-Century America: Essays in Honor of Paul H. Bergeron, 2005; Firebrand of Liberty: The Story of Two Black Regiments that Changed the Course of the Civil War, 2008; The Black Experience in the Civil War South, 2010. Contributor of articles to books and periodicals. **Address:** Department of History, University of Tennessee, 915 Volunteer Blvd., 6th Fl., Dunford Hall, Knoxville, TN 37996-4065, U.S.A. **Online address:** sash@utk.edu

ASH, **William Franklin.** British/American (born United States), b. 1917. **Genres:** Novels, History, Autobiography/Memoirs, Biography, Humanities. **Career:** British Broadcasting Corp., Radio Drama Department, senior script editor, 1948-80. **Publications:** The Lotus in the Sky, 1961; Choice of Arms, 1962; The Longest Way Round, 1963; Marxism and Moral Concepts, 1964; Ride a Paper Tiger, 1968; Take-Off, 1969; Pickaxe and Rifle: The Story of the Albanian People, 1974; Morals and Politics: The Ethics of Revolution, 1977; A Red Square (autobiography), 1978; Incorporated, 1979; Right Side

Up, 1984; The Way to Write Radio Drama, 1985; Bold Riot, 1992; What's the Big Idea, 1993; But My Fist Is Free, 1997; Rise Like Lions, 1998; Marxist Morality (philosophy), 1998; (with B. Foley) Under the Wire: The World War II Adventures of a Legendary Escape Artist and Cooler King, 2005. **Address:** Chenies House, Ste. 9, 43 Moscow Rd., London, GL W2 4SW, England.

ASHABRANNER, Melissa. American (born United States), b. 1950. **Genres:** Children's Non-fiction, How-to Books, Adult Non-fiction. **Career:** Association of American Medical Colleges, staff, 1972-77; Hill Rag Inc. (publisher of community newspaper), owner and editor, 1980-88, executive editor; Fagon Publishing Group (publisher of community newspapers), co-owner, 1989-; Capital Community News Inc., executive editor. **Publications:** (With B. Ashabranner) Into a Strange Land: Unaccompanied Refugee Youth in America, 1987; (with B. Ashabranner) Counting America: The Story of the United States Census, 1989. **Address:** Capital Community News Inc., 224 7th St. SE, Ste. 300, Washington, DC 20003, U.S.A. **Online address:** melissaashabranner@hillrag.com

ASHALL, Frank. American/British (born England), b. 1957. **Genres:** Medicine/Health, Sciences. **Career:** Eleanor Roosevelt Institute for Cancer Research, postdoctoral researcher, 1982-85; University of London, London School of Hygiene and Tropical Medicine, postdoctoral researcher, 1985-89, Imperial College of Science and Technology, senior research fellow, 1989-92; Washington University, assistant professor, 1992-94. Writer. **Publications:** Remarkable Discoveries!, 1994; (ed. with A.M. Goate) Plaques and Tangles in Alzheimer's Disease, 1995. Contributor of articles to journals. **Address:** 1 New Ballas Pl., Wellness Center, Saint Louis, MO 63146-8700, U.S.A.

ASHBERY, John (Lawrence). (Jonas Berry). American (born United States), b. 1927. **Genres:** Novels, Plays/Screenplays, Poetry, Translations, Essays, Art/Art History. **Career:** Oxford University Press, copywriter, 1951-54; McGraw-Hill Book Co., copywriter, 1954-55; New York University, instructor in elementary French, 1957-58; Locus Solus, Lans-en-Vercors, editor, 1960-62; New York Herald-Tribune, European Edition, art critic, 1960-65; Art Intl., art critic, 1961-64; Art and Literature, editor, 1963-66; Art News, Paris correspondent, 1964-65, executive editor, 1965-72; City University of New York, Brooklyn College, professor of English, 1974-, M.F.A. Program in Creative Writing, co-director, 1974-90, distinguished professor, 1980-90, distinguished emeritus professor, 1990; New York Magazine, art critic, 1975-80; Partisan Review, poetry editor, 1976-80; Newsweek, art critic, 1980-85; Harvard University, Charles Eliot Norton professor of poetry, 1989-90; Bard College, Charles P. Stevenson, Jr. professor of languages and literature, 1990-2008, Charles P. Stevenson Jr. professor emeritus of languages and literature, 2008-; Brooklyn Public Library, librarian. **Publications:** POETRY: Turandot and Other Poems, 1953; Some Trees, 1956; The Poems, 1960; The Tennis Court Oath, 1962; Rivers and Mountains, 1966; Selected Poems, 1967; Sunrise in Suburbia, 1968; Three Madrigals, 1968; Fragment, 1969; The Double Dream of Spring, 1970; Evening in the Country, 1970; The New Spirit, 1970; Three Poems, 1972; (with J. Brainard) The Vermont Notebook, 1975; The Serious Doll, 1975; Self-Portrait in a Convex Mirror, 1975; Houseboat Days, 1977; As We Know, 1979; Shadow Train, 1981; (co-author) Apparitions (poems), 1981; (co-author) Kitaj Paintings, Drawings, Pastels, 1983; Fairfield Porter: Realist Painter in an Age of Abstraction, 1983; A Wave, 1984; Selected Poems, 1985; April Galleons, 1987; The Ice Storm, 1987; Haibun, 1990; Flow Chart, 1991; Hotel Lautreamont, 1992; Three Books: Poems, 1993; And the Stars Were Shining, 1994; Can You Hear, Bird, 1995; Pistils (essays), 1996; The Mooring of Starting Out: The First Five Books of Poetry, 1997; Wakefulness, 1998; Girls on the Run, 1999; Your Name Here, 2000; Other Traditions: The Charles Eliot Norton Lectures, 2000; As Umbrellas Follow Rain, 2001; Chinese Whispers, 2002; Selected Prose, 2004; Where Shall I Wander, 2005; Giorgio Cavallon, 1904-1989: Paintings, 2005; A Worldly Country: New Poems, 2007; Notes from the Air: Selected Later Poems, 2007; Planisphere: New Poems, 2009. TRANSLATOR: J.J. Mayoux, Melville, 1960; (as Jonas Berry with L.G. Blochman) Murder in Montmartre, 1960; (as Jonas Berry with L.G. Blochman) G. Manceron, The Deadlier Sex, 1961; J. Dupin, Alberto Giacometti, 1963; The Dice Cup: Selected Prose Poems, 1979; M. Allain and P. Souvestre, Fantomas, 1986; P. Martory, Every Question but One, 1990; Selected Poems by Germaine Bree, 1991; P. Reverdy, Selected Poems, 1991; Hebdomeros and Other Writings by G. De Chirico, 1992; P. Martory, The Landscape Is behind the Door, 1994; (and intro.) Landscapist: Selected Poems, 2008; (and intro.) Illuminations, 2011. OTHERS: (with J. Schuyler) A Nest of Ninnies (novel), 1969; (with L. Harwood and T. Raworth) Penguin Modern Poets 19, 1971; Three Plays, 1978; Fairfield Porter (non-fiction), 1982; (co-author) R.B. Kitaj (non-fiction), 1983; Reported Sightings (essays and criticism), 1989; (foreword) Joan Mitchell 1992, 1993; (contrib.) 1995 Biennial Exhibition, 1995; Description of a Masque, 1998; (contrib.) Never Seek to Tell Thy Love, 1999; Other Traditions (essays and criticism), 2000; (contrib. with C. Ratcliff) Joe Brainard: A Retrospective, 2001; (co-author) Jane Hammond: The Ashbery Collaboration, 2001; (contrib.) If I Don't Hear from You Again, 2002; John Ashbery in Conversation with Mark Ford, 2003; (contrib.) The New York Poets, 2004; (with G. Bennett and B. Berkson) Walt Whitman, hom(m)age, 1855-1905, 2005; (contrib.) Another Sleep, 2005; (co-author) Seven American Poets in Conversation, 2008; (with T. Winkfield) Faster than Birds can Fly, 2009. EDITOR: (co-ed.) American Literary Anthology 1, 1968; (with T.B. Hess) Light, 1969; (with T.B. Hess) Light in Art, 1971; (with T.B. Hess) Painterly Painting, 1971; (with T.B. Hess) Avant-Garde Art, 1971; (with T.B. Hess) Art of the Grand Eccentrics, 1971; (with T.B. Hess) Painterly Painting, 1971; Penguin Modern Poets 24, 1974; Muck Arbour, 1975; The Funny Place, 1975; (and trans.) Max Jacob, The Dice Cup: Selected Prose Poems, 1979; (with D. Lehman) The Best American Poetry, 1988; John Ashbery: Collected Poems, 1956-1987, 2010. **Address:** Department of Languages & Literature, Bard College, 30 Campus Rd., PO Box 5000, Annandale-On-Hudson, NY 12504-5000, U.S.A.

ASHBY, Franklin C. American (born United States), b. 1954. **Genres:** Adult Non-fiction. **Career:** Dale Carnegie and Associates Inc., vice president and chief educational officer, 1984-98; host, 1986-87; Performance Resources Organization, director, 1998-99; Manchester Partners International Inc., director, 1998-2000, executive vice president, 1998-2000, chief learning officer; Manchester Training Inc., president, 1998-2000; Leadership Capital Group L.L.C., president, chief executive officer, chairman, 2000-, co-founder. Writer. **Publications:** (Ed.) Effective Leadership Programs: Twelve Case Studies from the Real World of Training, 1999; Revitalize Your Corporate Culture, 1999; The Complete Idiot's Guide to Team Building, 1999; (with A.R. Pell) Embracing Excellence, 2001. **Address:** Leadership Capital Group L.L.C., PO Box 361, Westport, CT 06881-0361, U.S.A. **Online address:** ellen6@aol.com

ASHBY, Godfrey W. British/Welsh (born Wales), b. 1930. **Genres:** inspirational/Motivational Literature, Theology/Religion. **Career:** Church of the Province of South Africa, priest to bishop, 1957-88; Rhodes University, faculty, 1969-75; University of the Witwatersrand, faculty, 1986-88, professor of divinity; Diocese of George, assistant bishop, 1988-95; Diocese of Portsmouth, honorary assistant bishop, 2008-. Writer. **Publications:** Theodoret of Cyrrhus as Exegete of the Old Testament, 1972; Sacrifice: Its Nature and Purpose, 1988; Go Out and Meet God: A Commentary on the Book of Exodus, 1997. **Address:** Bishops House, Edinburgh Rd., Portsmouth, PO1 3HG, England. **Online address:** gashby@cyberperk.co.za

ASHBY, Gwynneth Margaret. British (born England), b. 1922. **Genres:** Children's Fiction, Children's Non-fiction, Geography, Travel/Exploration, Human Relations/Parenting, Education, Social Sciences, Travel/Exploration, Travel/Exploration. **Career:** Teacher, 1943-47, 1950-52; A&C Black Ltd., editorial staff, 1948-50. **Publications:** Mystery of Coveside House, 1946; The Secret Ring, 1948; The Cruise of the Silver Spray, 1951; The Land and People of Sweden 1951; The Land and People of Belgium, 1955; (with J. Gadsby and D. Gadsby) Looking at the World Today, 1960, 3rd ed., 1965; Let's Look at Austria, 1966; Looking at Norway, 1967, 3rd ed., 1971; Looking at Japan, 1969, rev. ed., 1971; Take A Trip to Japan, 1980; Korean Village, 1986; A Family in South Korea, 1987; School by a Volcano, 1994; We Go to School in Japan, 2001. **Address:** 12D Blenheim Dr., De Havilland Way, Christchurch, DS BH23 4JH, England. **Online address:** gwyn@ashbybooks.co.uk

ASHBY, Ruth. American (born United States) **Genres:** Children's Non-fiction, Animals/Pets, Natural History, History, Biography, Children's Fiction. **Career:** Writer of children's books. **Publications:** Quest for King Arthur, 1988; Sea Otters, 1990; Tigers, 1990; The Orangutan, 1994; (ed. with D. Gore Ohrn) Her Story: Women Who Changed the World, 1995; Elizabethan England, 1999; T-Rex: Back to the Cretaceous, 2000; Steve Case: America Online Pioneer, 2002; Boss Tweed and Tammany Hall, 2002; Fury on Horseback, 2003; Victorian England, 2003; Gettysburg, 2003; How the Solar System Was Formed, 2003; 1800, 2003; The Outer Planets, 2003; Extraordinary People, 2003; Lincoln, 2003; The Earth and Its Moon, 2003; Lee vs. Grant: Great Battles of the Civil War, 2003; The Underground Railroad, 2003; (ed.) The Letters of Elinore Pruitt Stewart, Woman Homesteader, 2004; Rocket Man: The Mercury Adventure of John Glenn, 2004; (ed.) The Diary of Sam Watkins, A Confederate Soldier, 2004; The Amazing Mr. Franklin: Or, The Boy Who Read Everything, 2004; Ronald and Nancy Reagan, 2005; My Favorite Dinosaurs, 2005; Anne Frank: Young Diarist, 2005; Abraham and Mary Todd Lincoln, 2005; Woodrow and Edith Wilson, 2005; Bill and Hillary Rodham Clinton, 2005; John and Jacqueline Kennedy, 2005; Franklin and Eleanor Roosevelt, 2005; George W. and Laura Bush, 2005; James and Dolly Madison, 2005; John and Abigail Adams, 2005; Pteranodon: The Life Story of a Pterosaur, 2005; George and Martha Washington, 2005; Caedmon's Song, 2006; Rosa Parks: Freedom Rider, 2008; Young Charles Darwin and the Voyage of the Beagle, 2009. **Address:** c/o Author Mail, William B. Eerdmans Publishing, 255 Jefferson Ave. SE, Grand Rapids, MI 49503, U.S.A.

ASHE, Geoffrey Thomas. British (born England), b. 1923. **Genres:** History, Mythology/Folklore, Writing/Journalism. **Career:** Polish University College, lecturer, 1948-50; Newman Neame, industrial research assistant, 1949-51; Ford Motor Co., administrative assistant, 1952-54; Post Office Department, technical officer, 1954-55; Management Studies Polytechnic, lecturer, 1956-68; University of Southern Mississippi, visiting professor, 1982; University of Alabama, visiting professor, 1984; Union College, Thomas Lamont visiting professor, 1984; Wilfred Laurier University, visiting professor, 1985; University of Minnesota, visiting professor, 1986; Drew University, visiting professor, 1989; Portland State University, visiting professor, 1990-95; University of Northern Iowa, visiting professor, 1995. Writer. **Publications:** The Tale of the Tub, 1950; King Arthur's Avalon, 1957; From Caesar to Arthur, 1960; Land to the West, 1962; The Land and the Book, 1965; Gandhi: A Study in Revolution, 1968; (ed.) The Quest for Arthur's Britain, 1968; All about King Arthur in US as King Arthur in Fact and Legend, 1969; Camelot and the Vision of Albion, 1971; The Quest for America, 1971; The Art of Writing Made Simple, 1972; The Finger and the Moon, 1973, rev. ed., 2004; Do What You Will, 1974 as The Hell-Fire Clubs, 2000; The Virgin, 1976; The Ancient Wisdom, 1977; Miracles, 1978; A Guidebook to Arthurian Britain, 1980, as Traveller's Guide to Arthurian Britain, 1997; Kings and Queens of Early Britain, 1982; Avalonian Quest, 1982; The Discovery of King Arthur, 1985, rev. ed., 2003; The Arthurian Encyclopedia, 1986; The Landscape of King Arthur, 1987; The Virgin: Mary's Cult and the Re-emergence of the Goddess, 1988; (with N.J. Lacy and D.N. Mancoff) The Arthurian Handbook, 1988, 2nd ed., 1997; Mythology of the British Isles, 1990; King Arthur, the Dream of a Golden Age, 1990; (ed.) The New Arthurian Encyclopedia, 1991; Dawn behind the Dawn, 1992; Atlantis, 1992; (ed.) The Quest for Arthur's Britain, 1994; The Book of Prophecy, 1999; Gandhi: A Biography, 2000; Encyclopedia of Prophecy, 2001; The Glastonbury Tor Maze, 5th ed., 2001; Merlin, 2001; Labyrinths and Mazes, 2003; Merlin: The Prophet and His History, 2006; The Offbeat Radicals, 2007. Contributor to periodicals. **Address:** Chalice Orchard, Well House Ln., Glastonbury, SM BA6 8BJ, England. **Online address:** ashemail@tinyworld.co.uk

ASHE, Rebecca. *See* **MELUCH, R(ebecca) M.**

ASHENBURG, Katherine. Canadian (born Canada) **Genres:** History, Social Sciences. **Career:** Canadian Broadcasting System Inc. (CBS), radio producer; The Globe and Mail, arts and books editor; University of British Columbia, faculty; The New York Times, Sunday Travel Section, contributor; Toronto Life Magazine, columnist. Writer. **Publications:** Going to Town: Architectural Walking Tours in Southern Ontario, 1996; The Mourner's Dance: What We Do When People Die, 2002; The Dirt on Clean: An Unsanitized History, 2007 in UK as Clean: An Unsanitised History of Washing, 2008. Contributor of articles to periodicals and magazines. **Address:** Farrar, Straus & Giroux, 18 W 18th St., Newyork, NY 10011, U.S.A. **Online address:** katherine@ashenburg.com

ASHER, Bridget. *See* **BAGGOTT, Julianna.**

ASHER, Catherine B. (Catherine Ella Blanshard Asher). American (born United States), b. 1946. **Genres:** Architecture, History. **Career:** University of Minnesota, professor of art history and director of graduate studies. Writer and art historian. **Publications:** Architecture of Mughal India, 1992; (ed. with T.R. Metcalf) Perceptions of South Asia's Visual Past, 1994; (with C. Talbot) India before Europe, 2006. Contributor to books, periodicals and journals. **Address:** Department of Art History, University of Minnesota, 338 Heller Hall, 271 19th Ave. S, Minneapolis, MN 55455, U.S.A. **Online address:** asher001@umn.edu

ASHER, Catherine Ella Blanshard. *See* **ASHER, Catherine B.**

ASHER, Harry. *See* **FREEMANTLE, Brian (Harry).**

ASHER, Jane. British (born England), b. 1946. **Genres:** Food And Wine, Novellas/Short Stories, Children's Fiction, Literary Criticism And History. **Career:** Actress, 1957-; Jane Asher Party Cakes and Sugarcraft, founder and principal, 1990-; Arthritis Care, president; National Autistic Society, president; Parkinson's U.K., president. Writer. **Publications:** Jane Asher's Party Cakes, 1982; Jane Asher's Fancy Dress, 1983; Silent Nights for You and Your Baby, 1984; Jane Asher's Quick Party Cakes, 1985; The Moppy Stories, 1987; Easy Entertaining, 1987; Keep Your Baby Safe, 1988; Children's Parties, 1988; Calendar of Cakes, 1989; Eats for Treats, 1990; Jane Asher's Complete Book of Cake Decorating Ideas, 1993; Round the World Cookbook, 1994; Rhymes for All Seasons, 1995; Time to Play, 1995; 101 Things I Wish I'd Known Before..., 1996; The Longing, 1996; Decorated Cakes, 1997; The Best of Good Living, 1998; Good Living at Christmas, 1998; The Question, 1998; Tricks of the Trade, 1999; Losing It, 2002; Cakes For Fun, 2005; Beautiful Baking, 2008. **Address:** Jane Asher Party Cakes and Sugarcraft, 22-24 Cale St., London, GL SW3 3QU, England. **Online address:** info@jane-asher.co.uk

ASHER, Miriam. *See* **MUNDIS, Hester (Jane).**

ASHER, Neal. British (born England), b. 1961?. **Genres:** Novels, Mystery/Crime/Suspense, Science Fiction/Fantasy, Young Adult Fiction, Literary Criticism And History, Novellas/Short Stories. **Career:** Writer. **Publications:** Mindgames: Fools Mate, 1992; The Parasite, 1996; The Engineer, 1998; Runcible Tales, 1999; Masons Rats, 1999; Africa Zero, 2001; Cowl, 2005; Hilldiggers, 2007; The Gabble - and Other Stories, 2008; Shadow of the Scorpion, 2008. AGENT CORMAC/POLITY SERIES: Gridlinked, 2003; The Line of Polity, 2003; Prador Moon, 2006; Polity Agent, 2006; Brass Man, 2007; Line War, 2008. THE SPATTERJAY BOOKS: The Skinner, 2004; The Voyage of the Sable Keech, 2006; Orbus, 2009. Contributor to periodicals. **Address:** Tor Books, 175 5th Ave., New York, NY 10010, U.S.A. **Online address:** n.asher@virgin.net

ASHER, R. E. British (born England), b. 1926. **Genres:** Language/Linguistics, History, Literary Criticism And History, Reference, Translations. **Career:** University of London, School of Oriental and African Studies, assistant lecturer, 1953-56, lecturer in linguistics, 1956-67, lecturer in Tamil, 1957-65; University of Edinburgh, senior lecturer, 1965-70, reader, 1970-77, professor of linguistics, 1977-93, head of department, 1976-80, 1983-86, Faculty of Arts, associate dean, 1985-86, dean, 1986-89, Centre for Speech Technology Research, associate director, 1984-93, director, 1994, vice-principal, 1990-93, curator of patronage, 1991-93, honorary fellow and professor emeritus, 1993-. Writer. **Publications:** (With R. Radhakrishnan) A Tamil Prose Reader, 1971; Some Landmarks in the History of Tamil Prose, 1973; Tamil, 1989; Malayala Bhasa-Sahitya Pathanangal, 1989; National Myths in Renaissance France: Francus, Samothes, and the Druids, 1993; (with T.C. Kumari) Malayalam, 1997; Basir, Malayalattinte Sargavismayam: Pathanangal (critical studies), 1999; (with E. Annamalai) Colloquial Tamil, 2002; A Tamil Prose Reader, 2004. TRANSLATOR FROM MALAYALAM: (with A. Coilparampil) V.M. Basheer, Me Grandad 'ad an Elephant!: Three Stories of Muslim Life in South India, 1980; T.S. Pillai, Scavenger's Son (novel), 1986, rev. ed., 1993; (with N. Gopalakrishnan) What the Sufi Said, 2002. EDITOR: (with E.J.A. Henderson) Towards a History of Phonetics, 1981; (with C. Moseley) Atlas of the World's Languages, 1994, rev. ed., 2007; The Encyclopedia of Language and Linguistics, 10 vols., 1994; (with E.F.K. Koerner) Concise History of the Language Sciences: From the Sumerians to the Cognitivists, 1995; Bashir Svatantrya Samara Kathakal, 1998; (with R. Harris) Linguisticoliterary-A Festschrift for Professor D.S. Dwivedi, 2000; (with V. Abdulla) Wind Flowers: Contemporary Malayalam Short Fiction, 2004. **Address:** School of Philosophy, Psychology and Language Scie, University of Edinburgh, Dugald Stewart Bldg., 3 Charles St., Edinburgh, EH8 9AD, Scotland. **Online address:** r.e.asher@ed.ac.uk

ASHER, Sandy. American (born United States), b. 1942. **Genres:** Children's Fiction, Young Adult Fiction, Plays/Screenplays, Children's Non-fiction, Writing/Journalism, Young Adult Non-fiction, Picture/Board Books, Writing/Journalism, Writing/Journalism. **Career:** WFIU-Radio, scriptwriter, 1963-64; Ball Associates (advertising agency), copywriter, 1964; Spectator, drama critic, 1966-67; Drury University, instructor in creative writing, 1978-85, writer-in-residence, 1985-2003; Creative Writing for Children's Summer Programs, instructor, 1981-83; Institute of Children's Literature, instructor,

1986-96; Good Company Theater for All Ages, co-founder and managing director, 1997-2003; American Writes for Kids, co-founder and director, 1997-; USA Plays for Kids, co-founder and director, 1997-. **Publications:** NOVELS: Summer Begins, 1980 in US as Summer Smith Begins, 1986; Daughters of the Law, 1980 in UK as Friends and Sisters, 1982; Just Like Jenny, 1982; Things Are Seldom What They Seem, 1983; Missing Pieces, 1984; Teddy Teabury's Fabulous Fact, 1985; Everything Is Not Enough, 1987 in Germany as Sunnyboy und Aschenputtel, 1990; Teddy Teabury's Peanutty Problems, 1987; Out of Here: A Senior Class Yearbook, 1993. BALLET ONE SERIES: Best Friends Get Better, 1989; Mary-in-the-Middle, 1990; Pat's Promise, 1990; Can David Do It?, 1991. OTHERS: The Great American Peanut Book, 1977; Where Do You Get Your Ideas? Helping Young Writers Begin, 1987; Wild Words! How to Train Them to Tell Stories, 1989; Princess Bee and the Royal Goodnight Story (picture book), 1990; (ed.) But That's Another Story, 1996; (ed. and contrib.) With All My Heart, With All My Mind, 1999; Stella's Dancing Days (picture book), 2001; Discovering Cultures: China, 2002; Discovering Cultures: Mexico, 2002; (with J. Robinette and K. Brown) 125 Original Audition Monologues, 2003; (ed. and contrib.) On Her Way: Stories and Poems About Growing Up Girl, 2004; Why Rabbit's Nose Twitches, 2004; Too Many Frogs! (picture book), 2005; (ed. with D.L. Harrison and contrib.) Dude!: Stories and Stuff for Boys, 2006; What A Party (picture book), 2007; Here Comes Gosling (picture book), 2009; (ed. and contrib.) Writing It Right!: How Successful Children's Authors Revise and Sell Their Stories, 2009. Works appear in anthologies. Contributor of articles to books and magazines. **Address:** c/o Wendy Schmalz, Wendy Schmalz Agency, PO Box 831, Hudson, NY 12534, U.S.A. **Online address:** sasher@drury.edu

ASHFORD, Jane. *See* **LECOMPTE, N(ancy) Jane.**

ASHFORD, Jeffrey. *See* **JEFFRIES, Roderic.**

ASHFORD, Nigel (John Gladwell). American/British (born England), b. 1952. **Genres:** Politics/Government, Philosophy. **Career:** European Democrat Students, London, executive director, 1976-78; Paisley College, assistant professor, 1979-83; University of Strathclyde, assistant professor, 1983-84; Staffordshire Polytechnic, Stoke-on-Trent, associate professor, professor, 1984-2002; George Mason University, Institute for Humane Studies, senior program officer, 2002-; American Politics Group, chairman. Writer. **Publications:** (Ed. with S. Davies) A Dictionary of Conservative and Libertarian Thought, 1991; (ed. with G. Jordan) Public Policy and The Impact of The New Right, 1993; (with R. O'Quinn) The Kiwi Effect, 1996; (with E. Ashbee) U.S. Politics Today, 1999; Principles for a Free Society, 1999. **Address:** Institute for Humane Studies, George Mason University, 3301 N Fairfax Dr., Ste. 440, Arlington, VA 22201, U.S.A. **Online address:** nashford@gmu.edu

ASHLEY, Bernard. British (born England), b. 1935. **Genres:** Novellas/Short Stories, Children's Fiction, Children's Non-fiction, Novels, Young Adult Non-fiction, Picture/Board Books, Horror. **Career:** King's Farm Primary School, teacher, 1957-65; Hertford Heath Primary School, head teacher, 1965-71; Hartley Junior School, head teacher, 1971-76; Charlton Manor Junior School, head teacher, 1977-95, retired, 1995; Ashley Chappel Productions, producer. Writer. **Publications:** JUVENILE FICTION: The Trouble with Donovan Croft, 1974; Terry on the Fence, 1975; All My Men, 1977; A Kind of Wild Justice, 1978; Break in the Sun, 1980; I'm Trying to Tell You, 1981; Dinner Ladies Don't Count, 1981; Dodgem, 1981; Linda's Lie, 1982; High Pavement Blues, 1983; Your Guess Is as Good as Mine, 1983; A Bit of Give and Take, 1984; Janey, 1985; Running Scared, 1986; Bad Blood, 1988; The Country Boy, 1989; The Secret of Theodore Brown, 1989; Boat Girl, and Other Dockside School Stories, 1990; The Caretaker's Cat, 1990; Chrysalis, 1990; Dim Thin Ducks, 1990; Cleversticks, 1992; Dockside School Stories, 1992; More Stories from Dockside School, 1992; Seeing Off Uncle Jack, 1992; (with C. Ashley) Three Seven Eleven, 1993; Johnnie's Blitz, 1995; I Forgot! Said Troy, 1996; A Present for Paul, 1996; Justin and the Demon Drop Kick, 1997; Flash, 1997; A Present for Peter, 1997; Tiger without Teeth, 1998; King Rat, 1998; Hannibal Route, 1999; Growing Good, 1999; Justin and the Big Fight, 1999; Who Loves You, Billy?, 2000; Playing against the Odds, 2000; Justin Strikes Again, 2001; Little Soldier, 2002; Double the Love, 2002; Revenge House, 2002; Freedom Flight, 2003; The Bush, 2003; Torrent, 2004; Close Look, Quick Look: Playing Against the Odds: Copymasters, 2004; Smokescreen, 2006; That's the One!, 2007; Angel Boy, 2008; Solitaire, 2008; Justin and the Grandad War, 2009; No Way to Go, 2009; Ronnie's War, 2010; Aftershock, 2011. OTHERS: Don't Run Away, 1966; Wall of Death, 1966; Space Shot, 1967; The Big Escape, 1967; The Men and the Boats: Britain's Life-Boat Service, 1968; Weather Men, 1974; Dodgem, 1982; Running Scared, 1986; (ed.) The Puffin Book of School Stories, 1992; (co-author) Meetings with the Minister: Five Chidren's Authors on the National Literacy Strategy, 2003. CLIPPER STREET STORIES SERIES: Calling for Sam, 1987; Taller Than Before, 1987; Down-and-Out, 1988; The Royal Visit, 1988; All I Ever Ask..., 1988; Sally Cinderella, 1989. GRAFFIX SERIES: Roller Madonnas, 1997; Rapid, 1999; Respect, 2000. CITY LIMITS SERIES: Stitch-Up, 1997; The Scam, 1997; Framed, 1997; Mean Street, 1997. BEN MADDOX SERIES: Ten Days to Zero, 2005; Down to the Wire, 2006; Flashpoint, 2007. DOCKSIDE SCHOOL SERIES: Getting In, 1990; The Ghost of Dockside School, 1990. Contributor to journals and periodicals. **Address:** 128 Heathwood Gardens, London, GL SE7 8ER, England. **Online address:** bernardashley@talktalk.net

ASHLEY, Leonard R. N. American (born United States), b. 1928. **Genres:** Novels, Novellas/Short Stories, Poetry, Gay And Lesbian Issues, Language/Linguistics, Literary Criticism And History, Military/Defense/Arms Control, Paranormal, Social Sciences. **Career:** University of Utah, instructor in English, 1953-56; RCAF, assistant to the air historian, 1956-58; University of Rochester, instructor in English, 1958-61; New School for Social Research, lecturer, 1961-72; City University of New York, Brooklyn College, instructor, 1961-64, assistant professor, 1964-67, associate professor, 1967-71, professor of English, 1972-95, professor emeritus, 1995-. Writer. **Publications:** (With F.F. Liu) A Military History of Modern China, 1956; Colley Cibber, 1965, rev. ed., 1989; (ed.) Nineteenth-Century British Drama, 1967; British Short Stories: Classics and Criticism, 1968; Authorship and Evidence: A Study of Attribution and the Renaissance Drama, 1968; The History of the Short Story, 1968; George Peele, 1970; Other People's Lives: 34 Stories, 1970; Ripley's Believe It or Not Book of the Military, 1977; Tales of Mystery and Melodrama, 1977; The Wonderful World of Superstition, Prophecy and Luck, 1984; The Wonderful World of Magic and Witchcraft, 1986; The Amazing World of Superstition, Prophecy, Luck, Magic and Witchcraft, 1988; Elizabethan Popular Culture, 1988; What's in a Name?: Everything You Wanted to Know, 1989; The Complete Book of Superstition, Prophecy and Luck, 1995; The Complete Book of Magic and Witchcraft, 1995; The Complete Book of Devils and Demons, 1996; The Complete Book of the Devil's Disciples, 1996; The Complete Book of Spells, Curses and Magical Recipes, 1997; The Complete Book of Vampires, 1998; George Alfred Henty and the Victorian Mind, 1999; The Complete Book of Ghosts and Poltergeists, 2000; Language and Society, 2001; Complete Book of Werewolves, 2001; What I Know about You: 100 Lesbian & Gay New York Voices, 2001; Cornish Names, 2002; Complete Book of Dreams and What They Mean, 2002; Dictionary of Sexual Slang, 2002; Art Attack: Names in Satire, 2003; Complete Book of Sex Magic, 2003; Names in Popular Culture, 2003; The Complete Book of Sex Magic, 2003; Names of Places, 2003; Names in Literature, 2003; The Complete Book of Numerology, 2005. EDITOR/CO-EDITOR: (with S.L. Astor) British Short Stories, 1968; A Narrative of the Life of Mrs. Charlotte Clarke, 1969; Phantasms of the Living, 2 vols., 1970; Reliques of Irish Poetry: A Memoir of Miss Brooke, 1970; Shakespeare's Jest Book, 1970; Suhrab and Rustam, 1972; The Picture of Dorian Grey, 1972; The Ballad Poetry of Ireland, 1973; Tales of Mystery and Melodrama, 1977; Geolinguistic Perspectives, 1987; (with J. Levitt and K.H. Rogers) Language in Contemporary Society, 1993; (with K.H. Rogers and J. Levitt) Constructed Languages & Language Construction, 1996; (with J. Levitt and W.H. Finke) Language & Communication in the New Century, 1998; (with W.H. Finke) Languages across Borders, 2001; A Garland of Names, 2003; Language and Identity, 2004; Enriched Classics, 11 vols. Contributor of articles to periodicals. **Address:** Department of English, Brooklyn College, City University of New York, 2900 Bedford Ave., Brooklyn, NY 11210, U.S.A.

ASHLEY, Trisha. British (born England) **Genres:** Humor/Satire, Romance/Historical, Young Adult Fiction, Novels. **Career:** Novelist. **Publications:** NOVELS: Good Husband Material, 2000; The Urge to Jump, 2001; Every Woman for Herself, 2002; Singled Out, 2003; The Generous Gardener, 2005; Lord Rayven's Revenge, 2007; Sweet Nothings, 2007; Sowing Secrets, 2008; Happy Endings, 2008; A Winter's Tale, 2008; Wedding Tiers, 2009; Chocolate Wishes, 2010; Twelve Days of Christmas, 2010; The Magic of Christmas, 2011; Chocolate Shoes and Wedding Blues, 2012. **Address:** The Marsh Agency Ltd., 50 Albemarle St., London, GL W1S 4BD, England. **Online address:** trisha.ashley@tesco.net

ASHLIMAN, D. L. American (born United States), b. 1938. **Genres:** Novels, Literary Criticism And History. **Career:** University of Pittsburgh, Department of German, associate professor of German, 1977-86, professor, 1986-2000, chair, 1994-97, professor emeritus, 2000-; Semester at Sea, academic dean, 1994. Writer. **Publications:** A Guide to Folktales in the English Language: Based on the Aarne-Thompson Classification System, 1987; Once upon a Time: The Story of European Folktales, 1994; (comp.) Voices from the Past: The Cycle of Life in Indo-European Folktales, 1995; (intro.) Aesop's Fables, 2003; Folk and Fairy Tales: A Handbook, 2004; Fairy Lore: A Handbook, 2006. Contributor to periodicals. **Address:** Department of German, University of Pittsburgh, 1409 Cathedral of Learning, Pittsburgh, PA 15260, U.S.A. **Online address:** ashliman@hotmail.com

ASHMAN, Anastasia M. Indian/American (born United States), b. 1964. **Genres:** Adult Non-fiction, Biography, Social Sciences. **Career:** Wieser & Wieser (literary agency), director of operations, 1987-89; Metro-Goldwyn-Mayer, staff, 1990-92; Pierre Cossette Productions, executive producer's assistant, 1993-94. Writer. **Publications:** (Ed. with J.E. Gokmen) Tales from the Expat Harem: Foreign Women in Modern Turkey (nonfiction anthology), 2006. Contributor to books. **Address:** Seal Press, 1700 4th St., Berkeley, CA 94710, U.S.A. **Online address:** aashman@expatharem.com

ASHRAWI, Hanan (Mikhail). (Hanan Mikhail-Ashrawi). Palestinian (born Palestine), b. 1946. **Genres:** Literary Criticism And History, History, Autobiography/Memoirs. **Career:** Bir Zeit University, Department of English, founder, 1973, professor, 1973-95, chair, 1973-78, 1981-84, chair, 1974-95, dean of the faculty of arts, 1986-90; Palestinian National Authority, ministry of higher education, 1996-98; MIFTAH, Palestinian Initiative for the Promotion of Global Dialogue and Democracy, founder and secretary general, 1998-2006; Palestinian Independent Commission for Citizen's Rights, founder and commissioner. Writer, activist and politician. **Publications:** (As H. Ashrawi): (with Ṣ Shaḥrūrī) Al-Qisòsòah al-qasòīrah fī al-ardòal-muhòtallah, 1988; This Side of Peace: A Personal Account, 1995; (intro.) The Jerusalem Question (Radical History), 2006. OTHERS: Contemporary Palestinian Literature under Occupation, 1976; From Intifada to Independence, 1989. Contributor to books and periodicals. **Address:** MIFTAH, Simon & Schuster, PO Box 69647, Jerusalem, 95908, Israel.

ASHTON, Dianne. American (born United States), b. 1949. **Genres:** Theology/Religion, Literary Criticism And History, History, Bibliography, Cultural/Ethnic Topics. **Career:** La Salle University, lecturer in religion, 1986-88; Gratz College, lecturer, 1986-88; Netzky Institute, lecturer, 1986-88; University of Pennsylvania, teacher of general studies, 1987; Rowan University, professor of religion, 1987-, director of American studies, Department of Philosophy and Religion, chair; Rutgers University, lecturer, 1988. Writer. **Publications:** (Ed. and intro. with E.M. Umansky) Four Centuries of Jewish Women's Spirituality: A Sourcebook, 1992, rev. ed., 2009; The Philadelphia Group and Philadelphia Jewish History: A Guide to Archival and Bibliographic Collections, 1993; Rebecca Gratz: Women and Judaism in Antebellum America, 1997; Jewish Life in Pennsylvania, 1998. Contributor to books and periodicals. **Address:** Department of Philosophy and Religion, Rowan University, Bunce Hall, 201 Mullica Hill Rd., Glassboro, NJ 08028-1701, U.S.A. **Online address:** ashtond@rowan.edu

ASHTON, Dore. American (born United States), b. 1928. **Genres:** Art/Art History, Cultural/Ethnic Topics, History, Biography. **Career:** Arts Magazine, associate editor, 1951-54, contributing editor, 1965-; New York Times, associate art critic, 1955-60; writer, 1960-; Pratt Institute, art history instructor, 1962-63; School of Visual Arts, lecturer in philosophy of art, head of department of humanities, 1965-68; Cooper Union, professor of art history, 1969-; City University of New York, instructor, 1973, Columbia University, instructor, 1975; New School for Social Research, instructor, 1986-; Yale University, senior lecturer, 2000-, senior critic in painting/printmaking, 2002-. **Publications:** Abstract Art before Columbus, 1957; Poets and the Past, 1959; Philip Guston, 1960; (co-author) Redon, Moreau, Bresdin, 1961; The Unknown Shore, 1962; Rauschenberg's Dante, 1964; Modern American Sculpture, 1968; A Reading of Modern Art, 1969; Richard Lindner, 1969; The Sculpture of PolBury, 1971; Picasso on Art, 1972; The New York School: A Cultural Reckoning, 1973; A Joseph Cornell Album, 1974; Yes, But...A Critical Biography of Philip Guston, 1976; A Fable of Modern Art, 1980; (with D.B. Hare) Rosa Bonheur: A Life and a Legend, 1981; American Art Since 1945, 1982; About Rothko, 1983; Twentieth Century Artists on Art, 1985; Richard Diebenkorn: Small Paintings from Ocean Park, 1985; Out of the Whirlwind: Three Decades of Arts Commentary, 1987; Fragonard in the Universe of Painting, 1988; Noguchi East and West, 1992; Terence La Noue, 1992; (ed.) Monumental Propaganda, 1994; Joseph Solman, 1995; Arshile Gorky, 1995; Gunther Gerzso, 1995; The Delicate Thread: Teshigahara's Life in Art, 1996; Planes, 1996; Identi Kit, 1999; A Rebours, 1997; (contrib.) Bernard Maisner, 1999; The Walls of the Heart, 2000; Crossroads of American Sculpture, 2000; The Black Rainbow; The Work of Fernando de Szyszlo, 2002; (contrib.) Cuatro cuartetos, 2005; (ed. with J. Banach and intro.) Writings of Robert Motherwell, 2007; (contrib.) Bonevardi, 2007; (with L. Pittman) Cecily Brown, 2008; (contrib.) Manuel Felguérez, 2009. **Address:** Cooper Union, 30 Cooper Sq., 8th Fl., New York, NY 10003-7120, U.S.A.

ASHTON, Robert. British (born England), b. 1924. **Genres:** History, Military/Defense/Arms Control. **Career:** University of Nottingham, assistant lecturer in economic history, 1952-54, lecturer, 1954-61, senior lecturer in economic history, 1961-63; University of California, visiting associate professor of history, 1962-63; University of East Anglia, professor, 1963-89, professor emeritus, 1989-, School of English Studies, dean, 1964-67; Oxford University, All Souls College, visiting fellow, 1973-74, 1987, James Ford special lecturer in history, 1982. Writer. **Publications:** The Crown and the Money Market 1603-1640, 1960; (ed. and intro.) James I by His Contemporaries, 1969; (contrib.) English Civil War and After, 1642-1658, 1970; English Civil War: Conservatism and Revolution, 1603-1649, 1978, 2nd ed., 1989; The City and the Court, 1603-1643, 1979, 2nd ed., 1989; Reformation and Revolution, 1558-1660, 1984; Counter-revolution: The Second Civil War and Its Origins, 1646-48, 1994. Contributor of articles to journals. **Address:** University of East Anglia, Earlham Rd., Norwich, NF NR4 7TJ, England. **Online address:** robert.ashton@uea.ac.uk

ASHTON, Rosemary. British/Scottish (born Scotland), b. 1947. **Genres:** Literary Criticism And History, Biography, Novellas/Short Stories. **Career:** University College London, lecturer, 1974-86, reader, 1986-91, professor of English, 1991-2002, Quain professor of English language and literature, 2002-; University of Birmingham, lecturer. Writer. **Publications:** The German Idea: Four English Writers and the Reception of German Thought, 1800-1860, 1980; George Eliot, 1983; Little Germany: Exile and Asylum in Victorian England, 1986; Little Germany: German Refugees in Victorian Britain, 1989; The Mill on the Floss: A Natural History, 1990; G.H. Lewes: A Life, 1991; The Life of Samuel Taylor Coleridge: A Critical Biography, 1996; George Eliot: A Life, 1997; Thomas and Jane Carlyle: Portrait of a Marriage, 2002; 142 Strand: A Radical Address in Victorian London, 2006. EDITOR: George Eliot: Selected Critical Writings, 1992; Versatile Victorian: Selected Writings of G.H. Lewes, 1992; G. Eliot, The Mill on the Floss, 1992; Eliot, Silas Marner, 1993; Middlemarch, 1994. Contributor to periodicals. **Address:** Department of English, University College London, Gower St., London, GL WC1E 6BT, England. **Online address:** r.ashton@ucl.ac.uk

ASHWORTH, Andrea. British/American (born United States), b. 1969. **Genres:** Bibliography, Autobiography/Memoirs. **Career:** University of Oxford, Jesus College, lecturer, junior research fellow in English literature, 1997-. Writer. **Publications:** Once in a House on Fire: A Memoir, 1998. **Address:** Jesus College, University of Oxford, Turl St., Oxford, OX OX1 3DW, England. **Online address:** andrea.ashworth@ell.ox.ac.uk

ASHWORTH, Heidi. American (born United States), b. 1964?. **Genres:** Romance/Historical. **Career:** Writer. **Publications:** Miss Delacourt Speaks Her Mind, 2008; Miss Delacourt Has Her Day, 2011. **Address:** Avalon Books, 160 Madison Ave., 5th Fl., New York, NY 10016, U.S.A. **Online address:** write2me@heidiashworth.com

ASHWORTH, Jenn. British (born England), b. 1982?. **Genres:** Mystery/Crime/Suspense. **Career:** University of Central Lancashire, lecturer; University of Manchester, research fellow; Central Lancashire Writing Hub, coordinator. Writer and librarian. **Publications:** A Kind of Intimacy, 2010. **Address:** England. **Online address:** jenn.ashworth@gmail.com

ASHWORTH, (Lewis) William. American (born United States), b. 1942. **Genres:** Environmental Sciences/Ecology, Natural History, Sciences, Travel/Exploration, Autobiography/Memoirs. **Career:** Composer, 1966-; Washington State University, music theory, teaching assistant, 1968-69; writer, 1970-; Ashland Public Library, reference librarian, 1985-2002; Arts Council of Southern Oregon, Young Writers Workshop, instructor, 1998-2000; Three Rivers School District, Young Writers Workshop, instructor, 2000. **Publications:** Hells Canyon: The Deepest Gorge on Earth, 1977; The Wallowas: Coming of Age in the Wilderness, 1978; The Carson Factor, 1979; Under the Influence: Congress, Lobbies and the American Pork-Barrel System, 1981; Nor Any Drop to Drink: The American Water Crisis, 1982; The Late, Great Lakes: An Environmental History, 1986; The Encyclopedia of Environmental Studies, 1991; Bears of North America, 1992; (contrib.) Bears, Their Life and Behavior: A Photographic Study of The North American Species, 1992; (contrib.) Penguins, Puffins and Auks: Their Lives and Behavior, 1993; The Economy of Nature: Rethinking the Connections between Ecology and Economics, 1995; The Left Hand of Eden: Meditations on Nature and Human Nature, 1999; Great Lakes Journey: A New Look at America's Freshwater Coast, 2000; (with C.E. Little and J.M. Fowler) Encyclopedia of Environmental Studies, 2001; Ogallala Blue: Water and Life on the High Plains, 2006. Contributor to periodicals. **Address:** Max Gartenberg Literary Agent, 12 Westminster Dr., Livingston, NJ 07039, U.S.A. **Online address:** wa@williamashworth.net

ASIM, Jabari. American (born United States), b. 1962?. **Genres:** Children's Fiction, Literary Criticism And History, History, Humanities, Law, Popular Culture, Race Relations, Social Commentary, Writing/Journalism, Essays, Picture/Board Books, Poetry, Novellas/Short Stories, Film. **Career:** Mosby-Year Book, production editor, 1992; St Louis Post-Dispatch, copy editor, 1992-93, book editor, 1993-95, arts editor, 1995-96; Washington Post, staff, 1996-99, senior editor, 1996-2005, syndicated columnist, 2003-07, deputy editor, 2005-07; Crisis Magazine, editor-in-chief, 2007-; Emerson College, associate professor, 2010-. **Publications:** (Ed. with S. LeFlore) Wordwalkers, 1988; The Road to Freedom, 2000; (ed.) Not Guilty: Twelve Black Men Speak Out on Law, Justice, and Life, 2001; The N Word: Who Can Say It, Who Shouldn't, and Why, 2007; What Obama Means: ... for Our Culture, Our Politics, Our Future, 2009; Taste of Honey, 2010. CHILDREN'S BOOKS: Daddy Goes to Work, 2006; Whose Toes Are Those?, 2006; Whose Knees are These?, 2006; Nappy Days, 2010; Girl of Mine, 2010; Boy of Mine, 2010. **Address:** Department of Writing, Literature and Publishing, Emerson College, 120 Boylston St., Boston, MA 02116-4624, U.S.A. **Online address:** jabari_asim@emerson.edu

ASIMOV, Janet Jeppson. (J. O. Jeppson). American (born United States), b. 1926. **Genres:** Novels, Novellas/Short Stories, Children's Fiction, Writing/Journalism. **Career:** Philadelphia General Hospital, intern, 1952-53; physician, 1952-; Bellevue Hospital, psychiatric resident, 1953-56; W.A. White Psychoanalytic Institute, assistant director of clinical services, 1967-71, training and supervising analyst, 1969-71, director of training, 1974-82; Contemporary Psychoanalysis, associate editor, 1970-94; Los Angeles Times Syndicate, science columnist, 1992-; Tribune Media, bimonthly science columnist. **Publications:** (As J.O. Jeppson) The Second Experiment, 1974; (as J.O. Jeppson) The Last Immortal, 1980; (with I. Asimov) Norby, The Mixed-up Robot, 1983; (with I. Asimov) Norby's Other Secret, 1984; (with I. Asimov) Norby and the Lost Princess, 1985; (as J.O. Jeppson) The Mysterious Cure and Other Stories of Pshrinks Anonymous, 1985; (with I. Asimov) Norby and the Invaders, 1985; (with I. Asimov) Norby and the Queen's Necklace, 1986; (with I. Asimov) Norby Finds a Villain, 1987; (with I. Asimov) How to Enjoy Writing: A Book of Aid and Comfort, 1987; (with I. Asimov) Norby: Robot for Hire, 1987; (with I. Asimov) Norby through Time and Space, 1988; Mind Transfer, 1988; The Package in Hyperspace, 1988; (with I. Asimov) Norby Down to Earth, 1988; (with I. Asimov) Norby and Yobo's Great Adventure, 1989; (with I. Asimov) Norby and the Oldest Dragon, 1990; (with I. Asimov) Norby and the Court Jester, 1991; (with I. Asimov) Frontiers II: Frontiers II: More Recent Discoveries About Life, Earth, Space, and the Universe, 1993; Murder at the Galactic Writers' Society, 1995; Norby and the Terrified Taxi, 1997; (ed.) It's Been a Good Life, 2002; Notes for a Memoir: On Isaac Asimov, Life, and Writing, 2006. EDITOR: (as J.O. Jeppson with I. Asimov) Laughing Space, 1982. Contributor to periodicals. **Address:** c/o Ralph M. Vicinanza, 303 W 18th St., New York, NY 10011, U.S.A.

ASIMOW, Michael. American (born United States), b. 1939. **Genres:** Law, Social Sciences. **Career:** Irell & Manella, associate, 1964-66; University of California, School of Law, professor of law, 1967-, now professor emeritus of law, associate dean, 1992-93; Stanford University, visiting professor, 1972, Law School, visiting professor, 2010-11; University of Michigan, visiting professor, 1984; Loeb & Loeb, counsel, 1986-91; Jewish Community Foundation, board trustee, 1989-93; American Bar Association, Section on Administrative Law and Regulatory Practice, chair, 1991-93; Duke University, visiting professor, 1992; AME Church-Temple Isaiah, Public Counsel Legal Service Program, founder, 1993, supervising attorney, 1993-; University of the Witwatersrand, visiting professor, 1995. Writer. **Publications:** Advice to the Public from Federal Administrative Agencies, 1973; (contrib.) Income Tax II, 1973; (contrib.) Gilbert Law Summaries: Income Tax I, 1982; (contrib.) Gilbert Law Summaries: Income Tax II, 1982; (with A.E. Bonfield) State and Federal Administrative Law, 1989, (with R.M. Levin) 3rd ed., 2009; Impartial Adjudicators: Bias, Ex Parte Contacts, and Separation of Functions, 1991; (with P. Bergman) Reel Justice: The Courtroom Goes to the Movies, 1996; (ed. with W.P. Hogoboom and D.B. King) California Practice Guide: Family Law, 1995; (with D.L. Greenwald) California Practice Guide: Real Property Transactions, 1995; (with M. Cohen) California Administrative Law, 2002; (ed.) A Guide to Federal Agency Adjudication, 2003; (with S. Mader) Law and Popular Culture: A Course Book, 2004; Adjudication, 6 vols., 2008; (ed.) Lawyers in Your Living Room!: Law on Television, 2009. Contributor to books and journals. **Address:** School of Law, University of California, 1242 Law Bldg., 385 Charles E Young Dr., PO Box 951476, Los Angeles, CA 90024-8311, U.S.A. **Online address:** asimow@law.ucla.edu

ASKARI, Hossein G. American/Iranian (born Iran), b. 1945. **Genres:** Economics, Business/Trade/Industry. **Career:** Massachusetts Institute of Technology, instructor in economics, 1968-69; Tufts University, assistant professor of economics, 1969-73; Wayne State University, associate professor of economics, 1973-75; University of Texas, associate professor, professor of international business and Middle Eastern studies, 1975-81; International Monetary Fund, assistant, 1978-80; Cambridge University, Anglo-American Academy, honorary fellow, 1980; George Washington University, Department of International Business, professor, 1982, Iran Professor of International Business and International Affairs, chair, 1992-97, Institute for Global Management and Research, director, 1995-98, faculty director, 1998-2000; The Consulting Center, director, 1984-86; Clark University, adjunct professor; John Hopkins University, School of Advanced International Studies, adjunct professor. Writer. **Publications:** (With F. Modigliani) Reform of the International Payments System, 1971; (with J.T. Cummings) Middle East Economies in the 1970s: A Comparative Approach, 1976; (with J.T. Cummings) Agricultural Supply Response: A Survey of the Econometric Evidence, 1976; (with T. Ruefli and M. Kennedy) Horizontal Divestiture of Energy Companies, 1977; (with J.T. Cummings) Oil, OECD, and the Third World: A Vicious Triangle? (monograph), 1978; (with G. Kozmetsky) Evaluation of the Conversion of U.S. Industry and the National Energy Plan, 1978; (with G. Kozmetsky) Economics of Energy, Trade, and International Interdependence, 1978; (with J.T. Cummings and M. Salehizadeh) Economic Analysis of OPEC Aid, 1978; (with G. Kozmetsky and A.T. Reichert) Foreign Operations of Multinational Oil Companies, 1979; (with G. Kozmetsky) National and International Energy Stabilization Policies, 1980; (contrib.) Islam and Development, 1980; (with J.T. Cummings and M. Glover) Taxation and Tax Policies in the Middle East, 1982; (with B. Dastmaltschi) Saudi Arabia's Economy: Oil and the Search for Economic Development, 1990; Third World Debt and Financial Innovation: The Experiences of Chile and Mexico, 1991; (with V. Nowshirvani and M. Jaber) Economic Development in the Countries of the GCC: The Blessing and the Curse of Oil, 1997; (contrib.) Financial Crisis Management in Regional Blocs, 1998; (with J. Forrer, H. Teegen and J. Yang) Case Studies of U.S. Economic Sanctions: The Chinese, Cuban, and Iranian Experiences, 2003; (with J. Forrer, H. Teegen and J. Yang) Economic Sanctions: Examining Their Philosophy and Efficacy, 2003; Middle East Oil Exporters: What Happened to Economic Development?, 2006; (with S. Daneshvar and A. Mohseni) Militarization of the Persian Gulf: An Economic Analysis of Global Impacts, Adaptation and Distributional Effects, 2009; (with Z. Iqbal, N. Krichene and A. Mirakhor) Stability of Islamic Finance: Creating a Resilient Financial Environment for a Secure Future, 2010; (with S.S. Rehman and N. Arfaa) Corruption and its Manifestation in the Persian Gulf, 2010; (with Z. Iqbal and A. Mirakhor) Globalization and Islamic Finance: Convergence, Prospects and Challenges, 2010; (with A. Mirakhor) Islam and the Path to Human and Economic Development, 2010. Contributor of articles to books and periodicals. **Address:** Department of International Business, George Washington University, Funger Hall, Ste. 405, 2201 G St. NW, Washington, DC 20052, U.S.A. **Online address:** askari@gwu.edu

ASKEW, Thomas A(delbert). American (born United States), b. 1931. **Genres:** History, Regional/Urban Planning. **Career:** Wheaton College, instructor, 1960-62, assistant professor, 1962-68; National College of Education, professor of social science, 1968-72, associate dean of the college, 1971-72; Gordon College, professor of history, 1972-2000, assistant dean, 1975-76, 1993-94, chairman of department, 1976-, Centennial, director, 1986-89, East West Institute of International Studies, executive director, 1996-2005, now

Stephen Phillips professor of history emeritus; University of Illinois, visiting faculty, 1970-72; Christian Scholar's Review, publisher, 1979-86. Writer. **Publications:** (With J.M. Askew) Beverly, Massachusetts, and the American Revolution: One Town's Experience, 1974; (with P.W. Spellman) The Churches and the American Experience: Ideals and Institutions, 1984; (ed. and intro. With R.A. Wells) Liberty and Law: Reflections on the Constitution in American Life and Thought, 1987; (with J.M. Askew) Gordon College: A Centennial History, 1988; (with R.V. Pierard) The American Church Experience: A Concise History, 2004. Contributor of articles to journals. **Address:** Department of History, East West Institute of International Studies, Gordon College, 255 Grapevine Rd., Wenham, MA 01984, U.S.A.

ASLAM, Nadeem. British/Pakistani (born Pakistan), b. 1966?. **Genres:** Novels, Young Adult Fiction, Literary Criticism And History. **Career:** Writer. **Publications:** NOVELS: Season of the Rainbirds, 1993; Maps for Lost Lovers, 2004; The Wasted Vigil, 2008. Contributor to periodicals. **Address:** Alfred A. Knopf, 1745 Broadway, New York, NY 10019, U.S.A.

ASLAN, Reza. American/Iranian (born Iran), b. 1972. **Genres:** Film, Theology/Religion, History, Humanities, Literary Criticism And History. **Career:** Ploughshares Fund, board director; Abraham's Vision, director; PEN USA, director; Aslan Media Inc., president, chief executive officer; Daily Beast, contributing editor; AslanMedia.com, founder; BoomGen Studios, cofounder and chief creative officer; AppOvation Labs, president; University of California, associate professor. **Publications:** No God But God: The Origins Evolution and Future of Islam, 2005; Kein Gott ausser Gott: der Glaube der Muslime von Muhammad bis zur Gegenwart, 2006; How to Win a Cosmic War: God, Globalization and the End of the War on Terror, 2009; (ed.) Tablet & Pen: Literary Landscapes from the Modern Middle East, 2010; Beyond Fundamentalism: Confronting Religious Extremism in the Age of Globalization, 2010; (ed. with A.J.H. Tapper) Muslims and Jews in America: Commonalities, Contentions, and Complexities, 2011. **Address:** Random House Publishers, 1745 Broadway, New York, NY 10019, U.S.A. **Online address:** contact@rezaaslan.com

ASNER, Jules. (Julie White). American (born United States), b. 1968. **Genres:** Novels, Mystery/Crime/Suspense. **Career:** Hard Copy, production assistant, producer, 1989-; E! Entertainment Television, E! News Daily, cohost, 1999-2002. Journalist. **Publications:** Whacked, 2008. **Address:** William Morris Agency, 13625 Ave. of the Americas, New York, NY 10019, U.S.A.

ASPER, Kathrin. American/Swiss (born Switzerland), b. 1941. **Genres:** Psychology, Medicine/Health, Self Help. **Career:** C.G. Jung Institute, lecturer and supervisor, 1982-99. Writer. **Publications:** Verlassenheit und Selbstentfremdung: Neue Zugänge zum Therapeutischen Verständnis, 1987; Von der Kindheit zum Kind in uns: Lebenshilfeaus dem Unbewussten, 1988; Schritte im Labyrinth-Tagebuch Einer Psychotherapeutin, 1992; The Inner Child in Dreams, 1992; The Abandoned Child Within: On Losing and Regaining Self-Worth, 1993; Fenster im Alltag-Psychologisches Skizzenbuch, 1994. Contributor to journals. **Address:** Plattenstrasse 98, Meilen, CH-8706, Switzerland. **Online address:** kathrin.asper@bluewin.ch

ASPINALL, Edward. Australian (born Australia) **Genres:** Social Sciences. **Career:** University of New South Wales, lecturer in Indonesian studies, 1997-2001; University of Sydney, lecturer in Southeast Asian studies, 2003-05; Australian National University, Department of Political and Social Change, fellow in Indonesian politics, senior fellow. Writer. **Publications:** (Ed. with G. van Klinken and H. Feith) The Last Days of President Suharto, 1999; (ed. with G. Fealy) Local Power and Politics in Indonesia: Decentralisation and Democratisation, 2003; (with H. Crouch) The Aceh Peace Process: Why It Failed, 2003; The Helsinki Agreement: A More Promising Basis for Peace in Aceh?, 2005; Opposing Suharto: Compromise, Resistance and Regime Change in Indonesia, 2005; Islam and Nation: Separatist Rebellion in Aceh, Indonesia, 2009. **Address:** Australian National University, Research School of Pacific & Asian Studies, Australian Capital Territory, Canberra, AC 2601, Australia. **Online address:** edward.aspinall@anu.edu.au

ASQUITH, Christina. American (born United States) **Genres:** Autobiography/Memoirs. **Career:** Julia de Burgos Bilingual Middle Magnet School, teacher, 1999; Philadelphia Inquirer, journalist and staff writer; freelance journalist-Iraq, 2003-04; University of Vermont, adjunct professor; Solutions Journal, senior editor; Diverse Magazine, senior editor. Memoirist. **Publications:** The Emergency Teacher: The Inspirational Story of a New Teacher in an Inner-City School (memoir), 2007; Sisters in War: A Story of Love, Family, and Survival in the New Iraq, 2009. Contributor to newspapers and periodicals. **Address:** Burlington, VT , U.S.A. **Online address:** christinaasquith@hotmail.com

ASSAEL, Brenda. British/American (born United States), b. 1967. **Genres:** History, Theatre, Humanities, Literary Criticism And History. **Career:** City University of New York, Lehman College, lecturer, 1997-98; University of Wales, lecturer, 1998-; Swansea University, Department of History, lecturer, 1998-2010; University of Cincinnati, Charles Phelps Taft Research Center, visiting fellow, 2005. Academic and Writer. **Publications:** The Circus and Victorian Society, 2005. Contributor to books and journals. **Address:** Swansea University, Singleton Pk., Swansea, WG SA2 8PP, Wales. **Online address:** b.assael@swansea.ac.uk

ASSEFI, Nassim. American/Iranian (born Iran), b. 1972?. **Genres:** Novels. **Career:** University of Washington, School of Medicine, teaching assistant in anatomy and embryology course, 1993, junior faculty, 2000-03, Department of Internal Medicine, junior faculty, 2006-07, Department of Obstetrics and Gynecology, junior faculty, 2006-07; Harvard Medical School, preceptor, 1998-99; Faulkner Hospital, chief medical resident, 1999; Management Sciences for Health, senior program associate, 2004-05; Family Health Alliance, womens health adviser, 2006-; global health consultant, 2006-; Harborview Medical Center, clinical preceptor, 2006-07; Primary Care Curriculum for Gynecology Residents, director, 2006-07; Country Doctor Community Health Clinics, consultant. Writer and musician. **Publications:** Aria, 2007; Say I Am You, forthcoming. **Address:** Seattle, WA , U.S.A. **Online address:** nassim@nassimassefi.com

ASSMANN, Jan. German (born Germany), b. 1938. **Genres:** Archaeology/Antiquities, Theology/Religion. **Career:** University of Heidelberg, Institute of Egyptology, faculty, 1971-, professor of Egyptology, 1976-2003, professor emeritus, 2003-; Institute for Advanced Study-Berlin, staff, 1974-75; University of Konstanz, Department of History and Sociology, honorary professor, 2005-. Writer. **Publications:** Zeit und Ewigkeit im alten äegypten: ein Beitrag zur Geschichte der Ewigkeit, 1975; (comp.) Aegyptische Hymnen und Gebete, 1975; Funktionenund Leistungen des Mythos: Drei Altorientalische Beispiele, 1982; Re und Amun: die Krise des polytheistischen Weltbilds im äegypten der 18.-20. Dynastie, 1983; Sonnenhymnen in thebanischen Gräebern, 1983; äegypten: Theologie und Fröemmigkeit einer früehen Hochkultur, 1984; Ma'at: Gerechtigkeit und Unsterblichkeit im alten äegypten, 1990; Das Grab des Amenemope, 1991; Das Grab des Amenemope, TT 41, 1991; Das Kulturelle Gedäechtnis: Schrift, Erinnerung und politische Identität in frühen Hochkulturen, 1992; Politische Theologie zwischen äegypten und Israel, 1992; Akhanyati's Theology of Light and Time, 1992; Monotheismus und Kosmotheismus: äegyptische Formen eines Denkens des Einen und ihre Europäische Rezeptionsgeschichte, 1993; Egyptian Solar Religion in the New Kingdom: Re, Amun and the Crisis of Polytheism, 1995; äegypten Eine Sinngeschichte, 1996; Moses the Egyptian: The Memory of Egypt in Western Monotheism, 1997; Dasverschleierte Bild zu Sais: Schillers Ballade und ihre Griechischen undäegyptischen Hintergründe, 1999; Herrschaft und Heil: Politische Theologie in Altägypten, Israel und Europa, 2000; Weisheit und Mysterium: das Bild der Griechen von äegypten, 2000; Der Tod als Themader Kulturtheorie: Todesbilder und Totenriten im alten äegypten, 2000; Images et Rites de la Mort dans l'Egypte Ancienne: l'Apport des LiturgiesFunerires: Quatre Séminaires à l'Ecole Pratique des Hautesétudes, 2000; Tod und Jenseits im Alten ägypten, 2001; The Search for God in Ancient Egypt, 2001; The Mind of Egypt: History and Meaning in the Time of the Pharaohs, 2002; Die Mosaische Unterscheidung, Oder, DerPreis des Monotheismus, 2003; ägyptische Geheimnisse, 2004; Die Zauberflöte: Oper und Mysterium, 2005; Thomas Mann undägypten: Mythos und Monotheismus in den Josephsromanen, 2006; Of God and Gods: Egypt, Israel, and the Rise Of Monotheism, 2008; (contrib.) Europa der Akademien, 2010; Religio duplex, 2010; Mémoire culturelle, 2010; Cultural Memory and Early Civilization, 2011. EDITOR: (with E. Feucht and R. Grieshammer) Fragen an die Altäegyptische Literatur: Studien zum Gedenken an Eberhard Otto, 1977; (with C. Hardmeier) Schrift und Gedäechtnis: Beiträege zur Archäeologie der literarischen Kommunikation, 1983; (with A. Assmann) Kanon und Zensur, 1987; (with G. Burkard and V. Davies) Problems and Priorities in Egyptian Archaeology, 1987; (with T. Hölscher) Kultur und Gedächtnis, 1988; (with D. Harth) Kultur und Konflikt, 1990; (with T. Sundermeier) Das Fest und das Heilige: Religiöese Kontrapunkte zur Alltagswelt, 1991; (co-ed.)

Revolution und Mythos, 1992; Die Erfindung des inneren Menschen: Studienzur religiöesen Anthropologie, 1993; (with A.R.E. Agus) Ocular desire: Sehnsucht desAuges, 1994; Text und Kommentar, 1995; (with E. Dziobek, H. Guksch and F. Kampp) The banische Beamtennekropolen: neue Perspektiven archäeologischer Forschung, 1995; (with T. Sundermeier) Schuld, Gewissen, undPerson: Studien zur Geschichte des inneren Menschen, 1997; (with A.I. Baumgarten and G.G. Stroumsa) Self, Soul, and Body in Religious Experience, 1998; (with G.G. Stroumsa) Transformations of the Inner Self in Ancient Religions, 1999; (with A. Assmann) Einsamkeit, 2000; (with A.I. Baumgarten) Representation in Religion: Studies in Honor of Moshe Barasch, 2000; (with F. Maciejewski and A. Michaels) Abschied von den Toten, 2005; (with K.E. Müller) Der Ursprung der Geschichte: archaische Kulturen, das Alte ägypten und dasFrühe Griechenland, 2005; (with M. Mulsow) Sintflut und Gedächtnis, 2006; (with A. Assmann) Verwandlungen, 2006; (with A. Kucharek) ägyptische Religion, 2008. **Address:** Institute of Egyptology, University of Heidelberg, Marstallhof 4, Heidelberg, 69117, Germany. **Online address:** jan.assmann@urz.uni-heidelberg.de

ASSOULINE, Pierre. French (born France), b. 1953. **Genres:** History, Biography, Adult Non-fiction, Literary Criticism And History. **Career:** Quotidien de Paris, 1976-78; France Soir, staff, 1979-83; Center for Training of Journalists and collaborating, staff in history, 1979; France Inter, staff, 1986-90; RTL, staff, 1990-99; Lire (magazine), editor. Journalist and biographer. **Publications:** BIOGRAPHIES: Monsieur Dassault, 1983; Gaston Gallimard: un demi-siecle, 1984; Une eminence grise: Jean Jardin (1904-1976), 1986; L'homme de l'art: D.-H. Kahnweiler, 1884-1979, 1988; Albert Londres: vie et mort d'un grand reporter, 1884-1932, 1989; Simenon: biographie, 1992; Trois hommes d'influence, 1994; Herge: biographie, 1996; Henri Cartier-Bresson: L'oeil du siècle, 1999; Grâces lui soient rendues: Paul Durand-Ruel, le marchand des impressionnistes, 2002. NOVELS: La cliente, 1998; Double vie, 2000; Etat limite, 2003; Lutetia, 2005; Desiree Dolron, 2006; Rosebud, 2006; Portrait: Roman, 2007; (with P. Ardenne) Anselm Kiefer, 2007; Dans les Archives Secrètes de la Police, 2009; Hergé: The Man who Created Tintin, 2009; Invités: Roman, 2009. OTHER NONFICTION: (with P. Dampenon) De nos envoyes speciaux: les coulisses du reportage, 1977; Lourdes: histoires d'eau, 1980; Les nouveaux convertis: enquete sur les chretiens, des juifs et des musulmans pas comme las autres, 1982; L'epuration des intellectuels, 1944-1945 (history), 1985; Le fleuve Combelle, 1997; Le dernier des Camondo, 1997; Elles: Histoires de femmes, 1999. OTHERS: Discovering Impressionism, 2004; Lectures de Romain Gary, 2010; Vies de Job: roman, 2011. **Address:** 72 boulevard Flandrin, Paris, 75016, France.

ASTARITA, Tommaso. American/Italian (born Italy), b. 1961. **Genres:** History, Local History/Rural Topics, Social Commentary, Adult Non-fiction, Cultural/Ethnic Topics. **Career:** Wright State University, visiting assistant professor, 1988-89; Georgetown University, Department of History, associate professor, 1989-, professor, director of undergraduate studies. Writer. **Publications:** The Continuity of Feudal Power: The Caracciolo di Brienza in Spanish Naples, 1992; Village Justice: Community, Family and Popular Culture in Early Modern Italy, 1999; Between Salt Water and Holy Water: A History of Southern Italy, 2005. **Address:** Department of History, Georgetown University, 621 International Criminal Ct., 37th and O St. NW, PO Box 571035, Washington, DC 20057-1035, U.S.A. **Online address:** astaritt@georgetown.edu

ASTELL, Ann W. American (born United States) **Genres:** History, Theology/Religion. **Career:** Purdue University, professor of English and chair of Medieval Studies, director of graduate studies; University of Notre Dame, Department of Theology, professor, 2007-. Writer. **Publications:** The Song of Songs in the Middle Ages, 1990; Job, Boethius and Epic Truth, 1994; (ed.) Divine Representations: Postmodernism and Spirituality, 1994; Chaucer and the Universe of Learning, Cornell University Press 1996; Political Allegory in Late Medieval England, 1999; (ed.) Lay Sanctity, Medieval and Modern: A Search for Models, 2000; (ed. with B. Wheeler) Joan of Arc and Spirituality, 2003; Joan of Arc and Sacrificial Authorship, 2003; Eating Beauty: The Eucharist and the Spiritual Arts of the Middle Ages, 2006; (ed. with J.A. Jackson) Levinas and Medieval Literature: The Difficult Reading of English and Rabbinic Texts, 2009; Sacrifice, Scripture, and Substitution: Readings in Ancient Judaism and Christianity, 2011. **Address:** Department of Theology, University of Notre Dame, 333 Malloy Hall, Notre Dame, IN 46556, U.S.A. **Online address:** ann.w.astell.1@nd.edu

ASTIN, Anna. *See* **DUKE, Anna Marie.**

ASTLEY, Neil. British (born England), b. 1953. **Genres:** Novels, Poetry, Literary Criticism And History, Children's Fiction, Young Adult Fiction. **Career:** Warner Brothers Magazine, press officer; Stand (magazine), production editor, 1975-78; Morden Tower (poetry readings organization), publications editor, 1976-78; Bloodaxe Books Ltd., founder, editor and managing director, 1978-; Northern Territory News, sub-editor. **Publications:** POETRY: The Speechless Act, 1984; Darwin Survivor, 1988; Biting My Tongue, 1995. EDITOR: Ten North-East Poets, 1980; Bossy Parrot: Best Children's Poems from the Evening Chronicle Poetry Competition (anthology), 1987; Poetry with an Edge, 1988, rev. ed., 1993; Dear Next Prime Minister: Open Letters to Margaret Thatcher and Neil Kinnock (anthology), 1990; Tony Harrison (criticism), 1991; Wordworks: Poetry on T.V., 1992; (with A. Myers) North of the Word, 1993; New Blood, 1999; Staying Alive: Reqal Poems for Unreal Times, 2002; Pleased to See Me: 69 Very Sexy Poems, 2002; Do Not Go Gentle: Poems for Funerals, 2003; Bloodaxe Poems of the Year 2003, 2003; Being Alive: The Sequel to Staying Alive, 2004; Passionfood: 100 Love Poems, 2005; Bloodaxe Poetry Introductions 1, 2006; Bloodaxe Poetry Introductions 2, 2006; Bloodaxe Poetry Introductions 3, 2007; Earth Shattering: Ecopoems, 2007; Ten North-East Poets, 2007; The Heavy Bear Who Goes with Me, 2007; (with P. Robertson-Pearce) Soul Food: Nourishing Poems for Starved Minds, 2007; In Person: 30 Poets, 2008; Being Human, 2011. OTHERS: The End of My Tether (novel), 2002; The Sheep Who Changed the World, 2005; (co-author) Magnetic North: New Work from North East Writers, 2005. Contributor to periodicals. **Address:** Bloodaxe Books Ltd., Highgreen, Tarset, NM NE48 1RP, England. **Online address:** editor@bloodaxebooks.demon.co.uk

ATABAKI, Touraj. Iranian (born Iran), b. 1950. **Genres:** Novels. **Career:** Utrecht University, associate professor, 1987-2006; International Institute of Social History, senior research fellow, 1995-; European Council of the International Institute of Persian Speaking Societies, director, 2000-03; University of Amsterdam, department of history, chair, 2001- 06; University of Leiden, associate professor, 2006-. Writer. **Publications:** (ed. with others) Etymologisch woordenboek, 1989; (ed. with Margreet Dorlijn) Kurdistan in Search of Ethnic Identity, 1990; (ed.) Ayat-e Eshq, Tajiki Contemporary Poetry, 1992; Azerbaijan: Ethnicity and Autonomy in Twentieth-Century Iran, 1993, rev. ed., Azerbaijan: Ethnicity and the Struggle for Power in Iran, I.B., 2000; (with J. Versteeg) Centraal-Azie: Mensen, politiek, economie, cultuur, 1994; (with S. Rustamova-Towhidi) Baku Documents: Union Catalogue of Persian, Azerbaijani, Ottoman Turkish and Arabic Serials and Newspapers in the Libraries of the Republic of Azerbaijan, 1995; Azarbayjan dar Iran-e Mo aser, 1997; (ed. with John O'Kane) Post-Soviet Central Asia, 2003; Beyond Essentialism: Who Writes Whose Past in the Middle East and Central Asia?, 2003; (with E.J. Zurcher) Men of Order: Authoritarian Modernization under Ataturk and Reza Shah, 2004; (ed. with Sanjyot Mehendale) Central Asia and the Caucasus: Transnationalism and Diaspora, 2005; (ed.) Iran and the First World War: Battleground of the Great Powers, 2006; (ed.) The State and the Subaltern: Modernization, Society and Politics in Turkey and Iran, 2007; (ed.) Tajaddod Ameraneh, 2007; (ed.) Historiography and Political Culture in Twentieth-Century Iran. Contributor of numerous articles to journals. **Address:** International Institute of Social History, Cruquiusewg 31, Amsterdam, 1019, Netherlands. **Online address:** t.atabaki@let.leidenuniv.nl

ATHAS, Daphne. American (born United States), b. 1923. **Genres:** Novels, Young Adult Non-fiction. **Career:** Perkins School for the Blind, teacher of algebra, 1944-45; U.S. Air Force, service club director, 1952-58; Durham Technical Institute, coordinator of basic education, 1964-66; University of North Carolina, Department of English, lecturer, 1967-73, 1974-79, lecturer in the creative writing, 1968-; Tehran University, Fulbright professor of American literature, 1973-74. Writer. **Publications:** The Weather of the Heart, 1947; The Fourth World, 1956; (with G. Campbell) Sit on the Earth (play), 1957; Greece by Prejudice, 1963; Entering Ephesus, 1971; Cora, 1978; Crumbs for the Bogeyman, 1991; (with M.B. Gingher) Gram-O-Rama: Breaking the Rules, 2007; Chapel Hill in Plain Sight: Notes from the Other Side of the Track, 2010. Contributor of articles to magazines. **Address:** University of North Carolina, Greenlaw Hall, PO Box 3520, Chapel Hill, NC 27599-3520, U.S.A. **Online address:** dathas@mindspring.com

ATHERDEN, Margaret Ann. British (born England), b. 1947. **Genres:** Natural History. **Career:** York St. John College, principal lecturer in geography, 1971-2003, director of research, 1998-2003, research development officer, 2003-07, chief executive; University of Bradford, visiting lecturer and honorary research fellow, 1978-2007, retired, 2007. Writer. **Publications:** Upland Britain: A Natural History, 1992. EDITOR/CO-EDITOR: (with R.A. Butlin) Woodland in the Landscape: Past and Future Perspectives, 1998; Wetlands in the Landscape: Archaeology, Conservation, Heritage, 2001; Global Warming: A Yorkshire Perspective, 2003. Contributor to books and journals. **Address:** York St John University, Lord Mayor's Walk, York, YO31 7EX, England. **Online address:** m.atherden@yorksj.ac.uk

ATKEY, Mel. Canadian (born Canada), b. 1958. **Genres:** Music, Theatre, History. **Career:** Writer, composer and theatre critic. **Publications:** When We Both Got to Heaven: James At key among the Anishnabek at Colpoy's Bay, 2002; Broadway North: The Dream of a Canadian Musical Theater, 2006; A Million Miles from Broadway-the Musical Theatre from a Universal Perspective, forthcoming. **Address:** 247 Eversholt St., Flat 6, London, GL NW1 1BA, England. **Online address:** melatkey@hotmail.com

ATKIN, Flora B. American (born United States), b. 1919. **Genres:** Children's Fiction, Plays/Screenplays, Theatre, Young Adult Fiction. **Career:** Jewish Community Center, dance instructor, Recreational Arts Department, director, Camp JCC, founding director, 1940-44, instructor of creative dance, drama, music, director and choreographer, 1940-68; Howard University, instructor, 1942-43; Coast Guard Auxiliary, instructor, 1967-73; Jewish Community Center of Greater Washington, cultural arts chairperson, 1968-69, instructor in drama, 1979-82; Adventure Theatre, founding director and playwright of in-school players, 1969-79; National Park Service, instructor, 1973-74; Writer's Center, instructor in children's playwriting, 1980-81; Children's Theatre Association of America, play reader, 1983-84; University of Maryland, Writing Center, professional tutor, 1986-90; Matinee Lollipops (a children's entertainment guide), director, 1989-91. Writer and consultant. **Publications:** PLAYS: Tarradiddle Tales, 1969; Tarradiddle Travels, 1970; Golliwhoppers!, 1972; Skupper-Duppers, 1974; Dig 'n Tel, 1978; Grampo/Scampo, 1981; Hold that Tiger, 1984; Tales from the Rebbe's Table, 1994. Contributor to periodicals. **Address:** Dramatic Publishing, 311 Washington St., Woodstock, IL 60098-3308, U.S.A. **Online address:** matkin1@compuserve.com

ATKINS, Charles. American (born United States) **Genres:** Novels, Psychiatry, Psychology, Adult Non-fiction, Medicine/Health. **Career:** Yale University School of Medicine, clinical faculty in psychiatry, Department of Psychiatry, lecturer in psychiatry; Waterbury Hospital, director of behavioral health. Writer. **Publications:** The Portrait, 1998; Risk Factor, 1999; The Cadaver's Ball, 2005; The Bipolar Disorder Answer Book, 2007; The Prodigy: A Novel of Suspense, 2008; Ashes, Ashes, 2008; Alzheimer's Answer Book: Professional Answers to More than 250 Questions about Alzheimer's and Dementia, 2008; Mother's Milk, 2009; Vultures at Twilight, 2012. **Address:** Atkins Unlimited L.L.C., PO Box 833, Woodbury, CT 06798, U.S.A. **Online address:** atkinsunlimited@aol.com

ATKINS, E. Taylor. American (born United States), b. 1967. **Genres:** History, Music. **Career:** University of Iowa, visiting assistant professor, 1997; Northern Illinois University, Deparment of History, assistant professor, 1997-2003, associate professor, 2003-10, professor 2010-, director of undergraduate studies, 2005-, Anime Association, faculty advisor, 1998-2007, Fermi National Accelerator Laboratory Oral History Project, director, 1998; Bahai Institute for Higher Education, affiliated global faculty, 2009-. Writer. **Publications:** Blue Nippon: Authenticating Jazz in Japan, 2001; (ed.) Jazz Planet, 2003; Primitive Selves: Koreana in the Japanese Colonial Gaze, 1910-1945, 2010. Contributor to periodicals. **Address:** Department of History, Northern Illinois University, Zulauf 702, 231 N Annie Glidden Rd., DeKalb, IL 60115, U.S.A. **Online address:** etatkins@niu.edu

ATKINS, Leo. *See* **HARVEY, Clay.**

ATKINS, Russell. American (born United States), b. 1926. **Genres:** Plays/Screenplays, Poetry, Music. **Career:** Freelance Magazine, co-founder and editor, 1950-; University of Iowa, Iowa Workshop, affiliater, 1953-54; Sutphen School of Music, publicity manager, 1957-60; WVIZ-TV, consultant, 1969-72; Cleveland Board of Education, consultant, 1972-73; Karamu House and Theatre, creative writing instructor, 1972-86; Ohio Program in the Humanities, instructor, 1978. Writer. **Publications:** Psychovisual Perspective for Musical Composition, 1956-1958, 3rd ed., 1969; A Podium Presentation, 1960; Phenomena (poetry and play), 1961; Objects(poetry), 1961; Two by Atkins: The Abortionist and The Corpse, 1963; Objects 2, 1963; Spyrytual, 1966; Heretofore (poetry and play), 1968; Presentations, 1969; Sounds and Silences: Poetry for Now, 1969; Here In The (poetry), 1976; Celebrations, 1977; Whichever, 1978; Juxtapositions (poetry, criticism), 1991. Contributor to periodicals. **Address:** 6005 Grand Ave., Cleveland, OH 44104, U.S.A.

ATKINSON, Anthony Barnes. British (born England), b. 1944. **Genres:** Economics, Social Commentary. **Career:** St. John's College, fellow, 1967-71; University of Essex, professor of economics, 1971-76, chairman, 1974-76; Journal of Public Economics, editor, 1971-97; Massachusetts Institute of Technology, visiting professor of economics, 1973; University of London, London School of Economics and Political Science, Department of Political Economy, professor and head, 1976-79, Tooke professor of economic science and statistics, 1980-92, honorary fellow, 2004, Centennial professor, 2010-; Suntory-Toyota International Centre for Economics and Related Disciplines, chairman, 1981-87; Econometric Society, president, 1988; British Academy, vice president, 1988-90; European Economic Association, president, 1989; International Economic Association, president, 1989-92; Foundation for International Studies in Social Security, chairman, 1990-92; University of Cambridge, professor of political economy, 1992-94; Churchill College, fellow, 1992-94; University of Oxford, professor of economics, 2007-09, Nuffield College, warden, 1994-2005, fellow, senior research fellow, 2005-, now emeritus senior research fellow; Royal Economic Society, president, 1995-98; Nuffield Foundation, trustee, 1996-; British Association for the Advancement of Science, president, 1997; Harvard University, F W Taussig visiting professor of economics, 2009-11. Writer. **Publications:** Poverty in Britain and the Reform of Social Security, 1969; Unequal Shares: Wealth in Britain, 1972; The Tax Credit Scheme and the Redistribution of Income, 1973; (ed.) Wealth, Income, and Inequality, 1973; The Economics of Inequality, 1975, 2nd ed., 1983; (with A.J. Harrison) The Distribution of Personal Wealth in Britain, 1978; (with J.E. Stiglitz) Lectures on Public Economics, 1980; Social Justice and Public Policy, 1982; (with A. Maynard and C. Trinder) Parents and Children, 1983; (with J. Micklewright) Unemployment Benefits and Unemployment Duration, 1988; Poverty and Social Security, 1989; The Reform of Direct Taxation, 1990; (ed.) Modern Public Finance, 1991; Dilemmi della democrazia e strategie del riformismo, 1991; (ed. with R. Brunetta) Economics for the New Europe, 1991; (with J. Micklewright) The Distribution of Income in Eastern Europe, 1992; (ed.) Economics in a Changing World: Proceedings of the Tenth World Congress of the International Economic Association, Moscow, 1992; (with J. Micklewright) Economic Transformation in Eastern Europe and the Distribution of Income, 1992; (with F. Bourguignon and C. Morrisson) Empirical Studies of Earnings Mobility, 1992; (ed. with M. Rein) Age, Work and Social Security, 1993; (ed.) Welfare and Work Incentives: A North American Perspective, 1993; (ed.) Alternatives to Capitalism: The Economics of Partnership, 1993; Taux d'intérêt et chômage, 1993; (co-author) Pour l'emploi et la cohésion sociale, 1994; (with L. Rainwater and T.M. Smeeding) Income Distribution in OECD Countries: Evidence from the Luxembourg Income Study, 1995; Public Economics in Action, 1995; Incomes and the Welfare State, 1995; Poverty in Europe, 1998; The Economic Consequences of Rolling Back the Welfare State, 1999; Is Rising Income Inequality Inevitable?, 1999; Die Zukunft des Sozialstaats, 2000; Den glömda krisen, 2000; (ed. with F. Bourguignon) Handbook of Income Distribution, 2000; (co-author) Social Indicators, 2002; (ed.) Funding the Millennium Development Goals, 2004; (ed.) New Sources of Development Finance, 2005; (contrib.) Wider Perspectives on Global Development, 2005; (ed. with T. Piketty) Top Incomes Over the Twentieth Century: A Contrast Between Continental European and English-speaking Countries, 2007; Changing Distribution of Earnings in OECD Countries, 2008; (with E. Marlier) Analysing and Measuring Social Inclusion in a Global Context, 2010. **Address:** Nuffield College, University of Oxford, 1 New Rd., Oxford, OX OX1 1NF, England. **Online address:** tony.atkinson@nuffield.ox.ac.uk

ATKINSON, Elizabeth Jane. American (born United States), b. 1961?. **Genres:** Sports/Fitness. **Career:** Writer and educator. **Publications:** NONFICTION: Monster Vehicles, 1991; Glee! An Easy Guide to Gluten-Free Independence, 2009. FICTION: From Alice to Zen and Everyone in Between, 2008; I, Emma Freke, 2010. Contributor to periodicals. **Address:** West Newbury, MA , U.S.A. **Online address:** elizabethatkinson2@gmail.com

ATKINSON, James. British (born England), b. 1914. **Genres:** Theology/Religion. **Career:** Archbishop of Canterbury, theological adviser, 1955-79; University of Hull, reader in theology, 1956-67; Garret Theological Seminary, visiting professor, 1966-67; University of Sheffield, Department of Biblical Studies, professor, 1967-79, head, 1967-, canon theological emeritus, 1994-, now professor emeritus, Centre for Reformation Studies, founder and director; Canon Theologian of Sheffield Cathedral, 1970-; St John's College, honorary fellow. Writer. **Publications:** (Ed. and trans.) Luther's Early Theological Works, 1962; Rome and Reformation: A Stubborn Problem Re-Examined, 1966; (ed.) Luther's Works, vols. 44, 1967; Martin Luther and the Birth of Protestantism, 1968; The Reformation, 1968; The Great Light: Luther and Reformation, 1968; The Trial of Luther, 1971; Erasmus of Rotterdam (television script), 1974; Martin Luther, Prophet to the Church Catholic, 1983; Christianity and Judaism: New Understanding, New Relationship, 1984; (with M. Luther) The Darkness of Faith, 1987; Faith Lost: Faith Regained, 2005; Understanding the Incarnation, 2008. Contributor to books. **Address:** Department of Biblical Studies, University of Sheffield, 45 Victoria St., Sheffield, S3 7QB, England.

ATKINSON, Kate. Scottish/British (born England), b. 1951?. **Genres:** Novels, Novellas/Short Stories, Young Adult Fiction. **Career:** University of Dundee, Department of English, tutor. Writer. **Publications:** Behind the Scenes at the Museum, 1996; Human Croquet, 1997; Abandonment, 2000; Emotionally Weird: A Novel, 2000; Not the End of the World: Stories, 2002; Case Histories: A Novel, 2004; One Good Turn: A Novel, 2006; Jolly Murder Mystery, 2006; When Will There Be Good News, 2008; Started Early, Took My Dog, 2010. **Address:** Macmillan Picador, 25 Eccleston Pl., London, GL SW 1W 9NF, England. **Online address:** info@kateatkinson.co.uk

ATKINSON, Lawrence Rush. *See* **ATKINSON, Rick.**

ATKINSON, Michael (J.). American (born United States) **Genres:** Literary Criticism And History, Reference, Humanities. **Career:** Institute of Pathology, GSF-National Research Center for Environment and Health, staff. Writer. **Publications:** Plotinus, Ennead V.1: On the Three Principal Hypostases, 1983. **Address:** Oxford University Press, 198 Madison Ave., New York, NY 10016-4308, U.S.A. **Online address:** atkinson@gsf.de

ATKINSON, Rick. (Lawrence Rush Atkinson). American/German (born Germany), b. 1952. **Genres:** Military/Defense/Arms Control, History. **Career:** Pittsburg Morning Sun, reporter, 1976-77; Kansas City Times, reporter, 1977-83; Washington Post, general assignment reporter, investigative reporter, 1983-85, 1989-91, deputy national editor, 1985-87, Berlin bureau chief and Central Europe correspondent, 1993-96, assistant managing editor, 1996-. **Publications:** The Long Gray Line: The American Journey of West Point's Class of 1966, 1989; Crusade: The Untold Story of the Persian Gulf War, 1993; Long Gray Line, 1999; The Liberation Trilogy, vol. I: An Army at Dawn: The War in North Africa, 1942-1943, 2002, vol. II: The Day of Battle: The War in Sicily and Italy, 1943-1944, 2007, vol. III: The Normandy Invasion and the War in Western Europe, forthcoming; In the Company of Soldiers: A Chronicle of Combat, 2004; Where Valor Rests, 2007. **Address:** c/o Raphael Sagalyn, Sagalyn Literary Agency, 4922 Fairmont Ave., Ste. 200, Bethesda, MD 20814-7213, U.S.A.

ATLAS, James (Robert). American (born United States), b. 1949. **Genres:** Poetry, Novellas/Short Stories, Education, Biography, Literary Criticism And History. **Career:** Harvard Advocate, editor, 1969-70; Time, book reviewer and staff writer, 1977-78; New York Times Book Review, assistant editor, 1979-81; Atlantic Monthly, associate editor, 1981-85; Vanity Fair, contributing editor, 1985-87; New York Times Magazine, assistant editor, 1988-97, editor; New Yorker, staff writer, 1997-99; Lipper and Co., co-founder, 1999-; Lipper Publications, director, 1999-; The New Yorker, contributor; Atlas Books, publisher; Atlas & Co., president. **Publications:** Delmore Schwartz: The Life of an American Poet, 1977; The Great Pretender, 1986; The Book Wars: What It Takes to Be Educated in America, 1990 as Battle of the Books: The Curriculum Debate in America, 1992; (co-author) Life Overshadowing Art: A Literary Discussion at the First North American Reunion of Oxonians, 1992; Bellow: A Biography, 2000; My Life in the Middle Ages: A Survivor's Tale, 2005. EDITOR: (with G. Goemoeri) Attila Jozsef: Selected Poems and Texts, 1973; Ten American Poets: An Anthology of Poems by Alan Williamson, Jonathan Galassi, Paul Smyth, Peggy Rizza, James Martin, Richard Tillinghast, Robert B. Shaw, Jane Shore, Frank Bidart and John Koethe, 1973; (and intro.) In Dreams Begin Responsibilities, and Other Stories, 1978. Contributor of articles to periodicals. **Address:** Atlas & Co., 15 W 26th St., 2nd Fl., New York, NY 10010-1031, U.S.A.

ATLAS, Nava. American (born United States), b. 1955?. **Genres:** Food And Wine, Human Relations/Parenting. **Career:** Artist and author. **Publications:** Vegetariana: A Rich Harvest of Wit, Lore, and Recipes, 1984, 2nd ed., 1993; Nava Atlas and Chaim Tabak: A Collaborative Exhibition: The Radwaste and Stonehenge Series, Wichita Art Museum, March 31-May 1, 1985, 1985; American Harvest: Regional Recipes for the Vegetarian Kitchen, 1987; The Wholefood Catalog: A Complete Guide to Natural Foods, 1988; Vegetarian Celebrations: Menus for Holidays and Other Festive Occasions, 1990; Vegetarian Express: Easy, Tasty, and Healthy Menus in 28 Minutes or Less!, 1995; Vegetarian Celebrations: Festive Menus for Holidays and Other Special Occasions, 1996; Vegetarian Soups for All Seasons: A Treasury of Bountiful Low-Fat Soups and Stews, 1996, 4th ed. as Vegan Soups and Hearty Stews for All Seasons, 2009; Great American Vegetarian: Traditional and Regional Recipes for the Enlightened Cook, 1998; Pasta East to West: A Vegetarian World Tour, 1998; The Vegetarian 5- Ingredient Gourmet: 250 Simple Recipes and Dozens of Healthy Menus for Eating Well Every Day, 2001; The Vegetarian Family Cookbook, 2004; Everyday Traditions: Simple Family Rituals for Connection and Comfort, 2005; Vegan Express: Featuring 160 Recipes for Quick, Delicious, and Healthy Meals, 2008; Vegan Soups and Hearty Stews for All Seasons, 2009; Secret Recipes for the Modern Wife: All the Dishes You'll Need to Make from the Day You Say I Do until Death (or Divorce) Do You Part, 2009. Contributor to books and periodicals. **Address:** NY , U.S.A. **Online address:** navaatlas@mac.com

ATTALI, Jacques. French (born France), b. 1943. **Genres:** Novels, Poetry, Essays. **Career:** école Polytechnique, professor of economics, 1970-85, école des Mines, école des Ponts et Chaussées, lecturer in economics, 1971; Action contre la Faim, founder, 1980; European Bank for Reconstruction and Development, founder and president, 1991-93; Attali & Associates, founder, 1994, chief executive officer; PlaNet Finance, founder and president, 1998-; Grenoble University, Orchestra, co-director, 2010-; The Express, columnist; Dauphine University, faculty. Writer and economist. **Publications:** Les Modèles politiques, 1972; Analyse économique de la vie politique, 1972; (with M. Guillaume) L'anti- économique, 1974; La parole et l'outil, 1975; Conséquences sociales de la situation économique contemporaine: conférence à l'occasion du Cours international de stagiaires sur la mise en oeuvre d'une politique sociale active, organisé par l'Institut international d'études sociales, 1976; (ed.) Opinion européenne face aux multinationales, 1977; Bruits: essai sur l'économie politique de la musique, 1977; La nouvelle économie française, 1978; L'ordre cannibale: vie et mort de la médecine, 1979; Les trois mondes: pour une théorie de l'après-crise, 1981; Histoires du temps, 1982; La figure de Fraser, 1984; Un homme d'influence: Sir Siegmund Warburg, 1902-1982, 1985; Noise: The Political Economy of Music, 1985; Man of Influence: The Extraordinary Career of S.G. Warburg, 1987; Au propre et au figuré: une histoire de la propriété, 1988; Eternal Life, a Novel, 1989; Lines of Horizon, 1990; Le premier jour après moi: Roman, 1990; 1492, 1991; Millennium: Winners and Losers in the Coming World Order, 1991; Verbatim, vol. III, 1993; Il viendra: Roman, 1994; Europe(s), 1994; Economie de l'apocalypse: trafic et proliférations nucléaires, 1995; Chemins de sagesse: traité du labyrinthe, 1996; Au-delà de nulle part: Roman, 1997; Dictionnaire du XXIe siècle, 1998; Fraternités: une nouvelle utopie, 1999; Les portes du ciel: pièce en cinq actes, 1999; La femme du menteur: Roman, 1999; The Labyrinth in Culture and Society: Pathways to Wisdom, 1999; Blaise Pascal; ou, Le génie français, 2000; Les utopies, 2001; Nouv'elles: Roman, 2002; Les Juifs, le monde et l'argent: histoire économique du peuple juif, 2002; L'homme nomade, 2003; Français, langue du monde, 2003; Le confrérie des éveillés: Roman, 2004; Raison et foi: Averroès, Maïmonide, Thomas d'Aquin, 2004; La voie humaine: pour une nouvelle social-démocratie, 2004; Israël, les Juifs, l'antisémitisme, 2005; Karl Marx; ou, L'esprit du monde: biographie, 2005; C'était François Mitterrand, 2005; Israël, les Juifs, l'antisémitisme, 2005; Brève histoire de l'avenir, 2006; Conférence sur Marx, 2006; Amours: histoires des relations entre les hommes et les femmes, 2007; Gândhî, ou, L'éveil des humiliés: biographie, 2007; Avenir du travail, 2007; 300 décisions pour changer la France: rapport de la Commission pour la libération de la croissance française, 2008; Du cristal à la fumée: Théâtre, 2008; La Crise, et après, 2008; A Brief History of the Future, 2008; Survivre Aux Crises, 2009; Dictionnaire Amoureux du Judäsme, 2009; Sens Des Choses, 2009; Brief History of the Future: Abrave and Controversial Look at the Twenty-First Century, 2009; Tous Ruińs Dans Dix Ans: Dette Publique, La Dernīre Chance, 2010; Une ambition pour dix ans, 2010; Paris et la Mer: La Seine est Capitale, 2010; Phares, 2010. **Address:** Attali & Associates, 5 Ave. de Messine, Paris, 75008, France. **Online address:** j@attali.com

ATTEMA, Martha. Canadian/Dutch (born Netherlands), b. 1949. **Genres:** Children's Fiction, Young Adult Fiction, Picture/Board Books, History, Novels. **Career:** Kindergarten teacher-Giekerk, 1969-73; teacher of kindergarten and grade one-North Bay, 1987-. Writer. **Publications:** The Unhappy Pinetree (picture book), 1992. NOVELS FOR YOUNG ADULTS: A Time to Choose (historical), 1995; A Light in the Dunes, 1997; Daughter of Light (historical), 2001; When the War Is Over, 2002; Hero, 2003; Paper Wagon: A Folktale from Friesland, 2005. Contributor to periodicals. **Address:** 233 Peever Line, Powassan, ON P0H 1Z0, Canada. **Online address:** martatte@vianet.on.ca

ATTENBOROUGH, Richard (Samuel). British (born England), b. 1923. **Genres:** Philosophy, Biography, Essays, Film, Social Commentary. **Career:** Writer, actor and producer. **Publications:** In Search of Gandhi, 1982; (ed.) The Words of Gandhi, 1982, (ed. and intro.) 2nd ed., 2000; (afterword) Gandhi, a Pictorial Biography, 1983; (afterword) Richard Attenborough's Chorus Line, 1985; Richard Attenborough's Cry Freedom: A Pictorial Record, 1987; Pandora's Box?: Will the 1990s Bring Forth Feast or Famine?, 1989. **Address:** c/o Martin Baum, Creative Artists Agency, 9830 Wilshire Blvd., Beverly Hills, CA 90212, U.S.A.

ATTFIELD, Robin. Welsh/British (born England), b. 1941. **Genres:** Ethics, Intellectual History, Philosophy. **Career:** University of Wales, assistant lecturer, 1968-70, lecturer, 1971-77, senior lecturer, 1977-81, reader in philosophy, 1981-92; University of Ife, visiting lecturer, 1972-73; University of Nairobi, inter-university council visiting lecturer, 1975; Cardiff University, professor of philosophy, 1992-; Royal Institute of Philosophy, Cardiff Branch, chair. Writer. **Publications:** God and the Secular, 1978, 2nd ed., 1993; The Ethics of Environmental Concern, 1983, 2nd ed., 1991; A Theory of Value and Obligation, 1987; (ed. with K.J. Dell) Values, Conflict and the Environment, 1989, 2nd ed., 1996; (ed. with B. Wilkins) International Justice and the Third World, 1992; (ed. with A. Belsey and contrib.) Philosophy and the Natural Environment, 1994; Environmental Philosophy, 1994; Value, Obligation and Meta-Ethics, 1995; The Ethics of the Global Environment, 1999; Environmental Ethics: An Overview for the Twenty-First Century, 2003; Creation, Evolution and Meaning, 2006; (ed.) Ethics of the Environment, 2008; Ethics: An Overview, 2012. **Address:** Cardiff School of English, Communication, and Philosophy, Cardiff University, Humanities Bldg., Colum Dr., Cathays, Cardiff, CF10 3EU, Wales. **Online address:** attfieldr@cf.ac.uk

ATWILL, David G. American (born United States) **Genres:** Young Adult Non-fiction, History, Ethics. **Career:** Yunnan University, Department of Foreign Languages and Literature, visiting instructor, 1989-90; Juniata College, Department of History, assistant professor, 1999-2001; Humboldt University, Center of Islamic and Central Asian Studies, visiting fellow, 2001; University of Colorado, Department of History, assistant professor, 2001-02; Pennsylvania State University, Department of History and Religious Studies, lecturer, 2002-03, assistant professor, 2003-. Writer. **Publications:** The Chinese Sultanate: Islam, Ethnicity and the Panthay Rebellion in Southwest China, 1856-1873 (nonfiction), 2005; (ed. with Y.Y. Atwill) Sources in Chinese History: Diverse Perspectives from 1644 to the Present, 2010. Contributor of articles to books and journals. **Address:** Department of History and Religious Studies, Pennsylvania State University, 108 Weaver Bldg., University Park, PA 16802, U.S.A. **Online address:** dga11@psu.edu

ATWOOD, Craig D. American (born United States), b. 1960. **Genres:** History, Theology/Religion. **Career:** Moravian College, chaplain, 1986-88; Moravian Theological Seminary, assistant dean, 1988-89, adjunct faculty, 1994, 1999, Charles D. Couch associate professor of Moravian theology and ministry, director of the center for Moravian studies, 2010-; Third Moravian Church, pastor, 1992-94; Salem College, chaplain, 1994, assistant professor of religion, 1995, Starbuck chair of religion, 1997; Greensboro College, adjunct faculty, 1995; Home Moravian Church, Sunday school teacher, 1997; Wake Forest University, School of Divinity, John Comenius visiting professor of Moravian studies. Writer. **Publications:** Always Reforming: A History of Christianity since 1300, 2001; (ed.) Handbook of Denominations in the United States, 11th ed., 2001, (with F.S. Mead and S.S. Hill) 12th ed., 2005; (ed. with P. Vogt) The Distinctiveness of Moravian Culture: Essays and Documents in Moravian History in Honor of Vernon H. Nelson on His Seventieth Birthday, 2003; Community of the Cross: Moravian Piety in Colonial Bethlehem, 2004; The Theology of the Czech Brethren from Hus to Comenius, 2009. Contributor to books and periodicals. **Address:** School of Divinity, Wake Forest University, 1834 Wake Forest Rd., Winston-Salem, NC 27109-6000, U.S.A. **Online address:** atwoodcd@wfu.edu

ATWOOD, Margaret. (Margaret Eleanor Atwood). Canadian (born Canada), b. 1939. **Genres:** Novels, Novellas/Short Stories, Children's Fiction, Poetry, Literary Criticism And History, Young Adult Non-fiction. **Career:** University of British Columbia, lecturer in English, 1964-65; Sir George Williams University, instructor in English, 1967-68; University of Alberta, faculty, 1969-70; York University, assistant professor of English, 1971-72; University of Toronto, writer-in-residence, 1972-73; University of Alabama, M.F.A. Program, honorary chair, 1985; New York University, Berg chair, 1986; Macquarie University, writer-in-residence, 1987; Trinity University, writer-in-residence, 1989; Anansi, editor. **Publications:** Double Persephone (poetry), 1961; Kaleidoscopes Baroque: A Poem, 1965; Talismans for Children (poetry), 1965; The Circle Game (poetry), 1966; Speeches for Doctor Frankenstein (poetry), 1966; Expeditions (poetry), 1966; The Animals in That Country (poetry), 1968; The Edible Woman, 1969; What Was in the Garden (poetry), 1969; (co-author) Blewointmentpress Occupation Issew, 1970; The Journals of Susanna Moodie (poetry), 1970; Procedures for Underground (poetry), 1970; (co-author) Lobsticks: Lobstick, a Spruce Tree Trimmed of All But the Top Branches (poetry), 1970; Power Politics (poetry), 1971, 2nd ed., 1996; Surfacing, 1972; Survival: A Thematic Guide to Canadian Literature, 1972; You Are Happy (poetry), 1974; Lady Oracle, 1976; Selected Poems, 1965-1975, 1976; Days of the Rebels, 1815-1840, 1977; Dancing Girls and Other Stories, 1977; Marsh Hawk (poetry), 1977; Women on Women, 1978; Two-headed Poems, 1978; Up in the Tree, 1978; Life before Man, 1979; (intro.) To See Our World, 1979; (with J. Barkhouse) Anna's Pet, 1980; Bodily Harm, 1981; Notes towards a Poem That Can Never Be Written, 1981; True Stories (poetry), 1981; Encounters with the Element Man, 1982; Second Words: Selected Critical Prose, 1982; (ed. and intro.) The New Oxford Book of Canadian Verse in English, 1982; Unearthing Suite, 1983; Snake Poems, 1983; Bluebeard's Egg and Other Stories, 1983; Murder in the Dark: Short Fictions and Prose Poems, 1983; Interlunar (poetry), 1984; The Handmaid's Tale, 1985; (ed. with R. Weaver) The Oxford Book of Canadian Short Stories in English, 1986; (comp.) The Canlit Foodbook: From Pen To Palate: A Collection Of Tasty Literary Fare, 1987; Selected Poems II: Poems Selected and New, 1976-1986, 1987; Cat's Eye, 1988; (ed. with S. Ravenel) The Best American Short Stories, 1989; (with S. Tanaka) For the Birds, 1990; Wilderness Tips and Other Stories, 1991; Good Bones, 1992 in US as Good Bones and Simple Murders, 1994; The Robber Bride, 1993; (ed. with B. Callaghan and intro.) The Poetry of Gwendolyn MacEwen, vol. I: The Early Years, 1993, vol. II: The Later Years, 1994; The Morning in the Burned House, 1995; (ed. with R. Weaver) The New Oxford Book of Canadian Short Stories in English, 1995; Strange Things: The Malevolent North in Canadian Literature, 1995; Princess Prunella and the Purple Peanut, 1995; Alias Grace, 1996; The Labrador Fiasco, 1996; A Quiet Game: And Other Early Works, 1997; Some Things about Flying, 1997; Eating Fire: Selected Poetry, 1965-1995, 1998; Deux Sollicitudes, 1998; (intro.) Women Writers at Work: The Paris Review Interviews, 1998; The Blind Assassin, 2000; Juegos de poder, 2000; Second Words: Selected Critical Prose, 1960-1982, 2000; Story of a Nation: Defining Moments in our History, 2001; Negotiating with the Dead: A Writer on Writing, 2002; (intro.) Ground Works: Avant-garde for Thee, 2002; Oryx and Crake: A Novel, 2003; Rude Ramsay and the Roaring Radishes, 2003; Bashful Bob and Doleful Dorinda, 2004; Moving Targets: Writing with Intent, 1982-2004, 2004; Cibles Mouvantes: Essais, 1971-2004, 2004; Bottle, 2004; (co-author) New Beginnings: Sold in Aid of the Indian Ocean Tsunami Earthquake Charities, 2005; Writing With Intent: Essays, Reviews, Personal Prose, 1983-2005, 2005; (intro.) Works on Paper, 2005; The Penelopiad, 2005; (contrib.) Moments of Change: For Soprano and Piano, 2005; (contrib.) Ein neuer Anfang, 2005; Curious Pursuits: Occasional Writing, 1970-2005, 2005; (co-author) Don Quijote alrededor del mundo, 2005; Moral Disorder: Stories, 2006; The Tent, 2006; The Door, 2007; Payback: Debt and the Shadow Side of Wealth, 2008; The Year of the Flood: A Novel, 2009; (co-author) Crimespotting, 2009; (as Margaret Eleanor Atwood) Glances at Germany, Poland, and the Euxine, 2009; In Other Worlds: SF and the Human Imagination, 2011; (co-author) I'm with the Bears: Short Stories from a Damaged Planet, 2011. **Address:** McClelland & Stewart Ltd., 75 Sherbourne St., 5th Fl., Toronto, ON M5A 2P9, Canada.

ATWOOD, Margaret Eleanor. *See* **ATWOOD, Margaret.**

ATWOOD, William G(oodson). *See* **OBITUARIES**.

ATXAGA, Bernardo. (Joseba Irazu Garmendia). Spanish (born Spain), b. 1951. **Genres:** Novels, Children's Fiction, Novellas/Short Stories. **Career:** Writer and translator. **Publications:** Ziutateaz, 1976; Bi Anai, 1985; Sugeak Txoria'ri Begiratzen Dionean, 1985; Obabakoak, 1988; Ricardo Toja: Dibujos, 1952-1991, 1992; (co-author) Relatos urbanos, 1994; Nueva Etiopía:

Canciones, Conversaciones Y Poemas, 1996; (contrib.) Erase Una Vez La Paz, 1996; Esos cielos, 1996; (contrib.) Egungo Munduaren Globalizazio eta Fragmentazioa: Globalización y Fragmentación Del Mundo contemporáneo, 1997; (contrib.) Infancia De Escritor, 1997; Lista De locos Y Otros Alfabetos, 1998; Poemas & Híbridos: Selección Y Versiones Del Propio Autor, 1974-1989, 1999; (co-author) Cuentos apátridas, 1999; (with M. Valverde) Recuerdo De Mis Abuelos, 1999; (contrib.) Toros, 1999; Espía Llamado Sara, 2001; Two Brothers, 2002; Soinujolearen semea, 2003; El Hombre Solo, 2004; Hijo Del Acordeonista, 2004; Lekuak, 2005; Declaración de Guillermo, 2005; (co-author) Memoria Del Futuro, 2006; Markak: Gernika, 1937, 2007; Siete Casas En Francia, 2009; Zazpi Etxe Frantzian, 2009; Obabakoak: Stories from a Village, 2010; Seven Houses in France, 2011. **Address:** Random House Group Ltd., 20 Vauxhall Bridge Rd., London, GL SW1V 2SA, England.

AUBERT, Alvin. American (born United States), b. 1930. **Genres:** Plays/Screenplays, Poetry, Education, Literary Criticism And History, Young Adult Fiction. **Career:** Southern University, instructor, 1960-62, assistant professor, 1962-64, associate professor of English, 1965-70; State University of New York, associate professor, 1970-74, professor, 1974-79; poet, 1972-; Obsidian Journal, founder, editor and publisher, 1975-85; Wayne State University, professor of English, 1979-93, professor emeritus of English, 1993-, Center for Black Studies, interim director, 1988-90, Department of Africana Studies, interim chair, 1990-. **Publications:** Against the Blues: Poems, 1972; Feeling Through, 1975; A Noisesome Music, 1979; South Louisiana: New and Selected Poems: New and Selected Poems, 1985; Home from Harlem, 1986; If Winter Come: Collected Poems, 1994; Harlem Wrestler and Other Poems, 1995; The Way I Do, 2004. **Address:** Department of English, Wayne State University, 5057 Woodward, Ste. 9408, Detroit, MI 48202-4050, U.S.A. **Online address:** ad8722@wayne.edu

AUBERT, Jacques. French (born France), b. 1932. **Genres:** Literary Criticism And History, History, Philosophy, Novels. **Career:** University of Lyon, assistant, 1962-67, charge d'enseignement, 1967-71, professor, 1971-, Centre d'Etudes et de Recherches Anglaises et Nord-Americaines, director; University of Hawaii, visiting professor; University of Tulsa, visiting professor; University of Dublin, visiting professor; University of Torino, visiting professor; University of Fribourg, visiting professor; University of Seville, visiting professor. Writer. **Publications:** Introduction à l'esthétique de James Joyce, 1973; (trans.) The Dubliners, 1974, rev. ed., 1992; (with M. Jolas) Joyce and Paris, 1979; (co-author) état et sa police en France (1789-1914), 1979; (ed.) Oeuvres, vol. I, 1982, vol. II, 1995; (with F. Senn) Cahier James Joyce, 1986; (co-ed.) Joyce avec Lacan, 1987; The Aesthetics of James Joyce, 1992; (co-ed.) Virginia Woolf, identité, politique, écriture, 2008. Contributor to periodicals. **Address:** 16 rue de Tourvielle, Lyon, 69005, France.

AUCH, Mary Jane. American (born United States) **Genres:** Children's Fiction, Young Adult Fiction. **Career:** Pennywhistle Press, designer, graphic artist and illustrator. Writer. **Publications:** SELF-ILLUSTRATED PICTURE BOOKS: The Easter Egg Farm, 1992; Bird Dogs Can't Fly, 1993; Peeping Beauty, 1993; Monster Brother, 1994; Hen Lake, 1995; Eggs Mark the Spot, 1996; Bantam of the Opera, 1997; Noah's Aardvark, 1999; The Nutquacker, 1999. NOVELS: The Witching of Ben Wagner, 1987; Cry Uncle!, 1987; Mom is Dating Weird Wayne, 1988; Pick of the Litter, 1988; Glass Slippers Give You Blisters, 1989; Angel and Me and the Bayside Brothers, 1989; Kidnapping Kevin Kowalski, 1990; A Sudden Change of Family, 1990; Seven Long Years until College, 1991; Out of Step, 1992; The Latchkey Dog, 1994; Journey to Nowhere, 1997; I was a Third-Grade Science Project, 1998; Frozen Summer, 1998; The Road to Home, 2000; I was a Third-Grade Spy, 2001; Ashes of Roses, 2002; (with H. Auch) The Princess and the Pizza, 2002; I was a Third-Grade Bodyguard, 2003; (with H. Auch) Poultrygeist, 2003; (with H. Auch) Souperchicken, 2003; (as M.J. Auch) Wing Nut, 2005; (with H. Auch) Chickerella, 2005; (as M.J. Auch) One-Handed Catch, 2006; (with H. Auch) Beauty and the Beaks, 2007; Plot Chicken, 2008; Dog on His Own, 2008; (with H. Auch) Plot Chickens, 2009; Guitar Boy, 2010. Illustrator of books by others. **Address:** c/o Holiday House, 425 Madison Ave., New York, NY 10017, U.S.A. **Online address:** jmawebsite@aol.com

AUDEH, Azmi S. American/Palestinian (born Palestine), b. 1932. **Genres:** Adult Non-fiction, Race Relations, Autobiography/Memoirs, Architecture, History. **Career:** 3M Co., senior engineer, 1963-66; Ampex Corp., engineering manager, 1966-71; Burroughs Corp., vice-president for engineering, 1971-82; Storage Technology Corp., chief engineer, 1982-88, retired, 1998. Writer and consultant. **Publications:** Carpenter from Nazareth: A Palestinian Portrait, 1998. Contributor to journals. **Address:** Para Publishing, 530 Ellwood Ridge, PO Box 8206-240, Santa Barbara, CA 93117-1047, U.S.A. **Online address:** asaudeh@aol.com

AUDOUARD, Antoine. French (born France), b. 1956. **Genres:** History, Translations. **Career:** Laffont-Fixot (France), publishing director, through 1999; full-time writer, 2000-. **Publications:** Marie en quelques mots, 1977; Le voyage au Liban, 1979; Abeilles, vousavez changé de maltre, 1981; Farewell My Sole, 2000; (trans.) Adieu, mon unique, 2000 (title means: Farewell, My Only One), 2004; Inca, 2001; Une maison au bord du monde, 2001; La peau á l'envers, 2003; Un pont d'oiseaux: roman, 2006; (with M. Benchellali) Voyage vers l'enfer, 2006; Larabe, 2009; Le rendez-vous de Saigon, 2011. **Address:** c/o Author Mail, Adult Editorial, Houghton Mifflin Co., 222 Berkeley St., Boston, MA 02116, U.S.A.

AUEL, Jean M(arie). American (born United States), b. 1936. **Genres:** Novels. **Career:** Tektronix Inc., clerk, 1965-66, circuit board designer, 1966-73, technical writer, 1973-74, credit manager, 1974-76. **Publications:** EARTH'S CHILDREN SERIES: The Clan of the Cave Bear, 1980, 3rd ed., 1998; The Valley of Horses, 1982; The Mammoth Hunters, 1985; The Plains of Passage, 1990; The Shelters of Stone, 2002; The Land of Painted Caves, 2011. Contributor to periodicals. **Address:** Jean V. Naggar Literary Agency, 216 E 75th St., Ste. 1E, New York, NY 10021, U.S.A.

AUERBACH, Kimberlee. American (born United States), b. 1972?. **Genres:** Plays/Screenplays, Biography. **Career:** Fox Television News, producer; Mediabistro, faculty of memoir writing; Bank Street College of Education, faculty; Gotham Writers' Workshop, faculty. Author. **Publications:** The Devil, the Lovers and Me: My Life in Tarot, 2007. **Address:** Gotham Writers' Workshop, 555 8th Ave., Ste. 1402, New York, NY 10018-4358, U.S.A.

AUERBACH, Loyd. American (born United States), b. 1956. **Genres:** Paranormal, Adult Non-fiction, Communications/Media, Mythology/Folklore, Theology/Religion, Mystery/Crime/Suspense. **Career:** The Office of Paranormal Investigations, founder and director, 1989-; John F. Kennedy University, adjunct professor, 1983-; Rosebridge Graduate School for Integrative Psychology, faculty, 1996-98; FATE Magazine, consulting editor and Psychic Frontiers columnist, 1991-2004; American Society for Psychical Research, public information and media consultant, 1982-83; Lexis-Nexis, consultant, 1984-; HCH Institute, Parapsychological Studies, creator and Instructor; Psychic Entertainers Association, president, 2001-05; California Society for Psychical Study, president. **Publications:** ESP, Hauntings, and Poltergeists, 1986; Psychic Dreaming, 1991, rev. ed. 1999; Reincarnation, Channeling, and Possession: A Parapsychologist's Handbook, 1993; Mind over Matter, 1996; Ghost Hunting: How to Investigate the Paranormal, 2004; Hauntings and Poltergeists: A Ghost Hunter's Guide, 2004; A Paranormal Casebook: Ghost Hunting in the New Millennium, 2005; Haunted by Chocolate: How to Go from Chocoholic to Chocolate Gourmet, 2010. **Address:** Office of Paranormal Investigations, PO Box 875, Orinda, CA 94563, U.S.A. **Online address:** esper@sfo.com

AUERBACH, Michael. American (born United States), b. 1949. **Genres:** Medicine/Health. **Career:** Cleveland Clinic, internal medicine, 1978; Columbia University, faculty hematology and oncology, 1981; Franklin Square Hospital Center, chief of hematology and oncology, Comprehensive Cancer Center, director, 1986-; Georgetown University, clinical professor. Writer. **Publications:** Conversations about Cancer: A Patient's Guide to Informed Decision Making, 1997. Contributor to medical journals. **Address:** Oncology Cancer Care, Franklin Square Hospital Center, 9110 Philadelphia Rd., Ste. 314, 9000 Franklin Square Dr., Baltimore, MD 21237, U.S.A. **Online address:** michaela@helix.org

AUGENBRAUM, Harold. American (born United States), b. 1953. **Genres:** Cultural/Ethnic Topics, Bibliography. **Career:** Teacher of English, 1976-79; United Way of NYC, account executive, 1980; Bruce Porter Co., staff consultant, 1981-84; City University of New York, Hunter College, director of external affairs, 1984-87; Museum of the City of New York, deputy director for external affairs, 1987-89; Mercantile Library, 1990-2004; National Book Foundation, executive director, 2004-. Writer. **Publications:** Latinos in English: A Selected Bibliography of Latino Fiction Writers of the United States, 1992; (ed. with I. Stavans) Growing Up Latino: Memoirs and Stories, 1993; The Latino Reader, 1997; U.S. Latino Literature: A Critical Guide for Students and Teachers, 2000; (with S. Shillinglaw) How to Organize a

Steinbeck Book or Film Discussion Group, 2002; (with I. Stavans) Lengua Fresca: Latinos Writing on the Edge, 2006; (trans.) J. Rizal, Noli me tángere, 2006. Contributor to periodicals. **Address:** National Book Foundation, 95 Madison Ave., Ste. 709, New York, NY 10016, U.S.A. **Online address:** haugebraum@nationalbook.org

AUGER, C(harles) P(eter). British (born England), b. 1931. **Genres:** Language/Linguistics, Technology, Engineering, Reference, Law. **Career:** Lucas Industries, research manager, 1957-88; Peter Auger Research Services, information consultant, 1988-. Writer. **Publications:** Engineering Eponyms: An Annotated Bibliography of Some Named Elements, Principles and Machines in Mechanical Engineering, 1965, 2nd ed., 1975; (ed.) Use of Reports Literature, 1975; Information Sources in Grey Literature, 1989, 4th ed., 1998; (ed.) Information Sources in Patents, 1992. **Address:** 82 Malvern Rd., Redditch, Redditch, B97 5DP, England.

AUGUST, Bille. Danish (born Denmark), b. 1948. **Genres:** Plays/Screenplays. **Career:** Cinematographer, 1973-79. Screenwriter and film director. **Publications:** Bille August fortaller om sit liv og sine film til Anne Wolden, 1993; Miss Smilla's Feeling for Snow: The Making of a Film, 1997. **Address:** c/o Fred Specktor, Creative Artists Agency, 9830 Wilshire Blvd., Beverly Hills, CA 90212, U.S.A. **Online address:** fspecktor@caa.com

AUGUST, Oliver. British/German (born Germany), b. 1971. **Genres:** Business/Trade/Industry, Travel/Exploration. **Career:** The Times of London, New York correspondent, 1995, Beijing bureau chief, Middle East reporter; The Economist, Africa correspondent and editor. **Publications:** Along the Wall and Watchtowers: A Journey Down Germany's Divide, 1999; Inside the Red Mansion: On the Trail of China's Most Wanted Man, 2007. **Address:** Barbara J. Zitwer Agency, 525 West End Ave., Ste. 11H, New York, NY 10024, U.S.A. **Online address:** oaugust@gmail.com

AUGUSTINE, Dolores L. American (born United States), b. 1955. **Genres:** History. **Career:** Sweet Briar College, visiting professor, 1989-90; St. John's University, Department of History, instructor, associate professor, 1990-2008, chair, 1998-2001, professor, 2008-. Writer and historian. **Publications:** Patricians and Parvenus: Wealth and High Society in Wilhelmine Germany, 1994; Red Prometheus: Engineering and Dictatorship in East Germany, 1945-1990, 2007. Contributor of articles to books and journals. **Address:** Department of History, St. John's University, 8000 Utopia Pkwy., Jamaica, NY 11439, U.S.A. **Online address:** augustid@stjohns.edu

AUILER, Dan Rose. American (born United States) **Genres:** Film, Young Adult Non-fiction. **Career:** Critic, teacher of film and cinema, film historian. Writer. **Publications:** Vertigo: The Making of a Hitchcock Classic, 1998; Hitchcock's Notebooks: An Authorized and Illustrated Look inside the Creative Mind of Alfred Hitchcock, 1999; (contrib.) The Alfred Hitchcock Story, 1999; (with A. Castle) Some Like It Hot, 2001; (contrib.) Cold Mountain: The Journey From Book to Film, 2003. Contributor to periodicals. **Address:** c/o HarperCollins, 1350 Ave. of the Americas, New York, NY 10019, U.S.A.

AULICH, James. British (born England), b. 1952?. **Genres:** Art/Art History, History, Politics/Government. **Career:** Manchester Metropolitan University, Manchester Institute for Research and Innovation in Art and Design (MIRIAD), reader in visual culture, lecturer in the history of art and design, 1977, senior lecturer, research professor, faculty research degrees coordinator. Writer. **Publications:** (With M. Sylvestrova) Political Posters in Central and Eastern Europe 1945-95: Signs of the Times, 1999; War Posters: Weapons of Mass Communication, 2007; (with J. Hewitt) Seduction or Instruction?: First World War Posters in Britain and Europe, 2007. EDITOR: (with J. Walsh) Vietnam Images: War and Representation, 1989; Framing the Falklands War: Nationhood, Culture, and Identity, 1992; (with T. Wilcox) Europe without Walls: Art, Posters and Revolution 1989-93, 1993; (with J. Lynch) Critical Kitaj: Essays on the Work of R.B. Kitaj, 2000; (with L. Purbrick and G. Dawson) Contested Spaces: Sites, Representations and Histories of Conflict, 2007; (with L. Burke and S. Faulkner) Politics of Cultural Memory, 2010. **Address:** Manchester Institute, Research and Innovation in Art & Design, Manchester Metropolitan University, Rm. G11, Righton Bldg., Manchester, M15 6BG, England. **Online address:** j.aulich@mmu.ac.uk

AUNE, James Arnt. American (born United States), b. 1953. **Genres:** Economics. **Career:** St. Olaf College, instructor, 1979-80, assistant professor, associate professor, 1989-94; Tulane University, assistant professor, director of forensics, acting department head, 1980-81; University of Virginia, assistant professor, 1981-86; University of St. Thomas, associate professor, 1994-96, professor, 1996-; Texas A&M University, Department of Communication, associate professor, 1996-2003, professor, 2003-, department head; Penn State University, associate professor, 2000-01. Writer. **Publications:** The Rhetoric and Marxism, 1994; Selling The Free Market: The Rhetoric of Economic Correctness, 2001; (ed. with E.D. Rigsby) Civil Rights Rhetoric and the American Presidency, 2005; (ed. with M.J. Medhurst) Prospect of Presidential Rhetoric, 2008. **Address:** Department of Communication, Texas A&M University, 202F Bolton Hall, MS 4234 TAMU, College Station, TX 77843-4234, U.S.A. **Online address:** jaune@tamu.edu

AUSEON, Andrew. American (born United States), b. 1976?. **Genres:** Novels, Mystery/Crime/Suspense, Science Fiction/Fantasy. **Career:** PhotoAssist Inc., photo editor, 1999-2002; The History Factory, senior researcher, 2002-04; Words and Numbers, editor and staff writer; Big Huge Games, associate producer. **Publications:** Funny Little Monkey, 2005; Alienated, 2009; Jo-Jo and the Fiendish Lot, 2009; Freak Magnet, 2010. **Address:** c/o Author Mail, Harcourt International, 6277 Sea Harbor Dr., Orlando, FL 32887, U.S.A.

AUSLANDER, Shalom. American (born United States), b. 1970?. **Genres:** Novels, Novellas/Short Stories, Young Adult Non-fiction. **Career:** Writer. **Publications:** (With J. Beck) I Tawt I Taw a Puddy Tat: Fifty Years of Sylvester and Tweety, 1991; Beware of God: Stories, 2005; Holocaust Tips for Kids, 2006; Foreskin's Lament: A Memoir, 2007. Contributor of articals to periodicals. **Address:** c/o Jody Hotchkiss, Hotchkiss and Associates Inc., 611 Broadway, Ste. 741, New York, NY 10012, U.S.A. **Online address:** shalom@shalomauslander.com

AUSTEN, Catherine. Canadian (born Canada), b. 1965. **Genres:** Novels, Children's Fiction. **Career:** Freelance writer, 2000-. **Publications:** Walking Backward (novel), 2009; My Cat Isis, 2011. Contributor to journals. **Address:** QC , Canada. **Online address:** info@catherineausten.com

AUSTER, Paul. American (born United States), b. 1947. **Genres:** Novels, Novellas/Short Stories, Plays/Screenplays, Poetry, Literary Criticism And History, Translations, Young Adult Fiction, Autobiography/Memoirs, Essays. **Career:** Princeton University, teacher of creative writing, 1986-90; PEN American Center, president. Translator and writer. **Publications:** White Spaces (short prose), 1980; The Invention of Solitude, 1982; City of Glass, 1985; Ghosts, 1986; The Locked Room, 1986; In the Country of Last Things, 1987; Moon Palace, 1989; The Music of Chance, 1990; Leviathan, 1992; The Art of Hunger, 1992; Mr. Vertigo, 1994; Smoke & Blue in the Face, 1995; The Red Notebook and other Writings, 1995; Why Write? (literary criticism and history), 1996; Hand to Mouth (autobiography), 1997; Timbuktu (novel), 1999; The Book of Illusions, 2002; The Red Notebook (true stories), 2002; (with S. Messer) The Story of My Typewriter (essay), 2002; Oracle Night (novel), 2003; (intro.) Twenty Days with Julian & Little Bunny by Papa, 2003; Collected Prose (nonfiction), 2003; Three films, 2003; Auggie Wren's Christmas Story, 2004; (with J. Baldesarri) Yours in Food, John Baldessari, 2004; Reflections on a Cardboard Box, 2004; The Brooklyn Follies, 2006; Travels in the Scriptorium, 2006; The Intervention of Solitude, 2007; Inner Life of Martin Frost, 2007; The Man in Dark, 2008; Man in the Dark, 2008; Invisible, 2009; Sunset Park, 2010. POETRY: Unearth, 1974; Wall Writing, 1976; Fragments from Cold, 1977; Facing the Music, 1980; Disappearances, 1988; Collected Poems, 2004. EDITOR: The Random House Book of Twentieth-Century French Poetry, 1982; (and trans.) J. Joubert, The Notebooks of Joseph Joubert: A Selection, 1983; (with J. Legueil) Und Jabes: Hommage, 1994; (with G. de Cortanze) La Solitude du labyrinthe: Essais et Entretiens, 1997; I Thought My Father Was God and Other True Tales from NPR's National Story Project, 2001; (ed.) Samuel Beckett: The Grove Centenary Edition, 2006. TRANSLATIONS: A Little Anthology of Surrealist Poems, 1972; Fits and Starts: Selected Poems of Jacques Dupin, 1974; (with L. Davis) Arabs and Israelis: A Dialogue 1975; The Uninhabited: Selected Poems of Andre de Bouchet, 1976; (with L. Davis) J.P. Sartre, Life/Situations, 1978; (with L. Davis) J. Chesneaux, China: The People's Republic, 1979; (with L. Davis) J. Chesneaux, China from the 1911 Revolution to Liberation, 1979; (and ed.) The Notebooks of Joseph Joubert: A Selection, 1983; S. Mallarme, A Tomb for Anatole, 1983; M. Blanchot, Vicious Circles, 1985; P. Petit, On the High Wire, 1985; (with M. Rowell) J. Miro, Selected Writings, 1986; Selected Writings, 1986; (with S. Romer and D. Shapiro) Jacques Dupin: Selected Poems, 1992; Translations, 1996; P. Clastres, Chronicle of the Guuyaki Indians,

1998; Doubles-Jeux, 1998; Lulu on the Bridge, 1998; (with L. Davis and R. Lamberton) M. Blanchot, The Station Hill Blanchot Reader: Fiction and Literary Essays, 1999; (intro.) The Notebooks of Joseph Joubert: A Selection, 2005. Contributor to magazines. **Address:** Penguin Putnam Inc., 375 Hudson St., New York, NY 10014, U.S.A. **Online address:** info@paulauster.co.uk

AUSTERLITZ, Paul. American (born United States), b. 1957. **Genres:** Music, Social Sciences, Art/Art History. **Career:** City University, adjunct lecturer, 1990-; Wesleyan University, lecturer in music, 1992-; State University, lecturer, 1993-; University of Michigan, visiting assistant professor of music, 1993-94; Michigan State University, lecturer, 1993; Bowling Green State University, adjunct professor, 1995-; Autonomous University, Fulbright visiting professor of music, 1996-; Dominican Conservatory of Music, Fulbright visiting professor, 1996-; University of Miami, visiting professor of music, 1996-97; University of Connecticut, lecturer, 1997; Brown University, assistant professor of music and Africana studies, 1997-2005; University of Connecticut, lecturer, 1997-; Gettysburg College, Sunderman Conservatory of Music, assistant professor, 2006-. Writer. **Publications:** Merengue: Dominican Music and Dominican Identity, 1997; (contrib.) Island Sounds in the Global City: Caribbean Popular Musics and Identity in New York, 1998; (contrib.) Rhythms of Culture: Latin American Popular Music, 1998; Jazz Consciousness: Music, Race and Humanity, 2005. Contributor of articles to books and periodicals. **Address:** Department of Music, Brown University, Orwig Music Bldg., 1 Young Orchard Ave., PO Box 1924, Providence, RI 02912, U.S.A. **Online address:** paul_austerlitz@brown.edu

AUSTIN, Curtis J. American (born United States), b. 1969. **Genres:** History, Politics/Government. **Career:** University of Southern Mississippi, assistant professor and director of the Center for Black Studies, Black Graduate Student Organization, faculty advisor, Omega Psi Phi, faculty advisor. Writer. **Publications:** Up against the Wall: Violence in the Making and Unmaking of the Black Panther Party, 2006. **Address:** Department of History, University of Southern Mississippi, Rm. 5047, 118 College Dr., Hattiesburg, MS 39406-5047, U.S.A. **Online address:** curtis.j.austin@usm.edu

AUSTIN, Dan. American (born United States), b. 1971?. **Genres:** Film, History, Architecture, Sports/Fitness. **Career:** Writer and filmmaker. **Publications:** True Fans: A Basketball Odyssey, 2003; Lost Detroit: Stories Behind the Motor City's Majestic Ruins, 2010. **Address:** c/o Author Mail, Lyon's Press, 246 Goose Ln., PO Box 480, Guilford, CT 06437, U.S.A. **Online address:** dan@truefans.com

AUSTIN, Gareth. British (born England), b. 1956. **Genres:** History, Agriculture/Forestry. **Career:** Kiamuya Secondary School, instructor in mathematics, 1975; University of Birmingham, lecturer, 1981-82; University of Ghana, lecturer, 1982-85; London School of Economics, lecturer, senior lecturer, reader in economic history, 1988-. Writer, economist, historian and consultant. **Publications:** (ed. with K. Sugihara) Local Suppliers of Credit in the Third World, 1750-1960, 1993; (intro.) Migrant Cocoa Farmers of Southern Ghana, 1997; Labor, Land, and Capital in Ghana: From Slavery to Free Labor in Asante, 1807-1956, 2004. Contributor to books, periodicals and journals. **Address:** Department of Economic History, London School of Economics, Rm. C314, Houghton St., London, GL WC2A 2AE, England. **Online address:** g.m.austin@lse.ac.uk

AUSTIN, Guy. British (born England), b. 1966?. **Genres:** Film. **Career:** University of Sheffield, Department of French, lecturer, 1992-2000, senior lecturer, 2000-06, reader in French 2006-09, head, 2009, subdean, 2006-08; Newcastle University, School of Modern Languages, professor of French studies, 2009-, director of research, Research Centre in Film and Digital Media, director. Writer. **Publications:** Contemporary French Cinema: An Introduction, 1996, 2nd ed., 2008; Claude Chabrol, 1999; Stars in Modern French Film, 2003. Contributor of articles to periodicals. **Address:** School of Modern Languages, Newcastle University, Old Library Bldg., Newcastle upon Tyne, TW NE1 7RU, England. **Online address:** guy.austin@ncl.ac.uk

AUSTIN, Jeannette Holland. American (born United States), b. 1936. **Genres:** Genealogy/Heraldry. **Career:** Professional genealogists, owner, 1967; Genealogy-Books.com, owner and operator, 1996; Jonesboro Family History Center, staff training director, 1998-200; Georgia Pioneers.com, owner and operator, 2001. Writer. **Publications:** The Georgians, 1984; Index to Georgia Wills, 1985; Georgia Bible Records, 1985; Georgia Intestate Records, 1986; Alabama Bible Records, 1987; Abstracts of Some Revolutionary War Pensions, 1987; Virginia Bible Records, 1988; North Carolina, South Carolina Bibles, 1988; Emigrants from Great Britain to the Georgia Colony, 1990; Austin Collection, 1990; Georgia Pioneers and Their Times, 1990; Georgia Obituaries (1905-1910), 1991; Chambliss, 1630-1987, 1991; Holland, 1991; Deaths of Revolutionary War Soldiers Who Died in Georgia and Their Widows, 1991; (as Jeannette H. Austin) Ancient Families in the British Isles, 1991; Newton County, Georgia Newspapers, 1868-1904: The Georgia Enterprise and Covington Star, 1991; Abstracts of Georgia Wills, 1991; (as Jeannette H. Austin) Paulding County, Georgia Marriages, 1834-1906, 1991; Family History Center Research Handbook, 1994; 30638 Burials in Georgia, 1995; Colonial Georgians, 1997; McIntosh Co., Georgia Cemeteries, 1997; 1860 Paulding County, Georgia Census, 2000; DeKalb County, Georgia Probate Records, 2001; The Georgia Frontier, 2005. **Address:** PO Box 21701, St. Simons Island, GA 31522, U.S.A. **Online address:** jeannette@georgiapioneers.com

AUSTIN, Jim. *See* **REASONER, Livia Jane Washburn.**

AUSTIN, Linda Marilyn. American (born United States), b. 1951?. **Genres:** Literary Criticism And History, Economics, Art/Art History. **Career:** Oklahoma State University, professor of English. Writer, literary critic and historian. **Publications:** The Practical Ruskin: Economics and Audience in the Late Work, 1991; Nostalgia in Transition, 1780-1917, 2007. Contributor to books, periodicals and journals. **Address:** Department of English, College of Arts and Sciences, Oklahoma State University, 205 Morrill Hall, Stillwater, OK 74078-4068, U.S.A. **Online address:** linda.m.austin@okstate.edu

AUSTIN, M(ichel) M(ervyn). Scottish/Australian (born Australia), b. 1943. **Genres:** History, Economics. **Career:** University of St. Andrews, lecturer, 1968-85, senior lecturer in ancient history, 1985-2000, honorary lecturer. Writer. **Publications:** Greece and Egypt in the Archaic Age, 1970; (with P. Vidal-Naquet) Economies et societes en Grece ancienne, 1972, as Economic and Social History of Ancient Greece: An Introduction, 1977; The Hellenistic World from Alexander to the Roman Conquest, 1981, 2nd ed., 2006. **Address:** Department of Ancient History, University of St. Andrews, St. Andrews, FF KY16 8AJ, Scotland.

AUSTIN, Paul. (Paul Ethan Austin). American (born United States), b. 1955. **Genres:** Medicine/Health, Biography, Autobiography/Memoirs. **Career:** North Carolina Memorial Hospital, nursing assistant and physician. Writer and physician. **Publications:** Something for the Pain: One Doctor's Account of Life and Death in the ER, 2008. Contributor to periodicals and journals. **Address:** c/o Michelle Tessler, Tessler Literary Agency, 27 W 20th St., Ste. 1003, New York, NY 10011-3724, U.S.A. **Online address:** paul@paulethanaustin.com

AUSTIN, Paul Ethan. *See* **AUSTIN, Paul.**

AUSTIN, R. G. *See* **LAMB, Nancy.**

AUSTIN, Robyn M. American (born United States) **Genres:** inspirational/Motivational Literature, Trivia/Facts, Psychology, Medicine/Health. **Career:** Elan Publishing, publisher. Writer. **Publications:** LifeChimes: A Collection of Simple Truths, 2nd ed., 2007. **Address:** Elan Publishing L.L.C., 8408 E 24th St., PO Box 18350, Tucson, AZ 85710, U.S.A. **Online address:** ashdiville@cox.net

AUSTIN, Suzanne. *See* **ALCHON, Suzanne Austin.**

AUTRY, Curt. American (born United States) **Genres:** Novels, Mystery/Crime/Suspense, Young Adult Fiction. **Career:** WWBT-TV, Fox Richmond News, anchor, 1994-; KFOR-TV, broadcaster; KTEN-TV, broadcaster; WRAL-TV, broadcaster; WRLH-TV, anchor; NBC12, anchor and reporter. **Publications:** The Reunion, 2002. **Address:** c/o Author Mail, Poisoned Pen Press, 6962 E 1st Ave., Ste. 103, Scottsdale, AZ 85251, U.S.A. **Online address:** cautry@nbc12.com

AVAKIAN, Arlene Voski. American (born United States), b. 1939. **Genres:** History, Women's Studies And Issues, Autobiography/Memoirs, Biography. **Career:** University of Massachusetts, associate professor of women's studies, 1986-2001, director and professor of women's studies, 2001-, now director emeritus; Smith College, part-time faculty of social work, 1990-93. Writer. **Publications:** Lion Woman's Legacy: An Armenian-American Memoir, 1992; (ed.) Through the Kitchen Window: Women Explore the Intimate Meaning of Food & Cooking, 1997; (co-ed.) African American Women and the Vote 1837-1965, 1997; (comp. with A. Deschamps) Transdisciplinary Introduction to Women's Studies, 2002; (ed. with B. Haber) From Betty Crocker to Feminist Food Studies: Critical Perspectives on Women and Food, 2005. **Address:** Women's Studies Program, University of Massachusetts, 208 Bartlett Hall, Amherst, MA 01003-0530, U.S.A. **Online address:** avakian@wost.umass.edu

AVALOS, Hector. Mexican (born Mexico), b. 1958. **Genres:** History, Humanities, Theology/Religion. **Career:** Lowa State University, professor of religious studies, U.S. Latino Studies Program, chair. Writer. **Publications:** Illness and Health Care in the Ancient Near East: The Role of the Temple in Greece, Mesopotamia, and Israel, 1995; Health Care and the Rise of Christianity, 1999; Se Puede Saber Si Dios Existe?, 2003; (ed.) Introduction to the U.S. Latina and Latino Religious Experience, 2004; Fighting Words: The Origins of Religious Violence, 2005; Strangers in Our Own Land: Religion in Contemporary U.S. Latina/o Literature, 2005; (ed. with S.J. Melcher and J. Schipper) This Abled Body: Rethinking Disabilities in Biblical Studies, 2007; The End of Biblical Studies, 2007. Contributor to periodicals. **Address:** Department of Philosophy and Religious Studies, College of Liberal Arts and Sciences, Iowa State University, 402 Catt Hall, Ames, IA 50011, U.S.A. **Online address:** havalos@iastate.edu

AVANT, Deborah D. (Deborah Denise Avant). American (born United States), b. 1958. **Genres:** Public/Social Administration, Adult Non-fiction, Politics/Government, Law, International Relations/Current Affairs. **Career:** University of California, San Diego, instructor, 1988, 1991; State University of New York, assistant profesor, 1991-95; George Washington University, assistant profesor, 1995-98, Elliott School of International Affairs, Security Policy Studies Program, director, 1997-99, Institute for Global and International Studies, director, 2004-07, associate professor, 1998-2006, professor, 2006-07; University of California, Irvine, Center for Research on International and Global Studies, director of international studies, 2007-, professor of political science, 2007-, International Security Studies Section, chair; Pacific Council on International Policy, adjunct fellow. Writer. **Publications:** Political Institutions and Military Change: Lessons from Peripheral Wars, 1994; The Market for Force: The Consequences of Privatizing Security, 2005. (ed. with M. Finnemore and S.K. Sell) Who Governs the Globe?, 2010. Contributor of articles to journals. **Address:** Department of Political Science, University of California, 3151 Social Science Plz., PO Box 5100, Irvine, CA 92697-5100, U.S.A. **Online address:** davant@uci.edu

AVANT, Deborah Denise. *See* **AVANT, Deborah D.**

AVELLA, Steven M. American (born United States), b. 1951. **Genres:** Theology/Religion, Essays. **Career:** Saint Catherine's High School, instructor, 1973-75; Saint Joseph's High School, instructor, 1978-81; Carthage College, lecturer, 1979-81; St. Francis Seminary, assistant professor of historical studies, 1984-89; Cardinal Stritch College, lecturer, 1984-86, 1989-90, assistant professor of history, 1990-91; Sacred Heart School of Theology, lecturer, 1989-90; Marquette University, Department of History, visiting assistant professor of history, 1989-90, assistant professor of history, 1991-94, chair, 1994-99, associate professor, professor of history, 1994-; California State University, lecturer, 2002-. Writer. **Publications:** (Ed.) Milwaukee Catholicism: Essays on Church and Community, 1991; This Confident Church: Catholic Leadership and Life in Chicago, 1940-1965, 1992; (with E. Skerrett and E.R. Kantowicz) Catholicism, Chicago Style, 1993; (contrib.) Moment of Grace: One Hundred Years of Salvatorian Life and Ministry in the United States, 1994; (ed.) St. Francis Seminary: Sesquicentennial Essays, 1997; (ed. with E. McKeown) Public Voices: Catholics in the American Context, 1999; Like an Evangelical Trumpet: A History of the Mother of God Province of the Society of the Catholic Apostolate, 1999; In the Richness of the Earth: A History of the Archdiocese of Milwaukee, 1843-1958, 2002; Sacramento: Indomitable City, 2003; That All Might Be One: A History of the Diocese of Reno, Nevada, 2006; Good Life: Sacramento's Consumer Culture, 2008; Sacramento and the Catholic Church: Shaping a Capital City, 2008; Capital City: The Catholic Church and the Shaping of Sacramento, 1850-2000, 2008; I Lift My Eyes to the Mountains, 2008; Encountering the Living Christ, 2009. **Address:** Department of History, Marquette University, 308 Charles L. Coughlin Hall, 607 N 13th St., PO Box 1881, Milwaukee, WI 53201-1881, U.S.A. **Online address:** steven.avella@marquette.edu

AVERILL, Gage. Canadian/American (born United States), b. 1954. **Genres:** Music, Humanities, Popular Culture, Cultural/Ethnic Topics, Politics/Government, Sociology, Urban Studies, Anthropology/Ethnology, History. **Career:** Station WORT, world music programmer, 1979-82; Station KRAB, world music programmer, 1982-85; University of Washington, instructor in music, 1986-89; Columbia University, visiting assistant professor of music, 1989-90; Wesleyan University, assistant professor, 1990-96, Center for the Humanities, resident fellow, 1992, director of graduate studies in music, 1993, associate professor of music, 1996-97; New York University, Department of Music, associate professor, 1997-2001, head of Ethnomusicology Program, 1997-98, professor and department chair, 2001-04; Princeton University, visiting professor, 2001; University of Toronto, Faculty of Music, dean, 2004-07, professor of history and culture; University of Toronto-Mississauga, vice-principal academic and dean, 2007-11, professor history and culture. Writer. **Publications:** (Co-author) Zouk: World Music in the West Indies, 1993; (contrib.) Music and Black Ethnicity: The Caribbean and South America, 1994; (contrib.) The Reordering of Culture: Latin America, the Caribbean, and Canada in the Hood, 1995; (contrib.) Multicultural Musics of America, 1996; (co-ed.) Making and Selling Culture, 1996; A Day for the Hunter, a Day for the Prey: Popular Music and Power in Haiti, 1997; (contrib.) The African Diaspora: A Musical Perspective, 1998; Four Parts, No Waiting: A Social History of American Barbershop Harmony, 2003. Contributor to books and periodicals. **Address:** University of Toronto, 3359 Mississauga Rd. N, Mississauga, ON L5L 1C6, Canada. **Online address:** gage.averill@utoronto.ca

AVERY, Evelyn. American (born United States), b. 1940. **Genres:** Literary Criticism And History. **Career:** Towson University, professor of English, 1975-, coordinator of Jewish studies, 1997-, director of ethnic and Jewish studies, Writer. **Publications:** Rebels and Victims: The Fiction of Richard Wright and Bernard Malamud, 1979; (contrib.) Sex and the Modern Jewish Woman: An Annotated Bibliography, 1986; (ed.) The Magic Worlds of Bernard Malamud, 2001; (ed.) Modern Jewish Women Writers in America, 2007. **Address:** Department of English, Towson University, 219E Linthicum Hall, 8000 York Rd., Towson, MD 21252, U.S.A. **Online address:** eavery@towson.edu

AVERY, Fiona Kai. American (born United States), b. 1974. **Genres:** Agriculture/Forestry, Young Adult Fiction. **Career:** Writer; poet; archeologist; historian. **Publications:** (With B. Tan and S. Firchow) Witchblade, 2002; Thundercats: Hammerhand's Revenge, 2004; The Crown Rose, 2005. Contributor to periodicals. **Address:** c/o Author Mail, Top Cow Productions Inc., 10390 Santa Monica Blvd., Ste. 110, Los Angeles, CA 90025, U.S.A.

AVERY, Gillian (Elise). British (born England), b. 1926. **Genres:** Novellas/Short Stories, Children's Fiction, Literary Criticism And History, Children's Non-fiction, Social Sciences, Sociology, Politics/Government. **Career:** Surrey Mirror, journalist, junior reporter, 1944-47; Chambers Encyclopedia, journalist, 1947-50; Clarendon Press, assistant illustrations editor, 1950-54; Children's Books Historical Society, chair, 1987-89; Oxford University Press, journalist. **Publications:** The Warden's Niece, 1957; Trespassers at Charlcote, 1958; James without Thomas, 1959; The Elephant War, 1960; Mrs. Ewing, 1961; To Tame a Sister, 1961; The Greatest Gresham, 1962; The Peacock House, 1963; The Italian Spring, 1964; (with A. Bull) Nineteenth Century Children: Heroes and Heroines in English Children's Stories 1780-1900, 1965; Call of the Valley, 1968; Victorian People in Life and Literature, 1970; (co-author) Authors Choice 1, 1970; A Likely Lad, 1971; Ellen's Birthday, 1971; Jemima and the Welsh Rabbit, 1972; The Echoing Green: Memories of Victorian and Regency Youth, 1974; Ellen and the Queen, 1974; Book of Strange and Odd, 1975; Gillian Avery's Book of the Strange and Odd, 1975; Childhood's Pattern: A Study of the Heroes and Heroines of Children's Fiction 1770-1950, 1975; Freddie's Feet, 1976; Huck & Her Time Machine, 1977; Mouldy's Orphan, 1978; Sixpence, 1979; The Lost Railway, 1980; Onlookers, 1983; The Best Type of Girl: A History of Girls' Independent School, 1991; Maria Escapes, 1992; Maria's Italian Spring, 1993; Behold the Child: American Children and Their Books, 1621-1922, 1994; (comp.) The Everyman Anthology of Poetry for Children, 1994; (reteller) Russian Fairy Tales, 1995; Cheltenham Ladies: A History of Cheltenham Ladies's College, 2003; (intro.) The Wind in the Willows, 2005; (intro.) Five Children and It, 2005. EDITOR: A Flat Iron for Farthing, 1959; Jan of the Windmill, 1960; The Sapphire Treasury of Stories for Boys and Girls, 1960; In the Window Seat, 1960; Father Phim, 1962; Unforgettable Journeys, 1965; School Remembered, 1967; A Great Emergency and a Very Ill-Tempered Family, 1967; The Gold of Fairnilee and Other Stories, 1967; Village Children, 1967; Banning and Blessing, 1967; The Hole in the Wall and Other Stories, 1968; Victoria Bess and Others, 1968; The Wallypug of Why, 1968; Froggy's Little Brother, 1968; My New Home, 1968; The Life and Adventures of Lady Anne, 1969; Stephanie's Children, 1969; Anne's Terrible Good Nature and Other Stories for Children, 1970; The Rival Kings, 1970; Red Letter Days, 1971; (with J. Briggs) Children and Their Books, 1990; (with K. Reynolds) Representations of Childhood Death, 2000. Contributor to periodicals. **Address:** 32 Charlbury Rd., Oxford, OX OX2 6UU, England.

AVERY, Kevin J. American (born United States), b. 1950. **Genres:** Art/Art History. **Career:** Metropolitan Museum of Art, attendant and guard, 1973-75, Department of Greek and Roman Art, technician, 1975-77, Chester fellow, 1983-84, Andrew Mellon fellow, 1984-85, research associate, 1985-88, assistant curator of American paintings and sculpture, 1988-95, associate curator, 1995-; City University of New York, Hunter College, adjunct instructor, 1983-91, adjunct assistant professor, 1991-; Columbia University, adjunct instructor, 1994; Montclair Art Museum, occasional curator, 1997-; New York University, lecturer. Writer. **Publications:** (With P.L. Fodera) John Vanderlyn's Panoramic View of the Palace and Gardens of Versailles, 1988; Church's Great Picture; The Heart of the Andes, 1993; (with D.P. Fischer) American Tonalism: Selections from the Metropolitan Museum of Art and the Montclair Art Museum, 1999; American Drawings and Watercolors in the Metropolitan Museum of Art, 2002; (ed. with F. Kelly) Hudson River School Visions: The Landscapes of Sanford R. Gifford, 2003; (contrib.) Treasures from Olana: Landscapes by Frederic Edwin Church, 2005; (contrib. with T. Lovejoy) Alexis Rockman: A Fable for Tomorrow, 2010. Contributor to art journals. **Address:** Department of American Paintings & Sculpture, Metropolitan Museum of Art, 1000 5th Ave., New York, NY 10028, U.S.A.

AVERY, Martha. American (born United States), b. 1951. **Genres:** Business/Trade/Industry, Translations, History. **Career:** Avery Press Inc., president. Writer. **Publications:** Women of Mongolia, 1996; The Tea Road: China and Russia Meet across the Steppe, 2003; (ed. with Z. Min and C. Jinqin) China's Emerging Financial Markets: Challenges and Global Impact, 2009; (with L. Shiying) Alibaba: The Inside Story behind Jack Ma and the Creation of the World's Biggest Online Marketplace, 2009. TRANSLATOR: Z. Xianliang, Half of Man Is Woman, 1988; W. Anyi, Baotown (novel), 1989; (and intro.) Z. Xianliang, Getting Used to Dying (novel), 1991; Z. Xianliang, Grass Soup (novel), 1995; Z. Xianliang, My Bodhi Tree, 1996; H. Ying, Summer of Betrayal (novel), 1997; L. Zhijun, The Lenovo Affair: The Growth of China's Computer Giant and Its Takeover of IBM-PC, 2006. **Address:** Avery & Binford, 600 Kalmia Ave., Boulder, CO 80304-1736, U.S.A.

AVERY, Tom. British (born England), b. 1975. **Genres:** Travel/Exploration, Sports/Fitness, Autobiography/Memoirs. **Career:** Writer. **Publications:** Pole Dance: The Story of the Record-breaking British Expedition to the Bottom of the World, 2004; To the End of the Earth: Our Epic Journey to the North Pole and the Legend of Peary and Henson, 2009. **Address:** c/o Mel Berger, William Morris Agency, 1325 Ave. of the Americas, New York, NY 10019-6091, U.S.A. **Online address:** info@tomavery.net

AVI. American (born United States), b. 1937. **Genres:** Children's Fiction, Young Adult Fiction, Novels, Mystery/Crime/Suspense, Novellas/Short Stories. **Career:** New York Public Library, librarian in performing arts research center, 1962-70; Lambeth Public Library, exchange program librarian, 1968; Trenton State College, assistant professor and humanities librarian, 1970-86. Writer. **Publications:** Things That Sometimes Happen, 1970; Snail Tale: The Adventures of a Rather Small Snail, 1972; No More Magic, 1975; Captain Grey, 1977; Emily Upham's Revenge: Or, How Deadwood Dick Save the Banker's Niece: A Massachusetts Adventure, 1978; Night Journeys, 1979; American Children's Literature: A Bibliographic History, 1979; Encounter at Easton, 1980; The Man from the Sky, 1980; History of Helpless Harry: To Which Is Added a Variety of Amusing and Entertaining Adventures, 1980; A Place Called Ugly, 1981; Who Stole the Wizard of Oz?, 1981; Sometimes I Think I Hear My Name, 1982; Shadrach's Crossing, 1983; The Fighting Ground, 1984; S.O.R. Losers, 1984; Devil's Race, 1984; Bright Shadow, 1985, 2nd ed., 1994; Wolf Rider: A Tale of Terror, 1986, 2nd ed., 1993; Romeo and Juliet Together and Alive! At Last, 1987; Something Upstairs: A Tale of Ghosts, 1988; The Man Who Was Poe, 1989; The True Confessions of Charlotte Doyle, 1990; Windcatcher, 1991; Nothing but the Truth: A Documentary Novel, 1991; Who Was That Masked Man, Anyway?, 1992; Blue Heron, 1992; Emily Upham's Revenge: A Massachusetts Adventure, 1992; Punch with Judy, 1993; City of Light, City of Dark: A Comic Book Novel, 1993; The Barn, 1994; The Bird, the Frog and the Light: A Fable, 1994; Tom, Babette and Simon: Three Tales of Transformation, 1995; Poppy, 1995, rev. ed., 2005; Beyond the Western Sea: The Escape from Home, 1996; Beyond the Western Sea: Lord Kirkle's Money, 1996; What Do Fish Have to Do with Anything?: And Other Stories, 1997; Finding Providence: The Story of Roger Williams, 1997; Poppy and Rye, 1998; Perloo the Bold, 1998; Ragweed, 1999; (co-author) Second Sight: Stories for a New Millennium, 1999; Abigail Takes the Wheel, 1999; Midnight Magic, 1999; Ereth's Birthday, 2000; The Christmas Rat, 2000; Talk to Me and Other Stories, 2000; Prairie School, 2001; The Secret School, 2001; Don't You Know There's a War On?, 2001; The Good Dog, 2001; Crispin: The Cross of Lead, 2002; Silent Movie, 2003; Mayor of Central Park, 2003; End of the Beginning: Being the Adventures of a Small Snail, 2004; (with R. Vail) Never Mind!: A Twin Novel, 2004; The Book Without Words: A Fable of Medieval Magic, 2005; Poppy's Return, 2005; Strange Happenings: Five Tales of Transformation, 2005; Crispin: At the Edge of the World, 2006; (ed. with C. Shute) Best Shorts: Favorite Short Stories for Sharing, 2006; (co-author) Tripping Over the Lunch Lady, 2006; The Traitors' Gate, 2007; Iron Thunder, 2007; The Seer of Shadows, 2008; Hard Gold: The Colorado Gold Rush of 1859, a Tale of the Old West, 2008; A Beginning, a Muddle, and an End: The Right Way to Write Writing, 2008; (co-author) Acting Out, 2008; Poppy and Ereth, 2009; Murder at Midnight, 2009; Crispin: The End of Time, 2010; (intro.) Just so Stories, 2010; City of Orphans, 2011; Into the Storm, 2012. Contributor to books and periodicals. **Address:** Atheneum Publishing, 1230 Ave. of the Americas, New York, NY 10020, U.S.A. **Online address:** awortis@qwest.net

AVILA, Eric. American (born United States), b. 1968. **Genres:** Adult Nonfiction. **Career:** University of California, Department of Chicana/o Studies and History, instructor, 1997-2004, assistant professor, 1997-, associate professor, 2004-; Stanford University, Research Institute for Comparative Studies in Race and Ethnicity, visiting fellow, 2007-08. Writer. **Publications:** NONFICTION: (co-ed.) The Chicano Studies Reader: An Anthology of Aztlan, 1970-2000, 2001; Popular Culture in the Age of White Flight: Fear and Fantasy in Suburban Los Angeles, 2004. Contributor to books and journals. **Address:** Department of Chicana and Chicano Studies and, Department of History, University of California, 6265 Bunche Hall, PO Box 951473, Los Angeles, CA 90095-1473, U.S.A. **Online address:** eavila@ucla.edu

AVISE, John C. American (born United States), b. 1948. **Genres:** Natural History, Sciences, Zoology, Biography, Autobiography/Memoirs. **Career:** Savannah River Ecology Laboratory, research assistant, 1971-73; University of Georgia, assistant professor of zoology, 1975-79, associate professor, 1979-84, professor of genetics, 1984-, distinguished research professor, 1975-2005, distinguished research professor emeritus, 2005-; University of California, School of Biological Sciences, Department of Ecology and Evolutionary Biology, distinguished professor, 2005-. Writer. **Publications:** Molecular Markers: Natural History and Evolution, 1994 2nd ed. 2004; (ed. with J.L. Hamrick) Conservation Genetics: Case Histories from Nature, 1996; The Genetic Gods: Evolution and Belief in Human Affairs, 1998; Phylogeography: The History and Formation of Species, 2000; Captivating Life: A Naturalist in the Age of Genetics, 2001; Genetics in the Wild, 2002; The Hope, Hype & Reality of Genetic Engineering, 2004; Evolutionary Pathways in Nature: A Phylogenetic Approach, 2006; A Field Guide to Little Known Genetically Engineered Organisms, 2007; On Evolution, 2007; (ed. with F.J. Ayala) In the Light of Evolution I: Adaptation and Complex Design, 2007; Clonality: The Genetics, Ecology and Evolution of Sexual Abstinence in Vertebrate Animals, 2008; Inside the Human Genome: A Case for Non-intelligent Design, 2010; (ed.) Molecular Ecology and Evolution, 2010; Hermaphroditism, 2011. Contributor to journals. **Address:** Department of Ecology and Evolutionary Biology, School of Biological Sciences, University of Califonia, 425 Steinhaus Hall, PO Box 2525, Irvine, CA 92697, U.S.A. **Online address:** javise@uci.edu

AVISHAI, Bernard. Israeli (born Israel), b. 1949?. **Genres:** Novels, Politics/Government. **Career:** Harvard Business Review, technology editor, 1986-91; Monitor Group, head of product development; Klynveld Peat Marrwick Goerdeler L.L.P., international director of intellectual capital, 1998-2001; Interdisciplinary Center, director; Duke University, faculty; Massachusetts Institute of Technology, faculty. **Publications:** The Tragedy of Zionism: Revolution and Democracy in the Land of Israel, 1985 as The Tragedy of Zionism: How Its Revolutionary Past Haunts Israeli Democracy, 2002; A New Israel:

Democracy in Crisis, 1973-1988: Essays, 1990; The Hebrew Republic: How Secular Democracy and Global Enterprise Will Bring Israel Peace at Last, 2008. Contributor to periodicals. **Address:** Jerusalem, Israel.

AVNI, Haim. Israeli/Austrian (born Austria), b. 1930. **Genres:** Cultural/Ethnic Topics, History. **Career:** Hebrew University of Jerusalem, professor of contemporary Jewish history and head of division for Latin America, Spain, and Portugal, 1967-, head of institute, 1981-82, 1992-94, Institute for Contemporary Jewry, senior lecturer, 1974-79, associate professor, 1979-85, professor, 1985-, Saloman and Victoria Cohen professor emeritus, 1998-, Harman Institute of Contemporary Jewry, head, 1991-94, Division for Latin America, Spain and Portugal, head, 1968-2009; Intl. Center for University Teaching of Jewish Civilization, Latin American Project, director, 1983-, Intl. Center for University Teaching of Jewish Civilization Rabin Building for the World Center of Jewish Studies, academic chairman, 1997-98; Unversidad Iberoamericana, Judaic Studies Program, co-director, 1982-98; Ecole des Hautes Etudesen Sciences Sociales, visiting professor, 1988; Study Circle on World Jewry in the Home of the President of Israel, chair and editor, 1988-90, 1992-93. **Publications:** Le-Hora at Ha-Històoryah Be-Vet-Ha-Sefer Ha-Tikhon, 1961; Ha-No Ar Ha-Yehudi Ha-Universita, 1971; Yahadut Amerikah Ha-Latinit Be Idan Shel Temurot, 1972, trans. as Yahadut Argentòinah, 1972; Argentine Jewry: Its Socio-Political Status and Organizational Patterns, 1972; Argentine, the Promised Land: Baron de Hirschs Colonization Project in the Argentine Republic, 1973; Sefarad Vòeha-Yehudim Bi-Yeme Ha-Sho Ah Vòeha-Emantsipatsyah, 1975; Ha-Tsiyonut Vòe-Hanhòalatah Ba-Amerikòah Ha-Latòinit, 1976; Im Yehudim Be-Mahòanot-Ha-Akòurim: Rishme Shelihòut, 1945-1947, 1981; Spain, The Jews, and Franco, 1982; Mi-Bitòul Ha-Inkòvòizitsyah Vòe-Ad Hòokò Ha-Shevut: ToldotHa-Hagirah Ha-Yehudit Le-Argentòinah, 1982; Argentina y la historia dela immigración Judía, 1810-1950, 1983; Emancipation and Jewish Education: A Century of Argentinian Jewrys Experience, 1884-1984, 1985; Antòishemiyut Be-Mishtòarim Rodaniyim Vòe-Demokòratòiyim: Lekòahòim Mi-Nisyonah Shel Yahadut Amerikòah Ha-Latòinit, 1985, trans. as Antisemitism Under Democratic And Dictatorial Regimes: The Experience Of Latin American Jewry, 1986; Mexico: Immigration and Refuge, 1989; Ha-Tsiyonut U-Mitnagdeha Ba-Am Ha-Yehudi: Kòovets Ma Amarim, 1989; (with F.F. Goldberg) Jewish Civilization Studies in Latin American Universities, 1990; Argentina and the Jews: A History of Jewish Migration, 1991; Judíos en América: Cinco Siglos de Historia, 1992; (with L. Senkman) Del Campo Al Campo: Colonos De Argentina En Israel, 1993; (comp. with J. Mandl) Six Day War and Communal Dynamics in the Diaspora, 1994; (co-author) Makah tahat makah: lohem Yehudi-Ostri ba-Mahteret be-Tsarefat, 2003; Argentina y las migraciones judías: de la Inquisición al Holocausto y después, 2005; Temeim: sahar be-nashim be-Argentinah uve-Yisrael, 2009; (co-author) Pertenencia y alteridad, 2011. EDITOR: Estudios Judaicos en Universidades Latinoamericanas, 1985; (with R.P. Raicher) Memorias Del Uruguay: Holocausto Y Lucha Por La Fundación Del Estado De Israel, 1986; (co-author) Historia Viva: Memorias Del UruguayY De Israel, 1989; (with G. Shimoni) Zionism and Its Jewish Opponents, 1990; (with L. Senkman) Del campo al campo, colonos de Argentinaen Israel, 1993; La Comunidad Hebrea de Cuba: La Memoria y la Historia, 1996; (with S. Steindling) Hitting Back, an Austrian Jew in the French Resistance, 2000. **Address:** Division for Latin America, Spain, and Portugal, Institute of Contemporary Jewry, Hebrew University of Jerusalem, Mount Scopus, Jerusalem, 91905, Israel. **Online address:** heavni@h2.hum.huji.ac.il

AVOLIO, Bruce J. American (born United States) **Genres:** Business/Trade/Industry, Economics, Administration/Management. **Career:** State University of New York, Binghamton University, Center for Cognitive and Psycholinguistics Sciences, associate director, 1988-92, director of graduate programs, 1990-93, Kellogg Leadership Program, co-director, 1990-94, director of doctoral programs, 1993-94, Eisenhower Leadership Development Project, co-director, 1993-96, Global Center for Leadership Studies, director, 1998-2000, co-director, 2000-01; Queensland University of Technology, distinguished visiting professor, 2000-03; University of Nebraska, School of Business, Clifton Chair in Leadership, 2001-08, professor of management, 2001-08, Doctoral Program in Leadership, director, 2003-08, Gallup Leadership Institute, director, 2003-08, senior research scientist; Gallup Organization, senior research scientist; University of Washington, Michael G. Foster School of Business, Marion B. Ingersoll professor, 2008-, Department of Management and Organization, professor of management, Center for Leadership and Strategic Thinking, executive director. Writer. **Publications:** (With B.M. Bass) Transformational Leadership Development: Manual for the Multifactor Leadership Questionnaire, 1990; (ed. with B.M. Bass) Improving Organizational Effectiveness through Transformational Leadership, 1994; Full Leadership Development: Building the Vital Forces in Organizations, 1999; (ed. with B.M. Bass) Developing Potential across a Full Range of Leadership: Cases on Transactional and Transformational Leadership, 2002; (ed. with F.J. Yammarino) Transformational and Charismatic Leadership: The Road Ahead, 2002; Leadership Development in Balance: Made/Born, 2005; (with F. Luthans) The High Impact Leader: Moments Matter in Accelerating Authentic Leadership Development, 2006; (with C.M. Youssef and F. Luthans) Psychological Capital: Developing the Human Competitive Edge, 2007; Full Range Leadership Development, 2011; No People: Tribal Tales of Organizational Cliff Dwellers, 2011. **Address:** Department of Management and Organization, Michael G. Foster School of Business, University of Washington, 487 Paccar Hall, PO Box 353226, Seattle, WA 98195-3226, U.S.A. **Online address:** bavolio@u.washington.edu

AVORN, Jerome Lewis. *See* **AVORN, Jerry.**

AVORN, Jerry. (Jerome Lewis Avorn). American (born United States), b. 1948. **Genres:** Adult Non-fiction, Medicine/Health. **Career:** Harvard Medical School, instructor in preventive and social medicine, 1977-79, assistant professor of social medicine and health policy, 1979-85, associate professor of social medicine, 1985-90, associate professor of medicine, 1990-2005, professor, 2005-, Beth Israel Hospital, physician, 1977-81, physician, 1981-92, Department of Medicine, assistant in medicine, 1977-84, assistant physician, 1984-87, associate physician, 1987-89, physician, 1989-94, Brigham and Women's Hospital, associate physician, 1986-92, physician, 1992-, Division of Pharmacoepidemiology and Pharmacoeconomics, chief, 1998-, Program for the Analysis of Clinical Strategies, director. Writer, pharmacoepidemiologist and researcher. **Publications:** NONFICTION: (co-author as Jerry L. Avorn) Up Against the Ivy Wall: A History of the Columbia Crisis, 1968; (co-author as Jerry L. Avorn) University in Revolt: A History of the Columbia Crisis, 1969; Powerful Medicines: The Benefits, Risks, and Costs of Prescription Drugs, 2004. Contributor to periodicals. **Address:** Brigham and Women's Hospital, Department of Medicine, 1620 Tremont St., Ste. 3030, Boston, MA 02120-1613, U.S.A. **Online address:** javorn@partners.org

AVRAMIDES, Anita. American (born United States), b. 1952. **Genres:** Philosophy, History. **Career:** University of Oxford, Oriel College, lecturer, 1980, Exeter College, lecturer, 1981-82, Balliol College, lecturer, 1982, Queen's College, lecturer, 1983-90, St. Hilda's College, Southover Manor Trust fellow in philosophy, 1990-, reader in philosophy of mind; Bedford College, visiting lecturer, 1980-82. Writer. **Publications:** Meaning and Mind: An Examination of a Gricean Account of Meaning, 1989; (ed.) Women of Ideas, 1995; Other Minds, 2001; Skepticism About Knowledge of Other Minds, forthcoming; Abiding Intention, forthcoming. **Address:** Department of Philosophy, St. Hilda College, Oxford University, Cowley Pl., Oxford, OX OX1 1DY, England. **Online address:** anita.avramides@st-hildas.ox.ac.uk

AW, Tash. British/Taiwanese (born Taiwan), b. 1971. **Genres:** Novels, Young Adult Fiction. **Career:** Writer. **Publications:** The Harmony Silk Factory, 2005; Map of the Invisible World, 2009. **Address:** Riverhead Books, 375 Hudson St., New York, NY 10014, U.S.A. **Online address:** anna@davidgodwinassociates.co.uk

AWDRY, Christopher Vere. British (born England), b. 1940. **Genres:** Novellas/Short Stories, Children's Fiction, Transportation, Engineering, Picture/Board Books. **Career:** Writer. **Publications:** Really Useful Engines, 1983, rev. ed., 2001; James and the Diesel Engines, 1984; Great Little Engines, 1985; More about Thomas the Tank Engine, 1986; Gordon, the High-Speed Engine, 1987; Percy and the Postman: Sticker Book, 1988; Thomas and the Evil Diesel, 1988; Thomas and the Lost Cat: A Sticker Book, 1988; Thomas and the Missing Christmas Tree, 1988; Toby, Trucks and Trouble, 1988; Henry Pulls the Express Train, 1989; James and the Rescue Train, 1989; Meet Thomas the Tank Engine and His Friends, 1989; Percy, the Seaside Train, 1989; Thomas and the Twins, 1989; Thomas's Book of Colours, 1989; Thomas's Big Book of Games and Puzzles, 1989; Thomas and the Good Train, 1989; Thomas Gets Tricked and Other Stories, 1989; Thomas the Tank Engine and the Great Race, 1989; Thomas the Tank Engine's Noisy Trip, 1989; Trouble for Thomas and Other Stories, 1989; Up and Down with Percy, 1989; Thomas the Tank Engine's ABC's, 1990; Breakfast Time for Thomas, 1990; Jock the New Engine, 1990; Catch Me, Catch Me!, 1990; Happy Birthday, Thomas!, 1990; Henry and the Elephant, 1990; Encyclopedia of British

Railway Companies, 1990; Thomas Visits a Farm, 1991; Thomas and the Great Railway Show, 1991; Thomas's Big Book of Words, 1991; Thomas Comes Home, 1992; Thomas and the Hurricane, 1992; Brunel's Broad Gauge Railway, 1992; Tell the Time with Thomas, 1992; Henry and the Express, 1993; Over the Summitt, 1993; (with K. Stott) Learn with Thomas, 1993; Wilbert the Forest Engine, 1994; Thomas and the Fat Controller's Engines, 1995; Awdry's Steam Railways, 1995; Thomas the Tank Engine Easy to Read Treasury, 1995; Great Little Engines, 1995; More About Thomas the Tank Engine, 1995; Thomas and the Giant, 1995; Thomas and the Great Railway Show, 1995; Thomas and the Helicopter Rescue: A Revolving Picture Book with Flaps, 1995; Thomas and the Tank Engine and the Scrambled Eggs, 1995; Thomas and the Tank Engine Catches a Thief, 1995; Toby, Trucks and Trouble, 1995; Thomas Comes Home, 1995; New Little Engine, 1996; Railways Galore, 1996; Thomas and the Tank Engine's Big Blue Treasury, 1998; Thomas the Tank Engine's Big Yellow Treasury, 1998; Thomas and the Missing Christmas Tree: A Thomas the Tank Engine Storybook, 1999; Thomas and the Dinosaur, 2000; Tell the Time with Thomas, 2006; Thomas and Victoria, 2007; Thomas and His Friends, 2011. **Address:** Sodor Enterprises, 1 Hutton Close, Spalding, SU PE12 6UY, England.

AWE, Susan C. American (born United States), b. 1948. **Genres:** Business/Trade/Industry, Librarianship, Economics, Reference. **Career:** University of Wisconsin-Madison, information specialist, 1980-87; Northern Arizona University, Flagstaff, business reference librarian, 1987-90, senior reference librarian, 1988-90; Natrona County Public Library, Information Services Department, supervisor, 1990-91; Jefferson County Library System, Arvada Library, library manager, 1991-98; University of New Mexico, Library for Business and Economics, director, 1998-. Writer. **Publications:** (Ed.) The ARBA Guide to Subject Encyclopedias and Dictionaries, 2nd ed., 1997; Entrepreneur's Information Sourcebook, 2006; Going Global: An Information Sourcebook for Small and Medium-Sized Businesses, 2009. Contributor to periodicals. **Address:** Parrish Memorial Business & Economics Library, University of New Mexico, Ste. 203, PO Box 05 3020, Albuquerque, CO 87131-0001, U.S.A. **Online address:** sawe@unm.edu

AWIAKTA, Marilou. American (born United States), b. 1936. **Genres:** Anthropology/Ethnology, History, Women's Studies And Issues, Poetry, Essays. **Career:** U.S. Air Force, Laon Air Force Base, civilian liaison officer and translator, 1964-67; United Methodist Publishing House, consultant, 1982; Aaron Copeland Festival, consultant; Far-Away Cherokee Association (now Native American Inter-Tribal Association), co-founder, 1982, ambassador-at-large, 1986-90; Mayor's International Heritage Commission, commissioner, 1987-90; Brandeis University, lecturer; Tufts University, lecturer; University of New Mexico, lecturer; Far Away Cherokee Association, co-founder. Writer. **Publications:** Abiding Appalachia: Where Mountain and Atom Meet, 1978; (contrib.) Poets of the River City Poetry Competition, 1978; Rising Fawn and the Fire Mystery: A Story of Heritage, Family and Courage, 1833 (children's book), 1983, rev. ed., 1992; (contrib.) Confessing Conscience: Churched Women on Abortion, 1990; Selu: Seeking the Corn-Mother's Wisdom, 1993; (contrib.) Returning the Gift, 1994; (co-author) Always at Home Here: Poems and Insights from Six Tennessee Poets, 1996; (intro.) Settling: Poems, 2000. Works appear in anthologies. Contributor to periodicals. **Address:** Fulcrum Publishing, 16100 Table Mountain Pkwy., Ste. 300, Golden, CO 80403, U.S.A.

AWOONOR, Kofi. (George Awoonor-Williams). Ghanaian (born Ghana), b. 1935. **Genres:** Novels, Plays/Screenplays, Poetry, Novellas/Short Stories, Politics/Government, History. **Career:** University of Ghana, lecturer and research fellow, 1960-64; Ghana Ministry of Information, director of films, 1964-67; State University of New York, assistant professor of English, 1968-75; University of Texas, visiting professor, 1972-73; University of Cape Coast, Department of English, head, 1975-76, professor of English, 1977-82; Ghana ambassador-Brazil in Brasilia, 1983-88; Ghana ambassador-Cuba, 1988-90; Ghana ambassador-United States, 1990-94. Writer. **Publications:** AS GEORGE AWOONOR-WILLIAMS: Rediscovery, and Other Poems, 1964; (contrib.) The Writer in Modern Africa, 1969. OTHERS: (ed. with G. Adali-Martty) Messages: Poems from Ghana, 1970; This Earth, My Brother: An Allegorical Tale of Africa, 1971; Night of My Blood (poetry), 1971; Ride Me, Memory (poetry), 1973; (ed.) Guardians of the Sacred Word: Ewe Poetry, 1974; The Breast of the Earth: A Survey of the History, Culture, and Literature of Africa, 1975; (contrib.) In Person, 1975; Teatro Africano, 1976; The House by the Sea (poetry), 1978; (trans.) When Sorrow-Song Descends on You, 1981; Fire in the Valley: Ewe Folktales, 1983; The Ghana Revolution: Background Account from a Personal Perspective, 1984; Until the Morning After: Collected Poems, 1963-1985, 1987; Alien Corn, 1988; Ghana: A Political History from Pre-European to Modern Times, 1990; Comes the Voyager at Last: A Tale of Return to Africa, 1992; Latin American and Caribbean Notebook (poetry), 1992; Africa: The Marginalized Continent, 1994; The African Predicament: Collected Essays, 2006; (foreword) My Name, My Race: A Young African's Untold Story, 2008. Contributor to periodicals. **Address:** Harold Ober Associates Inc., 425 Madison Ave., New York, NY 10017-1110, U.S.A.

AWOONOR-WILLIAMS, George. *See* **AWOONOR, Kofi.**

AWRET, Irene. American (born United States), b. 1921. **Genres:** Children's Fiction, Young Adult Fiction, Autobiography/Memoirs. **Career:** Writer and painter. **Publications:** Days of Honey: The Tunisian Boyhood of Rafael Uzan (juvenile), 1984; They'll Have To Catch Me First: An Artist's Coming of Age in the Third Reich, 2004. **Address:** c/o Leona Schecter, 3748 Huntington St. NW, Washington, DC 20015, U.S.A. **Online address:** ireneawret@hotmail.com

AXELROD, Amy. American (born United States) **Genres:** Children's Fiction, Animals/Pets, Literary Criticism And History. **Career:** Writer. **Publications:** The News Hounds in the Great Balloon Race: A Geography Adventure, 2000; The News Hounds Catch a Wave: A Geography Adventure, 2001; My Last Chance Brother, 2002; They'll Believe Me When I'm Gone, 2003; Your Friend in Fashion, Abby Shapiro, 2011. PIGS WILL BE PIGS SERIES: Pigs Will Be Pigs, 1994; Pigs on a Blanket, 1996; Pigs Go to Market: Fun with Math and Shopping, 1997; Pigs in the Pantry: Fun with Math and Cooking, 1997; Pigs on the Ball: Fun with Math and Sports, 1998; Pigs on the Move: Fun with Math and Travel, 1999; Pigs at Odds: Fun with Math and Games, 2000; Pigs in the Corner: Fun with Math and Dance, 2001. Contributor to periodicals. **Address:** c/o Author Mail, Simon & Schuster Inc., 1230 Ave. of the Americas, New York, NY 10020-1513, U.S.A.

AXELROD, Mark (R.). American (born United States), b. 1946. **Genres:** Plays/Screenplays, Literary Criticism And History, Novels, Film. **Career:** University of Minnesota, Department of English, teaching assistant, 1978-88, Honors Department, teaching assistant, 1978-88, Department of Comparative Literature, lecturer, 1988-89; Edinburgh University, Department of English, Leverhulme fellow in creative writing, 1989-90; Chapman University, Department of English and Comparative Literature, assistant professor of comparative literature, 1990-95, associate professor of comparative literature, 1995-99, professor of comparative literature, 1999-, Screenwriter-in-Residence Program, director, 1993-94, graduate program coordinator, 1999-2002, chair, 2004-05, director of graduate studies, 2008-, Comparative Literature Program, assistant coordinator, 1993-97, John Fowles Center for Creative Writing, director, 1997-; University of Hamburg, Hamburg Media School, adjunct professor of screenwriting, 2001-04; Soka University, visiting writer-in-residence, 2007. **Publications:** Neville Chamberlain's Chimera: Or, Nine Metaphors of Vision, 1979; (co-ed.) C.L.A.M. Chowder, 1983; The Politics of Style in the Fiction of Balzac, Beckett, and Cortázar, 1992; Bombay California: Or, Hollywood, Somewhere West of Vine (novel), 1994; (ed., contrib. and intro.) Review of Contemporary Fiction, 1995; Cardboard Castles (novel), 1996; Cloud Castles (novel), 1998; (co-author) Babel Guide to Jewish Fiction, 1998; The Poetics of Novels (literary criticism), 1998; Capital Castles (novel), 2000; Aspects of the Screenplay: Techniques of Screenwriting, 2001; Character and Conflict: The Cornerstones of Screenwriting, 2004; Borges' Travel, Hemingway's Garage: Secret Histories, 2004; I Read It at the Movies: The Follies and Foibles of Screen Adaptation, 2007. Works appear in anthologies. Contributor of articles to books and periodicals. **Address:** Department of English, Chapman University, 226 Wilkinson Hall, 1 University Dr., Orange, CA 92866-1005, U.S.A. **Online address:** axelrod@chapman.edu

AXLER, Leo. *See* **LAZUTA, Gene.**

AYALA, Francisco J. American (born United States), b. 1934. **Genres:** Biology, Philosophy. **Career:** Rockefeller University, research associate, 1964-65, assistant professor, 1967-71; Providence College, research associate, 1964-65, assistant professor of biology, 1965-67; University of California, faculty, 1971, Institute of Ecology, director, 1977-81, associate dean of environmental studies, 1977-81, professor of genetics; University of California, distinguished professor of biology, 1987-89, Donald Bren professor of biological sciences, 1989-, university professor, 2003-. Writer. **Publications:**

(Ed. with T. Dobzhansky) Studies in the Philosophy of Biology, 1974; (ed.) Molecular Evolution, 1976; (with T. Dobzhansky) Humankind, a Product of Evolutionary Transcendence, 1977; (with J.W. Valentine) Evolving: The Theory and Processes of Organic Evolution, 1979; (with J.A. Kiger Jr.) Modern Genetics, 1980, 2nd ed., 1984; El Origen y evolucion del hombre, 1980; Population and Evolutionary Genetics: A Primer, 1982; Biologie moleculaire et evolution, 1982; (ed. with J.P. Gustafson and G.L. Stebbins) Genetics, Development, and Evolution: 17th Stadler Genetics Symposium, 1986; La Teoria de La Evolucion: De Darwin a los Ultimos Avances de la Genetica, 1994; (ed. with W.M. Fitch) Tempo and Mode in Evolution: Genetics and Paleontology 50 Years after Simpson, 1995; (co-author) El Metodo en las Ciencias: Epistemologia y darwinismo, 1998; (ed. with R.J. Russell and W.R. Stoeger) Evolutionary and Molecular Biology: Scientific Perspectives on Divine Action, 1998; (ed. with W.M. Fitch and M.T. Clegg) Variation and Evolution in Plants and Microorganisms: Toward a New Synthesis 50 Years after Stebbins, 2000; (with A. Barahona and S. Pinar) La genetica en Mexico Institucionalizacion de una disciplina, 2003; (ed. with J.H. and W.M. Fitch) Systematics and the Origin of Species: On Ernst Mayr's 100th Anniversary, 2005; (and ed. with F.M. Wuketits) Handbook of Evolution: The Evolution of Living Systems, 2005; Darwin and Intelligent Design, 2006; La piedra que se volvio palabra. Las claves evolutivas de la humanidad, 2006; (with C. Conde) Human Evolution: Trails from the Past, 2007; Darwin's Gift to Science and Religion, 2007; (ed. with J.C. Avise) In the Light of Evolution, vol. I: Adaptation and Complex Design, 2007, vol. II: Biodiversity and Extinction, 2008, vol. III: Two Centuries of Darwin, 2009, vol. IV: The Human Condition, 2010; (ed. with R. Arp) Contemporary Debates in Philosophy of Biology, 2010; Am I a Monkey? Six Big Questions about Evolution, 2010. **Address:** Department of Ecology & Evolutionary Biology, University of California, Irvine, 321 Steinhaus Hall, Irvine, CA 92697-2525, U.S.A. **Online address:** fjayala@uci.edu

AYARBE, Heidi. Colombian/American (born United States), b. 1973?. **Genres:** Mystery/Crime/Suspense. **Career:** Writer. **Publications:** Freeze Frame, 2008; Compromised, 2010. **Address:** Colombia. **Online address:** info@heidiayarbe.com

AYCKBOURN, Alan. (Roland Allen). British (born England), b. 1939. **Genres:** Plays/Screenplays, Theatre, Songs/Lyrics And Libretti, Young Adult Non-fiction, Art/Art History. **Career:** Stephen Joseph Theatre-in-the-Round Co. (now Stephen Joseph Theatre), acting assistant stage manager, 1957, actor, 1958-62, writer and director, 1959-61, artistic director, 1972-2009; Victoria Theatre, actor, writer and director, 1961-64; British Broadcasting Corp. (BBC), drama producer, 1965-70; Royal National Theatre, visiting director, visiting playwright, 1977, 1980, 1986-88, associate director, 1986-88; Oxford University, St. Catherine's College, Cameron Mackintosh professor of contemporary theatre, 1991-92. **Publications:** PLAYS: Relatively Speaking: A Comedy, 1968; Ernie's Incredible Illucinations, 1969; Mixed Doubles: An Entertainment on Marriage, 1970; Time and Time Again: A Comedy in Two Acts, 1973; Absurd Person Singular, 1974; Absent Friends, 1975; The Norman Conquests: A Trilogy of Plays, 1975; Table Manners, 1975; Living Together, 1975; Round and Round the Garden, 1975; Confusions: Five Interlinked One-act Plays, 1977; Bedroom Farce: A Comedy, 1977; Three Plays, 1977; Family Circles, 1978; Ten Times Table, 1979; Joking Apart, 1979; Taking Steps, 1981; Sisterly Feelings: A Related Comedy, 1981; Season's Greetings, 1982; Suburban Strains, 1982; Way Upstream, 1983; A Chorus of Disapproval, 1985; Intimate Exchanges, 1985; Woman in Mind, 1986; A Small Family Business, 1987; Henceforward, 1988; Mr. A's Amazing Maze Plays, 1989; Body Language, 1990; Invisible Friends, 1991; A Cut in the Rates, 1991; A Day in the Life of Tich Oldfield, 1991; Wildest Dreams, 1993; Time of My Life, 1993; The Alan Ayckbourn: Plays 1, 1995; This Is Where We Came In, 1995; My Very Own Story: A Play for Children, 1995; Callisto 5, 1995; By Jeeves, 1996; Family Circles: A Comedy, 1997; It Could Be Any One of Us: A Comedy, 1998; Things We do for Love, 1998; A Word from Our Sponsor: A Musical Play, 1998; The Champion of Paribanou, 1998; Comic Potential, 1999; Whenever, 2000; The Boy Who Fell into a Book, 2000; Gizmo, 2001; Gameplan, 2002; Flatspin, 2002; Roleplay, 2002; The Jollies, 2002; Orvin-Champion of Champions, 2003; My Sister Sadie, 2003; House & Garden, rev. ed., 2003; Snake in the Grass, 2004; Plays Three, 2005; Drowning on Dry Land, 2006. NON-FICTION: (with I. Watson) Conversations with Ayckbourn, 1981; Improbable Fiction: A Comedy, 2007. OTHERS: The Crafty Art of Playmaking, 2003; If I Were You, 2009; Life and Beth, 2009; Awaking Beauty, 2009; My Wonderful Day, 2011; (intro.) Plays Five, 2011. Contributor to periodicals. **Address:** Casarotto Ramsay & Associates Ltd., Waverley House, 7-12 Noel St., London, GL W1F 8GQ, England.

AYCLIFFE, Jonathan. *See* **MACEOIN, Denis.**

AYERS, William. American (born United States), b. 1944. **Genres:** Education, Essays. **Career:** Weather Underground, co-founder, 1969; Columbia University, Teachers College, Department of Curriculum and Teaching, instructor, 1985-87; University of Illinois-Chicago, Department of Curriculum, Instruction and Evaluation, assistant professor, 1987-92, associate professor, 1992-96, professor of education, 1996-99, distinguished professor of education, 1999-, adjunct professor, Small Schools Workshop, founder, co-director, 1992-2002, now retired; Nazareth College, doctor of humane letters, 1996; Center for Youth and Society, founder and director, 1999-2002; Vassar College, Randolph distinguished visiting professor, 2005-06; Childrens Community School, teacher. Writer. **Publications:** The Good Preschool Teacher: Six Teachers Reflect on Their Lives, 1989; To Teach: The Journey of a Teacher, 1993, 3rd ed., 2010; A Kind and Just Parent: The Children of Juvenile Court, 1997; (as Bill Ayers) Fugitive Days: A Memoir, 2001, rev. ed., 2003; On the Side of the Child: Summerhill Revisited, 2003; Teaching the Personal and the Political: Essays on Hope and Justice, 2004; Teaching Toward Freedom: Moral Commitment and Ethical Action in the Classroom, 2004; (with B. Dohrn) Race Course against White Supremacy, 2009; (with R. Alexander-Tanner) To Teach: The Journey in Comics, 2010; (co-author) Teaching Toward Democracy: Educators as Agents of Change, 2010; (with R. Ayers) Teaching the Taboo: Courage and Imagination in the Classroom, 2011. EDITOR: (with W.H. Schubert) Teacher Lore: Learning from Our Own Experience, 1992; To Become a Teacher: Making a Difference in Children's Lives, 1995; (with P. Ford) City Kids, City Teachers: Reports from the Front Row, 1996; (with J.L. Miller) A Light in Dark Times: Maxine Green and the Unfinished Conversation, 1998; (co-ed.) Teaching for Social Justice: A Democracy and Education Reader, 1998; (with M. Klonsky and G. Lyon) A Simple Justice: The Challenge of Small Schools, 2000; (with R. Ayers and B. Dohrn) Zero Tolerance: Resisting the Drive for Punishment in Our Schools: A Handbook for Parents, Students, Educators and Citizens, 2001; (with B. Dohm and J. Jones) Sing a Battle Song: The Revolutionary Poetry, Statements and Communiqués of the Weather Underground, 1970-1974, 2006; City Kids, City Schools: More Reports from the Front Row, 2008; (with T. Quinn and D. Stovall) Handbook of Social Justice in Education, 2009. **Address:** College of Education, University of Illinois at Chicago, Rm. 3404, 1040 W Harrison, PO Box 147, Chicago, IL 60607-7133, U.S.A. **Online address:** bayers@uic.edu

AYITTEY, George B. N. American/Ghanaian (born Ghana), b. 1945. **Genres:** Politics/Government, Writing/Journalism, Area Studies. **Career:** Wayne State College, faculty; Bloomsburg University, faculty; American University, distinguished economist and professor, visiting associate professor; Free Africa Foundation, founder and president, 1993-; Hudson Institute, fellow; Heritage Foundation, fellow. Writer. **Publications:** Indigenous African Institutions, 1991, 2nd ed., 2004; Africa Betrayed, 1992; The Blueprint For Ghana's Economic Recovery, 1997; Africa in Chaos, 1998; Africa Unchained: The Blueprint for Africa's Future, 2006; Contributor to periodicals. **Address:** The Free Africa Foundation, 910 17th St. NW, Ste. 419, Washington, DC 20006, U.S.A. **Online address:** ayittey@american.edu

AYLEN, Leo. British/South African (born South Africa), b. 1935. **Genres:** Plays/Screenplays, Poetry, Theatre. **Career:** BBC-TV, producer, 1965-70; Fairleigh Dickinson University, poet-in-residence, 1972-74; McMaster University, Hooker distinguished visiting professor, 1982. Actor and broadcaster. **Publications:** Greek Tragedy and the Modern World, 1964; Greece for Everyone, 1975; The Greek Theater, 1985; Rhymoceros, 1989. POETRY: Discontinued Design, 1969; I, Odysseus, 1971; Sunflower, 1976; Return to Zululand, 1980; (contrib.) The Apples of Youth, 1980; Jumping-Shoes, 1983; Red Alert: This is a God Warning, 1981; Dancing the Impossible: New and Selected Poems, 1997. Works appear in anthologies. **Address:** Aitken Alexander Associates Ltd., 18-21 Cavaye Pl., London, GL SW10 9PT, England. **Online address:** leo@leoaylen.com

AYLESWORTH, Jim. American (born United States), b. 1943. **Genres:** Children's Fiction. **Career:** Teacher, 1971-96; Concordia University, College of DuPage, professor of children's literature; University of Chicago, professor of children's literature; writer, 1980-. **Publications:** CHILDREN'S FICTION: Hush Up! 1980; Tonight's the Night, 1981; Mary's Mirror, 1982; Siren in the Night, 1983; The Bad Dream, 1985; Shenandoah Noah, 1985; Two Terrible Frights, 1987; One Crow, 1988; Hanna's Hog, 1988; Mother Halverson's New Cat, 1989; Mr. McGill Goes to Town, 1989; The Completed Hickory Dickory Dock, 1990; Country Crossing, 1991; The Folks in the Valley, 1991; Old Black Fly, 1992; The Cat and the Fiddle and More, 1992; The Good-Night Kiss, 1993; My Son John, 1994; McGraw's Emporium, 1995; Wake Up, Little Children, 1996; My Sister's Rusty Bike, 1996; Teddy Bear Tears, 1997; (reteller) The Gingerbread Man, 1998; Through the Night, 1998; Jim Aylesworth's Book of Bedtime Stories, 1998; (reteller) Aunt Pitty Patty's Piggy, 1999; The Full Belly Bowl, 1999; (reteller) The Tale of Tricky Fox, 2001; The Burger and the Hot Dog, 2001; Naughty Little Monkeys, 2003; (reteller) Goldilocks and the Three Bears, 2003; Jim Aylesworth and You, 2006; Little Bitty Mousie, 2007; (adapter) Our Abe Lincoln, 2009; (reteller) The Mitten, 2009: Cock-a-doodle-do Creak Pop-pop Moo, 2012. Contributor to periodicals. **Address:** 55 W Delaware Pl. 407, Chicago, IL 60610, U.S.A. **Online address:** oldfly@ayles.com

AYRES, E. C. (Gene Ayres). American (born United States), b. 1946. **Genres:** Mystery/Crime/Suspense, Plays/Screenplays, Literary Criticism And History, International Relations/Current Affairs, Sociology, Environmental Sciences/Ecology, Popular Culture, History, Politics/Government. **Career:** Producer, writer and director of educational films, 1969-72; Children's Television Workshop, producer, writer and director, 1973-74; Hanna Barbera Productions, staff writer, 1979-84; Jack Arnold Productions, writer and associate producer, 1980-82; Roll Over Beethoven Productions, feature film development writer, 1983-89; WTSP-TV, television film critic, 1990-91; 2020 Productions, writer and creative producer, 1992-94; Future Wave Inc., writer and creative producer, 1992-94; freelance novelist, 1994-; Harbin Shang Da University, instructor in English and creative writing, 2004-07. **Publications:** MYSTERIES: Hour of the Manatee, 1994; Eye of the Gator, 1995; Night of the Panther, 1997; Lair of the Lizard, 1998; Cry of the Heron, 2009; A Billion to One: An American Insider in the New China, 2009; Inside the New China, 2010. Contributor to periodicals. **Address:** 19230 Forest Park Dr. NE, G-222, Seattle, WA 98155, U.S.A. **Online address:** geneayres@juno.com

AYRES, Gene. *See* **AYRES, E. C.**

AYRES, Mary Jo. American (born United States), b. 1953?. **Genres:** Education, Reference. **Career:** Writer. **Publications:** Happy Teaching and Natural Learning, vol. I, 1992, vol. II, 1994; Natural Learning from A to Z, 1997, 2nd ed., 2002. **Address:** Natural Learning, 103 Sycamore St., Leland, MS 38756-3136, U.S.A. **Online address:** nlearn@naturallearning.com

AYRES, Pam. British (born England), b. 1947. **Genres:** Children's Fiction, Poetry, Humor/Satire, Literary Criticism And History. **Career:** BBC radio show, host, 1996-99. Broadcaster and Writer. **Publications:** FOR CHILDREN: Some of Me Poetry, 1976; All Pam's Poems, 1978; When Dad Cuts down the Chestnut Tree, 1988; When Dad Fills in the Garden Pond, 1988; Guess Who?, 1987; Guess What?, 1988; The Bear Who Was Left Behind, 1991; Piggo and the Nosebag, 1992; Piggo has a Train Ride, 1992; Jack Crater, 1992; Guess Where?, 1994; Guess Why?, 1994; The Nubbler, 1997. OTHER: The Works: Selected Poems (light verse), 1992; With These Hands (poetry), 1997. **Address:** Acorn Entertainments Ltd., PO Box 64, Cirencester, GL7 5YD, England. **Online address:** acornents@btconnect.com

AYRES, Philip. Australian (born Australia), b. 1944. **Genres:** Novels, Novellas/Short Stories, History, Literary Criticism And History. **Career:** Monash University, lecturer, 1972-79, senior lecturer in English, 1980-93, associate professor, 1994-2006-, professorial fellow, 2006-; Vassar College, visiting professorial fellow, 1993; Australian Council, Literature Board, deputy chair, 2000-02; Boston University, visiting professorial fellow, 2001. Writer. **Publications:** Tourneur, The Revenger's Tragedy, 1977; The English Roman Life, 1980; Malcolm Fraser: A Biography, 1987; Classical Culture and the Idea of Rome in Eighteenth-Century England, 1997; Douglas Mawson: A Biography, 1999; Mawson: A Life, 1999; Owen Dixon, 2003; The Worlds of Cardinal Moran, 2007; Prince of the Church: Patrick Francis Moran, 1830-1911, 2007. EDITOR: Sejanus His Fall, 1990; Characteristicks of Men, Manners, Opinions, Times, 1999; Climate and Its Discontents: The Richard James Chester Guest Spring Conversazione, 2008. Contributor to journals and periodicals. **Address:** Department of English, Monash University, PO Box 4, Clayton, VI 3800, Australia.

AYRES, Thomas (R.). American (born United States), b. 1936. **Genres:** History, Local History/Rural Topics, Mythology/Folklore, Trivia/Facts, Military/Defense/Arms Control, Social Sciences. **Career:** Writer. **Publications:** That's Not in My American History Book, 2000; Dark and Bloody Ground, 2001; Dammit Sam and Me, 2002; Military Miscellany: Important, Uncommon and Sometimes Forgotten Facts, Lists and Stories from America's Military History, 2006. Contributor to magazines and newspapers. **Address:** 1676 Beacon St., Ste. 3, Brookline, MA 02445, U.S.A. **Online address:** tayres@pineynet.com

AYUB, Awista. Afghani (born Afghanistan), b. 1979?. **Genres:** Young Adult Non-fiction, Travel/Exploration. **Career:** Embassy of Afghanistan, education and health officer; Afghan Youth Sports Exchange, founder, 2003-. Writer. **Publications:** However Tall the Mountain: A Dream, Eight Girls, and a Journey Home (nonfiction), 2009. **Address:** Afghanistan. **Online address:** awista@awistaayub.com

AZIMI, Fakhreddin. American/Iranian (born Iran), b. 1953. **Genres:** History. **Career:** University of Connecticut, faculty, 1991-, professor of history; Yale University, Iran Colloquium, fellow. Writer and historian. **Publications:** Iran: The Crisis of Democracy, 1941-1953, 1989, rev. ed. as Iran: The Crisis of Democracy: From the Exile of Reza Shah to the Fall of Musaddiq, 2009; Asnad sukhan mi'guyand: majmu'ah-i kamil-i asnad-i sirri-i marbut bih ruydadha dar ravabit-i khariji-i Iran ba Ayalat-i Muttahidah va Inglistan dar dawran-i nahz at-i milli-i Iran (1951-1945): mushtamil bar 508 sanad-i rasmi-i bi-kulli sirri vb sirri, 2004; Hakemiyat-e melli va doshmanan-e an, 2004; The Quest for Democracy in Iran: A Century of Struggle against Authoritarian Rule, 2008; Ta'ammoli dar binesh-e siasi-ye Mosaddeq, forthcoming. Contributor to books and journals. **Address:** Department of History, University of Connecticut, 241 Glenbrook Rd., Storrs, CT 06269-2103, U.S.A. **Online address:** fakhreddin.azimi@uconn.edu

AZOULAY, Dan. Canadian (born Canada), b. 1960. **Genres:** History. **Career:** Trent University, sessional instructor, 1989-2002; McMaster University, sessional instructor in history, 1992-; York University, sessional instructor in history, 1995-; University of Toronto, sessional instructor, 2002-03. Writer. **Publications:** Keeping the Dream Alive: The Survival of the Ontario CCF/NDP, 1950-1963, 1997; (ed.) Canadian Political Parties: Historical Readings, 1998; Only the Lonely: Finding Romance in the Personal Columns of the Western Home Monthly, 1905-1924, 2000; Hearts and Minds: Canadian Romance at the Dawn of the Modern Era, 1900-1930, 2011. Contributor to books and periodicals. **Address:** 1005 Lemar Rd., Newmarket, ON L3Y 1S2, Canada. **Online address:** dazoulay@yorku.ca

AZRIEL, Yakov. (Gerald Rosenkrantz). American (born United States), b. 1950?. **Genres:** Novels, Literary Criticism And History, Poetry. **Career:** Writer. **Publications:** Threads from a Coat of Many Colors: Poems on Genesis, 2005; In the Shadow of a Burning Bush: Poems on Exodus, 2008; Beads for the Messiah's Bride: Poems on Leviticus, 2009; Swimming in Moses' Well: Poems on Numbers, 2011. **Address:** Time Being Books, 10411 Clayton Rd., 201 203 Ste., St. Louis, MO 63131, U.S.A. **Online address:** yakovaz@hotmail.com

B

B., David. *See* **BEAUCHARD, Pierre François.**

B., Dick. *See* **BURNS, Richard Gordon.**

BAARS, Bernard J(oseph). American/Dutch (born Netherlands), b. 1946. **Genres:** Psychology. **Career:** University of Wisconsin, university fellow, 1975; State University of New York at Stony Brook, assistant professor of psychology, 1977, professor; University of California, Langley Porter Neuropsychiatric Institute, visiting scientist, 1985-86; Wright Institute, associate professor, 1986-, faculty professor, 1986; Consciousness & Cognition: An International Journal, co-editor, 1989, co-founder; Association for the Scientific Study of Consciousness, co-founder, president, 1994-96; Society for Philosophy and Psychology, director, 1998; The Neurosciences Institute, visiting fellow, 1999, senior fellow in theoretical neurobiology, 2001-, affiliated fellow; Science and Consciousness Review, founding editor, 2002. **Publications:** The Cognitive Revolution in Psychology, 1986; A Cognitive Theory of Consciousness, 1988; (ed.) The Experimental Psychology of Human Error: Implications for the Architecture of Voluntary Control, 1992; (ed.) Experimental Slips and Human Error, 1992; In the Theater of Consciousness: The Workspace of the Mind, 1997; (ed. with W.P. Banks and J.B. Newman) Essential Sources in the Scientific Study of Consciousness, 2003; (ed. with N.M. Gage) Cognition, Brain and Consciousness: Introduction to Cognitive Neuroscience, 2nd ed., 2010. Contributor to books and journals. **Address:** The Neurosciences Institute, 10640 John Jay Hopkins Dr., San Diego, CA 92121, U.S.A. **Online address:** baars@nsi.edu

BAAS, Jacquelynn. American (born United States), b. 1948. **Genres:** Architecture, History. **Career:** University of California, Berkeley Art Museum and Pacific Film Archive, director, 1988-99, now director emeritus, 1999-, interim director, 2007-; Awake: Art, Buddhism and the Dimensions of Consciousness Arts Consortium, founder and director, 1999-2005; University of Michigan Museum of Art, assistant director; Dartmouth College, Hood Museum, director. Writer. **Publications:** NONFICTION: (with R.S. Field) The Artistic Revival of the Woodcut in France 1850-1900, 1984; Treasures of the Hood Museum of Art, 1985; (with K. Tsujimoto) Art of Joan Brown, 1998; (contrib.) Ghosts, 2003; (ed. with M.J. Jacob) Buddha Mind in Contemporary Art, 2004; Smile of the Buddha: Eastern Philosophy and Western Art from Monet to Today, 2005; (contrib.) Measure of Time, 2007; (ed. with M.J. Jacob) Learning Mind: Experience Into Art, 2009; (ed. and contrib.) Fluxus and the Essential Questions of Life, 2011. **Address:** Berkeley Art Museum and Pacific Film Archive, 2625 Durant Ave., Ste. 2250, Berkeley, CA 94720, U.S.A.

BAATZ, Simon. American (born United States), b. 1952. **Genres:** History, Agriculture/Forestry, Sciences, Cultural/Ethnic Topics. **Career:** National Institutes of Health, researcher, 2000; George Mason University, visiting associate professor; City University of New York, John Jay College of Criminal Justice, Graduate Center, faculty, Department of History, associate professor, professor. Writer. **Publications:** Venerate the Plough: A History of the Philadelphia Society for Promoting Agriculture, 1785-1985, 1985; Knowledge, Culture and Science in the Metropolis: The New York Academy of Sciences, 1817-1970, 1990; For the Thrill of It: Leopold, Loeb and the Murder that Shocked Chicago, 2008. **Address:** Department of History, Jay College of Criminal Justice, City University of New York, Rm. 4324N, North Hall, 445 W 59th St., New York, NY 10019-1104, U.S.A. **Online address:** sbaatz@jjay.cuny.edu

BABB, Valerie (Melissa). American (born United States), b. 1955. **Genres:** Biography, Local History/Rural Topics, Cultural/Ethnic Topics, Literary Criticism And History, Young Adult Fiction. **Career:** Georgetown University, assistant professor of English, 1981-, associate professor of English, professor; University of Georgia, professor of English and of African American studies; Middlebury College, Bread Loaf School of English, faculty. Writer. **Publications:** Ernest Gaines, 1991; (with C.R. Gibbs) Black Georgetown Remembered: A History of Its Black Community from the Founding of The Town of George in 1751 to the Present Day, 1991; Whiteness Visible: The Meeting of Whiteness in American Literature and Culture, 1998. Contributor to books. **Address:** Department of English, University of Georgia, 312 Park Hall, Athens, GA 30602-6205, U.S.A. **Online address:** vbabb@uga.edu

BABBITT, Natalie. American (born United States), b. 1932. **Genres:** Children's Fiction, Young Adult Fiction, Illustrations, Novels. **Career:** Children's book writer and illustrator. **Publications:** SELF-ILLUSTRATED: VERSE: Dick Foote and the Shark, 1967; Phoebe's Revolt, 1968. SELF-ILLUSTRATED: FICTION: The Search for the Delicious, 1969; Kneeknock Rise, 1970; The Something, 1970; Goody Hall, 1971; The Devil's Storybook, 1974; Tuck Everlasting, 1975; The Eyes of the Amaryllis, 1977; Herbert Rowbarge, 1982; The Devil's Other Storybook, 1987; Nellie: A Cat on Her Own, 1989; Tuck Para Siempre, 1991; Bub: Or the Very Best Thing, 1994; Elsie Times Eight, 2001; Jack Plank Tells Tales, 2007; Knee Knock Rise, 2007. OTHERS: Phoebe's Revolt, 1968; The Search for Delicious, 1969; The Big Book for Peace, 1990; Ouch!: A Tale from Grimm, 1998; (with M.T. Anderson and C. Brown) The Exquisite Corpse Adventure: A Progressive Story Game, 2011; Moon over High Street, 2012. Illustrator of books by V. Worth. Contributor to periodicals and journals. **Address:** 81 Benefit St., Providence, RI 02904-2703, U.S.A.

BABBITT, Susan E. Canadian (born Canada), b. 1953. **Genres:** Philosophy. **Career:** Queen's University, assistant professor of philosophy, 1990-, associate professor. Writer. **Publications:** Impossible Dreams: Rationality, Integrity, and Moral Imagination, 1996; (ed. with S. Campbell) Racism and Philosophy, 1999; Artless Integrity: Moral Imagination, Agency, and Stories, 2001. Contributor of articles and to books and journals. **Address:** Department of Philosophy, Queen's University, Watson Hall, 49 Bader Ln., Kingston, ON K7L 3N6, Canada. **Online address:** babbitts@post.queensu.ca

BABICH, Babette E. American (born United States), b. 1956. **Genres:** Philosophy, Politics/Government, Archaeology/Antiquities, Art/Art History, Speech/Rhetoric. **Career:** Denison University, visiting assistant professor, 1987-88; Marquette University, assistant professor of philosophy, 1988-89; Fordham University, Department of Philosophy, professor of philosophy, 1989-, New Nietzsche Studies, executive editor, 1996-; State University of New York, adjunct assistant professor, 1990, adjunct professor, 2004; University of Tuebingen, Fulbright lecturer, 1991-92; Georgetown University, adjunct research professor, 1993-; University of California, visiting professor, 2005-07. **Publications:** Nietzsche's Philosophy of Science: Reflecting Science on the Ground of Art and Life, 1994; Words in Blood, Like Flowers: Philosophy and Poetry, Music and Eros in Hölderlin, Nietzsche, and Heidegger, 2006; Eines Gottes Glueck, voller Macht und Liebe, 2009; Nietzsches Wissenschaftsphilosophie, 2010. EDITOR: From Phenomenology to Thought, Errancy, and Desire: Essays in Honor of William J. Richardson, S.J., 1995; (with D.B. Bergoffen and S.V. Glynn) Continental and Postmodern Perspectives in the Philosophy of Science, 1995; Nietzsche, Theories of Knowledge and Critical Theory, 1999; Nietzsche, Epistemology, and Philosophy of Science, 1999; Hermeneutic Philosophy of Science, Van Gogh's Eyes, and God: Essays in Honor of Patrick A. Heelan, 2002; Habermas, Nietzsche, and Critical Theory, 2004. Contributor to books and journals. **Address:** Department of Philosophy, Fordham University, LL 925H Collins Hall, 441 E Fordham Rd., New York, NY 10458, U.S.A. **Online address:** babich@fordham.edu

BACA, Ana. American (born United States), b. 1967?. **Genres:** Novels, Social Sciences, Children's Fiction. **Career:** Public Relations, marketing and communications executive. Author. **Publications:** Benito's Bizcochitos, 1999; Chiles for Benito/Chiles para Benito, 2003; Mama Fela's Girls (novel), 2006; Benito's Sopaipillas/Las sopaipillas de Benito, 2006; Tia's Tamales, 2011. **Address:** Pinata Books/Arte Publico Press, University of Houston, 452 Cullen Performance Hall, Houston, TX 77204-2004, U.S.A. **Online address:** anawrite@msn.com

BACH, David. American (born United States), b. 1966. **Genres:** Economics, Environmental Sciences/Ecology. **Career:** Morgan Stanley, senior vice president; Bach Group, partner, 1993-2001; FinishRich Media, founder, chair, 2001-; FinishRich Seminars, creator; Redbook Magazine, columnist; Yahoo! Web site, columnist; FinishRich.com, founder. Speaker and financial advisor. **Publications:** Give What You Didn't Get, 1998; Smart Women Finish Rich: Seven Steps to Achieving Financial Security and Funding Your Dreams, 1999, rev. ed. as Smart Women Finish Rich: Nine Steps to Achieving Financial Security and Funding Your Dreams, 2002; Smart Couples Finish Rich: Nine Steps to Creating a Rich Future for You and Your Partner, 2001; The Finish Rich Workbook: Creating a Personalized Plan for a Richer Future, 2003; 1001 Financial Words You Need to Know, 2003; The Automatic Millionaire: A Powerful One-Step Plan to Live and Finish Rich, 2004; Start Late, Finish Rich: A No-Fail Plan for Achieving Financial Freedom at Any Age, 2005; The Automatic Millionaire Homeowner: A Powerful Plan to Finish Rich in Real Estate, 2005; The Automatic Millionaire Workbook: A Personalized Plan to Live and Finish Rich, 2005; The Automatic Millionaire Homeowner: A Lifetime Plan to Finish Rich in Real Estate, 2006; El millonario automático: un plan poderoso y sencillo para vivir y acabar rico, 2006, 2006; (with H. Rosner) Go Green, Live Rich: Fifty Simple Ways to Save the Earth and Get Rich Trying, 2008; (ed.) The Finish Rich Dictionary, 2009; Start Over, Finish Rich, 2009; Fight for your Money, 2009; Debt Free for Life, 2010. **Address:** FinishRich Media, 295 Greenwich St., Ste. 529, New York, NY 10007, U.S.A.

BACHE, Ellyn. American (born United States), b. 1942. **Genres:** Novels, Novellas/Short Stories, Children's Fiction, Young Adult Fiction, Social Commentary. **Career:** Novelist, editor and journalist. **Publications:** Culture Clash, 1982, 2nd ed., 1989; The Value of Kindness (short stories), 1993; (and ed.) What Locals Know About Wilmington and Its Beaches; The Art of Saying Goodbye, 2011. NOVELS: Safe Passage, 1988; Festival in Fire Season, 1992; The Activist's Daughter, 1997; (as E.M.J. Benjamin) Takedown, 1999; Holiday Miracles, 2001; Daddy and the Pink Flash, 2003; Riggs Park, 2005; Daughters of the Sea, 2005; Over 50's Singles Night, 2006; Raspberry Sherbet Kisses, 2007; The Power of Sharpe Thinking, 2008; On a Roll in the Suburbs, 2008; A South Carolina Mystery, 2009; What Lies Ahead, 2009. **Address:** c/o Homecourt Publishers, 2435 E North St., Ste. 245, Greenville, SC 29615, U.S.A. **Online address:** ellyn@ellynbache.com

BACHELDER, Thomas. Canadian (born Canada), b. 1958. **Genres:** Food And Wine. **Career:** Wine Tidings (magazine), assistant editor, 1988-92, columnist, 1988-; Hour Magazine, wine columnist, 1993-; Le Clos Jordanne, viniculture manager. Writer. **Publications:** For the Love of Wine, 1990; You Made This?!: A Guide to Making Wine No One Knows is Homemade, 1992; The Best B.Y.O.B. Restaurants of Montreal, 1994, 3rd ed., 2000. **Address:** Le Clos Jordanne, 2540 S Service Rd., Jordan Station, ON L0R 1S0, Canada. **Online address:** mabourgogne@sympatico.ca

BACHER, John. Canadian (born Canada), b. 1954. **Genres:** Environmental Sciences/Ecology. **Career:** McMaster University, instructor; University of Toronto, instructor; Ontario Drainage Tribunal, hearing officer, 1991-97; Preservation of Agricultural Lands Society, researcher. Writer. **Publications:** (Co-author) Niagara Conservation Strategy, 1988; Keeping to the Marketplace: The Evolution of Canadian Housing Policy, 1900-1990, 1993; (with W. Roberts and B. Nelson) Get a Life, 1994; Petrotyranny, 2000; Two Billion Trees and Counting: The Legacy of Edmund Zavitz, 2011. Contributor of articles to periodicals. **Address:** 134 Church St., St. Catharines, ON L2R 3E4, Canada. **Online address:** pals@becon.org

BACHMAN, Richard. *See* **KING, Stephen.**

BACHMAN, W. Bryant. *See* **BACHMAN, W(illiam) Bryant.**

BACHMAN, W(illiam) Bryant. (W. Bryant Bachman). American (born United States), b. 1941. **Genres:** Mythology/Folklore, Literary Criticism And History. **Career:** University of Southwestern Louisiana, professor of English, 1976-. Writer. **Publications:** Four Old Icelandic Sagas, 1985; (with G. Erlingsson) The Saga of Finnbogithe Strong, 1990; (with Erlingsson) The Sagas of King Half and King Hrolf, 1991; Forty Old Icelandic Tales, 1992; (with Erlingsson) Six Old Icelandic Sagas, 1993; (with G. Erlingsson) Svarfdale Sagas and Other Tales, 1994; (trans. and contrib.) Heidarviga Saga, 1995. **Address:** Department of English, University of Southwestern Louisiana, Lafayette, LA 70504, U.S.A.

BACHO, Peter. American (born United States), b. 1950?. **Genres:** Novels, Novellas/Short Stories. **Career:** University of Washington, assistant professor in the ethnic studies, professor of law and Philippine history, Interdisciplinary Arts and Sciences program, lecturer; Ninth Circuit Court of Appeals, staff attorney, 1989; freelance writer, 1991-; The News Tribune, full-time editorial writer, 1999-2004. **Publications:** Cebu (novel), 1991; Dark Blue Suit and Other Stories, 1997; Boxing in Black and White, 1999; Nelson's Run, 2002; Entrys, 2005; Leaving Yesler, 2010. Contributor to books and periodicals. **Address:** University of Washington Press, 4333 Brooklyn Ave. NE, PO Box 50096, Seattle, WA 98195-9570, U.S.A.

BACHORZ, Pam. American (born United States), b. 1973?. **Genres:** Science Fiction/Fantasy. **Career:** Author. **Publications:** Candor, 2009; Drought, 2010. **Address:** c/o Emily van Beek, Folio Literary, 505 8th Ave., Ste. 603, New York, NY 10018, U.S.A.

BACHRACH, Nancy. American (born United States), b. 1950?. **Genres:** Autobiography/Memoirs. **Career:** Grey Advertising, chief writer, advertising agency executive and educator; Brandeis University, teaching assistant. **Publications:** The Center of the Universe: A Memoir, 2009. **Address:** New York, NY , U.S.A. **Online address:** nancy@nancybachrach.com

BACIK, Ivana. Irish (born Ireland), b. 1968. **Genres:** Documentaries/Reportage, International Relations/Current Affairs, Area Studies. **Career:** University of North London, lecturer, 1991-93; University of Kent, seminar tutor, 1992-93; National College of Industrial Relations, lecturer, 1993-95; Trinity College Dublin, lecturer, 1995-96, professor of criminal law, criminology & penology, 1996-, fellow, 2005-, director of undergraduate teaching & learning; Seanad eireann (Irish Parliament), senator, 2007-. Writer. **Publications:** (with J. Kingston and A. Whelan) Abortion and the Law, 1997; (ed. with M. O'Connell) Crime and Poverty in Ireland, 1998; (with C. Maunsell and S. Gogan) The Legal Process and Victims of Rape: A Comparative Analysis of the Laws and Legal Procedures Relating to Rape, and Their Impact upon Victims of Rape, in the Fifteen Member States of the European Union, 1998; (with S. Livingstone) Towards a Culture of Human Rights in Ireland: From Black-Spot to Role Model?, 2001; (with C. Costello and E. Drew) Gender Injustice: Feminising the Legal Professions?, 2003; Kicking and Screaming: Dragging Ireland into the 21st Century, 2004. **Address:** Seanad Eireann, Leinster House, Kildare St., Dublin, 2, Ireland. **Online address:** ivana.bacik@oireachtas.ie

BACKER, Sara. American (born United States), b. 1957?. **Genres:** Novels, Poetry, Novellas/Short Stories. **Career:** Shizuoka University, visiting professor of English; University of Massachusetts, adjunct professor of English. Fiction and poetry writer. **Publications:** American Fuji: A Novel, 2001. Contributor to periodicals. **Address:** c/o Jennifer Unter, The Unter Agency L.L.C., 23 W 73rd St., Ste. 100, New York, NY 10023, U.S.A. **Online address:** saraebacker@gmail.com

BACKES, David James. American (born United States), b. 1957. **Genres:** Travel/Exploration, Biography, Natural History, Art/Art History. **Career:** Ely

Echo, reporter, 1979-80; University Bookstore, textbook information clerk, 1980-81; University of Wisconsin, College of Agriculture and Life Sciences, staff writer, 1982-83, Department of Agriculture Journalism, lecturer, 1984-88, Department of Mass Communications, assistant professor, 1988-94, associate professor, 1994-99, Department of Journalism and Mass Communication, professor, 1999-, chair, 1995-96. Writer. **Publications:** Canoe Country: An Embattled Wilderness, 1991; (comp. and intro.) The Wilderness Companion, 1992; A Wilderness Within: The Life of Sigurd F. Olson, 1997; (ed. and intro.) The Meaning of Wilderness: Essential Articles and Speeches, 2001; (ed.) Spirit of the North: The Quotable Sigurd F. Olson, 2004. Contributor to periodicals. **Address:** Department of Journalism and Mass Communication, University of Wisconsin, 130 Johnston Hall, 2200 E Kenwood Blvd., PO Box 413, Milwaukee, WI 53201-0413, U.S.A. **Online address:** backes@uwm.edu

BACKHOUSE, Constance B. Canadian (born Canada), b. 1952?. **Genres:** Business/Trade/Industry, History. **Career:** University of Western Ontario, faculty; University of Ottawa, distinguished university professor, university research chair, Human Rights Research and Education Centre, director, Common Law Exchange Program, director; Feminist History Society, co-founder, 2009-; Women's Education and Research Foundation of Ontario Inc., board director; Claire L'Heureux-Dubé Fund for Social Justice, board director. Writer. **Publications:** NONFICTION: (with L. Cohen) The Secret Oppression: Sexual Harassment of Working Women, 1978; (co-author) Fighting Sexual Harassment: An Advocacy Handbook, Graphics by Linda Hoffman, 1979; (co-author) London Battered Women's Legal Handbook, 1980; (with L. Cohen) Sexual Harassment on the Job: How to Avoid the Working Woman's Nightmare, 1981; (co-author) London Rape Victims' Legal Handbook, 1981; Petticoats and Prejudice: Women and Law in Nineteenth-Century Canada, 1991; Women and the Law in Nineteenth-Century Canada, 1991; (ed. with D.H. Flaherty) Challenging Times: The Women's Movement in Canada and the United States, 1992; Colour-Coded: A Legal History of Racism in Canada, 1900-1950, 1999; (ed. with J. Swainger) People and Place: Historical Influences on Legal Culture, 2003; (with M. McInnes, J.A. Vanduzer and C. Carmody) Managing the Law: The Legal Aspects of Doing Business, 2003, 2nd ed., 2005; (with N.L. Backhouse) The Heiress vs. the Establishment: Mrs. Campbell's Campaign for Legal Justice, 2004; (ed. with N. Finkelstein) The Laskin Legacy: Essays in Commemoration of Chief Justice Bora Laskin, 2007; Carnal Crimes: Sexual Assault Law in Canada, 1900-1975, 2008; (ed. with W.W. Pue) The Promise and Perils of Law: Lawyers in Canadian History, 2009. Contributor to periodicals. **Address:** University of Ottawa, Fauteux Hall, 57 Louis Pasteur St., Ottawa, ON K1N 6N5, Canada.

BACKSCHEIDER, Paula R(ice). American (born United States), b. 1943. **Genres:** Literary Criticism And History, Bibliography, History, Novels, Cultural/Ethnic Topics, Poetry. **Career:** Rollins College, assistant professor, 1973-75; University of Rochester, assistant professor, 1975-78, associate professor, 1978-87, vice provost for academic concerns, 1981-82, professor of English, 1987-, Roswell Burrows professor of English, 1992-; University of Edinburgh's Institute for Advanced Studies, associate, 1980-; Auburn University, Department of English, graduate faculty. Writer. **Publications:** NONFICTION: (with F. Nussbaum and P. Anderson) An Annotated Bibliography of Twentieth-Century Critical Studies of Women and Literature, 1660-1800, 1977; A Being More Intense: A Study of the Prose Works of Bunyan, Swift and Defoe, 1984; Daniel Defoe: Ambition and Innovation, 1986; Daniel Defoe: His Life, 1989; Spectacular Politics: Theatrical Power and Mass Culture in Early Modern England, 1993; Reflections on Biography, 1999; Eighteenth-Century Women Poets and their Poetry: Inventing Agency, Inventing Genre, 2005; Reading the Eighteenth-Century Novel, forthcoming; Obsessed by the Novel, forthcoming; Elizabeth Singer Rowe and the Development of the Mid-Eighteenth Century English Novel, forthcoming; Revising the History of the Novel: Elizabeth Singer Rowe's Place, forthcoming. EDITOR: Probability, Time and Space in 18th-Century Literature, 1979; (and intro.) The Plays of Charles Gildon, 1979; (and intro.) The Plays of Elizabeth Inchbald, 1980; Eighteenth-Century Drama, 69 vols., 1979-83; (with D. Howard) The Plays of Samuel Foote, 3 vols., 1983; Dictionary of Literary Biography, vol. LXXX: Restoration and Eighteenth-Century Dramatists: First Series 1989, vol. LXXXIV: Restoration and 18th-Century Dramatists: Second Series, 1989, vol. LXXXIX: Restoration and 18th-Century Dramatists: Third Series, 1989; Moll Flanders: The Making of a Criminal Mind, 1990; A Journal of the Plague Year: Authoritative Text, Backgrounds, Contexts, Criticism, 1992; (with T. Dystal) The Intersections of the Public and Private Spheres in Early Modern England, 1996; (with J.J. Richetti) Popular Fiction by Women, 1660-1730: An Anthology, 1996; (with H.D. Cotton) The Excursion, 1997; Selected Fiction and Drama of Eliza Haywood, 1999; Revising Women: Eighteenth-Century Women's Fiction and Social Engagement, 2000; (with C. Ingrassia) A Companion to the Eighteenth-Century English Novel and Culture, 2005; (with C.E. Ingrassia) British Women Poets of the Long Eighteenth Century: An Anthology, 2009. **Address:** Department of English, Auburn University, 9082 Haley Ctr., Auburn, AL 36849, U.S.A. **Online address:** pkrb@auburn.edu

BACKUS, George Edward. American (born United States), b. 1930. **Genres:** Earth Sciences, Physics, Sciences, Mathematics/Statistics. **Career:** University of Chicago, assistant examiner, 1949-50; Institute for Air Weapons Research, junior mathematician, 1951-54; Princeton University, Project Matterhorn, physicist, 1957-58; Massachusetts Institute of Technology, assistant professor of mathematics, 1959-60; University of California, research professor of geophysics, associate professor, 1960-62, professor of geophysics, 1962-, now professor emeritus; International Working Group on Magnetic Field Satellites, co-chairman, 1983-; Institut de France, Acadaemie des Sciences, foreign associate, 1989. Writer. **Publications:** Self-Sustaining Dissipative Kinematic Fluid Dynamo, 1958; Rotational Splitting of the Free Oscillations of the Earth, 1961; Propagation of Short Waves on a Slowly Rotating Earth, 1962; Possible Forms of Seismic Anistropy, 1962, 3rd ed., 1970; Magnetic Anomalies over Oceanic Ridges, 1964; Potentials for Tangent Tensor Fields in Spheroids, 1966; (with F. Gilbert) Inversion of Seismic Normal Mode Data, 1966; Geomagnetic Data and Core Motions, 1967; (with F. Gilbert) Inversion of Earth Normal Mode Data, 1968; Inference from Inaccurate and Inadequate Data, 1972; Mathematical Representation of Seismic Sources, 1976; Computing Extrema of Multidimensional Polynomials, 1980; Relative Importance of Tectonic Plate-Driving Forces, 1981; Construction of Geomagnetic Field Models, 1982; Mantle Conductivity, 1983; Core Motion, 1986; Statistical Inference, 1989. (with C. Constable and R.L. Parker) Foundations of Geomagnetism, 1996. **Address:** Scripps Institution of Oceanography, University of California, 9500 Gilman Dr., PO Box 2005, La Jolla, CA 92093-0225, U.S.A. **Online address:** gbackus@ucsd.edu

BACON, Charlotte. Indonesian/American (born United States), b. 1965?. **Genres:** Novellas/Short Stories, Novels. **Career:** University of New Hampshire, assistant professor, 1998, associate professor of English. Journalist. **Publications:** COLLECTION: A Private State: Stories, 1997. NOVELS: Lost Geography, 2000; There Is Room For You, 2004; Split Estate, 2008; The Twisted Thread, 2011. **Address:** Farrar, Straus & Giroux, 18 W 18th St., New York, NY 10011-4607, U.S.A. **Online address:** cbacon@cisunix.unh.edu

BACON, David. American (born United States), b. 1948. **Genres:** Social Sciences, Military/Defense/Arms Control. **Career:** Pacific News Service, associate editor; New America Media, associate editor. Photojournalist and activist. **Publications:** The Children of NAFTA: Labor Wars on the U.S./Mexico Border, 2004; Communities without Borders: Images and Voices from the World of Migration, 2006; Illegal People: How Globalization Creates Migration and Criminalizes Immigrants, 2008. Contributor of articles to periodicals and journals. **Address:** Beacon Press, 25 Beacon St., Boston, MA 02108, U.S.A. **Online address:** dbacon@igc.org

BACON, Donald C. *See* **BACON, Donald C(onrad).**

BACON, Donald C(onrad). (Donald C. Bacon). American (born United States), b. 1935. **Genres:** History, Politics/Government, Biography. **Career:** Wall Street Journal, staff writer, 1957-61; Washington Star, staff writer, 1962-63; Newhouse News Service, congressional correspondent, White House correspondent, senior correspondent, columnist, 1962-75; U.S. News and World Report, associate editor, 1975-79, senior editor, 1979-81, assistant managing editor, 1981-88; Nation's Business, senior editor, 1988-89; Encyclopedia of the U.S. Congress, project director and co-editor, 1989-. **Publications:** (Contrib.) The New Millionaires, 1961; Congress and You: A Primer for Participation in the Legislative Process, 1969; (with D.B. Hardeman) Rayburn: A Biography, 1987; (ed. with R.H. Davidson and M. Keller) Encyclopedia of the United States Congress, 1995. Contributor to periodicals and books. **Address:** Texas Monthly, PO Box 1569, Austin, TX 78767-1569, U.S.A. **Online address:** donbacon@erols.com

BACON, George Edward. *See* Obituaries.

BACON, Lauren. Canadian (born Canada), b. 1972?. **Genres:** Business/Trade/Industry, Administration/Management, Economics. **Career:** Musica Intima, founding member, marketing chair; Raised Eyebrow Web Studio Inc., co-founder and lead designer, 2000-; Soapboxgirls.com, co-editor, 2000-06. **Publications:** (With E. Mears) The Boss of You: Everything a Woman Needs to Know to Start, Run, and Maintain Her Own Business, 2008. **Address:** Raised Eyebrow Web Studio Inc., 209-163 W Hastings St., Vancouver, BC V6B 1H5, Canada. **Online address:** thebosses@laurenandemira.com

BACON, Margaret. British (born England) **Genres:** Novels, Children's Fiction, Travel/Exploration. **Career:** British Broadcasting Corp., broadcaster; educator, 1952-61; writer, 1961-. **Publications:** Journey to Guyana (travel), 1970; A Packetful of Trouble (children's fiction), 1974. NOVELS: The Episode, 1971; Kitty, 1972; The Unentitled, 1974; The Package, 1975; Snow in Winter, 1978; The Kingdom of the Rose, 1981; The Chain, 1984; The Serpent's Tooth, 1987; Other Women, 1994; Home Truths, 1995; (with F. Brown) Friends and Relations, 1996; The Ewe Lamb, 1999; Mother Nature, 2001; Northrop Hall, 2003; The Years Between, 2004; For Better, for Worse, 2005. **Address:** Bolt & Watson Ltd., 26 Charing Cross Rd., Ste. 8, London, GL WC2H 0DG, England.

BADA, Constantina. Greek (born Greece), b. 1950. **Genres:** Anthropology/Ethnology, Local History/Rural Topics. **Career:** University of Ioannina, assistant professor, 1978-83, curator of university museum, 1978-83, lecturer, 1983-90, senior lecturer, 1990-97, reader, 1997-2004, professor in popular culture and anthropology, 2004-. Writer. **Publications:** (With P.S. Cassia) The Making of the Modern Greek Family: Marriage and Exchange in Nineteenth Century Athens, 1992; Costume Codes of Childhood and Youth and Their Socio-Historical Equivalent (in Greek), 1993; The World of Work: The Fishermen of the Messologi Lagoon, 2004. **Address:** Department of History & Archaeology, University of Ioannina, G. Seferi 2, Ioannina, 30 100, Greece. **Online address:** kbada@cc.uoi.gr

BADAMI, Anita Rau. Canadian/Indian (born India), b. 1961. **Genres:** Novels, Women's Studies And Issues, Literary Criticism And History. **Career:** Novelist. **Publications:** Tamarind Mem, 1996 in US as Tamarind Woman, 2002; The Hero's Walk, 2000; Can you Hear the Nightbird Call?, 2006. Contributor to periodicals. **Address:** The Bukowski Agency, 14 Prince Arthur Ave., Ste. 202, Toronto, ON M5R 1A9, Canada. **Online address:** badami.anita@gmail.com

BADAWI, M. M. *See* **BADAWI, Mohamed Mustafa.**

BADAWI, Mohamed Mustafa. (M. M. Badawi). British/Egyptian (born Egypt), b. 1925. **Genres:** Novels, Novellas/Short Stories, Plays/Screenplays, Poetry, Literary Criticism And History. **Career:** Alexandria University, research fellow, 1947-54, lecturer, 1954-60, assistant professor of English, 1960-64; Oxford University, lecturer, Brasenose College, lecturer, 1964-92, St. Antony's College, fellow, 1967-, emeritus fellow; Journal of Arabic Literature, co-editor, 1970-96. **Publications:** Dirāsāt fī al-shir wa-al-masraḥ, 1960; Mukhtārātmin al-shir al-Arabī al-ḥadīth, 1969; Bud al-khāmis, 1970; Coleridge: Critic of Shakespeare, 1973; (as M.M. Badawi) A Critical Introduction to Modern Arabic Poetry, 1975; Aṭlāl wa-Rasāil min Landan, 1979; (as M.M. Badawi) Background to Shakespeare, 1981; (as M.M. Badawi) Modern Arabic Literature and the West, 1985; (as M.M. Badawi) Modern Arabic Drama in Egypt, 1987; (as M.M. Badawi) Early Arabic Drama, 1988; A Short History of Modern Arabic Literature, 1993. TRANSLATOR: The Saint's Lamp and Other Stories, by Yahya Haqqi, 1973; Sara, by A.M. El Aqqad, 1978; (with T.L. Gassick) N. Mahfouz, Liṣ ṣ wa-al-kilāb (title means: 'Thief and the Dogs, a Novel'), 1984; (as M.M. Badawi) Short History of Modern Arabic Literature, 1993; Gesellschaftlicher Umbruch und Historie imzeitgenössischen Drama der islamischen Welt, 1995. EDITOR: (intro.) An Anthology of Modern Arabic Verse, 1970; (as M.M. Badawi) Modern Arabic Literature, The Cambridge History of Arabic Literature, 1992; Short History of Modern Arabic Literature, 1993. Contributor to periodicals. **Address:** St Antony's College, Oxford University, 62 Woodstock Rd., Oxford, OX OX2 6JF, England.

BADCOCK, Christopher Robert. British (born England), b. 1946. **Genres:** Psychology, Sociology, Psychiatry. **Career:** Polytechnic of the South Bank, lecturer in sociology, 1969-73; University of London, London School of Economics and Political Science, lecturer in sociology, 1974-79, reader in sociology, 1979-2011. Writer. **Publications:** Levi-Strauss: Structuralism and Sociological Theory, 1975; The Psychoanalysis of Culture, 1980; Madness and Modernity: A Study in Social Psychoanalysis, 1983; The Problem of Altruism: Freudian-Darwinian Solutions, 1986; Essential Freud: A Modern Introduction to Classical Psychoanalysis, 1988; Oedipus in Evolution: A New Theory of Sex, 1989; Evolution and Individual Behavior: An Introduction to Recent Human Sociobiology, 1991; Psycho Darwinism: The New Synthesis of Darwin and Freud, 1994; Evolutionary Psychology: A Critical Introduction, 2000; The Imprinted Brain: How Genes Set the Balance Between Autism and Psychosis, 2009. **Address:** 36 Gilpin Ave., London, GL SW14 8QY, England. **Online address:** christopherbadcock@gmail.com

BADCOCK, Gary D. Canadian (born Canada), b. 1961. **Genres:** Theology/Religion, Education. **Career:** University of Aberdeen, teaching fellow, 1991-92; University of Edinburgh, lecturer, 1993-99, associate dean of divinity faculty, 1997-99; Huron University College, Peache chair of divinity, 1999-, associate professor of theology. Writer. **Publications:** Light of Truth and Fire of Love: A Theology of the Holy Spirit, 1997; The Way of Life: A Theology of Christian Vocation, 1998; House where God Lives, 2009. EDITOR: (with D.F. Wright) Disruption to Diversity: Edinburgh Divinity, 1846-1996, 1996; Theology after the Storm, 1997. **Address:** Huron University College, University of Western Ontario, 1349 Western Rd., London, ON N6G 1H3, Canada. **Online address:** gbadcock@julian.uwo.ca

BADDOCK, James. British (born England), b. 1950. **Genres:** Novels, Mystery/Crime/Suspense, Young Adult Fiction, Literary Criticism And History. **Career:** Training College, teacher, 1971-74; Bedfordshire Education Authority, teacher, 1974-; Queensbury School, teacher. Writer. **Publications:** The Faust Conspiracy, 1985; The Radar Job, 1986 as The Dutch Caper, 1990; (with R. Gordon) Gold Run, 1986; Emerald, 1987; The Alaska Project, 1989; Piccolo, 1992. Contributor to periodicals. **Address:** Queensbury School, Langdale Rd., Dunstable, BD LU6 3BU, England. **Online address:** jbaddock@hotmail.com

BADENI, June. (June Wilson). British (born England), b. 1925?. **Genres:** Novels, History, Biography, Sciences. **Career:** Writer. **Publications:** AS JUNE WILSON: The Bitter Journey, 1947; One Foolish Heart, 1948; Second Hearing, 1949; Green Shadows: A Life of John Clare, 1951. OTHERS: Wiltshire Forefathers, 1950; Green Shadows: the Life of John Clare, 1951; (with M.L. Beak) A Picture Book of Malmesbury, 1962; The Slender Tree: A Life of Alice Meynell, 1981; Past People in Wiltshire and Gloucestershire, 1992; The Primrose Wood, 2006. **Address:** Garden Cottage, Norton, Malmesbury, WT SN16 9EN, England.

BADERIN, Mashood A. British (born England) **Genres:** Theology/Religion, Law. **Career:** Brunel University, professor; Brunel Law School, professor; University of the West of England School of Law, reader; University of Nottingham, School of Law, instructor; University of Southampton, instructor; University of London, School of Oriental and African Studies, professor of law; Supreme Court of Nigeria, barrister & solicitor. Writer, educator and attorney. **Publications:** International Human Rights and Islamic Law, 2003; (ed. with M. Monshipouri, S. Mokhtari and L. Welchman) Islam and Human Rights: Advocacy for Social Change in Local Contexts, 2006; (ed. with R. McCorquodale) Economic, Social and Cultural Rights in Action, 2007; International Law and Islamic Law, 2008. Contributor of articles to journals. **Address:** School of Oriental & African Studies, University of London, Thornhaugh St., Russell Sq., London, GL WC1H 0XG, England. **Online address:** mashood.baderin@uwe.ac.uk

BADGER, Anthony J. (Tony Badger). British (born England), b. 1947. **Genres:** History, Politics/Government, Essays. **Career:** Newcastle University, instructor; Cambridge University, Paul Mellon Professor of American History, 1992-, Clare College, master. Writer, academic and historian. **Publications:** Prosperity Road: The New Deal, Tobacco, and North Carolina, 1980; North Carolina and the New Deal, 1981; (contrib.) The U.S. Constitution after 200 Years, 1988; The New Deal: The Depression Years, 1933-1940, 1989; (ed. with W. Edgar and J.N. Gretlund) Southern Landscapes, 1996; (ed. with B. Ward) The Making of Martin Luther King and the Civil Rights Movement, 1996; (ed. with B.E. Shafer) Contesting Democracy: Substance and Structure in American Political History, 1775-2000, 2001; (contrib.) The Role of Ideas in the Civil Rights South: Essays, 2002; New Deal/New South: An Anthony J. Badger Reader, 2007; FDR: The First Hundred Days, 2008. Contributor to periodicals and journals. **Address:** Clare College, Cambridge University, Cambridge, CB CB2 1TL, England. **Online address:** ajb1001@cam.ac.uk

BADGER, Tony. *See* **BADGER, Anthony J.**

BADGLEY, John Herbert. American (born United States), b. 1930. **Genres:** Novels, Politics/Government, Business/Trade/Industry, Economics, History. **Career:** Rangoon University, Rangoon-Hopkins Center, acting director, 1958; Miami University, assistant professor, 1962-66; Kyoto University, visiting professor, 1964-65; Johns Hopkins University, School of Advanced International Studies, associate professor of political science, 1967-70, director of Asian studies, 1970-73; Institute of the Rockies, president, 1973-94; Cornell University, Southeast Asia Collection, curator, 1986; Nargis Library Recovery, executive director; U.S. Agency for International Development, consultant. Writer. **Publications:** (With R. Osgood and G.R. Packard, III) Japan and the United States in Asia, 1968; Politics among Burmans, 1970; Asian Development: Problems and Prognosis, 1971; Intellectuals and the National Vision: The Burmese Case: In Literature and Society in Southeast Asia, 1981; The Foreign Policy of Burma in the Political Economy of Foreign Policy in Southeast Asia, 1990; Remodelling Myanmar in Myanmar Dilemmas and Options, 1990; A Clear Gathering of Miraculous Success in Peace and Security, vol. VII, No. 1, 1992; Cornell in the Killing Fields, A Play in Three Acts, 1994; Red Peacocks, 1995; The Strategist, 1996; (ed.) From The Class Of '48 with Love, 2003; (ed. with A. Kyaw) Red Peacocks: Commentaries on Burmese Socialist Nationalism. 2009. CONTRIBUTOR: Japan's Future in Southeast Asia, 1965; Policies Toward China, 1966; Garrisons and Governments, 1967; The Communist Revolution in Asia, 1968; Comparative Regional International Politics, 1971; Films and Popular Culture in Asia, 1972; (ed.) Peasant Rebellion and Communist Revolution in Asia, 1974. Contributor to periodicals. **Address:** Nargis Library Recovery, 9911 220th St. SW, PO Box 603, Edmonds, WA 98020-4563, U.S.A. **Online address:** john@myanmarbookaid.org

BADILLO, David A. American (born United States), b. 1956?. **Genres:** Theology/Religion, History. **Career:** University of Illinois, assistant professor; Brooklyn College, visiting associate professor; University of Notre Dame, visiting associate professor; City University of New York, Lehman College, associate professor of Latin American and Puerto Rican studies. Writer and historian. **Publications:** Latinos in Michigan, 2003; Latinos and the New Immigrant Church, 2006. **Address:** Department of Latin American & Puerto Rican, Studies, City University of New York, 280 Carman Hall, 250 Bedford Park Blvd., Bronx, NY 10468, U.S.A. **Online address:** david.badillo@lehman.cuny.edu

BADT, Karin L(uisa). American/Italian (born Italy), b. 1963. **Genres:** Novellas/Short Stories, Children's Fiction, Film, Writing/Journalism, Plays/Screenplays. **Career:** University of Chicago, Continuing Education Program, basic program instructor, 1989-90, open program instructor, 1993-94, lecturer, 1994-95; John Cabot University, lecturer, 1991-93; University of Rome, lecturer, 1992; American University of Paris, assistant professor, 1995-97; Sciences-Po, lecturer, 1996-2000; University of Paris VIII, associate professor of theater and cinema, 1999-, professor; New York University, visiting professor. Writer. **Publications:** The Mississippi Flood of 1993, 1994; Charles Eastman: Sioux Physician and Author, 1994; The Underground Railroad (play), 1995; (with M. Bartok) The Southeast Indians, 1995; (ed.) Indians of the Southwest, 1996; Indians of the Northeast, 1997. A WORLD OF DIFFERENCE SERIES: Good Morning, Let's Eat, 1994; Greetings!, 1994; Hair There and Everywhere, 1994; On Your Feet!, 1994; Pass the Bread!, 1995; Let's Go!, 1995. FORTHCOMING: The Drowning; The House; Out of the Dancing Village; Locked In Syndrome. Contributor to magazines. **Address:** Université Paris 8, 2 rue de la Liberté, St. Denis, 93526, France. **Online address:** karinbadt@yahoo.com

BAECHLE, Thomas R. American (born United States), b. 1943?. **Genres:** Medicine/Health. **Career:** University of Nebraska, teacher, 1968-; Briar Cliff College, staff, 1969-78, chair, 1971; Iowa AHPERD, Physical Education Public Information, Northwest District, representative, 1970-73, Iowa AHPERD, Local Physical Education Public Information, coordinator, 1972-73, Physical Education Public Information, state director, 1974, 1975; Creighton University, staff, 1978-, faculty senate, Department of Exercise Science and Athletic Training, chair, 1981-, professor; National Strength and Conditioning Association (NSCA), region director, 1979-83, executive director, 1982-83, president, 1983-85; Central Association for Physical Education in Higher Education, board director, 1980-90; Nebraska AHPERD, Physical Education and Sport, president, 1981, 1992; NSCA Certification Commission, executive director, 1985-2007; Journal of Strength and Conditioning Research, associate editor, 1987-97; Countryside Community Church, Board of Christian Education, chair, 1988-89; Recreation and Dance, Sports and Physical Education, student section advisor, 1988-91, vice-president, 1992-93; American Heart Association Nebraska Affiliate, president, 1992-93; National Organization for Competency Assurance, president, 1998; Wellness Council of America, medical advisory editor, 2002-; Sports Health Integrated Network, technical advisor, 2005-; National Strength and Conditioning Association, consultant to executive director; University of Pretoria, Department of Biokinetics, Sport and Leisure Sciences, honorary professor; National Commission for Certification Accreditation, commissioner; Physical Education, Recreation and Dance, Nebraska Alliance for Health, president. Writer. **Publications:** (With B.R. Groves) Weight Training: Steps to Success, 1992, 4th ed., 2012, as Weight Training Instruction: Steps to Success, 1994; (ed.) Essentials of Strength Training and Conditioning, 1994, 3rd ed., 2008; (with R.W. Earle) Fitness Weight Training, 1995, 2nd ed., 2005; (with W.L. Westcott) Strength Training Past 50, 1998, 2nd ed., 2007; (with W.L. Westcott) Strength Training for Seniors: An Instructor Guide for Developing Safe and Effective Programs, 1999; (ed. with R.W. Earle) NSCA's Essentials of Personal Training, 2004; (with W.L. Westcott) Fitness Professional's Guide to Strength Training Older Adults, 2010. **Address:** Department of Exercise Science, Creighton University, 2500 California Plz., Omaha, NE 68178, U.S.A. **Online address:** tbaech@creighton.edu

BAECQUE, Antoine de. French (born France), b. 1962. **Genres:** History, Novels. **Career:** Cahiers du cinéma, editor-in-chief, 1996-99; Musée ducinéma Henri Langlois, director, 2000-01; University of Versailles Saint-Quentin-en-Yvelines, professor; New York University, Institute of French Studies, visiting faculty. Writer. **Publications:** La caricature révolutionnaire, 1988; Ils ont pensé les droits delhomme: Textes et débats 1789-1793, 1989; Andrei Tarkovski, 1989; Dictionnaire des ministres de 1789 1989, 1990; Une Histoire de ladémocratie en Europe, 1991; Les cahiers du cinéma: histoire dunerevue, 1991; Recherches sur la révolution: un bilan des travauxscientifiques du bicentaire, 1991; Lespirit de lEurope, 1993; Le corps delhistoire: métaphores et politique (1770-1800), 1993; Le cinémades écrivains, 1995; Le retour du cinéma, 1996; François Truffaut, 1996; La gloire et leffroi: sept morts sous la terreur, 1997; LABCdaire de Prudhon et le néoclassicisme, 1997; Body Politic: Corporeal Metaphor in Revolutionary France, 1770-1800, 1997; De l'histoireau cinéma, 1998; La nouvelle vague: Portrait dune jeunesse, 1998; Lesécrivains face lhistoire (France 1920-1996): actes du colloqueorganisé la Bibliothéque publique dinformation le 22 mars 1997 enrelation avec le parcours littéraire de lexposition Face lhistoire, 1998; De lhistoire au cinéma, 1998; Truffaut, 1999; Les années 68: le temps de la contestation, 2000; Calembours et autres jeux sur les motsdesprit, 2000; Les éclats du rire: la culture des rieurs au XVIIIesicle, 2000; Glory and Terror: Seven Deaths Under the French Revolution, 2001; La cérémonie du pouvoir: Les duels sur la scne politiquefrançaise de la Révolution nos jours, 2002; La cinéphilie: invention dun regard histoire dune culture 1944-1968, 2003; Le Dictionnaire Truffaut, 2004; Lange exterminateur, 2006; Histoire dufestival dAvignon, 2007; (contrib.) Mes repas, ou, La vérité en riant et autres facéties, 2007; Les leçons de cinéma, 2007; Crises dans la culture française, 2008; Doisneau: portraits dartistes, 2008; Le dictionnaire Pialat, 2008; Histoire- caméra, 2008; (with J. Trey) Serment du jeu de paume: quand David réécrit lhistoire, 2008; Le bestiaire imaginaire, 2010; Godard: Biographie, 2010; Tim Burton, 2011; Vie de Jean Rossignol, 2011; Dictionnaire Eustache, 2011; Camera Historica, 2012. Contributor to periodicals. **Address:** Institute of French Studies, New York University, 15 Washington Mews, New York, NY 10003-6694, U.S.A.

BAEHR, Kingsley M. American (born United States), b. 1937. **Genres:** Novellas/Short Stories, Poetry, Ethics. **Career:** Adamsville School, English teacher, 1959-71; Cedarcroft Bible Chapel, teacher, preacher, youth worker and elder, 1971-; Timothy Christian School, Bible teacher, 1973-2004, middle school principal, 1987-2002. **Publications:** Bible Quest Devotional: Hope in a Scarlet Rope, 1994. **Address:** Cedarcroft Bible Chapel, 1512 Kenyon Ave., South Plainfield, NJ 07080, U.S.A. **Online address:** kbaehr@verizon.net

BAER, Greg. American (born United States), b. 1952?. **Genres:** Self Help, Administration/Management, Human Relations/Parenting, Romance/Historical, Business/Trade/Industry. **Career:** Full-time writer, educator, ophthalmologist, consultant and public speaker. **Publications:** The Wart King: The Truth about Love and Lies, 1997; The Truth about Relationships: A Simple and Powerfully Effective Way for Everyone to Find Real Love and Loving Relationships, 1998; The Wise Man: The Truth about Sharing Real Love, 2003. REAL LOVE SERIES: Real Love: The Truth About Finding Unconditional Love and Fulfilling Relationships, 2003; Real Love in Dating, 3rd ed., 2005; Real Love in Parenting, 2nd ed., 2005; Real Love in Marriage: The Truth

About Finding Genuine Happiness Now and Forever, 2006; Real Love for Wise Men and Women, 2006; The Essentials of Real Love Bible Workbook, 2006; The Essentials of Real Love Workbook, 2007; Real Love and Freedom for the Soul: Eliminating the Chains of Victimhood, 2007; Real Love in the Workplace: Eight Principles for Consistently Effective Leadership in Business, 2007. **Address:** c/o Author Mail, Gotham Books, 375 Hudson St., New York, NY 10014-3657, U.S.A. **Online address:** coaching@reallove.com

BAER, Richard K. American (born United States) **Genres:** Women's Studies And Issues. **Career:** Practicing psychiatrist, 1978-; Admina Star Medicare Services, medical director; University of Illinois Medical Center, Department of Psychiatry, faculty member. Psychiatrist and writer. **Publications:** Switching Time: A Doctor's Harrowing Story of Treating a Woman with 17 Personalities, 2007. **Address:** National Government Services, 225 N Michigan Ave., 22nd Fl., Chicago, IL 60601-7601, U.S.A.

BAERT, Barbara. Belgian (born Belgium), b. 1967. **Genres:** Business/Trade/Industry, History. **Career:** Catholic University of Leuven, professor of art history. Writer. **Publications:** Het Boec Van Den Houte, 1995; (with V. Fraeters) Aan de Vruchten Kent Men de Boom: De Boom in Tekst en Beeld in de Middeleeuwse Nederlanden, 2001; Een Erfenis Van Heilig Hout: De Neerslag Van Het Teruggevonden Kruis in Tekst en Beeld Tijdens de Middeleeuwen, 2001; (with B. Fraeters) Het Wellende Water: De Bron in Tekst en Beeld in de Middeleeuwse Nederlanden en Het Rijnland, 2005; (co-author) Noli Me Tangere: Maria Magdalena in Veelvoud: Tentoonstelling Maurits Sabbebibliotheek, 23 Februari 2006-30 April 2006, Faculteit Godgeleerdheid, K.U. Leuven, 2006, trans. as Noli Me Tangere: Mary Magdalene, One Person, Many Images: Exhibition, Maurits Sabbe Library, 23 February-30 April 2006, Faculty of Theology, K.U. Leuven, 2006; (ed. with K.M. Rudy) Weaving, Veiling, and Dressing: Textiles and Their Metaphors in the Late Middle Ages, 2007. **Address:** Onderzoekseenheid Kunstwetenschap, Katholieke Universiteit Leuven, Blijde-Inkomststraat 21-bus 03313, Leuven, BE-3000, Belgium. **Online address:** barbara.baert@arts.kuleuven.be

BAEZ, Annecy. Spanish/American (born United States) **Genres:** Novellas/Short Stories. **Career:** New York University School of Social Work, assistant professor; Lehman College Counseling Center, director; Julia Dyckman Andrus Memorial, Diagnostic Center, director; Latina writers group of Daisy Cocco De Filippis, member. Writer and social worker. **Publications:** My Daughter's Eyes and Other Stories, 2007. Contributor to periodicals. Works appear in anthologies. **Address:** Lehman College, 250 Bedford Park Blvd. W, Bronx, NY 10468, U.S.A. **Online address:** annecy.baez@lehman.cuny.edu

BAEZ, Fernando. Venezuelan/Spanish (born Spain), b. 1970. **Genres:** History, Anthropology/Ethnology, Poetry, Adult Non-fiction, Novellas/Short Stories. **Career:** United Nations Educational, Scientific, and Cultural Organization (UNESCO), advisor, 2003-11; National Library of Venezuela, director general, 2008. Writer and historian. **Publications:** El saqueo cultural de América Latina, 2010; Nueva historia universal de la destrucción de libros, 2011. **Address:** Venezuela. **Online address:** baez.fernando@gmail.com

BAGDIKIAN, Ben H(aig). American/Turkish (born Turkey), b. 1920. **Genres:** Communications/Media, Criminology/True Crime, Politics/Government, Race Relations, Sociology, Writing/Journalism, Autobiography/Memoirs, Documentaries/Reportage, Documentaries/Reportage. **Career:** Springfield Morning Union, general reporter, 1941-42; Periodical House Inc. (magazine publishers), associate editor, 1946; Providence Journal, chief Washington correspondent, 1947-61; Saturday Evening Post, contributing editor, writer, 1962-67; Rand News Media Study Project, director, 1967-69; Washington Post, assistant managing editor of national news, 1970-72; American University, research fellow, 1975-76; University of California, Graduate School of Journalism, professor, 1977-90, dean, 1985-88, professor emeritus, 1990-, dean emeritus. **Publications:** (Ed.) Man's Contracting World in an Expanding Universe, 1960; The Kennedy Circle, 1961; In the Midst of Plenty: The Poor in America, 1964; Behavioral Sciences and the Mass Media, 1968; (co-author) Media and the Cities, 1968; Newsman's Scope, 1968; U.S.A.: Almagt og Afmagt, 1969; The Information Machines: Their Impact on Men and the Media, 1971; (with L. Dash) The Shame of the Prisons, 1972; The Effete Conspiracy and Other Crimes by the Press, 1972; (contrib.) Evaluating the Press: The New England Daily Newspaper Survey, 1973; Caged: Eight Prisoners and Their Keepers, 1976; Bagdikian on Political Reporting, Newspaper Economics, Law and Ethics, 1977; The Media Monopoly, 1983, 6th ed., 2000; Double Vision: Reflections on My Heritage, Life and Profession, 1995; The New Media Monopoly, 2004. **Address:** Graduate School of Journalism, University of California, Northgate Hall, Berkeley, CA 94705, U.S.A. **Online address:** benmar@berkeley.edu

BAGEANT, Joe. American (born United States), b. 1946?. **Genres:** Social Commentary, Autobiography/Memoirs, Politics/Government. **Career:** Primedia History Magazine Group, senior editor. **Publications:** Deer Hunting with Jesus: Dispatches from America's Class War, 2007; Rainbow Pie: A Memoir of Redneck America, 2010. **Address:** Portobello Books Ltd., 12 Addison Ave., London, GL W11 4QR, England. **Online address:** joebageant@joebageant.com

BAGERT, Brod. American (born United States), b. 1947. **Genres:** Children's Fiction, Poetry, Young Adult Fiction, Humor/Satire. **Career:** Lawyer, attorney and writer. **Publications:** FOR CHILDREN: Let Me Be the Boss: Poems for Kids to Perform, 1992; Chicken Socks And Other Contagious Poems, 1994; Elephant Games and Other Playful Poems, 1995; (ed.) Edgar Allan Poe, 1995; The Gooch Machine, 1997; Giant Children, 2002; Shout!: Little Poems that Roar, 2007. FOR ADULTS: A Bullfrog at Café du Monde (poetry), 1986, 2nd ed., 2008; Steel Cables (poetry), 1992; Throw Me Somethin Mistuh, 1995; Rainbows, Head Lice, and Pea Green Tile (poetry), 1999; (ed. with F.S. Bolin and G.D. Schmidt) The Blackbirch Treasury of American Poetry, 2001; Hormone Jungle: Coming of Age in Middle School, 2006; School Fever, 2008; Steel Cables: The Poetry of Permanent Love, 2008. **Address:** Brod Bagert Poetry, 2413 Metairie Ct., 204 W 15th Ave., Metairie, LA 70003, U.S.A. **Online address:** brodbagert@aol.com

BAGGE, Peter (Christian Paul). American (born United States), b. 1957. **Genres:** Graphic Novels, Cartoons. **Career:** Weirdo Magazine, editor, 1983-86; Reason Magazine, contributing editor and cartoonist. Graphic artist. **Publications:** COLLECTIONS: SELF-ILLUSTRATED: The Bradleys, 1989; Studs Kirby: The Voice of America, 1989; Junior and Other Losers, 1990; Stupid Comics, 1991; Road Strips, 2005; Peter Bagge's Other Lives, 2010. HATE COLLECTIONS: SELF-ILLUSTRATED: Hate, 1990; Hey, Buddy!, 1993; Buddy the Dreamer, 1994; Fun with Buddy and Lisa, 1995; Buddy Go Home, 1997; Buddy's Got Three Moms, 1999; Buddy Bites the Bullet!, 2001; Buddy's at the End of the Line, 2003; Buddy Does Seattle, 2005; Buddy Does Jersey, 2007. OTHERS: (contrib.) Roadstrips: A Graphic Journey across America, 2005; Everybody Is Stupid Except for Me: And Other Astute Observations, 2009. Contributor to periodicals. **Address:** c/o Author Mail, Fantagraphics Books, 7563 Lake City Way NE, Seattle, WA 98115, U.S.A. **Online address:** peterbagge@earthlink.net

BAGGETT, Jennifer. American (born United States), b. 1978?. **Genres:** Biography, Autobiography/Memoirs. **Career:** Nickelodeon, manager of integrated marketing and partnerships. Sundance Channel, staff; VH1, staff; NBC Universal, staff. Writer. **Publications:** (With H.C. Corbett and A. Pressner) The Lost Girls: Three Friends, Four Continents, One Unconventional Detour around the World, 2010. Contributor to periodicals. **Address:** New York, NY , U.S.A. **Online address:** jenbaggett5@yahoo.com

BAGGINI, Julian. American (born United States), b. 1968. **Genres:** Ethics, Travel/Exploration, Philosophy. **Career:** Writer. **Publications:** Philosophy: Key Themes, 2002; (ed. with J. Stangroom) New British Philosophy, 2002; Making Sense: Philosophy behind the Headlines, 2002; Atheism: A Very Short Introduction, 2003; (with P.S. Fosl) The Philosopher's Toolkit: A Compendium of Philosophical Concepts and Methods, 2003; (ed. with J. Stangroom) What Philosophers Think, 2003; (ed. with J. Stangroom) Great Thinkers A- Z, 2004; The Pig That Wants to Be Eaten: And Ninety-nine Other Thought Experiments, 2005 in US as The Pig That Wants to Be Eaten: 100 Experiments for the Armchair Philosopher, 2006; What's It All About? Philosophy and the Meaning of Life, 2005; (with J. Stangroom) Do You Think What You Think You Think? The Ultimate Philosophical Quiz Book, 2006 in US as Do You Think What You Think You Think? The Ultimate Philosophical Handbook, 2007; (with P.S. Fosl) The Ethics Toolkit: A Compendium of Ethical Concepts and Methods, 2007; Welcome to Everytown: A Journey into the English Mind, 2007; (ed. with J. Stangroom) What More Philosophers Think, 2007; The Duck That Won the Lottery: 100 New Experiments for the Armchair Philosopher, 2008; Complaint: From Minor Moans to Principled Protests, 2008; Atheism, 2009. Contributor to periodicals. **Online address:** julian@julianbaggini.com

BAGGOTT, Julianna. Also writes as Bridget Asher, N. E. Bode. American (born United States), b. 1969. **Genres:** Novels, Poetry. **Career:** Florida State University, creative writing program instructor, assistant director, associate professor; Goucher College, Kratz Center for Creative Writing, writer-in-residence, 2004; University of North Carolina, associate professor; Kids in Need-Books in Deed, founder; Delaware Division of Arts, fellow; Virginia Center for the Creative Arts, fellow; Bread Loaf Writers' Conference, fellow. Writer. **Publications:** This Country of Mothers (poetry), 2001; Girl Talk, 2001; The Miss America Family, 2002; The Madam: A Novel, 2003; (with S. Almond) Which Brings Me To You: A Novel in Confessions, 2006; Lizzie Borden in Love: Poems in Women's Voices (poetry), 2006; Compulsions of Silkworms and Bees, 2007; Prince of Fenway Park, 2009; Ever Breath, 2009; Pure, 2012; The Ever Cure, forthcoming. AS BRIDGET ASHER: My Husband's Sweethearts, 2008; The Pretend Wife, 2009; The Provence Cure for the Broken-Hearted, forthcoming. AS N.E. BODE: The Nobodies, 2005; The Somebodies, 2006; The Slippery Map, 2007; Prequel Novel to the Movie Mr. Magorium's Wonder Emporium, 2007; The Prince of Fenway Park, 2008. Contributor to journals. **Address:** c/o Author Mail, Simon & Schuster, 1230 Ave. of the Americas, New York, NY 10020, U.S.A. **Online address:** jcbaggott@gmail.com

BAGLEY, Mary (C.). American (born United States), b. 1958. **Genres:** Literary Criticism And History, Adult Non-fiction, Business/Trade/Industry, Poetry, Education, Architecture. **Career:** St. Louis University, faculty; Maryville University, faculty; Southern Illinois University, faculty; University of Missouri, faculty; Missouri Baptist University, Department of English, instructor, professor of English, 1983-, Testing Center, director; KWMU Radio, features reporter; America Alive!, writer and broadcaster, 1983-85; Suburban Newspapers, stringer; St. Louis Post-Dispatch, freelancer; St. Louis Magazine, freelancer; St. Louis Bride Magazine, copy editor; Current Newspaper, features editor. **Publications:** The Front Row: Missouri's Grand Theatres, 1984; The Art of Writing Well, 1987; Handbook for Professional and Academic Writing, 1988; Professional Writing Types, 1989; Poetics of Realism, 1994; Willa Cather's Myths, 1996; (co-author) Parent Power: Energizing Home-school Communication, 1999; Business Communications and Art of Business Writing, forthcoming. Contributor of articles to journals and periodicals. **Address:** Department of English, Missouri Baptist University, 1 College Park Dr., St. Louis, MO 63141-8698, U.S.A. **Online address:** bagley@mobap.edu

BAGLEY, Tennent H. British/Belgian/American (born United States), b. 1925?. **Genres:** Food And Wine, Biography, Autobiography/Memoirs, History, Social Sciences. **Career:** CIA, Clandestine Services, agent, chief of Soviet bloc counter intelligence. Writer and researcher. **Publications:** (With P. Deriabin) KGB: Masters of the Soviet Union, 1990; Spy Wars: Moles, Mysteries and Deadly Games, 2007. **Address:** 47 Bedford Sq., London, GL WC1B 3DP, England.

BAHAL, Aniruddha. Indian (born India), b. 1967?. **Genres:** Novellas/Short Stories, Adult Non-fiction, Race Relations. **Career:** Tehelka.com Private Ltd., co-founder, editor-in-chief and chief executive officer; Cobrapost.com, founder and editor-in-chief. Journalist. **Publications:** A Crack in the Mirror, 1991; Bunker 13, 2003; The Emissary, 2010. Contributor to periodicals. **Address:** c/o Author Mail, Farrar Straus & Giroux Inc., 19 Union Sq. W, New York, NY 10003-3304, U.S.A. **Online address:** bunker13@cobrapost.com

BAHGAT, Gawdat G. American/Egyptian (born Egypt) **Genres:** Adult Non-fiction, International Relations/Current Affairs. **Career:** Radio Cairo, journalist, 1977-85; American University in Cairo, Department of Middle Eastern Studies, research assistant, 1984-85; Florida State University, Department Of Political Science, research assistant, 1987-88, teaching assistant, 1988-91, instructor, 1991-92; University of North Florida, visiting assistant professor of political science, 1992-95; Indiana University of Pennsylvania, Department of Political Science, assistant professor, 1995-99, associate professor, 1999-2002, professor, 2002-, Center for Middle Eastern Studies, director; IUP Center for Middle Eastern Studies, director, 1997-; George Mason University, Institute for Conflict Analysis and Resolution, fellow, 2005. Writer. **Publications:** NONFICTION: The Persian Gulf at the Dawn of the New Millennium, 1999; (contrib.) Oil and Water: Cooperative Security in the Persian Gulf, 2001; (contrib.) Oman in the 21st Century, 2001; American Oil Diplomacy in the Persian Gulf and the Caspian Sea, 2003; Israel and the Persian Gulf: Retrospect and Prospect, 2006; Proliferation of Nuclear Weapons in the Middle East, 2007; (ed. with X. Yi-chong) The Political Economy of Sovereign Wealth Funds, 2010; Energy Security: An Interdisciplinary Approach, 2011. Contributor to journals and periodicals. **Address:** Department of Political Science, Indiana University of Pennsylvania, 100 Keith Hall, Indiana, PA 15705-1069, U.S.A. **Online address:** gbahgat@grove.iup.edu

BAHLMANN, Shirley. American (born United States), b. 1958. **Genres:** Novellas/Short Stories, Adult Non-fiction, Social Commentary. **Career:** Reflections, school-to-community council chairperson; Sister and Me (musical duo with R. McGarry), singer and saxophonist; Write magazine, editor. **Publications:** Against All Odds: Amazing Pioneer Stories of Courage and Survival, 2002; Walkers Gold, 2002; Isn't That Odd?: Strange and Unusual Pioneer Stories, 2002; Even Love Is Odd: True Old-fashioned Stories of Love and Romance, 2003; Led by the Hand of Christ, 2004; Unseen Odds: Spiritual Happenings Ghostly Tales and Spooky Pranks from a Century or So Ago, 2004; Fools Gold, 2005; Dark of Day, 2005; How Odd Andapu Oyati: Friendships and Feuds between Pioneers and Native Americans, 2005; Haunted Dwellings of the West, 2005; Through The Window of Life, 2006; Friends From Beyond The Veil, 2007; Life is Like Riding A Unicycle: Fun Ways to Keep Your Balance When Life Gets A Little Bumpy, 2007; Oddly Enough: Touching and Humorous Stories From The Olden Days, 2007; The Pioneers: A Course in Miracles, 2008. **Address:** Spring Creek Book Co., PO Box 50355, Provo, UT 84605-0355, U.S.A. **Online address:** yoshirley@gmail.com

BAHN, Paul (Gerard). British (born England), b. 1953. **Genres:** Archaeology/Antiquities, Translations, Art/Art History. **Career:** University of Liverpool, postdoctoral research fellow in archaeology, 1979-82; University of London, V. Canada Blanch research fellow in archaeology, 1982-83; freelance writer, translator and broadcaster, 1986-; Easter Island Foundation, vice president. **Publications:** Pyrenean Prehistory, 1984; (with J. Hawkes) The Shell Guide to British Archaeology, 1986; (with G. Daniel) Ancient Places, 1987; (with J. Vertut) Images of the Ice Age, 1988; The Bluffer's Guide to Archaeology, 1989, rev. ed., 1999; (with C. Renfrew) Archaeology, 1991, 4th ed., 2004; (with C. Renfrew) Archaeology: Theories, Methods, and Practice, 1991, 5th ed., 2008; (with J. Flenley) Easter Island, Earth Island, 1992, rev. ed. as The Enigmas of Easter Island: Island on the Edge, 2003; (with A. Lister) Mammoths, 1994, rev. ed. as Mammoths: Giants of the Ice Age, 2007; Archaeology: A Very Short Introduction, 1996; The Cambridge Illustrated History of Prehistoric Art, 1997; (with J. Vertut) Journey through the Ice Age, 1997; The Easter Island Enigma, 1997; Geoglyphs, 1997; (with B. Tidy) Disgraceful Archaeology, 1999; (with J. Flenley) The Enigmas of Easter Island, 2003; (with P. Pettitt and D. Palmer) Unearthing the Past: The Great Archaeological Discoveries that Have Changed History, 2005; Chamanismes et arts préhistoriques: Vision Critique, 2006; Prehistoric Rock Art: Polemics and Progress, 2010. TRANSLATOR: P. Courbin, What Is Archaeology?, 1988; M. Rodna, The Bluffer's Guide to Modern Art, 1990; S. Gruzinski, The Aztecs, 1992; M. Krafft, Volcanoes, 1993; C. Bernand, The Incas, 1994; H. Thomas, The First Humans, 1995; M. Orliac, The Silent Gods, Mysteries of Easter Island, 1995; J.M. Chauvet and Others, Dawn of Art, 1996; Jean-Marie Chauvet, Eliette Brunel Deschamps and Christian Hillaire, Chauvet Cave: The Discovery of the World's Oldest Paintings, 1996; V. Berinstain, Mughal India, 1998; D. Vialou, Our Prehistoric Past, 1998; C. Debaine-Francfort, The Search for Ancient China, 1999, D. Lavallee, The First South Americans, 2000; P. Tort, Charles Darwin, 2001; J. Clottes, Chauvet Cave, 2003. EDITOR AND CONTRIBUTOR: The Collins Dictionary of Archaeology, 1992; Rock Art Studies: The Post-Stylistic Era, or, Where Do We Go From Here?: Papers Presented in Symposium A of the 2nd AURA Congress, Cairns 1992, 1993; 100 Great Archaeological Discoveries, 1995; The Cambridge Illustrated History of Archaeology, 1996; Tombs, Graves and Mummies, 1996; Rock Art Studies: News of the World I, 1996; Lost Cities, 1997; Wonderful Things, 1999; Dating and the Earliest Known Rock Art, 1999; Atlas of World Archaeology, 2000; Penguin Archaeology Guide, 2001; The Archaeology Detectives, 2001; The Archaeology Companion, 2001; The Definitive Guide: Archaeology, 2001; Written in Bones, 2003; (with A. Fossati) Rock Art Studies: News of the World. 2, Developments in Rock Art Research, 1995-1999, 2003; (with P. Pettitt and S. Ripoll) Palaeolithic Cave Art at Creswell Crags in European Context, 2007; Ancient Obscenities, or, Things You Shouldn't Know About the History of Mankind!, 2007; (with C. Renfrew) Archaeology Essentials: Theories, Methods and Practice, 2007; (ed. with N. Franklin and M. Strecker) Rock Art Studies: News of the World. 3, 2008; An Enquiring Mind: Studies in Honor of Alexander Marshack, 2010. Contributor to periodicals. **Address:** Watson Little Ltd., Capo Di Monte, London, GL NW3 6RJ, England.

BAHR, Alice Harrison. American (born United States), b. 1946. **Genres:** Librarianship, Bibliography, Technology. **Career:** Lehigh University, assistant reference librarian, 1970-74; Cedar Crest College, adjunct faculty, 1978-82, project librarian, 1980-88; Muhlenberg College, project librarian, 1980-88; Salisbury University, Spring Hill College, director of library, 1988-, adjunct faculty of English, 1989, associate professor, 1993-99, professor, 1999-, dean of enrollment management, dean of libraries and instructional resources, 2002-; The Haworth Press, College and Undergraduate Libraries, editor-in-chief, 1990-99. Writer. **Publications:** Book Theft and Library Security Systems, 1978-79, 1978; Microforms: The Librarian's View, 1978-79, 1978; Automated Library Circulation Systems, 1979-80, 1979; Video in Libraries: A Status Report, 1979-80, 1980; (comp. with M.J. McLane) In Print: Publishing Opportunities for College Librarians, 1997. EDITOR: Future Teaching Roles for Academic Librarians, 2000. Contributor of articles to journals and periodicals. **Address:** Blackwell Library, Salisbury University, 1101 Camden Ave., Salisbury, MD 21801, U.S.A. **Online address:** ahbahr@salisbury.edu

BAHR, Ehrhard. American/German (born Germany), b. 1932. **Genres:** Literary Criticism And History, Biography, Translations. **Career:** University of California, Department of Germanic Languages, teaching assistant, 1962-66, acting assistant professor, 1966-68, assistant professor, 1968-70, associate professor, 1970-72, professor of German, 1972-, chairman, 1981-84, 1993-98, distinguished professor emeritus, 2003-. Writer. **Publications:** Georg Lukács, 1970; Die Ironie im Spätwerk Goethes (criticism), 1972; Ernst Bloch (biography), 1974; (with W.K. Stewart) Internationales Verzeichnis der Goethe-Dissertationen, 1978; Nelly Sachs (biography), 1980; The Novel as Archive: The Genesis, Reception, and Criticism of Goethe's Wilhelm Meisters Wanderjahre, 1998; Weimar on the Pacific: German Exile Culture in Los Angeles and the Crisis of Modernism, 2007. EDITOR: Kant: What is Enlightenment, 1974; Was ist Aufklärung?: Thesen u. Definitionen, 1974; (with E.P. Harris and L.C. Lyon) Humanität und Dialog, 1982; (with F. Gaede and G. Hillen) Geschichte der deutschen Literatur, 1987; (with C. See) Literary Exiles & Refugees in Los Angeles, 1988, 2nd ed., 1999; (with T.P. Saine) The Internalized Revolution: German Reactions to the French Revolution, 1789-1989, 1992. **Address:** Department of Germanic Languages, University of California, 212 Royce Hall, PO Box 951539, Los Angeles, CA 90095-1539, U.S.A. **Online address:** bahr@humnet.ucla.edu

BAHR, Iris. American/Israeli (born Israel) **Genres:** Biography, Autobiography/Memoirs, Reference. **Career:** Stanford University, researcher; Tel Aviv University, researcher. Actor and writer. **Publications:** Dork Whore: A Totally True Account of My Travels through Asia as a Twenty-Year-Old Pseudo Virgin (memoir), 2006; DAI: (enough): A Play, 2009; Machu my Picchu, 2011. **Address:** Bahr None Films, 7510 Sunset Blvd., Ste. 177, Los Angeles, CA 90046, U.S.A. **Online address:** irisbbb@earthlink.net

BAHR, Robert. Also writes as Harold Litten. American (born United States), b. 1940. **Genres:** Novellas/Short Stories, Gay And Lesbian Issues, Medicine/Health, Psychology, Sex, Writing/Journalism, Biography. **Career:** Rodale Press, editor, 1964-72, Health Bulletin, managing editor, 1965-67, Prevention magazine, senior editor, 1967-69, Fitness for Living, managing editor, 1969-71; Spring Hill College, adjunct professor of creative writing; University of South Alabama, faculty. **Publications:** Man with a Vision (biography), 1961; Natural Way to a Healthy Skin, 1972; Physical Fitness in Business and Industry, 1973; The Virility Factor: Masculinity Through Testosterone, the Male Sex Hormone, 1976; Least of All Saints, 1979; Great Blizzard, 1979; The Blizzard, 1980; Blizzard at the Zoo, 1982; (contrib.) Eat Better, Live Better, 1982; (ghostwriter) Kreskin's Fun Way to Mind Expansion, 1984; Good Hands: Massage Techniques for Total Health, 1984; (with P. Whybrow) The Hibernation Response, 1988; The Joy of Solo Sex, 1990; Indecent Exposures (short stories), 1993; (ed.) Home Again, Home Again: An Anthology of Short Fiction, 1994; More Joy of Solo Sex, 1996; Harold Litten's Best Erotic Fantasies, 1998; Dramatic Technique in Fiction, 1998; Our Finest Hour, forthcoming. **Address:** 5204 Dove Point Ln., Salisbury, MD 21801, U.S.A. **Online address:** factorpress@earthlink.net

BAICKER-MCKEE, Carol. American (born United States), b. 1958?. **Genres:** Human Relations/Parenting, Illustrations. **Career:** Writer, child psychologist and educator. **Publications:** Mapped Out!: The Search for Snookums, 1997; Fussbusters at Home: Around-the-Clock Strategies and Games for Smoothing the Rough Spots in Your Preschooler's Day, 2002; Fussbusters on the Go: Strategies and Games for Stress-Free Outings, Errands and Vacations with Your Preschooler, 2002; Mimi, 2008; The Preschooler Problem Solver: Helping your Preschooler Cope with Everything from the New Baby and Starting School to Moving and Family Crises, 2009. Illustrator of books by J. Stiegemeyer. **Address:** c/o Author Mail, Peachtree Publishers Ltd., 1700 Chattahoochee Ave., Atlanta, GA 30318-2112, U.S.A. **Online address:** baickermckee@adelphia.net

BAIL, Murray. Australian (born Australia), b. 1941. **Genres:** Novels, Novellas/Short Stories. **Career:** Writer. **Publications:** Contemporary Portraits and Other Stories, 1975 in UK as The Drover's Wife and Other Stories, 1984; Erkundungen: 31 australische Erzähler, 1976; Homesickness (novel), 1980; Ian Fairweather, 1981; The Faber Book of Contemporary Australian Short Stories, 1988; Longhand: A Writer's Notebook, 1989; Holden's Performance (novel), 1989; (ed.) Fairweather, 1994; (ed.) Eucalyptus: A Novel, 1998; Camouflage, 2000; (with A. Sayers) Sidney Nolan's Ned Kelly: The Ned Kelly Paintings in the National Gallery of Australia, 2002; Notebooks: 1970-2003, 2005; Pages, 2008. Contributor to periodicals. **Address:** c/o Pat Kavanagh, Drury House, 34-43 Russell St., London, GL WC2B 5HA, England.

BAILEY, Anne C. American/Jamaican (born Jamaica), b. 1964?. **Genres:** Adult Non-fiction, Young Adult Fiction, Novels. **Career:** Coro Foundation, fellow, 1986-87; New York City Board of Education, Coro Foundation fellow, 1986-87, special assistant, 1987-89; A.C. Bailey and Associates, consultant, 1991-; University of Pennsylvania, teaching assistant, 1992-93, Annenberg visiting professor of history, 1999-2000; Albert G. Oliver Program, executive director, 1994-96; Rutgers University, instructor in history and visiting fellow, 1998; visiting professor of history, 1998-2000; Bryn Mawr College, professor of history, 1998-99; Harvard University, W.E.B. Dubois fellow and visiting professor of history, 2000; Spelman College, assistant professor of history, 2000-06, associate professor of history and Africana studies; State University of New York, associate professor. Writer. **Publications:** (With E. Packard) Return to the Cave of Time, 1985; You Can Make a Difference: The Story of Martin Luther King Jr., 1990; African Voices of the Atlantic Slave Trade: Beyond the Silence and the Shame, 2005; Anchors in the Sand, forthcoming; Beyond Boundaries, forthcoming, The Weeping Time: Anatomy of a Slave Auction, forthcoming. **Address:** Department of History, Binghamton University, Library Twr. 614, PO Box 6000, Binghamton, NY 13902-6000, U.S.A. **Online address:** abailey@binghamton.edu

BAILEY, Anthony. British (born England), b. 1933. **Genres:** Novels, Human Relations/Parenting, Travel/Exploration, Autobiography/Memoirs, Documentaries/Reportage, Biography, Architecture. **Career:** The New Yorker, staff writer, 1956-92; The Greenwich Society, chairman, 1979-81; The Burney St. Garden Project, chairman, 1981-90. **Publications:** Making Progress, 1959; The Mother Tongue, 1961; The Inside Passage, 1965; Through the Great City, 1967; The Thousand Dollar Yacht, 1968; The Light in Holland, 1970; In the Village, 1971; The Horizon Concise History of the Low Countries, 1972; Rembrandt's House, 1978; Acts of Union: Reports on Ireland, 1973-79, 1980; America, Lost & Found, 1980; Along the Edge of the Forest: An Iron Curtain Journey, 1983; (intro.) The Coast of Massachusetts, 1984; England, First and Last, 1985; Spring Jaunts: Some Walks, Excursions and Personal Explorations of Town, Country and Seashore, 1986; Major André, 1987; The Outer Banks, 1989; A Walk through Wales, 1992; Responses to Rembrandt, 1994; The Coast of Summer: Sailing New England Waters from Shelter Island to Cape Cod, 1994; Standing in the Sun: A Life of J.M.W. Turner, 1997; Vermeer: A View of Delft in UK as A View of Delft: Vermeer Then and Now, 2001; John Constable: A Kingdom of his Own, 2007; Velázquez: Surrendering at Breda, 2011. **Address:** c/o Candida Donadio, Donadio & Ashworth Inc., 121 W 27th St., Ste. 704, New York, NY 10001-6262, U.S.A.

BAILEY, Blake. American (born United States), b. 1963. **Genres:** History, Biography. **Career:** College of William & Mary, writer-in-residence, Mina Hohenberg Darden professor of creative writing. Writer. **Publications:** Sixties (history), 1992; A Tragic Honesty: The Life and Work of Richard Yates (biography), 2003; Cheever: A Life (biography), 2009. Contributor to periodicals. **Address:** c/o Author Mail, Picador USA, 175 5th Ave., New York, NY 10010, U.S.A.

BAILEY, Charles Waldo. American (born United States), b. 1929. **Genres:** Novels, History, Politics/Government, Ethics, Young Adult Fiction. **Career:** Minneapolis Tribune, reporter, 1950-54, Washington correspondent, 1954-72, Washington bureau chief, 1968-72, editor, 1972-82; Des Moines Register, Washington correspondent, 1954-67; Look, Washington correspondent, 1954-67; U.S. Congress, secretary, 1963; National Public Radio, Washington editor, 1983-87; American Society of Newspaper Editors, director; The Henry L. Stimson Center, director, now director emeritus. **Publications:** (With F.

Knebel) No High Ground, 1960; (with F. Knebel) Seven Days in May, 1962; (with F. Knebel) Convention, 1964; Conflicts of Interest: A Matter of Journalistic Ethics, 1984; The Land was Ours: A Novel of the Great Plains, 1991. Contributor to books. **Address:** The Henry L. Stimson Center, 1111 19th St. NW, 12th Fl., Washington, DC 20036, U.S.A.

BAILEY, Donna. British/Malaysian (born Malaysia), b. 1938. **Genres:** Children's Non-fiction, Medicine/Health, History, Animals/Pets, Environmental Sciences/Ecology, Natural History, Sports/Fitness. **Career:** University of Sussex, library assistant, 1962-64; Essex Education Authority, Margaret Tabor School, teacher of English, 1967; Essex University Library, senior library assistant and assistant Russian cataloger, 1967-69; N.V. Philips Language Teaching Centre, teacher of English as a foreign language, 1970-71; National Central Library, filing assistant, 1972; Macmillan, freelance editor, 1972-73, overseas book editor, 1974, senior overseas book editor, 1975-77, managing editor, 1978-79, secondary publishing manager, 1980, senior editor of children's books, 1980, publishing manager, 1981-84. Consultant. **Publications:** (With M. Rodgers) India, 1990; (with A. Sproule) Israel, 1990; Ships, 1990; Skiing, 1990; (with J. Chapman) Australia, 1990; Cities, 1990; Deserts: 1990; Farmers, 1990; Forests, 1990; (with J. Taylor) Hong Kong, 1990; (with T. Potter) Hens, 1990; (with T. Potter) Sheep, 1990; (with A. Sproule) Italy, 1990; (with A. Sproule) Japan, 1990; (with A. Sproule) Mexico, 1990; Mountains, 1990; Nigeria, 1990; Nomads, 1990; (with A. Sproule) Philippines, 1990; Planes, 1990; Reptiles, 1990; Rivers, 1990; (with J. Vaughan) Greece, 1990; (with J. Vaughan) Russia, 1990; Space, 1990; (with A. Wong) Trinidad, 1990; (with T. Potter) Cows, 1990; (with T. Potter) Donkeys, 1990; (with T. Potter) Ducks and Geese, 1990; (with T. Potter) Goats, 1990; (with A. Sproule) Bangladesh, 1991; (with A. Sproule) Brazil, 1991; Camels, 1991; Energy for Our Bodies, 1991; Energy from Oil and Gas, 1991; Energy from Wind and Water, 1991; (with A. Sproule) Kenya, 1991; Litter, 1991; Lizards, 1991; Canoeing, 1991; Conserving Energy, 1991; Cycling, 1991; Dancing, 1991; Dolphins, 1991; Energy All Around Us, 1991; Spiders, 1991; Swimming, 1991; Tennis, 1991; Far Out in Space, 1991; Far Planets, 1991; Fishing, 1991; (with A. Sproule) France, 1991; Giraffes, 1991; Hiking, 1991; (with A. Sproule) Ireland, 1991; Judo, 1991; Tiburones, 1991; Track and Field, 1991; Wasting Water, 1991; Looking at Stars, 1991; Near Planets, 1991; Noise and Fumes, 1991; Protecting Nature, 1991; Recycling Garbage, 1991; Sailing, 1991; Sharks, 1991; Skating, 1991; Águilas, 1992; Canada, 1992; Delfines, 1992; Germany, 1992; (with A. Sproule) My Home in Northern Nigeria, 1992; Netherlands, 1992; Osos, 1992; Ranas, 1992; Serpientes, 1992; Spain, 1992; Sweden, 1992; Thailand, 1992. HEALTH FACTS SERIES: All about Birth and Growth, 1991; All about Digestion, 1991; All about Your Heart and Blood, 1991; All about Your Skin, Hair, and Teeth, 1991; All about Your Brain, 1991; All about Your Lungs, 1991; All about Your Senses, 1991; All about Your Skeleton, 1991. WITH C. BUTTERWORTH: Birds, 1988; Cats, 1988; Dogs, 1988; Fish, 1988; Hamsters, 1988; Horses, 1988; Bears, 1990; Butterflies, 1990; Snakes, 1990; Eagles, 1990; Frogs, 1990; Kangaroos, 1990; Alligators, 1991; Chimpanzees, 1991; Foxes, 1991; Crabs, 1991; Deer, 1991; Owls, 1991. **Address:** Reeds Cottage, Appleshaw, North Andover, HM SP11 9AA, England.

BAILEY, Dulcie Winifred Catherine. *See* **GRAY, Dulcie.**

BAILEY, F(rancis) Lee. American (born United States), b. 1933. **Genres:** Novels, Law, Young Adult Fiction. **Career:** Bailey, Fishman and Leonard, senior partner; Gallery Magazine, publisher, 1972-; Enstrom Helicopter Corp., president, 1972-; Bailey, Alch & Gillis, partner; IMPAC Control Systems Inc., chief executive officer, chairman. Writer. **Publications:** (With H.B. Rothblatt) Complete Manual of Criminal Forms: Federal and State, 2 vols., 1968-74, 3rd ed., 1993; (with H.P. Rothblatt) Criminal Law Library, I-XI vols., 1969-82; (with H.B. Rothblatt) Defending Business and White Collar Crimes, 1969, 2nd ed., 1984; (with H.B. Rothblatt) Investigation and Preparation of Criminal Cases, Federal and State, 1970, 2nd ed., 1985; (with H. Aronson) The Defense Never Rests: The Art of Cross-Examination, 1971; (with H.B. Rothblatt) Successful Techniques for Criminal Trials, 1971, 2nd ed., 1985; (with H.B. Rothblatt) Handling Narcotic and Drug Cases, 1972; (with H.B. Rothblatt) Crimes of Violence, 1973; (with H.B. Rothblatt) Fundamentals of Criminal Advocacy, 1974; (with J. Greenya) For the Defense, 1975; (with K.J. Fishman) Handling Misdemeanor Cases, 1976, 2nd ed., 1992; (with J. Greenya) Cleared for the Approach: F. Lee Bailey in Defense of Flying, 1977; Secrets (novel), 1977; (with H.B. Rothblatt) Cross-Examination in Criminal Trials, 1978; How to Protect Yourself Against Cops in California and Other Strange Places, 1982; To Be a Trial Lawyer, 1982, 2nd ed., 1994; (with H.B. Rothblatt) Handling Juvenile Delinquency Cases, 1982; (with K.J. Fishman) Supplements to the Bailey-Rothblatt Criminal Law Series, 1986; (with K.J. Fishman) Complete Manual of Criminal Forms, 3rd ed., 1993; (with K.J. Fishman) Criminal Trial Techniques, 1994; (with J. Rabe) When the Husband is the Suspect, 2008. **Address:** IMPAC Control Systems Inc., 3300 Irvine Ave., Ste. 325, Newport Beach, CA 92660, U.S.A.

BAILEY, Frederick George. British (born England), b. 1924. **Genres:** Anthropology/Ethnology, Politics/Government, Social Commentary, Third World. **Career:** University of London, reader in Asian anthropology, 1960-63; University of Sussex, professor of anthropology, 1964-71; University of California, professor of anthropology, 1971-, now professor emeritus. Writer. **Publications:** Caste and the Economic Frontier: A Village in Highland Orissa, 1957; Tribe, Caste and Nation: A Study of Political Activity and Political Change in Highland Orissa, 1960; Politics and Social Change: Orissa in 1959, 1963; Stratagems and Spoils: A Social Anthropology of Politics, 1969; Les Règles du jeu politique; étude anthropologique, 1971; Morality and Expediency: The Folklore of Academic Politics, 1977; The Tactical Uses of Passion, 1983; Humbuggery and Manipulation: The Art of Leadership, 1988; The Prevalence of Deceit, 1991; The Kingdom of Individuals: An Essay on Self-Respect and Social Obligation, 1993; The Witch-Hunt, or, The Triumph of Morality, 1994; The Civility of Indifference: On Domesticating Ethnicity, 1996; The Need for Enemies: A Bestiary of Political Forms, 1998; Treasons, Stratagems and Spoils: How Leaders Make Practical Use of Values and Beliefs, 2001; The Saving Lie: Truth and Method in the Social Sciences, 2003; Morality and Expediency: The Folklore of Academic Politics, 2007; God-botherers and Other True Believers: Gandhi, Hitler and the Religious Right, 2008. EDITOR: Gifts and Poisons: The Politics of Reputation, 1971; Debate and Compromise: The Politics of Innovation, 1973. **Address:** Department of Anthropology, University of California at San Diego, 9500 Gilman Dr., La Jolla, CA 92093-0532, U.S.A. **Online address:** fbailey@ucsd.edu

BAILEY, Gordon (Keith). British (born England), b. 1936. **Genres:** Poetry, Education, Theology/Religion, Humor/Satire. **Career:** A.B.C. Television Ltd., film editor, 1956-59; Heywood Ltd., sales manager, 1959-63; freelance broadcaster, 1968-; ATV Network Ltd., Gordon Bailey Series, staff, 1973-75; Lightlines Ltd., director, 1980-83; Schools Outreach, founder, chief executive, 1986-. Writer. **Publications:** Plastic World, 1971; Moth-balled Religion, 1972; Patchwork Quill, 1975; Can a Man Change?, 1979; 100 Contemporary Christian Poets, 1983; I Want to Tell You How I Feel, God, 1983; Stuff and Nonsense, 1989; Mix and Match, 1999. Contributor of articles. **Address:** Schools Outreach, 109 Worcester Rd., Bromsgrove, B61 7HN, England. **Online address:** schoolsoutreach@aol.com

BAILEY, Greg. Australian (born Australia), b. 1948?. **Genres:** Theology/Religion, Cultural/Ethnic Topics, Mythology/Folklore, Sociology, Translations. **Career:** La Trobe University, School of Social Sciences, Faculty of Humanities and Social Sciences, associate professor, 1979-, Asian Studies Program, coordinator; Universität Tübingen, visiting research fellow, 1998. Writer and historian. **Publications:** The Mythology of Brahmā, 1983; (ed. with I. Kesarcodi-Watson) Bhakti Studies, 1992; Bhartrhari's Critique of Culture, 1994; (trans. and intro.) Gaṇeśapurāna, 1995; Mythologies of Change and Certainty in Late-Twentieth Century Australia, 2000; (ed. with M. Brockington) Epic Threads: John Brockington on the Sanskrit Epics, 2000; (with I. Mabbett) The Sociology of Early Buddhism, 2003; (trans. with R. Gombrich) Amaru and Bhartṛ hari, Love Lyrics, 2005; (contrib.) Hindu Nationalism and Governance, 2007. Contributor to books, periodicals and journals. **Address:** School of Social Sciences, La Trobe University, SS 418, Melbourne, VI 3086, Australia. **Online address:** greg.bailey@latrobe.edu.au

BAILEY, Hilary. British (born England), b. 1936?. **Genres:** Novels, Bibliography. **Career:** Writer and publicist. **Publications:** NOVELS: (with M. Moorcock) The Black Corridor, 1969; Polly Put the Kettle On, 1975; Mrs. Mulvaney, 1978; All the Days of My Life, 1984; Hannie Richards, or, The Intrepid Adventures of a Restless Wife in US as Hannie Richards, 1985; Vera Brittain, 1987; As Time Goes By, 1988; A Stranger to Herself, 1989; In Search of Love, Money and Revenge, 1990; The Cry from Street to Street, 1992; Cassandra: Princess of Troy, 1993; The Strange Adventures of Charlotte Holmes, 1994; Frankenstein's Bride, 1995; Miles and Flora, 1997; Mrs. Rochester, 1997; Elizabeth and Lily, 1997; After the Cabaret, 1998; Connections, 2000; (with E. Tennant) The Autobiography of the Queen, 2007; Fifty-First State, 2008; (with E. Tennant) Diana: The Ghost Biography, 2008. Contributor of articles to journals. **Address:** Simon & Schuster Inc., 1230 Ave. of the Americas, New York, NY 10020, U.S.A.

BAILEY, Jerry. (Jerry Dale Bailey). American (born United States), b. 1957. **Genres:** Sports/Fitness. **Career:** Professional jockey, 1974-2006, retired, 2006. Writer. **Publications:** (With T. Pedulla) Against the Odds: Riding for My Life, 2005. **Address:** Jockeys Guild, 250 W Main St., Lexington, KY 40507-1714, U.S.A. **Online address:** info@jerrybailey.com

BAILEY, Jerry Dale. *See* **BAILEY, Jerry.**

BAILEY, John. Australian (born Australia), b. 1944. **Genres:** Novels, Biography, History. **Career:** Lawyer and historian. Writer. **Publications:** The Wire Classroom, 1972; The Moon Baby, 1978; The White Divers of Broome: The True Story of a Fatal Experiment, 2001; The Lost German Slave Girl: The Extraordinary True Story of Sally Miller and Her Fight for Freedom in Old New Orleans, 2003; Mr Stuart's Track, 2006. Contributor to periodicals. **Address:** c/o Author Mail, Pan Macmillan Australia, Level 18, St. Martins Twr., 31 Market St., Sydney, NW 2000, Australia.

BAILEY, Julius H. American (born United States) **Genres:** Adult Non-fiction, Civil Liberties/Human Rights, Politics/Government. **Career:** Kenyon College, Department of Religious Studies, instructor, 2000-01; University of Redlands, Department of Religious Studies, assistant professor, 2001-07, associate professor of religion, 2007-. Writer. **Publications:** (Contrib.) Organizing Black America: An Encyclopedia of African American Associations, 2001; (contrib.) Encyclopedia of Fundamentalism, 2001; Around the Family Altar: Domesticity in the African Methodist Episcopal Church, 1865-1900, 2005; (contrib.) Encyclopedia of Slave Resistance and Rebellion, 2007; (contrib.) African American National Biography, 2008; Race Patriotism: Protest and Print Culture in the A.M.E. Church, 2012. Contributor to journals. **Address:** Department of Religious Studies, University of Redlands, 220 Larsen Hall, 1200 E Colton Ave., PO Box 3080, Redlands, CA 92373-0999, U.S.A. **Online address:** julius_bailey@redlands.edu

BAILEY, Kathleen C. American (born United States), b. 1949. **Genres:** Military/Defense/Arms Control, Novels, Young Adult Fiction, Politics/Government, History. **Career:** Lawrence Livermore National Laboratory, director of program, 1978-81, staff, 1992-98, senior fellow, 1992-; U.S. Information Agency, research director, 1983-85; U.S. Department of State, Bureau of Intelligence and Research, deputy assistant secretary, 1985-87; Arms Control and Disarmament Agency, assistant director, 1988-90; National Institute for Public Policy, senior analyst and vice-president, 1990-92, senior associate, 1998-, director of armed control studies. Writer. **Publications:** South Africa, Stability or Revolution?: A Political Risk Assessment, 1981; Doomsday Weapons in the Hands of Many: The Arms Control Challenge of the '90s, 1991; Strengthening Nuclear Nonproliferation, 1993; (ed. with R. Rudney) Proliferation and Export Controls, 1993; (ed.) Weapons of Mass Destruction: Costs Versus Benefits, 1994; The UN Inspections in Iraq: Lessons for On-Site Verification, 1995; Death for Cause (novel), 1995; (with G.N. Kinnas) Pyrenike Energeia & Diaspora, 1996. **Address:** National Institute for Public Policy, 3031 Javier Rd., Ste. 300, Fairfax, VA 22031-4662, U.S.A. **Online address:** kathleen.bailey@nipp.org

BAILEY, Kathryn. American (born United States) **Genres:** Music, Biography, Literary Criticism And History. **Career:** Editor, 1991-. **Publications:** NONFICTION: The Twelve-Note Music of Anton Webern: Old Forms in a New Language, 1991; (ed.) Webern Studies, 1996; The Life of Webern, 1998. Contributor to periodicals. **Address:** Cambridge University Press, 32 Ave. of the Americas, New York, NY 10013-2473, U.S.A.

BAILEY, Kathryn Ann. *See* **HUTCHISON, Kay Bailey.**

BAILEY, Lee W. American (born United States), b. 1943. **Genres:** Theology/Religion, Technology, Mythology/Folklore, Psychology. **Career:** Ithaca College, Department of Philosophy and Religion, associate professor of world religions and culture, 1983-2005. Writer. **Publications:** (Ed. with J. Yates) The Near-Death Experience: A Reader, 1996; The Enchantments of Technology, 2005; (ed.) Introduction to the World's Major Religions, 6 vols., 2006; Christianity, 2006; (ed. with M. Fisher) Anthology of Living Religions, 2011. Works appear in anthologies. Contributor to periodicals and journals. **Address:** 3333 Slaterville Rd., Brooktondale, NY 14817, U.S.A. **Online address:** bailey@ithaca.edu

BAILEY, Len. American (born United States) **Genres:** Bibliography, Children's Fiction. **Career:** Bagpipe player, voice-over actor and author. **Publications:** Clabbernappers, 2005; Fantasms, 2007. Contributor to periodicals. **Address:** c/o Tracy Grant, Leona Literary Agency, PO Box 835, Highland Park, IL 60035, U.S.A.

BAILEY, Linda. Canadian (born Canada), b. 1948?. **Genres:** Children's Fiction, Young Adult Fiction, Picture/Board Books, Novels. **Career:** Writer. **Publications:** How Come the Best Clues Are Always in the Garbage?, 1992; How Can I Be a Detective If I Have to Babysit?, 1993; Who's Got Gertie? And How Can We Get Her Back?, 1994; How Can a Frozen Detective Stay Hot on the Trail?, 1996; What's a Daring Detective Like Me Doing in the Doghouse?, 1997; Gordon Loggins and the Three Bears, 1997; Petula, Who Wouldn't Take a Bath, 1998; How Can a Brilliant Detective Shine in the Dark?, 1999; What's a Serious Detective Like Me Doing in Such a Silly Movie, 2002. FOR CHILDREN: Petula, Who Wouldn't Take a Bath, 1996; Gordon Loggins and the Three Bears, 1997; When Addie Was Scared, 1999; The Best Figure Skater in the Whole Wide World, 2001; Stanley's Party, 2003; Stanley's Wild Ride, 2006; The Farm Team, 2006; Goodnight, Sweet Pig, 2006; Stanley at Sea, 2008; Stanley's Beauty Contest, 2009; Stanley's Little Sister, 2010. GOOD TIMES TRAVEL AGENCY: Adventures in Ancient Egypt, 2000; Adventures in the Middle Ages, 2000; Adventures with the Vikings, 2001; Adventures in Ancient Greece, 2002; Adventures in Ancient China, 2003; Adventures in the Ice Age, 2004. **Address:** Kids Can Press Ltd., 29 Birch Ave., Toronto, ON M4V 1E1, Canada. **Online address:** linda@lindabaileybooks.com

BAILEY, Maria T. American (born United States), b. 1964. **Genres:** Business/Trade/Industry. **Career:** Bailey Innovative Marketing, president; Broward Community College, president of marketing and interim executive; Auto Nation USA, vice president of loyalty marketing; BSM Media Inc. (marketing and media Co.), founder and chief executive officer, 2000-; BlueSuitMom.com, founder; Broward County Library Foundation, Night of Literary Feasts, chair; Newbaby.com, co-founder. Writer, host and producer. **Publications:** The Women's Home-based Business Book of Answers: 78 Important Questions Answered by Top Women Business Leaders, 2001; Marketing to Moms: Getting Your Share of the Trillion-Dollar Market, 2002; (with B.W. Ulman) Trillion-Dollar Moms: Marketing to a New Generation of Mothers, 2005; Diaries of a Bluesuitmom, 2006; Mom 3.0: Marketing with Today's Mothers, 2008; The Ultimate Mom: Uplifting Stories, Endearing Photos, and the Best Experts' Tips on the Toughest Job You'll Ever Love, 2009; Power Moms: The New Rules for Engaging Mom Mavens Who Drive Brand Choice, 2011. Contributor to periodicals. **Address:** BSM Media Inc., 2335 E Atlantic Blvd., Ste. 300, Fort Lauderdale, FL 33062, U.S.A. **Online address:** maria@bsmmedia.com

BAILEY, Martha (J.). American (born United States), b. 1929. **Genres:** Librarianship, Administration/Management, Reference, Social Sciences. **Career:** Purdue University, assistant professor, 1970-75, physics librarian, 1970-75, associate professor, 1975-79, physics and geosciences librarian, 1975-79, professor of library service, 1980-95, life sciences librarian, 1980-95, professor emeritus, 1995-; Union Carbide Corp., technical librarian; E.I. DuPont and de Nemours and Co., library assistant; Eli Lilly and Co., staff. Writer. **Publications:** The Special Librarian as a Supervisor or Middle Manager, 1977, 2nd ed., 1986; Supervisory and Middle Managers in Libraries, 1981; American Women in Science: Colonial Times to 1950, a Biographical Dictionary, 1994; American Women in Science: 1950 to the Present, a Biographical Dictionary, 1998. Contributor to books and magazines. **Address:** 4039-C Willow Bend Dr., Beech Grove, IN 46107-3200, U.S.A.

BAILEY, Michael D. American (born United States), b. 1971. **Genres:** History, Theology/Religion. **Career:** St. Louis University, visiting assistant professor of history, 2002-03; Iowa State University, assistant professor of history, 2003-, associate professor; University of Pennsylvania, Mellon fellow in humanities, 2003-04. Writer. **Publications:** A Historical Dictionary of Witchcraft, 2003; Battling Demons: Witchcraft, Heresy, and Reform in the Late Middle Ages, 2003; Magic and Superstition in Europe: A Concise History from Antiquity to the Present, 2007. Contributor to periodicals. **Address:** Department of History, Iowa State University, 621 Ross Hall, Ames, IA 50011, U.S.A. **Online address:** mdbailey@iastate.edu

BAILEY, Nancy Fayrweather. American (born United States), b. 1940. **Genres:** Food And Wine. **Career:** Writer. **Publications:** Have Your Cake and Eat It Too!, 2004. **Address:** Elderberry Press Inc., 1393 Old Homestead Dr., Oakland, OR 97462-9690, U.S.A. **Online address:** nbailey4@cox.net

BAILEY, Norman (Alishan). American (born United States), b. 1931. **Genres:** Politics/Government, International Relations/Current Affairs, Economics, Politics/Government. **Career:** National Security Council, National Security Affairs, special assistant to the president, International Economic Affairs, senior director, 1981-84; Potomac Foundation, senior fellow, 2003-06; The Office of the Director of National Intelligence, mission manager, 2006-07; Institute for Global Economic Growth, president, 2007-. Writer. **Publications:** (With R. Linney and D. Cascio) Ten Plays for Radio: Adapted from the World's Masterpieces of Drama and Literature, 1954; (with R. Linney and D. Cascio) Radio Classics, 1956; (ed.) Latin America: Politics, Economics and Hemispheric Security, 1965; Latin America in World Politics, 1967; Portuguese Africa, 1969; (with S.M. Feder) Operational Conflict Analysis, 1973; Brazil as a Monetary Model, 1975; (trans.) L. Pirandello, Sicilian Comedies, 1983; (with R. Cohen) The Mexican Time Bomb, 1987; The Strategic Plan that Won the Cold War, 1993, 2nd ed., 1994; (with W. Perr) Venezuela, 1994: Challenges for the Caldera Administration, 1994. **Address:** 1020 16th St. NW, Ste. LL1, Washington, DC 20036, U.S.A. **Online address:** normanabailey@aol.com

BAILEY, Peter J. American (born United States), b. 1946. **Genres:** Literary Criticism And History, Art/Art History. **Career:** Time Magazine, Clip Desk, head, 1966-68; Red Diamond Brand, information specialist and assistant editor; Mountaineer, information specialist and assistant editor; The Boys' Latin School, The Upper School, master of English, 1971-73; University of Southern California, teaching assistant, 1973-75, Thematic Option Program, writing instructor and lecturer, 1975-79, Department of English, instructor, 1979-80, Thematic Option Program, instructor, 1979-80; St. Lawrence University, Department of English, visiting assistant professor, 1980-85, assistant professor, 1985-86, associate professor, 1986-92, professor, 1992, Piskor professor; Jeffrey Campbell Graduate Fellows Program, director. **Publications:** Reading Stanley Elkin, 1985; The Reluctant Film Art of Woody Allen, 2001; Rabbit (Un)Redeemed: The Drama of Belief in John Updike's Fiction, 2006. Contributor to periodicals. **Address:** Department of English, St. Lawrence University, 107 Richardson Hall, 23 Romoda Dri., Canton, NY 13617, U.S.A. **Online address:** pbailey@stlawu.edu

BAILEY, Robin W(ayne). American (born United States), b. 1952. **Genres:** Science Fiction/Fantasy, Novels. **Career:** Science Fiction and Fantasy Writers of America, South-central regional director, president, 2005-. Teacher, musician and writer. **Publications:** FANTASY NOVELS: Frost, 1983; Skull Gate, 1985; Bloodsongs, 1986; Enchanter, 1989; The Lake of Fire, 1989; Nightwatch, 1990; The Lost City of Zork, 1991; Brothers of the Dragon, 1992; Straight on Till Mourning, 1993 in US as Flames of the Dragon, 1994; Triumph of the Dragon, 1994; The Palace of Souls, 1995; The Shadowdance, 1996; Swords Against the Shadowland, 1998; Dragonkin, 2001; Night's Angel, 2002; (co-author) The Dungeon 2, 2003; Talisman, 2004; Undersky, 2005; Turn Left to Tomorrow, 2007; (contrib.) Lace and blade. 2, 2009; Swords in the Storm, forthcoming. **Address:** c/o Richard Curtis, Richard Curtis Associates Inc., 171 E 74th St., 2nd Fl., New York, NY 10021, U.S.A. **Online address:** robin@robinwaynebailey.net

BAILEY, Rosemary. French/British (born England), b. 1953?. **Genres:** Adult Non-fiction, Biography, Autobiography/Memoirs, Travel/Exploration. **Career:** Writer. **Publications:** Scarlet Ribbons: A Priest with AIDS, 1997; The National Geographic Traveler: France, 1999; Life in a Postcard: Escape to the French Pyrenees, 2002; The Man Who Married a Mountain: A Journey through the Pyrenees, 2005; Love and War in the Pyrenees, 2008. EDITOR: Tuscany, 1990; Loire Valley, 1991; Burgundy, 1992, rev. ed., 2000; Cote d'Azur, 1992; Eyewitness Travel Guide to France, 1998; The French Riviera, 2nd ed., 1999; Gascony and the Pyrenees, 2001. Contributor to periodicals. **Address:** c/o Author Mail, Transworld Publishers, 61-63 Uxbridge Rd., London, GL W5 5SA, England. **Online address:** info@rosemarybailey.com

BAILEY, Roz. (Carly Alexander). American (born United States) **Genres:** Children's Fiction, Psychology, Romance/Historical. **Career:** Simon & Schuster, editorial assistant. **Publications:** Party Girls, 2002; Girls' Night Out, 2003; Ghosts of Boyfriends Past, 2003; Retail Therapy, 2004; Eggnog Chronicles, 2004; Secret Life of Mrs. Claus, 2005; (with T. Alan and H. Chamberlain) Sex and the Single Witch, 2005; Postcards from Last Summer, 2006; Mommies Behaving Badly, 2007. **Address:** Kensington Publishing Corp., 119 W 40th St., New York, NY 10018, U.S.A.

BAILEY-WILLIAMS, Nicole. (Ivana B. Rich). American (born United States), b. 1971. **Genres:** Novels. **Career:** Ewing High School, instructor in English. Writer. **Publications:** NOVELS: A Little Piece of Sky, 2000; Floating: A Novel, 2004. OTHERS: (as Ivana B. Rich) The Gold Digger's Guide: How to Marry the Man and the Money, 2004; Love Child's Revenge, 2008. Contributor to periodicals. **Address:** c/o Author Mail, Harlem Moon, 1745 Broadway, New York, NY 10019-4368, U.S.A.

BAILIE, Grant. American (born United States), b. 1962?. **Genres:** Novels. **Career:** Writer. **Publications:** NOVELS: Cloud 8, 2003; Mortarville, 2008. Contributor to peridicals. **Address:** Sheffield Lake, OH , U.S.A. **Online address:** grantbailie@hotmail.com

BAILLIE, Allan. Australian (born Australia), b. 1943. **Genres:** Novels, Children's Fiction, Young Adult Fiction, History, Children's Fiction, Astronomy, Race Relations, Third World, Third World. **Career:** Sun News Pictorial, reporter and sub-editor, 1961-64; Middlesex Advertiser, sub-editor, 1966-67; Australian Associated Press, sub-editor, 1968-69; freelance writer, 1969-2004; Sunday Telegraph, sub-editor, 1970-73; Daily Telegraph, sub-editor, 1973-74; Australian Broadcasting Commission, staff, 1973-77; ABC, sub-editor, 1974-78; Women's Weekly, sub-editor, 1978-80; Sun Herald, sub-editor, 1980-87. **Publications:** YOUNG ADULT FICTION: Adrift, 1983, 2nd ed., 1992; Little Brother, 1985, 2nd ed., 1992; Riverman, 1986, 2nd ed., 1992; Eagle Island, 1987; Creature, 1987; Drac and the Gremlin, 1988, 2nd ed., 1989; Megan's Star, 1988; Mates, 1989; Hero, 1991; Bawshou Rescues the Sun: A Han Folktale, 1991; Little Monster, 1991; The China Coin, 1991; The Boss, 1992; The Bad Guys, 1993; Magician, 1993; Rebel, 1993, 2nd ed., 1994; Songman, 1994; Dream Catcher; 1995; Old Magic, 1996; Dragon Quest, 1996; Secrets of Walden Rising, 1997; Last Shot, 1997; The Excuse, 1997; Star Navigator, 1997; Wreck, 1997; (with J. Bentley) Archie: The Big Good Wolf, 1998; Legends: Stories of Australia, 1999; Saving Abbie, 2000; Heroes: Australians at Their Best, 2001; Foggy, 2001; Imp, 2002; Treasure Hunters, 2002; Villains: A Gallery of Australian Rogues, 2003; My Story: Riding with Thunderbolt, 2004; Castles, 2004; Cat's Mountain, 2006; Krakatoa Lighthouse, 2009; Outpost, 2012. ADULT FICTION: Mask Maker, 1975. Works appear in anthologies. Contributor to magazines. **Address:** 197 Riverview Rd., Avalon, NW 2107, Australia. **Online address:** baillie_allan@hotmail.com

BAILYN, Lotte. American/Austrian (born Austria), b. 1930. **Genres:** Administration/Management, Human Relations/Parenting, Social Sciences, Adult Non-fiction. **Career:** Harvard University, postdoctoral research associate in education, 1956-57, research associate, 1958-64, lecturer in social relations, 1963-67; Massachusetts Institute of Technology, instructor in economics and social science, 1957-58, research associate, 1969-70, lecturer, 1970-71, senior lecturer, 1971-72, associate professor, 1972-80, professor, 1980-91, T. Wilson professor of management, 1991-2005, professor of management, 2005-, now professor emeritus of organization studies; University of London, Imperial College of Science and Technology, Management School, academic visitor, 1991, 1995, 2000; University of Auckland, visiting university fellow in management studies, 1984. Writer. **Publications:** (With B. Bailyn) Massachusetts Shipping, 1697-1714: A Statistical Study, 1959; Mass Media and Children: A Study of Exposure Habits and Cognitive Effects (monograph), 1959; (with E.H. Schein) Living with Technology: Issues at Mid-Career, 1980; (with M.B. Arthur, D.J. Levinson and H.A. Shepard) Working with Careers, 1984; Breaking the Mold: Women, Men, and Time in the New Corporate World, 1993, 2nd ed. as Breaking the Mold: Redesigning Work for Productive and Satisfying Lives, 2006; (with R. Rapoport) Relinking Life and Work: Toward a Better Future, 1996; Work and Family: Beyond Work and Family: Adventures on the Fault Line, 1996; (with R. Rapoport, J.K. Fletcher and B.H. Pruitt) Beyond Work and Family Balance: Advancing Gender Equity and Workplace Performance, 2002. Contributor to books and periodicals. **Address:** Sloan School of Management, Massachusetts Institute of Technology, E62-377-1, 50 Memorial Dr., Cambridge, MA 02142, U.S.A. **Online address:** lbailyn@mit.edu

BAIN, David Haward. American (born United States), b. 1949. **Genres:** History, Social Commentary, Writing/Journalism, Travel/Exploration, Education. **Career:** Alfred A. Knopf Inc., editorial assistant, 1973-76; Stonehill Publishers, editor, 1976-77; Crown Publishers, editor, 1977-78; freelance writer, 1978-; Middlebury College, faculty, 1981-88, 2003, visiting lecturer, 1987-. **Publications:** Aftershocks: A Tale of Two Victims, 1980, rev. ed.,

1986; Sitting in Darkness: Americans in the Philippines, 1984, rev. ed., 1986; (ed. with M.S. Duffy) Whose Woods These Are: A History of the Bread Loaf Writers' Conference, 1926-1992, 1993; (ed. with S.L. Plum) At an Elevation: On the Poetry of Robert Pack, 1994; The College on the Hill: A Browser's History for the Bicentennial, Middlebury College, 1800-2000, 1999; Empire Express: Building the First Transcontinental Railroad, 1999; The Old Iron Road: An Epic of Rails, Roads, and the Urge to Go West, 2004; Best Be Getting Home: Essays on Place, Writers, and Writing, forthcoming. Contributor to periodicals. **Address:** Ellen Levine Literary Agency Inc., 41 Madison Ave., 36th Fl., New York, NY 10010, U.S.A.

BAIN, Kenneth (Ross). New Zealander (born New Zealand), b. 1923. **Genres:** History, Cultural/Ethnic Topics, Human Relations/Parenting, International Relations/Current Affairs, Politics/Government, Public/Social Administration, Race Relations, Third World, Autobiography/Memoirs. **Career:** Government of Fiji, assistant district commissioner for Palestine, 1946-48, administrative officer and clerk to executive and legislative councils, 1949-52; British colonial administrator, 1946-74; Government of Tonga, secretary, 1953-56; British South Pacific Office, commissioner, 1966-70; Fiji high commission, counselor and deputy high commissioner, 1970-74; Commonwealth Fund for Technical Cooperation, director of finance and field personnel services, 1974-79; Government of the British Virgin Islands, financial secretary and deputy governor, 1980-85; Government of St. Helena, budgetary aid and finance adviser, 1985-87; Commonwealth Consultants Ltd., chairman, 1985-96; Fulcrum Advertising Associates, director, 1987; Royal Institute of Public Administration, director of studies of financial management in government, 1989-; The Independent, contributor. Writer. **Publications:** Official Record of the Royal Visit to Tonga, 1954; Low Income Housing in the West Indies, 1958; The Friendly Islanders: A Story of Queen Salote and Her People, 1967; (ed.) A Guide to Pitcairn Island, 2nd ed., 1970; Treason at 10: Fiji at the Crossroads, 1989; The New Friendly Islanders, 1993; St. Helena: The Island, Her People and Their Ship, 1993; Treasured Islands: The British Virgins and Beyond, 2002. **Address:** South Rigg, 115 Kippington Rd., Sevenoaks, KT TN13 2LW, England.

BAIN, Trevor. American (born United States), b. 1931?. **Genres:** Business/Trade/Industry, Economics, Technology. **Career:** University of Arizona, assistant professor of economics, 1964-67; University of Michigan, visiting associate professor of economics, Institute of Industrial and Labor Relations, research associate, 1967-69; City University of New York, Queens College, associate professor of economics, 1969-74; University of Alabama, professor of labor economics and industrial relations, 1974-2000, Human Resources Institute, director, 1974-2000, John R. Miller professor of management, 1983-93, professor emeritus of management, 2000-. Writer. **Publications:** Defense Manpower and Contract Termination, 1968; Labor Market Experience of Engineers During Periods of Changing Demand, 1974; Banking the Furnace: Restructuring of the Steel Industry in Eight Countries, 1992. Contributor to journals. **Address:** Human Resource Institute, University of Alabama, PO Box 870225, Tuscaloosa, AL 35487-0225, U.S.A. **Online address:** tbain@cba.ua.edu

BAINS, William. British (born England), b. 1955. **Genres:** Technology, Science Fiction/Fantasy, Biology. **Career:** Stanford University, postdoctoral research fellow, 1982-85; University of Bath, Avon, lecturer in biochemistry, 1985-88; PA Consulting Group, technology consultant, 1988-96; Merlin Biosciences, specialist, 1996-2000; Imperial College, visiting professor, 1999; Cauis College, visiting fellow; Amedis Pharmaceuticals Ltd., founder, 1999-2002; Delta G Ltd., founder, 2002-; Choracle Ltd., chairman and co-founder, 2003-; University of Cambridge, senior associate faculty, 2006. Writer. **Publications:** Genetic Engineering for Almost Everybody, 1987; (with J. Raggett) Artificial Intelligence from A to Z, 1991; Biotechnology from A to Z, 1993, 3rd ed., 2004; Venture Capital and the European Biotechnology Industry, 2008. Contributor to scientific journals. **Address:** 101 Beechwood Ave., Melbourn, Royston, HM SG8 6DP, England. **Online address:** william@rufus-scientific.com

BAIR, Deirdre. American (born United States), b. 1935. **Genres:** Writing/Journalism, Biography, Autobiography/Memoirs, Photography. **Career:** Freelance journalist, 1957-69; University of Pennsylvania, assistant professor of English, 1976-; The Ohio State University, visiting professor and writer-in-residence; Macquarie University, visiting professor and writer-in-residence; Bennington College, visiting professor and writer-in-residence; New York University Institute for the Humanities, professor of contemporary literature and culture. Writer. **Publications:** BIOGRAPHIES: Samuel Beckett, 1978; Simone de Beauvoir, 1990; Anaïs Nin, 1995; Jung, 2003, new ed., 2005; Saul Steinberg, 2012. OTHERS: Calling It Quits: Late-Life Divorce and Starting Over, 2007. Contributor to journals. **Address:** Elaine Markson Literary Agency Inc., 44 Greenwich Ave., New York, NY 10011, U.S.A. **Online address:** deirdre_bair@earthlink.net

BAIRD, Alison. Canadian (born Canada), b. 1963?. **Genres:** Children's Fiction, Novels, Young Adult Fiction. **Career:** Writer. **Publications:** The Dragon's Egg, 1994; White as the Waves: A Novel of Moby Dick, 1999; The Hidden World, 1999; The Wolves of Woden, 2001; The Witches of Willowmere, 2002; The Warding of Willowmere, 2004; The Stone of the Stars, 2004; The Empire of the Stars, 2004; The Wyrd of Willowmere, 2005; The Archons of the Stars (Dragon Throne), 2005. SHORT FICTION: Changeling Child, 1993; The Dragon Door, 1993; Dragon Pearl, 1994; The Empty Sky, 1995; Moon Maiden, 1998; The Doom of Planet D, 2001; Walking with Wolves, 2005. Works appear in anthologies. Contributor to magazines. **Address:** Sternig & Byrne Literary Agency, 2370 S 107th St., Apt. 4, Milwaukee, WI 53227-2036, U.S.A.

BAIRD, Brian J. American (born United States), b. 1966. **Genres:** Librarianship. **Career:** Princeton University, assistant preservation librarian, conservator, 1991-94; University of Kansas, preservation librarian, 1994-2004; Heckman Bindery Inc. (now The HF Group L.L.C.), director of preservation services, 2004-; Bridgeport National Bindery Inc., vice president of library services. Writer. **Publications:** Preservation Strategies for Small Academic and Public Libraries, 2003; Library Collection Assessment through Statistical Sampling, 2004. **Address:** The HF Group L.L.C., 1010 N Sycamore St., North Manchester, IN 46962, U.S.A. **Online address:** brian_baird@heckmanbindery.com

BAIRD, Vanessa A. American (born United States), b. 1970. **Genres:** Law. **Career:** University of Colorado, Department of Political Science, assistant professor, 2000-07, associate professor of political science, 2007-, Faculty Teaching Excellence Program, director, 2006. Writer. **Publications:** Answering the Call of the Court: How Justices and Litigants Set the Supreme Court Agenda, 2007. Contributor of articles to periodicals and journals. **Address:** Department of Political Science, University of Colorado, Rm. 131D, Ketchum Arts and Sciences Bldg., PO Box 333, Boulder, CO 80309-0333, U.S.A. **Online address:** vanessa.baird@colorado.edu

BAITZ, Jon Robin. American (born United States), b. 1961. **Genres:** Plays/Screenplays, Social Sciences, Film. **Career:** Playwright, 1986-. Screenwriter and producer. **Publications:** The Film Society (play), 1987; Dutch Landscape, 1989; Substance of Fire, 1993; The End of the Day (play), 1993; Three Hotels (play), 1993; A Fair Country (play), 1996; Mizlansky/Zilinsky or Schmucks, 1998; Hedda Gabler, 2002; Ten Unknowns, 2003; Paris Letter: A Play in Two Acts, 2005. **Address:** Creative Artists Agency, 9830 Wilshire Blvd., Beverly Hills, CA 90212-1825, U.S.A.

BAJORIA, Paul. British (born England), b. 1964. **Genres:** Children's Fiction, Mystery/Crime/Suspense, Horror. **Career:** British Broadcasting Corp., radio producer, 1989. Writer. **Publications:** The Printer's Devil, 2005; Rastros De Tinta, 2005; Schwarze Spuren, 2005; L'Apprendista, 2005; The God of Mischief, 2006; Il Re degli Inganni, 2006; The City of Spirits, 2007. **Address:** Christopher Little Literary Agency, Eel Brook Studios, 125 Moore Park Rd., London, SW6 4PS, United Kingdom. **Online address:** paul.bajoria@bbc.co.uk

BAJWA, Rupa. Indian (born India), b. 1976?. **Genres:** Novels, Young Adult Fiction, Literary Criticism And History. **Career:** Writer. **Publications:** The Sari Shop, 2004. **Address:** c/o Author Mail, W.W. Norton & Co., 500 5th Ave., New York, NY 10110-0017, U.S.A.

BAKALIAN, Anny. American/Lebanese (born Lebanon), b. 1951. **Genres:** Sociology, Anthropology/Ethnology, Mystery/Crime/Suspense, Military/Defense/Arms Control. **Career:** American University of Beirut, sociology instructor, 1978-81; College of Notre Dame of Maryland, assistant professor of sociology, 1989-2001; Diocese of Armenian Church in America, consultant, 1991-93; St. Nersess Armenian Seminary, teacher, 1993; CUNY Graduate Center, Middle East and Middle Eastern American Center, associate director; TAMKEEN-Center for Arab American Empowerment, founding member and president, 2009. Writer. **Publications:** Armenian-Americans: From Being to

Feeling Armenian, 1993; (with M. Bozorgmehr) Backlash 9/11: Middle Eastern and Muslim Americans Respond, 2009. **Address:** MEMEAC Graduate Center, CUNY Graduate Ctr., 6304.24 Rm., 365 5th Ave., New York, NY 10016-4309, U.S.A. **Online address:** abakalian@gc.cuny.edu

BAKER, Alan. British (born England), b. 1939. **Genres:** Mathematics/Statistics. **Career:** University of Cambridge, Trinity College, fellow, 1964-, director of studies in mathematics, 1968-74, Centre for Mathematical Sciences, Department of Pure Mathematics and Mathematical Statistics, professor of pure mathematics, 1974-2006, professor emeritus of pure mathematics, 2006- . Writer and mathematician. **Publications:** Transcendental Number Theory, 1975; A Concise Introduction to the Theory of Numbers, 1984; (with G. Wustholz) Logarithmic Forms and Diophantine Geometry, 2007. EDITOR: (with D.W. Masser) Transcendence Theory: Advances and Applications, 1977; New Advances in Transcendence Theory, 1988; (with B. Bollobas and A. Hajnal) A Tribute to Paul Erdos, 1990. **Address:** Centre for Mathematical Sciences, University of Cambridge, Wilberforce Rd., Cambridge, CB CB3 0WB, England. **Online address:** a.baker@dpmms.cam.ac.uk

BAKER, Barbara. British (born England), b. 1952. **Genres:** Literary Criticism And History, Poetry, Homes/Gardens, Children's Fiction, Film, Theatre. **Career:** River Wye Booksellers, owner of antiquarian bookshop, 1977-79; Central Casting Ltd., casting agent, 1983-92; Waterstones Bookshop, bookseller, 1993-94; Oxford University Press, editor, 1995-98; Hong Kong Philharmonic Orchestra, editor, 1998-2000; freelance writer, 2000-. **Publications:** Shanghai: Electric and Lurid City, 1998; (with M. Slavick) Round: Poems and Photographs of Asia, 2000; Chinese Ink, Western Pen: Stories of China, 2000; Let the Credits Roll: Interviews with Film Crew, 2003; Why We Garden: Stories of a British Obsession, 2004; (ed.) Way We Write: Interviews with Award-winning Writers, 2006; (ed.) Backstage Stories, 2007; Dream Gardens of England, 2010. Contributor to magazines. **Address:** 8 Lower Mall, London, GL W6 9DJ, England. **Online address:** barbara.baker@spitfireuk.net

BAKER, Barbara. American (born United States), b. 1947. **Genres:** Children's Fiction, Animals/Pets. **Career:** Writer and educator. **Publications:** Third Grade Is Terrible, 1989; N-O Spells No!, 1990; Oh, Emma, 1991; Staying with Grandmother, 1994; The William Problem, 1994; Little Martin, 2003; Anna's Book, 2004; Anna Shares, 2004. DIGBY AND KATE SERIES: Digby and Kate, 1988; Digby and Kate Again, 1989; Digby and Kate and the Beautiful Day, 1998; Digby and Kate 1, 2, 3, 2004. SATURDAY SERIES: One Saturday Morning, 1994; One Saturday Afternoon, 1999; One Saturday Evening, 2007. **Address:** Dutton Children's Books, 375 Hudson St., New York, NY 10014-3657, U.S.A. **Online address:** barbaraabaker@yahoo.com

BAKER, Calvin. American (born United States), b. 1972?. **Genres:** Novels, Young Adult Fiction. **Career:** People Magazine, staff writer; Milton Avery Graduate School of the Arts, faculty; Bard College, Milton Avery Graduate School of the Arts, faculty; Columbia University, faculty; Life Magazine, staff. **Publications:** Naming the New World: A Novel, 1997; Once Two Heroes, 2003; Dominion, 2006. Contributor to periodicals. **Address:** People Weekly, 1271 6th Ave., New Time & Life Bldg., Rockefeller Ctr., New York, NY 10020, U.S.A.

BAKER, Christina Looper. American (born United States), b. 1939. **Genres:** Women's Studies And Issues, Biography, History, Autobiography/Memoirs. **Career:** Durham High School, English teacher, 1961-63; University of Maine-Bangor, assistant professor of English, 1978-84, associate professor, 1985-92, professor of English, 1993-2000; University of Maine-Augusta, professor of English, Writer. **Publications:** (With C.B. Kline) The Conversation Begins: Mothers and Daughters Talk About Living Feminism, 1996; In a Generous Spirit: A First-Person Biography of Myra Page, 1996. **Address:** Department of English, University of Maine-Augusta, Belfast Hall, 46 University Dr., Augusta, ME 04330-9410, U.S.A. **Online address:** cbaker@maine.edu

BAKER, Christopher W. American (born United States), b. 1952. **Genres:** Information Science/Computers, Technology, Education, Reference. **Career:** Brandslinger Naming Group, founder, creative director and chief executive officer, 1999-. Writer. **Publications:** Computer Illusion in Film and TV, 1994; Scientific Visualization: The New Eyes of Science, 1994; Let There Be Life!: Animating with the Computer, 1997; Virtual Reality: Experiencing Illusion, 2000; A New World of Simulators: Training with Technology, 2001; Robots among Us: The Challenges and Promises of Robotics, 2002; Quel avenir pour le capital social?, 2004. Contributor to periodicals. **Address:** Brandslinger Naming Group, 8770 Cider Springs Rd., Sebastopol, CA 95472-2521, U.S.A. **Online address:** inquiries@brandslinger.com

BAKER, Deb. American (born United States), b. 1953. **Genres:** Mystery/Crime/Suspense. **Career:** Writer. **Publications:** GERTIE JOHNSON MURDER MYSTERIES: Murder Passes the Buck, 2006; Murder Grins and Bears It, 2007; Murder Talks Turkey, 2008; Murder Bites the Bullet, forthcoming. DOLLS TO DIE FOR MYSTERY SERIES: Dolled Up for Murder, 2006; Goodbye Dolly, 2007; Dolly Departed, 2008; Ding Dong Dead, 2008. QUEEN BEE MYSTERIES AS HANNAH REED: Buzz Off, 2010; Mind Your Own Beeswax, 2011; Plan Bee, 2012. **Address:** North Lake, WI , U.S.A. **Online address:** debbkr1@gmail.com

BAKER, Deirdre. Canadian (born Canada), b. 1955?. **Genres:** Novels, Children's Fiction, Education. **Career:** Toronto Star, children's book reviewer, 1998-; Horn Book, children's book reviewer; University of Toronto, assistant professor of English. Writer. **Publications:** (With K. Setterington) A Guide to Canadian Children's Books in English, 2003; Becca at Sea (novel), 2007. Contributor to books. **Address:** Department of English, University of Toronto, 170 Saint George St., Toronto, ON M5R 2M8, Canada. **Online address:** df.baker@utoronto.ca

BAKER, Ellen. American (born United States), b. 1975?. **Genres:** Novels. **Career:** Curator and writer. **Publications:** Keeping the House: A Novel, 2007; I Gave My Heart to Know This: A Novel, 2011. **Address:** Marly Rusoff & Associates Inc., PO Box 524, Bronxville, NY 10708-0524, U.S.A.

BAKER, Elna. American (born United States), b. 1982?. **Genres:** Autobiography/Memoirs. **Career:** Writer and actress. **Publications:** The New York Regional Mormon Singles Halloween Dance (memoir), 2009. Contributor of articles to magazines. **Address:** New York, NY , U.S.A. **Online address:** elnabaker@elnabaker.com

BAKER, Geoffrey. British (born England), b. 1970. **Genres:** History. **Career:** University of London, Royal Holloway College, lecturer, 2005-. Writer. **Publications:** Imposing Harmony: Music and Society in Colonial Cuzco, 2008. Contributor of articles to journals. Works appear in anthologies. **Address:** Department of Music, Royal Holloway College, University of London, Egham, SR TW20 0EX, England. **Online address:** geoff.baker@rhul.ac.uk

BAKER, Hugh D(avid) R(oberts). British (born England), b. 1937. **Genres:** Anthropology/Ethnology, Cultural/Ethnic Topics, Language/Linguistics. **Career:** University of London, School of Oriental and African Studies, lecturer in Chinese, 1967-80, reader in modern Chinese, 1980-90, professor of Chinese, 1990-2002, dean (interface), 2001-04, professor emeritus, 2002-; Hong Kong Government, Chinese language training adviser, 1974-75; Chinese University of Hong Kong, professor of humanities, 2005-07. Writer. **Publications:** The Five Great Clans of the New Territories of Hong Kong, 1966; A Chinese Lineage Village: Sheung Shui, 1968; (ed.) City in Late Imperial China, 1977; Chinese Family and Kinship, 1979; Ancestral Images: A Hong Kong Album, 1979; More Ancestral Images: A Second Hong Kong Album, 1980; Ancestral Images Again: A Third Hong Kong Album, 1981; (with P.Y.L. Ng) New Peace County: A Chinese Gazetteer of the Hong Kong Region, 1983; The Overseas Chinese, 1987; (with S. Feuchtwang) An Old State in New Settings: Studies in the Social Anthropology of China in Memory of Maurice Freedman, 1991; (with P.C. T'ung) Chinese in Three Months, 1993; (with P.K. Ho) Teach Yourself Cantonese, 1995; (with P.K. Ho) Cantonese: A Complete Course for Beginners, 1996; (with P.C. T'ung) Chinese in Three Months, 1999; (with P.C. T'ung) Speak Chinese with Millions: The Language of Everyday Conversation, 2010; (with P.K. Ho) Complete Cantonese, 2010. **Address:** GL , England. **Online address:** hb3@soas.ac.uk

BAKER, Jeannie. Australian/British (born England), b. 1950. **Genres:** Children's Fiction, Art/Art History, Environmental Sciences/Ecology, Film, Travel/Exploration, Picture/Board Books, Young Adult Fiction. **Career:** Author, illustrator, artist, designer and filmmaker. **Publications:** Grandfather, 1977; Grandmother, 1978; Millicent, 1980; One Hungry Spider, 1981; Home in the Sky, 1984; Where the Forest Meets the Sea, 1987; Window, 1991; The Story of Rosy Dock, 1995; The Hidden Forest, 2000; Belonging in US as Home, 2004; Mirror, 2010. Contributor to periodicals. **Address:** Walker Books Australia, PO Box 22, Newtown, Sydney, NW 2042, Australia.

BAKER, John F. American (born United States), b. 1962. **Genres:** History. **Career:** Verizon Wireless, inventory specialist and call center supervisor. Independent historian and writer. **Publications:** The Washingtons of Wessyngton Plantation: Stories of My Family's Generational Journey to Freedom, 2009. **Address:** U.S.A. **Online address:** john@johnbakerbooks.com

BAKER, Kevin (Breen). American (born United States), b. 1958. **Genres:** Novels, Graphic Novels, Adult Non-fiction, Young Adult Fiction. **Career:** Gloucester Daily Times, staff writer, 1971-80; Foundation Center, compiler, 1980-85; Public Securities Association, freelance writer, 1986-87; freelance writer, 1988-; American Heritage, columnist, 1998-2007; Harper's Magazine, contributing editor. **Publications:** Sometimes You See It Coming, 1993; (with H. Evans and G. Buckland) American Century, 1998; Dreamland, 1999; Paradise Alley: A Novel, 2002; Strivers Row, 2006; Luna Park, 2009. Contributor to books and periodicals. **Address:** The Dunow, Carlson, and Lerner Literary Agency, 27 W 20th St., Ste. 1107, New York, NY 10011, U.S.A.

BAKER, Kyle. American (born United States), b. 1965. **Genres:** Graphic Novels, Children's Fiction, Young Adult Fiction, Art/Art History, Illustrations, Humor/Satire. **Career:** Kyle Baker Publishing, founder. Writer and illustrator. **Publications:** GRAPHIC NOVELS SELF-ILLUSTRATED: The Cowboy Wally Show, 1988; Why I Hate Saturn, 1993; You Are Here, 1999; What We Learned Today (graphic), 2001; Call (graphic), 2001; King David, 2002; Undercover Genie: The Irreverent Conjurings of an Illustrative Aladdin, 2003; My Special Plan, forthcoming. OTHERS: (with A. McGruder and R. Hudlin) Birth of a Nation: A Comic Novel, 2004; Plastic Man on the Lam!, 2004; Kyle Baker, Cartoonist, 2005; The Bakers: Do These Toys Belong Somewhere?, 2006; (contrib.) Scary Summer, 2007; Nat Turner, 2008; How to Draw Stupid and Other Essentials of Cartooning, 2008. **Address:** c/o Author Mail, DC Comics, 1700 Broadway, New York, NY 10019, U.S.A. **Online address:** kylebaker@kylebaker.com

BAKER, Larry. American (born United States), b. 1947?. **Genres:** Novels, Children's Fiction. **Career:** Iowa City, city councilor, 1993-; WaldenBooks, part-time staff. Novelist and educator. **Publications:** The Flamingo Rising (novel), 1997; (with B. Lyles) It's a God Thing: Inspiring Stories of Life-Changing Friends, 2000; Athens, America, 2004; A Good Man: A Novel, 2009; Love and Other Delusions, 2012. **Address:** 1217 Rochester Ave., Iowa City, IA 52245-3129, U.S.A. **Online address:** flamingo@avalon.net

BAKER, Lise S. American (born United States) **Genres:** Novels. **Career:** L. S. Baker Investigations, investigator. Writer. **Publications:** The Losers' Club, 2000. **Address:** L. S. Baker Investigations, PO Box 2298, Granite Bay, CA 95746-2298, U.S.A. **Online address:** bakerpi@jps.net

BAKER, Lori. American (born United States), b. 1962. **Genres:** Novels, Novellas/Short Stories, Medicine/Health, Psychiatry, Psychology, inspirational/Motivational Literature. **Career:** Massachusetts General Hospital, science writer in psychiatry research, 1989-90; Brown University, senior technical writer in psychiatry, 1990-91, adjunct lecturer in creative writing, 1993-; Wheaton College, visiting assistant professor of English, 1992-95; Baylor University, assistant professor of anthropology, associate professor of anthropology. **Publications:** (Ed. with R.P. Galea and B.F. Lewis) AIDS and IV Drug Abusers: Current Perspectives (nonfiction), 1988; (contrib.) Relapse: Conceptual, Research and Clinical Perspectives, 1988; Scraps (fiction), 1995; Crazy Water: Six Fictions (short stories), 1996. (contrib.) Feminist Literary Theory: A Dictionary, 1997. Contributor of articles to magazines and journals. **Address:** Department of Anthropology and Sociology, Baylor University, Rm. C313, Baylor Science Bldg., Marrs McLean Science, Ste. 300A, Waco, TX 76798-7024, U.S.A. **Online address:** lori_baker@baylor.edu

BAKER, Margaret J(oyce). British (born England), b. 1918. **Genres:** Children's Fiction, Biography. **Career:** Writer. **Publications:** The Fighting Cocks, 1949; Nonsense Said the Tortoise, 1949 in US as Homer the Tortoise, 1950; Four Farthings and a Thimble, 1950; A Castle and Sixpence, 1951; Benbow and the Angels, 1952; The Family That Grew and Grew, 1952; Treasure Trove, 1952; Homer Sees the Queen, 1953; The Young Magicians, 1954; Lions in the Potting Shed, 1954 in US as Lions in the Woodshed, 1955; The Wonderful Wellington Boots, 1955; Acorns and Aerials, 1956; Anna Sewell and Black Beauty, 1957; The Bright High Flyer, 1957; Tip and Run, 1958; Homer Goes to Stratford, 1958; The Magic Sea-shell, 1960; The Birds of Thimblepins, 1960; Homer in Orbit, 1961; Into the Castle, 1962; The Cats of Honeytown, 1962; Away Went Galloper, 1962; Castaway Christmas, 1963; Cut Off from Crumpets, 1964; The Shoe Shop Bears, 1965; Homer Goes West, 1965; Hannibal and the Bears, 1966; Bears Back in Business, 1967; Porterhouse Major, 1967; Hi-Jinks Joins the Bears, 1968; Home from the Hill, 1969; Snails' Place, 1970; Teabag and the Bears, 1970; The Boots and the Ginger Bears, 1972; The Sand Bird, 1973; Prickets Way, 1973; Last Straw, 1974; Lock Stock and Barrel, 1974; Sand in Our Shoes, 1976; The Gift Horse, 1982; Catch as Catch Can, 1983; Beware of the Gnomes, 1985; The Waiting Room Doll, 1986; Fresh Fields for Daisy, 1987; Controlling Movement: A Therapeutic Approach to Early Intervention, 1991; (with F.C. Eeles) St. Andrew's Church Old Cleeve: With the Architectural Description of the Church, 1995; Slow Coach: In a Nutshell, forthcoming. **Address:** Prickets, Old Cleeve, Minehead, SM TA24 6HW, England.

BAKER, Mark. American (born United States), b. 1950. **Genres:** Military/Defense/Arms Control, Law, Education, Business/Trade/Industry. **Career:** Freelance writer, 1979-. **Publications:** Nam: The Vietnam War in the Words of the Men and Women Who Fought There, 1981; I Hate Videos: Today the Arcade, Tomorrow the World, 1982; Cops: Their Lives in Their Own Words, 1985; Women: American Women in Their Own Words, 1990; What Men Really Think about Women, Love, Sex, and Themselves, 1992; Sex Lives: A Sexual Self-Portrait of America, 1994; Bad Guys: America's Most Wanted in Their Own Words, 1996; Insider's Book of Business School Lists, 1997; Insider's Book of Law School Lists, 1997; D.A.: Prosecutors in Their Own Words, 1999. Contributor to periodicals. **Address:** c/o Esther Newberg, International Creative Management, 825 8th Ave., 26th Fl., New York, NY 10019, U.S.A.

BAKER, Maureen. New Zealander/Canadian (born Canada), b. 1948. **Genres:** Sociology, Human Relations/Parenting. **Career:** Acadia University, assistant professor of sociology, 1974-76; University of Toronto, assistant professor of sociology, 1978-83; Parliament of Canada, senior researcher, 1984-90; McGill University, associate professor, professor of social work, 1990-97; University of Auckland, Department of Sociology, professor of sociology, 1998-, head of sociology, 1998-2004. Writer. **Publications:** (Co-ed.) Families: Changing Trends in Canada, 1984, 6th ed., 2009; What Will Tomorrow Bring? (monograph), 1985; Aging in Canadian Society, 1988; Families in Canadian Society, 1989, 2nd ed., 1993; (ed.) Canada's Changing Families: Challenges to Public Policy, 1994; Canadian Family Policies, 1995; (with D. Tippin) Poverty, Social Assistance, and the Employability of Mothers: Restructuring Welfare States, 1999; Families, Labour and Love, 2001; Restructuring Family Policies, 2006; Choices and Constraints in Family Life, 2007, 2nd ed. 2010. **Address:** Department of Sociology, University of Auckland, Rm. 952, Human Sciences Bldg., 9th Fl., 10 Symonds St., Auckland, 1010, New Zealand. **Online address:** ma.baker@auckland.ac.nz

BAKER, Nena. American (born United States), b. 1959. **Genres:** Medicine/Health, Sciences, Philosophy. **Career:** GQ, assistant copy editor; TV Guide, staff; United Press Intl., reporter and editor; Oregonian, staff, 1991-99; Arizona Republic, staff, 1999-2003. **Publications:** The Body Toxic: How the Hazardous Chemistry of Everyday Things Threatens Our Health and Well-Being, 2008. Contributor to periodicals. **Address:** Farrar, Straus & Giroux, 18 W 18th St., New York, NY 10011, U.S.A. **Online address:** nenabaker@thebodytoxic.com

BAKER, Paul R(aymond). American (born United States), b. 1927. **Genres:** Architecture, Area Studies, History, Young Adult Non-fiction, Social Sciences, Economics, Cultural/Ethnic Topics. **Career:** Encyclopedia Americana, staff writer and editor, 1952-55; Harvard University, history tutor, 1957-58, 1959-60; California Institute of Technology, instructor, assistant professor, 1960-63; University of California, lecturer in history, 1963-64; University of Oregon, lecturer in history, 1964-65; New York University, fellow, assistant professor, professor of history, director of American Civilization Program, 1965, now professor emeritus. **Publications:** The John Harvard Library, 1963; The Fortunate Pilgrims: Americans in Italy, 1800-1860, 1964; (with W. Hall) The American Experience, vol. I, The American People, 1976, vol. II, (with W.H. Hall) Growth of a Nation, 1977, vol. III, Organizing a Democracy, 1979, vol. IV, The American Economy, 1979, vol. V, The United States in World Affairs, 1979; Richard Morris Hunt, 1980, rev. ed., 1986; Master Builders, 1985; The Architecture of Richard Morris Hunt, 1986; Stanny: The Gilded Life of Stanford White, 1989; Insight and Inspiration II: The Italian Presence in American Art, 1860-1920, 1992; Greenwich Village: Culture and Counterculture, 1993. EDITOR: Views of Society and Manners in America, by F.W. D'Arusmont, 1963; The Atomic Bomb: The Great Decision, 1968, rev. ed., 1976. **Address:** Department of History, New York University, 53 Washington Sq. S, 7th Fl., New York, NY 10012, U.S.A. **Online address:** prb2@nyu.edu

BAKER, Raymond W. American (born United States), b. 1935?. **Genres:** Economics. **Career:** Global Financial Integrity, director. Writer and consultant. **Publications:** Capitalism's Achilles Heel: Dirty Money and How to Renew the Free-Market System, 2005. Contributor to periodicals. **Address:** Center for International Policy, 1717 Massachusetts Ave. NW, Ste. 801, Global Financial Integrity, 1319 18th St. NW, Ste. 200, Washington, DC 20036-2000, U.S.A. **Online address:** rbaker@gfip.org

BAKER, Raymond William. American (born United States), b. 1942. **Genres:** Theology/Religion, Politics/Government, Social Commentary, History, Social Sciences. **Career:** Williams College, professor of political science, 1973-96, Department Of Political Science, chair, 1988-91, third century professor of international relations, 1993, Williams Executive Program, professor of international and comparative politics, 1993-96, Williams College and the American University in Cairo, Williams-in-Cairo Program, director, 1985-96, Global Studies Program, co-founder and chair, African and Middle Eastern Studies Program, chair, 1992-96; American University in Cairo, adjunct professor of political science, 1990-; Trinity College, professor of international politics, 1996-, dean of faculty, 1996-99, director of Middle East Studies, 2001-03, 2004-; Global Partnership for the International University of Iraq, co-chair, 2003-; Sandia Laboratories, consultant; Pacific Sierra Research Corp., consultant; Rockefeller Foundation, consultant; Georgetown Center for International and Strategic Studies, consultant; U.S. State Department, consultant; U.S. Department of Defense, consultant; media analyst; International Council for Middle East Studies, director, 2009-; The Brussells Tribunal, advisory board, 2010-. Writer. **Publications:** NONFICTION: Egypt's Uncertain Revolution under Nasser and Sadat, 1978; Sadat and After: Struggles for Egypt's Political Soul, 1990; (contrib.) The Gulf War and the New World Order: International Relations in the Middle East, 1994; (contrib.) Political Islam: Revolution, Radicalism, or Reform?, 1997; (contrib.) Globalization: Policies, Challenges, and Responses, 1999; Islam without Fear: Egypt and the New Islamists, 2003; (contrib.) Religion, Social Practice and Contested Hegemonies: Reconstructing the Public Sphere in Muslim Majority Societies, 2005. Contributor to journals. **Address:** Department of International Studies, Trinity College, Hartford, CT 06106, U.S.A. **Online address:** raymond.baker@trincoll.edu

BAKER, Richard A(llan). American (born United States), b. 1940. **Genres:** Politics/Government, History, Biography. **Career:** Holy Apostles College, assistant professor of history, 1965-67; Library of Congress, American History for Legislative Reference Service, specialist, 1968-69; U.S. Senate, acting curator, 1969-70, director of Historical Office, 1975-, historian, now historian emeritus; Government Research Corp., director of research, 1970-75; University of Oklahoma, Carl Albert Congressional Studies Center, board director, 1980-; University of Maryland, adjunct instructor, 1983-84; University of Texas, Walter Prescott Webb lecturer, 1984; Cornell University, adjunct professor, 1987-90, 1992; Everett Dirksen Congressional Leadership Research Center, board director, 1988-; American University, Center for Presidential and Congressional Studies, board director, 1988-. Writer. **Publications:** (With F.R. Valeo) The United States Senate: A Historical Bibliography, 1977; Conservation Politics: The Senate Career of Clinton P. Anderson, 1985; The Senate of the United States: A Bicentennial History, 1988; 200 Notable Days: Senate Stories, 1787-2002, 2006; Traditions of the United States Senate, 2007. EDITOR: Proceedings: Conference on Research Use and Disposition of Senators' Papers, 1979; (with W. Wollf and contrib.) Historical Almanac of the United States Senate, 1989; (with R.H. Davidson) First among Equals: Senate Leaders of the Twentieth Century, 1991. Works appear in anthologies. **Address:** Historical Office, U.S. Senate, Washington, DC 20510-7108, U.S.A. **Online address:** historian@sec.senate.gov

BAKER, Richard E. American (born United States), b. 1950. **Genres:** Literary Criticism And History, Young Adult Fiction. **Career:** Front Range Community College, liberal arts, instructor, 1985-90; University of Colorado, instructor, 1988-91; Metropolitan State College, adjunct faculty, 1989-94; Adams State College, visiting assistant professor of Spanish, 1994-95, associate professor of English, 1995, professor of English. Writer. **Publications:** The Dynamics of the Absurd in the Existentialist Novel, 1993. Contributor to periodicals. **Address:** Department of Arts & Letters, Adams State College, 208 Edgemont Blvd., Rm. ES325, Alamosa, CO 81102, U.S.A. **Online address:** rebaker@adams.edu

BAKER, Rosalie F. American (born United States), b. 1945. **Genres:** History, Biography, Autobiography/Memoirs, Young Adult Non-fiction, Children's Fiction, Literary Criticism And History, Reference. **Career:** Ivy Close Publishing Co., co-founder, 1980-; Classical Calliope (now Calliope Magazine), co-editor and writer, 1981-. Publisher. **Publications:** WITH C.F. BAKER III: The Classical Companion, 1988; Myths and Legends of Mount Olympos, 1992; Classical Ingenuity: The Legacy of the Ancient Greek and Roman Architects Artists and Inventors, 1992; Ancient Greeks: Creating the Classical Tradition, 1997; Ancient Romans: Expanding the Classical Tradition, 1998; Ancient Egyptians: People of the Pyramids, 2001; (and W. Rembert) Don't Hold Me Back: My Life and Art, 2003; Ancient Greece: A Student Companion, 2006. OTHER: In a Word: 750 Words and Their Fascinating Stories and Origins, 2003. **Address:** 150 Page St., New Bedford, MA 02740, U.S.A. **Online address:** cfbakeriii@meganet.net

BAKER, Russell (Wayne). American (born United States), b. 1925. **Genres:** Autobiography/Memoirs, Humor/Satire, Literary Criticism And History, Biography, Young Adult Fiction, History. **Career:** Baltimore Sun, staff, 1947-53, London bureau chief, 1953-54; New York Times, Washington Bureau, staff, 1954-98; Public Broadcasting Service, host, through 2004. Writer. **Publications:** Washington: City on the Potomac, 1958; An American in Washington, 1961; No Cause for Panic, 1964; Baker's Dozen, 1964; All Things Considered, 1965; Our Next President: The Incredible Story Of What Happened In The 1968 Elections, 1968; Poor Russell's Almanac, 1972; (contrib.) Better Times, 1975; The Upside Down Man, 1977; So This Is Depravity, 1980; (co-author) Home Again, Home Again, 1979; Growing Up, 1982; The Rescue of Miss Yaskell and Other Pipe Dreams, 1983; (ed.) The Norton Book of Light Verse, 1986; (co-author) Inventing the Truth: The Art and Craft of Memoir, 1987, rev. ed., 1998; The Good Times, 1989; There's a Country in My Cellar: The Best of Russell Baker, 1990; (ed.) Russell Baker's Book of American Humor, 1993; Looking Back, 2002. **Address:** New York Review of Books, 435 Hudson St., Ste. 300, New York, NY 10014, U.S.A.

BAKER, Sharlene. American (born United States), b. 1954. **Genres:** Novels, Plays/Screenplays, Literary Criticism And History. **Career:** Paper Journey Press, founder, 1988-. Writer and lecturer. **Publications:** Finding Signs (novel), 1990; (ed.) As You May Never See Us Again: The Civil War Letters of George and Walter Battle, 4th North Carolina Infantry: Coming of Age on the Front Lines of the War between the States, 1861-1865, 2004; As You May Never See Us Again: The Civil War Letters of George and Walter Battle, 4th North Carolina Infantry, 2010. Contributor to periodicals. **Address:** Paper Journey Press, PO Box 1575, Wake Forest, NC 27588, U.S.A. **Online address:** sh9876@gmail.com

BAKER, Stephen. (Stephen L. Baker). American (born United States), b. 1955?. **Genres:** Business/Trade/Industry, Technology. **Career:** Black River Tribune, managing editor, 1978-80; Daily Journal, reporter, 1983-85; El Paso Herald-Post, reporter, 1985-86; BusinessWeek, Mexico bureau chief, 1987-92, Pittsburgh bureau chief, 1992-98, Europe technology correspondent, 1998-2002, acting senior editor, information technology, 2002-03, senior writer, 2003-. **Publications:** The Numerati, 2008. Contributor of journalism to magazine. **Address:** Montclair, NJ , U.S.A. **Online address:** steve@sbakermedia.com

BAKER, Stephen L. *See* **BAKER, Stephen.**

BAKER, Stuart Eddy. American (born United States), b. 1938. **Genres:** History, Theology/Religion, Young Adult Fiction. **Career:** Hunter College (now Hunter College of the City University of New York), adjunct lecturer, 1972-75, assistant professor of theatre history, 1977-82; Florida State University, College of Visual Arts, School of Theatre, associate professor, 1977-82, professor of theatre and drama, 1982-2004, professor emeritus, 2004-. Writer. **Publications:** Georges Feydeau and the Aesthetics of Farce, 1981; Bernard Shaw's Remarkable Religion: A Faith That Fits the Facts, 2002. **Address:** School of Theatre, College of Visual Arts, Florida State University, 600 W College Ave., Tallahassee, FL 32306-1058, U.S.A.

BAKER, Susan P. American (born United States) **Genres:** Novels. **Career:** Women's Resource and Crisis Center of Galveston County, founder & board member, 1970; Galveston County Community Supervision and Corrections Department Board, member. Writer. **Publications:** NONFICTION: (with B. O'Neill and R.S. Karpf) The Injury Fact Book, Lexington Books, 1992; Murdered Judges of the Twentieth Century: And Other Mysterious Deaths, 2003; Heart of Divorce: Advice from a Judge, 2004; MYSTERY NOVELS: My First Murder, 1989; Death of a Prince, 2005; The Sweet Scent of Murder, 2007. **Address:** Susan P. Baker Campaign, 4917 Alamo Dr., Galveston, TX 77552-4528, U.S.A. **Online address:** snana456@austin.rr.com

BAKER, Tom. American (born United States), b. 1959?. **Genres:** Money/Finance, Law. **Career:** United States Court of Appeals, First Circuit, law clerk, 1986-87; Covington and Burling, attorney, 1987-91; Neighborhood Legal Services Program, staff attorney, 1989; Office of Independent Counsel-Walsh, associate counsel, 1991-92; University of Miami Law School, associate professor, 1992-97; Hebrew University of Jerusalem, visiting law professor, 1996-97, Fulbright visiting law professor, 2001-02; University of Connecticut School of Law, Connecticut Mutual professor of law, 1997-2008, Insurance Law Center, director, 1997-2008; Yale Law School, visiting lecturer, 2002; University of Pennsylvania Law School, professor of Law, 2008-09, William Maul Measey Professor of Law and Health Sciences, 2009-, Department of the Wharton School, chair, 2009-, deputy dean, 2010-. Writer. **Publications:** (Ed. with J. Simon) Embracing Risk: The Changing Culture of Insurance and Responsibility, 2002; Insurance Law and Policy: Cases, Materials and Problems, 2003, 2nd ed., 2008; The Medical Malpractice Myth, 2005; (with S.J. Griffith) Ensuring Corporate Misconduct: How Liability Insurance Undermines Shareholder Litigation, 2011. **Address:** University of Pennsylvania Law School, 3400 Chestnut St., Philadelphia, PA 19104, U.S.A. **Online address:** tombaker@law.upenn.edu

BAKER, William. American (born United States), b. 1954. **Genres:** Poetry, Young Adult Fiction, Business/Trade/Industry, Economics, History. **Career:** College of the Ozarks, Beacon Hill Summer Stock Theater, associate director, 1979-81; Avila University, associate professor, 1982-96, chair of theater board, 1987-96. Writer. **Publications:** Celtic Mythological Influences on American Theatre, 1750-1875, 1994; A Solitary Frost, 1998; The Orphans of Carmarthen, 2001; Vault of the Griffin, 2004; The Crimson, forthcoming. Contributor to periodicals. **Address:** c/o Author Mail, Xlibris, 436 Walnut St., 11th Fl., Philadelphia, PA 19106-3703, U.S.A. **Online address:** drwbuck@comcast.net

BAKER, William. American/British (born England), b. 1944. **Genres:** Literary Criticism And History, Autobiography/Memoirs, Bibliography, Reference. **Career:** City Literary Institute, lecturer in English, 1967-71; Thurrock Technical College, lecturer, 1969-71; Ben-Gurion University of the Negev, lecturer, 1971-77; Hebrew University of Jerusalem, lecturer, 1973-75; University of Kent, lecturer, 1977-78; West Midlands College of Higher Education, senior lecturer, 1978-85; Pitzer College, visiting professor, 1981-82; Clifton College, housemaster, 1986-89; Northern Illinois University, associate professor, 1989-94, professor of English and library studies, 1994-2003, presidential research professor, 2004-07, distinguished research professor, 2007-; Sheffield Hallam University, Department of English, visiting professor of English, 2005-08; University Jean Moulin, Humanities Research Centre, 2006-07. Writer, consultant and advisor. **Publications:** Harold Pinter, 1973; Critics on George Eliot, 1973; George Eliot and Judaism, 1975; Some George Eliot Notebooks, 4 vols., 1976-85; The George Eliot-George Henry Lewes Library, 1977, vol. IV, forthcoming; The Libraries of George Eliot and G.H. Lewes, 1981; Shakespeare: The Merchant of Venice, 1985; Shakespeare: Antony and Cleopatra, 1985, rev. ed., 1991; (with J. Kimber and M.B. Kinch) F.R. Leavis and Q.D. Leavis: An Annotated Bibliography, 1989; The Early History of the London Library, 1992; (with K. Womack) Recent Work in Critical Theory, 1989-1995, 1996; 20th-Century Bibliography and Textual Criticism, 2000; Wilkie Collins's Library, 2002; (with J.C. Ross) George Eliot: A Bibliographical History, 2002; Harold Pinter: A Bibliographical History, 2005; (with E. Traherne and H. Lucas) The English Association: One Hundred Years On, 2006; A Wilkie Collins Chronology, 2007; A Critical Companion to Jane Austen, 2008; Harold Pinter, 2008; (with G.N. Wachs) Tom Stoppard, 2010; (with K. Womack) The Facts on File Companion to Shakespeare, 2011; The Literature of the Fox, forthcoming. EDITOR: The Letters of George Henry Lewes, 3 vols., 1995-1999; (with J.H. Alexander) Sir Walter Scott: Tales of a Grandfather; The History of France, 1996; (with J. Wolfreys) Literary Theories, 1996; New Dictionary of National Biography, 1996; (with K. Womack) Pre-Nineteenth-Century British Book Collectors and Bibliographers, 1997; (with W.M. Clarke) The Letters of Wilkie Collins, 1999; Year's Work in English Studies, 2001; G. Eliot, Felix Holt, the Radical, 2000; A Companion to the Victorian Novel, 2002; Fod Madox Ford: The Good Soldier, 2003; (with I.B. Nadel) Redefining the Modern, 2004; (with A. Gasson, G. Law and P. Lewis) The Public Face of Wilkie Collins, 2005; (with A.G.V.D. Broek) The Complete Shorter Poetry of George Eliot, 2005; (with B. Vickers) The Merchant of Venice, 2005; (with A. Gasson) Lives of Victorian Literary Figures V: Wilkie Collins, 2007; (with M. Lister) David Daiches: A Celebration of His Life and Work, 2008; Critical Companion to Jane Austen: A Literary Reference to Her Life and Work, 2008, A Wilkie Collins Chronology, 2008, Harold Pinter: Writers' Lives, 2008; William Shakespeare: Writers' Lives, 2009; (with J.R. Shumaker) Leonard Merrick: A Forgotten Novelist's Novelist, 2009. Contributor of articles to periodicals. **Address:** Department of English, University Libraries, Northern Illinois University, FO 207B, 1425 W Lincoln Hwy., DeKalb, IL 60115-2868, U.S.A. **Online address:** wbaker@niu.edu

BAKER-CRISTALES, Beth. American (born United States) **Genres:** History, Travel/Exploration. **Career:** California State University, assistant professor, 2002-. Writer, educator and anthropologist. **Publications:** Salvadoran Migration to Southern California: Redefining El Hermano Lejano, 2004. Contributor of articles and reviews to journals. **Address:** California State University, 5151 State University Dr., Los Angeles, CA 90032-8530, U.S.A. **Online address:** bbakerc@calstatela.edu

BAKEWELL, Kenneth (Graham Bartlett). *See* Obituaries.

BAKKE, Odd Magne. *See* **BAKKE, O. M.**

BAKKE, O. M. (Odd Magne Bakke). Norwegian (born Norway), b. 1962?. **Genres:** Theology/Religion, History, Politics/Government. **Career:** School of Mission and Theology, associate professor, 1998-2005, professor, 2005-. Writer. **Publications:** (As Odd Magne Bakke) "Concord and Peace": A Rhetorical Analysis of the First Letter of Clement with an Emphasis on the Language of Unity and Sedition, 2001; When Children Became People: The Birth of Childhood in Early Christianity, 2005. Contributor of articles to journals. **Address:** Misjonshgskolen, Misjonsveien 12, Stavanger, 4024, Norway. **Online address:** odd.magne.bakke@mhs.no

BAKKEN, Kerry Neville. American (born United States), b. 1972?. **Genres:** Young Adult Fiction. **Career:** Allegheny College, assistant professor, Environmental Writing Track, director. Writer. **Publications:** Necessary Lies, 2006. **Address:** Department of English, Allegheny College, Rm. 218 Oddfellows, 520 N Main St., Meadville, PA 16335, U.S.A. **Online address:** kerry.bakken@allegheny.edu

BAKKER, Robert T. American (born United States), b. 1945. **Genres:** Novels, Zoology, Sciences, Animals/Pets. **Career:** University of Colorado Museum, adjunct curator; Johns Hopkins University, associate professor, 1976-84; Tate Museum, dinosaur curator; Dinamation International Society and Sega Genesis, consultant; Houston Museum of Natural Science, visiting curator of paleontology. Writer. **Publications:** The Dinosaur Heresies: New Theories Unlocking the Mystery of the Dinosaurs and Their Extinction, 1986; Raptor Red (novel), 1995; The Great Dinosaur Debate, 2001; Raptor Pack, 2003; Maximum Triceratops, 2004; Dinosaurs!, 2005; Dactyls!: Dragons of the Air, 2005; Prehistoric Monsters!, 2008; Dino Babies, 2010; Dinosaurs: In Your Face!, 2012. **Address:** Houston Museum of Natural Science, 5555 Hermann Park Dr., Houston, TX 77030-1799, U.S.A.

BAL, Mieke (Maria Gertrudis). Dutch (born Netherlands), b. 1946. **Genres:** Literary Criticism And History, Theology/Religion, Women's Studies And Issues. **Career:** University of Amsterdam, research assistant, 1969-70, professor of theory of literature, 1991-, chair of the theory of literature, 1991-, Amsterdam School of Cultural Analysis (a research center) founder and co-director, 1993-98; University of Utrecht, Women's Studies Program, co-founder, 1981, director, 1982-; Harvard University Divinity School, research associate and visiting lecturer, 1985-86; University of Rochester, Department of Foreign Languages, professor of comparative literature and director of graduate studies, 1987-91, Susan B. Anthony professor of women's studies, 1987-91, Department of Art and Art History, professor of comparative literature and art history, 1990-91, adjunct visiting professor, 1991-96, Program in Comparative Arts (now Visual and Cultural Studies) co-founder and director; Royal Netherlands Academy of Arts and Sciences, academy professor, 2005-. Writer. **Publications:** NONFICTION: Complexite d'un roman populaire, 1974; Narratologie: Essaissur la signification narrative dans quatre romans modernes, 1977, trans. as Narratology: Introduction to the Theory of Narrative, 1985, 3rd ed., 2009; De Theorievan vertellen en verhalen, 1978, 3rd ed., 1985; (with J. van Luxemburg and W. Weststeijn) Inleiding in de literatuurwetenschap, 1981, rev. 5th ed., 1987; (with F. van Dijk and G. van Ginneken) En Sara in haar tent lachte: Patriarchaat en verzet in bijbelverhalen, 1984; Femmes imaginaires: L'Ancien Testament au risque d'une narratologie critique, 1986 in US as Lethal Love: Feminist Literary Readings of Biblical Love Stories, 1987; (with Luxemburg and Weststeijn) Over literatuur, 1987; Het Rembrandt Effect: Visies op kijken, 1987; Death and Dissymmetry: The Politics of Coherence in the Book of Judges, 1988; Murder and Difference: Gender, Genre, and Scholarship on Sisera's Death, 1988; Verkrachting verbeeld: Seksueel geweld in cultuur gebracht, 1988; On Storytelling: Essays in Narratology, 1991; Reading Rembrandt: Beyond the Word-Image Opposition: The Northrop Frye Lectures in Literary Theory, 1991; On Meaning-Making: Essays in Semiotics, 1994; Double Exposures: The Subject of Cultural Analysis, 1996; Images litt Traires, ou comment lire visuellement Proust, 1997; Schweben zwischen Gegenstand und Ereignis: Begegnungen mit Lili Dujourie/ Hovering Between Thing and Event: Encounters with Lili Dujourie, 1998; Jeannette Christensen's Time, 1998; Quoting Caravaggio: Contemporary Art, Preposterous History, 1999; Looking In: The Art of Viewing, 2001; Ann Veronica Janssens: Lichtspiel, 2001; Louise Bourgeois's Spider: The Architecture of Art-writing, 2001; Résurgences baroques, 2001; (contrib.) George Deem and Peter Angelo Simon, 2001; Mieke Bal Kulturanalyse, 2002; Travelling Concepts in the Humanities: A Rough Guide, 2002; (ed.) Narrative theory, 2004; Marthe Wéry, 2005; (ed.) The Artemisia Files, 2005; A Mieke Bal Reader, 2006; (contrib.) Take Your Time, 2007; (co-author) We All Laughed at Christopher Columbus, 2007; Balthus: Works and Interview, 2008; Loving Yusuf: Conceptual Travels from Present to Past, 2008; (with J. Sparagana) Sleeping Beauty, 2008; (ed. with E.V. Alphen and C. Smith) The Rhetoric Of Sincerity, 2009; (contrib.) Jussi Niva, 2010; Of What One Cannot Speak, 2010. **Address:** University of Amsterdam, Spuistraat 210, Amsterdam, 1012 VT, Netherlands. **Online address:** m.g.bal@uva.nl

BALAGURU, P(erumalsamy) N(aidu). American/Indian (born India), b. 1947. **Genres:** Engineering, Technology, Sciences. **Career:** Coimbatore Institute of Technology, associate lecturer, 1970-73; University of Illinois, teaching and research assistant, 1975-77; Rutgers University, assistant professor, 1977-82, associate professor, 1982-88, professor of civil engineering, 1988-2002, distinguished professor, 2002-, Graduate Program, director; Northwestern University, visiting professor, 1990; National Science Foundation, program director, 2001-04; American Concrete Institute, fellow. Writer. **Publications:** (With S.P. Shah) Fiber Reinforced Cement Composites, 1992; (with A.Nanni and J. Giancaspro) FRP Composites for Reinforced and Prestressed Concrete Structures: A Guide to Fundamentals and Design for Repair and Retrofit, 2009. EDITOR: (with V. Ramakrishnan) Computer Use for Statistical Analysis of Concrete Test Data, 1987; Thin Reinforced Concrete Products and Systems, 1994; (with A. Naaman and W. Weiss) Concrete: Material Science to Application: A Tribute to Surendra P. Shah, 2002. Contributor to books and periodicals. **Address:** Department of Civil & Environmental Engineering, Rutgers University, CAIT Bldg., Rm. 114, 623 Bowser Rd., Piscataway, NJ 08854-8014, U.S.A. **Online address:** balaguru@rci.rutgers.edu

BALAJI, Murali. American (born United States), b. 1979?. **Genres:** Novels. **Career:** Pioneer Press, journalist, 2000-02; News Journal, journalist; Temple University, instructor; Pennsylvania State University, lecturer & doctoral fellow; Maruthi Consulting Inc., founder. Writer. **Publications:** House of Tinder, 2003; The Professor and the Pupil: The Politics of W.E.B. Du Bois and Paul Robeson, 2007; (ed. with A. Nair) Desi Rap: Hip-Hop and South Asian America, 2008. Contributor to periodicals and magazines. **Address:** State College, PA , U.S.A. **Online address:** mub172@psu.edu

BALAKRISHNAN, N. Canadian/Indian (born India), b. 1956. **Genres:** Mathematics/Statistics, Engineering, Sciences. **Career:** McMaster University, post-doctoral fellow, 1982-83, research fellow, 1985-86, assistant professor, 1986-89, associate professor, 1989-95, professor of mathematics and statistics, 1995-, Graduate Program in Statistics, coordinator, 1993-96; University of Manitoba, post-doctoral fellow, 1983; University of Guelph, visiting faculty, 1984-85; University of Waterloo, visiting associate professor, 1992-93, visiting professor, 1996; Ain-Shams University, visiting professor, 1999; Statpro Consulting, proprietor; Universite de Le Havre, visiting professor, 2001; International Indian Statistical Association, vice president, 2001-03, president, 2004-06; Ankara University, visiting professor, 2002; King Saud University, visiting professor, 2003, distinguished visiting university professor, 2010-; Bowling Green State University, visiting distinguished Eugene Lukacs professor, 2005; University of Texas, visiting professor, 2006; Universidad Complutense Madrid, visiting distinguished Santalo lecturer, 2006; National Central University, visiting professor, 2007, adjunct professor, 2007-; Ren-Min University, visiting professor, 2007, distinguished visiting university professor, 2009-; University of Berne, visiting professor, 2008; University of Bologna, visiting professor, 2009; University of Vienna, visiting professor, 2009. Writer. **Publications:** (With M.L. Tiku and W.Y. Tan) Robust Inference, 1986; (with B.C. Arnold) Relations, Bounds, and Approximations for Order Statistics, 1989; (with A.C. Cohen) Order Statistics and Inference: Estimation Methods, 1991; (with B.C. Arnold and H.N. Nagaraja) A First Course in Order Statistics, 1992; (with N.L. Johnson and S. Kotz) Continuous Univariate Distributions, vol. I, 1994, vol. II, 1995; (with H.L. Harter) The CRC Handbook of Tables for the Use of Order Statistics in Estimation, 1996; The CRC Tables for the Use of Order Statistics in Tests of Hypotheses, 1997; (with H.L. Harter) The CRC Handbook of Tables for the Use of Range, 1997; (with N.L. Johnson and S. Kotz) Discrete Multivariate Distributions, 1997; (with W.W.S. Chen) CRC Handbook of Tables for Order Statistics from Inverse Gaussian Distributions with Applications, 1997; (with B.C. Arnold and H.N. Nagaraja) Records, 1998; (with R. Aggarwala) Progressive Censoring: Theory, Methods and Applications, 2000; (with N.L. Johnson and S. Kotz) Continuous Multivariate Distributions, vol. I, 2000; (with M.V. Koutras) Runs and Scans with Applications, 2002; (with V.B. Nevzorov) A Primer on Statistical Distribution, 2003; (co-author) Extreme Value and Related Models with Applications in Engineering and Science, 2005; (with H.K.T. Ng) Precedence-Type Tests and Applications, 2006; (with B.C. Arnold and H.N. Nagaraja) First Course in Order Statistics, 2008; (with C. Lai) Continuous Bivariate Distributions, 2nd ed., 2009; Methods and Applications of Statistics in the Life and Health Sciences, 2010; Methods and Applications of Statistics in Business, Finance, and Management Science, 2010. EDITOR: Handbook of the Logistic Distribution, 1992; Recent Advances in Life-Testing and Reliability, 1995; CRC Handbook of Applied Industrial Statistics, 1996; (with A.P. Basu) The Exponential Distribution: Theory, Methods and Applications, 1996; (with N.L. Johnson) Advances in the Theory and Practice of Statistics, 1997; (with S. Panchapakesan) Advances in Statistical Decision Theory and Applications, 1997; Advances in Combinatorial Methods and Applications to Probability and Statistics, 1997; (with C.R. Rao) Order Statistics: Theory and Mrthods, 1998; (with J. Glaz) Scan Statistics and Applications, 1999; (with V.B. Melas and S. Ermakov) Advances in Stochastic Simulation Methods, 2000; (with C.R. Rao) Advances in Reliability, 2001; (with I.A. Ibragimov and V.B. Nevzorov) Asymptotic Methods in Probability and Statistics with Applications, 2001; Advances on Methodological and Applied Aspects of Probability and Statistics, 2002; (with N. Kannan and M.R. Srinivasan) Statistical Methods and Practice: Recent Advances, 2003; (with C.R. Rao) Advances in Survival Analysis, 2004; (with N. Kannan and H.N. Nagarjuna) Advances in Ranking and Selection, Multiple Comparisons and Reliablility: Methodology and Applications, 2005; (with S. Kotz, C. Read and B. Vidakovic) Encyclopedia of Statistical Sciences, 2nd ed., 2006; (with E. Castillo and J.M. Sarabia) Advances in Distribution Theory, Order Statistics, and Inference, 2006; (co-ed.) Advances in Degradation Modeling, 2010; Methods and Applications of Statistics: Engineering, Quality Control, and the Physical Sciences, 2011. **Address:** Department of Mathematics and Statistics, McMaster University, 1280 Main St. W, Hamilton, ON L8S 4K1, Canada. **Online address:** bala@mcmaster.ca

BALBIRER, Nancy. American (born United States), b. 1965. **Genres:** Autobiography/Memoirs. **Career:** Pasita (wine bar), co-owner. Writer. **Publications:** I Slept with Jack Kerouac, 2001; Take Your Shirt off and Cry: A Memoir of Near-fame Experiences, 2009. **Address:** New York, NY , U.S.A.

BALBO, Ned Clark. American (born United States), b. 1959. **Genres:** Poetry, Essays, Music, Popular Culture, Literary Criticism And History. **Career:** Dundalk Community College, Writing Center, adjunct instructor, 1986-87; Towson University, adjunct instructor in composition, 1987-; Kirkwood Community College, adjunct instructor in composition, 1989-90; Loyola University, adjunct instructor, 1990-99, adjunct assistant professor, 2000-06, adjunct associate professor of writing, 2006-. Writer. **Publications:** Galileo's Banquet, 1998; Lives of the Sleepers, 2005; Something Must Happen, 2009; The Trials of Edgar Poe and Other Poems, 2010. **Address:** Department of Writing, Loyola University Maryland, 4501 N Charles St., Baltimore, MD 21210, U.S.A. **Online address:** nbalbo@loyola.edu

BALCH, James F. American (born United States), b. 1933. **Genres:** Medicine/Health, Food And Wine, Sports/Fitness. **Career:** Self-employed surgeon, 1960-96; Health Counseling Inc., physician and author, 1997-, president. Writer. **Publications:** WITH P.A. BALCH: Nutritional Outline for the Professional, 1987; Designer Diets for the Healing Force Within: Medically Proven Designed Diets for Permanent Weight Loss and Better Health, 1987; Prescription for Cooking and Rx Dietary Wellness, 1987; Prescription for Nutritional Healing, 1990, 3rd ed., 2000; Prescription for Cooking, 1991; Rx Prescription for Cooking and Dietary Wellness, 1992; Prescription for Nutritional Healing: An A-to-Z Guide to Supplements, 1998; Prescription for Dietary Wellness: Using Foods to Heal, 1998. OTHERS: The Super Antioxidants: Why They Will Change the Face of Healthcare in the 21st Century, 1998; (with M. Walker) Heartburn and What to Do about It: A Guide to Overcoming the Discomforts of Indigestion Using Drug Free Remedies, 1998; 10 Natural Remedies That Can Save Your Life, 1999, rev. ed., 2000; (with M. Stengler) Prescription for Natural Cures: A Self-Care Guide for Treating Health Problems with Natural Remedies, Including Diet and Nutrition, Nutritional Supplements, Bodywork and More, 2004, rev. ed. as Prescription for Natural Cures: A Self-Care Guide for Treating Health Problems With Natural Remedies Including Diet, Nutrition, Supplements and Other Holistic Methods, 2011; (with M. Stengler and R. Young-Balch) Prescription for Drug Alternatives: All-Natural Options for Better Health without the Side Effects, 2008. **Address:** 99 Trophy Club Dr., Trophy Club, TX 76262, U.S.A. **Online address:** balch33@aol.com

BALDASSARRI, Mario. Italian (born Italy), b. 1946. **Genres:** Economics, Social Sciences, Sociology, Money/Finance. **Career:** University of Turin, assistant professor of economics, 1970-74; Catholic University of Milan, associate professor of economics, 1974-78; University of Bologna, professor of economics, 1979-88; University of Rome, professor of economics, 1988-; Italian Government, deputy minister of economy and finance, 2001-06, Italian Republic, senator, Finance Commission of the Senate, president. Writer. **Publications:** Saggi di programmazione economica, 1977; Spesa Pubblica, Inflazione eCrescita: Uno Schema Teorico Per Un'economia Mista, 1979; (co-author) Partecipazione Ed Efficienza Nell'organizzazione e Gestione Dei ServiziSociali, 1980; Deficit, Debito Pubblico Ed Effetti Sul Sistema Economico: Aspetti Teorici Ed Evidenze Empiriche, 1990; La Politica Industriale in Italia Dal '45 Ad Oggi: Fasi, Intrecci, Prospettive '90, 1990; The Italian Economy: Heaven or Hell, 1990; (co-author) Risparmio, Accumulazione, Sviluppo, 1991; (with P. Annunziato) Il Ciclo Economico: Teoria, Evidenza Empiricae Politiche Congiunturali, 1992; (co-author) Problemi Fiscali Nell'europa Del Mercato Unico, 1992; Le Privatizzazioni Nell'est Europeo: Fondamenti Teorici ed Analisi Empiriche, 1992; World Savings, Inflation and Growth, 1992; The Italian Economy: A New Miracle, 1993; (co-author) Finanza, Moneta e Cambi: Il Sistema Internazionale Tra Nuova Integrazione E Neo-Protezionismo, 1994; (co-author) Equità, Efficienza E Crescita: Il Futuro Del Welfare State, 1995; L'italia Che Produce: Mappa Del Sistema Produttivo Italiano E Degli Strumenti Per Far Affari InItalia, 1996; Il Secondo Miracolo Possibile: Dalla Sconfitta Dell'inflazione Al Progetto Per La Piena Occupazione, 1999; (with S. Cararo) Cuba: Orgoglio e Pregiudizi, 2005; (with P. Capretta) The World Economy Towards Global Disequilibrium: American-Asian Indifference and European Fears, 2007; Un Anno Di Governo Prodi 5 bugie, 3 falsi, 5 tesoretti, 2007. EDITOR: Global Disequilibrium in the World Economy, 1992; (with L. Paganetto and E.S. Phelps) International Economic Interdependence, Patterns of Trade Balances and Economic Policy Coordination, 1992; Keynes and the Economic Policies of the 1980s, 1992; Oligopoly and Dynamic Competition: Firm, Market and Economic System, 1992; Industrial Policy in Italy, 1945-1990, 1993; (with R. Mundell) The Single Market and Monetary Unification, 1993; World Saving, Prosperity and Growth, 1993; (with L. Paganetto and E.S. Phelps) Privatization Processes in Eastern Europe: Theoretical Foundations and Empirical Results, 1993; (with R. Mundell and J. McCallum) Debt, Deficit and Economic Performance, 1993; Industrial Policy in Italy, 1945-1990, 1993; (with R. Mundell) Eastern Europe's Transition to a Market Economy, 1993; (with R. Mundell) Building a New Europe, 1993; (with L. Paganetto and E.S. Phelps) International Differences in Growth Rates: Market Globalization and Economic Areas, 1994; (with M.D. Matteo and R. Mundell) International Problems of Economic Interdependence, 1994; (with P. Annunziato) Is the Economic Cycle Still Alive? Theory, Evidence, and Policies, 1994; (with P. Roberti) Fiscal Problems in the Single-Market Europe, 1994; (with F. Modigliani) The Italian Economy: What Next?, 1995; (with C. Imbriani and D. Salvatore) The International System between New Integration and Neo-Protectionism, 1996; (with L. Paganetto and E.S. Phelps) The 1990s Slump: Causes and Cures, 1996; (with L. Paganetto and E.S. Phelps) Equity, Efficiency, and Growth: The Future of the Welfare State, 1996; Maffeo Pantaleoni: At the Origin of the Italian School of Economics and Finance, 1997; (with A. Macchiati and D. Piacentino) The Privatization of Public Utilities: The Case of Italy, 1997; (with L. Paganetto and E.S. Phelps) Institutions and Economic Organization in the Advanced Economies: The Governance Perspective, 1998; (with M. Bagella and L. Paganetto) Financial Markets: Imperfect Information and Risk Management, 2001; (with P. Ciocca) Roots of the Italian School of Economics and Finance: From Ferrara (1857) to Einaudi (1944), 2001; (with L. Lambertini) Antitrust, Regulation, and Competition, 2003; (with B. Chiarini) Studies in Labour Markets and Industrial Relations, 2003; The New Welfare: Unemployment and Social Security in Europe, 2003; How to Reduce Unemployment in Europe, 2003; (with F. Busato) Full Employment and High Growth in Europe: A New Cycle of Reforms to Play a Leading Role in the New World Economy, 2004. Contributor to magazines, newspapers and periodicals. **Address:** Department of Economics, University of Rome, Via del Castro Laurenziano 9, Rome, I-00161, Italy. **Online address:** mario.baldassarri@senato.it

BALDASTY, Gerald J. American (born United States) **Genres:** Writing/Journalism. **Career:** University of Washington, professor of communications and adjunct professor of women's studies, 1974-, Department of Communication, chair, vice provost, The Graduate School, dean, adjunct professor of women studies and of American ethnic studies, UW Teaching Academy, director. Writer. **Publications:** The Commercialization of News in the Nineteenth Century, 1992; E.W. Scripps and the Business of Newspapers, 1999; Vigilante Newspapers: A Tale of Sex, Religion, and Murder in the Northwest, 2005. Contributor to journals. **Address:** Department of Communications, University of Washington, CMU 233, PO Box 353740, Seattle, WA 98195-3740, U.S.A. **Online address:** baldasty@uw.edu

BALDEOSINGH, Kevin. Trinidadian (born Trinidad and Tobago), b. 1963. **Genres:** Novels, Romance/Historical, Humor/Satire. **Career:** Education Ministry, secondary school teacher, 1985-88; Trinidad Express Newspapers, editorial writer, 1989-92; Trinidad Guardian Newspapers, assistant features editor, 1992-96; freelance writer, 1996-. **Publications:** NOVELS: The Autobiography of Paras P, 1996; Virgin's Triangle, 1997; The Ten Incarnations of Adam Avatar, 2004; (with R. Mahase) Caribbean History for CSEC, 2011. **Address:** 3 Ali Lane Freeport Todd's Rd., Upper Carapichaima, Freeport, 675-6515, Trinidad and Tobago. **Online address:** kbaldeosingh@hotmail.com

BALDERSTON, Daniel. American (born United States), b. 1952. **Genres:** Translations, Literary Criticism And History, Bibliography, Novellas/Short Stories, History, Gay And Lesbian Issues. **Career:** Earlham College, assistant professor, 1980-82; Wittenberg University, assistant professor, 1982-83; Tulane University, assistant professor, 1983-87, associate professor, 1987-93, professor of Spanish and Portuguese, 1993-98; Universidade de Sao Paulo, visiting professor, 1987-; Universidade Estadual de Campinas, visiting professor, 1993-; Universidad de Buenos Aires, visiting professor, 1994-; University of California, visiting professor, 1998-; University of Bergen, visiting professor, 1998-; University of Iowa, professor of Spanish and Portuguese, 1999-2007; Universidad de La Habana, visiting professor, 2002-; Universidad Javeriana, visiting professor, 2004-; University of Pittsburgh, Mellon professor of Hispanic languages and literatures, 2008-, director of graduate studies, Variaciones Borges, editor. **Publications:** El precursor velado: R.L. Stevenson en la obra de Borges, 1985; The Literary Universe of Jorge Luis Borges: An Index to References and Allusions to Persons, Titles and Places in His Writings, 1986; (comp.) The Latin American Short Story: An Annotated Guide to Anthologies and Criticism, 1992; Out of Context: Historical Reference and the Representation of Reality in Borges, 1993; Borges: realidades y simulacros, 2000; El Deseo, enorme cicatriz luminosa: ensayos sobre homosexualidades latinoamericanas, 2004. TRANSLATOR: J. Bianco, Shadow Play and The Rats: Two Novellas, 1983; S. Oliver, Figari, 1984; S. Ocampo, Leopoldina's Dream, 1988; S. Molloy, Certificate of Absence, 1989; (and intro.) J.C. Onetti, Goodbyes and Stories, 1990; (and intro.) R. Piglia, Artificial Respiration, 1994; (with M. Benedetti) Blood Pact & Other Stories, 1997. OTHERS: (ed.) The Historical Novel in Latin America: A Symposium, 1986; (co-trans.) Ficción y política: la narrativa argentina durante elproceso militar, 1987; (ed. with D.J. Guy) Sex and Sexuality in Latin America, 1997; (with G. Gallo and N. Helft) Borges: Una Enciclopedia, 1999; (ed. with M. Gonzalez and A.M. Lopez) Encyclopedia of Contemporary Latin American and Caribbean Cultures, 2000, rev. ed., 2004; (ed.) Sexualidad y nación, 2000; (ed. with M. Schwartz) Voice-overs: Translation and Latin American Literature, 2002; (co-trans.) Escrito por los otros: Ensayos Sobre Los Libros deLuis Gusmán,

2004; (comp.) Literatura y Otras Artes En America Latina: Actas Del XXXIV Congreso del Instituto Internacional de Literatura Iberoamericana, 2004; Sexualidades en Disputa: Homosexualidades, Literatura y Medios de Comunicacion en America Latina, 2005; (ed.) Noé Jitrik Reader: Selected Essays on Latin American Literature, 2005; (comp.) Lecciones del Maestro: Homenaje A José Bianco, 2006; (ed. with F. Masiello) Approaches of Teaching Puig's Kiss of the Spider Woman, 2007; (ed.) Novelas cortas, 2009; Innumerables Relaciones: cómo Leer Con Borges, 2010. Contributor to periodicals and newspapers. **Address:** Department of Hispanic Literatures and Literatures, University of Pittsburgh, 1309G Cathedral of Learning, Pittsburgh, PA 15260, U.S.A. **Online address:** dbalder@pitt.edu

BALDWIN, Frank. American (born United States), b. 1963?. **Genres:** Novels, Mystery/Crime/Suspense. **Career:** Novelist and copy editor. **Publications:** Balling the Jack (novel), 1997; Jake & Mimi (novel), 2002. Contributor to periodicals. **Address:** c/o Author Mail, Simon & Schuster Inc., 1230 Ave. of the Americas, 11th Fl., New York, NY 10020-1513, U.S.A. **Online address:** shanerules@aol.com

BALDWIN, John. American (born United States), b. 1944. **Genres:** Novels, Young Adult Fiction, History. **Career:** Writer. **Publications:** Ice Pick, 1983; (with J.S. Marr) The Eleventh Plague: A Novel of Medical Terror, 1998; (with R. Powers) Last Flag Down: The Epic Journey of the Last Confederate Warship, 2007. Contributor to periodicals. **Address:** c/o John Talbot, Talbot Fortune Agency L.L.C., 980 Broadway, Ste. 664, Thornwood, NY 10594, U.S.A.

BALDWIN, Rosecrans. American (born United States), b. 1977?. **Genres:** Novels. **Career:** Morning News, co-founder and editor, 1999-. **Publications:** You Lost Me There, 2010. Contributor to periodicals. **Address:** Chapel Hill, NC , U.S.A. **Online address:** theinspectorlestrade@gmail.com

BALE, Don. American (born United States), b. 1937?. **Genres:** Money/Finance, Recreation. **Career:** Bale Books and Bale Publishers, president. Writer. **Publications:** Complete Guide for Profitable Coin Investing, 1963, 2nd ed. as Complete Guide for Profitable Coin Investing and Collecting, 1969; How to Invest in Singles, 1970; Fabulous Investment Potential of Singles, 1970; Fabulous Investment Potential of Uncirculated Singles, 1970; Fabulous Investment Potential of Liberty Walking Halves, 1971; A Gold Mine in Your Pocket, 1971; A Gold Mine in Gold, 1972; How to Invest in Uncirculated Singles, 1972; Out of Little Coins, Big Fortunes Grow, 1973, 3rd ed., 1982; (ed.) How to Find Valuable Old and Scarce Coins, 4th ed., 1980; The Fabulous Collecting and Investing Potential of U.S. Copper Cents, 2002. **Address:** 5121 St Charles Ave., Ste. 13, New Orleans, LA 70115-4900, U.S.A.

BALE, John R. British (born England), b. 1940. **Genres:** Sports/Fitness, Geography, Education. **Career:** Keele University, professor of sports geography; Aarhus University, visiting professor. Writer. **Publications:** (Ed. with N. Graves and R. Walford) Perspectives in Geographical Education, 1973; Industrial Estates: A Bibliography and Geographical Introduction, 1976; (ed. with D. Gowing) Geography and Football: The Use of Ideas from Football in the Teaching of Geography, 1976; The Development of Soccer as a Participant and Spectator Sport: Geographical Aspects, 1979; The Location of Manufacturing Industry: An Introductory Approach, 2nd ed., 1981; (with A. Coleman and M. Hewitt) Patterns on the Map: 3 Leeds and Rosedale/ Land Utilisation Survey Maps as Resources for Teaching and Learning, 1982; Sport and Place: A Geography of Sport in England, Scotland, and Wales, 1982; Patterns of Underdevelopment, 1982; Office Location, 1983; (ed. with C. Jenkins) Geographical Perspectives on Sport, 1983; (ed.) The Third World: Issues and Approaches: Papers Produced by a Working Party of the Geographical Association, 1983; Geography in the Primary School, 1987; Sports Geography, 1989; The Brawn Drain: Foreign Student-Athletes in American Universities, 1991; Sport, Space, and the City, 1993; Landscapes of Modern Sport, 1994; (ed.) Community, Landscape and Identity: Horizons in a Geography of Sports: Seminar on Space, Place, Landscape and Sport: New Directions in a Geography of Sport: Selected Papers, 1994; (ed. with J. Maguire) The Global Sports Arena: Athletic Talent Migration in an Interdependent World, 1994; (ed. with O. Moen) The Stadium and the City, 1995; (with J. Sang) Kenyan Running: Movement Culture, Geography, and Global Change, 1996; (ed. with C. Philo) Henning Eichberg, Body Cultures: Essays on Sport, Space, and Identity, 1998; Sportscapes, 2000; Sport, Space, and the City, 2001; Imagined Olympians: Body Culture and Colonial Representation in Rwanda, 2002; Sports Geography, 2003; (ed. with M. Cronin) Sport and Postcolonialism, 2003; Roger Bannister and the Four-Minute Mile, 2004; Running Cultures: Racing in Time and Space, 2004; (ed. with M.K. Christensen) Post-Olympism? Questioning Sport in the Twenty-first Century, 2004; (ed. with M.K. Christensen and G. Pfister) Writing Lives in Sport: Biographies, Life-Histories and Methods, 2004; (ed. with P. Vertinsky) Sites of Sport: Space, Place, Experience, 2004; Anti-sport Sentiments in Literature: Batting for the Opposition, 2007; (ed. with P.D. Howe) The Four-Minute Mile: Historical and Cultural Interpretations of a Sporting Barrier, 2008; (with A. Bateman) Sporting Sounds: Relationships between Sport and Music, 2009. Works appear in anthologies. Contributor to journals. **Address:** Department of Education, Keele University, Keele, ST ST5 5BG, England.

BALEN, Malcolm. British (born England), b. 1956. **Genres:** Biography, Politics/Government, History. **Career:** British Broadcasting Corp. (BBC), news trainee, 1978, regional journalist, 1980-82, news editor, 1994-97, executive editor, 1997-2000, editorial adviser, 2003-, senior news editor, senior editorial adviser, 2011; Manchester, regional journalist, 1980-82; Channel Four News/ Independent Television News (ITN), senior programme editor, 1989-94; Radio News Bulletin, executive editor, 1997-2000; Independent Television (ITV), head of news, 2000-03; Council of Europe, lecturer, 2003-; London News Network, head of news. **Publications:** Kenneth Clarke, 1994; A Very English Deceit: The Secret History of the South Sea Bubble and the First Great Financial Scandal, 2002 as The Secret History of the South Sea Bubble: The World's First Great Financial Scandal, 2003 as The King, the Crook and the Gambler: The True Story of the South Sea Bubble and the Greatest Financial Scandal in History, 2004; A Model Victory: Waterloo & the Battle for History, 2005. **Address:** British Broadcasting Corp., Television Ctr., Wood Ln., London, GL W12 7RJ, England. **Online address:** malcolm.balen@bbc.co.uk

BALES, Richard F. American (born United States), b. 1951. **Genres:** Novels, History. **Career:** Chicago Title Insurance Co., assistant vice president and assistant regional counsel, 1989-; Illinois Land Title Association, dean of title insurance school. Writer. **Publications:** The Great Chicago Fire and the Myth of Mrs. O'Leary's Cow, 2002; Cap Streeter: The Man Who Defied Chicago, forthcoming. Contributor to books and journals. **Address:** Chicago Title Insurance Co., 1725 S Naperville Rd., Ste. 100, Wheaton, IL 60189-5855, U.S.A. **Online address:** dbales@dickbales.com

BALESTER, Valerie M. American (born United States), b. 1952. **Genres:** Education, History, Cultural/Ethnic Topics. **Career:** Texas A&M University, Department of English, associate professor, 1988-2001, 2005-, Professor, director of English computer classroom, 1990-91, director of writing programs, 1995-2000, University Writing Center, executive director, 2001-, Writing Course Advisory Committee, chair, 2002-; International Writing Centers Association, director, 2008-; South Central Writing Centers Association, vice president, 2009-; Daedalus Group Inc., consultant. Writer. **Publications:** Cultural Divide: Case Studies of African American College-Level Writers, 1993; Holt Guide to Using Daedalus, 1995. EDITOR: (with B. Johnstone) Uses for Journal Keeping: An Ethnography of Writing in a University Science Class, 1994; (with M.H. Kells) Attending to the Margins: Writing, Researching, and Teaching on the Front Lines, 1999; (with M.H. Kells and V. Villanueva) Latino/a Discourses: On Language, Identity, and Literacy Education, 2004. Contributor to books and journals. **Address:** University Writing Center, Texas A&M University, 205D Blocker Bldg., PO Box 4227, College Station, TX 77843-5000, U.S.A. **Online address:** v-balester@tamu.edu

BALGASSI, Haemi. American/Korean (born Korea (South)), b. 1971?. **Genres:** Children's Fiction, Young Adult Fiction, History. **Career:** Writer. **Publications:** Peacebound Trains, 1996; Tae's Sonata, 1997. Contributor to magazines and journals. **Address:** c/o Author Mail, Clarion Books, 215 Park Ave. S, New York, NY 10003, U.S.A.

BALIAN, Lorna. American (born United States), b. 1929. **Genres:** Children's Fiction, Illustrations. **Career:** American Lace Co., artist, 1949-51. Author and illustrator, 1964-. **Publications:** SELF-ILLUSTRATED FOR CHILDREN: Humbug Witch, 1965; I Love You, Mary Jane, 1967; The Aminal, 1972; Where in the World is Henry?, 1972; Sometimes It's Turkey, Sometimes It's Feathers, 1973; Humbug Rabbit, 1974; The Sweet Touch, 1976; Bah! Humbug?, 1977; A Sweetheart for Valentine, 1979; Leprechauns Never Lie, 1980; Mother's Mother's Day, 1982; Humbug Potion: An A-B-Cipher, 1984; A Garden for a Groundhog, 1985; Amelia's Nine Lives, 1986; The Socksnatchers, 1988; Wilbur's Space Machine, 1990. **Address:** PO Box 107, Green Lake, WI 54941, U.S.A. **Online address:** leciabalian@gmail.com

BALIBAR, Sebastien. French (born France), b. 1947. **Genres:** Sciences, Physics. **Career:** école Normale Supérieure, researcher, 1970-83, director of research, 1985, 1992, 2008; Universität Konstanz, visiting professor, 1999; Harvard University, Loeb Lecturer, 1999-2000; Kyoto University, visiting professor, 2003. Writer and physicist. **Publications:** (Co-author) Demain, la physique, 2004; La pomme et l'atome, 2005; Je casse de l'eau, 2008; The Atom and the Apple: Twelve Tales from Contemporary Physics, 2008. Contributor of articles to books, journals and periodicals. **Address:** Directeur de Recherches au CNRS, Laboratoire de Physique Statistique de l'ENS, Rm. D8, 2nd Fl., 24 rue Lhomond, Paris, 75231, France. **Online address:** balibar@physique.ens.fr

BALINT, Ruth. Australian (born Australia) **Genres:** History, Young Adult Non-fiction. **Career:** SBS Television, reporter, 2004; ABC Radio National, producer of radio documentaries; University of New South Wales, School of History and Philosophy, lecturer, senior lecturer, Foundation Studies program, consultant. Writer. **Publications:** Troubled Waters: Borders, Boundaries and Possession in the Timor Sea, 2005; The Somerton Man: An Unsolved History, forthcoming. Contributor to periodicals. **Address:** School of History, University of New South Wales, Rm. No 345-Morven Brown, Sydney, NW 2052, Australia. **Online address:** r.balint@unsw.edu.au

BALIT, Christina. British (born England), b. 1961. **Genres:** Children's Non-fiction, Plays/Screenplays, Illustrations, History, Young Adult Fiction, Adult Non-fiction. **Career:** City and Guilds School of Art, tutor. Author. **Publications:** My Arabian Home: Leila and Mustapha's Story, 1988; (adapted) Atlantis: The Legend of a Lost City, 2000; (with J. Mitton) Once Upon a Starry Night: A Book of Constellation Stories, 2003; Escape from Pompeii, 2003; (with J. Mitton) Planet Gods: Myths and Facts About the Solar System, 2008. Illustrator of books by others. **Address:** Pym Lodge, Soles Hill Rd., Shottenden, KT CT4 8JU, England. **Online address:** christina@pymlodge.f9.co.uk

BALKEN, Debra Bricker. American/Canadian (born Canada), b. 1954. **Genres:** Art/Art History, Biography. **Career:** Independent curator, 1990-; Brown University, visiting associate professor, 1996-; Rhode Island School of Design, staff. Writer. **Publications:** John Marin's Berkshire landscapes: June 9 through August 4, 1985, the Berkshire Museum, 1985; Nancy Graves, Painting, Sculpture, Drawing, 1980-1985, 1986; Albert Eugene Gallatin and His Circle, 1986; Patricia Johanson: Drawings and Models for Environmental Projects, 1969-1986, 1987; (with D.M. Rothschild) Suzy Frelinghuysen and George L.K. Morris: American Abstract Artists: Aspects of Their Work and Collection, 1992; Philip Guston's Poem Pictures, 1994; (with B. Horrigan) Muntadas, 1994; (contrib.) Dimitri Hadzi, 1996; (with W.C. Agee and E.H. Turner) Arthur Dove, 1997; (contrib.) Edna Andrade, 1997; (contrib.) Ellen Lanyon, 1999; (ed.) Philip Guston's Poor Richard, 2001; (contrib.) The Park Avenue Cubists, 2002; Debating American Modernism: Stieglitz, Duchamp, and the New York Avant-Garde, 2003; Abstract Expressionism, 2005; (contrib.) Action/Abstraction, 2008; Dove/O'Keeffe: Circles of Influence, 2009; After Many Springs: Regionalism, Modernism, and the Midwest, 2009; (contrib.) John Moore, 2009; John Storrs: Machine-age Modernist, 2010; John Marin: Modernism at Midcentury, 2011. Contributor to books. **Address:** 183 Central St., Somerville, MA 02145, U.S.A. **Online address:** dbbalken@aol.com

BALL, Angela. American (born United States), b. 1952. **Genres:** Poetry. **Career:** University of Southern Mississippi, instructor, 1979-80, assistant professor, 1980-85, associate professor, 1985-91, professor of English, 1991-, Center for Writers, faculty, Mississippi Review, editor; University of Richmond, writer-in-residence; Le Chateau de Lavigny, writer-in-residence. **Publications:** Recombinant Lives (pamphlet), 1987; Vixie, 1988; Kneeling between Parked Cars, 1990; Quartet, 1995; Possession, 1995; The Museum of the Revolution, 1999; Night Clerk at the Hotel of Both Worlds, 2007; Thousands of Everything, forthcoming; (trans. with D. Pooey) J.C. Galeano, Amazonia, forthcoming. **Address:** Department of English, University of Southern Mississippi, 366 Liberal Arts Bldg., 118 College Dr., PO Box 5037, Hattiesburg, MS 39406, U.S.A. **Online address:** angela.ball@usm.edu

BALL, Donna Rochelle. Also writes as Taylor Brady, Donna Carlisle, Rebecca Flanders, Leigh Bristol, Donna Boyd. American (born United States), b. 1951. **Genres:** Romance/Historical, Young Adult Fiction. **Career:** Belle Books, co-owner and editorial director, 1999-. **Publications:** Summer Masquerade, 1982; Winners: A Love Story, 1982; Cry in the Woods, 1991; The Darkest Hour, 1992; Exposure, 1996; Just Before Dawn, 1997; Dark Angel, 1998; Sweet Tea and Jesus Shoes, 2000; Let's Dance: A Beginner's Guide to Dancing with Your Do, 2005; Rapid Fire: A Raine Stockton Dog Mystery, 2006; Smoky Mountain Tracks: A Raine Stockton Dog Mystery, 2006; Gun Shy, 2007; At Home on Ladybug Farm, 2009; Year on Ladybug Farm, 2009; Recipes From Ladybug Farm, 2010; Love Letters from Ladybug Farm, 2010; Keys to the Castle, 2011; Bone Yard, 2011; Silent Night, 2011; Christmas on Ladybug Farm, 2011. AS DONNA BOYD: The Passion, 1998, The Promise, 1999; The Alchemist, 2002; The Awakening, 2003; (ed. with E. Saccoman) Evolve Reach Admission Assessment Exam Review, 2nd ed., 2009; Renegade, 2011. AS DONNA CARLISLE: Under Cover, 1988; A Man Around the House, 1989; Interlude, 1989; Matchmaker, Matchmaker, 1990; For Keeps, 1991; The Stormriders, 1991; Cast Adrift, 1992; It's Only Make Believe, 1992; Stealing Savannah, 1994; The Message in the Miracles, 2003. AS REBECCA FLANDERS: (with L. Dano) Prom Twice in a Lifetime, 1983; A Matter of Trust, 1983; Falcone's Promise, 1983; Best of Friends, 1983; Morning Song, 1983; Falkone's Promise, 1984; Suddenly Love, 1984; Gilded Heart, 1984; Second Sight, 1984; Desert Fire, 1984; The Third Time, 1984; Daydreams, 1984; The Key, 1984; Silver Threads, 1984; A Modern Girl, 1984; The Growing Season, 1985; Easy Access, 1985; Prom Afterglow, 1985; Open Hands, 1985; Rainbows and Unicorns, 1985; Uncertain Images, 1985; The Last Frontier, 1985; The Straight Game, 1986; Minor Miracles, 1986; After the Storm, 1986; Satin Fires, 1986; Obsessions, 1986; Painted Sunsets, 1987; Search the Heavens, 1988; The Sensation, 1990; Earthbound, 1990; Under the Mistletoe, 1991; Yesterday Comes Tomorrow, 1992; Once Upon a Time, 1992; The Last Real Man, 1993; Sunchasers, 1993; Forever Always, 1994; Kissed by the Sea, 1994; Quinn's Way, 1994. MEN MADE IN AMERICA SERIES: After the Storm, 1994. HEART OF THE WOLF SERIES: Secret of the Wolf, 1995; Wolf in Waiting, 1995; Shadow of the Wolf, 1995. AS LEIGH BRISTOL: Hearts of Fire, 1989; Sunswept, 1990; Twice Blessed, 1991; Angel, 1992; Legacy, 1993. FIELDING TRILOGY: Scarlet Sunrise, 1987; (as Leigh Bristol) Amber Skies, 1987; Silver Twilight, 1987. AS TAYLOR BRADY: THE KINCAIDS SERIES: Raging Rivers, 1992; Prairie Thunder, 1993; Mountain Fury, 1993; Westward Winds, 1993. **Address:** Belle Books, PO Box 300921, Memphis, TN 38130, U.S.A.

BALL, Edward. American (born United States), b. 1958?. **Genres:** Documentaries/Reportage, Mystery/Crime/Suspense, Young Adult Non-fiction. **Career:** Yale University, lecturer in English. Journalist. **Publications:** Slaves in the Family (nonfiction), 1998; The Sweet Hell Inside: A Family History, 2001; Peninsula of Lies: A True Story of Mysterious Birth and Taboo Love, 2004; The Genetic Strand: Exploring a Family History through DNA, 2007; The Octopus and the Inventor: Eadweard Muybridge, the Killer Who Created the Movies, 2011. **Address:** Department of English, Yale University, Rm. 008, Linsly-Chittenden Hall, 63 High St., PO Box 208302, New Haven, CT 06511-8977, U.S.A. **Online address:** edward.ball@yale.edu

BALL, Gordon. American (born United States), b. 1944. **Genres:** Adult Non-fiction, Biography. **Career:** Allen Ginsberg's Farm, manager, 1968-71; Old Dominion University, literature professor, 1981-85; Wasedo, Sophia and Rikkyo Universities, Fulbright specialist lecturer in American literature, 1983-84; Tougaloo College, professor, 1985-89; Virginia Military Institute, professor of English and fine arts, 1989-, coordinator of the symposium. Filmmaker, photographer and writer. **Publications:** '66 Frames: A Memoir, 1999; Dark Music, 2006; His East Hill Farm: Seasons with Allen Ginsberg, 2011. EDITOR: Allen Verbatim: Lectures on Poetry, Politics, and Consciousness, 1974; (and contrib with J.H. Richards) An Introduction to Film Criticism: Prepared for English 42 and Christopher Brookhouse and Howard Harper, 3rd ed., 1977; Allen Ginsberg, Journals: Early Fifties, Early Sixties, 1977; Allen Ginsberg, Journals Mid-fifties, 1954-1958, 1995. Contributor to books. **Address:** Department of English & Fine Arts, Virginia Military Institute, Lexington, VA 24450, U.S.A. **Online address:** ballgv@mail.vmi.edu

BALL, Karen. American (born United States), b. 1957. **Genres:** Novels, Children's Fiction, Young Adult Fiction, Adult Non-fiction. **Career:** B&H Publishing Group, senior acquisitions editor. Writer. **Publications:** The Hazardous Homestead, 1992; (with K.L. Tornberg) Family Traditions That Last a Lifetime, 1993; The Overnight Ordeal, 1994; (with B.J. Hicks and L. McCourtney) Mistletoe, 1996; Reunion, 1996; (with J. Brooks and A. Jones) Fools for Love, 1998; (with B.J. Hicks and D. Noble) Hearts Delight, 1998; Wilderness, 1999; (comp.) The Storytellers' Collection: Tales from Home: Collection Two, 2001; (with L.C. Higgs and C. Zane) Three Weddings and a Giggle, 2001; The Breaking Point, 2003; (contrib.) Lively Bible Lessons for Preschoolers, 2004; A Test of Faith, 2004; Shattered Justice, 2005; (co-author) Writers on Writing, 2005; Kaleidoscope Eyes: A Novel, 2006; What Lies Within: A Novel, 2007. **Address:** Multnomah Publishers, PO Box 1720, Sisters, OR 97759-1720, U.S.A. **Online address:** kb4him@gmail.com

BALL, Nelson. Canadian (born Canada), b. 1942. **Genres:** Poetry. **Career:** Weed Flower Press, Kitchener and Toronto, founder, editor and publisher, 1965-74; University of Toronto Library, library technician, 1967-71; Village Book Store, cataloger, 1970-73; William Nelson Books, founder and proprietor, 1972-85; Nelson Ball, Bookseller, proprietor, 1985-. **Publications:** POETRY: Room of Clocks, 1965; Beaufort's Scale, 1967; Sparrows, 1968; Force Movements, 1969; Water-Pipes and Moonlight, 1969; The Pre-Linguistic Heights, 1970; Points of Attention, 1971; Round Stone, 1971; Dry Spell, 1973; Our Arms Are Featherless Wings, 1973; The Shore, 1974; With Issa: Poems 1964-71, 1991; Sightings, 1992; (ed.) Frank Harrington's Kristmiss Book, 1993; Bird Tracks on Hard Snow, 1994; Fifteen Poems, 1994; The Concrete Air, 1996; Round Table, 1996; Small Gardens, 1996; To Share That Yellow, 1998; Visitation, 1998; Almost Spring, 1999; At The Edge of The Frog Pond, 2004; (ed.) Konfessions of an Elizabethan Fan Dancer by bpNichol, 2004; With Held, 2004; Three-Letter Words, 2006. Contributor of articles to periodicals. **Address:** Mercury Press, PO Box 672, Sta. P, Toronto, ON M5S 2Y4, Canada. **Online address:** nbb@sympatico.ca

BALL, Stuart. British (born England), b. 1956. **Genres:** History, Politics/Government, Biography, Autobiography/Memoirs. **Career:** University of Leicester, lecturer in modern history, 1979-96, reader in modern history, 1996-. Writer. **Publications:** Baldwin and the Conservative Party: The Crisis of 1929-1931, 1988; The Conservative Party and British Politics 1902-1951, 1995; Winston Churchill, 2003. EDITOR: (and intro.) Parliament and Politics in the Age of Baldwin and MacDonald: The Headlam Diaries 1923-1935, 1992; (with A. Seldon) Conservative Century: The Conservative Party since 1900, 1994; The Conservative Party since 1945, 1998; (with A. Seldon) The Heath Government, 1970-1974: A Reappraisal, 1996; Parliament and Politics in the Age of Churchill and Attlee: The Headlam Diaries 1935-1951, 1999; (with I. Holliday) Mass Conservatism: The Conservatives and the Public since the 1880s, 2002; (with A. Seldon) Recovering Power: The Conservatives in Opposition since 1867, 2005. **Address:** School of Historical Studies, University of Leicester, Attenborough 511, University Rd., Leicester, LE LE1 7RH, England. **Online address:** bal@le.ac.uk

BALL, Terence. American (born United States), b. 1944. **Genres:** Mystery/Crime/Suspense, Politics/Government, Novels, Philosophy. **Career:** University of Minnesota, assistant professor, 1972-75, associate professor, 1975-82, professor of political science, 1982-98; Oxford University, visiting professor, 1978-79, 1993, 1995, 1998, Keeley-Rutherford fellow, 1988; University of California, visiting professor, 1984; Arizona State University, School of Government, Politics and Global Studies, Department of Political Science, professor, 1998-. Writer. **Publications:** Civil Disobedience and Civil Deviance, 1973; (ed.) Political Theory and Praxis: New Perspectives, 1977; (ed. with J. Farr) After Marx, 1984; (ed.) Idioms of Inquiry: Critique and Renewal in Political Science, 1987; Transforming Political Discourse: Political Theory and Critical Conceptual History, 1988; (ed. with J.G.A. Pocock) Conceptual Change and the Constitution, 1988; (co-author) Democracy, State, and Justice: Critical Perspectives and New Interpretations, 1988; (ed. with J. Farr and R.L. Hanson) Political Innovation and Conceptual Change, 1989; (with R. Dagger) Political Ideologies and the Democratic Ideal, 1990, 8th ed., 2011; (ed. with R. Dagger) Ideals and Ideologies: A Reader, 1991, 8th ed., 2011; (ed.) Political Writings, 1992; Reappraising Political Theory Revisionist Studies in the History of Political Thought, 1995; Rousseau's Ghost: A Novel, 1998; (ed. with J. Appleby) Thomas Jefferson: Political Writings, 1999; (ed. with R. Bellamy) The Cambridge History of Twentieth-Century Political Thought, 2003; (ed.) Federalist, 2003; (ed.) James Madison, 2008. Contributor to journals. **Address:** Department of Political Science, Arizona State University, 6780 Lattie Coor Hall, PO Box 3902, Tempe, AZ 85287-2001, U.S.A. **Online address:** terence.ball@asu.edu

BALLANTYNE, Tony. British (born England) **Genres:** Novels, Mystery/Crime/Suspense. **Career:** Blue Coat School, assistant head teacher, Mathematics and Information Technology, teacher. Writer. **Publications:** AI SERIES: Recursion, 2004; Capacity, 2005; Divergence, 2007. PENROSE SERIES: Twisted Metal, 2009; Blood and Iron, 2010. Works appear in anthologies. Contributor to periodicals. **Address:** c/o Simon Kavanagh, Mic Cheetham Literary Agency, 50 Albemarie St., London, GL W1S 4BD, England. **Online address:** tb@tonyballantyne.com

BALLANTYNE, Tony. New Zealander (born New Zealand), b. 1972. **Genres:** History, Sociology, Social Sciences. **Career:** University of Otago, Department of History and Art History, lecturer, associate professor; University of Illinois, faculty. Writer. **Publications:** Orientalism and Race: Aryanism in the British Empire, 2002; (ed.) Science, Empire and the European Exploration of the Pacific, 2004; (ed. with J.A. Bennett) Landscape/Community: Perspectives from New Zealand, 2005; (ed. with A. Burton) Bodies in Contact: Rethinking Colonial Encounters in World History, 2005; (with B. Moloughney) Disputed Histories: Imagining New Zealand's Pasts, 2006; Between Colonialism and Diaspora: Sikh Cultural Formations in an Imperial World, 2006; (ed.) Textures of the Sikh Past: New Historical Perspectives, 2007; (ed. with A. Burton) Moving Subjects: Gender, Mobility and Intimacy in an Age of Global Empire, 2009. Contributor to journals. **Address:** Department of History and Art History, University of Otagoof, Rm. 2S7, Arts 1 (Burns) Bldg., PO Box 56, Dunedin, 9016, New Zealand. **Online address:** tony.ballantyne@stonebow.otago.ac.nz

BALLARD, John R. American (born United States), b. 1957. **Genres:** Social Sciences. **Career:** Massey University, professor; National War College, professor. Writer. **Publications:** Upholding Democracy: The United States Military Campaign in Haiti, 1994-1997, 1998; Continuity during the Storm: Boissy d'Anglas and the Era of the French Revolution, 2000; Fighting for Fallujah: A New Dawn for Iraq, 2006; Triumph of Self- Determination: Operation Stabilise and United Nations Peacemaking in East Timor, 2008; From Storm to Freedom: America's Long War with Iraq, 2010. Contributor to periodicals. **Address:** National War College, 300 D St. SW, Fort Lesley J. McNair, Washington, WA 20319-5078, U.S.A.

BALLARD, Michael B. American (born United States), b. 1946. **Genres:** History, Novels. **Career:** Western Carolina University, project archivist, 1978-79; Mississippi State University, Department of History, research assistant, 1979-82, assistant professor, 1983-92, associate professor, 1992-95, professor, 1995, adjunct instructor in history, 2002-04, instructor, 2006, Mississippi State University Library, archivist, coordinator of the Congressional collection, 1999; Mary Holmes (Junior) College, adjunct instructor in history, 1992-93. Writer. **Publications:** A Long Shadow: Jefferson Davis and the Final Days of the Confederacy, 1986; Landscapes of Battle: The Civil War, 1988; Pemberton: A Biography, 1991; (co-ed.) A Mississippi Rebel in the Army of Northern Virginia, 1995; Campaign for Vicksburg, 1996; The Battle of Tupelo, 1996; Civil War Mississippi: A Guide, 2000; (co-author) Sonny Montgomery: The Veteran's Champion, 2003; Vicksburg: The Campaign that Opened the Mississippi, 2004; U.S. Grant: The Making of a General, 1861-1863, 2005; Chickasaw, a Mississippi Scout for the Union: The Civil War Memoir of Levi H. Naron, 2005; Maroon and White: Mississippi State University, 1878-2003, 2008; Civil War in Mississippi: Major Campaigns and Battles, 2011. **Address:** Mississippi State University Library, PO Box 5408, Mississippi State, MS 39762-5408, U.S.A. **Online address:** mballard@library.msstate.edu

BALLARD, Terry. American (born United States), b. 1946. **Genres:** Librarianship, Politics/Government. **Career:** Phoenix Public Library, library assistant, 1969-90; Adelphi University, systems librarian and assistant professor, 1990-95; John's University, assistant professor and adjunct reference librarian, 1992-95; Library Software Review, contributing editor, 1993-95; New York University, School of Law Library, automation coordinator, 1995-97; Palmer Library School, adjunct professor, 1995-; Information Today, columnist, 1996-2001; Quinnipiac University, automation librarian, 1997-2008, assistant professor, 1997-2002, associate professor, 2002-; Southern Connecticut State University, adjunct professor, 2000-; New York Law School, assistant director of technical services for library systems and automation librarian. **Publications:** INNOPAC: A Reference Guide to the System, 1995. Contributor to journals. **Address:** Quinnipiac University, 275 Mount Carmel Ave., Hamden, CT 06518-1908, U.S.A. **Online address:** terry.ballard@quinnipiac.edu

BALLENDORF, Dirk Anthony. American (born United States), b. 1939. **Genres:** Area Studies. **Career:** U.S. Peace Corps, associate director in Micronesia; College of Micronesia, president; University of Guam, RFT/Micronesian Area Research Center, director, interim director, 1979-84, 2004-, professor of history and Micronesian studies. Writer. **Publications:** (Ed. with F.P. King) Oceania Today: Towards New Directions and Political Self-Actualization, 1980; (with B.G. Karolle) Prospects for Economic Self-sufficiency in the New Micronesian States, 1986; Historical Dictionary of Guam and Micronesia, 1995; (co-author) Pete Ellis: Amphibious Warfare

Prophet, 1880-1923, 1997; Guam History Perspectives, vol. I, 1998; (with H.P. Willens) Secret Guam Study, 2004; Historical Dictionary of America in the Pacific, forthcoming. Contributor of articles to journals. **Address:** Micronesian Area Research Center, University of Guam, Rm. 207, Richard Flores Taitano MARC Bldg., UOG Sta., Mangilao, 96923, Guam. **Online address:** ballendo@uguam.uog.edu

BALLENTINE, Lee (Kenney). American (born United States), b. 1954. **Genres:** Poetry, Young Adult Fiction, Literary Criticism And History. **Career:** Osborne and Associates, software engineer, 1978-80; Triad Systems Corp., software engineer, 1981-84; Ocean View Press, publisher, 1981-86, Ocean View Books, publisher, 1986-2001, Ocean View Technical Publications, co-founder and president, 1989-91; Daisy Systems Corp., group leader in operating systems and communications, 1984-85; Schlumberger, Fairchild Semiconductor Division, software applications engineering manager, 1985-87; Professional Book Center, co-founder and president, 1987-2000; Documents of Colorado Art, editor, 1991-2001; Poeisis (Colorado poetry calendar), founder and publisher, 1992-97; Permanence Press, editor, 1992-2001; UR-VOX, editor, 2000-01; Gallup House Fine Art, staff. Consultant. **Publications:** Directional Information, 1981; Basements in the Music-Box, 1986; (ed.) Poly: New Speculative Writing, 1989; Dream Protocols, 1992; (ed.) High Fantastic, 1995; Phase Language, 1995; Renounce the Emerald Piety, 1998; (ed.) Urvox: Journal of the Underlying Voice 4, 2000; (with N. Balbulus) Medusas, 2002. Contributor to periodicals. **Address:** Gallup House Fine Art, PO Box 9249, Denver, CO 80209, U.S.A. **Online address:** lee@gallup-house.com

BALLIETT, Blue. American (born United States), b. 1955?. **Genres:** Novels, Young Adult Non-fiction, Adult Non-fiction, History. **Career:** University of Chicago Laboratory School, third-grade teacher, 1980-91. Freelance writer, art gallery director and researcher. **Publications:** The Ghosts of Nantucket: 23 True Accounts, 1984; Nantucket Hauntings: 21 Firsthand Encounters with the Supernatural, 1990; Chasing Vermeer, 2004; The Wright 3, 2006; Nantucket Ghosts: 44 True Hauntings, 2006; The Calder Game, 2008; Danger Box, 2010. **Address:** c/o Doe Coover, Doe Coover Agency, PO Box 668, Winchester, MA 01890, U.S.A.

BALLING, Robert C. American (born United States), b. 1952. **Genres:** Earth Sciences, Environmental Sciences/Ecology. **Career:** University of Nebraska, Department of Geography, assistant professor, 1979-84, research fellow, 1979-81, assistant professor, 1979-84; Arizona State University, visiting assistant professor, 1985-86, research associate, 1985-87, assistant professor, 1987-88, director, 1988-89, associate professor of geography, 1989-98, Office of Climatology, director, 1988-2004, professor of geography, 1998-2004, Masters of Advanced Study, Geographic Information Systems Program, professor, 2004-. Writer. **Publications:** The Heated Debate: Greenhouse Predictions Versus Climate Reality, Pacific Research Institute for Public Policy, 1992; (with M.A.J. Williams) Interactions of Desertification and Climate, 1994; (with P.J. Michaels) Satanic Gases: Clearing the Air about Global Warming, 2000; (with P.J. Michaels) Climate of Extremes: Global Warming Science They Don't Want You to Know, 2008. Contributor of articles to journals. **Address:** School of Geographical Sciences, Arizona State University, SCOB 233, PO Box 871508, Tempe, AZ 85287-0104, U.S.A. **Online address:** robert.balling@asu.edu

BALMAIN, Lydia. *See* **TURNER, Judith.**

BALMASEDA, Liz. American/Cuban (born Cuba), b. 1959. **Genres:** Novels, Autobiography/Memoirs. **Career:** Miami Herald, intern, 1980, general assignment reporter, 1981-85, feature writer, 1987-91, columnist, 1991-; Newsweek, Central America bureau chief, 1985-; NBC News, field producer; Palm Beach Post newspaper, writer; Home Box Office (HBO), associate producer and writer. **Publications:** (With P.J. Greer, Jr.) Waking Up in America: How One Doctor Brings Hope to Those Who Need It Most (memoir), 1999; (with M.E. Salinas) I Am My Father's Daughter: Living a Life without Secrets (memoir), 2006; Sweet Mary (novel), 2009. Contributor to periodicals. **Address:** Miami, FL , U.S.A. **Online address:** gosweetmary@aol.com

BALMER, Randall (Herbert). American (born United States), b. 1954. **Genres:** Theology/Religion, Humanities. **Career:** Columbia University, assistant professor, 1985-90, Tremaine associate professor of religion, 1990, Barnard College, associate professor, 1991-94, professor, 1994-, Ann Whitney Olin professor of American religion, 1996-; Yale University, Divinity School, visiting professor, 2004-08; Saint John's Episcopal Church, rector, 2008-09. Writer. **Publications:** A Perfect Babel of Confusion: Dutch Religion and English Culture in the Middle Colonies, 1989; Mine Eyes Have Seen the Glory: A Journey into the Evangelical Subculture in America, 1989, 3rd ed., 1999; (ed. with E.L. Blumhofer) Modern Christian Revivals, 1993; (with J.R. Fitzmier) The Presbyterians, 1993; Grant Us Courage: Travels along the Mainline of American Protestantism, 1996; Blessed Assurance: The History of Evangelicalism in America, 1999; Religion in Twentieth-Century America, 2001; Growing Pains: Learning to Love My Father's Faith, 2001; Encyclopedia of Evangelicalism, 2002; Thy Kingdom Come: How the Religious Right Distorts the Faith and Threatens America, 2006; God in the White House: How Faith Shaped the Presidency from John F. Kennedy to George W. Bush, 2008; The Making of Evangelicalism: From Revivalism to Politics and Beyond, 2010. Contributor of articles to newspapers and magazines. **Address:** Barnard College, Columbia University, 3009 Broadway, New York, NY 10027-6598, U.S.A. **Online address:** rb281@columbia.edu

BALOGH, Mary. Canadian/Welsh (born Wales), b. 1944. **Genres:** Novellas/Short Stories, Romance/Historical, Novels, Young Adult Non-fiction, Young Adult Fiction. **Career:** Kipling High School, English teacher, 1967-82; Windthorst High School, principal and English teacher, 1982-88; writer, 1988-. **Publications:** NOVELS: A Masked Deception, 1985; The Double Wager, 1985; A Chance Encounter, 1986; Red Rose, 1985; The Trysting Place, 1986; The First Snowdrop, 1987; The Wood Nymph, 1987; The Constant Heart, 1987; Gentle Conquest, 1987; Secrets of the Heart, 1988; The Ungrateful Governess, 1988; An Unacceptable Offer, 1988; Daring Masquerade, 1989; A Gift of Daisies, 1989; The Obedient Bride, 1989; Lady with a Black Umbrella, 1989; The Gilded Web, 1989; A Promise of Spring, 1990; Web of Love, 1990; The Incurable Matchmaker, 1990; Devil's Web, 1990; An Unlikely Duchess, 1990; A Certain Magic, 1991; Snow Angel, 1991; The Secret Pearl, 1991; The Ideal Wife, 1991; Christmas Beau, 1991; The Counterfeit Betrothal, 1992; The Notorious Rake, 1992; A Christmas Promise, 1992; Beyond the Sunrise, 1992; A Precious Jewel, 1993; Deceived, 1993; Courting Julia, 1993; Dancing with Clara, 1994; Tangled, 1994; Tempting Harriet, 1994; Dark Angel, 1994; A Christmas Belle, 1994; Longing, 1994; Lord Carew's Bride, 1995; Heartless, 1995; The Famous Heroine, 1996; Truly, 1996; The Plumed Bonnet, 1996; Indiscreet, 1997; Temporary Wife, 1997; Silent Melody, 1997; A Christmas Bride, 1997; Unforgiven, 1998; Thief of Dreams, 1998; Irresistible, 1998; The Last Waltz, 1998; One Night for Love, 1999; More than a Mistress, 2000; No Man's Mistress, 2001; A Summer to Remember, 2002; Slightly Married, 2003; Slightly Wicked, 2003; Slightly Scandalous, 2003; Slightly Tempted, 2004; Slightly Sinful, 2004; Slightly Dangerous, 2004; Simply Unforgettable, 2005; The Secret Pearl, 2005; The Gilded Web, 2006; Simply Love, 2006; Simply Magic, 2007; Web of Love, 2007; Simply Perfect, 2008; First Comes Marriage, 2009; Then Comes Seduction, 2009; At Last Love Comes, 2009; Seducing an Angel, 2009; A Matter of Class, 2010; A Secret Affair, 2010; The Secret Mistress, 2011. NOVELLAS: A Regency Christmas, 1989; A Regency Christmas II, 1990; A Regency Valentine, 1991; A Regency Christmas III, 1991; A Regency Valentine II, 1992; A Regency Summer, 1992; Full Moon Magic, 1992; A Regency Christmas IV, 1992; Tokens of Love, 1993; Rakes and Rogues, 1993; Moonlight Lovers, 1993; A Regency Christmas V, 1993; From the Heart, 1994; A Regency Christmas VI, 1994; Blossoms, 1995; Dashing and Dangerous, 1995; A Regency Christmas VII, 1995; An Angel Christmas, 1995; Love's Legacy, 1996; Timeswept Brides, 1996; A Regency Christmas Feast, 1996; (co-author) A Regency Christmas Carol, 1997; The Gifts of Christmas, 1998; Captured Hearts, 1999; Under the Mistletoe, 2003; Christmas Keepsakes, 2005; (with S. Laurens, J. 'Alessandro and C. Hern) It Happened One Night, 2008; (with N. Cornick and C. Milan) The Heart of Christmas, 2009. OTHERS: At Last Comes Love, 2009; Bespelling Jane Austen, 2010; The Proposal, 2012. **Address:** Maria Carvainis Agency, 1350 Ave. of the Americas, Ste. 2905, New York, NY 10019, U.S.A.

BALSWICK, Judith K. American (born United States), b. 1939. **Genres:** Human Relations/Parenting, Psychology, Ethics, Adult Non-fiction, Theology/Religion, Reference. **Career:** University of Iowa, Veterans' War Orphan Program, director, counselor, 1963-64; University of Georgia, University Testing and Evaluation Center, career counselor, 1974-75, University Health Services, Graduate Assistantship, counselor, 1975-76, University Housing Department, administrative assistant professor, 1977-78, Department of Child and Family Development, assistant professor, 1978-79; licensed marriage and family counselor, 1977-; Family Counseling Services of Athens, senior clinical counselor, 1979-82; Fuller Theological Seminary, School of Theology, Marriage and Family Ministries, director of practicum, 1982-83, School of

Psychology, Marriage and Family Therapy Department, assistant professor, 1987-93, associate professor of marriage and family therapy, professor of marital and family therapy and director of clinical training, 1993-, Therapy and Director of Clinical Training, professor of marriage and family, 2002-04, Department of Marriage and Family, senior professor of marital and family therapy, 2004-; AAMFT approved supervisor, 1983-; CAMFT certified supervisor, 1999-; marriage and family therapist in private practice. Writer. **Publications:** (With J.O. Balswick) The Family: A Christian Perspective on the Contemporary Home, 1989, 3rd. ed., 2007; (with J.O. Balswick) The Gift of Gender: Eight Sessions on the Roles of Men and Women, 1991; (with L. Brookside) Mothers and Daughters Making Peace: The Most Intimate, Tangled, Beautiful, and Frustrating Relationship Shared by Women, 1993; (with J.O. Balswick) Raging Hormones: What to Do When You Suspect Your Teen May Be Sexually Active, 1994; (with B. Piper) Life Ties: Cultivating Relationships That Make Life Worth Living, 1995; (with J.O Balswick) Dual-Earner Marriage: The Elaborate Balancing Act, 1995; (with J.O. Balswick) Families in Pain: Working Through the Hurts, 1997; (with B. Piper) Then They Leave Home: Parenting After the Kids Grow Up, 1997; (with J.O. Balswick) Authentic Human Sexuality: An Integrated Christian Approach, 1999, 2nd ed., 2008; (with J.O. Balswick) The Two-Paycheck Marriage: Making It Work, 1999; (with J.O. Balswick) Building Strong Family Life: A Study Guide, 2000; (with J.O. Balswick) Relationship Empowerment Parenting (REP): A Christian Model, 2001; (co-author) Relationship-Empowerment Parenting: Building Formative and Fulfilling Relationships with Your Children, 2003; (with J.O. Balswick) A Model for Marriage: Covenant, Grace, Empowerment and Intimacy, 2006; (with J.O. Balswick) Family: A Christian Perspective on the Contemporary Home, 2007. **Address:** Fuller Theological Seminary, 135 N Oakland Ave., Pasadena, CA 91182, U.S.A. **Online address:** jbalswic@fuller.edu

BALTER, Dave. American (born United States) **Genres:** Business/Trade/Industry, Marketing. **Career:** Kessler Financial Services, direct marketing and affinity program implementations manager; Webb & Co., circulation and fulfillment operations analyst; Bzz Agent, founder, 2001-, chief executive officer. Writer. **Publications:** (With J. Butman) Grapevine: The New Art of Word-of-Mouth Marketing, 2005. **Address:** BzzAgent Inc., 500 Harrison Ave., Boston, MA 02118, U.S.A.

BALUTANSKY, Kathleen M(arie). American/Haitian (born Haiti), b. 1954. **Genres:** Literary Criticism And History, Language/Linguistics, Novels, Young Adult Fiction. **Career:** University of Virginia, assistant dean, 1985-86, assistant professor of English, 1988-92; St. Michael's College, assistant professor of English, 1992-94, associate professor of English, professor of English, 1994-, associate dean for academic affairs, 2004-; Washington International School, vice principal, 1986-87. Writer. **Publications:** The Novels of Alex La Guma: The Representation of a Political Conflict, 1990; (ed. with M.A. Sourieau) Caribbean Creolization: Reflections on the Cultural Dynamics of Language, Culture, and Identity, 1998; Haiti: Writing under Siege, 2004. **Address:** Department of English, St. Michael's College, Klein Hall, 1 Winooski Pk., PO Box 242, Colchester, VT 05439, U.S.A. **Online address:** kbalutansky@smcvt.edu

BALZ, Dan. American (born United States), b. 1946?. **Genres:** Politics/Government, Young Adult Non-fiction. **Career:** National Journal, reporter and deputy editor; Philadelphia Inquirer, reporter; Washington Post, reporter, 1978-. **Publications:** NONFICTION: Ronald Reagan: A Trusty Script, 1976; (co-author) Interest Groups: Who They Are and How They Influence: Articles, 1977; (with R. Brownstein) Storming the Gates: Protest Politics and the Republican Revival, 1996; (with H. Johnson) The Battle for America 2008: The Story of an Extraordinary Election, 2009. **Address:** Bethesda, MD , U.S.A. **Online address:** balzd@washpost.com

BALZO, Sandra. American (born United States) **Genres:** Mystery/Crime/Suspense, Literary Criticism And History. **Career:** Balzo Communications, founder, independent public relations consultant, 1995-; Firstar Corp., assistant vice president and manager of special events. Writer. **Publications:** MAGGY THORSEN MYSTERY SERIES: Uncommon Grounds, 2004; Grounds for Murder, 2007; Bean There, Done That, 2008; Brewed, Crude and Tattooed, 2009; From the Grounds Up, 2010. Contributor to periodicals. **Address:** Severn House Publishers Ltd., 9-15 High St., Sutton, SR SM1 1DF, England. **Online address:** sandy@sandrabalzo.com

BAMBACH, Carmen C. American (born United States), b. 1959. **Genres:** Art/Art History, History, Humanities, Biography, Essays. **Career:** Connecticut Trust for Historic Preservation, assistant, 1982-83, Connecticut Preservation News, managing editor, 1983; Philadelphia Museum of Art, Department of Prints, Drawings, and Photographs, curatorial intern, 1988-89; Fordham University, assistant professor of art history, 1989-95; Metropolitan Museum of Art, associate curator of drawings and prints, 1995-; Harvard University, Center for Italian Renaissance Studies, Leopold S. Schepp fellow, 1996-97. **Publications:** (With N. Orenstein) Genoa: Drawings and Prints, 1530-1800, 1996; (with G.R. Goldner) The Drawings of Fillippino Lippi and His Circle, 1997; Drawing and Painting in the Italian Renaissance Workshop: Practice and Theory, 1300-1600, 1999; (ed.) Leonardo da Vinci, Master Draftsman, 2003; (with J. Cox-Rearick and G.R. Goldner) Drawings of Bronzino, 2010; (with L. Wolk-Simon) Italian Journey: Drawings from the Tobey Collection: Correggio to Tiepolo, 2010. Contributor of articles to books and journals. **Address:** Department of Drawings and Prints, Metropolitan Museum of Art, 1000 5th Ave., 82nd St., New York, NY 10028-0198, U.S.A. **Online address:** carmen.bambach@metmuseum.org

BAMBOLA, Sylvia. (Margaret Miller). American/Romanian (born Romania), b. 1945. **Genres:** Novels, Young Adult Fiction, Mystery/Crime/Suspense. **Career:** Novelist. **Publications:** NOVELS: (as Margaret Miller) A Vessel of Honor, 1997; Refiner's Fire, 2000; Tears in a Bottle, 2001, Waters of Marah, 2004; Return to Appleton, 2005. **Address:** c/o Publicity Director, Multnomah Publishers Inc., 204 W Adams., PO Box 1720, Sisters, OR 97759-1720, U.S.A. **Online address:** sylvia@sylviabambola.com

BAN, Thomas Arthur. American/Canadian/Hungarian (born Hungary), b. 1929. **Genres:** Psychiatry, Medicine/Health, Sciences, Translations. **Career:** McGill University, demonstrator, 1960-63, lecturer, 1963-65, assistant professor, 1965-70, associate professor of psychiatry, 1970-76, Division of Psychopharmacology, Department of Psychiatry, director, 1970-76; Douglas Hospital, senior research psychiatrist, 1961-66, associate director of research, 1966-70, chief of research services, 1970-72; Hospital des Laurentides, psychiatric research consultant, 1963-72; Lakeshore General Hospital, psychiatric research consultant, 1967-; World Health Organization International Reference Center Network for the Study of Psychotropic Drugs, National Reference Center, director, 1972-76; Neuropsychiatric Institute, Clinical Research Service, director, 1976-; Vanderbilt University, professor of psychiatry, 1976-94, professor emeritus of psychiatry, 1995-. Writer. **Publications:** Conditioning and Psychiatry, 1964 as Conditioning Behavior and Psychiatry, 2008; Psychopharmacology, 1969; (with H.E. Lehmann) Pharmacotherapy of Tension and Anxiety, 1970; (with H.E. Lehmann) Experimental Approaches to Psychiatric Diagnosis: Psychometric, Conditioning and Psychopharmacological Studies, 1971; Nicotinic Acid in the Treatment of Schizophrenias, 1971; Schizophrenia: A Psychopharmacological Approach, 1972; Recent Advances in the Biology of Schizophrenia, 1973; Depression and the Tricyclic Antidepressants, 1974; Introduction to the Psychopharmacology Doxepin, 1977; Psychopharmacology of Thiothixene, 1978; Psychopharmacology of Depression, 1981; Psychopharmacology for the Aged, 1980; (with M. Hollender) Psychopharmacology for Everyday Practice, 1981; Composite Diagnostic Evaluation of Depressive Disorders, 1989; Declino Cognitivo Nell' Anziano, 1991; Sostituire il Neurolettico, 1992; (with R.V. Udabe) Clasificacion delas Psicosis, 1995; (with P. Gaszner) Composite Diagnostic Evaluation of Hyperthymic Disorders, 1998. EDITOR: (with B. Silvestrini) Trazodone, 1974; (with F.A. Freyhan) Drug Treatment of Sexual Dysfunction, 1980; (co-ed.) Prevention and Treatment of Depression, 1981; (with W. Guy) The AMDP-System: Manual for the Assessment and Documentation of Psychopathology, 1982; (with H.E. Lehmann) The Butyrophenones in Psychiatry, 1964; Trimipramine: A New Anti-Depressant, 1965; (with H.E. Lehmann) Toxicity and Adverse Reaction Studies with Neuroleptics and Antidepressants: Skin-Eye Syndrome and Electrocardiographic Changes, 1967; (with H.E. Lehmann) The Thioxanthenes, 1969; Psychotherapy of Tension and Anxiety, 1970; (co-ed.) Psychopharmacology, Sexual Disorders and Drug Abuse, 1973; (trans. and co-ed.) The AMDP-System: Manual for the Assessment and Documentation of Psychopathology, 1982; (trans. and co-ed.) The AGP System: Manual for the Documentation of Psychopathology in Gerontopsychiatry, 1985; (with N.N. Sartorius) Assessment of Depression, 1986; (with F.J. McGuigan) Critical Issues in Psychology, Psychiatry and Physiology: A Memorial to W. Horsley Gantt, 1987; (co-ed.) Diagnosis and Treatment of Old Age Dementias: Symposium on Diagnosis and Treatment of Old Age Dementias, Milan, June 6, 1987, 1989. **Address:** School of Medicine, Vanderbilt University, 215 Light Hall, Nashville, TN 37232, U.S.A. **Online address:** fmcp@attcanada.ca

BANASH, Stan. American (born United States), b. 1940. **Genres:** Literary Criticism And History, Civil Liberties/Human Rights, History. **Career:** Daniel J. Edelman Inc., account executive, 1972-73; Office of the Lieutenant Governor, administrative assistant for press relations, 1973-74; self employed consultant, 1974-; Society of American Registered Architects, executive director, 1988-96. Writer. **Publications:** (Ed.) Best of Dee Brown's West: An Anthology, 1998; (and ed.) Dee Brown's Civil War Anthology, 1998. Contributor of articles to magazines. **Address:** 5940 N Neva Ave., Chicago, IL 60631, U.S.A.

BANAZEK, Jeanne M. *See* **BANAZEK, Jeanne M. (Carpenter).**

BANAZEK, Jeanne M. (Carpenter). Also writes as Jeanne Carpenter, Jeanne M. Banazek. American (born United States), b. 1943. **Genres:** Documentaries/Reportage, Psychology. **Career:** Onondaga County Department of Drainage and Sanitation, secretary, 1987-99. Writer. **Publications:** (As Jeanne Carpenter) Naked as We Stand, 1997. **Address:** 245 E Manchester Rd., Syracuse, NY 13219, U.S.A.

BANBURY, Jen(nifer Marie). American (born United States), b. 1966. **Genres:** Novels, Plays/Screenplays, Mystery/Crime/Suspense, Young Adult Fiction. **Career:** National Public Radio, reporter; Salon.com, reporter. Journalist. **Publications:** Ablaze, 1995; Like a Hole in the Head (novel), 1998. Contributor to periodicals. **Address:** c/o Paul Chung, The Paul Chung Literary Agency, 200 W 90th St., New York, NY 10024-1234, U.S.A. **Online address:** bittermews@aol.com

BANCROFT, Anne. British (born England), b. 1923. **Genres:** Theology/Religion, Women's Studies And Issues, Philosophy. **Career:** Writer and educator. **Publications:** Religions of the East, 1974; Twentieth Century Mystics & Sages, 1976; Zen: Direct Pointing to Reality, 1979; The Luminous Vision: Six Medieval Mystics and Their Teachings, 1982; Chinese New Year, 1984; Festivals of the Buddha, 1984; The Buddhist World, 1984; The New Religious World, 1985; Origins of the Sacred: The Way of the Sacred in Western Tradition, 1987; Weavers of Wisdom: Women of the Twentieth Century, 1989; The Spiritual Journey, 1991; Mystiker: Wegweiser für die Zukunft, 1992; Women in Search of the Sacred, 1996. EDITOR: (and intro.) The Dhammapada, 1997; (and comp.) Buddha Speaks, 2000; The Wisdom of Zen, 2001; (and comp.) The Pocket Buddha Reader, 2001. **Address:** Cobberton, Denys Rd., Totnes, DN TQ9 5TL, England.

BANDARAGE, Asoka. American (born United States), b. 1950. **Genres:** Politics/Government. **Career:** Yale University, teaching fellow, 1975-78; Brandeis University, Department of Sociology, assistant professor, 1979-85; Colorado College, visiting professor, 1988, 1989; Mount Holyoke College, associate professor of women's studies, 1989-2006, Women's Studies Program, chair, 1995-97; Johns Hopkins University, School for Advanced International Studies, Foreign Policy Institute, visiting fellow, 2002-04; Georgetown University, Department of Government, visiting associate professor, 2006-07, Georgetown Public Policy Institute, affiliated associate professor, 2008-. Writer. **Publications:** Colonialism in Sri Lanka: The Political Economy of the Kandyan Highlands, 1833-1886, 1983; Women, Population and Global Crisis: A Political-Economic Analysis, 1997; (contrib.) Theravada Women Regain Their Lost Legacy, 1999; Separatist Conflict in Sri Lanka: Terrorism, Ethnicity, Political Economy, 2008. **Address:** Georgetown Public Policy Institute, Georgetown University, 100 Old N, 37th & O St. NW, Washington, DC 20057-1034, U.S.A. **Online address:** ab479@georgetown.edu

BANDELE, Biyi. (Biyi Bandele-Thomas). American/Nigerian (born Nigeria), b. 1967. **Genres:** Novels, Plays/Screenplays, History. **Career:** Royal Court Theatre, associate writer, 1992-; Talawa Theatre Co., writer-in-residence, 1994-95; Royal National Theatre Studio, resident dramatist, 1996; Churchill College, Judith E. Wilson fellow, 2000-02; Bush Theatre, royal literary fund resident playwright, 2002-03. Novelist. **Publications:** AS BIYI BANDELE-THOMAS: NOVELS: (Biyi Bandele-Thomas)The Man Who Came in from the Back of Beyond, 1991; (Biyi Bandele-Thomas) The Sympathetic Undertaker and Other Dreams, 1991; The Street, 1999; (S.B. Iwanisziw) Oroonoko: Adaptations and Offshoots, 2006; Burma Boy, 2007; The King's Rifle, 2009. PLAYS: Marching for Fausa, 1993; Resurrections, 1994; Death Catches the Hunter, 1995. Contributor to periodicals. **Address:** c/o Leah Schmidt, The Agency, 24 Pottery Ln., Holland Pk., London, GL W11 4LZ, England. **Online address:** biyi@hotmail.com

BANDELE-THOMAS, Biyi. *See* **BANDELE, Biyi.**

BANDELIN, Oscar J. American (born United States), b. 1964. **Genres:** History. **Career:** Heritage Foundation, Salvatori fellow, 1994-96; University of Washington, instructor, 1999; Four Creeks Unincorporated Area Council, at-large representative, 2000-03, president, 2002-03; American Councils for International Education Regional Scholar Exchange Program to Moscow, program officer, 2000. Writer. **Publications:** Return to the NEP: The False Promise of Leninism and the Failure of Perestroika, 2002. **Address:** 17702 SE May Valley Rd., Renton, WA 98059-5305, U.S.A. **Online address:** bandelin@nwlink.com

BANDO, Mark. (Mark A. Bando). American (born United States), b. 1949. **Genres:** Military/Defense/Arms Control, Air/Space Topics, History. **Career:** Historian. **Publications:** The 101st Airborne at Normandy, 1994; The 101st Airborne: From Holland to Hitler's Eagle's Nest, 1995; Breakout at Normandy: The 2nd Armored Division in the Land of the Dead, 1999; 101st Airborne: Screaming Eagles at Normandy, 2001; Vanguard of the Crusade: The US 101st Airborne Division in World War II, 2003; Avenging Eagles: Forbidden Tales of the 101st Airborne Division in WW2, 2006; 101st Airborne: The Screaming Eagles in World War II, 2007. **Address:** U.S.A. **Online address:** markbando@aol.com

BANDO, Mark A. *See* **BANDO, Mark.**

BANDRAUK, Andre D. Canadian/German (born Germany), b. 1941. **Genres:** Physics, Sciences. **Career:** Loyola College, assistant professor of chemistry, 1963-65; Oxford University, Mathematical Institute, NATO fellow, 1968-70; Universite de Sherbrooke, Technische Hochschule Munchen, assistant, 1970, assistant professor of theoretical chemistry, professor of theoretical chemistry, Canada research chair in computational and photonic chemistry, IBM Center of Excellence, director, 1995-2000, Department of Chemistry, chair, 2005-07, Molecular Modelling-Visualization Center, director, 2010-; University of California-Berkeley, visiting professor, 1977-78; NRC, senior visiting scientist, 1985, 2001, 2002, 2004; Institute of Chemical Physics, foreign lecturer, 1985; University of British Columbia, CA McDowell lecturer, 1990; Institute for Molecular Science, foreign professor, 1992; Tohoku University, Japan Society for Promotion, science lecturer, visiting fellow, 1997-2000; University of Paris, visiting professor, 1998; University of Toronto, Centre for Quantum Control, external affiliate, 2005-10; The Governor General of Canada, Order of Canada for pioneering work in Attosecond Chemistry, officer, 2011-; University of Malaya, visiting professor, 2011-13. Writer. **Publications:** (Ed.) Atomic and Molecular Processes with Short Intense Laser Pulses, 1988; Atoms and Molecules in Laser Fields, 1988; (ed. with S.C. Wallace) Coherence Phenomena in Atoms and Molecules in Laser Fields, 1992; (ed.) Molecules in Laser Fields, 1994; (ed. with J. Laane and H. Takahashi) Structure and Dynamics of Electronic Excited States, 1999; (ed. with Y. Fujimura and R.J. Gordon) Laser Control and Manipulation of Molecules, 2002; (ed. with M.C. Delfour and C. Le Bris) High-Dimensional Partial Differential Equations in Science and Engineering, 2007; Molecular Physics in Intense Laser Fields, forthcoming. **Address:** Department of Chemistry, Universite de Sherbrooke, D1-3034, Sherbrooke, QC J1K 2R1, Canada. **Online address:** andre.bandrauk@usherbrooke.ca

BANDURA, Albert. American/Canadian (born Canada), b. 1925. **Genres:** Psychology. **Career:** Stanford University, instructor, 1953-, department chair, 1976-77, professor of psychology, David Starr Jordan professor of social science in psychology, now David Starr Jordan professor emeritus of social science in psychology, Center for Advanced Study in the Behavioral Sciences, fellow, 1969-70; American Psychological Association, chair and president, 1974; Western Psychological Association, chair and president, 1980; Canadian Psychological Association, honorary president, 1999. Writer. **Publications:** (With R.H. Walters) Adolescent Aggression, 1959; (with R.H. Walters) Social Learning and Personality Development, 1963; (contrib.) Research in Behavior Modification, 1965; Principles of Behavior Modification, 1969; Psychological Modeling: Conflicting Theories, 1971; Aggression: A Social Learning Analysis, 1973; Social Learning Theory, 1977; (contrib.) Experimente zur Sozialpsychologie, 1981; Social Foundations of Thought and Action: A Social Cognitive Theory, 1986; Self-Efficacy: The Exercise of Control, 1997; (with P. Yŏng-sin and K. Omgim) Chagi hyonŭnggam kwa sam ŭi chil, 2001. EDITOR: (with E. Ribes-Inesta) Analysis of Delinquency and Aggression, 1976; Self-Efficacy in Changing Societies, 1995; (co-ed.) Qu'est-ce-donc qu'apprendre?, 1999; Teoria social cognitiva: Conceitor basicos,

2008. **Address:** Department of Psychology, Stanford University, Rm. 134, Bldg. 420, Jordan Hall, 450 Serra Mall, Stanford, CA 94305-2130, U.S.A. **Online address:** albertob@stanford.edu

BANDYOPADHYAY, Bidisha. British (born England), b. 1978. **Genres:** Novels, Education, Travel/Exploration. **Career:** The London College, senior lecturer in political theory, journalism and ethics, 2003, 2004. Writer. **Publications:** AS BIDISHA: Seahorses, 1997; Too Fast to Live: The Second Coming, 2000; (as Bidisha Bandyopadhyay) Sudipa: Nirbachjita galpa, 2005; Venetian Masters: Under the Skin of the City of Love, 2008. Contributor to periodicals. **Address:** c/o Author Mail, International Publishers Marketing, PO Box 605, Herndon, VA 20172-0605, U.S.A.

BANERJEE, Asit. Indian (born India), b. 1940. **Genres:** Physics, Sciences, Astronomy. **Career:** Jadavpur University, lecturer, 1964-78, reader, 1978-86, professor of physics, 1986-2005, Relativity and Cosmology Research Centre, coordinator; Institute Henri Poincare, postdoctoral fellow, 1971-72; Federal University of Rio de Janeiro, visiting professor, 1979-81; Inter-University Centre for Astronomy and Astrophysics, senior associate. Writer. **Publications:** (With A.K. Raychaudhuri and S. Banerji) General Relativity, Astrophysics, and Cosmology, 1992; (co-author) The Special Theory of Relativity, 2002. Contributor to journals. **Address:** G1, Cluster 9, Purbachal, Salt Lake, Calcutta, WB 700091, India. **Online address:** asitb@cal3.vsnl.net.in

BANERJEE, Mukulika. British (born England) **Genres:** Anthropology/Ethnology, Theology/Religion, Social Sciences. **Career:** University College, lecturer in anthropology, 1996-2009; London School of Economics, Department of Anthropology, reader in social anthropology, 2009-. Writer. **Publications:** The Pathan Unarmed: Opposition and Memory in the North West Frontier, 2000; (with D. Miller) The Sari, 2003; (ed.) Muslim Portraits: Everyday Lives in India, 2008. **Address:** Department of Anthropology, London School of Economics, 6th Fl., Old Bldg., Houghton St., London, GL WC2A 2AE, England. **Online address:** m.banerjee@lse.ac.uk

BANERJI, S(iranjan). Indian (born India), b. 1938. **Genres:** Physics, Translations, Adult Non-fiction, Astronomy. **Career:** University of Burdwan, lecturer, 1961-74, reader, 1974-79, professor of physics, through 1979; Jadavpur University, department of physics, Relativity and Cosmology Research Center, professor, now professor emeritus. Writer. **Publications:** (Trans. with K. Mukherjee and R.S. Banerjee) Wolfgang Borchert, Duarer Bahirey (stories and a play), 1975; Apekshikata Tattva, 1982; Sudur Niharika, 1987; (with A. Banerjee and A.K. Raychaudhuri) General Relativity, Astrophysics, and Cosmology, 1992. Works appear in anthologies. Contributor to journals. **Address:** Relativity and Cosmology Research Centre, Department of Physics, Jadavpur University, Block-LB, Plot No. 8, Sector-III, Calcutta, WB 700091, India. **Online address:** sban@cal2.vsnl.net.in

BANFIELD, Stephen. British (born England), b. 1951. **Genres:** Music. **Career:** University of Keele, lecturer, 1978-88, senior lecturer in music, 1988-92, department head, 1988-90; University of Birmingham, head of school of performance studies, 1992-95, Elgar professor of music, 1992-2003; University of Bristol, Stanley Hugh Badock professor of music, 2003-, Centre for the History of Music in Britain the Empire and the Commonwealth, founding director, 2006-09, School of Arts, head, 2010-. **Publications:** Sensibility and English Song, 1985; Sondheim's Broadway Musicals, 1993; (ed. and contrib.) The Blackwell History of Music in Britain, vol. VI: The Twentieth Century, 1995; Gerald Finzi: An English Composer, 1997; (co-ed.) Concertos for Cello, Clarinet, Violin, 2001; Jerome Kern, 2006; (ed. and contrib.) The Sounds of Stonehenge, 2009; (co-ed. and contrib.) Music and the Wesleys, 2010. Contributor to periodicals. **Address:** School of Arts, University of Bristol, 43 Woodland Rd., Bristol, AV BS8 1UU, England. **Online address:** s.d.banfield@bristol.ac.uk

BANG, Garrett. *See* **BANG, Molly Garrett.**

BANG, Molly Garrett. (Garrett Bang). American (born United States), b. 1943. **Genres:** Children's Fiction, Illustrations, Picture/Board Books, Translations. **Career:** Doshisha University, English teacher, 1965-67; Asahi Shimbun, interpreter of Japanese, 1969; Baltimore Sun, reporter, 1970; Johns Hopkins University, Center for Medical Research and Training, illustrator and consultant; United Nations Children's Fund, illustrator and consultant; Harvard University, Institute for International Development, illustrator and consultant. **Publications:** SELF-ILLUSTRATED FOR CHILDREN: (trans. as Garrett Bang) Men from the Village Deep in the Mountains and Other Japanese Folk Tales, 1973; The Grey Lady and the Strawberry Snatcher, 1980; (adaptor) Tye May and the Magic Brush (Chinese folktale), 1981; One Fall Day, 1994; Sunshine's Book, 1994; When I Get Angry, 1998. OTHERS: Wiley and the Hairy Man: Adapted from an American Folktale, 1976; Ten, Nine, Eight, 1983; Dawn (Japanese folktale), 1983; The Paper Crane (Chinese folktale), 1985; Picture This: Perception and Composition, 1991; Delphine, 1988; Yellow Ball, 1991; Goose, 1996; Chattanooga Sludge, 1996; Common Ground: The Water, Earth, and Air We Share, 1997; When Sophie Gets Angry: Really, Really Angry..., 1999; Nobody Particular: One Woman's Fight to Save the Bays, 2000; Picture This: How Pictures Work, 2000; Tiger's Fall, 2001; My Light, 2004; In My Heart, 2005; All of Me!: A Book of Thanks, 2009. EDITOR: The Goblins Giggle, and Other Stories (folktales), 1973; The Buried Moon and Other Stories (folktales), 1977. Illustrator of books by others. **Address:** Blue Sky Press, 557 Broadway, New York, NY 10012, U.S.A. **Online address:** mgbbooks@gmail.com

BANG-CAMPBELL, Monika. American (born United States) **Genres:** Children's Fiction, Music, Animals/Pets. **Career:** Writer. **Publications:** Little Rat Sets Sail, 2002; Little Rat Rides, 2004; Little Rat Makes Music, 2007. Contributor to periodicals. **Address:** c/o Author Mail, Harcourt Children's Books, 525 B St., Ste. 1900, San Diego, CA 92101-4495, U.S.A.

BANGS, Nina. American (born United States) **Genres:** Romance/Historical, Young Adult Fiction. **Career:** Writer. **Publications:** ROMANCE FICTION: An Original Sin, 1999; (with M. Baker, A. Lawrence and K. Nance) Paradise, 1999; (with L. Cach, T. Devine and P. Neri) Seduction by Chocolate, 2000; (with C. Dain and S. Henke) Unwrapped, 2000; The Pleasure Master, 2001; (with J. Denison and E. McCarthy) Men at Work, 2001; Night Games, 2002; From Boardwalk with Love, 2003; (co-author) Burning Up: Four Novellas of Erotic Romance, 2003; Master of Ecstasy, 2004; Night Bites, 2005; Wicked Nights, 2005; Wicked Pleasure, 2006; (with M.J. Davidson and J. Denison) Surf's Up, 2006; A Taste of Darkness, 2006; Wicked Fantasy, 2007; One Bite Stand, 2008; (with S. Hill and D. Joy) This Year's Christmas Present, 2008; Eternal Pleasure, 2008; Eternal Craving, 2009; My Wicked Vampire, 2009; Eternal Prey, 2010; Wicked Edge, 2012. Contributor to periodicals. **Address:** c/o Author Mail, St. Martin's Press, 175 5th Ave., New York, NY 10010, U.S.A. **Online address:** ninabangs@aol.com

BANISADR, Abol-Hassan. French/Iranian (born Iran), b. 1933. **Genres:** Politics/Government, International Relations/Current Affairs. **Career:** Teacher, through, 1978; Republic of Iran, acting minister of foreign affairs, 1979, minister of economy and foreign affairs, 1979-80, president, 1980-81; Constituent Assembly, member, 1979; Revolutionary Council, president, 1980-81. Writer. **Publications:** (With P. Vieille) Pétrole et Violence: Terreur blanche et resistance en Iran, 1974; Uṣ ūl-i pāyah va zābiṭahhā-yi ḥukūmat-i Islāmī, 1975; Mawqiīyat-i īrān va naqsh-i Mudarris: sayrī dar tārīkh-i taḥavvul-i iqtiṣ ādī va siyāsī va ṭabī'ī-i īrān va andīshah va akhlāq-i siyāsī-i Mudarris, 1977; Bisat-i dāimī, 1979; Nigāhī bih tārīkh-i siyāsī-i īrān, 1979; Ta'mīm-i imāmat va mubārazah bā sānsūr, 1979; Kār va kārgar dar Islām: majmū'ah-'i sukhunrānī, 1979; Quelle revolution pour l'Iran, 1980; Nifāq dar Qur'ān: majmū'ah-i sukhanrānī, 1980; Rūz'hābar ra'īs-i jumhūr chigūnah mī-guzad, 1980; Nafṭ wa-al-sayṭarah, 1980; Ṣad maqālah, 1980; 'ā'ilah fī al-Islām, aw, Makānat al-mar'ah fī al-Islām, 1981; Chigūnagī-i intikhāb-i avvalīn nukhust vazīr-i Jumhūrī-i Islāmī-i īrān va mukātabāt-i Rajā'ī bāBanī ṣ adr, 1981; L'espérance trahie, 1982; Khiyānat bih umīd, 1982; (ed.) Bani Sadr racconta l'Iran, 1984; Sayr-i andīshah-i siyāsī dar sih qārrah, 1988; Le complot des ayatollahs, 1989; Usul-i hakem bar qazavat-i Islami: va Huquq-i bashar dar Islam, 1989; My Turn to Speak: Iran, the Revolution & Secret Deals with the U.S, 1991; Sayr-i taḥavvul-i siyāsat-i āmrīkā dar īrān, 1992; Le coran et le pouvoir, 1993; Nāmah'hā az āqā-yi Banī ṣ adr bih āqā-yi Khumaynī va dīgarān, 2006. **Address:** 5, rue du Gal Pershing, Versailles, 78000, France. **Online address:** ab_banisadr@yahoo.de

BANISH, Roslyn. American (born United States), b. 1942?. **Genres:** Novels, Photography, Human Relations/Parenting, Illustrations, Biography, Autobiography/Memoirs. **Career:** Photographer and author. **Publications:** SELF-ILLUSTRATED: I Want to Tell You about My Baby, 1982, rev. ed. as Let Me Tell You about My Baby, 1988; (with J. Jordan-Wong) A Forever Family, 1992; (and contrib.) Focus on Living: Portraits of Americans with HIV and AIDS, 2003. OTHER: City Families: Chicago and London, 1976. Contributor to periodicals. **Address:** c/o Author Mail, University of Massachusetts Press, 671 N Pleasant St., PO Box 429, Amherst, MA 01003, U.S.A.

BANKER, James R. American (born United States), b. 1938. **Genres:** History, Human Relations/Parenting, Essays, Photography. **Career:** North Carolina State University, assistant professor, 1971-76, associate professor, 1976-85, professor of history, 1988-2008; professor emeritus, 2008-. Writer. **Publications:** Death in the Community: Memorialization and Confraternities in an Italian Commune in the Late Middle Ages, 1988; Florentine Essays: Selected Writings of Marvin B. Becker, 2002; Culture of San Sepolcro during the Youth of Piero Della Francesca, 2003. **Address:** Department of History, North Carolina State University, Withers 248, 350 Withers Hall, PO Box 8108, Raleigh, NC 27695-8108, U.S.A. **Online address:** james_banker@ncsu.edu

BANKER, Mark T(ollie). American (born United States), b. 1951. **Genres:** Local History/Rural Topics, Cultural/Ethnic Topics, History. **Career:** Menaul School, teacher and head of social studies department, 1976-81, dean of students, 1981-83; University of New Mexico-Valencia Campus, instructor in history, 1986; Albuquerque Academy, history teacher, 1986-87; Webb School of Knoxville, history teacher, 1987-, department head, 1990-92, chair. Writer. **Publications:** Toward Frontiers Yet Unknown: A Ninetieth Anniversary History of Warren Wilson College, 1985; Presbyterian Missions and Cultural Interaction in the Far Southwest, 1850-1950, 1992; Warren Wilson College: A Centennial Portrait, 1994; Appalachians All: East Tennesseans and the Elusive History of an American Region, 2010. Works appear in anthologies. Contributor to journals. **Address:** Department of Social Studies, Webb School of Knoxville, 9800 Webb School Dr., Knoxville, TN 37923-3399, U.S.A. **Online address:** mark_banker@webbschool.org

BANKS, Geraldine. (Jeri Banks). American (born United States), b. 1942. **Genres:** Animals/Pets, Education, History, Young Adult Non-fiction, Biography. **Career:** Teacher of language arts, 1963-67; substitute elementary schoolteacher, 1967-70; teacher, 1970-80; John H. Kinzie Elementary School, replication specialist, 1985-86, teacher, 1986-92, assistant principal, 1992-, principal; St. Xavier University, Illinois Renewal Institute, instructor. Writer. **Publications:** All Animals, 1978; (as Jeri Banks) All of Us Together: The Story of Inclusion at the Kinzie School, 1994. Contributor to periodicals. **Address:** John H. Kinzie School, 5625 S Mobile Ave., Chicago, IL 60638, U.S.A.

BANKS, Jeri. *See* **BANKS, Geraldine.**

BANKS, Kate. French/American (born United States), b. 1960?. **Genres:** Young Adult Fiction, Novels, Picture/Board Books. **Career:** Alfred A. Knopf, assistant editor. **Publications:** Max's Words, 1980; Close Your Eyes, 1985; Walk Softly, Rachel, 1987; Alphabet Soup, 1988; Big, Bigger, Biggest Adventure, 1990; The Bunnysitters, 1991; Peter and the Talking Shoes, 1994; Spider, Spider, 1996; Baboon, 1997; Witch and Cat, 1997; And If the Moon Could Talk, 1998; Howie Bowles: Secret Agent, 1999; The Bird, the Monkey, and the Snake in the Jungle, 1999; Petit lapin, grandes oreilles, 1999; Small Rabbit, Large Ears, 1999; Kangaroo, 1999; Who Goes There?, 1999; One Crafty Fox, 1999; The Large One and the Small One, 1999; The Night Worker, 2000; Howie Bowles and Uncle Sam, 2000; A Gift from the Sea, 2001; Mama's Little Baby, 2001; Dillon, Dillon, 2002; The Turtle and the Hippopotamus, 2002; Mama's Coming Home, 2003; The Cat Who Walked across France, 2004; The Great Blue House, 2005; Friends of the Heart: Amici del Cuore, 2005; Fox, 2007; Lenny's Space, 2007; Monkeys and Dog Days, 2008; Max's Dragon, 2008; Monkeys and the Universe, 2009; What's Coming for Christmas?, 2009; That's Papa's Way, 2009; This Baby, 2010; Eraserheads, 2010; Max's Castle, 2011; The Bear in the Book, 2012; The Magician's Apprentice, 2012. **Address:** c/o Author Mail, Farrar, Straus and Giroux Books For Young Readers, 19 Union Sq. W, New York, NY 10003-3304, U.S.A.

BANKS, Leanne. American (born United States), b. 1959. **Genres:** Young Adult Fiction, Novels. **Career:** Writer. **Publications:** ROMANCE NOVELS: Where There's a Will, 1991; The Fairest of Them All, 1992; Guardian Angel, 1992; His Royal Pleasure, 1993; Dance with the Devil, 1993; More Than a Mistress, 1994; Playing with Dynamite, 1994; For the Love of Sin, 1994; A Date with Dr. Frankenstein, 1995; Expectant Father, 1996; Ridge: The Avenger, 1996; The Troublemaker Bride, 1997; The Five-Minute Bride, 1997; The You-Can't-Make-Me Bride, 1997; Thirty-Day Fiancé, 1998; The Lone-Ride Takes a Bride, 1999; Millionaire Dad, 1999; The Lone Rider Takes a Bride, 1999; The Secretary and the Millionaire, 1999; Bride of Fortune, 2000; Her Forever Man, 2000; The Doctor Wore Spurs, 2000; Expecting His Child, 2000; Expecting the Boss's Baby, 2000; Never a Bride, Meteor, 2001; Millionaire's Husband, 2001; The Millionaire's Secret Wish, 2001; Royal Dad, 2001; His Majesty, M.D., 2002; Tall, Dark and Royal, 2002; Princess in His Bed, 2003; Some Girls Do, 2003; When She's Bad, 2003; The Playboy & Plain Jane, 2003; Between Duty and Desire, 2004; Shocking the Senator, 2004; Trouble in High Heels, 2004; Feet First, 2005; Footloose, 2006; Underfoot, 2006; Billionaire's Proposition, 2006; Hot Stuff, 2007; Bedded By The Billionaire, 2008; The Billionaire's Marriage Bargain, 2008; Billionaire Extraordinaire, 2008; CEO's Expectant Secretary, 2010; From Playboy to Papa!, 2010; Playboy's Proposition, 2010; Secrets of the Playboy's Bride, 2010; Royal Holiday Baby, 2010; The Prince's Texas Bride, 2010; The Doctor Takes a Princess, 2011. **Address:** HQN Books, 233 Broadway, Ste. 1001, New York, NY 10279, U.S.A. **Online address:** leannebbb@aol.com

BANKS, Leslie. British (born England), b. 1920. **Genres:** History, Air/Space Topics, Travel/Exploration, Sciences, Earth Sciences. **Career:** Clerk for a local government service, 1935-40; International Business Machines Ltd., sales instructor, marketing representative, academic consultant, personnel, 1963-85; Jetbond Ltd. (conference management firm), chairperson, 1985-. Writer. **Publications:** Polar Air Navigation, 1947; Grid Navigation in All Latitudes, 1950; (with C.S. Stanley) Britain's Coastline: A History from the Air, 1986; (with C.S. Stanley) The Thames: A History from the Air, 1990. **Address:** 22 Minister Ct., Hillcrest Rd., Ealing, London, GL W5 1HH, England.

BANKS, Lynne Reid. British (born England), b. 1929. **Genres:** Novels, Children's Fiction, Young Adult Fiction, Plays/Screenplays, History, Writing/Journalism, Young Adult Non-fiction, Humor/Satire, Humor/Satire. **Career:** Actress, 1949-54; freelance journalist, 1954-55; Independent Television News, television news reporter, 1955-57, television news scriptwriter, 1958-62; Kibbutz Yasur School, teacher of English as a foreign language, 1963-71; Na'aman High School, teacher of English as a foreign language, 1963-71; writer, 1971-. **Publications:** JUVENILE FICTION: One More River, 1973, rev. ed., 1992; Sarah and After: The Matriarchs, 1975 in US as Sarah and After: Five Women Who Founded a Nation, 1977; The Adventures of King Midas, 1976; Farthest-Away Mountain, 1976; My Darling Villain, 1977; I, Houdini: The Autobiography of a Self-educated Hamster, 1978; The Indian in the Cupboard, 1980; Writing on the Wall, 1981; Maura's Angel, 1984; The Fairy Rebel, 1985; The Return of the Indian, 1986; Melusine: A Mystery, 1988; The Secret of the Indian, 1989; Magic Hare, 1993; Mystery of the Cupboard, 1993; Broken Bridge, 1994; Angela and Diabola, 1997; Harry the Poisonous Centipede: A Story to Make You Squirm, 1997; Fair Exchange, 1998; Key to the Indian, 1998; Alice by Accident, 2000; Harry the Poisonous Centipede's Big Adventure: Another Story to Make You Squirm, 2001; The Dungeon, 2002; Tiger, Tiger, 2005; Harry the Poisonous Centipede Goes to Sea, 2006. ADULT NOVELS: L-Shaped Room, 1960, rev. ed., 1977; House of Hope in UK as An End to Running, 1962; Children at the Gate, 1968; The Backward Shadow, 1970; Two Is Lonely, 1974; Dark Quartet: The Story of the Brontes, 1976; Path to the Silent Country: Charlotte Bronte's Years of Fame, 1977; Defy the Wilderness, 1981; The Warning Bell, 1984; Casualties, 1986. OTHERS: It Never Rains: A Play in Three Acts, 1954; (with V. Madden) Miss Pringle Plays Portia, 1955; All in a Row: A Comedy in Three Acts, 1956; The Killer Dies Twice: A Play in Three Acts, 1956; Already It's Tomorrow: A Play in One Act, 1962; The Kibbutz: Some Personal Reflections, 1972; Letters to My Israeli Sons: The Story of Jewish Survival, 1979; Torn Country: An Oral History of the Israeli War of Independence, 1982; The Magic Hare, 1992; Twelve Stories of the Magic Hare, 1992; Moses in Egypt: A Novel Inspired by the Price of Egypt and the Book of Exodus, 1998; Bad Cat, Good Cat, 2011. PICTURE BOOKS: Polly and Jake, 2010; The Spice Rack, 2010. **Address:** Harper Collins Publishers Ltd., 77-85 Fulham Palace Rd., Hammersmith, GL W6 8JB, England.

BANKS, Piper. *See* **GASKELL, Whitney.**

BANKS, Ray. British/Scottish (born Scotland), b. 1977?. **Genres:** Novels, Young Adult Fiction, Mystery/Crime/Suspense. **Career:** Writer. **Publications:** CRIME NOVELS CAL INNES SERIES: Saturday's Child, 2006; Donkey Punch, 2007 in US as Sucker Punch, 2009; No More Heroes, 2008; Beast of Burden, 2009. CRIME FICTION: The Big Blind, 2004; Gun (novella), 2008; California, 2011. Contributor of articles to periodicals. Works appear in anthologies. **Address:** Houghton Mifflin Harcourt, 222 Berkeley St., Boston, MN 02116, U.S.A. **Online address:** raybanks77@yahoo.co.uk

BANKS, Russell (Earl). American (born United States), b. 1940. **Genres:** Novels, Novellas/Short Stories, Poetry, Young Adult Non-fiction, Young

Adult Fiction. **Career:** Lillabulero Press Inc., publisher and editor; Lillabulero Magazine, co-editor, publisher and editor, 1966-75; Northwood Narrows, publisher and editor, 1966-75; Emerson College, instructor, 1968, 1971; University of New Hampshire, instructor, 1968-75; New England College, instructor, 1975, 1977-82; Princeton University, instructor, 1982-; University of Maryland, artist-in-residence. **Publications:** POEMS: (with W. Matthews and N. Smith) 15 Poems, 1967; 30/6, 1969; Waiting to Freeze, 1969. SHORT STORIES: Searching for Survivors, 1975; The New World, 1978; Success Stories, 1986; The Angel on the Roof: The Stories of Russell Banks, 2000. NOVELS: Snow: Meditations of a Cautious Man in Winter, 1974; Family Life, 1975; Hamilton Stark, 1978; The Book of Jamaica, 1980; Trailerpark, 1981; The Relation of My Imprisonment, 1984; Continental Drift, 1985; Affliction, 1989; The Sweet Hereafter, 1991; Rule of The Bone, 1995; Cloudsplitter, 1998; The Darling, 2004; The Reserve, 2008; The Lost Memory of Skin, 2011. OTHERS: (with P.C. Metcalf) Paul Metcalf: A Special Issue, 1973; (co-ed.) Brushes with Greatness: An Anthology of Chance Encounters with Greatness, 1989; (with A. Patten) The Invisible Stranger: The Patten, Maine, Photographs of Arturo Patten, 1998; (contrib.) Mark Twain, 2001; Le voyage en Palestine de la délégation du Parlement international des écrivains en réponse á un appel de Mahmoud Darwish, 2002; (ed. and intro.) Varieties of Exile, 2003; (ed. and intro.) Montreal Stories, 2004; Outer Banks, 2008; Beneath the Roses, 2008; Dreaming Up America, 2008; Conversations with Russell Banks, 2010. **Address:** Department of English, College of Arts & Humanities, University of Maryland, 1102 Francis Scott Key Hall, College Park, MD 20742-7311, U.S.A.

BANN, **Stephen.** British (born England), b. 1942. **Genres:** Cultural/Ethnic Topics, Archaeology/Antiquities, Essays. **Career:** University of Kent, professor of modern cultural studies, 1988-2001; University of Bristol, chair, 2000, professor of the history of art, 2001-, now professor emeritus, Institute for Advanced Studies, senior research fellow. Writer. **Publications:** Four Essays on Kinetic Art, 1966; Experimental Painting: Construction, Abstraction, Destruction, Reduction, 1967; (ed.) Concrete Poetry: An International Anthology, 1967; (trans.) F. Popper, Origins and Development of Kinetic Art, 1968; Experimental Painting: Construction, Abstraction, Destruction, Reduction, 1970; (ed. with J.E. Bowlt) Russian Formalism: A Collection of Articles and Texts in Translation, 1973; (ed. and intro.) The Tradition of Constructivism, 1974, rev. ed., 2001; (with I.H. Finlay) Heroic Emblems, 1977; Constructive Context, 1978; Ian Hamilton Finlay, 1972; (ed.) Les Pins, 1983; The Clothing of Clio: A Study of the Representation of History in Nineteenth-Century Britain and France, 1984; (contrib.) Yves Abrioux, 1985; The True Vine: On Visual Representation and Western Tradition, 1989; The Inventions of History: Essays on the Representation of the Past, Manchester, 1990; (ed. and contrib. with W. Allen) Interpreting Contemporary Art, 1991; (ed. with K. Kumar) Utopias and the Millennium, 1993; (ed.) Frankenstein, Creation and Monstrosity, 1994; Under the Sign: John Bargrave as Collector, Traveler and Witness, 1994; The Edge of Town, 1995; Romanticism and the Rise of History, 1995; (contrib.) The Sculpture of Stephen Cox, 1995; Paul Delaroche: History Painted, 1997; Parallel Lines: Printmakers, Painters and Photographers in Nineteenth-Century France, 2001; (co-author) Le witz: figures de l'esprit et formes de l'art, 2002; (contrib.) Crossing the Channel: British and French Painting in the Age of Romanticism, 2003; (co-author) Nouvelles curiosités=New Curiosities, 2003; Jannis Kounellis, 2004; (contrib.) Art of the Garden: The Garden in British Art, 1800 to the Present Day, 2004; (ed.) The Reception of Walter Pater in Europe, 2004; Ways Around Modernism (Theories of Modernism and Postmodernism in the Visual Arts), 2007; (ed.) The Coral Mind: Adrian Stokes's Engagement with Architecture, Art History, Criticism and Psychoanalysis, 2007; (contrib.) The Repeating Image: Multiples in French Painting from David to Matisse, 2007; Ways around Modermism, 2007; (contrib.) Francis Alÿs: Fabiola: An Investigation, 2008; (with L. Whiteley and J. Guy) Painting History: Delaroche and Lady Jane Gre, 2010; (ed.) Art and the Early Photographic Album, 2011; (ed.) Interlacing Words and Things, 2012. Contributor to periodicals. **Address:** Department of History of Art, School of Humanities, University of Bristol, 11 Woodland Rd., Bristol, GL BS8 1TB, England. **Online address:** s.bann@bristol.ac.uk

BANNATYNE-CUGNET, **(Elizabeth) Jo(-Anne).** Canadian (born Canada), b. 1951. **Genres:** Children's Fiction, Picture/Board Books. **Career:** Saskatchewan Ministry of Health, rural public health nurse, 1974-77; Souris Valley Regional Care Centre, part-time nursing supervisor, 1977-94; writer, 1980-. **Publications:** PICTURE BOOKS: A Prairie Alphabet, 1992; Estelle and the Self-Esteem Machine, 1993; A Prairie Year, 1994; From Far and Wide: A Canadian Citizenship Scrapbook, 2000; Heartland: A Prairie Sampler, 2002. FICTION: Grampa's Alkali, 1993; The Day I Became a Canadian, 2008. **Address:** PO Box 1150, Weyburn, SK S4H 2L5, Canada.

BANNER, **Catherine.** British (born England), b. 1989?. **Genres:** Novels, Science Fiction/Fantasy. **Career:** Novelist. **Publications:** The Eyes of a King (novel), 2008; Voices in the Dark: The Last Descendants 2 (novel), 2009; The Heart at War, 2011. **Address:** c/o Simon Trewin, United Agents, 12-26 Lexington St., London, GL W1F 0LE, England.

BANNER-HALEY, **Charles Pete.** *See* **BANNER-HALEY**, **Charles T.**

BANNER-HALEY, **Charles T.** (Charles Pete Banner-Haley). American (born United States), b. 1948. **Genres:** History, Race Relations. **Career:** Colby College, assistant professor of history, 1977-79; State University of New York College-Oneonta, assistant professor of history, 1979-80; State University of New York College, lecturer in history and Black studies, 1980-85; University of Rochester, Frederick Douglass Institute, postdoctoral fellow, 1985-86; Martin Luther King, Jr. Papers Project, assistant editor, 1988-89; Colgate University, assistant professor, 1989-93, associate professor of history and Africana and Latin American studies, 1994-, professor of history and Africana and Latin American studies. **Publications:** To Do Good and to Do Well: Middle Class Blacks and the Depression, Philadelphia, 1929-1941, 1993; Fruits of Integration: Black Middle-Class Ideology and Culture, 1960-1990, 1994; From Du Bois to Obama: African American Intellectuals in the Public Forum, 2010. **Address:** Department of History, Colgate University, 320 Alumni Hall, 13 Oak Dr., Hamilton, NY 13346, U.S.A. **Online address:** cbannerhaley@mail.colgate.edu

BANNISTER, **Patricia Valeria.** *See* **VERYAN**, **Patricia.**

BANNISTER, **Roger (Gilbert).** British (born England), b. 1929. **Genres:** Medicine/Health, Sports/Fitness, Education. **Career:** The Sports Council of Great Britain, chairman, 1971-74; International Council for Sport and Physical Recreation, president, 1976-83; Pembroke College, master, 1985-93, retired, 2001; Clinical Autonomic Research, chair of editorial board, 1990-; University of Oxford, Merton College, honorary fellow. Writer. **Publications:** The Four-Minute Mile, 1955 in UK as First Four Minutes, 1955; (ed.) Prospect: The Schweppes Book of the New Generation, 1962; Brain's Clinical Neurology, 4th ed., 1973, 7th ed. as Brain and Bannister's Clinical Neurology, 1992; Autonomic Failure: A Textbook of Clinical Disorders of the Autonomic Nervous System, 1983, (ed. with C.J. Mathias) 4th ed., 1999. Contributor to periodicals and journals. **Address:** c/o Author Mail, Sutton Publishing Ltd., Phoenix Mill, London Rd., Thrupp, Stroud, GC GL5 2BU, England.

BANNISTER RAY, **Sheila G.** *See* **RAY**, **Sheila G(raham).**

BANNOCK, **Graham.** British (born England), b. 1932. **Genres:** Business/Trade/Industry, Economics. **Career:** Economist Intelligence Unit, economist, 1956-58, managing director, 1981-84; Rover Co., market research manager, 1958-60, 1962-67; Organization for Economic Cooperation and Development, Economics Division, senior administrator, 1960-62; Ford, manager of market research, 1967-68; Ford of Europe Inc., advanced planning manager, 1967-69; Economists Advisory Group Ltd., managing director, 1971-81. Writer. **Publications:** (With A.J. Merrett) Business Economics and Statistics, 1962; The Juggernauts: The Age of the Giant Corporation, 1971; (with R.E. Baxter and R. Rees) The Penguin Dictionary of Economics, 1972, (with R.E. Baxter and E. Davis) 7th ed., 2003; How to Survive the Slump: A Guide to Economic Crisis, 1975; The Smaller Business in Britain and Germany, 1976; The Economics of Small Firms, 1981; The Economics of Small Firms: Return from the Wilderness, 1981; (with A. Doran) Going Public, 1987; (with A. Peacock) Governments and Small Business, 1989; (with W.A.P. Manser) A Dictionary of International Finance, 1989; VAT and Small Business Revisited, 1990; Taxation in the European Community, 1990; (with W. Manser) The Penguin International Dictionary of Finance, 1990; (with H. Albach) Small Business Policy in Europe, 1991; Międzynarodowy slownik finansów, 1992; (ed. with M. Daly) Small Business Statistics, 1994; (with R.E. Baxter and R. Rees) Dictionary of Economics, 1998, 4th ed., 2003; (with W. Manser) International Dictionary of Finance, 1999, 4th ed., 2003; (co-author) Dictionary of Business, 2003; The Economics and Management of Small Business: An International Perspective, 2005. Contributor of articles and reviews to journals. **Address:** Bannock Consulting, 47 Marylebone Ln., London, GL WIU 2LD, England.

BANNON, David Race. American (born United States), b. 1963?. **Genres:** History, Criminology/True Crime, Politics/Government. **Career:** Information Architects, computer trainer; Duke University, faculty; University of South Carolina, faculty; Wake Technical College, faculty; Interpol agent; college science instructor. Writer. **Publications:** Race against Evil: The Secret Missions of the Interpol Agent Who Tracked the World's Most Sinister Criminals: A Real Life Drama, 2003. **Address:** c/o Author Mail, New Horizon Press Publishers, PO Box 669, Far Hills, NJ 07931, U.S.A.

BANSEMER, Roger. American (born United States), b. 1948. **Genres:** Area Studies, Natural History, Art/Art History, Technology, Sports/Fitness, Illustrations. **Career:** Writer and artist. **Publications:** SELF-ILLUSTRATED: The Art of Hot-Air Ballooning, 1987; (with D. May) Rachael's Splendifilous Adventure, 1991. OTHERS: Southern Shores, 1989; (with B. Renc) At Water's Edge: The Birds of Florida, 1993; Mountains in the Mist: Impressions of the Great Smokies, 1993; Bansemer's Book of Florida Lighthouses, 1999; Bansemer's Book of Carolina and Georgia Lighthouses, 2000; Bansemer's Book of the Southern Shores, 2003; Journey to Titanic, 2003. **Address:** 2352 Alligator Creek Rd., Clearwater, FL 33765-2205, U.S.A. **Online address:** bansemer@bansemer.com

BANTA, Trudy W. American (born United States) **Genres:** Education, Young Adult Non-fiction. **Career:** University of Tennessee, assistant professor, professor of education, 1967-81, special assistant, 1979-82, Bureau of Educational Research, professor, National Assessment Resource Center, director, Research and Service, professor, 1981-86, Learning Research Center, 1986-89, Center for Assessment Research and Development, professor and director, 1989-92; Indiana University-Purdue University, professor of higher education and vice chancellor for planning and institutional improvement, 1992-. Writer. **Publications:** (With D.C. Towne) Interpretive Study of Cooperative Efforts of Private Industry and the Schools to Provide Job-Oriented Education Programs for the Disadvantaged, 1969; Description of School Plant Facilities in Tennessee, 1973; (with S.M. Bowlby) Bibliographical References from ERIC Citations, 1974; (co-author) Assessment in Practice: Putting Principles to Work on College Campuses, 1996; (with C.A. Palomba) Assessment Essentials: Planning, Implementing and Improving Assessment in Higher Education, 1999; (co-author) Designing Effective Assessment: Principles and Profiles of Good Practice, 2009. EDITOR AND CONTRIBUTOR: Performance Funding in Higher Education: A Critical Analysis of Tennessee's Experience, 1986; Implementing Outcomes Assessment: Promise and Perils, 1988; Making a Difference: Outcomes of a Decade of Assessment in Higher Education, 1993; (with V.M.H. Borden) Using Performance Indicators to Guide Strategic Decision Making, 1994; (with C.A. Palomba) Assessing Student Competence in Accredited Disciplines: Pioneering Approaches to Assessment in Higher Education, 2001; Building a Scholarship of Assessment, 2002; Portfolio Assessment: An Assessment Update Collection, 2003; Assessing Student Achievement in General Education: Assessment Update Collections, 2007; Assessing Student Learning in the Disciplines, 2007. Contributor to books and journals. **Address:** School of Education, Indiana University-Purdue University, 140 IUPUI Administration Bldg., 355 N Lansing St., Bloomington, IN 47405-1006, U.S.A. **Online address:** tbanta@iupui.edu

BANVILLE, John. (Benjamin Black). Irish (born Ireland), b. 1945. **Genres:** Novels, Novellas/Short Stories. **Career:** Irish Press, copy editor, 1969-83; Irish Times, sub-editor, 1986-88, literary editor, 1988-99. **Publications:** NOVELS: Nightspawn, 1971; Birchwood, 1973; Doctor Copernicus, 1976; Kepler, 1981; The Newton Letter, 1982; Mefisto, 1986; The Book of Evidence, 1989; Ghosts, 1993; The Broken Jug: After Heinrich von Kleist, 1994; Athena, 1995; The Untouchable, 1997; The Supreme Fictions of John Banville, 1999; God's Gift: A Version of Amphitryon by Heinrich von Kleist, 2000; The Revolutions Trilogy, 2000; Eclipse, 2001; Shroud, 2002; Prague Pictures: Portraits of a City, 2004; Love in the Wars: A Version of Penthesilea by Heinrich von Kleist, 2005; The Sea, 2005; (as Benjamin Black) Christine Falls, 2006; (as Benjamin Black) The Silver Swan, 2007; The Lemur, 2008; (as Benjamin Black) Elegy for April, 2010; (as Benjamin Black) A Death In Summer, 2011. OTHER: Long Lankin (short stories), 1970, rev. ed., 1984; (foreword) The Jugger, 2009; (foreword) The Score, 2009; The Infinities, 2009. **Address:** Gillon Aitken Associates, 18-21 Cavaye Pl., London, GL SW10 9PT, England.

BAOFU, Peter. American (born United States), b. 1962. **Genres:** Sciences, Education, Technology. **Career:** Center for Strategic and International Studies, research assistant, 1987; Massachusetts Institute of Technology, teaching assistant, 1990; Quinsigamond Community College, adjunct professor, 1991; Harvard University, teaching fellow, 1993-95; Eastern Mediterranean University, associate professor, 1998-99; Urban Institute, consultant, 2000; Bocconi University, visiting professor, 2001; U.S. Department of Agriculture, Graduate School, adjunct instructor, 2002; Eastern New Mexico University, assistant professor, 2003; University of Pittsburgh, semester-at-sea program visiting lecturer, 2005; Kazakhstan Institute of Management, Economics and Strategic Research, associate professor, 2005-06; International Black Sea University, post-doctoral fellow, 2006; Izmir University of Economics, associate professor, 2007; Karakurum International University, professor, 2007; South East European University, professor, 2008-09; Universiti Utara Malaysia, visiting professor, 2011. **Publications:** The Future of Human Civilization, 2 vols., 2000; The Future of Capitalism and Democracy, 2002; The Future of Post-Human Consciousness, 2004; Beyond Democracy to Post-Democracy: Conceiving a Better Model of Governance to Supercede Democracy, 2 vols., 2004; Beyond Captialism to Post-Capitalism: Conceiving a Better Model of Wealth Acquisition to Supersede Capitalism, 2005; Beyond Civilization to Post-Civilization: Conceiving a Better Model of Life Settlement to Supersede Civilization, 2006; The Future of Post-Human Space-Time: Conceiving a Better Way to Understand Space and Time, 2006; Beyond Nature and Nurture, 2006; Beyond the World of Titans, and the Remaking of World Order, 2007; Future of Complexity: Conceiving a Better Way to Understand Order and Chaos, 2007; Future of Aesthetic Experience: Conceiving a Better Way to Understand Beauty, Ugliness, and the Rest, 2007; Beyond the World of Titans, and the Remaking of World Order: A Preface to a New Logic of Empire Building, 2007; Rise of Authoritarian Liberal Democracy: A Preface to a New Theory of Comparative Political Systems, 2007; Future of Post-Human Unconsciousness: A Preface to a New Theory of Anomalous Experience, 2008; Future of Post-Human Mathematical Logic, 2008; Future of Post-Human Knowledge: A Preface to a New Theory of Methodology and Ontology, 2008; Future of Information Architecture: Conceiving a New Way to Understand Taxonomy, Network, and Intelligence, 2008; Future of Post-Human Geometry: A Preface to a New Theory of Infinity, Symmetry, and Dimensionality, 2009; Future of Post-Human Engineering: A Preface to a New Theory of Technology, 2009; Future of Post-Human Mass Media: A Preface to a New Theory of Communication, 2009; Future of Post-Human Creative Thinking: A Preface to a New Theory of Invention and Innovation, 2009; Future of Post-Human Martial Arts: A Preface to a New Theory of the Body and Spirit of Warriors, 2009; Future of Post-Human Organization: A Preface to a New Theory of Communication, Decision-Making, and Leadership, 2009; Future of Post-Human Language: A Preface to a New Theory of Structure, Context, and Learning, 2009; Future of Post-Human Urban Planning: A Preface to a New Theory of Density, Void, and Sustainability, 2009; Future of Post-Human Religion: A Preface to a New Theory of Spirituality, 2010; Future of Post-Human Chess: A Preface to a New Theory of Tactics and Strategy, 2010; Future of Post-Human Geology: A Preface to a New Theory of Statics and Dynamics, 2010; Beyond Cosmology to Post-Cosmology: A Preface to a New Theory of Different Worlds, 2010; Future of Post-Human Personality: A Preface to a New Theory of Normality and Abnormality, 2010; Future of Post-Human War and Peace: A Preface to a New Theory of Aggression and Pacificity, 2010; Future of Post-Human Formal Science: A Preface to a New Theory of Abstraction and Application, 2010; Future of Post-Human Law: A Preface to a New Theory of Necessity, Contingency, and Justice, 2010; Future of Post-Human Sexuality: A Preface to a New Theory of the Body and Spirit of Love Makers, 2010; Future of Post-Human Computing: A Preface to a New Theory of Hardware, Software, and the Mind, 2011; Future of Post-Human Gambling: A Preface to a New Theory of Risk and Caution, 2011; Future of Post-Human Acoustics: A Preface to a New Theory of Sound and Silence, 2011; Future of Post-Human Humor: A Preface to a New Theory of Joking and Laughing, 2011; Beyond Ethics to Post-Ethics: A Preface to a New Theory of Morality and Immorality, 2011; Future of Post-Human Education: A Preface to a New Theory of Teaching and Learning, 2011; Future of Post-Human Chemistry: A Preface to a New Theory of Substances and their Changes, 2011; Future of Post-Human Literature: A Preface to a New Theory of Fiction and Non-Fiction, 2011. **Address:** Los Angeles, CA , U.S.A. **Online address:** pbaofu@yahoo.com

BAPTIST, Edward (E.). American (born United States), b. 1970. **Genres:** History, Economics, Politics/Government. **Career:** University of Pennsylvania, lecturer, 1997-98; University of Miami, Charlton W. Tebeau assistant professor, 1998-2003; Cornell University, Department of History, assistant professor, 2003-05, associate professor, 2005-, Carl Becker House, dean. Writer. **Publications:** Creating an Old South: Middle Florida's Plantation

Frontier before the Civil War, 2002; (ed. with S.M.H. Camp) New Studies in the History of American Slavery, 2006; Encyclopedia of Slavery in the America's, 2011; The Half Has Never Been Told: The Migration That Made African America, the United States and the World, forthcoming. **Address:** Department of History, Cornell University, 433 McGraw Hall, Ithaca, NY 14850, U.S.A. **Online address:** eeb36@cornell.edu

BAR, Shmuel. Israeli (born Israel), b. 1954. **Genres:** Military/Defense/Arms Control, History, Politics/Government, Theology/Religion. **Career:** Israel Defense Forces, intelligence officer; Stanford University, Hoover Institution, Distinguished Koret Visiting Fellow; Institute of Policy and Strategy, director of studies. Author of nonfiction. **Publications:** The Yom Kippur War in the Eyes of the Arabs, 1986; The Jordanian Communist Party: A Historical Analysis, 1988; The Muslim Brotherhood in Jordan, 1998; Warrant for Terror: Fatwas of Radical Islam and the Duty of Jihad, 2006. Works appear in anthologies. Contributor to journals. **Address:** The Interdisciplinary Center, PO Box 167, Herzliya, 46150, Israel. **Online address:** shmuel-bar@idc.ac.il

BARABÁSI, Albert-László. American/Hungarian/Romanian (born Romania), b. 1967. **Genres:** Physics, Sciences. **Career:** Hungarian Academy of Sciences, Research Institute for Technical Physics, research assistant, 1989-91; Boston University, teaching assistant, 1991-92, research assistant, 1992-94; International Business Machines Corp., T.J. Watson Research Center, Department of Physical Sciences, postdoctoral associate, 1994-95; University of Notre Dame, assistant professor, 1995-99, associate professor, 1999-2000, Emil T. Hofman professor, 2000-07, Center for Complex Network Research, director, 2004-07, adjunct professor of computer science and engineering, 2007-; Institute of Advanced Studies, senior fellow, 2000; Harvard University, Dana Farber Cancer Institute, visiting professor, 2005-06, Department of Medicine, lecturer on medicine, 2007-; Northeastern University, distinguished professor, 2007-, Center for Complex Network Research, director, 2007-. Writer. **Publications:** (With H.E. Stanley) Fractal Concepts in Surface Growth, 1995; (co-ed.) Epitaxial Growth: Principles and Applications Symposium Held April 5-8, 1999, San Francisco, California, U.S.A., 1999; Linked: The New Science of Networks, 2002; Linked: How Everything is Connected to Everything else and What it Means for Business, Science, and Everyday Life, 2003; (ed. with M. Newman and D. Watts) The Structure and Dynamics of Networks, 2006; Bursts: The Hidden Pattern Behind Everything We Do, 2010. Contributor to periodicals. **Address:** Center for Complex Network Research, Northeastern University, 360 Huntington Ave., Boston, MA 02115, U.S.A. **Online address:** alb@neu.edu

BARABTARLO, Gennady. American/Russian (born Russia), b. 1949. **Genres:** Poetry, Literary Criticism And History, Translations, Essays, Novellas/Short Stories. **Career:** Pushkin Literary Museum, senior research fellow, 1970-78; University of Missouri, professor of Russian, 1984-90, associate professor of Russian, 1990-94, professor of Russian, 1994-, Graduate Studies in Russian and Slavonic Studies, director. Writer. **Publications:** (Trans.) Vladimir Nabokov, Pnin, 1983; Phantom of Fact: A Guide to Nabokov's Pnin, 1989; Aerial View: Essays on Nabokov's Art and Metaphysics, 1993; (with C. Nicol) Small Alpine Form: Studies in Nabokov's Short Fiction, 1993; In Every Place of His Dominion, 1999; Solzhenitsyn: What A Pity (short stories), 1999; (ed.) Cold Fusion: Aspects of the German Cultural Presence in Russia, 2000; Ebbing of Time (short stories), 2001; A Shimmering Hoop, On the Movement of Nabokov's Themes, 2003; (foreword) Laura i ee Original: Fragmenty Romana, 2010; Vladimir Nabokov: Collected Works, forthcoming. **Address:** Department of German and Russian Studies, University of Missouri, 456 GCB, 456 Strickland Hall, Columbia, MO 65211, U.S.A. **Online address:** barabtarlog@missouri.edu

BARACCHI, Claudia. American (born United States), b. 1962. **Genres:** Philosophy. **Career:** New School for Social Research, associate professor of philosophy. Philosopher and writer. **Publications:** Of Myth, Life and War in Plato's Republic, 2002; Aristotle's Ethics as First Philosophy, 2008. Contributor to periodicals. **Address:** Department of Philosophy, New School for Social Research, Rm. 1116, 6 E 16th St., New York, NY 10003, U.S.A. **Online address:** baracchc@newschool.edu

BARAKA, Imamu Amiri. ((Everett) LeRoi Jones). American (born United States), b. 1934. **Genres:** Novels, Plays/Screenplays, Poetry, Music, Race Relations, Essays. **Career:** Yugen Magazine, founder, 1958; Totem Press, founder, 1958; Kulchur, editor and critic, 1960-65; Floating Bar Magazine, founder and co-editor, 1961-63; New School for Social Research (now New School University), instructor, 1962-64; Black Arts Repertory Theatre/School, founder and director, 1964-66; San Francisco State University, visiting professor, 1967; Yale University, visiting professor, 1977-78; George Washington University, visiting professor, 1978-79; State University of New York, Department of Africana Studies, lecturer, 1979, assistant professor, 1980-83, associate professor, 1983-85, professor of African studies, 1985-, now professor emeritus; Columbia University, visiting professor, 1982-83; Rutgers University, professor, 1984, visiting professor, 1988. **Publications:** POETRY: April 13, 1959; Spring and So Forth, 1960; Preface to a Twenty Volume Suicide Note, 1961; The Disguise, 1961; The Dead Lecturer, 1964; (as LeRoi Jones) Black Art, 1966; (as LeRoi Jones) Baptism & The Toilet, 1967; (as LeRoi Jones) Black Magic, 1967; A Poem for Black Hearts, 1967; It's Nation Time, 1970; Spirit Reach, 1972; Afrikan Revolution, 1973; Hard Facts: Excerpts, 1975, 2nd ed., 1975; Spring Song, 1979; AM/TRAK, 1979; Selected Poetry of Amiri Baraka/LeRoi Jones, 1979; In the Tradition: For Black Arthur Blythe, 1980; Reggae or Not!, 1982; LeRoi Jones-Amiri, 1991; Transbluency: The Selected Poems of Amiri Baraka/LeRoi Jones (1961-1995), 1995; Funk Lore: New Poems, 1984-1995, 1996; Beginnings and Other Poems, 2003; Somebody Blew up America & Other Poems, 2003. ESSAYS: Cuba Libre, 1961; (as LeRoi Jones) Blues People: Negro Music in White America, 1963 as Negro Music in White America, 1965; (as LeRoi Jones) Home: Social Essays, 1966; Black Music, 1968; Raise, Race, Rays, Raze: Essays since 1965, 1971; Strategy and Tactics of a Pan-African Nationalist Party, 1971; Kawaida Studies: The New Nationalism, 1972; Crisis in Boston!, 1974; Daggers and Javelins: Essays, 1974-1979, 1984; (with A. Baraka) The Music: Reflections on Jazz and Blues, 1987; Jesse Jackson and Black People, 1996; The Essence of Reparation: Afro-American Self-Determination & Revolutionary Democratic Struggle in the United States of America, 2003. EDITOR: January 1st 1959: Fidel Castro, 1959; Four Young Lady Poets, 1962; (and intro. as LeRoi Jones) The Moderns: An Anthology of New Writing in America, 1963 as The Moderns: New Fiction in America, 1964; Gilbert Sorrentino, 1965; Edward Dorn, Hands Up!, 1965; (with L. Neal and A.B. Spellman) The Cricket: Black Music in Evolution, 1968 as Trippin': A Need for Change, 1969; (as LeRoi Jones with L. Neal) Black Fire: An Anthology of Afro-American Writing, 1968; A Black Value System, 1970; (with B. Abernathy as Fundi) In Our Terribleness, 1970; (and intro.) African Congress: A Documentary of the First Modern Pan-African Congress, 1972; (with D.D. Prima) The Floating Bear, 1961-1969, 1974; (with A. Baraka) Confirmation: An Anthology of African-American Women, 1983. OTHERS: (co-author) In-formation, 1965; (as LeRoi Jones) The System of Dante's Hell, 1965; (contrib.) Afro-American Festival of the Arts Magazine, 1966 as Anthology of Our Black Selves, 1969; (intro.) Felix of the Silent Forest, 1967; Striptease, 1967; Tales (short stories), 1967; (intro.) Black Boogaloo, 1969; (as LeRoi Jones) Dutchman and The Slave, 1971; Selected Plays and Prose of Amiri Baraka/LeRoi Jones, 1979; The Autobiography of LeRoi Jones/ Amiri Baraka, 1984; (intro.) Rebellion Is the Circle of a Lover's Hand, 1990; (intro.) Space, and Other Poems, 1990; The LeRoi Jones/ Amiri Baraka Reader, 1991, 2nd ed., 2000; Thornton Dial: Images of the Tiger, 1993; Jesse Jackson and Black People, 1994; Shy's Wise, Y's: The Griot's Tale, 1994; (with C. Reilly) Conversations with Amiri Baraka, 1994; Wise, Why's, Y's, 1995; Eulogies, 1996; The Fiction of LeRoi Jones, 2000; Tales of the Out & the Gone, 2006; Digging: The Afro-American Soul of American Classical Music, 2009; (contrib.) Eyeminded: Living and Writing Contemporary Art, 2011. **Address:** Celeste Bateman & Associates, PO Box 4071, Newark, NJ 07114-4071, U.S.A.

BARAKAT, Ibtisam. American (born United States), b. 1963. **Genres:** Biography, Children's Non-fiction. **Career:** Journalist. **Publications:** Tasting the Sky: A Palestinian Childhood, 2007. **Address:** Farrar, Straus and Giroux, 175 5th Ave., New York, NY 10010-7703, U.S.A.

BARAM, Amatzia. Israeli (born Israel), b. 1938?. **Genres:** Area Studies, History, Young Adult Non-fiction. **Career:** Kibbutz Kfar Menachem, high school science teacher, 1968-73; Hebrew University of Jerusalem, tutor, 1976-80; University of Haifa, lecturer, 1981, professor in modern history of the Middle East, 1982-, chairman, through 1997, Jewish-Arab Center and Gustav Heinemann Institute for Middle Eastern Studies, deputy director, 1992-93, director, 1999-2002; Oxford University, St. Antony's College, senior associate, 1989-90. Writer. **Publications:** Culture, History, and Ideology in the Formation of Ba'thist Iraq, 1968-1989, 1991; (ed. with B. Rubin) Iraq's Road to War, 1993; Building toward Crisis: Saddam Husayn's Strategy for Survival, 1998; State and Mosque in Iraq 1968-2006, 2007; (ed. with A. Rohde and R. Zeidel) Iraq Between Occupations: Perspectives from 1920 to the Present, 2010. Contributor to journals. **Address:** Department of Modern History of the Middle East, University of Haifa, Mount Carmel, Haifa, 31999, Israel. **Online address:** baram@research.haifa.ac.il

BARAŃCZAK, Stanisław. American/Polish (born Poland), b. 1946. **Genres:** Poetry, Politics/Government, Literary Criticism And History, Translations, Essays. **Career:** Adam Mickiewicz University, Institute of Polish Philology, assistant professor, 1969-77, associate professor of literature, 1980-81; Harvard University, associate professor of Slavic language and literature, 1981-84, Alfred Jurzykowski professor of Polish language and literature, 1984-; The Polish Review, editor, 1986-90. **Publications:** POETRY: Korekta twarzy, 1968; Jednym tchem, 1970; Dziennik poranny: Wiersze 1967-1971, 1972; Ja wiem, ze to niesluszne: Wiersze z lat 1975-1976, 1977; Sztuczne oddychanie, 1978; Tryptyk z betonu, zmeczenia isniegu, 1980; Wiersze prawie zebrane, 1981; Atlantyda i inne wiersze z lat 1981-1985, 1986; Widokowka z tego swiata i inne rymy zlat 1986-1988, 1988; 159 wierszy: 1968-1988, 1990; Poezjewybrane, 1990; Zwierzeca zajadlosc: Zzapiskow zneicheconego zoologa, 1991; Biografioly: Poczet 56 jednostek slawnych, slawetnych, i ostawionych, 1991; Zupelnezezwierzecenie, 1993; Podroz zimowa ('Winter Journey'), 1994; Bog, Traba i Ojczyzna: Slon a sprawa polskaoczami poetow od Reja do Rymkiewicza, 1995; Zegam cie Nosorozcze: Kompletne bestiarium zniecheconegozoologa, 1995. ESSAYS AND CRITICISM: Nieufni i zadufani: Romantyzm i klascycyzm w mlodej poezji latszescdziesiatych, 1971; Ironia i harmonia: Szkice o najnowszej literaturze polskiej, 1973; Jezykpoetycki Mirona Bialoszewskiego, 1974; Etyka i poetyka: Szkice 1970-1978, 1979; Ksiazki najgorsze 1975-80, 1981, rev. ed., 1990; Czytelnikubezwlasnowolniony: Perswazja w masowej kulturze literackiej PRL, 1983; Uciekinier z Utopii: O poezji Zbigniewa Herberta, 1984, 2nd ed., 1994, trans. as A Fugitive from Utopia: The Poetry of Zbigniew Herbert, 1987; Przed i po: Szkice o poezji krajowejprzelo mu lat siedemdziesiatych i osiemdziesiatych, 1988; Breathing under Water, and Other East European Essays, 1990; Tablica z Macondo: Osiem nascie prob wytlumaczenia, po co i dlaczego sie pisze, 1990; Ocalone w tlumaczeniu, 1992, 3rd ed., 2004; Zaufac nieufnosci: Osiemrozmow o sensie poezji 1990-1992 (interviews), 1993; Pomyslane przepascie: Osien interpretacij, 1995. EDITOR AND TRANSLATOR: D. Thomas, Wiersze wybrane, 1974; O. Mandelshtam, Pózne wiersze, 1977; J. Brodsky, Wiersze i poematy, 1979; G.M. Hopkins, Wybor poezji, 1981; Antologia angielskiej poezji metafizycznej XVII stulecia, 1982; J. Donne, Wiersze wybrane, 1984; (with R.A. Davies and J.M. Gogol) R. Krynicki, Citizen R. K. Does Not Live: Poems, 1985; T. Venclova, Rozmowa w zimie: Wybór wierszy, 1989; G. Herbert, Wierszewybrane, 1990; J. Merrill, Wybor poezji, 1990; Zwierze slucha zwierzen: Malebestiarium z angielskiego, 1991; Z Toba wiec ze Wszystkim: 222 arcydziela angielskiej i amerykanskiej liryki religijnej, 1992; (with C. Cavanagh) Polish Poetry of the Last Two Decades of Communist Rule: Spoiling Cannibals' Fun, 1991; C. Simic, Madonny z dorysowana szpicbrodka oraz inne wiersze, prozy poetyckie ieeseje, 1992; Milosc jest wszystkim, co istnieje: 300 najslawniejszych angielskich i amerykanskich wierszy milosnych, 1993; Fioletowa krowa: 333 najslawniejsze okazyangielskiej i amerykanskiej poezji niepowaznej od Williama Shakespeare'ado Johna Lennona, 1993; Od Chaucera do Larkina: 400 niesmiertelnych wieszy 125 poetow anglojezycznych z 8 stuleci, 1993; (with C. Cavanagh) Seventy-Seven Translations, 1995. TRANSLATOR: A.A. Milne, Nieposluszna mama (children's poetry), 1983; E.E. cummings, 150 wierszy, 1983; U.K. Le Guin, Czarnoksieznik z Archipelagu, 1983, 2nd ed., 1991; Milne, Nieposluszna mama I inne wierszyki dla dzieci, 1983; J. Brodsky, 82 wiersze I poematy, 1988; W. Shakespeare, Hamlet, 1990; W. Shakespeare, Romeo I Julia, 1990; E. Dickinson, 100 wierszy, 1990; P. Larkin, 44 wiersze, 1991; W. Shakespeare, Burza. Zimowaopowiesc, 1991; W. Shakespeare, Krol Lear, 1991; R. Herrick, 77 wierszy, 1992; R. Frost, 55 wierszy, 1992; W. Shakespeare, Makbet, 1992; W. Shakespeare, Sen nocy letniej. Kupiec wenecki, 1992; W. Shakespeare, Dwaj panowie z Werony. Pokromienie zlosnicy, 1992; W. Shakespeare, Sonety, 1993; W. Shakespeare, Juliusz Cezar, 1993; W. Shakespeare, Jak wam sie podoba, 1993; W. Shakespeare, Otello, 1993; A. Marvel, 24 wiersze, 1993; T. Hardy, 55 wiersze, 1993; Brodsky, Znakwodny, 1993; W. Shakespeare, Wiele halasu o nic. Wieczor Trzech Kroli, 1994; W. Shakespeare, Komedia omylek. Stracone zachody Milosci, 1994; W.H. Auden, 44 wiersze, 1994; S. Heaney, 44 wiersze, 1994; W. Shakespeare, Koriolan, 1994; T. Campion, 33 piesni, 1995; E. Dickinson, Drugie 100 wiersze, 1995; (with C. Cavanagh) W. Szymborska, View with a Grain of Sand: Selected Poems, 1995; T.S. Eliot, Koty, 1995; E. Bishop, 33 wiersze, 1995; (with S. Heaney) J. Kochanowski, Laments, 1995, rev. ed., 2009; (with C. Cavanagh and afterword) W. Szymborska, Nothing Twice: Selected Poems, 1997; (with C. Cavanagh) W. Szymborska, Poems, New and Collected, 1957-1997, 1998; J. Twardowski, When You Say, 2000; (with C. Cavanagh) W. Szymborska, Monologue of a Dog: New Poems, 2006; (with C. Cavanagh) W. Szymborska, Here: New Poems, 2010; (with C. Cavanagh) Three Great Polish Romantic Poets, forthcoming. EDITOR: Poeta pamieta: Antologia poezji swiadectwa I sprzeciwu 1944-1984, 1984; Wiktor Weintraub, O wspolczesnych I o sobie: Wyspomnienia, sylwetki, szkice literacki, 1994. OTHERS: Breathing under Water and other East European Essays, 1990; Wybór wierszy I przekladów, 1997; Zimy ipodróze, 1997; Chirurgiczna precyzja: elegie I piosenki z lat1995-1997, 1998; Geografioly: z notatek globtrottera-domatora, 1998; Uciekinier z Utopii: o poezji Zbigniewa Herberta, 2001; Chwila: Moment, 2003; Fin y principio, 2004; Zbigniew Herbert, 2005; Pokaz prozy, 2006; Wiersze zebrane, 2006; (trans. with C. Cavanagh) Three Great Polish Romantic Poets, forthcoming; Polish Poetry After 1944, forthcoming. Contributor of articles to periodicals. **Address:** Department of Slavic Languages & Literatures, Harvard University, Barker Ctr., 3rd Fl., 12 Quincy St., Cambridge, MA 02138-3804, U.S.A. **Online address:** barancz@fas.harvard.edu

BARASCH, Frances K. American (born United States), b. 1928. **Genres:** Literary Criticism And History, Romance/Historical, Essays, Bibliography. **Career:** New York University, administrative assistant, 1957-60, instructor in English, 1959-61; Pace College (now University), assistant professor of English, 1961-64; Long Island University, assistant professor of English, 1964-65; City University of New York, Bernard M. Baruch College, assistant professor, 1965-72, associate professor, 1972-77, professor of English, 1977, now professor emeritus. Writer. **Publications:** Review Notes and Study Guide to Shakespeare's Henry IV, Part II, 1964; Modern British Literature, vol. III, 1966; The Grotesque: A Study of Meanings, 1971; Academic Women and Unions, 1974; (contrib.) Reverse Discrimination, 1977; (with R.E. Helbling) New Essays on the Grotesque, forthcoming. EDITOR: Romantic Poets, 1966; A History of Caricature and the Grotesque in Literature and Art, 1968; The Critical Temper, vol. II: The Romantic Period, 1969; Home Life, 1971; PSC Clarion, 1972-73. Contributor of articles to periodicals. **Address:** Department of English, Bernard M. Baruch College, City University of New York, New York, NY 10010, U.S.A. **Online address:** fbarasch@aol.com

BARASH, David P(hilip). American (born United States), b. 1946. **Genres:** Biology, Psychology, Politics/Government, Military/Defense/Arms Control, Zoology, Sex, Human Relations/Parenting, Natural History, Natural History, Social Commentary. **Career:** State University of New York, assistant professor of biology, 1970-73; University of Washington, associate professor, 1973-80, professor of psychology and zoology, 1980-. Writer. **Publications:** Sociobiology and Behavior, 1977, rev. ed., 1982; The Whisperings Within, 1979; Stop Nuclear War!: A Handbook, 1982; Aging: An Exploration, 1983; The Caveman and the Bomb, 1985; The Hare and the Tortoise: Culture, Biology, and Human Nature, 1986; The Arms Race and Nuclear War, 1987; Marmots: Social Behavior and Ecology, 1989; The Great Outdoors, 1989; Introduction to Peace Studies, 1991; The L Word: An Unapologetic, Thoroughly Biased, Long-overdue Explication and Celebration of Liberalism, 1992; Beloved Enemies: Exploring Our Need for Opponents, 1994; Ideas of Human Nature, 1997; Approaches to Peace, 2000, 2nd ed., 2009; Peace and Conflict Studies, 2001, 2nd ed., 2008; Gender Gap, 2001; The Myth of Monogamy, 2002; The Survival Game, 2003; Madame Bovary's Ovaries: A Darwinian look at literature, 2005; Natural Selections: Honest Liars, Selfish Altruists and Other Realities of Evolution, 2007; How Women Got Their Curves and Other Just-So Stories, 2009; Strange Bedfellows: The Surprising Connection between Sex, Evolution and Monogamy, 2009; Payback: Why We Retaliate, Redirect Aggression and Seek Revenge, 2011. **Address:** Department of Psychology, University of Washington, PO Box 351525, Seattle, WA 98195, U.S.A. **Online address:** dpbarash@u.washington.edu

BARASH, Samuel T. (Samuel Theodore Barash). American (born United States), b. 1921. **Genres:** Money/Finance, Economics, Business/Trade/Industry. **Career:** Veterans Administration, assistant chief real estate appraiser, 1951-53, chief of construction, 1953-56, assistant chief appraiser, 1956-63, chief appraiser, 1963-72; independent real estate appraiser, 1972-. Writer. **Publications:** Standard Real Estate Appraising Manual, 1979; How to Reduce Your Real Estate Taxes, 1979; How to Cash in on Little-Known Local Real Estate Investment Opportunities, 1980; Complete Guide to Condominium and Cooperative Appraising, 1981; Encyclopedia of Real Estate Appraisal Forms and Model Reports, 1983. Contributor to magazines. **Address:** Prentice Hall, 1 Lake St., Upper Saddle River, NJ 07458, U.S.A. **Online address:** sambal@frontiernet.net

BARASH, **Samuel Theodore.** *See* **BARASH**, **Samuel T.**

BARATTA, **Joseph Preston.** American (born United States), b. 1943. **Genres:** History, Politics/Government. **Career:** Center for Global Community and World Law, co-director, 1994-; Boston College, instructor in international organization, 1994-95; Coalition for a Strong United Nations, founding member, 1994-99; Worcester State College, associate professor, 1999-. Writer. **Publications:** Strengthening the United Nations: A Bibliography on U.N. Reform and World Federalism, 1987; The World Federalist Movement: A Collection of Mainstream Journals, 1989; Human Rights: Improving U.N. Mechanisms for Compliance, 1990; The United Nations System: Meeting the World Constitutional Crisis, 1995; What Happened to One World, 2003; The Politics of World Federation: From World Federation to Global Governance, 2004. Contributor to periodicals. **Address:** History and Political Science Department, Worcester State College, Sullivan 327K, 486 Chandler St., Worcester, MA 01602-2597, U.S.A. **Online address:** jbaratta@worcester.edu

BARATZ-LOGSTED, **Lauren.** American (born United States) **Genres:** Novels, Novellas/Short Stories, Young Adult Fiction. **Career:** Klein's (independent bookstore), staff, 1983-94; writer, 1994-. **Publications:** The Thin Pink Line, 2003; Crossing the Line, 2004; (ed.) This is Chick-lit, 2005; A Little Change of Face, 2005; Angel's Choice, 2006; Dodo Lays an Egg: A Jane Taylor Story, Sort of, 2006; Stan and His Sisters: A Jane Taylor Story, Sort of, 2006; Bardolatry, 2006; Constance in Love, 2006; Of Ponies and Trolls, 2006; Emma Speaks Out, 2006; How Nancy Drew Saved My Life, 2006; Vertigo, 2006; Ren d'arc, 2007; Secrets of My Suburban Life, 2008; Me, In Between, 2008; (with G. Logsted and J. Logsted) Annie's Adventures, 2008; (with G. Logsted and J. Logsted) Durinda's Dangers, 2008; Baby Needs a New Pair of Shoes, 2008; (with G. Logsted and J. Logsted) Georgia's Greatness, 2009; Crazy Beautiful, 2009; (with G. Logsted and J. Logsted) Jackie's Jokes, 2009; The Twin's Daughter, 2010; The Education of Bet, 2010; (with G. Logsted and J. Logsted) Marcia's Madness, 2010; (with G. Logsted and J. Logsted) Petal's Problems, 2010; (with G. Logsted and J. Logsted) Rebecca's Rashness, 2011; (with G. Logsted and J. Logsted) Zinnia's Zaniness, 2011; Little Women (and Me), 2011; (with G. Logsted and J. Logsted) Final Battle, 2012. Contributor to periodicals. **Address:** Red Dress Ink, 233 Broadway, 10th Fl., New York, NY 10279-1099, U.S.A. **Online address:** lauren@laurenbaratzlogsted.com

BARBARESE, **J. T.** American (born United States), b. 1948. **Genres:** Novellas/Short Stories, Poetry, Literary Criticism And History, Young Adult Fiction. **Career:** Temple University, Conwell fellow, 1981-83; Friends Select School, chair of English department and director of writing center, 1984-; Rutgers University, adjunct professor, 1988-97, associate professor, 1999-2005. Writer. **Publications:** Under the Blue Moon, 1985; New Science, 1989; Euripides' Children of Herakles, 1999; A Very Small World, 2004; The Black Beach, 2005. **Address:** Friends Select School, 17th & Pkwy., Philadelphia, PA 19102, U.S.A. **Online address:** jt.barbarese@verizon.net

BARBAS, **Samantha.** American (born United States) **Genres:** Film, Biography. **Career:** Arizona State University, Interdisciplinary Studies Program, instructor; Chapman University, assistant professor of history; University of California, visiting assistant professor of history; State University of New York, University at Buffalo, Law School, faculty. Writer. **Publications:** Movie Crazy: Fans, Stars, and the Cult of Celebrity, 2001; The First Lady of Hollywood: A Biography of Louella Parsons, 2005. **Address:** c/o Author Mail, University of California Press, 2120 Berkeley Way, Berkeley, CA 94704-1012, U.S.A. **Online address:** barbas@chapman.edu

BARBASH, **Shepard.** American (born United States), b. 1957. **Genres:** Art/Art History, Earth Sciences, Photography, Essays. **Career:** Patriot Ledger, correspondent for music and film reviews, 1981-82; Associated Press, statistical worker-newsperson, 1982-83; Hudson Dispatch, court and county politics reporter, 1983-84; Euromoney's Latin Finance Magazine, stringer and freelance writer, 1986-89; Houston Chronicle, bureau chief, 1987-88; Barron's, stringer and freelance writer; AP-Dow Jones, stringer and freelance writer; Newsday, stringer and freelance writer; American Banker, stringer and freelance writer; New York Times, stringer, 1992-; Advocate, business reporter and real estate columnist. **Publications:** Oaxacan Woodcarving: The Magic in the Trees, 1993; (contrib.) The Edible Alphabet Book, 1995; Margarito's Carvings, 1996; (contrib.) Changing Dreams: A Generation of Oaxaca's Woodcarvers, 2007. Contributor to books. **Address:** 1732 Meadowdale Ave., Atlanta, GA 30306-3114, U.S.A.

BARBASH, **Tom.** American (born United States) **Genres:** Novellas/Short Stories, Natural History. **Career:** Syracuse Post Standard, reporter; University of Iowa, lecturer; Stanford University, Wallace Stegner and Scowcroft fellow and lecturer; California College of the Arts, Creative Writing Program, Jones lecturer, associate professor of writing and literature, associate professor of writing. **Publications:** The Last Good Chance, 2002; On Top of the World: The Remarkable Story of Howard Lutnick, Cantor Fitzgerald and The Twin Towers Attack, 2003. Contributor to periodicals. **Address:** Picador USA, 175 5th Ave., New York, NY 10010, U.S.A. **Online address:** tbarbash@cca.edu

BARBATO, **Joseph.** American (born United States), b. 1944. **Genres:** Adult Non-fiction, Environmental Sciences/Ecology, How-to Books, Writing/Journalism, Reference, Psychology, Environmental Sciences/Ecology. **Career:** New York University, news writer and editor, 1964-68, alumni communications director, 1969-74, senior development writer, 1976-78; Shell Oil Co., staff writer, 1968-69; City University of New York, public information director and manager of media relations office at La Guardia Community College, 1974-76; lecturer in journalism; independent consultant to nonprofit institutions, 1978-90; Nature Conservancy, director of development communications and special editorial project leader for Book Publishing Group, 1990-99; Barbato Associates, president, 1999-; Publishers Weekly, contributing editor. Writer. **Publications:** (With A. Luks) You Are What You Drink: The Authoritative Report on What Alcohol Does to Your Body, Mind and Longevity, 1989. EDITOR/CO-EDITOR: How Your Mind Affects Your Health, 1990; (co-ed.) Patchwork of Dreams: Voices from the Heart of the New America, 1994; (co-ed.) Heart of the Land: Essays on the Last Great Places, 1995; Off the Beaten Path, 1998; (with F. Gurlich) Writing for a Good Cause, 2000; How to Write Knockout Proposals: What You Must Know (And Say) To Win Funding Every Time, 2004; Attracting The Attention Your Cause Deserves, 2005; The Mercifully Brief, Real World Guide To: Attracting the Attention Your Cause Deserves, 2005. Contributor to magazines and newspapers. **Address:** Barbato Associates, 5420 Gary Pl., Alexandria, VA 22311, U.S.A. **Online address:** jb@barbatoassociates.com

BARBEAU, **Edward J(oseph).** Canadian (born Canada), b. 1938. **Genres:** Mathematics/Statistics, Adult Non-fiction, Education, Psychology. **Career:** University of Western Ontario, assistant professor of mathematics, 1964-66; Yale University, NATO research fellow, 1966-67; University of Toronto, assistant professor, associate professor, 1967-88, professor of mathematics, 1988, now professor emeritus; College Mathematics Journal, associate editor. Writer. **Publications:** Polynomials, 1989; After Math: Puzzles and Brainteasers, 1995; (with M. Klamkin and M. Moser) Five Hundred Mathematical Challenges, 1995; Power Play, 1997; Mathematical Fallacies, Flaws and Flimflam, 2000; Pell's Equation, 2003. **Address:** Department of Mathematics, University of Toronto, 6176 Bahen Ctr. BA, 40 St. George St., Toronto, ON M5S 1A5, Canada. **Online address:** barbeau@math.toronto.edu

BARBER, **Benjamin R(eynolds).** American (born United States), b. 1939. **Genres:** Novels, Plays/Screenplays, Politics/Government, Education, Philosophy, Economics, Business/Trade/Industry. **Career:** Albert Schweitzer College, lecturer in ethics and politics, 1963-65; University of Pennsylvania, assistant professor of political science, 1966-69; Haverford College, visiting assistant professor, 1968; Rutgers University, assistant professor, 1969-70, associate professor, 1971-75, professor of political science, 1975-, Walt Whitman professor of political science, now Walt Whitman professor emeritus of political science, Whitman Center for the Culture and Politics of Democracy, director, 1988-2001; City University of New York, Hunter College, visiting associate professor, 1970; New York Institute for the Humanities, visiting fellow, 1980-81; Princeton University, visiting professor, 1986-87, 1988; University of Maryland, Kekst Chair of Civil Society and distinguished professor, 2001-; Bodies Electric, chairman; New Jersey Academy for Community Service and Service Learning, executive director; Demos, distinguished senior fellow, CivWorld-NGO, president and director. Writer. **Publications:** (With C.J. Friedrich and M. Curtis) Totalitarianism in Perspective: Three Views, 1969; Superman and Common Men: Freedom, Anarchy and the Revolution, 1971; The Death of Communal Liberty: A History of Freedom in a Swiss Mountain Canton, 1974; Liberating Feminism, 1975; Marriage Voices: A Novel, 1981; Can America Be Democratic?: A Participatory Critique of the Liberal Consensus, 1981; (ed. with M.J.G. McGrath) The Artist and Political Vision, 1982; Strong Democracy: Participatory Politics for a New Age, 1984; The Conquest of Politics, 1988; (with P. Watson) The Struggle for Democracy, 1988; An Aristocracy of Everyone, 1992; (co-author) Visions of Service: The Future of the National and Community Service Act, 1993; (ed. with

R.M. Battistoni) Education for Democracy, 1993; Jihad vs. McWorld, 1995; A Place for Us: How to Make Society Civil and Democracy Strong, 1998; A Passion for Democracy (essays), 1998; My Affair with Clinton: An Intellectual Memoir, 2001; The Truth of Power: Intellectual Affairs in the Clinton White House, 2001; Fear's Empire: War, Terrorism, and Democracy, 2003; (ed. with S. Myers) The Interdependence Handbook: Looking Back, Living the Present, Choosing the Future, 2004; (co-author) Soziale Gerechtigkeit: Neue Antworten in Der Globalisierten Oekonomie?, 2004; Consumed: How Markets Corrupt Children, Infantilize Adults, and Swallow Citizens Whole, 2007. **Address:** CivWorld, 220 5th Ave., 2nd Fl., New York, NY 10001-7708, U.S.A. **Online address:** bbarber@sorosny.org

BARBER, Charles. American (born United States), b. 1962. **Genres:** Young Adult Non-fiction, Autobiography/Memoirs, Psychiatry. **Career:** Yale University, School of Medicine, Department of Psychiatry, lecturer in psychiatry; The Connection Inc. (social services agency), senior administrator, director of grantwriting and special projects, The Connection Institute for Innovative Practice, director; Wesleyan University, faculty. Writer. **Publications:** NONFICTION: Songs from the Black Chair: A Memoir of Mental Interiors, 2005; Comfortably Numb: How Psychiatry is Medicating a Nation, 2008. Contributor to periodicals. **Address:** Department of Psychiatry, School of Medicine, Yale University, 300 George St., Ste. 901, New Haven, CT 06511, U.S.A. **Online address:** charles.barber@yale.edu

BARBER, David. American (born United States), b. 1950. **Genres:** History. **Career:** University of Tennessee, associate professor of history. Writer and historian. **Publications:** A Hard Rain Fell: SDS and Why It Failed, 2008. Contributor to periodicals. **Address:** Department of History and Philosophy, University of Tennessee, 322 Humanities Bldg., Martin, TN 38238, U.S.A. **Online address:** dbarber@utm.edu

BARBER, E(lizabeth) J. W(ayland). American (born United States), b. 1940. **Genres:** Archaeology/Antiquities, Language/Linguistics, Mythology/Folklore, Anthropology/Ethnology, Dance/Ballet. **Career:** Princeton University, Chinese Linguistics Project, research associate, 1968-69; Occidental College, Department of Linguistics and Archaeology, professor, 1970-2007, now professor emeritus; Asia Foundation on Chinese machine translation project, consultant, 1974; Archaeological Institute of America, lecturer, 1974-76, 1983-84, 1993-99, 2002-03, Cotsen Institute of Archaeology, research associate. Writer. **Publications:** Archaeological Decipherment, 1974; Prehistoric Textiles: The Development of Cloth in the Neolithic and Bronze Ages, 1991; Women's Work: The First 20,000 Years, 1994; The Mummies of ürümchi, 1999; (with P.T. Barber) When They Severed Earth from Sky: How the Human Mind Shapes Myth, 2004. Contributor to books and periodicals. **Address:** Departments of Former Language/Anthro, Occidental College, Los Angeles, CA 90041, U.S.A. **Online address:** barber@oxy.edu

BARBER, John (Douglass). British (born England), b. 1944. **Genres:** History, Politics/Government, Social Sciences. **Career:** University of Birmingham, Center for Russian and East European Studies, research fellow, 1976-80; Cambridge University, King's College, fellow and director of studies in history, 1980-, university lecturer in politics, 1981-, acting lay dean, lay dean. Writer. **Publications:** Soviet Historians in Crisis 1928-1932, 1980; (co-author) Defended to Death: A Study of the Nuclear Arms Race, 1983; (with M. Harrison) The Soviet Home Front, 1941-1945: A Social and 1941-1945: A Social and Economic History of the USSR in World War II, 1991; (ed. with M. Harrison) The Soviet Defence-Industry Complex from Stalin to Khrushchev, 2000; (ed. with A. Dzeniskevich) Life and Death in Besieged Leningrad, 1941-44, 2005. Contributor to periodicals. **Address:** King's College, King's Parade, Rm. H2 (left), Cambridge, CB CB2 1ST, England. **Online address:** jdb6@cam.ac.uk

BARBER, Karin. British (born England) **Genres:** Cultural/Ethnic Topics, Language/Linguistics, Translations. **Career:** Saint Mary's Teacher Training College, 1967-68; University of Ife, assistant lecturer, 1977-79, lecturer in African languages and literatures, 1979-84; University of California, principal instructor in Yoruba, 1982; City Literary Institute, part-time instructor in Yoruba language, 1984-85; University of Birmingham, lecturer in West African studies, 1985-93, senior lecturer, 1993-97, professor of African cultural anthropology, 1999-, Centre of West African Studies, faculty; Northwestern University, Institute for Advanced Study and Research in the African Humanities, preceptor, 1993-94, Melville Herskovits distinguished visiting professor, 1999; Screenlife Ltd., British Academy Research Readership, consultant, 2001-03. **Publications:** Yorùbá Dùn ún Sọ: A Beginners' Course in Yoruba, vol. I, 1985; I Could Speak Until Tomorrow: Oriki, Women, and the Past in a Yoruba Town in UK as Could Speak Until Tomorrow: Oriki, Women and the Past in a Yoruba Town, 1991; (comp. with M. Wuttke) Bischofswerda, Tor zur Oberlausitz, 1992; (with J. Collins and A. Ricard) West African Popular Theatre, 1997; (contrib.) Running After Riches, 1999; The Generation of Plays: Yorùbá Popular Life in Theater, 2000; The Anthropology of Texts, Persons and Publics: Oral and Written Culture in Africa and Beyond, 2007. EDITOR: (with P.F. de Moraes Farias and contrib.) Discourse and Its Disguises: The Interpretation of African Oral Texts, 1989; (with P.F. de M. Farias and contrib.) Self-Assertion and Brokerage: Early Cultural Nationalism in West Africa, 1990; (and trans. with B. Ògúndíjọ) Yorùbá Popular Theatre, 1994; Readings in African Popular Culture, 1997; Africa's Hidden Histories: Everyday Literacy and Making the Self, 2006. Works appear in anthologies. Contributor of articles to journals. **Address:** Centre of West African Studies, University of Birmingham, Arts Bldg., Edgbaston, Birmingham, WM B15 2TT, England. **Online address:** k.j.barber@bham.ac.uk

BARBER, Katherine. Canadian/British (born England), b. 1959?. **Genres:** Language/Linguistics, Adult Non-fiction. **Career:** University of Ottawa, School of Translation and Interpretation, lecturer, 1984-91, Bilingual Canadian Dictionary project, research associate, 1989-91, instructor and reviser; Oxford University Press, Canadian Dictionaries, editor-in-chief, 1991-2008, Department of Dictionary, head, 1991-. Lexicographer and translator. **Publications:** (Ed.) Canadian Oxford Dictionary, 1998, 2nd ed., 2004; (ed.) Canadian Oxford High School Dictionary, 2001; (ed.) Canadian Oxford Dictionary of Current English, 2005; Six Words You Never Knew Had Something to Do with Pigs: And Other Fascinating Facts from Canada's Word Lady, 2006; Only in Canada You Say: A Treasury of Canadian Language, 2007; Six Words You Never Knew Had Something to do with Pigs: And Other Fascinating Facts about the English Language, 2007. **Address:** 70 Wynford Dr., Don Mills, ON M3C 1J9, Canada. **Online address:** katherine.barber@oup.com

BARBER, Lucy G(race). American (born United States), b. 1964. **Genres:** Civil Liberties/Human Rights. **Career:** U.S. National Archives and Records Administration, National Historical Publications and Records Commission, deputy executive director, director for technology initiatives; California State Archives, archivist; Brown University, faculty; Rhode Island School of Design, faculty; University of California, faculty. Writer and historian. **Publications:** Marching on Washington: The Forging of an American Political Tradition, 2002. Contributor to periodicals. **Address:** National Historical Publications and Records, Commission, U.S. National Archives and Records Administration, Rm. 106, 700 Pennsylvania Ave. NW, Washington, DC 20408-0001, U.S.A. **Online address:** lucy.barber@nara.gov

BARBER, Paul (Thomas). American (born United States), b. 1941. **Genres:** Novels, Mythology/Folklore. **Career:** Princeton University, instructor, 1967-68, assistant professor of Germanic languages and literatures, 1968-70; Pasadena City College, part-time instructor in creative writing, 1972-76; Glendale City College, part-time teacher, 1972-76; Occidental College, instructor in literature, mythology and folklore, 1974-78, lecturer; University of California, Fowler Museum of Cultural History, research associate; Ludwigsburg University, lecturer, 1992. Writer. **Publications:** Vampires, Burial, and Death: Folklore and Reality, 1988; (with E.W. Barber) When They Severed Earth from Sky: How the Human Mind Shapes Myth, 2005; (with E.W. Barber and M.F. Zirin) Two Thoughts with but a Single Mind: Crime and Punishment and the Writing of Fiction, forthcoming. Contributor to periodicals. **Address:** Fowler Museum of Cultural History, University of California, 405 Hilgard Ave., PO Box 951549, Los Angeles, CA 90024-1549, U.S.A. **Online address:** grendel33@hotmail.com

BARBER, Phyllis (Nelson). American (born United States), b. 1943. **Genres:** Novellas/Short Stories, Children's Fiction, Young Adult Fiction, Poetry, Literary Criticism And History, Autobiography/Memoirs, Essays. **Career:** Christina DeVore Dance Studio, pianist, 1958-61; Brigham Young University, part-time copy typist, 1961-63, student body vice president of culture, 1963-64; professional pianist, 1964-; piano teacher, 1965-70; Utah Symphony Guild, public relations director, 1970-71; Western Humanities Review and Quarterly West, reader and proof reader, 1984-86; Pioneer Craft House, creative writing instructor, 1985-88; Pioneer Craft House, creative writing instructor, 1985-88; Writers at Work Conference, co-founder, 1985, president, 1985-87, co-director, 1988-89; Utah State Literary Arts Panel, president, 1985-89; Utah Women's Art Project, executive co-chair, 1989-90;

Summit County Artist Series, founder, 1990-92; Antioch University, academic consultant, 1990; Vermont College, faculty, MFA Writing Program, faculty, 1991-; Colorado Mountain College, faculty member, 1992-94; University of Missouri, visiting writer, 1994; Mankato State University, visiting writer, 1996; Fourth Genre, contributing editor, 1998-2001; Community Education, teacher, 1999; Expanding Heart, sales personnel, 1999-2001; University of Utah, faculty, 2000-01; Utah Holiday magazine, feature writer. **Publications:** Smiley Snake's Adventure (juvenile), 1980; The School of Love (short stories), 1990; Legs: The Story of a Giraffe (juvenile), 1991; And the Desert Shall Blossom (novel), 1991; How I Got Cultured: A Nevada Memoir, 1992; Parting the Veil: Stories from the Mormon Imagination, 1999; Raw Edges: A Memoir, 2009. Works appears in anthologies. Contributor to journals. **Address:** Vermont College of Fine Arts, 38 College St., Montpelier, VT 05602, U.S.A. **Online address:** pb@phyllisbarber.com

BARBER, Richard (William). British (born England), b. 1941. **Genres:** Food And Wine, History, Literary Criticism And History, Mythology/Folklore, Travel/Exploration, Reference. **Career:** Boydell and Brewer Ltd., founder, 1969, managing director. Writer. **Publications:** Arthur of Albion: An Introduction to the Arthurian Literature and Legends of England, rev. ed. as King Arthur: Hero and Legend, 1986; Henry Plantagenet, a Biography, 1964, rev. ed., 2001; (with F.E. Camps) The Investigation of Murder, 1966; The Knight and Chivalry, 1970, rev. ed., 1995; Samuel Pepys Esquire, Secretary of the Admiralty to King Charles & King James the Second, 1970; (with A. Riches) A Dictionary of Fabulous Beasts, 1971; The Figure of Arthur, 1972; King Arthur; in Legend and History, 1973; Cooking and Recipes from Rome to the Renaissance, 1973; (ed.) Brief Lives, 1975; A Strong Land and a Sturdy: England in the Middle Ages, 1976; Companion Guide to South West France: Bordeaux and the Dordogne, 1977, rev. ed. as Companion Guide to Gascony and the Dordogne, 1991; The Devil's Crown: Henry II, Richard I, John, 1978; Tournaments, 1978; Edward, Prince of Wales and Aquitaine: A Biography of the Black Prince, 1978; The Arthurian Legends: An Illustrated Anthology, 1979; (ed. and trans.) Life and Campaigns of the Black Prince: From Contemporary Letters, Diaries, and Chronicles, Including Chandos Herald's Life of the Black Prince, 1979; The Reign of Chivalry, 1980; A Companion to World Mythology, 1980; Living Legends, 1980; (ed.) The Pastons: A Family in the Wars of the Roses, 1981; Penguin Guide to Medieval Europe, 1984; The Worlds of John Aubrey, 1986; (with T. Fuller) Fuller's Worthies: Selected from The Worthies of England, 1987; (with J. Barker) Tournaments: Jousts, Chivalry, and Pageants in the Middle Ages, 1989; Pilgrimages, 1991; Bestiary: Being an English Version of the Bodleian Library, Oxford M.S. Bodley 764: With all the Original Miniatures Reproduced in Facsimile, 1993; (ed.) Myths & Legends of the British Isles, 1999; Legends of King Arthur, 2001; (ed.) King Arthur in Music, 2002; The Holy Grail: Imagination and Belief, 2004; (with J. Munby and R. Brown) Edward III's Round Table at Windsor: The House of the Round Table and the Windsor Festival of 1344, 2007; Forty Books for Forty Years: An Informal History of the Boydell Press, 2009. **Address:** Stangrove Hall, Alderton, SU IP12 3BL, England.

BARBER, Ronde. American (born United States), b. 1975. **Genres:** Novels. **Career:** Tampa Bay Buccaneers, football player, 1997-. Broadcaster, radio show host and writer. **Publications:** WITH T. BARBER AND R. BURLEIGH: By My Brother's Side, 2004; Game Day, 2005; Teammates, 2006. WITH P. MANTELL and T. BARBER: Kickoff!, 2007; Go Long!, 2008; Wild Card, 2009; Red Zone, 2010; Goal Line, 2011. **Address:** Tampa Bay Buccaneers, 1 Buccaneer Pl., Tampa, FL 33607, U.S.A.

BARBIER, Patrick. French (born France), b. 1956. **Genres:** Music, History, Intellectual History. **Career:** Université Catholique de l'Ouest, professor of music history, managing director in cultural life. Writer. **Publications:** La vie quotidienne à l'Opéra au temps de Rossini et de Balzac, Paris, 1800-1850, 1987; Histoire de Castrats, 1989, trans. as The World of the Castrati, 1996; Graslin, Nantes et l'Opéra: deux siècles devie lyrique au Théâtre Graslin 1993; Farinelli, le castrat desLumièrs, 1994; La Maison des Italiens: les castrats à Versailles, 1998; La Venise de Vivaldi: musique et fêtes baroques, 2002; Pauline Viardot, 2009. **Address:** Université Catholique de l'Ouest, 3 Pl. André-Leroy, PO Box 10 808, Angers, 49008, France. **Online address:** patrick.barbier@uco.fr

BARBIERI, Elaine. (Elaine Rome). American (born United States), b. 1936. **Genres:** Novels, Young Adult Fiction, Romance/Historical. **Career:** Writer. **Publications:** Captive Ecstasy, 1980; Amber Fire (first novel in trilogy), 1981; Love's Fiery Jewel, 1982; Amber Treasure (second novel in trilogy), 1983; Sweet Torment, 1984; Amber Passion (third novel in trilogy), 1985; Race for Tomorrow, 1985; Passion's Dawn, 1985; Defiant Mistress, 1986; Ecstasy's Trail, 1987; Untamed Captive, 1987; Tarnished Angel, 1988; Wings of a Dove, 1990; Wishes on the Wind, 1991; (as Elaine Rome) Stark Lightning, 1991; Tattered Silk, 1991; More Precious than Gold, 1992; To Love a Stranger, 1993; Only For Love, 1994; Dance of the Flame, 1995; Midnight Rogue, 1995; Honesty, 1996, Purity, 1997, Chastity, 1998; Eagle, 1999; Hawk, 1999; Night Raven, 2000; The Wild One, 2001; To Meet Again, 2001; Miranda and the Warrior (young adult), 2002; Renegade Moon, 2003; Texas Star, 2004; Texas Glory, 2004; Texas Triumph, 2005; Silent Awakening, 2005; Hawk's Prize, 2006; Hawk's Passion, 2006; Sign of the Wolf, 2007; Night of the Wolf, 2007; The Redemption of Jake Scully, 2008; Cry of the Wolf, 2008; Getting Lucky, 2009; Rose & The Shield, 2009; Renegade, 2010. **Address:** PO Box 536, West Milford, NJ 07480, U.S.A.

BARBIERI-LOW, Anthony J. American (born United States), b. 1967. **Genres:** Art/Art History, History. **Career:** University of Pittsburgh, assistant professor, 2001-06, associate professor of early Chinese history, 2006-07, adjunct professor of the history of art and architecture, 2006-07; University of California, assistant professor, 2007-09, associate professor of history, 2009-. Writer. **Publications:** (With C.Y. Liu and M. Nylan) Recarving China's Past: Art, Archaeology, and Architecture of the Wu Family Shrines, 2005; Artisans in Early Imperial China, 2007. Contributor of articles to journals. **Address:** Department of History, University of California, HSSB 4225, Santa Barbara, CA 93106-9410, U.S.A. **Online address:** barbieri-low@history.ucsb.edu

BARBOUR, Douglas. Canadian (born Canada), b. 1940. **Genres:** Novellas/Short Stories, Poetry, Literary Criticism And History, Science Fiction/Fantasy. **Career:** Alderwood Collegiate Institute, teacher of English, 1968-69; University of Alberta, assistant professor, 1969-77, associate professor, 1977-82, professor of English, 1982, now professor emeritus. Writer. **Publications:** Land Fall, 1971; A Poem as Long as the Highway, 1971; White, 1972; Songbook, 1973; He. & She. &, 1974; Visions of My Grandfather, 1977; Worlds Out of Words: The SF Novels of Samuel R. Delany, 1979; Shore Lines, 1979; Vision/Sounding, 1980; (with S. Scobie) The Pirates of Pen's Chance: Homolinguistic Translations, 1981; The Harbingers, 1984; Visible Visions: The Selected Poems of Douglas Barbour, 1984; Canadian Poetry Chronicle, 1984: A Comprehensive Review of Canadian Poetry Books, 1985; Story for a Saskatchewan Night, 1990; John Newlove and His Works, 1992; Daphne Marlatt and Her Works, 1992; BpNichol and His Works, 1992; Michael Ondaatje, 1993; Fragmenting Body etc., 2000; Lyric/Anti-lyric: Essays on Contemporary Poetry, 2001; Breath Takes, 2001; A Flame on the Spanish Stairs, 2003; Transformations of Contemporary Canadian Poetry in English, 2005; (with S.E. Murphy) Continuations, 2006. EDITOR: The Story So Far Five, 1978; (and intro.) The 'Crow' Journals, 1980; (with S. Scobie) The League of Canadian Poets, 1980; (with Scobie) The Maple Laugh Forever: An Anthology of Canadian Comic Poetry, 1981; (with M. Stanley) Writing Right: New Poetry by Canadian Women, 1982; (and intro.) Three Times Five: Short Stories, 1983; (and intro.) Selected and New Poems, 1983; (with P. Gotlieb) Tesseracts 2: Canadian Science Fiction, 1987; Beyond Tish: New Writing Interviews, Critical Writing, 1991. **Address:** University of Alberta Press, Ring House 2, Edmonton, AB T6G 2E1, Canada. **Online address:** doug.barbour@ualberta.ca

BARBOUR, JoAnn. *See* **HICKS, Barbara.**

BARBOUR, John D. American (born United States), b. 1951. **Genres:** Literary Criticism And History, Theology/Religion. **Career:** University of Chicago, Divinity School, junior fellow in institute for the advanced study of religion and lecturer in religion and literature, 1980-82; St. Olaf College, Department of Religion, assistant professor, 1982-88, associate professor, 1988-94, professor, 1994-, professor of art, tutor in paracollege, 1985-90, chair, 1998-2001, Martin Marty Regents chair in religion and academy, 2004-08. Writer. **Publications:** Tragedy As a Critique of Virtue: The Novel and Ethical Reflection, 1984; The Conscience of the Autobiographer: Ethical and Religious Dimensions of Autobiography, 1992; Versions of Deconversion: Autobiography and the Loss of Faith, 1994; The Value of Solitude: The Ethics and Spirituality of Aloneness in Autobiography, 2004. **Address:** Department of Religion, St. Olaf College, Boe Memorial Chapel 302, 1520 St., Olaf Ave., Northfield, MN 55057, U.S.A. **Online address:** barbourj@stolaf.edu

BARBOUR, Julian B. British/Israeli (born Israel), b. 1937. **Genres:** Physics,

Sciences, Reference. **Career:** Independent researcher, translator and writer. **Publications:** Absolute or Relative Motion?: A Study from Machian Point of View of the Discovery and the Structure of Dynamical Theories, 1989; (ed. with H. Pfister) Mach's Principle: From Newton's Bucket to Quantum Gravity, 1995; The End of Time: The Next Revolution in Physics, 2000; Discovery of Dynamics: A Study from a Machian Point of View of the Discovery and the Structure of Dynamical Theories, 2001. Contributor to journals. **Address:** College Farm, South Newington, Banbury, OX OX15 4JG, England. **Online address:** julian@platonia.com

BARCLAY, Bill. *See* **MOORCOCK, Michael (John).**

BARCLAY, Donald A. American (born United States), b. 1958. **Genres:** Librarianship, Literary Criticism And History, Education. **Career:** New Mexico State University, Library Institute, co-ordinator, 1990-96; University of Houston, Electronic Publishing Center, coordinator, 1996-97; Houston Academy of Medicine-Texas Medical Center Library, assistant director for systems and informatics, 1997-2002; University of California, assistant university librarian, 2002-06, deputy university librarian, 2006-11, interim university librarian, 2011-. Writer. **Publications:** (Ed. with J.H. Maguire and P. Wild) Into the Wilderness Dream: Exploration Narratives of the American West, 1500-1805, 1994; (ed.) Teaching Electronic Information Literacy: A How-to-do-it Manual, 1995; (ed. with J.H. Maguire and P. Wild) A Rendezvous Reader: Tall, Tangled, and True Tales of the Mountain Men, 1997; Managing Public-Access Computers: A How-to-Do-It Manual for Librarians, 2000; (with D.D. Halsted) The Medical Library Association Consumer Health Reference Service Handbook, 2001; (ed. with J.H. Maguire and P. Wild) Different Travellers, Different Eyes; Artists' Narratives of the American West, 1810-1920, 2001; Teaching and Marketing Electronic Information Literacy: A How-to-do-it Manual for Librarians, 2003; (with E.D. Scott) The Library Renovation, Maintenance, and Construction Handbook, 2011. Contributor of articles to books and periodicals. **Address:** Kolligian Library, University of California, 5200 N Lake Rd., Merced, CA 95343-5001, U.S.A. **Online address:** dbarclay@ucmerced.edu

BARCLAY, Max. *See* **SHERWOOD, Ben.**

BARCLAY, Patrick. British (born England), b. 1947. **Genres:** Sports/Fitness, Architecture. **Career:** Guardian, sports reporter, 1970; Sunday Telegraph, soccer correspondent; The Times, writer; Independent, writer. **Publications:** Mourinho: Anatomy of a Winner, 2005; Wembley Stadium: Venue of Legends, 2007; Football-Bloody Hell!: The Biography of Alex Ferguson, 2010. Contributor to periodicals. **Address:** The Daily Telegraph, 1 Canada Sq., London, GL E14 5DT, England. **Online address:** patrick.barclay@telegraph.co.uk

BARCLAY, Robert. (Robert L. Barclay). Canadian/British (born England), b. 1946. **Genres:** Anthropology/Ethnology, Cultural/Ethnic Topics, Music. **Career:** Canadian Conservation Institute, senior conservator of instruments, 1975-. Writer. **Publications:** The Care of Musical Instruments in Canadian Collections, 1982; (ed. and contrib.) Anatomy of an Exhibition: The Look of Music, 1983; The Art of the Trumpet-Maker: The Materials, Tools, and Techniques of the Seventeeth and Eighteenth Centuries in Nuremberg, 1992; (ed.) The Care of Historic Musical Instruments, 1997; (with A. Bergeron and C. Dignard) Mount-making for Museum Objects, 1998; The Preservation and Use of Historic Musical Instruments: Display Case and Concert Hall, 2005. Contributor to periodicals. **Address:** Canadian Conservation Institute, 1030 Innes Rd., Ottawa, ON K1B 4S7, Canada. **Online address:** robert_barcaly@pch.gc.ca

BARCLAY, Robert L. *See* **BARCLAY, Robert.**

BARD, Mitchell G. (Mitchell Geoffrey Bard). American (born United States), b. 1959. **Genres:** Politics/Government, History. **Career:** California Employment Development Department, analyst, 1980-81; American Enterprise Institute for Public Policy Research, analyst, 1982; University of California-Los Angeles, Comparative Higher Education Research Group and Higher Education Research Institute, research assistant, 1984, Department of Political Science, teaching assistant, 1984-87; University of California-Irvine, postdoctoral fellow, 1986-87; George Bush for President Survey Research Group, senior analyst, 1988; Near East Report, editor, 1989-92; American-Israeli Cooperative Enterprise (AICE), executive director, 1993-; Jewish Virtual Library, director. **Publications:** The Water's Edge and Beyond: Defining the Limits to Domestic Influence on United States Middle East Policy, 1991; U.S.-Israel Relations: Looking to the Year 2000, 1991; (with J. Himelfarb) Myths and Facts: A Concise Record of the Arab-Israeli Conflict, 1992; Partners for Change: How U.S.-Israel Cooperation Can Benefit America, 1993; Forgotten Victims: The Abandonment of Americans in Hitler's Camps, 1994; (ed.) Learning Together, 1995; The Complete Idiot's Guide to Middle East Conflict, 1999, 4th ed., 2008; The Complete Idiot's Guide to World War II, 1999, 2nd ed., 2004; Encyclopedia of the Holocaust, 2000; (ed.) The Holocaust (Turning Points in History Series), 2001; 1001 Facts about Israel, 2001; (ed.) Complete History of the Holocaust, 2001; (ed.) Nuremberg Trials, 2001; From Tragedy to Triumph: The Politics behind the Rescue of Ethiopian Jewry, 2002; (with M. Schwartz) 1001 Facts Everyone Should Know About Israel, 2005; Will Israel Survive?, 2006; 48 Hours of Kristallnacht, 2008; Arab Lobby, 2010. Contributor of books to articles and magazines. **Address:** American-Israeli Cooperative Enterprise, 2810 Blaine Dr., Chevy Chase, MD 20815-3040, U.S.A. **Online address:** mgbard@aol.com

BARD, Mitchell Geoffrey. *See* **BARD, Mitchell G.**

BARDEN, Dan. American (born United States), b. 1960. **Genres:** Novels, Horticulture. **Career:** The George Washington University, Jenny McKean Moore writer-in-residence; Butler University, Department of English, associate professor. **Publications:** John Wayne: A Novel, 1997; Next Right Thing, 2012. **Address:** Department of English, Butler University, 308B Jordan Hall, 4600 Sunset Ave., Indianapolis, IN 46208, U.S.A. **Online address:** dan@danbarden.com

BARDEN, Thomas. American (born United States), b. 1946. **Genres:** Mythology/Folklore, Literary Criticism And History, Urban Studies, Area Studies. **Career:** University of Virginia, acting assistant professor of English, 1975-76; University of Toledo, assistant professor, 1976-80, associate professor, 1980-90, professor of English, 1990-, American Studies Program, director, 1991-97, director of graduate studies in English, 1997-99, College of Arts and Sciences, associate dean, 1999-2003, University of Toledo Press, general editor, 2004-, Honors College, dean, 2006-; University of Swansea, senior Fulbright lecturer, 1993-94. **Publications:** (Ed. with C.L. Perdue and R.K. Phillips) Weevils in the Wheat: Interviews with Virginia Ex-Slaves, 1976; (co-author) An Annotated Listing of the Virginia WPA Folklore, 1979; The Travels of Peter Woodhouse: Memoir of an American Pioneer, 1981; Virginia Folk Legends, 1991; Hungarian American Toledo: Life and Times in Toledo's Birmingham Neighborhood, 2002; Steinbeck in Vietnam: Dispatches from the War, 2012. **Address:** University of Toledo, 2801 Bancroft, PO Box 504, Toledo, OH 43606, U.S.A. **Online address:** thomas.barden@utoledo.edu

BARDHAN, Pranab Kumar. American/Indian (born India), b. 1939. **Genres:** Economics, Business/Trade/Industry. **Career:** Calcutta University, lecturer, 1961-62; Cambridge University, undergraduate supervisor, 1963-65; Massachusetts Institute of Technology, assistant professor, 1966-68, associate professor of economics, 1968-69, visiting professor, 1971-72; Indian Statistical Institute, professor, 1969-72; Quantitative Economics, co-editor, 1971-76; International Economic Review, associate editor, 1971-85; Delhi School of Economics, professor, 1973-76; University of California, visiting professor and visiting Ford professor, 1976-77, professor of economics, 1977-; Stanford University, visiting professor, 1977; Journal of Development Economics, chief editor, 1985-2003; Journal of Economic Perspectives, associate editor, 1989-94; St. Catherine's College, Christensen visiting fellow, 1991; MacArthur Foundation Research Network on Inequality and Economic Performance, co-leader, 1995-; London School of Economics, Sticerd Distinguished Visitor, 1998; London School of Economics, STICERD distinguished visitor, 1998, BP centennial professor, 2010, 2011; Trinity College, visiting fellow, 2002, 2004; University of Siena, distinguished Fulbright Siena Chair, 2008-09. **Publications:** Economic Growth, Development and Foreign Trade: A Study in Pure Theory, 1970; (with A. Rudra) On the Interlinkage of Land, Labour, Credit Relations in Agriculture: An Analysis of Village Survey Data in East India, 1978; (with A. Rudra) Agrarian Relations in West Bengal: Results of Two Surveys, 1983; Land, Labor and Rural Poverty: Essays in Development Economics, 1984; The Political Economy of Development in India, 1984; Rāshtòra, samāja byabasthā, o deśeraśrībrddhi, 1985; The State, Society and Economic Growth, 1985; (with R.Z. Prialé) Endogenous Growth Theory in a Vintage Capital Model, 1996; The Role of Governance in Economic Development: A Political Economy Approach, 1997; (with C. Udry) Development Microeconomics, 1999; The Political Economy of Reform in India, 1999; Social Justice in a Global Economy, 2000; International Trade, Growth and Development: Essays, 2003; Poverty, Agrarian Structure and Political Economy in India: Selected Essays, 2003; Scarcity, Conflicts and Cooperation: Essays in the Political and Institutional Economics of Development, 2005. EDITOR: (with T.N. Srinivasan) Poverty and Income Distribution in India, 1974; (with A. Fishlow and J. Behrman) International Trade, Investment, Macro Policies and History: Essays in Memory of Carlos F. Diaz Alejandro, 1987; (with T.N. Srinivasan) Rural Poverty in South Asia, 1988; The Economic Theory of Agrarian Institutions, 1989; Conversations between Economists and Anthropologists: Methodological Issues in Measuring Economic Change in Rural India, 1989; (with J. Roemer) Market Socialism: The Current Debate, 1993; (with M. Datta-Chaudhuri and T.N. Krishnan) Development and Change: Essays in Honour of K.N. Raj, 1993; (with C. Udry) Readings in Development Microeconomics, 2000; (with D. Mookherjee) Decentralization and Local Governance in Developing Countries: A Comparative Perspective, 2006; (ed. with S. Bowles and M. Wallerstein) Globalization and Egalitarian Redistribution, 2006; (with J. Baland and S. Bowles) Inequality, Cooperation and Environmental Sustainability, 2007; (with I. Ray) The Contested Commons: Conversations between Economists and Anthropologists, 2008; Awakening Giants, Feet of Clay: Assessing the Economic Rise of China and India, 2010. OTHERS: (contrib.) India's Democracy: An Analysis of Changing State-Society Relations, 1988. **Address:** Department of Economics, University of California, 508-1 Evans Hall, Ste. 3880, Berkeley, CA 94720, U.S.A. **Online address:** kalpanabardhan@worldnotes.org

BARDIGE, Betty S. American (born United States), b. 1950. **Genres:** Language/Linguistics, Human Relations/Parenting, Adult Non-fiction. **Career:** A.L. Mailman Family Foundation Inc., chair, vice president and director. Writer. **Publications:** (With M.M. Segal) Your Child at Play, Five to Eight Years: Building Friendships, Expanding Interests, and Resolving Conflicts, 2000; (with M.M. Segal) Building Literacy with Love: A Guide for Teachers and Caregivers of Children from Birth through Age 5, 2005; (with M.M. Segal) Poems to Learn to Read By: Building Literacy with Love, 2005; At a Loss for Words: How America Is Failing Our Children and What We Can Do about It, 2005; Talk to Me, Baby!: How You Can Support Young Children's Language Development, 2009. **Address:** A.L. Mailman Family Foundation Inc., 707 Westchester Ave., White Plains, NY 10604-3102, U.S.A. **Online address:** betty@mailman.org

BARDSLEY, Michele. American (born United States), b. 1970?. **Genres:** Horror. **Career:** Writer and speaker. **Publications:** BROKEN HEART SERIES: I'm the Vampire, That's Why, 2006; Don't Talk Back to Your Vampire, 2007; Because Your Vampire Said So, 2008; Wait till Your Vampire Gets Home, 2008; Over My Dead Body, 2009; Come Hell or High Water, 2010. OTHERS: Daddy in Training, 1998; Wild Women, 2003; Shadows Present, 2004; A Mother Scorned and Other Stories, 2005; Cupid, Inc., 2006; Fantasyland, 2007. **Address:** Tulsa, OK , U.S.A. **Online address:** michele.bardsley@gmail.com

BARDWICK, Judith M(arcia). American (born United States), b. 1933. **Genres:** Business/Trade/Industry, Institutions/Organizations, Psychology, Women's Studies And Issues. **Career:** University of Michigan, lecturer, 1964-66, assistant professor, 1966-69, associate professor, 1969-74, professor of psychology, 1974-83, College of Literature, Science and Arts, associate dean, 1977-80, Society of Fellows, senior fellow, 1975-80; Judith M. Bardwick Inc., management consultants, president, 1983-; In Transition, president, 1983-86; University of California, clinical professor of psychology, 1984-; Kielty, Goldsmith & Boone, partner, 1986-. Consultant and writer. **Publications:** (Co-author) Feminine Personality and Conflict, 1970; Psychology of Women: A Study of Bio-Cultural Conflicts, 1971; (ed. and contrib.) Readings on the Psychology of Women, 1972; In Transition: How Feminism, Sexual Liberation and the Search for Self-fulfillment have Altered America, 1979; Essays on the Psychology of Women, 1981; The Plateauing Trap, 1986; Danger in the Comfort Zone, 1991; In Praise of Good Business: How Optimizing Risk Rewards Both your Bottom Line and your People, 1998; Seeking the Calm in the Storm: Managing Chaos in Your Business Life, 2002; One Foot Out the Door: How to Combat the Psychological Recession that's Alienating Employees and Hurting American Business, 2008. Contributor to books. **Address:** 1389 Caminito Halago, La Jolla, CA 92037-7165, U.S.A. **Online address:** jmbwick@san.rr.com

BAREHAM, Lindsey. British/American (born United States), b. 1948. **Genres:** Food And Wine, Travel/Exploration, International Relations/Current Affairs. **Career:** Sell Out, editor, 1970-85; Time Out Magazine, restaurant critic, food writer and editor. **Publications:** The Time Out Guide to Shopping in London, 1983; Pauper's London, 1990; In Praise of the Potato: Recipes from Around the World, 1991; A Celebration of Soup: With Classic Recipes from around the World, 1994; (with S. Hopkinson) Roast Chicken and Other Stories, 1994; The Little Book of Big Soups, 1996; Onions without Tears, 1996; (with S. Hopkinson) The Prawn Cocktail Years, 1997; Supper Won't Take Long: Favourite Recipes from the Evening Standard, 1997; The Big Red Book of Tomatoes, 1999; A Wolf in the Kitchen: Easy Food for Hungry People, 2000; The Fish Store, 2006; Dinner in a Dash: 50 Dinners for 6 in 60 Minutes, 2007; Just One Pot, 2007; Pasties, 2008; Hungry?: Easy Food for Hungry People, 2008; The Trifle Bowl, 2013. Contributor to periodicals. **Address:** c/o Bruce Hunter, David Higham Associates Ltd., 5-8 Lower John St., Golden Sq., London, GL W1F 9HA, England. **Online address:** lindsey.bareham@mac.com

BAREHAM, Terence. (Tony Bareham). British (born England), b. 1937. **Genres:** Literary Criticism And History, Bibliography, Biography, Autobiography/Memoirs. **Career:** University of Rhodesia, lecturer in English, 1963-67; University of York, lecturer in English, 1967-68; New University of Ulster, senior lecturer in English, 1968-, professor of English, 1990-2001, now retired. Writer. **Publications:** George Crabbe: A Critical Study, 1977; (with S.J. Gatrell) A Bibliography of George Crabbe, 1978; Malcolm Lowry, 1989. EDITOR: (as Tony Bareham) Anthony Trollope, 1980; Robert Bolt's A Man for All Seasons, 1980; T.S. Eliot's: Murder in the Cathedral, 1981; Shakespeare's Two Gentlemen of Verona, 1982; Anthony Trollope, Barsetshire Novels, 1982; The Barsetshire Novels of Trollope, 1983; Tom Stoppard: A Casebook, 1987; Charles Lever: New Evaluations, 1991. **Address:** Barnes & Noble Books, 122 5th Ave., New York, NY 10011, U.S.A.

BAREHAM, Tony. *See* **BAREHAM, Terence.**

BARER, Burl (Roger). American (born United States), b. 1947. **Genres:** Communications/Media, Young Adult Non-fiction, Criminology/True Crime. **Career:** Creative consultant, radio personality and writer; Korean Journal of Radiology, on-air personality, 1967-68, 1974-76; KOL, staff, 1968-73; KYYX, staff, 1978-80; KXA, staff, 1981-; Mind Development Inc., teacher and consultant, 1973-74, vice president, 1978-; Barer/McManus, creative director and on-air personality, 1975-77; Merklingar Labs, regional vice president, 1977-; Barer/Goldblatt and Associates, president, 1978-; B. Barer and Sons Inc., director, 1980-; Barer Cable Advertising, president, 1982-. Writer. **Publications:** The Saint: A Complete History in Print, Radio, Film and Television of Leslie Charteris' Robin Hood of Modern Crime, Simon Templar, 1928-1992, 1993; Maverick: The Making of the Movie and the Official Guide to the Television Series, 1994; Murder in the Family, 1994; Saint: A Novel, 1997; Headlock, 2000; Head Shot, 2001; Body Count, 2002; Broken Doll, 2004; Mom Said Kill, 2008. **Address:** 1839 Crestline Dr., Walla Walla, WA 99362, U.S.A.

BARER, Helen. American (born United States) **Genres:** Novels, Mystery/Crime/Suspense, Literary Criticism And History. **Career:** Writer. **Publications:** Fitness Kills: A Nora Franke Mystery, 2007. Contributor to periodicals. **Address:** Five Star Publishing, 27500 Drake Rd., Farmington Hills, MI 48331-3535, U.S.A. **Online address:** helen@helenbarer.com

BARFIELD, Rhonda. American (born United States), b. 1953?. **Genres:** Food And Wine, Medicine/Health. **Career:** Lilac Publishing, founder, owner, chief executive officer, secretary. Writer. **Publications:** Eat Well: For Fifty Dollars a Week, 1993; 15-Minute Cooking, 1996; Eat Healthy for Fifty Dollars a Week: Feed Your Family Nutritious, Delicious Meals for Less, 1996; Feed Your Family for Twelve Dollars a Day: A Complete Guide to Nutritious, Delicious Meals for Less Money, 2002; Real Life Homeschooling: The Stories of Twenty-one Families Who Make It Work, 2002. Contributor to periodicals. **Address:** Lilac Publishing, PO Box 665, St. Charles, MO 63302, U.S.A. **Online address:** barfield@aol.com

BARFIELD, Woodrow. American (born United States), b. 1950. **Genres:** Information Science/Computers, Technology, Social Sciences, Engineering, Education. **Career:** George Washington University, assistant professor of engineering management, 1985-87; University of Washington, assistant professor, 1987-91, associate professor of industrial engineering, 1991-96, affiliate professor, 1997-98; Virginia Polytechnic Institute and State University, professor of industrial and systems engineering, 1996-; University of London, visiting professor of computer science, 1996. Writer. **Publications:** (Contrib.) Handbook of Human Factors/Ergonomics, 1986; (co-author) Human Aspects of Computer-Aided Design, 1987; (contrib.) Job Analysis Handbook, 1988; (ed. with T. Furness and contrib.) Virtual Environments and Advanced Interface Design, 1995; (co-ed.) Human Factors in the Design of Tactical Display Systems for the Individual Soldier, 1995; (ed. with T.A. Dingus and contrib.) Human Factors in Intelligent Transportation Systems, 1998; (ed. with T. Caudell) Fundamentals of Wearable Computers and Augumented Reality, 2001. Contributor to journals and books. **Address:** Department of Industrial and Systems Engineering, Virginia Polytech Institute and State University, 250 Durham Hall, Blacksburg, VA 24061, U.S.A. **Online address:** barfield@vt.edu

BARHAM, Patte B. American (born United States) **Genres:** Autobiography/Memoirs, Biography, Humor/Satire. **Career:** Acting secretary of State-California, 1980-81; Television International Magazine, senior editor, 2000-; Los Angeles Times, entertainment reporter; Los Angeles Council of International Visitors, president. **Publications:** Operation Nightmare, 1953; (with M. Rasputin) Rasputin: The Man behind the Myth: A Personal Memoir, 1977; Peasant to Palace, 1990; (with P.H. Brown) Marilyn: The Last Take, 1992. **Address:** Dutton Publishers, 375 Hudson St., New York, NY 10014-3657, U.S.A.

BARICCO, Alessandro. Italian (born Italy), b. 1958. **Genres:** Novels, Essays, Young Adult Fiction. **Career:** Musicologist; La Repubblica, music critic; La Stampa, cultural correspondent; Holden School of Writing, founder. Writer. **Publications:** Genio in fuga: due saggi sul teatro musicale di Gioachino Rossini, 1988; Castelli di rabbia, 1991; Oceano mare, 1993; Novecento: un monologo, 1994; Seta, 1996; Silk, 1997; Scrittura creativa, 1997; City, 1999; Ocean Sea, 1999; La leggenda del pianista sull'oceano, 1999; Punteggiatura, 2001; Senza Sangue, 2002; Lands of Glass, 2002; Next: piccolo libro sulla globalizzazione e sul mondo che verrà, 2002; Partita spagnola, 2003; Without Blood, 2004; La Fenice, 2004; Questa storia, 2005; Iliad, 2006; I Barbari: saggio sulla mutazione, 2006; Corpo a Corpo: interviste impossibili, 2008; Mondi al limite, 2008; Emmaus, 2009. **Address:** c/o Author Mail, Alfred A. Knopf Inc., 201 E 50th St., New York, NY 10022, U.S.A.

BARICH, Bill. American (born United States), b. 1943. **Genres:** Novels, Novellas/Short Stories, Travel/Exploration, Essays, Autobiography/Memoirs, History. **Career:** Somerset Hills School, teacher, 1967-69; L.S. Distributors, stock person and book salesperson, 1969-71; Friends of Books and Comics, president, 1971; Alfred A. Knopf, publicity assistant and editorial assistant, 1972-75; New Yorker, staff writer, 1981-94; Intersection for the Arts, director, 1987-91; Squaw Valley Community of Writers, faculty; University of California-Berkeley, instructor of creative writing; University of California-Santa Cruz, instructor of creative writing; Jack Kerouac School of Disembodied Poetics, instructor of creative writing; Naropa Institute, instructor of creative writing. **Publications:** Laughing in the Hills (autobiography), 1980; Traveling Light (essays), 1984; Hard to Be Good (short stories), 1987; Hat Creek and the McCloud, 1988; Big Dreams: Into the Heart of California, 1994; Carson Valley (novel), 1997; Crazy for Rivers (essay), 1999; The Sporting Life: Horses, Boxers, Rivers and a Soviet Ballclub, 1999; A Fine Place to Daydream, 2005; Pint of Plain: How the Irish Pub Lost its Magic But Conquered the World, 2009; Long Way Home: On the Trail of Steinbeck's America, 2010. Contributor to periodicals. **Address:** c/o Liz Darhansoff, Darhansoff, Verrill & Feldman, 236 W 26th St., New York, NY 10001-6736, U.S.A. **Online address:** barichbill@hotmail.com

BARILLEAUX, Ryan J. American (born United States), b. 1957. **Genres:** Politics/Government. **Career:** Senator J. Bennett Johnston, intern/aide, 1977-78; University of Texas, assistant professor, 1983-87; Miami University, associate professor, 1987-95, professor of political science, 1995-, chair, 2001-. Writer. **Publications:** NONFICTION: The Politics of Southwestern Water, 1984; (co-author) The Presidency and National Security Policy, 1984; The President and Foreign Affairs: Evaluation, Performance, and Power, 1985; The Post-Modern Presidency: The Office after Ronald Reagan, 1988; (with B. Kellerman) The President as World Leader, 1991; (ed. with M.E. Stuckey) Leadership and the Bush Presidency: Prudence or Drift in an Era of Change?, 1992; American Government in Action: Principle, Process, Politics, 1996; (ed.) Presidential Frontiers: Underexplored Issues in White House Politics, 1998; (with M.J. Rozell) Power and Prudence: The Presidency of George H.W. Bush, 2004; (ed. with C.S. Kelley) Unitary Executive and the Modern Presidency, 2010; Inside American Politics, 2010. **Address:** Department of Political Science, Miami University, 220 Harrison Hall, 501 E High St., Oxford, OH 45056, U.S.A. **Online address:** barillrj@muohio.edu

BARISH, Evelyn. (Evelyn Barish Greenberger). American (born United States), b. 1935. **Genres:** Literary Criticism And History, Biography. **Career:** Cornell University, instructor, 1964-66, assistant professor of English, 1966-69; Briarcliff College, assistant professor of English, 1970-; City University of New York, College of Staten Island, associate professor, 1971-75, professor of English, 1976-, professor emeritus of English, Graduate Center, professor, 1988-. Writer. **Publications:** (As E.B. Greenberger) Arthur Hugh Clough: Growth of a Poet's Mind, 1970; Emerson in Italy, 1989; Emerson: The Roots of Prophecy, 1989. Contributor to journals. **Address:** College of Staten Island, City University of New York, 2800 Victory Blvd., Staten Island, NY 10314, U.S.A. **Online address:** barish@i-2000.com

BAR-JOSEPH, Uri. Israeli (born Israel), b. 1949. **Genres:** International Relations/Current Affairs, Politics/Government, History, Social Sciences. **Career:** University of Haifa, School of Political Sciences, Division of International Relations, Department of Political Science, lecturer, 1992-2000, senior lecturer, 2000-, associate professor, 2007-, chair. Writer. **Publications:** (With A. Perlmutter and M. Handel) Two Minutes over Baghdad, 1982, 2nd ed., 2003; The Best of Enemies: Israel and Transjordan in the War of 1948, 1987; Intelligence Intervention in the Politics of Democratic States: The U.S.A., Britain and Israel, 1995; Ha-Tsofeh she-nirdam: Haftaat Yom ha-Kipurim u-mekoroteha, 2001, trans. as The Watchman Fell Asleep: The Surprise of Yom Kippur and Its Sources, 2005; (ed.) Israel's National Security towards the 21st Century, 2001; The Angel: Ashraf Marwan, the Mossad, and the War of Yom Kippur, 2011. Contributor to periodicals. **Address:** Department of Political Science, University of Haifa, Rm. 413, Terrace Bldg., Haifa, 31905, Israel. **Online address:** barjo@poli.haifa.ac.il

BARKAN, Joanne. (J. B. Wright). American (born United States) **Genres:** Children's Fiction, Adult Non-fiction. **Career:** Prentice-Hall Inc., editor of curriculum materials for teachers, 1976-78; Croft-NEI Publications, editor, 1976-78; Seven Days Magazine, national news editor, 1978; Jim Henson Productions, The Muppets, book editor and staff writer, 1985-87; Brooke-House Publishing, editor and project coordinator, 1988-92; Dissent Magazine, executive editor. **Publications:** Visions of Emancipation: The Italian Workers' Movement since 1945 (adult nonfiction), 1984; Baby Piggy and the Thunderstorm, 1987; The Christmas Toy, 1987; Kermit's Mixed-up Message, 1987; Baby Gonzo's Unfinished Dream, 1988; Baby Kermit's Old Blanket, 1988; Boober's Colorful Soup, 1988; Doozers Big and Little, 1988; My First Kitchen Gadget Books, 1989; My Cooking Pot, 1989; My Cooking Spoon, 1989; My Frying Pan, 1989; My Measuring Cup, 1989; My Rolling Pin, 1989; My Spatula, 1989; What's So Funny, 1989; The Girl Who Couldn't Remember, 1989; The Secret of the Sunken Treasure, 1989; My First Garden Tools, 1990; Abraham Lincoln and President's Day, 1990; Abraham Lincoln: A Biography, 1990; Air, Air All Around, 1990; Fire, Fire Burning Bright, 1990; Rocks, Rocks Big & Small, 1990; Water, Water Everywhere, 1990; My Pruning Shears, 1990; My Rake, 1990; My Trowel, 1990; My Watering Can, 1990; Whiskerville Bake Shop, 1990; Whiskerville Firehouse, 1990; Whiskerville Post Office, 1990; Whiskerville School, 1990; Anna Marie's Blanket, 1990; Spooky House, 1990; Creatures That Glow, 1991; My Birthday Adventure with Teddy O (a computer-personalized picture book), 1991; A Very Scary Haunted House, 1991; A Very Scary Jack O'Lantern, 1991; Easter Egg Fun, 1991; Easter Surprise, 1991; Where Do I Put My Toys?, 1991; Where Do I Put My Clothes?, 1991; Where Do I Put My Books?, 1991; Where Do I Put My Food?, 1991; Whiskerville Train Station, 1991; Whiskerville Theater, 1991; Whiskerville Grocery, 1991; Whiskerville Toy Shop, 1991; (as J.B. Wright) Dinosaurs, 1991; Boxcar, 1992; Caboose, 1992; Locomotive, 1992; Passenger Car, 1992; A Very Merry Santa Claus Story, 1992; A Very Merry Snowman Story, 1992; A Very Scary Ghost Story, 1992; A Very Scary Witch Story, 1992; That Fat Hat, 1992; Animal Car, 1993; Circus Locomotive, 1993; Clown Caboose, 1993; Performers' Car, 1993; The Magic Carpet's Secret, 1993; Elves for a Day, 1993; Numbers Add Up at Home, 1993; The Ballet Mystery, 1994; Home, Creepy Home, 1994; The Krystal Princess and the Grand Contest, 1994; Merry Christmas, Santa!, 1995; Big Wheels, 1996; Big Fire Trucks, 1996; Switching Hour, 1996; Textures, 1998; Pup in King Arthur's Court, 1998; Santa Claus Nutcracker, 1998; Splish! Splash!, 1998; Colors, 1998; Patterns, 1998; Tale of Two Sitters, 1998; Toy Soldier, 1999; Barnum's Animals: ABC Puzzle Pack, 1999; Riddle of the Lost Lake, 2000; What is Velocity?, 2004; Games We Play, 2005; Looking Good, 2005; Boy

Who Cried Wolf: A Tale about Telling the Truth, 2006; What is Density?, 2006; (reteller) Wild Swans: A Tale of Persistence, 2006; Celebrate!: Your Amazing Achievements, 2007; (reteller) King Midas and the Golden Touch: A Tale of Greed, 2007. Works appear in anthologies. Contributor to periodicals. **Address:** 711 W End Ave., Ste. 5AN, New York, NY 10025-0093, U.S.A.

BARKAN, Josh. American (born United States), b. 1969?. **Genres:** Novels, Novellas/Short Stories. **Career:** Harvard University, writing instructor; New York University, writing instructor; Boston University, writing instructor. Writer. **Publications:** Before Hiroshima: The Confession of Murayama Kazuo, and Other Stories, 2000; Blind Speed: A Novel, 2008. **Address:** New York, NY , U.S.A. **Online address:** josh@joshbarkan.com

BARKER, Clive. American/British (born England), b. 1952. **Genres:** Mystery/Crime/Suspense, Plays/Screenplays, Novels, Novellas/Short Stories, Horror, Young Adult Non-fiction, Young Adult Fiction, Illustrations, Illustrations. **Career:** Full-time writer, director and producer. **Publications:** SHORT FICTION: Clive Barker's Books of Blood, 6 vols., 1984-86; Clive Barker's A-Z of Horror, 1997; Books of Blood: Volumes One to Three, 1998; The Essential Clive Barker: Selected Fiction, 2000. NOVELS: The Damnation Game, 1985; Cabal, 1988; The Great and Secret Show: The First Book of the Art, 1989; Imajica, 1991, vol. I, Imajica I: The Fifth Dominion, 1995, vol. II, Imajica II: The Recibcukuatuib, 1995, rev. ed., 2002; The Thief of Always: A Fable, 1992; Everville: The Second Book of the Art, 1994; Sacrament, 1996; Galilee: A Romance, 1998; Coldheart Canyon: A Hollywood Ghost Story, 2001; Clive Barker's The Thief of Always, 2002; Mister B. Gone, 2007; Hellbound Hearts, 2009; Galilee II, 2009; Absolute Midnight, 2011. SELF-ILLUSTRATED, ABARAT QUARTET SERIES: Abarat, 2002; Days of Magic, Nights of War, 2004. CO-AUTHOR: Tapping the Vein, 1989, rev. ed., 2002; Hellraiser, 1989; Night Breed, vol. I, 1990; Weaveworld, 1991; The Yattring and Jack, 1991; Book of the Damned, 4 vol., 1991; Clive Barker's Hellraiser, 1991; Son of Celluloid, 1991; Dread, 1992; Epic, 1992; Revelations, 1992; Primal From the Cradle to the Grave, 1992; Razorline, 1993; Saint Sinner, vol. I, 1993; Ectokid, vol. I, 1993; Pinhead, vol. I, 1993; Hokum & Hex, vol. I, 1993; Pinhead vs Marshal Law in Hell, 1993; The Life of Death, 1993; The Harrowers: Raiders of the Abyss, vol. I, 1993; Hyperkind, vol. I, 1993; Night of the Living Dead: London Book One: Bloodline, 1993; Book Two: End of the Line, 1993; Rawhead Rex, 1994; Deady: The Malevolent Teddy, 2004. OTHERS: (intro.) Scared Stiff: Tales of Sex and Death, 1987; (intro.) Night Visions 4, 1987; (intro.) Taboo, 1988; Theatre Games, 1988; Clive Barker's Nightbreed: The Making of the Film, 1990; (intro.) H. R. Giger's Necronomicon, 1991; (intro.) Salem's Lot, 1991; Clive Barker's Shadows in Eden (autobiography), 1991; Pandemonium: The World of Clive Barker (autobiography), 1991; Incarnations: Three Plays, 1995; Forms of Heaven: Three Plays, 1996; The Inhuman Condition, 2001; (intro.) Dark Dreamers, 2001; (contrib.) Rare Flesh, 2003; Clive Barker: Visions of Heaven and Hell, 2005; The Painter, the Creature and the Father of Lies, 2010. Illustrator of books by F. Burke. **Address:** Creative Artists Agency, 9830 Wilshire Blvd., Beverly Hills, CA 90212-1825, U.S.A.

BARKER, David J. P. British (born England), b. 1938. **Genres:** Medicine/Health. **Career:** Royal South Hampshire Hospital, consultant physician; University of Birmingham, research fellow, 1963-66, clinical lecturer, 1966-69; University Makerere, lecturer, 1969-72; University of Southampton, senior lecturer, 1972-79, professor of clinical epidemiology, 1979-, now professor emeritus, Medical Research Council Environmental Epidemiology Unit, director, 1984-; Royal College of Obstetricians and Gynaecologists, honorary fellow, 1993; Royal College of Paediatrics and Child Health, honorary fellow, 2002; Oregon Health and Science University, Department of Cardiovascular Medicine, Heart Research Center, faculty, 2003, professor; Association of Physicians of Great Britain and Ireland, president, 2003; King Saud University, professor, 2009; Society for Social Medicine, president. Writer. **Publications:** Practical Epidemiology, 1972, 4th ed., 1990; (with G. Rose) Epidemiology in Medical Practice, 1976, 5th ed., 1997; (with G. Rose) Epidemiology for the Uninitiated, 1979, 3rd ed., 1993; (with M.J. Gardner and P.D. Winter) Atlas of Mortality from Selected Diseases in England and Wales, 1968-1978, 1984; (ed.) Fetal and Infant Origins of Adult Disease, 1992; Mothers, Babies and Disease in Later Life, 1994, 2nd ed. as Mothers, Babies and Health in Later Life, 1998; (co-ed.) Fetal Programming, 1999; (ed.) Fetal Origins of Cardiovascular and Lung Disease, 2001; (ed.) Type 2 Diabetes: The Thrifty Phenotype, 2001; The Best Start in Life, 2003; (ed. with R.L. Bergmann and P.L. Ogra) Window of Opportunity: Pre-pregnancy to 24 Months of Age, 2008; (ed. with G.J. Burton, A. Moffett and K. Thornburg) The Placenta and Human Developmental Programming, 2011. **Address:** Medical Research Council, Environmental Epidemiology Unit, University of Southampton, Southampton General Hospital, Southampton, HM SO16 6YD, England. **Online address:** d.j.barker@soton.ac.uk

BARKER, Dennis (Malcolm). British (born England), b. 1929. **Genres:** Novels, Plays/Screenplays, Communications/Media, Crafts, Military/Defense/Arms Control, Self Help, Social Commentary, Writing/Journalism, Documentaries/Reportage. **Career:** Suffolk Chronicle and Mercury, reporter, 1947-48; East Anglian Daily Times, reporter, feature writer and theater and film critic, 1948-58; Express and Star, estates and property editor, feature writer, theater critic and columnist, 1958-63; The Guardian, midlands staff, 1963-67, reporter, feature writer, columnist, media correspondent and obituarist, 1967-; BBC Radio Stop, broadcaster, 1974-77. **Publications:** Candidate of Promise, 1969; The Scandalisers, 1974; Soldiering On: An Unofficial Portrait of the British Army, 1981; One Man's Estate: The Preservation of an English Inheritance, 1983; Parian Ware, 1985; Ruling the Waves: An Unofficial Portrait of the Royal Navy, 1986; Winston Three Three Three, 1987; Guarding the Skies: An Unofficial Portrait of the Royal Air Force, 1989; Fresh Start, 1990; The Craft of the Media Interview, 1998; How to Deal with the Media, 2000; Tricks Journalists Play: How the Truth is Massaged, Distorted, Glamorized and Glossed over, 2007; Clients of Miss May, 2008. Contributor to books. **Address:** The Guardian, Kings Pl., 90 York Way, London, GL N1 9GU, England.

BARKER, Eileen (Vartan). British (born England), b. 1938. **Genres:** Theology/Religion, Sociology. **Career:** London School of Economics, lecturer, 1970-85, dean undergraduate studies, 1982-86, senior lecturer, 1985-90, reader, 1990-92, professor of sociology, 1992-, now professor emeritus; Brunel University, visiting part-time lecturer, 1974-75; Information Network Focus on Religious Movements, chair, founder, director, 1988-93, 1999-; University of London, Faculty of Economics, vice dean, 1986-88; University of New England, Department of Sociology, visiting professor, 1988; Society for the Scientific Study of Religion, president, 1991-93; Order of the British Empire, officer, 2000; Association for the Sociology of Religion, president, 2001-02. Writer. **Publications:** The Making of a Moonie: Choice or Brainwashing?, 1984; Sects and New Religious Movements, 1988; New Religious Movements: A Practical Introduction, 1989. EDITOR: New Religious Movements: A Perspective for Understanding Society, 1982; Of Gods and Men: New Religious Movements in the West, 1983; (with J.A. Beckford and K. Dobbelaere) Secularization, Rationalism and Sectarianism, 1993; 20 Years On: Changes in New Religions, 1995; LSE on Freedom, 1997; (with M. Warburg) New Religions and New Religiosity, 1998; (with J.A. Beckford and J.T. Richardson) Challenging Religion: Essays in Honour of Eileen Barker, 2003; The Centrality of Religion in Social Life: Essays in Honour of James A Beckford, 2008. **Address:** Department of Sociology, London School of Economics and Political Science, Houghton St., London, GL WC2A 2AE, England. **Online address:** e.barker@lse.ac.uk

BARKER, Elspeth. British/Scottish (born Scotland), b. 1940. **Genres:** Novels, Poetry, Literary Criticism And History. **Career:** Norwich School of Art, tutor and lecturer in creative writing, 1992; Kansas University, visiting professor of fiction, 1999. Writer. **Publications:** O Caledonia (novel), 1991; (ed.) Loss: An Anthology, 1998; Janet, 1999. Contributor to periodicals. **Address:** c/o Bill Hamilton, A. M. Heath & Company Ltd., 79 St. Martin's Ln., London, GL WC2N 4AA, England.

BARKER, Jonathan. British (born England), b. 1949. **Genres:** Literary Criticism And History, Bibliography, Librarianship, Reference. **Career:** Royal Borough of Kensington and Chelsea, library assistant, 1970-72; Arts Council of Great Britain, poetry librarian, 1973-88; Poetry Book Society, assistant secretary, 1973-83, selector of books, 1985-86; British Council, literature officer and deputy director of literature department, 1988-2006, senior literature consultant, 2007-09, assistant director of literature; Arts Council England, literative assessor, 2010. Writer. **Publications:** (Comp.) Short-Title Catalogue, 6th ed., 1981; A Bibliography of Poetry in Britain and Ireland since 1970, 1995. EDITOR: (and intro.) Selected Poems of W.H. Davies, 1985; (and intro.) Poetry Book Society Anthology, 1986/87, 1986; The Art of Edward Thomas, 1987; (and intro.) Thirty Years of the Poetry Book Society, 1956-1986, 1988; (with W. Hope) Collected Poems and Selected Translations, 1990. Work appears in anthologies. Contributor of articles to periodicals. **Address:** Arts Group, British Council, 10 Spring Gardens, London, GL SW1A 2BN, England. **Online address:** jonathan.barker@britishcouncil.org

BARKER, M. P. (Michele Plourde-Barker). American (born United States), b. 1960. **Genres:** Novels. **Career:** Connecticut Valley Historical Museum, archivist. Writer, archivist and historian. **Publications:** A Difficult Boy (historical novel), 2008. **Address:** c/o William Reiss, John Hawkins and Associates Inc., 71 W 23rd St., Ste. 1600, New York, NY 10010-4185, U.S.A. **Online address:** mpbarker@mpbarker.net

BARKER, Pat(ricia). British (born England), b. 1943. **Genres:** Novels, Young Adult Non-fiction. **Career:** Teacher, 1965-70. Writer. **Publications:** Union Street, 1982; Blow Your House Down, 1984; The Century's Daughter, 1986 in UK as Liza's England, 1996; The Man Who Wasn't There, 1989; Regeneration, 1991; The Eye in the Door, 1993; The Ghost Road, 1995; Another World, 1998; Border Crossing, 2001; Double Vision, 2003; War Talk, 2005; Life Class, 2007. **Address:** Aitken Alexander Associates Ltd., 18-21 Cavaye Pl., London, GL SW10 9PT, England.

BARKER, Paul. British (born England), b. 1935. **Genres:** Sociology, Economics, Social Sciences. **Career:** Times, journalist, staff, 1959-64; Economist, journalist; école Normale Supérieure, lecturer; New Society, deputy editor, 1965-68, editor, 1968-86; freelance writer and broadcaster, 1986-; Victoria and Albert Museum, Reyner Banham memorial lecturer, 1998; Institute of Community Studies, senior research fellow and fellow in the built environment, 2000-02; Young Foundation, senior research fellow. **Publications:** (Ed.) A Sociological Portrait: A Series from New Society, 1972; One for Sorrow, Two for Joy: Ten Years of New Society, 1972; (ed.) The Social Sciences Today, 1975; (ed.) Arts in Society, 1977, new ed., 2006; (ed.) The Other Britain: A New Society Collection, 1982; (ed.) Founders of the Welfare State: A Series from New Society, 1984; Gulliver and Beyond, 1996; (ed.) Living as Equals, 1996; (ed.) A Critic Writes, 1997; Town and Country, 1998; Non-Plan, 2000; From Black Economy to Moment of Truth, 2004; Porcupines in Winter, 2006; The Rise and Rise of Meritocracy, 2007; The Freedoms of Suburbia, 2009; The Banham Lectures: Designing the Future, 2009; Hebden Bridge: A Sense of Belonging, 2012. Contributor to books, magazines and newspapers. **Address:** Young Foundation, 18 Victoria Park Sq., London, GL E2 9PF, England.

BARKER, Philip. Canadian/British (born England), b. 1929. **Genres:** Psychiatry, Medicine/Health. **Career:** Hackney Hospital, house physician, 1954; Whittington Hospital, house surgeon, 1954; Royal Berkshire Hospital, pediatric house physician, 1957; Leicester Royal Infirmary, senior house officer, 1957-58; Royal Edinburgh Hospital, senior house officer and registrar in psychiatry, 1958-60; Newcastle-upon-Tyne Teaching Hospital, senior registar in child psychiatry, 1960-62; University of St. Andrews, lecturer in clinical child psychiatry, 1962-67; Dundee Child Psychiatry Service, consultant and child psychiatrist, Liff House Children's Unit, founder and psychiatrist, 1962-67; Ward End Child Guidance Center, consultant children's psychiatrist, Charles Burns Clinic, consultant in clinical charge, 1967-75; University of Birmingham, lecturer in child psychiatry, 1968-75; University of Toronto, assistant professor, 1975-76, associate professor, 1976-79, professor of psychiatry, 1979-80; Thistletown Regional Centre for Children and Adolescents, director of inpatient services, 1975-79, director of psychiatric education, 1979-80; Children's Assessment and Treatment Centre, consultant, 1976-80; University of Calgary, Department of Psychiatry, professor of psychiatry and pediatrics, 1980-99, professor emeritus of psychiatry, 1999-; Alberta Children's Hospital, psychiatrist, 1980-99, head, through 1999; Children's Service Centre, consultant psychiatrist, Alberta Mental Health Services, consultant psychiatrist, 1980-. Writer. **Publications:** Basic Child Psychiatry, 1971, 7th ed., 2004; Care Can Prevent, 1973; (ed.) The Residential Psychiatric Treatment of Children, 1974; Basic Family Therapy, 1981, 5th ed., 2007; Using Metaphors in Psychotherapy, 1985; Clinical Interviews with Children and Adolescents, 1990; (ed. with S. Baldwin) Ethical Issues in Mental Health, 1991; (with D. Fraser) The Nurse as Therapist: A Behavioral Model, 1991; Psychotherapeutic Metaphors: A Guide to Theory and Practice, 1996; (ed. with C. Stevenson) The Construction of Power and Authority in Psychiatry, 2000. CONTRIBUTOR: Occupational Therapy: Today-Tomorrow, 1971; Forward Trends in Special Education, 1974; Treating Families with Special Needs, 1982; Creating Adult Learning: Theoretical and Practical Communications on Educational Design for Adults, 1989. Contributor of articles to journals. **Address:** Department of Psychiatry, University of Calgary, 1403-29 St. NW, Calgary, AB T2N 2T9, Canada. **Online address:** jazz@canuck.com

BARKER, Raffaella. British (born England), b. 1964. **Genres:** Novels. **Career:** Freelance writer, 1988-; Burlington Danes Academy, Creative Writing, teacher; The Recovery Centre, Creative Writing, teacher; Arvon Foundation, Creative Writing, teacher; First Story, writer. **Publications:** NOVELS: Come and Tell Me Some Lies, 1994; The Hook, 1996; Hens Dancing, 1999; Summertime, 2001; Green Grass, 2003; Phosphorescence, 2005; A Perfect Life, 2006; Poppyland, 2008. **Address:** c/o Sarah Lutyens, Lutyens & Rubinstein, 231 Westbourne Park Rd., London, GL W11 1EB, England. **Online address:** coname@lutyensrubinstein.co.uk

BARKEY, Karen. American/Turkish (born Turkey), b. 1958. **Genres:** History, Sociology. **Career:** University of Wisconsin-Madison, assistant professor of sociology, 1988-89; Columbia University, assistant professor, 1989-93, associate professor of sociology, 1993-2006, professor of sociology, 2007-, Undergraduate Studies, director, Center for Historical Social Science, co-director, 2000-04; Amherst College, president. Writer. **Publications:** Bandits and Bureaucrats: The Ottoman Route to State Centralization, 1994; (ed. with M. von Hagen) After Empire: Multiethnic Societies and Nation-Building: The Soviet Union and the Russian, Habsburg, and Ottoman Empires, 1997; Empire of Difference: The Ottomans in Comparative Perspective, 2008; (with E. Ikegami and R.B. Wong) Alternative Routes to State Formation: A Relational Approach to Politics, Culture and Society in Japan, China and Turkey, forthcoming. **Address:** Department of Sociology, Columbia University, 601C Knox Hall, 1180 Amsterdam Ave., 6060 W 122nd St., PO Box 9649, New York, NY 10027, U.S.A. **Online address:** kb7@columbia.edu

BARKIN, Jill. *See* **JOHNSON, Susan (M.).**

BARKOW, Al. American (born United States), b. 1932. **Genres:** History, Sports/Fitness. **Career:** R.H. Donnelley Corp., assistant editor, 1960-63; McGraw-Hill Co., assistant editor, 1960-63; Shell's Wonderful World of Golf Television Series, chief writer, 1963-69; Golf Magazine, editor-in-chief, 1970-72; Golf Illustrated Magazine, editor-in-chief, 1985-90, 1994-96, editor-at-large; Al Barkow's Golf Report, editor and publisher; GolfWeb, columnist; The Journal of the Shivas Irons Society, editor, 2005-07. **Publications:** Golf's Golden Grind, 1974; (with B. Casper) The Good Sense of Golf, 1978; (with K. Venturi) The Venturi Analysis, 1981; The Venturi System, 1983; (with G. Low) The Master of Putting, 1983; (with P. Rodgers) Play Lower Handicap Golf, 1986; Gettin' to the Dance Floor: An Oral History of American Golf, 1986; (with R. Pace) Target Golf: Lower Scores by Visualizing Your Game, 1986; (with P. Rodgers) A Unique Teacher of the Pros Shows You How to Play Lower Handicap Golf, 1987; Getting' to the Dance Floor: An Oral History of American Golf, 1986; The History of the PGA Tour, 1989; (with C. Lohren) Getting Set for Golf, 1995; (with D. Stockton) Dave Stockton's Putt to Win, 1996; (with D. Barrett) Golf Legends of All Time, 1997; (with D. Barrett) Golf Greats, 1998; The Golden Era of Golf: How America Rose to Dominate the Old Scotsgame, 2000; That's Golf: The Best of Al Barkow, 2001; Gene Darazen and Shell's Wonderful World of Golf, 2003; Sam: The One and Only Sam Snead, 2005; Tom Crow, King of Clubs: Reflections on the Game from the Course to Cobra, 2005; (with D. Barrett and K. Janke) The Wit & Wisdom of Golf, 2007; Sam: The One and Only Sam Snead, 2010. **Address:** 410 Evelyn Ave., Ste. 303, Albany, CA 94706, U.S.A. **Online address:** abark@sbcglobal.net

BARKS, Coleman Bryan. American (born United States), b. 1937. **Genres:** Poetry, Translations. **Career:** University of Southern California, instructor in English, 1965-67; University of Georgia, assistant professor, 1967-72, associate professor, 1972-78, professor of English, 1978-97, professor emeritus, 1997-; University of Michigan, visiting professor, 1974. Writer. **Publications:** The Juice, 1971; New Words, 1976; We're Laughing at the Damage, 1977; Gourd Seed (poetry), 1993; Xenia (poetry), 1994; Tentmaking (poetry), 2001; Club: Granddaughter Poems, 2001; (with J. Moyne) Year with Rumi: Daily Readings, 2006. TRANSLATOR: (with R. Bly) Night and Sleep, 1981; (with J. Moyne) Open Secret: Versions of Rumi, 1984; (with J. Moyne) Unseen Rain: Quatrains of Rumi, 1986; We Are Three: New Rumi Poems, 1986; (with J. Moyne) These Branching Moments: Forty Odes by Rumi, 1988; (with J. Moyne) This Longing: Poetry Teaching Stories and Selected Letters, 1988; Delicious Laughter: Rambunctions Teaching Stories from the Mathnawi of Jelaluddin Rumi, 1990; Like This, 1990; Rumi: One-Handed Basket Weaving: Twenty Poems on the Theme of Work, 1991; Feeling the Shoulder of the Lion: Selected Poetry and Teaching Stories from the Mathnawi, 1991; Naked Song, 1992; Stallion on a Frozen Lake: Love Songs of the Sixth Dalai Lama, 1992; Say I Am You, 1992; One-Handed Basket Weaving: Twenty Poems on the Theme of Work, 1993; Birdsong: Fifty-Three Short Poems, 1993; The Hand of Poetry, 1993; The Essential Rumi, 1995; The Illuminated Rumi,

1997; (with J. Moyne) Whoever Brought Me Here Will Have to Take Me Home, 1998; The Glance: Songs of Soul-Meeting, 1999; (with M. Green) The Illuminated Prayer: The Five-Times Prayer of the Sufis as Revealed by Jellaludin Rumi and Bawa Muhaiyaddeen, 2000; Divan-i Shams-i Tabrizi, 2001; (co-author) The Soul of Rumi: A New Collection of Ecstatic Poems, 2001; (co-author) Rumi: The Book of Love: Poems of Ecstasy and Longing, 2003; The Drowned Book: Ecstatic and Earthy Reflections of Bahauddin, the Father of Rumi, 2004; Rumi: Bridge to the Soul: Journeys into the Music and Silence of the Heart, 2007; Winter Sky: New and Selected Poems, 1968-2008, 2008; Rumi: The Big Red Book, 2010. Contributor to books. **Address:** Department of English, Franklin College of Arts & Sciences, University of Georgia, 254 Park Hall, Athens, GA 30602-6205, U.S.A. **Online address:** maypopbooks@gmail.com

BARLETT, **Peggy F.** American (born United States), b. 1947. **Genres:** Anthropology/Ethnology, Economics, Local History/Rural Topics, Women's Studies And Issues, Business/Trade/Industry. **Career:** Columbia University, Department of Anthropology, research assistant, 1970-72; Carleton College, assistant professor of anthropology, 1974-76; Emory University, assistant professor, 1976-82, associate professor, 1982-89, professor of anthropology, 1989-2007, department head, 1991-94, Liaison to the Office of Sustainability Initiatives, faculty, 2006-, Goodrich C. White professor of anthropology, 2007-. Writer. **Publications:** (Ed.) Agricultural Decision Making: Anthropological Contributions to Rural Development, 1980; Agricultural Choice and Change: Decision Making in a Costa Rican Community, 1982; American Dreams, Rural Realities: Family Farms in Crisis, 1993; (ed. with G.W. Chase) Sustainability on Campus: Stories and Strategies for Changes, 2004; (ed.) Urban Place: Reconnecting with the Natural World, 2005. Contributor to journals. Works appear in anthologies. **Address:** Department of Anthropology, Emory University, Atlanta, GA 30322, U.S.A. **Online address:** pbarlett@emory.edu

BARLEY, **Janet Crane.** American (born United States), b. 1934. **Genres:** Literary Criticism And History, Biography, Autobiography/Memoirs. **Career:** Xenia Daily Gazette, women's editor, 1956-57; Freelance writer, 1968-. **Publications:** Winter in July: Visits with Children's Authors Down Under, 1995. **Address:** 846 Sandalwood Rd. W, Perrysburg, OH 43551, U.S.A.

BARLOW, **Aaron.** American (born United States), b. 1951. **Genres:** Adult Non-fiction, Technology. **Career:** University of Ouagadougou, lecturer, 1985-97; Kutztown University, assistant professor of English, 2004-06; New York City College of Technology, assistant professor of English, 2006-12, associate professor of English, 2012-; Skakespeare's Sister (a bookstore), owner and manager. Writer. **Publications:** The DVD Revolution: Movies, Culture, and Technology, 2005; Blogging America: The New Public Sphere, 2007; The Rise of the Blogosphere, 2007; Quentin Tarantino: Life at the Extremes, 2010; (ed.) One Hand Does Not Catch a Buffalo: 50 Years of Amazing Peace Corps Stories: vol. I, 2011; (with R. Leston) Beyond the Blogosphere, 2012. Contributor to periodicals. **Address:** Department of English, New York City College of Technology, Rm. N503, 300 Jay St., Brooklyn, NY 11201-1909, U.S.A. **Online address:** abarlow@citytech.cuny.edu

BARLOW, **Maude.** Canadian (born Canada), b. 1947. **Genres:** Economics, Education, Politics/Government, Natural History, Social Sciences. **Career:** Women Associates Consulting Inc., vice president, 1975-80; City of Ottawa, director of equal opportunities, 1980-83; senior adviser to Prime Minister Pierre Trudeau, 1983-84; Council of Canadians, national chairperson, 1988-. Writer. **Publications:** Women and Disarmament, 1988; Parcel of Rogues, 1990; (with B. Campbell) Take Back the Nation: Meeting the Threat of NAFTA, 1991, rev. ed. as Take Back the Nation 2: Meeting the Threat of NAFTA, 1993; (co-author) Meeting the Global Challenge: Competitive Position and Strategic Response, 1992; (with H-J. Robertson) Class Warfare, 1994; (with B. Campbell) Straight through the Heart: How the Liberals Abandoned the Just Society, 1995; (with J. Winter) The Big Black Book: The Essential Views of Conrad and Barbara Amiel Black, 1997; (with T. Clarke) MAI: The Multilateral Agreement on Investment and the Threat to Canadian Sovereignty, 1997; (with T. Clarke) MAI: The Multilateral Agreement on Investment and the Threat to American Freedom, 1998; The Fight of My Life, 1998; (with E. May) Frederick Street: Life and Death on Canada's Love Canal, 2000; (with T. Clarke) Global Showdown: How the New Activists are Fighting Global Corporate Rule, 2001; (with T. Clarke) Blue Gold: The Battle Against Corporate Theft of the World's Water, 2002; Profit Is not the Cure: A Citizen's Guide to Saving Medicare, 2002; Too Close for Comfort: Canada's Future within Fortress North America, 2005; (co-author) Voix rebelles du monde=Rebel Voices of the World, 2007; Blue Covenant: the Global Water Crisis and the Coming Battle for the Right to Water, 2008. Contributor to periodicals and journals. **Address:** Council of Canadians, 700-170 Laurier Ave. W, Ottawa, ON K1P 5V5, Canada. **Online address:** mbarlow@canadians.org

BARLOW, **Paul.** British (born England), b. 1962. **Genres:** Art/Art History, Young Adult Fiction, Institutions/Organizations. **Career:** University of Northumbria, senior lecturer in art history. Writer. **Publications:** NONFICTION: (ed. with C. Trodd and D. Amigoni) Victorian Culture and the Idea of the Grotesque, 1999; (ed. with C. Trodd) Governing Cultures: Art Institutions in Victorian London, 2000; Time Present and Time Past: The Art of John Everett Millais, 2005. Contributor to books and periodicals. **Address:** Visual Arts Division, School of Arts and Social Sciences, Northumbria University, 411 Lipman Bldg., Sandyford Rd., Newcastle upon Tyne, TW NE1 8ST, England. **Online address:** paul.barlow@northumbria.ac.uk

BARLOW, **Tani E.** American (born United States), b. 1950. **Genres:** Cultural/Ethnic Topics, Intellectual History, Women's Studies And Issues, Translations. **Career:** Shanghai Teachers University, lecturer in American culture, 1981-82; University of Missouri-Columbia, assistant professor of history, 1985-90, associate professor of history, 1990-92, university research fellow, 1987-88; San Francisco State University, associate professor, 1992-94; East Asia Cultures Critique, founding editor, 1992-, senior editor; University of Washington, Women Studies, associate professor, 1994-97, professor, 1997-2008, professor of history, 2004-08, affiliated doctoral professor, 2008-; Rockefeller Institutional Grants for the Humanities, co-director, 1996-2001; Luce Foundation, co-researcher, 1997-2000; Rice University, professor of history, Ting Tsung and Wei Fong Chao Professor of Asian Studies, 2008-, Chao Center for Asian Studies, director, 2008-; Henry Luce Foundation, The Ephemera Project, principle investigator, 2011-. Writer. **Publications:** (With D.M. Lowe) Chinese Reflections: Americans Teaching in the People's Republic, 1985; (with D.M. Lowe) Teaching China's Lost Generation: Foreign Experts in the People's Republic of China, 1987; (ed. with G.J. Bjorge) I Myself am a Woman: Selected Writings of Ding Ling, 1989; (ed.) Gender Politics in Modern China: Writing and Feminism, 1993; (ed. with A. Zito) Body, Subject & Power in China, 1994; (ed.) Formations of Colonial Modernity in East Asia, 1997; (ed.) New Asian Marxisms, 2002; Cinema and Desire, 2002; The Question of Women in Chinese Feminism, 2004; (with S. Chakravorty and S. Milevska) Conversations with Gayatri Chakravorty Spivak, 2006; (with I. Ruri and S. Hiroko) Modan gāru to shokuminchiteki kindai: Higashi Ajia ni okeru teikoku, shihon, jendā, 2010. **Address:** Department of History, Rice University, 321 Humanities, 6100 Main MS-42, PO Box 1892, Houston, TX 77005-1827, U.S.A. **Online address:** tb5@rice.edu

BARLOW, **William.** American (born United States), b. 1943. **Genres:** Adult Non-fiction, Communications/Media, Cultural/Ethnic Topics, Music, Theatre, History. **Career:** Howard University, Department of Radio, Television and Film, professor of communications, 1980-92; National Endowment for the Humanities, fellow, 1991-92; Smithsonian Institution, Blues Foundation, consultant; Pacifica Radio, music programmer and producer. Writer. **Publications:** (With P. Shapiro) An End to Silence: The San Francisco State College Student Movement in the '60s, 1971; Looking Up at Down: The Emergence of Blues Culture, 1989; (ed. with J.L. Dates) Split Image: African Americans in the Mass Media, 1990, 2nd ed., 1993; (with T.L. Morgan) From Cakewalks to Concert Halls: An Illustrated History of African American Popular Music from 1895 to 1930, 1991; (with C. Finley) From Swing to Soul: An Illustrated History of African American Popular Music from 1930 to 1960, 1994; Voice Over: The Making of Black Radio, 1999. Contributor to periodicals. **Address:** Temple University Press, 1852 N 10th St., Philadelphia, PA 19122, U.S.A. **Online address:** wbarlow@howard.edu

BARLOWE, **Raleigh (Bruce).** American (born United States), b. 1914. **Genres:** Novels, Economics. **Career:** American University, instructor in political science, 1937-38; Library of Congress, assistant, 1937-40; Southwestern Land Tenure Research Project, land economist, 1942-43; U.S. Department of Agriculture, economist, 1943-47; United Nations Food and Agriculture Organization, economist, 1947; Michigan State University, lecturer, 1948-50, associate professor, 1950-52, professor, 1952-81, Department of Resource Development, chairman, 1959-71, 1980-81, adjunct professor, 1981-84, now emeritus professor; University of Puerto Rico, consultant, 1958; Colombian Government, consultant, 1959; University of Nigeria, consultant, 1967; Korean Government, consultant, 1971-72; U.S. Agricultural Development Council, consultant, 1972-. Writer. **Publications:** (With V.W. Johnson) Land Problems and Policies, 1954; Land Resource Economics: The Political Economy of Rural and Urban Land Resource Use, 1958, 4th ed. as Land Resource Economics: The Economics of Real Estate, 1986; Valuation of Lands in Southcentral Iowa, 1839-1843: Royce Cession Area 262, 1973; Valuation of Lands in Eastern Iowa: Royce Areas 175, 226, and 244, 1833-1839, 1973; Spanish Land Grants in Royce's Cession 50 in Missouri, 1973; Appraisal of Sac and Fox Lands in Portions of Royce Area 50 in Wisconsin, Illinois, and Missouri, 1805, 1974; The Ancestral Heritage of George and Charlotte Barlow, 1992; Fain would I Climb: Sir Walter Raleigh Tells His Life Story, 1996; Saint's Second Season, 1999, 2nd ed. as The Blackening of Richard III, 2003; Mayflower Maid, 2006. **Address:** Department of Resource Development, Michigan State University, 450 Administration Bldg., East Lansing, MI 48824-1046, U.S.A.

BARLOWE, Wayne Douglas. American (born United States), b. 1958. **Genres:** Science Fiction/Fantasy, Young Adult Fiction, Children's Fiction, Illustrations. **Career:** Parson's School of Design, teacher of science fiction courses, 1979-80; artist, illustrator and writer, 1980-. **Publications:** (With I. Summer) Barlowe's Guide to Extraterrestrials, 1979, 2nd ed. 1987; (contrib.) Dawn for a Distant Earth, 1987; Expedition: Being an Account in Words and Artwork of the A.D. 2358 Voyage to Darwin IV, 1990; Barlowe's Guide to Fantasy, 1996; The Alien Life of Wayne Barlowe, 1996; Barlowe's Inferno, 1998; Brushfire: Illuminations from the Inferno, 2001; God's Demon, 2007; The Art of Avatar: James Cameron's Epic Adventure, 2009. **Address:** Writer's House Inc., 21 W 26th St., New York, NY 10010, U.S.A. **Online address:** wdbarlowe@aol.com

BARMACK, Erik S. American (born United States), b. 1973?. **Genres:** Novels, Humor/Satire. **Career:** Sporting News, vice president of fantasy games; ESPN, director of business development, senior director of business development. Writer. **Publications:** The Virgin: A Novel, 2005; (with M. Handelman) Why Fantasy Football Matters: And Our Lives Do Not, 2006. Contributor to periodicals. **Address:** ESPN, ESPN Plz., 545 Middle St., Bristol, CT 06010-1099, U.S.A.

BARMANN, Lawrence (Francis). American (born United States), b. 1932. **Genres:** History, Theology/Religion, Humanities. **Career:** St. Louis University, assistant professor, 1970-73, associate professor, 1973-78, professor of history, 1978-2002, professor of American studies, 1981-2002, professor of theological studies, 1996-2002, professor emeritus, 2002-. Writer. **Publications:** Baron Friedrich Von Hügel and the Modernist Crisis in England, 1972. EDITOR: Newman at St. Mary's 1962; Newman on God and Self, 1965; The Letters of Baron Friedrich Von Hügel and Professor Norman Kemp Smith, 1981; Sanctity and Secularity, 1999; (with H. Hill) Personal Faith and Institutional Commitments: Roman Catholic Modernist and Anti-Modernist Autobiography, 2002. Contributor to professional journals. **Address:** The Lindell Terr., 4501 Lindell Blvd., Ste. 12-A, St. Louis, MO 63108, U.S.A.

BARMASH, Pamela. American (born United States), b. 1966. **Genres:** Law. **Career:** Washington University, associate professor & director of Jewish, Islamic and Near Eastern Studies Program. Writer. **Publications:** Homicide in the Biblical World, 2005. **Address:** Dept. of Asian & Near Eastern Languages & Lit., University of Washington, Rm. 121, Busch Bldg., St. Louis, MO 63130, U.S.A. **Online address:** pbarmash@artsci.wustl.edu

BARNABY, Charles Frank. (Frank Barnaby). British (born England), b. 1927. **Genres:** International Relations/Current Affairs, Military/Defense/Arms Control, Young Adult Fiction. **Career:** U.K. Atomic Energy Authority, scientist, 1951-57; University College, lecturer, 1957-67, Medical Research Council, scientific staff, 1957-69, senior scientific staff; New Scientist Magazine, defense consultant, 1970-71; Stockholm International Peace Research Institute, director, 1971-81; Free University, World Disarmament Campaign, director, 1981-; VU University Amsterdam, professor, 1981-85; Oxford Research Group, nuclear issues consultant, 1982-2007; University of Minnesota, visiting professor, Stassen Chair, 1985; Oxford Research Group, consultant, 1995-. Freelance defense analyst and writer. **Publications:** AS FRANK BARNABY: (with A.L. Williams and G.L. Williams) The Nuclear Future, 1969; (co-author) The Supreme Folly: Chemical and Biological Weapons, 1970; Man and the Atom: The Uses of Nuclear Energy, 1972; The Nuclear Age/SIPRI, 1974; (with R. Huiskens) Arms Uncontrolled/SIPRI, 1975; Nuclear Disarmament or Nuclear War?, 1975; Preventing Nuclear-Weapon Proliferation: An Approach to the Non-Proliferation Treaty Review Institute, 1975; The Nuclear Age, 1976; Nuclear Proliferation and the South African Threat, 1977; Prospects for Peace, 1980; Krig Och Miljö, 1981; (with E. Boeker) Defensie zonder kernwapens, 1982; (with B. Jasani) Verification Technologies: The Case for Surveillance by Consent, 1984; The Automated Battlefield, 1986; What on Earth is Star Wars?: A Guide to the Strategic Defense Initiative, 1986; Military R&D: The Need for Information and Debate, 1988; The Invisible Bomb, 1989; The Role and Control of Armsin the 1990s, 1992; The Role and Control of Weapons in the 1990's, 1992; How Nuclear Weapons Spread, 1993; Instruments of Terror, 1996; How to Build A Nuclear Bomb: And Other Weapons of Mass Destruction, 2004; Future of Terror, 2007. EDITOR AS FRANK BARNABY: (with A. Boserup) Implications of Anti-Ballistic Missile Systems, 1969; (with C. Schaerf) Disarmament and Arms Control, Proceedings, 1970; Preventing the Spread of Nuclear Weapons, 1971; Tactical Nuclear Weapons: European Perspectives, 1978; (with C. Shaerf) Arms Control and Disarmament, 1972; (with G.P. Thomas) Nuclear Arms Race: Control or Catastrophe, 1982; Future Warfare, 1984; (with M.T. Borg) Emerging Technologies and Military Doctrine: A Political Assessment, 1986; (with P.T. Hopmann) Rethinking the Nuclear Weapons Dilemma in Europe, 1988; The Gaia Peace Atlas, 1988; A Handbook of Verification Procedures, 1990; Building a More Democratic United Nations: Proceedings of CAMDUN-1, International Conference on a More Democratic United Nations, 1991; Plutonium and Security: The Military Aspects of the Plutonium Economy, 1991; (with D. Holdstock) Hiroshima and Nagasaki: Retrospect and Prospect, Frank Cass, 1995; Instruments of Terror, 1996; (with D. Holdstock) British Nuclear Weapons Programme, 1952-2002, 2003; (with K. Booth) Future of Britain's Nuclear Weapons: Experts Reframe the Debate, 2006. EDITOR: (with C. Schaerf) Preventing the Spread of Nuclear Weapons, 1969; Radionuclides in Medicine, 1969. **Address:** Oxford Research Group, Development House, 56-64 Leonard St., London, GL EC2A 4LT, England. **Online address:** frank@barnabyc.fsnet.co.uk

BARNABY, Frank. *See* **BARNABY, Charles Frank.**

BARNACLE, Hugo. British (born England), b. 1958. **Genres:** Novels, Young Adult Fiction. **Career:** Writer. **Publications:** NOVELS: Promise, 1988; Day One, 1998. **Address:** Lisa Eveleigh Literary Agency, 11/12 Dover St., London, GL W1S 4LJ, England.

BARNAO, Jack. *See* **WOOD, Edward John.**

BARNARD, Frederick Mechner. Canadian/Czech (born Czech Republic), b. 1921. **Genres:** Intellectual History, Philosophy, Politics/Government, Sociology, Social Sciences. **Career:** University of Leicester, extra-mural lecturer, 1948-59; Leicester University and Leicester College of Technology, extra-mural lecturer, 1948-59; University of Salford, senior lecturer and director of social studies, 1959-64; University of Saskatchewan, associate professor, 1964-67, department chair, 1964-65, professor of political science, 1967-70; University of Western Ontario, professor of political science, 1970-86, professor emeritus, 1986-. Writer. **Publications:** Between Enlightenment and Political Romanticism, 1964; ZwischenAufklärung und Politischer Romantik, 1965; J.G. Herder's Social and Political Thought, 1965, 2nd ed., 1967; (ed.) J.G. Herder on Social and Political Culture, 1969; Socialism with a Human Face: Slogan and Substance, 1973; Unity, Plurality & Politics: Essays in Honour of F.M. Barnard, 1986; Self-Direction and Political Legitimacy, 1988; Pluralism, Socialism, and Political Legitimacy: Reflections on Opening Up Communism, 1991; Democratic Legitimacy: Plural Values and Political Power, 2001; Herder on Nationality, Humanity, and History, 2003; Reason and Self-Enactment in History and Politics: Themes and Voices of Modernity, 2006; Social and Political Bonds: A Mosaic of Contrast and Convergence, 2010. Contributor to books. **Address:** Department of Political Science, University of Western Ontario, Rm. 4154, Social Science Ctr., London, ON N6A 5C2, Canada.

BARNARD, Judith. (Judith Michael). American (born United States), b. 1932. **Genres:** Novels, Romance/Historical, Education. **Career:** Wilmette Community Concert Association, vice president, 1964-67. Writer. **Publications:** ROMANCE NOVELS AS JUDITH MICHAEL (with M. Fain): Deceptions, 1982; Possessions, 1984; Private Affairs, 1986; Inheritance, 1988; A Ruling Passion, 1990; Sleeping Beauty, 1991; Pot of Gold, 1993; A Tangled Web, 1994: Acts of Love, 1997; A Certain Smile, 1999; The Real Mother, 2005; The House on Webster Street, 2005. OTHER: (co-author) Beyond the Americas, 1963; The Past and Present of Solomon Sorge (novel), 1967. Contributor to periodicals. **Address:** Poseidon Press, Simon & Schuster Bldg., 1230 Ave. of the Americas, New York, NY 10020, U.S.A.

BARNARD, Nicholas. British (born England), b. 1958. **Genres:** Crafts, Design, Homes/Gardens, Art/Art History, Architecture. **Career:** Writer. **Publications:** (With A. Hull) Living with Kilims, 1988; Living with Decorative Textiles: Tribal Art from Africa, Asia and the Americas, 1989; (with J. Gillow) Traditional Indian Textiles, 1991; Living with Folk Art: Ethnic Styles from Around the World, 1991; (with P. Adler) Asafo!: African Flags of the Fante, 1992; (with P. Adler) African Majesty: The Textile Art of the Ashanti and Ewe, 1992; Arts and Crafts of India, 1993; The Complete Home Decorating Book, 1994; (with J. Barnard) New Decorator, 1999; The Step-by-Step Home Decorating Book, 2000; (with J. Gillow) Indian Textiles, 2008. **Address:** DK Publishing, 375 Hudson St., New York, NY 10014, U.S.A.

BARNARD, Robert. (Bernard Bastable). British (born England), b. 1936. **Genres:** Novellas/Short Stories, Mystery/Crime/Suspense, Literary Criticism And History, Novels. **Career:** University of New England, lecturer in English literature, 1961-66; Bergen University, lecturer, senior lecturer, 1966-76; University of Tromsoe, professor of English literature, 1976-83. Writer, 1983-. **Publications:** MYSTERIES: Death of an Old Goat, 1974; A Little Local Murder, 1976; Death on the High C's, 1977; Blood Brotherhood, 1977; Unruly Son, 1978; Death of a Mystery Writer, 1978; Posthumous Papers, 1979; Death of a Literary Widow, 1979; Death in a Cold Climate, 1980; Mother's Boys, 1981; Sheer Torture, 1981; Death of a Perfect Mother, 1981; Death and the Princess, 1982; The Missing Bronte, 1983; The Case of the Missing Brontë, 1983; Little Victims, 1983; School for Murder, 1983; A Corpse in a Gilded Cage, 1984; Out of the Blackout, 1985; The Disposal of the Living, 1985; Fête fatale, 1985; Political Suicide, 1986; Bodies, 1986; Death in Purple Prose, 1987; The Skeleton in the Grass, 1987; The Cherry Blossom Corpse, 1987; At Death's Door, 1988; Death of a Salesperson: And Other Untimely Exits (short stories), 1989; Death and the Chaste Apprentice, 1989; A City of Strangers, 1990; A Scandal in Belgravia, 1991; A Fatal Attachment, 1992; A Hovering of Vultures, 1993; Masters of the House: A Novel of Suspense, 1994; The Bad Samaritan: A Novel of Suspense Featuring Charlie Peace, 1995; The Habit of Widowhood (short stories), 1996; No Place of Safety, 1998; The Corpse at the Haworth Tandoori, 1999; Touched by the Dead, 2000; A Murder in Mayfair, 2000; The Bones in the Attic, 2001; Cywion Nell, 2001; Unholy Dying, 2001; The Mistress of Alderley, 2002; Cry from the Dark, 2003; The Graveyard Position: A Novel of Suspense, 2005; Dying Flames, 2006; A Fall from Grace, 2007; (with L. Barnard) A Brontë Encyclopedia, 2007; Last Post, 2008; The Killings on Jubilee Terrace, 2009; A Stranger in the Family, 2010; The Rogue's Gallery, 2011; A Charitable Body, 2012. LITERARY CRITICISM: Imagery and Theme in the Novels of Dickens, 1974; A Talent to Deceive: Appreciation of Agatha Christie, 1980; A Short History of English Literature, 1984; Emily Bronte, 2000. AS BERNARD BASTABLE: To Die Like a Gentleman, 1993; Dead, Mr. Mozart, 1995; Too Many Notes, Mr. Mozart, 1995; A Mansion and Its Murder, 1998. **Address:** Hazeldene, Houghley Ln., Leeds, LS13 2DT, England.

BARNARD, Toby Christopher. British (born England), b. 1945. **Genres:** History, Politics/Government. **Career:** University of Exeter, tutor, 1969-70; University of London, Royal Holloway College, tutor, 1970-76; University of Oxford, Hertford College, lecturer in modern history, 1976-. Writer. **Publications:** Cromwellian Ireland: English Government and Reform in Ireland 1649-1660, 1975; The English Republic, 1649-1660, 1982, 2nd ed., 1997; The Abduction of a Limerick Heiress: Social and Political Relations in Mid-Eighteenth-Century Ireland, 1998; Cromwellian Ireland: English Government and Reform in Ireland 1649-1660, 2000; (contrib.) The Cries of Dublin & C: Drawn from the Life by Hugh Douglas Hamilton, 1760, 2003; A New Anatomy of Ireland: The Irish Protestants, 1649-1770, 2003; Irish Protestant Ascents and Descents, 1641-1770, 2004; The Kingdom of Ireland, 1641-1760, 2004; Making the Grand Figure: Lives and Possessions in Ireland, 1641-1770, 2004; A Guide to Sources for the History of Material Culture in Ireland, 1500-2000, 2005; Improving Ireland? Projectors, Prophets and Profiteers, 1641-1786, 2008. EDITOR: (with J. Clark) Lord Burlington: Architecture, Art and Life, 1995; (with D. O'Croinin and K. Simms) A Miracle of Learning: Studies in Manuscripts and Irish Learning, Essays in Honour of William O'Sullivan, 1998; (with J. Fenlon) The Dukes of Ormonde, 1610-1745, 2000; (with W.G. Neely) The Clergy of the Church of Ireland, 1000-2000: Messengers, Watchmen, and Stewards, 2006. **Address:** Hertford College, University of Oxford, Catte St., Oxford, OX OX1 3BW, England. **Online address:** toby.barnard@hertford.ox.ac.uk

BARNARD, Tom. *See* **GELDENHUYS, Deon.**

BARNES, Annie S. American (born United States), b. 1932. **Genres:** Sociology, Race Relations, Education, Social Sciences, Human Relations/Parenting. **Career:** High school teacher of American history and government, 1954-65; Hampton Institute, instructor in sociology, 1965-67; Norfolk State University, associate professor, 1971-76, professor of anthropology and sociology, 1976-97, professor emeritus, 1997-; The Virginia Social Science Association, president, 1983-84; American Association of Black Anthropologists, president, 1992-93. Writer. **Publications:** The Black Middle Class Family: A Study of Black Subsociety, Neighborhood and Home in Interaction, 1985; (ed.) Social Science Research: Skills Handbook, 1985; Black Women: Interpersonal Relationships in Profile: A Sociological Study of Work, Home and the Community, 1986; Single Parents in Black America: A Study in Culture and Legitimacy, 1987; Retention of African-American Males in High School: A Study of African-American Male High School Dropouts, African-American Male Seniors and White Male Seniors, 1992; Research Skills in the Social Sciences, 1994; Say it Loud: Middle-Class Blacks Talk about Racism and What to Do about It, 2000; Everyday Racism: A Book for All Americans, 2000; Thorns Black Spousal Abuse, 2011. Contributor to journals. **Address:** Department of Sociology, Norfolk State University, 700 Park Ave., Norfolk, VA 23504, U.S.A. **Online address:** anniesbarnes@aol.com

BARNES, Burton V(erne). American (born United States), b. 1930. **Genres:** Environmental Sciences/Ecology, Natural History, Sciences. **Career:** U.S. Forest Service, forester, 1953-59, Intermountain Forest and Range Experiment Station, research forester, 1959-63; Baden-Wurttemberg Forest Research Station, NSF postdoctoral fellow, 1963-64; University of Michigan, School of Natural Resources and Environment, assistant professor, 1964-67, associate professor, 1967-70, professor, 1970-87, Stephen H. Spurr professor of forest ecology, 1987-2006, Arthur F. Thurnau professor, professor emeritus of forestry, 2006-. Writer. **Publications:** (With S.H. Spurr) Forest Ecology, 2nd ed., 1973, 4th ed., 1998; (with W.H. Wagner, Jr.) Michigan Trees: A Guide to the Trees of Michigan and the Great Lakes Region, 1981, rev. ed., 2004; Deciduous Forests of North America, 1991. **Address:** School of Natural Resources & Environment, University of Michigan, 2008 Dana, 440 Church St., Ann Arbor, MI 48109-1041, U.S.A. **Online address:** bvb@umich.edu

BARNES, Christopher J(ohn). Canadian/British (born England), b. 1942. **Genres:** Literary Criticism And History, Music, Biography, Translations, Autobiography/Memoirs, Art/Art History. **Career:** University of St. Andrews, lecturer in Russian language and literature, 1967-89; University of Toronto, professor of Slavic languages and literatures and chairman of the department, 1989-. Writer. **Publications:** Boris Pasternak: A Literary Biography, vol. I: 1890-1928, 1989, vol. II: 1928-1960, 1998; (trans.) The Jewish Lover, 1998; (trans.) The Russian Lover, 1998; (trans.) The Life and Art of Maria Olenina-d'Alheim, 2000. EDITOR: Studies in Twentieth-Century Russian Literature, 1976; (intro.) Collected Short Prose, 1977; (trans.) The Voice of Prose, vol. I, 1986, vol. II, 1990; (trans.) The Russian Seven, 1990; Boris Pasternak and European Literature, 1990; (with G.S. Smith) Proceedings of the Pasternak Centenary Conference 1990, 1991; (as C.J. Barnes) Russian Library Treasures: An Index of National and Academic Libraries, 2000; The Path to Perfection: Russian Pianists and Moscow Conservatoire Professors on the Art of the Piano, 2006; Journey from St. Petersburg, forthcoming. **Address:** Department of Slavic Languages and Literatures, University of Toronto, Rm. 425, Alumni Hall, 121 St. Joseph St.,, Toronto, ON M5S 1A1, Canada. **Online address:** chrjbarnes1942@yahoo.ca

BARNES, Douglas. British (born England), b. 1927. **Genres:** Education. **Career:** Teacher, 1950-66; University of Leeds, lecturer, 1966-73, senior lecturer, 1973-84, reader in education, 1984-89, retired, 1989; National Association for the Teaching of English, chairman, 1967-69. Writer. **Publications:** (With M.R. Genel) Los insectos y sus daños a los granos almacenados, 1958; (with J. Britton and H. Rosen) Language, The Learner and the School, 1969, 4th ed. (with J. Britton and M. Torbe), 1990; Language in the Classroom, 1973; From Communication to Curriculum, 1976, 2nd ed., 1992; (with F. Todd) Communication and Learning in Small Groups, 1977; (contrib.) Language Across the Curriculum, 1977; Practical Curriculum Study, 1982; (with D. Barnes and S.R. Clarke) Versions of English, 1984; (with Y. Sheeran) School Writing: Discovering the Ground Rules, 1991; (with K.M. Pierce and C.J. Gilles) Cycles of Meaning, 1993; (with F. Todd) Communication and Learning Revisited: Making Meaning through Talk, 1995; Becoming an English Teacher, 2000. EDITOR: (with R. Egford) Twentieth Century Short

Stories, 1958; Short Stories of Our Time, 1963; (and contrib.) Drama in the English Classroom, 1968. **Address:** 4 Harrowby Rd., Cholmeley Pk., Leeds, LS16 5HN, England. **Online address:** dougbarnes@dougbarnes.f9.co.uk

BARNES, Edward F. *See* **MARQUIS, Max.**

BARNES, Fred Wood. American (born United States), b. 1943. **Genres:** History, Politics/Government, Biography. **Career:** Charleston News Courier, reporter, 1965-67; Washington Star, reporter, 1967-79; Baltimore Sun, reporter and national political correspondent; New Republic, senior editor and White House correspondent, 1985-95; Weekly Standard, co-founder and executive editor, 1995-; Reader's Digest, writer and editor; New York Times, writer and editor; Los Angeles Times, writer and editor; Newsday, writer and editor; Wall Street Journal, writer and editor; Vogue, writer and editor. **Publications:** (Ed.) A Cartoon History of the Reagan Years, 1988; Rebel-in-Chief: Inside the Bold and Controversial Presidency of George W. Bush, 2006. Contributor to periodicals. **Address:** Weekly Standard, 1150 17th St. NW, Ste. 505, Washington, DC 20036-4627, U.S.A.

BARNES, H. Lee. American (born United States), b. 1944. **Genres:** Novellas/Short Stories, Novels, Young Adult Fiction, Cultural/Ethnic Topics. **Career:** College of Southern Nevada, professor of English, 1992-; University of Las Vegas, adjunct instructor, 1993-96. Writer. **Publications:** Gunning For Ho: Vietnam Stories, 2000; Dummy Up and Deal: Inside the Culture of Casino Dealing, 2002; The Lucky, 2003; Talk to Me, James Dean, 2003; Minimal Damage: Stories of Veterans, 2007; (co-author) Restless City, 2009; Car Tag, 2011; When We Walked above the Clouds: A Memoir of Vietnam, 2011. **Address:** Department of English, Community College, 6375 W Charleston Blvd., Las Vegas, NV 89146-1139, U.S.A. **Online address:** lee.barnes@csn.edu

BARNES, Hugh. British (born England), b. 1963?. **Genres:** History. **Career:** Soviet Union, journalist and political analyst; Nature, reporter; London Review of Books, assistant editor; The Times, reporter; Glasgow Herald, reporter; The Observer, reporter; Trinity College, part-time tutor, 1993-97; Penguin Books, executive editor; International Herald Tribune, deputy editor, 1998-99; Agence France Presse-Moscow, senior correspondent, 1999-2004; Agence France Presse-Paris, senior correspondent, 1999-2004; Foreign Policy Centre, Democracy and Conflict Programme, director, 2005-06; BBC World Service, commentator; CNN, commentator; Al-Jazeera, commentator; Ministry of Foreign Affairs, Institute for Political and International Studies, visiting fellow, 2006; University of Westminster, principal lecturer; openDemocracy, Russian editor, 2007-08; Financial Times, foreign correspondent; Independent on Sunday, foreign correspondent; New Statesman, foreign correspondent; Kingston University, senior lecturer; Oblomovism Ltd., managing director. Writer. **Publications:** Special Effects, 1994; Glasgow Victim, 1995; Gannibal: The Moor of Petersburg, 2005 as The Stolen Prince: Gannibal, 2006; (comp. with J. Owen) Russia in the Spotlight: G8 Scorecard, 2006; (co-author) Understanding Iran, 2006. Contributor to periodicals. **Address:** Oblomovism Ltd., 45 Wallingford Ave., London, GL W10 6PZ, England. **Online address:** h.barnes@kingston.ac.uk

BARNES, James J. American (born United States), b. 1931. **Genres:** History, Business/Trade/Industry, Politics/Government, Biography. **Career:** Amherst College, instructor in history, 1959-62; Wabash College, assistant professor to associate professor, 1962-76, professor of history, 1976-2006, Hadley professor and chairman of the department, 1979, professor of history emeritus, 2006-. Writer. **Publications:** Free Trade in Books: A Study of the London Book Trade Since 1800, 1964; Authors, Publishers and Politicians: The Quest for an Anglo-American Copyright Agreement, 1815-1854, 1974; WITH P.P. BARNES: Hitler's Mein Kampf in Britain and America 1930-39, 1980; James Vincent Murphy: Translator and Interpreter of Fascist Europe, 1880-1946, 1987; Private and Confidential: Letters from British Ministers in Washington to Their Foreign Secretaries in London, 1844-67, 1993; Nazi Refugee Turned Gestapo Spy: The Life of Hans Wesemann, 1895-1971, 2001; The American Civil War through British Eyes: Diplomatic Dispatches from British Diplomat, vol. I: Nov 1860-April 1862, 2003, vol. II: April 1862-February 1863, 2005, vol. III: February 1863-December 1865, 2005; Nazis in Pre-War London, 1930-1939: The Fate and Role of German Party Members and British Sympathizers, 2005. **Address:** Department of History, Wabash College, Baxter Hall 205, PO Box 352, Crawfordsville, IN 47933, U.S.A. **Online address:** barnesj@wabash.edu

BARNES, Jay. American (born United States), b. 1958. **Genres:** Meteorology/Atmospheric Sciences, History, Natural History. **Career:** North Carolina Aquarium, exhibits curator, 1980-86, exhibits consultant, director, 1989-2009, retired, 2009. Writer. **Publications:** North Carolina's Hurricane History, 1995, 3rd ed., 2001; Florida's Hurricane History, 1997, 2nd ed., 2007; (with R. Moore) Faces from the Flood, 2004; Hurricane Hazel in the Carolinas, 2010. **Address:** Arcadia Publishing, 420 Wando Park Blvd., Mount Pleasant, SC 29464, U.S.A. **Online address:** jay.barnes@ncmail.net

BARNES, Jennifer Lynn. American (born United States), b. 1984?. **Genres:** Children's Fiction. **Career:** Writer. **Publications:** Golden, 2006; Platinum, 2007; Tattoo, 2007; The Squad: Perfect Cover, 2008; The Squad: Killer Spirit, 2008; Fate, 2009; Raised by Wolves, 2010; Trial by Fire, 2011; Every Other Day, 2012; Taken by Storm: A Raised by Wolves Novel, 2012. Contributor to periodicals. **Address:** Delacorte Press Contest Random House Inc., 1745 Broadway, 9th Fl., New York, NY 10019, U.S.A. **Online address:** golden_or_non@yahoo.com

BARNES, John (Allen). American (born United States), b. 1957. **Genres:** Science Fiction/Fantasy, Westerns/Adventure, Young Adult Fiction, Theatre. **Career:** Middle South Services, systems analyst, 1982-84; computer consultant, 1985-94. Writer. **Publications:** The Man Who Pulled down the Sky, 1986; Sin of Origin, 1987; Orbital Resonance, 1991; A Million Open Doors, 1992; Wartide, 1992; Battle Cry, 1992; Union Fires, 1992; Mother of Storms, 1994; Kaleidoscope Century, 1995; One for the Morning Glory, 1996; (with B. Aldrin) Encounter with Tibor, 1996; Earth Made of Glass, 1997; Patton's Spaceship, 1997; Washington's Dirigible, 1997; Caesar's Bicycle, 1997; Finity, 1998; Apostrophes and Apocalypses, 1998; Candle, 2000; (with B. Aldrin) The Return, 2000; The Merchants of Souls, 2001; The Sky So Big and Black, 2002; The Duke of Uranium, 2002; A Princess of the Aerie, 2003; In the Hall of the Martian King, 2003; Gaudeamus, 2004; The Armies of Memory, 2006; Payback City, 2007; Tales of the Madman Underground, 2009; Directive 51, 2010; Daybreak Zero, 2011; The Last President, 2012; Losers in Space, 2012. Contributor to periodicals. **Address:** c/o Ashley Grayson, Ashley Grayson Literary Agency, 1342 18th St., San Pedro, CA 90732, U.S.A. **Online address:** johnbarnes@sprintmail.com

BARNES, Jonathan. British (born England) **Genres:** Philosophy, History. **Career:** University of Chicago, lecturer in philosophy, 1967; Oxford University, Oriel College, fellow, 1968-78, professor of ancient philosophy, Balliol College, fellow and tutor, 1978-94; University of Massachusetts, visiting professor, 1973; University of Texas, visiting professor, 1981; University of Geneva, professor of ancient philosophy, 1994-2002; University of Paris, faculty, 2002-06. Writer. **Publications:** (Trans.) Aristotle's Theory of the Syllogism, 1969; The Ontological Argument, 1972; The Presocratic Philosophers, 2 vols., 1975, rev. ed., 1982; Aristotle's Posterior Analytics, 1976; (comp.) Aristotle: A Selective Bibliography, 1977; Aristotle, 1982; Philosophers, 1982; Terms and Sentences: Theophrastus on Hypothetical Syllogisms, 1985; (with J. Annas) The Modes of Scepticism, 1985; Early Greek Philosophy, 1987, rev. ed., 2001; The Toils of Scepticism, 1990; Founders of Thought, 1991; (trans.) On Aristotle's Prior Analytics 1.1-7, 1991; (trans.) Sextus Empiricus: Outlines of Scepticism, 1994; (trans.) Posterior Analytics, 1994; Logic and the Imperial Stoa, 1997; Greek Philosophers, 1999; Aristotle: A Very Short Introduction, 2000; The Cambridge History of Hellenistic Philosophy, 2000; Porphyry: Introduction, 2003; Galien et la Philosophie: Huit Exposés Suivis de Discussions, 2003; Truth, etc.: Six Lectures on Ancient Logic, 2007. EDITOR: Articles on Aristotle, 1975; (with M. Schofield and M. Burnyeat) Doubt and Dogmatism, 1980; Science and Speculation: Studies in Hellenistic Theory and Practice, 1982; Complete Works of Aristotle: The Revised Oxford Translation, 1984; (ed. with M. Mignucci) Matter and Metaphysics: Fourth Symposium Hellenisticum, 1988; (ed. with M. Griffin) Philosophia Togata: Essays on Philosophy and Roman Society, 1989; Cambridge Companion to Aristotle, 1995; Philosophia Togata. II: Plato and Aristotle at Rome, 1997; (and comp. with V. Calzolari) L'oeuvre de David l'invincible et la Transmission de la Pensée Gecque dans la tradition Arménienne et Syriaque, 2009. **Address:** Les Charmilles, L'Auvergne, Ceaulmont, 36200, France. **Online address:** jonathanbarnes@wanadoo.fr

BARNES, Joyce Annette. American (born United States), b. 1958. **Genres:** Novels, Plays/Screenplays, Travel/Exploration. **Career:** Catonsville Community College, assistant professor of English, 1986-; Agitprov Players, creative director, 1991-. Writer. **Publications:** The Baby Grand, the Moon in July, and Me (adapted from the play The Baby Grand), 1994; Amistad (novel), 1997; Promise Me the Moon, 1997; Play the Game You Know, 2004. Contributor to periodicals. **Address:** c/o Author Mail, Dial Books, 345 Hudson St., New York, NY 10014, U.S.A.

BARNES, Linda (Joyce Appelblatt). American (born United States), b. 1949. **Genres:** Mystery/Crime/Suspense, Plays/Screenplays, Literary Criticism And History. **Career:** Chelmsford High School, teacher of theater, 1971-76; Lexington Public Schools, drama director, 1977-78. Writer. **Publications:** MYSTERY NOVELS: Blood Will Have Blood, 1982; Bitter Finish, 1983; DeadHeat, 1984; Cities of the Dead, 1986; A Trouble of Fools, 1987; The Snake Tattoo, 1989; Coyote, 1990; Steel Guitar, 1991; Snapshot, 1993; Hardware, 1995; Cold Case, 1997; Flashpoint, 1999; The Big Dig, 2001; Deep Pockets, 2004; Heart of the World, 2006; Lie Down with the Devil, 2008. PLAYS: Wings, 1973; Prometheus, 1974. **Address:** St. Martin's Press, 175 5th Ave., New York, NY 10010, U.S.A. **Online address:** linda@lindabarnes.com

BARNES, Linda L. American (born United States), b. 1953. **Genres:** Theology/Religion. **Career:** Boston Medical Center, director of Spirituality and Child Health Initiative, 1999-; Boston University, Department of Pediatrics, The Boston Healing Landscape Project, director, 2000-, School of Public Health, assistant professor, 2002-, School of Medicine, Department of Pediatrics, assistant professor, 1999-2004, associate professor, 2005-, Department of Social and Behavioral Sciences, associate professor, 2005-, Department of Family Medicine, associate professor, 2006-; Harvard University, visiting lecturer, 1996, senior thesis advisor, 1999-2004; Northeastern University, visiting scholar, 1996-98; Brown University, visiting assistant professor, 1998-99; Harvard Divinity School, visiting lecturer, 1999; Wake Forest University, visiting professor, 2004. Medical anthropologist, educator and editor. **Publications:** Variations on a Teaching/ Learning Workshop: Pedagogy and Faculty Development in Religious Studies, 1999; (ed. with S.S. Sered) Religion and Healing in America, 2005; Needles, Herbs, Gods and Ghosts: China, Healing and the West to 1848, 2005; (ed. with I. Talamantez and intro.) Teaching Religion and Healing, 2006. Contributor to books and journals. **Address:** Department of Family Medicine, Boston University Medical Center, Dowling 5, 1 Boston Medical Center Pl., Boston, MA 02118, U.S.A. **Online address:** linda.barnes@bmc.org

BARNES, Lynard. American (born United States), b. 1948. **Genres:** Science Fiction/Fantasy, Novels. **Career:** Department of Justice, program analyst; Trices Co., publisher. Writer. **Publications:** SCIENCE FICTION NOVELS: Phobos Lock, 1997; Rolun, 2000. **Address:** Trices Co., PO Box 12560, Chicago, IL 60612-0560, U.S.A. **Online address:** lynardbarnes@tricespublishing.com

BARNES, Michael (Anthony). British (born England), b. 1947. **Genres:** Theology/Religion, History. **Career:** Pontifical Gregorian University, lecturer in Buddhist studies, 1979-81; University of London, Heythrop College, lecturer in religious studies, 1982-, reader, senior tutor, 1983-91; Diocesan Interfaith Agency, Westminster Interfaith, director, 1991-95; The Way, editor, 1996-2001. **Publications:** Christian Identity and Religious Pluralism in UK as Religions in Conversation, 1989; God East and West, 1991; (co-author) Secrets of Lost Empires: Reconstructing the Glories of Ages Past, 1997; Walking the City: Christian Discipleship in a Pluralist World, 1999; Traces of the Other: Three Philosophers and Inter-Faith Dialogue, 2000; Theology and the Dialogue of Regions, 2002; Interreligious Learning: Dialogue, Spirituality and the Christian Imagination, 2012. Contributor to periodicals. **Address:** Department of Religious Studies, Heythrop College, University of London, Kensington Sq., London, GL W8 5HQ, England. **Online address:** m.barnes@heythrop.ac.uk

BARNES, Mike. Canadian/American (born United States), b. 1955. **Genres:** Poetry, Novels, Novellas/Short Stories, Literary Criticism And History. **Career:** Writer and educator. **Publications:** Calm Jazz Sea, 1996; Aquarium, 1999; Captain Beefheart: The Biography, 2002; The Syllabus, 2002; Contrary Angel, 2004; Catalogue Raisonne, 2005; A Thaw Foretold, 2006; Lily Pond: A Memoir of Madness, Memory, Myth and Metamorphosis, 2008; Wayward Guest, forthcoming. Works appear in anthologies. Contributor to periodicals. **Address:** 564 Eglinton Ave. W, Apt. 405, Toronto, ON M5N 1B7, Canada. **Online address:** mh.barnes@sympatico.ca

BARNES, Peter. American (born United States), b. 1942. **Genres:** Environmental Sciences/Ecology, History. **Career:** Lowell Sun, reporter; Newsweek, Washington correspondent, journalist; New Republic, West Coast correspondent, journalist; The New York Times, journalist; The Solar Center, co-founder and president, 1976-; Working Assets Money Fund, co-founder and vice president, 1983-; Working Assets Long Distance, co-founder and president, 1985-; National Cooperative Bank (now NCB), director; California State Assistance Fund for Energy, director; TechMar Inc., director; Tomales Bay Institute, senior fellow. **Publications:** Pawns: The Plight of the Citizen-Soldier, 1972; (ed.) The People's Land: A Reader on Land Reform in the United States, 1975; Who Owns the Sky?: Our Common Assets and the Future of Capitalism, 2001; Capitalism 3.0: A Guide to Reclaiming the Commons, 2006; Climate Solutions: A Citizen's Guide, 2008; Theological Controversies in the Presbyterian Church of New South Wales, 1865-1915, 2008; Cappy Tail's Capitol Tales, 2010. Contributor of articles to books and journals. **Address:** VSP Books Inc., 1903 Duffield Ln., Alexandria, VA 22307, U.S.A. **Online address:** peter@capanddividend.org

BARNES, Rory. Australian/British (born England), b. 1946. **Genres:** Adult Non-fiction. **Career:** Melbourne University, teacher; New South Wales Institute of Technology, teacher. Writer. **Publications:** NONFICTION: Teacher Learning, 1982; (with J. Birrell) Water from the Moon, 1989. FICTION: (with D. Broderick) Valencies, 1983; The Bomb-Monger's Daughter, 1984; (with D. Broderick) Zones, 1997; Horsehead Boy, 1998; Horsehead Man, 1999; (with D. Broderick) Stuck in Fast Forward, 1999; (with D. Broderick) The Book of Revelation, 1999 in US as Dark Gray, 2010; Horsehead Soup, 2000; Night Vision, 2006; (with D. Broderick) I'm Dying Here: A Comedy of Bad Manners, 2009. **Address:** Unley, SA , Australia. **Online address:** rory.barnes@optusnet.com.au

BARNES, Samuel Henry. American (born United States), b. 1931. **Genres:** Politics/Government, Social Sciences. **Career:** University of Michigan, Center for Political Studies, instructor, 1957-60, instructor, professor of political science and program director, 1957-91, assistant professor, 1960-64, associate professor, 1964-68, James Orin Murphy professor of political science, 1968-91, chairman, Institute for Social Research, program director, 1969-91; Georgetown University, Edmund A. Walsh School of Foreign Service, director, 1991-2002, Graf Goltz professor, 1999-, BMW Center for German and European Studies, director, 1999-2003, director emeritus, 2003-; Stanford University, Center for Advanced Study in the Behavioral Sciences, fellow. Writer. **Publications:** Party Democracy: Politics in an Italian Socialist Federation, 1967; Representation in Italy, 1977; (with M. Kaase and K.R. Allerbeck) Political Action, 1979; Politics and Culture, 1989; (co-author) Continuities in Political Action, 1990; (with R.M. Worcester) Dynamics of Societal Learning about Global Environmental Change, 1991; (contrib.) Italia fra crisi e transizione, 1994; (with A. Lopez-pina and P. McDonough) The Cultural Dynamics of Democratization in Spain, 1998; (co-author) Política Comparada: Entre lo Local y lo Global, 2005; (co-author) Governare Un Nuovo ordine Globale, 2005. **Address:** BMW Center for German and European Studies, Georgetown University, 501 Intercultural Ctr., 37th and O St. NW, Washington, DC 20057-1026, U.S.A. **Online address:** barness@georgetown.edu

BARNES, Simon. British (born England), b. 1951. **Genres:** Sports/Fitness, Biography, Novels, Environmental Sciences/Ecology, Children's Non-fiction. **Career:** The Times, sportswriter and ecological reporter, 1983-; The Spectator, sportswriter, 1996-, chief sportswriter. **Publications:** Phil Edmonds: A Singular Man, 1986; (ed.) There Was a Young Fellow Called Glover: Sporting Limericks, 1987; Horsesweat and Tears, 1989; A Sportswriter's Year, 1989; Sportswriter's Eye: An Anthology, 1989; Flying in the Face of Nature, 1991; Tiger!, 1994; Rogue Lion Safaris, 1998; Hong Kong Belongers, 1998; Rogue Lion Safaris, 1998; Miss Chance, 2000; Planet Zoo, 2000; How to Be a Bad Birdwatcher, 2005; The Meaning of Sport, 2006; How To Be Wild, 2007; (with R. Barnes) Horse: A Celebration of Horses in Art, 2008; My Natural History, 2010; The Horsey Life, 2010. **Address:** The Times, 3 Thomas More Sq., London, GL E98 1XY, England.

BARNET, Miguel. Cuban (born Cuba), b. 1940. **Genres:** Poetry, Mythology/Folklore, Theology/Religion, History, Social Sciences. **Career:** Escuela de Instruciones de Arte, professor of folklore, 1961-66; Institute of Ethnology and Folklore of the Academy of Science, researcher; Fernando Ortiz Foundation, head, 1995. Ethnologist and novelist. **Publications:** La piedra fina y el pavorreal, 1963; Isla de guijes, 1964; Biografía de un cimarrón, 1966; La sagrada familia (poems), 1967; Autobiografia di uno schiavo, 1968; Cancion de Rachel, 1969, 2nd ed., 1985; Akeké y la jutía, 1978; Orikis y otros poemas, 1981; Gallego, 1981; Carta de noche, 1982; La fuente viva, 1983; (ed.) Ensayos etnograficos, 1984; La vida real, 1986; Claves por Rita Montaner, 1987; Viendo mi vida pasar, 1987; Oficio de angel, 1989; Mapa del tiempo, 1989; Kubaner in New York: Roman, 1990; Autógrafos cubanos, 1990; Handwerk des Engels, 1993; Con pies de gato, 1993; Cultos afrocubanos: la Regla de Ocha, la Regla de Palo Monte, 1995; Actas del final, 2000; When Night is Darkest: Selected Poems, 2002; Vestido de fantasma y otros poemas, 2006; Itinerario inconcluso, 2007; (with A. de Juan and E. Pedroza) Reinas de corazones, 2008. Contributor to periodicals. **Address:** Smithsonian Institution Press, Rm. 7100, 470 L'Enfant Plz., Washington, DC 20560, U.S.A.

BARNETT, Anthony. British (born England), b. 1942. **Genres:** Politics/Government, Translations. **Career:** Author, 1982-; Charter 88, founder, 1988-, director, 1988-95; Town and Country Forum, co-founder, 1995; openDemocracy Ltd., co-founder, 2001-, editor, editor-in-chief, through 2007, Our Kingdom, co-editor; Convention on Modern Liberty, co-director, 2008-09. **Publications:** Iron Britannia, 1982; (contrib.) Revolution and Its Aftermath in Kampuchea: Eight Essays, 1983; (with N. Bielski) Soviet Freedom, 1988; (ed. with C. Ellis and P. Hirst) Debating the Constitution: New Perspectives on Constitutional Reform, 1993; (ed. and intro.) The Power and the Throne: The Monarchy Debate, 1994; This Time: Our Constitutional Revolution, 1997; (co-ed.) Town and Country, 1998; (with P. Carty) The Athenian Option: Radical Reform for the House of Lords, 1998, rev. ed., 2008; Lisa Lisa: Two Prosays, 2000; (co-trans.) T. Vesaas, Beyond the Moment: One Hundred and One Selected Poems, 2001; (ed.) Pure at Heart 2: Anecdotes & Interviews, 2002; (ed.) Type 2 Diabetes, 2008. Contributor of articles to periodicals. **Address:** openDemocracy Ltd., PO Box 49799, London, GL WC1X 8XA, England. **Online address:** info@opendemocracy.net

BARNETT, Correlli (Douglas). British (born England), b. 1927. **Genres:** Economics, Education, Engineering, History, Industrial Relations, Military/Defense/Arms Control, Politics/Government, Social Sciences, Technology, Biography. **Career:** East Anglian Writers, president, 1969-88; Eastern Arts Association, chairman, 1972, vice president, 1978-91; Churchill Archives Centre, keeper, 1977-95; Churchill College, fellow, 1977-; Cambridge University, president, defence lecturer, 1980-83. Writer. **Publications:** The Hump Organisation (novel), 1957; (with H. Slater) The Channel Tunnel, 1958; The Desert Generals, 1960, 2nd ed., 1982; The Swordbearers: Studies in Supreme Command in the First World War, 1963; The Battle of El Alamein: Din the Desert., 1964; (co-author) The Great War (TV series), 1964; (co-author) The Lost Peace (TV series), 1966; Britain and Her Army, 1509-1970: A Military, Political and Social Survey, 1970; The Collapse of British Power, 1972; The First Churchill: Marlborough, Soldier and Statesman, 1974; Marlborough, 1974; Strategy and Society, 1975; Bonaparte, 1978; The Great War, 1979; The Audit of War: The Illusion & Reality of Britain as a Great Nation, 1986; Old Battles and New Defences: Can We Learn from Military History?, 1986; The Pride and the Fall: The Dream and Illusion of Britain as a Great Nation, 1986; (ed.) Hitler's Generals, 1989; Engage the Enemy More Closely: The Royal Navy in the Second World War, 1991; The Lost Victory: British Dreams, British Realities, 1945-1950, 1995; The Verdict of Peace: Britain between Her Yesterday and the Future, 1945-1950, 2001. Contributor to periodicals. **Address:** Churchill College, Cambridge, CB3 0DS, England.

BARNETT, Cynthia. American (born United States), b. 1966?. **Genres:** Sciences. **Career:** Florida Trend Magazine, staff, 1998-. Journalist and writer. **Publications:** Mirage: Florida and the Vanishing Water of the Eastern U.S., 2007. Contributor of articles to newspapers and magazines. **Address:** Gainesville, FL , U.S.A. **Online address:** cynthiabarnett@gmail.com

BARNETT, John Le Page. Also writes as John Grant. American/Scottish (born Scotland), b. 1949. **Genres:** Novels, Young Adult Non-fiction, Translations. **Career:** Frederick Muller Ltd., editorial assistant, editorial director, 1969-75; Elsevier International Projects, science editor, 1976-77; David & Charles/Westbridge, sponsoring editor, 1978-80; Webb & Bower, commissioning editor, 1980; freelance editor and writer, 1980-; Paper Tiger, commissioning editor, 1996-2003; Artists' and Photographers' Press Ltd., part-time consultant editor; BeWrite, consultant editor; Infinity Plus, U.S. reviews editor. **Publications:** AS JOHN GRANT: (ed.) Aries I, 1979; (ed. with C. Wilson) The Book of Time, 1980; A Directory of Discarded Ideas, 1981; (ed. with C. Wilson) The Directory of Possibilities, 1981; Encyclopedia of Walt Disney's Animated Characters, 1987, 3rd ed., 1998; The Sword of the Sun, 1989; (ed. with R. Tiner) The Encyclopedia of Fantasy and Science Fiction Art Technique, 1996; Enchanted World: The Art of Anne Sudworth, 2000; Masters of Animation, 2001; (with B. Eggleton) Dragonhenge, 2002; Perceptualistics, 2002; The Hundredfold Problem, 2003; (with E. Humphrey and P.D. Scoville) The Chesley Awards for Science Fiction and Fantasy Art: A Retrospective, 2003; (with A. Vysniauskas) Renderosity: Digital Art for the 21st Century, 2004; Take No Prisoners, 2004; Denying science, 2011. LEGENDS OF LONE WOLF SERIES WITH J. DEVER: Eclipse of the Kai, 1989; The Dark Door Opens, 1989; Hunting Wolf, 1990; The Claws of Helgedad, 1991; The Sacrifice of Ruanon, 1991; The Birthplace, 1992; The Book of the Magnakai, 1992; The Tellings, 1993; The Lorestone of Varetta, 1993; The Secret of Kazan-Oud, 1994; The Rotting Land, 1994. DRAGONHENGE SERIES: (with B. Eggleton) The Stardragons, 2005. NOVELS: The Truth about the Flaming Ghoulies, 1984; Sex Secrets of Ancient Atlantis, 1985; (with D. Langford) Earthdoom, 1987; The World, 1992; (adaptor with F. Brooks) Doctor Jekyll and Mr. Hyde (graphic novel), 1995; (as Paul Barnett) Strider's Galaxy, 1997; (as Paul Barnett) Strider's Universe, 1998; Frankenstein, 1999; The Far-Enough Window, 2002; (with D. Langford) A Comedy of Manners, 2005. COLLECTIONS: (with C. Wilson) Qinmeartha & the Girl Child Lochi [and] The Tomb of the Old Ones, 2002; (co-author) Triquorum, 2006. NONFICTION: (trans. and adaptor as Paul Barnett) J. Vassal, Electric Children: Roots and Branches of Modern Folkrock, 1976; Book of Numbers, 1984; Travellers in the World of Dreams, 1984; The Depths of Cricket, 1986; Advanced Trivia Quiz Book, 1987; Great Unsolved Mysteries of Science, 1990; An Introduction to Viking Mythology, 1990; Unexplained Mysteries of the World, 1991; Great Mysteries: Monsters, 1992; (as Eve Devereaux) Book of World Flags, 1992; (as Eve Devereaux) The Ultimate Card Trick Book: Master the Magic of Over 70 Amazing Tricks, 1994; Great Mysteries, 1995; (co-ed.) The Encyclopedia of Fantasy, 1997; (as Eve Devereaux with G. Spelvin) Walking New York: 20 Original Walks Exploring New York City, 2001; (ed. as Paul Barnett) The Fantasy Art Gallery: Conversations with 25 of the World's Top Fantasy/SF Artists Conducted for the Paper Snarl, the Monthly E-Zine Associated with the Publisher Paper Tiger, 2002; (as Eve Devereaux with P. Eldin) Card & Magic Tricks, 2004; Faeries and Other Fantastical Folk: The Faery Paintings of Maxine Gadd, 2005; Noir Movies: Facts, Figures, and Fun, 2006; Sci-Fi Movies: Facts, Figures, and Fun, 2006; Life-Size Dragons, 2006. OTHERS: (ed. with M. Stocks) The Usborne Book of Classic Horror: The Stories of Dracula, Frankenstein, Jekyll & Hyde, 2004. **Address:** Usborne Publishing Ltd., Usborne House, 83-85 Saffron Hill, London, GL EC1N 8RT, England. **Online address:** realthog@optonline.net

BARNETT, Matthew. American (born United States), b. 1974?. **Genres:** Theology/Religion. **Career:** Los Angeles International Church, pastor, 1994-; Dream Center, co-founder, 1994-, senior pastor; Angelus Temple, senior pastor, 2001-. Writer and evangelist. **Publications:** The Church That Never Sleeps: The Amazing Story That Will Change Your View of Church Forever, 2000; (with G. Barna) The Cause Within You: Finding the One Great Thing You were Created to Do in This World, 2011. **Address:** Dream Center, 2301 Bellevue Ave., Los Angeles, CA 90026-4017, U.S.A. **Online address:** pastorsoffice@dreamcenter.org

BARNETT, Michael N. American (born United States), b. 1960. **Genres:** Politics/Government, International Relations/Current Affairs, History. **Career:** Wellesley College, assistant professor of political science, 1989-90; University of Wisconsin, assistant professor of political science, 1990-94, associate professor, 1994-98, professor of political science, 1998-2004, International Studies Program, director, 1996-2004; New York University, Center on International Cooperation, visiting fellow, 2003-04, visiting researcher, 2004-05; University of Minnesota, Hubert Humphrey School, Stassen chair of international affairs and professor of political science, 2004-10; Graduate Institute of International and Development Studies, Centre for Conflict, Development, and Peacebuilding, research fellow, 2009-10; George Washington University, Elliott School of International Affairs, university professor of international affairs and political science, 2010-. Writer. **Publications:** Confronting the Costs of War: Military Power, State, and Society in Egypt and Israel, 1992; (ed.) Israel in Comparative Perspective: Challenging the Conventional Wisdom, 1996; (ed. with E. Adler) Security Communities, 1998; Dialogues in Arab Politics: Negotiations in Regional Order, 1998; (ed. with S. Telhami) Identity and Foreign Policy in the Middle East, 2002; Eyewitness to a Genocide: The United Nations and Rwanda, 2002; (with M. Finnemore) Rules for the World: International Organizations in Global Politics, 2004; (ed. with R. Duvall) Power in Global Governance, 2005; (ed. with T. Weiss) Humanitarianism in Question: Politics, Power, Ethics, 2008; International Humanitarian Order, 2010; (with T.G. Weiss) Humanitarianism Contested: Where Angels Fear to

Tread, 2011; The Empire of Humanity: A History of Humanitarianism, 2011; (ed. with J. Stein) Sacred Aid: Faith and Humanitarianism, 2012. Contributor to periodicals. **Address:** Elliott School of International Affairs, George Washington University, 1957 E St. NW, Ste. 501J, Washington, DC 20052, U.S.A. **Online address:** barnett@gwu.edu

BARNETT, Paul. Australian (born Australia), b. 1935. **Genres:** Theology/Religion. **Career:** Moore College, faculty, 1963-73, visiting faculty, 2002-; St. Barnabas Broadway, rector, 1967-73; Holy Trinity, rector, 1973-79; Macquarie University, Robert Menzies College, master, 1980-90, honorary visiting fellow in ancient history, 1996-; Regent College, visiting professor, 1987-; Regent College, teaching fellow, 1987-; Anglican bishop of North Sydney, 1990-2001; Oak Hill College, visiting fellow, 1996. Writer. **Publications:** (With P. Jensen) The Quest for Power: Neo-pentecostals and the New Testament, 1973; Is the New Testament Reliable?: A Look at the Historical Evidence, 1992, rev. ed., 2003; The Message of 2 Corinthians: Power in Weakness, 1988; Behind the Scenes of the New Testament, 1990; (with P. Jensen and D. Peterson) Resurrection: Truth and Reality, 1994; The Second Epistle to the Corinthians, 1997; Jesus and the Logic of History, 1997; Jesus & the Rise of Early Christianity: A History of New Testament Times, 1999; Birth of Christianity: The First Twenty Years, 2005; Paul: Missionary of Jesus, 2008; Finding the Historical Christ, 2009. **Address:** Moore Theological College, 1 King St., Newtown, NW 2042, Australia. **Online address:** paul.barnett@moore.edu.au

BARNETT, Robert. *See* **SHAGAN, Steve.**

BARNETT, Sloan. American (born United States), b. 1968?. **Genres:** Medicine/Health. **Career:** Fox, legal and consumer expert; CNN, legal and consumer expert; ABC, legal and consumer expert; NBC Affiliate, consumer editor; New York Daily News, legal and consumer advice. Journalist and writer. **Publications:** Green Goes with Everything: Simple Steps to a Healthier Life and a Cleaner Planet, 2008. **Address:** Atria Books, 1230 Ave. of the Americas, New York, NY 10020, U.S.A. **Online address:** info@greengoeswitheverything.com

BARNETT, Victoria (Joan). American (born United States), b. 1950. **Genres:** History, Theology/Religion, Translations, Humanities. **Career:** Racine Community Action Program, neighborhood worker, 1969; ACTION, community worker, 1969-70; Center for University Ministry, ministry associate, 1975-76; Kilburn Presbyterian Church and Unified Vailsburg Services Organization, intern, 1977-78; freelance journalist and translator, 1979-92; University of Hamburg, World Council of Churches, fellow, 1979-80; U.S. Holocaust Memorial Museum, Church Relations Department, consultant, 1994-, director; Fortress Press, Dietrich Bonhoeffer Works Series, associate general editor. **Publications:** For the Soul of the People: Protestant Protest against Hitler, 1992; Bystanders: Conscience and Complicity during the Holocaust, 1999. EDITOR: (and trans.) W. Gerlach, And the Witnesses Were Silent: The Confessing Church and the Jews, 2000; Dietrich Bonhoeffer: Theologian, Christian, Man for His Times, 2000. Contributor of articles to periodicals. **Address:** Publicity Director, Oxford University Press, 198 Madison Ave., New York, NY 10016, U.S.A. **Online address:** vjbarnett@worldnet.att.net

BARNETTE, Martha. American (born United States), b. 1957. **Genres:** Language/Linguistics, Medicine/Health, Food And Wine. **Career:** Norton Psychiatric Clinic, psychiatric aide, 1977-78; Louisville Times, feature and medical writer, 1981-85; Washington Post, national news intern, 1981, special correspondent, reporter; Self Magazine, contributing editor; Allure Magazine, contributing editor; Courier-Journal, editorial writer. Freelance journalist and radio host. **Publications:** The Bill Schroeder Story: The Schroeder Family with Martha Barnette, 1987; A Garden of Words, 1992; Ladyfingers and Nun's Tummies: A Lighthearted Look at How Foods Got their Names, 1997; Dog Days and Dandelions, 2003. Contributor to periodicals. **Address:** c/o Russell Galen, Scovil, Chichak, Galen, Literary Agency Inc., 381 Park Ave. S, Ste. 1020, New York, NY 10016, U.S.A. **Online address:** martha@funwords.com

BARNHARDT, Deanna. *See* **KAWATSKI, Deanna.**

BARNHART, David K. American (born United States), b. 1941. **Genres:** Language/Linguistics, Art/Art History, Dance/Ballet. **Career:** Nyack Boys School, teacher; MacArther Military Academy, teacher; Office of Clarence L. Barnhart, dictionary editor, 1966-80; Lexik House Publishers, founder, proprietor/editor and lexicographer, 1980. **Publications:** Barnhart Dictionary Companion Index, 1987; Neo-Words: A Dictionary of the Newest and Most Unusual Words of Our times, 1991; The Barnhart New-Words Concordance, 1994; (with A. Metcalf) America in So Many Words: Words That Have Shaped America, 1997. **Address:** Lexik House Publishers, PO Box 2018, Hyde Park, NY 12538-0718, U.S.A. **Online address:** barnhart@lexikhouse.com

BARNHART, Terry A. American (born United States), b. 1952. **Genres:** Anthropology/Ethnology, History, Biography, Autobiography/Memoirs, Sociology, Social Sciences. **Career:** Eastern Illinois University, associate professor of history. Writer. **Publications:** Ephraim George Squier and the Development of American Anthropology, 2005; Albert Taylor Bledsoe: Defender of the Old South and Architect of the Lost Cause, 2011. **Address:** Department of History, Eastern Illinois University, 2566 - Coleman Hall, 600 Lincoln Ave., Charleston, IL 61920-3011, U.S.A. **Online address:** tabarnhart@eiu.edu

BARNHILL, David Landis. American (born United States), b. 1949. **Genres:** Literary Criticism And History, Translations. **Career:** Guilford College, Department of Religious Studies, Dana professor of religious studies, 1986-2003, chair, Interdisciplinary Studies, director, Environmental Studies Program, faculty; University of Wisconsin, Environmental Studies Program, director, 2003-, Department of English, professor of English, 2003-. Writer. **Publications:** (Ed.) At Home on the Earth: Becoming Native to Our Place: A Multicultural Anthology, 1999; (ed. with R.S. Gottlieb) Deep Ecology and World Religions: New Essays on Sacred Grounds, 2001; (trans. and intro.) Bashō's Haiku: Selected Poem by Matsuo Bashō, 2004; Engaging the Earth, 2004; (trans. and intro.) Basho's Journey: The Literary Prose of Matsuo Basho, 2005. Contributor to journals. **Address:** Environmental Studies Program, University of Wisconsin, 324 Swart Hall, 800 Algoma Blvd., Oshkosh, WI 54901-3551, U.S.A. **Online address:** barnhill@uwosh.edu

BARNIE, John. Welsh (born Wales), b. 1941. **Genres:** Poetry, History, Literary Criticism And History. **Career:** Copenhagen University, lecturer in English literature, 1969-82; Planet: The Welsh Internationalist, assistant editor, 1985-90, editor, 1990-2006. **Publications:** War in Medieval Society: Social Values and the Hundred Years War 1337-99, 1974; Borderland, 1984; Lightning Country, 1987; Clay, 1989; The King of Ashes, 1989; The Confirmation, 1992; Y Felan a Finnau, 1992; The City, 1993; Heroes, 1996; No Hiding Place, 1996; The Wine Bird, 1998; Ice, 2001; At the Salt Hotel, 2003; Sea Lilies: Selected Poems 1984-2003, 2006; Trouble in Heaven, 2007; Tales of the Shopocracy, 2009; The Forest Under the Sea, 2010; Fire Drill, 2010; A Year of Flowers, 2011. **Address:** Greenfields, Comins Coch, Aberystwyth, Ceredigion, SY23 3BG, England. **Online address:** john.barnie@googlemail.com

BARNOSKY, Anthony D. American (born United States), b. 1952. **Genres:** Natural History, Environmental Sciences/Ecology. **Career:** Trinity College, Department of Geology, Leverhulme postdoctoral fellow, 1983-84; Carnegie Museum of Natural History, assistant curator, associate curator of vertebrate paleontology, 1984-90; University of Pittsburgh, Department of Geology, adjunct assistant professor, 1987-90; University of California, Department of Integrative Biology, associate professor, professor, Museum of Paleontology, associate curator, curator, Museum of Vertebrate Zoology, research paleontologist, 1990-, Undergraduate Services, assistant dean, 1993-94; Montana State University, professor of earth sciences, professor of biology and director of Mountain Research Center, 1994-98; California Academy of Sciences, fellow, 1992-. Writer and paleontologist. **Publications:** Arikareean, Hemingfordian, and Barstovian Mammals from the Miocene Colter Formation, Jackson Hole, Teton County, Wyoming, 1986; (ed. and contrib. with R.A. Martin) Morphological Change in Quaternary Mammals of North America, 1993; (ed.) Biodiversity Response to Climate Change in the Middle Pleistocene: The Porcupine Cave Fauna from Colorado, 2004; Heatstroke: Nature in an Age of Global Warming, 2009. Contributor to books and journals. **Address:** Department of Integrative Biology, University of California, 3060 Valley Life Sciences Bldg., Ste. 3140, Berkeley, CA 94720-3140, U.S.A. **Online address:** barnosky@berkeley.edu

BARNUM, Barbara (J.) Stevens. American (born United States), b. 1937. **Genres:** Medicine/Health, Education, Humanities. **Career:** Mound Park Hospital, charge nurse in labor, delivery, and obstetrics, 1958-59; Augustana Hospital School of Nursing, instructor in medical-surgical nursing, 1959-62, instructor in medical-surgical nursing, 1963-68, associate director of nursing education, 1968-70, director of nursing services, 1970-71; Swedish Covenant Hospital, staff and supervisory nurse, 1962-63; University of Chicago, Chicago Hospitals and Clinics, director of nursing for staff education, 1971-

72, director of nursing for staff and community education, 1972-73; writer and consultant, 1973-74, 1987-88; University of Illinois, assistant professor, 1974-76, associate professor, 1976-78, professor of nursing service administration, 1978-79; Columbia University, Teachers College, professor of nursing and director of division of health services, sciences, and education, 1979-87, Department of Nursing, chair, 1979-85, professor of clinical nursing, 1995-98; Barnum Communications, chief executive officer, 1989-90, chairperson, 1989-92; Columbia-Presbyterian Medical Center, Division of Nursing, editor and consultant, 1992-95. **Publications:** (With K.M. Kerfoot) The Nurse as Executive, 1975, 4th ed., 1995; First-Line Patient Care Management, 1976, 2nd ed., 1983; (ed. with A.G. Rezler) The Nurse Evaluator in Education and Service, 1978; Nursing Administration, Present and Future, 1978; Nursing Theory: Analysis, Application, Evaluation, 1979, 4th ed., 1994; Educating the Nurse Manager: Case Studies and Group Work, 1982; (with C.O. Mallard) Essentials of Nursing Management: Concepts and Context of Practice, 1989; Writing and Getting Published: A Primer for Nurses, 1995; Spirituality in Nursing: From Traditional to New Age, 1996, 3rd ed., 2010; Teaching Nursing in the Era of Managed Care, 1999; The New Healers: Minds and Hands in Complementary Medicine, 2002. Contributor to periodicals. **Address:** 80 Park Ave., Ste. 15-G, New York, NY 10016-2547, U.S.A.

BARNWELL, Andrea D. *See* **BROWNLEE, Andrea Barnwell.**

BARNWELL, Tim. American (born United States), b. 1955. **Genres:** Photography, Art/Art History, Travel/Exploration, Social Sciences. **Career:** Professional photographer, 1977-; University of North Carolina, Learning Resources Media Center, chief photographer, 1974-75; Arts Journal, photographer and writer, 1977-81; Mountain Living, chief photographer and writer, 1978-81; Appalachian Photographic Workshops, director, 1980-88. **Publications:** The Face of Appalachia: Portraits from the Mountain Farm (monograph and photographs), 2003; On Earth's Furrowed Brow: The Appalachian Farm in Photographs (photographs and oral history interviews), 2006; Hands in Harmony: Traditional Crafts and Music in Appalachia, 2009. **Address:** Tim Barnwell Photography, 244 Coxe Ave., Asheville, NC 28801, U.S.A. **Online address:** barnwellphoto@hotmail.com

BARNWELL, William (Curtis). American (born United States), b. 1943. **Genres:** Science Fiction/Fantasy, Writing/Journalism, Novels, Adult Nonfiction. **Career:** University of South Carolina, assistant professor of English, 1971-77; Columbia College, writer-in-residence, 1979-. **Publications:** The Blessing Papers, 1980; The Sigma Curve, 1981; Imram, 1981; Writing for a Reason (non-fiction), 1983; The Spearman Novel, 1984; The Book of Romes, 1994; Supreme Candy, 1996; Our Lady of the Stars, 1999; Book of the Romes, 2001; The Scheme-of-the-Month Club, 2002. FORTHCOMING: The Green Fuse; The Dungeon Below Bling-Bling High; American Heat; Off Base. Contributor to journals. **Address:** Curtis Brown Ltd., 10 Astor Pl., Fl. 3, New York, NY 10003, U.S.A.

BAROLINI, Helen. American (born United States), b. 1925. **Genres:** Novels, Poetry, Food And Wine, Literary Criticism And History, Translations. **Career:** Author, lecturer, translator, 1948-; Trinity College, teacher, 1971-73, 1988; Kirkland College, instructor, 1974-75; Westchester Illustrated, associate editor, 1975-78; Dobbs Ferry Adult Education Program, teacher of oral history, 1976; Chappaqua, librarian, 1984-91; Westchester Community College, adjunct faculty, 1988; Elmira College, Quarry Farm Center, writer-in-residence, 1989; Pace University, lecturer, 1990-. Writer. **Publications:** Umbria, 1953; (with A. Barolini) Duet (poems), 1966; Umbertina (novel), 1979; (co-author) Images, A Pictorial History of Italian Americans, 1981; (ed. and intro.) The Dream Book: An Anthology of Writings by Italian American Women, 1985, rev. ed., 2000; Love in the Middle Ages (novel), 1986; Festa: Recipes and Recollections of Italian Holidays, 1988; Aldus and His Dream Book: An Illustrated Essay, 1991; Chiaroscuro: Essays of Identity, 1997, rev. ed., 1999; More Italian Hours, and Other Stories, 2001; Rome Burning, 2004; A Circular Journey, 2006; Their Other Side: Six American Women and the Lure of Italy, 2006. Hudson River Haiku, 2009; Making My Bones, 2009; Crossing the Alps, 2010. Contributor to periodicals. **Address:** 19 Maple Ave., Apt. 2B, Hastings on Hudson, NY 10706, U.S.A. **Online address:** helenbarolini@juno.com

BARON, Beth. American (born United States), b. 1958. **Genres:** Women's Studies And Issues, History, Area Studies, Poetry, Humanities. **Career:** Franklin and Marshall College, visiting assistant professor of history, 1988-89; City University of New York, City College, assistant professor of history, 1989-93, associate professor of history, 1994-, professor of history, Middle East and Middle Eastern American Center and Graduate Center, co-director. Writer. **Publications:** (Ed. with N.R. Keddie) Women in Middle Eastern History: Shifting Boundaries in Sex and Gender, 1991; The Women's Awakening in Egypt: Culture, Society and the Press, 1994; (ed. with R. Matthee) Iran and Beyond: Essays in Middle Eastern History in Honor of Nikki R. Keddie, 2000; Egypt as a Woman: Nationalism, Gender and Politics, 2005. Contributor to periodicals. **Address:** Department of History, City College, City University of New York, 160 Convent Ave., New York, NY 10031, U.S.A. **Online address:** bbaron@gc.cuny.edu

BARON, Denis Neville. (D. N. Baron). British (born England), b. 1924?. **Genres:** Medicine/Health. **Career:** Middlesex Hospital Medical School, teacher of chemical pathology, 1953-55; University of Chicago, Ben May Laboratory, fellow in medicine, 1960-61; University of London, Royal Free Hospital School of Medicine, professor, 1963-88, senator, 1985-88, professor emeritus of chemical pathology, 1988-; St. Mary's Hospital Medical School, tutor in medical ethics, 1989-96. Writer. **Publications:** AS D.N. BARON: Essentials of Chemical Pathology, 1957; (with K. Lee and J.T. Whicher) A New Short Textbook of Chemical Pathology, 2nd ed., 1969, 5th ed., 1989; Short Textbook of Clinical Biochemistry, 2nd ed., 1969, 3rd ed., 1973; (ed. with N. Compston and A.M. Dawson) Recent Advances in Medicine, 17th ed., 1977; (ed.) Units, Symbol and axAbbreviations, 6th ed., 2008. **Address:** 47 Holne Chase, London, GL N2 0QG, England. **Online address:** d.baron@btinternet.com

BARON, D. N. *See* **BARON, Denis Neville.**

BARON, Kathi. American (born United States), b. 1956. **Genres:** Children's Fiction. **Career:** Writer and therapist. **Publications:** Shattered, 2009. Contributor to journals, books and periodicals. **Address:** Oak Park, IL , U.S.A. **Online address:** kathi@kathibaron.com

BARON, Michael. *See* **KAHN, Michael A.**

BARON, Mike. American (born United States), b. 1949?. **Genres:** Graphic Novels, E-books, Plays/Screenplays, Young Adult Fiction. **Career:** Rocky Mountain College of Art and Design, self-publishing comics instructor, 2003-04. Writer and comic book creator. **Publications:** Badger, 1986; Robotech, the Graphic Novel: Genesis (based on a plot by Carl Macek), 1986; Original Nexus, 1986; The World of Ginger Fox, 1986; Hexbreaker: A Badger Graphic Novel, 1988; Stan Lee Presents the Punisher in Intruder, 1989; Dead Man: Book 1, 1990; Next Nexus, 1990; (co-author) The Punisher: G Force, 1992; (with J. Homan) The Complete Blankbook, 1993; Nexus: One, 1993; Nexus: Two, 1993; (with K. Jones and L. Dorscheid) Deadman: Lost Souls, 1995; Bruce Lee, 1995; Nexus: Alien Justice, 1996; (with T. Zahn) Star Wars: Heir to the Empire, 1996; (with T. Zahn) Star Wars: Dark Force Rising, 1998; Star Wars: The Last Command, 1999; Madman Boogaloo!, 1999; (with J. Herman and C. Macek) The Macross Saga, vol. I, 2003; Witchblade: Demons, 2003; (with S. Lobdell) Kiss: Men and Monsters, 2003; (with J. Herman and C. Macek) Robotech, the Macross Saga, 2003; Kiss: Unholy War, 2004; Faro Korbit, 2004; Complete Wordbook for Game Players: Winning Words for Word Freaks, 2004; Versus, 2007; Star Wars: The Thrawn Trilogy, 2010. **Address:** c/o Author Mail, Dark Horse Comics, 10956 SE Main St., Milwaukie, OR 97222, U.S.A. **Online address:** baron.m@attbi.com

BARON, Naomi S(usan). American (born United States), b. 1946?. **Genres:** Language/Linguistics, Technology. **Career:** Brown University, assistant professor, 1972-78, associate professor of linguistics, 1978-85, associate dean of the college, 1981-83; Rhode Island School of Design, visiting faculty member, 1982-83; Emory University, visiting National Endowment for the Humanities chair, 1983-84; Southwestern University, Brown visiting chair, 1985-87; American University, professor of linguistics, 1987-, associate dean for undergraduate affairs, 1987-92, associate dean for curriculum and faculty development, 1992-94, Department of Language and Foreign Studies, Center for Teaching, Research and Learning, executive director, chair, 1996-2000, AU TESOL Program, director, 1997-2009, presidential research fellow, 2007-, Guggenheim fellow, Swedish Fulbright fellow, 2007. Writer. **Publications:** Language Acquisition and Historical Change, 1977; Speech, Writing, and Sign, 1981; Computer Languages: A Guide for the Perplexed, 1986; Pigeon-Birds and Rhyming Words: The Role of Parents in Language Learning, 1990;

Growing Up with Language: How Children Learn to Talk, 1992; Alphabet to Email: How Written English Evolved and Where It's Heading, 2000; Always On: Language in an Online and Mobile World, 2008. Contributor to journals. **Address:** Department of Language & Foreign Studies, Center for Teaching, Research and Learning, Rm. 212, Hurst Hall, Washington, DC 20016-8045, U.S.A. **Online address:** nbaron@american.edu

BARON, Ora Wendy. *See* **BARON, Wendy.**

BARON, Wendy. Also writes as Ora Wendy Baron, Wendy Dimson. British (born England), b. 1937. **Genres:** Art/Art History, History, How-to Books, Young Adult Fiction. **Career:** Government Art Collection, Department of National Heritage, director, 1978-97; Public Art Communications Agency, trustee, 1990-99; Contemporary Art Society, staff, 1997-2000; Arts Research Ltd., 1998-2004; British Art Fair, staff, 2005-07; The Society of Antiquaries of London, fellow, 2007-; Ben Uri Art Gallery, staff, 2009-; Imperial College Healthcare Trust, staff, 2010-. Writer. **Publications:** Sickert, 1973; Miss Ethel Sands and Her Circle, 1977; (with M. Cormack) The Camden Town Group, 1979; (ed. with R. Shone) Sickert Paintings, 1992; Perfect Moderns: A History of the Camden Town Group, 2000; Sickert: Paintings and Drawings, 2006; (ed. with L. Tickner and B. Wright) Walter Sickert: Camden Town Nudes, 2006; (with R. Bongolan and E. Moir) Keys to the Secondary Classroom: A Teacher's Guide to the First Months of School, 2010. **Address:** Paul Holberton Publishing, 89 Borough High St., London, GL SE1 1NL, England.

BARON CHALFONT, Arthur Gwynne Jones. *See* **CHALFONT.**

BARON-COHEN, Simon. British (born England), b. 1958. **Genres:** Psychiatry, Sciences, Medicine/Health. **Career:** University of London, Institute of Psychiatry, Department of developmental psychology, staff psychologist, 1985-87, lecturer, 1988-91, senior lecturer, 1991-94, MRC Child Psychiatry Unit, joint head, 1992-94; University College London, Department of Psychology, lecturer in psychology, 1987-88; University of Cambridge, Department of psychopathology, lecturer, 1994-99, reader, 1999-2001, professor, 2001-; Trinity College, teaching fellow, 1995-2007, professorial fellow, 2007-, Autism Research Center, director; Molecular Autism, co-editor-in-chief. **Publications:** (Ed. with H. Tager-Flusberg and D.J. Cohen) Understanding Other Minds: Perspectives from Autism, 1993, 2nd ed., 2000; (with P. Bolton) Autism: The Facts, 1993; Mindblindness: An Essay on Autism and Theory of Mind, 1995; (ed.) The Maladapted Mind: Classic Readings in Evolutionary Psychopathology, 1997; (ed. with J.E. Harrison) Synaesthesia: Classic and Contemporary Readings, 1997; (with M.M. Robinson) Tourette Syndrome: The Facts, 1998; (with P. Howlin and J. Hadwin) Teaching Children With Autism to Mind-Read: A Practical Guide for Teachers and Parents, 1998; (co-author) All about Emotions, 2000; The Essential Difference: Male And Female Brains And The Truth About Autism, 2004; (with S. Wheelwright and P. Myers) An Exact Mind: An Artist with Asperger Syndrome, 2004; (with R. Knickmeyer and S. Lutchmaya) Prenatal Testosterone in Mind: Amniotic Fluid Studies, 2004; Autism and Asperger Syndrome, 2008; Teaching Children With Autism to Mind-Read: A Practical Guide for Teachers and Parents, 2011. Contributor to periodicals. **Address:** University of Cambridge, Douglas House, 18b Trumpington Rd., Cambridge, CB2 2AH, England. **Online address:** s.baron-cohen@psychol.cam.ac.uk

BARONE, Joe. American (born United States), b. 1942. **Genres:** Mystery/Crime/Suspense, Theology/Religion, Humanities. **Career:** Christian Church (Disciples of Christ), minister, now retired. Writer and ordained minister. **Publications:** About a Loving God: Twenty-four Meditations on the Funeral Scriptures, 1991; My Tomb Was Empty: Seven Monologues for Lent and Easter, 1993; (with J.M. Beer and W.R. Grimbol) Living in the Light: Twenty-two Creative Components Including Services, Dialogues, Monologues, Skits, Dramas, Meditations, and a Litany, 2008; The Body in the Record Room: A Mystery, 2008. **Address:** CSS Publishing Comp., 5450 N Dixie Hwy., Lima, OH 45807, U.S.A. **Online address:** thesunrisesaga@gmail.com

BAROT, Enrique. *See* **BAROT, Rick.**

BAROT, Rick. (Enrique Barot). American (born United States), b. 1969. **Genres:** Poetry. **Career:** Stanford University, Jones Lecturer in Poetry; Warren Wilson College, Program for Writers, teacher; Pacific Lutheran University, assistant professor of English. Poet and educator. **Publications:** The Darker Fall: Poems, 2002; Want: Poems, 2008. Works appear in anthologies. Contributor to periodicals. **Address:** Department of English, Pacific Lutheran University, Administration Bldg., Tacoma, WA 98447, U.S.A. **Online address:** barotrp@plu.edu

BARR, Alwyn. American (born United States), b. 1938. **Genres:** History, Race Relations. **Career:** Southwestern Historical Quarterly, editorial assistant, 1961-66; Purdue University, assistant professor, 1966-69; Texas Tech University, associate professor, 1969-75, professor of history, 1975-2009, chairman, 1978-85, now professor emeritus. Writer. **Publications:** Polignac's Texas Brigade, 1964; Reconstruction to Reform: Texas Politics, 1876-1906, 1971, 2nd ed. 2000; Black Texans: A History of Negroes in Texas, 1528-1971, 1973; Essays on Southern History: Written in Honor of Barnes F. Lathrop, 1980; Texans in Revolt: The Battle for San Antonio 1935, 1990; Black Texans: A History of African Americans in Texas, 1528-1995, 1996; The African Texans, 2004; (contrib.) Blacks in East Texas History, 2008. EDITOR: Charles Porter's Account of the Confederate Attempt to Seize Arizona and New Mexico, 1964; (with Calvert) Black Leaders: Texans for Their Times, 1981; N. Smithwick, The Evolution of a State or Recollections of Old Texas Days, 1995. **Address:** Department of History, Texas Tech University, 138 Holden Hall, PO Box 1013, Lubbock, TX 79409-1013, U.S.A. **Online address:** alwyn.barr@ttu.edu

BARR, Andrew. British (born England), b. 1961. **Genres:** Food And Wine, History, Social Sciences, Classics, Theology/Religion. **Career:** Time Out Magazine, wine correspondent, 1983-84; broadcaster; writer on food and drink, 1983-; Sunday (newspaper), correspondent, drinks correspondent, 1983-. **Publications:** Wine Snobbery: An Insider's Guide to the Booze Business, 1988; Wine Snobbery: An Exposé, 1992; Guide to Pinot Noir, 1992; Drink: An Informal Social History, 1995; Drink: A Social History of America, 1999; (with L. Barr) Jobs for the Boys?: Women Who Became Priests, 2001. Contributor to periodicals. **Address:** Carroll & Graff Publishers Inc., 19 W 21st St., Ste. 601, New York, NY 10010, U.S.A.

BARR, Donald A. American (born United States), b. 1946?. **Genres:** Young Adult Non-fiction. **Career:** Highland Health Center, 1974-82; Kaiser-Permanente Medical Center, 1982-93; Stanford University School of Medicine, assistant professor of emergency medicine, 1993-94; University of California, assistant professor of social and behavioral sciences, 1993-95; Stanford University, lecturer in human biology, 1994-2001, associate professor of sociology and human biology, 2001-. Writer and medical doctor. **Publications:** NONFICTION: Introduction to U.S. Health Policy: The Organization, Financing and Delivery of Health Care in America, 2002, 2nd ed., 2007; Health Disparities in the United States: Social Class, Race, Ethnicity and Health, 2008; Questioning the Premedical Paradigm: Enhancing Diversity in the Medical Profession a Century after the Flexner Report, 2010. Contributor of articles to periodicals. **Address:** Stanford University, Human Biology Program, Bldg. 20, Stanford, CA 94305-2160, U.S.A. **Online address:** barr@stanford.edu

BARR, Gonzalo. American (born United States) **Genres:** Air/Space Topics, Young Adult Fiction, Novellas/Short Stories. **Career:** Writer and attorney. **Publications:** The Last Flight of José Luis Balboa: Stories, 2006. Contributor of articles to periodicals. **Address:** Houghton Mifflin Harcourt Publishing Co., 222 Berkeley St., Boston, MA 02116-3748, U.S.A. **Online address:** gb@gonzalobarr.com

BARR, John. *See* **MUNSON, Noel J.**

BARR, N. A. *See* **BARR, Nicholas.**

BARR, Nevada. American (born United States), b. 1952. **Genres:** Mystery/Crime/Suspense, Novels, Horror, Children's Fiction, Young Adult Fiction. **Career:** Classic Stage Co., performer in shows off-broadway; Morgan Stanley, executive assistant; United States National Park Service, law enforcement ranger, 1989-. Writer. **Publications:** ANNA PIGEON MYSTERIES: Track of the Cat, 1993; A Superior Death, 1994; Ill Wind, 1995; Firestorm, 1996; Endangered Species, 1997; Blind Descent, 1998; Liberty Falling, 1999; Deep South, 2000; Blood Lure, 2001; Hunting Season, 2002; Flashback, 2003; High Country, 2004; Hard Truth, 2005; Deadly Housewives, 2006; Winter Study, 2008; Borderline, 2009. OTHER NOVELS: Bittersweet, 1984; (co-author) Naked Came the Phoenix, 2001; (ed. and intro.) Nevada Barr Presents Malice Domestic 10: An Anthology of Original Traditional Mystery Stories, 2001; Seeking Enlightenment-Hat by Hat: A Skeptic's Path to Religion, 2003; Winter Study, 2008; Borderline, 2009; 13 1/2, 2009; Burn 2010; The Rope, 2012. Contributor to periodicals. **Address:** Vanguard Press, 387 Park Ave. S, 12th Fl., New York, NY 10016, U.S.A. **Online address:** nevadabarr@comcast.net

BARR, Nicholas. (N. A. Barr). British (born England), b. 1943. **Genres:** Education, Money/Finance, Economics, Education, Social Sciences, Business/Trade/Industry. **Career:** University of London, London School of Economics and Political Science, lecturer, senior lecturer in economics, 1971-, professor of public economics; World Bank, consultant, 1990-92; Australian Economic Review, CESifo Economic Studies, associate editor. Writer. **Publications:** (With S.R. James and A.R. Prest) Self-Assessment for Income Tax, 1977; (with A.R. Prest) Public Finance in Theory and Practice, 1979, 7th ed., 1985; The Economics of the Welfare State, 1987, 4th ed., 2004; (with A.J.L. Barnes) Strategies for Higher Education: The Alternative White Paper, 1988; Student Loans: The Next Steps, 1989; State of Welfare: The Welfare State in Britian Since 1974, 1990; Income Transfers and the Social Safety Net in Russia, 1992; Poland: Income Support and the Social Safety Net during the Transition, 1993; (ed. with D. Whynes) Current Issues in the Economics of Welfare, 1993; (ed.) Labor Markets and Social Policy in Central and Eastern Europe: The Transition and Beyond, 1994; Welfare State as Piggy Bank: Information, Risk, Uncertainty and the Role of the State, 2001; (ed.) Economic Theory and the Welfare State, 2001; Pension Puzzle: Prerequisites and Policy Choices in Pension Design, 2002; Financing Higher Education: Answers from the U.K., 2005; (co-author) Social Security Reform in China: Issues and Options, 2005; (with P. Diamond) Reforming Pensions: Principles and Policy Choices, 2008; (with P. Diamond) Pension Reform: A Short Guide, 2009. Contributor to journals. **Address:** London School of Economics and Political Science, University of London, Rm. 4.09 Kingsway Bldg., Houghton St., London, GL WC2A 2AE, England. **Online address:** n.barr@lse.ac.uk

BARR, Pat. *See* **BARR, Patricia (Miriam).**

BARR, Patricia (Miriam). (Pat Barr). British (born England), b. 1934. **Genres:** Novels, History, Women's Studies And Issues, Biography, Romance/Historical, Literary Criticism And History. **Career:** Yokohama International School, teacher of English, 1959-61; University of Maryland, teacher of English for overseas program in Japan, 1961-62; National Old People's Welfare Council, assistant secretary, 1965-66; writer, 1966-. **Publications:** NONFICTION: The Coming of the Barbarians, 1967; The Dear Cry Pavilion, 1968; The Elderly: Handbook on Care and Services, 1968; Foreign Devils: Westerners in the Far East, 1970; Curious Life for a Lady (biography), 1970; To China with Love, 1972; The Memsahibs: Women of Victorian India, 1976; Taming the Jungle, 1977; The Framing of the Female, 1978; (with R. Desmond) Simla: A Hill Station in British India, 1978; Japan (guidebook), 1980; The New Sourcebook for the Disabled, 1981; The Dust in The Balance: British Women in India 1905-1945, 1989. NOVELS: Chinese Alice, 1981; Jade, 1982; Kenjiro, 1985; Coromandel, 1988; Snaring the Sun, forthcoming. Contributor to periodicals. **Address:** c/o Sara Menguc, 4 Hatch Pl., Kingston-upon-Thanes, SR KT2 5NB, England.

BARR, Sheldon. American (born United States), b. 1938. **Genres:** Art/Art History, Crafts. **Career:** Gardner & Barr Inc., co-owner, 1992-. Writer. **Publications:** Venetian Glass: Confections in Glass, 1855-1914, 1998; Venetian Glass Mosaics: 1860-1917, 2008. **Address:** Gardner & Barr Inc., 305 E 61st St., New York, NY 10065-8204, U.S.A. **Online address:** gardbar@aol.com

BARR, Stephen M. American (born United States), b. 1953?. **Genres:** Physics, Sciences, Natural History. **Career:** University of Washington, research assistant professor, 1980-85; Brookhaven National Laboratory, associate physicist, 1985-87; University of Delaware, Department of Physics and Astronomy, Bartol Research Institute, associate professor, professor of physics, 1987-. Writer and physicist. **Publications:** Modern Physics and Ancient Faith, 2003; A Student's Guide to Natural Science, 2006. **Address:** Bartol Research Institute, Department of Physics and Astronomy, University of Delaware, 209 Sharp Laboratory, Newark, DE 19716-2593, U.S.A. **Online address:** smbarr@bartol.udel.edu

BARRA, Allen. American (born United States) **Genres:** Sports/Fitness, History. **Career:** American Heritage magazine, contributing editor; Salon.com, columnist; Wall Street Journal, sports columnist. Commentator. **Publications:** Football by the Numbers, 1986, 1986; Football by the Numbers, 1987, 1987; That's Not the Way It Was: (Almost) Everything They Told You about Sports Is Wrong, 1995; Inventing Wyatt Earp: His Life and Many Legends, 1998; Clearing the Bases: The Greatest Baseball Debates of the Last Century, 2002; Brushbacks and Knockdowns: The Greatest Baseball Debates of Two Centuries, 2004; Big Play: Barra on Football, 2004; The Last Coach: A Life of Paul Bear Bryant, 2005; Inventing Wyatt Earp: His Life and Many Legends, 2008; Yogi Berra: Eternal Yankee, 2009; Rickwood Field: A Century in America's Oldest Ballpark, 2010. Contributor to periodicals. **Address:** Wall Street Journal, 200 Liberty St., New York, NY 10281, U.S.A.

BARRANGER, Milly S(later). American (born United States), b. 1937. **Genres:** Theatre, Biography, Literary Criticism And History. **Career:** Louisiana State University, special lecturer in English, 1964-69; Tulane University, assistant professor, associate professor of theatre, 1971-82, chair of department, 1973-82; University of Tennessee, visiting young professor of humanities, 1981-82; University of North Carolina, Department of Dramatic Art, professor of dramatic art and chairman, 1982-99, alumni distinguished professor, 1997-2003, alumni distinguished professor emerita, 2003-. Writer. **Publications:** Generations: An Introduction to Drama, 1971; Theatre: A Way of Seeing, 1980, 7th ed., 2013; Theatre: Past and Present, 1984, rev. ed., 2001; (ed. with A.M. Robinson and V.M. Roberts) Notable Women in the American Theatre, 1989; Understanding Plays, 1990, 3rd ed., 2004; Jessica Tandy: A Bibliography, 1991; Margaret Webster: A Bio-Bibliography, 1994; Margaret Webster: A Life in the Theater, 2004; Unfriendly Witnesses: Gender, Theater and Film in the McCarthy Era, 2008; A Gambler's Instinct: The Story of Broadway Producer Cheryl Crawford, 2010; Audrey Wood and the Playwrights, 2013. Contributor of articles to books and periodicals. **Address:** 245 W 107th St., Apt. 8F, New York, NY 10025-3057, U.S.A. **Online address:** mbarrang@mindspring.com

BARRATT, Barnaby B. American/British (born England), b. 1950?. **Genres:** Psychology, Philosophy, Sex. **Career:** Wayne State University, professor of family medicine, psychiatry and behavioral neurosciences, 1994, director of human sexuality; American Association of Sex Educators, president, counselor and therapist, 2004-06; Northcentral University, professor, director of clinical psychology and provost, 2009-; International University of Professional Studies, director of the MA/PhD program in somatic and spiritual psychology; Midwest Institute of Sexology, founder and director; Santa Barbara Graduate Institute, chair and core faculty in somatic and clinical psychology. Writer. **Publications:** Psychic Reality And Psychoanalytic Knowing, 1984; Psychoanalysis And The Postmodern Impulse: Knowing and Being since Freud's Psychology, 1993; The Way of the Body Prayer Path: Erotic Freedom And Spiritual Enlightenment, 2004; Sexual Health And Erotic Freedom, 2005; Ten Keys To Successful Sexual Partnering, 2005; What is Tantric Practice?, 2006; Emergence of Somatic Psychology and Bodymind Therapy, 2010. **Address:** AZ , U.S.A. **Online address:** bbbarratt@earthlink.net

BARRATT, Iris K. American (born United States), b. 1954. **Genres:** Paranormal, Self Help. **Career:** Writer. **Publications:** Divination for Decision Makers, 1989, rev. ed., 1999; The Power of Forgiveness, 1989; Advanced Investigative Techniques, 1996; The Divination Workbook: An Expert's Guide to Awakening the Power and Wisdom of Your Soul, 1998; Surgery: Before and After, 1999; The Joy of Synchronicity: Inspiring Short Stories 2008; Children's Celebrations and Ceremonies Workbook, 2011. **Address:** 13762 S Elk Creek, Pine, CO 80470, U.S.A. **Online address:** ourgoddessiris@juno.com

BARRATT BROWN, Michael. British (born England), b. 1918. **Genres:** Economics, Environmental Sciences/Ecology, History, Business/Trade/Industry. **Career:** United Nations Relief and Rehabilitation Administration, special assistant to chief of Balkan and Yugoslavian missions, 1944-47; Cambridge University, part-time tutor, 1947-61; University of Sheffield, lecturer, 1961-66, senior lecturer in extra-mural studies, 1966-77; University of Sussex, Institute for Developmental Studies, associate fellow, 1976; Northern College, principal, 1977-83; Sheffield City Polytechnic, fellow, 1984; Bertrand Russell Peace Foundation, board director. Writer. **Publications:** After Imperialism, 1963, rev. ed. 1970; Labour and Sterling, 1968; Opening the Books, 1968; (with K. Coates) The Big Flame; and, What is the I.W.C.?, 1969; What Economics is About, 1970; Essays on Imperialism, 1972; From Labourism to Socialism, 1972; Europe, Time to Leave and How to Go, 1973; The Economics of Imperialism, 1974; (ed.) Anatomy of Underdevelopment, 1974; (co-ed.) Resources and the Environment, 1976; (with K. Coates) Accountability and Industrial Democracy, 1977; (co-ed.) Full Employment, 1978; Information at Work, 1978; (co-author) What Went Wrong, 1979; How to Win?, 1981; Planning the Planners, How to Control the Recovery, 1983; Models in Political Economy, 1984, rev. ed., 1995; (contrib.) Joint Action for Jobs, 1986; (co-author) Perestroika, Global Challenge, 1988; European Union: Fortress or Democracy, 1990; Short Changed: Africa in World Trade, 1992; Fair Trade: Reforming the International Trading System, 1993; Africa's Choices: After 30 Years of the World Bank, 1995; (with K. Coates) The Blair Revelation: Deliverance for Whom?, 1996; Yugoslav Tragedy: Lessons for Socialists, 1996; Defending the Welfare State, 1998; Young Person's Guide to the Global Crisis, 1999; Arms for Oil, 2005. Contributor to books. **Address:** Robin Hood Farm, Baslow, DB NG21 9JA, England. **Online address:** robinh@globalnet.co.uk

BARRÉ, Jean-Luc. French (born France), b. 1957?. **Genres:** Adult Nonfiction, Autobiography/Memoirs, Biography. **Career:** Writer and historian. **Publications:** NONFICTION: (with R. Leygues) Delcassé, 1980; (with R. Leygues) Les Mutins de la mer Noire, 1981; Reconquérir, 1944- 1945, 1985; Le Seigneur-Chat: Philippe Berthelot, 1866-1934, 1988; La Ferveur et le Sacrifice: Indochine 1951, 1988; Jacques et Raïssa Maritain: Les Mendiants du ciel: Biographies Croisées, 1995, rev. ed., 2009; Algérie: L'espoir Fraternel, 1997; Devenir De Gaulle: 19391943, 2003; Dominique de Roux: Le Provocateur (1935-1977), 2005; (with J. Mauriac) L'Apres de Gaulle, 2006; Il faut Partir: Correspondances inédites, 1953-1977, 2007; Le Général et le Journaliste, 2008; Journal/Mémoires politiques, 2008; François Mauriac, 2009; (with J. Chirac) Mémoires, 2009. Contributor to books. **Address:** Fayard Publishers, 13 rue du Montparnasse, Paris, 75006, France. **Online address:** jean.luc.barre@wanadoo.fr

BARRE, Richard. American (born United States), b. 1943. **Genres:** Mystery/Crime/Suspense, Novels. **Career:** Barre Advertising, owner, copywriter and creative director, 1975-90; Capra Press, associate publisher, publisher and editor. **Publications:** MYSTERY NOVELS: The Innocents, 1995; Bearing Secrets, 1996; The Ghosts of Morning, 1998; Blackheart Highway, 1999; The Star, 2002; Bethany, 2003; Burning Moon, 2003; Echo Bay, 2004; Wind on the River, 2004. **Address:** Capra Press, 155 Canon View Rd., Santa Barbara, CA 93108, U.S.A. **Online address:** richardbarre@caprapress.com

BARRECA, Regina. American (born United States), b. 1957. **Genres:** Women's Studies And Issues, Humor/Satire, Social Commentary. **Career:** Queens College of the City University of New York, graduate assistant and adjunct lecturer, 1981-87; University of Connecticut, assistant professor, 1987-91, associate professor, 1991-97, professor of English, 1997-; The Hartford Courant, weekly columnist; The Washington Post, columnist. **Publications:** They Used to Call Me Snow White But I Drifted: Women's Strategic Uses of Humor, 1991; Perfect Husbands and Other Fairy Tales: Demystifying Marriage, Men and Romance, 1993; Untamed and Unabashed: Essays on Women and Comedy, 1994; Sweet Revenge: The Wicked Delights of Getting Even, 1995; Too Much of a Good Thing Is Wonderful, 2000; (intro.) Glimpses of the Moon, 2000; The ABC of Vice: An Insatiable Women's Guide, 2003; I'm with Stupid: One Man, One Woman: 10, 000 Years of Misunderstanding Between the Sexes Cleared Right Up, 2004; Babes in Boyland: A Personal History of Co-Education in the Ivy League, 2005; It's not that I'm Bitter: Or How I Learned to Stop Worrying about Visible Panty Lines and Conquered the World, 2009. EDITOR AND CONTRIBUTOR: Last Laughs: Perspectives on Women and Comedy, 1988; Sex and Death in Victorian Literature, 1990; New Perspectives on Women and Comedy, 1992; Women of the Century: Thirty Modern Short Stories, 1993; Penguin Book of Women's Humor, 1994; Fay Weldon's Wicked Fiction, 1994; Desire and Imagination: Twenty Classic Essays on Sexuality, 1995; The Erotics of Instruction, 1997; Signet Book of American Humor, 1999, rev. ed., 2004; (with L.A. Jacobus) Helene Cixous: Critical Impressions, 1999; A Sit-Down with the Sopranos: Watching Italian American Culture on TV's Most Talked about Series, 2002; (intro.) Don't Tell Mama!: The Penguin Book of Italian American Writing, 2002; (ed.) Make Mine a Double: Non-Tragic Stories of Women and Drink, 2010; Vital Ideas: Sex, 2011. Contributor to periodicals. **Address:** Department of English, University of Connecticut, CLAS Rm. 130, x2988, 215 Glenbrook Rd., PO Box U-4025, Storrs Mansfield, CT 06269-4025, U.S.A. **Online address:** gb@ginabarreca.com

BARRETO, Amilcar Antonio. American/Puerto Rican (born Puerto Rico), b. 1965. **Genres:** Politics/Government, Cultural/Ethnic Topics, Language/Linguistics. **Career:** State University of New York, Department of Political Science, lecturer, 1991-93; Alfred State College, Department of Social and Behavioral Sciences, assistant professor of political science, 1993-95; Northeastern University, Department of Political Science, assistant professor, 1996-2002, associate professor, 2002-, Department of African American Studies, affiliated faculty, 2011-, associate director for humanities center, Graduate School, interim associate dean and interim director; Ben Gurion University, visiting fellow, 2005. Writer. **Publications:** Language, Elites, and the State: Nationalism in Puerto Rico and Quebec, 1998; The Politics of Language in Puerto Rico, 2001; Vieques, the Navy and Puerto Rican Politics, 2002; (with R. Godoy and I. Redstone) Social, Economic, and Political Constraints to the Use of English in Puerto Rico, 2002; Nationalism and Its Logical Foundations, 2009. Contributor to books and journals. **Address:** Department of Political Science, Northeastern University, 301 Meserve Hall, Boston, MA 02115, U.S.A. **Online address:** a.barreto@neu.edu

BARRETO, Augusto Cassiano Neves da Sylveira Mascarenhas. *See* **BARRETO, Mascarenhas.**

BARRETO, Mascarenhas. (Augusto Cassiano Neves da Sylveira Mascarenhas Barreto). Portuguese (born Portugal), b. 1923. **Genres:** Poetry, History, Literary Criticism And History, Popular Culture, Translations, Natural History, Social Sciences. **Career:** Livros do Brasil, editor; Aster, editor. Educator. **Publications:** (Contrib.) Touros em Portugal, 1962; Lisboa Antiga, 1962; Portugal, Terra De Vinho, 1963; Origens liricas e motivacao poetica, 1970; História da polícia em Portugal: Polícia e Sociedade, 1979; O Português Cristóvão Colombo, Agente Secreto do Rei Dom João II, 1988; Português Salvador Fernandes Zarco, vulgo Cristovão Colombo, o redescobridor da América, 1993; Colombo português: Provas Documentais, 1997; A Verdadeira Identidade de Criostovao Colombo (The True Identity of Christopher Columbus-Documental Proof). TRANSLATOR: Gardner and E. Stanley, O Caso da Ninfa Nocturna (title means: 'The Case of the Negligent Nymph'), 1972; Gardner and E. Stanley, O Caso das Bebidas Drogadas (title means: 'The Case of the Gilded Lily'), 1973; Gardner and E. Stanley, O Caso do Casco de Arminbo (title means: 'The Case of the Moth-Eaten Mink'), 1974; Gardner and E. Stanley, Os Ciumes de Minerva (title means: 'Some Slips Don't Show'), 1975. **Address:** Avenida da Liberdade 262 c/e, Lisbon, 1150-279, Portugal.

BARRETT, Andrea. (Andrea Fuller Barrett). American (born United States), b. 1954. **Genres:** Novels, Novellas/Short Stories, How-to Books, Young Adult Fiction, Reference. **Career:** Skidmore College, New York State Summer Writers' Institute, senior fiction fellow, 1993; Warren Wilson College, instructor in the M.F.A. Program, 1993-98, 2000; University of Michigan, adjunct lecturer, 1995; Saint Mary's College, visiting writer, 1998; University of Virginia, visiting writer, 1999; Williams College, instructor, lecturer in English, 2004-; Bread Loaf Writers' Conference, faculty; New York Public Library, Center for Scholars and Writers, fellow. **Publications:** NOVELS: Lucid Stars, 1988; Secret Harmonies, 1989; The Middle Kingdom, 1991; The Forms of Water, 1993; The Voyage of the Narwhal, 1998; The Air We Breathe, 2007. SHORT FICTION: Ship Fever, 1996; Servants of the Map, 2002; (ed. with P. Turchi) The Story Behind the Story: 26 Writers and How They Work, 2004; Air We Breathe, 2007. OTHERS: (and comp.) The Diabetic's Brand Name Food Exchange Handbook, 1984, 2nd ed., 1991; (with P. Turchi) Kite in the Wind: Fiction Writers on their Craft, 2011. Works appear in anthologies. Contributor to periodicals. **Address:** Wendy Weil Literary Agency, 232 Madison Ave., Ste. 1300, New York, NY 10016, U.S.A.

BARRETT, Andrea Fuller. *See* **BARRETT, Andrea.**

BARRETT, Anthony A(rthur). British/Canadian (born Canada), b. 1941. **Genres:** Classics, History, Law. **Career:** Carleton University, lecturer in classics, 1965-66; University of British Columbia, assistant professor, 1968-73, associate professor of classics, 1973-, distinguished university professor, now professor emeritus. Writer. **Publications:** (With M. Havers and P. Shankland) Tragedy in Three Voices: The Rattenbury Murder, 1980; (with R.W. Liscombe) Francis Rattenbury and British Columbia: Architecture and Challenge in the Imperial Age, 1983; (ed. and trans. with C. Kiadó) Janus Pannonius, Epigrams, 1985; Caligula: The Corruption of Power, 1990; Agrippina: Sex, Power and Politics in the Early Empire, 1996; Livia: First Lady of Imperial Rome, 2002; (ed.) Lives of the Caesars, 2008; (intro.) Annals: The Reigns of Tiberius, Claudius and Nero, 2008. **Address:** Department of Classical, Near Eastern & Religious, University of British Columbia, 1866 Main Mall, BUCH C227, Vancouver, BC V6T 1Z1, Canada. **Online address:** aab@interchange.ubc.ca

BARRETT, Buckley Barry. American (born United States), b. 1948. **Genres:** Bibliography, Reference, Language/Linguistics, Education. **Ca-**

reer: South Dakota State Library, faculty, 1973-75; California State Library, faculty, 1975-78; Marymount Palos Verdes College, assistant director, director of library, 1978-82; California State University, Pfau Library, assistant head of materials services, 1982-87, head of technical services, 1987-94, chair of educational resources, 1989-90, head of automation services, 1994-, now emeritus. Writer. **Publications:** Barstow Printer: A Personal Name and Subject Index to the Years 1910-1920, 1985; (ed. with M. Bloomberg) Stalin: An Annotated Guide to Books in English, 1993; (with M. Bloomberg) The Jewish Holocaust: An Annotated Guide to Books in English, 2nd ed., 1995; World War I: A Cataloging Reference Guide, 1995; Churchill: An Annotated Guide to Books in English, 1998; World War II: A Cataloging Reference Guide, 1998; Churchill: A Concise Bibliography, 2000. Contributor to periodicals. **Address:** Pfau Library, California State University, 5500 University Pkwy., San Bernardino, CA 92407-2397, U.S.A. **Online address:** bbarrett@csusb.edu

BARRETT, Charles Kingsley. *See* Obituaries.

BARRETT, David M(arshall). American (born United States), b. 1951. **Genres:** History, Politics/Government, Biography. **Career:** WLOI-Radio, news director, 1974; WNIT Public Television, public affairs director, 1975-84; University of Wisconsin, visiting assistant professor of political science, 1989-90; Villanova University, assistant professor of political science, 1990-. Writer. **Publications:** (Contrib.) Making of U.S. Foreign Policy, 1990; Uncertain Warriors: Lyndon Johnson and His Vietnam Advisers, 1993; (ed.) Lyndon Johnson's Vietnam Papers: A Documentary Collection, 1997; CIA & Congress: The Untold Story from Truman to Kennedy, 2005. Contributor of articles to journals. Works appear in anthologies. **Address:** Department of Political Science, Villanova University, Rm. 262, Liberal Arts, St. Augustine Ctr., 800 Lancaster Ave., Villanova, PA 19085, U.S.A. **Online address:** david.barrett@villanova.edu

BARRETT, James R. American (born United States), b. 1950. **Genres:** Novels. **Career:** North Carolina State University, assistant professor of history, 1981-84; University of North Carolina, visiting assistant professor of history, 1983-84; University of Illinois, associate professor, professor of history, 1984-, associate chair, 1987-89, chair, director of graduate studies, 1991-93, chair, 1997-2000, professor of African American studies. Writer. **Publications:** (With S. Nelson and R. Ruck) Steve Nelson, American Radical, 1981; Work and Community in The Jungle: Chicago's Packing House Workers, 1894-1922, 1987; (and intro.) The Jungle, 1988; William Z. Foster and the Tragedy of American Radicalism, 1999; (and intro.) The Spirit of Labor, 2004; Irish Way: Becoming American in the Multi-ethnic City, 2012. Contributor to books. **Address:** Department of History, University of Illinois, 304A Gregory Hall, 810 S Wright St., Po Box 466, Urbana, IL 61801, U.S.A. **Online address:** jrbarret@illinois.edu

BARRETT, John G(ilchrist). American (born United States), b. 1921. **Genres:** History, Biography, Military/Defense/Arms Control, Autobiography/Memoirs. **Career:** Virginia Military Institute, instructor, 1953-56, assistant professor, 1956-58, associate professor, 1958-63, professor of history, 1963-87, professor emeritus, 1987-. Writer. **Publications:** Sherman's March through the Carolinas, 1956; North Carolina as a Civil War Battleground, 1861-1865, 1960; The Civil War in North Carolina, 1963; (with J.S. Moore) History of Manly Memorial Baptist Church, 1841-1966, 1966; So Much Water, So Little Land: Life in World War II's Waterbug Navy, 2001. EDITOR: (with R.K. Turner, Jr.) Letters of a New Market Cadet, 1961, 2nd ed., 2006; (and intro.) Yankee Rebel: The Civil War Journal of Edmund Dewitt Patterson, 1966; (with W.B. Yearns) North Carolina Civil War Documentary, 1980. CONTRIBUTOR: Writing Southern History, 1965; Perspectives in South Carolina History, the First 300 Years, 1973; North Carolina Government, 1585-1974: A Narrative and Statistical History, 1975; The Cincinnati-Dance Lectures on the American Revolution, 1976; Encyclopedia of Southern History, 1980; Dictionary of North Carolina Biography, 1980. Contributor to journals and newspapers. **Address:** Virginia Military Institute, 201 Smith Holw, Lexington, VA 24450-6639, U.S.A.

BARRETT, Joyce Durham. American (born United States), b. 1943. **Genres:** Novels, Children's Fiction, Natural History, Biography. **Career:** Pickens Sentinel, reporter, 1980-83; Tri-County Technical College, instructor in English, 1982; Easley Progress, reporter, 1983; Clemson University, Department of News Services, editor, 1983-86; Friends of the Arts of Pickens County, secretary, 1986; Lamar County Elementary School, author-in-residence, 1989-92; Gordon College, teacher of creative writing, 1993-; Heart of Georgia Resa, visiting author, 1990. **Publications:** JUVENILE FICTION: Willie's Not the Hugging Kind, 1989; Gift of the White Dolphin, 1998; After the Flood, 1998. ADULT FICTION: Quiet Crazy: A Novel, 1993; A Day in the Blue Ridge Mountains, 1995. Contributor to magazines. **Address:** 39 Ninety-Two Pl., Griffin, GA 30223, U.S.A. **Online address:** jbarr92371@aol.com

BARRETT, Julia. *See* **KESSLER, Julia Braun.**

BARRETT, Lorna. *See* **BARTLETT, L. L.**

BARRETT, Mark. British (born England), b. 1957. **Genres:** Theology/Religion, Young Adult Fiction. **Career:** Benedictine Abbey of Our Lady Help of Christians, monk. Writer. **Publications:** Crossing: Reclaiming the Landscape of Our Lives, 2002, 2nd ed., 2008. **Address:** Morehouse Publishing, PO Box 1321, Harrisburg, PA 17105, U.S.A. **Online address:** abbey@worth.org.uk

BARRETT, Michèle. British (born England), b. 1949?. **Genres:** Adult Non-fiction, Politics/Government. **Career:** City University London, teacher of humanities and social science; University of London, Queen Mary College, Department of English, professor of modern literary and cultural theory. Writer. **Publications:** NON-FICTION: (intro.) Women and Writing, 1979 in US as (ed. and intro.) Virginia Woolf: Women and Writing, 1980; Women's Oppression Today: Problems in Marxist Feminist Analysis, 1980, rev. ed. as Women's Oppression Today: The Marxist/Feminist Encounter, 1988; (with M. McIntosh) The Anti-social Family, 1982, 2nd ed., 1991; The Politics of Truth: From Marx to Foucault, 1991; Imagination in Theory: Culture, Writing, Words, and Things, 1999; (with D. Barrett) Star Trek: The Human Frontier, 2001; Casualty Figures: How Five Men Survived the First World War, 2007. EDITOR: NON-FICTION: (co-ed.) Ideology and Cultural Production, 1979; (with R. Hamilton) The Politics of Diversity: Feminism, Marxism, and Nationalism, 1986; (with A. Phillips) Destabilizing Theory: Contemporary Feminist Debates, 1992; (with B. Baker) Bobby Baker: Redeeming Features of Daily Life, 2007. **Address:** Department of English, Queen Mary College, University of London, Mile End Rd., London, GL E1 4NS, England. **Online address:** m.barrett@qmul.ac.uk

BARRETT, Nancy Smith. American (born United States), b. 1942. **Genres:** Economics, Politics/Government. **Career:** American University, Department of Economics, instructor, 1966-67, assistant professor, 1967-70, associate professor, 1970-74, professor, 1974-88, department chair, 1974-75, 1983-89; University of Gothenburg, visiting professor, 1973; Congressional Budget Office, Fiscal Analysis, deputy assistant director and deputy director, 1975-76; Carter-Mondale Transition, staff, 1976-77; Council of Economic Advisers, senior staff, 1977; The Urban Institute, principal research associate, 1977-79; Department of Labor, Policy, Evaluation and Research, deputy assistant secretary, 1979-81; Farleigh Dickinson University, Samuel J. Silberman College of Business Administration, dean, 1989-91; Western Michigan University, provost and vice president for academic affairs, 1991-96; University of Alabama, provost and vice president for academic affairs, 1996-2003; Wayne State University, provost and senior vice president for academic affairs, 2003-10, professor of economics, 2010-. Writer. **Publications:** The Theory of Macroeconomic Policy, 1972, 2nd ed., 1975; (with G. Gerardi and T.P. Hart) Prices and Wages in U.S. Manufacturing: A Factor Analysis, 1973. **Address:** Department of Economics, Wayne State University, 2133 Faculty/Administration Bldg., 4841 Cass Ave., 2155 Old Main, Detroit, MI 48202-3622, U.S.A. **Online address:** nancy.barrett@wayne.edu

BARRETT, Tracy. American (born United States), b. 1955. **Genres:** Children's Fiction, Young Adult Fiction, Children's Non-fiction. **Career:** Vanderbilt University, senior lecturer in Italian, 1984-. Writer. **Publications:** NON-FICTION FOR CHILDREN: Nat Turner and the Slave Revolt, 1993; Harpers Ferry: The Story of John Brown's Raid, 1994; Growing Up in Colonial America, 1995; Virginia, 1997; Tennessee, 1998; Kidding around Nashville: What to Do, Where to Go, and How to Have Fun in Nashville, 1998; Kentucky, 1999; The Trail of Tears: An American Tragedy, 2000; The Ancient Greek World, 2004; The Ancient Chinese World, 2005. FICTION FOR CHILDREN AND YOUNG ADULTS: The Reading Works, 1975; Anna of Byzantium, 1999; Cold in Summer, 2003; On Etruscan Time, 2005; The 100-Year-Old Secret, 2008; The Beast of Blackslope, 2009; King of Ithaka, 2010; The Case That Time Forgot, 2010. OTHER: (trans. and intro.) C. Angiolieri, Cecco, as I Am and Was: The Poems of Cecco Angiolieri, 1994. **Address:** Department of French and Italian, Vanderbilt University, 2301 Vanderbilt Pl., Ste. 356312, VU Sta. B, Nashville, TN 37235-6312, U.S.A. **Online address:** tracy.barrett@vanderbilt.edu

BARRIE, Alexander. British/German (born Germany), b. 1923. **Genres:** Children's Fiction, Children's Non-fiction, History, Transportation, Military/Defense/Arms Control. **Career:** Municipal Journal, assistant technical editor, 1951-53; New Liberty, assistant editor, 1953; Maclean Hunter Publishing Co., managing editor, editor, 1953-56; freelance writer, 1956-; House Information Services Ltd., managing director, 1970-86; Alexander Barrie Associates, principal, 1986-89. **Publications:** War Underground, 1961; Guide to Light Aircraft, 1973; Fly for Three Lives, 1974; Operation Midnight, 1974; Let Them All Starve, 1974; (with R.G. Smith) Aspro-How a Family Business Grew Up, 1976; Jonathan Kane's Jungle Run, 1977; Jonathan Kane Climbs High, 1978; Jonathan Kane Flares Out, 1978; Ben Goes for Gold, 1991; Flight: Age of Travel, 1994; Ships and Boats, 1994; Prehistoric World, 1995; War Underground: The Tunnellers of the Great War, 2000. Contributor to magazines. **Address:** 33 Manor Way, London, GL SE3 9XG, England.

BARRIE, Thomas (Matthew). American (born United States), b. 1955. **Genres:** Architecture, Urban Studies. **Career:** Architectural Resources Cambridge Inc., architect, 1980; Huygens and DiMella Inc., architect, 1981-83; Payette Associates Inc., architect, 1983-87; Roger Williams University, adjunct professor of design, 1987-90, 1993; Thomas Barrie Architects, architect, 1987-90, 1993-; Oasis Studio Inc., co-director, 1988-90; Boston Architectural Center, instructor in drawing, 1990; Manchester Metropolitan University, visiting lecturer, 1990-91; Victoria University of Manchester, visiting lecturer, 1991-92; Lawrence Technological University, associate professor of design, history and theory of architecture, professor, 1993-2002, head of faculty council, 1997-, Detroit Studio, founder, co-ordinator, 1999-2002; North Carolina State University, professor of architecture, 2002-, School of Architecture, director, 2002-07; Journal of Architectural Education, co-editor, 2008; Architecture, Culture and Spirituality, co-editor, 2009. **Publications:** Spiritual Path, Sacred Place: Myth, Ritual and Meaning in Architecture, 1996; The Sacred In-between: The Mediating Roles of Architecture, 2010. Contributor of articles to journals and periodicals. **Address:** School of Architecture, North Carolina State University, College of Design, 305-A Brooks Hall, PO Box 7701, Raleigh, NC 27695-7701, U.S.A. **Online address:** tom_barrie@ncsu.edu

BARRISH, Phillip. American (born United States), b. 1963?. **Genres:** Literary Criticism And History, History. **Career:** University of Texas, associate professor of English. Writer and literary critic. **Publications:** American Literary Realism, Critical Theory, and Intellectual Prestige, 1880-1995, 2001; White Liberal Identity, Literary Pedagogy, and Classic American Realism, 2005. Contributor of articles to journals. **Address:** Department of English, University of Texas, 1 University Sta. B5000, Austin, TX 78712, U.S.A. **Online address:** pbarrish@mail.utexas.edu

BARRON, Judy. American (born United States), b. 1939. **Genres:** Medicine/Health, Children's Non-fiction, Biography, Medicine/Health. **Career:** Road manager for performer Maureen Mcgovern, 1978-. Writer. **Publications:** (With S. Barron) There's a Boy in Here, 1992; I Want To Learn To Fly!, in Spanish as (with M. McGovern) Volar Yo Quiero, 1995. **Address:** c/o Jed Mattes, 200 W 22nd St., Ste. 50, New York, NY 10023, U.S.A.

BARRON, Laird. American (born United States), b. 1970?. **Genres:** Novellas/Short Stories, Novels. **Career:** Melic Review, managing editor. **Publications:** The Imago Sequence and Other Stories, 2007; Occultation, 2010; The Light is the Darkness, 2011; The Croning, 2012. Works appear in anthologies. Contributor to magazines. **Address:** Night Shade Books, 1661 Tennessee St., Ste. 3H, San Francisco, CA 94107, U.S.A. **Online address:** llairdsbarron@msn.com

BARRON, Stephanie. American (born United States), b. 1950. **Genres:** Art/Art History, Young Adult Fiction. **Career:** Solomon R. Guggenheim Museum, intern and curatorial assistant, 1971-72; Toledo Museum of Art, National Education Association, intern in education, 1973-74; Jewish Museum, exhibition coordinator, 1975-76; Los Angeles County Museum of Art, associate curator of modern art, 1976-80, curator, 1980-94, coordinator of curatorial affairs, 1993-96, senior curator of modern and contemporary art, 1995-, vice president of education and public programs, 1996-. Writer. **Publications:** California, 5 Footnotes to Modern Art History, 1977; (with M. Tuchman) Seven Artists in Israel, 1948-1978, 1978; The Museum as Site: Sixteen Projects, 1981; German Expressionist Sculpture, 1983; Gallery Guides to the Collection of Modern Art, 1987; German Expressionism 1915-1925: The Second Generation, 1988; (with M. Tuchman) David Hockney: A Retrospective, 1988; German Expressionist Prints and Drawings, 2 vols., 1989; (contrib.) German Expressionism: Documents from the End of the Wilhelmine Empire to the Rise of National Socialism, 1993; Exiles and Emigrés: The Flight of European Artists from Hitler, 1997; (with S. Bernstein and I.S. Fort) Made in California: Art, Image and Identity, 1900-2000, 2001; (with L. Zelevansky) Jasper Johns to Jeff Koons: Four Decades of Art from the Broad Collections, 2001; (with M. Draguet) Magritte and Contemporary Art: The Treachery of Images, 2006; (with S. Eckmann) Kunst und Kalter Krieg Deutsche Positionen 1945-89, 2009; (with S. Eckmann) Art of Two Germanys-Cold War Cultures, 2009. EDITOR: (with M. Tuchman) The Avant-Garde in Russia, 1910-1930: New Perspectives, 1980; German Expressionism 1915-1925: The Second Generation, 1988; Degenerate Art: The Fate of the Avant-Garde in Nazi Germany, 1991; (with W.D. Dube) German Expressionism: Art and Society, 1997; (with S. Bernstein and I.S. Fort and intro.) Reading California: Art, Image and Identity, 1900-2000, 2000, Contributor to books and periodicals. **Address:** Los Angeles County Museum of Art, 5905 Wilshire Blvd., Los Angeles, CA 90036, U.S.A. **Online address:** sbarron@lacma.org

BARRON, T. A. American (born United States), b. 1952. **Genres:** Novels, Children's Fiction, Young Adult Fiction, Natural History, Politics/Government, Popular Culture, Self Help, Young Adult Non-fiction, Picture/Board Books. **Career:** Venture Capital Firm, president; Sierra Ventures, general partner; Swiss Army Corp., chairman, through 1989; full-time writer, 1989-. **Publications:** Heartlight, 1990, rev. ed., 2003; The Ancient One, 1992, rev. ed., 2004; To Walk in Wilderness: A Rocky Mountain Journal, 1993; The Merlin Effect, 1994, rev. ed., 2004; (contrib.) Rocky Mountain National Park: A 100 Year Perspective, 1995; The Lost Years of Merlin, 1996, rev. ed., 1999; The Seven Songs of Merlin, 1997, rev. ed., 2000; The Fires of Merlin, 1998; The Mirror of Merlin, 1999, rev. ed., 2001; Where is Grandpa?, 1999; The Wings of Merlin, 2000, rev. ed., 2002; T.A. Barron Collection, 2001; Tree Girl, 2001; The Hero's Trail: A Guide for a Heroic Life, 2002; Child of the Dark Prophecy, 2003; High as a Hawk: A Brave Girl's Historic Climb, 2004; Shadows on the Stars, 2005; The Eternal Flame, 2006; Day the Stones Walked: A Fate of Easter Island, 2007; Merlin's Dragon: Basilgarrad, 2008; Doomraga's Revenge, 2009; Ultimate Magic, 2010; Ghost Hands: A Story Inspired by Patagonia's Cave of the Hands, 2011; Merlin: The Book of Magic, 2011. Contributor to periodicals. **Address:** Boulder Book Store, 1107 Pearl St., Boulder, CO 80302-5103, U.S.A.

BARRON-TIEGER, Barbara. American (born United States) **Genres:** Business/Trade/Industry, Film, Psychology, Self Help. **Career:** Author, consultant and trainer. **Publications:** WITH P.D. TIEGER: Do What You Are: Discover the Perfect Career for You through the Secrets of Personality Type, 1992, 4th ed., 2007; The Personality Type Tool Kit: The Career Professional's Guide to Do What You Are, 1995; Nurture by Nature: Understand Your Child's Personality Type-and Become a Better Parent, 1997; The Art of Speedreading People: Harness the Power of Personality Type and Create What You Want in Business and in Life, 1998 as The Art of Speedreading People: How to Size People Up and Speak Their Language, 1999; Just Your Type: Create the Relationship You've Always Wanted Using the Secrets of Personality Type, 2000. Contributor to periodicals. **Address:** Personality-Type.com, 20 Beverly Rd., West Hartford, CT 06119, U.S.A. **Online address:** info@personalitytype.com

BARROW, G. W. S. Scottish/British (born England), b. 1924. **Genres:** History. **Career:** University of London, University College, assistant lecturer in history, 1950-61; University of Newcastle upon Tyne, Kings College, professor of medieval history, 1961-74; University of St. Andrews, professor of Scottish history, 1974-79; Oxford University, Ford's Lecturer, 1977; University of Edinburgh, Sir William Fraser Professor of Scottish History and Paleography, 1979-92, professor emeritus, 1992-, School of History, Classics and Archaeology, honorary professorial fellow; Society of Antiquaries of Scotland, Rhind Lecturer, 1985. Writer. **Publications:** Scottish Rulers and the Religious Orders, 1070-1153, 1953; Feudal Britain: The Completion of the Medieval Kingdoms, 1066-1314, 1956; Acts of Malcolm IV, King of Scots, 1153-1165, 1960; Robert Bruce and the Community of the Realm of Scotland, 1965, 4th ed., 2005; (ed.) Acts of William I, King of Scots, 1165-1214, 1971; The Kingdom of the Scots: Government, Church and Society from the Eleventh to the Fourteenth Century, 1973, 2nd ed., 2003; (ed.) The Scottish Tradition: Essays in Honor of Ronald Gordon Cant, 1974; The Anglo-Norman Era in Scottish History, 1980; Kingship and Unity: Scotland, 1000-1306, 1981, 2nd ed., 2003; Robert the Bruce and the Scottish Identity, 1984; Scotland and Its Neighbours in the Middle Ages, 1992; (contrib.) Why Scottish History Matters, 1997; (ed.) The Charters of King David I: The Written Acts of David I King of Scots, 1124-53 and of His Son Henry Earl of Northumberland, 1139-52, 1999; (ed. as Geoffery Barrow) Declaration of Arbroath: History, Significance, Setting, 2003; St Ninian and Pictomania, 2004. Contributor to journals. **Address:** School of History, Classics and Archaeology, University of Edinburgh, Rm. 1M.30, William Robertson Wing, Doorway 4, Teviot Pl., Old Medical School, Edinburgh, EH8 9AG, Scotland. **Online address:** scottish.history@ed.ac.uk

BARROW, John D(avid). British (born England), b. 1952. **Genres:** Astronomy, Geography. **Career:** Ealing Grammar School, teacher, 1964-71; Durham University, Van Mildert College, faculty, 1971-74; Oxford University, Magdalen College, Department of Astrophysics, faculty, 1974-77, junior research lecturer, 1978-80; University of California, Department of Astronomy, Lindemann fellow, 1977-78, Department of Physics, Miller fellow, 1980-81; University of Sussex, Astronomy Centre, lecturer, 1981-88, senior lecturer, 1988-89, reader, 1989, professor, 1989-99, acting director, 1989-90, director, 1995-99, Nuffield Foundation Science Fellow, 1986-87, Royal Society Leverhulme fellow, 1992-93, PPARC senior fellow, 1994-99; University of Cambridge, Department of Applied Mathematics and Theoretical Physics, professor of mathematical sciences, 1999-, Millennium Mathematics Project, director, 1999-, Clare Hall, professorial fellow, 1999-, vice president, 2004-07; Gresham College, Gresham professor of astronomy, 2003-07, emeritus professor of astronomy, 2007-08, fellow, 2007-10, Gresham professor of geometry, 2008-; British Science Association, Physics and Astronomy Section, president, 2008-09. Writer. **Publications:** (With J. Silk) The Left Hand of Creation: The Origin and Evolution of the Expanding Universe, 1983; (with F. Tipler and M. Monchicourt) L'Homme et le Cosmos, 1984; (with F.J. Tipler) The Anthropic Cosmological Principle, 1986; The World within the World, 1988; Theories of Everything, 1991, 2nd ed. as New Theories of Everything: The Quest for Ultimate Explanation, 2007; (ed. with L. Mestel and P.A. Thomas) Texas/ESO-CERN Symposium on Relativistic Astrophysics, Cosmology, and Fundamental Physics, 1991; Pi in the Sky, 1992; The Origin of the Universe, 1994; The Artful Universe, 1995; Impossibility: The Limits of Science and the Science of Limits, 1998; Perché il Mondo è Matematico?, 1998; (contrib.) Limiti e frontiere della scienza, 1999; Between Inner Space and Outer Space, 1999; The Universe that Discovered Itself, 2000; The Book of Nothing, 2000; The Constants of Nature, 2002; (ed. with P.C.W. Davies and C.L. Harper, Jr.) Science and Ultimate Reality: Quantum Theory, Cosmology, and Complexity, 2004; The Infinite Book: A Short Guide to the Boundless, Timeless, and Endless, 2005; The Artful Universe Expanded, 2005; Cosmic Imagery: Key Images in the History of Science, 2008; (co-ed.) Fitness of the Cosmos for Life: Biochemistry and Fine-Tuning, 2008; 100 Essential Things You Didn't Know You Didn't Know: Math Explains Your World, 2009; The Book of Universes in US as The Book of Universes: Exploring the Limits of the Cosmos, 2011. Contributor of articles to books and journals. **Address:** Department of Applied Mathematics & Theoretical, Physics, Centre for Mathematical Sciences, Cambridge University, Wilberforce Rd., Cambridge, CB CB3 0WA, England. **Online address:** j.d.barrow@damtp.cam.ac.uk

BARROW, Robin (St. Clair). Canadian/British (born England), b. 1944. **Genres:** Classics, Education, History, Philosophy, Social Sciences, Sociology. **Career:** City of London School for Boys, assistant master in classics, 1969-72; University of Leicester, lecturer, 1972-80, reader in philosophy of education, 1980-85; Simon Fraser University, professor of education, 1982-, dean of education, 1990-2002, dean of applied science, chair of Hellenic studies, dean of arts. Writer. **Publications:** Athenian Democracy, 1973; Moral Philosophy for Education, 1975; (with R.G. Woods) An Introduction to Philosophy of Education, 1975, 5th ed., 2007; Plato, Utilitarianism and Education, 1975; Sparta, 1975; Common Sense and the Curriculum, 1976; Greek and Roman Education, 1976; Plato and Education, 1976; Plato's Apology: A Philosophical Commentary, 1976; Radical Education: A Critique of Free Schooling and Deschooling, 1978; The Canadian Curriculum: A Personal View, 1979; Happiness and Schooling, 1980; The Philosophy of Schooling, 1981; Injustice, Inequality and Ethics: A Philosophical Introduction to Moral Problems, 1982; Language and Thought, 1982; Giving Teaching Back to Teachers: A Critical Introduction to Curriculum Theory, 1984; (with G. Milburn) Critical Dictionary of Educational Concepts: An Appraisal of Selected Ideas and Issues in Educational Theory and Practice, 1986, 2nd ed., 1990; Understanding Skills: Thinking, Feeling and Caring, 1990; Utilitarianism: A Contemporary Statement, 1991; Language, Intelligence and Thought, 1993; (ed. with P. White) Beyond Liberal Education: Essays in Honour of Paul H. Hirst, 1993; Ring Some Alarm Bells in Ontario: Reactions to the Report of the Royal Commission on Learning, 1996; What Use in Educational Research? A Debate, 2006; (ed. with P. Keeney) Academic Ethics, 2006; Introduction to Moral Philosophy and Moral Education, 2007; Plato, 2007. **Address:** Faculty of Education, Simon Fraser University, 8888 University Dr., Burnaby, BC V5A 1S6, Canada. **Online address:** robin_barrow@sfu.ca

BARRUS, Tim. *See* **NASDIJJ.**

BARRY, Dave. American (born United States), b. 1947. **Genres:** Social Commentary, Humor/Satire, Novels. **Career:** Miami Herald, columnist, 1983-2005, syndicated newspaper, columnist. **Publications:** Taming of the Screw: Several Million Homeowner's Problems Sidestepped, 1983; Babies and Other Hazards of Sex: How to Make a Tiny Person in Only Nine Months with Tools You Probably Have around the Home, 1984; Bad Habits: A 100% Fact Free Book, 1985; Stay Fit and Healthy Until You're Dead, 1985; Claw Your Way to the Top: How to Become the Head of a Major Corporation in Roughly a Week, 1986; Dave Barry's Guide to Marriage and/or Sex, 1987; Dave Barry's Greatest Hits, 1988; Homes and Other Black Holes: The Happy Homeowner's Guide to Ritual Closing Ceremonies, Newton's First Law of Furniture Buying, the Lethal Chemicals Man, and Other Perils of the American Dream, 1988; Dave Barry Slept Here: A Sort of History of the United States, 1989; Dave Barry Turns 40, 1990; Dave Barry Talks Back, 1991; Dave Barry's Only Travel Guide You'll Ever Need, 1991; Dave Barry Does Japan=Deibu Barī ga Nihon o suru, 1992; Dave Barry is Not Making This Up, 1994; Dave Barry's Gift Guide to End all Gift Guides, 1994; World According to Dave Barry, 1994; Dave Barry's Complete Guide to Guys: A Fairly Short Book, 1995; Dave Barry in Cyberspace, 1996; Dave Barry is from Mars and Venus, 1997; Dave Barry's Book of Bad Songs, 1997; (co-author) Naked Came the Manatee, 1997; Dave Barry Turns 50, 1998; Big Trouble, 1999; (co-author) The Putt at the End of the World, 2000; Dave Barry is Not Taking This Sitting Down, 2000; Dave Barry Hits Below the Beltway, 2001; My Teenage Son's Goal in Life is to Make Me Feel 3, 500 Years Old: And Other Thoughts on Parenting from Dave Barry, 2001; Greatest Invention in the History of Mankind is Beer: And Other Manly Insights from Dave Barry, 2001; Dave Barry Hits below the Beltway: A Vicious and Unprovoked Attack on Our most Cherished Political Institutions, 2001; Tricky Business, 2002; Boogers Are My Beat: More Lies, but Some Actual Journalism, 2003; (with R. Pearson) Peter and the Starcatchers, 2004; (with R. Pearson) Missing Mermaid: A Neverland Island Book, 2005; Shepherd, the Angel, and Walter the Christmas Miracle Dog, 2006; (with R. Pearson) Peter and the Shadow Thieves, 2006; Dave Barry's Money Secrets: Like, Why is There a Giant Eyeball on the Dollar?, 2006; (with R. Pearson) Peter and the Secret of Rundoon, 2007; Dave Barry's History of the Millennium, 2007; Dave Barry on Dads, 2007; Cave of the Dark Wind: A Never Land Book, 2007; Science Fair: A Story of Mystery, Danger, International Suspense, and a Very Nervous Frog, 2008; Blood Tide: A Never Land Book, 2008; (with R. Pearson) Peter and the Sword of Mercy, 2009; I'll Mature When I'm Dead: Dave Barry's Amazing Tales of Adulthood, 2010; The Bridge to Never Land, 2011; Lunatics, 2012. **Address:** The Miami Herald, 1 Herald Plz., Miami, FL 33132-1609, U.S.A. **Online address:** nolowflow@davebarry.com

BARRY, James P(otvin). American (born United States), b. 1918. **Genres:** Environmental Sciences/Ecology, History, Marine Sciences/Oceanography, Social Sciences, Geography, Photography. **Career:** U.S. Army, artillery, colonel, 1940-66; photographer and book illustrator, 1968-; Capital University, administrator, 1967-71; freelance writer and editor, 1971-77; Ohioana Library Association, director, 1977-, Ohioana Quarterly, editor, 1977-88; Inland Seas, senior editor, 1984-. **Publications:** Georgian Bay: The Sixth Great Lake, 1968, 3rd ed., 1995; The Battle of Lake Erie, 1970; Bloody Kansas, 1985-65, 1972; The Noble Experiment, 1919-1933, 1972; The Fate of the Lakes: A Portrait of the Great Lakes, 1972; The Louisiana Purchase, 1973; Henry Ford and Mass Production, 1973; Ships of the Great Lakes: 300 Years of Navigation, 1973, rev. ed. 1996; The Berlin Olympics, 1936, 1975; The Great Lakes, 1976; Lake Erie, 1980; Wrecks and Rescues of the Great Lakes, 1981, 2nd ed., 1994; Georgian Bay: An Illustrated History, 1992; Old Forts of the Great Lakes: Sentinels in the Wilderness, 1994; Hackercraft, 2002; American Powerboats, 2003. Contributor of articles to journals and magazines. **Address:** 353 Fairway Blvd., Columbus, OH 43213, U.S.A.

BARRY, John M. American (born United States), b. 1947. **Genres:** Documentaries/Reportage, Young Adult Non-fiction. **Career:** Writer. **Publications:** Opportunities in Journalism Careers, 1967; The Ambition and the Power: A True Story of Washington, 1989; (with S.A. Rosenberg) The Transformed Cell: Unlocking the Mysteries of Cancer, 1992; Nautical Research Journal, Index of Volumes 1-40, 1996; Rising Tide: The Great Mississippi Flood of 1927 and How It Changed America, 1997; Power Plays: Politics, Football, and Other Blood Sports, 2001; The Great Influenza: The Epic Story of the Deadliest Plague in History, 2004; Roger Williams and The Creation of the American Soul: Church, State, and the Birth of Liberty, 2012. Contributor to periodicals. **Address:** c/o Rafael Sagalyn, 7201 Wisconsin Ave., Bethesda, MD 20814, U.S.A. **Online address:** jbarry@tulane.edu

BARRY, Kathleen M. British (born England), b. 1970. **Genres:** History, Humanities. **Career:** Gilder Lehrman Institute of American History, coordinator of special projects and publications; University of Cambridge, faculty of American history, Mellon research fellow in American history; New York University, faculty of American history, fellow, 2003-06. Writer. **Publications:** Femininity in Flight: A History of Flight Attendants, 2007. **Address:** London, GL , England. **Online address:** barry@femininityinflight.com

BARRY, Michael. American (born United States), b. 1948?. **Genres:** Art/Art History, Biography, Autobiography/Memoirs, History. **Career:** International Federation for Human Rights, Afghan affairs observer, 1979-85; Médecins du Monde, coordinating officer, 1985-89; United Nations, consultant and humanitarian team leader, 1989-91; Princeton University, Department of Near Eastern Studies, lecturer, 2004-; Metropolitan Museum of Art, Department of Islamic Art, chairman, consultative chairman, 2005-08. Writer. **Publications:** Afghanistan, 1974; Royaume de l'insolence: la résistance afghane du Grand Moghol à l'invasion soviétique, 1984, 3rd ed. as Le Royaume de l'insolence: l'Afghanistan, 1504-2001, 2002; (contrib.) Design and Color in Islamic Architecture: Eight Centuries of the Tile-Maker's Art, 1996; (trans.) N.H. Paykar, Seven Icons, (title means: 'Le Pavillon des sept princesses'), 2000; Massoud (biography), 2002; Figurative Art in Medieval Islam and the Riddle of Bihzâd of Herât (1465-1535), 2004; A History of Modern Afghanistan, 2004. Contributor to periodicals. **Address:** Department of Near Eastern Studies, Princeton University, 10 Dillon Ct. W, 110 Jones Hall, Princeton, NJ 08544-1008, U.S.A. **Online address:** mbarry@princeton.edu

BARRY, P(atricia) S(teepee). Canadian/American (born United States), b. 1926. **Genres:** Poetry, Songs/Lyrics And Libretti, Anthropology/Ethnology, Art/Art History, History, Literary Criticism And History, Military/Defense/Arms Control. **Career:** Rochester Democrat and Chronicle, journalist, 1943-53; Cornell University, School of Industrial and Labor Relations, research assistant; University of Alberta, instructor in English, 1968-69, 1974-75. Researcher. **Publications:** The King in Tudor Drama, 1977; The Canol Project: An Adventure of the U.S. War Department in Canada's Northwest, 1985, rev. ed., 1998; Snow Geese of the Western Arctic, 1958-1983, 1985; Mystical Themes in Milk River Rock Art, 1991. Contributor to periodicals. **Address:** 14322 Ravine Dr., Edmonton, AB T5N 3M3, Canada.

BARRY, Robert Everett. American (born United States), b. 1931. **Genres:** Children's Fiction, Education, Mystery/Crime/Suspense, Animals/Pets. **Career:** Pava Prints, partner, 1957-63; Averett College, instructor, 1967-68; Texas Woman's University, instructor in art, 1968-69; University of Massachusetts, professor, 1969-96, professor emeritus, 1996-, now retired. Writer. **Publications:** This is the Story of Faint George Who Wanted to be a knight, 1957; Just Pepper, 1958; Boo, 1957; Next Please, 1961; Mr. Willowby's Christmas Tree, 1963; The Musical Palm Tree, 1965; Animals Around the World, 1967; The Riddle of Castle Hill, 1968; Ramon and the Pirate Gull, 1971; Snowman's Secret, 1975. **Address:** Doubleday Books for Young Readers, 1745 Broadway, 10th Fl., New York, NY 10019, U.S.A.

BARRY, Spranger. *See* **KAUFFMANN, Stanley.**

BARRY, Susan R. American (born United States), b. 1954. **Genres:** Sciences, Biography. **Career:** University of Miami, Medical School, research neuroscientist; University of Michigan, research neuroscientist; National Aeronautics and Space Administration, Johnson's Space Center, research neuroscientist, Marine Biological Laboratory, research neuroscientist; Mount Holyoke College, Department of Biological Sciences, professor of neurobiology, 1992-. Writer. **Publications:** Fixing My Gaze: A Scientist's Journey into Seeing in Three Dimensions, 2009. **Address:** Mount Holyoke College, Rm. 119, Clapp Laboratory, 50 College St., South Hadley, MA 01075, U.S.A.

BARRY, Tom. American (born United States), b. 1950. **Genres:** Economics, Geography, International Relations/Current Affairs, Military/Defense/Arms Control, Politics/Government, Adult Non-fiction. **Career:** Seers Weekly, reporter and editor, 1971-77; Maricopa County Organizing Project, publicity coordinator, 1977; Navajo Times, investigative journalist, reporter, 1978; Inter-Hemispheric Education Resource Center, senior analyst and writer, 1978-, co-founded, 1979, editor, project director; CIP, staff, 2007; Georgetown University, analyst; International Relations Center, policy director. **Publications:** (With B. Wood and D. Preusch) Red Ribbons for Emma, 1981; (with B. Wood and D. Preusch) Dollars and Dictators: A Guide to Central America, 1982, 2nd ed., 1983; (with B. Wood and D. Preusch) The Other Side of Paradise: Foreign Control in the Caribbean, 1984; (with D. Preusch) The Central America Fact Book, 1986; Destabilization of Nicaragua, 1986; El Salvador, The Other War, 1986; Roots of Rebellion: Land and Hunger in Central America, 1987; Conflicto de Baja Intensidad: Un Nuevo Campo de Batalla EnCentroaméica, 1988; (with D. Preusch) The Soft War: The Uses and Abuses of U.S. Economic Aid in Central America, 1988; Guatemala: A Country Guide, 1989, 2nd ed., 1990; Costa Rica: A Country Guide, 1989, 3rd ed., 1991; Belize: A Country Guide, 1989, 2nd ed., 1990; (with R. Garst) Feeding the Crisis: U.S. Food Aid and Farm Policy in Central America, 1990; Honduras: A Country Guide, 1990; Panama: A Country Guide, 1990; El Salvador: A Country Guide, 1990; (with K. Norsworthy) Nicaragua: A Country Guide, 2nd ed., 1990; Central America Inside Out: The Essential Guide to Its Societies, Politics and Economies, 1991; (with D. Vernon) Inside Belize, 1992, 2nd ed., 1995; Inside Guatemala, 1992; (ed.) Mexico: A Country Guide, 1992; (with K. Norsworthy) Inside Honduras, 1993; (with B. Sims) On Foreign Soil: Government Programs in U.S.-Mexico Relations, 1993; (H. Browne and B. Sims) Crossing the Line: U.S.-Mexico Relations in the 1990s, 1993; (H. Browne and B. Sims) Crossing the Line: Immigrants, Economic Integration and Drug Enforcement on the U.S.-Mexico Border, 1994; (with B. Sims) The Challenge of Cross-Border Environmentalism: The U.S.-Mexican Integration, 1994; (with H. Browne and B. Sims) The Great Divide: The Challenge of U.S.-Mexico Relations in the 1990s, 1994; (with H. Browne and B. Sims) For Richer, For Poorer: Shaping U.S.-Mexican Integration, 1994; (with M. Gandásegui, P. Simonson and J. Lindsay-Poland) Inside Panama, 1995; (with K. Murray) Inside El Salvador, 1995; Zapata's Revenge, 1995; (with S. Lara and P. Simonson) Inside Costa Rica, 1995; (with E. Leaver) Next Fifty Years: The United Nations and the United States, 1996; (ed. with M. Honey) Global Focus: A New Foreign Policy Agenda, 1997-1998, 1997; (ed. with M. Honey) Global Focus: U.S. Foreign Policy at the Turn of the Millennium, 2000; Border Wars, 2011. **Address:** Interhemispheric Resource Center, 815 N Black St., PO Box 2178, Silver City, NM 88062-2178, U.S.A. **Online address:** tom@irc-online.org

BARSAMIAN, David. American (born United States) **Genres:** Novels, History, Young Adult Non-fiction, Politics/Government, Social Sciences. **Career:** Bilingual Community Radio Station, program director; Alternative Radio, founder, producer and director, 1978-. Educator and writer. **Publications:** Stenographers to Power: Media and Propaganda, 1992; (contrib.) Future of History: Interviews with David Barsamian, 1999; (contrib.) Eqbal Ahmad, Confronting Empire: Interviews with David Barsamian, 2000; (contrib.) Terrorism: Theirs and Ours, 2001; (with N. Chomsky) Propaganda and the Public Mind: Conversations with Noam Chomsky, 2001; The Decline and Fall of Public Broadcasting, 2001; (with E.W. Said) Culture and Resistance: Conversations with Edward W. Said, 2003; (contrib.) The Checkbook and the Cruise Missile: Conversations with Arundhati Roy, 2004; Louder than Bombs: Interviews from the Progressive Magazine, 2004; (contrib.) Imperial Ambitions: Conversations on the Post-9/11 World, 2005; (with T. Ali) Speaking of Empire and Resistance: Conversations with Tariq Ali, 2005; (with H. Zinn) Original Zinn: Conversations on History and Politics, 2006; Targeting Iran, 2007; (contrib.) What We Say Goes: Conversations on U.S. Power in a Changing World: Interviews with David Barsamian, 2007; (contrib.) The Pen and the Sword: Conversations with Edward Said, 2010. WITH N. CHOMSKY: Chronicles of Dissent: Interviews with David Barsamian, 1992; Prosperous Few and the Restless Many, 1993; Secrets, Lies and Democracy, 1994; Keeping the Rabble in Line: Interviews with David Barsamian, 1994; Pen and the Sword: Conversations with David Barsamian, 1994; Class Warfare: Interviews with David Barsamian, 1996. **Address:** Alternative Radio, PO Box 551, Boulder, CO 80306, U.S.A. **Online address:** dbarsamian@hotmail.com

BARSKY, Robert F(ranklin). Canadian/American (born United States), b. 1961. **Genres:** History, Bibliography, Literary Criticism And History, Humanities, Education, Reference. **Career:** Trans-Canada Social Policy Research Centre, content analysis researcher, 1985-91; Institut quebecois de recherche sur la culture, ethnic studies and refugee studies researcher, 1991-93; Institut national de la recherche scientifique, refugee studies researcher, 1993-95; University of Western Ontario, assistant professor, 1995-98, associate professor of English, 1998-; Yale University, visiting fellow, 2000, Canadian bicentennial visiting professor, 2002-. Writer. **Publications:** (Ed. with M. Holquist) Bakhtin and Otherness, 1991; Budapest Poems for Yzabelle Martineau, 1991; Constructing a Productive Other: Discourse Theory and the Convention Refugee Hearing (refugee study), 1994; Introduction a la theorie litteraire (literary theory), 1997; Noam Chomsky: A Life of Dissent (biography), 1997; Arguing and Justifying (refugee study), 2000; (trans. and intro.) Michel Meyer, Philosophy and the Passions, 2000; Zellig Harris: Linguistics, Zionism, Radical Politics, 2002; (ed. and intro.) Workers Councils, 2003; Dislocations/Relocations: Narratives of Displacement, 2005; The Chomsky Effect: A Radical Works beyond the Ivory Tower, 2007; Zellig Harris: From American Linguistics to Socialist Zionism, 2011. Contributor to periodicals. **Address:** Department of English, University of Western Ontario, Rm. 173, University College, London, ON N6A 3K7, Canada. **Online address:** rbarsky@uwo.ca

BART, Michael. American (born United States) **Genres:** Novellas/Short Stories. **Career:** Writer. **Publications:** (with L. Corona) Until Our Last Breath: A Holocaust Story of Love and Partisan Resistance, 2008. **Address:** Barbara Braun Associates Inc., 151 W 19th St., 4th Fl., New York, NY 10011, U.S.A. **Online address:** untilourlastbreath@roadrunner.com

BARTELL, Karen Hulene. Also writes as Karen West. American (born United States), b. 1948. **Genres:** Food And Wine, Romance/Historical, inspirational/Motivational Literature, Education. **Career:** Bartell Information-services Consulting, consultant and writer, 1984-, documentation project manager and senior technical editor, 2001-04; Soochow University, lecturer, 1992-97; Texas Workforce Commission, technical writer, editor and web-page designer, 1998-99; Motorola and Freescale, technical writer and editor, 2000-01; Cisco, senior technical editor, 2006-09; Kforce Government Solutions, technical writer, 2010-11; Artech for Life Technologies, technical writer, 2011-. **Publications:** AS KAREN WEST: Best of Polish Cooking: Recipes for Entertaining and Special Occasions, 5th ed., 1983; OTHERS: American Business English, 1995; Sovereignty of the Dragons, 1999; Best of Taiwanese Cuisine: Recipes and Menus for Holidays and Special Occasions, 2001; Best of Korean Cuisine, 2002; Fine Filipino Food, 2003; Untimely Partners, 2009; (with K. McLean) Bound for the Methow, 2009. **Address:** c/o Author Mail, Hippocrene Books Inc., 171 Madison Ave., New York, NY 10016, U.S.A. **Online address:** hulene1@austin.rr.com

BARTELS, Larry M. American (born United States), b. 1956. **Genres:** Economics. **Career:** University of Rochester, instructor, 1983, assistant professor, 1984-86, associate professor, 1986-91; Princeton University, 1991-, Woodrow Wilson School, Stuart professor of communications and public affairs, 1991-99, Donald E. Stokes professor of public and international affairs, 1999-. Author. **Publications:** Presidential Primaries and the Dynamics of Public Choice, 1988; (ed. with L. Vavreck) Campaign Reform: Insights and Evidence, 2000; Unequal Democracy: The Political Economy of the New Gilded Age, 2008. Contributor of articles to periodicals and journals. **Address:** Woodrow Wilson School, Princeton University, 212 Robertson Hall, Princeton, NJ 08544-1013, U.S.A. **Online address:** bartels@princeton.edu

BARTH, John (Simmons). American (born United States), b. 1930. **Genres:** Novels, Novellas/Short Stories, Essays, Translations. **Career:** Johns Hopkins University, junior instructor in English, 1951-53, alumni centennial professor of English and creative writing, 1973-95, professor emeritus of English and creative writing, 1995-; Pennsylvania State University, instructor, 1953-56, assistant professor, 1957-60, associate professor, 1960-65; State University of New York, professor, 1965-71, Edward H. Butler professor of English, 1972-73; Boston University, visiting professor, 1972-73. Writer. **Publications:** The Floating Opera, 1956, rev. ed., 1967; The End of the Road, 1958, rev. ed., 1967; The Sot-Weed Factor, 1960, rev. ed., 1980; Giles, Goat-Boy: Or, The Revised New Syllabus, 1966; Lost in the Funhouse: Fiction for Print, Tape, Live Voice, 1968; (contrib.) The Sense of the 60s, 1968; Chimera, 1972; (contrib.) Directions in Literary Criticism, 1973; (co-author) Writer's Choice, 1974; Letters: A Novel, 1979; Todd Andrews to the Author: A Letter from Letters, 1979; Sabbatical: A Romance, 1982; The Literature of Exhaustion, and The Literature of Replenishment, 1982; The Friday Book: Essays and Other Nonfiction, 1984; Don't Count on It: A Note on the Number of the 1001 Nights, 1984; The Tidewater Tales, 1987; Floating Opera and The End of the Road, 1988; The Last Voyage of Somebody the Sailor, 1991; Once Upon a Time: A Floating Opera, 1994; Further Fridays: Essays, Lectures and Other Nonfiction, 1984-1994, 1995; On with the Story, 1996; Coming Soon!!!: A Narrative, 2001; Book of Ten Nights and a Night: Eleven Stories, 2004; Where Three Roads Meet: Novellas, 2005; The Development: Nine Stories, 2008; (trans. and intro.) The Arabian Nights, vol. II: More Marvels and Wonders of the Thousand and One Nights, 2010; Every Third Thought, 2011; Final Fridays, 2012. Contributors to periodicals. **Address:** The Writing Seminars, Johns Hopkins University, 081 Gilman Hall, 3400 N Charles St., Baltimore, MD 21218, U.S.A.

BARTH, Kelly L. American (born United States), b. 1964?. **Genres:** Children's Non-fiction. **Career:** Writer. **Publications:** (Co-author) The Place that Holds Our History: The Missouri Writer's Biennial Anthology, 1990; Birds of Prey, 2000; Snakes, 2001; (with W. Dudley) Attacks on America September 11 2001, 2002; Native Americans of the Northwest Plateau, 2002; (ed.) Human Medical Trials, 2005; Environment, 2005; (ed.) Drug Abuse, 2007; (ed.) Automobiles, 2007; (with R. Winters) Education, 2007; (with U. Kukathas) Domestic Violence, 2008; (ed.) Domestic Violence, 2009; (ed.) Assimilation, 2010. AT ISSUE IN HISTORY SERIES: (ed.) The Delcaration of Independence, 2003; (ed.) The Tianamen Square Massacre, 2003; (ed.) The Rise and Fall of the Taliban, 2005. **Address:** c/o Author Mail, Lucent Books, 10911 Technology Pl., San Diego, CA 92127, U.S.A.

BARTH, R. L. *See* **BARTH, Robert Lawrence.**

BARTH, Robert Lawrence. (R. L. Barth). American (born United States), b. 1947. **Genres:** Poetry, History. **Career:** Writer and poet. **Publications:** AS R.L. BARTH: POETRY: Forced-Marching to the Styx: Vietnam War Poems, 1983; Anniversaries, Hours, and Occasions, 1984; Looking for Peace, 1985; A Soldier's Time: Vietnam War Poems, 1987; Lessons, with Turner Cassity, 1987; (with T. Cassity and W. Hope) Mainstreaming: Poems of Military Life, 1988; Simonides in Vietnam, and Other Epigrams, 1990; Small Arms Fire, 1998; Deeply Dug In, 2003. OTHER: (with S. Barth) A Bibliography of the Published Works of Charles Gullans, 1946-1986, 1986. EDITOR: The Selected Poems of Yvor Winters, 1999; The Selected Letters of Yvor Winters, 2000; The Selected Poems of Janet Lewis, 2000. Contributor to periodicals. **Address:** 3122 Royal Windsor Dr., Edgewood, KY 41017, U.S.A.

BARTHELME, Frederick. American (born United States), b. 1943. **Genres:** Novels, Novellas/Short Stories, Adult Non-fiction, Children's Fiction, Reference, Human Relations/Parenting. **Career:** Kornblee Gallery, assistant director, 1967-68; University of Southern Mississippi, professor of English, 1977-, Center for Writers program, director, 1978-. Writer. **Publications:** Double Down: Reflections on Gambling and Loss, 1999; Trip, 1999. NOVELS: War and War, 1971; Second Marriage, 1984; Tracer, 1985; Two Against One, 1988; Against One, 1989; Natural Selection, 1990; The Brothers, 1993; Painted Desert, 1995; Bob the Gambler, 1997; Elroy, 2003; Waveland: A novel, 2009. SHORT STORIES: Rangoon, 1970; Moon Deluxe, 1983; Chroma, 1987; The Law of Averages: New and Selected Stories, 2000. **Address:** Department of English, The University of Southern Mississippi, 118 College Dr., PO Box 5037, Hattiesburg, MS 39406, U.S.A. **Online address:** frederick.barthelme@usm.edu

BARTHELME, Steve(n). American (born United States), b. 1947. **Genres:** Novels, Novellas/Short Stories, Autobiography/Memoirs, Humor/Satire, Autobiography/Memoirs. **Career:** Texas Observer, review editor, 1972-73; Northeast Louisiana University, instructor, 1984-86; University of Southern Mississippi, faculty, 1986-, professor of English. **Publications:** And He Tells the Little Horse the Whole Story (poetry and stories), 1987; (with F. Barthelme) Double Down: Reflections on Gambling and Loss (memoir), 1999; Early Posthumous Work (essays), 2009; Hush Hush (stories), 2012. Contributor to periodicals and newspapers. **Address:** c/o Andrew Wylie, The Wylie Agency, 250 W 57th St., Ste. 2114, New York, MS 10107, U.S.A. **Online address:** steven.barthelme@usm.edu

BARTHOLET, Elizabeth. American (born United States), b. 1940. **Genres:** Law, Social Commentary. **Career:** President's Commission on Law Enforcement and Administration of Justice, Staff Counsel, 1966-67; National Association for the Advancement of Colored People Legal Defense and Educational Fund Inc., staff attorney, 1968-72; Vera Institute of Justice, counsel, 1972-73; Legal Action Center, founding director and president, 1973-77, board director, 1977-; Society of American Law Teachers, board director, 1977-89; Harvard University, Law School, faculty, 1977-, assistant professor, 1977-83, professor of law, 1983-, Morris Wasserstein professor of law, 1996-, Child Advocacy Program, director, 2004-; Both Ends Burning Campaign Inc., board director, 2010-. Writer. **Publications:** Family Bonds: Adoption and the Politics of Parenting, 1993; Family Bonds: Adoption, Infertility and the New World of Child Protection, 1999; Nobody's Children: Abuse and Neglect, Foster Drift and the Adoption Alternative, 1999. Works appear in anthologies. Contributor of articles to books and journals. **Address:** Law School, Harvard University, Hauser 422, Cambridge, MA 02138, U.S.A. **Online address:** ebarthol@law.harvard.edu

BARTHOLOMEW-FEIS, Dixee R. American (born United States) **Genres:** History. **Career:** Buena Vista University, 1966-, assistant professor, associate professor of history & director of international education. Writer. **Publications:** The OSS and Ho Chi Minh: Unexpected Allies in the War against Japan, 2006. **Address:** Buena Vista University, 610 W 4th St., Storm Lake, IA 50588, U.S.A. **Online address:** bartholomew@bvu.edu

BARTKY, Sandra Lee. American (born United States), b. 1935. **Genres:** Women's Studies And Issues, Philosophy. **Career:** University of Illinois, associate professor of philosophy, 1970-89, professor of philosophy, 1989-, Women's Studies Program, chairman, professor, now professor emeritus of philosophy. Writer. **Publications:** Femininity and Domination: Studies in the Phenomenology of Oppression, 1990; (ed. with N. Fraser) Revaluing French Feminism: Critical Essays on Difference, Agency, and Culture, 1992; Sympathy and Solidarity and Other Essays, 2002. Contributor to journals. **Address:** Department of Philosophy, University of Illinois, M/C 267, 1420 University Hall, 601 S Morgan St., Chicago, IL 60607, U.S.A. **Online address:** bartky@uic.edu

BARTLETT, Anne. Australian (born Australia) **Genres:** Biography, Novels, Children's Fiction, Autobiography/Memoirs, Young Adult Non-fiction. **Career:** University of Adelaide, honorary research fellow. Writer. **Publications:** Willow Grove, 1979; Daisy Bates: Keeper of Totems (biography), 1997; (co-ed.) Iron Lace: An Anthology of Writing by Students from the 1997 Graduate Diploma in Creative Writing the University of Adelaide, 1998; The Aboriginal Peoples of Australia (nonfiction), 2002; (reteller) The Chairman: The Story of Garnett Ian Wilson OAM, 2004; Knitting: A Novel, 2005. **Address:** c/o Joy Harris, Joy Harris Literary Agency Inc., 381 Park Ave. S, Ste. 428, New York, NY 10016, U.S.A. **Online address:** anne@annebartlett.com.au

BARTLETT, Eric George. Welsh (born Wales), b. 1920. **Genres:** Novels, Sports/Fitness, Young Adult Fiction, Mystery/Crime/Suspense. **Career:** Sakura Academy of Judo, instructor, 1953-74; Yudachi School of Judo, instructor, 1977-; writer, 1984-. **Publications:** The Case of the Thirteenth Coach, 1958; The Complete Body Builder, 1961; Judo and Self-Defense: One Hundred Lessons Arranged as a Two-year Practical Course, for Private or Class Study, 1963; Self Defence in the Home, 1967 in US as New Ways of Self Defense, 1968; Basic Judo, 1974; Basic Fitness, 1976; Smoking Flax, 1977; Summer Day at Ajaccio, 1979; Basic Karate, 1980; Weight Training, 1984; Healing without Harm: Pathways to Alternative Medicine, 1985; (with M. Southall) Weight Training for Women, 1986; (with M. Southall) Weight Training for the Over-35s, 1987; World of Sport-Judo, 1988; Strangers in Eden, 1989; Mysterious Stranger, 1990; Jungle Nurse, 1990; Clouded Love, 1991; Beloved Hostage, 1991; Master of Kung Fu, 1991; Traditional Judo, 1996. Contributor of articles to periodicals. **Address:** 5 Bryngwyn Rd., Cardiff, SG CF2 6PQ, Wales.

BARTLETT, Jennifer Losch. American (born United States), b. 1941. **Genres:** Art/Art History, Novels. **Career:** University of Connecticut, instructor in painting, 1968-72; Art Institute of Chicago, visiting artist, 1972; School of Visual Arts, instructor in painting, 1976-. Artist and writer. **Publications:** Cleopatra I-IV, Adventures in Poetry Press, 1971; In the Garden (drawing collection), 1982. Rhapsody, 1985. The History of the Universe (novel), 1985; Air, 24 hours, 1994; Jennifer Bartlett: Important Works, 1974-1995: March 1-April 6, 1996, 1996; Jennifer Bartlett: New Paintings, 1998. **Address:** 237 Lafayette St., New York, NY 10012-4017, U.S.A.

BARTLETT, L. L. (Lorna Barrett). American (born United States), b. 1960?. **Genres:** Mystery/Crime/Suspense. **Career:** Writer. **Publications:** Murder on the Mind, 2005; Dead in Red, 2008. AS LORNA BARRETT: BOOKTOWN MYSTERIES SERIES: Murder Is Binding, 2008; Bookmarked for Death, 2009; Bookplate Special, 2009. **Address:** c/o Jacky Sach, Bookends Literary Agency, 136 Long Hill Rd., Gillette, NJ 07933, U.S.A. **Online address:** lorna@lornabarrett.com

BARTLETT, Sarah. American (born United States), b. 1955. **Genres:** Money/Finance, Mythology/Folklore. **Career:** Fortune, reporter, 1981-83; Business Week, staff reporter and associate editor, 1983-88, assistant managing editor, 1992-98; New York Times, reporter, 1988-92; Oxygen Media, editor-in-chief, 1999-2000; Inc. magazine, contributing editor; U$A Inc., host; City University of New York, Baruch College, Bloomberg chair of business journalism, CUNY Graduate School of Journalism, professor, Urban Reporting Program, director. **Publications:** (Contrib.) Geldschieters van de wereld, 1980; The Money Machine: How KKR Manufactured Power and Profits (nonfiction), 1991; The Love Tarot: Use the Power of the Mystic Deck to Guide you in Love, Romance, and Sex, 1995; Mythical Lovers, Divine Desires: The World's Great Love Legends, 1998; The World of Myths & Mythology: A Source Book, 1998; Mythical Lovers, Divine Desires: The World's Great Love Legends, 1998; Feng Shui for Lovers, 1999; Auras and How to Read Them, 2000; Tarot Bible: The Definitive Guide to the Cards and Spreads, 2006; Zodiac Baby: An Astrological Guide to Your Little Star, 2006; Simply Feng Shui, 2010; Brief History of Angels and Demons, 2011. Contributor to periodicals. **Address:** Graduate School of Journalism, City University of New York, 219 W 40th St., New York, NY 10018, U.S.A. **Online address:** sarah.bartlett@journalism.cuny.edu

BARTLETT, Thomas. Scottish/British/Irish (born Ireland) **Genres:** History, Adult Non-fiction. **Career:** University of Michigan, visiting professor, 1982-83; University College Dublin, professor of modern Irish history, 1995-; University of Washington, visiting professor, 1997; University of Notre Dame, visiting professor, 1999; Magdalene College, Parnell fellow in Irish studies, 2001-02; University of Aberdeen, King's College, School of Divinity, History and Philosophy, chair in Irish history. Writer. **Publications:** Macartney in Ireland, 1768-72: A Calendar of the Chief Secretaryship Papers of Sir George Macartney, 1979; The Fall and Rise of the Irish Nation: The Catholic Question, 1690-1830, 1992; (contrib.) Men, Women, and War: Papers Read Before the XXth Irish Conference of Historians, held at Magee College, University of Ulster, 6-8 June 1991, 1993; Theobald Wolfe Tone, 1997; (with K. Dawson and D. Keogh) Rebellion: A Television History of 1798, 1998; (with K. Dawson and D. Keogh) The 1798 Rebellion: An Illustrated History, 1998; Ireland: A History, 2010. EDITOR: (with D.W. Hayton) Penal Era and Golden Age: Essays in Irish History, 1690-1800, 1979; (co-ed.) Irish Studies: A General Introduction, 1988; (with K. Jeffery) A Military History of Ireland, 1996; (with G. O'Brien) History and Environment: The Lord Edward Fitzgerald Memorial Fund Bursary: Selected Essays of Award Winners, 1998; Life of Theobald Wolfe Tone, 1998; (co-ed.) 1798: A Bicentenary Perspective, 2003; (and intro.) Revolutionary Dublin, 1795-1801: The Letters of Francis Higgins to Dublin Castle, 2004. Contributor to books. **Address:** School of Divinity, History and Philosophy, King's College, University of Aberdeen, Rm. 216, Crombie Annexe, Meston Walk, Aberdeen, AB24 3FX, Scotland. **Online address:** t.bartlett@abdn.ac.uk

BARTOLETTI, Susan Campbell. American (born United States), b. 1958. **Genres:** Education, Children's Non-fiction, Young Adult Non-fiction. **Career:** North Pocono School District, faculty, 1979-97; Northeast Education Intermediate Unit, instructor, 1984-88; Keystone College, Department of English, adjunct faculty, 1984-86; University of Scranton, Department of English, adjunct faculty, 1997-98; Binghamton University, doctoral teaching assistant, 1997-2002; Hollins University, Degree Program in Children Literature, visiting associate professor, 1999-2005; Spalding University, Master of Fine Arts, Brief Residency Program, graduate faculty, 2003-. Writer. **Publications:** Silver at Night (picture book), 1994; Growing Up in Coal Country (nonfiction), 1996; Dancing with Dziadziu (picture book), 1997; Kids on Strike!, 1999; No Man's Land: A Young Soldier's Story, 1999; Coal Miner's Bride: The Diary of Anetka Kaminska, 2000; Black Potatoes: The Story of the Great Irish Famine, 1845-1850, 2001; Christmas Promise, 2001; Journal of Finn Reardon: A Newsie, 2003; Nobody's Noisier than a Cat, 2003; Flag Maker, 2004; Hitler Youth: Growing Up in Hitler's Shadow, 2005; Nobody's Diggier Than a Dog, 2005; Jugend im Nationalsozialismus: zwischen Faszination und Widerstand, 2007; The Boy Who Dared, 2008; They Called Themselves the K.K.K.: The Birth of an American Terrorist Group, 2010; Naamah and the Ark at Night, 2011. **Address:** Master of Fine Arts, 851 S 4th St., Louisville, KY 40203, U.S.A. **Online address:** susan@scbartoletti.com

BARTOLOMEO, Joseph F(rancis). American (born United States), b. 1958. **Genres:** Literary Criticism And History. **Career:** University of Massachusetts, Department of English, assistant professor, 1986-92, associate professor of English, 1992-2004, professor, 2004-, associate chair, through 2007, chair, 2007-, chief undergraduate advisor and director of undergraduate studies; Twayne Publishers, eighteenth-century field editor. **Publications:** New Species of Criticism: Eighteenth-Century Discourse on the Novel, 1994; Matched Pairs: Gender and Intertextual Dialogue in Eighteenth-Century Fiction, 2002. Contributor to journals. **Address:** Departmentt of English, University of Massachusetts, 164 Bartlett Hall, 390 Whitmore Administration Bldg., Amherst, MA 01003-0515, U.S.A. **Online address:** bartolomeo@english.umass.edu

BARTON, Anne. British/American (born United States), b. 1933. **Genres:** Literary Criticism And History, Plays/Screenplays, Young Adult Fiction. **Career:** Ithaca College, lecturer in the history of art, 1958-59; Cambridge University, Rosalind Carlisle fellow of Girton College, 1960-62, official fellow in English, 1962-72, from assistant lecturer to lecturer, 1962-74, Grace professor of English, 1984-2000, Trinity College, fellow, 1986-, professor; University of London, Bedford College, Hildred Carlile professor of English and head of department, 1972-74; Oxford University, fellow of New College and tutor in English, 1974-84. Writer. **Publications:** Shakespeare and the Idea of the Play, 1962; Byron and the Mythology of Fact, 1968; Ben Jonson, Dramatist, 1984; The Names of Comedy, 1990; Byron: Don Juan, 1992; Essays, Mainly Shakespeare, 1994. Works appear in anthologies. Contributor to journals. **Address:** Trinity College, Cambridge University, Cambridge, GL CB2 1TQ, England. **Online address:** ab10004@hermes.cam.ac.uk

BARTON, Carlin A. American (born United States), b. 1948?. **Genres:** History, Theology/Religion, Literary Criticism And History. **Career:** University of Massachusetts, Department of History, professor of history. Writer and historian. **Publications:** The Sorrows of the Ancient Romans: The Gladiator and the Monster, 1993; Roman Honor: The Fire in the Bones, 2001. **Address:** Department of History, University of Massachusetts, 637 Herter Hall, 161 Presidents Dr., Amherst, MA 01003-9312, U.S.A. **Online address:** cbarton@history.umass.edu

BARTON, Dan. American (born United States) **Genres:** Mystery/Crime/Suspense, Novels, Literary Criticism And History, Young Adult Fiction. **Career:** Author and television producer. **Publications:** Banshee, 1988; Relife, 1991; Killer Material, 2000; Heckler, 2001; Dead Crowd, 2002. Contributor to periodicals. **Address:** Thomas Dunne Books, 175 5th Ave., New York, NY 10010, U.S.A.

BARTON, Greg. Australian (born Australia), b. 1962?. **Genres:** Theology/Religion, Popular Culture, History, Politics/Government. **Career:** Victoria College, lecturer of Indonesian history and politics, 1992; Point Cook Air Base, Australian Defence Force School of Languages, lecturer of Indonesian language, 1992; Deakin University, lecturer of Indonesian studies and religious studies, 1993-97, senior lecturer of religious studies and politics, 1997-2004, associate professor of politics, 2005-06; Asia Pacific Center for Security Studies, associate professor, 2006-07, adjunct professor, 2007-; Monash University, Herb Feith research professor for the study of Indonesia, 2007-. Writer. **Publications:** (Ed. with D. Kingsbury) Difference and Tolerance: Human Rights Issues in Southeast Asia, 1994; (ed. with G. Fealy) Traditional Islam, and Modernity in Indonesia, 1996; Gagasan Islam Liberal di Indonesia: Pemikiran Neo-Modernisme Nucholish Madjid, 1999; Neraca Gus Dur di Panggung Kekuasaan, 2002; Abdurrahman Wahid, Muslim Democrat, Indonesian President: A View from the Inside, 2002; Gus Dur: The Authorized Biography of Abdurrahman Wahid, 2002; Indonesia's Struggle: Jemaah Islamiyah and the Soul of Islam, 2004; Jemaah Islamiyah: Radical Islamism in Indonesia, 2005. Contributor to books and periodicals. **Address:** Center for Muslim Minorities and Islam Pol Studies, Monash University, Rm. H5.30, Level 5, Bldg. H, Caulfield Campus, PO Box 197, Caulfield East, VI 3145, Australia. **Online address:** greg.barton@monash.edu

BARTON, John. British (born England), b. 1948. **Genres:** Theology/Religion, Cultural/Ethnic Topics, Essays. **Career:** Oxford University, Oriel College, Faculty of Theology, lecturer, 1974-89, reader, 1989-91, Oriel and Laing professor of the interpretation of the holy scripture, 1991-, St. Cross College, vicemaster; Journal of Theological Studies, editor, 2004-10. **Publications:** Amos's Oracles against the Nations, 1980; (contrib.) Prophets, Worship, and Theodicy, 1984; Reading the Old Testament: Method in Biblical Study, 1984, rev. ed., 1996; Oracles of God: Perceptions of Ancient Prophecy in Israel after the Exile, 1986, new ed., 2007; People of the Book?: The Authority of the Bible in Christianity, 1988; (with R. Morgan) Biblical Interpretation, 1988; Love Unknown: Meditations on the Death and Resurrection of Jesus, 1990; What Is the Bible?, 1991; (ed. with S.E. Balentine) Language, Theology, and the Bible: Essays in Honour of James Barr, 1994; (ed. with D.J. Reimer) After the Exile: Essays in Honour of Rex Mason, 1996; Isaiah 1-39, 1996; The Spirit and the Letter: Studies in the Biblical Canon, 1997; Holy Writings, Sacred Text: The Canon in Early Christianity, 1998; How the Bible Came to Be, 1998; Making the Christian Bible, 1998; (ed.) The Cambridge Companion to Biblical Interpretation, 1998; Ethics and the Old Testament, 1998; (ed. with G. Sauter) Revelation and Story: Narrative Theology and the Centrality of Story, 2000; (ed. with G. Sauter) Offenbarung und Geschichten, 2000; (ed. with J. Muddiman) Oxford Bible Commentary, 2001; Joel and Obadiah: A Commentary, 2001; (ed.) The Biblical World, 2002; (ed. with C. Rowland) Apocalyptic in History and Tradition, 2002; Understanding Old Testament Ethics, 2003; (ed. with B.M. Metzger) The Holy Bible, Containing the Old and New Testaments: New Revised Standard Version, 2003; (ed. with M. Wolter) Einheit der Schrift und die Vielfalt des Kanons, 2003; Living Belief: Being Christian, Being Human, 2005; (with J. Bowden) The Original Story: God, Israel, and The World, 2005; The Nature of Biblical Criticism, 2007; The Old Testament: Canon, Literature and Theology: Collected Works of John Barton, 2007; Bible: The Basics, 2010; (ed. with J. Muddiman) Pentateuch, 2010; (ed. with J. Muddiman, L. Alexander and H. Wansborough) Gospels, 2010; (ed. with J. Muddiman, L. Alexander and H. Wansborough) Pauline Epistiles, 2010; Theology of the Book of Amos, 2012. Contributor to periodicals. **Address:** Faculty of Theology, Oriel College, University of Oxford, 34 St. Giles, Oxford, SY OX1 3LD, England. **Online address:** john.barton@oriel.ox.ac.uk

BARTON, Lee. *See* **FANTHORPE, R(obert) Lionel.**

BARTON, (Samuel) Wayne. American (born United States), b. 1944. **Genres:** Westerns/Adventure, Novels, Crafts. **Career:** Arco Oil and Gas Co., engineer, senior engineer, 1967-94; Roundup Magazine, Bookmarks for Westerns, columnist, 1985-88; Writer's Digest Schools, editorial associate, 1987-94; Writer, 1994-; The Alpine School of Wood Carving Ltd., founder; Chicago Art institute, visiting lecturer. **Publications:** WESTERNS: Ride down the Wind, 1981; Return to Phantom Hill, 1983; Chip Carving: Techniques and Patterns, 1984; High Country, 1993; New and Traditional Styles of Chip Carving: From Classic to Positive Imaging, 1994; Art of Chip Carving, 1998; Chip Carving: Design and Pattern Sourcebook, 2002; Complete Guide to Chip Carving, 2007. WESTERNS WITH S. WILLIAMS: Warhorse, 1988; Live by the Gun, 1989; Manhunt, 1992; High Country, 1993; Shadow of Doubt, 1994; Wildcat, 1995; Fairchild's Passage, 1997; Lockhart's Nightmare, 1998. OTHER: (ed.) What Do I Read Next? 1990-99. **Address:** Alpine School of Wood Carving Ltd., 225 Vine Ave., Park Ridge, IL 60068, U.S.A. **Online address:** wayne@chipcarving.com

BARTON, Tamsyn (S.). British (born England), b. 1962. **Genres:** History, Medicine/Health. **Career:** Cambridge University, Henry Sidgwick research fellow, 1989-92; Action Aid India, staff, 1993-94; Overseas Development Administration, Water and Sanitation Office, social development field manager, 1994-97; Intermediate Technology Development Group, head of technology and acting operations director, 1998-2001; Department for International Development, Rural Livelihoods and Infrastructure Departments, social development adviser, 2001-03, Trade and Development Team, head, 2003-05, Sustainable Development Group, joint head, 2005-06, Conflict, Humanitarian and Security Department, deputy head, 2006-07, European Union Department, head, 2007-10; European Investment Bank, alternate director, 2007-10. Writer. **Publications:** Power and Knowledge: Astrology, Physiognomics and Medicine Under the Roman Empire, 1994; Ancient Astrology, 1994; (intro.) Lives of the Twelve Caesars, 1997. Contributor of articles to journals. **Address:** Department for International Development, Rm. 8E22, 1 Palace St., London, GL SW1E 5HE, England. **Online address:** t-barton@dfid.gov.uk

BARTOSZEWSKI, Wladyslaw T(eofil). Ukranian/British/Polish (born Poland), b. 1955. **Genres:** History. **Career:** Catholic University of Lublin, Department of History and Culture, assistant, 1980; Columbia University, YIVO Institute for Jewish Research, Max Weinreich Center for Advanced Jewish Studies, research fellow, 1982-83; Hebrew University of Jerusalem, Department of Anthropology and Sociology, visiting fellow, 1984-85; University of Cambridge, Department of Social Anthropology, visiting lecturer, 1985; St. Antony's College, research fellow, 1985-89, senior associate, 1989-90; Institute of Polish-Jewish Studies, secretary, 1985-92, director, 1985-; Wadham College, Sarah Lawrence College Year Abroad Programme, tutor in modern history and politics, 1986-90; London School of Economics and Political Science, Department of International History, research assistant, 1987-91; War Crime Enquiry, historical adviser, 1988-89; Oxford Year Abroad, tutor in modern history and politics, 1988-90; University of Oxford, Institute of Russian, senior associate, 1988-90; University of London, tutor in Jewish history, 1989-90; University of Warwick, Department of History, lecturer, 1989-91; British and European Studies Group, lecturer in East European history, 1990; COBA-M.I.D., associate, 1990-91; Central Europe Trust, manager, 1991-93, senior manager, 1993-94, director, CIS, 1994-; ASTARTA Holding, board director. **Publications:** Warsaw Death Ring, 1939-1944, 1968; Polska podziemna a walka getta warszawskiego: wybrane zagadnienia, 1973; 1859 dni Warszawy, 1974; Das Warschauer Ghetto, wie es wirklich war: Zeugenbericht eines Christen, 1983; Los Zydów Warszawy 1939-1943, 1983; Herbst der Hoffnungen: es lohnt sich, anständig zu sein, 1983; Warto być przyzwoitym: szkic do pamietnika, 1986; Aus der Geschichte lernen?: Aufsätze und Reden zur Kriegsund Nachkriegsgeschichte Polens, 1986; The Warsaw Ghetto: A Christian's Testimony, 1987; Na drodze do niepodległości, 1987; The Convent at Auschwitz, 1991; (co-author) Los Zydow Warszawy, 1939-1943, 1993; Common European Responsibility: Selected Speeches and Interviews, 2001; Above Divisions: Selected Speeches and Interviews, July-December 2000, 2001; Die deutsch-p Dówiadczenia lat wojny 1939-1945 olnischen Beziehungen: gestern, heute und morgen, 2002; (with A. Bujak) Warsaw, the Unvanquished: A Historic, Patriotic, and Modern Capital, 2005; Moja Jerozolima, mój Izrael, 2005; (intro.) John Nowak, 2005; Warto być przyzwoitym: teksty osobiste i nieosobiste, 2005; (intro.) Oskarzony Kazimierz Moczarski, 2006; Dziennik z internowania: Jaworze 15.12.1981-19.04.1982, 2006; Pisma wybrane, 2007; (with M. Komar) Mimo wszystko: wywiadu rzeki księga druga, 2008; (with Z. Augustýski) Abandoned Heroes of the Warsaw Uprising, 2008; Dziennikarstwo I Polityka, 2009; (with A.K. Kunert) 1939-Polska byla pierwsza, 2009; (with M. Komar) środowisko naturalne. Korzenie, 2010; (with A. Friszke) Zycie trudne lecz nie nudne, 2010; O Niemcach I Polakach, 2010; Moj Auschwitz, 2010; Pod Prad, 2011. EDITOR: Righteous Among Nations: How Poles Helped the Jews, 1939-1945, 1969; The Blood Shed Unites Us, 1970; Surviving Treblinka, 1989; Dni walczacej stolicy: kronika Powstania Warszawskiego, 1989; (with A. Polonsky) The Jews of Warsaw, 1991; The Road to Katyn: A Soldier's Story, 1992. **Address:** ASTARTA Holding, 38/44 Pochaynynska St., Kyiv, 04070, Ukraine.

BARTOV, Omer. Israeli/American (born United States), b. 1954. **Genres:** Novels, History, Intellectual History, Military/Defense/Arms Control. **Career:** Tel-Aviv University, senior lecturer in modern history, 1983-92; Rutgers University, visiting Raoul Wallenberg professor for human rights, 1992-94, associate professor of modern European history, 1994-96, professor, 1996-2000; Brown University, John P. Birkelund distinguished professor of European history, 2000-, professor of German studies. Writer. **Publications:** The Eastern Front, 1941-1945: German Troops and the Barbarization of Warfare, 1985, 2nd ed., 2001; Ptikhat tsir, 1988; Karev Yom, 1989; Hitler's Army: Soldiers, Nazis, and War in the Third Reich, 1991; Murder in Our Midst: The Holocaust, Industrial Killing, and Representation, 1996; Mirrors of Destruction: War, Genocide, and Modern Identity, 2000; Germany's War and the Holocaust: Disputed Histories (essays), 2003; From the Holocaust in Galicia to Contemporary Genocide: Common Ground-Historical Differences, 2003; The Jew in Cinema: From The Golem to Don't Touch My Holocaust, 2005; Erased: Vanishing Traces of Jewish Galicia in Present-Day Ukraine, 2007. EDITOR/CO-EDITOR: The Holocaust: Origins, Implementation, Aftermath, 2000; In God's Name: Genocide and Religion in the Twentieth Century, 2000; Crimes of War: Guilt and Denial in the 20th Century, 2002. **Address:** Department of History, Brown University, Peter Green House, 79 Brown St., PO Box N, Providence, RI 02912, U.S.A. **Online address:** omer_bartov@brown.edu

BARTRUM, Giulia. British (born England) **Genres:** Art/Art History. **Career:** British Museum, Department of Prints and Drawings, curator, 1979-. Writer. **Publications:** (Ed. with J. Rowlands) The Age of Dürer and Holbein: German Drawings, 1400-1550, 1988; (ed. with J. Rowlands) Drawings by German Artists: In the Department of Prints and Drawings in the British Museum, London, 1993; German Renaissance Prints, 1490-1550, 1995; (ed.) Albrecht Dürer and His Legacy: The Graphic Work of a Renaissance Artist, 2002; German Romantic Prints and Drawings, 2011. Contributor to periodicals. **Address:** Department of Prints and Drawings, The British Museum, Great Russell St., London, GL WC1B 3DG, England. **Online address:** gbartrum@thebritishmuseum.ac.uk

BARTZ, Albert. (Albert E(dward) Bartz). American (born United States), b. 1933. **Genres:** Mathematics/Statistics, Psychology, Education. **Career:** Concordia College, instructor, 1957-59, assistant professor, 1961-64, associate professor, 1964-70, professor of psychology, 1970-2009, psychologist-in-residence, 2009-. Writer. **Publications:** AS ALBERT E. BARTZ: Basic Descriptive Statistics for Education and the Behavioral Sciences, 4th ed., 1971; Elementary Statistical Methods for Educational Measurement, 1958; (with R.H. Kolstoe) Workbook for Introduction to Statistics for the Behavioral Sciences, 1968, 2nd ed., 1973; Basic Statistical Concepts in Education and the Behavioral Sciences, 1976, 4th ed., 1999; Basic Statistical Concepts, 2nd ed., 1981, 4th ed., 1999; (with M.A. Sabolik) Computer and Software Use in Teaching the Beginning Statistics Course, 2001; (with E.A. Olson) Neuroticism and the Irrational Health Belief, 2002. **Address:** Department of Psychology, Concordia College, 901 8th St. S, Moorhead, MN 56562, U.S.A. **Online address:** bartz@cord.edu

BARTZ, Albert E(dward). *See* **BARTZ, Albert.**

BARUCH, Elaine Hoffman. American (born United States) **Genres:** Literary Criticism And History, Women's Studies And Issues, Biography, Adult Non-fiction. **Career:** Queens College, lecturer, 1960-62, instructor, assistant professor of English, 1967-77; City University of New York, York College, associate professor of English, 1978-, professor of English. Writer. **Publications:** NONFICTION: (with L.J. Serrano) Women Analyze Women: In France, England, and the United States, 1988; Women, Love, and Power: Literary and Psychoanalytic Perspectives, 1991; (with L.J. Serrano) She Speaks/He Listens: Women on the French Analyst's Couch, 1995. EDITOR: (and intro. with R. Rohrlich) Women in Search of Utopia: Mavericks and Mythmakers, 1984; (with A.F. D'Adamo, Jr. and J. Seager) Embryos, Ethics, and Women's Rights: Exploring the New Reproductive Technologies, 1988. Contributor to books and periodicals. **Address:** Department of English, York College, City University of New York, 94-20 Guy R. Brewer Blvd., Jamaica, NY 11451, U.S.A. **Online address:** baruch@york.cuny.edu

BARUCHELLO, Gianfranco. Italian (born Italy), b. 1924. **Genres:** Art/Art History, Natural History, Photography. **Career:** Writer and filmmaker. **Publications:** Multipurpose Object, 1966; Mi Viene in Mente, 1967; La Quindicesima Riga, 1968; Avventure Nell'armadio di Plexigass, 1968; Una Settantina di Idee, 1968; Baruchello. Galleria Schwarz, Milano, Dal 3 al 30 Aprile 1968, 1968; Come ho Dipinto Certi Miei Quadri, 1976; (with G. Lascault) Alphabersd'éros, 1976; (contrib.) Ballate della Signorina Richmond: Primo Libro, 1977; (with H. Martin) Fragments of a Possible Apocalypse, 1978; Sentito vivere, 1978; La stazione del Conte Goluchowsky, 1978; (contrib.) Extra Media: Esperienze Attuali di Comunicazione Estetica, 1978; Marcel Duchamp in 20 Photographs, 1978; L'Altra Casa, 1979; Agricola Cornelia S.p.A. 1973-'81, 1981; La Scomparsa Di Amanda Silvers, 1982; (with H. Martin) How to Imagine: A Narrative on Art and Agriculture, 1983; (with H. Martin) Why Duchamp: An Essay on Aesthetic Impact, 1985; Uomini di Pane, 1986; Mille Titoli, 1987; (contrib.) Ritorno Della Signorina Richmond: Terzo Libro, 1984-1986, 1987; Bellissimo Il Giardino, 1989; Baruchell: Bringer of Plurabilities, 1989; Se Tanto Mi Da Canto, 1990; Dall'archiviodei Cinque Cuori, 1991; Miss Omissis, 1991; Al Polo Nord, Rotolando, 1992; Gianfranco Baruchello: L'altopiano Dell'incerto, 1992; Baruchello: Secondo Natura, 1997; Baruchello, Fuoricampo, 1997; Petite Cuiller Dans Le Bol: Dusurréalisme à l'Externet En Passant Par l'individualisme Révolutionnaire: Entretiens Avec Gianfranco Baruchello, Renaud Ego, Malek Abbou, 1998. **Address:** Via di Santa Cornelia, m. 695 Prima Porta, Rome, 00100, Italy.

BARUTH, Philip Edward. American (born United States), b. 1962. **Genres:** Young Adult Fiction, Adult Non-fiction. **Career:** University of Vermont, faculty, 1993-, assistant professor, professor of English, chair of department; Vermont Public Radio (VPR), commentator, 1998-, Camel's Hump Radio, host, 2000-03. **Publications:** NONFICTION: (ed.) Introducing Charlotte Charke: Actress, Author, Enigma, 1998; (ed. with J. Citro) Vermont Air: Best of the Vermont Public Radio Commentaries, 2002. FICTION: The Millennium Shows (novel), 1994; The Dream of the White Village: A Novel in Stories, 1998; The X President: A Novel, 2003; The Brothers Boswell: A Novel, 2009. Contributor to periodicals. **Address:** Department of English, University of Vermont, 400 Old Mill, Burlington, VT 05405-4030, U.S.A. **Online address:** pbaruth@uvm.edu

BAR-YOSEF, Eitan. Israeli (born Israel), b. 1968. **Genres:** Theology/Religion, History, Cultural/Ethnic Topics. **Career:** Ben-Gurion University of the Negev, lecturer in foreign literature and linguistics. Writer. **Publications:** The Holy Land in English Culture, 1799-1917: Palestine and the Question of Orientalism, 2005; (ed. with N. Valman) The Jew in Late-Victorian and Edwardian Culture: Between the East End and East Africa, 2009. **Address:** Department of Foreign Literatures and Linguistics, Ben-Gurion University of the Negev, PO Box 653, Beer Sheva, 84105, Israel. **Online address:** eby@bgu.ac.il

BARZAK, Christopher. American (born United States), b. 1975. **Genres:** Novels. **Career:** Youngstown State University, assistant professor of creative writing. Writer. **Publications:** One for Sorrow, 2007; The Love We Share without Knowing, 2008; (ed. with D. Sherman) Interfictions 2: An Anthology of Interstitial Writing, 2009. Works appear in anthologies. Contributor to periodicals. **Address:** Barry Goldblatt, 320 7th Ave., Ste. 266, Brooklyn, NY 11215, U.S.A. **Online address:** christopherbarzak@gmail.com

BARZUN, Jacques. American/French (born France), b. 1907. **Genres:** History, Intellectual History, Literary Criticism And History, Adult Non-fiction, Philosophy, Social Commentary, Speech/Rhetoric, Biography, Reference, Translations, Language/Linguistics. **Career:** Columbia University, instructor, 1929-37, assistant professor, 1938-42, associate professor, 1942-45, professor of history, 1945-60, dean of graduate faculties, 1955-58, dean of faculties and provost, 1958-67, Seth Low professor of history, 1960-67, university professor of history, 1967-75, university professor emeritus, 1975-; Churchill College, Cambridge, extraordinary fellow, 1961-; Charles Scribner's Sons (publishers), literary advisor, 1975-93. Writer. **Publications:** NONFICTION: The French Race: Theories of Its Origins and Their Social and Political Implications Prior to the Revolution, 1932; Race: A Study in Modern Superstition, 1937, rev. ed. as Race: A Study in Superstition, 1956; Of Human Freedom, 1939, rev. ed., 1964; Darwin, Marx, Wagner: Critique of a Heritage, 1941, rev. ed., 1958; Romanticism and the Modern Ego, 1943, rev. ed. as Classic, Romantic and Modern, 1961; (co-author) Introduction to Naval History, 1944; The Teacher in America, 1945, rev. ed. as We Who Teach, 1946; Berlioz and the Romantic Century, 1950, rev. ed. as Berlioz and His Century: An Introduction to the Age of Romanticism, 1962; (trans.) G. Flaubert, Dictionary of Accepted Ideas, 1954; God's Country and Mine: A Declaration of Love Spiced with a Few Harsh Words, 1954; Music in American Life, 1956; (trans. with R.H. Bowen) D. Diderot, Rameau's Nephew and Other Works, 1956; The Energies of Art: Studies of Authors Classic and Modern, 1956; (trans. and intro.) H.L. Berlioz, Evenings with the Orchestra, 1956; (with H.F. Graff) The Modern Researcher, 1957, 6th ed., 2004; Lincoln the Literary Genius, 1959; The House of Intellect, 1959; (trans. with R. Lowell) Phaedra and (The Marriage of) Figaro, 1961; Science the Glorious Entertainment, 1964; The American University: How It Runs, Where It Is Going, 1968; On Writing, Editing and Publishing: Essays Explicative and Horatory, 1971; (with W.H. Taylor) A Catalogue of Crime, 1971, rev. ed., 1989; (contrib.) Education: Threatened Standards: Essays on the Reasons for the Present Decline in Educational Achievement and Suggestions for Its Improvement, 1972; The Use and Abuse of Art, 1974; Clio and the Doctors: Psycho-History, Quanto-History and History, 1974; Simple & Direct: A Rhetoric for Writers, 1975, 4th ed., 2001; A Stroll with William James, 1983; A Word or Two before You Go (essays), 1986; (with J. Pelikan and J.H. Franklin) Scholarship Today, 1987; The Culture We Deserve, 1989; An Essay on French Verse for Readers of English Poetry, 1991; Begin Here: The Forgotten Conditions of Teaching and Learning, 1991; From Dawn to Decadence: Five Hundred Years of Western Cultural Life, 1500 to the Present, 2000; (trans. with R.H. Bowen) Rameau's Nephew and Other Works, 2001; (co-author) A Company of Readers: Uncollected Writings of W.H. Auden, Jacques Barzun and Lionel Trilling from The Readers' Subscription and Mid-century Book Clubs, 2001; A Jacques Barzun Reader: Selections from His Works, 2002. EDITOR: Samplings and Chronicles, Being the Continuation of the Philolexian Society History, 1927; Pleasures of Music: A Reader's Choice of Great Writing about Music and Musicians from Cellini to Bernard Shaw, 1951; Selected Letters, 1953; (trans. and intro.) New Letters of Berlioz, 1830-1868, 1954; Goethe, Faust: A Tragedy, Part I, 1955; History of the Faculty of Philosophy, Columbia University, 1957; Selected Writings, 1957; The Delights of Detection, 1957; Modern American Usage: A Guide, 1966; (intro.) Burke and Hare: The Resurrection Men, 1974. OTHERS: (ed. and intro.) The Interpretation of History, 1943; (intro.) The Adventures of Sherlock Holmes, 1985; Contributor of articles to periodicals and magazines. **Address:** Columbia University, 116th and Broadway, New York, NY 10027, U.S.A.

BASCH, Rachel. American (born United States), b. 1959. **Genres:** Novels, Romance/Historical, Young Adult Fiction. **Career:** Fairfield University, faculty; Writer. **Publications:** Degrees of Love, 1998; The Passion of Reverend Nash, 2003. Contributor to magazines. **Address:** c/o Alice Fried Martell, The Martell Agency, 545 Madison Ave. 7th Fl., New York, NY 10022-4219, U.S.A. **Online address:** mail@rachelbasch.com

BASCOMB, Neal. American (born United States), b. 1971. **Genres:** Novels, Sports/Fitness, Law. **Career:** St. Martin's Press, editorial assistant, editor; Euromoney Magazine, columnist and writer; full-time writer, 2000-. **Publications:** Higher: A Historic Race to the Sky and the Making of a City, 2003; The Perfect Mile: Three Athletes, One Goal, and Less than Four Minutes to Achieve It, 2004; Red Mutiny: Eleven Fateful Days on the Battleship Potemkin, 2007; Angels of Justice, 2007; Hunting Eichmann: How a Band of Survivors and a Young Spy Agency Chased Down the World's Most Notorious Nazi, 2009; The New Cool: A Visionary Teacher, His FIRST Robotics Team, and the Ultimate Battle of Smarts, 2010. Contributor to magazines. **Address:** c/o Jill Browning, Random House Inc., 1745 Broadway, New York, NY 10019-4368, U.S.A. **Online address:** neal@nealbascomb.com

BASE, Graeme (Rowland). (Rowland W. Greasebeam). Australian/British (born England), b. 1958. **Genres:** Children's Fiction, Illustrations, Mystery/Crime/Suspense, Animals/Pets, Young Adult Fiction, Children's Non-fiction. **Career:** Author and illustrator. **Publications:** SELF-ILLUSTRATED BOOKS FOR CHILDREN: My Grandma Lived in Gooligulch, 1983; Animalia, 1986; The Eleventh Hour: A Curious Mystery, 1988; The Sign of the Seahorse: A Tale of Greed and High Adventure, 1992; (as Rowland W. Greasebeam) The Discovery of Dragons, 1996, rev. ed. as The Discovery of Dragons: New Research Revealed, 2007; Lewis Carroll's Jabberwocky: A Book of Brillig Dioramas, 1996; The Worst Band in the Universe, 1999; The Water Hole, 2001; Jungle Drums, 2004; Truck Dogs: A Novel in Four Bites, 2004; Uno's Garden, 2006; The Water Hole Board Book, 2008; Enigma: A Magical Mystery, 2008; The Art of Graeme Base, 2008; Legend of the Golden Snail, 2010; The Jewel Fish of Karnak, 2011. Illustrator of books by S. Burke, L. Carroll and M. Dann. Contributor to periodicals. **Address:** Penguin Books Australia Ltd., 250 Camberwell Rd., PO Box 701, Camberwell, VI 3124, Australia.

BASH, Frank N(ess). American (born United States), b. 1937. **Genres:** Astronomy. **Career:** Harvard University, Astronomy Department, teaching assistant, 1959-62, research assistant, 1960-61; Lincoln Laboratory, staff scientist, 1962; National Radio Astronomy Observatory, associate astronomer, 1962-64; University of Virginia, Astronomy Department, research assistant, 1964-67; University of Texas, Astronomy Department, faculty associate, 1967-69, research fellow, 1967-70, assistant professor, 1969-73, associate professor, 1973-81, professor, 1981-85, chairman, 1982-86, Edmonds Regents professor of astronomy, 1985-, McDonald Observatory, director, 1989-2003, now Frank N. Edmonds, Jr. Regents professor emeritus in astronomy; Leiden University, visiting professor, 1979; Cambridge University, visiting professor, 1979. Writer. **Publications:** (With D. Schiller and D. Balamore) Astronomy, 1977; (ed. with C. Sneden) Astronomical Instrumentation and the Birth and Growth of Astrophysics: A Symposium Held in Honor of Robert G. Tull: Proceedings of a Meeting Held at the University of Texas, Austin, Texas, 20-21 October 2000, 2002; (ed. with T.G. Barnes) Cosmic Abundances as Records of Stellar Evolution and Nucleosynthesis in Honor of David L. Lambert: Proceedings of a Symposium Held in Austin, Texas, USA, 17-19 June 2004. Contributor to journals. **Address:** Department of Astronomy, University of Texas, RLM 13.134, 1 University Sta., C1400, Austin, TX 78712-0259, U.S.A. **Online address:** fnb@astro.as.utexas.edu

BASHE, Philip (Scott). American (born United States), b. 1954. **Genres:** Administration/Management, Medicine/Health, Biography, Medicine/Health, Sports/Fitness, Social Sciences, Essays. **Career:** Foxtrot (magazine), publisher and editor-in-chief, 1975-77; WBUF-FM Radio, announcer, 1977-78; Buffalo Evening News, features writer, 1978-79; Good Times (magazine), managing editor, 1979-80; Circus (magazine), senior editor, 1980-84; International Musician and Recording World (magazine), managing editor, 1984-86; writer, 1986-. **Publications:** (With K. Barun, W. King and M. Shore) Rolling Stone Rock Almanac, 1983; Heavy Metal Thunder: The Music, Its History, Its Heroes, 1985; (with D. Snider) Dee Snider's Teenage Survival Guide: How to Be a Legend in Your Own Lunch Time, 1987; (with K. Barun) How to Keep the Children You Love Off Drugs, 1988; (with M. Blanc) That's not all Folks, 1988; Teenage Idol, Travelin' Man: The Complete Biography of Rick Nelson, 1992; (with Geralyn and C. Gaes) You Don't Have to Die, 1992; Dog Days:

The New York Yankees' Fall from Grace and Return to Glory, 1964 to 1976, 1994; (with S.J. Winawer and M. Shike) Cancer Free: The Comprehensive Prevention Program, 1995; (co-author) The Patient's Guide to Tests and Procedures, 1997; (with R. McFarlane) The Complete Bedside Companion: No-Nonsense Advice on Caring for the Seriously Ill, 1998; (with P. Teeley) Fight for Your Life: Take Charge of Your Cancer Care and Increase Your Chances for Survival, 1998; (with P. Teeley) The Complete Cancer Survival Guide, 2000, rev. ed., 2005; Caring for Your Teenager: The Complete and Authoritative Guide, 2003; (with G. Binder) Science Lessons: What the Business of Biotech Taught Me about Management, 2008. **Address:** c/o Jed Mattes, 175 W 73rd St., New York, NY 10023, U.S.A.

BASIL, John D. American/Chinese (born China), b. 1934. **Genres:** History. **Career:** University of South Carolina, distinguished professor of history emeritus. Writer and historian. **Publications:** The Mensheviks in the Revolution of 1917, 1984; Church and State in Late Imperial Russia: Critics of the Synodal System of Church Government (1861-1914), 2005. Contributor to periodicals. **Address:** Department of History, University of South Carolina, 145 Gambrell Hall, Columbia, SC 29208, U.S.A.

BASINGER, Jeanine (Deyling). American (born United States), b. 1936. **Genres:** Film, Art/Art History, Literary Criticism And History. **Career:** South Dakota State University, instructor in introductory English, 1958-59; American Education Publications, Weekly Reader Children's Book Club, copywriter, 1960-62, marketing director, 1960-69, advertising director, 1962-68, editorial consultant, 1969-79, assistant editor of young people's encyclopedia, 1973; Wesleyan University, teaching associate, 1971-72, adjunct lecturer, 1972-76, adjunct associate professor, 1976-80, associate professor, 1980-84, professor of art, 1984-, Department of Film Studies, chair and Corwin-Fuller professor of film studies and American studies, Wesleyan Cinema Archives, founder and curator. Writer and actress. **Publications:** Shirley Temple, 1975; Gene Kelly, 1976; Lana Turner, 1976; Anthony Mann: A Critical Analysis, 1979, new ed., 2007; World War II Combat Films: Anatomy of a Genre, 1985; American Cinema: 100 Years of Filmmaking, 1994; A Woman's View: How Hollywood Spoke to Women, 1930-1960, 1994; Silent Stars, 1999; The Star Machine, 2007; I Do and I Don't: Marriage in the Movies, 2012. EDITOR: (with J. Frazer and J.W. Reed) Working with Kazan, 1973; Young People's Encyclopedia, 1973; The It's a Wonderful Life Book, 1986. Contributor to books, magazines and newspapers. **Address:** Center for Film Studies, Wesleyan University, 301 Washington Terr., Middletown, CT 06459, U.S.A. **Online address:** jbasinger@wesleyan.edu

BASINSKI, Michael. American (born United States), b. 1950. **Genres:** Poetry, Songs/Lyrics And Libretti, Literary Criticism And History. **Career:** Poet, 1975-; University at Buffalo, State University of New York, The Poetry Collection, assistant curator, curator, 2004-. **Publications:** POETRY: B (text broadside), 1982; The Wicked Old Woman (broadside), 1983; The Women Are Called Girls, 1983; A-Part (broadside), 1991; (with B. Tedlock) Egyptian Gods 6 (broadside), 1991; Moon Bok, 1992; Red Rain Too, 1992; Her Roses (broadside), 1992; It Is an Open (Christmas broadside), 1992; Cnyttan, 1993; Flight to the Moon, 1993; Vessels, 1993; Worms, 1993; So Up, 1994; Sle Vep, 1995; Duende, 1995; Catachresis Mum, 1995; Odalesque, 1995; The Sink, 1995; Coupid (broadside), 1996; Barstokai, 1996; Wen, 1996; Empty Mirror, 1996; Heebie-Jeebies, 1996; Idyll, 1996; Words, 1997; Nome, 1997; Un Nome, 1997; From Wooden Unguent-Spoon in the Shape of a Girl Swimming and Reaching Out to Touch a Duck, 1998; By, 1999; Book of Two Cartouche, 1999; Fine White Out Lines, 1999; The Doors, 2000; Nighttime Poems, 2000; Beseechers, 2000; Shards ov Shampoo, 2000; Mool3 Ghosts, 2001; Strange Things Begin to Happen When a Meteor Crashes in the Arizona, 2001; The Lay of Fraya Wray, 2001; Mool, 2001; Heka, 2001; The Sound Pome Today Must Come to Bum Impoemvisational, 2001; A Poet Dreams about Poetry, 2002; Two Toons, 2002; Poemeserss, 2002; Abzu, 2003; The Idyllic Book, 2003; Entrails, 2004; It's Alieve, 2004; Poems Popeye Papyrus, 2004; All My Eggs Are Broken, 2007; Of Venus 93, 2007; Welcome to the Alphabet, 2008; Auxin, 2008; (ed.) Gerald Locklin: A Critical Introduction, 2009; Trailers, 2011. **Address:** The Poetry Collection, Universtiy at Buffalo, State University of New York, 420 Capen Hall, North Campus, Buffalo, NY 14260-1613, U.S.A. **Online address:** basinski@acsu.buffalo.edu

BASKIN, Judith R. American/Canadian (born Canada), b. 1950. **Genres:** Theology/Religion, Women's Studies And Issues. **Career:** University of Massachusetts, Department of Near Eastern and Judaic Studies, assistant professor of Judaic studies, 1976-84, associate professor of Judaic and Near Eastern studies, 1984-99; Yale University, visiting assistant professor of religious studies, 1981-83; State University of New York, associate professor of Judaic studies, 1988-95, chair, 1988-2000, professor, 1995-2000; Association for Jewish Studies, director, 1998-, vice president for program, 2000-03, president, 2004-06; University of Oregon, Department of Religious Studies, professor, 2000-09, head, 2005-08, Knight professor of humanities, Harold Schnitzer Family Program in Judaic Studies, director, 2000-09, College of Arts and Sciences, associate dean of humanities, 2009-. Writer. **Publications:** Pharaoh's Counsellors: Job, Jethro, and Balaam in Rabbinic and Patristic Tradition, 1983; Famous Jewish Women in History, 1997; Midrashic Women: Formations of the Feminine in Rabbinic Literature, 2002. EDITOR AND CONTRIBUTOR: Jewish Women in Historical Perspective, 1991, 2nd ed., 1998; Women of the Word: Jewish Women and Jewish Writing, 1994; (with S. Tenenbaum) Gender and Jewish Studies: A Curriculum Guide, 1994; (with K. Seeskin) The Cambridge Guide to Jewish History, Religion, and Culture, 2010; Cambridge Dictionary of Jewish History, Religion, and Culture, 2011. Works appear in anthologies. **Address:** College of Arts and Sciences, University of Oregon, 114 Friendly Hall, 1245 University of Oregon, Eugene, OR 97403-5228, U.S.A. **Online address:** jbaskin@uoregon.edu

BASS, Cynthia. American (born United States), b. 1949. **Genres:** Novels, History, Literary Criticism And History. **Career:** San Francisco Chronicle, contributor; San Francisco Examiner, columnist. **Publications:** NOVELS: Sherman's March, 1994; Maiden Voyage, 1996; Beyond Our Wishes. Contributor of articles to periodicals. **Address:** Margret McBride Literary Agency, 7744 Fay Ave., Ste. 201, La Jolla, CA 92037-4313, U.S.A. **Online address:** cynthia@cynthiabass.com

BASS, Diana Butler. American (born United States), b. 1959. **Genres:** Theology/Religion, History. **Career:** Westmont College, assistant professor of religious studies, 1991-95; University of California at Santa Barbara, lecturer, 1995-96; New York Times Syndicate, columnist, 1995-2000; Macalester College, visiting assistant professor, 1996-97; Rhodes College, associate professor, 1997-2000; Virginia Theological Seminary, adjunct instructor, 2001-06, senior research fellow and project director, 2002-06; Cathedral College, Washington National Cathedral, senior fellow; Sojourners Magazine, contributing editor. Consultant. **Publications:** Standing against the Whirlwind: Evangelical Episcopalians in Nineteenth-Century America, 1995; Strength for the Journey: A Pilgrimage of Faith in Community, 2002; The Practicing Congregation: Imagining a New Old Church, 2004; Broken We Kneel: Reflections on Faith and Citizenship, 2004; (ed. with J. Stewart-Sicking) From Nomads to Pilgrims: Stories from Practicing Congregations, 2006; Christianity for the Rest of Us: How the Neighborhood Church Is Transforming the Faith, 2006; A People's History of Christianity: The Other Side of the Story, 2009. Contributor of articles journals and periodicals. **Address:** 1602 Belle View Blvd., Ste. 630, Alexandria, VA 22307, U.S.A.

BASS, Gary J. (Gary Jonathan Bass). American (born United States), b. 1969. **Genres:** Politics/Government, Military/Defense/Arms Control, History. **Career:** Harvard University, Carr Center for Human Rights Policy, fellow, Harvard Law School, visiting professor; Princeton University, Elias Boudinot Bicentennial Preceptor, associate professor. Writer and economist. **Publications:** Stay the Hand of Vengeance: The Politics of War Crimes Tribunals, 2000; Freedom's Battle: The Origins of Humanitarian Intervention, 2008. Contributor to periodicals. **Address:** Program in Law and Public Affairs, Princeton University, 416A Robertson Hall, Princeton, NJ 08544-1013, U.S.A. **Online address:** gjbass@princeton.edu

BASS, Gary Jonathan. *See* **BASS, Gary J.**

BASS, Harold F. American (born United States), b. 1948. **Genres:** Politics/Government. **Career:** Ouachita Baptist University, Department of Political Science, instructor, 1976-78, assistant professor, 1978-83, associate professor, 1983-89, professor, 1989-96, 2003-, Moody professor of pre-law studies, 1996-2003, chair, 1979-2001, Maddox Public Affairs Center, director, 1986-2000, Division of Social Science, chair, 1990-2002, School of Social Sciences, dean, 2002-11; Arkadelphia First Baptist Church, moderator, 1982-; Merchants & Planters Bank, board director. Writer. **Publications:** Historical Dictionary of United States Political Parties, 2000, 2nd ed., 2009. **Address:** Department of Political Science, Ouachita Baptist University, 410 Ouachita St., PO Box 3737, Arkadelphia, AR 71998, U.S.A. **Online address:** bassh@obu.edu

BASS, Howard. British (born England), b. 1923. **Genres:** Sports/Fitness. **Career:** Programme Publications Ltd., sports editorial writer, 1947-48; Lea-Side Nursery Company Ltd., director, 1948-56; Howard Bass Publications Ltd., founder, managing director, Winter Sports (magazine), editor, 1948-69, winter sports correspondent, 1960-61; Daily Telegraph, winter sports correspondent, 1961-; Sunday Telegraph, winter sports correspondent, 1961-; Evening Standard, winter sports correspondent, 1973-; Toronto Star, winter sports correspondent, 1980-. **Publications:** The Sense in Sport, 1943; This Skating Age, 1958; The Magic of Skiing, 1959; Winter Sports, 1968; Success in Ice Skating, 1970; International Encyclopaedia of Winter Sports, 1971; Let's Go Skating, 1976; Tackle Skating, 1978; Ice Skating for Pleasure, 1979; Ice Skating, 1980; The Love of Skating and Speed Skating, 1980; Elegance on Ice, 1980; (with R. Cousins) Skating for Gold, 1980; Glorious Wembley: The Official History of Britain's Foremost Entertainment Centre, 1982; Super Book of Ice Skating, 1988; Ski Sunday, 1988. **Address:** Guinness Superlatives Ltd., 33 London Rd., Enfield, Middlesex, EX EN2 6DA, England.

BASS, Jack. American (born United States), b. 1934. **Genres:** History, Politics/Government, Social Commentary, Biography, Social Sciences. **Career:** State (newspaper), governmental affairs editor, 1963-66; Charlotte Observer, bureau chief, 1966-73; University of South Carolina, part-time lecturer in journalism, 1967-71, research fellow, American South Special Projects, director, 1979-85; Duke University, Institute of Policy Sciences and Public Affairs, visiting research fellow, 1973-75; South Carolina State College, writer-in-residence, 1975, research fellow, 1975-78; University of Mississippi, professor of journalism, 1987-98; College of Charleston, professor of humanities and social sciences, 1999-, now professor emeritus of humanities and social sciences; The Los Angeles Times, writer; Atlanta Constitution, writer; Washington Post, writer; The New Republic, writer; The Nation, writer; The New York Times, writer. **Publications:** (With J. Nelson) The Orangeburg Massacre, 1970, rev. ed., 1996; Porgy Comes Home, 1972; (with W. DeVries) The Transformation of Southern Politics, 1976; Widening the Mainstream of American Culture, 1978; (co-author) Emerging Coalitions in American Politics, 1978; Unlikely Heroes, 1981; (ed. with T.E. Terrill) The American South Comes of Age, 1985; Taming the Storm: The Life and Times of Judge Frank M. Johnson and the South's Fight over Civil Rights, 1993; (with M.W. Thompson) Ol' Strom: An Unauthorized Biography of Strom Thurmond, 1998; (with M.W. Thompson) Strom: The Complicated Personal and Political Life of Strom Thurmond, 2005; (foreword) Explorations in Charleston's Jewish History, 2005; (with W.S. Poole) Palmetto State: The Making of Modern South Carolina, 2009. Contributor to books and periodicals. **Address:** College of Charleston, 66 George St., Charleston, SC 29424-0001, U.S.A. **Online address:** jackbassauthor@gmail.com

BASS, Paul. American (born United States), b. 1960?. **Genres:** Novels. **Career:** Reporter, 1980-; New Haven Advocate, editor, 1989-2004; Yale University, Online Journalism Project, executive director, Department of Political Science, lecturer; New Haven Independent (online news Web site), founder and editor. **Publications:** (With D.W. Rae) Murder in the Model City: The Black Panthers, Yale, And the Redemption of a Killer, 2006. **Address:** Department of Political Science, Yale University, Rosenkranz Hall, 115 Prospect St., PO Box 208301, New Haven, CT 06520-8301, U.S.A. **Online address:** paul.bass@yale.edu

BASS, Ronald. American (born United States), b. 1942. **Genres:** Novels, Plays/Screenplays, Literary Criticism And History, Young Adult Fiction. **Career:** Lawyer; film producer; screenwriter. **Publications:** NOVELS: The Perfect Thief, 1978; Lime's Crisis, 1982; The Emerald Illusion, 1984. Contributor to periodicals. **Address:** Nancy Seltzer & Associates, 6220 Del Valle Dr., Los Angeles, CA 90048, U.S.A.

BASS, Thomas A. American (born United States), b. 1951. **Genres:** Business/Trade/Industry, Economics, Money/Finance, Sciences, History. **Career:** The New Yorker, contributor; Wired, contributor; The New York Times, contributor; Smithsonian, contributor; Discover, contributor; Hamilton College, faculty of literature and history; University of California, professor of literature and history; University at Albany, State University of New York, professor of English and journalism. Writer. **Publications:** The Eudaemonic Pie, 1985 in UK as The Newtonian Casino, 1990; Camping with the Prince and Other Tales of Science in Africa, 1990; Reinventing the Future: Conversations with the World's Leading Scientists, 1994; Vietnamerica: The War Comes Home, 1996; The Predictors, 1999; The Spy Who Loved Us: The Vietnam War and Pham Xuan An's Dangerous Game, 2009. **Address:** Department of English, College of Arts & Sciences, University at Albany, Humanities 328, 1400 Washington Ave., Albany, NY 12222, U.S.A. **Online address:** tbass@albany.edu

BASS, T. J. (Thomas J. Bassler). American (born United States), b. 1932. **Genres:** Science Fiction/Fantasy, Medicine/Health, Novels, Literary Criticism And History. **Career:** Deputy medical examiner, 1961-64; American Medical Joggers Newsletter, founder and editor, 1969-. **Publications:** SCIENCE-FICTION NOVELS: Half Past Human, 1971; The Godwhale, 1975; (with R.E. Burger as Thomas J. Bassler) The Whole Life Diet: An Integrated Program of Nutrition and Exercise for a Lifestyle of Total Health, 1979. Contributor of articles to journals. **Address:** 27558 Sunnyridge Rd., Palos Verdes Peninsula, CA 90274, U.S.A.

BASSETT, Elizabeth. American (born United States), b. 1950. **Genres:** Travel/Exploration, Sports/Fitness. **Career:** Teacher, 1972-73; Beacon Hill Travel, travel agent, 1973-75; Paul Browne Associates, travel agent and assistant manager, 1975-77; Thomas Cook Inc., manager of travel agency, 1977-79; Bank of New York, compensation manager and assistant vice president, 1981-82; Kanoo Travel, travel agent, 1983-85; freelance writer, 1985-; Cole Surveys Inc., project manager; Charlotte News, senior editor, 1994-95, contributing editor, 1995-97; Vermont Times, editor, 1994-95. **Publications:** Nature Walks in Northern Vermont and the Champlain Valley, 1998, rev. ed., 2009. Contributor to books and journals. **Address:** 1989 Mount Philo Rd., Charlotte, VT 05445, U.S.A.

BASSIL, Andrea. (Anna Nilsen). British (born England), b. 1948. **Genres:** Children's Fiction, Art/Art History, Children's Non-fiction, Illustrations, Picture/Board Books, Novels, Cartoons. **Career:** Mussleburgh Grammar School, assistant teacher of art, 1973-74; Saint Margaret's School, assistant teacher of art, 1974-85; Bournemouth and Poole College of Art and Design, course director in natural history illustration, 1985-90; Anglia Polytechnic University, head of graphic arts and illustration, 1990-94; full-time artist, writer and illustrator, 1995-; Pixel Magic, art director, screen designer and games consultant, 1995-96; Multimedia Corp., educational games consultant. **Publications:** CHILDREN'S BOOKS AS ANNA NILSEN: Jungle, 1994; Farm, 1994; Friends, 1994; Wheels, 1994; Dinosaurs, 1994; Terrormazia, 1995; Flying High, 1996; Fairy Tales, 1996; Under the Sea, 1996; Drive Your Car, 1996; Drive Your Tractor, 1996; Where Are Percy's Friends?, 1996; Where Is Percy's Dinner?, 1996; Percy the Park Keeper Activity Book, 1996; Follow the Kite, 1997; Let's all Dig and Burrow, 1998; Treasure Smuggler, 1998; Spycatcher, 1998; Let's all Hang and Dangle, 1998; Jewel Thief, 1998; Gold Robber, 1998; Insectoid Invasion, 1998; Leap and Jump, 1998; Swim and Dive, 1998; I Can Spell Three Letter Words, 1998; My Favorite Fairy Tales: A Sticker Book, 1999; I Can Count 10 to 20, 1999; I Can Count from 1-10, 1999; I Can Add, 2000; I Can Subtract, 2000; Mousemazia: An Amazing Dream House Maze, 2000; Art Fraud Detective, 2000; I Can Multiply, 2001; Magnificent Mazes, 2001; Let's Learn Great Art Scandal, 2003; Pirates, 2003; Busy Digger, 2003; Zooming Plane, 2003; Racing Car, 2003; Sailing Boat, 2003; The Amazing Journey of Charles Darwin, 2003; Moo Cow Moo!, 2003; Swim Duck Swim!, 2003; Tip Truck ! Tip!, 2004; Wave Baby! Wave!, 2004; Robotics Maths Games & Puzzles, 2004; My Best Dad, 2004; My Best Mum, 2005; Bella's Mid-summer Secret, 2005; Peepers Pet, 2005; Peepers Farm, 2005; Peepers People, 2005; Peepers Jungle, 2005; Magnificent Mazes, 2005; Magnificent Mazes Dinosaur Trails, 2005; My Best Friends, 2005; The Amazing Journey of Marco Polo, 2005; Art Auction Mystery. 2005; Jungle Safari, 2006; Counting Train, 2006; Little Helpers, 2006; Clap Your Hands, 2008; Give a Little Clap, 2008; Float and Flutter, 2008; Up and Away, 2008; Dart and Dive, 2008; Bath or Bed?, 2008; Wind or Rain?, 2008; Carrots or Peas?, 2008; Teddy or Train?, 2008; Pirates & Pirates Galore, 2010; Bella's Butterfly Ball, 2011. OTHERS: Jaguar Expedition to Belize, 1989; Design in Partnership, 1989. Contributor to journals. **Address:** 16 Emery St., Cambridge, CB CB1 2AX, England. **Online address:** anna.nilsen@ntlworld.com

BASSLER, Gerhard P. Canadian (born Canada), b. 1937. **Genres:** Area Studies, Cultural/Ethnic Topics, History, Social Sciences. **Career:** University of Kansas, assistant instructor in western civilization, 1963-65; Memorial University of Newfoundland, Department of History, lecturer, assistant professor, 1966-71, associate professor, 1971-79, professor, 1979-2002, professor emeritus, 2002-. Writer. **Publications:** (Ed., intro. and trans.) The German Canadians, 1750-1937: Immigration, Settlement & Culture, 1986; The German Canadian Mosaic Today and Yesterday: Identities, Roots and Heritage, 1991; Sanctuary Denied: Refugees from the Third Reich and Newfoundland

Immigration Policy, 1906-1949, 1992; Alfred Valdmanis and the Politics of Survival, 2000; Vikings to U-boats: The German Experience in Newfoundland and Labrador, 2006. Contributor to books. **Address:** Department of History, Memorial University of Newfoundland, Faculty of Arts, St. John's, NL A1C 5S7, Canada. **Online address:** gbassler@mun.ca

BASSLER, Thomas J. *See* **BASS, T. J.**

BASSO, Keith H(amilton). American (born United States), b. 1940. **Genres:** Language/Linguistics, Anthropology/Ethnology, Reference. **Career:** University of Arizona, assistant professor, 1967-71, associate professor, 1972-76, professor of cultural anthropology, 1977-81; Institute for Advanced Study, staff, 1975-76; School for American Research, weather head fellow, 1977-78; Yale University, professor of cultural anthropology, 1982-87; University of New Mexico, distinguished professor of anthropology, 1987, now professor emeritus. Writer and consultant. **Publications:** Western Apache Witchcraft, 1969; (co-author) Systems of North American Witchcraft and Sorcery, 1970; The Cibecue Apache, 1970; Portraits of The Whiteman: Linguistic Play and Cultural Symbols Among the Western Apache, 1979; Western Apache Language and Culture: Essays in Linguistic Anthropology, 1990; Wisdom Sits in Places: Landscape and Language Among the Western Apache, 1996; (with E.T. Watt) Don't Let the Sun Step Over You: A White Mountain Apache Family Life (1860-1975), 2004. EDITOR: (with M. Opler) Apachean Culture History and Ethnology, 1971; Western Apache Raiding and Warfare: From the Notes of Grenville Goodwin, 1971; (with H.A. Selby) Meaning in Anthropology, 1976; (with S. Feld) Senses of Place, 1996. Contributor to periodicals. **Address:** Department of Anthropology, University of New Mexico, Anthropology 1, MSC01-1040, Albuquerque, NM 87131-0001, U.S.A.

BASSOFF, Evelyn S(ilten). American (born United States), b. 1944. **Genres:** Human Relations/Parenting, Psychology. **Career:** Teacher, 1965-70; Fine and Folk Art Museum School, art teacher, 1973-74; Whittier Elementary School, project director, 1977-78; Boulder Valley Schools, teacher, 1977-80; University of Colorado, adjunct professor, 1981-, associate professor, 1981-87; Parents Magazine, contributing editor, columnist, 1992-98. **Publications:** Mothers and Daughters: Loving and Letting Go, 1988; Mothering Ourselves: Help and Healing for Adult Daughters, 1991; Between Mothers and Sons: The Making of Vital and Loving Men, 1994; Cherishing Our Daughters: How Parents Can Raise Girls To Become Strong And Loving Women, 1998. Contributor of articles to journals. **Address:** 2043 Pearl St., Boulder, CO 80302, U.S.A. **Online address:** eviboulder@aol.com

BASTA, Lofty L. American/Egyptian (born Egypt), b. 1933. **Genres:** Medicine/Health, Psychology. **Career:** Ains Shams University, intern at university hospital, 1955-56, resident, 1956-58, instructor in clinical medicine, 1958-63, lecturer in cardiology, 1963-70, assistant professor, 1970-71; Hammersmith Hospital, research fellow, 1960-61; University of Oklahoma, Tulsa Medical Center, clinical professor, 1966-93; University of Iowa, senior fellow, 1971-72, research associate in cardiology, 1972-73, assistant professor of medicine, 1973-74; University of Oklahoma Health Sciences Center, professor of medicine and head of cardiovascular section, 1974-76; St. John Medical Center, director of cardiology, 1976-83; Hillcrest Medical Center, director of cardiology, 1976-92; Tulsa Heart Center, founder, 1976, consulting cardiologist, 1976-93; Tampa General Hospital, chief of clinical cardiology, 1993-; University of South Florida, professor, Division of Cardiology, director, 1995-; University of Tennessee, visiting professor. Writer. **Publications:** Cardiovascular Disease: Essentials of Primary Care, 1983; (with C. Post) A Graceful Exit: Life and Death on Your Own Terms, 1996; Life and Death on Your Own Terms, 2001. Contributor to journals and books. **Address:** Department of Internal Medicine, College of Medicine, University of South Florida, 12901 Bruce B. Downs Blvd., Tampa, FL 33612-4742, U.S.A.

BASTA, Samir Sanad. French/Egyptian (born Egypt), b. 1943. **Genres:** Novels, Novellas/Short Stories, Humanities, Medicine/Health, Psychology, Writing/Journalism, Sciences. **Career:** National Institute of Nutrition-Mexico, researcher, 1968-70; National Institute of Nutrition-Bogor, researcher and field team leader, 1971-73; World Bank, nutrition expert, 1973-82; United Nations, UNICEF, representative, 1982-86, Evaluation Department, director, 1986-90, Office for Europe, director, 1990-95; Writer, 1995-. **Publications:** Culture, Conflict, and Children: Transmission of Violence to Children, 2000. Contributor to books and journals. **Address:** 41 Place des Muriers, Mougins, 06250, France. **Online address:** samirbasta@wanadoo.fr

BASTABLE, Bernard. *See* **BARNARD, Robert.**

BASTIANICH, Lidia Matticchio. American/Italian (born Italy), b. 1947. **Genres:** Food And Wine, Adult Non-fiction, Children's Fiction. **Career:** Buonavia Restaurant, owner, 1972-81; Villa Secondo, owner, 1979-81; Felidia Restaurant, owner, 1981-; United Nations International Children's Emergency Fund, chairperson of Roman holidays fund-raising benefit, 1991, co-chairperson of celebration of women charity event, 1998; Becco Restaurant, co-owner, 1993-; Frico Bar and Restaurant, co-owner, 1995-; Lidia's Flavors of Italy, partner; Esperienze Italian Travel, president, 1997-; Lidia's Kansas City, co-owner, 1998-; Lidia Matticchio Bastianich Foundation, founder, 1999; Lidia's Pittsburgh, co-owner, 2001-; Felidia Restaurant, co-owner. Writer and host. **Publications:** (With J. Jacobson) La Cucina di Lidia: Distinctive Regional Cuisine from the North of Italy, 1990; Lidia's Italian Table: More Than 200 Recipes from the First Lady of Italian Cooking, 1998; Lidia's Italian American Kitchen, 2001; (with M. Batali) Vino Italiano: The Regional Wines of Italy, 2002; (with J. Jacobs) La Cucina di Lidia: Recipes and Memories from Italy's Adriatic Coast, 2003; (with D. Nussbaum) Lidia's Family Table, 2004; (with T.B. Manuali and D. Nussbaum) Lidia's Italy, 2007; (with T.B. Manauli and D. Nussbam) Lidia Cooks from the Heart of Italy, 2009; Nonna Tell me a Story: Lidia's Christmas Kitchen, 2010; (with T.B. Manuali) Lidia's Italy in America, 2011. Contributor to periodicals. **Address:** c/o Jane Dystel, Dystel & Goderich Literary Management, 1 Union Sq. W, Ste. 904, New York, NY 10003, U.S.A. **Online address:** lidia@lidiasitaly.com

BASTIEN, Joseph William. American/Indian/French (born France), b. 1935. **Genres:** Anthropology/Ethnology, Mythology/Folklore. **Career:** Roman Catholic Mission, priest, 1963-69; Cornell University, teaching assistant, 1973; University of Texas-Permian Basin, Johnson State College, instructor of anthropology, 1973-74, assistant professor, 1974-77; University of Texas-Arlington, College of Liberal Arts, Department of Sociology and Anthropology, charter faculty, 1976-, assistant professor of anthropology, 1977-80, associate professor of anthropology, 1980-85, chair of graduate studies in anthropology and professor of anthropology, 1985-, Sociology and Anthropology Program, associate chair, 2002-, Anthropology Program, director, 2002-, distinguished scholar professor. Writer and consultant. **Publications:** Qollahuaya Rituals: An Ethnographic Account of the Symbolic Relations of Man and Land in an Andean Village, 1973; Mountain of the Condor: Metaphor and Ritual in an Andean Ayllu, 1978; (ed.) Health in the Andes, 1981; Las Plantas Medicinales de Los Callaways, 1983; Healers of the Andes: Kallawaya Herbalists and Their Medicinal Plants, 1987; Drum and Stethoscope: Integrating Ethnomedicine and Biomedicine in Bolivia, 1992; La Montaña del Condor: Metafora y Ritual en un Ayllu Andino, 1996; The Kiss of Death: Chaga's Disease in the Americas, 1998; People of the Water: Change and Continuity Among the Uru-Chipayans of Bolivia, 2012. **Address:** Department of Sociology and Anthropology, University of Texas, Rm. 444, 601 S Nedderman Dr., PO Box 19599, Arlington, TX 76019, U.S.A. **Online address:** bastien@uta.edu

BASTON, Lewis. British (born England) **Genres:** Politics/Government, Biography, Autobiography/Memoirs, History. **Career:** British Broadcasting Corp., historical consultant; Kingston University, Centre for the Understanding of Society and Politics, research fellow in history, 1998-2003; Electoral Reform Society, director of research, 2003-10; Democratic Audit, senior research fellow, 2010-. Election commentator and writer. **Publications:** (With A. Seldon) Major: A Political Life, 1997; (with S. Henig) Politico's Guide to the General Election, 2000; Sleaze: The State of Britain, 2000; (with S. Henig) The Political Map of Britain, 2002; Reggie: The Life of Reginald Maudling, 2004; Conservatives and the Electoral System, 2005; (with B. Blizzard) Eastern Approaches: How Labour can Win Back the East of England, 2011. Contributor to books. **Address:** Democratic Audit, Eleanor Rathbone Bldg., Bedford St. S, Liverpool, L69 7ZA, England. **Online address:** lbaston@democraticaudit.com

BASU, Alaka Malwade. American (born United States), b. 1949?. **Genres:** Cultural/Ethnic Topics, Sociology. **Career:** Cornell University, Department of Sociology, associate professor, professor; Jawaharlal Nehru University, Centre for the Study of Regional Development, visiting professor, 2010-. Researcher and writer. **Publications:** Culture, The Status of Women and Demographic Behavior, 1992; (ed. with R. Jeffery) Girls' Schooling, Women's Autonomy and Fertility Change in South Asia, 1996; (ed. with P. Aaby) The Methods and Uses of Anthropological Demography, 1998; The Sociocultural and Political Aspects of Abortion: Global Perspectives, 2003. **Address:** Department of Sociology, Cornell University, Rm. 331, Warren Hall, Ithaca, NY 14853-7601, U.S.A. **Online address:** ab54@cornell.edu

BASU, Kunal. British/Indian (born India), b. 1956?. **Genres:** Novels. **Career:** McGill University, associate professor of marketing and founding director of Centre for International Management Studies; Oxford University, Saïd Business School, reader in marketing, Templeton College, reader in marketing, fellow in strategic marketing, director of Oxford Advanced Management Program; Renmin University, distinguished visiting professor. **Publications:** The Opium Clerk, 2001; The Miniaturist, 2003; Racists, 2006; The Japanese Wife, 2008. Contributor of articles to magazines. **Address:** Said Business School, University of Oxford, Park End St, Oxford, OX OX1 1HP, England. **Online address:** kunal.basu@sbs.ox.ac.uk

BASWELL, Christopher. (Christopher C. Baswell). American (born United States), b. 1952. **Genres:** Literary Criticism And History, Classics. **Career:** Universite de Geneve, assistant, 1981-84; Barnard College, associate professor of English, 1984-, Ann Whitney Olin professor of English; University of California, professor of English, Center for Medieval and Renaissance Studies, associate director, 2000-08; Columbia University, English and Comparative Literature, professor. Writer. **Publications:** (Ed. with W. Sharpe) The Passing of Arthur: New Essays in Arthurian Tradition, 1988; Virgil in Medieval England: Figuring the Aeneid from the Twelfth Century to Chaucer, 1995; (ed.) Barnard Series of New Women Poets. Contributor to periodicals. **Address:** Department of English, Barnard College, 411A Barnard Hall, 3009 Broadway, New York, NY 10027, U.S.A. **Online address:** cbaswell@barnard.edu

BASWELL, Christopher C. *See* **BASWELL, Christopher.**

BASZILE, Jennifer Lynn. American (born United States), b. 1969. **Genres:** Autobiography/Memoirs, Biography. **Career:** Yale University, assistant professor of history, 1999-2007. Writer and historian. **Publications:** The Black Girl Next Door: A Memoir, 2009. **Address:** c/o Robert F. Levine, Levine Plotkin & Menin L.L.P., 1740 Broadway, New York, NY 10019, U.S.A. **Online address:** info@theblackgirlnextdoor.com

BATAILLE, Christophe. French (born France), b. 1971. **Genres:** Novels, Young Adult Fiction. **Career:** Writer. **Publications:** Annam, 1993; Absinthe, 1994; Hourmaster, 1998; Le Matre des Heures: roman, 1997; Vive l'enfer, 1999; J'envie la félicité des Bêtes: Roman, 2002; Quartier Général du Bruit: Roman, 2006; Le Rêve de Machiavel: Roman, 2008. **Address:** Editions Grasset, 61 rue des Saint-Près, Paris, 75006, France. **Online address:** cbatille@grasset.fr

BATALI, Mario. American (born United States), b. 1960. **Genres:** Food And Wine, Regional/Urban Planning. **Career:** Po', chef and co-owner, 1993-; Babbo Ristorante Enoteca, chef and co-owner, 1998-; Lupa, chef and co-owner, 1999-; Esca, chef and co-owner, 2000; Otto Enoteca Pizzeria, chef and co-owner, 2003-; Del Posto, chef and co-owner, 2005-; Osteria Mozza and Pizzeria Mozza, chef and co-owner, 2006-; B&B Ristorante e Enoteca and Enoteca San Marco, chef and co-owner, 2007-; Carnevino Italian Steakhouse, chef and co-owner, 2008-; The Tarry Lodge, chef and co-owner, 2008-; Mario Batali Foundation, founder, 2008-; Italian Wine Merchants, co-owner. Writer. **Publications:** Mario Batali Simple Italian Food: Recipes from My Two Villages, 1998; Holiday Food: Family Recipes for the Festive Time of the Year, 2000; The Babbo Cookbook, 2002; Vino Italiano: The Regional Wines of Italy, 2002; Molto Italiano: 327 Simple Italian Recipes to Cook at Home, 2005; Mario Tailgates NASCAR Style, 2006; (with J. Sutton) Italian Grill, 2008; (with G. Paltrow) Spain: A Culinary Road Trip, 2008; (with M. Ladner) Molto Gusto: Easy Italian Cooking, 2010. Contributor to periodicals. **Address:** Otto Enoteca Pizzeria, 1 5th Ave., New York, NY 10003, U.S.A.

BAT-AMI, Miriam. American (born United States), b. 1950. **Genres:** Children's Fiction, Novels, Young Adult Fiction. **Career:** University of Pittsburgh, teaching fellow in English, 1980-84; Southwest Missouri State University, instructor in English, 1984-89; Western Michigan University, Department of English, assistant professor, 1989-94, associate professor, 1994-2000, professor, 2001-, now emeritus; California State University, tutor. Writer. **Publications:** Sea, Salt and Air (picture book), 1993; When the Frost is Gone, 1994; Dear Elijah (middle-grade novel), 1995; Two Suns in the Sky (young adult novel), 1999. Contributor of articles to journals and periodicals. **Address:** Department of English, Western Michigan University, 6th Fl., Sprau Twr., Kalamazoo, MI 49008, U.S.A. **Online address:** miriam.bat-ami@wmich.edu

BATCHELOR, David. British (born England), b. 1943. **Genres:** Novels, Novellas/Short Stories, Adult Non-fiction, Art/Art History, Photography. **Career:** Royal College of Art, Department of Curating Contemporary Art, senior tutor in critical theory; artist and writer. **Publications:** Brogan & Sons, 1976; A Dislocated Man, 1978; Children in the Dark, 1982; Why Tilbury?, 1985; (with B. Fer and P. Wood) Realism, Rationalism, Surrealism: Art Between the Wars, 1993; Minimalism, 1997; (co-author) Gary Hume: British Pavilion, XLVIII Venice Biennale, 1999; Chromophobia, 2000; (with B. Fibicher, C. Doherty and E. Seifermann) Anne Katrine Dolven, 2001; (with R. Fuchs and N. Serota) Donald Judd, 2004; Colour (Whitechapel: Documents of Contemporary Art), 2008. Contributor to magazines. **Address:** 52 Onslow Sq., London, GL SW7 3NX, England.

BATCHELOR, John. British (born England), b. 1942. **Genres:** Novels, Art/Art History, Literary Criticism And History, Biography. **Career:** Birmingham University, lecturer in English, 1968-76; Oxford University, New College, fellow, 1976-90, senior tutor, 1985-87; Newcastle University, Joseph Cowen professor of English, 1990-2007, head of department, 1992-94, now professor emeritus of English and senior research investigator; University of Lancaster, honorary adjunct professor, 2002, now professor emeritus; Modern Language Review, editor; Yearbook of English Studies, editor. **Publications:** Breathless Hush, 1974; Mervyn Peake: A Biographical and Critical Exploration, 1974; The Edwardian Novelists, 1982; H.G. Wells, 1985; Lord Jim, 1988; Virginia Woolf: The Major Novels, 1991; The Life of Joseph Conrad: A Critical Biography, 1994; John Ruskin: No Wealth but Life, 2000; John Ruskin: A Life, 2000; Scott, William Bell (1811-1890), 2004; Edwardian Literature, in Edwardian to Georgian Fiction, 2005; Lady Trevelyan and the Pre-Raphaelite Brotherhood, 2006; (ed. and contrib.) Alfred Tennyson: Problems of Biography, 2006; Victorian Literature: An Introduction, 2006; Lord Jim at the Frontier, 2007; A New Life, forthcoming. EDITOR: Lord Jim, by Conrad, 1983; Victory: An Island Tale, 1986; The Art of Literary Biography, 1995; (with T. Cain and C. Lamont) Shakespearean Continuities: Essays in Honour of E.A.J. Honigman, 1997. **Address:** c/o Felicity Bryan, Felicity Bryan Literary Agency, 2A N Parade Ave., Oxford, OX OX2 6LX, England. **Online address:** j.b.batchelor@ncl.ac.uk

BATCHELOR, R. E. British (born England), b. 1934. **Genres:** Language/Linguistics, Literary Criticism And History, Adult Non-fiction. **Career:** University of Besancon, teacher of English, 1957-59; San Sebastian, English teacher, 1959-60; teacher of French and Spanish, 1961-62; University of Nottingham, Department of Modern Languages, teacher of French and Spanish, 1961-95, now retired; University of Paris, teacher and researcher; University of Salamanca, teacher and researcher; University of Valencia, teacher and researcher. Writer. **Publications:** Unamuno, Novelist: A European Perspective, 1972; (with M.Offord) Using French: A Guide to Contemporary Usage, 1982, 3rd ed., 1999; (with C. Pountain) Using Spanish: A Guide to Contemporary Usage, 1992, 2nd ed., 2003; (with M. Offord) Using French Synonyms, 1993; Using Spanish Synonyms, 1994, 2nd ed., 2006; (with M.C. Saadi) French for Marketing: Using French in Media and Communications, 1997; (with M.C. Saadi) Usage Pratique et courant des synonymes anglais, 1998; L'Uso dei sinonimi (spagnoli), 2000; (with M.A.S. Jose) Using Spanish Vocabulary, 2003; L'uso dei sinonimi inglese, 2003; A Student Grammar of Spanish, 2006; (with M.A.S. José) Reference Grammar of Spanish, 2010; (with M. Chebli-Saadi) Reference Grammar of French, 2011. Contributor to journals. **Address:** Department of French, University of Nottingham, Nottingham, NT NG7 2RD, England. **Online address:** ronald@ronald48.fsnet.co.uk

BATCHELOR, Stephen. French/Scottish (born Scotland), b. 1953. **Genres:** Theology/Religion, Translations. **Career:** Tibetisches Institute, translator; Gaia House, guiding teacher, 1990-2000; Sharpham Trust, coordinator, 1992-; Sharpham College, Buddhist Studies and Contemporary Equity, co-founder, 1996-. Photographer. **Publications:** (Trans.) A. Shantideva, A Guide to the Bodhisattva's Way of Life, 1979; Alone with Others: An Existential Approach to Buddhism, 1983; Echoes of Voidness, 1983; Flight: An Existential Conception of Buddhism, 1984; (ed. and intro.) The Way of Korean Zen, 1985; (ed. and intro.) The Jewel in the Lotus: A Guide to the Buddhist Traditions of Tibet, 1987; The Tibet Guide, 1987, rev. ed. (with B. Beresford and S. Jones), 1998; Song of the Profound View, 1989; The Faith to Doubt: Glimpses of Buddhist Uncertainty, 1990; The Mind and Its Functions: A Textbook of Buddhist Epistemology and Psychology, 1991; The Awakening of the West: The Encounter of Buddhism and Western Culture, 1994; Buddhism without Beliefs: A Contemporary Guide to Awakening, 1997; (ed. with G. Watson and G. Claxton) The Psychology of Awakening: Buddhism, Science, and Our Day-to-Day Lives, 2000; Verses from the Center: A Buddhist Vision of the Sublime, 2000; Meditation for Life, 2001; Living with the Devil: A Meditation on Good and Evil, 2004; Confession of a Buddhist Atheist, 2010. **Address:** Anne Edelstein Literary Agency, 20 W 22nd St., Ste. 1603, New York, NY 10010-5848, U.S.A. **Online address:** info@stephenbatchelor.org

BATCHEN, Geoffrey. American/Australian (born Australia) **Genres:** Photography, Art/Art History, History. **Career:** University of California, instructor; University of New Mexico, associate professor of art history and theory; City University of New York, Graduate Center, professor of history of photography and contemporary art, 2002-10; Victoria University of Wellington, School of Art History, Classics and Religious Studies, professor, 2010-. Writer. **Publications:** Burning with Desire: The Conception of Photography, 1997; (contrib.) Deep Storage: Collecting, Storing, and Archiving in Art, 1998; Each Wild Idea: Writing, Photography, History, 2001; Forget Me Not: Photography & Remembrance, 2004; (contrib.) Joan Fontcuberta: Landscapes Without Memory, 2005; (contrib.) Singular Images: Essays on Remarkable Photographs, 2005; (with P. Javault and P. Uklanski) Joy of Photography, 2007; (contrib.) Now is Then: Snapshots from the Maresca Collection, 2008; (contrib.) Way out West: Desert Landscapes, 2008; William Henry Fox Talbot, 2008; (ed.) Photography Degree Zero: Reflections on Roland Barthes's Camera Lucida, 2009; (contrib.) Living Man Declared Dead and Other Chapters, 2011. **Address:** School of Art History, Classics and Religious, Studies, Victoria University, Rm. 312, Old Kirk Bldg., PO Box 600, Wellington, 6140, New Zealand. **Online address:** geoffrey.batchen@vuw.ac.nz

BATE, Jonathan. British (born England), b. 1958. **Genres:** Literary Criticism And History, Novels, Biography, Adult Non-fiction, Essays, Politics/Government. **Career:** Cambridge University, St. Catharine's College, research fellow, 1983-85, honorary fellow, Trinity Hall, fellow and director of studies in English, 1985-90; University of Liverpool, King Alfred professor of English literature, 1990-2003, Leverhulme personal research professor, 1999-2004, 2010-11; University of Warwick, professor of Shakespeare and Renaissance literature, 2003-; Royal Shakespeare Co., governor, 2007-11; University of Oxford, Harris Manchester College, visiting fellow, 2010-11, Worcester College, provost, 2011-. Writer. **Publications:** Shakespeare and the English Romantic Imagination, 1986; Shakespearean Constitutions: Politics, Theater, Criticism, 1730-1830, 1989; Romantic Ecology: Wordsworth and the Environmental Tradition, 1991; Shakespeare and Ovid, 1993; The Genius of Shakespeare, 1998; The Cure for Love, 1998; The Song of the Earth, 2000; (contrib.) Ovid's Metamorphoses: The Arthur Golding Translation, 1567, 2000; I Am: The Selected Poetry of John Clare, 2003; John Clare: A Biography, 2003; (foreword) Wild Reckoning: An Anthology Provoked by Rachel Carson's Silent Spring, 2004; Shakespeare in the Elizabethan World Viking, 2008; Soul of the Age: The Life, Mind and World of William Shakespeare, 2008; Soul of the Age: A Biography of the Mind of William Shakespeare, 2009; English Literature: A Very Short Introduction, 2010; Ted Hughes: The Inner Life, forthcoming. EDITOR: (and intro.) Elia; 1987; The Last Essays of Elia, 1987; The Romantics on Shakespeare, 1991; The Arden Shakespeare: Titus Andronicus, 1995; (with R. Jackson) Shakespeare: An Illustrated Stage History, 1996; (with J.L. Levenson and D. Mehl) Shakespeare and the Twentieth Century: The Selected Proceedings of the International Shakespeare Association World Congress, Los Angeles, 1996, 1998; The Oxford English Literary History, 2002; John Clare, Selected Poetry, 2004; (with E. Rasmussen) Complete Works, 2007; (with E. Rasmussen and intro.) Midsummer Night's Dream, 2008; (with E. Rasmussen and intro.) Love's Labour's Lost, 2008; (with E. Rasmussen and intro.) Hamlet, 2008; (with E. Rasmussen and intro.) Richard III, 2008; (with E. Rasmussen and intro.) Tempest, 2008; (with E. Rasmussen and intro.) King Lear, 2009; (with E. Rasmussen and intro.) Henry IV, Part I, 2009; (with E. Rasmussen and intro.) Henry IV, Part II, 2009; (with E. Rasmussen and intro.) Antony and Cleopatra, 2009; (with E. Rasmussen and intro.) Macbeth, 2009; (with E. Rasmussen and intro.) Othello, 2009; (with E. Rasmussen and intro.) Romeo and Juliet, 2009; (with E. Rasmussen and intro.) Sonnets and Other Poems, 2009; (with E. Rasmussen and intro.) Much Ado about Nothing, 2009; (with E. Rasmussen and intro.) Winter's Tale, 2009; (with E. Rasmussen and intro.) Taming of the Shrew, 2010; (with E. Rasmussen and intro.) Henry V, 2010; (with E. Rasmussen and intro.) Richard II, 2010; (with E. Rasmussen and intro.) Troilus and Cressida, 2010; (with E. Rasmussen and intro.) Merchant of Venice, 2010; (with E. Rasmussen and intro.) Twelfth Night, 2010; (with E. Rasmussen and intro.) Measure for Measure, 2010; (with E. Rasmussen and intro.) As You Like It, 2010; (with E. Rasmussen and intro.) Two Gentlemen of Verona, 2011; (with E. Rasmussen and intro.) Titus Andronicus and Timon of Athens, 2011; (with E. Rasmussen and intro.) Merry Wives of Windsor, 2011; (with E. Rasmussen and intro.) All's Well that Ends Well, 2011; (with E. Rasmussen and intro.) Comedy of Errors, 2011; (with E. Rasmussen and intro.) Coriolanus, 2011; (with E. Rasmussen and intro.) Cymbeline, 2011; (with E. Rasmussen and intro.) Julius Caesar, 2011. Contributor of articles to journals and periodicals. **Address:** Worcester College, University of Oxford, Wellington Sq., Oxford, OX1 2JD, England. **Online address:** j.bate@warwick.ac.uk

BATEMAN, Robert L. American (born United States), b. 1967. **Genres:** Military/Defense/Arms Control, History, Military/Defense/Arms Control, Biography, Autobiography/Memoirs. **Career:** U.S. Military Academy, assistant professor of military history; Georgetown University, Center for Strategic and International Studies, military fellow, Security Studies Program, adjunct professor; DC Examiner, columnist. **Publications:** (Ed.) Digital War: A View from the Front Lines, 1999; No Gun Ri: A Military History of the Korean War Incident, 2002. **Address:** Security Studies Program, Georgetown University, 3600 N St. NW, Washington, DC 20007, U.S.A. **Online address:** robert.bateman@us.army.mil

BATEMAN, Tracey V. Also writes as Tracey Victoria Bateman. American (born United States) **Genres:** Romance/Historical, Novels, Novellas/Short Stories. **Career:** Writer. **Publications:** CHRISTIAN FICTION: AS TRACEY VICTORIA BATEMAN: Darling Cassidy, 2000; Tarah's Lessons, 2001; Laney's Kiss, 2003; But for Grace, 2003; Emily's Place, 2003. CHRISTIAN FICTION: (with J. Stengl) A Christmas Sleigh Ride, 2004; Torey's Prayer, 2004; Everlasting Hope, 2004; Timing Is Everything, 2004; Betrayal of Trust, 2005; Beside Still Waters, 2005; A Love So Tender, 2005; Second Chance, 2005; Suspicion of Guilt, 2005; Reasonable Doubt, 2005; (with C.M. Hake and K.E. Hake) California Chances, 2005; 365 Secrets of Beauty, 2006. CHRISTIAN FICTION AS TRACEY BATEMAN: The Color of the Soul, 2005; Freedom of the Soul, 2007. CLAIRE SERIES AS TRACEY BATEMAN: Leave It to Claire, 2006; Claire Knows Best, 2006; I Love Claire, 2007. OTHERS: (with S.K. Downs, J. Miller and J. Peterson) China Tapestry, 2002; Defiant Heart, 2007; Oregon Brides, 2007; Catch a Rising Star, 2007; You Had Me at Good-bye, 2008; Distant Heart, 2008; Dangerous Heart, 2008; That's Amore, 2008; Tarah's Lessons, 2008; Season for Grace, 2008; Thirsty, 2009; Tandem, 2010; (co-author) A Prairie Christmas Collection, 2010. **Address:** c/o Author Mail, Warner Faith, 1271 Ave. of the Americas, New York, NY 10020, U.S.A. **Online address:** tracey@traceybateman.com

BATEMAN, Tracey Victoria. *See* **BATEMAN, Tracey V.**

BATES, Craig D. American (born United States), b. 1952. **Genres:** Natural History, Anthropology/Ethnology, Classics. **Career:** National Park Service, Yosemite National Park, park technician in Division of Interpretation, 1973-76, Indian cultural specialist, 1976-80, assistant curator, 1980-82, curator of ethnography, 1982-, now retired; Merced Community College, instructor, 1974; California Department of Parks and Recreation, instructor, 1977-84; Point Reyes Field Seminars, instructor, 1978-88; Humboldt State University, instructor, 1980; Santa Barbara Museum of Natural History, research associate, 1983-. Consultant and writer. **Publications:** The Reflexed Sinew-Backed Bow of the Sierra Miwok, 1978; (comp. with F. La Pena) Legends of the Yosemite Miwok, 1981, 3rd ed. (comp. with S.P. Medley and F.La Pena), 2007; Coiled Basketry of the Sierra Miwok: A Study of Regional Variation, 1982; Feathered Regalia of Central California: Wealth and Power, 1982; The Indian Cultural Museum: A Guide to the Exhibits, 1985, rev. ed. (with M.J. Lee), 1987; (with M.J. Lee) Tradition and Innovation: A Basket History of the Indians of the Yosemite-Mono Lake Area, 1990; (with T. Hudson) People From the Water: Indian Art and Culture from Russian California, 1993; The Miwok in Yosemite: Southern Miwok Life, History and Language in the Yosemite Region, 1996; (with B.B. Kahn and B.L. Lanford) An Introduction to the Cheyenne-Arapaho Ledger Book from the Pamplin Collection, 1999; (with B.B. Kahn and B.L. Lanford) Cheyenne/Arapaho Ledger Book: From the Pamplin Collection, 2003. **Address:** Santa Barbara Museum of Natural History, 2559 Puesta Del Sol, Santa Barbara, CA 93105, U.S.A. **Online address:** craig_bates@nps.gov

BATES, Judy Fong. Canadian/Chinese (born China), b. 1949?. **Genres:** Novellas/Short Stories, Novels, Young Adult Non-fiction, Young Adult Fiction. **Career:** University of Toronto, faculty; Trent University, faculty; Diaspora Dialogues, faculty. Writer. **Publications:** China Dog and Other Tales from a Chinese Laundry, 1997; Midnight at the Dragon Café, 2003; The Year of Finding Memory, 2010. Contributor of short fiction to periodicals. **Address:** c/o Denise Bukowski, The Bukowski Agency, 14 Prince Arthur Ave., Ste. 202, Toronto, ON M5R 1A9, Canada. **Online address:** mail@judyfongbates.com

BATES, Karen Grigsby. American (born United States), b. 1951?. **Genres:** Novels, Children's Fiction. **Career:** People Magazine, news reporter and writer, 1990-; Los Angeles Times, writer, 1990-, contributing columnist; National Public Radio, Day to Day Magazine, commentator, reporter and correspondent for news, 2003-. **Publications:** (With K.E. Hudson) Basic Black: Home Training for Modern Times, 1996, rev. ed. as The New Basic Black: Home Training for Modern Times, 2006; (contrib.) Mothers Who Think: Tales of Real-Life Parenthood, 1999; Plain Brown Wrapper: An Alex Powell Novel, 2001; (contrib.) Gumbo: An Anthology of African American Writing, 2002; Chosen People: An Alex Powell Novel, 2006; (with A.N. Cooper) Century and Some Change: My Life Before the President Called My Name, 2010. Contributor to periodicals. **Address:** National Public Radio, 635 Massachusetts Ave. NW, Washington, DC 20001, U.S.A. **Online address:** kkandjbates@earthlink.net

BATES, Stephen. (Stephen John Bates). British (born England), b. 1954. **Genres:** Theology/Religion, Novels, Politics/Government, History. **Career:** British Broadcasting Corp., staff; Daily Telegraph, staff; Daily Mail, staff; Guardian, education editor, 1990-93, political correspondent, 1993-95, European affairs editor, 1995-99, religious affairs and royal correspondent, 1999- . Journalist. **Publications:** A Church at War: Anglicans and Homosexuality, 2004; Asquith, 2006; God's Own Country: Religion and Politics in the US, 2007. **Address:** The Guardian, King's Pl., 90 York Way, London, GL N1 9GU, England. **Online address:** stephen.bates@guardian.co.uk

BATES, Stephen John. *See* **BATES, Stephen.**

BATESON, Mary Catherine. American (born United States), b. 1939. **Genres:** Anthropology/Ethnology, Autobiography/Memoirs. **Career:** Harvard University, instructor in Arabic, 1963-66; Ateneo de Manila University, assistant professor, associate professor of anthropology, 1966-68; Brandeis University, senior research fellow in psychology and philosophy, 1968-69; Massachusetts Institute of Technology, research staff, 1969-71; Northeastern University, visiting professor of anthropology, 1969-71, 1974-75; Iranian National Character Study Group, organizer, 1972-74; Damavand College, professor of anthropology and dean of graduate studies, 1975-77; University of Northern Iran, professor of anthropology and dean of social science and humanities, 1977-79; Institute for Intercultural studies, president, 1979-2009; Amherst College, professor of anthropology, 1980-86, dean of faculty, 1980-83; George Mason University, Clarence J. Robinson professor in anthropology and English, 1986-2004, professor emeritus of anthropology and English, 2004-. Writer. **Publications:** (Ed. with T.A. Sebeok and A.S. Hayes) Approaches to Semiotics: Anthropology, Education, Linguistics, Psychiatry and Psychology, 1964; Arab Language Handbook, 1967, 2nd ed., 2003; Structural Continuity in Poetry: A Linguistic Study of Five Pre-Islamic Odes, 1970; Our Own Metaphor: A Personal Account of a Conference on the Effects of Conscious Purpose on Human Adaptation, 1972; (co-author) About Bateson: Essays on Gregory Bateson, 1977; With a Daughter's Eye: A Memoir of Margaret Mead and Gregory Bateson, 1984; (with G. Bateson) Angels Fear: Towards an Epistemology of the Sacred, 1987; (with R. Goldsby) Thinking AIDS, 1988; Composing a Life, 1989; Peripheral Visions: Learning along the Way, 1994; (with E. Freud and D. van Golden) Youth Is an Art, 1997; Full Circles, Overlapping Lives: Culture and Generation in Transition, 2000; Willing to Learn: Passages of Personal Discovery, 2004; Composing a Further Life: The Age of Active Wisdom, 2010. Contributor of articles to books and journals. **Address:** George Mason University, 4400 University Dr., Fairfax, VA 22030, U.S.A. **Online address:** mcb@marycatherinebateson.com

BATH, K. P. American (born United States), b. 1959. **Genres:** Children's Fiction, Science Fiction/Fantasy. **Career:** Asian Reporter, editorial staff, 2002-. Children's book author. **Publications:** The Secret of Castle Cant: Being An Account of the Remarkable Adventures of Lucy Wickwright, Maidservant and Spy, 2004; Escape from Castle Cant, 2006; The Black Arrow of Cant, 2007; Flip Side, 2009. Contributor to journals. **Address:** c/o Author Mail, Warner Books, 1271 Ave. of the Americas, New York, NY 10020, U.S.A.

BATNITZKY, Leora. (Leora Faye Batnitzky). American (born United States), b. 1966. **Genres:** Philosophy, Politics/Government, History, Young Adult Fiction. **Career:** Syracuse University, assistant professor of religion, 1996-97; Princeton University, Department of Religion, assistant professor, 1997-2003, associate professor, 2003-06, professor of religion, 2007-, Richard Stockton bicentennial preceptor, 2000-03, Laurence S. Rockefeller preceptor, 2001-04, director of graduate studies, 2003-05, Tikvah Project on Jewish Thought, director, 2007-, Program in Judaic Studies, acting director, 2007-08, chair, 2010-; Jewish Studies Quarterly, co-editor, 2004-; University of Tokyo, visiting professor, 2006; New York University Law School, Hauser fellow in global law, 2006-07. **Publications:** NONFICTION: Idolatry and Representation: The Philosophy of Franz Rosenzweig Reconsidered, 2000; Leo Strauss and Emmanuel Levinas: Philosophy and the Politics of Revelation, 2006; How Judaism Became a Religion: An Introduction to Modern Jewish Thought, 2011. Contributor to books and journals. **Address:** Department of Religion, Princeton University, 237 1879 Hall, 416A Robertson Hall, Princeton, NJ 08544-1013, U.S.A. **Online address:** batnitzk@princeton.edu

BATNITZKY, Leora Faye. *See* **BATNITZKY, Leora.**

BATORY, Joseph P. American (born United States), b. 1943. **Genres:** Novels, Education. **Career:** Teacher, 1964-70; La Salle University, director of sports information, 1970-75; Upper Darby School District, director of communications, 1975-80, assistant superintendent, 1980-84, superintendent of schools, 1984-99, now retired; Educational Enterprises, associate, 2003-. Writer. **Publications:** Joey's Story: A Portrait of a School Leader, (autobiography), 2002; Yo! Joey! (autobiography), 2000; Joey Lets It All Hang Out, 2003. **Address:** 2401 Pennsylvania Ave., Ste. 10C47, Philadelphia, PA 19130, U.S.A. **Online address:** batoryjoe1@verizon.net

BATT, Tanya Robyn. New Zealander (born New Zealand), b. 1970. **Genres:** Mythology/Folklore, Children's Fiction. **Career:** Imagined Worlds, owner, 1995-. Writer and art educator. **Publications:** The Fabrics of Fairytale: Stories Spun from Far and Wide; The Terrible Queue, 2001; Imagined Worlds: A Journey through Expressive Arts in Early Childhood, 2001; A Child's Book of Fairies, 2002; The Fairy's Gift, 2002; The Princess and the White Bear King, 2004; The Bearfoot Book of Faeries, 2009; Contributor to periodicals. **Address:** Imagined Worlds, PO Box 660, Auckland, 1840, New Zealand. **Online address:** tanya@imagined-worlds.net

BATTEN, Bruce L. (Bruce Loyd Batten). Japanese/American (born United States), b. 1958?. **Genres:** Geography. **Career:** J.F. Oberlin University, faculty, professor of Japanese history & vice-president for international relations, 1989-; Inter-University Center for Japanese Language Studies, director, 1991-95. Author and historian. **Publications:** To the Ends of Japan: Premodern Frontiers, Boundaries and Interactions, 2003; Gateway to Japan: Hakata in War and Peace, 500-1300, 2006. Contributor to periodicals and books. **Address:** J.F. Oberlin University, 3758 Tokiwa-machi, Machida-shi, Tokyo, 194-0294, Japan. **Online address:** bruce@obirin.ac.jp

BATTEN, Bruce Loyd. *See* **BATTEN, Bruce L.**

BATTENFIELD, Jackie. American (born United States), b. 1950?. **Genres:** Photography, Education. **Career:** Columbia University, faculty; Rotunda Gallery, founder, 1981. Writer. **Publications:** Ikat Technique, 1978; The Artist's Guide: How to Make a Living Doing What You Love, 2009; Moments of Change: Prints by Jackie Battenfield, 2009. Contributor to periodicals. **Address:** New York, NY , U.S.A. **Online address:** jbattenfield@gmail.com

BATTERSBY, Christine. British (born England), b. 1946. **Genres:** Philosophy, Art/Art History, Literary Criticism And History, Women's Studies And Issues, History, Ethics. **Career:** Greater London Council, administrative assistant, 1968-69; University of Warwick, lecturer in philosophy, 1972-, senior lecturer, reader in philosophy, 1972-2008, reader emeritus in philosophy, 2008-, The Centre for Research in Philosophy, Literature and The Arts, associate fellow. Writer. **Publications:** Gender and Genius: Towards a Feminist Aesthetics, 1990; The Phenomenal Woman: Feminist Metaphysics and the Patterns of Identity, 1998; The Sublime, Terror and Human Difference, 2007. Contributor of articles to books and journals. **Address:** Department of Philosophy, University of Warwick, Coventry, WM CV4 7AL, England. **Online address:** c.battersby@warwick.ac.uk

BATTESTIN, Martin Carey. American (born United States), b. 1930. **Genres:** Literary Criticism And History, Biography, History. **Career:** Wesleyan University, instructor, 1956-58, assistant professor, 1958-61; University of Virginia, assistant professor, 1961-63, associate professor, 1963-67, professor, 1967-75, Center for Advanced Studies, associate, 1970-71, 1974, 1975, Kenan professor of English literature, 1975-98, chairman of the department, 1983-86, professor emeritus of English, 1998-; Cambridge University, associate, 1972. Writer. **Publications:** The Moral Basis of Fielding's Art, 1959;

The Providence of Wit: Aspects of Form in Augustan Literature and the Arts, 1974; (contrib.) Literature and Society, 1978; (with J.P. Hunter) Henry Fielding in His Time and Ours, 1987; New Essays by Henry Fielding: His Contributions to the Craftsman (1734-1739) and Other Early Journalism, 1989; Henry Fielding: A Life, 1989; A Henry Fielding Companion, 2000; (intro.) The History and Adventures of the Renowned Don Quixote, 2003. EDITOR/CO-EDITOR: (with intro.) Joseph Andrews and Shamela, 1961; Joseph Andrews, 1967; Twentieth-Century Interpretations of Tom Jones, 1968; Tom Jones, 1975; Amelia, 1983; Joseph Andrews/Henry Fielding, 1984; British Novelists, 1660-1800, 1985; (with C.T. Probyn) The Correspondence of Henry and Sarah Fielding, 1993; The Journal of a Voyage to Lisbon, Shamela and Occasional Writings, 2008. **Address:** Department of English Language and Literature, University of Virginia, PO Box 400121, Charlottesville, VA 22904-4121, U.S.A. **Online address:** mcb9g@virginia.edu

BATTIE, David. British (born England), b. 1942. **Genres:** Antiques/Furnishings, Art/Art History. **Career:** Reader's Digest, book designer, 1963-67; Sotheby's, expert, 1967-, director, 1976-99, retired, 1999; BBC TV Antiques Roadshow, expert, 1977-; broadcaster on radio and television; Masterpiece Magazine, editor. **Publications:** (With M. Turner) The Price Guide to 19th and 20th Century British Porcelain, 1975; (with M. Turner) Price Guide to 19th and 20th Century British Pottery: Including Staffordshire Figures and Commemorative Wares, 1979; David Battie's Guide to Understanding 19th and 20th Century British Porcelain: Including Fakes, Techniques and Prices, 1994. EDITOR: Sotheby's Concise Encyclopedia of Porcelain, 1990; Sotheby's Concise Encyclopedia of Glass, 1991; Antiques Roadshow, 2005. **Address:** Sotheby's, 34/35 New Bond St., London, GL W1A 2AA, England.

BATTLE, Michael Jesse. American (born United States), b. 1963. **Genres:** Novels, Theology/Religion. **Career:** Anglican Church, ordained priest, 1993; Archbishop Desmond Tutu, adjutant, 1993-94; University of the South, assistant professor, 1995-99; Duke University School of Divinity, assistant professor, 1999-2004; St. Ambrose Episcopal Church, rector, 2001- 04; Virginia Theological Seminary, vice president, dean of academic studies and associate professor, 2005-07; Cathedral Center of St. Paul, provost and canon theologian, 2007-; Episcopal House of Bishops, chaplain; CREDO, spiritual director; Church of Our Saviour, rector. Writer. **Publications:** Reconciliation: The Ubuntu Theology of Desmond Tutu, 1997; The Wisdom of Desmond Tutu, 2000; Blessed Are the Peacemakers: A Christian Spirituality of Nonviolence, 2004; (ed.) The Quest for Liberation and Reconciliation: Essays in Honor of J. Deotis Roberts, 2005; Practicing Reconciliation in a Violent World, 2005; (with T. Campolo) The Church Enslaved: A Spirituality of Racial Reconciliation, 2005; The Black Church in America: African American Christian Spirituality, 2006. **Address:** Rector and Canon Theologian, Church of Our Saviour, Anglican/Episcopal Church, 535 W Roses Rd., San Gabriel, CA 91775, U.S.A. **Online address:** info@michaelbattle.com

BATTLE, Richard V. American (born United States), b. 1951. **Genres:** Business/Trade/Industry, Social Sciences, Self Help. **Career:** Burroughs Corp., Office Products Group, sales representative, 1973-76, zone sales manager, 1976-77; Bell & Howell Co., Microfilm Products Division, sales representative, 1977-88, western area sales manager, 1987-2001; Datatron Communication, sales representative, 1986-87; KeyTrak Inc., national sales manager, 2001-, vice president of sales. Writer. **Publications:** The Volunteer Handbook: How to Organize and Manage a Successful Organization, 1988; Surviving Grief by God's Grace, 2002; The Four Letter Word that Builds Character, 2006. **Address:** KeyTrak Inc., 200 Quality Cir., College Station, TX 77845, U.S.A. **Online address:** rbat1@attglobal.net

BATTLES, Brett. American (born United States), b. 1962?. **Genres:** Novels, Mystery/Crime/Suspense. **Career:** Writer. **Publications:** JONATHAN QUINN THRILLER SERIES: The Cleaner, 2005; The Deceived, 2008; Shadow of Betrayal in UK as The Unwanted, 2009; The Silenced, 2011; The Sick, 2011; Every Precious Thing, 2011; The Pull of Gravity, 2011; Here Comes Mr. Trouble, 2011; Little Girl Gone, 2011; No Return: A Novel, 2012. Works appear in anthologies. **Address:** Random House Inc., 1745 Broadway, New York, NY 10019-4368, U.S.A. **Online address:** brett_battles@mail.vresp.com

BATTLES, Matthew. American (born United States) **Genres:** Librarianship. **Career:** Harvard University, Widener Library, librarian, Houghton Library, librarian, Harvard Library Bulletin, assistant editor, 1999-, coordinating editor, Harvard Depository Project Push, coordinator, 1998-. **Publications:** Library: An Unquiet History, 2003; Widener: Biography of a Library, 2004; (ed.) El Greco to Velazquez: Art During the Reign of Philip III, 2008. Contributor to Magazines. **Address:** Houghton Library, Harvard University, Massachusetts Hall, Cambridge, MA 02138, U.S.A. **Online address:** mbattles@fas.harvard.edu

BAUCKHAM, Richard J. Scottish/British (born England), b. 1946. **Genres:** Theology/Religion, History, Bibliography, Cultural/Ethnic Topics, Environmental Sciences/Ecology. **Career:** St. John's University, fellow, 1972-75; University of Manchester, reader in the history of Christian thought, 1977-92; University of St. Andrews, St. Mary's College, professor of New Testament studies, 1992-, Bishop Wardlaw Professor, 2000-, now professor emeritus; St. Mellitus College, visiting professor. Theologian and author. **Publications:** (With D. Bebbington) History & Christianity: A Bibliography, 1977; (ed.) Tudor Apocalypse: Sixteenth Century Apocalypticism, Millennarianism and the English Reformation: From John Bale to John Foxe and Thomas Brightman: Illustrative Texts from the Lanterne of Lyght, 1978; Jude, 2 Peter, 1983; Moltmann: Messianic Theology in the Making, 1987; (ed. with B. Drewery) Scripture, Tradition and Reason: A Study in the Criteria of Christian Doctrine: Essays in Honour of Richard P.C. Hanson, 1988; (ed. with R.J. Elford) The Nuclear Weapons Debate: Theological and Ethical Issues, 1989; (co-editor) Jesus 2000, 1989; The Bible in Politics: How to Read the Bible Politically, 1989, 2nd ed., 2011; Jude and the Relatives of Jesus in the Early Church, 1990; The Climax of Prophecy: Studies on the Book of Revelation, 1993; The Theology of the Book of Revelation, 1993; (contrib.) Hermias: Satire des Philosophes Pa Iens. Sources Chretiennes, 1993; (ed.) The Book of Acts in Its Palestinian Setting, 1995; The Theology of J. Urgen Moltmann, 1995; (ed.) The Gospels for All Christians: Rethinking the Gospel Audiences, 1998; The Fate of the Dead: Studies on the Jewish and Christian Apocalypses, 1998; God Crucified: Monotheism and Christology in the New Testament, 1999; (with T. Hart) Hope against Hope: Christian Eschatology at the Turn of the Millennium, 1999; (ed.) God Will Be All in All: The Eschatology of JUrgen Moltmann, 1999; (with T. Hart) At the Cross: Meditations on People Who Were There, 1999; James: Wisdom of James, Disciple of Jesus the Sage, 1999; (co-editor) Dictionary of Historical Theology, 2000; God and the Crisis of Freedom: Biblical and Contemporary Perspectives, 2002; Gospel Women: Studies of the Named Women in the Gospels, 2002; Bible and Mission: Christian Witness in a Postmodern World, 2003; Jesus and the Eyewitnesses: The Gospels as Eyewitness Testimony, 2006; The Testimony of the Beloved Disciple: Narrative, History and Theology in the Gospel of John, 2007; (ed. with C. Mosser) The Gospel of John and Christian Theology, 2008; The Fate of the Dead: Studies on the Jewish and Christian Apocalypses, 2008; Jesus and the God of Israel: God Crucified and Other Studies on the New Testament's Christology of Divine Identity, 2008; The Jewish World Around the New Testament: Collected Essays I, 2008; (ed.) A Cloud of Witnesses: The Theology of Hebrews in its Ancient Contexts, 2008; (co-editor) Epistle to the Hebrews and Christian Theology, 2008; Bible and Ecology: Rediscovering the Community of Creation, 2010; Jesus: A Very Short Introduction, 2011; Living with Other Creatures, 2011. **Address:** St. Mary's College, University of St. Andrews, South St., St. Andrews, FF KY16 9JU, Scotland. **Online address:** rjb@st-andrews.ac.uk

BAUCOM, Donald R. American (born United States), b. 1940. **Genres:** Military/Defense/Arms Control. **Career:** Strategic Defense Initiative Organization (now Ballistic Missile Defense Organization), Air Force historian, 1987-90, civilian historian, 1990-; International Military and Defense Encyclopedia, editorial staff, 1990; U.S. Air Force Academy, teacher of military history; Air War College, faculty; Airpower Research Institute, director of research; Air University Review, editor. **Publications:** The Origins of SDI, 1944-1983, 1992. **Address:** U.S. Department of Defense, Ballistic Missile Defense Organization, Rm. IE 1008, The Pentagon, Washington, DC 20301, U.S.A.

BAUDE, Jeannine. French (born France), b. 1946. **Genres:** Poetry, Songs/Lyrics And Libretti, Young Adult Fiction. **Career:** Writer. **Publications:** POETRY COLLECTIONS: Les feux de l'été, 1977; Ouessanes, 1989; Parabole de l'éolienne, 1990; C'était un paysage, 1992. OTHERS: (intro.) Correspondance, 1935-1970, 1993; Concerto pour une roche, 1995; Océan, 1995; (contrib.) Louis Guillaume, 1997; Incarnat désir, 1998; (co-author) Labiales, 2000; Venise, Venezia, Venessia, 2001; Île corps océan, 2001; L'adresse à la voix, 2003; New York is New York, 2006; Le chant de Manhattan: suivi de, Piano words, précédé de L'avancée dans le texte, 2006. **Address:** c/o Author Mail, Editions Rougerie, Route de Nouic, Mortemart, 87330, France.

BAUER, Belinda. Welsh/British (born England), b. 1962. **Genres:** Novels. **Career:** Scriptwriter and novelist. **Publications:** Blacklands, 2010; Darkside: A Novel, 2011. **Address:** Cardiff, SG , Wales.

BAUER, Caroline Feller. American (born United States), b. 1935. **Genres:** Novellas/Short Stories, Children's Fiction, Children's Non-fiction, Literary Criticism And History, Poetry, Reference. **Career:** New York Public Library, children's librarian, 1958, 1959, 1961; Colorado Rocky Mountain School, librarian, 1963-66; University of Oregon, associate professor of library science, 1966-79; Caroline's Corner, KOAP-TV, producer, 1973-74. Writer. **Publications:** Children's Literature: A Teletext, 1973; Storytelling, 1974; Caroline's Corner, 1974; Handbook for Storytellers, 1977; Children's Literature, 1978; My Mom Travels a Lot, 1981; This Way to Books, 1983; Too Many Books!, 1984; Getting It Together with Books, 1984; Celebrations: Read-Aloud Holiday and Theme Book Program, 1985; Presenting Reader's Theater Plays and Poems to Read Aloud, 1987; Midnight Snowman, 1987; Read For the Fun of It, 1992; Putting on a Play, 1993; Caroline Feller Bauer's New Handbook for Storytellers, 1993; The Poetry Break: An Annotated Anthology with Ideas for Introducing Children to Poetry, 1995; Bangladesh at Work, 2006. LEADING KIDS TO BOOKS THROUGH... SERIES: Magic, 1996; Puppets, 1997; Crafts, 2000. EDITOR: Rainy Day: Stories and Poems, 1986; Snowy Day: Stories and Poems, 1986; Halloween: Stories and Poems, 1989; Valentines Day, 1993; Windy Day: Stories and Poems, 1988; Valentine's Day: Stories and Poems, 1993; Thanksgiving, 1994. **Address:** 10150 Collins Ave., Miami, FL 33154-1654, U.S.A.

BAUER, Douglas. American (born United States), b. 1945. **Genres:** Local History/Rural Topics, Food And Wine. **Career:** Better Homes and Gardens, advertising copywriter; Playboy, associate editor; freelance journalist; Bennington College, MFA program in writing and literature, core faculty; Harvard University, faculty; Rice University, faculty; Smith College, faculty. **Publications:** Prairie City, Iowa: Three Seasons at Home, 1979; Dexterity, 1989; The Very Air, 1993; The Book of Famous Iowans, 1997; Stuff of Fiction: Advice on Craft, 2000, rev. ed., 2006; (ed.) Prime Times, 2004; Stuff of Fiction: Advice on Craft, 2006; (ed.) Death by Pad Thai: And Other Unforgettable Meals, 2006. Contributor to periodicals. **Address:** c/o Al Lowman, 19 W 44th St., Ste. 1602, New York, NY 10036, U.S.A. **Online address:** debauer@erols.com

BAUER, Henry H. (Josef Martin). American/Austrian/Australian (born Australia), b. 1931. **Genres:** Education, Sciences. **Career:** University of Sydney, Department of Agricultural Chemistry, lecturer, senior lecturer in agricultural chemistry, 1958-65; University of Michigan, Department of Chemistry, visiting scientist, 1965-66; University of Kentucky, associate professor, 1966-69, professor of chemistry, 1969-78; University of Southampton, visiting professor of chemistry, 1972-73; Virginia Polytechnic Institute and State University, professor of chemistry and science studies, 1978-99, College of Arts and Sciences, dean, 1978-86, Center for the Study of Science in Society, founding member, 1979, editor, 1993-99, professor and dean emeritus, 1999-; Journal of Scientific Exploration, editor-in-chief, 2000-07. **Publications:** (With B. Breyer) Alternating Current Polarography and Tensammetry, 1963; Electrodics-Modern Ideas Concerning Electrode Reactions, 1972; (ed. with G.D. Christian and J.E. O'Reilly) Instrumental Analysis, 1978; Beyond Velikovsky: The History of a Public Controversy, 1984; The Enigma of Loch Ness: Making Sense of a Mystery, 1986; (as Josef Martin) To Rise above Principle: The Memoirs of an Unreconstructed Dean, 1988; Scientific Literacy and the Myth of the Scientific Method, 1992; Science or Pseudoscience, 2001; Fatal Attractions: The Troubles with Science, 2001; Origin, Persistence and Failings of HIV/AIDS Theory, 2007; Dogmatism in Science and Medicine, 2011. Contributor to periodicals and journals. **Address:** 207 Woods Edge Ct., Blacksburg, VA 24060-4015, U.S.A. **Online address:** hhbauer@vt.edu

BAUER, Marion Dane. American (born United States), b. 1938. **Genres:** Children's Fiction, Young Adult Fiction, Children's Non-fiction, Picture/Board Books, Children's Non-fiction, Novels. **Career:** High school teacher, 1962-64; Hennepin Technical Center, instructor in creative writing for adult education program, 1975-78; Norwich University, Vermont College of Fine Arts, faculty, 1976-, Vermont College, faculty chair, 1997-2000, Union Institute and University, faculty, 2000-09; University of Minnesota, instructor of continuing education for women, 1978-85, Institute for Children's Literature, staff, 1982-85, The Loft, staff, 1987-95; Crestwood House, editor, 1989. **Publications:** FOR YOUNG ADULTS FICTION: Shelter from the Wind, 1976; Foster Child, 1977; Tangled Butterfly, 1980; Rain of Fire, 1983; Like Mother, Like Daughter, 1985; On My Honor, 1986; Touch the Moon, 1987; A Dream of Queens and Castles, 1990; Face to Face, 1991; Ghost Eye, 1992; A Taste of Smoke, 1993; A Question of Trust, 1994; (ed. and contrib.) Am I Blue? Coming out from the Silence, 1994; An Early Winter, 1999; Runt, 2002; Land of the Buffalo Bones, 2003; Grand Canyon, 2006; I'm Not Afraid of Halloween!: A Pop-Up and Flap Book, 2006; Niagara Falls, 2006; Rocky Mountains, 2006; Killing Miss Kitty and Other Sins, 2007; Mama for Owen, 2007; Mighty Mississippi, 2007; Mount Rushmore, 2007; Secret of the Painted House, 2007; Statue of Liberty, 2007; Baby Bear Discovers the World, 2007; Floods!, 2008; One Brown Bunny, 2008; Red Ghost, 2008; Volcanoes!, 2008; Yellowstone, 2008; Green Ghost, 2008; How Do I Love You?, 2009; Have You Heard? A Baby!, 2009; One Brown Bunny, 2009; Very Little Princess, 2009; Longest Night, 2009; Earthquake, 2009. NONFICTION: What's Your Story?: A Young Person's Guide to Writing Fiction, 1992; A Writer's Story: From Life to Fiction, 1995; Our Stories: A Fiction Workshop for Young Authors, 1996. FOR CHILDREN: PICTURE BOOKS: When I Go Camping with Grandma, 1995; Alison's Wings, 1996; Alison's Fierce and Ugly Halloween, 1997; Alison's Puppy, 1997; Turtle Dreams, 1997; If You Were Born a Kitten, 1997; Bear's Hiccups, 1998; Christmas in the Forest, 1998; Sleep, Little One, Sleep, 1999; Jason's Bears, 2000; Grandmother's Song, 2000; My Mother Is Mine, 2001; If You Had a Nose Like an Elephant's Trunk, 2001; Frog's Best Friend, 2002; Love Song for a Baby, 2002; The Kissing Monster, 2002; Uh-Oh, 2002; Toes, Ears and Nose, 2003; Snow, 2003; Clouds, 2003; Wind, 2003; Why Do Kittens Purr?, 2003; The Very Best Daddy, 2004; Rain, 2004; Double-digit Club, 2004; Bear named Trouble, 2005; Blue Ghost, 2005; Easter is Coming, 2005; If Frogs Made Weather, 2005; Recipe for Valentine's Day: A Rebus Lift-The-Flap Story, 2005; The Christmas Baby, 2009; Martin Luther King, Jr., 2009; Christopher Columbus, 2009; Thank You For Me!, 2010; The Golden Ghost, 2011; In Like a Lion, Out Like a Lamb, 2011; The Very Little Princess: Rose's Story, 2011; The Halloween Forest, 2012; Dinosaur Thunder, 2012; Little Dog, Lost, 2012. Contributor to books and periodicals. **Address:** 508 Montcalm Pl., St. Paul, MN 55116, U.S.A. **Online address:** mdb@mariondanebauer.com

BAUER, Susan Wise. American (born United States), b. 1968. **Genres:** Education. **Career:** Rita Welsh Adult Literacy Center, reading tutor and librarian; Peace Hill Press, editor-in-chief, co-owner, editorial director; College of William and Mary, instructor of writing and American literature, 1993-, visiting assistant professor of English. **Publications:** The Revolt, 1996; Though the Darkness Hide Thee, 1998; (with J. Wise) The Well-Trained Mind: A Guide to Classical Education at Home, 1999; The Story of the World: History for the Classical Child, vol. I: Ancient Times, 2002, vol. II: The Middle Ages, 2003; The Well-Educated Mind, 2003; The History of the Ancient World: From the Earliest Accounts to the Fall of Rome, 2007; Writing with Ease: Strong Fundamentals, 2008; The Art of the Public Grovel, 2008; The History of the Medieval World: From the Conversion of Constantine to the First Crusade, 2010. **Address:** c/o Rich Henshaw, Richard Henshaw Group, 22 W 23rd St., 5th Fl., New York, NY 10010, U.S.A.

BAUER, Tricia. American (born United States) **Genres:** Novels, Novellas/Short Stories, Young Adult Fiction, Literary Criticism And History. **Career:** Redbook Magazine, fiction reader and manuscript evaluator, 1990-94; Millbrook Press Inc., editor, manager of special sales and director of special sales and rights, 1992-98; Rosen Publishing, director for special markets, 1998-2005, vice president of special markets, 2005-. **Publications:** Working Women and Other Stories (short stories), 1995. Boondocking (novel), 1997; Hollywood & Hardwood, 1999; Shelterbelt, 2000; Father Flashes, 2010, The World is Red, forthcoming. Contributor to periodicals. **Address:** The Rosen Publishing Group, 29 E 21st St., New York, NY 10010, U.S.A.

BAUER, Yehuda. Israeli/Czech (born Czech Republic), b. 1926. **Genres:** History, Theology/Religion. **Career:** Hebrew University, Harman Institute of Contemporary Jewry, Department of Holocaust Studies, lecturer, 1961-68, senior lecturer, 1968-73, associate professor, 1973-77, professor, 1977-94, head, 1968-95, Jonah M. Machover professor emeritus of Holocaust studies, Pela and Adam Starkopf professor emeritus, 1994-, Institute of Contemporary Jewry, head, 1973-77, International Center for the Study of Antisemitism, head, 1985-95; Yale University, visiting professor, 1993; International Institute for Holocaust Studies, chair, 1995; International Institute for Holocaust Research, director, 1996-; Brandeis University, visiting professor; International Task Force for Holocaust Education, academic advisor. Writer. **Publications:** From Diplomacy to Resistance, 1970; (ed. with J. Robinson) Guide to Unpublished Materials of the Holocaust Period, 1970; Flight and Rescue, 1970; They Chose Life, 1973; My Brother's Keeper, 1974; The Holocaust in Historical Perspective, 1978; The Jewish Emergence from Powerlessness, 1979; American Jewry and the Holocaust: The American Jewish Joint Distribution Committee, 1939-1945, 1981; (ed. with N. Rotenstreich and M. Lowe) The Holocaust as Historical Experience: Essays and a Discussion, 1981; (with N. Keren) A History of the Holocaust, 1982, rev. ed., 2001; Sho'ah, hebeṭim hisṭoriyim, 1982; Teguvot be-'et ha-Sho'ah, 1983; Anti-Semitism in the 1980s, 1983; Ha-Gal ha-anṭishemi ba-'olam shel yamenu, 1985; Antisemitism Today: Myth and Reality, 1985; (ed. with M.Z. Rosensaft) Antisemitism: Threat to Western Civilization, 1988; (ed.) Present-day Antisemitism, 1988; (co-ed.) Remembering for the Future, 1989; Out of the Ashes: The Impact of American Jews on Post-Holocaust European Jewry, 1989; (ed.) The Danger of Antisemitism in Central and Eastern Europe in the Wake of 1989-1990, 1991; Jews for Sale?: Nazi-Jewish Negotiations, 1933-1945, 1994; (ed. with C. Rittner, S.D. Smith and I. Steinfeldt) Holocaust and the Christian World, 2000; Yehudim li-mekhirah?, 2001; Rethinking the Holocaust, 2001; (co-author) Extrema derecha, 2003; (intro.) Preludiu la asasinat, 2005; On the Holocaust and Other Genocides, 2007; Hirhurim 'al ha-sho'ah, 2008; Death of the Shtetl, 2009; (ed. with C. Rittner, S.D. Smith and I. Steinfeldt) A holokauszt és a keresztény világ, 2009. **Address:** Department of Holocaust Studies, Hebrew University, Mt. Scopus, Jerusalem, 91905, Israel. **Online address:** yehuda.bauer@huji.ac.il

BAUERLEIN, Mark (Weightman). American (born United States), b. 1959. **Genres:** Literary Criticism And History, Psychology. **Career:** University of California, lecturer in English, 1988-89; Emory University, assistant professor of English, 1989-2003, professor, 2005-; National Endowment for the Arts, Office of Research and Analysis, director, 2003-05. Writer. **Publications:** Whitman and the American Idiom, 1991; (ed.) Purloined Letters; (ed. and intro.) The Turning Word: American Literary Modernism and Continental Theory, 1996; The Pragmatic Mind: Explorations in the Psychology of Belief, 1997; Literary Criticism: An Autopsy, 1997; Negrophobia: A Race Riot in Atlanta, 1906, 2001; (with X.J. Kennedy and D. Gioia) Handbook of Literary Terms: Literature, Language, Theory, 2005, 2nd ed., 2009; (with X.J. Kennedy and D. Gioia) Longman Dictionary of Literary Terms: Vocabulary for the Informed Reader, 2006; Dumbest Generation: How The Digital Age Stupefies Young Americans and Jeopardizes Our Future (or, Don't Trust Anyone Under 30), 2008; (ed. with E. Grantham) National Endowment for the Arts: A History, 1965-2008, 2009; (ed.) Digital Divide, 2011. **Address:** Department of English, Emory University, N 302 Callaway Ctr., 537 Kilgo Cir., Atlanta, GA 30322, U.S.A. **Online address:** engmb@emory.edu

BAUERMEISTER, Erica. American (born United States), b. 1959?. **Genres:** Education, Women's Studies And Issues. **Career:** University of Washington, instructor; Antioch University, instructor. Writer. **Publications:** (With J. Larsen and H. Smith) 500 Great Books by Women: A Reader's Guide, 1994; (with H. Smith) Let's Hear It for the Girls: 375 Great Books for Readers 2-14, 1997; The School of Essential Ingredients, 2009. **Address:** Seattle, WA , U.S.A. **Online address:** ericabauermeister@gmail.com

BAUERSCHMIDT, Frederick Christian. American (born United States), b. 1961. **Genres:** Theology/Religion, History. **Career:** Duke University, Department of Religion, lecturer, 1993; Loyola College, assistant professor of theology, 1994-2000, associate professor, 2000-; Loyola International Nachbahr Huis, director, 2001-03; Katholieke Universiteit, visiting professor, 2001-03; Journal Modern Theology, co-editor, 2001-. **Publications:** NONFICTION: Julian of Norwich and the Mystical Body Politic of Christ, 1999; Why the Mystics Matter Now, 2003; (ed. with J. Fodor) Aquinas in Dialogue: Thomas for the Twenty-first Century, 2004; Holy Teaching: Introducing the Summa Theologiae of St. Thomas Aquinas, 2005; (ed. with J.J. Buckley and T. Pomplun) The Blackwell Companion to Catholicism, 2007; The Blackwell Introduction to Catholic Theology, 2008; Thomas Aquinas: Faith, Reason and Following Christ, 2009. Contributor to periodicals. **Address:** Department of Theology, Loyola College in Maryland, HU 042G, 4501 N Charles St., Baltimore, MD 21210, U.S.A. **Online address:** fbauerschmidt@loyola.edu

BAUGHAN, Peter Edward. British (born England), b. 1934. **Genres:** History, Area Studies, Transportation. **Career:** British Railways, Parliamentary Office, North-Eastern Region Estate and Rating Surveyor's Department, technical assistant, 1956-60, Chief Civil Engineer's Department, technical assistant, 1960-66; Greater London Council, Department of Transportation and Development, technical officer, 1966-86; Civil Engineers Institution, technician engineer. Writer. **Publications:** North of Leeds: The Leeds-Settle-Carlisle Line and Its Branches, 1966 as The Midland Railway: North of Leeds, 1987; The Railways of Wharfedale, 1969; The Chester & Holyhead Railway, 1972; A Regional History of the Railways of Great Britain, vol. XI: North and Mid Wales, 1980; The North Wales Coast Railway, 1988. Contributor to journals. **Address:** 55 Coulstock Rd., Burgess Hill, Sussex, WS RH15 9XZ, England.

BAUGHMAN, John Russell. American (born United States) **Genres:** Politics/Government, International Relations/Current Affairs. **Career:** Bates College, associate professor of politics. Writer. **Publications:** Common Ground: Committee Politics in the U.S. House of Representatives, 2006. **Address:** Department of Political Science, Bates College, 174 Pettengill Hall, Lewiston, ME 04240, U.S.A. **Online address:** jbaughma@bates.edu

BAUGHMAN, Michael. American (born United States), b. 1937. **Genres:** Adult Non-fiction, Philosophy, History, Politics/Government. **Career:** Writer. **Publications:** NONFICTION: The Perfect Fishing Trip, 1985; Ocean Fishing: A Basic Guide for the Saltwater Angler, 1986; Mohawk Blood, 1995; A River Seen Right, 1995; (with C. Hadella) Warm Springs Millennium: Voices from the Reservation, 2000. Contributor to magazines. **Address:** c/o John Ware, 392 Central Pk. W, New York, NY 10025, U.S.A.

BAUGHMAN, T. H. American (born United States), b. 1947. **Genres:** History, Autobiography/Memoirs. **Career:** CBS Inc., marketing and sales, 1976-84; John Wiley and Sons Inc., manager, 1984-85, 1988-90; Wesleyan College, instructor, 1985-88; Benedictine College, Department of History, assistant professor, associate professor, professor, chair, 1990-2000; University of Central Oklahoma, dean of the college of liberal arts, 2000-04, professor of history, 2004-; Faculty Global Competencies, officer, 2008-10. Writer. **Publications:** How to Get the Most out of Europe, 1984; Before the Heroes Came: Antarctica in the 1890s, 1994; (ed.) Ice: The Antarctic Diary of Charles Passel, 1995; Pilgrims on the Ice: Robert Falcon Scott's First Expedition, 1999; Shackleton of the Antartic, 2002; A Companion to Modern World History, 2003; Book Length Manuscripts: Antarctica, 1922 to 1941, forthcoming. Contributor to periodicals. **Address:** Department of History, University of Central Oklahoma, 100 N University Dr., Edmond, OK 73034, U.S.A. **Online address:** thb@thbaughman.com

BAULENAS, Lluís-Anton. Spanish (born Spain), b. 1958?. **Genres:** Novellas/Short Stories. **Career:** Writer, critic and theater director. **Publications:** Qui al cel escup-(a la cara li cau) (short stories), 1987; Neguit, 1988; Sus scrofa (porcs), 1988; Rampoines/451, 1990; Cálida nit (short stories), 1990; No hi ha illes meravelloses, 1992; (comp. and intro.) Poemes d'ausiás march: Antologia, 1993; Melosa Fel: Tragicomèdia urbana, 1993; Noms a la sorra, 1995; El pont de Brooklyn, 1995; Alfons XIV: Un crim d'estat, 1997; Els caníbals, 1998; El fil de Plata, 1998; La felicitat, 2001; Amor d'idiota, 2003; El Cataláno morirá: Un moment decisiu per al futur de la llengua, 2004; (co-author) Lux Mundi: Relats de la ribagorca, 2005; Per un sac d'ossos, 2005; área de servei, 2007; Un amor a cada bar, 2007; El nas de Mussolini, 2009. **Address:** Pontas Literary & Film Agency, Sèneca 31, Barcelona, 08006, Spain.

BAUMAN, Beth Ann. American (born United States), b. 1964?. **Genres:** Novels, Novellas/Short Stories. **Career:** University of California, Extension Writers' Program, online instructor in writing; New York University, instructor in writing. Writer. **Publications:** Beautiful Girls (short stories), 2002; Rosie and Skate (young-adult novel), 2009. Contributor to periodicals. **Address:** New York, NY , U.S.A. **Online address:** bethbau@aol.com

BAUMAN, Bruce. American (born United States) **Genres:** Novels, Literary Criticism And History. **Career:** Black Clock, senior editor; CalArts, instructor, adjunct professor in creative writing program; Virginia Center for the Creative Arts, fellow. **Publications:** (Contrib.) Fodor's I-95, Maine to Miami, 1986; And the Word Was, 2005; Broken Sleep, 2012. Contributor to periodicals. Works appear in anthologies. **Address:** California Institute of the Arts, Rm. D206A, 24700 McBean Pkwy., Valencia, CA 91355, U.S.A. **Online address:** bbauman@calarts.edu

BAUMAN, Christian. American (born United States), b. 1970. **Genres:** Novels, Young Adult Fiction, Social Sciences. **Career:** Writer, musician, songwriter and editor. **Publications:** NOVELS: The Ice beneath You, 2002; Voodoo Lounge, 2005; In Hoboken, 2008. Contributor to periodicals. **Address:** Publicity Department, Simon & Schuster Inc., 1230 Ave. of the Americas, New York, NY 10020-1513, U.S.A. **Online address:** christianbauman@pobox.com

BAUMAN, Richard. American (born United States), b. 1940. **Genres:** Politics/Government, Theology/Religion, Art/Art History. **Career:** University of Texas, faculty, 1968-86, Center for Intercultural Studies in Folklore and Ethnomusicology, director, 1970-86, professor, 1976-86; Indiana University, Department of Folklore and Ethnomusicology, chair, 1986-91, professor, 1986-, distinguished professor, 1991-, now distinguished professor emeritus, Department of Anthropology, professor, now distinguished professor emeritus, Department of Communication and Culture, professor, now professor emeritus, Research Center for Language and Semiotic Studies, director, 1992. Writer. **Publications:** For the Reputation of Truth; Politics, Religion, and Conflict among the Pennsylvania Quakers, 1750-1800, 1971; Verbal Art as Performance, 1978; Let Your Words Be Few: Symbolism of Speaking and Silence among Seventeenth-Century Quakers, 1983; Story, Performance, and Event: Contextual Studies of Oral Narrative, 1986; (with C.L. Briggs) Voices of Modernity: Language Ideologies and the Politics of Inequality, 2003; A World of Others' Words: Cross-Cultural Perspectives on Intertextuality, 2004. EDITOR: (with A. Paredes) Toward New Perspectives in Folklore, 1972; (with J. Sherzer) Explorations in the Ethnography of Speaking, 1974, 2nd ed., 1989; (with J. Sherzer) Language and Speech in American Society: A Compilation of Research Papers in Sociolinguistics, 1980; (with R.D. Abrahams) And Other Neighborly Names: Social Process and Cultural Image in Texas Folklore, 1981; Folklore, Cultural Performances, and Popular Entertainments: A Communications-Centered Handbook, 1992; (and intro.) Folklore and Culture on the Texas-Mexican Border, 1993. **Address:** Department of Anthropology, Indiana University, 130 Student Bldg., 701 E Kirkwood Ave., Bloomington, IN 47405-7100, U.S.A. **Online address:** bauman@indiana.edu

BAUMAN, Richard W. Canadian (born Canada), b. 1951. **Genres:** Law. **Career:** Dalhousie University, assistant professor, 1984-85; Alberta Law Reform Institute, counsel, 1987-88; University of Alberta, professor of law, 1988-, McCalla research professor, 1998-99, Osler professor of corporate law, Centre for Constitutional Studies, Management Board, chair, Faculty of Law, Graduate Programs, director, 1990-92. Writer. **Publications:** (Ed. with J. Hart) Explorations in Difference: Law, Culture, and Politics, 1996; Critical Legal Studies: A Guide to the Literature, 1996; Aristotle's Logic of Education, 1998; Ideology and Community in the First Wave of Critical Legal Studies, 2002; (ed. with T. Kahana) Least Examined Branch: The Role of Legislatures in the Constitutional State, 2006. **Address:** Faculty of Law, University of Alberta, 111 St. and 89 Ave., Edmonton, AB T6G 2H5, Canada. **Online address:** rbauman@law.ualberta.ca

BAUMAN, Zygmunt. British/Polish (born Poland), b. 1925. **Genres:** Sociology, Psychology, History, Social Sciences. **Career:** University of Warsaw, senior lecturer, 1956-59, docent in general sociology, 1960-, chair of the department, 1966-68, now professor emeritus; University of Tel Aviv, dozent to professor of sociology, 1968-71; University of Leeds, professor of sociology, 1971-, now emeritus professor of sociology, 1990-. Writer. **Publications:** Between Class and Elite, 1972; Culture as Praxis, 1973; Towards a Critical Sociology, 1976; Socialism: The Active Utopia, 1976; Hermeneutics and Social Science, 1978; Memories of Class, 1982; Legislators and Interpreters: On Modernity, Postmodernity and Intellectuals, 1987; Freedom, 1988; Modernity and the Holocaust, 1989; Thinking Sociologically: An Introduction for Everyone, 1990, (with T. May) 2nd ed., 2001; Modernity and the Ambivalence, 1991; Intimations of Postmodernity, 1992; Mortality, Immortality and Other Life Strategies, 1992; Postmodern Ethics, 1994; Life in Fragments, 1995; Ansichten der Postmoderne, 1995; Postmodernity and Its Discontents, 1997; Work, Consumerism and the New Poor, 1998, 2nd ed., 2005; Globalization: The Human Consequences, 1998; In Search of Politics, 1999; Liquid Modernity, 2000; Individualized Society, 2000; Community: Seeking Safety in an Uncertain World, 2001; (with D. Filipov) Conversations with Zygmunt Bauman, 2001; Society Under Siege, 2002; Liquid Love: On the Frailty of Human Bonds, 2003; Identity: Conversations with Benedetto Vecchi, 2004; Europe: An Unfinished Adventure, 2004; Globalizŭm, regionalizŭm i antiglobalizŭm, 2005; Liquid Life, 2005; Liquid Fear, 2006; Liquid Times: Living in an Age of Uncertainty, 2007; Consuming Life, 2007; Futuryzm miast przemyslowych, 2007; Does Ehics Have a Chance in a World of Consumers?, 2008; The Art of Life, 2008; Does Ethics have a Chance in a World of Consumers?, 2008; Living on Borrowed Time, 2009; (with R. Kubicki and A. Zeidler-Janiszewska) Życie w kontekstach, 2009; (contrib.) 17 x 23, 5 x 1, 6, 2009; 44 Letters from the Liquid Modern World, 2010; Collateral Damage, 2011. **Address:** Department of Sociology, University of Leeds, Woodhouse Ln., Leeds, WY LS2 9JT, England.

BAUMANN, Carol Edler. American (born United States), b. 1932. **Genres:** International Relations/Current Affairs. **Career:** University of Wisconsin-Madison, instructor in political science, 1957-61, National Security Studies Group, project associate, 1958-61; University of Wisconsin-Milwaukee, lecturer, 1961-62, assistant professor, 1962-67, associate professor, 1967-72, professor of political science, 1972-95, professor emeritus, 1995-, Institute of World Affairs, director, 1964-97, director emeritus, 1997-; United Nations Association, Wisconsin Division, vice-chairman, 1971-; U.S. Department of State, deputy assistant secretary for assessments and research, 1979-82. Writer. **Publications:** Political Co-operation in NATO (monograph), 1960; (ed. and intro.) Western Europe: What Path to Integration?, 1967; (with K. Wahner) Great Decisions, 1968: A Survey of Participants in Milwaukee County, 1969; The Diplomatic Kidnappings: A Revolutionary Tactic of Urban Terrorism, 1973; (ed.) Europe in NATO: Deterrence, Defense, and Arms Control, 1987. Contributor to books. **Address:** Department of Political Science, University of Wisconsin, NWQ B, Rm. 5450, 2025 E Newport Ave., PO Box 413, Milwaukee, WI 53201, U.S.A. **Online address:** cbaumann@excel.net

BAUMBACH, Jonathan. American (born United States), b. 1933. **Genres:** Novels, Novellas/Short Stories, Literary Criticism And History, Biography. **Career:** Stanford University, instructor, 1958-60; Ohio State University, instructor, 1961-62, assistant professor, 1962-64; New York University, assistant professor, 1964-66; City University of New York, Brooklyn College, associate professor, 1966-70, 1971-72, professor of English, 1972-, professor and director of MFA in creative writing, 1973-2001, adjunct professor and professor emeritus, 2001-; Tufts University, visiting professor, 1970-71; Partisan Review, film critic, 1974-83; University of Washington, visiting professor, 1978-79, 1985-86; Princeton University, visiting professor, 1990-91; Brown University, visiting professor, 1994; The New School University, lecturer in fiction writing, 2001-07. Writer. **Publications:** NOVELS: A Man to Conjure With, 1965; (contrib.) Man and the Movies, 1967; What Comes Next, 1968; Reruns, 1974; Babble, 1976; Chez Charlotte and Emily, 1979; My Father More or Less, 1982; Separate Hours, 1990; Seven Wives: A Romance, 1994; D-Tours, 1998; B: A Novel, 2002; YOU or The Invention of Memory, 2008. SHORT STORIES: The Return of Service, 1979; The Life and Times of Major Fiction, 1986; On the Way to My Father's Funeral: New and Selected Stories, 2004. CRITICISM: The Landscape of Nightmare: Studies in the Contemporary American Novel, 1965; Statements: New Fiction from the Fiction Collective, 1975. EDITOR: (with A. Edelstein) Moderns and Contemporaries: Nine Masters of the Short Story, 1968, 2nd ed., 1977; Writers as Teachers, Teachers as Writers, 1970; (with P. Spielberg) Statements 2: New Fiction, 1977. Contributor to periodicals. **Address:** Department of English, Brooklyn College, City University of New York, 2308 Boylan Hall, 2900 Bedford Ave., Brooklyn, NY 11210, U.S.A. **Online address:** jquartz@panix.com

BAUMGARDNER, Jennifer. American (born United States), b. 1970?. **Genres:** Women's Studies And Issues, Medicine/Health, Social Sciences. **Career:** Ms., editor, 1993-97; Oxygen Network, She-Span, commentator; Soapbox Inc: Speakers Who Speak Out, founder; AlterNet, columnist; Honor the Earth, writer, organizer; Planned Parenthood Federation of America, writer, organizer; Third Wave Foundation, writer, organizer; Dartmouth College, fellow, 2004. **Publications:** (With A. Richards) Manifesta: Young Women, Feminism, and the Future, 2000, rev. ed., 2010; Abortion from a Global Perspective, 2002; (intro.) The Female Eunuch, 2002; Recipe-Tested, 2004; (with A. Richards) Grassroots: A Field Guide for Feminist Activism, 2005; Look Both Ways: Bisexual Politics, 2007; Abortion & Life, 2008; F 'em!: Goo Goo, Gaga, and Some Thoughts on Balls, 2011. Contributor to books, periodicals and magazines. **Address:** Soapbox Inc: Speakers Who Speak Out, 106 Suffolk St., Ste. 2A, New York, NY 10002-3351, U.S.A. **Online address:** jennifer@manifesta.net

BAUMGARTNER, Frank R. American (born United States), b. 1958. **Genres:** Politics/Government, Social Sciences. **Career:** University of Michigan, research assistant, research associate, teaching assistant, instructor, lecturer, 1981-86; Institute for Public Policy Studies, research assistant, research associate, 1981-86; National Election Studies, research assistant, research associate, 1981-86; Center for Political Studies, research assistant, research associate, 1981-86; Inter-university Consortium for Political and Social Research, research assistant, research associate, 1981-86; University of Iowa, visiting assistant professor, 1986-87; Texas A&M University, assistant professor, 1987-92, associate professor, 1992-97; California Technical Institute, professor, 1998-99; Pennsylvania State University, Department of Political Science, professor, 1998-2005, interim head, 1999-2000; department head,

2000-04, distinguished professor, 2005-07, Bruce R. Miller and Dean D. LaVigne professor of political science, 2007-09; Center for European Studies, visiting researcher, 2006-; University of North Carolina, Richard J. Richardson distinguished professor of political science, 2009-; CEVIPOF-Sciences Po, ongoing researcher. Writer. **Publications:** Conflict and Rhetoric in French Policymaking, 1989; (with B.D. Jones) Agendas and Instability in American Politics, 1993; (with B.L. Leech) Basic Interests: The Importance of Groups in Politics and in Political Science, 1998; (ed. with B.D. Jones) Policy Dynamics, 2002; (with B.D. Jones) The Politics of Attention: How Government Prioritizes Problems, 2005; (with S.L. De Boef and A.E. Boydstun) The Decline of the Death Penalty and the Discovery of Innocence, 2008; (co-author) Lobbying and Policy Change: Who Wins, Who Loses and Why, 2009. Contributor to journals. **Address:** Department of Political Science, University of North Carolina at Chapel Hill, 358 Hamilton Hall, PO Box 3265, Chapel Hill, NC 27599-3265, U.S.A. **Online address:** frankb@psu.edu

BAUMOL, William J. American (born United States), b. 1922. **Genres:** Economics, Business/Trade/Industry. **Career:** U.S. Department of Agriculture, junior economist, 1942-43, 1946; University of London, London School of Economics and Political Science, assistant lecturer in economics, 1947-49; Princeton University, assistant professor, 1949-52, associate professor, 1952-54, professor of economics, 1954-92, Joseph Douglas Green, 1895, professor emeritus of economics, 1992-, senior research economist, 1992-; State of New Jersey, chairman, 1967-75; New York University, professor of economics, 1971-, C.V. Starr Center for Applied Economics, director, 1972-2000, Leonard N. Stern School of Business, Harold Price professor of entrepreneurship, Berkley Center for Entrepreneurship and Innovation, academic director. Writer and consultant. **Publications:** Economic Dynamics, 1951, 3rd ed., 1970; Welfare Economics and the Theory of the State, 1952, 2nd ed., 1965; (with L.V. Chandler) Economic Processes and Policies, 1954; Business Behavior, Value and Growth, 1959, rev. ed., 1967; (with K. Knorr) What Price Economic Growth?, 1961; Economic Theory and Operations Analysis, 1961, 4th ed., 1977; The Stock Market and Economic Efficiency, 1965; (with W.G. Bowen) Performing Arts, The Economic Dilemma: A Study of Problems Common to Theater, Opera, Music, and Dance, 1966; 1969 Economic Outlook for New Jersey, 1968; Teoriaeconomica e analisi Operative, 1968, 4th ed., 1977; (co-author) A New Rationale for Corporate Social Policy, 1970; Portfolio Theory: The Selection of Asset Combinations, 1970; Environmental Protection, International Spillovers and Trade, 1971; (with M. Marcus) Economics of Academic Libraries, 1973; 1975 Economic Outlook for New Jersey, 1974; (with W.E. Oates) Theory of Environmental Policy; Externalities, Public Outlays, and the Quality of Life, 1975, 2nd ed., 1988; Selected Economic Writings of William J. Baumol, 1976; Quasi Optimality: The Price We Must Pay for a Price System, 1977; Economics, Environmental Policy, and the Quality of Life, 1979; Some Principles for the Operation of Public Enterprise; Subsidies to New Energy Sources as a Threat to Energy Supplies, 1981; (with A.S. Blinder) Economics: Principles and Policy, 1982, 10th ed. as Essentials of Economics: Principles and Policy, 2006, 11th ed., 2009; (with J.C. Panzar and R.D. Williq) Contestable Markets and the Theory of Industry Structure, 1982, rev. ed., 1988; Superfairness: Applications and Theory, 1986; Microtheory: Applications and Origins, 1986; (co-author) Productivity and American Leadership: The Long View, 1989; (co-author) Economics of Mutual Fund Markets: Competition Versus Regulation, 1990; Growth, the Market, and Dissemination of Technology, 1991; Entrepreneurship, Management, and the Structure of Payoffs, 1993; (ed. with R.R. Nelson and E.N. Wolff) Convergence of Productivity: Cross-national Studies and Historical Evidence, 1994; (with J.G. Sidak) Toward Competition in Local Telephony, 1994; (with A.S. Blinder) Macroeconomics: Principles and Policy, 6th ed., 1994, 11th ed. as Macroeconomics: Policy & Practice, 2010; (with A.S. Blinder) Microeconomics: Principles and Policy, 6th ed., 1994, 11th ed., 2009; (with G. Sidak) Transmission Pricing and Stranded Costs in the Electric Power Industry, 1995; (ed. with W.E. Becker) Assessing Educational Practices: The Contribution of Economics, 1996; (with R.E. Gomory) Global Trade and Conflicting National Interests, 2000; (ed. with C.A. Wilson) Welfare Economics, 2001; Free-market Innovation Machine: Analyzing the Growth Miracle of Capitalism, 2002; (with A.S. Blinder and E.N. Wolff) Downsizing in America: Reality, Causes, and Consequences, 2003; (with J. Jeffri and D. Throsby) Making Changes: Facilitating the Transition of Dancers to Post-performance Careers, 2004; Regulation Misled by Misread Theory, 2006; (with D. Robyn) Toward an Evolutionary Regime for Spectrum Governance, 2006; (ed. with E. Sheshinski and R.J. Strom) Entrepreneurship, Innovation, and the Growth Mechanism of the Free-enterprise Economies, 2007; (with R.E. Litan and C.J. Schramm) Good Capitalism, Bad Capitalism, and the Economics of Growth and Prosperity, 2007; Microtheory of Innovative Entrepreneurship, 2009; (ed. with D.S. Landes and J. Mokyr) Invention of Enterprise: Entrepreneurship from Ancient Mesopotamia to Modern Times, 2010. Contributor of articles to periodicals. **Address:** Leonard N. Stern School of Business, New York University, Kaufman Management Ctr., Rm. 7-98, 44 W 4th St., New York, NY 10012-1106, U.S.A. **Online address:** william.baumol@nyu.edu

BAUMS, Roosevelt. American (born United States), b. 1946. **Genres:** Inspirational/Motivational Literature, Theology/Religion, Politics/Government. **Career:** Preacher. PEACE Inc., program director, 1973-75; Longley-Jones Restate, property manager, 1975-77; Onondaga Sheriff's Department, deputy sheriff, 1977-84; United States Postal Service, distribution clerk, 1984-2005; Worldwide Love and Brotherhood Ministry, founder; Thomas Memorial African Methodist Episcopal Zion Church, pastor; City-County Youth Bureau, affiliate; North Point Continuum Coalition, affiliate; Henry Barr Underground Railroad Society, chief executive officer. Writer. **Publications:** A Minority View of How to Campaign for Political Office, 1981; In Search of the Dove That Brings Love (children's prayers), 1997. Contributor to newspapers. **Address:** Thomas Memorial African Methodist Episcopal Zion, 715 Morrison St., PO Box 6002, Watertown, NY 13601-1318, U.S.A. **Online address:** r.baums@worldnet.att.net

BAUMSLAG, Naomi. American (born United States), b. 1936. **Genres:** Medicine/Health. **Career:** Megaloblastic Anemia South African Medical Research, principal investigator, 1957; Baragwanath Hospital, staff, 1959-62; Emory University, Medical School, professor of community medicine, 1972-77; Department of Health and Human Services, International Health Nutrition Division, director, 1979-84; Women's International Public Health Network, founder and president, 1987-; Georgetown University, Medical School, clinical professor of pediatrics, 1987-. Writer. **Publications:** (Ed.) Family Care: A Guide, 1973; (with C.D. Williams and D.B. Jelliffe) Mother and Child Health: Delivering the Services, 1985, 3rd ed., 1994; (with D.L. Michels) A Woman's Guide to Yeast Infections, 1992; (with D.L. Michels) Milk, Money, and Madness: The Culture and Politics of Breastfeeding, 1995; Murderous Medicine: Nazi Doctors, Human Experimentation, and Typhus, 2005. **Address:** Women's International Public Health Network, 7100 Oak Forest Ln., Bethesda, MD 20817, U.S.A. **Online address:** baumslag@gmail.com

BAUR, Gene. American (born United States), b. 1961?. **Genres:** Animals/Pets. **Career:** Farm Sanctuary, founder. Writer, film producer and environmental activist. **Publications:** Farm Sanctuary: Changing Hearts and Minds about Animals and Food, 2008. **Address:** Farm Sanctuary, PO Box 150, Watkins Glen, NY 14891, U.S.A.

BAUSCH, Richard. American (born United States), b. 1945. **Genres:** Novels, Novellas/Short Stories, Adult Non-fiction. **Career:** George Mason University, professor of English and Heritage chair of creative writing, 1980-; University of Virginia, visiting professor, 1985, 1988; Wesleyan University, visiting professor, 1986, 1990, 1992, 1993; University of Memphis, professor of English and Lillian and Morrie A. Moss chair of excellence. Writer. **Publications:** NOVELS: Real Presence, 1980; Take Me Back, 1981; The Last Good Time, 1984; Mr. Field's Daughter, 1989; Violence, 1992; Rebel Powers, 1993; Aren't You Happy for Me?, 1995; Good Evening Mr. & Mrs. America and All the Ships at Sea, 1996; In the Night of the Season, 1998; In the Night Season, 1999; (with R.V. Cassill) Norton Anthology of Short Fiction, 2000, 7th ed., 2006; (ed.) Cry of An Occasion, 2001; Hello to the Cannibals, 2002; Wives & Lovers, 2004; Thanksgiving Night, 2006; Peace, 2008. STORIES: Spirits and Other Stories, 1987; Firemans Wife and Other Stories, 1990; Rare and Endangered Species, 1994; Someone to Watch over Me, 1999; (intro.) Collected stories of Peter Taylor, 2009; These Extremes, 2009; Something Is Out There, 2010. Works appear in anthologies. Contributor to periodicals. **Address:** Department of English, University of Memphis, TBA, 467 Patterson Hall, Memphis, TN 38152-3530, U.S.A. **Online address:** rcbausch@gmail.com

BAUSELL, R. Barker. American (born United States), b. 1942. **Genres:** Education, Sciences, Social Sciences. **Career:** Medical College of Pennsylvania, research methodologist, 1975-76; University of Maryland, professor of coordinated faculty research, 1976-91, director of office research methodology, 1991-94, research professor, 1994-98, Complementary Medicine Program, director of research, 1998-; Delmarva Foundation for Medical Care, senior scientist, 1994-98; Rodale Press Inc., Prevention Research Center, director. Academic and research methodology educator. **Publications:** (with

C.R. Bausell and N.B. Bausell) The Bausell Home Learning Guide: Teach Your Child to Write, 1980; (with C.R. Bausell and N.B. Bausell) The Bausell Home Learning Guide: Teach Your Child to Read, 1980; (with C.F. Waltz) Nursing Research: Design, Statistics, and Computer Analysis, 1981; (with C.R. Bausell and N.B. Bausell) Teach Your Child Math: The Bausell Home Learning Guide, 1981; A Practical Guide to Conducting Empirical Research, 1986; (with M.A. Rooney and C.B. Inlander) How to Evaluate and Select a Nursing Home, 1988; Advanced Research Methodology: An Annotated Guide to Sources, 1991; Conducting Meaningful Experiments: 40 Steps to Becoming a Scientist, 1994; (with Y. Li) Power Analysis for Experimental Research: A Practical Guide for the Biological, Medical, and Social Sciences, 2002; Snake Oil Science: The Truth about Complementary and Alternative Medicine, 2007. Contributor to journals and periodicals. **Address:** School of Nursing, University of Maryland, 655 W Lombard St., Baltimore, MD 21201-1512, U.S.A. **Online address:** bausell@son.umaryland.edu

BAUSUM, Ann. American (born United States) **Genres:** Children's Non-fiction, Adult Non-fiction. **Career:** Beloit College, public relations staff. Writer. **Publications:** NONFICTION: Dragon Bones and Dinosaur Eggs: A Photobiography of Roy Chapman Andrews, 2000; Our Country's Presidents, 2001; With Courage and Cloth: Winning the Fight for a Woman's Right to Vote, 2004; Freedom Riders: John Lewis and Jim Zwerg on the Front Lines of the Civil Rights Movement, 2006; Muckrakers: How Ida Tarbell, Upton Sinclair, and Lincoln Steffens Helped Expose Scandal, Inspire Reform, and Invent Investigative Journalism, 2007; Our Country's First Ladies, 2007; Denied, Detained, Deported: Stories from the Dark Side of American Immigration, 2009. OTHERS: Unraveling Freedom: The Battle for Democracy on the Home Front During World War I, 2010; Marching to the Mountaintop: How Poverty, Labor Fights, and Civil Rights Set the Stage for Martin Luther King, Jr.'s Final Hours, 2012. Contributor to periodicals. **Address:** 408 S Main St., Apt. 5, Janesville, WI 53545-4881, U.S.A. **Online address:** ann.bausum@gmail.com

BAVLY, Dan A(braham). (Dan Bawly). Israeli (born Israel), b. 1929. **Genres:** Economics, International Relations/Current Affairs. **Career:** Jerusalem Post, economics journalist, 1955-57; Bavly Millner & Co. (Horwath Bavly Millner & Co.), partner, executive partner, 1957-95; Harvard University, Kennedy School of Government, fellow; Tel-Hai Academic College, chairman, through 1999; University of Haifa, Jewish-Arab Center, chairman, 2003-09. **Publications:** AS DAN BAWLY: (with D. Kimche) The Sandstorm: The Arab-Israeli War of June 1967; Prelude and Aftermath, 1968; Israël Face Aux Arabes, Hier, Demain, Aujourd'hui, 1968; The Subterranean Economy, 1982; (with E. Salpeter) Fire in Beirut: Israel's War in Lebanon with the PLO, 1984; Ḥalomot Ṿe-hizdamnuyot She-huhȯmetsu: 1967-1973, 2002. AS DAN BAVLY: (with D. Farhi) Israel and the Palestinians, 1971; Corporate Governance and Accountability: What Role for the Regulator, Director, and Auditor?, 1999. Contributor to periodicals. **Address:** Harashin, Galilee, 24954, Israel. **Online address:** dan_b@netvision.net.il

BAWCUTT, Priscilla (June). British (born England), b. 1931. **Genres:** Literary Criticism And History, Language/Linguistics, History, Young Adult Fiction. **Career:** University of Liverpool, Department of English Language and Literature, honorary professor. Writer. **Publications:** Gavin Douglas: A Critical Study, 1974; Dunbar the Makar, 1992; The Poems of William Dunbar, 1998. EDITOR: The Shorter Poems of Gavin Douglas, 1967, 2nd ed. 2003; (with F. Riddy) Longer Scottish Poems, 1987; (with F. Riddy) Selected Poems of Henryson and Dunbar, 1992; Poems of William Dunbar, 1998. Contributor to periodicals. **Address:** School of English, University of Liverpool, Cypress Bldg., Chatham St., Liverpool, L69 7ZR, England.

BAWDEN, Nina (Mary). British (born England), b. 1925. **Genres:** Novels, Mystery/Crime/Suspense, Children's Fiction, Picture/Board Books, Children's Non-fiction. **Career:** Town and Country Planning Associates, assistant, 1946-47; writer, 1952-; Surrey Justice of the Peace, staff, 1968-76. **Publications:** Someone at a Distance, 1953; Eyes of Green, 1953 in UK as Who Calls the Tune, 1953; The Odd Flamingo, 1954; Change Here for Babylon, 1955; The Solitary Child, 1956; Devil by the Sea, 1957; Glass Slippers Always Pinch in UK as Just Like a Lady, 1960; In Honour Bound, 1961; Tortoise by Candlelight, 1963; The Secret Passage, 1963; Under the Skin, 1964; The House of Secrets, 1964; On the Run, 1964; Three on the Run, 1965; A Little Love, a Little Learning, 1965; The White Horse Gang, 1966; The Witch's Daughter, 1966; A Handful of Thieves, 1967; A Woman of My Age, 1967; The Grain of Truth, 1968; The Runaway Summer, 1969; The Birds on the Trees, 1970; Squib, 1971; Anna Apparent, 1972; Carrie's War, 1973; George beneath a Paper Moon, 1974; The Peppermint Pig, 1975; Afternoon of a Good Woman, 1976; Rebel on a Rock, 1978; Familiar Passions, 1979; The Robbers, 1979; William Tell, 1981; Kept in the Dark, 1982; Walking Naked, 1982; The Ice House, 1983; Saint Francis of Assisi, 1983; The Finding, 1985; Princess Alice, 1985; Circles of Deceit, 1987; Henry, 1988; The Outside Child, 1989; Family Money, 1991; Humbug, 1992; The Real Plato Jones, 1993; In My Own Time: Almost an Autobiography, 1994; Welcome to Tangier, 1996; Granny the Pag, 1996; A Nice Change, 1997; Off the Road, 1998; The Ruffian on the Stair, 2001; Dear Austen, 2005; My Mum and My Bum, 2008. Contributor to newspapers. **Address:** 22 Noel Rd., Islington, London, GL N1 8HA, England.

BAWLY, Dan. *See* **BAVLY, Dan A(braham).**

BAX, Martin (Charles Owen). British (born England), b. 1933. **Genres:** Children's Fiction, Medicine/Health, Novels, Autobiography/Memoirs. **Career:** Ambit Magazine, editor, 1959-; St George's Hospital, Paediatric Unit, senior house officer, 1962; The Mac Keith Press, editor, 1963, senior editor, 1978-2005; University of London, lecturer, 1965-; Guy's Hospital, Paediatrician in Charge Salamon's Centre, Department of Paediatrics, senior lecturer, 1968-74; Salomon Centre of Guy's Hospital, medical officer, 1969-74; Charing Cross/Westminster Medical School, research community pediatrician, 1974-; St Mary's Hospital Medical School, Community Paediatric Research Unit, medical director, 1982-85; Castang Foundation, scientific director, 1990-2009; Imperial College School of Medicine, emeritus reader; Chelsea & Westminster Hospital, honorary consultant. **Publications:** The Hospital Ship, 1959; (with J. Bernal) Your Child's First Five Years, 1974; Edmund Went Far Away (children's story book), 1988; (with H. Hart and S.M. Jenkins) Child Development and Child Health, 1990; Love on the Borders, 2005; Memoirs of a Gone World, 2010. **Address:** 17 Priory Gardens, Highgate, London, GL N6 5QY, England. **Online address:** m.bax@imperial.ac.uk

BAXTER, John. French/Australian (born Australia), b. 1939. **Genres:** Novels, Science Fiction/Fantasy, Film, Biography, Autobiography/Memoirs, History. **Career:** New South Wales State Government, staff writer, 1957-67; Australian Commonwealth Film Unit, director of publicity, 1968-70; Hollins College, lecturer in film and theatre, 1974-78; freelance TV producer and screenwriter, 1978-87; Australian Broadcasting Corp., producer, 1984-, consultant; Mitchell College, visiting lecturer, 1987; freelance journalist and broadcaster, 1989-. **Publications:** The Off Worlders, 1966 in Australia as The God Killers, 1968; (adaptor) Adam's Woman, 1968; Hollywood in the Thirties, 1968; (ed.) The Pacific Book of Science Fiction, 1969; The Australian Cinema, 1970; Science Fiction in the Cinema, 1970; The Gangster Film, 1970; The Cinema of Josef von Sternberg, 1971; The Cinema of John Ford, 1971; The Second Pacific Book of Science Fiction, 1971; Hollywood in the Sixties, 1972; Sixty Years of Hollywood, 1973; An Appalling Talent: Ken Russell, 1973; Stunt: The Story of the Great Movie Stunt Men, 1973; The Hollywood Exiles, 1976; (with T.R. Atkins) The Fire Came By: The Riddle of the Great Siberian Explosion, 1976; King Vidor, 1976; The Hermes Fall, 1978; The Bidders in UK as Bidding, 1979; The Kid, 1981; (with B. Norris) The Video Handbook, 1982; The Black Yacht, 1982; Who Burned Australia? The Ash Wednesday Fires, 1984; Filmstruck, 1987; Bondi Blues, 1992; Fellini, 1994; Buñuel, 1994; Steven Spielberg: The Unauthorized Biography, 1997; Stanley Kubrick: A Biography, 1997; George Lucas, 1999; Mythmaker: The Life and Work of George Lucas, 1999; Woody Allen: A Biography, 2000; Pound of Paper: Confessions of a Book Addict, 2003; We'll Always have Paris: Sex and Love in the City of Light, 2006; Immoveable Feast: A Paris Christmas, 2008; Carnal Knowledge: Baxter's Concise Encyclopedia of Modern Sex, 2009; The Inner Man: The Life of J.G. Ballard, 2011; The Most Beautiful Walk in the World, 2011. **Address:** Curtis Brown Ltd., 27 Union St., Paddington, NW 2021, Australia.

BAXTER, Mary Lynn. American (born United States), b. 1943. **Genres:** Romance/Historical, Young Adult Fiction. **Career:** Houston Independent Schools, librarian, 1965-72. Writer. **Publications:** ROMANCE NOVELS: All Our Tomorrows, 1982; Shared Moments, 1982; Autumn Awakening, 1982; Tears of Yesterday, 1982; Another Kind of Love: Arkansas, 1983; Memories That Linger, 1984; Everything But Time, 1984; A Handful of Heaven, 1985; Price Above Rubies, 1986; When We Touch, 1986; Between the Raindrops, 1986; Moonbeams Aplenty, 1987; Fool's Music, 1987; Knight Sparks, 1988; Winter Heat, 1989; Wish Giver, 1989; Added Delight, 1989; Slow Burn, 1990; Tall in the Saddle, 1991; Marriage, Diamond Style, 1991; And Baby

Makes Perfect, 1992; A Day in April, 1992; Mike's Baby, 1993; Dancler's Woman, 1993; Sweet Justice, 1994; Priceless, 1995; Hot Texas Nights, 1996; Saddle Up, 1996; Southern Fries, 1996; Tight-fitting Jeans, 1997; Lone Star Heat, 1997; Raw Heat, 1998; Hard Candy, 1998; Slow-talking Texan, 1998; One Summer Evening, 1999; Heart of Texas, 1999; Sultry, 2000; Her Perfect Man, 2000; Tempting Janey, 2001; The Millionaire Comes Home, 2001; Like Silk, 2002; His Touch, 2003; Pulse Points, 2003; Without You, 2004; In Hot Water, 2005; Evening Hours, 2005; Totally Texan, 2006; To Claim His Own, 2006; At The Texan's Pleasure, 2006; Meant to Be, forthcoming. **Address:** c/o Karen Solem, Writers House Inc., 21 W 26th St., New York, NY 10010, U.S.A.

BAXTER, Paula A. American (born United States), b. 1954. **Genres:** Art/Art History, Adult Non-fiction, Design, Popular Culture, Social Sciences. **Career:** State University of New York College, visual arts librarian, 1981-83; Museum of Modern Art, Reference Department, associate librarian, 1983-87; New York Public Library, curator of art and architecture collection, 1987-2009; Berkeley College, adjunct professor, 2010-; State University of New York, Purchase College, lecturer, 2010-. Writer and public speaker. **Publications:** International Bibliography of Art Librarianship: An Annotated Compilation, 1987; (with A. Bird-Romero) Encyclopedia of Native American Jewelry, 2000; Southwest Silver Jewelry, 2001; Southwestern Indian Rings, 2012. Contributor of articles to periodicals. **Address:** Purchase College, State University of New York, 735 Anderson Hill Rd., Purchase, NY 10577, U.S.A.

BAXTER, Stephen. British (born England), b. 1957. **Genres:** Science Fiction/Fantasy, Novellas/Short Stories, Information Science/Computers, Young Adult Fiction, Young Adult Non-fiction, Novels. **Career:** Teacher; full-time writer, 1995-. **Publications:** SCIENCE FICTION NOVELS: Anti-Ice, 1993; The Time Ships, 1995; Web 2027, 1999; (with A.C. Clarke) The Light of Other Days, 2000; Evolution, 2002; The H-bomb Girl, 2007; (with T. Pratchett) The Long Earth, 2012. NASA TRILOGY: Voyage, 1996; Titan, 1997; Moonseed, 1998; Mayflower II, 2004. MAMMOTH TRILOGY: Silverhair, 1999; Long Tusk, 1999; Icebones, 2001. MANIFOLD SERIES: Time, 1999; Space, 2000; Origin, 2001. NONFICTION: Angular Distribution Analysis in Acoustics, 1986; (with D. Lisburn) Reengineering Information Technology: Success through Empowerment, 1994; The Role of the IT/IS Manager, 1996; Deep Future, 2001; Omegatropic, 2001. THE WEB: Gulliver Zone, 2027, 1994; Ice Bones, 2001; Futures, 2001; Origin, 2001; Revolutions In The Earth: Jame Hutton And the Evolution of Modern Geology, 2003; Coalescent, 2003; Exultant, 2004; Transcendent, 2005; The Third Expansion, 2005; Resplendent, 2006; Conqueror, 2007; Starfall, 2009. TIME ODYSSEY SERIES: SCIENCE FICTION: WITH A.C. CLARKE: Time's Eye, 2004; Sunstorm, 2005; Firstborn, 2007. TIME'S TAPESTRY SERIES: SCIENCE FICTION: Emperor, 2006; Conqueror, 2007; Navigator, 2007; Weaver, 2008. XEELEE SEQUENCE: SCIENCE FICTION: Raft, 1991; Flux, 1995; Ring, 1996; Vacuum Diagrams, 1997. OTHERS: Timelike Infinity, 1992; Gulliverzone (young adult novel), 1997; Webcrash (young adult novel), 1998; Traces (science fiction stories), 1998; Phase Space, 2002; True Age of the Earth, 2003; Ages in Chaos: James Hutton and the Discovery of Deep Time, 2004; The Hunters of Pangaea, 2004; (co-author) Time Pieces, 2005; Flood, 2008; Ark, 2009; Stone Spring, 2010; The Science of Avatar, 2010; Bronze Summer, 2011; Iron Winter, 2012; Last And First Contacts: Imaginings, 2012. Contributor to journals and magazines. Works appear in anthologies. **Address:** The Ralph Vicinanza Agency, 303 W 18th St., New York, NY 10011-4440, U.S.A. **Online address:** sbaxter100@aol.com

BAXTER(-WRIGHT), Keith (Stanley). British/Welsh (born Wales), b. 1935. **Genres:** Plays/Screenplays, Illustrations, Biography. **Career:** Writer and director. **Publications:** Barnaby and the Old Boys (play), 1991; My Sentiments Exactly, 1998. Illustrator of books by T. Yule. **Address:** Chatto & Linnit Ltd., 123A Kings Rd., London, GL SW3 4PL, England.

BAY, Jeanette Graham. American (born United States), b. 1928. **Genres:** Novellas/Short Stories, Education, Social Sciences. **Career:** Bay's Nursery School, founder and teacher, 1963-74; YMCA Preschool, director and teacher, 1974-85; Wee Wonders, teacher, 1987-89; Child Time Children's Center, teacher, 1990-93. Writer. **Publications:** Alleyside Book of Flannelboard Stories, 1991; A Treasury of Flannelboard Stories, 1995. **Address:** 770 Victor Rd., Macedon, NY 14502, U.S.A.

BAYARD, Pierre. French (born France), b. 1954. **Genres:** Young Adult Non-fiction, Mystery/Crime/Suspense. **Career:** University of Paris, professor of French literature. Writer. **Publications:** NONFICTION: Balzac et le troc de l'imaginaire: lecture de la peau de chagrin, 1978; Il était deux fois Romain Gary, 1990; Maupassant, juste avant Freud, 1994; (co-author) Esthétique plurielle, 1996; Le Hors-sujet: Proust et la digression, 1996; (ed.) Lire avec Freud: Pour Jean Bellemin-Noël, 1998; Qui a tué Roger Ackroyd?, 1998; Comment améliorer les oeuvres ratées, 2000; Enquète sur Hamlet: Le dialogue de sourds, 2002; Peut-on appliquer la littérature à la psychanalyse?, 2004; Demain est écrit, 2005; L'affaire du chien des Baskerville, 2007; Comment parler des livres que l'on n'a pas lus?, 2007; Sherlock Holmes Was Wrong: Reopening the Case of the Hound of the Baskervilles, 2008; Le plagiat par anticipation, 2009; Et si les œuvres changeaient d'auteur?, 2010. **Address:** Les Editions de Minuit, 7 rue Bernard-Palissy, Paris, 75006, France. **Online address:** bayard.sakai@wanadoo.fr

BAYBARS, Taner. (Timothy Bayliss). French/Cypriot (born Cyprus), b. 1936. **Genres:** Novels, Poetry, Autobiography/Memoirs, Translations, Literary Criticism And History. **Career:** British Council, staff, 1956-66, book exhibition assistant, 1966-67, periodicals assistant, 1967-72, head of overseas reviews scheme, 1972-81, book promotion officer, 1983-88; Writer, 1988-. **Publications:** To Catch a Falling Man, 1963; A Trap for the Burglar (novel), 1965; Plucked in a Far-Off Land, 1970; (ed. with O. Turkay) Modern Poetry in Translation: Turkey, 1971; Susila in the Autumn Woods, 1974; Narcissus in a Dry Pool, 1978; Pregnant Shadows, 1981; A Sad State of Freedom, 1990; Selected Poems, 1997; Fox and the Cradle Makers, 2001; Collected Poems, 2005. TRANSLATOR: Selected Poems of Nazim Hikmet, 1967; Moscow Symphony, 1970; Day before Tomorrow, 1972; E.J. Keats, The Snowy Day, 1980; E.J. Keats, Peter's Chair, 1980; M. Yashin, Don't Go Back to Kyrenia (poems), 2001. **Address:** 2 rue de l, Saint-Chinian, 34360, France. **Online address:** tbaybars@wanadoo.fr

BAYDA, Ezra. American (born United States) **Genres:** Young Adult Fiction, inspirational/Motivational Literature. **Career:** Zen Center of San Diego, teacher, 1995-; Santa Rosa Zen Group, founder, 1995-. Writer. **Publications:** Being Zen: Bringing Meditation to Life, 2002; At Home in the Muddy Water: A Guide to Finding Peace Within Everyday Chaos, 2003; (with J. Bartok) Saying Yes to Life (even the Hard Parts), 2005; Zen Heart: Simple Advice for Living With Mindfulness and Compassion, 2008; Beyond Happiness: The Zen Way to True Contentment, 2010. **Address:** Zen Center San Diego, 2047 Felspar St., San Diego, CA 92109-3551, U.S.A. **Online address:** ezra@zencentersandiego.org

BAYER, William. (David Hunt). American (born United States), b. 1939. **Genres:** Novels, Mystery/Crime/Suspense, Plays/Screenplays, Film, Adult Non-fiction. **Career:** United States Information Agency, foreign service officer, staff filmmaker, 1963-68. Freelance writer and film maker. **Publications:** NOVELS: In Search of a Hero, 1966; Stardust, 1974; Visions of Isabelle, 1976; Tangier, 1978; Punish Me with Kisses, 1980; Peregrine, 1981; Switch, 1984; Pattern Crimes, 1987; Blind Side, 1989; Wallflower, 1991; Mirror Maze, 1994; Tarot, 2001; The Dream of the Broken Horses, 2002; City Of Knives, forthcoming. NOVELS AS DAVID HUNT: The Magician's Tale, 1996; Trick of Light, 1998. NONFICTION: Breaking Through, Selling Out, Dropping Dead and Other Notes on Filmmaking, 1971, rev. ed., 1989; The Great Movies, 1973. **Address:** 1160 Dance Dr., Sonoma, CA 95476, U.S.A. **Online address:** crimenovelist@aol.com

BAYLEY, John (Oliver). British/Pakistani (born Pakistan), b. 1925. **Genres:** Novels, Poetry, Literary Criticism And History, Biography. **Career:** St. Anthony's and Magdalen College, member, 1951-55; New College, lecturer, 1955-74; Oxford University, St. Catherine's College, Warton professor of English literature and fellow, 1974-92. Writer. **Publications:** El Dorado: The Newdigate Prize Poem, 1950; In Another Country (novel), 1955; The Romantic Survival: A Study in Poetic Evolution, 1957; The Characters of Love: A Study in the Literature of Personality, 1960; Keats and Reality, 1963; Tolstoy and the Novel, 1966; Pushkin: A Comparative Commentary, 1971; The Uses of Division: Unity and Disharmony in Literature, 1976; An Essay on Hardy, 1978; Selected Essays, 1980; Shakespeare and Tragedy, 1981; The Line Order of Battle at Trafalgar, 1985; The Short Story: Henry James to Elizabeth Bowen, 1987; (intro.) The Terrible News: Russian Stories from the Years Following the Revolution, 1990; (intro.) Mrs. Bathurst and Other Stories, 1991; (intro.) Russian Short Stories, 1992; Housman's Poems, 1992; Alice (novel), 1994; The Queer Captain (novel), 1995; George's Lair (novel), 1996; The Red Hat (novel), 1997; (intro.) Tales of Belkin and Other Prose Writings, 1998; Elegy for Iris, 1999; Iris and Her Friends, 2000; Widower's House: A Study in Bereavement, or, How Margot and Mella Forced Me To Flee My Home, 2001; Hand Luggage: A Personal Anthology, 2001; (ed.) Good Companions: A Personal Anthology, 2002; The Power of Delight: A Lifetime in Literature: Essays, 1962-2002, 2005. **Address:** W.W. Norton & Co., 500 5th Ave., New York, NY 10110, U.S.A.

BAYLEY, P. C. *See* **BAYLEY, Peter (Charles).**

BAYLEY, Peter (Charles). (P. C. Bayley). Scottish/British (born England), b. 1921. **Genres:** Literary Criticism And History. **Career:** Oxford University, fellow, 1947-72, paelector in English, 1949-72, lecturer in English, 1952-72; London Times, correspondent, 1960-63; University of Durham, Collingwood College, master, 1972-78; University of St. Andrews, Berry professor and head of English department, 1978-85, Berry professor emeritus, 1985-; University College, emeritus fellow. Writer. **Publications:** Edmund Spenser: Prince of Poets, 1971; An ABC of Shakespeare, 1985; University College, Oxford: A Guide and Brief History, 1992. EDITOR: (as P.C. Bayley) The Faerie Queene, 1966; Loves and Deaths: Novelists Tales of the Nineteenth Century From Scott to Hardy, 1972; A Casebook on Spenser's Faerie Queene, 1977; Poems of Milton, 1981. CONTRIBUTOR: Patterns of Love and Courtesy, 1966; English Poetry: Select Bibliographical Guides, 1971; C.S. Lewis at the Breakfast Table, 1979. **Address:** Department of English, University of St. Andrews, Castle House, St. Andrews, FF KY169AL, Scotland.

BAYLEY, Stephen. British/Welsh (born Wales), b. 1951. **Genres:** Architecture, Art/Art History, Design, Sex, Physics, Photography. **Career:** Liverpool Polytechnic, lecturer in art history, 1972-74; Open University, lecturer in art history, 1974-76; University of Kent, lecturer in art history, 1977-80; Victoria and Albert Museum, Conran Foundation, director, Design Museum, chief executive, 1981-90; Eye-Q Ltd., principal, 1990-. Writer. **Publications:** (Ed.) In Good Shape: Style in Industrial Products 1900-1960, 1979; The Albert Memorial: The Monument in its Social and Architectural Context, 1981; Harley Earl and the Dream Machine, 1983; (and ed.) Taste: An Exhibition about Values in Design, 1983; (ed. with J. Ward) Kenneth Grange at the Boilerhouse, 1983; (ed.) The Conran Directory of Design, 1985; (with P. Garner and D. Sudji) Twentieth-Century Style and Design, 1986; Sex, Drink and Fast Cars: The Creation and Consumption of Images, 1986; Commerce and Culture: From Pre-Industrial art to Post-Industrial Value, 1989; (contrib.) Raymond Loewy, 1990; Harley Earl, 1991; Taste: The Secret Meaning of Things, 1992; Labour Camp: The Failure of Style over Substance, 1998; Moving Objects, 1999; General Knowledge, 2000; (ed.) Sex, 2001; (with T. Conran) Design: Intelligence Made Visible, 2007; Cars: Freedom, Style, Sex, Power, Motion, Colour, Everything, 2009; Liverpool: Shaping the City, 2010; (with T. Conran) Design A-Z, 2010. **Address:** 176 Kennington Park Rd., London, GL SE11 4BT, England. **Online address:** guru@stephenbayley.com

BAYLIS, Janice H(inshaw). American (born United States), b. 1928. **Genres:** Psychology, Paranormal. **Career:** School teacher, 1950-60; Santa Ana Unified Schools, reading specialist, 1964-86; Cypress Community College, instructor in dream study, now retired. Writer. **Publications:** Sleep on It!: The Practical Side of Dreaming, 1977; Dream Dynamics and Decoding: An Interpretation Manual, 1977; (with A. Bartlow) Palmistry Dictionary with Illustrations, 1986; (with A. Bartlow) Dowsing Dictionary with Illustrations, 1986; Sex, Symbols, and Dreams, 1997. **Address:** 1180 Oakmont Rd., Ste. 51-J, Seal Beach, CA 90740-3640, U.S.A. **Online address:** jbaylis@earthlink.net

BAYLIS, John. British (born England), b. 1946. **Genres:** International Relations/Current Affairs, Military/Defense/Arms Control, Politics/Government. **Career:** University of Liverpool, lecturer, 1969-71; University of Wales, lecturer, 1971-83, senior lecturer in international politics, 1983-83, reader, 1989-92, professor and dean of social sciences, 1989-2000; National Defence College, academic advisor, 1975-82; Swansea University, Department of Politics and International Relations, professor, 2000-, head, 2001-05, pro-vice-chancellor, 2002-08. Writer. **Publications:** (Co-author) Contemporary Strategy: Theories and Policies, 1975, 2nd ed., 1987; Anglo-American Defence Relations 1939-80: The Special Relationship, 1981, 2nd ed., 1984; (co-author) Nuclear War and Nuclear Peace, 1983; Anglo-American Defence Relations, 1939-1984, 1984; (co-author) Contemporary Strategy, vol. I: Theories and Concepts, 1987, vol. II: The Nuclear Powers, 1987; (with K. Booth) Britain, NATO and Nuclear Weapons, 1989; Britain and the Formation of NATO: A Study of Diplomatic Vision, Pragmatism and Patience, 1989; British Defence Policy: Striking the Right Balance, 1990; Diplomacy of Pragmatism, 1993; Ambiguity and Deterrence: British Nuclear Strategy, 1945-64, 1995; Strategy in the Contemporary World: An Introduction to Strategic Studies, 2002, 3rd ed., 2009. EDITOR: British Defence Policy in a Changing World, 1977; (with G. Segal) Soviet Strategy, 1981; Alternative Approaches to British Defense Policy, 1984; (with J. Garnett) Makers of Nuclear Stategy, 1991; (ed. with N.J. Rengger) Dilemmas of World Politics: International Issues in a Changing World, 1992; Anglo-American Relations Since 1939: The Enduring Alliance, 1997; (with S. Smith) The Globalization of World Politics: An Introduction to International Relations, 1997, 5th ed., 2011; (with R. O'Neil) Alternative Nuclear Futures: The Role of Nuclear Weapons in the Post-Cold War World, 2000; (with J. Roper) The United States and Europe: Beyond the Neo-conservative Divide?, 2006. **Address:** Department of Politics and International Relations, Swansea University, Singleton Pk., Swansea, DY SA2 8PP, United Kingdom. **Online address:** j.baylis@swansea.ac.uk

BAYLISS, Timothy. *See* **BAYBARS, Taner.**

BAYLY, C. A. (Christopher Alan Bayly). British (born England), b. 1945. **Genres:** History, Politics/Government, Military/Defense/Arms Control. **Career:** Cambridge University, St. Catharine's College, Vere Harmsworth professor of imperial and naval history, Centre of South Asian studies, director. Writer. **Publications:** The Local Roots of Indian Politics: Allahabad, 1880-1920, 1975; (co-author) Reappraisals in Overseas History: Essays on Post-War Historiography about European Expansion, 1979; Rulers, Townsmen, and Bazaars: North Indian Society in the Age of British Expansion, 1770-1870, 1983; (ed. with D.H.A. Kolff) Two Colonial Empires, 1986; (ed.) The Peasant Armed: The Indian Revolt of 1857, 1986; Indian Society and the Making of the British Empire, 1987; (ed. with J.F. Richards and G. Johnson) The New Cambridge History of India, 1987; Imperial Meridian: The British Empire and the World, 1780-1830, 1989; (ed.) Atlas of the British Empire, 1989; (ed.) Raj: India and the British, 1600-1947, 1990; Empire and Information: Intelligence Gathering and Social Communication in India, 1780-1870, 1996; Origins of Nationality in South Asia: Patriotism and Ethical Government in the Making of Modern India, 1998; (ed. with L.T. Fawaz and R. Ilbert) Modernity and Culture: From the Mediterranean to the Indian Ocean, 1890- 1920, 2002; The Birth of the Modern World, 1780- 1914: Global Connections and Comparisons, 2004; (with T. Harper) Forgotten Armies: The Fall of British Asia, 1941-1945, 2005; (with T. Harper) Forgotten Wars: Freedom and Revolution in Southeast Asia, 2007; (ed. with E.F. Biagini) Giuseppe Mazzini and the Globalisation of Democratic Nationalism 1830-1920, 2008; The C.A. Bayly Omnibus, 2009; (contrib.) The Indian Public Sphere: Readings in Media History, 2009; (ed. with P.F. Bang) Tributary Empires in Global History, 2011; Indian Thought in the Age of Liberalism and Empire, 2011. **Address:** St. Catharine's College, Cambridge University, Trumpington St., Laundress Ln., Cambridge, CB CB2 1RL, England. **Online address:** cab1002@cam.ac.uk

BAYLY, Christopher Alan. *See* **BAYLY, C. A.**

BAYME, Steven. American (born United States), b. 1950. **Genres:** Cultural/Ethnic Topics, Theology/Religion, Essays, History, Sociology. **Career:** Yeshiva University, visiting lecturer, 1973-75, instructor, 1975-77, assistant professor of history, 1977-79, adjunct assistant professor, 1979-87, Wurzweiler School of Social Work, adjunct professor, 1991-99; Jewish Theological Seminary, lecturer, 1973-74, visiting associate professor, 1999-; Hebrew Union College, lecturer, 1976, 1981; Hadassah, national Jewish education director, 1979-82; City University of New York, Queens College, adjunct assistant professor, 1986; Contemporary Jewish Life Department and Koppelman Institute on American Jewish-Israeli Relations, director. Writer. **Publications:** (With G. Rubin) American Jewry and Judaism in the Twentieth Century, 1980; (with G. Rubin and E.N. Dorff) Poor Among Us: Jewish Tradition and Social Policy, 1986; Spotlight on the Family: Public Policy and Private Responsibility, 1988; (ed.) Facing the Future: Essays on Contemporary Jewish Life, 1989; (ed. with D. Blankenhorn and J.B. Elshtain and contrib.) Rebuilding the Nest: A New Commitment to the American Jewish Family, 1990; (ed. with D. Ellenson and contrib.) Religious Pluralism: Implications for Israel-Diaspora Relations, 1992; (ed. with G. Rosen) The Jewish Family and Jewish Continuity, 1994; Understanding Jewish History: Texts and Commentaries, 1997; Jewish Arguments and Counterarguments, 2002. Contributor of articles to books and periodicals. **Address:** 3720 Independence Ave., Apt. 1E, Bronx, NY 10463, U.S.A.

BAYNE, Nicholas (Peter). British (born England), b. 1937. **Genres:** Economics, International Relations/Current Affairs, Politics/Government, Social Sciences. **Career:** British Foreign and Commonwealth Office, staff, 1963-66, 1969-72, treasurer, 1974-75, financial counselor, 1975-79, Economic Relations Department, head, 1979-82, economic director, 1988-92, Royal Institute of International Affairs, staff, 1982-83, British ambassador to Zaire, 1983-84, Civil Service Selection Board, diplomatic service chairman, 1985, Foreign and Commonwealth Office, deputy under secretary for economic affairs, 1988-92; Organization for Economic Co-Operation and Development, ambassador, 1985-88; British High Commissioner to Canada, 1992-96; Queen's University, School of Policy Studies, faculty; London School of Economics and Political Science, International Trade Policy Unit, fellow. Writer. **Publications:** (With R.D. Putnam) Hanging Together: The Seven-Power Summits, 1984, rev. ed., 1987; Hanging in There: The G7 and G8 Summit in Maturity and Renewal, 2000; Grey Wares of North-West Anatolia, 2000; (ed. with S. Woolcock) The New Economic Diplomacy: Decision-Making and Negotiation in International Economic Relations, 2002, 3rd., 2011; Staying Together: The G8 Summit Confronts the 21st Century, 2005. **Address:** International Trade Policy Unit, London School of Economics and Political Science, Houghton St., London, GL WC2A 2AE, England. **Online address:** nicholas.bayne@ukgateway.net

BAYNES, Ken. British (born England), b. 1934. **Genres:** Design, Art/Art History, Biography. **Career:** Editor; Royal College of Art, research associate, 1974, Design Education Unit, head; Loughborough University, Department of Design and Technology, visiting professor, professor. **Publications:** Industrial Design and the Community, 1967; Attitudes in Design Education, 1969; (with B. Langslow and C.C. Wade) Evaluating New Hospital Buildings, 1969; War, 1970; Work, 1970; (ed.) Scoop, Scandal, and Strife: A Study of Photography in Newspapers, 1971; Worship, 1971; Sex, 1972; (with K. Baynes and A. Robinson) Art in Society, 1975; About Design, 1976; The Railway Cartoon Books, 1976; (with F. Pugh) The Art of the Engineer, 1978; (with K. Baynes) The Shoe Show: British Shoes since 1790, 1979; Gordon Russell, 1981; (with K. Brochocka and B. Saunders) Fashion and Design, 1990. **Address:** Department of Design and Technology, Loughborough University, Loughborough, Loughborough, LE LE11 3TU, England. **Online address:** k.baynes@lboro.ac.uk

BAYNES, Kenneth R(ichard). American (born United States), b. 1954. **Genres:** Philosophy, Politics/Government, Social Sciences, Humanities. **Career:** University of Massachusetts, instructor, 1982-85; Boston University, assistant professor of philosophy, 1986-87; State University of New York, assistant professor, 1987-93, associate professor of philosophy, 1993-2002, director of undergraduate studies in philosophy, 1993-94, graduate director, 1998-2000; Syracuse University, Department of Philosophy, professor, 2003-. Writer. **Publications:** (Ed. with J. Bohman and T. McCarthy) After Philosophy: End or Transformation?, 1987; (trans.) Axel Honneth, The Critique of Power, 1991; The Normative Grounds of Social Criticism: Kant, Rawls and Habermas, 1992; (ed. with R. von Schomberg) Discourse and Democracy: Essays on Habermas's between Facts and Norms, 2002. Works appear in anthologies. Contributor of articles to journals. **Address:** Department of Philosophy, Syracuse University, 541 Hall of Languages, 208 Tolley Humanities Bldg., 805 South Crouse Ave., Syracuse, NY 13244-1170, U.S.A. **Online address:** krbaynes@syr.edu

BAZELL, Josh. American (born United States), b. 1978?. **Genres:** Novels. **Career:** Writer and physician. **Publications:** Beat the Reaper: A Novel, 2009. **Address:** Department of Psychiatry, University of California, 401 Parnassus Ave., PO Box 0984, San Francisco, CA 94143-0984, U.S.A.

BAZZANA, Kevin. Canadian (born Canada), b. 1963?. **Genres:** Music, Biography, Adult Non-fiction. **Career:** The Beethoven Journal, editor, 1990-92, 1999, 2007; University of Victoria, School of Music, sessional lecturer, 1993-94, 2011; University of Victoria, continuing-studies lecturer, 1993-; Glenn Gould (magazine), editor, 1995-2005, 2007-08; Toronto Symphony Orchestra, program annotator, 1996-; Times Colonist, classical-music columnist, 2009-; Orchestre symphonique de Montreal, program annotator, 2010-. Musicologist. **Publications:** Glenn Gould: The Performer in the Work-A Study in Performance Practice, 1997; Wondrous Strange: The Life and Art of Glenn Gould, 2003; Lost Genius: The Story of a Forgotten Musical Maverick, 2007. **Address:** 7227 Brentview Dr., Brentwood Bay, BC V8M 1B9, Canada. **Online address:** kevinbazzana@shaw.ca

BAZZONI, Jana O'Keefe. American (born United States), b. 1941. **Genres:** Film, Theatre, Humor/Satire. **Career:** J. Walter Thompson, casting associate, 1964-65; Doyle, Dane, Bernbach, casting director, 1965-67; Guinness-Harp Corp., administrative assistant for advertising and public relations, 1969-72, office manager for Wine Division, 1972-73; Images Unlimited (casting consultants), founding partner, 1975-77; Elizabeth Seton College, instructor in language and literature, 1975-86, academic adviser, 1981-87; City University of New York Readers Theatre, founding member, producer, writer and performer, 1979-90; City University of New York, Bernard M. Baruch College, adjunct assistant professor, 1980-85, assistant professor, 1985-94, associate professor of speech, 1995-98, associate dean, 1998-2000, chair and director of undergraduate programs in communication studies, 2000-, full professor, 2004; PSA, editor, 2002-. **Publications:** (With N.D. Nichols) Pirandello and Film, 1995; (trans. and intro.) Edoardo Sangheti, Natural Stories No. 1, 1998. Contributor to books and periodicals. **Address:** Weissman School of Arts & Sciences, Bernard M. Baruch College-CUNY, VC 8241, 1 Bernard Baruch Way, 55 Lexington 24th St., New York, NY 10010, U.S.A. **Online address:** jana.oKeefe.bazzoni@baruch.cuny.edu

BEACH, Hugh. Swedish/American (born United States), b. 1949. **Genres:** Cultural/Ethnic Topics. **Career:** Swedish National Immigration Board, researcher; National Labor Market Board, researcher; Uppsala University, research assistant in cultural anthropology, 1981-84, lecturer, 1984-90, departmental dean, 1985-86, Minority Interest Group, founder and leader, 1985-90, associate professor of cultural anthropology, 1990-2001, professor, 2001-; Minority Rights Group, board director, 1985-, chairperson, 1989-91; Umeaa University, Center for Arctic Cultural Research, researcher, 1987-90. Writer. **Publications:** Reindeer-Herd Management in Transition: The Case of Tuorpon Saameby in Northern Sweden, 1981; A New Wave on a Northern Shore: The Indochinese Refugees in Sweden, 1982; (co-ed.) Contributions to Circumpolar Studies, 1986; Gaest hos samerna, 1988; A Year in Lapland: Guest of the Reindeer Herders, 1993; The Saami of Lapland, 1994; (with N. Gurr) Flattering the Passions: Or, The Bomb and Britain's Bid for a World Role, 1997; (ed. with D. Funk and L. Sillanpää) Post-Soviet Transformations: Politics of Ethnicity and Resource Use in Russia, 2009. Work represented in anthologies. Contributor to books and periodicals. **Address:** Department of Cultural Anthropology, Uppsala University, PO Box 631, Uppsala, 75126, Sweden. **Online address:** hugh.beach@antro.uu.se

BEACHAM, Richard C. British (born England), b. 1946. **Genres:** Theatre, Humor/Satire. **Career:** Yale University, Yale Repertory Theatre, dramaturge, 1969-72, teaching associate, visiting lecturer in theater studies, 1970-72, resident fellow and visiting professor, 1979, 1982-83, Yale/Theatre Magazine, associate editor; Hiram College, assistant professor of theater studies and chairperson of department, 1972-74; University of Warwick, lecturer, senior lecturer, reader and professor in theater studies, 1976-2005, Joint School of Theatre Studies, acting chairperson, professor; University of California, visiting professor, 1989; American Institute for Foreign Study, lecturer; British Broadcasting Corp., World Service, German language broadcaster; Kings College, professor of digital culture, 2005-, Centre for Computing in the Humanities, Visualisation Lab, director. **Publications:** Adolphe Appia, Theatre Artist, 1987; (ed.) Adolphe Appia, Essays, Scenarios, and Designs, 1989; The Roman Theatre and Its Audience, 1992; (ed.) Adolphe Appia: Texts on Theatre, 1993; Adolphe Appia: Artist and Visionary of the Modern Theatre, 1994; Spectacle of Entertainment in Eatly Imperial Rome, 1999; Four Roman Comedies, 2003. Work represented in anthologies. Contributor of articles to journals. **Address:** School of Arts & Humanities, Kings College, 26-29 Drury Ln., London, GL WC2B 5RL, England. **Online address:** r.beacham@warwick.ac.uk

BEACHY, Kyle. American (born United States), b. 1978. **Genres:** Novels. **Career:** School of the Art Institute of Chicago, faculty; University of Chicago, Graham School of Continuing Liberal and Professional Studies, faculty. Writer. **Publications:** The Slide: A Novel, 2009. **Address:** The Dial Press, 1745 Broadway, New York, NY 10019, U.S.A. **Online address:** kyle@kylebeachy.com

BEAGLE, J. Robert. *See* **REGALBUTO, Robert J.**

BEAGLE, Peter S(oyer). American (born United States), b. 1939. **Genres:** Novels, Novellas/Short Stories, Plays/Screenplays, Songs/Lyrics And Libretti. **Career:** University of Washington, visiting professor, 1988. Author, editor, screenwriter, journalist and musician. **Publications:** FANTASY FICTION: A Fine & Private Place, 1960; The Last Unicorn: A Fantastic Tale, 1968; Lila the Werewolf, 1974, rev. ed., 1976; The Fantasy Worlds of Peter Beagle, 1978; The Folk of the Air (novel), 1986; The Innkeeper's Song: A Novel, 1993; The Unicorn Sonata (novel), 1996; Giant Bones (stories), 1997; Tamsin, 1999; A Dance for Emilia, 2000; The Line Between, 2006; Your Friendly Neighborhood Magician: Songs and Early Poems, 2006; I'm Afraid You've Got Dragons, 2007; Sweet Lightning, 2007; The Last Unicorn: The Lost Version, 2007; Strange Roads, 2008; We Never Talk About My Brother, 2009. NONFICTION: I See by My Outfit, 1965; The California Feeling, 1969; (with H.N. Abrams) American Denim: A New Folk Art, 1975; (with P. Derby) The Lady and Her Tiger, 1976; The Garden of Earthly Delights, 1982; (with P. Derby and G. Molina) In the Presence of Elephants, 1995. PLAYS AND SCREENPLAYS: The Zoo, 1973; (with A. Kennedy) The Dove, 1974; The Greatest Thing That Almost Happened, 1977; The Lord of the Rings, 1978; The Last Unicorn, 1982; The Midnight Angel (opera libretto), 1993. OTHERS: (intro.) The Tolkien Reader, 1966; (intro.) Evening Song, 1973; (intro.) Portrait of Jennie, 1976; (foreword) Adventures of Yemima and Other Stories, 1979; (foreword) The Best of Avram Davidson, 1979; (foreword) Davy, 1990; (foreword) Adventures in Unhistory: Conjectures on the Factual Foundation of Several Ancient Legends, 1993; (ed. with J. Berliner) Peter S. Beagle's Immortal Unicorn, vol. I, 1995, vol. II, 1999; The Rhinoceros Who Quoted Nietzsche and Other Odd Acquaintances, 1997; (contrib.) Songs of Love & Death, 2010. Contributor to periodicals. **Address:** Sebastian Literary Agency, 172 6th St. E, Ste. 2005, St. Paul, MN 55101, U.S.A. **Online address:** unclefox1@juno.com

BEAGLEY, Brenda E. Also writes as Amy Leigh, Marin Thomas. American (born United States), b. 1962. **Genres:** Romance/Historical, Novels, Mystery/Crime/Suspense. **Career:** Writer. **Publications:** (Contrib. as Amy Leigh) The Chipmunks in Alvin's Big Ideas: A Treasury of Chipmunk Stories, 1985; (as Amy Leigh) Chance of a Lifetime, 2001. ROMANCE FICTION AS MARIN THOMAS: The Cowboy and the Bride, 2004; Daddy by Choice, 2005; Homeward Bound, 2005; Aaron under Construction, 2006; Nelson in Command, 2006; Ryan's Renovation, 2007; (with A. Roth and L.M. Altom) Summer Lovin', 2007; For the Children, 2007; In a Soldier's Arms, 2008; A Coal Miner's Wife, 2008; The Cowboy and the Angel, 2008; A Cowboy's Promise, 2009; A Cowboy Christmas, 2009; Samanthas Cowboy, 2009; Dexter: Honorable Cowboy, 2010; Roughneck Cowboy, 2011; Rodeo Daddy, 2011; The Bull Rider's Secret, 2011; A Rodeo Man's Promise, 2011; Aeizona Cowboy, 2012. **Address:** c/o Paige Wheeler, Folio Literary Agency, 505 8th Ave., Ste. 603, New York, NY 10018, U.S.A. **Online address:** marin@marinthomas.com

BEAHRS, Andrew. American (born United States), b. 1973?. **Genres:** Novels. **Career:** Writer. **Publications:** Strange Saint, 2005; Sin Eaters, 2008; Twain's Feast: Searching for America's Lost Foods in the Footsteps of Samuel Clemens, 2010. Contributor to periodicals and journals. **Address:** c/o Author Mail, The Toby Press, 2 Great Pasture Rd., Danbury, CT 06810-8128, U.S.A. **Online address:** andrew@andrewbeahrs.com

BEAL, Peter. British (born England), b. 1944. **Genres:** Literary Criticism And History, Bibliography, Poetry, Education. **Career:** Bowker Publishing, research editor, 1974-79; Mansell Publishing Ltd., research editor, 1974-79; Sotheby's, Department of Printed Books and Manuscripts, English manuscripts expert, 1980-2005, deputy director, 1990-96, director, 1996-2005, consultant, 2005-, director and English manuscript expert; University of Reading, Department of English, visiting professor, 2000-02; University of London, School of Advanced Study, Institute of English Studies, senior research fellow, 2002-. Writer. **Publications:** Bishop Percy's Notes on a Voyage to Abyssinia, 1975; (contrib.) Index of English Literary Manuscripts, vol. I: 1450-1625, 1980, vol. II: 1625-1700, 1987; English Manuscript Studies, 1100-1700, 11 vols., 1989-2001; (contrib.) Parnassus Biceps, or, Severall Choice Pieces of Poetry, 1990; In Praise of Scribes: Manuscripts and Their Makers in Seventeenth Century England, 1998; Dictionary of English Manuscript Terminology, 1450-2000, 2008. EDITOR: English Verse Miscellanies of the Seventeenth Century, 5 vols., 1990. Contributor to periodicals. **Address:** Institute of English Studies, School of Advanced Study, University of London, Rm. 239, Senate House, Malet St., London, GL WC1E 7HU, England. **Online address:** peter.beal@sas.ac.uk

BEAL, Timothy. American (born United States), b. 1963?. **Genres:** Theology/Religion. **Career:** Eckerd College, assistant professor of religious studies and adjunct faculty in women's and gender studies and environmental studies, 1994-99; Case Western Reserve University, Harkness associate professor of Biblical literature, 1999-2002, Harkness professor of Biblical literature, 2002-04, Florence Harkness professor of religion, 2002-, Baker-Nord Center for Humanities, associate director, 2002-03, director, 2003-07. Writer. **Publications:** Identity and Subversion in Esther Microform, 1995; The Book of Hiding: Gender Ethnicity Annihilation and Esther, 1997; (ed. with D.M. Gunn) Reading Bibles Writing Bodies: Identity and the Book, 1997; (ed. with T. Linafelt) God in the Fray: A Tribute to Walter Brueggemann, 1998; Esther, Berit Olam, 1999; Religion and Its Monsters, 2002; (with W.E. Deal) Theory for Religious Studies, 2004; Roadside Religion: In Search of the Sacred the Strange and the Substance of Faith, 2005; (ed. with T. Linafelt) Mel Gibson's Bible: Religion, Popular Culture, and The Passion of the Christ, 2006; Religion in America: A Very Short Introduction, 2008; Biblical Literacy: The Essential Bible Stories Everyone Needs to Know, 2009; (ed. with T. Linafelt and C.V. Camp) The Fate of King David: The Past and Present of a Biblical Icon, 2010; Rise and Fall of the Bible: The Unexpected History of an Accidental Book, 2011; (ed.) The Oxford Encyclopedia of the Bible and the Arts, forthcoming. Contributor to periodicals. **Address:** Department of Religious Studies, Case Western Reserve University, 10900 Euclid Ave., Cleveland, OH 44106-7112, U.S.A. **Online address:** timothy.beal@case.edu

BEALE, Elaine. American/British (born England), b. 1962. **Genres:** Novels. **Career:** San Francisco Women against Rape, developer and teacher; International Media Project, board director. Writer, educator and consultant. **Publications:** Murder in the Castro (novel), 1997; Another Life Altogether (novel), 2010. Contributor to books. Works appear in anthologies. **Address:** Oakland, CA , U.S.A. **Online address:** info@elainebeale.com

BEALE, Fleur. New Zealander (born New Zealand), b. 1945. **Genres:** Novels, Adult Non-fiction, Young Adult Fiction, Novellas/Short Stories. **Career:** Melville High School, teacher, 1985-; Dunedin College of Education, writer-in-residence, 1999. Novelist and short-story writer. **Publications:** The Great Pumpkin Battle, 1988; A Surprise for Anna, 1990; Against the Tide, 1993; Slide the Corner, 1993; Over the Edge, 1994; Driving a Bargain, 1994; The Fortune Teller, 1995; Fifteen and Screaming, 1995; The Rich and Famous Body and the Empty Chequebook, 1995; Dear Pop, 1995; Rockman, 1996; I Am Not Esther, 1998; Further Back than Zero, 1998; Keep Out, 1999; Destination Disaster, 1999; Playing to Win, 1999; Deadly Prospect, 2000; Trucker, 2000; Ambushed, 2001; Seven Readers for Pearson Education, 2001; Lucky for Some, 2002; Red Dog in Bandit Country: A True Story as Told by Bill Redding to Fleur Beale, 2003; Walking Lightly, 2004; My Story: A New Song in the Land The Writings of Atapo Paihia c. 1840, 2004; Lacey and the Drama Queens, 2004; A Respectable Girl, 2006; Transformation of Minna Hargreaves, 2007; My Life of Crime, 2007; Juno of Taris: Self, 2008; Quin Majik and the Marvellous Machine, 2008; Sins of the Father: The Long Shadow of a Religious Cult: A New Zealand Story, 2009; (contrib.) Women of Shimshal, 2010. Contributor to periodicals. **Address:** Longacre Press, Level 2 Moray Chambers, 30 Moray Pl., PO Box 5340, Dunedin, 9016, New Zealand.

BEALES, D(erek) E(dward) D(awson). British (born England), b. 1931. **Genres:** History, Politics/Government. **Career:** University of Cambridge, Sidney Sussex College, research fellow, 1955-58, fellow, 1958-, now emeritus fellow in history, tutor, 1961-70, vice-master, 1973-75, assistant lecturer, 1962-65, lecturer, 1965-80, professor of modern history, 1980-97, professor emeritus of modern history, 1997-, Faculty Board of History, chairman, 1979-81; Harvard University, visiting lecturer, 1965; Historical Journal, editor, 1971-75; Gladstone's Library, memorial lecturer, 1990; Reading University, Stenton lecturer, 1992; Trinity College, Birkbeck lecturer, 1993; Central European University, visiting professor, 1995-97. **Publications:** England and Italy 1859-60, 1961; From Castlereagh to Gladstone, 1815-1885, 1969; The Risorgimento and the Unification of Italy, 1971; The Political Parties of Nineteenth-Century Britain, 1971; Joseph II, vol. I: In the Shadow of Maria Theresa, 1741-80, 1987, vol. II: Against the World, 1780-90, 2009; Mozart and the Habsburgs, 1993; Prosperity and Plunder: European Catholic Monasteries in the Age of Revolution, 1650-1815, 2003; Enlightenment and Reform in Eighteenth-Century Europe, 2005. EDITOR: (with G. Best) History, Society, and the Churches: Essays in Honour of Owen Chadwick, 1985; (with H.B. Nisbet) Sidney Sussex College, Cambridge: Historical Essays: In Commemoration of the Quatercentenary, 1996; Cassell's Companion to Twentieth-century Britain, 2001; Cassell's Companion to Eighteenth-Century Britain, 2001. Contributor of articles to books. **Address:** Sidney Sussex College, University of Cambridge, Sidney St., Cambridge, CB CB2 3HU, England. **Online address:** deb1000@cam.ac.uk

BEALEY, **Frank (William).** Scottish/British (born England), b. 1922. **Genres:** Industrial Relations, Politics/Government. **Career:** University of Manchester, lecturer, 1951-52; University of Keele, lecturer, 1952-64; University of Aberdeen, Department of Politics & International Relations, founding head, 1964-, professor of politics, 1964-90, professor emeritus, 1990-. Writer. **Publications:** (With H. Pelling) Labour and Politics, 1958; (with S. Parkinson) Unions in Prosperity, 1960; (with J. Blondel and W.P. McCann) Constituency Politics, 1965; (ed. and intro.) The Social and Political Thought of the British Labour Party, 1970; The Post Office Engineering Union, 1976; (with J. Sewel) The Politics of Independence, 1981; Democracy in the Contemporary State, 1988; (with R.A. Chapman and M. Sheehan) Elements in Political Science, 1999; The Blackwell Dictionary of Political Science, 1999; Power in Business and the State: An Historical Analysis of its Concentration, 2001. **Address:** Department of Politics & International Relations, University of Aberdeen, Edward Wright Bldg., Aberdeen, AB24 3QY, Scotland. **Online address:** fwsbealey@btopenworld.com

BEALL, **Anne E.** American (born United States), b. 1966. **Genres:** Psychology, Business/Trade/Industry, Economics. **Career:** National Analysts, project manager, 1994-; The Boston Consulting Group, staff; Beall Research & Training Inc., president. Writer. **Publications:** (Ed. with R.J. Sternberg) The Psychology of Gender, 1993, (ed. with R.J. Sternberg and A.H. Eagly) 2nd ed., 2004; Strategic Market Research: A Guide to Conducting Research that Drives Businesses, 2008; Reading the Hidden Communications Around You: A Guide to Reading Body Language in the Workplace, 2009. Contributor to periodicals. **Address:** Beall Research & Training Inc., 333 N Michigan Ave., Ste. 1120, Chicago, IL 60601-4001, U.S.A. **Online address:** anne@beallresearchandtraining.com

BEALMEAR, **Robert Fate.** *See* **FATE**, **Robert.**

BEAM, **Matt.** Canadian (born Canada), b. 1970. **Genres:** Human Relations/Parenting, Novels. **Career:** Papatoetoe Intermediate School, teacher, 1998. Journalist and photographer. **Publications:** Getting to First Base With Danalda Chase, 2005; Can You Spell Revolution?, 2006; Earth to Nathan Blue, 2007; Last December, 2009. **Address:** Dutton Children's Books, 375 Hudson St., New York, NY 10014-3657, U.S.A. **Online address:** info@mattbeam.com

BEAMAN, **Joyce Proctor.** American (born United States), b. 1931. **Genres:** Young Adult Fiction, Education, Psychology, Self Help, Reference. **Career:** Snow Hill High School, English and French teacher, 1953-59; Saratoga Central High School, English and French teacher and librarian, 1959-71, full-time librarian, 1971-77; Wilson Technical Institute, creative writing teacher, 1971-. Writer. **Publications:** Broken Acres, 1971; All for the Love of Cassie, 1973; Bloom Where You Are Planted, 1975; You Are Beautiful: You Really Are, 1981; Teaching: Pure and Simple: One Way of Looking at Teaching, 1998. Contributor of articles and and essays to journals. **Address:** PO Box 187, Saratoga, NC 27873, U.S.A.

BEAN, **Gregory (K.).** American (born United States), b. 1952. **Genres:** Mystery/Crime/Suspense, Novels, Literary Criticism And History. **Career:** Wyoming News, reporter, associate editor, 1978-80; University of Wyoming, instructor, 1979-85; Howard Publications, police reporter for casper star tribune, 1980-83, assistant city editor; Wyoming Horizons, staff, 1983-85; Freeport Journal Standard, editor, 1985-86; Community Newspapers Co., North Shore Sunday, editor, 1986-91; Merrimack Valley Sunday, editor, 1991-92, Seacoast Sunday, editor, 1991-92; Greater Media Newspapers, executive editor, 1993-. **Publications:** MYSTERY NOVELS: No Comfort in Victory, 1995; Long Shadows in Victory: A Harry Starbranch Mystery, 1996; A Death in Victory, 1997; Grave Victory, 1998. **Address:** c/o Helen Rees, 308 Commonwealth Ave., Boston, MA 02115, U.S.A.

BEAN, **Jonathan J.** American (born United States), b. 1962. **Genres:** Business/Trade/Industry, History, Politics/Government, Race Relations. **Career:** Saint Michael's College, lecturer, 1994; Juniata College, visiting assistant professor, 1995; Southern Illinois University, assistant professor, 1995-99, associate professor, 1999-2003, Undergraduate Studies, director, 1999-2005, professor of history, 2003-; H-Business, senior editor. Writer. **Publications:** Beyond the Broker State: Federal Policies toward Small Business, 1936-1961, 1996; Big Government and Affirmative Action: The Scandalous History of the Small Business Administration, 2001; (ed.) Race and Liberty In America: The Essential Reader, 2009. Contributor of articles to books. **Address:** Department of History, Southern Illinois University, 3266 Faner Hall, 1900 N Illinois Ave., PO Box 4519, Carbondale, IL 62901, U.S.A. **Online address:** jonbean@siu.edu

BEAR, **Elizabeth.** American (born United States), b. 1971. **Genres:** Novels, Young Adult Fiction, Adult Non-fiction. **Career:** Writer. **Publications:** JENNY CASEY TRILOGY: Hammered, 2005; Scardown, 2005; Worldwired, 2005. THE PROMETHEAN AGE CYCLE: Blood and Iron, 2006; Whiskey & Water, 2007. OTHERS: Carnival, 2006; The Chains That You Refuse, 2006; (with S. Monette) Companion to Wolves, 2007; Undertow, 2007; Ink and Steel: A Novel of the Promethean Age, 2008; Hell and Earth: A Novel of the Promethean Age, 2008; Dust, 2008; All the Windwracked Stars, 2008; By the Mountain Bound, 2009; Chill, 2009; (ed. with D.G. Hartwell) Year's Best SF 14, 2009; Grail, 2010; A Reckoning of Men, 2011; The Sea thy Mistress, 2011; (with S. Monette) Tempering of Men, 2011; Range of Ghosts, 2012; An Apprentice to Elves, 2013. Contributor of articles to books. Works appear in anthologies. **Address:** c/o Jennifer Jackson, Donald Maass Literary Agency, 121 W 27th St., Ste. 801, New York, NY 10001, U.S.A. **Online address:** elizabeth@elizabethbear.com

BEAR, **Greg(ory Dale).** American (born United States), b. 1951. **Genres:** Science Fiction/Fantasy, Novels, Novellas/Short Stories. **Career:** Aerospace Museum, lecturer, 1969-72; Fleet Space Theatre, writer and planetarium operator, 1973; writer, 1975-; Association of Science Fiction Artists, founding member; Central Intelligence Agency, consultant; Microsoft Corp., consultant; Callison Architects, consultant; Sandia National Laboratories, consultant. **Publications:** SCIENCE FICTION: Hegira, 1979; Psychlone, 1979; Beyond Heaven's River, 1980; Strength of Stones, 1981; Corona, 1984; The Infinity Concerto, 1984; Blood Music, 1985; Eon, 1985; The Serpent Mage, 1986; The Forge of God, 1987; Sleepside Story, 1988; Eternity, 1988; Queen of Angels, 1990; Heads, 1990; Anvil of Stars, 1992; Songs of Earth and Power, 1992; Moving Mars, 1993; Legacy, 1995; (ed. with M.H. Greenberg) New Legends, 1995; Slant, 1997; Country of the Mind, 1998; Dinosaur Summer, 1998; Foundation and Chaos, 1998; Darwin's Radio, 1999; Rogue Planet, 2000; Vitals, 2002; Darwin's Children, 2003; Dead Lines, 2004. COLLECTIONS: The Wind from a Burning Woman, 1983; Early Harvest, 1988; Tangents, 1989; Sisters, 1992; The Venging, 1992; Bear's Fantasies: Six Stories in Old Paradigms, 1992; The Collected Stories of Greg Bear, 2002; W3: Women in Deep Time, 2003; Sleepside: The Collected Fantasies of Greg Bear, 2004. OTHERS: Hardfought, 1993; The White Horse Child, 1993; Greatest Science Fiction Stories of the 20th Century, 1998; (intro.) Psycho Shop, 1998; (ed.) The Last War: A World Set Free, 2001; (intro.) The Time Machine, 2002; Quantico, 2005; City at the End of Time, 2008; Mariposa, 2009; Hull Zero Three, 2010; Halo: Cryptum, 2011. Contributor to periodicals. **Address:** Alderwood Manor, 506 Lakeview Rd., Lynnwood, WA 98087-2141, U.S.A.

BEAR, **Ray A. Young.** American (born United States), b. 1950. **Genres:** Poetry, Cultural/Ethnic Topics. **Career:** The Institute of American Indian Art, faculty, 1984; Eastern Washington University, visiting writer and lecturer, 1987; Meskwaki Indian Elementary School, teacher, 1988-89; University of Iowa, Native American Literature, instructor, 1989; Iowa State University, visiting writer and lecturer, 1993, 1998. **Publications:** Waiting to Be Fed: (poem), 1975; Winter of the Salamander: The Keeper of Importance, 1980; The Invisible Musician: Poems, 1990; Black Eagle Child: The Facepaint Narratives, 1992; Remnants of the First Earth, 1996; The Rock Island Hiking Club: Poems, 2001. Contributor to periodicals. **Address:** 202 Red Earth Dr., Tama, IA 52339, U.S.A.

BEARANGER, **Marie.** American (born United States), b. 1956. **Genres:** Zoology, Young Adult Non-fiction, Natural History, Children's Fiction, Animals/Pets. **Career:** Gareth Stevens Inc., national sales manager, 1987-2000; Horizon Travel, travel consultant, 1988-99; Central Programs Inc., staff, 2001-; Breakthrough Promotions, staff, 2001-. Writer. **Publications:** COLORS OF THE SEA SERIES WITH E. ETHAN: Coral Reef Builders, 1997; Coral Reef Feeders, 1997; Coral Reef Hunters, 1997; Coral Reef Partners, 1997; Coral Reef Survival, 1997. **Address:** Gareth Stevens Publishing, 330 W Olive St., Ste. 100, Milwaukee, WI 53212-1068, U.S.A. **Online address:** clairem@tds.net

BEARD, **Darleen Bailey.** American (born United States), b. 1961. **Genres:** Novels, Children's Fiction, Humor/Satire, Young Adult Fiction. **Career:** McGraw-Hill, freelance writer, 1989-90. **Publications:** The Pumpkin Man from Piney Creek, 1995; The Flimflam Man, 1998; Twister (picture book), 1999. NOVELS: The Babbs Switch Story, 2002; Operation: Clean Sweep, 2004; Annie Glover is NOT a Tree Lover, 2009. Works appear in anthologies. Contributor to magazines. **Address:** 1627 Briarcliff Ct., Norman, OK 73071-3811, U.S.A. **Online address:** darleen@darleenbaileybeard.com

BEARD, Geoffrey. British (born England), b. 1929?. **Genres:** Architecture, Art/Art History, Crafts. **Career:** Leeds City Art Gallery, assistant, 1957-61; Cannon Hall Art Gallery, director, 1961-66; Manchester Polytechnic, senior lecturer in history of design, 1966-72; University of Lancaster, visual arts center, director, 1972-82; writer, 1982-. **Publications:** (With A.R. Billington) English Abbeys, 1949; Nineteenth Century Cameo Glass, 1956; Collecting Antiques on a Small Income, 1957; Georgian Craftsmen and Their Work, 1966; Modern Glass, 1968; Modern Ceramics, 1969; Decorative Plasterwork in Great Britain, 1975; International Modern Glass, 1976; (with J. Wardman) Thomas H. Mawson, 1861-1933: The Life and Work of a Northern Landscape Architect, 1976; The Work of Robert Adam, 1978; The Greater House in Cumbria, 1978; (with G. Berry) The Lake District: A Century of Conservation, 1980; Robert Adam's Country Houses, 1981; Craftsmen and Interior Decoration 1660-1820, 1981; The Work of Christopher Wren, 1982; Stucco and Decorative Plasterwork in Europe, 1983; The National Trust Book of English Furniture, 1985; The Work of John Vanbrugh, 1986; (ed. with C.G. Gilbert) Dictionary of English Furniture Makers, 1660-1840, 1986; (with J. Goodison) English Furniture, 1500-1840, 1987; The Work of Grinling Gibbons, 1990; The National Trust Book of the English House Interior, 1990; The Compleat Gentleman: Five Centuries of Aristocratic Life, 1993; Upholsterers and Interior Furnishing in England, 1530-1840, 1997. **Address:** Yale University Press, 23 Pond St., Hampstead, London, GL NW3 2PN, England.

BEARD, Jo Ann. American (born United States), b. 1955. **Genres:** Novels, Literary Criticism And History. **Career:** Writer. **Publications:** The Boys of My Youth, 1998; In Zanesville, 2011. Contributor to periodicals. **Address:** Little Brown and Co., 1271 Ave. of the Americas, New York, NY 10020, U.S.A.

BEARD, Patricia. American (born United States), b. 1947?. **Genres:** Animals/Pets, Business/Trade/Industry. **Career:** Elle, editor-at-large; Town & Country, editor; Mirabella, editor. **Publications:** (Ed. and intro.) The Voice of the Wild: An Anthology of Animal Stories, 1992; Growing up Republican: Christie Whitman, the Politics of Character, 1996; Good Daughters: Loving Our Mothers as They Age, 1999; Class Action, 2000; After the Ball: Gilded-Age Secrets, Boardroom Betrayals, and the Party That Ignited the Great Wall Street Scandal of 1905, 2003; Blue Blood and Mutiny: The Fight for the Soul of Morgan Stanley, 2007. Contributor to periodicals. **Address:** Harper Collins, 10 E 53rd St., New York, NY 10022, U.S.A.

BEARD, Philip. American (born United States), b. 1963?. **Genres:** Novels, Young Adult Fiction. **Career:** Stonecipher, Cunningham, Beard and Schmitt (law firm), partner, 1990-2000. Writer. **Publications:** Dear Zoe, 2005; Lost in the Garden, 2006. **Address:** c/o Jane Dystel, Dystel & Goderich Literary Management, 1 Union Sq. W, Ste. 904, New York, NY 10003, U.S.A. **Online address:** author@philipbeard.net

BEARD, Richard. British/American (born United States), b. 1967?. **Genres:** Novels, Young Adult Non-fiction, Travel/Exploration, Reference. **Career:** Dragon School, games teacher; National Library, staff; National Academy of Writing, director; University of Tokyo, visiting professor, 2003-06. Writer. **Publications:** X20: A Novel of Not Smoking, 1996; Damascus: A Novel, 1999; The Cartoonist, 2000; Muddied Oafs: The Last Days of Rugger, 2003; Muddied Oafs: The Soul of Rugby, 2003; Dry Bones, 2004; Manly Pursuits: Beating the Australians, 2006; Becoming Drusilla: One Life, Two Friends, Three Genders, 2008. **Address:** Arcade Publishing, 141 5th Ave., New York, NY 10010, U.S.A.

BEARD, William. Canadian (born Canada), b. 1946. **Genres:** Film. **Career:** University of Alberta, professor of English and film, 1976-. Writer. **Publications:** Persistence of Double Vision: Essays on Clint Eastwood, 2000; The Artist as Monster: The Cinema of David Cronenberg, 2001, rev. ed., 2006; (with J. White) North of Everything: English Canadian Cinema Since 1980, 2002; Into the Past: The Cinema of Guy Maddin, 2010. **Address:** Department of English and Film, University Alberta, 3-5 Humanities Ctr., Edmonton, AB T6G 2E5, Canada. **Online address:** william.beard@ualberta.ca

BEARDEN, Milton. American (born United States), b. 1940. **Genres:** Mystery/Crime/Suspense, Novels. **Career:** Central Intelligence Agency, staff, 1964-, station chief, field officer, 1986-89, chief of the Soviet/East European division, retired, 1994. Writer and film consultant. **Publications:** The Black Tulip: A Novel, 1998; (contrib.) How Did This Happen?: Terrorism and The New War, 2001; (with J. Risen) The Main Enemy: The Inside Story of the CIA's Final Showdown with the KGB, 2003. Contributor to periodicals. **Address:** Random House Inc., 1745 Broadway, New York, NY 10019, U.S.A.

BEARDSELL, Peter R. British (born England), b. 1940. **Genres:** Cultural/Ethnic Topics, Literary Criticism And History, Translations, Poetry, Theatre. **Career:** University of Manchester, lecturer in Spanish, 1965-66; University of Sheffield, lecturer in Hispanic studies, 1966-93; Manchester Hispanic Texts, general editor, 1990-2002; University of Hull, chair of Hispanic studies, 1993-, professor of Hispanic studies, now professor emeritus. **Publications:** Critical Edition of Ricardo Guiraldes: Don Segundo Sombra, 1973; (intro.) Don Segundo Sombra, 1973; Winds of Exile: The Poetry of Jorge Carrera Andrade, 1977; Quiroga: Cuentos de amor, de locura y de muerte, 1986; A Theatre for Cannibals: Rodolfo Usigli and the Mexican Stage, 1992; (trans. and intro.) H.D. Cincotta, El Pesaroso: Man of Sorrows (poems), 1992; Critical Edition of Julio Cortazar: Siete cuentos, 1993; Gods and Demons, Self and Other, 1994; (ed. and intro.) Siete Cuentos, 1994; Europe and Latin America: Returning the Gaze, 2000. **Address:** University of Hull, Cottingham Rd., Hull, HB HU6 7RX, England. **Online address:** p.r.beardsell@hull.ac.uk

BEARDSLEE, Karen E. American (born United States), b. 1965. **Genres:** Literary Criticism And History, Social Sciences, Mythology/Folklore. **Career:** Burlington County College, adjunct professor, 1991-99, lecturer in English, 1999-2002; Camden County College, adjunct professor, 1992; Rowan College of New Jersey, adjunct professor, 1995; teacher of history and English, 1998-99; Moorestown Barnes and Noble Monthly Senior Memoirs Writing Group, co-facilitator, 2000; independent folklorist, 2002-. **Publications:** Literary Legacies, Folklore Foundations: Selfhood and Cultural Tradition in Nineteenth and Twentieth-Century American Literature, 2001; (ed.) Translating Tradition: A Longman Topics Reader, 2004; From San Quentin Gumbo to Fried Green Tomatoes at the Whistlestop Café: Foodways in Life and Literature, 2004; Translating Tradition: A Family Folklore Reader, 2004; Variety Shows: An American Family Reader and Writer, 2004. Contributor of articles to periodicals. Works appear in anthologies. **Address:** University of Tennessee Press, 110 Conference Ctr., 600 Henley St., Knoxville, TN 37996, U.S.A. **Online address:** leejogger@aol.com

BEARDSLEY, Theodore S. (Theodore Sterling Beardsley). American (born United States), b. 1936. **Genres:** Songs/Lyrics And Libretti, Literary Criticism And History, Language/Linguistics. **Career:** Rider College, instructor, 1957-59, assistant professor of modern languages and chairman of the department, 1959-61; Southern Illinois University, assistant professor of Spanish, 1961-62; University of Wisconsin, assistant professor of Spanish, 1962-65; Hispanic Society of America, director, 1965-95, president, 1995-; New York University, visiting professor, 1967-69; Columbia University, faculty, 1969. Museums Council of New York, chairman, 1972-73; Spanish Institute, director. Writer. **Publications:** Hispano-Classical Translations, 1482-1699, 1970; Tomás Navarro Tomas: A Tentative Bibliography 1908-1970, 1971; (trans.) Maria Sabina (libretto), 1973; Ponce de Leon (libretto), 1973; The Hispanic Impact on the United States, 1990. EDITOR: Enric Madriguera, 1994; (co-ed.) Celestina, Early Texts, 1997; Carlos Molina, 2000; Chuy Reyes, 2004. Contributor to journals. **Address:** Hispanic Society of America, 613 W 155th St., New York, NY 10032, U.S.A.

BEARDSLEY, Theodore Sterling. *See* **Beardsley, Theodore S.**

BEARMAN, Peter. (Peter Shawn Bearman). American (born United States), b. 1956?. **Genres:** Sociology, Social Sciences. **Career:** Harvard University, lecturer, 1985-86; University of North Carolina, assistant professor, 1986-91, associate professor, 1991-96, professor of sociology, 1996-97, adjunct professor, 1998-2001; Columbia University, Department of Sociology, professor of sociology, 1998-2006, chair, 2001-05, Jonathan Cole professor of the social sciences, 2006-, Jonathan Cole chair of sociology, faculty fellow, Paul F. Lazarsfeld Center for the Social Sciences, director, 1999-, Institute for Social and Economic Research and Policy, founding director, 2000-08, Project on the Social Determinants of Autism, director, Adolescent Health Project, director, Robert Wood Johnson Foundation, Health & Society Scholars Program, co-director, 2001-, Global Health Research Center of Central

Asia, founding co-director, 2006-, Mellon Interdisciplinary Training Program in the Social Sciences, director, 2006-, Department of Statistics, chair, 2007-08, Understanding Autism Project, principal investigator and researcher; University of Genova, visiting professor of sociology, 2002-03; Nuffield College, faculty, 2005-; Sociologica, international editor, 2010-. **Publications:** (As Peter S. Bearman) Relations into Rhetorics: Local Elite Social Structure in Norfolk, England, 1540-1640, 1993; Doormen, 2005; (ed. with K.M. Neckerman and L. Wright) After Tobacco: What Would Happen If Americans Stopped Smoking?, 2011. **Address:** Paul F. Lazarsfeld Center for the Social Sciences, Columbia University, International Affairs Bldg., 8th Fl., 420 W 118th St., PO Box 3355, New York, NY 10027, U.S.A. **Online address:** psb17@columbia.edu

BEARMAN, Peter Shawn. *See* **BEARMAN, Peter.**

BEARY, Michael J. American (born United States), b. 1956. **Genres:** Biography, Race Relations, Theology/Religion. **Career:** Writer and historian. **Publications:** Black Bishop: Edward T. Demby and the Struggle for Racial Equality in the Episcopal Church (biography), 2001. **Address:** c/o Danielle Wilberg, University of Illinois Press, 1325 S Oak St., Champaign, IL 61820-6903, U.S.A.

BEASER, Richard S. American (born United States), b. 1951. **Genres:** Medicine/Health. **Career:** Harvard University, Joslin Diabetes Center, senior staff physician, 1982-, medical executive director of professional education and continuing medical education, 2000-; Harvard Medical School, associate clinical professor of medicine; CeQur Ltd., consultant. Writer. **Publications:** (With L.P. Krall) Joslin Diabetes Manual, 12th ed., 1989; Outsmarting Diabetes: A Dynamic Approach for Reducing the Effects of Insulin-dependent Diabetes, 1994; Joslins Diabetes Deskbook, 2003; (with J.V.C. Hill) The Joslin Guide to Diabetes: A Program for Managing Your Treatment, 1995, (with A.P. Campbell) 2nd ed., 2005. **Address:** Joslin Diabetes Ctr., 1 Joslin Pl., Boston, MA 02215-5306, U.S.A. **Online address:** richard.beaser@joslin.harvard.edu

BEASLEY, Bruce. American (born United States), b. 1958. **Genres:** Poetry. **Career:** Western Washington University, professor of English, 1992-. Writer. **Publications:** POETRY: Spirituals, 1988; The Creation, 1994; Summer Mystagogia, 1996; Signs & Abominations, 2000; Lord Brain: Poems, 2005; Corpse Flower: New and Selected Poems, 2007. Contributor to periodicals. **Address:** Department of English, Western Washington University, Humanities 265, 516 High St., Bellingham, WA 98225, U.S.A. **Online address:** bruce.beasley@wwu.edu

BEASLEY, Faith E(velyn). American (born United States), b. 1958. **Genres:** History, Autobiography/Memoirs, Essays, Humanities, Intellectual History, Literary Criticism And History. **Career:** Dartmouth College, professor of French, women's and gender studies, 1986-. Writer. **Publications:** Revising Memory: Women's Fiction and Memoirs in Seventeenth-Century France, 1990; (co-ed.) Approaches to Teaching Lafayette's the Princess of Cleves, 1998; Salons, History and the Creation of 17th-Century France: Mastering Memory, 2006; (ed.) Options for Teaching Seventeenth and Eighteenth-Century French Women Writers, 2011. **Address:** Department of French and Italian, Dartmouth College, HB 6087, Hanover, NH 03755-3511, U.S.A. **Online address:** faith.e.beasley@dartmouth.edu

BEASLEY, Sandra. American (born United States), b. 1980. **Genres:** Poetry. **Career:** University of Mississippi, summer poet-in-residence. Writer. **Publications:** Theories of Falling (poetry), 2008; I Was the Jukebox: Poems, 2010; Don't Kill the Birthday Girl: Tales from an Allergic Life, 2011. Contributor to periodicals. **Address:** Washington, DC , U.S.A.

BEASLEY, Vanessa B. American (born United States), b. 1966. **Genres:** Adult Non-fiction, Public/Social Administration, Politics/Government. **Career:** Southern Methodist University, Division of Corporate Communication and Public Affairs, associate professor; Texas A&M University, associate professor; University of Georgia, instructor; Vanderbilt University, Department of Communication Studies, associate professor, Program in Career Development, director. Writer. **Publications:** You, the People: American National Identity in Presidential Rhetoric, 2004; (ed.) Who Belongs in America?: Presidents, Rhetoric, and Immigration, 2006. **Address:** Department of Communication Studies, Vanderbilt University, 213G Calhoun Hall, 2301 Vanderbilt Pl., PO Box 351505, VU Sta. B, Nashville, TN 37235-1505, U.S.A. **Online address:** vanessa.b.beasley@vanderbilt.edu

BEASON, Doug. American (born United States), b. 1953?. **Genres:** Novels, Adult Non-fiction, Military/Defense/Arms Control. **Career:** Air Force Weapons Laboratory, Airblast and Cloudrise Section, physicist, chief, 1977-80, Advanced Concepts Branch, chief, 1986-88, High Energy Plasma Division, chief, 1988-90; U.S. Air Force Academy, Department of Physics, assistant professor, 1983-86, associate professor of physics and director of faculty research, 1993-95; NASA, Department of Defense, deputy for science and technology, 1990-91, Department of Energy Space Exploration Initiative (the Synthesis Group), deputy for science and technology, 1990-91; White House, Executive Office of the President, Office of Science and Technology Policy, senior policy analyst, 1991-93; Industrial College of the Armed Forces, research fellow, 1995-96; Defense Special Weapons Agency, Lawrence Livermore National Laboratory Detachment, chief, 1996-98; Air Force Research Laboratory, Directed Energy Directorate, deputy director, 1998-2001, Phillips Research Site, commander, 1998-2001; Los Alamos National Laboratory, Threat Reduction, deputy associate laboratory director, 2001-03, associate laboratory director, 2005-08, International Space and Response Division, division director, 2003-05; Auburn University, freelance writer and special advisor, 2009-10; United States Army Force, Headquarters Air Force Space Command, Peterson Air Force Base, chief scientist and technology adviser, 2010-. Writer. **Publications:** NOVELS: Return to Honor, 1989; Assault on Alpha Base, 1990; Strike Eagle, 1991; DOD Science and Technology: Strategy for the Post-Cold War Era, 1997; E-Bomb: How America's New Directed Energy Weapons Will Change the Way Future Wars Will Be Fought, 2005; Wild Blue U, 2009. NOVELS WITH K.J. ANDERSON: Lifeline, 1990; The Trinity Paradox, 1991; Assemblers of Infinity, 1993; Ill Wind, 1995; Virtual Destruction, 1996; Ignition, 1996; Fallout, 1997; Lethal Exposure, 1998. Works appear in anthologies. Contributor to periodicals. **Address:** Peterson Air Force Base, Air Force Space Command, 150 Vandenberg St., Ste. 1105, Colorado Springs, CO 80914-4500, U.S.A. **Online address:** doug@dougbeason.com

BEATIE, Thomas. American (born United States), b. 1974?. **Genres:** Gay And Lesbian Issues. **Career:** Writer. **Publications:** Labor of Love: The Story of One Man's Extraordinary Pregnancy, 2008. **Address:** Bend, OR , U.S.A. **Online address:** definenormal2000@aol.com

BEATLEY, Timothy. American (born United States), b. 1957?. **Genres:** Natural History, Administration/Management, Environmental Sciences/Ecology, Politics/Government, Bibliography. **Career:** University of Virginia, School of Architecture, faculty, 1991-, Teresa Heinz professor of sustainable communities, 2002-. Writer. **Publications:** A Bibliography of Growth Management Sources (1970 Foreword), 1985; (with D.J. Brower and D.J.L. Blatt) Reducing Hurricane and Coastal Hazards through Growth Management: A Guidebook for North Carolina Coastal Localities, 1987; (with D.R. Godschalk and D.J. Brower) Catastrophic Coastal Storms: Hazard Mitigation and Development Management, 1989; (with P.R. Berke) Planning for Earthquakes: Risk, Politics, and Policy, 1992; (co-author) Coastal Erosion: Has Retreat Sounded?, 1992; Ethical Land Use: Principles of Policy and Planning, 1994; Habitat Conservation Planning: Endangered Species and Urban Growth, 1994; (with D.J. Brower and A.K. Schwab) An Introduction to Coastal Zone Management, 1994, 2nd ed., 2002; (with K. Manning) The Ecology of Place: Planning for Environment, Economy and Community, 1997; (with P.R. Berke) After the Hurricane: Linking Recovery to Sustainable Development in the Caribbean, 1997; Green Urbanism: Learning from European Cities, 2000; (ed. with S.M. Wheeler) The Sustainable Urban Development Reader, 2004, 2nd ed., 2008; Native to Nowhere: Sustaining Home and Community in a Global Age, 2004; (with P. Newman) Green Urbanism Down Under: Learning from Sustainable Communities in Australia, 2009; Planning for Coastal Resilience: Best Practices for Calamitous Times, 2009; (with P. Newman and H. Boyer) Resilient Cities: Responding to Peak Oil and Climate Change, 2009; Biophilic Cities: integrating Nature Into Urban Design and Planning, 2011; (ed.) Green Cities of Europe: Global Lessons on Green Urbansim, 2012. **Address:** School of Architecture, University of Virginia, 109 Campbell Hall, PO Box 400122, Charlottesville, VA 22904-4122, U.S.A. **Online address:** tb6d@virginia.edu

BEATTIE, Ann. American (born United States), b. 1947. **Genres:** Novels, Novellas/Short Stories, Art/Art History, Autobiography/Memoirs, Education, Literary Criticism And History. **Career:** University of Virginia, visiting assistant professor, 1976-77, visiting writer, 1980, Edgar Allan Poe professor of creative writing, 2001-; Harvard University, Briggs-Copeland lecturer in English, 1977-78; Northwestern University, Center for the Writing Arts, writer-in-residence, 1994. **Publications:** NOVELS: Chilly Scenes of Winter, 1976;

Falling in Place, 1980; Love Always, 1985; Spectacles, 1985; Picturing Will, 1989; Another You, 1995; My Life, Starring Dara Falcon, 1997; The Doctor's House, 2002; Follies: And New Stories, 2005. STORIES: Distortions, 1976; Secrets and Surprises, 1978; The Burning House, 1982; Where You'll Find Me and Other Stories, 1986; What Was Mine, 1991; (with B. Adelman) Americana, 1992; (with A. Grundberg) Flesh Blood: Photographer's Images of Their Own Families, 1992; (intro.) With This Ring: A Portrait of Marriage, 1997; Park City: New and Selected Stories, 1998; Perfect Recall: New Stories, 2001. OTHERS: Alex Katz (art criticism), 1987; The Pleasures of Perplexity, 2005; Lincoln Perry's Charlottesville, 2005; Walks with Men, 2010; Ann Beattie: The New Yorker Stories, 2010; Mrs. Nixon: A Novelist Imagines a Life, 2011. **Address:** Janklow & Nesbit Ltd., 445 Park Ave., 13th Fl., New York, NY 10022-8628, U.S.A.

BEATTIE, Judith Hudson. (Judith Valenzuela). Canadian (born Canada), b. 1944. **Genres:** History, Genealogy/Heraldry. **Career:** Archives of Ontario, archivist, 1969-73; University of Ottawa, Center for Research on Canadian-French Civilization, archivist, 1977-81; Hudson's Bay Company Archives, head of research and reference, 1981-91, keeper, 1991-2003. Writer. **Publications:** (With B. Pothier) Battle of the Restigouche, 1977; (ed. with H.M. Buss and contrib.) Undelivered Letters to Hudson's Bay Company Men on the Northwest Coast of America, 1830-57, 2002; The Colinda: The Hudson's Bay Company-Chile Connection, 1853-1856, forthcoming. **Address:** c/o Author Mail, University of British Columbia Press, 2029 W Mall, Vancouver, BC V6T 1Z2, Canada. **Online address:** jhbval@mts.net

BEATTIE, L(inda) Elisabeth. American (born United States), b. 1953. **Genres:** Women's Studies And Issues, Food And Wine, Essays, Law, Social Sciences. **Career:** Home for the Handicapped Elderly, director, 1974; George Washington University, administrative assistant in Oral History Program, 1978-79; Alston Wilkes Society, public information specialist, 1980-81; Bruccoli Clark Research, editor and copy editor, 1981-82; Retired Senior Volunteer Program, assistant director, 1982-84; Bellarmine College, adjunct instructor in English literature and composition, 1988-89; high school teacher of English and journalism, 1989-90; Kentucky Writers' Oral History Project, director, 1990-; Elizabethtown Community College, instructor, 1990-91, assistant professor, 1991-97, associate professor of English and journalism, 1997-99; University of Kentucky, Appalachian Center, associate, 1996-99; Midway College, associate professor of English, writer-in-residence and Robert L. Botkin chair, 1999-2002; Jefferson County Public Schools, editor, 2002-06; self-employed writer, 2006-. **Publications:** (Ed.) Conversations with Kentucky Writers, 1996; (ed.) Savory Memories, 1998; (ed.) Conversations with Kentucky Writers II, 1999; (with M.A. Shaughnessy) Sisters in Pain: Battered Women Fight Back, 2000. Contributor to periodicals. **Address:** The University Press of Kentucky, 663 S Limestone St., Lexington, KY 40508, U.S.A. **Online address:** lebeattie@ntr.net

BEATTIE, Melody (Lynn). American (born United States), b. 1948. **Genres:** Psychology, Social Sciences, Medicine/Health, Autobiography/Memoirs. **Career:** Lecturer. Freelance author of articles and books, 1979-. **Publications:** (With C. Owens) A Promise of Sanity, 1982; Denial, 1985; Codependent No More: How to Stop Controlling Others and Start Caring for Yourself, 1987, 2nd ed., 1992; Crack: The Facts, 1987; Beyond Codependency: And Getting Better All the Time, 1989; The Language of Letting Go: Daily Meditations for Codependents, 1990; Codependents' Guide to the Twelve Steps: How to Find the Right Program for You and Apply Each of the Twelve Steps to Your Own Issues, 1990; (ed.) A Reason to Live, 1991; Talk, Trust, and Feel: Keeping Codependency Out of Your Life, 1991; Gratitude: Affirming the Good Things in Life, 1992; The Lessons of Love: Rediscovering Our Passion for Life When It All Seems Too Hard to Take, 1994; Journey to the Heart: Daily Meditations on the Path to Freeing Your Soul, 1996; Stop Being Mean to Yourself: A Story about Finding the True Meaning of Self-Love, 1997; Codependent No More/Beyond Codependency, 1997; Language of Letting Go, 1997, rev. ed. as The Language of Letting Go Journal: A Meditation Book and Journal for Daily Reflection, 2003; Finding Your Way Home: A Soul Survivial Kit, 1998; Playing It by Heart: Taking Care of Yourself No Matter What, 1999; More Language of Letting Go: 366 New Daily Meditations, 2000; Choices: Taking Control of Your Life and Making It Matter, 2002; 52 Weeks of Conscious Contact: Meditations for Connecting with God, Self & Others, 2003; The Grief Club: The Secret to Getting Through all Kinds of Change, 2006; Gratitude: Inspirations, 2007; New Codependency: Help and Guidance for the Today's Generation, 2009; Make Miracles in Forty Days: Turning What You Have into What You Want, 2010; Codependent No More Workbook, 2011. Contributor to periodicals. **Address:** Ballantine Books, 201 E 50th St., New York, NY 10022, U.S.A. **Online address:** melody@melodybeattie.com

BEATTY, Barbara (R.). (Barbara Rachel Beatty). American (born United States), b. 1946. **Genres:** Education, History, Cultural/Ethnic Topics, Philosophy. **Career:** Boston Public Schools, kindergarten teacher, 1968-72; Education Development Center, Child Care Project, coordinator, 1973; Lesley Ellis School, administrative director, 1973-78; Lesley College, assistant professor of education, 1973-81; Wellesley College, Department of Education, assistant professor, 1981-93, associate professor of education, 1994-2007, professor of education, 2007-, department chair, 1995-96, 1999-2001, 2002-. Writer. **Publications:** Preschool Education in America: The Culture of Young Children From the Colonial Era to the Present, 1995; (ed. with E.D. Cahan and J. Grant) When Science Encounters the Child: Education, Parenting, and Child Welfare in 20th-Century America, 2006. Contributor of articles to books, periodicals and journals. **Address:** Department of Education, Wellesley College, Rm. 152, Pendleton Hall E, 106 Central St., Wellesley, MA 02481-8203, U.S.A. **Online address:** bbeatty@wellesley.edu

BEATTY, Barbara Rachel. *See* **BEATTY, Barbara (R.).**

BEATTY, Jack. American (born United States), b. 1945. **Genres:** History, Biography, Business/Trade/Industry. **Career:** Atlantic Monthly, senior editor, 1983-; On Point, news analyst; Newsweek, book reviewer; The New Republic, literary editor; Yale University, Poynter Fellow. **Publications:** The Rascal King: The Life and Times of James Michael Curley, 1874-1958: An Epic of Urban Politics and Irish America, 1992; The World According to Peter Drucker, 1998; (ed.) Colossus: How the Corporation Changed America, 2001; (ed.) Pols: Great Writers on American Politicians from Bryan to Reagan, 2004; Age of Betrayal: The Triumph Of Money In America, 1865-1900, 2007. Contributor to periodicals. **Address:** The Atlantic Monthly, 77 N Washington St., Boston, MA 02114, U.S.A.

BEATY, Andrea. American (born United States) **Genres:** Children's Fiction, Picture/Board Books, Novels. **Career:** Writer. **Publications:** When Giants Come to Play, 2006; Iggy Peck, Architect, 2007; Cicada Summer, 2008; Doctor Ted, 2008; Firefighter Ted, 2009; Hush, Baby Ghostling, 2009; Attack of the Fluffy Bunnies, 2010; Hide and Sheep, 2011; Artist Ted, 2012; Dorko the Magnificent, 2013; The Fractious Cat, 2015. **Address:** Margaret K. Mcelderry Books, 1230 Ave. of the Americas, New York, NY 10020, U.S.A. **Online address:** andreabeaty@gmail.com

BEATY, Betty Campbell. *See* **BEATY, Betty (Smith).**

BEATY, Betty (Smith). Also writes as Karen Campbell, Betty Campbell Beaty, Catherine Ross. British (born England), b. 1919?. **Genres:** Novels, Biography, Romance/Historical. **Career:** British European Airways, London, stewardess, 1946-47; St. Leonards Shoreditch, London, almoner, 1947-48; writer, 1953-; Pembury Hospital, Tunbridge Wells, medical social worker, 1971-72. **Publications:** Maiden Flight, 1956; South to the Sun, 1956; The Atlantic Sky, 1957; Amber Fire, 1958; The Butternut Tree, 1958; Top of the Climb, 1962; The Path of the Moonfish, 1964; Miss Miranda's Walk, 1967; The Swallows of San Fedora, 1974; Love and the Kentish Maid, 1975; Head of Chancery, 1976; Master at Arms, 1977; Fly Away, Love, 1977; Harlequin Romance: South to the Sun, 1979; Exchange of Hearts, 1980; Doctor on Board, 1980; (with D. Beaty) Wings of the Morning, 1982; Twice in a Lifetime, 1983; The Missionary's Daughter, 1983; Matchmaker Nurse, 1984; Airport Nurse, 1986; Romance Treasury: Head of Chancery, 1986; Wings of Love, 1988; That Special Joy, 1992; Just for the Love of Flying, 1997. AS CATHERINE ROSS: From This Day Forward, 1959; The Colours of the Night, 1962; The Trysting Tower, 1966; Battle Dress, 1979; The Shadow of the Peak, 1985; (with G. Richard and B. Porterfield) The Body Knows, 1986; Stella Mere, 2000. AS KAREN CAMPBELL: Suddenly, in the Air, 1969; Thunder on Sunday, 1972; Wheel Fortune, 1973; Death Descending, 1976; The Bells of St. Martin, 1979; Fatal Union, 1994. AS BETTY CAMPBELL BEATY: Winged Life: A Biography of David Beaty, 2001. **Address:** Curtis Brown Ltd., 162-168 Regent St., London, GL W1R 5TB, England.

BEAUCHAMP, Cari. American (born United States), b. 1949. **Genres:** Film, Westerns/Adventure, Art/Art History. **Career:** National Public Radio, reporter. **Publications:** (With H. Behar) Hollywood on the Riviera: The Inside Story of the Cannes Film Festival, 1992; Without Lying Down: Frances Marion and the Powerful Women of Early Hollywood, 1997; (ed.) Anita Loos

Rediscovered: Film Treatments and Fiction, 2003; (ed.) Adventures of a Hollywood Secretary: Her Private Letters from Inside the Studios of the 1920s, 2006; Joseph P. Kennedy Presents: His Hollywood Years, 2009. **Address:** Simon & Schuster Inc., 1230 Ave. of the Americas, New York, NY 10020, U.S.A. **Online address:** info@caribeauchamp.com

BEAUCHAMP, Kenneth. American (born United States), b. 1939. **Genres:** Psychology. **Career:** California State Polytechnic University, instructor, 1965-67, assistant professor of psychology, 1967-69; University of the Pacific, College of the Pacific, associate professor of psychology, 1969-78, acting dean, 1974-76, associate dean, 1974-77, professor of psychology, 1978-2007, department chair, 1987-94, 2001-04, acting chair, 2007-08, faculty fellow, professor emeritus, 2007-, Center of Social and Emotional Competence, consulting faculty. Writer. **Publications:** (Ed. with J.L. Philbrick) Readings in Contemporary Scientific Psychology, 1966, 2nd ed., 1967; (ed. with D.W. Matheson and R.L. Bruce) Current Topics in Experimental Psychology, 1970, 3rd ed., 1978; (with D.W. Matheson and R.L. Bruce) Introduction to Experimental Psychology, 1970, 3rd ed. as Experimental Psychology: Research Design and Analysis, 1978. **Address:** Psychology Department, College of the Pacific, University of the Pacific, 3601 Pacific Ave., Stockton, CA 95211, U.S.A. **Online address:** kbeauchamp@pacific.edu

BEAUCHARD, Pierre François. (David B.). French (born France), b. 1959. **Genres:** Graphic Novels, Novels. **Career:** L'Association, co-founder, 1990. Graphic novelist. **Publications:** La Bombe Familiale, 1991; Le Cheval Blême, 1992; Le Cercueil De course, 1993; Le Livre Somnambule, 1994; (co-author as David B.) Le Retour De Dieu, 1994; Les 4 Savants, 1996; Lascension Du Haut-mal, 1996; Mésopotamie, 1997; Hiram Lowatt Placido, 1997; Le Tengû Carré, 1997; Les Incidents De Lanuit, 1999; Maman a Des Problmes, 1999; Le Capitaine écarlate, 2000; Urani, 2000; Sagesses Et Malices De Nasreddine Le Fou Qui était Sage, 2000; La Lecture Des Ruines, 2001; Les Chercheurs De Trésor, 2003; Babel, 2004; Leonora, 2004; (as David B.) Epileptic, 2005. **Address:** Pantheon Books Inc., 1745 Broadway, 3rd Fl., New York, NY 10019-4368, U.S.A.

BEAUCLERK, Charles. British (born England), b. 1965. **Genres:** Biography, Young Adult Fiction. **Career:** Shakespeare Oxford Society, president, 1995-97; The Oxfordian, founder; Norroy & Ulster King of Arms, research assistant; Freedom in Action, director; Otley Hall, literary secretary to Nicholas Hagger; De Vere Society, librarian. Writer and lecturer. **Publications:** Nell Gwyn: Mistress to a King, 2005; Shakespeare's Lost Kingdom: The True History of Shakespeare and Elizabeth, 2010; Shakespeare's Identity Crisis, forthcoming. **Address:** A.P. Watt Ltd., 20 John St., London, GL WC1N 2DR, England.

BEAUD, Michel. French (born France), b. 1935. **Genres:** Economics, History, Essays. **Career:** University of Lille, assistant professor, 1965-66, associate professor of economics, 1966-69; University of Paris VIII, associate professor, 1969-70, professor of economics, 1970-91, department head; GIS Economie Mondiale, Tiers-Monde, Developpement (GEMDEV), co-founder, 1983, chairperson, 1983-90, honorary chairperson, 1993-; Vezelay Group, co-founder, 1988; French Ministry of the Environment, ECLAT Commission on Climate and Atmospheric Changes, vice chairperson, 1989-93; University of Paris VII, professor of economics, 1991-98, department head, retired, 1998. Writer. **Publications:** Histoire du capitalisme, 1981; Le Socialisme à l'épreuve de l'histoire, 1982; (with G. Dostaler) Le Pensee economique depuis Keynes, 1993. UNTRANSLATED WORKS: Commerce extérieur du Maroc, 1960; (with P. Danjou and J. David) Une multinationale française, 1975; (co-author) Dictionnaire des groupes industriels et financiers en France, 1978; (ed. with G. de Bernis and J. Masini) La France et le Tiers-Monde, 1979; Capitalisme et économie politique dans l'histoire, 1981; La Politique economique de la gauche, vol. I: Le mirage de la croissance, 1983, vol. II: Le grand ecart, 1985; L'Art de la these, 1985; Le Systeme national/mondial hierarchise, 1987; L'économie mondiale dans les années quatre-vingt, 1989; (with R. Alvayay and G. Marin) El Socialismo, en el umbral del Siglo XXI, 1990; (ed. with L. Bouguerra and C. Beaud) L'Etat de l'environnement dans le monde, 1993; Le Basculement du monde, 1997; Le Journal du Basculement du monde: 2000, 2001; Naissance d'un siecle: 2001, l'Amérique foudroyée dans un monde en désarroi, 2004; Art de la thèse: comment préparer et rédiger un mémoire de master, une thèse de doctorat ou tout autre travail universitaire à l'ère du net, 2006. Contributor to books and periodicals. **Address:** GEMDEV, Centre Malher, 9 Rue Malher, Paris, 75181, France. **Online address:** m.beaud@wanadoo.fr

BEAUDOIN, Tom. American (born United States), b. 1969?. **Genres:** Theology/Religion. **Career:** Boston College, Department of Theology, postdoctoral teaching fellow, 2001-02, adjunct assistant professor, 2001-02, Institute of Religious Education and Pastoral Ministry, visiting assistant professor, 2002-04; Santa Clara University, Department of Religious Studies, assistant professor, 2004-. Writer. **Publications:** Virtual Faith: the Irreverent Spiritual Quest of Generation X, 1998; Consuming Faith: Integrating Who We are with What we Buy, 2003; Witness to Dispossession: The Vocation of a Postmodern Theologian, 2008. Contributor of articles to periodicals. **Address:** Department of Religious Studies, Santa Clara University, Bannan 353, 500 El Camino Real, Santa Clara, CA 95053, U.S.A. **Online address:** tbeaudoin@scu.edu

BEAUFORT, Simon. *See* **GREGORY, Susanna.**

BEAUFOY, Simon. British (born England), b. 1966. **Genres:** Plays/Screenplays. **Career:** Screenwriter and director. **Publications:** Slumdog Millionaire: The Shooting Script, 2008. **Address:** Creative Artists Agency L.L.C., 9830 Wilshire Blvd., Beverly Hills, CA 90212-1825, U.S.A.

BEAUMAN, Nicola. (Nicola Catherine Beauman). American (born United States), b. 1944?. **Genres:** Literary Criticism And History, Biography, Novels, History. **Career:** Persephone Books, founder, 1999-. Writer. **Publications:** A Very Great Profession: The Woman's Novel, 1914-39, 1983; Cynthia Asquith (biography), 1987; Morgan: A Biography of the Novelist E.M. Forster, 1993 in US as E.M. Forster: A Biography, 1994; The Other Elizabeth Taylor, 2009. **Address:** c/o Amanda Urban, International Creative Management, 40 W 57th St., New York, NY 10019, U.S.A.

BEAUMAN, Nicola Catherine. *See* **BEAUMAN, Nicola.**

BEAUMAN, Sally. (Vanessa James). British (born England), b. 1944. **Genres:** Novels, Adult Non-fiction, Literary Criticism And History. **Career:** New York Magazine, critic and contributing editor; Sunday Telegraph Magazine, arts editor, 1970-73, 1976-78; New Yorker, staff; Vogue Magazine, staff; Daily Telegraph, staff; Queen Magazine, staff; Sunday Times, staff; Observer Magazine, staff. **Publications:** NOVELS: Destiny, 1987; Dark Angel, 1990; Lovers and Liars, 1994; Secret Lives, 1994; Danger Zones, 1996; Sextet, 1997; Decepton and Desire, 1998; Rebecca's Tale, 2001; The Landscape of Love, 2005 in US as The Sisters Mortland, 2006. OTHERS: (ed.) The Royal Shakespeare Company's Production of Henry V for the Centenary Season at the Royal Shakespeare Theatre, 1976; King Henry V, 1976; The Royal Shakespeare Company: A History of Ten Decades, 1982. AS VANESSA JAMES: Piers Clarendon, 1980; The Dark One, 1982; The Fire and the Ice, 1982; The Devil's Advocate, 1983; Ever After, 1983; Chance Meetings, 1984; The Object of the Game, 1985; Give Me This Night, 1985; Prisoner, 1986; Try to Remember, 1986; Genealogy of Greek Mythology, 2003; Shakespeare's Genealogies: Plots And Illustrated Family Trees For All 42 Works, 2007. Contributor to periodicals. **Address:** Peters Fraser and Dunlop Group Ltd., Drury House, 34-43 Russell St., London, GL WC2B 5HA, England.

BEAUMONT, Maria. (Jessie Jones). British (born England), b. 1965?. **Genres:** Novels. **Career:** Dancer, writer and teacher. **Publications:** NOVELS: Marsha Mellow and Me, 2004; Miss Fit, 2004; Motherland, 2007 in US as 37, 2008; (as Jessie Jones) Rubbish Boyfriends, 2008. **Address:** London, England. **Online address:** maria@letstalkaboutme.com

BEAUMONT, Matthew. British (born England), b. 1972. **Genres:** History. **Career:** University College of London, senior lecturer in English. Scholar, educator and writer. **Publications:** Utopia Ltd: Ideologies of Social Dreaming in England, 1870-1900, 2005; (ed.) Adventures in Realism, 2007; (ed. and contrib. with A. Hemingway, E. Leslie and J. Roberts) As Radical as Reality Itself: Essays on Marxism and Art for the 21st Century, 2007; (ed. and intro.) Edward Bellamy, Looking Backward, 2000-1887, 2007; (ed. and intro. with M. Freeman) The Railway and Modernity: Time, Space and the Machine Ensemble, 2007. Contributor to books and periodicals. **Address:** University College London, Gower St., London, GL WC1E 6BT, England. **Online address:** m.beaumont@ucl.ac.uk

BEAUREGARD, Robert A. American (born United States), b. 1945. **Genres:** Young Adult Non-fiction, History, Economics, Bibliography, Politics/Government. **Career:** Rutgers University, assistant professor, 1975-80, associate professor, 1980-89; University of Pittsburgh, Graduate School of Public and International Affairs, professor, 1990-95, director of doctoral studies program, 1990-94; University of California, visiting professor, 1994; New School, professor in graduate program in management and urban policy, 1995-2006; Columbia University, Graduate School of Architecture, Planning, and Preservation, professor of urban planning; Helsinki University of Technology, visiting professor, 2001; University of Helsinki, Department of Social Policy, docent professor, 2003; King's College, visiting professor, 2007-10. Writer. **Publications:** NONFICTION: (with B.P. Indik) Labor Market Planning to Serve the Developmentally Disabled: A Literature Review and Bibliography, 1977; (with B.P. Indik) A Human Service Labor Market: Developmental Disabilities, 1979; (with H.B. Holcomb) Revitalizing Cities, 1981; (ed.) Economic Restructuring and Political Response, 1989; (ed.) Atop the Urban Hierarchy, 1989; Voices of Decline: The Postwar Fate of U.S. Cities, 1993, 2nd ed., 2003; (ed. with S. Body-Gendrot) The Urban Moment: Cosmopolitan Essays on the Late-20th-Century City, 1999; When America Became Suburban, 2006. Contributor to books and periodicals. **Address:** Grad School of Architecture, Planning and, Preservation, Columbia University, 413 Avery Hall, 1172 Amsterdam Ave., New York, NY 10027, U.S.A. **Online address:** rab48@columbia.edu

BEAUSEIGNEUR, James. American (born United States), b. 1953?. **Genres:** Science Fiction/Fantasy, Novels, Mystery/Crime/Suspense. **Career:** University of Tennessee, Department of political science, teacher; National Security Agency, intelligence analyst, 1976-81, security analyst. Writer. **Publications:** In His Image, 1997; Birth of an Age, 1997; Acts of God, 2004. Contributor to periodicals. **Address:** c/o Author Mail, Warner Books, 1271 Ave. of the Americas, New York, NY 10020, U.S.A. **Online address:** sr@selectivehouse.com

BEAVAN, Colin. American (born United States), b. 1963?. **Genres:** Criminology/True Crime. **Career:** Liverpool Echo, theater critic; No Impact lifestyle, researcher and experimenter, 2007. Journalist. **Publications:** Fingerprints: The Origins of Crime Detection and the Murder Case That Launched Forensic Science, 2001; Operation Jedburgh: D-Day and America's First Shadow War, 2006; No Impact Man: The Adventures of a Guilty Liberal Who Attempts to Save the Planet, and the Discoveries He Makes About Himself and Our Way of Life in the Process, 2009. Contributor to periodicals. **Address:** Hyperion Books, 77 W 66th St., 11th Fl., New York, NY 10023-6201, U.S.A. **Online address:** info@colinbeavan.com

BEAVER, James N. *See* **BEAVER, Jim Norman.**

BEAVER, Jim Norman. (James N. Beaver). American (born United States), b. 1950. **Genres:** Film, Art/Art History, Plays/Screenplays. **Career:** Writer and actor. **Publications:** (As James N. Beaver, Jr.) John Garfield: His Life and Films, 1978; (with S. Scheuer) Movie Blockbusters, 1982, rev. ed., 1983; Life's That Way: A Memoir, 2009. **Address:** Triad Artists Inc., 1173 N Ardmore Ave., Apt. 2, Los Angeles, CA 90029-1443, U.S.A. **Online address:** jim@lifesthatway.com

BEAVIS, Mary Ann. Canadian (born Canada), b. 1955. **Genres:** Theology/Religion, Literary Criticism And History, Young Adult Non-fiction, Bibliography. **Career:** University of Saskatchewan, associate professor of religious studies; Canadian Corporation for the Study of Religion, publications officer; Journal of Religion and Popular Culture, founding editor; Canadian Journal of Urban Research, founding editor; Catholic Biblical Quarterly, associate editor; Journal of Religion and Popular Culture, academic editor. **Publications:** NONFICTION: Mark's Audience: The Literary and Social Setting of Mark 4.11-12, 1989; (ed.) Municipal Development in Northeastern Ontario: Copper Cliff and Sudbury, 1991; (with J. Patterson) A Select, Annotated Bibliography on Sustainable Cities, 1992; (ed.) Colloquium on Sustainable Housing and Urban Development: Papers Presented (November 16, 1991), 1992; (co-author) Literature Review: Aboriginal Peoples and Homelessness, 1997; (ed.) The Lost Coin: Parables of Women, Work and Wisdom, 2002; Jesus and Utopia: Looking for the Kingdom of God in the Roman World, 2006; (ed. with E. Guillemin and B. Pell) Feminist Theology with a Canadian Accent, 2008. Contributor to journals. **Address:** St. Thomas More College, University of Saskatchewan, 1437 College Dr., Saskatoon, SK S7N 0W6, Canada. **Online address:** mbeavis@stmcollege.ca

BEBBINGTON, D(avid) W(illiam). Scottish/British (born England), b. 1949. **Genres:** History, Theology/Religion. **Career:** Fitzwilliam College, research fellow, 1973-76; University of Stirling, lecturer, 1976-89, senior lecturer in history, 1989-91, reader in history, 1991-99, professor of history and chair, 1999-; University of Alabama, visiting professor, 1990; Regent College, visiting professor, 1992; Oxford Dictionary of National Biography, associate editor, 1993-2004, consultant, 2004-; Notre Dame University, Graduate School, visiting professor, 1994; University of Pretoria, Faculty of Theology, visiting professor, 1995; Baylor University, Department of History, distinguished visiting professor of history, 2003, 2005, 2007, 2009, Institute for the Study of Religion, senior fellow, 2006-; Ecclesiastical History Society, president, 2006-07. **Publications:** (With R. Bauckham) History & Christianity: A Bibliography, 1977; Patterns in History: A Christian View, 1979; The Nonconformist Conscience: Chapel and Politics, 1870-1914, 1982; Evangelicalism in Modern Britain: A History from the 1730s to the 1980s, 1989; Patterns in History: A Christian Perspective on Historical Thought, 1990; Victorian Nonconformity, 1992, rev. ed., 2011; William Ewart Gladstone: Faith and Politics in Victorian Britain, 1993; Holiness in Nineteenth-Century England, 2000; Mind of Gladstone: Religion, Homer, and Politics, 2004; Dominance of Evangelicalism: The Age of Spurgeon and Moody, 2005; Baptists Through the Centuries: A History of a Global People, 2010. EDITOR: The Baptists in Scotland: A History, 1988; Evangelicalism in Modern Britain: A History from the 1730s to the 1980s, 1989; (with M.A. Noll and G.A. Rawlyk) Evangelicalism: Comparative Studies of Popular Protestantism in North America, the British Isles, and Beyond, 1700-1990, 1994; (with R. Swift) Gladstone Centenary Essays, 2000; (with T. Larsen) Modern Christianity and Cultural Aspirations, 2003; (with T. Larsen, M.A. Noll and S. Carter) Biographical Dictionary of Evangelicals, 2003; (with K. Dix and A. Ruston) Protestant Nonconformist Texts, 2006. **Address:** Department of History, University of Stirling, A62 Pathfoot Bldg., Stirling, FK9 4LA, Scotland. **Online address:** d.w.bebbington@stir.ac.uk

BECHARD, Margaret. American/Canadian (born Canada), b. 1953. **Genres:** Young Adult Fiction, Novels, Science Fiction/Fantasy. **Career:** Writer. **Publications:** FOR YOUNG ADULTS: My Sister, My Science Report, 1990; Tory & Me and the Spirit of True Love, 1992; Really No Big Deal, 1994; Star Hatchling, 1995; My Mom Married the Principal, 1998; If It Doesn't Kill You, 1999; Hanging on to Max, 2002; Spacer and Rat, 2005. **Address:** 12180 SW Ann Pl., Tigard, OR 97223, U.S.A. **Online address:** margaret@margaretbechard.com

BECHLER, Curt. American (born United States), b. 1958?. **Genres:** Communications/Media. **Career:** Camp Friedenswald Inc., executive director, 1984-90; Denison University, assistant professor of communication, 1990-; Aquinas College, associate professor, 1998-; Whirlpool Corp., consultant; Christian Camping Intl., consultant; Venture International L.L.C, managing partner. Writer. **Publications:** (With R.L. Weaver) Listen to Win: A Manager's Guide to Effective Listening, 1994. Contributor to books and journals. **Address:** Venture International L.L.C., PO Box 461, Hudsonville, MI 49426, U.S.A. **Online address:** bechler@vianswers.com

BECHTEL, Stefan D. American (born United States), b. 1951. **Genres:** Sex, Adult Non-fiction, Sciences, Autobiography/Memoirs. **Career:** Triad, executive editor, 1978-79; Burlington Daily Times-News, reporter, 1979-81; Rodale Press, associate editor, 1981-82, senior editor, 1982-85, executive editor, 1985-87, Newsletter Group, managing editor, 1986-87; freelance writer, 1988-; Men's Health magazine, founding editor. **Publications:** (With K. Castle) Katherine, It's Time, 1989; The Practical Encyclopedia of Sex and Health, 1993; Keeping your Company Green, 1993; Sex Encyclopedia, 1993; (with L.R. Stains) Sex: A Man's Guide, 1996; (with L.R. Stains) The Good Luck Book, 1997; (with L.R. Stains) What Women Want: What Every Man Needs to Know about Sex, Romance, Passion, and Pleasure, 2000; Growing A Fortune: 12 Investment Secrets to Financial Prosperity, 2002; Roar of the Heavens: Surviving Hurricane Camille, 2006; (with T. Samras) Tornado Hunter: Getting Inside the Most Violent Storms on Earth, 2009; Dogtown: Tales of Rescue, Rehabilitation and Redemption, 2009; Mr. Hornaday's War, 2012; Shopping For Eden, forthcoming. Contributor to periodicals. **Address:** 302 Park St., Charlottesville, VA 22902, U.S.A. **Online address:** stefan@stefanbechtel.com

BECHTOL, Bruce E. American (born United States), b. 1959?. **Genres:** History. **Career:** National security specialist, professor and writer. Defense Intelligence Agency, senior analyst, 1997-2003; Joint Military Intelligence College, thesis advisor for master of science in strategic intelligence program, 1998-2003; United States Air University, Air Command and Staff College, assistant professor of national security studies, 2003-05; Marine Corps University, Marine Corps Command and Staff College, associate professor, 2005-07, professor of international relations, 2007-; American Military University, adjunct professor of national security studies and international relations, 2001-03; Korea University, visiting professor at Graduate School of International Studies, 2006-07; Norwich University, served as adjunct professor. **Publications:** Avenging the General Sherman: The 1871 Battle of Kang Hwa Do (master's thesis), 2002; Red Rogue: The Persistent Challenge of North Korea, 2007; (ed.) The Quest for a Unified Korea: Strategies for the Cultural and Interagency Process, 2007. Contributor to books. **Address:** Fredericksburg, VA , U.S.A. **Online address:** brucebechtoljr@verizon.net

BECK, Edward L. American (born United States), b. 1959. **Genres:** Theology/Religion. **Career:** Wall Street, staff; ABC NEWS, religion correspondent; The Sunday Mass, executive producer; ABC Television, host; CNN, commentator; Fox News, commentator. Consultant and writer. **Publications:** God Underneath: Spiritual Memoirs of a Catholic Priest, 2001; Unlikely Ways Home: Real- Life Spiritual Detours, 2004; Soul Provider: Spiritual Steps to Limitless Love, 2007. **Address:** Random House Inc., 1745 Broadway, New York, NY 10019, U.S.A. **Online address:** soulproviderbook@aol.com

BECK, Ian. (Ian Archibald Beck). British (born England), b. 1947?. **Genres:** Children's Fiction, Novels, Novellas/Short Stories, Young Adult Fiction, Science Fiction/Fantasy. **Career:** Children's book illustrator, 1982-; Saturday Express (magazine), gardening column illustrator; screenwriter, 2005-. **Publications:** SELF-ILLUSTRATED: Little Miss Muffet, 1989; The Teddy Robber, 1989; Emily and the Golden Acorn, 1990; Five Little Ducks, 1993; The Orchard ABC, 1994; Ian Beck's Picture Book, 1994; Away in a Manger: A Christmas Carousel Book, 1994; (reteller) Peter and the Wolf, 1995; Oxford Nursery Book, 1995; ABC, 1995; Tom and the Island of Dinosaurs, 1995; Poppy and Pip, 1995; Poppy and Pip's Bedtime, 1996; Poppy and Pip's Walk, 1996; (reteller) Hans Christian Andersen's The Ugly Duckling, 1997; (reteller) Cinderella, 1999; Hansel & Gretel, 1999; Blue Book, 2000; Green Book, 2000; The Oxford Nursery Story Book, 2000; The Oxford Nursery Treasury, 2000; Alone in the Woods, 2000; Home before Dark, 2001; Teddy's Snowy Day, 2002; Lost on The Beach, 2002; The Happy Bee, 2002; The Twelve Days of Christmas, 2002; Little Red Riding Hood, 2002; The Three Little Pigs, 2002; Chicken Licken, 2003; The Tortoise and the Hare, 2003; (reteller) The Christmas Story, 2003; Kitten Cat, 2003; Kitten Cat: Rainy Day Play, 2004; Jack and the Beanstalk, 2004; The Elves and the Shoemaker, 2005; The Princess and the Pea, 2005; The Secret History of Tom Trueheart: Boy Adventurer, 2006; Tom Trueheart and the Land of Dark Stories, 2008; Pastworld: A Mystery of the Near Future: A Novel, 2009; Tom Trueheart and the Land of Myths and Legends, 2010; The Hidden Kingdom: A Novel, 2011; The Haunting of Charity Delafield: A Novel, 2011. **Address:** Greenwillow Books, Harper Collins Publishers, New York, NY 10012, U.S.A. **Online address:** ian@ibeck.freeserve.co.uk

BECK, Ian Archibald. *See* **BECK, Ian.**

BECK, John C. American (born United States) **Genres:** Economics. **Career:** Harvard University, lecturer; University of Western Ontario, Ivey School of Business, adjunct professor; Asian Business Information, president; Asian Century, editor; Monitor Co., Far-East advisor; United Nations, co-director; Cambodian Prime Minister's office, senior strategic advisor; Accenture Institute for Strategic Change, associate partner and director of international research; University of California, visiting professor; IMD, visiting professor; IPADE, visiting professor; Thunderbird Graduate School, professor, visiting professor and dean of research; North Star Leadership Group, president; Globis University, dean; Harvard University, faculty; Dartmouth University, faculty; Kellogg University, faculty; Waseda University, faculty; University of Southern California, Annenberg Center of the Digital Future, senior research fellow; Monitor Group, senior advisor. **Publications:** (With T.H. Davenport) The Attention Economy: Understanding the New Currency of Business, 2001; (with M.E. Wade) DoCoMo: Japan's Wireless Tsunami: How One Mobile Telecom Created a New Market and Became a Global Force, 2003; (with M.E. Wade) Got Game: How The Gamer Generation is Reshaping Business Forever, 2004; (with M.B. Fuller) Japan's Business Renaissance: How The World's Greatest Economy Revived, Renewed, and Reinvented Itself, 2006. **Address:** 1601 Broadway, PO Box 55870, Phoenix, AZ 85022, U.S.A. **Online address:** johnbeck@gotgamebook.com

BECK, Mary L. (Giraudo). American (born United States), b. 1924. **Genres:** Mythology/Folklore, Sociology, Young Adult Non-fiction, History, inspirational/Motivational Literature, Biography, Autobiography/Memoirs, Young Adult Fiction, Young Adult Fiction. **Career:** University of Alaska, instructor, 1954-69, assistant professor, 1969-74, associate professor of English, 1974, professor emeritus, 1983-. Writer. **Publications:** Heroes and Heroines: Tlingit-Haida Legend and Their Counterparts in Classical Mythology, 1989; Shamans and Kushtakas: North Coast Tales of the Supernatural, 1991; Potlatch: Native Ceremony and Myth on the Northwest Coast, 1993; Ka.gun.da: George James Beck, Alaskan Pioneer Teacher, Missionary, Leader, 1999; Holy Name Catholic Church: A History of the Parish of the Holy Name in Ketchikan from 1904 to 2002, 2002. Contributor to magazines. **Address:** Rocky Point Publishing, 2855 Tongas Ave., Ketchikan, AK 99901, U.S.A.

BECK, Nina. *See* **CORNIER, Nadia.**

BECK, Peggy. American (born United States), b. 1949. **Genres:** Education, Reference, Adult Non-fiction. **Career:** Cherry Hill High School, English teacher, 1971-88, media department chair, 1989-95, media facilitator, 2001-03, librarian, 2003-07, media specialist; Cooper Elementary School, librarian, 1995-2001; New Jersey English Journal, editor; Educational Media Asssociation of New Jersey, Signal Tab, editor. **Publications:** GlobaLinks: Resources for World Studies, Grades K-8, 2001; GlobaLinks: Resources for Asian Studies, Grades K-8, 2001. **Address:** Cherry Hill High School East, 1750 Kresson Rd., Cherry Hill, NJ 08003, U.S.A.

BECK, Robert J. American (born United States), b. 1961. **Genres:** International Relations/Current Affairs, Law, Social Sciences. **Career:** University of Virginia, visiting assistant professor of government, 1989-90; University of Minnesota-Twin Cities, visiting assistant professor of political Science, 1990-91; University of Virginia, assistant professor of government, 1991-98; Tufts University, director and adjunct associate professor of political science, 1998-2000; University of Wisconsin-Milwaukee, director and adjunct associate professor of political science, 2000-08, director and associate professor of political science, 2008-. Writer. **Publications:** The Grenada Invasion: Politics, Law, and Foreign Policy Decisionmaking, 1993; (with A.C. Arend) International Law and the Use of Force: Beyond the UN Charter Paradigm, 1993; (ed.) International Rules: Approaches from international law and International Relations, 1996; (ed. with T. Ambrosio) International Law and the Rise of Nations: The State System and the Challenge of Ethnic Groups, 2002. **Address:** Department of Political Science, University of Wisconsin-Milwaukee, Rm. 5410, NWQ B, 2025 E Newport Ave., PO Box 413, Milwaukee, WI 53201, U.S.A. **Online address:** rjbeck@suwm.edu

BECKEL, Bob. American (born United States), b. 1950?. **Genres:** Social Sciences, Military/Defense/Arms Control, Politics/Government, International Relations/Current Affairs. **Career:** The Carter Administration, deputy assistant, 1977; George Washington University, professor of political strategy. Writer. **Publications:** (With C. Thomas) Common Ground: How to Stop the Partisan War That Is Destroying America, 2007. **Address:** Grad School of Political Management, George Washington University, 805 21st St. NW, Washington, DC 20052, U.S.A. **Online address:** rgbeckel@earthlink.net

BECKER, Charles M(axwell). American (born United States), b. 1954. **Genres:** Economics, Urban Studies, Demography. **Career:** Princeton University, assistant in instruction, 1979-81; Vanderbilt University, assistant professor of economics, 1981-86; Economics Institute, deputy director of academic program, 1987-89, associate professor of economics, 1987-96, president, 1990-96, professor of economics, 1996-98; University of Colorado, Institute of Behavioral Science, Program in Population Processes, research associate, 1987-2007, Department of Economics, adjunct associate professor, 1987-96, adjunct professor, 1996-2003, research professor, 1999-2003, Program in International Business and Economic Studies, co-director, 1999-2002, American Economic Association Summer Minority Program, director, 2000-03; Harvard University, CAER Project, consultant, 1998-99; International Management and Communications Corp., senior economist and director, 1998-2001; Government of the Republic of Kazakhstan, Ministry of Labor and Social Protection, senior advisor, 1999-2001, National Bank of the Republic of Kazakhstan, senior advisor, 1999-2001, Kazakhstan Actuarial Center, senior advisor, 2001-06; Duke University, American Economic Association Summer Program and Minority Scholarship Program, academic director, 2003-07, MA Program, academic director, 2003-, Department of Economics, research professor, 2004-, associate chair, 2009-, Center for Chinese Populations and Socioeconomic Studies, faculty associate, 2005-; World Bank, consultant. Writer. **Publications:** (With E.S. Mills and J.G. Williamson) Indian Urbanization, 1960-2000, 1984; (with E.S. Mills) Studies in Indian Urban Development, 1986; (with T. Bell, H.A. Khan and P. Pollard) The Impact of Sanctions on South Africa, vol. I: The Economy, 1990; (with E.S. Mills and J.G. Williamson) Indian Urbanization and Economic Growth since 1960, 1992; (with A.M. Hamer and A.R. Morrison) Beyond Urban Bias: African Cities in an Age of Structural Adjustment, 1994; (co-author) Social Security Reform in Transition Economies: Lessons from Kazakhstan, 2009. Contributor to journals. **Address:** Department of Economics, Duke University, 312 Social Sciences Bldg., 419 Chapel Dr., PO Box 90097, Durham, NC 27708-0097, U.S.A. **Online address:** cbecker@econ.duke.edu

BECKER, Elizabeth. American (born United States), b. 1947. **Genres:** Military/Defense/Arms Control, History. **Career:** Reporter, 1972-; Newsweek, war correspondent; National Broadcasting Corporation (NBC) Radio, war correspondent, 1973-74; Washington Post, reporter, correspondent, 1975-78, Maryland desk, editor, 1978-80; Center for International Policy, Indochina Project, creator and director, 1978-80; freelance writer on international diplomacy, 1986-90; National Public Radio, senior foreign editor, 1993-95; New York Times, assistant Washington editor, 1996-98, Washington correspondent, 1999-; Arthur F. Burns Foundation, director; Joan Shorenstein Center, fellow; Pearl S. Buck Foundation, director. **Publications:** When the War Was Over: The Voices of Cambodia's Revolution and Its People, 1986; When the War was Over: Cambodia and the Khmer Rouge Revolution, 1998; America's Vietnam War: A Narrative History, 1992. Contributor to periodicals. **Address:** c/o David Halpern, The Robbins Office, 405 Park Ave., 9th Fl., New York, NY 10022, U.S.A. **Online address:** info@elizabethbecker.com

BECKER, Ethan. American (born United States), b. 1945. **Genres:** Food And Wine. **Career:** Becker Knife and Tool Corp., owner. Writer. **Publications:** COOKBOOKS WITH I.S. ROMBAUER AND M.R. BECKER: Joy of Cooking Christmas Cookies, 1996; Joy of Cooking, 1997; Quick Weeknight Meals, 1999; Great Chicken Dishes, 1999; Joy of Cooking Cookie Kit, 2001. JOY OF COOKING SERIES WITH I.S. ROMBAUER AND M.R. BECKER: All about Soups & Stews, 2000; All About Vegetarian Cooking, 2000; All About Pasta & Noodles, 2000; All About Chicken, 2000; All about Cookies, 2001; All about Grilling, 2001; All about Salads & Dressings, 2001; All about Breakfast & Brunch, 2001; All about Party Foods & Drinks, 2002; All about Canning & Preserving, 2002; All about Pies & Tarts, 2002. **Address:** The Joy Kitchen, 2335 Buttermilk Crossing, Ste. 340, Crescent Springs, KY 41017, U.S.A. **Online address:** joyofc@aol.com

BECKER, Gary S. American (born United States), b. 1930. **Genres:** Economics, Money/Finance, Education, Essays, Reference. **Career:** University of Chicago, Department of Economics, assistant professor of economics, 1954-57, Ford Foundation visiting professor of economics, 1969-70, university professor of economics, 1970-83, professor of economics and sociology, 1983-, chairman, 1984-85, Graduate School of Business, and Sociology, university professor, 1983-, National Opinion Research Center, Economics Research Center, research associate, 1980-; Columbia University, assistant professor, 1957-58, associate professor, 1958-60, professor of economics, 1960-68, Arthur Lehman Professor of Economics, 1968-69; Business Week Magazine, columnist, 1985-2004; Hoover Institution, Rose-Marie and Jack R. Anderson Senior Fellow, 1990-; Manhattan Institute, director, 1997-2003; The New Center for Accelerating Medical Innovations, director, 2003-. Writer. **Publications:** The Economics of Discrimination, 1957, 2nd ed., 1971; Human Capital: A Theoretical and Empirical Analysis, with Special Reference to Education, 1964, 3rd ed., 1993; Human Capital and the Personal Distribution of Income: An Analytical Approach, 1967; Economic Theory, 1971; (with G.R. Ghez) The Allocation of Time and Goods over the Life Cycle, 1975; The Economic Approach to Human Behavior, 1976; A Treatise on the Family, 1981; Der Okonomische Ansazt zur Erklärung Menschlichen Verhaltens, 1982; (contrib.) Discrimination, Affirmative Action, and Equal Opportunity: An Economic and Social Perspective, 1982; (with N. Tomes) Human Capital and the Rise and Fall of Families, 1985; An Economic Analysis of the Family, 1986; (contrib.) The Essence of Becker, 1995; Accounting for Tastes, 1996; (with G.N. Becker) The Economics of Life: From Baseball to Affirmative Action to Immigration, How Real-world Issues Affect our Everyday Life, 1997; Economic Way of Looking at Behavior: The Nobel Lecture, 1996; Familie, Gesellschaft und Politik, 1996; Gary Beckerv Praze: Brezen 1995, 1996; (with K.M. Murphy) Social Economics: Market Behavior in a Social Environment, 2000; (afterword) Milton Friedman on Economics: Selected Papers, 2007; (with R.A. Posner) Uncommon Sense: Economic Insights, from Marriage to Terrorism, 2009. EDITOR: (with W.M. Landes) Essays in the Economics of Crime and Punishment, 1974; Essays in Labor Economics in Honor of H. Gregg Lewis, 1976. Contributor to periodicals. **Address:** Department of Economics, University of Chicago, 305C Rosenwald, 1126 E 59th St., Chicago, IL 60637-1580, U.S.A. **Online address:** gbecker@midway.uchicago.edu

BECKER, Jasper. British (born England), b. 1956. **Genres:** International Relations/Current Affairs, History, Travel/Exploration, Politics/Government, Ghost Writer, E-books, Adult Non-fiction. **Career:** Journalist, 1980-83; Associated Press, journalist, 1983-85; Guardian, journalist, 1985-91; British Broadcasting Corp., journalist; South China Morning Post, Beijing bureau chief, 1995-2002; The Independent, Beijing correspondent; Asia Weekly Magazine, publisher, 2007-09. Writer. **Publications:** The Lost Country: Mongolia Revealed, 1991; Hungry Ghosts: China's Secret Famine, 1996; The Chinese, 2000; Rogue State: The Continuing Threat of North Korea, 2005; Dragon Rising: An Inside Look at China Today, 2006; Mongolia: Travels in the Untamed Land, 2008; City of Heavenly Tranquility: Beijing in the History of China, 2008; CC Lee: Textile man, 2011. Works appear in anthologies. **Address:** 30 Green Pk., Bath, CI BA1 1HZ, England. **Online address:** jsprjas@aol.com

BECKER, Josh. American (born United States), b. 1958. **Genres:** Essays, Film. **Career:** Writer. **Publications:** The Complete Guide to Low-budget Feature Filmmaking, 2006; Rushes, 2008; Going Hollywood, 2009. **Address:** Panoramic Pictures, 3315 Little Applegate Rd., Jacksonville, OR 97530, U.S.A.

BECKER, Jürgen. German (born Germany), b. 1932. **Genres:** Poetry, Novellas/Short Stories, Young Adult Fiction. **Career:** Westdeutscher Rundfunk (radio), writer, 1959-64; Rowohlt Verlag, reader, 1964-65; Suhrkamp-Theaterverlag, director, 1974; Deutschlandfunk Koeln, head of drama department, 1975-94; Warwick University, writer-in-residence, 1988. **Publications:** (With W. Vostell) Phasen, 1960; Felder (title means: 'Fields'), 1964; Raender (short stories), 1968, trans. as Margins in Dimension, vol. I, 1968; Bilder, Haeuser: Hausfreunde: Drei Hoerspiel, 1969; Umgebungen (title means: 'Surroundings'), 1970; Eine Zeit ohne Woerter (title means: 'A Time without Words'), 1971; Die Zeit nach Harrimann: 29 Szenen fuer Nora, Helen, Jenny und den stummen Diener Moltke, 1971; Schreiben & Leben, 1974; ?In der verbleibenden Zeit: Gedichte, 1979; Erzaehlen bis Ostende (title means: 'Narration until Ostende'), 1981; Die Tuere zum Meer (title means: 'The Door to the Sea'), 1983; Die Abwesenden, 1983; Gedicht von der wiedervereinigten Landschaft, 1988; (with R. Bohne) Frauen mit dem Rucken zum Betrachter, 1989; Frauen mit dem Ruecken zum Betrachter, 1989; Kulturradio: Erinnerungen und Erwartungen, 1996; Gegend mit Spuren: Horspiel, 1996; Fehlende Rest: Erzahlung, 1997; Kaleidoskop der Stimmen: ein Gesprach mit Leo Kreutzer, 1998; Aus der Geschichte der Trennungen: Roman, 1999; Journal der Wiederholungen: Gedichte, 1999; Häuser und Häuser, 2002; Dorfrand mit Tankstelle: Gedichte, 2007; Im Radio das Meer: Journalsätze, 2009. EDITOR: (with W. Vostell) Happenings; Fluxus; Pop Art; Nouveau Realisme: Eine Dokumentation, 1965; Elisabeth Borchers, Gedichte (poetry), 1976. POETRY: Schnee: Gedichte, 1971; Das Ende der Landschaftsmalerei: Gedichte, 1974; Erzaehl mir nichts vom Kreig: Gedichte, 1977; In derverbleibenden Zeit: Gedichte, 1979; Gedichte 1965-1980 (title means: 'Poems, 1965-1980'), 1981; Fenster und Stimmen: Gedichte, 1982; Odenthals Kuenste, 1986; Das englische Fenster, 1990; Foxtrott im Erfurter Stadion: Gedichte, 1993; Schnee in den Ardennen Journalroman, 2003; Die folgenden Seiten Journalgeschichten, 2006. **Address:** 84 Am Klausenberg, Koeln-Brueck, 51109, Germany.

BECKER, Palmer (Joseph). American (born United States), b. 1936. **Genres:** Theology/Religion. **Career:** Relief worker, 1958-63; First Mennonite Church, pastor, 1965-69; Commission on Home Ministries, administrative executive, 1969-79; Peace Mennonite Church, founding pastor, 1979-88; Point Grey Fellowship, founding pastor, 1988-91; Mennonite Simons Center, chaplain 1988-91; Bethel Mennonite Church, senior pastor, 1991-94; Calvary Mennonite Church, senior pastor, 1994-98; Hesston College, Pastoral Ministries Program, director, 1998-, bible instructor. **Publications:** Daily Thoughts, 4 vols., 1961; Congregational Goals Discovery Plan, 1976; You and Your Options, 1979; Creative Family Worship, 1984; Called to Care: A Training Manual for Small Group Leaders, 1993; Called to Equip: A Small Group Training and Resource Manual for Pastors, 1993; Called to Lead: A Training Video and Guide for Small Group Leaders, 1994; The Ministry of Membership Preparation, 1995. **Address:** Bible & Ministry Department, Hesston College, 325 S College Dr., PO Box 3000, Hesston, KS 67062, U.S.A. **Online address:** palmerb@southwind.net

BECKER, Patti Clayton. American (born United States), b. 1951. **Genres:** Librarianship, History, Military/Defense/Arms Control. **Career:** Drew University, catalogue librarian, 1981-85; British Columbia Ministry of Consumer and Corporate Affairs, librarian, 1985-86; Vancouver Island Regional Library, area librarian, 1986; Marquette University, head cataloguer, 1987-93; University of Wisconsin-Milwaukee, adjunct instructor, 1992, 1995, 2004; University of Wisconsin-Stevens Point, assistant professor and reference and instruction librarian, 1993-96, associate professor and co-ordinator of reference, 1996-2006, professor and co-ordinator of reference and reference collection development, 2006-; University of Wisconsin-Madison, adjunct professor, 2003. Writer. **Publications:** Books and Libraries in American Society during World War II: Weapons in the War of Ideas, 2005; (contrib.) Tradition and Vision: Library and Information Studies, a Centennial History, 2006. Contributor to periodicals. **Address:** University Library, University of Wisconsin, 900 Reserve St., Stevens Point, WI 54481-1962, U.S.A. **Online address:** p2becker@uwsp.edu

BECKER, Robin. American (born United States), b. 1967. **Genres:** Novels, Autobiography/Memoirs. **Career:** University of Central Arkansas, creative writing teacher; Truman State University, faculty; Conway Twitties (punk rock band), leader. Writer. **Publications:** Brains: A Zombie Memoir (novel), 2010. Contributor to periodicals. **Address:** Toad Suck, AR , U.S.A. **Online address:** becker.robin@gmail.com

BECKER, Suzanne (Rose). (Suzy Becker). American (born United States), b. 1962?. **Genres:** Children's Fiction, Autobiography/Memoirs, Cartoons. **Career:** The Widget Factory, founder and owner, 1987-93; Harvard University, Radcliffe College, fellow, 1999-2000. Writer. **Publications:** SELF ILLUSTRATED AS SUZY BECKER: All I Need to Know I Learned from My Cat, 1990; The All Better Book, 1992; My Dog's the World's Best Dog, 1995; I Had Brain Surgery What's Your Excuse?, 2004; Manny's Cows: The Niagara Falls Tale, 2006; Books Are for Reading, 2009; Kids Make it Better Book, 2010. **Address:** Workman Publishing, 225 Varick St., New York, NY 10014, U.S.A. **Online address:** suzy@suzybecker.com

BECKER, Suzy. *See* **BECKER, Suzanne (Rose).**

BECKERMAN, Paul. American (born United States), b. 1948. **Genres:** Economics, Area Studies. **Career:** University of Illinois, assistant professor of economics, 1977; Boston University, assistant professor of economics; Fordham University, assistant professor of economics, through 1984; Marine Midland Bank, economist, 1984-85; Federal Reserve Bank of New York, economist, 1985-88; World Bank, economist, 1988-2001; independent consultant, 2001-. Writer. **Publications:** The Economics of High Inflation, 1992; Public Sector Debt Distress in Argentina, 1988-89, 1992; How Small Should an Economy's Fiscal Deficit Be?: A Monetary-Programming Approach, 2000; Dolarization and Semi-Dollarization in Ecuador, 2001; (ed. with A. Solimano) Crisis and Dollarization in Ecuador: Stability, Growth, and Social Equity, 2002; Multiannual Macroeconomic Programming Techniques for Developing Economies, 2010. Works appear in anthologies. Contributor to journals. **Address:** 7705 Massena Rd., Bethesda, MD 20817, U.S.A. **Online address:** pbeckerman@alum.mit.edu

BECKERMAN, Wilfred. British (born England), b. 1925. **Genres:** Economics, Philosophy. **Career:** University of Nottingham, lecturer in economics, 1950-52; Balliol College, fellow and tutor in economics, 1964-69, 1975-92, now emeritus fellow; British Department of Economic Affairs, economic consultant, 1964-65; Board of Trade, economic advisor, 1967-69; University College London, professor of political economy and head of department, 1969-75, honorary visiting professor of economics 2001-. Consultant and Writer. **Publications:** EDITOR: Labour Government's Economic Record, 1964-70, 1972; Slow Growth In Britain: Causes and Consequences, 1979; Wage Rigidity and Unemployment, 1986. OTHERS: (co-author) The British Economy in 1975, 1965; International Comparisons of Real Income, 1966; An Introduction to National Income Analysis, 1968; In Defence of Economic Growth, 1974 in US as Two Cheers for the Affluent Society, 1974; Pricing for Pollution, 1975; Measures of Equality, Leisure and Welfare, 1979; Poverty and the Impact of Income Maintenance Payments, 1979; (with S. Clark) Poverty and Social Security in Britain since 1961, 1982; Economic Development and the Environment: Conflict or Complementarity?, 1992; Small Is Stupid, 1995 in US as Through Green-Colored Glasses, 1996; Growth, The Environment and the Distribution of Incomes, 1995; (with J. Pasek) Justice, Posterity and the Environment, 2001; Poverty of Reason: Sustainable Development and Economic Growth, 2003; Economics as Applied Ethics, 2010. **Address:** 1C Norham Gardens, Oxford, OX OX2 6PS, England. **Online address:** wilfred.beckerman@economics.ox.ac.uk

BECKERT, Jens. German (born Germany), b. 1967. **Genres:** Economics, Sociology, Politics/Government. **Career:** Freie Universität, junior faculty, 1993-99, research fellow, 1999-2001; Harvard University, John F. Kennedy Memorial Fellow, 2001-02; International University, associate professor, 2002-03; Georg-August-Universität, professor, 2003-05; Cologne University, professor of sociology, 2005-; Max Planck Institute for the Study of Societies, director, 2005-. Writer. **Publications:** (Co-author) Transnationale Solidarität: Chancen Und Grenzen, 2004; (with M. Zafirovski) International Encyclopedia of Economic Sociology, 2011. Works appear in anthologies. Contributor of articles to periodicals. **Address:** Max-Planck-Institut für Gesellschaftsforschung, Paulstr. 3, Cologne, 50676, Germany.

BECKET, Henry S. A. *See* **GOULDEN, Joseph C.**

BECKETT, Francis. British (born England), b. 1945. **Genres:** Plays/Screenplays, Young Adult Non-fiction. **Career:** Writer and political historian. **Publications:** PLAY: Money Makes You Happy: A Play, 2008. NONFICTION: Paying the Piper: Power and Freedom in the Media, 1980; Enemy Within: The Rise and Fall of the British Communist Party, 1995; Clem Attlee, 1997; The Rebel Who Lost His Cause: The Tragedy of John Beckett, 1999; (with C. Beckett) Bevan, 2004; Stalin's British Victims, 2004; (with D. Hencke) The Blairs and Their Court, 2005; Olivier, 2005; Macmillan, 2006; The Great City Academy Fraud, 2007; Gordon Brown, 2007; (with D. Hencke) Marching to the Fault Line: The 1984 Miners' Strike and the Death of Industrial Britain, 2009. **Address:** London, GL , England. **Online address:** francis@francisbeckett.co.uk

BECKHORN, Susan Williams. American (born United States), b. 1953?. **Genres:** Novels, Children's Fiction, Illustrations. **Career:** Illustrator and writer. **Publications:** FOR CHILDREN SELF-ILLUSTRATED: In the Morning of the World: Six Woodland Why Stories, 2000; Sarey by Lantern Light, 2003. FOR YOUNG ADULTS: Wind Rider, 2006; Moose Eggs; or, Why Moose Has Flat Antlers, 2007; Moose Power!: Muskeg Saves the Day, 2010. OTHER: The Kingfisher's Gift, 2002. Contributor to periodicals. **Address:** National Book Network, 4501 Forbes Blvd., Ste. 200, Lanham, MD 20706, U.S.A. **Online address:** susb@zoominternet.net

BECKLEY, Harlan R. American (born United States), b. 1943. **Genres:** Ethics, Theology/Religion, Economics. **Career:** Minister of United Methodist churches, 1971-74; Washington and Lee University, instructor, assistant professor, associate professor, 1974-89, adjunct professor of business ethics, 1984-91, professor of religion, 1989-99, Department of Religion, chair, 1989-99, Shepherd Program for the Interdisciplinary Study of Poverty, director, 1997-, Fletcher Otey Thomas professor of religion, 1999-, Fletcher Otey Thomas professor, 2002, acting president, 2005-06; Lynchburg College, consultant, 1992; Roanoake College, consultant, 1992; Lilly Foundation, consultant, 1992; Society of Christian Ethic, vice president and president, 1999-2001. Writer. **Publications:** (Ed. with C.M. Swezey) James M. Gustafson's Theocentric Ethics: Interpretations and Assessments, 1988; Passion for Justice: Retrieving the Legacies of Walter Rauschenbusch, John A. Ryan, and Reinhold Niebuhr, 1992; (ed. and intro.) Economic Justice: Selections from Distributive Justice and A Living Wage, 1996. Contributor of articles to journals. **Address:** Department of Religion, Washington and Lee University, 206 Holekamp Hall, Lexington, VA 24450, U.S.A. **Online address:** beckleyh@wlu.edu

BECKMAN, John. American (born United States), b. 1967. **Genres:** Novels. **Career:** United States Naval Academy, assistant professor of English, associate professor of English. Novelist. **Publications:** The Winter Zoo, 2002. **Address:** Department of English, United States Naval Academy, 250 Sampson, 107 Maryland Ave., Annapolis, MD 21402-5044, U.S.A. **Online address:** beckman@usna.edu

BECKWITH, Harry. American (born United States), b. 1949. **Genres:** Business/Trade/Industry, Economics. **Career:** Gearin, Cheney, Landis, Aebi and Kelly (law firm), associate attorney, 1976-77; City of Portland, assistant city attorney, 1977-82; Carmichael-Lynch, writer, 1982-85, creative supervisor, 1985-88; Beckwith Advertising and Marketing, principal, 1988-. University of Saint Thomas, lecturer; University of Minnesota-Twin Cities, lecturer;

Snowmass Institute, founding partner and board director. **Publications:** Selling the Invisible: A Field Guide to Modern Marketing, 1997; The Invisible Touch: The Four Keys to Modern Marketing, 2000; What Clients Love: A Field Guide to Growing Your Business, 2003; (with C.C. Beckwith) You Inc: The Art of Selling Yourself, 2007; Unthinking: The Surprising Forces Behind Why We Buy, 2011. Contributor to periodicals. **Address:** Beckwith Partners, Lumber Exchange Bldg., Ste. 600, 10 S 5th St., Minneapolis, MN 55402, U.S.A. **Online address:** invisible@bitstream.net

BECKWITH, Jon. *See* **BECKWITH, Jonathan R(oger).**

BECKWITH, Jonathan R(oger). (Jon Beckwith). American (born United States), b. 1935. **Genres:** Medicine/Health, Sciences, Literary Criticism And History. **Career:** University of Illinois, teaching assistant, 1960; Harvard University Medical School, Department of Bacteriology and Immunology, associate, 1965-66, assistant professor, 1966-68, associate professor, 1968-69, professor, 1969-, Department of Microbiology and Molecular Genetics, professor, 1969-, chairman, 1971-73, director of genetics training grant, 1975-2000, American Cancer Society, research professor, 1980-; University of California, visiting professor, 1985, Roger Stanier Memorial lecturer, 1999; American Academy of Arts and Science, fellow, 1986-; Institut Pasteur, Jacques Monod Memorial lecturer, 1988; Science for the People, board president, 1990-93; Columbia University, College of Physicians and Surgeons, Samuel Rudin visiting professor, 1991; Case Western Reserve University, Lester O. Krampitz lecturer in microbiology, 1991; American Academy of Microbiology, fellow, 1992; Genentech Corp., consultant, 1994-98; University of Washington, Helen R. Whiteley Memorial lecturer, 2000; Brown University, Frank and Joan Rothman Commencement Forum, lecturer, 2001. Writer. **Publications:** (Ed. with D. Zipser) The Lactose Operon, 1970; (ed. with J. Davies and J.A. Gallant) Gene Function in Prokaryotes, 1983; (ed. with T.J. Silhavy) The Power of Bacterial Genetics: A Literature-based Course, 1992; (as Jon Beckwith) Making Genes, Making Waves: A Social Activist in Science (memoir), 2002; (ed. as Jon Beckwith) The Double-edged Helix: Social Implications of Genetics in a Diverse Society, 2002. Contributor of articles and reviews to periodicals. **Address:** Department of Microbiology & Molecular Genetics, Harvard Medical School, 200 Longwood Ave., Boston, MA 02115, U.S.A. **Online address:** jon_beckwith@hms.harvard.edu

BEDARD, Anthony. (Tony Bedard). American (born United States), b. 1968?. **Genres:** Children's Non-fiction, Horror. **Career:** Valient/Acclaim Comics, executive editor and writer; Crusade Entertainment, senior editor; DC Comics, editor of Vertigo imprint; Cross Generation Comics, writer, 2001-. **Publications:** AS TONY BEDARD: (with K. Moline and J. Dell) Route 666: Highway to Horror, 2003; (with J. Torres) Green Arrow and Black Canary, 2008; Birds of Prey. Platinum Flats, 2008; Birds of Prey: Club Kids, 2008; (with S.T. Seagle and J. Thomas) JSA Presents Green Lantern, 2008; (with M.W. Barr) Batman: The Wrath, 2009; (with K. Van Hook) Oracle. The Cure, 2010; R.E.B.E.L.S.: The Son and the Stars, 2010; Green Lantern Corps: Revolt of the Alpha-lanterns, 2011. NEGATION SERIES AS TONY BEDARD: (with M. Waid) Negation 1: BOHICA! 2002; Negation 2: Baptism of Fire, 2003; Negation 3: Hounded, 2002. MYSTIC SERIES AS TONY BEDARD: (with R. Marz) Mystic 3: Siege of Scales, 2002; Mystic 4: Out All Night, 2003. **Address:** Marvel Comics, W 42nd St., New York, NY 10036, U.S.A.

BEDARD, Michael. Canadian (born Canada), b. 1949. **Genres:** Children's Fiction, Novels, Biography, Young Adult Non-fiction, Adult Non-fiction. **Career:** St. Michael's College Library, library assistant, 1971-78; writer, 1982-. **Publications:** JUVENILE: Woodsedge and Other Tales (fairy tales), 1979; Pipe and Pearls: A Gathering of Tales (fairy tales), 1980; A Darker Magic (novel), 1987; The Lightning Bolt, 1989; Redwork (novel), 1990; Painted Devil (novel), 1994; Sitting Ducks, 1998; The Clay Ladies, 1999; The Wolf of Gubbio, 2000; Stained Glass (novel), 2001; Painted Wall and Other Strange Tales: Selected and Adapted from the Liao-chai of Pu Sung-ling, 2003; Bill Hatches an Egg, 2005. BIOGRAPHY: Emily, 1992; The Divide, 1997; Glass Town, 1997. OTHERS: (with L. Gottlieb and M. Viseltear) You Know Things are Tough When or, Inflation with Honor, 1973; Quacking Up!: Wacky Jokes for Feathered Folks, 2004; William Blake: The Gates of Paradise, 2006. Contributor to periodicals. **Address:** c/o Author Mail, Penguin Group, 375 Hudson St., New York, NY 10014, U.S.A. **Online address:** bedardstudio@aol.com

BEDARD, Tony. *See* **BEDARD, Anthony.**

BEDAU, Hugo Adam. American (born United States), b. 1926. **Genres:** Civil Liberties/Human Rights, Criminology/True Crime, Ethics, Humanities, Law, Philosophy, Politics/Government. **Career:** Dartmouth College, instructor, 1953-54; Princeton University, lecturer, 1954-61; Reed College, associate professor of philosophy, 1962-66; Tufts University, professor of philosophy, 1966-, Austin B. Fletcher professor of philosophy, through 1999, Austin B. Fletcher professor of philosophy emeritus, 1999-; Cambridge University, visiting fellow, 1980; Wolfson College, visiting fellow, 1988. Writer. **Publications:** (With E.M. Schur) Victimless Crimes: Two Views, 1974; The Courts, the Constitution, and Capital Punishment, 1977; Death is Different, 1987; (with M.L. Radelet and C.E. Putnam) In Spite of Innocence, 1992; Making Mortal Choices, 1997; Thinking and Writing about Philosophy, 1997, 2nd ed., 2002; Killing as Punishment: Reflections on the Death Penalty in America, 2004. CO-AUTHOR: Nomos VI: Justice, 1963; Nomos IX: Equality, 1967; The Concept of Academic Freedom, 1972; Philosophy and Political Action, 1972; Philosophy, Morality, and International Affairs, 1974; Justice and Punishment, 1977; Human Rights and U.S. Foreign Policy, 1979; Making Decisions, 1979; The Imposition of Law, 1979; Matters of Life and Death, 1980; Ethical Issues in Government, 1981; And Justice for All, 1982; Social Justice, 1982; Group Decision Making, 1984; Human Rights, 1984; Nomos XXVII: Criminal Justice, 1985; Current Issues and Enduring Questions, 1987, 8th ed., 2008; Critical Thinking, Reading, and Writing, 1993, 6th ed., 2008; From critical thinking to argument: A Portable Guide, 2005, 3rd ed. 2011. EDITOR: The Death Penalty in America, 1964, 4th ed., 1997; Civil Disobedience: Theory and Practice, 1969; Justice and Equality, 1971; (with C.M. Pierce) Capital Punishment in the United States, 1976; Current Issues and Enduring Questions: Methods and Models of Argument from Plato to the Present, 1987, 9th ed., 2011; Civil Disobedience in Focus, 1991; (with S. Barnet) Critical Thinking, Reading, and Writing: A Brief Guide to Argument, 1993, 7th ed., 2011; (P.G. Cassell) Debating the Death Penalty: Should America have Capital Punishment?: The Experts on Both Sides Make Their Best Case, 2004; (with S. Barnet) Contemporary & Classic Arguments: A Portable Anthology, 2005. **Address:** Department of Philosophy, Tufts University, Miner Hall 222, Medford, MA 02155, U.S.A. **Online address:** habedau@aol.com

BEDER, Sharon. New Zealander/Australian (born Australia), b. 1956. **Genres:** Young Adult Non-fiction. **Career:** University of Sydney, education coordinator, 1990-91; University of Wollongong, lecturer, senior lecturer, assistant professor, 1992-2001, visiting professor, 2002-. Writer. **Publications:** NONFICTION: Toxic Fish and Sewer Surfing: How Deceit and Collusion Are Destroying Our Great Beaches, 1989; The Hole Story: Recent Ozone Depletion Research in the Areas of Medical, Biological and Veterinary Science, Physics, Pharmacy and Physiology, 1992; The Nature of Sustainable Development, 1993; Global Spin: The Corporate Assault on Environmentalism, 1998, rev. ed., 2002; The New Engineer: Management and Professional Responsibility in a Changing World, 1998; Selling the Work Ethic: From Puritan Pulpit to Corporate PR, 2000; Noses to the Grindstone: Shaping Industrial Servitude, 2000; Power Play: The Fight to Control the World's Electricity, 2003; Free Market Missionaries: The Corporate Manipulation of Community Values, 2006; Suiting Themselves: How Corporations Drive the Global Agenda, 2006; Environmental Principles and Policies: An Interdisciplinary Introduction, 2006. **Address:** Faculty of Arts, University of Wollongong, Wollongong, NW 2522, Australia. **Online address:** sharonb@uow.edu.au

BEDERMAN, Gail. American (born United States), b. 1952. **Genres:** History, Humanities. **Career:** University of Notre Dame, assistant professor of history, 1992-97, associate professor of history, 1997-. **Publications:** The Women Have Had Charge of the Church Work Long Enough: The Men and Religion Forward Movement of 1911-1912 and the Masculinization of Middle-class Protestantism, 1989; Civilization, the Decline of Middle-Class Manliness, and Ida B. Wellss Anti-Lynching Campaign 1892-1894, 1992; Manliness & Civilization: A Cultural History of Gender and Race in the United States, 1880-1917, 1995; Teaching the U.S. Womens History Survey at a Catholic University, 1996; Revisiting Nashoba: Slavery, Utopia and Frances Wright in America, 1818-1826, 2005; Sex, Scandal, Satire, and Population in 1798: Revisiting Malthuss First Essay, 2008; Sex Politics and Contraception in England and the United States, 1793-1831: A Pre-History of the Reproductive Rights Movement, forthcoming. Contributor to books and periodicals. **Address:** Department of History, University of Notre Dame, 255 Decio, 219 O'Shaughnessy Hall, Notre Dame, IN 46556, U.S.A. **Online address:** gbederman@ias.edu

BEDFORD, Deborah. American (born United States), b. 1958. **Genres:** Romance/Historical, Novels, Theology/Religion, Young Adult Fiction. **Career:** Evergreen Today, editor; Jackson Hole Writers Conference, president and co-founder. **Publications:** Touch the Sky, 1985; A Distant Promise, 1986; Passages, 1988; To Weave Tomorrow, 1989; Just Between Us, 1992; Blessing, 1993; After the Promise, 1993; Chickadee, 1995; Timberline, 1996; A Child's Promise, 1997; Harvest Dance, 1997; (with R.L. Hatcher and A.E. Hunt) The Story Jar, 2001; A Rose by the Door, 2001; On Wings of Morning, 2002; A Morning Like This, 2002; When You Believe, 2003; A Time to Keep, 2004; If I Had You, 2004; Remember Me: A Novel, 2005; (with J. Meyer) The Penny: A Novel, 2007; Only You, 2007; Family Matters, 2008; His Other Wife, 2009; (with J. Meyer) Any Minute, 2009; (with L. Goodnight) Mothers & Daughters: An Anthology, 2009. Contributor to periodicals. **Address:** c/o Author Mail, Warner Books, 1271 Ave. of the Americas, New York, NY 10020, U.S.A. **Online address:** deborah.bed@bresnan.net

BEDFORD, Henry Frederick. American (born United States), b. 1931. **Genres:** History, Sociology, Politics/Government, Economics. **Career:** Bedford Gas Inc., vice-president and treasurer, 1955-57; Phillips Exeter Academy, Department of History, teacher, 1957-66, chairman, 1966-69, dean of the faculty, 1969-73, Cowles professor in the humanities, 1973-82, librarian, 1973-77, vice-principal, 1979-82; Amherst College, 1982-87; Albuquerque Academy, history teacher, 1988-90. Writer. **Publications:** The Union Divides: Politics and Slavery, 1850-1861, 1963; Socialism and the Workers in Massachusetts, 1886-1912, 1966; A New Library at Exeter, 1968; From Versailles to Nuremburg, 1969; (contrib.) Main Problems in American History, 1969; (with T. Colbourn) The Americans: A Brief History, 1972, 4th ed., 1985; Trouble Downtown: The Local Context of Twentieth-Century America, 1978; Seabrook Station: Citizen Politics and Nuclear Power, 1990; (ed. and intro.) Their Lives and Numbers: The Condition of Working People in Massachusetts, 1870-1900, 1995. Contributor of articles to magazines. **Address:** 4 Gill St., Exeter, NH 03833-2620, U.S.A.

BEDFORD, Martyn. British (born England), b. 1959. **Genres:** Novels, Young Adult Fiction. **Career:** South London Press, reporter and features writer, 1980-85; South Wales Echo, sports writer, 1985-87; Citizen Gloucester, reporter, 1988; Oxford Mail and Times, features writer and sub-editor, 1988-93; Bradford Telegraph and Argus, sub-editor, 1994-95; freelance writer, 1995-; University of Manchester, lecturer in creative writing, 2001-, director of novel writing programme; Royal Literary Fund, academic writer-in-residence, 2008-10; University of Leeds, faculty; Leeds Metropolitan University, faculty; Leeds Trinity University college, associate senior lecturer in creative writing. **Publications:** (Ed. and contrib.) Matrix, 1994. NOVELS: Acts of Revision, 1996; Exit, Orange and Red, 1997; The Houdini Girl, 1998; Black Cat, 2000; Island of Lost Souls, 2006; Flip, 2011; The Fallen One, 2012. Contributor to short stories. Works appear in anthologies. **Address:** Department of English, Leeds Trinity University College, Rm AS9, Brownberrie Ln., Leeds, WY LS18 5HD, England. **Online address:** m.bedford@leedstrinity.ac.uk

BEDINGFIELD, M. Bradford. American (born United States), b. 1971?. **Genres:** History, Bibliography, Literary Criticism And History. **Career:** Wilmer Cutler Pickering Hale and Dorr, LLP, associate, 2005-, senior associate; Tokyo Metropolitan University, lecturer; Rikkyo University, lecturer; Oxford University, lecturer; University of Connecticut, lecturer. Writer. **Publications:** The Dramatic Liturgy of Anglo-Saxon England, 2002; (ed. with H. Gittos) The Liturgy of the Late Anglo-Saxon Church, 2005. **Address:** Wilmer Cutler Pickering Hale and Dorr L.L.P., 60 State St., Boston, MA 02109-1800, U.S.A. **Online address:** brad.bedingfield@wilmerhale.com

BEE, Ronald J. American (born United States), b. 1955. **Genres:** Novels, History, International Relations/Current Affairs, Military/Defense/Arms Control. **Career:** International Atomic Energy Agency, public information assistant, 1981; Congressional Research Service, foreign-affairs analyst, 1982; Palomar Corp., special assistant for national security affairs, 1982-87; System Planning Corp., consultant, 1987-89; Urban Institute, consultant, 1988-89; National Security Archive, consultant, 1989; ACCESS, director of publications and research, 1990-92; Youth for Understanding Freedom Support Act, consultant, 1992-94; University of California, Institute on Global Conflict and Cooperation, senior analyst, 1994-2003, director of special projects, 2003-; San Diego State University, lecturer, 1994-, Charles A. Hostler Institute on World Affairs, director, 2005-; Hansen Summer Institute on Leadership and International Cooperation, managing director, 2006-07. Writer. **Publications:** (With C.B. Feldbaum) Looking the Tiger in the Eye: Confronting the Nuclear Threat, 1988; (with B. Seymore and S. Young) One Nation Becomes Many: The ACCESS Guide to the Former Soviet Union, 1992; Russia and the Central Asian Republics: After Independence, New Directions?, 1993; Nuclear Proliferation: The Post Cold War Challenge, 1995; Seven Minutes to Midnight: Nuclear Weapons after 9/11, 2006; Terrorism by the Numbers: Separating Fact from Fiction, 2008. Contributor to periodicals. **Address:** San Diego State University, MC 0518, 9500 Gilman Dr., 5500 Campanile Dr., San Diego, CA 92182-4427, U.S.A. **Online address:** rbee@mail.sdsu.edu

BEE, Samantha. Canadian (born Canada), b. 1969. **Genres:** Biography. **Career:** Atomic Fireballs, founding member. Writer and actor. **Publications:** I Know I Am, But What Are You?, 2010. Contributor to periodicals. **Address:** The Daily Show, 604R W 52nd St., New York, NY 10019-5013, U.S.A.

BEEBE, Ralph K. (Ralph Kenneth Beebe). American (born United States), b. 1932. **Genres:** History, Theology/Religion, Social Sciences. **Career:** George Fox College, dean of men and director of athletics, 1955-57, professor, 1974-96, professor emeritus, 1997-; Willamette High School, teacher, 1957-66; Churchill High School, teacher, 1966-74. Writer. **Publications:** A Garden of the Lord: A History of Oregon Yearly Meeting of Friends Church, 1968; The Worker and Social Change: The Pullman Strike of 1894, 1970; Thomas Jefferson, the Embargo and the Decision for Peace, 1972; (with J. Lamoreau) Waging Peace: A Study in Biblical Pacifism, 1980; (with A.G. Rantisi) Blessed Are the Peacemakers: A Palestinian Christian in the Occupied West Bank, 1990, rev. ed., 2003; George Fox College, 1891-1991: A Heritage of Honor, A Future to Fulfill, 1991. **Address:** Department of History, George Fox University, 414 N Meridian St., Newberg, OR 97132, U.S.A. **Online address:** rbeebe@georgefox.edu

BEEBE, Ralph Kenneth. *See* **BEEBE, Ralph K.**

BEEBY, Dean. Canadian (born Canada), b. 1954. **Genres:** Adult Non-fiction, Military/Defense/Arms Control. **Career:** Canadian Press, deputy bureau chief, 1983-, reporter and editor, 1983-88, business editor, 1988-90, news editor, 1990-96, bureau chief, 1996-2003. **Publications:** NONFICTION: (ed. and intro. with W. Kaplan) Moscow Despatches: Inside Cold War Russia, 1987; In a Crystal Land: Canadian Explorers in Antarctica, 1994; Cargo of Lies: The True Story of a Nazi Double Agent in Canada, 1996; Deadly Frontiers: Disaster and Rescue on Canada's Atlantic Seaboard, 2001. **Address:** Canadian Press, 165 Sparks St., Ste. 800, PO Box 595, Sta. B, Ottawa, ON K1P 5B9, Canada. **Online address:** dbeeby@cp.org

BEEBY, James M. American (born United States), b. 1969. **Genres:** History, Humanities. **Career:** Indiana University Southeast, associate professor of history, 2005-. Writer and historian. **Publications:** Revolt of the Tar Heels: The North Carolina Populist Movement, 1890-1901, 2008. Contributor to periodicals. **Address:** Department of History, Indiana University, SE, 4201 Grant Line Rd., New Albany, IN 47150, U.S.A. **Online address:** jbeeby@ius.edu

BEECH, Harold Reginald. *See* **BEECH, H. R(eginald).**

BEECH, H. R(eginald). (Harold Reginald Beech). British (born England), b. 1925. **Genres:** Psychology, Economics, Business/Trade/Industry. **Career:** Institute of Psychiatry, lecturer, 1957-66, senior lecturer, 1963-69; S.W. Metropolitan Region, consultant psychologist, 1969-72; Netherne Hospital, Department of psychology, head, 1969-73; North West Regional Health Authority, consultant psychologist; University of Manchester, professor of clinical psychology; British Journal of Social and Clinical Psychology, editor; University Hospital of South Manchester, Department of Psychology and Training Program in Clinical Psychology, head, 1973. **Publications:** (With F. Fransella) Research and Experiment in Stuttering, 1968; Changing Man's Behaviour, 1969; (ed.) Obsessional States, 1974; (with M. Vaughan) Behavioural Treatment of Obsessional States, 1978; A Behavioural Approach to the Management of Stress: A Practical Guide to Techniques, 1982; (with L.E. Burns and B.F. Sheffield) Behavioural Approaches to the Management of Stress; Staying Together, 1986. Contributor of articles to journals. **Address:** Department of Psychology, University Hospital of South Manchester, Nell Ln., West Didsbury, M20 8LR, England.

BEECHER, Donald A(llen). Canadian (born Canada), b. 1942. **Genres:** Humanities, Intellectual History, Literary Criticism And History, Music, Theatre. **Career:** Carleton University, lecturer, 1967-69, assistant professor, 1969-80, associate professor, 1980-87, professor of English, 1987-, Centre for Renaissance Studies, director, 1978-; Dovehouse Editions, director; Chiba University, visiting lecturer, 1999-2001; Jacksonville State University, visiting lecturer, 2001; Tulane University, visiting lecturer, 2003, University of Bologna, Institute for Advanced Studies, fellow, 2009; University of California, distinguished visiting professor, 2011. Writer. **Publications:** EDITOR: Fantazias for altus and bassus, 1978; (with B. Gillingham) Divisions for Treble, Bass Viol, and Keyboard, 1979; (and trans. with M. Ciavolella and intro.) A. Caro, The Scruffy Scoundrels: Gli straccioni, 1981; (with B. Gillingham) Sonatas in A Major and G Major for Two Violins, Viola da gamba (cello) nd basso continuo, 1983; (with M. Ciavolella) Comparative Critical Approaches to Renaissance Comedy, 1986; (with M. Ciavolella and trans.) J. Ferrand, A Treatise on Love, vol. I: Jacques Ferr and and the Tradition of Erotic Melancholy in Western Culture, vol. II: Jacques Ferrand, Of Lovesickness or Erotic Melancholy, 1989; (with M. Ciavolella) Eros and Anteros, 1992; (and intro.) Barnabe Riche, His Farewell to Military Profession, 1992; (and trans. with M. Ciavolella) L. de Sommi, The Three Sisters, 1993; (with U. Rappen) W. Young, 29 Movements in the French Style for Bass Viol Solo, 1993; Anon, The Dialogue between Solomon and Marcolphus, 1994; T. Lodge, Rosalind, 1996; Ariosto/Gascoigne, Supposes, 1998; G.B.D. Porta, The Sister, 2000; T. Overbury, Characters, 2002; (and trans.) P. Calderon, The Phantom Lady, 2001; (with J. Butler and C. Di Biase) The Fables of Bidpai, 2002; (with H. Janzen) A Margarite of America, 2005; Renaissance Comedy: The Italian Master, 2008; Greene in Conceit, 2008; Renaissance Comedy: The Italian Masters, vol. I, 2008, vol. II, 2009; The Jacques Ferrand, De la Maladie D'amour ou Melancolie Erotique, 2010. OTHERS: (intro. and trans.) O. de Turnèbe, Satisfaction All Around: Les contens, 1979; (intro. and trans. with M. Ciavolella) G.L. Bernini, The Impresario, 1985. **Address:** Department of English, Carleton University, 1908 Dunton Twr., 1125 Colonel By Dr., Ottawa, ON K1S 5B6, Canada. **Online address:** donald_beecher@carleton.ca

BEECHER, Maureen Ursenbach. American/Canadian (born Canada), b. 1935. **Genres:** Theology/Religion, Autobiography/Memoirs, Biography, History. **Career:** McGill University, lecturer, 1963-68; Western Humanities Review, managing editor, 1969-72; Church of Jesus Christ of Latter-day Saints, editor and senior research associate, history division, 1972-80; Cornerstone: Mormon Architectural Heritage, president, 1972-73; Brigham Young University, associate professor, 1981-89, professor of English, 1990-97; Joseph Fielding Smith Institute for Church History, research historian, 1981-. **Publications:** (Ed. with L.F. Anderson) Sisters in Spirit: Mormon Women in Historical and Cultural Perspective, 1987; (ed. with D. Bitton) New Views of Mormon History: A Collection of Essays In Honor of Leonard J. Arrington, 1987; Eliza and Her Sisters, 1991; (ed. with J.R. Canon and J.M. Derr) Women of Covenant: The Story of Relief Society, 1992; (ed.) The Personal Writings of Eliza Roxey Snow, 1995. Contributor to periodicals. **Address:** University of Utah Press, 1795 East South Campus Dr., Ste. 101, Salt Lake City, UT 84112-9402, U.S.A.

BEEMAN, Robin. American (born United States), b. 1940. **Genres:** Novellas/Short Stories, Plays/Screenplays, Young Adult Non-fiction. **Career:** Sonoma State University, adjunct professor, 1990-95. Writer. **Publications:** A Parallel Life and Other Stories, 1992; A Minus Tide: Novella, 1995; The Lost Art of Desire, 2001. Contributor to periodicals. Works appear in anthologies. **Address:** Chronicle Books, 680 2nd St., San Francisco, CA 94107, U.S.A. **Online address:** robinbee@comcast.net

BEEMAN, William O. American (born United States), b. 1947. **Genres:** Cultural/Ethnic Topics, Language/Linguistics. **Career:** Pacific News Service, associate editor; Brown University, professor, 1983; New York University, visiting professor, 1984-85; Institute for Research in Information and Scholarship, associate director of program analysis, 1985, director of Middle Eastern studies, 1999; University of Minnesota, professor and chair of anthropology; Institute of Intercultural Studies, director; Opera Chemnitz, vocalist, 1996-99; U.S. State Department and the Department of Defense, consultant. Writer. **Publications:** Culture, Performance, and Communication in Iran, 1982; Language, Status, and Power in Iran, 1986; (with E. Bakewell) Object, Image, Inquiry: The Art Historian at Work: Report on a Collaborative Study by the Getty Art History Information Program (AHIP) and the Institute for Research in Information and Scholarship (IRIS), Brown University, AHIP, 1988; (co-author) Intermedia: A Case Study in Innovation in Higher Education, 1988; (with D. Helfgot) The Third Line: The Opera Performer as Interpreter, 1993; (ed. with M. Mead and R. Metraux) The Study of Culture at a Distance, Berghahn Books 2000; The "Great Satan" vs. the "Mad Mullahs": How the United States and Iran Demonize Each Other, 2005; Iranian Performance Traditions, 2011. **Address:** PO Box 2603, Costa Mesa, CA 92628, U.S.A. **Online address:** wbeeman@umn.edu

BEER, Anna R. British (born England), b. 1964. **Genres:** History, Biography. **Career:** University of Oxford, Kellogg College, Department for Continuing Education, lecturer in literature, 2003-10, fellow, 2003, joint dean of degrees, 2005-07, deputy chamberlain, 2005-09, joint secretary to governing body, 2006-08, chair, 2007-09, chamberlain, 2009-10; visiting fellow, 2010-. Writer. **Publications:** Sir Walter Ralegh and His Readers in the Seventeenth Century: Speaking to the People, 1997; My Just Desire: The Life of Bess Ralegh, Wife to Sir Walter, 2003; Milton: Poet, Pamphleteer, and Patriot, 2008. **Address:** Kellogg College, Banbury Rd., Oxford, OX OX2 6PN, United Kingdom. **Online address:** anna.beer@kellogg.ox.ac.uk

BEER, Gillian Patricia Kempster. British (born England), b. 1935. **Genres:** Literary Criticism And History, Romance/Historical, Novels. **Career:** Bedford College, assistant lecturer, 1959-62; University of Liverpool, lecturer, 1962-64; University of Cambridge, Girton College, fellow, 1965-94, honorary fellow, now emeritus fellow, assistant lecturer, 1966-71, lecturer and reader in literature and narrative, 1971-89, King Edward VII professor of English literature, 1989-2002, emeritus professor of English literature, King Edward VII professor emeritus, 2002-, Clare Hall, president, 1994-2001; British Comparative Literature Association, president. St Anne's College, honorary fellow. Writer. **Publications:** Meredith: A Change of Masks, 1970; The Romance, 1970; (ed. with J. Beer) Delights and Warnings: A New Anthology of Poems, 1979; Darwin's Plots: Evolutionary Narrative in Darwin, George Eliot, and Nineteenth-Century Fiction, 1983, 3rd ed., 2009; Meredith's Unpublished Notebooks, 1984; George Eliot, 1986; Arguing with the Past, 1989; Forging the Missing Link: Interdisciplinary Stories, 1992; (ed. and intro.) The Waves, 1992; Impact of Changes in the Personal Income Tax and Family Payment Systems on Australian Families, 1964 to 1994, 1995; (ed.) Modern Love, 1995; Open Fields: Science in Cultural Encounter, 1996; Virginia Woolf: The Common Ground, 1996; (ed. and intro.) The Origin of Species, 1996; (ed. and intro.) Persuasion, 1998; (ed.) The Wolfman and Other Case-Histories, 2002; (ed. with M. Bowie and B. Perrey) In(ter) Discipline: New Languages for Criticism, 2007; (ed. and intro.) On the Origin of Species, 2008; (ed. and intro.) Waves, 2008. **Address:** Clare Hall, University of Cambridge, Herschel Rd., Cambridge, CB CB3 9AL, England. **Online address:** gpb1000@cam.ac.uk

BEERE, Peter. British (born England), b. 1951. **Genres:** Science Fiction/Fantasy, Mystery/Crime/Suspense, Young Adult Fiction, Romance/Historical, Humor/Satire, Horror. **Career:** Writer, 1980-. **Publications:** SCIENCE FICTION NOVELS: Urban Prey, 1984; The Crucifixion Squad, 1984; Silent Slaughter, 1985. CRIME NOVELS: The Squad, 1987; The Fifth Man, 1987; The Sixth Day, 1988. JUVENILE SUSPENSE NOVELS: Crossfire, 1991; Underworld, 1992; Underworld II, 1992; Underworld III, 1992. JUVENILE CRIME NOVELS: School for Death, 1993 in US as School for Terror, 1994; Kiss of Death, 1994. JUVENILE FANTASY NOVELS: Doom Sword, 1993; Star Warriors, 1995. OTHERS: Riot (juvenile drama), 1995; Bod's Mum's Knickers (juvenile humor), 1995; At Gehenna's Door, 1997; Death House, forthcoming. **Address:** 12 Sherman Dr., Rainhill, Prescot, MS L35 6PW, England.

BEERLING, David. (D. J. Beerling). British (born England), b. 1965. **Genres:** Sciences, Natural History, Social Sciences. **Career:** University of Wales, research assistant, 1990-93; University of Sheffield, research assistant, 1993-94; Royal Society University, research fellow, 1994-2002, honorary lecturer, 1994-99, Department of Animal and Plant Sciences, honorary reader, 1999-2002, personal chairman in palaeoclimatology, 2002-; University of California, visiting lecturer; Pennsylvania State University, visiting lecturer; Manchester University, visiting lecturer; Cambridge University, visiting lecturer; Yale University, visiting lecturer; University of Utrecht, visiting lecturer. Writer. **Publications:** (AS D.J. Beerling with F.I. Woodward) Vegetation and the Terrestrial Carbon Cycle: Modelling the First 400 Million Years, 2001; The Emerald Planet: How Plants Changed Earth's History, 2007. Contributor to periodicals. **Address:** Department of Animal and Plant Sciences, University of Sheffield, Alfred Denny Bldg., Sheffield, SY S10 2TN, England. **Online address:** d.j.beerling@sheffield.ac.uk

BEERLING, D. J. *See* **BEERLING, David.**

BEERS, Burton Floyd. American (born United States), b. 1927. **Genres:** History, International Relations/Current Affairs, Young Adult Non-fiction, Politics/Government. **Career:** North Carolina State University, instructor,

1955-57, assistant professor, 1957-61, associate professor, 1961-66, professor of history, 1966-96, alumni distinguished professor, 1970-96, professor emeritus, 1997-, head of department, 1981-86, National Endowment for the Humanities, director of Asian materials projects, 1974, 1976; National Taiwan University, Fulbright professor of history, 1966-67; Writer. **Publications:** Vain Endeavour: Robert Lansing's Attempts to End the American-Japanese Rivalry, 1962; (with P.H. Clyde) The Far East: A History of Western Impacts and Eastern Responses, 6th ed. 1976; China in Old Photographs, 1978; World History: Patterns of Civilization, 1983, 6th ed. 1993; (with M.S. Downs) North Carolina State: A Pictorial History, 1986; (ed.) Living in Our World, vol. IV, 1998. **Address:** Department of History, North Carolina State University, Withers 248, PO Box 8108, Raleigh, NC 27695-8108, U.S.A. **Online address:** burtbeers@aol.com

BEERS, Diane L. American (born United States) **Genres:** Adult Non-fiction, Animals/Pets, History, Sociology. **Career:** Holyoke Community College, Department of History, associate professor, 1999-. Writer. **Publications:** For the Prevention of Cruelty: The History and Legacy of Animal Rights Activism in the United States, 2006. **Address:** Department of History, Holyoke Community College, 303 Homestead Ave., Holyoke, MA 01040, U.S.A. **Online address:** dbeers@hcc.mass.edu

BEGBIE, Jeremy. British (born England), b. 1957?. **Genres:** Music. **Career:** St John's Church, Egham, Assistant Curate, 1982-85; University of London, Royal Holloway College, honorary chaplain, 1985-85; Ridley Hall, Cambridge, chaplain and tutor, 1985-87; Ridley Hall, Cambridge, Director of Studies, lecturer in Christian doctrine, 1987-93; Ridley Hall, Cambridge, Vice Principal, lecturer in Christian doctrine, 1993-2000; University of Cambridge, Faculty of Divinity, affiliated lecturer, 1994-; University of Cambridge, Director, Theology Through the Arts (TTA), Centre for Advanced Religious and Theological Studies, Faculty of Divinity, 1997-2000; Ridley Hall, Cambridge, Associate Principal, lecturer in Christian doctrine, 2000-08; University of St Andrews, School of Divinity, honorary reader, director, Theology Through the Arts, associate director, Institute of Theology, Imagination and the Arts (ITIA), 2000-08; University of St Andrews, School of Divinity, honorary professor, 2003-08; University of Cambridge, Faculty of Music, affiliated lecturer, 2007-; Duke University, Duke Divinity School, Thomas A. Langford research professor of theology, Duke Initiatives in Theology and the Arts (DITA), director, 2008-. Writer, theologian, and musician. **Publications:** NONFICTION: Music in God's Purposes, 1989; Voicing Creation's Praise: Towards a Theology of the Arts, 1991; (ed.) Beholding the Glory: Incarnation through the Arts, 2000; Theology, Music and Time, 2000; (ed.) Sounding the Depths: Theology through the Arts, 2002; Resounding Truth: Christian Wisdom in the World of Music, 2007; (ed. with S.R. Guthrie) Resonant Witness: Conversations in Music and Theology, 2010. **Address:** Duke Divinity School, Duke University, 407 Chapel Drive, PO Box 90968, Durham, NC 27708-0968, U.S.A. **Online address:** jeremy.begbie@duke.edu

BEGELMAN, Mitchell C. *See* **BEGELMAN, Mitchell (Craig).**

BEGELMAN, Mitchell (Craig). (Mitchell C. Begelman). American (born United States), b. 1953. **Genres:** Astronomy, Sciences, Physics. **Career:** Cambridge University, Institute of Astronomy, fellow, 1978-79, 1981-82; University of California, postgraduate research astronomer, 1979-82; N. Copernicus Astronomical Center, visiting scientist, 1980; University of Colorado at Boulder, Department of Astrophysical and Planetary Sciences, assistant professor, 1982-87, fellow, 1984-, associate professor, 1987-91, associate chair, 1989-90, 1992-95, professor of astrophysical, planetary and atmospheric sciences, 1991-, department head, 1995-98, 2008-. Writer. **Publications:** (With M. Rees) Gravity's Fatal Attraction: Black Holes in the Universe, 1996, 2nd ed., 2010; (with M. Rees) Schwarze Löcher Im Kosmos: Die Magische Anziehungskraft Der Gravitation, 1997; (with M. Rees) L'Attrazione Fatale Della Gravità: I Buchi Neri Dell' Universo, 1997; (with M. Rees) Zwarte Gaten In Het Heelal, 1998; (with M. Rees) Ta Sila Fatalna, Czarne Dziury we Wszechświecie, 1999; Turn Right at Orion: Travels through the Cosmos, 2000. Contributor to books and journals. **Address:** Joint Institute for Laboratory Astrophysics, University of Colorado at Boulder, PO Box 440, Boulder, CO 80309-0440, U.S.A. **Online address:** mitch@jila.colorado.edu

BEGLEY, Dan. American (born United States), b. 1968. **Genres:** Novels. **Career:** University of Missouri, adjunct professor; Elsevier Publishing, editor; Cor Jesu Academy, English teacher. Writer. **Publications:** Ms. Taken Identity, 2009. **Address:** Hachette Book Group, 237 Park Ave., New York, NY 10017, U.S.A. **Online address:** dan@danbegley.com

BEGLEY, Ed James. American (born United States), b. 1949. **Genres:** Environmental Sciences/Ecology, Biography. **Career:** Begley's Best, owner and chief executive officer. Writer and actor. **Publications:** (With R. McLean and D. Suzuki) Grassroots Rising: Protecting Your Family in Our Changing Environment, 2006; Living Like Ed: A Guide to the Eco-friendly Life, 2008; Ed Begley, Jr.'s Guide to Sustainable Living: Learning to Conserve Resources and Manage an Eco- conscious Life, 2009. Contributor to periodicals. **Address:** William Morris Agency, 1 William Morris Pl., Beverly Hills, CA 90212, U.S.A.

BEGLEY, Louis. American/Polish (born Poland), b. 1933. **Genres:** Novels. **Career:** Debevoise & Plimpton (law firm), associate, 1959-67, partner, 1968-2004, retired, 2004; University of Pennsylvania, senior visiting lecturer, 1985-86; American PEN, president, 1993-95. Writer. **Publications:** NOVELS: Wartime Lies, 1991; The Man Who Was Late, 1993; As Max Saw It, 1994; About Schmidt, 1996; Mister's Exit, 1998; Schmidt Delivered, 2000; Shipwreck, 2003; (with A. Muhlstein) Venice for Lovers, 2005; Matters of Honor, 2007; Tremendous World I Have Inside My Head: Franz Kafka, A Biographical Essay, 2008; Why the Dreyfus Affair Matters. 2009. OTHER: Mistler's Exit, 1998. Contributor to periodicals. **Address:** Georges Borchardt Inc., 136 E 57th St., New York, NY 10022, U.S.A. **Online address:** lbegley@louisbegley.com

BEHA, Christopher R. American (born United States), b. 1980?. **Genres:** Young Adult Fiction, Novellas/Short Stories. **Career:** Harper's magazine, assistant editor. **Publications:** (With J.C. Oates) The Ecco Anthology of Contemporary American Short Fiction, 2008; The Whole Five Feet: What the Great Books Taught Me about Life, Death and Pretty Much Everything Else, 2009. Contributor to periodicals. **Address:** Harper's Magazine, 666 Broadway, 11th Fl., New York, NY 10012, U.S.A. **Online address:** christopher.beha@gmail.com

BEHAR, Ruth. American/Cuban (born Cuba), b. 1956. **Genres:** Anthropology/Ethnology, Social Sciences, Women's Studies And Issues, Sociology. **Career:** University of Michigan, Department of Anthropology, assistant professor, 1986-89, associate professor, 1989-94, professor of anthropology, 1994-, Victor Haim Perera collegiate professor of anthropology, Center for Latin American and Caribbean Studies, faculty. Writer. **Publications:** Santa María del Monte: The Presence of the Past in a Spanish Village, 1986; Translated Woman: Crossing the Border With Esperanza's Story, 1993, 2nd ed., 2003; Las Visiones de una Bruja Guachichil en 1599: Hacia una Perspectiva Indígena Sobre la Conquista de San Luis Potosí, 1995; The Vulnerable Observer: Anthropology That Breaks Your Heart, 1996; Cortada, 2004; Island Called Home: Returning to Jewish Cuba, 2007. EDITOR: Bridges to Cuba/Puentes a Cuba (anthology), 1995; (with D.A. Gordon) Women Writing Culture, 1995; The Color of Privilege: Three Blasphemies on Race and Feminism, 1996; (with L.M. Suárez) Portable Island: Cubans at Home in the World, 2008. Contributor of articles to magazines and journals. Works appear in anthologies. **Address:** Department of Anthropology, University of Michigan, 228-A West Hall, 1085 S University Ave., Ann Arbor, MI 48109, U.S.A. **Online address:** rbehar@umich.edu

BEHDAD, Sohrab. American/Iranian (born Iran), b. 1943?. **Genres:** History, Theology/Religion. **Career:** Syracuse University, Department of Economics, lecturer, 1972-73; University of Tehran, Department of Economics, assistant professor, 1973-83, director of program of faculty of economics, 1979-80, Institute of Economic Development Studies, director, 1980-81; Denison University, assistant professor, associate professor of economics, 1985-95, professor of economics, 1996-, department chair, 1992-96, John E. Harris Chair in Economics, 2002-; Middle East Studies Association Bulletin, associate editor of economics, 1996-2000. **Publications:** (ed. with S. Rahnema) Iran after the Revolution: Crisis of an Islamic State, 1995; (ed. with F. Nomani) Islam and the Everyday World: Public Policy Dilemmas, 2006; (with F. Nomani) Class and Labor in Iran: Did the Revolution Matter?, 2006. **Address:** Department of Economics, Denison University, Higley Hall 206, Granville, OH 43023, U.S.A. **Online address:** behdad@denison.edu

BEHE, Michael J. American (born United States), b. 1952. **Genres:** Earth Sciences, Sciences, Theology/Religion. **Career:** City University of New York, Queens College, assistant professor of chemistry, 1982-85; Lehigh University, faculty, associate professor, professor of biological sciences, 1985-;

Discovery Institutes Center for Science and Culture, senior fellow. Writer. **Publications:** NONFICTION: Darwins Black Box: The Biochemical Challenge to Evolution, 1996; (with W.A. Dembski and S.C. Meyer) Science and Evidence for Design in the Universe: Papers Presented at a Conference Sponsored by the Wethersfield Institute, 2000; (with T.D. Singh) God, Intelligent Design and Fine-Tuning: A Discussion between Michael J. Behe and T.D. Singh, 2005; The Edge of Evolution: The Search for the Limits of Darwinism, 2007. Contributor of articles to books. **Address:** Department of Biological Sciences, Lehigh University, Rm. D-221, Iacocca Hall, 111 Research Dr., Bethlehem, PA 18015, U.S.A. **Online address:** mjb1@lehigh.edu

BEHN, Robert Dietrich. American (born United States), b. 1941. **Genres:** Public/Social Administration, Economics. **Career:** Massachusetts Institute of Technology, Lincoln Laboratory, engineer, 1964-65; RAND Corp., consultant, 1966; Ripon Society, research director, 1968-69, executive director, 1970-73; Commonwealth of Massachusetts, assistant for urban affairs to the governor, 1969-70; Harvard University, John F. Kennedy School of Government, lecturer in business administration, 1972-73, lecturer in public policy, 2007-, Driving Government Performance Program, faculty chair; Duke University, associate professor, 1973-88, professor of policy sciences and public affairs, 1988-, Institute of Policy Sciences and Public Affairs, director, 1982-85, Governors Center, director, 1984-; Whippoorwill Youth Athletic Association, baseball coach, 1982-84; Holt Athletic Association, baseball coach, 1985, 1987; Carrboro Recreation Department, baseball coach, 1989; State University of New York, New York State Department of Social Services, chairman, 1991-92; Urban Academy and Ford Foundation, consultant; National Academy of Public Administration, fellow. Writer. **Publications:** (Ed.) The Lessons of Victory, 1969; (with M.A. Clark) Termination II: How the National Park Service Annulled Its Commitment to a Beach Erosion Control Policy at the Cape Hatteras National Seashore, 1976; (with J.W. Vaupel) Quick Analysis for Busy Decision Makers, 1982; Case Commentaries, Robert F. Kennedy High School, 1984; (ed.) Governors on Governing, 1991; Leadership Counts: Lessons for Public Managers from the Massachusetts Welfare, Training, and Employment Program, 1991; (ed. with A.A. Altshuler) Innovation in American Government: Challenges, Opportunities, and Dilemmas, 1997; Rethinking Democratic Accountability, 2001; (with E.K. Keating) Facing the Fiscal Crises In State Governments: National Problem; National Responsibilities, 2004. Works appear in anthologies. Contributor to periodicals. **Address:** John F. Kennedy School of Government, Harvard University, 360 Taubman Ctr., 79 John F. Kennedy St., PO Box 114, Cambridge, MA 02138, U.S.A. **Online address:** redsox@hks.harvard.edu

BEHR, Ira Steven. American (born United States), b. 1953. **Genres:** Novels, Science Fiction/Fantasy, Young Adult Fiction. **Career:** Star Trek, showrunner and executive producer, supervising producer, 1993; Starz TV, head writer; Syfy Channel, head writer, show runner, executive producer, 2010; United Paramount Network, executive producer. **Publications:** (Contrib.) The Search, 1993; The Ferengi Rules of Acquisition (science fiction), 1995; (with D. Carey and R.H. Wolf) Star Trek: The Way of the Warrior, 1995; (with R.H. Wolf) Legends of the Ferengi, 1997. **Address:** c/o Author Mail, Pocket Books, 1230 Ave. of the Americas, New York, NY 10020-1513, U.S.A.

BEHRENS, Ellen. American (born United States), b. 1957. **Genres:** Novels, Novellas/Short Stories, Business/Trade/Industry, How-to Books, Education, E-books, Young Adult Fiction. **Career:** Delphi Automotive, educational development counselor, 1994-2000; Ohio Arts Council, artist-in-residence, 1991-2000; Novations Learning Technologies, manager of Instructional design, 2000-04; National Association of College and University Food services (NACUFS), director of education, 2004-09; independent e-learning consultant and writer, 2009-. **Publications:** None But the Dead and the Dying (novel), 1996; e-Learning: A Trail Guide to Association e-Learning (non-fiction), 2009; Road Tales: Short Stories About Full-Time RVing (fiction), 2010. Works appear in anthologies. Contributor to periodicals. **Address:** 3700 S Westport Ave., PO Box 2229, Sioux Falls, SD 57106, U.S.A. **Online address:** ellenbehr@aol.com

BEHRENS, John C. American (born United States), b. 1933. **Genres:** Business/Trade/Industry, History, How-to Books, Money/Finance, Music, Writing/Journalism. **Career:** Pacific Stars and Stripes, journalist, 1957-58; Seoul Education Center, instructor, 1957-58; Lancaster Eagle-Gazette, sports editor, 1958-62; Ohio Wesleyan University, Department of Journalism, chairman, 1962-63; Marshall University, assistant professor of journalism, 1963-65; Syracuse University, Utica College, associate professor, professor of journalism, 1965-97, professor emeritus, coordinator of journalism studies and public relations, Student Press Archives, curator, 1967-2006, Pioneer Magazine, editor, 1968-85, PR/J Programs, director, 1986-92; Commerce Commentary, editor, 1967-2008; Mohawk Valley Council of Churches, treasurer, 1969-72; The Elks, business columnist, 1976-2000; American Printer, columnist, 1978-99; Laubach's Literary Advance, editor, 1984-86; Home Business Journal, editor, 1995-2001; CBS/UC/WIBX Sunday Roundtable, founder and moderator, 1993-2003. **Publications:** Magazine Writer's Workbook: A Worktext of Instruction and Exercises for the Beginning Magazine Article Writer, 1968, 3rd ed., 1983; (ed.) Wood and Stone: Landmarks of the Upper Mohawk, 1972; Reporting Worktext, 1974; Typewriter Guerrillas: Closeups of 20 Top Investigative Reporters, 1976; Student Press Archives Directory, 1987; The Writing Business: How to be a Successful Magazine Writer, 1991; Pioneering Generations: The Utica College Story, 1997; The Big Band Days: A Memoir and Source Book, 2003; Presidential Profiles: An Intimate Collection of Portraits and Documents, 2003; The Writing Life, 2006; Big Bands and Great Ballrooms: America Is Dancing-Again, 2006; America's Music Makers: Big Bands and Great Ballrooms, 1912-2011, 2011. Contributor to books and periodicals. **Address:** 57 Stebbins Dr., Clinton, NY 13323, U.S.A. **Online address:** jbehrens@roadrunner.com

BEHRINGER, Wolfgang. German (born Germany), b. 1956?. **Genres:** Psychology, History. **Career:** Ludwigs-Maximilians University, magister, 1981, instructor, 1998; Thurn und Taxis, München/Regensburg, project manager, 1988-90; Rheinische Friedrich-Wilhelms University, researcher, 1991-96; Max-Planck Institute for History, researcher, 1998; University of York, instructor, 1999; University of the Saarland, instructor, chair of early modern times department, 2003-. Writer. **Publications:** Hexenverfolgung in Bayern: Volksmagie, Glaubenseifer und Staatsrason in der fruhen Neuzeit, 1987, 4th ed., 2000; Mit dem Feuer vom Leben zum Tod: Hexengesetzgebung in Bayern, 1988; Thurn und Taxis: Die Geschichte ihrer Post und ihrer Unternehmen, 1990; Löwenbrau: Von den Anf Angen des Munchner Brauwesens bis zur Gegenwart, 1991; (with C. Ott-Koptschalijski) Der Traum vom Fliegen: Zwischen Mythos und Technik, 1991; Chonrad Stoeckhlin und die Nachtschar: Eine Geschichte aus frUhen Neuzeit, 1994; Die Spaten-Brauerei, 1397- 1997: Die Geschichte eines Munchner Unternehmens vom Mittelalter bis zur Gegenwart, 1997; (ed. with B. Roeck) Das Bild der Stadt in der Neuzeit, 1400-1800, 1999; Im Zeichen des Merkur: Reichspost und Kommunikationsrevolution in der frUhen Neuzeit, 2003; Witches and Witch-Hunts: A Global History, 2004; (co-ed.) Kulturelle Konsequenzen der "Kleinen Eiszeit", 2005; Kulturgeschichte des Klimas: Von der Eiszeit bis zur Globalen Erw Armung, 2007; Cultural History of Climate, 2010. CONTRIBUTOR: Zeit der Postkutschen: Drei Jahrhunderte Reisen, 1600-1900, 1992; Kommunikation im Kaiserreich: der Generalpostmeister Heinrich von Stephan, 1997; Melancholie: Epochenstimmung, Krankheit, Lebenskunst, 2000; Kartenwelten: Der Raum und seine Repräsentation in der Neuzeit, 2006. Contributor to journals. **Address:** University of the Saarland, Campus Saarbrücken, SaarbrUcken, D-66041, Germany. **Online address:** behringer@mx.uni-saarland.de

BEHRMAN, Greg. Also writes as Greg Marc Behrman. American (born United States), b. 1976?. **Genres:** Travel/Exploration, Novels. **Career:** Harvard University, Carr Center for Human Rights, fellow; Aspen Institute, Henry Kissinger Fellow; Goldman Sachs Co., staff; Heartbeat, board of directors. Writer. **Publications:** The Invisible People: How the U.S. Has Slept Through the Global AIDS Pandemic the Greatest Humanitarian Catastrophe of Our Time, 2004; The Most Noble Adventure: The Marshall Plan and the Time When America helped Save Europe, 2007; Most Noble Adventure: The Marshall Plan and How America Helped Rebuild Europe, 2008. Contributor to periodicals. **Address:** ICM Inc., 825 8th Ave., New York, NY 10019, U.S.A.

BEHRMAN, Greg Marc. *See* **BEHRMAN, Greg.**

BEHUNIAK, James. American (born United States), b. 1969. **Genres:** Biography, Sciences, History. **Career:** Colby College, Department of Philosophy, assistant professor, associate professor of philosophy. Writer. **Publications:** (Ed.) Introduction to Eastern Thought, 2002; (with R.T. Ames) Mengzi xin xing zhi xue, 2005; Mencius on Becoming Human, 2005. **Address:** Colby College, Department of Philosophy, 252 Lovejoy, 4559 Mayflower Hill, Waterville, ME 04901-8845, U.S.A. **Online address:** jim.behuniak@colby.edu

BEI DAO. American/Chinese (born China), b. 1949. **Genres:** Novellas/Short Stories, Poetry. **Career:** Jintian, staff member, 1978-80, editor-in-chief; Today Magazine, co-founder, 1978; Esperanto Ribao, editor, 1985; University of

California, instructor; University of Alabama, faculty; Beloit College, faculty. **Publications:** (Contrib.) Jin tian=Today, 1978; (as Beidao Zhu) Beidao shi xuan, 1986; Gui lai di mo sheng ren, 1986; The August Sleepwalker (poetry), 1990; Waves (short stories), 1990; Old Snow (poetry), 1991; Strasse des Glücks Nr. 13: die Kurzgeschichten, 1992; Forms of Distance (poetry), 1994; Landscape over Zero (poetry), 1995; At the Sky's Edge: Poems 1991-1996, 1996; Lan fang zi, 1998; 13, rue du bonheur, 1999; Unlock (poetry), 2000; Blue House (essay), 2000; Chuan yue chou hen de hei an, 2005; Midnight's Gate, 2005; Qi shi nian dai, 2008; The Rose of Time: New and Selected Poems, 2009; Cheng men kai, 2010. Contributor to periodicals. **Address:** 1862 Imperial Ave., Davis, CA 95616, U.S.A.

BEIDERWELL, Bruce. American (born United States), b. 1952. **Genres:** Literary Criticism And History. **Career:** University of California, Writing Programs, director, lecturer in writing, 1985-. Writer. **Publications:** Power and Punishment in Scott's Novels, 1992; (ed. with J.M. Wheeler) The Literary Experience, 2008. Contributor of articles to journals. **Address:** Writing Programs, University of California, 144 Humanities Bldg., Los Angeles, CA 90095, U.S.A. **Online address:** beiderwe@humnet.ucla.edu

BEIDLER, Peter G. (Peter Grant Beidler). American (born United States), b. 1940. **Genres:** Literary Criticism And History, Novels, Race Relations, Classics. **Career:** Lehigh University, assistant professor, 1968-72, associate professor, 1972-77, professor, 1977-78, Lucy G. Moses distinguished professor of English, 1978-, Freshman Writing Program, director, 1989-90, retired, 2006; University of Kent, research professor, 1983-84; Sichuan University, Fulbright professor, 1987-88; Baylor University, Robert Foster Cherry visiting distinguished teaching professor, 1995-96. Writer. **Publications:** Fig Tree John: An Indian in Fact and Fiction, 1977; (with M.F. Egge) The American Indian in Short Fiction: An Annotated Bibliography, 1979; Distinguished Teachers on Effective Teaching, 1986; Ghosts, Demons and Henry James, 1989; Writing Matters, 1990, rev. ed., 2010; Henry James, The Turn of the Screw: Text and Five Contemporary Critical Essays, 1995, 3rd ed., 2010; Geoffrey Chaucer, The Wife of Bath: Complete, Authoritative Text with Biographical and Historical Contexts, Critical History and Essays from Five Contemporary Critical Perspectives, 1996; (with E.M. Biebel) The Wife of Bath's Prologue and Tale: An Annotated Bibliography, 1998; (with G. Barton) A Reader's Guide to the Novels of Louise Erdrich, 1999, rev. ed., 2006; (with Egge) The Native American in the Saturday Evening Post, 1897-1969, 2000; (with Egge and H.J. Brown) The Native American in Short Fiction in the Saturday Evening Post, 2001; Why I Teach, 2002; A Reader's Companion to J. D. Salinger's The Catcher in the Rye, 2009, 2nd ed., 2011; Self-Reliance Inc.: A Twentieth-Century Walden Experiment, 2009. EDITOR: (and contrib.) John Gower's Literary Transformations in the Confessio Amantis, 1982; (and contrib.) Masculinities in Chaucer, 1998; Turn of the Screw: Complete, Authoritative Text with Biographical, Historical and Cultural Contexts, Critical History and Essays from Contemporary Critical Perspectives, 2004; (with K.C. Reed) Approaches to Teaching Henry James's Daisy Miller and The Turn of the Screw, 2005; Self-Reliance, Inc.: A Twentieth-Century Walden Experiment, 2009; The Collier's Weekly Version of Henry James's The Turn of the Screw, 2010; Chaucer's Canterbury Comedies: Origins and Originality, 2011. **Address:** 1204 NW 73rd St., Seattle, WA 98117, U.S.A. **Online address:** pbeidler@gmail.com

BEIDLER, Peter Grant. *See* **BEIDLER, Peter G.**

BEIFUSS, John. American (born United States), b. 1959. **Genres:** Documentaries/Reportage, Children's Fiction, Young Adult Fiction. **Career:** The Memphis Press-Scimitar, newspaper reporter, 1981-83; The Commercial Appeal-Memphis, movie reviewer. Writer. **Publications:** Armadillo Ray, 1995. Contributor to periodicals. **Address:** The Commercial Appeal, 495 Union Ave., Memphis, TN 38103-3217, U.S.A. **Online address:** beifuss@gomemphis.com

BEINHART, Larry. American (born United States), b. 1947. **Genres:** Novels, Young Adult Non-fiction. **Career:** Co-host, producer, writer and co-creator, Big Orange Production Co., Founder and president; Woodstock Guild of Artists, staff; Oxford University, faculty; Wadham College, Detective and Crime Fiction Writing, Raymond Chandler Fulbright fellow; Belleayre Mountain, instructor; Hunter Mount Ski School, instructor, Kölner Club, instructor; Trois Valleés, instructor; Sheinkopf Communications, director/writer/producer for political commercials. Commentator and screenwriter. **Publications:** No One Rides for Free, 1987; You Get What You Pay For, 1988; Foreign Exchange, 1991; American Hero, 1993; (As Gillian Farrell) Alibi for an Actress, 1993; (As Gillian Farrell) Murder and a Muse, 1995; How to Write a Mystery, 1996; Librarian, 2004; Wag the Dog: A Novel, 2004; Fog Facts: Searching for Truth in the Land of Spin, 2005; Salvation Boulevard, 2008. **Address:** c/o Joy Harris, Chantz-Harris, 888 7th Ave., New York, NY 10106, U.S.A. **Online address:** beinhart@fogfacts.com

BEISNER, Robert L. (Robert Lee Beisner). American (born United States), b. 1936. **Genres:** History, Politics/Government, Biography, Autobiography/Memoirs. **Career:** University of Chicago, instructor in social science, 1962-63; Colgate University, instructor of history, 1963-65; American University, assistant professor, 1965-67, associate professor, 1967-71, professor of history, 1971-97, department chair, 1981-90, director of general education, 1993-97, emeritus professor, 1997-. Writer. **Publications:** Twelve against Empire: The Anti-Imperialists, 1898-1900, 1968; From the Old Diplomacy to the New, 1865-1900, 1975, 1986; (ed. with J.R. Challinor) Arms at Rest: Peacemaking and Peacekeeping in American History, 1987; (ed.) American Foreign Relations Since 1600: A Guide to the Literature, 2nd ed., 2003; Dean Acheson: A Life in the Cold War, 2006. **Address:** 3851 Newark St. NW, Washington, DC 20016-3026, U.S.A. **Online address:** huskerindc@rcn.com

BEISNER, Robert Lee. *See* **BEISNER, Robert L.**

BEISSEL, Henry (Eric). Canadian/German (born Germany), b. 1929. **Genres:** Plays/Screenplays, Poetry, Geography, Travel/Exploration, Essays, Translations. **Career:** Canadian Broadcasting Corp., stage hand, 1953-54, filmmaker, 1954-55; University of Munich, lecturer in English literature, 1960-62; University of Alberta, lecturer in department of English, 1962-64; University of the West Indies, visiting professor in department of English, 1964-66; Sir George Williams University, associate professor of English, 1966-69; Concordia University, associate professor, 1969-76, professor of English, 1976-96, emeritus professor of English, distinguished emeritus professor, 1996-; Montreal Theater Laboratory, chairman of board of directors; University of Toronto, teaching fellow. Writer. **Publications:** Introduction to Spain, 1955; Witness the Heart (poems), 1963; New Wings for Icarus: A Poem in Four Parts (poems), 1966; The World Is a Rainbow (poems), 1968; My Funny Little Clock (poems), 1968; (contrib.) The New Romans: Candid Canadian Opinions of the U.S., 1968; (ed., trans. and intro.) The Price of Morning, 1968; Face on the Dark (poems), 1970; (intro.) Winter in Paradise, 1972; Inook and the Sun, 1974; The Salt I Taste (poems), 1975; (trans. and intro.) A Different Sun (poems), 1976; (adapted) Three Plays, 2nd ed., 1976; (ed.) Cues and Entrances: Ten Canadian One-act Plays, 1977; Goya: A Play, 1978; (contrib.) Farewell to the Seventies, 1979; Cantos North (poems), 1980; Under Coyote's Eye: A Play About Ishi, 1980; Kanada, 1981; The Boar and the Dromedar (poems), 1982; Season of Blood: A Suite of Poems, 1984; Poems New and Selected, 1987; (trans.) Thistle in His Mouth: Poems, 1987; Dying I Was Born, 1992; (ed. with J. Bennett) Raging Like a Fire: A Celebration of Irving Layton, 1993; Stones to Harvest, 1993; (ed.) Magic Prison, Letters From Edward Lacey, 1995; Inuk, 2000; (trans.) Briefe auf Birkenbast, 2000; Letters on Birch bark, 2000; Dragon and the Pearl: Poems, 2002; Across the Sun's Wrap: A Poem, 2003; Coming to Terms with a Child, 2011; Seasons of Blood, 2011; Winter Crossing and The Sniper, forthcoming; Ayorama Elegies, forthcoming. **Address:** School of Graduate Studies, Concordia University, 2145 Mackay St., Montreal, QC H3G 2J2, Canada. **Online address:** beifran@glen-net.ca

BEISSINGER, Steven R. American (born United States), b. 1953. **Genres:** Environmental Sciences/Ecology, Biology. **Career:** National Institute for Urban Wildlife, field biologist, 1978; Florida Game and Fresh Water Fish Commission, contract biologist, 1979; University of Michigan, lecturer in ecology and environmental science, 1984-85; U.S. National Park Service, International Seminar on National Parks and Equivalent Reserves, staff, 1984; Smithsonian Institution, research associate, 1985-; University of Florida, adjunct assistant professor of wildlife science, 1986-88; Yale University, assistant professor, 1988-91, associate professor of ecology and conservation biology, 1991-; U.S. Fish and Wildlife Service, population biologist, 1993-; Universidad de Cordoba, lecturer; University of Puerto Rico, lecturer, 1994; University of California, A. Starker Leopold chair of wildlife biology, A. Starker Leopold professor of wildlife ecology and professor of conservation biology. Writer. **Publications:** (Ed. with N.F.R. Snyder) New World Parrots in Crisis: Solutions from Conservation Biology, 1992; (ed. with D.R. McCullough) Population Viability Analysis, 2002; (co-author) Modeling Approaches in Avian Conservation and the Role of Field Biologists, 2006. Contributor of articles to journals. **Address:** Department Environmental Science Policy, and Management, University of California, 29 Mulford Hall, Berkeley, CA 94720-3110, U.S.A. **Online address:** beis@berkeley.edu

BEJA, Morris. American (born United States), b. 1935. **Genres:** Film, Literary Criticism And History. **Career:** Ohio State University, from instructor to professor of English, 1961-94, chairman of English, 1983-94, professor emeritus, 2001-; University of Thessaloniki, visiting professor, 1965-66; University College Dublin, faculty, 1972-73; Northwestern University, faculty, 2007; Beijing Foreign Studies University, faculty, 2007. Writer. **Publications:** Epiphany in the Modern Novel, 1971; Film and Literature, 1979; Joyce, the Artist Manque, and Indeterminacy: A Lecture and an Essay, 1989; James Joyce: A Literary Life, 1992; Virginia Woolf's Mrs. Dalloway, 1996; Tell Us About . . . A Memoir, 2011. EDITOR: Virginia Woolf's To the Lighthouse: A Selection of Critical Essays, 1970; Psychological Fiction, 1971; James Joyce's Dubliners and A Portrait of the Artist as a Young Man: Selection of Critical Essays, 1973; (with S.E. Gontarski and P. Astier) Samuel Beckett: Humanistic Perspectives, 1982; Critical Essays on Virginia Woolf, 1985; (co-ed.) James Joyce: The Centennial Symposium, 1987; (with S. Benstock) Coping with Joyce, 1989; Perspectives on Orson Welles, 1995; (co-ed.) Joyce in the Hibernian Metropolis, 1996; (with E.C.l. Jones) Twenty-First Joyce, 2004; (with A. Fogarty) Bloomsday 100, 2009. **Address:** Department of English, Ohio State University, 164 W 17th Ave., Columbus, OH 43210, U.S.A. **Online address:** beja.1@osu.edu

BEKER, Avi. Israeli (born Israel), b. 1951. **Genres:** Politics/Government, History. **Career:** World Jewish Congress, secretary general, 1983-2003, Israel Office, international director and head, 1985-2001, Israel Council on Foreign Relations, founder and head, Institute for Research, founder and head; Tel Aviv University, Harold Hartog School of Government, professor, 2004-07, lecturer, U.N.-Israel Institute, Jewish Public Project, head; College of Kiryat Ono, lecturer; Georgetown University, Department of Government, Goldman Visiting Israeli Professor; Jewish Diaspora Museum, board director; Yad Vashem, board director. Writer, political scientist and historian. **Publications:** Disarmament without Order: The Politics of Disarmament at the United Nations, 1985; The United Nations and Israel: From Recognition to Reprehension, 1988; (with Y. Ro'i) Jewish Culture and Identity in the Soviet Union, 1991; (ed.) Arms Control without Glasnost: Building Confidence in the Middle East, 1993; (with L. Weinbaum) Post-Zionism, Post-Judaism? Israel's Crisis of Continuity, 1995; Unmasking National Myths: Europeans Challenge Their History, 1997; (ed.) Jewish Communities of the World, 1998; Dispersion and Globalization: The Jews and the International Economy, 2001; (ed.) The Plunder of Jewish Property during the Holocaust: Confronting European History, 2001; UNRWA, Terror and the Refugee Conundrum: Perpetuating the Misery, 2003; Chosen: The History of an Idea, the Anatomy of an Obsession, 2008. **Address:** International Master's Program in Security and, Diplomacy, Tel Aviv University, Naftali Bldg., Ramat Aviv, Tel Aviv, 69978, Israel.

BELAND, Pierre. Canadian (born Canada), b. 1947. **Genres:** Novels, Animals/Pets. **Career:** Glacialis Productions, screenplay writer; St. Lawrence National Institute of Ecotoxicology, senior research scientist, 1987-, head scientist. **Publications:** Beluga: A Farewell to Whales, 1996; Trois Jours en Juin (Three days in June), 1998: Passagers Clandestines (Stowaways), 2005. **Address:** St. Lawrence National Institute of Ecotoxicology, 3974 Saint-Hubert St., Montreal, QC H2L 4A5, Canada. **Online address:** belandp@sympatico.ca

BELASEN, Amy. American (born United States), b. 1983?. **Genres:** Social Sciences, Young Adult Fiction. **Career:** Writer. **Publications:** (With J. Osborn) Jenny Green's Killer Junior Year, 2008. **Address:** c/o Alex Glass, Trident Media Group L.L.C., 41 Madison Ave., 36th Fl., New York, NY 10010, U.S.A. **Online address:** bendyamy@gmail.com

BELBIN, David. British (born England), b. 1958. **Genres:** Children's Fiction, Young Adult Fiction, Novels. **Career:** Teacher of English, drama and media studies, 1985-94; writer, 1994-; Nottingham Trent University, senior lecturer in creative writing, 2002-. **Publications:** FOR YOUNG ADULTS: The Foggiest, 1990; Shoot the Teacher, 1993 in US as Deadly Secrets, 1994; Final Cut, 1994; Avenging Angel, 1994; Break Point, 1995; Deadly Inheritance, 1996; Dark Journey, 1997; The David Belbin Collection: Three Degrees of Murder, 1997; Haunting Time (stories), 1998; Love Lessons, 1998; Dying for You, 1999; Festival, 2000; The Last Virgin, 2002; Denial, 2004; Shouting At The Stars, 2006; Stray, 2006; China Girl, 2009. FOR CHILDREN: Runaway Train, 1999; The Right Moment, 2000; Boy King, 2002. THE BEAT SERIES: Missing Person, 1995; Black and Blue, 1995; Smokescreen, 1996; Asking for It, 1996; Dead White Male, 1996; Losers, 1997; Sudden Death, 1997; Night Shift, 1998; Victims, 1998; Suspects, 1999; Fallen Angel, 2000. FOR ADULTS: The Pretender, 2008; Bone and Cane, 2011. EDITOR FOR ADULTS: City of Crime (stories), 1997; (with J. Lucas) Stanley Middleton at Eighty, 1999; Harris's Requiem, 2006. Works appear in anthologies. Contributor to periodicals. **Address:** School of Arts, Communication & Culture, Nottingham Trent University, Clifton Ln., Nottingham, NT NG11 8NS, England. **Online address:** david.belbin@ntu.ac.uk

BELGUM, Erik. American (born United States), b. 1960?. **Genres:** Young Adult Fiction. **Career:** VOYS, co-editor. Speech-language pathologist. **Publications:** PRINT FICTION: Star Fiction, 1996. Contributor to periodicals. **Address:** VOYS, PO Box 580547, Minneapolis, MN 55458-0547, U.S.A. **Online address:** belgu003@gold.tc.umn.edu

BELIEU, Erin. American (born United States), b. 1965?. **Genres:** Poetry. **Career:** AGNI, managing editor; Kenyon College, visiting instructor, 1998-; Ohio University, faculty; Washington University, faculty; Boston University, faculty; Florida State University, Department of English, associate professor, Creative Writing Program, director. **Publications:** Infanta (poetry), 1995; One Above & One Below: Poems, 2000; (ed. with S. Aizenberg and J. Countryman) The Extraordinary Tide: New Poetry by American Women, 2001; Black Box, 2006. Works appear in anthologies. Contributor to periodicals. **Address:** Copper Canyon Press, Bldg. 313, Fort Worden State Pk., PO Box 271, Port Townsend, WA 98368, U.S.A. **Online address:** ebelieu@fsu.edu

BELIN, Esther G. American (born United States), b. 1968. **Genres:** Poetry, Young Adult Fiction. **Career:** Writer. **Publications:** (Co-ed.) Both Sides: New Work from the Institute of American Indian Arts, 1993-1994, 1994; From the Belly of My Beauty: Poems 1999. **Address:** c/o Author Mail, University of Arizona Press, 1510 E University Blvd., 5th Fl., PO Box 210055, Tucson, AZ 85721-0055, U.S.A. **Online address:** bitterwater@hotmail.com

BELKAOUI, Ahmed R. (Ahmed Riahi-Belkaoui). American/Tunisian (born Tunisia), b. 1943. **Genres:** Money/Finance, Novels, Administration/Management, Politics/Government, Business/Trade/Industry, Economics. **Career:** University of Ottawa, assistant professor, associate professor, 1973-79, associate professor, 1980-81; University of Chicago, visiting associate professor, 1979-80; University of Illinois, professor of accounting, 1981-2004, CBA distinguished professor of accounting, 1996-2001, emeritus professor of accounting, 2004-; Honors College, fellow, 1982-84; University of Quebec, lecturer; Syracuse University, lecturer; Carleton University, lecturer; Sherbrooke University, lecturer; University of Venice, lecturer; University of Kuwait, lecturer; Irbid University, lecturer; U.S. Army Corps of Engineers, consultant; U.S. Office of Personnel Management, consultant; Institute for International Cooperation, consultant. Writer. **Publications:** The Conceptual Foundations of Management Accounting, 1980; Accounting Theory, 1981, 2nd ed., 1985; Cost Accounting: A Multidimensional Emphasis, 1983; Industrial Bond Ratings and the Rating Process, 1983; Socio-Economic Accounting, 1984; Théorie Comptable, 2nd ed., 1984; Public Policy and the Problems and Practices of Accounting, 1985; International Accounting: Issues and Solutions, 1985; The Learning Curve: A Management Accounting Tool, 1986; Handbook of Management Control Systems, 1986; Quantitative Models in Accounting: A Procedural Guide for Professionals, 1987; Inquiry and Accounting: Alternate Methods and Research Perspectives, 1987; The New Environment in International Accounting: Issues and Practices, 1988; The Coming Crisis in Accounting, 1989; Behavioral Accounting: The Research and Practical Issues, 1989; Human Information Processing in Accounting, 1989; Judgment in International Accounting: A Theory of Cognition, Cultures, Language, and Contracts, 1990; (with E. Pavlik) Determinants of Executive Compensation: Corporate Ownership, Performance, Size, and Diversification, 1991; Accounting in the Dual Economy, 1991; Multinational Management Accounting, 1991; Multinational Financial Accounting, 1991; Handbook of Cost Accounting Theory and Techniques, 1991; (with J. Monti-Belkaoui) Accounting for Dual Economic, 1991; Value Added Reporting: Lessons for the United States, 1992; The New Foundations of Management Accounting, 1992; (with E.L. Pavlik) Accounting for Corporate Reputation, 1992; Morality in Accounting, 1992; Quality and Control: An Accounting Perspective, 1993; Accounting in the Developing Countries, 1994; Organizational and Budgetary Slack, 1994; (with J. Monti-Belkaoui) Human Resource Valuation: A Guide to Strategies and Techniques, 1995; Cultural Shaping of Accounting, 1995; Linguistic Shaping of Accounting, 1995; Nature and Consequences of the Multidivisional Structure, 1995; (with J. Monti-Belkaoui) Fairness in Accounting, 1996; (with J. Monti-Belkaoui) Qaddafi: The Man and His Policies, 1996; Accounting, a Multiparadigmatic Science, 1996; (with J. Monti-Belkaoui) Sherazade and Her Two Lovers, 1996; Multinationality and Firm Performance, 1996; Performance Results in Value Added Reporting, 1996; Nature and Determinants of Disclosure Adequacy: An International Perspective, 1997; Research Perspectives in Accounting, 1997; (with J. Monti-Belkaoui) Nature, Estimation, and Management of Political Risk, 1998; Critical Financial Accounting Problems: Issues and Solutions, 1998; Financial Analysis and the Predictability of Important Economic Events, 1998; Long Term Leasing-Accounting, Evaluation, Consequences, 1998; Significant Current Issues in International Taxation, 1998; Capital Structure: Determination, Evaluation, and Accounting, 1999; Corporate Social Awareness and Financial Outcomes, 1999; Earnings Measurement, Determination, Management, and Usefulness: An Empirical Approach, 1999; Performance Results of Multinationality, 1999; Value Added Reporting and Research: State of the Art, 1999; Accounting and the Investment Opportunity Set, 2000; Advanced Management Accounting, 2000; Evaluating Capital Projects, 2001; Financial Statements: Present and Future Scope, 2001; Role of Corporate Reputation for Multinational Firms: Accounting, Organizational, and Market Considerations, 2001; Behavioral Management Accounting, 2002; International Accounting and Economic Development: The Interaction of Accounting, Economic and Social Indicators, 2002; International Financial and Managerial Accounting, 2002; Multinationality: Earnings, Efficiency, and Market Considerations, 2002; Accounting-by Principle or Design?, 2003. Works appear in anthologies. Contributor of articles to periodicals. **Address:** Department of Accounting, College of Business Administration, University of Illinois, MC 006, 601 S Morgan St., PO Box 802451, Chicago, IL 60607-7183, U.S.A. **Online address:** belkaoui@uic.edu

BELKIN, Aaron. American (born United States), b. 1966?. **Genres:** Novels, Politics/Government, Adult Non-fiction. **Career:** Stanford University, visiting lecturer, 1998; University of California, assistant professor, 1998-, associate professor, Center for the Study of Sexual Minorities in the Military (now Michael D. Palm Center), director and founder, 1999-; San Francisco State University, Department of Political Science, associate professor; City University of New York, associate professor of psychology. Writer. **Publications:** (Ed. with P.E. Tetlock) Counterfactual Thought Experiments in World Politics: Logical, Methodological, and Psychological Perspectives, 1996; (ed. with G. Bateman) Don't Ask, Don't Tell: Debating the Gay Ban in the Military, 2003; United We Stand?: Divide-and-Conquer Politics and the Logic of International Hostility, 2005; Bring Me Men, 2012. **Address:** Department of Political Science, San Francisco State University, HSS 132, 1600 Holloway Ave., San Francisco, CA 94132, U.S.A. **Online address:** belkin@sfsu.edu

BELKIN, Lisa. (Lisa Beth Belkin). American (born United States), b. 1960?. **Genres:** Medicine/Health, Regional/Urban Planning, Women's Studies And Issues, Autobiography/Memoirs, Human Relations/Parenting. **Career:** New York Times, reporter, 1982-87, national correspondent, 1987-91, health care reporter, 1991-93, contributing writer; Fresh Air, reporter; National Public Radio, reporter. Writer. **Publications:** First Do No Harm, 1993; Show Me a Hero: A Tale of Murder, Suicide, Race, and Redemption, 1999; Life's Work: Confessions of an Unbalanced Mom, 2002; (ed.) Tales from the Times: Real-Life Stories to Make you Think, Wonder, and Smile from the Pages of the New York Times, 2004. Contributor to periodicals. **Address:** The New York Times, 620 8th Ave., New York, NY 10018, U.S.A.

BELKIN, Lisa Beth. *See* **BELKIN, Lisa.**

BELKNAP, Robert L. American (born United States), b. 1929. **Genres:** Education, Literary Criticism And History, History, Reference. **Career:** Columbia University, instructor, 1957-60, assistant professor, 1960-63, associate professor, 1963-68, chairman freshman humanities, 1963, 1967-68, 1988-91, professor of Slavic languages, 1968-2001, associate dean student affairs, 1968-69, professor of Russian, 1970-2001, acting dean of college, 1976-77, chair of Slavic department, dean of students, dean of the college, director of university seminars, now professor emeritus of slavic languages, University Seminars, director, 2001; Russian Institute, director, 1977-80; Indiana University, Russian and East European Institute, associate professor, 1966-67; Russian Yale University, adjunct professor, 1967. Writer. **Publications:** The Structure of The Brothers Karamazov, 1967, trans. as The Structure of the Brothers Karamazov, 1990; (with R. Kuhns) Tradition and Innovation, General Education and the Reintegration of the University: A Columbia Report, 1977; (contrib.) Literature and Society in Imperial Russia, 1800-1914, 1978; (ed.) Russianness, In Memoriam Rufus Mathewson, 1984; The Genesis of the Brothers Karamazov: The Aesthetics, Ideology and Psychology of Text Making, 1990. **Address:** Department of Slavic Languages and Literatures, Columbia University, 400 W 117 St., 305 Faculty House, PO Box 2302, New York, NY 10027, U.S.A. **Online address:** rb12@columbia.edu

BELL, Albert A. American (born United States), b. 1945. **Genres:** Mystery/Crime/Suspense, Children's Fiction, History, Theology/Religion, Bibliography. **Career:** Hope College, professor of history and classics, 1978-, Department of History, chair, 1994-2004. Writer. **Publications:** An Historiographical Analysis of the De Excidio Hiero Solymitano of Pseudo-Hegesippus Microform, 1977; Daughter of Lazarus, 1988; (with J.B. Allis) Resources in Ancient Philosophy: An Annotated Bibliography of Scholarship in English, 1965-1989, 1991; A Guide to the New Testament World, 1994; Exploring the New Testament World, 1998; Kill Her Again, 2000; All Roads Lead to Murder: A Case from the Notebooks of Pliny the Younger, 2002; Death Goes Dutch, 2006; Perfect Game, Imperfect Lives: A Memoir Celebrating The 50th Anniversary of Don Larsen's Perfect Game, 2006; The Secret of the Lonely Grave, 2007; The Blood of Caesar: A Second Case from the Notebooks of Pliny the Younger, 2008; Corpus Conundrum: A Third Case From the Notebooks of Pliny the Younger, 2011. Contributor to periodicals. **Address:** Department of History, Hope College, 331 Lubbers Hall, 126 E 10th St., PO Box 9000, Holland, MI 49423, U.S.A. **Online address:** bell@hope.edu

BELL, Betty Louise. American (born United States), b. 1949. **Genres:** Novels, Science Fiction/Fantasy, Children's Fiction. **Career:** University of Michigan, Department of English, assistant professor, 1993-, associate professor, Native American Studies Program, director. Writer. **Publications:** Faces in the Moon, 1994; White Houses, forthcoming. **Address:** Department of English, University of Michigan, 3187 Angell Hall, 435 S State St., Ann Arbor, MI 48109-1003, U.S.A. **Online address:** blbell@umich.edu

BELL, Cathleen Davitt. American (born United States), b. 1971?. **Genres:** Science Fiction/Fantasy, Children's Fiction. **Career:** Writer and reporter. **Publications:** Slipping, 2008. **Address:** Brooklyn, NY , U.S.A. **Online address:** cbell1@nyc.rr.com

BELL, David Owen. American (born United States), b. 1949. **Genres:** Children's Non-fiction, Environmental Sciences/Ecology, Marine Sciences/Oceanography, Picture/Board Books, Sports/Fitness. **Career:** Photographer, 1977-; master mariner, 1981-; Environmental Fund for Maryland, president, 1996-. Writer. **Publications:** The Celestial Navigation Mystery: Solved, 1977; Dockmanship, 1992; Awesome Chesapeake: A Kid's Guide to the Bay, 1994; (ed.) Hands On! Feet Wet!, 1997; If Dads Can Eat, Dads Can Cook!, 1997; Chesapeake Bay Walk, 1998. **Address:** Tidewater Publishers, PO Box 456, Centreville, MD 21617, U.S.A.

BELL, David S. British (born England), b. 1947. **Genres:** Politics/Government, Social Sciences, Biography. **Career:** University of Sussex, lecturer, 1975-79; University of Leeds, professor of French government and politics, 1979-, director of teaching and learning. Writer. **Publications:** (Ed. with M. Kolinsky) Divided Loyalties: British Regional Assertion and European Integration, 1978; Eurocommunism and the Spanish Communist Party, 1979; Eurocommunism, 1979; (ed.) Labour into the Eighties, 1980; (ed.) Contemporary French Political Parties, 1982; (ed.) Democratic Politics in Spain: Spanish Politics after Franco, 1983; (ed. with E. Shaw) The Left in France: Towards the Socialist Republic, 1983; (with B. Criddle) The French Socialist Party: Resurgence and Victory, 1984, (with B. Criddle) 2nd ed. as The French Socialist Party: The Emergence of a Party of Government, 1988; (ed.) The Conservative Government, 1979-84: An Interim Report, 1985; (with B.W. Kim and C.B. Lee) Administrative Dynamics and Development: The Korean Experience, 1985; (ed. with D. Johnson and P. Morris) Biographical Dictionary of French Political Leaders since 1870, 1990; (ed. with R. East) Communist and Marxist Parties of the World, 2nd ed., 1990; (ed.) Western European Communists and the Collapse of Communism, 1993; (ed. with E. Shaw) Conflict and Cohesion in Western European Social Democratic Parties, 1994; (with B. Criddle) The French Communist Party in the Fifth Republic, 1994; (ed.) France, 1995; (with C. Lord) Transnational Parties in the European Union, 1998; Parties and Democracy in France: Parties under Presidentialism, 2000; Presidential Power in Fifth Republic France, 2000; French Politics Today, new ed., 2002; François Mitterrand: A Political Biography, 2005. Contributor to periodicals and journals. **Address:** School of Politics & International Studies, University of Leeds, SSB 13.29, Leeds, WY LS2 9JT, England. **Online address:** d.s.bell@leeds.ac.uk

BELL, Dean Phillip. American (born United States), b. 1967. **Genres:** Theology/Religion, History. **Career:** Spertus Institute of Jewish Studies, professor of history, associate dean, 1998-2001, dean and chief academic officer, 2001-; DePaul University, faculty; Northwestern University, faculty; University of Illinois, faculty; Hebrew Theological College, faculty; University of California, faculty. Writer. **Publications:** Sacred Communities: Jewish and Christian Identities in Fifteenth-Century Germany, 2001; (ed. with S.G. Burnett) Jews, Judaism, and the Reformation in Sixteenth-Century Germany, 2006; Jewish Identity in Early Modern Germany: Memory, Power and Community, 2007; Jews in the Early Modern World, 2008. **Address:** Spertus Institute of Jewish Studies, 610 S Michigan Ave., Chicago, IL 60605, U.S.A. **Online address:** dbell@spertus.edu

BELL, Hazel K(athleen). British (born England), b. 1935. **Genres:** Biography, History, Children's Fiction. **Career:** National Housewives Register, National Newsletter, editor, 1976-80; Society of Indexers, The Indexer, editor, 1978-95; Association of Learned and Professional Publishers, Learned Publishing, editor, 1984-96; Malaysian Rubber Research and Development Association, Rubber Developments, editor, 1990; Journal of the Angela Thirkell Society, editor, 1997-98; Barbara Pym Society, Green Leaves, editor, 1999-. **Publications:** Situation Books for Under-Sixes, 1970; Indexing Biographies and Other Stories of Human Lives, 1992, 3rd ed., 2004; (ed.) Indexers and Indexes in Fact and Fiction, 2001; (ed.) Kay Macaulife: Women Take the Stage, 2003; A Stage Mother's Story: We're Not All Mrs. Worthingtons!, 2006; (comp.) The Frederica Indexes, 2007; From Flock Beds to Professionalism: A History of Index-Makers, 2008. Contributor of articles to periodicals. **Address:** HKB Press, 139 The Ryde, Hatfield, HF AL9 5DP, England.

BELL, Hilari. American (born United States), b. 1958?. **Genres:** Novels. **Career:** Writer. **Publications:** NOVELS: Navohar, 2000; Songs of Power, 2000; A Matter of Profit, 2001; The Goblin Wood, 2003; Flame, 2003; The Wizard Test, 2004; Rise of a Hero, 2005. OTHERS: Fall of a Kingdom, 2005; Prophecy, 2006; Shield of Stars, 2007; Forging the Sword, 2007; Last Knight, 2007; Sword of Waters, 2008; Rogue's Home: A Knight and Rogue, 2008; Crown of Earth, 2009; Player's Ruse: A Knight and Rogue, 2010; Goblin Gate, 2010; Trickster's Girl, 2011; Traitor's Son, 2012. Contributor to periodicals. **Address:** c/o Author Mail, HarperCollins, 10 E 53rd St., New York, NY 10022, U.S.A. **Online address:** hilaribell@myspace.com

BELL, Hilary. Australian/British (born England), b. 1966. **Genres:** Music, Plays/Screenplays, Literary Criticism And History, Young Adult Fiction. **Career:** Playwright, librettist and screenwriter; University of the South, Tennessee Williams fellow, 2003-04. **Publications:** Mirror, Mirror, 1996; Wolf Lullaby, 1997; Der Zorn der Kobolde, 2006. **Address:** RGM Associates, PO Box 128, Surry Hills, NW 2010, Australia.

BELL, Ian Mackay. Scottish (born Scotland) **Genres:** Literary Criticism And History, Area Studies, Biography, Novels, Film. **Career:** The Scotsman, literary editor; The Daily Record, staff; The Times Literary Supplement, staff; The Herald, columnist. Journalist. **Publications:** The Dominican Republic, 1980; Dreams of Exile: Robert Louis Stevenson, A Biography, 1993; (ed. and intro.) The Complete Short Stories, 1994; Whistling in the Dark, 1995; (with N. Abrams and J. Udris) Studying Film, 2001, 2nd ed., 2011. **Address:** Henry Holt & Company Inc., 115 W 18th St., New York, NY 10011, U.S.A.

BELL, James Edward. American (born United States), b. 1941. **Genres:** Psychology, How-to Books, Social Sciences. **Career:** University of Minnesota, instructor, 1965-66; Hanover College, assistant professor of psychology, 1966-68; Elmira College, assistant professor of psychology, 1968-71; Howard Community College, associate professor of psychology, 1971-, professor of psychology. Writer. **Publications:** A Guide to Library Research in Psychology, 1971; Evaluating Psychological Information: Sharpening Your Critical Thinking Skills, 4th ed., 2005; (ed.) Ideas and Issues in Psychology, 9th ed., 2006. Contributor to journals. **Address:** Howard Community College, Rm. ST 160, 10901 Little Patuxent Pkwy., Columbia, MD 21044, U.S.A. **Online address:** jbell@howardcc.edu

BELL, Madison Smartt. American (born United States), b. 1957. **Genres:** Novels, Novellas/Short Stories, Biography, Social Sciences, Sports/Fitness, Travel/Exploration, Young Adult Fiction. **Career:** Unique Clothing Warehouse, security guard, 1979; Gomes-Lowe Associates, production assistant, 1979; Radiotelevisione Italiana, sound man, 1979; Franklin Library, picture research assistant, 1980, writer of reader's guides, 1980-83; Berkley Publishing Corp., manuscript reader and copywriter, 1981-83; Poetry Center, visiting writer, 1984-86; Goucher College, Department of English, assistant professor of English, 1984-86, writer-in-residence, creative writing program, director, 1988-, professor of English, Kratz Center for Creative Writing, director, 1999-2008; Iowa Writers Workshop, visiting writer, 1987-88; Johns Hopkins University, writing seminars, visiting associate professor, 1989-93; WebDelSol, writer-in-residence. **Publications:** History of the Owen Graduate School of Management, 1985; Zero DB and Short Stories, 1987; (co-author) George Garrett: An Interview, 1988; Barking Man and Other Stories, 1990; New Millennium Writings, Spring & Summer 1996, 1996; Narrative Design: A Writer's Guide to Structure, 1997; (intro.) The King of Babylon Shall Not Come Against You, 1998; Doctor Sleep, 2003; Lavoisier in the Year One: The Birth of a New Science in an Age of Revolution, 2005; Charm City: A Walk through Baltimore, 2007; Toussaint Louverture: A Biography, 2007. NOVELS: The Washington Square Ensemble, 1983; Waiting for the End of the World, 1985; Straight Cut, 1986; The Year of Silence, 1987; Soldier's Joy, 1989; Doctor Sleep, 1991; Save Me, Joe Louis, 1993; All Soul's Rising, 1994; Ten Indians, 1996; Master of the Crossroads, 2000; Anything Goes, 2002; Stone that the Builder Refused, 2004; Devil's Dream, 2009; The Color of Night: A Novel, 2011. **Address:** c/o Jane Gelfman, John Farquharson Ltd., 250 W 57th St., New York, NY 10107, U.S.A. **Online address:** mbell@goucher.edu

BELL, Marvin (Hartley). American (born United States), b. 1937. **Genres:** Poetry, Literary Criticism And History, Autobiography/Memoirs, Essays. **Career:** Statements Magazine, editor and publisher, 1959-64; North American Review, poetry editor, 1964-69; University of Iowa, visiting lecturer, 1965, assistant professor, 1967-69, associate professor, 1969-75, professor of English, 1975-85, Flannery O'Connor professor of letters, 1986-2005, now professor emeritus; Oregon State University, visiting lecturer, 1969; Iowa Review, poetry editor, 1969-71; Goddard College, visiting lecturer, 1972; American Poetry Review, columnist, 1975-78, 1990-92; University of Hawaii, visiting lecturer, 1981; University of Washington, visiting lecturer, 1982; University of Redlands, Lila Wallace-Reader's Digest writing fellow, 1991-93; St. Mary's College of California, Woodrow Wilson visiting fellow, 1994-95; Nebraska-Wesleyan University, Woodrow Wilson visiting fellow, 1996-97; Pacific University, Woodrow Wilson visiting fellow, 1996-97; Hampden-Sydney College, Woodrow Wilson visiting fellow, 1999; West Virginia Wesleyan College, Woodrow Wilson visiting fellow, 2000-01; Birmingham-Southern College, Woodrow Wilson visiting fellow, 2000-01; Illinois College, Woodrow Wilson visiting fellow, 2001-02; Bethany College, visiting fellow, 2003-04; Wichita State University, distinguished poet-in-residence, 2004; Pacific Lutheran University, Low-Residency MFA Program, faculty, 2004-05; Pacific University, Brief-Residency MFA Program, core faculty, 2004-; Portland State University, distinguished visiting professor, 2007; Morningside College, visiting fellow, 2008-09; Augustana College, visiting fellow, 2008-09; Hiram College, visiting fellow, 2008-09. **Publications:** (Ed.) Iowa Workshop Poets 1963, 1963; Two Poems, 1965; Things We Dreamt We Died For, 1966; Poems for Nathan and Saul, 1966; A Probable Volume of Dreams: Poems, 1969; The Escape into You: A Sequence, 1971, 2nd ed., 1995; Woo Havoc, 1971; Residue of Song: Poems, 1974; Stars Which See, Stars Which Do Not See, 1977; (contrib.) Heinecken, 1980; These Green-Going-to-Yellow: Poems, 1981; (with W. Stafford) Segues: A Correspondence in Poetry, 1983; Old Snow Just Melting: Essays and Interviews, 1983; Drawn by Stones, by Earth, by Things that Have Been in the Fire: Poems, 1984; New and Selected Poems, 1987; (with W. Stafford) Annie-Over: Poems, 1988; Iris of Creation (poetry), 1990; (intro.) Hat Dancer Blue, 1992; (intro.) Whose Woods These Are: A History of the Bread Loaf Writers' Conference, 1926-1990, 1993; The Book of the Dead Man (poetry), 1994; A Marvin Bell Reader: Selected Poetry and Prose, 1994; Ardor: The Book of the Dead Man, vol. II, 1997; Wednesday: Selected Poems, 1966-1997, 1998; Poetry for a Midsummer's Night: In The Spirit Of William Shakespeare's A Midsummer Night's Dream, 1998; Nightworks: Poems, 1962-2000, 2000; Rampant: Poems, 2004; Mars Being Red, 2007; (co-author) 7 Poets, 4 Days, 1 Book, 2009; A Primer about the Flag (for children), 2011; Whiteout: Dead Man Poems by Marvin Bell in Response to Photographs by Nathan Lyons, 2011; Vertigo: The Living Dead Man Poems, 2011. **Address:** Writers' Workshop, The University of Iowa, Dey House, Iowa City, IA 52242, U.S.A. **Online address:** marvin-bell@uiowa.edu

BELL, Mary Reeves. American (born United States), b. 1946. **Genres:** Children's Fiction, Novels, Sciences. **Career:** Romanian Christian Enterprises (relief organization), executive director. Writer. **Publications:** PASSPORT TO DANGER SERIES: The Secret of the Mezuzah, 1995, rev. ed., 1999; The Sagebrush Rebellion, 1999; Checkmate in the Carpathians, 2000. OTHER: Oceans (Water Worlds), 2001. Contributor of articles to periodicals. **Address:** Romanian Christian Enterprises, 21058 Unison Rd., Middleburg, VA 20117-3806, U.S.A. **Online address:** snarkhunt2@aol.com

BELL, Nancy. American (born United States), b. 1932. **Genres:** Mystery/Crime/Suspense, Novels. **Career:** Novelist. **Publications:** NOVELS: Biggie and the Poisoned Politician, 1996; Biggie and the Mangled Mortician, 1997; Biggie and the Fricasseed Fat Man, 1998; Biggie and the Meddlesome Mailman, 1999; Biggie and the Quincy Ghost, 2001; Biggie and the Devil Diet, 2002; Restored to Death, 2003; Death Splits a Hair: A Judge Jackson Crain Mystery, 2005; Paint the Town Dead: A Judge Jackson Crain Mystery, 2008. Contributor to journals. **Address:** St. Martin's Press, 175 5th Ave., Rm. 1715, New York, NY 10010, U.S.A.

BELL, Richard H. American (born United States), b. 1938. **Genres:** Philosophy, Theology/Religion, Young Adult Non-fiction. **Career:** Yale University, Berkeley College, dean, 1966-69, lecturer in religious studies, 1967-69; College of Wooster, Department of Philosophy, assistant professor, 1969-75, associate professor, 1975-81, professor, 1981-84, Frank Halliday Ferris professor of philosophy, 1984-, now Frank Halliday Ferris professor emeritus of philosophy. Writer. **Publications:** (Ed. with R.E. Hustwit and intro.) Essays on Kierkegaard and Wittgenstein: On Understanding the Self, 1978; Sensing the Spirit, 1984; (ed.) Spirituality and the Christian Life Series, 1984; (ed.) The Grammar of the Heart: New Essays in Moral Philosophy and Theology, 1988; (ed. and intro.) Simone Weil's Philosophy of Culture: Readings Toward a Divine Humanity, 1993; Provoked to Jealousy: The Origin and Purpose of the Jealousy Motif in Romans 9-11, 1994; (ed. with B.L. Battin and intro.) Seeds of the Spirit: Wisdom of the Twentieth Century, 1995; Simone Weil: The Way of Justice as Compassion, 1998; Understanding African Philosophy: A Cross-Cultural Approach to Classical and Contemporary Issues, 2002; Rethinking Justice: Restoring Our Humanity, 2007. Contributor to periodicals. **Address:** Department of Philosophy, College of Wooster, Scovel Hall, 944 College Mall, Wooster, OH 44691-2363, U.S.A. **Online address:** rbell@wooster.edu

BELL, Robin. Scottish/British/American (born United States), b. 1945. **Genres:** Plays/Screenplays, Poetry, Military/Defense/Arms Control. **Career:** Poetry Association of Scotland, secretary, 1983-. Writer. **Publications:** POETRY: The Invisible Mirror, 1965; Culdee, Culdee, 1966; Sawing Logs, 1980; Strathinver: A Portrait Album, 1945-1953, 1984; Radio Poems, 1989; Scanning the Forth Bridge, 1994. EDITOR: Collected Poems of James Graham, Marquis of Montrose, 1970; Guide Book Series to Scottish Ancient Monuments, 1978; Best of Scottish Poetry: An Anthology of Contemporary Scottish Verse, 1989; (and trans.) Bittersweet within My Heart: The Love Poems of Mary, Queen of Scots, 1993; Civil Warrior: The Extraordinary Life and Complete Poetical Works of James Graham, First Marquis of Montrose, Warrior and Poet, 1612-1650, 2002. **Address:** The Orchard, Muirton, Achterarder, Perthshire, PH3 1ND, Scotland.

BELL, Susan. American (born United States), b. 1958?. **Genres:** Politics/Government, Art/Art History, Language/Linguistics, Reference, Essays. **Career:** Random House, editor; Conjunctions (magazine), editor; New School University, instructor; Tin House Writers Workshop, instructor. Editor and writer. **Publications:** (With J. West) Dare to Hope: Saving American Democracy (essays), 2005; The Artful Edit: On the Practice of Editing Yourself, 2007. **Address:** c/o Sarah Burnes, The Gernet Company Literary Agency, 136 E 57th St., New York, NY 10022, U.S.A. **Online address:** susanbell@artfuledit.com

BELL, Suzanne. American (born United States) **Genres:** Chemistry, Sciences. **Career:** The Facts on File Dictionary of Forensic Science, 2004, Rev. ed., 2008; Encyclopedia of Forensic Science, 2004; Forensic Chemistry, 2006; Crime And Circumstance: Investigating The History Of Forensic Science, 2008; Fakes And Forgeries, 2009; Drugs, Poisons, And Chemistry, 2009; (with K. Morris) Introduction To Microscopy, 2010; Dictionary of Forensic Science, 2012; Forensic Chemistry, 2013. **Publications:** The Facts on File Dictionary of Forensic Science, 2004, Rev. ed., 2008; Encyclopedia of Forensic Science, 2004; Forensic Chemistry, 2006; Crime And Circumstance: Investigating The History Of Forensic Science, 2008; Fakes And Forgeries, 2009; Drugs, Poisons, And Chemistry, 2009; (with K. Morris) Introduction To Microscopy, 2010. **Address:** C. Eugene Bennett Department of Chemistry, West Virginia University, 306 Oglebay Hall, Morgantown, WV 26506, U.S.A. **Online address:** suzanne.bell@mail.wvu.edu

BELL, Thornton. *See* **FANTHORPE, R(obert) Lionel.**

BELL, William. Canadian (born Canada), b. 1945. **Genres:** Young Adult Fiction, Romance/Historical, Humor/Satire, Novels. **Career:** High school English teacher, 1970-2000; Innisdale Secondary School, Department of English, head; Orillia District Collegiate and Vocational Institute, Department of English, head, 1970-2000; Harbin University of Science and Technology, English instructor, 1982-83; Foreign Affairs College of China, English instructor, 1985-86; University of British Columbia, instructor. Writer. **Publications:** FOR YOUNG ADULTS: Crabbe in US as Crabbe's Journey, 1986; Metal Head, 1987; Absolutely Invincible, 1987; Absolutely Invincible, 1988; Five Days of the Ghost, 1989; Death Wind, 1989; Forbidden City, 1990; No Signature, 1992; Speak to the Earth, 1994; Zack, 1998; Stones, 2001; Alma, 2003; (with T. Ye) Throwaway Daughter, 2003; Just Some Stuff I Wrote, 2005; The Blue Helmet, 2006; Only in the Movies, 2010; Fanatics, 2011. FOR CHILDREN: The Golden Disk, 1995; River My Friend, 1996. Contributor to periodicals. **Address:** Doubleday Canada Ltd., 1 Toronto St., Ste. 300, Toronto, ON M5C 2V6, Canada. **Online address:** greenleaf@orillia.org

BELLAMY, Alex J. Australian (born Australia), b. 1975. **Genres:** History, Military/Defense/Arms Control, Adult Non-fiction. **Career:** King's College London, lecturer in defense studies; University of Queensland, School of Political Science and International Studies, senior lecturer in peace and conflict studies, professor of international relations, 2002-, honorary professor, Asia-Pacific Centre for the Responsibility to Protect, executive director, 2008-; Griffith University, GAI, research staff, professor. Writer. **Publications:** NONFICTION: Kosovo and International Society, 2002; The Formation of Croatian National Identity: A Centuries-Old Dream?, 2003; (with P. Williams and S. Griffin) Understanding Peacekeeping, 2004, 2nd ed., 2010; Security Communities and Their Neighbours: Regional Fortresses or Global Integrators?, 2004; (ed.) International Society and Its Critics, 2005; (ed. with P. Williams) Peace Operations and Global Order, 2005; Just Wars: From Cicero to Iraq, 2006; (ed. with R. Bleiker, S.E. Davies and R. Devetak) Security and the War on Terror, 2007; (with M. Beeson) Securing Southeast Asia: The Politics of Security Sector Reform, 2007; Fighting Terror: Ethical Dilemmas, 2008; (ed.) War, 2008; Responsibility to Protect: The Global Effort to End Mass Atrocities, 2009. OTHERS: (ed. with K. Booth) The Kosovo Tragedy, 2000; (ed. with S.E. Davies and L. Glanville) The Responsibility to Protect and International Law, 2011; Global Politics and the Responsibilty to Protect, 2011; UN Peacekeeping in Bosnia, 2013; Towards Human Security, forthcoming; Massacres and Morality, forthcoming; (with S.E. Davies and S. McLoughlin) Preventing Genocide and Mass Atrocities, forthcoming. Contributor to journals. **Address:** Griffith University, N50 1.27, 170 Kessels Rd., GAI, Nathan Campus, Nathan, QL 4111, Australia. **Online address:** a.bellamy@griffith.edu.au

BELLAMY, Christopher (David). British (born England), b. 1955. **Genres:** History, Military/Defense/Arms Control, Humanities. **Career:** British Ministry of Defence, 1978-87; Independent, defense correspondent, 1990-97, analyst, 2003; Institute of Linguists, associate, 1981; Cranfield University, Defence College of Management and Technology, faculty, 1997-2000, professor of military science and doctrine, 2007-, Security and Resilience Group, head, 2007-, Security Studies Institute, director, academic leader. Writer. **Publications:** Red God of War, 1986; The Future of Land Warfare, 1987; The Times Atlas of the Second World War, 1989; The Evolution of Modern Land Warfare, 1990; Expert Witness, 1993; Knights in White Armour, 1996; (ed.) Oxford Companion to Military History, 2001; Absolute War: Soviet Russia in the Second World War, 200; The Gurkhas, 2011. Contributor to books. **Address:** Peters, Fraser & Dunlop, 34-43 Russell St., London, GL WC2B 5HA, England. **Online address:** c.bellamy@independent.co.uk

BELLAMY, David James. British (born England), b. 1933. **Genres:** Botany, Natural History. **Career:** University of Durham, senior lecturer in botany, 1960-80, honorary professor of adult and continuing education, 1980-82; WATCH, president, 1982-91; Youth Hostels Association, president, 1983; University of Nottingham, special professor, 1987-; Massey University, visiting professor of natural heritage studies, 1988-89; David Bellamy Associates, director, 1988-; Population Concern, president, 1989-; National Association for Environmental Education, president, 1989-; Association of Master Thatchers, president, 1991-; P-E Intl., associate director, 1993-; O.B.E., 1994; Conservation Foundation, founding director; Institute of Biology, fellow. Writer. **Publications:** Bellamy on Botany, 1972; Peatlands, 1974; World of Plants, 1975; Life Giving Sea, 1975; Green Worlds: Plants and Forest Life, 1976; (with C. Smallman) Bellamy's Europe, 1976; Botanic Action with David Bellamy, 1978; Half of Paradise, 1979; Botanic Man: A Journey through Evolution, 1979; Forces of Life: The Botanic Man, 1979; The Great Seasons, 1981; Discovering the Countryside with David Bellamy, vols. IV, 1983; Bellamy's New World: A Botanical History of America, 1983; The Mouse Book, 1983; The Queen's Hidden Garden, 1984; (with B. Quayle) Turning the Tide: Exploring the Options for Life on Earth, 1986; The Vanishing Bogs of Ireland, 1986; Wild Boglands: Bellamy's Ireland, 1987; Forest, 1988; River, 1988; Rock Pool, 1988; Roadside, 1988; Bellamy's Changing Countryside, vols. IV, 1988; (with B. Springett and P. Hayden) Moa's Ark: The Voyage of New Zealand, 1990; Wilderness Britain, 1990; Britain's Last Wilderness Wetlands, 1990; How Green Are You?, 1991; Tomorrow's Earth: A Squeaky-Green Guide, 1992; (with A. Pfister) World Medicine: Plants, Patients, and People, 1992; (intro.) Trees: A Celebration in Photographs, 1993; Blooming Bellamy, 1993; Trees of the World, 1994; Por You and the Potoroo's Loo, 1997. **Address:** The Conservation Foundation, 1 Kensington Gore, London, GL SW7 2AR, England.

BELLAMY, Richard (Paul). British/Scottish (born Scotland), b. 1957. **Genres:** History, Philosophy, Politics/Government. **Career:** University of Pisa, lecturer in history, 1981-82; Oxford University, Nuffield College, postdoctoral research fellow, 1983-86; Christ Church, lecturer in political studies, 1984-86; Cambridge University, Jesus College, Trinity College, fellow and lecturer in history, 1986-88; University of Edinburgh, lecturer in politics, 1988-92; University of East Anglia, professor of politics, 1992-96; University of Reading, professor of politics and international relations, 1996-2002; University of Essex, professor of government, 2002-05; Critical Review of International Social and Political Philosophy, co-editor, 2002-; European Consortium for Political Research, academic director, 2002-06; University College London, Social & Historical Sciences, faculty, School of Public Policy, director, 2005-10, professor of political science, 2005-, director of European Institute, 2010-, founding head and director. Writer. **Publications:** Modern Italian Social Theory: Ideology and Politics from Pareto to the Present, 1987; (co-author) La Filosofia politica, oggi, 1990; Liberalism and Modern Society: An Historical Argument, 1992; (with D. Schecter) Gramsci and the Italian State, 1993; Liberalism and Pluralism: Towards a Politics of Compromise, 1999; Political Constitutionalism: A Republican Defence of the Constitutionality of Democracy, 2007; Citizenship: A Very Short Introduction, 2008. EDITOR: (and intro.) Future of democracy, 1987; (and intro.) Which socialism?, 1987; Liberalism and Recent Legal and Social Philosophy, 1989; Victorian Liberalism: Nineteenth Century Political Thought and Practice, 1990; Theories and Concepts of Politics: An Introduction, 1993; Theories and Concepts of Politics, 1993; Antonio Gramsci, Pre-Prison Writings, 1994; On Crimes and Punishments and Other Writings, 1995; (with V. Bufacchi and D. Castiglione) Democracy and Constitutional Culture in the Union of Europe, 1995; Constitutionalism, Democracy and Sovereignty: American and European Perspectives, 1996; (with D. Castiglione) Constitiutionalism in Transformation: European and Theoretical Perspectives, 1996; (with A. Ross) A Textual Introduction to Social and Political Theory, 1996; (with D. Castiglione) Constitutionalism in Transformation: European and Theoretical Perspective, 1996; (with M. Hollis) Pluralism and Liberal Neutrality, 1999; Rethinking Liberalism, 2000; (with A. Warleigh) Citizenship and Governance in the European Union, 2001; (with A. Mason) Political Concepts, 2003; (with T. Ball) The Cambridge History of Twentieth Century Political Thought, 2003; (with D. Castiglione and E. Santoro) Lineages of European Citizenship: Rights, Belonging and Participation in Eleven Nation States, Palgrave, 2004; The Rule of Law and the Separation of Powers, 2005; Constitutionalism and Democracy, 2006; (with D. Castiglione and J. Shaw) Making European Citizens: Civic Inclusion in a Transnational Context, 2006; (with A. palumbo) Political Accountability, 2010; (with A. Palumbo) Citizenship, 2010; (ed. with A. Palumbo) Public Ethics, 2010; (ed. with A. Palumbo) From Government to Governance, 2010. Contributor of articles to journals. **Address:** Department of Political Science, School of Public Policy, University College London, Rm. 4.01, 29/30 Tavistock Sq., London, GL WC1H 9QU, England. **Online address:** r.bellamy@ucl.ac.uk

BELLAVIA, David Gregory. American (born United States), b. 1975. **Genres:** Novels. **Career:** Writer. **Publications:** (with J. Bruning) House to House: An Epic Memoir of War, 2007. **Address:** Vets for Freedom, 1200 Eton Ct. NW, Ste. 300, Washington, DC 20007, U.S.A. **Online address:** david@davidbellavia.com

BELLER, Susan Provost. American (born United States), b. 1949. **Genres:** Genealogy/Heraldry, History. **Career:** Fairfax City Adult Education, genealogy instructor, 1980-82; Christ the King School, librarian, 1982-86; Bristol Elementary School, librarian, 1986-93; University of Vermont, instructor, 1993-. Writer, 1993-. **Publications:** Roots for Kids: A Genealogy Guide for Young People, 1989; Cadets at War: The True Story of Teenage Heroism at the Battle of New Market, 1991; Woman of Independence: The Life of Abigail Adams, 1992; Medical Practices in the Civil War, 1992; Mosby and His Rangers: Adventures of the Gray Ghost, 1992; To Hold This Ground: A Desperate Battle at Gettysburg, 1995; Never Were Men So Brave: The Irish Brigade during the Civil War, 1998; Confederate Ladies, 1999; Billy Yank and Johnny Reb: Soldiering in the Civil War, 2000; Revolutionary War: Letters from the Home Front, 2001; American Voices from the Revolutionary War, 2002; American Voices from the Civil War, 2002; Yankee Doodle and the Redcoats! Soldiering in the Revolutionary War, 2003; The History Puzzle: How We Know What We Know About the Past, 2006; John Paul II and Benedict XVI: Keepers of the Faith, 2006; Roots for Kids: A Genealogy Guide for Young People, 2007; Billy Yank and Johnny Reb: Soldiering in the Civil War, 2008; Yankee Doodle and the Redcoats: Soldiering in the Revolutionary War, 2008; The Doughboys Over There: Soldiering in World War I, 2008; Battling in the Pacific: Soldiering in World War II, 2008; The Siege of the Alamo: Soldiering in the Texas Revolution, 2008; Roman Legions on the March: Soldiering in the Ancient Roman Army, 2008; The Aftermath of the Mexican Revolution, 2009; Four Generations, One Story, 2010. **Address:** 187 Stone Wall Ln., Charlotte, VT 05445, U.S.A. **Online address:** kidsbks@msn.com

BELLER, Thomas. *See* **BELLER, Tom.**

BELLER, Tom. (Thomas Beller). American (born United States), b. 1965. **Genres:** Novellas/Short Stories, Sex, Romance/Historical. **Career:** Open City (magazine), co-founder and co-editor; Cambodia Daily, contributing editor; Travel+ Leisure, contributing editor; Tulane University, faculty; The New Yorker, staff writer; The Cambodia Daily newspaper, staff. **Publications:** Seduction Theory: Stories, 1995 as Seduction Theory, 1996; (ed.) Personals: Dreams and Nightmares from the Lives of 20 Young Writers, 1998; The Sleep-Over Artist, 2000; (ed. with K. Kotzen) With Love and Squalor: 14 Writers Respond to the Work of J.D. Salinger, 2001; (co-author) Cabinet 9: Childhood, 2004; How to Be a Man: Scenes from a Protracted Boyhood, 2005. Contributor to periodicals. **Address:** Mary Evans Inc., 242 E 5th St., New York, NY 10003, U.S.A. **Online address:** tom@opencity.org

BELLESILES, Michael A. American (born United States) **Genres:** History, Documentaries/Reportage. **Career:** University of California, staff; Emory University, associate professor, through 2002. Educator, historian and writer. **Publications:** Revolutionary Outlaws: Ethan Allan and the Struggle for Independence in the Early American Frontier, 1993; (ed.) Lethal Imagination: Violence and Brutality in History, 1999; (contrib.) The Second Amendment in Law and History: Historians and Constitutional Scholars on the Right to Bear Arms, 2000; Arming America: The Origins of a National Gun Culture, 2000, rev. ed., 2003; (ed. with C. Waldrep) Documenting American Violence: A Sourcebook, 2006; 1877: America's Year of Living Violently, 2010. Contributor to periodicals. **Address:** c/o Author Mail, Soft Skull Press, 71 Bond St., Brooklyn, NY 11217, U.S.A.

BELLETTO, René. French (born France), b. 1945. **Genres:** Novels. **Career:** Lyon-Poche, film critic, 1976-82. Writer, musician and sculptor. **Publications:** L'homme de main: et autres nouvelles, 1974; La vie rêvée: et autres nouvelles, 1974; Le temps mort: récits fantastiques, 1974; Les traîtres mots, ou, Sept aventures de Thomas Nylkan: récit, 1976; Livre d'histoire..., 1978; Film noir, 1980; Le revenant, 1981; Sur la terre comme au ciel, 1982; Loin de Lyon: XLVII sonnets, 1986; L'enfer, 1986; La machine: roman, 1990; Eclipse, 1990; Remarques, 1991; Les grandes espérances de Charles Dickens (criticism), 1994; Régis Mille l'éventreur, roman, 1996; Ville de la peur: roman, 1997; Histoire d'une vie: Remarques II (reprenant nombres des premières Remarques), 1998; Créature: roman, 2000; Mourir, 2002; Petit traité de la vie et de la mort: Remarques III, 2003; Coda, 2005; Revenant, 2006; Hors la loi: roman, 2010; Dying, 2010; Somme toute, 2011. **Address:** c/o Author Mail, Editions P.O.L., 33, rue Saint-Andre-des-Arts, Paris, 75006, France.

BELLI, Gioconda. American (born United States), b. 1948. **Genres:** Poetry, Novels, Children's Fiction, Young Adult Fiction. **Career:** Alfa Omega Advertising Co., account executive, 1973-75; Garnier Advertising, creative director, 1976-78; Sandinista National Liberation Front, diplomat, 1978-79, international press liaison, 1982-83, executive secretary and spokesperson, 1983-84; Ministry of Economic Planning, director of communications and public relations, 1979-82; Nicaragua Writer's Union, foreign-affairs secretary, 1983-88; Sistema Nacional de Publicidad, managing director, 1984-86; Writer, 1986-. **Publications:** POETRY IN ENGLISH TRANSLATION: De la costilla de Eva, 1987; Nicaragua under Fire, 1989. OTHER POETRY: Sobre la grama, 1972; Línea de fuego, 1978; Truenos y arco iris, 1982; Amor insurrecto, 1984; (co-author) Nicaragua in Reconstruction and At War, 1985; El ojo de la mujer, 1991; Sortilegio contra el frio, 1992. NOVELS IN ENGLISH TRANSLATION: La mujer habitada, 1988. OTHERS: Tochter des Vulkans: Roman, 1990; Sofía de las presagios, 1990; The Workshop of the Butterflies (for children), 1994; Inhabited Woman, 1994; Waslala: memorial del futuro, 1996; El Taller de las mariposas, 1996; Apogeo, 1998; érase una vez una mujer, 1998; El País bajo mi piel: memorias de amor y guerra, 2001; Mi íntima multitud, 2002; El Esto es amor: poesía erótica reunida, 1970-2005, 2005; El Pergamino de la seducción: Juana la Loca: qué oculta su historia?, 2005; Fuego soy, apartado y espada puesta lejos, 2007; El Infinito en la palma de la mano, 2008. Works appear in anthologies. Contributor to periodicals. **Address:** 703 12th St., Santa Monica, CA 90402-2911, U.S.A. **Online address:** gioconda@giocondabelli.com

BELLIOTTI, Raymond A(ngelo). American (born United States), b. 1948. **Genres:** Law, Philosophy, Social Sciences. **Career:** Miami-Dade Community College South, adjunct instructor, 1976-78; Florida International University, adjunct assistant professor, 1977-78; Virginia Commonwealth University, assistant professor of philosophy, 1978-79; Harvard University, teaching fellow, 1980-82; Phillips, Nizer, Benjamin, Krim and Ballon, associate, 1981; Barrett, Smith, Schapiro, Simon and Armstrong, attorney, 1982-84; Brooklyn Law School, adjunct associate professor, 1983-84; State University of New York College, assistant professor, 1984-86, associate professor, 1986-91, professor of philosophy, 1991-, head of faculty council, 1989-90, distinguished teaching professor of philosophy, vice president for academics. Writer. **Publications:** Justifying Law: The Debate over Foundations, Goals, and Methods, 1992; Good Sex: Perspectives on Sexual Ethics, 1993; Seeking Identity: Individualism versus Community in an Ethnic Context, 1995; Stalking Nietzsche, 1998; What Is the Meaning of Human Life?, 2001; Happiness Is Overrated, 2004; Philosophy of Baseball: How to Play the Game of Life, 2006; Watching Baseball, Seeing Philosophy: The Great Thinkers at Play on the Diamond, 2008; Roman Philosophy and the Good Life, 2009; Niccolò Machiavelli: The Laughing Lion and the Strutting Fox, 2009; Dante's Deadly Sins, 2011; Posthumous Harm, 2012. Contributor to journals. **Address:** Department of Philosophy, State University of New York College, 289 Fenton Hall, 280 Central Ave., Fredonia, NY 14063, U.S.A. **Online address:** raymond.belliott@fredonia.edu

BELLM, Dan. American (born United States), b. 1952. **Genres:** Poetry, Education, Translations. **Career:** Writer and translator. **Publications:** (With M.L. Carson) On the Safe Side: Preventing Child Abuse in Residential Care, 1989; Story in a Bottle (poetry), 1991; (ed.) Family Day Care Handbook, 1993; (trans.) A. Blanco, Angel's Kite/Estrella de Angel, 1994; (with M. Whitebook and P. Hnatiuk) The Early Childhood Mentoring Curriculum: A Handbook for Mentors, 1997; Making Work Pay in the Child Care Industry: Promising Practices for Improving Compensation, 1997; (with M. Whitebook) Taking on Turnover: An Action Guide for Child Care Center Teachers and Directors, 1999; (with M. Fisk and F. Hamer) Terrain (poetry), 1998; One Hand on the Wheel (poetry), 1999; Buried Treasure: Poems, 1999; (with P. Haack) Working for Quality Child Care: Good Child Care Jobs Equals Good Care for Children, 2001; (trans.) L.G. Garcia, Legend of the Wandering King, 2005; Practice: A Book of Midrash, 2008. Contributor of articles to books. **Address:** Sixteen Rivers Press, PO Box 640663, San Francisco, CA 94164-0663, U.S.A. **Online address:** dan@danbellm.com

BELLOLI, Andrea P. A. American (born United States), b. 1947. **Genres:** Art/Art History, History, Translations. **Career:** Detroit Institute of Arts, managing editor and editor-in-chief; Los Angeles County Museum of Art, managing editor and editor-in-chief, 1978-92; Macmillan Publishers, editor, 1992-93; Prestel-Verlag, editorial director and consulting editor, 1993-. **Publications:** Oriental Ceramics from the Collection of Justice and Mrs. G. Mennan Williams, 1980; (ed.) A Day in the Country: Impressionism and the French Landscape, 1984; (with E. Savage-Smith) Islamicate Celestial Globes, 1984; (ed. with S.K. Morgan) The J. Paul Getty Museum Handbook of the Collections, 1986; (ed.) Artists of Michigan from the Nineteenth Century: A Sesquicentennial Exhibition Commemorating Michigan Statehood, 1837-1987, 1987; Guide to the Museum and Its Gardens, 1990; (with K. Godard) Make Your Own Museum: An Activity Package for Children, 1994; (ed. and trans.) D. Kutschbach, The Blue Rider: The Yellow Cow Sees the World in Blue, 1996; (ed.) Radix-Matrix: Architecture and Writings, 1997; Exploring World Art, 1999. **Address:** 5 Hosford House, 48 Devonshire Rd., London, GL SE23 3SU, England.

BELLOS, Alex. British (born England), b. 1969. **Genres:** Autobiography/Memoirs. **Career:** Guardian, reporter, 1994-98, South American correspondent in Rio de Janeiro, 1998-2003; Observer, reporter, 1994-98, South American correspondent in Rio de Janeiro, 1998-2003. **Publications:** Futebol: The Brazilian Way of Life, 2002; (co-author) Pelé: The Autobiography, 2006; Here's Looking at Euclid: A Surprising Excursion through the Astonishing World of Math in UK as Alex's Adventures in Numberland: Dispatches from the Wonderful World of Mathematics, 2010. **Address:** London, GL , England. **Online address:** alexanderbellos@gmail.com

BELLOS, David. British (born England), b. 1945?. **Genres:** Literary Criticism And History, Translations, Language/Linguistics. **Career:** University of Edinburgh, lecturer in French, 1972-82; University of Southampton, professor of French, 1982-85; University of Manchester, professor of French, 1986-96; Princeton University, professor of French and comparative literature, 1997-, Program in Translation and Intercultural Communication, director, 2007-. Writer. **Publications:** TRANSLATOR: (and ed.) G. Haupt, J-J Marie, Makers of the Russian Revolution, 1974; Leo Spitzer, Essays on Seventeenth-Century French Literature, 1983; Georges Perec, Winter Journey, 1985; Perec, Life A User's Manual, 1987; W or The Memory of Childhood, 1988; Things: A Story of the Sixties, 1990; 53 days: A Novel, 1992; Ismail Kadare, The Pyramid, 1995; The File on H, 1996; Georges Ifrah, The Universal History of Numbers: From Prehistory to the Invention of the Computer, 2000; Kadare, Spring Flowers, Spring Frost: A Novel, 2002; Fred Vargas, Have Mercy On Us All, 2003; Kadare, The Successor: A Novel, 2005; Agamemnon's Daughter: A Novella and Stories, 2006; The Siege, 2008; Helene Berr, Journal, 2008; Thoughts of Sorts, 2009; Romain Gary, Hocus Bogus, 2010; Is that a Fish in Your Ear?, 2011; Art and Craft of Approaching Your Head of Department to Submit a Request for a Raise, 2011. MONOGRAPHS: Balzac Criticism in France, 1850-1900: The Making of a Reputation, 1976; Honore de Balzac, La Cousine Bette, 1980; Balzac, Old Goriot, 1987; Georges Perec: A Life in Words, 1993; Jacques Tati: His Life and Art (biography), 1999. Romain Gary; A Tall Story, 2010. OTHERS: (co-ed.) Myth and Legend in French Literature: Essays in Honour of A.J. Steele, 1982; (ed.and intro.) Kadare Chronicle in Stone: A Novel, 2007; Le poisson et le bananier, 2012. **Address:** c/o Claire Paterson, Janklow & Nesbit Literary Agency, 33 Drayson Mews, London, GL W8 4LY, England. **Online address:** dbellos@princeton.edu

BELLOTTI, Laura Golden. American (born United States), b. 1947. **Genres:** Human Relations/Parenting, Psychology, Ghost Writer, Social Sciences, Sociology, Novellas/Short Stories. **Career:** Jeremy P. Tarcher Inc., developmental book editor, 1980-85; freelance writer, 1985-. **Publications:** (Ed.) Women Who Love Too Much: When You Keep Wishing and Hoping He'll Change, 1985; (ed.) Letters from Women Who Love Too Much: A Closer Look at Realtionship Addiction and Recovery, 1988; (with L. Levin) You Can't Hurry Love: An Intimate Look at First Marriages After 40, 1992; (with L. Levin) Creative Weddings: An Up-To-Date Guide For Making Your Wedding as Unique as You Are, 1994; (with A. Nogales) Dr. Ana Nogales's Book of Love, Sex, and Relationships: A Guide For Latino Couples, 1998; (with A. Nogales) Latina Power!: Using 7 Strengths You Already Have To Create The Success You Deserve, 2003; (with J. Friedman) Emotionally Healthy Twins, 2008; (with A. Nogales) Parents Who Cheat: How Children and Adults Are Affected When Their Parents Are Unfaithful, 2009. **Address:** Health Communications Inc., 3201 SW 15th St., Deerfield Beach, FL 33442, U.S.A. **Online address:** lgbellotti@hotmail.com

BELLOW, Adam. American (born United States), b. 1957?. **Genres:** History, Social Sciences, Sociology. **Career:** Free Press, editorial director; Doubleday Press, editor-at-large, 1997-. **Publications:** In Praise of Nepotism: A Natural History, 2003. Contributor to periodicals. **Address:** Doubleday, A Division of Random House Inc., 1745 Broadway, New York, NY 10019, U.S.A.

BELLOWS, Barbara L(awrence). (Barbara Bellows Rockefeller). American (born United States), b. 1950. **Genres:** History, Literary Criticism And History, Social Sciences. **Career:** University of Tennessee, research assistant, 1972-73; Spring Valley High School, teacher, 1973-77; University of South Carolina, teaching assistant, 1977-80; Middlebury College, assistant professor, 1983-90, associate professor of history, 1990-; Hollins College, trustee, 1992-, Academic Affairs Committee, chair, 1994-. Writer. **Publications:** (With T.L. Connelly) God and General Longstreet: Essays on the Lost Cause and the Southern Mind, 1982; Benevolence Among Slaveholders: Assisting the Poor in Charleston, 1760-1860, 1993; Talent for Living: Josephine Pinckney and the Charleston Literary Tradition, 2006. Work appears in anthologies. Contributor of articles and reviews to history journals. **Address:** 260 Stone Hill Rd., Pound Ridge, NY 10576-1421, U.S.A.

BELLOWS, Melina Gerosa. American (born United States), b. 1965?. **Genres:** Novels, Women's Studies And Issues, Human Relations/Parenting. **Career:** Ladies Home Journal, senior editor; National Geographic, executive vice president and chief creative officer; National Geographic Kids, vice president and editor-in-chief, 2000-; National Geographic Little Kids, editor-in-chief, 2007-; Entertainment Weekly & Premiere Magazines, staff writer. freelance writer. **Publications:** The Fun Book: 102 Ways for Girls to Have Some, 1998; The Fun Book for Couples: 102 Ways to Celebrate Love, 2003; Wish, 2005; The Fun Book for Moms: 102 Ways to Celebrate Family, 2007; The Fun Book for Christmas: New Ways to Have Fun for the Holidays, 2009; The Fun Book for Girlfriends: 102 Ways for Girls to Have Fun, 2009; Nat Geo Amazing!: 100 People, Places, and Things that Will Wow You, 2010. Contributor to magazines. **Address:** National Geographic Kids Magazine, National Geographic Society, 1145 17th St. NW, Washington, DC 20036-4688, U.S.A. **Online address:** melina@melinabellows.com

BELLOWS, Nathaniel. American (born United States), b. 1972?. **Genres:** Novels, Poetry, Illustrations, Songs/Lyrics And Libretti. **Career:** Writer and artist. **Publications:** On This Day: A Novel, 2003; Why Speak?: Poems, 2007. Contributor to periodicals and journals. **Address:** Harmon Blunt Publishing, PO Box 250111, New York, NY 10025, U.S.A. **Online address:** nathaniel@nathanielbellows.com

BELLUSH, Bernard. American (born United States), b. 1917. **Genres:** International Relations/Current Affairs, Organized Labor, Biography. **Career:** Hunter College, tutor, 1946-49; City College of the City University of New York, assistant professor, 1951-61, associate professor and sub-chairman of department, 1961-68, professor, 1968-78, resident professor of history, 1978-81; Ballard School, lecturer, 1950-53; Columbia University, Teachers College, lecturer, 1960, visiting associate professor, 1964-66; Cooper Union, lecturer, 1961; State University of Utrecht, Fulbright professor, 1966-67, 1970-71; New York State chapter, chair, 1971-73; Henry George School of Social Science, faculty, 1978-81; The Forward, roving correspondent, 1986-. Writer. **Publications:** Franklin D. Roosevelt as Governor of New York, 1955; (contrib.) Great American Liberals, 1956; (contrib.) Festschrift for Allan Nevins, 1961; He Walked Alone: A Biography of John Gilbert Winant, 1968; The Failure of the NRA, 1975; (with J. Bellush) Union Power and New York: Victor Gotbaum and District Council 37, 1984. **Address:** Forward Association Inc., 125 Maiden Ln., New York, NY 10038, U.S.A.

BELMONTE, Kevin Charles. American (born United States) **Genres:** Biography, Mystery/Crime/Suspense. **Career:** Gordon College, Wilberforce Project, director, 1998-2002; Wilberforce Forum, fellow. Film consultant, lecturer and writer. **Publications:** (Ed.) A Practical View of Christianity, 1996; Hero for Humanity: A Biography of William Wilberforce, 2002; Journey through the Life of William Wilberforce: The Abolitionist who Changed the Face of a Nation, 2006; William Wilberforce: A Hero for Humanity, 2007; (ed.) Quotable Chesterton, 2010; D.L. Moody, 2010; John Bunyan, 2010; Defiant Joy: The Remarkable Life & Impact of GK Chesterton, 2011. Contributor to periodicals. **Address:** Wilberforce Forum, Prison Fellowship Ministries, PO Box 5484, Baltimore, MD 21285, U.S.A.

BELNAP, Nuel. American (born United States), b. 1930. **Genres:** Philosophy. **Career:** Yale University, instructor, 1958-60, assistant professor of philosophy, 1960-63; University of Pittsburgh, faculty, 1961-, associate professor, 1963-66, director of graduate studies in philosophy, 1964-67, 1970-72, professor of philosophy, sociology and history and philosophy of science, 1966-, Center for the Philosophy of Science, fellow, senior research associate, 1964-78, Alan Ross Anderson lecturer, 1983-84, Alan Ross Anderson distinguished professor, 1984-, professor in intelligent systems program, 1988-; University of California, visiting professor, 1973. Writer. **Publications:** Entailment: The Logic of Relevance and Necessity, (with A.R. Anderson) vol. I, 1975, (with A.R. Anderson and J.M. Dunn) vol. II, 1992; (with T.B. Steel) The Logic of Questions and Answers, 1976; (with A. Gupta) The Revision Theory of Truth, 1993; (with M. Perloff and M. Xu) Facing the Future: Agents and Our Choices in Our Indeterminist World, 2001; (contrib.) Logic, Thought and Action, 2005. Works appear in anthologies. Contributor of articles to journals. **Address:** Department of Philosophy, University of Pittsburgh, 1028-A Cathedral of Learning, Pittsburgh, PA 15260, U.S.A. **Online address:** belnap@pitt.edu

BELSEY, Catherine. Welsh/British (born England), b. 1940. **Genres:** Literary Criticism And History, Essays. **Career:** New Hall (now Murray Edwards College), fellow in English, 1969-75; Cardiff University (University College), lecturer in English, 1975-89, professor of English, 1989-, Centre for Critical and Cultural Theory, chair; McMaster University, visiting professor, 1986; Swansea University, Department of English Language and Literature, research professor; University of Wales, professor of English. Writer. **Publications:** Critical Practice, 1980, 2nd ed., 2002; The Subject of Tragedy: Identity and Difference in Renaissance Drama, 1985; John Milton: Language, Gender, Power, 1988; (ed. with J. Moore) The Feminist Reader: Essays in Gender and the Politics of Literary Criticism, 1989, 2nd ed., 1997; Desire: Love Stories in Western Culture, 1994; Shakespeare and the Loss of Eden: The Construction of Family Values in Early Modern Culture, 1999; Post-structuralism: A Very Short Introduction, 2002; (ed.) Privileging Difference, 2002; Culture and the Real: Theorizing Cultural Criticism, 2005; Shakespeare in Theory and Practice, 2008; Future for Criticism, 2011. Contributor to periodicals. **Address:** College of Arts and Humanities, Swansea University, Singleton Pk., Swansea, SA2 8PP, Wales. **Online address:** c.belsey@btinternet.com

BELSHAW, Patrick. British (born England), b. 1936. **Genres:** Novels, Novellas/Short Stories, Poetry, Biography, Education, Autobiography/Memoirs. **Career:** Teacher, 1958-66; advisory teacher, 1966-69; Darlington College of Education, senior lecturer, 1969-76; Local Education Authority, adviser, 1976-80, Her Majesty's inspector of schools, 1980-91, retired, 1991. Writer. **Publications:** (Contrib.) Physical Education for Special Needs, 1979; A Kind of Private Magic (group biography), 1994. **Address:** Hilltop Cottage, Whashton, Richmond, NY DL11 7JN, England.

BELTING, Hans. German (born Germany), b. 1935. **Genres:** Art/Art History, Young Adult Fiction. **Career:** University of Hamburg, professor, 1966; University of Heidelberg, professor of art history, 1970-80, honorary professor, 1992-2002; University of Munich, professor of art history and chair, 1980-92; Karlsruhe College, professor of art history and media history, 1992-2002; School for New Media, founder, professor of art history and new media, 1993-2002; College de France, European chair, 2002-03; Buenos Aires University, Getty Visiting professor; Northwestern University, Mary Jane Crowe professor; State College of Design in Karlsruhe, Institute for Art Research, professor, 1992-2002, professor emeritus, 2002-. Writer. **Publications:** Die Oberkirche von San Francesco in Assisi: ihre Dekoration als Aufgabe u.d. Genese e. neuen Wandmalerei, 1977; (with C. Mango and D. Mouriki) The Mosaics and Frescoes of St. Mary Pammakaristos (Fethiye Camii) at Istanbul, 1978; (G. Cavallo) Die Bibel des Niketas: ein Werk der höfischen Buchkunst in Byzanz und sein antikes Vorbild, 1979; Das Bild und sein Publikum im Mittelalter: Form und Funktion fruher Bildtafeln der Passion, 1981; (with D. Eichberger) Jan van Eyck als Erzähler: fruhe Tafelbilder im Umkreis der New Yorker Doppeltafel, 1983; Das Ende der Kunstgeschichte, 1983; Il Medio Oriente e l'Occidente nell'arte del XIII secolo, 1982; Max Beckmann: die Tradition als Problem in der Kunst der Moderne, 1984; (co-author) Der Mensch und seine Gefuhle: Beitrage, 1985; Giovanni Bellini, Pieta: Ikone und Bilderzahlung in der venezianischen Malerei, 1985; The End of the History of Art?, 1987; (with D. Blume) Malerei und Stadtkultur in der Dantezeit: die Argumentation der Bilder, 1989; Bild und Kult: eine Geschichte des Bildes vor dem Zeitalter der Kunst, 1990; The Image and its Public in the Middle Ages: Form and Function of Early Paintings of the Passion, 1990; Die Deutschen und ihre Kunst: ein schwieriges Erbe, 1992; Thomas Struth: Museum Photographs, 1993; (contrib.) Gary Hill, 1995; Das unsichtbare Meisterwerk: die modernen Mythen der Kunst, 1998; (with L. Haustein) Das Erbe der Bilde, 1998; Identität im Zweifel: Ansichten der deutschen Kunst, 1999; (co-author) Qu'est-ce qu'un chef-d'oeuvre?, 2000; (with D. Kamper) Der zweite Blick, 2000; Bild-Anthropologie, 2001; (contrib.) Andrea Pozzo und die Videokunst, 2001; Jakob Broder: das grosse Triptychon: Katharsis,

Gezeitengesang, Kairos, 1975-2001, 2002; (ed. with D. Kamper and M. Schulz) Quel corps?, 2002; (contrib.) Ebenbilder, 2002; (trans.) Hieronymus Bosch, Garden of Earthly Delights, 2002; (contrib.) Bill Viola, 2003; Das echte Bild: Bildfragen als Glaubensfragen, 2005; Szenarien der Modern: Kunst und ihre offenen Grenzen, 2005; Bilderfragen: die Bildwissenschaften im Aufbruch, 2007; La vera immagine di Cristo, 2007; Florenz und Bagdad: eine westystliche Geschichte des Blicks, 2008; Hommage à Jovánovics, 2009. **Address:** The University of Chicago Press, 1427 East 60th St., Chicago, IL 60637, U.S.A. **Online address:** hans.belting@hfg-karlsruhe.de

BELTMAN, Brian W. American (born United States), b. 1945. **Genres:** History, Biography, Social Sciences. **Career:** Wisconsin State Historical Society, historical researcher, 1974-76; Hamilton College, professor of American history, 1975-80; Dartmouth College, professor of American history, 1975-80; Arizona State University, professor of American history, 1975-80; University of Mid-America, professor of American history, 1975-80; University of South Carolina, professor of American history, 1975-80, adjunct professor, 1980-; South Carolina Electric and Gas Co., coordinator of regulatory affairs, 1980-. Writer. **Publications:** (Contrib.) Dictionary of Literary Biography Yearbook 1985, 1986; Dutch Farmer in the Missouri Valley: The Life and Letters of Ulbe Eringa, 1866-1950, 1996. Contributor of articles to periodicals and books. Works appear in anthologies. **Address:** 3950 Rockbridge Rd., Columbia, SC 29206, U.S.A. **Online address:** bbeltman@scana.com

BELTON, Sandra (Yvonne). American (born United States), b. 1939. **Genres:** Children's Fiction, Adult Non-fiction, Picture/Board Books, Novels, Biography. **Career:** District of Columbia Public Schools, West Elementary School, elementary teacher, 1964-69; Scott, Foresman, associate editor, 1969-72, executive editor and editorial manager, 1978-2001; Lyons & Carnahan, editor, 1972-74; Encyclopaedia Britannica Educational Corp., senior editor; City Colleges of Chicago, reading teacher, 1976-78. **Publications:** Sparks (nonfiction for adults), 1973. CHILDREN'S FICTION: From Miss Ida's Porch, 1993; May'naise Sandwiches and Sunshine Tea, 1994; Ernestine & Amanda, 1996; Ernestine & Amanda: Summer Camp, Ready or Not, 1997; Ernestine & Amanda: Members of the C.L.U.B., 1997; Ernestine & Amanda: Mysteries on Monroe Street, 1998; McKendree, 2000; Pictures for Miss Josie, 2003; Beauty, Her Basket, 2004; Store Bought Baby, 2006; If Houses Could Sing, 2007; Tallest Tree: The Paul Robeson Story, 2008. **Address:** HarperCollins Publishers, 10 E 53rd St., New York, NY 10022-5244, U.S.A. **Online address:** contact@sandrabelton.com

BELUE, Ted Franklin. American (born United States), b. 1954. **Genres:** History, Biology, Sports/Fitness. **Career:** Murray State University, senior lecturer in history, 1991-; Muzzleloader, staff writer, 1993-. **Publications:** The Long Hunt: Death of the Buffalo East of the Mississippi, 1996; (ed.) A Sketch of the Life and Character of Daniel Boone, 1997; (ed.) The Life of Daniel Boone, 1998; The Hunters of Kentucky: A Narrative History of America's First Far West, 1750-1792, 2003. Contributor to books and periodicals. **Address:** Department of History, Murray State University, 6B16 Faculty Hall, Murray, KY 42071, U.S.A. **Online address:** ted.belue@murraystate.edu

BEMROSE, John. Canadian (born Canada), b. 1947?. **Genres:** Novels, Poetry, Young Adult Non-fiction, Literary Criticism And History, Young Adult Fiction. **Career:** Journalist, poet, playwright. **Publications:** Going Under, 1979; Imagining Horses: Poems of John Bemrose, 1984; The Island Walkers: A Novel, 2003; The Last Woman, 2010. **Address:** c/o Author Mail, Henry Holt & Co., 115 W 18th St., New York, NY 10011, U.S.A.

BENAÏSSA, Slimane. French (born France), b. 1943?. **Genres:** Plays/Screenplays, Novels, Young Adult Fiction. **Career:** Writer, actor and director. **Publications:** NOVELS: Les Fils de L'amertume: Roman, 1999; Le Silence de la Falaise: A Roman, 2001; La Dernière Nuit d'un Damné: Roman, 2003; Les colères du Silence: Roman, 2005. **Address:** c/o Author Mail, Grove/Atlantic Press, 841 Broadway, 4th Fl., New York, NY 10003, U.S.A. **Online address:** info@slimanebenaissa.com

BENARDE, Melvin Albert. American (born United States), b. 1923. **Genres:** Environmental Sciences/Ecology, Medicine/Health, Travel/Exploration. **Career:** Rutgers University, faculty, 1962-67; Hahnemann University, Department of Community Medicine and Environmental Health, professor and chairman, 1967-83; Drexel University, Environmental Studies Institute, associate director, 1983-87; Temple University, Asbestos-Lead Center, professor and director, 1987-; Mercer County Community College, Center for Continuing Studies, faculty of creative writing. Writer. **Publications:** Race against Famine, 1968; Our Precious Habitat, 1970, rev. ed., 1989; The Chemicals We Eat, 1973, rev. ed., 1975; Beach Holidays: Portugal to Israel, 1974; The Food Additives Dictionary, 1981; Global Warning/Global Warming, 1992; You've Been Had!: How the Media and Environmentalists Turned America into a Nation of Hypochondriacs, 2002; Our Precarious Habitat, It's in Your Hands, 2007. EDITOR AND CONTRIBUTOR: Disinfection, 1970; Asbestos: The Hazardous Fiber, 1990. **Address:** 6 Thorngate Ct., Princeton, NJ 08540-7807, U.S.A. **Online address:** dickiedare1a@comcast.net

BENAVIDES, O. Hugo. American (born United States), b. 1968. **Genres:** History. **Career:** Fordham University, associate professor of anthropology, Latin American and Latino studies and international political economy and development, director of the M.A. program in humanities and sciences. Writer. **Publications:** Making Ecuadorian Histories: Four Centuries of Defining Power, 2004; The Politics of Sentiment: Imagining and Remembering Guayaquil, 2006; Drugs, Thugs and Divas: Telenovelas and Narco-Dramas in Latin America, 2008. Contributor to journals. **Address:** Department of Sociology & Anthropology, Fordham University, 441 E Fordham Rd., Dealy Hall 402E, Bronx, NY 10458-9993, U.S.A. **Online address:** benavides@fordham.edu

BENBASSA, Esther. French/Turkish (born Turkey), b. 1950. **Genres:** History, Natural History, Theology/Religion. **Career:** Centre National de la Recherche Scientifique (CNRS), research professor, 1989-2000; Ecole pratique des hautes études, Modern Jewish History, professor, 2000-; Alberto Benveniste Center, founder, 2002; Nertherlands Institute for Advanced Study, fellow, 2004-05. Writer. **Publications:** Cuisine judéo-espagnole: recettes et traditions, 1984; Un grand rabbin sépharade en politique: 1892-1923, 1990; Une vie judéo-espagnole l'Est: autobiographie journal et correspondance, 1992; Juifs des Balkans: espaces judéo-ibériques XIVe-XXe sicles, 1993; Une diaspora sépharade en transition: Istanbul XIXe-XXe sicle, 1993; Le judaisme Ottoman entre occidentalisation et sionisme 1908-1920, 1996; Mámoires juives d'Espagne et du Portugal, 1996; Dictionnaire de civilisation juive: auteurs oeuvres notions, 1997; Transmission et passages en monde juif, 1997; Histoire des juifs de France, 1997, rev. ed. as Histoire des juifs sépharades, 2002; Israël imaginaire, 1998; Les Juifs ont-ils un avenir?, 2001; Israël, la terre et le sacré, 2001; Le Juif et l'autre, 2002; Israel, the Impossible Land, 2003; Toldot Yehude Tsarefat: meha-et ha-'atiḳah 'ad yemenu, 2004; (with J.C. Attias) Jew and the Other, 2004; La souffrance comme identité, 2007; (with J.C. Attias) Dictionnaire des mondes juifs, 2008; Etre juif après Gaz, 2009; Suffering as Identity, 2010. **Address:** Secretariat, The Sorbonne, Stair I, 3rd Fl., Rm. H 617, 1 rue Victor Cousin, Paris, 75230, France. **Online address:** attben@noos.fr

BENCHLEY, Rob. American (born United States), b. 1950?. **Genres:** Local History/Rural Topics, Documentaries/Reportage, Novels. **Career:** Freelance writer and photographer. **Publications:** (With J. Patrick) Scallop Season: A Nantucket Chronicle, 2002. Contributor to periodicals. **Address:** 50 Baxter Rd., PO Box 600, Siasconset, MA 02564-0600, U.S.A. **Online address:** benchley@comcast.net

BENDALL, Molly. American (born United States), b. 1961. **Genres:** Poetry, Anthropology/Ethnology. **Career:** University of Virginia, Department of English, training assistant, 1985-86; The Johns Hopkins University, The Writing Seminars, training assistant, 1986-87, instructor, 1987-88; Loyola College, Department of Writing and Media, instructor, 1987-88; University of Southern California, Department of English, lecturer, assistant professor, 1988-; Loyola Marymount University, instructor, 2003-07; University of California, Extension Program, instructor. Writer. **Publications:** Black Tulips, 1990; (co-author) Calamity & Belle: A Cowgirl Correspondence, 1992; After Estrangement (poetry), 1992; Dear Calamity-Love, Belle, 1994; Dark Summer, 1999; Ariadne's Island, 2002; Under the quick, 2009; (with G. Wronsky) Bling & Fringe, 2009. Work appears in anthology. **Address:** English Department, University of Southern California, THH 402J, 2337 Beach Ave., Venice, CA 90291, U.S.A. **Online address:** bendall@usc.edu

BENDER, Bert. (Bert Arthur Bender). American (born United States), b. 1938. **Genres:** Young Adult Fiction, Sex. **Career:** Junior high-school teacher, 1962-63; Arizona State University, professor of English, 1971-, now professor emeritus. Writer. **Publications:** Sea-Brothers: The Tradition of American Sea Fiction from Moby-Dick to the Present, 1988; The Descent of Love: Darwin and the Theory of Sexual Selection in American Fiction 1871-1926, 1996; Evolution and the Sex Problem: American Narratives during the

Eclipse of Darwinism, 2004; Catching the Ebb: Drift-Fishing for a Life in Cook Inlet, 2008. **Address:** Department of English Language & Literature, Arizona State University, Rm. 543B, Language and Literature Bldg., 851 S Cady Mall, PO Box 870302, Tempe, AZ 85287-0302, U.S.A. **Online address:** bert.bender@asu.edu

BENDER, Bert Arthur. *See* **BENDER, Bert.**

BENDER, Sheila. American (born United States), b. 1948. **Genres:** Poetry, Writing/Journalism, Autobiography/Memoirs. **Career:** Pima Community College, instructor in writing and literature; Loyola Marymount University, instructor in writing and literature; Writer's Digest Magazine, personal essay columnist; Writing it Real, founder. Writer. **Publications:** Love Along the Coastal Route (poems), 1983; Near the Light, 1983; (with C. Killien) Writing in a Convertible with the Top Down: A Unique Guide for Writers, 1992; (ed. with P. Tobin) The Poem & The World: An International Anthology, 1993; Writing Personal Essays: How to Shape Your Life Experiences for the Page, 1995; (ed.) The Writer's Journal: 40 Contemporary Authors and Their Journals, 1997; Writing Personal Poetry: Creating Poems From Your Life Experiences, 1998; Sustenance: New and Selected Poems, 1999; A Year in the Life: Journaling for Self-Discovery, 2000; Keeping a Journal You Love, 2001; Perfect Phrases for College Application Essays: Hundreds of Ready-to-use Phrases to Write a Compelling Essay and Catch the Attention of an Admissions Committee, 2008; New Theology: Turning to Poetry in a Time of Grief, 2009; Creative Writing Demystified, 2010; Writing and Publishing Personal Essays, 2011. **Address:** Wales Literary Agency, 1508 10th Ave. E, Seattle, WA 98102, U.S.A. **Online address:** sbender@writingitreal.com

BENDER, Thomas. American (born United States), b. 1944. **Genres:** History, Intellectual History, Urban Studies. **Career:** University of Wisconsin, assistant professor of history and urban studies, 1971-74; New York University, Department of History, assistant professor, 1974-76, associate professor, 1976-77, Samuel Rudin professor of humanities, 1977-82, professor of history, 1977-, university professor of humanities, 1982-, chair, 1986-89, dean for the humanities, 1995-98, interim chair, 2003-04, Society of Fellows, chair, 1991-94; New York Institute for the Humanities, co-director, 1978-80, acting director, 1982-83; Intellectual History Group Newsletter, founding editor, 1979-86; International Center for Advanced Studies, director, 1997-2007. **Publications:** Toward an Urban Vision, 1975; Community and Social Change in America, 1978; (with E.C. Rozwenc) The Making of American Society, 1978; New York Intellect: A History of Intellectual Life in New York City, from 1750 to the Beginnings of Our Own Time, 1987; Intellect and Public Life, 1993; The Unfinished City: New York and the Metropolitan Idea, 2002; (co-author) The Education of Historians for the Twenty-First Century, 2004; A Nation Among Nations: America's Place in World History, 2006. EDITOR: (and intro.) Democracy in America, 1981; The University and the City: From Medieval Origins to the Present, 1989; The Antislavery Debate, 1992; (with C.E. Schorske) Budapest and New York: Studies in Metropolitan Transformation, 1870-1930, 1994; American Academic Culture in Transformation, 1998; (with P. Smith) City and Nation: Rethinking Place and Identity, 2001; Rethinking American History in a Global Age, 2002; (with A. Çinar) Urban Imaginaries: Locating the Modern City, 2007; (with W. Smith) American Higher Education Transformed, 1940-2005: Documenting the National Discourse, 2008; (with I. Farias) Urban Assemblages: How Actor-Network Theory Changes Urban Studies, 2010. Contributor to books, journals and magazines. **Address:** Department of History, New York University, Rm. 601, King Juan Carlos I of Spain Bldg., 53 Washington Sq. S, 7th Fl., New York, NY 10012, U.S.A. **Online address:** thomas.bender@nyu.edu

BENDIS, Brian Michael. American (born United States), b. 1967. **Genres:** Graphic Novels. **Career:** Portland State University, faculty; Hillel Foundation, staff, illustrator; MTV, co-executive producer; YTV, co-executive producer. Writer. **Publications:** Goldfish, 1998; The Jinx Essential Collection, 1998; (with M. Andreyko) Torso: A True Crime Graphic Novel, 1998; Powers: Who Killed Retro Girl?, 2000; Fortune and Glory: A True Hollywood Comic Book Story, 2000; Jinx: The Definitive Collection, 2001; (with M.A. Oeming) Powers Scriptbook, 2001; Powers, vol. II: Role Play, 2001, vol. III: Little Deaths, 2002; vol. IV: Supergroup, 2003; Ultimate Spider-Man, vol. I: Power and Responsibility, 2002, vol. II: Learning Curve, 2002, vol. III, 2006, vol. IV, 2006, vol. V, 2006, vol. VI: Venom, 2006, vol. VII, 2006, vol. VIII, 2007, vol. IX, 2008, vol. X, 2009, vol. XI, 2010; Alias, Book 1, 2003; Come Home: Alias, Book 2, 2003; The Underneath: Alias, Book 3, 2003; Total Sell Out, 2003; Ultimate Spiderman, 15 vols., 2006; Pulse, 2vols., 2006; (with S. Niles) Hellspawn: The Ashley Wood Collection, 2006; Sam and Twitch: The Brian Michael Bendis Collection, 2006; The New Avengers, 2007; Daredevil, 2008; Secret Invasion: Dark Reign, 2009. SELF-ILLUSTRATOR: Fire: A Spy Graphic Novel, 1999. **Address:** Jinxworld Inc., 4110 SE Hawthorn Blvd., Ste. 438, Portland, OR 97214, U.S.A. **Online address:** brian1138@aol.com

BENDIX, Deanna Marohn. American (born United States), b. 1938. **Genres:** Art/Art History, Design. **Career:** Waseca Daily Journal, photojournalist and arts and education reporter, 1971-78; University of Minnesota, instructor, 1977, 1980; art historian, researcher, artist and writer, 1989-96; Minneapolis Institute of Arts, instructor, 1997. **Publications:** Diabolical Designs: Paintings, Interiors and Exhibitions of James McNeill Whistler, 1995. Contributor to periodicals. **Address:** 36078 Clear Lake Dr., Waseca, MN 56093-4649, U.S.A.

BENDIXSON, Terence. British (born England), b. 1934. **Genres:** Transportation, Urban Studies, Social Sciences. **Career:** Planning correspondent, 1963-69; Environment Directorate, OECD, principal administrator, 1971-73; freelance writer and broadcaster, 1971-; Transportation, News editor, 1972-; land use and transport consultant, 1974-2000; University of Southampton, Department of Civil and Environmental Engineering, visiting fellow; Independent Transport Commission, secretary, 1999-2010; The Guardian, policy analyst and writer. Consultant. **Publications:** Instead of Cars, 1974, rev. ed., 1977; Without Wheels: Alternatives to the Private Car, 1975; (ed.) The Management of Urban Growth: A Report on Policy Instruments for Influencing the Form and Structure of Urban Development and the Location and Distribution of Urban Growth, 1977; The Peterborough Effect, 1988; Milton Keynes: Image and Reality, 1991. **Address:** 39 Elm Park Gardens, Chelsea, GL SW10 9AA, England. **Online address:** t.bendixson@pobox.com

BENDROTH, Margaret Lamberts. American (born United States), b. 1954. **Genres:** Human Relations/Parenting, Theology/Religion, Women's Studies And Issues. **Career:** Northern Virginia Community College, instructor in history, 1983-86; Northeastern University, religion and history faculty, 1987-92; Divinitas Books, assistant manager, 1992-93; Gordon-Conwell Theological Seminary, Center for Urban Ministerial Education, adjunct faculty, 1992-; Andover Newton Theological School, adjunct lecturer in church history, 1993-; Calvin College, professor of history, 1994-; Women and Twentieth-Century Protestantism, project co-director, 1995-98; Congregational Library, librarian and executive director, 2004-. Writer. **Publications:** Fundamentalism and Gender, 1875 to the Present, 1993; (ed. with P. Airhart) Families: Past, Present and Future, 1996; (ed. with P.D. Airhart) Faith Traditions and the Family, 1996; Growing up Protestant: Parents, Children and Mainline Churches, 2002; (ed. with V.L. Brereton) Women and Twentieth-century Protestantism, 2002; Fundamentalists in the City: Conflict and Division in Boston's Churches, 1885-1950, 2005; A School of the Church: Andover Newton Across Two Centuries, 2008. Contributor to books and journals. **Address:** Congregational Library, 14 Beacon St. 2 Fl., Boston, MA 02108, U.S.A. **Online address:** mbendrot@calvin.edu

BENECKE, Mark. German (born Germany), b. 1970?. **Genres:** Sciences. **Career:** Office of the Chief Medical Examiner, forensic biologist, 1997-99; University of Cologne, professor of zoology, 1999; University of Medicine and Pharmacy, visiting assistant professor, 1999; Institute for Legal Medicine, visiting assistant professor, 1999; Federal Bureau of Investigation, scientific consultant; International Forensic Research and Consulting, consultant, 2000- . Writer. **Publications:** The Dream of Eternal Life: Biomedicine, Aging, and Immortality, 2002; Murderous Methods: Using Forensic Science to Solve Lethal Crimes, 2005. Contributor of articles to journals. **Address:** International Forensic Research & Consulting, Postfach 250411, Cologne, 50520, Germany. **Online address:** forensic@benecke.com

BENEDETTI, Jean (Norman). British (born England), b. 1930. **Genres:** Translations, Young Adult Non-fiction. **Career:** Rose Bruford College, principal, 1970-87, honorary professor, 1987-, fellow, 1991; Queen Margaret University College Edinburgh, honorary professor. Actor, director, writer and translator. **Publications:** TRANSLATIONS: A Sunday Walk, 1968; Edward II, A Respectable Wedding, 1970; The Architect and the Emperor of Assyria, Plays, vol. III, 1971. NONFICTION: Gilles de Rais: The Authentic Bluebeard, 1971 in US as Gilles de Rais, 1972; Stanislavski: An Introduction, 1982; Stanislavski, 1988; Stanislavski: A Biography, 1988; Stanislavski and the Actor, 1998; David Garrick and the Birth of Modern Theatre, 2001. EDITOR AND TRANSLATOR: The Moscow Art Theatre Letters, 1991; Dear

Writer, Dear Actress: The Love Letters of Olga Knipper and Anton Chekhov, 1997; K. Stanislavsky, Actor's Work: A Student's Diary, 2008; K. Stanislavsky, My Life in Art, 2008; K. Stanislavsky, Actor's Work on a Role, 2009. OTHERS: Dramatist and or Translator of Scripts: The Good Shoemaker and the Poor Fish Peddler, 1965; File on Harry Jordan, 1966; These Men Are Dangerous (trilogy), 1968; Lily, 1969; The Architect and the Emperor of Assyria, 1971; A Respectable Wedding, The Open Space, 1980; The Art of the Actor, 2007. Contributor to periodicals and books. **Address:** Rose Bruford College, Lamorbey Pk., Burnt Oak Ln., Sidcup, KT DA15 9DF, England.

BENEDICT, Barbara M. American (born United States), b. 1955. **Genres:** Literary Criticism And History, History, Intellectual History, Natural History. **Career:** University of California, teaching assistant, 1978-80, teaching associate, 1980-83; Trinity College, instructor, 1984-85, assistant professor, 1985-91, associate professor, 1991-96, professor of English, 1996-, Charles A. Dana professor of English literature, 2002-, Watkinson Rare Book Library, trustee, 2008-. Writer. **Publications:** University of California, teaching assistant, 1978-80, teaching associate, 1980-83; Trinity College, instructor, 1984-85, assistant professor, 1985-91, associate professor, 1991-96, professor of English, 1996-, Charles A. Dana professor of English literature, 2002-, Watkinson Rare Book Library, trustee, 2008-. Writer. **Address:** Department of English, Trinity College, Rm. 208, 115 Vernon St., Hartford, CT 06106-3100, U.S.A. **Online address:** barbara.benedict@trincoll.edu

BENEDICT, Elizabeth. American (born United States), b. 1954. **Genres:** Novels, Writing/Journalism. **Career:** Mexican American Legal Defense and Educational Fund, legislative advocate and publicist, 1978-82; George Mason University, part-time instructor, 1985; Swarthmore College, visiting writer, 1987-89, 1991, 1996; Haverford College, visiting writer, 1990; University of Iowa, faculty, 1993; Princeton University, lecturer, 1994-98; New York State Summer Writers Institute, faculty, 1997-; Harvard Extension School, faculty, 2002-03; Barnard College, faculty, 2008; Brooklyn College, faculty, 2008; Brandeis University, faculty, 2010-11. National Public Radio, book reviewer. Essayist and commentator. **Publications:** NOVELS: Slow Dancing, 1985; The Beginner's Book of Dreams, 1988; Safe Conduct, 1993; Almost, 2001; The Practice of Deceit, 2005. OTHER: The Joy of Writing Sex, 1996; The Joy of Writing Sex: A Guide for Fiction Writers, 2002; (with N. Connolly) In the Kennedy Kitchen: Recipes and Recollections of a Great American Family, 2007; Mentors, Muses & Monsters: 30 Writers on the People Who Changed their Lives, 2009. ESSAYS IN BOOKS: These United States: Leading American Writers on Their State Within the Union, 2003; The Dictionary of Failed Relationships, 2003; Bad Girls: 26 Writers Misbehave, 2007. **Address:** c/o Gail Hochman, Brandt & Hochman Literary Agents, 1501 Broadway, Ste. 2310, New York, NY 10036, U.S.A. **Online address:** info@elizabethbenedict.com

BENEDICT, Helen. American/British (born England), b. 1952. **Genres:** Novels, History, Writing/Journalism, International Relations/Current Affairs, Military/Defense/Arms Control, Race Relations, Social Commentary, Women's Studies And Issues, Documentaries/Reportage, Young Adult Fiction, Plays/Screenplays, Cultural/Ethnic Topics. **Career:** New Wings, managing editor, 1979; Independent and Gazette, reporter and feature writer, 1980; Columbia University, professor of journalism, 1986-; University of California, visiting lecturer, 1991. **Publications:** NONFICTION: (co-author) Women Making History: Conversations with Fifteen New Yorkers, 1985; Recovery: How to Survive Sexual Assault for Women, Men, Teenagers, Their Friends and Families, 1985, rev. ed., 1994; Safe, Strong and Streetwise (for young adults), 1987; Portraits in Print, 1991; Virgin or Vamp: How the Press Covers Sex Crimes, 1992; The Lonely Soldier: The Private War of Women Serving in Iraq, 2009. NOVELS: A World Like This, 1990; Bad Angel, 1996; The Sailor's Wife, 2000; The Opposite of Love, 2007; The Edge of Eden, 2009; Sand Queen, 2011. Works appear in anthologies. Contributor to periodicals. **Address:** Graduate School of Journalism, Columbia University, 2950 Broadway, 116th St., New York, NY 10027, U.S.A. **Online address:** hb22@columbia.edu

BENEDICT, Jeff. American (born United States), b. 1966. **Genres:** Criminology/True Crime, Business/Trade/Industry, Young Adult Non-fiction. **Career:** Northeastern University, Center for the Study of Society, director; Southern Virginia University, Division of Humanities, professor of advanced writing, distinguished professor of writing and mass media; Sports Illustrated, writer; Deseret News Newspaper, columnist. **Publications:** NONFICTION: Public Heroes, Private Felons: Athletes and Crimes against Women, 1997; Athletes and Acquaintance Rape, 1998; (with D. Yaeger) Pros and Cons: The Criminals Who Play in the NFL, 1998; Without Reservation: The Making of America's Most Powerful Indian Tribe and the World's Largest Casino, 2000; Without Reservation: How a Controversial Indian Tribe Rose to Power and Built the World's Largest Casino, 2001; No Bone Unturned: The Adventures of a Top Smithsonian Forensic Scientist and the Legal Battle for America's Oldest Skeletons, 2003; Out of Bounds: Inside the NBA's Culture of Rape, Violence, and Crime, 2004; The Mormon Way of Doing Business: Leadership and Success through Faith and Family, 2007; Little Pink House: A True Story of Defiance and Courage, 2009; How to Build a Business Warren Buffett Would Buy: The R.C. Willey Story, 2009, 2nd ed., 2011; Poisoned: The True Story of the Deadly E. Coli Outbreak That Changed the Way Americans Eat, 2011. **Address:** Division of Humanities, Southern Virginia University, 1 University Hill Dr., Buena Vista, VA 24416, U.S.A. **Online address:** jeff.benedict@svu.edu

BENEDICT, Laura Philpot. American (born United States), b. 1962. **Genres:** Novels. **Career:** Corporate Ink, owner, 1992-2003; Busch Creative Services, sales and promotion. Writer. **Publications:** Isabella Moon: A Novel, 2007; (ed. with P. Benedict) Surreal South: An Anthology of Short Fiction, 2007; Calling Mr. Lonely Hearts, 2008. Contributor to the magazines. Works appear in anthologies. **Address:** c/o Susan Raihofer, David Black Literary Agency, 156 5th Ave., New York, NY 10010, U.S.A. **Online address:** laura@laurabenedict.com

BENEDICT, Philip (Joseph). Swiss/American (born United States), b. 1949. **Genres:** History. **Career:** Cornell University, visiting assistant professor of history, 1975-76; University of Maryland, assistant professor of history, 1976-78; Brown University, assistant professor, 1978-82, associate professor, 1982-92, professor of history, 1992-2001, William Prescott and Annie McClelland Smith professor of history and religion, 2001-05; Ecole des Hautes Etudes en Sciences Sociales, director, 1986, 2002; Ecole Pratique des Hautes Etudes, director, 1999; Oxford University, All Souls College, visiting fellow, 2001-02; Université de Genève, professor, 2005-, Institut d'histoire de la Réformation, director, 2006-. Writer. **Publications:** Rouen during the Wars of Religion, 1981; The Huguenot Population of France, 1600-1685, 1991; The Faith and Fortunes of France's Huguenots, 1600-85, 2001; Christ's Churches Purely Reformed: A Social History of Calvinism, 2002; History through Images in the Sixteenth Century: The Wars, Massacres and Troubles of Tortorel and Perrissin, 2007; (with S.S. Menchi and A. Tallon) La Réforme en France et en Italie: Contacts, Comparaisons et Contrastes, 2007; Graphic History: The Wars, Massacres and Troubles of Tortorel and Perrissin, 2007. EDITOR: Cities and Social Change in Early Modern France, 1989; (co-ed.) Reformation, Revolt and Civil War in France and the Netherlands 1555-1585, 1999; (with M.P. Gutmann) Early Modern Europe: From Crisis to Stability, 2005; (with I. Backus) Calvin and His Influence: 1509-2009, 2011. Contributor to books and journals. **Address:** Institut d'histoire de la Réformation, Université de Genève, 5 rue de-Candolle, Geneva, 1211, Switzerland. **Online address:** philip.benedict@unige.ch

BENEDICT, Pinckney. American (born United States), b. 1964. **Genres:** Novellas/Short Stories, Novels, Young Adult Fiction, Reference. **Career:** Writer, 1987-; Hope College, associate professor of English, 1996-99; Hollins University, professor of English, 1999-2005; Southern Illinois University, Department of English, professor, 2005-; Princeton University, faculty; Oberlin College, faculty; Warren Wilson College, faculty; Queens University, faculty. **Publications:** Town Smokes (stories), 1987; The Wrecking Yard and Other Stories (stories), 1992; Dogs of God (novel), 1994; Dictionary of Literary Biography: American Short-Story Writers Since World War II, 2001; Miracle Boy and Other Stories, 2010. Contributor of articles to books. **Address:** Department of English, Southern Illinois University at Carbondale, 2244 Faner, 1000 Faner Dr., PO Box 4503, Carbondale, IL 62901, U.S.A. **Online address:** pinckney@siu.edu

BENERIA, Lourdes. Spanish/American (born United States), b. 1939. **Genres:** Women's Studies And Issues. **Career:** Rutgers University, assistant professor, 1975-81, associate professor of economics, 1981-86, Institute for Research on Women, executive officer, 1982-83, acting director, 1985-86; Cornell University, professor of city and regional planning and women's studies, 1987-, Program on International Development and Women, director, 1988-93, Latin American Studies Program, director, 1993-96, International Studies in Planning, director, 2001-03, 2007-08. Writer. **Publications:** (Trans.) J.M. Albertini, Los Engranajes de la Economia Nacional, 1965; (co-author) Planificacion y Desarrollo, 1965; Mujer, Economia, y Patriarcado Durante el Periodo Franquista, 1977; (co-author) Mujeres: Ciencia y Practica Politica, 1987; (with M. Roldan) The Crossroads of Class and Gender: Homework, Subcontracting, and Household Dynamics in Mexico City, 1987. EDITOR: Women and Development: The Sexual Division of Labor in Rural Societies, 1982; (with C. Stimpson) Women, Households, and the Current Economy, 1987; (with S. Feldman) Unequal Burden: Economic Crises, Persistent Poverty, and Women's Work, 1992; (with M.J. Dudley) Economic Restructuring in the Americas, 1996; (with S. Bisnath) Gender and Development: Theoretical, Empirical, and Practical Approaches, 2001; Gender, Development and Globalization: Economics as if All People Mattered, 2003; (with S. Bisnath) Global Tensions: Challenges and Opportunities in the World Economy, 2004; (with A.M. May and D. Strassmann) Feminist Economics, 2011. Works appear in anthologies. Contributor of articles to magazines and newspapers. **Address:** Department of City & Regional Planning, Cornell University, 209 W Sibley Hall, Ithaca, NY 14853, U.S.A. **Online address:** lb21@cornell.edu

BENES, Rebecca C. American (born United States), b. 1939. **Genres:** Art/Art History. **Career:** Denver Public Library Friends Foundation, trustee. Writer, librarian and educator. **Publications:** Native American Picture Books of Change: The Art of Historic Children's Editions, 2004. **Address:** c/o Author Mail, Museum of New Mexico Press, 1312 Basehart Rd. SE, PO Box 2087, Albuquerque, NM 87106-4363, U.S.A. **Online address:** rcbenes@aol.com

BENEZRA, Neal. American (born United States), b. 1953. **Genres:** Art/Art History, History, Photography. **Career:** Des Moines Art Center, curator, 1983-85; Art Institute of Chicago, associate curator, 1985-86, curator, 1986-91, deputy director and Frances and Thomas Dittmer curator of modern and contemporary art, 2000-02; University of Illinois-Urbana-Champaign, visiting lecturer, 1988; University of Chicago, visiting associate professor, 1990; Smithsonian Institution, Hirshhorn Museum and Sculpture Garden, chief curator, 1991-96, assistant director for art and public programs, 1996-99; San Francisco Museum of Modern Art, director, 2002-. Writer. **Publications:** Robert Arneson: A Retrospective, 1985; (ed.) Affinities and Intuitions: Gerald Elliott Collection of Contemporary Art, 1990; (with C. Schreiber) Ed Paschke, 1990; Martin Puryear, 1991; Stephan Balkenhol, 1995; Distemper, 1996; Franz West, 1999; Regarding Beauty: A View of the Late Twentieth Century, 1999; Ed Ruscha, 2000; Juan Munoz, 2001. **Address:** San Francisco Museum of Modern Art, 151 3rd St., San Francisco, CA 94103-3159, U.S.A.

BENFORD, Gregory (Albert). (Sterling Blake). American (born United States), b. 1941. **Genres:** Mystery/Crime/Suspense, Science Fiction/Fantasy. **Career:** Lawrence Radiation Laboratory, fellow, 1967-69, research physicist, 1969-72; University of California, Department of Physics and Astronomy, assistant professor, 1971-73, associate professor, 1973-79, professor of physics, 1979-, now professor emeritus; Cambridge University, visiting fellow, 1976, 1979, Woodrow Wilson fellow; Torino University, visiting fellow, 1979; MIT, visiting fellow, 1992; Physics International Co., Department of Energy, consultant; National Aeronautics and Space Administration, consultant. Writer. **Publications:** Deeper Than the Darkness, 1970, rev. ed. as The Stars in Shroud, 1978; Threads of Time, 1974; Jupiter Project, 1975, 2nd ed., 1980; (with G. Eklund) If the Stars Are Gods, 1977; In the Ocean of Night, 1977; (with G. Eklund) Find the Changeling, 1980; Timescape, 1980; (with W. Rotsler) Shiva Descending, 1980; Against Infinity, 1983; Time's Rub, 1984; Of Space-Time and the River, 1985; Artifact, 1985; In Alien Flesh, 1986; (with D. Brin) Heart of the Comet, 1986; Great Sky River, 1987; (co-author) Under the Wheel, 1987; New Hugo Winners: Award-Winning Science Fiction Stories, 1989; (with A.C. Clarke) Beyond the Fall of Night, 1990; Centigrade 233, 1990; (as Sterling Blake) Chiller, 1993; Foundation's Fear, 1997; Cosm, 1998; The Martian Race, 1999; Eater, 2000; Beyond Infinity, 2004; (with E. Malartre) Beyond Human: Living with Robots and Cyborgs, 2007. GALACTIC CENTER SAGA SERIES: Across the Sea of Suns, 1984; Tides of Light, 1989; Furious Gulf, 1994; Sailing Bright Eternity, 1995, new ed., 2005. EDITOR: (with M.H. Greenberg) Hitler Victorious: Eleven Stories of the German Victory in World War II, 1987, (with M.H. Greenberg), 1988; (with M.H. Greenberg) What Might Have Been, vol. I: Alternate Empires, 1989; (with M.H. Greenberg) What Might Have Been?, vol. II: Alternate Heroes, 1992; (with M.H. Greenberg) What Might Have Been?, vol. IV: Alternate Americas, 1992; Far Futures, 1995; (and intro.) Skylife: Space Habitats in Story and Science, 2000. OTHERS: Matter's End, 1994; Man-kzin Wars VI, 1995; Foundation and Chaos, 1998; We Could Do Worse, 1998; Deep Time: How Humanity Communicates across Millennia, 1999; Science Fiction Theatre, 1999; Worlds Vast and Various, 2000; Immersion and Other Short Novels, 2002; Microcosms, 2004; The Sunborn, 2005; Wonderful Future that Never Was: Flying Cars, Mail Delivery by Parachute and Other Predictions from the Past, 2010. Contributor of articles and stories to magazines. **Address:** Department of Physics and Astronomy, University of California, 4176 Frederick Reines Hall, PO Box 4575, Irvine, CA 92697-4575, U.S.A. **Online address:** gbenford@uci.edu

BENGTSON, Vern L. American (born United States), b. 1941. **Genres:** Sociology, Sciences, Psychology. **Career:** University of Chicago, research coordinator, 1965-67; University of Southern California, assistant professor, 1967-70, associate professor, 1970-71, professor of sociology, 1977-, university chair in gerontology, AARP/University professor of gerontology and sociology, AARP/University professor of gerontology emeritus, 1989-, Laboratory of Social Organization and Behavior, preceptor in sociology, chief, 1971-77, Socio-Cultural Contexts of Aging, principal investigator, 1972-, Division of Social and Behavioral Sciences, director; California Institute of Technology, visiting faculty associate in social sciences, 1975-76; Sociology of Education, associate editor, 1979-82; Gerontological Society of America, president, 1989-90; University of Bristol, Benjamin Meaker professor, 1997; University of Stockholm, visiting professor, 2006; Karolinska Institute, visiting professor, 2006. Writer. **Publications:** The Social Psychology of Aging, 1973; (co-author) Psychosocial Needs of the Aged, 1973; (comp. with K. Edwards and G.A. Baffa) Intergenerational Relations and Aging, 1975; (with R.A. Harootyan) Intergenerational Linkages: Hidden Connections in American Society, 1994; (with T.J. Biblarz and R.E.L. Roberts) How Families Still Matter: A Longitudinal Study of Youth in Two Generations, 2002. EDITOR: (co-editor) Aging, 1975; (with J.F. Robertson) Grandparenthood, 1985; (with J.E. Birren) Emergent Theories of Aging, 1988; (with K.W. Schaie) The Course of Later Life: Research and Reflections, 1989; (with D.J. Mangen and P.H. Landry, Jr.) Measurement of Intergenerational Relations, 1989; (with A.W. Achenbaum) The Changing Contract Across Generations, 1993; (with K.W. Schaie and L.M. Burton) Adult Intergenerational Relations: Effects of Societal Change, 1995; Adulthood and Aging: Research on Continuities and Discontinuities, 1996; (K.W. Schaie) Handbook of Theories of Aging, 1999, (co-ed.) 2nd ed., 2009; (co-ed.) Aging in East and West: Families, States, and the Elderly, 2000; (with A. Lowenstein) Global Aging and Challenges to Families, 2003; (co-ed.) Sourcebook of Family Theory & Research, 2005. Contributor of articles to journals. **Address:** Davis School of Gerontology, University of Southern California, Ethel Percy Andrus Gerontology Ctr., 3715 McClintock Ave., Los Angeles, CA 90089-0191, U.S.A. **Online address:** bengtson@usc.edu

BENIDICKSON, Jamie. Canadian (born Canada) **Genres:** Adult Non-fiction. **Career:** University of Ottawa, faculty of law, 1994-, professor, through 1997, Common Law Section, vice dean; IUCN Academy of Environmental Law, co-director; Council of Canadian Law Deans and Council of Canadian Administrative Tribunals, executive director. Writer. **Publications:** NONFICTION: (contrib.) Essays in Canadian Legal History, vol. II, 1983; (with B.W. Hodgins) The Temagami Experience: Recreation, Resources and Aboriginal Rights in the Northern Ontario Wilderness, 1989; (with G.B. Doern and N. Olewiler) Getting the Green Light: Environmental Regulation and Investment in Canada, 1994; (contrib.) Inside the Law: Canadian Law Firms in Historical Perspective, 1996; Environmental Law, 1997, 3rd ed., 2009; Idleness, Water and a Canoe: Reflections on Paddling for Pleasure, 1997; The Culture of Flushing: A Social and Legal History of Sewage, 2007. Contributor of articles to journals. **Address:** IUCN Academy of Environmental Law, University of Ottawa, Rm. 124, Fauteux Hall, 57 Louis Pasteur St., Ottawa, ON K1N 6N5, Canada. **Online address:** jamie.benidickson@uottawa.ca

BENIG, Irving. American (born United States), b. 1944. **Genres:** Novels, Poetry, Children's Fiction. **Career:** School teacher, 1967-71; Avon Books, editor, 1971-72; advertising executive, 1972-84; business executive, 1984-. **Publications:** The Children: Poems and Prose from Bedford-Stuyvesant (children's anthology), 1971; The Messiah Stones (novel), 1995. **Address:** c/o Barbara Lowenstein, Lowenstein Associates Inc., 121 W 27th St., Ste. 601, New York, NY 10001-6262, U.S.A.

BENISON, C. C. *See* **WHITEWAY, Doug(las) Alfred.**

BENITEZ, Sandra (Ables). American (born United States), b. 1941. **Genres:** Novels, Young Adult Non-fiction, Biography. **Career:** Gaunt High School, ninth-grade Spanish and English teacher, 1963-68; Northeast Missouri State University, teaching assistant, 1974; Wilson Learning Corp., freelance Spanish/English translator, 1975-76, marketing liaison in international division, 1977-80; The Loft and the University of Minnesota, fiction writer and creative writing teacher, 1980-; Loft Inroads Program, Hispanic mentor, 1989-92; University of Minnesota, Keller-Edelstein distinguished writer-in-residence, 1997. Writer. **Publications:** A Place Where the Sea Remembers, 1993; Home Views, A Place Called Home: Twenty Writing Women Remember, 1996; Bitter Grounds, 1997; Fire, Wax, Smoke, Sleeping with One Eye Open: Women Writers and the Art of Survival, 1999; The Weight of All Things, 2000; Night of the Radishes, 2003; Bag Lady: A Memoir, 2005. Contributor articles and periodicals. **Address:** c/o Ellen Levine, Ellen Levine Literary Agency, Trident Media Group, 41 Madison Ave., Fl. 36, New York, NY 10010-2257, U.S.A. **Online address:** benitezbooks@msn.com

BENJAMIN, Carol Lea. American (born United States) **Genres:** Animals/Pets, Mystery/Crime/Suspense, Novels, Young Adult Non-fiction, Children's Fiction. **Career:** Writer. **Publications:** NONFICTION: Dog Training for Kids, 1976, 2nd ed., 1988; (with A.J. Haggerty) Dog Tricks: New Tricks for Old Dogs, Old Tricks for New Dogs, and Ageless Tricks That Give Wise Men Paws, 1978; Running Basics, 1979; Dog Problems: A Professional Trainer's Guide to Preventing and Correcting Aggression, 1981; Cartooning for Kids, 1982; Mother Knows Best: The Natural Way to Train Your Dog, 1985; Writing for Kids, 1985; Second-hand Dog: How to Turn Yours into a First-Rate Pet, 1988; The Chosen Puppy: How to Select and Raise a Great Puppy from an Animal Shelter, 1990; Surviving Your Dog's Adolescence: A Positive Training Program, 1993; Dog Training in 10 Minutes, 1997; Dog Smarts: The Art of Training Your Dog 2007; See Spot Sit: 101 Illustrated Tips for Training the Dog You Love, 2008; Do Border Collies Dream of Sheep?, 2010. FICTION: The Wicked Stepdog, 1982; Nobody's Baby Now, 1984. RACHEL ALEXANDER AND DASH MYSTERIES: This Dog for Hire, 1996; The Dog Who Knew Too Much, 1997; Dash P.I., 1997; A Hell of a Dog, 1998; Lady Vanishes, 1999; The Wrong Dog, 2000; The Long Good Boy, 2001; Fall Guy, 2004; Without a Word, 2005; The Hard Way, 2006. **Address:** Brandt & Brandt Literary Agents, 1501 Broadway, Ste. 2310, New York, NY 10036, U.S.A. **Online address:** clb@carolleabenjamin.com

BENJAMIN, Denis R(ichard). American/South African (born South Africa), b. 1945. **Genres:** Medicine/Health, Sciences, Botany. **Career:** Johannesburg General Hospital, intern in surgery, 1969; Non-European Hospital, intern in medicine, 1969; Transvaal Memorial Hospital for Children, intern in pediatrics, 1970; University of Washington, resident in anatomic pathology, 1970-72, clinical pathology, 1972-74, chief resident in laboratory medicine, 1973-74, assistant professor, 1975-80, associate professor, 1980-90, professor of laboratory medicine and pathology, adjunct professor of pediatrics, 1990-; Cook Children's Orthopedic Hospital and Medical Center, assistant pathologist, 1974, Division of Laboratory Medicine, head, 1975, School of Medical Technology, director, 1975, Department of Laboratories, associate director, 1977-84, director, 1984-; Children's Cancer Study Group, pathologist for acute myeloid leukemia, 1980-90; Paediatric Pathology Society, president; Project Hope and Harvard Medical Intl., consultant. Writer. **Publications:** Mushrooms: Poisons and Panaceas: A Handbook for Naturalists, Mycologists and Physicians, 1995. Contributor to medical books, medical journals and popular magazines. **Address:** Department of Laboratories and Pathology, Cook Children's Medical Center, 801 7th Ave., Fort Worth, TX 76104, U.S.A. **Online address:** dbenjamin@cookchildrens.org

BENJAMIN, Floella. British/Trinidadian (born Trinidad and Tobago), b. 1949. **Genres:** Food And Wine, Novellas/Short Stories, Children's Fiction. **Career:** Floella Benjamin Productions, founder, chief executive, 1987-; Floella Benjamin's Caribbean Kitchen (food company), founder; Dulwich College, governor; Exeter University, chancellor; National Film and Television School, governor; Touching Success (children's charity), founder. Writer. **Publications:** FOR CHILDREN: Fall about with Flo: A Collection of Zany Jokes, 1984; Floella's Fun Book, 1984; Why the Agouti Has No Tail: And Other Stories, 1984; Floella's Fabulous Bright Ideas Book, 1985; Floella's Funniest Jokes, 1985; Floella's Cardboard Box Book, 1987; How Will We Go?, 1987; Snotty and the Rod of Power, 1987; Where's the Giraffe?, 1987; How Do You Eat It?, 1988; For Goodness Sake! A Guide to Choosing Right from Wrong, 1994; Skip across the Ocean: Nursery Rhymes from around the World, 1995; Coming to England (autobiographical picture book), 1997; My Two Grannies, 2007. OTHERS: Caribbean Cookery, 1986; Exploring Caribbean Food in Britain, 1988. **Address:** Benjamin-Taylor Associates, 73 Palace Rd., London, GL SW2 3LB, England. **Online address:** website@floellabenjamin.com

BENJAMIN, Joan. American (born United States), b. 1956. **Genres:** Homes/Gardens, Children's Fiction, Crafts, Horticulture. **Career:** Flower and Garden Magazine, editorial assistant, 1977; Shelter Insurance Co., gardener, 1978-80; Apple Valley Farm, farm manager, 1981-82; Columbia Parks and Recreation Department, landscape technician, 1982-88; Callaway Gardens, interpretive horticulturist, 1990-92; Rodale Press Inc., associate editor, 1992-. **Publications:** (With B.W. Ellis) Rodale's No-Fail Flower Garden: How to Plan, Plant and Grow a Beautiful, Easy-Care Garden, 1994, 2nd ed., 1997; (with B.W. Ellis and D.L. Martin) Rodale's Low-Maintenance Gardening Techniques: Shortcuts and Time-Saving Hints for Your Greatest Garden Ever, 1995, 2nd ed., 1999; (ed.) Great Garden Shortcuts: Hundreds of All-New Tips and Techniques that Guarantee You'll Save Time, Save Money, Save Work, 1996; (ed. with D.L. Martin) Great Garden Formulas: The Ultimate Book of Mix-It-Yourself Concoctions for Your Garden, 1998. **Address:** Rodale Press Inc., 33 E Minor St., Emmaus, PA 18098-0099, U.S.A.

BENJAMIN, Saragail Katzman. American (born United States), b. 1953. **Genres:** Children's Fiction, Animals/Pets, Novels. **Career:** Lincoln Center Institute, teaching artist, 1986-87, artist-in-residence; The Music of Business Inc., founder and facilitator. Writer and musician. **Publications:** CHILDREN'S FICTION: My Dog Ate It, 1994. Contributor to periodicals. **Address:** The Music of Business Inc., 27 Kewanee Rd., New Rochelle, NY 10804-1323, U.S.A. **Online address:** saragail@joyfulnoiseprograms.com

BENKLER, Yochai. American/Israeli (born Israel), b. 1964?. **Genres:** Business/Trade/Industry, Economics. **Career:** Kibbutz Shizafon, treasurer, 1984-87; Harvard College, teaching fellow, 1992-94; Ropes & Gray, associate, 1994- 95; United States Supreme Court, law clerk to Justice Stephen Breyer, 1995-96; New York University School of Law, assistant professor of law, 1996-99, faculty codirector of JSD Program, 1997-2001, associate professor of law, 1999-2001, professor of law, 2001-03, Engleberg Center for Innovation Law and Policy and of the Information Law Institute, director, 2000-03; Yale Law School, visiting professor of law, 2001-02, Joseph M. Field professor of law, 2003-07; Harvard Law School, visiting professor of law, 2002- 03, Jack N. and Lillian R. Berkman professor of entrepreneurial legal studies, 2007-; Berkman Center for Internet and Society, faculty codirector, 2007-. Writer and lawyer. **Publications:** Rules of the Road for the Information Superhighway: Electronic Communications and the Law, 1996; The Wealth of Networks: How Social Production Transforms Markets and Freedom, 2006; The Penguin and the Leviathan: The Triumph of Cooperation over Self-Interest, 2011. Contributor to books, journals and periodicals. **Address:** Harvard Law School, 1563 Massachusetts Ave., Cambridge, MA 02138, U.S.A. **Online address:** ybenkler@law.harvard.edu

BENMALEK, Anouar. French (born France), b. 1956. **Genres:** Novels. **Career:** Novelist. **Publications:** Cortge d'Impatience: Poésie et Prose, 1984; La Barbarie: lettre Madame Simone de Beauvoir que Feraient Bien de Lire M. Claude Lanzmann M. Bernard-Henri Lévy M. André Glucksmann et autres, 1986; Ludmila ou Le violon la mort lente, 1986; L'amour loup, 1994; Les amants dé Sunis, 1998; L'enfant du peuple ancien, 2000; The Lovers of Algeria, 2001; Chroniques de l'Algérie amre: 1985-2002, 2003; The Child of an Ancient People, 2003; Ma plante me monte la tête: historiettes hue et dia pour briser le coeur humain, 2005; O Mariá: Roman, 2006; Anneé de la putain: petits romans et autres nouvelles, 2006; Rapt: Roman, 2009. **Address:** Librairie Arthme Fayard, 75 rue des Saints-Pres, Paris, 75278, France.

BENN, Tony. British (born England), b. 1925. **Genres:** Politics/Government, History, Essays. **Career:** British Broadcasting Corp. North American Service, political talks producer, 1949-50; British Parliament, House of Commons for Bristol Southeast, labour member, 1950-60, 1963-83, 1984-; writer and educator, 1961-63; British Labour Party, vice-chair of party, 1970, chair, 1971-72; Government of England, Minister of technology, 1966-70, shadow minister of trade and industry, 1970-74, secretary of state for industry and minister of posts and telecommunications, 1974-75, secretary of state for energy, 1975-79. **Publications:** The Privy Council as a Second Chamber, 1957; The Regeneration of Britain, 1965; The Government's Policy for Technology, Special Lecture given at Imperial College of Science & Technology, 17th October 1967, 1967; The New Politics: A Socialist Reconnaissance, 1970; Speeches, 1974; Labour and the Slump: The Text of a Letter to the Bristol South East Constituency Labour Party, 1975; (with F. Morrell and F. Cripps) Ten-year Industrial Strategy for Britain, 1975; New Course for Labour, 1976; (contrib.) New Worker Co-Operatives, 1976; (co-author) Report of the Inquiry into Serious Gas Explosions, 1977; Right to Know: The Case for Freedom of Information to Safeguard our Basic Liberties, 1978; Why America needs Democratic Socialism, 1978; Industry, Technology and Democracy, 1978; Arguments for Socialism, 1979; Energy Crisis: One Man's View, 1980; (contrib.) The Crisis and the Future of the Left: The Debate of the Decade, 1980; Arguments for Democracy, 1981; Parliament, People and Power: Agenda for a Free Society: Interviews with New Left Review, 1982; (ed.) Writings on the Wall: A Radical and Socialist Anthology, 1215-1984, 1984; Sizewell Syndrome, 1984; (contrib.) Benn Inheritance: The Story of a Radical Family, 1984; Out of the Wilderness: Diaries 1963-67, 1987; Office without Power: Diaries 1968-72, 1988; Fighting Back: Speaking Out for Socialism in the Eighties, 1988; Against the Tide: Diaries, 1973-1976, 1989; Conflicts of Interest: Diaries, 1977-80, 1990; The End of an Era: Diaries 1980-90, 1992; (with A. Hood) Common Sense: A New Constitution for Britain, 1993; Speaking Up in Parliament, 1993; Benn Tapes, 1994; Years of Hope: Diaries 1940-1962, 1994; The Benn Diaries 1940-1990, 1995; (ed. and forword) Common Sense and The Rights of Man, 2000; Free at Last!: Diaries, 1990-2001, 2002; Free Radical: New Century Essays, 2003; Dare to be a Daniel: Then and Now, 2004. **Address:** c/o Anne McDermid, Curtis Brown Group Ltd., Haymarket House, 28-29 Haymarket, London, GL SW1Y 4SP, England. **Online address:** thebennites@yahoo.co.uk

BENNAHUM, David S. (David Solomon Bennahum). American/French (born France), b. 1968?. **Genres:** Music, Biography, Technology. **Career:** Writer, 1991-; Wired Magazine, staff, 1994-2004; Lingua Franca Magazine, staff, 1994-2004; I.D. Magazine, staff, 1995-99; Slate, columnist, 1996-2004; TV and radio commentator, 1996-; MEME, founder, 1995-; The American Independent News Network, president and chief executive officer. **Publications:** In Their Own Words: The Beatles after the Breakup, 1991; In Her Own Words: k.d. lang, 1995; Extra Life: Coming of Age in Cyberspace, 1998. Contributor to periodicals. **Address:** American Independent News Network, 1825 Connecticut Ave. NW, Ste. 625, Washington, DC 20009, U.S.A. **Online address:** davidsol@panix.com

BENNAHUM, David Solomon. *See* **BENNAHUM, David S.**

BENNAHUM, Judith Chazin. American (born United States), b. 1937. **Genres:** Dance/Ballet, Fash Ion/Costume. **Career:** Professional ballet dancer, 1954-64; University of New Mexico, head of dance program, 1987-92, Department of Theatre and Dance, chair, professor of theater and dance, 1988-, distinguished professor, distinguished professor emerita of dance, 2006-; Santa Fe Opera, teacher of body movement; Metropolitan Opera Ballet Co., principal; The Opera Academy, choreographer; The South West Ballet Co., choreographer. Writer. **Publications:** Dance in the Shadow of the Guillotine, 1988; The Ballets of Antony Tudor: Studies in Psyche and Satire, 1994; The Living Dance: An Anthology of Essays on Movement and Culture, 2003; The Lure of Perfection: Fashion and Ballet, 1780-1830, 2004; (ed.) Teaching Dance Studies, 2005; René Blum and the Ballets Russes: In Search of a Lost Life, 2011. Contributor of articles to journals. **Address:** Department of Theatre and Dance, University of New Mexico, MSC04 2570, Albuquerque, NM 87131-0001, U.S.A. **Online address:** gigiben@unm.edu

BENNASSAR, Bartolomé. French (born France), b. 1929. **Genres:** Novels, History, Literary Criticism And History. **Career:** Lyceé Ageh, teacher, 1950-56; College M. T. Rodez, teacher, 1950-56; Lyceé Périer Marseille, teacher, 1950-56; Casa de Velázquez, fellow resident, 1955-56; University of Toulouse, professor, professor of Spanish history, 1956-90, rector, 1978-80, now professor emeritus; Oxford University, visiting professor, 1973. Writer. **Publications:** Le Dernier Saut (novel), 1962; Le coup de midi (novel), 1964; Valladolidet Ses Campagnes au Sied d'or, 1967; Une fille en Janner (novel), 1968; (with J. Jacquart) Le XVIe Siecle, 1972; L'Homme Espagñol: Attitudes et Mentalites du XVIe auXIXe Siécle, 1975; (with P. Chaunu) L'Ouverture du Monde: XIVe-XVIe Siécles, 1977; L'inquisition Espagnole: XVe-XIXe Siécle, 1979; Un Siecle d'or Espagnol: Vers 1525-Vers 1648, 1982; Viure a la intempèrie, 1985; Histoire des Espagnols (series), 1985-92; La America Espagnola y la America Portuguesa, 1986; La Europa del Renacimiento, 1988; La Europa del siglo XVII, 1989; (with L. Bennassar) Les Chretiens D'Allah: L'histoire Extraordinaire des Renégats, XVIe et XVIIeSiécles, 1989; (with L. Bennassar) Los cristianos de Alá: la fascinante aventura de los renegrados, 1989; (co-author) Estado, hacienda y sociedad en la historia de España, 1989; (co-author) Le Premier âge de l'état en Espagne: 1450-1700, 1989; Valladolid, 1752: Según de Oru: Una Ciudadde Castilla y Su Entorno Agrario en el Siglo XVI, 1989; (with B. Bessiere) Le Défi Espagnol, 1991; (with L. Bennassar) 1492: Un monde nouveau?, 1991; Pouvoirs et Société dans L'Espagne Moderne: Hommage áBartolomé Bennasar, 1993; Histoire de la Tauromachie: Une Societe duSpectacle, 1993; (with P. Fullana) Carlisme i integrisme a Mallorca (1887-1889), 1993; Histoire du syndicalisme dans le monde, 1994; Franco, 1995; Les Tribulations de Mustafa des Six-Fours (novel), 1995; Les catastrophes naturelles dans l'Europe médiévale et moderne, 1996; (with J. Carpentier and F. Lebrun) Histoire de la Mediterranee, 1998; (with L. Bennassar) Le voyage en Espagne: Anthologiedes Voyageurs Francais et francophones du XVI au XIX Siécle, 1998; (with B. Vincent) Le Temps de L'Espagne, 1999; Franco: enfance et adolescence, 1999; (with V. Bernard) Le tempsde L'Espagne: XVI-XVII Síles, 1999; (with R. Marin) Histoire du Brisil 1500-2000: Don Juan de Austria: Un Heroe Para Un Imperio, 2000; (intro.) Young Charles V, 1500-1531, 2000; Cortes: le Conquérant de l'impossible, 2001; Toutes les Colombies: Roman, 2002; Miqueleta: une Femme des Annees '30 au Coeur de la Tauromachie, 2002; L'inquisition espagnole et la construction de la monarchie confessionnelle, 1478-1561, 2002; Vivir el Siglo de Oro: Poder, Cultura e Historia en la Epoca Moderna: Estudios en Homenaje al Profesor Angel Rodriguez Sanchez, 2003; Guerre d'Espagne et ses lendemains, 2004; Todas Las Colombias, 2004; Lit, le Pouvoir et la Mort: Reines et Princess d'Europe de la renaissance Aux Lumiéres, 2006; Les Chrétiens d'Allah: L'histoire Extraordinaire des Renégats, XVIe et XVIIe Siécles, 2006; Rivieres de ma vie: Memoires d'un pecheur de Truites, 1947-2006, 2008. **Address:** Université de Toulouse, 15 rue des Lois, Toulouse, 31000, France. **Online address:** bennassar@univ-tlse2.fr

BEN-NER, Yitzhak. Israeli (born Israel), b. 1937. **Genres:** Children's Fiction, Novels. **Career:** Journalist and film critic. **Publications:** Be-Ikvot Mavir Ha-Sadot, 1966; Ha-Ish Mi-Sham, 1967; The Man From There, 1970; Sheḳiah kafrit, 1976; ḳishonah: alilot a-lah-Yaaḳov ya-ḥavurato, 1978; Aḥare ha-geshem: sheloshah sipurim, 1979; Megamot Be-Siporet Ha-Hoveh: Ha-Sipur He Havui: Sipurim ve-Novelot, 1979; Yedidi Imanuel ya-ani, 1980; Be-iḳmavir ha-śadot, 1980; Erets reḥTEroman be-sipurim, 1981; Proṭoḳroman, 1982; Davar aḥ, 1986; Malakhim baim: roman, 1987; Ta'tu'on, 1989; Ugins: Kalba Lo Mikhnasayim, 1991; Jeans, 1991; Boḳhel shoṭ, 1992; After the Rain, 1992; Sipurim, 1993; Dubim ya-yaar, 1995; Rustic Sunset, 1997; Mitḥam oyev, 1997; Ir miḳlat, 2000; Sufat ḥol omedet le-hagia: ha-ḳolot ha-baim ba-siporet ha-Yiśreelit, 2005; Af eḥad od lo met ba-halikhah, 2007. **Address:** c/o Author Mail, Lynne Rienner Publishers Inc., 1800 30th St., Ste. 314, Boulder, CO 80301, U.S.A.

BENNETT, Alan. British (born England), b. 1934. **Genres:** Novellas/Short Stories, Plays/Screenplays, History, Young Adult Non-fiction. **Career:** Playwright and screenwriter, 1959-; Oxford University, Magdalen College, junior lecturer in history, 1960-62; North Craven Heritage Trust, president, 1968-93. **Publications:** (Co-author) Beyond the Fringe: A Revue, 1963; Forty Years On, 1969; Getting On, 1972; Habeas Corpus: A Play in Two Acts, 1973; The Old Country, 1978; Enjoy, 1980; Office Suite (2 plays), 1981; An Englishman Abroad, 1982; Forty Years On, Getting On, Habeas Corpus and Enjoy, 1985; A Private Function, 1985; The Writer in Disguise, 1985; Kafka's Dick, 1986; Two Kafka Plays: Kafka's Dick and The Insurance Man, 1987; Prick Up Your Ears, 1988; The Lady in the Van, 1990; Plays One, 1991; The Wind in the Willows, 1991; The Madness of George III, 1992, as The Madness of King George, 1995; (co-author) Poetry in Motion 2, 1992; Writing Home, 1995, rev. ed., 2006; Bed Among the Lentils: A Monologue from Talking Heads, 1998; A Cream Cracker Under the Settee: A Monologue from Talking Heads, 1998; Her Big Chance: A Monologue from Talking Heads, 1998; Plays Two, 1998; The Complete Talking Heads, 1998; Father! Father! Burning Bright, 2000; A Box of Alan Bennett, 2000; The Laying on of Hands (Stories), 2000; The Clothes They Stood Up In, 2001; Alan and Thora, 2004; Four Stories, 2006; The History Boys, 2006; Untold Stories, 2006; The Uncommon Reader, 2007; Habit of Art, 2009; Captain Roy Brown: The Definitive Biography, Including His Encounter With the Red Baron, Manfred Von Richthofen, 2010; A Life Like Other People's, 2010; (contrib.) Hogarth's Marriage à la mode, 2010; Smut: Two Unseemly Stories, 2011. NON-FICTION: A Working Life: Child Labour Through the Nineteenth Century, 1990; (with N. Franks) The Red Baron's last Flight: A Mystery Investigated, 1997: (with N. Sherrin and D. Thompson) Loose Canon: A Portrait of Brian Brindley, 2004. Contributor to periodicals. **Address:** United Agents, 12-26 Lexington St., London, GL W1F 0LE, England.

BENNETT, Charles A. American (born United States), b. 1947. **Genres:** Adult Non-fiction, Physics, Sciences. **Career:** Volunteer Central, founder. Writer, advertising and marketing specialist and motivational speaker. **Publications:** Volunteering: The Selfish Benefits: How to Achieve Deep-Down

Satisfaction and Create That Desire in Others, 2001; (with D.E. Pressey) Ojai Valley's Veterans Stories: 33 Stories from Military Veterans of the Ojai Valley's VFW Post 11461, 2003; Principles of Physical Optics, 2008. **Address:** Tom Brennan Media, 1119 Colorado Ave., Ste. 1, Santa Monica, CA 90401, U.S.A. **Online address:** bennettasc@aol.com

BENNETT, Cherie. Also writes as Zoey Jeffrey, C. J. Anders. American (born United States), b. 1960. **Genres:** Young Adult Fiction, Plays/Screenplays. **Career:** Playwright, columnist and director. **Publications:** SUNSET ISLAND SERIES: Sunset Island, 1991; Sunset Kiss, 1991; Sunset Dreams, 1991; Sunset Farewell, 1991; Sunset Reunion, 1991; Sunset Heat, 1992; Sunset Paradise, 1992; Sunset Promises, 1992; Sunset Scandal, 1992; Sunset Secrets, 1992; Sunset Whispers, 1992; Sunset after Dark, 1993; Sunset after Hours, 1993; Sunset after Midnight, 1993; Sunset Deceptions, 1993; Sunset Embrace, 1993; Sunset on the Road, 1993; Sunset Surf, 1993; Sunset Wishes, 1993; Sunset Touch, 1993; Sunset Wedding, 1993; Sunset Fantasy, 1994; Sunset Fire, 1994; Sunset Glitter, 1994; Sunset Heart, 1994; Sunset Illusions, 1994; Sunset Magic, 1994; Sunset Passion, 1994; Sunset Revenge, 1994; Sunset Sensation, 1994; Sunset Stranger, 1994; Sunset Fling, 1995; Sunset Holiday, 1995; Sunset Love, 1995; Sunset Spirit, 1995; Sunset Tears, 1995; Sunset Forever, 1997. YOUNG ADULT NOVELS: Good-Bye, Best Friend, 1993; Girls in Love, 1996; Bridesmaids, 1996; Searching for David's Heart, 1998; Life in the Fat Lane, 1998; Zink, 1998; The Haunted Heart, 1999; And the Winner Is, 1999; The Wedding That Almost Wasn't, 1999; Love Him Forever, 1999; (with J. Gottesfeld) Anne Frank and Me, 2001; (with J. Gottesfeld) A Heart Divided, 2004. PUBLISHED PLAYS: John Lennon and Me, 1993; Sex Anne Frank and Me, 1995; Cyra and Rocky, 1996. SURVIVING SIXTEEN TRILOGY: Did You Hear about Amber?, 1993; The Fall of the Perfect Girl, 1993; Only Love Can Break Your Heart, 1994. CLUB SUNSET ISLAND TRILOGY: Too Many Boys!, 1994; Dixie's First Kiss, 1994; Tori's Crush, 1994. WILD HEARTS SERIES: Hot Winter Nights, 1994; On the Edge, 1994; Passionate Kisses, 1994; Wild Hearts, 1994; Wild Hearts Forever, 1994; Wild Hearts on Fire, 1994. TEEN ANGELS SERIES WITH JEFF GOTTESFELD: Heaven Can't Wait, 1996; Love Never Dies, 1996; Angel Kisses, 1996; Heaven Help Us!, 1996; Nightmare in Heaven, 1996; Love without End, 1996. HOPE HOSPITAL SERIES: Get Well Soon, Little Sister, 1996; The Initiation, 1996; The Accident, 1997. TRASH SERIES WITH JEFF GOTTESFELD: Trash, 1997; Trash: Love, Lies and Video, 1997; Trash: Good Girls, Bad Boys, 1997; Dirty Big Secrets, 1997; Trash: The Evil Twin, 1997; Trash: Truth or Scare, 1998. PAGEANT SERIES: The National Pageant, 1998; Southern Girls, 1999; The Midwest Girls, 1999; Northeast Girls, 1999; West Coast Girls, 1999; Winners on the Road, 1999. MIRROR IMAGE SERIES WITH JEFF GOTTESFELD: Stranger in the Mirror, 1999; Rich Girls in the Mirror, 2000; Star in the Mirror, 2000; Flirt in the Mirror, 2000. WITH JEFF GOTTESFELD AS C.J. ANDERS: Shifting into Overdrive, 2008; Double Exposure, 1999; Too Hot to Handle, 1999; Trouble in Paradise, 1999; Tough Enough, 2000; Don't Scream, 2000; Playing for Keeps, 2000; A Capeside Christmas, 2000; Running on Empty, 2000. Samantha Tyler's Younger Sister. UNIVERSITY HOSPITAL SERIES WITH JEFF GOTTESFELD: University Hospital, 1999; Condition Critical, 1999; Crisis Point, 2000; Heart Trauma, 2000; Prognosis, Heart Break, 2002. WITH JEFF GOTTESFELD: Anne Frank and Me, 2001; See no Evil, 2002; Speed, 2003; Greed, 2003; Flight, 2002; Sparks, 2004; Amen, L.A., 2011; Wrestlemaniac, 2011. AS ZOEY DEAN: (with J. Gottesfeld) The A-List, 2003; Blonde Ambition, 2004; Girls on Film, 2004; Back in Black, 2005; Tall Cool One, 2005; Some like it Hot, 2006; American Beauty, 2006; How to Teach Filthy rich Girls, 2007; Heart of Glass, 2007; Beautiful Stranger, 2007; California Dreaming, 2008; Privileged, 2008; Talent, 2008; Zoey Dean's Almost Famous, 2008; Hollywood is like High School with Money, 2009; Zoey Dean's Star Power, 2009; Sunset Boulevard, 2009; City of Angels, 2010. OTHER: Reviving Ophelia, 2006. **Address:** c/o Ricki Olshan, Don Buchwald & Associates, 10 E 44th St., New York, NY 10017, U.S.A. **Online address:** authorchik@aol.com

BENNETT, Clinton. American/British (born England), b. 1955. **Genres:** Education, Theology/Religion. **Career:** Government of New South Wales, clerical officer, 1972-74; Baptist Missionary Society, minister and distance education tutor, 1978-83; Birmingham Ethnic Education and Advisory Service, tutor, 1983-86; Aston University, free church chaplain, 1986-87; British Council of Churches, executive secretary, 1987-92; King Alfred's College, lecturer, 1992-98; Westminster College, senior lecturer, 1992-98; Baylor University, associate professor, 1998-2001; Birchfield Community School, principal officer and clerk, 2001-05; Birmingham University, Graduate Institute for Theology and Religion, visiting fellow, 2002-05; Center for the Study of Jewish-Christian Relations, affiliated lecturer, 2003-05; UTS, associate professor, 2005-07; New World Encyclopedia, history and biography editor, 2005-09; State University of New York, adjunct faculty, 2008-; Marist College, adjunct faculty, 2009-; Royal Asiatic Society, fellow; Royal Anthropological Institute, fellow; American Biographical Institute, fellow. Writer. **Publications:** Victorian Images of Islam, 1992; In Search of the Sacred: Anthropology and the Study of Religions, 1996; (with C. Higgins and L. Foreman-Peck) Researching Teaching Methods in Colleges and Universities, 1996; In Search of Muhammad, 1998; In Search of Jesus: Insider and Outsider Images, 2001; Muslims and Modernity: An Introduction to the Issues and Debates, 2005; Understanding Christian-Muslim Relations, 2008; In Search of Solutions: The Problem of Religion and Conflict, 2008; Interpreting the Qur'an: A Guide for the Uninitiated, 2009; (intro.) Christianity and Islam: The Bible and the Koran, 2009; Studying Islam, 2010; Understanding the Qur'an, 2010; Interpreting the Qur'an: A Guide for the Uninitiated, 2010. **Address:** 89 Oval Rd., Erdington, Birmingham, B24 8PY, England. **Online address:** cb@clintonbennett.net

BENNETT, Colin J. Canadian/British (born England), b. 1955. **Genres:** Politics/Government, Social Sciences. **Career:** University of Victoria, assistant professor, 1986-91, Department of Political Science, associate professor, 1991-, professor, chair; Harvard's Kennedy School of Government, fellow, 1999-2000; University of California, Center for the Study of Law and Society, visiting fellow, 2007. Writer. **Publications:** Regulating Privacy: Data Protection and Public Policy in Europe and the United States, 1992; (ed. with R. Grant) Visions of Privacy: Policy Choices for the Digital Age, 1999; (with C.D. Raab) Governance of Privacy: Policy Instruments in Global Perspective, 2003, 2nd ed., 2006; Privacy Advocates: Resisting the Spread of Surveillance, 2008; (ed. with D. Lyon) Playing the Identity Card: Surveillance, Security and Identification in Global Perspective, 2008; (ed. with K.D. Haggarty) Security Games, 2011. Contributor to journals. **Address:** Department of Political Science, University of Victoria, Rm. SSM A336, STN CSC, Cornett Bldg., PO Box 3060, Victoria, BC V8W 3R4, Canada. **Online address:** cjb@uvic.ca

BENNETT, Edward M. American (born United States), b. 1927. **Genres:** International Relations/Current Affairs, History, Medicine/Health. **Career:** Texas A&M University, instructor, 1960-61; Washington State University, assistant professor of history, 1961-66, associate professor of history, 1966-71, professor of U.S. diplomatic history, 1971-94, professor emeritus of history, 1994-, Pacific-Eight Conference, president, 1972. Writer. **Publications:** (With J.W. Wulfeck) The Language of Dynamic Psychology, As Related to Motivation Research, 1954; (with H.M. Goodwin) Emotional Aspects of Political Behavior: The Woman Voter, 1958; (ed.) Polycentrism: Growing Dissidence in the Communist Bloc?, 1967; Recognition of Russia: An American Foreign Policy Dilemma, 1970; (with H.C. Payne and R. Callahan) As the Storm Clouds Gathered: European Perceptions of American Foreign Policy in the 1930s, 1979; German Rearmament and the West, 1932-1933, 1979; Mental Health Information Systems: Problems and Prospects, 1983; Franklin D. Roosevelt and the Search for Security: American-Soviet Relations, 1933-1939, 1985; Theoretical and Empirical Advances in Community Mental Health, 1985; Social Intervention: Theory and Practice, 1987; Franklin D. Roosevelt and the Search for Victory: American-Soviet Relations, 1939-1945, 1990; Separated by a Common Language: Franklin Delano Roosevelt and Anglo-American Relations, 1933-1939, 2002; (with N.A. Graebner) The Versailles Treaty and Its Legacy: The Failure of the Wilsonian Vision, 2011. EDITOR: Polycentrism: Growing Dissidence in the Communist Bloc?, 1967; (with R.D. Burns) Franklin D. Roosevelt Diplomats in Crisis: United Stetes-Chinese-Japanese Relations, 1919-1941, 1974. **Address:** Department of History, Washington State University, 301 Wilson-Short Hall, 173 Bohler, PO Box 644030, Pullman, WA 99164-0001, U.S.A. **Online address:** embennet@wsunix.wsu.edu

BENNETT, Elizabeth. *See* **HARROD-EAGLES, Cynthia.**

BENNETT, Emma. *See* **HARROD-EAGLES, Cynthia.**

BENNETT, Georgette. American/Hungarian (born Hungary), b. 1946. **Genres:** Civil Liberties/Human Rights, Criminology/True Crime, International Relations/Current Affairs. **Career:** City University of New York, assistant professor of sociology, 1970-77; New York City Office of Management and Budget, deputy assistant director for administration of justice, 1977-78; NBC News, network correspondent, 1978-80; MacNeil-Lehrer News, story development consultant; Bennett Associates, owner and president, 1980-87, 1992-; First New York Bank for Business (formerly First Women's Bank), vice president and marketing director, 1987, first vice president and chief marketing officer, 1987-88, senior vice president and division executive of domestic and international and private banking, 1988-92; Rabbi Marc H. Tanenbaum Foundation, president, 1992-; Tanenbaum Center for Interreligious Understanding, founder and president, 1992-. Writer. **Publications:** (Co-author) Women in Policing: A Manual, 1975; (co-author) Law Enforcement and Criminal Justice: An Introduction, 1979; Unlocking America: Commercial Union's Keys to Community Crime Prevention, 1981; Protecting against Crime, 1982; A Safe Place to Live, 1982; Crimewarps: The Future of Crime in America, 1987, rev. ed., 1989. Contributor of articles to books and periodicals. **Address:** Tanenbaum Center for Interreligious Understanding, 254 W 31st St., 7th Fl., New York, NY 10001-2813, U.S.A. **Online address:** gfbennett@bennettny.com

BENNETT, G. H. British (born England), b. 1967. **Genres:** History, Politics/Government, Biography, Military/Defense/Arms Control. **Career:** University of Plymouth, head of American studies and head of humanities, School of Humanities and Performing Arts, associate professor in history, reader in history. Writer. **Publications:** British Foreign Policy during the Curzon Period, 1919-24, 1995; (with R. Bennett) Survivors: British Merchant Seamen in the Second World War, 1999; (with M. Gibson) The Later Life of Lord Curzon of Kedleston-Aristocrat, Writer, Politician, Statesman: An Experiment in Political Biography, 2000; The American Presidency 1945-2000: Illusions of Grandeur, 2000; An American Regiment in Devon: The U.S. Army's 116th Infantry Regiment, Omaha Beach and the Photography of Olin Dows, 2003; (ed.) Roosevelt's Peacetime Administrations, 1933-41: A Documentary History of the New Deal Years, 2004; (with R. Bennett) Hitler's Admirals, 2004; Destination Normandy: Three American Regiments on D-Day, 2007; (with G.S. Guinn) British Naval Aviation in World War II: The U.S. Navy and Anglo-American Relations, 2007; RAF's French Foreign Legion 1940-45, 2011; Hitler's Ghost Ships, 2011; Hunting Tirpitz, 2011; The Policeman and the Painter, 2011; (ed.) Raiding Support Regiment: A Memoir, 2011; Killing Time, forthcoming; The Policman and the Painter: Holocaust, Truth and Justice in the Ukraine, forthcoming. **Address:** University of Plymouth, Rm. 1, 6 Portland Villas, Drake Circus, Plymouth, DN PL4 8AA, England. **Online address:** h.bennett-1@plymouth.ac.uk

BENNETT, Hal Z(ina). American (born United States), b. 1936. **Genres:** Self Help, Writing/Journalism, Medicine/Health, Adult Non-fiction. **Career:** Consulting psychologist, 1989-. Writer, teacher and publishing consultant. **Publications:** Behind the Scenes, 1967; The Vanishing Pirate, 1967; Battle of Wits, 1968; Brave the Dragon, 1969; No More Public School, 1972; (with M. Samuels) The Well Body Book, 1972; (with M. Samuels) Spirit Guides: Access to Secret Worlds, 1973; (with M. Samuels) Be Well, 1973; Cold Comfort: Colds and Flu-Everybody's Guide to Self-Treatment, 1977; The Doctor Within, 1978; Sewing for the Outdoors, 1979; (with J. Marino) John Marino's Bicycling Book, 1980; The Complete Bicycle Commuter, 1982; (with M. Samuels) Well Body, Well Earth, 1984; (with C.A. Garfield) Peak Performance: Mental Training Techniques of the World's Greatest Athletes, 1984; Mind Jogger: A Problem-Solving Companion, 1986; Inner Guides, Visions, Dreams, 1987; Lens of Perception: A Users Guide to Higher Consciousness, 1987, 3rd ed., 2007; (with M. Larsen) How to Write with a Collaborator, 1988; (with S.J. Sparrow) Follow Your Bliss: Let the Power of What You Love Guide You to Personal Fulfillment in Your Work and Relationships, 1990; (with S. Grof) The Holotropic Mind: Three Levels of Human Consiousness and How They Shape Our Lives, 1992; The Zuni Fetishes, 1993; (with R.T. Kiyosaki) If You Want to Be Rich & Happy, Don't Go to School: Ensuring Lifetime Security for Yourself and Your Children, 1993; (with L.N. Topf) You Are Not Your Illness: Seven Principles for Meeting the Challenge, 1995; Write from the Heart: Unleashing the Power of Your Creativity, 1995, rev. ed., 2001; (with S.J. Sparrow) Spirit Guides: What They are, How to Meet Them, and How to Make Use of Them in Every Area of Your Life, 1997; Invitation to Success: An Allegory about Creativity, 1997; White Mountain Blues, 1997; Spirit Circle: A Story of Adventure and Shamanic Revelation, 1998; Spirit Animals and the Wheel of Life, 2001; First Light, the Queit: Poems and Other Writings, 2002; Writing Spiritual Books: A Best-Selling Writer's Guide to Successful Publication, 2004; Backland Graces: Four Novellas, 2008; Write Starts: Prompts, Quotes, and Exercises to Jumpstart Your Creativity, 2010. EDITOR: The Tooth Trip, 1974; The New Dimensions Books Series, 1994; Emerging from Invisibility, 1997. **Address:** 9827 Irvine Ave., Upper Lake, CA 95485, U.S.A. **Online address:** halbooks@halzinabennett.com

BENNETT, Holly. Canadian (born Canada), b. 1957. **Genres:** Young Adult Fiction, Human Relations/Parenting, Writing/Journalism. **Career:** Wanepuhnud Corp., project coordinator, 1980-81; Wandering Spirit Survival School, secretary; Todays Parent (magazine), editorial trainee, 1986-, junior editor, editor-in-chief of special editions, 1994-2011; Trent University, instructor. **Publications:** The Bonemender, 2005; The Bonemender's Oath, 2006; The Warrior's Daughter, 2007; The Bonemender's Choice, 2007; Shapeshifter, 2010. **Address:** 606 Walkerfield Ave., Peterborough, ON K9J 4W4, Canada. **Online address:** hbennett27@cogeco.ca

BENNETT, James B. American (born United States), b. 1967. **Genres:** Novels, Theology/Religion. **Career:** Pew Notes, editor, 1994-96; University of Oklahoma, assistant professor, 2000-02; Santa Clara University, assistant professor of religious studies, 2002-08, associate professor of religious studies, 2008-. **Publications:** Religion and the Rise of Jim Crow in New Orleans, 2005. Contributor to journals. **Address:** Religious Studies Department, Santa Clara University, 500 El Camino Real, Santa Clara, CA 95053, U.S.A. **Online address:** jbbennett@scu.edu

BENNETT, James Richard. American (born United States), b. 1932. **Genres:** Civil Liberties/Human Rights, Communications/Media, Humanities, Literary Criticism And History, Military/Defense/Arms Control, Politics/Government, History. **Career:** University of Montana, assistant professor, 1960-62; Style, founder and editor, 1966-82; University of Western Washington, assistant professor, 1962-65; University of Arkansas, assistant professor, 1965-66, associate professor, 1966-71, professor, 1971-98, professor emeritus, 1998-; Myers Center for the Study of Human Rights, founder and director, 1984-98; Whistleblowers Research Center, founder and director, 1998-2002; Peace Research Center, director, 1998-; Omni Center for Peace, Justice and Ecology, founder and director. **Publications:** Prose Style: A Historical Approach through Studies, 1972; Guide to European Museums of the Anti-Nazi and Anti-Fascist Resistance and the Concentration and Extermination Camps, 1976; Bibliographies: Stylistics and Related Criticism, 1986; Control of Information in the United States, 1987; Control of the Media in the United States, 1991; Political Prisoners and Trials, 1995; Peace Movement Directory, 2001. **Address:** 2582 Jimmie Ave., Fayetteville, AR 72703, U.S.A. **Online address:** jbennet@uark.edu

BENNETT, Joe. New Zealander/British (born England), b. 1957. **Genres:** Travel/Exploration, Young Adult Fiction, Animals/Pets. **Career:** Christ Church College, faculty; The Press, columnist. **Publications:** Just Walking the Dogs, 1998; Fun Run and Other Oxymorons: Singular Reflections of an Englishman Abroad, 2000; So Help Me Dog, 2000; Sit, 2001; Bedside Lovers, 2002; Doggone, 2002; Barking, 2003; A Land of Two Halves: An Accidental Tour of New Zealand, 2004; Unmuzzled, 2004; Dogmatic, 2005; Down Boy, 2006; Mustn't Grumble: An Accidental Return to England, 2007; Eyes Right (and They's Wrong): Joe Bennett Sets the World Straight, Again, 2007; Love, Death, Washing-Up, Etc.: Joe Bennett Sorts It Out, 2007; Where Underpants Come From: From Checkout to Cotton, Field Travels through the New China, 2008; Laugh?: I Could have Cried, 2008; Alive and Kicking, 2008; The World's Your Lobster, 2009; Hello Dubai, 2010; Celebrity Cat Recipes, 2010. **Address:** c/o James Gill, United Agents, 12-26 Lexington St., London, GL W1F 0LE, England. **Online address:** joe@caverock.net.nz

BENNETT, John M(ichael). American (born United States), b. 1942. **Genres:** Poetry. **Career:** Ohio State University, assistant professor of Hispanic literature, 1969-76, University Libraries, Latin American Bibliographic assistant and special collections editor, 1976-98; Luna Bisonte Prods, publisher, 1974-; National Association for Poetry, board director, 1983-84; Association for Applied Poetry, vice-president, 1984-86; poetry therapist, 1985; Avant Writing Collection, curator, 1998-. **Publications:** Found Objects, 1973; Works, 1973; (with P. Virumbrales) La Revolucion, 1976; (ed. and intro. With P. Virumbrales) El Pensamiento político latinoamericano: selecciones, 1976; White Screen, 1976; Meat Dip, 1976; Do Not Cough, 1976; Meat Watch, 1977; Contents, 1978; Time Release, 1978; Nips Poems, 1980; (with C.M. Bennett) Pumped Gravel, 1980; Main Road, 1980; Motel Moods, 1980; (with R. Crozier) Meat Click, 1980; Puking Horse, 1980; Jerks, 1980; (with C.M. Bennett) Applied Appliances, 1981; (with C.M. Bennett) Some Blood, 1982; Blender, 1983; Burning Dog, 1983; Antpath, 1984; Nose Death, 1984; No Boy, 1985; 13 Splits, 1986; The Poems, 1987; Cascade, 1987; Stones in the Lake, 1987; Twitch, 1988; Swelling, 1988; Regression, 1988; Lice, 1989; Live Chains, 1990; Milk, 1990; (with S.E. Murphy) Lens Rolled in a Heart, 1990; Span, 1990; Bell-Nail, 1991; Was Ah, 1991; Fenestration, 1991; Johnee's Box, 1991; (with J. Berry) The Lemurs, 1991; (with J. Brewton) Somation, 1992; Neuf Poemes, 1992; Bleached, 1992; (with D. Clark and C. Culhane) Bag Talk, 1992; Leg, 1992; Wave, 1993; Blind on the Temple, 1993; Dry, 1993; Blanksmanship, 1994; (with D. Metcalf) Bone-flag, 1994; Just Feet, 1994; Infused, 1994; Spinal Speech, 1995; Fish, Man, Control, Room, 1995; Eddy, 1995; Prime Sway: A Transduction of Primero Sueno by Sor Juana Ines de la Cruz, 1996; Ridged, Poeta, 1996; Door Door, 1997; Cul Lit, 1997; The Seasons, 1997; Clown Door, 1997; Know Other, 1998; Sendero Luminoso in Context, 1998; Loose Watch: A Lost And Found Times Anthology, 1998; Mailer Leaves Ham, 1999; Rolling Combers, 2001; (with I. Arguelles) Decima Mucho, 2001; (with I. Arguelles) Chac Prostibulario, 2001; (with K.S. Ernst) Pon a Time Falme, 2001; (with R. Altemus) Yr Cream Dip, 2001; Ditch Clith, 2001; (with S. Helmes) Clunk, 2001; Greatest Hits 1978-2000, 2001; (with R. Crozier) The Chapters, 2002; Historietas Alfabeticas, 2003; Public Cube, 2003; The Peel, 2004; (co-ed.) Everything Lost: The Latin American Notebook of William S. Burroughs, 2008; Spitting Ddreams, 2008; Rrêves, 2009; (contrib.) Franticham's Assembling Box Nr 10: Visual Poetry & Fluxus Inspired Works. From 23 Artists from 13 Countries, 2011. **Address:** Luna Bisonte Prods, 137 Leland Ave., Columbus, OH 43214, U.S.A. **Online address:** bennett.23@osu.edu

BENNETT, Lerone. American (born United States), b. 1928. **Genres:** History, Social Sciences, Adult Non-fiction. **Career:** Atlanta Daily World, newspaper journalist, reporter, 1949-52, city editor, 1952-53; Jet Magazine, city editor, 1952-53, associate editor, 1953; Ebony Magazine, editorial staff, associate editor, 1954-57, senior editor, 1958-87, executive editor, 1987-; Northwestern University, visiting professor of history, 1968-69; Institute of the Black World, senior fellow, 1969. **Publications:** NONFICTION: Before the Mayflower: A History of the Negro in America, 1619-1962, 1962, 7th ed., 2003; The Negro Mood and Other Essays, 1964; What Manner of Man: A Biography of Martin Luther King, Jr., 1929-1968, 1964, 4th ed., 1976; Confrontation: Black and White, 1965; Black Power USA: The Human Side of Reconstruction, 1867-1877, 1967; Pioneers in Protest, 1968; The Challenge of Blackness, 1970; The Shaping of Black America, 1975; Wade in the Water: Great Moments in Black History, 1979, 2nd ed., 2000; (with J.H. Johnson) Succeeding Against the Odds, 1989; The Shaping of Black America, 1993; Forced into Glory: Abraham Lincoln's White Dream, 2000; National Visionary Leadership Project Oral History, 2004-04-15: Lerone Bennett, Jr., 2009. Contributor to books. **Address:** Ebony Magazine, 820 S Michigan Ave., Chicago, IL 60605, U.S.A.

BENNETT, Merit. American (born United States), b. 1947. **Genres:** Law, Medicine/Health, Psychology, Social Sciences. **Career:** Tinkler and Bennett (law firm), partner, 1975-; Dukes v. Wal-Mart Stores Inc., co-counsel. Writer. **Publications:** Law and the Heart: A New Paradigm for Lawyer-Client Relationships, 1994; Law and the Heart: A Practical Guide for Successful Lawyer/Client Relationships, 1997. **Address:** The Bennett Firm, 460 St. Michael's Dr., Ste. 703, Santa Fe, NM 87505, U.S.A.

BENNETT, Neville. British (born England), b. 1937. **Genres:** Education. **Career:** International Marine Radio Co., radio officer, 1965-61; British Aerospace, radar engineer, 1961-65; University of Lancaster, research officer, 1969-70, lecturer, 1970-76, senior lecturer, 1977-78, Centre for Educational Research and Development, director, 1978-85, Department of Educational Research, professor, head, 1981-85; University of Exeter, professor of primary education, 1985-, Centre for Research on Teaching and Learning, director, 1987-, now professor emeritus. Writer. **Publications:** Research design, 1973; Teaching Styles and Pupil Progress, 1976; Focus on Teaching: Readings in the Observation and Conceptualisation of Teaching, 1979; Open Plan Schools, 1980; The Quality of Pupil Learning Experiences, 1984; Recent Advances in Classroom Research, 1985; A Good Start: Four Year Olds in Infant Schools, 1989; (with A. Cass) From Special to Ordinary Schools: Case Studies in Integration, 1989; Learning and Instruction, vol. II-III, 1989; Talking and Learning in Groups, 1990; Managing Classroom Groups, 1992; (ed. with C. Carré)Learning to Teach, 1993; Teaching through Play, 1996; (with E. Dunne and C. Carré) Skills Development in Higher Education and Employment, 2000. **Address:** School of Education, University of Exeter, Streatham Campus, Northcote House, Exeter, DN EX4 4QJ, England. **Online address:** s.n.bennett@exeter.ac.uk

BENNETT, R.G. Stephen. (Elliot Long). British (born England), b. 1928?. **Genres:** Westerns/Adventure, Young Adult Fiction, Novels. **Career:** Writer. **Publications:** AS ELLIOT LONG: The Brothers Grant, 1990; Savage Land, 1990; Incident at Ryker's Creek, 1990; Death on High Mesa, 1991; Wassala Valley Shootout, 1991; Marshal of Gunsight, 1991; A Killing at Tonto Springs, 1992; Lawless Range, 1992; Showdown at Crazy Man Creek, 1992; Trail to Nemesis, 1993; Stopover at Rever, 1993; Warpath, 1994; Mankiller, 1995; Death Trail, 1995; Sixgun Predator, 1996; The Hanging Man, 1996; Last Texas Gun, 1996; Meet at Ipona Basin, 1997; Return to Callyville, 1997; Bushwhack at Wolf Valley, 1997; Welcome to Hell, 1998; Scallon's Law, 1999; Retribution Day, 1999; Guntalk at Catalee, 1999; Wolf, 2000; Hot Day at Noon, 2001; Hard-Dying Man, 2002; Killer on the Loose, 2007; Blood on the Sky, 2008; Death Range, 2009; Big Trouble at Flat Rock, 2010. **Address:** 61 Heathfield Nook Rd., Harpur Hill, Buxton, DB SK17 9SA, England.

BENNETT, Robert S. (Robert Stephen Bennett). American (born United States), b. 1939. **Genres:** Law. **Career:** United States District Court for the District of Columbia, law clerk, 1965-67; United States Department of Justice, assistant United States attorney, 1967-70; Hogan & Hartson L.L.P., associate, 1970-75; Dunnells, Duvall, Bennett, & Porter, founding partner, 1975-90; George Washington University, adjunct professor, 1975-79; District of Columbia Commission on Judicial Disabilities and Tenure, special counsel, 1976-82; Skadden, Arps, Slate Meagher & Flom L.L.P., partner, 1990-; Court of Arbitration for Sport, judge, 2002-. Writer. **Publications:** (Co-author) American Bar Association National Institute on Parallel Grand Jury and Administrative Agency Investigations, the Criminal and Civil Implications for Corporations and Their Officers: Phoenix, Arizona, Thursday, Friday, Saturday, November 2, 3, and 4, 1978, 1978; (co-author) A Report on the Crisis in the Catholic Church in the United States, 2004; In the Ring: The Trials of a Washington Lawyer, 2008. **Address:** Skadden, Arps, Slate Meagher & Flom L.L.P., 1440 New York Ave. NW, Washington, DC 20005-2111, U.S.A. **Online address:** robert.bennett@skadden.com

BENNETT, Robert Stephen. *See* **BENNETT, Robert S.**

BENNETT, Robert W. American (born United States), b. 1941. **Genres:** Law. **Career:** Chicago Legal Aid Bureau, OEO Reginald Heber Smith Fellow, 1967-68; Mayer, Brown & Platt, attorney, 1968-69; Chicago Council of Lawyers, co-founder, director, 1969-74, 1977-79, president, 1971-72; Northwestern University, School of Law, assistant professor, 1969-71, associate professor, 1971-74, professor, 1974-2002, dean, 1985-95, Nathaniel L. Nathanson professor of law, 2002-; United States Department of Justice, Community Relations Service, consultant, 1970-72; Administrative Conference of the United States, consultant, 1971-72; professional arbitrator, 1974-; University of Southern California, Law Center, visiting professor, 1982-83; American Bar Foundation, director, 1986-95, treasurer, 1986-87, vice president, 1990-92, president, 1992-94; George M. Pullman Educational Foundation, board director, 1986-96, 1997-; National Association for the Advancement of Colored People Legal Defense and Educational Fund Inc., co-chair, 1988-94; Chicago Appleseed Foundation, director, 2002-; Brooklyn Law School, visiting professor, 2004-05. Writer. **Publications:** (With A.B. LaFrance, M.R. Schroeder and W.E. Boyd) Hornbook on Law of the Poor, 1973; Representing the Audience in Broadcast Proceedings, 1974; (co-author) Harvard Child Health Project Report, vol. I: Toward a Primary Medical Care System Responsive to Children's Needs, 1977; Visions of the First Amendment for a New Millennium: Americans Speak Out on the Future of Free Expression, 1992; Talking It Through: Puzzles of American Democracy, 2003; Taming the Electoral College, 2006; (with L.B. Solum) Constitutional Originalism: A Debate. 2011. Contributor of articles to books, periodicals and journals. **Address:** School of Law, Northwestern University, 357 E Chicago Ave., Chicago, IL 60611-3059, U.S.A. **Online address:** r-bennett@law.northwestern.edu

BENNETT, Robin K. American/Cuban (born Cuba), b. 1964. **Genres:** Animals/Pets. **Career:** All About Dog Care L.L.C., co-owner and dog trainer, 1993-; Dream Dog Productions, owner. Writer. **Publications:** All about Dog Daycare: A Blueprint for Success, 2005; (with S. Briggs) Off-Leash Dog Play: A Complete Guide to Safety & Fun, 2008. **Address:** Dream Dog Productions, PO Box 4221, Woodbridge, VA 22194, U.S.A. **Online address:** robin@allaboutdogdaycare.com

BENNETT, Ronan. British/Irish (born Ireland), b. 1956. **Genres:** Novels, Film, Adult Non-fiction. **Career:** The Guardian, contributor; The Observer, contributor; Institute of Historical Research, research fellow, 1986-87; University of Bolton, School of Arts, Media and Education, staff. Writer. **Publications:** NOVELS: The Second Prison, 1992; Overthrown by Strangers, 1992; A Man You Don't Meet Every Day, 1994; Cinema e Libertà, 1995;

The Catastrophist, 1998; The Catastrophist: A Novel, 1999; Do Armed Robbers Have Love Affairs?, 2001; Havoc, in Its Third Year: A Novel, 2004; Zugzwang: A Novel, 2007. NON FICTION: Stolen Years: Before And After Guildford, 1990; Double Jeopardy: The Retrial of the Guildford Four, 1993; William Harvey and the Human Heart: How Harvey Revolutionized the Way We Think About the Body And Its Soul, 2004. Contributor to periodicals. **Address:** Tessa Sayle Agency, 1 Petersfield, Cambridge, GL CB1 1BB, England.

BENNETT, Ruth. *See* **WELLS, Shirley.**

BENNETT, Shelley M. American (born United States), b. 1947. **Genres:** Art/Art History, History, Bibliography, Photography. **Career:** University of Illinois, assistant professor of art history, 1977-78; University of Iowa, assistant professor of art history, 1978-80; Henry E. Huntington Art Gallery, assistant curator, 1980-83, associate curator of British and continental art, 1983-91, curator, 1991-; University of California, visiting professor, 1981-93; California Institute of Technology, lecturer in art history, 1987-; University of Southern California, faculty, 1990-. Writer. **Publications:** (Contrib.) Drawings From the Turner Shakespeare, 1973; (with P. Crown) English Book Illustration circa 1800, 1979; Prints by the Blake Followers (exhibition catalog), 1981; (contrib.) Essays on the Blake Followers, 1983; British Narrative Drawings and Watercolors, 1660-1880: Twenty-Two Examples From The Huntington Collection, 1985; Thomas Stothard: The Mechanisms of Art Patronage in England circa 1800, 1988; (ed. with M. Leonard and S. West) A Passion for Performance: Sarah Siddons and Her Portraitists, 1999; (ed.) British Paintings at the Huntington, 2001; (ed. with C. Sargentson) French Art of the Eighteenth-Century At The Huntington, 2008. Contributor to books and periodicals. **Address:** Division of the Humanities and Social Sciences, California Institute of Technology, MC 228-77, 1200 E California Blvd., Pasadena, CA 91125, U.S.A.

BENNETT, Vanora. British (born England), b. 1962. **Genres:** Novels, Economics, Young Adult Non-fiction. **Career:** Times, leader-writer; Reuters, Moscow correspondent; Los Angeles Times, Moscow correspondent. Journalist. **Publications:** Crying Wolf: The Return of War to Chechnya, 2001; The Taste of Dreams: An Obsession with Russia and Caviar, 2003; Portrait of an Unknown Woman, 2007; Figures in Silk in UK as Queen of Silks, 2008; Blood Royal in US as Queen's Lover, 2009; How to Get Over Love by Reading Russian Novels, 2010; The People's Queen, 2010. Contributor to periodicals. **Address:** c/o Natasha Fairweather, AP Watt Ltd., 20 John St., London, WC1N 2DR, England. **Online address:** vanora@vanorabennett.com

BENNETT, W. Lance. American (born United States), b. 1948. **Genres:** Politics/Government, Cultural/Ethnic Topics, Money/Finance, History. **Career:** University of California, lecturer in social sciences, 1973-74; University of Washington, Department of Political Science, assistant professor, 1974-76, associate professor, 1976-82, professor, 1982-, chair, 1993-96, acting chair, 1997-98, Ruddick C. Lawrence professor of communication, 2000-, Center for Communication and Civic Engagement, founding director, 2000-; TVW (Washington State public affairs network), director; Harvard University, Kennedy School of Government, Laurence M. Lombard visiting professor. Writer. **Publications:** The Political Mind and the Political Environment: An Investigation of Public Opinion and Political Consciousness, 1975; Public Opinion in American Politics, 1980; (with M.S. Feldman) Reconstructing Reality in the Courtroom: Justice and Judgment in American Culture, 1981; News: The Politics of Illusion, 1983, 9th ed., 2012; The Governing Crisis: Media, Money, and Marketing in American Elections, 1992, 2nd ed., 1996; (with E. Asard) Regulating the Marketplace of Ideas: Tax Reform and Election Rhetoric in Sweden and the United States, 1992; (ed. with D.L. Paletz) Taken by Storm: The Media, Public Opinion, and U.S. Foreign Policy in the Gulf War, 1994; Inside the System: Culture, Institutions, and Power in American Politics, 1994; (with E. Asard) Democracy and the Marketplace of Ideas: Communication and Government in Sweden and the United States, 1997; (ed. with R.M. Entman) Mediated Politics: Communication in the Future of Democracy, 2001; (with R.G. Lawrence and S. Livingston) When the Press Fails: Political Power and the News Media from Iraq to Katrina, 2007; (ed.) Civic Life Online: Learning How Digital Media Can Engage Youth, 2008. Contributor to books and journals. **Address:** Department of Political Science, University of Washington, 115 GWN, PO Box 353530, Seattle, WA 98195-3530, U.S.A. **Online address:** lbennett@u.washington.edu

BENNETT-ENGLAND, Rodney (Charles). British (born England), b. 1936. **Genres:** Writing/Journalism, Communications/Media, Fash Ion/Costume, Food And Wine, Homes/Gardens, Medicine/Health, Sports/Fitness. **Career:** Sunday Express, reporter and columnist, 1961-68; The Journal, editor, 1965-67, 1996-2003; Lords and Penthouse magazines, contributing editor, 1967-70; National Council in the Training of Journalists, chairman, 1968-69, 1977-79, 1984-85, 2001-04, director, 1994-; RBE Associates Ltd., chairman and managing director, 1968-81; Men Only, 1970-73; B&E Intl., editor, 1977-79; Connections Ltd., chairman, 1982, managing director, 1985-87; Media Society, secretary, 1984-96; Chartered Institute of Journalists, president, 1985-86; Newsline U.K., editor-in-chief, 1993-98; Journalism Training, editor, 1994-. Writer. **Publications:** (Contrib.) Faith in Fleet Street, 1967; (ed.) Inside Journalism, 1967; Dress Optional: The Revolution in Menswear, 1967; As Young As You Look: Male Grooming and Rejuvenation, 1970. Contributor to periodicals and books. **Address:** Church in Danger, Church Cottage, PO Box 132, East Rudham, NF PE31 8QT, England. **Online address:** rodney.bennettengland@virgin.net

BENNETT-GOLEMAN, Tara. American (born United States) **Genres:** Medicine/Health, Psychology, Self Help, Sciences. **Career:** Omega Institute, psychotherapist and workshop teacher. Writer. **Publications:** (Co-author) The Relaxed Body Book: A High-Energy Anti-Tension Program, 1986; Emotional Alchemy: How the Mind Can Heal the Heart, 2001. **Address:** Omega Institute, 150 Lake Dr., Rhinebeck, NY 12572-3252, U.S.A.

BENNIS, Phyllis. American (born United States), b. 1951?. **Genres:** Politics/Government, History. **Career:** United Nations (UN), journalist; Institute for Policy Studies, New Internationalism Project, director; U.S. Campaign to End Israeli Occupation, co-founder, 2001; Transnational Institute, fellow. Journalist and peace activist. **Publications:** From Stones to Statehood: The Palestinian Uprising, 1990; Calling the Shots: How Washington Dominates Today's UN, 2000; Before and After: U.S. Foreign Policy and the September 11th Crisis, 2003; Challenging Empire: How People, Governments, and the UN Defy U.S. Power, 2006; Understanding the Palestinian-Israeli Conflict: A Primer, 2007; Ending the Iraq War: A Primer, 2009; Understanding the US-Iran Crisis: A Primer, 2009; (with D. Wildman) Ending the U.S. War in Afghanistan: A Primer, 2009. EDITOR: (with M. Moushabeck) Beyond the Storm: A Gulf Crisis Reader, 1991; (with M. Moushabeck) Altered States: A Reader in the New World Order, 1993; War with No End, 2007. **Address:** Institute for Policy Studies, 1112 16th St. NW, Ste. 600, Washington, DC 20036, U.S.A. **Online address:** phyllis@ips-dc.org

BENOIT, Charles. American (born United States) **Genres:** Mystery/Crime/Suspense, Travel/Exploration, Novels. **Career:** Dixon Schwabl Inc., senior copywriter and producer. **Publications:** Relative Danger, 2004; Out of Order, 2006; Noble Lies, 2007; You, 2010. **Address:** c/o Author Mail, Poisoned Pen Press, 6962 E 1st Ave., Ste. 103, Scottsdale, AZ 85251, U.S.A. **Online address:** crbenoit@hotmail.com

BENOIT, William L. American (born United States), b. 1953. **Genres:** Communications/Media, Adult Non-fiction, Politics/Government. **Career:** Miami University of Ohio, visiting assistant professor of communication, 1979-80; Bowling Green State University, assistant professor, 1980-84; University of Missouri, assistant professor, professor of communication, 1984-; Journal of Communication, editor, 2002-05; Hong Kong Baptist University, fellow, 2006; Communication Studies, editor, 2007-09; Ohio University, School of Communication Studies, professor. **Publications:** (Ed. with P.J. Benoit and D. Hample) Readings in Argumentation, 1992; Accounts, Excuses and Apologies: A Theory of Image Restoration Strategies, 1995; (with W.T. Wells) Candidates in Conflict: Persuasive Attack and Defense in the 1992 Presidential Debates, 1996; (with J.R. Blaney and P.M. Pier) Campaign '96: A Functional Analysis of Acclaiming, Attacking and Defending, 1998; Seeing Spots: A Functional Analysis of Presidential Television Advertisements, 1952-1996, 1999; (with J.R. Blaney) The Clinton Scandals and the Politics of Image Restoration, 2001; (co-author) The Primary Decision: A Functional Analysis of Debates in Presidential Primaries, 2002; (co-author) Campaign 2000: A Functional Analysis of Presidential Campaign Discourse, 2003; (co-author) Bush Versus Kerry: A Functional Analysis of Campaign 2004, 2007; Communication in Political Campaigns, 2007; (with P.J. Benoit) Persuasive Messages: The Process of Influence, 2008. Contributor to periodicals. **Address:** Department of Communication, University of Missouri-Columbia, 127 Switzler Hall, 115 Switzler Hall, Columbia, MO 65211-2310, U.S.A. **Online address:** benoitw@missouri.edu

BEN-RAFAEL, Eliezer. Israeli/Belgian (born Belgium), b. 1938. **Genres:**

Cultural/Ethnic Topics, Language/Linguistics, Sociology. **Career:** Harvard University, Department of Sociology, research fellow, 1973-74; Hebrew University of Jerusalem, Department of Sociology and Social Anthropology, lecturer, 1973-74; Tel-Aviv University, Department of Sociology, senior lecturer, 1981, associate professor, 1986, professor of sociology, 1992-, Department of Sociology and Anthropology, Institute for Social Research, director, 1981-84, head, 1985-87, Zelman and Zima Weinberg Chair in Political Sociology, 1997-2007, professor emeritus, 2006-; Stanford University, Department of Sociology, visiting professor, 1984-85; Ecole des Hautes Etudes en Sciences Sociales, Centre de Sociologie Rurale, associate director of studies, 1984-85; The Kibbutz at the Turn of the Century, Yad Tabenkin Research Project, head, 1990-94; International Peace Research Association, consultant, 1991-93; Israeli Social Sciences Research, co-editor, 1993-98; International Institute of Sociology, vice-president, 1997-2001, president, 2001-05; Israeli Association for the Study of Language and Society, chair, 2001-04; Klal-Israel Project, co-founder and co-director, 2001-. **Publications:** Mahpekhot ha-sṭudenṭim, 1973; (with M. Lissak) Social Aspects of Guerilla and Anti-Guerilla Warfare, 1979; (with M. Konopnicki and P. Rambaud) Le Nouveau Kibboutz, 1979; The Emergence of Ethnicity, 1982; (with M. Konopnicki and P. Rambaud) Le Kibboutz, 1983; Israel-Palestine: A Guerrilla Conflict in International Politics, 1987; Status, Power, and Conflict in the Kibbutz, 1988; (with S. Sharot) Ethnicity, Religion, and Class in Israeli Society, 1991; (with I. Gaiș t) Tefisot shel shinui ba-ḳibuts, 1993; (with H. Ayalon and A. Yogev) Community in Transition, 1993; (with E. Avrahami) ḥoshvim ḳibuts: 'siaḥ anshe aḳademyah, ḥoḳrim ve-rashe ha-tenuah, 1994; (with with I. Gaiș t and E. Olsḥtain) Hebeṭim shel zehut ve-śafah bi-ḳeliṭat ole ḥever ha-Medinot ha-Atsmaiyot, 1994; Language, Identity, and Social Division: The Case of Israel, 1994; (with E. Avrahami) ḥoshvim ḳibuts, 1994; Mahpekhah lo ṭoṭalit, 1996; Crisis and Transformation, 1997; Zehuyot Yehudiyot, 2001; Jewish Identities, 2002; Jewish Identities: Fifty Intellectuals Answer Ben Gurion, 2002; (with Y. Peres) Is Israel One?: Religion, Nationalism, and Multiculturalism Confounded, 2005; (with L. Ben ḥayim) Zehuyot Yehudiyot be-'idan rav-moderni, 2006; (co-author) Building a Diaspora: Russian Jews in Israel, Germany, and the USA, 2006; (with Y. Peres) ḳirvah u-merivah: shesa'im ba-ḥevrah ha-Yiśreelit, 2006; Eliṭot ḥadashot be-Yiśra'el, 2007; (co-author) Ha-ḳibuts 'al derakhim mitpatslot, 2008; (co-author) Yehudim ba-hoveh, 2009; (with O. Glöckner and Y. Sternberg) Jews and Jewish Education in Germany Today, 2011. EDITOR: (with E. Olshtain) Language and Society in Israel, 2 vols., 1994; (with H. Herzog) Language & Communication in Israel, 2001; (with Y. Sternberg) Identity, Culture, and Globalization, 2001; Sociology and Ideology, 2003; (with Y. Gorny and Y. Ro'i) Contemporary Jewries: Convergence and Divergence, 2003; (with Y. Sternberg) Comparing Modernities: Pluralism Versus Homogenity: Essays in Homage to Shmuel N. Eisenstadt, 2005; Cleavages in Israeli Society, 2006; Jewish Identities in a Era of Multiple Modernities, 2006; (with T. Gergely and Y. Gorny) Jewry Between Tradition and Secularism: Europe and Israel Compared, 2006; (with Y. Sternberg) Transnationalism, 2009; (with Y. Sternberg) World Religions and Multiculturalism A Dialectic Relation, 2010; (with E. Shohamy and M. Barni) Linguistic Landscape in the City, 2010. **Address:** Department of Sociology, Tel Aviv University, Rm. 629, Naftali Bldg., Tel Aviv, 69978, Israel. **Online address:** saba@post.tau.ac.il

BENSEL, Richard Franklin. American (born United States), b. 1949. **Genres:** History, Politics/Government. **Career:** Texas A&M University, assistant professor, 1977-82; University of Texas, assistant professor, 1982-84; New School for Social Research, associate professor, 1984-88, acting director, 1987-88, 1991-92, chairman, 1990-91, professor, 1990-93; Cornell University, professor, 1993-2011, Gary S. Davis professor of government, 2011-, director of placement, 1995-98, 2001-02, director of graduate studies, 2003-06, Department of Government, associate chair, 2008-. Writer. **Publications:** Sectionalism and American Political Development, 1880-1980, 1984; Yankee Leviathan: The Origins of Central State Authority in America, 1859-1877, 1990; The Political Economy of American Industrialization, 1877-1900, 2000; The American Ballot Box in the Mid-Nineteenth Century, 2004; Passion and Preferences: William Jennings Bryan and the 1896 Democratic National Convention, 2008. Contributor to books and journals. **Address:** Government Department, Cornell University, White Hall, Ithaca, NY 14853, U.S.A. **Online address:** rfb2@cornell.edu

BENSLEY, Connie. British (born England), b. 1929. **Genres:** Poetry, Plays/Screenplays, Young Adult Fiction, Animals/Pets. **Career:** Writer. **Publications:** Progress Report, 1981; Moving In, 1984. POEMS: Central Reservations, 1990; Choosing to Be a Swan, 1994; The Back and the Front of It, 2000; The Covetous Cat, 2006; Private Pleasures, 2007. **Address:** 49 Westfields Ave., Barnes, London, GL SW13 0AT, England.

BENSMAN, David. American (born United States), b. 1949. **Genres:** History, Documentaries/Reportage, Politics/Government, Young Adult Fiction. **Career:** Rutgers State University, director of graduate program in labor studies, 1985-89, School of Management and Labor Relations, Department of Labor Studies and Employment Relations, associate professor, 1989-94, professor, 1994-. Writer. **Publications:** The Practice of Solidarity: American Hat Finishers in the Nineteenth Century, 1985; (with R. Lynch) Rusted Dreams: Hard Times in a Steel Community, 1987; (co-author) Who Built America?, vol. II, 1992; Lives of the Graduates: What Did They Do? What Did They Learn?, 1994; Learning to Think Well: Graduates of Central Park East Secondary School, 1995; Building Home-School Partnerships in a South Bronx Classroom, 1999; Central Park East and Its Graduates, 2000; Globalisation and Labour: The New 'Great Transformation, 2002. Contributor to books and periodicals. **Address:** Department of Labor Studies, School of Management & Labor Relations, Rutgers State University, Rm. 151, Labor Education Ctr., 50 Labor Center Way, New Brunswick, NJ 08901, U.S.A. **Online address:** dbensman@rci.rutgers.edu

BENSON, Ann. American (born United States) **Genres:** Crafts, Mystery/Crime/Suspense, History, Homes/Gardens. **Career:** Beads East (craft store), owner. Writer. **Publications:** Beadweaving: New Needle Techniques and Original Designs, 1993; Ann Benson's Beadwear: Making Beaded Accessories and Adornments, 1994; Beadwork Basics, 1994; Two-Hour Beaded Projects: More than 200 Designs, 1996; The Plague Tales (thriller), 1997; Burning Road: A Novel, 1999; Beading For the First Time, 2001; Thief of Souls: A Novel, 2002; Beadpoint: Beautiful Bead Stitching on Canvas, 2003; New Beadweaving: Great Projects with Innovative Materials, 2004; Designer Beadwork: Beaded Crochet Designs, 2005; Physician's Tale, 2006; Tapestry Bead Crochet: Projects & Techniques, 2010. Contributor to periodicals. **Address:** Beads East, 35 Oakland St., Manchester, CT 06042, U.S.A.

BENSON, Frank Atkinson. British (born England), b. 1921?. **Genres:** Technology, Engineering, Information Science/Computers, Sciences. **Career:** University of Sheffield, lecturer, 1949-59; senior lecturer, 1959-61; reader in electronics, 1961-67; professor, 1967-87, pro-vice-chancellor, 1972-76, professor emeritus of electronic and electrical engineering, 1987-. Writer. **Publications:** Electrical Engineering Problems with Solutions, 1954; Voltage Stabilized Supplies, 1957; Problems in Electronics with Solutions, 1958, 5th ed., 1976; (with D. Harrison) Electric Circuit Theory, 1959, 3rd ed., 1975; Voltage Stabilization, 1965; Electric Circuit Problems with Solutions, 1967, 2nd ed., 1975; (ed.) Millimetre and Submillimetre Waves, 1969; (with T.M. Benson) Fields, Waves and Transmission Lines, 1991. **Address:** 64 Grove Rd., Sheffield, SY S7 2GZ, England.

BENSON, Gerard. British (born England), b. 1931. **Genres:** Poetry, Autobiography/Memoirs, Children's Fiction, Literary Criticism And History. **Career:** Central School of Speech and Drama, senior lecturer, 1965-85; Wordsworth Trust: Center for British Romanticism, poet-in-residence, 1994. **Publications:** Name Game, 1971; Gorgon, 1984; The Magnificent Callisto, 1992; Evidence of Elephants, 1995; In Wordsworth's Chair, 1995; Bradford and Beyond: A Sonnet Journal, 1997; Help! 15 Poems, 2001; To Catch an Elephant (poetry for children), 2002; Omba Bolomba, 2005; A Good Time (poetry collection), 2010. EDITOR: (with W.B. Wright and C. Herbert) Barrow Poems, 1976; This Poem Doesn't Rhyme (for young people), 1990; Does W Trouble You?, 1994; (comp.) Nemo's Almanac (annual), 1997, rev. ed., 2000. WITH J. CHERNAIK AND C. HERBERT: 100 Poems on the Underground, 1991 as Poems on the Underground, 10th ed., 2001; London Poems on the Underground, 1996; Comic Poems on the Underground, 1996; Love Poems on the Underground, 1996; (ed.) New Poems on the Underground 2006; (ed.) Best Poems on the Underground, 2009. **Address:** Campbell Thomson & McLaughlin Ltd., 1 King's Mews, London, GL WC1N 2JA, England. **Online address:** gerardjbenson@hotmail.com

BENSON, Jackson J. American (born United States), b. 1930. **Genres:** Novellas/Short Stories, Literary Criticism And History, Biography, Young Adult Fiction, Novels, Essays. **Career:** Orange Coast College, instructor, 1956-62, associate professor of English, 1962-66; San Diego State University, assistant professor, 1966-69, associate professor, 1969-71, professor of English and American literature, 1971-97, professor emeritus, 1997-. Writer. **Publications:** Hemingway: The Writer's Art of Self-Defense, 1969; The True Adventures of John Steinbeck, Writer: A Biography, 1984; Looking for Steinbeck's Ghost, 1988; John Steinbeck, Writer: A Biography, 1990; Steinbeck's Cannery Row: A Reconsideration, 1991; Wallace Stegner: His

Life and Work, 1996; Wallace Stegner: A Study of the Short Fiction, 1998; Down by the Lemonade Springs: Essays on Wallace Stegner, 2001; The Ox-Bow Man: A Biography of Walter van Tilburg Clark, 2004; Under the Big Sky: A Biography of A.B. Guthrie Jr., 2009. EDITOR: (with R. Astro and intro.) Hemingway in Our Time, 1974; The Short Stories of Ernest Hemingway: Critical Essays, 1975; (with R. Astro) The Fiction of Bernard Malamud, 1977; The Short Novels of John Steinbeck: Critical Essays with a Checklist to Steinbeck Criticism, 1990; New Critical Approaches to the Short Stories of Ernest Hemingway, 1990; (with S. Shilliglaw) America and Americans and Selected Nonfiction, 2002. **Address:** Department of English, San Diego State University, 5500 Campanile Dr., San Diego, CA 92182-8140, U.S.A. **Online address:** jjbenson@inreach.com

BENSON, John. British (born England), b. 1945. **Genres:** Economics, History. **Career:** Sunderland Polytechnic, lecturer in history, 1973-74; Lady Mabel College of Education, lecturer in history, 1974-76; Wolverhampton University, Wolverhampton Polytechnic, lecturer, 1976-77, senior lecturer, 1977-86, professor of history, 1986-, professor emeritus of history, School of Law, social science and communications, research group coordinator. Writer. **Publications:** EDITOR: (with R.G. Neville) Studies in the Yorkshire Coal Industry, 1976; (with R.G. Neville and C.H. Thompson) Bibliography of the British Coal Industry, 1981; The Working Class in England: 1875-1914, 1984; (with G. Shaw) The Evolution of Retail Systems, 1800-1914, 1992; (with L. Ugolini) Cultures of Selling: Perspectives on Consumption and Society Since 1700, 2006. OTHERS: (comp. with R.G. Neville) Rotherham As It Was, 1976; (comp. with T. Raybould) Walsall As It Was, 1978; West Riding: Unique Photographs of a Bygone Age, 1978; British Coal Miners in the Nineteenth Century, 1980; British Coalminers in the Nineteenth Century: A Social History, 1980; The Penny Capitalists: A Study of Nineteenth-Century Working-Class Entrepreneurs, 1983; The Working Class in Britain: 1850-1939, 1989, rev. ed., 2003; Entrepreneurism in Canada, 1990; The Rise of Consumer Society in Britain 1880-1980, 1994; Prime Time: A History of the Middle Aged in Twentieth-Century Britain, 1997; Working Class in Britain, 1850-1939, 2003; Affluence and Authority: A Social History of Twentieth-Century Britain, 2005. **Address:** School of Humanities, Language & Soc Sciences, University of Wolverhampton, Millennium City Bldg. Rm. MC211, Wultruna St., Wolverhampton, WV1 1LY, England. **Online address:** j.benson@wlv.ac.uk

BENSON, Judi. American (born United States), b. 1947. **Genres:** Poetry, Human Relations/Parenting, Young Adult Fiction. **Career:** Jacksonville Symphony Orchestra, public relations director, 1975-78; Antioch University Intl., assistant director, 1980-87; Foolscap Magazine, editor, 1987; freelance writer, 1987-92; Royal London Hospital, bereavement counselor, 1992-94; Dumfries and Galloway Royal Infirmary, writer-in-residence, 2004-06. **Publications:** Somewhere Else, 1990; In the Pockets of Strangers, 1993; Call It Blue (poetry), 2000; The Thin Places (poetry), 2006. EDITOR: (with K. Smith) Klaonica: Poems for Bosnia, 1993; What Poets Eat (poems and recipes), 1994; (with A. Falk) The Long Pale Corridor (bereavement poems), 1995; (with K. Smith) You Again-Last Poems and Other Words, 2004. Contributor of poems to periodicals. **Address:** 78 Friars Rd., E Ham, London, GL E6 1LL, England. **Online address:** judi_benson2001@yahoo.com

BENSON, Ophelia. American (born United States) **Genres:** Anthropology/Ethnology, Psychology. **Career:** Butterflies and Wheels website, cofounder and editor; The Philosophers' Magazine, deputy editor. **Publications:** (With J. Stangroom) The Dictionary of Fashionable Nonsense: A Guide for Edgy People, 2004; (with J. Stangroom) Why Truth Matters, 2006; (with J. Stangroom) Does God Hate Women?, 2009. Contributor to periodicals. **Address:** The Continuum International Publishing Group, 80 Maiden Ln., Ste. 704, New York, NY 10038, U.S.A. **Online address:** opheliabenson@msn.com

BENSON, Peter. British (born England), b. 1956. **Genres:** Novels, Novellas/Short Stories, Young Adult Fiction. **Career:** Writer. **Publications:** The Levels (novel), 1987; A Lesser Dependency (novel), 1989; The Other Occupant (novel), 1990; Odo's Hanging (novel), 1993; Riptide (novel), 1994; A Private Moon, 1995; The Shape of Clouds, 1996. Works appear in anthologies. **Address:** Tessa Sayle Agency, 11 Jubilee Pl., London, GL SW3 3TD, England.

BENSON, Richard. British (born England), b. 1966. **Genres:** Novels, Young Adult Fiction, Sociology, Environmental Sciences/Ecology. **Career:** Beverley Guardian, reporter, 1988-89; Independent, freelance journalist, 1991-92; Face, associate editor, 1992-95, editor, 1995-98, consultant and development director, 1998; Arena, consultant and development director, 1998, editor, 1998-; Arena Homme Plus, editor, 1998-; Frank, editor, 1998-; Bug, consultant; Telegraph Magazine, journalist; Vogue, journalist; Sleaze Nation, journalist; Blueprint, journalist; Observer, journalist. **Publications:** (Ed.) Night Fever: Club Writing in The Face, 1980-1997, 1997; The Farm: The Story of One Family and the English Countryside, 2005. Contributor to periodicals. **Address:** c/o Author Mail, Hamish Hamilton, 80 Strand, London, GL WC2R 0RL, England.

BENSTOCK, Shari. American (born United States), b. 1944. **Genres:** Literary Criticism And History, Biography. **Career:** Drake University, instructor in English, 1970-72; Kent State University, instructor in English, 1972-74; University of Illinois, Departments of Political Science, affiliate, 1975-77, Departments of Clinical Medicine, affiliate, 1979-82; University of Tulsa, associate professor, 1982-86; University of Miami, Department of English, professor, 1987-, chair, 1996-2000, College of Arts and Science, associate dean, 2000-03. Writer. **Publications:** (With B. Benstock) Who's He When He's at Home, 1980; Women of the Left Bank: Paris 1900-1940, 1986; (ed.) Feminist Issues in Literary Scholarship, 1987; (ed. with M. Beja) Coping with Joyce: Essays from the Copenhagen Symposium, 1988; (ed.) The Private Self, 1988; Textualizing the Feminine, 1991; No Gifts from Chance: A Biography of Edith Wharton, 1994; (ed.) House of Mirth: Complete, Authoritative Text with Biographical and Historical Contexts, Critical History and Essays from Five Contemporary Critical Perspectives, 1994; (ed. with S. Ferriss) On Fashion, 1994; (ed. with S. Ferris) Footnotes: On Shoes, 2001; (with S. Ferris and S. Woods) A Handbook of Literary Feminism, 2002. **Address:** Department of English, University of Miami, Rm. 321, Ashe Bldg., 1252 Memorial Dr., Coral Gables, FL 33124, U.S.A. **Online address:** sbenstock@umiami.iv.miami.edu

BENT, Timothy (David). American (born United States), b. 1955. **Genres:** Translations, Literary Criticism And History. **Career:** Penguin USA (publisher), assistant, 1990-91; Arcade Publishing, senior editor, 1991-99; St. Martin's Press, senior editor, 1999-. **Publications:** (Ed.) Selected Poems, 1991. TRANSLATOR: Henry Miller: The Paris Years, 1996; The Lost Museum, 1997; Memoir in Two Voices, 1999; The Character of Rain, 2002; I Am Alive and You Are Dead: A Journey into the Mind of Philip K. Dick, 2004; Green Mountain, White Cloud: A Novel of Love in the Ming Dynasty, 2004; The Theory of Clouds, 2007. **Address:** St. Martin's Press, 175 5th Ave., 18th Fl., New York, NY 10010, U.S.A.

BENTLEY, C. F. *See* **RADFORD, Irene.**

BENTLEY, Joanne. American (born United States), b. 1928. **Genres:** Biography, Autobiography/Memoirs. **Career:** Psychologist, 1974-80; Asthmatic Children's Foundation, director, 1974-88; writer, 1980-; Volunteer Counseling Service of Rockland County, supervisor, 1993-. Educator. **Publications:** Hallie Flanagan: A Life in the American Theatre, 1988. Contributor of articles to journals. **Address:** 2 Castle Heights Ave., Upper Nyack, NY 10960, U.S.A.

BENTLEY, Joyce. (Josie Collins). British (born England), b. 1928. **Genres:** Novels, Romance/Historical, Biography, Food And Wine, Autobiography/Memoirs, Mystery/Crime/Suspense. **Career:** Law clerk, 1944-49; Blackburn and Darwen, freelance writer, 1958-; Constable Trophy for Northern Writers (now absorbed by North West Arts Council), founder and secretary, 1975-83; Blackburn Adult Centre, lecturer in creative writing, 1983-; Open University, lecturer in creative writing. **Publications:** NOVELS: Dangerous Refuge, 1974 in US as Secret of Strangeways, 1976; Ring of Fate, 1979; (as Josie Collins) The Mad Major, 1980; Proud Riley's Daughter, 1988; Sing Me a New Song, 1990; Peterloo Shadows, 1995. OTHERS: The Importance of Being Constance: A Biography of Oscar Wilde's Wife, 1983; Kenya, 2005; Wet, 2005; Soft, 2005; Smooth, 2005; Norway, 2005; Caribbean, 2005; Rough, 2006; Potatoes, 2006; Pasta, 2006; Hard, 2006; Eggs, 2006; Milk, 2006; Bread, 2006; Beans, 2006. **Address:** Silk Hall, Tockholes, Darwen, LC BB3 0NQ, England.

BENTLEY, Michael (John). Scottish/British (born England), b. 1948. **Genres:** History, Politics/Government, Philosophy. **Career:** University of Sheffield, professor of history, 1977-95; University of St. Andrews, School of History, professor of modern history, 1995-. Writer. **Publications:** The Liberal Mind, 1914-1929, 1977; (ed. with J. Stevenson) High and Low Politics in Modern Britain: Ten Studies, 1983; Politics without Democracy; Great Britain, 1815-1914: Perception and Preoccupation in British Government, 1985, 2nd ed. as Politics without Democracy, 1815-1914: Perception and Preoccupation in British Government, 1999; The Climax of Liberal Politics: British

Liberalism in Theory and Practice, 1868-1918, 1987; (ed.) Public and Private Doctrine: Essays in British History Presented to Maurice Cowling, 1993; (ed.) Companion to Historiography, 1997; Modern Historiography: An Introduction, 1999; Lord Salisbury's World: Conservative Environments in Late-Victorian Britain, 2001; Modernizing England's Past: English Historiography in the Age of Modernism, 1870-1970, 2005; Life and Thought of Herbert Butterfield: History, Science, and God, 2011. **Address:** School of History, University of St. Andrews, Rm. 1.17, St Katharine's Lodge, The Scores, St. Andrews, FF KY16 9AR, Scotland. **Online address:** mjb6@st-and.ac.uk

BENTLEY, Nancy. American (born United States), b. 1946. **Genres:** Children's Fiction, Plays/Screenplays, Children's Non-fiction, How-to Books, Reference. **Career:** Dancer-Fitzgerald-Sample, Department of Production, assistant, 1968-70; San Mateo Educational Resources Center, educational research assistant, 1972-74; Colorado Springs School District, media specialist, 1974-78, teacher, 1979-95, coordinator of information and technology, 1995-2002. Writer. **Publications:** I've Got Your Nose!, 1991; (with D. Guthrie) The Young Author's Do-It-Yourself Book, 1994; (with D. Guthrie) The Young Producer's Video Book, 1995; (with D. Guthrie) Putting on a Play, 1996; (with D. Guthrie) The Young Journalist's Book, 1998; (with D. Guthrie) Writing Mysteries, Movies, Monsters, and More, 2001; The Case of the Sneaky Stinger, 2003; The Case of the Garden Monster, 2003; The Case of the Missing Bluebirds, 2003; Don't be a Copycat!: Write a Great Report without Plagiarizing, 2008. BUSY BODY BOARD BOOK SERIES: Let's Go, Feet!, 1987; Do This, Hands!, 1987; Listen to This, Ears!, 1987; What's on Top, Head?, 1987. **Address:** 1220 W High Point Ln., Colorado Springs, CO 80904, U.S.A. **Online address:** info@nancybentley.freeservers.com

BENTLEY, Nancy Ann. American (born United States), b. 1961. **Genres:** Literary Criticism And History. **Career:** University of Pennsylvania, Department of English, associate professor and chair. Writer. **Publications:** The Ethnography of Manners: Hawthorne, James, Wharton, 1995; (ed. with S. Gunning) The Marrow of Tradition, 2002; Frantic Panoramas: American Literature and Mass Culture, 1870-1920, 2009. Contributor to books, journals and periodicals. **Address:** Department of English, University of Pennsylvania, Rm. 127, Fisher-Bennet Hall, 3340 Walnut St., Philadelphia, PA 19104-6273, U.S.A. **Online address:** nbentley@english.upenn.edu

BENTLEY, Peter J. British (born England), b. 1972. **Genres:** Sciences, Technology, Information Science/Computers, Biology. **Career:** University College London, honorary senior research fellow, Digital Biology Interest Group, head; Korean Advanced Institute for Science and Technology, collaborating professor. Writer. **Publications:** (Ed.) Evolutionary Design by Computers, 1999; Digital Biology: How Nature Is Transforming Our Technology and Our Lives, 2001; (with D.W. Corne) Creative Evolutionary Systems, 2002; (ed. with S. Kumar) On Growth, Form and Computers, 2003; (ed. with J. Timmis and E. Hart) Artificial Immune Systems: Second International Conference, ICARIS 2003, Edinburgh, UK, September 1-3, 2003: Proceedings, 2003; The Ph.D. Application Handbook, 2006; The Undercover Scientist: Investigating the Mishaps of Everyday Life, 2008, published in US as Why Sh*t Happens: The Science of a Really Bad Day, 2009; The Book of Numbers: The Secret of Numbers and How They Changed the World, 2008. **Address:** Department of Computer Science, University College London, Malet Pl., London, GL WC1E 6BT, England. **Online address:** p.bentley@cs.ucl.ac.uk

BENTON, D(ebra) A. American (born United States), b. 1953. **Genres:** Administration/Management, Business/Trade/Industry. **Career:** Benton Management Resources, founder, owner, public speaker and consultant, 1976-; Rocky Mountain News, contributing editor, 1993; KMGH-TV, career expert. **Publications:** Lions Don't Need to Roar: Using the Leadership Power of Professional Presence to Stand Out, Fit In and Move Ahead, 1992; How to Think Like a CEO: The 22 Vital Traits You Need to be the Person at the Top, 1996; $100, 000 Club: How to Make Six Figure Income, 1998; Secrets of a CEO Coach: Your Personal Training Guide to Thinking like a Leader and Acting like a CEO, 1999; How to Act Like a CEO: 10 Rules for Getting to the Top and Staying There, 2001; From Biotech to Hollywood: New Career Opportunities in Technology, 2002; Executive Charisma, 2003; CEO Material: How to be a Leader in Any Organization, 2009. Contributor to journals and newspapers. **Address:** Benton Management Resources Inc., 521 Rattlesnake Rd., Livermore, CO 80536, U.S.A. **Online address:** debra@debrabenton.com

BENTON, Jim. American (born United States), b. 1960. **Genres:** Young Adult Fiction, Novels, Children's Fiction, Education. **Career:** J.K. Benton Design Studio, owner, president. Artist, cartoonist and writer. **Publications:** Dealing with the Idiots in Your Life, 1993; My Pants are Haunted, 2004; It's Happy Bunny: Life. Get One and Other Words of Wisdom and Junk That Will Make You Wise or Something, 2005; It's Happy Bunny: Love Bites, 2005; It's Happy Bunny: What's Your Sign?, 2006; Problem with Here is that It's Where I'm From, by Jamie Kelly: Jim Benton's Tales from Mackerel Middle School, 2007; Cherise the Niece, 2007; Never Underestimate Your Dumbness, 2008; Three-headed Book, 2009. FRANNY K. STEIN: MAD SCIENTIST SERIES: Lunch Walks among Us, 2003; Attack of the 50-Foot Cupid, 2004; The Invisible Fran, 2004; The Fran That Time Forgot, 2005; Frantastic Voyage, 2006; It's Happy Bunny: The Good, The Bad and the Bunny, 2006; Fran with Four Brains, 2006; Frandidate, 2007; Franny K. Stein, Mad Scientist, 2007; Spooky Science, 2007. DEAR DUMB DIARY SERIES: Let's Pretend This Never Happened: By Jamie Kelly, 2004; My Pants Are Haunted: By Jamie Kelly, 2004; Am I the Princess or the Frog?: Jim Benton's Tales from Mackerel Middle School, 2005; Can Adults Become Human?, 2006; Never Do Anything Ever, 2006; It's Not My Fault I Know Everything, 2009; Worst Things in Life are also Free, 2010; Dear Dumb Diary, That's What Friends aren't for, 2010; Okay, So Maybe I Do Have Superpowers, 2011; Me!, 2011. DEAR DUMB DIARY YEAR TWO: School: Hasn't This Gone on Long Enough?, 2012; The Super-Nice Are Super-Annoying, 2012. **Address:** c/o Author Mail, Simon & Schuster, 1230 Ave. of the Americas, New York, NY 10020, U.S.A. **Online address:** jkbenton@aol.com

BENTON, Megan L. American (born United States), b. 1954. **Genres:** Literary Criticism And History. **Career:** Institute of Early American History and Culture, editorial apprentice, 1978-79; freelance editor, 1979-86; Pacific Lutheran University, adjunct professor, 1986-94, Publishing and Printing Arts Program, director, 1986-2002, assistant professor, 1994-98, associate professor of English, 1998-2002, fellow, 2002-, co-editor. **Publications:** (Ed. with B. Hutchinson) Nothing Rich, but Some things Rare: The South in Poetry from the Black Warrior Review, 1984; Beauty and the Book: Fine Editions and Cultural Distinction in America, 2000; (ed. with P. Gutjahr) Illuminating Letters: Typography and Literary Interpretation, 2001. Contributor to books and periodicals. **Address:** Humanities Division, Pacific Lutheran University, Tacoma, WA 98447, U.S.A. **Online address:** bentonml@plu.edu

BENTOS, Carlos. American/Uraguayian (born Uruguay), b. 1941. **Genres:** Romance/Historical, Environmental Sciences/Ecology, Essays. **Career:** El Caribe (restaurant chain), owner, 1974-2004; Fathoms Grill, general manager and co-owner; Voice of America, commentator. Writer. **Publications:** A Crew of One: The Odyssey of a Solo Marlin Fisherman, 2002. **Address:** c/o Author Mail, Tarcher Publicity, 375 Hudson St., New York, NY 10014, U.S.A.

BENTSEN, Cheryl. American (born United States), b. 1950. **Genres:** Cultural/Ethnic Topics, Biography, Sports/Fitness, Technology, History, Social Sciences. **Career:** Change (magazine), assistant editor, 1971-72; Los Angeles Times, feature and sports writer, 1973-76; New York Post, feature writer, 1976-77; freelance writer, 1977-; CIO (magazine), senior editor, 2001; Darwin (magazine), senior editor, 2001. **Publications:** Maasai Days, 1989. Contributor of articles to periodicals. **Address:** c/o Amanda Urban, ICM Artists Ltd., 40 W 57th St. 17th Fl., New York, NY 10019-4001, U.S.A. **Online address:** cherylbentsen@yahoo.com

BENVENUTO, Christine. American (born United States) **Genres:** Novels, Young Adult Fiction. **Career:** Amherst College, Excel Program, instructor in journalism; Mount Holyoke College, Five College Women's Studies Research Center, associate; Putney Student Travel, journalist. Freelance journalist. **Publications:** Shiksa: The Gentile Woman in the Jewish World, 2004; Virginia Dare, forthcoming. Contributor to periodicals. **Address:** St. Martin's Press, 175 5th Ave., New York, NY 10010-7703, U.S.A.

BEN-YEHUDA, Nachman. Israeli (born Israel), b. 1948. **Genres:** Sociology. **Career:** Hebrew University of Jerusalem, Department of Sociology, staff, 1978-; State University of New York-Stony Brook, visiting assistant professor, 1983-84; University of Toronto, visiting professor, 1990-91; London School of Economics and Political Science, visiting professor, 1996-97; Hebrew University, Department of Sociology, chair, 1991-94, dean of faculty of social sciences, 1999-2005. Writer. **Publications:** The Myth of the Junkie: Towards A Natural Typology of Drug Addicts, 1977; Sekirat Matsav Ha-Samim Be-Yisrael, 1979; Samim, 1980; Deviance and Moral Boundaries: Witchcraft, the Occult, Deviant Sciences and Scientists, 1985; The Politics and Morality of Deviance: Moral Panics, Drug Abuse, Deviant Science, and

Reversed Stigmatization, 1989; Political Assassinations by Jews: A Rhetorical Device for Justice, 1993; (with E. Goode) Moral Panics: The Social Construction of Deviance, 1994, 2nd ed., 2009; The Masada Myth: Collective Memory and Mythmaking in Israel, 1995; Betrayals and Treason: Violations of Trust and Loyalty, 2001; Sacrificing Truth: Archaeology and the Myth of Masada, 2002; (with P.L. Kohl and M. Kozelsky) Selective Remembrances: Archaeology in the Construction, Commemoration, and Consecration of National Pasts, 2008; Theocratic Democracy, 2010. **Address:** Department of the Sociology and Anthropology, Hebrew University of Jerusalem, Rm. 4514, Jerusalem, 91905, Israel. **Online address:** msnahman@pluto.mscc.huji.ac.il

BENZ, Derek. American (born United States), b. 1971. **Genres:** Young Adult Fiction, Science Fiction/Fantasy. **Career:** Writer. **Publications:** GREY GRIFFINS SERIES WITH J.S. LEWIS: The Revenge of the Shadow King, 2005; The Rise of the Black Wolf, 2007; The Fall of the Templar, 2008; Brimstone Key, 2010; Relic Hunters, 2011; The Paragon Prison, 2012. **Address:** PO Box 2431, Chandler, AZ 85244, U.S.A. **Online address:** derekbenz@greygriffins.com

BEN-ZVI, Rebecca Tova. *See* **O'CONNELL, Rebecca.**

BERAN, Michael Knox. American (born United States), b. 1966?. **Genres:** Biography, Autobiography/Memoirs, Politics/Government. **Career:** Davis Polk and Wardwell, associate. Attorney and writer. **Publications:** The Last Patrician: Bobby Kennedy and the End of American Aristocracy, 1998; Jefferson's Demons: Portrait of a Restless Mind, 2003; Forge of Empires, 1861-1871: Three Revolutionary Statesmen and the World They Made, 2007; Pathology of the Elites: How the Arrogant Classes Plan to Run Your Life, 2010. Contributor to periodicals. **Address:** c/o Author Mail, Free Press, 1230 Ave. of the Americas, New York, NY 10020, U.S.A.

BERBERIAN, Viken. American (born United States) **Genres:** Novels, Literary Criticism And History. **Career:** Writer. **Publications:** The Cyclist, 2002; Das Kapital: A Novel of Love and Money Markets, 2007. Contributor to periodicals. **Address:** c/o Author Mail, Simon & Schuster Inc., 1230 Ave. of the Americas, New York, NY 10020, U.S.A.

BERBERICK, Nancy Varian. American (born United States), b. 1951. **Genres:** Science Fiction/Fantasy, Novels, Novellas/Short Stories, Children's Fiction. **Career:** Writer. **Publications:** FANTASY NOVELS: Stormblade, 1988; The Jewels of Elvish, 1989; A Child of Elvish, 1992. GARROC SERIES: Shadow of the Seventh Moon, 1991; The Panther's Hoard, 1994; (with L.P. Baker) Tears of the Night Sky, 1998; Dalamar the Dark, 1999; (with S.S. Brown and P.B. Thompson) Bertrem's Guide to the Age of Mortals, 2000; (with J. Crook, J. Grubber and M.H. Herbert) Bertrem the Aesthetic, 2001; The Inheritance, 2001; Lioness, 2002; Prisoner of Haven, 2004. **Address:** Maria Carvainis Agency Inc., 235 W End Ave., New York, NY 10023, U.S.A. **Online address:** nancy_berberick@yahoo.com

BERCK, Judith. American (born United States), b. 1960. **Genres:** Social Commentary, Writing/Journalism, Young Adult Non-fiction. **Career:** Coalition for the Homeless, consultant, 1986; Citizen's Committee for Children, consultant, 1987-90; New York Civil Liberties Union, consultant, 1991; Nike Inc., web site designer and project manager, 1995-96; Intel Corp., senior technical staff, 1996-97, editor and website manager, 1998-99, writer, 1999-, editor, 2000-01; Microsoft Corp., writer, 1999-; Blakely Sokoloff Taylor & Zafman, writer and editor, 1999-2000; PSC, writer, 2003-; Judith Berck Communications Inc., owner. **Publications:** No Place to Be: Voices of Homeless Children, 1992. Contributor of articles. **Address:** Judith Berck Communications Inc., 2441 41st Ave. NE, Portland, OR 97212-5424, U.S.A. **Online address:** judyb@judyb.com

BERCOVITCH, Jacob. *See* Obituaries.

BERDANIER, Carolyn D. American (born United States), b. 1936. **Genres:** Medicine/Health, Food And Wine. **Career:** U.S. Department of Agriculture, Nutrition Institute, research nutritionist, 1968-75; Hebrew University of Jerusalem, visiting scientist, 1970-72; University of Maryland, assistant professor, 1970-75; University of Nebraska, associate professor of biochemistry and medicine, 1975-77; University of Georgia, Department of Foods and Nutrition, head, 1977-88, professor of nutrition, 1977-, now professor emeritus of food and nutrition; Guy's Hospital Medical School, visiting professor, 1976; University of Vermont, visiting professor, 1994; Oregon State University, visiting professor, 1994; University of Washington, visiting professor, 1994; National Yang-Ming Medical College, visiting professor, 1994; University of Pennsylvania, visiting professor, 1995. Writer. **Publications:** Advanced Nutrition, 1995, 2nd ed. as Advanced Nutrition: Macronutrients, 2000, (with J. Zempleni) rev. ed. as Advanced Nutrition: Macronutrients, Micronutrients and Metabolism, 2009; CRC Desk Reference for Nutrition, 1998, 2nd ed., 2005; (with L. Berdanier) Case Studies in Physiology and Nutrition, 2010. EDITOR: Carbohydrate Metabolism: Regulation and Physiological Role, 1976; (with J.L. Hargrove) Nutrition and Gene Expression, 1992; Nutrients and Gene Expression: Clinical Aspects, 1996; (with N. Moustaïd-Moussa) Nutrient-Gene Interactions in Health and Disease, 2001; (ed. with E.B. Feldman and J. Dwyer) Handbook of Nutrition and Food, 2002, 2nd ed., 2008; (with N. Moustaïd-Moussa) Genomics and Proteomics in Nutrition, 2004; Mitochondria in Health and Disease, 2005. Contributor to books and journals. **Address:** Department of Foods and Nutrition, University of Georgia, 278 Dawson Hall, Athens, GA 30602-3622, U.S.A.

BERDESHEVSKY, Margo Ann. French/American (born United States), b. 1945. **Genres:** Poetry. **Career:** Writer, actress and photographer. **Publications:** But a Passage in Wilderness (poetry), 2007; Beautiful Soon Enough (short stories), 2009. Works appear in anthologies. Contributor to periodicals. **Address:** Paris, France. **Online address:** margomargo1@hotmail.com

BEREBITSKY, Julie. American (born United States) **Genres:** History. **Career:** University of the South, Department of History, assistant professor, professor, Women's Studies Program, director, chair; Hopewell-Furnace National Historic Site, consultant. Writer. **Publications:** Like Our Very Own: Adoption and the Changing Culture of Motherhood, 1851-1950, 2000; Sex and the Office: A History of Gender, Power, and Desire, 2012. Works appear in anthologies. **Address:** Department of History, University of the South, Walsh Ellet 209, 735 University Ave., Sewanee, TN 37383, U.S.A. **Online address:** jberebit@sewanee.edu

BERENBAUM, Michael. American (born United States), b. 1945. **Genres:** History, Theology/Religion, Biography. **Career:** Park Avenue Synagogue, instructor, 1966-67, 1968-69; Colby-Sawyer College, Department of Philosophy and Religion, instructor in philosophy and religion, 1969-71; Wesleyan University, university Jewish chaplain and adjunct assistant professor of religion, 1973-80; Zachor: The Holocaust Resource Center, associate director, 1978; President's Commission on the Holocaust, deputy director, 1979-80; Jewish Community Council of Greater Washington, executive director, 1980-83; George Washington University, Department of Religion, associate professorial lecturer in religion, 1981-83; University of Maryland, visiting professor of Hebrew studies, 1983; Washington Jewish Week, opinion page editor, 1983-86, acting editor, 1985; Georgetown University, Department of Theology, Hyman Goldman adjunct orofessor of theology, 1983-97; Together, editor, 1986-89; U.S. Holocaust Memorial Museum, research fellow, 1987-88, project director, 1988-93, United States Holocaust Research Institute, director, 1993-97; American University, adjunct professor of Judaic studies, 1987; Gannett Center for Media Studies, associate, 1987-; Survivors of the Shoah Visual History Foundation, president and chief executive officer, 1997-99; Richard Stockton College, Ida E. King Distinguished Visiting Professor of Holocaust Studies, 1999-2000; Clark University, Center for Holocaust Studies, Strassler Family distinguished visiting professor of Holocaust studies, 2000; University of Judaism (now The American Jewish University), adjunct professor of theology, 2002-07, professor of Jewish studies, 2002-, Sigi Ziering Institute, director, 2002-; Berenbaum Group, president. **Publications:** After Tragedy and Triumph: Modern Jewish Thought and the American Experience, 1990; The World Must Know: A History of the Holocaust, 1993; The Vision of the Void: Theological Reflections on the Works of Elie Wiesel, 1979 as Elie Wiesel: God, the Holocaust and the Children of Israel, 1994; A Holocaust Reader, 1995; (intro.) The Willing Executioners/Ordinary Men Debate, 1996; Promise to Remember: The Holocaust in the Words and Voices of Its Survivors, 2003; (with Y. Mais) Memory and Legacy, 2008. EDITOR: From Holocaust to New Life, 1985; (with J.K. Roth) Holocaust: Religious and Philosophical Implications, 1989; A Mosaic of Victims: Non-Jews Persecuted and Murdered by the Nazis, 1990; (with Y. Gutman) Anatomy of the Auschwitz Death Camp, 1994; (with B.R. Rubenstein) What Kind of God?: Essays in Honor of Richard L. Rubenstein, 1995; Witness to the Holocaust, 1997; (with A.J. Peck) The Holocaust and History: The Known, the Unknown, the Disputed and the Re-examined, 1998; (with M.J. Neufeld) The Bombing of Auschwitz: Should the Allies have Attempted It?, 2000; (with J.S. Landres) After The Passion is Gone: American Religious Consequences,

2004; Murder Most Merciful: Essays on the Ethical Conundrum Occasioned by Sigi Ziering's Judgment of Herbert Bierhoff, 2005; (with F. Skolnik) Encyclopedia Judaica, 2007; (with F. Skolnik) Encyclopaedia Judaica, 2007; Not Your Father's Antisemitism: Hatred of the Jews in the 21st Century, 2008; (with R. Lichtenstein and A.J. Edelheit) Witness to History, 2009; George's Kaddish for Kovno and the Six Million, 2009. **Address:** The Berenbaum Group, 1124 S Orlando Ave., Los Angeles, CA 90035-2512, U.S.A. **Online address:** michael@berenbaumgroup.com

BERENDT, John. American (born United States), b. 1939. **Genres:** Local History/Rural Topics, Young Adult Non-fiction, Social Sciences. **Career:** Harvard University, Harvard Lampoon, staff; Esquire, associate editor, 1961-69, columnist, 1982-94; Holiday, senior staff editor, 1969; New York Magazine, editor, 1977-79. Producer. **Publications:** Midnight in the Garden of Good and Evil: A Savannah Story (nonfiction), 1994; (intro.) Hiding My Candy: The Autobiography of the Grand Empress of Savannah, 1997; (intro.) The Lady and Sons: Savannah Country Cookbook, 1998; (intro.) The Adventures and Memoirs of Sherlock Holmes, 2001; (intro.) Other Voices, Other Rooms, 2004; The City of Falling Angels, 2005. Contributor to periodicals. **Address:** International Creative Management, 40 W 57th St., New York, NY 10019, U.S.A.

BERENZY, Alix. American (born United States), b. 1957. **Genres:** Children's Fiction, Illustrations, Mythology/Folklore. **Career:** Glassman Advertising Agency, assistant art director, 1977-78; Mark Color Studios, art director, 1978-79; freelance illustrator, 1982-; Hussian School of Art, part-time art instructor, 1989-90; University of the Arts, part-time art instructor, 1990-91. Writer. **Publications:** SELF-ILLUSTRATED: A Frog Prince, 1989; (and reteller) Rapunzel, 1995; What's the Matter, Sammy?, 2005; Sammy the Classroom Guinea Pig, 2005. Contributor to periodicals. **Address:** Henry Holt and Company Inc., 175 5th Ave., New York, NY 10010, U.S.A.

BERESFORD, Anne. British (born England), b. 1929. **Genres:** Plays/Screenplays, Poetry, Translations, Natural History. **Career:** Actress, 1948-70; British Broadcasting Corp., broadcaster, 1960-70; Wimbledon Girls High School, drama teacher, 1969-73; Arts Educational School, drama teacher, 1973-76; Cockpit Theatre, Poetry Workshop, teacher, 1970-72. Writer. **Publications:** Walking without Moving, 1967; The Lair, 1968; Footsteps on Snow, 1972; The Courtship, 1972; Modern Fairy Tale, 1972; (trans.) V. Lungu, Alexandros: Selected Poems, 1974; The Curving Shore, 1975; (with M. Hamburger) Words, 1977; Unholy Giving, 1977; Songs a Thracian Taught Me, 1980; The Songs of Almut from God's Country, 1980; The Sele of the Morning, 1988; Snapshots from an Album 1884-1895, 1992; Landscape with Figures, 1994; Selected Poems, 1997; Duet for Three Voices, 1997; No Place for Cowards, 1998; Hearing Things, 2002; Collected Poems, 1967-2006, 2006. **Address:** Marsh Acres, Middleton, Saxmundham, SU IP17 3NH, England.

BERESFORD-KROEGER, Diana. Canadian/British (born England), b. 1944. **Genres:** Young Adult Non-fiction, Novellas/Short Stories. **Career:** Educator, 1969-82; WINGS WorldQuest Inc., fellow; Canadian Department of Agriculture, scientist; University of Ottawa, scientist; Carleton University, research scientist in molecular biology and hemodilution. Writer. **Publications:** Bioplanning a North Temperate Garden, 1999; Arboretum America: A Philosophy of the Forest, 2003; Time Will Tell, 2004; A Garden for Life: The Natural Approach to Designing, Planting, and Maintaining a North Temperate Garden, 2004; Arboretum Borealis: A Lifeline of the Planet, 2010; Global Forest, 2010. **Address:** PO Box 253, Merrickville, ON K0G 1N0, Canada.

BERG, A. Scott. American (born United States), b. 1949. **Genres:** Biography, Autobiography/Memoirs. **Career:** Full-time writer. **Publications:** BIOGRAPHIES: Max Perkins: Editor of Genius, 1978; Goldwyn, 1989; Lindbergh, 1998; Kate Remembered, 2003. **Address:** Janklow and Nesbit Associates, 445 Park Ave., New York, NY 10022-2606, U.S.A.

BERG, Carol. American (born United States) **Genres:** Novels. **Career:** Hewlett-Packard, software engineer, 1985-2002. Educator and writer. **Publications:** THE RAI-KIRAH SERIES: Transformation, 2000; Revelation, 2001; Restoration, 2002. BRIDGE OF D'ARNATH SERIES: Son of Avonar, 2004; Guardians of the Keep, 2004; The Soul Weaver, 2005; Daughter of Ancients, 2005. THE LIGHTHOUSE DUET SERIES: Flesh and Spirit, 2007; Breath and Bone, 2008. Elemental Magic, 2007. NOVELS: The Spirit Lens, 2010; The Soul Mirror, 2011; The Daemon Prism, 2012. OTHER: Song of the Beast, 2003. **Address:** c/o Anne Sowards, Penguin Putnam USA, 375 Hudson St., New York, NY 10014, U.S.A. **Online address:** carolberg@sff.net

BERG, Elizabeth. American (born United States), b. 1948. **Genres:** Novels, How-to Books. **Career:** Radcliffe College, teacher. Writer. **Publications:** Family Traditions: Celebrations for Holidays and Everyday, 1992; Durable Goods, 1993, 3rd ed. 2003; Talk Before Sleep, 1994; Range of Motion, 1995; Pull of the Moon, 1996; Joy School, 1997; We Keep, 1998; Escaping into the Open: The Art of Writing True, 1999; What We Keep, 1999; Until the Real Thing Comes Along, 1999; Open House, 2000; You Gotta Have Heart: The Art of Writing True, 2000; Never Change, 2001; Ordinary Life: Stories, 2002; True to Form, 2002; Say When, 2003; Art of Mending, 2004; Year of Pleasures, 2005; We Are All Welcome Here, 2006; Handmaid and the Carpenter, 2006; Dream When You're Feeling Blue, 2007; The Day I Ate Whatever I Wanted: And Other Small Acts of Liberation, 2008, new ed. 2011; Home Safe: A Novel, 2009; Last Time I Saw You: A Novel, 2010; Egypt, 2010; United States, 2010; Pull of the Moon, 2010; Mexico, 2011; Once Upon a Time, There Was You, 2011. Contributor to periodicals. **Address:** c/o Arlynn Greenbaum, Authors Unlimited, 31 E 32nd St., Ste. 300, New York, NY 10016, U.S.A.

BERG, John C. American (born United States), b: 1943. **Genres:** Politics/Government. **Career:** Suffolk University, instructor, 1974-75, assistant professor, 1975-80, associate professor, 1980-85, professor of government, 1985-, director of graduate studies, 1993-2000, chair, 2003-10; Boston Center for International Visitors, lecturer, 1993-94; New Political Science, reviews editor, 1998-2003. **Publications:** Unequal Struggle: Class, Gender, Race, and Power in the U.S. Congress, 1994; (ed.) Teamsters and Turtles?: U.S. Progressive Political Movements in the 21st Century, 2002. Contributor to books and journals. **Address:** Department of Government, Suffolk University, Rm. 1085, 73 Tremont St., Boston, MA 02108, U.S.A. **Online address:** jberg@suffolk.edu

BERG, Leila. British (born England), b. 1917. **Genres:** Novellas/Short Stories, Children's Fiction, Children's Non-fiction, Civil Liberties/Human Rights, Education, Human Relations/Parenting, Mythology/Folklore, Theology/Religion, Autobiography/Memoirs, inspirational/Motivational Literature, Literary Criticism And History. **Career:** Methuen & Company Ltd., children's book editor, 1958-60; Thomas Nelson & Sons Ltd., general editor of salamander books, 1965; freelance editor, 1966-. **Publications:** FOR CHILDREN: Fourteen What-Do-You-Know Stories, 1948; The Adventures of Chunky, 1950; The Nightingale and Other Stories, 1951; The Tired Train and Other Stories, 1952; Trust Chunky, 1954; The Story of the Little Car, 1955, rev. ed. as The Little Car Has a Day Out, 1970 as The Little Car, 1974; Fire Engine by Mistake, 1955; Lollipops: Stories and Poems, 1957; Andy's Pit Pony, 1958; The Hidden Road, 1958; Little Pete Stories, 1959, rev. ed., 1970; Three Men Went to Work, 1960; The Jolly Farm Book, 1960; A Box for Benny, 1961; See How They Work, 1962; A Newt for Roddy, 1965; Folk Tales for Reading and Telling, 1966; Penguin Who Couldn't Paddle, 1967; My Dog Sunday, 1968; A Day Out, 1968; Finding a Key, 1968; Fish and Chips for Supper, 1968; Jimmy's Story, 1968; The Jumble Sale, 1968; Lesley's Story, 1968; The Nippers and Little Nippers (series 24 titles), 1968-76; Julie's Story, 1970; Letters, 1970; Paul's Story, 1970; Robert's Story, 1970; Susan's Story, 1970; Bouncing, 1970; Doing the Pools, 1971; The Doctor, 1972; Hospital Day, 1972; Knitting, 1972; My Brother, 1972; Put the Kettle On!, 1972; That Baby, 1972; Tracy's Story, 1972; Well, I Never!, 1972; A Band in School, 1975; Plenty of Room, 1975; Granddad's Clock, 1976; Snaps Series, (4 titles), 1977; Tales for Telling, 1983; Topsy Turvy Tales, 1984; Hanukka, 1985; Christmas, 1985; Time for One More, 1986. SERIES: Chatterbooks, (4 titles), 1981; Small World, (8 titles), 1983-85; Steep Street Stories, (4 titles), 1987. FOR ADULTS: Risinghill: Death of a Comprehensive School, 1968; Children's Rights, 1971; (with P. Chapman) The Train Back: A Search for Parents, 1972; Look at Kids, 1972; Reading and Loving, 1977; Time for One More, 1986; Mr. Wolf and His Tail, 1990; The Knee-High Man, 1990; Dear Billy and Other Stories, 1992; Flickerbook, 1997; The God Stories, 1999. **Address:** Alice's Cottage, Brook St., Wivenhoe, Colchester, EX C07 9DS, England.

BERG, Manfred. German (born Germany), b. 1959. **Genres:** History, Medicine/Health, Law. **Career:** Free University of Berlin, John F. Kennedy-Institute for North American Studies, Department of History, assistant professor of American history, 1989-92, adjunct professor, 1998-2000, visiting professor, 2001-02; University of Cologne, visiting professor of Anglo-American history, 2000-01; University of Erlangen, visiting professor of American history, 2002-03; German Historical Institute, deputy director; Universität Halle-Wittenberg, Leucorea Foundation, Center for U.S. Studies, executive director, 2003-05; Heidelberg University, Department of History, Curt Engelhorn

Professor of American History, 2005-, chair, 2007-08, Faculty of Philosophy, dean, 2010-; Wofford College, Lewis P. Jones visiting professor, 2009. Writer and historian. **Publications:** Gustav Stresemann und die Vereinigten Staaten von Amerika: Weltwirtschaftliche verflechtung und Revisionspolitik 1907-1929, 1990; Gustav Stresemann: Eine politische Karriere zwischen Reich und Republik, 1992; (ed. with J.S. Micunek) German-American Scholarship Guide: Exchange Opportunities for Historians and Social Scientists, 1994/95, 1994; (ed. with G. Cocks) Medicine and Modernity: Public Health and Medical Care in Nineteenth-and Twentieth-Century Germany, 1997; (co-ed.) Macht und Moral: Beiträge zur Ideologie und Praxis amerikanischer Aussenpolitik im 20. Jahrhundert, 1999; The Ticket to Freedom: Die NAACP und das Wahlrecht der Afro-Amerikaner, 2000, trans. as The Ticket to Freedom: The NAACP and the Struggle for Black Political Integration, 2005; (ed. with M.H. Geyer) Two Cultures of Rights: The Quest for Inclusion and Participation in Modern America and Germany, 2002; (ed. with S. Kapsch and F. Streng) Criminal Justice in the United States and Germany: History, Modernization, and Reform, 2006; (ed. with A. Etges) John F. Kennedy and the Thousand Days: New Perspectives on the Foreign and Domestic Policies of the Kennedy Administration, 2007; (ed. with B. Schaefer) Historical Justice in International Perspective: How Societies are Trying to Right the Wrongs of the Past, 2009; (ed. with S. Wendt) Racism in the Modern World, 2011; (ed. with S. Wendt) Globalizing Lynching History, 2011; Popular Justice: A History of Lynching in America, 2011. **Address:** Department of History, Heidelberg University, Rm. 042, Grabengasse 3-5, Heidelberg, 69047, Germany. **Online address:** manfred.berg@uni-hd.de

BERG, Scott W. American (born United States) **Genres:** History, Adult Non-fiction, Architecture, Writing/Journalism, Biography. **Career:** George Mason University, Department of English, term assistant professor. Writer. **Publications:** Grand Avenues: The Story of the French Visionary Who Designed Washington, D.C., 2007; Grand Avenues: The Story of Pierre Charles L'Enfant, the French Visionary Who Designed Washington, D.C., 2008; 38 Nooses: Lincoln, Little Crow, and the Beginning of the Frontier's End, 2012. **Address:** Department of English, George Mason University, Robinson Hall A487, 4400 University Dr., Fairfax, VA 22030, U.S.A. **Online address:** scottwberg@scottwberg.com

BERG, Stephen. American (born United States), b. 1934. **Genres:** Poetry, Translations. **Career:** Philadelphia College of Art, assistant professor; Haverford College, instructor; Saturday Evening Post, poetry editor, 1961-62; Temple University, instructor in English, 1963-; University of the Arts, professor of humanities, 1967-; Princeton University, poet-in-residence, 1979-81; The American Poetry Review, founder and co-editor. **Publications:** Berg Goodman Mezey: Poems, 1957; Bearing Weapons: Poems, 1963; The Queen's Triangle: A Romance, 1970 (Frank O'Hara Prize) The Daughters: Poems, 1971; Grieve Like This, 1974; Grief: Poems and Versions of Poems, 1975; With Akhmatova at the Black Gates, 1981; Singular Voices: American Poetry Today, 1985; In It: Poems, 1986; Crow with No Mouth: Ikkyu Fifteenth Century Zen Master, 1989; First Song, Bankei, 1653, 1989; Homage to the Afterlife, 1991; New and Selected Poems, 1992; Oblivion: Poems, 1995; The Steel Cricket: Versions 1958-1997, 1997; Shaving, 1998; Footnotes to an Unfinished Poem, 2000; Porno Diva Numero Uno: An Anonymous Confession, 2000; Halo, 2000; X=: Poems, 2002; Rimbaud Versions & Inventions: Still Unilluminated I, 2005; Elegy on Hats, 2005; Cuckoo's Blood: Versions of Zen Masters, 2008. TRANSLATOR: (co-trans.) Cantico: Selections, by Jorge Guillen, 1965; Nothing in the Word, 1972; (with S. Polgar and S.J. Marks) M. Radnoti, Clouded Sky, 1973, rev. ed., 2003; (with D. Clay) Sophocles, Oedipus the King, 1978. EDITOR: (with S.J. Marks and J.M. Pilz) Between People, 1972; (with R. Mezey) Naked Poetry: Recent American Poetry in Open Forms, and Naked Poetry 2, 1969, 1974; (with S.J. Marks) Doing the Unknown, 1974; (with R. Mezey) The New Naked Poetry, 1976; In Praise of What Persists, 1983; Singular Voices: American Poetry Today, 1985; (with D. Bonanno and A. Vogelsang) The Body Electric: America's Best Poetry from the American Poetry Review, 2000; My Business is Circumference, 2001. **Address:** The American Poetry Review, 1700 Sansom St., Ste. 800, Philadelphia, PA 19103, U.S.A. **Online address:** sberg@aprweb.org

BERGEIJK, Jeroen van. Dutch (born Netherlands), b. 1965?. **Genres:** Travel/Exploration. **Career:** Freelance journalist, 1996-2002; New York Times, journalist; Wired, journalist; Vrijzinnig Protestantse Radio Omroep (VPRO), radio documentarian. **Publications:** U.S. 1: Amerika Na 11 September, 2003; (with H. Ceelen) Meer Dan De Feiten: Gesprekken Met Auteurs Van Literaire Non-fictie, 2007; My Mercedes Is Not for Sale: From Amsterdam to Ouagadougou... An Auto-Misadventure across the Sahara, 2008. **Address:** Amsterdam, Netherlands. **Online address:** us1@xs4all.nl

BERGEIJK, Peter A.G. van. Dutch (born Netherlands), b. 1959. **Genres:** Economics, International Relations/Current Affairs, Adult Non-fiction, Institutions/Organizations. **Career:** Teacher, 1983-85; ABN Bank, economist country risk department, 1985-87; Groningen University, assistant professor of international economics, 1988-90; Ministry of Economic Affairs, senior economist of international economic relations directorate, 1990-92, senior economist of economic policy directorate (research unit), 1992-97; De Nederlandsche Bank, head of monetary and economic policy department, 1997-98; Erasmus University, professor of economic policy in the research center for economic policy, 1998-2004; WIIW University of Zurich, visiting professor of monetary policy, 1999-2001; UBS Group Economic Research, director, 1999; NMA (Dutch competition authority), Economic Counsel, staff, 2001-06; Economic Policy Directorate Ministry of Economic Affairs, chief trade economist, 2006-; University of Utrecht, CERES, deputy director, 2009-; Erasmus University, International Institute of Social Studies, professor of international economics and macroeconomics, 2009-. Writer. **Publications:** Handel en diplomatie, 1990; Handel, politiek & handelspolitiek, 1991; (with J. van Sinderen and E.W.M.T. Westerhout) Anticiperenen reageren op de Europese uitdaging (title means: 'The European Challenge: Strategies'), 1992; (ed. with L.A. Geelhoed and J. van Sinderen) Met distantie: J.E. Andriessen en het economische bestuur, 1993; Economic Diplomacy, Trade and Commercial Policy: Positive and Negative Sanctions in a New World Order, 1994; Economic Policy, Technology and Growth, 1995; (with R.C.G. Haffner) Privatization, Deregulation and the Macroeconomy: Measurement, Modelling and Policy, 1996; (co-ed.) Economic Science and Practice: The Roles of Academic Economists and Policymakers, 1997; (ed. with J. van Sinderen and B.A. Vollaard) Structural Reform in Open Economies: A Road to Success?, 1999; (ed. with R.J. Berndsen and W.J. Jansen) Economics of the Euro Area: Macroeconomic Policy and Institutions, 2000; (ed. with E. Kloosterhuis and S. Bremer) Modelling European Mergers: Theory, Competition Policy and Case Studies, 2005; (co-ed.) A Wealth of Creations: A Catalogue of an Exceptional Exhibition, 2007; (ed. with S. Brakman) The Gravity Model in International Trade: Advances and Applications, 2010; On the Brink of Deglobalization: An Alternative Perspective on the Causes of the World Trade Collapse, 2010; (ed. with M. Okano-Heijmans and J. Melissen) Economic Diplomacy: Economic and Political Perspectives, 2011; (ed. with A.D. Haan and R.V.D. Hoeven) Financial Crisis and Developing Countries, 2012. Contributor to books, periodicals and journals. **Address:** Economic Policy Directorate, Ministry of Economic Affairs, PO Box 20101, The Hague, 2500 EC, Netherlands. **Online address:** p.a.g.vanbergeijk@minez.nl

BERGEN, Candice. (Candice Patricia Bergen). American (born United States), b. 1946. **Genres:** Plays/Screenplays, Autobiography/Memoirs, Art/Art History. **Career:** Writer. **Publications:** Knock Wood (autobiography), 1984. Contributor to periodicals. **Address:** 955 S Carillo Dr., Ste. 200, Los Angeles, CA 90048, U.S.A.

BERGEN, Candice Patricia. *See* **BERGEN, Candice.**

BERGER, Arthur A(sa). American (born United States), b. 1933. **Genres:** Anthropology/Ethnology, Communications/Media, Film, Literary Criticism And History, Humor/Satire, Social Sciences, Sociology, Cultural/Ethnic Topics, Politics/Government. **Career:** University of Minnesota, faculty of English and American studies, 1960-65; University of Milan, Fulbright lecturer, 1963-64, Fulbright fellow, 1963-64; San Francisco State University, Department of Broadcast and Electronic Communication Arts, assistant professor, associate professor, professor, 1965-2003, emeritus professor, 2003-; University of Southern California, Annenberg School of Communication, visiting professor, 1984-85. Writer. **Publications:** SELF-ILLUSTRATED: Signs in Contemporary Culture: An Introduction to Semiotics, 1984, 2nd ed., 1999; Seeing Is Believing: An Introduction to Visual Communication, 1989, 4th ed., 2011; Ads, Fads, and Consumer Culture: Advertising's Impact on American Character and Society, 2000, 4th ed., 2011; The Kabbalah Killings: A Murder Mystery Introduction to Jewish Mysticism: A Solomon Hunter Educational Murder Mystery, 2004; Shop 'til You Drop: Consumer Behavior and American Culture, 2005; 50 Ways to Understand Communication: A Guided Tour of Key Ideas and Theorists In Communication, Media, and Culture, 2006; Academic Writer's Toolkit: A User's Manual, 2008. OTHERS: (with S.I. Hayakawa and A. Chandler) Language in Thought and Action, 1968, 4th ed., 1978;

Li'l Abner: A Study in American Satire, 1970; The Evangelical Hamburger, 1970; Pop Culture, 1973; The Comic-Stripped American: What Dick Tracy, Blondie, Daddy Warbucks, and Charlie Brown Tell Us about Ourselves, 1973; The TV-Guided American, 1976; Television as an Instrument of Terror: Essays on Media, Popular Culture, and Everyday Life, 1980; Media Analysis Techniques, 1982, 4th ed., 2012; Agit-Pop: Political Culture and Communication, 1989; Scripts: Writing for Radio and Television, 1990; Media Research Techniques, 1991, 2nd ed., 1998; Reading Matter: Multidisciplinary Perspectives on Material Culture, 1992; Popular Culture Genres: Theories and Texts, 1992; An Anatomy of Humor, 1993; Improving Writing Skills: Memos, Letters, Reports, and Proposals, 1993; Blind Men and Elephants: Perspectives on Humor, 1995; Cultural Criticism: A Primer of Key Concepts, 1995; Essentials of Mass Communication Theory, 1995; Manufacturing Desire: Media, Popular Culture and Everyday Life, 1995; Narratives in Popular Culture, Media and Everyday Life, 1997; The Genius of the Jewish Joke, 1997; Bloom's Morning: Coffee, Comforters, and the Secret Meaning of Everyday Life, 1997; The Art of Comedy Writing, 1997; Postmortem for a Postmodernist, 1997; The Postmodern Presence, 1997; Media and Communication Research Methods: An Introduction to Qualitative and Quantitative Approaches, 2000, 2nd ed., 2011; Jewish Jesters: A Study in American Popular Culture, 2000; Die Laughing, 2000; Murder Ad Nauseum, 2000; The Hamlet Case, 2000; Video Games: A Popular Culture Phenomenon, 2002; The Agent in The Agency: Media, Popular Culture, and Everyday Life in America, 2003; The Mass Comm Murders: Five Media Theorists Self-Destruct, 2002; Media and Society: A Critical Perspective, 2003, 2nd ed., 2007; Durkheim is Dead!: Sherlock Holmes is Introduced to Sociological Theory, 2003; The Portable Postmodernist, 2003; Deconstructing Travel: Cultural Perspectives on Tourism, 2004; Games and Activities For Media, Communication, and Cultural Studies Students, 2004; Ocean Travel and Cruising: A Cultural Analysis, 2004; Mistake in Identity: A Cultural Studies Murder Mystery, 2005; Vietnam Tourism, 2005; The Genius of the Jewish Joke, 2006; Thailand Tourism, 2007; Bali Tourism, 2008; The Golden Triangle: An Ethno-Semiotic Tour of Present-Day India, 2008; What Objects Mean: An Introduction to Material Culture, 2009; Cultural Theorist's Book of Quotations, 2010; The Objects of Affection: Semiotics and Consumer Culture, 2010; Tourism in Japan: An Ethno-semiotic Analysis, 2010; Understanding American Icons: An Introduction to Semiotics, 2012. EDITOR: About Man: An Introduction to Anthropology, 1974; Film in Society, 1980; Television in Society, 1986; Humor, the Psyche and Society, 1987; Visual Sociology and Semiotics, 1987; Media USA: Process and Effect, 1988, 2nd ed., 1991; Political Culture and Public Opinion, 1989; The Postmodern Presence: Readings on Postmodernism in American Culture and Society, 1998; Making Sense Of Media: Key Texts in Media and Cultural Studies, 2005. Contributor of articles to periodicals. **Address:** Department of Broadcast and Electronic, Communication Arts, San Francisco State University, 1600 Holloway Ave., San Francisco, CA 94132-1722, U.S.A. **Online address:** aberger@sfsu.edu

BERGER, Barbara Helen. American (born United States), b. 1945. **Genres:** Children's Fiction, Autobiography/Memoirs, Essays, Illustrations, Picture/Board Books. **Career:** Freelance artist, author and illustrator. **Publications:** SELF-ILLUSTRATED: Animalia: Thirteen Small Tales, 1982; Grandfather Twilight, 1984; The Donkey's Dream, 1985; When the Sun Rose, 1986; Gwinna, 1990; The Jewel Heart, 1994; A Lot of Otters, 1997; Angels on a Pin, 2000; All the Way to Lhasa: A Tale from Tibet, 2002. OTHER: Thunder Bunny, 2007. Works appear in anthologies. Contributor to periodicals. **Address:** Philomel Books, 375 Hudson St., New York, NY 10014-3657, U.S.A. **Online address:** bhb3@bhberger.com

BERGER, Bruce. American (born United States), b. 1938. **Genres:** Poetry, Environmental Sciences/Ecology, Natural History, Travel/Exploration, Psychology. **Career:** Professional pianist, 1965-74; Aspen Recycling Center, operator, 1976-78; American Way, contributing editor, 1991-94. **Publications:** The Telling Distance: Conversations with the American Desert, 1990; There Was A River, 1994; Facing the Music (poetry), 1995; Almost an Island, 1998; Sierra, Sea and Desert: El Vizcaino, Baja California, 1998; Music in the Mountains: The First Fifty Years of the Aspen Music Festival, 1999; The Complete Half-Aspenite, 2005; Oasis of Stone: Visions of Baja California Sur, 2006. Contributor of articles to magazines. **Address:** PO Box 482, Aspen, CO 81612, U.S.A. **Online address:** bberger@rof.net

BERGER, Charles R. American (born United States) **Genres:** Language/Linguistics, Communications/Media. **Career:** Illinois State University, assistant professor of psychology, 1968-71; Northwestern University, assistant professor, 1971-74, associate professor, 1974-78, professor of communication, 1978-87, 1989-90, Van Zelst research professor of communication, 1987-88; Stanford University, visiting professor, 1983; University of California, visiting professor of communication, 1989-90, professor of communication, 1991-95, 1999-2005, head of department, 1995-2005, 2005-08, distinguished professor, 2009-; West Virginia University, lecturer; University of Turin, lecturer; Marquette University, lecturer; Arizona State University, lecturer; University of Oklahoma, lecturer. Writer. **Publications:** (With J.J. Bradac) Language and Social Knowledge: Uncertainty in Interpersonal Relations, 1982; (ed. with M.E. Roloff) Social Cognition and Communication, 1982; (ed. with S.H. Chaffee) Handbook of Communication Science, 1987, 2nd ed., (ed. with M.E. Roloff and D.R. Roskos-Ewoldsen), 2010; (ed. with M. Burgoon) Communication and Social Influence Processes, 1995; Planning Strategic Interaction: Attaining Goals Through Communicative Action, 1997. **Address:** Department of Communication, University of California, 108 Sproul Hall, 377 Kerr Hall, Davis, CA 95616, U.S.A. **Online address:** crberger@ucdavis.edu

BERGER, Fredericka. (Fredericka Nolde Berger). American (born United States), b. 1932. **Genres:** Plays/Screenplays, Young Adult Non-fiction, Novels, Technology, Engineering. **Career:** Haverford College, librarian, 1954-55; Friends' school, English teacher, 1955-56; Riverdale Presbyterian Church, founder, 1979-; Wesley Theological Seminary, team teacher in theology and the arts, 1983-, adjunct professor of drama, 1987-, religion and drama lecturer, 1995. Writer. **Publications:** Nuisance (young adult novel), 1983; Robots: What They Are, What They Do, 1992; The Green Bottle and the Silver Kite, 1993. **Address:** 4209 Sheridan St., University Park, MD 20782, U.S.A.

BERGER, Fredericka Nolde. *See* **BERGER, Fredericka.**

BERGER, John (Peter). French/British (born England), b. 1926. **Genres:** Novels, Novellas/Short Stories, Art/Art History, Literary Criticism And History, Sociology, Essays, Politics/Government, Young Adult Fiction, Photography. **Career:** Writer. **Publications:** NON-FICTION: A Painter of Our Time, 1958; Permanent Red: Essays in Seeing, 1960 in US as Towards Reality: Essays in Seeing, 1962; The Success and Failure of Picasso, 1965; Art and Revolution: Ernst Neizvestny and the Role of the Artist in the U.S.S.R, 1969; Moment of Cubism and Other Essays, 1969; Selected Essays and Articles: The Look of Things, 1972; Ways of Seeing, 1972; About Looking, 1980; (with J. Mohr) Une Autre Facon Deraconter, 1981 in US as Another Way of Telling, 1982; About Time, 1985; The Sense of Sight: Writings, 1985; The White Bird: Writings, 1985; A Question of Geography, 1987; Goya's Last Portrait, 1989; Paul Hogarth: Cold War Reports, 1947-67, 1989; Pequod: A Special Issue, 1990; (with J. Mohr) At the Edge of the World, 1999; Rays of the Rising Sun: Japan's Asian Allies 1931-45, 2001; Selected Essays, 2001; The Shape of a Pocket, 2001; Hold Everything Dear: Dispatches on Survival and Resistance, 2007; From A to X: A Story in Letters, 2008; Why Look at Animals?, 2009; Bento's Sketchbook, 2011. NOVELS: Marcel Frishman, 1958; The Foot of Clive, 1962; Corker's Freedom, 1964; A Fortunate Man: The Story of a Country Doctor, 1967; G, 1972; (with J. Mohr) A Seventh Man, 1975; Keeping a Rendezvous, 1991; To the Wedding, 1995; Isabelle: A Story in Shorts, 1998; King: A Street Story, 1999; (with K.B. Andreadakis) Titian: Nymph And Shepherd, 2003; Here Is Where We Meet, 2005; Forest, 2005; SERIES: Pig Earth, 1979; Once in Europa, 1987; Lilac and Flag: An Old Wives Tale of a City, 1990; Into Their Labours: Pig Earth, Once in Europa, Lilac And Flag: A Trilogy, 1991. COLLECTIONS: And Our Faces, My Heart, Brief as Photos, 1984; Pages of the Wound: Poems, Drawings, Photographs, 1956-96, 1994; Photocopies, 1996. OTHERS: Renato Guttuso, 1957; (trans. with A. Bostock) Bertolt Brecht, Poems on the Theatre, 1961; (trans. with A. Bostock) Bertolt Brecht, Great Art of Living Together--Poems on the Theatre, 1972; Poems in Voix, 1977; Artista and Writers: Ways of Seeing Art in Small Countries, 1981; Once in Europa, 1987; (with N. Bielski) Dernier Portrait De Franciso Goya: Le Peintre Joué aujourd'hui, 1989; (trans. with J. Steffen) Nella Bielski, After Arkadia, 1992; (with J. Christie) I Send You This Cadmium Red, 2000; (with N. Bielski) Oranges for the Son of Alexander Levy/Isabelle, 2001; (with M. Hofmann and C. Lloyd) Arturo Di Stefano, 2002; (intro.) Between the Eyes: Essays on Photography and Politics, 2003; (trans. with L. Appignanesi) Nella Bielski, Year is '42, 2004; (contrib.) Juan Muñoz: A Retrospective, 2008; (with K. Ghaddab) Jean-Marc Cerino: dans les laniéres des seuils, 2008; (intro. and trans. with R. Hammami) Mural, 2009; Face au silence, 2010; (intro.) The Necessity of Art, 2010. **Address:** Anna Arthur PR, Ground Fl., 3 Charlotte Mews, London, GL W1T 4DZ, England. **Online address:** info@johnberger.org

BERGER, Joseph. American/Russian (born Russia), b. 1945. **Genres:** Adult Non-fiction, Education. **Career:** Bronx junior high school, English teacher, 1967-71; New York Post, reporter, 1971-78; Newsday, reporter, 1978-84; New York Times, religion correspondent, 1985-87, national education correspondent, 1987-90, New York City education reporter, 1990, Westchester bureau chief, 1993-. **Publications:** The Young Scientists: America's Future and the Winning of the Westinghouse, 1994; Displaced Persons: Growing Up American After the Holocaust, 2001; World in a City: Traveling the Globe Through the Neighborhoods of the New New York, 2007. Contributor to periodicals. **Address:** c/o Jane Dystel, Dystel Literary Agency, 1 Union Sq., New York, NY 10003, U.S.A. **Online address:** joeberg@nytimes.com

BERGER, Samantha (Allison). American (born United States), b. 1969. **Genres:** Children's Fiction, Children's Non-fiction, Picture/Board Books. **Career:** City and Country School, teacher, 1994; C.O.L.L.A.G.E. Comics, designer, editor and writer, 1994-97; Scholastic, editor and writer, 1997-2000; Nickelodeon, head writer, 2000-02, editorial director, 2002-04, creative director, 2004-; Nicktoons TV, editorial director, 2000-; Nick Junior, editorial director; Creative for the On-Air Brand Image Group, director; Nick Animation Studio, vice president. **Publications:** Baby Bird, 1999; Light, 1999; Honk! Toot! Beep!, 2000; (with A. Kennedy) Fifi Ferret's Flute, 2001; (with M. Phillips) Worm's Wagon, 2001; (with M. Chambliss) Hide-and-Seek Hippo, 2001; (with L.E. Huberman) Junior in the City, 2002; (with L.E. Huberman) Junior on the Farm, 2002; Please Don't Tell about Mom's Bell, 2002; Spend a Day in Backwards Bay, 2002; Nighttime Noises, 2002; Where is Polka Dots?, 2002; Jan and Stan, 2002; Please Don't Tell about Mom's Bell, 2002; Ride and Slide, 2002; Dora's Search for the Seasons, 2002; (with L.H. Viscardi) Junior Goes to School, 2003; Doctor Dora, 2003; Martha Doesn't Say Sorry, 2009; Martha Doesn't Share, 2010; Pirate Potty, 2010; Princess Potty, 2010; Santa's Reindeer Games, 2011. WITH P. CHANKO: Markets, 1998; Big and Little, 1998; Scientists, 1999; School, 1999; The Boat Book, 1999; Electricity, 1999; Festivals, 1999; It's Spring!, 2000. WITH S. CANIZARES; Clay Art with Gloria Elliot, 1998; What Do Artists Use?, 1998; Tedd & Huggly, 1998; Pelé, the King of Soccer, 1999; Canada, 1999; Building Shapes, 1999; Meet Jim Henson, 1999; (co-author) Puppets, 1999; The Voyage of Mae Jemison, 1999; Tools, 1999; Restaurant, 2000; At Home, 2000. WITH D. MORETON: Why Write?, 1998; Patterns, 1998; Then & Now, 1998; It's a Party, 1998; Celebrations, 1999; A Day in Japan, 1999; Games, 1999. WITH B. CHESSEN: Hello, 1998; Apples, 1998; In the Air, 1999. **Address:** c/o Brenda Bowen, Sanford J. Greenburger Associates, 55 5th Ave., New York, NY 10003, U.S.A. **Online address:** samantha@samanthaberger.com

BERGER, Sidney. American (born United States), b. 1936. **Genres:** Plays/Screenplays, Songs/Lyrics And Libretti, Theatre. **Career:** University of Kansas, assistant instructor, 1958-63; Speech and Drama Service Center Bulletin, senior staff editor, 1959-64; Michigan State University, assistant professor, 1964-66, associate professor, 1966-69, faculty, director of Graduate Studies; University of Houston, professor, John and Rebecca Moores professor of theatre, 1969-, director of plays, 1969-; Alley Theatre, associate artist, 1989-; Shakespeare Theatre Association of America, cofounder and president; Public Broadcasting Service, producer and director, 1991-94; Stages Repertory Theatre, artistic director, 1992-96; University of Houston School of Theatre & Dance, director. Writer. **Publications:** The Little Match Girl: The Musical, 1985; Bird Boy, 1988; Rapunzel: A Dramatization of the Tale by the Brothers Grimm, 1991; (ed. with J. Luere) The Playwright versus the Director, 1994; (with J. Luere) The Theatre Team, 1998. **Address:** School of Theatre, University of Houston, 133G CWM, 4800 Calhoun Rd., Houston, TX 77204-4016, U.S.A. **Online address:** sberger@uh.edu

BERGER, Stefan. German (born Germany), b. 1964. **Genres:** History, Organized Labor, Politics/Government, Business/Trade/Industry, Economics. **Career:** University of Plymouth, lecturer in British social history, 1990-91; University of Wales, lecturer, senior lecturer in European studies, 1991-2000, Hefcw-funded Centre for Border Studies, co-founder and co-director, 2000-05; University of Glamorgan, professor of history, 2000-05; Labour History Society, international secretary, 2002-06; University of Manchester, professor of modern German and comparative European history, 2005-11, Manchester Jean-Monnet-Centre of Excellence, director; Freiburg Institute for Advanced Studies School of History, senior research fellow, 2009-10; Ruhr-University Bochum, professor of social history, Institute of Social Movements, director. Writer. **Publications:** The British Labour Party and the German Social Democrats, 1900-1931, 1994; (ed. with D. Broughton) The Force of Labour, 1995; The Search for Normality: National Identity and Historical Consciousness in Germany since 1800, 1997; Ungleiche Schwestern?: Die Britische Labour Party und Die Deutsche Sozialdemokratie im Vergleic, 1997; (ed. with A. Smith) Nationalism, Labour and Ethnicity 1870-1939, 1999; (ed. with M. Donovan and K. Passmore) Writing National Histories: Western Europe Since 1800, 1999; Social Democracy and the Working Class in 19th & 20th Century Germany, 2000; (ed. and contrib.) Social Partnership in the 1990s: The West European Experience in Historical Perspective, 2001; (ed. with H. Compston) Policy Concentration and Social Partnership in Western Europe: Lessons for the 21st Century, 2002; Labour and Social History in Great Britain, 2002; (with P. Lambert and P. Schumann) Historikerdialoge: Geschichte, Mythos und Gedachtnis imdeutsch-britischen kulturellen Austausch 1750-2000, 2003; (ed. with H. Feldner and K. Passmore) Writing History: Theory and Practice, 2003; Germany, 2004; (ed. with N. LaPorte) The Other Germany: Perceptions and Influences in British-East German Relations, 1945-1990, 2005; (ed. with A. Croll and N. LaPorte) Towards a Comparative History of Coalfield Societies, 2005; (ed.) Companion to Nineteenth-Century Europe, 1789-1914, 2006; (ed. with L. Eriksonas and A. Mycock) Narrating the Nation: Representations in History, Media and the Arts, 2008; (ed. with C. Lorenz) Contested Nation: Ethnicity, Class, Religion and Gender in National Histories, 2008; (ed. with C.Lorenz) Nationalizing the Past: Historians as Nation Builders in Modern Europe, 2010; (with N. LaPorte) Friendly Enemies: Britain and the GDR, 1949-1990, 2010. Contributor to journals and newspapers. **Address:** Ruhr-University Bochum, Clemensstrasse 17-19, Bochum, 44789, Germany. **Online address:** stefan.berger@rub.de

BERGER, Thomas (Louis). American (born United States), b. 1924. **Genres:** Novels, Westerns/Adventure, Plays/Screenplays, Language/Linguistics, Literary Criticism And History, Classics, Humanities. **Career:** Rand School of Social Science, librarian, 1948-51; New York Times Index, staff, 1951-52; Popular Science Monthly, associate editor, 1952-54; Esquire Magazine, film critic, 1972-73; University of Kansas, writer-in-residence, 1974; Southampton College, distinguished visiting professor, 1975-76; Yale University, visiting lecturer, 1981-82; University of California, regent's lecturer, 1982. Writer. **Publications:** NOVELS: Crazy in Berlin, 1958; Reinhart in Love, 1962; Little Big Man, 1964; Killing Time, 1967; Vital Parts, 1970; Regiment of Women, 1974; Sneaky People, 1975; Who is Teddy Villanova?, 1977; Arthur Rex: A Legendary Novel, 1978; Neighbors, 1980; Reinhart's Women, 1981; The Feud, 1983; Nowhere, 1985; Being Invisible, 1987; The Houseguest, 1988; Changing the Past, 1989; Orrie's Story, 1990; Meeting Evil, 1992; Robert Crews, 1994; Suspects, 1996; The Return of Little Big Man, 1999; Best Friends, 2003; Adventures of the Artificial Woman, 2004. OTHERS: Granted Wishes, 1984; (with W.C. Bradford and S.L. Sondergard) An Index of Characters in Early Modern English Drama: Printed Plays, 1500-1660, 1998; (ed. with L.E. Maguire) Textual Formations and Reformations, 1999; (ed. with J.L. Levenson and B. Gaines) Romeo and Juliet, 1597, 2000; (afterword) The Pathfinder or The Inland Sea, 2006. Contributor to periodicals. **Address:** Don Congdon Associates Inc., 156 5th Ave., Ste. 625, New York, NY 10010-7782, U.S.A.

BERGER, Thomas R(odney). Canadian (born Canada), b. 1933. **Genres:** Law, Civil Liberties/Human Rights, Biography, Autobiography/Memoirs. **Career:** Shulman, Tupper and Co., lawyer, 1957-62; member of Parliament for Vancouver-Burrard, 1962-63; Thomas R. Berger and Co., lawyer, 1963-71; Legislative Assembly for Vancouver-Burrard, member, 1966-69; Supreme Court of BC, judge, 1971-83; Royal Commission on Family and Children's Law, chair, 1973-75; Mackenzie Valley Pipeline Inquiry, commissioner, 1974-77; Simon Fraser University, adjunct professor, 1979-; Indian and Inuit Health Consultation, commissioner, 1979-80; University of British Columbia, honorary lecturer, 1979-82, adjunct professor of law, 1983-; University of Victoria, sessional lecturer, 1982-83; International Defense and Aid Fund for Southern Africa in Canada, president, 1982-. Writer. **Publications:** Northern Frontier, Northern Homeland: The Report of the Mackenzie Valley Pipeline Inquiry, 1977, rev. ed., 1989; Fragile Freedoms: Human Rights and Dissent in Canada, 1981; Village Journey: The Report of the Alaska Native Review Commission, 1985, rev. ed., 1995; (co-author) Arctic: Choices for Peace and Security: Proceedings of a Public Inquiry, 1989; A Long and Terrible Shadow: White Values, Native Rights in the Americas, 1492-1992, 1991, 3rd ed., 1999; Report of the Special Counsel Regarding Claims Arising Out of Sexual Abuse at Jericho Hill School, 1995; Village Journey: The Report of the Alaska Native Review Commission, 1995; One Man's Justice: A Life in the Law, 2002. Contributor to journals and periodicals. **Address:** 1440-355 Burrard St., Vancouver, BC V6C 2G8, Canada.

BERGER-KISS, Andres. American/Hungarian (born Hungary), b. 1927. **Genres:** Novels, Novellas/Short Stories, Poetry, Autobiography/Memoirs, Humor/Satire, Translations, Young Adult Fiction, Science Fiction/Fantasy, Science Fiction/Fantasy. **Career:** State of Oregon, chief psychologist director of mental health education, 1965-67. Writer. **Publications:** Hijos de la Madrugada (novel), 1987, trans. as Children of the Dawn, 1999; Voices from the Earth, 1997; Mis 3 patrias y Un puñado de polvo (Poetry), 2004; Donalejo y sus 186 Hijos, 2005; The Sharpener and Other Stories, 2005; Secret Memoirs of a Born-again Preacher, 2006. Contributor of periodicals. Works appear in anthologies. **Address:** Latin American Literary Review Press, PO Box 17660, Pittsburgh, PA 15235, U.S.A. **Online address:** berger-kiss@att.net

BERGERUD, Eric M. American (born United States), b. 1948. **Genres:** Military/Defense/Arms Control, History, Technology, Natural History. **Career:** Lincoln University, associate professor, 1983-, professor of history and humanities, Department of General Education, chairman; San Francisco PC Users Group, OS/2 SIG leader. Writer. **Publications:** The Dynamics of Defeat, 1991; Red Thunder, Tropic Lightning, 1993; Touched with Fire, 1996; Fire in the Sky, 2000. **Address:** Lincoln University, 401 15th St., Oakland, CA 94612, U.S.A. **Online address:** bergerud@lincolnuca.edu

BERGES, Emily Trafford. American (born United States), b. 1937. **Genres:** Novels, Sex, Self Help, Young Adult Fiction. **Career:** New Jersey City University (formerly Jersey City State College), assistant professor of English, 1969-, professor of English, now professor emeritus. Writer. **Publications:** (Co-author) Children and Sex: The Parents Speak, 1983; The Flying Circus (novel), 1985. **Address:** Department of English, Jersey City State College, K304, 2039 Kennedy Blvd., Jersey City, NJ 07305-1597, U.S.A. **Online address:** eberges@njcu.edu

BERGHAHN, Volker R. American/German (born Germany), b. 1938. **Genres:** History, Politics/Government, International Relations/Current Affairs, Translations. **Career:** University of East Anglia, lecturer, 1969-71, reader in European history, 1971-75; University of Warwick, professor of history, 1975-88; Brown University, faculty, 1988-98, J.P. Birkelund professor, 1992-97; Columbia University, Seth Low professor of history and director of Institute for the Study of Europe, 1998-, The London School of Economics Dual Master's Degree Program in International and World History, program chair, 2010. Writer. **Publications:** Der Stahlhelm, Bund der Frontsoldaten 1918-1935, 1966; Der Tirpitz-Plan. Genesis und Verfall einer innenpolitischen Krisenstrategie unter Wilhelm II, 1971; Ruestung und Machtpolitik. Zur Anatomie des Kalten Krieges vor 1914, 1973; Germany and the Approach of War in 1914, 1973, 2nd ed., 1993; Militarismus, 1975; Militarism: The History of an International Debate, 1861-1979, 1981, 3rd ed., 1984; (ed. with M. Kitchen) Germany in the Age of Total War, 1981; Modern Germany: Society, Economy, and Politics in the Twentieth Century, 1982, 2nd ed., 1987; Unternehmer und Politik in der Bundesrepublik, 1985; The Americanization of West German Industry, 1945-1973, 1986; (with D. Karsten) Industrial Relations in West Germany, 1987; (ed. with H. Schissler) Perceptions of History: International Textbook Research on Britain, Germany, and the United States, 1987; (comp. with W. Deist) Ruestung im Zeichen der wilhelminischen Weltpolitik: Grundlegende Dokumente 1890-1914, 1988; (with P.J. Friedrich) Otto A. Friedrich, ein politischer Unternehmer: Sein Leben und seine Zeit, 1902-1975, 1993; Imperial Germany, 1871-1914: Economy, Society, Culture and Politics, 1994; (ed.) Quest for Economic Empire: European Strategies of German Big Business in the Twentieth Century, 1996; Sarajewo, 28. Juni 1914: Der Untergang des alten Europa, 1997; America and the Intellectual Cold Wars in Europe: Shepard Stone Between Philanthropy, Academy and Diplomacy, 2001; Europa und die beiden Weltkriege. Die Entfesselung und Entgrenzung der Gewalt, 2002; (with S. Unger and D. Ziegler) Deutsche Wirtschaftselite im 20. Jahrhundert: Kontinuitaet und Mentalitaet, 2003; Der Erste Weltkrieg, 2003, 4th ed. 2009; Imperial Germany, 1871-1918: Economy, Society, Culture, and Politics, 2005; (trans.) Europe in the Era of Two World Wars: From Militarism and Genocide to Civil Society, 1900-1950, 2005; (ed. with S. Vigols) Gibt es einen deutschen Kapitalismus?: Tradition und globale Perspektiven der Sozialen Marktwirtschaft, 2006; (ed. with S. Laessig) Biography Between Structure and Agency: Central European Lives in International Historiography, 2008; Industriegesellschaft und Kulturtransfer. Die deutsch-amerikanischen Beziehungen im 20. Jahrhundert, 2010. **Address:** Department of History, Columbia University, 501 Fayerweather Hall, 435 W 116th St., PO Box 2520, New York, NY 10027-2520, U.S.A. **Online address:** vrb7@columbia.edu

BERGIN, Thomas J. American (born United States), b. 1940. **Genres:** History, Information Science/Computers, Engineering. **Career:** U.S. Veterans Administration, systems manager, 1966-82; American University, professor of computer science, 1982-, now professor emeritus, Computing History Museum, curator and director; IEEE Annals of the History of Computing, editor-in-chief, 1999-2003. Consultant. **Publications:** (With J. Lefter) Microcomputer Based Primer on Structural Behavior, 1986; (ed.) Computer Aided Software Engineering, 1993; (ed. with R.G. Gibson) History of Programming Languages, 1996; Fifty Years of Army Computing from ENIAC to MSRC, 2000. **Address:** Department of Computer Science, American University, Clark Hall 118, Washington, DC 20016, U.S.A. **Online address:** tbergin@american.edu

BERGLAND, Martha. American (born United States), b. 1945. **Genres:** Novels, Poetry, Young Adult Fiction, Literary Criticism And History. **Career:** St. Matthew Grade School, teacher, 1967-68; Institute for Advanced Study, teaching disadvantaged youth, editor, 1968; University of Illinois, Press, assistant editor, 1968-70; Santiago College, teacher, 1971-72; U.S. Office of Education, Institute on Educational Reform, editor, 1972; University of Wisconsin, teaching assistant, 1974-77, lecturer in English, 1981; University of Wisconsin, Division of Urban Outreach, research associate, 1977-78; State University of New York, lecturer in freshman composition, 1979-80; Marquette University, lecturer in English and journalism, 1981-82; Milwaukee Area Technical College, part-time lecturer, 1982-84; Milwaukee Center for Photography, lecturer in English, 1983-85; Milwaukee Area Technical College, instructor in English, 1984-2001; Wisconsin Arts Board, literature panelist, 1985-89. Writer. **Publications:** Fish (chapbook), 1975. NOVELS: A Farm under a Lake, 1989; Idle Curiosity, 1997. Contributor to periodicals. **Address:** 7460 N Longview Ave., Milwaukee, WI 53209-2152, U.S.A.

BERGLAND, Renee L. American (born United States), b. 1963. **Genres:** Sciences, Astronomy, Young Adult Non-fiction. **Career:** Simmons College, Department of English, assistant professor, 1999-, professor; University of the District of Columbia, faculty; Marymount University, faculty; University of New Hampshire, faculty; Boston University, faculty; Dartmouth College, faculty. Writer. **Publications:** NONFICTION: The National Uncanny: Indian Ghosts and American Subjects, 2000; Maria Mitchell and the Sexing of Science: An Astronomer among the American Romantics, 2008. OTHERS: (ed. with G. Williams) Philosophies of Sex: Critical Essays on The Hermaphrodite, 2012. Contributor to periodicals. **Address:** Department of English, Simmons College, C-310E, 300 The Fenway, Boston, MA 02115, U.S.A. **Online address:** renee.bergland@simmons.edu

BERGMAN, Andrew. (Warren Bogle). American (born United States), b. 1945. **Genres:** Novels, Plays/Screenplays, Film, Adult Non-fiction. **Career:** Writer and director. **Publications:** We're in the Money: Depression America and Its Films (nonfiction), 1971; James Cagney (monograph), 1973; The Big Kiss-Off of 1944: A Jack LeVine Mystery (novel), 1974; Hollywood and LeVine (novel), 1975; (with D. Rogers) The In-laws a Novel, 1979; Sleepless Nights (novel), 1994; Tender is LeVine (novel), 2001. PLAYS: Social Security: A Play in Two Acts, 1986. **Address:** c/o Sam Cohn, International Creative Management, 40 W 57th St., New York, NY 10019, U.S.A.

BERGMAN, Eugene. American/Polish (born Poland), b. 1930. **Genres:** Theatre, Biography, Novels. **Career:** Galludet University, associate professor of English, 1971-91, now retired. Writer. **Publications:** (Ed. with T.W. Batson) The Deaf Experience: An Anthology of Literature by and about the Deaf, 2nd ed., 1976; (with B. Bragg) Tales from a Club Room, 1981; (ed. with T. Batson) Angels and Outcasts: An Anthology of Deaf Characters in Literature, 1985; (with B. Bragg) Lessons in Laughter: The Autobiography of a Deaf Actor, 1989; Survival Artist: A Memoir of the Holocaust, 2009. **Address:** 5225 Pooks Hill Rd., Bethesda, MD 20814, U.S.A. **Online address:** eecbergman@aol.com

BERGMAN, Ronen. Israeli (born Israel), b. 1972. **Genres:** History, Military/Defense/Arms Control. **Career:** Haaretz (newspaper), senior staff writer; Yedioth Ahronoth (newspaper), senior security and intelligence correspondent and analyst; Tel-Aviv University, faculty. Writer. **Publications:** Vehareshut Netunah: 'Efoh T'ainu? Kakh Hafkhah ha-Rashut ha-Palestinit le-pas Yitsur Shel Shehitut U-teror, 2002; Milhemet Yom Kippur, 2003; Nekudat ha-al-hazor: ha- modi'in ha-Yisre'eli mul Iran ve-Hizbalah, 2007. **Address:** Israel. **Online address:** ronen@thesecretwarwithiran.com

BERGMAN, Tamar. Israeli (born Israel), b. 1939. **Genres:** Children's Fiction, Children's Non-fiction, Young Adult Fiction, Novels, Biography. **Career:** Israeli Broadcasting Authority, radio play writer, 1970-82. **Publications:** FOR CHILDREN: Hamassa Legan Hashoshanim, 1976; Danny Holeh Lemirpe'at Hashina'in, 1976; Al Shumklum ve-'al Shumakom, 1976; Mi Rotze Lehitarev?, 1977; Beshabat Baboker, 1979; Shinayim tsohakot, 1980; Simlat Haksamim, 1980; (with C. Gutman) Kol Ehad Ha'ya Pa'am Yeled, 1983; Ha Yeled mi-shamah, 1983; Mehapsim Et Osnat, 1985; Gozal Shel Aba Ve'ima, 1987; Leoreh Hamessila, 1987; Rav Hovel Shav Ela'ich, 1990; Kunchiat Hassodot, 1996; Eifo?, 1998; Ina Afa im Hatziporim, 1999; Mook, 2003. FOR ADULTS: Kemara Letusha, 1996. **Address:** 6 Hanassi St., Jerusalem, 92188, Israel. **Online address:** zevtamar@netvision.net.il

BERGNER, Daniel. American (born United States), b. 1960. **Genres:** Biography, Adult Non-fiction. **Career:** New York Times, contributing writer. Freelance journalist. **Publications:** Moments of Favor, 1991; God of the Rodeo: The Search for Hope, Faith, and a Six-Second Ride in Louisiana's Angola Prison, 1998; In the Land of Magic Soldiers: A Story of White and Black in West Africa, 2003; The Other Side of Desire: Four Journeys into the Far Realms of Lust and Longing, 2009. Contributor of articles to periodicals. **Address:** c/o Author Mail, HarperCollins Publishers Inc., 10 E 53rd St., New York, NY 10022, U.S.A. **Online address:** bergnerdaniel@gmail.com

BERGON, Frank. American (born United States), b. 1943. **Genres:** Literary Criticism And History, Novels, Natural History, Young Adult Fiction. **Career:** Vassar College, professor of English, 1972-, professor emeritus of English; University of Washington, visiting associate professor, 1980-81. Writer. **Publications:** Stephen Crane's Artistry, 1975. NOVELS: Shoshone Mike, 1987; The Temptations of St. Ed and Brother S, 1993; Wild Game, 1995. EDITOR: (with Z. Papanikolas) Looking Far West: The Search for the American West in History, Myth and Literature, 1978; The Western Writings of Stephen Crane, 1979; The Wilderness Reader, 1980, rev. ed., 1994; A Sharp Lookout: Selected Nature Essays of John Burroughs, 1987; (intro.) The Journals of Lewis and Clark, 1989. **Address:** c/o Peter Matson, Sterling Lord Literistic Inc., 65 Bleecker St., New York, NY 10012, U.S.A. **Online address:** bergon@vassar.edu

BERGONZI, Bernard. British (born England), b. 1929. **Genres:** Novels, Poetry, Literary Criticism And History, Essays, History. **Career:** University of Manchester, assistant lecturer, lecturer in English, 1959-66; University of Warwick, senior lecturer, 1966-71, professor, 1971-92, professor emeritus of English, 1992-, pro-vice chancellor, 1979-82; Brandeis University, visiting lecturer, 1964-65. Writer. **Publications:** The Early H.G. Wells, 1961; Heroes' Twilight A Study of the Literature of the Great War, 1965, 2nd ed., 1980; (intro.) Tono-Bungay, 1966; An English Sequence, 1966; The Situation of the Novel, 1970, 2nd ed., 1979; Anthony Powell, 1971; T.S. Eliot, 1972, 2nd ed., 1978; The Turn of a Century, 1973; Gerard Manley Hopkins, 1977; Reading the Thirties: Texts and Contexts, 1978; Years: Sixteen Poems, 1979; The Roman Persuasion (novel), 1981; (co-author) Why I am still a Catholic, 1982; The Myth of Modernism and Twentieth Century Literature, 1986; Exploding English: Criticism, Theory, Culture, 1990; Wartime and Aftermath: English Literature and Its Background, 1939-60, 1993; David Lodge, 1995; War Poets and Other Subjects, 1999; A Victorian Wanderer: The Life of Thomas Arnold the Younger, 2003; A Study in Greene: Graham Greene and the Art of the Novel, 2006. EDITOR: Innovations: Essays on Art and Ideas, 1968; T.S. Eliot: Four Quartets: A Casebook, 1969; The Twentieth Century, 1970; Tales of East and West, 1973; H.G. Wells: Collection of Critical Essays, 1976; Poetry 1870-1914, 1980; (and intro.) Napoleon of Notting Hill, 1994. **Address:** Department of English and, Comparative Literary Studies, University of Warwick, Humanities Bldg., Coventry, CV4 7AL, England.

BERGQUIST, Charles. American (born United States), b. 1942. **Genres:** History, Translations. **Career:** Duke University, assistant professor, 1972-77, associate professor, 1978-85, professor of history, 1985-88, University of Washington, professor of history, 1989-, Harry Bridges professor of labor studies, 1994-96, coordinator of Latin-American studies, 1989-92, Harry Bridges Center for Labor Studies, chair, 1994-95, 1995-96, director, 1994-96, now professor emeritus of Modern Latin America and Labor; Fulbright lecturer in Colombia, 1988-89, 1997. Writer. **Publications:** Coffee and Conflict in Colombia, 1886-1910, 1978, trans. as Café y conflicto en Colombia, 1886-1910: la Guerra de los Mil Días, sus antecedentes y consecuencias, 1999; (ed.) Alternative Approaches to the Problem of Development: A Selected, Annotated Bibliography, 1979; (ed.) Labor in the Capitalist World-Economy, 1984; Labor in Latin America: Comparative Essays on Chile, Argentina, Venezuela, and Colombia, 1986; (ed. with R. Peñaranda and G. Sánchez) Violence in Colombia: The Contemporary Crisis in Historical Perspective, 1992; Labor and the Course of American Democracy: US History in Latin-American Perspective, 1996; (ed. with R. Peñaranda and G. Sánchez) Violence in Colombia, 1990-2000: Waging War and Negotiating Peace, 2001. Contributor to books and periodicals. **Address:** Department of History, University of Washington, SMI 10, 315 Smith Hall, PO Box 353560, Seattle, WA 98195-3560, U.S.A. **Online address:** caramba@uw.edu

BERGQUIST, William Hastings. American (born United States), b. 1940. **Genres:** Psychology, Education, Business/Trade/Industry, Economics, Institutions/Organizations, Reference. **Career:** University of Idaho, assistant professor of psychology, 1969-72; Western Interstate Commission for Higher Education, director of special higher education programs, 1972-74; William Bergquist and Associates, director, 1974-; Professional School of Psychology, president, 1986-, senior tutor. Writer. **Publications:** (Ed. with W.A. Shoemaker) A Comprehensive Approach to Institutional Development, 1976; (co-ed.) Designing Teaching Improvement Programs, 1979; (ed. with E. Greenberg and K.M. O'Donnell) Educating Learners of All Ages, 1980; (with R.A. Gould and E.M. Greenberg) Designing Undergraduate Education, 1981; (with J.L. Armstrong) Planning Effectively for Educational Quality, 1986; (with S.R. Phillips) Solutions: A Guide to Better Problem Solving, 1987; The Four Cultures of the Academy: Insights and Strategies for Improving Leadership in Collegiate Organizations, 1992; The Postmodern Organization: Mastering the Art of Irreversible Change, 1993; (with G.A. Klaum and E.M. Greenberg) In Our Fifties: Voices of Men and Women Reinventing Their Lives, 1993; (with B. Weiss) Freedom!: Narratives of Change in Hungary and Estonia, 1994; (with R. McLean and B.A. Kobylinski) Stroke Survivors, 1994; (with J. Betwee and D. Meuel) Building Strategic Relationships: How to Extend Your Organization's Reach through Partnerships, Alliances, and Joint Ventures, 1995; (co-author) Quality Through Access, Access with Quality: The New Imperative for Higher Education, 1995; (with S.R. Phillips) The Six Principles of Successful Self-Management: A Guidebook for Using the Domain Preference Scale, 1996; (with C.J. Bland) The Vitality of Senior Faculty Members: Snow on the Roof, Fire in the Furnace, 1997; (with K. Pawlak) Engaging the Six Cultures of the Academy: Revised and Expanded Edition of The Four Cultures of the Academy, 2008; Quality and Access: An Essential Unity in Higher Education, forthcoming. **Address:** Professional School of Psychology, 3550 Watt Ave., Ste. 140, Sacramento, CA 95821-2666, U.S.A. **Online address:** from.website.2008@williambergquist.com

BERGREEN, Laurence. American (born United States), b. 1950. **Genres:** Writing/Journalism, Biography, History, Travel/Exploration. **Career:** Museum of Broadcasting, assistant, 1977-78; writer, lecturer and teacher, 1980-; New School for Social Research, faculty, 1981-82. **Publications:** Look Now, Pay Later: The Rise of Network Broadcasting, 1980; James Agee: A Life, 1984, 2nd ed., 1985; As Thousands Cheer: The Life of Irving Berlin, 1990; Capone: The Man and the Era, 1994; Louis Armstrong: An Extravagant Life, 1997; Voyage to Mars: NASA's Search for Life Beyond Earth, 2000; Over the Edge of the World: Magellan's Terrifying Circumnavigation of the Globe, 2003; Marco Polo: From Venice to Xanadu, 2007. Contributor to magazines and newspapers. **Address:** c/o Suzanne Gluck, William Morris Endeavor Entertainment L.L.C., 1325 Ave. of the Americas, New York, NY 10019, U.S.A. **Online address:** lbergreen@yahoo.com

BERGSTROM, Elaine. (Marie Kiraly). American (born United States), b. 1946. **Genres:** Mystery/Crime/Suspense, Romance/Historical, Novels, inspirational/Motivational Literature. **Career:** Novelist. **Publications:** NOVELS: Shattered Glass, 1989; Blood Alone, 1990; Blood Rites, 1991; Daughter of the Night, 1992; Tapestry of Dark Souls, 1993; Baroness of Blood, 1995; The Rose Wallpaper, 1995; The Door through Washington Square, 1998; Blood to Blood: The Dracula Story Continues, 2000; Mina, 2000; Nocturne, 2003. NOVELS AS MARIE KIRALY: Leanna: Possession of a Woman, 1996; (with E.A. Poe) Madeline: After the Fall of Usher, 1996. Works appear in anthologies. **Address:** 2918 S Wentworth Ave., Milwaukee, WI 53207, U.S.A. **Online address:** ebergstrom2@wi.rr.com

BERGUNDER, Michael. German (born Germany), b. 1966?. **Genres:** History. **Career:** University of Halle, adjunct lecturer in ecumenics, Christian confessions and religious studies, 1998-2002; University of Heidelberg, professor of religions and mission studies, 2002-, Philosophy for the Religious Studies Program, faculty, 2004-. Writer, historian and theologian.

Publications: Die Südindische Pfingstbewegung im 20. Jahrhundert: eine historische und systematische Untersuchung, 1999; (ed.) Missionsberichte aus Indien im 18. Jahrhundert: ihre Bedeutung für die europäische Gesitesgeschichte und ihr wissenschaftlicher Quellenwert für die Indienkunde, 1999; Religiöser Pluralismus und das Christentum: Festgabe für Helmut Obst zum 60. Geburtstag, 2001; (ed. with D. Cyranka) Esoterik Und Christentum: Religionsgeschichtliche Und Theologische Perspektiven: Helmut Obst Zum 65. Geburtstag, 2005; The South Indian Pentecostal Movement in the Twentieth Century, 2008. Contributor to books. **Address:** Universitat Heidelberg, Grabengasse 1, Heidelberg, 69117, Germany. **Online address:** michael.bergunder@wts.uni-heidelberg.de

BERINSKY, Adam J. American (born United States), b. 1970. **Genres:** History, Politics/Government. **Career:** Princeton University, instructor of politics, 1999-2000, assistant professor of politics, 2000-03; Massachusetts Institute of Technology, Department of Political Science, assistant professor, 2003-04, associate professor, 2004-; Public Opinion Quarterly, book review editor, 2008-12. **Publications:** Silent Voices: Public Opinion and Political Participation in America, 2004; In Time of War: Understanding American Public Opinion from World War II to Iraq, 2009; (ed.) New Directions in Public Opinion, 2011. Contributor to books and journals. **Address:** Department of Political Science, Massachusetts Institute of Technology, 77 Massachusetts Ave., E53-459, Cambridge, MA 02139, U.S.A. **Online address:** berinsky@mit.edu

BERINSTEIN, Paula. American (born United States), b. 1950. **Genres:** Engineering, How-to Books, Mathematics/Statistics, Adult Non-fiction, Information Science/Computers, Librarianship, Technology, Travel/Exploration, Travel/Exploration, Reference. **Career:** Rockwell Intl., Rocketdyne Division, programmer and analyst; Berinstein Research, principal, 1987-2002; Paula Hollywood Inc., software developer, executive vice-president; The Writing Show, producer and host; Mechnicality Inc., vice president of marketing, chief operating officer; The Writing Show, producer and host. Freelane writer, 1994-. **Publications:** Communicating with Library Users, 1994; Finding Images Online: Online User's Guide to Image Searching in Cyberspace, 1996; Finding Statistics Online: How to Locate the Elusive Numbers You Need, 1998; The Statistical Handbook on Technology, 1999; Alternative Energy: Facts, Statistics and Issues, 2001; Making Space Happen: Private Space Ventures and the Visionaries behind Them, 2002; Business Statistics on the Web: Find Them Fast-At Little or No Cost, 2003. Contributor to magazines and newspapers. **Address:** c/o Author Mail, Information Today Inc., 143 Old Marlton Pke., Medford, NJ 08055, U.S.A. **Online address:** paula@writingshow.com

BERKENSTADT, Jim. American (born United States), b. 1956. **Genres:** Music, Autobiography/Memoirs. **Career:** Pollina & Phelan, associate, 1982-85; Axley Brynelson, associate, 1985-86; Wisconsin Cheeseman Inc., vice president and general counsel, 1987-. Writer and consultant. **Publications:** (With Belmo) Black Market Beatles: The Story behind the Lost Recordings, 1995; (co-ed.) John, Paul and Me: Before the Beatles, 1997; (with C.R. Cross) Nevermind: Nirvana, 1998; The Goldmine Beatles Digest, 2000. Contributor to periodicals. **Address:** Collectors Guide Publishing Inc., PO Box 62034, Burlington, ON L7R 4K2, Canada. **Online address:** nelsonwills@worldnet.att.net

BERKEY, Jonathan P. American (born United States), b. 1959. **Genres:** History. **Career:** Schutz American School, teacher, 1981-82; Princeton University, lecturer in history, 1988-90; Mount Holyoke College, assistant professor of religion, 1990-93; Davidson College, John D. and Catherine T. MacArthur assistant professor, 1993-95, assistant professor, 1993-96, associate professor, 1996-2004, E. Craig Wall Jr. distinguished professor in humanities, 2001-03, semester-in-India program, director, 2004; American Research Center, director, 1998-2001. Writer. **Publications:** The Transmission of Knowledge in Medieval Cairo: A Social History of Islamic Education, 1992; Popular Preaching and Religious Authority in the Medieval Islamic Near East, 2001; The Formation of Islam: Religion and Society in the Near East, 600-1800, 2003. **Address:** Department of History, Davidson College, 3252 Chambers, PO Box 6911, Davidson, NC 28035-6911, U.S.A. **Online address:** joberkey@davidson.edu

BERKMAN, Michael B. American (born United States), b. 1960. **Genres:** Sciences, Politics/Government. **Career:** Pennsylvania State University, Department of Political Science, assistant professor, 1989-94, associate professor, 1995-2006, professor of political science, 2006-, director of undergraduate studies, 2000-, director of the minor in liberal arts and business, 2006-; Penn State Hillel, board director, 1991-94; American Political Science Association, State Politics Section, secretary, treasurer and newsletter editor, 1999-2002; American Journal of Education, contributing editor, 2004. **Publications:** The State Roots of National Politics: Congress and the Tax Agenda, 1978-1986, 1993; (with E.Plutzer) Ten Thousand Democracies: Politics and Public Opinion in America's School Districts, 2005; (with E. Plutzer) Evolution, Creationism and the Battle to Control America's Classrooms, 2010. Contributor to periodicals and journals. **Address:** Department of Political Science, Pennsylvania State University, 321 Pond Lab, University Park, PA 16802-6200, U.S.A. **Online address:** mberkman@la.psu.edu

BERKMAN, Pamela Rafael. American (born United States) **Genres:** Novellas/Short Stories. **Career:** Jossey-Bass/Pfeiffer, editor. Writer. **Publications:** Her Infinite Variety: Stories of Shakespeare and the Women He Loved, 2001; The Falling Nun, and Other Stories, 2003; The Courtesan of Verona: Mercutio's Story, forthcoming; His Dark Lady and Christopher Marlowe, forthcoming. **Address:** c/o Jenny Bent, The Bent Agency, 204 Park Pl., PO Box 2, Brooklyn, NY 11238, U.S.A. **Online address:** pberkman@josseybass.com

BERKOFF, Steven. British (born England), b. 1937. **Genres:** Novels, Novellas/Short Stories, Plays/Screenplays, Travel/Exploration, Autobiography/Memoirs, Young Adult Fiction. **Career:** London Theater Group, founding director, 1973-. Writer and actor. **Publications:** East and Agamemnon and The Fall of the House of Usher, 1977, rev. ed., 1982; Gross Intrusion and Other Stories, 1979; Greek, 1980; The Trial and Metamorphosis: Two Theatre Adaptations from Franz Kafka, 1981; Decadence: A New Play, 1981; Decadence and Greek, 1983; West, Lunch and Harry's Christmas: Three Plays, 1985; Kvetch and Acapulco: Two Plays, 1987; Sink the Belgrano!, with, Massage, 1987; The Trial, Metamorphosis, In the Penal Colony: Three Theatre Adaptations from Franz Kafka, 1988; Steven Berkoff's America, 1988; I Am Hamlet, 1989; A Prisoner in Rio (memoir), 1989; Decadence and Other Plays: East-West-Greek, 1989; (intro.) Salome, 1989; Greek: Opera in Two Acts, 1990; Coriolanus in Deutschland, 1992; The Theatre of Steven Berkoff, 1992; Overview, 1994; Collected Plays, 1994; Meditations on Metamorphosis, 1995; Free Association: An Autobiography, 1996; Graft: Tales of an Actor, 1998; Shopping in the Santa Monica Mall: The Journals of a Strolling Player, 2000; Plays One, 2000; Plays Three, 2000; The Secret Love Life of Ophelia, 2001; Requiem for Ground Zero, 2002; Tough Acts, 2003; Sit and Shiver, 2006; My Life in Food, 2007; Richard II in New York, 2008; Diary of a Juvenile Delinquent, 2010. **Address:** c/o Joanna Marston, Rosica Colin Ltd., 1 Clareville Grove Mews, London, GL SW7 5AH, England.

BERKOVITCH, Nitza. Israeli (born Israel), b. 1955. **Genres:** Sociology, Women's Studies And Issues. **Career:** Tel-Aviv University, Department of Sociology, adjunct lecturer, 1986-88, School of Management, adjunct lecturer, 1986-88; Stanford University, Department of Sociology, research assistant, 1989-92, Libraries and Information Resources, statistical consultant, 1991-93, adjunct lecturer, 1992-94; National Institutes of Health, consultant, 1991-93; Western Washington University, Department of Sociology, adjunct lecturer, 1993; Hebrew University, post doctoral fellow, 1994-95; Ben-Gurion University of the Negev, Department of Behavioral Sciences, lecturer, 1995-2002, senior lecturer, 2002-, chair. Writer. **Publications:** (Ed. with V. Moghadam) Middle East Politics: Feminist Challenges, 1999; From Motherhood to Citizenship: Women's Rights and International Organizations, 1999; (ed. with H. Dahan-Kalev, N. Yanay and Henriette) Gender, Space and Periphery: Women of the Negev, 2004; (with H. Dahan-Kalev) Nashim ba-darom: merḥav, periferyah, migdar, 2005. (ed. with U. Ram) In/Equality, 2006; (ed. with U. Ram) I/shivyon, 2006. Contributor to books and periodicals. **Address:** Department of Behavioral Sciences, Ben-Gurion University of the Negev, PO Box 653, Beer-Sheva, 84105, Israel. **Online address:** nberko@bgumail.bgu.ac.il

BERKOVITZ, Jay R. American (born United States), b. 1951. **Genres:** History, Cultural/Ethnic Topics. **Career:** Spertus College, faculty; University of Massachusetts, assistant professor, 1982-88, associate professor of Jewish history, 1988-2000, 2000-, adjunct professor of history, Center for Jewish Studies, director, 1989-, Department of Judaic and Near Eastern Studies, chairman, 1990-95, professor, Department of History, adjunct faculty, Department of French and Italian Studies, adjunct faculty; Bar Ilan University, visiting professor; Boston Hebrew College, visiting professor; Hebrew University of Jerusalem, visiting professor; Touro College, visiting professor; Trinity College, visiting professor; University of Connecticut, visiting professor.

Writer. **Publications:** The Shaping of Jewish Identity in Nineteenth-Century France, 1989; Rites and Passages: The Beginnings of Modern Jewish Culture in France, 1650-1860, 2004; Tradition and Revolution: Jewish Culture in Early Modern France, 2007. **Address:** Department of Judaic & Near Eastern Studies, University of Massachusetts, 744 Herter Hall, 161 Presidents Dr., Amherst, MA 01003-9312, U.S.A. **Online address:** jrb@judnea.umass.edu

BERKOWITZ, Edward D. American (born United States), b. 1950. **Genres:** History, Medicine/Health. **Career:** Department of Health, Education, and Welfare, Office of the Secretary, policy analyst, 1975-76; Northwestern University, Department of History, instructor, 1976-77; University of Massachusetts, assistant professor of history and John F. Kennedy fellow, 1977-80; Harvard Business School, research associate, 1979; President's Commission for a National Agenda for the Eighties, senior staff, 1980-81; Brandeis University, director of corporate and foundation relations, 1982; George Washington University, Department of History, associate professor, 1982-89, professor of history, 1989-, chair, 1993-97, 2000-02, Elliott School of International Affairs, professor of public policy and public administration, 2003-, Program in History and Public Policy, director, 1982-2006; Johns Hopkins Medical Institutes, Robert Wood Johnson found faculty fellow, 1987-88. Writer and historian. **Publications:** (Ed.) Disability Policies and Government Programs, 1979; (with K. McQuaid) Creating the Welfare State: The Political Economy of Twentieth-Century Reform, 1980, rev. ed., 1992; Disabled Policy: America's Programs for the Handicapped, 1987; (ed.) Social Security after Fifty: Successes and Failures, 1987; (with W. Wolff) Group Health Association: A Portrait of a Health Maintenance Organization, 1988; (with E.R. Kingson and F. Pratt) Social Security in the USA: A Discussion Guide to Social Insurance with Lesson Plans, 1989; America's Welfare State: From Roosevelt to Reagan, 1991; (with E.R. Kingson) Social Security and Medicare: A Policy Primer, 1993; Mr. Social Security: The Life of Wilbur J. Cohen, 1995; To Improve Human Health: A History of the Institute of Medicine, 1998; (with M.J. Santangelo) The Medical Follow-Up Agency: The First Fifty Years, 1946-1996, 1999; Robert Ball and the Politics of Social Security, 2003; Something Happened: A Political and Cultural Overview of the Seventies, 2006; (with L.W. DeWitt and D. Béland) Social Security: A Documentary History, 2008; Mass Appeal: The Formative Age of the Movies, Radio, and Tv, 2010. Contributor of articles to journals and periodicals. **Address:** Department of History, George Washington University, 801 22nd St. NW, Ste. 319, Washington, DC 20052-0058, U.S.A. **Online address:** ber@gwu.edu

BERKOWITZ, Peter. American (born United States), b. 1959. **Genres:** Ethics, Politics/Government, History, Philosophy, Humanities. **Career:** Harvard University, assistant professor, 1990-94, associate professor of government, 1994-99; Stanford University, Hoover Institution, research fellow, 2002-05, Tad and Dianne Taube senior fellow, 2005-, Koret-Taube Task Force on National Security and Law, chair, Boyd and Jill Smith Task Force on Virtues of a Free Society, co-chair; George Mason University, School of Law, associate professor of law, 1999-2007; Israel Program on Constitutional Government, co-founder, director; Interdisciplinary Center, Tikvah Program in Political Leadership, co-founder, co-director. Writer. **Publications:** Nietzsche: The Ethics of an Immoralist, 1995; Virtue and the Making of Modern Liberalism, 1999; (ed.) Never a Matter of Indifference: Sustaining Virtue in a Free Republic, 2003; (ed.) Varieties of Conservatism in America, 2004; (ed.) Varieties of Progressivism in America, 2004; (ed.) Terrorism, the Laws of War, and the Constitution: Debating the Enemy Combatant Cases, 2005; (ed.) Future of American Intelligence, 2005. EDITOR WITH T. LINDBERG: Preventing Surprise Attacks: Intelligence Reform in the Wake of 9/11, 2005; Confirmation Wars: Preserving Independent Courts in Angry Times, 2006; Warrant for Terror: Fatwas of Radical Islam and the Duty to Jihad, 2006; Fight Club Politics: How Partisanship is Poisoning The House of Representatives, 2006; Uncertain Shield: The U.S. Intelligence System in the Throes of Reform, 2006; Countering Terrorism: Blurred Focus, Halting Steps, 2007; Race, Wrongs, and Remedies: Group Justice in the 21st Century, 2009; Advancing Democracy Abroad: Why We Should and How We Can, 2009; Unchecked and Unbalanced: How the Discrepancy between Knowledge and Power Caused the Financial Crisis and Threatens Democracy, 2009; Victorious and Vulnerable: Why Democracy won in the Twentieth Century and How It Is Still Imperiled, 2009. Contributor of articles to periodicals. **Address:** Hoover Institution, 21 Dupont Cir. NW, Ste. 300, Washington, DC 20036-1109, U.S.A. **Online address:** berkowitz@hoover.stanford.edu

BERKSON, Bill. American (born United States), b. 1939. **Genres:** Poetry, Art/Art History, Literary Criticism And History. **Career:** Portfolio and Art News Annual, editorial associate, 1960-63; WNDT-TV, associate producer, 1964-65; New School for Social Research, teacher, 1964-69; Poets in the Schools, poet, teacher, 1968-84; Best and Co. Magazine, editor, 1969; Yale University, Ezra Stiles College, teaching fellow, 1969-70; Southampton College, adjunct professor, 1979-80; Big Sky Magazine, editor, 1971-78; Big Sky Books, editor, 1971-78; San Francisco Art Institute, professor, 1984-2008, director of letters and science, 1994-98, professor emeritus, 2011-; Art in America, correspondent editor, 1988-; Modern Painters, editorial board member, 2002-05; artcritical.com, poetry editor, 2009-. **Publications:** Saturday Night: Poems 1960-61, 1961; Shining Leaves, 1969; (with L. Fagin) Two Serious Poems and One Other, 1972; Recent Visitors, 1973; Ants, 1974; (with F. O'Hara) Hymns of St. Bridget, 1974; 100 Women, 1975; Enigma Variations, 1975; Blue is the Hero, 1976; Start Over, 1983; Red Devil, 1983; Lush Life, 1984; Ronald Bladen: Early and Late, 1991; A Copy of the Catalogue, 1999; (with A. Waldman) Young Manhattan, 2000; Serenade: Poems and Prose, 1975-1989, 2000; Fugue State, 2001; (with F. O'Hara) Hymns of St. Bridget and Other Writings, 2001; The Sweet Singer of Modernism and Other Art Writings, 2004; (with B. Mayer) What's Your Idea of a Good Time?, 2006; Sudden Address: Selected Lectures 1981-2006, 2007; (with C. Jacobsen) BILL, 2008; Goods & Services, 2009; Portrait and Dream: New & Selected Poems, 2009; Costanza, 2009; (with G. Schneeman) Ted Berrigan, 2010; Lady Air, 2010; For the Ordinary Artist, 2010; Not an Exit, 2011. EDITOR: In Memory of My Feelings, 1967; Best & Company, 1969; (with I. Sandler) Alex Katz, 1971; (with J. LeSueur) Homage to Frank O'Hara, 1978; What's With Modern Art?, 1998. **Address:** CA , U.S.A. **Online address:** berkson@pacbell.net

BERLFEIN, Judy Reiss. American (born United States), b. 1958. **Genres:** Young Adult Non-fiction, Adult Non-fiction, Science Fiction/Fantasy. **Career:** KPBS Radio, science reporter, 1984-87; KUNC Radio, science reporter, 1985; Bernardo News, editorial assistant, 1986; Holt, Rinehart and Winston Inc., science editor and writer, 1987; freelance science writer and reporter, 1987-. **Publications:** Teen Pregnancy, 1992. Contributor of articles for magazines and newspapers. **Address:** 1145 Stratford Dr., Encinitas, CA 92024, U.S.A.

BERLIN, Eric. American (born United States) **Genres:** Plays/Screenplays. **Career:** PC Magazine, editorial researcher, 1990-92; Mecklermedia, editor, 1995-97; Uproar, game designer, 1998-2000; Skillgames, game designer, 2000-01; Vtech, producer, 2002-03; Penny Publications, assistant publisher, 2004-. Writer, publisher and puzzle creator. **Publications:** The Puzzling World of Winston Breen (novel), 2007; The Potato Chip Puzzles (novel), 2008. PLAYS: Babes and Brides: Two One-Act Plays (contains The Line That's Picked Up 1,000 Babes and The Midnight Moonlight Wedding Chapel), 1993. **Address:** Milford, CT , U.S.A. **Online address:** ericberlin@gmail.com

BERLIN, Leslie. American (born United States), b. 1969. **Genres:** Adult Non-fiction, Biography, Autobiography/Memoirs. **Career:** Stanford University, Silicon Valley Archives, project historian. Educator and writer. **Publications:** The Man Behind the Microchip: Robert Noyce and the Invention of Silicon Valley, 2005. **Address:** Silicon Valley Archives, Stanford University Libraries, Green Library - HASRG, 557 Escondido Mall, Stanford, CA 94305-6004, U.S.A. **Online address:** leslie@leslieberlinauthor.com

BERLINER-GLUCKMAN, Janet. (Janet Gluckman). American/South African (born South Africa), b. 1939. **Genres:** Novels, Novellas/Short Stories, Mystery/Crime/Suspense, Horror, Science Fiction/Fantasy, Biography, Literary Criticism And History. **Career:** Professional Media Services (editorial consulting service), founder, 1978-; Berliner Productions (media production company), founder, 1995; Horror Writers Association, president, 1997-98. Educator and writer. **Publications:** NOVELS AS JANET GLUCKMAN: (with W. Greer) The Execution Exchange, 1980; Rite of the Dragon, 1981, rev. ed. as Janet Berliner, 2001; (co-author) Artifact, 2003. MADAGASCAR MANIFESTO SERIES: (with G. Guthridge as Janet Gluckman): Child of the Light, 1991, rev. ed. as Janet Berliner, 1996; Child of the Journey, 1996; Children of the Dusk, 1997; The Horror Writers Association Presents Whitley Strieber's Aliens, 1999. EDITOR: (with P.S. Beagle) Peter S. Beagle's Immortal Unicorn, 1995; (with D. Copperfield) David Copperfield's Tales of the Impossible, 1995; (with M.H. Greenberg and U. Luserke) Desire Burn: Women's Stories from the Dark Side of Passion, 1995; (with P.S. Beagle) Peter S. Beagle's Immortal Unicorn, 1995; (with D. Copperfield) David

Copperfield's Beyond Imagination, 1996; (with J.C. Oates) Snapshots: 20th Century Mother-Daughter Fiction, 2000; (with J.C. Oates) Snapshots: Mothers and Daughters: An Outstanding and Vibrant Collection of Stories from Internationally Acclaimed Women Writers, 2001; (with M. Crichton) Michael Crichton Companion, forthcoming. Contributor of articles to periodicals. **Address:** 1320 S 13th St., Las Vegas, NV 89104-3317, U.S.A. **Online address:** subscribe@janetberliner.com

BERLINGER, Joe. American (born United States), b. 1961. **Genres:** Plays/Screenplays, Biography, Music, Novels. **Career:** McCann-Erickson, staff, 1983-84; Ogilvy and Mather, staff, 1984-; Maysles Films, executive producer; Creative Thinking Intl., owner; director, producer and writer. **Publications:** (With G. Milner) Metallica: This Monster Lives, 2004. Contributor to periodicals. **Address:** c/o Innovative Artists, 3000 W Olympic Blvd., Bldg. 4, Ste. 1200, Santa Monica, CA 90404, U.S.A.

BERLO, Janet Catherine. American (born United States) **Genres:** Art/Art History. **Career:** University of Rochester, Susan B. Anthony chair of gender and women's studies, 1997-, Department of Art and Art History, professor of art history and visual and cultural studies, 2003-; Harvard University, visiting professor, 2002. Writer and historian. **Publications:** Teotihuacan Art Abroad: A Study of Metropolitan Style and Provincial Transformation in Incensario Workshops, 1984; The Art of Pre-Hispanic Mesoamerica: An Annotated Bibliography, 1985; (co-author) Native Paths: American Indian Art from the Collection of Charles and Valerie Diker, 1998; (with R.B. Phillips) Native North American Art, 1998; Spirit Beings and Sun Dancers: Black Hawk's Vision of the Lakota World, 2000; Transforming Images, 2000; Quilting Lessons: Notes from the Scrap Bag of a Writer and Quilter, 2001; (with P.C. Crews) Wild by Design: Two Hundred Years of Innovation and Artistry in American Quilts, 2003; (contrib.) A Kiowa's Odyssey, 2007; (with Bettelheim) Transcultural Pilgrim, 2011. EDITOR: (with R.A. Diehl) Mesoamerica after the Decline of Teotihuacan, A.D. 700-900, 1989; (with M.B. Schevil and E.B. Dwyer) Textile Traditions of Mesoamerica and the Andes: An Anthology, 1991; Art, Ideology, and the City of Teotihuacan: A Symposium at Dumbarton Oaks, 8th and 9th October 1988, 1992; The Early Years of Native American Art History: The Politics of Scholarship and Collecting, 1992; (with L.A. Wilson) Arts of Africa, Oceania, and the Americas, 1993; Plains Indian Drawings, 1865-1935: Pages from a Visual History, 1996. Contributor to books. **Address:** Department of Art and Art History, University of Rochester, 305 Morey Hall, Rochester, NY 14627, U.S.A. **Online address:** brlo@mail.rochester.edu

BERLOW, Alan. American (born United States), b. 1950. **Genres:** Documentaries/Reportage, Young Adult Non-fiction. **Career:** National Public Radio, reporter, 1979-89, Southeast Asia correspondent; freelance writer, 1989-. Writer. **Publications:** Dead Season: A Story of Murder and Revenge on the Philippine Island of Negros, 1996. **Address:** 9 E Melrose St., Chevy Chase, MD 20815, U.S.A.

BERMAN *See* **Strother, Ruth.**

BERMAN, Brooke. American (born United States), b. 1970?. **Genres:** Autobiography/Memoirs, Humor/Satire. **Career:** MCC Theater Youth Co., Playwrights Unit, director. Playwright and screenwriter. **Publications:** Playing House: A Comedy, 2002; Wonderland: A Dark Comedy, 2007; Hunting and Gathering, 2008; No Place Like Home: A Memoir in 39 Apartments, 2010. **Address:** c/o Swanna MacNair, Fletcher & Co., 78 5th Ave., 3rd Fl., New York, NY 10011, U.S.A. **Online address:** brooke@brookeberman.net

BERMAN, Claire. American (born United States), b. 1936. **Genres:** Gerontology/Senior Issues, Human Relations/Parenting, Psychology. **Career:** Cosmopolitan, senior editor, 1958-63; New York Magazine, contributor editor, 1972-78; Child Welfare League of America, Permanent Families for Children, director of public education; New York Times, senior editor. **Publications:** A Great City for Kids: A Parent's Guide to a Child's New York, 1969; We Take This Child: A Candid Look at Modern Adoption, 1974; Making It as a Stepparent: New Roles/New Rules, 1980; What Am I Doing in a Stepfamily?, 1982; Stepfamilies: A Growing Reality, 1982; Raising an Adopted Child, 1983; Preparing to Remarry, 1987; Adult Children of Divorce Speak Out: About Growing Up With and Moving Beyond Parental Divorce, 1991; A Hole in My Heart: Adult Children of Divorce Speak Out, 1991; (with A. Elgart) Golden Cradle: How the Adoption Establishment Works and How to Make It Work for You, 1992; Caring for Yourself While Caring for Your Aging Parents: How to Help, How to Survive, 1996, 3rd ed., 2006; (with K. Steele) The Day the Voices Stopped: A Memoir of Madness and Hope, 2001; When a Brother or Sister Dies: Looking Back, Moving Forward, 2009. Contributor to periodicals. **Address:** c/o Julian Bach, Julian Bach Literary Agency Inc., 747 3rd Ave., New York, NY 10017, U.S.A. **Online address:** claire@claireberman.com

BERMAN, David. (David R. Berman). American (born United States), b. 1939?. **Genres:** Politics/Government, History, Social Sciences, Humanities. **Career:** American University, lecturer in political science, 1962-64; National League of Cities, research associate, 1964-66; Arizona State University, assistant professor, associate professor, 1966-80, professor of political science, 1981-, professor emeritus of political science, Morrison Institute for Public Policy, senior research fellow; Institute of Public Administration, acting director, 1966-67, assistant director, 1966-69; KTSP-TV, political consultant, 1990, 1992. Writer. **Publications:** AS DAVID R. BERMAN: State and Local Politics, 1975, 9th ed., 2000; American Government: Politics and Policy-Making, 1979, 3rd ed., 1988; Reformers, Corporations and the Electorate: An Analysis of Arizona's Age of Reform, 1992; Arizona Politics and Government: The Quest for Autonomy, Democracy and Development, 1998; Local Government and the States: Autonomy, Politics and Policy, 2003; Restrictions, Mandates and the Arizona Budget, 2004; Effects of Legislative Term Limits in Arizona, 2004; (with N. Welch) Can't Stand Still: Issues and Ideas for Workforce Governance in Arizona, 2004; Radicalism in the Mountain West, 1890-1920: Socialists, Populists, Miners and Wobblies, 2007. EDITOR AS DAVID R. BERMAN: Government Finances, 1967-70; (with J.C. Bollens and contrib.) American Government: Ideas and Issues, 1981; (and contrib.) County Governments in an Era of Change, 1993. Contributor to books and journals. **Address:** Department of Political Science, Arizona State University, Coor Hall, 6th Fl., PO Box 873902, Tempe, AZ 85287-3902, U.S.A. **Online address:** david.berman@asu.edu

BERMAN, David. American (born United States), b. 1942. **Genres:** History, Philosophy, Psychology, Essays, Young Adult Non-fiction. **Career:** University of Dublin, Trinity College, Department of Philosophy, lecturer, senior lecturer, associate professor, head, 1968-. Writer. **Publications:** (With R.W. Houghton and M.T. Lapan) Images of Berkeley, 1986; A History of Atheism in Britain: From Hobbes to Russell, 1988; George Berkeley: Idealism and the Man, 1994; Berkeley: Experimental Philosophy, 1999; Berkeley and Irish Philosophy, 2005. EDITOR: George Berkeley's Alciphron in Focus, 1986; George Berkeley: Eighteenth-Century Responses, 1989; Alciphron, or, The Minute Philosopher: In Focus, 1993; World as Will and Idea: Abridged in One Volume, 1995; Atheism in Britain: A Collection of Key Works, 1996; (and intro. with P. O'Riordan) Irish Enlightenment and Counter-Enlightenment, 2001. **Address:** Trinity College, University of Dublin, Rm. 5005, Arts Bldg., Dublin, 2, Ireland. **Online address:** dberman@tcd.ie

BERMAN, David R. *See* **BERMAN, David.**

BERMAN, Jeffrey. American (born United States), b. 1945. **Genres:** Literary Criticism And History, Writing/Journalism, Education, Language/Linguistics, Reference. **Career:** Cornell University, lecturer in English, 1971-73; State University of New York, assistant professor, 1973-79, associate professor, 1979-88, professor of English, 1988-2007, distinguished teaching professor, 2007-. Writer. **Publications:** Joseph Conrad: Writing as Rescue, 1977; The Talking Cure: Literary Representations of Psychoanalysis, 1985; Narcissism and the Novel, 1990; Diaries to an English Professor: Pain and Growth in the Classroom, 1994; Surviving Literary Suicide, 1999; Risky Writing: Self-Disclosure and Self-Transformation in the Classroom, 2001; Empathic Teaching: Education for Life, 2004; Dying to Teach: A Memoir of Love, Loss, and Learning, 2007; (with P.H. Wallace) Cutting and the Pedagogy of Self-Disclosure, 2007; Death in the Classroom: Writing about Love and Loss, 2009; Companionship in Grief: Love and Loss in the Memoirs of C.S. Lewis, John Bayley, Donald Hall, Joan Didion, and Calvin Trillin, 2010; Death Education in the Writing Classroom, 2011. Contributor to periodicals. **Address:** Department of English, State University of New York at Albany, 348 Humanities, 1400 Washington Ave., Albany, NY 12222, U.S.A. **Online address:** jberman@albany.edu

BERMAN, Morris. American (born United States), b. 1944. **Genres:** Anthropology/Ethnology, History, Humanities, Intellectual History, Psychology, Social Commentary, Theology/Religion. **Career:** Rutgers University, assistant professor of history, 1970-75; Concordia University, assistant professor of history, 1980-82; University of Victoria, Lansdowne professor of history, 1982-88; Seattle University, visiting professor, 1990; Evergreen State College, visiting professor, 1991; University of Kassel, visiting professor, 1991-92; Simon Fraser University, visiting professor, 1997; DC Writing Services, founder and director, 1998-; Johns Hopkins University, visiting professor, 1999-2000; Catholic University of America, visiting professor of sociology, 2003-, adjunct professor; Incarnate Word College, visiting endowed chair; University of New Mexico, visiting endowed chair; Weber State University, visiting endowed chair. Freelance cultural historian and writer. **Publications:** Social Change and Scientific Organization: The Royal Institution, 1799-1844, 1978; The Reenchantment of the World, 1981; Coming to Our Senses: Body and Spirit in the Hidden History of the West, 1989; Wandering God: A Study in Nomadic Spirituality, 2000; The Twilight of American Culture, 2000; Colossus Adrift, 2005; Dark Ages America: The Final Phase of Empire, 2006; Why America Failed: the Roots of Imperial Decline, 2011. Contributor of articles to periodicals. **Address:** Department of Sociology, Catholic University of America, 620 Michigan Ave. NE, Washington, DC 20064, U.S.A. **Online address:** mberman@flash.net

BERMAN, Russell A. American (born United States), b. 1950. **Genres:** History. **Career:** Stanford University, Department of German Studies, assistant professor, 1979-85, associate professor of German studies, 1985-88, professor of German and comparative literature, 1988-, chair, 1991, 1994-2000, Walter A. Haas professor in the humanities, 1997-, Overseas Studies Program, director, 1992-2000, Hoover Institution, senior fellow, 2002-; Columbia University, professor of German and comparative literature, 1990-91; Telos, editor. **Publications:** Between Fontane and Tucholsky: Literary Criticism and Public Sphere in Imperial Germany, 1983; The Rise of the Modern German Novel: Crisis and Charisma, 1986; Paul Von Hindenburg, 1987; Modern Culture and Critical Theory: Art, Politics, and the Legacy of the Frankfurt School, 1989; Cultural Studies of Modern Germany: History, Representation, and Nationhood, 1993; Enlightenment or Empire: Colonial Discourse in German Culture, 1998; (ed. with C.M. Gross) Political and Religious Ideas in the Works of Arnold Schoenberg, 2000; (ed. with C.M. Gross) Schoenberg and Words: The Modernist Years, 2000; (with K. Kenkel and A. Strum) Oeffentlichkeit: Geschichte Eines Kritischen Begriffs, 2000; Anti-Americanism in Europe: A Cultural Problem, 2004, 2nd ed., 2008; Fiction Sets You Free: Literature, Liberty and Western Culture, 2007. Contributor of articles to books and journals. **Address:** Department of German Studies, Stanford University, Bldg. 260, Rm. 201, Stanford, CA 94305-2030, U.S.A. **Online address:** berman@stanford.edu

BERMAN, Sanford. American (born United States), b. 1933. **Genres:** Communications/Media, Cultural/Ethnic Topics, Librarianship, Sex, Bibliography, Young Adult Fiction. **Career:** District of Columbia Public Library, assistant chief of acquisitions department, 1957-62; U.S. Army Special Services Libraries, administrative librarian in Karlsruhe, Worms and Mannheim-Sandhofen, 1962-66; Schiller College, librarian, 1966-67; University of California, periodicals librarian in research library, 1967-68; University of Zambia, assistant librarian in charge of periodicals section, 1968-70; Makerere University, Makerere Institute of Social Research, assistant librarian, 1971-72; Hennepin County Library, head cataloguer, 1973-99. Writer. **Publications:** Spanish Guinea: An Annotated Bibliography, 1961; Prejudices and Antipathies: A Tract on the LC Subject Heads Concerning People, 1971; The Joy of Cataloging: Essays, Letters, Reviews and Other Explosions, 1981; Alternative Library Literature, 1984; Worth Noting: Editorials, Letters, Essays, an Interview and Bibliography, 1988. CONTRIBUTOR: Educated African, 1962; Magazines for Libraries, 1969, 2nd ed., 1972; Book Selection and Censorship in the Sixties, 1969; Readings and Development, 1971; Revolting Librarians, 1972; Library Lit. 2: The Best of 1971, 1972; Library Lit. 5: The Best of 1974, 1975; Expanding Media, 1977; On Equal Terms: A Thesaurus for Non-Sexist Indexing and Cataloging, 1977; Requiem for the Card Catalog, 1978; A Dialogue on the Subject Catalogue: J.M. Perreault, A Representative of the New Left in American Subject Cataloguing: A Review Essay on Sanford Berman's The Joy of Cataloging, with Response by Sanford Berman, 1984. COMPILER: African Liberation Movements and Support Groups: A Directory, 1972; Subject Headings Employed at the Makerere Institute of Social Research Library, 1972; Alternative Library Publications, 1977. EDITOR/CO-EDITOR: Subject Cataloging: Critiques and Innovations, 1984; Alternative Library Literature, Biennially, 1984; Cataloging Special Materials: Critiques and Innovations, 1986. OTHER: Everything You Always Wanted to Know About Sandy Berman But Were Afraid to Ask, 1995. **Address:** 4400 Morningside Rd., Edina, MN 55416-5043, U.S.A. **Online address:** sandy-mdougla@pclink.com

BERMANN, Sandra L. American (born United States), b. 1947. **Genres:** Literary Criticism And History. **Career:** Princeton University, Department of Comparative Literature, professor, 1976-, chair, Cotsen professor of the humanities, Program in Translation and Intercultural Communication, co-founder; Columbia University, fellow. Writer. **Publications:** (Trans. and intro.) Alessandro Manzoni, On the Historical Novel, 1984; The Sonnet over Time: A Study in the Sonnets of Petrarch, Shakespeare and Baudelaire, 1988; (ed. with M. Wood) Nation, Language and the Ethics of Translation, 2005. **Address:** Department of Comparative Literature, Princeton University, 107 E Pyne, Princeton, NJ 08544, U.S.A. **Online address:** sandralb@princeton.edu

BERMEO, Nancy G(ina). American (born United States), b. 1951. **Genres:** Politics/Government. **Career:** Gladstone Associates, research assistant, 1973-75; Yale University, teaching assistant, 1980; Dartmouth College, instructor, 1981-82; Princeton University, assistant professor, 1983-89, associate professor of politics, 1989-2001, professor, 2001, now professor emeritus; Institute of Advanced Study, visiting fellow, 1993, 1995, 1998, 2001; Oxford University, Nuffield professor of comparative politics, visiting fellow, 1996. Writer. **Publications:** The Revolution within the Revolution: Workers' Control in Rural Portugal, 1986; Ordinary People in Extraordinary Times: The Citizenry and the Breakdown of Democracy, 2003. EDITOR: Liberalization and Democratization: Change in the Soviet Union and Eastern Europe, 1992; (with P. Nord) Civil Society before Democracy: Lessons from Nineteenth-Century Europe, 2000; Unemployment in Southern Europe: Coping with the Consequences, 2000; Unemployment in the New Europe, 2001; (ed. with P.T. Almeida and A.C. Pinto) Who Governs Southern Europe?: Regime Change and Ministerial Recruitment, 1850-2000, 2003; (with U.M. Amoretti) Federalism and Territorial Cleavages, 2004. **Address:** Department of Politics, Princeton University, 331 Aaron Burr Hall, PIIRS, 144 Constitution Dr., New Rd., Princeton, NJ 08540, U.S.A. **Online address:** nancy.bermeo@nuffield.ox.ac.uk

BERNARD, Andre. American (born United States), b. 1956. **Genres:** Writing/Journalism, Literary Criticism And History. **Career:** Viking Penguin, member of editorial department; David R. Godine Publishers Inc., executive editor; Simon and Schuster Inc., Touchstone Books, senior editor and director; Guggenheim Foundation, vice president and secretary; Harcourt, Brace & Co., publisher. **Publications:** (Ed.) Rotten Rejections: A Literary Companion, 1990. (ed. with Bill Henderson) The Complete Rot, 1991; Now All We Need is a Title: Famous Book Titles and How They Got That Way, 1995; (ed. with C. Fadiman) Bartlett's Book of Anecdotes, 2000; Madame Bovary, c'est moi!: The Great Characters of Literature and Where They Came From, 2004. **Address:** Pushcart Press, PO Box 380, Wainscott, NY 11975-0380, U.S.A.

BERNARD, G. W. British (born England), b. 1950. **Genres:** Essays, History, Social Commentary, Adult Non-fiction. **Career:** University of Southampton, professor of early modern history. Writer and historian. **Publications:** HISTORY: The Power of the Early Tudor Nobility: A Study of the Fourth and Fifth Earls of Shrewsbury, 1985; War, Taxation and Rebellion in Early Tudor England: Henry VIII, Wolsey and the Amicable Grant of 1525, 1986; (ed.) The Tudor Nobility, 1992; Power and Politics in Tudor England, 2000; (ed. with S.J. Gunn) Authority and Consent in Tudor England: Essays Presented to C.S.L. Davies, 2002; Studying at University: How to Adapt Successfully to College Life, 2003; The King's Reformation: Henry VIII and the Remaking of the English Church, 2005; Anne Boleyn: Fatal Attractions, 2010; Late Medieval English Church: Vitality and Vulnerability Before the Break With Rome, 2012. Contributor to periodicals. **Address:** Department of History, School of Humanities, University of Southampton, Rm. 2049, University Rd., Southampton, HM S017 1BJ, England. **Online address:** gwb@soton.ac.uk

BERNARD, Kenneth. Also writes as Otis Bernard. American (born United States), b. 1930. **Genres:** Novels, Novellas/Short Stories, Plays/Screenplays, Poetry, Young Adult Fiction. **Career:** Long Island University, Department of English, instructor, 1959-62, assistant professor, 1962-66, associate professor, 1967-70, professor, 1971-2003; New York Theatre Strategy, vice-president, 1974-80. Writer and consultant. **Publications:** The Maldive Chronicles (novel and short fiction), 1970; Night Club and Other Plays, 1971; Two Stories, 1973; (contrib.) Theatre of the Ridiculous, 1979; How We Danced While We Burned and La Justice, or the Cock that Crew (plays), 1990; Curse of Fool (plays), 1992; From the District File (fiction), 1992; The Baboon in the Night Club (poetry), 1993; Clown at Wall: A Kenneth Bernard Reader (fiction, poetry, plays, collage), 1996; The Qui Parle Plays and Poems, 1999; Nullity (short fiction), 2000; The Man in the Stretcher: Previously Uncollected Short Fiction

(fiction), 2005. Contributor to periodicals. **Address:** 800 Riverside Dr., Ste. 8H, New York, NY 10032, U.S.A. **Online address:** k.bernard@verizon.net

BERNARD, Oliver. British (born England), b. 1925. **Genres:** Poetry, Autobiography/Memoirs, Translations. **Career:** Teacher, 1948-50, 1954-55; Eye Grammar School, senior English master, 1964-. Writer. **Publications:** Country Matters and Other Poems, 1960; Moons and Tides, 1978; Poems, 1983; Five Peace Poems, 1985; (trans. and intro.) G. Apollinaire, Selected Poems, 1986; The Finger Points at the Moon, 1989; Getting Over It (autobiography), 1992; Verse & c., 2001. EDITOR: (trans. and intro.) Rimbaud, 1962; Apollinaire: Selection Poems, 1965, rev. ed., 1986. **Address:** The Walnut Tree, Banham, Norwich, NF NR16 2EP, England.

BERNARD, Otis. *See* **BERNARD, Kenneth.**

BERNARD, Patricia. Also writes as Judy Bernard-Waite, P. Scot-Bernard. Australian (born Australia), b. 1942. **Genres:** Young Adult Fiction, Mystery/Crime/Suspense, Picture/Board Books, Adult Non-fiction. **Career:** Writer and educator. **Publications:** FOR CHILDREN: We Are Tam, 1983; Aida's Ghost, 1988; Kangaroo Kids, 1989; (as Judy Bernard-Waite) Riddle of the Trumpalar, 1990; (as Judy Bernard-Waite) Challenge of the Trumpalar, 1990; Monkey Hill Gold, 1992; The Outer Space Spy, 1992; Dream Door of Shinar, 1992; Jacaranda Shadow, 1993; JB and the Worry Dolls, 1994; Outerspace Spy, 1994; Monster Builder, 1996; Duffy: Everyone's Dog Story (picture book), 1997; Spook Bus, 1997; The Outcast, 1997; The Punisher, 1997; The Rule Changer, 1998; No Sooks on the Starship, 1998; Wolf-Man, Pizza-Man, Jumping Dogs and Jellyfish, 1998; Into the Future, 2000; Techno Terror, 2000; Greening the Earth, 2001; Temple of Apis, 2001; Fords and Flying Machines, 2002; Duffy and the Invisible Crocodile, 2003; Stegosaurus Stone, 2003; The Mask, 2005; Basil Bigboots, 2005; Claw of the Dragon, 2006. FOR ADULTS: Sex is a Deadly Exercise, 1987; Sex is a Deadly Weapon, 1990; (as P. Scot-Bernard) Deadly Sister Love, 1998; With the Kama Sutra under My Arm, 2005. **Address:** 54 Birrell St., Queens Pk., Sydney, NW 2022, Australia. **Online address:** patriciabernard@iinet.net.au

BERNARDI, Adria. American/Italian (born Italy), b. 1957?. **Genres:** Novels. **Career:** Clark University, teacher. Writer. **Publications:** Houses with Names: The Italian Immigrants of Highwood, 1990; Abandoned Places: Poems, 1999; The Day Laid on the Altar, 2000; (trans.) G. Celati, Adventures in Africa, 2000; In the Gathering Woods, 2000; Carta Canta, 2001; Openwork, 2007; (trans.) R. Baldini, Small Talk, 2009; (trans.) R. Caddeo, Siren's Song, 2009. **Address:** c/o Author Mail, University of Pittsburgh Press, 5th Fl. 3400 Forbes Ave., Eureka Bldg., Pittsburgh, PA 15260, U.S.A. **Online address:** gtomao@gmail.com

BERNARDI, Daniel (Leonard). American (born United States), b. 1964. **Genres:** Film. **Career:** University of California-Riverside, assistant professor, 1996-98; Sci-Fi Channelc creative consultant, 1997-99; Arizona State University, assistant professor of new media, 1998, associate professor of film and media studies, director, professor, through 2011; University of California-Los Angeles, faculty, 1999, 2000; San Francisco State University, Department of Cinema, professor and chair, 2011-, Documentary Film Institute, director. Writer. **Publications:** Birth of Whiteness: Race and the Emergence of U.S. Cinema, 1996; Star Trek and History: Race-ing Toward a White Future, 1998; (ed.) Classic Hollywood, Classic Whiteness, 2001; (ed.) The Persistence of Whiteness: Race and Contemporary Hollywood Cinema, 2008; (ed.) Filming Difference: Actors, Directors, Producers and Writers on Gender, Race and Sexuality in Film, 2009; (co-author) Narrative Landmines, 2012. **Address:** Department of Cinema, San Francisco State University, FA 245, 1600 Holloway Ave., San Francisco, CA 94132, U.S.A. **Online address:** bernardi@u.arizona.edu

BERNARDINI, Joe. American (born United States), b. 1937. **Genres:** Novels, Young Adult Fiction. **Career:** Writer. **Publications:** Singapore: A Novel of the Bronx, 1983. **Address:** Gunther Stuhlmann, PO Box 276, Becket, MA 01223, U.S.A. **Online address:** bernardi@optonline.net

BERNARDO, Anilu. American/Cuban (born Cuba) **Genres:** Young Adult Fiction. **Career:** Writer. **Publications:** Un día con mis tías/A Day with My Aunts (bilingual picture book), 2006. FOR YOUNG ADULTS: Jumping Off to Freedom, 1996; Fitting In (short stories), 1996; Loves Me, Loves Me Not, 1998. Contributor to periodicals. **Address:** Reynold Public Relations Inc., 7301 SW 7th St., Plantation, FL 33317, U.S.A. **Online address:** anilu_bernardo@comcast.net

BERNARD-WAITE, Judy. *See* **BERNARD, Patricia.**

BERNHARDT, William. American (born United States), b. 1960. **Genres:** Mystery/Crime/Suspense, Picture/Board Books, Novels, Novellas/Short Stories, Adult Non-fiction, Romance/Historical, Young Adult Fiction. **Career:** Hall, Estill, Hardwick, Gable, Golden and Nelson (law firm), trial lawyer, 1986-95; Arts and Humanities Council of Tulsa, board director, 1994-; Hawk Publishing Group, founder and owner, 1999-; Oklahoma Arts Institute, Thomas H. Gilcrease Museum of Western Art, board director. Writer. **Publications:** Primary Justice, 1991; Blind Justice, 1992; The Code of Buddyhood, 1993; Deadly Justice, 1993; Perfect Justice, 1994; Double Jeopardy, 1995; Cruel Justice, 1996; Naked Justice, 1997; (ed. and contrib.) Legal Briefs: Stories by Today's Best Legal Thriller Writers, 1998; The Midnight before Christmas (novel), 1998; Extreme Justice, 1998; Dark Justice, 1999; Silent Justice, 2000; (ed. and contrib.) Natural Suspect (anthology), 2001; Murder One, 2001; Final Round, 2002; Bad Faith, 2002; Criminal Intent, 2002; Death Row, 2003; Hate Crime, 2004; Dark Eye (novel), 2005; (with K. Henry) Equal Justice: The Courage of Ada Sipuel, 2006; Capitol Murder, 2006; Capitol Threat, 2007; Strip Search (novel), 2007; Princess Alice and the Dreadful Dragon, 2007; Capitol Conspiracy: A Novel, 2008; Nemesis: The Final Case of Eliot Ness, 2009; Capitol Offense, 2009; Capitol Betrayal: A Novel, 2010. Works appear in anthologies. Contributor to magazines. **Address:** c/o Lauren Williams, William Bernhardt Writing Foundation, 7107 S Yale Ave., Ste. 345, Tulsa, OK 74136-1619, U.S.A. **Online address:** wb@williambernhardt.com

BERNHEIM, Emmanuèle. French (born France), b. 1955. **Genres:** Novels, Plays/Screenplays. **Career:** French television networks, reader of motion picture scripts, 1983-93. Writer. **Publications:** Le Cran d'arrêt, 1985; Un Couple, 1987; Sa Femme, 1993; Vendredi Soir (novel), 1998; Stallone, 2002. **Address:** 56 rue de l'Universite, Paris, 75007, France.

BERNIKOW, Louise. American (born United States), b. 1940. **Genres:** Human Relations/Parenting, Literary Criticism And History, Women's Studies And Issues, Writing/Journalism, Food And Wine. **Career:** Times of London, journalist; Columbia University, research fellow, 1962; City University of New York, Queens College, faculty, 1963; The Juilliard School, instructor in writing, 1965-70, Barnard College, faculty; Hunter College, curriculum consultant and founder of women's studies programs, 1970, faculty, 1973-75; New York University, faculty, 1978-81; NBC News Magazine, consultant, 1982; Jersey City State College, curriculum consultant and founder of women's studies programs. **Publications:** Abel, 1970; (ed. and intro.) The World Split Open: Four Centuries of Women Poets in England and America, 1552-1950, 1974; Among Women, 1980; Let's Have Lunch: Games of Sex and Power, 1981; Alone in America: The Search for Companionship, 1986; The American Women's Almanac: An Inspiring and Irreverent Women's History, 1997; (with G. Null) Food-Mood-Body Connection: Nutrition-based and Environmental Approaches to Mental Health and Physical Well-being, 2000; Bark if You Love Me: A Woman-Meets-Dog Story, 2000; Dreaming in Libro: How a Good Dog Tamed a Bad Woman, 2007. Contributor to magazines and periodicals. **Address:** 318 W 105 St., Ste. 4A, New York, NY 10025-3463, U.S.A.

BERNSTEIN, Burton. American (born United States), b. 1932. **Genres:** Novels, Biography, Documentaries/Reportage, Literary Criticism And History, Air/Space Topics, Autobiography/Memoirs, Humor/Satire. **Career:** DuMont Television, writer, 1956; The New Yorker, staff writer, 1957-92; freelance writer and editor, 1992-. **Publications:** The Grove, 1961; The Lost Art, 1963; The Sticks, 1972; Thurber: A Biography, 1975; (ed. and comp.) Look, Ma, I am Kool! and Other Casuals, 1977; Sinai: The Great and Terrible Wilderness, 1979; Family Matters, Sam, Jennie, and the Kids, 1982, rev. ed., 2000; Plane Crazy: A Celebration of Flying, 1985; (with B.B. Haws) Leonard Bernstein: American Original, 2008. Contributor of articles to magazines. **Address:** Candida Donadio & Associates Inc., 231 W 22nd St., New York, NY 10011-2765, U.S.A.

BERNSTEIN, Charles. American (born United States), b. 1950. **Genres:** Poetry, Songs/Lyrics And Libretti, Essays. **Career:** University of Auckland, visiting lecturer, 1986; University of California, visiting lecturer, 1987; City University of New York, Queens College, visiting professor, 1988; Princeton University, lecturer, 1989, 1990; State University of New York, Butler Chair professor, 1989, David Gray professor of poetry and letters, 1989-2003, distinguished professor, 2002-03, Poetics Program, director, Electronic Poetry Center, co-founder and executive editor; City College of the City of New

York, visiting professor, 1998; Columbia University, visiting professor, 2002; University of Pennsylvania, Donald T. Regan professor of English and comparative literature, 2003-; New York University, Paul McGhee Division, visiting distinguished writer, 2007. Writer. **Publications:** Asylums, 1975; Parsing, 1976; Shade, 1978; Poetic Justice, 1979; Senses of Responsibility, 1979; (co-author) Legend, 1980; Controlling Interests, 1980; Disfrutes, 1981; The Occurrence of Tune, 1981; Stigma, 1981; Islets/Irritations, 1983; Resistance, 1983; (ed. with B. Andrews) The L=A=N=G=U=A=G=E Book, 1984; (co-author) On Equal Terms: Poems, 1984; Content's Dream: Essays 1975-1984, 1985; The Sophist, 1987; (with S. Bee) The Nude Formalism, 1989; (ed.) The Politics of Poetic Form: Poetry and Public Policy, 1990; Rough Trades, 1991; The Absent Father in Dumbo, 1991; A Poetics, 1992; Dark City, 1994; Log Rhythms, 1998; (ed.) Close Listening: Poetry and the Performed Word, 1998; My Way: Speeches and Poems, 1999; Republics of Reality: Poems 1975-1995, 2000; With Strings, 2001; Some of These Daze, 2005; (ed.) Selected Poems, 2006; Girly Man, 2006; (trans.) O. Mandelstam, Modernist Archaist: Selected Poems, 2008; All the Whiskey in Heaven, 2010; Attack of the Difficult Poems, 2011. **Address:** Department of English, University of Pennsylvania, 221 Fisher-Bennett Hall, 3340 Walnut St., Philadelphia, PA 19104-6293, U.S.A. **Online address:** charles.bernstein@english.upenn.edu

BERNSTEIN, David E(liot). American (born United States), b. 1967. **Genres:** Civil Liberties/Human Rights, History. **Career:** U.S. Court of Appeals, law clerk, 1991-92; Crowell & Moring (law firm), associate, 1992-94; Columbia University, Law School, Julius Silver Program in Law, Science and Technology, Mellon Foundation research fellow, 1994-95; George Mason University, School of Law, assistant professor, 1995-98, associate professor of law, 1998-2003, professor of law, 2003-09, foundation professor, 2009-; University of Michigan, School of Law, visiting professor, 2005-06. Writer. **Publications:** (Ed. with K.R. Foster and P.W. Huber) Phantom Risk: Scientific Inference and the Law, 1993; Only One Place of Redress: African Americans, Labor Regulations, and the Courts from Reconstruction to the New Deal, 2001; (with D. Kaye and J. Mnookin) The New Wigmore: Expert Evidence, 2002, 2nd ed., 2010; You Can't Say That!: The Growing Threat to Civil Liberties from Antidiscrimination Laws, 2003; Rehabilitating Lochner: Defending Individual Rights against Progressive Reform, 2011; Equality at Any Price?: The Growing Conflict between Civil Rights and Civil Liberties, forthcoming. Contributor of articles to books, journals and periodicals. **Address:** School of Law, George Mason University, Rm. 416, Arlington Campus, 3301 N Fairfax Dr., Arlington, VA 22201, U.S.A. **Online address:** dbernste@gmu.edu

BERNSTEIN, Ellen. American (born United States), b. 1953?. **Genres:** Environmental Sciences/Ecology, Theology/Religion. **Career:** Turtle River Educational Journeys, Outdoor Education Program, co-founder and co-director, 1974-80; Berkeley Community Health Project, producer of educational and self helpmaterials, education director, 1975-77; teacher, 1977-79; physical therapist, 1983-87; Shomrei Adamah: Keepers of the Earth (Jewish environmental organization), founder and director, 1988-96; Jewish Federation of Greater Philadelphia, Jewish Continuity Initiative, director, 1996-2001; Hebrew College, teacher, 2001-08. Writer. **Publications:** Let the Earth Teach You Torah, 1992; Ecology and the Jewish Spirit, 1998; An American Tu B'Sh'vat, 1999; The Splendor of Creation, 2005. Works appear in anthologies. Contributor to periodicals. **Address:** 22 Liberty St., Holyoke, MA 01040, U.S.A. **Online address:** ellen@ellenbernstein.org

BERNSTEIN, Frances Lee. American (born United States) **Genres:** History. **Career:** Drew University, associate professor of history. Writer and historian. **Publications:** The Dictatorship of Sex: Lifestyle Advice for the Soviet Masses, 2007; (ed. with C. Burton and D. Healey) Soviet Medicine: Culture, Practice, and Science, 2010. Contributor to books. **Address:** Department of History, Drew University, 36 Madison Ave., Madison, NJ 07940, U.S.A. **Online address:** fbernste@drew.edu

BERNSTEIN, Jake. American (born United States) **Genres:** Politics/Government. **Career:** Pasadena Citizen, staff writer; Texas Observer, executive editor; Miami New Times, journalist; San Francisco Examiner, journalist; Dallas Morning News, journalist; Pro Publica Inc., investigative reporter. **Publications:** (With L. Dubose) Vice: Dick Cheney and the Hijacking of the American Presidency, 2006. **Address:** Pro Publica Inc., 1 Exchange Plz., 55 Broadway, 23rd Fl., New York, NY 10006, U.S.A. **Online address:** jake@jakebernstein.net

BERNSTEIN, Jared. American (born United States), b. 1955. **Genres:** Economics, Organized Labor, Social Sciences, Business/Trade/Industry, Politics/Government. **Career:** Howard University, teacher; Columbia University, teacher; New York University, teacher; Economic Policy Institute, labor economist, 1992-, senior economist, Living Standards Program, director; Department of Labor, deputy chief economist, 1995-96; White House, Middle Class Working Families Task Force, executive director, 2009; Center on Budget and Policy Priorities, senior fellow, 2011-. Writer. **Publications:** (With L.R. Mishel and S. Allegretto) The State of Working America, 1993, 9th ed., 2008; Examining the Puzzle: The Gap Between Black Educational and Labor Market Progress, 1995; All Together Now: Common Sense for a Fair Economy, 2006; Crunch: Why Do I Feel so Squeezed? (and Other Unsolved Economic Mysteries), 2008. **Address:** Economic Policy Institute, 1333 H St. NW, Ste. 300, East Twr., Washington, DC 20005-4707, U.S.A.

BERNSTEIN, Laurie. American (born United States) **Genres:** History, Humanities. **Career:** Vassar College, assistant professor, 1987-89; Swarthmore College, lecturer, 1988, visiting assistant professor, 1989-90; Drew University, assistant professor, 1991-92; Rutgers University, assistant professor, 1992-97, associate professor of history, 1997-, Women's Studies Program, director, 2001-. Writer. **Publications:** Sonia's Daughters: Prostitutes and Their Regulation in Imperial Russia, 1995; (ed.) My Life in Stalinist Russia: An American Woman Looks Back, 2001; (with R. Weinberg) Revolutionary Russia: A History in Documents, 2011. Contributor to books and periodicals. **Address:** Department of History, Rutgers University, Rm. 354, Armitage Hall, 311 N 5th St., Camden, NJ 08102, U.S.A. **Online address:** lbernste@camden.rutgers.edu

BERNSTEIN, Mark. American (born United States), b. 1950. **Genres:** Communications/Media, History, Romance/Historical, Information Science/Computers. **Career:** Writer. **Publications:** Paper with Presence: A Gilbert Century, 1987; Miami Valley Hospital: A Centennial History, 1990; Grand Eccentrics: Turning the Century: Dayton and the Inventing of America, 1996; (contrib.) Discover Columbus, 1997; New Bremen, 1999; (contrib.) New Bremen 2000, 2000; (with A. Lubertozzi) World War II on the Air: Edward R. Murrow and The Broadcasts that Riveted a Nation, 2003; The Tinderbox Way, 2007. Contributor to periodicals. **Address:** 830 Xenia Ave., Yellow Springs, OH 45387, U.S.A.

BERNSTEIN, Patricia. American (born United States), b. 1944. **Genres:** Novellas/Short Stories, Medicine/Health. **Career:** Bernstein & Associates Inc. (public relations firm), founder and principal, 1983-; Smith College, teacher of English. Writer. **Publications:** Having a Baby: Mothers Tell Their Stories, 1993; The First Waco Horror: The Lynching of Jesse Washington and the Rise of the NAACP, 2005. Contributor to periodicals. **Address:** Bernstein & Associates Inc., 6300 W Loop S, Ste. 218, Bellaire, TX 77401, U.S.A. **Online address:** marie.wright@bernsteinandassoc.com

BERNSTEIN, Paula. American (born United States), b. 1968. **Genres:** Biography, Autobiography/Memoirs. **Career:** Variety, reporter; The Hollywood Reporter, reporter; CNN, reporter. **Publications:** (With E. Schein) Identical Strangers: A Memoir of Twins Separated and Reunited, 2007. Contributor to periodicals. **Address:** Random House Inc., 1745 Broadway, 3rd Fl., New York, NY 10019-4368, U.S.A. **Online address:** paulabernstein@gmail.com

BERNSTEIN, Richard. American (born United States), b. 1944. **Genres:** Documentaries/Reportage, History, Social Sciences. **Career:** Washington Post, foreign correspondent; Time Magazine, staff, 1973-, foreign correspondent, Beijing bureau chief, 1979-; New York Times, staff, 1982-, United Nations bureau chief, Paris bureau chief, Berlin bureau chief, national cultural correspondent, 1987-95, daily book critic, 1995-; International Herald Tribune, columnist. **Publications:** From the Center of the Earth: The Search for the Truth about China, 1982; Fragile Glory: A Portrait of France and the French, 1990; Dictatorship of Virtue: Multiculturalism and the Battle for America's Future, 1994; (with R.H. Munro) The Coming Conflict with China, 1997; Ultimate Journey: Retracing the Path of an Ancient Buddhist Monk Who Crossed Asia in Search of Enlightenment, 2001; (co-author) Out of the Blue: A Narrative of September 11, 2001, from Jihad to Ground Zero, 2002; (contrib.) New York Times: The Complete Front Pages 1851-2008, 2008; East, the West, and Sex: A History of Erotic Encounters, 2009; A Girl Named Faithful Plum, 2011. **Address:** New York Times, 229 W 43rd St., New York, NY 10036-3913, U.S.A.

BERNSTEIN, Richard B. American (born United States), b. 1956. **Genres:** History, Politics/Government, Law. **Career:** The New York Public Library, Constitution Bicentennial Project, research curator, 1984-87; U.S. Constitution, New York City Commission on the Bicentennial, historian, 1987-90, research director, 1989-90; New York Law School, adjunct assistant professor of law, 1991-2000, adjunct professor of law, 2000-07, distinguished adjunct professor of law, 2007-; City University of New York, Brooklyn College, Daniel M. Lyons visiting professor of history, 1997-98, City College of New York, adjunct professor, 2011-; Heights Books Inc., director of online operations, 2002-11. Writer. **Publications:** Are We to Be a Nation?: The Making of the Constitution, 1987; Into the Third Century: The Congress, 1989; Into the Third Century: The Supreme Court, 1989; Into the Third Century: The Presidency, 1989; (ed. with S.L. Schechter) Well Begun: Chronicles of the Early National Period, 1989; Where The Experiment Began: New York City and the Two Hundredth Anniversary of the Inauguration of George Washington, 1990; (ed. with S.L. Schechter and D.S. Lutz) Roots of the Republic: American Founding Documents Interpreted, 1990; (ed. with S.L. Schechter) Contexts of the Bill of Rights, 1990; (ed. with S.L. Schechter) New York and the Union: Contributions to the American Constitutional Experience, 1990; (ed. with S. L. Schechter) New York and the Bicentennial: Contributions to the American Constitutional Experience, 1990; Amending America: If We Love the Constitution So Much, Why Do We Keep Trying to Change It? 1993; Of the People by the People for the People: The Congress, the Presidency, and the Supreme Court in American History, 1993; (ed. with B. Schwartz and B.W. Kern) Thomas Jefferson and Bolling v. Bolling: Law and the Legal Profession in Pre-Revolutionary America, 1997; (ed. and intro.) The Constitution of the United States of America: With the Declaration of Independence and the Articles of Confederation, 2002; (ed. and intro.) The Wisdom of John and Abigail Adams, 2002; Thomas Jefferson, 2003; Thomas Jefferson: The Revolution of Ideas, 2004; The Founding Fathers Reconsidered, 2009. **Address:** New York Law School, 185 W Broadway, New York, NY 10013-2921, U.S.A. **Online address:** rbernstein@nyls.edu

BERRA, Tim M. American (born United States), b. 1943. **Genres:** Natural History, Bibliography, Zoology. **Career:** University of Papua New Guinea, instructor; Ohio State University, Department of Evolution, Ecology, and Organismal Biology, professor, 1972-; University of Concepción, visiting professor, 1992; University of Otago, visiting professor, 1996; Museum and Art Gallery of the Northern Territory, research associate, 2001-; Ohio Journal of Science, editor, biologist; Charles Darwin University, University professorial fellow, 2010-. **Publications:** William Beebe: An Annotated Bibliography, 1977; (with R.M. McDowall) An Atlas of Distribution of the Freshwater Fish Families of the World, 1981; A Chronology of the American Society of Ichthyologists and Herpetologists through 1982-1984; Evolution and the Myth of Creationism: A Basic Guide to the Facts in the Evolution Debate, 1990; A Natural History of Australia, 1998; Freshwater Fish Distribution, 2001; Charles Darwin: The Concise Story of an Extraordinary Man, 2009. **Address:** Bellville, OH , U.S.A. **Online address:** berra.1@osu.edu

BERRES, Thomas Edward. American (born United States), b. 1953. **Genres:** Archaeology/Antiquities, History. **Career:** University of Illinois, staff archaeologist, 1981-85, Illinois Transportation Archaeological Research Program, staff archaeologist, 1986-95, Museum of Natural History, staff, 1995-96, Public Service Archaeology Program, project archaeologist, 1996-99; Northern Illinois University, assistant professor of anthropology and project director, 1999-2004; Our Heritage Archaeological Services, president, 2004-. Writer. **Publications:** (Contrib.) The Marge Site: Late Archaic and Emergent Mississippian Occupations in the Palmer Creek Locality, 1996; Power and Gender in Oneota Culture: A Study of a Late Prehistoric People, 2001. Contributor of articles to periodicals. **Address:** Our Heritage Archaeological Services Inc., 983 Quail Run, DeKalb, IL 60115-6117, U.S.A.

BERRIDGE, G. R. British (born England), b. 1947. **Genres:** Politics/Government, International Relations/Current Affairs. **Career:** Metropolitan Police College, assistant lecturer, 1969-71; University of Leicester, lecturer, 1978-89, reader, 1989-93, professor of politics, 1993-2001, emeritus professor of international politics, 2001-; Oxford Dictionary of National Biography, associate editor; DiploFoundation, senior fellow, 2004. Writer. **Publications:** Economic Power in Anglo-South African Diplomacy: Simontown, Sharpeville and After, 1981; (ed. with A. Jennings and contrib.) Diplomacy at the U.N., 1985; The Politics of the South Africa Run: European Shipping and Pretoria, 1987; International Politics: States, Power and Conflict since 1945, 1987, 2nd ed., 1992; Return to the U.N.: United Nations Diplomacy in Regional Conflicts, 1991; South Africa, the Colonial Powers and African Defence: The Rise and Fall of the White Entente, 1948-60, 1992; (with D. Heater) An Introduction to International Politics, 1993; Talking to the Enemy: How States without Diplomatic Relations Communicate, 1994; Guicciardini's Ricordi: The Counsels and Reflections of Francesco Guicciardini, 2000; (ed. with M. Keens-Soper and T.G. Otte) Diplomatic Theory from Machiavelli to Kissinger, 2001; Machiavelli's Legations, 2001; (with A. James) Dictionary of Diplomacy, 2001, 2nd ed., 2003; Diplomacy: Theory and Practice, 2002, 4th ed., 2010; (ed. and intro.) Diplomatic Classics: Selected Texts from Commynes to Vattel, 2004; Gerald Fitzmaurice (1865-1939), Chief Dragoman of the British Embassy in Turkey, 2007; (ed.) Tilkidom and the Ottoman Empire: The Letters of Gerald Fitzmaurice to George Lloyd, 1906-1915, 2007; British Diplomacy in Turkey, 1583 to the Present: A Study in the Evolution of the Resident Embassy, 2009; The Counter-Revolution In Diplomacy and Other Essays, 2011; Embassies In Armed Conflict, 2012; (with A. James and L. Lloyd) Palgrave Macmillan Dictionary of Diplomacy, 2012. Works appear in anthologies. Contributor to journals. **Address:** Department of Politics and International Relations, University of Leicester, University Rd., Leicester, LE LE1 7RH, England. **Online address:** grberridge@diplomacy.edu

BERRIGAN, Daniel J. American (born United States), b. 1921. **Genres:** Plays/Screenplays, Poetry, Social Commentary, Theology/Religion, Autobiography/Memoirs, Art/Art History, Writing/Journalism. **Career:** Ordained Roman Catholic priest, 1952; teacher, 1954-57; Le Moyne College, professor of New Testament studies, 1957-63; Cornell University, United Christian Work, director, 1967-68; Fordham University, poet-in-residence. Writer, and political activist. **Publications:** Time Without Number, 1957; The Bride: Essays in the Church, 1959; Encounters: Poems, 1960; The Bow in the Clouds: Man's Covenant with God, 1961; The World for Wedding Ring: Poems, 1962; No One Walks Waters: New Poems, 1966; They Call Us Dead Men: Reflections on Life and Conscience, 1966; Consequences: Truth and..., 1967; Go from Here: A Prison Diary, 1968; Love, Love at the End: Parables, Prayers and Meditations, 1968; Night Flight to Hanoi: War Diary with 11 Poems, 1968; False Gods, Real Men: New Poems, 1969; Crime Trial, 1970; (with T. Lewis) Trial Poems, 1970; The Trial of the Catonsville Nine (play), 1970; No Bars to Manhood, 1970; The Dark Night of Resistance, 1971: The Geography of Faith: Conversations Between Daniel Berrigan, When Underground and Robert Coles, 1971; (with L. Lockwood) Absurd Convictions, Modest Hopes: Conversations after Prison with Lee Lockwood, 1972; America is Hard to Find, 1972; Jesus Christ, 1973; Selected and New Poems, 1973; Prison Poems, 1973; (with N. Hanh) Contemplation and Resistance, 1973; Lights on in the House of the Dead: A Prison Diary, 1974; (with T.N. Hanh) The Raft Is Not the Shore: Conversations toward Buddhist/Christian Awareness, 1975; A Book of Parables. 1977; Uncommon Prayer, 1978, Beside the Sea of Glass: The Song of the Lamb, 1978; The Discipline of the Mountain: Dante's Purgatorio in a Nuclear World, 1979; We Die Before We Live: Talking with the Very Ill, 1980; Ten Commandments for the Long Haul, 1981; Portraits: Of Those I Love, 1982; The Nightmare of God, 1983; Journey to Black Island, 1984; May All Creatures Live, 1984; Steadfastness of the Saints: A Journal of Peace and War in Central and North America, 1985; Block Island, 1985; The Mission: A Film Journal, 1986; To Dwell in Peace: An Autobiography, 1987; (with M. Parker) Stations, 1988; Daniel Berrigan: Poetry, Drama, Prose, 1988; Lost & Found, 1989; Sorrow Built a Bridge: Friendship and AIDS, 1989; Whereon to Stand, 1991; Jubilee: Poems, 1991; Tulips in the Prison Yard: Selected Poems, 1992; Minor Prophets, Major Themes, 1995; Apostle of Peace: Essays in Honor of Daniel Berrigan, 1996; Isaiah: Spirit of Courage, Gift of Tears, 1996; Ezekiel: Vision in the Dust, 1997; And the Risen Bread: Selected Poems 1957-1997, 1998; Daniel, Under the Siege of the Divine, 1998; Jeremiah: The World, the Wound of God, 1999; Bride: Images of the Church, 2000; Job: And Death no Dominion, 2001; (with G. Levinson) Consolation: For Voice and Piano, 2000; Job: Why Forsake Me?, 2001; (with R. Coles) The Geography of Faith: Underground Conversations on Religious, Political and Social Change, 2001; Wisdom: The Feminine Face of God, 2001; Lamentations: From New York to Kabul and Beyond, 2002; Testimony: The Word Made Fresh, 2004; The Trial of the Catonsville Nine, 2004; Genesis: Fair Beginnings, Then Foul, 2006; Sunday in Hell: Fables & Poems, 2006; Kings and Their Gods: The Pathology of Power, 2008; Prayer for the Morning Headlines, 2007; No Gods but One, 2009; Essential Writings, 2009. **Address:** 220 W 98th St., Ste. 11-L, New York, NY 10025, U.S.A.

BERRINGTON, John. *See* **BROWNJOHN, Alan (Charles).**

BERRY, Adrian M. British (born England), b. 1937. **Genres:** Science Fiction/Fantasy, Astronomy, Sciences, Novels. **Career:** Time Magazine, correspondent, 1965-67; Daily Telegraph, science correspondent, 1977-97; consulting Editor. Writer. **Publications:** The Next Ten Thousand Years: A Vision of Man's Future in the Universe, 1974; The Iron Sun: Crossing the Universe through Black Holes, 1977; From Apes to Astronauts, 1981; The Super Intelligent Machine, 1983; High Skies and Yellow Rain, 1983; Koyama's Diamond (fiction), 1984; Labyrinth of Lies (fiction), 1985; Ice with Your Evolution, 1986; Harrap's Book of Scientific Anecdotes, 1989; Eureka: The Book of Scientific Anecdotes, 1993; The Next 500 Years: Life in the Coming Millennium, 1996; Galileo and the Dolphins: Amazing But True Stories from Science, 1997; The Giant Leap: Mankind Heads for the Stars, 1999. **Address:** 11 Cottesmore Gardens, Kensington, London, GL W8, England. **Online address:** adrianspage@safe-mail.net

BERRY, Andrew. American/British (born England), b. 1963. **Genres:** Animals/Pets, History. **Career:** Harvard University, Museum of Comparative Zoology, research associate, harvard junior fellow, undergraduate advisor in the life sciences and lecturer on organismic and evolutionary biology, assistant head tutor. Writer. **Publications:** (Ed.) Infinite Tropics: An Alfred Russel Wallace Anthology, 2002; (with J.D. Watson) DNA: The Secret of Life, 2003; (with B. Wallace and D. Cave) Teaching Problem-Solving and Thinking Skills Through Science: Exciting Cross-Curricular Challenges for Foundation Phase, Key Stage One and Key Stage Two, 2008. **Address:** Organismic & Evolutionary Biology, Harvard University, Rm. 1082b BioLabs, 16 Divinity Ave., Cambridge, MA 02138, U.S.A. **Online address:** berry@oeb.harvard.edu

BERRY, Brian Joe Lobley. American/British (born England), b. 1934. **Genres:** Novels, Economics, Geography, Regional/Urban Planning, Autobiography/Memoirs. **Career:** University of Washington, teaching and research assistant, 1955-56, pre-doctoral associate, 1957, instructor in geography and research instructor in civil engineering, 1958; University of Chicago, assistant professor, 1958-62, associate professor, 1962-65, director of training programs, 1963-73, professor, 1965-72, Irving B. Harris professor of urban geography, 1972-76, Department of Geography, chairman, 1972-76, Center for Urban Studies, director, 1974-76, Center for Policy Studies, fellow; City of Chicago, consultant, 1961-65; Ford Foundation, consultant, 1962; Canada Land Inventory, consultant, 1964; Brookings Institution, Advanced Study Program in Urban Policy, faculty, 1964-76; U.S. Department of Agriculture, consultant, 1965-66; U.S. Bureau of Public Roads, consultant, 1965-66; Regional Science Association, vice president, 1966; Economic Development Administration, consultant, 1966-70; World Bank, consultant, 1970-74; U.S. Department of Housing and Urban Development, consultant, 1972-; U.S. Environmental Protection Agency, consultant, 1972-; Urban Land Institute, research fellow, 1974; Harvard University, professor in sociology, Laboratory for Computer Graphics and Spatial Analysis, director and Frank Backus Williams professor of city and regional planning, 1976-81, Faculty of Arts and Sciences, Ph.D. Program in Urban Planning, chairman, 1976-81, Harvard Institute for International Development, consultant, 1976-, faculty fellow, 1976-81; U.S. Corps of Engineers, consultant, 1977-80; U.S. Geological Survey, consultant, 1977-81; Association of American Geographers, vice president, 1977-78, president, 1978-79; Carnegie-Mellon University, Heinz College, School of Urban and Public Affairs, university professor and dean, 1981-86; University College, fellow, 1983; Urban Geography(journal), editor-in-chief 1986-2004; University of Texas, professor of political economy, 1986-2004, founders professor, 1986-91, Polykarp Kusch lecturer, 1991; Bruton Center for Development Studies, director, chair, 1988-95, Lloyd Viel Berkner regental professor, 1991-, School of Economic, Political and Policy Sciences, dean, 2005-10; Weimer School of Advanced Studies in Real Estate and Land Economics, honorary fellow, 1990; Homer Hoyt Institute, honorary fellow, 1990; The Academy of Medicine, Engineering and Science of Texas, founding member, 2004. **Publications:** (Co-author) Studies of Highway Development and Geographic Change, 1959; (co-author) Commercial Structure and Commercial Blight: Retail Patterns and Processes in the City of Chicago, 1963; The Science of Geography, 1965; (co-author) Essays on Commodity Flows and the Spatial Structure of the Indian Economy, 1966; Geography of Market Centers and Retai Distribution, 1967; (ed. with J. Meltzer) Goals for Urban America, 1967; (with D.F. Marble) Spatial Analysis: A Reader in Statistical Geography, 1968; (with S.J. Parsons and R.H. Platt) The Impact of Urban Renewal on Small Business: The Hyde Park-Kenwood Case, 1968; (co-author) A Strategic Approach to Urban Research and Development, 1969; (ed. with F.E. Horton) Geographic Perspectives on Urban Systems, 1970; (ed. with K.B. Smith) City Classification Handbook: Methods and Applications, 1972; The Human Consequences of Urbanisation: Divergent Paths in the Urban Experience of the Twentieth Century, 1973; Growth Centers in the American Urban System, 1973, vol. I: Community Development and Regional Growth in the Sixties and Seventies, vol. II: Working Materials on the U.S. Urban Hierarchy and on Growth Center Characteristics Organized by Economic Regions; (with Horton) Urban Environmental Management: Planning for Pollution Control, 1974; Land Use, Urban Form and Environmental Quality, 1974; Towards an Understanding of Metropolitan America, 1974; A Framework for Regional Planning in Indonesia, 3 vols., World Bank, 1974; (with E. Conkling and M. Ray) The Geography of Economic Systems, 1976; Urbanization and Counter-Urbanization, 1976; Chicago: Transformations of an Urban System, 1976; (with J. Kasarda) Contemporary Urban Ecology, 1977; (with Q. Gillard) The Changing Shape of Metropolitan America: Commuting Patterns, Urban Fields and Decentralization Processes, 1960-1970, 1977; (with D. Dahmann) Population Redistribution in the United States in the 1970s, 1977; (co-author) The Social Burdens of Environmental Pollution: A Comparative Metropolitan Data Source, 1977; (ed.) Perspectives in Geography 3: The Nature of Change in Geographical Ideas, 1979; The Open Housing Question: Race and Housing in Chicago, 1966-1976, 1979; (ed. with L.P. Silverman) Population Redistribution and Public Policy, 1980; (ed. with L.P. Silverman) Population Redistribution and Public Policy, 1980; (co-author) Explorations in Public Policy: Essays in Celebration of the Life of John Osman, 1980; Comparative Urbanization: Divergent Paths in the Twentieth Century, rev. ed., 1981; (ed. with E. Teicholz) Computer Graphics and Environmental Planning, 1983; (with S.W. Sanderson) Growth and Adjustment in an Economy Undergoing Structural Transformation, 1985; (with E.C. Conkling and D.M. Ray) Economic Geography: Resource Use, Locational Choices and Regional Specialization in the Global Economy, 1987; Westward the American Shapleys: The Family and Descendants of David Shapley, a Seventeenth Century Marblehead Fisherman, with Pedigrees of the Spouses (Atwater, Berry, Chapman, Coleman, French, Parks, Talmage, Utter and Connecting Lines): English Ancestry and American Descent of Five Additional Shapley Immigrants, Alexander, John, Nicholas, Philip and Reuben, 1987; (co-author) Market Centers and Retail Location: Theory and Applications, 1988; The Ancestry of Elizabeth Yanconish Berry, 1989; The Ancestry of Fanny Barnes and Her Husband Thomas Knight: Family Relationships in Connecticut, Massachusetts and Long Island, 1620-1820, 1989; The Rufus Parks Pedigree: Seventeen Centuries of One Family's Ancestry, 1989; Strengthened Urban-Rural Linkages as Instruments of Rural Development, 1989; Northern Neck Families: The Ancestors of Susan Frances Chapman: Alexander, Chapman and Pearson, Plus Connecting Lines Including the Balls, Macraes and Washingtons, 1990; The McNeills, 1990; The MacAlisters, 1990; The Hontz Family, 1990; Concluding Discoveries, 1990; The Cary Family in England and America, 1990; The Berry Family of New Jersey, 1990; Venturing to Develop Forces that Promote Economic Transformation at the Leading Edge and on the Far Periphery, 1990; Long-Wave Rhythms in Economic Development and Political Behavior, 1991; Understanding the Metroplex: The Regional Business Cycle, 1991; Deeper Societal Structures: Glimpses Through a Macroscope, 1991; Ten Generations of Descendants of Fisherman David Shapley of Marblehead, 1991; Yankee Heritage: A Sisson Ancestry, 1991; America's Utopian Experiments: Communal Havens from Long-Wave Crises, 1992; The Shapleigh, Shapley and Shappley Families: A Comprehensive Genealogy, 1635-1993, 1993; (with E.C. Conkling and D.M. Ray) The Global Economy: Resource Use, Locational Choice, and International Trade, 1993; Long Term Economic Cycles and American Politics, 1993; (with E.C. Conkling and D.M. Ray) The Global Economy in Transition, 2nd ed., 1997; Berry Roots: Origins and Dispersals in Lancashire and Yorkshire, 1997; (co-author) The Rhythms of American Politics, 1998; (co-author) John Littleton of Accomack Co., VA: His Family and Descendants, 1999; Aaron's Ancestry: Claunch, Littleton and Connections, 2000; Hastingleigh 1000-2000 A.D., 2002; (ed. with J.O. Wheeler) Urban Geography in America, 1950-2000: Paradigms and Personalities, 2005; Nihil Sine Labore: An Autobiography, 2006. **Address:** School of Economic, Political & Policy Sciences, University of Texas, Rm. GR 3.813, Green Hall, 800 W Campbell Rd., Richardson, TX 75080-3021, U.S.A. **Online address:** brian.berry@utdallas.edu

BERRY, Carmen Renee. American (born United States), b. 1953?. **Genres:** Theatre, Self Help, Psychology. **Career:** Motivational lecturer, certified massage therapist and author. **Publications:** When Helping You is Hurting Me: Escaping the Messiah Trap, 1988, rev. ed., 2003; (with M.L. Taylor) Loving Yourself As Your Neighbor: A Recovery Guide for Christians Escaping Burnout and Codependency, 1990; Are You Having Fun Yet? How to Bring the Art of Play into Your Recovery, 1992; Your Body Never Lies, 1993; (with

J. Ryan) Coming Home to Your Body: 365 Simple Ways to Nourish Yourself Inside and Out, 1996; (with M.W. Baker) Who's to Blame?: Escape the Victim Trap and Gain Personal Power in Your Relationship, 1996; Is Your Body Trying to Tell You Something? Why It Is Wise to Listen to Your Body and How Massage and Body Work Can Help, 1997; (with L. Barrington) Daddies and Daughters, 1998; (with M.E. Berry) Reawakening to Life: Renewal after a Husband's Death, 2002; The Unauthorized Guide to Choosing a Church, 2003; Unauthorized Guide to Sex and the Church, 2005; (with M. Brunetz) Take the U Out of Clutter, 2010. WITH TAMARA TRAEDER: Girlfriends: Invisible Bonds, Enduring Ties, 1995; The Girlfriends Keepsake Book: The Story of Our Friendship, 1996; Girlfriends Talk about Men: Sharing Secrets for a Great Relationship, 1997; Women's Rites: Girlfriends' Rituals, 1998; Girlfriends Are Forever, 1998; Girlfriends for Life: Friendships Worth Keeping Forever, 1998; A Friendship Meant to Be, 2000; True Blue Friends, 2000; A Girlfriend's Gift: Reflections on the Extraordinary Bonds of Friendship, 2000; (with J. Hazen) Girlfriends Get Together: Food, Frolic and Fun Times, 2001; Girlfriends Talk About Men: Sex, Money, Power, 2003; Girlfriends, 2004. Contributor to periodicals. **Address:** c/o Author Mail, HarperCollins Publishers, 10 E 53rd St., 7th Fl., New York, NY 10022, U.S.A.

BERRY, Carole. American (born United States) **Genres:** Mystery/Crime/Suspense, Novels, Young Adult Fiction, Psychology. **Career:** Writer. **Publications:** BONNIE INDERMILL MYSTERY NOVELS: The Letter of the Law, 1987; The Year of the Monkey, 1988; Goodnight, Sweet Prince, 1990; Island Girl, 1991; The Death of a Difficult Woman, 1994; The Death of a Dancing Fool, 1996; Death of a Dimpled Darling, 1997; Death of a Downsizer, 1999. SUSPENSE NOVEL: Nightmare Point, 1993. **Address:** Berkley Publishing Group, Berkley Prime Crime, 375 Hudson St., New York, NY 10014, U.S.A.

BERRY, Chad. American (born United States), b. 1963. **Genres:** History, Dance/Ballet. **Career:** Maryville College, assistant professor, associate professor of history, 1995-2006; Berea College, Loyal Jones Appalachian Center, director, 2006-11, Center for Excellence in Learning through Service, director, Goode professor of Appalachian studies and professor of history, academic vice president and dean of the faculty, 2011-. Writer. **Publications:** Southern Migrants, Northern Exiles, 2000; (ed.) Hayloft Gang: The Story of the National Barn Dance, 2008. Contributor to periodicals. **Address:** Office of the Academic Vice President, Berea College, 331 Lincoln Hall, PO Box 2204, Berea, KY 40404, U.S.A. **Online address:** chad_berry@berea.edu

BERRY, Cicely. British (born England), b. 1926. **Genres:** Speech/Rhetoric. **Career:** Central School of Speech and Drama, teacher of voice and speech, 1948-65; Royal Shakespeare Co., voice director, 1969-; British Ministry of Education, teacher; St. Patrick's College, teacher; BBC-Radio, teacher; City University of New York, Brooklyn College, lecturer; New York University, lecturer; University of North Carolina, lecturer; University of Denver, lecturer; University of Nebraska, lecturer; Oberlin College, lecturer. Writer. **Publications:** Voice and the Actor, 1973, rev. ed., 1991; Your Voice and How to Use It, 1975; The Actor and His Text, 1988, rev. ed. as Actor and the Text, 1992; Text in Action, 2001; From Word to Play: A Handbook for Directors, 2008. **Address:** Royal Shakespeare Co., The Courtyard Theatre, Southern Ln., Stratford-upon-Avon, WW CV37 6BB, England.

BERRY, Faith D. American (born United States), b. 1939. **Genres:** Literary Criticism And History, Biography, Translations, Humanities, Essays, Cultural/Ethnic Topics, Writing/Journalism, Race Relations, Race Relations. **Career:** New Yorker, editorial assistant, 1962-64; freelance writer, editor, and translator, 1964-70; Business and Professional Women's Foundation, career advancement fellow, 1970; National Gallery of Art, assistant editor, 1972-75; Dispatch News Service Intl., senior editor, 1972; WETA-TV, staff writer, 1975-78; U.S. Department of Labor, speech writer for Women's Bureau, 1980; Faith Berry and Associates, partner, 1980-82; Florida Atlantic University, associate professor of American literature and comparative literature, 1988-93; University of California, professor of Afro-American literature and gender studies, 1993-. **Publications:** Langston Hughes: Before and beyond Harlem; A Biography, 1983. EDITOR AND AUTHOR OF INTRODUCTION: Good Morning Revolution: Uncollected Social Protest Writings by Langston Hughes, 1973; A Scholar's Conscience: Selected Writings, 1991. (ed.) From Bondage to Liberation: Writings By and About African-Americans from 1700 to 1918, 2001. Contributor of articles, newspapers and magazines. **Address:** Department of Black Studies, University of California, 6046 HSSB, South Hall 3631, 552 University Ave., Santa Barbara, CA 93106, U.S.A. **Online address:** berryf@alishaw.ucsb.edu

BERRY, J. Bill. American (born United States), b. 1945. **Genres:** Literary Criticism And History, History, Autobiography/Memoirs. **Career:** University of Central Arkansas, associate professor of history, dean of faculty and vice president for academic affairs, 1989-98; University of Tennessee, provost and vice chancellor for academic affairs, 1998-2001; Butler University, administrative staff, provost and senior vice president for academic affairs, 2001-08; University of Dallas, provost, executive vice president and chief academic officer, 2008-, interim chancellor, 2009-10. Writer. **Publications:** (Ed.) Located Lives: Place and Idea in Southern Autobiography, 1989; (ed. and intro.) Home Ground: Southern Autobiography, 1991. **Address:** University of Dallas, 1845 E Northgate Dr., Irving, TX 75062, U.S.A.

BERRY, Jeffrey M. American (born United States), b. 1948. **Genres:** Politics/Government, Law. **Career:** Tufts University, Department of Political Science, assistant professor, 1974-, chairman, 1990-93, 2006, professor of political science, John Richard Skuse, class of 1941 chair, 2001-, John Richard Skuse, class of 1941, professor of political science, Graduate Program in Public Policy and Citizen Participation, co-founder and director, 1980-82, 1984-85; U.S. Department of State, American specialist lecturer, 1978; Citizen Participation Magazine, associate editor, 1979-86; Harvard University, Department of Government, visiting professor, 1988; American Political ScienceAssociation, Section on Political Organizations and Parties, president, 1999-2001; Alzheimer's Association of Massachusetts and New Hampshire, treasurer, 2004-06, vice chair, 2006-08, chair, 2008-09. Writer. **Publications:** (With R.L. Peabody, W.G. Frasure and J. Goldman) To Enact a Law: Congress and Campaign Financing, 1972; Lobbying for the People: The Political Behavior of Public Interest Groups, 1977; The Interest Group Society, 1984, (with C. Wilcox) 5th ed., 2009; Feeding Hungry People: Rulemaking in the Food Stamp Program, 1984; (with K. Janda and J. Goldman) The Challenge of Democracy: Government in America, 1987, 11th ed., 2011; (with K.E. Portney and K. Thomson) The Rebirth of Urban Democracy, 1993; (with K. Janda and J. Goldmeni) Amerikuli demokratia: ASS xelisup'leba da politikuri proc'esi, 1995; (with K. Janda and J. Goldman) The Challenge of Democracy: The Essentials, 1999; The New Liberalism: The Rising Power of Citizen Groups, 1999; (with D.F. Arons) A Voice for Nonprofits, 2003; (co-author) Surveying Nonprofits: A Methods Handbook, 2003; (co-author) Democracy at Risk: How Political Choices Undermine Citizen Participation and What We Can Do About It, 2005; (co-author) Lobbying and Policy Change: Who Wins, Who Loses, and Why, 2009; (ed. with L.S. Maisel) The Oxford Handbook of American Political Parties and Interest Groups, 2010. Contributor of articles to journals, newspapers and magazines. **Address:** Department of Political Science, Tufts University, Packard Hall, Medford, MA 02155, U.S.A. **Online address:** jeffrey.berry@tufts.edu

BERRY, Joanne. Welsh (born Wales), b. 1971. **Genres:** Young Adult Nonfiction, History. **Career:** Swansea University, instructor in archaeology. Writer. **Publications:** NON-FICTION: Cultural Identity in the Roman Empire, 1998; Unpeeling Pompeii: Studies in Region I of Pompeii, 1998; The Complete Pompeii, 2007; (with P. Matyszak) Lives of the Romans, 2008. Contributor of articles to periodicals. **Address:** School of Humanities, Swansea University, Singleton Pk., Swansea, SA2 8PP, Wales.

BERRY, John Stevens. American (born United States), b. 1938. **Genres:** Poetry, History. **Career:** Berry Law Firm, founder, 1965-; Berry, Anderson, Creager & Wittstruck (law firm), senior partner, 1977-. Writer. **Publications:** Darkness of Snow (poems), 1973; Those Gallant Men: On Trial in Vietnam, 1984. Contributor to journals and magazines. **Address:** Berry Law Firm, 2650 N 48th St., Lincoln, NE 68504-3631, U.S.A. **Online address:** jsberry@jsberrylaw.com

BERRY, John W. *See* **BERRY, J. W.**

BERRY, Jonas. *See* **ASHBERY, John (Lawrence).**

BERRY, Julie. American (born United States), b. 1974?. **Genres:** Novels. **Career:** MetroWest Daily News, humor columnist, 2004-. **Publications:** NOVELS: The Amaranth Enchantment, 2009; Secondhand Charm, 2010; The Colossal Fossil Freakout, 2011. SPLURCH ACADEMY FOR DISRUPTIVE BOYS SERIES: The Rat Brain Fiasco, 2010; Curse of the Bizarro Beetle, 2010. **Address:** Stow, MA , U.S.A. **Online address:** julie@julieberrybooks.com

BERRY, J. W. (John W. Berry). Canadian (born Canada), b. 1939. **Genres:** Psychology, Social Sciences, Anthropology/Ethnology. **Career:** University of Sydney, lecturer in psychology, 1966-69; Queen's University, professor of psychology, 1969-99, now professor emeritus; University de Nice, Institut d'Etudes et de Recherches Interethniques et Interculturelles, visiting professor, 1979-80; University de Geneva, Facult de Psychologie et Sciences de l'Education, visiting professor, 1986-87; Cross-Cultural/Multicultural Associates Inc., president. Writer. **Publications:** (Ed. with P.R. Dasen) Culture and Cognition: Readings In Cross-Cultural Psychology, 1974; (co-author as John W. Berry) Multiculturalism and Ethnic Attitudes in Canada, 1976; (as John W. Berry) Human Ecology And Cognitive Style: Comparative Studies In Cultural and Psychological Adaptation, 1976; (ed. with S.H. Irvine as John W. Berry) Human Assessment and Cultural Factors, 1983; (ed. with R.J Samuda and M. Laferrière as John W. Berry) Multiculturalism in Canada: Social and Educational Perspectives, 1984; On the Edge of the Forest: Cultural Adaptation and Cognitive Development in Central Africa, 1986; (ed. with W.J. Lonner as John W. Berry) Field Methods in Cross-cultural Research, 1986; (co-ed.) Indigenous Cognition: Functioning in Cultural Context, 1988; (co-ed.) Health and Cross-cultural Psychology: Toward Applications, 1988; (ed. with S.H. Irvine) Human Abilities in Cultural Context, 1988; (with J.A. Bennett) Cree Syllabic Literacy: Cultural Context and Psychological Consequences, 1991; (co-author as John W. Berry) Cross-cultural Psychology: Research and Applications, 1992, 3rd ed., 2011; (ed. with U. Kim as John W. Berry) Indigenous Psychologies: Research and Experience in Cultural Context, 1993; (co-ed.) Ethnicity and Culture in Canada, 1994; (with R.C. Mishra as John Widdup Berry) Ecology, Acculturation, and Psychological Adaptation, 1996; Cultures in Contact: Acculturation and Change, 1997; Handbook of Cross-Cultural Psychology, 3 vols., 1997; (co-author) Cross-Cultural Psychology: Research and Applications, 2002; (with R.C. Mishra and R.C. Tripathi) Psychology in Human And Social Development: Lessons From Diverse Cultures: A Festschrift for Durganand Sinha, 2003; (co-ed. as John W. Berry) Immigrant Youth in Cultural Transition: Acculturation, Identity, And Adaptation Across National Contexts, 2006; (ed. with D.L. Sam as John W. Berry) Cambridge Handbook of Acculturation Psychology, 2006; (ed. with C. Leong as John W. Berry) Intercultural Relations in Asia: Migration and Work Effectiveness, 2010. **Address:** Queen's University, 154 Albert St., Kingston, ON K7L 3N6, Canada. **Online address:** berryj@kos.net

BERRY, Linda. American (born United States), b. 1940. **Genres:** Mystery/Crime/Suspense, Novels, Young Adult Fiction, Literary Criticism And History. **Career:** Colorado Tennis Association/Intermountain Tennis Association, writer and editor, 1981-88; Accent Newspaper, weekly columnist, 1991-93. **Publications:** Death and the Easter Bunny, 1998; Death and the Hubcap, 2000; Death and the Icebox: A Trudy Roundtree Mystery, 2003; Death and the Walking Stick: A Trudy Roundtree Mystery, 2005; Death and the Family Tree, 2007; Death and the Crossed Wires, 2009. **Address:** 11558 E Wesley Ave., Aurora, CO 80014, U.S.A. **Online address:** jerryberry@juno.com

BERRY, Philippa. British (born England), b. 1955. **Genres:** Literary Criticism And History, Young Adult Fiction. **Career:** University of Fès, research assistant, 1980-84; University of East Anglia, lecturer, 1984-85; West London Institute of Higher Education, lecturer, 1985-88; Cambridge University, King's College, fellow and director of studies in English, 1988-. Writer. **Publications:** Of Chastity and Power: Elizabethan Literature and the Unmarried Queen, 1989; (ed. with A. Wernick) Shadow of Spirit: Postmodernism and Religion, 1992; Shakespeare's Feminine Endings, 1999; (ed. with M. Tudeau-Clayton) Textures of Renaissance Knowledge, 2003. **Address:** King's College, Cambridge University, Cambridge, CM CB2 1ST, England.

BERRY, Stephen W. American (born United States) **Genres:** History. **Career:** Stanley H. Kaplan Inc., instructor, 1990-99; Center for the Study of the American South, designer, developer and maintainer, 1995-99; freelance web designer, 1997-2001; University of North Carolina, assistant professor and coordinator of the American studies program, 2001-07; University of Georgia, associate professor of history, codirector of center for virtual history and coordinator of war and society workshop, 2007-. Writer. **Publications:** All That Makes a Man: Love and Ambition in the Civil War South, 2003; (ed.) Princes of Cotton: Four Diaries of Young Men in the South, 1848-1860, 2007; House of Abraham: Lincoln and the Todds, A Family Divided by War, 2007; (ed.) Weirding the War: Stories from the Civil War's Ragged Edges, 2011; Jingle-Man: The Death and Times of Edgar Allan Poe, forthcoming. Contributor of articles to books and periodicals. **Address:** Department of History, University of Georgia, 235 LeConte Hall, Athens, GA 30602, U.S.A. **Online address:** berry@uga.edu

BERRY, Steve. American (born United States), b. 1955. **Genres:** Novels, Mystery/Crime/Suspense. **Career:** Writer, 1990-. Attorney. **Publications:** The Amber Room, 2003; The Romanov Prophecy: A Novel, 2004; The Third Secret: A Novel, 2005; The Templar Legacy: A Novel, 2006; The Venetian Betrayal: A Novel, 2007; The Alexandria Link: A Novel, 2007; The Charlemagne Pursuit, 2008; The Paris Vendetta, 2009; Emperor's Tomb, 2010; The Balkan Escape, 2010; The Devil's Gold, 2011; Jefferson Key: A Novel, 2011; The Columbus Affair, 2012. **Address:** c/o Pamela G. Ahearn, Ahearn Literary Agency, 2021 Pine St., New Orleans, LA 70118, U.S.A.

BERRYMAN, Jack W. American (born United States), b. 1947. **Genres:** History, Medicine/Health, Sports/Fitness. **Career:** University of Massachusetts, Department of Physical Education, instructor and varsity soccer coach, 1971-72; University of Washington, College of Arts and Sciences, acting assistant professor, 1975-76, Department of Kinesiology, assistant professor, 1976-81, associate professor of kinesiology, 1981-84, Department of Medical History and Ethics, associate professor of medical history, 1984-95, professor of medical history, 1995-2009, acting chairman, 1999-2000, School of Medicine, adjunct professor of orthopaedics and sports medicine, 2001-, Department of Bioethics and Humanities, professor of medical history, 2009-, Minor Program, director; Ball State University, Phi Alpha Theta lecturer, 1981; writer, 1986-; American College of Sports Medicine, fellow, D.B. Dill historical lecturer, 1994, 2004, Museum, History, and Archives, chair. Writer. **Publications:** (Ed. with R.J. Park) Sport and Exercise Science: Essays in the History of Sports Medicine, 1992; Out of Many, One: A History of the American College of Sports Medicine, 1995; Fly-Fishing Pioneers and Legends of the Northwest, 2006. Contributor to journals. **Address:** Department of Bioethics & Humanities, School of Medicine, University of Washington, Rm. A-204, Health Science Bldg., Seattle, WA 98195, U.S.A. **Online address:** berryman@u.washington.edu

BERRYMAN, Phillip E. American (born United States), b. 1938. **Genres:** Area Studies, Theology/Religion, Politics/Government, Economics, Translations, Cultural/Ethnic Topics. **Career:** St. Philip Church, administrator and counselor, 1963-65; Parroquia de Fatima, pastoral worker, 1965-73; Opportunities Industrialization Center, counselor, 1973-76; consultant, translator and writer, 1981-; Villanova University, teacher, 1987; Rosemont College, teacher, 1989; University of Notre Dame, Kellogg fellow, 1990; Stockton State College, teacher, 1990; Temple University, teacher, 1993-95, 2000-. Writer. **Publications:** What's Wrong in Central America and What to Do About it, 1983, rev. ed., 1984; The Religious Roots of Rebellion: Christians in Central American Revolutions, 1984; Christians In Guatemala's Struggle, 1984; Inside Central America: The Essential Facts Past and Present on El Salvador, Nicaragua, Honduras, Guatemala and Costa Rica, 1985; Liberation Theology: The Essential Facts about the Revolutionary Movement in Latin America and Beyond, 1987; Our Unfinished Business: The U.S. Catholic Bishops Letters on Peace and the Economy, 1989; Stubborn Hope: Religion, Politics and Revolution in Central America, 1994; Religion in the Megacity: Catholic and Protestant Portraits from Latin America, 1996. TRANSLATOR: J. Sobrion, Juan Hernandez Pico, Theology of Christian Solidarity, 1985; T. Cabestrero, Revolutionaries for the Gospel: Testimonies of Fifteen Christians in the Nicaraguan Government, 1986; F. Hinkelammert, The Ideological Weapons of Death: A Theological Critique of Capitalism, 1986; P. Casaldaliga, Prophets in Combat: The Nicaraguan Journal of Bishop Pedro Casaldaliga, 1987; P. Richard, Death of Christendoms, Birth of the Church, 1987; C. Boff, Feet-on-the-Ground Theology, 1987; E.F. Mignone, Witness to the Truth: The Complicity of Church and Dictatorship in Argentina, 1987; National Conference of Catholic Bishops, Justicia Economica para Todos: Carta Pastoral Sobre la Ensenanza Social Catolica y la Economia de los E.U.A., 1987; R.G. Treto, The Church and Socialism in Cuba, 1988; Path from Puebla: Significant Documents of the Latin American Bishops Since 1979, 1989; Resonancias de Puebla: Documentos Significativos de Los Obispos Latinoamericanos Desde 1979, 1990; I. Gebara and M.C.L. Bingemer, Mary, Mother of God and Mother of the Poor, 1990; N. Jaen, Toward a Spirituality of Liberation, 1991; J. Hasset and H. Lacey, (and ed.) Towards a Society that Serves Its People: The Intellectual Contribution of El Salvador's Murdered Jesuits, 1991; J.L. Segundo, The Liberation of Dogma: Faith, Revelation and Dogmatic Teaching Authority, 1992; L. Boff, The Path to Hope: Fragments from a Theologian's Journey, 1993; Report of the Chilean National Commission on Truth and Reconciliation, 2 vols., 1993; Fourth General Conference of Latin American Bishops, Santo Domingo Conclusions, 1993; (and ed.) People of God, 2004. Contributor to periodicals and newspapers. **Address:** 3818 Hamilton St., Philadelphia, PA 19104, U.S.A. **Online address:** pberrymn@philly.infi.net

BERT, Norman A(llen). American (born United States), b. 1942. **Genres:** Theatre, Plays/Screenplays, Film. **Career:** Choma Secondary School, teacher and deputy headmaster, 1969-70; Messiah College, assistant professor of drama, 1975-81; Eastern Montana College, assistant professor, 1981-, Communication Arts/Theater Department, professor, graduate faculty, chair, 1991-; Texas Tech University, Department of Theatre and Dance, professor, head of playwriting. Writer. **Publications:** One-Act Plays for Acting Students: An Anthology of Short One-Act Plays for One, Two, or Three Actors, 1987; A History and Genealogy of Peter Bert, 1987; (and ed.) The Scene book for Actors: Great Monologs and Dialogs from Contemporary & Classical Theater, 1990; (intro. and ed.) Theater Alive!: An Introductory Anthology of World Drama, 1991, rev. ed., 1995; Adventure in Discipleship, 1992; (and ed.) Scenes from Classic Plays, 1993; (with D. Bert) Play It Again!: More One-Act Plays for Acting Students, 1993; (ed. with D. Bert) New One-Act Plays for Acting Students: A New Anthology of Complete One-Act Plays for One, Two, or Three Actors, 2003; (ed. with D. Bert) More One-Act Plays for Acting Students: An Anthology of Short One-Act Plays for One to Three Actors, 2003; (with S. Smiley) Playwriting: The Structure of Action, 2005. PLAYS: Dayspring, 1974; Woolman, 1976; Jeremiah of Anathoth, 1978; Pilgrimage, 1988; Contributor to journals. **Address:** Department of Theatre & Dance, Texas Tech University, 2500 Broadway, Lubbock, TX 79409, U.S.A. **Online address:** norman.bert@ttu.edu

BERTAGNA, Julie. Scottish (born Scotland), b. 1962?. **Genres:** Young Adult Fiction, Children's Fiction, Illustrations, Picture/Board Books. **Career:** Freelance writer and educator. **Publications:** The Spark Gap, 1996; The Ice-Cream Machine, 1998; Clumsy Clumps and the Baby Moon, 1999; Soundtrack, 1999; Dolphin Boy, 1999; Bungee Hero, 1999; Exodus, 2002; The Opposite of Chocolate, 2003; Zenith, 2007; Aurora, 2010. Works appear in anthologies. **Address:** c/o Caroline Walsh, David Higham Associates Ltd., 5-8 Lower John St., Golden Sq., London, GL W1F 9HA, England. **Online address:** julie@juliebertagna.com

BERTEMATTI, Richard. American (born United States), b. 1971. **Genres:** Mystery/Crime/Suspense, Young Adult Fiction. **Career:** National Discount Brokers, compliance officer, 1996-; Bertematti-Henriquez, L.L.C., executive director. Writer. **Publications:** Project Death: A Tito Rico Mystery, 1997; The Undead, 2008; Virginia: A Story of the Civil War, 2009; Be The Dream; Puerto Rican Paradise, forthcoming. **Address:** Arte Publico Press, University of Houston, 452 Cullen Performance Hall, Houston, TX 77204-2004, U.S.A. **Online address:** bertematti@mail.com

BERTLING, Tom. American (born United States), b. 1956. **Genres:** Language/Linguistics, Education. **Career:** Kodiak Media Group, president, 1989-; LexieCannes.com Productions L.L.C, producer, director. Writer. **Publications:** A Child Sacrificed: To the Deaf Culture, 1994; No Dignity for Joshua: More Vital Insight Into Deaf Children, Deaf Education and Deaf Culture, 1997. EDITOR: American Sign Language: Shattering the Myth, 1998; Intellectual Look At American Sign Language: Clear Thinking On American Sign Language, English and Deaf Education, 2001; Communicating with Deaf Children, 2002. **Address:** LexieCannes.com Productions L.L.C., PO Box 644, Wilsonville, OR 97070, U.S.A.

BERTOLINO, James. American (born United States), b. 1942. **Genres:** Novellas/Short Stories, Poetry, Writing/Journalism, Autobiography/Memoirs, Literary Criticism And History. **Career:** Abraxas Press, editor, 1968-72; Washington State University, teaching assistant; Stone Marrow Press, editor, 1970-76; Epoch Magazine, assistant editor, 1971-73; Cornell University, teaching assistant, 1971-73, lecturer in creative writing, 1973-74; Print Center Inc., board director, 1972-74; University of Cincinnati, assistant professor, 1974-77, associate professor of English, 1977-84; Cincinnati Poetry Review, co-editor, 1975-82; Eureka Review, poetry editor, 1975-81; Cincinnati Area Poetry Project, founder, 1977; Skagit Valley College, instructor, 1984-89; Western Washington University, instructor, 1991-; Willamette University, writer-in-residence and Hallie Ford chair of creative writing, 2005-06. **Publications:** Day of Change, 1968; Drool, 1968; Mr. Nobody, 1969; Ceremony: A Poem, 1969; Maize: A Poem, 1969; Stone Marrow, 1969; Becoming Human: Poems, 1970; The Interim Handout, 1972; Employed: Poems, 1972; Edging Through, 1972; Soft Rock, 1973; Making Space for Our Living, 1975; Terminal Placebos, 1975; The Gestures, 1975; The Alleged Conception, 1976; New and Selected Poems, 1978; Are You Tough Enough for the Eighties?, 1979; Precinct Kali and the Gertrude Spicer Story, 1981; Drool, 1986; First Credo, 1986; Like a Planet, 1993; Snail River, 1995; Greatest Hits: 1965-2000, 2000; Pocket Animals, 2002; Finding Water, Holding Stone: Poems, 2009. EDITOR: Quixote: Northwest Poets, 1968; The Abraxas/Five Anthology, 1972. Works appear in anthologies. Contributor of articles to magazines and newspapers. **Address:** Department of English, Western Washington University, HU269, 516 High St., Bellingham, WA 98225, U.S.A. **Online address:** james.bertolino@wwu.edu

BERTOZZI, Nick. American (born United States), b. 1970. **Genres:** Novels, Graphic Novels. **Career:** ACT-I-VATE, founding member, 2006-; School of Visual Arts, teacher; Rhode Island School of Design, teacher; The Center for Cartoon Studies, teacher. Writer, graphic artist and programmer. **Publications:** Boswash (graphic story/map), 2000; The Masochists, 2001; Rubber Necker, 2002; The Salon, 2007; (with J. Lutes) Houdini: The Handcuff King, 2007; (with G. Eichler) Stuffed!, 2009; Lewis & Clark, 2011. **Address:** c/o Author Mail, Alternative Comics, 644 NE 9th Ave., Gainesville, FL 32601-4440, U.S.A. **Online address:** nub@nickbertozzi.com

BERTRAND, Diane Gonzales. American (born United States), b. 1956. **Genres:** Children's Fiction, Young Adult Fiction, Essays, Poetry. **Career:** St. Mary's University, English and Communication Studies Department, visiting lecturer in creative writing and English composition, professor, writer-in-residence; Pecan Grove Review, faculty advisor, writer-in-residence. **Publications:** Touchdown for Love, 1990; Close to the Heart, 1991; Carousel of Dreams, 1992; Sweet Fifteen, 1995; Alicia's Treasure, 1996; Sip, Slurp, Soup, Soup/Caldo, Caldo, Caldo (picture book), 1996; Lessons of the Game, 1998; Trino's Choice, 1999; Family, Familia (picture book), 1999; The Last Doll, 2000; Uncle Chente's Picnic, 2001; Trino's Time, 2001; Close to the Heart, 2002; The Empanadas that Abuela Made, 2003; My Pal, Victor, 2004; Upside Down and Backwards: De cabeza y al revés, 2004; The Ruiz Street Kids: Los muchachos de la calle Ruiz, 2006; We Are Cousins, 2007; Ricardo's Race, 2007; Party for Papá Luis, 2010; F Factor, 2010; Park Our Town Built: El parque que nuestro pueblo construyó, 2011; Adelita and the Veggie Cousins, 2012. Contributor to books and magazines. **Address:** Deparment of English, St. Mary's University, Chaminade Tower 412, 1 Camino Santa Maria, San Antonio, TX 78228, U.S.A. **Online address:** dbertrand@stmarytx.edu

BERTRAND, Jacques. Canadian (born Canada), b. 1965?. **Genres:** Civil Liberties/Human Rights, Adult Non-fiction. **Career:** Princeton University, lecturer in political science, 1994-95; North-South Institute, researcher, 1996-98; University of Toronto, assistant professor, 1998-2003, associate professor of political science, 2003-, Social Sciences and Humanities, vice-chair, 2003-04, chair, 2004-05, Asian Institute, faculty. Writer. **Publications:** L'Indonesie: La Prevention des conflits ethniques, 1997; Nationalism and Ethnic Conflict in Indonesia, 2004; (ed. with A. Laliberté) Multination States in Asia: Accommodation or Resistance, 2010. CONTRIBUTOR: Managing Change in Southeast Asian Communities: Local Identities, Global Connections, 1995; Canadian Development Report 1999: Civil Society and Global Change, 1999; Good Governance and Conflict Resolution in Indonesia, 2000; Democracy, Human Rights and Civil Society in Eastern Asia, 2001; Fighting Words: Language Policy and Ethnic Relations in Asia, 2003; Development and Security in Southeast Asia, 2003; Democracy and Identity: Regimes and Ethnicity in East and Southeast Asia, 2004. Contributor to books and periodicals. **Address:** Asian Institute, Munk School of Global Affairs, University of Toronto, Rm. 107N, 1 Devonshire Pl., Toronto, ON M5S 3K7, Canada. **Online address:** jacques.bertrand@utoronto.ca

BERTRAND, Lynne. American (born United States), b. 1963. **Genres:** Children's Fiction, Social Sciences, Humor/Satire. **Career:** Freelance journalist, 1987-. **Publications:** One Day, Two Dragons, 1992; Good Night, Teddy Bear, 1992; Let's Go! Teddy Bear, 1993; Who Sleeps in the City?, 1994; Dragon Naps, 1996; Granite Baby, 2005. Contributor to periodicals. **Address:** PO Box 761, Williamsburg, MA 01096, U.S.A.

BERTRAND, Marsha. American (born United States), b. 1950. **Genres:** Money/Finance, How-to Books, Marketing, Business/Trade/Industry, Economics. **Career:** Coopers & Lybrand, personnel specialist and director of training and development, 1971-83; Allnet Communication Services Inc., shareholder relations administrator, 1983-85; VMS Realty Partners, assistant vice-president for investor relations, 1985-88; freelance writer, 1988-. **Publications:** Consumer Guide to the Stock Market, 1993; A Woman's Guide to Savvy Investing, 1998; Fraud!: How to Protect Yourself from Schemes, Scams and Swindles, 2000; Getting Started in Investment Clubs, 2001. Contributor to magazines. **Address:** c/o Nicholas Smith, Altair Literary Agency, 141 5th Ave., Ste. 8N, New York, NY 10010, U.S.A. **Online address:** mbertrand@orlinter.com

BERTSCHINGER, Claire. British/Swiss (born Switzerland), b. 1952?. **Genres:** Autobiography/Memoirs. **Career:** International Committee of the Red Cross, nurse, 1984-90; London School of Hygiene and Tropical Medicine, instructor in tropical nursing, director, 1990-. Writer. **Publications:** (With F. Blake) Moving Mountains (memoir), 2005. **Address:** c/o Author Mail, Doubleday Press, 1745 Broadway, New York, NY 10019-4368, U.S.A.

BERTULANI, C. A. *See* **Bertulani, Carlos A.**

BERTULANI, Carlos A. (C. A. Bertulani). American (born United States) **Genres:** Sciences, Physics. **Career:** Federal University of Rio de Janeiro, assistant professor, 1980-83, professor, 1988-2000, chair of the Physics Graduate Program, 1997-99; Michigan State University, faculty, 1991-92, 2002-04; University of Wisconsin, 1993; GSI/Darmstadt, staff, 1994; Brookhaven National Laboratory, staff, 2000-01; University of Arizona, faculty, 2004-06; University of Tennessee, research professor, 2006-07; Oak Ridge National Laboratory, research professor, 2006-07; Texas A&M University, associate professor of physics, 2007-. Writer. **Publications:** (ed. with L.F. Canto and M.S. Hussein) Proceedings of the First International Workshop on Physics of Unstable Nuclear Beams: Topics on the Structure and Interactions of Nuclei far from the Stability Line; 28-31 August 1996, Serra Negra, Sao Paulo, Brazil, 1997; (co-ed.) Nuclear Physics: Proceedings of the VIII Jorge Andre Swieca Summer School, Campos do Jordado, Brazil, January 26-February 7, 1997, 1997; (ed. with L.F. Canto and M.S. Hussein) International Workshop on Collective Excitations in Fermi and Bose Systems, Serra Negra, Brazil, 1998; (As C. A. Bertulani with M.S. Hussein and G. Munzenberg) Physics of Radioactive Beams (textbook), 2001; (with H. Schechter) Introduction to Nuclear Physics (textbook), 2002; (with P. Danielewicz) Introduction to Nuclear Reactions (textbook), 2004; Nuclear Physics in a Nutshell (textbook), 2007. **Address:** Department of Physics, Texas A&M University, PO Box 3011, Commerce, TX 75429-3011, U.S.A. **Online address:** carlos_bertulani@tamu-commerce.edu

BERUBE, David M. American (born United States), b. 1953?. **Genres:** Sciences, Technology. **Career:** Seton Hall University, adjunct instructor, 1975-81, Public Policy Research Institute, director, 1979-81; Weber State University, instructor, 1982-86, Center for Policy Studies, director, 1984-86; Trinity University, instructor, 1986-87; University of Vermont, instructor, 1987-90, World Debate Institute, co-director, 1988-2004; Burlington Free Press, dance and music critic, 1988-; University of South Carolina, professor of speech communication studies, 1990-2007, Nanoscience and Technology Studies, associate director, 2002-05, Industrial and Governmental Relations of Nanoscience and Technology Studies, associate, research director and coordinator, 2004-05; Ketchum Communications, contributing editor, 2006; International Council on Nanotechnology, communications director, 2006-07; North Carolina State University, Department of Communication, professor of communication, 2008-; Public Communication of Science and Technology, director, 2008-; Center for Emerging Technologies L.L.C., manager, 2008-; Soros Foundation, consultant; Food Products Association, consultant; Grocery Manufacturers Association, consultant. **Publications:** (With A.C. Snider and K. Pray) Non-Policy Debating, 1994; (contrib.) Reading Nanoscience, 2004; (contrib.) Societal Implications of Nanoscience and Nanotechnology II: Maximizing Human Benefit, Report of the National Nanotechnology Initiative Workshop, 2004; Nano-Hype: The Truth behind the Nanotechnology Buzz, 2006; (contrib.) Nanoethics: Examining the Societal Impact of Nanotechnology, 2007; (contrib.) Nanoethics: Emerging Debates, 2008; (contrib.) Nano- Predictions: Big Thinkers on the Smallest Technology, 2008; (contrib.) Nanotechnology: Ethics and Society, 2008; (contrib.) Nanotechnology Applications: Solutions for Improving Water Quality, 2008; (contrib.) Nanomedicine, 2008. Contributor to periodicals. **Address:** Department of Communication, North Carolina State University, 201 Winston Hall, PO Box 8104, Raleigh, NC 27695-8104, U.S.A. **Online address:** dmberube@ncsu.edu

BERUBE, Maurice R. American (born United States), b. 1933. **Genres:** Education, Essays, Reference. **Career:** United Federation of Teachers, assistant editor, 1964-67; Queens College of the City University of New York, Institute of Community Studies, faculty, 1968-73, assistant professor of urban studies, 1971-76; Old Dominion University, professor of education, 1979-, now professor emeritus of educational leadership. Writer. **Publications:** The Urban School Crisis: An Anthology of Essays, 1966; Educational Achievement and Community Control, 1968; (ed. with M. Gittell) Confrontation at Ocean Hill Brownsville: The New York School Strikes of 1968, 1969; (co-author) Demonstration for Social Change: An Experiment in Local Control, 1971; (co-author) Local Control in Education: Three Demonstration School Districts in New York City, 1972; (co-author) School Boards and School Policy, 1973; The Urban University in America, 1978; Education and Poverty: Effective Schooling in the United States and Cuba, 1984; Teacher Politics: The Influence of Unions, 1988; American Presidents and Education, 1991; American School Reform: Progressive, Equity and Excellence Movements, 1883-1993, 1994; Eminent Educators: Studies in Intellectual Influence, 2000; Beyond Modernism and Postmodernism, 2002; Radical Reformers: The Influence of the Left in American Education, 2004; (with C.T. Berube) The End of School Reform, 2007; (with C.T. Berube) Moral University, 2010. Contributor to periodicals. **Address:** Department of Educational Leadership, Old Dominion University, ED 165-10, Norfolk, VA 23529-0157, U.S.A. **Online address:** mberube@odu.edu

BERZENSKY, Steven Michael. *See* **BURRS, Mick.**

BESNER, Hilda F. American (born United States), b. 1950. **Genres:** Gay And Lesbian Issues, Human Relations/Parenting, Psychology, Medicine/Health. **Career:** Washington University, Malcolm Bliss Mental Health Center, intern in clinical psychology, 1975-76; Bessette, Farinacci and Associates, clinical psychologist, 1977-81; Dade County Department of Youth and Family Development, clinical psychologist, 1977-78; Nova University, Florida School of Professional Psychology, adjunct professor, 1979-82; Southeast Biosocial Institute, director of clinical internship, 1980-81; OptimaCare, vice-president, 1994-; Besners' Psychological Care Center, psychologist; American Psychological Association, president; Biofeedback Society of Florida, president; Broward County Psychological Association, president. Writer. **Publications:** (With S.J. Robinson) Understanding and Solving Your Police Marriage Problems, 1982; (with A. Besner and T.L. Perez) Rebuilding, 1992; (with A. Besner and Perez) After the Storm, 1992; (with C.I. Spungin) Gay and Lesbian Students: Understanding Their Needs, 1995; (with C.I. Spungin) Training for Professionals Who Work with Gays and Lesbians in Educational and Workplace Settings, 1997. Contributor to periodicals. **Address:** Besners' Psychological Care Center, 915 Middle River Dr., Ste. 204, Fort Lauderdale, FL 33304-3559, U.S.A. **Online address:** hilda@psychsolutionbuilders.com

BESNER, Neil K. Canadian (born Canada), b. 1949. **Genres:** Literary Criticism And History, Poetry, Art/Art History, Young Adult Fiction. **Career:** University of Regina, teaching assistant, 1972-73, instructor in English, 1973-74, sessional lecturer in English, 1975-76; Epicenter Language Academy, instructor, 1975; Plains Community College, instructor, 1975-76; University of British Columbia, sessional lecturer, 1976-78, teaching assistant, 1978-79, teaching assistant, 1982-83, Centre for Continuing Education, instructor, 1978-80; Okanagan College, instructor in English, 1980-81; Kwantlen College, instructor in English, 1982-83; Mount Royal College, instructor in English, 1983-87, coordinator of composition, 1983-85, chairman of academic council, 1984-86; University of Winnipeg, Department of English, assistant professor, 1987-90, associate professor, 1990-95, professor of English, 1995-, chair, 1993-2000, dean of humanities, 2002-05, dean of arts, 2005-, vice president of research and international. Writer. **Publications:** The Light of Imagination: Mavis Gallant's Fiction, 1988; Introducing Lives of Girls and Women, 1990; (ed. with D. Staines) The Short Story in English, 1991; A Reader's Guide to Alice Munro's Lives of Girls and Women, 1991; (ed. with D. Schnitzer and A. Turner) Uncommon Wealth: An Anthology of Poetry in English, 1997; Rare and Commonplace Flowers: The Story of Elizabeth Bishop and Lota de Macedo Soares, 2001; Carol Shields: The Arts of a Writing Life, 2003. Contributor of articles to journals. Works appear in anthologies. **Address:** Department of English, University of Winnipeg, 515 Portage Ave., Winnipeg, MB R3B 2E9, Canada. **Online address:** n.besner@uwinnipeg.ca

BESSEL, Richard. British/American (born United States), b. 1948. **Genres:** History. **Career:** University of Southampton, Parkes fellow, 1977-79; Open University, lecturer to reader in history, 1979-98; University of York, professor of twentieth-century history, 1998-. Writer. **Publications:** Political Violence and the Rise of Nazism: The Storm Troopers in Eastern Germany, 1925-1934, 1984; Germany after the First World War, 1993; Nazism and War, 2004; Germany 1945: From War to Peace, 2009. EDITOR: (with E.J. Feuchtwanger) Social Change and Political Development in Weimar Germany, 1981; (intro.) Life in the Third Reich, 1987; Fascist Italy and Nazi Germany: Comparisons and Contrasts, 1996; (with R. Jessen) Die Grenzen der Diktatur: Staat und Gesellschaft in der DDR, 1996; (with C. Emsley) Patterns of Provocation: Police and Public Disorder, 2000; (with D. Schumann) Life After Death: Approaches to a Cultural and Social History during the 1940s and 1950s, 2003; (with C. Haake) Removing Peoples: Forced Removal in the Modern World, 2009; (with N. Guyatt and J. Rendall) War, Empire and Slavery, 1770-1830, 2010. **Address:** Department of History, University of York, Vanbrugh College V/218, Heilington, York, NY YO10 5DD, England. **Online address:** richard.bessel@york.ac.uk

BESSETTE, Roland L. American (born United States) **Genres:** Bibliography, Autobiography/Memoirs. **Career:** Attorney and writer. **Publications:** Mario Lanza: Tenor in Exile, 1999. **Address:** Amadeus Press, 133 SW 2nd Ave., Ste. 450, Portland, OR 97204, U.S.A.

BES-SHAHAR, Eluki. (Rosemary Edghill). American (born United States), b. 1956?. **Genres:** Romance/Historical, Mystery/Crime/Suspense, Novellas/Short Stories, Novels. **Career:** Romance, science fiction, occult novelist and short story writer. **Publications:** NOVELS AS ROSEMARY EDGHILL: Turkish Delight, or, The Earl and the Houri, 1987; Two of a Kind: An English Trifle, 1988; The Ill-bred Bride or The Inconvenient Marriage, 1990; Fleeting Fancy, 1992; Speak Daggers To Her, 1994; The Sword of Maiden's Tears, 1994; The Cup of Morning Shadows, 1995; Book of Moons: A Bast Mystery, 1995; The Bowl of Night, 1996; The Cloak of Night and Daggers, 1997; Met by Moonlight, 1998; Bell, Book, and Murder, 1998; (with A. Norton) The Shadow of Albion, 1999; (with A. Norton) A Heart for Every Fate, 2000; (with M. Lackey) Beyond World's End, 2001; (with A. Norton) Leopard in Exile, 2001; (ed. with M. Lackey) Spirits White as Lightning, 2001; The Warslayer, 2002; Paying the Piper at the Gates of Dawn, 2003; Vengeance of Masks, 2003; (ed. with M. Lackey) Mad Maudlin, 2003; (ed.) Murder and Magic, 2004; (with M. Lackey) Music to My Sorrow, 2005; (ed. with M. Lackey) Bedlam's Edge, 2007; (with M. Lackey) Legacies, 2010; Conspiracies, 2011; (with M. Lackey) Dead Reckoning, 2012. AS ELUKI BES SHAHAR: Hellflower, 1990; Darktraders, 1992; Archangel Blues, 1993; X-Men: Smoke and Mirrors, 1997; (with T. Defalco) Time's Arrow: The Future, 1998. **Address:** St. Martin's Press, 175 5th Ave., New York, NY 10010, U.S.A. **Online address:** eluki@aol.com

BESSLER, John D. American (born United States), b. 1967?. **Genres:** Law. **Career:** Indiana University, Indiana Law Journal, senior managing editor, 1991; Faegre & Benson L.L.P., associate, 1991-96; Leonard, Street & Deinard, associate, 1996; Kelly & Berens P.A., partner, 1998-2007; University of Minnesota, School of Law, adjunct professor, 1998-2006; George Washington University, Law School, visiting associate professor of law, 2007-09; University of Baltimore, School of Law, associate professor, 2009-. **Publications:** Death in the Dark: Midnight Executions in America, 1997; Kiss of Death: America's Love Affair with the Death Penalty, 2003; Legacy of Violence: Lynch Mobs and Executions in Minnesota, 2003; Writing for Life: The Craft of Writing for Everyday Living, 2007; Cruel and Unusual: The American Death Penalty and the Founders' Eighth Amendment, 2012. Contributor to periodicals. **Address:** School of Law, University of Baltimore, LC 104A, 1420 N Charles St., Baltimore, MD 21201-5779, U.S.A. **Online address:** jbessler@ubalt.edu

BESSON, Luc. French (born France), b. 1959. **Genres:** Plays/Screenplays. **Career:** Les Films du Loup, founder, 1982-. Film director, producer, cinematographer and screenwriter. **Publications:** Le Grand bleu, 1988; Atlantis, 1991; Story of the Fifth Element, 1997; L'histoire de Subway, 2000; Arthur and the Forbidden City, 2005; Arthur and the Minimoys, 2005; Arthur and the Invisibles, 2006; Qu'est-ce qu'une star aujourd'hui?, 2009. **Address:** Ne le 18 Mars, Lieu, Signe Poissons, Paris, 1959, France.

BEST, Antony. British (born England), b. 1964?. **Genres:** History, Military/Defense/Arms Control. **Career:** University of London, London School of Economics and Political Science, Department of International History, lecturer in international history, 1989-, senior lecturer in international history. Writer. **Publications:** Britain, Japan, and Pearl Harbor: Avoiding War in East Asia, 1936-41, 1995; (ed. with P. Preston and M. Partridge) British Documents on Foreign Affairs-Reports and Papers from the Foreign Office Confidential Print, vol. III: From 1940 through 1945, 1997, vol. IV, 1999, vol. V: From 1951 through 1956, 2005; (contrib.) Pearl Harbor and the Coming of the Pacific War, 1999; British Intelligence and the Japanese Challenge in Asia, 1914-1941, 2002; (contrib.) The Origins of World War Two: The Debate Continues, 2003; (contrib.) The Anglo-Japanese Alliance, 2004; (with J. Hanhimaki, J. Maiolo and K.E. Schulze) International History of the Twentieth Century, 2004, 2nd ed. as International History of the Twentieth Century and Beyond, 2008; (ed.) The International History of East Asia, 1900-1968, 2010; (ed.) Imperial Japan and the World, 1931-1945, 2010; We are Virtually at War with Russia: Britain and the Cold War in East Asia, 1923-40, 2011; (ed. with J. Fisher) On the Fringes of Diplomacy, 2011. **Address:** Department of International History, London School of Economics and Political Science, University of London, Rm. EAS.E405, Houghton St., London, GL WC2A 2AE, England. **Online address:** a.best@lse.ac.uk

BEST, Don(ald M.). (John Lawless). American (born United States), b. 1949. **Genres:** How-to Books, Architecture, Sciences. **Career:** Oklahoma Daily, executive editor and sports editor, 1967-72; Brazil Herald, managing editor and business editor, 1974-75; Data News, founder, 1975, editor-in-chief, 1975-77; Corpus Christi Sun, associate editor, 1977-78; freelance writer, 1978-80, 1986-; Solar Age (now Custom Builder), senior editor, 1981-86; editor, 1986-; Energy Design Update, editor, 1997-. **Publications:** (With R. Trethewey) This Old House: Heating, Ventilation and Air Conditioning: A Guide to the Invisible Comforts of Your Home, 1994; The Do-It-Yourself Guide to Home Emergencies: From Breakdowns and Leaks to Cracks and Critters: Step-by-Step Solutions to the Toughest Problems a Homeowner Will Ever Face, 1996; The Handy Guide to Home Emergencies: From Breakdowns and Leaks to Cracks and Critters, Step-by-Step Solutions to the Toughest Problems a Homeowner Will Ever Face, 1996; Moonlight on the Amazon: Truth-Telling and Laughter from a Missionary Life, 2009. Contributor to books, magazines and newspapers. **Address:** Letters Ltd., 65 Hallwood Dr., Surry, NH 03431, U.S.A.

BEST, Geoffrey (Francis Andrew). (G. F. A. Best). British (born England), b. 1928. **Genres:** History, Military/Defense/Arms Control, Biography, Autobiography/Memoirs, Politics/Government, Law. **Career:** Harvard University, Choate fellow, 1954-55; Cambridge University, assistant lecturer and fellow of Trinity Hall, 1955-61; Edinburgh University, lecturer, 1961-66, Sir Richard Lodge professor of history, 1966-74, Richard Lodge chair of history, 1966-74; University of Chicago, visiting professor, 1964; Oxford University, All Souls College, visiting fellow, 1969-70, St. Antony's College, faculty, senior associate; Cambridge University, Lee Knowles Lecturer, 1970; Sussex University, professor of history, 1974-85, School of European Studies, dean, 1980-82, now chair of history; Woodrow Wilson International Center for Scholars, fellow, 1978-79; University of Western Ontario, Joane Goodman Lecturer, 1981; University of London, visiting professor, 1983-88; Australian National University, visiting fellow, 1984. Writer. **Publications:** Protestant Constitution and Its Supporters, 1800-1829, 1958; Temporal Pillars: Queen Anne's Bounty, the Ecclesiastical Commissioners and the Church of England, 1964; (as G.F.A. Best) Shaftesbury, 1964; Bishop Westcott and the Miners, 1967; History, Politics and Universities: Inaugural Lecture Delivered on Tuesday 4th March 1969, 1969; Mid-Victorian Britain, 1851-1875, 1971, rev. ed., 1973; Humanity in Warfare: The Modern History of the International Law of Armed Conflicts, 1980; Honour among Men and Nations: Transformations of an Idea, 1981; Seventeenth Century Europe, 1982; War and Society in Revolutionary Europe, 1770-1870, 1982; Nuremberg and After: The Continuing History of War Crimes and Crimes Against Humanity, 1984; (contrib.) Armed Conflict and the New Law: Aspects of 1977 Geneva Protocols and the 1981 Weapons Convention, 1989; War and Law since 1945, 1994; Churchill: A Study in Greatness, 2001; Churchill and War, 2005. EDITOR: (with J. Clive and intro.) Oxford Movement: Twelve Years, 1833-45, 1970; (with A. Wheatcroft) War, Economy and the Military Mind, 1976; (with D. Beales) History, Society, and the Churches: Essays in Honour of Owen Chadwick, 1985; The Permanent Revolution: The French Revolution and Its Legacy, 1789-1989, 1988. **Address:** St. Antony's College, Oxford University, 62 Woodstock Rd., Oxford, OX OX2 6JF, England. **Online address:** geefab@fish.co.uk

BEST, G. F. A. *See* **BEST, Geoffrey (Francis Andrew).**

BEST, Wallace D. American (born United States), b. 1960. **Genres:** Cultural/Ethnic Topics, Social Sciences, History, Theology/Religion. **Career:** University of Virginia, Department of Religious Studies, assistant professor, 2000-; Princeton University, Center for the Study of Religion, fellow, 2002-03, professor, 2007-; Harvard University, W.E.B. Du Bois Institute for African and African American Research, fellow, 2003-04, Harvard Divinity School, assistant professor of African American religious studies, 2004-. Writer. **Publications:** Passionately Human, No Less Divine: Religion and Culture in Black Chicago, 1915-1952, 2005. Contributor to books and periodicals. **Address:** Ctr. for African American Studies, Princeton University, Stanhope Hall, Princeton, NJ 08544, U.S.A. **Online address:** wbest@princeton.edu

BETANCOURT, Ingrid. (Ingrid Betancourt Pulecio). Colombian (born Colombia), b. 1961. **Genres:** Area Studies, Biography. **Career:** Activist, author and politician. **Publications:** Sí sabía: viaje a través del expediente de Ernesto Samper, 1996; (with L. Duroy) La rage au coeur, 2001; (L. Delloye-Betancourt and M. Delloye-Betancourt) Letters to My Mother: A Message of Love, A Plea for Freedom, 2008; Even Silence has an End: My Six Years of Captivity in the Colombian Jungle, 2010; Même le silence a une fin, 2010. Contributor to periodicals. **Address:** c/o Author Mail, Ecco Press, 18 W 30th St., New York, NY 10001-4447, U.S.A.

BÉTEILLE, André. Indian (born India), b. 1934. **Genres:** Sociology. **Career:** University of Delhi, Department of Sociology, professor, 1972-2003, professor emeritus, 2003-; Cambridge University, Commonwealth Visiting Professor, 1978-79; Wolfson College, visiting fellow, 1978-79; Centre for Studies in Social Sciences, chairman. Writer. **Publications:** Caste, Class and Power: Changing Patterns of Stratification in a Tanjore Village, 1965; Castes: Old and New, 1969; Harmonic and Disharmonic Social Systems, 1971; Studies in Agrarian Social Structure, 1974; Six Essays in Comparative Sociology, 1974, rev. ed. as Essays in Comparative Sociology, 1987; (trans.) The Structure of Hindu Society, by Nirmal K. Bose, 1976; Inequality among Men, 1977; Ideologies and Intellectuals, 1980; The Backward Classes and the New Social Order, 1981; The Idea of Natural Inequality and Other Essays, 1983, rev. ed., 1987; Some Observations on the Comparative Method, 1990; Society and Politics in India: Essays in a Comparative Perspective, 1991; The Backward Classes in Contemporary India, 1992; How Philosophy Makes the Stoic Sage Tranquil, 1997; Chronicles of Our Times, 2000; Antinomes of Society, 2000; Sociology: Essays on Approach and Method, 2002; Equality and Universality, 2002; Social Class, 2005; Ideology and Social Science, 2006; Marxism and Class Analysis, 2007; Present Significance of Caste, 2008; Remembered Childhood, 2010; Universities at the Crossroads, 2010. EDITOR: Social Inequality: Selected Readings, 1969; (with T.N. Madan) Encounter and Experience: Personal Accounts of Fieldwork, 1975; Equality and Inequality: Theory and Practice, 1983; Anti-Utopia: Essential Writings of André Beteillé, 2005. Contributor to periodicals. **Address:** Department of Sociology, University of Delhi, New Delhi, DH 110 007, India.

BETHELARD, Faith. American (born United States), b. 1953?. **Genres:** Animals/Pets, Psychology, Race Relations. **Career:** Business consultant and writer. **Publications:** (With E. Young-Bruehl) Cherishment: A Psychology of the Heart, 2000. Contributor to periodicals. **Address:** Free Press, Simon & Schuster, 1230 Ave. of the Americas, New York, NY 10020, U.S.A.

BETTEY, J(oseph) H(arold). British (born England), b. 1932. **Genres:** History, Theology/Religion, Cultural/Ethnic Topics. **Career:** Boys' Grammar School, teacher in history, 1957-60, head of history department, 1960-66; University of Bristol, lecturer, 1966-73, senior lecturer, 1973-, reader in local history, 1989-96. Writer. **Publications:** (Ed.) English Historical Documents, 1906-1939, 1967; The Island and Royal Manor of Portland: Some Aspects of Its History, with Particular Reference to the Period, 1750-1851, 1970; Dorset, 1974; Rural Life in Wessex, 1500-1900, 1977; The Rise of a Gentry Family: The Smyths of Aston Court, c. 1500-1642, 1978; Church & Community: The Parish Church in English Life, 1979; The Landscape of Wessex, 1980; (with C.W.G. Taylor) Sacred & Satiric: Medieval Stone Carving In The West Country, 1982; The Casebook of Sir Francis Ashley, J.P., 1982; (ed.) The Calendar of the Correspondence of the Smyth Family of Ashton Court, 1548-1642, 1982; Bristol Observed, 1986; Wessex from AD 1000, 1986; Church and Parish: An Introduction for Local Historians, 1987; Suppression of the Monasteries in the West Country, 1989; Estates and the English Countryside, 1993; Man and the Land: Farming in Dorset 1846-1996, 1996; (ed.) Historic Churches and Church Life in Bristol: Essays in Memory of Elizabeth Ralph 1911-2000, 2001; (ed.) Archives & Local History In Bristol & Gloucestershire: Essays In Honour Of David Smith, 2007. Contributor to history and archeology journals. **Address:** Clayley Cottage, Compton Dando, Bristol, GL BS39 4NX, England.

BETTINI, Maurizio. Italian (born Italy), b. 1947. **Genres:** Anthropology/Ethnology, Archaeology/Antiquities, Classics, Young Adult Fiction, Translations. **Career:** University of Pisa, assistant instructor of Latin literature, 1974, professor of Greek and Latin grammar, 1975-80; University of Venice, professor of Latin American literature, 1981-84; University of Siena, professor of Greek and Latin philology, 1985-, Faculty of Arts and Sciences, dean, 1986-95, Doctoral Program Anthropology and the Ancient World, chairman, 1990-, 2005, School of Humanities Studies, chair, president, 2003-, Doctoral Program Anthropology, history and theory of culture, chairman, 2005-; Center for the Study of Anthropology and the Ancient World, director, 1987-; Johns Hopkins University, visiting professor, 1990-; University of California, chair for Italian culture, 1992, visiting professor of classics, 1994, 1995, 1998. Writer. **Publications:** Studi e note su Ennio, 1979; Antropologia e cultura Romana, 1986, (trans.) Anthropology and Roman Culture: Kinship, Time, Images of the Soul, 1991; Verso un antropologia dellintreccio, 1991; Il Ritratto dellamante, 1992; I classici nelletàdellindiscrezione, 1994, (trans.) Classical Indiscretions, trans., 2001; (preface) Poet, Public, and Performance in Ancient Greece, 1997; Nascere: storie di donne, donnole, madri ed eroi, 1998; Con i libri, 1998; Le orecchie di Hermes: studi di antropologia e letterature classiche, 2000; (co-author) Cult of Vespa, 2001; In fondo al cuore, eccellenza, 2001; Francesco Petrarca sulle arti figurative: tra Plinio e SantAgostino, 2002; Il sonno della ragione: manifesti politici di Andrea Rauch, 2002; Bizzarra Mente: eccentrici e stravaganti dal mondo antico allamodernità, 2002; Il mito di Elena: immagini e racconti dalla Grecia aoggi, 2002; Il mito di Narciso: immagini e racconti dalla Grecia a oggi, 2003; Il corpo a pezzi: orizzonti simbolici a confronto, 2004; Il mito diEdipo: immagini e racconti dalla Grecia a oggi, 2004; Le coccinelle diRedún, 2004; Siena mostra Duccio: mostra Siena, 2004; Il mito delle sirene: immagini e racconti dalla Grecia a oggi, 2007; Autenticoassassinio, 2007; Cera una volta il mito, 2007; Voci: antropologia sonora del mondo antico, 2008; Alle porte dei sogni, 2009; Affari di famiglia: la parentela nella letteratura e nella cultura antica, 2009; (with C. Francoll) mito di Circe: immagini e racconti dalla Grecia a oggi, 2010. EDITOR: Plauto. Mostellaria e Persa, 1981; Las maschera, il doppio e il ritratto, 1991; Lo straniero, ovvero lidentita culturale aconfronto, 1992; Maschile/femminile: genere e ruoli nella cultura antica, 1993; Letteratura Latina: Storia letteraria e antropologia romana, 3 vols., 1995; I signori della memoria e delloblio, 1996; (with M. Boldrini, O. Calabrese and G. Piccinni) Miti di città, 2010. FICTION: Ilbizantino, 1981; Successo, 1984; Le bollicine della vita interiore, 1988; Arianna, 1995; Il cavaliere e il fantaccino, 1995, 2nd ed., 1996; Con ilibri, 1998; Il viaggiatore invisibile, 2004. Contributor to periodicals. **Address:** Faculty of Arts and Sciences, University of Siena, Centro AMA, Sede del Glicine, Via Roma 56, Siena, 53100, Italy. **Online address:** bettini@unisi.it

BETTIS, Jerome Abram. American (born United States), b. 1972. **Genres:** Novels. **Career:** National Broadcasting Co., television announcer, 2006-; The Bus Stops Here Foundation, Founder, 1997. Writer. **Publications:** (with T. Varley) Driving Home: My Unforgettable Super Bowl Run, 2006; (with G. Wojciechowski) The Bus: My Life in and out of a Helmet, 2007. **Address:** Jerome Bettis Enterprises, Inc., 2615 W 12 Mile Rd., Berkley, MI 48072, U.S.A.

BETTS, Clive. Welsh/British (born England), b. 1943. **Genres:** History, Language/Linguistics, Politics/Government, Regional/Urban Planning, Transportation, Documentaries/Reportage, Education. **Career:** National Assembly, Western Mail, staff, 1999-2002, National Assembly Press Gallery, staff. Writer. **Publications:** Culture in Crisis: The Future of the Welsh Language, 1976; A Oedd Heddwch?, 1978; Cardiff and the Eisteddfod, 1978; The Political Conundrum, 1993. **Address:** Western Mail, National Assembly, Pier Head St., Cardiff, SG CF99 1NA, Wales. **Online address:** cbetts@btconnect.com

BETTS, Doris. American (born United States), b. 1932. **Genres:** Novels, Novellas/Short Stories, Writing/Journalism, Essays. **Career:** Statesville Daily Record, journalist, 1950-51, Chapel Hill Weekly, staff, 1953-54; News-Leader, staff, 1953-54; Sanford Daily Herald, editorial staff, 1956-57; North Carolina Democrat, editorial staff, 1960-62; Sanford News Leader (weekly), editor, 1962; University of North Carolina, lecturer, 1966-74, associate professor, 1974-78, professor of creative writing, 1978-, alumni distinguished professor, 1980-, now alumni distinguished professor emeritus, director of freshman-sophomore English, 1972, director of fellows program, 1975-76, assistant dean of honors program, 1979-81, faculty chairperson, 1982-85; Duke University, visiting lecturer in creative writing, 1971. **Publications:** NOVELS: Tall Houses in Winter, 1954; The Scarlet Thread, 1964; The River to Pickle Beach, 1972; Heading West, 1981; Souls Raised from the Dead, 1994; The Sharp Teeth of Love, 1997; My Love Affair with Carolina, 1998.

STORY COLLECTIONS: The Gentle Insurrection and Other Stories, 1954; The Astronomer and Other Stories, 1966; Beasts of the Southern Wild & Other Stories, 1973. OTHER: Creative Writing: The Short Story, 1970. Contributor to periodicals. **Address:** Department of English and Comparative Literature, University of North Carolina, Greenlaw Hall, PO Box 3520, Chapel Hill, NC 27599-3520, U.S.A. **Online address:** dorisbetts@unc.edu

BETTS, William Wilson. American (born United States), b. 1926. **Genres:** Literary Criticism And History, Humor/Satire, Young Adult Non-fiction. **Career:** Teacher, 1950-52; Ohio University, instructor, 1954-55; Indiana University of Pennsylvania, associate professor, 1955-57, assistant basketball coach, 1955-68, 1971-, professor of English, 1957-, assistant dean, associate dean of graduate school, 1968-71, now emeritus; Indiana Evening Gazette, outdoors editor, 1973-80. Writer. **Publications:** (Ed. with P.A. Shelley and A.O. Lewis) Anglo-German and American-German Crosscurrents, vol. I, 1957; Lincoln and the Poets, 1965; A Docketful of Wry (humor), 1970; (comp. with R.M. Kurtz) Thomas Betts of Guilford and His Descendants (1615-2001), 2001; Slips that Pass in the Night, the King's English Adrift on the Campus (humor), 2002; Bombardier John Arris and the Rivers of the Revolution, 2006. Contributor of articles to magazines. **Address:** Department of English, Indiana University of Pennsylvania, 1011 South Dr., Indiana, PA 15701, U.S.A. **Online address:** wwjjbetts@earthlink.net

BEUMERS, Birgit. British/German (born Germany), b. 1963. **Genres:** Theatre, Film, Cartoons. **Career:** University of Cambridge, Slavonic Department, lecturer, 1992-94; University of Bristol, lecturer, 1994-2001, senior lecturer in Russian, 2001-06, reader in Russian, 2006-, Centre for Russian and East European Cultural Studies, founder, Department of Drama, Theater, Film, Television, teacher; Modern Language Review, Slavonic Editor, 2001-06; KinoKultura, editor. **Publications:** Yury Lyubimov at the Taganka Theatre, 1964-1994, 1997; (ed.) Russia on Reels: The Russian Idea in Post-Soviet Cinema, 1999; Burnt by the Sun, 2000; Nikita Mikhalkov: Between Nostalgia and Nationalism, 2005; Pop Culture Russia!: Media, Arts and Lifestyle, 2005; (ed.) 24 Frames: The Cinema of Russia and the Former Soviet Union, 2007; (ed. with S. Hutchings and N. Rulyova) The Post-Soviet Russian Media: Conflicting Signals, 2009; (ed. with V. Bocharov and D. Robinson) Alexander Shiryaev: Master of Movement, 2009; (co-ed.) Globalisation, Freedom and the Media after Communism, 2009; A History of Russian Cinema, 2009; (with M. Lipovetsky) Performing Violence, 2009. Contributor to books. **Address:** Department of Russian Studies, School of Modern Languages, University of Bristol, Rm. 1.55, 17 Woodland Rd., Bristol, BS8 1TE, England. **Online address:** birgit.beumers@bris.ac.uk

BEVAN, James (Stuart). British (born England), b. 1930. **Genres:** Medicine/Health, Sex. **Career:** St. Mary's Hospital, house physician, 1955-77, deputy medical superintendent, 1977-; Addenbrooke's Hospital, house surgeon, 1977; Automobile Association, senior medical consultant; Foundation of Nursing Studies, chairman; Charity Trustee Network, trustee. Writer. **Publications:** Preliminary Questions and Answers for Nurses, 1963; Sex: The Plain Facts, 1966; State Final Questions and Answers for Nurses, 4th ed., 1968, 5th ed., 1971; Simon and Schuster Handbook of Anatomy and Physiology, 1978; A Pictorial Handbook of Anatomy and Physiology, 1979, rev. ed., 1998; The Pocket Medical Encyclopedia and First Aid Guide, 1979; Your Family Doctor, 1980; The Family First Aid and Medical Guide: Emergencies, Symptoms, Treatments: In the Home, on the Road, on Vacation, 1984; (ed.) Sex and Your Health, 1990. Contributor to magazines. **Address:** 9 Hill Rd., London, GL NW8 9QE, England.

BEVANS, Stephen B(ennett). American (born United States), b. 1944. **Genres:** Theology/Religion. **Career:** Catholic Theological Union, faculty, 1986-, Louis J. Luzbetak, SVD professor of mission and culture, 1998-; Mission Studies, editor, 1997-2004; American Society of Missiology, president, 2006; Catholic Theological Society of America, board director, 2007-09; International Bulletin of Missionary Research, contributing editor; Yarra Theological Union, visiting lecturer, 2009; Society of the Divine Word, Roman Catholic priest. **Publications:** (Ed. with J.A. Scherer) New Directions in Mission and Evangelization, 1992; John Oman and His Doctrine of God, 1992; Models of Contextual Theology, 1992, rev. ed., 2002; Dictionary of Mission: Theology, History, Perspectives, 1997; (ed. with R. Schroeder) Word Remembered, Word Proclaimed: Selected Papers from Symposia Celebrating the SVD Centennial in North America, 1997; New Directions in Mission and Evangelization, 1999; (with R.P. Schroeder) Constants in Context: A Theology of Mission for Today, 2004; (with J. Gros) Evangelization and Religious Freedom: Ad Gentes, Dignitatis Humanae, 2009; Introduction to Theology in Global Perspective, 2009. Contributor to periodicals. **Address:** Catholic Theological Union, 5401 S Cornell Ave., Chicago, IL 60615, U.S.A. **Online address:** sbevans@ctu.edu

BEVERLEY, Jo. British (born England), b. 1947. **Genres:** Romance/Historical, Novels, Young Adult Fiction, Novellas/Short Stories. **Career:** Writer. **Publications:** Lord Wraybourne's Betrothed, 1988; The Stanforth Secrets, 1989; The Stolen Bride, 1990; If Fancy Be the Food of Love, 1991; Emily and the Dark Angel, 1991; The Fortune Hunter, 1991; Deirdre and Don Juan, 1993; Moonlight Lovers, 1993; An Arranged Marriage, 1991, 2nd ed., 1999; The Christmas Angel, 1992, 2nd ed., 2001; An Unwilling Bride, 1992, 2nd ed., 2000; Lord of My Heart, 1992, 2nd ed., 2002; My Lady Notorious, 1993, 2nd ed., 2002; Dark Champion, 1993, 2nd ed., 2003; Forbidden, 1994, 2nd ed., 2003; Tempting Fortune, 1995, 2nd ed., 2002; Dangerous Joy, 1995, 2nd ed., 2004; The Shattered Rose, 1996; Black Satin, 1997; Something Wicked, 1997, 2nd ed., 2005; Lord of Midnight, 1998; Forbidden Magic, 1998; Secrets of the Night, 1999, 2nd ed., 2004; (co-author) Star of Wonder, 1999; Devilish, 2000; The Devil's Heiress, 2001; The Dragon's Bride, 2001; (co-author) In Praise of Younger Men, 2001; Hazard, 2002; St. Raven, 2003; Winter Fire, 2003; Skylark, 2004; Three Heroes, 2004; The Trouble With Heroes in Irresistible Forces, 2004; A Most Unsuitable Man, 2005; (forward) Civil Contract, 2005; The Rogue's Return, 2006; To Rescue a Rogue, 2006; Lady Beware, 2007; (co-author) Dragon Lovers, 2007; Lady's Secret, 2008; The Secret Wedding, 2009; Lord Wraybourne's Bethrothed: A Romance of Regency England, 2009; (co-author) Chalice of Roses, 2010; (contrib.) Songs of Love & Death, 2010; The Secret Duke, 2010; Songs of Love and Death, 2010; The Unlikely Countess, 2011; An Invitation to Sin, 2011; A Scandalous Countess, 2012. Works appear in anthologies. **Address:** c/o Margaret Ruley, The Rotrosen Agency, 318 E 51st St., New York, NY 10022, U.S.A. **Online address:** jo@jobev.com

BEVIS, William W. American (born United States), b. 1941. **Genres:** Literary Criticism And History, Environmental Sciences/Ecology, Travel/Exploration, Novels. **Career:** University of Montana, associate professor of English, 1974-78, professor of English, 1978-99, professor emeritus, 1999-. Writer. **Publications:** Mind of Winter: Wallace Stevens, Meditation, and Literature, 1988; Ten Tough Trips: Montana Writers and the West, 1990; Borneo Log: The Struggle for Sarawak's Forests, 1995; Shorty Harris, or, The Price of Gold, 1999; (ed. with W.E. Farr) Fifty Years after The Big Sky: New Perspectives on the Fiction and Films of A.B. Guthrie, Jr., 2001. **Address:** Department of English, University of Montana, 133 Liberal Arts, 32 Campus Dr., Missoula, MT 59812-0003, U.S.A. **Online address:** wbevis@msn.com

BEW, Paul Anthony. Irish (born Ireland), b. 1950. **Genres:** Area Studies, History, Politics/Government. **Career:** Ulster College, Northern Ireland Polytechnic, lecturer, 1975-79; Queen's University, School of Politics, International Studies and Philosophy, lecturer, 1979-86, Department of Political Science, reader, 1986-, professor of politics, 1991-; University of Pennsylvania, visiting lecturer, 1982-83; Pembroke College, honorary fellow. Writer. **Publications:** Land and the National Question in Ireland, 1858-82, 1979; (with P. Gibbon and H. Patterson) The State in Northern Ireland, 1921-72: Political Forces and Social Classes, 1979; C.S. Parnell (biography), 1980; (with H. Patterson) Seán Lemass and the Making of Modern Ireland, 1945-66, 1982; (with H. Patterson) The British State and the Ulster Crisis: From Wilson to Thatcher, 1985; Conflict and Conciliation in Ireland, 1890-1910: Parnellites and Radical Agrarians, 1987; (with E. Hazelkorn and H. Patterson) The Dynamics of Irish Politics, 1989; (with G. Gillespie) Northern Ireland: A Chronology of the Troubles, 1968-1993, 1993, rev. ed., 1999; (ed. with K. Darwin and G. Gillespie) Passion and Prejudice: Nationalist/Unionist Conflict in Ulster in the 1930s and the Origins of the Irish Association, Institute of Irish Studies, 1993; Ideology and the Irish Question: Ulster Unionism and Irish Nationalism, 1912-1916, 1994; (with P. Gibbon and H. Patterson) Northern Ireland, 1921-1994: Political Forces and Social Classes, 1995, new ed. as Northern Ireland 1921-2001: Political Forces and Social Classes, 2002; (with G. Gillespie) Northern Ireland Peace Process, 1993-1996: A Chronology, 1996; John Redmond, 1996; (with H. Patterson and P. Teague) Northern Ireland-Between War and Peace: The Political Future of Northern Ireland, 1997; Ireland: The Politics of Enmity, 1789-2006, 2007; Making and Remaking of the Good Friday Agreement, 2008; (ed. with P. Maume) Journey in Ireland, 1921, 2009. **Address:** School of Politics, International Studies and Philosophy, Department of Political Science, Queens University, Rm. 20.205, 21 University Sq., Belfast, BT7 1PA, Northern Ireland. **Online address:** p.bew@qub.ac.uk

BEWES, Richard. British/Kenyan (born Kenya), b. 1934. **Genres:** Theology/Religion, Reference. **Career:** Church of England, ordained minister, 1959, assistant minister, 1959-65, vicar, 1965-74; BBC-Radio, host, 1969-74; Emmanuel Church, vicar, 1974-83; All Souls Church, rector, 1983-2004; African Enterprise, U.K. chairman. Writer. **Publications:** God in Ward 12, 1974; Advantage Mr. Christian, 1975; Talking about Prayer, 1979; John Wesley's England, 1981; The Church Reaches Out, 1981; The Pocket Handbook of Christian Truth, 1981; (with R.F. Hicks) The Creative Pocket Handbook of Christian Truth, 1981; The Church Overcomes, 1984; On the Way, 1984; Quest for Truth, 1985; Quest for Life, 1985; The Church Marches On, 1986; When God Surprises, 1986; New Beginning, 1989; The Resurrection: Fact or Fiction?, 1989; Does God Reign?, 1995; Speaking in Public Effectively, 1998; Great Quotations of the 20th Century, 1999; The Lamb Wins, 2000; Ten Steps in Prayer, 2001; The Stone That Became a Mountain, 2001; Words That Circled the World, 2002; The Top 100 Questions, 2002; Wesley Country, 2003; Beginning the Christian Life, 2004; 150 Pocket Thoughts, 2004. **Address:** 50 Curzon Rd., London, GL W5 1NF, England.

BEYFUS, Drusilla. British (born England), b. 1927?. **Genres:** Human Relations/Parenting, Social Commentary. **Career:** Sunday Express, women's editor, 1952-53; Queen Magazine, associate editor, 1959-63; The Observer, home editor, 1962-64; Weekend Telegraph Magazine, associate editor, 1963-71; Brides and Setting Up Home Magazine, editor, 1971-79; Vogue Magazine, associate editor, 1979-86; Sunday Telegraph, columnist, 1989-90; Central St. Martin's College of Art, visiting tutor, 1989-2007; Telegraph Magazine, contributing editor, 1991-2008; You, columnist, 1994-2002. **Publications:** (With A. Edwards) Lady Behave, 1956, rev. ed., 1969; The English Marriage, 1968; The Brides Book, 1981; (contrib.) The Art of Giving, 1987; Modern Manners: The Essential Guide to Living in the 90s, 1992; Courtship Parties, 1992; Sex, Business, 1993; (co-author) Photographs by Snowdon: A Retrospective, 2000. **Address:** 51g Eaton Sq., London, GL SW1 W9RE, England. **Online address:** drusy@clara.co.uk

BEYNON, Huw. Welsh (born Wales), b. 1942. **Genres:** Industrial Relations, Sociology, Business/Trade/Industry, Economics. **Career:** University of Bristol, lecturer in sociology, 1968-73; Victoria University of Manchester, Simon Marks fellow, 1973-75; University of Southern Illinois, visiting associate professor of sociology, 1975-76; University of Durham, lecturer, 1976-81, reader in sociology, 1981-; Strong Words, founder, 1977; University of Manchester, Department of Sociology, professor and chair, 1987-99; Cardiff University, Cardiff School of Social Science, director, 1999, professor; Wales Institute of Social & Economic Research, Data & Methods, professor, director, 2009-10, retired, 2010. Writer. **Publications:** (With R.M. Blackburn) Perceptions of Work: Variations Within a Factory, 1972; Working for Ford, 1973, 2nd ed., 1982; (with T. Nichols) Living with Capitalism: Class Relations and the Modern Factory, 1977; What Happened at Speke?, 1978; (contrib.) Work and Society, 1978; (with H. Wainwright) The Workers Report on Vickers: The Vickers Shop Stewards Combine Committee Report on Work, Wages, Rationalisation, Closure and Rank-and-File Organisation in a Multinational Company, 1979; (with N. Hedges) Born to Work: Images of Factory Life, 1982; Shop Floor Trade Unionism, 1983; (with T. Austrin) The Hope of the World: Class and Politics on the Durham Coalfield, 1983; (with R. Hudson and D. Sadler) A Tale of Two Industries: The Decline of Coal and Steel in the Northeast, 1991; (with H. Hudson and D. Sadler) A Place Called Teesside: A Locality in a Global Economy, 1994; (with T. Austrin) Masters and Servants: Class and Patronage in the Making of a Labour Organisation, 1994; Neoliberalismo, Trabalho e Sindicatos: Reestruturação Produtiva na Inglaterra e no Brasil, 1997; (with A. Cox and R. Hudson) Digging up Trouble: Opencast Coal Mining, the Environment and Social Protest, 2000; (co-author) Managing Employment Change: The New Realities of Work, 2002; (with M. Harvey and S. Quilley) Exploring the Tomato: Transformations of Nature, Society and Economy, 2003. EDITOR: (ed. with K. Armstrong) Hello, Are You Working? Memories of the Thirties in the North East of England, 1977; Digging Deeper: Issues in the Miners Strike, 1985; (with P. Glavanis) Patterns of Social Inequality, 1999; (with S. Rowbotham) Looking at Class, 2001; (with T. Nichols) Patterns of Work in the Post-Fordist Era: Fordism and Post-Fordism, 2006; (with T. Nichols) The Fordism of Ford and Modern Management: Fordism and Post-Fordism, 2006. **Address:** School of Social Sciences, Cardiff University, 1.01, 46 Park Pl., Glamorgan Bldg., King Edward VII Ave., Cardiff, SG CF10 3WT, Wales. **Online address:** beynonh@cf.ac.uk

BHABHA, Homi K. American/Indian (born India), b. 1949. **Genres:** Young Adult Non-fiction. **Career:** Harvard University, Department of English, Anne F. Rothenberg professor of English and American literature and language, 2001-06, Anne F. Rothenberg professor of the humanities, 2006-, Humanities Center, director, 2005-; University College, distinguished visiting professor, 2004-. Writer. **Publications:** NONFICTION: (ed.) Nation and Narration, 1990; The Location of Culture, 2004; (contrib.) Negotiating Rapture: The Power of Art to Transform Lives, 1996; (with P.L. Tazzi) Anish Kapoor, 1998; (with C.A. Breckenridge, S. Pollock and D. Chakrabarty) Cosmopolitanism, 2002; (with W.J.T. Mitchell) Edward Said: Continuing the Conversation, 2005; (contrib.) Without Boundary: Seventeen Ways of Looking, 2006; (contrib.) Naciones Literarias, 2006; Georges Adéagbo: Grand Tour di un Africano, 2008. **Address:** Humanities Center, Harvard University, 134 Barker Ctr., 12 Quincy St., Cambridge, MA 02138, U.S.A. **Online address:** hbhabha@fas.harvard.edu

BHAGAT, Chetan. Indian (born India), b. 1974. **Genres:** Novels, Information Science/Computers, Human Relations/Parenting. **Career:** Goldman Sachs (investment bank), associate, 1998-; Deutsche Bank, investment banker. Writer. **Publications:** Five Point Someone: What Not to Do at IIT (novel), 2004; One Night @ the Call Center (novel), 2005; The 3 Mistakes of My Life, 2008; 2 States: The Story Of My Marriage, 2009; Revolution 2020, 2011. Contributor to journals and periodicals. **Address:** c/o Bhavna Sharma, Corporate Voice/Weber Shandwick Private Ltd., 212, 2nd Fl., Okhla Industrial Estate, Phase-III, New Delhi, DH 110 020, India. **Online address:** info@chetanbhagat.com

BHALA, Raj. American/Canadian (born Canada), b. 1962. **Genres:** Law, Money/Finance, Business/Trade/Industry. **Career:** Federal Reserve Bank of New York, Legal Department, attorney, 1989-93; College of William and Mary, Marshall-Wythe School of Law, associate professor, 1993-98; George Washington University, School of Law, professor, 1998-2003, Patricia Roberts Harris research professor, 2000-03, associate dean for international and comparative legal studies, 2001-03; World Bank, consultant; International Monetary Fund, consultant; University of Kansas, School of Law, Rice distinguished professor, 2003-, associate dean for international and comparative law, 2011-; Heenan Blaikie (Canada), foreign legal consultant, 2009-. Writer. **Publications:** Perspectives on Risk-Based Capital, 1989; (with E.T. Patrikis and T.C. Baxter, Jr.) Wire Transfers: A Guide to U.S. and International Laws Governing Funds Transfers, 1993; Foreign Bank Regulation after BCCI, 1994; Towards a Payments System Law for Developing and Transition Economies, 1995; International Trade Law: Cases and Materials, 1996, 3rd ed. as International Trade Law: Interdisciplinary Theory and Practice, 2008; Global Foreign Exchange Trading: Fundamentals, Market Practice, Law, and Policy, 1996; International Payments and Five Foundations of Wire Transfer Law, 1996; The Law of Foreign Exchange, 1997; World Trade Law: The GATT-WTO System, Regional Arrangements, and U.S. Law, 1998; Global Business Law: Principles and Practice, 1999; Trade, Development and Social Justice, 2003; Modern GATT Law: A Treatise on the General Agreement on Tariffs and Trade, 2005, 2nd ed., 2013; Dictionary of International Trade Law, 2008; Understanding Islamic Law (Shari'a), 2011. Contributor to books and journals. **Address:** School of Law, University of Kansas, Green Hall, 1535 W 15th St., Lawrence, KS 66045, U.S.A. **Online address:** bhala@ku.edu

BHATIA, June. *See* **FORRESTER, Helen.**

BHATT, Jagdish J(eyshanker). (J. J. Bhatt). American/Indian (born India), b. 1939. **Genres:** Earth Sciences, Marine Sciences/Oceanography, Education. **Career:** Jackson Community College, instructor in physical science and chemistry, 1964-65; Panhandle State University, instructor in physical science and geology, 1965-66; Stanford University, scientist in geology, 1971-72; State University of New York, assistant professor, 1972-74; geo-resources and environmental consultant, 1972-75; Community College of Rhode Island, assistant professor, 1974-79, associate professor, 1979-84, professor of geology and oceanography, 1984-, now professor emeritus, Applied Oceanography Student Workshop, project director, 1976-81; University of Rhode Island, School of Oceanography, visiting professor, 1995. Writer. **Publications:** Laboratory Manual on Physical Geology, 1966; Laboratory Manual on Physical Science, 1966; Cretaceous History of Himalayan Geosyncline, 1966; (contrib.) Mineral Exploitation and Economic Geology, 1971; Environmentology: Earth's Environment and Energy Resources, 1975; Geochemistry and Petrology of South Wales Main Limestone, 1976; Geologic Exploration of Earth, 1976; Introduction to Geochemistry and Geology of South Wales' Main Limestones, Lower Carboniferous, 1976; (as J.J. Bhatt) Oceanography: Exploring the Planet Ocean, 1978, 2nd ed., 1983; Applied Oceanography:

Mining, Energy and Management, 1979; Applied Oceanography Manuals, vol. I: Mineral Resources and Geologic Process, vol. II: Marine Fisheries, vol. III: Sea-Farming, vol. IV: Ocean Energy, vol. V: Sea Mammals, vol. VI: Marine Pollution, vol. VII: Underwater Habitat by Man, 1983; Ocean Enterprise: Domain of Resources, Policies and Conflicts, 1984; Oceanography Year 2000 and Beyond, 1988; Odyssey of the Damned (novel), 1992; Oceanography-Concepts and Applications, 1994; Laboratory in Historical Geology, 1995; Spinning Mind, Spinning Time, c'est la vie, 1999; Oceanography Textbook; Geolab Studies; Exploring the Earth's History: Laboratory Manual; Odyssey of Perception: Selected Poems; Human Endeavor: Essence & Mission: A Call for Global Awakening, 2010. Contributor to journals. **Address:** Department of Physics, Community College of Rhode Island, Rm. 2288, Knight Campus, 400 E Ave., Warwick, RI 02886-1807, U.S.A. **Online address:** jbhatt@ccri.edu

BHATT, J. J. *See* **BHATT, Jagdish J(eyshanker).**

BHATT, Sujata. German/Indian (born India), b. 1956. **Genres:** Poetry, Plays/Screenplays. **Career:** University of Victoria, writer-in-residence; Dickinson College, visiting fellow, 1992. Freelance writer and translator. **Publications:** POETRY: Brunizem, 1988; Monkey Shadows, 1991; Freak Waves (chapbook), 1992; The Stinking Rose, 1995; Point No Point: Selected Poems, 1997; Augatora, 2000; My Mother's Way of Wearing a Sari, 2000; A Colour for Solitude, 2002. OTHERS: (trans.) Mickle Makes Muckle: Poems, Mini Plays and Short Prose, 2007; Pure Lizard, 2008. **Address:** c/o Author Mail, Carcanet Press, Alliance House, 30 Cross St., 4th Fl., Manchester, GM M2 7AQ, England.

BHATTACHARYA, Nalinaksha. Indian (born India), b. 1949. **Genres:** Novels, Young Adult Fiction, Literary Criticism And History. **Career:** National Society for the Prevention of Blindness, proofreader of opthalmic journals, 1972-73; Directorate of Estates, Ministry of Works and Housing, assistant, 1973-81; Ministry of Agriculture, section officer, 1981-85; Ministry of Environment and Forests, section officer, 1985-94, under secretary, 1994-. Writer. **Publications:** NOVELS: Hem and Football, 1992; Hem and Maxine, 1995; A Fistful of Desire, 1997; Im Himmel spielen die Götter Fubball, 2005. Contributor to books. **Address:** Ministry of Environment & Forests, Paryavaran Bhavan, CGO Complex, Lodhi Rd., New Delhi, DH 110 003, India. **Online address:** bhattach@ms.umanitoba.ca

BHIKSHU, Cheng Chien. *See* **POCESKI, Mario.**

BHOTE, Keki R. American/Indian (born India), b. 1925. **Genres:** Administration/Management, Business/Trade/Industry, Economics. **Career:** Glencoe Board of Education, president, 1969-73; Motorola, director of quality and value assurance, 1970-80, Quality and Productivity Improvement Group, director of quality, 1980-85, senior corporate consultant, 1985-92; New Trier Township, president, 1977-85; Keki R. Bhote Associates, president, 1992-; Illinois Institute of Technology, associate professor; University of San Diego, visiting professor. Writer. **Publications:** (Co-author) Value Analysis Methods, 1974; Supply Management: How to Make U.S. Suppliers Competitive, 1987; World Class Quality: Design of Experiments Made Easier, More Cost Effective than SPC, 1988, 2nd ed. as World Class Quality: Using Design of Experiments to Make it Happen, 2000; Strategic Supply Management, 1989; The Next Operation as Customer (NOAC), 1991; Beyond Customer Satisfaction to Customer Loyalty, 1996; The Ultimate Six Sigma: Beyond Quality Excellence to Total Business Excellence, 2002; The Power of Ultimate Six Sigma: Keki Bhote's Proven System for Moving beyond Quality Excellence to Total Business Excellence, 2003; (with A.K. Bhote) World Class Reliability: Using Multiple Environment Overstress Tests to Make it Happen, 2004. **Address:** Keki R. Bhote Associates, 493 Woodlawn Ave., Glencoe, IL 60022, U.S.A. **Online address:** krbhote@msn.com

BI, Feiyu. Also writes as Bi Feiyu zhu. Chinese (born China), b. 1964. **Genres:** Novels, Novellas/Short Stories. **Career:** Nanjing Daily, journalist; Yu Hua, editor. Poet. **Publications:** IN CHINESE: (co-author) Shanghai Triad, 1996; Nan Ren Hai Sheng Xia Shen Mo, 2001; Di Qiu Shang De Wang JiaZhuang, 2002; Bi Feiyu Xiao Shuo (short stories), 2006. AS BI FEIYU ZHU: Ping yuan, 2009; Qing yi, 2010. Contributor to periodicals. **Address:** Susijn Agency Ltd., 64 Great Titchfield St., 3rd Fl., London, GL W1W 7QH, England.

BIAGINI, Eugenio F. British (born England), b. 1958. **Genres:** History, Politics/Government. **Career:** Princeton University, faculty; University of Cambridge, Robinson College, faculty, Sidney Sussex College, professor and fellow. Writer. **Publications:** Liberty, Retrenchment and Reform: Popular Liberalism in the Age of Gladstone, 1860-1880, 1992; Progressisti e puritani: aspetti della tradizione liberal-laburista in Gran Bretagna: 1865-1992, 1995; Gladstone, 2000; (with D. Beales) The Risorgimento and the Unification of Italy, 2nd ed., 2002; British Democracy and Irish Nationalism, 1876-1906, 2007. EDITOR: (with A.J. Reid) Currents of Radicalism: Popular Radicalism, Organised Labour and Party Politics in Britain, 1850-1914, 1991; (with T. Raffaelli and R.M. Tullberg) Alfred Marshall's Lectures to Women: Some Economic Questions Directly Connected to the Welfare of the Laborer, 1995; Citizenship and Community: Liberals, Radicals and Collective Identities in the British Isles, 1865-1931, 1996; (with C.A. Bayly) Giuseppe Mazzini and the Globalisation of Democratic Nationalism 1830-1920, 2008. Works appear in anthologies. **Address:** Cambridge, CB , England. **Online address:** efb21@cam.ac.uk

BIAGIOLI, Mario. American/Italian (born Italy), b. 1955. **Genres:** Sciences. **Career:** University of California, lecturer, associate professor, 1988-92; Stanford University, visiting professor, 1992; École des Hautes Études en Sciences Sociales, visiting professor, 1992, 1999; Harvard University, professor of the history of science, 1995-2010, distinguished professor of law and science and technology studies, Center for Innovation Studies, director; UC Davis School of Law, King Hall, professor of law, professor of science and technology studies; University of Aberdeen, faculty, visiting sixth century chair of modern thought, 2007-08. Writer, historian and biographer. **Publications:** (With P. Pellagalli, N. Poli and A. Stuppini) Contrattazione Aziendale e Retribuzione: Un'indagine Empirica Sull'esperienza Dell'Emilia Romagna, 1984; Galileo, Courtier: The Practice of Science in the Culture of Absolutism, 1993; (ed.) The Science Studies Reader, 1999; (ed. with P. Galison) Scientific Authorship: Credit and Intellectual Property in Science, 2003; Galileo's Instruments of Credit: Telescopes, Images, Secrecy, 2006; (ed.) Making and Unmaking Intellectual Property, 2011; The Author as Vegetable, forthcoming. Contributor to books, periodicals and journals. **Address:** Department of Science, Harvard University, 457 Science Ctr., Cambridge, MA 02138, U.S.A. **Online address:** biagioli@fas.harvard.edu

BIAL, Raymond. American (born United States), b. 1948. **Genres:** Children's Non-fiction, Photography. **Career:** Parkland College Library, library director, 1988-2004. Writer. **Publications:** FICTION FOR CHILDREN: The Fresh Grave and Other Ghostly Stories, 1997; The Ghost of Honeymoon Creek, 1999; Shadow Island: A Tale of Lake Superior, 2006. NONFICTION FOR CHILDREN: Corn Belt Harvest, 1991; County Fair, 1992; Amish Home, 1993; Frontier Home, 1993; Shaker Home, 1994; The Underground Rairoad, 1995; Portrait of a Farm Family, 1995; With Needle and Thread, 1996; Mist over the Mountains: Appalachia and Its People, 1997; The Strength of These Arms: Life in the Slave Quarters, 1997; Where Lincoln Walked, 1997; Cajun Home, 1998; One-Room School, 1999; A Handful of Dirt, 2000; Ghost Towns of the American West, 2001; A Book Comes Together: From Idea to Library, 2002; Tenement: Immigrant Life on the Lower East Side, 2002; The Long Walk: The Story of Navajo Captivity, 2003; Where Washington Walked, 2004; Nauvoo: Mormon City on the Mississippi River, 2006. LIFEWAYS SERIES: The Navajo, 1999; The Cherokee, 1999; The Iroquois, 1999; The Sioux, 1999; The Ojibwe, 2000; The Pueblo, 2000; The Seminole, 2000; The Comanche, 2000; The Apache, 2001; The Huron, 2001; The Haida, 2001; The Cheyenne, 2001; The Inuit, 2002; The Shoshone, 2002; The Powhatan, 2002; The Nez Perce, 2002; The Blackfeet, 2003; The Tlingit, 2003; The Mandan, 2003; The Choctaw, 2003; The Delaware, 2004; The Chumash, 2004; The Arapaho, 2004; The Wampanoag, 2004; The Shawnee, 2004; The Menominee, 2006; The Crow, 2006; The Cree, 2006. BUILDING AMERICA SERIES: The Mills, 2002; The Houses, 2002; The Forts, 2002; The Farms, 2002; The Canals, 2002. AMERICAN COMMUNITY SERIES: Missions and Presidios, 2004; Longhouses, 2004; Frontier Settlements, 2004; Early American Villages, 2004; Cow Towns, 2004. OTHER: Ivesdale: A Photographic Essay, 1982; In All My Years: Portraits of Oalder Blacks in Champaign-Urbana, 1983, rev. ed. 1985; (ed. with F.A. Schlipf) Upon a Quiet Landscape: The Photographs of Frank Sadorus, 1983; There is a Season, 1984; Common Ground: Photographs of Rural and Small Town Life, 1986; Stopping By: Portraits from Small Towns, 1988; (with L.L. Bial) The Carnegie Library in Illinois, 1988; From the Heart of the Country: Photographs of the Midwestern Sky, 1991; Looking Good: A Guide to Photographing Your Library, 1991; Champaign: A Pictorial History, 1993; Urbana: A Pictorial History, 1994; Visit to Amish Country, 1995; Zoom Lens Photography, 1996; The Super

Soybean, 2007; Champaign, 2008; The Shaker Village, 2008; Ellis Island, 2009; Rescuing Rover: A Book About Saving Our Dogs, 2011. **Address:** First Light Photography, PO Box 593, Urbana, IL 61801, U.S.A. **Online address:** ray@raybial.com

BIALE, Rachel (Korati). Israeli (born Israel), b. 1952. **Genres:** Children's Fiction, Law. **Career:** Jewish Family and Children's Services of the East Bay, clinical social worker and psychotherapy senior clinician, 1990-97; Jewish studies lecturer; Progressive Jewish Alliance, regional director; Osher Marin JCC, director of community education; Bible by the Bay, director. Writer. **Publications:** SELF-ILLUSTRATOR: LET'S MAKE A BOOK ABOUT IT SERIES: We Are Moving, 1996; My Pet Died, 1997. OTHER: Women in Jewish Law: An Exploration of Women's Issues in Halakhic Sources, 1984, 2nd ed. as Women and Jewish Law: The Essential Texts, Their History and Their Relevance for Today, 1995. **Address:** Jewish Family & Children's Services, 2484 Shattuck Ave., Ste. 210, Berkeley, CA 94704, U.S.A. **Online address:** biale@socrates.berkeley.edu

BIALER, Uri. Israeli (born Israel), b. 1944. **Genres:** History, Social Commentary, International Relations/Current Affairs, Theology/Religion, Adult Non-fiction. **Career:** Israeli Foreign Ministry, senior research officer, 1973-74; The Hebrew University of Jerusalem, Department of International Relations, faculty, 1975-, professor of international relations, Maurice B. Hexter chair in international relations Middle Eastern studies, chair, 1990-93, dean of students, 1994-98, Shaltiel Center for Pre-Academic Studies, director, 2007-10, professor emeritus, 2011-; Oxford University, St. Antony's College, visiting fellow, 1979-80, research fellow; University of Chicago, visiting professor, 1993-94; Harvard University, visiting fellow, 1999-2000; Yad Ben-Zvi Institute, Center for the Study of the Land of Israel, director. Writer. **Publications:** NONFICTION: Armed Forces in Foreign Territories under the Terms of Peace Agreements: Historical Implications, 1979; The Shadow of the Bomber: The Fear of Air Attack and British Politics, 1932-1939, 1980; Our Place in the World: Mapai and Israel's Foreign Policy Orientation, 1947-1952, 1981; Between East and West: Israel's Foreign Policy Orientation, 1948-1956, 1990; Oil and the Arab-Israeli Conflict, 1948-63, 1999; Cross on the Star of David: The Christian World in Israel's Foreign Policy, 1948-1967, 2005; Tselav be-magen Daṿid: ha-'olam ha-Notsri bi-mediniyut ha-ḥuts shel Yiśra'el, 1948-1967, 2006. **Address:** Department of International Relations, The Hebrew University of Jerusalem, Mt. Scopus, Jerusalem, 91905, Israel. **Online address:** msbialer@mscc.huji.ac.il

BIANCHI, Eugene Carl. American (born United States), b. 1930. **Genres:** Theology/Religion, Young Adult Fiction. **Career:** St. Ignatius High School, instructor, 1955-58; American Magazine, international correspondent, 1958-62, assistant editor, 1963-66; University of Santa Clara, assistant professor of religion and director of center for study of contemporary values, 1966-68, visiting fellow, 1973; Emory University, professor of religion, 1968-, now professor emeritus, Graduate Department of Theological Studies, chair, 1976-81, Emeritus College, director, 2001-; University of San Francisco, visiting fellow, 1966, 1968; Stanford University, visiting fellow, 1969; Federation of Christian Ministries, founder and president, 1969-71; University of California, Danforth Underwood fellow, 1972-73; Graduate Theological Union, Center for Ethics and Social Policy, visiting fellow, 1974; California State University, distinguished visiting professor, 1975; National AAR, Religion and Ecology Group, coordinator, 1992-94. **Publications:** John XXIII and American Protestants, 1968; Reconciliation: The Function of the Church, 1969; The Religious Experience of Revolutionaries, 1972; (with Rosemary R. Ruether) From Machismo to Mutuality, 1975; Aging as a Spiritual Journey, 1982; On Growing Older, 1985; (ed. with R.R. Ruether) A Democratic Catholic Church, 1992; Elder Wisdom: Crafting Your Own Elderhood, 1994; (with P. McDonough) Passionate Uncertainty: Inside the American Jesuits, 2002; Bishop of San Francisco: Romance, Intrigue and Religion, 2005. **Address:** Department of Religion, Emory University, 1111 Clairmont Ave. J6, S214 Callaway Ctr., 537 Kilgo Cir., PO Box 1535/002/1AA, Atlanta, GA 30322, U.S.A. **Online address:** releb@emory.edu

BIANCO, Anthony. American (born United States), b. 1953. **Genres:** Business/Trade/Industry, Biography, Economics. **Career:** Minneapolis Tribune, reporter, 1977; Willamette Week, business writer, 1978-80; Business Week, San Francisco correspondent, 1980-82, staff editor, 1982, department editor in markets and investments, 1983-84, associate editor, 1984-85, senior writer, 1985-92, 1996-2005, national correspondent, 2005. **Publications:** Rainmaker: The Saga of Jeff Beck, Wall Street's Mad Dog, 1991; The Reichmanns: Family, Faith, Fortune and the Empire of Olympia and York, 1997; Ghosts of 42nd Street: A History of America's Most Infamous Block, 2004; Wal-Mart: The Bully of Bentonville: How the High Cost of Everyday Low Prices is Hurting America, 2006; Big Lie: Spying, Scandal and Ethical Collapse at Hewlett-Packard, 2010. Contributor to periodicals. **Address:** Business Week, 1221 Ave. of the Americas, 43rd Fl., New York, NY 10020, U.S.A. **Online address:** tony_bianco@businessweek.com

BIANK, Tanya. American (born United States) **Genres:** Military/Defense/Arms Control, Autobiography/Memoirs, Biography, Adult Non-fiction. **Career:** Fayetteville Observer, reporter; Military.com, columnist. Educator and writer. **Publications:** Under the Sabers: The Unwritten Code of Army Wives, 2006; Army Wives: The Unwritten Code of Military Marriage, 2006. **Address:** c/o Rachel Ekstrom, St. Martin's Press, 175 5th Ave., New York, NY 10010, U.S.A. **Online address:** tanya@tanyabiank.com

BICÂT, Tony. British (born England), b. 1945. **Genres:** Plays/Screenplays, Education, Film, Communications/Media. **Career:** Portable Theatre, co-founder and director, 1968-72; writer, director and lyricist, 1972-. **Publications:** Dinosaur, 1974; Trotsky Is Dead, 1975; It's Only Rock 'n Roll, 1975; Glitter, 1976; Devil's Island, 1977; (co-author) All's Well That Ends, 1978; Zigomania, 1978; Face Lift, 1982; Star Trap, 1988; The Laughter of God, 1990; The Wordsworth Murders, 1991; (with T. MacNabb) Creative Screen Writing, 2002; A Buyer's Market, 2002; Robin of Wychwood, 2003; Creative TV Writing, 2007. **Address:** Berlin Associates, 7 Tyers Gate, London, GL SE1 3HX, England.

BICCHIERI, Cristina. American/Italian (born Italy), b. 1950. **Genres:** Philosophy, Social Sciences, Natural History. **Career:** Harvard University, Ford Foundation fellow, 1980-81; Columbia University, Barnard College, assistant professor of economics and philosophy, 1984-86; University of Notre Dame, assistant professor of philosophy, 1986-89; University of Chicago, Center for Ethics, Rationality and Society, research fellow, 1987-89; University of Pittsburgh, Center for Philosophy of Science, research associate, 1989-, Department of History and Philosophy of Science, associate professor, 1989-94, adjunct professor, 1994-2004; Carnegie Mellon University, Department of Philosophy and Social and Decision Sciences, associate professor, 1989-94, professor, 1994-2004; Wissenschaftskolleg zu Berlin, fellow, 2001-02; University of Pennsylvania, Carol and Michael Lowenstein professor of philosophy and legal studies, 2004-, Philosophy, Politics and Economics Program, director, 2004-, Graduate Group in Psychology, faculty, 2006-; UNICEF Human Rights Program, consultant. Writer. **Publications:** (Co-author) Modelli di Razionalita Nelle Scienze Economico-Sociali, 1982; Ragioni per Crederem Ragioni per Fare: Convenzioni e Vincoli nel Metodo Scientifico, 1988; Rationality and Coordination, 1993; The Grammar of Society: The Nature and Dynamics of Social Norms, 2006; Why Does Game Theory Matter to Philosophy, forthcoming. EDITOR: (with M.L.D. Chiara) Knowledge, Belief and Strategic Interaction, 1992; (with R. Jeffrey and B. Skyrms) The Dynamics of Norms, 1995; (with R. Jeffrey and B. Skyrms) The Logic of Strategy, 1999. **Address:** Department of Philosophy, University of Pennsylvania, 491 Claudia Cohen Hall, 249 S 36th St., Philadelphia, PA 19104-6304, U.S.A. **Online address:** cb36@sas.upenn.edu

BICERANO, Jozef. American/Turkish (born Turkey), b. 1952. **Genres:** Chemistry, Engineering. **Career:** University of California, postdoctoral research associate, 1981-82; Energy Conversion Devices Inc., senior research scientist, 1982-86; Dow Chemical Co., researcher, 1986-2004; Bicerano & Associates L.L.C., president and founder; Eastern Michigan University, College of Technology, adjunct faculty; American Physical Society, fellow, 1996. Writer, scientist and consultant. **Publications:** Prediction of Polymer Properties, 1993, 3rd ed., 2002. EDITOR: (with D. Adler) Proceedings of the International Conference on the Theory of the Structures of Non-Crystalline Solids, 1985; Computational Modeling of Polymers, 1992. Contributor to scientific journals. **Address:** Bicerano & Associates Consulting Inc., 1208 Wildwood St., Midland, MI 48642, U.S.A. **Online address:** bicerano@polymerexpert.biz

BICKERSTAFF, Steve. American (born United States), b. 1946. **Genres:** Law, History. **Career:** Texas Constitutional Revision Commission and Texas Constitutional Convention, legal counsel, 1973-74, director of Legislative Council Office of Constitutional Research, 1974-75; parliamentarian for Texas Senate and for Texas Senate Sitting as a Court of Impeachment, 1974-76; assistant attorney general, 1976-79; Oppenheimer, Rosenberg, Kelleher and

Wheatley (law firm), associate, 1979-80; Bickerstaff, Heath and Smiley (law firm), founder and partner, 1980-99; University of Texas, Law School, adjunct professor, 1992-97, visiting and adjunct professor, 2000-07; University of St. Gallen, Executive Masters of European and International Business Law Programme, professor, 2000-05; University of Goettingen, visiting professor, 2000; Texas Legislative Redistricting Board on Reapportionment and Voting Rights, special consultant, 2000-01; Corporate Systems Inc., chairman, 2003-04. Writer. **Publications:** (co-author) The Constitution of the State of Texas: An Annotated and Comparative Analysis, 1976; Reapportionment by State and Local Governments: A Guide for the 1980s, 1981; Lines in the Sand: Congressional Redistricting in Texas and the Downfall of Tom DeLay, 2007. Contributor to journals. **Address:** 41571 State Hwy. 118, Fort Davis, TX 79734-2523, U.S.A. **Online address:** sbickerstaff@law.utexas.edu

BICKERTON, David M. British/French (born France), b. 1944. **Genres:** Language/Linguistics, Communications/Media, Biography, Translations, History. **Career:** University of Glasgow, lecturer, 1969-86, senior lecturer in French, 1986-93, Language Centre, director, 1983-93; Satellite Materials in Language Education, project director, 1989-93; University of Bergamo, Produzione di Materiali Didattici in Lingue inglese perorientatori nei Centri Informagiovani, partner, 1992-94; Rapid Authoring of Packages Using Innovative Development Tools, coordinator, 1997-98; University of Plymouth, professor of modern languages, 1993-98, director of modern languages, 1993-98, research professor, 1999-2001; Subject Centre for Languages, Linguistics and Area Studies, chair of specialist advisory group, 2000-; University of Southampton, visiting professor, 2002-05, consultant. **Publications:** Marc-Auguste and Charles Pictet, the Biblioth Fque britannique (1796-1815) and the Dissemination of British Literature and Science on the Continent, 1986. EDITOR: (with J. Proud) The Transmission of Culture in Western Europe, 1750-1850: Papers Celebrating the Bicentenary of the Foundation of the Bibliotheque Britannique (1796-1815) in Geneva, 1999; (with M. Gotti) Language Centres: Integration through Innovation, 1999; (with R. Sigrist) Marc-Auguste Pictet 1752-1825, Correspondance Sciences et Techniques, vol. II, The British Correspondents, 2000. Contributor to books and periodicals. **Address:** Dremmwel, Valanec, Hanvec, 29460, France. **Online address:** davidbick01@hotmail.com

BICKFORD-SMITH, Vivian. South African/British (born England), b. 1955. **Genres:** Area Studies, Third World, History. **Career:** Rhodes University, assistant lecturer in history, 1980-81; University of Cape Town, temporary lecturer, 1982-87, lecturer, 1987-95, senior lecturer in history, 1995-, Department of Historical studies, professor, head; University of London, Institute of Historical Research, Centre for Metropolitan History, visiting professor of comparative metropolitan history. Writer. **Publications:** (Ed. with E.V. Heyningen) The Waterfront, 1994; Ethnic Pride and Racial Prejudice in Victorian Cape Town, 1995; (with N. Worden and E.V. Heyningen) Cape Town: The Making of a City, 1998; (with N. Worden and E.V. Heyningen) Cape Town in the Twentieth Century: An Illustrated Social History, 1999; (ed. with R. Mendelsohn) Black and White in Colour: African History on Screen, 2007. Contributor to books. **Address:** Department of History, University of Cape Town, Rondebosch 7700, Rm. 230, Beattie Bldg., Cape Town, 021, South Africa. **Online address:** vivian.bickford@sas.ac.uk

BICKS, Caroline. American (born United States), b. 1966?. **Genres:** Literary Criticism And History, History. **Career:** Ohio State University, assistant professor; Boston College, associate professor of English. Writer. **Publications:** Midwiving Subjects in Shakespeare's England, 2003. Contributor to books. **Address:** Boston College, Carney Hall 429, Chestnut Hill, MA 02467, U.S.A. **Online address:** bicks@bc.edu

BIDART, Frank. American (born United States), b. 1939. **Genres:** Poetry. **Career:** Wellesley College, Department of English, faculty, 1972-; Brandeis University, faculty; Academy of American Poets, chancellor. Writer. **Publications:** Poetry Collections: Golden State, 1973; The Book of the Body, 1977; The Sacrifice, 1983; In the Western Night: Collected Poems, 1965-90, 1990; Desire, 1997; Music Like Dirt, 2002; (ed. with D. Gewanter) Robert Lowell: Collected Poems, 2003; Star Dust, 2005; Watching the Spring Festival, 2008. **Address:** Department of English, Wellesley College, FND 124B, 103 Founders Hall, 106 Central St., Wellesley, MA 02481, U.S.A.

BIDDISS, Michael Denis. British (born England), b. 1942. **Genres:** History, Intellectual History, International Relations/Current Affairs. **Career:** Downing College, fellow, 1966-73, director of studies in history, 1970-73; University of Victoria, visiting professor, 1973; University of Leicester, lecturer, 1973-78, reader in history, 1978-79; University of Cape Town, visiting professor, 1976, 1978; University of Reading, professor of history, 1979-2004, dean, faculty of letters and social sciences, 1982-85, emeritus professor, 2004-; Monash University, visiting professor, 1989; Historical Association, president, 1991-94, fellow, 2006-; Society of Apothecaries, Faculty of the History and Philosophy of Medicine, president, 1994-98; Royal Historical Society, vice president, 1995-99; Nanjing University, visiting professor, 1997. Writer. **Publications:** Father of Racist Ideology: The Social and Political Thought of Count Gobineau, 1970; (with F.F. Cartwright) Disease and History, 1972, rev. ed., 2000; The Age of the Masses: Ideas and Society in Europe since 1870, 1977; The Nuremberg Trial and the Third Reich, 1992; (with N. Atkin and F. Tallett) The Wiley-Blackwell Dictionary of Modern European History since 1789, 2010. EDITOR: (intro.) Gobineau: Selected Political Writings, 1970; (intro.) Images of Race, 1979; (with K. Minogue) Thatcherism: Personality and Politics, 1987; (with M. Wyke) The Uses and Abuses of Antiquity, 1999; (with S. Peters and I. Roe) The Humanities in the New Millennium, 2002; (with N. Atkin) Themes in Modern European History, 1890-1945, 2008. **Address:** Department of History, University of Reading, Whiteknights, PO Box 217, Reading, BR RG6 6AH, England. **Online address:** m.d.biddiss@reading.ac.uk

BIDDLE, Bruce Jesse. American (born United States), b. 1928. **Genres:** Education, Psychology, Sociology, Economics, Self Help. **Career:** Wayne State University, research associate in education, 1953, 1956-57; University of Kentucky, assistant professor of sociology, 1957-58; University of Kansas City (now University of Missouri at Kansas), associate professor of education, 1958-60; University of Missouri, associate professor, 1960-66, professor of psychology and sociology, 1966-2000, emeritus professor, 2000-, Center for Research in Social Behavior, director, 1966-; University of Queensland, visiting associate professor, 1965. Consultant and writer. **Publications:** (With J.P. Twyman and E.R. Rankin, Jr.) Concept of Role Conflict, 1960; (with H.A. Rosencranz and E.F. Rankin) Studies in the Role of the Public School Teacher, 5 vols., 1961; The Present Status of Role Theory, 1961; (co-author) Essays on the Social Systems of Education, 1966; (with R.S. Adams) An Analysis of Classroom Activities; A Final Report, 1967; (with R.S. Adams) Realities of Teaching: Explorations with Videotape, 1970; (with M.J. Dunkin) The Study of Teaching, 1974; (with T.L. Good and J.E. Brophy) Teachers Make a Difference, 1975; Role Theory: Expectations, Identities and Behaviors, 1979; (with D.C. Berliner) The Manufactured Crisis: Myths, Fraud and The Attack On America's Public Schools, 1995; (with L.J. Saha) The Untested Accusation: Principals, Research Knowledge and Policy Making in Schools, 2002. EDITOR: (and contrib. with W.J. Ellena) Contemporary Research on Teacher Effectiveness, 1964; (with E.J. Thomas) Role Theory: Concepts and Research, 1966; (with P.H. Rossi) The New Media and Education: Their Impact Society, 1966; (with D.S. Anderson) Knowledge for Policy: Improving Education Through Research, 1991; (with T.L. Good and I.F. Goodson) International Handbook of Teachers and Teaching, 1997; Social Class, Poverty and Education: Policy and Practice, 2001. Contributor of articles of professional journals. **Address:** Department of Sociology, University of Missouri, 312 Middlebush Hall, Columbia, MO 65211-6100, U.S.A. **Online address:** biddleb@missouri.edu

BIDDLE, Cordelia Frances. (Nero Blanc). American (born United States), b. 1947. **Genres:** Novels, Mystery/Crime/Suspense, Adult Non-fiction. **Career:** Writer. **Publications:** (With M.K. Levenstein) Caring for Your Cherished Possessions: The Experts' Guide to Cleaning, Preserving and Protecting Your China, Silver, Furniture, Clothing, Paintings and More, 1989; Beneath the Wind, 1993; (with P. Hearst) Murder at San Simeon, 1996; Conjurer, 2007; Deception's Daughter, 2008; Without Fear, 2010; (with E.S. Brown, A.J. Heavens and C. Peitz) St. Peter's Church, 2011. AS NERO BLANC WITH S. ZETTLER: The Crossword Murder, 1999; Two Down, 2000; The Crossword Connection, 2001; A Crossword to Die For, 2002; A Crossworder's Holiday, 2002; Corpus de Crossword, 2003; A Crossworder's Gift, 2003; Wrapped up in Crosswords, 2004; Anatomy of a Crossword, 2004; Crossworder's Delight, 2005; Another Word for Murder, 2005; Death on the Diagonal, 2006. **Address:** c/o Alice Martell, 1350 Ave. of Americas, Ste. 1205, New York, NY 10019, U.S.A. **Online address:** cordelia@cordeliafrancesbiddle.com

BIDDLE, Martin. British (born England), b. 1937. **Genres:** Archaeology/Antiquities. **Career:** Ministry of Public Buildings and Works, assistant inspector of ancient monuments, 1961-63; University of Exeter, lecturer in medieval archeology, 1963-67; All Souls College, visiting fellow, 1967-

68; Winchester Research Unit, director, 1968-; University of Pennsylvania, University Museum, director and professor of anthropology and history of art, 1977-81; Christ Church, lecturer of the house, 1983-86; University of Oxford, professor of medieval archeology, 1997-2002, emeritus professor of medieval archeology, 2002-, emeritus fellow, 2002-; The Leverhulme Trust, Leverhulme emeritus fellow, 2005-06, director and secretary; director of several excavations and investigations, 1959-60; Repton, staff, 1974-88, 1993; Canterbury Cathedral, St. Alban's Abbey and Cathedral Church, consultant; Royal Commission on Historical Monuments of England, 1984-95. British archeologist, writer and educator. **Publications:** (With J. Dent) Nonsuch, 1960: The Banqueting House, 1960; (with D.M. Hudson and C.M. Heighway) The Future of London's Past: A Survey of the Archaeological Implications of Planning and Development in the Nation's Capital, 1973; (ed.) Winchester in the Early Middle Ages, 1977; (co-author) Object and Economy in Medieval Winchester, 2 vols., 1990; The Tomb of Christ, 1999; (co-author) The Church of the Holy Sepulchre, 2000; (co-author) King Arthur's Round Table: An Archaeological Investigation, 2001; (with J. Hiller and I. Scott) Henry VIII's Artillery Fort at Camber Castle, 2001; (co-author) Nonsuch Palace: The Material Culture of a Noble Restoration Household, 2005. Contributor to journals. **Address:** Oxford University, Hertford College, Catte St., Oxford, OX OX1 3BW, England. **Online address:** martin.biddle@hertford.ox.ac.uk

BIDDULPH, Steve. Australian (born Australia), b. 1956?. **Genres:** Human Relations/Parenting, Adult Non-fiction, Biography. **Career:** Writer, 1984-; Cairnmillar Institute, School of Psychology, adjunct professor, 2011-; Manhood Online, advisor and contributor. **Publications:** NONFICTION: The Secret of Happy Children: A New Guide for Parents, 1984; (with S. Biddulph) The Making of Love, 1988 in US as The Secret of a Happy Family: Stay in Love as a Couple Through Thick and Thin-and Even with Kids, 1989; More Secrets of Happy Children, 1996; Raising Boys: Why Boys Are Different-And How to Help Them Become Happy and Well-Balanced Men, 1998, 2nd ed., 2008; Manhood: An Action Plan for Changing Men's Lives, 1999; (ed.) Stories of Manhood: Journeys into the Hidden Hearts of Men, 2000; (with S. Biddulph) Love, Laughter and Parenting: In the Years from Birth to Six, 2000; Secret of Happy Children: Why Children Behave the Way They Do and What You Can Do to Help Them to Be Optimistic, Loving, Capable and Happy, 2002; (with S. Biddulph) New Secrets of Happy Children: Embrace Your Power as a Parent and Help Your Children Be Confident, Positve, Well Adjusted and Happy, 2003; Secret Life of Men: A Practical Guide to Helping Men Discover Health, Happiness and Deeper Personal Relationships, 2003; The Complete Secrets of Happy Children, 2003; (with S. Biddulph) Secret of Happy Children, 2004; Raising Babies: Should Under 3s Go to Nursery?, 2006. **Address:** Manhood Online, PO Box 231, Saint Leonards, NW 2065, Australia.

BIDINI, Dave. Canadian (born Canada), b. 1963. **Genres:** Autobiography/Memoirs, Documentaries/Reportage, Sports/Fitness. **Career:** Musician and writer. **Publications:** On a Cold Road: Tales of Adventure in Canadian Rock, 1998; Tropic of Hockey: My Search for the Game in Unlikely Places, 2000; Baseballissimo: My Summer in the Italian Minor Leagues, 2004; The Greatest Hockey Stories Ever, 2004; For Those About to Rock: A Road Map for Being in a Band, 2004; The Best Game You Can Name, 2005; The Five Hole Stories, 2006; For Those About to Write: How I Learned to Love Books and Why I Had to Write Them, 2007; Around the World in 57 1/2 Gigs, 2007; Dingers: Contemporary Baseball Writing, 2008; Home and Away: The Story of the 2008 Homeless World Cup, forthcoming. Contributor to periodicals. **Address:** c/o Author Mail, McClelland & Stewart Ltd., 481 University Ave., Ste. 900, Toronto, ON M5G 2E9, Canada.

BIDNER, Jenni. American (born United States), b. 1963. **Genres:** Photography. **Career:** Petersen's Photographic magazine, editor; Outdoor & Travel Photography, editor; BetterPhoto.com, instructor. Author and photographer. **Publications:** Great Photos with the Advanced Photo System, 1996; The Lighting Cookbook: Foolproof Recipes for Perfect Glamour, Portrait, Still Life and Corporate Photographs, 1997; Digital Photography, 1998; Yearbook Photography, 1998; Digital Photography: A Basic Guide to New Technology, 2000; Digital Camera Basics: Getting the Most from Your Digital Camera, 2002; (with M. Wegner) The Best of Nature Photography: Images and Techniques from the Pros, 2003; Making Family Websites: Fun and Easy Ways to Share Memories, 2003; (with E. Bean) Complete Guide for Models: Inside Advice from Industry Pros, 2004; The Kids Guide to Digital Photography: How to Shoot, Save, Play with and Print Your Digital Photos, 2004; Amphoto's Complete Book of Photography: How to Improve Your Pictures with a Film or Digital Camera, 2004; (with E. Bean) Lighting Cookbook for Fashion and Beauty: Foolproof Recipes for Taking Perfect Portraits, 2005; Is My Dog a Wolf? How Your Pet Compares to Its Wild Cousin, 2006; Kodak Most Basic Book of Digital Printing, 2006; Love Your Dog Pictures: How to Photograph Your Dog with Any Camera, 2006; Is My Cat a Tiger? How Your Pet Compares to Its Wild Cousins, 2006; Dog Heroes: Saving Lives and Protecting America, 2006; Capture the Portrait: How to Create Great Digital Photos, 2008. Contributor of articles to periodicals. **Address:** WI , U.S.A.

BIDNEY, Martin. American (born United States), b. 1943. **Genres:** Literary Criticism And History, Poetry, Romance/Historical. **Career:** Cornell University, lecturer, 1996; State University of New York, instructor, 1969-71, assistant professor, 1971-77, associate professor, 1977-89, professor of English and comparative literature, 1989-2004, professor emeritus of English and comparative literature, 2004-. Writer. **Publications:** Blake and Goethe: Psychology, Ontology, Imagination, 1988; (intro.) Theoretical Anthropology, 2nd ed., 1996; Patterns of Epiphany: From Wordsworth to Tolstoy, Pater and Barrett Browning, 1997; (intro.) Shaped Notes: Stories of 20th Century Georgia, 2001; (contrib.) A Poetic Dialogue with Adam Mickiewicz, 2007; East-West Poetry, 2009; Ronald Gonzalez Black Figures, 2010; (trans. with P.A. von Arnim and intro.) The West-East Divan, 2010; Theorizing Epiphanies: From Byron and Bronte to Chekhov and Biely, forthcoming. Contributor to books. Contributor of articles to journals. **Address:** Department of English, State University of New York, Binghamton University, 4400 Vestal Pkwy. E, PO Box 6000, Binghamton, NY 13902, U.S.A. **Online address:** mbidney@binghamton.edu

BIEDER, Robert E. American (born United States), b. 1938. **Genres:** Anthropology/Ethnology, Sciences, History. **Career:** Grinnell College, assistant professor of history, 1972-73; Newberry Library, Center for the History of the American Indian, assistant director, 1973-74, associate director, 1974-75; University of Illinois, assistant professor of Native American studies, 1977-80; University of Mainz, senior Fulbright lecturer in ethnology and American studies, 1980-81; Indiana University, visiting associate professor of history, 1985-87, Malaysian Program, associate professor, 1987, associate professor of history, 1995-, School of Public and Environmental Affairs, adjunct associate professor, 1996-2000, visiting assistant professor, visiting professor, 2001, now professor emeritus; Free University of Berlin, senior Fulbright lecturer in history, 1988-89; L. Kossuth University, Soros Foundation professor of American civilization, 1991, 1992, senior Fulbright lecturer in history, 1992-94; University of Tampere, senior Fulbright lecturer, 1997-98, finnish academy professor, 2001; University of Debreceu, external doctoral faculty, 2001. Writer. **Publications:** (Ed. and intro.) Kitchi-Gami: Life Among the Lake Superior Ojibway, 1985; Science Encounters the Indian: A Study of the Early Years of American Ethnology, 1820-1880, 1986; A Brief Historical Survey of the Expropriation of American Indian Remains, 1990; Contemplating Others: Cultural Contacts in Red and White America, 1990; Native American Communities in Wisconsin, 1600-1960: A Study of Tradition and Change, 1995; Bear, 2005; A Social, Cultural History of the Concept of the Zoo, forthcoming. Contributor of articles to books and journals. **Address:** Department of History, Indiana University, 742 Ballantine Hall, 1020 E Kirkwood Ave., Bloomington, IN 47405-7103, U.S.A.

BIEDERMAN, Lynn. American (born United States), b. 1962?. **Genres:** Social Sciences, Novels. **Career:** Writer. **Publications:** (With M. Baldini) Unraveling, 2008; (with L. Pazer) Teenage Waistland: A Novel, 2010. **Address:** Delacorte Press, 1745 Broadway, New York, NY 10019, U.S.A. **Online address:** unraveling@lynnbiederman.com

BIEK, David E. American (born United States), b. 1952. **Genres:** Horticulture, Sciences. **Career:** Tacoma Public Library, manager, 1976-. Writer. **Publications:** Mushrooms of Northern California, 1984; Flora of Mount Rainier National Park, 2000. **Address:** Tacoma Public Library, 1102 Tacoma Ave. S, Tacoma, WA 98402, U.S.A. **Online address:** dbiek@tpl.lib.wa.us

BIEL, Steven. American (born United States), b. 1960. **Genres:** History, Humanities. **Career:** Harvard University, lecturer in history and literature, 1990-93, 1998-, preceptor, expository writing, 1994-96, director of studies in history and literature, 1999-2006, Mahindra Humanities Center, executive director, 2005-, senior lecturer on history and literature; Brandeis University, lecturer, 1997-98. Writer. **Publications:** Independent Intellectuals in the United States, 1910-1945, 1992; Down with the Old Canoe: A Cultural History of the Titanic Disaster, 1996; (ed.) Titanica: The Disaster of the Century in Poetry, Prose, and Song, 1998; (ed.) American Disasters, 2001; American Gothic: A Life of America's Most Famous Painting, 2005. Contributor to periodicals. **Address:** Mahindra Humanities Center, Harvard University, Barker Ctr., 12 Quincy St., Cambridge, MA 02138, U.S.A. **Online address:** biel@fas.harvard.edu

BIELEFELD, Wolfgang. American (born United States), b. 1947. **Genres:** Business/Trade/Industry, Economics. **Career:** Indiana University-Purdue University, professor in the School of Public and Environmental Affairs (SPEA) & Center on Philanthropy, adjunct professor, 1999-; University of Texas, faculty; University of Minnesota, faculty; Stanford University, faculty; Lutheran Child and Family Services of Indiana/Kentucky, director. Scholar, social scientist, educator and writer. **Publications:** (with J. Galaskiewicz) Nonprofit Organizations in an Age of Uncertainty: A Study of Organizational Change, 1998; (with S.S. Kennedy) Charitable Choice at Work: Evaluating Faith-based Job Programs in the States, 2006. Contributor to periodicals. **Address:** Indiana University, 425 University Blvd., Indianapolis, IN 46202-5143, U.S.A. **Online address:** wbielefe@iupui.edu

BIELER, Andreas. British/German (born Germany), b. 1967. **Genres:** Economics, Social Sciences. **Career:** University of Cambridge, Newnham College, lecturer in social and political sciences, 1998-2001; University of Nottingham, professor of political economy, 2001-, Centre for the Study of Social and Global Justice, fellow; British Journal of Politics and International Relations, assistant editor, 2007-09. **Publications:** The Single European Act & Economic & Monetary Union: Theories of Integration Revisited, 1995; Austria's and Sweden's Accession to the European Community: A Comparative Neo-Gramscian Case Study of European Integration, 1998; Globalisation and Enlargement of the European Union: Austrian and Swedish Social Forces in the Struggle over Membership, 2000; Labour and the Struggle for a Social Europe: A Comparative Analysis of British and German Trade Unions, 2001; Transnational Class Formation and the Demise of the Swedish Model, 2002; The Struggle for a Social Europe: Trade Unions and EMU in Times of Global Restructuring, 2006; (with W. Bonefeld, P. Burnham and A.D. Morton) Global Restructuring, State, Capital and Labour: Contesting Neo-Gramscian Perspectives, 2006. EDITOR: (with R.A. Higgott and G.R.D. Underhill) Non-state Actors and Authority in the Global System, 2000; (with A.D. Morton) Social Forces in the Making of the New Europe: The Restructuring of European Social Relations in the Global Political Economy, 2001; (with I. Lindberg) Blagult fack och gränslöst kapital: vägval för svensk fackföreningsrörelse, 2006; (with A.D. Morton) Images of Gramsci: Connections and Contentions in Political Theory and International Relations, 2006; (with I. Lindberg and D. Pillay) Labour and the Challenges of Globalization: What Prospects for Transnational Solidarity?, 2008; (with I. Lindberg) Global Restructuring, Labour, and the Challenges for Transnational Solidarity, 2010. Contributor to journals. **Address:** School of Politics and International Relations, University of Nottingham, University Pk., Nottingham, NT NG7 2RD, England. **Online address:** andreas.bieler@nottingham.ac.uk

BIELSKI, Alison (Joy Prosser). British (born England), b. 1925. **Genres:** Poetry, Mythology/Folklore, Local History/Rural Topics. **Career:** British Red Cross, secretary; Yr Academi Gymreig, English Language Section, secretary, 1969-74. Writer. **Publications:** Twentieth-Century Flood, 1964; The Story of the Welsh Dragon, 1969; Across the Burning Sand, 1970; Flower Legends of Wales, 1972; Flower Legends of the Wye Valley, 1972; Chwedlau'r Cymry am Flodau, 1973; Eve, 1973; Shapes and Colours, 1973; Zodiacpoems, 1973; Mermaid Poems, 1974; The Lovetree, 1974; Seth, 1980; Tales and Traditions of Tenby, 1981; Eagles, 1983; The Story of St. Mellons, 1985; That Crimson Flame: Selected Poems, 1996; Green-Eyed Pool, 1997; Sacramental Sonnets, 2003; One of Our Skylarks, 2010. **Address:** 92 Clifton Rd., Paignton, DN TQ3 3LD, England.

BIEMAN, Elizabeth. Canadian (born Canada), b. 1923. **Genres:** Poetry, Literary Criticism And History, Writing/Journalism, Autobiography/Memoirs, Young Adult Fiction, Humor/Satire. **Career:** Ottawa Journal, reporter, 1944-46; University of Western Ontario, instructor and professor, 1966-88, coordinating secretary, 1978-79, professor emeritus, 1988-. Writer. **Publications:** Plato Baptized: Towards the Interpretation of Spenser's Mimetic Fictions, 1988; William Shakespeare: The Romances, 1990; The Reach of Winter Branches, 2005. Contributor of articles to periodicals. **Address:** 250 Sydenham St., Apt. 205, London, ON N6A 5S1, Canada. **Online address:** ebieman@sympatico.ca

BIEN, Peter. American (born United States), b. 1930. **Genres:** Language/Linguistics, Literary Criticism And History, Translations. **Career:** Dartmouth College, professor of English, 1961-97, professor emeritus, 1997-; Harvard, visiting professor, 1983; Princeton University, visiting professor, 2001; Columbia University, visiting professor, 2004; Brown University, visiting professor, 2005; University of Crete, visiting professor, 2007. Writer. **Publications:** L.P. Hartley, 1963; Constantine Cavafy, 1964; Kazantzakis and the Linguistic Revolution in Greek Literature, 1972; (ed. with E. Keeley) Modern Greek Writers, 1972; (with J. Rassias and C. Bien) Demotic Greek, 1972; Nikos Kazantzakis, 1972; (with N. Stangos) Yannis Ritsos: Selected Poems, 1974; Antithesi kai synthesi sti poiisi tou Yanni Ritsou, 1980; (with J. Rassias, C. Bien and C. Alexiou) Demotic Greek II: O IptamenosThalamos, 1982; Three Generations of Greek Writers: Introductions to Cavafy, Kazantzakis, Ritsos, 1983; Tempted by Happiness: Kazantzakis' Post-Christian Christ, 1984; Kazantzakis: Politics of the Spirit, vol. I, 1989, 2007; Nikos Kazantzakis, Novelist, 1989; Words, Wordlessness, and the Word, 1992; (with D.J.N. Middleton) God's Struggler: Religion in the Writings of Nikos Kazantzakis, 1996; (with C. Fager) In Stillness There is Fullness, 2000; On Retiring to Kendal (and Beyond), 2003; (with P. Constantine, E. Keeley and K. Van Dyck and intro.) A Century of Greek Poetry 1900-2000, 2004; (co-ed.) Greek Today, 2004; The Mystery of Quaker Light, 2006; Kazantzakis: Politics of the Spirit, vol. II, 2007; Eight Essays on Kazantzakis, 2007; Oktō kephalaia gia ton Niko Kazantzake, 2007; (ed. and trans.) The Selected Letters of Nikos Kazantzakis, 2012. TRANSLATOR N: Kazantzakis, The Last Temptation of Christ, 1960; Saint Francis, 1962; Report to Greco, 1965; S. Myrivilis, Life in the Tomb, 1977. **Address:** 80 Lyme Rd., Apt. 171, Hanover, NH 03755, U.S.A. **Online address:** peter.a.bien@dartmouth.edu

BIEN, Thomas (H.). American (born United States), b. 1953. **Genres:** Psychology. **Career:** United Methodist minister, 1978-86; University of New Mexico, faculty, 1988-90, 1993-94; Veterans Administration Medical Center, clinical trainee, 1987, therapist, 1993-94; Albuquerque Technical-Vocational Institute, faculty, 1990-92; Health Psychology Associates, intern, 1992-93, clinical psychologist, 1994-96; Samaritan Counseling Center, psychotherapist, 1993-94. Writer. **Publications:** (With B. Bien) Mindful Recovery: A Spiritual Path to Healing from Addiction, 2002; (with B. Bien) Finding the Center Within: The Healing Way of Mindfulness Meditation, 2003; Mindful Therapy: A Guide for Therapists and Helping Professionals, 2006; (ed. with S.F. Hick) Mindfulness and the Therapeutic Relationship, 2008; Buddha's Way of Happiness: Healing Sorrow, Transforming Negative Emotion & Finding Well-Being in the Present Moment, 2010. Contributor to books and periodicals. **Address:** 2501 San Pedro Dr. NE, Ste. 205, Albuquerque, NM 87110, U.S.A. **Online address:** tom@mindfulpsychology.com

BIENES, Nicholas Peter. (Judith Gould). American/Austrian (born Austria), b. 1952. **Genres:** Novels, Documentaries/Reportage, Romance/Historical, Young Adult Fiction, Travel/Exploration, Literary Criticism And History. **Career:** Programming Methods Inc., GTE Division, technical software publishing, 1973-76; freelance writer, 1976-. **Publications:** NOVELS AS JUDITH GOULD (with W.R. Gallaher, Jr.) Sins, 1982; Love-Makers, 1985; Dazzle, 1989; (with R. Koretsky) Brew Cuisine: Cooking with Beer, 1989; The Texas Years, 1989; Never Too Rich, 1990; Texas Born, 1992; Forever, 1992; Too Damn Rich, 1995; Second Love, 1997; Till the End of Time: A Love Story, 1998; Rhapsody: A Love Story, 1999; Time to Say Good-Bye, 2000; Moment in Time, 2001; Best is Yet to Come, 2002; Greek Villa, 2003; Parisian Affair, 2004; Dreamboat, 2005; Secret Heiress, 2006; Greek Winds of Fury, 2008. **Address:** c/o Judith Gould, Dutton Publicity, 375 Hudson St., New York, NY 10014, U.S.A. **Online address:** judithgould001@yahoo.com

BIENVENU, Marcelle. American (born United States), b. 1945. **Genres:** Food And Wine. **Career:** Times-Picayune, feature writer, 1967-71; Time-Life Books, researcher and consultant, 1971-; Chez Marcelle, owner and operator, 1981-84; Times-Picayune, columnist, 1984-; Times of Acadiana, food writer, 1986-; Emeril's Restaurant, cookbook writer, 1993-. Consultant. **Publications:** (Ed.) The Picayune's Creole Cook Book, 1987; Who's Your Mama, Are You Catholic, and Can You Make a Roux? (cookbook), 1991; Cajun Cooking for Beginners, 1996; (with E. Lagasse) Louisiana Real and Rustic, 1996; (with E. Lagasse) Emeril's Creole Christmas, 1997; (E. Lagasse and F. Willett) Emeril's TV Dinners, 1998; (E. Lagasse and F. Willett) Every Day's a Party, 1999; (with E.M. Dore) Eula Mae's Cajun Kitchen, 2002; (with C.A. Brasseaux and R.A. Brasseaux) Stir the Pot: The History of Cajun Cuisine, 2005; (ed. with J. Walker) Cooking Up a Storm, 2008; (with K. Courrege) Pecans from Soup to Nuts, 2009; (with C. Hohorst, Jr.) Wings of Paradise:

Birds of the Louisiana Wetlands, 2009; No Baloney on My Boat!, 2011. Contributor to books, magazines and newspapers. **Address:** 1056 Mimosa Ln., St. Martinville, LA 70582, U.S.A.

BIERDS, Linda. American (born United States), b. 1945. **Genres:** Poetry, Biography, Autobiography/Memoirs, Sciences, Young Adult Fiction. **Career:** Credit Northwest Corp., editor, 1971-80; University of Washington, information specialist and part-time lecturer, 1981-91, lecturer in English, 1991-94, senior lecturer, 1994-96, associate professor of English, 1996-98, Creative Writing Program, director, 1997-2000, professor of English, 1998-, Byron W. and Alice L. Lockwood professor in the humanities. **Publications:** POETRY: Snaring the Flightless Birds, 1982; Flights of the Harvest-Mare, 1985; Off the Aleutian Chain, 1985; The Stillness, the Dancing, 1988; Heart and Perimeter, 1991; Companions for the Slow Rowing, 1991; The Ghost Trio, 1994; The Profile Makers, 1997; The Seconds, 2001; First Hand, 2005; Flight: New and Selected Poems, 2008. Works appear in anthologies. Contributor to periodicals. **Address:** Department of English, University of Washington, PDL B-403, PO Box 354330, Seattle, WA 98195-4330, U.S.A. **Online address:** lbierds@u.washington.edu

BIERHORST, John. American (born United States), b. 1936. **Genres:** Cultural/Ethnic Topics, Language/Linguistics, Mythology/Folklore, Natural History, Translations, Social Sciences. **Career:** Writer, translator and concert pianist. **Publications:** A Cry from the Earth: Music of the North American Indians, 1979; (trans.) C. Perrault, The Glass Slipper: Charles Perraults Tales from Times Past, 1981; (trans.) Spirit Child: A Story of Nativity, 1984, rev. ed., 2001; The Mythology of North America, 1985; A Nahuatl-English Dictionary with a Concordance to the Cantares Mexicanos: With an Analytic Transcription and Grammatical Notes, 1985; The Mythology of South America, 1988, rev. ed. as The Mythology of South America, with a New Afterword, 2002; The Mythology of Mexico and Central America, 1990, rev. ed. as The Mythology of Mexico and Central America with a New Afterword 2002; (trans.) History and Mythology of the Aztecs: The Codex Chimalpopoca: The Text in Nahuatl with a Glossary and Grammatical Notes, 1992; The Way of the Earth: Native America and the Environment, 1994; Mythology of the Lenape: Guide and Texts, 1995; The Ashokan Catskills: A Natural History, 1995; Is My Friend at Home?: Pueblo Fireside Tales, 2001; (trans.) Niño espíritu: Una Historia de la Natividad, 2001; (trans.) Nahuatl, Ballads of the Lords of New Spain: The codex Romances de los señores de la Nueva España, 2009. EDITOR: The Fire Plume: Legends of the American Indians, 1969; The Ring in the Prairie: A Shawnee Legend, 1970; In the Trail of the Wind: American Indian Poems and Ritual Orations, 1971; (trans.) Four Masterworks of American Indian Literature: Quetzalcoatl, The Ritual of Condolence, Cuceb, The Night Chant, 1974; Songs of the Chippewa, 1974; (trans.) Black Rainbow: Legends of the Incas and Myths of Ancient Peru, 1976; The Red Swan: Myths and Tales of the American Indians, 1976, rev. ed., 1992; The Girl Who Married a Ghost: Tales from the North American Indian, 1978; The Whistling Skeleton: American Indian Tales of the Supernatural, 1982; (trans.) The Sacred Path: Spells, Prayers, & Power Songs of the American Indians, 1983; The Hungry Woman: Myths and Legends of the Aztecs, 1984; (trans. and intro.) Cantares Mexicanos, 1985; (trans.) The Monkeys Haircut and Other Stories Told by the Maya, 1986; (ed.) The Naked Bear: Folktales of the Iroquois, 1987; Doctor Coyote: A Native American Aesops Fables, 1987; Lightning inside You and Other Native American Riddles, 1992; (reteller) The Woman Who Fell from the Sky: The Iroquois Story of Creation, 1993; (ed.) On the Road of Stars: Native American Night Poems and Sleep Charms, 1994; The White Deer and Other Stories Told by the Lenape, 1995; (ed.) The Dancing Fox: Arctic Folktales, 1997; The Deetkatoo: Native American Stories About Little People, 1998; (ed.) The Norton Anthology of World Literature, 2001; (intro.) Latin American Folktales: Stories from Hispanic and Indian Traditions, 2002. Contributor to periodicals. **Address:** PO Box 10, West Shokan, NY 12494, U.S.A.

BIERINGER, R(eimund). American/German (born Germany), b. 1957. **Genres:** Theology/Religion. **Career:** Catholic University of Leuven, professor of theology, 1990-. Writer. **Publications:** (With J. Lambrecht) Studies on 2 Corinthians, 1994; (ed.) The Corinthian Correspondence, 1996; (ed. with D. Pollefeyt and F. Vanneuville) Anti-Judaism and the Fourth Gospel, 2001; (ed. with V. Koperski and B. Lataire) Resurrection in the New Testament: Festschrift J. Lambrecht, 2002; (with M. Elsbernd) When Love Is Not Enough: A Theo-Ethic of Justice, 2002; (ed. with G.V. Belle and J. Verheyden) Luke and His Readers: Festschrift A. Denaux, 2005; (ed. with C.R. Koester) The Resurrection of Jesus in the Gospel of John, 2008; (ed.) The New Testament and Rabbinic Literature, 2009; (with M. Elsbernd) Normativity of the Future: Reading Biblical and Other Authoritative Texts in an Eschatological Perspective, 2010; Dialoog En Participatie: Over Hedendaagse Uitdagingen Van Het Christelijk Geloof, 2010. **Address:** Catholic University of Louvaine, St-michielsstr 6, Louvain, 3000, Belgium. **Online address:** reimund.bieringer@theo.kuleuven.ac.be

BIERMANN, Pieke. German (born Germany), b. 1950. **Genres:** Novels, Mystery/Crime/Suspense, Novellas/Short Stories, Documentaries/Reportage, Essays, Humor/Satire, Translations, Literary Criticism And History, Literary Criticism And History. **Career:** Translator and writer. **Publications:** NOVELS: Herz der Familie, 1977; Wir sind Frauen wie andere auch!: Prostituierte u ihre Kaempfe, 1980; Potsdamer Ableben, 1990; Violetta, 1990; Herzrasen, 1993; Vier, Fuenf, Sechs, 1997. STORIES: Berlin, Kabbala, 1997; Herta and Doris, 2002; Gojisch gesehen: Feuilletons, 2004; Der Asphalt unter Berlin: Kriminalreportagen aus der Metropole, 2008. Work appears in anthologies. Contributor of articles. **Address:** POBox 311628, Berlin, 10653, Germany. **Online address:** pieke.biermann@gmail.com

BIESECKER-MAST, Gerald. *See* **MAST, Gerald J.**

BIESEL, David B. American (born United States), b. 1931. **Genres:** Sports/Fitness, Reference, How-to Books, Art/Art History. **Career:** American Institute of Physics, Editorial Department, manager, 1962-69; R.R. Bowker, managing editor, editor of reference books, 1969-73, Book Division, editor-in-chief, 1984-86; Macmillan Publishing Company Inc., Professional and Reference Book Division, senior editor, 1973-82; Elsevier Science Publishing Co., senior editor, 1982-84; M.E. Sharpe Inc., vice-president and editorial director, 1986-88; St. Johann Press, president, 1988-; Scarecrow Press Inc., Association Publishing Program, director, 1991-98. **Publications:** Can You Name That Team?: A Guide to Professional Baseball, Football, Soccer, Hockey, and Basketball Teams and Leagues, 1991. **Address:** St. Johann Press, 315 Schraalenburgh Rd., PO Box 241, Haworth, NJ 07641-1200, U.S.A.

BIGELOW, Brian J(ohn). Canadian (born Canada), b. 1947. **Genres:** Criminology/True Crime, Psychology. **Career:** University of Windsor, faculty, 1970-71; University of Dundee, faculty, 1971-73; Lakehead University, faculty, 1973-75; Laurentian University, assistant professor, 1978-82, associate professor, 1982-96, professor, 1996-2010, professor emeritus, 2010-; Northern Ontario School of Medicine, part-time assistant professor of medicine, 2005-08. Writer. **Publications:** (With G. Tesson and J.H. Lewko) Learning the Rules: The Anatomy of Children's Relationships, 1996. **Address:** Department of Psychology, Laurentian University, Rm. A217, Ramsey Lake Rd., Sudbury, ON P3E 2C6, Canada. **Online address:** bbigelow@laurentian.ca

BIGER, Gideon. Israeli (born Israel), b. 1945. **Genres:** History, Area Studies, Geography, Politics/Government. **Career:** Tel Aviv University, lecturer, 1979-83, senior lecturer, 1983-96, head of department, 1987-90, 1998-, associate professor, 1996-2006, professor, 2006-. Writer. **Publications:** Crown Colony or National Homeland?, 1983; Gevul Iran-Iraḳ: anatomyahshel kav gevul ba-Mizrah-ha-tikhon, 1989; (ed. with A.R. Baker) Ideology and Landscape in Historical Perspective: Essays on the Meanings of Some Places in the Past, 1992; An Empire in the Holy Land-Historical Geography of the British Administration in Palestine, 1994; The Encyclopedia of International Boundaries, 1995; Erets rabat gevulot: meah ha-shanimha-rishonot shel tihum gevuloteha shel Erets-Yisrael, 1840-1947, 2001; Green Dress for a Country, 2003; The Boundaries of Modern Palestine, 2004. **Address:** Department of Geography & the Human Environment, Tel Aviv University, Yad Avner Bldg., 10 Zelig St., Afeka, Tel Aviv, 69970, Israel. **Online address:** biger@post.tau.ac.il

BIGG, Patricia Nina. *See* **AINSWORTH, Patricia.**

BIGGS, Brian. American (born United States), b. 1968?. **Genres:** Novels. **Career:** Writer. **Publications:** GRAPHIC NOVELS: Frederick and Eloise: A Love Story, 1993; Dear Julia, 2000; ILLUSTRATOR: Stephen Mooser, Follow That Flea!, 2005; Stephen Mooser, Smell That Clue!, 2006; Garth Nix, One Beastly Beast: Two Aliens, Three Inventors, Four Fantastic Tales, 2007; Lynn Brunelle, Camp Out! The Ultimate Kids' Guide from the Backyard to the Backwoods, 2007; Judy Sierra, Beastly Rhymes to Read after Dark, 2008; Cynthia Rylant, Brownie and Pearl Step Out, 2009; Cynthia Rylant, Brownie and Pearl Get Dolled Up, 2009; ILLUSTRATOR SHREDDERMAN SERIES: Wendelin Van Draanen, Secret Identity, 2004; Wendelin Van Draanen, Attack of the Tagger, 2004; Wendelin Van Draanen, Meet the Gecko, 2005; Wendelin Van Draanen, Enemy Spy, 2005; ILLUSTRATOR ROSCOE RILEY RULES SERIES: Katherine Applegate, Never Glue Your Friends to Chairs, 2008; Katherine Applegate, Never Swipe a Bully's Bear, 2008; Katherine Applegate, Never Swap Your Sweater for a Dog, 2008; Katherine Applegate, Never Swim in Applesauce, 2008; Katherine Applegate, Never Walk in Shoes That Talk, 2009. Contributor of illustrations to periodicals. **Address:** PO Box 25922, Philadelphia, PA 19128, U.S.A. **Online address:** brian@mrbiggs.com

BIGGS, Chester M(axwell). American (born United States), b. 1921. **Genres:** Military/Defense/Arms Control, Autobiography/Memoirs, History, Humanities, Biography. **Career:** Teacher, 1963-69; Southeastern Community College, coordinator for audiovisual and printing services, director of audiovisual and printing services, 1969-86, retired, 1986. Writer. **Publications:** A Boot Marine (monograph), 1993; Behind the Barbed Wire: Memoir of a World War II U.S. Marine Captured in North China in 1941 and imprisoned by the Japanese until 1945, 1995; The United States Marines in North China, 1894-1942, 2003. Contributor to journals, magazines and periodicals. **Address:** 8532 Independence Dr., Hope Mills, NC 28348-9156, U.S.A.

BIGGS, John Burville. (Sally Leigh). Australian (born Australia), b. 1934. **Genres:** Education, Psychology, Novels, Autobiography/Memoirs, Romance/Historical, Novellas/Short Stories, History. **Career:** Teacher, 1957-58; National Foundation for Educational Research, research officer, 1958-62; University of New England, lecturer in psychology, 1962-66; Monash University, education research officer, 1966-69; University of Alberta, associate professor, 1969-72, professor of educational psychology, 1972; University of Newcastle, professor of education, 1973-87; University of Hong Kong, professor of education, 1987-95; honorary professor of psychology, educational consultant, writer, 1995-. **Publications:** Anxiety and Primary Mathematics, 1963; Mathematics and the Conditions of Learning, 1967; Information and Human Learning, 1968; (ed. with J.R. Kirby) Cognition, Development, and Instruction, 1980; (with K.F. Collis) Evaluating the Quality of Learning, 1982; Student Approaches to Learning and Studying, 1987; (with R. Telfer) Psychology of Flight Training, 1988; (ed.) Teaching for Learning: The View from Cognitive Psychology, 1991; (with P. Moore) The Process of Learning, 1993; Teaching for Quality Learning at University, 1999, 2nd ed., 2003; (ed. with D.A. Watkins) Teaching the Chinese Learner: Psychological and Pedagogical Perspectives, 2001; Girl in the Golden House, 2003; Project Integrens, 2006; Disguises, 2007; Tin Dragons, 2008; Tasmania over Five Generations, 2011. **Address:** PO Box 1083, Sandy Bay, Hobart, TA 7006, Australia. **Online address:** jbiggs@bigpond.com

BIGGS, Mary. American (born United States), b. 1944. **Genres:** Literary Criticism And History, Women's Studies And Issues, Gay And Lesbian Issues, Education, Librarianship, Poetry, Young Adult Fiction. **Career:** University of Evansville, humanities librarian, 1977-79; University of Chicago, assistant professor, 1982-87, The Library Quarterly, editor, 1982-87; Columbia University, assistant professor of library service, 1987-89; Mercy College, director of libraries, 1989-92; Trenton State College (now The College of New Jersey), professor of English, 1992-, dean of the library, 1992-95, dean of library and information services, 1995-98. **Publications:** (Ed.) Publishers and Librarians, 1984; (ed. with M. Sklar) Editor's Choice II: Fiction, Poetry, and Art from the U.S. Small Press, 1987; (ed. with M. Sklar) Men and Women: Together and Alone (poems), 1988; A Gift That Cannot Be Refused: The Writing and Publishing of Contemporary American Poetry, 1990; Women's Words: The Columbia Book of Quotations by Women, 1996; (ed. with R. Andrews and M. Seidel) Columbia World of Quotations, 1996. Contributor of articles to journals. **Address:** Department of English, The College of New Jersey, 211 Bliss Hall, 2000 Pennington Rd., PO Box 7718, Ewing, NJ 08618-1104, U.S.A. **Online address:** mbiggs@tcnj.edu

BIGHAM, Darrel E. American (born United States), b. 1942. **Genres:** Local History/Rural Topics, History, Politics/Government. **Career:** University of Southern Indiana, assistant professor, 1970-75, associate professor, 1975-81, professor of history, 1981-, Historic Southern Indiana Program, director, 1986-; Indiana State University, co-director of regional archives, 1972-74. Writer. **Publications:** Reflections on a Heritage: The German Americans in Southwestern Indiana, 1980; We Ask Only a Fair Trial: A History of the Black Community of Evansville, Indiana, 1987; An Evansville Album: Perspectives on a River City, 1812-1988, 1988; Indiana Resource Book, 1997; Towns and Villages of the Lower Ohio, 1998; Evansville, 1998; (co-author) Shared Lives, One Community, 1998; Images of America: Evansville, 1999; Images of America: Southern Indiana, 2000; (ed.) Indiana Territory, 1800-2000: A Bicentennial Perspective, 2001; (ed.) Proceedings of the Indiana Territory Bicentennial Symposium, June 2000, 2001; Evansville: The World War II Years, 2005; On Jordan's Banks: Emancipation and Its Aftermath in the Ohio River Valley, 2006. Contributor of articles to journals and books. **Address:** Department of History, University of Southern Indiana, 8600 University Blvd., Evansville, IN 47712, U.S.A. **Online address:** dbigham@usi.edu

BIGNELL, Jonathan (Charles). British (born England), b. 1963. **Genres:** Film. **Career:** University of Reading, lecturer in English, 1989-99, Department of Film, Theatre and Television, reader, 2002-, School of Arts, English and Communication Design, head, Centre for Television Drama Studies, director, professor; Royal Holloway College, senior lecturer in media arts, 1999-2002. Writer. **Publications:** Media Semiotics: An Introduction, 1997, 2nd ed., 2002; (ed.) Writing and Cinema, 1999; Postmodern Media Culture, 2000; (ed. with S. Lacey and M. Macmurraugh-Kavanagh) British Television Drama: Past, Present and Future, 2000; An Introduction to Television Studies, 2003, 2nd ed., 2008; (with A. O'Day) Terry Nation, 2004; Big Brother: Reality TV in the Twenty-First Century, 2005; (with J. Orlebar) Television Handbook, 2005; (ed. with A. Fickers) European Television History, 2009; Beckett on Screen: The Television Plays, 2009. Contributor to books. **Address:** Department of Film, Theatre and Television, University of Reading, Rm. 201 Minghella Bldg., Shinfield Rd., Reading, BR RG6 6BT, England. **Online address:** j.bignell@reading.ac.uk

BIGSBY, C. W. E. British (born England), b. 1941. **Genres:** Novels, Literary Criticism And History, Theatre, Botany, History, Cultural/Ethnic Topics. **Career:** University of Wales, lecturer in English and American literature, 1966-69; University of East Anglia, lecturer, 1969-73, senior lecturer, 1973-85, professor of American literature, 1985-, Arthur Miller Centre, director. Writer. **Publications:** AS CHRISTOPHER BIGSBY: (ed.) Essays and Poems, 1992; (ed.) Deerslayer, 1993; (ed.) Sketch book of Geoffrey Crayon, gent, 1993; Hester: A Novel about the Heroine of the Scarlet Letter, 1994; Pearl (novel), 1995; (ed. and intro.) The Portable Arthur Miller, 1995, rev. ed., 2003; (ed.) The Cambridge Companion to Arthur Miller, 1997, 2nd ed., 2010; (ed.) Cambridge History of American Theatre, 1998; Contemporary American Playwrights, 1999; (intro.) All My Sons: A Drama in Three Acts, 2000; Beautiful Dreamer (novel), 2002, 2nd ed., 2006; Cambridge Companion to David Mamet, 2004; Arthur Miller: A Critical Study, 2004; (ed. with H. Temperley) New Introduction to American Studies, 2005; (ed.) The Cambridge Companion to Modern American Culture, 2006; (ed.) The Cambridge Companion to August Wilson, 2006; Beautiful Dreamer, 2006; Remembering and Imagining the Holocaust: The Chain of Memory, 2006; Neil LaBute, 2007; Arthur Miller: 1915-1962, 2008; Arthur Miller, 1962-2005, 2011. OTHERS: Confrontation and Commitment: Study of Contemporary American Drama, 1959-1966, 1967; Edward Albee, 1969 in US as Albee, 1978; (ed.) The Black American Writer, 2 vols., 1969; Three Negro Plays, 1969; Dada & Surrealism, 1972; (ed.) Superculture: The Impact of American Popular Culture on Europe, 1974; Edward Albee: A Collection of Critical Essays, 1975; (ed.) Edward Albee, 1975; (ed.) (ed.) Approaches to Popular Culture, 1976; Tom Stoppard, 1976; The Second Black Renaissance: Essays in Black Literature, 1980; Contemporary English Drama, 1981; Joe Orton, 1982; A Critical Introduction to Twentieth-Century American Drama, 3 vols., 1982-85; (ed. with H. Ziegler) The Radical Imagination and the Liberal Tradition: Interviews with English and American Novelists, 1982; David Mamet, 1985; (ed. with M. Gonnaud and S. Perosa) Cultural Change in the United States since World War II, 1986; (ed. and intro.) Plays, 1987; (comp.) File on Miller, 1988; Miller on File, 1988; Miller and Company, 1990; (ed.) Arthur Miller and Company: Arthur Miller Talks about His Work, 1990; Modern American Drama: 1945-1990, 1992, rev. ed., Modern American Drama, 1945-2000, 2000; Nineteenth-Century American Short Stories, 1995; Still Lives (novel), 1996; The Cambridge History of the American Theatre, 3 vols., 1998-2000; Writers in Conversation with Christopher Bigsby, 2001; One Hundred Days, One Hundred Nights (novel), 2008; Arthur Miller (biography), 2008. **Address:** School of American Studies, University of East Anglia, 1.22 Arts Bldg., Norwich Research Pk., Norwich, AV NR4 7TJ, England. **Online address:** c.bigsby@uea.ac.uk

BIHLER, Penny. *See* **HARTER, Penny.**

BILBY, Joanne Stroud. Also writes as Joanne H. Stroud, Joanne Stroud. American (born United States), b. 1927. **Genres:** Literary Criticism And History, History, Psychology. **Career:** University of Dallas, Department of Literature, faculty, 1972-84, Department of Psychology, faculty, 1977-82; Dallas Institute of Humanities and Culture, founding fellow and lecturer, 1981-, director of publications, 1981-. Writer. **Publications:** (Ed. as Joanne Stroud with G. Thomas) Images of the Untouched: Virginity in Psyche, Myth and Community, 1982. AS JOANNE H. STROUD: The Bonding of Will and Desire, 1994; (ed.) The Olympians, 1995. **Address:** Dallas Institute of Humanities and Culture, 2719 Routh St., Dallas, TX 75201-1968, U.S.A.

BILDNER, Phil. American (born United States) **Genres:** Novels, Picture/Board Books, Children's Fiction, Sports/Fitness. **Career:** New York City Public Schools, elementary and middle school teacher, 1994-2005; Manhattan School for Children, teacher of English and American history, through 2006; full-time writer, 2006-. Attorney. **Publications:** PICTURE BOOKS: Shoeless Joe & Black Betsy, 2002; Twenty-One Elephants, 2004; The Shot Heard 'round the World, 2005; The Greatest Game Ever Played: A Football Story, 2006; The Hallelujah Flight, 2010; The Unforgettable Season: Joe DiMaggio, Ted Williams and the Record-Setting Summer of 1941, 2011. NOVELS: Playing the Field, 2006; Busted, 2007; Turkey Bowl, 2008; (with L. Long) Water, Water Everywhere, 2009; (with L. Long) Magic in the Outfield, 2009; (with L. Long) Horsin' Around, 2009; (with L. Long) Great Balls of Fire, 2009; (with L. Long) Blastin' the Blues, 2010; (with L. Long) Home of the Brave, 2010. BARNSTORMERS SERIES WITH L. LONG: Game 1, 2007; Game 2: The River City, 2007; Game 3: The Windy City, 2008. **Address:** c/o Jennifer Flannery, Flannery Literary, 1140 Wickfield Ct., Naperville, IL 60563-3300, U.S.A. **Online address:** phil@philbildner.com

BILGRAMI, Akeel. American/Indian (born India), b. 1950. **Genres:** Philosophy, Politics/Government, History, Cultural/Ethnic Topics. **Career:** University of Michigan, assistant professor; Columbia University, Department of Philosophy, associate professor, 1985-, chairman, 1994-98, professor, 1995-, Johnsonian professor of philosophy, The Heyman Center for the Humanities, director, 2004-11; Oxford University, visiting faculty; Yale University, visiting faculty; Australian National University, visiting faculty; Jawaharlal Nehru University, visiting faculty; New York Public Library, Writers and Scholars Programme, fellow, 2008-09; Journal of Philosophy, editor. **Publications:** Belief and Meaning: The Unity and Locality of Mental Content, Basil Blackwell, 1992; (co-author) Lire Davidson: Interprétation et Holisme, 1994; Self-Knowledge and Resentment, 2006; Politics and The Moral Psychology of Identity, 2012; What is a Muslim?, forthcoming; Gandhi the Philosopher, forthcoming. **Address:** Department of Philosophy, Columbia University, 719 Philosophy Hall, PO Box 4971, New York, NY 10027, U.S.A. **Online address:** ab41@columbia.edu

BILINKOFF, Jodi. American (born United States), b. 1955?. **Genres:** Adult Non-fiction, History. **Career:** Princeton University, assistant in instruction, 1979-80; University of North Carolina, Department of History, instructor, 1982-83, assistant professor, 1983-89, associate professor, 1989-2005, professor, 2005-; Harvard Divinity School, Department of History, visiting lecturer, 1985-86; Radcliffe College, Mary Ingraham Bunting Institute fellow, 1989-90; American Association of University Women, American Postdoctoral Research Leave fellow, 1999-2000; National Humanities Center, Mellon fellow, 1999-2000. Writer. **Publications:** The Avila of Saint Teresa: Religious Reform in a Sixteenth-Century City, 1989; (contrib.) Crossing Boundaries: Attending to Early Modern Women, 2000; (ed. with A. Greer) Colonial Saints: Discovering the Holy in the Americas, 1500-1800, 2003; Related Lives: Confessors and Their Female Penitents, 1450-1750, 2005. Contributor to periodicals. **Address:** Department of History, University of North Carolina, MHRA 2127, PO Box 26170, Greensboro, NC 27402-6170, U.S.A. **Online address:** jodi_bilinkoff@uncg.edu

BILLETDOUX, Marie. *See* **BILLETDOUX, Raphaële.**

BILLETDOUX, Raphaële. (Marie Billetdoux). French (born France), b. 1951. **Genres:** Novels, Plays/Screenplays, Autobiography/Memoirs, Essays. **Career:** Novelist and screenwriter. **Publications:** NOVELS: Jeune fille en silence, 1971; L'ouverture des bras de l'homme, 1973; Prends garde a la douceur des choses, 1976; Lettre d'excuse, 1981; Mes nuits sont plus belles que vos jours, 1985, trans. as Night without Day, 1987; Entrez et fermez la porte, 1991; Melanie dans un vent terrible, 1994; Chere madame ma fille cadette, 1997; Je fremis en le racontant (essay), 2000; De l'air, 2001; (as Marie Billetdoux) Un peu de désir sinon je meurs, 2006; (as Marie Billetdoux) C'est fou, une fille-: Roman, 2007; (as Marie Billetdoux) C'est encore moi qui vous écris, 1968-2008, 2010. OTHER: La Femme-enfant, 1979. **Address:** Editions Grasset, 61 rue des St. Peres, Paris, 75006, France.

BILLIAS, George Athan. American (born United States), b. 1919. **Genres:** History, Essays, Politics/Government. **Career:** University of Maine, associate professor of history, 1954-62; Clark University, Department of History, associate professor of history, 1962-, now Jacob and Frances Hiatt professor of history emeritus. Writer. **Publications:** Massachusetts Land Bankers of 1740, 1959; General John Glover and His Marblehead Mariners, 1960; George Washington's Generals, 1964; Elbridge Gerry: Founding Father and Republican Statesman, 1976; (with H.J. Bass and E.J. Lapsansky) Our American Heritage, 1979; The Republican Synthesis Revisited: Essays in Honor of George Athan Billias, 1992; American Constitutionalism Heard Round the World, 1776-1989: A Global Perspective, 2009. EDITOR: George Washington's Generals, 1964; The American Revolution: How Revolutionary Was It?, 1965, 4th ed., 1990; Law and Authority in Colonial America: Selected Essays, 1965; George Washington's Opponents: British Generals and Admirals in the American Revolution, 1969; (with G.N. Grob) Interpretations of American History: Patterns and Perspectives, 2 vols., 1967, 6th ed., 1992; The Federalists: Realists or Idealogues?, 1970; (with G.N. Grob) American History: Retrospect and Prospect, 1971; (with T. Balch) The Examination of Joseph Galloway, Esq., by a Committee of the House of Commons, 1972; (with C.K. Balton) Letters of Hugh, Earl of Percy, from Boston and New York, 1774-1776, 1972; (with W.C. Ford) General Orders Issued by Major-General Israel Putnam, 1972; (with V.H. Palsits) Minutes of the Commissioners for Detecting and Defeating Conspiracies in the State of New York, 1972; (with W.O. Raymond) The Winslow Papers, 1972; The Naval Biography of Great Britain, 1972; (with A. Vaughan) Perspectives on Early American History: Essays in Honor of Richard B. Morris, 1973; Eldridge Gerry: Founding Father and Republican Statesman, 1976; The History of the British Empire, from the Year 1765, to the End of 1783, 1979; The Revolution of America, 1979; American Constitutionalism Abroad: Selected Essays in Comparative Constitutional History, 1990; George Washington's Generals and Opponents: Their Exploits and Leadership, 1994. Contributor to periodicals. **Address:** Department of History, Clark University, Jefferson Academic Ctr., 3rd Fl., 950 Main St., Worcester, MA 01610-1400, U.S.A.

BILLINGER, Robert D. American (born United States), b. 1944?. **Genres:** History. **Career:** Palm Beach Atlantic College, assistant professor, associate professor of history, 1973-79; Wingate University, 1979-, associate professor, professor of history, Ruth Davis Horton professor of history, 1997-; United Way of Union County, board director, 1998-2000. Historian, writer and academic. **Publications:** Metternich and the German Question: States' Rights and Federal Duties, 1820-1834, 1991; Hitler's Soldiers in the Sunshine State: German POWs in Florida, 2000; Nazi POWs in the Tar Heel State, 2008. **Address:** Department of History, Wingate University, PO Box 3023, Wingate, NC 28174, U.S.A. **Online address:** billingr@wingate.edu

BILLINGSLEY, (Kenneth) Lloyd. American/Canadian (born Canada), b. 1949. **Genres:** Theology/Religion, Film, Art/Art History, Business/Trade/Industry, Economics, History, Politics/Government, Photography, Photography. **Career:** Spectator Magazine, correspondent; Washington Times, correspondent; Pacific Research Institute for Public Policy, editorial director. Writer. **Publications:** The Generation that Knew Not Josef: A Critique of Marxism and the Religious Left, 1985; The Absence of Tyranny: Recovering Freedom in Our Time, 1986; A Year for Life, 1986; Religion's Rebel Son: Fanaticism in Our Time, 1986; The Seductive Image: A Christian Critique of the World of Film, 1989; From Mainline to Sideline: The Social Witness of the National Council of Churches, 1991; (ed.) Voices on Choice: The Education Reform Debate, 1994; Hollywood Party: The Untold Story of How Communism Seduced the American Film Industry in the 1930s and 1940s, 1998. Contributor to periodicals. **Address:** Pacific Research Institute for Public Policy, 660 J St., Ste. 250, Sacramento, CA 95814, U.S.A. **Online address:** lbillingsley@pacificreseach.org

BILLINGSLEY, Scott. American (born United States), b. 1968. **Genres:** Race Relations, History. **Career:** Fort Worth Christian High School, history instructor, 1991-93; Middle Tennessee State University, adjunct instructor, 1997-98; Motlow State Community College, adjunct instructor, 1997-98; Auburn University, graduate teaching assistant, 1998-99, 2002, Alabama Review, graduate research assistant, 1999-2001, senior graduate teaching assistant, 2002-03; Southern Union State Community College, adjunct instructor, 2001; University of North Carolina, visiting assistant professor, 2003-04, assistant professor of history, 2004-09, associate professor, 2009-, Graduate Social Studies Education, program director, 2004-. Writer and historian. **Publications:** It's a New Day: Race and Gender in the Modern Charismatic

Movement, 2008. Contributor to books and journals. **Address:** Department of History, University of North Carolina, 1 University Dr., Pembroke, NC 28372-1510, U.S.A. **Online address:** scott.billingsley@uncp.edu

BILLINGTON, David P(erkins). American (born United States), b. 1927. **Genres:** Art/Art History, Engineering, History. **Career:** Roberts and Schaefer Co., structural engineer, 1952-60; Princeton University, visiting lecturer, 1958-60, associate professor, 1960-64, professor of civil engineering, 1964-, Gordon Y.S. Wu professor of engineering, 1996-, Princeton Program on Architecture and Engineering, director, 1990-2008, School of Engineering, visiting researcher, 1996-98, now Gordon Y.S. Wu professor emeritus of engineering, now professor emeritus of civil and environmental engineering; Delft University of Technology, visiting professor, 1966-67; Institute for Advanced Studies, visiting professor, 1974-75, 1978-79; Smithsonian Institution, research assistant, 1985-86; Cornell University, A.D. White professor-at-large, 1987-93; Grinnell College, Robert Noyce visiting professor, 2006. Writer and consultant. **Publications:** Thin Shell Concrete Structures, 1965, 2nd ed., 1982; Robert Maillart's Bridges: The Art of Engineering, 1979; The Tower and the Bridge: The New Art of Structural Engineering, 1983; Technique and Aesthetics in the Design of Tall Buildings, 1986; Robert Maillart and the Art of Reinforced Concrete, 1990; The Innovators: The Engineering Pioneers Who Made America Modern, 1996; Robert Maillart: Builder, Designer, and Artist, 1997; The Art of Structural Design: A Swiss Legacy, 2003; The History of Large Federal Dams: Planning, Design, and Construction in the Era of Big Dams, 2005; (with D.C. Jackson) Big Dams of the New Deal Era: A Confluence of Engineering and Politics, 2006; Lothian, 2006; (with D.P. Billington, Jr.) Power, Speed, and Form: Engineers and the Making of the Twentieth Century, 2006; (with M.E. Garlock) Félix Candela: Engineer, Builder, Artist, 2008. **Address:** Department of Civil and Environmental Engineering, Princeton University, E-323 Engineering Quad, Princeton, NJ 08544, U.S.A. **Online address:** billington@princeton.edu

BILLINGTON, James H(adley). American (born United States), b. 1929. **Genres:** Cultural/Ethnic Topics, History, Social Sciences, Young Adult Fiction. **Career:** Harvard University, instructor, 1957-58, assistant professor of history, 1958-61, Russian Research Center, fellow, 1958-59; Princeton University, associate professor, 1961-64, professor, 1964-73; Chase Manhattan Bank, consultant, 1971-73; Fulbright-Hays Foreign Scholarships, director, 1971-76, chair, 1973-75; Woodrow Wilson International Center for Scholars, director, 1973-87; Atlantic Council's Working Group, vice chair, 1982-86; Library of Congress, librarian, 1987-; Kennan Institute for Advanced Russian Studies, founder. Writer. **Publications:** Mikhailovsky and Russian Populism, 1956; The Icon and the Axe: An Interpretive History of Russian Culture, 1966; (intro.) The Horizon Book of the Arts of Russia, 1970; Fire in the Minds of Men: Origins of the Revolutionary Faith, 1980; Books and the World, 1988; Russian Transformed: Breakthrough to Hope, Moscow, August 1991, 1992; Face of Russia: Anguish, Aspiration and Achievement in Russian Culture, 1999; Russia in Search of Itself, 2004. **Address:** Office of the Librarian, The Library of Congress, LM-608, 101 Independence Ave. SE, Washington, DC 20540-1000, U.S.A.

BILLINGTON, Rachel. British (born England), b. 1942. **Genres:** Novels, Children's Fiction, Children's Non-fiction, Young Adult Fiction, Adult Nonfiction. **Career:** PEN, vice-president, president. Writer. **Publications:** All Things Nice, 1969; The Big Dipper, 1970; Lilacs out of the Dead Land, 1971; Cock Robin, 1973; Beautiful, 1974; A Painted Devil, 1975; A Woman's Age, 1979; Occasion of Sin, 1982; The Garish Day, 1985; Loving Attitudes, 1988; Theo and Matilda, 1990; The Family Year (non-fiction), 1992; Bodily Harm, 1992; The Great Umbilical (non-fiction), 1994; Magic and Fate: Being the not Quite Believable Adventures of Sissie Slipper, 1996; Perfect Happiness (sequel to Emma), 1996; The Life of Jesus, 1996; Tiger Sky, 1998; The Life of St. Francis, 1999; Saint Francis of Assisi, 1999; (with M. Mewshaw) Spain: The Best Travel Writing from the New York Times, 2001; A Woman's Life, 2002; Chapters of Gold: The Life of Mary in Mosaics, 2003; The Space Between, 2004; One Summer, 2006; Emma & Knightley: Perfect Happiness in Highbury, 2008; Lies and Loyalties, 2008; The Missing Boy, 2010; Maria and the Admiral, 2010. FOR CHILDREN: Rosanna and the Wizard-Robot, 1981; The First Christmas, 1983; Star-Time, 1984; The First Easter, 1987; (with B. Brown) The First Miracles, 1990; Far Out!, 2002; There's More to Life, 2006. **Address:** David Higham Associates Ltd., 5-8 Lower John St., Golden Sq., Golden Sq, London, GL W1F 9HA, England.

BILLINGTON, Ray(mond John). British (born England), b. 1930. **Genres:** Philosophy, Theology/Religion. **Career:** Methodist minister, 1952-68; pastor, 1952-66; Bristol Polytechnic, lecturer, 1968-70, senior lecturer, 1970-72, principal lecturer in humanities, 1972; University of the West of England, principal lecturer in humanities, 1972-95, head of philosophy; Open University, tutor, lecturer in philosophy, 1972-; University of Oxford, faculty, 1995-; University of Cardiff, lecturer; State University of California, exchange professor and visiting professor. Writer. **Publications:** The Basis of Pacifist Conviction, 1961; The Teaching of Worship, 1962; Concerning Worship, 1963, (with S. Hopkinson and J. Foster) rev. ed., 1967; (with T.M. Morrow) Worship and Preaching, 1967; The Liturgical Movement and Methodism, 1969; The Christian Outsider, 1971; A New Christian Reader, 1974; Living Philosophy: An Introduction to Moral Thought, 1988, 3rd ed., 2003; East of Existentialism: The Tao of the West, 1990; Understanding Eastern Philosophy, 1997; Religion without God, 2002. **Address:** University of Oxford, Rewley House, 1 Wellington Sq., Oxford, OX OX1 2JA, England. **Online address:** philosophylive@aol.com

BILLONE, Amy Christine. American (born United States), b. 1972. **Genres:** Novels. **Career:** Princeton University, teaching assistant and lecturer, 1996-2001; University of Tennessee, Department of English, assistant professor, 2001-07, associate professor, 2007-. Writer. **Publications:** (Ed. and intro.) Peter Pan (novel), 2005; Little Songs: Women, Silence, and the Nineteenth-Century Sonnet (nonfiction), 2007. Contributor of articles to journals and books. **Address:** Department of English, University of Tennessee, 416 McClung Twr., Knoxville, TN 37996-0430, U.S.A. **Online address:** abillone@utk.edu

BILLSON, Anne. British (born England), b. 1954. **Genres:** Novels, Film, Adult Non-fiction, Young Adult Fiction, Young Adult Non-fiction. **Career:** Time Out Ltd., literary editor, 1985-86; Sunday Correspondent, film critic, 1989-90; New Statesman & Society, film critic, 1991-92; Sunday Telegraph, film critic, 1992-2001; British GQ, contributing editor. **Publications:** Screen Lovers, 1988; Dream Demon, 1989; My Name is Michael Caine: A Life in Film, 1991; Suckers (novel), 1993; Stiff Lips (novel), 1996; The Thing, 1997; The Ex, 2008; Spoilers, 2008; Let the Right One In, 2011. Contributor to periodicals. **Address:** c/o Antony Harwood, Curtis Brown Group Ltd., 162-168 Regent St., London, GL W1R 5TB, England.

BILLSON, Janet Mancini. American/Canadian (born Canada), b. 1941. **Genres:** Poetry, Sociology, Urban Studies, Women's Studies And Issues, Social Sciences. **Career:** Peace Corps Training Program, graduate assistant/field assessment officer, 1966; Harvard University, Harvard Graduate School of Education, Pathways to Identity Project, chief research associate, 1967-69; National Institute of Mental Health Field Work Fellow, 1966-68; Rhode Island College, professor of sociology and women's studies, 1973-91, acting associate dean of students and director of student life, 1984, assistant dean of faculty of arts and sciences, 1984-86; Danforth Associate, 1979-; University of Exeter, honorary research fellow, 1981; American Sociological Association, assistant executive officer and director of the academic and professional affairs program, 1991-95; George Washington University, adjunct professor of sociology and women's studies, 1993-95, 1997-, professor of sociology, 1995-97, visiting professor of sociology, 1995-97; Group Dimensions Intl., director, 1981-; Writer. **Publications:** (Ed. with F.A.M. Robbins) Encountering Society: Introductory Readings in Sociology, 1980; Strategic Styles: Coping in the Inner City, 1980; (with R. Majors) Cool Pose: Dilemmas of Black Manhood in America, 1992; Keepers of the Culture: The Power of Tradition in Women's Lives, 1995; Pathways to Manhood: Young Black Males Struggle for Identity, 1996; The Power of Focus Groups for Social Policy and Research, 2002; (with K.M. Ries) Their Powerful Spirit: Inuit Women, a Century of Change, 2001; (ed. with C. Fluehr-Lobban) Female Well-Being: Toward a Global Theory of Social Change, 2005; (with K. Mancini) Inuit Women: Their Powerful Spirit in a Century of Change, 2007. Work appears in anthologies. **Address:** Group Dimensions Intl., 16 Otis Shores, Woolwich, ME 04579, U.S.A. **Online address:** jmbillson@gdiworld.com

BINA, Cyrus. American/Iranian (born Iran), b. 1946. **Genres:** Poetry, Economics, Philosophy, Politics/Government, Industrial Relations, Environmental Sciences/Ecology, Essays, Third World, Third World. **Career:** Plan and Budget Organization, foreign exchange analyst, 1966-68; General Gendarmerie Headquarters, Division of Pension and Social Security, senior auditor, 1969-71; American University, Department of Economics, instructor, 1978-79, Center for Technology and Administration, lecturer, 1982; Towson State University, Department of Economics, lecturer, 1979-80; EMAY Corp., associate, 1980-81; Washington International College, lecturer in economics and statistics, 1981-82; Olivet College, Department of Business and Economics, professor of economics, 1982-87; Providence College, Department of Economics, associate professor of economics, 1987-90; Harvard University, research fellow and research associate, 1990-93, affiliate in research, 1994-95; University of Redlands, Department of Management and Business, associate professor of business and management, 1996-98; California State University, Department of Economics, faculty, 1999-2000, Department of Finance, faculty, 1999-2000; University of Minnesota, Division of the Social Sciences, associate professor of economics and management, 2000-02, professor of economics and management, 2002-04, distinguished research professor of economics and management, 2004-. Writer. **Publications:** Accounting Manual for Community Development, 1980; The Economics of the Oil Crisis, 1985; (ed. with H. Zangeneh and contrib.) Modern Capitalism and Islamic Ideology in Iran, 1992; (ed. with L. Clements and C. Davis) Beyond Survival: Wage Labor in the Late Twentieth Century, 1996; The Sun and the Earth (poetry), 1998; Khurshid va khak: majmu-i she'r, 1998; Encyclopedia of Life in the Islamic Republic, 2008; Oil: A Time Machine-Journey Beyond Fanciful Economics and Frightful Politics, 2011; Encyclopedia of Global Studies, 2012; Behind the High Seas, forthcoming. Works appear in anthologies. **Address:** Division of the Social Science, University of Minnesota, 109 Camden Hall, 600 E 4th St., Morris, MN 56267, U.S.A. **Online address:** binac@umn.edu

BINCHY, Maeve. Irish (born Ireland), b. 1940. **Genres:** Novels, Novellas/Short Stories, Adult Non-fiction, Young Adult Fiction, Plays/Screenplays. **Career:** Zion Schools, French teacher; Pembroke School, history and Latin teacher, 1961-68; Irish Times, columnist, 1968-2000. **Publications:** My First Book, 1970; The Central Line (short stories), 1978; The Half-Promised Land (play), 1979; Maeve's Diary (journalism), 1979; Victoria Line (short stories), 1980; Maeve Binchy's Dublin 4, 1982; Dublin Four (short stories), 1982; Light a Penny Candle, 1982; London Transports (short stories), 1983; The Lilac Bus, 1984; Echoes, 1985; Firefly Summer, 1987; Silver Wedding, 1988; Circle of Friends, 1990; Story Teller: Collection of Short Stories, 1990; Short Stories, 1992; The Copper Beech, 1992; Dublin People, 1993; The Glass Lake, 1994; Dear Maeve, 1995; This Year It Will Be Different and Other Stories: A Christmas Treasury, 1996; Cross Lines, 1996; Evening Class, 1996; The Return Journey, 1998; Tara Road, 1998; Ladies' Night at Finbar's Hotel, 1999; Aches & Pains, 1999; Scarlet Feather, 2000; Quentins, 2002; The Builders, 2002; Nights of Rain and Stars, 2004; Deeply Regretted By, 2005; A Time to Dance, 2006; Star Sullivan, 2006; Whitethorn Woods, 2006; (afterword) Of Human Bondage, 2007; Na tógálaithe, 2007; Heart and Soul, 2008; The Maeve Binchy Writers' Club, 2008; (co-author) Over the Moon: How Children Changed My Life, 2009; End of Term, 2009; (co-author) From the Republic of Conscience: Stories Inspired by the Universal Declaration of Human Rights, 2009; Minding Frankie, 2010. Contributor to periodicals. **Address:** Christine Green Authors' Agent, 6 Whitehorse Mews, Westminster Bridge Rd., London, GL SE1 7QD, England.

BINDING, Paul. British (born England), b. 1943. **Genres:** Novels, Literary Criticism And History, Plays/Screenplays, Poetry, Autobiography/Memoirs, Sciences, History. **Career:** Freelance writer, 1990-; Oxford University Press, editor; New Statesman, deputy literary editor. Educator. **Publications:** NONFICTION: Robert Louis Stevenson (juvenile biography), 1974; Separate Country: A Literary Journey Through the American South, 1979, 2nd ed., 1988; (ed. and intro.) Weir of Hermiston and Other Stories, 1979; Lorca: The Gay Imagination, 1985; St. Martin's Ride (autobiography), 1990; The Still Moment: Eudora Welty: Portrait of a Writer, 1994; An Endless Quiet Valley: A Reappraisal of John Masefield, 1998; (with R. Keenoy and P. Curry) Babel Guide to Scandinavian and Baltic Fiction, 1999. NOVELS: Harmonica's Bride Groom, 1984; Kingfisher Weather, 1990. OTHERS: (with J. Horder) Dreams and Speculations (poetry); My Cousin the Writer, 2002; Imagined Corners: Exploring the World's First Atlas, 2003; With Vine-Leaves in His Hair: The Role of the Artist in Ibsen's Plays, 2006. **Address:** Logaston Press, Little Logaston, Woonton, Hereford, HF HR3 6QH, England.

BINDING, Tim. British/German (born Germany), b. 1947?. **Genres:** Novels, Children's Fiction. **Career:** Penguin, editorial director. Simon & Schuster, senior editor, 2000-05, part-time commissioning editor. **Publications:** In the Kingdom of Air, 1993; A Perfect Execution, 1996; Island Madness, 1998; Lying with the Enemy, 1999; On Ilkley Moor: The Story of an English Town, 2001; Anthem, 2003; Man Overboard, 2005; Sylvie and the Songman, 2008; Cliffhanger, 2008; Champion, 2011. **Address:** c/o Author Mail, Picador/Pan Macmillan, 20 New Wharf Rd., London, GL N1 9RR, England.

BING, Leon. American (born United States), b. 1950?. **Genres:** Adult Non-fiction, Criminology/True Crime. **Career:** Fashion model and freelance journalist. **Publications:** Do or Die, 1991; Smoked, 1993; Wrongful Death: One Child's Fatal Encounter with Public Health and Private Greed, 1997; Swans and Pistols: Modeling, Motherhood, and Making It in the Me Generation, 2009. Contributor to periodicals. **Address:** Donadio & Olson Inc., 121 W 27th St., Ste. 704, New York, NY 10001, U.S.A.

BINGHAM, Charlotte. British (born England), b. 1942. **Genres:** Novels, Plays/Screenplays, Autobiography/Memoirs, Biography, Adult Non-fiction, Literary Criticism And History. **Career:** Writer. **Publications:** Coronet among the Weeds (autobiography), 1963; Coronet among the Grass, 1972. WITH T. BRADY: Victoria (novel), 1972; Rose's Story (novel), 1972; Victoria and Company, 1974; No Honestly (biography), 1975. NOVELS: Lucinda, 1965; Yes, Honestly, 1977; Belgravia, 1984; Country Life, 1985; At Home, 1986; To Hear a Nightingale, 1988; The Business, 1989; In Sunshine or in Shadow, 1991; Stardust, 1993; Nanny, 1993; By Invitation, 1993; Change of Heart, 1994; Debutantes, 1995; The Nightingale Sings, 1996; Grand Affair, 1997; Love Song, 1998; Country Wedding, 1999; The Kissing Garden, 1999; The Love Knot, 2000; The Blue Note, 2000; The Season, 2001; Summertime, 2001; The Chestnut Tree, 2002; Distant Music, 2002; The Moon At Midnight, 2003; The Wind Off The Sea, 2003; Daughters of Eden, 2004; The House of Flowers, 2004; Friday's Girl, 2005; The Magic Hour, 2005; In Distant Fields, 2006; Out of the Blue, 2006; The White Marriage, 2007; Goodnight Sweetheart, 2007; The Enchanted, 2008; The Land of Summer, 2008; The Daisy Club, 2009; Mums on the Run, 2010. Contributor to periodicals. **Address:** United Authors Ltd., Garden Studios, 11/15 Betterton St., London, GL WC2 9BP, England. **Online address:** charlottebrady@btconnect.com

BINGHAM, Howard L. American (born United States), b. 1939. **Genres:** Biography, Autobiography/Memoirs. **Career:** Freelance photographer, 1960-; Sony Pictures, executive producer, 2001. Writer. **Publications:** Muhammad Ali: A Thirty-Year Journey, 1993; (with M. Wallace) Muhammad Alis Greatest Fight: Cassius Clay vs. the United States of America, 2000; (co-author) Ali: The Movie and the Man, 2001; (with G. Moore) Black Panthers 1968, 2008. Contributor to periodicals. **Address:** PO Box 5385, Gardena, CA 90249-5385, U.S.A. **Online address:** alicos@mac.com

BINGHAM, Sallie. (Sarah (Montague) Bingham). American (born United States), b. 1937. **Genres:** Novels, Novellas/Short Stories, Plays/Screenplays, Autobiography/Memoirs. **Career:** National Book Critics Circle, director; University of Louisville, teacher of English and creative writing; College of Santa Fe, teacher. Writer. **Publications:** NOVELS: After Such Knowledge, 1960; Small Victories, 1992; Upstate, 1993; Matron of Honor, 1994; Straight Man, 1996; Nick of Time: A Novel, 2006. STORIES: The Touching Hand and Six Short Stories, 1967; The Way It Is Now, 1972; Transgressions, 2002; Red Car, 2008. OTHERS: Passion and Prejudice: A Family Memoir, 1989; Cory's Feast, 2005; Hub of the Miracle: Poems, 2006; If in Darkness, 2009. Contributor to books and anthologies. Contributor of fiction to periodicals. **Address:** 369 Montezuma, Ste. 316, Santa Fe, NM 87501, U.S.A. **Online address:** salliebingham@earthlink.net

BINGHAM, Sarah (Montague). *See* **BINGHAM, Sallie.**

BINGLE, Donald J. American (born United States) **Genres:** Novels, Science Fiction/Fantasy. **Career:** KL/Gates LLP (formerly Bell, Boyd & Lloyd, LLP), staff, 1979-92, partner, 1999-; Boston Chicken Inc., vice president, general counsel and secretary, 1992-96; freelance writer, consultant and investor, 1996-99. **Publications:** Forced Conversion (novel), 2004; Greensword: A Tale of Extreme Global Warming (novel), 2009. Works appear in anthologies. Contributor to periodicals and journals. **Address:** K&L Gates L.L.P., 70 W Madison St., Ste. 3100, Chicago, IL 60602-4207, U.S.A. **Online address:** orphyte@aol.com

BINKLEY, Christina. American (born United States) **Genres:** History. **Career:** Times Leader, reporter, 1990-93; Tallahassee Democrat, reporter, 1993-94; Wall Street Journal, real estate & general assignment reporter, 1994-97, hotels and gambling reporter, 1997-2006, style columnist, 2007-. **Publications:** Winner Takes All: Steve Wynn, Kirk Kerkorian, Gary Loveman and the Race to Own Las Vegas, 2008. **Online address:** christina.binkley@wsj.com

BINNEMA, Theodore. Canadian (born Canada), b. 1963. **Genres:** History,

Anthropology/Ethnology, Area Studies, Young Adult Fiction. **Career:** University of Northern British Columbia, assistant professor of history, 2000-, associate professor, 2003-, professor and graduate student coordinator, 2008-, chair. Writer. **Publications:** (Ed. with G. Ens and R.C. Macleod) From Rupert's Land to Canada, 2001; Common and Contested Ground: A Human and Environmental History of the Northwestern Plains, 2001; (ed. with S. Neylan) New Histories for Old: Changing Perspectives on Canada's Native Pasts, 2007. Contributor to periodicals. **Address:** University of Northern British Columbia, Rm. ADM 3020, 3333 University Way, Prince George, BC V2N 4Z9, Canada. **Online address:** binnemat@unbc.ca

BINNS, Michael Ferrers Elliott. British (born England), b. 1923?. **Genres:** Theology/Religion, Literary Criticism And History, Young Adult Fiction. **Career:** Church Assembly, assistant secretary, 1949-63; legal secretary, 1963-70; assistant secretary to General Synod, 1970-76; charity consultant, 1983-. Writer. **Publications:** The Layman in Church Government, 1956; Guide to the Pastoral Measure, 1968; The Layman and His Church, 1970; North Downs Church, 1983; Realisation, 1993; Finding through War, 1995. **Address:** Quest Cottage, High St., N Cadbury, Yeovil, SM BA22 7DH, England.

BINSKI, Paul. British (born England), b. 1956. **Genres:** Art/Art History, History. **Career:** Yale University, assistant professor of art history, 1988-91; University of Manchester, lecturer in art history, 1991-95; Cambridge University, Gonville and Caius College, fellow, 1995-, director of studies in history of art, lecturer in art history, 1996-, reader, Department of History of Art, head, 1999-2001, professor; Oxford University, Slade professor, 2006-07; British Academy, fellow, 2007. Writer. **Publications:** The Painted Chamber at Westminster, 1986; (with C. Norton and D. Park) Dominican Painting in East Anglia: The Thornham Parva Retable and the MusTe de Cluny Frontal, 1987; Painters, 1991; Westminster Abbey and the Plantagenets, 1995; Medieval Death: Ritual and Representation, 1996; (ed. with M. Pointon) Image, Music, Text, 1996; (ed. with W. Noel) New Offerings, Ancient Treasures: Studies in Medieval Art for George Henderson, 2001; Becket's Crown: Art and Imagination in Gothic England, 1170-1300, 2004; (ed. with S. Panayotova) The Cambridge Illuminations: Ten Centuries of Book Production in the Medieval West, 2005; (with M. Bunker) Peterborough Cathedral, 2001-2006: From Devastation to Restoration, 2006; (with P. Zutshi and S. Panayotova) Western Illuminated Manuscripts, 2011; (ed. with A. Massing) The Westminster Retable: History, Technique, Conservation, forthcoming. **Address:** Department of History of Art, Cambridge University, 1-5 Scroope Terr., Cambridge, CB CB2 1PX, England. **Online address:** pb214@cam.ac.uk

BINSTOCK, Robert H. American (born United States), b. 1935. **Genres:** Politics/Government, Social Sciences, History. **Career:** Brandeis University, lecturer, 1963-65, assistant professor, 1965-69, associate professor, 1969-72, Stulberg Professor of Law and Politics, 1972-84, Policy Center on Aging, director, 1979-84; White House Task Force on Older Americans, director, 1967-68; Case Western Reserve University, Department of Epidemiology and Biostatistics, professor of aging, health and society, 1985-, Henry R. Luce Professor, 1985-92, School of Medicine, Department of Medicine, professor of aging, Department of Bioethics, professor of bioethics, College of Arts and Sciences, professor of political science, professor of sociology, University Center on Aging and Health, faculty associate, Center for Genetic Research, Ethics and Law, faculty associate. Writer. **Publications:** A Report on Politics in Worcester, Massachusetts, 1960; (with R. Morris and M. Rein) Feasible Planning for Social Change, 1966; (ed. with K. Ely) The Politics of the Powerless, 1971; (with P. Woll) America's Political System: State and Local, 1972, 2nd ed. as America's Political System: Urban, State, and Local, 1975, 3rd ed., 1979; (with P. Woll) America's Political System: People, Government, Policies, 1972; (with P. Woll) America's Political System, 1972, 5th ed. as America's Political System: A Text with Cases, 1991; (ed. with E. Shanas) Handbook of Aging and the Social Sciences, 1976, 7th ed., 2010; (ed. with S.G. Post) Too Old for Health Care? Controversies in Medicine, Law, Economics, and Ethics, 1991; (ed. with S.G. Post and P.J. Whitehouse) Dementia and Aging: Ethics, Values, and Policy Choices, 1992; (ed. with L.E. Cluff and O. von Mering) The Future of Long-term Care: Social and Policy Issues, 1996; (ed. with L.E. Cluff) Home Care Advances: Essential Research and Policy Issues, 2000; (ed. with L.E. Cluff) The Lost Art of Caring: A Challenge to Health Professionals, Families, Communities, and Society, 2001; (ed. with S.G. Post) The Fountain of Youth: Cultural, Scientific, and Ethical Perspectives on a Biomedical Goal, 2004; (with J.H. Schulz) Aging Nation: The Economics and Politics of Growing Older in America, 2006; (ed. with T.R. Prohaska and L.A. Anderson) Public Health for an Aging Society, 2012. Contributor of articles to books and journals. **Address:** School of Medicine, Case Western Reserve University, Rm. WG-43A, Wood Bldg., Cleveland, OH 44106-4945, U.S.A. **Online address:** rhb3@case.edu

BINZEN, Peter (Husted). American (born United States), b. 1922. **Genres:** Writing/Journalism, History, Biography, Education. **Career:** United Press Intl., reporter, 1947; Passaic Herald-News, reporter, 1947-50; Philadelphia Bulletin, reporter and editor, 1951-82; Philadelphia Inquirer, reporter, 1982-86, business columnist, 1986-; Philadelphia Daily News, inquirer columnist and journalist. **Publications:** Whitetown, U.S.A., 1970; (with J.R. Daughen) The Wreck of the Penn Central, 1971; (with J.R. Daughen) The Cop Who Would Be King: The Honorable Frank Rizzo, 1977; (ed.) Odyssey of Gold, 1995; (ed.) Nearly Everybody Read It: Snapshots of the Philadelphia Bulletin, 1998. Contributor to periodicals. **Address:** Philadelphia Inquirer, 400 N Broad St., Philadelphia, PA 19101, U.S.A.

BIRCH, Anthony Harold. Canadian/British (born England), b. 1924. **Genres:** Politics/Government. **Career:** Manchester University, lecturer, senior lecturer in government, 1947-61; Harvard University, commonwealth fund fellow, 1951-52; University of Chicago, commonwealth fund fellow, 1951-52; University of Hull, professor of political studies, 1961-70; University of Exeter, professor of political science, 1970-77; University of Victoria, professor, 1977-89, head and chair of political science, 1981-87, professor emeritus of political science, 1989-. Writer. **Publications:** AS A.H. BIRCH: Federalism, Finance and Social Legislation in Canada, Australia, and the United States, 1955; Small-Town Politics, 1959; Representative and Responsible Government, 1964; The British System of Government, 1967, (as Anthony H. Birch) 10th ed., 1998; Representation, 1971; Political Integration and Disintegration in the British Isles, 1977; Nationalism and National Integration, 1989. OTHER: (as Anthony H. Birch) The Concepts and Theories of Modern Democracy, 1993, 3rd ed., 2007. **Address:** University of Victoria, PO Box 1700, Victoria, BC V8W 2Y2, Canada.

BIRCHMORE, Daniel A. American (born United States), b. 1951. **Genres:** Children's Fiction. **Career:** Vanderbilt University, Medical Center, residency in internal medicine, 1976-79, assistant professor of medicine; U.S. Veterans Hospital-Elsmere, Division of Rheumatology, chief, 1990-97; U.S. Veterans Hospital-Nashville, physician, 1997-. Writer. **Publications:** The Rock, 1996; Harry, the Happy Snake of Happy Hollow, 1996; The Reluctant Santa, or, Christmas Has Been Cancelled!, 1996; The White Curtain, 1996; Little Fish, 1996; Pilly, Polly, and Wee, 1996. **Address:** Department of Medicine, Medical Center, Vanderbilt University, D-3100, Medical Ctr. N, Nashville, TN 37232-2358, U.S.A. **Online address:** daniel.a.birchmore@vanderbilt.edu

BIRD, Brad. American (born United States), b. 1957. **Genres:** Plays/Screenplays, Film, Criminology/True Crime. **Career:** Walt Disney Co., staff animator, 1970-80; Turner Featured Animation, staff, 1990; Pixar Animation Studios, staff, 2000-. Writer and director. **Publications:** (With R. Curtis and R. Perez) The Incredibles, 2005. **Address:** Pixar Animation Studios, 1200 Park Ave., Emeryville, CA 94608-3677, U.S.A.

BIRD, Christiane. American (born United States) **Genres:** Music, Military/Defense/Arms Control, History, Travel/Exploration, Essays, Mystery/Crime/Suspense, Biography, Autobiography/Memoirs, Autobiography/Memoirs. **Career:** New York Daily News, travel and general assignment freelance reporter, editor; Wall Street Journal, freelance reporter; Washington Post, freelance reporter; Chicago Tribune, freelance reporter. **Publications:** Below the Line: Living Poor in America, 1987; The Jazz and Blues Lover's Guide to the U.S.: With More than 900 Hot Clubs, Cool Joints, Landmarks and Legends from Boogie-Woogie to Bop and Beyond, 1991; New York City Handbook, 1997; The Da Capo Jazz and Blues Lover's Guide to the United States, 3rd ed., 2001; Neither East nor West: One Woman's Journey through the Islamic Republic of Iran, 2001; A Thousand Sighs, a Thousand Revolts: Journeys in Kurdistan, 2004; New York State, 2006; The Sultan and the Princess: A Story of Romance, Religion and the Arab Slave Trade, 2010; The Sultan's Shadow: One Family's Rule at the Crossroads of East and West, 2010. **Address:** c/o Neeti Madan, Sterling Lord Literistic Inc., 65 Bleecker St., New York, NY 10012, U.S.A. **Online address:** chbird@aol.com

BIRD, Edward J. (Edward Castronova). American (born United States), b. 1963?. **Genres:** Politics/Government, Social Sciences, Economics. **Career:** University of Rochester, assistant professor, 1991-97, associate professor of public policy and political science, 1997-2000; California State University, associate professor of economics; Indiana University, Department of Telecommunications, associate professor, 2004-, cognitive science program faculty. University of California, Center for Governance, fellow; University of Munich, CESifo, research fellow. Writer and consultant. **Publications:** Synthetic Worlds: The Business and Culture of Online Games, 2005; Exodus to the Virtual World: How Online Fun Is Changing Reality, 2007. Contributor to journals and periodicals. **Address:** Department of Telecommunications, Indiana University, 1229 E 7th St., Bloomington, IN 47405, U.S.A. **Online address:** castro@indiana.edu

BIRD, Richard. Canadian (born Canada), b. 1938. **Genres:** Economics, Sociology, Money/Finance. **Career:** Harvard University, instructor in economics, 1961-63, lecturer, 1966-68, visiting professor of law, 2001-04; Columbia University, senior research fellow, 1963-64; University of Toronto, Rotman School of Management, associate professor of economics, 1968-69, professor of economics, 1969-99, professor emeritus, 1999-, Institute for Policy Analysis, director, 1981-85; International Monetary Fund, Tax Policy Division, chief, 1972-74; Erasmus University, Tinbergen professor, 1988; Georgia State University, Andrew Young School of Public Policy, distinguished visiting professor, 1999-; Harvard Law School, visiting professor, 2001-04; University of New South Wales, ARC international fellow, 2007, Australian School of Taxation, Faculty of Law, visiting professional fellow, 2010. Writer. **Publications:** (Ed. with O. Oldman) Readings on Taxation in Developing Countries, 1964; Sales Tax and the Carter Report, 1967; (co-author) Financing Urban Development in Mexico City, 1967; (with A.O. Hirschman) Foreign Aid: A Critique and a Proposal, 1968; Bibliography on Taxation in Developing Countries, 1968; (with O. Oldman) Tax Research and Tax Reform in Latin America: A Survey and Commentary, 1968; (with D.G. Hartle) Criteria for the Design of Governmental Decision-Making Units, 1969; Taxation and Development: Lessons from Colombian Experience, 1970; The Growth of Government Spending in Canada, 1970; (ed. with J.G. Head) Modern Fiscal Issues: Essays in Honor of Carl S. Shoup, 1972; Taxing Agricultural Land in Developing Countries, 1974; Charging for Public Services: A New Look at an Old Idea, 1976; A New Look at Benfit Taxation, 1976; (with M.W. Bucovetsky) Canadian Tax Reform and Private Philanthropy, 1976; (with E. Slack) Residential Property Tax Relief in Ontario, 1978; Intergovernmental Fiscal Relations in Developing Countries, 1978; Financing Canadian Government: A Quantitative Overview, 1979; (with M.W. Bucovetsky and D.K. Foot) The Growth of Public Employment in Canada, 1979; Taxing Corporations, 1980; Tax Incentives for Investment: The State of the Art, 1980; (ed.) Fiscal Dimensions of Canadian Federalism, 1980; Central-Local Fiscal Relations and Provision of Urban Public Services, 1980; (with R.D. Fraser) Commentaries on the Hall Report, 1981; (with E. Slack) Urban Public Finance in Canada, 1983; Intergovernmental Finance in Colombia: Final Report of the Mission on Intergovernmental Finance, 1984; (co-author) Industrial Policy in Ontario, 1985; Federal Finance in Comparative Perspective, 1986; (with R.A. Musgrave and P.B. Musgrave) Public Finance in Theory and Practice, 1987; (ed. with S. Horton) Government Policy and the Poor in Developing Countries, 1989; (ed. with S. Cnossen) The Personal Income Tax: Phoenix from the Ashes?, 1990; (with O. Oldman) Taxation in Developing Countries, 1990; (ed.) More Taxing than Taxes?: The Taxlike Effects of Nontax Policies in LDCs, 1991; (with D. Brean and M. Krauss) Taxing International Portfolio Investment, 1991; (ed. with M.C. de Jantscher) Improving Tax Administration in Developing Countries, 1992; Tax Policy and Economic Development, 1992; (ed. with J.M. Mintz) Taxation to 2000 and Beyond, 1992; (with C.I. Wallich) Financing Local Government in Hungary, 1992; (with C.I. Wallich) Fiscal Decentralization and Intergovernmental Relations in Transition Economies: Toward a Systemic Framework of Analysis, 1993; Decentralizing Infrastructure: For Good or For Ill?, 1994; Where Do We Go from Here?: Alternative to the GST, 1994; (ed. with R.D. Ebel and C.I. Wallich) Decentralization of The Socialist State: Intergovernmental Finance in Trasition Economies, 1995; (with J.I. Litvack and M.G. Rao) Intergovernmental Fiscal Relations and Poverty Alleviation in Viet Nam, 1995; Pourquoi Imposer les Sociétés?, 1996; (with J. Litvack and J. Ahmad) Rethinking Decentralization in Developing Countries, 1998; (with F. Vaillancourt) Fiscal Decentralization in Developing Countries, 1998; (ed. with E. Slack) International Handbook of Land and Property Taxation, 2004; (ed. with J.M. Poterba and J. Slemrod) Fiscal Reform in Colombia: Problems and Prospects, 2005; (ed. with F. Vaillancourt) Perspectives on Fiscal Federalism, 2006; (with P. Gendron) VAT in Developing and Transitional Countries, 2007; (with E. Slack and A. Tassonyi) A Tale of Two Taxes, 2012. Contributor of articles to periodicals. **Address:** Rotman School of Management, University of Toronto, 105 St. George St., Toronto, ON M5S 3E6, Canada. **Online address:** rbird@rotman.utoronto.ca

BIRDSALL, Jeanne. American (born United States), b. 1952?. **Genres:** Children's Fiction. **Career:** Writer and photographer. **Publications:** The Penderwicks: A Summer Tale of Four Sisters, Two Rabbits, and a Very Interesting Boy, 2005; The Penderwicks on Gardam Street, 2008; Flora's Very Windy Day, 2010; (intro.) Nancy and Plum, 2010; The Penderwicks at Point Mouette, 2011; Lucky and Squash Run Away, 2012. Contributor to periodicals. **Address:** Barbara S. Kouts Literary Agency, PO Box 560, Bellport, NY 11713, U.S.A.

BIRDSELL, Sandra. Canadian (born Canada), b. 1942. **Genres:** Novels, Novellas/Short Stories, Young Adult Fiction. **Career:** University of Waterloo, writer-in-residence, 1987; University of Alberta, writer-in-residence, 1991; University of Prince Edward Island, writer-in-residence, 1991; Saskatoon Public Library, writer-in-residence, 1995; Regina Public Library, writer-in-residence, 2000; McMaster University, writer-in-residence; University of British Columbia, instructor; University of Winnipeg, writer-in-residence, 2007; Humber College, mentor/instructor, 2010; Manitoba Writers' Guild, founder. **Publications:** Night Travellers (short stories), 1982; Ladies of the House (short stories), 1984; Agassiz Stories, 1987; The Missing Child (novel), 1989; Agassiz: A Novel in Stories, 1991; The Chrome Suite (novel), 1992; The Town That Floated Away, 1997; The Two-Headed Calf, 1997; The Russländer, 2001; Katya, 2004; Children of the Day, 2005; (contrib.) A Feast of Longing, 2007; (contrib.) Long after Fathers, 2007; Waiting for Joe, 2010. Contributor to periodicals. Works appear in anthologies. **Address:** 2741 Thornton Ave., Regina, SK S4S 1J2, Canada. **Online address:** sandylou@sasktel.net

BIRDSEYE, Tom. American (born United States), b. 1951. **Genres:** Children's Fiction. **Career:** Ocean Lake School, teacher, 1977-83; Washington Elementary School, teacher, 1985-88. Writer. **Publications:** FOR CHILDREN: I'm Going to Be Famous, 1986; Airmail to the Moon, 1988; A Song of Stars: An Asian Legend, 1990; Tucker, 1990; Waiting for Baby, 1991; Soap! Soap! Don't Forget the Soap!: An Appalachian Folktale, 1993; A Kids Guide to Building Forts, 1993; Just Call Me Stupid, 1993; A Regular Flood of Mishap, 1994; (with D.H. Birdseye) She'll Be Coming Round the Mountain, 1994; Tarantula Shoes, 1995; (with D.H. Birdseye) What I Believe: Kids Talk About Faith, 1996; (with D.H. Birdseye) Under Our Skin: Kids Talk About Race, 1997; The Eye of the Stone, 2000; Look Out Jack! The Giant Is Back!, 2001; Oh Yeah!, 2003; Attack of the Mutant Underwear, 2003; A Tough Nut to Crack, 2006; Storm Mountain, 2010; Revenge of the Mutant Underwear, forthcoming. **Address:** 511 NW 12th St., Corvallis, OR 97330, U.S.A. **Online address:** birdseye@proaxis.com

BIRDWELL, Cleo. *See* **DELILLO, Don.**

BIRDWELL, Michael E. American (born United States), b. 1957. **Genres:** History. **Career:** Tennessee Tech University, Department of History, assistant professor, associate professor, professor. Writer. **Publications:** Celluloid Soldiers: The Warner Bros. Campaign against Nazism, 1999; (with W.C. Dickinson and H.D. Kemp) Upper Cumberland Historic Architecture, 2002; (ed. with W.C. Dickinson) Rural Life and Culture in the Upper Cumberland, 2004. Contributor of articles. **Address:** Department of History, Tennessee Tech University, Henderson (HH) 110, PO Box 5064, Cookeville, TN 38505, U.S.A. **Online address:** birdie@tntech.edu

BIRELEY, Robert. American (born United States), b. 1933. **Genres:** History. **Career:** St. Ignatius High School, teacher of European and American history, 1958-61; Loyola University, instructor, 1971-72, assistant professor, 1972-76, associate professor, 1976-82, professor of history, 1982-; Catholic Historical Review, advisory editor, 1979-85. Writer. **Publications:** Maximilian von Bayern, Adam Contzen, S.J., und die Gegenreformation in Deutschland, 1624-1635, 1975; Politics and Religion in the Age of the Counterreformation: Emperor Ferdinand II, William Lamormaini, S.J., and the Formation of Imperial Policy, 1981; The Counter-Reformation Prince: Antimachiavellianism or Catholic Statecraft in Early Modern Europe, 1990; The Refashioning of Catholicism, 1450-1700: A Reassessment of the Counter Reformation, 1999; The Jesuits and the Thirty Years War: Kings, Courts, and Confessors, 2003. Work represented in anthologies. Contributor to history journals. **Address:** Department of History, Loyola University, Crown Ctr. 531, 1032 W Sheridan Rd., Chicago, IL 60660, U.S.A. **Online address:** rbirele@luc.edu

BIRENBAUM, Barbara. American (born United States), b. 1941. **Genres:** Children's Fiction, Poetry, Songs/Lyrics And Libretti, Children's Non-fiction,

Self Help, Humor/Satire, Illustrations, Human Relations/Parenting, Literary Criticism And History. **Career:** Richland County Schools, elementary teacher, 1961-62, school psychologist, 1963-65; South Carolina Department of Vocational Rehabilitation, rehabilitation psychologist, 1965; Clayton Schools, school psychologist, 1966; University City Schools, elementary teacher, 1966-67; Huntington Schools, teacher of creative writing workshops, 1976-78; Melville Center, Board of Cooperative Educational Services, school psychologist, 1978; Pinellas County, poet-in-schools, 1980-82; Peartree Publications, founder, 1985; Free-lance author and illustrator, 1985-. **Publications:** SELF-ILLUSTRATED: Light after Light, 1985; The Gooblins' Night, 1985; Lady Liberty's Light, 1986; The Hidden Shadow, 1986; The Lost Side of the Dreydl, 1987; Candle Talk, 1991; The Lighthouse Christmas, 1991. OTHERS: Up Til Now, Yet..., 1964; (with G. Hoagland and N. Carter) Breaking through to Poetry, 1982; (with G. Hoagland and N. Carter) A Dance of Words, 1982; The Birthday Wish, 1986; The Olympic Glow, 1988; The Cupdeer, 1993; Amazing Bald Eaglet, 1999; The Groundhog Message, 2000; Quipnotes About Uncles, 2001; Quipnotes About Aunts, 2001; Groundhog Willie's Shadow, 2001; Quipnotes About Moms, 2003; Quipnotes About Dads, 2003; Groundhog Phil's Message, 2003; A Nation Stands United, 2005; Great Lives of the 21st Century, 2005; Top 100 Writers, 2005. ANTHOLOGIES: A Voyage to Remember, 1996; Best Poems of the 90s, 1996; Lyrical Heritage, 1997; Best Poems of 1997; Embedded Dreams, 1997; The Best Poems of 1998; Outstanding Poets of 1998; The Rustling Leaves, 1998; Captured Moments, 1999; Hearts of Glass, 1999; Poetic Voices of America, 2000; America in the Millennium, 2000; In-Between Days, 2001; America-Voices Coming Together, 2002; The Best Poems and Poets of 2002, 2003. **Address:** Peartree Books & Music, PO Box 14533, Clearwater, FL 33766-4533, U.S.A.

BIRKBY, Robert Corrie. American (born United States), b. 1950. **Genres:** Communications/Media. **Career:** Southwest Missouri State University, instructor in English; Philmont Scout Ranch, director. Writer, educator and mountaineer. **Publications:** KMA Radio, the First Sixty Years, 1985; Learn How to Canoe in One Day: Quickest Way to Start Paddling, Turning, Portaging and Maintaining, 1990; Boy Scout Handbook, 10th ed., 1990; Lightly on the Land: The SCA Manual of Backcountry Work Skills: Mission Statement of the Student Conservation Association, 1995; Lightly on the Land: The SCA Trail-Building and Maintenance Manual, 1996, 2nd ed., 2005; Mountain Madness, 2008. **Online address:** robertbirkby@earthlink.net

BIRKERTS, Sven. American (born United States), b. 1951. **Genres:** Literary Criticism And History. **Career:** Harvard University, lecturer in expository writing, 1984-91; Boston Review, contributing editor, 1988-; Boston University, Agni Review, contributing editor, 1988-, editor, 2002-; Bennington Writing Seminars, core faculty, 1995-, director, 2008-; Mount Holyoke College, lecturer, 1996-2004; Harvard University, Briggs-Copeland lecturer in creative writing, 2006-08; Emerson College, faculty; Amherst College, faculty. **Publications:** An Artificial Wilderness: Essays on Twentieth-Century Literature, 1987; The Electric Life: Essays on Modern Poetry, 1989; American Energies: Essays on Fiction, 1992; The Longwood Introduction to Fiction, 1992; Literature: The Evolving Canon, 1993; The Gutenberg Elegies: The Fate of Reading in an Electronic Age, 1994; (ed.) Tolstoy's Dictaphone: Technology and the Muse, 1996; (with D. Hall) Writing Well, 9th ed., 1998; Readings, 1999; My Sky Blue Trades: Growing Up Counter in a Contrary Time (memoir), 2002; (foreword) The Inspector Barlach Mysteries, 2006; Reading Life: Books for the Ages, 2007; Art of Time in Memoir: Then, Again, 2008; (contrib.) Gunnar Birkerts: Metaphoric Modernist, 2009; The Other Walk, 2011. Contributor to periodicals. **Address:** AGNI Magazine, Boston University, 236 Bay State Rd., Boston, MA 02215, U.S.A. **Online address:** cyberbirk@aol.com

BIRKLAND, Thomas A. American (born United States), b. 1961. **Genres:** Public/Social Administration, Politics/Government, Regional/Urban Planning, Environmental Sciences/Ecology, Sociology, Administration/Management, History, Social Sciences, Social Sciences. **Career:** University at Albany, Nelson A. Rockefeller College of Public Affairs, assistant professor, associate professor, 1995-2007, Center for Policy Research, director, 2001-05; National Science Foundation, program officer, 2006; North Carolina State University, School of Public and International Affairs, William T. Kretzer distinguished professor, 2007-, College of Humanities and Social Sciences, associate dean for research, 2011-. Writer. **Publications:** After Disaster: Agenda Setting, Public Policy, and Focusing Events, 1997; An Introduction to the Policy Process: Theories, Concepts, and Models of Public Policy Making, 2001, 3rd ed., 2011; Lessons of Disaster: Policy Change after Catastrophic Events, 2006; (with T. Schaefer) Encyclopedia of Media and Politics, 2006. Contributor of articles to periodicals. **Address:** School of Public & International Affairs, North Carolina State University, 211 Caldwell, 2221 Hillsborough St., 135 Western Ave., Raleigh, NC 27695-8102, U.S.A. **Online address:** tom_birkland@ncsu.edu

BIRMINGHAM, John. (Harrison Biscuit). Australian/British (born England), b. 1964. **Genres:** Novels, Biography, Adult Non-fiction. **Career:** Australian Department of Defense, Office of Special Clearances and Records, researcher. Writer and film maker. **Publications:** He Died with a Felafel in His Hand, 1994; (as Harrison Biscuit) The Search for Savage Henry, 1995; (with D. Flinthart) How to Be a Man, 1995, rev. ed., 1998; The Tasmanian Babes Fiasco, 1997; Leviathan: The Unauthorized Biography of Sydney, 1999; Hell Has Harbour Views, 2001; Appeasing Jakarta: Australia's Complicity in the Timor Tragedy, 2001; Off One's Tits: Ill-considered Rants and Raves from a Graceless Oaf Named John Birmingham, 2002; The Felafel Guide to Getting Wasted, 2002; The Felafel Guide to Sex, 2002; Dopeland: Taking the High Road through Australia's Marijuana Culture, 2003; Weapons of Choice, 2004; Designated Targets, 2005; Final Impact, 2007; Without Warning, 2009; After America, 2010. Contributor to periodicals. **Address:** Pan Macmillan Australia, Level 25, 1 Market St., Sydney, NW 2000, Australia.

BIRMINGHAM, Maisie. British/Indian (born India), b. 1914. **Genres:** Mystery/Crime/Suspense, Young Adult Fiction. **Career:** John Lewis Partnership (retail stores), personnel assistant, 1936-38; Rowntree and Company Ltd., (wholesale manufacturers), personnel manager, 1938-41; British Government, inspector of factories, 1941-43; Anglo-Iranian Oil Co., in-personnel, 1943-45; University of Wales, lecturer in social science, 1945-49; University of Ghana, lecturer in social science, 1958-60; Kate Weatherly, creator. Writer. **Publications:** You Can Help Me, 1974; The Heat of the Sun, 1976; Sleep in a Ditch, 1978; The Mountain by Night, 1997. **Address:** Castle Hill House, Shaftesbury, DS SP7 8AX, England.

BIRN, Raymond Francis. American (born United States), b. 1935. **Genres:** History, Intellectual History. **Career:** University of Oregon, Department of History, instructor, assistant professor, 1961-66, associate professor, 1966-72, head, 1971-78, professor, 1972-2001, professor emeritus of history, 2001-; école des hautes études en sciences sociales, visiting professor, 1992; Washington University, Center for the History of Freedom, fellow, 1992; College de France, visiting professor, 2001. Writer. **Publications:** Crisis, Absolutism, Revolution: Europe, 1648-1789/91, 1977, 3rd ed. as Crisis, Absolutism, Revolution: Europe and the World, 1648-1789, 2005; (ed.) The Printed Word in the Eighteenth Century, 1984; Forging Rousseau: Print, Commerce and Cultural Manipulation in the Late Enlightenment, 2001; La censure royale des livres dans la France des lumières, 2007; Royal Censorship of Books in Eighteenth-century France, 2012. Contributor to journals. **Address:** Department of History, University of Oregon, 363 McKenzie Hall, 1288 University of Oregon, Eugene, OR 97403-1288, U.S.A. **Online address:** rbirn@oregon.uoregon.edu

BIRNBAUM, Jeffrey H. American (born United States), b. 1955?. **Genres:** Documentaries/Reportage, Business/Trade/Industry, Law, Social Sciences. **Career:** Miami Herald, staff reporter, 1978; The Wall Street Journal, staff, 1979, White House correspondent, 1992, tax reporter, through 1995; National Public Radio, commentator, 1994-; Time, senior correspondent, 1995-97; Fortune Magazine, Washington bureau chief, 1997-2004; The Washington Post, columnist, 2004-; Fox News Channel, contributor; Washington Times, columnist, managing editor-digital, 2008-10; Washington Insight/Energy, founder; BGR Public Relations, president, 2010-, head of the public relations division. **Publications:** (With A. Murray) Showdown at Gucci Gulch: Lawmakers, Lobbyists and the Unlikely Triumph of Tax Reform, 1987; The Lobbyists: How Influence Peddlers Work Their Way in Washington, 1992; Madhouse: The Private Turmoil of Working for the President, 1996; The Money Men: The Real Story of Fund-raising's Influence on Political Power in America, 2000. **Address:** BGR Group, The Homer Bldg., 11th Fl. S, 601 13th St. NW, Washington, DC 20005, U.S.A. **Online address:** jbirnbaum@bgrpr.com

BIRNEY, Alice Lotvin. American (born United States), b. 1938. **Genres:** Literary Criticism And History, Plays/Screenplays, Bibliography, History, Poetry. **Career:** Billboard, assistant editor, 1959-61; Mansfield State College, associated professor of English, 1968-69; University of California, lecturer in literature, 1970-72; Library of Congress, English literature and world theater cataloger, 1973-89; Library of Congress, literary manuscript specialist, 1990-. **Publications:** Satiric Catharsis in Shakespeare: A Theory of Dramatic

Structure, 1973; The Literary Lives of Jesus: An International Bibliography of Poetry, Drama, Fiction and Criticism, Garland, 1989; (with J. Bates and J. Baker) Holland Point, 2008. Contributor of articles to journals. **Address:** The Library of Congress, 101 Independence Ave. SE, Washington, DC 20540, U.S.A. **Online address:** alicebirney@gmail.com

BIRNEY, Betty G. American (born United States), b. 1947. **Genres:** Children's Fiction. **Career:** Disneyland, advertising copywriter, 1977-79; Walt Disney Co., publicist, 1979-81; freelance television writer, 1982-; Disney StudioBurbank, writer and producer of television and radio commercials; Disney Channel, writer and story editor. **Publications:** Someone's Fibbing!, 1991; Disneys Chip n Dale Rescue Rangers: The Rescue Rangers Save Little Red, 1991; No One's Listening!, 1991; Riddle Flap Book, 1992; Who Am I?: A Riddle Flap Book, 1992; Oh Bother, Someone's Grumpy, 1992; Walt Disney's Winnie the Pooh Half a Haycorn Pie, 1992; Walt Disneys Winnie the Pooh and the Missing Pots, 1992; Oh Bother, Someone's Messy, 1992; Disneys The Little Mermaid, 1992; Disneys Beauty and the Beast: The Tale of Chip the Teacup, 1992; Walt Disney's Bambi: Snowy Day, 1992; Whats My Job?: A Riddle Flap Book, 1992; Walt Disney's Winnie the Pooh and the Little Lost Bird, 1993; (adaptor) Disney's Beauty and the Beast, 1993; Oh Bother, Someone Wont Share, 1993; Raja's Story, 1993; Walt Disneys Sleeping Beauty, 1993; Walt Disneys Winnie the Pooh: The Merry Christmas Mystery, 1993; Oh Bother, Oh Bother, Somebodys Afraid of the Dark, 1993; Walt Disneys I Am Winnie the Pooh, 1994; (adaptor) Black Beauty, 1994; Tyrannosaurus Tex, 1994; Someone Jealous, 1994; (adaptor) Disneys Toy Story, 1995; Meltdown at the Wax Museum, 1995; Pies in the Oven, 1996; Lets Play Hide and Seek: A Lift-The-Flap Book, 1997; The World According to Humphrey, 2004; Friendship According to Humphrey, 2005; Seven Wonders of Sassafras Springs, 2005; Trouble According to Humphrey, 2007; The Princess and The Peabodys, 2007; Surprises According to Humphrey, 2008; Adventure According to Humphrey, 2009; Summer According to Humphrey, 2010; School Days According to Humphrey, 2011; Mysteries according to Humphrey, 2012; Back To School According to Humphrey, forthcoming. **Address:** c/o Todd Koerner, Writers & Artists Agency Inc., 8383 Wilshire Blvd., Ste. 550, Beverly Hills, CA 90211-3136, U.S.A. **Online address:** bettybirney@bettybirney.com

BIRO, Andrew William. Canadian (born Canada), b. 1969?. **Genres:** Politics/Government, International Relations/Current Affairs, Philosophy. **Career:** York University, Department of Political Science, teaching assistant, 1993-99, lecturer, 1998, 2001; University of Western Ontario, Department of Political Science, lecturer, 2000-01, post-doctoral research associate, 2001-02; Acadia University, Department of Political Science, assistant professor, 2002-08, Canada research chair, 2002-, associate professor, 2008-. Writer. **Publications:** Denaturalizing Ecological Politics: Alienation from Nature from Rousseau to the Frankfurt School and Beyond, 2005. Contributor to books and periodicals. **Address:** Department of Political Science, Acadia University, Wolfville, NS B4P 2R6, Canada. **Online address:** andrew.biro@acadiau.ca

BIRO, Val. British/Hungarian (born Hungary), b. 1921. **Genres:** Children's Fiction, Education, Illustrations, Picture/Board Books, Literary Criticism And History. **Career:** Sylvan Press, studio manager, 1944-46; C and J Temple, production manager, 1946-48; John Lehmann Publishers, art director, 1948-53; freelance artist and illustrator, 1953. Writer. **Publications:** SELF-ILLUSTRATED: (with A. Baines) Val Biro's Discovering Chesham, 1968; The Honest Thief: A Hungarian Folktale, 1972; Hungarian Folk-Tales, 1980; The Magic Doctor, 1982; Hansel and Gretel, 1983; Fables from Aesop, 18 vols., 1983-88; (reteller) The Pied Piper of Hamelin, 1985; Tales from Hans Christian Andersen, 4 vols., 1986; Drango Dragon, 1989; Jack and the Beanstalk, 1989; Tobias and the Dragon: A Hungarian Folk Tale, 1989; Miranda's Umbrella, 1990; The Three Little Pigs, 1990; Rub-a-Dub-Dub: Val Biro's 77 Favourite Nursery Rhymes, 1991; The Donkey That Sneezed, 1998; The Hobyahs, 1998; Jack And The Robbers, 1998; The Three Billy-Goats Gruff, 1998; Jennings Sounds the Alarm, 1999; Little Red Riding Hood, 2000; Aesop's Fables, 2001; The Joking Wolf, 2001. GUMDROP SERIES SELF-ILLUSTRATED: Gumdrop: The Adventures of a Vintage Car, 1966; Gumdrop and the Farmer's Friend, 1967; Gumdrop on the Rally, 1968; Gumdrop on the Move, 1969; Gumdrop Goes to London, 1971; Gumdrop Finds a Friend, 1973, 2nd ed., 1978; Gumdrop in Double Trouble, 1975; Gumdrop and the Steamroller, 1976; Gumdrop on the Brighton Run, 1976; Gumdrop Posts a Letter, 1976 in US as Gumdrop and the Birthday Surprise, 1986; Gumdrop Has a Birthday, 1977; Val Biro's Gumdrop Annual, 1979; Gumdrop Gets His Wings, 1979; Gumdrop Finds a Ghost, 1980; Gumdrop and the Secret Switches, 1981; Gumdrop and Horace, 1982; Gumdrop Makes a Start, 1982; Gumdrop Races a Train, 1982; Gumdrop Goes to School, 1982; Gumdrop at the Zoo, 1982; Gumdrop at Sea, 1983; Gumdrop Gets a Lift, 1983; Gumdrop in a Hurry, 1983 in US as Gumdrop Beats the Clock, 1986; Gumdrop's Magic Journey, 1984; Gumdrop Goes Fishing, 1984; Gumdrop Has a Tummy-Ache, 1984; Gumdrop Is the Best Car, 1984 in US as Gumdrop Is the Best, 1985; Gumdrop on the Farm, 1984; Gumdrop and the Monster, 1985; Gumdrop and the Farmyard Caper, 1985; Gumdrop and the Great Sausage Caper, 1985; Gumdrop Catches a Cold, 1985; Gumdrop Floats Away, 1985; Gumdrop to the Rescue, 1986; Gumdrop For Ever!, 1987; Gumdrop and the Dinosaur, 1988; The Bumper Gumdrop Omnibus, 1989; Gumdrop and the Pirates, 1989; Gumdrop and the Elephant, 1990; (comp.) Rub-a-Dub-Dub, 1991; Gumdrop and the Bulldozer, 1991. Illustrator of books by others. **Address:** Bridge Cottage, Brook Ave., Bosham, WS PO18 8LQ, England. **Online address:** valbiro@lineone.net

BIRRELL, Anne (Margaret). British (born England) **Genres:** Poetry, Anthropology/Ethnology, Area Studies, Classics, Literary Criticism And History, Mythology/Folklore, Theology/Religion, Women's Studies And Issues, Women's Studies And Issues. **Career:** University of Cambridge, faculty of Chinese. Sinologist and writer. **Publications:** Chinese Love Poetry: New Songs from a Jade Terrace: A Medieval Anthology, 1982, rev. ed., 1995; Popular Songs and Ballads of Han China, 1988, rev. ed., 1993; Chinese Mythology: An Introduction, 1993; (trans. and intro.) The Classic of Mountains and Seas, 1999; Chinese Myths: The Legendary Past, 2000; Games Poets Play: Readings in Medieval Chinese Poetry, 2004. Contributor to periodicals. **Address:** University of Cambridge, Clare Hall, Herschel Rd., Cambridge, CB3 9AL, England.

BIRRELL, James Peter. Australian (born Australia), b. 1928?. **Genres:** Architecture, History, Autobiography/Memoirs, Biography, Literary Criticism And History. **Career:** Brisbane City Council, architect, 1955-61; University Queensland, staff architect, 1961-66, now retired. Writer. **Publications:** Walter Burley Griffin, 1964; (with R. Barnes) Water from the Moon, 1989. **Address:** 104 Duporth Ave., Maroochydore, QL QLD 4558, Australia.

BIRRINGER, Johannes (H.). German (born Germany), b. 1953. **Genres:** Theatre, Literary Criticism And History, Art/Art History. **Career:** Yale University, lecturer, 1982-85; University of Texas, visiting professor, 1985-87; Rice University, visiting professor, 1989-90; Northwestern University, assistant professor, 1990-; Ohio State University, New Dance and Technology Program, head, 1999-2003; Alien Nation Co., artistic director; Interaktionslabor Goettelborn, founder, 2003-; Nottingham Trent University, Live Art and Performance, principal research fellow, 2003-06; Brunel University, Drama & Performance Technologies, chair, professor of performance technologies, 2006-, Design And Performance-Lab, director, Centre for Contemporary and Digital Performance, acting director; Contemporary Art Museum, media and arts consultant; Southwest Alternate Media Project, media consultant. Writer. **Publications:** Marlowe's Dr. Faustus and Tamburlaine: Theological and Theatrical Perspectives, 1984; Theatre, Theory, Postmodernism, 1991; Media & Performance: Along the Border, 1998; Performance on the Edge: Transformations of Culture, 2000; (with J. Fenger) Tanz im Kopf=Dance and Cognition, 2005; (with K. Behringer) Spielsysteme: Internationales Interaktionslabor Göttelborn 2005-2006: eine Dokumentation, 2006; Performance, Technology, and Science, 2008. Contributor of articles to periodicals. **Address:** Department of Drama, School of Arts, Brunel University, Rm. GB022, Uxbridge, UB8 3PH, England. **Online address:** johannes.birringer@brunel.ac.uk

BIRSTEIN, Ann. American (born United States), b. 1927. **Genres:** Novels, Novellas/Short Stories, Writing/Journalism, Biography, Autobiography/Memoirs, Essays. **Career:** Queens College, The New School, lecturer, 1953-54; City College of New York, writer-in-residence, 1960; University of Iowa, Writers Workshop, visiting lecturer, 1966, 1972; Hofstra University, adjunct professor, 1980; Barnard College, adjunct professor of English, 1981-93, Writers on Writing Program, founder and director, 1988; Columbia University, lecturer, 1985-87; State University of New York, Albany, visiting professor of English; Browning School, teacher of creative writing. Writer. **Publications:** NOVELS: Star of Glass, 1950; The Troublemaker, 1955; The Sweet Birds of Gorham, 1966; Summer Situations, 1972; Dickie's List, 1973; American Children, 1980; The Last of the True Believers, 1988; Vanity Fare, 2009. OTHER: (co-ed.) The Works of Anne Frank, 1959; (contrib.) The Open Form,

1970; (contrib.) On the Job: Fiction about Work by Contemporary American Writers, 1977; Rabbi on Forty-Seventh Street: The Story of Her Father, 1982; What I Saw at the Fair (autobiography), 2002. Contributor to magazines. **Address:** c/o Mildred Marmur, 2005 Palmer Ave., PO Box 127, Larchmont, NY 10538, U.S.A. **Online address:** abirstein@aol.com

BIRYUKOV, Nikolai (Ivanovich). Russian (born Russia), b. 1949. **Genres:** Politics/Government. **Career:** U.S.S.R. Trade Mission in Egypt, interpreter, 1972-74; Moscow State Institute for International Relations, research scientist, 1977-79, teacher, 1979-83, senior teacher, assistant professor, 1983-88, associate professor in philosophy, 1994-; All-Russia Knowledge Society, lecturer, 1984-88; Russian Academy of Sciences, Center for the Analysis of Scientific and Industrial Policies, senior research scientist, 1991-. Writer. **Publications:** (With V. Sergeyev) Russia's Road to Democracy: Parliament, Communism, and Traditional Culture, 1993; (with V. Sergeyev) Russian Politics in Transition, 1997; (with V. Sergeyev) Stanovlenie institutov predstavitel'noi vlasti v sovremennoi Rossii, 2004; Rossiĭskaia gosudarstvennost', 2006; Contributor to journals. **Address:** Department of Philosophy, Moscow State Institute for International Relations, 76, Prospekt Vernadskogo, Moscow, 119454, Russia. **Online address:** nibiryukov@newmail.ru

BIRZER, Bradley J. American (born United States), b. 1967. **Genres:** History, Biography, Autobiography/Memoirs. **Career:** OAH Magazine of History, assistant editor, 1994-97; St. Francis College, adjunct lecturer, 1995-96; Montana: The Magazine of Western History, associate editor, 1997-98; Carroll College, adjunct lecturer, 1998; University of Texas, visiting assistant professor, 1998-99; Hillsdale College, Russell Amos Kirk Chair in History and director of the American Studies Program, 1999-. **Publications:** (ed. and intro. with J. Willson) The American Democrat and Other Political Writings, 2000; J.R.R. Tolkien's Sanctifying Myth: Understanding Middle-Earth, 2002; (with L. Schweikart) The American West, 2003; Sanctifying the World: The Augustinian Life and Mind of Christopher Dawson, 2007; American Cicero: The Life of Charles Carroll, 2010. Contributor to periodicals. **Address:** Department of History, Hillsdale College, 33 E College, Hillsdale, MI 49242-1205, U.S.A. **Online address:** bradleybirzer@me.com

BISCUIT, Harrison. *See* **BIRMINGHAM, John.**

BISHOP, Bill. American (born United States), b. 1953. **Genres:** Politics/Government, Sociology. **Career:** The Mountain Eagle, reporter; Lexington Herald-Leader, columnist; Austin American-Statesman, special projects staff; Bastrop County Times, co-owner and operator; Daily Yonder (web publication), editor. **Publications:** (With R.G. Cushing) The Big Sort: Why the Clustering of Like-Minded America Is Tearing Us Apart, 2008. **Address:** Houghton Mifflin Co., 222 Berkeley St., Boston, MA 02116, U.S.A. **Online address:** bbish@austin.rr.com

BISHOP, Courtney. *See* **RUEMMLER, John D(avid).**

BISHOP, Holley. American (born United States), b. 1966?. **Genres:** Novels, Biography, Natural History, Sciences. **Career:** Writer and literary agent. **Publications:** Robbing the Bees: A Biography of Honey the Sweet Liquid Gold That Seduced the World, 2005. **Address:** c/o Author Mail, Free Press, 1230 Ave. of the Americas, New York, NY 10020, U.S.A.

BISHOP, Jacqueline Kay. American (born United States), b. 1955?. **Genres:** Business/Trade/Industry, Economics, Marketing. **Career:** Tulane University, teaching assistant, 1981-82, Newcomb College, adjunct professor, painting and drawing, 1982-84, adjunct professor, 1993, Art and Environment MFA Graduate Seminar, adjunct professor, 2003; Loyola University, adjunct professor of advanced painting, 1990, Department of Visual Arts, senior class external assessor, 1999-2002, Practicum in Environmental Studies Program, supervisor, 2002-03, Art and Environment Graduate Seminar, adjunct professor, 2003-05, 2008, Costa Rica Study Abroad Program, adjunct professor, 2010; Norwich University, Vermont College, MFA Program, artist-teacher, 1998-99; Contemporary Arts Center, ArtSpeak program, founder and organizer. Writer. **Publications:** Effective Marketing: Principles and Practice, 2002; Living Color: Photographs by Judy Cooper, 2007. Illustrator of books by others. **Address:** Arthur Roger Gallery, 432 Julia St., New Orleans, LA 70130, U.S.A.

BISHOP, Michael. (Philip Lawson). American (born United States), b. 1945. **Genres:** Novels, Novellas/Short Stories, Mystery/Crime/Suspense, Science Fiction/Fantasy, Plays/Screenplays, Poetry, Essays, Young Adult Fiction, Young Adult Fiction. **Career:** Air Force Academy Preparatory School, faculty, 1968-72; University of Georgia, instructor of English, 1972-74; freelance writer, 1974-; LaGrange College, writer-in-residence, 1996-; United Methodist Men's Club, president. **Publications:** NOVELS: A Funeral for the Eyes of Fire, 1975 as Eyes of Fire, 1980; And Strange at Ecbatan the Trees, 1976 as Beneath the Shattered Moons, 1977; Stolen Faces, 1977; A Little Knowledge, 1977; Catacomb Years, 1979; Transfigurations, 1979; (with I. Watson) Under Heaven's Bridge, 1981; No Enemy but Time, 1982; Who Made Stevie Crye?, 1984; Ancient of Days, 1985; Philip K. Dick Is Dead, Alas, 1987; Unicorn Mountain, 1988; Count Geiger's Blues, 1992; Brittle Innings, 1994; Ancient of Days, 1995; Blue Kansas Sky: Four Short Novels of Memory, Magic, Surmise & Estrangement, 2000; The Door Gunner, 2011; The City Quiet as Death, 2011. NOVELS AS PHILIP LAWSON (with P. Di Filippo): Would It Kill You to Smile?, 1998; Muskrat Courage, 2000. POETRY: Windows and Mirrors, 1977; Time Pieces, 1998. STORIES: Blooded on Arachne, 1982; One Winter in Eden, 1984; Close Encounters with the Deity, 1986; Emphatically Not SF, Almost, 1990; At the City Limits of Fate, 1996; Brighten to Incandescence, 2003. NOVELLAS: Apartheid, Superstrings and Mordecai Thubana, 1989; Blue Kansas Sky, 2000. OTHER: Seven Deadly Sins, 1999. EDITOR: (with I. Watson) Changes (anthology), 1983; Light Years and Dark (anthology), 1984; Nebula Awards (anthologies), vol. II3-25, 1989-91; A Reverie for Mister Ray: Reflections on Life, Death, and Speculative Fiction, 2005; A Cross of Centuries (anthology), 2007. Contributor to periodicals. **Address:** LaGrange College, 601 Broad St., LaGrange, GA 30240, U.S.A. **Online address:** mlbishop@juno.com

BISHOP, Nic. American/New Zealander (born New Zealand), b. 1955. **Genres:** Travel/Exploration, Natural History, Animals/Pets. **Career:** Massey University, research fellow, 1977-80; University of Canterbury, tutor and researcher, 1980-86; writer and photographer, 1988-. **Publications:** AUTHOR: Untouched Horizons: Photographs from the South Island Wilderness, 1989; Natural History of New Zealand, 1992; From the Mountains to the Sea: The Secret Life of New Zealand's Rivers and Wetlands, 1994; New Zealand Wild: The Greenest Place on Earth, 1995; Backyard Detective: Critters Up Close, 2002; Forest Explorer: A Life-size Field Guide, 2004. FOR CHILDREN: Leap Frog, 1994; Ready, Steady, Jump, 1995; The Secrets of Animal Flight, 1997; Strange Plants, 1997; The Green Snake, 1998; The Katydids, 1998; Gecko Flies, 1998; Mudskipper, 1998; Canoe Diary, 1998; Caught in a Flash, 1998; Digging for Bird-dinosaurs: An Expedition to Madagascar, 2000. OTHERS: Spiders, 2007; Frogs, 2008; Marsupials, 2009; Nic Bishop Butterflies and Moths, 2009; Lizards, 2010; Nic Bishop Snakes, 2012. Contributor to books, magazines and periodicals. **Address:** Houghton Mifflin Harcourt Co., 222 Berkeley St., 9th Fl., Boston, MA 02116-3764, U.S.A.

BISKUPIC, Joan. American (born United States), b. 1956?. **Genres:** Law. **Career:** Tulsa Tribune, bureau chief and reporter, 1985-87; Congressional Quarterly, legal affairs reporter, 1989-92; Washington Post, supreme court reporter, 1992-2000; USA Today, reporter, 2000-. **Publications:** The Supreme Court Yearbook: 1989-1990, 1990; The Supreme Court Yearbook: 1990-1991, 1991; The Supreme Court at Work, 2nd ed., 1997; (with E. Witt) The Supreme Court and the Powers of the American Government, 1997, 2nd ed., 2009; (with E. Witt) The Supreme Court and Individual Rights, 4th ed., 2004; (with E. Witt) Guide to the U.S. Supreme Court, 4th ed., 2004; Sandra Day O'Connor: How the First Woman on the Supreme Court Became Its Most Influential Justice (biography), 2005; American Original: The Life and Constitution of Supreme Court Justice Antonin Scalia, 2009. **Address:** USA Today, 7950 Jones Branch Dr., McLean, VA 22102-3302, U.S.A. **Online address:** jbiskupic@usatoday.com

BISSELL, Sallie. American (born United States) **Genres:** Novels, Mystery/Crime/Suspense, Ghost Writer. **Career:** Tennessee Writers Alliance, director. Writer. **Publications:** NOVELS: In the Forest of Harm, 2001; A Darker Justice, 2002; Call the Devil by His Oldest Name, 2004; A Legacy of Masks, 2005. **Address:** c/o Author Mail, Bantam Books, 1540 Broadway, New York, NY 10036, U.S.A. **Online address:** sallie@salliebissell.com

BISSETT, Bill. Canadian (born Canada), b. 1939. **Genres:** Poetry, Songs/Lyrics And Libretti, Biography, Young Adult Fiction. **Career:** Blue Ointment Press, editor and printer, 1962-83. **Publications:** SELF ILLUSTRATED: We Sleep Inside Each Other All, 1965; The Jinx Ship nd Othr Trips: Pomes-drawings-collage, 1966; Fires in the Tempul, 1967; Where Is Miss Florence Riddle, 1967, 2nd ed., 1973; Lebanon Voices, 1967; What Poetiks, 1967; Gossamer Bed Pan, 1967, rev. ed., 1974; Of the Land/Divine Service Poems, 1968; Awake in the Red Desert!, 1968; Liberating Skies: Th Sic Tree Of Life Sings, 1968; Killer Whale, 1969; Sunday Work?, 1969; The Lost Angel Mining Company, 1969; A Marvellous Experience, 1969; IBM, 1970; Sth Story I To: Trew Adventure, 1970; The Outlaw, 1970; Tuff Shit Loves Pomes, 1970; Blew Trewz, 1971; Rush what Fukin Thery, 1971; Nobody Owns th(sic) Earth, 1971; Air 6, 1971; Dragon Fly, 1971; Drifting Into War, 1971; (co-author) Four Parts Sand: Concrete Poems, 1972; Air 10-11-12, 1972; Th Ice Bag, 1972; Ice, 1972; Pomes For Yoshi, 1972, 2nd ed., 1977; Th High Green Hill, 1972; Polar Bear Hunt, 1972; Words in the Fire, 1972; Pass th Food, Release th Spirit Book, 1973; The First Sufi Line, 1973; What, 1974; Vancouver Mainland Ice & Cold Storage, 2nd ed., 1974; Medicine: My Mouth's On Fire, 1974; Space Travl, 1974; Living with the Vishyun, 1974; Drawings, 1974; You can Eat it at th Opening, 1974; The Fifth Sun, 1975; Image Being, 1975; Stardust, 1975; Venus, 1975; Plutonium Missing, 1976; An Allusyun to Macbeth, 1976; The Wind Up Tongue, 1976; Sailor, 1978, 2nd ed., 1982; Th First Snow, 1979; (and ed.) Selected Poems: Beyond Even Faithful Legends, 1980; Sa n th monkey, 1980; Beyond Even Faithful Legends, 1980; Soul Arrow, 1981; Northern Birds In Color, 1981; S n His Crystal Ball, 1981; Ready for Framing, 1981; Seagull on Yonge Street, 1983; Canada Gees Mate For Life, 1985; The Last Blew Ointment Anthology: 1963-1983, 1986; Animal Uproar, 1987; What We Have, 1988; Inkorrect Thots, 1992, 2nd ed., 1994; The Last Photo uv th Human Soul, 1993; Th Influenza uv Logik, 1995; Loving Without Being Vulnrabul, 1997; Scars on the Seehors, 1999; B leev abul char ak trs, 2000; Lunaria, 2001; Peter Among th Towring Boxes, Text Bites, 2002; Th Oranges uv Orantangua, 2002; Narrativ Enigma: Rumours uv hurricane, 2004; Northern Wild Roses: Deth Interrupts Th Dansing, 2005; Ths is erth thees ar peopul, 2007; Sublingual, 2008; (with C. Malyon) Griddle Talk: A Yeer uv Bill n Carol Dewing Brunch, 2009; Time, 2010; Novel, 2011. **Address:** 152 Carleton St., PO Box 92516, Toronto, ON M5A 2K1, Canada. **Online address:** centralianwings@sympatico.ca

BISSETTE, Stephen. American (born United States), b. 1955. **Genres:** Cartoons, Novels, Young Adult Non-fiction. **Career:** SpiderBaby Grafix, publisher; First Run Video, co-manager, 1998-2005, buyer; The Center for Cartoon Studies, teacher; White River Independent Film, board director; The Center for Digital Art, consultant; Professional cartoonist, comics writer and publisher. **Publications:** Goreshriek, 1988; Shriek, 1989; Aliens: Tribes, 1993; (ed.) From Hell: The Complete Scripts, vol. I, 1993; (with S. Waiter) Comic Book Rebels: Conversations with the Creators of the New Comics, 1993; (co-author) The Monster Book: Buffy the Vampire Slayer, 2000; We Are Going to Eat You!: The Third World Cannibal Movies and the Inside Story of the Goona-Goona Films, 2003; (with H. Wagner and C. Golden) Prince of Stories: The Many Worlds of Neil Gaiman, 2008; Saga of the Swamp Thing, 2009. Contributor of articles. **Address:** The Center for Cartoon Studies, PO Box 125, White River Junction, VT 05001, U.S.A. **Online address:** mbleier@sover.net

BITTLESTONE, Robert. British (born England), b. 1952?. **Genres:** Geography, Money/Finance, Administration/Management. **Career:** Roneo Vickers, head of financial analysis and group information, 1976-78; Metapraxis Ltd., founder, managing director and chairman, 1979-. Writer. **Publications:** (With J. Diggle and J. Underhill) Odysseus Unbound: The Search for Homer's Ithaca, 2005; Financial Management for Business: Cracking the Hidden Code, 2010. **Address:** Metapraxis Ltd., Kingstons House, Coombe Rd., Kingston-upon Thames, SR KT2 7AB, England. **Online address:** robert.bittlestone@metapraxis.com

BITTNER, F. Rosanne. *See* **BITTNER, Rosanne.**

BITTNER, Rosanne. (F. Rosanne Bittner). American (born United States), b. 1945. **Genres:** Romance/Historical, Novellas/Short Stories, Young Adult Fiction, Novels. **Career:** Writer, 1984-. **Publications:** HISTORICAL ROMANCES, SAVAGE DESTINY SERIES: Sweet Prairie Passion, 1983; (as F. Rosanne Bittner) Ride the Free Wind, 1984; (as F. Rosanne Bittner) River of Love, 1984; (as F. Rosanne Bittner) Embrace the Wild Land, 1984; (as F. Rosanne Bittner) Climb the Highest Mountain, 1985; Meet the New Dawn, 1986; Eagle's Song, 1996. HISTORICAL ROMANCES, SAVAGE DESTINY SERIES: Sweet Prairie Passion, 1983; Ride the Free Wind, 1984; River of Love, 1984; Embrace the Wild Land, 1984; Climb the Highest Mountain, 1985; Meet the New Dawn, 1986; Eagle's Song, 1996. ROMANCE NOVELS: Savage Horizons, 1987; Frontier Fires, 1987; (as F. Rosanne Bittner) Destiny's Dawn, 1987; (as F. Rosanne Bittner) Tennessee Bride, 1988; (as F. Rosanne Bittner) Texas Bride, 1988; This Time Forever, 1989; (as F. Rosanne Bittner) Oregon Bride, 1990; Love Me Tomorrow, 1998; Texas Passions, 1999; Where Heaven Begins, 2004; Walk By Faith, 2005; Follow Your Heart, 2005. OTHER HISTORICAL ROMANCES: (as F. Rosanne Bittner) Arizona Bride, 1985; (as F. Rosanne Bittner) Lawless Love, 1985; Rapture's Gold, 1986; Prairie Embrace, 1987; Heart's Surrender, 1988; Ecstasy's Chains, 1989; Arizona Ecstasy, 1989; Sweet Mountain Magic, 1990; Sioux Splendor, 1990; (as F. Rosanne Bittner) Comanche Sunset, 1991; Caress, 1992; Shameless, 1993; Unforgettable, 1994; Full Circle, 1994; Until Tomorrow, 1995; Texas Embrace, 1997; Mystic Dreamers, 1999. HISTORICAL SAGAS: (as F. Rosanne Bittner) Montana Woman, 1990; Embers of the Heart, 1990; In the Shadow of the Mountains, 1991; Song of the Wolf, 1992; Thunder on the Plains, 1992; Outlaw Hearts, 1993; Tender Betrayal, 1993; Wildest Dreams, 1994; The Forever Tree, 1995; Chase the Sun, 1995; Tame the Wild Wind, 1996. ANTHOLOGIES: (with A. Mills and A. Lamb) Cherished Moments, 1994; (co-author) Love by Chocolate, 1997; (with D. Domning and V. Vaughan) Cherished Love, 1997. MYSTIC INDIAN SERIES: Mystic Dreamers, 1999; Mystic Visions, 2000; Mystic Warriors, 2001. AMERICA WEST SERIES: Into the Wilderness, 2002; Into The Valley, 2003; Into the Prairie, 2004. OTHER: Love's Bounty, 2000. **Address:** PO Box 1044, Coloma, MI 49038, U.S.A. **Online address:** bittner@parrett.net

BITTON-ASHKELONY, Brouria. (Bruria Bitton-Ashkelony). Israeli (born Israel), b. 1956. **Genres:** Theology/Religion. **Career:** The Hebrew University, Department of Comparative Religion, lecturer, 1999-2005; Center for the Study of Christianity, acting director, 1999-2001, director, 2010-, Joint Center for Eretz-Israel Studies, director, 2002-06, senior lecturer, 2005-, chair, 2005-08, Honors Program for the Training of Jewish Studies Teachers, director and academic head of revivim, 2006-08. Writer. **Publications:** Aliyah Le-regel: Tefisot U-teguvot Be-sifrut Avot Ha-kenesiyah Uva-sifrut Ha-nezirit Ba-me'ot Ha- revi'it-shishit, 1995; (ed. with A. Kofsky) Christian Gaza in Late Antiquity, 2004; Encountering the Sacred: The Debate on Christian Pilgrimage in Late Antiquity, 2005; (with A. Kofsky) The Monastic School of Gaza, 2006. Contributor to books and periodicals. **Address:** Department of Comparative Religion, The Hebrew University of Jerusale, Rm. 6603, Faculty of Humanities, Mt. Scopus, 91905, Israel. **Online address:** ashkelon@mscc.huji.ac.il

BITTON-ASHKELONY, Bruria. *See* **BITTON-ASHKELONY, Brouria.**

BITTON-JACKSON, Livia E(lvira). American/Israeli (born Israel), b. 1931. **Genres:** Young Adult Non-fiction, Autobiography/Memoirs, Literary Criticism And History, History. **Career:** City University of New York, Hunter College, lecturer in Hebrew literature, 1965-68; Long Island University, adjunct assistant professor of Hebrew language and literature, 1965-68; Herbert H. Lehman College, professor of Hebrew and Judaic studies, 1968-2003, professor emeritus, 2003-; Academy for Jewish Religion, associate professor, 1970-71, dean of students, 1972-75; Brooklyn College, assistant professor of Judaic studies, 1972-76; Tel Aviv University, professor of Jewish history, 1979-82. Writer. **Publications:** AS LIVIA ELVIRA BITTON: A Decade of Zionism in Hungary, 1918-1928, 1971. AS LIVIA BITTON-JACKSON: Elli: Coming of Age in the Holocaust, 1980; Madonna or Courtesan?: The Jewish Woman in Christian Literature, 1982; I Have Lived a Thousand Years: Growing Up in the Holocaust, 1997; My Bridges of Hope: Searching for Life and Love After Auschwitz, 1999; Hello, America, 2005; Towards Freedom, 2006; Saving What Remains, 2009. Contributor to journals. **Address:** City University of New York, Lehman College, 250 Bedford Park Blvd. W, Bronx, NY 10468, U.S.A. **Online address:** lbj@013.net

BIVINS, Jason C. American (born United States), b. 1969. **Genres:** Theology/Religion, Politics/Government. **Career:** North Carolina State University, Department of Philosophy and Religion, assistant professor, 2000-04, associate professor of religion, 2004-, associate department head, 2005-. Writer. **Publications:** (With M.J. Weaver and D.B. Brakke) Introduction to Christianity, 1998; The Fracture of Good Order: Christian Antiliberalism and the Challenge to American Politics, 2003; Religion of Fear: The Politics of Horror in Conservative Evangelicalism, 2008. **Address:** Department of Philosophy and Religious Studies, North Carolina State University, 340B Withers Hall, PO Box 8103, Raleigh, NC 27695-8103, U.S.A. **Online address:** jcbivins@unity.ncsu.edu

BIZZARRO, Tina Waldeier. American (born United States), b. 1950.

Genres: Architecture, Art/Art History, History. **Career:** Canadian Consulate, bilingual public relations representative, 1972-74; Rosemont College, assistant professor of art history, 1977-, Arts Division, head, 1986-91, Mediterranean Studies Summer Program, co-director, 2000-, discipline coordinator; Franklin and Marshall College, art history teacher, 1981; Beaver College, faculty, 1981. Writer. **Publications:** Romanesque Architectural Criticism: A Pre-History, 1992. Works appear in anthologies. Contributor to books and periodicals. **Address:** Department of History of Art, Rosemont College, 1400 Montgomery Ave., Rosemont, PA 19010-1699, U.S.A. **Online address:** tbizzarro@rosemont.edu

BIZZELL, Patricia. *See* **BIZZELL, Patricia (Lynn).**

BIZZELL, Patricia (Lynn). (Patricia Bizzell). American (born United States), b. 1948. **Genres:** Education, Writing/Journalism, Bibliography, Language/Linguistics, Social Sciences. **Career:** Rutgers University, assistant professor of English, 1975-78, director of remedial writing program, 1975-77, teacher training program, director, 1977-78; College of the Holy Cross, assistant professor, 1978-81, associate professor, 1981-88, director of writing across the curriculum, 1981-94, director of Writing Workshop, 1982-87, 1992-94, professor of English, 1988-, director of honors program, 1994-98, director of English honors program, 1999-2000; English department, chair, 2001-05, Reverend John E. Brooks professor of humanities, 2010-; Rhetoric Society of America, president, 2004-06. Writer. **Publications:** (As Patricia Bizzell): (with B. Herzberg and R. Gorrell) The Bedford Bibliography for Teachers of Writing, 1983, 6th ed., 2004; (with B. Herzberg and N. Reynolds) 5th ed., 2000; (with B. Herzberg) The Rhetorical Tradition: Readings from Classical Times to the Present, 1990, 2nd ed., 2001; Academic Discourse and Critical Consciousness, 1992; (ed. with B. Herzberg) Negotiating Difference: Cultural Case Studies for Composition, 1996; (ed. with C. Schroder and H. Fox) ALT DIS: Alternative Discourses and the Academy, 2002; (ed.) Rhetorical Agendas: Political, Ethical, Spiritual, 2006. Contributor to journals. Works appear in anthologies. **Address:** Department of English, College of the Holy Cross, 1 College St., Worcester, MA 01610, U.S.A. **Online address:** pbizzell@holycross.edu

BJARKMAN, Peter C(hristian). American (born United States), b. 1941. **Genres:** History, Sports/Fitness, Biography, Young Adult Fiction, Novellas/Short Stories. **Career:** Wethersfield Connecticut High School, instructor of English, 1963-68; Colegio Panamericano Bucaramanga, instructor in English, 1968-69; Colegio Americano Guayaquil, U.S. Program, director, 1971-72; George Mason University, assistant professor of English, 1976-79; Purdue University, assistant professor of English, 1979-86, director of English-as-a-second-language programs, 1979-85; Butler University, adjunct associate professor, 1986; Ball State University, visiting assistant professor, 1986; University of Colorado, visiting assistant professor, 1987; Indiana University-Purdue University, visiting assistant professor, 1988; free-lance author, 1989-. **Publications:** (Co-ed.) The Real-World Linguist: Linguistic Applications in the 1980s, 1986; (co-ed.) American Spanish Pronunciation: Theoretical and Applied Perspectives, 1989; The Toronto Blue Jays, 1990; Baseball's Great Dynasties-The Dodgers, 1990; (ed. and contrib.) Encyclopedia of Major League Baseball Team Histories: The American League, 1991, rev. ed., 1993; (ed. and contrib.) Encyclopedia of Major League Baseball Team Histories: The National League, 1991, rev. ed., 1993; Baseball Great Dynasties: The Reds, 1991; Roberto Clemente (juvenile), 1991; The History of the NBA, 1991; (ed. and contrib.) Baseball and the Game of Life: Stories for the Thinking Fan, 1991; The Baseball Scrapbook: The Men and Magic of America's National Pastime, 1991, 5th ed., 2008; Duke Snider (juvenile), 1991; Ernie Banks (juvenile) 1991; Warren Spahn (juvenile), 1991; The History of the NBA, 1991; Baseball Great Dynasties: The Reds, 1991; The Baseball Scrapbook: The Men and Magic of America's National Pastime, 1991, 2nd ed., 2000; (ed. and contrib.) The Inter-National Pastime: A Review of Baseball History, 1992; The Brooklyn Dodgers, 1992; (ed. and contrib.) Baseball and the Game of Ideas: Essays for the Serious Fan, 1993; The Encyclopedia of Pro Basketball Team Histories, 1994; Shaq: The Making of a Legend, 1994; Slam Dunk Superstars, 1994; Baseball with a Latin Beat: A History of the Latin American Game, 1994; Big Ten Basketball, 1995; Top Ten Baseball Base Stealers (juvenile), 1995; Top Ten Basketball Slam Dunkers (juvenile), 1995; ACC: Atlantic Coast Conference Basketball, 1996; Hoopla: A Century of College Basketball, 1896-1996, 1996; Sports Great Scottie Pippin (juvenile), 1996; Sports Great Dominique Wilkins (juvenile), 1996; Sports Great Scottie Pippen (juvenile), 1996; Reggie Miller (juvenile), 1998; Biographical History of Basketball, 1998; (with M. Rucker) Smoke: The Romance and Lore of Cuban Baseball, 1999; The Boston Celtics Encyclopedia, 2000; The New York Mets Encyclopedia, 2001; Diamonds Around the Globe: The Encyclopedia of International Baseball, 2005; A History of Cuban Baseball, 1864-2006, 2007; Who's Who In Cuban Baseball, 1962-2011, forthcoming; Baseball's Other Big Red Machine: A History of the Cuban National Team, forthcoming; Cuba Today, forthcoming. **Address:** PO Box 2199, West Lafayette, IN 47996-2199, U.S.A. **Online address:** bjarkman@mindspring.com

BJORGE, Gary J(ohn). American (born United States), b. 1940. **Genres:** History, Military/Defense/Arms Control, Translations, Literary Criticism And History. **Career:** University of Wisconsin, library associate in Chinese, 1973-80; University of Kansas, East Asian librarian in Chinese, 1980-84; U.S. Army Command and General Staff College, military historian and researcher, 1984-. Writer. **Publications:** Deception Operations, 1986; (ed. with T.E. Barlow) I Myself Am a Woman: Selected Works of Ding Ling, 1989; Merrill's Marauders: Combined Operations in Northern Burma in 1944, 1996; Moving the Enemy: Operational Art in the Chinese PLA's Huai Hai Campaign, 2004. Contributor to periodicals. **Address:** 1321 Jana Dr., Lawrence, KS 66049, U.S.A. **Online address:** gbjorge@sunflower.com

BJORK, Daniel W. American (born United States), b. 1940. **Genres:** Biography, History, Sciences, Autobiography/Memoirs, Psychology. **Career:** Southeast Missouri University, professor, through 1974; University of Alabama, assistant professor of history, 1974-81; Mercy College, professor of history, 1983-91; St. Mary's University, professor of history, 1991-. Writer. **Publications:** The Victorian Flight, 1978; The Compromised Scientist, 1983; William James: The Center of His Vision, 1988; B.F. Skinner: A Life, 1993. **Address:** Department of History, St. Mary's University, Rm. 501 Chaminade Twr., 5th Fl., 1 Camino Santa Maria, San Antonio, TX 78228, U.S.A. **Online address:** dbjork@stmarytx.edu

BJORKLUND, David F. American (born United States), b. 1949. **Genres:** Psychology, Human Relations/Parenting. **Career:** Florida Atlantic University, instructor, 1976-86, professor of psychology, 1986-; Max Planck Institute for Psychological Research, staff, 1988, 1990; University of Georgia, visiting professor, 1994; Emory University, visiting professor, 1994; James I University, visiting professor, 2001; University of Würzburg, Alexander von Humboldt Research Professor, 2002, 2003; University of Canterbury, Visiting Erskine Fellow, 2004. Writer, psychologist, researcher and consultant. **Publications:** Children's Thinking: Developmental Function and Individual Differences, 1989, 4th ed. as Children's Thinking: Cognitive Development and Individual Differences, 2005; (ed.) Children's Strategies: Contemporary Views of Cognitive Development, 1990; (with B.R. Bjorklund) Parents Book of Discipline, 1990; (with B.R. Bjorklund) Looking at Children: An Introduction to Child Development, 1992; (with A.D. Pellegrini) Applied Child Study: A Developmental Approach, 3rd ed., 1998; (ed.) False-Memory Creation in Children and Adults: Theory, Research, and Implications, 2000; (with A.D. Pellegrini) The Origins of Human Nature: Evolutionary Developmental Psychology, 2002; (ed. With B.J. Ellis) Origins of the Social Mind: Evolutionary Psychology and Child Development, 2005; Why Youth Is Not Wasted on the Young: Immaturity in Human Development, 2007. Contributor to books, periodicals and journals. **Address:** Department of Psychology, Florida Atlantic University, 112 Behavioral Science, 77 Glades Rd., Boca Raton, FL 33431-0991, U.S.A. **Online address:** dbjorklu@fau.edu

BJORNERUD, Marcia. American (born United States) **Genres:** Autobiography/Memoirs. **Career:** University of Wisconsin, National Science Foundation, graduate fellow, 1983-86, Department of Geology and Geophysics, university graduate fellow, 1986-87; Ohio State University, Byrd Polar Research Center, First Byrd postdoctoral fellow, 1987-88; Miami University, Department of Geology, assistant professor, 1989-94, associate professor, 1994-95; Lawrence University, Department of Geology, associate professor of geology, 1995-2002, chair, 1995-, professor of geology, 2002-, Environmental Studies, director, 2002-; Michigan Technological University, Department of Geological Engineering and Sciences, adjunct research professor, 1996-99. Writer. **Publications:** Reading the Rocks: The Autobiography of the Earth, 2005. **Address:** Department of Geology, Lawrence University, 711 E Boldt Way, PO Box 599, Appleton, WI 54911-5690, U.S.A. **Online address:** marcia.bjornerud@lawrence.edu

BLACK, Arthur (Raymond). Canadian (born Canada), b. 1943. **Genres:** Essays, Humor/Satire, Children's Fiction. **Career:** CBC-Radio, host, 1976-

85, Basic Black, host, 1985-2001; Kitchener Public Library, writer-in-residence, 1992; Global Television, commentator, 1992-94; Weird Homes, host, 1998-; Weird Wheels, host, 2000-. **Publications:** Basic Black, 1981; Old Fort William: A History, 1985; Back to Black, 1986; That Old Black Magic (essays), 1989; Arthur! Arthur!, 1991; Black by Popular Demand, 1993; (comp. with L. Raymond) Blackmail!: Exemplary Epistles, Delightful Dispatches, and Fanciful Faxes Sent to Basic Black, 1995; Black in the Saddle Again, 1996; Black Tie and Tales, 1999; Flashback!, 2002; Black & White And Read All Over, 2004; Pitch Black, 2005; Black Gold: Nuggets From a Lifetime of Laughs, 2006; Black to the Grindstone, 2007; Black is the New Green, 2009; A Chip Off the Old Black, 2010; Plaudits, Kudos and Huzzahs. **Address:** Harbour Publishing, 4437 Rondeview Rd., PO Box 219, Madeira Park, BC V0N 2H0, Canada. **Online address:** arblack43@shaw.ca

BLACK, Benjamin. *See* **BANVILLE, John.**

BLACK, Brian. (Brian C. Black). American (born United States), b. 1966. **Genres:** Natural History, Environmental Sciences/Ecology. **Career:** Gettysburg College, visiting assistant professor, 1994-97; Skidmore College, visiting assistant professor, 1997-99; Pennsylvania State University, Department of History, associate professor, 1999-. Writer. **Publications:** Petrolia: The Landscape of America's First Oil Boom, 2000; Nature and the Environment in Nineteenth-Century American Life, 2006; Nature and the Environment in Twentieth-Century American Life, 2006; (with D.L. Lybecker) Great Debates in American Environmental History, 2008. Contributor to periodicals. **Address:** Department of History, Pennsylvania State University, Ivyside Pk., Altoona, PA 16601, U.S.A. **Online address:** bcb4@psu.edu

BLACK, Brian C. *See* **BLACK, Brian.**

BLACK, Charlene Villasenor. American (born United States), b. 1962?. **Genres:** Art/Art History, Sociology, Theology/Religion. **Career:** University of California, associate professor of art history. Writer. **Publications:** Creating the Cult of St. Joseph: Art and Gender in the Spanish Empire, 2006. Contributor to journals. **Address:** Department of Art History, University of California, 247C, Dodd Hall, Los Angeles, CA 90095-1417, U.S.A. **Online address:** cvblack@humnet.ucla.edu

BLACK, Conrad. (Conrad Moffat Black). Canadian (born Canada), b. 1944. **Genres:** History, Biography. **Career:** Sherbrooke Record, owner, 1969; Sterling Newspapers Ltd. (chain of daily and weekly periodicals), owner; Argus Corporation Ltd. (holding company), chairman of board and chairman of executive committee, 1978-86; Hollinger International Inc. (media company), founder and chief executive officer, 1978-2003; Sotheby's Holdings Inc., director; Brascan Corp., director; Canadian Imperial Bank of Commerce, director; CanWest Global Communications, director; Jerusalem Post, director; Daily Telegraph, owner; Chicago Sun-Times, owner. Writer and politician. **Publications:** Duplessis, 1977; A Life in Progress, 1993; Render Unto Caesar: The Life and Legacy of Maurice Duplessis, 1998; Franklin Delano Roosevelt: Champion of Freedom, 2003; Richard M. Nixon: A Life in Full, 2007; The Invincible Quest, 2009. **Address:** Janklow Nesbitt Literary Agency, 445 Park Ave., New York, NY 10022, U.S.A.

BLACK, Conrad Moffat. *See* **BLACK, Conrad.**

BLACK, D(avid) M(acleod). British/South African (born South Africa), b. 1941. **Genres:** Poetry, Social Sciences. **Career:** Writer. **Publications:** The Rocklestrakes, 1960; From the Mountain, 1963; Theory of Diet, 1966; With Decorum, 1967; A Dozen Short Poems, 1968; (with D.M. Thomas and P. Redgrove) Penguin Modern Poets 11, 1968; The Educators, 1969; The Old Hag, 1971; (with J.S. Kirkaldy) Social Reporting and Educational Planning: A Feasibility Study, 1972; The Happy Crow, 1974; Gravitations, 1979; A Place for Exploration, 1991; Collected Poems, 1964-87, 1991. Contributor of articles and poems to periodicals. **Address:** 30 Cholmley Gardens, London, GL NW6 IAG, England.

BLACK, Donald. American (born United States), b. 1941. **Genres:** Sociology, Law, Criminology/True Crime, Ethics. **Career:** Yale University, Yale Law School, Russell Sage fellow, 1968-70, assistant professor of sociology and lecturer in law, 1970-74, junior faculty fellow, 1973-74, associate professor of sociology, 1974-79; Harvard University, Center for Criminal Justice, research associate, 1979-85, lecturer in law, 1980-85; Academic Press, series editor, 1977-86; University of Virginia, professor of sociology, 1985-88, chairman of Sociology, 1986-89, university professor of the social sciences, 1988-, Press, series editor, 2005-; Oxford University Press, series editor, 1986-; American Anthropological Association, fellow, 1986; JAI Press, Virginia Review of Sociology, Founder and General Editor, 1989-99; American Society of Criminology, fellow, 1991; Sage Publications, Advisory Editor, 2000-07. **Publications:** (Contrib.) Studies in Crime and Law Enforcement in Major Metropolitan Areas, 1967; The Behavior of Law, 1976, Special Edition, 2010; The Manners and Customs of the Police, 1980; Sociological Justice, 1989; The Social Structure of Right and Wrong, 1993, rev. ed., 1998; Moral Time, 2011. EDITOR: (with M. Mileski) The Social Organization of Law, 1973; Toward a General Theory of Social Control, 2 vols., 1984. **Address:** Department of Sociology, University of Virginia, 310 Dynamics, Cabell Hall, PO Box 400766, Charlottesville, VA 22904, U.S.A. **Online address:** black@virginia.edu

BLACK, Ethan. (Bob Reiss). American (born United States), b. 1951?. **Genres:** Novels, Young Adult Non-fiction, Mystery/Crime/Suspense. **Career:** Chicago Tribune, reporter; Outside Magazine, correspondent; Glamour Magazine, columnist. Journalist. **Publications:** CONRAD VOORT SERIES: The Broken Hearts Club, 1999; Irresistible, 2000; All the Dead Were Strangers, 2001; Dead for Life, 2003; At Hell's Gate, 2004. AS BOB REISS: Summer Fires, 1980; The Casco Deception, 1983; Divine Assassin, 1985; Saltmaker, 1988; Flamingo, 1989; The Last Spy, 1992; The Road to Extrema, 1992; Frequent Flyer: One Plane, One Passenger, and the Spectacular Feat of Commercial Flight, 1994; The Coming Storm: Extreme Weather and Our Terrifying Future, 2001; The Side Effect, 2006; Black Monday, 2007. Contributor to periodicals. **Address:** c/o Author Mail, Simon & Schuster Inc., 1230 Ave. of the Americas, 10th Fl., New York, NY 10020-1513, U.S.A. **Online address:** bobreiss@hotmail.com

BLACK, Jeremy (Martin). British (born England), b. 1955. **Genres:** History, Military/Defense/Arms Control, Politics/Government. **Career:** University of Durham, lecturer in history, 1980-90, senior lecturer, 1990-91, reader, 1991-95, University Research Foundation and Society of Fellows, director, 1991-95, professor, 1994-95; University of Exeter, professor of history, 1996-, established chair in history, 1996-; Foreign Policy Research Institute, Center for the Study of America and the West, senior fellow. Writer. **Publications:** The British and the Grand Tour, 1985; British Foreign Policy in the Age of Walpole, 1985; The English Press in the 18th Century, 1986; Natural and Necessary Enemies, 1986; Collapse ofthe Anglo-French Alliance, 1727-1731, 1987; 18th Century Europe, 1700-1789, 1990; Culloden and the '45, 1990; The Rise of the European Powers, 1679-1793, 1990; Robert Walpole and the Nature of Politics in Early 18th-Century Britain, 1990; War for America, 1991; A Military Revolution?, 1991; A System of Ambition?, 1991; The Grand Tour, 1992; Pitt the Elder, 1992; The British Abroad, 1993; British Foreign Policy in an Age of Revolutions, 1783-1793, 1994; Convergence or Divergence?: Britain and the Continent, 1994; European Warfare, 1660-1815, 1994; European Warfare, 1660-1815, 1994; Divergence?, 1994; Cambridge Illustrated Atlas, Warfare: Renaissance to Revolution, 1492-1792, 1996; History of the British Isles, 1996; Illustrated Historyof Eighteenth-Century Britain, 1688-1793, 1996; Maps and History: Constructing Images of the Past, 1997; Maps and Politics, 1997; America or Europe?: British Foreign policy, 1739-63, 1998; War and the World: Military Power and the Fate of Continents, 1450-2000, 1998; Why Wars Happen, 1998; America or Europe?: British Foreign Policy, 1739-63, 1998; Warfare in the 18th Century, 1999; Britain as a Military Power, 1688-1815, 1999; New History of Wales, 2000; War and the World, 2000; War: Past, Present, and Future, 2000; Eighteenth-century Britain, 1688-1783, 2001, 2nd ed., 2008; English Press, 1621-1861, 2001; Politics of James Bond: From Fleming's Novels to the Big Screen, 2001; Walpole in Power, 2001; War in the New Century, 2001; Western Warfare, 1775-1882, 2001; America as a Military Power: From the American Revolution to the Civil War, 2002; Europe and the World, 1650-1830, 2002; European International Relations, 1648-1815, 2002; Warfare in the Western World, 1882-1975, 2002; France and the Grand Tour, 2003; History of the British Isles, 2003; Italy and the Grand Tour, 2003; (with D.M. MacRaild) Nineteenth-Century Britain, 2003; Visions of the World: A History of Maps, 2003; World War Two, 2003; British Seaborne Empire, 2004; Hanoverians: The History of a Dynasty, 2004; Kings, Nobles and Commoners: States and Societies in Early Modern Europe, a Revisionist History, 2004; War and The New Disorder in the 21st Century, 2004; Rethinking Military History, 2004; Parliament and Foreign Policy in the Eighteenth Century, 2004; Kings, Nobles and Commoners: States and Societies in Early Modern Europe, A Revisionist History, 2004; The Hanoverians: The History of a Dynasty, 2004; Using History,

2005; A Subject For Taste: Culture In Eighteenth-Century England, 2005; The Continental Commitment: Britain, Hanover and Interventionism, 1714-1793, 2005; Introduction to Global Military History: 1775 to the Present Day, 2005; George III: America's Last King, 2006; Age of Total War, 1860-1945, 2006; European Question and the National Interest, 2006; Slave Trade, 2006; Warfare in the Eighteenth Century, 2006; War in European History, 1494-1660: The Essential Bibliography, 2006; Military History of Britain: From 1775 to the Present, 2006; Second World War Seven Volume Set, 2007; Trade, Empire and British Foreign Policy, 1689-1815: Politics of a Commercial State, 2007; Tools of War, 2007; Short History of Britain, 2007; George II: Puppet of the Politicians?, 2007; European Warfare in a Global Context, 1660-1815, 2007; (with D.M. Macraild) Studying History, 3rd ed., 2007; Great Powers and the Quest for Hegemony: The World Order Since 1500, 2008; Holocaust, 2008; Curse of History, 2008; What If?: Counterfactualism and the Problem of History, 2008; Crisis of Empire: Britain and America in the Eighteenth Century, 2008; (with S. Morillo and P. Lococo) War in World History: Society, Technology and War from Ancient Times to the Present, 2009; The Politics of World War Two, 2009; War Since 1990, 2009; Defence: Policy Issues for a New Government, 2009; War in European History, 1660-1792: The Essential Bibliography, 2009; War: A Short History, 2009; The War of 1812 in the Age of Napoleon, 2009; London: A History, 2009; Naval Power: A History of Warfare and the Sea from 1500 Onwards, 2009; War in the Nineteenth Century: 1800-1914, 2009; A History of Diplomacy, 2010; Battle of Waterloo, 2010; Brief History of Slavery, 2011; Debating Foreign Policy in Eighteenth-century Britain, 2011; Elite Fighting forces: From the Praetorian Guard to the Green Berets, 2011; Beyond the Military Revolution: War in the Seventeenth-century World, 2011; Cold War, 2011; Fighting for America: The Struggle for Mastery in North America, 1519-1871, 2011; Great War: And the Making of the Modern World, 2011; Historiography: Contesting the Past; Claiming the Future, 2011; War in the World 1450-1600, 2011; Fighting for America: The Struggle for Mastery in North America, 1519-1871, 2011; War in the World: A Comparative History, 1450-1600, 2011; War and the Cultural Turn, 2012. EDITOR: Britain in the Age of Walpole, 1984; (with K. Schweizer) Essays in European History in Honour of Ragnhild Hatton, 1985; The Causes of War in Early Modern Europe, 1987; (with E. Cruickshanks) The Jacobite Challenge, 1988; (with P. Woodfine) The British Navy and the Use of Naval Power in the 18th Century, 1988; Knights Errant and True Englishmen, 1989; (with K. Schweizer) Press and Politics in Hanoverian Britain, 1989; British Politics and Society from Walpole to Pitt, 1742-1789, 1990; (with J. Gregory) Culture, Politics and Society in Britain, 1660-1800, 1991; Culture and Society in Britain, 1660-1800, 1997; War in the Early Modern World, 1999; Atlas of World History, 2000; European Warfare 1494-1660, 2002; Race, Radicalism, Religion, and Restriction: Immigration in the Pacific Northwest, 1890-1924, 2003; War in the Modern World, 1815-2000, 2003; Seventy Great Battles in History, 2005; Warfare in Europe 1650-1792, 2005; Atlantic Slave Trade, 2006; Revolutions in the Western World, 1775-1825, 2006; Second World War, 2007; (with A. Fazackerley and H.D. Burgh) Can the Prizes still Glitter?: The Future of British Universities in a Changing World, 2007; Great Military Leaders and Their Campaigns, 2008; (with T.G. Otte) Coalition Government in British Politics: From Glorious Revolution to Cameron-Clegg, 2011. **Address:** Department of History, University of Exeter, Amory Bldg., Rennes Dr., Exeter, DN EX4 4RJ, England. **Online address:** ejeremy@jeremyblack.co.uk

BLACK, Keith Lanier. American (born United States), b. 1957. **Genres:** Medicine/Health. **Career:** University of California, assistant professor, 1987-91, associate professor, 1991-93, professor of neurosurgery, 1994-97, Department of Surgery, Ruth and Raymond Stotter chair, 1992; Institute of Neurosurgery, Cedars-Sinai Medical Center, Maxine Duniz Neurosurgical Institute, director, 1997-, Ruth and Lawrence Harvey chair in neuroscience, 1997-; Microsurgeon Inc., founder, 1997; Imagine Pharmaceuticals, founder, 2003; Johnnie L. Cochran, Jr., Brain Tumor Center, founder, 2007. Writer. **Publications:** NONFICTION: (with A. Mann) Brain Surgeon: A Doctor's Inspiring Encounters with Mortality and Miracles (memoir), 2009. Contributor to books and journals. **Address:** Cedars-Sinai Medical Center, Maxine Duniz Neurosurgical Institute, PO Box 48750, Los Angeles, CA 90048-1869, U.S.A.

BLACK, Merle. American (born United States), b. 1942. **Genres:** Politics/Government, History. **Career:** University of North Carolina, instructor, 1970-71, assistant professor, 1972-77, associate professor, 1978-88, professor, 1988-89; Emory University, Emory College of Arts and Sciences, Department of Political Science, Asa Griggs Candler professor of politics and government, 1989-; political scientist. Writer. **Publications:** (With D.M. Kovenock and W.C. Reynolds and contrib.) Political Attitudes in the Nation and the States: Comparative State Elections Project, 1974; (ed. with T.L. Beyle and contrib.) Politics and Policy in North Carolina, 1975; (ed. with J.S. Reed) Perspectives on the American South, vol. I, 1981, vol. II, 1984; (with E. Black) Politics and Society in the South, 1987; (with E. Black) The Vital South: How Presidents Are Elected, 1992; (with E. Black) The Rise of Southern Republicans, 2002; (with E. Black) Divided America: The Ferocious Power Struggle in American Politics, 2007. **Address:** Department of Political Science, Emory University, 311 Tarbutton Hall, 1555 Dickey Dr., Atlanta, GA 30322, U.S.A. **Online address:** pblac01@emory.edu

BLACK, Michael A. American (born United States) **Genres:** Mystery/Crime/Suspense, Novels. **Career:** Illinois Police Department, sergeant on the Matteson. Writer. **Publications:** Tanks: The M1A1 Abrams, 2000; Volunteering to Help Kids, 2000; A Killing Frost, 2002; Windy City Knights, 2004; Heist, 2005; Freeze Me, Tender, 2006; A Final Judgment: A Ron Shade Novel, 2006; Melody of Vengeance, 2007; (with J. Hyzy) Dead Ringer: A Ron Shade and Alex St. James Mystery, 2008; Random Victim, 2008; (with R. Belzer) I am not a Psychic!, 2009; Hostile Takeovers, 2009. **Address:** c/o Author Mail, Five Star, 295 Kennedy Memorial Dr., Waterville, ME 04901, U.S.A. **Online address:** mike@michaelablack.com

BLACK, Robert Perry. American (born United States), b. 1927. **Genres:** Economics, Money/Finance, Business/Trade/Industry, Social Sciences. **Career:** Federal Reserve Bank of Richmond, research associate, 1954-55, associate economist, 1956-58, economist, 1958-60, assistant vice president, 1960-62, vice president, 1962-68, first vice president, 1968-73, president, 1973-92; University of Tennessee, assistant professor of finance, 1955-56. Writer. **Publications:** (With B.U. Ratchford) The Federal Reserve at Work, 1961, 6th ed., 1974; The Federal Reserve Today, 1964, 5th ed., 1971; (with D.E. Harless) Non-Bank Financial Institutions, 1965, 3rd ed., 1969. Contributor to journals. **Address:** 2842 Waterford Way W, Richmond, VA 23233, U.S.A.

BLACK, Roger David. American (born United States), b. 1948. **Genres:** Design. **Career:** L.A. (weekly newspaper), art director, 1972; Rolling Stone, art director, 1976-78; New York Magazine, design director, 1978-81; New West Magazine, design director, 1978-81; New York Times Magazine, art director, 1982-84, director of editorial art, 1984-85; Newsweek, art director, 1985-87; Smart Magazine, design director, 1988-90, 1993-; Roger Black Studio Inc., president, 1981-; Interactive Bureau, co-founder and president, 1994-; Font Bureau, founder; Nomad Editions, design director; Cooper Union, Department of Continuing Education, faculty. **Publications:** Roger Black's Desktop Design Power, 1991; (with S. Elder) Web Sites That Work, 1997; (foreword) Don't Make Me Think! A Common Sense Approach to Web Usability, 2000. **Address:** Roger Black Studio Inc., Rm. 2345, 245 5th Ave., New York, NY 10016, U.S.A. **Online address:** roger@rogerblack.com

BLACK, Shane. American (born United States), b. 1961. **Genres:** Plays/Screenplays, Novels. **Career:** Writer. **Publications:** Last Action Hero: A Novel, 1993. **Address:** Intertalent Agency, 131 S Rodeo Dr., Ste. 300, Beverly Hills, CA 90212, U.S.A.

BLACK, Shayla. *See* **BRADLEY, Shelley.**

BLACK, Tank. *See* **BLACK, William H.**

BLACK, William H. (Tank Black). American (born United States), b. 1957. **Genres:** Autobiography/Memoirs. **Career:** Professional Management Inc., staff, 1988-2000; Greenville High School, assistant coach; University of Tennessee Chattanooga, assistant coach; University of South Carolina, assistant coach. Writer. **Publications:** (As Tank Black) Tanked! The Tank Black Story, 2009. **Online address:** tank@thetankblackstory.com

BLACKABY, Richard. American/Canadian (born Canada), b. 1961. **Genres:** Theology/Religion, History. **Career:** Friendship Baptist Church, senior pastor; Canadian Southern Baptist Seminary, president, 1993-2006; Blackaby Ministries Intl., president, 2006-. Writer. **Publications:** (With H.T. Blackaby) Experiencing God Day-by-Day: The Devotional and Journal, 1997; (with H.T. Blackaby) Cross Seekers: Discipleship Covenant for a New Generation, 1998; (with H.T. Blackaby) Experiencing God Day-by-Day: Devotional, 1998; (with H.T. Blackaby) Spiritual Leadership: Moving People on to God's Agenda, 2001; (with H.T. Blackaby) Hearing God's Voice, 2002; (with H.T. Blackaby) Called to Be God's Leader: How God Prepares His

Servants for Leadership, 2004; (with H.T. Blackaby) TQ120A, 2005; (with H.T. Blackaby) TQ120B, 2005; (with H.T. Blackaby) TQ120C, 2005; (with H.T. Blackaby) Spiritual Leadership: The Interactive Study, 2006; Putting a Face on Grace, 2006; (with H.T. Blackaby and C. King) Experiencing God: Knowing and Doing the Will of God, 2007; (with H.T. Blackaby) God in the Marketplace: 45 Questions Fortune 500 Executives Ask about Faith, Life & Business, 2008; Unlimiting God: Increasing Your Capacity to Experience the Divine, 2008; (with H.T. Blackaby and C. King) Fresh Encounter: God's Pattern for Spiritual Awakening, 2009; (with H.T. Blackaby and C. King) Fresh Encounter: Experiencing God's Power for Spiritual Awakening, 2009; (with H.T. Blackaby) Spiritual Leadership: Moving People on to God's Agenda, 2011. **Address:** Blackaby Ministries International, PO Box 1035, Jonesboro, GA 30237-1035, U.S.A.

BLACKBOURN, David. American/British (born England), b. 1949. **Genres:** Area Studies, History, Local History/Rural Topics, Social Sciences. **Career:** Cambridge University, Jesus College, research fellow in history, 1973-76; University of London, Queen Mary College, lecturer, 1976-79, Birkbeck College, lecturer, 1979-85, reader in history, 1985-89, professor, 1989-92; Alexander von Humboldt Foundation, research fellow, 1984-85; Stanford University, visiting professor, 1989-90; Harvard University, professor of history, 1992-97, Coolidge professor of history, 1997-, Center for European Studies, chair, 1998-99, 2000-02, director, 2007-, faculty associate; Guggenheim Foundation, research fellow, 1994-95; American Historical Association, Conference Group for Central European History, president, 2003-04; Friends of the German Historical Institute, chair. Writer. **Publications:** (Contrib.) Society and Politics in Wilhelmine Germany, 1978; Class, Religion and Local Politics in Wilhelmine Germany: The Centre Party in Wuerttemberg before 1914, 1980; (with G. Eley) Mythen deutscher Geschichtsschreibung: Die gescheiterte buergerliche Revolution von 1848, 1980; (contrib.) Nationalist and Racialist Movements in Britain and Germany before 1914, 1981; (with G. Eley) The Peculiarities of German History: Bourgeois Society and Politics in Nineteenth-Century Germany, 1984; (contrib.) Shopkeepers and Master Artisans in Nineteenth-Century Europe, 1984; (contrib.) Nineteenth-Century Liberalism: An International Perspective, 1985; Populists and Patricians: Essays in Modern German History, 1987; (ed. with R.J. Evans) The German Bourgeoisie, 1991; Marpingen: Apparitions of the Virgin Mary in Bismarckian Germany, 1993; The Long Nineteenth Century: A History of Germany, 1780-1918, 1997, 2nd ed., 2003; Volksfrömmigkeit und Fortschrittsglaube im Kulturkampf, 1998; History of Germany, 1790-1918: The Long Nineteenth Century, 2003; The Conquest of Nature: Water, Landscape and the Making of Modern Germany, 2006; Localism, Landscape and the Ambiguities of Place: German Speaking Central Europe, 1860-1930, 2007. **Address:** Center for European Studies, Harvard University, Rm. 401, 27 Kirkland St., Cambridge, MA 02138, U.S.A. **Online address:** dgblackb@fas.harvard.edu

BLACKBURN, Fred M(onroe). American (born United States), b. 1950. **Genres:** Archaeology/Antiquities, History, Travel/Exploration, Social Sciences, Young Adult Non-fiction. **Career:** Bureau of Land Management, ranger, chief ranger, 1974-79; Crow Canyon Archaeological Center, interpretive guide, 1979-81; interpreter, educator, guide and researcher, 1981-. Writer and consultant. **Publications:** The Hiker's Guide to Utah, 1982; (with R. Williamson) An Approach to Vandalism of Archaeological Resources, 1990; (with V. Atkins) Handwriting on the Wall, 1993; (with R. Williamson) Cowboys and Cave Dwellers: Basketmaker Archaeology in Utah's Grand Gulch, 1997; Inscription History and Discover of Balcony House, 2000; Historical Inscriptions and the Expeditionary History of Balcony House, Cliff Palace, Hemenway House, Little Hemenway House, Honeymoon House, and Spruce Tree House, 2005; The Wetherills: Friends of Mesa Verde, 2006. **Address:** 104 E Carpenter, Cortez, CO 81321, U.S.A. **Online address:** blackburn104@msn.com

BLACKBURN, Julia. (Julia Karen Eugenie Blackburn). British (born England), b. 1948. **Genres:** Novels, Autobiography/Memoirs, Literary Criticism And History, Young Adult Non-fiction. **Career:** Writer. **Publications:** BIOGRAPHICAL FICTION: The White Men: The First Response of Aboriginal Peoples to the White Man, 1979; Charles Waterton, 1782-1865: Traveller and Conservationist, 1989; The Emperor's Last Island: A Journey to St. Helena, 1991; Daisy Bates in the Desert: One Woman's Life among the Aborigines, 1994; Charles Waterton: 1782-1865, 1997; Leper's Companions, 1999; Old Man Goya, 2002; With Billie, 2005; Three of Us: A Family Story, 2008. NOVELS: The Book of Colour, 1995; The Leper's Companion, 1999; My Animals and Other Family, 2007. **Address:** Pantheon Publicity, 1540 Broadway, New York, NY 10036-4039, U.S.A. **Online address:** blackburnmakkink@gmail.com

BLACKBURN, Julia Karen Eugenie. *See* **BLACKBURN, Julia.**

BLACKFORD, Mansel G(riffiths). American (born United States), b. 1944. **Genres:** Business/Trade/Industry, History, Politics/Government, Economics. **Career:** Ohio State University, assistant professor, 1972-78, associate professor, 1979-84, professor, 1984-, senior Fulbright lecturer to Japan, 1980-81, 1985-86. Writer. **Publications:** Politics of Business in California, 1890-1920, 1977; Pioneering a Modern Small Business: Wakefield Seafoods and the Alaskan Frontier, 1979; A Portrait Cast in Steel: Buckeye International and Columbus, Ohio, 1881-1980, 1982; (with K.A. Kerr) Business Enterprise in American History, 1986, 3rd ed., 1994; The Rise of Modern Business in Great Britain, the United States, Japan and China, 1988, rev. ed., 2008; (with K.A. Kerr and A.J. Loveday) Local Businesses: Exploring their History, 1990; A History of Small Business in America, 1991, 2nd ed., 2003; The Lost Dream: Businessmen and City Planning on the Pacific Coast, 1890-1920, 1993; (ed.) On Board the USS Mason: The World War II Diary of James A. Dunn, 1996; (with K.A. Kerr) BF Goodrich: Tradition and Transformation, 1870-1995, 1996; Fragile Paradise: The Impact of Tourism on Maui, 1959-2000, 2001; Pathways to the Present: U.S. Development and Its Consequences in the Pacific, 2007. **Address:** Department of History, Ohio State University, 173 Dulles Hall, 230 W 17th Ave., Columbus, OH 43210, U.S.A. **Online address:** blackford.1@osu.edu

BLACKLOCK, Dianne. Australian (born Australia) **Genres:** Young Adult Fiction. **Career:** Writer. **Publications:** Call Waiting, 2002; Wife for Hire, 2003; Almost Perfect, 2004; False Advertising, 2007; Crossing Paths, 2008; Threes a Crowd, 2009; The Right Time, 2010; The Secret Ingredient, 2011. **Address:** Faye Bender Literary, 337 W 76th St., Ste. E1, New York, NY 10023-8010, U.S.A. **Online address:** dianne.blacklock@gmail.com

BLACKMAN, Malorie. British (born England), b. 1962. **Genres:** Children's Fiction, Young Adult Fiction, Children's Non-fiction, Young Adult Non-fiction, Novels, Picture/Board Books, Novellas/Short Stories. **Career:** Reuters, computer programmer, 1983-85, database manager, 1986-90; Digital Equipment, software specialist, 1985-86. Writer. **Publications:** NOVELS FOR YOUNG ADULTS: Not So Stupid!: Incredible Short Stories, 1990; Elaine, You're a Brat!, 1991; Trust Me, 1992; Hacker, 1992; Girl Wonder to the Rescue, 1994; Rachel and the Difference Thieves, 1994; My Friend's a Gris-Quok!, 1994; Eddie and the Treasure Hunt Rap, 1995; A.N.T.I.D.O.T.E., 1996; Grandma Gertie's Haunted Handbag, 1996; The Quasar Quartz Quest, 1996; Peril on Planet Pellia, 1996; Space Race, 1997; Don't Be Afraid, 1997; Fangs, 1998; Words Last Forever, 1998; The Naughts and Crosses Series: Naughts & Crosses, 2001; An Eye for an Eye, 2003; Knife Edge, 2004; Checkmate, 2005; The Stuff of Nightmares, 2007; (ed.) Unheard Voices: An Anthology of Stories and Poems to Commemorate the Bicentenary Anniversary of the Abolition of the Slave Trade, 2007; Double Cross, 2008. SHORT STORIES FOR YOUNG ADULTS: Hacker, 1992; Operation Gadgetman!, 1993; Jack Sweettooth the 73rd, 1995; The Space Stowaway, 1995; Whizziwig, 1995; Thief!, 1996; Pig-Heart Boy, 1997; Animal Avengers, 1999; Dangerous Reality, 1999; Don't Be Afraid, 1999; Forbidden Game, 1999; Hostage, 1999; Tell Me No Lies, 1999; Whizziwig Returns, 1999; Dead Gorgeous, 2002; Cloud Busting, 2004; The Deadly Dare Mysteries, 2005; Whizziwig and Whizziwig Returns, 2005; Shining On: A Collection of Stories in Aid of the Teen Cancer Trust, 2006; Boys Don't Cry, 2010. SHORT STORIED FOR CHILDREN: Out of This World: Stories of Virtual Reality, 1997; Aesop's Fables, 1998; Dare to be Different, 1999; Peacemaker and Other Stories, 1999. NEW READERS: Elaine You're a Brat!, 1991; Girl Wonder and the Terrific Twins, 1991; Girl Wonder's Winter Adventures, 1992; Betsey Biggalow the Detective, 1992; Betsey Biggalow is Here!, 1992; Hurricane Betsy, 1993; Magic Betsey, 1994; My Friend'sa Gris-Quok, 1994; Rachel versus Bonecrusher the Mighty, 1994; Rachel and the Difference Thief, 1994; (with A.M. Smith and S. Lever) Crazy Crocs, 1994; Girl Wonder to the Rescue, 1994; Betsey's Birthday Surprise, 1996; Peril on Planet Pellia, 1996; The Secret of the Terrible Hand, 1996; Grandma Gertie's Haunted Handbag, 1996; Space Race, 1997; Fangs, 1998; Marty Monster, 1999; Snow Dog, 2001; Anansi and the Rubber Man, 2001; The Monster Crisp-Guzzler, 2002; The Amazing Adventures of Girl Wonder, 2003; Ellie and the Cat, 2005. PICTURE BOOKS: That New Dress, as A New Dress for Maya, 1991; Mrs Spoon's Family, 1995; Dizzy's Walk, 1999; Marty Monster, 1999; I Want a Cuddle!, 2001; (with A. Bartlett) Jessica Strange Hodder, 2002; Sinclair, Wonder Bear, 2005. Works appear in anthologies. **Address:** c/o Children's Publicity Department, Random House Children's Books, 61-63 Uxbridge Rd., Holland Pk., London, GL W5 5SA, England.

BLACKMER, Donald L. M. American (born United States), b. 1929. **Genres:** International Relations/Current Affairs, Social Sciences, Politics/Government. **Career:** Massachusetts Institute of Technology, lecturer, 1960-61, assistant professor, 1961-67, Center for International Studies, faculty, 1956, assistant director, 1961-68, associate professor, 1967-73, professor of political science, 1973-, now professor emeritus, School of Humanities and Social Sciences, associate dean, 1973-80, Science, Technology and Society Program, director, 1977-80, Political Science Department, head, 1980-88, Council for European Studies, chairman; Harvard University, faculty, 1973-. Writer. **Publications:** (Ed. with M.F. Millikan and contrib.) The Emerging Nations: Their Growth and United States Policy, 1961; Unity in Diversity: Italian Communism and the Communist World, 1968; (ed. with S. Tarrow) Communism in Italy and France, 1975; (with A. Kriegel) The International Role of the Communist Parties of Italy and France, 1975. **Address:** Department of Political Science, Massachusetts Institute of Technology, E53-470, 77 Massachusetts Ave., Cambridge, MA 02139-4307, U.S.A. **Online address:** blackmer@mit.edu

BLACKMORE, Susan (Jane). British (born England), b. 1951. **Genres:** Paranormal, Psychology, Autobiography/Memoirs, Biology. **Career:** North East London Polytechnic, Department of Architecture, part-time lecturer, 1974-78; University of Surrey, Department of General Studies, associate lecturer in parapsychology, 1975-80; Thames Polytechnic, Department of Architecture, part-time lecturer, 1977-78; University of Utrecht, Parapsychology Laboratory, temporary research fellow, 1980; University of Bristol, The Medical School, Brain and Perception Laboratory, visiting research fellow, 1980-88, Department of Mental Health, tutor in behavioral sciences, 1989-90, lecturer in psychology, 1990-91; University of Bath, Department Social Sciences, part-time lecturer, 1990-91; University of the West of England, senior lecturer in psychology, 1992-98, reader in psychology, 1998-2001; University of Plymouth, visiting professor. Writer and host. **Publications:** Parapsychology and Out-of-the-Body Experiences, 1978; Beyond the Body: An Investigation of Out-of-the-Body Experiences, 1982, rev. ed., 1992; The Adventures of a Parapsychologist, 1986, rev. ed., 1996; (contrib.) Not Necessarily the New Age: Critical Essays, 1988; (contrib.) The Hundredth Monkey and Other Paradigms of the Paranormal, 1991; (contrib.) Reincarnation: Fact or Fable?, 1991; Dying to Live: Near-Death Experiences, 1993; In Search of the Light, 1996; (with A. Hart-Davis) Test Your Psychic Powers, 1997; The Meme Machine, 1999; (co-author) Ciencia y sociedad: diversidad humana, 2002; Consciousness: An Introduction, 2003, 2nd ed., 2010; Consciousness: A Very Short Introduction, 2005; Conversations on Consciousness, 2005; Conversations on Consciousness: What the Best Minds Think about the Brain, Free Will and What It Means to be Human, 2006; Ten Zen Questions, 2009; Zen and the Art of Consciousness, 2011. Contributor of articles to periodicals. **Address:** Thornham Bridge, Ivybridge Rd., Ermington, Plymouth, DN PL21 0LG, England. **Online address:** susan.blackmore@virgin.net

BLACKSTOCK, Terri. Also writes as Tracy Hughes, Terri Herrington. American (born United States), b. 1957. **Genres:** Novels, Mystery/Crime/Suspense, Romance/Historical, inspirational/Motivational Literature. **Career:** Writer. **Publications:** Emerald Windows, 2001. AS TERRI HERRINGTON: Blue Fire, 1984; Head over Heels, 1986; Lovers' Reunion, 1986; Tender Betrayer, 1986; A Secret Stirring, 1986; Stolen Moments, 1987; Tangled Triumphs, 1987; Ticket to a Fantasy, 1987; Wife Wanted, 1987; Her Father's Daughter, 1991; Flashback, 1993; One Good Man, 1993; Silena, 1993; Winner Take All, 1995. AS TRACY HUGHES: Impressions, 1986; Quiet Lightning, 1986; Above the Clouds, 1988; White Lies & Alibis, 1990; Honorbound, 1991; Second Chances, 1991; Father Knows Best, 1992; Sand Man, 1992; Jo (Calloway Corner Series), 1993; Delta Dust, 1993; Catch a Falling Star, 1994; Heaven Knows, 1994; The Princess and the Pauper, 1994; To Heaven and Back, 1995; Daniel-Return to Calloway Corners, 1996. SEASONS SERIES WITH BEVERLY LAHAYE: Seasons under Heaven, 1999; Showers in Season, 2000; Times and Seasons, 2001; Season of Blessing, 2002. CAPE REFUGE SERIES: Cape Refuge, 2002; Southern Storm, 2003; River's Edge, 2004; Breaker's Reef, 2005. RESTORATION SERIES: Last Light, 2005; Night Light, 2006; True Light, 2007; Dawns Light, 2007. INTERVENTION SERIES: Intervention, 2009; Vicious Cycle, 2011, Downfall, 2012. STAND-ALONES: The Listener, 2000; The Heart Reader, 2000; The Heart Reader of Franklin High, 2000; Seaside: A Novella, 2001; Covenant Child, 2002; The Gifted, 2002; The Gifted Sophmores, 2002; Soul Restoration: Hope for the Weary, 2005; Emerald Windows, 2008; Double Minds, 2009; Predator, 2010; Miracles, 2010; Shadow in Serenity, 2011. **Address:** c/o Author Mail, The Zondervan Corp., 5300 Patterson Ave. SE, Grand Rapids, MI 49530, U.S.A. **Online address:** tblkstk@yahoo.com

BLACKSTONE. (Tessa Blackstone). British (born England), b. 1942. **Genres:** Education, Politics/Government, Social Commentary. **Career:** University of London, London School of Economics and Political Science, assistant lecturer, 1966-69, lecturer in social administration, 1969-75, Institute of Education, professor of educational administration, 1978-83; Cabinet Office, advisor of central policy review staff, 1975-78; Inner London Education Authority, deputy education officer, 1983-86, clerk, 1986; Policy Studies Institute, Rowntree special research fellow, 1986-87; Birkbeck College, master, 1987-97; minister of state for education and employment, 1997-2001; Department of Culture, Media and Sport, minister of state for the arts, 2001-03; University of Greenwich, vice-chancellor, 2004-11. Writer. **Publications:** AS TESSA BLACKSTONE: (with K. Gales and R. Hadley) Students in Conflict: L.S.E. In 1967, 1970; A Fair Start: The Provision of Pre-School Education, 1971; First Schools of the Future, 1972; Education and Day Care for Young Children in Need: The American Experience, 1973; (with G. Williams and D. Metcalf) The Academic Labour Market: Economic and Social Aspects of a Profession, 1974; (with P. Vines) Social Policy and Administration in Britain: A Bibliography, 1975; (contrib.) Education for the Inner City, 1980; (with P. Lodge) Educational Policy and Education Inequality, 1982; How Many Teachers?, 1982; (with J. Mortimore) Disadvantage and Education, 1982; (with G. Williams) Response to Adversity, 1983; (co-author) Testing Children, 1983; (co-author) Educational Policy Making, 1985; (with W. Plowden) Inside the Think Tank: Advising the Cabinet 1971-83, 1990; (contrib.) Counter Blast No. 11, 1990; Prisons and Penal Reform, 1990; (ed. with B. Parekh and P. Sanders) Race Relations in Britain: A Developing Agenda, 1998. **Address:** House of Lords, London, GL SW1A OPW, England. **Online address:** blackstonet@parliament.uk

BLACKSTONE, Tessa. *See* **BLACKSTONE.**

BLACKTHORNE, Thomas. *See* **MEANEY, John.**

BLACKWELL, Joyce. (Joyce Blackwell-Johnson). American (born United States), b. 1954. **Genres:** History, International Relations/Current Affairs, Gay And Lesbian Issues, Education. **Career:** Meredith College, assistant professor of history; North Carolina State University, adjunct assistant professor of history; University of North Carolina, assistant professor of history; North Carolina Central University, assistant professor of history; Saint Augustine's College, Department of History and Political Science, assistant professor, associate professor, professor, chair, Division of Social Sciences, dean. Writer. **Publications:** No Peace without Freedom: Race and the Women's International League for Peace and Freedom, 1915-1975, 2004; (contrib.) Black Women in America: A Historical Encyclopedia, 2005; (ed.) The Encyclopedia of Violence, Peace and Conflict, 2nd ed., 2008; (contrib.) Conflict and Allegiance: Black Religious Activism and the U.S. Middle East Crisis, 2008. Contributor to periodicals. **Address:** Department of History and Political Science, St. Augustine's College, 300-A Boyer Hall, 1315 Oakwood Ave., Raleigh, NC 27610, U.S.A. **Online address:** jblackwell-johnson@st-aug.edu

BLACKWELL, Richard J. American (born United States), b. 1929. **Genres:** Sciences, Bibliography, Translations. **Career:** John Carroll University, instructor, 1954-57, assistant professor, 1957-61; St. Louis University, associate professor, 1961-66, professor of philosophy, 1966-, Danforth chair in the humanities, 1986-, now professor emeritus; The Modern Schoolman, associate editor, 1961-. **Publications:** (Trans. with R.J. Spath and W.E. Thirlkel) Commentary on Aristotle's Physics, 1963: (trans.) Preliminary Discourse on Philosophy in General, 1963; Discovery in the Physical Sciences, 1969; (contrib.) Concept of Matter in Modern Philosophy, 1978; (comp.) Bibliography of the Philosophy of Science 1945-1981, 1983; (trans.) The Pendulum Clock, 1986; Galileo, Bellarmine, and the Bible, 1991; (trans.) T. Campanella, A Defense of Galileo, 1994; Science, Religion and Authority: Lessons from the Galileo Affair, 1998; Behind the Scenes at Galileo's Trial, 2006. Contributor to journals. **Address:** Department of Philosophy, St. Louis University, Humanities Bldg., 3800 Lindell Blvd., Ste. 130, St. Louis, MO 63108, U.S.A. **Online address:** rblackwe@worldnet.att.net

BLACKWELL-JOHNSON, Joyce. *See* **BLACKWELL, Joyce.**

BLACKWILL, Robert D. American (born United States), b. 1939. **Genres:** International Relations/Current Affairs, Politics/Government, Social Sciences, Humanities. **Career:** Career diplomat, 1967-; U.S. State Department, Bureau of Personnel, training officer, 1968-69, associate watch officer, 1969-70, Executive Secretariat, staff officer, 1972-73; National Security Council, director of west European affairs; Harvard University, John F. Kennedy School of Government, associate dean and faculty, 1983-85, Executive Program for Senior Chinese Military Officers, faculty chairman, Belfer lecturer in international security, through 2001; American Ambassador to India, 2001-03; Barbour Griffith & Rogers Intl., president, 2004-08; RAND Corp., senior fellow, 2008-; U.S. ambassador, chief negotiator. Writer. **Publications:** (Ed. with F.S. Larrabee) Conventional Arms Control and East-West Security, 1989; (ed. with G.T. Allison and A. Carnesale) A Primer for the Nuclear Age, 1990; (ed. with A. Carnesale) New Nuclear Nations: Consequences for U.S. Policy, 1993; (ed. with S.A. Karaganov) Damage Limitation or Crisis?: Russia and the Outside World, 1994; (with R. Braithwaite and A. Tanaka) Engaging Russia: A Report to the Trilateral Commission, 1995, trans. as Russland einbinden: Ein Bericht für die Trilaterale Kommission, 1996; Arms Control and the U.S.-Russian Relationship: Problems, Prospects and Prescriptions: Report of an Independent Task Force, 1996; (with M. Stürmer) Allies Divided: Transatlantic Policies for the Greater Middle East, 1997; The Future of Transatlantic Relations, 1999; (ed. with P. Dibb) America's Asian Alliances, 2000. Contributor of articles to periodicals. **Address:** John F. Kennedy School of Government, Harvard University, 79 John F. Kennedy St., Cambridge, MA 02138, U.S.A. **Online address:** robert_blackwill@harvard.edu

BLADES, Ann. Canadian (born Canada), b. 1947. **Genres:** Children's Fiction, Illustrations, Humor/Satire, Animals/Pets. **Career:** Peace River North School District, school teacher, 1967-68; Department of Indian Affairs and Northern Development, staff, 1969; Surrey School District, teacher, 1969-71; Vancouver General Hospital, part-time nurse, 1974-75; Mount St. Joseph Hospital, part-time nurse, 1975-80; artist, 1976-. Writer and illustrator. **Publications:** SELF-ILLUSTRATED: Mary of Mile 18, 1971; A Boy of Taché, 1973, rev. ed., 1995; The Cottage at Crescent Beach, 1977; By the Sea: An Alphabet Book, 1985; Back to the Cabin, 1996; Wolf and the Seven Little Kids, 1999; Too Small, 2000. SEASONS BOARD BOOK SERIES SELF-ILLUSTRATED: Summer, 1989; Fall, 1989; Winter, 1989; Spring, 1989. Illustrator of books by others. **Address:** c/o Bella Pomer, Bella Pomer Agency Inc., 355 St. Clair Ave. W, Ste. 801, Toronto, ON M5P 1N5, Canada.

BLADES, John D. American (born United States), b. 1936. **Genres:** Novels, Plays/Screenplays, Essays, Humor/Satire, Literary Criticism And History. **Career:** Illinois State Register, reporter, 1959; Miami Herald, reporter, 1961-64; Chicago Sun-Times, midwest magazine copy editor, 1964-65, managing editor, 1965-69; Chicago Tribune, daily book editor, 1969-71, staff writer and articles editor for Sunday magazine, 1969-77, book editor, 1977-85, book critic, 1985-88, staff writer and book columnist for Tempo section, 1988-97. **Publications:** NOVELS: James Joyce, A Portrait of the Artist as a Young Man, 1991; Small Game, 1992; How to Study James Joyce, 1996; John Keats: The Poems, 2002; Wordsworth and Coleridge: Lyrical Ballads, 2004; Shakespeare: The Sonnets, 2007. Contributor to periodicals. **Address:** 2111 Maple, Evanston, IL 60201, U.S.A. **Online address:** jdblades@comcast.net

BLAGOJEVIC, Ljiljana. American (born United States), b. 1960?. **Genres:** Architecture, History. **Career:** University of Belgrade, faculty of architecture, lecturer; School for History and Theory of Images, teacher. Writer, architect, architectural historian and theoretician. **Publications:** Modernism in Serbia: The Elusive Margins of Belgrade Architecture, 1919-1941, 2003; Novi Beograd: Osporeni Modernizam, 2007. Contributor to periodicals. **Address:** c/o Author Mail, MIT Press, 5 Cambridge Ctr., Cambridge, MA 02142-1493, U.S.A.

BLAINE, Celia. *See* **MURPHEY, Cecil B(laine).**

BLAINE, Chris. *See* **MASSIE, Elizabeth.**

BLAINE, Michael. American (born United States) **Genres:** Novels, Young Adult Fiction. **Career:** New York Stories Magazine, founder and editor-in-chief; City University of New York, assistant professor of English. Writer. **Publications:** Whiteouts, 1999; The Desperate Season, 1999; The Midnight Band of Mercy, 2004; The King of Swings: Johnny Goodman, the Last Amateur to Beat the Pros at Their Own Game, 2006. Works appear in anthologies. Contributor to periodicals. **Address:** c/o Author Mail, Soho Press Inc., 853 Broadway, New York, NY 10003-4703, U.S.A. **Online address:** michael@mpblaine.com

BLAINEY, Geoffrey Norman. Australian (born Australia), b. 1930. **Genres:** History, Biography, Autobiography/Memoirs. **Career:** Freelance writer, 1951-61; University of Melbourne, senior lecturer, 1962-63, reader, 1963-68, professor of economic history, 1968-77, chair of economic history, 1968-77, Ernest Scott professor of history, 1977-88, chair of history, 1977-88, now professor emeritus, Faculty of Arts, dean, 1982-88, Queen's College, fellow, senior fellow, Council, president; Commonwealth Literary Fund, chair, 1971-73; Australia Council, chairman, 1979-84; Australia-China Council, 1979-84; Harvard University, professor, 1982-83; University of Ballarat, chancellor, 1994-98; National Council for the Centenary of Federation, chairman, 2001; Farrago, editor. **Publications:** The Peaks of Lyell, 1954; University of Melbourne: A Centenary Portrait, 1956; A Centenary History of the University of Melbourne, 1957; Gold and Paper, 1958; Mines in the Spinifex, 1960; The Rush That Never Ended, 1963, 5th ed., Rush that Never Ended: A History of Australian Mining, 2003; A History of Camberwell, 1964; (ed.) If I Remember Rightly: The Memoirs of W.S. Robinson, 1966; (co-author and ed.) Wesley College: The First Hundred Years, 1967; The Tyranny of Distance, 1966; Across a Red World, 1968; The Rise of Broken Hill, 1968; The Steel Master, 1971; The Causes of War, 1973, 3rd ed., 1988; Triumph of the Nomads, 1975; Land Half Won, 1980; The Blainey View, 1982; Our Side of the Country, 1984; All for Australia, 1984; (with M. Clark and R.M. Crawford) Making History, 1985; (co-author) Weltwirtschafts probleme Mitte der 80er Jahre, 1985; (contrib.) Birth of Australia, 1987; The Great Seesaw, 1988; Australian Universities, 1989; A Game of Our Own: The Origins of Australian Football, 1990; Eye on Australia, 1991; Odd Fellows, 1992; (with I. Crombie) Sites of the Imagination, 1992; The Golden Mile, 1993; Jumping over the Wheel, 1993; A Shorter History of Australia, 1994; (ed. with R. Jamieson) Charles Court, the Early Years: An Autobiography, 1995; Steel Master: A Life of Essington Lewis, 1995; White Gold: The Story of Alcoa of Australia, 1997; In Our Time, 1999; This Land is All Horizons, 2001; A Short History of the World, 2002; Black Kettle and Full Moon, 2003; A Very Short History of the World, 2004; Short History of the 20th Century, 2006; A History of Victoria, 2006; Sea of Dangers: Captain Cook and His Rivals, 2008; Sea of Dangers: Captain Cook and His Rivals in the South Pacific, 2009. **Address:** Queen's College, University of Melbourne, 1-17 College Cres., Parkville, VI 3052, Australia.

BLAIR, Ann. American (born United States), b. 1961?. **Genres:** Art/Art History. **Career:** Harvard University, lecturer and acting head tutor, 1991-93, assistant professor, 1996-99, John L. Loeb associate professor of the social sciences, 1999-2001, professor of history, 2001-, Henry Charles Lea professor of history; University of California, assistant professor, 1992-96. Writer. **Publications:** (Ed. with A. Grafton) The Transmission of Culture in Early Modern Europe, 1990; The Theater of Nature: Jean Bodin and Renaissance Science, 1997; Too Much to Know: Managing Scholarly Information Before the Modern Age, 2010; Coping With Information Overload in Early Modern Europe, forthcoming. **Address:** Department of History, Harvard University, Center for Government and International Studies, Rm. S437, S Bldg., 1730 Cambridge St., Cambridge, MA 02138, U.S.A. **Online address:** amblair@fas.harvard.edu

BLAIR, E(lizabeth) Anne. Australian (born Australia), b. 1946. **Genres:** History, Politics/Government, Biography, Military/Defense/Arms Control, Autobiography/Memoirs. **Career:** Monash University, National Center for Australia Studies, research associate, instructor; University of Victoria, lecturer in international relations. Writer. **Publications:** Lodge in Vietnam: A Patriot Abroad, 1995; There to the Bitter End: Ted Serong in Vietnam, 2001; Ted Serong: The Life of an Australian Counter-Insurgency Expert, 2002; Ruxton: A Biography, 2004. **Address:** 41 Swallow St., Port Melbourne, VI 3207, Australia. **Online address:** jablair@smartchat.net.au

BLAIR, Jessica. *See* **SPENCE, William John Duncan.**

BLAIR, L. E. *See* **APPLEGATE, Katherine (Alice).**

BLAIR, L. E. *See* **CALHOUN, B. B.**

BLAIR, Sheila. American/Canadian (born Canada), b. 1948. **Genres:** Art/Art History, Adult Non-fiction, Theology/Religion, Social Commentary. **Career:** Massachusetts Institute of Technology, Aga Khan lecturer on Islamic art and architecture; Harvard University, Aga Khan lecturer on Islamic art and architecture, 1980-81, Department of Fine Arts, research associate, 1987-88, The Dictionary of Art, area editor for Islam and Central Asia, 1987-96; Smith College, faculty, 2000; Virginia Commonwealth University, Hamad bin Khalifa endowed dhair of Islamic art, 2006-; Boston College, Fine Arts Department, Norma Jean Calderwood chair of Islamic and Asian art, 2000-; Norma Jean Calderwood professor, 2007-; Macmillan Dictionary of Art, Islamic section, editor. Art historian. **Publications:** (With O. Grabar) Epic Images and Contemporary History: The Illustrations of the Great Mongol Shahnama, 1980; The Ilkhanid Shrine Complex at Natanz, Iran, 1986; (with O. Grabar) The Art and Architecture of Islam, 1987; (ed. with J.M. Bloom) Images of Paradise in Islamic Art, 1991; The Monumental Inscriptions from Early Islamic Iran and Transoxiana, 1992; (with J.M. Bloom) The Art and Architecture of Islam, 1250-1800, 1994; Compendium of Chronicles: Rashid Al-Din's Illustrated History of the World, 1995; Islamic Arts, 1997; Islamic Inscriptions, 1998; (with K. Otavsky) Entlang Der Seidenstrasse: Früh mittelalterliche Kunst Zwischen Persien und Chinain Der Abegg-Stiftung, 1998; (with J. Bloom) Islam: A Thousand Years of Faith and Power, 2001; (with J.M. Bloom) Cosmophilia: Islamic Art from the David Collection, Copenhagen, 2006; Islamic Calligraphy, 2006; (ed. with J.M. Bloom) Rivers of Paradise: Water in Islamic Art and Culture, 2009; (ed. with J.M. Bloom) Grove Encyclopedia of Islamic Art and Architecture, 2009. **Address:** Fine Arts Department, Boston College, Devlin Hall 433, 140 Commonwealth Ave., Chestnut Hill, MA 02467, U.S.A. **Online address:** sheila.blair@bc.edu

BLAIR, Steven N. (Steven Noel Blair). American (born United States), b. 1939. **Genres:** Medicine/Health, Sports/Fitness, Sciences, Biology, Administration/Management. **Career:** Kansas Wesleyan University, instructor in physical education and athletic coach, 1962-63; University of South Carolina, instructor, professor, 1966-84, Human Performance Laboratory, founder and director, 1966-78, adjunct professor of epidemiology and biostatistics, 1989-, Arnold School of Public Health, Departments of Exercise Science and Epidemiology and Biostatistics, professor, 2006-, Prevention Research Center, faculty; Cooper Institute for Aerobics Research, director of epidemiology and clinical applications and director of research, 1980-2002, Fred and Barbara Meyer chair in preventive medicine, president and chief executive officer, 2002-06; University of Texas Health Science Center, adjunct professor of epidemiology, 1989-; University of North Texas, Academy for Research and Development, adjunct professor, 1996-, Department of Kinesiology, executive lecturer, 2006-08, School of Public Health, visiting professor, 2007; University of Houston, adjunct professor, 1998-2007; University of Bristol, Benjamin Meaker fellow and visiting professor, 2001. Writer. **Publications:** (Co-ed.) Resource Manual for Guidelines for Exercise Testing and Prescription, 1988; Living with Exercise, 1991; (with W.H. Ettinger, Jr. and B.S. Mitchell) Fitness after 50: It's Never Too Late to Start!, 1996; (co-author) The Life Style Counselor's Guide for Weight Control, 1996; (co-author) Active Living Every Day: 20 Weeks to Lifelong Vitality, 2001, 2nd ed., 2011; (with W.H. Ettinger, B.S. Wright) Fitness after 50: Add Years to Your Life and Life to Your Years, 2006; (ed. with C. Bouchard and W.L. Haskell) Physical Activity and Health, 2007. **Address:** Department of Exercise Science, Arnold School of Public Health, University of South Carolina, 225 Public Health Research Bldg., 921 Assembly St., Columbia, SC 29208, U.S.A. **Online address:** sblair@mailbox.sc.edu

BLAIR, Steven Noel. *See* **BLAIR, Steven N.**

BLAIRMAN, Jacqueline. *See* **PINTO, Jacqueline.**

BLAIS, André. Canadian (born Canada), b. 1947. **Genres:** Politics/Government, Social Commentary, Sociology. **Career:** University of Ottawa, lecturer in political science, 1972-74; Laval University, lecturer in political science, 1974-75; University of Montreal, lecturer, 1975-78, assistant professor, 1978-83, associate professor, 1983-89, professor of political science, 1989-; Royal Commission on the Economic Union and Development Prospects for Canada, research coordinator, 1983-85. Writer. **Publications:** (With C. Andrew and R. Des Rosiers) élites Politiques, lesbas-salariés et la Politique du Logement à Hull, 1976; Industrial Policy, 1986; (with C. Desranleau and Y. Vanier) A Political Sociology of Public Aid to Industry, 1986; (ed. with S. Dion) The Budget Maximizing Bureaucrat: Appraisals and Evidence, 1991; (with E. Gidengil) Making Representative Democracy Work: The Views of Canadians, 1991; (with R. Johnston, H.E. Brady and J. Crete) Letting the People Decide: The Dynamics of a Canadian Election, 1992; (with E. Gidengil, N. Nevitte and R. Johnston) The Challenge of Direct Democracy: The 1992 Canadian Referendum, 1996; (with D.E. Blake and S. Dion) Governments, Parties and Public Sector Employees: Canada, United States, Britain and France, 1997; A Question of Ethics, 1998, 2nd ed. as A Question of Ethics: Canadians Speak Out, 2006; (N. Nevitte, E. Gidengil and R. Nadeau) An Unsteady State: The 1997 Canadian Federal Election, 2000; To Vote or Not to Vote?: The Merits and Limits of Rational Choice Theory, 2000; (with E. Gidengil, R. Nadeau and N. Nevitte) Anatomy of a Liberal Victory: Making Sense of the Vote in the 2000 Canadian Election, 2002; (with A. Yoshinaka and L. Massicotte) Establishing the Rules of the Game: Election Laws in Democracies, 2004; (with N. Nevitte, R. Nadeau and G. Elisabeth) Citizens, 2004; (with P. Martin) Dynamiques Partisanes etréalignements électoraux au Canada: 1867-2004, 2005; (ed. with P. Howe and R. Johnston) Strengthening Canadian Democracy, 2005; (with C.J. Anderson and S. Bowler) Losers' Consent: Elections and Democratic Legitimacy, 2005; (ed.) To Keep or to Change First Past the Post?: The Politics of Electoral Reform, 2008; (ed. with S. Bowler and B. Grofman) Mechanical and Psychological Effects of Duverger's Law: Evidence from Canada, India, the U.K. and the U.S., 2009; (ed. with B. Grofman and S. Bowler) Duverger's Law of Plurality Voting: The Logic of Party Competition in Canada, India, the United Kingdom and the United States, 2009; (ed. with K. Aarts and H. Schmitt) Political Leaders and Democratic Elections, 2011. Contributor to books and periodicals. **Address:** Département de science politique, Université de Montréal, Rm. C-4040, Lionel-Groulx, 3150 Jean-Brillant, PO Box 6128, Station Centre-ville, Montreal, QC H3T 1N8, Canada. **Online address:** andre.blais@umontreal.ca

BLAISDELL, Bob. American (born United States), b. 1959. **Genres:** Children's Fiction, Poetry, Education, Biography, Social Sciences. **Career:** City University of New York, Kingsborough Community College, assistant professor, associate professor of English, professor. Writer. **Publications:** Favorite Greek Myths, 1995; The Story of Hercules, 1997. EDITOR: Hardy's Selected Poems, 1995; Snake and Other Poems, 1999; Tolstoy as Teacher: Leo Tolstoy's Writings on Education, 2000; Thoreau: A Book of Quotations, 2000; Great Speeches by Native Americans, 2000; Decameron, 2000; Selected Federalist papers, 2001; (and intro.) Classic Tales and Fables for Children, 2002; Poems of Faith, 2002; Communist Manifesto and Other Revolutionary Writings, 2003; The Civil War: A Book of Quotations, 2004; Selected Writings and Speeches of Marcus Garvey, 2004; Great English Essays, 2005; Wit and Wisdom of Abraham Lincoln, 2005; Famous Documents and Speeches of the Civil War, 2006; Shakespeare's Great Soliloquies, 2006; (and intro.) Abraham Lincoln Tribute, 2009; Great Short Stories By African-American Writers, 2009; The United States Constitution: The Full Text with Supplementary Materials, 2009; Infamous Speeches: From Robespierre to Osama bin Laden, 2011; Great Speeches of the Twentieth Century, 2011; (with O. Blaisdell) Wit and Wisdom of Oscar Wilde, 2011; Great Short Poems from around the World, 2011; Civil War Short Stories and Poems, 2011; New York: The Big Apple Quote Book, 2011; (and intro.) Selected Poems of Gerard Manley Hopkins, 2011; Civil War Letters, 2012. Contributor to periodicals. **Address:** Department of English, Kingsborough Community College, City University of New York, F315, 2001 Oriental Blvd., Brooklyn, NY 11235-2398, U.S.A. **Online address:** robert.blaisdell@kbcc.cuny.edu

BLAISE, Bulot. *See* **HORNE, R(alph) A(lbert).**

BLAISE, Clark. American (born United States), b. 1940. **Genres:** Novels, Novellas/Short Stories, Travel/Exploration, Young Adult Fiction. **Career:** University of Wisconsin, acting instructor in English, 1964-65; Concordia University, Sir George Williams University, lecturer, 1966-67, assistant professor, 1968-73, associate professor, 1973-76, professor of English, 1976-78; York University, professor of humanities, 1978-80; Skidmore College, professor of English, 1980-84; David Thompson University Centre, visiting professor, 1984; Emory University, visiting professor, 1985-87; Columbia University, adjunct professor, 1985-89, visiting professor, 1987-90; New York University, adjunct professor, 1985-89; Sarah Lawrence College, adjunct professor, 1987-90; University of Iowa, professor of English, 1990-98, International Writing Program, director, professor emeritus, 1998-; University of California-Berkeley, visiting professor of writing, 1998-2000; California College of Arts and Crafts, distinguished visiting professor, 2001-. Writer. **Publications:** (With D.L. Stein and D. Godfrey) New Canadian Writing, 1968; A North American Education (short stories), 1974; Tribal Justice (short stories), 1974: (with B. Mukherjee) Days and Nights in Calcutta (travel memoir), 1977; (ed. with J. Metcalf) Here & Now, 1977; Lunar Attractions (novel), 1979; Lusts, 1983; Resident Alien, 1986; Border as Fiction, 1990; Man and His World, 1992; I Had a Father, 1993; If I Were Me, 1997; Time

Lord: Sir Sandford Fleming and the Creation of Standard Time, 2000; New and Selected Stories, 4 vols., 2000-05; Southern Stories, 2000; Pittsburgh Stories, 2001; Montreal Stories, 2003; World Body, 2006; Selected Essays, 2008; Meagre Tarmac, 2011. **Address:** c/o Eric Simonoff, Janklow & Nesbit Associates, 445 Park Ave., New York, NY 10022, U.S.A. **Online address:** clarquito@aol.com

BLAKE, Jennifer. *See* **MAXWELL, Patricia Anne.**

BLAKE, Jon. Welsh/British (born England), b. 1954. **Genres:** Children's Fiction, Plays/Screenplays, Novellas/Short Stories, Novels, Young Adult Fiction. **Career:** Bretton Woods School, English and drama teacher, 1979-80; Chilwell Comprehensive, English teacher, 1980-81; International Community Centre, teacher; Broxtowe College, lecturer in communications, 1982-84; University of Glamorgan, lecturer in creative writing, 1994-. Writer. **Publications:** YOUNG ADULT NOVELS: Yatesy's Rap, 1986; Geoffrey's First, 1988; Trick or Treat?, 1988; Holiday in Happy Street, 1989; Oddly, 1989; Roboskool, 1990; The King of Rock and Roll, 1991; The Likely Stories, 1991; The Melody of Oddly, 1992; You're a Hero, Daley B.!, 1994; How I Became a Star, 1995; The Sandbag Secret, 1997; Sid's War, 1998; The Supreme Dream Machine, 1998; Stop, Thief!, 1999; One Girl School, 2002; True Beautiful Game, 2002; The Deadly Secret of Dorothy W., 2003; The Mad Mission of Jasmin J., 2004; Feela, 2008; The Last Free Cat, 2008; Stinky Finger's Deadly Doll of Death, 2008; Mutiny on the School Ship Bounty, 2010; Oshie, 2011. CHILDREN'S BOOKS: Binka and the Banana Boat, 1991; Impo, 1991; Pilot Bird and Gums, 1991; Wriggly Pig, 1992; Daley B., 1992; The Ghost of Joseph Coney, 1994; FS3, 1995; Danger Eyes, 1999. LITTLE STUPENDO SERIES: Little Stupendo, 1995; Little Stupendo Rides Again, 1999; Little Stupendo Flies High, 2001. DOGSBOTTOM SCHOOL SERIES: Dogsbottom School Goes Totally Mental, 2005; Dogsbottom School Loses the Plot, 2005; I Rule Dogsbottom School, 2005. HOUSE OF FUN SERIES: Stinky Finger's House of Fun, 2005; Crazy Party At the House of Fun, 2005; Mystery Guest at the House of Fun, 2006; Holiday Mania At the House of Fun, 2007; Peace and Love at the House of Fun, 2007; Stinky Finger's Peace and Love Thing, 2007. OTHERS: Net (play), 1986; Showdown (stories), 1988; The Birdwoman of Normal Street (play), 1991; The Hell Hound of Hooley Street (stories), 1993; Life (play), 1995; Broken Hearts and Rock and Roll (novel), 2002. **Address:** David Higham Associates, 5-8 Lower John St., Golden Sq., London, GL W1F 9HA, England. **Online address:** penderyn2000@yahoo.co.uk

BLAKE, Justin. *See* **BOWEN, John (Griffith).**

BLAKE, Laurel. *See* **PALENCIA, Elaine Fowler.**

BLAKE, Mark R. (David Harrington). British (born England), b. 1965. **Genres:** Novels, Young Adult Fiction. **Career:** Metal Forces, writer, 1988; Q, assistant editor, editor-in-chief; Mojo (magazine), editor-in-chief. **Publications:** Pearl Jam, 1995; (as D. Harrington) REM: Fully Illustrated Book and Interview Disc, 1996; (ed.) Dylan: Visions, Portraits and Back Pages, 2005; (ed.) Punk: The Whole Story, 2006; Pigs Might Fly: The Inside Story of Pink Floyd, 2007 in US as Comfortably Numb: The Inside Story of Pink Floyd, 2008; (comp.) Stone Me, 2008; Is this the Real Life?, 2011. Contributor to periodicals. **Address:** Da Capo Press, 11 Cambridge Ctr., Cambridge, MA 02142, U.S.A. **Online address:** info@markrblake.com

BLAKE, Michael. American (born United States), b. 1945. **Genres:** Westerns/Adventure, Novels. **Career:** Public Information Office, The Strategian, assistant editor. **Publications:** Dances with Wolves (novel), 1988; (with K. Costner and J. Wilson) Dances with Wolves: The Illustrated Story of the Epic Film, 1990; Airman Mortensen (novel), 1991, 2nd ed., 2002; Marching to Valhalla: A Novel of Custer's Last Days, 1996; The Holy Road: A Novel, 2001; Like a Running Dog: An Autobiography, 2002; Indian Yell: The Heart of an American Insurgency, 2006; Twelve the King, 2009. **Address:** 2918 Gilmerton Ave., Los Angeles, CA 90064, U.S.A.

BLAKE, Nick. *See* **HUTSON, Shaun P.**

BLAKE, Norman Francis. British/Brazilian (born Brazil), b. 1934. **Genres:** Language/Linguistics, Literary Criticism And History, Biography, Translations, Bibliography, History, Education. **Career:** University of Liverpool, lecturer, senior lecturer, 1959-73; University of Sheffield, professor of English language, 1973-99, chair of English language, through 1999, head of the department; De Montfort University, English department and Centre for Technology and the Arts, research professor. Writer. **Publications:** Caxton and His World, 1969; Caxton's Quattros Sermones, 1973; The English Language in Medieval Literature, 1977; Non-Standard Language in English Literature, 1981; Shakespeare's Language: An Introduction, 1983; Textual Tradition of the Canterbury Tales, 1985; William Caxton: A Bibliographical Guide, 1985; Traditional English Grammar and Beyond, 1988; The Language of Shakespeare, 1989; An Introduction to the Language of Literature, 1990; William Caxton and English Literary Culture, 1991; The Language of Literature, 1993; Essays on Shakespeare's Language, 1996; A History of the English Language, 1996; A Grammar of Shakespeare's Language, 2001; Shakespeare's Non-Standard English: A Dictionary of His Informal Language, 2004. EDITOR: (trans. and intro.) The Saga of the Jomsvikings, 1962; The Phoenix, 1964; W. Caxton, History of Reynard the Fox, 1970; (comp.) Middle English Religious Prose, 1972; (intro.) Selections from William Caxton, 1973; Caxton's Own Prose, 1973; Quattuor Sermons, 1975; Caxton: England's First Publisher, 1976; The Canterbury Tales, 1980; English Historical Linguistics: Studies in Development, 1984; The Index of Printed Middle English Prose, 1985; Cambridge History of the English Language, vol. II, 1066-1476, 1992. Contributor to journals. **Address:** De Montfort University, The Gateway, Sheffield, LE LE1 9BH, England. **Online address:** n.f.blake@sheffield.ac.uk

BLAKE, Quentin. British (born England), b. 1932. **Genres:** Children's Fiction, Illustrations, History. **Career:** Freelance illustrator, 1957-; French Lycee, teacher in English, 1962-65; Royal College of Art, School of Graphic Design, tutor, 1965-78, Department of Illustration, head, 1978-86, visiting tutor, 1986-89, senior fellow, 1988, visiting professor, 1989-. Writer and artist. **Publications:** Patrick, 1969; Jack and Nancy, 1969; A Band of Angels, 1969; Angelo, 1970; Snuff, 1973; Lester at the Seaside, 1975; (comp. with J. Yeoman) The Puffin Book of Improbable Records, 1975 as The Improbable Book of Records, 1976; Lester and the Unusual Pet, 1975; The Adventures of Lester, 1978; (comp.) Custard and Company: Poems by Ogden Nash, 1980; Mister Magnolia, 1980; Quentin Blake's Nursery Rhyme Book, 1983; The Story of the Dancing Frog, 1984; Smell Jelly Smelly Fish, 1986; (with M. Rosen) Under the Bed, 1986; (with M. Rosen) Hard Boiled Legs, 1987; (with M. Rosen) Spollyollydiddlytiddlyitis, 1987; Mrs. Armitage on Wheels, 1987; Quentin Blake's ABC, 1989; All Join In, 1990; (with J. Yeoman) Bear's Winter House, 2009; Quentin Blake's Ten Frogs; Quentin Blake's diez Ranas, 2010. WITH Y. JEOMAN: Old Mother Hubbard's Dog Dresses Up, 1990; Old Mother Hubbard's Dog Learns to Play, 1990; Old Mother Hubbard's Dog Needs a Doctor, 1990; Old Mother Hubbard's Dog Takes Up Sport, 1990; Quentin Blake's Nursery Collection, 1991; Cockatoos, 1992; Simpkin, 1993; (comp.) The Quentin Blake Book of Nonsense Verse, 1994; Quentin Blake Agenda, 1994; Simpkin, 1994; La Vie de la Page, 1995; (comp.) The Quentin Blake Book of Nonsense Stories, 1996; Clown, 1996; Dix Grenouilles, 1997; Mrs. Armitage and the Big Wave, 1997; The Green Ship, 1998; (with J. Yeoman) Up with Birds, 1998; Zagazoo, 1998; (with J. Cassidy) Drawing for the Artistically Undiscovered, 1998; Zap! The Quentin Blake Guide to Electrical Safety, 1998; Fantastic Daisy Artichoke, 1999; Words and Pictures, 2000; Un Bateau Dans le Ciel, 2000; The Laureate's Party, 2000; Fantastic Daisy Artichoke, 2001; Loveykins, 2002; Laureate's Progress, 2002; (ed.) Magic Pencil, 2002; Tell Me a Picture, 2003; A Sailing Boat in the Sky, 2003; Mrs. Armitage: Queen of the Road, 2003; (ed.) Promenade de Quentin Blake aupaysde la Poesie Francaise, 2003; Angel Pavement, 2004; (foreword) In the Land of Illustration, 2005; Quentin Blake et les Demoiselles des Bords deSeine, 2005; (ed.) In All Directions: Travel and Illustration, 2005; You're Only Young Twice, 2008; Daddy Lost His Head, 2009; Sixes and Sevens, 2011; The Heron and the Crane, 2011; Le Drole d'Hiver d'Ours, 2011; (with M. Rosen) Sad Book, 2011. Illustrator of books by others. Contributor to periodicals. **Address:** A. P. Watt Ltd., 20 John St., London, GL WC1N 2DR, England.

BLAKE, Raymond B. Canadian (born Canada), b. 1958. **Genres:** History, Local History/Rural Topics, Essays. **Career:** Teacher of social studies and history, 1979-83, 1984-86; Canadian Historical Review, bibliographer, 1988-91, proofreader, 1991; Brock University, course director for Canadian social history, 1991; York University, course director for Canadian economic history, 1991-92; University of Alberta, visiting assistant professor of history, 1992-93; St. Thomas University, assistant professor of history, 1993-94; Mount Allison University, professor of Canadian studies, 1994-, Centre for Canadian Studies, Winthrop Pickard Bell Fellow, 1994-95, director, 1995-; University of Regina, Saskatchewan Institute of Public Policy, director, 2001-04, Faculty of Arts, Department of History, professor of history, acting associate dean. Writer. **Publications:** Canadians at Last: Canada Integrates Newfoundland as a Province, 1994; From Fishermen to Fish: The Evolution of Canadian Fishery Policy, 2000; From Rights to Needs: A History of Family Allowances in Canada, 1929-92, 2009. EDITOR: (with J.A. Keshen) Social Welfare Policy in Canada: Historical Readings, 1995; (with J. Keshen) A History of Social Welfare in Canada: Selected Readings, 1995; (with P.E. Bryden and J.F. Strain) The Welfare State in Canada, 1997; (with M.J. Tucker and P.E. Bryden) Canada and the New World Order: Facing the New Millennium, 2000; (with A. Nurse) Trajectories of Rural Life: New Perspectives on Rural Canada, 2003; (with J.A. Keshen) Social Fabric or Patchwork Quilt: The Development of Social Policy in Canada, 2006; Transforming the Nation: Canada and Brian Mulroney, 2007; (with A. Nurse) Beyond National Dreams: Essays on Canadian Citizenship and Nationalism, 2009. Contributor of articles to books and journals. **Address:** Department of History, University of Regina, AH.350.2, 3737 Wascana Pkwy., Regina, SK S4S 0A2, Canada. **Online address:** raymond.blake@uregina.ca

BLAKE, Sally. *See* **SAUNDERS, Jean (Innes).**

BLAKE, Sarah. American (born United States), b. 1960?. **Genres:** Novels, Poetry. **Career:** Writer and educator. **Publications:** Full Turn (chapbook of poems), 1989; (with R. Kahn) Runaway Girls, 1997; Grange House (novel), 2000; The Postmistress (novel), 2010. Contributor to periodicals. **Address:** Washington, DC , U.S.A. **Online address:** sarah@sarahblakebooks.com

BLAKE, Stephen P. American (born United States), b. 1942. **Genres:** Geography, Local History/Rural Topics, Adult Non-fiction, History. **Career:** University of Minnesota, visiting professor of history, 1974-84, administrator; Saint Olaf College, assistant professor of history, associate professor of history of India, Middle East, 1986, associate professor emeritus of history, 2003-. Writer. **Publications:** Dar-ul-Khilafat-i-Shahjahanabad: The Padshahi Shahar in Mughal India, 1556-1739, 1974; Shahjahanabad: The Sovereign City in Mughal India, 1991; Half the World: The Social Architecture of Safavid Isfahan, 1590-1722, 1999. **Address:** Department of History, Saint Olaf College, 1520 St. Olaf Ave., Northfield, MN 55057, U.S.A. **Online address:** blake@stolaf.edu

BLAKE, Sterling. *See* **BENFORD, Gregory (Albert).**

BLAKELY, Mary Kay. American (born United States), b. 1948. **Genres:** Novels, Autobiography/Memoirs, Essays. **Career:** Indiana University-Purdue University, instructor in women's studies, 1976-80; Vogue, contributing editor, 1981-84; Ms., contributing editor, 1981-2001; New School for Social Research, lecturer and instructor in writing, 1984-97; Lear's, contributing editor, 1989-91; Los Angeles Times Magazine, contributing editor, 1994-97; Missouri School of Journalism, associate professor, 1997-. **Publications:** (With G. Kaufman) Pulling Our Own Strings: A Collection of Feminist Humor and Satire, 1980; Wake Me When It's Over: A Journey to the Edge and Back, 1989; American Mom: Motherhood, Politics and Humble Pie, 1994; Red, White and Oh So Blue: A Memoir of a Political Depression, 1996. Contributor to periodicals. **Address:** Missouri School of Journalism, 211 Lee Hills Hall, Columbia, MO 65211-1200, U.S.A. **Online address:** blakelym@missouri.edu

BLAKEMORE, Colin (Brian). British (born England), b. 1944. **Genres:** Biology, Medicine/Health, Psychology, Sciences, Psychiatry. **Career:** Cambridge University, Physiological Laboratory, university demonstrator, 1968-72, lecturer, 1972-; New York University, visiting professor, 1970; Massachusetts Institute of Technology, visiting professor, 1971; British Broadcasting Corp., writer and broadcaster, Reith lecturer, 1976; Downing College, fellow, director of medical studies and lecturer in physiology, 1977-79; Royal College of Art, Lethaby professor, 1978; Oxford University, Waynflete professor of physiology, 1979-2007, Centre for Cognitive Neuroscience, director, 1996-2003, Magdalen College, professorial fellow, 1979-, professor of neuroscience, Perspectives in Vision Research, series editor, 1981-; Salk Institute, visiting scientist, 1982, 1983, 1992; IBRO News, editor-in-chief, 1986-2000; Neuro Report, associate editor, 1989-2003; McMaster University, McLaughlin visiting professor, 1992; Royal Society, fellow, 1992-; Academy of Medical Sciences, fellow, 1992-; University of California, Harkness fellow, Regents' Professor, 1995-96; Institute of Biology, honorary fellow, chartered biologist, 1996-; European Dana Alliance for the Brain, vice-chairman, 1997-; Medical Research Council, chief executive, 2003-07; University of Warwick, professor of neuroscience; British Technology Group, director; British Neuroscience Association, president; Physiological Society, president; Biosciences Federation, president; Association of British Science Writers, president; Motor Neurone Disease Association, president; SANE, vice chairman; Progressive Supranuclear Palsy Association, vice president; Understanding Animal Research, chairman; British Science Association, president and chairman; Royal College of Physicians, honorary fellow. **Publications:** (Contrib.) Illusion in Nature and Art, 1973; Mechanics of the Mind, 1977; The Mind Machine, 1988; (with S.D. Iversen) Sex and Society, 1999. EDITOR: (with M.S. Gazzaniga) Handbook of Psychobiology, 1975; Mindwaves, 1987; (with H. Barlow and M. Weston-Smith) Images and Understanding, 1990; Vision: Coding and Efficiency, 1990; The Cognitive Neurosciences, 1995; (with S. Iversen) Gender and Society, 2000; (with S. Jennett) The Oxford Companion to the Body, 2001; (with A. Parker and A. Derrington) The Physiology of Cognitive Processes, 2003; (with C.A. Heywood and A.D. Milner) The Roots of Visual Awareness: A Festschrift in Honour of Alan Cowey, 2003. **Address:** Department of Physiology, Anatomy and Genetics, University of Oxford, Sherrington Bldg., Parks Rd., Oxford, OX OX1 3PT, England. **Online address:** colin.blakemore@ndm.ox.ac.uk

BLAKESLEE, Matthew. American (born United States) **Genres:** Adult Non-fiction, Psychology, Medicine/Health. **Career:** Writer. **Publications:** (With S. Blakeslee) The Body Has a Mind of Its Own: How Body Maps in Your Brain Help You Do (Almost) Everything Better (nonfiction), 2007. **Address:** Random House Inc., 1745 Broadway, New York, NY 10019, U.S.A. **Online address:** mattblakeslee@yahoo.com

BLAKESLEE, Sandra. American (born United States), b. 1943. **Genres:** Medicine/Health, Sciences, Psychology. **Career:** New York Times, news assistant, staff writer, 1968-, science correspondent, 1983-. **Publications:** (Co-ed.) Human Heart Replacement: A New Challenge for Physicians and Reporters, 1986; (with L. Gillespie) You Don't Have to Live With Cystitis, 1986; (with J.S. Wallerstein) Second Chances: Men, Women and Children a Decade After Divorce, 1989; (with J.S. Wallerstein) The Good Marriage: How and Why Love Lasts, 1995; (with W.S. Ramachardan) Phantoms in the Brain, 1998; (with J. Wallerstein and J. Lewis) The Unexpected Legacy of Divorce: A 25 Year Landmark Study, 2000; (with J.S. Wallerstein) What About the Kids?: Raising Your Children Before, During and After Divorce, 2003; (with J. Hawkins) On Intelligence, 2004; (with M. Blakeslee) Body Has a Mind of Its Own: New Discoveries About How the Mind-Body Connection Helps Us Master the World, 2008; (with S.L. Macknik and S. Martinez-Conde) Sleights of Mind: What the Neuroscience of Magic Reveals about Our Everyday Deceptions, 2010. **Address:** Santa Fe, NM , U.S.A. **Online address:** blakes@nytimes.com

BLAKESLEY, Christopher L. American (born United States), b. 1945. **Genres:** Law, Social Sciences, Politics/Government, Humanities. **Career:** U.S. Department of State, Office of the Legal Adviser, attorney and advisor, 1973-75; Louisiana State University, assistant professor, associate professor of law, 1977-82, professor, 1987-2002, Paul M. Hebert Law Center, J.Y. Sanders professor of law, 1991-2002, chair, 1991, J.Y. Sanders professor of law emeritus, 2002-; University of the Pacific, professor of law, 1982-87; University of Nevada Las Vegas, The Boyd School of Law, Beckley Singleton professor, Cobeaga Tomlinson professor, 2005-06, Cobeaga Law Firm professor of law; American Society of Comparative Law, board director; Association International de Droit Pénal, board director, vice-president, 2001-09; Revue Internationale de Droit Pénal, co-editor-in-chief. **Publications:** (With L.D. Wardle and J.Y. Parker) Contemporary Family Law: Principles, Policy and Practice, 4 vols., 1988; Terrorism, Drugs, International Law and the Protection of Human Liberty, 1992; Louisiana Family Law, 1993; (co-author) The International Legal System, 6th ed., 2008; (co-author) Cases and Materials on the International Legal System, 2001; (with A. Eser and O. Lagodny) The Individual as Subject of International Cooperation in Criminal Matters: A Comparative Study, 2002; Terrorism and Anti-Terrorism: A Normative and Practical Assessment, 2006; (with L.E. Carter and P.J. Hening) Global Issues in Criminal Law, 2007; (with E.B. Firmage and T.B. McAffee) The Most Dangerous Branch: Why the Constitution Gave the War Power to Congress and Not to Rogue Presidents, forthcoming. Works appear in anthologies. Contributor of articles and reviews to journals. **Address:** William S. Boyd School of Law, University of Nevada, 451 BSL, 4505 S Maryland Pk., PO Box 451003, Las Vegas, NV 89154-1003, U.S.A. **Online address:** chris.blakesley@unlv.edu

BLAKEY, Nancy. American (born United States), b. 1955. **Genres:** How-to

Books, Self Help, Children's Fiction, Human Relations/Parenting. **Career:** Seattle's Child Magazine, columnist, 1987. **Publications:** The Mudpies Activity Book: Recipes for Invention, 1993; More Mudpies: 101 Alternatives to Television, 1994; Lotions, Potions and Slime: Mudpies and More!, 1996; The Mudpies Book of Boredom Busters, 1999; Go Outside!: Over 130 Activities for Outdoor Adventures, 2002. Works appear in anthologies. Contributor to magazines. **Address:** 15890 Euclid Ave. NE, Bainbridge Island, WA 98110, U.S.A. **Online address:** mail@nancyblakey.com

BLAMIRES, Alcuin (Godfrey). British (born England), b. 1946. **Genres:** Literary Criticism And History, Women's Studies And Issues, Classics. **Career:** University of Wales, St. David's University College, senior lecturer, 1970-99; Medieval Illuminated Manuscripts in Wales Project, co-director; University of London, Goldsmiths College, Department of English and Comparative Literature, reader, 1999-, professor, 2004-, emeritus professor of English. Writer. **Publications:** The Canterbury Tales (criticism), 1987; (ed. with K. Pratt and C.W. Marx) Woman Defamed and Woman Defended: An Anthology of Medieval Texts, 1992; The Case for Women in Medieval Culture, 1997; (with G.C. Holian) The Romance of the Rose Illuminated: Manuscripts at the National Library of Wales, Aberystwyth, 2002; (ed. with S. Ellis) Sexuality, in Chaucer: An Oxford Guide, 2005; Chaucer, Ethics, and Gender, 2006; Philosophical Sleaze? The Stroke of Thought in the Miller's Tale and Chaucerian Fabliau, 2007. Contributor to journals. **Address:** Department of English and Comparative Literature, Goldsmiths College, University of London, Rm. 401, 4th Fl., Warmington Twr., London, GL SE14 6NW, England. **Online address:** a.blamires@gold.ac.uk

BLAMIRES, Harry. British (born England), b. 1916. **Genres:** Novels, Language/Linguistics, Literary Criticism And History, Theology/Religion, Young Adult Fiction, Science Fiction/Fantasy. **Career:** King Alfred's College, principal lecturer in English, 1948-76, dean of degrees, 1972-74, dean of arts, 1974-76, head of department; Wheaton College, visiting professor of English literature, 1987. Writer. **Publications:** Repair the Ruins: Reflections on Educational Matters from the Christian Point of View, 1950; English in Education, 1951; The Devil's Hunting Grounds: A Fantasy, 1954; Cold War in Hell, 1955; Blessing Unbounded, 1955 as Highway to Heaven, 1984; The Faith and Modern Error: An Essay on the Christian Message in the Twentieth Century, 1956 as The Secularist Heresy, 1980; The Will and the Way: A Study of Divine Providence and Vocation, 1957 as A God Who Acts, 1981; The Kirkbride Conversations: Six Dialogues of the Christian Faith, 1958; Kirkbride and Company, 1959; The Offering of Man, 1960; The Christian Mind: How Should a Christian Think?, 1963; A Defence of Dogmatism in US as The Tyranny of Time: A Defence of Dogmatism, 1965; The Bloomsday Book: Guide through Joyce's Ulysses, 1966, 3rd ed. as The New Bloomsday Book: A Guide Through Ulysses, 1996; Word Unheard: A Guide through Eliot's Four Quartets, 1969; Milton's Creation: A Guide through Paradise Lost, 1971; A Short History of English Literature, 1974, 2nd ed., 1984; Where Do We Stand?: An Examination of the Christian's Position in the Modern World, 1980; Twentieth-Century English Literature, 1982, 2nd ed., 1986; (ed.) A Guide to Twentieth-Century Literature in English, 1983; On Christian Truth, 1983; Notes on A Portrait of the Artist as a Young Man, 1984; Words Made Flesh: God Speaks to Us in the Ordinary Things of Life, 1985 in UK as The Marks of the Maker, 1987; Studying James Joyce, 1987; Meat not Milk in US as Recovering the Christian Mind, 1988; Knowing the Truth About Heaven and Hell: Our Choices and Where they Lead Us, 1988; The Victorian Age of Literature, 1988; The Age of Romantic Literature, 1989; A History of Literary Criticism, 1991; Notes on John Betjeman: Selected Poems, 1992; The Queen's English, 1994; The Cassell Guide to Common Errors in English, 1999; The Post-Christian Mind: How Should a Christian Think?, 1999; The Penguin Guide to Plain English: Express Yourself Clearly and Effectively, 2000; Compose Yourself-and Write Good English, 2003; New Town: A Fable-Unless You Believe, 2005. **Address:** Rough Close, Keswick, CM CA12 5QQ, England.

BLANC, Nero. *See* **BIDDLE, Cordelia Frances.**

BLANC, Nero. *See* **ZETTLER, Steve.**

BLANCHARD, J. *See* **BLANCHARD, James G.**

BLANCHARD, James G. (J. Blanchard). Canadian (born Canada), b. 1948. **Genres:** History, Librarianship. **Career:** Winnipeg Public Library, librarian, 1981-82; Canadian Grain Commission, librarian, 1982-87; Manitoba Department of Culture, director of public library services, 1988-91; University of Manitoba, reference librarian, 1992-, Elizabeth Dafoe Library, head of reference services, 1992-. Writer. **Publications:** (As J. Blanchard) A History of the Canadian Grain Commission, 1912-1987, 1987; 1000 Miles of Prairie: The Manitoba Historical and Scientific Society and the History of Western Canada, 2002; Winnipeg 1912: A Year in the Life of a City, 2005; Winnipeg's Great War: A City Comes of Age, 2010. **Address:** University of Manitoba Libraries, Rm. 156, Elizabeth Dafoe Library, University of Manitoba, Winnipeg, MB R3T 2N2, Canada. **Online address:** blanchd@ms.umanitoba.ca

BLANCHARD, Melinda. American (born United States), b. 1952?. **Genres:** Food And Wine. **Career:** Blanchard's Restaurant, owner. Writer. **Publications:** WITH ROBERT BLANCHARD: A Trip to the Beach: Living on Island Time in the Caribbean (memoir), 2000; At Blanchard's Table: A Trip to the Beach Cookbook, 2003; Live What You Love: Notes from an Unusual Life (memoir), 2005; Cook What You Love: Simple Flavorful Recipes to Make Again and Again, 2005; Changing Your Course: The 5-Step Guide to Getting the Life you Want, 2008; Live What You Love: Notes from a Passionate Life, 2010. **Address:** Blanchard's Restaurant, Meads Bay, PO Box 898, Anguilla, MS 38721, U.S.A. **Online address:** blanchards@lwyl.com

BLANCHARD, Olivier Jean. French (born France), b. 1948. **Genres:** Economics. **Career:** Massachusetts Institute of Technology, instructor in economics, 1977, associate professor, 1983-85, professor of economics, 1985-93, chairman, 1998-2003; Harvard University, assistant professor, 1977-81, associate professor of economics, 1981-83, visiting Taussig professor, 1997-98; National Bureau of Economic Research, research associate, 1979-; Center for Economic Performance, research associate, 1992-; International Monetary Fund, economic counsellor and director, chief economist, 2008-. Writer. **Publications:** (With R. Dornbusch) U.S. Deficits, the Dollar, and Europe, 1983; (contrib.) Economic Equilibrium: Model Formulation and Solution, 1985; (with R. Dornbusch and R. Layard) Restoring Europe's Prosperity: Macroeconomic Papers From the Centre for European Policy Studies, 1986; (with S. Fischer) Lectures on Macroeconomics, 1989; World Imbalances, 1989; Suggestions for a New Set of Fiscal Indicators, 1990; (co-author) Reform in Eastern Europe, 1991; La desinflation competitive, le mark et les politiques budgetaires en Europe, 1991; East-West Migration, 1992; (ed. with K. Froot and J. Sachs) The Transition in Eastern Europe, 1993; (with P. Aghion and R. Burgess) The Behaviour of State Firms in Eastern Europe, 1993; (with P. Aghion) On the Speed of Transition in Central Europe, 1993; Post-Communist Reform: Pain and Progress, 1993; Spanish Unemployment: Is there a Solution?, 1995; Revisiting European Unemployment: Unemployment, Capital Accumulation and Factor Prices, 1997; Macroeconomics, 1997, 5th ed., 2009; Economics of Post-Communist Transition, 1997; European Unemployment: The Role of Shocks and Institution, 1999; (with A. Amighini and F. Giavazzi) Macroeconomics: A European Perspective, 2010; (ed. with Sakong Il) Reconstructing the World Economy, 2010. Works appear in anthologies. Contributor to journals. **Address:** International Monetary Fund, 700 19th St. NW, Washington, DC 20431, U.S.A. **Online address:** oblanchard@imf.org

BLANCHARD, Robert. American (born United States), b. 1951?. **Genres:** Food And Wine, How-to Books, Autobiography/Memoirs. **Career:** Blanchard's Restaurant, owner. Writer. **Publications:** WITH M. BLANCHARD: A Trip to the Beach: Living on Island Time in the Caribbean (memoir), 2000; At Blanchard's Table: A Trip to the Beach Cookbook, 2003; Live What You Love: Notes from an Unusual Life (memoir), 2005; Cook What You Love: Simple, Flavorful Recipes to Make Again and Again, 2005; Changing Your Course: The 5-step Guide to Getting the Life You Want, 2008; Working For Yourself: The 5-Step Guide to Becoming Your Own Boss, 2011. **Address:** Blanchard's Restaurant, PO Box 898, Meads Bay, Anguilla, 2640, England. **Online address:** blanchards@lwyl.com

BLANCHARD, Stephen (Thomas). British (born England), b. 1950. **Genres:** Novels, Young Adult Fiction, Literary Criticism And History, Young Adult Fiction. **Career:** Writer. **Publications:** NOVELS: Gagarin and I, 1995; Wilson's Island, 1997; The Paraffin Child, 1999. Contributor of stories and articles to magazines. **Address:** c/o Rachel Calder, Tessa Sayle Agency, 11 Jubilee Pl, London, GL SW3 3TE, England.

BLANCHET, Pascal. Canadian (born Canada), b. 1980?. **Genres:** Translations. **Career:** Writer. **Publications:** La Fugue, 2005; Rapide blanc, 2005, trans. as White Rapids, 2007; Bologne: Conte en 3 actes symphoniques, 2007. **Address:** QC , Canada. **Online address:** billblanchet@sympatico.ca

BLANCO, Jodee. American (born United States), b. 1964. **Genres:** Self Help, Young Adult Non-fiction. **Career:** Blanco Group, public relations executive. Writer and consultant. **Publications:** (With C. Lanigan) The Evolving Woman, 2000; The Complete Guide to Book Publicity, 2000, 2nd ed., 2004; Please Stop Laughing at Me: One Woman's Inspirational Story, 2003; Please Stop Laughing at Us: One Survivor's Extraordinary Quest to Prevent School Bullying, 2008; (with R. O'Neal and K. Carroll) Both Of Us: My Life With Farrah, 2012. **Address:** Blanco Group, 16531 106th Ct., Orland Park, IL 60467, U.S.A. **Online address:** jodee@jodeeblanco.com

BLANCO, Richard. American/Spanish (born Spain), b. 1968. **Genres:** Poetry. **Career:** Butterfly Lightning (a poetry reading series), co-founder, founder and coordinator, 1993; Young Men's Christian Association, founder and coordinator, 1994; Florida International University, instructor of creative writing program, 1998-99; Miami Dade College, Department of English, instructor, 1998; Central Connecticut State University, poet-in-residence, assistant professor of English and director of creative writing, 1999-2002; Hudson Valley Writers' Center, staff instructor; Georgetown University, lecturer of creative writing, 2003-04; American University, lecturer of creative writing, 2003-04. Writer. **Publications:** City of a Hundred Fires, 1998; Nowhere But Here, 2004; Directions to the Beach of the Dead, 2005. Contributor to periodicals. Works appear in anthologies. **Address:** c/o Stuart Bernstein, Representation For Artists, 63 Carmine St. 3D, New York, NY 10014, U.S.A. **Online address:** rblanco@att.net

BLAND, Peter. British (born England), b. 1934. **Genres:** Plays/Screenplays, Poetry, Children's Fiction. **Career:** New Zealand Broadcasting Corp., editor poetry program, 1960-64; Downstage Theatre Co., co-founder and artistic director, 1964-68; London Magazine, contributor, 1964-99. **Publications:** POETRY: (with J. Boyd and V. O'Leary) Three Poets, 1958; My Side of the Story: Poems, 1960-1964, 1964; Domestic Interiors. 1964; Passing Gods, 1970; (with B. MacSweeney) Joint Effort, 1970; The Man with the Carpet-Bag, 1972; Mr. Maui, 1976; Primitives, 1979; Stone Tents, 1981; The Crusoe Factor, 1985; Selected Poems, 1987; Paper Boats, 1991; Let's Meet: Poems, 1985-2000, 2003; The Night Kite: Poems for Children, 2004; Sorry, I'm a Stranger Here Myself, 2004. PLAYS: Ports of Call, 2003; Mr Maui's Monologues, 2008. **Address:** c/o Maureen Vincent, Peters Fraser and Dunlop Group Ltd., Drury House, 34-43 Russell St., London, GL WC2B 5HA, England.

BLANK, G(regory) Kim. Canadian (born Canada), b. 1952. **Genres:** Poetry, Literary Criticism And History, Essays, Humor/Satire, Language/Linguistics, Humanities. **Career:** University of Victoria, lecturer in English, 1978-80, assistant professor, 1986-90, associate professor, 1990-96, director of graduate studies, 1994-99, professor of English, 1996-, director of writing, 2002-05; University of Southampton, instructor in English, 1980-83; Open University, tutor, 1983-85; University of Namibia, lecturer in English, 1984-86. **Publications:** Shelley and the Problem of Wordsworth's Influence, 1983; Wordsworth's Influence on Shelley: A Study of Poetry Authority, 1988; (ed.) The New Shelley: Later Twentieth-Century Views, 1991; (ed. with M.K. Louis) Influence and Resistance in Nineteenth-Century English Poetry, 1993; Wordsworth and Feeling: The Poetry of an Adult Child, 1995; Sex, Life Itself, and the Original Nanaimo Bar Recipe, 1999; (co-author) The Writer's Block Calendar, 2000, rev. ed., 2004; Rant, 2002; The University of Victoria Writer's Guide, 2006; Perspectives on Contemporary Issues, 2007; Being Frank, 2007. Contributor of articles to books, journals and newspapers. **Address:** Department of English, University of Victoria, Rm. C354, 3800 Finnerty Rd., PO Box 3070, STN CSC, Victoria, BC V8W 3P4, Canada. **Online address:** gkblank@uvic.ca

BLANK, Harrod. American (born United States), b. 1963?. **Genres:** Transportation, Art/Art History, Photography. **Career:** Artcar Fest Ltd., co-founder, president. Producer, photographer, director and author. **Publications:** Wild Wheels, 1994, 2nd ed., 2001; Art Cars: The Cars, the Artists, the Obsession, the Craft, 2002, 2nd ed., 2007. **Address:** ArtCar Fest Inc., 393 Rutland Ave., San Jose, CA 95128, U.S.A. **Online address:** excentrix@aol.com

BLANK, Jessica. American (born United States), b. 1975. **Genres:** Young Adult Fiction, Novels, Plays/Screenplays, Romance/Historical. **Career:** The Fire Department (theater Co.), co-artistic director. Writer and actress. **Publications:** WITH HUSBAND E. JENSEN: The Exonerated: A Play, 2004; Living Justice: Love, Freedom, and the Making of the Exonerated, 2005. NOVELS: Almost Home, 2007; Karma for Beginners, 2009. **Address:** c/o Author Mail, Atria Books, 1230 Ave. of the Americas, New York, NY 10020-1513, U.S.A.

BLANK, Paula. (Paula Carin Blank). American (born United States), b. 1959. **Genres:** Literary Criticism And History, Politics/Government. **Career:** Hofstra University, assistant professor, 1991-92; College of William and Mary, assistant professor, associate professor, 1992, Margaret L. Hamilton Professor. Writer. **Publications:** Broken English: Dialects and the Politics of Language in Renaissance Writings, 1996; Shakespeare and the Mismeasure of Renaissance Man, 2006. **Address:** Department of English, College of William and Mary, PO Box 8795, Williamsburg, VA 23187-8795, U.S.A. **Online address:** pcblan@wm.edu

BLANK, Paula Carin. *See* **BLANK, Paula.**

BLANK, Rebecca M. American (born United States), b. 1955. **Genres:** Business/Trade/Industry, Economics. **Career:** Data Resources Inc., consultant and educational co-ordinator; Princeton University, assistant professor of economics and public affairs, 1983-89; Massachusetts Institute of Technology, visiting assistant professor of economics, 1988-89; Northwestern University, associate professor, 1989-94, professor of economics, 1994-99, Northwestern University/University of Chicago Joint Center for Poverty Research, director, 1996-97; University of Michigan, Henry Carter Adams collegiate professor of public policy and professor of economics, 1999-, Gerald R. Ford School of Public Policy, Joan and Sanford Weill dean, 1997-2007; National Poverty Center, co-director, 2002-08; Brookings Institution, Robert V. Kerr visiting fellow, 2007-08, faculty, 2008-09; United States Department of Commerce, under secretary, 2009-10, deputy secretary, 2010-11; University of Wisconsin, Department of Economics, visiting fellow, Institute for Research on Poverty, visiting fellow; National Bureau of Economic Research, faculty affiliate. Writer. **Publications:** Disaggregating the Effects of Economic Growth on the Distribution of Income, 1985; How Important Is Welfare Dependence?, 1986; The Effect of Medical Need on AFDC and Medicaid Participation, 1987; Do Justice: Linking Christian Faith and Modern Economic Life, 1992; (ed.) Social Protection versus Economic Flexibility: Is There a Trade-off?, 1994; It Takes a Nation: A New Agenda for Fighting Poverty, 1997; (ed. with D.E. Card) Finding Jobs: Work and Welfare Reform, 2000; (with D.T. Ellwood) A Working Nation: Workers, Work, and Government in the New Economy, 2000; (ed. with R. Haskins) The New World of Welfare, 2001; (with W. McGurn) Is the Market Moral? A Dialogue on Religion, Economics, and Justice, 2004; (ed. with M. Dabady and C.F. Citro) Measuring Racial Discrimination, 2004; (ed. with S.H. Danziger and R.F. Schoeni) Working and Poor: How Economic and Policy Changes Are Affecting Low-Wage Workers, 2006; (ed. with M.S. Barr) Insufficient Funds: Savings, Assets, Credit and Banking Among Low-Income Households, 2009. Contributor to journals and periodicals. **Address:** Department of Commerce, 1401 Constitution Ave. NW, Deputy Secretary's Office, Washington, DC 20230, U.S.A. **Online address:** rblank55@gmail.com

BLANKENHORN, David (George). American/German (born Germany), b. 1955. **Genres:** Sociology. **Career:** Citizen Action, community organizer, 1978-84; Institute for American Values, founder, 1985, president, 1985-; National Fatherhood Initiative, founding chairman; National Parenting Association, board director. Writer. **Publications:** Fatherless America: Confronting Our Most Urgent Social Problem, 1995; The Future of Marriage, 2007; Thrift: A Cyclopedia, 2008. EDITOR: (with S. Bayme and J.B. Elshtain) Rebuilding the Nest: A New Commitment to the American Family, 1990; (with M.A. Glendon) Seedbeds of Virtue: Sources of Competence, Character and Citizenship in American Society, 1995; (with D. Popenoe and J.B. Elshtain) Promises to Keep: Decline and Renewal of Marriage in America, 1996; American Idea, 1999; (with W.F. Horn and M.B. Pearlstein) The Fatherhood Movement: A Call to Action, 1999; (with D. Mack) The Book of Marriage: The Wisest Answers to the Toughest Questions, 2001; (with O. Clayton and R.B. Mincy) Black Fathers in Contemporary American Society: Strengths, Weaknesses and Strategies for Change, 2003; (with D. Browning and M.S.V. Leeuwen) Does Christianity Teach Male Headship?: The Equal-Regard Marriage and Its Critics, 2004; (co-ed.) Islam/West Debate: Documents from a Global Debate on Terrorism, U.S. Policy and the Middle East, 2005; (with B.D. Whitehead and S. Brophy-Warren) Franklin's Thrift: The History of a Lost American Virtue, 2009. **Address:** Institute for American Values, 1841 Broadway, Ste. 211, New York, NY 10023, U.S.A. **Online address:** info@americanvalues.org

BLANKLEY, Tony. American/British (born England), b. 1948?. **Genres:**

Politics/Government, Social Sciences. **Career:** California Attorney General's Office, prosecutor, 1972-82; Ronald Reagan Presidential Administration, policy analyst and speechwriter, 1982-88; Congresswoman Bobbi Fiedler, staff writer, 1988-90; U.S. Congress, House Speaker Newt Gingrich, press secretary, 1990-97; George Magazine, contributing editor, 1997-99; Washington Times, staff, 1990-2002, weekly political columnist and editorial page editor, 2002-07, weekly columnist, 2007-; Edelman, executive vice president of global public affairs, 2007-. Journalist, columnist, radio and television broadcaster. **Publications:** The West's Last Chance: Will We Win the Clash of Civilizations?, 2005; American Grit: What It Will Take to Survive and Win in the 21st Century, 2009. **Address:** Great Falls, VA , U.S.A. **Online address:** tonyblankley@gmail.com

BLANNING, T. C. W. British (born England), b. 1942. **Genres:** History, Essays. **Career:** University of Cambridge, Sidney Sussex College, research fellow, 1965-68, fellow, 1968, assistant lecturer in history, 1972-76, lecturer in history, 1976-87, reader in modern European history, 1987-92, professor of modern European history, 1992-. Writer. **Publications:** Joseph II and Enlightened Despotism, 1970; Reform and Revolution in Mainz, 1743-1803, 1974; The French Revolution in Germany: Occupation and Resistance in the Rhineland, 1792-1802, 1983; The Origins of the French Revolutionary Wars, 1986; The French Revolution: Aristocrats Versus Bourgeois?, 1987, 2nd ed. as The French Revolution: Class War or Culture Clash?, 1998; Joseph II, 1994; The French Revolutionary Wars, 1787-1802, 1996; The Culture of Power and the Power of Culture: Old Regime Europe, 1660-1789, 2002; The Pursuit of Glory: Europe, 1648-1815, 2007; Triumph of Music: The Rise of Composers, Musicians and Their Art, 2008; The Romantic Revolution: A History, 2011. EDITOR: (with D. Cannadine) History and Biography: Essays in Honour Derek Beales, 1996; The Rise and Fall of the French Revolution, 1996; The Oxford Illustrated History of Modern Europe, 1996; (with P. Wende) Reform in Great Britain and Germany, 1750-1850, 1999; The Short Oxford History of Europe: The Eighteenth Century: Europe, 1688-1815, 2000; The Short Oxford History of Europe: The Nineteenth Century: Europe, 1789-1914, 2000; (with H. Schulze) Unity and Diversity in European Culture c. 1800, 2006. **Address:** Sidney Sussex College, University of Cambridge, West Rd., Cambridge, CB CB3 9EF, England. **Online address:** tcb1000@cam.ac.uk

BLASHFORD-SNELL, John Nicholas. British (born England), b. 1936. **Genres:** Animals/Pets, Archaeology/Antiquities, Military/Defense/Arms Control, Natural History, Travel/Exploration, Autobiography/Memoirs. **Career:** Royal Military Academy, instructor, 1963-66; The Scientific Exploration Society, founder and president, 1969-; Discovery Expeditions Ltd., chair. Writer. **Publications:** (With G.R. Snailham) The Expedition Organisers Guide, 1969; (with T. Wintringham) Weapons and Tactics, 1973; Where the Trails Run Out, 1974; In the Steps of Stanley, 1975; (ed. with A. Ballantine) Expeditions: The Experts' Way, 1977; A Taste for Adventure, 1978; (with M. Cable) In the Wake of Drake, 1980; (with M. Cable) Operation Drake, 1981; Mysteries: Encounters with the Unexplained, 1984; Operation Raleigh: The Start of an Adventure, 1987; (with A. Tweedy) Operation Raleigh: Adventure Challenge, 1988; (with A. Tweedy) Operation Raleigh: Adventure Unlimited, 1990; Something Lost behind the Ranges, 1994; (with R. Lenska) Mammoth Hunt, 1996; (with R. Snailham) Kota Mama, 2000; (with R. Snailham) East to the Amazon: In Search of Great Paititi and the Trade Routes of the Ancients, 2003. **Address:** The Scientific Exploration Society, Expedition Base, Motcombe, Shaftesbury, DS SP7 9PB, England. **Online address:** jbs@ses-explore.org

BLASI, Anthony J(oseph). American (born United States), b. 1946. **Genres:** Sociology, Theology/Religion, Social Sciences, Cultural/Ethnic Topics, Bibliography. **Career:** St. Anselm's College, lecturer, 1973-74; DePauw University, assistant professor, 1975-76; University of Alabama, visiting assistant professor, 1975-76; University of Louisville, assistant professor of sociology, 1976-78; Daemen College, associate professor of sociology and chairperson of department, 1978-80; University of Hawaii, assistant professor of sociology, 1986-90; Muskingum College, associate professor of sociology, 1990-94; Tennessee State University, associate professor, 1994-99, professor of sociology, 2000-. Writer. **Publications:** (With F.B Dasilva and A.J. Weigert) Toward an Interpretive Sociology, 1978; Segregationist Violence and Civil Rights Movements in Tuscaloosa, 1980; (with F. Dasilva and D. Dees) The Sociology of Music, 1984; A Phenomenological Transformation of the Social Scientific Study of Religion, 1985; (with M.W. Cuneo) Issues in the Sociology of Religion: A Bibliography, 1986; Moral Conflict and Christian Religion, 1988; Early Christianity as a Social Movement, 1988; (with M.W. Cuneo) The Sociology of Religion: An Organizational Bibliography, 1990; Making Charisma: The Social Construction of Paul's Public Image, 1991; A Sociology of Johannine Christianity, 1996; Organized Religion and Seniors' Mental Health, 1999; (ed. with P. Turcotte and J. Duhaime) Handbook of Early Christianity: Social Science Perspectives, 2002; (with B.F. Donahoe) A History of Sociological Teaching and Research at Catholic Notre Dame University, 2002; (with J.F. Zimmerman) Transition from Vowed to Lay Ministry in American Catholicism, 2004; (ed.) Diverse Histories of American Sociology, 2005; (ed. and trans. with A.K. Jacobs and M. Kanjirathinkal) G. Simmel, Sociology: Inquiries into the Construction of Social Forms, 2009; (ed. with D.P. Sullins) Catholic Social Thought: American Reflections on the Compendium, 2009; (ed.) Toward a Sociological Theory of Religion and Health, 2011. **Address:** Department of Sociology, Tennessee State University, 212c Women's Bldg., Elliott Hall, 3500 John A. Merritt Blvd., Nashville, TN 37209-1561, U.S.A. **Online address:** ablasi@tnstate.edu

BLASING, Randy. American (born United States), b. 1943. **Genres:** Poetry, Translations. **Career:** Randolph-Macon College, instructor in English, 1966-67; College of William and Mary, instructor in English, 1967-69; Community College of Rhode Island, instructor, 1969-72, assistant professor, 1972-80, associate professor, 1980-88, professor of English, 1988-; Pomona College, lecturer, 1977-79. Writer. **Publications:** POEMS: Light Years: Poems, 1977; To Continue: Poems, 1983; The Particles: Poems, 1983; The Double House of Life: Poems, 1989; Graphic Scenes, 1994; Second Home: Poems, 2001; Choice Words: Poems, 1970-2005, 2007. TRANSLATOR: (with M. Konuk) N. Hikmet, Things I Didn't Know I Loved: Selected Poems of Nâzim Hikmet, 1975; (with M. Konuk) N. Hikmet, The Epic of Sheik Bedreddin and Other Poems, 1977; (with M. Konuk) N. Hikmet, Human Landscapes, 1982; (with M. Konuk) N. Hikmet, Rubáiyát, 1985; (with M. Konuk) N. Hikmet, Selected Poetry, 1986; (with M. Konuk) N. Hikmet, Poems of Nazim Hikmet, 1994, 2nd ed., 2002; (with M. Konuk) Human Landscapes from My Country, 2002. Contributor of articles to magazines. **Address:** Department of English, Community College of Rhode Island, 400 E Ave., Warwick, RI 02886-1807, U.S.A. **Online address:** rblasing@ccri.edu

BLASS, Thomas. American/Hungarian (born Hungary), b. 1941?. **Genres:** Psychology, Social Sciences, Autobiography/Memoirs. **Career:** American Psychological Association, G. Stanley Hall lecturer, 2001; University of Maryland Baltimore County, Department of Psychology, professor of social psychology. Writer. **Publications:** Contemporary Social Psychology: Representative Readings, 1976; (ed.) Personality Variables in Social Behavior, 1977; (ed.) Obedience to Authority: Current Perspectives on the Milgram Paradigm, 2000; The Man Who Shocked the World: The Life and Legacy of Stanley Milgram, 2004. **Address:** Department of Psychology, University of Maryland, MP 334, 1000 Hilltop Cir., Baltimore, MD 21250, U.S.A. **Online address:** blass@umbc.edu

BLATANIS, Konstantinos. Greek (born Greece), b. 1966. **Genres:** Novels, Cultural/Ethnic Topics. **Career:** National and Kapodistrian University of Athens, lecturer in American literature and modern drama. Writer. **Publications:** Popular Culture Icons in Contemporary American Drama, 2003. **Address:** Fairleigh Dickinson University Press, M-GH2-01, 285 Madison Ave., Madison, NJ 07940-1006, U.S.A. **Online address:** kblatanis@yahoo.gr

BLATCHFORD, Claire H. American (born United States), b. 1944. **Genres:** Children's Fiction, Children's Non-fiction, Education, inspirational/Motivational Literature, Theology/Religion, Self Help. **Career:** Caritas Day Classes for Deaf Children, teacher of kindergarten and art, 1970-72; writer, 1972-; teacher, 1980-94; Clarke School for the Deaf, art teacher, 2000-. **Publications:** Listening: Notes from a Kindergarten Journal, 1973; Yes, I Wear a Hearing Aid, 1976; All Alone (Except for My Dog Friday), 1983; Down the Path, 1992; A Surprise for Reggie, 1992; Shawna's Bit of Blue Sky, 1992; Nick's Mission, 1995; Turning, 1994; Full Face: A Correspondence about Becoming Deaf in Mid-Life, 1997; Many Ways of Hearing, 1997; Going with the Flow, 1998; Friend of My Heart: Meeting Christ in Everyday Life, 1999; Nick's Secret, 2000; Becoming: A Call to Love, 2004; (comp. and ed.) What Works for Me, 2005; Experiences with the Dying and the Dead: Waking to Our Connections with Those Who Have Died, 2007; 101 Ways to Encourage Self-Advocacy, 2010. Contributor of articles. **Address:** Clarke Schools for Hearing and Speech, 1 Whitman Rd., Canton, MA 02021, U.S.A.

BLATNER, David. American (born United States), b. 1966. **Genres:** Information Science/Computers, Education. **Career:** Afterlife, executive director; InDesign Magazine, editorial director; Moo.com (computer desktop publishing consulting firm), president; CreativePro.com, contributing editor. Consultant. **Publications:** (With K. Stimely) The QuarkXpress Book, 1991; The Desktop Publisher's Survival Kit, 1991; (with E. Taub) QuarkXpress Tips and Tricks, 1992; (with S. Aukstakalnis) Silicon Mirage: The Art and Science of Virtual Reality, 1992; (with S.F. Roth) Real World Scanning and Halftones, 1993, (with G. Fleishman and S. Roth) 2nd ed. as Real World Scanning and Halftones: The Definitive Guide to Scanning and Halftones from the Desktop World, 1998; Real World Quarkimmedia, 1997; The Joy of Pi, 1997; QuarkXPress 4 Book for Macintosh and Windows, 1998; (with T. Falcon) Judaism for Dummies, 2001; The Flying Book: Everything You Wanted to Know About Flying on Airplanes, 2002; QuarkXPress Power Shortcuts, 2002; Real World QuarkXPress 5: For Macintosh and Windows, 2002; (C. Smith and S. Werner) InDesign for QuarkXPress Users, 2003; (co-author) Real World Scanning & Halftones: Industrial Strength Production Techniques, 2004; Real world QuarkXPress 6 for Macintosh and Windows, 2004; (with C. Chavez) Adobe Photoshop CS/CS2 Breakthroughs, 2005; (with C. Smith and S. Werner) Moving to InDesign, 2005; (with C. Chavez) Real World Adobe Photoshop CS4 for Photographers: Industrial-strength Imaging Techniques, 2009. WITH O.M. KVERN: Real World Adobe InDesign 2, 2003; Real World Adobe InDesign CS, 2004; Real World Adobe InDesign CS2, 2006; Real World Adobe InDesign CS3, 2008; Real World Adobe InDesign CS4, 2009. WITH B. FRASER: Real World Photoshop 3, 1992; Real World Photoshop 4: Industrial Strength Production Techniques, 1997; Real world Photoshop 5: Industrial Strength Production Techniques, 1999; Real World Photoshop 6: Industrial Strength Production Techniques, 2001; Real world Adobe Photoshop 7: Industrial Strength Production Techniques, 2003; Real World, Adobe Photoshop CS: Industrial Strength Production Techniques, 2004; Real World Adobe Photoshop CS2: Industrial-Strength Production Techniques, 2006; (and C. Chavez) Real World Adobe Photoshop CS3: Industrial-Strength Production Techniques, 2008. Contributor to periodicals. **Address:** Reid Boates Literary Agency, 274 Crooks Crossroad, PO Box 328, Pittstown, NJ 08867-0328, U.S.A. **Online address:** david@moo.com

BLAU, Francine D. American (born United States), b. 1946. **Genres:** Economics, Women's Studies And Issues. **Career:** National Bureau of Economic Research Inc., research associate, 1988; Cornell University, School of Industrial and Labor Relations, Frances Perkins professor of industrial and labor relations, 1994-, professor of economics, 2011-; Center for Economic Studies/Ifo Institute for Economic Research, research fellow, 2001-; Institute for the Study of Labor, research fellow, 2004-; Stanford University, Center for the Study of Poverty and Inequality, fellow, 2006-; Compensation Research Initiative, research fellow, 2009-. **Publications:** (With A. Simmons, A. Freedman and M. Dunkle) Exploitation from 9 to 5: Report of the Twentieth Century Fund Task Force on Women and Employment, 1975; Equal Pay in the Office, 1977; (with M.A. Ferber) The Economics of Women, Men and Work, 1st ed., 1986, 2nd ed., 1992; (with M.A. Ferber and A.E. Winkler) The Economics of Women, Men and Work, 1986, 6th ed. 2010; (with L.M. Kahn) Wage Inequality: International Comparisons of its Sources, 1996; (ed. with R.G. Ehrenberg) Gender and Family Issues in the Workplace, 1997; (with L.M. Kahn) At Home and Abroad: U.S. Labor Market Performance in International Perspective, 2002; (ed. with M.C. Brinton and D.B. Grusky) Declining Significance of Gender, 2006. Contributor of articles to books and periodicals. **Address:** School of Industrial and Labor Relations, Cornell University, 268 Ives Faculty Bldg., Ithaca, NY 14853-3901, U.S.A. **Online address:** fdb4@cornell.edu

BLAU, Joel. American (born United States), b. 1945. **Genres:** Social Work, Public/Social Administration. **Career:** New York City Human Resources Administration, policy analyst, 1983-86, project manager, 1986-87; Columbia University, adjunct lecturer, 1983-87; State University of New York, Department of Social Welfare, assistant professor, 1987-93, associate professor, 1993-2000, professor of social policy, 2000-, School of Social Welfare, Ph.D. Program, director, 1996-2000, 2000-. Writer. **Publications:** The Visible Poor: Homelessness in the United States, 1992; Illusions of Prosperity: America's Working Families in an Age of Economic Insecurity, 1999; (with M. Abramovitz) The Dynamics of Social Welfare Policy, 2004, 3rd ed., 2010. Contributor to journals. **Address:** School of Social Welfare, State University of New York, Health Sciences Ctr., L2-093, Stony Brook, NY 11794-8231, U.S.A. **Online address:** Jblau@notes.cc.sunysb.edu

BLAUFARB, Rafe. American (born United States), b. 1967. **Genres:** Military/Defense/Arms Control, History. **Career:** Université Paul-Valéry III, visiting professor; Auburn University, associate professor of history, 1999-2006; Florida State University, Department of History, professor, 2006-. Writer. **Publications:** The French Army, 1750- 1820: Careers, Talent, Merit, 2002; Bonapartists in the Borderlands: French Exiles and Refugees on the Gulf Coast, 1815- 1835, 2005; Napoleon, Symbol for an Age: A Brief History with Documents, 2008; (with D.D. Bien and J.M. Smith) Caste, Class and Profession in Old Regime France: The French Army and The Ségur Reform of 1781, 2010; Napoleonic Footsoldiers and Civilians: A Brief History with Documents, 2011; Politics of Fiscal Privilege in Provence, 1530s -1830s, 2012. Contributor to journals. **Address:** Department of History, Florida State University, 408 Bellamy Bldg., Tallahassee, FL 32306, U.S.A. **Online address:** rblaufarb@fsu.edu

BLAUNER, Bob. American (born United States), b. 1929. **Genres:** Race Relations, Sociology, Autobiography/Memoirs, Adult Non-fiction. **Career:** San Francisco State University, assistant professor of sociology, 1961-62; University of Chicago, assistant professor of sociology, 1962-63; University of California, assistant professor, 1963-67, associate professor, 1967-78, professor of sociology, 1978-93, professor emeritus of sociology, 1993-. Writer. **Publications:** Alienation and Freedom: The Factory Worker and His Industry, 1964; Racial Oppression in America, 1972; (ed.) Black Lives, White Lives: Three Decades of Race Relations in America, 1989; (ed.) Our Mothers' Spirits: On the Death of Mothers and the Grief of Men, 1997; Still the Big News: Racial Oppression in America, 2001; Resisting McCarthyism: To Sign or Not to Sign California's Loyalty Oath, 2009. Contributor to journals and periodicals. **Address:** Department of Sociology, University of California, 410 Barrows Hall, Berkeley, CA 94720-1980, U.S.A. **Online address:** kebb@berkeley.edu

BLAUNER, Peter. American (born United States), b. 1959. **Genres:** Novels, Mystery/Crime/Suspense, Novellas/Short Stories, Young Adult Fiction. **Career:** Norwich Bulletin, general assignment reporter, 1980; Newark Star-Ledger, general assignment reporter, 1981; New York Magazine, contributing editor, 1982-92; Law & Order: Criminal Intent, staff writer, 2008; Law & Order: Los Angeles, staff writer, 2010. **Publications:** NOVELS: Slow Motion Riot, 1991; Casino Moon, 1994; The Intruder, 1996; Man of the Hour, 1999; The Last Good Day, 2003; Slipping Into Darkness, 2006. Contributor to periodicals. **Address:** c/o Richard Pine, InkWell Management, 521 5th Ave., 26th Fl., New York, NY 10175-0003, U.S.A. **Online address:** peter@peterblauner.com

BLAUVELT, Martha Tomhave. American (born United States), b. 1948?. **Genres:** History. **Career:** College of Saint Benedict, professor. Writer. **Publications:** The Work of the Heart: Young Women and Emotion, 1780-1830, 2007. Contributor of articles to periodicals. Works appear in anthologies. **Address:** College of Saint Benedict, 37 S College Ave., St. Joseph, MN 56374, U.S.A. **Online address:** mtomhave@csbsju.edu

BLAUW, Wim. Dutch (born Netherlands), b. 1942. **Genres:** Sociology, Adult Non-fiction, Social Sciences, Law, Politics/Government. **Career:** High school teacher of commercial sciences, 1965-66; Erasmus University, assistant professor, 1971-77, associate professor of economic sociology, 1977-; Rotterdam School of Architecture, assistant professor, 1972-80. Writer. **Publications:** (Co-author) Luchtverontreiniging: Laten de Industriele Leiders Ons Stikken?, 1970; (with J.H. Elich) Emigreren (Emigration), 1983; Suburbanisatie en Sociale Contacten (Suburbanisation and Social Contacts), 1986; De ontsluiting Van Tweewaarden: Een Kleine Gaschiedenis Van Verkeer En vervoer in de Krimpener: En Lopikerwaard, 1989; Progress in Social Ecology, 1991; The Use and Meaning of Home and Neighborhood: Methodological Issues, 1992. EDITOR: (with C. Pastor and cont.) Soort Bij Soort. Beschouwingen Over Ruimtelijke Segregatie Alsmaatschappelijk Probleem (Essays on Spatial Segregation as a Social Problem), 1980; Ruimte Voor Openbaarheid (Space for Public Life), 1989. UNDER NAME WIM BLAUW: (ed. with E.D. Huttman and J. Saltman and contrib.) Urban Housing Segregation of Minorities in Western Europe and the United States, 1991; (co-authorl) Tempora Mutantur: Over Maatschappelijke Verandering En ontwikkelingen in Hetsociale Denken (Tempora Mutantur: On Social Change and Developments of Social Thoughts), 1992. CO-EDITOR: Netherlands Journal of Housing and Environmental Research, 1988, 1989. TRIALOG: Zeitschrift Fuer Das Planenund Bauen in Der Dritten Welt, 1989. **Address:** Faculty of Economic Sciences, Erasmus University, 6000 Dr., PO Box 1738, Rotterdam, 3000 DR, Netherlands. **Online address:** blauw@few.eur.nl

BLAYNE, Diana. *See* **KYLE, Susan S(paeth).**

BLECH, Susan. American (born United States), b. 1965. **Genres:** Novels. **Career:** Brookdale Hospital, senior care coordinator in the live light. Writer. **Publications:** (with C. Bock) Confessions of a Carb Queen: The Lies You Tell Others & the Lies You Tell Yourself, 2008. **Address:** New York, NY , U.S.A. **Online address:** info@susanblech.com

BLECHMAN, Elaine A(nn). American (born United States), b. 1943. **Genres:** Medicine/Health. **Career:** Brentwood Veterans Administration Hospital, intern in clinical psychology, 1969-71; University of Maryland, assistant professor of psychology, 1971-73; Yale University, assistant professor of psychiatry, 1973-77; Wesleyan University, research associate professor, 1977-83, research professor, 1983-84; Yeshiva University, Albert Einstein College of Medicine, professor of psychiatry, 1984-89; New York City, Department of Health, senior research scientist, 1990; University of Colorado, professor of psychology, 1990-; State University of New York, Health Sciences Center, professor, 1990; Boulder County District Attorney, consultant, 1995-. Writer. **Publications:** EDITOR AND CONTRIBUTOR: Behavior Modification with Women, 1984; (with K.D. Brownell) Handbook of Behavioral Medicine for Women, 1988; Emotions and the Family: For Better or for Worse, 1990; (with E.M. Hetherington) Stress, Coping, and Resiliency in Children and Families, 1996; (with K.D. Brownell) Behavioral Medicine for Women: A Comprehensive Handbook, 1998. OTHERS: Solving Child Behavior Problems: At Home and at School, 1985; Como resolver problemas de comportamiento en la escuela y en casa, 1985; (co-author) Caregiver Alliances for At-Risk and Dangerous Youth: Establishing School and Agency Coordination and Accountability, 2004. Contributor of books to journals. **Address:** Department of Psychology, University of Colorado, Muenzinger Psychology Bldg., PO Box 345, Boulder, CO 80309-0345, U.S.A. **Online address:** elaine.blechman@colorado.edu

BLECKER, Robert A. American (born United States), b. 1956. **Genres:** Economics, Politics/Government, Law. **Career:** Fulbright fellow in Mexico, 1978-79; American University, instructor, 1985-86, assistant professor, 1986-92, associate professor, 1992-98, professor of economics, 1998-, economic department chair, 2008-, School of International Service, affiliated faculty; Economic Policy Institute, visiting fellow, 1989-90, 1998-99, research associate, 1991-; Center for Economic and Policy Research, senior research fellow. Writer. **Publications:** Beyond the Twin Deficits: A Trade Strategy for the 1990s, 1992; (with S.D. Cohen and J.R. Paul) Fundamentals of U.S. Foreign Trade Policy: Economics, Politics, Laws, and Issues, 1996, 2nd ed., 2003; (ed.) U.S. Trade Policy and Global Growth: New Directions in the International Economy, 1996; Taming Global Finance: A Better Architecture for Growth and Equity, 1999. CONTRIBUTOR: The Imperiled Economy: Left Perspectives on Macroeconomics, 1987; Are Americans on a Consumption Binge? The Evidence Reconsidered, 1990; Growth and Equity: Tax Policy Challenges for the 1990s, 1990; (contrib.) Economic Problems of the 1990s: Europe, the Developing Countries, and the United States, 1991; Essays in Honour of Paul Davidson, vol. I: Keynes, Money and the Open Economy, 1996; The Macroeconomics of Finance, Saving and Investment, 1997; Competitiveness Matters: U.S. Industry, Industrial Policy, and Economic Performance, 1999; Foundations of International Economics: Post Keynesian Perspectives, 1999; International Capital Markets: Systems in Transition, 2002; The Economics of Demand-Led Growth: Challenging the Supply-Side Vision of the Long Run, 2002; A Post Keynesian Perspective on Twenty-First Century Economic Problems, 2002; The Bridge to a Global Middle Class: Development, Trade and International Finance, 2003; The Elgar Companion to Post Keynesian Economics, 2003; Financialization and the World Economy, 2005; Contemporary Cases in U.S. Foreign Policy: From Terrorism to Trade, 3rd ed., 2008; The Princeton Encyclopedia of the World Economy, 2009. Contributor of articles to books and journals. **Address:** Department of Economics, American University, 104B Kreeger, 4400 Massachusetts Ave. NW, Washington, DC 20016-8029, U.S.A. **Online address:** blecker@american.edu

BLEDIN, David. American (born United States) **Genres:** Novels. **Career:** Writer and economic consultant. **Publications:** Bank: A Novel, 2007. Contributor to periodicals. **Address:** c/o Matt McGowan, Frances Goldin Literary Agency Inc., 57 E 11th St., Ste. 5B, New York, NY 10003-4605, U.S.A. **Online address:** free_mumbles@hotmail.com

BLEDSOE, Alex. American (born United States), b. 1963?. **Genres:** Young Adult Fiction. **Career:** Writer. **Publications:** EDDIE LaCROSSE MYSTERY SERIES: The Sword-Edged Blonde, 2007; Burn Me Deadly, 2009; Dark Jenny, 2009 . RUDOLFO ZGINSKI SERIES: Blood Groove, 2006; The Girls with Games of Blood, 2010. **Address:** c/o Marlene Stringer, Stringer Literary Agency, Naples, FL 34107, U.S.A. **Online address:** alex@alexbledsoe.com

BLEDSOE, Glen. *See* **BLEDSOE, Glen L(eonard).**

BLEDSOE, Glen L(eonard). (Glen Bledsoe). American (born United States), b. 1951. **Genres:** Young Adult Fiction, Air/Space Topics, Literary Criticism And History. **Career:** U.S. Steel Co., chemical technician, 1972-78; Rubino's Music Center, luthier and seller of musical instruments, 1976-80; Keizer Elementary School, teacher, 1991-, team leader, 1995-; Lansing Art Gallery, interim director, 1981; web page designer and webmaster, 1995-; Willamette University, co-chair of education consortium, 1996. Writer. **Publications:** JUVENILES COMPILED WITH K. BLEDSOE: Classic Ghost Stories II, 1998; Classic Sea Stories, 1999; (ed.) Creepy Classics III: More Hair-Raising Horror from the Masters of the Macabre, 1999; Classic Mysteries II: A Collection of Mind-Bending Masterpieces, 1999; Classic Adventure Stories, 1999; Ballooning Adventures, 2001. OTHERS: (with E.H. Hopkins) The Blue Angels: The U.S. Navy Flight Demonstration Squadron, 2001; (with K. Bledsoe and E.H. Hopkins) The Golden Knights: The U.S. Army Parachute Team, 2001; (with K. Bledsoe) World's Fastest Indy Cars, 2002; (with K. Bledsoe) Airplane Adventures, 2002; (with K. Bledsoe) Bicycling Adventures, 2002; (with K. Bledsoe) World's Fastest Helicopters, 2002; (with K. Bledsoe) World's Fastest Trucks, 2002; (with K. Bledsoe) World's Fastest Dragsters, 2003; (with K. Bledsoe) Fighter Planes: Fearless Fliers, 2006; (with K. Bledsoe) Helicopters: High-Flying Heroes, 2006; The Charity of Ebenezer Scrooge: A Christmas Carol II, 2009. Contributor of articles to periodicals. **Address:** 4230 12th St. SE, Salem, OR 97302, U.S.A. **Online address:** glenbledsoe@mac.com

BLEDSOE, Jerry. American (born United States), b. 1941. **Genres:** Criminology/True Crime, Adult Non-fiction, Documentaries/Reportage, Literary Criticism And History. **Career:** Greensboro News and Record, reporter and columnist, 1966-77, 1981-89; Louisville Times, feature writer, 1971; Esquire, contributing editor, 1972-76; Charlotte Observer, columnist, 1977-81; Down Home Press, publisher and editor, 1989-. **Publications:** TRUE CRIME BOOKS: Bitter Blood: A True Story of Southern Family Pride, Madness, and Multiple Murder, 1988; Blood Games: A True Account of Family Murder, 1991; Before He Wakes: A True Story of Money, Marriage, Sex, and Murder, 1994; Death Sentence: The True Story of Velma Barfield's Life, Crimes and Execution, 1998. OTHER NONFICTION: The World's Number One, Flat-Out, All-Time Great, Stock Car Racing Book, 1975; You Can't Live on Radishes: Some Funny Things Happened on the Way Back to the Land, 1976; Just Folks: Visitin' with Carolina People, 1980; North Carolina Curiosities: Jerry Bledsoe's Outlandish Guide to the Dadblamedest Things to See and Do in North Carolina, 1984; From Whalebone to Hot House: A Journey Along North Carolina's Longest Highway, U.S. 64, 1986; Country Cured: Reflections from the Heart, 1989; The Bare-Bottomed Skier: And Other Unlikely Tales, 1990; Blue Horizons: Faces and Places from a Bicycle Journey Along the Blue Ridge Parkway, 1993; The Angel Doll: A Christmas Story, 1996; Gift of Angels, 1999; (with B. Timberlake) Partial to Home: A Memoir of the Heart, 2000. **Address:** Down Home Press, PO Box 4126, Asheboro, NC 27204, U.S.A. **Online address:** jerry@jerrybledsoe.com

BLEDSOE, Karen E(lizabeth). American (born United States), b. 1962. **Genres:** Young Adult Fiction, Biology, Sciences, Education. **Career:** Willamette University, Department of Biology, laboratory teaching assistant, 1984-85; Oregon State University, assistant to herbarium curator, 1985-88, graduate assistant, 2000-06, Department of Science and Mathematics Education, 2001-02, curriculum coordinator, School Science and Mathematics Journal, managing editor; U.S. Forest Service, seasonal biological technician, 1985; City of Salem, Youth Interpretive Program, seasonal recreational leader and environmental educator, 1989-90; North Salem High School, teacher, 1990-91; Salem-Keizer School District, teacher, 1991-92, 1993-95; Western Oregon University, adjunct instructor in biology, 1995-2000, adjunct assistant professor, 2006-; Oregon Academy of Science, science education co-chairperson and web page designer, 1996-; Oregon Collaborative for Excellence in the Preparation of Teachers, faculty fellow, 1997-; Oregon Public Education Network, team coach, 1998-99; Linn-Benton Community College, Department of Biology, part-time instructor, 2004-06, instructor, adjunct faculty; Northwest Evaluation Association, freelance item writer, 2010-. **Publications:** JU-

VENILES WITH G.L. BLEDSOE: (comp.) Classic Ghost Stories II, 1998; (ed. and comp.) Creepy Classics III, 1999; (comp.) Classic Sea Stories, 1999; (comp.) Classic Mysteries II, 1999; (comp.) Classic Adventures, 2000; Blue Angels: The U.S. Navy Flight Demonstration Squadron, 2001; Ballooning Adventures, 2001; Airplane Adventures, 2002; World's Fastest Trucks, 2002; World's Fastest Helicopters, 2002; Bicycling Adventures, 2002; World's Fastest Indy Cars, 2003; World's Fastest Dragsters, 2003; Fighter Planes: Fearless Fliers, 2006; Helicopters: High-Flying Heroes, 2006. OTHER JUVENILES: (with C. Norvall) 365 Nature Crafts & Activities, 1997; Best Friends, 1997; Pocketful of Memories, 1998; Millennium Album, 1998; (with M. Birmingham and K.M. Halls) 365 Outdoor Activities, 2000; Daredevils of the Air: Thrilling Tales of Pioneer Aviators, 2003; (with M. Birmingham and K.H. Halls) Habitat Destruction, 2004; Consumption and Waste, 2004; Keeping Our Food and Water Safe, 2004; Energy Sources, 2004; Global Warming, 2004; Hanukkah Crafts, 2004; Chinese New Year Crafts, 2005; Genetically Engineered Foods, 2005; Divides and Watersheds, 2007; Human Reproduction, Growth and Development, 2007; Heredity, 2007; Tissues, Organs, Systems, 2007; Cell Processes, 2007; Immunity, forthcoming. **Address:** Department of Biology, Division of Natural Science, Western Oregon University, 220 NS, 345 Monmouth Ave., Monmouth, OR 97361, U.S.A. **Online address:** bledsoek@wou.edu

BLEDSOE, Timothy. American (born United States), b. 1953. **Genres:** Politics/Government, Young Adult Non-fiction, International Relations/Current Affairs. **Career:** University of South Carolina, assistant professor of political science, 1984-89; Wayne State University, associate professor, 1989-96, professor of political science, 1996-2008; University of Nebraska, faculty; Michigan State House of Representatives, democrat, 2008-. Writer. **Publications:** (With S. Welch) Urban Reform and Its Consequences: A Study in Representation, 1988; Careers in City Politics: The Case for Urban Democracy, 1993. **Address:** Department of Political Science, Wayne State University, 2007 Faculty Administration Bldg., Detroit, MI 48202, U.S.A. **Online address:** t.bledsoe@wayne.edu

BLEE, Kathleen M. American (born United States), b. 1953?. **Genres:** Sociology, Women's Studies And Issues, History, Race Relations. **Career:** University of Kentucky, instructor, professor, 1981-96, Women's Studies Program, director, 1987-89, College of Arts and Sciences, associate dean, 1989-91, 1992, research professor, 1994-95; Sociological Focus, associate editor, 1992-94; University of Pittsburgh, Women's Studies Program, director, 1996-2001, Department of Sociology, professor of sociology, 1996-2006, distinguished professor of sociology, 2007-, chair, 2008-, Department of History, faculty, 1997-, Center on Race and Social Problems, faculty associate, 2005-, Department of Psychology, faculty, 2007-, School of Arts and Sciences, associate dean for graduate studies and research, 2011-. **Publications:** Women of the Klan: Racism and Gender in the 1920s, 1991; (with D.B. Billings) The Road to Poverty: The Making of Wealth and Hardship in Appalachia, 2000; Inside Organized Racism: Women in the Hate Movement, 2002; Democracy in the Making: How Activist Groups Form, 2011. EDITOR: No Middle Ground: Women and Radical Protest, 1998; (with F.W. Twine) Feminism and Antiracism: International Struggles for Justice, 2001; (with S.M. Deutsch) Women of the Right: Comparisons and Interplay across Borders, 2012. **Address:** Department of Sociology, University of Pittsburgh, 2417 Wesley W. Posvar Hall, 230 Bouquet St., Pittsburgh, PA 15260, U.S.A. **Online address:** kblee@pitt.edu

BLEGEN, Daniel M. American (born United States), b. 1950. **Genres:** History, Plays/Screenplays, Young Adult Fiction, Biography. **Career:** Lutheran High School, teacher, 1973-75; Vikan Junior High School, teacher and chair of language arts department, 1975-83; Brighton High School, teacher, 1983-; Aims Community College, teacher. Writer. **Publications:** (With M. Bacon) Bent's Fort: Crossroads of Cultures on the Santa Fe Trail, 1995; Bob Sakata: American Farmer, 2009. Contributor to periodicals. **Address:** 1624 Adkinson Ave., Longmont, CO 80501, U.S.A. **Online address:** danblegen@aol.com

BLEI, Norbert. American (born United States), b. 1935. **Genres:** Poetry, Essays, Novels. **Career:** City News Bureau, reporter, 1958-59; high school English teacher, 1960-68; Cross + Roads Press, owner, 1994; writer, 1969-; Forkroads, contributing editor, Peninsula Pulse, columnist. **Publications:** POETRY: The Watercolored Word, 1968; Door Steps (prose poems), 1983; Paint Me a Picture, Make Me a Poem, 1987. FICTION: The Second Novel: Becoming a Writer, 1978; The Hour of the Sunshine Now (short stories), 1978; Adventures in an American's Literature (novel), 1982; The Ghost of Sandburg's Phizzog and Other Stories (short stories), 1986. NONFICTION: Door Way: The People in the Landscape, 1981; Door to Door, 1985; Neighborhood, 1987; Meditations on a Small Lake: (Requiem for a Diminishing Landscape) (essays), 1987; Chi Town, 1990; Chronicles of a Rural Journalist in America (essays), 1990; The Watercolor Way (essays), 1990. OTHER: Charles L. Peterson: Of Place and Time, 1994. Works appear in anthologies. Contributor to periodicals. **Address:** PO Box 33, Ellison Bay, WI 54210, U.S.A.

BLENK, Katie. American (born United States), b. 1954. **Genres:** Education, Adult Non-fiction. **Career:** Kids Are People Elementary School, speech director and founder, 1980-, administrator, 1992-; Massachusetts State Department of Education, consultant, 1993-94; Kenmore Community and Economic Development Corp., vice president. Writer. **Publications:** (With D.L. Fine) Making School Inclusion Work: A Guide To Everyday Practice, 1995. **Address:** Kids Are People Elementary School, 530 Commonwealth Ave., PO Box 15656, Boston, MA 02215-2606, U.S.A.

BLENKINSOPP, Joseph. American/British (born England), b. 1927. **Genres:** Theology/Religion, History. **Career:** Chicago Theological Seminary, teacher of Biblical studies, 1968-69; Hartford Seminary Foundation, associate professor, 1969-70; University of Notre Dame, associate professor, 1970-85, John A. O'Brien professor of the Hebrew Bible, 1985-, John A. O'Brien professor Emeritus of Old Testament studies; Vanderbilt University, visiting lecturer, 1968. Writer. **Publications:** The Corinthian Mirror, 1964: The Promise to David, 1964; From Adam to Abraham: Introduction to Sacred History, 1965; Jesus is Lord: Paul's Life in Christ, 1967; Sketchbook of Biblical Theology, 1968; Celibacy, Ministry, Church: An Enquiry into the Possibility of Reform in the Present Self-Understanding of the Roman Catholic Church and Its Practice of Ministry, 1968; Men Who Spoke Out: The Old Testament Prophets, 1969; Sexuality and the Christian Tradition, 1970; Pentateuch, 1971; Gibeon and Israel: the Role of Gibeon and the Gibeonites in the Political and Religious History of Early Israel, 1972; Prophecy and Canon: A Contribution to the Study of Jewish Origins, 1977; A History of Prophecy in Israel, 1983, rev. ed., 1996; Ezra-Nehemiah: A Commentary, 1988; Wisdom and Law in the Old Testament: The Ordering of Life in Israel and Early Judaism, 1990, rev. ed., 1995; Ezekiel, 1990; The Pentateuch: Introduction to the First Five Books of the Bible, 1992; (co-ed.) Priests, Prophets, and Scribes: Essays on the Formation and Heritage of Second Temple Judaism in Honour of Joseph Blenkinsopp, 1992; Sage, Priest, Prophet: Religious and Intellectual Leadership in Ancient Israel, 1995; Isaiah 1-39: A New Translation with Introduction and Commentary, 2000; (co-ed.) HarperCollins Bible Commentary, 2000; Isaiah 40-55: A New Translation with Introduction and Commentary, 2002; Isaiah 56-66: A New Translation with Introduction and Commentary, 2003; (ed. with O. Lipschits) Judah and the Judeans in the Neo-Babylonian Period, 2003; Treasures Old and New: Essays in the Theology of the Pentateuch, 2004; Opening the Sealed Book: Interpretations of the Book of Isaiah in Late Antiquity, 2006; Judaism, the First Phase: The Place of Ezra and Nehemiah in the Origins of Judaism, 2009. **Address:** Department of Theology, University of Notre Dame, 130 Malloy Hall, Notre Dame, IN 46556, U.S.A.

BLESSINGTON, Francis C(harles). American (born United States), b. 1942. **Genres:** Novels, Novellas/Short Stories, Poetry, Classics, Literary Criticism And History, Translations, Essays, Young Adult Fiction, Young Adult Fiction. **Career:** Teacher, 1963-64; Northeastern University, Department of English, instructor, 1967-72, assistant professor, 1972-75, associate professor, 1975-84, professor of English, 1984-. Writer. **Publications:** Paradise Lost and the Classical Epic, 1979; (ed. with G.L. Rotella) The Motive for Metaphore: Essays on Modern Poetry in Honor of Samuel French Morse, 1983; Lantskip (poetry), 1987; Paradise Lost: Ideal and Tragic Epic, 1988; Lorenzo de' Medici, 1992; (trans. and ed.) Euripides: The Bacchae and Aristophanes: The Frogs, 1993; Wolf Howl (poetry), 2000; The Last Witch of Dogtown (novel), 2001. Contributor of articles to magazines and journals. **Address:** Department of English, Northeastern University, 360 Huntington Ave., Boston, MA 02115-5005, U.S.A. **Online address:** f.blessington@neu.edu

BLETHEN, H(arold) Tyler. American (born United States), b. 1945?. **Genres:** History. **Career:** Western Carolina University, professor of history, 1972-, now professor emeritus of history, Mountain Heritage Center, director, 1985-; Appalachian Consortium, chair, 1997-99. Writer. **Publications:** (With C.W. Wood) A Mountain Heritage: The Illustrated History of Western Carolina University, 1989; (ed. with C.W. Wood) Ulster and North America: Transatlantic Perspectives on the Scotch-Irish, 1997; (with Wood) From Ulster to Carolina: The Migration of the Scotch-Irish to South Western North Carolina, 1998; (ed. with R.A. Straw) High Mountains Rising: Appalachia in Time and Place, 2004. **Address:** Department of History, Western Carolina University, 227B McKee Bldg., 107 State Hwy., Cullowhee, NC 28723, U.S.A. **Online address:** blethen@email.wcu.edu

BLEVINS, David. American/Italian (born Italy), b. 1955. **Genres:** Adult Non-fiction, Sports/Fitness. **Career:** Writer. **Publications:** The Almanac of UFO Organizations and Publications, 1990, 2nd ed., 1992; Almanac of World Governments, 1992; Seven Angels, Seven Horns, 1994; The Doonesbury Trivia Book, 1995; UFO Directory International: 1, 000 Plus Organizations and Publications in Forty Plus Countries, 2003; Halls of Fame: An International Directory, 2004; Encyclopedia of Television and Cable Networks, 2005; American Political Parties in the 21st Century, 2006; Television Networks: More Than 750 American and Canadian Broadcasters and Cable Networks, 2006; The Sports Hall of Fame Encyclopedia: Baseball, Basketball, Football, Hockey Soccer, 2009. **Address:** PO Box 1241, San Bruno, CA 94066, U.S.A. **Online address:** mytitles@aol.com

BLEVINS, Meredith. American (born United States), b. 1952. **Genres:** Young Adult Fiction, Mystery/Crime/Suspense, Women's Studies And Issues. **Career:** Santa Rosa Junior College, Department of Community Services, music therapist and founder of intergenerational program, 1987-93; F&M Business Finance, marketing/program director, 1992-98; writer and consultant, 1998-; TOR/Forge, writer, 2002-05; Rodale Publishers, writer, 2002-05; Authentic Ireland Travel, chief communications officer, 2005-; Authentic Travel Group, chief communications officer, 2006-; Authentic Hawaii, chief communications officer, 2009-. **Publications:** ANNIE SZABO MYSTERY SERIES: The Hummingbird Wizard, 2003; The Vanished Priestess, 2004; The Red Hot Empress, 2005. **Address:** c/o Author Mail, Forge, Tom Doherty Associates L.L.C., 175 5th Ave., New York, NY 10010-7703, U.S.A. **Online address:** meredith@meredithblevins.com

BLEWETT, Daniel K(eith). American (born United States), b. 1957. **Genres:** History, Librarianship, Bibliography. **Career:** Louisiana State University, Troy H. Middleton Library, reference librarian, 1984-86; Johns Hopkins University, Milton S. Eisenhower Library, reference librarian, 1986-90; Loyola University of Chicago, Elizabeth M. Cudahy Memorial Library, reference librarian and bibliographer for history, political science, international studies, geography and maps, 1990-2000, head of government documents, 1992-2000; College of DuPage Library, reference librarian, 2000-. Writer. **Publications:** American Military History: A Guide to Reference and Information Sources, 1995, 2nd ed., 2009. Contributor to books. **Address:** College of DuPage Library, 425 Fawell Blvd., Glen Ellyn, IL 60137-6599, U.S.A. **Online address:** blewett@conet.cod.edu

BLICKLE, Peter. American/German (born Germany), b. 1938. **Genres:** History. **Career:** University of Saarbruecken, professor of modern history, 1972-80; University of Berne, professor of history, 1980-2004; Western Michigan University, associate professor of German, professor and advisor of German. Writer. **Publications:** Die Revolution von 1525, 1975, 4th ed., 2004, trans. as The Revolution of 1525: The German Peasants War from a New Perspective, 1981; Landgemeinde und Stadtgemeinde in Mitteleuropa: ein struktureller Vergleich, 1981; (co-author) Deutsche Bauernkrieg, 1984; (with H. Rublack and W. Schulze) Religion, Politics, and Social Protest: Three Studies on Early Modern Germany, 1984; Der Deutsche Bauernkrieg von 1525, 1985; Gemeindereformation: Die Menschen des 16. Jahrhunderts auf dem Weg zum Heil, 1985, trans. as Communal Reformation, Humanities, 1992; Zugänge zur bäuerlichen Reformation, 1987; (with J. Kunisch) Kommunalisierung und Christianisierung: Voraussetzungen und Folgen der Reformation, 1400-1600, 1989; Thomas Müntzer e la rivoluzione dell'uomo comune, 1990; Communal Reformation: The Quest for Salvation in Sixteenth-Century Germany, 1992; Politische Kultur in Oberschwaben, 1993; Theorien kommunaler Ordnung in Europa, 1996; Oberschwaben: Politik als Kultur einer deutschen Geschichtslandschaft, 1996; (with P. Witschi) Appenzell-Oberschwaben: Begegnungen zweier Regionen in sieben Jahrhunderten, 1997; (ed.) Resistance, Representation, and Community, 1997; Obedient Germans?: A Rebuttal: A New View of German History, 1997; From the Communal Reformation to the Revolution of the Common Man, 1998; Kommunalismus: Skizzen einer gesellschaftlichen Organisationsform, 2000; Landschaften und Landstände in Oberschwaben: bäuerliche und bürgerliche Repräsentation im Rahmen des frühen europäischen Parlamentarismu, 2000; Macht und Ohnmacht der Bilder: reformatorischer Bildersturm im Kontext der europäischen Geschichte, 2002; Bauernkrieg: die Revolution des Gemeinen Mannes, 2002; Heimat: A Critical Theory of the German Idea of Homeland, 2002; Von der Leibeigenschaft zu den Menschenrechten: eine Geschichte der Freiheit in Deutschland, 2003; (with T. Adam) Bundschuh: Untergrombach 1502, das unruhige Reich und die Revolutionierbarkeit Europas, 2004; (with R. Schlög) Säkularisation im Prozess der Säkularisierung Europas, 2005; Alte Europa: vom Hochmittelalter bis zur Moderne, 2008. IN GERMAN: Memmingen, 1967; Kempten, 1968; Landschaften im Alten Reich: Die staatliche Funktion des gemeinen Mannes in Oberdeutschland, 1973; Deutsche ländliche Rechtsquellen: Probleme u. Wege d. Weistumsforschung, 1977; (with R. Blickle) Dokumente zur Geschichte von Staat und Gesellschaft in Bayern, 1979; Aufruhr und Empörung?: Studien zum bäuerl. Widerstand im Alten Reich, 1980; Deutsche Untertanen: Ein Widerspruch, 1981; Die Reformation im Reich: Uni-Taschenbuecher 1181, 1982, 3rd ed., 2000; Unruhen in der ständischen Gesellschaft 1300-1800, 1988; Studien zur geschichtlichen Bedeutung des deutschen Bauernstandes, 1989; Agrarverfassungsverträge, 1996; Agrargeschichte: Positionen und Perspektiven, 1998. Contributor to periodicals. **Address:** Department of Foreign Languages, Western Michigan University, 414 Sprau Twr., 1903 W Michigan Ave., Kalamazoo, MI 49008-5338, U.S.A. **Online address:** peter.blickle@wmich.edu

BLIGHT, David W. American (born United States), b. 1949. **Genres:** History. **Career:** Flint Northern High School, staff, 1971-78; Saginaw Valley State College, Department of History, instructor, 1977-78; University of Wisconsin, Department of History, teaching assistant, 1979-82; North Central College, instructor, 1982-85, assistant professor, 1985-87; Harvard University, assistant professor of history and Afro-American studies, 1987-89; Amherst College, assistant professor, 1989-92-, associate professor of history and Afro-American studies, 1992-97, professor, 1998-99, Class of 1959 professor of history and Black studies, 1999-2002; University of Munich, Amerika Institut, senior Fulbright professor in American studies, 1992-93; Yale University, Class of '54 professor of American history, 2003-, Yale Center for International and Area Studies, Gilder Lehrman Center for the Study of Slavery, Resistance and Abolition, director, 2003-; African American Programs, director, 2004-; Bedford Books, series advisor and editor. **Publications:** Frederick Douglass' Civil War: Keeping Faith in Jubilee, 1989; (contrib.) Why the Civil War Came, 1996; Race and Reunion: The Civil War in American Memory, 2001; Frederick Douglass and Abraham Lincoln, 2001; Beyond the Battlefield: Race, Memory and the American Civil War, 2002; (contrib.) Accepting the Prize: Three Laureates Speak, 2003; A Slave No More: Two Men Who Escaped to Freedom: Including Their Own Narratives of Emancipation, 2007; A People and a Nation: A History of the United States, 8th ed., 2008; (contrib.) Great Lincoln Documents: Historians Present Treasures from the Gilder Lehrman Collection, 2009; American Oracle: The Civil War in the Civil Rights Era, 2011; Frederick Douglass: A Life, 2013; Gods and Devils Aplenty, forthcoming. EDITOR: (and intro.) When This Cruel War Is Over: The Civil War Letters of Charles Harvey Brewster, 1992; (and intro.) Narrative of the Life of Frederick Douglass, an American Slave, 1993, 2nd ed., 2003; (with B.D. Simpson) Union and Emancipation: Essays on Politics and Race in the Civil War Era, 1997; (and intro. with R. Gooding-Williams) The Souls of Black Folk, 1997; (and intro.) The Columbian Orator: Containing a Variety of Original and Selected Pieces Together with Rules, Which Are Calculated to Improve Youth and Others, in the Ornamental and Useful Art of Eloquence, 1998; Passages to Freedom: The Underground Railroad in History and Memory, 2001; (with R. Harms and B. Fraeman) Slavery and the Slave Trade in the Indian Ocean, 2010. Contributor to journals and periodicals. **Address:** Gilder Lehrman Center for the Study of Slavery,, Resistance and Abolition, Yale University, Rm. 300, 230 Prospect St., PO Box 208206, New Haven, CT 06511, U.S.A. **Online address:** david.blight@yale.edu

BLIGHT, James G. American (born United States) **Genres:** International Relations/Current Affairs, Politics/Government, History. **Career:** Grand Valley State University, assistant professor of psychology and history of science, 1974-80; Harvard University, Andrew W. Mellon faculty fellow, John F. Kennedy School of Government, lecturer, 1984-90; National Endowment for the Humanities, research fellow; Kennedy School of Government's Project on Avoiding Nuclear War, director, 1985-90; Brown University, Watson Institute for International Studies, Center for Foreign Policy Development, research fellow, 1990-95, research professor of international relations, 1995-. Writer. **Publications:** Beyond Deterrence or beyond Utopian Ideology?: Thought Experiments for Antinuclear Movements in Crisis, 1986; (with D.A. Welch) On the Brink: Americans and Soviets Reexamine the Cuban Missile Crisis, 1989, 2nd ed., 1990; (co-author) Superpowers and Regional Conflict in a Post-Cold War World: The Caribbean Basin and Southern Africa, 1990; The Shattered Crystal Ball: Fear and Learning in the Cuban Missile Crisis, 1990; (with B.J. Allyn and D.A. Welch) Cuba on the Brink: Castro, the Missile Crisis, and the Soviet Collapse, 1993, rev. ed., 2002; (with R.S. McNamara and R.K. Brigham) Argument without End: In Search of Answers to the Vietnam Tragedy, 1999; (with R.S. McNamara) Wilson's Ghost: Reducing the Risk of Conflict, Killing, and Catastrophe in the 21st Century, 2001; (with P. Brenner) Sad and Luminous Days: Cuba's Struggle with the Superpowers after the Missile Crisis, 2002; (with J.M. Lang) Fog of War: Lessons from the Life of Robert S. McNamara, 2005; (contrib.) Li Shi de Jiao Xun: Meiguo Guo Jia an Quan Zhan Lüe Jian Yan Shu, 2005; (with J.M. Lang and D.A. Welch) Vietnam if Kennedy had Lived: Virtual JFK, 2009. EDITOR: (with T.G. Weiss) The Suffering Grass: Superpowers and Regional Conflict in Southern Africa and the Caribbean, 1992; (with B.J. Allyn and D.A. Welch) Back to the Brink: Proceedings of the Moscow Conference on the Cuban Missile Crisis, January 27-28, 1989, 1992; (with D.A. Welch) Intelligence and the Cuban Missile Crisis, 1998; (with P. Kornbluh) Politics of Illusion: The Bay of Pigs Invasion Reexamined, 1998. Contributor to journals and periodicals. **Address:** Watson Institute, Brown University, 71 George St., PO Box 1970, Providence, RI 02912-9025, U.S.A. **Online address:** james_blight@brown.edu

BLINDER, Alan S(tuart). American (born United States), b. 1945. **Genres:** Economics, Business/Trade/Industry. **Career:** Rider College, instructor in finance, 1968-69; Boston State College, instructor in economics, 1969-; Princeton University, Department of Economics, assistant professor, 1971-76, associate professor, 1976-79, professor, 1979-82, chairman, 1988-90, bicentennial preceptor, 1975-78, Center for Economic Policy Studies, founder, co-director, director, 1989-93, 1996-2011, Gordon S. Rentschler Memorial professor of economics, 1982-2007, Gordon S. Rentschler Memorial professor of economics and public affairs, 2007-; Congressional Budget Office, Fiscal Analysis Division, deputy assistant director, 1975-, National Bureau of Economic Research, research associate, 1978-; Hebrew University of Jerusalem, Institute for Advanced Studies, fellow, 1976-77; National Policy Exchange chairman of economic policy, 1981-85; Boston Globe columnist, 1981-85; Institute for Advanced Studies, visiting professor, 1982; Brookings Panel on Economic Activity, senior adviser, 1982-; Business Week, 1985-92; Brookings Institution, visiting fellow, 1985-86, 1999-2000; Promontory Financial Group, Partner, 2000-; Council of Economic Advisers, consultant; Board of Governors of Federal Reserve System, consultant; Wall Street Journal, columnist; American Economic Association, vice president; Eastern Economic Association, president. Writer. **Publications:** Micro Estimating a Wage Equation: Pitfalls and Some Provisional Estimates, 1971; Model of Inherited Wealth, 1971; Are Income Taxes or Deflationary Inflationary? An Expository Note, 1972; (with R.M. Solow) Fiscal Policy Does Matter?, 1972; (co-author) The Economics of Public Finance, 1974; Toward an Economic Theory of Income Distribution, 1974; Budget wirkungen und Budget politik, 1977; (with W.J. Newton) 1971-1974 The Program and Controls the Price Level: An Econometirc Post-Mortem, 1978; (with W.J. Baurmol) Economics: Principles and Policy, 1979, 12th ed., 2012; Economic Policy and the Great Stagflation, 1979; The Truce in the War on Poverty: Where Do We Go from Here? 1981; Macroeconomics, Income Distribution and Poverty, 1986; Hard Heads, Soft Hearts: Tough-Minded Economics for a Just Society, 1987; Economic Opinion, 1989; Macroeconomics Under Debate, 1989; Inventory Theory and Consumer Behavior, 1990; Growing Together, 1991; Maintaining Competitiveness with High Wages, 1992; (with W.J. Baumol) Macroeconomics: Principles and Policy, 1994, 11th ed., 2009; (with W.J. Baumol) Microeconomics: Principles and Policy, 6th ed., 1994, 11th ed., 2009; Central Banking in Theory and Practice, 1998; (co-author) Asking about Prices: A New Approach to Understanding Price Stickiness, 1998; (with J.L. Yellen) The Fabulous Decade: Macroeconomic Lessons from the 1990s, 2001; (co-author) How Do Central Banks Talk?, 2001; (with W.J. Baumol and E.N. Wolff) Downsizing in America: Reality, Causes and Consequence, 2003; (with A.B. Krueger) What Does The Public Know about Economic Policy and How Does It Know It?, 2004; Quiet Revolution: Central Banking Goes Modern, 2004; (with W.J. Baumol) Essentials of Economics: Principles and Policy, 10 ed., 2006; (with J. Bhagwati) Offshoring of American Jobs: What Response from U.S. Economic Policy?, 2009. EDITOR: (with P. Friedman and contrib.) Natural Resources, Uncertainty and General Equilibrium Systems: Essays in Memory of Rafael Lusky, 1977; Paying for Productivity: A Look at the Evidence, 1990; Bank Management and Regulation: A Book of Readings, 1992. Contributor to periodicals. **Address:** Department of Economics, Center for Economic Policy Studies, Princeton University, 105 Fisher Hall, Princeton, NJ 08544-1021, U.S.A. **Online address:** blinder@princeton.edu

BLINN, William Frederick. American (born United States), b. 1937. **Genres:** Novels. **Career:** Writer and producer. **Publications:** Brian's Song, 1972; A Cold Place in Hell (novel), 2009. **Address:** c/o Len Rosenberg, William Morris Agency, 151 S El Camino Dr., Beverly Hills, CA 90212, U.S.A.

BLISS, Harry. American (born United States), b. 1964. **Genres:** Children's Fiction, Children's Non-fiction, Cartoons. **Career:** New Yorker, cartoonist and cover artist. Writer and illustrator. **Publications:** Death by Laughter, 2008; Luke on the Loose: A Toon Book, 2009; Bailey, 2011. Contributor to periodicals. **Address:** Joanna Cotler Books, HarperCollins Childrens, 1350 Ave. of the Americas, New York, NY 10019, U.S.A.

BLISS, Michael (J.). American (born United States), b. 1947. **Genres:** Film, Biography, Art/Art History. **Career:** University of Minnesota, instructor in English and film, 1979-91; Metropolitan Community College, instructor in English and film, 1979-91; Hamline University, instructor in English and film, 1979-91; Minneapolis public schools, instructor in English and film, 1979-91; Minneapolis Film Festival, associate director and programmer, 1979-80; Cinemaland Theatres, copywriter, 1979-81; Virginia Polytechnic Institute and State University, instructor in English and film, 1991-, senior instructor. **Publications:** Brian De Palma, 1983; Martin Scorsese and Michael Cimino, 1985; Justified Lives: Morality and Narrative in the Films of Sam Peckinpah, 1993; (ed. and intro.) Doing It Right: The Best Criticism on Sam Peckinpah's The Wild Bunch, 1994; The Word Made Flesh: Catholicism and Conflict in the Films of Martin Scorsese, 1995; (with C. Banks) What Goes Around Comes Around: The Films of Jonathan Demme, 1996; Dreams Within a Dream: The Films of Peter Weir, 2000; Between the Bullets: The Spiritual Cinema of John Woo, 2002; Green Worlds and Political Landscapes: The Films of 1985 in The Films of the 80s, forthcoming; For a Spiritual American Cinema, forthcoming. **Address:** Department of English, Virginia Polytechnic Institute, 200 E Eggleston Hall, Blacksburg, VA 24061, U.S.A. **Online address:** mbliss@vt.edu

BLITZER, Wolf. American/German (born Germany), b. 1948. **Genres:** International Relations/Current Affairs, Documentaries/Reportage, History. **Career:** Reuters News Agency, Tel Aviv Bureau, staff, 1972; The Jerusalem Post, Washington correspondent, 1973-90; CNN, cable network's military affairs reporter, 1990; White House correspondent, 1992-99; The Situation Room, host and anchor, 2005-. Writer. **Publications:** Between Washington and Jerusalem: A Reporter's Notebook, 1985; Territory of Lies: The Exclusive Story of Jonathan Jay Pollard, the American Who Spied on His Country for Israel and How He Was Betrayed, 1989. Contributor of articles to periodicals. **Address:** CNN Washington Bureau, 820 1st St. NE, Washington, DC 20002, U.S.A.

BLIX, Jacqueline. American (born United States), b. 1949. **Genres:** Documentaries/Reportage, Money/Finance, Business/Trade/Industry. **Career:** Mademoiselle, manager, 1975-79; Pacific Telephone, market administrator, 1979-80; American Telephone and Telegraph Co., market administrator, 1980-81, technical consultant, 1981-88. Writer and advocate. **Publications:** (With D.A. Heitmiller) Getting a Life: Real Lives Transformed by Your Money or Your Life, 1997. Contributor to journals. **Address:** 1745 NW 59th St., Seattle, WA 98107-3050, U.S.A. **Online address:** jacque@gettingalife.org

BLIXT, David. American (born United States) **Genres:** Novels, Young Adult Fiction, Literary Criticism And History. **Career:** A Crew of Patches (a Shakespearean repertory co.), co-founder, actor, director and choreographer. Writer and educator. **Publications:** PIETRO ALIGHIERI SERIES: The Master of Verona (novel), 2007; Voice of the Falconer (novel), 2010. **Address:** St. Martin's Press, 175 5th Ave., New York, NY 10010-7703, U.S.A. **Online address:** greyhoundverona@aol.com

BLOCH, Douglas. American (born United States), b. 1949. **Genres:** Self Help, How-to Books, Psychology, inspirational/Motivational Literature. **Career:** Writer, educator and counselor. **Publications:** (With D. George) Asteroid Goddesses, 1986; (with D. George) Astrology for Yourself: How to Understand and Interpret Your Own Birth Chart: A Workbook for Personal Transformation, 1987; (with S. Warren) Bus Touring: A Guide to Charter Vacations, U.S.A, 1989; Words That Heal: Affirmations and Meditations for Daily Living, 1990; Listening to your Inner Voice: Discover the Truth Within You and Let it Guide and Direct your Way, 1991; (comp.) I Am with You Always:

A Treasury of Inspirational Quotations, Poems, and Prayers, 1992; (with J. Merritt) Positive Self-Talk for Children: Teaching Self-Esteem through Affirmations: A Guide for Parents, Teachers, and Counselors, 1993; When Going through Hell... Don't Stop!: A Survivor's Guide to Overcoming Anxiety and Clinical Depression, 2000; Healing from Depression: 12 Weeks to a Better Mood: A Body, Mind, and Spirit Recovery Program, 2001; (with J. Merritt) Power of Positive Talk: Words to Help Every Child Succeed: A Guide for Parents, Teachers, and Other Caring Adults, 2003; Words that Heal the Blues: Affirmations & Meditations for Living Optimally with Mood Disorders: A Daily Mental Health Recovery Program, 2004. **Address:** 4226 NE 23rd Ave., Portland, OR 97211, U.S.A. **Online address:** dbloch@teleport.com

BLOCK, Brett Ellen. American (born United States), b. 1973?. **Genres:** Novellas/Short Stories, Novels. **Career:** Writer. **Publications:** Destination Known, 2001; The Grave of God's Daughter, 2004; The Lightning Rule, 2006; Language of Sand: A Novel, 2010; The Definition of Wind: A Novel, 2011. Contributor to journals. Works appear in anthologies. **Address:** c/o Author Mail, William Morrow, 10 E 53rd St., New York, NY 10022, U.S.A. **Online address:** info@ellenblock.net

BLOCK, Cathy Collins. American (born United States), b. 1948. **Genres:** Education, Language/Linguistics. **Career:** Teacher, 1970-74; University of Wisconsin-Madison, Wisconsin Research and Development Center for Cognitive Development, research assistant, 1974-76; Southern Illinois University, graduate faculty, assistant professor, 1976-77; Texas Christian University, instructor, 1977-78, School of Education, assistant professor, 1978-82, associate professor, 1982-90, professor of education, 1990-; University of Notre Dame, national faculty, 1997-. Educational advisor, consultant and writer. **Publications:** Time Management for Teachers: Techniques and Skills That Give You More Time to Teach, 1987; (ed. with J.N. Mangieri) Teaching Thinking: An Agenda for the Twenty-first Century, 1992; 126 Strategies to Build Language Arts Abilities: A Month-by Month-Resource, 1992; Teaching the Language Arts: Expanding Thinking Through Student-Centered Instruction, 1993 (ed. with J.N. Mangieri) Creating Powerful Thinking in Teachers and Students: Diverse Perspectives, 1994; (with J.A. Zinke) Creating a Culturally Enriched Curriculum for Grades K-6, 1995; (with J.N. Mangieri) Reason to Read: Thinking Strategies for Life through Literature, 1995; (with J.N. Mangieri) Power Thinking for Success, 1996; Literacy Difficulties: Diagnosis and Instruction, 1997, 2nd ed. as Literacy Difficulties: Diagnosis and Instruction for Reading Specialists and Classroom Teachers, 2003; (co-author) Learning to Read: Lessons from Exemplary First-Grade Classrooms, 2001; (ed. with M. Pressley) Comprehension Instruction: Research-based Best Practices, 2001, (with S.R. Parris) 2nd ed., 2008; (ed. with L. Gambrell and M. Pressley) Improving Comprehension Instruction: Rethinking Research, Theory and Classroom Practice, 2002; (with J.N. Mangieri) Exemplary Literacy Teachers: Promoting Success for All Childrenin Grades K-5, 2003; (with J.N. Mangieri) Yale Assessment of Thinking: A Self-Assessment of Your Skill in the Areas of Reasoning, Insight, and Self-Knowledge, 2003; (with L.L. Rodgers and R.B. Johnson) Comprehension Process Instruction: Creating Reading Success in Grades K-3, 2004; Teaching Comprehension: The Comprehension Process Approach, 2004; (with J.N. Mangieri) Power Thinking: How the Way You Think Can Change the Way You Lead, 2004; (with S.E. Israel) Reading First and Beyond: The Complete Guide for Teachers and Literacy Coaches, 2005; (with S.E. Israel) Quotes to Inspire Great Reading Teachers: A Reflective Tool for Advancing Students Literacy, 2006; (with J.N. Mangieri) The Vocabulary-Enriched Classroom: Practices for Improving the Reading Performance of all Students in Grades 3 and Up, 2006; (with S.E. Israel and D.A. Sisk) Collaborative Literacy: Using Gifted Strategies to Enrich Learning for Every Student, 2007; (with J.N. Mangieri) Exemplary Literacy Teachers: What Schools Can do to Promote Success for All Students, 2009. Contributor to periodicals. **Address:** College of Education, Texas Christian University, PO Box 297900, Fort Worth, TX 76129, U.S.A. **Online address:** c.block@tcu.edu

BLOCK, Daniel I. American/Canadian (born Canada), b. 1943. **Genres:** Theology/Religion, Adult Non-fiction, inspirational/Motivational Literature, Cultural/Ethnic Topics. **Career:** Providence College and Theological Seminary, professor of Old Testament, 1973-83; Bethel Theological Seminary, professor of Old Testament, 1983-95; Southern Baptist Theological Seminary, professor of Old Testament, 1995-; Wheaton College, Gunther H. Knoedler professor of Old Testament, 2005-. Writer. **Publications:** Bny-cmwn: The Sons of Ammon, 1984; Israel-Sons of Israel: A Study in Hebrew Eponymic Usage, 1984; The Gods of the Nations: Studies in Ancient Near Eastern National Theology, 1988, 2nd ed., 2000; The New Living Translation, 1996; The Book of Ezekiel 1-24, 1997; The Book of Ezekiel 25-48, 1998; Judges, Ruth, 1999; Theology and Anthropology, 2000; Deuteronomy: A Commentary, 2000; Marriage and Family in Ancient Israel, 2003; The New Living Translation, 2004; The Privilege of Calling: The Mosaic Paradigm for Missions, 2005; The Burden of Leadership: The Mosaic Paradigm of Kingship, 2005; The Joy of Worship: The Mosaic Invitation to the Presence of God, 2005; The Grace of Torah: The Mosaic Prescription for Life, 2005; (ed.) Israel: Ancient Kingdom or Late Invention?, 2008; (ed. with N.J. Toly) Keeping God's Earth: The Global Environment in Biblical Perspective, 2010; Revising The Gods of the Nations, forthcoming. **Address:** Wheaton College, 288 BGC, 501 College Ave., Wheaton, IL 60187-5593, U.S.A. **Online address:** daniel.block@wheaton.edu

BLOCK, David. American (born United States), b. 1944?. **Genres:** Sports/Fitness. **Career:** Writer. **Publications:** Baseball before We Knew It: A Search for the Roots of the Game, 2005. **Address:** c/o Author Mail, University of Nebraska Press, 1111 Lincoln Mall, Lincoln, NE 68588-0630, U.S.A. **Online address:** info@baseballbeforeweknewit.com

BLOCK, Francesca (Lia). American (born United States), b. 1962. **Genres:** Science Fiction/Fantasy, Novels, Novellas/Short Stories, Young Adult Fiction, Plays/Screenplays, Poetry. **Career:** Writer. **Publications:** WEETZIE BAT SERIES: Weetzie Bat, 1989; Witch Baby, 1991; Cherokee Bat and the Goat Guys, 1992; Missing Angel Juan, 1993; Baby Be-Bop, 1995; Dangerous Angels: The Weetzie Bat Books, 1998; Beautiful Boys: Two Weetzie Bat Books, 2004; Goat Girls: Two Weetzie Bat Books, 2004; Necklace of Kisses, 2005; Pink Smog, 2012. NOVELS: Ecstasia, 1993; Primavera, 1994; The Hanged Man, 1994; I was a Teenage Fairy, 1998; (with H. Carlip) Zine Scene, 1998; Violet and Claire, 1999; Nymph, 2000; Echo, 2001; Wasteland, 2003; Psyche in a Dress, 2006; (with C. Staton) Ruby: A Novel, 2006; (with S. Scalora) Evidence of Angels, 2009; Pretty Dead, 2009; The Frenzy, 2010; House of Dolls, 2010; Roses and Bones, 2011. OTHER: Moon Harvest (poetry), 1978; Season of Green (poetry), 1979; Girl Goddess 9: Nine Stories, 1996; The Rose and the Beast: Fairy Tales Retold, 2000; Guarding the Moon: A Mother's First Year (autobiography), 2003; How to (Un) Cage a Girl, 2008; Blood Roses, 2008; Quakeland, 2008; The Waters and the Wild, 2009; Open Letter to Quiet Light, 2009; Wood Nymph Seeks Centaur: A Mythological Dating Guide, 2009; (co-author) Kisses from Hell, 2010; Fairy Tales in Electri-City, 2011. Works appear in anthologies. **Address:** Lydia Willis Artist, 230 W 55th St., Ste. 29D, New York, NY 10019, U.S.A.

BLOCK, Geoffrey (Holden). American (born United States), b. 1948. **Genres:** Music, Theatre. **Career:** Thacher School, director of music, 1977-80; University of Puget Sound, assistant professor, professor of music, 1980-, distinguished professor 2008-. Writer. **Publications:** Charles Ives: A Bio-Bibliography, 1988; Ives: Concord Sonata, 1996; Enchanted Evenings: The Broadway Musical from Show Boat to Sondheim, 1997; Yale Broadway Masters: Richard Rodgers, 2003; Enchanted Evenings: The Broadway Musical from Show Boat to Sondheim and Lloyd Webber, 2009. EDITOR: (with J.P. Burkholder) Charles Ives and the Classical Tradition, 1996; The Richard Rodgers Reader, 2002; Yale Broadway Masters: Andrew Lloyd Webber, 2004; Jerome Kern, 2006; Sigmund Romberg, 2007; Frank Loesser, 2008; John Kander and Fred Ebb, 2009; George Gershwin, 2010; Oxford's Broadway Legacies: South Pacific, 2010; Dorothy Fields, 2010; Jerry Bock and Sheldon Harnick, 2011. **Address:** School of Music, University of Puget Sound, 1500 N Warner St., PO Box 1076, Tacoma, WA 98416-1076, U.S.A. **Online address:** block@ups.edu

BLOCK, Jennifer. American (born United States) **Genres:** Adult Nonfiction, Medicine/Health. **Career:** Ms. magazine, editor; Plenty, senior editor; Our Bodies, Ourselves, editor. **Publications:** Pushed: The Painful Truth About Childbirth and Modern Maternity Care (nonfiction), 2007. Contributor of articles to periodicals. **Address:** Brooklyn, NY , U.S.A. **Online address:** jennifer@jenniferblock.com

BLOCK, Joyce. American (born United States), b. 1951. **Genres:** Psychology, Women's Studies And Issues, Medicine/Health. **Career:** University of Notre Dame, St. Mary's College, adjunct professor. Writer. **Publications:** Motherhood as Metamorphosis: Change and Continuity in the Life of a New Mother, 1990; Family Myths: Living Our Roles, Betraying Ourselves, 1994. **Address:** 300 N Michigan St., South Bend, IN 46601, U.S.A. **Online address:** joyceblock1951@yahoo.com

BLOCK, Lawrence. Also writes as Paul Kavanagh, Sheldon Lord, Jill Emerson, Andrew Shaw, Chip Harrison. American (born United States), b. 1938. **Genres:** Novels, Novellas/Short Stories, Mystery/Crime/Suspense, Recreation, Writing/Journalism, Young Adult Non-fiction, Young Adult Fiction. **Career:** Scott Meredith Inc., editor, 1957-58; freelance writer, 1958-; Whitman Publishing Co., editor, 1964-66; Hofstra University, instructor, 1981-82. **Publications:** MYSTERY NOVELS: Cinderella Sims, 1961; Death Pulls a Double Cross, 1961: Mona, 1961; The Case of the Pornographic Photos, 1961 in UK as Marham: The Case of the Pornographic Photos, 1965; The Girl with the Long Green Heart, 1965; Deadly, 1967; After the First Death, 1969; The Specialists, 1969; Burglars Can't Be Choosers, 1977; The Burglar in the Closet, 1978; T he Burglar Who Liked to Quote Kipling, 1979; Aniel, 1980; The Burglar Who Studied Spinoza, 1980; The Burglar Who Painted Like Mondrian, 1983; Like a Lamb to Slaughter in UK as Five Little Rich Girls, 1984; (with C. Woolrich) Into the Night, 1987; Coward's Kiss, 1987; Random Walk, 1988; Spider Spin Me a Web, 1988; You Could Call It Murder, 1989; A Ticket to the Bone Yard, 1990; The Burglar Who Traded Ted Williams, 1994; The Burglar Who Thought He Was Bogart, 1995; The Burglar in the Library, 1997; Murder on the Run, 1998; Keller's Greatest Hits: Adventures in the Murder Trade, 1998; Hit Man, 1998; The Burglar in the Rye: A Bernie Rhodenbarr Mystery, 1999; Hit List, 2000; Small Town, 2003; The Burgler on the Prowl, 2004; Hit and Run, 2008. NOVELS: Ronald Rabbit is a Dirty Old Man, 1971; Ariel, 1980; (with H. King) Code of Arms, 1981. AS SHELDON LORD: Kept, 1960. AS JILL EMERSON: Warm and Willing, 1964; Enough of Sorrow, 1965; Threesome, 1970; Sensuous, 1972; The Trouble with Eden, 1973; A Week as Andrea Benstock, 1975. EDITOR: (J. Hitt) The Perfect Murder: Five Great Mystery Writers Create the Perfect Crime, 1991; Death Cruise: Crime Stories on the Open Seas, 1999; Master's Choice: Mystery Stories by Today's Top Writers and the Masters Who Inspired Them, 1999; Speaking of Greed: Stories of Envious Desire, 2001; Opening Shots: Great Mystery and Crime Writers Share Their First Published Stories, 2001; Speaking of Lust: Stories of Forbidden Desire, 2001; Blood on Their Hands, 2003; Gangsters, Swindlers, Killers, and Thieves: The Lives and Crimes of Fifty American Villains, 2004; Manhattan Noir, 2006; Manhattan Noir 2: The Classics, 2008. AS CHIP HARRISON: No Score, 1970; Chip Harrison Scores Again, 1971; Make Out with Murder, 1974; The Topless Tulip Caper, 1975. NOVELS AS PAUL KAVANAGH: Such Men Are Dangerous, 1969; The Triumph of Evil, 1971; Not Comin' Home to You, 1974. EVAN TANNER SERIES: The Thief Who Couldn't Sleep, 1966; The Cancelled Czech, 1966; Tanner's Twelve Swingers, 1967; Two for Tanner, 1967 as The Scoreless Thai, 2001; Tanner's Tiger, 1968; Here Comes a Hero, 1968; Me Tanner, You Jane, 1970; Tanner on Ice, 1998. MATTHEW SCUDDER SERIES: In the Midst of Death, 1976; Sin of the Fathers, 1977; Time to Murder and Create, 1977; A Stab in the Dark, 1981; Eight Million Ways to Die, 1982; When the Sacred Ginmill Closes, 1986; Out on the Cutting Edge, 1989; A Ticket to the Boneyard, 1990; A Dance at the Slaughterhouse, 1991; A Walk among the Tombstones, 1992; The Devil Knows You're Dead, 1993; A Long Line of Dead Men, 1994; Even the Wicked, 1997; Everybody Dies, 1998; Hope to Die, 2001; All the Flowers are Dying, 2005; A Drop of the Hard Stuff, 2011. NONFICTION: Writing the Novel: From Plot to Print, 1979; Telling Lies for Fun and Profit, 1981; Write for Your Life, 1986; Spider, Spin Me a Web: A Handbook for Fiction Writers, 1988; After Hours: Conversations with Lawrence Block, 1995; Step by Step: A Pedestrian Memoir, 2009; Introducing Myself & Others, 2010. OTHERS: (as Andrew Shaw) Campus Tramp, 1958; (with W. Ard) Babe in the Woods, 1960; A Guide Book to Australian Coins, 1964; (with D.R. Krause) Swiss Shooting Talers and Medals, 1965; Deadly Honeymoon, 1967; Writing the Novel from Plot to Print, 1979; Mr. Rhodenbarr, Bookseller, Advises a Young Customer on Seeking a Vocation, 1979; Telling Lies for Fun and Profit, 1981; (with C. Morrison) Real Food Places, 1981; Sometimes They Bite (short stories), 1983; Write for Your Life, 1985; Spider, Spin Me a Web, 1988; Some Days You Get the Bear (stories), 1993; After Hours: Conversations with Lawrence Block, 1995; Canceled Czech, 1996; Mary Higgins Clark Presents The Plot Thickens, 1997; As Dark as Christmas Gets: A Christmas Story, 1997; The Burglar Who Dropped in on Elvis, 1999; One Night Stands, 1999; The Lost Cases of Ed London, 2001; The Scoreless Thai, 2001; Enough Rope, 2002; The Burglar on the Prowl, 2004; Hit Parade, 2006; Lucky at Cards, 2007; Hit and Run, 2008; A Diet of Treacle, 2008; Killing Castro, 2009; Grifter's Game, 2011; (foreword) Backflash, 2011; (foreword) Butcher's Moon, 2011; (foreword) Comeback, 2011; Strange Embrace/69 Barrow Street, 2012. **Address:** c/o Author Mail, HarperCollins Publishers, 10 E 53rd St., 7th Fl., New York, NY 10022-5244, U.S.A. **Online address:** lb@lawrenceblock.com

BLOCK, Sharon. American (born United States), b. 1968. **Genres:** Adult Non-fiction, Humanities, History, Sex. **Career:** University of Iowa, assistant professor of history; University of California, associate professor of history; Omohundro Institute of Early American History and Culture, National Endowment for the Humanities fellow. Historian and writer. **Publications:** Rape and Sexual Power in Early America, 2006. Contributor to periodicals. **Address:** Department of History, University of California, 133 Krieger Hall, PO Box 3275, Irvine, CA 92697, U.S.A. **Online address:** sblock@uci.edu

BLOCK, Thomas H(arris). American (born United States), b. 1945. **Genres:** Novels, Young Adult Fiction, History, Theology/Religion. **Career:** U.S.Airways, airline pilot, 1964-; Flying Magazine, columnist, 1970-. **Publications:** (With N. DeMille) Mayday, 1980; Orbit, 1982: Forced Landing, 1983; Airship Nine, 1984; Sky Fall, 1987; Open Skies, 1990; Shalom/Salaam: A Story of a Mystical Fraternity, 2010. **Address:** Joseph Elder Agency, 150 W 87th St., New York, NY 10024, U.S.A.

BLOCK, Valerie. American (born United States), b. 1964?. **Genres:** Novels, Mystery/Crime/Suspense, Young Adult Fiction, Humor/Satire. **Career:** Writer. **Publications:** Was It Something I Said?, 1998; None of Your Business, 2003; Don't Make a Scene: A Novel, 2007. **Address:** c/o Patty Park, Random House Publishing Group, 1745 Broadway, New York, NY 10019, U.S.A.

BLOCKSMA, Mary. American (born United States), b. 1942. **Genres:** Children's Fiction, Adult Non-fiction, Children's Non-fiction, Natural History, Illustrations. **Career:** Junior high school English teacher, 1964-65; U.S. Peace Corps, University of Nigeria, lecturer, 1965-67; De Paul University, research librarian, 1968-69; Albany County Public Library, director, 1970-76; Addison-Wesley Publishing Co., staff writer, 1977-79; freelance writer, 1980-; Baltimore Junior College, teacher; Eastern Nigeria University, teacher; Delta College, teacher; Chicago Public Library, reference librarian; DePaul University Library, reference librarian; Albany County Library, director; Bay City Public Library, part-time reference librarian. **Publications:** SELF-ILLUSTRATED: Lake Lover's Year, 2001; What's On the Beach? A Great Lakes Treasure Hunt, 2003; What's in the Woods? A Great Lakes Treasure Hunt, 2005; What's on the Beach in Florida?, forthcoming. OTHERS: The Pup Went Up, 1983; Did You Hear That?, 1983; Apple Tree! Apple Tree!, 1983; Grandma Dragon's Birthday, 1983; (with D. Blocksma) Easy-to-Make Spaceships That Really Fly, 1983, 2nd ed., 1988; Marvelous Music Machine: A Story of Piano, 1984; The Best-Dressed Bear, 1984; Rub-a-Dub-Dub: What's in the Tub?, 1984; (with D. Blocksma) Easy-to-Make Water Toys That Really Work, 1985; (with D. Blocksma) Space Crafting: Invent Your Own Flying Spaceships, 1986; Amazing Mouths and Menus, 1986; Where's That Duck?, 1987; All My Toys Are on the Floor, 1986; (with D. Blocksma) Action Contraptions: Easy-To-Make Toys that Really Move, 1987; Reading the Numbers: A Survival Guide to the Measurements, Numbers, and Sizes Encountered in Everyday Life, 1989; Yoo Hoo Moon!, 1990; Naming Nature: A Seasonal Guide for the Amateur Naturalist, 1992; Ticket To the Twenties: A Time Traveler's Guide, 1993; The Fourth Coast: Exploring the Great Lakes Coastline from The St. Lawrence Seaway to the Boundary Waters of Minnesota, 1995; Great Lakes Solo, 2001; Necessary Numbers: An Everyday Guide to Sizes, Measures, and More, 2002; Great Lakes Nature: An Outdoor Year, 2003, rev. ed., 2004. Contributor of articles to magazines. **Address:** Beaver Island Arts, PO Box 40, Bay City, MI 48707-0040, U.S.A. **Online address:** mblocksma@yahoo.com

BLOCKSON, Charles L(eRoy). American (born United States), b. 1933. **Genres:** Cultural/Ethnic Topics, History, Librarianship, Bibliography, Literary Criticism And History. **Career:** Norristown High School, advisor, 1970; author, 1975-; Pennsylvania Afro-American Historical Board, director, 1976-; Afro-American Historical and Cultural Museum in Philadelphia, co-founder, 1976; Pennsylvania Afro-American Historical Board, director, 1976-; Governor's Heritage Affairs Commission, Afro-American commissioner, 1983-; Temple University, Charles L. Blockson Afro-American Collection, curator, 1984-; Valley Forge African-American Revolutionary Soldier Monument, chairman, 1990-; Pennsylvania State Historical and Record Advisory Board and Black History Advisory Board, director; Afro-American Historical and Cultural Museum in Philadelphia, co-founder; Johnson C. Smith University, historian and curator; lecturer. **Publications:** Pennsylvania's Black History, 1975; (with R. Fry) Black Genealogy, 1977, rev. ed., 1991; Handbook of Black Librarianship, 1977; The Underground Railroad in Pennsylvania, 1981; The Underground Railroad: First Person Narratives of Escapes to Freedom in the North, 1987; A Commented Bibliography of One Hundred and One Influential Books By and About People of African Descent, 1556-1982: A

Collector's Choice, 1989; (ed.) Catalogue of the Charles L. Blockson Afro-American Collection, 1990; Philadelphia's Guide: African-American State Historical Markers, 1992; The Journey of John W. Mosley: An African-American Pictorial, 1993; The Hippocrene Guide to the Underground Railroad, 1994; African-Americans in Pennsylvania: A History and Guide, 1994; Damn Rare: The Memoirs of an African American Bibliophile, 1998; Philadelphia: 1639-2000, 2000; African Americans in Pennsylvania: Above Ground and Underground: An Illustrated Guide, 2001; Haitian Revolution: Celebrating the First Black Republic, 2004; Ballad of the Underground Railroad: A Story for All Ages, 2008. Contributor to books, magazines and journals. **Address:** Johnson C. Smith University, 100 Beatties Ford Rd., Charlotte, NC 28216, U.S.A.

BLODGETT, (Anita) Jan. American (born United States), b. 1954. **Genres:** Literary Criticism And History, Local History/Rural Topics. **Career:** West Texas A&M University, assistant reference librarian, 1980-82; Texas Tech University, assistant archivist, 1982-89; Dickinson College, college archivist, 1987-89; St. Mary's County Public Library, county archivist, 1989-94; Davidson College, college archivist and records management coordinator, 1994-, adjunct faculty of humanities, 1998-99. Writer. **Publications:** Land of Bright Promise: Advertising the Texas Panhandle and South Plains, 1870-1971, 1988; Protestant Evangelical Literary Culture and Contemporary Society, 1997; (co-author) One Town, Many Voices: A History of Davidson, North Carolina, 2012. **Address:** E.H. Little Library, Davidson College, PO Box 7200, Davidson, NC 28035, U.S.A. **Online address:** jablodgett@davidson.edu

BLODGETT, Peter J. American (born United States), b. 1954. **Genres:** History, Librarianship, Social Sciences. **Career:** Yale University, teaching and research assistant in history, 1979-84; Huntington Library, curator of western manuscripts, 1985-. Writer. **Publications:** Land of Golden Dreams: California in the Gold Rush Decade, 1848-1858, 1999. Contributor to books and periodicals. **Address:** Manuscripts Department, Huntington Library, 1151 Oxford Rd., San Marino, CA 91108, U.S.A. **Online address:** pblodgett@huntington.org

BLOEMBERGEN, Nicolaas. American/Dutch (born Netherlands), b. 1920. **Genres:** Physics, Sciences, Technology. **Career:** University of Utrecht, part-time teaching fellow, 1942-45; University of Leiden, research associate, 1947-48; Harvard University, part-time research assistant, 1946-47, Society of Fellows, junior fellow, 1949-51, associate professor of applied physics, 1951-57, Gordon McKay professor of applied physics, 1957-74, Rumford professor of physics, 1974-80, Gerhard Gade University professor, 1980-90, professor emeritus, 1990-, Pforzheimer House, honorary associate; Ecole Normale Superieure, visiting professor, 1957; University of California, visiting professor, 1965, Hitchcock lecturer, 1984; College de France, visiting professor, 1980; University of Central Florida, Center for Research and Education in Optics and Lasers, visiting scientist, 1995; University of Arizona, College of Optical Sciences, professor, 2001-. Writer. **Publications:** Nuclear Magnetic Relaxation, 1948; (with P. Grivet) Quantum Electronics: Proceedings of the Third International Congress. électronique Quantique: Comptes-rendus de la 3e conférence Internationale, Paris, 1964; Nonlinear Optics: A Lecture Note and Reprint Volume, 1965; (contrib.) Quantum Electronics: A Treatise, 1975; (contrib.) High-Resolution Laser Spectroscopy, 1976; Topics in Nonlinear Optics: Selected Papers of N. Bloembergen, Raman Professor, 1979, 1982; Nonlinear Optics, 1992, 4th ed., 1996. EDITOR: Nonlinear Spectroscopy, 1977; Encounters in Nonlinear Optics: Selected Papers of Nicolaas Bloembergen, with Commentary, 1996; Encounters in Magnetic Resonances: Selected Papers of Nicolaas Bloembergen: With Commentary, 1996; (with N. Rahman and A. Rizzo) Atoms, Molecules, and Quantum Dots in Laser Fields: Fundamental Processes: Pisa, 12-16 June 2000, 2001. **Address:** College of Optical Sciences, University of Arizona, Meinel Bldg., 1630 E University Blvd., Tucson, AZ 85721, U.S.A. **Online address:** nbloembergen@optics.arizona.edu

BLOM, Philipp. German (born Germany), b. 1970. **Genres:** Novels, History, Philosophy, Intellectual History, Food And Wine. **Career:** Historian, novelist, translator and journalist. **Publications:** The Simmons Papers (novel), 1995; The Wines of Austria, 2000; To Have and to Hold: An Intimate History of Collectors and Collecting, 2003; Encyclopédie: The Triumph of Reason in an Unreasonable Age, 2004; Enlightening the World: Encyclopédie, the Book that Changed the Course of History, 2005; Luxor, 2006; The Vertigo Years: Europe, 1900-1914, 2008; Der taumelnde Kontinent, 2009; A Wicked Company: The Forgotten Radicalism of the European Enlightenment, 2010; Wicked Company: Freethinkers and Friendship in pre-Revolutionary Paris, 2011. **Address:** c/o Victoria Hobbs, A M Heath & Company Ltd., 6 Warwick Ct., London, GL WC1R 5DJ, England. **Online address:** info@philipp-blom.eu

BLONDEL, Jean (Fernand Pierre). Italian/British/French (born France), b. 1929. **Genres:** Politics/Government, Social Sciences. **Career:** University of Keele, assistant lecturer, lecturer in government, 1958-63; Yale University, visiting fellow, 1963-64; University of Essex, professor of government, 1963-84, dean of school of comparative studies, 1967-69; Institut d'Etudes Politiques, visiting professor, 1969-; Carleton University, visiting professor, 1969-70; European University Institute, professor of political science, 1985-94, external professor, 1994-2000, emeritus professor, 2000-; University of Siena, visiting professor, 1996-. Writer. **Publications:** As condicões da vida política no Estado da Paraíba, 1957; Voters, Parties and Leaders: The Social Fabric of British Politics, 1963, rev. ed., 1967; (with F. Ridley) Public Administration in France, 1964, 2nd ed., 1969; Société politique britannique, 1964; (with F. Bealey and W.P. McCann) Constituency Politics: A Study of Newcastle-under-Lyme, 1965; Government of France, 1968, 4th ed., 1974; Comparative Government: A Reader, 1969; Democracy in Crisis: New Challenges to Constitutional Democracy in the Atlantic Area, 1971; Sociologia dei partiti politici, 1971; Comparing Political Systems, 1972; (with V. Herman) A Workbook for Comparative Government, 1972; Comparative Legislatures, 1973; The Government of France, 1974; Contempoaray France: Politics, Society and Institutions, 1974; Thinking Politically, 1976; Political Parties, 1977; Political Parties: A Genuine Case of Discontent?, 1978; (with G. Gordon and J. Gombeaud) Vérités: Est-ce à dire?, 1978; (ed. and comp. with C. Walker) Directory of European Political Scientists, 1979; World Leaders: A Study of Heads of Government in the Postwar Period, 1979; Political Leadership, 1979, 2nd ed., 1987; Lei eleitoral e os partidos no Brasil, 1980; The Discipline of Politics, 1981; The Organization of Governments: A Comparative Analysis of Governmental Structures, 1982; Government Ministers in the Contemporary World, 1985; Political Leadership: Towards a General Analysis, 1987; (ed. with F. Müller-Rommel) Cabinets in Western Europe, 1988; Comparative Government, 1990; Developing Democracy: Comparative Research in Honour of J.F.P. Blondel, 1994; Comparative Government: An Introduction, 1995; (with R. Sinnott and P. Svensson) People and Parliament in the European Union: Participation, Democracy and Legitimacy, 1998; (with F.M. Rommel) Cabinets in Eastern Europe, 2001; (with T. Inoguchi) Political Cultures in Asia and Europe: Citizens, States and Societal Values, 2006; (co-author) Governing New European Democracies, 2007; (with T. Inoguchi) Citizens and The State: Attitudes in Western Europe and East and Southeast Asia, 2007. EDITOR: Comparative Government, 1969; Introduction to Comparative Government, 1969, (co-ed.) 5th ed., 2003; (with F.M. Rommel) Cabinets in Western Europe, 1988, 2nd ed., 1997; (with J.L. Thiebault) The Profession of Government Minister in Western Europe, 1991; (with F.M. Rommel) Governing Together: The Extend and Limits of Joint Decision-Making in Western European Cabinets, 1993; (with M. Cotta) Party and Government: An Inquiry Into the Relationship Between Governments and Supporting Parties in Liberal Democracies, 1996; (with C. Cansino) Political Leadership in Changing Societies, 1998; (with I. Marsh and T. Inoguchi) Democracy, Governance, and Economic Performance: East and Southeast Asia, 1999; (with M. Cotta) The Nature of Party Government: A Comparative European Perspective, 2000; (with P. Segatti) Italian Politics: The Second Berlusconi Government, 2003; (co-ed.) Political Leadership, Parties and Citizens: The Personalisation of Leadership, 2010. **Address:** European University Institute, Convento, SD011 ground fl., Via delle Fontanelle 19, San Domenico di Fiesole, I-50014, Italy. **Online address:** jean.blondel@eui.eu

BLOODWORTH-THOMASON, Linda. American (born United States), b. 1947. **Genres:** Novels, Children's Fiction, Young Adult Fiction. **Career:** Mozark Productions, co-founder; Claudia Co., founder; Clinton Presidential Library, director of films; teacher; producer; Los Angeles Daily Journal, reporter; The Wall Street Journal, staff. **Publications:** The Man from Hope, 1992; Liberating Paris, 2004. **Address:** c/o Author Mail, William Morrow Co., 10 E 53rd St., Fl. 7, New York, NY 10022, U.S.A.

BLOOM, Clive. British (born England), b. 1953. **Genres:** Mystery/Crime/Suspense, Romance/Historical, Cultural/Ethnic Topics, History, Literary Criticism And History, Politics/Government, Sociology, Adult Non-fiction, Adult Non-fiction. **Career:** Middlesex University, Middlesex Polytechnic, senior lecturer in English, 1980-, professor of English and American Studies, now professor emeritus; Libris Press, consultant editor; Palgrave Macmillan, consultant editor; Lumiere Press Ltd., chair of cooperative; Fullwood School, governor. **Publications:** The Occult Experience and the New Criticism, 1986;

Reading Poe, Reading Freud, 1988; (with G.S. McCue) Dark Knights, 1993; Cult Fiction, 1996; Bestsellers, 2002, 2nd ed., 2008; Literature, Politics, and Intellectual Crisis in Britain Today, 2001; Violent London: 2000 Years of Riots, Rebels and Revolts, 2003, rev. ed., 2010; Terror Within: Terrorism and the Dream of a British Republic, 2007; Haunted Castle: Adventures in the Gothic, 2009; Gothic Histories: The Taste for Terror, 1764 to the Present, 2010; Restless Revolutionaries, 2011. EDITOR: (with G. Day) Perspectives on Pornography, 1988; (and contrib.) Jacobean Poetry and Prose, 1988; (co-ed.) Nineteenth-Century Suspense, 1988; (and contrib.) Twentieth-Century Suspense, 1990; (and contrib.) Spy Thrillers, 1990; (with M. Roberts) Arcane Worlds, 1990; (with D. Zadworna-Fjellerstad) Criticism towards 2000, 1990; (and contrib.) Voices from the Vault, 1991; Creepers, 1993; Literature and Culture in Modern Britain, 1993; American Drama, 1995; (with B. Docherty) American Poetry: The Modernist Ideal, 1995; Gothic Horror, 1998. Contributor to books and periodicals. **Address:** School of Arts, Middlesex University, White Hart Ln., London, GL N17 8HR, England. **Online address:** cbloom4189@aol.com

BLOOM, Elizabeth. *See* **SAULNIER, Beth.**

BLOOM, Harold. American (born United States), b. 1930. **Genres:** Novels, Literary Criticism And History, Poetry. **Career:** Yale University, instructor, 1955-60, assistant professor, 1960-63, associate professor, 1963-65, professor of English, 1965-74, DeVane professor of humanities, 1974-77, professor of humanities, 1977-, Sterling professor of the humanities and English, 1983-; Hebrew University, visiting professor, 1959; Breadloaf Summer School, visiting professor, 1965-66; Cornell University, society for humanities visiting professor, 1968-69; New School for Social Research, visiting professor, 1982-84; Harvard University, Charles Eliot Norton Professor of Poetry, 1987-88; New York University, Berg Visiting Professor of English, 1998-2004. Writer. **Publications:** NON-FICTION: Shelley's Mythmaking, 1959; The Visionary Company: A Reading of English Romantic Poetry, 1961, rev. ed., 1971; Blake's Apocalypse, 1963; Yeats, 1970; (comp.) Romanticism and Consciousness: Essays in Criticism, 1970; The Ringers in the Tower: Studies in Romantic Tradition, 1971; The Anxiety of Influence: A Theory of Poetry, 1973, rev. ed., 2001; A Map of Misreading, 1975, rev. ed., 2003; Kabbalah and Criticism, 1975; Poetry and Repression: Revisionism from Blake to Stevens, 1976; Figures of Capable Imagination, 1976; Wallace Stevens: The Poems of Our Climate, 1977; The Flight to Lucifer: A Gnostic Fantasy, 1979; (with J.H. Miller, P. de Man and J. Derrida) Deconstruction and Criticism, 1979; Agon: Towards a Theory of Revisionism, 1982; The Breaking of the Vessels, 1982; (intro.) The Poetry and Prose of William Blake, The Complete Poetry and Prose of William Blake, 1982; The Strong Light of the Canonical: Kafka, Freud, and Scholem as Revisionists of Jewish Culture and Thought, 1987; Poetics of Influence, 1989; Ruin the Sacred Truths: Poetry and Belief from the Bible to the Present, 1989; (contrib.) The Book of J, 1990; The American Religion: The Emergence of the Post-Christian Nation, 1992; (contrib.) The Gospel of Thomas: The Hidden Sayings of Jesus, 1992; (comp. with P. Kane) Collected Poems and Translations, 1994; The Western Canon: The Books and School of the Ages, 1994; Omens of Millennium: The Gnosis of Angels, Dreams, and Resurrection, 1996; Shakespeare: The Invention of the Human, 1998; How to Read and Why, 2000; Genius: A Mosaic of One Hundred Exemplary Creative Minds, 2002; Hamlet: Poem Unlimited, 2003; Hamlet: Poem Unlimited, 2003; Where Shall Wisdom Be Found?, 2004; Eudora Welty, 2004, rev. ed., 2007; Italian Renaissance, 2004; Short Story Writers and Short Stories, 2005; Novelists and Novels, 2005; Jesus and Yahweh: The Names Divine, 2005; Essayists and Prophets, 2005; Epic, 2005; Dramatists and Dramas, 2005; (intro.) Bloom's How to Write About Nathaniel Hawthorne, 2008; (intro.) Bloom's How to Write About Emily Dickinson, 2008; (intro.) Bloom's How to Write About John Steinbeck, 2008; (intro.) Bloom's How to Write About J.D. Salinger, 2008; (intro.) Bloom's How to Write About William Shakespeare, 2008; (intro.) Bloom's How to Write About Toni Morrison, 2008, new ed., 2011; (intro.) Bloom's How to Write About Edgar Allan Poe, 2008; (intro.) Bloom's How to Write about Mark Twain, 2008; (intro.) Bloom's How to Write About F. Scott Fitzgerald, 2008; (intro.) Bloom's How to Write about Tennessee Williams, 2009; (intro.) Bloom's How to Write about William Faulkner, 2009; (intro.) Bloom's How to Write about Amy Tan, 2009; (intro.) Bloom's How to Write About Gabriel García Márquez's, 2009; (intro.) Bloom's How to Write about Oscar Wilde, 2009; (intro.) Bloom's How to Write about Walt Whitman, 2009; (intro.) Bloom's How to Write about Shakespeare's Histories, 2010; (intro.) Bloom's How to Write about Langston Hughes, 2010; (intro.) Bloom's How to Write about Robert Frost, 2010; (intro.) Bloom's How to Write about Homer, 2010; (intro.) Bloom's How to Write about Joseph Conrad, 2010; (intro.) Bloom's How to Write about Shakespeare's Comedies, 2010; (intro.) Bloom's How to Write about Shakespeare's Tragedies, 2010; (intro.) Bloom's How to Write about George Orwell, 2010; (intro.) Bloom's How to Write about Shakespeare's Romances, 2010; (intro.) Bloom's How to Write about Geoffrey Chaucer, 2010; (intro.) Bloom's How to Write about James Joyce, 2010; The King James Bible: A Literary Appreciation, 2011; (intro.) Bloom's How to Write about Kurt Vonnegut, 2011; (intro.) Bloom's How to Write about Harper Lee, 2011; (intro.) Bloom's How to Write about Maya Angelou, 2012. EDITOR: English Romantic Poetry, An Anthology, 1963; (with J. Hollander) The Wind and the Rain, 1961; (with F.W. Hilles) From Sensibility to Romanticism: Essays Presented to Frederick A. Pottle, 1965; Selected Poetry, 1966; Marius the Epicurean: His Sensations and Ideas, 1970; Selected Poetry, 1972; The Romantic Tradition in American Literature, 1972; (with L. Trilling) Romantic Prose and Poetry, 1973; (with L. Trilling) Victorian Prose and Poetry, 1973; (co-ed.) Oxford Anthology of English Literature, 1973; (with A. Munich) Robert Browning: A Collection of Critical Essays, 1979; (with D. Lehman) The Best of the Best American Poetry, 1988-1997, 1998; Selected Poems/Walt Whitman, 2003; The Best Poems of the English Language: From Chaucer through Robert Frost, 2004; Till I End My Song, 2010. STUDY GUIDES: EDITOR AND AUTHOR OF INTRODUCTION: The Literary Criticism of John Ruskin, 1965; Samuel Beckett, 1985, new ed., 2011; William Shakespeare: Tragedies, 1985, new ed., 2010; Samuel Taylor Coleridge, 1986, new ed., 2010; William Shakespeare's The Merchant of Venice, new ed., 2010; Contemporary Poets, 1986, new ed., 2010; William Shakespeare's A Midsummer Night's Dream, 1987, new ed., 2010; Zora Neale Hurston's Their Eyes were Watching God, 1987, new ed., 2008; William Shakespeare's King Lear, 1987, new ed., 2010; William Shakespeare's Othello, 1987, new ed., 2010; William Shakespeare's Macbeth, 1987, new ed., 2011; Thomas Hardy, 1987, new ed., 2010; William Shakespeare's Julius Caesar, 1988, new ed., 2010; William Shakespeare's Antony and Cleopatra, 1988, new ed., 2011; William Shakespeare's The Tempest, 1988, new ed., 2011; Selected Writings of Walter Pater, 1974; Hamlet, 1990; Caddy Compson, 1990; Cleopatra, 1990; French Poetry: The Renaissance through 1915, 1990; Edwardian and Georgian Fiction, 1880 to 1914, 1990; French Prose and Criticism, 1790 to World War II, 1990; French Prose and Criticism through 1789, 1990; Holden Caulfield, 1990; Huck Finn, 1990; Clarissa Dalloway, 1990; Modern Latin American Fiction, 1990; Bigger Thomas, 1990; Toni Morrison, 1990; Sophocles, 1990; Shylock, 1991; Odysseus/Ulysses, 1991; Ahab, 1991; Antonia, 1991; Brett Ashley, 1991; Macbeth, 1991; Willy Loman, 1991; Gatsby, 1991; Joan of Arc, 1992; Falstaff, 1992; David Copperfield, 1992; Iago, 1992; Caliban, 1992; Marlow, 1992; Isabel Archer, 1992; King Lear, 1992; Rosalind, 1992; Heathcliff, 1993; Lolita, 1993; Classic Science-Fiction Writers, 1994; Science-Fiction Writers of the Golden Age, 1994; Modern Fantasy Writers, 1994; Modern Mystery Writers, 1994; Classic Fantasy Writers, 1994; Julius Caesar, 1994; Black American Prose Writers of the Harlem Renaissance, 1994; Black American Prose Writers: Before the Harlem Renaissance, 1994; Black American Poets and Dramatists: Before the Harlem Renaissance, 1994; Contemporary Horror Writers, 1994; Major Modern Black American Writers, 1994; Contemporary Black American Fiction Writers, 1994; Classic Horror Writers, 1994; Modern Horror Writers, 1994; Modern Black American Poets and Dramatist, 1994; Emma Bovary, 1994; Contemporary Black American Poets and Dramatists, 1994; Major Black American Writers through the Harlem Renaissance, 1994; Black American Women Fiction Writers, 1994; Modern Black American Fiction Writers, 1995; Classic Mystery Writers, 1995; Classic Crime and Suspense Writers, 1995; Robinson Crusoe, 1995; Black American Poets and Dramatists of the Harlem Renaissance, 1995; Modern Crime and Suspense Writers, 1995; Beowulf, 1996, rev. ed., 2007; Dante's Divine Comedy: The Inferno, 1996; Emily Brontë's Wuthering Heights, 1996, rev. ed., 2007; Charles Dickens' Great Expectations, 1996; Harper Lee's To Kill a Mockingbird, 1996, new ed., 2010; Arthur Miller's The Crucible, 1996, new ed., 2010; Mark Twain's Adventures of Huckleberry Finn, 1996; F. Scott Fitzgerald's The Great Gatsby, 1996, new ed., 2010; Joseph Conrad's Heart of Darkness and The Secret Sharer, 1996; George Orwell's 1984, 1996, rev. ed., 2007; Homer's the Odyssey, 1996, rev. ed., 2007; John Milton's Paradise Lost, 1996; Sophocles' Oedipus Plays: Oedipus the King, Oedipusat Colonus, and Antigone, 1996; John Steinbeck's the Grapes of Wrath, 1996, rev. ed., 2007; Charles Dickens' A Tale of Two Cities, 1996; Alex Haley and Malcolm X's The Autobiography of Malcolm X, 1996; Nathaniel Hawthorne's The Scarlet Letter, 1996, new ed., 2011; Harriet Beecher Stowe's Uncle Tom's Cabin, 1996; George Orwell's Animal Farm, 1996; George Eliot's Silas Marner, 1996; William Shakespeare's Romeo and Juliet, 1996, new ed., 2010; Charlotte Bronte's Jane Eyre, 1996, rev. ed., 2006; Herman Melville's Billy Budd,

Benito Cereno, and Bartleby the Scrivener, 1996; Maya Angelou's I Know Why the Caged Bird Sings, 1996; Black American Women Poets and Dramatists, 1996; Fyodor Dostoevsky's Crime and Punishment, 1996; Homer's Iliad, 1996; Ernest Hemingway's The Sun Also Rises, 1996, new ed., 2011; Ralph Ellison's Invisible Man, 1996; Ernest Hemingway's The Old Man and the Sea, 1996; Richard Wright's Native Son, 1996, new ed., 2009; Thomas Hardy's Tess of the D'Urbervilles, 1996; Aldous Huxley's Brave New World, 1996, new ed., 2011; Mary Shelley's Frankenstein, 1996, rev. ed., 2007; Jane Austen's Pride and Prejudice, 1996, rev. ed., 2007; Jonathan Swift's Gulliver's Travels, 1996; Vergil's Aeneid, 1996; Herman Melville's Moby Dick, 1996, rev. ed., 2007; Arthur Miller's The Crucible, 1996; Charles Dickens's Great Expectations, 1996, new ed., 2010; Stephen Crane's The Red Badge of Courage, 1996, new ed., 2010; William Shakespeare's Henry IV, Part 1, 1996; Ernest Hemingway's A Farewell to Arms, 1996, new ed., 2009; William Golding's Lord of the Flies, 1996, new ed., 2010; John Steinbeck's of Mice and Men, 1996; J.D. Salinger's The Catcher in the Rye, 1996, new ed., 2009; Caribbean Women Writers, 1997; American Women Fiction Writers, 1997; Asian American Women Writers, 1997; British Women Fiction Writers, 1900-1960, 1997; Lesbian and Bisexual Fiction Writers, 1997; Native American Writers, 1998, new ed., 2010; Henrik Ibsen, 1999, new ed., 2011; Toni Morrison's The Bluest Eye, 1999, new ed., 2007; Scholarly Look at The Diary of Anne Frank, 1999, new ed. as Anne Frank's The Diary of Anne Frank, 2010; Shakespeare's Romances: Comprehensive Research and Study Guide, 2000, new ed. as William Shakespeare: Romances, 2010, new ed., 2011; Ben Johnson, 2001; Cervantes' Don Quixote, 2001, new ed. as Miguel de Cervantes's Don Quixote, 2010; D.H. Lawrence, 2001; Edgar Allan Poe, 2001, new ed., 2012; Elie Wiesel's Night, 2001, new ed., 2010; Erich Maria Remarque's All Quiet on the Western Front, 2001; Henry James, 2001; Homer, 2001; Italio Calvino, 2001; Jack London, 2001, new ed., 2011; Jean Paul Sartre, 2001; John Irving, 2001; John Keats, 2001, rev. ed., 2007; John Updike, 2001; Anton Chekov, 2001; Joseph Conrad, 2001, new ed., 2010; Katherine Anne Porter, 2001; Kurt Vonnegaut's Slaughterhouse Five, 2001; Maya Angelou, 2001; Nathaniel Hawthorne, 2001, rev. ed., 2007; Percy Bysshe Shelley, 2001; Ray Bradbury, 2001, new ed., 2010; Ray Bradbury's Fahrenheit 451, 2001; Robert Browning, 2001; Samuel T. Coleridge, 2001; Shirley Jackson, 2001; Hero's Journey, 2001; Sylvia Plath, 2001, rev. ed., 2007; Tom Wolfe, 2001; W.E.B. Dubois, 2001; William B. Yeats, 2001; Margaret Atwood's The Handmaid's Tale, 2001; Chinua Achebe's Things Fall Apart, 2002, new ed., 2010; Christopher Marlowe, 2002; Cormac McCarthy, 2002; E.L. Doctorow, 2002; Edith Wharton, 2002; Elizabeth Barrett Browning, 2002; William Shakespeare, 2002; Elizabeth Bishop, 2002; H.D., 2002; James Joyce, 2002, new ed., 2009; Leo Tolstoy, 2002; Moliére, 2002; Neil Simon, 2002; Octavio Paz, 2002; Oscar Wilde, 2002, new ed., 2011; Poets of World War I: Wilfred Owen and Issac Rosenberg, 2002; Raymond Carver, 2002; Robert Frost, 2002, new ed., 2011; Stendhal, 2002; Ken Kesey's One Flew over the Cuckoo's Nest, 2002; Kurt Vonnegut's Cat's Cradle, 2002; Tennessee Williams's Cat on a Hot Tin Roof, 2002, new ed., 2010; Thomas Mann, 2002; Upton Sinclair's The Jungle, 2002, new ed., 2010; Virginia Woolf, 2002; William Styron's Sophie's Choice, 2002; Albert Camus's the Stranger, 2002, new ed., 2011; Amy Tan's The Joy Luck Club, 2002, new ed., 2009; African-American Poets, 2003, new ed., 2009; American Renaissance, 2003; Bram Stoker's Dracula, 2003; Cormac McCarthy's All the Pretty Horses, 2003; Dante Alighieri, 2003, new ed., 2011; David Guterson's Snow Falling on Cedars, 2003; Derek Walcott, 2003; Don Delillo, 2003; Don Delillo's White Noise, 2003; Doris Lessing, 2003; E. E. Cummings, 2003; The Eighteenth-Century English Novel, 2003; Eugene Ionesco, 2003; Euripides, 2003; Franz Kafka, 2003, new ed., 2010; Gabriel García Márquez's One Hundred Years of Solitude: Essays, 2003, new ed., 2009; George Eliot, 2003; Gwendolyn Brooks, 2003; Hart Crane, 2003; Herman Melville, 2003; Hermann Hesse, 2003; Honoré de Balzac, 2003; Sandra Cisneros's The House on Mango Street, 2003, new ed., 2010; Huck Finn, 2003; Isabel Allende, 2003; Christina Rossetti, 2004; Alan Paton's Cry, the Beloved Country, 2004, new ed., 2010; William Shakespeare's Taming of the Shrew, 2005; London, 2005; Shakespeare's The Merchant of Venice, 2005; Tony Kushner, 2005; Tim O'Brien's The Things They Carried, 2005; Tennessee Williams's A Streetcar Named Desire, 2005, new ed., 2009; Satan, 2005; Robert Musil's The Man Without Qualities, 2005; Nathanael West's Miss Lonelyhearts, 2005; Modern American Poetry, 2005; Modern American Drama, 2005; Edith Wharton's The Age of Innocence, 2005; Chaim Potok's The Chosen, 2005; Carson McCullers' The Member of the Wedding, 2005; Carson McCullers' The Ballad of the Sad Cafe, 2005; American Fiction Between the Wars, 2005; Miguel de Cervantes, 2005; Robert Louis Stevenson, 2005; Robert Hayden, 2005; Hans Christian Andersen, 2005; Gabriel Garcia Márquez, 2005, rev. ed., 2007; Fyodor Dostoevsky, 2005; James Baldwin, 2006, rev. ed., 2007; G.K.Chesterton, 2006; Richard Wright's Black Boy, 2006; Lewis Carroll's Alice's Adventures in Wonderland, 2006; Emerson's Essays, 2006; The Bible, 2006; Homer's The Iliad, rev. ed., 2007; Tennessee Williams's The Glass Menagerie, 2007; T.S. Eliot's The Waste Land, 2007; Ralph Waldo Emerson, 2007; Kate Chopin, 2007; George Orwell, 2007; Franz Kafka's The Metamorphosis, 2007; Eugene O'Neill, 2007; Kurt Vonnegut's Slaughterhouse-five, 2007; Sophocles' Oedipus Rex, 2007; Arthur Miller's Death of a Salesman, 2007, new ed., 2011; Kate Chopin's The Awakening, 2008; Joseph Heller's Catch-22, 2008; John Donne and the Metaphysical Poets, 2008, new ed., 2010; John Knowles's A Separate Peace, 2008, new ed., 2009; Jamaica Kincaid, 2008; Geoffrey Chaucer's The Canterbury Tales, 2008; Grotesque, 2009; Death and Dying, 2009; Labyrinth, 2009; American Dream, 2009; Asian-American Writers, 2009; Alienation, 2009; Eugene O'neill's Long Day's Journey Into Night, 2009; Erich Maria Remarque's All Quiet On The Western Frnt, 2009; Truman Capote, 2009; Rebirth And Renewal, 2009; Edgar Allan Poe's The Tell-tale Heart and Other Stories, 2009; African-American poets, vol. I, 1700s-1940s, 2009; Percy Shelley, 2009; Jonathan Swift, 2009; Alfred, Lord Tennyson, 2010; Bloom's Literary Themes: Civil Disobedience, 2010; Bloom's Literary Themes: Dark humor, 2010; Bloom's Literary Themes: Enslavement and Emancipation, 2010; Much Ado about Nothing, 2010; Sin and Redemption, 2010; Sublime, 2010; Bloom's Literary Themes: The Taboo, 2010; The Comedy of Errors, 2010; Exploration and Colonization, 2010; Richard III, 2010; All's Well that Ends Well, 2010; Henry V, 2010; Winter's Tale, 2010; Jane Austen's Emma, 2010; Bloom's Literary Themes: The Trickster, 2010; American Modernist Poets, 2011; Charles Dickens's A Christmas Carol, 2011; Cormac McCarthy's The Road, 2011; George Bernard Shaw, 2011; John Steinbeck's Short Stories, 2011; Mark Twain's The Adventures of Tom Sawyer, 2011; Victorian Poets, 2011; The Anatomy of Influence: Literature as a Way of Life, 2011. STUDY GUIDES: EDITOR AND AUTHOR OF INTRODUCTION: JUVENILE: Stories and Poems for Extremely Intelligent Children of All Ages, 2001; F. Scott Fitzgerald, 2001; William Shakespeare, 2002; William Faulkner, 2002; Maya Angelou, 2002, new ed., 2009; Langston Hughes, 2002; Jorge Luis Borges, 2002; Jane Austen, 2002; Stephen Crane, 2002; Stephen King, 2003, rev. ed., 2007; Walt Whitman, 2003; William Blake, 2003; William Wordsworth, 2003, rev. ed., 2007; Zora Neale Hurston, 2003; A. E. Housman, 2003; Albert Camus, 2003; Aldous Huxley, 2003, new ed., 2010; Arthur Miller, 2003; Charles Dickens, 2003, rev. ed., 2006; Emily Dickinson, 2003; Ernest Hemingway, 2003, new ed., 2011; Geoffrey Chaucer, 2003; Henry David Thoreau, 2003, rev. ed., 2007; James Joyce, 2003; John Milton, 2003; John Steinbeck, 2003; Marcel Proust, 2003; Mark Twain, 2003; Nathaniel Hawthorne, 2003; Tennessee Williams, 2003, rev. ed., 2007; The Brontë Sisters, 2003; Lord Byron, 2004; Mark Twains' The Adventures of Huckleberry Finn, 2007; Human Sexuality, 2009; Margaret Atwood, 2009; Mary Wollstonecraft Shelley, 2009; Hispanic American Writers, 2009; Richard Wright, 2009; The Brontës, 2009; Kurt Vonnegut, 2009; Lorraine Hansberry's A Raisin in the Sun, 2009; Sylvia Plath's The Bell Jar, 2009; Carson McCullers, 2009; Escuela de Wallace Stevens, 2011; F. Scott Fitzgerald's Short Stories, 2011. OTHERS: Johann Wolfgang von Goethe, 2003; John Cheever, 2003; Leo Tolstoy, 2003; Marianne Moore, 2003; Mark Strand, 2003; Milan Kundera, 2003; Norman Mailer, 2003; A Passage to India, 2003; Philip Roth, 2003; Poets of World War I: Rupert Brooke & Siegfried Sassoon, 2003; Ralph Ellison, 2003, new ed., 2010; Salman Rushdie, 2003; Sam Shepard, 2003; Seamus Heady, 2003; Sherwood Anderson, 2003; Sir John Falstaff, 2003; T.S. Eliot, 2003, new ed., 2011; The Tale of Genji, 2003; Thomas Pynchon, 2003; Aeschylus, 2003; Agatha Christie, 2003; American and Canadian Women Poets, 1300 to Present, 2003; American Women Poets, 1650-1950, 2003, new ed., 2011; Aristophanes, 2003; August Wilson, 2003; Bertolt Brecht, 2003; American Naturalism, 2004; Arthur Koestler's Darkness at Noon, 2004; E.L. Doctorow's Ragtime, 2004; Edward Fitzgerald's The Rubaiyat of Omar Khayyam, 2004; Elizabethan Drama, 2004; English Romantic Poets, 2004; Greek Drama, 2004; Jack Kerouac's On the Road, 2004; James Joyce's Ulysses, 2004; Jane Austen's Persuasion, 2004; Literature of the Holocaust, 2004; David Mamet, 2004; Alan Tate, 2004; Philip Roth's Portnoy's Complaint, 2004; William Shakespeare's As You Like It, 2004; Elizabeth Bennet, 2004; Emile Zola, 2004; George F. Babbitt, 2004; Guy de Maupassant, 2004; Hester Prynne, 2004; Issac Babel, 2004; John Ashbery, 2004; Julio Cortázar, 2004; King Arthur, 2004; Leopold Bloom, 2004; Nick Adams, 2004; William Gaddis, 2004; Nikolai Gogol, 2004; Paul Auster, 2004; Raskolnikov and Svidrigailov, 2004; Rudyard Kipling, 2004; W.S.Merwin, 2004; William Gaddis, 2004; American Religious Poems: An Anthology, 2006; Fallen Angels, 2007; Twelfth Night, or, What you Will, 2007; J.D. Salinger's Short Stories, 2011; J.R.R. Tolkien's The hobbit, 2011; Mark Twain's Short Stories, 2011; Romantic Poets, 2011;

Twentieth-century British poets, 2011; The Shadow of a Great Rock, 2011. **Address:** Department of English, Yale University, Rm. 109, 105 WLH, 63 High St., PO Box 208302, New Haven, CT 06511-8963, U.S.A. **Online address:** harold.bloom@yale.edu

BLOOM, Howard. American (born United States), b. 1943. **Genres:** History, Sciences. **Career:** Roswell Park Memorial Cancer Research Institute, laboratory assistant, 1958; Middlesex County Mental Health Clinic, writer and editor, 1963-64; Cloud Studio, co-founder, 1968-71; Circus Magazine, editor, 1971-73; ABC Records, national director for artist and public relations, 1974-75; Howard Bloom Organization Ltd., publicist, 1976-88. Writer, researcher, paleopsychologist and publicist. **Publications:** The Lucifer Principle: A Scientific Expedition into the Forces of History, 1995; The Global Brain: The Evolution of Mass Mind from the Big Bang to the 21st Century, 2000; The Genius of the Beast: A Radical Re-vision of Capitalism, 2010. Contributor of articles to books and periodicals. **Address:** International Paleopsychology Project, 705 President St., Brooklyn, NY 11215, U.S.A.

BLOOM, James D. American (born United States), b. 1951?. **Genres:** Literary Criticism And History. **Career:** Muhlenberg College, professor of English and American studies, 1982-. Writer. **Publications:** The Stock of Available Reality: R.P. Blackmur and John Berryman, 1984; Left Letters: The Culture Wars of Mike Gold and Joseph Freeman, 1992; The Literary Bent: In Search of High Art in Contemporary American Writing, 1997; Gravity Fails: The Comic Jewish Shaping of Modern America, 2003; Gravity Fails: The Comic Jewish Shaping Of Modern America, 2003; Hollywood Intellect, 2009. Contributor to periodicals. **Address:** Department of English, Muhlenberg College, Baker Center for Arts 255, 2400 Chew St., Allentown, PA 18104, U.S.A. **Online address:** bloom@muhlenberg.edu

BLOOM, Jonathan M(ax). American (born United States), b. 1950. **Genres:** Architecture, Art/Art History, History, Theology/Religion. **Career:** University of California, visiting assistant professor, 1980; Harvard University and Massachusetts Institute of Technology, Aga Khan lecturer, 1980-81; Harvard University, assistant professor of fine arts, 1981-87, research associate, 1987-88, Center for Middle Eastern Studies, faculty associate, 1988-93, affiliate in research, 1993-; Trinity College, visiting associate professor, 1995; University of Bamberg, visiting professor, 1995-96; Gardner Films, principal consultant, 1998-2000; Boston College, Norma Jean Calderwood University professor of Islamic and Asian art, 2000-; Smith College, visiting professor of art history, 2000-01; Grove Encyclopaedia of Islamic Art and Architecture, co-editor, 2005-08; Virginia Commonwealth University, Hamad Bin Khalifa endowed chair of Islamic art, 2006-. Writer. **Publications:** Minaret: Symbol of Islam, 1989; (ed. with S.S. Blair) Images of Paradise in Islamic Art, 1991; (with S.S. Blair) The Art and Architecture of Islam, 1250-1800, 1994; (with S.S. Blair) Islamic Arts, 1996; (co-author) The minbar from the Kutubiyya Mosque, 1998; (with S.S. Blair) Islam, a Thousand Years of Faint and Power, 2000; Paper before Print: The History and Impact of Paper in the Islamic Lands, 2001; Early Islamic Art and Architecture, 2002. (with S.S. Blair) Cosmophilia: Islamic Art from the David Collection Copenhagen, 2006; Arts of the City Victorious, 2007; (ed. with S.S. Blair) Rivers of Paradise: Water in Islamic Art and Culture, 2009; Grove Encyclopedia of Islamic Art and Architecture, 2009. Contributor of articles to books and journals. **Address:** Department of Fine Arts, Boston College, Rm. 433, Devlin Hall, 140 Commonwealth Ave., Chestnut Hill, MA 02467, U.S.A. **Online address:** jonathan.bloom@bc.edu

BLOOM, Lisa E. American (born United States), b. 1958. **Genres:** Art/Art History, Cultural/Ethnic Topics, Humanities, Photography, Travel/Exploration, Women's Studies And Issues. **Career:** Tuscarora Intermediate Unit, special education teacher, 1981-83; Valley Mental Health Center, teacher, 1983-84; Marion County Board of Education, special education teacher, 1984-87; West Virginia University, Learning Disabilities Clinic, graduate assistant, 1986-87, research instructor 1987-89, program evaluation essistant and rural behavior disorders project assistant, 1987-88, rural behavior disorders project coordinator and program evaluation coordinator, 1988-89, professor and head of department, 1989-; University of California, lecturer in art history, 1989-91; University of California, lecturer in art history, 1991-92; Brown University, postdoctoral fellow, 1992-93; Rhode Island School of Design, lecturer in liberal arts, 1993; Stanford University, visiting assistant professor of art history and Mellon research fellow, 1993-94. Writer. **Publications:** Gender on Ice: American Ideologies of Polar Expeditions, 1993; (ed.) With Other Eyes: Looking at Race and Gender in Visual Culture, 1999; Jewish Identities in American Feminist Art: Ghosts of Ethnicity, 2006. Contributor of articles to journals. **Address:** The Visual Arts Department, University of California, 9500 Gilman Dr., La Jolla, CA 92093-0327, U.S.A. **Online address:** bloom@email.wcu.edu

BLOOM, Lynn (Marie Zimmerman). American (born United States), b. 1934. **Genres:** Literary Criticism And History, Women's Studies And Issues, Writing/Journalism, Autobiography/Memoirs, Bibliography, Biography, Essays. **Career:** Western Reserve University, lecturer in English, 1962-63, instructor, 1963-65, associate, 1965-67; Butler University, assistant professor, 1970-73, associate professor, 1973-74; University of New Mexico, associate professor, 1975-78, director of freshman English, 1976-78; College of William and Mary, associate professor of English, 1978-82, director of writing, 1979-81, Eastern Virginia Writing Project, co-director, 1979-81; Virginia Commonwealth University, Department of English, professor of English, 1982-90, chair, 1982-83; University of Connecticut, board of trustees distinguished professor, professor of English and Aetna chair of writing, 1988-. Writer. **Publications:** Doctor Spock: Biography of a Conservative Radical, 1972; (co-author) The New Assertive Woman, 1975, rev. ed., 2000; (co-author) American Autobiography: A Bibliography, 1945-1980, 1982; Strategic Writing, 1983; Fact and Artifact: Writing Non-Fiction, 1985, 2nd ed., 1994; Composition Studies as a Creative Art: Teaching, Writing, Scholarship, Administration, 1998; The Seven Deadly Virtues and Other Lively Essays, 2008; Writers Without Borders: Writing and Teaching Writing in Troubled Times, 2008. EDITOR: Forbidden Diary, 1980, rev. ed., 2001; The Essay Connection, 1984, 10th ed., 2013; The Lexington Reader, 1987; Forbidden Family, 1989, rev. ed., 1998. CO-EDITOR: Bear, Man and God: 7 Approaches to Faulkner's The Bear, 1964; (and comp.) Symposium, 1969; Symposium on Love, 1970; Bear, Man and God: 8 Approaches to Faulkner's The Bear, 1971; Inquiry, 1993, rev. ed., 2004; Composition in the 21st Century: Crisis and Change, 1996; The St. Martin's Custom Reader, 2001; The Arlington Reader, 2003, 3rd ed., 2011; Composition Studies in the New Millennium: Rereading the Past, Rewriting the Future, 2004; The Arlington Shorter Reader, 2004. Contributor to books and periodicals. **Address:** Department of English, University of Connecticut, PO Box 4025, Storrs Mansfield, CT 06269-4025, U.S.A. **Online address:** lynn.bloom@uconn.edu

BLOOM, Miriam. American (born United States), b. 1934. **Genres:** Biology, Medicine/Health, Sciences, Young Adult Non-fiction. **Career:** University of Utah, assistant research professor of biology, 1973-74; University of South Florida, biology research associate, 1974-75; Hillsborough Community College, adjunct professor of biology, 1975-77; Georgetown University, U.S. Public Health service research fellow, 1977-79; U.S. Consumer Product Safety Commission, geneticist, 1979-88; SciWrite, president, 1989-; Hinds Community College, instructor, 1991; University Press of Mississippi, series editor, 1995-; Journal of the National Cancer Institute, senior editor. **Publications:** Understanding Sickle Cell Disease, 1995. Contributor to books and magazines. **Address:** SciWrite, 4433 Wedgewood St., Jackson, MS 39211-6219, U.S.A.

BLOOM, Paul. American/Canadian (born Canada), b. 1963. **Genres:** Language/Linguistics. **Career:** University of Arizona, Department of Psychology, assistant professor, 1990-96, associate professor, 1996-99; University College London, Cognitive Development Unit, visiting professor, 1997-98; Yale University, Department of Psychology, professor, 1999-2011, Brooks and Suzanne Ragen professor of psychology and cognitive science, 2011-. Writer. **Publications:** (Ed.) Language Acquisition: Core Readings, 1994; (co-ed.) Language and Space, 1996; (ed. with R. Jackendoff and K. Wynn) Language, Logic, and Concepts: Essays in Memory of John Macnamara, 1999; How Children Learn the Meanings of Words, 2000; Descartes' Baby: How the Science of Child Development Explains What Makes Us Human, 2004; (contrib.) Belief & Doubt, 2006; How Pleasure Works, 2010; (with S.J. Shettleworth and L. Nadel) Fundamentals of Comparative Cognition, 2013; Just Babies, forthcoming. Contributor of articles to periodicals. **Address:** Department of Psychology, Yale University, 202 Strathcona Hall, PO Box 208205, New Haven, CT 06520-8205, U.S.A. **Online address:** paul.bloom@yale.edu

BLOOM, Rebecca (S.). American (born United States), b. 1975. **Genres:** Novels, Young Adult Fiction. **Career:** Speckles by Rebecca Bloom (jewelry and fashion design company), owner, 2001-; Los Angeles Confidential magazine, author and editor. **Publications:** Girl Anatomy (novel), 2002; Tangled up in Daydreams (novel), 2003; Have I Got a Guy for You, 2008. Contributor to periodicals. **Address:** c/o Jan Miller, Dupree/Miller, 100 Highland

Park Village, Ste. 350, Dallas, TX 75205-2722, U.S.A. **Online address:** rebecca@rebeccabloom.com

BLOOM, Steven. American/German (born Germany), b. 1942. **Genres:** Novels, Young Adult Fiction. **Career:** University of Heidelberg, part-time teacher, 1992-, professor of English, lecturer in American studies; New York University, part-time teacher; Fordham University, part-time teacher; University of Maryland's European Division, part-time teacher. Writer. **Publications:** No New Jokes (novel), 1997; Immer Dieselben Witze, 2000; Offene Ehe und Anderer New York (short stories), 2004; Stellt mir eine Frage, 2009. contributor to periodicals. **Address:** Bogenstrasse 5, Heidelberg, 69124, Germany. **Online address:** gloomof@aol.com

BLOOMFIELD, Lincoln P(almer). American (born United States), b. 1920. **Genres:** International Relations/Current Affairs, History. **Career:** Massachusetts Institute of Technology, professor of political science, professor emeritus of political science, 1963-. Writer. **Publications:** Evolution or Revolution?, 1957; The United Nations and U.S. Foreign Policy, 1960, rev. ed., 1967; (co-author and ed.) Outer Space: Prospects for Man and Society, 1962, rev. ed., 1968; International Military Forces, 1964, (co-author) rev. ed. as The Power to Keep Peace, 1971; (co-author) Khrushchev and the Arms Race, 1966; (with A.C. Leiss) Controlling Small Wars, 1967; In Search of American Foreign Policy, 1974; What Future for the U.N.?, 1977; The Foreign Policy Process, 1982; (ed. with H. Cleveland) Prospects for Peacemaking, 1987; (ed.) The Management of Global Disorder, 1987; Managing International Conflict, 1997; Accidental Encounters with History, 2005. **Address:** Department of Political Science, Massachusetts Institute of Technology, Rm. E53-371, 77 Massachusetts Ave., Cambridge, MA 02139, U.S.A. **Online address:** linc37@aol.com

BLOOMFIELD, Louis A(ub). American (born United States), b. 1956. **Genres:** Physics, Sciences. **Career:** American Telephone and Telegraph Bell Laboratories, technical staff, 1983-85; Stanford University, postdoctoral research associate, 1983; University of Virginia, assistant professor, 1985-91, associate professor, 1991-96, professor of physics, 1996-. **Publications:** How Things Work: The Physics of Everyday Life, 1997, 4th ed., 2008; How Everything Works: Making Physics Out of the Ordinary, 2007. **Address:** Department of Physics, University of Virginia, 382 McCormick Rd., 133 Physics Bldg., PO Box 400714, Charlottesville, VA 22904-4714, U.S.A. **Online address:** lab3e@virginia.edu

BLOOR, Edward (William). American (born United States), b. 1950. **Genres:** Young Adult Fiction, Plays/Screenplays, Novellas/Short Stories. **Career:** Teacher, 1983-86; Harcourt Brace School Publishers (now HMH), senior editor, 1986-. **Publications:** Tangerine, 1997; Crusader, 1999; Story Time, 2004; London Calling, 2005; Taken, 2007; Memory Lane, 2010; A PLague Year, 2011. **Address:** 12021 Windstone St., Winter Garden, FL 34787, U.S.A. **Online address:** ebloor@edwardbloor.net

BLOS, Joan W. American (born United States), b. 1928. **Genres:** Children's Fiction, Children's Non-fiction, Novels, Biography, Education, Young Adult Fiction, Novellas/Short Stories. **Career:** Jewish Board of Guardians, research assistant, 1949-50; City College, teaching assistant, 1950-51; Yale University, Child Study Center, research assistant, 1951-53; Bank Street College of Education, editor and instructor, 1958-70; University of Michigan, Medical Center, research assistant, 1970-72, lecturer in education, 1972-80. **Publications:** In the City, 1964; (with B. Miles) People Read, 1964; (with B. Miles) Joe Finds a Way, 1967; It's Spring, She Said, 1967; (with B. Miles) Just Think!, 1971; A Gathering of Days: A New England Girl's Journal, 1830-32: A Novel, 1979, 2nd ed., 1990; Martin's Hats, 1984; Brothers of the Heart: A Story of the Old Northwest, 1837-1838, 1985; Old Henry, 1987; Lottie's Circus, 1989; The Grandpa Days, 1989; One Very Best Valentine's Day, 1989; The Heroine of the Titanic: A Tale Both True and Otherwise of the Life of Molly Brown, 1991; A Seed, a Flower, a Minute, an Hour, 1992; Brooklyn Doesn't Rhyme, 1994; The Hungry Little Boy, 1995; Nellie Bly's Monkey: His Remarkable Story in His Own Words, 1996; Bedtime!, 1998; Hello, Shoes!, 1999; Letters from the Corrugated Castle: A Novel of Gold Rush California, 1850-1852, 2007. Contributor of articles to periodicals. **Address:** Curtis Brown Ltd., 10 Astor Pl., New York, NY 10003-6935, U.S.A.

BLOSSER, Susan Sokol. American (born United States), b. 1944. **Genres:** Food And Wine, History, Autobiography/Memoirs. **Career:** Sokol Blosser Vineyard, co-founder, 1971, president, 1991-2008. Writer. **Publications:** (With C.N. Wilson, Jr.) The Southern Historical Collection: A Guide to Manuscripts, 1970; At Home in the Vineyard: Cultivating a Winery, an Industry, and a Life, 2006. **Address:** Sokol Blosser Winery, 5000 Sokol Blosser Ln., PO Box 399, Dundee, OR 97115-0399, U.S.A. **Online address:** info@sokolblosser.com

BLOSSFELD, Hans Peter. German (born Germany), b. 1954. **Genres:** Mathematics/Statistics, Sociology. **Career:** University of Mannheim, research scientist, 1980-84; Max Planck Institute for Human Development and Education, senior research scientist, 1984-89; European University Institute, professor of political and social sciences, 1989-92, external professor, 1992-95; University of Bremen, professor of sociology and social statistics, 1992-98; University of Bielefeld, professor of sociology and department chair, 1998-2000; Fakultät Sozial und Wirtschaftwissenschaften, staff; Bamberg University, chair of sociology, 2001-, professor of sociology, 2002-, State Institute for Family Research, director, 2003-; Institute of Longitudinal Studies in Education, director; National Educational Panel Study, principal investigator; Netherlands Institute for the Advanced Study in the Humanities and Social Sciences, research fellow; European Sociological Review, editor-in-chief. **Publications:** Bildungsexpansion und Berufschancen: Empirische Analysen zur Lage der Berufsanfänger in der Bundesrepublik, 1985; (with A. Hamerle and K.U. Mayer) Ereignisanalyse: Statistische Theorie und Anwendung in den Wirtschafts und Sozialwissenschaften, 1986; Kohortendifferenzierung und Karriereprozess: Eine Längsschnittstudie über die Veränderungder Bildungs-und Berufschancen im Lebenslauf, 1989; (co-author) Lebensverläufe und Wohlfahrtsentwicklung: Konzeption, Design und Methodik der Erhebung von Lebensverläufen der Geburtsjahrgänge, 1929-1931, 1939-1941, 1949-1951, 1989; (with A. Hamerle and K.U. Mayer) Event History Analysis: Statistical Theory and Application in the Social Sciences, 1989; Ökonomie und Politik beruflicher Bildung: europäische Entwicklungen, 1992; Bildung, Bildungsfinanzierung und Einkommensverteilung, 1993; (ed. with Y. Shavit and contrib.) Persistent Inequality: Changing Educational Attainment in Thirteen Countries, 1993; (with G. Rohwer) Techniques of Event History Modeling: New Approaches to Causal Analysis, 1995, 2nd ed., 2002; (ed.) The New Role of Women: Family Formation in Modern Societies, 1995; (ed. with C. Hakim) Between Equalization and Marginalization: Womens Part-Time Work in Europe and the United States of America, 1997; (ed. with G. Prein and contrib.) Rational Choice Theory and Large-Scale Data Analysis, 1997; (with R. Stockmann) Globalization and Changes in Vocational Training Systems in Developing and Advanced Industrialized Societies, 1999; (ed. with S. Drobnič) Careers of Couples in Contemporary Societies: From Male Breadwinner to Dual-Earner Families, 2001; (ed. with A. Timm) Who Marries Whom?: Educational Systems as Marriage Markets in Modern Societies, 2003; (ed. with K. Kurz) Home Ownership and Social Inequality in Comparative Perspective, 2004; (ed.) Globalization, Uncertainty and Youth in Society, 2005; (ed. with M. Mills and F. Bernardi) Globalization, Uncertainty and Mens Careers: An International Comparison, 2006; (ed. with S. Buchholz and D. Hofacker) Globalization, Uncertainty and Late Careers in Society, 2006; (ed. with H. Hofmeister) Globalization, Uncertainty and Womens Careers: An International Comparison, 2006; (ed.) Young Workers, Globalization and the Labor Market: Comparing Early Working Life in Eleven Countries, 2008. Contributor to journals and books. **Address:** Lehrstuhl für Soziologie I, Otto-Friedrich-Universität Bamberg, Lichtenhaidestrasse 11, PO Box 1549, Bamberg, D-96045, Germany. **Online address:** soziologie1@sowi.uni-bamberg.de

BLOUET, Olwyn M(ary). American/British (born England), b. 1948. **Genres:** International Relations/Current Affairs, History, Humanities. **Career:** University of Nebraska, administrative assistant, 1977, Division of Continuing Studies, faculty, 1978-80, visiting assistant professor of history, 1979-80, 1981-83; Doane College, visiting assistant professor of history, 1977-79; Texas A&M University, visiting assistant professor of history, 1983-89; College of William and Mary, visiting assistant professor of history, 1990-91; Virginia State University, professor of history, 1992-. Writer. **Publications:** The Contemporary Caribbean: History, Life and Culture since 1945, 2007. EDITOR: (with B.W. Blouet) Latin America: An Introductory Survey, 1982; (with B.W. Blouet) Latin America and the Caribbean: A Systematic and Regional Survey, 1993, 5th ed., 2006. Contributor of articles to periodicals. **Address:** Department of History, Virginia State University, Colson Hall, Rm. 101F, PO Box 9070, Petersburg, VA 23806, U.S.A. **Online address:** oblouet@vsu.edu

BLOUIN, Lenora P. American (born United States), b. 1941. **Genres:** Librarianship, Literary Criticism And History. **Career:** San Jose Public Library, reference librarian, 1976-86, senior librarian and head of reference department, 1986-96; writer and bibliographer, 1978-. **Publications:** May Sarton: A Bibliography, 1978, 2nd ed., 2000. Contributor to books and periodicals. **Address:** 1484 Pompey Dr., San Jose, CA 95128, U.S.A. **Online address:** lpblouin@earthlink.net

BLOUNT, Brian K. American (born United States), b. 1955. **Genres:** Adult Non-fiction, Theology/Religion, Cultural/Ethnic Topics. **Career:** Ordained Presbyterian minister; Carver Presbyterian Church, pastor, 1982-88; Emory University, Woodruff fellow, 1988; Princeton Theological Seminary, Richard J. Dearborn professor of New Testament, 1992-2007; Union Presbyterian Seminary, president, 2007-, Walter W. Moore and Charles E. S. Kraemer presidential chairs, professor of New Testament, 2007-. Writer and theologian. **Publications:** Cultural Interpretation: Reorienting New Testament Criticism, 1995; Go Preach!: Mark's Kingdom Message and the Black Church Today, 1998; (ed. with L.T. Tisdale) Making Room at the Table: An Invitation to Multicultural Worship, 2000; Then the Whisper Put on Flesh: New Testament Ethics in an African American Context, 2001; (with G.W. Charles) Preaching Mark in Two Voices, 2002; (with W. Brueggemann and W.C. Placher) Struggling with Scripture, 2002; Can I Get a Witness?: Reading Revelation through African American Culture, 2005; (co-ed.) True to Our Native Land: An African American New Testament Commentary, 2007; Revelation: A Commentary, 2009. Contributor to periodicals. **Address:** Union Presbyterian Seminary, Watts Hall, 3401 Brook Rd., Richmond, VA 23227, U.S.A. **Online address:** bblount@upsem.edu

BLOUNT, Roy (Alton). American (born United States), b. 1941. **Genres:** Novels, Poetry, Sports/Fitness, Humor/Satire, Young Adult Fiction, Young Adult Non-fiction, Literary Criticism And History, Photography, Photography. **Career:** Decatur-DeKalb News, reporter and sports columnist, 1958-59; Morning Telegraph, reporter, 1961; New Orleans Times-Picayune, reporter, 1963; Atlanta Journal, reporter, editorial writer and columnist, 1966-68; Georgia State College, instructor, 1967-67; Sports Illustrated, staff writer, 1968-74, associate editor, 1974-75; freelance writer, 1975-; The Atlantic, contributing editor, 1979; Men's Journal, contributing editor, 1993. **Publications:** About Three Bricks Shy of a Load; A Highly Irregular Lowdown on the Year the Pittsburgh Steelers were Super But Missed the Bowl, 1974, rev. ed. as About Three Bricks Shy and the Load Filled Up: The Story of the Greatest Football Team Ever, 1989; Crackers: This Whole Many-Sided Thing of Jimmy, More Carters, Ominous Little Animals, Sad-Singing Women, My Daddy and Me (humor), 1980; One Fell Soup, or, I'm Just a Bug on the Windshield of Life (humor), 1982; The Best of Modern Humor, 1983; What Men Don't Tell Women (humor), 1984; Not Exactly What I Had in Mind (humor), 1985; It Grows on You: A Hair-Raising Survey of Human Plumage (semiotics), 1986; Soupsongs/Webster's Ark (poetry), 1987; Laughing Matters, 1987; (contrib.) The Norton Book of Light Verse, 1987; (contrib.) The Baseball Hall of Fame 50th Anniversary Book, 1988; Now, Where Were We? (humor), 1988; First Hubby (novel), 1990; Camels Are Easy, Comedy Is Hard (humor), 1991; (ed.) Roy Blount's Book of Southern Humor, 1994; (with D. Marsh, K.K. Glodmark and G. Shields) The Great Rock 'n' Roll Joke Book, 1997; If Only You Knew How Much I Smell You: True Portraits of Dogs, 1998; (intro.) The Wit & Wisdom of the Founding Fathers: Benjamin Franklin, George Washington, John Adams, Thomas Jefferson, 1998; Be Sweet: A Conditional Love Story, 1998; (intro.) Mark Twain's Library of Humor, 2000; I Am Puppy, Hear Me Yap: Ages of a Dog, 2000; (with W. Iooss) Gladiators: 40 Years of Football Photographs, 2000; Am I Pig Enough for You Yet?: Voices of the Barnyard, 2001; Robert E. Lee: A Penguin Life, 2003; I Am the Cat, Don't Forget That: Feline Expressions, 2004; Feet on the Street: Rambles around New Orleans, 2005; Long Time Leaving: Dispatches from Up South, 2007; Alphabet Juice: The Energies, Gists, and Spirits of Letters, Words, and Combinations thereof: Their Roots, Bones, Innards, Piths, Pips, and Secret Parts, Tinctures, Tonics, and Essences, with Examples of Their Usage Foul and Savory, 2008; (ed. with M. Twain) A Tramp Abroad, Following the Equator, Other Travels, 2010; Hail, Hail, Euphoria!: Presenting the Marx Brothers in Duck Soup, the Greatest War Movie Ever Made, 2010; Alphabetter Juice or the Joy of Text, 2011. Contributor of articles to periodicals. **Address:** c/o Esther Newberg, International Creative Management, 730 5th Ave., New York, NY 10019, U.S.A.

BLOXHAM, Donald. Scottish (born Scotland) **Genres:** History, Social Sciences. **Career:** Holocaust Educational Trust, research director; University of Edinburgh, lecturer, 2002-06, reader, 2006-07, professor, 2007-. United States Holocaust Memorial Museum, J.B. and Maurice C. Shapiro Senior Scholar-in-Residence, 2007-08. Author, editor, genocide scholar and professor. **Publications:** Genocide on Trial: War Crimes Trials and the Formation of Holocaust History and Memory, 2001; (ed. with B. Flanagan) Remembering Belsen: Eyewitnesses Record the Liberation, 2005; The Great Game of Genocide: Imperialism, Nationalism and the Destruction of the Ottoman Armenians, 2005; (with T. Kushner) The Holocaust: Critical Historical Approaches, 2005; Genocide, the World Wars and the Unweaving of Europe, 2008. Contributor to books. **Address:** School of History, Classics & Archaeology, University of Edinburgh, William Robertson Bldg., 50 George Sq., Edinburgh, CN EH8 9JY, Scotland. **Online address:** donald.bloxham@ed.ac.uk

BLUEMEL, Kristin. American (born United States), b. 1964. **Genres:** Literary Criticism And History, Politics/Government. **Career:** Wesleyan University, teaching assistant, 1985; Rutgers University, Rutgers College, teaching assistant, 1991-94, Douglass College, teaching assistant, 1991-94; Monmouth University, assistant professor of English, 1994-2000, associate professor of English, 2000-07, professor of English, 2007-. Writer. **Publications:** Experimenting on the Borders of Modernism: Dorothy Richardson's Pilgrimage, 1997; George Orwell and the Radical Eccentrics: Intermodernism in Literary London, 2004; (ed.) Intermodernism: Literary Culture in Mid-Twentieth-Century Britain, 2009. **Address:** Department of English, Monmouth University, Wilson Annex 509, West Long Branch, NJ 07764, U.S.A. **Online address:** kbluemel@monmouth.edu

BLUESTEIN, Eleanor. American (born United States), b. 1941. **Genres:** Novellas/Short Stories. **Career:** Crawl Out Your Window, co-editor; Harcourt, editor; Curriculum Concepts, editor. **Publications:** Tea & Other Ayama Na Tales: Stories, 2008. Contributor to periodicals. **Address:** La Jolla, CA , U.S.A. **Online address:** elblue@gmail.com

BLUM, Bruce I(van). American (born United States), b. 1931. **Genres:** Information Science/Computers, Medicine/Health. **Career:** Fairleigh Dickinson University, instructor in history and social science, 1955-60; Johns Hopkins University, Applied Physics Laboratory, senior staff mathematician, 1962-67; National Space Science Data Center, systems analyst and deputy project director, 1967-69, manager of information systems department, project director for Earth Resources Technology Satellite, 1969-70; Wolf Research and Development Corp., vice-president, manager of information systems department, 1970-73; TRW Systems, senior systems engineer, assistant manager of fleet command support center program, 1973-74; Johns Hopkins University, School of Medicine, senior staff mathematician with applied physics laboratory, 1974-79, assistant professor, 1975-83, assistant professor of oncology, associate professor of biomedical engineering, 1983-94; Beijing Medical University, visiting professor, 1988. Writer. **Publications:** Clinical Information Systems, 1986; TEDIUM and the Software Process, 1990; Software Engineering: A Holistic View, 1992; Beyond Programming to a New Era of Design, 1996. EDITOR: Proceedings: Sixth Annual Symposium on Computer Applications in Medical Care, 1982; Information Systems for Patient Care, 1984; (with R. Salamon and M. Jorgensen) MED INFO-86, 2 vols., 1986; ACM Conference on the History of Medical Informatics, 1987; (with H.F. Orthner) Implementing Health Care Information Systems, 1989; (with J.P. Enterline and R.E. Lenhard) A Clinical Information System for Oncology, 1989; (with K. Duncan) A History of Medical Informatics, 1990; (with T. Timmers) Software Engineering in Medical Informatics, 1991. Contributor of articles to journals. **Address:** Oxford University Press, 198 Madison Ave., New York, NY 10016, U.S.A. **Online address:** biblum@verizon.net

BLUM, Deborah (Leigh). American (born United States), b. 1954. **Genres:** Adult Non-fiction, Social Sciences, Biography, Autobiography/Memoirs. **Career:** The Times, general assignment reporter, 1976-77; The Macon Telegraph, general assignment reporter, 1977-79; The St. Petersburg Times, general assignment reporter, 1979-81; The Fresno Bee, science writer, 1982-84; The Sacramento Bee, science writer, 1984-97; University of Wisconsin-Madison, professor of journalism, 1997-. Journalist and nonfiction writer. **Publications:** Bad Karma: A True Story of Obsession and Murder, 1986; The Monkey Wars, 1994; (ed. with M. Knudson) Field Guide for Science Writers: The Official Guide of the National Association of Science Writers, 1997, (ed. with M. Knudson and R.M. Henig), 2nd ed., 2006; Sex on the Brain: The Biological Differences Between Men and Women, 1997; Love at Goon Park: Harry Harlow and the Science of Affection, 2002; Ghost Hunters: William James and the Search for Scientific Proof of Life After Death, 2006; Poisoner's Handbook: Murder and the Birth of Forensic Medicine in Jazz Age

New York, 2010. **Address:** School of Journalism & Mass Communication, University of Wisconsin, 5154 Vilas Hall, 821 University Ave., Madison, WI 53706, U.S.A. **Online address:** dblum@wisc.edu

BLUM, Edward J. American (born United States), b. 1977. **Genres:** History, Humanities, Race Relations, Intellectual History, Literary Criticism And History, Adult Non-fiction. **Career:** Kean University, assistant professor of history, 2006-07; University of Notre Dame, W.E.B. Du Bois Center for the Advanced Study of Race and Religion, fellow; San Diego State University, assistant professor, associate professor of history, 2007-; Lilly Foundation, consultant. Writer. **Publications:** (Ed. with W.S. Poole) Vale of Tears: New Essays in Religion and Reconstruction, 2005; Reforging the White Republic: Race, Religion and American Nationalism, 1865-1898, 2005; W.E.B. DuBois, American Prophet, 2007; (ed. with J.R. Young) The Souls of W.E.B. DuBois: New Essays and Reflections, 2009; (ed. with P. Harvey) Columbia Guide to Religion in American History, forthcoming; Jesus Christ in Red, White, and Black, forthcoming. **Address:** Department of History, San Diego State University, 5500 Campanile Dr., San Diego, CA 92182, U.S.A. **Online address:** eblum@mail.sdsu.edu

BLUM, Howard. American (born United States), b. 1948. **Genres:** Novels, Adult Non-fiction, Mystery/Crime/Suspense, Biography. **Career:** New York Times, reporter, 1986; Village Voice, journalist; Vanity Fair, contributing editor, 1994-. **Publications:** Wanted!: The Search for Nazis in America, 1977; Wishful Thinking (novel), 1985; I Pledge Allegiance: The True Story of the Walkers: An American Spy Family, 1987; Out There: The Government's Secret Quest for Extraterrestrials, 1990; Gangland: How the FBI Broke the Mob, 1993; The Gold of Exodus: The Discovery of the True Mount Sinai, 1998; Brigade: An Epic Story of Vengeance, Salvation and World War II, 2001; Eve of Destruction: The Untold Story of the Yom Kippur War, 2003; American Lightning: Terror, Mystery, Movie-Making and the Crime of the Century, 2008; Floor of Heaven: A True Tale of the American West and the Yukon Gold Rush, 2010. Contributor to periodicals. **Address:** c/o Lynn Nesbit, Janklow & Nesbit Associates, 445 Park Ave., Fl. 13, New York, NY 10022-2606, U.S.A.

BLUM, Kristen Raub. American (born United States), b. 1967. **Genres:** Travel/Exploration, Young Adult Non-fiction, Regional/Urban Planning, Reference. **Career:** Wanderlust Publishing, editor and publisher, 1997-; Rezworks, editor, 1999-. Educator. **Publications:** The Greater Evergreen Area Guide: Including the Communities, Bailey, Conifer, Evergreen, Genesee, Indian Hills, Kittredge, Lookout Mountain, Morrison and Pine, 1999; Last Night I Slept with a Gecko in My Room, forthcoming. **Address:** 4213 2nd Ave. NE, Seattle, WA 98105-6509, U.S.A.

BLUM, Lenore (Carol). American (born United States), b. 1942. **Genres:** Mathematics/Statistics. **Career:** Air Force Office of Science and Research, fellow, 1968-69; University of California, lecturer in mathematics, 1969-71, adjunct professor of computer science, 1989-, postdoctoral fellow, Mathematical Sciences Research Institute, deputy director, 1992-96; Mills College, research associate in mathematics, 1973-77, Department of Mathematics and Computer Science, founder, 1974, chair, 1974-86, associate professor of mathematics, 1977-, Letts-Villard chair of mathematics and computer science, 1978-, Letts-Villard professor, 1978-88; International Computer Science Institute, Theory Group, research scientist, 1988-; City University of Hong Kong, visiting professor, 1996-98; Carnegie Mellon University, distinguished career professor of computer science, 1999-. Writer. **Publications:** (With S. Smale and M. Shub) Complexity and Real Computation, 1997. Contributor to journals. **Address:** Department of Computer Science, School of Computer Science, Carnegie Mellon University, Wean 4105, Pittsburgh, PA 15213-3891, U.S.A. **Online address:** lblum@cs.cmu.edu

BLUM, Louise A(gnes). (Louise A(gnes) Sullivan-Blum). American (born United States), b. 1960?. **Genres:** Gay And Lesbian Issues, Novels, Biography. **Career:** University of Iowa, teaching assistant and instructor of creative writing, 1987-88; University of Nebraska, assistant professor of creative writing, 1988-89; Mansfield University, associate professor of English, 1989-. Writer. **Publications:** Good Girls, 1993; Amnesty (novel), 1995; You're Not from around Here, Are You?, A Lesbian in Smalltown America (memoir), 2001. Works appear in anthologies. Contributor to journals. **Address:** Department of English and Modern Languages, Mansfield University, 207B Belknap Hall, Mansfield, PA 16933, U.S.A. **Online address:** lblum@mnsfld.edu

BLUMBERG, Phillip Irvin. American (born United States), b. 1919. **Genres:** Law, Social Sciences, Reference. **Career:** Szold, Brandwen, Meyers & Blumberg, partner, 1949-66; Boston University School of Law, professor of law, 1968-74; University of Connecticut, School of Law, professor of law and business, 1974-89, dean, 1974-84, emeritus professor, emeritus dean, 1989-; Federated Development Co. (formerly Federated Mortgage Investors), president. Writer. **Publications:** Corporate Responsibility in a Changing Society, 1972; The Megacorporation in American Society: The Scope of Corporate Power, 1975; The Multinational Challenge to Corporation Law: The Search for a New Corporate Personality, 1993. THE LAW OF CORPORATE GROUPS: Procedural Problems in the Law of Parent and Subsidiary Corporations, 1983; Problems in the Bankruptcy or Reorganization of Parent and Subsidiary Corporations, Including the Law of Corporate Guaranties, 1985; Tort, Contract and Other Common Law Problems in the Substantive Law of Parent and Subsidiary Corporations, 1987; Substantive Common Law, 1987; Problems of Parent and Subsidiary Corporations Under Statutory Law of General Application, 1989; General Statutory Law, 1989; Specific Statutory Law, 1992; (with K.A. Strasser) Problems of Parent and Subsidiary Corporations Under Statutory Law Specifically Applying Enterprise Principles, 1992; The Multinational Challenge To Corporation Law: The Search for a New Corporate Personality, 1993; State Statutory Law, 1995; (with K.A. Strasser) Problems of Parent and Subsidiary Corporations Under State Statutory Law, 1995; (with K.A. Strasser) Enterprise Liability in Commercial Relationships: Including Franchising, Licensing, Health Care Enterprises, Successor Liability, Lender Liability and Inherent Agency, 1998; (co-author) The Law of Corporate Groups: Jurisdiction, Practice and Procedure, 2007; Repressive Jurisprudence in the Early American Republic: The First Amendment and the Legacy of English Law, 2010. Contributor to journals. **Address:** University of Connecticut School of Law, Hosmer Hall 130, 45 Elizabeth St., Hartford, CT 06105-2290, U.S.A. **Online address:** pblumber@law.uconn.edu

BLUMBERG, Rhoda. American (born United States), b. 1917. **Genres:** Children's Non-fiction, Biography, Travel/Exploration. **Career:** CBS Radio, writer and researcher, 1940-44; NBC Radio, talent scout, 1945-46; Simon & Schuster, executive editor, 1973-74. **Publications:** Simon & Schuster Travel Guides, 1974; Sharks, 1976; Fire Fighters, 1976; UFO, 1977; First Ladies, 1977; Famine, 1978; Backyard Bestiary, 1978; Witches, 1979; The Truth about Dragons, 1980; The First Travel Guide to the Moon: What to Pack, How to Go, and What to See When You Get There, 1980; More Freaky Facts, 1981; Southern Africa: South Africa, Namibia, Swaziland, Lesotho, and Botswana, 1981; Devils & Demons, 1982; (with L. Blumberg) Dictionary of Misinformation, 1982; First Travel Guide to the Bottom of the Sea, 1983; Monsters, 1983; (with L. Blumberg) The Simon and Schuster Book of Facts and Fallacies, 1983; Commodore Perry in the Land of the Shogun, 1985; (with L. Blumberg) Lovebirds, Lizards, and Llamas: Strange and Exotic Pets, 1986; The Incredible Journey of Lewis and Clark, 1987; The Great American Gold Rush, 1989; The Remarkable Voyages of Captain Cook, 1991; Jumbo, 1992; Bloomers!, 1993; Full Steam Ahead: The Race to Build a Transcontinental Railroad, 1996; What's the Deal?: Jefferson, Napoleon, and the Louisiana Purchase, 1998; Shipwrecked!: The True Adventures of a Japanese Boy, 2001; York's Adventures with Lewis and Clark: An African-American's Part in the Great Expedition, 2004. **Address:** 1 Rockefeller Plz., New York, NY 10020-2003, U.S.A.

BLUME, Harvey. American (born United States), b. 1946. **Genres:** Cultural/Ethnic Topics, Sciences, Autobiography/Memoirs. **Career:** Literary critic and writer. **Publications:** (With P.V. Bradford) OTA Benga: The Pygmy in the Zoo, 1992. Contributor to periodicals. **Address:** 1267 Cambridge St., Cambridge, MA 02139, U.S.A. **Online address:** hblume@globe.com

BLUME, Judy. American (born United States), b. 1938. **Genres:** Novels, Children's Fiction, Young Adult Fiction, Human Relations/Parenting, Literary Criticism And History, Humor/Satire, Social Commentary. **Career:** Kids fund, founder, 1981. Writer. **Publications:** CHILDREN'S FICTION: The One in the Middle Is the Green Kangaroo, 1969, rev. ed., 1991; Iggie's House, 1970; Freckle Juice, 1971, rev. ed., 2004; Then Again, Maybe I Won't, 1971; Tales of a Fourth Grade Nothing, 1972; It's Not the End of the World, 1972; Otherwise Known as Sheila the Great, 1972; Deenie, 1973; Blubber, 1974, 2nd ed., 2005; Starring Sally J. Freedman as Herself, 1977; Superfudge, 1980; Judy Blume Diary, 1981; La ballena, 1983; The Pain and the Great One, 1984; Just as Long as We're Together, 1987; Fudge-a-Mania, 1990, rev. ed., 2003; Are You There God? It's Me, Margaret, 1990; Here's to You, Rachel Robinson, 1993; Double Fudge, 2002; A Judy Blume Collection: Three Novels by

Best-selling Author Judy Blume, 2003; Going, Going, Gone, 2009. YOUNG ADULT FICTION: Forever..., 1975; Tiger Eyes, 1981. ADULT FICTION: Wifey, 1978; Smart Women, 1984, rev. ed., 2004; Summer Sisters, 1998. OTHERS: Letters to Judy: What Kids Wish They Could Tell You (nonfiction), 1986; The Judy Blume Memory Book, 1988; (ed.) Places I Never Meant to Be: Original Stories by Censored Writers, 1999; (co-author) Author Talk: Conversations with Judy Blume, 2000; Soupy Saturdays with The Pain and The Great One, 2007; BFF: Best Friends Forever: Two Novels, 2007; Cool Zone with the Pain & the Great One, 2008; Going, Going, Gone! With the Pain and the Great One, 2008; Friend or Fiend? With the Pain and the Great One, 2009. **Address:** c/o Suzzane Gluck, William Morris Agency Inc., 1325 Ave. of the Americas, New York, NY 10019-6026, U.S.A. **Online address:** judyb@judyblume.com

BLUMENFELD, Robert. American (born United States), b. 1943. **Genres:** Film, Area Studies. **Career:** Dialect coach, actor and writer. **Publications:** Accents: A Manual for Actors, 1998, rev. ed., 2002; (ed.) Acting with the Voice: The Art of Recording Books, 2004; Tools and Techniques for Character Interpretation: A Handbook of Psychology for Actors, Writers, and Directors, 2006; (with A. Spivak) How to Rehearse When There is No Rehearsal: Acting and the Media, 2007; Blumenfeld's Dictionary of Acting and Show Business, 2009; Blumenfeld's Dictionary of Musical Theater: Opera, Operetta, Musical Comedy, 2010; Stagecraft: Stanislavsky and External Acting Techniques, 2011. **Address:** 321 W 105th St., New York, NY 10025-3400, U.S.A. **Online address:** rblume8300@aol.com

BLUMENFELD-KOSINSKI, Renate. American (born United States), b. 1952. **Genres:** Novels. **Career:** University of Pittsburgh, departments of Romance languages and Germanic language, lecturer, 1980-81, associate professor, 1994-98, professor, 1998-, director of the Medieval & Renaissance Studies Program, 1996-2003, director of graduate studies, 2002-; Columbia University, Mellon Fellow & lecturer in the Society of Fellows in the Humanities, 1981-83, assistant professor, 1983-89, associate professor, 1989-93. Scholar, educator, writer and editor. **Publications:** Not of Woman Born: Representations of Caesarean Birth in Medieval and Renaissance Culture, 1990; (ed. with T. Szell) Images of Sainthood in Medieval Europe, 1991; (ed.) The Selected Writings of Christine de Pizan: New Translations, Criticism, 1997; Reading Myth: Classical Mythology and Its Interpretations in Medieval French Literature, 1997; (ed. with K. Brownlee, M. Speer and L. Walters) Translatio Studii: Essays by His Students in Honor of Karl D. Uitti for His Sixty-fifth Birthday, 2000; (ed. with L. von Flotow and D. Russell) The Politics of Translation in the Middle Ages and the Renaissance, 2001; (ed. with D. Robertson and N.B. Warren) The Vernacular Spirit: Essays on Medieval Religious Literature, 2002; Poets, Saints and Visionaries of the Great Schism, 1378-1417, 2006. Contributor to books. **Address:** Department of French & Italian, University of Pittsburgh, 1328 Cathedral of Learning, Pittsburgh, PA 15260, U.S.A. **Online address:** renate@pitt.edu

BLUMHOFER, Edith L. Also writes as Edith Waldvogel Blumhofer, Edith Waldvogel Blumhofer. American (born United States), b. 1950. **Genres:** Theology/Religion, Music. **Career:** Wheaton College, professor of history, Institute for the Study of American Evangelicals (ISAE), project director, 1987-95, 1999-. Writer. **Publications:** (As Edith Waldvogel Blumhofer) The Assemblies of God: A Popular History, 1985; The Assemblies of God: A Chapter in the Story of American Pentecostalism, 1989; Pentecost in My Soul: Explorations in the Meaning of Pentecostal Experience in the Assemblies of God, 1989; (with J.A. Carpenter) Twentieth-Century Evangelicalism: A Guide to the Sources, 1990; Aimee Semple McPherson: Everybody's Sister, 1993; (ed. with R. Balmer) Modern Christian Revivals, 1993; Restoring the Faith: The Assemblies of God Pentecostalism and American Culture, 1993; (ed. with R.P. Spittler and G.A. Wacker) Pentecostal Currents in American Protestantism, 1999; (ed.) Religion Politics and the American Experience: Reflections on Religion and American Public Life, 2002; (ed.) Religion Education and the American Experience: Reflections on Religion and American Public Life, 2002; (with R.M. Fowler and F.F. Segovia) New Paradigms for Bible Study: The Bible in the Third Millennium, 2004; (ed. with M.A. Noll) Singing the Lords Song in a Strange Land: Hymnody in the History of North American Protestantism, 2004; Her Heart Can See: The Life and Hymns of Fanny J. Crosby, 2005; (ed. with P.V. Bohlman and M.M. Chow) Music in American Religious Experience, 2006; (ed. with M.A. Noll) Sing them Over Again to Me: Hymns and Hymnbooks in America, 2006. **Address:** Department of History, Wheaton College, 215 Blanchard, 501 College Ave., Wheaton, IL 60187, U.S.A. **Online address:** edith.l.blumhofer@wheaton.edu

BLUMHOFER, Edith Waldvogel. *See* **BLUMHOFER, Edith L.**

BLUNDELL, Derek (John). American/British (born England), b. 1933. **Genres:** Earth Sciences, Sciences, Humanities. **Career:** University of Birmingham, research fellow, 1957, lecturer, 1959-70; University of Lancaster, Department of Environmental Sciences, senior lecturer, 1970, reader, 1971-75; University of Ghana, Geology Department, visiting professor, 1974; University of London, Chelsea College, professor of environmental geology, 1975-85, head of geology department, 1975-85; University of London, Royal Holloway, professor of environmental geology, 1985-98, head of geology department, 1992-97, emeritus professor of geophysics, 1998-, Leverhulme emeritus fellow, 1998-2000. Writer. **Publications:** Geological Predictions, 1977; (ed.) Tectonic Evolution of the North Sea Rifts, 1990; (ed. with R. Freeman and S. Mueller) A Continent Revealed: The European Geotraverse, 1992; (ed. with A.C. Scott) Lyell: The Past is the Key to the Present, 1998; (ed. with F. Neubauer and A. von Quadt) The Timing and Location of Major Ore Deposits in an Evolving Orogen, 2002; (ed. with R. Hall) Tectonic Evolution of Southeast Asia, 2006. **Address:** Department of Earth Sciences, Royal Holloway, University of London, Rm. 006 ,New Science Block, Egham, SR TW20 0EX, England. **Online address:** d.blundell@gl.rhul.ac.uk

BLUNDELL, Sue. British (born England), b. 1947. **Genres:** History, Women's Studies And Issues, Civil Liberties/Human Rights. **Career:** University of London, Birkbeck College, part-time lecturer in classical civilization, 1979-; Open University, part-time lecturer, 1979-; Architectural Association School of Architecture, tutor; British Museum, lecturer; Bonnington Playwrights, playwright. **Publications:** The Origins of Civilization in Greek and Roman Thought, 1986; Women in Ancient Greece, 1995; (ed. with M. Williamson) The Sacred and the Feminine in Ancient Greece, 1998; Women in Classical Athens, 1998. Contributor to books. **Address:** Bonnington Playwrights, Bonnington Sq., London, GL SW8, England. **Online address:** sue@bonningtonplaywrights.co.uk

BLUNDY, Anna. British (born England), b. 1970?. **Genres:** Autobiography/Memoirs, Mystery/Crime/Suspense. **Career:** London Times, Moscow correspondent; Time Magazine, columnist. Journalist. **Publications:** Every Time We Say Goodbye: The Story of a Father and a Daughter (memoir), 1998; Only My Dreams, 2001. FAITH ZANETTI MYSTERY SERIES: The Bad News Bible, 2004; Faith without Doubt, 2005; Vodka Neat, 2008; Double Shot, 2008; My Favorite Poison, 2008. **Address:** London, GL , England. **Online address:** anna@faithzanetti.com

BLUNT, Giles. Canadian (born Canada), b. 1952. **Genres:** Novels, Poetry. **Career:** Writer. **Publications:** NOVELS: Cold Eye, 1989; Forty Words for Sorrow, 2000; The Delicate Storm, 2003; Black Fly Season, 2005; By the Time You Read This, 2006; No Such Creature: A Novel, 2008; Breaking Lorca, 2009; Crime Machine, 2010. Contributor to periodicals. **Address:** c/o Helen Heller, Helen Heller Agency Inc., 4-216 Heath St. W, Toronto, ON M5P 1N7, Canada. **Online address:** books2@gilesblunt.com

BLUSTEIN, Paul. American/Japanese (born Japan), b. 1951?. **Genres:** International Relations/Current Affairs, Politics/Government. **Career:** Forbes Magazine, researcher, associate editor, 1975-79, writer, 1976-79, affiliated; Wall Street Journal, staff reporter, 1979-87, chief economics correspondent, 1983-87, affiliated, staff writer; Washington Post, staff writer, 1987-2006, Tokyo Bureau, Asian economics correspondent, 1990-95, international economics correspondent, 1995, retired; Institute for International Economics, visiting fellow, 1999, 2000; Brookings Institution, journalist-in-residence, 2006, Global Economy and Development Program, fellow, nonresident fellow; Centre for International Governance Innovation (CIGI), senior visiting fellow, 2010-. **Publications:** The Chastening: Inside the Crisis That Rocked the Global Financial System and Humbled the IMF, 2001; And the Money Kept Rolling In (and Out): Wall Street the IMF and the Bankrupting of Argentina, 2005; Misadventures of the Most Favored Nations: Clashing Egos, Inflated Ambitions and the Great Shambles of the World Trade System, 2009. **Address:** Brookings Institution, 1775 Massachusetts Ave. NW, Washington, DC 20036-2188, U.S.A. **Online address:** info@cigionline.org

BLY, Robert (Elwood). American (born United States), b. 1926. **Genres:** Poetry, Adult Non-fiction, Mythology/Folklore, Essays, Translations, How-to Books, Natural History. **Career:** University of Iowa, Writers Workshop, staff, 1954-56; The Fifties, founder, publisher and editor, 1958-; The Sixties, founder; The Seventies, founder. **Publications:** POETRY: (with J. Wright and W. Duffy) The Lion's Tail and Eyes: Poems Written Out of Laziness and Silence, 1962; Silence in the Snowy Fields: And Other Poems, 1962; (with D. Ray) A Poetry Reading against the Vietnam War, 1966; The Light Around the Body, 1967; Chrysanthemums, 1967; Ducks, 1968; The Morning Glory: Another Thing That Will Never Be My Friend, 1969, rev. ed., 1973; The Teeth Mother Naked at Last, 1970; (with W.E. Stafford and and W. Matthews) Poems for Tennessee, 1971; Christmas Eve Service at Midnight at St. Michael's, 1972; Water Under the Earth, 1972; The Dead Seal Near McClure's Beach, 1973; Jumping Out of Bed, 1973; Sleepers Joining Hands, 1973; The Hockey Poem, 1974; Point Reyes Poems, 1974; Old Man Rubbing His Eyes, 1975; The Loon, 1977; This Body Is Made of Camphor and Gopherwood: Prose Poems, 1977; Visiting Emily Dickinson's Grave and Other Poems, 1979; This Tree Will Be Here for a Thousand Years, 1979, rev. ed., 1992; The Man in the Black Coat Turns, 1981; Finding an Old Ant Mansion, 1981; Four Rumages, 1983; The Whole Moisty Night, 1983; Out of the Rolling Ocean, 1984; Mirabai Versions, 1984; In the Month of May, 1985; A Love of Minute Particulars 1985; Selected Poems, 1986; Loving a Woman in Two Worlds, 1987; The Moon on a Fence Post, 1988; The Apple Found in Plowing, 1989; Angels of Pompeii, 1991; What Have I Ever Lost by Dying? (prose poems), 1992; Gratitude to Old Teachers, 1993; Meditations on the Insatiable Soul, 1994; Morning Poems, 1997; Holes the Crickets Have Eaten in Blankets, 1997; Saturday Nights in Marietta, 1999; The Night Abraham Called to the Stars, 2001; My Sentence was a Thousand Years Of Joy: Poems, 2005; The Urge To Travel Long Distances: Poems, 2005. TRANSLATOR: H. Hvass, Reptiles and Amphibians of the World, 1960; (with J. Wright) Twenty Poems of Georg Trakl, 1961; S. Lager, The Story of Gosta Berling, 1962; (with J. Wright and J. Knoepfle) Twenty Poems of Cesar Vallejo, 1962; (with E. Sellin and T. Buckman) T. Tranströmer, Three Poems, 1966; K. Hamsun, Hunger, 1967; (with C. Paulston) G. Ekeloef, I Do Best Alone at Night, 1967; (with C. Paulston) Late Arrival on Earth: Selected Poems of Gunnar Ekel of, 1967; I. Goll, Selected Poems, 1968; (with J. Wright) Twenty Poems of Pablo Neruda, 1968; Forty Poems of Juan Ramon Jimenez, 1969; I. Kobayashi, Ten Poems, 1969; (with J. Wright and J. Knoepfle) Neruda and Vallejo: Selected Poems, 1971; T. Tranströmer, Twenty Poems of Thomas Tranströmer, 1971; The Fish in the Sea Is Not Thirsty, 1971; T. Tranströmer, Night Vision, 1972; R.M. Rilke, The First Ten Sonnets of Orpheus, 1972; Lorca and Jimenez: Selected Poems, 1973; Martinson, Ekeloef, Tranströmer: Selected Poems, 1973; Basho, 1974; Selected Poems of Rainer Maria Rilke, 1981; Time Alone: Selected Poems of Antonio Machado, 1983; Tomas Tranströmer: Selected Poems, 1954-86, 1987; Trusting Your Life to Water and Eternity: 20 Poems of Olav H. Hague, 1987; Ten Poems of Francis Ponge, 1990; (with S. Dutta) The Lightning Should Have Fallen on Ghalib: Selected Poems of Ghalib, 1999; The Half-Finished Heaven: The Best Poems of Tomas Tranströmer, 2001; (with R. Hedin and R. Greenwald) The Roads Have Come to an End Now: Selected and Last Poems of Rolf Jacobsen, 2001; Tomas Tranströmer, Air Mail: Brev 1964-1990, 2001; The Winged Energy of Delight: Selected Translations, 2004; (with J. Hirshfield) Mirabai: Ecstatic Poems, 2004; Kabir, Kabir: Ecstatic Poems, 2004; I Explain A Few Things: Selected Poems, 2007; (with L. Lewisohn) The Angels Knocking On The Tavern Door: Thirty Poems Of Hafez, 2008; (with R. Hedin) Dream We Carry: Selected and Last Poems of Olav H. Hauge, 2008; J. Harbison, Madrigal, 2008. EDITOR: The Sea and the Honeycomb (poems), 1966; Forty Poems Touching on Recent American History, 1970; Leaping Poetry, 1975; Selected Poems, 1975; News of the Universe (poems), 1979; 10 Love Poems, 1981; (with W. Duffy) The Fifties and the Sixties, 1982; The Winged Life: The Poetic Voice of Henry David Thoreau, 1986; (co-ed.) The Rag and Bone Shop of the Heart: Poems for Men, 1992; (and intro.) The Darkness around Us is Deep: Selected Poems of William Stafford, 1993; The Soul Is Here for Its Own Joy, 1995; Eating the Honey of Words, 1999; The Best American Poetry, 1999, 1999; (with A. Wright) Selected Poems, 2005. OTHERS: A Broadsheet against the New York Times Book Review, 1961; Talking All Morning (interviews), 1980; A Little Book on the Human Shadow, 1986; The Pillow and the Key, 1987; American Poetry, 1990; Iron John: A Book about Men, 1990; (contrib.) Men Healing Shame: An Anthology, 1995; The Sibling Society, 1996; (with M. Woodman) The Maiden King: The Reunion of Masculine and Feminine (prose), 1998; The Science In Science Fiction: 83 SF Predictions That Became Scientific Reality, 2005; (with E. Yaverbaum and I. Benun) Public Relations For Dummies, 2nd ed., 2006; Turkish Pears In August: Twenty-Four Ramages, 2007; Reaching Out to the World: New and Selected Prose Poems, 2009; Talking into the Ear of a Donkey: Poems, 2011. **Address:** 1904 Girard Ave. S, Minneapolis, MN 55403-2945, U.S.A.

BLYTH, John. *See* **HIBBS, John.**

BLYTHE, Martin. American/New Zealander (born New Zealand), b. 1954. **Genres:** Film, History. **Career:** University of California, Film and Television Archive, programmer, 1988-89; Buena Vista Intl., senior marketing manager, 1989-95; Buena Vista Home Video, director of public relations, 1995-; University of California, lecturer. Writer. **Publications:** Naming the Other: Images of the Maori in New Zealand Film and Television, 1994. Contributor of articles to periodicals. **Address:** Buena Vista Home Video, 350 S Buena Vista St., Burbank, CA 91521, U.S.A. **Online address:** martin.blythe@gmail.com

BLYTHE, Ronald (George). British (born England), b. 1922. **Genres:** Novels, Novellas/Short Stories, History, Literary Criticism And History, Local History/Rural Topics. **Career:** Penguin Classics, editor; Librarian, 1947-54; writer, 1960-. **Publications:** A Treasonable Growth (novel), 1960; Immediate Possession (short stories), 1961; The Age of Illusion 1963; Akenfield: Portrait of an English Village, 1969; The View in Winter, 1979; Places, 1981; From the Headlands, 1982; Age of Illusion: Glimpses of Britain Between the Wars, 1919-1940, 1983; Characters and Their Landscapes, 1983; Visitors, 1985; The Stories of Ronald Blythe, 1985; Divine Landscapes, 1986; Each Returning Day, 1989; Private Words: Letters and Diaries from the Second World War, 1991; England: The Four Seasons (essays), 1993; Word from Wormingford: A Parish Year, 1997; First Friends (biography), 1997; Out of the Valley (essays), 2000; The Circling Year: Perspectives from a Country Parish, 2001; Talking to the Neighbours, 2002; The Assassin, 2004; Field Work: Selected Essays, 2007; Outsiders: A Book of Garden Friends, 2008; River Diary, 2008; (foreword) Private Diaries of Alison Uttley: Author of Little Grey Rabbit and Sam Pig, 2009; Aftermath: Selected Writings 1960-2010, 2010. EDITOR: Emma, 1966; (and intro.) Components of the Scene: An Anthology of the Prose and Poetry of the Second World War, 1966; (and intro.) William Hazlitt: Selected Writings, 1970; Aldeburgh Anthology, 1972; T. Hardy, A Pair of Blue Eyes, 1976; The Death of Ivan Ilyich, 1977; (and intro.) Far from the Madding Crowd, 1978; My Favourite Village Stories, 1979; The Awkward Age, 1987; George Herbert: The Country Person, 2003. **Address:** Bottengom Farm, Wormingford, Colchester, EX C06 3AP, England.

BO, Zhiyue. Singaporean/American/Chinese (born China), b. 1958. **Genres:** History, Cultural/Ethnic Topics. **Career:** Beijing Nonferrous Metals Corp., instructor in English, 1985-88; Peking University, assistant professor, 1988-90; Roosevelt University, instructor, 1993-94, visiting assistant professor, 1995-96; Urban Innovation Analysis, research director and postdoctoral fellow, 1996-98; American University, assistant professor, World Capitals Program, director, 1997-98; University of Chicago, lecturer, 1997-98; Saint John Fisher College, assistant professor of international studies, 1998-2003, department chair, 1998-2003, 2004-, associate professor, 2004-, International Studies Program, director, 2004; Rochester Institute of Technology, Center for International Business and Economic Growth, research fellow, 2003; National University of Singapore, East Asian Institute, visiting research fellow, 2004, senior research fellow; Beijing University, faculty; Tarleton State University, faculty; Chinese University of Hong Kong, faculty. Writer. **Publications:** (Trans.) M.A. Kaplan, Guojizhengzhi de Xitong he Guocheng (title means: 'System and Process in International Politics'), 1989; Chinese Provincial Leaders: Economic Performance and Political Mobility since 1949, 2002; The History of Modern China, 2004; China's Elite Politics: Political Transition and Power Balancing, 2007; China's Elite Politics: Governance and Democratization, 2010; (ed. with J. Wong) China's Reform in Global Perspective, 2010; Leaders and Institutions in Chinese Politics: From Mao Zedong to Hu Jintao, forthcoming; Who's Who in China: Provincial Leaders, 1949-2003, forthcoming. **Address:** East Asian Institute, National University of Singapore, 469 Bukit Timah Rd., Bukit Timah, 259756, Singapore. **Online address:** zbo@sjfc.edu

BOAG, Peter G. American (born United States), b. 1961?. **Genres:** Environmental Sciences/Ecology, History, Sex, Social Commentary, Medicine/Health, Adult Non-fiction. **Career:** Oregon Historical Society, researcher, 1982; University of Oregon, adjunct assistant professor of history, 1989, visiting associate professor, 1994-95; Idaho State University, assistant professor, 1989-94, associate professor of history, 1994-2002; University of Colorado, professor and chair for department of history; Washington State University, endowed chair, 2009-, Columbia chair in the history of the American west. Writer. **Publications:** (Foreword) Boys of Boise: Furor, Vice & Folly in An American City, 1966; Environment and Experience: Settlement Culture in Nineteenth-Century Oregon, 1992; Same-sex Affairs: Constructing and Controlling Homosexuality in the Pacific Northwest, 2003; Re-Dressing America's Frontier Past, 2011. Contributor to journals. **Address:** Department of

History, Washington State University, PO Box 644030, Pullman, WA 99164-4030, U.S.A. **Online address:** boag@wsu.edu

BOALER, Jo. British (born England), b. 1964. **Genres:** Mathematics/Statistics, Education. **Career:** Teacher, 1986-89; London University, King's College, deputy director of math assessment project, 1989-93; lecturer and researcher, 1993-98; Stanford University, associate professor, 2000-06; University of Sussex, Marie Curie professor of mathematics education, 2006-. Writer. **Publications:** Experiencing School Mathematics: Teaching Styles, Sex, and Setting, 1997, rev. ed. as Experiencing School Mathematics: Traditional and Reform Approaches to Teaching and Their Impact on Student Learning, 2002; (ed.) Multiple Perspectives on Mathematics Teaching and Learning, 2000; (with C. Humphreys) Connecting Mathematical Ideas: Middle School Video Cases to Support Teaching and Learning, 2005; What's Math Got to Do with It? Helping Children Learn to Love Their Most Hated Subject-and Why It's Important for America, 2008 in UK as The Elephant in the Classroom: Helping Children Learn and Love Maths, 2009. Contributor of articles to books and journals. **Address:** University of Sussex, Sussex House, Brighton, ES BN1 9RH, England. **Online address:** jo.boaler@sussex.ac.uk

BOARDMAN, Alonzo. *See* **WAGNER, Ralph D.**

BOARDMAN, John. British (born England), b. 1927. **Genres:** Archaeology/Antiquities, Art/Art History, Classics, History, Translations. **Career:** British School-Athens, assistant director, 1952-55; Oxford University, Ashmolean Museum, assistant keeper, 1955-59, reader in classical archaeology, 1959-78, Lincoln professor of classical archaeology and art, 1978-94, emeritus Lincoln professor of classical archaeology and art, 1994-, Environmental Change Institute, deputy director and director, through 2008, now emeritus fellow; University of Aberdeen, Geddes-Harrower professor, 1974; Royal Academy of Arts, professor of ancient history, 1990-; Merton College, fellow, 1963-78, subwarden, 1975-78, honorary fellow, 1978; Lincoln College, fellow, 1978; Columbia University, visiting professor, 1965; Magdalene College, honorary fellow, 1984; Australian Institute of Archaeology, visiting professor, 1987; Lincoln College, honorary fellow, 1995. Writer. **Publications:** (Trans.) S.N. Marinatos, Crete and Mycenae, 1960; The Cretan Collection in Oxford: The Dictaean Cave and Iron Age Crete, 1961; (with M. Pope) Greekvases in Cape Town, 1961; Island Gems: A Study of Greek Seals in the Geometric and Early Archaic Periods, 1963; (with L.R. Palmer) On the Knossos Tablets, 1963; Greek Art, 1964, 4th ed., 1996; The Greeks Overseas: The Archaeology of Their Early Colonies and Trade, 1964, 4th ed. as The Greeks Overseas: Their Early Colonies and Trade, 1999; (co-author) Die Griechische Kunst, 1966; Greek Art and Architecture, 1967 as The Art and Architecture of Ancient Greece, 1967; (with J. Hayes) Excavations at Tocra, 1963-1965, vol. I: The Archaic Deposits, 1966, vol. II: Archaic Deposits II and Later Deposits, 1973; Excavations in Chios, 1952-1955: Greek Emporio, 1967; Pre-Classical: From Crete to Archaic Greece, 1967; Archaic Greek Gems: Schools and Artists in the Sixth and Early Fifth Centuries B.C., 1968; Engraved Gems: The Ionides Collection, 1968; Greek Painted Vases: Catalogue of an Exhibition in the Mappin Art Gallery, 1968; Greek Gems and Finger Rings: Early Bronze Age to Late Classical, 1970; (with D.C. Kurtz) Greek Burial Customs, 1971; Athenian Black Figure Vases: A Handbook, 1974; (with E.L. Rocca) Eros in Greece, 1975; Intaglios and Rings: Greek, Etruscan, and Eastern, from a Private Collection, 1975; Ashmolean Museum, 1975; Athenian Red Figure Vases: The Archaic Period: A Handbook, 1975; Corpus Vasorum Antiquorum, 1975; (with D. Scarisbrick) The Ralph Harari Collection of Finger Rings, 1977; (with M.L. Vollenweider) Catalogue of the Engraved Gems and Finger Rings: Ashmolean Museum, Oxford, vol. I: Greek and Etruscan, 1978; Greek Sculpture: The Archaic Period: A Handbook, 1978, rev. ed., 1988; (with M. Robertson) Corpus Vasorum Antiquorum: Great Britain, 1979; (with M. Astruc and J.H. Hernandez) Escarabeos De Piedraprocedentes De Ibiza, 1984; Greek Sculpture: The Classical Period: A Handbook, 1985; The Parthenon and Its Sculptures, 1985; Athenian Red Figure Vases: The Classic Period: A Handbook, 1989; The Diffusion of Classical Art in Antiquity, 1994; Greek Sculpture: The Late Classical Period and Sculpture in Colonies and Overseas, 1994; The Great God Pan: The Survival of an Image, 1998; Early Greek Vase Painting: 11th-6th Centuries BC: A Handbook, 1998; Greek Gems and Finger Rings: Early Bronzeto Late Classical, 2000; Persia and the West: An Archaeological Investigation of the Genesis of Achaemenid Art, 2000; The History of Greek Vases: Potters, Painters and Pictures, 2001; (ed. with S.L. Solovyov and G.R. Tsetskhladze) Northern Pontic Antiquities in the State Hermitage Museum, 2001; (ed. with J. Griffin and O. Murray) Oxford Illustrated History of Greece and the Hellenistic World, 2001; (ed. with J. Griffin and O. Murray) Oxford Illustrated History of the Roman World, 2001; Cyprus Between East and West, 2001; The Archaeloogy of Nostalgia, 2002; (co-ed.) Lewes House Collection of Ancient Gems, 2002; Archaeology of Nostalgia: How the Greeks Re-created Their Mythical Past, 2002; (co-author) Ancient Art from Cyprus: In the Collection of George and Nefeli Giabra Pierides, 2002; (with C. Wagner) Collection of Classical and Eastern Intaglios, Rings, and Cameos, 2003; Classical Phoenician Scarabs, 2003; (with C. Wagner) A Collection of Classical and Eastern Engraved Gems and Cameos, 2003; World of Ancient Art, 2006; (with K.A. Piacenti) Ancient and Modern Gems and Jewels: In the Collection of Her Majesty The Queen, 2008; (with C. Wagner) Gem Mounts and the Classical Tradition, 2009; (co-author) The Marlborough Gems, 2009; Relief Plaques of Eastern Eurasia and China: The Ordos Bronzes, Peter the Great's Treasure, and Their Kin, 2010. **Address:** University of Oxford, Wellington Sq., Oxford, OX OX1 2JD, England. **Online address:** john.boardman@ashmus.ox.ac.uk

BOAST, Philip. (Philip James Boast). British (born England), b. 1952. **Genres:** Romance/Historical, History, Novels, Young Adult Fiction, Literary Criticism And History. **Career:** Norrice Green Farms Ltd., chief executive. Writer. **Publications:** The Assassinators, 1976; London's Child, 1987; The Millionaire, 1989; Watersmeet, 1990; Pride, 1991; London's Daughter, 1992; Gloria, 1994; London's Millionaire, 1994; City, 1995; The Foundling, 1995; Resurrection, 1996; Deus, 1997; Sion, 1999; Era, 2000; The Third Princess, 2005; The Son of Heaven, 2007. Works appear in anthologies. **Address:** Dorian Literary Agency, 27 Church Rd., Torquay, DN TQ1 4QY, England. **Online address:** philipboast@beeb.net

BOAST, Philip James. *See* **BOAST, Philip.**

BOATWRIGHT, Mary T. (Mary Taliaferro Boatwright). American (born United States), b. 1952. **Genres:** Novels, History. **Career:** University of Michigan, trench supervisor, 1976; Duke University, Intercollegiate Center for Classical Studies, graduate assistant, 1976-77, Department of Classical Studies, A.W. Mellon assistant professor, 1979-82, assistant professor, 1982-85, associate professor, 1985-95, A.W. Mellon professor-in-charge, 1992-93, professor of classical studies, 1995-, chair, 1996-99, 2010-11, director of undergraduate studies, 1985-86, 1987-89, 1990, director of graduate studies, 2004-08, Department of History, professor, 2005-. Writer. **Publications:** (Contrib. as Mary Taliaferro Boatwright) I Volusii Saturnini: Una famiglia romana della prima età imperiale, 1982; (as Mary Taliaferro Boatwright) Hadrian and the City of Rome, 1987; (ed. with H.B. Evans) The Shapes of City Life in Rome and Pompeii: Essays in Honor of Lawrence Richardson, Jr. on the Occasion of His Retirement, 1998; Hadrian and the Cities of the Roman Empire, 2000; (with D.J. Gargola and R.J.A. Talbert) The Romans: From Village to Empire, 2004, 2nd ed., 2012; (with D.J. Gargola and R.J.A. Talbert) A Brief History of Ancient Rome: Politics, Society, and Culture, 2005; (ed. with B.C. Ewald and C.F. Norena) Antonine Rome: Security in the Homeland: The Emperor and Rome: Space, Representation and Ritual, 2010; (ed. with M. Gagarin) Oxford Encyclopedia of Ancient Greece and Rome, 2010; Peoples of the Roman World, 2011. Contributor to periodicals. Works appear in anthologies. **Address:** Department of Classical Studies, Duke University, 231 Allen Bldg., PO Box 90103, Durham, NC 27708-0103, U.S.A. **Online address:** tboat@duke.edu

BOATWRIGHT, Mary Taliaferro. *See* **BOATWRIGHT, Mary T.**

BOAZ, David. American (born United States), b. 1953. **Genres:** Politics/Government, Education. **Career:** Council for a Competitive Economy, research director, 1978-80, executive director; Cato Institute, executive vice president, 1981-; New Guard Magazine, editor, 1976-78; Liberty, contributing editor. **Publications:** Libertarianism: A Primer, 1997; (contrib.) Cato Handbook for Congress, 1999; (contrib.) Cato Handbook on Policy, 2005; The Politics of Freedom: Taking on the Left, the Right, and Threats to Our Liberties, 2008. EDITOR: (with E.H. Crane) Beyond the Status Quo: Policy Proposals for America, 1985; Left, Right, and Babyboom: America's New Politics, 1986; Assessing the Reagan Years, 1988; (with E.H. Crane) American Vision: Policies for the '90s, 1989; The Crisis in Drug Prohibition, 1990; Liberating Schools: Education in the Inner City, 1991; (with E.H. Crane) Market Liberalism: A Paradigm for the 21st Century, 1993; The Libertarian Reader: Classic and Contemporary Readings from Lao-tzu to Milton Friedman, 1997; Toward Liberty: The Idea that is Changing the World: 25 Years of

Public Policy from the Cato Institute, 2002. Contributor to periodicals. **Address:** Cato Institute, 1000 Massachusetts Ave. NW, Washington, DC 20001-5403, U.S.A. **Online address:** dboaz@cato.org

BOAZ, David Douglas. *See* **BREDERO, Adriaan H(endrik).**

BOAZ, Noel T(homas). American (born United States), b. 1952. **Genres:** Anthropology/Ethnology, Sociology. **Career:** University of California-Berkeley, staff research associate, 1972, senior museum scientist, 1975-77; University of California-Los Angeles, lecturer in anthropology, 1977-78; New York University, assistant professor of anthropology, 1978-83; Virginia Museum of Natural History, founding director and curator, 1983-90, president, 1984-89; Blue Ridge-Piedmont Cultural Consortium, president, 1987-88; International Foundation for Human Evolutionary Research, president, 1991-; George Washington University, research professor, 1991-94; International Institute for Human Evolutionary Research, foundation president, founder and director, 1991-; Weizmann Institute of Science, Meyerhoff visiting professor, 1993-94; Saba University, professor, 1995-98, course director for gross anatomy and chair of anatomy 1996-98; Paleoanthropology of Zhoukoudian, affiliate, 1999-2000; Physicians for Human Rights, forensic anthropologist and scientific planning director, 1999; Dominica Centenarian Study, affiliate, 2001-02; Ross University, School of Medicine, professor of anatomy, 2001-, director of research development, 2002-, course director for gross anatomy, 2005-; Old Dominion University, adjunct professor, 2003-05; New Mexico State University, adjunct professor, 2004-; Portland State University, adjunct professor/principal investigator; Washington State University, adjunct professor; University of Oregon, adjunct professor. Consultant and writer. **Publications:** Paleoecology of Plio-Pleistocene Hominidae in the Lower Omo Basin, Ethiopia, 1977; Quarry: Closing in on the Missing Link, 1993; (with A.J. Almquist) Biological Anthropology: A Synthetic Approach to Human Evolution, 1997, 2nd ed., 2002; Eco Homo: How the Human Being Emerged from the Cataclysmic History of the Earth, 1997; (with A.J. Almquist) Essentials of Biological Anthropology, 1999; Evolving Health: The Origins of Illness and How the Modern World is Making Us Sick, 2002; (with R.L. Ciochon) Dragon Bone Hill: An Ice-Age Saga of Homo Erectus, 2004. EDITOR: (co-ed.) Neogene Paleontology and the Geology of Sahabi, 1987; The Evolution of Environments and Hominidae in the African Western Rift Valley, 1990; (with L. Wolfe and contrib.) Biological Anthropology: The State of the Science, 2nd ed., 1995. **Address:** Department of Anatomy, Ross University School of Medicine, PO Box 266, Portsmouth, 266, England. **Online address:** nboaz@rossmed.edu.dm

BOBER, Natalie S. American (born United States), b. 1930. **Genres:** History, Young Adult Non-fiction, Biography, Picture/Board Books, Poetry. **Career:** Writer, educator, reading consultant and historian. **Publications:** William Wordsworth: The Wandering Poet, 1975; A Restless Spirit: The Story of Robert Frost, 1981, rev. ed., 1991; Breaking Tradition: The Story of Louise Nevelson, 1984; (comp.) Let's Pretend: Poems of Flight and Fancy, 1986; Thomas Jefferson: Man on a Mountain, 1988; Marc Chagall: Painter of Dreams, 1991; Abigail Adams: Witness to a Revolution, 1995; Countdown to Independence: A Revolution of Ideas in England and Her American Colonies: 1760-1776, 2001; Thomas Jefferson: Draftsman of a Nation, 2007. Contributor to periodicals. **Address:** 500 E 77th St., Apt. 1832, New York, NY 10162-0020, U.S.A. **Online address:** nsbober@nyc.rr.com

BOBINSKI, George S. (George Sylvan Bobinski). American (born United States), b. 1929. **Genres:** Librarianship. **Career:** Cleveland Public Library, Business Information Bureau, reference assistant, 1954-55; Royal Oak Public Library, assistant director, 1955-59; State University College, director of libraries, 1960-67; University of Kentucky, College of Library Science, professor and assistant dean, 1967-70; State University at Buffalo, School of Information Studies, dean and professor, 1970-99, professor emeritus and dean emeritus, 1999-. Writer. **Publications:** A Brief History of the Libraries of Western Reserve University, 1826-1952, 1955; Carnegie Libraries: Their History and Impact on American Public Library Development, 1969; (ed. with J.H. Shera and B.S. Wynar) Dictionary of American Library Biography, 1978; (ed. with J.H. Shera and B.S. Wynar) Current and Future Trends in Library and Information Science Education, 1986; Libraries in the Democratic Process, 1994; (ed. with M. Kocójowej) Rola bibliotek w rozwoju demokracji: praca zbiorowa, 1995; The School of Information and Library Studies of SUNY at Buffalo, 1919-1999, 2002; Libraries and Librarianship: Sixty Years of Challenge and Change, 1945-2005, 2007. **Address:** Graduate School of Education, State University of New York, 549 Baldy Hall, Buffalo, NY 14260, U.S.A. **Online address:** bobinski@buffalo.edu

BOBINSKI, George Sylvan. *See* **BOBINSKI, George S.**

BOBIS, Merlinda Carullo. Australian (born Australia), b. 1959. **Genres:** Poetry, Novellas/Short Stories. **Career:** University of Wollongong, lecturer. Writer. **Publications:** POETRY: Ang Lipad Ay Awit Sa Apat Na Hangin/Flight Is Song on Four Winds, 1990; Rituals: Selected Poems, 1985-1990, 1990; Summer Was a Fast Train without Terminals, 1998. Pag-uli=Pag-uwi=Homecoming: Poetry in Three Tongues, 2004. PROSE: White Turtle Spinifex, 1993; The Kissing: A Collection of Short Stories, 2001; Banana Heart Summer (novel), 2005; The Solemn Lantern Maker, 2009. CANTATA OF THE WOMAN WARRIOR PERFORMANCE SERIES: Cantata of the Warrior Woman, Daragang Magayon: An Epic, 1993; (with V. Hilyard, J. Ulman and P. Ulman) Cantata: Sound-Screen Montage, 1998. **Address:** University of Wollongong, Wollongong, NW 2522, Australia. **Online address:** merlinda_bobis@uow.edu.au

BOBRICK, Benson. American (born United States), b. 1947?. **Genres:** History, Theology/Religion, Biography. **Career:** Writer and historian. **Publications:** Labyrinths of Iron: A History of the World's Subways, 1981; Parsons Brinckerhoff: The First Hundred Years, 1985; Labyrinths of Iron: Subways in History, Myth, Art, Technology, and War, 1986; Fearful Majesty: The Life and Reign of Ivan the Terrible, 1987; East of the Sun: The Epic Conquest and Tragic History of Siberia, 1992; Knotted Tongues: Stuttering in History and the Quest for a Cure, 1995; Angel in the Whirlwind: The Triumph of the American Revolution, 1997; Making of the English Bible, 2001; Wide as the Waters: The Story of the English Bible and the Revolution It Inspired, 2001; Testament: A Soldier's Story of the Civil War, 2003; Fight for Freedom: The American Revolutionary War, 2004; The Fated Sky: Astrology in History, 2005; Master of War: The Life of General George H. Thomas, 2009; Battle of Nashville: General George H. Thomas & the Most Decisive Battle of the Civil War, 2010; Passion for Victory: The Story of the Olympics in Ancient and Early Modern Times, 2012; Caliph's Splendor: Islam and the West in the Golden Age of Baghdad, 2012. Contributor to periodicals. **Address:** c/o Author Mail, Simon & Schuster Inc., 1230 Ave. of the Americas, New York, NY 10020, U.S.A. **Online address:** shiloh98@sover.net

BOCARDO, Claire. American (born United States), b. 1939. **Genres:** Novels, Novellas/Short Stories, Young Adult Fiction. **Career:** Plano Morning Press, writer and editor, 1976-77; Rockwell Intl., editor of technical documentation, 1978-83; freelance writer, 1984-89; real estate editor and business writer, 1990. **Publications:** NOVELS: Maybe Later, Love, 1992; A Patchwork Holiday, 1992; Sweet Nothings, 1993; (co-author) Home for Christmas, 1994; (co-author) Joy of Christmas, 1994; Lovers and Friends, 1995. OTHER: Becoming Sarah, 2004. Works appear in anthologies. **Address:** Adele Leone Agency Inc., 26 Nantucket Pl., Scarsdale, NY 10583-4720, U.S.A. **Online address:** clairebocardo@msn.com

BOCHIN, Hal W(illiam). American (born United States), b. 1942. **Genres:** History, Speech/Rhetoric, Bibliography. **Career:** California State University, Department of Speech Communication, graduate adviser, assistant professor, 1969-74, associate professor, 1974-78, professor, 1978-2005, professor emeritus, 2005-, Speech Communication Program, chair, 1980-83; Venture Capital and Private Equity, staff. Writer. **Publications:** (With M. Weatherson) Hiram Johnson: A Bio-Bibliography, 1988; Richard Nixon: Rhetorical Strategist, 1990; (with M.A. Weatherson) Hiram Johnson: Political Revivalist, 1995. Works appear in anthologies. Contributor to journals and periodicals. **Address:** Department of Speech Communication, California State University, Fresno, CA 93740, U.S.A. **Online address:** hal_bochin@csufresno.edu

BOCHNER, Mel. American (born United States), b. 1940?. **Genres:** Photography. **Career:** School of the Visual Arts, instructor, 1965; Yale University, senior critic painting/printmaking, 1979-2001, adjunct professor, 2001-. Writer. **Publications:** Scott Rothkopf, Mel Bochner: Photographs, 1966-1969, 2002; Johanna Burton, James Rondeau, and James Meyer, Mel Bochner: Language, 1966-2006, 2007; (With Y. Bois) Solar System & Rest Rooms: Writings and Interviews, 1965-2007, 2008. Contributor of articles to periodicals and journals. **Address:** New York, NY , U.S.A. **Online address:** info@melbochner.net

BOCK, Charles. American (born United States), b. 1970?. **Genres:** Novels, Young Adult Fiction. **Career:** Gotham Writers Workshop, faculty. Writer and educator. **Publications:** Beautiful Children: A Novel, 2008. Contributor to periodicals. **Address:** PFD, Drury House, 34-43 Russell St., London, GL WC2B 5HA, England.

BOCK, Gisela. German (born Germany), b. 1942. **Genres:** History, Intellectual History, Women's Studies And Issues, Social Sciences. **Career:** Free University of Berlin, John F. Kennedy Institute for North American Studies, research fellow, 1971-76, Zentralinstitut fur Sozialwissenschaft, assistant professor of history, 1977-83, professor of western European history, 1997-2007, retired, 2007; Harvard University, Center of European Studies, Kennedy fellow, 1974-75; European University Institute, professor of European history, 1985-89, European Culture Research Center, director, 1987-89; University of Bern, lecturer, 1985; University of Bielefeld, professor of history, 1989-97; University of Basel, lecturer; Institute for Advanced Study, fellow, 1995-96. Writer. **Publications:** Thomas Campanella: Politische Intention und philosophische Spekulation, 1974; Die andere Arbeiterbewegung in den USA, 1905-1922, 1976; Zwangssterilisation im Nationalsozialismus, 1986; Storia, storia delle donne, storia di genere, 1988; Frauen in der europaischen Geschichte, 2000 as Women in European History, 2001; Genozid und Geschlecht: jüdische Frauen im nationalsozialistischen Lagersystem, 2005; (with D. Schönpflug) Friedrich Meinecke in seiner Zeit: Studien zu Leben und Werk, 2006. EDITOR: (trans.) E. Flexner, Hundert Jahre Kampf, 1978; (with G.N. Schiera) Il corpo delle donne, 1988; (with Q. Skinner and M. Viroli) Machiavelli and Republicanism, 1990; (with P. Thane) Maternity and Gender Policies, 1991; (with S. James) Beyond Equality and Difference, 1992; Lebenswege von Frauen im Ancien Regime, 1992; Rassenpolitik und Geschlechterpolitik im Nationalsozialismus, 1993; (with A. Cova) Writing Women's History in Southern Europe, 2003. Works appear in anthologies. Contributor to journals. **Address:** Routledge, 711 3rd Ave., 8th Fl., New York, NY 10017, U.S.A. **Online address:** gisela.bock@fu-berlin.de

BOCK, Philip Karl. American (born United States), b. 1934. **Genres:** Anthropology/Ethnology, Plays/Screenplays, Songs/Lyrics And Libretti. **Career:** PALL Corp., technical writer, 1960; University of New Mexico, assistant professor, 1962-66, associate professor, 1966-71, professor of anthropology, 1971-, now professor emeritus; Journal of Anthropological Research, editor, 1982-94; Columbia University, visiting professor; Stanford University, visiting professor; Universidad Ibero-Americana, visiting professor; Random House Dictionaries, consultant. **Publications:** The Micmac Indians of Restigouche, 1966; Modern Cultural Anthropology, 1969, 3rd ed., 1978; (contrib.) Handbook of American Indians, 1978; Continuities in Psychological Anthropology, 1980; Shakespeare and Elizabethan Culture, 1984; The Formal Content of Ethnography, 1986; Rethinking Psychological Anthropology, 1988, 2nd ed., 1999. EDITOR: Peasants in the Modern World, 1968; Culture Shock, 1970; (ed.) Handbook of Psychological Anthropology, 1994. Contributor to books and journals. **Address:** Department of Anthropology, University of New Mexico, MSC01 1040, 1 University of New Mexico, Albuquerque, NM 87131-0001, U.S.A. **Online address:** pbock@unm.edu

BOCZKOWSKI, Pablo J. Argentine (born Argentina), b. 1965. **Genres:** Information Science/Computers. **Career:** Massachusetts Institute of Technology, assistant professor, 2001-05; Columbia University, visiting professor, 2002-; Universidad Torcuato Di Tella, visiting professor, 2004-; Northwestern University, Department of Communication Studies, associate professor, 2005-10, professor, 2010-11, Department of Sociology, affiliate faculty, 2010-, Science in Human Culture, faculty, 2010-, Institute for Policy Research, faculty associate, 2010-; Writer. **Publications:** Digitizing the News: Innovation in Online Newspapers, 2004; News at Work: Imitation in an Age of Information Abundance, 2010. **Address:** Department of Communication Studies, Northwestern University, Rm. 2-146, Frances Searle Bldg., 2240 Campus Dr., Evanston, IL 60208, U.S.A. **Online address:** pjb9@northwestern.edu

BODANSKY, Yossef. American/Israeli (born Israel) **Genres:** Novels, History, Biography, Autobiography/Memoirs, Military/Defense/Arms Control, Politics/Government. **Career:** United States House of Representatives, Congressional Task Force on Terrorism and Unconventional Warfare, director, 1988-2004; International Strategic Studies Association, director of research; Freeman Center for Strategic Studies, special consultant on international terrorism; United States Department of State, senior consultant, Department of Defense, senior consultant. Writer. **Publications:** Target America: Terrorism in the U. S. Today, 1993; Terror!: The Inside Story of the Terrorist Conspiracy in America, 1994; Crisis in Korea: The Emergence of a New Nuclear Power, 1994; Offensive in the Balkans: The Potential for a Wider War as a Result of Foreign Intervention in Bosnia-Herzegovina, 1995; Some Call It Peace: Waiting for War in the Balkans, 1996; Islamic Anti-Semitism as a Political Instrument, 1999; Bin Laden: The Man Who Declared War on America, 1999; The High Cost of Peace: How Washington's Middle East Policy Left America Vulnerable to Terrorism, 2002; The Secret History of the Iraq War, 2004; Chechen Jihad: Al Qaeda's Training Ground and the Next Wave of Terror, 2007. Contributor to books and periodicals. **Address:** International Strategic Studies Association, PO Box 320608, Alexandria, VA 22320, U.S.A. **Online address:** ybodansky@strategicstudies.org

BODDY, Janice. Canadian (born Canada), b. 1951. **Genres:** Anthropology/Ethnology, Biography, Women's Studies And Issues, History, Politics/Government. **Career:** University of Toronto, lecturer in anthropology, 1978-79, lecturer, 1981-82, assistant professor, 1982-85, Department of Anthropology, assistant professor, 1985-90, associate professor, 1990-96, professor of anthropology, 1997-, graduate chair, 2006-, St. George undergraduate chair; University of Manitoba, lecturer in anthropology, 1979-80; Lakehead University, lecturer in anthropology, 1980-81; Horizons of Friendship Development Organization, director. Writer. **Publications:** (Contrib.) In Her Prime: A New View of Middle Aged Women, 1985; Wombs and Alien Spirits: Women, Men, and the Zar Cult in Northern Sudan, 1989; (co-author) Aman: The Story of a Somali Girl, 1994; Civilizing Women: British Crusades in Colonial Sudan, 2007. Contributor to journals and periodicals. **Address:** Department of Anthropology, University of Toronto, AP 270, 19 Russell St., Toronto, ON M5S 2S2, Canada. **Online address:** janice.boddy@utoronto.ca

BODE, N. E. *See* **BAGGOTT, Julianna.**

BODEK, Richard. American (born United States), b. 1961. **Genres:** Cultural/Ethnic Topics, History, Art/Art History, Social Sciences. **Career:** College of Charleston, assistant professor of history, 1990-97, associate director, Jewish Studies, 1994-99, associate professor of history, 1997-2006, professor of history, 2006-, chair, director of postgraduate fellowships, 2004-06. Writer. **Publications:** Proletarian Performance in Weimar Berlin: Agitprop, Chorus, and Brecht, 1997; Hampton Park: Charleston's Reflection on the Ashley, 1997; (ed. with S. Lewis) The Fruits of Exile: Central European Intellectual Imigration to America in the Age of Fascism, 2010; (trans. and intro.) What Will Become of the Children?: A Novel of a German Family in the Twilight of Weimar Berlin, 2010; (trans.) Claire Bergmann, Was wird aus deinen Kindern, Pitt?, forthcoming. Contributor to periodicals. **Address:** Department of History, College of Charleston, Rm. 221, Maybank Hall, 66 George St., Charleston, SC 29424, U.S.A. **Online address:** bodekr@cofc.edu

BODEN, Margaret A(nn). British (born England), b. 1936. **Genres:** Information Science/Computers, Philosophy, Psychology, Social Sciences, Art/Art History. **Career:** University of Birmingham, lecturer in philosophy, 1959-65; University of Sussex, lecturer and reader, 1965-80, professor of philosophy and psychology, 1980-2002, School of Cognitive and Computing Sciences, founding dean, Department of Informatics, research professor of cognitive science, 2002-, precursor; Harvester Press, director. Writer. **Publications:** Purposive Explanation in Psychology, 1972; Artificial Intelligence and Natural Man, 1977, 2nd ed., 1987; Piaget, 1979, 2nd ed., 1984; Jean Piaget, 1980; Minds and Mechanisms. 1981; Computer Models of Mind, 1988; Artificial Intelligence in Psychology, 1989; (contrib.) Mente umana, 1989; The Creative Mind, 1991, 2nd ed., 2004; (contrib.) Informatik und Philosophie, 1993; Mind as Machine, 2 vols., 2006; Creativity And Art: Three Roads To Surprise, 2010. EDITOR: The Philosophy of Artificial Intelligence, 1990; Dimensions of Creativity, 1994; The Philosophy of Artificial Life, 1996; Artificial Intelligence, 1996; (with M. Wheeler and J. Ziman) Evolution of Cultural Entities, 2002. Contributor to journals. **Address:** Department of Informatics, University of Sussex, Rm. 3r347b, Chichester 3, Falmer, Brighton, ES BN1 9QJ, England. **Online address:** m.a.boden@sussex.ac.uk

BODENHAMER, David J(ackson). American (born United States), b. 1947. **Genres:** History, Geography, Humanities, Social Sciences, Politics/Government, Civil Liberties/Human Rights. **Career:** University of Southern Mississippi, professor of history and associate vice-president for academic affairs, 1976-88; Indiana University-Purdue University, professor of history and founding executive director of Polis Center, 1989-; International Journal of Humanities and Arts Computing, editor, 2005-. **Publications:** The Pursuit of Justice: Crime and Law in Antebellum Indiana, 1986; Fair Trial: Rights of the Accused in American History, 1992; (with E.B. Monroe and L. Hulse) The Main Stem: The History and Architecture of North Meridian Street, 1992; (intro.) Voices of Faith: Making a Difference in Urban Neighborhoods, 1998; Our Rights, 2007; The Revolutionary Constitution, 2011. EDITOR: (with J.W. Ely, Jr.) Ambivalent Legacy: A Legal History of the South, 1984; (with J.W. Ely, Jr.) The Bill of Rights in Modern America: After Two Hundred

Years, 1993, rev, ed., 2008; (with R.G. Barrows and David G. Vanderstel) The Encyclopedia of Indianapolis, 1994; (with R.T. Shepard) The History of Indiana Law, 2006; (with J. Corrigan and T. Harris) The Spatial Humanities: GIS and the Future of Humanities Scholarship, 2010. Contributor to journals. **Address:** Polis Center, Indiana University-Purdue University, 1200 Waterway Blvd., Ste. 100, Indianapolis, IN 46202, U.S.A. **Online address:** intu100@iupui.edu

BODETT, Tom. American (born United States), b. 1955. **Genres:** Novels, Essays, History, Young Adult Fiction. **Career:** Bodett Construction Inc., owner, 1977-85; National Public Radio, commentator, 1984-86; Alaska Public Radio, commentator, 1984-87; Anchorage Daily News, columnist, 1985-88; Loose Leaf Book Co., founder, 1999; Bodett and Co., host. **Publications:** As Far as You Can Go without a Passport: The View from the End of the Road, 1985; Small Comforts: More Comments and Comic Pieces (essays), 1987; The End of the Road, 1989; The Big Garage on Clear Shot: Growing Up, Growing Old and Going Fishing at the End of the Road, 1990; (with A.M. Herb) Alaska A to Z: The Most Comprehensive Book of Facts and Figures Ever Compiled about Alaska, 1993; (foreword) J.K. Pierce, America's Historic Trails with Tom Bodett, 1997; The Free Fall of Webster Cummings, 1996; Williwaw, 1999; Norman Tuttle on the Last Frontier: A Novel in Stories, 2004. Contributor to periodicals. **Address:** International Creative Management, 10250 Constellation Blvd., Los Angeles, CA 90067, U.S.A. **Online address:** tbodett@gmail.com

BODMER, Walter (Fred). British/German (born Germany), b. 1936. **Genres:** Biology, Medicine/Health. **Career:** University of Cambridge, Clare College, research fellow, 1958-60, official fellow, 1961, Department of Genetics, demonstrator, 1960-61; Stanford University, School of Medicine, fellow and visiting assistant professor, 1961-62, Department of Genetics, assistant professor, 1962-66, associate professor, 1966-68, professor of genetics, 1968-70; Oxford University, professor of genetics, 1970-79, Cancer and Immunogenetics Laboratory, head; Imperial Cancer Research Fund, research director, 1979-91, director general, 1991-96; Hertford College, principal, 1996-2005; University of Salford, chancellor, 1995-2005, now retired. Writer. **Publications:** (With L. Cavalli-Sforza) The Genetics of Human Population, 1971; (with A. Jones) Our Future Inheritance: Choice or Chance?, 1974; (with L.L. Cavalli-Sforza) Genetics, Evolution and Man, 1976; (ed.) Inherited Susceptibility to Cancer in Man, 1983; (ed. with A.J. McMichael) New Look at Tumour Immunology, 1992; (with R. McKie) The Book of Man: The Quest to Discover Our Genetic Heritage, 1994; (with R. McKie) The Book of Man: The Human Genome Project and The Quest to Discover Our Genetic Heritage, 1995; (ed. with M.J. Owen) Molecular Mechanisms of the Immune Response, 1995; (with L.L. Cavalli-Sforza) Genetics of Human Populations, 1999. **Address:** John Radcliffe Hospital, Manor House, Mill Ln., Oxford, OX OX3 9DS, England. **Online address:** walter.bodmer@hertford.ox.ac.uk

BOEGEHOLD, Alan L(indley). American (born United States), b. 1927. **Genres:** Classics, History. **Career:** University of Illinois, instructor, assistant professor of classics, 1957-60; Brown University, assistant professor, professor, 1960-68, chairperson of department, 1966-71, director of ancient studies program, 1985-91, professor emeritus of classics, 2001-; American School of Classical Studies, visiting professor, 1968-69, research fellow, 1974-75, Agora Excavations, research fellow, 1980-81, director of summer sessions, 2001-, now professor emeritus; Yale University, visiting professor, 1971; University of California, visiting professor, 1978; Amherst College, visiting professor, 2001-03, 2005. Writer. **Publications:** In Simple Clothes: Translations of 11 Poems, 1993; Law Courts at Athens: Sites, Buildings, Equipment, Procedure and Testimonia, 1995; When a Gesture Was Expected: A Selection of Examples from Archaic and Classical Greek Literature, 1999; Constantine Cavafy. 166 Poems, 2009. EDITOR AND CONTRIBUTOR: C.A. Robinson Jr., Ancient History from Prehistoric Times to the Death of Justinian, 2nd ed., 1967; Studies Presented to Sterling Dow, 1984; In Simple Clothes: Eleven Poems, 1992; (with A.C. Scafuro) Athenian Identity and Civic Ideology, 1994. Contributor of articles to books, periodicals and journals. **Address:** Department of Classics, Brown University, Macfarlane House, 48 College St., PO Box 1937, Providence, RI 02912, U.S.A. **Online address:** alan_boegehold@brown.edu

BOEHLING, Rebecca L. American (born United States), b. 1955. **Genres:** History. **Career:** Franklin and Marshall College, visiting instructor in history, 1986-87; University of Dayton, assistant professor of history, 1987-89; University of Maryland, instructor, 1989-90, assistant professor, 1990-96, associate professor of history, 1996-, director, 1996-. Writer. **Publications:** A Question of Priorities: Democratic Reforms and Economic Recovery in Postwar Germany; Frankfurt am Main, Munich, and Stuttgart under U.S. Occupation, 1945-49, 1996; Life and Loss in the Shadow of the Holocaust: A Jewish Family's Untold Story, 2011; Gender and Party Politics in Postwar West Germany, forthcoming. Contributor of articles to periodicals. **Address:** Department of History, University of Maryland, 714 Administration Bldg., 1000 Hilltop Cir., Baltimore, MD 21250, U.S.A. **Online address:** boehling@umbc.edu

BOEHMER, Elleke. British (born England), b. 1961. **Genres:** Novels, Humanities, Literary Criticism And History, inspirational/Motivational Literature. **Career:** University of Leeds, lecturer, 1990-2000; Nottingham Trent University, chair of colonial and postcolonial studies, 2000-04; University of London, Hildred Carlile professor in literatures in English, 2004-. Writer. **Publications:** NOVELS: Screens against the Sky, 1990; An Immaculate Figure, 1993; Bloodlines, 2000. NONFICTION: Colonial and Postcolonial Literature: Migrant Metaphors, 1995, 2nd ed., 2005. EDITOR: (with L. Chrisman and K. Parker) Altered State?: Writing and South Africa, 1994; (and intro.) Empire Writing: An Anthology of Colonial Literature, 1870-1918, 1998; (and intro.) Scouting for Boys, 2004; C. Sorabji, India Calling, 2004; (with S. Morton) Terror and the Postcolonial: A Concise Companion, 2009; (with K. Iddiols and R. Eaglestone) J.M. Coetzee in Context and Theory, 2009; (with S. Morton) Terror and the Postcolonial: A Concise Companion, 2010; (with R. Chaudhuri) Indian Postcolonial: A Critical Reader, 2010. OTHERS: Empire, the National, and the Postcolonial, 1890-1920, 2002; Stories of Women: Gender and Narrative in the Postcolonial Nation, 2005; Nelson Mandela: A Brief Insight, 2008; Nelson Mandela: A Very Short Introduction, 2008; Nile Baby, 2008; (contrib.) 90 the Nelson Mandela Years, 2009; Sharmilla and Other Portraits, 2010. **Address:** Department of English, University of London, Egham Hill, Egham, SR TW20 0EX, England. **Online address:** elleke.boehmer@rhul.ac.uk

BOEHMER, Ulrike. American/German (born Germany), b. 1959. **Genres:** Adult Non-fiction, Medicine/Health. **Career:** Boston University, School of Public Health, Department of Community Health Sciences, instructor, 1997-2000, assistant professor, 2000-, associate professor, Department of Social and Behavioral Sciences, associate professor, Center for Health Quality, Outcomes and Economic Research, researcher. Writer. **Publications:** (With I. Kokula) Die Welt gehort uns doch! Zusammenschluss lesbischer Frauen in der Schweiz der 30er Jahre, 1991; The Personal and the Political: Women's Activism in Response to the Breast Cancer and AIDS Epidemics, 2000. **Address:** School of Public Health, Boston University, CT454, Crosstown Ctr., 715 Albany St., Talbot Bldg., Boston, MA 02118, U.S.A. **Online address:** boehmer@bu.edu

BOELLSTORFF, Tom. American (born United States), b. 1969. **Genres:** Gay And Lesbian Issues, Anthropology/Ethnology, History. **Career:** Institute for Community Health Outreach, regional co-ordinator, 1993-94; University of California, instructor, 2000-01, assistant professor, 2002-06, associate professor of anthropology, 2006-. Writer. **Publications:** (ed. with W.L. Leap) Speaking in Queer Tongues: Globalization and Gay Language, 2004; The Gay Archipelago: Sexuality and Nation in Indonesia, 2005; A Coincidence of Desires: Anthropology, Queer Studies, Indonesia, 2007; Coming of Age in Second Life: An Anthropologist Explores the Virtually Human, 2008. Contributor to periodicals. **Address:** Department of Anthropology, University of California, Irvine, CA 92697-5100, U.S.A. **Online address:** tboellst@uci.edu

BOELTS, Maribeth. American (born United States), b. 1964. **Genres:** Children's Non-fiction. **Career:** St. John/St. Nicholas School, preschool teacher, 1988-. Writer. **Publications:** With My Mom, with My Dad, 1992; Tornado, 1993; Dry Days, Wet Nights, 1994; Grace and Joe, 1994; Lullaby Babes, 1994; The Lulla-Book, 1994; Summer's End, 1995; Little Bunny's Preschool Countdown, 1996; Little Bunny's Cool Tool Set, 1997; Little Bunny's Pacifier Plan, 1999; When Big Daddy Was Famous, 2000; Big Daddy, Frog Wrestler, 2000; You're a Brother, Little Bunny, 2001; Lullaby Lullabook, 2002; Sloths Get a Pet, 2003; Sarah's Grandma Goes to Heaven, 2004; Looking for Sleepy, 2004; Sometimes I'm Afraid, 2004; When It's the Last Day of School, 2004; Firefighters' Thanksgiving, 2004; Why Did You Bring Home a New Baby?, 2005; Starlight Lullaby, 2006; Those Shoes, 2007; Before You Were Mine, 2007; Dogerella, 2008; Sweet Dreams, Little Bunny!, 2010; P.S. Brothers, 2010; Sleeping Bootsie, 2011; Happy Like Soccer, 2011. NONFICTION: Kids to the Rescue!: First Aid Techniques for Kids, 1992, rev. ed., 2003; Kid's Guide to Staying Safe Around Fire, 1997; Kid's Guide to Staying Safe at Playgrounds, 1997; Kid's Guide to Staying Safe at School, 1997; Kid's Guide to Staying Safe on Bikes, 1997; A Kid's Guide to Staying Safe on the Streets, 1997; Kid's Guide to Staying Safe Around Water, 1997. **Address:** 3815 Clearview Dr., Cedar Falls, IA 50613-6107, U.S.A. **Online address:** maribeth@maribethboelts.com

BOERS, Arthur Paul. Canadian (born Canada), b. 1957. **Genres:** Theology/Religion, Autobiography/Memoirs, Social Sciences. **Career:** Church Community Services, client counselor, 1981-82; Lombard Mennonite Peace Center, director, 1983; Alternative High School for Latino Youth, history teacher, business manager, 1984-85; United Methodist church, associate pastor, 1985-87; Mennonite Fellowship, pastor, 1988-92; Associated Mennonite Biblical Seminary, assistant professor of pastoral theology and coordinator of spiritual formation program, 2002; Bloomingdale Mennonite Church, pastor, 1992-2002; Tyndale University College and Seminary, associate professor, R.J. Bernardo Family chair of leadership. Writer. **Publications:** On Earth as in Heaven: Justice Rooted in Spirituality, 1991; Justice That Heals: A Biblical Vision for Victims and Offenders, 1992; Lord, Teach Us to Pray: A New Look at the Lord's Prayer, 1992; Never Call Them Jerks: Healthy Responses to Difficult Behavior, 1999; The Rhythm of God's Grace: Uncovering Morning and Evening Hours of Prayer, 2003; Take Our Moments and Our Days: An Anabaptist Prayer Book: A Four-Week Cycle of Morning and Evening Prayers for Ordinary Time, 2006, rev. ed., 2007; The Way is Made by Walking: A Pilgrimage Along the Camino de Santiago, 2007; Day By Day These Things We Pray: Uncovering Ancient Rhythms of Prayer, 2010; Living Into Focus: Choosing What Matters in an Age of Distractions, 2012. Contributor of articles to periodicals. **Address:** Tyndale University College & Seminary, 25 Ballyconnor Ct., Toronto, ON M2M 4B3, Canada. **Online address:** aboers@tyndale.ca

BOERSMA, Hans. Canadian/Dutch (born Netherlands), b. 1961. **Genres:** Theology/Religion, Mystery/Crime/Suspense, History. **Career:** Theologian and pastor, 1994-98; Trinity Western University, professor, 1999-2005, Geneva Society for Reformational Worldview Studies, endowed chair, 1999-2005; Regent College, James I. Packer Professor of Theology, 2005-. Writer. **Publications:** A Hot Pepper Corn: Richard Baxter's Doctrine of Justification in Its Seventeenth-Century Context of Controversy, 1993; Eating God's Words: The Life of Jeremiah: A Study Guide, 1998; The Visions of Zechariah: Lighting the Darkness: A Study Guide, 1999; (ed.) Living in the Lamblight: Christianity and Contemporary Challenges to the Gospel, 2001; Richard Baxter's Understanding of Infant Baptism, 2002; Violence, Hospitality, and the Cross: Reappropriating the Atonement Tradition, 2004; (ed.) Imagination and Interpretation: Christian Perspectives, 2005; Nouvelle Théologie and Sacramental Ontology: A Return to Mystery, 2009; Heavenly Participation: The Weaving of a Sacramental Tapestry, 2011. **Address:** Regent College, 5800 University Blvd., Vancouver, BC V6T 2E4, Canada.

BOESCHE, Roger. American (born United States), b. 1948?. **Genres:** Politics/Government, Young Adult Non-fiction, Social Sciences. **Career:** Stanford University, assistant professor, 1976-77; Occidental College, assistant professor, 1977-82, associate professor, 1982-88, professor, 1988-, Arthur G. Coons Distinguished Professor of the History of Ideas, 1996-. Writer. **Publications:** (ed.) Alexis de Tocqueville, Selected Letters on Politics and Society, 1985; The Strange Liberalism of Alexis de Tocqueville, 1987; Theories of Tyranny from Plato to Arendt, 1996; The First Great Political Realist: Kautilya and His Arthashastra, 2002; Tocqueville's Road Map: Methodology, Liberalism, Revolution and Despotism, 2006. Contributor of articles to journals. **Address:** Department of Politicals, Occidental College, 1600 Campus Rd., M-22, Los Angeles, CA 90041, U.S.A. **Online address:** boesche@oxy.edu

BOESSENECKER, John. American (born United States), b. 1953. **Genres:** History, Biography, Criminology/True Crime. **Career:** Attorney in private practice, 1985-; PBS, historical commentator; The History Channel, historical commentator; A&E, historical commentator. Writer. **Publications:** Badge and Buckshot: Lawlessness in Old California, 1988; (with M. Dugan) The Grey Fox: The True Story of Bill Miner, Last of the Old-Time Bandits, 1992; Lawman: The Life and Times of Harry Morse, 1835-1912, 1998; Gold Dust and Gunsmoke: Tales of Gold Rush Outlaws, Gunfighters, Lawmen and Vigilantes, 1999; Against the Vigilantes: The Recollections of Dutch Charley Duane, 1999; Bandido: The Life and Times of Tiburcio Vasquez, 2010. Contributor to books. **Address:** 220 Montgomery St., Ste. 600, San Francisco, CA 94104, U.S.A.

BOFF, Leonardo (Genezio Darci). Brazilian (born Brazil), b. 1938. **Genres:** Theology/Religion, Natural History, History. **Career:** Roman Catholic priest, 1964-92; Franciscan Philosophical and Theological Institute of Petrópolis, titular professor of basic, systematical and ecumenical theology, 1970-91; Franciscan Centers for Pastoral Studies for Latin America, professor of spiritual theology and Franciscanism, 1970, 1980; Institute Teologico Franciscano, professor of systematic theology, Franciscan spirituality, and theology of liberation, 1971-92; Centre for Theological and Spiritual Studies of the National Conference of Religious, professor of theology, 1975-90; Catholic University of Lisbon, visiting professor, 1976; Mexican American Cultural Center, visiting professor, 1977-78; Centre for the Defence of Human Rights (CDDH), co-founder and honorary president, 1979; University of Salamanca, visiting professor, 1980; National Movement for the Human Rights, co-founder, 1981; Ecumenical Centre of Services for Evangelization and Popular Education, professor and co-founder, 1981-93; University of Basel, visiting professor, 1987-88, 1997-98; Theology and Organic Assessorship, co-founder, 1988; Bonn-Potsdam-Petrópolis Partnership, co-founder, 1992; University of Rio de Janeiro, professor of theology, 1992-; Superior Institute for the Study of Religion, visiting professor, 1993; Rio de Janeiro State University, Philosophy and Human Sciences Institute, visiting professor, 1993, professor of ethics, 1993-2001, professor emeritus of ethics, philosophy of religion and ecology, 2001-; Barcelona University, visiting professor, 1997; Juiz de Fora Federal University, visiting professor, 2000; University of Heidelberg, visiting professor, 2001. Writer. **Publications:** O Evangelho do Cristo cósmico: A Realidade de um mito e o mito de umarealidade, 1971; The Question of Faith in the Resurrection of Jesus, 1971; Vida Religiosa e secularizacao, 1971; (co-author) A Oração nomundo secular: Desafio e chance, 1971; Die Kirche als Sakrament im Horizont der Welterfahrung: Versuch einer Legitimation und einerstruktur-funktionalistischen Grundlegung der Kirche im Anschluss an das II. Vatikanische Konzil, 1972; Jesus Cristo libertador: Ensaio decristologia crítica para o nosso tempo, 1972; A Ressurreicao de Cristo e a nossa na morte: A Dimensao antropologica da esperanca crista, 1972; (co-author) Credo para amamha, 1972; O Destino do homem e domundo, 1973; A Atualidade da experiencia de Deus, 1973; Vida para alem damorte: O Futuro, a festa e a contestacao do presente, 1974; (co-author) Experimentar Deus hoje, 1974; Minima Sacramentalia: Os Sacramentos da vidae a vida dos sacramentos, 1975; A Vida religiosa e a Igreja no processo delibertação, 1975; Teologia desde el cautiverio, 1975; Pobreza, obediencia, realizacion personal en la vida religiosa, 1975; (co-author) A Mulher na Igreja: Presenca e acao hoje, 1975; (co-author) Nosso Irmao Francisco de Assis, 1975; (co-author) Quem é Jesus Cristo no Brasil?, 1975; Teologia da libertacao e do cativeiro, 1976; A Graç alibertadora no mundo, 1976; Paixao de Cristo-paixao do mundo: Os Fatos as interpretacoes e o significado ontem ehoje, 1976; Encarnação: A Humanidade e a jovialidade de nosso Deus, 1976; Testigos de Dios en el corazon del mundo, 1977; Eclesiogênese: As Comunidades eclesiais de base reinventam a Igreja, 1977; Quées hacer teología desde Amréica Latina, 1977; A Fé naperiferia do mundo, 1978; Via-Sacra da justiça, 1978; (co-author) Die lateinamerikanische Befreiungstheologie, 1978; (co-author) Religiosita popolare e cammino diliberazione, 1978; (co-author) Jesucristo: Fe y historia, 1978; (co-author) Responsabilidades eclesiales y sociales de los religiosos, 1978; (co-author) Renovacao carismatica catolica, 1978; O Rosto materno de Deus: Ensaio interdisciplinar sobre o feminino e suas formas religiosas, 1979; O Pai-nosso: A Oração de libertação integral, 1979; Die Anliegen der Befreiungstheologie, 1979; (co-author) Da libertação: O Teológico das libertações sócio-históricas, 1979; Pueblas Herausforderung an die Franziskaner (Berichte, Dokumente, Kommentare), 1979; (co-author) Frontiers of Theology in Latin America, 1979; (co-author) Roberto Burle Marx: Homenagem à natureza, 1979; EmPreparo: O Homem, o nao-homem, o homem novo: Ensaio de antropologia apartir do oprimido, 1980; Em Preparo: A Ave-Maria, o espirito santo e ofeminino, 1980; O caminhar da Igreja com os oprimidos: do vale delágrimas à terra prometida, 1980; Igreja, carisma e poder, 1981; Vida segundo o espírito, 1982; Saint Francis: A Model for Human Liberation, 1982; (with C. Boff) Salvation and Liberation, 1984; (with P. Eicher) Theologie der Befreiung im Gespräch, 1985; (with C. Boff) Bedrohte Befreiung, 1985; Francisco de Assis: Homem do paraíso, 1985; (with C. Boff) Teologia dalibertação no debate atual, 1985; Como pregar a cruz hoje numasociedade de crucificados?, 1986; (ed. with V. Elizondo) The People of God Amidst the Poor, 1986; (ed. with V. Elizondo) Option for the Poor: Challenge to the Rich Countries, 1986; (co-author) Teólogos de la liberación hablan sobre la mujer, 1986; A Trindade, a sociedade e a libertacao, 1986; E a Igreja se fez povo: Eclesiogenese a Igreja que nasce defe do povo, 1986; (with C. Boff) Como fazer teologia dalibertação, 1986; (with C. Boff) Liberation Theology: From Dialogue to Confrontation, 1986; Sacraments of Life: Life of the Sacraments, 1987; Trinidad, la sociedad yla liberación, 1987; A Santíssima Trindade é a melhorcomunidade, 1988; (with B. Kern and A. Muller) Werkbuch Theologie der Befreiung: Anliegen, Streitpunkte, Personen: Materialien, und Texte, 1988; (ed. with V. Elizondo) Convergences and Differences, 1988; When Theology Listens to the Poor, 1988; Faith on the Edge: Religion and Marginalized Existence, 1989; (with F. Betto and A.H. Dávalos) Launidad de cristianos y marxistas: una utopía realizable?, 1989; (ed. with V. Elizondo) 1492-1992: The Voice of the Victims, 1990; Novaevangelização: Perspectiva dos oprimidos, 1990; (co-author) Direitos humanos, direitos dos pobres, 1991; (co-author) Sobre la opción por los pobres, 1991; Die Utopie Jesu: Neuevangelisierung nach 500 Jahren Lateinamerika, 1992; América Latina: Da Conquista à nova evangelização, 1992; Brasa sob cinzas: Estórias do anti-cotidiano, 1992; Ecologia, mundialização, espiritualidade: a emergência de um novoparadigma, 1993; (ed. with V. Elizondo) Is There Room for Christ in Asia?, 1993; The Path to Hope: Fragments from a Theologian's Journey, 1993; (co-author) Die Entdeckung der Eroberung: Reflexionen zum Bedenkjahr 500 Jahre Lateinamerika, 1993; (ed. with V. Elizondo) Any Room for Christ in Asia?, 1993; Igreja: Carisma e poder: Ensaios de eclesiologia militante, 1994; Jem'explique: Entretiens avec Christian Dutilleux, 1994; (with F. Betto) Mística e espiritualidade, 2nd ed., 1994; Nova Era: Acivilização planetária: Desafios à sociedade e aocristianismo, 1994; (ed. with V. Elizando) Ecology and Poverty: Cry of the Earth, Cry of the Poor, 1995; Princípio-Terra: A volta à Terracomo pátria comum, 1995; A teologia da libertação: Balançoe perspectives, 1996; Ecologia: Grito da terra, grito dos pobres, 1997; A voz doarco-írism, 2000; Santíssima Trinidade e a melhor comunidade, 2000; Saber cuidar: éticado humano, compaixão pela terra, 2000; Tempo de transcendência, 2000; Depois de 500 anos: Que Brasil queremos?, 2000; (co-author) Conversando em casa, 2000; (with M. Arruda) Globalização: Desafiossocioeconômicos, éticos e educativos: Uma visão a partir dosul, 2001; O casamento entre o céu e a terra: Contos dos povosindígenas do Brasil, 2001; Oracao de Sao Francisco, 2001; Espiritualidade: Um caminho de transformação, 2001; Fundamentalismo: A globalização e o futuro da humanidade, 2002; Doiceberg à arca de Noé: O nascimento de uma éticaplanetária, 2002; Crise: Oportunidade de crescimento, 2002; (with M.A. De Miranda) Terra América: imagens, 2003; Etica & Eco-Espiritualidade, 2003; Ethos mundial: Um consenso miñimo entre os humanos, 2003; Responder Florindo: Crise da civilização e revoluçãoradicalmente humana, 2004; Novas fronteiras da Igreja: O futuro de um povoa caminho, 2004; São José: A personificação do pai, 2005; Praying with Jesus and Mary: Our Father, Hail Mary, 2005; (with L. Ribeiro) Masculino, feminino: experiências vividas, 2007; Evangelho do Cristo cosmico: a busca da unidade do Todo na ciencia e na religiao, 2008; Homem: sata ou anjo bom?, 2008; (with M. Hathaway) Tao of Liberation: Exploring the Ecology of Transformation, 2009. Contributor of articles to periodicals. **Address:** Rio de Janeiro State University, 95 Rua Evaristo da Veiga, Lapa, Rio de Janeiro, RJ 20031-040, Brazil.

BOGACKI, Tomek. American/Polish (born Poland), b. 1950. **Genres:** Children's Fiction, Illustrations, Picture/Board Books, Literary Criticism And History. **Career:** Writer. **Publications:** FOR CHILDREN: (with A. Matthews) Crackling Brat, 1993; Cat and Mouse, 1996; Cat and Mouse in the Rain, 1997; I Hate You! I Like You!, 1997; Cat and Mouse in the Night, 1998; The Story of a Blue Bird, 1998; Cat and Mouse in the Snow, 1999; My First Garden, 2000; Circus Girl, 2001; (with E. Jenkins) Up, Up, Up!: A Bea and Haha Book, 2006; (with E. Jenkins) Num, Num, Num!: A Bea and Ha Ha Book, 2006; (with E. Jenkins) Plonk, Plonk, Plonk!: A Bea and Haha Book, 2006; Champion of Children, 2009; Monkeys and the Universe, 2009. Illustrator of books by K. Banks, E. Jenkins and W. Kreye. **Address:** Farrar, Straus & Giroux Inc., 19 Union Sq. W, New York, NY 10003, U.S.A.

BOGART, Eleanor A(nne). American (born United States), b. 1928. **Genres:** Writing/Journalism, Military/Defense/Arms Control, Reference. **Career:** Freelance writer and educator. **Publications:** (With W.M. Smith) The Wars of Peggy Hull: The Life and Times of a War Correspondent, 1991. Contributor to magazines and newspapers. **Address:** 2924 Walnut St., Hays, KS 67601-1721, U.S.A.

BOGART, Jo Ellen. American/Canadian (born Canada), b. 1945. **Genres:** Children's Fiction, Children's Non-fiction, Literary Criticism And History. **Career:** Austin Independent School District, teacher, 1968; Margaret Roane Center, teacher of educable mentally retarded teenagers, 1973; Wellington County Board, teacher, 1983-92. Writer, 1993-. **Publications:** Dylan's Lullaby, 1988; Malcolm's Runaway Soap, 1988; 10 for Dinner, 1989; Daniel's Dog, 1990; Sarah Saw a Blue Macaw, 1991; Mama's Bed, 1993; Two Too Many, 1994; Gifts, 1994; Jeremiah Learns to Read, 1997; Money, Make It, Spend It, Save It, 2001; The Night the Stars Flew, 2001; Capturing Joy: The Story of Maud Lewis, 2002; Emily Carr: At the Edge of the World, 2003, The Big Tree Gang, 2005; Crazy for Puppies, 2006; Out and about with the Big Tree Gang, 2006; Big and Small, Room for All, 2009. **Address:** 172 Palmer St., Guelph, ON N1E 2R6, Canada. **Online address:** joellenbogart@rogers.com

BOGART, Stephen Humphrey. American (born United States), b. 1949. **Genres:** Mystery/Crime/Suspense, Autobiography/Memoirs, Biography. **Career:** ESPN, producer, 1979-; National Broadcasting Co., staff, 1984-; WFLA-TV, executive producer, 1988-; Court TV, studio line producer, 1991-; author, 1995-; WPIX-TV, head writer and news editor; CBS TV, field producer; MODA Entertainment Inc., president. **Publications:** Play It Again (mystery), 1995; (with G. Provost) Bogart: In Search of My Father (biography/autobiography), 1995; Remake: As Time Goes By, 1997; (foreword) Bogie: A Celebration of the Life and Films of Humphrey Bogart, 2006. **Address:** MODA Entertainment Inc., 1325 Ave. of the Americas, 27th Fl., New York, NY 10019, U.S.A. **Online address:** sbogart@modaentertainment.com

BOGDAN, Radu J. American/Romanian (born Romania) **Genres:** Philosophy, Humanities, Adult Non-fiction. **Career:** Institute for Teachers Training, assistant professor, 1970-74; Academy of Economic Sciences, lecturer, 1972-74; Stanford University, teaching assistant, 1976-79, instructor, 1979-80, visiting assistant professor, 1981; Tulane University, assistant professor, 1980-86, associate professor, 1986-95, professor, 1995-, Cognitive Studies Program, founder and director, 1984-, adjunct professor of psychology, 2004-; University of Bucharest, The Cognitive Science Program, coordinator, 2003-; Université Catholique de Louvain, professor, 2001-02; Bilkent University, visiting professor. Writer. **Publications:** (With A. Milcoveanu) Logic: An Introduction (in Romanian), 1974; Grounds for Cognition: How Goal-Guided Behavior Shapes the Mind, 1994; Interpreting Minds: The Evolution of a Practice, 1997; Minding Minds: Evolving a Reflexive Mind by Interpreting Others, 2000; Predicative Minds: The Social Ontogeny of Propositional Thinking, 2008; Our Own Minds: Executive and Social Grounds of Self-Consciousness and Self-Understanding, 2009; Our Own Minds: Sociocultural Grounds for Self-Consciousness, 2010. EDITOR: Logic, Methodology and Philosophy of Science (in Romanian), 1971; Jaakko Hintikka (in Romanian), 1972; Mario Bunge (in Romanian), 1973; (with I. Niiniluoto) Logic, Language and Probability, 1973; (with A. Milcoveanu) Logică, pe înțelesul elesul tuturor, 1974; Local Induction, 1976; Patrick Suppes, 1979; Keith Lehrer, 1981; Henry E. Kyburg and Isaac Levi, 1982; D.M. Armstrong, 1984; Roderick M. Chisholm, 1986; Belief, 1986; Mind and Common Sense, 1991. SERIES EDITOR: Profiluri si Sinteze, 1971-74; Profiles: An International Series on Contemporary Philosophers and Logicians, 1977-90. Contributor to journals. **Address:** Department of Philosophy, Tulane University, Rm. 105 I, Newcomb Hall, New Orleans, LA 70118, U.S.A. **Online address:** bogdan@tulane.edu

BOGDANICH, Walt. American (born United States), b. 1950. **Genres:** Medicine/Health. **Career:** Compass, reporter, editor, 1974-75; Dayton Daily News, reporter, 1977; Cleveland Press, reporter, 1977-79; Cleveland Plain Dealer, reporter, 1980-84; Wall Street Journal, reporter, 1984-88, Washington correspondent, 1989-93; ABC-TV, producer of Day One, 1993; CBS News, investigative producer for 60 Minutes; New York Times, investigative editor of finance and business desk, 2001-, assistant editor, 2003-; Columbia University Graduate School of Journalism, adjunct professor. **Publications:** The Great White Lie: How Americas Hospitals Betray Our Trust and Endanger Our Lives, 1991. **Address:** The New York Times Co., 229 W 43rd St., New York, NY 10036, U.S.A.

BOGDANOR, Vernon. British (born England), b. 1943. **Genres:** Politics/Government. **Career:** Oxford University, Brasenose College, fellow and tutor in Politics, 1966, senior tutor, 1979-85, 1996-97, reader in government, 1990-96, professor of government, 1996-, vice-principal, acting principal, 2002-03, now emeritus fellow; Gresham College, professor of law, 2004-08; King's College, Institute for Contemporary History, research professor, visiting professor; Institute for Advanced Legal Studies, honorary fellow; Queen's College, honorary fellow. Writer. **Publications:** Who Commands the Heights?: Socialism and Industry, 1974; Devolution, 1979; The People and the Party System, 1981; Multi-Party Politics and the Constitution, 1983; What is Proportional Representation?, 1984; (with S.E. Finer and B. Rudden) Comparing Constitutions, 1995; The Monarchy and the Constitution, 1995; Politics and the Constitution, 1996; Power and the People: A Guide to Constitutional

Reform, 1997; Devolution in the United Kingdom, 1999. EDITOR: (with R. Skidelsky) The Age of Affluence 1951-1964, 1970; Lothair, by Disraeli, 1975; Liberal Party Politics, 1983; (with D. Butler) Democracy and Elections: Electoral Systems and Their Political Consequences, 1983; Coalition Government in Western Europe, 1983; Parties and Democracy in Britain and America, 1984; Science and Politics, 1984; Representatives of the People?, 1985; Blackwell's Encyclopaedia of Political Institutions, 1987; Constitutions in Democratic Politics, 1988; The Blackwell Encyclopaedia of Political Science, 1991; (with D. Butler and R. Summers) The Law, Politics, and the Constitution: Essays in Honour of Geoffrey Marshall, 1999; The British Constitution in the Twentieth Century, 2003; (and intro.) Joined-up Government, 2005; New British Constitution, 2009; The Coalition and the Constitution, 2011. **Address:** Department of Politics & International Relations, Brasenose College, Oxford, OX OX1 4AJ, England.

BOGEN, David S. (David Skillen Bogen). American (born United States), b. 1941. **Genres:** Law. **Career:** University of Maryland, School of Law, professor, 1969-2006, professor emeritus, 2006-, associate dean for academic affairs, 1992-94, 1997-99; University of Sydney, Parsons research fellow; California Western School of Law, visiting professor; University of Denver, School of Law, visiting professor; Villanova University, Law School, Harold Gill Reuschlein visiting professor. Writer. **Publications:** Bulwark of Liberty: The Court and the First Amendment, 1984; (as David Skillen Bogen) Privileges and Immunities: A Reference Guide to the United States Constitution, 2003. **Address:** School of Law, University of Maryland, Rm. 445, 500 W Baltimore St., Baltimore, MD 21201-1786, U.S.A. **Online address:** dbogen@law.umaryland.edu

BOGEN, David Skillen. *See* **BOGEN, David S.**

BOGGS, Belle McQuade. American (born United States), b. 1977. **Genres:** Literary Criticism And History. **Career:** Writer and educator. **Publications:** Mattaponi Queen, 2010. Contributor to periodicals. **Address:** Hawbridge School, 1735 Saxapahaw-Bethlehem Church Rd., Saxapahaw, NC 27340, U.S.A. **Online address:** belleboggs@hotmail.com

BOGIN, Magda. (Meg Bogin). American (born United States), b. 1950. **Genres:** Novels, Translations, Women's Studies And Issues. **Career:** City University of New York, City College, writing program faculty, 1984-; Columbia University, School of the Arts, faculty, 1994-; Princeton University, faculty; Under the Volcano, founder and director. Writer. **Publications:** (As Meg Bogin) The Women Troubadours, 1976; (as Meg Bogin) The Path to Pain Control, 1982; (intro.) Trobairitz: Poetes Occitanes del Segle XII, 1983; (trans.) I. Allende, The House of the Spirits (novel), 1985; (trans. with C. Vicuna and ed.) The Selected Poems of Rosario Castellanos, 1988; (trans., intro. and ed.) Selected Poems of Salvador Espriu, 1989; (trans. and ed.) M. de Cervantes Saavedra, Don Quixote, 1991; Natalya, God's Messenger (novel), 1994; (trans.) My name is Victoria, 2010. **Address:** 425 Riverside Dr., Apt. 14H, New York, NY 10025, U.S.A. **Online address:** director@underthevolcano.org

BOGIN, Meg. *See* **BOGIN, Magda.**

BOGLE, Donald. American (born United States) **Genres:** Film, Biography, Art/Art History. **Career:** Ebony Magazine, staff writer, assistant editor; New York University, Tisch School of the Arts, instructor; University of Pennsylvania, instructor. Historian and editor. **Publications:** Toms, Coons, Mulattoes, Mammies and Bucks: An Interpretive History of Blacks in American Films, 1973, 4th ed., 2001; Brown Sugar: Eighty Years of America's Black Female Superstars, 1980; Blacks in American Films and Television: An Encyclopedia, 1988; (ed.) Black Arts Annual 1987/88, 1989; Louis Armstrong: A Cultural Legacy, 1994; Dorothy Dandridge: A Biography, 1997; Primetime Blues: African Americans on Network Television, 2001; Bright Boulevards, Bold Dreams: The Story of Black Hollywood, 2005; Brown Sugar: Over One Hundred Years of America's Black Female Superstars, 2007; Heat Wave: The Life and Career of Ethel Waters, 2011. Contributor to books. **Address:** c/o Author Mail, Farrar Straus & Giroux, 19 Union Sq. W, New York, NY 10001, U.S.A.

BOGLE, Warren. *See* **BERGMAN, Andrew.**

BOGOSIAN, Eric. American (born United States), b. 1953. **Genres:** Plays/Screenplays, Novels. **Career:** Woburn Drama Guild, co-founder. Actor and writer. **Publications:** PLAYS: (With M. Zwack) Drinking in America, 1987; Talk Radio, 1988; Pounding Nails in the Floor With My Forehead, 1994; The Essential Bogosian: Talk Radio, Drinking in America, Funhouse and Men Inside, 1994; SubUrbia, 1995, rev. ed., 2009; Love's Fire: Seven New Plays Inspired by Seven Shakespearean Sonnets: Original Works, 1998; Griller, 1998. OTHERS: Notes from Underground (novel), 1997; Physiognomy: The Mark Seliger Photographs, 1999; Mall: A Novel, 2000; 31 Ejaculations, 2000; Wake Up and Smell the Coffee, 2002; Ararat, 2002; Humpty Dumpty, 2004; Red Angel, 2005; Wasted Beauty, 2005; (afterword) One Day in the Life of Ivan Denisovich, 2008; Perforated Heart: A Novel, 2009. Contributor to periodicals. **Address:** c/o George Lane, Creative Artists Agency, 162 5th Ave. 6th Fl., New York, NY 10010, U.S.A. **Online address:** eric@ericbogosian.com

BOGUE, Gary L. American/Argentine (born Argentina), b. 1938?. **Genres:** Young Adult Non-fiction, Children's Fiction. **Career:** Lindsay Wildlife Museum, curator, 1967-79; Contra Costa Newspapers, columnist, 1970-; Animal Rescue Foundation, executive director, 1992-93; Western Interpreters Association, co-founder and president. **Publications:** NONFICTION: (with D. Garcelon) Raptor Rehabilitation (textbook), 1972; It's a Wild Life, 1989; Isis, 1989; FOR CHILDREN: The Raccoon Next Door, 2003; There's an Opossum in My Backyard, 2007; There's a Hummingbird in My Backyard, 2010. **Address:** PO Box 8099, Walnut Creek, CA 94596-8099, U.S.A. **Online address:** garybug@infionline.net

BOGUS, Diane Adams. *See* **ADAMZ-BOGUS, S. Diane.**

BOGUS, S. Diane. *See* **ADAMZ-BOGUS, S. Diane.**

BOHJALIAN, Chris. (Christopher A. Bohjalian). American (born United States), b. 1960. **Genres:** Novels, Adult Non-fiction, Military/Defense/Arms Control. **Career:** Burlington Free Press, book critic, 1987-2004, columnist, 1992-; Vermont Life Magazine, book critic, 1991-2000. Freelance journalist. **Publications:** A Killing in the Real World, 1988; Hangman, 1991; Past the Bleachers, 1992; Water Witches, 1995; Midwives, 1997; The Law of Similars, 1999; Trans-Sister Radio, 2000; The Buffalo Soldier, 2002; Idyll Banter: Weekly Excursions to a Very Small Town, 2003; Before You Know Kindness: A Novel, 2004; The Double Bind: A Novel, 2007; Skeletons at the Feast: A Novel, 2008; Secrets of Eden: A Novel, 2010; The Night Strangers: A Novel, 2011. Contributor to periodicals and magazine. **Address:** c/o Jane Gelfman, Gelfman Schneider, 250 W 57th St., New York, NY 10107-0001, U.S.A. **Online address:** chris@chrisbohjalian.com

BOHJALIAN, Christopher A. *See* **BOHJALIAN, Chris.**

BOHLMEIJER, Arno. Dutch (born Netherlands), b. 1956. **Genres:** Novels, Adult Non-fiction, Literary Criticism And History, History, Translations, Young Adult Fiction. **Career:** Sprengerloo High School, teacher of English and French, 1978-92; freelance writer, 1993-; Christian High School, teacher. **Publications:** NOVELS: Breekpunt, 1991; De Luwte, 1992; Aan een engel die nieuw is, 1994; Het Vermoeden, 1995; (and trans.) Something Very Sorry, 1996; Rubbish in My Head, 1999; Help Me, 1999. OTHERS: The Intruder: A Jungian Study of Henry James, 1987; The Secret of the Truth, 2000; Little Freedom, 2002; To An Angel Who is New, 2004; Minnie & Flo: Beesten en meisjes, 2006; Minnie & Flo-Per ongeluk, 2007. Contributor to periodicals. **Address:** 208 De Waarden, Zutphen, 7206, Netherlands.

BOHM, Arnd. Canadian (born Canada), b. 1953. **Genres:** Literary Criticism And History, Adult Non-fiction. **Career:** Carleton University, associate professor of English, professor; Queen's University, adjunct associate professor of German. Writer. **Publications:** Goethe's Faust and European Epic: Forgetting the Future (nonfiction), 2007. Contributor of articles to books and journals. **Address:** Department of English Language and Literature, Carleton University, 1907 Dunton Twr., 1125 Colonel By Dr., Ottawa, ON K1S 5B6, Canada. **Online address:** arnd_bohm@carleton.ca

BOHMAN, James F. American (born United States) **Genres:** Philosophy, Social Sciences. **Career:** Boston University, visiting assistant professor, 1985-86; Saint Louis University, assistant professor, 1986-91, associate professor, 1991-96, professor of philosophy, 1996-, Danforth I chair in the humanities, 1996-, Danforth professor in the humanities, professor of international studies, 2000-; University of Frankfurt, visiting professor, 2002, 2004. Writer. **Publications:** NONFICTION: New Philosophy of Social Science: Problems of Indeterminacy, 1991; Public Deliberation: Pluralism, Complexity, and Democracy, 1996; Democracy Across Borders: From Dêmos to Dêmoi, 2007; Decentered Democracy: From Pluralism to Cosmopolitanism, forthcoming; Living without Freedom: Republican Cosmopolitanism and the Rule of Law, forthcoming. EDITOR: (with K. Baynes and T. McCarthy) After Philosophy: End or Transformation?, 1987; (with D.R. Hiley and R. Shusterman) The Interpretive Turn: Philosophy, Science, Culture, 1991; (with M. Lutz-Bachmann) Frieden durch Recht, 1996; (with W. Rehg) Deliberative Democracy: Essays on Reason and Politics, 1997; (with M. Lutz-Bachmann) Perpetual Peace: Essays on Kant's Cosmopolitan Ideal, 1997; (with W. Rehg) Pluralism and the Pragmatic Turn: The Transformation of Critical Theory, 2001; (ed. with M. Lutz-Bachmann) Weltstaat oder Staatenwelt?: Für und wider die Idee einer Weltrepublik, 2002; (co-ed.) Cosmopolitismo, 2009; Contributor to books and periodicals. **Address:** Department of Philosophy, Saint Louis University, 204 Adorjan Hall, 221 N Grand Blvd., St. Louis, MO 63103, U.S.A. **Online address:** bohmanjf@slu.edu

BOHNHOFF, Maya Kaathryn. American (born United States), b. 1954. **Genres:** Romance/Historical, Science Fiction/Fantasy, Poetry, Novels, Young Adult Fiction. **Career:** Kelly Services, manager of instructional design, 1994-95; ComTrain Inc., director of development. Writer. **Publications:** MERI SERIES: The Meri, 1992; Taminy, 1993; The Crystal Rose, 1995. NOVELS: The Spirit Gate, 1996; (with M. Reaves) Mr. Twilight, 2006. OTHERS: (with M.S. Zicree) Magic Time: Angelfire, 2002; (adaptor) Kino no tabi, 2006; (contrib.) Missing, 2007; Star Wars: Shadow Games, 2011. Contributor of articles to periodicals. Works appear in anthologies. **Address:** Mystic Fig Records, 14708 Echo Ridge Dr., Nevada City, CA 95959-9631, U.S.A. **Online address:** syntax@oro.net

BOHN-SPECTOR, Claudia. American (born United States) **Genres:** Photography, Art/Art History. **Career:** Curator and writer. **Publications:** (With J.A. Watts) The Great Wide Open: Panoramic Photographs of the American West, 2001. **Address:** c/o Author Mail, Rizzoli/Universe International Publications, 300 Park Ave. S, Fl. 3, New York, NY 10010, U.S.A.

BOHNTINSKY, Dori. American (born United States), b. 1951. **Genres:** Speech/Rhetoric, Poetry, Social Sciences, Young Adult Non-fiction, Education. **Career:** Alameda County Medical Center, Department of Speech Pathology and Audiology, manager, 1980-2002; freelance writer, 2002-. **Publications:** Standard American English Pronunciation Training (workbook with audiotapes), 1994; Pragmatics for Effective Speaking (workbook), 1998; Once upon a Lunar Eclipse (poetry), 2000; The Healing Room: Discovering Joy through the Journal (nonfiction), 2002. **Address:** PO Box 20248, Castro Valley, CA 94546, U.S.A. **Online address:** inwordbound@aol.com

BOHRER, Frederick Nathaniel. American (born United States), b. 1956. **Genres:** Adult Non-fiction, History. **Career:** National Gallery of Art, Center for Advanced Study in the Visual Arts, Samuel H. Kress predoctoral fellow, 1985-87; Getty Grant Program postdoctoral fellow in the history of art and the humanities, 1992-93; Clark Art Institute, fellow, 2002; Hood College, associate professor of art and archaeology and department chair, 2007-, professor. Writer. **Publications:** (Ed.) Sevruguin and the Persian Image: Photographs of Iran, 1870-1930, 1999; Orientalism and Visual Culture: Imagining Mesopotamia in Nineteenth-Century Europe, 2003. Contributor to periodicals and journals. **Address:** Department of Art & Archaeology, Hood College, Rm. 102, Tatem Arts Ctr., 401 Rosemont Ave., Frederick, MD 21701, U.S.A. **Online address:** bohrer@od.edu

BOICE, James. American (born United States), b. 1982. **Genres:** Novels. **Career:** Writer. **Publications:** MVP (novel), 2007; Nova, 2009; The Good and the Ghastly, 2011. **Address:** Nancy Yost Literary Agency, 350 7th Ave., Ste. 2003, New York, NY 10001, U.S.A. **Online address:** james.boice@jamesboice.com

BOIES, David. American (born United States), b. 1941. **Genres:** Law. **Career:** Cravath, Swaine & Moore, partner, 1973-97; United States Department of Justice, special trial counsel, 1998-2000; Boies, Schiller & Flexner LLP, chairman, founder and managing partner, 2011-. Writer. **Publications:** (With P.R. Verkuil) Public Control of Business: Cases, Notes, and Questions, 1977; (co-author) CBS's Reply to Plaintiff's Memorandum in Opposition to CBS's Motion to Dismiss and for Summary Judgment, 1984; (co-author) Memorandum in Support of Defendant CBS's Motion to Dismiss and for Summary Judgment, 1984; Courting Justice: From NY Yankees v. Major League Baseball to Bush v. Gore, 1997-2000, 2004. **Address:** Boies, Schiller & Flexner L.L.P., 333 Main St., Armonk, NY 10504, U.S.A. **Online address:** dboies@bsfllp.com

BOISSEAU, Michelle. American (born United States), b. 1955. **Genres:** Poetry, Literary Criticism And History. **Career:** Virginia Intermont College, assistant professor of English, 1985-87; Morehead State University, associate professor of English and creative writing, 1988-95; University of Missouri, associate professor of English and creative writing, professor of English, 1995-, BkMk Press, associate editor. **Publications:** POETRY: No Private Life, 1990; Understory, 1996; Trembling Air, 2003; Sunday in Godyears: Poems, 2009. OTHER: (with R. Wallace) Writing Poems (textbook), 4th ed., 1996, (with H. Bar-Nadav and R. Wallace) 8th ed., 2012. Contributor of articles to periodicals. **Address:** Department of English, University of Missouri, 16C Cockefair Hall, 5100 Rockhill Rd., Kansas City, MO 64110, U.S.A. **Online address:** boisseaum@umkc.edu

BOISVERT, Raymond D. American (born United States), b. 1947. **Genres:** Philosophy, Physics, Politics/Government. **Career:** Clark College, instructor, assistant professor of philosophy, 1978-84; Siena College, professor of philosophy, 1984-, coordinator of the college core; Universite Lumiere, Fulbright professor in American studies, 1991-92. Writer. **Publications:** Dewey's Metaphysics, 1988; John Dewey: Rethinking Our Time, 1998; From Soil to Spirit: Food Transforms Philosophy, forthcoming. **Address:** Department of Philosophy, Siena College, Siena Hall 423, 515 Loudon Rd., Loudonville, NY 12211-1462, U.S.A. **Online address:** boisvert@siena.edu

BOITANI, Piero. Italian (born Italy), b. 1947. **Genres:** Literary Criticism And History, Translations. **Career:** Cambridge University, lecturer in Italian, 1971-74; University of Pescara, lecturer in English literature, 1974-79; University of Perugia, professor of English literature, 1979-85; University of Rome, chair of English literature, 1985-98, chair of comparative literature, 1998-, professor of conservation biology and animal ecology, 2000-, Department of Animal and Human Biology, head, 2001-, professor of comparative literature; University of Connecticut, visiting professor, 1987-89; European Society for English Studies, president, 1989-95; University of California, chair of Italian culture, 1990-; University of Italian, chair of comparative literature, 2007-; Universities of Cambridge, visiting professor; British Academy, fellow; Academia Europaea, fellow. Writer. **Publications:** Prosatori negrí Americani, 1973; Chaucer and Boccaccio, 1977; Narrativa del Medioevo inglese, 1980; English Medieval Narrative in the Thirteenth and Fourteenth Centuries, 1982; Chaucer and the Imaginary World of Fame, 1984; The Tragic and the Sublime in Medieval Literature, 1989; L'ombra di Ulisse, 1992, trans. as The Shadow of Ulysses, 1994; Ri-Scritture, 1997, trans. as Re-Scriptures: The Bible and Its Rewritings, 1999; Sulle orme di Ulisse, 1998; Ulisse: archeologia dell'uomo moderno, 1998; Il genio di migliorare un'invenzione, 1999; Bible and its Rewritings, 1999; Genius to Improve an Invention: Literary Transitions, 2002; Parole alate: voci nella poesia e nella storia da Omero all'11 settembre, 2004; Dante's Poetry of the Donati, 2007; Letteratura europea e Medioevo volgare, 2007; Winged Words: Flight in Poetry and History, 2007; Prima lezione sulla letteratura, 2007; (intro.) Il viaggio dellanima, 2007; Vangelo Secondo Shakespeare, 2009. TRANSLATOR: Sir Gawain and the Green Knight; The Cloud of Unknowing, 1998. EDITOR: Humane Medievalist: And Other Essays in English Literature and Learning, from Chaucer to Eliot, 1982; Chaucer and the Italian Trecento, 1983; (with J. Mann) The Cambridge Chaucer Companion, 1986; The European Tragedy of Troilus, 1989; (with A. Torti) Religion in the Poetry and Drama of the Late Middle Ages in England, 1991; (with A. Torti) Poetics: Theory and Practice in Medieval English Literature, 1991; (with A. Torti) Interpretation, Medieval and Modern, 1993; (with A. Torti) Mediaevalitas: Reading the Middle Ages, 1996; (with J. Mann) Cambridge Companion to Chaucer, 2003. Contributor to periodicals. **Address:** Department of English Literature, University of Rome, Vle dell, Rome, 00185, Italy. **Online address:** pboitani@uniroma1.it

BOJANOWSKI, Marc. American (born United States), b. 1977?. **Genres:** Novels, Young Adult Fiction. **Career:** Writer. **Publications:** The Dog Fighter, 2004. Contributor to periodicals. **Address:** c/o Author Mail, William Morrow/HarperCollins Publishers, 10 E 53rd St., 7th Fl., New York, NY 10022, U.S.A.

BÖK, Christian. Canadian (born Canada), b. 1966. **Genres:** Novels, Sciences, Young Adult Fiction. **Career:** York University, professor of English; University of Calgary, associate professor, Undergraduate Student Program, associate head. Poet and conceptual artist. **Publications:** Crystallography: Book One of Information Theory, 1994, 2nd. ed. as Crystallography, 2003; Eunoia, 2001; Pataphysics: The Poetics of an Imaginary Science, 2002; (ed.) Ground Works: Avant-Garde for Thee, 2002; The Cyborg Opera, forthcoming. Contributor to periodicals. **Address:** Department of English, University of Calgary, 1140 Social Sciences, 2500 University Dr. NW, Calgary, AB T2N 1N4, Canada. **Online address:** cbok@ucalgary.ca

BOK, Derek Curtis. American (born United States), b. 1930. **Genres:** Education, Law, Politics/Government. **Career:** Harvard University, assistant professor, 1958-61, professor of law, 1961-68, Harvard Law School, dean, 1968-71, president of university, 1971-91, now university president emeritus, 300th anniversary university research professor, 1991-, interim president, 2006-07, Hauser Center for Nonprofit Organizations, acting director, faculty chair, Harvard Graduate School of Education, faculty, Harvard Kennedy School, faculty; American Council on Education, chair, 1981-82; Citizens Democracy Corps, director, 1990-. Lawyer and writer. **Publications:** The First Three Years of the Schuman Plan, 1955; (ed. with A. Cox and R.A. Gorman) Cases and Materials on Labor Law, 1962, 10th ed., 1986; (with M.D. Kossoris) Methods of Adjusting to Automation and Technological Change, 1964; Automation, Productivity and Manpower Problems, 1964; (with J.T. Dunlop) Labor and the American Community, 1970; Beyond the Ivory Tower: Social Responsibilities of the Modern University, 1982; Higher Learning, 1986; Universities and the Future of America, 1990; The Improvement of Teaching, 1991; The Cost of Talent: How Executives and Professionals Are Paid and How It Affects America, 1993; The State of the Nation: Government and the Quest for a Better Society, 1996; (with W.G. Bowen) The Shape of the River: Long-Term Consequences of Considering Race in College and University Admissions, 1998; (contrib.) Between Friends: Perspectives on John Kenneth Galbraith, 1999; The Trouble with Government, 2001; Universities in the Marketplace: The Commercialization of Higher Education, 2003; Estados Unidos y el fin de la hegemonía, 2004; Our Underachieving Colleges: A Candid Look at How Much Students Learn and Why They Should be Learning More, 2006; The Politics of Happiness: What Government Can Learn from the New Research on Well-being, 2010. Contributor to journals. **Address:** John F. Kennedy School of Government, Harvard University, 79 JFK St., PO Box 50, Cambridge, MA 02138-5801, U.S.A. **Online address:** derek_bok@harvard.edu

BOK, Sissela. American/Swedish (born Sweden), b. 1934. **Genres:** Ethics, Philosophy, Social Commentary, Autobiography/Memoirs, Intellectual History, Psychology, Writing/Journalism, Translations, Translations. **Career:** Simmons College, lecturer, 1971-72; Harvard University, Interfaculty Program in Medical Ethics, fellow, 1972-73, faculty, 1982-84; Harvard-Massachusetts Institute of Technology, Division of Health Sciences and Technology, lecturer in medical ethics, 1975-80, lecturer in university core curriculum, 1982-84, visiting professor, 1986; Brandeis University, associate professor, 1985-89, professor of philosophy, 1989-92; Harvard University, Harvard School of Public Health, Harvard Center for Population and Development Studies, distinguished fellow, 1993-, senior visiting fellow. Writer. **Publications:** (Ed. with J.A. Behnke) The Dilemmas of Euthanasia, 1975; Lying: Moral Choice in Public and Private Life, 1978, 3rd ed., 1999; (ed. with D. Callahan) Ethics Teaching in Higher Education, 1980; Secrets: On the Ethics of Concealment and Revelation, 1983; Alva: Ett kvinnoliv, 1987; A Strategy for Peace: Human Values and the Threat of War, 1989; Alva Myrdal: A Daughter's Memoir, 1991; TV Violence, Children and the Press: Eight Rationales Inhibiting Public Policy Debates, 1994; Common Values, 1995, rev. ed., 2002; (intro.) An American Dilemma: The Negro Problem and Modern Democracy, 1996; Mayhem: Violence as Public Entertainment, 1998; (with G. Dworkin and R. Frey) Euthanasia and Physician-Assisted Suicide, 1998; Exploring Happiness: From Aristotle to Brain Science, 2010. **Address:** Harvard Ctr. for Population & Dev. Studies, Harvard University, 9 Bow St., Cambridge, MA 02138, U.S.A. **Online address:** sbok@hsph.harvard.edu

BOKINA, John. American (born United States), b. 1948. **Genres:** Politics/Government, History, Classics, Intellectual History, Music, Philosophy. **Career:** University of Illinois, teaching assistant, 1971; University of Illinois-Urbana-Champaign, teaching assistant, 1972-74, 1975-76, instructor, 1973-76; University of Detroit, visiting assistant professor, 1976-77, instructor, 1977-79, director of the honors program, 1977-80, assistant professor, 1979-81; University of Texas, assistant professor, 1982-85, associate professor, 1986-92, professor, 1992-2011, professor emeritus, 2011-; Central Michigan University, Department of Political Science, visiting professor. Writer. **Publications:** (With J.P. Friedman and J. Miller) Contemporary Political Theory, 1977; (ed. with T.J. Lukes) Marcuse: From the New Left to the Next Left, 1994; Opera and Politics: From Monteverdi to Henze, 1997. Contributor to journals. Works appear in anthologies. **Address:** Department of Political Science, Central Michigan University, 234 Anspach Hall, Mount Pleasant, MI 48859, U.S.A. **Online address:** bokin1jr@cmich.edu

BOLAM, Robyn. (Marion Lomax). British (born England), b. 1953. **Genres:** Poetry, Songs/Lyrics And Libretti, Literary Criticism And History, Theatre, Women's Studies And Issues, Writing/Journalism, Education, Reference, Reference. **Career:** University of Reading Library, senior library assistant, 1975-77; King Alfred's College, part-time lecturer in English, 1983-86; Open University, part-time tutor and counselor, 1983-88; University of Reading, part-time lecturer in English, 1983-87; St. Mary's College, lecturer, 1987-89, senior lecturer in English, 1989-95, professor of literature, 1995-; National Association of Writers in Education, chair, 1998-2003; University of Southampton, royal literary fund fellow. Writer. **Publications:** AS MARION LOMAX: Stage Images and Traditions: Shakespeare to Ford, 1987; The Peepshow Girl (poems), 1989; Beyond Men and Dreams (libretto), 1991; Tis Pity She's a Whore and Other Plays, J. Ford, 1995; Raiding the Borders (poems), 1996. EDITOR: Time Present and Time Past: Poets at the University of Kent at Canterbury, 1965-1985, 1985; (with D. Constantine) New Worlds: The 1992 Berkshire Literature Festival Anthology, 1992; The Rover, A. Behn, 1995, rev. ed., 2005. AS ROBYN BOLAM: (ed.) Eliza's Babes: Four Centuries of Women's Poetry in English, 2005; New Wings: Poems 1977-2007, 2007. Works appear in anthologies. Contributor to periodicals. **Address:** School of Communication, Culture & Creative Arts, St. Mary's College, Waldegrave Rd., Twickenham, SR TW1 4SX, England. **Online address:** bolamr@smuc.ac.uk

BOLAND, Eavan (Aisling). (Eavan Casey). Irish (born Ireland), b. 1944. **Genres:** Poetry, Literary Criticism And History. **Career:** Trinity College, junior lecturer, 1967-68, writer-in-residence; School of Irish Studies, lecturer, 1975-88; Washington University St Louis, Hurst professor, 1993; National Maternity Hospital, poet-in-residence, 1994; Stanford University, Bella Mabury and Eloise Mabury Knapp professor in humanities, Stanford and Lane professor, 1995-, Creative Writing Program, Melvin and Bill Lane Professor, director, 1997-2000, 2002-; University College Dublin, writer-in-residence; University of California, regent's lecturer; University of Utah, faculty. Writer. **Publications:** POETRY: 23 Poems, 1962; Autumn Essay, 1963; Poetry, 1963; New Territory, 1967; The War Horse, 1975; In Her Own Image, 1980; Introducing Eavan Boland, 1981; Night Feed, 1982; The Journey, 1983; The Journey and Other Poems, 1987; Selected Poems, 1989; Outside History: Selected Poems, 1980-90, 1990; In a Time of Violence, 1994; (co-author) Dozen Lips, 1994; An Origin Like Water: Collected Poems 1967-87, 1995; Persephone, 1996; Anna Liffey, 1997; The Lost Land: Poems, 1998; Against Love Poetry, 2001. Domestic Violence, 2007. OTHER: (with M.M. Liammoir) W.B. Yeats and His World, 1971; A Kind of Scar: The Woman Poet in a National Tradition, 1989; Object Lessons, 1995; (ed. with M. Strand) The Making of a Poem: A Norton Anthology of Poetic Forms, 2001; Code, 2001; Three Irish Poets, 2003; A Look in the Mirror, 2003; After Every War, 2004; (ed.) Irish Writers on Writing, 2007; The Making of a Sonnet: A Norton Anthology of the Sonnet (with E. Hirsch), 2008; New Collected Poems, 2008; A Journey With Two Maps 2011. Works appear in anthologies. Contributor to newspapers and journals. **Address:** Department of English, Stanford University, Rm. 460-223C, Stanford, CA 94305-2087, U.S.A. **Online address:** boland@stanford.edu

BOLAND, Janice. American (born United States) **Genres:** Children's Fiction, Education, Biography. **Career:** Richard C. Owen Publishers Inc., director of children's books, 1990-. Writer, illustrator, graphic artist and educator. **Publications:** Annabel, 1993; Annabel Again, 1995; A Dog Named Sam, 1996; The Fox, 1996; The Strongest Animal, 1996; El Zorro, 1996; The Pond, 1997; Zippers, 1997; Breakfast with John, 1997; Sunflowers, 1998; Mrs. Murphy's Crows, 1999; I Meowed, 2000; So Sleepy, 2001; My Dog Fuzzy, 2001; Alley Cat, 2002; Strange Things, 2005. **Address:** Richard C. Owen Publishers Inc., PO Box 585, Katonah, NY 10536, U.S.A.

BOLDEN, Abraham. American (born United States), b. 1935?. **Genres:** Novels, Biography, Autobiography/Memoirs. **Career:** U.S. Secret Service, agent, 1960-64. Writer. **Publications:** The Echo from Dealey Plaza: The True Story of the First African American on the White House Secret Service Detail and His Quest for Justice after the Assassination of JFK (memoir), 2008. **Ad-**

dress: Echo from Dealey Plaza L.L.C., PO Box 20416, Chicago, IL 60620, U.S.A. **Online address:** author@echofromdealeyplaza.com

BOLDEN, Tonya. American (born United States), b. 1959. **Genres:** Young Adult Fiction, Cultural/Ethnic Topics, Food And Wine, History, How-to Books. **Career:** Charles Alan Inc., salesperson, 1981-83; Raoulfilm Inc., office coordinator, 1985-87; MTA Arts for Transit Office, editorial consultant, 1987-88; Malcolm-King College, English instructor, 1988-89; Harlem River Press, Writers and Readers Publishing Inc., editorial consultant, 1987, 1989-90; College of New Rochelle, School of New Resources, English instructor, 1989-90, 1996-2000. **Publications:** The Family Heirloom Cookbook, 1990; (with V. Higginsen) Mama, I Want to Sing, 1992; Starting a Business from Your Home, 1993; Mail-Order and Direct Response, 1994; Just Family, 1996; The Book of African-American Women: 150 Crusaders, Creators and Uplifters, 1996; Through Loona's Door: A Tammy and Owen Adventure with Carter G. Woodson, 1997; And Not Afraid to Dare: The Stories of Ten African-American Women, 1998; (with M. Love) Forgive or Forget: Never Underestimate the Power of Forgiveness, 1999; Strong Men Keep Coming: The Book of African-American Men, 1999; (with E. Kitt) Rejuvenate!: It's Never Too Late, 2001; Tell All the Children Our Story: Memories and Mementos of Being Young and Black in America, 2001; Rock of Ages: A Tribute to the Black Church, 2001; (with C. Khan) Chaka! Through the Fire, 2003; (contrib.) American Patriots: The Story of Blacks in the Military from the Revolution to Desert Storm, 2003; Portraits of African-American Heroes, 2003; The Champ: The Story of Muhammad Ali, 2004; Wake Up Our Souls: A Celebration of Black American Artists, 2004; Cause: Reconstruction America, 1863-1877, 2005; Maritcha: A Nineteenth Century American Girl, 2005; (with M. Love) Half the Mother, Twice the Love: My Journey to Better Health with Diabetes, 2006; (contrib.) Weddings Valentine Style, 2006; MLK: Journey of a King, 2007; Take-Off: America All-Girl Bands During World War II, 2007; George Washington Carver, 2008; W.E.B. Du Bois: A Twentieth-Century Life, 2008; FDR's Alphabet Soup: New Deal America, 1932-1939, 2010; Finding Family, 2010. EDITOR: Rites of Passage: Stories about Growing Up by Black Writers from around the World, 1994; 33 Things Every Girl Should Know: Stories, Songs, Poems and Smart Talk by 33 Extraordinary Women, 1998; 33 Things Every Girl Should Know About Women's History, 2002. Contributor of articles to periodicals. **Address:** Jennifer Lyons Literary Agency, 151 W 19th St., 3rd Fl., New York, NY 10011, U.S.A. **Online address:** tonya@tonyabolden.com

BOLDRIN, Michele. American/Italian (born Italy), b. 1956. **Genres:** Business/Trade/Industry, History. **Career:** University of Chicago, Department of Economics, postdoctoral fellow, 1986-87, visiting professor, 1996-99; University of California, Department of Economics, assistant professor, associate professor, 1987-94, visiting professor, 1996-99; Santa Fe Institute, external assistant and associate professor, 1987-94; Autonomous University of Barcelona, visiting professor, 1990-94; Universidad Carlos III de Madrid, visiting professor, 1990-94, Marc Rich professor, 1994-99, Master en Analisis Financiero, director, 1994-97, visiting professor, 2002-03; University Bocconi Milano, visiting professor, 1990-94; Northwestern University, associate professor, 1990-94; International Economic Review, associate editor, 1994-2000; Journal of Nonlinear Economic Dynamics, associate editor, 1994-2003; Economic Theory, associate editor, 1995-97; Cuadernos Economicos, editor, 1995-2002; University of Pennsylvania, visiting professor, 1996-99; Macroeconomic Dynamics, advisory editor, book review editor, 1996-2009; Review of Economic Dynamics, associate editor, editor, 1996-; Abdus Salam International Centre for Theoretical Physics, School on the Mathematics of Economics, co-director, 1997-2002; University of Minnesota, professor, 1999-2006; Econometrica, associate editor, 2003-09; Washington University, Department of Economics, professor, 2006-, chair, 2008-, Joseph Gibson Hoyt distinguished professor in arts and sciences. Economist. **Publications:** (Ed. with B. Chen and P. Wang) Human Capital, Trade, and Public Policy in Rapidly Growing Economies: From Theory to Empirics, 2004; (with D.K. Levine) Against Intellectual Monopoly, 2008. Contributor to books, periodicals and journals. **Address:** Department of Economics, Washington University, 338 Seigle Hall, 1 Brookings Dr., PO Box 1208, St. Louis, MO 63130-4899, U.S.A. **Online address:** mboldrin@artsci.wustl.edu

BOLDT, Laurence G. American (born United States), b. 1954?. **Genres:** Novels, Young Adult Fiction, Social Work, Self Help. **Career:** Author, consultant and educator. **Publications:** Manifest Your Destiny, 1986; Zen and the Art of Making a Living in the Post-Modern World: A Career Guide for Dharma Bums, Social Activists, and Reformed Yuppies, 1990, rev. ed. as Zen and the Art of Making a Living: A Practical Guide to Creative Career Design, 1993, rev. ed., 2009; How to Find the Work You Love, 1996, new ed., 2004; Zen Soup: Tasty Morsels of Wisdom from Great Minds East and West, 1997; The Tao of Abundance: Eight Ancient Principles of Abundant Living, 1999; How to Be, Do, or Have Anything: A Practical Guide to Creative Empowerment, 2001. Contributor to periodicals. **Address:** c/o Author Mail, Tricycle Press, PO Box 7123, Berkeley, CA 94707-0123, U.S.A.

BOLES, Philana Marie. American (born United States) **Genres:** Novels, Young Adult Fiction. **Career:** 40 Acres and a Mule Filmworks, staff; Glamour Magazine, staff; Toledo Free Press, staff. Writer and artist. **Publications:** Blame It on Eve: A Novel, 2002; In the Paint: A Novel, 2005; Little Divas, 2005; Glitz, 2011. **Address:** c/o Author Mail, Random House Inc., 1745 Broadway, New York, NY 10019, U.S.A. **Online address:** contactphilana@pmarie.com

BOLGER, Dermot. Irish (born Ireland), b. 1959. **Genres:** Novels, Poetry, Education, Plays/Screenplays, Novellas/Short Stories. **Career:** Raven Arts Press, founder and editor, 1979-92; New Island Books, executive editor, 1992-. Editor, poet and novelist. **Publications:** NOVELS: Night Shift, 1985; The Woman's Daughter, 1987, rev. ed., 1991; The Journey Home, 1990; Emily's Shoes, 1992; A Second Life, 1994, rev. ed., 2010; Tinbars Hotel, 1997; Father's Music, 1997; Temptation, 2000; Valparaiso Voyage, 2001; From These Green Heights, 2005; The Family on Paradise Pier, 2005; New Town Soul, 2010. POETRY: The Habit of Flesh, 1980; Finglas Lilies, 1981; No Waiting America, 1982; Internal Exiles, 1986; Leinster Street Ghosts, 1989; Taking My Letters Back: New and Selected Poems, 1998; The Chosen Moment, 2004, External Affairs: New Poems, 2008. EDITOR: (and intro.) Madeleine Stuart, Manna in the Morning: A Memoir 1940-1958, 1986; The Dolmen Book of Irish Christmas Stories, 1986; The Bright Wave: Poetry in Irish Now, 1986; 16 on 16: Irish Writers on the Easter Rising, 1988; Invisible Cities: The New Dubliners: A Journey through Unofficial Dublin, 1988; Invisible Dublin: A Journey through Dublin's Suburbs, 1991; Francis Ledwidge: Selected Poems, 1992; Wexford through Its Writers, 1992; The Picador Book of Contemporary Irish Fiction, 1993; (with A. Murphy) 12 Bar Blues, 1993; Greatest Hits: Four Irish One-Act Plays, 1997; The New Irish Fiction, 2000; Ladies Night at Finbar's Hotel, 1999; Druids, Dudes and Beauty Queens: The Changing Face of Irish Theatre, 2001; (with C. Carty) New Hennessy Book of Irish Fiction, 2005; County Lines: A Portrait of Life in South Dublin County, 2006; Ledwidge Treasury: Selected Poems/Francis Ledwidge, 2007; Night & Day: Twenty Four Hours in the Life of Dublin City, 2008. PLAYS: The Lament for Arthur Cleary, 1989; Blinded by the Light, 1990; In High Germany, 1990; The Holy Ground, 1990; One Last White Horse, 1991; A Dublin Quartet, 1992; The Dublin Bloom (adapted from Ulysses by J. Joyce), 1994; Crack in the Emerald: New Irish Plays, 1994; April Bright, 1997; Blinded by the Light, 1997; The Passion of Jerome, 1999; Consenting Adults, 2000; Plays, 2000; Ranelagh Bus, 2007; Walking the Road: A Play In One Act, 2007; The Townlands of Brazil, 2007; The Consequences of Lightning, 2008; Ballymun Trilogy, 2010; The Parting Glass, 2011. OTHER: (with M. O'Loughlin) A New Primer for Irish Schools, 1985. Works appear in anthologies. **Address:** A. P. Watt Ltd., 20 John St., London, GL WC1N 2DR, England. **Online address:** debolger@iol.ie

BOLGIANO, Chris(tina). American (born United States), b. 1948. **Genres:** Environmental Sciences/Ecology, Local History/Rural Topics, Natural History, Essays. **Career:** National Agricultural Library, faculty, 1970-72; James Madison University Library, faculty, 1974-2005, now professor emeritus. Freelance Writer. **Publications:** Mountain Lion: An Unnatural History of Pumas and People, 1995; The Appalachian Forest: A Search for Roots and Renewal, 1998; Living in the Appalachian Forest: True Tales of Sustainable Forestry, 2002; (ed. with J. Roberts) Eastern Cougar: Historic Accounts, Scientific Investigations, and New Evidence, 2005; (ed.) Mighty Giants: An American Chestnut Anthology, 2008; Southern Appalachian Celebration, Univ. of NC Press, Aug., 2011. Contributor to magazines. Works appear in anthologies. **Address:** 10375 Genoa Rd., Fulks Run, VA 22830, U.S.A. **Online address:** bolgiace@jmu.edu

BOLINO, August C. American (born United States), b. 1922. **Genres:** Economics, Education, Reference. **Career:** University of Washington, instructor, 1951; Idaho State University, instructor, 1952-55; Saint Louis University, assistant professor of economics, associate professor of economics, 1955-62; Economic Studies, Office of Manpower, Automation, and Training, director, 1962-64; Evaluation of Manpower Branch, U.S. Office of Education, director,

1964-66; Catholic University of America, professor of economics, 1966-90, professor emeritus of business and economics, 1990-. Writer. **Publications:** The Development of the American Economy, 1961, 2nd ed., 1966; Manpower and the City, 1969; Career Education: Contributions to Economic Growth, 1973; The Ellis Island Source Book, 1985, 2nd ed., 1990; The Watchmakers of Massachusetts, 1987; A Century of Human Capital by Education and Training, 1989; From Depression to War: American Society in Transition-1939, 1998; Thomas Angel, American, 2001; A Century of Human Capital Development by Education and Training, forthcoming. **Address:** Department of Economics and Business, Catholic University of America, 620 Michigan Ave., NE, Washington, DC 20064, U.S.A.

BOLLER, Paul F. American (born United States), b. 1916. **Genres:** History, Intellectual History, Autobiography/Memoirs. **Career:** U.S. Navy Department, civilian analyst, 1947-48; Southern Methodist University, assistant professor, professor of history, 1948-66; University of Texas, visiting professor, 1963-64; University of Massachusetts, professor of history, 1966-76; Texas Christian University, L.B.J. professor of history, 1976-83, emeritus professor of history, 1983-. Writer. **Publications:** (With J. Tilford) This is Our Nation, 1961; George Washington and Religion, 1963; Quotemanship: The Use and Abuse of Quotations for Polemical and Other Purposes, 1967; American Thought in Transition: The Impact of Evolutionary Naturalism, 1865-1900, 1969; American Transcendentalism 1830-1860: An Intellectual Inquiry, 1974; Freedom and Fate in American Thought: From Edwards to Dewey, 1978; Presidential Anecdotes, 1981, rev. ed., 1996; Presidential Campaigns, 1984, rev. ed., 1996; (comp. with R. Story) A More Perfect Union: Documents in American History, 1984, 6th ed., 2005; (with R.L. Davis) Hollywood Anecdotes, 1987; Presidential Wives, 1988, 2nd ed., 1998; (with J. George) They Never Said It: A Book of Fake Quotes, Misquotes, and Misleading Attributions, 1989; Congressional Anecdotes, 1991; Memoirs of an Obscure Professor and Other Essays, 1992; Not So! Popular Myths from Columbus to Clinton, about the American Past, 1995; Presidential Inaugurations, 2001; Presidential Diversions: Presidents at Play from George Washington to George W. Bush, 2007. Contributor to periodicals. **Address:** Department of History & Geography, AddRan College of Liberal Arts, Texas Christian University, Reed Hall 308, Fort Worth, TX 76129, U.S.A.

BOLLES, Edmund Blair. American (born United States), b. 1942. **Genres:** Language/Linguistics, Natural History, Psychology, Essays, Travel/Exploration, Education, Reference. **Career:** Writer. **Publications:** (With P. Rosenthal) Readings in Psychology 1973/74, 1973; (with J. Sommer and J.F. Hoy) The Language Experience (essays), 1974; (with R. Fisher) Fodor's Old West (travel guide), 1976; (ed. with J. Fireman) Cat Catalog (essays), 1976; (with J. Fireman) TV Book (essays), 1977; Fodor's Animal Parks of Africa, 1979; The Beauty of America, 1979; The Love of America, 1979; So Much to Say: How to Help Your Child Learn to Talk, 1982; The Penguin Adoption Handbook: A Guide to Creating Your New Family, 1984, rev. ed., 1993; Who Owns America?, 1984, rev. ed., 1993; (with D.E. Papalia and S.W. Olds) A Child's World: Infancy Through Adolescence, 1987; Remembering and Forgetting: An Inquiry into the Nature of Memory, 1988; (with L.W. Weisberg and R. Greenberg) When Acting Out Isn't Acting, 1988; Learning to Live with Chronic Fatigue Syndrome, 1990; Relief from Chronic Back Pain, 1990; A Second Way of Knowing: The Riddle of Human Perception, 1990; (ed.) Galileo's Commandment: An Anthology of Great Science Writing, 1997, rev. ed. as Galileo's Commandment: 2500 Years of Great Science Writing, 1997; The Ice Finders: How a Poet, a Professor and a Politician Discovered the Ice Age, 1999; Einstein Defiant: Genius versus Genius in the Quantum Revolution, 2004; Babel's Dawn: A Natural History of the Origins of Speech, 2011. Contributor to periodicals. **Address:** c/o John Thornton, Spieler Literary Agency, 154 W 57th St., New York, NY 10019, U.S.A. **Online address:** blair@ebbolles.com

BOLLES, Richard Nelson. American (born United States), b. 1927. **Genres:** How-to Books, Education. **Career:** Episcopal Church, ordained priest, 1953; St. James Church, vicar, 1955-58; St. John's Episcopal Church, rector, 1958-66; Grace Cathedral, canon pastor, 1966-68; National Career Development Project, director, 1974-87; United Ministries in Higher Education, national staff, 1978-87. Writer and educator. **Publications:** What Color Is Your Parachute?: A Practical Manual for Job-Hunters and Career Changers, 1971, (with J.E. Nelson) 2nd ed., 2010; (with J. Crystal) Where Do I Go from Here with My Life?, 1974; The Three Boxes of Life: And How to Get Out of Them, 1978; New Quick Job-Hunting Map, 1985; (co-author) Your Next Pastorate: Starting the Search, 1990; How to Find Your Mission in Life, 1991; Job-hunting Tips for the So-Called Handicapped or People Who Have Disabilities: A Supplement to What Color is Your Parachute?, 1991; Job-Hunting on the Internet, 1997, (with M.E. Bolles) 4th ed., 2005; (with H.E. Figler) Career Counselor's Handbook, 1999, 2nd ed., 2007; The What Color Is Your Parachute Workbook, 2000; Job-Hunting for the So-Called Handicapped or People Who Have Disabilities, 2001; (foreword) Mapping your Career, 2002; (with M.E. Bolles) Job-hunting Online: A Guide to Job Listings, Message Boards, Research Sites, the Underweb, Counseling, Networking, Self-Assessment Tools, Niche Sites, 5th ed., 2008; The Job-Hunter's Survival Guide: How to Find Hope and Rewarding Work, Even When There Are No Jobs, 2009. **Address:** 10 Stirling Dr., Danville, CA 94526-2921, U.S.A. **Online address:** rnb25@aol.com

BOLLIER, David. American (born United States), b. 1955. **Genres:** Young Adult Non-fiction. **Career:** Public Knowledge, co-founder. Writer, activist and consultant. **Publications:** NONFICTION: Liberty & Justice for Some: Defending a Free Society from the Radical Right's Holy War on Democracy, 1982; (with J. Claybrook) Freedom from Harm: The Civilizing Influence of Health, Safety and Environmental Regulation, 1986; Crusaders & Criminals, Victims & Visionaries: Historic Encounters between Connecticut Citizens and the United States Supreme Court, 1986; (with H.S. Cohn) The Great Hartford Circus Fire: Creative Settlement of Mass Disasters, 1991; Aiming Higher: 25 Stories of How Companies Prosper by Combining Sound Management and Social Vision, 1996; Beyond Bureaucracy: New Roles for Government, Civil Society and the Private Sector, 1997; The Networked Society: How New Technologies Are Transforming Markets, Organizations and Social Relationships: A Report of the Fifth Annual Aspen Institute Roundtable on Information Technology, Aspen, Colorado, August 15-18, 1996, 1997; The Global Advance of Electronic Commerce: Reinventing Markets, Management and National Sovereignty: A Report of the Sixth Annual Aspen Institute Roundtable on Information Technology, 1998; How Smart Growth Can Stop Sprawl: A Fledgling Citizen Movement Expands, 1998; Work and Future Society: Where Are the Economy and Technology Taking Us?, 1998; Media Madness: The Revolution So Far, 1999; The Global Wave of Entrepreneurialism: Harnessing the Synergies of Personal Initiative, Digital Technologies and Global Commerce: A Report of the Seventh Annual Aspen Institute Roundtable on Information Technology, 1999; Ecologies of Innovation: The Role of Information and Communications Technologies: A Report of the Eighth Annual Aspen Institute Roundtable on Information Technology, 2000; Values for the Digital Age: The Legacy of Henry Luce, 2000; Public Assets, Private Profits: Reclaiming the American Commons in an Age of Market Enclosure, 2001; Silent Theft: The Private Plunder of Our Common Wealth, 2002; Why the Public Domain Matters: The Endangered Wellspring of Creativity, Commerce and Democracy, 2002; (with T. Watts) Saving the Information Commons: A Public Interest Agenda in Digital Media, 2002; (with T.O. McGarity and S. Shapiro) Sophisticated Sabotage: The Intellectual Games Used to Subvert Responsible Regulation, 2004; Brand Name Bullies: The Quest to Own and Control Culture, 2005; (with C. Cox and M. Gluck) Ready to Share: Fashion & the Ownership of Creativity, 2006; When Push Comes to Pull: The New Economy and Culture of Networking Technology: A Report of the Fourteenth Annual Aspen Institute Roundtable on Information Technology, 2006; Viral Spiral: How the Commoners Built a Digital Republic of Their Own, 2008. **Address:** Amherst, MA , U.S.A. **Online address:** david@bollier.org

BOLLINGER, Lee C. American (born United States), b. 1946. **Genres:** Law, Social Commentary, Civil Liberties/Human Rights. **Career:** U.S. Court of Appeals for the Second Circuit, law clerk, 1971-72; U.S. Supreme Court, law clerk to chief justice Warren E. Burger, 1972-73; University of Michigan, assistant professor, 1973-76, associate professor, 1976-78, professor of law, 1979-, dean of law school, 1987-94, Davis-Markert-Nickerson lecturer, 1992, president, 1996-2002; Rockefeller Foundation, fellow, 1980; Cambridge University, Clare Hall, visiting associate, 1983; College of William and Mary, George Wythe lecturer, 1984; Capital University, John E. Sullivan lecturer, 1988; Center for the Continuing Education of Women, board director, 1989-; Columbia University, Rubin lecturer, 1989, president, 2002-; Southern Methodist University, Atwell lecturer in constitutional law, 1992; American Academy of Arts and Sciences, fellow, 1992; Dartmouth College, provost and professor of government, 1994-96; Columbia Law School, faculty; Federal Reserve Bank of New York, chair; Washington Post Co., director; American Academy of Arts and Sciences, fellow; American Philosophical Society, fellow; Law Review, articles editor; National Association for Public Interest Law, board director. **Publications:** (With J.H. Jackson) Contract Law in Modern Society, 2nd ed., 1980; The Tolerant Society: Freedom of Speech and

Extremist Speech in America, 1986; Images of a Free Press, 1991; (ed. with J.C. Dann) Events of My Life: An Autobiographical Sketch by John Marshall, 2001; (with G.R. Stone) Eternally Vigilant: Free Speech in the Modern Era, 2002; Uninhibited, Robust, and Wide-open: A Free Press for a New Century, 2010. Work appears in anthologies. Contributor of articles to journals. **Address:** Columbia University, Office of the President, 202 Low Library, 535 W 116th St., PO Box 4309, New York, NY 10027, U.S.A. **Online address:** bollinger@columbia.edu

BOLMAN, Lee G. American (born United States), b. 1941. **Genres:** Administration/Management, Education. **Career:** Carnegie-Mellon University, Graduate School of Industrial Administration, assistant professor, 1967-72, Department of Psychology, assistant professor, 1967-72; Harvard University, Graduate School of Education, lecturer in education, 1972-93, Institute for Educational Management, educational chairperson, 1983-88, Management Development Program, educational chairperson, 1986-88, National Center for Educational Leadership, director and principal investigator, 1988-94. Harvard School Leadership Academy, principal investigator, 1991-93; Yale School of Organization and Management, lecturer, 1983; University of Missouri, Henry W. Bloch School of Business and Public Administration, Marion H. Bloch Missouri professor of leadership and Marion H. Bloch/Missouri chair in leadership, 1993-, interim dean, 2008-09, Center for Leadership Development, director, 1993-, Department of Organizational Leadership and Marketing, interim chair, 2003-04. Writer. **Publications:** (With T.E. Deal) Modern Approaches to Understanding and Managing Organizations, 1984; (with T.E. Deal) Reframing Organizations: Artistry, Choice, and Leadership, 1991, 4th ed., 2008; (with T.E. Deal) The Path to School Leadership, 1993; (with T.E. Deal) Becoming a Teacher Leader: From Isolation to Collaboration, 1994; (with T.E. Deal and E.G. de Aldaz) Liderazgo, Arte y Decision, 1995; (with T.E. Deal and S.F. Rallis) Becoming a School Board Member, 1995; (with T.E Deal) Leading with Soul: An Uncommon Journey of Spirit, 1995, 3rd ed., 2011; (with T.E. Deal) Escape from Cluelessness: A Guide for the Organizationally Challenged, 2000; (with T.E. Deal) Reframing the Path to School Leadership: A Guide for Teachers and Principals, 2002, 2nd ed., 2010; (with T.E. Deal) The Wizard and the Warrior: Leading with Passion and Power, 2006; (with J.V. Gallos) Reframing Academic Leadership, 2011. Contributor of articles to books and journals. **Address:** Henry W. Bloch School of Business and Public, Administration, University of Missouri, 322 Bloch School, 5100 Rockhill Rd., Kansas City, MO 64110-2499, U.S.A. **Online address:** bolmanl@umkc.edu

BOLOTIN, Norman (Phillip). American (born United States), b. 1951. **Genres:** History, Military/Defense/Arms Control. **Career:** Publishers Professional Services, editorial director, 1973-77; Alaska NW Publishing, editor and book division director, 1978-84; KC Aly and Company Communications, partner and vice president, 1984; Laing Communications, president, 1985-99; University of Chicago, Business of Publishing Program, director, 1995-2000; The History Bank, managing partner, 2000-. **Publications:** Klondike Lost, 1980; (comp.) A Klondike Scrapbook: Ordinary People, Extraordinary Times, 1987; (with C. Laing) The World's Columbian Exposition: The Chicago World's Fair of 1893, 1992; (with A. Herb) For Home and Country: A Civil War Scrapbook, 1995; Civil War A to Z: A Young Readers' Guide to Over 100 People, Places, and Points of Importance, 2002; The World's First and Grandest Midway, 2009. **Address:** The History Bank, PO Box 1568, Woodinville, WA 98072-1568, U.S.A. **Online address:** norm@thehistorybank.com

BOLSTER, Richard (H.). British (born England) **Genres:** Literary Criticism And History, Biography, Autobiography/Memoirs, History. **Career:** University of Kano, senior lecturer in French studies; University of Bristol, Department of French, senior lecturer. Writer. **Publications:** Stendhal, Balzac, et le féminisme romantique, 1970; (intro.) La Vie de Balzac, 1981; Stendhal: Le Rouge et le Noir, 1994; Balzac: Le père Goriot, 2000; Marie d'Agoult: The Rebel Countess (biography), 2000. EDITOR: Documents littéraires de l'époque romantique (nonfiction), 1982; La Vie extraordinaire du Baron de Trenck (autobiography), 1985; Histoire d'Eléonore de Parme (fiction), 1997. **Address:** Department of French, University of Bristol, 17 Woodland Rd., Bristol, GL BS8 1TE, England. **Online address:** r.bolster@bristol.ac.uk

BOLSTER, W(illiam) Jeffrey. American (born United States), b. 1954. **Genres:** History, Marine Sciences/Oceanography. **Career:** Dirigo Cruises, seaman, 1977-78; Southampton College, instructor and schoolship captain, 1977-83; Sea Education Association, instructor and schoolship captain, 1978-85; Northeastern University, instructor and schoolship captain, 1982; Ocean World Institute, historic vessel captain, 1987-90; Living Classroom Foundation, schoolship relief captain, 1987-90; WGBH PBS-TV, consultant, 1990; University of New Hampshire, assistant professor of history, 1991-97, associate professor of history, 1997-, James H. Hayes and Claire Short chair in the humanities, 2002-07; New England Cable News, consultant, 1992; Northern Lights Productions, consultant, 1993-94; The National Park Service, consultant, 1993-94; Howard University, consultant, 1993-94; Syddansk University, Fulbright distinguished chair in American studies, 2002-03. Writer. **Publications:** Black Jacks: African American Seamen in the Age of Sail, 1997; (with H. Anderson) Soldiers, Sailors, Slaves and Ships: The Civil War Photographs of Henry P. Moore, 1999; (ed. and intro.) Cross-Grained and Wiley Waters: A Guide to the Puscataqua Maritime Region, 2002; (with A. Roland and A. Keyssar) The Way of the Ship: America's Maritime History Reenvisioned, 2007. Contributor to periodicals. **Address:** History Department, University of New Hampshire, 301B Horton Social Science Ctr., Durham, NH 03824, U.S.A. **Online address:** jeff.bolster@unh.edu

BOLTON, Charles C. American (born United States), b. 1960. **Genres:** Education, History, Race Relations, Reference. **Career:** University of Southern Mississippi, Mississippi Oral History Program, director, 1990-94, Department of History, assistant professor, 1990-94, associate professor, 1994-2000, professor of history and chair, 2000-05, director of graduate studies, 1994-94, Center for Oral History and Cultural Heritage, director, 1994-2000, co-director, 2000-05; University of North Carolina, Department of History, professor, 2005-, head, 2005-. Writer. **Publications:** Poor Whites of the Antebellum South: Tenants and Laborers in Central North Carolina and Northeast Mississippi, 1994; (with N.R. McMillen) A Synopsis of American History, 1997; (ed. with S.P. Culclasure) The Confessions of Edward Isham: A Poor White Life of the Old South, 1998; The Hardest Deal of All: The Battle over School Integration in Mississippi, 1870-1980, 2005; (ed. with B.J. Daugherity) With All Deliberate Speed: Implementing Brown v. Board of Education, 2008. Contributor to journals. **Address:** Department of History, University of North Carolina, 2135 MHRA, PO Box 26170, Greensboro, NC 27402-6170, U.S.A. **Online address:** ccbolton@uncg.edu

BOLTON, Evelyn. *See* **BUNTING, (Anne) Eve(lyn Bolton).**

BOLTON, Ruthie. American (born United States), b. 1961. **Genres:** Biography, Autobiography/Memoirs, Regional/Urban Planning. **Career:** Writer. **Publications:** Gal: A True Life, 1994. **Address:** Harriet Wasserman Literary Agency Inc., 137 E 36th St., New York, NY 10016, U.S.A.

BONADIO, Felice A(nthony). American (born United States) **Genres:** History, Politics/Government, Biography, Military/Defense/Arms Control. **Career:** University of California-Santa Barbara, professor of history, emeritus professor of history. Writer. **Publications:** North of Reconstruction: Ohio Politics, 1865-1870, 1970; (ed.) Political Parties in American History, vol. II: 1828-1890, 1974; A.P. Giannini: A Biography, 1994. Works appear in anthologies. Contributor to periodicals. **Address:** Department of History, University of California-Santa Barbara, HSSB 3253, 4th Fl., Santa Barbara, CA 93106-9410, U.S.A.

BONADIO, William. American (born United States), b. 1955?. **Genres:** Autobiography/Memoirs, Medicine/Health. **Career:** Children's Health Care, pediatric ED staff physician; University of Minnesota, Amplatz Children's Hospital, assistant clinical professor of pediatrics and attending physician of pediatric medicine, 1984-, Division of Pediatric Emergency Medicine, professor of pediatrics, 2008, Department of Pediatric Emergency, staff physician. Writer. **Publications:** Julia's Mother: Life Lessons in the Pediatric ER, 2000. **Address:** Amplatz Children's Hospital, University of Minnesota, D580 Mayo Bldg., 420 Delaware St. SE, Minneapolis, MN 55455-0341, U.S.A. **Online address:** bonadio@umn.edu

BONANSINGA, Jay R. American (born United States) **Genres:** Mystery/Crime/Suspense, Horror, Plays/Screenplays, Novels, Young Adult Fiction. **Career:** Northwestern University, Creative Writing for the Media program, visiting professor; DePaul University, graduate writing program, visiting professor; suspense and horror novelist, screenwriter and film director. **Publications:** The Black Mariah, 1994; Sick, 1995; The Killer's Game, 1997; Head Case, 1998; Bloodhound, 1999; Sleep Police, 2001; Oblivion, 2003; The Sinking of the Eastland: America's Forgotten Tragedy, 2004; Frozen, 2005; Twisted, 2006; Shattered, 2007; Perfect Victim, 2008; (with R. Kirkman) The Walking Dead: Rise of the Governor, 2011; The Miniaturist, forthcoming.

Contributor to magazines. **Address:** Simon and Schuster Children's Publishing, 1230 Ave. of the Americas, New York, NY 10020, U.S.A. **Online address:** jaybona@aol.com

BONCOMPAGNI, Tatiana. American (born United States), b. 1977?. **Genres:** Novels. **Career:** Freelance writer, 2003-. **Publications:** Gilding Lily, 2008; Hedge Fund Wives, 2009. **Address:** New York, NY , U.S.A. **Online address:** tatiana@boncompagni.net

BOND, C. G. *See* **BOND, C(hristopher Godfrey).**

BOND, C(hristopher Godfrey). (C. G. Bond). British (born England), b. 1945?. **Genres:** Novels, Plays/Screenplays, Music. **Career:** Victoria Theatre, actor, 1968-70, resident dramatist, 1970-71; Everyman Theatre, artistic director, 1976-; Half Moon Theatre, artistic director; Liverpool Playhouse, artistic director. Writer. **Publications:** The Food of Love: The Sweetest Canticle, 1955; A Policeman's Lot, 1957; (as C.G. Bond) You Want Drink Something Cold (novel), 1969; (as C.G. Bond) Sweeney Todd: The Demon Barber of Fleet Street, 1974. **Address:** Blanche Marvin Agency, 21A St. John's Wood High St., London, GL NW8 7NG, England.

BOND, Edward. British (born England), b. 1934. **Genres:** Plays/Screenplays, Poetry, Songs/Lyrics And Libretti, Philosophy, Politics/Government, Social Commentary, Theatre, Translations, Translations, Humor/Satire. **Career:** University of Essex, resident theatre writer, 1982-83. Poet. **Publications:** FICTION FOR ADULTS: The Happy Sadist, 1962. PUBLISHED PLAYS: Saved, 1965; Narrow Road to the Deep North: A Comedy, 1968; Early Morning, 1968; The Pope's Wedding, 1971; Lear, 1972; (with B. Mauer and A. Röhl) Passion: Schwarze Messe, 1972; The Sea; A Comedy, 1973; Bingo: Scenes of Money and Death, 1974; Bingo and the Sea: Two Plays, 1975; Wir Erreichen den Fluss: Handlungen für Musik, 1976; We Come to the River: Actions for Music, 1976; The Fool and We Come to the River, 1976; A-A-America! & Stone, 1976, rev. ed., 1981; A Paápa Lakodalma: Négy Dráma, 1977; Plays, 1977; The Bundle, 1978; (intro.) Plays Two, 1978; The Fool: A Full Length Play, 1978; The Woman: Scenes of War and Freedom, 1979; The Worlds, with The Activists Papers, 1980; Restoration, 1981; Summer, 1982; Derek: And, Choruses from After the Assassinations, 1983; Human Cannon, 1985; War Plays (Red, Black and Ignorant; The Tin Can People; Great Peace), 1985; Jackets, 1989; In the Company of Men, 1990; September, 1990; Olly's Prison, 1993; Tuesday, 1993; Coffee: A Tragedy, 1995; At the Inland Sea: A Play for Young People, 1996; (with J. Mulligan) Eleven Vests & Tuesday, 1997; The Children: and, Have I None, 2000; Chair, 2000; Existence, 2002; Plays 7, 2003; Born, 2003; The Balancing Act, 2003; Collected Plays 1977-2003, vol. VII, 2003; Plays 8, 2006. LIBRETTOS: We Come to the River: Actions for Music, 1976; The English Cat, 1983. TRANSLATOR: A. Chekhov, The Three Sisters, 1967; F. Wedekind, Spring Awakening, 1980; (with E. Bond-Pable) F. Wedekind, Lulu, 1992. OTHERS: The Swing Poems, 1976; Theatre Poems and Songs, 1978; Poems 1978-1985, 1987; Notes on Post-Modernism, 1990; Letters, vol. VI, 1994-2000; The Hidden Plot: Notes on Theatre and the State, 2000. **Address:** Casarotto Ramsay & Associates Ltd., National House, 60-66 Wardour St., London, GL W1F 0TA, England.

BOND, George C(lement). American (born United States), b. 1936. **Genres:** Anthropology/Ethnology, Language/Linguistics. **Career:** University of East Anglia, lecturer, 1966-68; Columbia University, Teachers College, assistant professor, 1968-74, associate professor, 1974-82, professor of anthropology, 1982-, Institute of African Studies, director, 1989-99, Center for African Education, director, 2004-, William F. Russell professor of anthropology and education; Association for Africanist Anthropology, president, 1994-97. Writer. **Publications:** The Politics of Change in a Zambia Community, 1976. EDITOR: (with W. Johnson and S.S. Walker) African Christianity: Patterns of Religious Continuity, 1978; (with A. Gilliam) Social Construction of the Past: Representation as Power, 1994; (co-ed.) AIDS in Africa and the Caribbean, 1997; (with D.M. Ciekawy) Witchcraft Dialogues: Anthropological and Philosophical Exchanges, 2001; (with N.C. Gibson) Contested Terrains and Constructed Categories: Contemporary Africa in Focus, 2002; (with J.A. Kleifgen) Languages of Africa and the Diaspora: Educating for Language Awareness, 2009. **Address:** Teachers College, Columbia University, 375B Grace Dodge Hall, 525 W 120th St., PO Box 211, New York, NY 10027, U.S.A. **Online address:** gcb1@columbia.edu

BOND, Larry. American (born United States), b. 1952. **Genres:** Mystery/Crime/Suspense. **Career:** Officer Candidate School, staff. Computer game designer, computer programmer, naval analyst and writer. **Publications:** (With T. Clancy) Red Storm Rising, 1986; Red Phoenix, 1989; Vortex, 1991; Cauldron, 1993; The Enemy Within, 1996; Day of Wrath, 1998; (with J. DeFelice) Larry Bond's First Team, 2004; Dangerous Ground, 2005; (with J. DeFelice) Larry Bond's First Team: Angels of Wrath, 2006; (with J. DeFelice) Fires of War, 2006; (with J. DeFelice) Larry Bond's First Team: Soul of the Assassin, 2008; (with J. DeFelice) Shadows of War, 2009; Cold Choices, 2009; (with J. DeFelice) Larry Bond's Red Dragon Rising: Shadows of War, 2009; (ed.) Crash Dive, 2010; (with J. DeFelice) Larry Bond's Red Dragon Rising: Edge of War, 2010; (with J. DeFelice) Shock of War, 2012; Exit Plan, 2012. **Address:** c/o Author Mail, Warner Books, 1271 Ave. of the Americas, New York, NY 10020, U.S.A. **Online address:** authorbond@aol.com

BOND, Nancy. American (born United States), b. 1945. **Genres:** Children's Fiction, Children's Non-fiction, Young Adult Fiction, Literary Criticism And History. **Career:** Oxford University Press, promotional staff, 1967-68; Lincoln Public Library, assistant children's librarian, 1969-71; Heywood Library, director, 1974-75; Massachusetts Audubon Society, administrative assistant, 1976-77; Simmons College, Center for the Study of Children's Literature, instructor in children's literature, 1978-2001; Barrow Bookstore, salesperson, 1980-. Writer. **Publications:** A String in the Harp, 1976; The Best of Enemies, 1978; Country of Broken Stone, 1980; The Voyage Begun, 1981; A Place to Come Back To, 1984; Another Shore, 1988; Truth to Tell, 1994; The Love of Friends, 1997; (foreword) A Little Princess, 2001. Illustrator of books by D.L. Reeves. Contributor to periodicals. **Address:** 109 Valley Rd., Concord, MA 01742-4900, U.S.A.

BOND, Peter. British (born England), b. 1948. **Genres:** Adult Non-fiction. **Career:** Royal Astronomical Society, space science advisor and press officer, 1995-2007; European Space Agency, Science Communication Office, consultant writer, 1998-. **Publications:** NONFICTION: Population and Settlement, 1989; Heroes in Space: From Gagarin to Challenger, 1989; People and the Environment, 1990; Reaching for the Stars: The Illustrated History of Manned Spaceflight, 1993, rev. ed., 1996; DK Guide to Space: A Photographic Journey through the Universe (for children), 1999; Zero G: Life and Survival in Space, 1999; The Continuing Story of the International Space Station, 2002; (with J. Redfearn and A. Wilson) The Space Dimension: European Space Agency, 2003; (with A. Wilson) Benefits of Human Spaceflight, 2005; Distant Worlds: Milestones in Planetary Exploration, 2007; (with B. Gallagher) Jane's Space Recognition Guide, 2008; Exploring the Solar System, 2011. Contributor to newspapers and magazines. **Address:** Sterling Publishing Company Inc., 387 Park Ave. S, New York, NY 10016, U.S.A. **Online address:** peterrbond@aol.com

BOND, Ruskin. Indian (born India), b. 1934. **Genres:** Novels, Novellas/Short Stories, Children's Fiction, Poetry, Children's Non-fiction, Autobiography/Memoirs, Biography, Essays, Essays. **Career:** Freelance writer, 1956-; Imprint magazine, managing editor, 1975-79. **Publications:** The Room on the Roof, 1956; Neighbour's Wife and Other Stories, 1967; Grandfather's Private Zoo, 1967; My First Love and Other Stories, 1968; Strange Men, Strange Places, 1969; Tales Told At Twilight, 1970; The Last Tiger, 1971; Angry River, 1972; It Isn't Time that's Passing: Poems, 1970-1971, 1972; Axe for the Rani, 1972; The Blue Umbrella, 1974; Once upon a Monsoon Time (memoirs), 1974; Man Eater of Manjari, 1975; Lone Fox Dancing: Lyric Poems, 1975; Love is a Sad Song, 1975; Man of Destiny: A Biography of Jawaharlal Nehru, 1976; Girl from Copenhagen, 1977; The Hidden Pool, 1978; Night of the Leopard, 1979; Big Business, 1979; The Little Book of Comfort, 1980; The Cherry Tree, 1980; The Road to the Bazaar, 1980, 1991; A Flight of Pigeons, 1980; The Young Vagrants, 1981; Flames in the Forest, 1981; Tales and Legends from India, 1982; A Garland of Memories (essays), 1982; Tigers Forever, 1983; Earthquake, 1984; Getting Granny's Glasses, 1985; To Live in Magic: A Book of Nature Poems, 1985; Cricket for the Crocodile, 1986; The Adventures of Rusty, 1986; The Eyes of the Eagle, 1987; The Adventures of Rama and Sita, 1987; The Night Train at Deoli and Other Stories, 1988; Beautiful Garhwal: Heaven in Himalayas, 1988; Ghost Trouble, 1989; Time Stops at Shamli and Other Stories, 1989; Dust on the Mountain, 1990; Snake Trouble, 1991; Cherry Tree, 1991; Panther's Moon and Other Stories, 1991; Our Trees Still Grow in Dehra, 1991; Ganga Descends, 1992; (with G. Saili) Mussoorie and Landour: Days of Wine and Roses, 1992; Island of Trees: Nature Stories and Poems, 1992; Rain in the Mountains: Notes from the Himalayas (memoirs), 1993; Delhi is not Far: The Best of Ruskin Bond, 1994; Tiger Roars, Eagle Soars, 1994; Quakes and Flames, 1994; Binya's

Blue Umbrella, 1995; The Ruskin Bond Children's Omnibus, 1995; When the Trees Walked and Other Stories, 1996; (ed.) Penguin Book of Classical Indian Love Stories and Lyrics, 1996; Strangers in the Nights: Two Novellas, 1996; Scenes from a Writer's Life, 1997; Bond with the Mountains: Stories, Thoughts, and Poems, 1998; Leopard On the Mountain, 1998; The Lamp is Lit: Leaves from a Journal, 1998; Seasons of Ghosts, 1999; Friends in Small Places: Ruskin Bond's Unforgettable People, 2000; Ruskin Bond's Treasury of Stories for Children, 2000; Granny's Tree Climbing and Other Poems, 2000; When Darkness Falls and Other Stories, 2001; Days of Innocence: Stories for Ruskin Bond, 2002; (ed.) Ghost Stories from the Raj, 2002; Landour Days: A Writer's Journal, 2002; Rusty, the Boy from the Hills, 2002; Rupa Book of Ruskin Bond's Himalayan Tales, 2003; Vagrants in the Valley, 2003; Rusty and the Leopard, 2003; Rusty Runs Away, 2003; Rusty Comes Home, 2004; Rusty Goes to London, 2004; A Face in the Dark and Other Hauntings: Collected Stories of the Supernatural, 2004; India I Love, 2004; Little Night Music, 2004; Ruskin Bond's Book of Nature, 2004; (ed.) Post Box No. 99 and Other Stories, 2005; Roads to Mussoorie, 2005; Tales of the Open Road, 2006; (ed.) Once Upon a Time in the Doon: Writings from the Green Valley, 2007; Potpourri, 2007; Ruskin Bond's Book of Verse, 2007; Ruskin Bond's Book of Humour, 2008; Town Called Dehra, 2008; Notes from a Small Room, 2009; Classic Ruskin Bond: Complete & Unabridged, 2010; Susanna's Seven Husbands, 2011; The Kitemaker, 2011. **Address:** Ivy Cottage, Landour Cantt, Mussoorie, UP 248179, India.

BOND, **Tess.** *See* **GALLAGHER**, **Tess.**

BOND, **(Thomas) Michael.** British (born England), b. 1926. **Genres:** Novels, Children's Fiction, Biography, Young Adult Non-fiction. **Career:** British Broadcasting Corp., engineer's assistant and television camera operator, 1947-66; Paddington and Company Ltd., director. Writer. **Publications:** FOR CHILDREN: FICTION: A Bear Called Paddington, 1958; More about Paddington, 1959; Paddington Helps Out, 1960; Paddington Abroad, 1961; Paddington at Large, 1962, rev. ed., 2002; Paddington Marches On, 1964; Adventures of Paddington, 1965; Here Comes Thursday!, 1966; Paddington at Work, 1966, rev. ed., 2001; Paddington Goes to Town, 1968, rev. ed., 2001; Thursday Rides Again, 1968; Parsley's Good Deed, 1969; The Story of Parsley's Tail, 1969; Thursday Ahoy!, 1969; Paddington Takes the Air, 1970; Parsley's Last Stand, 1970; Parsley's Problem Present, 1970; Thursday in Paris, 1971; Parsley the Lion, 1972; Parsley Parade, 1972; (with F. Banbery) Paddington Bear, 1972, rev. ed., 1998; (with F. Banbery) Paddington's Garden, 1972; The Day the Animals Went on Strike, 1972; Paddington at the Circus, 1973, rev. ed., 2000; Paddington Goes Shopping, 1973 in US as Paddington's Lucky Day, 1974; Paddington on Top, 1974, rev. ed., 2000; Paddington's Blue Peter Story Book in US as Paddington Takes to TV, 1974, rev. ed., 2002; Paddington Goes to School, 1974; Mr. Cram's Magic Bubbles, 1975; Windmill, 1975; Paddington at the Seaside, 1975 in US as Paddington at the Seashore, 1992; Paddington at the Tower, 1975; Parsley and the Herbs, 1976; Paddington at the Station, 1976; Paddington Takes a Bath, 1976; Paddington Goes to the Sales, 1976; Paddington's New Room, 1976; Paddington Carpenter, 1977; Paddington Conjurer, 1977; Paddington Cook, 1977; Paddington Golfer, 1977; Paddington Does It Himself, 1977; Paddington Hits Out, 1977; Paddington in the Kitchen, 1977; Paddington's Birthday Party, 1977; Paddington's First Book, 1978; Paddington's Picture Book (collection), 1978; Paddington's Play Book, 1978; Paddington's Counting Book, 1978; Paddington's Cartoon Book, 1979; Paddington Takes the Test, 1979, rev. ed., 2002; Paddington for Christmas, 1979; J.D. Polson and the Liberty Head Dime, 1980; Paddington in Touch, 1980; Paddington and Aunt Lucy, 1980; Paddington Weighs In, 1980; Paddington at Home, 1980; Paddington Goes Out, 1980; Paddington and the Snowbear, 1981; Paddington at the Launderette, 1981; Paddington's Shopping Adventure, 1981; Paddington's Birthday Treat, 1981; J.D. Polson and the Dillogate Affair, 1981; Paddington On Screen: A Second Blue Peter Storybook, 1981; Paddington Has Fun, 1982; Paddington Works Hard, 1982; J.D. Polson and the Great Unveiling, 1982; The Caravan Puppets, 1983; Paddington's Storybook, 1983; Paddington on the River, 1983; Paddington and the Knickerbocker Rainbow, 1984; Paddington at the Zoo, 1984, rev. ed., 1998; Great Big Paddington Bear Picture Book, 1984; Paddington at the Fair, 1985, rev. ed., 1998; Paddington's Painting Exhibition, 1985 in US as Paddington's Art Exhibition, 1986; Paddington at the Palace, 1986, rev. ed., 1999; Paddington Minds the House, 1986, rev. ed., 1999; Paddington Spring Cleans, 1986 in US as Paddington Cleans Up, 1986; The Hilarious Adventures of Paddington, 1986; (with K. Bond) Paddington Posts a Letter, 1986 in US as Paddington Mails a Letter, 1986; (with K. Bond) Paddington's Clock Book, 1986; Paddington at the Airport, 1986; (with K. Bond) On Four Wheels: Paddington's London, 1986 in US as Paddington's Wheel Book, 1986; (with P. Parnes) Oliver the Greedy Elephant, 1986; Paddington and the Marmalade Maze, 1987, rev. ed., 1999; Paddington's Busy Day, 1987, rev. ed., 1999; A Mouse Called Thursday, 1988; Paddington's Magical Christmas, 1988; Paddington's ABC, 1990; Paddington's 123, 1990; Paddington's Colors, 1990; Paddington's Opposites, 1990; Paddington Meets the Queen, 1991; Paddington Rides On!, 1991; Paddington's Jar of Jokes, 1992; A Day by the Sea, 1992; Paddington at the Seashore, 1992; Paddington Breaks the Peace, 1992; Something Nasty in the Kitchen, 1992; Paddington Book and Bear Box, 1993; Paddington's First Word Book, 1993; Paddington's Picnic, 1993; Paddington Does the Decorating, 1993; Paddington's Disappearing Trick, 1993; Paddington's Things I Do, 1994; Paddington's Things I Feel, 1994; Bears and Forebears: A Life So Far, 1996; Paddington and the Christmas Surprise, 1997; Paddington A Classic Collection, 1998; Paddington at the Carnival, 1998; Paddington Bear All Day, 1998; Paddington Bear and the Busy Bee Carnival, 1998; Paddington Bear Goes to Market, 1998; Paddington and the Tutti Frutti Rainbow, 1998; Paddington Treasury, 1999; Paddington up and About, 1999; Paddington Bear: My Scrapbook, 1999; Paddington's Party Tricks, 2000; (with K. Jankel) Paddington Bear Goes to the Hospital, 2001; Olga Follows Her Nose, 2002; Paddington Bear in the Garden, 2002; Paddington and the Grand Tour, 2003; Paddington Rules the Waves, 2008; Paddington Here and Now, 2008; Paddington at the Beach, 2009; Paddington Buggy Book, 2011; Paddington Cook Book, 2011. OLGA DA POLGA PICTURE BOOKS: The Tales of Olga da Polga, 1971; Olga Meets Her Match, 1973; Olga Carries On, 1976; Olga Counts Her Blessings, 1977; Olga Makes a Friend, 1977; Olga Makes a Wish, 1977; Olga Makes Her Mark, 1977; Olga Takes a Bite, 1977; Olga's New Home, 1977; Olga's Second House, 1977; Olga's Special Day, 1977; Olga Takes Charge, 1982; First Big Olga da Polga Book, 1983; Second Big Olga da Polga Book, 1983; The Complete Adventures of Olga Da Polga, 1983; Olga Moves House, 2001. MYSTERIES FORADULTS: Monsieur Pamplemousse, 1983; Monsieur Pamplemousse and the Secret Mission, 1984; Monsieur Pamplemousse on the Spot, 1986; Monsieur Pamplemousse Takes the Cure, 1987; Monsieur Pamplemousse Aloft, 1989; Monsieur Pamplemousse Investigates, 1990; Monsieur Pamplemousse Rests His Case, 1991; Monsieur Pamplemousse Stands Firm, 1992; Monsieur Pamplemousseon Location, 1992; Monsieur Pamplemousse Takes the Train, 1993; Monsieur Pamplemousse Afloat, 1998; Monsieur Pamplemousse on Probation, 1999; Paddington Bear at the Circus, 2000; Monsieur Pamplemousse on Vacation, 2002; Monsieur Pamplemousse Hits the Headlines, 2003; Monsieur Pamplemousse and the Militant Midwives, 2006; Monsieur Pamplemousse and the French Solution, 2007; Monsieur Pamplemousse and the Carbon Footprint, 2010. OTHERS: Herbs Annual, 1969; The Parsley Annual, 1970; (ed.) Michael Bond's Book of Mice, 1972; (ed.) Michael Bond's Book of Bears, 1973; (trans. with B. Johnson) The Motormalgamation, 1974; How to Make Flying Things, 1975; Paddington's Loose-End Book: An ABC of Things to Do, 1976; Paddington's Party Book, 1976; The Great Big Paddington Book, 1976; Fun and Games with Paddington, 1977; Paddington's Pop-Up Book, 1977; Paddington's Colouring Books, 4 vols., 1977; Paddington Pastime Series, 4 vols., 1977; Picnic on the River, 1980; Paddington's Suitcase, 1983; (with K. Bond) Paddington's First Puzzle Book, 1987; (with K. Bond) Paddington's Second Puzzle Book, 1987; (contrib.) The Pleasures of Paris, 1987; Paddington at the Rainbow's End, 2009; The Paddington Treasury for the Very Young, 2010; Paddington, 2011; Paddington's London Treasury, 2011; Paddington's Guide to London, 2011; Paddington's Cookery Book, 2011; Paddington Races Ahead, 2012; Paddington Goes for Gold, 2012. **Address:** The Agency, 24 Pottery Ln., London, GL W11 4LZ, England.

BONDER, **Nilton.** Brazilian (born Brazil), b. 1957. **Genres:** Theology/Religion, Philosophy, Psychology, Business/Trade/Industry, Money/Finance, Economics, Ethics. **Career:** Rabbi, 1987-. Writer. **Publications:** Cabala do Dinheiro, 1991; Cabala da Inveja, 1992; Arte de se Salvar: Sobre Desespero e Morte, 1993; Idiche Kop: O Segredo Judaico de Resolucão de Problemas: A Utilização da Ignorância na Resolução de Problemas, 1995; Kabbalah of Money, 1996; The Kabbalah of Envy, 1997; Alma Imoral: Traição e Tradição Através dos Tempos, 1998; Kabbalah of Food: Conscious Eating for Physical, Emotional and Spiritual Health, 1998; Cabala: Da Comida, do Dinheiro e da Inveja, 1999; Yiddishe Kop, 1999; Exercícios d'alma: A Cabala como Sabedoria em Movimento, 2000; Fronteiras da Inteligência: A Sabedoria da Espiritualidade, 2001; (with B. Sorj) Judaísmo para o Século XXI: O Rabino e o Sociólogo, 2001; Our Immoral Soul, 2001; Tirando os Sapatos: O Caminho de Abraão, um Caminho para o Outro, 2008; The Kabbalah of Time: Teachings on the Inexistence of God, 2009; To Have Or Not To Have That Is The

Question, 2010; Taking Off Your Shoes: The Abraham Path, A Path to the Other, 2010; Boundaries Of Intelligence: Senses And Spirituality In Management, 2010; Heaven's Criminal Code, 2010. **Address:** Rua Professor Milward 65, Barra da Tijula, Rio de Janeiro, 22611-070, Brazil. **Online address:** nbonder@globo.com

BONDS, Alexandra B. American (born United States), b. 1950. **Genres:** Art/Art History, Theatre. **Career:** University of Oregon, Department of Theatre Arts, professor. Writer. **Publications:** Beijing Opera Costumes: The Visual Communication of Character and Culture, 2008. Contributor of articles to journals. **Address:** Department of Theatre Arts, University of Oregon, 219 Villard Hall, Eugene, OR 97403, U.S.A. **Online address:** abonds@uoregon.edu

BONDY, Andy. American (born United States) **Genres:** Education, Human Relations/Parenting, Medicine/Health. **Career:** Delaware Autistic Program, director; Pyramid Educational Consultants Inc., co-founder, president and consultant, 1992-. Writer and teacher. **Publications:** (With L. Frost) A Pictures Worth: PECS and Other Visual Communication Strategies in Autism, 2001, 2nd ed., 2011; (with B. Sulzer-Azaroff) The Pyramid Approach to Education in Autism, 2002; (with L. Frost) Autism 24/7: A Family Guide to Learning at Home and in the Community, 2008. Contributor to periodicals. **Address:** Pyramid Educational Consultants Inc., 13 Garfield Way, Newark, DE 19713, U.S.A. **Online address:** abondy@pecs.com

BONDY, Filip. American (born United States) **Genres:** Sports/Fitness. **Career:** New York Daily News, sports columnist, 1993; New York Times, contributor. **Publications:** (With H. Araton) The Selling of the Green: The Financial Rise and Moral Decline of the Boston Celtics, 1992; (with W.R. Coffey) Dreams of Gold: The Nancy Kerrigan Story, 1994; Tip-Off: How the 1984 NBA Draft Changed Basketball Forever, 2007; Chasing the Game: America and the Quest for the World Cup, 2010. **Address:** New York Daily News, 4 New York Plz., New York, NY 10004, U.S.A. **Online address:** fbondy@nydailynews.com

BONE, Eugenia. American/Italian (born Italy), b. 1959. **Genres:** Food And Wine. **Career:** Freelance journalist and author, 1985-. **Publications:** At Mesa's Edge: Cooking and Ranching in Colorado's North Fork Valley, 2004; (with E. Giobbi) Italian Family Dining, 2005; Well Preserved: Recipes and Techniques for Putting Up Small Batches of Seasonal Foods, 2009; Mycophilia: New Revelations from the Weird World of Mushrooms, 2011. **Address:** 121 Wooster St., Ste. R, New York, NY 10012, U.S.A. **Online address:** egbone@aol.com

BONEKEMPER, Edward H. American (born United States), b. 1942. **Genres:** History, Military/Defense/Arms Control. **Career:** Hirschberg, Pettengill & Strong, associate, 1967-68; Churchland Childhood Opportunity Inc., president, 1970-71; CAB, Bureau of Consumer Protection, senior trial attorney, 1979-80; Bureau of Domestic Aviation, Legal Processing Division, acting and assistant chief, 1980-81; Office of Solicitor, Department of the Interior, assistant solicitor, 1981-86; Department of Transportation, assistant chief counsel of hazardous materials safety, 1986-91; Muhlenberg College, adjunct lecturer in military history, 2003-; Civil War News, book review editor, 2010-. Historian. **Publications:** (Ed.) Update 1976: Hatfield History (Township and Borough) 1742-Incorporated-1898, 1976; How Robert E. Lee Lost the Civil War, 1997; A Victor, Not a Butcher: Ulysses S. Grant's Overlooked Military Genius, 2004; McClellan and Failure: A Study of Civil War Fear, Incompetence, and Worse, 2007; Grant and Lee: Victorious American and Vanquished Virginian, 2008. **Address:** PA , U.S.A. **Online address:** ebonekemper@comcast.net

BONELLO, Frank J. American (born United States), b. 1939. **Genres:** Economics, Business/Trade/Industry. **Career:** Michigan State University, lecturer of economics, 1967-68; University of Notre Dame, assistant professor, 1968-74, associate professor of economics, 1974-, director of undergraduate studies, 1996-, College of Arts and Letters, fellow. Writer. **Publications:** The Formulation of Expected Interest Rates, 1969; (with W.I. Davisson) Computer-Assisted Instruction in Economic Education: A Case Study, 1976; (with K.P. Jameson) Macroeconomic Assessment of the Economy of Guyana, 1978; (ed. with T.R. Swartz) Alternative Directions in Economic Policy, 1978; (ed. and intro. with T. Swartz) Taking Sides: Clashing Views of Alternative Economic Issues, 1982, 14th ed., 2010; Supply Side Economics, 1985; (ed. with T.R. Swartz) Urban Finance Under Siege, 1993. **Address:** Department of Economics and Policy Studies, University of Notre Dame, 408 Decio Faculty Hall, Notre Dame, IN 46556, U.S.A. **Online address:** frank.j.bonello.1@nd.edu

BONIFACE, William. American (born United States), b. 1963. **Genres:** Children's Fiction, Law, Humor/Satire. **Career:** Publisher and children's author. **Publications:** Welcome to Dinsmore, the World's Greatest Store, 1995; Mystery in Bugtown, 1997; The Adventures of Max the Minnow, 1997; The Treasure Hunter, 1998; Trim the Tree for Christmas!, 2000; What do You Want on Your Sundae?, 2001; Christmastime is Cookie Time, 2001; Santa's Sleigh is Full!: A Top This! Book, 2002; The Stars Came out on Christmas, 2002; What Do You Want in Your Cereal Bowl?, 2002; Five Little Ghosts, 2002; Five Little Pumpkins, 2002; Five Little Eagle Eggs, 2003; Five Little Christmas Trees, 2003; Five Little Christmas Angels, 2003; Five Little Candy Hearts, 2003; Five Little Bunny Rabits, 2003; Easter Bunnies Everywhere: A Top This! Book, 2003; Five Little Easter Eggs, 2003; Five Little Turkeys, 2003; Max Makes Millions: The Adventures of Max Continue, 2005; Hero Revealed, 2006; Treasure Hunter, 2006; The Return to Meteor Boy?, 2007; Great Powers Outage, 2008; Lights Out, Night's Out, 2009. **Address:** c/o Jon Anderson, 313 W 22nd St., Ste. 2B, New York, NY 10011, U.S.A.

BONINGTON, Chris(tian). British (born England), b. 1934. **Genres:** Travel/Exploration, Autobiography/Memoirs. **Career:** Unilever, management trainee, 1961-62; freelance writer, photographer and mountaineer, 1962-; University of Manchester, Institute of Science and Technology, fellow, 1976; LEPRA, president, 1985-; British Orienteering Federation, president, 1986-; National Trust Lake District Appeal, president, 1986-; The Alpine Club, president, 1996-98; Outward Bound, trustee, 1997-2009; Himalayan Environment Trust, trustee, 1997-2009; Mount Everest Foundation, chairman, 1999-2001; Mountain Heritage Trust of the BMC, trustee, 2000, chairman, 2000-06; Lancaster University, chancellor, 2005-; Army Mountaineering Association, vice president, 2009-; Young Explorers Trust, vice president, 2009-; Youth Hostels Association (England & Wales), vice president, 2009-; British Lung Foundation, vice president, 2009-; Cranfield School of Management, fellow. **Publications:** I Chose to Climb, 1966; Annapurna South Face, 1971; Next Horizon, 1973; Everest Southwest Face: Ultimate Challenge, 1973; (co-author) Changabang, 1975; Everest the Hard Way, 1976; Quest for Adventure, 1981; Kongur: China's Elusive Summit, 1982; (with C. Clarke) Everest: The Unclimbed Ridge, 1983; The Everest Years: A Climbers Life, 1986; Mountaineer: 30 Years of Climbing, 1990; The Climbers: A History of Mountaineering, 1992; (with R. Knox-Johnston) Sea, Ice and Rock, 1993; (ed. with A. Salkeld) Great Climbs: A Celebration of World Mountaineering, 1994; (ed. with A. Salkeld) Heroic Climbs: A Celebration of World Mountaineering, 1994; (co-author) Tibet's Secret Mountain, 1999; Boundless Horizons, 1999; Quest for Adventure: 1950-2000, 2000; Chris Bonington's Everest, 2002. **Address:** Badger Hill Nether Row, Hesket Newmarket, Wigton, CM CA7 8LA, England. **Online address:** chris@bonington.com

BONJOUR, Laurence Alan. American (born United States), b. 1943. **Genres:** Philosophy, Humanities. **Career:** University of Washington, Department of Philosophy, professor of philosophy. Writer. **Publications:** The Structure of Empirical Knowledge, 1985; In Defense of Pure Reason: A Rationalist Account of A Priori Justification, 1997; Epistemology: Classic Problems and Contemporary Responses, 2002, 2nd ed., 2010; (with E. Sosa) Epistemic Justification: Internalism vs. Externalism, Foundations vs. Virtues, 2003; (ed. with A. Baker) Philosophical Problems: An Annotated Anthology, 2005, 2nd ed., 2008. Contributor to books and periodicals. **Address:** Department of Philosophy, University of Washington, Savery M282, 4333 Brooklyn Ave. NE, PO Box 353350, Seattle, WA 98105-1016, U.S.A. **Online address:** bonjour@u.washington.edu

BONNER, Arthur. American (born United States), b. 1922. **Genres:** Area Studies, Biography, Documentaries/Reportage, Social Sciences, History. **Career:** CBS Radio News, news writer, 1944-53; freelance foreign correspondent in Asia, 1953-61; CBS News, documentary producer, foreign correspondent, 1961-68; NBC-TV News, documentary producer, 1968; WNBC-TV News, news writer, producer, 1970-84; freelance writer, 1986-. Journalist. **Publications:** (Co-author) The Place-Names of Surrey, 1934; Jerry McAuley and His Mission, 1967, rev. ed., 1990; Among the Afghans, 1987; Averting the Apocalypse: Social Movements in India Today, 1990; (with K. Ilaiah) Democracy in India: A Hollow Shell, 1994; Alas! What Brought Thee Hither: The Chinese in New York 1800-1950, 1997; We Will not Be Stopped: Evangelical Persecution, Catholicism and Zapatistas in Chiapas, Mexico, 1998; Enacted Christianity: Evangelical Rescue Missions In the United States and Canada,

2002. Contributor to periodicals. **Address:** 40 W 106th St., Apt. 1, New York, NY 10025-3805, U.S.A. **Online address:** arthur_bonner@msn.com

BONNER, Jeffrey P. American (born United States) **Genres:** Sociology. **Career:** University of Michigan, Department of Behavioral Sciences, professor; Saint Louis Science Center, vice president for research and special projects, 1983-93; Indianapolis Zoo, president and chief executive officer, 1993-2002; White River Gardens, president and chief executive officer, 1993-2002; Saint Louis Zoo, president and chief executive officer, 2002; Madagascar Fauna Group, chair, 2003-06; National Elephant Center, founding member, 2007; Zoo's Institute for Conservation Medicine, founder, 2011; Conservation Breeding Specialist Group of the Species Survival Commission of IUCN, director; International Species Information System, director; Madagascar Fauna Group, chair. Writer. **Publications:** Land Consolidation and Economic Development in India: A Study of Two Haryana Villages, 1987; Sailing with Noah: Stories from the World of Zoos, 2006. Contributor to periodicals. **Address:** St. Louis Zoo, 1 Government Dr., St. Louis, MO 63110, U.S.A.

BONNER, John Tyler. American (born United States), b. 1920. **Genres:** Biology, Sciences. **Career:** Princeton University, assistant professor, 1947-50, associate professor, 1950-58, professor, 1958-66, Department of Biology, chairman, 1965-77, 1983-84, 1987-88, Department of Biological Sciences, acting chairman, 1983-84, George M. Moffett professor, 1966-90, George M. Moffett professor emeritus, 1990-; Dodd Mead & Co., advisory editor, 1962-69; Oxford Surveys in Evolutionary Biology, editorial board staff, 1982-93. **Publications:** Morphogenesis: An Essay on Development, 1952; Cells and Societies, 1955; The Evolution of Development, 1958; The Cellular Slime Molds, 1959, 2nd ed., 1967; (ed.) On Growth and Form, rev. ed., 1961; The Ideas of Biology, 1962; Size and Cycle, 1965; The Scale of Nature, 1969; (contrib.) Chemical Ecology, 1970; On Development: The Biology of Form, 1974; The Evolution of Culture in Animals, 1980; (with T.A. McMahon) On Size and Life, 1983; (ed.) On Growth and Form, 1984; The Evolution of Complexity by Means of Natural Selection, 1988; Researches on Cellular Slime Molds: Selected Papers of J.T. Bonner, 1991; Life Cycles: Reflections of an Evolutionary Biologist, 1993; Sixty Years of Biology: Essays on Evolution and Development, 1996; First Signals: The Evolution of Multicellular Development, 2000; Lives of a Biologist: Adventures in a Century of Extraordinary Science, 2002; Why Size Matters: From Bacteria to Blue Whales, 2006; Social Amoebae: The Biology of Cellular Slime Molds, 2009. Contributor to books and periodicals. **Address:** Department of Ecology and Evolutionary Biology, Princeton University, 305 Guyot Hall, Princeton, NJ 08544-1003, U.S.A. **Online address:** jtbonner@princeton.edu

BONNER, Kieran (Martin). Canadian/Irish (born Ireland), b. 1951. **Genres:** Sociology. **Career:** Augustana University College, assistant professor, 1987-93, associate professor, 1993-99, professor of sociology, 1999, Centre for Interdisciplinary Research in the Liberal Arts, founding member, 1990-97, chairperson of division of interdisciplinary studies and international programs, 1997-99; York University, visiting professor, 1987; Kings College, visiting assistant professor, 1988; National University of Ireland, University College, visiting fellow in the humanities, 1993-94; University of Waterloo, professor of sociology, 1999-, St. Jerome's University, Department of Sociology and Legal Studies, professor, 1999-, chair, Human Sciences Initiative, director, vice-president and academic dean, 1999-2003, professor of sociology, 2005-; University of Queensland, associate doctoral supervisor, 1999; University of Alberta, adjunct professor, 1999-2003. Writer. **Publications:** A Great Place to Raise Kids: Interpretation, Science, and the Urban-Rural Debate, 1997; Power and Parenting: A Hermeneutic of the Human Condition, 1998. EDITOR: Space, Place and the Culture of Cities, Special Issue of The Canadian Journal of Urban Research, 2002; Continuity, Contradiction and Change in Contemporary Dublin, Special Issue of The Canadian Journal of Irish Studies, 2004. Contributor of articles to journals. **Address:** Department of Sociology, St. Jerome's University, University of Waterloo, Waterloo, ON N2L 3G3, Canada. **Online address:** kmbonner@watarts.uwaterloo.ca

BONNER, Robert E. American (born United States), b. 1967?. **Genres:** Social Sciences. **Career:** Michigan State University, assistant professor of history; Dartmouth College, associate professor of history. Writer. **Publications:** Colors and Blood: Flag Passions of the Confederate South, 2002; The Soldier's Pen: Firsthand Impressions of the Civil War, 2006; Mastering America: Southern Slaveholders and the Crisis of American Nationhood, 2009. **Address:** Department of History, Michigan State University, 301 Morrill Hall, 450 Administration Bldg., East Lansing, MI 48824-1234, U.S.A. **Online address:** bonnerro@msu.edu

BONNER, Terry Nelson. *See* **YARBRO, Chelsea Quinn.**

BONNOR, William Bowen. British (born England), b. 1920. **Genres:** Astronomy, Mathematics/Statistics, Physics, Sciences. **Career:** University of Liverpool, lecturer, 1949-57; University of London, Queen Elizabeth College, reader, 1957-61, professor of mathematics, 1962-84, Queen Mary College, visiting professorial research fellow, 1987-, now emeritus staff; University of Cape Town, senior research officer, 1984-87. Writer. **Publications:** (Co-author) Rival Theories of Cosmology, 1960; The Mystery of the Expanding Universe, 1964; Status of General Relativity, 1969; (ed. with J.N. Islam and M.A.H. Maccallum) Classical General Relativity, 1984. **Address:** 1 S Bank Terr., Surbiton, GL KT6 6DG, England. **Online address:** 100571.2247@compuserve.com

BONOMELLI, Charles J(ames). American (born United States), b. 1948. **Genres:** Novels, Poetry, Literary Criticism And History, Young Adult Fiction. **Career:** Police officer, sergeant, now retired. Writer. **Publications:** Of Life and Ecstasy, 1989; Season of Discord: War-Peace-Confusion, 2000; A Poet's Soul and Heart: Of Reality and Mortality, 2009. Contributor to magazines. Works appear in anthologies. **Address:** 1610 Kings Royal Blvd., Pueblo, CO 81005, U.S.A. **Online address:** bonomelc@live.com

BONSIGNORE, Joan. American (born United States), b. 1959. **Genres:** Children's Non-fiction. **Career:** Teacher, 1984-; Center for Human Resources Development, case manager for adults with developmental disabilities, 1994-99; National Council on Alcoholism and Drug Dependence/Westchester Inc., executive director. Writer. **Publications:** Stick out Your Tongue!: Fantastic Facts, Features, and Functions of Animal and Human Tongues, 2001. **Address:** National Council on Alcoholism and Drug Dependence, Westchester Inc., 5 Waller Ave., Ste. 105, White Plains, NY 10601-5421, U.S.A. **Online address:** bonsignorej@easthampton.k12.ma.us

BONTA, Marcia Myers. American (born United States), b. 1940. **Genres:** Environmental Sciences/Ecology, Natural History, Women's Studies And Issues, Social Sciences. **Career:** Pennsylvania Game News, columnist; freelance nature writer, 1977-. **Publications:** Escape to the Mountain: A Family's Adventures in the Wilderness, 1980; Outbound Journeys in Pennsylvania, 1987; Appalachian Spring, 1991; Women in the Field: America's Pioneering Women Naturalists, 1991; Appalachian Autumn, 1994; (ed.) American Women Afield: Writings by Pioneering Women Naturalists, 1995; More Outbound Journeys in Pennsylvania, 1995; Appalachian Summer, 1999; Appalachian Winter, 2005. Contributor to magazines. **Address:** PO Box 68, Tyrone, PA 16686, U.S.A. **Online address:** marciabonta@hotmail.com

BOOKCHIN, Debbie. American (born United States) **Genres:** Medicine/Health, History, Sciences, Sports/Fitness. **Career:** Journalist, 1979-; Rutland Herald, reporter, 1980; Barre-Montpelier Times Argus, reporter, 1980; Burlington Free Press, reporter, 1980. **Publications:** (With J. Schumacher) The Virus and the Vaccine: The True Story of a Cancer-Causing Monkey Virus, Contaminated Polio Vaccine, and the Millions of Americans Exposed, 2004. Contributor to periodicals. **Address:** c/o Author Mail, St. Martins Press, 175 5th Ave., New York, NY 10010-7703, U.S.A.

BOOKER, Christopher. British (born England), b. 1937. **Genres:** History, Documentaries/Reportage, Literary Criticism And History, Humor/Satire, Mythology/Folklore, Psychology, Politics/Government. **Career:** Freelance journalist, 1960; Sunday Telegraph, jazz critic, 1961; Private Eye, founding editor, 1961-63; British Broadcasting Co., resident scriptwriter, 1962-64; Daily Telegraph, monthly columnist, 1973-90, columnist, 1987-90; Read All about It, contributor, 1975-77; Sunday Telegraph, editorial page columnist, 1990-. **Publications:** (With W. Rushton and R. Ingrams) Private Eye on London, 1962; Private Eye's Romantic England, 1963; The Neophiliacs: A Study of the Revolution in English Life in the Fifties and Sixties, 1969 in US as The Neophiliacs, 1970; (with C.L. Green) Goodbye London: An Illustrated Guide to Threatened Buildings, 1973; The Booker Quiz, 1976; The Seventies: The Decade That Changed the Future in UK as The Seventies: Portrait of a Decade, 1980; The Games War: A Moscow Journal, 1981; (with A. Cowgill and L. Brimelow) The Repatriations from Austria in 1945: The Report of an Inquiry, 1990; The Seven Basic Plots: Why We Tell Stories, 2004; The Real Global Warming Disaster: Is the Obsession with Climate Change Turning Out to be the Most Costly Scientific Blunder in History?, 2009. WITH R. NORTH: The Mad Officials, 1994; Off the Rails: The New Authoritarians Who Have Hijacked Britain, 1995; The Castle of Lies: Why Britain Must

Get Out of Europe, 1996; Scared to Death: An Anatomy of the Food Scare Phenomenon, 1998; The Great Deception: A Secret History of the European Union, 2003, 2nd ed. as The Great Deception: Can the European Union Survive?, 2005; Scared to Death: From BSE to Global Warming: How Scares are Costing us the Earth, 2007. Contributor to periodicals. Works appear in anthologies. **Address:** The Old Rectory, Litton, Bath, SM BA3 4PW, England.

BOOKER, Sue. *See* **THANDEKA.**

BOOKMAN, Charlotte. *See* **ZOLOTOW, Charlotte.**

BOOKMAN, Terry Allen. American (born United States), b. 1950. **Genres:** Theology/Religion, History. **Career:** Temple Sinai, rabbi/educator, 1984-95; Hebrew Union College, Jewish Institute of Religion, rabbi, 1984; Temple Beth Am, senior rabbi, 1995-; Eitzah Center for Congregational Leadership, co-founder. Writer. **Publications:** The Busy Soul: Ten-minute spiritual Workouts Drawn From Jewish Tradition, 1999; God 101: Jewish Ideals, Beliefs and Practices for Renewing Your Faith, 2001; A Soul's Journey, 2004; This House We Build: Lessons for Healthy Synagogues and the People Who Dwell There, 2006. **Address:** Temple Beth Am, The Richard and Janet Yulman Campus, 5950 N Kendall Dr., Pinecrest, FL 33156, U.S.A. **Online address:** rebbeaid@aol.com

BOOKSTABER, Richard. (Richard Michael Bookstaber). American (born United States), b. 1950. **Genres:** Business/Trade/Industry, Information Science/Computers, Money/Finance, Economics. **Career:** Data Resources, research associate, 1975; Boston University, assistant professor, 1977-78; University of Utah, visiting professor, 1979-80; Brigham Young University, associate professor, 1980; Hebrew University, visiting professor, 1981-82; Morgan Stanley & Co., research manager, 1984-94; Salomon Brothers, managing director and manager of firm-wide risk, 1994-98; Moore Capital Management, head of risk management, 1998-2002; Ziff Brothers Investments, managing director, risk manager and quantitative portfolio manager, 2002-04; FrontPoint Partners, portfolio manager, 2004-07; Bridgewater Associates, staff, 2007-08; U.S. Securities and Exchange Commission, senior policy adviser to the director, 2009-, Department of Treasury, senior policy adviser, 2011. Writer. **Publications:** (As Richard M. Bookstaber) Option Pricing and Strategies in Investing, 1981, rev. ed. as Option Pricing & Investment Strategies, 1987, 3rd ed., 1991; (with R.G. Clarke as Richard M. Bookstaber) Option Strategies for Institutional Investment Management: A Guide for Improving Portfolio Performance, 1983; The Complete Investment Book: Trading Stocks, Bonds and Options with Computer Applications, 1985; A Demon of Our Own Design: Markets, Hedge Funds and the Perils of Financial Innovation, 2007. **Address:** Department of Treasury, U.S. SEC Headquarters, 100 F St., NE, Washington, DC 20549, U.S.A. **Online address:** rick@bookstaber.com

BOOKSTABER, Richard Michael. *See* **BOOKSTABER, Richard.**

BOON, Debbie. British (born England), b. 1960. **Genres:** Children's Fiction, Poetry, Picture/Board Books, Illustrations. **Career:** Roy Walker Design Associates, illustrator-designer, 1980-83; Pencil Box Design, co-founder and co-managing director, 1983-97; Aspire Design, co-founder and co-managing director, 1997-. Writer. **Publications:** SELF-ILLUSTRATED POETRY FOR CHILDREN: My Gran, 1998; Aunt Sal, 1998; Gio's Pizzas, 1998. Illustrator of books by others. **Address:** Artist Partners Ltd., 2E The Chandlery, 50 Westminster Bridge Rd., London, GL SE1 7QY, England. **Online address:** debbieboon@btinternet.com

BOONE, Daniel R. American (born United States), b. 1927. **Genres:** Medicine/Health, Speech/Rhetoric, Self Help. **Career:** Case Western Reserve University, assistant professor, 1960-63; University of Kansas, Medical School, associate professor, 1963-66; University of Denver, professor, 1966-73; U.S. Office of Education, consultant, 1968-; University of Arizona, Department of Speech, Language and Hearing, professor, 1973-88, professor emeritus, 1988-; American Speech-Language-Hearing Association, president. Writer. **Publications:** An Adult Has Aphasia, 1965, 5th ed., 1995; The Voice and Voice Therapy, 1971, 8th ed., 2010; Cerebral Palsy, 1972; Human Communication and Its Disorders, 1987, 2nd ed., 1993; Is Your Voice Telling on You?, 1991, 2nd ed., 1997; The Boone Voice Program for Children, 1993; Communication and Communication Disorders, 1999; The Boone Voice Program for Adults, 2nd ed., 2000; Damn Shoes, 2009. **Address:** 5715 N Genematas Dr., Tucson, AZ 85704-5935, U.S.A. **Online address:** boonvoz@msn.com

BOORSTEIN, Sylvia. American (born United States) **Genres:** inspirational/Motivational Literature, How-to Books, Theology/Religion. **Career:** Washburn University, faculty of chemistry; University of California, psychotherapist; College of Marin, faculty of psychology, 1970-84; Spirit Rock Meditation Center, founding teacher, 1985-; Insight Meditation Society, teacher. Writer. **Publications:** It's Easier than You Think: The Buddhist Way to Happiness, 1995; Don't Just Do Something, Sit There: A Mindfulness Retreat with Sylvia Boorstein, 1996; That's Funny, You Don't Look Buddhist: On Being a Faithful Jew and a Passionate Buddhist, 1997; (contrib.) The Buddha Smiles: A Collection of Dharmatoons, 1999; Pay Attention, for Goodness' Sake: Practicing the Perfections of the Heart-the Buddhist Path of Kindness, 2002; Happiness Is an Inside Job: Practicing for a Joyful Life, 2008; (with N. Fischer and T. Rinpoche) Solid Ground: Buddhist Wisdom for Difficult Times, 2011. Contributor to periodicals. **Address:** Spirit Rock Meditation Ctr., 5000 Sir Francis Drake Blvd., PO Box 169, Woodacre, CA 94973, U.S.A.

BOOS, Ben. American (born United States), b. 1971?. **Genres:** Art/Art History. **Career:** Blizzard North (computer gaming company), senior artist, 1997-2004; Flagship Studios (computer gaming company), freelance illustrator and artist. Writer. **Publications:** SELF-ILLUSTRATED: Swords: An Artist's Devotion, 2008. **Address:** CA , U.S.A. **Online address:** swords@benboos.com

BOOSTROM, Robert E(dward). American (born United States), b. 1949. **Genres:** Education, Young Adult Non-fiction, Social Sciences. **Career:** Laidlaw Brothers, editor, 1981-86; University of Southern Indiana, College of Education and Human Services, assistant professor, 1993-, associate professor of education, professor and chair; Journal of Curriculum Studies, editor, 1997-. **Publications:** The Moral Significance of Classroom Rules, 1991; Developing Creative and Critical Thinking: An Integrated Approach, 1992; (with P.W. Jackson and D.T. Hansen) The Moral Life of Schools, 1993; Thinking: The Foundation of Critical and Creative Learning in the Classroom, 2005. Contributor to periodicals. **Address:** Teacher Education Department, College of Education and Human Services, University of Southern Indiana, EDUC3118, 8600 University Blvd., Evansville, IN 47712-3596, U.S.A. **Online address:** rboostro@usi.edu

BOOT, John C. G. American/Indonesian (born Indonesia), b. 1936. **Genres:** Economics, Mathematics/Statistics. **Career:** Netherlands School of Economics, Econometric Institute, research associate, 1960-64; U.S. Army Mathematics Research Center, visiting associate professor, 1962; State University of New York, University at Buffalo, School of Management, Department of Management Science and Systems, associate professor, 1964-65, professor of management science, 1965-, now professor emeritus, chairman; Marine Midland Banks, consultant, 1965-; University of Wyoming, Bugas professor, 1972. Writer. **Publications:** Quadratic Programming, 1964; Voorspellen en Beslissen, 1964; (with H. Thiel and T. Kloek) Operations Research and Qualitative Economics: An Elementary Introduction, 1965; Mathematical Reasoning in Economics and Management Science, 1967; (with E.B. Cox) Statistical Analysis for Managerial Decisions, 1970, 2nd ed., 1974; Common Globe or Global Commons, 1974. Contributor to journals. **Address:** Department of Management Science and Systems, School of Management, University at Buffalo, 341 Jacobs Management Ctr., Buffalo, NY 14260-4000, U.S.A. **Online address:** jboot@buffalo.edu

BOOTH, Brian. American (born United States), b. 1936. **Genres:** History, Literary Criticism And History, Local History/Rural Topics, Biography. **Career:** Stoel Rives Boley Jones & Grey, partner, 1962-74; Tonkon, Torp, Galen, Marmaduke & Booth (now as Tonkon Torp L.L.P.), partner and corporate attorney, 1974-; Oregon State Bar, Securities Section, chair; Portland Art Museum, chair, 1976-78; Oregon Institute of Literary Arts, founder, 1986, chair, 1986-; Oregon Health Sciences University Foundation, chair, 1986-89; Oregon State Parks and Recreation Commission, chair, 1989-; American Bar Foundation, fellow; Stanford Law Review, editor. **Publications:** (Ed. and intro.) Wildmen, Wobblies, and Whistle Punks: Stewart Holbrook's Lowbrow Northwest, 1992; (ed. with G.A. Love) Davis Country: H.L. Davis's Northwest, 2009. **Address:** Tonkon Torp L.L.P., 1600 Pioneer Twr., 888 SW 5th Ave., 888 SW 5th Ave., Portland, OR 97204, U.S.A. **Online address:** brianb@tonkon.com

BOOTH, Edward. German/British (born England), b. 1928. **Genres:** History, Philosophy, Theology/Religion. **Career:** Pontifical Beda College, lecturer, 1978-80; Pontifical University of St. Thomas (Angelicum), lecturer, 1980-88; Chico Enterprise-Record, sportswriter and copy editor. Priest, researcher, and writer. **Publications:** Aristotelian Aporetic Ontology in Islamic and Christian Thinkers, 1983; (contrib.) La Production Du Livre Universitaire Au Moyen Age: Exemplar Et Pecia, 1988; Saint Augustine and the Western Tradition of Self-Knowing: The Saint Augustine Lecture 1986, 1989; (contrib.) Historisch-Systematisch Untersuchungen Zum Begriff Der Kategorie Im Philosophischen Denken, 1990; (with K. Johnson, J. Nopel and C. Davis) Chico, 2005. Contributor to periodicals. **Address:** Monastery of the Dominikanerinnen, Maria Viktoria, Vellarsweg 2, Wetten, Kevelaer, D-47625, Germany. **Online address:** edward.booth@t-online.de

BOOTH, Stanley. American (born United States), b. 1942. **Genres:** Mystery/Crime/Suspense, Plays/Screenplays, Songs/Lyrics And Libretti, Art/Art History, Literary Criticism And History, Music, Photography, Theology/Religion, Autobiography/Memoirs, Young Adult Fiction. **Career:** Teacher and writer. **Publications:** Furry's Blues, 1970; Dance with the Devil: The Rolling Stones and Their Times, 1984; The True Adventures of the Rolling Stones, 1984; Rythm Oil: A Journey Through the Music of the American South, 1991; Keith: Till I Roll Over Dead (biography), 1994; Keith, 1995; Keith: Standing in the Shadows, 1996; Tree Full of Owls, forthcoming. Contributor to periodicals. **Address:** c/o George Borchardt, 136 E 57th St., New York, NY 10022, U.S.A. **Online address:** sbooth@ktc.com

BOPP, Mary S. American (born United States), b. 1946. **Genres:** Dance/Ballet, Reference. **Career:** Indiana University, librarian, 1989-. Writer. **Publications:** Research in Dance: A Guide to Resources, 1994. **Address:** HPER Library, Indiana University, HPER Bldg 029, 107 S Indiana Ave., Bloomington, IN 47405, U.S.A. **Online address:** mstrow@indiana.edu

BORAINE, Alex(ander). American/South African (born South Africa), b. 1931?. **Genres:** International Relations/Current Affairs, Biography, Autobiography/Memoirs, History. **Career:** Ordained Methodist minister, 1956; Methodist Church of South Africa, president, 1970-72; South African Parliament, member of parliament, 1974-86; Institute for a Democratic Alternative in South Africa, co-founder, 1986-95; Truth and Reconciliation Commission, vice chair, 1995-98; University of Cape Town, visiting professor, 1998; New York University, School of law, professor of law (dignitary in permanent residence), 1998-2001, Justice in Transition Program, director, Hauser Global Law School Program, global visiting professor of law, 2001-; International Center for Transitional Justice, co-founder, 2001-, president, 2001-04, chairperson, 2004-. Writer. **Publications:** A Country Unmasked: Inside South Africa's Truth and Reconciliation Commission, 2000; Life in Transition, 2008. EDITOR: (with P.H. Baker and W. Krafchik) South Africa and the World Economy in the 1990s, 1993; (with J. Levy and R. Scheffer) Dealing with the Past: Truth and Reconciliation in South Africa, 1994; (with J. Levy) The Healing of a Nation?, 1995. **Address:** International Center for Transitional Justice, 5 Hanover Sq., Fl. 24, New York, NY 10004, U.S.A. **Online address:** alexboraine@ictj.org.za

BORAY, Paul. *See* **KENNEALY, Jerry.**

BORCHARD, Therese Johnson. American (born United States) **Genres:** Children's Fiction, Young Adult Fiction, Self Help, Theology/Religion. **Career:** U.S. Catholic Magazine, editor; Paulist Press, editor; Catholic Herald, Catholic News Service, columnist. **Publications:** (Ed.) Women, Why Are You Weeping?: A Lenten Companion for Women, 1997; Everyone's Problem: Addiction & Recovery: Director's Manual, 1997; (ed.) Woman, Why Are You Weeping?, 1997; (ed.) Let It Be: Advent and Christmas Meditations for Women, 1998; Our Catholic Devotions: A Popular Guidebook, 1998; Our Blessed Mother: Mary in Catholic Tradition, 1999; Our Catholic Prayer: A Popular Guidebook, 1999; Taste and See the Goodness of the Lord, 2000; (ed. with M. Leach) I Like Being Catholic: Treasured Traditions, Rituals, and Stories, 2000; Winging It: Meditations of a Young Adult, 2001; (ed. with M. Leach) I Like Being Married: Treasured Traditions, Rituals, and Stories, 2002; (ed.) I Love Being a Mom: Treasured Stories, Memories, and Milestones, 2004; (ed.) The Imperfect Mom: Candid Confessions of Mothers Living in the Real World, 2006; Beyond Blue: Surviving Depression & Anxiety and Making the Most of Bad Genes, 2010; The Pocket Therapist: An Emotional Survival Kit, 2010. EMERALD BIBLE SERIES FOR CHILDREN: Whitney Coaches David on Fighting Goliath: And Learns to Stand up for Herself, 1999; Whitney Rides the Whale with Jonah and Learns She Can't Run Away, 1999; Whitney Sews Joseph's Many-Colored Coat: And Learns a Lesson about Jealousy, 1999; Whitney Solves a Dilemma with Solomon: And Learns the Importance of Honesty, 1999; Whitney Climbs the Tower of Babel and Learns What Happens to Snobs, 2000; Whitney Stows Away on Noah's Ark: And Learns How to Deal with Peer Pressure, 2000. **Address:** Catholic News Service, Catholic Herald, 3211 4th St. NE, Washington, DC 20017, U.S.A. **Online address:** comment@thereseborchard.com

BORCH-JACOBSEN, Mikkel. American/French (born France), b. 1951?. **Genres:** Psychology, Philosophy, History, Translations. **Career:** University of Washington, professor of comparative literature and French. Writer. **Publications:** Le Sujet Freudien, 1982, trans. as The Freudian Subject, 1988; (with E. Michaud and J.L Nancy) Hypnoses, 1984; Le Lien Affectif, 1991, trans. As The Emotional Tie: Psychoanalysis, Mimesis and Affect, 1993; Lacan: The Absolute Master, 1991; Souvenirs d'Anna O.: une mystification centenaire, 1995, trans. As Remembering Anna O.: A Century of Mystification, 1996; (with S. Shamdasani) Dossier Freud: enquête sur l'histoire de la psychanalyse, 2006; Making Minds and Madness: From Hysteria to Depression, 2009; Freud Files: An Inquiry Into the History of Psychoanalysis, 2012. **Address:** Department of Comparative Literature, University of Washington, Padelford B-530, Stevens Way, PO Box 354361, Seattle, WA 98195, U.S.A. **Online address:** mbj@u.washington.edu

BORCZ, Geri. (Geri Buckley). American (born United States) **Genres:** Novels. **Career:** Writer. **Publications:** HISTORICAL ROMANCE NOVELS: Devil's Knight, 1999; Loving Glory, 2000; Asking for Trouble, 2001; One Wild Rose, 2002; Driven, 2011; Rambling Rose, 2011. CONTEMPORARY ROMANCE NOVELS AS GERI BUCKLEY: For Pete's Sake, 2005; Can't Catch This, 2006; Hot Ticket, 2006; Stormy Weather, 2008; (co-author) Fall in Love Like a Romance Writer: Your Favorite Novelists Share Their Secret Keys to a Long and Lasting Love, 2011. **Address:** c/o Stephanie Kip Rostan, Levine Greenberg Literary Agency, 307 7th Ave., Ste. 1906, New York, NY 10001, U.S.A. **Online address:** geri@geribuckley.com

BORDEN, Debra. American (born United States), b. 1957?. **Genres:** Novels, Literary Criticism And History. **Career:** Counseling2Go, founder. Writer. **Publications:** Lucky Me: A Novel, 2005; A Little Bit Married: A Novel, 2007. **Address:** Counseling2Go, 1 International Dr., Ste. 400, Mahwah, NJ 07495-0025, U.S.A. **Online address:** debra@debraborden.com

BORDEWICH, Fergus M. American (born United States), b. 1947?. **Genres:** Novels, History, Travel/Exploration. **Career:** Writer. **Publications:** Cathay: A Journey in Search of Old China, 1991; Peach Blossom Spring: Adapted from a Chinese Tale, 1994; Killing the White Man's Indian: Reinventing of Native Americans at the End of the Twentieth Century, 1996; My Mother's Ghost, 2001; Bound for Canaan: The Epic Story of the Underground Railroad, America's First Civil Rights Movement, 2005; Bound for Canaan: The Underground Railroad and the War for the Soul of America, 2005; Washington: The Making of the American Capital, 2008; Washington: How Slaves, Idealists, and Scoundrels Created the Nation's Capital, 2008; America's Great Debate: Henry Clay, Stephen A. Douglas, and the Compromise that Preserved the Union, 2012. Contributor to newspapers and periodicals. **Address:** Amistad Press, 10 E 53rd St., 7th Fl., New York, NY 10022-5244, U.S.A. **Online address:** fergus.bordewich@yahoo.com

BORDO, Susan (Rebecca). American (born United States), b. 1947. **Genres:** Philosophy, History, Young Adult Fiction, Adult Non-fiction. **Career:** Duke University, visiting associate professor, graduate faculty of women's studies, 1989; Le Moyne College, associate professor of philosophy, 1987-93, Joseph C. Georg professor, 1991-94; University of Kentucky, Otis A. Singletary chair in the humanities, professor of philosophy, 1994-. Writer. **Publications:** The Flight to Objectivity: Essays on Cartesianism and Culture, 1987; Unbearable Weight: Feminism, Western Culture and the Body, 1993; Twilight Zones: The Hidden Life of Cultural Images from Plato to O.J., 1997; The Male Body: A New Look at Men in Public and in Private, 1999; My Father's Body and Other Unexplored Regions of Masculinity, forthcoming. EDITOR: (with A.M. Jaggar) Gender/Body/Knowledge: Feminist Reconstructions of Being and Knowing, 1989; Feminist Interpretation of René Descartes, 1999. **Address:** Department of Philosophy, University of Kentucky, 111 Breckinridge, 1415 Paterson Office Twr., Lexington, KY 40506-0027, U.S.A. **Online address:** bordo@uky.edu

BORDOWITZ, Hank. Also writes as Dr. Rock. American (born United States), b. 1959. **Genres:** Music, Law, Popular Culture, Trivia/Facts, Writing/Journalism, Biography, Ghost Writer, Novels, Novellas/Short Stories, Songs/Lyrics And Libretti, Adult Non-fiction, Communications/Media, Advertising/

Public Relations, Education, Film. **Career:** Cannings Recording Studio, engineer, producer and musician, 1978-81; WEVD, engineer, 1978-79; Record World, writer, editor and chart researcher, 1979; Ben El Distributors/Crazy Eddie's Records, manager, 1981-84; Publishers Packaging Corp., Concert Shots, Metal Mania, and Rock Scene, managing editor, Rock Fever, Focalpoint, Heavy Metal Hall of Fame, Hot Metal, and Cream Specials, senior editor, 1985-90; Fama, writer and copy editor, 1992-94; Wizard: Guide to Comics, managing editor, 1994; Interactive Quarterly, editor, 1995-96; Sheet Music, editor, 1996-97; Baruch College, adjunt professor, 1998-2005; MCY.com, Editorial Content, director, 1999-2001; Bergen Community College, adjunt professor, 2001; Ramapo College, adjunct professor of music, 2004-07, 2010; Colorado State University, adjunt professor, 2005-; Western Illinois University, Music Business Program, director, assistant professor, 2007-08. **Publications:** Bad Moon Rising: The Unauthorized History of Creedence Clearwater Revival, 1998, 2nd ed., 2008; (ed. and intro.) Every Little Thing Gonna Be Alright: The Bob Marley Reader, 2004; The Bruce Springsteen Scrapbook, 2004; Turning Points in Rock and Roll: The Key Events that Affected Popular Music in the Latter Half of the 20th Century, 2004; Noise of the World: Non-Western Artists in Their Own Words, 2004; Billy Joel: The Life and Times of an Angry Young Man, 2005, 2nd ed., 2011; Dirty Little Secrets of the Record Business: Why So Much Music You Hear Sucks, 2007. Contributor of articles to periodicals. **Address:** c/o James Fitzgerald, James Fitzgerald Agency, 165 Christopher St., New York, NY 10014, U.S.A. **Online address:** hank@bordowitz.com

BORDWELL, David. American (born United States), b. 1947. **Genres:** Film, Art/Art History. **Career:** University of Wisconsin-Madison, faculty, 1973-, Wisconsin Center for Film and Theater Research, director, 1985-87, 2000-, Department of Communication Arts, associate chair, 1988-89, Jacques Ledoux professor of film studies, 1990-, now professor emeritus. Writer. **Publications:** Filmguide to La Passion de Jeanne d'Arc, 1973; (with K. Thompson) Film Art: An Introduction, 1979, 9th ed., 2010; French Impressionist Cinema: Film Culture, Film Theory, Film Style, 1980; The Films of Carl-Theodor Dreyer, 1981; (with K. Thompson and J. Staiger) The Classical Hollywood Cinema: Film Style and Mode of Production to 1960, 1985; Narration in the Fiction Film, 1985; Ozu and the Poetics of Cinema, 1988; Making Meaning: Inference and Rhetoric in the Interpretation of Cinema, 1989; The Cinema of Eisenstein, 1993; (with K. Thompson) Film History: An Introduction, 1994, 3nd ed., 2010; (ed. with N. Carroll) Post-Theory: Reconstructing Film Studies, 1996; On the History of Film Style, 1997; (co-author) Filmgespenster der Postmoderne, 1998; Planet Hong Kong: Popular Cinema and the Art of Entertainment, 2000; Xianggang dian yingwang guo: yu le de yi shu: Planet Hong Kong: Popular Cinema and the Art of Entertainment, 2001; Figures Traced in Light: On Cinematic Staging, 2005; Way Hollywood Tells It: Story and Style in Modern Movies, 2006; Poetics of Cinema, 2008; (with K. Thompson) Minding Movies: Observations on the Art, Craft and Business of Filmmaking, 2011. Contributor to film journals. **Address:** Department of Communication Arts, University of Wisconsin, 4045 Vilas Hall, 821 University Ave., Madison, WI 53706, U.S.A. **Online address:** bordwell@wisc.edu

BOREL, Kathryn. Canadian (born Canada), b. 1979. **Genres:** Autobiography/Memoirs. **Career:** CBC Radio, One's Q, founding producer. Radio and television producer and journalist. **Publications:** Corked: A Memoir, 2010. Contributor to periodicals. **Address:** Canada. **Online address:** kathryn.borel@gmail.com

BORELLI, John. American (born United States), b. 1946?. **Genres:** Theology/Religion. **Career:** Fordham University, Department of Theology, instructor, 1975-76; College of Mount St. Vincent, professor of religious studies, 1976-87; United States Conference of Catholic Bishops, Secretariat for Ecumenical and Interreligious Affairs, associate director, 1987-2003, director of interreligious relations, 1987-2003; Georgetown University, special assistant; Vatican's Pontifical Council for Interreligious Dialogue, consultant, 1991-2007. Writer and theologian. **Publications:** (Ed.) Handbook for Interreligious Dialogue, 2nd ed., 1990; (ed. with J.H. Erickson) The Quest for Unity: Orthodox and Catholics in Dialogue: Documents of the Joint International Commission and Official Dialogues in the United States, 1965-1995, 1996; (with M.L. Fitzgerald) Interfaith Dialogue: A Catholic View, 2006. Contributor to journals. **Address:** Catholic Studies Program, Georgetown University, PO Box 571058, Washington, DC 20057-1058, U.S.A. **Online address:** borellij@georgetown.edu

BORENSTEIN, Emily. *See* **BORENSTEIN, Emily Schwartz.**

BORENSTEIN, Emily Schwartz. (Emily Borenstein). American (born United States), b. 1923. **Genres:** Poetry. **Career:** Times Herald-Record, music, drama and dance reviewer, 1956-60; Middletown Psychiatric Center, supervisor of hospital volunteer service, 1958-68; writer, 1972-; Orange County Council for the Arts, poetry advisor, 1972-76. **Publications:** Cancer Queen, 1977; Woman Chopping, 1978; Finding My Face, 1979; Night of the Broken Glass, 1981; From a Collector's Garden, 2001; Night Of The Broken Glass and Transformations, 2007; Enigma Variations, 2009; Neruda Dropped Out of The Sky, 2009. Contributor of articles to magazines. Works appear in anthologies. **Address:** Timberline Press, 6281 Red Bud, Fulton, MO 65251, U.S.A. **Online address:** eboren@warwick.net

BORG, Marcus J(oel). American (born United States), b. 1942. **Genres:** Philosophy, Theology/Religion. **Career:** Concordia College, instructor, 1966-69, assistant professor, 1972-74; South Dakota State University, assistant professor, 1975-76; Carleton College, assistant professor, 1976-79; Oregon State University, professor, 1979-, faculty council president, 1985-86, 1992-93, Hundere distinguished professor and Hundere Endowed Chair of Religion and Culture, 1993-2007, now professor emeritus; University of Puget Sound, Chism distinguished visiting professor, 1986-87; Pacific School of Religion, visiting professor, 1989-91; Trinity Episcopal Cathedral, canon theologian. Writer. **Publications:** Conflict and Social Change, 1971; Conflict, Holiness & Politics in the Teachings of Jesus, 1984; Jesus, a New Vision: Spirit, Culture and the Life of Discipleship, 1987; Jesus in Contemporary Scholarship, 1994; Meeting Jesus Again for the First Time: The Historical Jesus & the Heart of Contemporary Faith, 1994; (with J.D. Crossan and S. Patterson) The Search for Jesus: Modern Scholarship Looks at the Gospels, 1994; God We Never Knew: Beyond Dogmatic Religion to a More Authentic Contemporary Faith, 1997; (with J. Kornfield and R. Riegert) Jesus and Buddha: The Parallel Sayings, 1997; (with N.T. Wright) Meaning of Jesus: Two Visions, 1999; Reading the Bible Again for the First Time: Taking the Bible Seriously but Not Literally, 2001; The Heart of Christianity: Rediscovering a Life of Faith, 2003; (with J.D. Crossan) Last Week: The Day-by-Day Account of Jesu's Final Week in Jerusalem, 2006; (with T. Scorer) Living The Heart of Christianity: A Guidebook for Putting Your Faith into Action, 2006; Jesus: Uncovering the Life, Teachings and Relevance of a Religious Revolutionary, 2006; (with J.D. Crossan) First Christmas: What the Gospels Really Teach about Jesus's Birth, 2007; (with J.D. Crossan) First Paul: Reclaiming the Radical Visionary behind the Church's Conservative Icon, 2009; Conversations with Scripture: The Gospel of Mark, 2009; Putting Away Childish Things, 2010; Speaking Christian, 2011; Evolution of the Word, 2012. EDITOR: (with M. Powelson and R. Riegert) The Lost Gospel Q: The Original Sayings of Jesus, 1996; Jesus at 2000, 1997; (with R. Mackenzie) God at 2000, 2000. **Address:** The Center for Spiritual Development, Trinity Episcopal Cathedral, 147 NW 19th Ave., Portland, OR 97209, U.S.A. **Online address:** mborg@orst.edu

BORGENICHT, David. American (born United States), b. 1968?. **Genres:** Children's Fiction, Children's Non-fiction, Humor/Satire, Novels. **Career:** Quirk Productions (formerly Book Soup Publishing), founder. president and publisher. Writer. **Publications:** FOR CHILDREN: (comp.) A Treasury of Children's Poetry, 1994; (reteller) Bible Stories: Four of the Greatest Stories Ever, 1994; (reteller) Brer Rabbit, 1995; (reteller) The Legend of King Arthur: A Young Reader's Edition of the Classic Story by Howard Pyle, 1996; Grimm's Fairy Tales: The Children's Classic Edition, 1997; Whose Nose Is This?: A Create-a-Creature Drawing Book, 2001; Whose Tail Is This?, 2001. WITH J. PIVEN: The Worst-Case Scenario Survival Handbook, 1999; (and J. Worick) The Worst-Case Scenario Survival Handbook: Dating and Sex, 2001; (and D. Concannon) The Worst-Case Scenario Survival Handbook: Travel, 2001; (and J. Grace) The Worst-Case Scenario Survival Handbook: Holidays, 2002; (and J. Grace) Worst-Case Scenario Survival Handbook: Golf, 2002; (and S. Jordan) Worst-Case Scenario Survival Handbook. Parenting, 2003; Worst-Case Scenario Survival Handbook: Work, 2003; (and J. Worick) Worst-Case Scenario Survival Handbook: College, 2004; (and S. Jordan) Worst-Case Scenario Survival Handbook: Weddings, 2004; Worst-Case Scenario Book of Survival Questions, 2005; Worst-Case Scenario Survival Handbook: Extreme Edition, 2005; Worst-Case Scenario Survival Handbook: Life, 2006; Worst-Case Scenario Survival Handbook: Junior Edition, 2007; (and J. Heimberg) Worst-Case Scenario Survival Handbook: Extreme Junior Edition, 2008; Worst-Case Scenario Survival Handbook: Middle School, 2009; (and B.H. Winters) Complete Worst-case Scenario Survival Handbook: Man Skill, 2010. OTHER: Smile! Twenty-five Happy Reminders, 1995; Bytes of Wisdom: A User's Guide to the World, 1996; (comp.) Mom Always Said, Don't Play Ball in the House, 1996; Sesame Street Unpaved: Scripts, Stories, Secrets, Songs, 1998; The Little Book of Stupid Questions: 300 Hilarious, Bold, Embarrassing, Personal, and Basically Pointless Queries, 1999; The Jewish Mother Goose: Modified Rhymes for Meshugennah Times, 2000; (with J. Borgenicht) The Action Hero's Handbook: How to Catch a Great White Shark, Perform the Jedi Mind Trick, Track a Fugitive, and Dozens of Other TV and Movie Skills, 2002; The Little Book of Stupid Questions: 200 Hilarious, Bold, Embarrassing, Personal, and Basically Pointless Queries, 2005; (with M.T. Nobleman and J. Borgenicht) How to do a Belly Flop!: And Other Tricks, Tips, and Skills No Adult Will Teach You, 2005; (with J. Borgenicht) How to Give a Wedgie: And Other Tricks, Tips, & Skills No Adult Will Teach You, 2005; (with J. Grace) How to Con Your Kid: Simple Scams for Mealtime, Bedtime, Bathtime -anytime!, 2006; (with B. Winters) Meetings, 2009; (with M. Joyner) The Worst-Case Scenario Business Survival Guide, 2009; (with V. De Silverio) Worst-case Scenario Pocket Guide. Breakups, 2009; (with D. Ramsey and J. Ramsey) Worst-case Scenario Pocket Guide. Retirement, 2009; (with N. Marunas and R. Epstein) Worst-case Scenario Survival Handbook: Gross Junior Edition, 2010; (with J. Heimberg) Worst-Case Scenario Survival Handbook: Weird Junior Edition, 2010; (with H. Khan) Mars, 2011; (co-author) Worst-case Scenario Survive-o-pedia: Junior Edition, 2011; (with B. Doyle) Everest, 2011. EDITOR: The Best Little Book of One Liners, 1992; Golf: Great Thoughts on the Grand Game, 1995. **Address:** Quirk Books, 215 Church St., Philadelphia, PA 19106, U.S.A. **Online address:** david@quirkproductions.com

BORGESON, **Jess.** *See* **WINFIELD**, **Jess M.**

BORINSKY, **Alicia.** American/Argentine (born Argentina), b. 1946. **Genres:** Poetry, Literary Criticism And History. **Career:** Boston University, Department of Romance Studies, College of Arts and Sciences, fellow of the university professors, professor of Spanish, director of the writing in the Americas program; Harvard University, visiting professor. Writer. **Publications:** La Ventrilocua Y Otras Canciones, 1975; Ver/Ser Visto: Notas Para Una analítica Poética, 1978; Mujeres Tímidas Y La Venus De China, 1987; Mina Cruel, (Novel), 1989; Theoretical Fables: The Pedagogical Dream in Contemporary Latin American Fiction (Literary Criticism), 1993; Mean Woman, 1993; Lapareja Desmontable, 1994; Sueños Del Seductor Abandonado: Novelavodevil (Novel), 1995; Madres Alquiladas, 1996; Cine Continuado (novel), 1997; Dreams of the Abandoned Seducer, 1998; Golpes Bajos: Instantáneas, 1999; La Mujer De Mi Marido, 2000; All Night Movie, 2002; Las Ciudades Perdidas Van Al Paraíso, 2003; Frivolous Women And Other Sinners/Frívolas Y Pecadoras, 2009; One-Way Tickets: Writers and the Culture of Exile, 2011. Contributor to periodicals. **Address:** Modern Foreign Languages & Literatures, Boston University, 718 Commonwealth Ave., Boston, MA 02215, U.S.A. **Online address:** borinsky@bu.edu

BORITT, **Gabor.** American (born United States), b. 1940. **Genres:** History, Military/Defense/Arms Control, Biography, Civil Liberties/Human Rights. **Career:** Gettysburg College, Robert Fluhrer professor of Civil War studies, 1981, Civil War Institute, founder and director, 1983-. **Publications:** Lincoln and the Economics of the American Dream, 1978; (with H. Holzer and M.E. Neely, Jr.) The Lincoln Image: Abraham Lincoln and the Popular Print, 1984; (with H. Holzer and M.E. Neely, Jr.) Changing the Lincoln Image, 1985; Confederate Image, 1987; Abraham Lincoln: War Opponent and War President, 1987; Historian's Lincoln: Rebuttals, 1988; Gettysburg Gospel: The Lincoln Speech that Nobody Knows, 2006. EDITOR: (with N.O. Forness) The Historian's Lincoln: Pseudohistory, Psychohistory, and History, 1988; Lincoln: The War President, 1992; Why the Confederacy Lost, 1992; Lincoln's Generals, 1994; War Comes Again: Comparative Vistas on the Civil War and World War II, 1995; Of the People, by the People, for the People, 1996; Why the Civil War Came, 1996; The Gettysburg Nobody Knows, 1997; Jefferson Davis's Generals, 1999; The Lincoln Enigma, 2000; (with S. Hancock) Slavery, Resistance, Freedom, 2007; Gettysburg Auto Tour. Contributor of articles to journals. **Address:** Department of History and Civil War Institute, Gettysburg College, 300 N Washington St., Gettysburg, PA 17325, U.S.A. **Online address:** gboritt@gettysburg.edu

BORJAS, **George J(esus).** American/Cuban (born Cuba), b. 1950. **Genres:** Economics, Money/Finance, Business/Trade/Industry, Politics/Government. **Career:** National Bureau of Economic Research, senior research analyst, 1972-78, research associate, 1983-; City University of New York, Queens College, assistant professor of economics, 1975-77; University of Chicago, post-doctoral fellow, 1977-78; University of California-Santa Barbara, assistant professor of economics, 1978-80, associate professor, 1980-82, professor, 1982-90; University of California-San Diego, professor of economics, 1990-95; Quarterly Journal of Economics, staff, 1992-98; Harvard University, professor of public policy, 1995-97, Pforzheimer professor of public policy, 1998-, Robert W. Scrivner professor of economics and social policy; Review of Economics and Statistics, editor, 1997-98, 1998-; The World Bank, consultant. **Publications:** Union Control of Pension Funds: Will the North Rise Again?, 1979; Wage Policy in the Federal Bureaucracy, 1980; The Sensitivity of Labor Demand Functions to Choice of Dependent Variable, 1985; (with M. Tienda) The Economic Consequences of Immigration, 1986; International Differences in the Labor Market Performance of Immigrants, 1988; Friends or Strangers: The Impact of Immigrants on the U.S. Economy, 1990; Labor Economics, 1996, 5th ed., 2010; (and intro.) Heaven's Door: Immigration Policy and the American Economy, 1999; Economic Research on the Determinants of Immigration: Lessons for the European Union, 1999. EDITOR: (with M. Tienda) Hispanics in the U.S. Economy, 1985; (with R.B. Freeman) Immigration and the Work Force: Economic Consequences for the United States and Source Areas, 1992; Issues in the Economics of Immigration, 2000; (with J. Crisp) Poverty, International Migration and Asylum, 2005; Mexican Immigration to the United States, 2007. Contributor to books, professional publications and journals. **Address:** Kennedy School of Government, Harvard University, 79 John F. Kennedy St., Cambridge, MA 02138, U.S.A. **Online address:** gborjas@harvard.edu

BORK, **Lisa.** American (born United States), b. 1964?. **Genres:** Mystery/Crime/Suspense. **Career:** Writer. **Publications:** For Better, for Murder, 2009; For Richer, for Danger: A Broken Vows Mystery, 2010. **Address:** New York, NY , U.S.A. **Online address:** lisa@lisabork.com

BORK, **Robert H(eron).** American (born United States), b. 1927. **Genres:** Law, Politics/Government, Young Adult Non-fiction. **Career:** University of Chicago, research associate, 1953-54; Kirkland, Ellis, Hodson, Chaffetz & Masters, staff, 1955-62, partner, 1981-82; Yale University Law School, associate professor of law, 1962-65, professor of law, 1965-75, Chancellor Kent professor of law, 1977-79, Alexander M. Bickel professor of public law, 1962-81; United States Department of Justice, acting attorney general, 1973-74, solicitor general, 1973-77; U.S. Court of Appeals for the District of Columbia Circuit, circuit judge, 1982-88; University of Richmond, School of Law, visiting professor; Ave Maria School of Law, professor of law. Writer. **Publications:** NON FICTION: (ed. with R.R. Bowie and E.V. Rostow) Government Regulation of Business: Cases from the National Reporter System, 1963; (with H.G. Krane and G.D. Webster) Political Activities of Colleges and Universities: Some Policy and Legal Implications, 1970; (with intro.) The Antitrust Paradox: A Policy at War with Itself, 1978; The Tempting America: The Political Seduction of the Law, 1990; (with W. Nielsen) Donor Intent, 1993; War in the Culture, 1994; Slouching Towards Gomorrah: Modern Liberalism and American Decline, 1996, rev. ed., 2003. OTHERS: Constitutionality of the President's Busing Proposals, 1972; (contrib.) Welfare Reform: Why?: A Round Table Held on May 20, 1976, 1976; (co-author) Professors, Politicians, and Public Policy, 1977; Tradition and Morality in Constitutional Law, 1984; The Tempting of America: The Political Seduction of the Law, 1990; Coercing Virtue: The Worldwide Rule of Judges, 2002; (ed.) Country I Do Not Recognize: The Legal Assault on American Values, 2005; Time to Speak: Selected Writings and Arguments, 2008. **Address:** Ave Maria School of Law, 1025 Commons Cir., Naples, FL 34119, U.S.A.

BORKO, **Harold.** American (born United States), b. 1922. **Genres:** Information Science/Computers, Librarianship, Language/Linguistics. **Career:** University of California, lecturer in psychology, Graduate School of Education and Information Studies, professor, 1967-. Writer. **Publications:** Computer Applications in the Behavioral Sciences, 1962; (ed.) Automated Language Processing, 1967; Study of the Needs for Research in Library and Information Science Education, 1970; (ed. with H. Sackman) Computers and the Problems of Society, 1972; (ed.) Targets for Research in Library Education, 1973; (with C.L. Bernier) Abstracting Concepts and Methods, 1975; (with K. Samuelson and G.X. Amey) Information Systems and Networks: Design and Planning Guidelines of Informatics for Managers, Decision Makers and Systems Analysts, 1976; (with C.L. Bernier) Indexing Concepts and Methods, 1978. Contributor of articles to journals. **Address:** Graduate School of Education and Information Studi, University of California, 405 Hilgard Ave., Los Angeles, CA 90095-1521, U.S.A. **Online address:** hborko@ucla.edu

BORKOWSKI, **Mark.** British (born England), b. 1959?. **Genres:** Business/Trade/Industry, Art/Art History, History. **Career:** Borkowski PR, president.

Writer and consultant. **Publications:** Improperganda: Art of the Publicity Stunt, 2001; The Fame Formula: How Hollywood's Fixers, Fakers, and Star Makers Created the Celebrity Industry, 2008. **Address:** Borkowski PR, 65 Clerkenwell Rd., London, GL EC1R 5BL, England. **Online address:** sarahb@borkowski.co.uk

BORNEMAN, John W. American (born United States), b. 1952. **Genres:** Anthropology/Ethnology, Politics/Government. **Career:** Harvard University, lecturer in social studies, 1989-90; University of California, Department of Anthropology and Political Science, assistant professor and visiting lecturer, 1990-91; Cornell University, assistant professor of anthropology, 1991-98, associate professor, 1998-99, professor, 1999-2001; Princeton University, professor of anthropology, 2001-, acting chair, 2009-. Writer. **Publications:** Narratives of Belonging in the Two Berlins: Kinship Formation and Nation-Building in the Contex, 1989; After the Wall: East Meets West in the New Berlin, 1991; (ed. and intro.) Gay Voices from East Germany, 1991; United the German Nation: Law and Narrations of History, 1991; Belonging in the Two Berlins: Kin, State, Nation, 1992; (with J.M. Peck) Sojourners: The Return of German Jews and the Question of Identity, 1995; Retribution and Judgement: Violence, Democratic Accountability and the Invocation Of the Rule, 1997; Settling Accounts: Violence, Justice and Accountability in Post-socialist Europe, 1997; (ed.) National Audubon Society the Poetry of Flowers, 1997; Subversions of International Order: Studies in the Political Anthropology of Culture, 1998; (ed.) Death of the Father: An Anthropology of the End in Political Authority, 2004; The Case of Ariel Sharon and the Fate of Universal Jurisdiction, 2004; Syrian Episodes: Sons, Fathers and an Anthropologist in Aleppo, 2007; (ed. with A. Hammoudi) Being There: The Fieldwork Encounter and the Making of Truth, 2009; Political Crime and the Memory of Loss, 2011. Contributor to books and periodicals. **Address:** Department of Anthropology, Princeton University, 126 Aaron Burr Hall, Princeton, NJ 08543, U.S.A. **Online address:** borneman@princeton.edu

BORNHOLDT, Jenny. New Zealander (born New Zealand), b. 1960. **Genres:** Poetry. **Career:** Unity Books, staff, 1989-92; Haines Recruitment Advertising, copywriter, 1992-; Victoria University, writer-in-residence. Anthologist. **Publications:** This Big Face, 1988; Moving House, 1989; Waiting Shelter, 1991; How We Met, 1995; (ed. with G. O'Brien) My Heart Goes Swimming: New Zealand Love Poems, 1996; Miss New Zealand: Selected Poems, 1997; (ed. with G. O'Brien and M. Williams) An Anthology of New Zealand Poetry in English, 1997; These Days, 2000; (ed. with G. O'Brien) Colour of Distance: New Zealand Writers in France, French Writers in New Zealand, 2005; Shards of Silver, 2006; Mrs. Winter's Jump, 2007; The Rocky Shore, 2008; The Hill of Wool, 2011. **Address:** Victoria University Press, 49 Rawhiti Terr., Kelburn, PO Box 600, Wellington, 6015, New Zealand.

BORNSTEIN, David Neil. American/Canadian (born Canada), b. 1963. **Genres:** Social Sciences. **Career:** Dowser.org, founder. Journalist. **Publications:** The Price of a Dream: The Story of the Grameen Bank and the Idea That Is Helping the Poor to Change Their Lives, 1996; How to Change the World: Social Entrepreneurs and the Power of New Ideas, 2004, rev. ed., 2007; So You Want to Change the World? The Emergence of Social Entrepreneurship and the Rise of the Citizen Sector, 2005; (with Y. Pierron) Missionnaire Sous La Dictature, 2007; (with S. Davis) Social Entrepreneurship: What Everyone Needs to Know, 2010. Contributor to periodicals. **Address:** Oxford University Press, 198 Madison Ave., New York, NY 10016, U.S.A. **Online address:** manuel.rosaldo@gmail.com

BORNSTEIN, George. American (born United States), b. 1941. **Genres:** Literary Criticism And History, Poetry. **Career:** Massachusetts Institute of Technology, assistant professor of English, 1966-69; Rutgers University, assistant professor of English, 1969-70; University of Michigan, associate professor, 1970-75, professor of English, 1975-95, C.A. Patrides professor of English, language and literature, 1995-2006, professor emeritus, 2006-. Writer. **Publications:** Yeats and Shelley, 1970; (with D. Fader) British Periodicals of the 18th and 19th Centuries, 1972; (with D. Fader) Two Centuries of British Periodicals, 1974; Transformations of Romanticism in Yeats, Eliot, and Stevens, 1976; The Postromantic Consciousness of Ezra Pound, 1977; Poetic Remaking: The Art of Browning, Yeats, and Pound, 1988; Material Modernism: The Politics of the Page, 2001; Colors of Zion: Blacks, Jews, and Irish From 1845 to 1945, 2011; (intro.) The Winding Stair and Other Poems: A Facsimile Edition, 2011. EDITOR: Romantic and Modern; Revaluations of Literary Tradition, 1977; Ezra Pound among the Poets, 1985; The Early Poetry, vol. I, 1987, vol. II, 1994; Mosada, 1987; (with H. Witemeyer) Letters to the New Island, 1989; Representing Modernist Texts: Editing as Interpretation, 1991; (with R.G. Williams) Palimpsest: Editorial Theory in the Humanities, 1993; Wanderings of Oisin, and Other Early Poems to 1895, 1994; (with H.W. Gabler and G.B. Pierce) Contemporary German Editorial Theory, 1995; Under the Moon, 1995; (with T. Tinkle) The Iconic Page in Manuscript, Print, and Digital Culture, 1998. **Address:** Department of English Language and Literature, University of Michigan, 5216 Angell Hall, 435 S State St., Ann Arbor, MI 48109-1003, U.S.A. **Online address:** georgeb@umich.edu

BORNTRAGER, Mary Christner. American (born United States), b. 1921. **Genres:** Children's Fiction, Children's Non-fiction, Novels, Poetry. **Career:** Youth social worker, 1966-78. Full-time poet. **Publications:** Ellie, 1988; Rebecca, 1989; Rachel: A Sequel to Ellie and Rebecca, 1990; Daniel, 1991; Reuben, 1992; Andy, 1993; Polly, 1994; Sarah, 1995; Mandy, 1996; Annie, 1997. **Address:** c/o Author Mail, Herald Press, 616 Walnut Ave., Scottdale, PA 15683, U.S.A.

BOROVIK, Genrikh (Aviezerovich). Russian (born Russia), b. 1929. **Genres:** Plays/Screenplays, Novels, International Relations/Current Affairs. **Career:** Literary Gazette and Novosti Press Agency, chief correspondent, 1966-72; Writers Union of the U.S.S.R., secretary, 1976-89; International Federation for Peace and Conciliation, president; Theater, editor in chief; Passport to the New orld, editor in chief; World Peace Council, vice president, 1987-93; Soviet Union, people's deputy, 1989-91; Vashe-TV, president. Writer. **Publications:** Reportazh iz novŏi Birmy, 1958; Povest? o zelenoĭ i a shcherits e, 1962; Vash spetsial nyi korrespondent vstretilsia, 1967; Odin god nespokŏinogo solnts a, 1971; Tri minuty Martina Grou, 1971; Tragediia Chili, 1974; Reportaj s fashistskih granits, 1974; Maĭ v Lissabone, 1975; Kontora na Ulits e Montéra, 1978; Interv'I u v Buénos Aĭrese, 1980; Istorii a odnogo ubiĭystva, 1980; Agonía de una dictadura, 1980; Moment Istiny, 1981; Prolog, 1984; Agent 00 (play), 1986; Izbrannoe, vol. II, 1987; The Philby Files: The Secret Life of Master Spy Kim Philby, 1994; (co-author) Artëm, 2000. Contributor to periodicals. **Address:** Vashe TV, 12 ul Koroleva, Moscow, 1, Russia.

BOROWITZ, Andy. American (born United States), b. 1958. **Genres:** Adult Non-fiction, Humor/Satire. **Career:** National Broadcasting Co., The Fresh Prince of Bel Air, executive producer and creator, 1990-96. Writer and producer. **Publications:** (With H. Beard and J. Boswell) Rationalizations to Live By, 2000; The Trillionaire Next Door: The Greedy Investor's Guide to Day Trading, 2000; Who Moved My Soap?: The CEO's Guide to Surviving in Prison, 2003; Governor Arnold: A Photodiary of His First 100 Days in Office, 2004; The Borowitz Report: The Big Book of Shockers, 2004; The Republican Playbook, 2006. Contributor to periodicals. **Address:** c/o Morton Janklow, 445 Park Ave., Fl. 13, New York, NY 10022, U.S.A. **Online address:** andy@borowitzreport.com

BORSCH, Stuart J. American (born United States), b. 1964?. **Genres:** History. **Career:** Assumption College, assistant professor, 2002-. Historian, author and scholar. **Publications:** The Black Death in Egypt and England: A Comparative Study, 2005. Contributor to books and periodicals. **Address:** Assumption College, 500 Salisbury St., Worcester, MA 01609, U.S.A.

BORTHWICK, J. S. *See* **CREIGHTON, Joan Scott.**

BORTNIK, Aida (Beatriz). Argentine (born Argentina), b. 1938. **Genres:** Plays/Screenplays, Film, Young Adult Fiction, Children's Fiction, Art/Art History. **Career:** Writer. **Publications:** Doldados y Soldaditos, 1972; Tres por Chejov, 1974; La Tregua, 1974; Dale Nomas, 1975; Una Mujer, 1975; Crecer de Golpe, 1976; La Isla, 1979; Papa Querido, 1981; Domesticados, 1981; Guiones Cinematográficos, 1981; Volver, 1983; No habra mas penas ni olvido, 1984; Primaveras, 1985; (with L.Puenzo) La Historia oficial, 1985; Pobre mariposa, 1986; Old Gringo, 1989; (with M. Pineyro) Tango feroz: la leyenda de Tanguito, 1993; Caballos salvajes, 1995; Cenizas del paráso, 1997; La soledad era esto, 2000; Noticia de un secuestro, forthcoming. **Address:** 595 Salta St., Buenos Aires, 1074, Argentina.

BORTOLOTTI, Dan. Canadian (born Canada), b. 1969. **Genres:** Environmental Sciences/Ecology, Money/Finance, Human Relations/Parenting, Sciences. **Career:** Shift, reviews editor, 1992-94; Paragraph: The Canadian Fiction Review, reviews editor, 1993-98; Equinox, editorial assistant, 1994-96; Today's Parent, managing editor, 1996-2002; writer and editor, 2002-.

Publications: Exploring Saturn, 2003; Panda Rescue, 2003; Tiger Rescue, 2003; Hope in Hell: Inside the World of Doctors Without Borders, 2004, 3rd ed., 2010; What Makes What Makes a Planet a Planet?, 2007; Baseball Now, 2008; Wild Blue: A Natural History of the World's Largest Animal, 2009; Auroras: Fire in the Sky, 2011; The MoneySense Guide to the Perfect Portfolio, 2011. Contributor of articles to periodicals and journal. **Address:** c/o Frontier Distributing, Firefly Books, 1000 Young St., Ste. 160, Tonawanda, NY 14150, U.S.A. **Online address:** dan@danbortolotti.com

BORTON, D. B. *See* **CARPENTER, Lynette.**

BORTON, Della. *See* **CARPENTER, Lynette.**

BORTON, Lady. American (born United States), b. 1942. **Genres:** Autobiography/Memoirs, Children's Fiction, Translations, History. **Career:** Westtown School, teacher of mathematics, 1964-67; Friends School, teacher of history, 1967-68; Quaker Service, assistant director, 1969-71, interim director, 1990-91, field director, 1993-; freelance writer and photographer, 1972-; Careline Inc., executive director, 1975-77; Pulau Bidong Refugee Camp, Red Cross, health administrator, 1980; independent radio producer, 1987-; Akron Beacon Journal, columnist, 1989-; University of Ohio, Southeast Asian Studies, adjunct professor. **Publications:** Sensing the Enemy: An American Woman Among the Boat People of Vietnam, 1984; Voyage of the Mekong Dragon, 1986; Boat People and Vietnamese Refugees in the United States, 1991; Fat Chance!, 1993; The Perfect Gift, 1996; After Sorrow: An American Among the Vietnamese, 1995; Junk Pile, 1997; Boat Boy; Bác Hô vói thiêu nhi và phuò nũ/Uncle Ho With Children and Women, 2002; (trans.) Hô Chí Minh, 2003; (trans. and contrib.) Hô Chí Minh, 2003; (ed. with H. Ngọc) Dô gôm, 2004; (ed. with H. Ngọc) Hôi họa Viêt Nam, hiên dại thuo ban dâu, 2004; (ed. with H. Ngọc) Chèo, 2004; (with C. Biên and H. Ngọc) Vietnamese Lunar New Year, 2004; (ed. with H. Ngọc) Thi cu nho giáo, 2004; (ed. with H. Ngọc) Phô cô Hà Nôi, 2004; (ed. with H. Ngọc) Trâu cau, 2004; (ed. with H. Ngọc) Võ dân tôc, 2004; (ed. with H. Ngọc) Y học cô truyên, 2004; (ed. with H. Ngọc) Têt trung thu, 2004; (trans.) Diên Biên Phu: Rendezvous with History: A Memoir, 2004; (ed. with H. Ngoc) Frequently Asked Questions about Vietnamese Culture, 2006; (co-ed. and intro.) Vietnamese Feminist Poems from Antiquity to the Present, 2007; Hô, Chí Minh: A Journey, 2007; Water Puppets, 2008; (with H. Ngọc) Pho a Specialty of Hanoi, 2008. Contributor to books and periodicals. **Address:** 12800 Stella Rd., Millfield, OH 45761-9766, U.S.A.

BORTZ, Alfred B. *See* **BORTZ, Fred.**

BORTZ, Fred. (Alfred B. Bortz). American (born United States), b. 1944. **Genres:** Children's Non-fiction, Sciences, Technology. **Career:** Bowling Green State University, assistant professor of physics, 1970-73; Yeshiva University, research associate, 1973-74; Westinghouse Electric Co., senior engineer, 1974-77; Essex Group Inc., staff scientist, 1977-79; Carnegie Mellon University, scientist, 1979-83, Data Storage Systems Center, assistant director, 1983-90, Special Projects for Engineering Education, director, 1990-92, science and technology education, senior fellow, 1992-94; Duquesne University, School of Education, senior research fellow, 1994-96; Institute of Children's Literature, staff, 1996-; freelance writer, 1996-; Chatham College, lecturer in English and science, 2000-. **Publications:** Superstuff!: Materials That Have Changed Our Lives, 1990; Mind Tools: The Science of Artificial Intelligence, 1992; Catastrophe!: Great Engineering Failure--and Success, 1995; Martian Fossils on Earth?: The Story of Meteorite ALH 84001, 1997; (as Alfred B. Bortz) To the Young Scientist: Reflections on Doing and Living Science, 1997; (with J.M. Shepherd) Dr. Fred's Weather Watch: Create and Run Your Own Weather Station, 2000; Collision Course!: Cosmic Impacts and Life on Earth, 2001; Techno-Matter: The Materials behind the Marvels, 2001; Quark, 2004; Proton, 2004; Neutrino, 2004; Electron, 2004; Photon, 2004; Neutron, 2004; Beyond Jupiter: The Story of Planetary Astronomer Heidi Hammel, 2005; Physics: Decade by Decade, 2007; Astrobiology, 2008; Seven Wonders of Exploration Technology, 2010; Meltdown!: The Nuclear Disaster in Japan and Our Energy Future, 2012. Contributor of articles to magazines. **Address:** 1312 Foxboro Dr., Monroeville, PA 15146-4441, U.S.A. **Online address:** bortz@duq3.cc.duq.edu

BORUCH, Marianne. American (born United States), b. 1950. **Genres:** Poetry, Essays. **Career:** Tunghai University, lecturer in English, 1979-81; University of Maine, assistant professor of English, 1983-87; Warren Wilson College, teacher, 1988-; Purdue University, Department of English, professor of English, 1987-, Master of Fine Arts Program, director, 1987-2005. Poet. **Publications:** View from the Gazebo, 1985; Descendant, 1989; Moss Burning: Poems, 1993; Poetry's Old Air, 1995; A Stick That Breaks and Breaks, 1997; Poems: New & Selected, 2004; In the Blue Pharmacy: Essays on Poetry and Other Transformations, 2005; Ghost and Oar, 2007; Grace, Fallen From, 2008; Glimpse Traveler, 2011; Book of Hours, 2011. Contributor to books. **Address:** Department of English, Purdue University, 204C Heavilon Hall, 500 Oval Dr., West Lafayette, IN 47907-2038, U.S.A. **Online address:** mboruch@purdue.edu

BORYSENKO, Joan. (Joan Z. Borysenko). American (born United States), b. 1945. **Genres:** Medicine/Health, inspirational/Motivational Literature. **Career:** Tufts University, College of Medicine, faculty; Mind/Body Health Sciences, co-founder, president; Claritas Institute, Interspiritual Inquiry and the Interspiritual Mentor Training Program, co-founder, director; Harvard University, Harvard Medical School, instructor, National Institutes of Health, research fellow; Prevention magazine, columnist; psychologist; health-care consultant, yoga instructor, biologist, organizational official and writer. **Publications:** (With L. Rothstein) Minding the Body, Mending the Mind, 1987; Guilt Is the Teacher, Love Is the Lesson, 1990; (with J. Drescher) On Wings of Light: Meditations for Awakening to the Source, 1992; Fire in the Soul: A New Psychology of Spiritual Optimism, 1993; Pocketful of Miracles: Prayers, Meditations, and Affirmations to Nurture your Spirit Every Day of the Year, 1994; (with M. Borysenko) The Power of the Mind to Heal, 1994; A Woman's Book of Life: The Biology, Psychology and Spirituality of the Feminine Life Cycle, 1996; The Ways of the Mystic: Seven Paths to God, 1997; A Woman's Journey to God: Finding the Feminine Path, 1999; (foreword) Healing Back Pain Naturally: The Mind-Body Program Proven to Work, 1999; Inner Peace for Busy People: 52 Simple Strategies for Transforming your Life, 2001; Inner Peace for Busy Women: Balancing Work, Family and Your Inner Life, 2003; (with J. Drescher) On Wings of Light: Finding Hope when the Heart Needs Healing, 2003; Minding the Body, Mending the Mind, 2007; Your Soul's Compass: What is Spiritual Guidance?, 2007. AS JOAN Z. BORYSENKO: (with G.F. Dveirin) Saying Yes to Change: Essential Wisdom for Your Journey, 2006; It's not the End of the World: Developing Resilience in times of Change, 2009; Fried: Why You Burn Out and How to Revive, 2011. Contributor to newsletters and a variety of lectures, workshops and audiotapes. **Address:** Mind-Body Health Sciences L.L.C.., New Dimensions in Health and Healing, 393 Dixon Rd., Boulder, CO 80302, U.S.A.

BORYSENKO, Joan Z. *See* **BORYSENKO, Joan.**

BORZUTZKY, Silvia. American/Chilean (born Chile), b. 1946. **Genres:** Politics/Government. **Career:** Carnegie Mellon University, H. John Heinz III School of Public Policy and Management, faculty, 1989, teaching professor of social and decision sciences, Department of Social and Decision Science, International Relations and Politics Program, faculty advisor, Political Science Undergraduate Major, director; Heinz College, Trade and Development Concentration, co-director, Heinz Journal, faculty advisor. Writer. **Publications:** Vital Connections: Politics, Social Security Policies and Inequality in Chile, 2002; (ed. with L.H. Oppenheim) After Pinochet: The Chilean Road to Democracy and the Market, 2006; (ed. with G.B. Weeks) Bachelet Government, 2010. **Address:** Department of Social & Decision Sciences, H. John Heinz III College of Public, Policy and Management, Carnegie Mellon University, 208 Porter Hall, 5000 Forbes Ave., PO Box 208, Pittsburgh, PA 15213-3890, U.S.A. **Online address:** sb6n@andrew.cmu.edu

BOSCHKEN, Herman L. American (born United States), b. 1944. **Genres:** Novels, Business/Trade/Industry, Economics, Social Sciences, Reference. **Career:** Ford Motor Co., strategic financial analyst for product development group, 1967-69; San Diego State University, assistant professor of management, 1973-77; University of Southern California, assistant professor of policy, planning and development, 1977-81; University of California, Haas School of Business, visiting professor, 1981-82; San José State University, College of Business, professor of organization and management, 1982-; University of New Brunswick, Fulbright New Brunswick distinguished chair in property studies, 2000-01; Vail Resorts, consultant; Scholastic Corp., consultant. Writer. **Publications:** Corporate Power and the Mismarketing of Urban Development, 1974; Port Authorities as Public Enterprises: Organizational Adjustment to Conflicting Demands, 1982; Land Use Conflicts: Organizational Design and Resource Management, 1982; Strategic Design and Organizational Change: Pacific Rim Seaports in Transition, 1988; Social Class, Politics, and Urban Markets: The Makings of Bias in Policy Outcomes, 2002;

Impacts of the American Upper Middle Class and Government Structure on Global-City Development, forthcoming. Contributor to books and periodicals. **Address:** Department of Organization and Management, San José State University, 656 Business Twr., 1 Washington Sq., San José, CA 95192-0070, U.S.A. **Online address:** herman.boschken@sjsu.edu

BOSCO, Dominick. American (born United States), b. 1948. **Genres:** Medicine/Health, Ghost Writer, Criminology/True Crime. **Career:** Prevention Magazine, editor. **Publications:** Confessions of a Medical Heretic, 1979; The People's Guide to Vitamins and Minerals: From A to Zinc, 1980, rev. ed., 1989; (with M.E. Rosenbaum) Super Fitness Beyond Vitamins: The Bible of Super Supplements, 1987; (with R.A. Markman) Alone with the Devil: Famous Cases of a Courtroom Psychiatrist, 1989; Bedlam: A Year in the Life of a Mental Hospital, 1992; My Perfect Crimes, 2009. Contributor to magazines. **Address:** c/o Russell Galen, Scovil Chichak Galen Literary Agency Inc., 381 Park Ave. S, Ste. 1020, New York, NY 10016, U.S.A. **Online address:** dbosco@comcast.net

BOSCO, Monique. *See* Obituaries.

BOSE, Purnima. American (born United States), b. 1962. **Genres:** History. **Career:** Indiana University, associate professor of English and gender studies, adjunct professor of American studies, comparative literature, cultural studies and history and director of cultural studies. Writer. **Publications:** Organizing Empire: Individualism, Collective Agency, and India, 2003. Contributor to books and journals. **Address:** Department of English, Indiana University, 442 Ballantine Hall, 10-20 E Kirkwood Ave., Bloomington, IN 47405-7103, U.S.A. **Online address:** pbose@indiana.edu

BOSKIN, Joseph. American (born United States), b. 1929. **Genres:** History, Race Relations, Social Commentary, Humor/Satire. **Career:** University of Minnesota, teaching assistant and instructor, 1954-59; State University of Iowa, adjunct professor of history, 1959-60; University of Southern California, associate professor of history, 1960-69, American Studies Program, co-director, Honors Program, coordinator, Institute on Law and Urban Studies, director, 1970-71; Boston University, professor of history and Afro-American studies and director of urban studies and public policy program, 1969, now professor emeritus. Writer. **Publications:** (With F. Krinsky) The Oppenheimer Affair: A Political Play in Three Acts, 1968; (with F. Krinsky) The Welfare State: Who is My Brother's Keeper?, 1968; Urban Racial Violence in the 20th Century, 1969; (with R.A. Rosenstone) Seasons of Rebellion: Protest and Radicalism in Recent America, 1971; Into Slavery: Racial Decisions in the Virginia Colony, 1976; Issues in American Society, 1978; Humor and Social Change in 20th Century America, 1979; Sambo: The Rise and Demise of an American Jester, 1986; Rebellious Laughter: People's Humor in American Culture, 1997; Corporal Boskin's Cold Cold War, 2011. EDITOR: Opposition Politics: The Anti-New Deal Tradition, 1968; (with F. Krinsky) Problems of American Foreign Policy, 1968; Is American Democracy Exportable?, 1968; Protest from the Right, 1968; Ferment in Labor, 1968; Politics and Antipolitics of the Young, 1969; (with R.A. Rosenstone) Protest in the Sixties, 1969; Black Power: The Radical Response to White America, 1969; (with R.A. Rosenstone) Seasons of Rebellion: Protest and Radicalism in Recent America, 1972; The Humor Prism in 20th Century America, 1997. **Address:** Department of History, Boston University, 226 Bay State Rd., Boston, MA 02215, U.S.A. **Online address:** jboskin@bu.edu

BOSKOFF, Alvin. American (born United States), b. 1924. **Genres:** Politics/Government, Sociology, Urban Studies, Regional/Urban Planning. **Career:** University of Illinois, instructor in sociology, 1950-51; Drake University, assistant professor of sociology, 1951-54; College of William and Mary, Department of Sociology, associate professor and head, 1955-58; Emory University, professor of sociology, 1958-, now emeritus. Writer. **Publications:** (With H. Becker) Modern Sociological Theory, 1957; The Sociology of Urban Regions, 1962, 2nd ed., 1970; (with W.J. Cahnman) Sociology and History, 1964; (with H. Zeigler) Voting Patterns in a Local Election, 1964; Theory in American Sociology, 1969; The Mosaic of Sociological Theory, 1972; (with J. Doby and W. Pendleton) Sociology: The Study of Man in Adaptation. 1973. Contributor to sociological journals. **Address:** Department of Sociology, Emory University, 225 Tarbutton Hall, 1555 Dickey Dr., Atlanta, GA 30322, U.S.A.

BOSMAJIAN, Haig. American (born United States), b. 1928. **Genres:** Civil Liberties/Human Rights, Language/Linguistics, Speech/Rhetoric, Social Sciences. **Career:** University of Connecticut, assistant professor of speech, 1961-65; University of Washington, assistant professor, 1965-73, professor of speech, 1973, now professor emeritus. Writer. **Publications:** (Comp. with H. Bosmajian) The Rhetoric of the Civil-rights Movement, 1969; (comp.) The Rhetoric of Nonverbal Communication, 1971; (comp.) Dissent: Symbolic Behavior and Rhetorical Strategies, 1972; The Language of Oppression, 1974; (comp. and intro.) Justice Douglas and Freedom of Speech, 1980; (comp. and intro.) Censorship, Libraries, and the Law, 1983; Metaphor and Reason in Judicial Opinions, 1992; The Freedom Not to Speak, 1999; Burning Books, 2006; Anita Whitney, Louis Brandeis, and the First Amendment, 2010. EDITOR: Readings in Speech, 1965, 2nd ed., 1971; The Rhetoric of the Speaker, 1967; Readings in Parliamentary Procedure, 1968; The Principles and Practice of Freedom of Speech, 1971, 2nd ed., 1983; (with H. Bosmajian) This Great Argument: The Rights of Women, 1972; (and comp.) Obscenity and Freedom of Expression, 1976. EDITOR: FIRST AMMENDMENT IN THE CLASSROOM SERIES: vol. I: The Freedom to Read, 1987, vol. II: Freedom of Religion, 1987, vol. III: Freedom of Expression, 1988, vol. IV: Academic Freedom, 1989, vol. V: Freedom to Publish, 1989. Contributor to journals. **Address:** Department of Communication, University of Washington, PO Box 353740, Seattle, WA 98195-3740, U.S.A.

BOSS, Alan Paul. American (born United States), b. 1951. **Genres:** Astronomy. **Career:** University of California, postdoctoral researcher, 1979; NASA Ames Research Center, Space Science Division, research associate, 1979-81; Carnegie Institution of Washington, Department of Terrestrial Magnetism, staff associate, 1981-83, staff, 1983-. Writer. **Publications:** Looking for Earths: The Race to Find New Solar Systems, 1998; Protostars and Planets IV, 2000; The Crowded Universe: The Search for Living Planets, 2009. **Address:** Lakewood, OH , U.S.A. **Online address:** boss@dtm.ciw.edu

BOSS, Pauline G. American (born United States), b. 1934. **Genres:** Human Relations/Parenting, Bibliography. **Career:** University of Wisconsin, lecturer, 1973-75, assistant professor, 1975-80, associate professor of child and family studies, 1980-81; University of Minnesota, associate professor, 1981-84, professor of family social science, 1984-2005, professor emeritus, 2005-, director of marital and family therapy program, 1984-87, director of graduate studies, 1987-91. Writer. **Publications:** (Co-author) The Father's Role in Family Systems: An Annotated Bibliography, 1979; Family Stress Management, 1988, 2nd ed. as Family Stress Management: A Contextual Approach, 2002; (co-ed.) Sourcebook of Family Theories and Methods: A Contextual Approach, 1993; (ed.) Family Structures and Child Health in the Twenty-first Century, Maternal and Child Health Leadership Conference, 1993; Ambiguous Loss: Learning to Live with Unresolved Grief, 1999; Losing a Way of Life: Ambiguous Loss in Farm Families, 2001; (ed. with C. Mulligan) Family Stress: Classic and Contemporary Readings, 2003; Loss, Trauma, and Resilience: Therapeutic Work with Ambiguous Loss, 2006; Loving Someone Who Has Dementia, 2011. Contributor of articles to books and periodicals. **Address:** Department of Family Social Science, University of Minnesota, 299H McNeal Hall, 1985 Buford Ave., St. Paul, MN 55108-6140, U.S.A. **Online address:** pboss@umn.edu

BOSSELAAR, Laure Anne. American/Belgian (born Belgium), b. 1943?. **Genres:** Poetry, Literary Criticism And History. **Career:** Emerson College, faculty; Sarah Lawrence College, teacher; International School of Brussels, French poetry faculty, 1983-86; Hamilton College, writer-in-residence; Vermont Studio Center, writer-in-residence; Georgia Tech University, McEver chair for visiting writers; Pine Manor College, Low-Residency MFA in Creative Writing Program, founding faculty. Poet and translator. **Publications:** POETRY: Artemis, 1982; The Hour between Dog and Wolf, 1997; Small Gods of Grief, 2001; (trans. with K. Brown) Plural of Happiness: Selected Poems of Herman de Coninck, 2006; A New Hunger, 2007. EDITOR: (with K. Brown) Night Out: Poems about Hotels, Motels, Restaurants and Bars, 1997; Outsiders: Poems about Rebels, Exiles & Renegades (anthology), 1999; Urban Nature: Poems about Wildlife in the Cities (anthology), 2000; Never Before: Poems about First Experiences (anthology), 2005. Contributor to periodicals. **Address:** Low Residency MFA in Creative Writing, Pine Manor College, 400 Heath St., Chestnut Hill, MA 02467, U.S.A. **Online address:** loranneke@gmail.com

BOSTDORFF, Denise M. American (born United States), b. 1959. **Genres:** Politics/Government, Speech/Rhetoric, Military/Defense/Arms Control, History, International Relations/Current Affairs. **Career:** Purdue University, visiting assistant professor, 1987-88, assistant professor, 1988-93, associate professor of communication, 1994; College of Wooster, assistant professor,

1994-97, associate professor, 1997-2007, professor of communication, 2007-, chair, 1998-2002, associate dean for the Class of 2012, 2008. Writer. **Publications:** The Presidency and The Rhetoric of Foreign Crisis, 1994; Proclaiming The Truman Doctrine: The Cold War Call to Arms, 2008. Works appear in anthologies. Contributor to journals and periodicals. **Address:** Department of Communication, College of Wooster, 103 Wishart Hall, 1189 Beall Ave., 303 E University St., Wooster, OH 44691, U.S.A. **Online address:** dbostdorff@wooster.edu

BOSTICCO, (Isabel Lucy) Mary. British (born England), b. 1922?. **Genres:** Administration/Management, Business/Trade/Industry, Novellas/Short Stories, Novels, Economics, Education. **Career:** Cement and Concrete Association, staff writer and editor, 1968-71; Commonwealth War Graves Commission, editor, 1972; International Management, associate editor, 1973-74; Bracknell Development Corp., press officer, 1974-. **Publications:** Modern Personnel Management, 1964; Personal Letters for Businessmen, 1965, 3rd ed., 1986; Etiquette for the Businessman: At Home and Abroad, 1967; Instant Business Letters, 1968, 3rd ed., 1988; Top Secretary, 1970; (trans.) Modern Filing Methods and Equipment, 1970; Creative Techniques for Management, 1971; The Businessman's Wife, 1972; Teach Yourself Secretarial Practice, 1984; Personal Letters for Business People, 1986; Uncle Ginger: Tales of Italy and Other Places, 1990; Autumn Leaves, 1996; Cartas de Negocios Eficaces, 2001. **Address:** The Oasis, 7A Telston Close, Bourne End, BK SL8 5TY, England.

BOSTOCK, David. British (born England), b. 1936?. **Genres:** Philosophy, Sciences. **Career:** Merton College, fellow and tutor in philosophy, emeritus fellow; University of Leicester, temporary lecturer in philosophy, 1963; Australian National University, lecturer in philosophy, 1964-67; Oxford University, lecturer in philosophy, 1968-, now emeritus. Writer. **Publications:** Logic and Arithmetic, 2 vols., 1974-79; Plato's Phaedo, 1986; Plato's Theaetetus, 1988; (trans.) Aristotle: Metaphysics, 1994; (intro.) Physics, 1996; Intermediate Logic, 1997; Aristotle's Ethics, 2000; Space, Time, Matter and Form: Essays on Aristotle's Physics, 2006; Philosophy of Mathematics: An Introduction, 2009. **Address:** Faculty of Philosophy, University of Oxford, 10 Merton St., Oxford, OX OX1 4JD, England.

BOSTOCK, Donald Ivan. British (born England), b. 1924?. **Genres:** Music. **Career:** Ashford Methodist Church, musical director, 1947-87; The Echelforde Singers, assistant conductor, 1950-53. Writer. **Publications:** Choirmastery: A Practical Handbook, 1966. **Address:** Kerridge, Gorse Hill Ln., Virginia Water, SR GU25 4AJ, England.

BOSTON, Jonathan. New Zealander/British (born England), b. 1957. **Genres:** Politics/Government, Administration/Management. **Career:** New Zealand Treasury, investigating officer, 1984; Victoria University of Wellington, School of Government, Institute of Policy Studies, senior lecturer, 1987-93, associate professor, 1994-97, professor and personal chair in public policy, 1997-, Institute of Policy Studies, fellow, 1984, executive, senior associate, deputy director, 2005-08, director, 2008-; University of Canterbury, lecturer, 1985-87. Writer. **Publications:** Incomes Policy in New Zealand, 1968-1984, 1984; The Future of New Zealand Universities, 1988; (co-author) Public Management: The New Zealand Model, 1996; (co-author) New Zealand under MMP: A New Politics?, 1996; Governing Under Proportional Representation: Lessons from Europe, 1998; (with P. Callister and A. Wolf) Policy Implications of Diversity, 2006. EDITOR: (with M. Holland) The Fourth Labour Government: Radical Politics in New Zealand, 1987, 2nd ed. as Fourth Labour Government: Politics and Policy in New Zealand, 1992; (co-ed.) Reshaping the State: New Zealand's Bureaucratic Revolution, 1991; (with P. Dalziel) The Decent Society: Essays in Response to National's Economic and Social Policies, 1992; (with A. Cameron) Voices for Justice: Church, Law, and State in New Zealand, 1994; The State under Contract, 1995; (co-ed.) From Campaign to Coalition: New Zealand's First General Election under Proportional Representation, 1997; (with P. Dalziel and S. John) Redesigning the Welfare State in New Zealand: Problems, Policies, Prospects, 1999; (co-ed.) Electoral and Constitutional Change in New Zealand: An MMP Sourcebook, 1999; (co-ed.) Left Turn: The New Zealand General Election of 1999, 2000; (co-ed.) New Zealand Votes: The General Eelection of 2002, 2003; (with J.A. Davey) Implications of Population Ageing: Opportunities and Risks, 2006; (with R. Chapman and M. Schwass) Confronting Climate Change: Critical Issues for New Zealand, 2006; Eliminating World Poverty: Global Goals and Regional Progress, 2009; (with P. Nel and M. Righarts) Climate Change and Security: Planning for the Future?, 2009; (ed. with A. Bradstock and D. Eng) Public Policy: Why Ethics Matters, 2010. **Address:** School of Government, Victoria Univ. of Wellington, Rm. 825, Pipitea Campus, Rutherford House, 23 Lambton Quay, Level 8, PO Box 600, Wellington, 1, New Zealand. **Online address:** jonathan.boston@vuw.ac.nz

BOSWELL, Angela. American (born United States), b. 1965. **Genres:** Women's Studies And Issues, History, Social Sciences. **Career:** Texas Women's Political Caucus, executive director, 1988-91; University of Iowa, Center for Advanced Studies, professor of history and research assistant, 1994-95; Journal of Southern History, graduate editorial assistant, 1992-95; Del Mar College, adjunct instructor, 1996; Henderson State University, professor of history, 1997-. Writer. **Publications:** Her Act and Deed: Women's Lives in a Rural Southern County, 1837-1873, 2001; (ed. with T.H. Appleton Jr.) Searching for Their Places: Women in the South across Four Centuries, 2003; (ed. with J.N. McArthur) Women Shaping the South: Creating and Confronting Change, 2006; Black Women in Texas History, 2008. Contributor of articles to periodicals. **Address:** Department of History, Henderson State University, 1100 Henderson St., PO Box 7754, Arkadelphia, AR 71999-0001, U.S.A. **Online address:** boswela@hsu.edu

BOSWELL, Robert. American (born United States), b. 1953. **Genres:** Novels, Novellas/Short Stories, Plays/Screenplays, Essays. **Career:** University of Arizona, graduate assistant, 1981-84, teaching assistant, 1982-86, instructor in English, 1984-86; Northwestern University, assistant professor of creative writing, 1986-89; New Mexico State University, professor of English, 1989-2009; University of Houston, Cullen chair of creative writing, 2001-. Writer. **Publications:** SHORT STORIES: Dancing in the Movies, 1986; Living to Be 100, 1994; The Heyday of the Insensitive Bastards, 2009. NOVELS: Crooked Hearts, 1987; The Geography of Desire, 1989; Mystery Ride, 1993; (as S. Aaron) Virtual Death, 1995; American Owned Love, 1997; Century's Son, 2003; PLAY: Tongues, 1996. NONFICTION: Half-Known World: On Writing Fiction, 2008; (with D. Schweidel) What Men Call Treasure: The Search for Gold at Victorio Peak, 2008. **Address:** University of Houston, Rm. 234B, Roy Cullen Bldg., 4800 Calhoun Rd., Houston, TX 77004, U.S.A. **Online address:** robertboswell@sbcglobal.net

BOSWORTH, R(ichard) J(ames) B(oon). Australian (born Australia), b. 1943. **Genres:** History, International Relations/Current Affairs. **Career:** University of Sydney, lecturer, 1969-73, senior lecturer, 1974-81, associate professor, 1981-86; F. May Foundation for Italian Studies, deputy director, 1981-85, acting director, 1982-83, 1986; University of Western Australia, professor of history, 1987-2007, head of department, 1988-90, part-time professor, 2007-11, professor emeritus, 2011-; University of Trento, visiting professor, 2004-; University of Reading, part-time professor, 2007-; University of Oxford, Jesus College, senior research fellow, 2011-. Writer. **Publications:** Benito Mussolini and the Fascist Destruction of Liberal Italy, 1900-1945, 1973; Italy, The Least of the Great Powers: Italian Foreign Policy Before the First World War, 1979, rev. ed., 1985; Italy and the Approach of the First World War, 1983; (with J. Wilton) Old Worlds and New Australia: A History of Non-British Migration to Australia since the Second World War, 1984: (with J. Wilton) Old Worlds and New Australia: The Post-War Migrant Experience, 1984; (with M. Bosworth) Fremantle's Italy, 1993; Explaining Auschwitz and Hiroshima: History Writing and the Second World War 1945-1990, 1993; Italy and the Wider World 1860-1960, 1996; The Italian Dictatorship: Problems and Perspectives in the Interpretation of Mussolini and Fascism, 1998; Mussolini, 2002; Mussolini's Italy: Life Under the Dictatorship, 1915-1945, 2006; Nationalism a Critical History, 2007; Whispering city: Rome and its histories, 2011. EDITOR: (with G. Cresciani) Altro Polo: A Volume of Italian Studies, 1979; (with G. Rizzo and contrib.) Altro Polo: A Study of Intellectuals and Ideas in Contemporary Italy, 1983; (with S. Romano and contrib.) La Politicaestera italiana, 1860-1985, 1991; (with M. Melia) Aspects of Ethnicity in Western Australia, 1991; (with S. Romano) Il Problema dellapolitica estera italiana, 1991; (with R. Ugolini and contrib.) War, Internment and Mass Migration: The Italo-Australian Experience, 1940-1990, 1992; (and trans. with M. Melia) L. Zunini, Western Australia As It Is Today, 1906, 1997; (with P. Dogliani) Italian Fascism: History, Memory and Representation, 1999; Oxford Handbook of Fascism, 2009. Contributor to books and journals. **Address:** Jesus College, Turl St., Oxford, OX OX1 3DW, United Kingdom. **Online address:** richard.bosworth@uwa.edu.au

BOTEACH, Shmuley. American (born United States), b. 1966. **Genres:** Theology/Religion, Psychology, Romance/Historical. **Career:** L'Chaim Society, founder; Heal the Kids Foundation, co-founder; Love prophet.com (dating Web site), founder. Rabbi, writer and public speaker. **Publications:** The Wolf Shall Lie with the Lamb: The Messiah in Hasidic Thought, 1993; Wrestling with the Divine: A Jewish Response to Suffering, 1995; Wisdom, Understanding and Knowledge: Basic Concepts of Hasidic Thought, 1996; An Intelligent Person's Guide to Judaism and Jewish Guide to Adultery, 1998; Kosher Sex: A Recipe for Passion and Intimacy, 1999; Dating Secrets of the Ten Commandments, 2000; Why Can't I Fall in Love: A Twelve-Step Program, 2001; (with U. Geller and D. Chopra) The Psychic and the Rabbi: A Remarkable Correspondence, 2001; Kosher Adultery: Seduce and Sin with Your Spouse, 2002; Private Adam: Becoming a Hero in a Selfish Age, 2003; Face Your Fear: Living with Courage in an Age of Caution, 2004; Intelligent Person's Guide to Judaism, 2005; Hating Women: America's Hostile Campaign against the Fairer Sex, 2005; Parenting with Fire: Lighting up the Family with Passion and Inspiration, 2006; 10 Conversations You Need to Have with Your Children, 2006; Shalom in the Home, 2007; Broken American Male: And how to Fix Him, 2008; Kosher Sutra: Eight Sacred Secrets for Reigniting Desire and Restoring Passion for Life, 2009; The Michael Jackson Tapes: A Tragic Icon Reveals His Soul in Intimate Conversation, 2009; Judaism for Everyone: Renewing Your Life Through the Vibrant Lessons of Jewish Faith, 2010; Renewal: A Guide to the Values-filled Life, 2010; Honoring the Child Spirit: Inspiration and Learning from Our Children, 2010; Kosher Jesus, 2011. Contributor to periodicals. **Address:** Random House, 1745 Broadway, New York, NY 10019, U.S.A.

BOTHA, Ted. American (born United States), b. 1958?. **Genres:** Adult Non-fiction, Criminology/True Crime, Social Sciences, Young Adult Non-fiction. **Career:** Journalist. **Publications:** Apartheid in My Rucksack, 1990; Mongo: Adventures in Trash, 2004; (with J. Baxter) The Expat Confessions: South Africans Abroad Speak Out!, 2005; The Girl with the Crooked Nose: A Tale of Murder, Obsession, and Forensic Artistry, 2008. Contributor to magazines and newspapers. **Address:** c/o Author Mail, Bloomsbury Publishing, 175 5th Ave., New York, NY 10010, U.S.A. **Online address:** tedbotha@gmail.com

BOTHWELL, Robert (Selkirk). Canadian (born Canada), b. 1944. **Genres:** History, Biography, Social Commentary, Adult Non-fiction. **Career:** University of Toronto, lecturer, 1970-72, assistant professor, 1972-75, associate professor, 1975-81, professor of history, 1981-; Canadian Historical Review, co-editor and editor, 1972-80; CJRT-FM, academic broadcaster, 1989-99. **Publications:** (With B. Alexandrin) A Bibliography of the Material Culture of New France, 1970; (with Hillmer) Canada's Foreign Policy, 1919-1939, 1978; Pearson, His Life and World, 1978; (with W. Kilbourn) C.D. Howe: A Biography, 1979; (with I. Drummond and J. English) Canada since 1945: Power, Politics, and Provincialism, 1981, rev. ed., 1989; Eldorado: Canada's National Uranium Company, 1984; (with D.J. Bercuson and J.L. Granatstein) The Great Brain Robbery: Canada's Universities on the Road to Ruin, 1984; Short History of Ontario, 1986; (with I. Drummond and J. English) Canada, 1900-1945, 1987; Years of Victory, 1987; Loring Christie: The Failure of Bureaucratic Imperialism, 1988; Nucleus: This History of Atomic Energy of Canada Limited, 1988; (with Granatstein) Pirouette: Pierre Trudeau and Canadian Foreign Policy, 1990; Laying the Foundations, 1991; Canada and the United States: The Politics of Partnership, 1992; Canada and Quebec: One Country, Two Histories, 1995, rev. ed., 1998; History of Canada Since 1867, 1996; (with D. Bercuson) Petrified Campus: The Crisis in Canada's Universities, 1997; The Big Chill: Canada and the Cold War, 1998; (with J.L. Granatstein) Our Century: The Canadian Journey in the Twentieth Century, 2000; Traveller's History of Canada, 2001, 2nd ed., 2010; The Penguin History of Canada, 2006; Alliance and Illusion: Canada and the World, 1945-1984, 2007. EDITOR: (with M. Cross) Policy by Other Means, 1972; (with N. Hillmer) The In-Between Time, 1975; (with J.L. Granatstein) Gouzenko Transcripts: The Evidence Presented to the Kellock-Taschereau Royal Commission of 1946, 1982; (with J. Daudelin) Canada among Nations 2008, 2009; (with J. Daudelin) 100 Years of Canadian Foreign Policy, 2009. **Address:** International Relations Program, Trinity College, University of Toronto, MU 307N, Sidney Smith Hall, 100 St. George St., Toronto, ON M5S 3G3, Canada. **Online address:** bothwell@chass.utoronto.ca

BOTKIN, Daniel B. American (born United States), b. 1937. **Genres:** Agriculture/Forestry, Environmental Sciences/Ecology, Natural History, Earth Sciences. **Career:** University of Wisconsin News Service, science writer, 1959-62; Yale University, assistant professor, associate professor, 1968-75; Ecosystems Center, associate scientist, 1976-78; University of California, professor of biology and environmental studies, 1978-92, Environmental Studies Program, chairman, 1979-85, Department of Ecology, Evolution and Marine Biology, research professor, 1999-, now professor emeritus; Center for the Study of the Environment, founder and president, 1992-; George Mason University, professor of biology and director of program on global change, 1993-99; Worldwide Medical News Service, science writer, 1994. **Publications:** (With R.S. Miller and G.S. Hochbaum) Simulation Model for the Management of Sandhill Cranes, 1972; (with E.A. Keller) Environmental Studies: Earth As a Living Planet, 1982, 8th ed., 2011; Discordant Harmonies: A New Ecology for the 21st Century, 1990; Forest Dynamics: An Ecological Model, 1993; (with E.A. Keller) Environmental Science: Earth as a Living Planet, 1995, 8th ed., 2011; Our Natural History: The Lessons of Lewis and Clark, 1995; Passage of Discovery: The American Rivers Guide to the Missouri River of Lewis and Clark, 1999; (with B.J. Skinner and S.C. Porter) Blue Planet: An Introduction to Earth System Science, 1999; (co-author) Forces of Change: A New View of Nature, 2000; No Man's Garden: Thoreau and a New Vision for Civilization and Nature, 2001; Strange Encounters: Adventures of a Renegade Naturalist, 2003; Beyond the Stony Mountains: Nature in the American West from Lewis and Clark to Today, 2004; The Restless Earth: An Atlas of Global Change, 2005; (with E.A. Keller) Essential Environmental Science, 2008; Powering the Future: A Scientist's Guide to Energy Independence, 2010; The Moon in the Nautilus Shell: Discordant Harmonies Reconsidered, 2012; Energy Forever: A Voter's Guide to Energy, forthcoming. EDITOR: (with D.C. West and H.H. Shugart) Forest Succession: Concepts and Applications, 1981; (co-ed.) Changing the Global Environment: Perspectives on Human Involvement, 1989. **Address:** Department of Ecology, Evolution and Marine, Biology, University of California, Life Sciences Bldg., 552 University Rd., Santa Barbara, CA 93106-9620, U.S.A. **Online address:** dan@danielbbotkin.com

BOTSMAN, Daniel V. American/Papua New Guinean (born Papua New Guinea), b. 1968. **Genres:** Adult Non-fiction, Public/Social Administration, Politics/Government, Law, Criminology/True Crime. **Career:** Tokyo University, Historiographical Institute, research fellow; Hokkaido University, lecturer in the faculty of law; University of North Carolina, faculty, 2006, associate professor of history; Harvard University, Edwin O. Reischauer Institute of Japanese Studies, Center for Government and International Studies, associate professor of history; Yale University, Department of History, professor. Writer. **Publications:** Saburo Okita: A Life in Economic Diplomacy, 1993; Punishment and Power in the Making of Modern Japan, 2005. **Address:** Edwin O. Reischauer Institute of Japanese Studies, Center for Government & International Studies, Harvard University, 1730 Cambridge St., Cambridge, MA 02138, U.S.A. **Online address:** dbotsman@fas.harvard.edu

BOTT, Caroline G. British/Malaysian (born Malaysia), b. 1940. **Genres:** Biography, Autobiography/Memoirs. **Career:** Writer and educator. **Publications:** The Life and Works of Alfred Bestall: Illustrator of Rupert Bear, 2003. **Address:** Rake Ct., Milford, Godalming, SR GU8 5AD, England. **Online address:** bottcg@supanet.com

BOTTING, Douglas. British (born England), b. 1934. **Genres:** History, Natural History, Travel/Exploration, Biography, Adult Non-fiction, Children's Fiction, Novels, Military/Defense/Arms Control, Technology. **Career:** British Broadcasting Corp., writer and independent producer for television, 1958-. Explorer and photographer. **Publications:** Island of the Dragon's Blood, 1958; The Knights of Bornu (travel), 1961; One Chilly Siberian Morning (travel), 1965; Humboldt and the Cosmos (biography), 1973; Pirates of the Spanish Main, 1973; Shadow in the Clouds, 1974; Wilderness Europe, 1976; Rio de Janeiro (reportage), 1977; The Pirates (history), 1978; The Second Front (war), 1978; The U-Boats (war), 1979; The Giant Airships (history), 1980; The Aftermath: Europe, 1983; (with I. Sayer) Nazi Gold: The Story of the World's Greatest Robbery-And Its Aftermath, 1984; In the Ruins of the Reich, 1985; From the Ruins of the Reich: Germany, 1945-1949, 1985; Wild Britain: A Traveller's and Naturalist's Handbook, 1988, 2nd ed., 1994; (with I. Sayer) Hitler's Last General: The Case Against Wilhelm Mohnke, 1989; (with I. Sayer) America's Secret Army: The Untold Story of the Counter Intelligence Corps, 1989; Gavin Maxwell: The Life of the Man Who Wrote Ring of Bright Water, 1994, rev. ed. as The Saga of Ring of Bright Water: The Enigma of Gavin Maxwell, 2000; (ed.) Wild France: A Traveller's Guide, 1994; (with K. Botting) Sex Appeal: The Art and Science of Sexual Attraction, 1996; The D-Day Invasion, 1998; Gerald Durrell: The Authorized Biography, 1999; Dr. Eckener's Dream Machine: The Great Zeppelin and the Dawn of Air Travel, 2001; (ed. with I. Sayer) Hitler's Bastard: Through Hell and Back in Nazi Germany and Stalin's Russia, 2003; (with I. Sayer) The Women Who Knew Hitler: The Private Life of Adolf Hitler, 2004; Hitler and Women: The

Love Life of Adolf Hitler, 2004; The Whisky Ship (fiction), forthcoming; Lost Horizons, Forbidden Worlds (non-fiction), forthcoming; My Darling Enemy (novel), forthcoming; Island of the Dragon's Blood, forthcoming. Contributor to books. **Address:** c/o Andrew Hewson, Johnson & Alcock Ltd., Clerkenwell House, 45-47 Clerkenwell Green, London, GL EC1R 0HT, England.

BOTTKE, Allison Gappa. American (born United States), b. 1955. **Genres:** Novels, Human Relations/Parenting, Young Adult Fiction, Young Adult Non-fiction. **Career:** Writer. **Publications:** (With H. Gemmen) Jingles and Joy, 2003; (with H. Gemmen) Picnics and Peace, 2003; (with H. Gemmen) Laughter and Love, 2003; (with H. Gemmen) Friend or Freak, 2004; (with H. Gemmen) Get Real!, 2004; (with H. Gemmen) Pastrami Project, 2004; (ed. with C. Hutchings and J. Devlin) God Answers Prayers, 2005; (with C. Hutchings) God Answers Moms' Prayers, 2005; A Stitch in Time (novel), 2006; (with T. Peterson and D. O'Brian) I Can't Do It All!: Breaking Free from the Lies That Control Us, 2006; One Little Secret (novel), 2007; Setting Boundaries with Your Adult Children, 2008; You Make Me Feel Like Dancing, 2009; Setting Boundaries with Your Aging Parents, 2010; What a Wonderful World, 2011; Setting Boundaries With Difficult People, 2011. GOD ALLOWS U-TURNS SERIES: God Allows U-turns, 1998; (comp. with C. Hutchings and E. Regan) God Allows U-turns: True Stories of Hope and Healing, 2001; (with C. Hutchings and E. Regan) More God Allows U-turns: True Stories of Hope and Healing, 2001; (with C. Hutchings) God Allows U-turns: American Moments, True Stories of Hope and Healing from Times of National Crisis, 2002; (with C. Hutchings) God Allows U-turns for Women: The Choices We Make Change the Story of Our Life, 2006. Contributor to periodicals. **Address:** c/o Author Mail, Steve Laube Agency, 5025 N Central Ave., Ste. 635, Phoenix, AZ 85012-1502, U.S.A. **Online address:** allison@allisonbottke.com

BOTTOMS, David. American (born United States), b. 1949. **Genres:** Poetry, Novels, Literary Criticism And History, Young Adult Fiction. **Career:** Teacher, 1974-78; Georgia State University, Department of English, assistant professor, 1982-86, associate professor, through 1987, professor in creative writing, poetry, associate dean for fine arts, John B. and Elena Diaz-Verson Amos distinguished chair; University of Montana, poet-in-residence, 1986. Writer. **Publications:** Jamming with the Band at the VFW, 1978; Shooting Rats at the Bibb County Dump, 1980; In a U-Haul North of Damascus, 1983; (ed. with D. Smith) The Morrow Anthology of Younger American Poets, 1985; Any Cold Jordan, 1987; Under the Vulture-Tree, 1987; Easter Weekend, 1990; Armored Hearts: Selected and New Poems, 1995; Vagrant Grace: Poems, 1999; Oglethorpe's Dream: A Picture of Georgia, 2001; Waltzing Through the Endtime, 2004; Onion's Dark Core, 2010; We Almost Disappear, 2011. Contributor to perioidicals. **Address:** Department of English, Georgia State University, 33 Gilmer St., Ste. 200, PO Box 3970, Atlanta, GA 30303, U.S.A. **Online address:** engdhb@aol.com

BOUCHER, Bruce (Ambler). American (born United States), b. 1948. **Genres:** Art/Art History. **Career:** University of London, lecturer, 1976-92, reader in art history, 1992-98, professor, 1998-; Art Institute of Chicago, Eloise Martin curator of European decorative arts and sculpture, 2002-; University of Virginia, University Art Museum, director, 2009-. Writer. **Publications:** The Sculpture of Jacopo Sansovino, 1991; (ed.) Piero di Cosimo de'Medici: Art in the Service of the Medici, 1993; Andrea Palladio: The Architect in His Time, 1994, 2nd ed., 2007; Italian Baroque Sculpture, 1998; (co-ed.) Earth and Fire: Italian Terracotta Sculpture from Donatello to Canova, 2001. **Address:** University Art Museum, University of Virginia, Thomas H. Bayly Bldg., 155 Rugby Rd., PO Box 400119, Charlottesville, VA 22904-4119, U.S.A. **Online address:** b.boucher@ucl.ac.uk

BOUCHER, Philip P. American (born United States), b. 1944. **Genres:** History, Social Sciences, Politics/Government. **Career:** University of North Carolina, instructor, 1973-74; University of Alabama, Department of History, assistant professor, 1974-80, associate professor, 1980-89, professor of history, 1989-96, distinguished professor of history, 1996-2007, distinguished professor emeritus of history, 2007-, chair. Writer. **Publications:** Shaping of the French Colonial Empire: A Bio-bibliography of the Careers of Richelieu, Fouquet and Colbert, 1985; Les Nouvelles Frances: France in America, 1500-1815, an Imperial Perspective, 1989; Cannibal Encounters: Europeans and Island Caribs, 1492-1763, 1992; France and the American Tropics to 1700: Tropics of Discontent?, 2008. **Address:** Department of History, University of Alabama, 323 Roberts Hall, 301 Sparkman Dr. NW, Huntsville, AL 35899, U.S.A. **Online address:** boucherp22@hotmail.com

BOUDREAU, Kristin. American (born United States), b. 1965. **Genres:** Literary Criticism And History. **Career:** University of Georgia, professor of English and graduate co-ordinator. Writer. **Publications:** Sympathy in American Literature: American Sentiments from Jefferson to the Jameses, 2002; The Spectacle of Death: Populist Literary Responses to American Capital Cases, 2006. **Address:** Department of English, Franklin College of Arts & Sciences, University of Georgia, 254 Park Hall, Athens, GA 30602-6205, U.S.A. **Online address:** boudreau@uga.edu

BOUDREAU, R(obert) L(ouis). Canadian (born Canada), b. 1951. **Genres:** Young Adult Non-fiction, Biography. **Career:** Newport Yachts Intl., chief executive officer; Sailing Holidays Ltd., chief executive officer; Yachting Holidays Ltd., chief executive officer. Writer. **Publications:** The Man Who Loved Schooners (biography), 2000. **Address:** 1852 Crescent Rd., Victoria, BC V8S 2G8, Canada.

BOUGHTON, Doug(las Gordon). American/Australian (born Australia), b. 1944. **Genres:** Education, Art/Art History. **Career:** Teacher, 1963-64, 1965-67, 1971-72; Riverina Area Office of Education, art adviser, 1968-70; art teacher and department head, 1973-74; University of Lethbridge, assistant professor of education, 1976-78; University of British Columbia, assistant professor of art education, 1978-79; Salisbury College of Advanced Education, senior lecturer, 1979-81, principal lecturer in art and art education, 1981-82, school of art and design education, department chair and head; South Australian College of Advanced Education, principal lecturer in art and design education, 1982-90, School of Art and Design Education, head, 1985-90; University of South Australia, associate professor, 1991-92, professor of art and design education, 1993-, School of Art and Design Education, head, 1993; Northern Illinois University, professor of art and education, School of Art, director; International Society for Education through Art, president; Australian Institute of Art Education, National Art Education Research Council, foundation director; Institute of Education, consulting professor in art education; National Art Education Association, distinguished fellow. Writer. **Publications:** Evaluation and Assessment of Visual Arts Education, 1994. EDITOR: (with J. Cunningham and D.C. Wilson) Curriculum Policies and the Expressive Arts (monograph), 1979; (with E.W. Eisner and J. Ligtvoet) Evaluating and Assessing the Visual Arts in Education: International Perspectives, 1996; (with K. Congdon) Evaluating Art Education Programs in Community Centers: International Perspectives of Conception and Practice, 1998; (with R. Mason) Beyond Multicultural Art Education: International Perspectives, 1999. Contributor of articles to books and journals. **Address:** School of Art, Northern Illinois University, Rm. 215A, Jack Arends Hall, DeKalb, IL 60115-2883, U.S.A. **Online address:** dboughton@niu.edu

BOULEZ, Pierre. French/German (born Germany), b. 1925. **Genres:** Music, Biography. **Career:** Compagnie Renaud/Barrault, theater music director, 1946-56; Music Academy, music teacher, 1960-62; British Broadcasting Corp. (BBC-TV) Symphony Orchestra, chief conductor, 1971-77; New York Philharmonic Orchestra, music director, 1971-77; College de France, professor, 1976-95; Institut de recherche et coordination-acoustique/musique, director, 1976-92; Ensemble Intercontemporain, president, 1977-99. Writer. **Publications:** Musikdenken heute, 1963; Penser la Musique Aujourd'hui, 1964; Eclat: pour orchestre, 1965; Releves d'apprenti, 1966; Par Volonte et Par Hasard: Entretiens avec Celestin Deliege, 1975; Messagesquisse: pour 7 violoncelles, 1977; Notations: pour orchestre, 1978; Dérive: pour six instruments, 1984; Douze notations: pour piano, 1985; Points de Repere, 1985; Jalons (Pour une Decennie), 1990; Anthèmes: pour violon seul, 1992; Incises: pour piano, 1994, 1994; L'écriture du Geste: Entretiens avec Cécile Gilly sur la direction d'orchestre, 2002; (with J. Cage) Correspondance et documents, 2002. Contributor to books. **Address:** Institut de Recherche, 1 Place Igor Stravinsky, Paris, 75004, France.

BOULLATA, Issa J. American (born United States), b. 1929. **Genres:** Novels, Novellas/Short Stories, Humanities, Intellectual History, Language/Linguistics, Literary Criticism And History, Theology/Religion, Translations, Translations. **Career:** De La Salle College, senior teacher of Arabic literature, 1949-52; Ahliyyah College, senior teacher of Arabic literature, 1952-53; Saint George's School, senior teacher of Arabic literature and deputy headmaster, 1953-68; Hartford Seminary, professor of Arabic literature and language, 1968-75; McGill University, professor of Arabic literature and language, 1975-99, now professor emeritus. Writer and translator. **Publications:** Outlines of Romanticism in Modern Arabic Poetry (in Arabic), 1960; Badr Shakir al Sayyab: His Life and Poetry (in Arabic), 1971; Trends and Issues in Contemporary Arab Thought, 1990; 'A'id ila al-Quds, 1998; A Retired Gentleman and Other Stories, 2007. EDITOR: (and trans.) Modern Arab Poets, 1950-1975, 1976; Critical Perspectives on Modern Arabic Literature, 1980; (with T. DeYoung) Tradition and Modernity in Arabic Literature, 1997; Literary Structures of Religious Meaning in the Qur'an, 2000. TRANSLATOR: A. Amin, My Life, 1978; E. Nasrallah, Flight against Time, 1987; J.I. Jabra, The First Well: A Bethlehem Boyhood, 1995; M. Berrada, The Game of Forgetting, 1996; G. Samman, The Square Moon, 1998; M. Berrada, Fugitive Light, 2002; J.I. Jabra, Princesses Street, 2005; H. Sharabi, Embers and Ashes: Memoirs of an Arab Intellectual, 2008; I.A. Rabbih, The Unique Necklace, 3 vols., 2006-11. Contributor of articles to books and journals. **Address:** Institute of Islamic Studies, McGill University, 319 Morrice Hall, 3485 McTavish St., Montreal, QC H3A 1Y1, Canada. **Online address:** issa.boullata@mcgill.ca

BOULTON, James T(hompson). British (born England), b. 1924. **Genres:** Literary Criticism And History, Politics/Government. **Career:** University of Nottingham, assistant lecturer, 1951-53, lecturer, 1953-62, senior lecturer, 1962-63, reader in English, 1963-64, professor of English literature, 1964-75, Faculty of Arts, dean, 1970-73; Hofstra University, John Cranford Adams professor of English, 1967; University of Birmingham, Department of English, professor of English studies and head of department, 1975-88, professor emeritus, 1989-, Faculty of Arts, dean, 1981-84, Institute for Advanced Research in Arts and Social Sciences, director, 1987-, emeritus director; Fircroft College, chairman of governors, 1985-92; Bangor University, School of English, honorary professor; British Academy and of the Royal Society of Literature, fellow. Writer. **Publications:** The Language of Politics in the Age of Wilkes and Burke, 1963; Arbitrary Power: An Eighteenth-Century Obsession, 1967. EDITOR: The Condition of England, 1960; (and intro.) Of Dramatick Poesie, 1964; Daniel Defoe: Prose and Verse, 1965; (with J. Kinsley) English Satiric Poetry: Dryden to Byron, 1966; (intro.) Lawrence in Love: Letters from D.H. Lawrence to Louie Burrows, 1968; (with S.T. Bindoff) Research in Progress in English and Historical Studies, 1971, vol. II, 1976; Samuel Johnson: The Critical Heritage, 1971; Selected Writings of Daniel Defoe, 1975; (and intro.) Memoirs of a Cavalier, 1978; The Letters of D.H. Lawrence, vol. I, 1979, vol. II, 1982, vol. III, 1984, vol. IV, 1987, vol. V, 1989, vol. VI, 1991, vol. VII, 1993, vol. VIII, 2000; Edmund Burke: Philosophical Enquiry into Sublime and Beautiful, 1958, 1987; (and comp.) Selected Letters of D.H. Lawrence, 1997; Last Essays and Articles, 2004; (and intro. with T.O. McLoughlin) An Account of Corsica, 2005. Contributor to periodicals. **Address:** School of English, Bangor University, Ysgol Saesneg Prifysgol Cymru, Bangor, LL57 2DG, England.

BOUQUET, Mary (Rose). Dutch/British (born England), b. 1955. **Genres:** Anthropology/Ethnology. **Career:** University of Lisbon, lecturer, 1983-87; National Museum of Ethnology, exhibition developer, 1986-88; University of Amsterdam, lecturer, 1989; National Museum of Natural History, exhibition developer, 1992-93; Utrecht University College, Cultural Anthropology and Museum Studies, lecturer. Writer. **Publications:** Family, Servants and Visitors: The Farm Household in Nineteenth and Twentieth Century Devon, 1985; (ed. with M. Winter) Who from Their Labours Rest?: Conflict and Practice in Rural Tourism, 1987; Reclaiming English Kinship, 1993; Man-Ape, Ape-Man: Pithecanthropus in Het Pesthuis, Leiden, 1993; (ed.) Academic Anthropology and the Museum: Back to the Future, 2001; (ed. with N. Porto) Science, Magic and Religion: The Ritual Process of Museum Magic, 2004. Author of exhibition catalogues. **Address:** Utrecht University, PO Box 80125, Utrecht, 3508, Netherlands. **Online address:** m.r.bouquet@uu.nl

BOURDEAUX, Michael Alan. British (born England), b. 1934. **Genres:** History, Theology/Religion, Politics/Government. **Career:** Ordained priest in Episcopalian church, 1960; Enfield Parish Church, assistant curate, 1960-64; Centre de Recherches, research associate, 1965-68; University of London, London School of Economics and Political Science, research fellow, 1968-70; Oxford University, Keston Institute, founder and director, 1969-, president, now director emeritus; St. Bernard's Seminary, visiting professor, 1969; Royal Institute of International Affairs, research fellow, 1970-72; Wellesley College, Kathryn C. Davis professor of Slavic studies, 1981. Writer. **Publications:** Opium of the People, 1965, 2nd ed., 1977; Religious Ferment in Russia, 1968; (contrib.) URSS: Dibattito nella communita cristiana, 1968; (contrib.) The Religious Situation in 1969, 1969; (intro.) Christian Appeals from Russia, 1969; Patriarch and Prophets: Persecution of the Russian Orthodox Church Today, 1969; (contrib. with P. Reddaway) Religion and the Soviet State, 1969; (ed.) Religious Minorities in the Soviet Union, 1960-70, 1970, 4th ed., 1984; (contrib. and ed. with G. Schoepflin) The Soviet Union and Eastern Europe: A Handbook, 1970; Faith on Trial in Russia, 1971; (ed. with Howard-Johnston) The Evidence That Convicted Aida Skripnikove, 1971; (ed. with X.H. Johnston) Aida of Leningrad: The Story of Aida Skripnikova, 1972; (with K. Murray) Young Christians in Russia, 1976; White Book on Restrictions of Religion in the U.S.S.R, 1977; Land of Crosses: The Struggle for Religious Freedom in Lithuania, 1979; Risen Indeed: Lessons in Faith from the U.S.S.R, 1983; (with L. Bourdeaux) Ten Growing Soviet Churches, 1987; Gorbachev, Glasnost and the Gospel, 1990 in US as The Gospel's Triumph over Communism, 1991; The Politics of Religion in Russia and the New States of Eurasia, 1995; (with J. Witte, Jr.) Proselytism and Orthodoxy in Russia, 1999; Sovremennaia religioznaia zhizn Rossii: opytsistematicheskogo opisaniia, 2003; Atlas sovremennoĭ religioznoĭzhizni Rossii, 2005. Contributor to periodicals. **Address:** Keston Institute, PO Box 752, Oxford, OX OX1 9QF, England. **Online address:** michael.bourdeaux@keston.org

BOURGEAULT, Cynthia. Canadian (born Canada), b. 1947. **Genres:** Theology/Religion, Romance/Historical. **Career:** Contemplative Society, founding director and principal teacher; Aspen Wisdom School, founding director; Vancouver School of Theology, adjunct faculty. Episcopal priest and writer. **Publications:** (Trans.) The Wakefield Resurrection Play: A Fourteenth-Century Play, 1974; (ed.) The Music of the Medieval Church Dramas, 1980; Love Is Stronger Than Death: The Mystical Union of Two Souls, 1999; Mystical Hope: Trusting in the Mercy of God, 2001; The Wisdom Way of Knowing: Reclaiming an Ancient Tradition to Awaken the Heart, 2003; Centering Prayer and Inner Awakening, 2004; Chanting the Psalms: A Practical Guide with Instructional CD, 2006; The Wisdom Jesus: Transforming Heart and Mind-A New Perspective on Christ and His Message, 2008; The Meaning of Mary Magdalene: Discovering the Woman at the Heart of Christianity, 2010. Contributor to periodicals. **Address:** Contemplative Society, Cook St. RPO, PO Box 23031, Victoria, BC V8V 4Z8, Canada.

BOURGEOIS, Michael. Canadian/American (born United States), b. 1956. **Genres:** Theology/Religion, History. **Career:** St. Andrew's College, faculty; University of Toronto, Victoria University, Emmanuel College, associate professor of theology and director of basic degree studies, 2001-, vice-principal. Writer. **Publications:** All Things Human: Henry Codman Potter and the Social Gospel in the Episcopal Church, 2004. **Address:** Emmanuel College, Victoria University, University of Toronto, Rm. 111, 73 Queen's Park Cres., Toronto, ON M5S 1K7, Canada. **Online address:** michael.bourgeois@utoronto.ca

BOURGEOIS, Paulette. Canadian (born Canada), b. 1951. **Genres:** Children's Fiction, Novels, Young Adult Non-fiction, Young Adult Fiction. **Career:** Royal Ottawa Hospital, staff occupational therapist, 1975-76; Canadian Broadcasting Corp., reporter, 1977-78, 1980-81; Home Maker's Magazine, columnist; freelance writer, 1981-; Ottawa Citizen, reporter. **Publications:** FRANKLIN SERIES: Franklin in the Dark, 1986; Hurry Up, Franklin, 1989; Franklin Fibs, 1991; Franklin Is Lost, 1992; Franklin Is Bossy, 1993; Franklin Is Messy, 1994; Franklin and Me: A Book about Me, 1994, rev. ed. as Franklin and Me: My First Record of Favourite Things, Personal Facts, and Special Memories, 1997; Franklin Goes to School, 1995; Franklin Plays the Game, 1995; Franklin Wants a Pet, 1995; Franklin's Blanket, 1995; Franklin and the Tooth Fairy, 1996; Franklin Has a Sleepover, 1996; Franklin's Halloween, 1996; Franklin's School Play, 1996; Franklin Rides a Bike, 1997; Franklin's Bad Day, 1997; Franklin's New Friend, 1997; Franklin's Valentine, 1998; Finders Keepers for Franklin, 1998; Franklin and the Thunderstorm, 1998; Franklin's Club, 1998; Franklin's Christmas Gift, 1998; Franklin's Class Trip, 1999; Franklin and the Baby, 1999; Franklin's Classic Treasury, 1999, vol. II, 2000; Franklin Goes to the Hospital, 2000; Franklin's Baby Sister, 2000; Franklin's Friendship Treasury, 2000; Franklin's Pet Problem, 2000; Franklin Says Sorry, 2000; Franklin's First Day at School, 2000; Franklin's Baby Sister, 2000; Franklin in the Dark, 2000; Franklin's Bicycle Helmet, 2000; (with B. Clark) Franklin's Special Blanket, 2000; Franklin Helps Out, 2000; Franklin and Harriet, 2001; Franklin's School Treasury, 2001; Franklin's Birthday Party, 2001; Franklin Says I Love You, 2002; Franklin's Holiday Treasury, 2002; Franklin's Family Treasury, 2003; Franklin the Detective, 2004; Franklin's Library Book, 2005. JUVENILE: Big Sarah's Little Boots, 1987; On Your Mark, Get Set: All about the Olympic Games, Then and Now, 1987; The Amazing Apple Book, 1987; The Amazing Paper Book, 1987; Grandma's Secret, 1989; The Amazing Dirt Book, 1990; Too Many Chickens, 1990; Amazing Potato Book, 1991; Canadian Fire Fighters, 1991, rev. ed. as Fire Fighters, 1998; Canadian Garbage Collectors, 1991, rev. ed. as Garbage Collectors, 1998; Canadian Police Officers, 1991, rev. ed. as Police Officers, 1998; Canadian Postal Workers, 1992, rev. ed. as Postal Workers, 1998; (with M. Wolfish) Changes in You and Me: A Book about Puberty, Mostly for Boys, 1994; Too Many Hats of Mr.Minches, 1994; The Sun, 1995; The Moon, 1995; Oma's Quilt, 2001. OTHERS: Franklin's Secret Club, 1998; Franklin es un mandón, 1998; Franklin va a la escuela, 1998; Franklin juega al fútbol, 1998; (with B. Clark) Franklin's Thanksgiving, 2001; (with B. Clark) Franklin Plants a Tree, 2001; (contrib.) Franklin and the Babysitter, 2001; (contrib.) Franklin runs Away, 2001; (with B. Clark) Franklin's Birthday Party, 2001; (contrib.) Franklin and the Big Kid, 2002; (co-author) Franklin Snoops, 2003; (contrib.) Franklin Forgives, 2004; (contrib.) Franklin's Nickname, 2004. Contributor to periodicals. **Address:** c/o Author Mail, Kids Can Press, 25 Dockside Dr., Toronto, ON M5A 0B5, Canada. **Online address:** contact@paulettebourgeoiswriter.com

BOURKE, Angela. Irish (born Ireland), b. 1952?. **Genres:** Literary Criticism And History. **Career:** University College Dublin, senior lecturer in Irish, Naughton Fellow, 2004-05; Harvard University, visiting professor; University of Minnesota, visiting professor. Writer. **Publications:** Caoineadh na dTrí Muire: Téama na Paise I bhFiliocht Bheil na Gaeilge, 1983; Inion Ri na Cathrach Deirge, 1989; Inion Ri an Oileain Dhorcha, 1991; Caoineadh na Marbh: Siceoilfhiliocht, 1992; By Salt Water, 1996; The Burning of Bridget Cleary, 1999; (ed.) Field Day Anthology: Irish Women's Writings and Tradition, 2002; Maeve Brennan: Homesick at The New Yorker, 2004. **Address:** School of Irish & Celtic Studies, University College Dublin, John Henry Newman Bldg., Rm. C206, Dublin, 4, Ireland. **Online address:** angela.bourke@ucd.ie

BOURKE, Dale Hanson. American (born United States), b. 1953. **Genres:** Women's Studies And Issues. **Career:** Marketing of World Relief, senior vice president; Christian College Consortium, director of public relations, 1975-77; Continental Marketing Association, consultant, 1977-79; Today's Christian Woman, editor, 1979; International Marketing Group, vice president, 1979-82; Publishing Directions, Inc. (PDI), president, 1982-; Possibilities (magazine), publisher, 1983; Religion News Service, publisher, 1994-; Center for Infectious Disease Research in Zambia (CIDRZ) Foundation, president, 2007-; Center for Interfaith Action, consultant. **Publications:** You Can Make Your Dreams Come True, 1985; Everyday Miracles: Holy Moments in a Mother's Day, 1989, 2nd ed. as Everyday Miracles: Glimpses of Grace in a Mother's Day, 1999; The Sleep Management Plan, (foreword by W.B. Mendelson), 1990; Sacred Surprises, 1991; Turn toward the Wind: Embracing Change in Your Life, 1995; The Skeptic's Guide to the Global AIDS Crisis: Tough Questions, Direct Answers, 2004, rev. ed., 2006; Second Calling: Finding Passion and Purpose for the Rest of Your Life, 2006, rev. ed. as Embracing Your Second Calling: Find Passion and Purpose for the Rest of Your Life; A Woman's Guide, 2009; The Skeptic's Guide to Global Poverty, 2007. Contributor to periodicals. **Address:** CIDRZ Foundation NW, 5335 Wisconsin Ave., Ste. 440, Washington, DC 20015-2054, U.S.A.

BOURNE, Joyce. British (born England), b. 1933. **Genres:** Music, Photography. **Career:** Medical assistant and anesthetist, 1962-87. Writer. **Publications:** Who's Who in Opera: A Guide to Opera Characters, 1998. EDITOR: The Oxford Dictionary of Music, 1994, rev. ed., 2006; The Concise Oxford Dictionary of Music, 2004, 5th ed., 2007; Who Married Figaro?: A Book of Opera Characters, 2008; Dictionary of Opera Characters, 2010. **Address:** The Bungalow, Edilom Rd., Manchester, GM M8 4HZ, England.

BOURNE, Russell. American (born United States), b. 1928. **Genres:** History. **Career:** Life, reporter, 1950-53; American Heritage Publishing Co., editor of Junior Library and Horizon Caravel Books, 1960-69, publisher and editor, 1981-84; National Geographic Book Service, associate chief of book service, 1969-71; U.S. News and World Report Books, consulting editor, 1975-76; Bourne-Thompson and Associates, partner, 1975-77; Smithsonian Books, senior editor of exposition books, 1977-79; Hearst Books, publisher of general books, 1980-81. **Publications:** (Co-ed.) A Bicentennial Portrait of the American People, 1975; The View from Front Street: Travels through Historic New England Fishing Communities, 1989; The Red King's Rebellion: Racial Politics in New England, 1675-1678, 1990; Big Golden Book of Christopher Columbus and Other Early Adventurers, 1991; Floating West: The Erie and Other American Canals, 1992; Americans on the Move: A History of Waterways, Railways and Highways, 1995; Invention in America, 1996; The Best of the Best Sparkman and Stephens Designs, 1996; Rivers of America: Birthplaces of Culture, Commerce and Community, 1998; Gods of War, Gods of Peace: How the Meeting of Native and Colonial Religions Shaped Early America, 2002; Cradle of Violence: How Boston's Waterfront Mobs Ignited the American Revolution, 2006. **Address:** Curtis Brown Ltd., 10 Astor Pl., New York, NY 10003, U.S.A. **Online address:** rbourne@compuserve.com

BOURQUE, Antoine. *See* **BRASSEAUX, Carl A(nthony).**

BOUSON, J. Brooks. American (born United States) **Genres:** Literary Criticism And History. **Career:** Mundelein College, assistant professor, 1980-86, associate professor of English, 1986-91; Loyola University, associate professor, 1991-2000, undergraduate programs director, 1998-2001, professor of English, 2000-, assistant department chair, 2002-. Writer. **Publications:** The Empathic Reader: A Study of the Narcissistic Character and the Drama of the Self, 1989; Brutal Choreographies: Oppositional Strategies and Narrative Design in the Novels of Margaret Atwood, 1993; Quiet as It's Kept: Shame, Trauma, and Race in the Novels of Toni Morrison, 2000; Jamaica Kincaid: Writing Memory, Writing Back to the Mother, 2005; Embodied Shame: Uncovering Female Shame in Contemporary Women's Writings, 2009; Critical Insights: Margaret Atwood's The Handmaid's Tale, 2009; Margaret Atwood: The Robber Bride, The Blind Assassin, and Oryx and Crake, 2010; Critical Insights: Emily Dickinson, 2010; Critical Insights: Margaret Atwood, 2012. Contributor to books and periodicals. **Address:** Department of English, Loyola University of Chicago-Lake Shore Campus, Crown Center for the Humanities, 1032 W Sheridan Rd., Chicago, IL 60660, U.S.A. **Online address:** jbouson@luc.edu

BOUTILIER, Robert. Canadian (born Canada), b. 1950. **Genres:** Marketing. **Career:** Freelance research consultant, 1981-85; Criterion Research Corp., vice president and partner, 1985-87; Boutilier and Associates (independent marketing research consultants), president, partner, 1987-; University of British Columbia, adjunct faculty of psychology, part-time teacher of psychology; Simon Fraser University, Center for Innovation in Management, director, Centre for Sustainable Community Development, associate; Atzingo Institute for Stakeholder Network Studies, executive director. Writer. **Publications:** Children's Understanding to Systems, Educational Research Institute of British Columbia, 1980; Targeting Families: Marketing to and Through the New Family, 1993; Stakeholder Politics: Social Capital, Sustainable Development and the Corporation, 2009. **Address:** Robert Boutilier and Associates, 3611 Kingsway, Ste. 201, Vancouver, BC V5R 5M1, Canada. **Online address:** boutilir@boutilierassoc.com

BOUTON, Gary David. American (born United States), b. 1953. **Genres:** How-to Books, Information Science/Computers, Technology, Graphic Novels. **Career:** Writer. **Publications:** CorelDRAW! for Non-Nerds, 1993; (with B.M. Bouton) Inside Adobe Photoshop for Windows, 1994; CorelDRAW! 5 for Beginners, 1994; Adobe Photoshop Now!, 1994; (with G. Kubicek) Adobe Photoshop 3 Filters and Effects, 1995; (with B.M. Bouton) Inside Adobe Photoshop 3, 1995; CorelDRAW! 6, 1996; Official Multimedia Publishing for Netscape: Make Your Web Pages Come Alive!, 1996; Extreme 3D Fundamentals, 1997; (with B.M. Bouton and G. Kubicek) Inside Adobe Photoshop 4, 1997; Inside Extreme 3D 2, 1997; (with B.M. Bouton and G. Kubicek) Inside Adobe Photoshop 5.0, 1998; (with B.M. Bouton and G. Kubicek) Inside Adobe Photoshop 5, 1999; Inside Adobe Photoshop 5.5, 2000; Adobe Photoshop 5.5 Fundamentals with ImageReady 2, 2000; Inside Adobe Photoshop 6, 2001; Inside Adobe Photoshop 6 Limited Edition, 2002; Inside Photoshop 7, 2003; Inside Photoshop CS, 2004; Photoshop Elements: All-in-One Desk Reference for Dummies, 2006; Microsoft Graphic Designer for Graphic Artists Only, 2006; Adobe Photoshop CS3 Extended: Retouching Motion Pictures, 2008; CorelDRAW X4: The Official Guide, 2008; (with C. Matthews) Photoshop CS4 Quicksteps, 2009; Xara Xtreme 5: The Official Guide, 2010; CorelDRAW X5: The Official Guide, 2011. **Address:** Macmillan Computer Publishing, 201 W 103rd St., Indianapolis, IN 46290, U.S.A. **Online address:** gary@garydavidbouton.com

BOUTON, Marshall M. (Marshall Melvin Bouton). American (born United States), b. 1942. **Genres:** History. **Career:** Asia Society, executive vice president and chief operating officer, 1990-2001; Northwestern University, adjunct professor of political science; Chicago Council on Global Affairs, president, 2001-. Writer. **Publications:** Agrarian Radicalism in South India, 1985; (ed. with P. Oldenburg) India Briefing: A Transformative Fifty Years, 1988; (with F.G. Wisner and N. Platt) New Priorities in South Asia: U.S. Policy toward India, Pakistan, and Afghanistan: Chairmen's Report of an Independent Task Force Cosponsored by the Council on Foreign Relations and the Asia Society, 2003; (with B.I. Page) The Foreign Policy Disconnect: What Americans Want from Our Leaders but Don't Get, 2006. **Address:** Chicago Council on Global Affairs, 332 S Michigan Ave., Ste. 1100, Chicago, IL 60604-4416, U.S.A.

BOUTON, Marshall Melvin. *See* **BOUTON, Marshall M.**

BOUTROS-GHALI, Boutros. Egyptian (born Egypt), b. 1922. **Genres:** International Relations/Current Affairs. **Career:** Al-Ahram Al-Iktisadi, editor, 1960-75; University of Cairo, professor of international law and international relations, 1974-77; Al-Siyasa Al-Dawlyya (a foreign affairs journal), editor; State for Foreign Affairs, minister, 1977-91; Egyptian Parliament, deputy prime minister for foreign affairs, 1991-; Socialist Intl., vice president, 1990-91; United Nations, secretary general, 1992-96; International Panel on Democracy and Development, UNESCO, chairperson, 1997-; Society for International Development, president, 1997-2000; International Organisation of the Francophonie, secretary-general, 1998-2002; Institute for Mediterranean Political Studies, Club de Monaco, president, 2002. **Publications:** Reflexions sur le dialogue afro-arabe, 1975; Qaḍ āyā Arabīyah, 1977; (with M.K. Isa) al-Madkhal fī ilm al-siyāsah, 1982; al-Alāqāt al-dawlīyah fī iṭār Munaẓẓamat al-Waḥdah al-Ifrīqīyah, 1987; Achievements of Egyptian diplomacy, 1987, 1988; Masīrat al-diblūmāsīyah al-Miṣ rīyah fī ām 1989, 1990; Aḥādīth siyāsīyah, 1990; al-Siyāsah al-khārijīyah al-Miṣ rīyah, 1983-1990, 1991; al-ḥukūmah al-ālamīyah, 1992; New Dimensions Of Arms Regulation and Disarmament in the Post-Cold War Era: Report of the Secretary-General, 1993; L'ordre du jour de la communauté internationale en matière de désarmement pour l'année 1994 et au-dela, 1994; An Agenda For Peace 1995, 1995; The United Nations and the Advancement of Women, 1945-1996, 1995, rev. ed., 1996; An Agenda for Development 1995; An Agenda for Democratization, 1996; The United Nations and apartheid, 1996; The United Nations and the Iraq-Kuwait conflict, 1990-1996, 1996; Egypt's Road to Jerusalem: A Diplomat's Story of the Struggle for Peace in the Middle East, 1997; Unvanquished: A U.S.-U.N. saga, 1999; 5 sanawāt fī bayt min zujāj, 1999; Emanciper la francophonie, 2002; Démocratiser la mondialisation: entretiens avec Yves Berthelot, 2002; Khiṭaṭ lil-salām wa-al-tanmiyah wa-al-dīmuqrātīyah, 2003; En attendant la prochaine lune: carnets 1997-2002, 2004; Bi-intiz'ār badr al-budūr-: yawmīyāt 1997-2002, 2005; Sittūnāman min al-s'irāīal-sharq al-awsat, 2007; Entre le Nil et Jérusalem: Journal d'un Diplomate égyptien, 1981-1991, 2011. INTRODUCTION: The United Nations and apartheid, 1948-1994, 1994; The United Nations and Human Rights, 1945-1995, 1995; The United Nations and the Independence of Eritrea, 1996; ṭarīq ilá al-Quds: qiṣ ṣ at al-sirā min ajli al-salām fī al-Sharq al-Awsaṭ, 1997; Droits de l'homme: une universalitémenacée, 2010. **Address:** Egyptian National Commission for UNESCO, 7, Shareh Ibrahim Abou-Al Naja, Block 1, Hayy Al-Sifarat, Cairo, 38408064, Egypt.

BOUVARD, Marguerite Guzman. American (born United States), b. 1937. **Genres:** Poetry, Organized Labor, Politics/Government, Psychology, Women's Studies And Issues, Biography. **Career:** Regis College, professor of political science and creative writing, 1966-90, department head, director; University of Maryland, writer-in-residence, Virginia Center for the Creative Arts, fellow. **Publications:** The Labor Movements in the Common Market Countries, 1972; Intentional Community Movement: Labor Movements in the Common Market Countries, 1975; The Search for Community: Building a New Moral World, 1975; Journeys over Water, 1982; Voices from an Island, 1985; (ed.) Landscape and Exile, 1985; The Path through Grief, 1988, rev. ed., 1997; Of Light and Silence, 1990; With the Mothers of the Plaza de Mayo, 1993; Revolutionizing Motherhood: The Mothers of the Plaza de Mayo, 1994; Women Reshaping Human Rights, 1996; The Body's Burning Fields, 1997; (ed.) Grandmothers: Granddaughters Remember, 1998; (with E. Gladu) The Path through Grief: A Compassionate Guide, 1998; Wind, Frost and Fire, 2001; Prayers for Comfort in Difficult Time, 2004; (contrib.) Canticles, 2005; Healing: A Life with Chronic Illness, 2007; he Unpredictability of Light, 2009. Works appear in anthologies. Contributor of articles to periodicals. **Address:** 6 Brookfield Cir., Wellesley, MA 02481, U.S.A. **Online address:** bouvard@brandeis.edu

BOVA, Ben(jamin William). American (born United States), b. 1932. **Genres:** Novels, Novellas/Short Stories, Science Fiction/Fantasy, Sciences, Social Commentary, Young Adult Non-fiction. **Career:** Upper Darby News, editor, 1953-56; Martin Aircraft Co., Vanguard Project, technical editor, 1956-58; Avco-Everett Research Laboratory, marketing manager, 1960-71; Analog (science fiction magazine), editor, 1971-78; Omni, fiction editor, 1978-80, editorial director, 1980-81, vice president, 1981-82; Harvard University, teacher of science fiction; CBS, Morning News Television Program, science and technology consultant, 1982-84; National Space Society, now president emeritus. **Publications:** WATCHMEN SERIES: The Star Conquerors, 1959; Star Watchman, 1964; The Dueling Machine, 1969; The Watchmen. 1994. EXILES SERIES: Exiled from Earth, 1971; Flight of Exiles, 1972; End of Exile, 1975; The Exiles Trilogy, 1980. KINSMAN SERIES: Millennium, 1976; Kinsman, 1979; The Kinsman Saga, 1987. VOYAGERS SERIES: Voyagers, 1981; The Alien Within, 1986; Star Brothers, 1990; The Return, 2009. ORION SERIES: Orion, 1984; Vengeance of Orion, 1988; Orion in the Dying Time, 1990; Orion and the Conqueror, 1994; Orion Among the Stars, 1995; Orion and King Arthur, 2012. PRIVATEERS SERIES: Privateers, 1985; Empire Builders, 1993. SAM GUNN SERIES: Sam Gunn, Unlimited, 1992; Sam Gunn Forever, 1998. TO SAVE THE SUN SERIES WITH A.J. AUSTIN: To Save the Sun, 1992; To Fear the Light, 1994. MOONRISE SERIES: Moonrise, 1996; Moonwar, 1997. BEN BOVA'S GRAND TOUR OF THE UNIVERSE SERIES: Venus, 2000; Jupiter, 2000; Saturn, 2003; Mercury, 2005; Powersat, 2005; Titan, 2006; Mars Life, 2008; Leviathans of Jupiter, 2011. ASTEROID WARS SERIES: The Precipice, 2001; The Rock Rats, 2002; The Silent War, 2004; The Aftermath, 2007. MARS SERIES: Mars, 1992; Return to Mars, 1999. NOVELS: The Weathermakers, 1967; Out of the Sun, 1968; Escape!, 1970; THX 1138, 1971; The Winds of Altair, 1972; As on a Darkling Plain, 1972; When the Sky Burned, 1973; (with G.R. Dickson) Gremlins, Go Home!, 1974; The Starcrossed, 1975; City of Darkness, 1976; The Multiple Man, 1976; Colony, 1978; Test of Fire, 1982; Peacekeepers, 1988; Cyberbooks, 1989; (with B. Pogue) The Trikon Deception, 1992; Triumph, 1993; Death Dream, 1994; Brothers, 1995; The Green Trap, 2006; The Immortality Factor, 2009; Able One, 2010; The Hittite, 2010; Power Play, 2012. COLLECTIONS: Forward in Time, 1973; Maxwell's Demons, 1978; Escape Plus, 1984; The Astral Mirror, 1985; Prometheans, 1986; Battle Station, 1987; Future Crime, 1990; Challenges, 1993; (with F. Pohl, J. Pournelle and C. Sheffield) The Future Quartet: Earth in the Year 2042, 1994; Twice Seven, 1998; Tales of the Grand Tour, 2004. NONFICTION: Milky Way Galaxy, 1961; Giants of the Animal World, 1962; Reptiles Since the World Began, 1964; Uses of Space, 1965; Planets- Life and LGM, 1970; In Quest of Quasars, 1971; Man Changes the Weather, 1973; The New Astronomies, 1973; The Weather Changes Man, 1973; Starflight and Other Improbabilities, 1973; The Fourth State of Matter: Plasma Dynamics and Tomorrow's Technology, 1974; Analog Science Fact Reader, 1974; Workshops in Space, 1974; Through Eyes of Wonder, 1975; Notes to a Science Fiction Writer, 1975; Science: Who Needs It?, 1975; (with T.E. Bell) Closeup: New Worlds, 1977; Viewpoint, 1977; The Seeds of Tomorrow, 1977; The High Road, 1981; Vision of the Future: The Art of Robert McCall, 1982; Assured Survival: Putting the Star Wars Defense in Perspective, 1984; Star Peace: Assured Survival, 1986; Welcome to Moonbase, 1987; (with S. Glashow) Interactions: A Journey Through the Mind of a Particle Physicist and the Matter of This World, 1988; The Beauty of Light, 1988; Immortality: How Science is Extending Your Life Span and Changing the World, 1990; Are We Alone in the Cosmos?: The Search for Alien Contact, 1992; The Craft of Writing Science Fiction That Sells, 1994; (with S. Schmidt) Aliens and Alien Societies: A Writer's Guide to Creating Extraterrestial Life-forms, 1996; (with S. Gillett) World Building, 1996; (with A.R. Lewis) Space Travel: A Writer's Guide to the Science of Interplanetary and Interstellar Travel, 1997; The Story of Light, 2001; The Living Universe: The Science and Politics of Finding Life Beyond Earth, 2002; Faint Echoes, Distant Stars: The Science and Politics of Finding Life Beyond Earth, 2004; (with J. Paul) Visions of Lake Tahoe, 2004; Laugh Lines, 2008. OTHER: The Next Logical Step, 2011. EDITOR: The Many Worlds of Science Fiction, 1971; Analog 9, 1973; SFWA Hall of Fame, vol. II, 1973; Analog Annual, 1976; Analog Yearbook, 1978; Aliens: 3 Novellas, 1978; Best of Analog, 1978; (with D. Myrus) Best of Omni Science Fiction, 1980; Best of the Nebulas, 1989; (with B. Preiss) First Contact: The Search for Extraterrestrial Intelligence, 1990; The Science Fiction Hall of Fame, 2003. Contributor to periodicals. **Address:** National Space Society, 1155 15th St. NW, Ste. 500, Washington, DC 20005-2725, U.S.A.

BOVAIRD, Anne E(lizabeth). American (born United States), b. 1960. **Genres:** Language/Linguistics, Children's Fiction, Young Adult Fiction. **Career:** Grassroots Research, journalist, 1989-; Universite de Paris X, teacher and instructor, 1991-; Universite de Paris XIII, teacher and instructor, 1991-; Oxford Intelligence, senior business writer; Smartcardstrends, translator. Journalist and consultant. **Publications:** GOODBYE U.S.A. SERIES: Goodbye U.S.A., Bonjour la France: A Language Learning Adventure, 1993, vol. II, 1994; Goodbye U.S.A.-Hola México!, 1994. OTHER: (with L. Potier) Dictionnaire anglais-francais, 1990. **Address:** 521 Walnut St., Winnetka, IL 60093, U.S.A. **Online address:** bovaird@wharton.upenn.edu

BOVELL, Andrew (John). American/Australian (born Australia), b. 1962. **Genres:** Novels, Biography, Essays, Plays/Screenplays. **Career:** Ensemble Theatre Project, writer-in-residence, 1986; Jigsaw Theatre Co., writer-in-residence, 1987; Melbourne Workers Theatre, writer-in-residence, 1987-88; Melbourne Theatre Co., writer-in-residence, 1989-90. **Publications:** An Ocean out My Window, 1986; State of Defence, 1987; Ship of Fools, 1987; The Ballad of Lois Ryan, 1988; Gulliver's Travels, 1992; Like Whiskey on the Breath of a Drunk You Love, 1992; Strictly Ballroom, 1992; Seven Deadly Sins, 1993; Distant Lights from Dark Places, 1994; Shades of Blue, 1996; After Dinner, 1997; Scenes from a Separation, 1997; Head On, 1997; Speaking in Tongues, 1998, rev. ed., 2003; Confidentially Yours-Jane and Paula, 1998; Who's Afraid of the Working Class, 1998; Holy Day, 2001; Lantana, 2001; When the Rain Stops Falling, 2009. **Address:** Currency Press, 164 James St., PO Box 2287, Redfern, NW 2016, Australia.

BOVON, François. Swiss (born Switzerland), b. 1938. **Genres:** Theology/Religion, Art/Art History. **Career:** Université de Genève, professor, 1967-93, dean, 1976-79, honorary professor; Harvard University, New Testament and Early Christian Literature, teacher, 1993, New Testament Department, chair, 1993-98, 2001-02, The Divinity School, Frothingham research professor of the history of religion; Harvard Theological Review, editor, 2000-10. Writer. **Publications:** De vocatione gentium, 1967; Introduction Aux évangiles Synoptiques, 1970; Les derniers jours de Jésus: textes et événements, 1974; Exegesis: problèmes de méthode et exercices de lecture (Genèse22 et Luc 15): travaux, 1975; Luc le théologien: vingt-cinq ans derecherches (1950-1975), 1978; (co-author) Les Actes apocryphes desapôtres: Christianisme et monde païen, 1981; (co-author) Schriftauslegung als theologische Aufklärung: Aspektegegenwärtiger Fragestellungen in der neutestamentlichen Wissenschaft, 1984; Lukas in neuer Sicht, 1985; Loeuvre de Luc: études dexégèse et de théologie, 1987; Luke the Theologian, 1987, 2nd ed., Luke the Theologian: Fifty-five Years of Research (1950-2005), 2006; Das Evangelium Nach Lukas, 1989; (co-author) Die Sprache der Bilder: Gleichnis und Metapher in Literatur und Theologie, 1989; Evangile Selon Saint Luc, 1991; Genése de Lécriture Chrétienne, 1991; Révélations et écritares, 1993; New Testament Traditions and Apocryphal Narratives, 1995; (ed. with A.G. Brock and C.R. Matthews) The Apocryphal Acts of the Apostles: Harvard Divinity School Studies, 1999; (with B. Bouvier and F. Amsler) Acta Philippi, 1999; Luke 1: A Commentary on the Gospel of Luke 1: 1-9: 50 (Hermenia), 2002; Studies in Early Christianity, 2003; Early Christian Voices: In Texts, Traditions, and Symbols: Essays in Honor of Francois Bovon, 2003; Last Days of Jesus, 2006; Lévangile selon saint Luc (1, 1 - 9, 50), 2007; New Testament and Christian Apocrypha: Collected Studies II, 2009. **Address:** The Divinity School, Harvard University, 45 Francis Ave., Cambridge, MA 02138, U.S.A. **Online address:** francois_bovon@harvard.edu

BOWDEN, Charles. American (born United States), b. 1945?. **Genres:** Environmental Sciences/Ecology, Literary Criticism And History. **Career:** Tucson Citizen, reporter; City Magazine, editor; Harper's Magazine, contributing editor. **Publications:** The Impact of Energy Development on Water Resources in Arid Lands: Literature Review and Annotated Bibliography, 1975; Killing the Hidden Waters, 1977; (with L. Kreinberg) Street Signs Chicago: Neighborhood and Other Illusions of Big City Life, 1981; Blue Desert (essays), 1986; Frog Mountain Blues, 1987; Mezcal (autobiography), 1988; Red Line, 1989; Desierto: Memories of the Future, 1991; The Sonoran Desert: Arizona, California, and Mexico, 1992; The Secret Forest, 1993; (with M. Binstein) Trust Me: Charles Keating and the Missing Billions, 1993; (contrib.) Seasons of the Coyote: The Legend and Lore of an American Icon (essays), 1994; Blood Orchid: An Unnatural History of America, 1995; Chihuahua: Pictures from the Edge, 1996; Stone Canyons of the Colorado Plateau, 1996; Juárez: Laboratory of Our Future, 1998; (contrib.) Sierra Pinacate, 1998; (contrib.) Paul Dickerson, 1961-1997, 2000; Eugene Richards, 2001; Down by the River: Drugs, Money, Murder, and Family, 2002; Blues for Cannibals: The Notes from Underground, 2002; Killing the Hidden Waters, 2003; Shadow in the City: Confessions of an Undercover Drug Warrior, 2005; Inferno, 2006; (contrib.) Exodus/Exodo, 2008; Some of the Dead are still Breathing: Living in the Future, 2009; (contrib.) Trinity, 2009; Charles Bowden Reader, 2010; Dreamland: The Way out of Juárez, 2010; Murder City: Ciudad Juárez and the Global Economy's New Killing Fields, 2010; (ed. with M. Molloy) El Sicario: The Autobiography of a Mexican Assassin, 2011. Contributor to books. **Address:** c/o Kathleen Anderson, Anderson Grinberg Literary Management Inc., 12 W 19th St., New York, NY 10011, U.S.A.

BOWDEN, Jim. *See* **SPENCE, William John Duncan.**

BOWDEN, Keith. American (born United States), b. 1957. **Genres:** Autobiography/Memoirs. **Career:** Laredo Community College, English teacher; Laredo Morning Times, writer. **Publications:** The Tecate Journals: Seventy Days on the Rio Grande (memoir), 2007. **Address:** Laredo, TX , U.S.A. **Online address:** tktkeith@hotmail.com

BOWDEN, Mark. American (born United States), b. 1951. **Genres:** Documentaries/Reportage, Adult Non-fiction. **Career:** Baltimore News American, staff writer, 1973-79; Philadelphia Inquirer, staff writer, 1979-2003; Atlantic Monthly, national correspondent; Loyola College, adjunct professor of creative writing and journalism; National Public Radio, commentator; Harvard University, Kennedy School of Government, visiting lecturer; Yale University Law School, visiting lecturer; Georgetown University, visiting lecturer; United States Military Academy, visiting lecturer; U.S. Central Intelligence Agency, visiting lecturer; Vanity Fair, contributing editor. **Publications:** NON FICTION: Doctor Dealer, 1987; Bringing the Heat, 1994, as Bringing the Heat: A Pro Football Team's Quest for Glory, Fame, Immortality and a Bigger Piece of the Action, 2000; Black Hawk Down: A Story of Modern War, 1999; Killing Pablo: The Hunt for the World's Greatest Outlaw, 2001; Finders Keepers: The Story of a Man Who Found One Million, 2002; Our Finest Day: D-Day: June 6, 1944, 2002; Black Hawk Down: The Shooting Script, 2002; Road Work: Among Tyrants, Heroes, Rogues and Beasts, 2004; Guests of the Ayatollah: The First Battle in America's War with Militant Islam, 2006; The Best Game Ever: Giants vs. Colts, 1958 and the Birth of the Modern NFL, 2008; Winning Body Language, 2010. Contributor to periodicals. **Address:** Atlantic Monthly, 600 New Hampshire Ave. NW, Washington, DC 20037, U.S.A.

BOWDEN, Martha F. American/Irish (born Ireland) **Genres:** Adult Nonfiction, Social Commentary. **Career:** Kennesaw State University, Department of English, associate professor, 1992-, professor; The Aphra Behn Society, executive president; Southeastern American Society for Eighteenth Century Studies, president. Writer. **Publications:** (Ed.) The Reform'd Coquet: or, Memoirs of Amoranda; Familiar Letters Betwixt a Gentleman and a Lady; and, the Accomplish'd Rake, or, Modern Fine Gentleman, 1999; Yorick's Congregation: The Church of England in the Time of Laurence Sterne, 2007. **Address:** Department of English, Kennesaw State University, Rm. 167, 27 English Bldg., 1000 Chastain Rd., Kennesaw, GA 30144, U.S.A. **Online address:** mbowden@kennesaw.edu

BOWDRING, Paul (Edward). Canadian (born Canada), b. 1946. **Genres:** Novels, Poetry, Travel/Exploration, Literary Criticism And History. **Career:** College of the North Atlantic, instructor in English, 1975-99; Cabot Institute of Applied Arts and Technology, instructor in English, 1975-; Tickle Ace literary magazine, editor and co-publisher, 1979-87; The Fiddlehead literary magazine, associate editor; Editors & Co., editor. **Publications:** NOVELS: The Roncesvalles Pass, 1989; The Night Season, 1997. Contributor to periodicals. **Address:** Writers' Alliance of Newfoundland & Labrador, PO Box 2681, St. John's, NL A1C 5M5, Canada.

BOWE, John. American (born United States) **Genres:** Sociology. **Career:** Journalist and writer. **Publications:** (ed. with M. Bowe and S. Streeter) Gig: Americans Talk about Their Jobs at the Turn of the Millennium, 2000; Gig: Americans Talk about Their Jobs, 2001; Nobodies: Modern American Slave Labor and the Dark Side of the New Global Economy, 2007. Contributor to periodicals. **Address:** New York, NY , U.S.A.

BOWE, Julie. American (born United States), b. 1962. **Genres:** Human Relations/Parenting. **Career:** Augsburg Fortress Publishers, curriculum writer and editor. **Publications:** My Last Best Friend, 2007; My New Best Friend, 2008; My Best Frenemy, 2010; My Forever Friends, 2011; My Extra Best Friend, 2012. **Address:** The Chudney Agency, 72 N State Rd., Ste. 501, Briarcliff Manor, NY 10510, U.S.A. **Online address:** juliebowe@frontiernet.net

BOWEN, Barbara C(herry). British (born England), b. 1937. **Genres:** Intellectual History, Literary Criticism And History. **Career:** University of Illinois, instructor, 1962-63, assistant professor, 1963-66, associate professor, 1966-72, professor, 1973-87; Vanderbilt University, professor of French and comparative literature, 1987-2002, now professor emeritus of French and comparative literature. Writer. **Publications:** Les Caracteristiques essentielles de la farce francaise, et leur survivance dans les annees 1550-1620, 1964; The Age of Bluff: Paradox & Ambiguity in Rabelais and Montaigne, 1972; Words and the Man in French Renaissance Literature, 1983; Enter Rabelais, Laughing, 1998; Humour and Humanism in the Renaissance, 2004. EDITOR: Four Farces, 1967; The French Renaissance Mind: Studies Presented to W.G. Moore, L'Esprit Createur, 1976; One Hundred Renaissance Jokes: A Critical Anthology, 1988; Lapidary Inscriptions: Renaissance Studies for Donald A. Stone, Jr., 1991; Rabelais in Context: Proceedings of the 1991 Vanderbilt Conference, 1993. **Address:** Vanderbilt University, 1211 Medical Center Dr., Nashville, TN 37232, U.S.A. **Online address:** barbara.c.bowen@vanderbilt.edu

BOWEN, Gail. Canadian (born Canada), b. 1942. **Genres:** Mystery/Crime/Suspense, Novellas/Short Stories, Novels. **Career:** University of Saskatchewan, instructor, 1976-79; Gabriel Dumont Institute, instructor, 1979-85; University of Regina, Department of English, lecturer, 1979-85, assistant professor of English, 1986-97, associate professor of English, 1997-, department head, 1997-; Canadian Broadcasting Corp., arts columnist, 1991-97; First Nations University of Canada, English department, associate professor, head. Writer. **Publications:** JOANNE KILBOURN MYSTERY NOVELS: Deadly Appearances, 1990; Murder at the Mendel, 1991 as Love and Murder, 1993; The Wandering Soul Murders, 1992; A Colder Kind of Death, 1994; A Killing Spring, 1996; Verdict in Blood, 1998; Burying Ariel, 2000; The Glass Coffin, 2003; Early Investigations of Joanne Kilbourn, 2004; Last Good Day, 2004; Endless Knot, 2006; Further Investigations of Joanne Kilbourn, 2006; Brutal Heart, 2008. OTHER: (with R. Marken) 1919: The Love Letters of George and Adelaide (novella), 1987; (with R. Marken) Dancing in Poppies, 2002; Love You to Death, 2010; The Nesting Dolls, 2010; Kaleidoscope, 2012. Contributor to periodicals. **Address:** First Nations University of Canada, 1 First Nations Way, University of Regina, Regina, SK S4S 7K2, Canada. **Online address:** gbowen@sifc.edu

BOWEN, Huw. *See* **BOWEN, H. V.**

BOWEN, H. V. (Huw Bowen). Welsh/British (born England), b. 1959. **Genres:** Military/Defense/Arms Control, History. **Career:** University of Newcastle-upon-Tyne, Sir James Knott Research Fellow, 1985, instructor, 1988-92; University of Leicester, lecturer and senior lecturer, 1992-2006, personal chair, 2006; Swansea University, professor, 2007-. Writer and historian. **Publications:** Revenue and Reform: The Indian Problem in British Politics, 1757-1773, 1991; (ed. with R.A. Barlow) A Dear and Noble Boy: The Life and Letters of Louis Stokes, 1897-1916, 1995; Elites, Enterprise, and the Making of the British Overseas Empire, 1688-1775, 1996; War and British Society, 1688-1815, 1998; (ed. with M. Lincoln and N. Rigby) The Worlds of the East India Company, 2002; (ed. with A.G. Enciso) Mobilising Resources for War: Britain and Spain at Work, 1650-1815, 2006; The Business of Empire: The East India Company and Imperial Britain, 1756-1833, 2006. Contributor of articles to books and journals. **Address:** Department of History, Swansea University, Singleton Pk., Swansea, SA2 8PP, Wales. **Online address:** h.v.bowen@swansea.ac.uk

BOWEN, Jeremy. British/Welsh (born Wales), b. 1960. **Genres:** Adult Nonfiction. **Career:** British Broadcasting Corp., staff, 1984-, foreign correspondent, 1987, war correspondent, television reporter, Middle East correspondent, 1995-2000, host of breakfast program, 2000-02, special correspondent, 2003-, Middle East editor, 2005-. **Publications:** Six Days: How the 1967 War Shaped the Middle East, 2005. **Address:** Thomas Dunne Books, 175 5th Ave., New York, NY 10010, U.S.A.

BOWEN, John (Griffith). (Justin Blake). British/Indian (born India), b. 1924. **Genres:** Novels, Children's Fiction, Plays/Screenplays, Young Adult Fiction. **Career:** Sketch Magazine, assistant editor, 1953-56; J. Walter Thompson Co., copywriter, 1956-58; S.T. Garland Advertising Co., head of copy department, 1958-60; Associated Television, script consultant, 1960-67; London Academy of Music and Dramatic Art, stage director, 1967-; Thames Television, drama producer, 1978-79; London Weekend Television, producer, 1981-83; British Broadcasting Corp., producer, 1984. **Publications:** The Truth Will Not Help Us; Embroidery on an Historical Theme, 1956; Pegasus, 1957; The Mermaid and the Boy, 1958; After the Rain, 1959, new ed. as After the Rain: A Play in Three Acts, 1972; The Centre of the Green, 1960; Storyboard: A Novel, 1960; Pegasus, 1960; The Birdcage: A Novel, 1962; The Essay Prize, with A Holiday Abroad and The Candidate: Plays for Television, 1962; I Love You, Mrs. Patterson, 1964; (with J. Bullmore as Justin Blake) Garry Halliday, 5 vols., 1964; A World Elsewhere: A Novel, 1965; The Fall and Redemption of Man, 1968; Little Boxes, 1968; The Disorderly Women, 1969; The Corsican Brothers, 1970; The Waiting Room: A Play, 1971; Heil Caesar!, 1974; Florence Nightingale: A Play, 1976, Squeak, 1983; The McGuffin, 1984; The Girls: A Story of Village Life, 1987; Fighting Back, 1989; The Precious Gift, 1992; No Retreat, 1994; Cold Salmon: A Play, 1998; Plays One, 1999. **Address:** Old Lodge Farm, Sugarswell Ln., Edgehill, Banbury, OX OX15 6HP, England.

BOWEN, John R. (John Richard Bowen). American (born United States), b. 1951?. **Genres:** Social Sciences. **Career:** Washington University, Dunbar-Van Cleve professor in arts and sciences. Writer and anthropologist. **Publications:** (Ed. with J.W. Bennett) Production and Autonomy: Anthropological Studies and Critiques of Development, 1988; Sumatran Politics and Poetics: Gayo History, 1900-1989, 1991; Muslims through Discourse: Religion and Ritual in Gayo Society, 1993; (ed.) Religion in Culture and Society, 1998; Religions in Practice: An Approach to the Anthropology of Religion, 1998, 5th ed., 2011; (with R. Petersen) Critical Comparisons in Politics and Culture, 1999; Islam, Law, and Equality in Indonesia: An Anthropology of Public Reasoning, 2003; (with C. O'Brien) Cork Silver and Gold: Four Centuries of Craftsmanship, 2005; Why the French Don't Like Headscarves: Islam, the State, and Public Space, 2006; (with C. O'Brien) Celebration of Limerick's Silver, 2007; Can Islam Be French?: Pluralism and Pragmatism in a Secularist State, 2010. Contributor to journals. **Address:** Department of Anthropology, Washington University, 133 McMillan Hall, PO Box 1114, St. Louis, MO 63130, U.S.A. **Online address:** jbowen@wustl.edu

BOWEN, John Richard. *See* **BOWEN, John R.**

BOWEN, Mark. (Mark Stander Bowen). American (born United States) **Genres:** Environmental Sciences/Ecology, Earth Sciences, Sciences, Adult Non-fiction. **Career:** Journalist and photographer. **Publications:** Thin Ice: Unlocking the Secrets of Climate in the World's Highest Mountains, 2005; Censoring Science: Inside the Political Attack on Dr. James Hansen and the Truth of Global Warming, 2008. Contributor to periodicals. **Address:** c/o Jessica Firger, Henry Holt & Co., 175 5th Ave., New York, NY 10010, U.S.A. **Online address:** thinice@mark-bowen.com

BOWEN, Mark Stander. *See* **BOWEN, Mark.**

BOWEN, Michael. Also writes as Hillary Bell Locke. American (born United States), b. 1951. **Genres:** Mystery/Crime/Suspense, Law. **Career:** Foley & Lardner L.L.P., partner, 1976-. Writer. **Publications:** MYSTERY NOVELS: Badger Game, 1989; Washington Deceased, 1990; Fielder's Choice, 1991; Faithfully Executed, 1992; Act of Faith, 1993; Corruptly Procured, 1994; Worst Case Scenario, 1996; Collateral Damage, 1999; The Fourth Glorious Mystery, 2000; Screenscam, 2001; Unforced Error, 2004; Putting Lipstick on a Pig, 2006; Shoot the Lawyer Twice, 2008; Service Dress Blues, 2009; (as Hillary Bell Locke) But Remember Their Names, 2011. OTHERS: (with G. Marshall and K. Freeman) Passing By: The United States and Genocide in Burundi, 1973; Discovery in Patent Interference Proceedings, 1976; (comp. and ed.) Can't Miss, 1987; (with B.E. Butler) The Wisconsin Fair Dealership Law, 1988, 3rd ed., 2003; Entry on the American Legal System in the Oxford Companion to Crime and Mystery Fiction, 1999; Hillary! How America's First Woman President Won the White House, 2003. Contributor to journals and periodicals. **Address:** Foley & Lardner L.L.P., 777 E Wisconsin Ave., Milwaukee, WI 53202, U.S.A. **Online address:** mbowen@foley.com

BOWEN, Roger W. American (born United States), b. 1947. **Genres:** History, Biography. **Career:** St. Mary's University, visiting professor, 1978; Colby College, assistant professor, 1978-82, associate professor, 1982-87, professor, 1987-91; Japan Institute of Harvard University, associate in research, 1980; Hollins College, vice president for academic affairs, 1992-96; State University of New York, New Paltz, president, 1996-2001; Milwaukee Public Museum, head, 2002-03; American Association of University Professors, general secretary, 2004-. Writer. **Publications:** Rebellion and Democracy in Meiji Japan: A Study of Commoners in the Popular Rights Movement, 1980; (ed.) E.H. Norman: His Life and Scholarship, 1984; Innocence Is Not Enough: The Life and Death of Herbert Norman, 1986; Japan's Dysfunctional Democracy: The Liberal Democratic Party and Structural Corruption, 2003. **Address:** American Association of University Professors, 1133 19th St. NW, Ste. 200, Washington, DC 20036, U.S.A.

BOWEN, William (Gordon). American (born United States), b. 1933. **Genres:** Economics, Education. **Career:** Princeton University, professor of Economics and public affiars, 1958-88, president, 1972-88; The Andrew W.

Mellon Foundation, president, 1988-2006, now president emeritus. Writer. **Publications:** The Wage-Price Issue: A Theoretical Analysis, 1960; Wage Behavior in the Postwar Period: An Empirical Analysis, 1960; Economic Aspects of Education: Three Essays, 1964; (ed. and intro.) Labor and the National Economy, 1965; (ed. with F.H. Harbison) Unemployment in a Prosperous Economy, 1965; (with W.J. Baumol) Performing Arts: The Economic Dilemma, 1966; Economics of the Major Private Universities, 1968; (with T.A. Finegan) The Economics of Labor Force Participation, 1969; Ever the Teacher, 1987; (with J.A. Sosa) Prospects for Faculty in the Arts and Sciences: A Study of Factors Affecting Demand and Supply, 1987 to 2012, 1989; (with N.L. Rudenstine) In Pursuit of the PhD, 1992; (with T.I. Nygren, S.E. Turner and E.A. Duffy) The Charitable Nonprofits: An Analysis of Institutional Dynamics and Characteristics, 1994; Inside the Boardroom: Governance by Directors and Trustees, 1994; (with D. Bok) The Shape of the River: Long Term Consequences of Considering Race in College and University Admissions, 1998; (ed. with H.T. Shapiro) Universities and Their Leaderships, 1998; (with J.L. Shulman) Game of Life: College Sports and Educational Values, 2001; (with S.A. Levin) Reclaiming the Game: College Sports and Educational Values, 2003; (with M.A. Kurzweil and E.M. Tobin) Equity and Excellence in American Higher Education, 2006; Board Book: An Insider's Guide for Directors and Trustees, 2008; (with M.M. Chingos and M.S. McPherson) Crossing the Finish Line: Completing College at America's Public Universities, 2009; Targer, 2010; Lessons Learned: Reflections of a University President, 2011. **Address:** Andrew W. Mellon Foundation, 140 E 62nd St., New York, NY 10065, U.S.A.

BOWER, John Morton. (John S.M. Bower). British (born England), b. 1942. **Genres:** Animals/Pets, Medicine/Health. **Career:** Associate veterinary surgeon, 1965-69; Veterinary Hospital, principal veterinarian, senior partner, 1969-; British Small Animal Veterinary Association, president, 1984-85; Cornish Cat Club, vice-president, 1986-; British Veterinary Association, president, 1989-90; Pet Plan Insurance Co., consultant-adviser, 1991-; Veterinary Drug Co., director, 1993-98; Veterinary Practice Management Association, president, 1998-2000; Genusxpress plc., consultant, 1998-. Writer. **Publications:** (With D. Youngs) The Health of Your Dog, 1989; (as John S.M. Bower with J. Gripper and D. Gunn) Veterinary Practice Management, 1989, 3rd ed., 2001; The Dog Owners Veterinary Handbook, 1994; (with C. Bower) The Dog Owner's Problem Solver, 1998; (with C. Bower) The Cat Owner's Problem Solver, 1998. Contributor to periodicals. **Address:** Veterinary Hospital, Colwill Rd., Plymouth, DN PL6 8RP, England. **Online address:** johnbower@plymouthvets.co.uk

BOWER, John S.M. *See* **BOWER, John Morton.**

BOWER, Tom. British (born England), b. 1946. **Genres:** Writing/Journalism, Documentaries/Reportage, Politics/Government. **Career:** British Broadcasting Corp., television documentary producer and correspondent; Panorama, reporter; London Evening Standard, editor. **Publications:** Blind Eye to Murder: Britain, America and the Purging of Nazi Germany-A Pledge Betrayed, 1981 in US as The Pledge Betrayed: America and Britain and the Denazification of Postwar Germany, 1982; Klaus Barbie, Butcher of Lyons, 1984, rev. ed., 1985; Klaus Barbie: Itineraire D'un Bourreau Ordinaire, 1984; The Paperclip Conspiracy: The Hunt for the Nazi Scientists in UK as The Paperclip Conspiracy: The Battle for the Spoils and Secrets of Nazi Germany, 1987; Maxwell, the Outsider, 1992; Tiny Rowland: A Rebel Tycoon, 1993; The Red Web: MI6 and the KGB Mastercoup, 1993; Perfect English Spy: Sir Dick White and the Secret War, 1935-1990, 1995; Maxwell: The Final Verdict, 1995; Blood Money: The Swiss, The Nazis and The Looted Billions, 1997; Nazi Gold: The Full Story of the Fifty-Year Swiss-Nazi Conspiracy to Steal Billions from Europe's Jews and Holocaust Survivors, 1997; Branson, 2000; Broken Dreams: Vanity, Greed and the Souring of British Football, 2003; Gordon Brown, 2004; Outrageous Fortune: The Rise and Ruin of Conrad and Lady Black, 2006; Squeeze: Oil, Money and Greed in the Twenty-First Century, 2009; Oil: Money, Politics, and Power in the 21st Century, 2010; No Angel: The Secret Life of Bernie Ecclestone, 2011. **Address:** Curtis Brown Group Ltd., Haymarket House, 28-29 Haymarket, London, GL SW1Y 4SP, England.

BOWERING, George. Canadian (born Canada), b. 1935. **Genres:** Novels, Novellas/Short Stories, Young Adult Fiction, Plays/Screenplays, Poetry, Essays. **Career:** University of Calgary, instructor, assistant professor, 1963-66; Sir George Williams University, instructor, writer-in-residence, 1967-68, assistant professor of English, 1968-72; Simon Fraser University, professor of English, 1972-2001, now professor emeritus; Imago Magazine, editor. **Publications:** A Home for Heroes (play), 1962; Baseball, 1967; Mirror on the Floor, 1967; Rocky Mountain Foot, 1969; The Gangs of Kosmos, 1969; Al Purdy, 1970; George, Vancouver, 1970; Sitting in Mexico, 1970; Geneve, 1971; Autobiology, 1971; The Sensible, 1972; Layers 1-13, 1973; Curious, 1973; In the Flesh, 1974; At War with the U.S., 1974; Allophanes, 1976; The Catch, 1976; The Concrete Island, 1977; A Short Sad Book, 1977; Concentric Circles, 1977; Protective Footwear, 1978; Another Mouth, 1979; Burning Water, 1980; West Window, 1982; Smoking Mirror, 1982; Errata (literary theory), 1987; Urban Snow, 1991; George Bowering Selected, 1993; Bowering's B.C. (history), 1996; Blonds on Bikes, 1997; Egotists and Autocrats (history), 1999; Stone Country: An Unauthorized History of Canada, 2003. NOVELS: Caprice, 1987; Harry's Fragments, 1990; Shoot!, 1994; Parents from Space (young adult), 1994; Diamondback Dog (young adult), 1998; Piccolo Mondo, 1998; Pin Boy 2010. POETRY: Sticks and Stones, 1963; Points on the Gril, 1964; The Man in Yellow Boots, 1965; The Silver Wire, 1966; Two Police Poems, 1968; Selected Poems, 1971; Touch: Selected Poems 1960-1970, 1971; Poem and Other Baseballs, 1976; Particular Accidents: Selected Poems, 1981; Kerrisdale Elegies, 1984; Seventy-one Poems for People, 1985; Delayed Mercy, 1986; His Life, a Poem, 2000; Changing on the Fly, 2004; Vermeer's Light, 2006; My Darling Nellie Grey, 2010. STORIES: Flycatcher, 1974; A Place to Die, 1984; The Rain Barrel, 1994; Standing on Richards, 2004; The Box. 2009; ESSAYS: A Way with Words, 1982; The Mask in Place, 1983; Craft Slices, 1985-71; Imaginary Hand, 1988; Left Hook, 2005; Horizontal Surfaces, 2010. MEMOIRS: The Moustache (memoir), 1993; A Magpie Life (memoir), 2001; (with R. Knighton) Cars (memoir), 2002; Rewriting My Grandfather, 2005; Baseball Love (memoir) 2006. EDITOR: Vibrations, 1970; The Story So Far, 1971; (and foreword) Sheila Watson and The Double Hook, 1985; Likely Stories, 1992; (with M. Ondaatje) An H in the Heart: A Reader, 1994; And Other Stories, 2001; The Heart Does Break (with Jean Baird), 2010. **Address:** Simon Fraser University, 8888 University Dr., Burnaby, BC V5A 1S6, Canada. **Online address:** bowering@sfu.ca

BOWERING, Marilyn (Ruthe). Canadian (born Canada), b. 1949. **Genres:** Novels, Plays/Screenplays, Poetry, Children's Fiction, Young Adult Fiction, Adult Non-fiction, Young Adult Non-fiction, Autobiography/Memoirs, Autobiography/Memoirs. **Career:** Teacher in public schools at Masset, 1974-75; freelance writer and book reviewer, 1975-77; University of British Columbia, extension lecturer in poetry writing, 1977; Gregson/Graham, British Columbia, editor and writer, 1978-80; University of Victoria, visiting lecturer, 1978-82, lecturer in creative writing, 1982-86, 1989-, visiting associate professor of creative writing, 1993-94; Noel Collins and Blackwells, freelance editor, 1980-82; freelance writer, 1990-92; Banff Centre, faculty, 1992, writer-in-electronic-residence, 1993-94; Memorial University of Newfoundland, writer-in-residence. Writer. **Publications:** POETRY: The Liberation of Newfoundland, 1973; One Who Became Lost, 1976; The Killing Room, 1977; Third Child & Zian, 1978: The Book of Glass, 1978; Sleeping with Lambs, 1980; Giving Back Diamonds, 1982; The Sunday before Winter, 1984; Anyone Can See I Love You, 1987; Grandfather was a Soldier, 1987; Calling All the World, 1989; Love as It Is, 1993; Interior Castle, 1994; Autobiography, 1996; Human Bodies, New and Selected Poems 1987-1999, 1999; The Alchemy of Happiness, 2003; Green, 2007; A Commonplace of Hills, forthcoming. NOVELS: The Visitors Have All Returned, 1979; To All Appearances a Lady, 1989; Visible Worlds, 1998; (co-author) Breaking the Surface, 2000; Cat's Pilgrimage, 2004; What It Takes to Be Human, 2007. EDITOR: (with D.A. Day) Many Voices: An Anthology of Contemporary Canadian Indian Poetry, 1977; Guide to the Labor Code of British Columbia, 1980. Contributor to books and periodicals. **Address:** The Writers' Union of Canada, 40 Wellington St. E, 3rd Fl., Toronto, ON M5E 1C7, Canada. **Online address:** info@marilynbowering.com

BOWERS, Jane Palatini. American (born United States), b. 1945. **Genres:** Literary Criticism And History, Women's Studies And Issues, Plays/Screenplays. **Career:** University of California, Extencion Division, program coordinator, 1977-82, lecturer in English, 1981-87, assistant director of composition, 1983-85; University of Florence, visiting professor, 1986; City University of New York, John Jay College of Criminal Justice, assistant professor, 1987-91, associate professor, 1991-93, professor of English, 1993-, dean of undergraduate studies and professor of English, 2005-07, provost and senior vice president for academic affairs, 2007-, Graduate School and University Center, professor, 1995-, Hunter college, Women's Studies Program, director, 1997-2001, professor of English, 1997-2005, Honors College, director of academic affairs, 2001-05; Writing on the Edge, consulting editor, 1991. **Publications:** They Watch Me as They Watch This: Gertrude Stein's Metadrama, 1991;

Gertrude Stein, 1993. Works appear in anthologies. Contributor to journals. **Address:** Department of English, John Jay College of Criminal Justice, Rm. 621T, 445 W 59th St., New York, NY 10019-1104, U.S.A. **Online address:** jbowers@jjay.cuny.edu

BOWERS, Janice Emily. American (born United States), b. 1950. **Genres:** Botany, Horticulture, Essays, Natural History, Earth Sciences. **Career:** University of Arizona, research assistant and coordinator, 1976-82; U.S. Geological Survey, Desert Laboratory, hydrological assistant and botanist, 1982-. Writer. **Publications:** Seasons of the Wind: A Naturalist's Look at the Plant Life of Southwestern Sand Dunes, 1986; 100 Roadside Wildflowers of Southwest Woodlands, 1987; A Sense of Place: The Life and Work of Forrest Shreve, 1988; Chiricahua National Monument, 1988; 100 Desert Wildflowers of the Southwest, 1989; One Hundred Desert Wildflowers of the Southwest, 1989; The Mountains Next Door, 1991; Shrubs and Trees of the Southwest Deserts, 1993; A Full Life in a Small Place: And Other Essays from a Desert Garden, 1993; (with R.M. Turner and T.L. Burgess) Sonoran Desert Plants: An Ecological Atlas, 1995; Fear Falls Away and Other Essays from Hard and Rocky Places, 1997; Dune Country: A Naturalist's Look at the Plant Life of Southwestern Sand Dunes, 1998; Desert: The Mojave and Death Valley, 1999; Flowers and Shrubs of the Mojave Desert, 1999; The Desert, 2000; Frequently Asked Questions About the Saguaro, 2003; The Best Spring Ever: Why El Niño Makes the Desert Bloom, 2004. Contributor to periodicals. **Address:** Desert Laboratory, U.S. Geological Survey, 1675 W Anklam Rd., Tucson, AZ 85745, U.S.A. **Online address:** jebowers@usgs.gov

BOWERS, John. American (born United States), b. 1928. **Genres:** Novels, Autobiography/Memoirs, Biography, Local History/Rural Topics, Young Adult Fiction. **Career:** U.S. Department of State, personnel officer, 1955-62; freelance writer, 1962-; Magazine Management, editor; Columbia University, professor in the writing program; New York State University, faculty; East Tennessee State University, faculty; Wilkes University, faculty. **Publications:** The Colony (autobiography), 1971; The Golden Bowers, 1971; No More Reunions (novel), 1973; Helene, 1975; In the Land of Nyx: Night and its Inhabitants, 1984; Stonewall Jackson: Portrait of a Soldier, 1989; Chickamauga and Chattanooga: The Battles that Doomed the Confederacy, 1994; Love in Tennessee, 2009. **Address:** PO Box 373, Phoenicia, NY 12464, U.S.A. **Online address:** jwb@johnbowersauthor.com

BOWERS, Terrell L. (Terry Bowers). American (born United States), b. 1945. **Genres:** Westerns/Adventure, Young Adult Fiction, Romance/Historical. **Career:** City Market Stores, clerk, 1966-70; Safeway Stores Inc., Grocery Department, manager, 1970-74; Bold Petroleum, store-station manager, 1975-81; Desert Gateway, store owner, 1981-85; Questar, emergency dispatcher, 1985-98. Writer. **Publications:** Noose at Big Iron, 1979; A Man Called Banker, 1980; Rio Grande Death Ride, 1980; Crossfire at Twin Forks, 1980; Gunfire at Flintlock, 1981; Frozen Trail, 1981; Last Stand at Rio Blanco, 1981; Banyon's War, 1982; Chase into Mexico, 1982; Avery's Vengeance, 1982; Maverick Raid, 1983; The Fighting Peacemaker, 1983; Death at Devil's Gap, 1983; The Fighting McBride, 1983; Gold Trail, 1983; Dakota Bullets, 1984; Job for a Gunman, 1984; Culhane's Code, 1984; Deadly Bounty, 1985; Sinclair's Double War, 1985; Blood Vengeance, 1985; Dark Reunion, 1985; The Devils Rope, 1985; Banshee Raiders, 1985; The Masked Cowpoke, 1985; Skull Mountain Bandit, 1985; Petticoat War, 1985; Vendetta, 1985; The Fighting Lucanes, 1986; Cheyenne Brothers, 1986; Trail to Justice, 1986; Armageddon at Gold Butte, 1986; Delryan's Draw, 1986; Destiny's Trail, 1987; Lassito's Last War, 1988; The Railroad War, 1988; Black Cloud over Gunstock, 1988; Iron Claw's Revenge, 1988; The Shadow Killer, 1989; Justice at Black Water, 1989; Doctor Totes a Six-Gun, 1990; Tanner's Last Chance, 1991; Winter Vendetta, 1991; Secret of Snake Canyon, 1993; Rio Grande Death Ride, 1996; Ride Against the Wind, 1996; Noose at Sundown, 1997; Feud at Broken Spoke, 1997; Gun Law at Broken Spoke, 1998; Crossfire at Broken Spoke, 1998; Destiny at Broken Spoke, 1998; Yancy's Luck, 2002; Battle at Lost Mesa, 2002; Mystery at Gold Vista, 2002; A Man Called Sundown, 2003; The Shadow Killers, 2003; Spencer's Law, 2003; The Guns at Three Forks, 2004; The Last Revenge, 2005; High Gun at Surlock, 2006; The Trail to Yuma, 2007; Warrick's Battle, 2007; A Reckoning at Orphan Creek, 2008; The Killer's Brand, 2008; Judgment at Gold Butte, 2008; The Switchback Trail, 2010; Konniger's Woman, 2010; Death Comes Riding, 2010; The Legend of Tornado Tess, 2010; Ambush at Lakota Crossing, 2011; No Quarter at Devil's Fork, 2011. **Address:** PO Box 651, West Jordan, UT 84084, U.S.A. **Online address:** tlbowers@compuserve.com

BOWERS, Terry. *See* **BOWERS, Terrell L.**

BOWIE, Andrew (S.). British (born England), b. 1952. **Genres:** Philosophy, Music, Literary Criticism And History. **Career:** Free University of Berlin, instructor in aesthetics, 1980-81; Anglia Polytechnic University, lecturer in philosophy, professor of philosophy, 1981-99; Tübingen University, Department of Philosophy, Alexander von Humboldt research fellow; University of London, Royal Holloway, professor of philosophy and German, 1999-, Royal Holloway Humanities and Arts Research Centre (HARC), founding director. Writer. **Publications:** Aesthetics and Subjectivity: From Kant to Nietzsche, 1990, 2nd ed., 2003; (trans. and intro.) F.W.J. Schelling, Lectures on the History of Modern Philosophy, 1993; Schelling and Modern European Philosophy: An Introduction, 1993; From Romanticism to Critical Theory: The Philosophy of German Literary Theory, 1997; Introduction to German Philosophy: From Kant to Habermas, 2003; Music, Philosophy, and Modernity, 2007; German Philosophy, 2010; Philosophical Variations: Music as Philosophical Language, 2010. EDITOR: (intro.) Manfred Frank, The Subject and the Text: Essays on Literary Theory and Philosophy, 1998; (and trans.) F.D.E. Schleiermacher, Hermeutics and Criticism and Other Texts, 1998. **Address:** Royal Holloway, University of London, Egham Hill, Egham, SR TW20 0EX, England. **Online address:** a.bowie@rhul.ac.uk

BOWIE, Phil. American (born United States) **Genres:** Novels. **Career:** City Magazine, editor; Neuse River Foundation, water quality researcher; writer. **Publications:** JOHN HARDIN SERIES NOVELS: Guns, 2006; Diamondback, 2007; KLLRS, 2008. Contributor of short stories and articles to periodicals. **Address:** New Bern, NC , U.S.A. **Online address:** philbowie@always-online.com

BOWKER, Gordon. British (born England), b. 1934. **Genres:** Literary Criticism And History, Biography, Young Adult Fiction. **Career:** University of London, Goldsmiths' College, teacher, 1966-90. Freelance journalist, biographer and literary critic. **Publications:** Education of Coloured Immigrants, 1968; (contrib.) Apparently Incongruous Parts: The Worlds of Malcolm Lowry, 1990; Pursued by Furies: A Life of Malcolm Lowry, 1993; Through the Dark Labyrinth: A Biography of Lawrence Durrell, 1997; (intro.) Hear Us O Lord from Heaven Thy Dwelling Place, 2000; George Orwell, 2003; Inside George Orwell, 2003; James Joyce: A Biography, 2011. EDITOR: Freedom: Reason or Revolution?, 1970; (with J. Carrier) Race and Ethnic Relations: Sociological Readings, 1976; Malcolm Lowry Remembered, 1985; Malcolm Lowry: Under the Volcano, 1988. Contributor to books, periodicals and magazines. **Address:** c/o Anthony Goff, David Higham Associates, 5-8 Lower John St., Golden Sq., London, GL W1F 9HA, England.

BOWKETT, Stephen. British/Welsh (born Wales), b. 1953. **Genres:** Novels, Plays/Screenplays, Novellas/Short Stories, Horror, Poetry, Science Fiction/Fantasy, Children's Fiction, Education, Education. **Career:** Lutterworth High School, teacher, 1976-94. Writer. **Publications:** Spellbinder, 1985; The Copy Cat Plan (two plays), 1986; Gameplayers, 1986; Dualists, 1987; Catch and Other Stories, 1987; Frontiersville High, 1990; The Community, 1993; The Bidden, 1994; For the Moon There Is a Cloud, 1996; A Rare Breed, 1996; Panic Station, 1996; Dinosaur Day, 1996; The World's Smallest Werewolf, 1996; Meditations for Bus People: How to Stop Worrying and Stay Calm, 1996; A Little Book of Joy: 365 Inspirations for Daily Serenity, 1996; Dreamcastle, 1997; Imagine That: A Handbook of Creative Learning Activities for the Classroom, 1997; Imagine That, 1997; Roy Kane TV Detective, 1998; Dino Discoveries, 1999; Horror at Halloween, 1999; Self Intelligence, 1999; Dreamcatcher, 2000; The Planet Machine, 2000; What's the Story?: Games and Activities for Creative Storymaking, 2001; Ice, 2001; The Frankenstein Steps and Other Adventures, 2001; ALPS Story Maker: Using Fiction as a Resource for Accelerated Learning, 2001; The Allotment Ghost and Other Stories, 2001; Thaw, 2002; Storm, 2002; Catch Minitales: Short Horror Stories with a Sting!, 2003; Story Maker Catch Pack, 2003; The Passenger and Other Adventures, 2003; (with S. Stanley) But Why?, 2004; 100 Ideas for Teaching Creativity, 2005; Boys and Writing, 2006; 100 Ideas for Teaching Thinking Skills, 2007; Emotional Intelligence, 2007; Jumpstart! Creativity: Games & Activities for Ages 7-14, 2007; 100 Ideas for Creative Development in Preschool, 2007; (with W. Bowkett) 100 ideas for Developing Good Practice in the Early Years, 2008; 100 Ideas for Good Practice in Preschool, 2008; (co-author) Happy Families-Insights into Parenting, 2008; (with W. Bowkett) 100 Ideas for Teaching Creative Development, 2008; Success in the Creative Classroom, 2008; Countdown to Creative Writing: Step by Step Approach to Writing Techniques for 7-12 years, 2008; Countdown to Poetry Writing: Step by Step Approach to Writing Techniques for 7-12 years, 2009; Countdown to Non-Fiction Writing: Step by Step Approach to Writing Techniques for 7-12 years, 2009; (with S. Percival) Coaching Emotional Intelligence in the Classroom: A Practical Guide for 7-14, 3rd ed., 2011; Using Comic Art to improve Speaking, Reading and Writing: Kapow!, 2011. **Address:** c/o Sheila Watson, Watson Little Ltd., 12 Egbert St., London, GL NW1 8LJ, England. **Online address:** steve@sbowkett.freeserve.co.uk

BOWLBY, Rachel. British (born England), b. 1957. **Genres:** Literary Criticism And History, Women's Studies And Issues, Mythology/Folklore, Biography, Translations, Essays. **Career:** University of Sussex, lecturer in English, 1984-93, professor of English, 1994-97; Oxford University, professor of English, 1997-99; York University, professor of English and French, 1999-2004; University College London, professor of modern English, 2004-, Lord Northcliffe professor of modern English literature, 2007-; Cornell University, visiting professor; Rutgers University, visiting professor; Otago University, visiting professor; Université Sorbonne Nouvelle, visiting professor. Writer. **Publications:** Just Looking: Consumer Culture in Dreiser, Gissing, and Zola, 1985; (ed. and intro.) Virginia Woolf: Feminist Destinations, 1988; Still Crazy After All These Years: Women, Writing, and Psychoanalysis, 1992; (ed. and intro.) A Woman's Essays, 1992; Shopping with Freud, 1993; (ed. and intro.) The Crowded Dance of Modern Life, vol. II, 1993; Feminist Destinations and Further Essays on Virginia Woolf, 1997; (ed., intro. and contrib.) Orlando, 1998; Carried Away: The Invention of Modern Shopping, 2000; (trans.) J. Derrida, Of Hospitality, 2000; (trans.) E. Roudinesco, Why Psychoanalysis?, 2001; (trans.) Questions for Judaism, 2004; (trans.) J. Derrida, Paper Machine, 2005; Freudian Mythologies: Greek Tragedy and Modern Identities, 2007. Contributor to journals. **Address:** Department of English Language and Literature, University College London, Gower St., London, GL WC1E 6BT, England. **Online address:** r.bowlby@ucl.ac.uk

BOWLER, Tim. British (born England), b. 1953. **Genres:** Young Adult Fiction, Children's Fiction. **Career:** Writer. **Publications:** Midget, 1995; Dragon's Rock, 1995; River Boy, 1997; Shadows, 1999; Storm Catchers, 2001; Starseeker, 2004; Apocalypse, 2005; Walking with the Dead, 2005; Blood on Snow, 2005; Higher Ground, 2005; Frozen Fire, 2007; Bloodchild, 2008. BLADE SERIES: Playing Dead, 2008; Closing In, 2008; Breaking Free, 2009; Running Scared, 2009; Fighting Back, 2009; Mixing It, 2010; Cutting Loose, 2010; Risking All, 2010; Buried Thunder, 2011. **Address:** c/o Caroline Walsh, David Higham Associates Ltd., 5-8 Lower John St., Golden Sq., London, GL W1R 4HA, England. **Online address:** tim@timbowler.co.uk

BOWLES, Samuel. American (born United States), b. 1939?. **Genres:** Education, Economics, Politics/Government. **Career:** Harvard University, assistant professor of economics, 1965-71, associate professor of economics, 1971-74; University of Massachusetts, Department of Economics, professor of economics, 1974-2002, chair, 2000, professor emeritus of economics, 2002-; University of Siena, visiting professor, 1982-, William Fulbright distinguished visiting professor, 1993, professor of economics, 2002-10; University of California, Ford visiting professor, 1988; MacArthur Foundation, Research Network on Inequality and Economic Performance, founder and co-director, 1993-2007; Santa Fe Institute, research associate, 2000-, Economics Program, director, 2000-03, Behavioral Sciences Program, director and Arthur Spiegel Research Professor, 2003-. Writer and economist. **Publications:** Planning Educational Systems for Economic Growth, 1969; (with D. Kendrick, L. Taylor and M. Roberts) Notes and Problems in Microeconomic Theory, 1970; (with H. Gintis) Schooling in Capitalist America: Educational Reform and the Contradictions of Economic Life, 1976; (with D.M. Gordon and T.E. Weisskopf) Beyond the Waste Land: A Democratic Alternative to Economic Decline, 1983; (with R. Edwards) Understanding Capitalism: Competition, Command, and Change in the U.S. Economy, 1985, (with R. Edwards and F. Roosevelt) 3rd ed. as Understanding Capitalism: Competition, Command, and Change, 2005; (with H. Gintis) Democracy and Capitalism: Property, Community, and the Contradictions of Modern Social Thought, 1986; (with D.M. Gordon and T.E. Weisskopf) After the Waste Land: A Democratic Economics for the Year 2000, 1990; (with H. Gintis) Recasting Egalitarianism: New Rules for Communities, States, and Markets, 1998; Microeconomics: Behavior, Institutions, and Evolution, 2004; (with H. Gintis) Schooling in Capitalist America, 2011; (with H. Gintis) Cooperative Species, 2011. EDITOR: (co-ed.) Studies in Development Planning, 1971; (with R. Edwards and W.G. Shepherd) Unconventional Wisdom: Essays on Economics in Honor of John Kenneth Galbraith, 1989; (with R. Edwards) Radical Political Economy, 1990; (with H. Gintis and B. Gustafsson) Markets and Democracy: Participation, Accountability, and Efficiency, 1993; (with T.E. Weisskopf) Economics and Social Justice: Essays on Power, Labor, and Institutional Change, 1998; (with M. Franzini and U. Pagano) The Politics and Economics of Power, 1999; (with K. Arrow and S. Durlauf) Meritocracy and Economic Inequality, 2000; (with H. Gintis and M.O. Groves) Unequal Chances: Family Background and Economic Success, 2005; (with P. Bardhan and M. Wallerstein) Globalization and Egalitarian Redistribution, 2006; (with S.N. Durlauf and K. Hoff) Poverty Traps, 2006; (with J. Baland and P. Bardhan) Inequality, Cooperation, and Environmental Sustainability, 2007. Contributor to periodicals and journals. **Address:** Santa Fe Institute, 1399 Hyde Park Rd., Santa Fe, NM 87501-8943, U.S.A. **Online address:** bowles@santafe.edu

BOWLEY, Rex Lyon. British (born England), b. 1925. **Genres:** Education, History, Local History/Rural Topics, Theology/Religion, Travel/Exploration. **Career:** Bancroft's School, senior history master and housemaster, 1970-85. Writer. **Publications:** Fortunate Islands, a History of the Isles of Scilly, 9th ed., 2004; Tresco: The Standard Guidebook to the Isle of Tresco, 1970; Teaching without Tears: A Guide to Teaching Technique, 4th ed., 1973; Scillonian Quiz-Book, 1974; Readings for Assembly, 1976; The Study: The Story of a Wimbledon Girls' School, 1996; The Isles of Scilly Standard Guidebook, 55th ed., 2004; Scilly at War, 2002. **Address:** Bowley Publications Ltd., PO Box 1, St. Mary's, Isles of Scilly, CW TR21 0PR, England.

BOWLING, Lewis. American (born United States), b. 1959. **Genres:** History, Medicine/Health, Sports/Fitness. **Career:** North Carolina Central University, instructor, 1996-, Department of Physical Education and Recreation, adjunct instructor; Aerobics and Fitness Association of America, personal trainer certification examiner, 1999-; Durham Herald Sun, fitness columnist. **Publications:** (Co-author) Lifetime Physical Fitness, 1999; Granville County: Images of America, 2002; Granville County Revisited, 2003; Oxford, 2005; Wallace Wade: Championship Years at Alabama and Duke, 2006; Resistance Training: The Total Approach, 2007; Granville County, North Carolina: Looking Back, 2007; Duke University Basketball, 2008; Duke Basketball: A Pictorial History, 2008. **Address:** Department of Physical Education and Recreation, North Carolina Central University, C227 LeRoy T. Walker Physical Education Complex, 1801 Fayetteville St., Durham, NC 27707, U.S.A. **Online address:** lbowling@nccu.edu

BOWLT, John E(llis). American/British (born England), b. 1943. **Genres:** Art/Art History, Translations. **Career:** University of St. Andrews, lecturer in Russian, 1968-69; University of Birmingham, lecturer in Russian language and literature, 1970; University of Kansas, assistant professor of Russian, 1970-71; University of Texas, Department of Slavic, assistant professor, associate professor, 1971-81, professor of Russian, 1981-88; Yale University, National Humanities Institute, research fellow, 1977-78; University of Southern California, Department of Slavic Languages and Literatures, adjunct professor, professor, 1988-, Institute of Modern Russian Culture, director, 1979-; Metropolitan Museum of Art, consultant; M.H. de Young Museum, consultant; Thames & Hudson Ltd., consultant. Writer. **Publications:** (Ed. with S. Bann) Russian Formalism: A Collection of Articles and Texts in Translation, 1973; Russian Art, 1875-1975: A Collection of Essays, 1976; (ed. and trans.) Russian Art of the Avant Garde: Theory and Criticism, 1902-1934, 1976, rev. ed., 1986; (intro.) Stage Designs and the Russian Avant Garde, 1911-1929: A Loan Exhibition of Stage and Costume Designs from the Collection of Mr. and Mrs. Nikita D. Lobanov-Rostovsky, 1976; (ed.) Benedikt Livshits, 1977; (ed. and trans.) B. Livshits, The One-and-a-Half-Eyed Archer, 1977; (with D.V. Sarabianov) Russian and Soviet Painting, 1977; Russian Theater and Costume Design from the Fine Arts Museums, 1979; (trans.) V. Krasovskaya, Nijinsky, 1979; (trans.) E.S. Sizov, Treasures from the Kremlin, 1979; The Silver Age: Russian Art of the Early Twentieth Century and the World of Art Group, 1979, 2nd ed., 1982; Journey into Non-Objectivity, 1980; (ed. with R.C.W. Long and trans.) The Life of Vasilii Kandinsky in Russian Art, 1982; Russian Stage Design: Scenic Innovation, 1900-1930: From the Collection of Mr. and Mrs. Nikita D. Lobanov-Rostovsky, 1982; (ed. and trans. with N. Misler) Pavel Filonov: A Hero and His Fate, Collected Writings on Art and Revolution, 1910-40, 1984; (co-author) Russian Samizdat Art: Essays, 1986; (with A.E. Senn and D. Straševičius) Mikalojus Konstantinas čiurlionis: Music of the Spheres, 1986; (ed. and intro.) Varvara Stepanova: The Complete Work, 1988; Russkoeteatralno-dekoratsionnoe iskusstvo, 1880-1930: iz kollektsii Nikity i Niny Lobanovykh-Rostovskikh: katalog vystavki, 1988; (ed. with V. Misiano) Ten Plus Ten: Contemporary Soviet and American Painters, 1989; (intro.) The Quest for Self-Expression: Painting in Moscow and Leningrad, 1965-1990, 1990; (with O. Matich) Laboratory of Dreams: The Russian Avant-Garde and Cultural Experiment, 1990; (contrib.) Theatre in Revolution: Russian Avant-garde Stage Design, 1913-1935, 1991; (with N. Kasak) From Action to Dynamic Silence: The Art of Nikolai Kasak, 1991; (contrib.) Sakharoff, un mito della danza: fra teatro e avanguardie artistiche, 1991; (comp. with N. Misler) Pawel Filonow in den 1920er Jahren: Die Physiologiede Malerei, 1992; Khudozhniki teatra. Kollektsiia Niny i Nikity Lobanovykh-Rostovskikh, 1993; (contrib.) Wassili Kandinsky: tra Oriente e Occidente: capolavori dai musei russi, 1993; (with N. Misler) Russian and East European Painting in the Thyssen-Bornemisza Collection, 1993; (with B. Hernad) Aus vollem Halse: russische Buchillustration und Typographie1900-1930: aus den Sammlungen der Bayerischen Staatsbibliothek München, 1993; (contrib.) Khudozhniki russkogo teatra: 1880-1930: sobranie Nikity i Niny Lobanovykh-Rostovskikh, 1994; Artists of the Russian Theater, vol. II, 1994; (ed. and trans.) The Salon Album of Vera Sudeikin-Stravinsky, 1995; Forbidden Art: Soviet Nonconformist Art 1956-1988, 1997; Theater of Reason, Theater of Desire: The Art of Alexandre Benois and Léon Bakst, 1998; (ed. with M. Drutt) Amazons of the Avant-garde: Alexandra Exter, 2000; (co-author) Dmitri Plavinsky, 2000; (ed. with M.T. Lampard and W.R. Salmond) The Uncommon Vision of Sergi Konenkov, 1874-1971: A Russian Sculptor and His Times, 2001; (ed. with M. Konecny and E. Petrova) A Legacy Regained: Nikolai Khardzhiev and the Russian Avant-garde, 2002; (co-author) Il libro dell'avanguardia russa: operedella collezione Marzaduri a Ca' Foscari, 2004; (contrib.) Working for Diaghilev, 2004; (intro.) Aleksandr Rodchenko: Experiments for the Future: Diaries, Essays, Letters, and Other Writings, 2005; Pavel Filonov: Seer of the Invisible: Catalogue of the Exhibition at the Russian Museum, The Pushkin Museum of Fine Arts, 2006; Moscow & St. Petersburg 1900-1920: Art, Life, and Culture of the Russian Silver Age, 2008; (intro.) Visual resources from Russia and Eastern Europe in the New York Public Library, 2008; A Feast of Wonders, 2009; (co-author) Cosmos de la vanguardia rusa, 2010. Contributor to journals. **Address:** Department of Slavic Languages, University of Southern California, 255 THH, University Pk., PO Box 4353, Los Angeles, CA 90089-4353, U.S.A. **Online address:** bowlt@usc.edu

BOWMAN, Christian. (Christian Miller). British/Scottish (born Scotland), b. 1920. **Genres:** Novels, Travel/Exploration, Autobiography/Memoirs, History. **Career:** Ministry of Production, technical adviser, 1939-45. Writer. **Publications:** AS CHRISTIAN MILLER: The Champagne Sandwich, 1969; Daisy, Daisy, 1980; A Childhood in Scotland, 1981. Contributor to periodicals. **Address:** The Walled Garden, Chamberlain St., Wells, SM BA5 2PE, England.

BOWMAN, Crystal. American (born United States), b. 1951. **Genres:** Children's Fiction, Songs/Lyrics And Libretti, Picture/Board Books. **Career:** FJH Music Co., children's lyricist, 1990-; Little Angels Nursery School, teacher; Lollipop Preschool, teacher and director. Writer. **Publications:** JUVENILES: Cracks in the Sidewalk (poems), 1993, rev. ed., 2001; Jonathan James Says: I Can Be Brave, 1995; Let's Be Friends, 1995; I Can Help, 1995; Let's Play Ball, 1995; School's Out, 1997; I Can Hardly Wait, 1997; Happy Birthday to Me, 1997; Christmas Is Coming, 1997; Ivan and the Dynamos, 1997; If Peas Could Taste like Candy (poems), 1998; Windmills and Wooden Shoes, 1999; The M.O.P.S. series, 1999-2002; See the Country, See the City, 2000; Morning, Mr. Ted!, 2000; Mommy, May I Hug the Fishes?, 2000, rev. ed., 2007; My ABC Bible/ My ABC Prayers, 2001; Boxes, Boxes, Everywhere!, 2001; Room in the Stable, 2001; My Cowboy Boots, 2002; (with N. Faber) Dinosaur Stomp, 2003; I'm Jack!: I Am Made to Run and Play, 2003; I'm Kaitlyn!: I Have Important Jobs To Do, 2003; I'm Parker!: I Like to Think About It, 2003; My 1-2-3 Bible; My 1-2-3 Bible Promises, 2004; My Color Bible; My Color Praises, 2004; One Year Book of Devotions for Preschoolers, 2004; My 1-2-3 Bible; My 1-2-3 Bible Promises, 2004; Is God Always with Me?, 2005; My Cowboy Boots, 2008; Jake Learns to Share, 2008; Jake's New Friend, 2008; Otter and Owl and the Big Ah-Choo!, 2008; Otter and Owl Set Sail, 2008; Otter and Owl's Helpful Hike, 2008; (with C. Kennedy) My Read and Rhyme Bible Storybook, 2009; Little David Sings for the King, 2010; Little David's Brave Day, 2010; Little David's Big Heart, 2010; Boy on the Yellow Bus, 2010; Little David and His Best Friend, 2010. ADULT NON-FICTION: (with T. Goyer) Mealtime Moments: 164 Faith-Filling Entrees to Stir Family Discussions, 2000; Meditations for Moms, 2001; A Mom's Guide to Making Memories Last: Simple, Inexpensive Ways to Scrapbook and Journal Revell, 2006. OTHERS: J Is for Jesus: The Sweetest Story Ever Told, 2005; Jesus, Me, and My Christmas Tree, 2005; Amazing Women of West Michigan, 2006; My Christmas stocking: Filled With God's Love, 2006; Star for Jesus, 2006; Is God Always with Me?, 2006; Jake's Brave Night, 2007; Jake Plays Ball, 2007; Jake Helps Out, 2007; Jake Goes Fishing, 2007; An Easter Gift for Me, 2007; The House in the Middle of Town, 2007; What Do I See?, 2008; (with A. Pennington) Do You Love Me More?, 2010; Prodigal Son, 2011; Joshua Crosses the Jordan River, 2011; Jesus Raises Lazarus, 2011; Jesus Feeds the Five Thousand, 2011; Zacchaeus, 2012; Story of the Resurrection Eggs, 2013. **Address:** Cygnet Publishing, 2153 Wealthy SE, Grand Rapids, MI 49506, U.S.A. **Online address:** info@crystalbowman.com

BOWMAN, David. American/Greek (born Greece), b. 1957. **Genres:** Novels, Novellas/Short Stories, Mystery/Crime/Suspense, Children's Fiction, Plays/Screenplays, Adult Non-fiction, Film, History, Information Science/Computers, Institutions/Organizations, Music, Literary Criticism And History, Social Commentary, Writing/Journalism, Young Adult Non-fiction. **Career:** Strand Bookstore, staff, 1976-78; freelance writer, 1978-; Scholastic Inc., editor, 1979-83; Holt, Rinehart & Winston, project editor, 1987-89; Sony Wonder, designer, 1993-94. **Publications:** Let the Dog Drive, 1992; Bunny Modern, 1998; This Must Be the Place: The Adventures of Talking Heads in the 20th Century, 2001. Contributor to periodicals. **Address:** c/o Author Mail, HarperCollins, 10 E 53rd St., 7th Fl., New York, NY 10022, U.S.A.

BOWMAN, Eric. *See* **FROST, Mark C.**

BOWMAN, James. American (born United States), b. 1948. **Genres:** History. **Career:** Lebanon Valley College, Department of Public Relations, assistant, 1971, director of publications, 1971-73; Westminster School, assistant master, 1980; Portsmouth Grammar School, teacher, 1980-89; American Spectator, American correspondent, 1989-91, film critic, 1990-; Times Literary Supplement, American editor, 1991-2002; New Criterion, media critic, 1993-. **Publications:** Honor: A History, 2006; Media Madness: The Corruption of Our Political Culture, 2008. Contributor to books and periodicals. **Address:** Ethics and Public Policy Center, 1730 M St. NW, Ste. 910, Washington, DC 20036, U.S.A. **Online address:** jamesbowman@comcast.net

BOWMAN, J. Wilson. American (born United States) **Genres:** Cultural/Ethnic Topics, Education, Gerontology/Senior Issues, How-to Books, Race Relations. **Career:** Merritt College, professor and department head; Diablo Valley College, assistant dean; Compton College, dean and assistant supervisor; Mars Hill College, professor; R.J. Enterprises (consultancy and publisher), president; Young Women's Christian Association, executive director, 1994-96; Black Women Leadership Institute, co-founder. National public speaker and writer. **Publications:** America's Black Colleges: The Comprehensive Guide to Historically and Predominantly Black 4-Year Colleges and Universities, 1992; America's Black and Tribal Colleges, 1994, 3rd ed., 1999. **Address:** 24 Bevlyn Dr., PO Box 1034, Asheville, NC 28803, U.S.A. **Online address:** rjeanc@earthlink.net

BOWN, Deni. British (born England), b. 1944. **Genres:** Homes/Gardens, Horticulture, Natural History, Botany, Medicine/Health, Sports/Fitness, Sciences. **Career:** Laurence Urdang Associates, etymologist, 1972-77; Newbury College, lecturer, 1982-84; The Herb Society, chairman, 1997-; Deni Bown Associates, writer and photographer; Photolibrary, consultant editor; Collins English Dictionary, editor. **Publications:** Aroids: Plants of the Arum Family, 1988, 2nd ed., 2000; Fine Herbs, 1988 as Ornamental Herbs for Your Garden, 1993; Alba: The Book of White Flowers, 1989; Through the Seasons, a Series of Six Nature Books for Children Titled Pond, Stream, Wood, Park, Garden, Field and Hedgerow, 1989; Westonbirt Arboretum, 1990; Orchids: A Volume In The Green World Series, 1991; Four Gardens in One: The Royal Botanic Garden, Edinburgh, 1992; The Encyclopedia of Herbs and Their Uses, 1995; Growing Herbs, 1995; Garden Herbs, 1998; Healing Garden: Nature's Remedies and Cures, 1998; New Encyclopedia of Herbs and Their Uses, 2001. Contributor to books. **Address:** Herb Society, Sulgrave Manor, Banbury, OX OX17 2SD, England. **Online address:** denibown@aol.com

BOWNESS, Alan. British (born England), b. 1928. **Genres:** Art/Art History, Literary Criticism And History. **Career:** University of London, Courtauld Institute of Art, lecturer, 1957-, reader, 1967-, professor of art history, 1978-79; Tate Gallery, director, 1980-88; Henry Moore Foundation, director, 1988-. Writer. **Publications:** Lynn Chadwick, 1962; Henry Moore: Complete Sculpture, 6 vols., 1965-88; Impressionists and Post-impressionists, 1965; (ed. and intro.) William Scott: Paintings, 1965; (intro.) Contemporary British Painting,

1967; Modern Sculpture, 1967; (ed.) Alan Davie, 1967; (ed. and intro.) Recent British Paintings: Peter Stuyvesant Foundation Collection, 1968; (comp.) Alfred Wallis, 1968; (comp.) Vincent van Gogh, 1968; (contrib.) Matisse and the Nude, 1968; (ed.) Complete Sculpture of Barbara Hepworth, 1960-69, 1971; (contrib.) Gauguin, 1971; William Scott-Paintings, Drawings and Gouaches, 1938-71, 1972; Modern European Art, 1972; Courbet's L'Atelier du Peintre, 1972; (ed.) Ivon Hitchens, 1973; (intro.) Jackson Pollock: Paintings and Drawings, 1934 to 1952, 1989; The Condition of Success: How the Modern Artist Rises to Fame, 1990; (co-author) British Contemporary Art, 1910-1990: Eighty Years of Collecting by the Contemporary Art Society, 1991; Poetry and Painting: Baudelaire, Mallarmé, Apollinaire, and Their Painter Friends, 1994; Modern European Art, 1995; (with A. Garrould) Bernard Meadows: Sculpture and Drawings, 1996. **Address:** The Henry Moore Foundation, Dane Tree House, Perry Green, Much Hadham, HF SG10 6EE, England.

BOWSER, Benjamin P(aul). American (born United States), b. 1946. **Genres:** Race Relations, Sociology, Cultural/Ethnic Topics, Urban Studies, Medicine/Health. **Career:** Cornell University, graduate school, assistant dean, 1975-82; Western Interstate Commission for Higher Education, Minority Education Office, director, 1982-83; University of Santa Clara, Office of Black Student Affairs, director, 1983-85; Stanford University, assistant, 1985-86; California State University, Department of sociology and social services, associate professor, 1987-94, professor, 1994-, College of Arts, Letters and Social Sciences, interim dean, 2006-08, chair, 2008-, California State East Bay Urban Institute, director, College of Engineering, dean; Bayview Hunter's Point Community Foundation, director of multicultural inquiry and research on AIDS, 1990-91. Writer. **Publications:** (With G. Auletta and T. Jones) Dealing with Diversity in the University, 1993; (with G.S. Auletta and T. Jones) Confronting Diversity Issues on Campus, 1993; Black Middle Class: Social Mobility and Vulnerability, 2007. EDITOR: (with E. Mann and M. Oling) Census Data with Maps for Small Areas of New York City, 1910-1960, 1981; (with R.G. Hunt) Impacts of Racism on White Americans, 1981, 2nd ed., 1996; Black Male Adolescents: Parenting and Education in Community Context, 1991; (with T. Jones and G. Auletta) Toward the Multicultural University, 1995; (ed.) Racism and Anti-Racism in World Perspective, 1995; (with L. Kushnick) Against the Odds: Scholars Who Challenged Racism in the 20th Century, 2002; (co-ed.) Preventing AIDS: Community-Science Collaborations, 2004; (co-ed.) When Communities Assess Their AIDS Epidemics: Results of Rapid Assessment of HIV/AIDS in Eleven U.S. Cities, 2007; The Black Middle Class, 2007. Contributor to books and journals. **Address:** Department of Sociology and Social Services, California State University East Bay, 3103 Meiklejohn Hall, Hayward, CA 94542, U.S.A. **Online address:** benjamin.bowser@csueastbay.edu

BOWYER, Mathew Justice. American (born United States), b. 1926. **Genres:** Young Adult Fiction, Novellas/Short Stories, Local History/Rural Topics, Essays, Humor/Satire, History, Literary Criticism And History. **Career:** Dulles Intl. Airport Mail Facility, supervisor. Writer. **Publications:** They Carried the Mail: A Survey of Postal History and Hobbies, 1972; How to Become an Expert on Stamp Collecting and Other Postal Hobbies, 1974; Collecting Americana, 1977; Encyclopedia of Mystical Terminology, 1979; (with P.J. Lyons) Real Estate Investor's Desk Encyclopedia, 1982; General George Washington's Great Secret, 1998; Return to Memory, 1999; St. Elmo's Fire, 1999; The Post Office Delivers: Humor, 1999; Love on the Bridge, 2000; George Washington's Boy, 2001; A Generation Apart, 2003. **Address:** 3504 Pinnacle Ridge Rd. NE, Roanoke, VA 24012-6562, U.S.A. **Online address:** matbowyer@matbowyerbooks.com

BOX, Edgar. *See* **VIDAL, Gore.**

BOXER, Arabella. British (born England), b. 1934. **Genres:** Food And Wine, Travel/Exploration, Medicine/Health, Food And Wine. **Career:** Sunday Times Magazine, contributor; Vogue magazine, food correspondent, 1965-67, 1975-91. Writer. **Publications:** First Slice Your Cookbook, 1964; A Second Slice, 1966; (ed.) Seven Centuries of English Cooking, 1973; Nature's Harvest: The Vegetable Cookbook, 1974; Arabella Boxer's Garden Cookbook, 1974; Christmas Food and Drink, 1975; Bon appétit Summer Cookbook, 1980; Bon appétit Winter Cookbook, 1980; (with P. Back) Herb Book, 1980; Mediterranean Cookbook, 1981; Wind in the Willows Country Cookbook, 1983; Sunday Times Complete Cookbook, 1983; Arabella Boxer's Book of Elegant Cooking and Entertaining: The Planning, Preparation, and Presentation of 350 Delicious Dishes, 1984; (co-author) Encyclopedia of Herbs, Spices, and Flavourings, 1984; Starters With Style, 1986; Fashionable First Courses, 1987; Book of English Food, 1991; (with T. Traeger) A Visual Feast, 1991; Seven Centuries of English Cooking, 1992; The Hamlyn Herb Book, 1996; The Hamlyn Spice Book, 1997; The New First Slice Your Cookbook, 1998; Herb and Spice Handbook, 1999. **Address:** 44 Elm Park Rd., London, GL SW3 6AX, England.

BOYARIN, Daniel. American/Israeli (born Israel), b. 1946. **Genres:** Theology/Religion. **Career:** Jewish Theological Seminary of America, teaching staff member, 1973-, assistant professor, 1975- 81; Ben Gurion University, senior lecturer, 1978-87, associate professor, 1985; Hebrew University, Institute for Advanced Studies, fellow, 1979-80; Bar-Ilan University, senior lecturer, 1983-90, associate professor, 1986; University of California, professor, 1990-, Herman P. and Sophia Taubman Chair; Yale University, visiting associate professor, 1984-85; Yeshiva University, visiting professor, 1985, 1988; Pontifical Gregorian University, Harvard Divinity School, visiting professor; Memorial Foundation in Jewish Studies, project evaluator, 1991-92, 1995-96, 1996-97, 1997-98, 1998-99; Center for Hermeneutical Studies, co-director, 1992-96. Writer. **Publications:** The Loss of Final Consonants in Babylonian Jewish Aramaic (BJA), 1976; Ha-'Iyun ha-Sefaradi: le-farshanut ha-Talmud shel megorshe Sefarad, 1989; Intertextuality and the Reading of Midrash, 1990; Carnal Israel: Reading Sex in Talmudic Culture, 1993; A Radical Jew: Paul and the Politics of Identity, 1994; Unheroic Conduct: The Rise of Heterosexuality and the Invention of the Jewish Man, 1997; (with J. Boyarin) Jews and Other Differences: The New Jewish Cultural Studies, 1997; Dying for God: Martyrdom and the Making of Christianity and Judaism, 1999; Atiarah le-Hiayim: mehikiarim ba-sifrut ha-Talmudit vieha-rabanit li-khevod Profesor Hiayim Zalman Dimitrovski, 2000; (with J. Boyarin) Powers of Diaspora: Two Essays on the Relevance of Jewish Culture, 2002; (ed.) Queer Theory and the Jewish Question, 2003; Sparks of the Logos: Essays in Rabbinic Hermeneutics, 2003; Border Lines: The Partition of Judaeo-Christianity, 2004. Contributor to books. **Address:** University of California, Department of Near Eastern Studies, 250 Barrows Hall, Berkeley, CA 94720-1940, U.S.A. **Online address:** boyarin@socrates.berkeley.edu

BOYD, Blanche McCrary. American (born United States), b. 1945?. **Genres:** Novels, Essays, Literary Criticism And History, Young Adult Fiction. **Career:** Connecticut College, teacher of creative writing, writer-in-residence, Roman and Tatiana Weller professor of English. **Publications:** NOVELS: Nerves; A Novel, 1973; Mourning the Death of Magic, 1977; The Revolution of Little Girls, 1991; Terminal Velocity, 1997. NONFICTION: The Redneck Way of Knowledge: Down-Home Tales (essays), 1982. Contributor to periodicals. **Address:** Connecticut College, 270 Mohegan Ave., PO Box 5421, New London, CT 06320, U.S.A.

BOYD, Brian (David). New Zealander/British/Irish (born Ireland), b. 1952. **Genres:** Literary Criticism And History, Biography, Psychology, Philosophy. **Career:** Victoria University, junior lecturer, 1974; University of Auckland, postdoctoral fellow, 1979-80, lecturer, 1980-85, senior lecturer, 1986-91, associate professor, 1992-98, professor, 1998-2001, university distinguished professor, 2001-; Universite de Nice-Sophia Antipolis, visiting professor, 1994-95; Nabokov Museum, visiting professor, 2002. Writer. **Publications:** Nabokov's Ada: The Place of Consciousness (criticism), 1985, 2nd ed., 2001; Vladimir Nabokov: The Russian Years (biography), 1990; Vladimir Nabokov: The American Years (biography), 1991; (ed.) Nabokov: Novels and Memoirs, 1941-1951, 1996; (ed.) Nabokov: Novels 1955-1962, 1996; (ed.) Nabokov: Novels 1969-1974, 1996; The Presents of the Past: Literature in English before 1900, 1998; Nabokov's Pale Fire: The Magic of Artistic Discovery, 1999; (intro.) Speak, Memory: An Autobiography Revisited, 1999; (ed. with R.M. Pyle and intro.) Nabokov's Butterflies: Unpublished and Uncorrected Writings, 2000; Vladimir Nabokov: Russkie Gody: Biografiia, 2001; (ed.) Words that Count: Essays on Early Modern Authorship in Honor of MacDonald P. Jackson, 2004; (foreword) Alphabet in Color, 2005; (ed. with S. Shvabrin and intro.) Verses and Versions: Three Centuries of Russian Poetry, 2008; On the Origin of Stories: Evolution, Cognition and Fiction, 2009; (ed. with J. Carroll and J. Gottschall) Evolution, Literature, and Film: A Reader, 2010; (co-ed.) Nabokov: Oeuvres Romanesques Completes, vol. II, 2010; (ed. and intro.) Pale Fire: A Poem in Four Cantos by John Shade, 2011; Stalking Nabokov: Selected Essays, 2011; Why Lyrics Last: Evolution, Cognition, and Shakespeare's Sonnets, 2012. Contributor to periodicals. **Address:** Department of English, University of Auckland, 14A Symonds St., PO Box 92019, Auckland, 1142, New Zealand. **Online address:** b.boyd@auckland.ac.nz

BOYD, Candy Dawson. American (born United States), b. 1946. **Genres:** Children's Fiction, Social Sciences, Young Adult Fiction, Human Relations/Parenting. **Career:** Overton Elementary School, teacher, 1968-71; Longfellow School, teacher, 1971-73; University of California, extension instructor in the language arts, 1972-79; Saint Mary's College of California, extension instructor in language arts, 1972-79, lecturer, 1975, assistant professor, 1976-87, associate professor, 1983-91, professor of education, 1991-, director of reading leadership and teacher effectiveness programs, 1976-87, director of elementary education, 1983-88; Berkeley Unified School District, district teacher trainer in reading and communication skills, 1973-76. Writer. **Publications:** Circle of Gold, 1984; Breadsticks and Blessing Places, 1985 as Forever Friends, 1986; Charlie Pippin, 1987; Chevrolet Saturdays, 1993; Fall Secrets, 1994; Daddy, Daddy Be There, 1995; Different Beat, 1996; (co-author) Scot Foresman Social Studies: The United States: Grade 5, 2005. Contributor of articles and essays to journals. **Address:** St. Mary's College of California, School of Education, PO Box 4350, Moraga, CA 94575, U.S.A. **Online address:** cboyd@stmarys-ca.edu

BOYD, Carl. American (born United States), b. 1936. **Genres:** History, International Relations/Current Affairs, Military/Defense/Arms Control, Young Adult Fiction. **Career:** Ohio State University, instructor to assistant professor of history, 1969-75; Old Dominion University, assistant professor, associate professor, 1975-85, professor of history, 1985-2001, director of graduate program in history, 1991-94, Louis I. Jaffe Professor and eminent scholar emeritus, 1995-2001, Louis I. Jaffe Emeritus Professor, 2001-. Writer. **Publications:** The Extraordinary Envoy: General Hiroshi Ōshima and Diplomacy in the Third Reich, 1934-1939, 1980; Hitler's Japanese Confidant: General Ōshima Hiroshi and MAGIC Intelligence from Berlin, 1941-1945, 1993; The Japanese Submarine Force and World War II, 1995; American Command of the Sea through Carriers, Codes, and the Silent Service: World War II and Beyond, 1995. Contributor of articles to periodicals and journals. **Address:** 1229 Rockbridge Ave., Norfolk, VA 23508-1337, U.S.A. **Online address:** cboyd31480@aol.com

BOYD, Claude E. American (born United States), b. 1939. **Genres:** Environmental Sciences/Ecology. **Career:** Mississippi State University, instructor, 1963; Federal Water Pollution Control Administration, aquatic biologist, 1966; Auburn University, assistant professor, 1967, associate professor, 1971-77, professor, 1977-; University of Georgia, Savannah River Ecology Laboratory, ecologist, 1968-70. Writer. **Publications:** (Co-author) Effects of Phytoplankton on Dissolved Oxygen Concentration in Catfish Ponds, 1977; Water Quality in Warmwater Fish Ponds, 1979; Water Quality Management in Pond Aquaculture, 1982, rev. ed., 1998; Water Quality in Ponds for Aquaculture, 1990; (with C.S. Tucker) Water Quality and Pond Soil Analyses for Aquaculture, 1992; Hydrology and Water Supply for Pond Aquaculture, 1994; Bottom Soils, Sediment and Pond Aquaculture, 1995; (ed. with H.S. Egna) Dynamics of Pond Aquaculture, 1997; Water Quality, an Introduction, 2000. **Address:** Department of Fisheries and Allied Aquacultures, Auburn University, 203B Swingle Hall, PO Box 3074, Auburn, AL 36849, U.S.A. **Online address:** ceboyd@acesag.auburn.edu

BOYD, Donna. *See* **BALL, Donna Rochelle.**

BOYD, Joe. American/British (born England), b. 1942. **Genres:** Music. **Career:** Warner Brothers Films, head of music; UFO (a music club), co-founder, 1966; Hannibal Records (a music recording label), founder; Witchseason (a production company), founder. Writer. **Publications:** White Bicycles: Making Music in the 1960s (memoir), 2006. **Address:** Meryl Zegarek Public Relations, 255 W 108th St., Ste. 9D1, New York, NY 10025-2927, U.S.A.

BOYD, Malcolm. American (born United States), b. 1923. **Genres:** Novellas/Short Stories, Civil Liberties/Human Rights, Gay And Lesbian Issues, Race Relations, Sex, Theology/Religion, Autobiography/Memoirs. **Career:** Foote, Cone and Belding Advertising Agency, copywriter, 1945-46; film writer and producer, 1947-49; Pickford, Rogers and Boyd, founder, 1949, vice president and general manager, 1949-51; Episcopal priest, 1955-; World Council of Churches, lecturer, 1955, 1964; Saint George's Episcopal Church, rector, 1957-59; Colorado State University, Episcopal chaplain, 1959-61; Wayne State University, Episcopal chaplain, 1961-64; Grace Episcopal Church, assistant priest, 1961-64; Church of the Atonement, assistant pastor, 1964-68; Yale University, Calhoun College, resident fellow, 1968-71, associate fellow, 1971-75; Saint Augustine-by-the-Sea Episcopal Church, writer priest-in-residence, 1980-96; PEN Center USA West, president, 1984-87; Modern Maturity Magazine, columnist, 1990-2000; AIDS Commission, chaplain, 1990-; Episcopal Cathedral Center, poet-in-residence, 1996-. **Publications:** Crisis in Communication: The Church in Mass Culture, 1957; Christ and Celebrity Gods, 1958; Focus: Rethinking the Meaning of Our Evangelism, 1960; If I Go Down to Hell: Man's Search for Meaning in Contemporary Life, 1962; The Hunger, The Thirst: The Questions of Students and Young Adults, 1964; Four Plays on Race, 1965; Are You Running with Me Jesus?, 1965; Free to Live, Free to Die, 1967; Book of Days, 1968; You can't Kill the Dream, 1968; The Fantasy Worlds of Peter Stone and and Other Fables, 1969; As I Live and Breathe: Stages of an Autobiography, 1969; My Fellow Americans, 1970; Human Like Me, Jesus: Prayers with Notes on the Humanistic Revolution, 1971; The Lover, 1972; (with P. Conrad) When in the Course of Human Events, 1973; The Runner, 1974; The Alleluia Affair, 1975; Christian: Its Meaning in an Age of Future Shock, 1975; Am I Running with You, God?, 1977; Take Off the Masks, 1978, rev. ed., 1993; Look Back in Joy: Celebration of Gay Lovers, 1981, rev. ed., 1990; Half Laughing, Half Crying, 1986; Gay Priest: An Inner Journey, 1986; Edges, Boundaries, and Connections, 1992; Rich with Years: Daily Meditations on Growing Older, 1993; Go Gentle into That Good Night, 1998; Running with Jesus: The Prayers of Malcolm Boyd, 2000; Simple Grace: A Mentor's Guide to Growing Older, 2001; Prayers for the Later Years, 2002; Samuel Joseph for President: Media, Politics, Religion, Race: Timeless Satire Stories, 2008; A Prophet in His Own Land: A Malcolm Boyd Reader, 2008. EDITOR: On the Battle Lines, 1964; The Underground Church, 1968; (with N. Wilson) Amazing Grace: Stories of Lesbian and Gay Faith, 1991; (with C. Talton) Race and Prayer, 2003; (with J.J. Bruno) In Times Like These: How We Pray, 2005. **Address:** PO Box 512164, Los Angeles, CA 90051-2145, U.S.A. **Online address:** info@malcolmboyd.com

BOYD, Nan Alamilla. American (born United States), b. 1963?. **Genres:** History. **Career:** University of Colorado, assistant professor of women's studies, 1999-2003; Sonoma State University, assistant professor, 2003-; San Francisco State University, Department of Women and Gender Studies, associate professor, professor and department chair. Writer. **Publications:** Wide-Open Town: A History of Queer San Francisco to 1965, 2003. **Address:** Department of Women and Gender Studies, San Francisco State University, HUM 314, 1600 Holloway Ave., San Francisco, CA 94132, U.S.A. **Online address:** alamilla@sfsu.edu

BOYD, Steven R(ay). American (born United States), b. 1946. **Genres:** History, Politics/Government, Social Commentary, Adult Non-fiction, Photography. **Career:** St. Olaf College, instructor, 1974-75; University of Texas, assistant professor, 1975-81, associate professor, 1981-94, professor of history, 1994-. Writer. **Publications:** The Politics of Opposition: Antifederalists and the Acceptance of the Constitution, 1979; (ed.) The Whiskey Rebellion: Past and Present Perspectives, 1985; Constitution in State Politics: From the Calling of the Constitutional Convention to the First Federal Elections, 1990; (ed.) Alternative Constitutions for the United States: A Documentary History, 1992; Patriotic Envelopes of the Civil War: The Iconography of Union and Confederate Covers, 2010. Contributor to books and periodicals. **Address:** Department of History, University of Texas, HSS 4.04.28, 1 UTSA Cir., San Antonio, TX 78249-1644, U.S.A. **Online address:** steven.boyd@utsa.edu

BOYDEN, Amanda. American (born United States) **Genres:** Novels, Literary Criticism And History. **Career:** University of New Orleans, Department of English, creative writing professor and writer-in-residence. Writer. **Publications:** Pretty Little Dirty: A Novel, 2006; L'Enfant Terrible (novel), 2008; Babylon Rolling (novel), 2008. Contributor to periodicals. **Address:** Department of English, College of Liberal Arts, University of New Orleans, 201 Liberal Arts Bldg., 2000 Lakeshore Dr., New Orleans, LA 70148, U.S.A. **Online address:** aeboyden@hotmail.com

BOYDEN, Joseph. Canadian (born Canada), b. 1966. **Genres:** Novels. **Career:** Northern College, instructor in communications; University of New Orleans, teacher of writing and literature, MFA Creative Writing Program, writer-in-residence. **Publications:** Born with a Tooth, 2001; The Three Day Road, 2005; She Takes You Down, 2006; Through Black Spruce: A Novel, 2008. Contributor to periodicals. **Address:** Westwood Creative Artists, 94 Harbord St., Toronto, ON M5S 1G6, Canada. **Online address:** josephboyden@yahoo.com

BOYER, Jay. American (born United States), b. 1947. **Genres:** Plays/Screenplays, Novellas/Short Stories, Biography, Writing/Journalism, Literary Criticism And History, Theatre. **Career:** St. Louis University, student Instructor, 1969; State University of New York, teaching assistant, 1969-71, instructor, 1974-76; Arizona State University, faculty member, 1976-, Department of English, assistant professor, 1976-81, associate professor, 1981-95, professor, 1995-, Film Studies Program, chair, coordinator, 1984-2005. Writer. **Publications:** Richard Brautigan, 1987; Ishmael Reed, 1993; Sidney Lumet, 1993; Bob Rafelson: Hollywood Maverick, 1996; Wollicotts Traveling Rabbit's Foot Minstrels, 2002; Time Went By, But Slowly, 2002; Poaching Deer in Northern Arizona, 2003; Five New York Biker Chics, Out of Control, 2004; Suicide Gal, Won't You Come Out Tonight, Come Out Tonight, 2006; The Crown Prince of Perfect, 2007; For Some Reason Comma She Laughed, 2008; Love in the Time of Paris Hilton and Other Stories, 2009. **Address:** Department of English, Arizona State University, MC 0302, 1151 S Forest Ave., Tempe, AZ 85287, U.S.A. **Online address:** j.boyer@asu.edu

BOYER, Richard Lewis. *See* **BOYER, Rick.**

BOYER, Rick. (Richard Lewis Boyer). American (born United States), b. 1943. **Genres:** Mystery/Crime/Suspense, Anthropology/Ethnology, Travel/Exploration, Novels, Horror. **Career:** New Trier Township High School, English teacher, 1968-70; Little Brown and Co., text book representative, 1971-73, acquisitions editor, 1973-78; Places Rated Partnership, founding partner, 1978-; Western Carolina University, writer-in-residence, 1988-, assistant professor of English, 1988-, associate professor, professor. **Publications:** NOVELS: The Giant Rat of Sumatra, 1976; Billingsgate Shoal, 1982; The Penny Ferry, 1984; The Daisy Ducks, 1986; Moscow Metal, 1987; The Whale's Footprints, 1988; Gone to Earth, 1990; Yellow Bird, 1991; Pirate Trade, 1995; Runt, 1997; The Man Who Whispered, 1998; A Sherlockian Quartet, 1998; Mzungu Mjinga: Swahili for Crazy White Man, 2004; Buck Gentry, 2005; Take Back the Land, 2011. NONFICTION: (with D. Savageau) Places Rated Almanac: Your Guide to Finding the Best Places to Live in America, 1981; (with D. Savageau) Places Rated Retirement Guide: Finding the Best Places in America for Retirement Living, 1983; Yes, They're All Ours: Six of One, Half a Dozen of the Other, 1984; Retirement Places Rated: All You Need to Plan Your Retirement, 1987; Fun Projects for Hands on Character Building, 1996; Home Educating With Confidence, 1996; What About Socialization: Answering the Questions About Homeschooling And Social Interaction, 2001; Mzengu Mfinga: Swahili for Crazy White Man (memoir), 2004. Contributor to periodicals. **Address:** Department of English, Western Carolina University, 305 Coulter Bldg., Cullowhee, NC 28723, U.S.A. **Online address:** boyer@email.wcu.edu

BOYERS, Robert. American (born United States), b. 1942. **Genres:** Literary Criticism And History, Novellas/Short Stories, Essays. **Career:** Bernard Baruch College of the City University of New York, faculty, 1967-68; Sullivan County Community College, faculty, 1968-69; Skidmore College, assistant professor, 1969-73, associate professor, 1973-78, professor of English, 1979-, New York State Summer Writers Institute, founder and director, 1987, Tisch professor of arts and letters, editor-in-chief; Fordham University, Lincoln Center, Cultural Affairs Programs, co-chairman, 1971-72; Bennington Review, editor, 1977-83; Salmagundi Magazine, founder and editor-in-chief; Eugene Lang College, The New school for Liberal Arts, visiting senior lecturer in liberal studies. **Publications:** (Ed. with M. London) Robert Lowell: A Portrait of the Artist in His Time, 1970; (ed. with R. Orrill and comp.) R.D. Laing and Anti-Psychiatry, 1971; (ed.) The Legacy of the German Refugee Intellectuals, 1972; (ed.) Contemporary Poetry in America: Essays and Interviews, 1974; (ed. with R. Orrill) Psychological Man: Approaches to an Emergent Social Type, 1975; Excursions: Selected Literary Essays, 1977; Lionel Trilling: Negative Capability and the Wisdom of Avoidance, 1977; F.R. Leavis: Judgment and The Discipline of Thought, 1978; R.P. Blackmur, Poet-Critic: Toward a View of Poetic Objects, 1980; (ed. with P. Boyers) The Salmagundi Reader, 1983, rev. ed. as The New Salmagundi Reader, 1996; Atrocity and Amnesia: The Political Novel since 1945, 1985; After the Avant-Garde: Essays on Art and Culture, 1988; Book of Common Praise, 2002; Dictator's Dictation: The Politics of Novels and Novelists, 2005; Excitable Women, Damaged Men: Short Stories, 2005; A Friend of Dr. Reis (fiction), 2005; Impudence and Subversion: On Witold Gombrowicz, 2006; Populism & Politics in Salmagundi, 2006; (ed. and intro.) George Steiner at the New Yorker, 2009. CONTRIBUTOR: The Young American Writers, 1968; The Perverse Imagination, 1970; Modern American Poetry: Essays in Criticism, 1970; Profile of Robert Lowell, 1970; One Flew over the Cuckoo's Nest: A Casebook, 1973; (E. Kusturica and V.S. Turchin) Vojo Stanić: Sailing on Dreams, 2007. Contributor to periodicals. **Address:** Department of English, Skidmore College, 325 Palamountain, 815 N Broadway, Saratoga Springs, NY 12866-1632, U.S.A. **Online address:** rboyers@skidmore.edu

BOYES, Vivien (Elizabeth). British (born England), b. 1952. **Genres:** Children's Fiction, Writing/Journalism, History. **Career:** British Broadcasting Corp., radio studio manager, 1974-79, technical instructor, 1979-82; freelance writer, 1982-; St. John's Primary School, governor, 1989-98. Broadcast trainer and photographer. **Publications:** The Druid's Head, 1997; The Raven's Son, forthcoming. Contributor to periodicals. **Address:** London, GL , England. **Online address:** info@vivienboyes.co.uk

BOYETT, Jimmie T. American (born United States), b. 1948. **Genres:** Administration/Management, Business/Trade/Industry, Economics. **Career:** Management and systems analyst, 1976-80; Tarkenton Software, account executive, 1982-85; Bank South N.A., assistant vice president, 1985-90; Boyett & Associates, co-founder. Writer and consultant. **Publications:** WITH J.H. BOYETT: Beyond Workplace 2000: Essential Strategies for the New American Corporation, 1995; The Guru Guide: The Best Ideas of the Top Management Thinkers, 1998; Guru Guide to Entrepreneurship: A Concise Guide to the Best Ideas from the World's Top Entrepreneurs, 2001; Guru Guide to the Knowledge Economy: The Best Ideas for Operating Profitably in a Hyper-Competitive World, 2001; Guru Guide to Money Management: The Best Advice from Top Financial Thinkers on Managing your Money, 2003; Guru Guide To Marketing: A Concise Guide to the Best Ideas from Today's Top Marketers, 2003. **Address:** Boyett & Associates, 125 Stepping Stone Ln., Alpharetta, GA 30004-4009, U.S.A. **Online address:** jimmie@jboyett.com

BOYETT, Joseph H. American (born United States), b. 1945. **Genres:** Administration/Management, Business/Trade/Industry, Politics/Government, Economics, Industrial Relations. **Career:** U.S. Department of Education, Office for Civil Rights, deputy assistant secretary, principal advisor; Tarkenton, Conn & Co., director on consulting, vice-president, chief administrative officer, 1981-90; A.T. Kearney Inc., principal, 1990-92, Executive Issues Center of Excellence, co-founder; Boyett & Associates, co-founder and president, 1992-. Writer. **Publications:** Background Characteristics of Delegates to the 1972 Conventions: A Summary Report of Findings from a National Sample, 1973; (ed. with J.D. Weeks) Handbook for Georgia Mayors & Councilmen, 1974; (with H.P. Conn) Maximum Performance Management: How to Manage and Compensate People to Meet World Competition, 1988, 3rd ed., 1995; (with H.P. Conn) Workplace 2000: The Revolution Reshaping American Business, 1991; (with F. Tarkenton) The Competitive Edge: Essential Business Skills for Entrepreneurs, 1991; (co-author) The Quality Journey: How Winning the Baldrige Sparked the Remaking of IBM, 1993; (with J.T. Boyett) Beyond Workplace 2000: Essential Strategies for the New American Corporation, 1995; (with J.T. Boyett) The Guru Guide: The Best Ideas of the Top Management Thinkers, 1998; (with J.T. Boyett) Guru Guide to Entrepreneurship: A Concise Guide to the Best Ideas from the World's Top Entrepreneurs, 2001; (with J.T. Boyett) Guru Guide to the Knowledge Economy: The Best Ideas for Operating Profitably in a Hyper-Competitive World, 2001; (with J.T. Boyett) Guru Guide to Money Management: The Best Advice from Top Financial Thinkers on Managing Your Money, 2003; (with J.T. Boyett) Guru Guide to Marketing: A Concise Guide to the Best Ideas from Today's Top Marketers, 2003; The Gainsharing Design Manual, 2004; The Skill-Based Pay Design Manual, 2004; Won't Get Fooled Again: A Voter's Guide to Seeing through the Lies, Getting Past the Propaganda and Choosing the Best Leaders, 2008; Getting Things Done in Washington, forthcoming. **Address:** Boyett & Associates, 125 Stepping Stone Ln., Alpharetta, GA 30004-4009, U.S.A. **Online address:** joe@jboyett.com

BOYKIN, J. Robert. American (born United States), b. 1944. **Genres:** History. **Career:** Arts Council of Wilson, president, 1973-75; Friends of Wilson County Public Library, president, 1979-81; Boykin Antiques and Appraisals Inc., owner, 1980-; Wilson Historic Properties Commission, chair, 1984-86; Indiana University, instructor in appraisal, 1986-92; Wilson County Chamber of Commerce, director, 1997-99, vice president, 1999. Writer. **Publications:** (Comp.) Wilson County, North Carolina 1880 Census, 1984; (comp.) Marriages of Wilson County, North Carolina, 1855-1899, 1988; (comp.) Abstracts of Wills, Wilson County, North Carolina, 1855-1899, 1992; Historic Wilson: In Vintage Postcards, 2003. Contributor to journals. **Address:** Boykin Antiques and Appraisals Inc., 2013 US Hwy. 301 S, PO Box 7440, Wilson, NC 27893-6833, U.S.A. **Online address:** boykinappraisals@coastalnet.com

BOYKIN, Keith. American (born United States), b. 1965. **Genres:** Politics/Government, Race Relations, Law, Gay And Lesbian Issues, Social Sciences. **Career:** High school teacher, 1989; The White House, staff, 1993-95; public speaker, 1995-; American University, adjunct professor of government, 1999-

2000; BET J TV, host, 2006-08; BET News, contributor, 2008-09; CNBC, contributor, 2008-; The Daily Voice, editor, 2008-09. Broadcaster. **Publications:** One More River to Cross: Black and Gay in America, 1996; Respecting the Soul: Daily Reflections for Black Lesbians and Gays, 1999; Beyond The Down Low, 2005. Contributor to books and periodicals. **Address:** PO Box 1505, New York, NY 10027, U.S.A. **Online address:** kb@keithboykin.com

BOYLE, Brian. American (born United States), b. 1986?. **Genres:** Autobiography/Memoirs. **Career:** Writer. **Publications:** (With B. Katovsky) Iron Heart: The True Story of How I Came Back from the Dead (memoir), 2009. **Online address:** bjboyle@smcm.edu

BOYLE, David (Courtney). British (born England), b. 1958. **Genres:** Business/Trade/Industry, Economics, Politics/Government, Regional/Urban Planning, History, Money/Finance. **Career:** Oxford Star, arts editor, 1983-85; Town and Country Planning, editor, 1985-88; New Economics, editor, 1987-98, New Economics Foundation, associate, fellow, senior associate, 1998-; Community Network, editor, 1987-88; Rapide Productions, manager, 1988-92; New Democrat Intl., editor, 1989-91; Liberal Democrat News, editor, 1992-98; Radical Economics, editor; London Time Bank, founder; Time Banks UK, co-founder. **Publications:** Building Futures: A Layman's Guide to the Inner City Debate, 1989; (ed.) The New Economics of Information, 1989; What Is New Economics?, 1993; World War II: A Photographic History, 1998; Funny Money: In Search of Alternative Cash, 1999; Virtual Currencies, 1999; Why London Needs Its Own Currency, 2000; The Tyranny of Numbers: Why Counting Can't Make Us Happy, 2000; Renaissance Art: A Crash Course, 2001; Impressionist Art: A Crash Course, 2001; The Sum of Our Discontent, 2002; (ed.) The Money Changers: Currency Reform from Aristotle to E-Cash, 2002; Authenticity: Brands, Fakes, Spin and the Lust for Real Life, 2003; The Little Money Book, 2003; African Americans, 2003; News from Somewhere, 2003; The Communist Manifesto, 2004; The Sum of Our Discontent: One Two Three Four Five, How Numbers Make Us Irrational, 2004; (with S. Sandford) Side by Side: Young People in Divide Communities, a Guide for Donors and Grant Makers, 2004; (with A. Roddick) Numbers, 2004; Blondel's Song: The Capture, Imprisonment and Ransom of Richard the Lionheart, 2005; Power, Actually, 2007; Who's the Entrepreneur?, 2007; Toward the Setting Sun: Columbus, Cabot, Vespucci, and the Race for America, 2008; (with A. Simms) The New Economics: A Bigger Picture, 2009; Understanding the Communist Manifesto, 2010; (with A. Simms and N. Robins) Eminent Corporations: The Rise and Fall of the Great British Corporation, 2010; Voyages of Discovery, 2011; Human Element: Ten New Rules to Kickstart Our Failing Organizations, 2012. **Address:** New Economics Foundation, 3 Jonathan St., London, GL SE11 5NH, England. **Online address:** davidboyle1958@aol.com

BOYLE, Gerry. American (born United States), b. 1956. **Genres:** Novels. **Career:** Rumford Falls Times, reporter and editor, 1979; Central Maine Morning Sentinel, reporter and editor, 1981-87, columnist, 1987-99, managing editor, Colby College magazine, 1999-. **Publications:** NOVELS: Dead Line: A Jack McMorrow Mystery, 1993; Bloodline, 1995; Lifeline, 1996; Potshot, 1997; Borderline, 1998; Cover Story, 2000; Pretty Dead, 2003; Home Body, 2004; Port City Shakedown, 2008; Damaged Goods, 2010; Port City Black and White, 2011. **Address:** Helen Brann Agency, 94 Curtis Rd., Bridgewater, CT 06752, U.S.A. **Online address:** gerry@gerryboyle.com

BOYLE, Josephine. British (born England), b. 1935. **Genres:** Mystery/Crime/Suspense, Local History/Rural Topics, Novels, Adult Non-fiction, Literary Criticism And History, Young Adult Fiction, Horror. **Career:** Augener's Music Publisher, staff; British Broadcasting Corp., Music Library, staff, 1956-59, writer, 1984-. **Publications:** NOVELS: A Spectre in the Hall, 1984; Summer Music, 1986; Maiden's End, 1988; Knock, Knock, Who's There?, 1989; Holy Terror, 1993; The Spirit of the Family, 2000. NON-FICTION: Builders of Repute: The Story of Reader Bros., 2002. **Address:** c/o Anne Dewe, Andrew Mann Ltd., 1 Old Compton St., London, GL W1V 5PH, England.

BOYLE, Kevin. American (born United States), b. 1960. **Genres:** History, Politics/Government, Literary Criticism And History. **Career:** University of Toledo, assistant professor, 1990-94; University of Massachusetts, assistant professor, 1994-97, associate professor, 1997-, professor, through 2002, Graduate Program in History, director, 1999; Ohio State University, professor of history, 2002-, humanities distinguished professor; University College Dublin, chair in American history, Mary Ball Washington professor. Writer and historian. **Publications:** The UAW and the Heyday of American Liberalism, 1945-1968, 1995; (with V. Getis) Muddy Boots and Ragged Aprons: Images of Working-Class Detroit, 1900-1930, 1997; (ed.) Organized Labor and American Politics, 1894-1994: The Labor-Liberal Alliance, 1998; Arc of Justice: A Saga of Race, Civil Rights, and Murder in the Jazz Age, 2004. Contributor to periodicals. **Address:** Department of History, Ohio State University, 144 Dulles Hall, 230 W 17th Ave., Columbus, OH 43210, U.S.A. **Online address:** boyle.145@osu.edu

BOYLE, Nicholas. British (born England), b. 1946. **Genres:** Literary Criticism And History. **Career:** Cambridge University, Magdalene College, research fellow, 1968-, official fellow, 1972, reader, 1993-2000, lecturer in modern languages, professor of German literary and intellectual history, 2000-, Department of German and Dutch, Schröder professor, 2006-; Institute of Advanced Study, faculty, 1994-95. Writer. **Publications:** (Ed. with M. Swales) Realism in European Literature: Essays in Honor of J.P. Stern, 1986; Goethe, Faust, Part One, 1987; Goethe, the Poet and the Age, vol. I: The Poetry of Desire (1749-1790), 1991, vol. II: Revolution and Renunciation (1790-1803), 1999; Who are We Now? Christian Humanism and the Global Market from Hegel to Heaney, 1998; (ed. with J. Guthrie) Goethe and the English-Speaking World: Essays from the Cambridge Symposium for his 250th Anniversary, 2002; Sacred and Secular Scriptures: A Catholic Approach to Literature, 2005; German Literature: A Very Short Introduction, 2008; 2014: How to Survive the Next World Crisis, 2010. **Address:** Department of German and Dutch, Magdalene College, Cambridge University, Magdalene St., Cambridge, CB3 OAG, England. **Online address:** nb215@cam.ac.uk

BOYLE, Susan Silsby. American/Belgian (born Belgium), b. 1955. **Genres:** History, Biography. **Career:** AMIDEAST, program officer, 1980-81; U.S. Department of State, international visitor programs, and languages services, consultant, 1984-89; Institute of International Education, program officer and proposal writer, 1989-90; University of Maryland, lecturer, 1989; World Bank, consultant, 1990-; U.S. Government, consultant, 1990-; George Mason University, lecturer, 1990; Council on Public Relations, lecturer, 2001; Third World Studies Center, research fellow, 2004-. Writer. **Publications:** Betrayal of Palestine: The Story of George Antonius, 2001. **Address:** Westview Press, Perseus Books Group, 5500 Central Ave., Boulder, CO 80301-2877, U.S.A. **Online address:** nboyle@eastern.com.ph

BOYLE, Thomas A. American (born United States), b. 1922. **Genres:** Information Science/Computers, Sciences, Education. **Career:** Fenn College, laboratory instructor in physics, 1942-43; U.S. Naval Academy, instructor in marine engineering, 1945; Lafayette College, instructor in mechanical engineering, 1947-49; University of Michigan, instructor, assistant professor of mechanical engineering, 1949-56; Duke University, associate professor of mechanical engineering, 1956-67; J.G. Hoad and Associates, staff engineer, 1966-67; Purdue University, associate professor, professor of engineering, 1967-88, retired, 1988; Indiana University, faculty, 189-95; South Georgia College, faculty, 189-95; Francis Marion College, faculty, 189-95; Horry-Georgetown Technical College, faculty, 189-95; Coastal Carolina College, faculty, 189-95. Writer. **Publications:** Enough Fortran, 1974, 3rd ed., 1980; Fortran 77 PDQ, 1985, 2nd ed., 1989; Precursory Physical Science: The Science You Need Before Taking Science in School, 1997. **Address:** 226 Lander Dr., Conway, SC 29526, U.S.A. **Online address:** tboyle@sccoast.net

BOYLL, (James) Randall. American (born United States), b. 1962?. **Genres:** Novels, Science Fiction/Fantasy, Psychology, Horror, Mystery/Crime/Suspense. **Career:** Novelist. **Publications:** After Sundown, 1989; Mongster, 1990; Shocker: No More Mr. Nice Guy, 1990; Wes Craven's Shocker, 1990; Chiller, 1992; The Hangman, 1994; The Price of Fear, 1994; The Gods of Hell, 1994; In the Face of Death, 1995; Tales from the Crypt: Demon Knight, 1995; The Long Kiss Goodnight, 1996; Mission: Impossible, 1996; Katastrophe, 2000. Contributor to periodicals. **Address:** c/o Author Mail, HarperCollins Publishers, 10 E 53rd St., New York, NY 10022, U.S.A.

BOYM, Svetlana. Russian (born Russia), b. 1959. **Genres:** Novellas/Short Stories, Plays/Screenplays, Young Adult Fiction, Philosophy. **Career:** Harvard University, instructor in Slavic and comparative literature, 1984-88, assistant professor of comparative literature and of history and literature (Russian studies), 1988-93, John L. Loeb associate professor of humanities, 1993-, Curt Hugo Reisinger professor of Slavic languages and literatures, professor of comparative literature. Writer. **Publications:** Death in Quotation Marks: The Cultural Myths of the Modern Poet, 1991; Common Places: Mythologies of Everyday Life in Russia, 1994; (contrib.) Kosmos: A Portrait of the Russian Space Age, 2001; The Future of Nostalgia, 2001; Ninochka, 2003; (contrib.) Space is the Place, 2006; (contrib.) Territories of Terror: Mythologies and Memories of the Gulag in Contemporary Russian-American art, 2006; Architecture of the Off-Modern, 2008; Another Freedom: The Alternative History of an Idea, 2010; The Other Freedom: Between Aesthetics and Politics, forthcoming. Work represented in anthologies. Contributor to journals. **Address:** Department of Slavic Languages and Literatures, 311 Barker Ctr., 3rd Fl., Harvard University, 12 Quincy St., Cambridge, MA 02138, U.S.A. **Online address:** boym@fas.harvard.edu

BOYNE, Daniel J. American (born United States), b. 1959. **Genres:** Recreation, Biography. **Career:** Tufts University, coach; Harvard University, instructor, 1986-, director of recreational rowing. **Publications:** Essential Sculling, 2000; Red Rose Crew: A True Story of Women, Winning, and the Water, 2000; Kelly: A Father, A Son, An American Quest, 2007. Contributor to periodicals. **Address:** Department of Athletics, Faculty of Arts and Sciences, Harvard University, Murr Ctr., 65 N Harvard St., Allston, MA 02134, U.S.A. **Online address:** boyne@fas.harvard.edu

BOYNE, Walter J(ames). American (born United States), b. 1929. **Genres:** Novels, Air/Space Topics, Cultural/Ethnic Topics, Military/Defense/Arms Control, History, Adult Non-fiction, Young Adult Fiction. **Career:** Writer, 1962-; United States Air Force, officer, colonel, through 1974, retired, 1974; Smithsonian Institution, National Air and Space Museum, assistant curator, 1974-75, curator, 1975-78, executive officer, 1978-80, assistant director, 1980-82, acting director, 1981-83, director, 1983-86, chief of preservation and restoration, chief of exhibits and production, deputy director, retired, 1986; consultant, 1986-; Air & Space, founder. **Publications:** German Aircraft and Armament: Informational Intelligence, 1944; (ed. with D.S. Lopez) The Jet Age: Forty Years of Jet Aviation, 1979; Flying: An Introduction to Flight, Airplanes and Aviation Careers, 1980; Messerschmitt Me 262: An Arrow to the Future, 1980; Boeing B-52: A Documentary History, 1981; Aircraft Treasures of Silver Hill: The Behind-the-Scences Workshop of Our Nation's Air Museums, 1982; The McDonnell Douglas F-4 in Combat, 1983; De Havilland DH-4: From Flaming Coffin to Living Legend, 1984; Jet Combat History: Phantom, 1984; (ed. with D.S. Lopez) Vertical Flight: The Age of the Helicopter, 1984; Phantomin Combat, 1985; Phantom in Combat, 1985; The Leading Edge, 1986; (with S.L. Thompson) The Wild Blue: The Novel of the U.S. Air Force, 1986; The Smithsonian Book of Flight, 1987; Power behind the Wheel: Creativity and the Evolution of the Automobile, 1988; The Smithsonian Book of Flight for Young People, 1988; (co-ed.) Last Flight, 1988; Trophy for Eagles, 1989; Flight, 1990; (intro.) Weapons of Desert Storm, 1991; Gulf War: A Comprehensive Guide to People, Places and Weapons, 1991; Eagles at War, 1991; Art in Flight, 1991; Air Force Eagles, 1992; Silver Wings: A History of the USAF, 1993; Clash of Wings: Air Power in World War II, 1994; (ed.) The Army Times Book of Great Land Battles: From the Civil War to the Gulf War, 1994; Clash of Titans: World War II at Sea, 1995; (ed.) Fly Past, Fly Present: A Celebration of Preserved Aviation, 1995; (ed.) Encyclopedia of Modern U.S. Military Weapons, 1995; Classic Aircraft, 1996; Eagles at War: Demonology, 1996; (ed.) Clash of Chariots: The Great Tank Battles, 1996; (ed.) Generals in Muddy Boots: A Concise Encyclopedia of Combat Commanders, 1996; Beyond the Wild Blue: A History of the USAF, 1947-1997, 1997, 2nd ed. as Beyond the Wild Blue: A History of the United States Air Force, 1947-2007, 2007; (contrib.) Legends of Flight: With the National Aviation Hall of Fame, 1997; (ed.) The Navy Times Book of Submarines: A Political, Social and Military History, 1997; Beyond the Horizons: The Lockheed Story, 1998; B-2 Spirit: The Most Capable War Machine on the Planet, 1999; (ed. with P. Handleman) Brassey's Air Combat Reader, 1999; B-17 Flying Fortress: The Symbol of Second World War Air Power, 2000; Kua yue cang qiong: Meiguokong jun shi: 1947-1997, 2000; Pushing the Limits, 2000; Hitler's Squadron: The Fuehrer's Personal Aircraft and Transportation Unit, 1933-1945, 2001; (with J.C. Fredriksen) International Warbirds: An Illustrated Guide to World Military Aircraft, 1914-2000, 2001; Aces in Command: Fighter Pilots as Combat Leaders, 2001; The Best of Wings Magazine, 2001; Two O'Clock War: The 1973 Yom Kippur Conflict and the Airlift That Saved Israel, 2002 as The Yom Kippur War and the Airlift Strike That Saved Israel, 2003; The 451st Bomb Group in World War II: A Pictorial History, 2002; (with L.O. Nordeen) Air Warfare in the Missile Age, 2002; (ed.) Air Warfare: An International Encyclopedia, 2002; The Influence of Air Power Upon History, 2003; Dawn over Kitty Hawk: A Novel of the Wright Brothers, 2003; (with G.E. Weir) Rising Tide: The Untold Story of the Russian Submarines That Fought the Cold War, 2003; Operation Iraqi Freedom: What Went Right, What Went Wrong, and Why, 2003; Chronicle of Flight, 2003; (ed.) Today's Best Military Writing: The Finest Articles on the Past, Present, and Future of the U.S. Mlitary, 2004; Roaring Thunder: A Novel of the Jet Age, 2006; (foreword) Winged Crusade, 2006; Soaring to Glory: The United States Air Force Memorial, 2007; Supersonic Thunder: A Novel of the Jet Age, 2007; (foreword) AirCraft: The Jet as Art, 2007; Hypersonic Thunder: A Novel of the Jet Age, 2009; How the Helicopter Changed Modern Warfare, 2011. Contributor of articles to magazines. **Address:** 21028 Starflower Way, Ashburn, VA 20147-4700, U.S.A. **Online address:** wboyne@cqi.com

BOYNTON, Susan. American (born United States), b. 1966. **Genres:** History, Theology/Religion. **Career:** Brandeis University, teaching associate, 1994-96; University of Oregon, School of Music, assistant professor, 1996-2000; Columbia University, Department of Music, assistant professor of historical musicology, 2000-06, associate professor of historical musicology, 2006-. Writer and musicologist. **Publications:** (Ed. with I. Cochelin) From Dead of Night to End of Day: The Medieval Customs of Cluny, 2005; (ed. with R. Kok) Musical Childhoods & the Cultures of Youth, 2006; Shaping a Monastic Identity: Liturgy and History at the Imperial Abbey of Farfa, 1000-1125, 2006; (ed. with E. Rice) Young Choristers, 650-1700, 2008; Silent Music: Medieval Song and the Construction of History in Eighteenth-Century Spain, 2011; (ed. with D.J. Reilly) Practice of the Bible in the Middle Ages: Production, Reception, and Performance in Western Christianity, 2011. Contributor of articles to books and periodicals. **Address:** Department of Music, Columbia University, 607 Dodge Hall, 2960 Broadway, PO Box 1813, New York, NY 10027, U.S.A. **Online address:** slb184@columbia.edu

BOYSEN, Sally T. American (born United States), b. 1949?. **Genres:** Animals/Pets, Zoology. **Career:** Ohio State University, professor, Comparative Cognition Project, director. Writer. **Publications:** (With D. Custance) The Smartest Animals on the Planet: Extraordinary Tales of the Natural World's Cleverest Creatures, 2009. Contributor to books and periodicals. **Address:** 209 Psychology Bldg., 1835 Neil Ave. Mall, Columbus, OH 43210, U.S.A. **Online address:** boysen.1@osu.edu

BOYT, Susie. British (born England), b. 1969. **Genres:** Autobiography/Memoirs. **Career:** Writer and counselor. **Publications:** The Normal Man, 1995; The Characters of Love, 1996; The Last Hope of Girls, 2001; Only Human, 2004; My Judy Garland Life: A Memoir, 2009. **Address:** c/o Caroline Dawnay, United Agents, 12-26 Lexington St., London, GL W1F OLE, England. **Online address:** susie.boyt@ft.com

BOZAI, ágota. Hungarian (born Hungary), b. 1965?. **Genres:** Novels, Translations. **Career:** Writer and translator. **Publications:** NOVELS: Tranzit Glória, 1999; Irren is göttlich, 2001; Mi az ábra?, 2003. **Address:** c/o Author Mail, Counterpoint Press, 387 Park Ave. S, New York, NY 10016-8810, U.S.A. **Online address:** abozai@axelero.hu

BOZÓKI, András. Hungarian (born Hungary), b. 1959. **Genres:** Politics/Government, History, Law. **Career:** Eötvös University, assistant professor, 1983-93, associate professor, 1993-2005, professor, 2005-; Hungarian Academy of Sciences, research fellow, 1991-93; Nottingham University, visiting professor, 1993; Central European University, associate professor, 1993-; Smith College, visiting lecturer, 1999-2000; Hampshire College, visiting professor; Columbia University, visiting professor, 2004, 2009; Minister of Culture of Hungary, 2005-06; Bologna University, visiting professor, 2008. **Publications:** IN ENGLISH TRANSLATION: (ed. with J. Bak and M. Sukosd) Liberty and Socialism, 1991; (ed. with A. Korosenyi and G. Schopflin and contrib.) Post-Communist Transition: Emerging Pluralism in Hungary, 1992; (ed.) Zsolt Béla: A végzetes toll, 1992; (ed. and contrib.) Democratic Legitimacy in Post-Communist Societies, 1994; (ed. with B.K. Kiraly and contrib.) Lawful Revolution in Hungary, 1989 1994, 1994; (ed. and contrib.) Intellectuals and Politics in Central Europe, 1999; (ed. and contrib.) The Roundtable Talks of 1989: The Genesis of Hungarian Democracy, 2002; (ed. with J. Ishiyama and contrib.) The Communist Successor Parties of Central and Eastern Europe, 2002; (with B. Bosze) Migrants, Minorities, Belonging, and Citizenship: The Case of Hungary, 2004; (co-author) The Future of Democracy in Europe: Trends Analyses, and Reforms, 2004; Culture of Freedom: Cultural Policy for Hungary in the 21st Century, 2005. OTHERS: (ed.) A Szép Szó, 1936-39, 1987; (ed. with M. Sukosd and contrib.) Anarchizmus, 1991; (co-ed. and contrib.) Csendes? Forradalom? Volt?, 1991; (with G. Peli) Társadalomismeret, 1991, 2nd ed., 1995; (ed. and contrib.) A Fidesz a magyar politikában 1988-1991, 1992; (ed. with G. Nagy) Vannak-e emberi jogaik? Aszínesbörü diákok helyzete a fövárosban és askinhead-jelenség, 1992; (with A. Heller and F. Feher) Polgárosodás, civiltársadalom és demokrácia, 1993; (ed. with L. Seres, M. Sukosd and contrib.) Anarchizmus ma, 1994; (with M. Sukosd) Az anarchizmus elmélete ésmagyarországi története, 1994; Konfrontáció éskonszenzus: a demokratizálás stratégiái, 1995; Magyar panoptikum, 1996; (ed. and contrib.) Vissza az értelemhez, 1997, 2nd ed., 1998; (ed. with M. Sukosd) Magyar anarchizmus, 1998; (with I. Javorniczky and Istvan Stumpf) Magyar politikusi arcképscarnok, 1998; (ed.) Arendszerváltás forgatókönyve: kerekasztaltárgyálasok 1989-ben, vol. I-IV, 1999, (with M. Elbert) vol. VIII as Portrék éséletrajzok: A rendszerváltás forgatókönyve, 1999, (with M. Elbert and Zoltan Ripp) vol. V-VI, 2000, (ed. and contrib.) vol. VII as Alkotmányos forraldalom: Arendszerváltás forgatókönyve, 2000; Politikai pluralizmus Magyarországon, 1987-2002, 2003; Ignotus Pál, 2003; Ars Politica, 2007; (co-author) Anarcho-demokraták, 2007; (co-ed.) Az anarchizmus klasszikusai, 2009. **Address:** Department of Political Science, Central European University, 1051 Budapest, Nador, 9, Hungary. **Online address:** bozokia@ceu.hu

BRACE, Paul (R.). American (born United States), b. 1954. **Genres:** Politics/Government, Social Sciences. **Career:** Colorado State University, Department of Political Science, assistant professor, 1982-86; New York University, assistant professor of political science, 1986-90; State Politics and Policy Newsletter, editor, 1990-91; American Political Science Association, secretary-treasurer, 1990-91, president; University of Illinois, Institute of Government and Public Affairs, Department of Political Science, associate professor of political science, 1990-93; Florida State University, Department of Political Science, professor of political science, 1993-96; Southern Political Science Association, section organizer, 1995; Rice University, Baker Institute for Public Policy, research fellow, 1996-, Department of Political Science, Clarence L. Carter chair and professor, 1996-; Western Political Science Association, section organizer, 1998; Midwest Political Science Association, section organizer, 1998; American Political Science Association, section organizer, 2003; Western Political Science Association, section organizer, 2004. **Publications:** (Ed. with C.B. Harrington and G. King) The Presidency in American Politics, 1989; (with B. Hinckely) Follow the Leader, 1992; State Government and Economic Performance, 1993; (ed. with R.E. Weber) American State and Local Politics: Directions for the 21st Century, 1999; (co-ed.) Change and Continuity in American State and Local Government, 1999. **Address:** Department of Political Science, Baker Institute for Public Policy, Rice University, 208 Baker Hall, Houston, TX 77005-1892, U.S.A. **Online address:** pbrace@rice.edu

BRACEGIRDLE, Brian. British (born England), b. 1933. **Genres:** Archaeology/Antiquities, Biology, Photography, Sciences. **Career:** ICI, technician in research department, 1950-57; Erith Grammar School, biology master, 1958-61; Saint Katharine's College, senior lecturer in biology, 1961-64; College of All Saints, Department of Natural Science and Learning Resources, head, 1964-77; Institute of Medicine and Biological Illustration, secretary, chairman, 1971-75; Wellcome Museum of the History of Medicine, keeper, 1977-87; Science Museum, assistant director and head of collections management, 1987-89, research consultant in microscopy and fellow, 1990-; Institute of Medical and Biological Illustration, chairman. Writer. **Publications:** (With W.H. Freeman) An Atlas of Embryology, 1963; (with W.H. Freeman) An Atlas of Histology, 1966; Photography for Books and Reports, 1970; (with W.H. Freeman) An Atlas of Invertebrate Structure, 1971; (with P.H. Miles) An Atlas of Plant Structure, vol. I, 1971, vol. II, 1973; (with B. Bowers) The Archaeology of the Industrial Revolution, 1973; (with P.H. Miles) Thomas Telford, 1973; (with P.H. Miles) The Darbys and the Ironbridge Gorge, 1974; (with P.H. Miles) The Darbys and the Ironbridge Gorge, 1974; (with W.H. Freeman) An Advanced Atlas of Histology, 1976; (with P.H. Miles) An Atlas of Chordate Structure, 1978; The Evolution of Microtechnique, 1978; History of Micro Technique, 1978; (ed.) Beads of Glass: Leeuwenhoek and the Early Microscope, 1983; (ed.) Proceedings of the Second Symposium of the European Association of Museums of History of Medical Sciences: 10, 11, 12 September 1984, Wellcome Museum of the History of Medicine Science Museum, London, 1987; (ed.) Microscopal Papers from the Quekett, 1989; (with J.B. McCormick) The Microscopic Photographs of J.B. Dancer, 1993; (ed.) Cumulative Index to the Quekett Journals, 1994; Scientific PhotoMACROgraphy, 1995; (with S. Bradbury) Modern PhotoMICROgraphy, 1995; Notes on Modern Microscope Manufacturers, 1996; (with S. Bradbury) An Introduction to the Light Microscope, 1997; Microscopical Mounts and Mounters, 1998. Contributor to periodicals. **Address:** Cold Aston Lodge, Cheltenham, GC GL54 3BN, England.

BRACEWELL-MILNES, (John) Barry. British (born England), b. 1931. **Genres:** Economics, Business/Trade/Industry. **Career:** Iron and Steel Board, economist, 1960-63; Federation of British Industries, Confederation of British Industry, economist, 1964-65, assistant economic director, 1965-67, deputy economic director, 1967-68, economic director, 1968-73; Institute of Directors, economic adviser, 1973-96; Erasmus University, advisor, 1973-80; Institute of Economic Affairs, senior research fellow, 1989-; freelance writer and economic consultant. **Publications:** The Cost of Cutting Taxes, 1969; (with V. Tanzi and D.R. Myddelton) Taxation: A Radical Approach, A Reassessment of the High Level of British Taxation and the Scope for Its Reduction, 1970; The Measurement of Fiscal Policy: An Analysis of Tax Systems in Terms of the Political Distinction between 'Right' and 'Left', 1971; Saving and Switching, 1971; Pay and Price Control Guide, 1973; The Counter-Inflation Act, 1973, 1973; Is Capital Taxation Fair?: The Tradition and the Truth, 1974; Redistribution in Reverse: More Equal Shares of Wealth Mean Less Equal Shares of Spending, 1974; Eastern and Western Economic Integration, 1976 in UK as Economic Integration in East and West, 1976; The Camel's Back: An International Comparison of Tax Burdens, 1976; Industry for the People: Investment Financing through Partially Guaranteed Securities, 1976; (with J.C.L. Huiskamp) Investment Incentives: A Comparative Analysis of the Systems in the EEC, the USA and Sweden, 1977; Short Measure from Whitehall: How CSO Statistics Understate the British Tax Burden, 1977; (co-author) International Tax Avoidance, vol. I: General Report, 1978, vol. II: Country Reports, 1979; Tax Avoidance and Evasion: The Individual and Society, 1979; The Economics of International Tax Avoidance: Political Power versus Economic Law, 1980; The Taxation of Industry: Fiscal Barriers to the Creation of Wealth, 1981; Land and Heritage: The Public Interest in Personal Ownership, 1982; A Market in Corporation Tax Losses, 1983; Smoking and Personal Choice: The Problem of Tobacco Taxation, 1985; The Public Sector Borrowing Requirement: The Scope of Privatising Taxation, 1985; Are Equity Markets Short-Sighted?: Short-Termism and Its Critics, 1987; Caring for the Countryside: Public Dependence on Private Interests, 1987; Taxes on Spending: The Assault on Personal Responsibility, 1988; (with B. Sutherland) A Capital Offence, 1989; Capital Gains Tax: Reform through Abolition, 1989; A Tax on Trade: U.K. Tax Prejudice against Trading Abroad: The Problem of Surplus ACT and Its Solution, 1989; The Wealth of Giving: Every One in His Inheritance, 1989; An ACT Against Trade, 1992; False Economy, 1993; (with R. Carnaghan) Testing the Market, 1993; A Disorderly House, 1993; Will to Succeed, 1994; A House Divided, 1994; Captive Capital, 1995; A Pool of Resources, 1996; Capital Punishment, 1998; Is a Mast a Must?, 2001; (co-author) International Evidence on the Effects of Having No Capital Gains Taxes, 2001; Euthanasia for Death Duties, 2002. Contributor to books. **Address:** Institute of Economic Affairs, 2 Lord North St., Westminster, GL SW1P 3LB, England.

BRACEY, Christopher Alan. American (born United States), b. 1970. **Genres:** Politics/Government, International Relations/Current Affairs, History. **Career:** Washington University, School of Law, associate professor, 2001-08, associate professor of African and African American studies, 2005-08; George Washington University, School of Law, visiting associate professor, 2007, law faculty, 2008-; Northwestern University School of Law, visiting assistant professor, through 2008; United States District Court, Honorable Royce C. Lamberth, clerk; Jenner & Block, associate. Writer and attorney. **Publications:** Saviors or Sellouts: The Promise and Peril of Black Conservatism, from Booker T. Washington to Condoleezza Rice, 2008. Contributor to books. **Address:** Washington University School of Law, Anheuser-Busch Hall, Rm. 585, 1 Brookings Dr., St. Louis, MO 63130, U.S.A. **Online address:** bracey@wulaw.wustl.edu

BRACH, Tara. American (born United States), b. 1953. **Genres:** Animals/Pets, Psychology. **Career:** Meditation teacher, 1975-; psychotherapist, 1980-; clinical psychologist, 1994-; Insight Meditation Community of Washington, founder. **Publications:** Radical Acceptance: Embracing Your Life with the Heart of a Buddha, 2003. **Address:** Insight Meditation Community of Washington, PO Box 3, Cabin John, MD 20818, U.S.A. **Online address:** info@tarabrach.com

BRACK, Bruno. *See* **HUMPHRYS, Leslie George.**

BRACKEN, James K. American (born United States), b. 1952. **Genres:** Librarianship, Technology. **Career:** Knox College, reader services librarian, 1979-85; Purdue University, humanities bibliographer and assistant professor of library science, 1985-88; Ohio State University, head of second floor main library information services, 1988-2000, professor and assistant director for collections, instruction, and main library research and reference services, 2005-, Department of English, adjunct professor; Choice Magazine, reviewer-consultant; Kent State University Libraries, dean, 2010-. Writer. **Publications:** Reference Works in British and American Literature, vol. I: English and American Literature, 1990, vol. II: English and American Writers, 1991, 2nd ed., 1998; (with E.S. Block) Communication and the Mass Media: A Guide to the Reference Literature, 1991; (with C.H. Sterling) Telecommunications Research Resources: An Annotated Guide, 1995; (ed. with C.H. Sterling and S.M. Hill) Mass Communications Research Resources: An Annotated Guide, 1998; (with L.G. Hinman) Undergraduate's Companion to American Writers and Their Web Sites, 2001; (with K.A. Dean and M. Conteh-Morgan) Undergraduate's Companion to Women Writers and Their Web Sites, 2002. EDITOR: (with J. Silver): The British Literary Book Trade, 1700-1820, 1995; The British Literary Book Trade, 1475-1700, 1996. Works appear in anthologies. Contributor of articles and to journals. **Address:** University Libraries, Ohio State University, 1858 Neil Avenue Mall, 5820 Ackerman Library, Columbus, OH 43210-1286, U.S.A. **Online address:** bracken.1@osu.edu

BRACKEN, Len. American (born United States), b. 1961. **Genres:** Novels, History, Politics/Government, Biography, Literary Criticism And History, Social Sciences. **Career:** Bureau of National Affairs, Daily Report for Executives, copy editor, 2000-. Translator and writer. **Publications:** Freeplay, 1989, 2nd ed., 2007; The East Is Black, 1992, rev. ed., 2006; Secret City, 1994; The Neo-Cataline Conspiracy, 1996; Guy Debord: Revolutionary, 1997; (trans.) G. Sanguinetti, The Real Report on the Last Chance to Save Capitalism in Italy, 1997; The Arch Conspirator, 1999; (trans.) Paul Lafargue, The Right to Be Lazy, 1999; Shadow Government: 9-11 and State Terror, 2002; Snitch Jacket, 2006; (trans.) O. Khayyam, Persian Love, 2006. **Address:** PO Box 5585, Arlington, VA 22205, U.S.A. **Online address:** lenbracken@hotmail.com

BRACKENBURY, Alison. British (born England), b. 1953. **Genres:** Poetry. **Career:** Gloucestershire College of Arts and Technology, librarian, 1976-83; Polytechnics Central Admissions System, clerical assistant, 1985-89; Electro-plater, 1990-. Writer. **Publications:** Journey to a Cornish Wedding, 1977; Two Poems, 1979; Dreams of Power and Other Poems, 1981; Breaking Ground and Other Poems, 1984; Christmas Roses and Other Poems, 1988; Selected Poems, 1991; 1829, 1995; After Beethoven and Other Poems, 2000; The Story of Sigurd, 2003; Bricks and Ballads, 2004; Singing in the Dark, 2008; Shadow, 2009. **Address:** Carcanet Press, Alliance House, 30 Cross St., 4th Fl., Manchester, GM M2 7AQ, England.

BRACKETT, Peter. *See* **COLLINS, Max Allan.**

BRACKMAN, Barbara. American (born United States), b. 1945. **Genres:** Antiques/Furnishings, Crafts, Reference. **Career:** University of Kansas, educator in special education, 1970-85; University of Illinois, educator in special education, 1970-85. Museum curator and writer. **Publications:** (With M. Shirer) Creature Comforts: A Quilter's Animal Alphabet Book, 1986; Clues in the Calico: A Guide to Identifying and Dating Antique Quilts, 1989; Encyclopedia of Applique, 1993; (comp.) Encyclopedia of Pieced Quilt Patterns, 1993; (with M. Waldvogel) Patchwork Souvenirs of the 1933 World's Fair, 1993; (co-author) Kansas Quilts and Quilters, 1993; (with M. Waldvogel) Patchwork Souvenirs, 1993; Quilts From the Civil War, 1997; Kansas Trivia, 1997; Patterns of Progress: Quilts in the Machine Age, 1997; (ed. with C. Dwigans) Backyard Visionaries: Grassroots Art in the Midwest, 1999; Civil War Women: Their Quilts, Their Roles, Activities for Re-Enactors, 2000; Prairie Flower: A Year on the Plains, 2001; America's Printed Fabrics 1770-1890, 2004; Facts and Fabrications: Unraveling the history of Quilts and Slavery, 2006; Borderland in Butternut and Blue, 2007; The Lincoln Museum Quilt: A Reproduction for Abe's Frontier Family, 2008; Making History, 2008; Carrie Hall's Sampler, 2008; Juniper and Mistletoe, 2009; Barbara Brackman's Encyclopedia of Appliqué, 2009; Flora Botanica, 2009; Sew into Sports, 2010. **Address:** 3115 W 6th St., Ste. C-237, Lawrence, KS 66049, U.S.A. **Online address:** bbrackman@sunflower.com

BRAD. *See* **EPPS, Bradley S.**

BRADBURD, Rus. American (born United States), b. 1959?. **Genres:** Autobiography/Memoirs. **Career:** Von Steuben High School, head basketball coach, 1981-82; University of Texas El Paso, assistant basketball coach, 1983-91; New Mexico State University, assistant basketball coach, 1994-2000, assistant professor of English; Frosties Tigers, head coach, 2002; Taos Summer Writers Workshop, instructor. Writer. **Publications:** Paddy on the Hardwood: A Journey in Irish Hoops (memoir), 2006; Forty Minutes of Hell: The Extraordinary Life of Nolan Richardson, 2010. Contributor to periodicals. **Address:** Department of English, New Mexico State University, MSC 3E, PO Box 30001, Las Cruces, NM 88003, U.S.A. **Online address:** coachrus@hotmail.com

BRADBURY, Edward P. *See* **MOORCOCK, Michael (John).**

BRADBURY, J. C. American (born United States), b. 1973. **Genres:** Sports/Fitness, Recreation. **Career:** George Mason University, J.M. Buchanan Center, C.G. Koch and J.M. Buchanan research fellow, 1997-2000, Mercatus Center, Regulatory Studies Program, research associate, 1999-2000, instructor in economics, 1999-2000; North Georgia College and State University, assistant professor of business administration, 2000-01; Sewanee: The University of the South, visiting assistant professor of economics, 2001-03, assistant professor of economics, 2003-06, associate professor of economics, 2006; Kennesaw State University, Department of Health, Physical Education, and Sport Science, associate professor of health, physical education and sport science, 2006-10, professor and chair, 2010-, faculty advisor. Writer. **Publications:** The Baseball Economist: The Real Game Exposed, 2007; Hot Stove Economics: Understanding Baseball's Second Season, 2010. Contributor to books and periodicals. **Address:** Department of Health, Physical Education, and, Sport Science, Kennesaw State University, 3014 Convocation Ctr., MD 0202, 1000 Chastain Rd., Kennesaw, GA 30144-5591, U.S.A. **Online address:** jbradbu2@kennesaw.edu

BRADBURY, Jim. British (born England), b. 1937. **Genres:** History, Literary Criticism And History, Humanities. **Career:** Shoreditch Comprehensive School, school teacher, 1959-61; Manhood Secondary School, school teacher, 1961-69; West London Institute of Higher Education (now Borough Road College), history lecturer, 1969-89, part-time lecturer, 1989-93. Writer. **Publications:** Shakespeare and His Theatre (for children), 1975, 2nd ed., 1990; The Medieval Archer, 1985; Introduction to Buckinghamshire Domesday, 1986; Jig Fishing for Steelhead, Salmon, and Other Species, 1991; The Medieval Siege, 1992; Stephen and Matilda: The Civil War of 1139-53, 1996; Philip Augustus: King of France, 1180-1223, 1998; The Battle of Hastings, 1998; The Routledge Companion to Medieval Warfare, 2004; The Capetians: Kings of France, 987-1328, 2007; Robin Hood, 2010. Contributor of articles to books and journals. **Address:** St. Martin's Press, 175 5th Ave., New York, NY 10010, U.S.A. **Online address:** jim@bradbury21.fsnet.co.uk

BRADBURY, Ray (Douglas). American (born United States), b. 1920. **Genres:** Novels, Science Fiction/Fantasy, Children's Fiction, Plays/Screenplays, Poetry, Novellas/Short Stories. **Career:** Writer, 1943-. **Publications:** Dark Carnival, 1947, rev. ed. as The October Country, 1955; The Martian Chronicles, 1950; The Illustrated Man, 1951; Fahrenheit 451, 1953; The Golden Apples of the Sun, 1953; Switch on the Night, 1955; Dandelion Wine, 1957; Sun and Shadow, 1957; A Medicine for Melancholy in UK as The Day It Rained Forever, 1959; (intro.) The Mysterious Island, 1959; The Ghoul Keepers, 1961; In The Dead of Night: An Anthology Of Horror Stories, 1961; R is for Rocket, 1962; Something Wicked This Way Comes, 1962; The Anthem Sprinters and Other Antics (play), 1963; The Machineries of Joy: Short Stories, 1964; The Vintage Bradbury: Ray Bradbury's Own Selection of His Best Stories, 1965; The Wonderful Ice-Cream Suit (play), 1965; The Autumn People, 1965; The Silver Locusts, 1965; Tomorrow Midnight, 1966; The Pedestrian (play), 1966; S is for Space, 1966; Twice Twenty-Two: The Golden Apples of the Sun. A Medicine for Melancholy, 1966; I Sing the Body Electric! Stories, 1969; Bloch and Bradbury: Ten Masterpieces of Science Fiction, 1969, rev. ed. as Fever Dreams and Other Fantasies, 1970 as Whispers from Beyond, 1972; Christus Apollo, 1969; The Small Assassin, 1970; Old Ahab's Friend and Friend to Nosh, Speaks His Piece: A Celebration, 1971; The Halloween Tree, 1972; When Elephants Last in the Dooryard Bloomed: Celebrations For Almost Any Day In The Year, 1973; Zen and the Art of Writing And The Joy of Writing: Two Essays, 1973; Mars and the Mind of Man, 1973; That Son of Richard III, 1974; Pillar of Fire and Other Plays For Today, Tomorrow, and Beyond Tomorrow, 1975; Selected Stories, 1975; Ray Bradbury, 1975; That Ghost, That Bride of Time: Excerpts From A Play-In-Progress Based On The Moby Dick Mythology and Dedicated To Herman Melville, 1976; The Best of Bradbury, 1976; Long after Midnight (stories), 1976; Where Robot Mice and Robot Men Run Round in Robot Towns: New Poems, Both Light and Dark, 1977; The Bike Repairman, 1978; The Mummies of Guanajuato, 1978; Twin Hieroglyphs That Swim The River Dust, 1978; About Norman

Corwin, 1979; The Author Considers His Resources, 1979; The Aqueduct, 1979; Beyond 1984: Remembrance of Things Future, 1979; This Attic Where The Meadow Greens, 1979; The Last Circus & The Electrocution, 1980; The Stories of Ray Bradbury, 1980; The Ghosts of Forever, 1981; The Haunted Computer and the Android Pope: Poems, 1981; The Last Circus, 1981; The Complete Poems of Ray Bradbury, 1982; Fahrenheit 451, 1982; The Love Affair, 1983; Dinosaur Tales, 1983; A Memory of Murder, 1984; Forever and the Earth: Radio Dramatization, 1984; The Last Good Kiss: A Poem, 1984; Los Angeles, 1984; The Art of Playboy, 1985; Death Is a Lonely Business, 1985; Frost And Fire: A Story, 1985; Orange County, 1985; A Device Out Of Time, 1986; Death Has Lost Its Charm for Me, 1987; Fever Dream, 1987; The Other Foot, 1987; The Veldt, 1987; The April Witch, 1988; The Dragon, 1988; The Fog Horn, 1988; Ray Bradbury's Falling Upward, 1988; Ray Bradbury's To the Chicago Abyss, 1988; The Toynbee Convector: Stories, 1988; The Climate of Palettes, 1989; Urban Horrors: Stories, 1990; A Graveyard for Lunatics: Another Tale Of Two Cities, 1990; Zen In The Art Of Writing, 1990; Folon's Folons, 1990; The Bradbury Chronicles: Stories In Honor Of Ray Bradbury, 1991; Yestermorrow: Obvious Answers to Impossible Futures, 1991; The Smile, 1991; On Stage: A Chrestomathy Of His Plays, 1991; Green Shadows, White Whale: A Novel, 1992; Journey To Far Metaphor: Further Essays On Creativity, Writing, Literature and The Arts, 1994; Quicker than the Eye, 1996; With Cat for Comforter, 1997; Dogs Think that Every Day Is Christmas, 1997; Driving Blind, 1997; Ahmed and the Oblivion Machines: A Fable, 1998; Christus Apollo: Cantata Celebrating the Eighth Day of Creation and the Promise of the Ninth, 1998; (co-author) You Are Here: The Jerde Partnership International, 1999; A Chapbook For Burnt-Out Priests, Rabbis And Ministers, 2001; From the Dust Returned: A Family Remembrance, 2001; Ray Bradbury Collected Short Stories, 2001; I Live By The Invisible: New & Selected Poems, 2002, new ed., 2008; One More for the Road: A New Story Collection, 2002; Let's All Kill Constance: A Novel, 2003; Bradbury Stories: 100 Of His Most Celebrated Tales, 2003; The Cat's Pajamas: Stories, 2004; It Came From Outer Space, 2004; Conversations with Ray Bradbury, 2004; Bradbury Speaks: Too Soon from the Cave, Too Far from the Stars, 2005; (contrib.) Kong Unbound: The Cultural Impact, Pop Mythos and Scientific Plausibility Of a Cinematic Legend, 2005; A Sound of Thunder and Other Stories, 2005; The Homecoming, 2006; The Best of Ray Bradbury: The Graphic Novel, 2006; Farewell Summer, 2006; Match to Flame: The Fictional Paths to Fahrenheit 451, 2006; Futuria Fantasia, 2007; Now and Forever, 2007; We'll Always Have Paris: Stories, 2009; (intro.) Ray Bradbury's Fahrenheit 451: The Authorized Adaptation, 2009; (foreword) Comic-con: 40 Years of Artists, Writers, Fans & Friends, 2009; Bullet Trick, 2009; Marionettes, Inc., 2009; Summer Morning, Summer Night, 2010; (with S. Weller) Listen to the Echoes, 2010; A Pleasure to Burn, 2010; (intro.) Ray Bradbury's The Martian Chronicles, 2011; (intro.) Ray Bradbury's Something Wicked this Way Comes, 2011. EDITOR: Timeless Stories for Today and Tomorrow, 1952; The Circus of Dr. Lao: And Other Improbable Stories, 1956; A Day in the Life of Hollywood, 1992. Contributor to journals. **Address:** William Morrow, 10 E 53rd St., New York, NY 10022, U.S.A. **Online address:** raybradbury@harpercollins.com

BRADBY, Rachel. *See* **ANDERSON, Rachel.**

BRADEN, Donna R. American (born United States), b. 1953. **Genres:** Social Commentary, History, Art/Art History, Food And Wine, Humanities. **Career:** Henry Ford Museum and Greenfield Village (The Henry Ford), curator in historical resources unit and developer, 1977-; Domestic Technology, lecturer; National Endowment for the Humanities, exhibition project director, proposal writer, proposal reviewer, content expert, exhibition, program developer, consultant. Writer. **Publications:** Leisure and Entertainment in America, 1988; (intro.) Eagle Tavern Cookbook, 1988; (with J. Endelman) Americans on Vacation, 1990; (ed. with G.W. Overhiser and contrib.) Old Collections New Audiences: Decorative Arts and Visitor Experience for the 21st Century, 2000; (with K.A. Marling) Behind the Magic: 50 Years of Disneyland, 2005. Contributor to books and periodicals. **Address:** Henry Ford Museum and Greenfield Village, 20900 Oakwood Blvd., PO Box 1148, Dearborn, MI 48124-5029, U.S.A. **Online address:** donnab@thehenryford.org

BRADEN, Nate. American (born United States), b. 1968. **Genres:** History, Military/Defense/Arms Control. **Career:** America and the World Inc., founder, owner, chief executive officer, 2002. Writer. **Publications:** (With G.D. Young) The Last Sentry: The True Story That Inspired the Hunt for Red October, 2005. **Address:** America and the World Inc., 518 17th St., Ste. 1390, Denver, CO 80202, U.S.A. **Online address:** nbraden@americaandtheworld.com

BRADFIELD, Scott (Michael). American (born United States), b. 1955. **Genres:** Novellas/Short Stories, Novels. **Career:** University of Connecticut, Department of English, assistant professor, professor, 1989-96; University of California, assistant professor of English, 1989-94; Kingston University, reader in creative writing. Writer. **Publications:** NOVELS: The History of Luminous Motion, 1989; What's Wrong with America?, 1994; Animal Planet, 1995; The Anti-Santa, 2002; Good Girl Wants It Bad, 2004. COLLECTIONS: Greetings from Earth, 1985; The Secret Life of Houses, 1997; Hot Animal Love: Tales of Modern Romance, 2005. NON FICTION: Dreaming Revolution: Transgression in the Development of American Romance, 1993. SHORT STORIES: The Dream of the Wolf, 1984; Unmistakably the Finest, 1984; The Darling, 1988; Didn't She Know, 1991; The Parakeet and the Cat, 1993; Animals Behind Bars!, 1994; Penguins for Lunch, 1995; The Queen of the Apocalypse, 1996; Goldilocks Tells All, 2000. OTHERS: The People Who Watched Her Pass By, 2010. Contributor to periodicals. **Address:** c/o A. D. Peters, The Chambers, Chelsea Harbor, Lots Rd., London, GL SW10 OXF, England. **Online address:** s.bradfield@kingston.ac.uk

BRADFORD, Barbara Taylor. American/British (born England), b. 1933. **Genres:** Novels, How-to Books, Young Adult Non-fiction, Young Adult Fiction, Literary Criticism And History. **Career:** Yorkshire Evening Post, reporter, 1949-51, women's page editor, 1951-53; Woman's Own, fashion editor, 1953-54; London Evening News, columnist, 1955-57; The London American, executive editor, 1959-62; Today Magazine, columnist, 1962-63; National Design Center, editor-in-chief, 1965-69; Newsday, syndicated columnist, 1966-70; Chicago Tribune-New York News Syndicate, columnist, 1970-75; Los Angeles Times Syndicate, columnist, 1975-81; March of Dimes, ambassador, 1999. **Publications:** NOVELS: Children's Stories of the Bible from the Old Testament, 1966; Children's Stories of Jesus from the New Testament, 1966; A Garland of Children's Verse, 1968; Voice of the Heart, 1983; Act of Will, 1986; The Women in His Life, 1990; Remember, 1991; Angel, 1993; Everything to Gain, 1994; Dangerous to Know, 1995; Love in Another Town, 1995; Her Own Rules, 1996; A Secret Affair, 1996; Power of a Woman, 1997; A Sudden Change of Heart, 1999; Where You Belong, 2000; The Triumph of Katie Byrne, 2001; Barbara Taylor Bradford's Living Romantically Every Day, 2002; Three Weeks in Paris, 2002; Playing the Game, 2010; Letter from a Stranger, 2011; Secrets from the Past, 2012. EDITOR: The Dictionary of 1001 Famous People, 1966. OTHERS: Easy Steps to Successful Decorating, 1971; How to Solve Your Decorating Problems, 1976; Decorating Ideas for Casual Living, 1977; Making Space Grow, 1979; Luxury Designs for Apartment Living, 1981. EMMA HARTE SERIES: A Woman of Substance, 1979; Hold the Dream, 1985; To Be the Best, 1988; Emma's Secret, 2003; Unexpected Blessings, 2005; Just Rewards, 2005; Breaking the Rules, 2009. HOUSE OF DERAVENEL SERIES: The Ravenscar Dynasty, 2006; Heirs of Ravenscar in US as The Heir, 2007; Being Elizabeth, 2008. Contributor to periodicals. **Address:** St. Martin's Press, 175 5th Ave., New York, NY 10010, U.S.A. **Online address:** btbweb@barbarataylorbradford.com

BRADFORD, Chris. British (born England), b. 1974?. **Genres:** Novels. **Career:** Writer, martial artist and musician. **Publications:** YOUNG SAMURAI NOVEL SERIES: The Way of the Warrior, 2008; The Way of the Sword, 2009; The Way of the Dragon, 2010; The Ring of Earth, 2010. OTHERS: Heart and Soul: Revealing the Craft of Songwriting, 2005; Record Deals Outloud, 2006; Artist Management Outloud, 2006; Music Publishing Outloud, 2006; Virtual Kombat, 2010. **Address:** Viney Agency, 23 Erlanger Rd., Telegraph Hill, London, GL SE14 5TF, England. **Online address:** fanmail@youngsamurai.com

BRADFORD, Karleen. Canadian (born Canada), b. 1936. **Genres:** Children's Fiction, Young Adult Fiction, Children's Non-fiction, Young Adult Non-fiction. **Career:** T. Eaton Co., advertising copywriter, 1959; Canadian Government, foreign service officer; teacher of creative writing; Writers in Electronic Residence (WIER), writer-in-residence; writer, 1963-. **Publications:** FICTION FOR YOUNG ADULTS: The Nine Days Queen, 1986; Windward Island, 1989; There Will Be Wolves, 1992; Thirteenth Child, 1994; Shadows on a Sword, 1996; Dragonfire, 1997; Lionheart's Scribe, 1999; Whisperings of Magic, 2001; Angeline, 2004; Ghost Wolf, 2005; The Nine Days Queen, 2005; The Scarlet Cross, 2006; Dragonmaster, 2009. FOR CHILDREN: A Year for Growing, 1977 as Wrong Again, Robbie, 1983; The Other Elizabeth, 1982; I Wish There Were Unicorns, 1983; The Stone in the Meadow, 1984; The Haunting at Cliff House, 1985; Write Now!, 1988, rev. ed., 1996; Animal Heroes, 1995, rev. ed., 2000; More Animal Heroes, 1996; A Different Kind of Champion, 1998; With Nothing but Our Courage, 2002;

(with L.E. Watts) You Can't Rush a Cat, 2003; A Desperate Road to Freedom: The Underground Railroad Diary of Julia May Jackson, 2009. Contributor to magazines. **Address:** Writers Union of Canada, 40 Wellington St. E, 3rd Fl., Toronto, ON M5E 1C7, Canada. **Online address:** karleenbradford@bell.net

BRADFORD, Sarah (Mary Malet). British (born England), b. 1938. **Genres:** Food And Wine, History, Biography, Art/Art History. **Career:** Christie's, manuscript expert, 1974-80; Sotheby's, manuscript consultant, 1980-82; Times Literary Supplement, book and manuscript consultant, 1982-85. Writer. **Publications:** The Englishman's Wine, 1969 in UK as The Story of Port, 1978; Portugal and Madeira: A Guide and Gazetteer: Where to Stay, What to See, What to Eat, What to Buy, 1969; Portugal, 1973; Cesare Borgia, His Life and Times, 1976; The Borgias, 1981; Disraeli, 1982; Princess Grace, 1984; King George VI in US as The Reluctant King: The Life & Reign of George VI, 1895-1952, 1989; Splendours and Miseries: A Life of Sacheverell Sitwell in UK as Sacheverell Sitwell: Splendours and Miseries, 1993; Harriet Tubman, the Moses of Her People, 1993; (co-author) The Sitwells and the Arts of the 1920s and 1930s, 1996; Elizabeth: A Biography of Britain's Queen, 1996; Elizabeth: A Biography of Her Majesty the Queen, 1996; America's Queen: The Life of Jacqueline Kennedy Onassis, 2000; George VI, 2002; Lucrezia Borgia: Life, Love and Death in Renaissance Italy, 2004; Diana, 2006; Queen Elizabeth II: Her Life in Our Times, 2011. Contributor to periodicals. **Address:** Gillon Aitken Associates Ltd., 29 Fernshaw Rd., London, GL SW10 0TG, England.

BRADING, D. A. British (born England), b. 1936. **Genres:** Area Studies, Cultural/Ethnic Topics, History, Theology/Religion. **Career:** University of California, assistant professor, 1965-71; Yale University, associate professor, 1971-73; Cambridge University, lecturer in history, 1973-92, reader in Latin American history, 1991-98, professor of Mexican history, 1999-2003, emeritus professor of Mexican history, Centre of Latin American Studies, director, 1975-90; University of Lima, honorary professor, 1993. Writer. **Publications:** Miners and Merchants in Bourbon Mexico, 1763-1810, 1971; Orígenes del nacionalismo mexicano, 1973; Haciendas and Ranchos in Mexican Bajío, Léon, 1700-1860, 1978; (ed.) Caudillo and Peasant in the Mexican Revolution, 1980; Classical Republicanism and Creole Patriotism: Simon Bolivar (1783-1830) and the Spanish American Revolution, 1983; Myth and Prophecy in Mexican History, 1984; The Origins of Mexican Nationalism, 1985; First America: The Spanish Monarchy, Creole Patriots and the Liberal State, 1492-1867, 1991; (trans. and ed.) Generals and Diplomats: Great Britain and Peru, 1820-40, 1991; Church and State in Bourbon Mexico: The Diocese of Michoacán, 1749-1810, 1994; Ocaso Novohispano: Testimonios Documentales, 1996; Marmoreal Olympus: José Enrique Rodó and Spanish American Nationalism, 1998; Cinco miradas británicas a la historia de México, 2000; Mexican Phoenix: Our Lady of Guadalupe: Image and Tradition across Five Centuries, 2001; Octavio Paz y la poética de la historia mexicana, 2002; (intro.) Letter to the Spanish Americans: A Facsimile of the Second English Edition (London, 1810), 2002; (intro.) Nueve sermones guadalupanos (1661-1758), 2005; El Gran Michoacán en 1791: Sociedad e Ingreso Eclesiástico en una diócesis Novohispana, 2009. Contributor to periodicals. **Address:** History Faculty Building, Cambridge University, West Rd., Cambridge, CB3 9AL, England.

BRADLEE, Benjamin (Crowninshield). American (born United States), b. 1921. **Genres:** International Relations/Current Affairs, Autobiography/Memoirs, Biography. **Career:** New Hampshire Sunday News, reporter, 1946-48; Washington Post, reporter, 1948-51, managing editor, 1965-68, executive editor, 1968-91, vice president at large; U.S. Foreign Service, press attache, 1951-53; Newsweek, European bureau chief, 1953-57, reporter, 1957, Washington bureau chief, 1957-65. **Publications:** That Special Grace, 1964; Conversations with Kennedy, 1975; The Theodore H. White Lecture, 1991; A Good Life: Newspapering and Other Adventures, 1995; Reflections on Lying: A Lecture, 1997; A Life's Work: Fathers and Sons, 2010. **Address:** Washington Post, 1150 15th St. NW, Washington, DC 20071-0001, U.S.A.

BRADLEY, Alan. Canadian (born Canada), b. 1938. **Genres:** Literary Criticism And History, Novels, Autobiography/Memoirs, Mystery/Crime/Suspense. **Career:** Ryerson Polytechnical Institute (now Ryerson University), staff; University of Saskatchewan, director of television engineering in media centre, teacher of scriptwriting and television production courses, 1969-94. Writer. **Publications:** (With W.A.S. Sarjeant) Ms. Holmes of Baker Street: The Truth about Sherlock (literary criticism), 2nd ed., 2004; The Shoebox Bible (memoir), 2006; The Sweetness at the Bottom of the Pie (mystery), 2009; A Red Herring Without Mustard (novel), 2011; I Am Half-Sick of Shadows (novel), 2011. Contributor to periodicals. **Address:** The Bukowski Agency Ltd., 14 Prince Arthur Ave., Suite 202, Toronto, ON M5R 1A9, Canada. **Online address:** info@flaviadeluce.com

BRADLEY, Blythe. *See* **WAGNER, Sharon Blythe.**

BRADLEY, David (Henry). American (born United States), b. 1950. **Genres:** Novels, Novellas/Short Stories, Plays/Screenplays, Adult Non-fiction, History, Intellectual History, Autobiography/Memoirs, Essays, Essays. **Career:** Lippincott Publishers, reader and assistant editor, 1974-76; Temple University, assistant professor, 1977-82, associate professor, 1982-89, professor of English, 1989-96; University of Pennsylvania, visiting lecturer, 1975; Colgate University, visiting professor, 1988; Massachusetts Institute of Technology, visiting professor, 1989; University of Oregon, visiting professor, 2000, Creative Writing Program, associate professor of fiction, 2003-; University of Texas, visiting professor, 2000; Austin Peay University, visiting professor, 2001. **Publications:** South Street, 1975; The Chaneysville Incident, 1981; Sweet Sixteen, 1983; The Lodestar Project, 1986; (ed. with S.F. Fishkin) Encyclopedia of Civil Rights in America, 1998; (ed. and intro. with S.F. Fishkin) Sport of the Gods: And Other Essential Writings, 2005; The Bondage Hypothesis: Meditations on Race and History, forthcoming. Contributor of articles to magazines and newspapers. **Address:** Creative Writing Program, University of Oregon, 208 Alder Bldg., 818 E 15th Ave., 5243 University of Oregon, Eugene, OR 97401, U.S.A. **Online address:** dbradley@uoregon.edu

BRADLEY, Ernestine. American/German (born Germany), b. 1935?. **Genres:** Humanities. **Career:** Spelman College, teacher; State University New York, teacher; Yale University, visiting professor; Columbia University, visiting professor; Montclair State College, visiting professor of liberal studies, now professor emeritus of German and comparative literature; New York University, New School for Social Research, part-time faculty, visiting associate professor of humanities. Writer. **Publications:** Die Philosophie Hermann Brochs and Hermann Broch, 1971; Hermann Broch, 1978; (co-ed.) Legacies and Ambiguities: Postwar Fiction and Culture in West Germany and Japan, 1991; The Language of Silence: West German Literature and the Holocaust, 1999; The Way Home: A German Childhood, an American Life, 2005. **Address:** New School University, 6 E 16th St., New York, NY 10003, U.S.A. **Online address:** misslbeck@comcast.net

BRADLEY, John Ed(mund). American (born United States), b. 1958. **Genres:** Novels, Novellas/Short Stories, Sports/Fitness, Young Adult Fiction. **Career:** Washington Post, staff writer, 1983-87, contributing writer, 1988-89; Esquire, contributing writer, 1991-; Sports Illustrated, contributing writer, 1993-. **Publications:** NOVELS: Tupelo Nights, 1988; The Best There Ever Was, 1990; Love & Obits, 1992; Smoke, 1994; My Juliet, 2000; Restoration: A Novel, 2003; It Never Rains in Tiger Stadium, 2007. **Address:** c/o Esther Newberg, International Creative Management, 730 5th Ave., New York, NY 10019, U.S.A.

BRADLEY, John Lewis. British (born England), b. 1917. **Genres:** Literary Criticism And History, Autobiography/Memoirs. **Career:** Wellesley College, instructor, 1948-51; University of Maryland, instructor, 1952-53, professor, 1976-77, 1978-82, professor emeritus, 1982-; Clark University, assistant professor of English, 1953-55; Mount Holyoke College, assistant professor, 1955-58, associate professor of English, 1958-64; Smith College, visiting lecturer, 1962-63; Ohio State University, visiting associate professor, 1963-64, professor of English, 1964-65; University of South Carolina, Graduate Division, professor, 1965-69; University of Durham, professor, 1969-78, professor emeritus, 1978-. Writer. **Publications:** An Introduction to Ruskin, 1971; A Shelley Chronology, 1993; A Ruskin Chronology, 1997. EDITOR: Ruskin's Letters from Venice, 1851-1852, 1955; Letters of John Ruskin to Lord and Lady Mount-Temple, 1964; (and intro.) Selections From London Labour and the London Poor, 1965; (and intro.) Rogue's Progress: The Autobiography of Lord Chief Baron Nicholson, 1965; Unto This Last, and Traffic, 1967; (with M. Stevens) Masterworks of English Prose, 1968; Ruskin, The Critical Heritage, 1984; Lady Curzon's India, 1986; (with I. Ousby) The Correspondence of John Ruskin and Charles Eliot Norton, 1987. Contributor of articles to journals. **Address:** University of Durham, Elvet Hill Rd., Durham, DU DH1 3LR, England.

BRADLEY, Michael R. (Michael Raymond Bradley). American (born United States), b. 1940. **Genres:** Theology/Religion, Civil Liberties/Human Rights, Military/Defense/Arms Control, History. **Career:** Motlow State Community College, professor of history. Writer and historian. **Publications:** On the Job: Safeguarding Workers' Rights, 1992; Old Times There Are Not Forgotten: A Family Saga of the Civil War, 1992; A Country Christmas: Holiday Stories about Times Gone By, 1993; Early on a Frosty Morn: Stories of the Great Depression, 1995; Tullahoma: The 1863 Campaign for the Control of Middle Tennessee, 2000; It Happened in the Civil War, 2002; It Happened in the Revolutionary War, 2003; With Blood and Fire: Life behind Union Lines in Middle Tennessee, 1863-65, 2003; It Happened in the Great Smokies, 2004; Nathan Bedford Forrest's Escort and Staff, 2006. **Address:** Department of Social Sciences, Motlow State Community College, Rm. 210, PO Box 8500, Lynchburg, TN 37352-8500, U.S.A.

BRADLEY, Michael Raymond. *See* **BRADLEY, Michael R.**

BRADLEY, Patricia. American/British (born England), b. 1941?. **Genres:** History, Art/Art History, Social Sciences. **Career:** KMJ-TV, anchor and reporter; Temple University, School of Communications and Theater, Department of Journalism, chair, professor, now professor emeritus of journalism, College of Arts and Sciences, American Studies Program, director, 1994-98. **Publications:** Slavery, Propaganda, and the American Revolution, 1998; Mass Media and the Shaping of American Feminism, 1963-1975, 2003; Women and the Press: The Struggle for Equality, 2005; Making American Culture: A Social History, 1900-1920, 2009. **Address:** School of Communications and Theater, Department of Journalism, Temple University, Rm. 316, 011-00 Annenberg Hall, 2020 N 13th St., Philadelphia, PA 19122, U.S.A. **Online address:** patricia.bradley@temple.edu

BRADLEY, Richard. British (born England), b. 1946. **Genres:** Art/Art History, Young Adult Non-fiction, Adult Non-fiction. **Career:** University of Reading, assistant lecturer, professor of archaeology, 1971-. Writer. **Publications:** NONFICTION: (with A. Ellison, J. Barrett and J. Evans) Rams Hill: A Bronze Age Defended Enclosure and Its Landscape, 1975; The Prehistoric Settlement of Britain, 1978; (ed. with J. Barrett) Settlement and Society in the British Later Bronze Age, 2 vols., 1980; (ed. with J. Gardiner) Neolithic Studies: A Review of Some Current Research, 1984; The Social Foundations of Prehistoric Britain: Themes and Variations in the Archaeology of Power, 1984; The Passage of Arms: An Archaeological Analysis of Prehistoric Hoards and Votive Deposits, 1990, 2nd ed., 1998; (co-author) Landscape, Monuments, and Society: The Prehistory of Cranborne Chase, 1991; Altering the Earth: The Origins of Monuments in Britain and Continental Europe: The Rhind Lectures, 1991-1992, 1993; (with M. Edmonds) Interpreting the Axe Trade: Production and Exchange in Neolithic Britain, 1993; Rock Art and the Prehistory of Atlantic Europe: Signing the Land, 1997; The Significance of Monuments: On the Shaping of Human Experience in Neolithic and Bronze Age Europe, 1998; An Archaeology of Natural Places, 2000; (co-author) The Good Stones: A New Investigation of the Clava Cairns, 2000; The Past in Prehistoric Societies, 2002; (co-author) The Moon and the Bonfire: An Investigation of Three Stone Circles in Northeast Scotland, 2005; Ritual and Domestic Life in Prehistoric Europe, 2005; The Prehistory of Britain and Ireland, 2007; Image and Audience: Rethinking Prehistoric Art, 2009. Contributor to journals. **Address:** Department of Archaeology, University of Reading, Whiteknights, PO Box 226, Reading, BR RG6 6AB, England. **Online address:** r.j.bradley@reading.ac.uk

BRADLEY, Shelley. (Shayla Black). American (born United States), b. 1968. **Genres:** Romance/Historical, Young Adult Fiction, Novels. **Career:** Writer. **Publications:** HISTORICAL ROMANCES: The Lady and the Dragon, 1999; Sweet Enemy, 1999; One Wicked Night, 2000; His Stolen Bride, 2000; His Lady Bride, 2000; His Rebel Bride, 2001; A Christmas Promise, 2001; Strictly Seduction, 2002; Strictly Forbidden, 2002; Strictly Wanton, 2003. CONTEMPORARY: Bound and Determined, 2006; (as Shayla Black) Strip Search, 2006; Naughty Little Secret, 2006; Watch Me, 2007; A Perfect Match, 2009; A Dangerous Little Secret, 2010. FORTHCOMING: Undercover Stranger; Naughty Business. **Address:** PO Box 270126, Flower Mound, TX 75027, U.S.A. **Online address:** shelley@shelleybradley.com

BRADMAN, Tony. British (born England), b. 1954. **Genres:** Children's Fiction, Novels, Young Adult Non-fiction, Picture/Board Books. **Career:** Music Week Magazine, chief sub-editor, 1978; Parents Magazine, music writer, children's book reviewer and deputy editor, 1979-87; writer, 1987-. **Publications:** FOR CHILDREN: A Kiss on the Nose (poetry), 1984; The Bad Babies' Counting Book, 1985; John Lennon, 1985; One Nil, 1985; Let's Pretend, 1985; The Bad Babies' Book of Colors, 1986; See You Later, Alligator, 1986; At the Park, 1986; Hide and Seek, 1986; Play Time, 1986; Through My Window, 1986; The Lonely Little Mole (based on a story by P. Alen), 1986; Night-Time, 1986; Will You Read Me a Story?, 1986; Baby's Best Book, 1987; The Baby's Bumper Book, 1987; The Bad Babies' Book of Months, 1987; Smile, Please!, 1987; I Need a Book!, 1987; The Little Cake Maker and the Greedy Magician (based on a story by Alen), 1987; Look Out, He's Behind You!, 1988; Wait and See, 1988; Not Like That, Like This!, 1988; Bedtime, 1988; The Cuddle, 1988; Our Cat, 1988; All Together Now! (poetry), 1989; Who's Afraid of the Big Bad Wolf?, 1989; Bub, 1989; Gary and the Magic Cat, 1989, rev. ed. as The Magic Cat, 1992; Tracey's Wish, 1989; The Sandal: A Story, 1989; This Little Baby, 1990; Michael, 1990; Let's Go, Ben, 1990; Gerbil Crazy, 1990; Miranda the Magnificent, 1990; In a Minute, 1990; Five Minutes More!, 1991; Morning, 1991; That's Not a Fish!, 1991; Tommy Niner and the Planet of Danger, 1991; Billy and the Baby, 1992; It Came from Outer Space, 1992; Has Anyone Seen Jack?, 1992; Frankie Makes a Friend, 1992; My Family, 1992; My Little Baby Brother, 1992; That's Not My Cat!, 1992; Wally's New Face, 1992; Winnie's New Broom, 1992; A Bad Week for the Three Bears, 1993; The Invaders, 1993; Tommy Niner and the Mystery Spaceship, 1994; Night, Night, Ben!, 1994; Two Minute Puppy Tales, 1994; Teddy Bear Tales, 1994; Wow! I'm a Whale, 1996; Help! I'm a Hamster, 1996; The Magnificent Mummies, 1997; Here Come the Heebie-Jeebies, 2000; Midnight in Memphis, 2002; Daddy's Lullaby, 2002; Bad Boys, 2003; Orchard Book of Swords, Sorcerors & Superheroes, 2003; Final Cut, 2004; This is the Register, 2004; The Talent Contest, 2004; Home Sweet Home, 2004; Arthur and the King's Sword, 2004; (with N. Fisk) Two Tales from the Future, 2005; The Surprise Party, 2005; Robin Hood and the Silver Arrow, 2005; Three Terrifying Tales of Terror!, 2005; The Big Race, 2005; Flora the Fairy, 2005; The Mummy Family Find Fame, 2006; Tom's Dragon Trouble, 2007; Elvis the Squirrel, 2007; Tommy Niner and the Moon of Doom, 2007; Under Pressure, 2009; Flora the Fairy's Magic Spells, 2009; Red Riding Hood takes Charge, 2009; Betrayal, 2009; Young Merlin, 2009; Richard III, 2009; Merlin and the Ring of Power, 2010; (with T. Ross) The Orchard Book of Swords, Sorcerers and Superheroes, 2010; Football Fever, 2010; The Perfect Baby, 2010; Doomsday, 2010; Sleeping Nasty, 2010; Julius Caesar, 2011; Wait and See, 2011; Don't Bother Ben!, 2011; In a Minute, 2011. SPACE SCHOOL SERIES WITH T. BRADMAN: Blast Off, 2011; Bug Wars, 2011; Crash Course, 2011; Ice Breaker, 2011; Dilly and the Birthday Treat, 2011. GREATEST ADVENTURES IN THE WORLD SERIES WITH T. ROSS: Beowulf the Hero, 2010; Robinson Crusoe, Shipwrecked!, 2010; David and Goliath, 2011; Gulliver in Lilliput, 2011. NOVELS: Spooky Teachers, 2005; Assassin, 2007. HAPPY EVER AFTER SERIES: Jack's Bean Snacks, 2006; Rapunzel Cuts Loose, 2006; The Wicked Stepmother Helps Out, 2010; The Three Little Pigs Go Camping, 2010; Mr. Giant and the Beastly Baron, 2011; Snow White and the Magic Mirror, 2011; The Ugly Duckling Returns, 2011. AFTER HAPPILY EVER AFTER SERIES: Mr. Wolf Bounces Back, 2006; Cinderella and the Mean Queen, 2009; The Fairy Godmother takes a Break, 2009; The Frog Prince Hops to It, 2009; Goldilocks and the Just Right Club, 2009; Jack and the Bean Snacks, 2009; Rapunzel lets Her Hair Down, 2009; Mr. Bear Gets Alarmed, 2011. RETELLER: The Ugly Duckling, 1990; The Gingerbread Man, 1991; Goldilocks and the Three Bears, 1991; The Little Red Hen, 1991. DILLY THE DINOSAUR SERIES: Dilly the Dinosaur, 1985; Dilly Visits the Dentist in US as Dilly Goes to the Dentist, 1986; Dilly Tells the Truth, 1986; Dilly and the Horror Film in US as Dilly and the Horror Movie, 1987; Dilly's Muddy Day, 1987; Dilly and the Tiger, 1988; Dilly, 1988; Dilly and the Ghost, 1989; Dilly Dinosaur, Superstar, 1989; Dilly Speaks Up, 1990; Dilly Goes on Holiday, 1990; Dilly the Angel, 1990; Dilly and His Swamp Lizard, 1991; Dilly and the Big Kids, 1991; Dilly's Birthday Party, 1991; Dilly Goes to School, 1992; Dilly and the Pirates, 1993; Dilly-The Worst Day Ever, 1993; Dilly Goes Swamp Wallowing, 1994; Dilly's Day Out, 1994; Dilly Dinosaur, Detective, 1994; Dilly and the Goody Goody, 1996; Dilly and the Vampire, 1996; Dilly Party Kit, 1997; Dilly At the Funfair, 1999; Dilly Gets Muddy!, 1999; Dilly Saves the Day, 1999; Dilly and the School Report, 2001; Dilly's Bumper Book of Stories, 2008. DAISY TALES: Daisy and the Babysitter, 1986; Daisy and the Crying Baby, 1986; Daisy and the Washing Machine, 1986; Daisy Feels Ill, 1988; Daisy Goes to Playgroup, 1988; Daisy Goes Swimming, 1989. THE BLUEBEARDS SERIES: Adventure on Skull Island, 1988; Mystery at Musket Bay, 1989; Contest at Cutlass Cove, 1990; Search for the Saucy Sally, 1990; Peril at the Pirate School, 1990; Revenge at Ryan's Reef, 1991. SAM, THE GIRL DETECTIVE SERIES: Sam, the Girl Detective, 1989. EDITOR: The Magic Kiss, 1987; Animals Like Us, 1987; The Mad Family, 1987; The Best of Friends, 1988; What a Wonderful Day, 1988; Things That Go, 1989; You're Late, Dad, 1989; That Spells Magic, 1989; The

Parents' Book of Bedtime Stories, 1990; Love Them, Hate Them, 1991; Our Side of the Playground, 1991; Hissing Steam and Whistles Blowing, 1991; Good Sports!, 1992; A Stack of Story Poems, 1992; Amazing Adventure Stories, 1994; Fantastic Space Stories, 1994; The Kingfisher Treasury of Pirate Stories, 1999; My Dad's a Punk: 12 Stories About Boys and Their Fathers, 2006. OTHERS: The Essential Father, 1985; So You Want to Have a Baby?, 1985; Reading for Enjoyment, 0-6, 6th ed., 1989; The Cash Box Caper, 1990; The Case of the Missing Mummy, 1990; The Secret of the Seventh Candle, 1992; The Great Rock 'n' Roll Ransom, 1994; (with C. Scruton) A Goodnight Kind of Feeling, 1998. Contributor to periodicals. **Address:** c/o Pat White, Rogers, Coleridge & White Ltd., 20 Powis Mews, London, GL W11 1JN, England. **Online address:** tbradman@ntlworld.com

BRADSHAW, Anne. American/British (born England), b. 1942. **Genres:** Novels, Young Adult Fiction, Genealogy/Heraldry, Adult Non-fiction, How-to Books. **Career:** Writer. **Publications:** NOVELS: Terracotta Summer, 2000; Chamomile Winter, 2002. OTHERS: LDS Storymakers: Publishing Secrets, 2004; (comp.) Famous Family Nights, 2009; Please, No Zits & Other Short Stories for LDS Youth, 2010; Dingo, 2010; True Miracles with Genealogy, vol. I, 2011, vol. II, 2012. Contributor to magazines. **Address:** 255 East 1300 North, Mapleton, UT 84664, U.S.A. **Online address:** xtrafam@yahoo.com

BRADSHAW, Michael. British (born England), b. 1935. **Genres:** Geography, Earth Sciences, Regional/Urban Planning, Natural History. **Career:** Teacher of geography and geology, 1959-68; The University College of St. Mark and St. John, teacher of geography and geology and department head, 1968-93, Department of Geography, chair, dean of humanities course, retired, 1993. Writer. **Publications:** AS MICHAEL J. BRADSHAW: (with E.A. Jarman) Reading Geological Maps: Geological Map Exercises, 1969; Earth, The Living Planet, 1977; (with A.J. Abbott and A.P. Gelsthorpe) Earth's Changing Surface, 1978. OTHERS: A New Geology, 1968, 2nd ed., 1973; Earth: Past, Present and Future, 1981; (with P. Guinness) North America: A Human Geography, 1985; Regions and Regionalism in the United States, 1988; Industrial Change: New England and Appalachia, 1988; The Appalachian Regional Commission: Twenty-Five Years of Government Policy, 1992; (with R. Weaver) Physical Geography: An Introduction to Earth Environments, 1993; (with R. Weaver) Foundations of Physical Geography, 1995; A World Regional Geography: The New Global Order, 1997, 3rd ed., 2002; (with G.W. White and J.P. Dymond) Contemporary World Regional Geography: Global Connections, Local Voices, 2004, (co-author) 4th ed., 2012; (co-author) Essentials of World Regional Geography, 2007, 2nd ed., 2011. **Address:** 57 Frensham Ave., Glenholt, Plymouth, DN PL6 7JN, England.

BRADSHAW, Timothy. British (born England), b. 1950. **Genres:** Theology/Religion. **Career:** Church of England, curate, 1976-79; University of Cambridge, Trinity College, lecturer, 1979-90; Oxford University, Regent's Park College, senior tutor, 1990-, dean, university research lecturer in theology, admissions tutor and tutorial fellow in Christian doctrine. Writer. **Publications:** Purity and Orthodoxy, 1984; The Olive Branch, 1992; Trinity and Ontology, 1992; (ed.) The Way Forward?: Christian Voices on Homosexuality and the Church, 1997, 2nd ed., 2003; (ed.) Grace and Truth in the Secular Age, 1998; Praying as Believing, 1998; Pannenberg: A Guide for the Perplexed, 2009; Chaos or Control: Change and Authority in the Church and Society, 2010. **Address:** Regent's Park College, Oxford University, Pusey St., Oxford, OX OX1 2LB, England. **Online address:** timothy.bradshaw@theology.ox.ac.uk

BRADY, Catherine. American (born United States), b. 1955?. **Genres:** Novellas/Short Stories, Sciences. **Career:** University of San Francisco, professor of creative writing. Writer. **Publications:** The End of the Class War, 1999; Curled in the Bed of Love: Stories, 2003; Elizabeth Blackburn and the Story of Telomeres: Deciphering the Ends of DNA, 2007; The Mechanics of Falling and Other Stories, 2009; Story Logic and the Craft of Fiction, 2010. **Address:** Master of Fine Arts in Writing Program, University of San Francisco, 302 Kalmanovitz Hall, 2130 Fulton St., San Francisco, CA 94117-1080, U.S.A. **Online address:** bradyc@usfca.edu

BRADY, Joan. British/American (born United States), b. 1939. **Genres:** Novels, Young Adult Non-fiction, Mystery/Crime/Suspense. **Career:** Dancer, 1955-58, 1960. Writer. **Publications:** The Imposter, 1979; The Unmaking of a Dancer, 1982 in UK as Prologue: an Unconventional Life, 1994; Theory of War, 1992; Death Comes for Peter Pan, 1996; God on a Harley, 1995; Heaven in High Gear, 1997; I Don't Need a Baby To Be Who I Am, 1998; The ?Emigré, 1999; Joyride, 2003; Bleedout, 2005; Venom, 2010; The Ghost of Mt. Soledad, 2010; Thirst, 2012. **Address:** 59a Marlborough Rd., Oxford, OX OX1 4LW, England. **Online address:** joanbradybooks@aol.com

BRADY, John (Mary). Canadian/Irish (born Ireland), b. 1955. **Genres:** Novels, Mystery/Crime/Suspense. **Career:** Bank of Ireland, bank official, 1972-75; Royal Canadian Mounted Police, Northwest Territories, police officer, 1975-76; St. Patrick's School, teacher, 1988-. Writer. **Publications:** A Stone of the Heart (mystery novel), 1988; Unholy Ground (mystery novel), 1989; Kaddish in Dublin, 1990; All Souls, 1993; The Good Life, 1994; A Carra King, 2001; Wonderland, 2003; Islandbridge: A Matt Minogue Mystery, 2005; Poacher's Road, 2006; The Going Rate, 2008; A Long Hard Look, 2009; The Coast Road: A Matt Minogue Mystery, 2010; A Rebel Hand, forth coming. Contributor to periodicals. **Address:** St. Patrick, 51 W Ave. SS1, Schomberg, ON L0G 1T0, Canada.

BRADY, Kimberley S(mith). American (born United States), b. 1953. **Genres:** Adult Non-fiction, Children's Fiction. **Career:** Tempe Unified School District, elementary school teacher, 1977-81; Clovis Unified School District, substitute teacher, 1996-, now retired. Writer. **Publications:** Keeper for the Sea, 1996. **Address:** 55 Antrim Rd., Hancock, NH 03449, U.S.A. **Online address:** ksbrady@aol.com

BRADY, Patricia. Also writes as Patricia Mary Brady, Patricia Brady Schmit. American (born United States), b. 1943. **Genres:** Anthropology/Ethnology, Cultural/Ethnic Topics, Biography. **Career:** Louisiana Historical Association, president; New Orleans/Gulf South Booksellers Association, president; Dillard University, instructor, 1969-73, assistant professor of history, 1973-80; Historic New Orleans Collection, editor, 1980-82, founder, director of publications department, 1982-2002; DivaBooks Publication Consulting, president, 2001-. **Publications:** Martha Washington: An American Life, 2005; A Being So Gentle: The Frontier Love Story of Rachel and Andrew Jackson, 2011. EDITOR (as Patricia Brady Schmit and intro.): Nelly Custis Lewis's Housekeeping Book, 1982; Encyclopaedia of New Orleans Artists, 1718-1918, 1987; George Washington's Beautiful Nelly: The Letters of Eleanor Parke Custis Lewis to Elizabeth Bordley Gibson, 1794-1851, 1991; (co-ed.) Complementary Visions of Louisiana Art, 1996; (with J.H. Lawrence) Haunter of Ruins: The Photography of Clarence John Laughlin, 1997; (co-ed.) Queen of the South: New Orleans, 1853-1862, 1999; Arts and Entertainment in Louisiana, 2006; (contrib.) In Search of Julien Hudson: Free Artist of Color in Pre-Civil War New Orleans, 2011. Contributor of articles to journals and newspapers. **Address:** c/o Author Mail, Viking Publicity, 375 Hudson St., New York, NY 10014, U.S.A. **Online address:** historianpatriciabrady@gmail.com

BRADY, Patricia Mary. *See* **BRADY, Patricia.**

BRADY, Rachel. American (born United States), b. 1975?. **Genres:** Literary Criticism And History. **Career:** Lyndon B. Johnson Space Center, engineer. Writer. **Publications:** Final Approach, 2009; Dead Lift, 2010. Contributor to periodicals. **Address:** c/o Victoria Skurnick, Levine Greenberg Literary Agency Inc., 307 7th Ave., Ste. 2407, New York, NY 10001, U.S.A. **Online address:** rachel@rachelbrady.net

BRADY, Rose. American (born United States), b. 1956?. **Genres:** Economics, Social Sciences. **Career:** Hartford Courant, staff reporter; Business Week, staff editor, 1986-89, Moscow bureau chief, 1989-93, European and Latin American editions, editor, 1995-2000, senior writer; Alliance of American and Russian Women Inc., director, 2000-01. **Publications:** Kapitalizm: Russia's Struggle to Free Its Economy, 1999. Contributor to periodicals. **Address:** Business Week, 1221 Ave. of the Americas, 43rd Fl., New York, NY 10020-1001, U.S.A.

BRADY, Taylor. *See* **BALL, Donna Rochelle.**

BRADY, William S. *See* **HARVEY, John.**

BRAFFET, Kelly. American/British (born England), b. 1976?. **Genres:** Novels, Mystery/Crime/Suspense, Young Adult Fiction. **Career:** Sackett Street Writing Workshop, instructor. Writer. **Publications:** Josie and Jack in UK as Fabulous Things: A Slightly Twisted Love Story, 2005; Last Seen Leaving, 2006. **Address:** Adult Editorial Department Trade Division, Houghton Mifflin Co., 222 Berkeley St., 8th Fl., Boston, MA 02116-3764, U.S.A.

BRAFMAN, Ori. American/Israeli (born Israel) **Genres:** Business/Trade/Industry, Advertising/Public Relations, Sports/Fitness. **Career:** Courtroom Connect, co-founder. Writer. **Publications:** (With R.A. Beckstrom) The Starfish and the Spider: The Unstoppable Power of Leaderless Organizations, 2006; (with R. Brafman) Sway: The Irresistible Pull of Irrational Behavior, 2008; (with R. Brafman) Click: The Magic of Instant Connections, 2010. **Address:** Esther Newberg, International Creative Management, 730 5th Ave., New York, NY 10019-7416, U.S.A. **Online address:** ori@oribrafman.com

BRAGA, Newton C. Brazilian (born Brazil), b. 1946. **Genres:** Information Science/Computers, Sciences. **Career:** Electronics in Focus, technical director and columnist, 1967-74; Instituto Monitor, consultant, 1969-, professor, 1972; Canadian Broadcasting Corp., correspondent, 1970-72; Escola Paulista de Medicina, Bionic researcher, 1970; SWL Magazine, correspondent, 1970; Guarulhos University, professor of college advancement, 1971-76, professor of ethics, 1976-81; Know magazine, columnist, 1976-98; State of Sao Paulo, Writers Union, secretary, 1986-87; Computer Guarulhos, columnist, 1995-96; Colegio Mater Amabilis, instructor in mechatronics, 1999-; Editoria Saber Ltd., technical director; Community Technical School, consultant; Mechatronics Teaching and Technology, professor, 2000-; McGraw Hill, technical writer. **Publications:** Fun Projects for the Experimenter, 1998; CMOS Projects and Experiments: Fun with the 4093 Integrated Circuit, 1999; Sourcebook for Electronics Calculations, Formulas, and Tables, 1999; Electronics for the Electrician, 2000; Electronics Projects from the Next Dimension: Paranormal Experiments for Hobbyists, 2001; CMOS Sourcebook, 2001; Pirate Radio and Video: Experimental Transmitter Projects, 2001; Robotics, Mechatronics, and Artificial Intelligence: Experimental Circuit Blocks for Designers, 2002; Mechatronics Sourcebook, 2003; Mechatronics for the Evil Genius, 2006; Bionics for the Evil Genius: 25 Build-It-Yourself Projects, 2006. UNTRANSLATED WORKS: Eletronica Para Eletricistas, 2001; Instalacoes Eletricas Domiciliares, 2003; Curso de Eletronica Digital, 2003. Contributor to periodicals. **Address:** Rua Vera 247, Guarulhos, Sao Paulo, 07096, Brazil. **Online address:** newtoncbraga@sili.com.br

BRAGDON, Kathleen J. American (born United States) **Genres:** Anthropology/Ethnology, History. **Career:** College of William and Mary, Department of Anthropology, associate professor, professor. Writer. **Publications:** (With I. Goddard) Native Writings in Massachusetts, 1988; Native People of Southern New England, 1500-1650, 1996; Columbia Guide to American Indians of the Northeast, 2001; Native People of Southern New England, 1650-1775, 2009. Contributor to journals. **Address:** Department of Anthropology, College of William and Mary, 118 Washington Hall, PO Box 8795, Williamsburg, VA 23187-8795, U.S.A. **Online address:** bkbrag@wm.edu

BRAGG, Melvyn. British (born England), b. 1939. **Genres:** Novels, Plays/Screenplays, Biography, Songs/Lyrics And Libretti. **Career:** British Broadcasting Corp., producer, 1961-67, 1974-77, presenter of Second House series, 1973-77, presenter and editor of Read All About It series, 1976-77; BBC2, editor New Release program, 1964-, The Darwin Debate, chair, 1999; ITV, London Weekend Television, presenter and editor of South Bank Show, 1978-, head of arts, 1982-90, controller of arts, 1992-, presenter of Two Thousand Years series; Cumbrians for Peace, president, 1982-90; Northern Arts, president, 1983-87; Border Television, deputy chairperson, 1985-90, chairperson, 1990-; National Campaign for the Arts, president, 1986-; Radio 4, writer and presenter of Start the Week, 1988-98, presenter of Giants' Shoulders, 1999; WETA-TV, staff, 1990; London School of Economics, governor, 1997-; University of Leeds, chancellor, 1999-; LWT Productions, director and controller of arts; In Our Time series, writer and presenter. Writer. **Publications:** NOVELS: For Want of a Nail, 1965; The Second Inheritance, 1966, rev. ed., 1989; Without a City Wall, 1968; The Hired Man, 1969; A Place in England, 1969; The Nerve, 1971; Josh Lawton: A Novel, 1972; The Hunt, 1972; The Silken Net, 1974; Speak for England: An Essay on England, 1900-1975: Based on Interviews with Inhabitants of Wigton, Cumberland, 1976, rev. ed. as Autumn Manoeuvres, 1978; Kingdom Come, 1980; Love and Glory, 1983; The Cumbrian Trilogy (includes The Hired Man, A Place in England and Kingdom Come), 1984; The Maid of Buttermere, 1987; A Time to Dance: A Novel, 1990; Crystal Rooms, 1992; The Seventh Seal: Det sjunde inseglet, 1993; Credo, 1996; The Sword and the Miracle: A Novel, 1996; The Soldier's Return: A Novel, 1999; A Son of War, 2001; Crossing the Lines: A Novel, 2003; Remember Me, 2008. OTHER: (and intro.) John Peel: The Man, the Myth and the Song: A Book to Celebrate his Bi-Centenary, 1976; Mardi Gras (play), 1976; A Christmas Child, 1976; (ed.) My Favorite Stories of Lakeland, 1981; Land of the Lakes, 1983, 2nd ed., 1990; Laurence Olivier (biography), 1984; (ed.) Cumbria in Verse, 1984; (with H. Goodall) The Hired Man: A Musical, 1986; Rich: The Life of Richard Burton, 1988 in US as Richard Burton: A Life, 1988; (intro.) Enid J. Wilson's Country Diary, 1989; (with R. Gardiner) On Giants Shoulders: Great Scientists and Their Discoveries: From Archimedes to DNA, 1998; (contrib.) Vision: 50 Years of British Creativity, 1999; The Adventure of English: The Biography of a Language, 2004; Twelve Books that Changed the World, 2006; In Our Time, 2009; The Book of Books: The Radical Impact of the King James Bible, 1611-2011, 2011. **Address:** University of Leeds, Leeds, WY LS2 9JT, England.

BRAGG, Steven M. American (born United States), b. 1960. **Genres:** Business/Trade/Industry, Administration/Management, Economics, Money/Finance. **Career:** Teague Equipment Co., controller; Isolation Technologies, chief operating officer; Ernst & Young, consulting manager; Deloitte & Touche, auditor. Accountant and writer. **Publications:** (With J.D. Willson and J.M. Roehl-Anderson) Controllership: The Work of the Managerial Accountant, 1995, 8th ed. 2009; (with J.M. Roehl-Anderson) The Controller's Function: The Work of the Managerial Accountant, 1996, 4th ed., 2011; Just-in-Time Accounting: How to Decrease Costs and Increase Efficiency, 1996, 3rd ed. 2009; Advanced Accounting Systems, 1997; Outsourcing: A Guide To Selecting the Correct Business Unit, Negotiating the Contract, Maintaining Control of the Process, 1998, 2nd ed. 2006; Accounting Best Practices, 1999, 6th ed. 2010; Managing Explosive Corporate Growth, 1999; Financial Analysis: A Controller's Guide, 2000; Just-in-time Accounting: How to Decrease Costs and Increase Efficiency, 2001; Cost Accounting: A Comprehensive Guide, 2001; (with E.J. Burton) Accounting and Finance for Your Small Business, 2001, 2nd ed. 2006; (with E.J. Burton) Sales and Operations for your Small Business, 2001; Business Ratios and Formulas: A Comprehensive Guide, 2002, 3rd ed., 2012; Accounting Reference Desktop, 2002; (with H.L. Brown) Design and Maintenance of Accounting Manuals: A Blueprint for Running an Effective and Efficient Department, 2003; Essentials of Payroll: Management and Accounting, 2003; New CFO Financial Leadership Manual, 2003, 3rd ed. 2011; Controllership, the Work of the Managerial Accountant, 2004, 8th ed., 2009; GAAP Implementation Guide, 2004; Inventory Best Practices, 2004, 2nd ed., 2011; Run the Rockies: Classic Trail Runs in Colorado's Front Range, 2004; Controller's Guide to Planning and Controlling Operations, 2004; Accounting for Payroll: A Comprehensive Guide, 2004; Billing and Collections: Best Practices, 2005; Controller's Guide: Roles and Responsibilities for the First Years, 2005; Ultimate Accountants' Reference: Including GAAP, IRS & SEC Regulations, Leases, and More, 2005, 2nd ed. 2006; Controller's Guide to Costing, 2005; Payroll Best Practices, 2005; Fast Close: A Guide to Closing the Books Quickly, 2005, 2nd ed., 2009; Inventory Accounting: A Comprehensive Guide, 2005; Throughput Accounting: A Guide to Constraint Management, 2007; Revenue Recognition, 2007; Management Accounting Best Practices: A Guide for the Professional Accountant, 2007; Willey GAAP Policies and Procedures, 2007; Financial Analysis: A Controller's Guide, 2007; Accounting Policies and Procedures Manual: A Blueprint for Running an Effective and Efficient Department, 2007; Mergers & Acquisitions: A Condensed Practitioner's Guide, 2009; Accounting Control Best Practices, 2009; (with B.J. Epstein and R. Nach) Wiley Wiley GAAP 2010: Interpretation and Application of Generally Accepted Accounting Principles, 2009; Running a Public Company: From IPO to SEC Reporting, 2009; Cost Reduction Analysis: Tools and Strategies, 2010; Treasury Management: The Practitioner's Guide, 2010; Running an Effective Investor Relations Department: A Comprehensive Guide, 2010; The Vest Pocket Controller, 2010; The Vest Pocket Guide to IFRS, 2010; Wiley Revenue Recognition: Rules and Scenarios, 2010; Bookkeeping Essentials: How to Succeed as a Bookkeeper, 2011; IFRS Made Easy, 2011; New CEO Corporate Leadership Manual: Strategic and Analytical Tools for Growth, 2011; Vest Pocket Guide to GAAP, 2011; Essential Controller: An Introduction to What Every Financial Manager Must Know, 2012. **Address:** 6727 E Fremont Pl., Englewood, CO 80112, U.S.A. **Online address:** brasto@aol.com

BRAGINSKY, Vladimir B. (Vladimir Borisovich Braginsky). Russian (born Russia), b. 1931. **Genres:** Physics, Sciences, Education. **Career:** Moscow State University, senior lecturer, 1955-56, assistant professor, 1956-64, senior research scientist, 1964-68, professor of physics, 1968-, chair of department, 1986-; California Institute of Technology, research associate, 1993-96, visiting associate. Writer. **Publications:** Physical Experiments with Test Bodies, 1970; Fizicheskie ėksperimenty s probnymi telami, 1970; Izmerenie malykh sil v fizicheskikh ėksperimentakh, 1974; (with A.B. Manukin) Measurement of Weak Forces in Physics Experiments, 1977; (with V.P. Mitrofanov and V.I. Panov) Sistemy s maloi dissipatsiei, 1981; Teoriia i metody makroskopicheskikh izmerenii, 1989; (with F.Y. Khalili) Quantum Measurement, 1992. **Address:** Department of Physics, Moscow State University, Leninskie Gory, Moscow, 119991, Russia. **Online address:** brag@mol.phys.msu.su

BRAGINSKY, Vladimir Borisovich. *See* **BRAGINSKY, Vladimir B.**

BRAHAM, (E.) Jeanne. American (born United States), b. 1940. **Genres:** Literary Criticism And History, Poetry, Medicine/Health, Autobiography/Memoirs. **Career:** Allegheny College, professor, 1970-90; Clark University, professor, 1994-2002, retired, 2002; Chautauqua Writers Center, creative writing teacher; Smith College, visiting professor; Hampshire College, visiting professor; University of New Hampshire, visiting professor; College of the Holy Cross, visiting professor; Heatherstone Press, founding editor and chief. Writer. **Publications:** One Means of Telling Time (poems), 1981; Primary Sources: Poems, 1981; A Sort of Columbus: The American Voyages of Saul Bellow's Fiction, 1984; Crucial Conversations: Interpreting Contemporary American Literary Autobiographies by Women, 1995; (with P.P. Peterson) Starry, Starry Night: Provincetown's Response to the AIDS Crisis, 1998; Made by Hand: Art and Craft in the Heartland of New England, 2004; The Light Within the Light: Portraits of Donald Hall, Richard Wilbur, Maxine Kumin, and Stanley Kunitz, 2007; Another Language: Portraits of Assistance Dogs and their People, 2012. **Address:** Bauhan Publishing L.L.C., 7 Main St., Peterborough, NH 03458, U.S.A. **Online address:** ejbraham@aol.com

BRAINARD, Cecilia Manguerra. American/Filipino (born Philippines), b. 1947. **Genres:** Novels, Women's Studies And Issues, Novellas/Short Stories, Third World, Essays. **Career:** Fiction writer, communications specialist, 1969-81; freelance writer, 1981-; University of California, instructor in writing program, 1989-; Santa Monica College, instructor, 1991-; Philippine American Literary House, partner, 1994-. **Publications:** Woman with Horns and Other Stories, 1988; The Philippine Woman in America: Essays, 1991; Song of Yvonne, 1991, as When the Rainbow Goddess Wept, 1994, rev. ed., 1999; Acapulco at Sunset and Other Stories, 1995; Magdalena (novel), 2002; Cecilia's Diary 1962-1969, 2003; Fundamentals of Creative Writing, 2009; Angelica's Daughters: A Dugtungan Novel, 2010; Vigan and Other Stories, 2011; Out of Cebu: Essays and Personal Prose, 2012. EDITOR: Seven Stories from Seven Sisters: A Collection of Philippine Folktales, 1992; Fiction by Filipinos in America, 1993; The Beginning and Other Asian Folktales, 1995; Contemporary Fiction by Filipinos in America, 1997; (with E.F. Litton) Journey of 100 Years: Reflections on the Centennial of Philippine Independence, 1999; Growing up Filipino: Stories for Young Adults, 2003; Behind the Walls: Life of Convent Girls, 2005; (with M.Y. Orosa) Ala Carte Food and Fiction, 2007; (with M.Y. Orosa) Finding God: True Stories of Spiritual Encounters, 2009. Works appear in anthologies. Contributor of articles to periodicals. **Address:** PO Box 5099, Santa Monica, CA 90409, U.S.A. **Online address:** cbrainard@aol.com

BRAINE, David. Scottish/British (born England), b. 1940. **Genres:** Medicine/Health, Ethics, Philosophy, Natural History, Psychology. **Career:** University of Aberdeen, Department of Philosophy, lecturer, 1965-89, honorary lecturer, 1989-2002, honorary research fellow, 2002-. Writer. **Publications:** Medical Ethics and Human Life, 1982, 2nd ed., 1983; The Reality of Time and the Existence of God: The Project of Proving God's Existence, 1988; (ed. with H. Lesser) Ethics, Technology and Medicine, 1988; The Human Person: Animal and Spirit, 1992. **Address:** Philosophy, School of Philosophy, Divinity and Religious Studies, University of Aberdeen, Old Brewery, High St., Aberdeen, AB24 3UB, Scotland. **Online address:** d.braine@abdn.ac.uk

BRAKE, Laurel. American (born United States), b. 1941. **Genres:** Literary Criticism And History. **Career:** University of London, Birkbeck College, research assistant in English, 1970-73, reader in literature, 1988-, professor of literature and print culture, senior research fellow, now professor emeritus; University of Wales, University College of Wales, lecturer in English, 1973-88; Pater Newsletter, co-editor, 1978-98. **Publications:** The Special Art of the Modern World, 1993; Subjugated Knowledges, 1994; Walter Pater, 1994; Print in Transition, 1850-1910, 2001. EDITOR: The Year's Work in English Studies, vols. 62-69, 1984-91; (with A. Jones and L. Madden) Investigating Victorian Journalism, 1990; (with I. Small) Pater in the 1990s, 1991; (with B. Bell and D. Finkelstein) Nineteenth-Century Media and the Construction of Identity, 2000; (with L. Higgins and C. Williams) Walter Pater: Transparencies of Desire, 2002; (with J.F. Codell) Encounters in the Victorian Press: Editors, Authors, Readers, 2005; (contrib.) Au bonheur du feuilleton, 2007; (ed. with M. Demoor) Lure of Illustration in the Nineteenth Century: Picture and Press, 2009. **Address:** Department of English and Humanities, Birkbeck College, University of London, 43-46 Gordon Sq., London, GL WC1H, England. **Online address:** l.brake@bbk.ac.uk

BRAKE, Mark L. Welsh (born Wales) **Genres:** Young Adult Fiction. **Career:** University of Glamorgan, Department of Science Communication, professor, Centre for Astronomy and Science Education, director; Science Shops Wales, director, Robotic Cyberspace Community Telescope and Observatory, project director, SETPOINT Wales Centre for Astronomy and Science Education, director; NASA Astrobiology Institute, Science Communication Group, founder member; Science Fiction Museum in Seattle and the Australian Centre for Astrobiology, consultant. Writer, academic and science consultant. **Publications:** (with N. Hook) Different Engines: How Science Drives Fiction and Fiction Drives Science, 2008; (with N. Hook) FutureWorld: Where Science Fiction Becomes Science, 2008. **Address:** University of Glamorgan, Pontypridd, CF37 1DL, Wales. **Online address:** profmbrake@gmail.com

BRAKKE, David Bernhard. American (born United States), b. 1961. **Genres:** Theology/Religion. **Career:** Concordia College, visiting assistant professor, 1992-93; Indiana University, assistant professor, 1993-. Writer. **Publications:** Athanasius and the Politics of Asceticism, 1995; (with M.J. Weaver and J. Bivins) Introduction to Christianity, 3rd ed., 1998; (ed.) Pseudo-Athanasius on Virginity, 2002; (ed. with C.A. Bobertz) Reading in Christian Communities: Essays on Interpretation in the Early Church, 2002; (ed. with M.L. Satlow and S. Weitzman) Religion and the Self in Antiquity, 2005; (ed. with A.C. Jacobsen and J. Ulrich) Beyond Reception: Mutual Influences between Antique Religion, Judaism and Early Christianity, 2006; Demons and the Making of the Monk: Spiritual Combat in Early Christianity, 2006; (trans. and intro.) Talking Back: A Monastic Handbook for Combating Demons, 2009; (ed. with A.C. Jacobsen and J. Ulrich) Critique and Apologetics: Jews, Christians, and Pagans in Antiquity, 2009; Gnostics: Myth, Ritual and Diversity in Early Christianity, 2010; (ed. with A.C. Jacobsen and J. Ulrich) Narrated Reality: The Historia Ecclesiastica of Eusebius of Caesarea, 2011; (ed. with D. Deliyannis and E. Watts) Shifting Cultural Frontiers in Late Antiquity, 2012. Contributor to books. **Address:** Department of Religious Studies, College of Arts & Sciences, Indiana University, Sycamore Hall 230, Bloomington, IN 47405, U.S.A. **Online address:** dbrakke@indiana.edu

BRALLIER, Kate. American (born United States) **Genres:** Romance/Historical, Young Adult Fiction, Literary Criticism And History. **Career:** New York publisher, senior editor. **Publications:** Seal Island, 2005; The Boundless Deep, 2008. Contributor to periodicals. **Address:** c/o Kay McCauley, The Pimlico Agency Inc., PO Box 20447, Cherokee Sta., New York, NY 10021, U.S.A.

BRAME, Charles L. American (born United States), b. 1926. **Genres:** Biography, History. **Career:** Educator, 1961-84; radio show producer; artist for advertisements. Writer. **Publications:** Honestly Abe: A Cartoon Biography of Abraham Lincoln, 1998, rev. ed., 2000. FORTHCOMING: Who Painted My Taters Green; Three Little Pigs: Pete, Prunelli, and Loulabel; The War and Charlie B, The Education of Charlie B, and The Works. Contributor of articles to periodicals. **Address:** PO Box 521, Alta Loma, CA 91701, U.S.A. **Online address:** cbrame@abepress.com

BRAMLY, Serge. French/Tunisian (born Tunisia), b. 1949. **Genres:** Biography, Novels, Translations, Young Adult Fiction. **Career:** Journalist, publisher, art critic and historian. **Publications:** Terre Wakan: Univers sacré des Indiens d'Amerique du Nord, 1974; (ed. and comp.) Macumba, forces noires du Brésil: Les Enseignements deMaria-José, mere des dieux, 1975, trans. as Macumba: The Teachings of Maria-Jose, Mother of the Gods, 1977, rev. ed. as Macumba: Forces noires du Bresil, 1981; Rudolf Steiner, prophete de l'homme nouveau, 1976; (with E. de Smedt and V. Bardet) La Pratique des arts divinatoires: Astrologie, tarots, chiromancie, geomancie, Yi-king, 1976; L'Itineraire du fou: Roman (novel), 1978; Un Piège a lumière: Roman (novel), 1979; Man Ray, 1980; (with J-P.I. Amunategui) Le Livre des dates, 1981; La Danse du loup, 1982; Un Poisson muet, surgi de la mer, 1985; Léonard de Vinci, 1988, (trans.) S. Reynolds as Leonardo: Discovering the Life of Leonardo da Vinci, 1991; L. de Vinci: Manuscrit sur le vol des oiseaux, 1989; Le grand cheval de Leonard: Le Projet monumental de Leonard de Vinci, 1990; Madame Satan (novel), 1992; Chambre Close, 1992; La Terreur dans le boudoir (novel), 1992; Le Terreur dans le Boudoir, 1994; Leonardo: The Artist and the Man, 1994; Mona Lisa, 1994; (contrib.) Photo dessin, dessin photo, 1994; Le réseau Melchior, 1996; I.N.R.I., 1998; (with B. Rheims) Chambre

Close: Fiction, 1999; (with G. Lévy) Fleurs de peau=Skin Flowers, 1999; Ragots: Pour Servir àl'histoire de Bussy-Rabutin, de sa fille de Coligny, et du chevalier de LaRivière, 2000; Shanghai, 2004; Le Voyage de Shanghai, 2005; (contrib.) BTK, 2006; Le Premier Principe, le Second Principe: Roman, 2008; Rose, c'est Paris, 2010. **Address:** c/o Publicity Director, Jean Claude Lattes, 17 rue Jacob, Paris, F-75006, France.

BRAMPTON, Sally Jane. British (born England), b. 1955. **Genres:** Novels, Writing/Journalism. **Career:** Vogue, fashion writer, 1978; Observer, fashion editor, 1981; Elle, editor, 1985-89; Mirabella, associate editor, 1990-91; Red, editor, 2000; Central St. Martins College of Art and Design, visiting professor; Fashion Institute, teacher. **Publications:** Good Grief, 1992; Lovesick, 1995; Concerning Lily, 1998; Love, Always, 1999; Shoot the Damn Dog: A Memoir of Depression, 2008. **Address:** Bloomsbury Publishing, 36 Soho Sq., London, GL W1D 3QY, England.

BRAMSEN, Paul D. American (born United States), b. 1957. **Genres:** Theology/Religion, Adult Non-fiction, Young Adult Non-fiction. **Career:** Self-employed teacher, writer, producer and missionary, 1981-; ROCK Intl., president, 2007-. Writer. **Publications:** The Way of Righteousness, 1999; One God One Message, 2007; Your Story, 2009; King of Glory, 2011. **Address:** ROCK Intl., PO Box 4766, Greenville, SC 29608-4766, U.S.A. **Online address:** pb@rockintl.org

BRAMSON, Leon. American (born United States), b. 1930. **Genres:** Sociology, Humanities, Social Sciences, Politics/Government. **Career:** Harvard University, teaching fellow, 1956-57, 1958-59, Department of Social Relations, instructor, 1959-61, assistant professor, 1961-65; Swarthmore College, associate professor, 1965-70, Department of Sociology and Anthropology, chairman, 1965-77, professor of sociology, 1971-78; Exxon Education Foundation, program officer, 1978-80; Exxon Corp., Corporate Planning Department, coordinator for social analysis, 1980-82; National Endowment for the Humanities, Division of Research, senior program officer, 1982-. Writer. **Publications:** The Political Context of Sociology, 1961; (ed.) Examining in Harvard College: A Collection of Essays by Members of the Harvard Faculty, 1963; (ed. with G.W. Goethals) War: Studies from Psychology, Sociology, Anthropology, 1964, rev. ed., 1968; (ed.) Robert MacIver: On Community, Society and Power, 1970. **Address:** National Endowment for the Humanities, 1100 Pennsylvania Ave. NW, Washington, DC 20506, U.S.A. **Online address:** lbramson@neh.gov

BRANAGH, Kenneth (Charles). British/Irish (born Ireland), b. 1960. **Genres:** Plays/Screenplays, Film, Theatre. **Career:** Renaissance Theater Co., founder, producer and director, 1987-. Actor, playwright and screenwriter. **Publications:** Tell Me Honestly (play), 1985; Public Enemy (play), 1987; (Adapted) Henry V (film), 1989; Beginning (autobiography), 1989; (Adapter) Much Ado about Nothing (film), 1993; The Making of Mary Shelley's Frankenstein, 1994; Shakespeare and Macbeth, 1994; Mary Shelley's Frankenstein: The Classic Tale of Terror Reborn on Film, 1994; In the Bleak Midwinter, 1995; A Midwinter's Tale (film), 1995; A Midwinter's Script, 1995; Hamlet: The Making of the Movie Including the Screenplay, 1996; Shakespeare on the Screen: Kenneth Branagh's Adaptations of Henry V, Much Ado About Nothing And Hamlet, 2000. Contributor to periodicals. **Address:** 83 Berwick St., London, GL W1V 3PJ, England.

BRANCH, Alan E(dward). British (born England), b. 1933. **Genres:** Business/Trade/Industry, Economics, Marketing, Transportation, Reference, Humanities. **Career:** Basingstoke College of Technology, senior lecturer, now retired; European Institute of Maritime Studies, visiting professor; University of Leicester, lecturer; University of Reading, lecturer. Writer and marketing, shipping and export consultant. **Publications:** The Elements of Shipping, 1964, 7th ed., 1995; A Dictionary of Shipping/International Business Trade Terms and Abbreviations, 1976, 4th ed., 1995; Elements of Export Practice, 1979, 3rd ed. as Export Practice and Management, 1994; Economics of Shipping Practice and Management, 1982, 2nd ed., 1988; Elements of Export Marketing and Management, 1984, 2nd ed., 1990; Dictionary of Commercial Terms and Abbreviations, 1984; Elements of Port Operation and Management, 1986; (with J.A. Hakmeh) Dictionary of English-Arabic Commercial, International Trade and Shipping Terms, 1988; Import/Export Documentation, 1990, 2nd ed. as Shipping and Air Freight Documentation For Importers and Exporters and Associated Terms, 2000; Elements of Import Practice, 1990; (co-author) Multi-Lingual Dictionary of Commercial International Trade and Shipping Terms, 1990; Maritime Economics, Management and Marketing, 1998; International Purchasing and Management, 2001; Global Supply Chain Management and International Logistics, 2009. **Address:** 19 The Ridings, Emmer Green, Reading, BR RG4 8XL, England.

BRANCH, Muriel Miller. American (born United States), b. 1943. **Genres:** Children's Fiction, Children's Non-fiction, Education, History, Bibliography. **Career:** Maggie L. Walker High School, teacher; American Tobacco Co., Department of Research and Development, research librarian; Richmond Public Schools, library media specialist, 1967-98, retired, 1998; full-time writer, 1998-. **Publications:** (With D. Rice) Miss Maggie: The Story of Maggie Lena Walker, 1984; (comp. with E.G. Evans) Hidden Skeletons and Other Funny Stories, 1995; (with E.G. Evans) A Step Beyond: Multimedia Activities for Learning American History, 1995; The Water Brought Us: The Story of the Gullah-speaking People, 1995; (with D.M. Rice) Pennies to Dollars: The Story of Maggie Lena Walker, 1997; Juneteenth: Freedom Day, 1998; (with E.G. Evans) 3-D Displays for Libraries, Schools, and Media Centers, 2000; (with M.E. Lyons) Dear Ellen Bee: A Civil War Scrapbook of Two Union Spies, 2000; Fine Arts and Crafts, 2001; Tin Tubs and Tinsel, forthcoming. Contributor to journals. **Address:** 9315 Radborne Rd., Richmond, VA 23236-2752, U.S.A. **Online address:** mmbranch@stories-plus.com

BRANCH, Taylor. American (born United States), b. 1947. **Genres:** Novels, Autobiography/Memoirs, History, Politics/Government. **Career:** Washington Monthly, assistant editor, 1970-73; Harper's, Washington editor, 1973-76; Esquire Magazine, Washington columnist, 1976-77; Goucher College, lecturer, 1998-2000. Journalist and civil rights activist. **Publications:** (And ed. with C. Peters) Blowing the Whistle: Dissent in the Public Interest, 1972; (with B. Russell) Second Wind: The Memoirs of an Opinionated Man, 1979; The Empire Blues (novel), 1981; (with E.M. Propper) Labyrinth, 1982; Parting the Waters: America in the King Years, 1954-63, 1988; Pillar of Fire: America in the King Years, 1963-65, 1998; Nonviolent Leadership: The Essence of Democracy, 2005; At Canaan's Edge: America in the King Years, 1965-68, 2006; Clinton Tapes: Wrestling History with the President, 2009. Contributor to periodicals. **Address:** Simon & Schuster Inc., 1230 Ave. of the Americas, New York, NY 10020, U.S.A. **Online address:** info@taylorbranch.com

BRAND, Alice Glarden. American (born United States), b. 1938. **Genres:** Poetry, Psychology, Writing/Journalism, Essays, Social Sciences, Humanities, Literary Criticism And History. **Career:** New Jersey Public Schools, creative writing, 1960-78; Rutgers University, writing instructor, 1978-80; Middlesex County College, writing instructor, 1978-80; Somerset County College, writing instructor, 1978-80; Rider College, writing instructor, 1978-80; University of Missouri, assistant professor, associate professor of English, 1980-87, director of communications programs and program director of the gateway writing project, 1980-87; Clarion University of Pennsylvania, associate professor of English and director of writing, 1987-89; State University of New York, associate professor, 1989-91, director of composition, 1989-92, professor of English, 1992-99, professor emeritus, 2000-. Writer. **Publications:** Therapy in Writing: A Psycho-Educational Enterprise, 1980; As it Happens (poetry), 1983; Studies on Zone (poetry), 1989; The Psychology of Writing: The Affective Experience, 1989; (ed. with R.L. Graves) Presence of Mind: Writing and the Domain Beyond the Cognitive, 1994; Court of Common Pleas (poetry), 1996. Contributor to periodicals. **Address:** State University of New York, 350 New Campus Dr., 180 Holley St., Brockport, NY 14420-2989, U.S.A. **Online address:** abrand@brockport.edu

BRAND, Dionne. Canadian/Trinidadian (born Trinidad and Tobago), b. 1953. **Genres:** Poetry, Race Relations, Novels, Young Adult Fiction. **Career:** Agency for Rural Transformation, information and communications officer, 1983; University of Toronto, writer-in-residence, 1990-91; University of Guelph, assistant professor of English, 1992-94, writer-in-residence, 2003-04; Simon Fraser University, Ruth Wynn Woodward professor in women's studies, 2000-02, Ruth Wynn Wodward chair in women's studies; Saint Lawrence University in New York, distinguished visiting professor, writer-in-residence, 2004-05; University of Guelph, research chair, English professor. Writer and journalist. **Publications:** POETRY: Fore Day Morning, 1978; Earth Magic, 1980; Primitive Offensive, 1982; Winter Epigrams and Epigrams to Ernesto Cardenal in Defense of Claudia, 1983; Chronicles of the Hostile Sun, 1984; No Language Is Neutral, 1990; Sisters in Struggle, 1991; In Another Place, Not Here, 1996; Land to Light On, 1997; Thirsty, 2002; Inventory, 2006; Fierce Departures, 2009; Ossuaries, 2010. OTHER: Sans Souci and Other Stories, 1983; (with K.S. Bhaggiyadatta) Rivers Have Sources, Trees Have Roots: Speaking of Racism, 1986; A Conceptual Analysis of How Gender Roles are

Racially Constructed: Black Women, 1988; (with L. De Shield) No Burden to Carry: Narratives of Black Working Women in Ontario, 1920s-1950s, 1991; Long Time Comin, 1993; Bread Out of Stone: Recollections, Sex, Recognitions, Race, Dreaming, Politics, 1994, rev. ed., 1998; Grammar of Dissent: Poetry and Prose by Claire Harris, M. Nourbese Philip and Dionne Brand, 1994; At the Full and Change of the Moon: A Novel, 1999; Vintage Book of International Lesbian Fiction, 1999; A Map to the Door of No Return: Notes to Belonging, 2001; What We All Long For: A Novel, 2005; Chronicles: Early Years, 2011. Contributor to books and periodicals. **Address:** McClelland and Stewart Ltd., 481 University Ave., Ste. 900, Toronto, ON M5G 2E9, Canada.

BRAND, Oscar. American/Canadian (born Canada), b. 1920. **Genres:** Children's Fiction, Plays/Screenplays, Songs/Lyrics And Libretti, Adult Nonfiction, Communications/Media, Music, Documentaries/Reportage, Humor/Satire, Humor/Satire. **Career:** Bellevue Hospital, research associate, through 1942; Harlequin Productions Inc., president; Gypsy Hill Music Inc., president; Hofstra University, lecturer on dramatic writing, social Research, 1970-; WNYC, co-coordinator of folk music; Songwriters Hall of Fame, curator; host of television folk-song program, freelance writer and composer. **Publications:** Courting Songs, 1952; Singing Holidays, 1957; The Ballad Mongers (autobiography), 1957; Bawdy Songs, 1958; Bawdy Songs and Backroom Ballads, 19960; Folksongs for Fun, 1961; Oscar Brand's Easiest Folk Song Book, 1964; (ed.) Words about Music, 1969; Celebrate; The Feast Days of the Christian Calendar, 1970; Songs of '76 (music history), 1972; When I First Came to This Land (children), 1974; Sing America Sing, 1975; Schirmer's Easy Five String Banjo Book: Famous Contemporary Folk Songs, 1978; Party Songs, 1985; Bunyan and the Termites, 1996; The High Road, 1998; The Gender Gap, 1999. **Address:** Gypsy Hill Music, PO Box 1362, Manhasset, NY 11030, U.S.A. **Online address:** oscarbrand@oscarbrand.com

BRAND, Rebecca. *See* **CHARNAS, Suzy McKee.**

BRANDEN, Nathaniel. American/Canadian (born Canada), b. 1930. **Genres:** Literary Criticism And History, Psychology, Self Help, inspirational/Motivational Literature, Social Sciences, Sciences. **Career:** Psychotherapist in private practice and author, 1956-; Nathaniel Branden Institute, founder and president, 1958-68; The Objectivist Newsletter, with Ayn Rand, contributor, co-founder and co-editor, 1962-65, 1966-68; The Biocentric Institute (now the Branden Institute for Self-Esteem), owner and director, 1968-; University of Southern California, lecturer in biology and psychology, 1969. **Publications:** Who Is Ayn Rand?: An Analysis of the Novels of Ayn Rand, 1962; The Virtue of Selfishness: A New Concept of Egoism, 1964; Capitalism: The Unknown Ideal, 1966; The Psychology of Self-Esteem, 1970, as The Psychology of Self-Esteem: A Revolutionary Approach to Self-Understanding That Launched a New Era in Modern Psychology, 2001; Breaking Free, 1970; The Disowned Self, 1972; The Psychology of Romantic Love, 1980; (with E.D. Branden) The Romantic Love Question & Answer Book, 1982, rev. ed. (with E.D. Branden) as What Loves Asks of Us, 1987; If You Could Hear What I Cannot Say, 1983; Honoring the Self, 1984; To See What I See and Know What I Know, 1986; How to Raise Your Self-Esteem, 1987; Experience High Self-Esteem, 1988; Judgment Day, 1989 as My Years with Ayn Rand, 1999; The Power of Self-Esteem, 1992; Tharte Six Pillars of Self-Esteem, 1993; The Art of Self-Discovery, 1993; Nathaniel Branden's Little Blue Book of Self-Esteem, 1995; Taking Responsibility: Self-Reliance and the Accountable Life, 1996; The Art of Living Consciously, 1997; Self-Esteem Everyday, 1998; Self-Esteem at Work: How Confident People Make Powerful Companies, 1998; Woman's Self-Esteem: Struggles and Triumphs in the Search for Identity, 1998; My Years with Ayn Rand, 1999; The Art Of Living Consciously: The Power of Awareness to Transform Everyday Life, 1999; The Moral Revolution in Atlas Shrugged, 2000; The Vision of Ayn Rand: The Basic Principles of Objectivism, 2009. Contributor to books and periodicals. **Address:** c/o Nat Sobel, Sobel Weber Associates, 146 E 19th St., New York, NY 10003, U.S.A. **Online address:** nathaniel@nathanielbranden.com

BRANDENBERG, Franz. British/Swiss (born Switzerland), b. 1932. **Genres:** Children's Fiction, Young Adult Fiction, Human Relations/Parenting, Children's Non-fiction, Social Commentary. **Career:** Literary agent, 1960-72; writer, 1970-. **Publications:** I Once Knew a Man, 1970; Fresh Cider and Pie, 1973; A Secret for Grandmother's Birthday, 1975; No School Today, 1975; A Robber! A Robber!, 1976; I Wish I Was Sick Too!, 1976 in UK as I Don't Feel Well, 1977; Nice New Neighbors, 1977; What Can You Make of It?, 1977; A Picnic, Hurrah!, 1978; Six New Students, 1978; Everyone Ready?, 1979; It's Not My Fault, 1980; Leo and Emily, 1981; Leo and Emily's Big Ideas, 1982; Aunt Nina and Her Nephews and Nieces, 1983; Aunt Nina's Visit, 1984; Leo and Emily and the Dragon, 1984; The Hit of the Party, 1985; Cock-a-Doodle-Doo, 1986; What's Wrong with a Van?, 1987; Aunt Nina, Good Night!, 1989. OTHERS: Otto is Different, 1985; Leo and Emily's Zoo, 1988; A Fun Weekend, 1991; (co-author) Home: A Collaboration of Thirty Distinguished Authors and Illustrators of Children's Books to Aid the Homeless, 1992. **Address:** 17 Regent's Park Terr., London, GL NW1 7ED, England.

BRANDENBURG, Jim. American (born United States), b. 1945. **Genres:** Zoology, Environmental Sciences/Ecology, Photography, Animals/Pets, Sciences. **Career:** Daily Globe, picture editor, 1970, photojournalist; National Geographic, contract photographer, 1978-92, co-producer, director and cinematographer of documentary films, 1998; Brandenburg Prairie Foundation, owner. Writer. **Publications:** White Wolf: Living with an Arctic Legend, 1988; Brother Wolf: A Forgotten Promise, 1993; To the Top of the World: Adventures with Arctic Wolves, 1993; Sand and Fog: Adventures in Southern Africa, 1994; (ed.) An American Safari: Adventures on the North American Prairie, 1995; Scruffy: A Wolf Finds His Place in the Pack, 1996; Chased by the Light, 1998, 2nd ed., 2001; Looking for the Summer, 2003; (with J. Brandenburg) Face to Face with Wolves, 2008. Contributor of books and periodicals. **Address:** Brandenburg Prairie Foundation, c/o Brandenburg Gallery, 11 E Sheridan St., Ely, MN 55731, U.S.A. **Online address:** brthrwolf@aol.com

BRANDES, Joseph. American/Polish (born Poland), b. 1928. **Genres:** History. **Career:** Teacher, 1950-53, 1956-57; New York University, university fellow, 1953-54, 1957-58; City University of New York, City College, lecturer in economics, 1955; William Paterson University, professor of history, 1958-92, professor emeritus, 1992-; U.S. Department of Commerce, consulting economist, 1958-61; U.S. Department of Commerce, consultant, 1958-61; Passaic County Committee on Economic Opportunities for Youth, chairperson, 1959-60; Passaic County Citizens' Association on Correction, chairperson, 1960-61; American Jewish History Center, research associate, 1965-71. Writer. **Publications:** (Ed.) Pictorial History of the World, 1956; Herbert Hoover and Economic Diplomacy, 1962; (with M. Douglas) Immigrants to Freedom, 1971; (with M. Douglas) Immigrants to Freedom: Jews as Yankee Farmers!: 1880-1960's, 2009. **Address:** Department of History, William Paterson University of New Jersey, 300 Pompton Rd., Wayne, NJ 07470-2103, U.S.A. **Online address:** marjoe26@juno.com

BRANDES, Stanley H. American (born United States), b. 1942. **Genres:** Intellectual History, Adult Non-fiction, Local History/Rural Topics. **Career:** Michigan State University, assistant professor of anthropology, 1971-74; University of California, assistant professor, 1974-78, associate professor, 1978-81, professor of anthropology, 1982-, Barcelona Study Center, director, 1981-82, Department Of Anthropology, chair, 1990-93, 1998-2000, Mexico City Study Center, director, 1995-96; Universitat Central de Barcelona, director, 1981-82. Writer. **Publications:** Migration, Kinship and Community: Tradition and Transition in a Spanish Village, 1975; (ed. with M.L. Foster) Symbol as Sense: New Approaches to the Analysis of Meaning, 1980; Metaphors of Masculinity: Sex and Status in Andalusian Folklore, 1980; Forty: The Age and the Symbol, 1985; Power and Persuasion: Fiestas and Social Control in Rural Mexico, 1988; (co-author) Los Españoles vistos por los antropólogos, 1991; Staying Sober in Mexico City, 2002; Skulls to the Living, Bread to the Dead: The Day of the Dead in Mexico and Beyond, 2006. Contributor to periodicals. **Address:** Department of Anthropology, University of California, 309 Kroeber Hall, Berkeley, CA 94720, U.S.A. **Online address:** brandes@berkeley.edu

BRANDES, Stuart D. American (born United States), b. 1940. **Genres:** History, Military/Defense/Arms Control. **Career:** University of Wisconsin-Rock County, professor of history, 1967-99, department chair of history, 1981-84, American Association of University Professors, president, 1996-99; Wisconsin Association of Scholars, treasurer, 1991-; Social Science Division, chair, 1993-99; University of Wisconsin-Madison, professor of history, now professor emeritus. Writer. **Publications:** American Welfare Capitalism: 1880-1940 (historical monograph), 1976; Warhogs: A History of War Profits in America (historical monograph), 1997. **Address:** Department of History, University of Wisconsin-Madison, 3211 Mosse Humanities Bldg., 455 N Park St., Madison, WI 53706-1483, U.S.A. **Online address:** sbrandes@uwc.edu

BRANDEWYNE, Rebecca. American (born United States), b. 1955. **Genres:** Novels, Novellas/Short Stories, Mystery/Crime/Suspense, Horror, Romance/Historical, Science Fiction/Fantasy, Westerns/Adventure, Young Adult Fiction, Young Adult Fiction. **Career:** National Dental Warranty, editor, 1974-76; International Business Machines (IBM) Corp., Data Processing Division, executive secretary to branch manager, 1976-77; Alliance Corp. (life insurance firm), office manager, executive secretary, 1977-80; Glaves, Weil & Evans (attorneys), legal secretary, 1980; freelance writer, 1980-; Novelists Inc., founder. **Publications:** FATE SERIES: Love, Cherish Me, 1983; And Gold Was Ours, 1984. CHRONICLES OF TINTAGEL: Passion Moon Rising, 1988; Beyond the Starlit Frost, 1991. HIGHCLYFFE HALL: Upon a Moon-Dark Moor, 1988; Across a Starlit Sea, 1989. NOVELS: No Gentle Love, 1980; Forever My Love, 1982; Rose of Rapture, 1984; The Outlaw Hearts, 1986; Desire in Disguise, 1987; Heartland, 1990; Rainbow's End, 1991; Desperado, 1992; (co-author) Bewitching Love Stories, 1992; Swan Road, 1994; Wildcat, 1995; The Jacaranda Tree, 1996; Dust Devil, 1996; Presumed Guilty, 1996; Glory Seekers, 1997; The Lioness Tamer, 1998; High Stakes, 1999; Destiny's Daughter, 2001; (co-author) At the Edge, 2002; The Love Knot, 2003; The Ninefold Key, 2004; The Crystal Rose, 2006; From the Mists of Wolf Creek, 2009. OTHERS: (contrib.) Hired Husband, 1996; (contrib.) A Spring Bouquet, 1996. Contributor to magazines and newspapers. **Address:** 2203 Winstead Cir., Wichita, KS 67226, U.S.A. **Online address:** rebecca@brandewyne.com

BRANDI, John. American (born United States), b. 1943. **Genres:** Novellas/Short Stories, Poetry. **Career:** State of New Mexico, poet-in-residence, 1973-86; Tooth of Time Books, founder and editor, 1978-89; Carlsbad Caverns and Guadalupe Mountains, poet-in-residence, 1979; Aleknagik, Ekwok, New Stuyahok, Alaska poet-in-residence, 1986, 1991; Just Buffalo/Literary Center, writer-in-residence, 1989; Roswell Museum, poet-in-residence, 2000; Just Buffalo, poet-in-residence, 2004. **Publications:** POETRY: Tehachapi Fantasy, 1964; A Nothing Book, 1964; Poem Afternoon in a Square of Guadalajara, 1970; Empty lots: Poems of Venice and L.A., 1971; Field Notes from Alaska, 1971; Three Poems for Spring, 1973; August Poems, 1973; San Francisco Last Day Homebound Hangover Highway Blues, 1973; A Partial Exploration of Palo Flechado Canyon, 1973; Smudgepots: For Jack Kerouac, 1973; Firebook, 1974; The Phoenix Gas Slam, 1974; Turning Thirty Poem, 1974; In a December Storm, 1975; Looking for Minerals, 1975; In a September Rain, 1976; The Guadalupes: A Closer Look, 1978; Poems from Four Corners, 1978; Andean Town, 1979; As It Is These Days, 1979; Poems for the People of Coyote, 1980; Sky House/Pink Cottonwood, 1980; That Crow That Visited Was Flying Backwards, 1982; At the World's Edge, 1983; Poems at the Edge of Day, 1984; Zuleika's Book, 1983; Rite for the Beautification of All Beings, 1983; That Back Road In, 1985; Circling, 1988; Hymn for a Night Feast: Poems 1979-1987, 1989; Shadow Play: Poems 1987-1991, 1992; Turning 50 Poem, 1993; Weeding the Cosmos: Selected Haiku, 1994; Heartbeat Geography, 1995; No Reason at All, 1995; No Other Business Here, 1999; Stone Garland A Haiku Journey, Northern Vietnam, 2000; Visits to the City of Light, 2000; Empty Moon, Bellyfull: Asian Haiku, 2001; In What Disappears, 2003; One Cup and Another, 2004; Too Short the Long Night, 2006; Staff in Hand, Wind in Pines, 2008; Facing High Water, 2008; Other Roads, 2009. SHORT STORIES: The Cowboy from Phantom Banks, 1982; In the Desert We Do not Count the Days, 1991; A Question of Journey, 1995; Unmasking the Fire: Bali Journals, 1999; Reflections in the Lizard's Eye, 2000; One Cup and Another, 2004; Empty Moon, Belly Full, 2004. OTHER: Desde Alla, 1971; One Week of Mornings at Dry Creek, 1971; Towards a Happy Solstice, 1971; Y Aun Hay Mas, 1972; Narrowgauge to Riobamba, 1975; Memorandum from a Caribbean Isle, 1977; Diary from Baja, California, 1978; Diary from a Journey to the Middle of the World, 1979. Water Shining Beyond the Fields, 2006; Seeding the Cosmos: New & Selected Haiku, 2010. **Address:** PO Box 2553, Corrales, NM 87048, U.S.A. **Online address:** johnbrandi@cybermesa.com

BRANDON, Alicia. *See* **CAMERON, Stella.**

BRANDON, Laura. Canadian/British (born England), b. 1951. **Genres:** History, Art/Art History. **Career:** Canadian War Museum, chief curator and historian for art and war, 1992-. Writer. **Publications:** Pegi by Herself: The Life of Pegi Nicol MacLeod, Canadian Artist, 2005; Art or Memorial?: The Forgotten History of Canada's War Art, 2006; Art and War, 2007. **Address:** Canadian War Museum, 1 Vimy Pl., Ottawa, ON K1A 0M8, Canada. **Online address:** laura.brandon@warmuseum.ca

BRANDON, Ruth. British (born England), b. 1943?. **Genres:** Adult Nonfiction, Young Adult Fiction, Mystery/Crime/Suspense, Novels, Business/Trade/Industry. **Career:** British Broadcasting Corp., trainee producer. Writer. **Publications:** NON-FICTION: Seventy Plus, 1971; Houses and Homes, 1972; (with C. Davies) Wrongful Imprisonment: Mistaken Convictions and Their Consequences, 1973; Central Government, 1975; A Capitalist Romance: Singer and the Sewing Machine, 1977; The Lost World of the Great Spas, 1979; The Dollar Princesses: Sagas of Upward Nobility 1870-1914, 1980; Dollar Princesses: American Invasion of the European Aristocracy, 1870-1914, 1980; Marie Curie: A Life for Science, 1981; The Spiritualists: The Passion for the Occult in the Nineteenth and Twentieth Centuries, 1982; The Burning Question: The Anti-Nuclear Movement since 1945, 1987; The New Women and the Old Men: Love Sex and the Woman Question, 1990; Being Divine: A Biography of Sarah Bernhardt, 1991; The Life and Many Deaths of Harry Houdini, 1993; Surreal Lives: The Surrealists 1917-1945, 1999; Auto Mobile: How the Car Changed Life, 2002; Automobile, 2002; The Peoples Chef: The Culinary Revolutions of Alexis Soyer, 2004; Governess: The Lives and Times of the Real Jane Eyres, 2008; Other People's Daughters: The Life and Times of the Governess, 2008; Ugly Beauty: Helena Rubinstein, L'Oreal and the Blemished History of Looking Good, 2011. FICTION: Left Right and Centre (mystery novel), 1986; Out of Body out of Mind (mystery novel), 1987; Mind Out, 1991; The Gorgon's Smile, 1992; Tickling the Dragon, 1995; The Uncertainty Principle, 1996; Caravaggio's Angel, 2008. Contributor to periodicals. **Address:** Gillon Aitken Associates, 18-21 Cavaye Pl., London, GL SW10 9PT, England. **Online address:** info@ruthbrandon.co.uk

BRANDS, Hal. American (born United States), b. 1983?. **Genres:** Military/Defense/Arms Control, History. **Career:** Institute for Defense Analyses, researcher and senior defense analyst; History News Service, writer. Historian. **Publications:** From Berlin to Baghdad: America's Search for Purpose in the Post-Cold War World, 2008; Mexico's Narco-Insurgency and U.S. Counterdrug Policy, 2009; Crime, Violence, and the Crisis in Guatemala: A Case Study in the Erosion of the State, 2010; Latin America's Cold War, 2010. **Address:** U.S.A. **Online address:** henry.brands@gmail.com

BRANDS, Henry William. *See* **F, H. W.**

BRANDS, H. W. (Henry William Brands). American (born United States), b. 1953. **Genres:** History, Biography, Autobiography/Memoirs. **Career:** Austin Community College, instructor, 1981-86; Vanderbilt University, visiting assistant professor, 1986-87; Texas A&M University, assistant professor, 1987-89, associate professor, 1990-92, professor of history, 1992-98, Ralph R. Thomas '21 professor of liberal arts, History of the Americas Research Program, coordinator, 1998-2001, distinguished professor, 2000-04, Melbern G. Glasscock chair in American history, 2001-04; University of Texas, visiting assistant professor, 1990, Dickson Allen Anderson centennial professor of history and professor of government, 2005-; Society for Historians of American Foreign Relations, Bernath lecturer, 1992. Writer. **Publications:** Cold Warriors, 1988; The Specter of Nationalism, 1989; India and the United States, 1990; Inside the Cold War, 1991; Bound to Empire, 1992; The Devil We Knew, 1993; Into the Labyrinth, 1994; The United States in the World, 1994; The Wages of Globalism, 1995; The Reckless Decade, 1995, 2nd ed., 2002; Since Vietnam, 1995; The Last Romantic, 1997; What America Owes the World, 1998; Masters of Enterprise, 1999; The First American, 2000; The Strange Death of American Liberalism, 2001; The Age of Gold, 2002; Woodrow Wilson, 2003; Lone Star Nation: How a Ragged Army of Volunteers Won the Battle for Texas Independence and Changed America, 2004; (with R.A. Divine) America Past and Present, 7th ed., 2004; (with R.A. Divine) The American Story, 2005; Andrew Jackson: A Life and Times, 2005; The Money Men: Capitalism, Democracy and the Hundred Years' War Over the American Dollar, 2006; Traitor to His Class: The Privileged Life and Radical Presidency of Franklin Delano Roosevelt, 2008; American Dreams: The United States Since 1945, 2010; American Colossus: The Triumph of Capitalism, 1865-1900, 2010. EDITOR: The Foreign Policies of Lyndon Johnson, 1999; The Use of Force After the Cold War, 2000; Critical Reflections on the Cold War, 2000; Selected Letters of Theodore Roosevelt, 2001. Contributor to periodicals. **Address:** Department of History, University of Texas, BUR 526, Garrison Hall 1.104, 1 University Sta., B7000, Austin, TX 78712-0220, U.S.A. **Online address:** hwbrands@hwbrands.com

BRANDSTETTER, Alois. Austrian (born Austria), b. 1938. **Genres:** Novels, Novellas/Short Stories, Young Adult Fiction. **Career:** University of Saarland, research assistant for altgermanistik and linguistics, 1962-, professor,

1971-74; University of Klagenfurt, professor of old German language and literature, 1974-2007, professor emeritus, 2007-. Writer. **Publications:** (With R. Rath) Zur Syntax des Wetterberichtes und des Telegrammes, 1968; über Untermieter, 1970; Stille Grösse, 1971; überwindung der Blitzangst, 1971 as Von den Halbschuhen der Flachländer und Der Majestät der Alpen, 1980; Prosaauflösung; Studien zur Rezeption der höfischen Epik imfrühnerhoch deutschen Prosaroman, 1971; Ausfälle: Natur und Kunstgeschichten, 1972 as Von den Halbschuhen der Flachländer und Der Majestät der Alpen, 1980; (with L. Aichinger) Daheim ist daheim, 1973; Zu Lasten der Brieftrager: Roman (novel), 1974; Start: Erzählungen, 1976; Der Leumund des Löwen: Geschichten von grossen Tieren und Menschen (short stories), 1976; Die Abtei: Roman (novel), 1977; Vom Schnee der vergangenen Jahre (short stories), 1979; Von den Halbschuhen der Flachländer und der Majestät derAlpen: frühe prosa, 1980; Die Mühle: Roman (novel), 1981; über den grünen Klee der Kindheit (short stories), 1982; Altenehrung: Roman (novel), 1983; (contrib.) Buch der alten Mühlen, 1984; Die Burg: Roman (novel), 1986; Landessäure: starke Stücke und schöne Geschichten, 1986; Kleine Menschenkunde, 1987; So wahr ich Feuerbach heise: Roman (novel), 1988; Romulus und WörtherSEE: Ein poetiches Wörterbuch, 1989; Vom Manne aus Eicha: Roman (novel), 1991; Vom Hören Sagen: Eine poetische Akustik, 1992; Almträume: eine Erzählung, 1993; Herbert Wochinz: Vom Endspiel zum Theater der Freude, 1994; Hier kocht der Wirt: Roman (novel), 1995; Schönschreiben, 1997; Gross in Fahrt, 1998; Die Rampe: Porträt, 1998; Gros in Fahrt: Roman (novel), 1998; Abbey: A Novel, 1998; Meine Besten Geschichten (selected short stories), 1999; Die Zärtlichkeit des Eisenkeils: Roman, 2000; Der Geborene Gärtner: Roman, 2005; (co-author) Freund und Feind: über ihreliterarischen Vorbilder, Widersacher und Nebenbuhler, 2006; Vandale Ist Kein Hunne: Roman, 2007; Cant lässt grüssen, 2009; Zur Entlastung der Briefträger, 2011. EDITOR: (with R. Malter) Saarbrüker Beiträge zur ästhetik, 1966; Daheim istdaheim. Neue Heimatgeschichten (short stories), 1973; Katzenmusik: Prosa, 1974; Gegenwartsliteratur als Bildungswert, 1982; österreichische Erzählungen des 20. Jahrhunderts, 1984; (with György Sebestyén) Der Ort, an dem wir uns befinden: ungarische Erzählerder Gegenwart, 1985; österreichische Erzählungen des 19, Jahrhunderts, 1986; (and foreword) Ich Brauch Einen Wintermantel Etz.: Briefe an Herbert Wochinz, 2005. Contributor to books. **Address:** University of Klagenfurt, Universityersitasstrasse 65-67, Klagenfurt, A-9020, Austria. **Online address:** alois.brandstetter@uni.klu.ac.at

BRANDT, Allan M(orris). American (born United States), b. 1953. **Genres:** Medicine/Health, History, Business/Trade/Industry. **Career:** Hastings Center, intern, 1977; Columbia University, College of Physicians and Surgeons, research associate, 1977-82, faculty of medicine and teaching fellow in the humanities, 1979-82; Smith College, lecturer in American history, 1982; Harvard University, instructor, 1982, assistant professor of history of medicine and science, 1983-87, associate professor, 1987-90, President's fellow, 1989-90, Amalie Moses Kass professor of history of medicine and professor of history of science, 1992-, chair, 2000-06, Harvard Medical School, Department of Social Medicine and Health Policy, instructor, 1982, division of medical ethics, director, 1996-2003, Harvard Medical School MD/PhD Program, Social Science Track, director, 2004-08, Graduate School of Arts and Science, dean, 2008-; University of North Carolina, department of social medicine and history, associate professor, 1990-92. Writer. **Publications:** No Magic Bullet: A Social History of Venereal Disease in the United States Since 1880, 1985, rev. ed., 1987; (ed. with P. Rozin) Morality and Health, 1997; The Cigarette Century: The Rise, Fall and Deadly Persistence of the Product That Defined America, 2007. Contributor to periodicals. **Address:** Office of the Dean, Graduate School of Arts and Sciences, Harvard University, University Hall 3 N, Cambridge, MA 02138, U.S.A. **Online address:** brandt@fas.harvard.edu

BRANDT, Clare. American (born United States), b. 1934?. **Genres:** Biography, Young Adult Non-fiction. **Career:** Writer. **Publications:** (Comp. with A. Kelly) A Livingston Genealogy, 1982; An American Aristocracy: The Livingstons, 1986; The Man in the Mirror: A Life of Benedict Arnold, 1994; (contrib.) A Livingston Genealogical Register, 1995. **Address:** Random House Inc., 1745 Broadway, New York, NY 10019-4343, U.S.A.

BRANDT, Deborah. American (born United States), b. 1951. **Genres:** Language/Linguistics, Humanities, Education. **Career:** University of Wisconsin, assistant professor, 1983-89, associate professor of English, 1990-95, professor, 1995-. Writer. **Publications:** Literacy as Involvement: The Acts of Writers, Readers and Texts, 1990; Literacy in American Lives, 2001; Literacy and Learning: Reflections on Writing, Reading and Society, 2009. Contributor to language and communication journals. **Address:** Department of English, University of Wisconsin, 7195 Helen C. White, 600 N Park St., Madison, WI 53706, U.S.A. **Online address:** dlbrandt@wisc.edu

BRANDT, Di. (Diana Brandt). Canadian (born Canada), b. 1952?. **Genres:** inspirational/Motivational Literature, Women's Studies And Issues, Poetry, Literary Criticism And History, Adult Non-fiction, History, Reference. **Career:** University of Manitoba, lecturer, 1981-95; University of Winnipeg, assistant professor of English, 1986-95; University of Alberta, writer-in-residence, 1995-96, SSHRC research fellow, 1995-96; University of Windsor, associate professor in English, 1997-2005, adjunct professor, 2005-07; Brandon University, professor, Canada research chair, 2005-. Writer. **Publications:** POETRY: Questions I Asked My Mother, 1987; Agnes in the Sky, 1990; Mother Not Mother, 1992; Jerusalem Beloved, 1995; Now You Care, 2003; Bouquet for St. Mary, 2004. OTHERS: The Bridge: Or What's Wrong with Jim McKenzie, 1973; (ed. as Diana Brandt) Being Brothers and Sisters: Stories of Personal Need in the Church, 1984; What's a Nice Feminist?, 1993; Wild Mother Dancing: Maternal Narrative in Canadian Literature, 1993; Dancing Naked: Narrative Strategies for Writing across Centuries, 1996; Now You Care, 2003; (ed. with B. Godard) Re: Generations: Canadian Women Poets in Conversation, 2005; (after word) Speaking of Power: The Poetry of Di Brandt, 2006; So This is the World & Here I Am in It, 2007; (after word) Watermelon Syrup, 2007; Walking to Mojácar: Poems, 2010. **Address:** Department of English, Brandon University, Brandon, MB R7A 6A9, Canada. **Online address:** brandtd@brandonu.ca

BRANDT, Diana. *See* **BRANDT, Di.**

BRANNEN, Julia (M.). British (born England), b. 1944. **Genres:** Human Relations/Parenting, Sociology, Social Sciences, Women's Studies And Issues, Reference. **Career:** Middlesex Hospital, Marriage Research Centre, research officer, 1978-80; University of London, Bedford College, Social Research Unit, research officer, 1980-82, Thomas Coram Research Unit, research officer, 1982-86, 1985-91, project director, 1985-91, Institute of Education, senior research officer, 1991-94, reader in sociology of the family, 1994-98, professor in sociology of the family, 1998-; University of Bergen, visiting professor, 1997, adjunct professor in sociology, 2005-. Writer. **Publications:** (With J. Collard) Marriages in Trouble: The Process of Seeking Help, 1982; (with P. Moss) New Mothers at Work: Employment and Childcare, 1988; Cross-National Studies of Household Resources After Divorce, 1989; (with P. Moss) Managing Mothers: Dual Earner Households after Maternity Leave, 1991; (co-author) Young People, Health and Family Life, 1994; (with M. O'Brien) Children, Research and Policy, 1996; (with E. Heptinstall and K. Bhopal) Connecting Children: Care and Family Life in Later Childhood, 2000; (with P. Moss and A. Mooney) Working and Caring Over the Twentieth Century: Change and Continuity in Four-Generation Families, 2004; (with J. Statham, A. Mooney and M. Brockmann) Coming to Care: The Work and Family Lives of Workers Caring for Vulnerable Children, 2007. EDITOR: (with G. Wilson) Give and Take in Families: Studies in Resource Distribution, 1987; Mixing Methods: Qualitative and Quantitative Research, 1992; (with M. O'Brien) Parenthood and Childhood, 1995; (with M. O'Brien) Children in Families: Research and Policy, 1996; (co-author) Young Europeans, Work and Family: Futures in Transition, 2001; (with P. Moss) Rethinking Children's Care, 2002; (with P. Alasuutari and L. Bickman) SAGE Handbook of Social Research Methods, 2008; (with S. Lewis and A. Nilsen) Work, Families, and Organisations in Transition: European Perspectives, 2009. Contributor to periodicals. **Address:** Thomas Coram Research Unit, Institute of Education, University of London, Rm. 35, 27/28 Woburn Sq., London, GL WC1H 0AA, England. **Online address:** j.brannen@ioe.ac.uk

BRANNIGAN, Augustine. Canadian (born Canada), b. 1949. **Genres:** Social Sciences, Criminology/True Crime, Law, Politics/Government, Social Work. **Career:** University of Western Ontario, assistant professor, 1977-79; University of Calgary, assistant professor, 1979-83, associate professor, 1983-90, professor of sociology, 1990, MacKimmie Library, Prairie Regional Research Data Centre, academic director, 2003-05. **Publications:** NONFICTION: The Social Basis of Scientific Discoveries, 1981; Crimes, Courts, and Corrections: An Introduction to Crime and Social Control in Canada, 1984; Social Responses to Technological Change, 1985; Studying Runaways and Street Youth in Canada: Conceptual and Research Design Issues, 1993; The Rise and Fall of Social Psychology: The Use and Misuse of the Experimental Method, 2004; Social Interaction: Process and Products, 2006. EDITOR: (with S. Goldenberg) Social Responses to Technological Change, 1985; (with C. Reasons) Law and Society: A Critical Perspective, 1989; (with G. Pavlich)

Governance and Regulation in Social Life: Essays in Honour of W.G. Carson, 2007. Contributor of articles to books and journals. **Address:** Department of Sociology, University of Calgary, Rm. SS 1060, 2500 University Dr. NW, Calgary, AB T2N 1N4, Canada. **Online address:** brannigangus@yahoo.com

BRANNIGAN, Gary G(eorge). American (born United States), b. 1947. **Genres:** Education, Psychology. **Career:** Veterans Administration Hospital, clinical psychologist, 1971-72; Devereux Foundation, clinical psychologist, 1972-73; State University of New York, assistant professor, 1973-76, associate professor, 1976-82, professor of psychology, 1982-, Psychological Services Clinic, director, 1975-80; Sibley Educational Research and Demonstration Center, school psychologist, 1978-80; Plattsburgh Little League, board director, 1979-81; Young Men's Christian Association, Youth Basketball Program, coordinator, 1980-85; Northern New York Center for the Emotionally Disturbed, consultant; Psychological Corp., consultant; Riverside Publishing, consultant. Writer. **Publications:** (With A. Tolor) Research and Clinical Applications of the Bender-Gestalt Test, 1980; (with N.A. Brunner) The Modified Version of the Bender-Gestalt Test for Preschool and Primary School Children, 1989, rev. ed., 1996; (with M.R. Merrens) Experiences in Personality, 1998; Experiencing Psychology: Active Learning Adventures, 2000; Experiences in Social Psychology: Active Learning Adventures, 2000; (with N.A. Brunner) Guide to the Qualitative Scoring System for the Modified Version of the Bender-Gestalt Test, 2002; (with S.L. Decker) Bender Gestalt II: Bender Visual Motor Gestalt Test, 2nd ed., 2003; (with H. Margolis) Reading Disabilities: Beating The Odds, 2009. EDITOR: Psychoeducational Perspectives: Readings in Educational Psychology, 1982; (with M.R. Merrens) The Undaunted Psychologist: Adventures in Research, 1992; (with M.R. Merrens) The Social Psychologists: Research Adventures, 1995; The Enlightened Educator: Research Adventures in the Schools, 1996; (with M.R. Merrens) The Developmental Psychologists: Research Adventures across the Life Span, 1996; (with E.R. Allgeier and A.R. Allgeier) The Sex Scientists, 1998; The Sport Scientists, 1999. Works appear in anthologies. Contributor of articles to journals and newspapers. **Address:** Department of Psychology, State University of New York, 213A Beaumont Hall, 101 Broad St., Plattsburgh, NY 12901, U.S.A. **Online address:** gary.brannigan@plattsburgh.edu

BRANOVER, Herman. (Yirmeyahu (Herman) Branover). American (born United States), b. 1931. **Genres:** Engineering, Physics, Theology/Religion, Autobiography/Memoirs. **Career:** Technical School, lecturer in fluid mechanics, 1953-59; Academy of Sciences, senior scientific worker, 1959-70; Institute of Technology, professor of fluid mechanics, 1970-71; Ben-Gurion University of the Negev, professor, 1973-, Center for Magnetohydrodynamics, head, Joint Israeli-Russian Laboratory for Energy Research, head, Lady Davis chair of magnetohydrodynamics, now professor emeritus; New York University, adjunct professor of applied science, 1987-; Solmecs Corp., scientific director, 1980-; SHAMIR Advanced Technologies Engineering Center Ltd., scientific director, SHAMIR Association of Religious Professionals, president, Publishing House, editor-in-chief. **Publications:** Textbook of Elementary Hydraulics and Pump Theory, 1960; (with O. Lielausis) Foundations of Hydraulics, 1963; Turbulent Magnetohydrodynamic Flows in Pipes, 1963; Elementary Hydrodynamics, 1967; Iz glubin: filosofskie nabroski, 1970; (with A. Cinober) Magnetohydrodynamics of Incompressible Media, 1970; (as Yirmeyahu Branover) Mi-máamaḳim: darki el ha-Yahadut, 1973; Vozvrashchenie, 1977; Magnetohydrodynamic Flow in Ducts, 1978; Return: A Philosophical Autobiography, 1983; (as Yirmeyahu Branover) Derekh ḥazarah, 1984; (with A. Naveh) Be-'en ha-lev: 'al ha-Rabi mi-Lubavits', 1989; (with Eidelman, Golbraikh and Moisev) Turbulence and Structures, 1999; (with J. Ginsburg) How Great are Thy Works God, 2000; (with A. Naveh) The Vision of the Heart, 2002; Navi mi-ḳirbekha: ha-biyografyah shel ha-rabi mi-Lubavits', 2006. EDITOR: MHD-Flows and Turbulence, 1976, (with A. Yakhot) vol. II, 1979; (with P.S. Lykoudis and Yakhot) Liquid-Metal Flows and Magnetohydrodynamics, 1983; (with Lykoudis and M. Mond) Single and Multi-Phase Flows in an Electromagnetic Field, 1985; (with M. Mond and Y. Unger) Liquid Metal Flows, 1988; (with M. Mond and Yakhot) Current Trends in Turbulent Research, 1988; (with A. Gottfryd and S. Lipskar) Fusion: Absolute Standards in a World of Relativity, 1989; (with Y. Unger) Metallurgical Technologies, Energy and Conversion, and Magnetohydrodynamic Flows, 1993; (with Y. Unger) Advances in Turbulence Studies, 1993; (with I. Coven-Attia) Science in the Light of Torah, 1994; (with Y. Unger) Progress in Turbulence Research, 1995. **Address:** Department of Mechanical Engineering, Center for MHD Studies, Ben Gurion University of the Negev, PO Box 653, Beer-Sheva, 84 105, Israel. **Online address:** ammi@bgu.ac.il

BRANOVER, Yirmeyahu (Herman). *See* **BRANOVER, Herman.**

BRANSON, Gary D. *See* Obituaries.

BRANT, James. *See* **KENNEALY, Jerry.**

BRANT, Jo-Ann A. American (born United States), b. 1956?. **Genres:** Young Adult Fiction. **Career:** Canadian Mennonite Bible College, assistant professor, 1991-93; Goshen College, professor, 1993. Writer and educator. **Publications:** Dialogue and Drama: Elements of Greek Tragedy in the Fourth Gospel, 2004; (ed. with C.W. Hedrick and C. Shea) Ancient Fiction: The Matrix of Early Christian and Jewish Narrative, 2005. Contributor to books. **Address:** Goshen College, 1700 S Main St., Goshen, IN 46526, U.S.A. **Online address:** joannab@goshen.edu

BRANT, Marley. American (born United States), b. 1950. **Genres:** Biography, History, Music, Politics/Government, Social Commentary, Novels, Criminology/True Crime. **Career:** Chrysalis Records, assistant national director of artist development, 1976-78; Paramount Television, publicist, 1980-81; ICPR Public Relations, publicist, 1981-83; freelance writer and author, 1986-. **Publications:** The Outlaw Youngers: A Confederate Brotherhood, 1992; Outlaws: The Illustrated History of the James-Younger Gang, 1997; Jesse James: The Man and the Myth, 1998; Southern Rockers: The Roots and Legacy of Southern Rock, 1999; Freebirds: The Lynyrd Skynyrd Story, 2002; Tales from the Rock and Roll Highway, 2004; Lightning in a Bottle: Paramount Television's Golden Sitcoms, 1973-1983, 2005; Join Together: Forty Years of the Rock Music Festival, 2008. **Address:** c/o Author Mail, Billboard Books, 770 Broadway, New York, NY 10003, U.S.A. **Online address:** marley@marleybrant.com

BRANTENBERG, Gerd. Norwegian (born Norway), b. 1941. **Genres:** Novels, Literary Criticism And History, Plays/Screenplays, Novellas/Short Stories. **Career:** Tårnby Gymnasium, high school teacher, 1971-74; Women's Houses, feminist activist, 1972-83; Sinsen Gymnasium, high school teacher, 1974-82; Writer, 1982-. **Publications:** NOVELS: Opp alle jordens homofile, 1973; Egalia's døtre, 1977; Ja, vi slutter, 1978; Sangem om St. Croix, 1979; Favntak, 1983; Ved fergestedet, 1985; For alle vinder, 1989; Four Winds, 1996; Augusta og Bjørnstjerne: roman, 1997. MUSICALS: Egalia, 1982. LITERARY HISTORY AND CRITICISM: (co-author) På sporet av den tapte lyst: Kjurlighet mellom kvinner som litterurt motiv, 1986; Eremitt og entertainer: Forfatteren moter sitt publikum, 1991. **Address:** c/o Aschehougs Forlag, Schestedsgt. 3, Oslo, 0855, Norway.

BRANTLEY, Richard E. American (born United States), b. 1944. **Genres:** Literary Criticism And History, Theology/Religion. **Career:** University of Florida, professor of English, 1969-, distinguished alumni professor, 1993-96. Writer. **Publications:** Wordsworth's Natural Methodism, 1975; Locke, Wesley, and the Method of English Romanticism, 1984; Coordinates of Anglo- American Romanticism: Wesley, Edwards, Carlyle & Emerson, 1993; Anglo-American Antiphony: The Late Romanticism of Tennyson and Emerson 1994; Experience and Faith: The Late-Romantic Imagination of Emily Dickinson, 2004. Contributor to journals. **Address:** Department of English, University of Florida, 4008 Turlington Hall, PO Box 117310, Gainesville, FL 32611-7310, U.S.A. **Online address:** brantley@english.ufl.edu

BRANTLINGER, Patrick (Morgan). American (born United States), b. 1941. **Genres:** Literary Criticism And History, Essays, Cultural/Ethnic Topics, Politics/Government, Social Sciences. **Career:** Indiana University, Department of English, assistant professor, 1968-72, associate professor, 1972-78, professor of English, 1978-, chair of department, 1990-94, director of Victorian Studies Graduate Program, 1978-90, now professor emeritus, James Rudy Professor Emeritus of English; Victorian Studies, editor, 1980-90. **Publications:** The Spirit of Reform: British Literature and Politics, 1832-1867, 1977; Bread and Circuses: Theories of Mass Culture as Social Decay, 1983; Rule of Darkness: British Literature and Imperialism, 1830-1914, 1988; (ed.) Energy and Entropy: Science and Culture in Victorian Britain; Essays from Victorian Studies, 1989; Crusoe's Footprints: Cultural Studies in Britain and America, 1990; (ed. with J. Naremore) Modernity and Mass Culture (essays), 1991; Fictions of State: Culture and Credit in Britain, 1694-1994, 1996; The Reading Lesson: The Threat of Mass Literacy in Nineteenth-Century British Fiction, 1998; (ed. and intro.) P.M. Taylor, Confessions of a Thug, 1998; Who Killed Shakespeare?: What's Happened to English since the Radical Sixties, 2001; (ed. and intro.) She: A History of Adventure, 2001; (ed. with W.

Thesing) The Blackwell Companion to the Victorian Novel, 2002; Dark Vanishings: Discourse on the Extinction of Primitive Races, 1800-1930, 2003; Victorian Literature and Postcolonial Studies, 2009; Taming Cannibals: Race and The Victorians, 2011. Contributor to periodicals. **Address:** Department of English, Indiana University, 442 Ballantine Hall, 1020 E Kirkwood Ave., Bloomington, IN 47405-7103, U.S.A. **Online address:** brantli@indiana.edu

BRASCHI, Giannina. American/Puerto Rican (born Puerto Rico), b. 1953. **Genres:** Poetry, Humor/Satire, Novellas/Short Stories, Cultural/Ethnic Topics, Women's Studies And Issues, Social Sciences, Novels. **Career:** Rutgers University, faculty; City University of New York, faculty; Colgate University, faculty, distinguished chair of creative writing, 1997; Grazie magazine, foreign correspondent, 2001-02. Writer. **Publications:** Asalto al Tiempo (poems), 1981; La Poesia de Becquer (criticism), 1982; La Comedia Profana (poems), 1985; El Imperio de los Suenos (poems and a novella), 1988, 2nd. ed., 1999, trans. as Empire of Dreams, 1994; Yo-Yo Boing! (bilingual novel), 1998. **Address:** Publicity Department, Yale University Press, PO Box 209040, New Haven, CT 06520-9040, U.S.A.

BRASHEAR, Jean. American (born United States), b. 1949. **Genres:** Romance/Historical, Novels, Young Adult Fiction. **Career:** Romance novelist. **Publications:** The Bodyguard's Bride, 1998; Millionaire in Disguise, 2001; What the Heart Wants, 2002; The Healer, 2002; Sweet Child of Mine, 2004; Forgiveness, 2005; Coming Home, 2005; Mercy, 2005; Sweet Mercy, 2006; Love is Lovelier, 2006; Return to West Texas, 2007; (with L. Cardillo) A Valentine Gift, 2008; The Way Home, 2008; Go With the Flow, 2008; The Man She Once Knew, 2009; The Goddess of Fried Okra, 2009; Crossing the Line, 2010; On His Honor, 2012; A Texas Chance, 2012. MORNING STAR TRILOGY: A Family Secret, 1999; Lonesome No More, 2000; Texas Royalty, 2000. DEEP IN THE HEART SERIES: What the Heart Wants, 2002; The Healer, 2003; The Good Daughter, 2003; A Real Hero, 2004; Most Wanted, 2004. NASCAR SERIES: (co-author) Holiday 3, 2008; A Family For Christmas, 2008; Extreme Caution, 2008; Black Flag White Lies, 2009. Contributor to magazines. **Address:** c/o Author Mail, Harlequin Enterprises, PO Box 5190, Buffalo, NY 14240-5190, U.S.A. **Online address:** jean@jeanbrashear.com

BRASSEAUX, Carl A(nthony). (Antoine Bourque). American (born United States), b. 1951. **Genres:** History, Bibliography, Translations, Translations. **Career:** University of Louisiana at Lafayette, Center for Cultural and Eco-Tourism, assistant director, 1975-2001, director, 2001-, Center for Louisiana Studies Colonial Records Collection, curator, 1980-, adjunct assistant professor, 1987-90, assistant professor, 1990-94, associate professor, 1994-98, professor of history and geography, 1998-, Center for Louisiana Studies, director, 2003-, Center for Louisiana Studies Publications Program, editor and associate manager; Macmillan Publishing Co., Scribner's Reference Book Division, freelance editor, 1991-92; John Muir Publications, freelance editor, 1994; Universite Laval, visiting professor, 1994; Louisiana Historical Association, fellow, 2000; Louisiana History, managing editor, 2003-. **Publications:** HISTORY: (with G.R. Conrad and R.W. Robison) The Courthouses of Louisiana, 1977, 2nd ed., 1998; (comp. with Conrad) Gone but Not Forgotten, vol. I: St. Peter's Cemetery, New Iberia, LA, 1983; Denis-Nicolas Foucault and the New Orleans Rebellion of 1768, 1987; The Founding of New Acadia, 1987; (ed. and trans. with E. Garcia and J.K. Voorhies) Quest for the Promised Land, 1989; In Search of Evangeline, 1989; Lafayette, Where Yesterday Meets Tomorrow, 1990; The Foreign French: French Immigration into the Mississippi Valley, 1820-1900, vol. I: 1820-1839, 1990, vol. II: 1840-1848, 1992, vol. III: 1820-1900, 1993; Scattered to the Wind, 1991; Acadian to Cajun, 1992; Crevasse: The 1927 Flood in Acadiana, 1994; (with C. Oubre and K.P. Fontenot) Creoles of Color in the Bayou Country, 1995; A Refuge for All Ages, 1996; France's Forgotten Legion, 2000; Steamboats on Louisiana's Bayous, 2004; French, Cajun, Creole, Houma, 2005; (with C.A. Brasseaux and R.A. Brasseaux) Stir the Pot: The History of Cajun Cuisine, 2005; (with M. Bienvenu and R.A. Brasseaux) A History of Cajun Cuisine, 2008; Acadiana: Louisiana's Historic Cajun Country, 2011. REFERENCE WORKS: (with Conrad) A Selected Bibliography of Scholarly Literature on Colonial Louisiana and New France, 1982; (with M.J. Foret) A Bibliography of Acadian History, Literature and Genealogy, 1955-1985, 1986; (with Conrad) Louisiana History: The Journal of the Louisiana Historical Association: Index to vol. I-XXV, 1985, Index to vol. XXVI-XXX, 1990; (with Conrad) A Bibliography of Scholarly Literature on Colonial Louisiana and New France, 1992. OTHER: (as Antoine Bourque) Trois Saisons: Nouvelles, contes, et fables, 1988. EDITOR: (trans.) A Comparative View of French Louisiana: The Journals of Pierre Le Moyne d'Iberville and Jean-Jacques-Blaise d'Abbadie, 1979, 2nd ed., 1980; (with M. Allain) A Franco-American Overview: Louisiana, vol. V, 1981, vol. VI, 1981, vol. VII: The Postbellum Period, 1982, vol. VIII: French Louisiana in the 20th Century, 1982; (with Conrad) M. de V. du Terrage, The Last Years of French Louisiana, 1982; Dictionary of Louisiana Biography, 1988; (with Conrad) The Road to Louisiana: The Saint-Domingue Refugees, 1792-1809, 1992; (with J.D. Wilson) Ten-Year Supplement, 1988-1998, 1998. Works appear in anthologies. Contributor to periodicals. **Address:** Center for Cultural & Eco-Tourism, University of Louisiana, PO Box 40831, Lafayette, LA 70504, U.S.A. **Online address:** brasseaux@louisiana.edu

BRASWELL, Elizabeth. Also writes as J. B. Stephens, Tracy Lynn, Celia Thomson. American/British (born England) **Genres:** Novels, Young Adult Fiction. **Career:** Microsoft Corp., technical support engineer; Harcourt Brace, assistant editor; Simon & Schuster Inc., Interactive Division, video game producer. **Publications:** AS TRACY LYNN: Snow, 2003; Rx, 2006; The Five Rules of Girls, forthcoming. AS J.B. STEPHENS: The Big Empty, 2004; Desolation Angels, 2004; Paradise City, 2004; No Exit, 2005. AS CELIA THOMSON: The Stolen, 2004; The Fallen, 2004; The Chosen, 2005. Contributor of articles to periodicals. **Address:** Simon & Schuster Inc., 1230 Ave. of the Americas, New York, NY 10020, U.S.A. **Online address:** me@lizbraswell.com

BRATT, James D. American (born United States), b. 1949. **Genres:** History, Theology/Religion. **Career:** University of Pittsburgh, assistant professor, associate professor of religious studies, 1978-87; Calvin College, professor of history, 1987-; Calvin Center for Christian Scholarship, director, 1999-2008; Grand Rapids Area Council on the Humanities, consultant. Writer. **Publications:** Dutch Calvinism in Modern America, 1984; (ed.) Viewpoints: Exploring the Reformed Tradition, 1991; (with C. Meehan) Gathered at the River: Grand Rapids, Michigan, and Its People of Faith, 1993; (ed.) Abraham Kuyper: A Centennial Anthology, 1998; (ed.) Antirevivalism in Antebellum America: A Collection of Religious Voices, 2005; (ed. with E. Dommen and J. Calvin) Rediscovered: The Impact of His Social and Economic Thought, 2007; (ed.) By the Vision of Another World: Worship in American History, 2011; (ed. with R.A. Wells) Best of The Reformed Journal, 2012. **Address:** Department of History, Calvin College, 1845 Knollcrest Cir. SE, Hiemenga Hall 478, Grand Rapids, MI 49546-4402, U.S.A. **Online address:** jbratt@calvin.edu

BRAUDE, Stephen E. American (born United States), b. 1945. **Genres:** Philosophy. **Career:** University of Maryland, Department of philosophy, professor of philosophy and chair; Journal of Scientific Exploration, editor-in-chief; Journal of the Society for Scientific Exploration, editor-in-chief. **Publications:** ESP and Psychokinesis: A Philosophical Examination, 1979, rev. ed., 2002; The Limits of Influence: Psychokinesis and the Philosophy of Science, 1986, rev. ed., 1997; First Person Plural: Multiple Personality and the Philosophy of Mind, 1991, rev. ed., 1995; Immortal Remains: The Evidence for Life after Death, 2003; The Gold Leaf Lady and Other Parapsychological Investigations, 2007. Contributor to books. **Address:** Department of Philosophy, University of Maryland, 1000 Hilltop Cir., Baltimore, MD 21250, U.S.A. **Online address:** braude@umbc.edu

BRAUDIS, Bob. American (born United States), b. 1944?. **Genres:** Novels, Biography, Autobiography/Memoirs. **Career:** Pitkin County Sheriff's Office, deputy sheriff, 1977-79, patrol director, 1979-81, jail administrator, 1981-83, director of operations, 1983-86, sheriff, 1986-2011. Writer. **Publications:** (With M. Cleverly) The Kitchen Readings: Untold Stories of Hunter S. Thompson, 2008. **Address:** Committee to Re-elect Braudis, PO Box 9860, Aspen, CO 81612, U.S.A. **Online address:** bob@sheriffbobbraudis.com

BRAUDY, Leo. American (born United States), b. 1941. **Genres:** Film, History, Literary Criticism And History, Social Commentary. **Career:** Yale University, instructor, 1966-68; Columbia University, assistant professor, 1968-70, associate professor, 1970-73, professor, 1973-76; University of California, professor of cinema studies, 1974-80; Johns Hopkins University, professor, 1976-83; University of Southern California, professor, 1983-85, Leo S. Bing professor of English, 1985-, university professor, 1997-. Writer. **Publications:** Narrative Form in History and Fiction: Hume, Fielding, and Gibbon, 1970, 2nd ed., 2003; Jean Renoir: The World of His Film, 1972, 2nd ed., 1989; The World in a Frame: What We See in Films, 1977, 3rd ed., 2002; The Frenzy of Renown: Fame and Its History, 1986, 2nd ed., 1997; Native Informant: Essays on Film, Fiction and Popular Culture, 1991; From Chivalry to Terrorism: War and the Changing Nature of Masculinity, 2003;

Plot of Time: Narrative Form in Hume, Fielding, and Gibbon, 2003; On the Waterfront, 2005; The Hollywood Sign: Fantasy and Reality of an American Icon, 2011. EDITOR: Norman Mailer: A Collection of Critical Essays, 1972; Focus on Shoot the Piano Player, 1972; (with M. Dickstein) Great Film Directors, 1978; Harvard Guide to Contemporary American Writing, 1979; (with M. Cohen and G. Mast) Film Theory and Criticism: Introductory Readings, 5th ed., 1998, 7th ed., 2008. **Address:** Department of English, University of Southern California, THH 447, Los Angeles, CA 90089-0354, U.S.A. **Online address:** braudy@usc.edu

BRAUER, Jurgen. American (born United States), b. 1957. **Genres:** Economics, Adult Non-fiction. **Career:** Augusta State University, assistant professor, 1991-96, associate professor, 1996-2001, professor of economics, 2001-. Writer. **Publications:** NONFICTION: Economic Issues of Disarmament: Contributions from Peace Economics and Peace Science, 1993; (with W.G. Gissy) Economics of Conflict and Peace, 1997. (ed. with K. Hartley) The Economics of Regional Security: NATO, the Mediterranean, and Southern Africa, 2000; (ed. with J.P. Dunne) Arming the South: The Economics of Military Expenditure, Arms Production, and Arms Trade in Developing Countries, 2002; (ed. with J.P. Dunne) Arms Trade and Economic Development: Theory, Policy and Cases in Arms Trade Offsets, 2004; (with H.V. Tuyll) Castles, Battles, and Bombs: How Economics Explains Military History, 2008; War and Nature: The Environmental Consequences of War in a Globalized World, 2009. Contributor of articles to periodicals. **Address:** James. M. Hull College of Business, Augusta State University, Augusta, GA 30904, U.S.A. **Online address:** jbrauer@aug.edu

BRAUER, Ralph. American (born United States) **Genres:** History, Social Sciences, Politics/Government. **Career:** Transforming Schools Consortium, executive director. Writer, consultant and educator. **Publications:** (With D. Brauer) The Horse, the Gun, and the Piece of Property: Changing Images of the TV Western, 1975; The Strange Death of Liberal America, 2006. Contributor to periodicals. **Address:** Transforming Schools Consortium, 14419 Waco St. NW, Ramsey, MN 55303-6179, U.S.A.

BRAULT, Jacques. Canadian (born Canada), b. 1933. **Genres:** Poetry, Plays/Screenplays, Literary Criticism And History, Illustrations, Young Adult Fiction. **Career:** University of Montreal, professor, 1960, now professor emeritus. Writer. **Publications:** POETRY: (with R. Perusse and C. Mathieu) Trinome, 1957; (co-author) La Poesie et Nous, 1958; Mémoire, 1965; Miron Lemagnifique, 1966; Suite Fraternelle, 1969; La Poésie ce Matin, 1971; Trois Partitions, 1972; L'en Dessous, L'admirable, 1975; Poèmes des Quatre côtés, 1975; Chemin Faisant: Essais, 1975; Droits des Salaries et Autogestion: Propositions Concretes Pour les Entreprises Francaises, 1975; Les Hommesde Paille, 1978; Migration, 1979; Vingt-quatre Murmures en Novembre, 1980; (with M. Beaulieu) P.V. Beaulieu, 1981; Trois fois Passera: Précédé de Jour et Nuit, 1981; Moments Fragiles, 1981; La Naissance des Nuages, 1984; Ductus, 1985; Poemes I, 1986; La Poussièredu Chemin: Essais, 1988; La Solitude: Communications de la Seizième Rencontre québécoise Internationale des écrivains, Tenue àMontréal du 16 au 19 Avril 1988, 1989; Il n'y a Plus de Chemin, 1990; (with R. Melancon) Au Petit Matin, 1993; (contrib.) La Beauté: Communications de la XXe Rencontre Québécoise Internationale des écrivains Tenue à Sainte-Adèle et à Montréal du 24 au 28 Avril 1992, 1993; Poèmes Choisis, 1965-1990, 1996; Au Bras des Ombres, 1997; (with E.D. Blodgett) Transfiguration, 1998; Poèmes, 2000; L'artisan, 2006. PROSE: (with A. Brochu and A. Major) Nouvelles, 1963; Agonie: Récit, 1984. OTHERS: Alain Grandbois, 1958, rev. ed., 1967; (ed. with B. Lacroix) Saint-Denys Garneau: Oeuvres, 1971; Au fonds du jardin, 1996; Au bras de ombres, 1997; (with E.D. Blodgett) At the Bottom of the Garden: Accompaniments, 2001; Au coeur du bois, 2005. Illustrations of books by E.D. Blodgett. Contributor to periodicals. **Address:** Université de Montréal, 2900 boul édouard-Montpetit, Montreal, QC H3T 1J4, Canada.

BRAUN, Marta (A.). Canadian (born Canada), b. 1946. **Genres:** Film, Photography. **Career:** Ryerson University, professor of film and photography, 1975-, research chair, 2005-; Ontario College of Art, visiting professor, 1978-79; University of Waterloo, visiting professor, 1981-82; Opera Atelier, board directors, 1988-91. Writer. **Publications:** Picturing Time: The Work of Etienne-Jules Marey (1830-1904), 1992; (contrib.) Eadweard Muybridge: The Kingston Museum Bequest, 2004; (contrib.) Moving Pictures: American Art and Early Film, 1880-1910, 2005; (contrib.) Helios: Eadweard Muybridge in a Time of Change, 2010; Contributor to periodicals. **Address:** Ryerson Polytechnic University, 350 Victoria St., Toronto, ON M5B 1K3, Canada. **Online address:** mbraun@ryerson.ca

BRAUN, Matt(hew). Also writes as W. Burke, Tom Lord. American (born United States), b. 1932. **Genres:** Westerns/Adventure, Young Adult Nonfiction, Novels, Children's Fiction, Young Adult Fiction, Literary Criticism And History, Children's Non-fiction. **Career:** Journalist and writer. **Publications:** Mattie Silks, 1972 as The Gamblers, 1997; Black Fox, 1972; The Savage Land, 1973; El Paso, 1973; Noble Outlaw, 1975; Bloody Hand, 1975; Cimarron Jordan, 1975; Kinch, 1975; Buck Colter, 1976; The Kincaids, 1976; The Second Coming of Lucas Brokaw, 1977; Hangman's Creek, 1979; Lords of the Land, 1979; The Stuart Women, 1980 as This Loving Promise, 1984; Jury of Six, 1980; Tombstone, 1981; The Spoilers, 1981; Manhunter, 1981; Deadwood, 1981; Deadwood, No. 6, 1981; The Judas Tree, No. 7, 1982; (as W. Burke) The Killing Touch, 1983; Santa Fe, 1983 as Bloodstorm, 1985; The Wages of Sin, 1984; Indian Territory, 1985, 2nd ed., 1999; The Brannocks, 1986; (as W. Burke) A Time of Innocence, 1986; Rio Hondo, 1987; Windward West, 1987; A Distant Land, 1988; Tenbow, 1991; Westward of the Law, 1991; Wyatt Earp, 1994; Outlaw Kingdom, 1995; Texas Empire, 1996; One Last Town, 1997; Doc Holliday, 1997; The Last Stand, 1998; Rio Grande, 1998; Gentleman Rogue, 1999; Bloodsport, 1999; You Know My Name, 1999; Death Walk, 2000; Shadow Killers, 2000; Kinch Riley, 2000; Hickok & Cody, 2001; The Wild Ones, 2002; The Overlords, 2003; The Warlords, 2003; Black Gold, 2004; Dakota, 2005; Dodge City, 2006. AS TOM LORD: Highbinders, 1984; Crossfire, 1984; The Wages of Sin, 1984. NONFICTION: The Save-Your-Life Defense Handbook, 1977; Matt Braun's Western Cooking, 1988, 2nd ed., 1996; How to Write Western Novels, 1988. **Address:** Richard Curtis Associates Inc., 171 E 74th St., 2nd Fl., New York, NY 10021, U.S.A. **Online address:** info@mattbraun.com

BRAUN, Richard Emil. Canadian/American (born United States), b. 1934. **Genres:** Poetry, Translations, Young Adult Fiction. **Career:** University of Alberta, Department of Classics, lecturer, 1962-64, assistant professor, 1964-69, associate professor, 1969-76, professor, 1976-96, professor emeritus, 1996-; Modern Poetry Studies, poetry editor, 1970-77. **Publications:** Companions to Your Doom, 1961; Children Passing, 1962; (ed. and intro.) Decimus Junius Juvenalis, Satires, 1965; Bad Land, 1971; The Foreclosure, 1972; (trans.) Sophocles, Antigone, 1973; (trans.) Rhesos, 1978; Last Man In, 1990; The Snow Man is No One, 2001. Contributor to Poetry. **Address:** Department of History & Classics, University of Alberta, 201 N Power Plant, Edmonton, AB T6G 2H4, Canada. **Online address:** krbraun@bcsupernet.com

BRAUN, Stephen R. American (born United States), b. 1957. **Genres:** Adult Non-fiction, Sciences, Social Sciences. **Career:** New England Research Institutes, executive producer, 1994-. Writer. **Publications:** Buzz: The Science and Lore of Alcohol and Caffeine, 1996; The Science of Happiness: Unlocking the Mysteries of Mood, 2000; (with D.S. Charney and C.B. Nemeroff) The Peace of Mind Prescription: An Authoritative Guide to Finding the Most Effective Treatment for Anxiety and Depression, 2004; (with H. Fisch) Male Biological Clock: The Startling News about Aging, Sexuality, and Fertility in Men, 2005; (with D. Farah) Merchant of Death: Money, Guns, Planes, and the Man Who Makes War Possible, 2007; Coping with Depression and Anxiety in Uncertain Times, forthcoming. **Address:** New England Research Institutes, 9 Galen St., Watertown, MA 02472-4515, U.S.A. **Online address:** stephenb@neri.org

BRAUND, Kathryn E. Holland. American (born United States), b. 1955. **Genres:** History, Young Adult Fiction. **Career:** Auburn University, associate professor of history, Hollifield professor of southern history; Friends of Horseshoe Bend, president. Writer. **Publications:** Deerskins and Duffels: Creek Indian Trade with Anglo-America, 1685-1815, 1993, rev. ed., 2008; (ed. with G.A. Waselkov) William Bartram of the Southeastern Indians, 1995; (ed. and intro.) A Concise Natural History of East and West Florida, 1999; (ed. and intro.) History of the American Indians, 2005; (ed. with C.M. Porter) Fields of Vision: Essays on the Travels of William Bartram, 1739-1823, 2010; Tohopeka: Rethinking the Creek War, 2012; Creek War of 1813-1814, forthcoming. **Address:** University of Nebraska Press, 1111 Lincoln Mall, Lincoln, NE 68588-0630, U.S.A.

BRAUNMULLER, A(lbert) R(ichard). American (born United States), b. 1945. **Genres:** Literary Criticism And History, History, Young Adult Fiction. **Career:** University of California, assistant professor, 1971-76, associate professor, 1976-81, professor of English, 1982-, distinguished professor; University of Zurich, visiting professor, 1990. Writer. **Publications:** The Captive Lady, 1982; George Peele, 1983; Natural Fictions: George Chapman's Major Tragedies, 1992. EDITOR: (intro.) The Rise and Fall of the City of Mahagonny, 1976; A Seventeenth-Century Letter Book: A Facsimile Edition of Folger MS Va321, 1983; (ed. with J.C. Bulman) Comedy from Shakespeare to Sheridan: Change and Continuity in the English and European Tradition, 1986; Life and Death of King John, 1989; (with M. Hattway) Cambridge Companion to English Renaissance Drama, 1990, 2nd ed., 2003; Macbeth, 1997, 2nd ed., 2008; Antony and Cleopatra, 1999; The Merchant of Venice, 2000; Tragical History of Hamlet Prince of Denmark, 2001; (with S. Orgel) Complete Works, 2002. **Address:** Department of English, University of California, Humanities Bldg. 280, PO Box 951530, Los Angeles, CA 90095-1530, U.S.A. **Online address:** barddoc@humnet.ucla.edu

BRAUNTHAL, Gerard. American/German (born Germany), b. 1923. **Genres:** International Relations/Current Affairs, Politics/Government, Social Commentary. **Career:** National Bureau of Economic Research, research assistant, 1953-54; University of Massachusetts, instructor, 1954-57, assistant professor, 1957-62, associate professor, 1962-67, professor, 1967-88, professor emeritus, 1988-; Mt. Holyoke College, visiting lecturer, 1957-58; Columbia University, visiting lecturer, 1968; University of Freiburg, visiting lecturer, 1970. Writer. **Publications:** The Federation of German Industry in Politics, 1965; (contrib.) Cases in Comparative Politics, 1965, 2nd ed., 1969; The West German Legislative Process: A Case Study of Two Transportation Bills, 1972; Socialist Labor and Politics in Weimar Germany: The General Federation of German Trade Unions, 1978; The West German Social Democrats 1969-82: Profile of a Party in Power, 1983; The German Social Democrats since 1969: A Party in Power and Opposition, 2nd ed., 1994; (ed. with M.J. Holler) Albert Lauterbach, The Odyssey of Rationality, 1989; Political Loyalty and Public Service in West Germany: The 1972 Decree against Radicals and Its Consequences, 1990; Parties and Politics in Modern Germany, 1996; Right-Wing Extremism in Contemporary Germany, 2009. Contributor to journals. **Address:** Department of Political Science, University of Massachusetts-Amherst, 338 Thompson, 200 Hicks Way, Amherst, MA 01003, U.S.A. **Online address:** gbraunth@polsci.umass.edu

BRAVEBOY-WAGNER, Jacqueline Anne. American (born United States), b. 1948. **Genres:** International Relations/Current Affairs, Politics/Government, Third World, Area Studies, Social Sciences. **Career:** Bowling Green State University, assistant professor of political science, 1979-81; Friends World College (now part of Long Island University), Latin American program, coordinator, 1983-84; City College of New York, Graduate School of CUNY, associate professor, 1984-91, professor of political science, 1991-; Tokyo Metropolitan University, visiting professor, 1988; Caribbean Studies Association, president, 1992-93; International Studies Association, president, 1995-2009; Caricom/UNDP, Latin American agencies, consultant. Writer. **Publications:** The Venezuela-Guyana Border Dispute: Britain's Colonial Legacy in Latin America, 1984; Interpreting the Third World: Politics, Economic and Social Issues, 1985; The Caribbean in World Affairs: Foreign Policies of the English-Speaking Caribbean, 1989; (co-author) The Caribbean in the Pacific Century: Prospects for Caribbean-Pacific Cooperation, 1993; Caribbean Diplomacy: Focus on Washington, Cuba, and the Post Cold War Era, 1995; (ed. with D.J. Gayle) Caribbean Public Policy: Regional, Cultural, and Socioeconomic Issues for the Twenty-First Century, 1997; The Foreign Policies of the Global South: Re-Thinking Conceptual Frameworks, 2003; Small States In Global Affairs: The Foreign Policies of the Caribbean Community (CARICOM), 2007; Institutions of the Global South, 2009. **Address:** Department of Political Science, Graduate School of CUNY, City College of New York, NAC R4/152, 160 Convent Ave., New York, NY 10031, U.S.A. **Online address:** jbraveboy-wagner@gc.cuny.edu

BRAVERMAN, Melanie. American (born United States), b. 1960. **Genres:** Novels, Poetry, Young Adult Fiction. **Career:** Dartmouth College, visiting writer, 2003; Brandeis University, lecturer in creative writing, Jacob Ziskind visiting poet-in-residence. **Publications:** East Justice (novel), 1996; Red (poetry), 2002. Contributor to periodicals. **Address:** Department of English and American Literature, Brandeis University, Rabb 249, 415 South St., PO Box 549110, Waltham, MA 02454-9110, U.S.A. **Online address:** braver@brandeis.edu

BRAVERMAN, Terry. American (born United States), b. 1953. **Genres:** Self Help, Humor/Satire, Psychology. **Career:** Musician, 1984-87; professional speaker and humorist, 1992-; professional standup comic, 1988-91; Terry Braverman & Co., owner. Writer. **Publications:** When the Going Gets Tough, The Tough Lighten Up!: How to be Happy in Spite of It All, 1997. Contributor to magazines. **Address:** Terry Braverman & Co., PO Box 11571, Marina Del Rey, CA 90295, U.S.A. **Online address:** tbraverman@ca.rr.com

BRAWLEY, Ernest. French/American (born United States), b. 1937. **Genres:** Novels. **Career:** Buenos Aires Herald, translator, 1963; Berlitz School, English teacher, 1964; University of Hawaii, instructor in English, 1969; City University of New York, adjunct lecturer, 1985-97, Hunter College, International English Language Institute, faculty. Writer. **Publications:** The Rap, 1974; Selena, 1979; The Alamo Tree: A Novel, 1984. Contributor to magazines. **Address:** c/o John Hawkins, John Hawkins and Associates Inc., 71 W 23rd St., Ste. 1600, New York, NY 10010-4185, U.S.A.

BRAWLEY, Robert L. American (born United States), b. 1939. **Genres:** Theology/Religion, Social Sciences, Reference. **Career:** Seminario Teologico Presbiteriano Asociado Reformado, teacher, 1965-; Beaver College, teacher; Princeton Theological Seminary, teacher; Memphis Theological Seminary, professor of the new testament, 1979-92; McCormick Theological Seminary, professor of new testament, 1992-, Albert G. McGraw professor of the New Testament, 1995-, Albert G. McGaw professor emeritus of New Testament. Writer. **Publications:** Luke-Acts and the Jews: Conflict, Apology, and Conciliation, 1987; Centering on God: Method and Message in Luke-Acts, 1990; Text to Text Pours Forth Speech: Voices of Scripture in Luke-Acts, 1995; (ed. and contrib.) Biblical Ethics and Homosexuality: Listening to Scripture, 1995; (ed.) Character Ethics and the New Testament: Moral Dimensions of Scripture, 2007. **Address:** McCormick Theological Seminary, 5460 S Universityersity Ave., Chicago, IL 60615, U.S.A. **Online address:** rbrawley@mccormick.edu

BRAXTON, Joanne M(argaret). American (born United States), b. 1950. **Genres:** Literary Criticism And History, Poetry, Humanities. **Career:** College of William and Mary, assistant professor, 1980-86, associate professor, 1986-89, Frances L. and Edwin L. Cummings professor of American studies and English and professor of English, 1989-; Harvard University, W.E.B. DuBois Institute for African and African American Studies, artist-in-residence, 1998; University of Muenster, senior Fulbright professor, 2000-01; Morgan State University, artist-in-residence, 2006. Writer. **Publications:** Sometimes I Think of Maryland, 1977; Black Women Writing Autobiography: A Tradition within a Tradition, 1989; (ed. with A.N. McLaughlin) Wild Women in the Whirlwind: Afra-American Culture and the Contemporary Literary Renaissance (anthology), 1990; (ed.) The Collected Poetry of Paul Laurence Dunbar, 1993; (ed.) Maya Angelou's I know Why the Caged Bird Sings: A Casebook, 1999; (ed.) Monuments of the Black Atlantic: Slavery and Memory, 2004. Works appear in anthologies. Contributor to periodicals. **Address:** Department of English, College of William and Mary, PO Box 8795, Williamsburg, VA 23187, U.S.A. **Online address:** jmbrax@wm.edu

BRAY, Libba. American (born United States), b. 1964. **Genres:** Novels. **Career:** Penguin Putnam, Publicity Department, staff; Spier (advertising agency), staff. Novelist. **Publications:** Kari, 2000; A Great and Terrible Beauty, 2003; Rebel Angels, 2005; (ed.) The Restless Dead: Ten Original Stories of the Supernatural, 2007; The Sweet Far Thing, 2007; (co-author) Up All Night, 2008; Going Bovine, 2009; (co-author) Vacations from Hell, 2009; Beauty Queens, 2011. Work appears in anthologies. **Address:** c/o Author Mail, Delacorte Press, Dell Publishing, 1540 Broadway, New York, NY 10036, U.S.A.

BRAY, Patricia. American (born United States) **Genres:** Novels. **Career:** Information Technology project manager and writer. **Publications:** HISTORICAL ROMANCE NOVELS: A London Season, 1997; (with J. Bennett and C. Clare) Bewitching Kittens, 1998; An Unlikely Alliance, 1998; Lord Freddie's First Love, 1999; The Irish Earl, 2000; A Most Suitable Duchess, 2001. FANTASY NOVELS: SWORD OF CHANGE TRILOGY: Devlin's Luck, 2002; The Wrong Mr. Wright, 2002; Devlin's Honor, 2003; Devlin's Justice, 2004. OTHERS: First Betrayal, 2006; Sea Change, 2007; Final Sacrifice, 2008; (ed. with J. Palmatier) After Hours, 2011. **Address:** c/o Author Mail, Bantam Dell Books, 1745 Broadway, New York, NY 10019, U.S.A. **Online address:** patriciabray@sff.net

BRAY, Robert C. American (born United States), b. 1944. **Genres:** Biography, History. **Career:** Illinois Wesleyan University, professor, R. Forest Colwell professor of American literature, 1970-; Read Illinois, chair, 1983-92. Writer. **Publications:** In Pursuit of a Distinctive Utterance: Realistic Novels in the Midwest, 1871-1914, 1971; (ed. with P.E. Bushnell) Diary of a Common Soldier in the American Revolution, 1775-1783: An Annotated Edition of the Military Journal of Jeremiah Greenman, 1978; Rediscoveries: Literature and Place in Illinois, 1982; A Reader's Guide to Illinois Literature, 1985; (ed. and intro.) The Valley of Shadows: Sangamon Sketches, 1990; Peter Cartwright, Legendary Frontier Preacher, 2005; Reading with Lincoln, 2010. **Address:** Department of American Literature, Illinois Wesleyan University, Rm. 103, English House, 1312 Park St., Bloomington, IL 61701-2900, U.S.A. **Online address:** bbray@iwu.edu

BRAYFIELD, Celia. British (born England), b. 1945. **Genres:** Novels, Language/Linguistics, Art/Art History, Human Relations/Parenting, Young Adult Fiction, Children's Fiction, Social Sciences. **Career:** Nova, trainee journalist, 1968; Observer, fashion writer, 1969; Daily Mail, features writer, 1969-71; freelance writer, 1971-74; Evening Standard, TV columnist, 1974-82; The Times, TV critic, 1982-88, feature writer, 1998-; Sunday Telegraph, columnist, 1989; Brunel University, senior lecturer in creative writing, 2005-, reader in creative writing, Creative Enterprise Centre, director. Writer. **Publications:** NON-FICTION: (with Y. Ocampo) Body Show Book, 1982; Glitter: The Truth about Fame, 1985; Bestseller: Secrets of Successful Writing, 1996; Deep France: A Writer's Year in the Béarn, 2004; Arts Reviews: And How to Write Them, 2008. NOVELS: Pearls, 1987; The Prince, 1990; The Princess, 1991; White Ice, 1994; Getting Home, 1998; Harvest, 1999; Sunset, 2000; Heartswap, 2001; Mister Fabulous and Friends, 2003; Wild Weekend, 2004. Contributor to periodicals. **Address:** c/o Jonathan Lloyd, Curtis Brown Group Ltd., Haymarket House, 28-29 Haymarket, 4th Fl., London, GL SW1Y 4SP, England. **Online address:** celia.brayfield@brunel.ac.uk

BRAZAITIS, Mark. American (born United States), b. 1966. **Genres:** Novellas/Short Stories, History, Young Adult Non-fiction, Poetry, Children's Fiction. **Career:** Bowling Green Junior High School, creative writing instructor, 1993-94; Bowling Green State University, English instructor, 1993-95; Farmer-to-Farmer Program, U.S. AID, technical consultant, 1995; World Learning Center, technical trainer, 1995-96; Helene Fuld College of Nursing, adjunct English professor, 1996-; Fordham University, adjunct English professor, 1998-; West Virginia University, Department of English, associate professor, director of creative writing, researcher. Writer. **Publications:** Qué Onda Vos?, 1996; The River of Lost Voices: Stories from Guatemala, 1998; Steal My Heart: A Novel, 2000; (ed.) Pinnick Kinnick Hill: An American Story=Las colinas sueñan en español, 2003; An American Affair, 2005. Contributor of articles and periodicals. **Address:** Department of English, Eberly College of Arts and Sciences, West Virginia University, 458 Stansbury Hall, Morgantown, WV 26506-6296, U.S.A. **Online address:** mark.brazaitis@mail.wvu.edu

BREAKWELL, Glynis M(arie). British (born England), b. 1952. **Genres:** Psychology, Social Sciences, Sociology. **Career:** University of Bradford, lecturer in social psychology, 1976-78; University of Oxford, Nuffield College, prize fellow, 1978-81, tutor in external studies, 1978-85, tutor in social psychology, 1978-82; University of Surrey, lecturer in social psychology, 1981-87, senior lecturer in psychology, 1987-88, reader, 1988-91, Department of Psychology, head, 1990-95, professor of psychology, 1991-2001, pro-vice-chancellor, 1994-2001, School of Human Sciences, head, 1997-2001; University of Bath, vice-chancellor, 2001-, academic leader and chief executive, Universities Superannuation Scheme, director; University of Shandong, honorary professor, 2004-; Theatre Royal, director; Bath Technology Centre, director; Cheltenham Ladies College, governor; Daphne Jackson Trust, chairman. Writer. **Publications:** (With C. Rowett) Social Work: The Social Psychological Approach, 1982; The Quiet Rebel: Women at Work in a Man's World, 1985; Coping with Threatened Identities, 1986; Quiet Rebel: How to Survive as a Woman & Businessperson, 1986; Facing Physical Violence, 1989; Interviewing, 1990; (with C. Rowett) Managing Violence at Work, 1992; (co-author) Careers and Identities, 1992; (with L. Millward) Basic Evaluation Methods, 1995; Coping with Aggressive Behaviour, 1997; Psychology of Risk, 2007. EDITOR: (with H. Foot and R. Gilmour) Social Psychology, 1982; Threatened Identities, 1983; (with H. Foot and R. Gilmour) Doing Social Psychology: Laboratory and Field Exercises, 1988; Social Psychology of Political and Economic Cognition, 1992; Social Psychology of Identity and the Self Concept, 1992; (D.V. Canter) Empirical Approaches to Social Representations, 1993; (with S. Hammond and C. Fife-Schaw) Research Methods in Psychology, 1994, 2nd ed., 2000; (with E. Lyons) Changing European Identities, 1996; Doing Social Psychology Research, 2004; Research Methods in Psychology, 2006. **Address:** Vice-Chancellor's Office, University of Bath, Bath, SM BA2 7AY, England. **Online address:** g.breakwell@bath.ac.uk

BREARS, Peter C. D. British (born England), b. 1944. **Genres:** Crafts, Food And Wine, History. **Career:** Curtis Museum, curator, 1967-69; Shibden Hall, keeper, 1969-72; Clarke Hall, curator, 1972-75; The Castle Museum, curator, 1975-79; Leeds City Museums, director, 1979-94. Writer and museum consultant. **Publications:** Catalogue of English Country Pottery Housed in the Yorkshire Museum, York, 1968; The English Country Pottery: Its History and Techniques, 1971; The Collector's Book of English Country Pottery, 1974; Yorkshire Probate Inventories 1542-1685, 1972; St. Mary's Heritage Centre, York, 1976; York Castle Museum, 1978; Yorkshire Farmhouse Fare, 1978; The Castle Museum, York, Guidebook, 1978; The Kitchen Catalogue, 1979; The Dairy Catalogue, 1979; Horse Brasses, 1981; The Gentlewoman's Kitchen: Great Food in Yorkshire, 1650-1750, 1984; Food and Cooking in Britain, 1985; Traditional Food in Yorkshire, 1987; North Country Folk Art, 1989; Of Curiosities and Rare Things, 1989; Treasures for the People, 1989; (co-author) Traditional Food East and West of the Pennines: Papers, 1991; Images of Leeds, 1992; Leeds Describ'd, 1993; (co-author) Taste of History: 10, 000 Years of Food in Britain, 1993; Leeds Waterfront, 1994; (ed. with P.A. Sambrook) The Country House Kitchen, 1650-1900: Skills and Equipment for Food Provisioning, 1996; The Old Devon Farmhouse, 1998; Ryedale Recipes, 1998; (with R. Weir and C. Liddell) Recipes From the Dairy, 1998; A Taste of Leeds, 1998; All the King's Cooks: The Tudor Kitchens of King Henry VIII at Hampton Court Palace, 1999; The Compleat Housekeeper, 2000; The Boke of Kervynge, 2003; Tudor Cookery: Recipes & History, 2003; Stuart Cookery: Recipes & History, 2004; Cooking and Dining in Medieval England, 2008; Traditional Food in Shropshire, 2009; Traditional Food in Shropshire, 2009; Jellies & their Moulds, 2010. **Address:** Laurence Pollinger Ltd., 9 Staple Inn, Holborn, London, GL WC1V 7QH, England.

BREBNER, Philip. Portuguese/British (born England), b. 1955. **Genres:** Adult Non-fiction, Travel/Exploration, Literary Criticism And History. **Career:** King Abdulaziz University, assistant professor of architecture and planning, 1982-84; Universidade do Porto, adjunct professor of architecture and planning, 1985-90. Writer. **Publications:** A Country of Vanished Dreams, 1992; Maghrib-Mashriq: Travels in the Mind, 1993; The Fabulous Road, 1997. Contributor to periodicals. **Address:** Peters Fraser and Dunlop Group Ltd., Drury House, 34-43 Russell St., London, GL WC2B 5HA, England.

BRECHER, Michael. Canadian (born Canada), b. 1925. **Genres:** International Relations/Current Affairs, Politics/Government, Social Sciences. **Career:** McGill University, lecturer, 1952-54, assistant professor, 1954-58, associate professor, 1958-63, professor, 1963-93, R.B. Angus professor of political science, 1993-; University of Chicago, visiting professor, 1963; Hebrew University of Jerusalem, visiting professor, 1970-75; University of California Berkeley, visiting professor, 1979; Stanford University, visiting professor, 1980. Writer. **Publications:** The Struggle for Kashmir, 1953; Nehru: A Political Biography, 1959; The New States of Asia, 1963; Succession in India: A Study in Decision-Making, 1966; India and World Politics: Krishna Menon's View of the World, 1968; Political Leadership in India: An Analysis of Elite Attitudes, 1969; The Foreign Policy System of Israel: Setting, Images, Process, 1972; Israel, the Korean War and China, 1974; Decisions in Israel's Foreign Policy, 1974; Studies in Crisis Behavior, 1979; Decisions in Crisis: Israel 1967 and 1973, 1980; Crisis and Change in World Politics, 1986; Crises in the Twentieth Century, 2 vols., 1988; Crisis, Conflict, and Instability, 1989; Crises in World Politics, 1993; A Study of Crisis, 1997, 2000; Millennial Reflections on International Studies, 5 vols., 2002; International Political Earthquakes 2008. **Address:** Department of Political Science, McGill University, 855 Sherbrooke St. W, Montreal, QC H3A 2T7, Canada. **Online address:** michael.brecher@mcgill.ca

BRECKENRIDGE-HAYWOOD, Mae. American (born United States), b. 1940. **Genres:** Philosophy, Politics/Government, History. **Career:** John F. Kennedy High School, librarian, 1963-71; Norfolk State University, Circulation Department, assistant librarian, 1971; Portsmouth Public School, librarian, 1972; Brighton Elementary School, librarian, 1972-90; Churchland Academy Elementary School, librarian, 1972-90; Emily Spong, librarian; Woodrow Wilson High School, librarian; I. C. Norcom High School, librarian, 1992-2001, retired, 2001; African American Historical Society of Portsmouth, president. Writer. **Publications:** (With D. Walters) Inscriptions in Triumph: Tombstone Inscriptions from the African American Cemeteries of MT. Calvary, MT. Olive, Fisher's Hill and Potter's Field, 2001; (with C. Newby-Alexander) Black America: Portsmouth, Virginia, 2003. Contributor to periodicals. **Address:** African American Historical Society of Portsmouth, Park View United Church, 1131 Crawford Pkwy., Portsmouth, VA 23704-

2217, U.S.A. **Online address:** maehaywood@msn.com

BREDERO, Adriaan H(endrik). (David Douglas Boaz). Dutch (born Netherlands), b. 1921. **Genres:** History, Translations. **Career:** St, Bonifatiuscollege, professor of history, 1948-66; Theological Faculty, professor of church history, 1967-75; Free University, professor of medieval history, 1976-86, now professor emeritus. Writer. **Publications:** Etudes sur la Vita Prima de Saint Bernard, 1960; Bernhard von Clairvaux im Wilderstreit der Historie, 1966; Cluny et Cîteaux au douzième siècle: l'histoire d'une controverse monastique: avec des résumés en allemand et en anglais, une bibliographie et un index, 1975; (ed. with L. de Blois) Kerk en vrede, in oudheid en middeleeuwen, 1980; Christenheid en christendom in de middeleeuwen: over de verhouding van godsdienst, kerk en samenleving, 1986, 3rd rev. ed., 2000; Bernardus van Clairvaux (1091-1153): tussen cultus en historie: de ontoegankelijkheid van een hagiografisch levensverhaal, 1993, trans. as Bernard of Clairvaux: Between Cult and History, 1996; The Dechristianization of the Middle Ages (in Dutch), 2000; Ontkerstening der middeleeuwen: een terugblik op de geschiedenis van twaalf eeuwen christendom, 2000. **Address:** Amsterdam Free University, De Boelelaan 1105, Amsterdam, 1081 HV, Netherlands.

BREDSDORFF, Bodil. Danish (born Denmark), b. 1951. **Genres:** Novels, Children's Fiction. **Career:** Tarnby Kindergarten College, teacher; Glostrup Hospital, Department of Child Psychiatric, gestalt therapist and educator. Writer. **Publications:** CHILDREN OF CROW COVE SERIES: Krageungen, 1993; Eidi, 2009; Tink, 2011; Alek, 2012. **Address:** c/o Louise Langhoff Koch, Gyldendal Group Agency, 3 Klareboderne, Copenhagen K, 1001, Denmark. **Online address:** bodilbredsdorff@mail.tele.dk

BREEDEN, Joann Elizabeth. American (born United States), b. 1934. **Genres:** Human Relations/Parenting, Medicine/Health, Self Help. **Career:** Serenity Lane, lecturer, 1977-, supervisor of family program, 1977-87, director of family education services, 1987-. Writer. **Publications:** Chemical Family, 1984; Love, Hope and Recovery: Healing the Pain of Addiction, 1994. **Address:** Serenity Ln., 616 E 16th, Eugene, OR 97401, U.S.A.

BREEN, Steve. American (born United States), b. 1970. **Genres:** Children's Fiction, Humor/Satire. **Career:** Asbury Park Press, editorial cartoonist, 1996-2001; San Diego Union-Tribune, editorial cartoonist, 2001-. Writer. **Publications:** Your Grandma Rocks, Mine Rolls: A Grand Avenue Collection, 2001; Stick, 2007; Violet the Pilot, 2008; Secret of Santa's Island, 2009. **Address:** San Diego Union-Tribune, 350 Camino de la Reina, PO Box 120191, San Diego, CA 92108-3003, U.S.A. **Online address:** steve.breen@uniontrib.com

BREEN, Susan. (Susan Zelony). American (born United States), b. 1956. **Genres:** Novels, Architecture. **Career:** Gotham Writers Workshop, teacher; Fortune magazine, staff; Foreign Policy Association, editor. Journalist, writer and educator. **Publications:** Come Play at the Park: A Little Sturdy Page Book, 1999; Come Play at Home: A Little Sturdy Page Book, 1999; Entertaining for Wimps, 2003; Creating Your Dream Bathroom: How to Plan and Style the Perfect Space, 2005; Creating Your Dream Kitchen: How to Plan and Style the Perfect Space, 2005; The Fiction Class (novel), 2006. Contributor to periodicals. **Address:** Irvington, NY , U.S.A. **Online address:** susan@susanjbreen.com

BREHONY, Kathleen A. American (born United States), b. 1949. **Genres:** Self Help, Human Relations/Parenting, Sex, Young Adult Non-fiction. **Career:** University of Mississippi Medical Center, Department of Psychiatry and Human Behavior, chief resident, 1979-80; Virginia Tech, Department of Psychology and Extension Specialist in Human Ecology, assistant professor, 1981-83; The Media Works of Virginia Inc., president, 1983-88, director and chair, 1986-88; The Center for Women's Health Community Hospital, consulting psychologist, 1985-86; Comprehensive Back School, Downtown West Wellness and Fitness Center, consulting psychologist, 1985-86; The Acting Co., director, 1986-88; Health Care Marketing Programs Inc., director, 1986-88; Southern Shores Realty, director of marketing and human resources, 1988-89; Virginia Beach Psychiatric Center, adjunct medical staff, 1990-92; Full Potential Living, personal and organizational coach, 1998-, Full Potential Organizations, organizational consultant, 1999-; Jones Brehony Seminars, writing instructor, 2000-; Arthur Young and Co. (now Ernst and Young), management and marketing consultant; Outer Banks Media L.LC., executive producer. **Publications:** Awakening at Midlife: Realizing Your Potential for Growth and Change, 1996; Ordinary Grace: An Examination of the Roots of Compassion, Altruism, and Empathy, and the Ordinary Individuals Who Help Others in Extraordinary Ways, 1999; (with R. Gass) Chanting: Discovering Spirit in Sound, 1999; After the Darkest Hour: How Suffering Begins the Journey to Wisdom, 2000; (with K. Jones) Up the Bestseller Lists!: A Hands-On Guide to Successful Book Promotion, 2001; Living a Connected Life: Creating and Maintaining Relationships that Last, 2003. EDITOR: (with L.W. Frederiksen and L.J. Solomon) Marketing Health Behavior: Principles, Techniques, and Applications, 1984; (with E.D. Rothblum) Boston Marriages: Romantic but Asexual Relationships among Contemporary Lesbians, 1993. **Address:** Full Potential Living, 1118 Burnside Rd., Manteo, NC 27954, U.S.A. **Online address:** kbrehony@earthlink.net

BREINER, Laurence A. American (born United States) **Genres:** Poetry, Literary Criticism And History. **Career:** University of Pennsylvania, Center for Study of Black Literature and Culture, Rockefeller fellow, 1991-92; University of Tokyo, American Studies, visiting professor, 2004; Boston University, professor of English, African Studies Program, faculty. Writer. **Publications:** An Introduction to West Indian Poetry, 1998; Orality and Decolonization in West Indian Poetry: The Chemistry of Presence, 2005; Black Yeats: Eric Roach and the Politics of Caribbean Poetry, 2008. Contributor to books and periodicals. **Address:** Department of English, Boston University, Rm. 421, 236 Bay State Rd., Boston, MA 02215-1403, U.S.A. **Online address:** lbrei@bu.edu

BREIVIK, Patricia Senn. American (born United States), b. 1939. **Genres:** Librarianship, Education, Literary Criticism And History. **Career:** School librarian, 1969-70; City University of New York, Brooklyn College, humanities reference librarian, 1970; Pratt Institute, lecturer, 1971-72, Graduate School of Library and Information Science, assistant professor and assistant dean of 1972-76; Sangamon State University, dean of library services and associate professor, 1976-79; University of Colorador, director of Auraria Library and professor, 1979-90, special assistant to the president, 1984-90; Columbia University, visiting professor, 1988; National Forum on Information LIteracy, chair, 1989-2005; Towson State University, associate vice-president for information resources, 1990-95; dean of university libraries, 1995-; San Jose State University, dean of the University Library, through 2005; Nehemiah Communications, vice-president, 2005-. Writer. **Publications:** Open Admissions and the Academic Library, 1977; Planning the Library Instruction Program, 1982; (with E.G. Gee) Information Literacy: Revolution in the Library, 1989; (with J.A. Senn) Information Literacy: Educating Children for the Twenty-First Century, 1994, 2nd ed., 1998; Student Learning in the Information Age, 1997; (with E.G. Gee) Higher Education in the Internet Age: Libraries Creating a Strategic Edge, 2006. EDITOR and CONTRIBUTOR: The Political Science of Information, 1975; (with E.B. Gibson) Funding Alternatives for Libraries, 1979; Managing Programs for Learning Outside the Classroom, 1986; (with R. Wedgeworth) Libraries and the Search for Academic Excellence, 1988. Contributor of articals to journals. **Address:** Nehemiah Communications, 101 Rice Bent Way, Ste. 6, 3100 David Adamany Undergraduate Library, 5155 Anthony Wayne Dr., Columbia, SC 29229, U.S.A. **Online address:** p.breivik@wayne.edu

BREMER, L. Paul. American (born United States), b. 1941. **Genres:** Politics/Government, Biography, History, Adult Non-fiction. **Career:** U.S. Department of State, diplomat, 1966-89, secretary of state, executive assistant, 1973-76, U.S. Embassy-Norway, deputy chief of mission, 1976-79, executive secretary and special assistant, 1981-83, U.S. ambassador to the Netherlands, 1983-86, ambassador-at-large for counterterrorism, 1986-89; Kissinger Associates, managing director, 1989-2000; Air Products and Chemicals Corp., director; Harvard Business School Club of New York, director, 1990-2003; Netherland-America Foundation, director, 1990-2003; Connor Peripherals, director, 1990-97; Lincoln-Douglas Scholarship Foundation, co-founder and president, 1995-; Bipartisan National Commission on Terrorism, chairman, 1999-2000; March Crisis Consulting, chairman and chief executive officer, 2000-03; Catholic Charities of Washington, director; Coalition Provisional Authority-Iraq, head, administrator, 2003-04; presidential envoy to Iraq, 2003-04. Writer. **Publications:** (With M. McConnell) My Year in Iraq: The Struggle to Build a Future of Hope, 2006. **Address:** c/o Marvin Josephson, ICM Talent, 40 W 57th St., New York, NY 10019-4001, U.S.A.

BRENAMAN, Miriam. American (born United States) **Genres:** Young Adult Non-fiction, Military/Defense/Arms Control. **Career:** Writer. **Publications:** Evvy's Civil War, 2002. Contributor to periodicals. **Address:** c/o Author Mail, G.P. Putnam's Sons, 345 Hudson St., New York, NY 10014, U.S.A.

BRENDON, Piers. British (born England), b. 1940. **Genres:** Biography, History. **Career:** Cambridgeshire College of Arts and Technology, Department of History, lecturer, 1966-79, head, 1977-79; Cambridge University, Churchill College, fellow, 1994-, Archives Center, Churchill Archives, keeper, 1995-2001. Writer. **Publications:** (Comp. with W. Shaw) Reading They've Liked, 1967; Hurrell Froude and the Oxford Movement, 1974; Hawker of Morwenstow: Portrait of a Victorian Eccentric, 1975; Eminent Edwardians, 1979; The Life and Death of the Press Barons, 1982; Winston Churchill, 1984; Our Own Dear Queen, 1986; Ike: His Life and Times, 1986; Thomas Cook: 150 Years of Popular Tourism, 1991; (with P. Whitehead) The Windsors: A Dynasty Revealed, 1994; The Motoring Century: The Story of the Royal Automobile Club, 1997; The Dark Valley: A Panorama of the 1930s, 2000; (with P. Whitehead) The Windsors-A Dynasty Revealed 1917-2000, 2000; Eminent Edwardians: Four Figures Who Defined their Age, Northcliffe, Balfour, Pankhurst, Baden-Powell, 2003; Decline and Fall of the British Empire, 1781-1997, 2007. EDITOR WITH W. SHAW: Reading Matters, 1969; By What Authority?, 1972. Contributor to periodicals. **Address:** Churchill College, Storey's Way, Cambridge, CB CB3 0DS, England. **Online address:** pb204@cam.ac.uk

BRENER, Milton E(rnest). American (born United States), b. 1930. **Genres:** Anthropology/Ethnology, Art/Art History, Psychology, Documentaries/Reportage, History, Social Sciences, Paranormal. **Career:** Orleans Parish, assistant district attorney, 1956-58, part-time attorney, 1962-63; Garon, Brener and McNeely, trial lawyer, 1958-91; partner, 1958-. Writer. **Publications:** The Garrison Case: a Study of the Abuse of Power, 1969; The Other Side of the Airport: The Private Pilot's World, 1982; Opera Offstage: Passion and Politics behind the Great Operas, 1996; Faces: The Changing Look of Humankind, 2000; Vanishing Points: Three Dimensional Perspectives in Art and History, 2004; Richard Wagner and the Jews, 2006; Evolution and Empathy: The Genetic Factor in the Rise of Humanism, 2008; Our Interplanetary Future: A UFO Primer for Skeptics, 2009. **Address:** 201 W 72nd St., Apt. 17 H, New York, NY 10023, U.S.A. **Online address:** mebrener@aol.com

BRENNA, Beverley. Canadian (born Canada), b. 1962. **Genres:** Novels, Novellas/Short Stories. **Career:** Border Land School Division, elementary school teacher; Outlook School Division, elementary school teacher; Saskatchewan Valley School Division, elementary school teacher and educational consultant; University of Saskatchewan, assistant professor of curriculum studies. Writer. **Publications:** NOVELS: Spider Summer, 1998; The Keeper of the Trees, 1999; Wild Orchid, 1999; The Moon Children, 2007; Waiting for No One, 2010; Falling for Henry, 2011. OTHERS: Daddy Longlegs at Birch Lane, 1996; Something to Hang On To (stories), 2009. Contributor to books and periodicals. **Address:** College of Education, University of Saskatchewan, ED 3121, 28 Campus Dr., Saskatoon, SK S7N 0X1, Canada. **Online address:** beverley.brenna@gmail.com

BRENNA, Duff. American (born United States) **Genres:** Novels, Young Adult Fiction. **Career:** California State University, associate professor of literature and creative writing, now professor emeritus of English literature and creative writing. Writer. **Publications:** The Book of Mamie (novel), 1989; The Holy Book of the Beard, 1996; Too Cool, 1998; The Altar of the Body, 2001; The Willow Man, 2005; The Law of Falling Bodies, 2007; Murdering the Mom: A Memoir, 2012. **Address:** Sobel Weber Associates Inc., 146 E 19th St., New York, NY 10003-2404, U.S.A. **Online address:** info@duffbrenna.com

BRENNAN, Christine. American (born United States), b. 1958. **Genres:** Sports/Fitness, Recreation, Autobiography/Memoirs, Biography. **Career:** Miami Herald, sportswriter, 1981-84; Washington Post, reporter and sportswriter, 1984-86; USA Today, sports columnist, 1997-; American Broadcasting Co., on-air Olympics commentator, 1996, 1998, 2000; Entertainment and Sports Network (ESPN), on-air Olympics commentator, 2002; National Public Radio, Morning Edition, commentator; ESPN Radio, commentator; WMAL Radio, commentator. **Publications:** The Miracle of Miami: The Inside Story of the Hurricanes' Championship Season, 1984; (with T. Austin) Beyond Center Court: My Story, 1992; Inside Edge: A Revealing Journey into the Secret World of Figure Skating, 1996; Edge of Glory: The Inside Story of the Quest for Figure Skating's Olympic Gold Medals, 1998; Champions on Ice, 2002; Best Seat in the House: A Father, a Daughter, a Journey Through Sports, 2006. **Address:** Scribner Publishing, 1230 Ave. of the Americas, New York, NY 10020, U.S.A. **Online address:** christine@christinebrennan.com

BRENNAN, Frank. Australian (born Australia), b. 1954. **Genres:** Civil Liberties/Human Rights, Humanities, Law, Politics/Government, Young Adult Fiction. **Career:** Australian Catholic University, professor of law; University of Notre Dame, professor of human rights and social justice; Uniya Jesuit Social Justice Centre, founding director, director, through 2004; Australian National University, Research School of Pacific and Asian Studies, adjunct fellow; Australia and New Zealand Studies Center, visiting fellow; Jesuit Refugee Service, director, 2001-02; Boston College, Jesuit institution fellow, 2004-05. Lawyer, jesuit priest and writer. **Publications:** Too Much Order with Too Little Law, 1983; Queensland Aboriginal Land Tenure Becomes a Reality, 1984; (with J. Egan and J. Honner) Finding Common Ground: An Assessment of the Bases of Aboriginal Land Rights, 1984; (with R. Scruton and J. Hyde) Land Rights and Legitimacy: Three Views, 1985; Aboriginal Aspirations to Land, 1986; (with J. Crawford) Aboriginality, Recognition and Australian Law: Where To from Here, 1989; Looking for the Moonlight on the Land: Land Issues in Palau, 1989; Rights and Duties, 1990; The Rights to Protest and the Law: An Australian Perspective: The Role of the Peaceful Protest in the Democratic Process: An Address to the EARC Seminar, 1990; Aboriginal Customary Law and Community Justice: Mechanisms in Light of the Royal Commission into Aboriginal Deaths in Custody, 1991; Criminal Justice: A Christian Perspective: Address to the Prison-The Last Option Conference 1991, 1991; Land Law: Current Legislative Provisions in Queensland, 1991; Opting to Take a Stand: The Preferential Option for the Poor in Catholic Social Teaching, 1991; Reconciling the Unreconciled: Accommodating the Irreconcilable: Public Issue Dispute Resolution, 1991; Self-Determination for Aborigines: Limits and Possibilities, 1991; We Know What You Want but Tell Us What You'll Accept: Address to Yalga-Binbi Institute, 1991; Sharing the Country, 1991, 2nd ed., 1994; The Mabo Case and Terra Nullius, 1992; Social Justice-From Rhetoric to Action, 1992; The 1988 Referendum: A Lost Opportunity for an Australian Declaration on Religious Freedom, 1992; The Church's Mission and Social Justice, 1992; The Ethics of Sustainable Development: Coronation Hill, 1992; The Growth Points and Pre-Determined Limits of Aboriginal Self-Determination under the New Partnership of the 1990s, 1992; How Best to Promote Civil and Political Rights in Queensland, 1992; Land Rights Queensland Style: The Struggle for Aboriginal Self-Management, 1992; The Law, Politics and Religion of Land Rights in the Post-Mabo Era, 1993; Mabo and the Racial Discrimination Act 1975: The Limit of Native Title and Fiduciary Duty under Australia's Sovereign Parliaments, 1993; PRC Nationals: Some Problems and Responsibilities, 1993; Putting Mabo in Perspective, 1993; Self-Determination: The Limits of Allowing Aboriginal Communities to Be a Law unto Themselves, 1993; Sharing the Country, the Real Truth about Mabo Catholic Commission for Justice, 1993; The Vocation of Careers: A Talk to the Society of St. Vincent de Paul, 1993; Catholic Social Teaching and Bills of Rights, 1993; The Ethics of Migration, Asylum and Refuge, 1993; The Implications for Australia of Mabo v. Queensland, 1993; Land Rights: The Religious Factor, 1993; Controlling Destinies: Greater Opportunities for Indigenous Australians to Control Their Destinies, 1994; Pastoral Leases, Mabo and the Native Title Act 1993, Australian Institute of Aboriginal and Torres Strait Islander Studies, 1994; The Position of Indigenous People in National Constitutions, 1994; Securing a Bountiful Place for Aborigines and Torres Strait Islanders in a Modern, Free and Tolerant Australia, 1994; One Land, One Nation: Mabo, towards 2001, 1995; The Pulpit, the Parliament and the Public Domain, 1996; A Critique of the Native Title Amendment Bill 1997, 1997; Indigenous People and Constitutional Recognition in Australia, 1997; Submission and Evidence to Parliamentary Joint Committee on Native Title Amendment Bill 1997, 1997; Uniya Position Paper: A Critique of the Ten Point Plan, 1997; Wik and Beyond: The Coming Debate, 1997; The 1998 Revisiting of Wik and the Ten Point Plan, Queensland Law Society Symposium, 7 March 1998, 1998; The Wik Debate: Its Impact on Aborigines, Pastoralists and Miners, 1998; Legislating Liberty: A Bill of Rights for Australia? A Provocative and Timely Proposal to Balance the Public Good with Individual Freedom, 1998; (co-author) Refugees, Morality and Public Policy: The Jesuit Lenten Seminars 2002 & 2000, 2002; Tampering with Asylum: A Universal Humanitarian Problem, 2003, rev. ed., 2007; The Timor Sea's Oil and Gas: What's Fair?, 2004; Acting on Conscience: How Can We Responsibly Mix Law, Religion and Politics?, 2007. Contributor to periodicals. **Address:** Australian Catholic University, 40 Edward St., North Sydney, NW 2060, Australia. **Online address:** frank.brennan@acu.edu.au

BRENNAN, Herbie. *See* **BRENNAN, J(ames) H(erbert).**

BRENNAN, Herbie. Also writes as Maria Palmer, Jan Brennan, Cornelius Rumstuckle, James Herbert Brennan. Irish (born Ireland), b. 1940. **Genres:**

Children's Fiction. **Career:** Full-time author, 1973-. Educator. **Publications:** CHILDREN'S FICTION: (as J.H. Brennan) Marcus Mustard, 1994; (as J.H. Brennan) The Mystery Machine, 1995; (as J.H. Brennan) Blood Brothers, 1996; Bad Manners Day, 1996; Dorothy's Ghost, 1996; Little House, 1996; The Thing from Knucker Hole, 1996; Mario Scumbini and the Big Pig Swipe, 1996; Kookabura Dreaming, 1997; Letters from a Mouse, 1997; Jennet's Tale: A Story about the Great Plague, 2000; Final Victory, 2000; Zartog's Remote, 2000; Fairy Nuff: A Tale of Bluebell Wood, 2001; Nuff Said: The New Bluebell Wood Adventure in US as Nuff Said: Another Tale of Bluebell Wood, 2002; Frankenstella and the Video Shop Monster in US as Frankenstella and the Video Store Monster, 2002; Emily and the Werewolf, 2003; (as Cornelius Rumstuckle) The Book of Wizardry: The Apprentice's Guide to the Secrets of the Wizard's Guild, 2003; (ed. with L. Wilson) Strange Powers of the Human Mind, 2006; The Restless Dead: Ten Original Stories of the Supernatural; (ed. with L. Wilson) Through the Wardrobe: Your Favorite Authors on C.S. Lewis's Chronicles of Narnia, 2008; BARMY JEFFERS SERIES UNDER NAME J.H. BRENNAN: Barmy Jeffers and the Quasimodo Walk, 1988; Return of Barmy Jeffers and the Quasimodo Walk, 1988; Barmy Jeffers and the Shrinking Potion, 1989. ADVENTURE OF THE ICE AGE NOVEL SERIES: UNDER NAME J.H. BRENNAN: Shiva, 1989; The Crone, 1990 in US as Shiva Accused, 1991; Ordeal by Poison in US as Shiva's Challenge, 1992. HORRORSCOPE NOVEL SERIES AS J.H. BRENNAN EXCEPT WHERE NOTED: (as Maria Palmer) Capricorn's Children, 1995; Cancer: The Black Death, 1995; The Gravediggers, 1996. EDDIE THE DUCK SERIES: Eddie the Duck, 1998; Eddie and the Bad Egg, 1998; Eddie and the Dirty Dogs, 2001. FAERIE WARS CHRONICLES: Faerie Wars, 2003; The Purple Emperor, 2004; Ruler of the Realm, 2006; Faerie Lord, 2007. CHILDREN'S NONFICTION: (as J.H. Brennan) Mindpower 1: Succeed at School, 1990; (as J.H. Brennan) Mindpower 2: Make Yourself a Success, 1990; (as J.H. Brennan) The Young Ghost Hunter's Guide, 1990; Memory, 1997; Seriously Weird True Stories, 1997; Seriously Weird True Stories 2, 1998; Alien Contact, 1998; The Internet, 1998; Techno-Future, 2000; Space Quest: 111 Peculiar Questions Answered, 2003; A Spy's Handbook, 2003; (ed.) The Ghosthunter's Handbook, 2004; The Alien's Handbook, 2005; The Codebreaker's Handbook, 2006; The Wizard's Apprentice: Your Secret Path to Making Magic, 2007. FORBIDDEN TRUTHS CHILDREN'S NONFICTION SERIES: Atlantis and Other Lost Civilizations, 2006; The Secret Powers of the Mind, 2006; Time Travel, 2007; Parallel Worlds, 2007. EDUCATIONAL BOOKS FOR CHILDREN: The Death of the Dinosaurs, 2001; Dr. Jenner and the Cow Pox, 2001; How to Remember Absolutely Everything, 2001; Leonardo da Vinci: The Greatest Genius Who Ever Lived?, 2001; Why Do Cats Purr?, 2001. SAGAS OF THE DEMONSPAWN SERIES FANTASY GAME BOOKS UNDER NAME J.H. BRENNAN: Demonspawn, 1984; Fire Wolf, 1984; The Crypts of Terror, 1984; Demonstration, 1984; Ancient Evil, 1985; Demondoom, 1985. GRAILQUEST SERIES FANTASY GAME BOOKS UNDER NAME J.H. BRENNAN: The Castle of Darkness, 1984; The Den of Dragons, 1984; The Gateway of Doom, 1984; Voyage of Terror, 1985; Kingdom of Horror, 1985; Realm of Chaos, 1986; Tomb of Nightmares, 1986; Legion of the Dead, 1987. FANTASY GAME BOOKS: (as J.H. Brennan) The Curse of Frankenstein, 1986; (as J.H. Brennan) Dracula's Castle, 1986; (as J.H. Brennan) Monster Horrorshow, 1987; Aztec Quest, 1997; Egyptian Quest, 1997. ADULT FICTION: (as J.H. Brennan) The Greythorn Woman, 1979; (as J.H. Brennan) Dark Moon, 1980; (as Jan Brennan) Dream of Destiny, 1980. ADULT NONFICTION UNDER NAME J.H. BRENNAN, EXCEPT WHERE NOTED: Discover Astral Projection: How to Achieve Out-of-Body Experiences, 1970 as The Astral Projection Workbook, 1989; Astral Doorways, 1971, 2nd rev.ed., 1991; Five Keys to Past Lives, 1971, rev. ed. as Reincarnation: Five Keys to Past Lives, 1981; Experimental Magic, 1972; The Occult Reich, 1974; Beyond the Fourth Dimension, 1975; An Occult History of the World, vol. I, 1976; Power Play, 1977; Getting What You Want: Power Play Techniques for Achieving Success, 1977, rev. ed. as How to Get Where You Want to Go, 1991; The Good Con Guide (humor), 1978; Mindreach, 1985; Getting Rich: A Beginner's Manual, 1988; The Reincarnation Workbook: A Complete Course in Recalling Past Lives, 1989; (with E. Campbell) Aquarian Guide to the New Age, 1990 rev. ed. as Dictionary of Mind, Body, and Spirit: Ideas, People, and Places, 1994; Nostradamus: Visions of the Future, 1992; Discover Reincarnation, 1992 in US as Discover Your Past Lives: A Practical Course, 1994; A Guide to Megalithic Ireland, 1994; Ancient Spirit, 1995; Time Travel: A New Perspective, 1997; (as Herbie Brennan) Martian Genesis: The Extraterrestrial Origins of the Human Race, 1998; Magick for Beginners: The Power to Change Your World, 1998; (as Herbie Brennan) The Little Book of Nostradamus: Prophecies for the 21st Century, 1999; The Atlantis Enigma, 1999; The Secret History of Ancient Egypt: Electricity, Sonics, and the Disappearance of an Advanced Civilization, 2000; The Magical I Ching, 2000; (with D. Ashcroft-Nowicki) Magical Use of Thought Forms: A Proven System of Mental and Spiritual Empowerment, 2001; Death: The Great Mystery of Life, 2002; Occult Tibet: Secret Practices of Himalayan Magic, 2002; Tibetan Magic and Mysticism, 2006. Contributor to periodicals. **Address:** c/o Sophie Hicks, Ed Victor Ltd., 6 Bayley St., Bedford Sq., London, GL WC1B 3HE, England. **Online address:** herbie@eircom.net

BRENNAN, James Herbert. *See* **BRENNAN, Herbie.**

BRENNAN, J(ames) H(erbert). Also writes as Cornelius Rumstuckle, Maria Palmer, Herbie Brennan. British/Irish (born Ireland), b. 1940. **Genres:** Children's Fiction, Children's Non-fiction, Science Fiction/Fantasy, Paranormal, Horror, Novels, Young Adult Non-fiction, Romance/Historical, Young Adult Fiction, Adult Non-fiction, History, Self Help, Humor/Satire, E-books, Reference. **Career:** Full-time author, 1958-. Educator. **Publications:** FOR CHILDREN: Marcus Mustard, 1994; The Mystery Machine, 1995; Blood Brothers, 1996; (as Cornelius Rumstuckle) The Book of Wizardry: The Apprentice's Guide to the Secrets of the Wizard's Guild, 2003. BARMY JEFFERS SERIES: Barmy Jeffers and the Quasimodo Walk, 1988; Return of Barmy Jeffers and the Quasimodo Walk, 1988; Barmy Jeffers and the Shrinking Potion, 1989. ICE AGE SERIES: Shiva: An Adventure of the Ice Age, 1989; The Crone: An Adventure of the Ice Age, 1990 in US as Shiva Accused: An Adventure of the Ice Age, 1991; Ordeal by Poison in US as Shiva's Challenge: An Adventure of the Ice Age, 1992. FANTASY GAME BOOKS: SAGAS OF THE DEMONSPAWN SERIES: Demonspawn, 1984; Fire Wolf, 1984; The Crypts of Terror, 1984; Demonstration, 1984; Ancient Evil, 1985; Demondoom, 1985. GRAILQUEST SERIES: The Castle of Darkness, 1984; The Den of Dragons, 1984; The Gateway of Doom, 1984; Voyage of Terror, 1985; Kingdom of Horror, 1985; Realm of Chaos, 1986; Tomb of Nightmares, 1986; Legion of the Dead, 1987. OTHER FANTASY GAME BOOKS: The Curse of Frankenstein, 1986; Dracula's Castle, 1986; Monster Horrorshow, 1987. NONFICTION: Mindpower 1: Succeed at School, 1990; Mindpower 2: Make Yourself a Success, 1990; The Young Ghost Hunter's Guide, 1990. FOR ADULTS: PARAPSYCHOLOGY: Discover Astral Projection: How to Achieve Out-of-Body Experiences, 1970 as The Astral Projection Workbook, 1989; Mindreach, 1985; Discover Reincarnation, 1992 in US as Discover Your Past Lives: A Practical Course, 1994. ESOTERIC WRITINGS: Astral Doorways, 1971, rev. ed., 1991; Five Keys to Past Lives, 1971 as Reincarnation: Five Keys to Past Lives, 1981; Experimental Magic, 1972; Beyond the Fourth Dimension, 1975; The Reincarnation Workbook: A Complete Course in Recalling Past Lives, 1989; (with E. Campbell) Aquarian Guide to the New Age, 1990, rev. ed. as Dictionary of Mind, Body, and Spirit: Ideas, People, and Places, 1994; Nostradamus: Visions of the Future, 1992; Ancient Spirit, 1993; Magick for Beginners: The Power to Change Your World, 1998; The Magical I Ching, 2000; (with D. Ashcroft-Nowicki) Magical Use of Thought Forms: A Proven System of Mental and Spiritual Empowerment, 2001; Occult Tibet: Secret Practices of Himalayan Magic, 2002. NONFICTION: The Occult Reich, 1974; An Occult History of the World, vol. I, 1976; Power Play, 1977; Getting What You Want: Power Play Techniques for Achieving Success, 1977 in UK as How to Get Where You Want to Go, 1991; The Good Con Guide (humor), 1978; A Guide to Megalithic Ireland, 1994; Time Travel: A New Perspective, 1997. FICTION: The Greythorn Woman 1979; Dark Moon, 1980; (as J. Brennan) Dream of Destiny, 1980. FOR CHILDREN: FANTASY GAME BOOKS: Aztec Quest, 1997; Egyptian Quest, 1997. NONFICTION FOR CHILDREN: Memory, 1997; Alien Contact, 1998; The Internet, 1998; Space Quest: 111 Peculiar Questions Answered, 2003; A Spy's Handbook, 2003. INFORMATIONAL BOOKS FOR SCHOOLS: The Death of the Dinosaurs, 2001; Dr. Jenner and the Cow Pox, 2001; How to Remember Absolutely Everything, 2001; Leonardo da Vinci: The Greatest Genius Who Ever Lived?, 2001; Why Do Cats Purr?, 2001. FICTION: Dorothy's Ghost, 1996; Little House, 1996; The Thing from Knucker Hole, 1996; Letters from a Mouse, 1997; Jennet's Tale: A Story about the Great Plague, 2000; Final Victory, 2000; Zartog's Remote, 2000. AS MARIA PALMER HORRORSCOPE SERIES: Capricorn's Children, 1995; Cancer: The Black Death, 1995; The Gravediggers, 1996. AS HERBIE BRENNAN: BLUEBELL WOOD SERIES: Fairy Nuff: A Tale of Bluebell Wood, 2001; Nuff Said: The New Bluebell Adventure in US as Nuff Said: Another Tale of Bluebell Wood, 2002. FAERIE WARS SERIES: Faerie Wars, 2003; The Purple Emperor, 2004; Ruler of the Realm, 2006; Faerie Lord, 2007. CHAPBOOKS: Emily and the Werewolf, 1993; Bad Manners Day, 1996; Mario Scumbini and the Big Pig Swipe, 1997; Eddie the Duck, 1998; Eddie and the Bad Egg, 2000;

Zartog's Remote, 2000; Eddie and the Dirty Dogs, 2001; Frankenstella and the Video Shop Monster in US as Frankenstella and the Video Store Monster, 2002; Tibetan Magic and Mysticism, 2006. NOVEL: Kookaburra Dreaming, 1997. HERBIE BRENNAN'S FORBIDDEN TRUTHS: Atlantis and Other Lost Civilizations, 2006; The Secret Powers of the Mind, 2006; Time Travel, 2006; Parallel Worlds, 2007. NON FICTION: Getting Rich: A Beginner's Manual, 1988; Seriously Weird True Stories, 1997; Seriously Weird True Stories 2, 1998; Martian Genesis: The Extraterrestrial Origins of the Human Race, 1998; The Atlantis Enigma, 1999; Techno-Future: Sci-fi Explained, 2000; The Secret History of Ancient Egypt, 2000; Death: The Great Mystery of Life, 2002; The Spy's Handbook, 2003; Space Quest, 2003; Ghost Hunter's Handbook, 2004; The Aliens Handbook, 2005; The Codebreaker's Handbook, 2006; The Wizard's Apprentice, 2007; The Restless Dead: Ten Original Stories of the Supernatural, 2007; Madame de Gaulles Penis, 2009; The Shadow Project, 2010; The Doomsday Box, 2011; Through the Wardrobe, 2010; The Faeman Quest, 2011. **Address:** c/o Sophie Hicks, Ed Victor Ltd., 6 Bayley St., Bedford Sq., London, GL WC1B 3HB, England. **Online address:** herbie@eircom.net

BRENNAN, Jan. *See* **BRENNAN, Herbie.**

BRENNAN, Kate. American (born United States), b. 1950?. **Genres:** Autobiography/Memoirs, Medicine/Health. **Career:** Freelance writer and educator. **Publications:** In His Sights: A True Story of Love and Obsession, 2008. **Address:** Marly Rusoff & Associates Inc., PO Box 524, Bronxville, NY 10708, U.S.A.

BRENNAN, Mary C. American (born United States), b. 1959. **Genres:** History, Women's Studies And Issues. **Career:** Miami University, teaching fellow, 1984-87; Ohio State University, instructor in history, 1988-90; Texas State University, Department of History, assistant professor, associate professor, professor, 1990-, undergraduate advisor, 1993-2002, associate professor of history, 1996-, Phi Alpha Theta advisor, 1996-2004, graduate director, 2002-, professor, graduate advisor. Writer. **Publications:** Turning Right in the Sixties: The Conservative Capture of the GOP, 1995; Wives, Mothers and the Red Menace: Conservative Women and the Crusade against Communism, 2008; Pat Nixon: Embattled First Lady, 2011. Contributor to journals. **Address:** Department of History, Texas State University, TMH-209, San Marcos, TX 78666, U.S.A. **Online address:** mb18@txstate.edu

BRENNAN, Matthew C. American (born United States), b. 1955. **Genres:** Literary Criticism And History, Poetry. **Career:** University of Minnesota, Department of English, teaching assistant, 1978-79, teaching associate, 1979-82; visiting assistant professor, 1984-85; Golle & Holmes, editor, 1982-84; Indiana State University, assistant professor of English, 1985-88, associate professor of English, 1988-92, professor of English, 1992-, director of graduate studies, 1994-96, 1998-99, 2007-. Writer. **Publications:** LITERARY CRITICISM: Wordsworth, Turner and Romantic Landscape: A Study of the Traditions of the Picturesque and the Sublime, 1987; The Gothic Psyche: Disintegration and Growth in Nineteenth-Century English Literature, 1997; The Poet's Holy Craft: William Gilmore Simms and Romantic Verse Tradition, 2010. POETRY: Seeing in the Dark: Poems, 1993; The Music of Exile, 1994; American Scenes: Poems on WPA Artworks, 2001; The Sea-Crossing of Saint Brendan, 2008; The House with the Mansard Roof, 2009; The Light of Common Day, forthcoming. Contributor of articles to periodicals. **Address:** Department of English, Indiana State University, Root Hall A-222, Terre Haute, IN 47809, U.S.A. **Online address:** matthew.brennan@indstate.edu

BRENNAN, Michael G. British (born England) **Genres:** Travel/Exploration, Literary Criticism And History, History, Humanities. **Career:** Leeds University, reader in renaissance studies, professor of renaissance studies. Writer. **Publications:** Literary Patronage in the English Renaissance: The Pembroke Family, 1988; (with N.J. Kinnamon) A Sidney Chronology 1554-1654, 2003; The Sidneys of Penshurst and the Monarchy: 1500- 1700, 2006; Graham Greene: Fictions, Faith and Authorship, 2010. EDITOR: Lady Mary Wroth's Loves Victory: The Penshurst Manuscript, 1988; (and intro.) The Travel Diary (1611-1612) of an English Catholic, 1993; (with M.P. Hannay and N.J. Kinnamon) The Collected Works of Mary Sidney Herbert Countess of Pembroke, 1998; The Travel Diary of Robert Bargrave Levant Merchant 1647-1656, 1999; The Origins of the Grand Tour: The Travels of Robert Montagu, Lord Mandeville (1649-1651) William Hammond (1655-1658) and Banaster Maynard (1660-1663), 2004; (with M.P. Hannay and N.J. Kinnamon) Domestic Politics and Family Absence: The Correspondence (1588-1621) of Robert Sidney First Earl of Leicester and Barbara Gamage Sidney, 2005; (ed. with M.P. Hannay and N.J. Kinnamon) The Selected Works of Mary Sidney Herbert Countess of Pembroke, 2005; (co-ed.) The Sidney Psalter: The Psalms of Sir Philip and Mary Sidney, 2009; (ed. with N.J. Kinnamon and M.P. Hannay) The Correspondence (c.1626-1659) of Dorothy Percy Sidney, Countess of Leicester, 2010. **Address:** School of English, University of Leeds, Rm. 8.1.04, Cavendish Rd., Leeds, LS2 9JT, United Kingdom. **Online address:** m.g.brennan@leeds.ac.uk

BRENNAN, Sarah Rees. Irish (born Ireland), b. 1983. **Genres:** Science Fiction/Fantasy, Novels. **Career:** Author and librarian. **Publications:** FANTASY NOVELS: The Demon's Lexicon, 2009; The Demon's Covenant, 2010; The Demon's Surrender, 2011. Works appear in anthologies. **Address:** Dublin, DU , Ireland. **Online address:** sarahreesbrennan@gmail.com

BRENNAN, Wendy. (Emma Darcy). Australian (born Australia), b. 1940. **Genres:** Romance/Historical, Literary Criticism And History. **Career:** Wingham Department of Education, teacher of French and English, 1960-61; Macksville Department of Education, staff member, 1962-63; IBM, computer programmer, 1963-66; CAS, computer programmer, 1966-67. Writer. **Publications:** The Emma Darcy Duet, 1976; Twisting Shadows, 1983; A World Apart, 1983; Tangle of Torment, 1983; The Impossible Woman, 1985; Point of Impact, 1985; Song of a Wren, 1985; Don't Play Games, 1985; Fantasy, 1985; Blind Date, 1986; The Unpredictable Man, 1986; Dont Ask Me Now, 1986; The Wrong Mirror, 1986; Man in the Park, 1986; Woman of Honour, 1986; Mistress of Pillatoro, 1987; The Positive Approach, 1987; Strike at the Heart, 1987; The One That Got Away, 1987; Whirlpool of Passion, 1987; A Priceless Love, 1988; The Falcons Mistress, 1988; The Aloha Bride, 1988; Always Love, 1988; The Ultimate Choice, 1989; The Power and the Passion, 1989; Pattern of Deceit, 1989; Bride of Diamonds, 1990; Too Strong to Deny, 1990; One Woman Crusade, 1990; The Colour of Desire, 1990; Ride the Storm, 1991; Ride the Storm, 1991; Sunsational, 1991; The Wedding, 1992; Breaking Point, 1992; High Risk, 1992; To Tame a Wild Heart, 1992; The Seduction of Keira, 1992; The Velvet Tiger, 1992; Dark Heritage, 1992; Dark Heritage, 1992; The Last Grand Passion, 1993; The Sheikhs Revenge, 1993; A Very Stylish Affair, 1993; The Upstairs Lover, 1993; No Risks No Prizes, 1993; An Impossible Dream, 1993; Heart of the Outback, 1993; The Shining of Love, 1994; A Wedding to Remember, 1994; In Need of a Wife, 1994; The Emma Darcy Collection, 1994; The Ultimate Choice and Too Strong to Deny, 1995; Last Stop Marriage, 1995; The Secrets of Successful Romance Writing, 1995; Burning with Passion, 1995; The Fatherhood Affair, 1995; Climax of Passion, 1995; Father Knows Last: High Risk Guilty Passion, 1996; Jacks Baby, 1996; Their Wedding Day, 1996; Mischief and Marriage, 1996; The Father of Her Child, 1996; The Wedding and Whirlpool of Passion and The One That Got Away, 1996; Craving Jamie, 1997; The Secrets Within, 1997; Marriage Meltdown, 1997; Merry Christmas, 1997; Seducing the Enemy, 1997; Passion with a Vengeance, 1998; The Sheikhs Seduction, 1998; Storm over Mandargi and The Unpredictable Man; Knight to the Rescue, 1998; The Collection, 1998; Outback Heat, 1998; Fatherhood Fever!, 1998; Inherited One Nanny, 1998; Desert Heat, 1999; Mothers-to-Be, 1999; The Secret Mistress, 1999; The Marriage Decider, 1999; Having Leos Child, 1999; Conveniently Yours, 1999; A Marriage Betrayed, 1999; Bride of His Choice, 1999; The Man She Married, 1999; The Cattle Kings Mistress, 2000; Father and Child, 2000; The Marriage Risk, 2000; The Pleasure Kings Bride, 2000; The Playboy Kings Wife, 2000; Desert Destinies, 2001; Mistress to a Tycoon, 2001; Claiming His Mistress, 2001; The Hot-blooded Groom, 2001; The Sweetest Revenge, 2001; Who Killed Angelique?, 2001; A Christmas Seduction, 2001; An Australian Christmas, 2002; The Bridal Bargain, 2002; The Honeymoon Contract, 2002; Seduced, 2002; The Arranged Marriage, 2002; Latin Liaisons, 2002; Who Killed Bianca?, 2002; The Blind-Date Bride, 2003; His Boardroom Mistress, 2003; The Bedroom Surrender, 2003; Boardroom Baby, 2003; Red-Hot Passion, 2003; The Bedroom Surrender; Mistress to a Millionaire, 2003; The Billionaire Bridegroom, 2003; The Pregnancy Surprise, 2003; Who Killed Camilla?, 2003; The Outback Bridal Rescue, 2004; The Outback Wedding Takeover, 2004; Seduced by a Sultan, 2004; Pregnant Brides, 2004; Australian Tycoons, 2004; Man in the Park; Point, 2004; Burning with Passion; The Power and the Passion, 2004; The Outback Marriage Ransom, 2004; Kings of the Outback, 2004; His Bought Mistress, 2004; The Greeks Convenient Wife; Mistress to a Tycoon, 2005; The Italians Stolen Bride, 2005; The Ramirez Bride, 2005; Risque Business, 2005; Mistress to a Tycoon; Jacks Baby, 2005; The Playboy Boss's Chosen Bride, 2006; The Secret Baby Revenge, 2006; The Billionaire's Scandalous Marriage, 2007; Hot Blooded Affairs, 2007; Filling All the Holes, 2007; Ruthlessly Bedded

By the Italian Billionaire, 2008; Three's Never a Crowd, 2008; Bought For Revenge, Bedded For Pleasure, 2008; Outback Grooms, 2008; Ruthless Billionaire, Forbidden Baby, 2009; Master Player, 2009; Billionaires' Marriages, 2010. Contributor to periodicals. **Address:** c/o Author Mail, Harlequin, PO Box 5190, Buffalo, NY 14240-5190, U.S.A.

BRENNER, Joël Glenn. American (born United States), b. 1966. **Genres:** Documentaries/Reportage. **Career:** Des Moines Register, intern reporter, 1988; Washington Post, business reporter, 1989-95; freelance journalist, 1995-; Mars Co., staff; Financial News, reporter. **Publications:** The Emperors of Chocolate: Inside the Secret World of Hershey and Mars, 1999. Contributor to periodicals. **Address:** 425 New York Ave., Ste. 209, Huntington, NY 11743, U.S.A. **Online address:** jgbrennr@aol.com

BRENNER, Mayer Alan. (Rick North). American (born United States), b. 1956. **Genres:** Novels, Science Fiction/Fantasy, Sciences, Young Adult Fiction. **Career:** Software designer and writer. **Publications:** FANTASY NOVELS: DANCE OF THE GODS SERIES: Catastrophes Spell, 1989; Spell of Intrigue, 1990; Spell of Fate, 1992; Spell of Apocalypse, 1994. OTHER: (as Rick North) Space Pioneers (novel), 1991. **Address:** 1815 Westholme Ave., Ste. 4, Los Angeles, CA 90025-4953, U.S.A.

BRENNER, Michael. German (born Germany), b. 1964. **Genres:** History, Theology/Religion. **Career:** Indiana University, visiting assistant professor of Jewish history, 1993-94; Brandeis University, assistant professor of modern Jewish history, 1994-97; Tauber Institute for the Study of European Jewry, assistant director, 1995-97; University of Munich, professor of Jewish history and culture, 1997-, Faculty of History and Art, vice dean, 2001-03, Department of History, chair, 2002-03. Writer. **Publications:** Am Beispiel Weiden: Jüdischer Alltag im Nationalsozialismus, 1983; Nach dem Holocaust: Juden in Deutschland, 1945-1950, 1995; The Renaissance of Jewish Culture in Weimar Germany, 1996; (ed. with M.A. Meyer) German-Jewish History in Modern Times, vol. II: 1780-1871, 1996; After the Holocaust, 1997; Propheten des Vergangenen: Jüdische Geschichtsschreibung im 19. und 20. Jahrhundert, 2006; Short History of the Jews, 2010; Prophets of the Past: Interpreters of Jewish History, 2010. EDITOR: (with D. Penslar) Circles of Community: Collective Jewish Identities in Germany and Austria, 1918-1932, 1998; (with D. Penslar) In Search of Jewish Community: Jewish Identities in Germany and Austria, 1918-1933, 1998; (with R. Liedtke and D. Rechter) Two Nations: British and German Jews in Comparative Perspective, 1999; (with Y. Weiss) Zionistische Utopie, israelischeRealität: Religion und Nation in Israel, 1999; (with S. Rohrbacher) Wissenschaft vom Judentum: Annäherungen nach dem Holocaust, 2000; (ed. with V. Caron and U.R. Kaufmann) Jewish Emancipation Reconsidered: The French and German Models, 2003; Derbrennende Dornbusch: Glanz Und Elend Der Juden in Europa, 2004; Jüdisches München: Vom Mittelalter Bis Zur Gegenwart, 2006; (with G. Reuveni) Emancipation through Muscles: Jews and Sports in Europe, 2006; The Same History is Not the Same Story: Jewish History and Jewish Politics, 2006; (with L.B. Strauss) Mediating Modernity: Challenges and Trends in the Jewish Encounter with the Modern World: Essays in Honor of Michael A. Meyer, 2008; (with R. Höpfinger) Juden in der Oberpfalz, 2009. **Address:** Abteilung fur Jedische Geschichte und Kultur, Historisches Seminar, Universitat Munchen, 1 Geschwister-Scholl-Platz, Munich, 80539, Germany. **Online address:** michael.brenner@lrz.uni-muenchen.de

BRENNER, Neil. American (born United States), b. 1969?. **Genres:** History, Humanities. **Career:** New York University, Department of Sociology and Metropolitan Studies Program, assistant professor, 1999-2005, associate professor, 2005-06, professor, 2007-11, Department of Sociology and Department of Social and Cultural Analysis, associate professor, 2005-06, professor, 2007-11, director of the metropolitan studies program; University of Bristol, visiting professor; National University, visiting professor; University of Urbino, visiting professor; Harvard University, Graduate School of Design, professor, 2011-, Urban Theory Lab GSD, coordinator. Writer. **Publications:** (Ed. with N. Theodore) Spaces of Neoliberalism: Urban Restructuring in North America and Western Europe, 2002; (ed. with B. Jessop, M. Jones and G. Macleod) State/Space: A Reader, 2003; New State Spaces: Urban Governance and the Rescaling of Statehood, 2004; (ed. with R. Keil) The Global Cities Reader, 2006; (trans. and ed. with S. Elden) State, Space, World: Selected Essays, 2009; (ed. with P. Marcuse and M. Mayer) Cities for People, Not For Profit: Critical Urban Theory and The Right to The City, 2012. Contributor to journals. **Address:** Graduate School of Design, Harvard University, 48 Quincy Gund Hall, Cambridge, MA 02138, U.S.A. **Online address:** neil.brenner@nyu.edu

BRENNER, Philip (Joseph). American (born United States), b. 1946. **Genres:** International Relations/Current Affairs, Politics/Government, Business/Trade/Industry, Economics, Adult Non-fiction, Social Sciences. **Career:** Institute for Policy Studies, associate fellow, 1972-85; Trinity College, instructor in political science, 1973-75; University of Maryland, assistant professor of political science, 1975; National Security Archive, researcher, 1985-; American University, professor of international relations and history, Inter-Disciplinary Council on the Americas, chair, U.S. Foreign Policy Program, senior professor, director, senior associate dean for academic affairs, Department of International Politics and Foreign Policy, chair; United States Congress, staff; John F. Kennedy Library, consultant. Writer. **Publications:** (Ed. with R. Borosage and B. Weidner) Exploring Contradictions: Political Economy in the Corporate State, 1974; The Limits and Possibilities of Congress, 1983; From Confrontation to Negotiation: U.S. Relations with Cuba, 1988; (ed. with W.M. LeoGrande, D. Rich and D. Siegel) The Cuba Reader: The Making of a Revolutionary Society, 1989; (with J.G. Blight) Sad and Luminous Days: Cuba's Struggle with the Superpowers after the Missile Crisis, 2002; (ed. with M.R. Jimenez, W.M. LeoGrande and J.M. Kirk) A Contemporary Cuba Reader: Reinventing the Revolution, 2007. **Address:** School of International Service, American University, SIS-307, 4400 Massachusetts Ave. NW, Washington, DC 20016-8071, U.S.A. **Online address:** pbrenne@american.edu

BRENNER, Reuven. Canadian/Israeli/French (born France), b. 1947. **Genres:** History, Law, Money/Finance, Social Sciences, Economics, Business/Trade/Industry. **Career:** Bank of Israel, economist, 1974-75; University of Chicago, Department of Economics, lecturer, 1977-79; New York University, instructor in economics, 1979-80; McGill University, assistant professor of economics, 1980-82, School of Management, REPAP chair of economics, 1991-; C.D. Howe Institute Consumers and Corporate Affairs, consultant, 1981-84; Economic Council of Canada, consultant, 1981-91; Universite de Montreal, assistant professor, 1982-84, associate professor, 1984-89, professor of economics, 1989-91; Centre de recherche et développement en économique, associate fellow; Hebrew University, lecturer. Writer. **Publications:** (With G.A. Brenner) Why do Productivity and Profits Decline?: Theory and Evidence History, 1981; Theory of Wealth Distribution and of Attitudes toward Risks, 1981; On Politics and Inflation or Why do Central Banks Gamble on Inflationary Policies?, 1982; (with G.A. Brenner) Easy Case for Progressive Taxation?, 1982; Meaning of Causality, or, Why do People Believe in "Demons"?, 1982; Why does the U.S. Export New Technologies and Import Older, Perfected Products?: An Alternative View of International Trade, 1982; The Human Gamble, 1983, trans. as La Historia, Albur del Hombre, 1989; Betting on Ideas: Wars, Invention, Inflation, 1985; Rivalry: In Business, Science, Among Nations, 1987; (with G.A. Brenner) Gambling and Speculation: A Theory, a History, and a Future of Some Human Decisions, 1990, trans. as Les Jeux et la Speculation, 1993; (ed. with D. Colander) Educating Economists, 1992; Labyrinths of Prosperity, 1994; The Financial Century: From Turmoils to Triumphs, 2001; Forces of Finance, 2002; World of Chance: Betting on Religion, Games, Wall Street, 2008. Contributor to books and periodicals. **Address:** School of Management, McGill University, Rm. 483, Bronfman Bldg., 1001 Sherbrooke St. W, Montreal, QC H3A 1G5, Canada. **Online address:** reuven.brenner@mcgill.ca

BRENNER, Robert. American (born United States), b. 1945?. **Genres:** Antiques/Furnishings, History, Crafts. **Career:** Princeton High School, English teacher, 1968-; Galloway Village, Smithsonian Institution and Sheboygan Historical Society, consultant. Writer. **Publications:** Maineville, Ohio, History: 100 Years as an Incorporated Town, 1850-1950, 1950; So leben wir morgen: der Roman unserer Zukunft, 1972; Christmas Past: A Collectors's Guide to Its History and Decorations, 1985; Christmas Revisited, 1986, 3rd ed., 2004; Christmas through the Decades, 1993, rev. ed., 2000; Christmas Past, 1996, rev. ed., 1998; Valentine Treasury, 1997; Depression Glass, 1998; Celluloid: Collectibles from the Dawn of Plastics, 1999; Christmas: 1940-1959, 2002, 3rd. ed., 2007; Christmas 1960-Present, 2002, rev. ed., 2005. Contributor to periodicals. **Address:** 316 W Main St., Princeton, WI 54968, U.S.A. **Online address:** bob@christmasinprinceton.com

BRENNER, Wendy. American (born United States), b. 1966. **Genres:** Novellas/Short Stories. **Career:** University of Florida, writer and creative writing teacher, 1993-96; State University of New York, writer and creative writing teacher, 1996-97; University of North Carolina, writer and creative writing teacher, 1997-, associate professor. **Publications:** STORIES: Large Animals in Everyday Life, 1997; Phone Calls from the Dead: Stories, 2001. Contributor to periodicals. **Address:** Department of Creative Writing, University of North Carolina, 1223 Kenan Hall, 601 S College Rd., Wilmington, NC 28403-3201, U.S.A. **Online address:** brennerw@uncw.edu

BRENT, Allen. British/Australian (born Australia), b. 1940?. **Genres:** Theology/Religion, History, Humanities, Classics, Philosophy, Art/Art History. **Career:** Huddersfield University, principal lecturer of philosophy of education, 1974-80; James Cook University of North Queensland, professor of early Christian literature and history, 1980-95; Cambridge University, Clare Hall, visiting fellow, 1994-95, St. Edmund's College, doctor of divinity, 2008-, affiliated lecturer, 2008-10; King's College London, visiting professor, 2011-. Writer, theologian and historian. **Publications:** Philosophical Foundations for the Curriculum, 1978; Philosophy and Educational Foundations, 1983; Cultural Episcopacy and Ecumenism: Representative Ministry in Church History from the Age of Ignatius of Antioch to the Reformation, 1992; Hippolytus and the Roman Church in the Third Century: Communities in Tension before the Emergence of a Monarch-Bishop, 1995; The Imperial Cult and the Development of Church Order: Concepts and Images of Authority in Paganism and Early Christianity before the Age of Cyprian, 1999; Ignatius of Antioch and the Second Sophistic: A Study of an Early Christian Transformation of Pagan Culture, 2006; (trans. and intro.) St. Cyprian of Carthage, On the Church: Select Letters, 2006; (trans. and intro.) St. Cyprian of Carthage, On the Church: Select Treatises, 2006; Ignatius of Antioch: A Martyr Bishop and the Origin of Monarchial Episcopacy, 2007; Political History of Early Christianity, 2009; Cyprian and Roman Carthage, 2010. **Address:** King's College, University of London, Strand, London, GL WC2R 2LS, England. **Online address:** alb13@hermes.cam.ac.uk

BRENTON, Howard. British (born England), b. 1942. **Genres:** Novels, Plays/Screenplays, Poetry, Songs/Lyrics And Libretti, Humor/Satire, inspirational/Motivational Literature. **Career:** Brighton Combination, writer and actor, 1968; Portable Theatre, staff, 1969; Royal Court Theatre, resident dramatist, 1972-73; University of Warwick, resident writer, 1978-79; British Broadcasting Corp. TV, spooks episodes, 2002-03. **Publications:** Notes from a Psychotic Journal and Other Poems, 1969; Revenge, 1970; Christie in Love and Other Plays, 1970; Scott of the Antarctic, 1971; (co-author) Lay By, 1972; Plays for Public Places: Gum & Goo, Wesley, Scott of the Antarctic, 1972; Magnificence, 1973; (with D. Hare) Brassneck, 1974; Churchill Play, 1974; Weapons of Happiness, 1976; Epsom Downs, 1977; Saliva Milkshake, 1977; Sore Throats, with Sonnets of Love and Opposition, 1979; The Romans in Britain, 1980; Plays for the Poor Theatre, 1980; Thirteenth Night, 1981; A Short Sharp Shock, 1981; Hitler Dances, 1982; The Genius, 1983; (with T. Ikoli) Sleeping Policemen, 1984; Bloody Poetry, 1985; (with D. Hare) Pravda: A Fleet Street Comedy, 1985; Plays, One, 1986; Dead Head, 1987; Greenland, 1988; (with T. Ali) Iranian Nights, 1989; Diving for Pearls (novel), 1989; H.I.D (Hess Is Dead), 1989; (with T. Ali) Moscow Gold, 1990; Berlin Bertie, 1992; Hot Irons: Diaries, Essays, Journalism, 1995; Goethe, Faust, 1995; (with T. Ali) Ugly Rumours, 1998; (with T. Ali and A. de la Tour) Collateral Damage, 1999; (with T. Ali and A. de la Tour) Snogging Ken, 2000; Paul, 2005; In Extremis: The Story of Abelard and Heloise, 2006; Never So Good, 2008; (adaptor) Ragged Trousered Philanthropists, 2010; Anne Boleyn, 2010. **Address:** Casarotto Ramsay & Associates Ltd., Waverley House, 7-12 Noel St., London, GL W1F 8GQ, England.

BRESKIN, David. American (born United States), b. 1958?. **Genres:** Poetry. **Career:** Rolling Stone Magazine, staff; Poetic Justice L.L.C., staff. Music producer and freelance writer. **Publications:** We Are the World, 1985; The Real Life Diary of a Boomtown Girl, 1989; Inner Views: Filmmakers in Conversation, 1992; Fresh Kills: Poems, 1997; (ed.) Richter 858, 2002; Escape Velocity, 2004; Supermodel, 2006. Contributor to periodicals. **Address:** 1061 Francisco St., San Francisco, CA 94109-1126, U.S.A.

BRESLIN, Cathy. Irish (born Ireland) **Genres:** How-to Books, Self Help. **Career:** Monread Clinic, counselor and hypnotherapist; Powerful Perspectives Ltd., chief executive officer; Phoenix Medical Clinic, staff. Writer and life coach. **Publications:** (With J.M. Murphy) Your Life Only a Gazillion Times Better: A Practical Guide to Creating the Life of Your Dreams, 2005. **Address:** Phoenix Medical Clinic, 5A Sycamore House, Osberstown, Naas, KL 01, Ireland. **Online address:** info@cathybreslin.com

BRESLIN, Jimmy. American (born United States), b. 1930. **Genres:** Novels, Documentaries/Reportage, Social Sciences, Criminology/True Crime, Theology/Religion, History, Young Adult Non-fiction. **Career:** New York Journal-American, sportswriter, 1950-63; New York Herald Tribune, sportswriter, columnist, 1963-66; New York Post, columnist, 1968-69; New York Magazine, contributing editor and initiating writer, 1968-71; WABC-TV, commentator, 1968-69; author and freelance journalist, 1969-; New Times Magazine, contributing editor and initiating writer, 1973; WNBC-TV, commentator, 1973; The Daily News, writer, 1976-88; New York Daily News, columnist, 1978-88; ABC-TV, host, 1987; Newsday, columnist, 1988-2004. **Publications:** Sunny Jim, The Life of America's Most Beloved Horseman, James Fitzsimmons, 1962; Can't Anybody Here Play this Game?, 1963; The World of Jimmy Breslin, 1968; The Gang that Couldn't Shoot Straight, 1969; World without End, Amen, 1973; How the Good Guys Finally Won: Notes from an Impeachment Summer, 1975; Fire!, 1977; (with D. Schaap) Queens Peoples and Places, 1984; The World According to Breslin, 1984; Table Money, 1985; He Got Hungry and Forgot His Manners: A Fable, 1988; Damon Runyon: A Life, 1991; I Want to Thank My Brain for Remembering Me: A Memoir, 1996; I Don't Want to Go to Jail: A Good Novel, 2001; The Short Sweet Dream of Eduardo Gutiérrez, 2002; Church That Forgot Christ, 2004; The Good Rat: A True Story, 2008; Mafia Rat: A True Story, 2009; Branch Rickey, 2010. Contributor to magazines. **Address:** Joan Brandt, Sterling Lord Literistic Inc., 65 Bleecker St., New York, NY 10012-2420, U.S.A.

BRESLOW, Susan. (Susan B(reslow) Sardone). American (born United States), b. 1951. **Genres:** Travel/Exploration, Reference. **Career:** American Society for the Prevention of Cruelty to Animals, head of publications, 1981-83; New York Magazine, marketing director, 1983-91. Writer. **Publications:** (With S. Blakemore) I Really Want a Dog, 1990; (as Susan Breslow Sardone) Destination Weddings for Dummies, 2007. **Address:** 111 Woodland Clove, PO Box 32, Phoenicia, NY 12464, U.S.A. **Online address:** susan@writingthatsells.com

BRESSOUD, David M(arius). American (born United States), b. 1950. **Genres:** Mathematics/Statistics, Sciences. **Career:** Pennsylvania State University, assistant professor, 1977-82, associate professor, 1982-86, professor of mathematics, 1986-94; University of Wisconsin, visiting professor, 1980-82; University of Minnesota, visiting professor, 1983, 1998; University of Strasbourg, visiting professor, 1985-86; Macalester College, professor in mathematics and computer science, 1994-96, chair of the department, 1995-2001, DeWitt Wallace professor of mathematics, 1996-. Writer. **Publications:** Analytic and Combinatorial Generalizations of the Rogers-Ramanujan Identities, 1980; Factorization and Primality Testing, 1989; Second Year Calculus from Celestial Mechanics to Special Relativity, 1991; Radical Approach to Real Analysis, 1994, 2nd ed., 2007; (ed. with G.E. Andrews and L.A. Parson) Rademacher Legacy to Mathematics: The Centenary Conference in Honor Hans Rademacher, July 21-25, 1992, The Pennsylvania State University, 1994; Proofs and Confirmations: The Story of the Alternating Sign Matrix Conjecture, 1999; (with S. Wagon) A Course in Computational Number Theory, 2000; A Radical Approach to Lebesgue's Theory of Integration, 2008; Queen of the Sciences: A History of Mathematics, 2008 Contributor to journals. **Address:** Department of Mathematics and Computer Science, Macalester College, 1600 Grand Ave., St. Paul, MN 55105, U.S.A. **Online address:** bressoud@macalester.edu

BRETON, Albert. Canadian (born Canada), b. 1929. **Genres:** Economics, Human Relations/Parenting, Social Sciences, Politics/Government. **Career:** The Social Research Group, director of research, 1956-65; University of Montreal, assistant professor of economics, 1957-65; Carleton University, visiting associate professor, 1964-65; London School of Economics and Political Science, lecturer, 1966-67, reader in economics, 1967-69; Catholic University, visiting professor, 1968-69; Harvard University, visiting professor of Canadian studies, 1969-70; University of Toronto, professor of economics, 1970-, now professor emeritus; University of Paris, visiting professor, 1990, 1993; Università di Torino, research professor. Writer. **Publications:** CONTRIBUTOR: Social Purpose for Canada, 1961; Le Role de L'Etat, 1962; Canada: An Appraisal of Its Needs and Resources, 1965; Canadian Economic Problems and Policies, 1970; A Challenge to Social Scientists, 1970; Canadian Perspectives in Economics, 1972; Issues in Canadian Economics, 1974. EDITOR: Economic Approaches to Language and to Bilingualism, 1998; Exploring the Economics of Language, 1999. CO-EDITOR: The Competitive State: Villa Colombella Papers on Competitive Politics, 1988; Preferences and Democracy: Villa Colombella Papers, 1993; Nationalism and Rationality, 1995; (with P. Salmon, R. Wintrobe) Competition and Structure: The Political Economy of Collective Decisions: Essays in Honor of Albert Breton, 2000; Political Extremism and Rationality, 2002; Rational Foundations of Democratic Politics, 2003; (with M. Trebilcock) Bijuralism: An Economic Approach, 2006; The Economics of Transparency in Politics, 2006; Environmental Governance and Decentralisation, 2007; Governing the Environment: Salient Institutional Issues, 2009; Multijuralism: Manifestations, Causes and Consequences, 2009. OTHERS: Discriminatory Government Policies in Federal Countries, 1967; Lefondement théorique d'une stratégie industrielle, 1974; The Economic Theory of Representative Government, 1974; A Conceptual Basis for an Industrial Strategy, 1974; The Federal-Provincial Dimensions of the 1973-74 Energy Crisis in Canada, 1975; The Regulation of Private Economic Activity, 1976; (with A. Scott) The Economic Constitution of Federal States, 1978; Bilingualism: An Economic Approach, 1978; (with A. Scott) The Design of Federations, 1980; (with R. Breton) Why Disunity?: An Analysis of Linguistic and Regional Cleavages in Canada, 1980; (with R. Wintnobe) The Logic of Bureaucratic Conduct: An Economic Analysis of Competition, Exchange and Efficiency in Private and Public Organizations, 1982; Marriage, Population and the Labour Force Participation of Women, 1984; Competitive Governments: An Economic Theory of Politics and Public Finance, 1996; (co-author) Understanding Democracy: Economic and Political Perspectives, 1997. Contributor to books, periodicals and journals. **Address:** Department of Economics, University of Toronto, Max Gluskin House, Sidney Smith Hall, 150 St. George St., 254, Toronto, ON M5S 3G7, Canada. **Online address:** albert@albertbreton.com

BRETON, William. *See* **GURR, David.**

BRETT, Brian. Canadian (born Canada), b. 1950. **Genres:** Novellas/Short Stories, Poetry, Autobiography/Memoirs, Novels. **Career:** The Globe and Mail, freelance journalist and critic; The Toronto Star, freelance journalist and critic; The Vancouver Sun, freelance journalist and critic; The New Reader, freelance journalist and critic; Books In Canada, freelance journalist and critic; The Victoria Times-Colonist, freelance journalist and critic; The Vancouver Province, freelance journalist and critic; The Writer's Union of Canada, vice chair, chair, 2005, 2006; Yukon News, CultureWatch, columnist. **Publications:** POETRY: Fossil Ground at Phantom Creek, 1976; Greenlight, 1977; Savage People Dressed in Skins, 1978; Monster, 1981; Smoke without Exit, 1984; Evolution in Every Direction, 1987; Poems: New and Selected, 1993; Allegories of Love and Disaster, 1993; The Colour of Bones in a Stream, 1998; Uproar's Your Only Music, 2004; Wind River Elegies, forthcoming. NOVELS: The Fungus Garden, 1988; Coyote: A Mystery, 2003. OTHERS: Tanganyika (short stories), 1991; Trauma Farm: A Rebel History of Rural Life, 2009; Trauma Farm: An Unnntural History of Small Farming from Babylon to Globalization, forthcoming; The Wind River Variations, forthcoming. Works appear in anthologies. Contributor to periodicals. **Address:** 191 Meyer Rd., Salt Spring Island, BC V8K 1X4, Canada. **Online address:** brett@saltspring.com

BRETT, Catherine. *See* **HUMPHREYS, Helen (Caroline).**

BRETT, Donna W(hitson). American (born United States), b. 1947. **Genres:** International Relations/Current Affairs, Writing/Journalism, Documentaries/Reportage, Essays, Biography, Autobiography/Memoirs, Theology/Religion. **Career:** Louisiana Training Institute, purchasing agent, 1976-79; Computer School of Sante Fe, administrative assistant, 1981-84; Santa Fe Research Corp., administrative assistant, 1981-84; University of Pittsburgh, academic adviser, 1988-, senior advisor. Writer. **Publications:** (With E.T. Brett) Murdered in Central America: The Stories of Eleven U.S. Missionaries, 1988. Contributor to periodicals. **Address:** School of Arts & Sciences Undergraduate Studies, University of Pittsburgh, 140 Thackeray Hall, Pittsburgh, PA 15260, U.S.A. **Online address:** brett@as.pitt.edu

BRETT, Edward T(racy). American (born United States), b. 1944. **Genres:** Novellas/Short Stories, History, Theology/Religion, Third World, Writing/Journalism, Biography, Criminology/True Crime. **Career:** College of Santa Fe, assistant professor of history, 1980-83; Santa Fe Community College, instructor in history, 1983-84; St. John's College, National Endowment for the Humanities, visiting tutor, 1984; La Roche College, associate professor, 1984-90, professor and chair of history, 1990-; Duquesne University, visiting professor, 1987-89. Writer. **Publications:** Humbert of Romans: His Life and Views of Thirteenth-Century Society, 1984; The U.S. Catholic Press on Central America: From Cold War Anticommunism to Social Justice, 2003. WITH WIFE D.W. BRETT: Murdered in Central America: The Stories of Eleven U.S. Missionaries, 1988; American Catholic Studies, 2007. Contributor of articles to books and periodicals. **Address:** Department of History, La Roche College, 9000 Babcock Blvd., Pittsburgh, PA 15237, U.S.A. **Online address:** edward.brett@laroche.edu

BRETT, Jan. *See* **BRETT, Jan (Churchill).**

BRETT, Jan (Churchill). (Jan Brett). American (born United States), b. 1949. **Genres:** Children's Fiction, Illustrations. **Career:** Painter, author and illustrator of children's books. **Publications:** SELF-ILLUSTRATED: Fritz and the Beautiful Horses, 1981; Good Luck Sneakers, 1981; Annie and the Wild Animals, 1985; The Wild Christmas Reindeer, 1990; Berlioz the Bear, 1991; Christmas Trolls, 1993; Armadillo Rodeo, 1995; Comet's Nine Lives, 1996; Hedgie's Surprise, 2000; Knockety-Knock, It's Christmas Eve, 2002; Big Sparkler, 2006. OTHERS: The First Dog, 1988; (reteller) Goldilocks and the Three Bears, 1987; (reteller) Beauty and the Beast, 1989; The Mitten, 1989; The Trouble With Trolls, 1992; Town Mouse, Country Mouse, 1994; The Hat, 1997; Gingerbread Baby, 1999; Jan Brett's Christmas Treasury, 2001; Daisy Comes Home, 2002; Who's that Knocking on Christmas Eve?, 2002; On Noah's Ark, 2003; The Umbrella, 2004; Honey, Honey: Lion!: A Story of Africa, 2005; Hedgie Blasts Off!, 2006; The Three Snow Bears, 2007; Gingerbread Friends, 2008; Jan Brett's Snowy Treasury, 2009; Easter Egg, 2010; Three Little Dassies, 2010; Home for Christmas, 2011. Illustrator of books by others. **Address:** 132 Pleasant St., PO Box 366, Norwell, MA 02061-2523, U.S.A.

BRETT, Leo. *See* **FANTHORPE, R(obert) Lionel.**

BRETT, Peter V. American (born United States), b. 1973. **Genres:** Young Adult Fiction. **Career:** Pharmaceutical publisher and fiction writer. **Publications:** DEMON CYCLE SERIES: The Painted Man, 2008 in US as The Warded Man, 2009; The Great Bazaar and Other Stories, 2010; The Desert Spear, 2010. **Address:** Brooklyn, NY , U.S.A. **Online address:** peat@petervbrett.com

BRETT, Simon (Anthony Lee). British (born England), b. 1945. **Genres:** Mystery/Crime/Suspense, Plays/Screenplays, Novels, Novellas/Short Stories. **Career:** BBC Radio, producer, 1967-77; London Weekend Television, producer, 1977-79. Writer. **Publications:** NOVELS: Cast, In Order of Disappearance: A Crime Novel, 1975; So Much Blood, 1976; Star Trap: A Crime Novel, 1977; An Amateur Corpse, 1978; A Comedian Dies, 1979; The Dead Side of the Mike, 1980; Murder Unprompted: A Charles Paris Novel, 1982; Molesworth Rites Again, 1983; Murder in the Title: A Charles Paris Novel, 1983; Not Dead, Only Resting: A Charles Paris Novel, 1984; A Shock to the System, 1985; Dead Romantic, 1986; A Nice Class of Corpse, 1986; The 3 Detectives and the Missing Super Star, 1986; Dead Giveaway, 1986; What Bloody Man is That?: A Charles Paris Novel, 1987; The Three Detectives and the Knight-in-Armour, 1987; Mrs. Pargeter, Presumed Dead, 1989; A Series of Murders, 1989; Mrs. Pargeter's Package, 1991; The Christmas Crimes at Puzzle Manor, 1991; Corporate Bodies: A Charles Paris Mystery, 1992; Mrs. Pargeter's Pound of Flesh: A Mrs. Pargeter Mystery, 1993; A Reconstructed Corpse: A Charles Paris Mystery, 1994; Sicken and So Die, 1995; Singled Out: A Novel of Suspense, 1995; Mrs. Pargeter's Plot: A Mrs. Pargeter Mystery, 1998. STORIES: A Box of Tricks: Short Stories, 1985; Tickled to Death, and Other Stories of Crime and Suspense, 1985; Crime Writers and Other Animals, 1997; A Crime in Rhyme: and Other Mysterious Fragments, 2000. OTHERS: (with F. Muir) Frank Muir Goes Into-, 1978; (with F. Muir) Second Frank Muir Goes Into-, 1979; Frank Muir on Children, 1980; Situation Tragedy: A Charles Paris Mystery, 1981; The Childowner's Handbook, 1983; Bad Form, or How not to Get Invited Back, 1984; People-Spotting: The Human Species Laid Bare, 1985; After Henry, 1987; Booker book, 1989; Four Complete Mysteries, 1993; Sicken and So Die, 1995; Dead Room Farce, 1997; Mrs. Pargeter's Point of Honour, 1998; Body on the Beach: A Fethering Mystery, 2000; Death on the Downs: A Fethering Mystery, 2001; Torso in the Town: A Fethering Mystery, 2002; Murder in the Museum: A Fethering Mystery, 2003; Hanging in the Hotel: A Fethering Mystery, 2004; Witness at the Wedding, 2005; The Stabbing in the Stables: A Fethering Mystery, 2006; Penultimate Chance Saloon, 2006; On Second Thoughts, 2006; Death under the Dryer: A Fethering Mystery, 2007; Blood at the Bookies, 2008; Poisoning in the Pub, 2009; Blotto, Twinks, and the Ex-King's Daughter, 2009; Blotto, Twinks and the Dead Dowager Duchess, 2009; The Shooting in the Shop, 2010; Bones Under the Beach Hut, 2011; Blotto, Twinks and the Rodents of the Riviera, 2011. PLAYS: Murder in Play, 1994; Mr. Quigley's Revenge,

1995; Silhouette, 1998; Tale of Little Red Riding Hood: An Untraditional Pantomime, 1998; Sleeping Beauty, 1999; Putting the Kettle On, 2002; A Bad Dream, 2004; A Small Family Murder, 2008; A Healthy Grave, 2010. EDITOR: (and intro.) The Faber Book of Useful Verse, 1981; The Faber Book of Parodies, 1984; The Faber Book of Diaries, 1987. Contributor to books and periodicals. **Address:** Michael Motley Ltd., The Old Vicarage, Trendington, Tewkesbury, GC GL20 7BP, England.

BRETTON, Barbara. American (born United States), b. 1950. **Genres:** Novels, Romance/Historical, Autobiography/Memoirs. **Career:** Cross Country, computer programmer, 1974-82; Writer, 1983-. **Publications:** ROMANCE NOVELS: Love Changes, 1983; The Sweetest of Debts, 1984; No Safe Place, 1985; Starfire, 1985; The Edge of Forever, 1986; Promises in the Night, 1986; Shooting Star, 1986; Second Harmony, 1987; Mother Knows Best, 1989; Somewhere in Time, 1992; Tomorrow and Always, 1994; One and Only, 1994; The Invisible Groom, 1994; Destiny's Child, 1995; Maybe This Time, 1995; Operation: Husband, 1995; Guilty Pleasures, 1996; Operation: Baby, 1997; Sleeping Alone, 1997; Always, 1998; Operation: Family, 1998; Once Around, 1998; The Day We Met, 1999; At Last, 2000; A Soft Place to Fall, 2001; Because You Loved Me, 2003; Shore Lights, 2003; Girls of Summer, 2003; Chances Are, 2004; Someone Like You, 2005; Just Desserts, 2008; Casting Spells, 2008. HISTORICAL NOVELS: Playing for Time, 1987; Nobody's Baby, 1987; Honeymoon Hotel, 1988; A Fine Madness, 1988; Fire's Lady, 1989; Mrs. Scrooge, 1989; Midnight Lover, 1989; 1950's Stranger in Paradise, 1990 as Stranger in Paradise, 2004; All We Know of Heaven, 1990; Sentimental Journey, 1990; Bundle of Joy, 1991; The Reluctant Bride, 1992; Renegade Lover, 1993; The Bride Came C.O.D.: Sentimental Journey, 1993; Daddy's Girl, 1996; The Perfect Wife, 1997. ANTHOLOGY: (R.C. Estrada, S. James and D. Macomber) To Have And To Hold - I Do, I Do, 1992; (with M. Jensen and D. Macomber) Little Matchmakers, 1994; (co-author) The Christmas Cat, 1996; (with L. Logan and A. McAllister) New Year's Resolution, 1998; (with L. Small and E. Title) Love and Laughter, 1998; (with E. Rose and I. Sharpe) And the Envelope, Please: Ever After/An Affair to Remember/It Happened One Night, 2006; (with M. Ferrarella and C. Myers) A Wedding In Paris, 2007; Laced With Magic, 2009. OTHER: Spun by Sorcery, 2010; Spells & Stitches, 2011; Charmed: A Sugar Maple Short Story, 2011. Contributor of articles to books and periodicals. **Address:** 601 Rte. 206, Ste. 26442, PO Box 5655, Hillsborough, NJ 08844, U.S.A. **Online address:** barbara@barbarabretton.com

BREWARD, Christopher. British (born England), b. 1965. **Genres:** Fash Ion/Costume. **Career:** Manchester Metropolitan University, lecturer in the history of art and design, 1992-94; Royal College of Art, tutor in the history of design, 1994-98; London College of Fashion, professor in historical and cultural studies, 1999-, head of research; Manchester University Press Series 'Studies in Design', general editor; Victoria and Albert Museum, head of research; Royal Society of Arts, fellow. **Publications:** The Culture of Fashion: A New History of Fashionable Dress, 1995; Masculinity and Consumption in Gender and Material Culture, 1996; (ed. with J. Aynsley and M. Kwint) Material Memories, 1999; The Hidden Consumer, 1999; (ed. with B. Conekin and C. Cox) The Englishness of English Dress, 2002; Fashion, 2004; Fashioning London: Clothing and the Modern Metropolis, 2004; (co-author) The London Look: Fashion from Street to Catwalk, 2004; (with A. Cicolini) 21st Century Dandy, 2005; (ed. with C. Evans) Fashion and Modernity, 2005; (ed. with D. Gilbert) Fashion's World Cities, 2006; (ed. with P. Crang and R. Crill) Asian Style: Indian Textiles & Fashion in Britain, 2010. **Address:** Department of Research, Victoria & Albert Museum, Cromwell Rd., London, GL SW7 2RL, England. **Online address:** c.breward@lcf.linst.ac.uk

BREWARD, Ian. Australian/New Zealander (born New Zealand), b. 1934. **Genres:** History, Theology/Religion. **Career:** Knox College, professor of church history, 1965-82; Presbyterian Church of New Zealand, moderator, 1975; Radio N.Z., deputy chairman, 1976-77; Ormond College, professor of church history, 1982-2000; University Melbourne, Department of History, senior fellow, honorary senior fellow, emeritus professor of church history. Writer. **Publications:** Godless Schools? A Study in Protestant Reactions to the Education Act of 1877, 1968; Authority and Freedom, 1969; Grace and Truth: A History of Theological Hall, Knox College, Dunedin, 1876-1975, 1975; The Future of Our Heritage, 1984; Australia: The Most Godless Place under Heaven?, 1988; A History of the Australian Churches, 1993; A History of the Churches in Australasia, 2001. EDITOR: (and intro.) The Work of William Perkins, 1970; John Bunyan, 1988; Thomas Cranmer, 1991; A Man of Grace, 2002; Reforming the Reformation, 2004. **Address:** University Melbourne, 500 Yarra Blvd., Richmond, VI 3121, Australia. **Online address:** ibreward@unimelb.edu.au

BREWER, Bob. American (born United States) **Genres:** Poetry, Young Adult Non-fiction, History. **Career:** Writer. **Publications:** (With W. Getler) Shadow of the Sentinel: One Man's Quest to Find the Hidden Treasure of the Confederacy, 2003. Contributor to periodicals. **Address:** c/o Author Mail, Simon & Schuster Inc., 1230 Ave. of the Americas, 11th Fl., New York, NY 10020-1513, U.S.A.

BREWER, Carolyn. Australian (born Australia), b. 1946?. **Genres:** Social Sciences, History, Theology/Religion. **Career:** Australian National University, Research School of Pacific and Asian Studies, editor intersections and research fellow Gender Relations Centre, faculty. **Publications:** (Contrib.) Keeping Our Heads above Water: Reflections on the Ecumenical Decade of Churches in Solidarity with Women, 1998; (contrib.) Other Pasts: Women, Gender and History in Early Modern Southeast Asia, 2000; (ed. with Anne-Marie Medcalf) Researching the Fragments: Histories of Women in the Asian Context, 2000; Holy Confrontation: Religion, Gender and Sexuality in the Philippines, 1521-1685, 2001, rev. ed. as Shamanism, Catholicism and Gender Relations in Colonial Philippines, 1521-1685, 2004. **Address:** Gender Relations Centre, College of Asia and the Pacific, Australian National University, 7230 H.C. Coombs Bldg., Canberra, AC 0200, Australia. **Online address:** carolyn.brewer@anu.edu.au

BREWER, David Allen. American (born United States), b. 1969?. **Genres:** Literary Criticism And History. **Career:** Ohio State University, associate professor. Writer. **Publications:** The Afterlife of Character, 1726-1825, 2005. **Address:** Department of English, Ohio State University, 514 Denney Hall, 164 W 17th Ave., Columbus, OH 43210-1326, U.S.A. **Online address:** brewer.126@osu.edu

BREWER, Garry D(wight). American (born United States), b. 1941. **Genres:** Politics/Government, Sociology, Environmental Sciences/Ecology, Business/Trade/Industry. **Career:** RAND Corp., staff, 1970-72, senior staff, 1972-74; University of California, assistant professor of political science, 1970-71; University of California, lecturer, 1971; University of Southern California, lecturer in public administration, 1972-73; Rand Graduate Institute of Policy Studies, faculty, 1973-75; Center for Advanced Studies in the Behavioral Sciences, staff, 1974-75; Yale University, associate professor, 1975-78, professor, 1978-84, Frederick K. Weyerhaeuser professor, 1984-90, chair, 2001-, Edwin W. Davis professor, 1990-91; University of Michigan, School of Natural Resources and Environment, professor and dean, 1992-95, Frederick A. Erb Environmental Management Institute, director, 1996-; Swedish Agricultural University, King Carl XVI Gustaf Professor of Environmental Sciences, 1998-99; University of California, Berkeley, Energy and Resource Group, professor of resource policy, 1999-2001. Writer. **Publications:** (With R.D. Brunner) Organized Complexity: Empirical Theories of Political Development, 1971; (with M. Shubik) Questionnaire: Models, Computer Machine Simulations, Games and Studies, 1971; (with M. Shubik) Systems Simulation and Gaming as an Approach to Understanding Organizations, 1971; (with M. Shubik) Methodological Advances in Political Gaming: The One-Person Computer Interactive, Quasi-Rigid Rule Game, 1971; (with M. Shubik and E. Savage) Gaming Literature Review: A Critical Survey of Literature on Gaming and Allied Topics, 1971; Accommodating Increased Demands for Public Participation in Urban Renewal Decisionmaking, 1972; (with O.P. Hall) Policy Analysis by Computer Simulation, 1972; On Innovation, Social Change and Reality, 1972; A Policy Approach to the Study of Political Development and Change, 1972; A Book Review of New Tools for Urban Management by R.S. Rosenbloom and J.R. Russell, for Science, 1972; Dealing with Complex Social Problems: The Potential of the Decision Seminar, 1972; (with M. Shubik and E. Savage) The Literature of Gaming, Simulation and Model-Building: Index and Critical Abstracts, 1972; (with G.D. Brewer) Policy and the Study of the Future: Given Complexity, Trends or Processes?, 1972; (with G.D. Brewer) Reviews of Selected Books and Articles on Gaming and Simulation: A Report, 1972; (with G.D. Brewer) Models, Simulations and Games: A Survey, 1972; Documentation: An Overview and Design Strategy, 1973; Politicians, Bureaucrats and the Consultant: A Critique of Urban Problem-Solving, 1973; (with Shubik and Savage) A Partially Annotated Bibliography of Urban Models, 1973; Systems Analysis in the Urban Complex: Potential and Limitations, 1973; Analysis of Complex Systems: An Experiment and Its Implications for Policymaking, 1973; What's the Purpose? What's the Use?, 1973; (with J.S. Kakalik) Serving Handicapped Children: The Road Ahead,

1974; (with J.S. Kakalik) Serving the Deaf-Blind Population: Planning for 1980, 1974; (ed. with R.D. Brunner) Political Development and Change: A Policy Approach, 1975; An Analyst's View of the Uses and Abuses of Modeling for Decisionmaking, 1975; (with J.S. Kakalik) Mental Health and Mental Retardation Services, 1976; (with M. Shubik) The War Game: A Critique of Military Problem Solving, 1979; (with J.S. Kakalik) Handicapped Children: Strategies for Improving Services, 1979; Decision-Making and the Limits of Technique, 1980; (with P. deLeon) The Foundations of Policy Analysis, 1983; (co-author) Caught Unawares: The Energy Decade in Retrospect, 1983; (ed. with C.S. Binkley and V.A. Sample) Redirecting the RPA: Proceedings of the 1987 Airlie House Conference on the Resources Planning Act, 1988; (ed. with P.C. Stern) Decision Making for the Environment: Social and Behavioral Science Research Priorities, 2005. CONTRIBUTOR: Bureaucracy and Political Development, 1967; International Biographical Directory of Southeast Asian Specialists, 1969; Symposium on Computer Simulation as Related to Manpower and Personnel Planning, 1971; Organized Social Complexity: Challenge to Politics and Policy, 1974; Values and Development: Appraising Asian Experience, 1974; Improving the Quality of Urban Management, 1974; 1980 is Now, 1974; Education Yearbook 1974-1975, 1975; Forecasting in International Relations, 1977; New Trends in Mathematical Modeling, 1978; Utility and Use of Large-Scale Mathematical Models, 1979; The 1978 Energy Update Series, 1979; Verification and SALT, 1980; Marine Policy Papers, 1982; Organizational Effectiveness, 1983; Children, Families and Government, 1983; Special Education Policies, 1983; Global Fisheries, 1983; The Costs of Federalism, 1984. Contributor of articles to journals and periodicals. **Address:** School of Management, University of Michigan, Rm. 202, 56 Hillhouse Ave., New Haven, CT 06511, U.S.A. **Online address:** garry.brewer@yale.edu

BREWER, Heather. American (born United States), b. 1973. **Genres:** Mystery/Crime/Suspense. **Career:** Writer. **Publications:** CHRONICLES OF VLADIMIR TOD SERIES: Eighth Grade Bites, 2007; Ninth Grade Slays, 2008; Tenth Grade Bleeds, 2009; Eleventh Grade Burns, 2010; Twelfth Grade Kills, 2010. **Address:** c/o Michael Bourret, Dystel & Goderich Literary Management, 1 Union Sq. W, Ste. 904, New York, NY 10003, U.S.A.

BREWER, Holly. American (born United States), b. 1964. **Genres:** Adult Non-fiction. **Career:** North Carolina State University, Department of History, associate professor of history, professor and advisor; University of Maryland, Department of History, associate professor of history, Burke chair; American Society for Legal History, co-editor; National Council for History Education, state coordinator, 2010. **Publications:** By Birth or Consent: Children, Law and the Anglo-American Revolution in Authority, 2005. Contributor to periodicals. **Address:** Department of History, University of Maryland, 2115 Francis Scott Key, College Park, MD 20742, U.S.A. **Online address:** holly_brewer@ncsu.edu

BREWER, Jeannie A. American (born United States), b. 1960. **Genres:** Novels, Young Adult Fiction. **Career:** University of Chicago Medical School, teaching assistant, 1983-86; University of Pennsylvania Medical School, resident and instructor, 1989; University of California, general internal medicine instructor, 1991-92; University of Southern California Medical School, Introduction to Clinical Medicine, instructor, 1993-. Writer. **Publications:** A Crack in Forever (novel), 1996. **Address:** c/o Elizabeth Pomada, 1029 Jones St., San Francisco, CA 94109, U.S.A.

BREWER, John. British/American (born United States), b. 1947. **Genres:** Social Sciences, Politics/Government. **Career:** Washington University, visiting professor, 1972-73; Cambridge University, assistant lecturer in history, 1973-76; Yale University, associate professor of history, 1976-80; University of California, Clark Lecturer, 1977, Clark Library, director, 1987-91, Center for Seventeenth and Eighteenth-Century Studies, director, 1987-91, professor of history, 1987-94; Harvard University, professor of history and literature, 1980-87; European University Institute, professor of cultural history, 1993-99; University of Chicago, John and Marion Sullivan professor in English and history, 1999-2001; California Institute of Technology, professor of history and literature, 2002-, Eli and Edye Broad professor of humanities and social sciences, 2003-. Writer and consultant. **Publications:** Party Ideology and Popular Politics at the Accession of George III, 1976; (ed. with J. Styles) An Ungovernable People: The English and Their Law in the Seventeenth and Eighteenth Centuries, 1980; (with N. McKendrick and J.H. Plumb) The Birth of a Consumer Society: The Commercialization of Eighteenth-Century England, 1982; The Common People and Politics, 1750-1790s, 1986; The Sinews of Power: War, Money, and the English State, 1688-1783, 1989; (ed. with R. Porter) Consumption and the World of Goods, 1993; (ed. with S. Staves) Early Modern Conceptions of Property, 1995; (ed. with A. Bermingham) The Consumption of Culture, 1600-1800: Image, Object, Text, 1995; The Pleasures of the Imagination: English Culture in the Eighteenth Century, 1997; (ed. with E. Hellmuth) Rethinking Leviathan: The Eighteenth-Century State in Britain and Germany, 1999; I Piaceri dell'Immaginazione. La cultura inglese nel settecento, 1999; A Sentimental Murder: Love and Madness in the Eighteenth Century, 2004; (ed. with F. Trentmann) Consuming Cultures, Global Perspectives: Historical Trajectories, Transnational Exchanges, 2006; Un Crimen sentimental. Amor y locura en lo siglo XVIII, 2006; American Leonardo: A Tale of Obsession, Art and Money, 2009. **Address:** Division of the Humanities and Social Sciences, California Institute of Technology, MC 228-77, 313 Dabney Hall, 1200 E California Blvd., Pasadena, CA 91125, U.S.A. **Online address:** jbrewer@hss.caltech.edu

BREWER, Mark D. American (born United States), b. 1971. **Genres:** Politics/Government, History. **Career:** Colby College, visiting assistant professor; University of Maine, assistant professor. Writer. **Publications:** (with J.M. Stonecash and M.D. Mariani) Diverging Parties: Social Change, Realignment, and Party Polarization, 2003; Relevant No More? The Catholic/Protestant Divide in American Electoral Politics, 2003; (with J.M. Stonecash) Split: Class and Cultural Divides in American Politics, 2007; (with L.S. Maisel) Parties and Elections in America: The Electoral Process, 5th ed., 2008; Party Images in the American Electorate, 2009. Contributor of articles to journals. **Address:** Department of Political Science, University of Maine, 229 N Stevens Hall, Orono, ME 04469, U.S.A. **Online address:** mark.brewer@umit.maine.edu

BREWER, Sonny. American (born United States), b. 1949. **Genres:** Novels. **Career:** Mobile Bay Monthly, editor-in-chief; Eastern Shore Quarterly, publisher and editor; Red Bluff Review, editor; University of South Alabama, Southern Bard (literary magazine), co-editor; Over the Transom Bookstore, owner, 1997-; Fairhope Center for Writing Arts, founder. **Publications:** Stories from the Blue Moon Café: Anthology of Southern Writers, 2002-04; The Poet of Tolstoy Park, 2005; A Sound Like Thunder: A Novel, 2006; Cormac: One Dog's Fabled Tale (novel), 2007; Widow and the Tree: a Novel, 2009; Forty Hats: The Day Jobs in a Writer's Life, 2010; Don't Quit Your Day Job, 2010; The Alumni Grille, forthcoming. Contributor to periodicals. **Address:** Over the Transom Bookstore, 9 N Church St., Fairhope, AL 36532, U.S.A. **Online address:** sonny@sonnybrewer.com

BREWER, William D(ean). American (born United States), b. 1955. **Genres:** Literary Criticism And History, Essays. **Career:** Appalachian State University, Department of Language, associate professor, professor of English, 1987-. Writer. **Publications:** The Shelley-Byron Conversation, 1994; (ed.) New Essays on Lord Byron, 1996; (ed. with J. Losey) Mapping Male Sexuality: Nineteenth Century England, 2000; (ed. with C.J. Lambert) Essays on the Modern Identity, 2000; (ed.) Contemporary Studies on Lord Byron, 2001; The Mental Anatomies of William Godwin and Mary Shelley, 2001; (ed.) St. Leon: A Tale of the Sixteenth Century, 2006. Contributor to books and periodicals. **Address:** Department of English, Appalachian State University, 307D Sanford Hall, Boone, NC 28608, U.S.A. **Online address:** brewerwd@appstate.edu

BREWERTON, Derrick (Arthur). British (born England), b. 1924. **Genres:** Medicine/Health, Sciences, Sports/Fitness. **Career:** Consultant rheumatologist in London, 1957-89; Royal National Orthopaedic Hospital, consultant physician, 1957-73; Westminster Hospital, consultant physician, 1958-89; University of London, professor, 1982-89. Writer. **Publications:** (Ed.) Immunogenetics in Rheumatic Diseases, 1977; All About Arthritis: Past, Present, Future, 1992. Contributor to journals. **Address:** 173 Ashley Gardens, London, GL SW1P 1PD, England. **Online address:** derrick.brewerton@btinternet.com

BREWSTER, David (C.). American (born United States), b. 1939. **Genres:** Communications/Media, Cultural/Ethnic Topics, Intellectual History, Politics/Government, Biography, Autobiography/Memoirs, Travel/Exploration. **Career:** University of Washington, acting assistant professor of English, 1965-68; Seattle Times, copy editor and writer, 1968, columnist, 1997-2000; Seattle Magazine, associate editor, 1968-70; KING-TV News, assignment editor, 1971; Argus, managing editor, 1972-76; Sasquatch Publishing Company Inc., founder, president and publisher, 1976-94; Seattle Weekly, editorial director, editor and publisher, 1976-97; Town Hall Seattle, founder, creator and executive director, 1998-; Crosscut.com, publisher; Crosscut Public Media, editor-in-chief and board president. **Publications:** Best Places, 1975, 4th ed., 1984; (ed. with R. Earnest): The Seattle Book: The Weekly's Guide to Seattle, 1978; The Seattle Book, 1982; Northwest Best Places: Restaurants Lodgings, and Tourism in Washington, Oregon, and British Columbia, 1986, 12th ed., 1997; British Columbia Best Places: A Guide to Restaurants, Lodgings and Tourism, 1986; (ed. with D.M. Buerge) Washingtonians: A Biographical Portrait of the State, 1988; Seattle Best Places, 1990, 6th ed., 1993. **Address:** Crosscut Public Media, 105 S Main St., Ste. 330, Seattle, WA 98104, U.S.A. **Online address:** david.brewster@crosscut.com

BREWSTER, Elizabeth (Winifred). Canadian (born Canada), b. 1922. **Genres:** Novels, Novellas/Short Stories, Poetry, Autobiography/Memoirs, Essays, Literary Criticism And History. **Career:** Carleton University Library, cataloguer, 1953-57; Indiana University Library, cataloguer, 1957-58; University of Victoria, Department of English, faculty, 1960-61; Mount Allison University Library, reference librarian, 1961-65; New Brunswick Legislative Library, cataloguer, 1965-68; University of Alberta, Alberta Library, cataloguer, 1968-70, visiting assistant professor of English, 1970-71; University of Saskatchewan, Department of English, assistant professor, 1972-75, associate professor, 1975-80, professor, 1980-90, professor emeritus of English, 1990-. Writer. **Publications:** East Coast, 1951; Lillooet, 1954; Roads, and Other Poems, 1957; Passage of Summer: Selected Poems, 1969; Sunrise North, 1972; In Search of Eros, 1974; The Sisters: A Novel, 1974; Sometimes I Think of Moving, 1977; Poems, 1977; It's Easy to Fall on the Ice: Ten Stories, 1977; The Way Home: New Poems, 1982; Digging In: New Poems, 1982; Junction (novel), 1982; A House Full of Women (short stories), 1983; Visitations (short stories), 1987; Entertaining Angels (poetry), 1988; Spring Again: Poems, 1990; Invention of Truth (essays and stories), 1991; Wheel of Change (poems), 1993; Away from Home (essays and stories), 1995; Footnotes to the Book of Job (poems), 1995; Garden of Sculpture, 1998; Burning Bush (poems), 2000; Jacob's Dream (poems), 2002; Bright Centre, 2005; Time & Seasons, 2009. **Address:** Department of English, University of Saskatchewan, 320 Arts Bldg., 9 Campus Dr., Saskatoon, SK S7N 5A5, Canada.

BREWSTER, Gurdon. American (born United States), b. 1937?. **Genres:** Autobiography/Memoirs. **Career:** Ordained Episcopalian priest, 1962; Ebenezer Baptist Church, assistant minister, 1961, 1966; Madras Christian College, American history, instructor, director of student volunteer program and art department, founder, 1962-64; Cornell University, assistant to chaplain, 1965-69, Episcopal chaplain, 1969-99, university chaplain emeritus, 1999; Stuart Little Cooperative, founder. Writer. **Publications:** No Turning Back: My Summer with Daddy King (memoir), 2007. **Address:** 376 Shaffer Rd., Newfield, NY 14867-9607, U.S.A. **Online address:** gurdonbrewster@gmail.com

BREWSTER, Hugh. Canadian/British (born England), b. 1950. **Genres:** Children's Non-fiction, Adult Non-fiction, History. **Career:** Scholastic Inc., editor, 1972-84; Madison Press Books, editorial director, 1984-2004; Banff Publishing Workshop, instructor, 1993-95; freelance writer, 2005-. **Publications:** The Complete Hoser's Handbook, 1983; Anastasia's Album, 1996; Inside the Titanic, 1997; (with L. Coulter) 882 1/2 Answers to All Your Questions about the Titanic, 1998; (with L. Coulter) To Be a Princess: The Fascinating Lives of Real Princesses, 2001; Canada's D-Day Heroes on Juno Beach, 2004; At Vimy Ridge: Canada's Greatest World War I Victory, 2006; The Other Mozart: The Life of the Famous Chevalier de Saint-George, 2007; Carnation, Lily, Lily, Rose: The Story of a Painting, 2007; Breakout Dinosaurs: Canada's Coolest Scariest Ancient Creatures Return!, 2007; Dinosaurs in Your Backyard, 2009; DIEPPE: Canada's Darkest Day of World War II, 2009; I Am Canada: Prisoner of Dieppe, 2010; Gilded Lives, Fatal Voyage, 2011; I Am Canada: A Deadly Voyage, 2011; Titanic's First-Class Passengers and their World, 2012. Contributor to periodicals. **Address:** c/o Rights Manager, Scholastic Canada Ltd., 604 King St. W, Toronto, ON M5V 1E1, Canada. **Online address:** hbrewster@sympatico.ca

BREYFOGLE, Nicholas B. American (born United States), b. 1968. **Genres:** History. **Career:** Ohio State University, professor of history. Historian, educator and editor. **Publications:** Heretics and Colonizers: Forging Russia's Empire in the South Caucasus, 2005; (ed. with A. Schrader and W. Sunderland) Peopling the Russian Periphery: Borderland Colonization in Eurasian History, 2007. **Address:** Department of History, Ohio State University, 230 W 17th Ave., 106 Dulles Hall, Columbus, OH 43210-1367, U.S.A. **Online address:** breyfogle.1@osu.edu

BREYMAN, Steve. American (born United States), b. 1960. **Genres:** Engineering, History. **Career:** Marquette University, visiting assistant professor, 1991-93; Rensselaer Polytechnic Institute, School of Humanities, Arts and Social Science, Department of Science and Technology Studies, assistant professor, 1993-, associate professor. Writer. **Publications:** Movement Genesis: Social Movement Theory and the 1980s West German Peace Movement, 1998; Why Movements Matter: The West German Peace Movement and U.S. Arms Control Policy, 2001. **Address:** Department of Science and Technology Studies, School of Humanities and Social Science, Rensselaer Polytechnic Institute, SA5207, 110 8th St., Troy, NY 12180-3590, U.S.A. **Online address:** breyms@rpi.edu

BREZIANU, Andrei. American/Romanian (born Romania), b. 1934. **Genres:** Novels, Literary Criticism And History, Area Studies, History. **Career:** University of Bucharest, lecturer, 1970-79; Voice of America, international radio broadcaster, Romanian service chief, chief editor, 1986-, Romanian radio station, head, 1991-2001; Catholic University of America, lecturer, 1990-91; University of Cluj-Napoca, lecturer, 1998; Free International University of Moldova, lecturer, 1998, 1999, 2000. **Publications:** Odiseu în Atlantic: Studii Critice, 1977; Scrisori din războiulindependentei, 1877-1878; 1977; Iesirea La Tărmuri, 1978; Castelul Romanului: Etymologicum Parvum, 1981; Translatii, 1982; Laureatii Premiului Nobel pentru literatură: Almanah Contemporanul, 1983; (co-author) Romania: A Case in Dynastic Communism, 1989; The Historical Dictionary of the Republic of Moldova, 2000; Itinerarii Euro-Americane, 2004; între Washington Si Bucuresti: Tablete Transatlantice, 2006; (with V. Spânu) The Historical Dictionary of Moldova, 2nd ed., 2007. Contributor to periodicals. **Address:** Scarecrow Press, 4720 Boston Way, Ste. A, Lanham, MD 20706-6321, U.S.A.

BREZNITZ, Shlomo. Israeli/Slovak (born Slovakia), b. 1936. **Genres:** Psychology, Biography, Autobiography/Memoirs, Psychology, History. **Career:** Israeli Air Force, consultant, 1969-71; University of Haifa, professor of psychology, 1974-99, professor emeritus, 1999-, rector, 1975-77, president, R.D. Wolfe Center for the Study of Psychological Stress, founding director, 1979-; New School for Social Research, professor, 1985-; University of California, London School of Economics, Lady Davis professor of psychology and visiting professor; National Institute of Mental Health, visiting scientist; National Institutes of Health, visiting professor; Rockefeller University, visiting professor. Writer. **Publications:** (Ed. with L. Goldberger) Handbook of Stress: Theoretical and Clinical Aspects, 1982, 2nd ed., 1993; (ed.) Stress in Israel, 1983; Denial of Stress, 1983; Cry Wolf: The Psychology of False Alarms, 1984; Eḳronot ha-lemidah: pereḳ bi-psikhologyah, 1986; (ed. with O. Zinder) Molecular Biology of Stress: Proceedings of a Director's Sponsors-UCLA Symposium Held at Keystone, Colorado, April 10-17, 1988, 1989; Memory Fields, 1993; Sedot ha-zikaron, 1993. **Address:** Department of Psychology, University of Haifa, Mt Carmel, Haifa, 31905, Israel. **Online address:** shlomo@cognifit.com

BRIAN, Cynthia. American (born United States), b. 1975. **Genres:** inspirational/Motivational Literature, Novellas/Short Stories, Homes/Gardens, How-to Books, Self Help, Human Relations/Parenting, Women's Studies And Issues, Young Adult Non-fiction, Young Adult Non-fiction, Design, Film, Communications/Media. **Career:** StarStyle Productions L.L.C., actor, 1976-, coach, 1980-, publisher and freelance writer, 1984-, public speaker and lecturer, 1990-, creator and host, 1996-2002; Starstyle Interiors and Design, interior designer and consultant, 1986-2006; Star Searchers Express, editor; Be the Star You Are! (literacy and media charity), founder, president and executive director, 1999-; Lamorinda Weekly Newspaper, columnist and teen scene editor, 2008-; Express Yourself!, founder and adult coordinator, 2011-. **Publications:** Miracle Moments, 1997; (ed. with J. Canfield and M.V. Hansen) Chicken Soup for the Gardener's Soul: 101 Stories to Sow Seeds of Love, Hope, and Laughter, 2001; Be the Star You Are!: 99 Gifts for Living, Loving, Laughing, and Learning to Make a Difference, 2001; The Business of Show Business: A Comprehensive Career Guide for Actors and Models, 13th ed., 2002; Be the Star You Are! for Teens, 2010. **Address:** StarStyle Productions L.L.C., PO Box 422, Moraga, CA 94556, U.S.A. **Online address:** cynthia@star-style.com

BRIBIESCAS, Richard G. American (born United States) **Genres:** History, Human Relations/Parenting. **Career:** Yale University, Department of Anthropology, associate professor of anthropology, chair and professor of anthropology, Reproductive Ecology Laboratory, director and principal investigator. Writer. **Publications:** Men: Evolutionary and Life History, 2006. **Address:** Department of Anthropology, Yale University, Rm. 202, 10 Sachem St., PO Box 208277, New Haven, CT 06511-3707, U.S.A. **Online address:** richard.bribiescas@yale.edu

BRICE, Carleen. American (born United States), b. 1963. **Genres:** Novels, Young Adult Fiction. **Career:** Writer. **Publications:** Walk Tall: Affirmations for People of Color, 1994; Lead Me Home: An African American's Guide through the Grief Journey, 1999; (ed.) Age Ain't Nothing but a Number: Black Women Explore Midlife, 2003; Orange Mint and Honey: A Novel, 2008; Children of the Waters (novel), 2009; Every Good Wish, forthcoming. **Address:** Victoria Sanders & Associates, 241 Ave. of the Americas, Ste. 11H, New York, NY 10014, U.S.A. **Online address:** carleen@carleenbrice.com

BRICHOUX, Karen. American (born United States) **Genres:** Novels, Human Relations/Parenting, Young Adult Fiction. **Career:** Writer. **Publications:** Coffee & Kung Fu, 2003; Separation Anxiety, 2004; The Girl She Left Behind, 2005; Falling into the World, 2006. **Address:** Trident Media Group L.L.C., 41 Madison Ave., 36th Fl., New York, NY 10010-2257, U.S.A. **Online address:** email@karenbrichoux.com

BRIDE, Johnny Mack. Scottish/British (born England), b. 1926?. **Genres:** Westerns/Adventure, Young Adult Fiction, Novels. **Career:** Educator and writer. **Publications:** Lame Dog Lawman, 1990; Tenderfoot Veteran, 1990; Dutch Pensey Can Ride, 1991; The Men and the Boys, 1991; This Savage Land, 1992; Ride for Your Life, 1992; Bad Times at Blake's Canyon, 1993; Snakebite, 1997; Horse Thieves, 1997; Riders of the Plugged Nickel, 1998; Renegade Blood, 1999. **Address:** 84 Broompark Cres., Airdrie, Lanarkshire, ML6 6DA, Scotland.

BRIDE, Nadja. *See* **NOBISSO, Josephine.**

BRIDGE, Andrew. American (born United States) **Genres:** Autobiography/Memoirs, Biography. **Career:** Judge David L. Bazelon Center for Mental Health Law, staff lawyer; Alliance for Children's Rights, executive director, 1996-2002; Los Angeles County's Blue Ribbon Foster Care Task Force, chair; New Village Charter School, founding director; Broad Foundation, child welfare reform, managing director, 2002. Writer. **Publications:** Hope's Boy: A Memoir, 2008. **Address:** New York, NY , U.S.A. **Online address:** andrewbridgeauthor@gmail.com

BRIDGERS, Lynn. American (born United States), b. 1956?. **Genres:** Biography, History, Theology/Religion, Humanities. **Career:** University of San Francisco, faculty, 1992-93, lecturer, 1996-98; Scottsdale Community College, Department of English, adjunct faculty, 1994-95; Spring Hill College, assistant professor, 2004-05; St. Thomas University, Institute for Pastoral Ministries, assistant professor, 2005-07, graduate program coordinator, 2005-, Department of Religion, assistant professor; St. Norbert College, Master of Theological Studies, adjunct professor, 2008-11, associate director, 2010-11; University of New Mexico, Religious Studies Program, lecturer, 2009-. Writer. **Publications:** Death's Deceiver: The Life of Joseph P. Machebeuf, 1997; Contemporary Varieties of Religious Experience: James's Classic Study in Light of Resiliency, Temperament, and Trauma, 2005; The American Religious Experience: A Concise History, 2006. **Address:** Institute for Pastoral Ministries, St. Thomas University, 16401 NW 37th Ave., Miami Gardens, FL 33054-6313, U.S.A. **Online address:** lbridgers@stu.edu

BRIDGERS, Sue Ellen (Hunsucker). American (born United States), b. 1942. **Genres:** Novels, Young Adult Fiction, Children's Fiction, Social Sciences. **Career:** Writer, 1970-; North Carolina Center for Public Television, board director, 1984-; Jackson County Library, board director, 1985-. **Publications:** CHILDREN'S FICTION: Home Before Dark, 1976; All Together Now, 1979; Notes for Another Life, 1981; Permanent Connections, 1987, rev. ed., 1999; Keeping Christina, 1993. ADULT FICTION: Sara Will, 1985; All We Know of Heaven, 1996; Out with the Boys, forthcoming. Contributor to magazines. **Address:** 64 Savannah Dr., PO Box 248, Sylva, NC 28779, U.S.A.

BRIDGES, Ben. *See* **WHITEHEAD, David (Henry).**

BRIDGES, Laurie. American (born United States), b. 1921. **Genres:** Science Fiction/Fantasy, Young Adult Fiction, Horror, Sciences. **Career:** New Haven Regional Center for the Retarded, public relations officer, 1965-66; Bruck Industries Inc., marketing and public relations officer, 1968-77; Southbury Press Inc., projects coordinator and writer, 1980-82, vice president, 1982-86; The Bruck Corp., vice president, 1982-86; TWN Communications Inc., president, 1984-. Writer. **Publications:** DARK FORCES SERIES FOR JUVENILES: WITH P. ALEXANDER: Devil Wind, 1983; Magic Show, 1983; Swamp Witch, 1983. OTHER: The Ashton Horror, 1984. Contributor to periodicals. **Address:** 4500 Claire Chennault, Dallas, TX 75248, U.S.A.

BRIDGLAND, Fred. British (born England), b. 1941. **Genres:** Area Studies, Earth Sciences, Natural History, Travel/Exploration. **Career:** Reuters News Agency, foreign correspondent, 1969-78; Scotsman, diplomatic editor, 1978-88, assistant editor, 1995-97, Africa correspondent, 2001-; Sunday Telegraph, Southern Africa correspondent, 1988-95; Melbourne Age, Africa correspondent, 2001-. **Publications:** Jonas Savimbi: A Key to Africa, 1986; The War for Africa: Twelve Months That Transformed a Continent, 1990; Katiza's Journey: The True Story of Winnie Mandela, 1997; (with R. Harper) Dear Mr Harper: Britain's First Green Parliamentarian, 2011. **Address:** c/o Giles Gordon, Curtis Brown, 162-168 Regent St., London, GL W1R 5TB, England. **Online address:** fredk.bridgland@wol.co.za

BRIDWELL, Norman (Ray). American (born United States), b. 1928. **Genres:** Children's Fiction, Illustrations, Animals/Pets. **Career:** Raxon Fabrics, artist and designer, 1951-53; HD Rose Co. (filmstrips), artist, 1953-56; freelance commercial artist, 1956-70. Writer. **Publications:** Clifford the Big Red Dog, 1962; Zany Zoo, 1963; Bird in the Hat, 1964; Clifford Gets a Job, 1965; The Witch Next Door, 1965; Clifford Takes a Trip, 1966; Clifford's Halloween, 1966; A Tiny Family, 1968; The Country Cat, 1969; What Do They Do When It Rains?, 1969; Clifford's Tricks, 1969; How to Care for Your Monster, 1970; The Witch's Christmas, 1970; Monster Jokes and Riddles, 1972; Clifford the Small Red Puppy, 1972; The Witch's Vacation, 1973; Merton, the Monkey Mouse, 1973; The Dog Frog Book, 1973; Clifford's Riddles, 1974; Monster Holidays, 1974; Clifford's Good Deeds, 1974; Ghost Charlie, 1974; My Pet the Rock, 1975; Boy on the Ceiling, 1976; The Witch's Catalog, 1976; The Big Water Fight, 1977; Clifford at the Circus, 1977; Kangaroo Stew, 1978; The Witch Grows Up, 1979; Clifford Goes to Hollywood, 1980; Clifford's ABC's, 1983; Clifford's Story Hour, 1983; Clifford's Family, 1984; Clifford's Kitten, 1984; Clifford's Christmas, 1984; Clifford's Grouchy Neighbors, 1985; Clifford's Pals, 1985; Count on Clifford, 1985; Clifford's Manners, 1987; Clifford's Birthday Party, 1988; Clifford's Puppy Days, 1989; Fun with Clifford Activity Book, 1989; Clifford's Word Book, 1990; Where Is Clifford?, 1990; Clifford, We Love You!, 1991; Clifford's Bedtime, 1991; The Witch Goes to School, 1992; Clifford Follows His Nose, 1992; Clifford's Peeka Boo, 1992; Clifford's Bathtime, 1992; Clifford Counts Bubbles, 1992; Clifford's Noisy Day, 1992; Clifford's Animal Noises, 1992; Clifford's Thanksgiving Visit, 1993; Clifford's Happy Easter, 1994; Clifford the Firehouse Dog, 1994; Clifford's First Christmas, 1994; Clifford and The Big Storm, 1995; Clifford's First Halloween, 1996; Clifford's Sports Day, 1996; Clifford's Happy Christmas Lacing Book, 1996; Clifford's Furry Friends, 1996; Clifford's First Valentine's Day, 1997; Clifford's Spring Clean-Up, 1997; Clifford's First Autumn, 1997; Clifford Makes a Friend, 1998; Clifford's ABC Coloring Book, 1998; Sidekicks Clifford Nest Blocks, 1998; Clifford's First Snow Day, 1998; The Story of Clifford, 1998; Clifford's First School Day, 1999; Clifford Keeps Cool, 1999; Clifford Grows Up, 1999; Clifford's Big Book of Things to Know, 1999; Cooking with Clifford, 1999; Clifford and the Halloween Parade, 1999; Oops, Clifford!, 1999; Tiny Family, 1999; Clifford to the Rescue, 2000; Cat and the Bird in the Hat, 2000; Clifford Barks!, 2000; Clifford's Opposites, 2000; Clifford Visits the Hospital, 2000; Clifford's Best Friend, 2000; Clifford's Schoolhouse, 2000; Clifford's Happy Mother's Day, 2001; Clifford's Valentines, 2001; (with K. Weinberger) Clifford the Big Red Dog: the Stormy Day Rescue, 2001; (with L. Mills) Clifford's Teacher's Pets, 2001; (with T.S. Margulies and S. Haefele) Clifford the Big Red Dog: the Show-and-Tell Surprise, 2001; (with T.S. Margulies) Clifford the Big Red Dog: The Runaway Rabbit, 2001; Clifford's Puppy Fun, 2001; Glow-in-the-Dark Christmas, 2001; Cleo Cooperates, 2002; Clifford the Big Red Dog Magnet Math: 3 Bones, 2002; Clifford the Big Red Dog Spelling, 2002; Clifford's Neighborhood: Lots to Learn All around Town, 2002; Clifford Celebrates the Year, 2002; T-Bone Tells the Truth, 2002; (with S. Weyn and J. Durk) The Big Egg Hunt, 2002; (co-author) Clifford Saves the Whales, 2002; (co-author) The Mystery of the Kibble Crook, 2002; (with W.C. Lewison and J. Kurtz) Clifford's Loose Tooth, 2002; (with S. Fry) Take Me to School with You!, 2002; (with S. Fry and J. Kurtz) The Spring Carnival Sticker Storybook, 2002; Missing Beach Ball, 2002; Go, Clifford, Go!, 2002; Clifford's Busy Week, 2002; Clifford Goes to Dog School, 2002; Phonics

Fun Reading Program, Pack 2, 2002; (contrib.) The Big Snowfall, 2003; (co-author) Cookie Crazy!, 2003; (with G. Herman) The Big White Ghost, 2003; Phonics Fun Reading Program, Pack 4, 2003; Clifford's Day with Dad, 2003; Clifford's Class Trip, 2003; Clifford y los Sonidos de los Animales/Clifford's Animal Sounds, 2003; Clifford y los Opuestos/Clifford's Opposites, 2003; Clifford y la Hora de dormir/Clifford's Bedtime, 2003; Clifford y la Hora del Baño/Clifford's Bathtime, 2003; Clifford the Big Red Dog Camera Book, 2003; (contrib.) Camping Out, 2003; (with G. Maccarone) Magic Matt and the Jack O'Lantern, 2003; (with G. Maccarone) Magic Matt and the Skunk in the Tub, 2003; (G. Herman and M. McLaughlin) Clifford Finds A Clue, 2003; Clifford's First Sleepover, 2004; (contrib.) Magic Matt and the Dinosaur, 2004; (contrib.) Clifford for President, 2004; (contrib.) Snow Dog, 2004; Clifford Goes to Washington, 2005; (with S. Fisch) Backpack Puppy, 2005; (contrib.) Christmas Angel, 2005; (contrib.) Clifford, The Big Red Dog: Let's Spell!, 2006; (with D. Denega) Pumpkin Patch Puppy, 2006; (contrib.) The Snow Champion, 2006; (with A. Nye and S. Sander) The Biggest Easter Egg, 2006; (contrib.) Little Blue Easter Egg, 2006; (contrib.) Clifford Helps Santa, 2006; Clifford's Noisy Day, 2007; Clifford's First Christmas, 2007; (contrib.) Clifford Makes a Splash, 2007; Clifford's Happy New Year, 2008; (contrib.) Lots of Love, 2008; (contrib.) Earth Day Puppy, 2009; Clifford the Champion, 2009; Cliffords First Easter with Flaps, 2010; (contrib.) Happy St. Patrick's Day, Clifford!, 2010; Clifford's Big Dictionary, 2010; Clifford is a Star, 2010; Clifford Goes to School, 2010; (contrib.) Thanksgiving Parade, 2010; Clifford and the Big Parade, 2011; Clifford and the Dinosaurs, 2011; Clifford Goes to the Doctor, 2011; Clifford Makes the Team, 2011; Cliffords Class Trip, 2011; Clifford Sees America, 2012; Clifford Shares, 2012; Clifford's Field Day, 2012. Contributor to books and periodicals. Illustrator of books by others. **Address:** PO Box 869, High St., Edgartown, MA 02539-0869, U.S.A.

BRIEFEL, Aviva. American/French (born France) **Genres:** History, Art/Art History. **Career:** Bowdoin College, associate professor of English, Gay and Lesbian Studies Program, director. Writer and historian. **Publications:** The Deceivers: Art Forgery and Identity in the Nineteenth Century, 2006; (ed. with S.J. Miller) Horror after 9/11: World of Fear, Cinema of Terror, 2011; Amputations: The Colonial Hand at the Fin de Siècle Horror after 9/11, forthcoming. Contributor to periodicals. **Address:** Department of English, Bowdoin College, 205 Massachusetts Hall, Brunswick, ME 04011, U.S.A. **Online address:** abriefel@bowdoin.edu

BRIERLEY, Barry. American (born United States), b. 1937. **Genres:** Romance/Historical, Novels. **Career:** Jostens Inc., staff artist, 1969-79; Wincraft Inc., manager of special graphics, 1983-87, tee shirt designer and illustrator, through 1989; writer, 1993-. **Publications:** Washichu, 1993; Timeless Interlude at Wounded Knee, 1995; White Horse, Red Rider, 1996; Wasichu's Return, 1996; Yesterday's Bandit: Butch Cassidy's Pursuit of Life and Honor, 2003; Spirit Riders: A Novel of the West, 2006. **Address:** 1720 Stonehouse Ln., Cincinnati, OH 45255-2422, U.S.A. **Online address:** brierleybarry@yahoo.com

BRIGG, Peter. Canadian (born Canada), b. 1942?. **Genres:** Science Fiction/Fantasy, History, Literary Criticism And History. **Career:** Picton High school teacher, 1964-65; University of Guelph, lecturer, 1970-72, assistant professor, 1972-80, associate professor of English and theater studies, 1980-2004, professor, 2004, professor emeritus, 2004-; Shanghai Institute of International Economic Management, teacher, 1984-85; University of Canterbury, teacher, 1990. Gryphon Press, operator of antique hand press, 1973-84. Birmingham Repertory Theater, archivist, 1975-81; Massey College, Quarter Century Fund, trustee, 1995-97; Science Fiction Research Association, vice president, president. Writer. **Publications:** J. G. Ballard, 1985; Shanghai Year: A Westerner's Life in the New China, 1987; The Span of Mainstream and Science Fiction: A Critical Study of a New Literary Genre, 2003. **Address:** School of English and Theatre Studies, University of Guelph, 50 Stone Rd., Guelph, ON N1G 2W1, Canada. **Online address:** pbrigg@uoguelph.ca

BRIGGS, Asa. British (born England), b. 1921. **Genres:** Economics, History, Young Adult Fiction, Politics/Government. **Career:** Nuffield College, faculty fellow, 1953-55; Oxford University, Worcester College, reader in recent social and economic history, 1950-55, fellow, 1975-55, provost, 1976-91; University of Leeds, professor of modern history, 1955-61; University of Sussex, dean of school of social studies, 1961-65, pro-vice chancellor, 1961-67, vice-chancellor, 1967-76, honorary fellow, 1968-; British Film Institute, governor, 1970-77; United Nations University Council, chairman, 1974-80; European Institute of Education, president, 1975-96; Heritage Education Group, chairman, 1976-86; consultant, 1977-78; Open University, chancellor, 1978-94. Writer. **Publications:** (With D. Thomson and E. Meyer) Patterns of Peacemaking, 1945; 1851, 1951; History of Birmingham, 1952; Victorian People: Some Reassessments of People, Institutions, Ideas, and Events, 1851-1867, 1954, rev. ed., 1986; Victorian People: A Reassessment of Persons and Themes, 1851-67, 1955, rev. ed. 1973; Friends of the People, 1956; The Age of Improvement, 1959, 2nd ed., 2000; Essays in Labour History, 1960; Historians and the Study of Cities, 1960; Social Thought and Social Action, 1961; History of Broadcasting in the United Kingdom, 5 vols., 1961-95; Victorian Cities, 1963, rev. ed., 1996; Saxons, Normans and Victorians, 1966; Victorians and Victorianism, 1966; William Cobbett, 1967; (contrib.) Rhetoric and World Politics; An Interdisciplinary Analysis of Political Speeches, 1974; Social Thought and Social Action; A Study of the Work of Seebohm Rowntree, 1871-1954, 1974; Communications and Culture, 1823-1973: A Tale of Two Centuries, 1975; Governing the BBC, 1979; Iron Bridge to the Crystal Palace: Impact and Image of the Industrial Revolution, 1979; The Power of Steam: An Illustrated History of the World's Stream Age, 1982; (with J. Dekker and J. Mair) Marx in London: An Illustrated Guide, 1982; A Social History of England, 1983, rev. ed., 1999; Social History and Human Experience, 1984; (with A. Macartney) Tonybee Hall: The First Hundred Years, 1984; The BBC: The First Fifty Years, 1985; The Collected Essays of Asia Briggs, 1985; Wine for Sale: Victoria Wine and Liquor Trade, 1860-1984, 1985; (with J. Spicer) The Franchise Affair: Creating Fortunes and Failures in Independent Television, 1986; (foreword) Changes in China: The Role of Cooperatives in the New Socialism, 1987; Victorian Things, 1988, rev. ed., 2003; Haut-Brion, 1994; Channel Islands: Occupation and Liberation 1940-1945, 1995; (with P. Clavin) Modern Europe 1789-1989, 1997; Chartism, 1998; Who's Who in the Twentieth Century, 1999; Go to It: Working for Victory on the Home Front, 1939-45, 2000; Michael Young: Social Entrepreneur, 2001; (with P. Burke) A Social History of the Media: From Gutenberg to the Internet, 2001, 3rd., 2009; Modern Europe, 1789-Present, 2nd ed., 2003; History of Longmans and Their Books, 1724-1990: Longevity in Publishing, 2008; The History of Broadcasting in the United Kingdom, forthcoming. EDITOR: Chartist Studies, 1959; They Saw It Happen: An Anthology of Eyewitnesses Accounts of Events in British History, 1897-1940, 1960; (with J. Saville) Essays in Labour History: In Memory of G.D.H. Cole, 1967; (and contrib.) The Nineteenth Century: The Contradictions of Progress, 1970; (with S. Briggs) Cap and Bell: Punch's Chronicle of English History in the Making, 1972; (intro.) William Morris: Selected Writings and Designs, 1973; Essays in the History of Publishing, 1974; (and intro.) Gladstone's Bosewell: Late Victorian Conversations, 1984; Longman Dictionary of 20th Century Biography, 1985; (with J.H. Shelley) Science, Medicine, and the Community: The Last Hundred Years, 1986; A Dictionary of Twentieth-Century World Biography, 1992; (with D. Snowman) Fins de Siecle: How Centuries End, 1400-2000, 1996; (co-ed.) The History of Bethlem, 1997; Social and Economic History of England, forthcoming. **Address:** c/o Veronica Humphrey, 26 Oakmede Way, Ringmer, ES BN8 5JL, England.

BRIGGS, John. (John P. Briggs). American (born United States), b. 1945. **Genres:** Novellas/Short Stories, Literary Criticism And History, Writing/Journalism. **Career:** The Tarrytown Daily News, reporter, 1962-63; The Hartford Courant, reporter, 1965-68, copy editor, 1978-79; Patchogue High School, teacher, 1968-71; Irvington High School, teacher, 1968-71; The Academy, managing editor, 1970-76; New York Quarterly, managing editor, 1972-77; New School for Social Research, faculty, 1973-87; Mercy College, adjunct faculty, 1974-87; Brooklyn College, Department of English, adjunct faculty, 1974; freelance professional photographer, 1975-85; WNYC Public Radio, co-host, 1977-79; Herman Smith Associates, consulting editor, 1979-80; freelance science writer, 1981-; Western Connecticut State University, journalism co-ordinator, 1987-, Department of English Language, Comparative Literature and Writing, associate professor of English, 1987-95, professor of English, 1995-, distinguished professor, co-chair, 1999-2001, 2003; Norwich University, Vermont College, adjunct faculty, 1995-98; Connecticut Review, assistant fiction editor, 1997-, senior editor. **Publications:** (With R. Monaco) The Logic of Poetry, 1974; (with F.D. Peat) Looking Glass Universe, 1984; Fire in the Crucible: The Alchemy of Creative Genius, 1988; (with F.D. Peat) Turbulent Mirror, 1989; (comp. with R. Monaco) Metaphor: The Logic of Poetry, 1990; Fire in the Crucible: The Self-creation of Creativity and Genius, 1990; Fractals: The Patterns of Chaos, 1992; (with F.D. Peat) The Seven Life Lessons of Chaos, 1999; Fire in the Crucible: Understanding the Process of Creative Genius, 2000; (with J.R. Scrimgeour) Entangled Landscapes, 2003; (foreword) Art of Layering, 2004; Trickster Tales, 2005. Contributor of articles to books and periodicals. **Address:** Department of English, Western Connecticut State University, Rm. BR 214, 181 White St., Danbury, CT 06810-6639, U.S.A. **Online address:** briggsjp@wcsu.ctstateu.edu

BRIGGS, John P. *See* **BRIGGS, John.**

BRIGGS, Patricia. American (born United States), b. 1965?. **Genres:** Novels, Young Adult Non-fiction, Horror, Graphic Novels. **Career:** Writer. **Publications:** Giant Book of the Dog (nonfiction), 1998; The Hob's Bargain (novel), 2001; Hunting Ground, 2009; Fair Game: An Alpha and Omega Novel, 2012. SIANIM SERIES: Masques, 1993; Steal the Dragon, 1995; When Demons Walk, 1998; Wolfsbane, 2010. HUROG SERIES: Dragon Bones, 2002; Dragon Blood, 2003. RAVEN DUOLOGY SERIES: Raven's Shadow, 2004; Raven's Strike, 2005. MERCEDES THOMPSON SERIES: Moon Called, 2006, vol. II, 2011; Blood Bound, 2007; Iron Kissed, 2008; Bone Crossed, 2009; (with D. Lawrence) Homecoming, 2009; Silver Borne, 2010; River Marked, 2011; Frost Burned, 2013. ANNA AND CHARLES SERIES: Cry Wolf, 2008. **Address:** c/o Linn Prentis, Linn Prentis Literary, 155 E 116th St., Ste. 2F, New York, NY 10029, U.S.A. **Online address:** patricia@hurog.com

BRIGGS, Raymond (Redvers). British (born England), b. 1934. **Genres:** Children's Fiction, Illustrations, Picture/Board Books, Poetry. **Career:** Writer and illustrator, 1957-; Brighton College of Art, part-time lecturer, 1961-87; Slade School of Fine Art, teacher; Central Art School, teacher. **Publications:** SELF-ILLUSTRATED: Jim and the Beanstalk, 1970. SNOWMAN SERIES: The Snowman, 1978; Building the Snowman, 1985; Dressing Up, 1985; Walking in the Air, 1985; Party, 1985; (with R.V. der Meer) The Snowman: A Pop-Up Book with Music, 1986; The Snowman Storybook, 1990; The Snowman Flap Book, 1991; The Snowman Tell-the-Time Book, The Snowman Clock Book, 1992; Snowman: Songbook, 1993; The Snowman: Things to Touch and Feel, See and Sniff, 1994; The Snowman: A Fun-shaped Play Book, 1999. OTHERS: The Strange House, 1961; Midnight Adventure, 1961; Ring-a-Ring O' Roses (poems), 1962; Sledges to the Rescue, 1963; The White Land: A Picture Book of Traditional Rhymes and Verses, 1963; Fee Fi Fo Fum: A Picture Book of Nursery Rhymes, 1964; (ed.) The Mother Goose Treasury, 1966; Jimmy Murphy and the White Duesenberg, 1968, new ed., 2006; Nuvolari and the Alfa Romeo, 1968, new ed., 2006; Father Christmas, 1973; Father Christmas Goes on Holiday, 1975; Fungus the Bogeyman, 1977; Gentleman Jim, 1980; When the Wind Blows, 1982; The Tin-Pot Foreign General and the Old Iron Woman, 1984; (co-author) All in a Day, 1986; Unlucky Wally, 1987; Unlucky Wally Twenty Years On, 1989; Father Christmas Having a Wonderful Time, 1993; The Bear, 1994; The Man, 1995; Ethel & Ernest, 1998; Ug: Boy Genius of the Stone Age and His Search for Soft Trousers, 2001; (with A. Ahlberg) The Adventures of Bert, 2001; Ivor: The Invisible, 2001; (with A. Ahlberg) A Bit More Bert, 2002; Even More Revolting Recipes, 2002; Blooming Books, 2003; The Fungus Big Green Bogey Book: Snot for the Faint-Hearted, 2003; The Puddleman, 2004; Christmas Little Library, 2010; Mother Goose Nursery Rhymes, 2011; The Snowman Storybook and Magical Pop-up Snowglobe, 2011; Mother Goose, 2012. Illustrator of books by others. **Address:** The Agency Ltd., 24 Pottery Ln., Holland Pk., London, GL W11 4LZ, England.

BRIGGS, Ward W(right). American (born United States), b. 1945. **Genres:** Classics, Language/Linguistics, Literary Criticism And History, Biography. **Career:** University of South Carolina, instructor and professor of classics, 1973-, Carolina distinguished professor of classics, 1996-, now Carolina distinguished professor of emeritus, Louise Fry Scudder professor of humanities, 1996-, interim associate provost, 1996-97, professor and director of classics; University of Colorado, visiting professor, 1988. Writer. **Publications:** Narrative and Simile from the Georgics in the Aeneid, 1980. EDITOR: Concordantiain in Varronis Libros, De Re Rustica, 1983; Concordantia in Catonis Librum De Agri Cultura, 1983; (with H.W. Benario) Basil Lanneau Gildersleeve: An American Classicist, 1986; The Letters of Basil Lanneau Gildersleeve, 1987; (with W.M. Calder III) Classical Scholarship: A Biographical Encyclopedia, 1990; Selected Classical Papers of Basil Lanneau Gildersleeve, 1992; Biographical Dictionary of North American Classicists, 1994; (with E.C. Kopff) The Roosevelt Lectures of Paul Shorey (1913-1914), 1995; Ancient Greek Authors, 1997; Soldier and Scholar: Basil Lanneau Gildersleeve and the Civil War, 1998; Ancient Roman Writers, 1999; (with C.W. Kallendorf, J. Gaisser and C. Martindale) Companion to the Classical Tradition, 2007. Contributor to periodicals. **Address:** Department of French and Classics, University of South Carolina, 813A Welsh Humanities Bldg., 816 Bull St., Columbia, SC 29208, U.S.A. **Online address:** wardbriggs@sc.edu

BRIGHAM, Robert K. American (born United States), b. 1960?. **Genres:** History. **Career:** Vassar University, professor, 1994-, Shirley Ecker Boskey professor of history and international relations, chair of international relations; Johns Hopkins University, Albert Shaw endowed lecturer; Brown University, Watson Institute for International Studies, visiting professor of international relations; University College Dublin, Mary Ball Washington professor of American history, Clinton Institute, visiting professor. Writer. **Publications:** Guerrilla Diplomacy: The NLF's Foreign Relations and the Vietnam War, 1998; (with R.S. McNamara and J.G. Blight) Argument without End: In Search of Answers to the Vietnam Tragedy, 1999; ARVN: Life and Death in the South Vietnamese Army, 2006; Is Iraq Another Vietnam?, 2006; Iraq, Vietnam and the Limits of American Power, new ed., 2008; America and Iraq since 1990, 2012; The Global Ho Chi Minh, 2013; American Foreign Relations: A History, 2015; (with M. Bradley and L.H. Nguyen) The Wars for Vietnam, forthcoming. **Address:** Department of History, Vassar University, 39 Swift Hall, 124 Raymond Ave., PO Box 64, Poughkeepsie, NY 12604-0711, U.S.A. **Online address:** robrigham@vassar.edu

BRIGHT, Elizabeth. *See* **MYERS, Tim.**

BRIGHT, Freda. American (born United States), b. 1929. **Genres:** Novels, Advertising/Public Relations, Literary Criticism And History, Young Adult Fiction. **Career:** RCA Victor, literary editor, 1957-60; Batton, Barton, Durstine and 1960-63; West, Weir and Bartel, advertising copywriter, 1963-65; McCann Erikson, advertising copywriter, 1965-67; freelance advertising writer, 1967-. **Publications:** Options: A Novel, 1982; Futures, 1983; Decisions, 1984; Infidelities, 1986; Singular Women, 1989; Consuming Passions, 1991; Parting Shots, 1993; Masques, 1994. **Address:** c/o Carole Abel, 160 W 87th St., New York, NY 10024, U.S.A.

BRIGHT, Myron H. American (born United States), b. 1919. **Genres:** Law, Civil Liberties/Human Rights, Young Adult Fiction. **Career:** Wattam, Vogel, Bright and Peterson, lawyer, 1947-68; U.S. Court of Appeals, judge, 1968-85, senior judge 1985-; St. Louis University, distinguished professor of law, 1985-89, emeritus professor of law, 1989-95; North Dakota University, distinguished jurist-in-residence. Writer. **Publications:** (Co-author) New Jersey Objections at Trial, 1992. WITH R.L. CARLSON: Objections at Trial, 1990, 5th ed., 2008; Maine Objections at Trial, 1991; (with R.H. Aronson) Washington Objections at Trial, 1991; (with E.J. Imwinkelried) California Objections at Trial, 1992; (with W. Eleazer) Florida Objections at Trial, 1992; (with A.D. Montgomery) Minnesota Objections at Trial, 1993; New Hampshire Objections at Trial, 1992; Oregon Objections at Trial, 1992; (with S. Crump) Texas Objections at Trial, 1992; (with J.H. Young) Virginia Objections at Trial, 1993; (with J.C. O'Brien) Missouri Objections at Trial, 1993. Contributor of articles. **Address:** U.S. Court of Appeals, 8th Circuit, 655 1st Ave. N, Ste. 340, PO Box 2707, Fargo, ND 58108-2707, U.S.A.

BRIGHTMAN, Carol. American (born United States), b. 1939. **Genres:** International Relations/Current Affairs, Social Commentary, Biography, Documentaries/Reportage. **Career:** Central YMCA College, adjunct instructor, 1962-63; New York University, graduate assistant, 1964-65; New School College, instructor, 1965-67; Viet-Report: An Emergency News Bulletin on Southeast Asia Affairs, founder and editor, 1965-68; Southeastern Massachusetts University, instructor, 1969; Leviathan, co-editor, 1969-70; Brooklyn College, instructor, 1973-76; freelance writer, 1976-; GEO Magazine, associate editor, 1982-85; University of Maine, adjunct instructor, 1989-92. **Publications:** NONFICTION: (with L. Rivers) Drawings and Digressions, 1979; Writing Dangerously: Mary McCarthy and Her World, 1992; Sweet Chaos: The Grateful Dead's American Adventure, 1998; Total Insecurity: The Myth of American Omnipotence, 2004; Scouting the Perimeter, forthcoming. EDITOR: (with S. Levinson) Venceremos Brigade: Young Americans Sharing the Life and Work of Revolutionary Cuba: Diaries, Letters, Interviews, Tapes, Essays, Poetry, by the Venceremos Brigade, 1971; (and intro.) Between Friends: The Correspondence of Hannah Arendt and Mary McCarthy, 1949-1975, 1995. Contributor of articles to periodicals. **Address:** Barbara Hogenson Agency Inc., 165 W End Ave., Ste. 19C, New York, NY 10023-5511, U.S.A. **Online address:** cdmbrightman@gmail.com

BRIGNALL, Richard. Canadian (born Canada), b. 1977?. **Genres:** Biography, Sports/Fitness. **Career:** Kenora Daily Miner and News, sports reporter. Journalist, sports historian and biographer. **Publications:** (With J. Danakas) Small Town Glory: The Story of the Kenora Thistles' Remarkable Quest for the Stanley Cup, 2006; Forever Champions: The Enduring Legacy of the Record-Setting Edmonton Grads, 2007; Big Train: The Legendary Ironman of Sport, Lionel Conacher, 2009; Fearless: The Story of George Chuvalo, Canada's Greatest Boxer, 2009; China Clipper: Pro Football's First Chinese-Canadian Player, Normie Kwong, 2010; Big League Dreams, 2010. Contributor to periodicals. **Address:** Kenora, ON , Canada. **Online address:** richard@richardbrignall.com

BRILL, Marlene Targ. American (born United States), b. 1945. **Genres:** Children's Fiction, Adult Non-fiction, Children's Non-fiction, Medicine/Health, Politics/Government, Cultural/Ethnic Topics, Biology, Communications/Media, History, Art/Art History, Education, Human Relations/Parenting, Medicine/Health, Women's Studies And Issues, Young Adult Non-fiction, E-books, Picture/Board Books, Graphic Novels. **Career:** Teacher, 1967-80; Marlene Targ Brill Communications, speaker, writer and editor for businesses and textbook publishers, 1980-. **Publications:** JUVENILE: (with K. Checker) Unique Listening/Mainstreaming Stories, 1980; John Adams: Second President of the United States, 1986; I Can Be a Lawyer, 1987; Libya, 1987; James Buchanan: Fifteenth President of the United States, 1988; Hide-and-Seek Safety, 1988; Rainy Days and Rainbows, 1989; Algeria, 1990; Why Do We Have To?, 1990; Mongolia, 1992; Daniel in the Lion's Den, 1992; David and Goliath, 1992; Jonah and the Whale, 1992; Joseph's Coat of Many Colors, 1992; Noah's Ark, 1992; Allen Jay and the Underground Railroad, 1993; (with H.R. Targ) Guatemala, 1993; Guyana, 1994; Trail of Tears: The Cherokee Journey from Home, 1995; (with H.R. Targ) Honduras, 1995; Small Paul and the Big Bully, 1996; Building the Capital City, 1996; Let Women Vote!, 1996; Extraordinary Young People, 1996; Journey for Peace: The Story of Rigoberta Menchu, 1996; Illinois, 1997, 2nd ed., 2006; Women for Peace, 1997; Indiana, 1997, 2nd ed., 2006; Tooth Tales from Around the World, 1998; Diary of a Drummer Boy, 1998; Michigan, 1998, 2nd ed., 2007; Winning Women in Soccer, 1999; Winning Women in Ice Hockey, 1999; Winning Women in Baseball/Softball, 2000; Shoes Through the Ages, 2000; Winning Women in Basketball, 2000; Margaret Knight: Girl Inventor, 2001; Minnesota, 2004, (with E. Kaplan) 2nd ed., 2011; Broncho Charlie and the Pony Express, 2004; Doctors, 2005; Veteran's Day, 2005; Autism, 2008; Marshall Major Taylor: World Champion Bicyclist, 2008; America in the 1900s, 2009; America in the 1910s, 2009; America in the 1970s, 2009. OTHERS: Washington, D.C., Travel Guide, 1982; Infertility and You, 1984; Keys to Parenting a Child with Down Syndrome, 1994; Keys to Parenting a Child with Autism, 1994, rev. ed., 2001; The AMA Book of Asthma, 1998; Tourette Syndrome, 2002; Raising Smart Kids for Dummies, 2003; Garbage Trucks, 2005; Lung Cancer, 2005; Nurses, 2005; Barack Obama: Working to Make a Difference, 2006; Down Syndrome, 2007; Concrete Mixers, 2007; Diabetes, 2008; Multiple Sclerosis, 2008; Barack Obama: President for a New Era, 2009; Michelle Obama: From Chicago's South Side to the White House, 2010; America in the 1900s, 2010; America in the 1910s; America in the 1980s, 2010; America in the 1990s, 2010; Annie Shapiro and the Clothing Workers' Strike, 2010; The Rough-riding Adventure of Bronco Charlie, Pony Express Rider, 2011; Underground Railroad Adventure of Allen Jay, Antislavery Activist, 2011. **Address:** Marlene Targ Brill Communications, 314 Lawndale, Wilmette, IL 60091, U.S.A. **Online address:** marlenetbrill@comcast.net

BRILLIANT, Richard. American (born United States), b. 1929. **Genres:** Archaeology/Antiquities, Art/Art History. **Career:** University of Pennsylvania, assistant professor, 1962-64, associate professor, 1964-69, professor, 1969-70; Columbia University, Anna S. Garbedian professor in the humanities, art history and archaeology, 1970-, now Anna S. Garbedian professor emeritus in the humanities; University of Pittsburgh, visiting professor of fine arts, 1971. Writer. **Publications:** Gesture and Rank in Roman Art: The Use of Gestures To Denote Status In Roman Sculpture and Coinage, 1963; The Arch of Septimus Severus in the Roman Forum, 1967; Arts of the Ancient Greeks, 1973; Roman Art from the Republic to Constantine, 1974; (contrib.) Pompeii A.D. 79: The Treasure of Rediscovery, 1979; Visual Narratives: Storytelling in Etruscan and Roman Art, 1984; (with J.M. Borgatti) Likeness and Beyond: Portraits from Africa and the World, 1990; Portraiture, 1991; (contrib.) Campagna Romana: The Countryside of Ancient Rome, 1992; Commentaries on Roman Art: Selected Studies, 1994; (ed.) Facing the New World: Jewish Portraits in Colonial and Federal America, 1997; My Laocoön: Alternative Claims in the Interpretation of Artworks, 2000; Un Americano A Roma, 2000; (contrib.) Wlodzimierz Ksiazek: Paintings 1990-2001, 2001; (contrib.) Rhetorik des Ornaments, 2001; Miller Collection of Roman Sculpture: Mythological Figures and Portraits, 2004; (with A. Weinstein) Group Dynamics: Family Portraits & Scenes of Everyday Life at the New-York Historical Society, 2006; (ed. with D. Kinney) Reuse Value, 2011; Eric Fischl Portraits, 2012. Contributor of articles to journals. **Address:** Department of Art History and Archaeology, Columbia University, 826 Schermerhorn Hall, 8th Fl., 1190 Amsterdam Ave., New York, NY 10027, U.S.A.

BRIMSON, Dougie. British (born England), b. 1959?. **Genres:** Young Adult Fiction, Sports/Fitness. **Career:** British Royal Air Force, staff. Writer. **Publications:** (with E. Brimson) Everywhere We Go: Behind the Matchday Madness, 1996; (with E. Brimson) England, My England: The Trouble with the National Football Team, 1996; (with E. Brimson) Capital Punishment: London's Violent Football Following, 1997; The Geezers' Guide to Football: A Lifetime of Lads and Lager, 1998; (with E. Brimson) Derby Days: The Games We Love to Hate, 1998; The Crew (fiction), 1999; Billy's Log: The Hilarious Diary of One Man's Struggle with Life, Lager and the Female Race (fiction), 2000; Barmy Army: The Changing Face of Football Violence, 2000; Top Dog (fiction), 2001; Eurotrashed: The Rise and Rise of Europe's Football Hooligans, 2003; Kicking Off: Why Hooliganism and Racism Are Killing Football, 2006; (ed.) Rebellion: The Inside Story of Football's Protest Movement, 2006; March of the Hooligans: Soccer's Bloody Fraternity, 2007. **Address:** Jacque Evans Management Ltd., 14 Holmesley Rd., Ste. 1, London, GL SE23 1PJ, England. **Online address:** dbrimson@uk2.net

BRIN, David. American (born United States), b. 1950. **Genres:** Science Fiction/Fantasy, Sciences, Technology, Novels, Novellas/Short Stories. **Career:** Hughes Aircraft Research Laboratory, research engineer, 1973-77; Journal of the Laboratory of Comparative Human Cognition (UCSD), managing editor, 1980-81; Heritage Press, book reviewer and science editor, 1980-; University of California, California Space Institute, associate and post-doctoral research fellow, 1982-85; San Diego State University, faculty in physics and writing, 1982-85; Science Fiction Writers of America, secretary, 1982-84; San Diego community college, faculty, 1984-85; University of London, Westfield College, visiting artist, 1986-87; consultant, 1990-. **Publications:** Sundiver, 1980; Startide Rising, 1983; The Practice Effect, 1984; The Postman, 1985; (with G. Benord) Heart of the Comet, 1986; The River of Time, 1986; Earthclan, 1986; The Uplift War, 1987; Dr. Pak's Preschool, 1989; (with T. Kuiper) Extraterrestrial Civilization (non-fiction/science), 1989; Earth, 1990; Piecework, 1991; Glory Season, 1993; Otherness, 1994; Brightness Reef, 1995; Infinity's Shore, 1996; Heaven's Reach, 1997; Transparent Society: Will Technology Force Us to Choose Between Privacy and Freedom?, 1998; Tribes: It's 50, 000 B.C. Where Are Your Children?, 1998; Foundation's Triumph, 1999; (with K. Lenagh) Contacting Aliens, 2002; Kiln People, 2002; (with D. Geisler and J. Burns) Tomorrow Happens, 2003; The Life Eaters, 2003; (ed. with L. Wilson) King Kong is Back!: An Unauthorized Look at One Humongous Ape, 2005; Free the Mississippi?, 2005; The Other Culture War, 2005; Doing a Slow Turn, 2006; Singularities and Nightmares: The Range of Our Futures, 2006; (ed.) Star Wars on Trial, 2006; Sky Horizon, 2007; Through Stranger Eyes, 2008. Contributor to periodicals. **Address:** SFWA Inc., PO Box 877, Chestertown, MD 21620-0877, U.S.A. **Online address:** davidbrin@sbcglobal.net

BRINDLEY, John. British (born England), b. 1954. **Genres:** Novels. **Career:** Greater London Council, electrical engineer. Writer. **Publications:** NOVELS: The Terrible Quin: A Thriller, 1998; Pillars of Salt, 1999; Turning to Stone, 1999; Rhino Boy, 2000; Scissorman, 2001; Changing Emma, 2002; The Rule of Claw, 2007; The City of Screams, 2008; Legend, 2009; Blood Crime, 2010. AMY PEPPERCORN SERIES: Amy Peppercorn: Starry-eyed and Screaming, 2003, new ed. 2006; Amy Peppercorn: Living the Dream, 2006; Amy Peppercorn: Beyond the Stars, 2006; Amy Peppercorn: Out of Control, 2006. **Address:** Orion Publishing Group, Orion House, 5 Upper St. Martin's Ln., London, GL WC2H 9EA, England. **Online address:** johnbrindley@onetel.net

BRINGHURST, Robert. Canadian/American (born United States), b. 1946. **Genres:** Poetry, Art/Art History, Design, Literary Criticism And History, Translations. **Career:** Journalist, 1965-66, 1970-71; Judge Advocate General's Corps, staff, 1968-69; Panama Canal Zone, law clerk, 1968-69; University of British Columbia, visiting lecturer in creative writing, 1975-77, Department of English, lecturer in English, 1979-80; Simon Fraser University, adjunct lecturer in typographical history, 1983-84; Banff Centre School of Fine Arts, poet-in-residence, 1983; Ojibway & Cree Cultural Centre Writers' Workshops, poet-in-residence, 1985; University of Winnipeg, writer-in-residence, 1986; University of Edinburgh, writer-in-residence, 1989-90; Trent University, lecturer, 1994, Ashley Fellow, 1994, Traill College, Frost Centre for Canadian Studies and Indigenous Studies, adjunct professor, 1998-;

University of Western Ontario, writer-in-residence, 1998-99. **Publications:** POETRY: The Shipwright's Log, 1972; Cadastre, 1973; Deuteronomy, 1974; Pythagoras, 1974; Eight Objects, 1975; Bergschrund, 1975; Jacob Singing, 1977; The Stonecutter's Horses, 1979; Tzuhalem's Mountain, 1982; The Beauty of the Weapons: Selected Poems 1972-82, 1982; Tending the Fire, 1985; The Blue Roofs of Japan, 1986; Pieces of Map, Pieces of Music, 1986; Conversations with Toad, 1987; The Calling: Selected Poems, 1970-1995, 1995; Elements, 1995; The Book of Silences, 2001; Ursa Major: A Polyphonic Masque for Speakers & Dancers, 2003; Prosodies of Meaning: Literary Form in Native North America, 2004; New World Suite Number Three: A Poem in Four Movements for Three Voices, 2006. TRANSLATOR: Ghandl, Nine Visits to the Mythworld, 2000; (and ed.) Being in Being: The Collected Works of Skaay of the Qquuna Qiighawaay, 2001; The Fragments of Parmenides, 2003; Skaay, Floating Overhead, 2007. EDITOR: (co-ed.) Visions: Contemporary Art in Canada, 1983; (and intro.) Solitary Raven: Selected Writings of Bill Reid, 2000. OTHERS: (with B. Reid) The Raven Steals the Light: Stories, 1984; Ocean/Paper/Stone, 1984; Shovels, Shoes, and the Slow Rotation of Letters, 1986; (with C. McClellan) Part of the Land, Part of the Water: A History of the Yukon Indians, 1987; The Black Canoe: Bill Reid and the Spirit of Haida Gwaii, 1991; The Elements of Typographic Style, 1992, 3rd ed., 2004; Diogenes, 1994; Boats Is Saintlier than Captains: Thirteen Ways of Looking at Morality, Language and Design, 1997; Word 97 Essentials, Level II, 1997; A Story as Sharp as a Knife: The Classical Haida Mythtellers and Their World, 1999; (with W. Chappell) A Short History of the Printed Word, 1999; Thinking and Singing: Poetry and the Practice of Philosophy, 2002; The Solid Form of Language: An Essay on Writing and Meaning, 2004; The Tree of Meaning: Language, Mind, and Ecology, 2008; Surface of Meaning: Books and Book Design in Canada, 2008; Everywhere Being is Dancing: Twenty Pieces of Thinking, 2008; What is Reading For?, 2011. Contributor to books and periodicals. **Address:** Frost Center for Canadian/Indigenous Studies, Traill College, Trent University, Kerr House, Ste. 103, 299 Dublin St., Peterborough, ON K9H 7P4, Canada.

BRINK, André (Philippus). South African (born South Africa), b. 1935. **Genres:** Novels, Plays/Screenplays, Literary Criticism And History, Translations. **Career:** Rhodes University, lecturer, 1963-73, senior lecturer, 1974-75, associate professor, 1976-79, professor of Afrikaans and Dutch literature, 1980-90; University of Cape Town, professor of English, 1991-2000, professor emeritus of English, 2000-, Theoretical Productions, director. Writer. **Publications:** FICTION: Die meul teen die hang, 1958; Die gebondenes, 1959; Die eindelose weë, 1960; Lobola vir die lewe, 1962; Die Ambassadeur, 1963, trans. as File on a Diplomat, 1965, rev. ed. as The Ambassador, 1985; Orgie, 1965; (co-author) Rooi, 1965; Miskien nooit: 'n Somerspel, 1967; A Portrait of Woman as a Young Girl, 1973; Oom Kootjie Emmer (short stories), 1973; Kennis van die aand (novel), 1973, trans. as Looking on Darkness, 1974; Die Geskiedenis van oom Kootjie Emmer van Witgratworteldraai, 1973; 'n Oomblik in die wind, 1975, trans. as An Instant in the Wind, 1976; Gerugte van Reen, 1978, trans. as Rumours of Rain, 1978; 'n Droe wit seisoen, 1979, trans. as A Dry White Season, 1979; 'n Emmertjie wyn: 'n versameling dopstories, 1981; Houd-den-bek (title means: 'Shut Your Trap'), 1982, trans. as A Chain of Voices, 1982; Oom Kootjie Emmer en die nuwe bedeling: 'n stinkstorie, 1983; Die Muur van die pes, 1984, trans. as The Wall of the Plague, 1984; Loopdoppies: Nog dopstories, 1984; States of Emergency, 1988; Die Eerstelewe van Adamastor, 1988, trans. as Cape of Storms: The First Life of Adamastor: A Story, 1993; Mal en ander stories: 'n omnibus vanhumor, 3 vols., 1990; Die kreef raak gewoond daaraan, 1991; An Act of Terror, 1991; Inteendeel, 1993; On the Contrary: A Novel: Being the Life of a Famous Rebel, Soldier, Traveler, Explorer, Reader, Builder, Scribe, Latinist, Lover, and Liar, 1993; Sandkastele, 1995, trans. as Imaginings of Sand, 1996; Duiwelskloof, 1998, trans. as Devil's Valley, 1999; Donkermaan, 2000, trans. as The Rights of Desire, 2000; The Other Side of Silence, 2002; Anderkant die stilte: roman, 2002. OTHERS: Die band om ons harte (title means: 'The Bond around Our Hearts'), 1959; Caesar, 1961; (co-author) Die beskermengel en ander eenbedrywe (title means: 'The Guardian Angel and Other One-Act Plays'), 1962; Bagasie: Triptiek virdietoneel, 1964; Elders mooiweer en warm, 1965; Die verhoor: Verhoogstuk in drie bedrywe, 1970; Afrikaners is plesierig, 1973; Pavane, 1974; Bobaas van die Boendoe, 1974; Die hamer vandie hekse, 1976; Die Jogger, 1997; The Blue Door, 2006; Other Lives, 2008, trans. as Ander Lewens: 'n Roman in Drie Dele, 2008; (co-author) Should I Stay or Should I Go?: To Live in or Leave South Africa, 2010. FOR CHILDREN: Die bende, 1961; Platsak, 1962; Dieverhaal van Julius Caesar, 1963. LITERARY HISTORY AND CRITICISM: Orde en chaos: 'n studie oor Germanicus en die tragedies van Shakespeare, 1962; Aspekte van die nuweprosa, 1967, rev. ed., 1975; Die Poësie van Breyten Breytenbach, 1971; Inleiding tot die Afrikaanseletterkunde, onder Redaksie van E. Lindenberg, 1973; Aspekte vandie nuwe Drama, 1974; Voorlopige Rapport: Beskouings oor die Afrikaanse Literatuur van Sewentig, 1976; Tweede voorlopige Rapport: Nog beskouingsoor die Afrikaanse Literaturevan sewentig, 1980; Why Literature? Waaromliteratuur?, 1980; (co-author) Perspektief enprofiel: 'ngeskiedinis van die Afrikaanse letterkunde, 1982; Literatuur in diestrydperk, 1985; Vertelkunde: 'n inleiding tot die lees van verhalendetekste, 1987; The Novel: Language and Narrative from Cervantes to Calvino, 1998. TRANSLATOR: Pierre Boulle, Die Brug oor die rivier Kwaï, 1962; AndréDhôtel, Reisigers na die Groot Land, 1962; Joseph Kessel, Die Wonderhande, 1962; L.N. Lavolle, Nuno, die Visserseun, 1962; Léonce Bourliaguet, Verhale uit Limousin, 1963; Léonce Bourliaguet, Dieslapende Berg, 1963; Leonard Cottrell, Land van die Farao's, 1963; Michel Rouzé, Die Bos van Kokelunde, 1963; Marguerite Duras, Moderato Cantabile, 1963; Paul-Jacques Bonzon, Die Goue kruis, 1963; Leonard Cottrell, Land van die Twee Riviere, 1964; C.M. Turnbull, Volke van Afrika, 1964; Lewis Carroll, Alice se Avonture in Wonderland, 1965; Diemooisteverhale uit die Arabiese Nagte, 1966; James Reeves, Die Avonturevan Don Quixote, 1966; Elyesa Bazna, Ek was Cicero, 1966; Jean de Brunhoff, Koning Babar, 1966; Colette, Die Swerfling, Afrikaanse Pers, 1966; Miguel Cervantes, Die vindingryke ridder, Don Quijote de la Mancha, 1966; Simenon, Speuder Maigret, Maigret en sy Dooie, Maigret en die Lang Derm, and Maigret en die Spook, 4 vols., 1966-69; Charles Perrault, Die mooiste Sprokies van Moeder Gans, 1967; Ester Wier, Die Eenspaaier, 1967; Graham Greene, Die Eendstert, 1967; P.L. Travers, Mary Poppins in Kersieboomlaan, 1967; C.S. Lewis, Die Leeu, die Heks en die Hangkas, 1967; (co-author) Diegroot Boek oor ons Dieremaats, 1968; (co-author) Koning Arthur en sy Ridders van die Ronde Tafel, 1968; Lucy Boston, Die Kindersvan Groenkop, 1968; Lewis Carroll, Alice deur die Spieël, 1968; Ian Serraillier, Die Botsende rotse, Die Horing van Ivoor, and Die Kop van de Gorgoon, 4 vols., 1968; Dhan Gopal Mukerji, Bontnek, 1968; Henry James, Die Draaivan die Skroef, 1968; Oscar Wilde, Die Gelukkige Prins enander Sprokies, 1969; William Shakespeare, Richard III, 1969; Charles Perrault, Die Gestewelde kat, 1969; Pearl S. Buck, Die groot Golf, 1969; Hans Christian Andersen, Die Nagtegaal, 1969; Albert Camus, Die Terroriste, 1970; Michelde Ghelderode, Eskoriaal, 1971; Nada Curcija-Prodanovic, Ballerina, 1972; Anton Chekhov, Die Seemeeu, 1972; Synge, Die Bobaas van die Boendoe, 1973; Richard Bach, Jonathan Livingston Seemeeu, 1973; Henrik Ibsen, Hedda Gabler, 1974; Kenneth Grahame, Die Windin die Wilgers, 1974; William Shakespeare, Die Tragedie van Romeo en Juliet, 1975; Claude Desailly, Die Tierbrigade, 1978; Claude Desailly, Nuwe Avontuur van die Tierbrigade, 1979; Oscar Wilde, Die Nagtegaal en die Roos, 1980; Kenneth Grahame, Rotop Reis, 1981; Elizabeth Janet Gray, Adamvan die Pad, 1981; Charles Perrault, Klein Duimpie, 1983; Dan Sleigh, Eilande, 2004. OTHERS: Pot-pourri: Sketse uit Parys (title means: 'Pot-pourrie: Sketches from Paris'), 1962; Sèmpre diritto: Italiaan series joernaal (title means: 'Always Straight Ahead: Italian Travel Journal'), 1963; Olé: Reisboekoor Spanje (title means: 'Olé: A Travel Book on Spain'), 1966; Midi: Op reis deur Suld-Frankyrk (title means: 'Midi: Traveling through the South of France'), 1969; Parys-Parys: Return, 1969; Fado: 'n reis deurNoord-Portugal (title means: 'Fado: A Journey through Northern Portugal'), 1970; Portret van di vrou as 'nmeisie (title means: 'Portrait of Woman as a Young Girl'), 1973; Brandewynin Suid-Afrika, 1974, trans. as Brandy in South Africa, 1974; Dessertwynin Suid-Afrika, 1974, trans. as Dessert Wine in South Africa, 1974; (co-author) Ik ben er geweest: Gesprekken in Zuid-Afrika (title means: 'I've Been There: Conversations in South Africa'), 1974; Die Wyn van bowe (title means: 'The Wine from up There'), 1974; Die Klap van die meul (title means: 'A Stroke from the Mill'), 1974; Jan Rabie se 21, 1977; (ed.) Oggendlied: 'n bundel vir Uys Krige op syverjaardag 4 Februarie 1977, 1977; (ed.) Top Naeff, Klein Avontuur, 1979; Heildronk uit Wynboer Saamgestel deur AB ter viering van die Blad se 50 stebestaansjaar, 1981; Die Fees van die Malles: 'n keur uit die humor, 1981; Mapmakers: Writing in a State of Siege (essays), 1983, rev. ed. as Writing in a State of Siege: Essays on Politics and Literature, 1983; (ed. with J.M. Coetzee) A Land Apart: A South African Reader, 1986; Latynse reise: 'n keur uit diereisbeskrywings van André P. Brink, 1990; The Essence of the Grape, 1993; (comp.) SA, 27 April 1994: An Author's Diary, 1994; (comp.) 27 April: One Year Later/Een Jaar later, 1995; Reinventing a Continent: Writing and Politics in South Africa (essays), 1996, rev. ed., 1998; Destabilising Shakespeare, 1996; (comp.) Groot Verseboek 2000, 2000; Jan Vermeiren: A Flemish Artist in South Africa, 2000; (trans.) D. Sleigh, Islands, 2004; Bidsprinkaan: 'nware storie, 2005; Praying Mantis, 2005; Die blou deur: 'n storie, 2006; (foreword) Marjorie Wallace: Drif en Vreugde, 2006; Met 'n glimlag, 2006; Before I Forget, 2007; (trans.) I. Jonker, Black Butterflies, 2007; (comp.) Groot verseboek, 2008; Rumors of Rain, 2008; Fork in the Road, 2009, trans. as Vurk in Die Pad: A Memoir, 2009; Eerste lewe van Adamastor: 'n novelle, 2009. **Address:** Department of English Language & Literature, University of Cape Town, Arts Block, University Ave., PO Box X3, Rodebosch, 7701, South Africa. **Online address:** abrink@humanities.uct.ac.za

BRINK, Jean R. (J. R. Brink). American (born United States), b. 1942. **Genres:** Education, History. **Career:** San Jose State University, visiting assistant professor, 1971-72, 1973-74; Arizona State University, Department of English, assistant professor, 1974-79, associate professor, 1979-84, professor, 1984-, now professor emeritus, Arizona Center for Medieval and Renaissance Studies, founding director, 1981-94; Huntington Library, research fellow. Writer. **Publications:** Michael Drayton Revisited, 1990; National Traditions: England and the European Renaissance, 1992. EDITOR: Female Scholars: A Tradition of Learned Women, 1980; (with C.R. Haden and C. Burawa) The Computer and the Brain: Perspectives on Human and Artificial Intelligence, 1989; (with P.R. Baldini) Italian Renaissance Studies in Arizona, 1989; (with A.P. Coudert and M.C. Horowitz) The Politics of Gender in Early Modern Europe, 1989; (with A.P. Coudert and M.C. Horowitz) Playing with Gender: A Renaissance Pursuit, 1991; Privileging Gender in Early Modern England, 1991; (with C.R. Haden) Innovative Models for University Research, 1992; (with W.F. Gentrup) Renaissance Culture in Context: Theory and Practice, 1993; Privileging Gender in Early Modern England, 1993. **Address:** Department of English, Arizona State University, LL 302B, 851 S Cady Mall, PO Box 870302, Tempe, AZ 85287-0302, U.S.A. **Online address:** jean.brink@asu.edu

BRINK, J. R. *See* **BRINK, Jean R.**

BRINKBÄUMER, Klaus. German (born Germany), b. 1967. **Genres:** History. **Career:** Der Spiegel, reporter, editor, correspondent, 1993-, deputy editor, deputy editor-in-chief; Hamburg College of Journalism, lecturer; The Institute for the Advancement Journalistic Talent, lecturer. **Publications:** (With H. Leyendecker and H. Schimmöller) Reiche Steffi, Armes Kind-Die Akte Graf, 1986; 11. September, 2002; Irak (nonfiction), 2004; (with C. Höges) Die letzte Reise: Der Fall Christoph Columbus, 2004; Tsunami, 2005; Der Traum vom Leben, 2006; Unter dem Sand (novel), 2007. **Address:** Der Spiegel, Ericusspitze 1, Hamburg, 20457, Germany. **Online address:** klaus_brinkbaeumer@spiegel.de

BRINKLEY, Alan. American (born United States), b. 1949. **Genres:** History, Biography, Social Commentary. **Career:** Massachusetts Institute of Technology, assistant professor of history, 1978-82; Harvard University, Dunwalke associate professor of American history, 1982-88; City University of New York, Graduate School, professor of history, 1988-91; Columbia University, professor, 1991-98, Allan Nevins professor of history, 1998-, provost, 2003-09; Oxford University, Harmsworth professor of American history, 1998-99. Writer. **Publications:** America in the Twentieth Century, 1982; Voices of Protest: Huey Long, Father Coughlin, and the Great Depression, 1982; The Unfinished Nation: A Concise History of the American People, 1993, 6th ed., 2009; The End of Reform: New Deal Liberalism in Recession and War, 1995; Liberalism and Its Discontents, 1998; American History: A Survey, 13th ed., 2009; Franklin Delano Roosevelt, 2010; Publisher: Henry Luce and His American Century, 2010, American History: Connecting With the Past, 2011, John F. Kennedy, 2012. CO-AUTHOR: Eyes of the Nation: A Visual History of the United States, 1997; New Federalist Papers, 1997; America in Modern Times, Since 1890, 1997; American Journey, 1998; The Chicago Handbook for Teachers, 1999, 2nd ed., 2010, American Vision: Modern Times, 2006. CO-EDITOR: The Reader's Companion to the American Presidency, 2000; Days of Destiny: Crossroads in American History: America's Greatest Historians Examine Thirty-One Uncelebrated Days that Changed the Course of History, 2001; (intro.) Campaigns: A Century of Presidential Races from the Photo Archives of the New York Times, 2001; The American Presidency, 2004. **Address:** Department of History, Columbia University, 622 Fayerweather Hall, 535 W 116th St., New York, NY 10027-7041, U.S.A. **Online address:** ab65@columbia.edu

BRINKLEY, Douglas. American (born United States), b. 1960. **Genres:** History, Documentaries/Reportage, Young Adult Non-fiction, Biography. **Career:** University of Louisiana, associate professor; Georgetown University, Department of History, graduate teaching assistant; United States Naval Academy, Department of History, instructor; Woodrow Wilson School of Public Policy and International Affairs, visiting research fellow; Hofstra University, New College, associate professor of history and teaching fellow, 1989-94; University of New Orleans, Stephen E. Ambrose professor of history, 1994-2005; Eisenhower Center for American Studies, director, 1994-2005, Department of History, professor, 1994-2005; Tulane University, Theodore Roosevelt Center for American Civilization, director, 2005-07, Department of American History, professor, 2005-07; Rice University, James A. Baker Institute, fellow in history, 2007-, Department of History, professor, 2007-. Writer. **Publications:** NONFICTION: Dean Acheson: The Cold War Years, 1953-1971, 1992; (with T. Hoopes) Driven Patriot: The Life and Times of James Forrestal, 1992; The Majic Bus: An American Odyssey, 1993; (with T. Hoopes) FDR and the Creation of the United Nations, 1997; (with S.E. Ambrose) Rise to Globalism, 9th ed., 2011; The Unfinished Presidency: Jimmy Carter's Journey beyond the White House, 1998; American Heritage History of the United States, 1998; (contrib. with R.N. Smith) Who's Buried in Grant's Tomb?: A Tour of Presidential Gravesites, 1999; Rosa Parks, 2000; (intro.) 36 Days: The Complete Chronicle of the 2000 Presidential Election Crisis, 2001; (with S.E. Ambrose) The Mississippi and the Making of a Nation, 2002; Wheels for the World: Henry Ford, His Company, and a Century of Progress, 1903-2003, 2003; Tour of Duty: John Kerry and the Vietnam War, 2004; (with R.J. Drez) Voices of Valor: D-Day, June 6, 1944, 2004; The Boys of Pointe Du Hoc: Ronald Reagan, D-Day, and the U.S. Army 2nd Ranger Battalion, 2005; (with R.J. Drez) Voices of Courage: The Battle for Khe Sanh, Vietnam, 2005; The Great Deluge: Hurricane Katrina, New Orleans, and the Mississippi Gulf Coast, 2006; (with J.M. Fenster) Parish Priest: Father Michael McGivney and American Catholicism, 2006; Gerald R. Ford, 2007; (foreword) 100 Days in Photographs: Pivotal Events that Changed the World, 2007; (foreword) Jazzocracy: Jazz, Democracy, and the Creation of a New American Mythology, 2008; Wilderness Warrior: Theodore Roosevelt and the Crusade for America, 2009. EDITOR: (with C. Hackett) Jean Monnet: The Path to European Unity, 1991; (with N.A. Naylor and J.A. Gable) Theodore Roosevelt: Many-Sided American, 1992; Dean Acheson and the Making of U.S. Foreign Policy, 1993; The Proud Highway: Saga of a Desperate Southern Gentleman, 1955-1967, 1997; (with D.R. Facey-Crowther) The Atlantic Charter, 1994; (with R. Griffiths) John F. Kennedy and Europe, 1999; (with S.E. Ambrose) Witness to America: An Illustrated Documentary History of the United States From the Revolution To Today, 1999; Fear and Loathing in America: The Brutal Odyssey of an Outlaw Journalist, 1968-1976, 2000; (with P.N. Limerick) The Western Paradox: A Conservation Reader/The Bernard DeVoto Reader, 2001; The Penguin Encyclopedia of American History, 2003; The New York Times Living History, World War II: The Axis Assault, 1939-1942, 2003; (with intro.) Windblown World: The Journals of Jack Kerouac, 1947-1954, 2004; (ed.) World War II Memorial, 2004; (ed.) Road Novels, 1957-1960, 2007; The Reagan Diaries, 2007. OTHERS: Quiet World, 2011; Notes: Ronald Reagan's Private Collection of Stories and Wisdom, 2011; Cronkite, 2012. Contributor to periodicals. **Address:** Department of History, Rice University, 220 Baker Hall, 6100 Main MS-42, Houston, TX 77005-1827, U.S.A. **Online address:** douglas.brinkley@rice.edu

BRINKMAN, Kiara. American (born United States), b. 1979. **Genres:** Novels, Literary Criticism And History. **Career:** Educator and writer. **Publications:** Up High in the Trees: A Novel, 2007. Contributor to periodicals. **Address:** Grove Press, 841 Broadway, 4th Fl., New York, NY 10003, U.S.A. **Online address:** kb.inthetrees@gmail.com

BRISCOE, Connie. American (born United States), b. 1952. **Genres:** Novels, Biography. **Career:** Analytic Services Inc., research analyst, 1976-80; Joint Center for Political and Economic Studies, associate editor, 1981-90; Gallaudet University, American Annals of the Deaf, managing editor, 1990-94; novelist, 1994-. **Publications:** Sisters & Lovers, 1994; Big Girls Don't Cry, 1996; A Long Way From Home, 1999; P.G. County, 2002; Can't Get Enough: A Novel, 2005; (with A. Bunkley and L. Files) You Only Get Better: Three Brilliant New Novellas, 2007; (with M. Cunningham) Jewels: 50 Phenomenal Black Women Over 50, 2007; Sisters and Husbands, 2009; Money Can't Buy Love, 2011. **Address:** HarperCollins Publishers Inc., 10 E 53rd St., New York, NY 10022-5244, U.S.A.

BRISKIN, Jacqueline. American/British (born England), b. 1927. **Genres:** Novels, Romance/Historical, Young Adult Fiction, Literary Criticism And History. **Career:** Writer. **Publications:** California Generation, 1970, rev. ed., 1980; After Love, 1974; Rich Friends, 1976; Paloverde, 1978; Decade, 1981; The Onyx, 1982; Everything and More, 1983; Too Much, Too Soon, 1985; Dreams Are Not Enough, 1987; The Naked Heart, 1987; The Other Side of

Love, 1991; Crimson Palace, 1995. Contributor to periodicals. **Address:** 10580 Wilshire Blvd., Ste. 53, Los Angeles, CA 90024, U.S.A.

BRISKIN, Mae. American (born United States), b. 1924. **Genres:** Novels, Novellas/Short Stories, History, Criminology/True Crime. **Career:** Brooklyn College (now of the City University of New York), instructor in economics, 1944-45; New York State Department of Labor, investigator, 1945-47; New York City Housing Authority, management staffs of housing projects, 1947-50. Writer, 1973-. **Publications:** A Boy Like Astrid's Mother (stories), 1988; The Tree Still Stands (novel), 1991; A Hole in the Water (novel), 2002. Contributor to periodicals. **Address:** John Daniel & Co., PO Box 7290, McKinleyville, CA 95519, U.S.A.

BRISSENDEN, Alan (Theo). Australian (born Australia), b. 1932. **Genres:** Dance/Ballet, Literary Criticism And History, Theatre. **Career:** Education Department of New South Wales, teacher, 1955, research officer, 1956-59; University of Adelaide, Department of English, lecturer, 1963-68, senior lecturer, 1968-82, reader, 1982-94, chairman of the department, 1985-86, honorary visiting research fellow; critic, 1980-; Adelaide Festival of Arts, governor, 1981-94, 1998; Bibliographical Society of Australia and New Zealand, president, 1983-85; The Australian, dance critic, 1990-. Writer. **Publications:** Rolf Boldrewood, 1972; Shakespeare and the Dance, 1981; (with M. Harris) The Angry Penguin: Selected Poems of Max Harris: Selected Poems of Max Harris, 1996; (with K. Glennon) Australia Dances: Creating Australian Dance, 1945-1965, 2010; (with M. Carroll and J. Albert) Ballets Russes in Australia and Beyond, 2011. EDITOR: (with C. Higham) They Came to Australia, 1961; A Chaste Maid in Cheapside, 1968; Henry Lawson's Australia, 1973; The Drover's Wife and Other Stories by Henry Lawson (prose anthology), 1974; (and contrib.) Shakespeare and Some Others: Essays on Shakespeare and Some of His Contemporaries, 1976; Rolf Boldrewood (prose anthology), 1979; Aspects of Australian Fiction: Essays Presented to John Colmer, 1990; As You Like It, 1993; What Makes a Masterpiece?, 2002. CONTRIBUTOR: Shakespeare in the New World, 1972; The Australian Experience, 1974; Innovation No Stranger, 1982; From Colonel Light into the Footlights, 1988. Contributor to encyclopedia. **Address:** Curtis Brown Ltd., 86 William St., Paddington, NW 2021, Australia.

BRISSON, Pat. American (born United States), b. 1951. **Genres:** Children's Fiction. **Career:** St. Anthony of Padua School, elementary school teacher, 1974-75; Phillipsburg Free Public Library, library clerk, 1978-81, reference librarian, 1990-2000; Easton Area Public Library, library clerk, 1981-88. Writer. **Publications:** Your Best Friend, Kate, 1989; Kate Heads West, 1990; The Magic Carpet, 1991; Kate on the Coast, 1992; Benny's Pennies, 1993; Wanda's Roses, 1994; Hot Fudge Hero, 1997; The Summer My Father Was Ten, 1998; Little Sister, Big Sister, 1999; Sky Memories, 1999; Bertie's Picture Day, 2000; Hobbeldy-Clop, 2002; Star Blanket, 2003; Beach Is to Fun: A Book of Relationships, 2004; (contrib.) Don't Cramp My Style: Stories about that Time of the Month, 2004; Mama Loves Me from Away, 2004; Tap-Dance Fever, 2005; Melissa Parkington's Beautiful, Beautiful Hair, 2006; I Remember Miss Perry, 2006; The Best and Hardest Thing, 2010; Sometimes We were Brave, 2010. Contributor to periodicals. **Address:** 94 Bullman St., Phillipsburg, NJ 08865, U.S.A. **Online address:** patbrisson51@gmail.com

BRISTOL, Leigh. *See* **BALL, Donna Rochelle.**

BRISTOW, Robert O'Neil. American (born United States), b. 1926. **Genres:** Novels, Young Adult Fiction, Science Fiction/Fantasy. **Career:** Altus Times-Democrat, assistant advertising manager, 1951-53; full-time writer, 1953-60; Winthrop College, writer-in-residence, 1961-, assistant professor, 1961-65, associate professor, 1966-74, professor, 1974-88, professor emeritus, 1988-. **Publications:** Time for Glory, 1968; Night Season, 1970; A Faraway Drummer: A Novel, 1973; Laughter in Darkness: A Novel, 1974. Contributor of articles to magazines. **Address:** Department of English, Winthrop University, 250 Bancroft Hall, Rock Hill, SC 29733-0001, U.S.A. **Online address:** rbristow@cetlink.net

BRITAIN, Ian (Michael). Australian/Indian (born India), b. 1948. **Genres:** Art/Art History, Cultural/Ethnic Topics, Education, History, Intellectual History, Biography. **Career:** Monash University, research fellow, 1980-82, lecturer in literature and film, 1994, Department of History, senior research fellow, 1997-2002; Webbers Magazine, editor; University of Melbourne, lecturer in modern British history, 1982-91, research associate, 1992; National Library of Australia, Harold White research fellow, 1992; Meanjin Literary Magazine, editor, 2001-07. **Publications:** Fabianism and Culture: A Study in British Socialism and the Arts, 1884-1918, 1982; Once an Australian: Journeys with Barry Humphries, Clive James, Germaine Greer and Robert Hughes, 1997; (ed. with B. Niall) The Oxford Book of Australian Schooldays, 1997; (ed.) The Donald Friend Diaries: Chronicles and Confessions of an Australian Artist, 2010. **Address:** 5 Tyson St., Richmond, Melbourne, VI 3121, Australia. **Online address:** i.britainats@unimelb.edu.au

BRITE, Poppy Z. American (born United States), b. 1967. **Genres:** Novels, Novellas/Short Stories, Horror, Food And Wine, Gay And Lesbian Issues, Biography. **Career:** Writer. **Publications:** NOVELS: Lost Souls, 1992; Drawing Blood, 1993; Exquisite Corpse, 1996; The Lazarus Heart, 1998; The Value of X, 2002; Liquor, 2004; (with C. Faust) Triads, 2004; Prime, 2005; Soul Kitchen: A Novel, 2006; D*u*c*k, 2007; Second Line: Two Short Novels of Love and Cooking in New Orleans, 2009. STORIES: Swamp Foetus, 1993 as Wormwood: A Collection of Short Stories, 1995; Are You Loathsome Tonight?, 1998; (with C.R. Kiernan) Wrong Things, 2001; Con Party at Hotel California, 2002; The Devil You Know, 2003; Used Stories, 2004; Crown of Thorns, 2005; Antediluvian Tales, 2007. OTHER: (ed.) Love in Vein (anthology), 1994; Love in Vein II (anthology), 1997; Courtney Love: The Real Story (biography), 1997; Seed of Lost Souls, 1999; Plastic Jesus, 2000; Guilty but Insane, 2001; The Value of X, 2002; The Feast of St. Rosalie, 2003; Waiting for Bobby Hebert, 2006. Works appears in anthologies. **Address:** Donadio & Olson, 121 W 27th St., Ste. 704, New York, NY 10001, U.S.A.

BRITLAND, Karen. British (born England), b. 1970. **Genres:** Women's Studies And Issues, History, Art/Art History. **Career:** University of Keele, senior lecturer in English; University of Leeds, faculty; University of Hull, faculty; University of Wisconsin, Department of English, professor. Writer. **Publications:** Drama at the Courts of Queen Henrietta Maria, 2006; (ed.) Tragedy of Mariam, the Fair Queen of Jewry, 2010. Contributor to books. **Address:** Keele University, Keele, ST ST5 5BG, England. **Online address:** k.r.britland@keele.ac.uk

BRITNELL, R(ichard) H. (Richard Hugh Britnell). British (born England), b. 1944. **Genres:** History, Sociology, Agriculture/Forestry. **Career:** University of Durham, lecturer in economic history, 1966-85, lecturer in history, 1985-86, senior lecturer in history, 1986-94, reader, 1994-97, professor, 1997-2003, emeritus, 2003-; Van Mildert College, tutor, 1967-70; St Cuthbert's Society, tutor, 1973-83; Durham Medieval Theatre Co., treasurer, 1976-; Durham Shakespeare Group, treasurer, 1991-; Surtees Society, joint-editor, 1999-. **Publications:** Growth and Decline in Colchester, 1300-1529, 1986; The Commercialisation of English Society, 1000-1500, 1993, 2nd ed., 1997; (ed. with B.M.S. Campbell) A Commercialising Economy: England 1086 to c. 1300, 1995; (ed. with A.J. Pollard) The McFarlane Legacy: Studies in Late Medieval Politics and Society, 1995; (ed. with J. Hatcher) Progress and Problems in Medieval England: Essays in Honour of Edward Miller, 1996; The Closing of the Middle Ages? England, 1471-1529, 1997; (ed.) Pragmatic Literacy, East and West, 1200-1330, 1997; Daily Life in the Late Middle Ages, 1998; (ed. with J. Britnell) Vernacular Literature and Current Affairs in the Early Sixteenth Century: France, England and Scotland, 2000; (co-ed.) Thirteenth Century England VI-X, 2001; (ed.) Winchester Pipe Rolls and Medieval English Society, 2003; (ed.) Britain and Ireland 1050-1530: Economy and Society, 2004; (ed. with C.D. Liddy) North-East England in the Later Middle Ages, 2005; (ed. with B. Dodds) Agriculture and Rural Society after the Black Death, 2008; (ed.) Records of the Borough of Crossgate, Durham, 2008; Markets, Trade and Economic Development in England and Europe, 1050-1550, 2009; (with J. Mullan) Land and Family: Trends and Local Variations in the Peasant Land Market on the Winchester Bishopric Estates, 1263-1415, 2010. **Address:** 25 Orchard House, New Elvet, DU DH1 3DB, England. **Online address:** r.h.britnell@durham.ac.uk

BRITNELL, Richard Hugh. *See* **BRITNELL, R(ichard) H.**

BRITT, Brian (Michael). American (born United States), b. 1964. **Genres:** History, Theology/Religion. **Career:** Wesleyan College, assistant professor of religion and philosophy, 1992-96; Center for Interdisciplinary Studies, assistant professor of religious studies, 1996-2001; Virginia Polytechnic Institute and State University, Department of Religion and Culture, associate professor, director, 2001-06, professor religious study program, 2006-; University of Oklahoma, The Pride of Oklahoma Marching Band, associate director. director and coordinator of undergraduate studies; Lumberjack Marching Band, director. Writer. **Publications:** The Book of Life [microform]: The Hebrew Bible As Sacred Text in Deuteronomy 31-34 and in the Philosophy of Walter Benjamin, 1992; Walter Benjamin and the Bible, 1996; Rewriting Moses: The Narrative Eclipse of the Text, 2003; (co-ed.) Religion, Gender and Culture in the Pre-Modern World, 2007. Contributor of articles and reviews to periodicals. **Address:** Ctr. for Interdisciplinary Studies, Virginia Polytechnic Institute, 207 Major Williams, Blacksburg, VA 24061, U.S.A.

BRITTAIN, C. Dale. American (born United States), b. 1948. **Genres:** Science Fiction/Fantasy, Novels, Young Adult Fiction. **Career:** Writer and educator. **Publications:** FANTASY NOVELS: A Bad Spell in Yurt, 1991; The Wood Nymph and the Cranky Saint, 1993; Mage Quest, 1993; Voima, 1995; The Witch and the Cathedral, 1995; Daughter of Magic, 1996; (with R.A. Bouchard) Count Scar, 1997; Is This Apocalypse Necessary?, 2000; The Starlight Raven, forthcoming. **Address:** The Wooster Book Co., 205 West Liberty St., Downtown Wooster, Wooster, OH 44691-4831, U.S.A. **Online address:** bouchard@bright.net

BRITTAIN, William (E.). *See* Obituaries.

BRITTAN, Samuel. British (born England), b. 1933. **Genres:** Economics, Politics/Government, Business/Trade/Industry. **Career:** Financial Times, editorial staff, 1955-61, economics writer, 1966-, economic commentator, 1966-, principal economic commentator, 1970, assistant editor, 1978-, British columnist; Observer, economics editor, 1961-64; British Department of Economic Affairs, economics adviser, 1965; Nuffield College, research and visiting fellow, 1973-82; Jesus College, honorary fellow; Chicago Law School, visiting professor; Warwick University, honorary professor of politics. **Publications:** The Treasury Under the Tories, 1964 as Steering the Economy: The Role of the Treasury, 1969; Left or Right: The Bogus Dilemma, 1968; The Price of Economic Freedom: A Guide to Flexible Rates, 1970; Capitalism and the Permissive Society, 1973, new ed. as A Restatement of Economic Liberalism, 1988; Is There An Economic Consensus? An Attitude Survey, 1973; Second Thoughts on Full Employment Policy, 1975; (with P. Lilley) The Delusion of Incomes Policy, 1977; The Economic Consequences of Democracy, 1977; (co-ed.) The Future that Doesn't Work: Social Democracy's Failures in Britain, 1977; How to End the Monetarist Controvery, 1981; The Role and Limit of Government, 1983; Two Cheers for Self-interest: Some Moral Prerequisites of a Market Economy, 1985; Beyond the Welfare State: An Examination of Basic Incomes in a Market Economy, 1990; Capitalism with a Human Face, 1995; (ed. with A. Hamlin) Market Capitalism and Moral Values: Proceedings of Section F (Economics) of the British Association for the Advancement of Science, Keele, 1993, 1995; Essays, Moral, Political and Economic, 1998; Towards a Humane Individualism, 1998; Against the Flow: Reflections of an Individualist, 2005. Contributor to periodicals. **Address:** Financial Times, 1 Southwark Bridge, London, GL SE1 9HL, England.

BRITTO, Paulo Henriques. Brazilian (born Brazil), b. 1951. **Genres:** Poetry. **Career:** Writer and translator. **Publications:** (Contrib.) Pantanal, 1985; (trans.) F. Süssekind, Cinematograph of Words: Literature, Technique, and Modernization in Brazil, 1997; (ed.) O meio do mundo e outros contos, 1999; Macau, 2003; Paraísos artificiais: Contos, 2004; Eu quero é botar meu bloco na rua de Sérgio Sampaio, 2009; (contrib.) Estrelas de couro, 2010; Claudia Roquette-Pinto, 2010. POETRY: Liturgia da matéria: Poesia, 1982; Mínima lírica, 1982-1989, 1989; Trovar claro: Poemas, 1997; Tarde: Poemas, 2007. **Address:** Língua Geral, Rua Jd. Botânico, 600-cj. 502, Rio de Janeiro, 22461000, Brazil. **Online address:** phbritto@hotmail.com

BRITTON, Celia (Margaret). British/Scottish (born Scotland), b. 1946. **Genres:** Literary Criticism And History, Language/Linguistics, History, Young Adult Fiction, Politics/Government. **Career:** King's College, lecturer in French, 1972-74; University of Reading, lecturer in French, 1974-91; University of Aberdeen, professor of French, 1991-2002; University College, professor of French and chair, 2003-. Writer. **Publications:** Claude Simon: Writing the Visible, 1987; The Nouveau Roman: Fiction, Theory and Politics, 1992; (ed. and intro.) Claude Simon, 1993; Edouard Glissant and Postcolonial Theory: Strategies of Language and Resistance, 1999; Race and the Unconscious: Freudianism in French-Caribbean Thought, 2002; The Sense of Community in French Caribbean Fiction, 2008; The Cambridge History of French Literature, 2009. Contributor to books. **Address:** Department of French, University College London, Rm. 105, 1-4 Malet Pl., Gower St., London, GL WC1E 6BT, England. **Online address:** celiabritton@talk21.com

BRITTON, Hannah E. American (born United States), b. 1970. **Genres:** Women's Studies And Issues, Politics/Government, Humanities. **Career:** Tusculum College, communication skills instructor, 1992-93; Syracuse University, Department of Political Science, teaching assistant, 1994-96, instructor, 1997-98, Maxwell School of Citizenship and Public Affairs, teaching associate, 1998-99; Winthrop University, assistant professor of political science, 1999-2001; Mississippi State University, assistant professor of political science, 2001-05; University of Kansas, Department of Political Science, assistant professor, 2005-07, associate professor, 2007-, Institute for Policy and Social Research, Center for International Political Analysis, director, 2009-. Writer. **Publications:** Women in the South African Parliament: From Resistance to Governance, 2005; (ed. with G. Bauer) Women in African Parliaments, 2006; (ed. with S. Meintjes and J. Fish) Women's Activism in South Africa: Working Across Divides, 2009. Contributor of articles to journals. **Address:** Department of Political Science, University of Kansas, 504E Blake Hall, 1541 Lilac Ln., Lawrence, KS 66044-3177, U.S.A. **Online address:** britton@ku.edu

BRIZENDINE, Louann. American (born United States), b. 1952?. **Genres:** Psychiatry, Medicine/Health, Social Sciences. **Career:** Harvard University, faculty, 1985-88; University of California, Langley Porter Psychiatric Institute, researcher, instructor, clinician, faculty, 1988-, Lynne and Marc Benioff endowed chair in psychiatry, Department of Psychiatry, clinical professor, Women's Mood and Hormone Clinic, founder, director, 1994-. Writer. **Publications:** The Female Brain, 2006; The Male Brain, 2010. Contributor to periodicals. **Address:** University of California, 401 Parnassus Ave., LangPorter 274, PO Box 0984, San Francisco, CA 94143-0984, U.S.A. **Online address:** drlouann@louannbrizendine.com

BRKIC, Courtney Angela. American (born United States), b. 1972?. **Genres:** Mystery/Crime/Suspense, Autobiography/Memoirs. **Career:** United Nations International War Crimes Tribunal, forensic staff; United States Agency for International Development, staff; Kenyon College, faculty, visiting assistant professor of English, Richard L. Thomas chair in creative writing, 2006; New York University, teacher of creative writing; Cooper Union, faculty; George Mason University, MFA Program, faculty. Writer. **Publications:** Stillness and Other Stories, 2003; The Stone Fields: An Epitaph for the Living (memoir), 2004; The Sun in Another Sky, 2010. Works appear in anthologies. Contributor to journals. **Address:** Graduate Creative Writing Program, George Mason University, 3E4, 4400 University Dr., Fairfax, VA 22030, U.S.A.

BROACH, Elise. American (born United States), b. 1963. **Genres:** Children's Fiction, Novels, Picture/Board Books. **Career:** NBC, telemarketing; Yale University, faculty. Writer. **Publications:** PICTURE BOOKS: Wet Dog!, 2005; What the No-Good Baby Is Good For, 2005; Hiding Hoover, 2005; Cousin John Is Coming!, 2006; When Dinosaurs Came with Everything, 2007; Seashore Baby, 2010; Gumption!, 2010. NOVELS: Shakespeare's Secret, 2005; Desert Crossing, 2006; Masterpiece, 2008; Missing on Superstition Mountain, 2011; Snowflake Baby, 2011. Contributor to periodicals. **Address:** PO Box 24, Redding, CT 06896, U.S.A. **Online address:** hidinghoover@optonline.net

BROAD, Kendal L. American (born United States), b. 1966. **Genres:** Sociology, Politics/Government, Criminology/True Crime. **Career:** University of Florida, Department of Sociology and Criminology and Law, assistant professor of sociology and women's studies, 1998-, associate professor of sociology and women's studies and gender research. Writer. **Publications:** (With V. Jenness) Hate Crimes: New Social Movements and the Politics of Violence, 1997. **Address:** Department of Sociology and Criminology & Law, University of Florida, 301 Ustler Hall, PO Box 117352, Gainesville, FL 32611-7352, U.S.A. **Online address:** klbroad@ufl.edu

BROAD, Robin. American (born United States), b. 1954. **Genres:** Economics, Social Sciences. **Career:** Xavier University, Henry Luce Foundation, fellow of economic development and environmental studies and research associate, university professor, 1977-78; Chulalongkorn University, economic researcher, 1979; University of the Philippines, visiting research associate, 1980-81, 1988-89; U.S. Treasury Department, Office of Multilateral Development Banks, international economist, 1983-84, Inter-American Development Bank, desk officer, 1984-85; U.S. Congressman Charles E. Schumer, senior staff economist, 1985-87; Carnegie Endowment for International Peace, resident associate, 1987-88; American University, School of International Service, assistant professor of environment and development, 1990-96, associate professor, 1996-2006, professor, 2006-. Writer. **Publications:** Unequal Alliance: The World Bank, the International Monetary Fund, and the Philippines, 1988; (with J. Cavanagh) The Philippine Challenge: Sustainable and Equitable Development in the 1990s (monograph), 1991; (with J. Cavanagh) Plundering Paradise: The Struggle for the Environment in the Philippines, 1993; (ed.) Global Backlash: Citizen Initiatives for a Just World Economy, 2002; (with J. Cavanagh) Development Redefined: How the Market Met its Match, 2009. Works appear in anthologies. Contributor to journals and newspapers. **Address:** International Development Program, School of International Service, American University, Rm. 225, 4400 Massachusetts Ave. NW, Washington, DC 20016-8071, U.S.A. **Online address:** rbroad@american.edu

BROADHURST, Kent. American (born United States), b. 1940. **Genres:** Plays/Screenplays, Film, Humor/Satire. **Career:** Playwright, actor and screenwriter, 1961-; Actors Theatre of Louisville (ATL), playwright-inresidence, 1981. **Publications:** The Eye of the Beholder: A Perspective in One Act, 1982; The Habitual Acceptance of the Near Enough, 1983; Lemons, 1984; They're Coming to Make It Brighter: A Full-length Comedy, 1986; Art Who and Quest, 1995. Contributor to periodicals. **Address:** c/o Samuel Liff, William Morris Agency, 1325 Ave. of Americas, New York, NY 10019, U.S.A.

BROADMAN, Harry G. American (born United States), b. 1954. **Genres:** Economics, Business/Trade/Industry. **Career:** RAND Corp., economist, 1979; Brookings Institution, research fellow, 1980-81; Resources for the Future Inc., assistant director and fellow, 1981-84; Johns Hopkins University, professorial lecturer; Harvard University, Department of Economics, faculty, Kennedy School of Government, faculty, 1985-87; President's Council of Economic Advisors, chief of staff and senior economist, 1991-93; Executive Office of President, assistant U.S. trade representative, 1993-97; World Bank, senior economist for China operations, 1997-2005, lead economist on Russia, Europe, and Central Asia operations, 2005-08, economic advisor-African region, 2008-; Albright Stonebridge Group L.L.C., managing director, Albright Capital Management L.L.C., chief economist. **Publications:** (With W.D. Montgomery and M.B. Zimmerman) Natural Gas Markets after Deregulation: Methods of Analysis and Research Needs, 1983; Meeting the Challenge of Chinese Enterprise Reform, 1995; (ed.) Policy Options for Reform of Chinese State-Owned Enterprises: Proceedings of a Symposium in Beijing, June 1995, 1996; (with X. Sun) The Distribution of Foreign Direct Investment in China, 1997; (ed.) Russian Trade Policy Reform for WTO Accession, 1998; (ed.) Russian Enterprise Reform: Policies to Further the Transition, 1998; (ed.) Case-by-Case Privatization in the Russian Federation: Lessons from International Experience, 1998; (ed.) Unleashing Russia's Business Potential: Lessons from the Regions for Building Market Institutions, 2002; (co-author) Building Market Institutions in South Eastern Europe: Comparative Prospects for Investment and Private Sector Development, 2004; (ed. with T. Paas and P.J.J. Welfens) Economic Liberalization and Integration Policy: Options for Eastern Europe and Russia, 2005; (ed.) From Disintegration to Reintegration: Eastern Europe and the Former Soviet Union in International Trade, 2005; Africa's Silk Road: China and India's New Economic Frontier, 2007. Contributor to journals. **Address:** Albright Stonebridge Group, 555 13th St. NW, Ste. 300 W, Washington, DC 20004-1109, U.S.A.

BROADWATER, Robert P. American (born United States), b. 1958. **Genres:** Military/Defense/Arms Control, Biography, Bibliography. **Career:** Dixie Dreams Press, founder, 2003-, publisher. Writer. **Publications:** The Bronze and the Granite: Stories and Anecdotes of the Civil War Leaders, 1983; Campfires and Campaigns, 1986; Leaders in Liberty: Stories of the Revolution, 1988; Daughters of the Cause: Women in the Civil War, 1996; Of Men and Muskets: Stories of the Civil War, 1998; Desperate Deliverance: African Americans in the Civil War, 1998; From beyond the Battlefields: Civil War Side Shows and Little Known Events, 2003; Battle of Despair: Bentonville and the North Carolina Campaign, 2004; Liberty Belles: Women of the American Revolution, 2004; The Battle of Perryville, 1862: Culmination of the Failed Kentucky Campaign, 2005; The Source Book of the American Revolution, 2005; The Battle of Olustee, 1864: The Final Union Attempt to Seize Florida, 2006; (ed.) Chickamauga, Andersonville, Fort Sumter, and Guard Duty at Home: Four Civil War Diaries by Pennsylvania Soldiers, 2006; Boy Soldiers and Soldier Boys: Children in the Civil War, 2006; American Generals of the Revolutionary War: A Biographical Dictionary, 2007; Civil War Medal of Honor Recipients: A Complete Illustrated Record, 2007; The Luckiest Regiment in the Army of the Potomac: With Corporal John A. Rhode and the 137th Pennsylvania Infantry from South Mountain through the Gettysburg Campaign, 2007; WWII: GI Joe Remembers, 2007; Did Lincoln and the Republican Party Create the Civil War?: An Argument, 2008; General George H. Thomas: A Biography of the Union's Rock of Chickamauga, 2009; (ed.) Gettysburg as the Generals Remembered It: Postwar Perspectives of Ten Commanders, 2010; Battle of Fair Oaks: Turning Point of McClellan's Peninsula Campaign, 2011. **Address:** Dixie Dreams Press, 333 S 2nd St., Bellwood, PA 16617-2105, U.S.A.

BROBECK, Stephen. American (born United States), b. 1944. **Genres:** Business/Trade/Industry, Economics. **Career:** Case Western Reserve University, assistant professor of American studies, 1970-79; Consumer Federation of America, executive director, 1980-; Cornell University, visiting associate professor, 1989; University of Maryland, adjunct associate professor, 1990-92. Richmond Federal Reserve Bank, board director, 1990-96. Writer. **Publications:** (With A.C. Averyt) The Product Safety Book: The Ultimate Consumer Guide to Product Hazards, 1983; (with N. Hoffman) The Bank Book: How to Get the Most for Your Banking Dollars: The Consumer Federation of America's Guide to the New Financial Marketplace, 1986; (with J. Gillis) How to Fly: The Consumer Federation of America's Airline Survival Guide, 1987; The Modern Consumer Movement: References and Resources, 1990; (with K. Brunette) Money in the Bank: How to Get the Most for Your Banking Dollar, 1993; Encyclopedia of the Consumer Movement, 1997. **Address:** Consumer Federation of America, 1620 I St. NW, Ste. 200, Washington, DC 20006, U.S.A.

BROCH, Harald Beyer. Norwegian (born Norway), b. 1944. **Genres:** Anthropology/Ethnology, Social Sciences. **Career:** University of Oslo, Ethnographic Museum, conservator, 1975-94, associate professor of anthropology, 1975-89, associate professor of social anthropology, 1990-. Writer. **Publications:** Woodland Trappers: Hare Indians of Northwestern Canada, 1986; Growing up Agreeably: Bonerate Childhood Observed, 1990; Jangan Lupa: An Experiment in Cross Cultural Understanding: The Effort of Two Norwegian Children and Timpaus Indonesian Villagers to Create Meaning in Interaction, 2002. Contributor of articles to periodicals. **Address:** Department of Social Anthropology, University of Oslo, Eilert Sundt's House, 6th Fl., Moltke Moes vei 31 , PO Box 1091, Oslo, N-0851, Norway. **Online address:** h.b.broch@sai.uio.no

BROCHU, André. Canadian (born Canada), b. 1942. **Genres:** Novels, Poetry, Literary Criticism And History, Essays, Autobiography/Memoirs. **Career:** University of Montreal, Department of French Studies, professor of literature, 1963-97; writer, 1997-. **Publications:** POETRY: (with J.-A. Constant and Y. Dube) Etranges domaines, 1957; Privileges de l'ombre, 1961; Delit contre delit, 1965; Les matins nus, le vent, 1989; Dans les chances de l'air, 1990; Particulierement la vie change, 1990; Dela, 1994; L'inconcevable, 1998; Je t'aime, je t'ecris, 2001; élègies de lumière: poemes, 2005. NOVELS: Adéodat I, 1973; La vie aux trousses, 1993; Les epervieres, 1996; Le maitre reveur, 1997; Matamore premier, 2000; Anthológies de lumîre, 2005. NOVELLAS: La Croix du nord, 1991; L'Esprit ailleurs, 1992; Fievres blanches, 1994; Adele intime, 1996; Devil's Paintbrush, 2003. ESSAYS: (ed.) La Litterature par elle-meme, 1962; Hugo: Amour, Crime, Révolution: Essai sur Les Miserables, 1974; (with L. Mailhot and A. Le Grand) Le Reel, le realisme et la litterature quebecoise, 1974; (with G. Marcotte) La Littérature et le reste: Livre de lettres, 1980; L'Evasion Tragique-essai sur les romans d'Andre Langevin, 1985; La Visée critique: Essais autobiographiques et litteraires, 1988; Le Singulier pluriel, 1992; La Grande Langue: Eloge de l'anglais, 1993; Roman et enumeration De Flaubert a Perec, 1996; Une etude de Bonheur d'occasion de Gabrielle Roy, 1998; Anne Hebert, 2000; Rêver la lune, 2002. OTHER: (with J. Brault and A. Major) Nouvelles (short stories), 1963; L'Instance critique: 1961-1973 (collected articles), 1974; Littérature et le reste: livre de letters, 1980; Tableau du poeme, 1994; Saint-Denys Garneau, 1999; Jours à vif: poésie, 2004; Cahiers d'Icare, 2009. Contributor to periodicals. **Address:** 53 Ave. Wicksteed, Mont-Royal, QC H3P 1P9, Canada. **Online address:** andrebroc@hotmail.com

BROCK, Delia. *See* **EPHRON, Delia.**

BROCK, James. American (born United States), b. 1958. **Genres:** Poetry. **Career:** Indiana University, associate instructor of English, 1982-88; Belmont University, assistant professor of English, 1988-93; Idaho State University, visiting assistant professor of English, 1993-96; East Stroudsburg University, instructor of English, 1996-97; University of Miami, lecturer of English, 1997-98; Florida Gulf Coast University, assistant professor, associate professor in English, professor, 1998-. Writer. **Publications:** The Sunshine Mine Disaster (poems), 1995; Nearly Florida, 2000; Pictures That Got Small: Poems, 2005; (with R. Brock and O. Brock) Ex-bachelor's Roost: Letters and Memories of Life on an Alaskan Homestead, 2005; Gods & Money: Poems, 2010. Work appears in anthologies. Contributor of articles to journal. **Address:** College of Arts & Sciences, Florida Gulf Coast University, RH - 227, 10501 FGCU, Blvd. S, Ft. Myers, FL 33965-6565, U.S.A. **Online address:** jbrock@fgcu.edu

BROCK, Michael (George). British (born England), b. 1920. **Genres:** History, Politics/Government, Philosophy. **Career:** Oxford University, Corpus Christi College, fellow and tutor in modern history and politics, 1950-66, university lecturer in modern history, 1951-70, emeritus fellow, 1977, Nuffield College, warden, 1978-; Wolfson College, vice-president and bursar, 1967-76, honorary fellow, 1977; University of Exeter, professor of education, 1977-78; School of Education, director, 1977-78; St. George's House, warden, 1988-93. Writer. **Publications:** The Great Reform Act, 1973; (ed. with E. Brock) H.H. Asquith, Letters to Venetia Stanley, 1982; Nineteenth-Century Oxford (History of Oxford University, vol. VI-VII), vol. I, 1997, vol. II, 2000. Contributor of articles to journals. **Address:** 380 Banbury Rd., Ritchie Ct., Ste. 1, Oxford, OX OX2 7PW, England.

BROCK, Pope. American (born United States), b. 1950?. **Genres:** Mystery/Crime/Suspense, History. **Career:** Marymount College, creative writing faculty; Eastern Washington University, creative writing faculty; Horace Greeley School, creative writing faculty; University of Nebraska, MFA creative writing faculty; Beekman School, creative writing faculty; Westchester County public school system, creative writing faculty. Writer, freelance journalist and actor. **Publications:** Indiana Gothic: A Story of Adultery and Murder in an American Family (fiction), 1999; Charlatan: America's Most Dangerous Huckster, the Man who Pursued Him, and the Age of Flimflam, 2008. Contributor to periodicals. **Address:** c/o Author Mail, Nan A. Talese/Doubleday, 1540 Broadway, New York, NY 10036, U.S.A.

BROCK, William Hodson. British (born England), b. 1936. **Genres:** History, Sciences. **Career:** University of Leicester, lecturer, 1961-74, reader, 1974-92, Victorian Studies Centre, director, 1974-90, professor of history of science, 1992-98, head of history department, 1995-97, professor emeritus, 1998-; University of Toronto, Institute for History of Science and Technology, visiting fellow, 1977; Royal Institution, Centre for the History of Science and Technology, chair, 1984-90; University of Melbourne, visiting fellow in history and philosophy of science, 1985, 1989; Chemical Heritage Foundation, Edelstein international fellow in the history of chemical sciences, 1990-91, visiting fellow, 1993-; Hebrew University of Jerusalem, Edelstein fellow, 1992-; Dibner Institute for History of Science and Technology, senior fellow, 1999-; University of Canterbury, honorary visiting professor, 1999-2002; Science Museum, senior research fellow, 1999-2002; Max-Planck-Institut für Wissenschaftsgeschichte, research visitor, 2000. Writer. **Publications:** (With M. Chapple and M.A. Howson) Studies in Physics, 1972; (with R. MacLeod) Natural Knowledge in Social Context: The Journals of Thomas Archer Hirst FRS, 1980; (with A.J. Meadows) The Lamp of Learning: Taylor & Francis and the Development of Science Publishing, 1984, rev. ed. as The Lamp of Learning: Two Centuries of Publishing at Taylor & Francis, 1998; From Protyle to Proton: William Prout and the Nature of Matter, 1785-1985, 1985; Fontana History of Chemistry, 1992 as The Norton History of Chemistry, 1993 as The Chemical Tree: A History of Chemistry, 2000; Science for All: Studies in the History of Victorian Science and Education, 1996; Science for All: Studies in the History of Victorian Science and Education, 1996; Justus von Liebig: The Chemical Gatekeeper, 1997; William Crookes (1832-1919) and the Commercialization of Science, 2008; The Case of the Poisonous Socks: Tales from Chemistry, 2011. EDITOR: (and contrib.) The Atomic Debates: Brodie and the Rejection of the Atomic Theory, 1967; Science Case Histories, 1972; H.E. Armstrong and the Teaching of Science 1880-1930, 1973; (with N.D. McMillan and R.C. Mollan) John Tyndall: Essays on a Natural Philosopher, 1981; Liebig und Hofmann in ihren Briefen, 1984; Justus von Liebig und August Wilhelm Hofmann in ihren Briefen, 1841-1873, 1984; (with R.L. Hills) Chemistry and the Chemical Industry in the Nineteenth Century: The Henrys of Manchester and Other Studies: Wilfred Vernon Farrar 1920-1977, 1997; Oxford Dictionary of National Biography, 2004. Contributor to periodicals. **Address:** 29 Letheren Pl., Eastbourne, ES BN21 1HL, England. **Online address:** william.brock@btinternet.com

BROCK, William Ranulf. British/Scottish (born Scotland), b. 1916. **Genres:** History, Politics/Government. **Career:** Cambridge University, Trinity College, fellow, 1940-41, Selwyn College, fellow, 1947-67, lecturer in history, 1949-67, life fellow, 1967-, Class E fellow; University of Glasgow, professor of history, 1967-81, chair, now professor emeritus; British Academy, fellow, 1990-; Eton College, assistant. Writer. **Publications:** Lord Liverpool and Liberal Toryism, 1941, 2nd ed., 1967; Britain and the Dominions, 1951; The Character of American History, 1960, 2nd ed., 1965; An American Crisis, 1963; (ed.) The Civil War, 1969; The Evolution of American Democracy, 1970; Conflict and Transformation, the United States, 1844-1877, 1973; The United States, 1789-1890: Sources of History, 1975; (contrib.) A Bibliography of Research Aids, Bibliographies, Periodicals, and Government Documents Relating to the History of the United States and Held by the University and Major Reference Libraries of Scotland, 1977; Parties and Political Conscience: American Dilemmas, 1840-1850, 1979; Scotus Americanus, 1982; Investigation and Responsibility, 1984; Welfare, Democracy, and the New Deal, 1988; Selwyn College: A History, 1994; (ed. and intro.) Federalist, or, The New Constitution, 2000. **Address:** University of Glasgow, St. Andrews Bldg., 11 Eldon St., Kelvingrove, Glasgow, G3 6NH, Scotland. **Online address:** wrb20@cam.ac.uk

BROCK-BROIDO, Lucie. American (born United States), b. 1956. **Genres:** Poetry. **Career:** Harvard University, Briggs-Copeland assistant professor in poetry, 1988-93, creative writing program, director, 1992-93; Bennington Writing Seminars, associate professor in poetry, 1993-95; Columbia University, School of Arts, associate professor, professor, Writing Division, director of poetry, 1993-; Princeton University, visiting professor of poetry, 1995. Writer. **Publications:** POETRY: A Hunger, 1988; The Master Letters, 1995; Trouble in Mind, 2004; Soul Keeping Company: Selected Poems, 2010. **Address:** School of the Arts, Writing Division, Columbia University, 413 Dodge Hall, New York, NY 10027, U.S.A. **Online address:** lb89@columbia.edu

BROCKETT, Charles D. American (born United States), b. 1946. **Genres:** Civil Liberties/Human Rights, Politics/Government. **Career:** Southeastern Massachusetts State University, assistant professor, 1973-79; Sewanee: The University of the South, professor, 1979-2011, Biehl professor of international studies, university senate, 2010-11. Writer. **Publications:** (Co-ed.) Agrarian Reform in Reverse: The Food Crisis in the Third World, 1987; Land, Power, and Poverty: Agrarian Transformation and Political Conflict in Central America, 1988, 2nd ed., 1998; Political Movements and Violence in Central America, 2005; (ed. with H. Tosteson) Families: The Frontline of Pluralism, 2008; (ed. with H. Tosteson and K. Langan) Shifting Balance Sheets: Women's Stories of Naturalized Citizenship & Cultural Attachment, 2011. Contributor of articles to journals. **Address:** Sewanee: The University of the South, 735 University Ave., Sewanee, TN 37383, U.S.A. **Online address:** cbrocket@sewanee.edu

BROCKEY, Liam Matthew. American (born United States), b. 1972. **Genres:** Travel/Exploration, History, Social Sciences. **Career:** Princeton University, assistant professor of history. Historian, educator and editor. **Publications:** Journey to the East: The Jesuit Mission to China, 1579-1724, 2007; (ed.) Portuguese Colonial Cities in the Early Modern World, 2008. Contributor to books and periodicals. **Address:** Department of History, Princeton University, 129 Dickinson Hall, Princeton, NJ 08544-1017, U.S.A. **Online address:** lbrockey@princeton.edu

BROCKINGTON, J(ohn) L(eonard). Scottish/British (born England), b. 1940. **Genres:** Theology/Religion, Language/Linguistics, Area Studies. **Career:** University of Edinburgh, assistant lecturer, 1965-67, lecturer, 1967-82, director of studies, 1969-75, department head, 1975-99, senior lecturer, 1982-89, reader in Sanskrit, 1989-98, Centre for South Asian Studies, convenor, 1989-93, School of Asian Studies, head, 1998-99, professor of Sanskrit, 1998-2005, professor emeritus, 2005-, honorary fellow; International Association of Sanskrit Studies, secretary general, 2000-; Kyoto University, visiting professor, 2006; Royal Society of Edinburgh, fellow. Writer. **Publications:** The Sacred Thread: Hinduism in Its Continuity and Diversity, 1981; Righteous Rama: The Evolution of an Epic, 1985; Hinduism and Christianity, 1992; The Sanskrit Epics, 1998; (ed. with A.S. King) The Intimate Other: Love Divine in Indic Religions, 2005; (trans. with Mary Brockington) Rama the Steadfast: An Early Form of the Ramayana, 2006. Contributor to books and learned journals. **Address:** School of Asian Studies, University of Edinburgh, 7-8 Buccleuch Pl., Edinburgh, EH8 9LW, Scotland. **Online address:** j.l.brockington@ed.ac.uk

BROCKWAY, Connie. American (born United States), b. 1954. **Genres:** Romance/Historical, Novels, inspirational/Motivational Literature, Young Adult Fiction. **Career:** University of Minnesota-Duluth, School of Medicine, graphic artist, 1976-78; Bachman's Nursery, staff, 1978-80; Novel Ideas, editor, 1995-97; University of Minnesota, master gardener. **Publications:** HISTORICAL ROMANCE NOVELS: Promise Me Heaven, 1994; Anything for Love, 1994; A Dangerous Man, 1996; As You Desire, 1997; All through the Night, 1997; My Dearest Enemy, 1998; McClairen's Isle: The Passionate One, 1999; The Reckless One, 2000, The Ravishing One, 2000; (co-author) My Scottish Summer (short fiction) 2001; The Bridal Season, 2001; (with C. Dodd) Once upon a Pillow (short fiction), 2002; Bridal Favors, 2002; My Pleasure, 2004; My Seduction, 2004; (with B. Metzger, C. Claybourne and C. Anderson) True Love Wedding Dress, 2005; My Surrender, 2005, Hot Dish, 2006; Skinny Dipping, 2008; So Enchanting, 2009; The Golden Season, 2010; The Lady Most Likely..., 2010; The Other Guy's Bride, 2011; Cat Scratch Fever, 2011. Contributor to periodicals. **Address:** PO Box 828, Hopkins, MN 55343, U.S.A. **Online address:** connie@conniebrockway.com

BROD, Harry. American/German (born Germany), b. 1951. **Genres:** Philosophy, Women's Studies And Issues, Social Sciences. **Career:** University of Southern California, lecturer, 1982-84, associate professor of philosophy, 1984-87; Men's Studies Review (now masculinities), founding editor, 1983-85, consulting editor, 1985-86, associate editor, 1992-94; University of Delaware, assistant professor, 1994-2003; University of Northern Iowa, Department of Philosophy and World Religions, professor of philosophy and humanities, 2003-, director, 2003-05. Consultant. **Publications:** (Ed.) The Making of Masculinities: The New Men's Studies, 1987; (ed.) A Mensch among Men: Explorations in Jewish Masculinity, 1988; Hegel's Philosophy of Politics: Idealism, Identity, and Modernity, 1992; (ed. with M. Kaufman) Theorizing Masculinities, 1994; (C. Thompson and E. Schaefer) White Men Challenging Racism: 35 Personal Stories, 2003; (ed. with S.I. Zevit) Brother Keepers: New Perspectives on Jewish Masculinity, 2010. CONTRIBUTOR: Feminism and Psychoanalysis: A Critical Dictionary, 1982; History and System: Hegel's Philosophy of History, 1984; The Fathers' Book, 1986; Hegel's Philosophy of Spirit, 1987; Changing Men: New Directions in Research on Men and Masculinity, 1987. Works appear in anthologies. Contributor to books and periodicals. **Address:** Department of Philosophy and World Religions, University of Northern Iowa, 1227 W 27th St., Cedar Falls, IA 50614-0501, U.S.A. **Online address:** harry.brod@uni.edu

BRODE, Patrick. Canadian (born Canada), b. 1950. **Genres:** Criminology/True Crime, History, Adult Non-fiction. **Career:** City Solicitor's Office, attorney, 1980-; University of Windsor, lecturer, 1985-94. Writer. **Publications:** Sir John Beverley Robinson: Bone and Sinew of the Compact, 1984; The Odyssey of John Anderson, 1989; The Charter of Wrongs, 1990; Casual Slaughters and Accidental Judgements: Canadian War Crimes Prosecutions, 1944-1948, 1997; Courted and Abandoned: Seduction in Canadian Law, 2002; Death in the Queen City: Clara Ford on Trial, 1895, 2005; Slasher Killings: A Canadian Sex-Crime Panic, 1945-1946, 2009. **Address:** 243 Buckingham Dr., Windsor, ON N8S 2C5, Canada.

BRODERICK, Colin. American/Irish (born Ireland), b. 1968?. **Genres:** Autobiography/Memoirs. **Career:** Writer, memoirist and documentary filmmaker. **Publications:** Orangutan (memoir), 2009. Contributor to newspapers and periodicals. **Address:** c/o Jane Dystel, Dystel & Goderich Literary Management, 1 Union Sq. W, Ste. 904, New York, NY 10003, U.S.A.

BRODERICK, Damien. American/Australian (born Australia), b. 1944. **Genres:** Science Fiction/Fantasy, Novellas/Short Stories, Plays/Screenplays, Paranormal, Sciences, Young Adult Fiction. **Career:** Go-Set, journalist, 1967; freelance writer, 1967-, 1971-73; David Syme Private Ltd., journalist, 1970; Man, editor, 1971; Walkabout, assistant editor, 1973; Deakin University, writer-in-residence, 1986; University of Melbourne, School of Culture and Communication, Department of English and Cultural Studies, honorary senior research fellow; Cosmos Magazine, founding science fiction editor, 2005-10. **Publications:** A Man Returned (short stories), 1965; Sorcerer's World, 1970; The Dreaming Dragons, 1980; The Judas Mandala, 1982, rev. ed., 1990; (with R. Barnes) Valencies, 1983; Transmitters, 1984; The Black Grail, 1986; Striped Holes, 1988; The Dark Between the Stars (short stories), 1991; The Lotto Effect (parapsychology), 1992; The Sea's Furthest End, 1993; The Architecture of Babel: Discourse of Literature and Science, 1994; Reading By Starlight: Post Modern Science Fiction, 1995; (with R. Barnes) Zones, 1997; The Spike, 1997, rev. ed. as The Spike: How Our Lives Are Being Transformed by Rapidly Advancing Technologies, 2001; Theory and Its Discontents, 1997; The White Abacus, 1997; The Last Mortal Generation, 1999; (with R. Barnes) Stuck in Fast Forward, 1999; (with R. Barnes) The Book of Revelation, 1999; Transrealist Fiction: Writing in the Slipstream of Science, 2000; (contrib.) To Mars and Beyond, 2001; Transcension, 2002; Jack and the Aliens, 2002; Jack and the Skyhook, 2003; Godplayers, 2005; K-Machines, 2006; (with R. Barnes) I Suppose a Root's Out of the Question?, 2006; Outside the Gates of Science: Why It's Time for the Paranormal to Come in from the Cold, 2007; Uncle Bones, 2009; (with R. Barnes) I'm Dying Here, 2009; The Dreaming, 2009; Unleashing the Strange, 2009; (with R. Barnes) Dark Gray, 2010; Climbing Mount Implausible, 2010; Embarrass My Dog, 2011; The Qualia Engine, 2011; (with P.D. Filippo) Science Fiction, 2012. EDITOR: The Zeitgeist Machine, 1977; Strange Attractors, 1985; Matilda at the Speed of Light, 1988; Not the Only Planet, 1998; (with D.G. Hartwell) Centaurus, 1999; Earth is But a Star: Excursions through Science Fiction to the Far Future, 2001. Contributor to the books. **Address:** Department of English, University of Melbourne, John Medley Bldg., 2nd Fl., Parkville, VI 3010, Australia. **Online address:** d.broderick@english.unimelb.edu.au

BRODERICK, Tim. American (born United States), b. 1962?. **Genres:** Children's Fiction, Novels. **Career:** Writer and cartoonist. **Publications:** ODD JOBS SERIES: Something to Build Upon: Odd Jobs 2, 2005; Cash & Carry: Odd Jobs 3, 2008. Contributor to books. **Address:** FinePrint Literary Management, 240 W 35th St., Ste. 500, New York, NY 10001, U.S.A. **Online address:** aabroder@yahoo.com

BRODEUR, Adrienne. American (born United States), b. 1967?. **Genres:** Novels, Human Relations/Parenting. **Career:** Paris Review, reader; Zoetrope: All-Story, founding co-editor, editor-in-chief, 1997-2002. Novelist. **Publications:** (Ed. with S. Schnee) Francis Ford Coppolas Zoetrope All-Story, 2000; Man Camp: A Novel, 2005; Motherload, forthcoming. **Address:** c/o Patty Park, Ballantine Books, 1745 Broadway, 17-1, New York, NY 10019-4368, U.S.A. **Online address:** adrienne@gotomancamp.com

BRODEUR, Paul (Adrian). American (born United States), b. 1931. **Genres:** Novels, Environmental Sciences/Ecology, Novellas/Short Stories, Social Sciences, Young Adult Fiction, Sciences. **Career:** New Yorker, staff writer, 1958-; Columbia University graduate school of journalism, lecturer, 1969-80. **Publications:** The Sick Fox, 1963; The Stunt Man, 1970; Downstream (short stories), 1972; Asbestos and Enzymes, 1972; Expendable Americans, 1974; The Zapping of America: Microwaves, Their Deadly Risk, and the Cover up, 1977; The Asbestos Hazard, 1980; An Industry on Trial, 1984; Outrageous Misconduct: The Asbestos Industry on Trial, 1985; Restitution: The Land Claims of the Mashpee, Passamaguoddy and Penobscot Indians of New England, 1985; Currents of Death: Power Lines, Computer Terminals, and the Attempt to Cover Up Their Threat to Your Health, 1989; The Great Power Line Cover-Up: How the Utilities and the Government are Trying to Hide the Cancer Hazards Posed by Electromagnetic Fields, 1993; Secrets: A Writer in the Cold War, 1997. **Address:** c/o Sterling Lord, Sterling Lord Agency Inc., 660 Madison Ave., New York, NY 10021, U.S.A. **Online address:** paulbrodeur@juno.com

BRODIE, Leanna. Canadian (born Canada), b. 1966. **Genres:** Theatre, Women's Studies And Issues, History, Institutions/Organizations, Local History/Rural Topics, Gay And Lesbian Issues, Plays/Screenplays. **Career:** Playwright, translator and librettist. **Publications:** The Vic (play), 2002; For Home and Country (play), 2004; Schoolhouse (play), 2007; The Book of Esther (play), 2012. **Address:** Michael Petrasek, Kensington Literary Representation, 34 St. Andrew St., Toronto, ON M5T 1K6, Canada. **Online address:** leanna.brodie@sympatico.ca

BRODY, Jane E(llen). American (born United States), b. 1941. **Genres:** Food And Wine, How-to Books, Medicine/Health. **Career:** Minneapolis Tribune, reporter, 1963-65; New York Times, science writer, 1965-76, personal health columnist and writer, 1976-. **Publications:** (With R. Engquist) Secrets of Good Health, 1970; (with R. Engquist) Women and Smoking, 1972; (with A.I. Holleb) You Can Fight Cancer and Win, 1977; Jane Brody's Nutrition Book: A Lifetime Guide to Good Eating for Better Health and Weight Control, 1981, rev. ed., 1987; Jane Brody's The New York Times Guide to Personal Health, 1982; Jane Brody's Good Food Book: Living the High-Carbohydrate Way, 1985; Jane Brody's Good Food Gourmet: Recipes and Menus for Delicious and Healthful Entertaining, 1990; (with R. Flaste) Jane Brody's Good Seafood Book, 1994; Jane Brody's Cold and Flu Fighter, 1995; Jane

Brody's Allergy Fighter, 1997; The New York Times Book of Health: How to Feel Fitter, Eat Better, and Live Longer, 1997; (ed. with D. Grady) The New York Times Book of Women's Health: The Latest on Feeling Fit, Eating Right and Staying Well, 2000; (with D. Grady) The New York Times Guide to Alternative Health: A Consumer Reference, 2001; Jane Brody's Guide to the Great Beyond: A Practical Primer to Help You and Your Loved Ones Prepare Medically, Legally and Emotionally for the End of Life, 2009. Contributor to periodicals. **Address:** New York Times, 229 W 43rd St., New York, NY 10036, U.S.A. **Online address:** inquiries@janebrody.net

BRODY, Jean. *See* Obituaries.

BRODY, Jessica. American (born United States), b. 1979?. **Genres:** Novels. **Career:** MGM Studies, manager of acquisitions and business development, 2001-05. Novelist, producer and vocalist. **Publications:** NOVELS: The Fidelity Files, 2008; Love Under Cover, 2009; The Good Girl's Guide to Bad Men, 2009; The Karma Club, 2010; My Life Undecided, 2011. **Address:** Los Angeles, CA , U.S.A. **Online address:** email@jessicabrody.com

BRODY, Miriam. American (born United States), b. 1940. **Genres:** Writing/Journalism. **Career:** Ithaca College, Department of Writing, associate professor of writing program, professor of writing program. Writer. **Publications:** (With E. Goldman) Living My Life, 1970; (ed.) A Vindication of the Rights of Women, 1975; Manly Writing: Gender, Rhetoric and the Rise of Composition, 1993; Mary Wollstonecraft: Mother of Women's Rights, 2000; Victoria Woodhull: Free Spirit for Women's Rights, 2003; (ed. with B. Buettner) Prison Blossoms, 2011. **Address:** School of Humanities & Sciences, Ithaca College, 201 Muller Ctr., 953 Danby Rd., Ithaca, NY 14850, U.S.A. **Online address:** miriambrody@aol.com

BRODY, Richard. American (born United States), b. 1958. **Genres:** Biography, Autobiography/Memoirs, Film, Humor/Satire. **Career:** Forward, book editor, 1996-99; New Yorker, editor, film critic, 1999-, movie-listings editor, 2005-. Film critic and independent filmmaker. **Publications:** Everything Is Cinema: The Working Life of Jean-Luc Godard, 2008. **Address:** New Yorker, 4 Times Sq., New York, NY 10036-6518, U.S.A.

BRODY, Stuart. American (born United States), b. 1959. **Genres:** Medicine/Health. **Career:** Veterans Administration Hospital, staff psychologist, 1984-88; New York Family Court, senior psychologist, 1990-92; University of Tuebingen, research associate professor, 1992-97, adjunct research associate professor, 1997-2004; consultant, 1997-; University of Trier, senior research fellow, 1999-2001; University of the West of Scotland, professor of psychology. Writer. **Publications:** Sex at Risk: Lifetime Number of Partners, Frequency of Intercourse, and the Low AIDS Risk of Vaginal Intercourse, 1997. Contributor to journals. **Address:** School of Social Sciences, University of the West of Scotland, Paisley, PA1 2BE, Scotland. **Online address:** stuartbrody@hotmail.com

BROER, Lawrence R(ichard). American (born United States), b. 1938. **Genres:** Literary Criticism And History, Women's Studies And Issues, Sex, Politics/Government, Poetry, Young Adult Fiction. **Career:** University of South Florida, College of Arts and Sciences, instructor, 1965-68, adjunct instructor, assistant professor, 1968-73, associate professor, 1973-79, professor of English, 1979-2003, professor emeritus, 2003-. Writer. **Publications:** Hemingway's Spanish Tragedy, 1973; Counter Currents, 1973; (with H. Karl and C. Weingartner) The First Time, 1974; Sanity Plea: Schizophrenia in the Novels of Kurt Vonnegut, 1989, rev. ed., 1994; (ed. with J. Walther) Dancing Fools and Weary Blues: The Great Escape of the Twenties, 1990; (ed.) Rabbit Tales: Poetry and Politics in the Novels of John Updike, 1997; (ed. with G. Holland) Hemingway and Women: Female Critics and the Female Voice, 2002. Contributor to journals. **Address:** Department of English, University of South Florida, CPR 358-H, 4202 E Fowler Ave., Tampa, FL 33620, U.S.A. **Online address:** lbroer@usf.edu

BROGAN, Elise. *See* **URCH, Elizabeth.**

BROGAN, Hugh. British (born England), b. 1936. **Genres:** History, Biography, Autobiography/Memoirs, Social Sciences. **Career:** The Economist, staff, 1960-63; Saint John's College, fellow, 1963-74; University of Essex, lecturer in history, 1974-92, reader, R.A. Butler professor of history, 1992-98, research professor, 1998-. Writer. **Publications:** Tocqueville, 1973; The Life of Arthur Ransome, 1984; The Longman History of the United States of America, 1985; Mowgli's Sons: Kipling and Baden-Powell's Scouts, 1987; (with C. Mosley) American Presidential Families, 1993; (with A.P. Kerr) Conversations et Correspondance d'Alexis de Tocqueville et Nassau William Senior, 1991; Kennedy, 1996; Penguin History of the United States of America, 2001; Alexis de Tocqueville: A Life, 2007. EDITOR: (and intro.) Times Reports The American Civil War: Extracts from The Times, 1860-1865, 1975; (and intro.) The War of the Birds and the Beasts and Other Russian Tales, 1984; Coots in the North and Other Stories, 1988; (and intro.) Signalling From Mars: The Letters of Arthur Ransome, 1997. Contributor of reviews to periodicals and books. **Address:** Department of History, University of Essex, Rm. 5 NW.8.6, Wivenhoe Pk., Colchester, CO4 3SQ, England. **Online address:** hbrogan@essex.ac.uk

BROGAN, Jan. American (born United States), b. 1958?. **Genres:** Mystery/Crime/Suspense, Novels. **Career:** News Tribune, staff; Worcester Telegram and Gazette, staff writer; Providence Journal, staff writer; Boston Globe, correspondent; Brown University, Learning Community, teacher of novel writing; The Learning Connection, teacher of novel writing; Boston Learning Society, teacher of novel writing; Cape Cod Writer's Center, teacher of novel writing. **Publications:** Final Copy, 2001; A Confidential Source, 2005; Yesterday's Fatal, 2007; Teaser, 2008. Contributor to periodicals. **Address:** c/o Author Mail, Minotaur Books, 175 5th Ave., New York, NY 10010, U.S.A. **Online address:** jan@janbrogan.com

BROKS, Paul. British (born England), b. 1955?. **Genres:** Psychology, Self Help. **Career:** Merck, Sharp & Dohme, research scientist; St. James' University Hospital, clinical neuropsychologist; Royal Hallamshire Hospital, clinical neuropsychologist; Bradford Hospitals NHS Trust, clinical neuropsychologist; University of Birmingham, professor of psychology; University of Sheffield, professor of psychology; University of Plymouth, School of Psychology, lecturer, senior clinical lecturer in psychology, 2000-, honorary consultant. Writer. **Publications:** Into the Silent Land: Travels in Neuropsychology, 2003; (with M. Gordon) On Emotion, 2008; The Laws of Magic, forthcoming. Contributor to books. **Address:** Department of Psychology, School of Psychology, University of Plymouth, A202, Portland Sq., Drake Circus, Plymouth, DN PL4 8AA, England. **Online address:** pbroks@plymouth.ac.uk

BROM, Gerald. American (born United States), b. 1965. **Genres:** Novels. **Career:** Commercial illustrator, 1985-. Writer. **Publications:** Darkwërks: The Art of Brom, 2000; Offerings: The Art of Brom, 2001. SELF-ILLUSTRATED NOVELS: The Plucker, 2005; The Devil's Rose, 2007; The Child Thief, 2009. **Online address:** bromwerks@comcast.net

BROMANN, Jennifer. American (born United States), b. 1972. **Genres:** Essays, Adult Non-fiction, Social Sciences. **Career:** Prairie Trails Public Library, head of youth services, 1996-2002; Lincoln-Way Central and West High Schools, Library Department, chair, 2002, librarian, 2002-; Joliet Junior College, adjunct instructor, 2003-; Northern Illinois University, instructor, 2004-10; Illinois State University, School Library Media Program, adjunct instructor, 2007-. Writer. **Publications:** Booktalking That Works, 2001; Storytime Action!: 2000+ Ideas for Making 500 Picture Books Interactive, 2003; More Booktalking That Works, 2005; More Storytime Action!: 2000+ More Ideas for Making 500+ Picture Books Interactive, 2009. Contributor to journals. **Address:** Neal-Schuman Publishers Inc., 100 William St., Ste. 2004, New York, NY 10038-4512, U.S.A. **Online address:** bromannj@hotmail.com

BROMBERG, Nicolette A. American (born United States) **Genres:** Local History/Rural Topics, Essays. **Career:** Lower Columbia College, director of media center and photography instructor, 1979-83; University of Kansas, photo archivist, 1983-93; Wisconsin Historical Society, visual materials curator, 1993-2000; University of Washington, University of Washington Libraries, Special Collections Division, visual materials curator, 2000-. Writer. **Publications:** Wisconsin Revisited: A Rephotographic Essay, 1998; Wisconsin Then and Now: The Wisconsin Sesquicentennial Rephotography Project, 2001; Picturing the Alaska-Yukon-Pacific Exposition: The Photographs of Frank H. Nowell, 2009; (D.F. Martin) Shadows of a Fleeting World: Pictorial Photography and the Seattle Camera Club, 2011. Contributor to journals. **Address:** Special Collections Division, University of Washington Libraries, University of Washington, PO Box 352900, Seattle, WA 98195-2900, U.S.A. **Online address:** nxb@u.washington.edu

BROMBERT, Victor (Henri). American/French (born France), b. 1923. **Genres:** Literary Criticism And History, Novels, History, Essays. **Career:** Yale University, instructor, 1951-55, assistant professor, 1955-58, associate professor, 1958-62, professor of French, 1962-75, department of romance languages, chairman, 1964-73, Benjamin F. Barge professor of romance languages, 1969-75; Princeton University, Henry Putnam University professor of romance and comparative literatures, 1975-, Christian Gauss Seminars in Criticism, director, 1984-, Henry Putnam University professor of romance languages and literatures and comparative literature emeritus. Writer. **Publications:** The Criticism of T.S. Eliot, 1949; Stendhal Et La Voie Oblique: L'auteurdevant Son Monde Romanesque, 1954; The Intellectual Hero: Studies in the French Novel, 1961; (ed.) Stendhal: A Collection of Critical Essays, 1962; The Novels of Flaubert: A Study of Themes and Techniques, 1966; Stendhal: Fiction and the Themes of Freedom, 1968; (intro.) Gustave Flaubert, Madame Bovary, 1969; (ed.) The Hero in Literature, 1969; (intro.) Stendhal, Travels in the South of France, 1971; Flaubert Par Lui-même, 1971; La Prison Romantique: Essai Sur L'imaginaire as The Romantic Prison, 1978; (Contrib.) The Author in His Work, 1978; Victor Hugo and the Visionary Novel, 1984; (ed.) Gustave Flaubert, Madame Bovary, 1985; The Hidden Reader: Stendhal, Balzac, Hugo, Baudelaire, Flaubert, 1988; In Praise of Antiheroes: Figures and Themes in Modern European Literature, 1830-1980, 1999; Trains of Thought: Memories of a Stateless Youth, 2002. Contributor to periodicals. **Address:** Princeton University, 303 East Pyne, Princeton, NJ 08544, U.S.A. **Online address:** brombert@princeton.edu

BROMER, Anne C. American (born United States) **Genres:** Novels, How-to Books, Crafts. **Career:** Bromer Booksellers, owner, operator, rare book dealer, 1968-. Writer. **Publications:** (With D. Bromer) 35 Miniature Books in Designer Bindings, 1987; Strings Attached: Dorothy Abbe, Her Work and Wad, 2001; (with J.I. Edison) Miniature Books: 4,000 Years of Tiny Treasures, 2007. **Address:** Bromer Booksellers, 607 Boylston St., on Copley Sq., Boston, MA 02116-3604, U.S.A.

BROMKE, Adam. Canadian/Polish (born Poland), b. 1928. **Genres:** International Relations/Current Affairs, Politics/Government, Social Sciences, History. **Career:** University of Montreal, lecturer, 1953-54; McGill University, Department of Economics and Political Science, lecturer, 1957-60; Harvard University, Russian Research Centre, research fellow, 1960-62; Canadian Slavic Papers, managing editor, 1961-63; Carleton University, Department of Political Science, associate professor of political science, 1962-66, professor and chairman, 1968-71, Soviet and East European Studies Program, chairman, 1962-66; Canadian Council, senior fellow, 1967-68; McMaster University, professor of political science, 1973-89, professor emeritus, 1989-; Polish Academy of Sciences, professor of humanities, 1990. Writer. **Publications:** Poland's Politics, Idealism vs. Realism, 1967; Detente or Cold War II: East-West Relations After Afghanistan, 1980; Poland: The Last Decade, 1981; (co-author) Canada's Response to the Polish Crisis, 1982; Poland: The Protracted Crisis, 1983; Eastern Europe in the Aftermath of Solidarity, 1985; The Meaning and Uses of Polish History, 1987; Stosunki Wschód-Zachód w Latach Osiemdziesiatych, 1989; Polak w świecie (memoirs in Polish), 1995; Polska u Progu XXI Wieku, 2000. EDITOR: The Communist States at the Crossroads, 1965; (with P.E. Uren) The Communist States and the West, 1967; (with T.H. Rakowski-Harmstone) The Communist States in Disarray, 1972; (with J.W. Strong) Gierek's Poland, 1973; (with D. Novak) The Communist States in the Era of Détente: 1971-77, 1978. **Address:** Department of Political Science, McMaster University, 527 Kenneth Taylor Hall, 1280 Main St. W, Hamilton, ON L8S 4M4, Canada.

BROMLEY, Simon. British (born England), b. 1961. **Genres:** Politics/Government. **Career:** University of Leeds, international political economy, lecturer; Open University, faculty, 1999-, Department of Politics and International Studies, senior lecturer, Department of Curriculum Planning, associate dean, dean and director of studies. Writer. **Publications:** (With B. Jessop, K. Bonnett and T. Ling) Thatcherism, 1988; American Hegemony and World Oil, 1991; Rethinking Middle East Politics, 1994. EDITOR: Governing the European Union, 2001; (co-ed.) Making the International: Economic Interdependence and Political Order: A World of Whose Making?, 2004; (with W. Brown and S. Athreye) Ordering the International: History, Change and Transformation, 2004; American Power and the Prospects for International Order, 2008. **Address:** Faculty of Social Sciences, The Open University, Walton Hall, Milton Keynes, BK MK7 6AA, England. **Online address:** s.j.bromley@open.ac.uk

BRONLEEWE, Matt Ryan. American (born United States), b. 1973?. **Genres:** Mystery/Crime/Suspense. **Career:** Jars of Clay, co-founder. Novelist and musician. **Publications:** Illuminated, 2007; House of Wolves, 2008. **Address:** c/o Lydia Wills, Paradigm Literary Talent Agency, 360 Park Ave. S, 16th Fl., New York, NY 10010, U.S.A. **Online address:** matt@mattbronleewe.com

BRONNER, Leila Leah. American/Czech (born Czech Republic), b. 1930. **Genres:** Theology/Religion, Biography, History. **Career:** Witwaterstrand University, tenured associate professor, professor of Bible and Jewish history, 1960-84; Hebrew Teachers' College, senior lecturer, 1966-78; Harvard University, visiting fellow, 1984; Yeshiva University, visiting professor, 1985-87; University of Judaism, adjunct associate professor, 1987-90; Institute of Bible and Jewish Studies, professor, 1991-. Writer. **Publications:** Sects and Separatism During the Second Jewish Commonwealth, 1967; The Stories of Elijah and Elisha, 1968; Biblical Personalities and Archaeology, 1974; From Eve to Esther: Rabbinic Reconstructions of Biblical Women, 1994; Stories of Biblical Mothers: Maternal Power in the Hebrew Bible, 2004; Journey to Heaven, forthcoming. Contributor to books and periodicals. **Address:** 180 N Las Palmas Ave., Los Angeles, CA 90004, U.S.A. **Online address:** leilaleah@aol.com

BRONSKY, Alina. German/Russian (born Russia), b. 1978?. **Genres:** Novels. **Career:** Novelist and journalist. **Publications:** Scherbenpark: Roman, 2008. **Address:** Frankfurt, Germany. **Online address:** alinabronsky@t-online.de

BRONSON, Po. American (born United States), b. 1964?. **Genres:** Novels, Sex, Young Adult Non-fiction, Psychology. **Career:** Citi Respect (San Francisco Politics), staff, 1988-89; Mercury House (non-profit publishing Co.), associate publisher, 1989-95; The Grotto, co-founder, 1994-; Newsweek.com, writer. **Publications:** NOVELS: Bombardiers, 1995; The First $20 Million is Always the Hardest, 1997; The Nudist on the Late Shift: And Other True Tales of Silicon Valley, 1999; (with D. Liss and A. Parsons) Men Seeking Women: Love and Sex On-line, 2000; What Should I Do With My Life?, 2002; Why Do I Love These People?, 2005; (with A. Merryman) NurtureShock: New Thinking about Children, 2009. Contributor of articles to magazines and periodicals. **Address:** c/o Peter Ginsberg, Curtis Brown Ltd., 10 Astor Pl., New York, NY 10003-6935, U.S.A. **Online address:** pobronson@pobronson.com

BRONZINO, Joseph D. American (born United States), b. 1937. **Genres:** Engineering, Ethics, Medicine/Health, Technology. **Career:** U.S. Naval Postgraduate School, instructor, 1959-61; New York Telephone Co., transmission engineer, 1960-61, central office engineer, 1963-64; University of New Hampshire, instructor, 1964-66, assistant professor of electrical engineering, 1966-67; National Science Foundation, faculty fellow, Worcester Foundation for Experimental Biology, National Science Foundation, faculty fellow, 1967-68, cooperating staff, 1968-90; Trinity College, associate professor, 1968-75, professor of engineering, 1975-, Vernon Roosa professor of applied science, 1977-, now Vernon Roosa professor emeritus of applied science, Department of Engineering and Computer Science, chair, 1982-90; Hartford Graduate Center, director and chair of biomedical engineering program, 1969-2000; University of Connecticut Health Center, clinical associate, 1971-77, project manager, 1980, administrative assistant, 1981, management and computer consultant, 1981-97; Aetna Institute, educational consultant, 1985-88; Connecticut Science Museum, scientific advisor, 1985-2008; Boston University Medical School, adjunct faculty, 1989-98, cooperating staff, 1990-2005; BEACON, Biomedical Engineering Alliance for Connecticut, director, 1997-2000, founder and president, 2000-. Writer. **Publications:** Technology for Patient Care: Applications for Today, Implications for Tomorrow, 1977; Computer Applications for Patient Care, 1982; Biomedical Engineering and Instrumentation: Basic Concepts and Applications, 1986; (with V. Smith and M.L. Wade) Medical Technology and Society: An Interdisciplinary Perspective, 1990; Expert Systems: Basic Concepts and Applications, 1990; (ed.) Management of Medical Technology, 1992; (ed.) Biomedical Engineering Handbook, 1995, 3rd ed., 2006; (ed. with S.M. Blanchard and J.D. Enderle) Introduction to Biomedical Engineering, 2000, 3rd ed., 2012; (ed. with J.B. Park) Biomaterials: Principles and Applications, 2002; (ed. with K.M. Murdy and R. Plonsey) Biomedical Imaging, 2003; (ed. with D.J. Schneck) Biomechanics: Principles and Applications, 2003; (ed.) Medical Devices and Systems, 2006; (ed. with J.P. Fisher and A.G. Mikos) Tissue Engineering and Artificial Organs, 2006; (ed.) Biomedical Engineering Fundamentals, 2006; (ed. with A.G. Mikos) Tissue Engineering, 2007; (ed. with J.Y. Wong) Biomaterials, 2007; (ed. with D.J. DiLorenzo) Neuroengineering, 2008; (ed. with N.A. Diakides) Medical Infrared Imaging, 2008. **Address:** Department of Engineering, Trinity College, MCEC 309, 300 Summit St., Hartford, CT 06106, U.S.A. **Online address:** joseph.bronzino@beaconalliance.org

BROOK, Elaine (Isabel). British (born England), b. 1949. **Genres:** Anthropology/Ethnology, Cultural/Ethnic Topics, Environmental Sciences/Ecology, Mythology/Folklore, Natural History, Philosophy, Travel/Exploration, History, History. **Career:** Gaia Partnership, director. Writer. **Publications:** (With J. Donnelly) The Wind Horse, 1986; Land of the Snow Lion: Adventure in Tibet, 1987; In Search of Shambhala, 1996. Contributor to periodicals. **Address:** Jonathan Cape Ltd., 20 Vauxhall Bridge Rd., London, GL SW1V 2SA, England. **Online address:** elaine@gaiacooperative.org

BROOK, Stephen. British (born England), b. 1947. **Genres:** Food And Wine, Travel/Exploration. **Career:** Atlantic Monthly, staff editor, 1970-73; David R. Godine Inc., editorial director, 1973-75; Routledge and Kegan Paul Ltd., commissioning editor, 1976-80; writer, 1982-; Decanter, contributing editor, 1996-. **Publications:** Bibliography of the Gehenna Press: 1942-1975, 1976; New York Days, New York Nights, 1984; Honkytonk Gelato: Travels in Texas, 1984; The Dordogne, 1985; Maple Leaf Rag: Travels across Canada, 1987; Liquid Gold: Dessert Wines of the World, 1987; The Double Eagle: Vienna, Budapest, Prague, 1988; Vanished Empire, 1988; The Club: The Jews of Modern Britain, 1989; Winner Takes All: A Season in Israel, 1990; The Veneto, 1991; Prague, 1992; L.A. Lore, 1992; Sauvignon Blanc and Semillon, 1992; Claws of the Crab: Georgia and Armenia in Crisis, 1992; L.A. Days, L.A. Nights, 1993; Eyewitness Travel Guide to Vienna, 1994; (contrib.) Vienna, 1994; Sauternes and the Other Sweet Wines of Bordeaux, 1995; Southern France: Provence, Midi and South Rhone, 1997; Class, 1997; Pauillac, 1998; The Wines of California, 1999; Pocket Guide to Sweet and Fortified Wines, 2000; A Century of Wine, 2000; (with J. Radford) Fortified and Sweet Wines, 2000; Bordeaux: People, Power and Politics, 2001; Pocket Guide to California Wine, 2002; The Wines of Germany, 2003; Hugh Johnson's Wine Companion, 2003; National Geographic Traveler Guide To The Czech Republic, 2004; Bordeaux: Medoc and Graves, 2006; The Complete Bordeaux, 2007; Finest Wines of California: A Regional Guide to the Best Producers and their Wines, 2011. EDITOR: The Oxford Book of Dreams, 1983; The Penguin Book of Infidelities, 1994; The Penguin Book of Opera, 1995; Opera, 1996; Wine People, 2001. Contributor of articles to periodicals. **Address:** Decanter, Blue Fin Bldg., 110 Southwark St., London, GL SE1 0SU, England. **Online address:** info@stephenbrook.com

BROOK, Timothy (James). Canadian (born Canada), b. 1951. **Genres:** Civil Liberties/Human Rights, History, Third World. **Career:** Needham Research Institute, research associate, 1978-79; University of Alberta, MacTaggart Fellow, 1984-86; University of Toronto, assistant professor, professor history, 1986-97, 1999-2004, Joint Center for Asia Pacific Studies, China documentation project, director, 1989; Stanford University, professor of history, 1997-99; University of British Columbia, St. John's College, principal, 2004-, Department of History, professor, 2004-, Contemporary Tibetan Studies Program, Institute of Asian Research, academic director, 2004-, Republic of China, chair; University of Oxford, Shaw professor, Shaw chair, 2007-09. Writer. **Publications:** Geographical Sources of Ming-Qing History, 1988, 2nd. ed., 2002; Quelling the People: The Military Suppression of the Beijing Democracy Movement, 1992; Praying for Power: Buddhism and the Formation of Gentry Society in Late-Ming China, 1993; The Confusions of Pleasure: Commerce and Culture in Ming China, 1998; (with C.S. yi) Chinese State in Ming Society, 2005; Collaboration: Japanese Agents and Local Elites in Wartime China, 2005; Zhongguo yu lishi zi ben zhu yi: Han xue zhi shi de xi pu xue, 2005; Vermeer's Hat: The17th Century and The Dawn of the Global World, 2008; (with J. Bourgon and G. Blue) Death By a Thousand Cuts, 2008; Gong zhong wai jiao: ruan xing guo li, li lun yu ce lue=Public Diplomacy: Soft Power, Theory and Strategy, 2009; The Troubled Empire: China in the Yuan and Ming Dynasties, 2010. EDITOR: The Asiatic Mode of Production in China, 1989; (with P.A. Kuhn) National Polity and Local Power: The Transformation of Late Imperial China, 1989; (ed. with K. Robinson) Science and Civilisation in China, vol. VII, Part 1: The Social and Economic Background, 1993; (with Hy V. Luong) Culture and Economy: The Shaping of Capitalism in Eastern Asia, 1997; (with B.M. Frolic) Civil Society in China, 1997; (with G. Blue) China and Historical Capitalism: Genealogies of Sinological Knowledge, 1999; (co-ed.) Documents on the Rape of Nanking, 1999; (with A. Schmid) Nation Work: Asian Elites and National Identities, 2000; (with B.T. Wakabayashi) Opium Regimes: China, Britain and Japan, 1839-1952, 2000. Works appear in anthologies. Contributor of articles to periodicals. **Address:** Institute of Asian Research, University of British Columbia, 1855 West Mall, C.K. Choi Bldg., Vancouver, BC V6T 1Z2, Canada. **Online address:** tim.brook@ubc.ca

BROOK, Vincent. American (born United States), b. 1946. **Genres:** Novels. **Career:** International Television Film Production, documentary film editor and writer, 1976-80; Family Home Entertainment, film editor, 1980-84; Los Angeles Pierce College, adjunct professor, 1986-; Columbia College, adjunct professor, 1986-93; Los Angeles City College, adjunct professor, 1989-90; Argus Entertainment, screenwriter, 1991-95; Watterson College, instructor, 1994-96; Silver Lake Improvement Association, president, 1997-2003; California State University, adjunct professor, 1999-; California State University-Fullerton, adjunct professor, 2000-01; Pasadena City College, adjunct professor, 2000-02; Silver Lake Film Festival, advisor, 2000-02; Silver Lake Neighborhood Council, organizer, 2000-; California State University-Northridge, adjunct professor, 2001; University of Southern California, adjunct professor, 2003-; University of California, School of Theater, Film and Television, visiting assistant professor. **Publications:** Something Ain't Kosher Here: The Rise of the Jewish Sitcom, 2003; (ed.) You Should See Yourself: Jewish Identity in Postmodern American Culture, 2006; Driven to Darkness: Jewish émigré Directors and the Rise of Film Noir, 2009. Contributor to books. **Address:** School of Theater, Film and Television, University of California, 2319 Macgowan, 102 E Melnitz Hall, Los Angeles, CA 90095, U.S.A. **Online address:** vbrook@earthlink.net

BROOKE, Christopher N. L. British (born England), b. 1927. **Genres:** History. **Career:** Cambridge University, Gonville and Caius College, fellow, 1949-56, assistant lecturer, 1953-54, lecturer in history, 1954-56; University of Liverpool, professor of medieval history, 1956-67; University of London, Westfield College, professor of history, 1967-77; Cambridge University, Dixie professor of ecclesiastical history, 1977-94, Gonville and Caius College, fellow, 1977-, now Dixie professor emeritus of ecclesiastical history. Writer. **Publications:** (Intro.) The Book of William Morton, Almoner of Peterborough Monastery, 1448-1467, 1954; (with W.J. Millor and H.E. Butler) The Letters of John of Salisbury, 2 vols., 1955; The Dullness of the Past, an Inaugural Lecture, 1957; (co-author) Studies in the Early British Church, 1958; (ed. with M. Postan) Carte Nativorum: A Peterborough Abbey Cartulary of the 14th Century, 1960; From Alfred to Henry III, 871-1272, 1961; The Saxon & Norman Kings, 1963, 3rd ed., 2001; (co-author) Celt and Saxon, 1963; Europe in the Central Middle Ages, 1964, 3rd. ed., 2000; (with A. Morey) Gilbert Foliot and His Letters, 1965; (contrib.) The Flowering of the Middle Ages, 1966; (with D.A. Morey) The Letters and Charters of Gilbert Foliot, 1967; The Twelfth Century Renaissance, 1969; The Structure of Medieval Society: Collected Essays, 1971; Medieval Church and Society: Collected Essays, 1971; (ed. with D. Knowles and V.C.M. London) The Heads of Religious Houses, England and Wales, 940-1216, 1972, 2nd ed., 2001; (with W. Swaan) The Monastic World, 1000-1300, 1974; Monasteries of the World: The Rise and Development of the Monastic Tradition, 1974; (with G. Keir) London, 800-1216: The Shaping of a City, 1975; Europe in the Central Middle Ages, 962-1154, 1975, 3rd ed., 2000; (co-ed.) Church and Government in the Middle Ages: Essays Presented to C.R. Cheney on His 70th Birthday, 1976; Marriage in Christian History: An Inaugural Lecture, 1978; (with D. Whitelock and M. Brett) Councils and Synods, I, 871-1204, 1981; (co-ed.) Studies in Numismatic Method Presented To Philip Grierson, 1983; (contrib.) De nugis curialium=Courtiers' trifles, 1983; (co-ed.) De nugiscurialium/Courtiers' trifles, 1983; (with Rosalind) Popular Religion in the Middle Ages, 1984; A History of Gonville and Caius College, 1985; (with D.N. Dumville) The Church and the Welsh Border in the Central Middle Ages, 1986; (with R. Highfield and W. Swaan) Oxford and Cambridge, 1988; (with D.E. Luscombe) Evolution of Medieval Thought, 1988; The Medieval Idea of Marriage, 1989; (with M. Brett and M. Winterbottom) Hugh the Chanter: History of the Church of York, 1990; (co-author) David Knowles Remembered, 1991; (contrib.) Church and City, 1000-1500: Essays in Honour of Christopher Brooke, 1992; (ed.) A History of the University of Cambridge, IV: 1870-1990, 1993; Jane Austen: Illusion and Reality, 1999; (with S. Bendall and P. Collinson) A History of Emmanuel College Cambridge, 1999; Churches and Churchmen in Medieval Europe, 1999; The Age of the Cloister: The Story of Monastic Life in the Middle Ages, 2003; (co-author) II: 1546-1750, 2004. Contributor to journals. **Address:** Gonville & Caius College, University of Cambridge, Trinity St., Cambridge, CB CB2 1TA, England. **Online address:** cnlb2@cam.ac.uk

BROOKE, Heather. British (born England) **Genres:** How-to Books. **Career:** Spokesman- Review, reporter; Spartanburg Herald- Journal, reporter; British Broadcasting Corp. (BBC) Television, assistant publicist; City University, Department of Journalism, visiting fellow. Writer. **Publications:** Your Right to Know: How to Use the Freedom of Information Act and Other Access Laws, 2005, 2nd ed. as Your Right to Know: A Citizen's Guide to the Freedom of Information Act, 2007. **Address:** London, England. **Online address:** heather@yrtk.org

BROOKE, Jill. American (born United States), b. 1959?. **Genres:** Adult Non-fiction, Self Help. **Career:** ABC's Nightline, reporter; New York Post, columnist; CNN, correspondent; Daily News, columnist; Avenue Magazine, editor-in-chief; Travel Savvy, editor-in-chief; Hamptons Magazine, editor-in-chief; FirstWivesWorld.com, editor-in-chief and writer. **Publications:** Don't Let Death Ruin Your Life: A Practical Guide to Reclaiming Happiness After the Death of a Loved One, 2001; The Wacky World of Divorce, forthcoming. Contributor to publications. **Address:** c/o Travel Savvy, 72 Madison Ave., 5th Fl., New York, NY 10016, U.S.A.

BROOKE, Rosalind B(eckford). British (born England), b. 1925. **Genres:** History, Politics/Government, Theology/Religion. **Career:** Mitcham County Grammar School for Girls, temporary senior history mistress, 1949-50; Cambridge University, history supervisor, 1951-56, 1977-92, lecturer in history, 1977-92; Birkenhead High School, history mistress, 1958-59; Liverpool University, lecturer in palaeography, 1963, tutor, 1964-66; University College, part-time lecturer in medieval history, 1968-73, honorary research fellow, 1973-77. Writer. **Publications:** Early Franciscan Government: Elias to Bonaventure, 1959; (ed. and trans.) Scripta Leonis, Rufini et Angeli, Sociorum S. Francisci, 1970, rev. ed., 1990; The Coming of the Friars, 1975; (with C. Brooke) Popular Religion in the Middle Ages: Western Europe, 1000-1300, 1984; The Image of St Francis: Responses to Sainthood in the Thirteenth Century, 2006. Contributor to periodicals. **Address:** c/o C.N.L. Brooke, Gonville and Caius College, Trinity St., Cambridge, CB CB2 1TA, England.

BROOKE, William J. American (born United States), b. 1946. **Genres:** Children's Fiction, Young Adult Fiction, Humor/Satire, Novellas/Short Stories. **Career:** Word processor, 1987-90. Actor, director and writer. **Publications:** FOR CHILDREN: Operantics: Fun and Games for the Opera Buff, 1986; A Telling of the Tales, 1990; Untold Tales, 1992; A Brush with Magic, Based on a Traditional Chinese Story, 1993; Teller of Tales, 1994; A Is for Aarrgh!, 1999. **Address:** 215 W 78th St., Ste. 5C, New York, NY 10024-6629, U.S.A. **Online address:** billbrooke@nyc.rr.com

BROOKER, Jewel Spears. American (born United States), b. 1940. **Genres:** Poetry, Humanities, Intellectual History, Literary Criticism And History, Novellas/Short Stories, Education. **Career:** Yale University, postdoctoral research fellow in English, 1980-81; Eckerd College, associate professor, professor of English, professor emeritus, 1981-; Columbia University, visiting professor, 1988; Doshisha University, visiting professor, 1992-94; Harvard University, Stanley J. Kahrl fellow in literary manuscripts, 1999; University of London, Institute of United States Studies, John Adams fellow, 2000; Colorado School of Mines, Hennebach professor of humanities, 2003-04; T.S. Eliot International Summer School, professor, 2009-12; Hebrew University of Jerusalem, visiting professor, 2012. Writer. **Publications:** (With J. Bentley) Reading The Waste Land: Modernism and the Limits of Interpretation, 1990; Mastery and Escape: T.S. Eliot and the Dialectic of Modernism, 1994; Violence, Imagination and Modern Literature, 2003. EDITOR: (contrib.) Approaches to Teaching T.S. Eliot's Poetry and Plays, 1988; (contrib.) The Placing of T.S. Eliot, 1991; Conversations with Denise Levertov, 1998; (contrib.) T.S. Eliot and Our Turning World, 2001; (contrib.) T.S. Eliot: The Contemporary Reviews, 2004; (with R. Schuchard) T.S. Eliot's Complete Prose, vol. I, 2012. Contributor to books and journals. **Address:** Eckerd College, 4200 54th Ave. S, St. Petersburg, FL 33711, U.S.A. **Online address:** jsbrooker@aol.com

BROOKE-ROSE, Christine. British/French/Swiss (born Switzerland), b. 1923. **Genres:** Literary Criticism And History, Novels, Novellas/Short Stories, Autobiography/Memoirs, Poetry. **Career:** Freelance journalist, 1956-68; University of Paris VIII, Department of English and American Literature, lecturer in Anglo-American literature and literary theory, 1968-75, professor, 1975-88. Writer. **Publications:** NOVELS: The Languages of Love, 1957; A Grammar of Metaphor, 1958, 2nd ed., 1970; The Sycamore Tree, 1958; The Dear Deceit, 1960; The Middlemen: A Satire, 1961; Out, 1964; Such, 1966; Between, 1968; Thru, 1975; Amalgamemnon, 1984; Xorandor, 1986, 2nd ed., 1988; The Christine Brooke-Rose Omnibus: Four Novels, 1986; Verbivore, 1990; Textermination: A Novel, 1992; Remake, 1996; Next, 1998; Subscript, 1999; Life, End of, 2006. COLLECTIONS: Go When You Seethe Green Man Walking (short stories), 1970. CHAPBOOKS: Gold: A Poem, 1955. NON-FICTION: A ZBC of Ezra Pound, 1971; A Structural Analysis of Pound's Usura Canto: Jakobson's Method Extended and Applied to Free Verse, 1976; A Rhetoric of the Unreal: Studies in Narrative and Structure, Especially of the Fantastic, 1981; Stories, Theories and Things, 1991; Invisible Author: Last Essays, 2002. OTHERS: (trans.) Juan Goytisolo, Children of Chaos, 1959; (trans.) Alfred Sauvy, Fertility and Survival: Population Problems from Malthus to Mao Tse Tung, 1960; (trans.) Alain Robbe-Grillet, In the Labyrinth, Calder & Boyars, 1968; (contrib.) Reconstructing Individualism: Autonomy, Individuality and the Self in Western Thought, 1986; Poems, Letters, Drawings, 2000. **Address:** Carcanet Press Ltd., 30 Cross St., 4th Fl., Manchester, GM M2 7AQ, England.

BROOKES, Beth. *See* **MCKENNA, Lindsay Gvhdi.**

BROOKES, John A. British (born England), b. 1933. **Genres:** Homes/Gardens, Horticulture, How-to Books, Architecture. **Career:** John Brookes Design, principal, 1964-; Inchbald School of Interior Design, founder, 1978; John Brookes Landscape Design, founder, 1980; Royal Botanic Garden Kew, School of Garden Design, principal lecturer; Institute of Park Administration, lecturer; Regent Street Polytechnic, lecturer; Inchbald School of Landscape Design, director; Architectural Design, assistant editor. **Publications:** Room Outside, 1969; Gardens for Small Spaces, 1970; Garden Design and Layout, 1970; Living in the Garden, 1971; The Financial Times Book of Garden Design, 1975; Improve Your Lot, 1977; The Small Garden, 1977; The Garden Book, 1984; A Place in the Country, 1984; The Indoor Garden Book, 1986; Gardens of Paradise, 1987; (with K.A. Beckett and T.H. Everett) The Gardener's Index of Plants & Flowers, 1987; The Country Garden, 1987; The Small Garden Book, 1989; The Book of Garden Design in UK as John Brookes' Garden Design Book, 1991; (ed.) Garden Planning, 1992; Garden Design Workbook, 1994; (with E. Price) Home and Garden Style, 1996; John Brookes' Natural Landscapes, 1998; Planting the Country Way: A Hands-On Approach, 1998; Garden Masterclass, 2002; Well-Designed Garden, 2007; The Essentials Of Garden Design, 2008. **Address:** John Brookes Landscape Design, Clock House, Denmans Ln., Fontwell, WS BN18 0SU, England. **Online address:** jbrookes@denmans-garden.co.uk

BROOKES, Martin. American (born United States), b. 1967?. **Genres:** Biology, Biography, Sciences, Genealogy/Heraldry. **Career:** University College London, Galton Laboratory, biological researcher. Writer. **Publications:** Genetics, 1998; Fly: The Unsung Hero of Twentieth-Century Science, 2001; Fly: An Experimental Life, 2001; Extreme Measures: The Dark Visions and Bright Ideas of Francis Galton, 2004. Contributor to periodicals. **Address:** c/o Author Mail, Bloomsbury Publishing, 175 5th Ave., Ste. 300, New York, NY 10010-7703, U.S.A.

BROOKES, Tim. British (born England), b. 1953. **Genres:** Medicine/Health, Travel/Exploration. **Career:** University of Vermont, instructor in English, 1974-99, Professional Writing Program, director; Tim Brooks Inc., owner. Writer. **Publications:** Catching My Breath: An Asthmatic Explores His Illness, 1994; (co-author) The Blair Handbook: Instructor's Edition, 1994; Signs of Life: A Memoir of Dying and Discovery, 1997; A Hell of a Place to Lose a Cow: An American Hitchhiking Odyssey, 2000; (with O.A. Khan) Behind The Mask: How The World Survived SARS, The First Epidemic Of The 21st Century, 2004; Driveway Diaries, 2005; Guitar: An American Life, 2005; A Warning Shot: Influenza and the 2004 Flu Vaccine Shortage, 2005; (with O.A. Khan) The End of Polio?: Behind the Scenes of the Campaign to Vaccinate Every Child on the Planet, 2006; Thirty Percent Chance of Enlightenment, 2009. Contributor to periodicals. **Address:** Champlain College, 204 Wick, 163 S Willard St., Burlington, VT 05401, U.S.A. **Online address:** brookes@champlain.edu

BROOKHISER, Richard. American (born United States), b. 1955. **Genres:** History, Politics/Government, Social Commentary. **Career:** National Review, senior editor, 1979-85, 1988-, managing editor, 1986-87; Vice President George Bush, speechwriter, 1982-. **Publications:** The Outside Story: How Democrats and Republicans Re-elected Reagan, 1986; (intro.) Right Reason, 1986; The Way of the WASP: How It Made America and How It Can Save It, So to Speak, 1991; Founding Father: Rediscovering George Washington, 1996; (ed.) Rules of Civility, 1997; Alexander Hamilton, American, 1999; America's First Dynasty: The Adamse, 2002; Gentleman Revolutionary: Gouverneur Morris, the Rake Who Wrote the Constitution, 2003; What Would the Founders Do? Our Questions, Their Answers, 2006; George Washington on Leadership, 2008; Right Time, Right Place: Coming of Age with

William F. Buckley Jr. and the Conservative Movement, 2009. Contributor of articles and reviews to periodicals. **Address:** National Review, 215 Lexington Ave., 4th Fl., New York, NY 10016, U.S.A.

BROOKNER, Anita. British (born England), b. 1928. **Genres:** Novels, Novellas/Short Stories, Art/Art History, inspirational/Motivational Literature, Translations. **Career:** University of Reading, lecturer in history, 1959-64; Courtauld Institute of Art, lecturer, 1967-77, reader, 1977-88, now retired; Cambridge University, Slade Professor of Art, 1967-68; art historian and novelist, 1981-; British Empire, commander, 1990; King's College, fellow; Murray Edwards College, fellow. Writer. **Publications:** ART HISTORY AND CRITICISM: J.A. Dominique Ingres, 1965; Watteau, 1968; The Genius of the Future: Studies in French Art Criticism, 1971 in US as The Genius of the Future: Essays in French Art Criticism, 1998; Greuze: The Rise and Fall of an Eighteenth-Century Phenomenon, 1972; Jacques-Louis David: A Personal Interpretation: Lecture on Aspects of Art, 1974; Jacques-Louis David, 1980; Soundings: Studies in Art and Literature, 1997; Romanticism and Its Discontents, 2000. NOVELS: A Start in Life in US as The Debut, 1981; Providence, 1982; Look at Me, 1983; Hotel du Lac, 1984; Family and Friends, 1985; A Misalliance, 1986 in US as The Misalliance, 1987; A Friend from England, 1987; Latecomers, 1988; Lewis Percy, 1989; Brief Lives, 1990; A Closed Eye, 1991; Fraud, 1992; A Family Romance, 1993; Dolly, 1993; A Private View, 1994; Incidents in the Rue Laugier, 1996; Altered States, 1996; Visitors, 1997; Falling Slowly, 1998; Undue Influence, 1999; The Bay of Angels, 2001; Making Things Better in UK as The Next Big Thing, 2002; The Rules of Engagement, 2003; Leaving Home, 2005; Strangers, 2009. OTHERS: An Iconography of Cecil Rhodes, 1956. AUTHOR OF INTRODUCTIONS: Troy Chimneys, 1985; The Island of Desire, 1985; Summer in the Country, 1985; Living on Yesterday, 1986; The House of Mirth, 1987; (and ed.) The Stories of Edith Wharton, 1988; (and ed.) The Collected Stories of Edith Wharton, 1998; Eustace and Hilda: A Trilogy, 2001. TRANSLATOR: W. George, Utrillo, 1960; J.P. Crespelle, The Fauves, 1962; M. Gauthier, Gauguin, 1963. Contributor to periodicals. **Address:** 68 Elm Park Gardens, London, GL SW10 9PB, England.

BROOKS, Andrée (Nicole) Aelion. American/British (born England), b. 1937. **Genres:** Psychology, Writing/Journalism, History, Politics/Government, Biography, Young Adult Fiction, Adult Non-fiction. **Career:** Hampstead News, reporter, 1954-58; Ladies Home Journal, editorial staff, 1957-58; Photoplay, story editor, 1958-60; freelance journalist, 1960-; Australian Broadcasting Co., correspondent, 1961-68; Hertsmere Council, conservative representative from Elstree, 1973-74; New York Times, columnist, regular contributor, 1977-95; Fairfield University, adjunct professor of journalism, 1983-87; Yale University, associate fellow, 1989-, Women's Campaign School, founder. **Publications:** NON-FICTION: Children of Fast-Track Parents: Raising Self-Sufficient and Confident Children in an Achievement-Oriented World, 1989; The Woman Who Defied Kings: The Life and Times of Doña Gracia Nasi-A Jewish Leader during the Renaissance, 2002; Russian Dance: A True Story of Intrigue and Passion in Stalinist Moscow, 2004. Contributor to periodicals. **Address:** c/o Carolyn French, Fifi Oscard Agency, 110 W 40th St., New York, NY 10018, U.S.A. **Online address:** andreebrooks@hotmail.com

BROOKS, Arthur C. American (born United States), b. 1964. **Genres:** Social Sciences, Politics/Government, Business/Trade/Industry, Economics, Law. **Career:** City Orchestra of Barcelona, French hornist, 1983-92; Lynn University, Harid Conservatory of Music, professor of French horn, 1992-95; RAND Corp., doctoral fellow, 1996-98, consultant, 1998-2008; Georgia State University, assistant professor of public administration and economics, 1998-2000; Syracuse University, Maxwell School of Citizenship and Public Affairs, Center for Policy Research, senior research associate, 2001-03, associate professor of public administration, 2001-05, professor, 2006-08, Louis A. Bantle professor of business and government policy, 2007-09, Nonprofit Studies Program, director, 2003-07, Alan K. Campbell Public Affairs Institute, senior research associate, 2003-08, Whitman School of Management, Louis A. Bantle professor of business and government policy, 2007-09; American Enterprise Institute, president, 2009-; William E. Smith Institute for Association Research, research director. Writer. **Publications:** Economic Strategies for Orchestras, 1997; (co-author) The Performing Arts in a New Era, 2001; (ed.) Gifts of Time and Money: The Role of Charity in America's Communities, 2005; (co-author) Gifts of the Muse: Reframing the Debate about the Benefits of the Arts, 2005; (co-author) A Portrait of the Visual Arts: Meeting the Challenges of a New Era, 2005; Who Really Cares: The Surprising Truth about Compassionate Conservatism: America's Charity Divide-Who Gives, Who Doesn't, and Why It Matters, 2006; Gross National Happiness: Why Happiness Matters for America-and How We can Get More of It, 2008; Social Entrepreneurship: A Modern Approach to Social Value Creation, 2009; The Virtue of Vice: Why Bad Things Are Good for Us, 2009; The Battle: How The Fight Between Free Enterprise and Big Government Will Shape America's Future, 2010; (with P. Wehner) Wealth and Justice: The Morality of Democratic Capitalism, 2011. **Address:** American Enterprise Institute, 1150 17th St. NW, Washington, DC 20036, U.S.A. **Online address:** abrooks@aei.org

BROOKS, Betty. American (born United States), b. 1936. **Genres:** Romance/Historical, Young Adult Fiction, Reference, Novels. **Career:** Writer. **Publications:** HISTORICAL NOVELS: Savage Flame, 1987; Passion's Angel, 1987; Passion's Siren, 1988; Apache Sunset, 1988; Warrior's Embrace, 1989; Wild Texas Magnolia, 1990; Apache Captive, 1990; Comanche Embrace, 1991; Heart of the Mountains, 1991; Comanche Passion, 1992; Love's Endless Flame, 1992; Beloved Viking, 1994; Viking Mistress, 1994; Warrior's Destiny, 1995; Jade, 1997; Comanche Sunset, 1998; Sweet Words of Love, 1998; A Place in My Heart, 1999; Mail Order Love, 1999; The Wayward Heart, 1999; Texas Treasure, 2000. **Address:** PO Box 1504, Mineral Wells, TX 76068, U.S.A. **Online address:** lovescenes1@yahoo.com

BROOKS, Bill. American (born United States), b. 1943?. **Genres:** Mystery/Crime/Suspense, Animals/Pets. **Career:** Author. **Publications:** The Badmen, 1992; Buscadero, 1993; Moon's Blood, 1994; Old Times, 1995; The Last Law There Was, 1995; Deadwood, 1997; Dust On The Wind, 1998; Leaving Cheyenne, 1999; Return to No Man's Land, 2000; The Stone Garden: The Epic Life of Billy the Kid, 2001; Pretty Boy, 2003; Law for Hire: Protecting Hickok, 2003; Law for Hire: Defending Cody, 2003; Bonnie and Clyde: A Love Story, 2004; Law for Hire: Saving Masterson, 2004; Dakota Lawman. Killing Mr. Sunday, 2005; Dakota Lawman: Last Stand at Sweet Sorrow, 2005; Dakota Lawman: The Big Gundown, 2005; Rides a Stranger, 2007; A Bullet for Billy, 2007; Horses, 2008; The Messenger: A Western Story, 2009; Blood Storm: A John Henry Cole Story, 2012. **Address:** c/o Author Mail, Tor/Forge, 175 5th Ave., New York, NY 10010-7703, U.S.A.

BROOKS, Brooke. *See* **BROOKS-GUNN, Jeanne.**

BROOKS, Bruce (Delos). American (born United States), b. 1950. **Genres:** Novels, Natural History, Young Adult Fiction, Young Adult Non-fiction, Essays, Picture/Board Books, Social Commentary, Sports/Fitness, Sports/Fitness. **Career:** Newspaper reporter, newsletter editor, lecturer and writer. **Publications:** INTRODUCTION: World Series, 1989; Keystone Kids, 1990; Rookie of the Year, 2006; Kid from Tomkinsville, 2006. FICTION: Pilgrims in the Zoo and Other Stories, 1960; The Moves Make the Man, 1984; Midnight Hour Encores, 1986; No Kidding, 1989; Everywhere, 1990; What Hearts, 1992; Asylum for Nightface, 1996; Each a Piece, 1998; Vanishing, 1999; Throwing Smoke, 2000; All That Remains, 2001; Dolores: Seven Stories about Her, 2002. WOLFBAY WINGS SERIES: Woodsie, 1997; Zip, 1997; Cody, 1997; Boot, 1998; Prince, 1998; Shark, 1998; Billy, 1998; Dooby, 1998; Reed, 1998; Subtle, 1999; Barry, 1999; Woodsie, Again, 1999. NONFICTION: On the Wing: The Life of Birds: From Feathers to Flight, 1989; Predator!, 1991; Nature by Design, 1991; Making Sense: Animal Perception and Communication, 1993; (with G. Rivers) Those Who Love the Game: Glenn Doc Rivers on Life in the NBA and Elsewhere, 1993; NBA by the Numbers, 1997. ESSAYS: Boys will Be, 1993; (ed.) The Red Wasteland: A Personal Selection of Writings about Nature for Young Readers, 1998. Contributor to books and periodicals. **Address:** HarperCollins Children's Books, 1350 Ave. of the Americas, New York, NY 10019-4702, U.S.A.

BROOKS, David. American (born United States), b. 1961. **Genres:** Novels, Sciences. **Career:** City News Bureau, police reporter, 1980-; Wall Street Journal, book review editor, movie critic, foreign correspondent and op-ed editor, 1986-95; Weekly Standard, senior editor, 1995-2003; New York Times, op-ed columnist, 2003-; Newsweek, contributing editor; Atlantic Monthly, contributing editor; National Public Radio, commentator; Public Broadcasting Service, NewsHour, commentator; Duke University, Terry Sanford Institute of Public Policy, visiting professor of public policy. **Publications:** (Ed. and intro.) Backward and Upward: The New Conservative Writing, 1996; Bobos in Paradise: The New Upper Class and How They Got There, 2000; On Paradise Drive: How We Live Now (and Always Have) in the Future Tense, 2004; The Social Animal: The Hidden Sources of Love, Character, and Achievement, 2011; The Paradise Suite: Bobos in Paradise and On Paradise Drive, 2011. Contributor to periodicals. **Address:** New York Times Company, 620 8th Ave., New York, NY 10018, U.S.A. **Online address:** dabrooks@nytimes.com

BROOKS, David (Gordon). Australian (born Australia), b. 1953. **Genres:** Novels, Novellas/Short Stories, Poetry, Literary Criticism And History, Essays. **Career:** Open Door Press, founder, editor and printer, 1974-77; New Poetry, overseas and associate editor, 1976-82; University of Toronto, fellow, 1976-80, instructor in bibliography and operation of hand press, 1976-78, teaching assistant of twentieth-century literature, 1978-79; Helix Magazine, corresponding editor, 1977-78, general editor, 1983-86; University of New South Wales, lecturer, 1981; University of Western Australia, senior tutor, 1982-85; Australian National University, lecturer in English literature, 1986-91; Phoenix Review, founder and editor, 1987-91; University of Sydney, lecturer in Australian literature, 1991-, senior lecturer in Australian literature, Department of English, associate professor 2005-; Southerly, co-editor, 1999-. **Publications:** POETRY: Five Poems, 1981; The Cold Front, 1983; Walking to Point Clear: Poems, 1983-2002, 2005; Urban Elegies, 2007; The Balcony, 2008. STORIES: The Book of Sei and Other Stories, 1986, rev. 1988; Sheep and the Diva, 1990; Black Sea, 1997. OTHERS: The Necessary Jungle: Literature and Excess (essays), 1990; The House of Balthus (novel), 1995; De/Scription (art criticism), 2001; The Fern Tattoo: A Novel, 2007; The Umbrella Club, 2009. EDITOR: New South: Australian Poetry of the Late 1970s, 1980; (with B. Walker) Poetry and Gender: Statements and Essays in Australian Women's Poetry and Poetics, 1989; (and intro.) Selected Poems, 1991; (and intro.) Suddenly Evening: Selected Poems of R.F. Brissenden, 1991; Selected Poetry and Prose, 2000; The Double Looking Glass: New and Classic Essays on the Poetry of A.D. Hope, 2000; (with B. Kiernan) Running Wild, 2004. Works appears in anthologies. Contributor to periodicals. **Address:** Department of English, University of Sydney, A20 John Woolley Bldg., Sydney, NW 2006, Australia. **Online address:** david.brooks@sydney.edu.au

BROOKS, Edwin. Australian/Welsh (born Wales), b. 1929. **Genres:** Geography, Urban Studies, History. **Career:** University of Liverpool, lecturer, 1954-66, 1970-72, senior lecturer in geography, 1972-77, dean of college studies, 1975-77; Wagga Wagga, N.S.W., Birkenhead, councilor, 1958-67; Bebington, Labour M.P., 1966-70; Charles Sturt University (formerly Riverina-Murray Institute of Higher Education), Riverina College of Advanced Education, dean of business and liberal studies, 1977, dean of commerce, 1982-88, deputy principal, 1988-89, dean emeritus; England Government, member of parliament. Writer. **Publications:** (Co-author) Labour and Israel, 1968; This Crowded Kingdom: An Essay on Population Pressure in Great Britain., 1973; (ed.) Tribes of the Amazon Basin in Brazil, 1973. **Address:** Inchnadamph, Gregadoo Rd., Wagga Wagga, NW 2650, Australia.

BROOKS, Erik. American (born United States), b. 1972?. **Genres:** Children's Fiction, Illustrations. **Career:** Carleton College, cross-country and track coach. Writer and illustrator. **Publications:** SELF-ILLUSTRATED: The Practically Perfect Pajamas, 2000; Polar Opposites, 2010. OTHERS: Octavius Bloom and the House of Doom, 2003; Slow Days, Fast Friends, 2005; Slow Days for Howard, 2005. Illustrator of books by others. **Address:** 18 Aspen Ln., Wolf Creek, PO Box 731, Winthrop, WA 98862, U.S.A. **Online address:** brooks@methownet.com

BROOKS, Fairleigh. American (born United States), b. 1953. **Genres:** Novels, Young Adult Fiction, Air/Space Topics, Humor/Satire, Cultural/Ethnic Topics, Film. **Career:** Writer. **Publications:** Notes of a Would-Be Astronaut, 2002; Lady Chatterley's Pool Boy, 2012. **Address:** 7811 Circle Crest Rd., Louisville, KY 40241, U.S.A. **Online address:** fairbrooks@att.net

BROOKS, George E. (George Edward Brooks). American (born United States), b. 1933. **Genres:** History, Social Sciences, Anthropology/Ethnology, Business/Trade/Industry, Economics, Natural History. **Career:** Boston University, instructor in English; Indiana University, assistant professor, 1962-68, associate professor, 1968-75, professor of history, 1975-2006, professor emeritus; International Journal of African Historical Studies, editorial advisory board, 1968-97; Liberian Studies Journal, staff, 1968-77. **Publications:** (Ed. with N.R. Bennett) New England Merchants in Africa: A History through Documents, 1802-1865, 1965; Yankee Traders, Old Coasters and Africa Middlemen: A History of American Legitimate Trade with West Africa in the Nineteenth Century, 1970; The Kru Mariner in the Nineteenth Century: An Historical Compendium, 1972; Themes in African and World History, 1973; Luso-African Commerce And Settlement in the Gambia and Guinea-Bissau Region, 1980; Western Africa to c. 1860 A.D.: A Provisional Historical Schema Based on Climate Periods, 1985; African Studies Scholarship and Teaching In India, Japan, South Korea and the People's Republic of China, 1985; Landlords and Strangers: Ecology, Society and Trade in Western Africa, 1000-1630, 1993; Eurafricans in Western Africa: Commerce Social Status, Gender and Religious Observance from the Sixteenth to the Eighteenth Century, 2003; Western Africa and Cabo Verde, 1790s-1830s; Symbiosis of Slave and Legitimate Trades, 2010. **Address:** 1615 E University St., Bloomington, IN 47401, U.S.A. **Online address:** brooksg@indiana.edu

BROOKS, George Edward. *See* **BROOKS, George E.**

BROOKS, James F. American (born United States), b. 1955. **Genres:** Archaeology/Antiquities, History. **Career:** School for Advanced Research, president and chief executive officer, 2005-, School for Advanced Research Press, editor; University of California-Santa Barbara, professor of history; University of Maryland, faculty; University of California-Berkeley, faculty. Ethnohistorian. **Publications:** (With S. Elliott) The Timber Frame Planning Book, 1978; (ed.) Confounding the Color Line: The Indian-Black Experience in North America, 2002; Captives & Cousins: Slavery, Kinship, and Community in the Southwest Borderlands, 2002; (ed. with M.A. Irwin) Women and Gender in the American West, 2004; Mesa of Sorrows: Archaeology, Prophecy, and the Ghosts of Awat'ovi Pueblo, 2007; (ed. with C.R.N. DeCorse and J. Walton) Small Worlds: Method, Meaning, and Narrative in Microhistory, 2008. **Address:** School for Advanced Research, PO Box 2188, Santa Fe, NM 87504-2188, U.S.A.

BROOKS, Joanna. American (born United States), b. 1971. **Genres:** Area Studies, Language/Linguistics. **Career:** University of Texas-Austin, faculty; San Diego State University, associate professor. Writer. **Publications:** (Ed. and intro. with J. Saillant) "Face Zion Forward": First Writers of the Black Atlantic, 1785-1798, 2002; American Lazarus: Religion and the Rise of African-American and Native American Literatures, 2003; (ed.) The Life of Olaudah Equiano: The Interesting Narrative of the Life of Olaudah Equiano, or Gustavus Vassa, the African, 2004; (ed.) The Collected Writings of Samson Occom, Mohegan: Leadership and Literature in Eighteenth-Century Native America, 2006; (ed. with L.L. Moore and C. Wigginton) Transatlantic Feminisms in the Age of Revolutions, 2011. **Address:** Department of English & Comparative Literature, San Diego State University, 5500 Campanile Dr., San Diego, CA 92182-6020, U.S.A. **Online address:** jmbrooks@mail.sdsu.edu

BROOKS, Karl Boyd. American (born United States), b. 1956. **Genres:** Law, Social Sciences. **Career:** Boise Cascade Corp., associate general counsel, 1983-90; Idaho State Senator, 1986-92; Holland & Hart, attorney, 1990-93; Idaho Conservation League, executive and legislative director, 1993-96; University of Kansas, associate professor, 2000-06, Environmental Studies Program, director, 2003-04. Writer, lawyer and historian. **Publications:** Public Power, Private Dams: The Hells Canyon High Dam Controversy, 2006; Before Earth Day: The Origins of American Environmental Law, 1945-1970, 2009. Contributor of articles to books, periodicals and journals. **Address:** Department of History, University of Kansas, 3001 Wescoe Hall, 1445 Jayhawk Blvd., Lawrence, KS 66045-7590, U.S.A. **Online address:** kbrooks@ku.edu

BROOKS, Kevin M. British (born England), b. 1959. **Genres:** Young Adult Fiction, Novels. **Career:** Writer and musician. **Publications:** Martyn Pig, 2002; Lucas, 2002; Kissing the Rain, 2004; Bloodline, 2004; (with C. Forde) I See You, Baby..., 2005; Candy, 2005; The Road of the Dead, 2006; Being, 2007; Black Rabbit Summer, 2008; Killing God, 2009; iBoy, 2010; Summary of All, 2010; A Dance of Ghosts, 2011; Naked, 2011. JOHNNY DELGADO SERIES: Like Father, Like Son, 2006; Private Detective, 2006. **Address:** c/o Author Mail, Scholastic Inc., 557 Broadway, New York, NY 10012, U.S.A. **Online address:** fairbrooks@att.net

BROOKS, Martha. Canadian (born Canada), b. 1944. **Genres:** Children's Fiction, Novellas/Short Stories, Human Relations/Parenting. **Career:** Writer, 1972-. Creative writing teacher and lyricist. **Publications:** A Hill for Looking, 1982; Paradise Cafe and Other Stories, 1990; Two Moons in August, 1991; Traveling on into the Light, 1994; (with M. Hunter) I Met a Bully on the Hill, 1995; Bone Dance, 1997; Being with Henry, 1999; True Confessions of a Heartless Girl, 2002; Mistik Lake, 2007; Queen of Hearts, 2010. **Address:** 58-361 Westwood Dr., Winnipeg, MB R3K 1G4, Canada. **Online address:** bbm@mts.net

BROOKS, Mary R. Canadian (born Canada) **Genres:** Transportation. **Career:** Dalhousie University, faculty, 1979-, Centre for International Trade and Transportation, director, 1993-2001, School of Business Administration, professor, William A. Black chair of commerce; Canadian Journal of Administrative Sciences, editor, 2003-05. **Publications:** Fleet Development and the Control of Shipping in Southeast Asia, 1985; (ed.) Seafarers in the ASEAN Region, 1989; (with H.M. Kindred) Multimodal Transport Rules, 1997; Sea Change in Liner Shipping: Regulation and Managerial Decision-Making in a Global Industry, 2000; (ed. with K. Button and P. Nijkamp) Maritime Transport, 2002; North American Freight Transportation: The Road to Security and Prosperity, 2008. Contributor of articles to magazines. **Address:** School of Business Administration, Dalhousie University, Rm. 5118, 6100 University Ave., Halifax, NS B3H 1W7, Canada. **Online address:** m.brooks@dal.ca

BROOKS, Michael. (Michael Edward Brooks). American (born United States), b. 1970. **Genres:** Novels, Mystery/Crime/Suspense. **Career:** New Scientist Magazine, senior features editor, through 2006, consultant, 2006-. **Publications:** (ed.) Quantum Computing and Communications, 1999; Entanglement (novel), 2007; 13 Things That Don't Make Sense: The Most Baffling Scientific Mysteries of Our Time, 2008. Contributor to periodicals. **Address:** U.S.A. **Online address:** info@michaelbrooks.org

BROOKS, Michael Edward. *See* **BROOKS, Michael.**

BROOKS, Peter Newman. British (born England), b. 1931. **Genres:** History, Theology/Religion, Biography, Essays, Autobiography/Memoirs. **Career:** Cambridge University, lecturer in divinity, professor of reformation studies, 1970-98, Downing College, fellow, 1970-82, proctor of the university, 1977-78, dean, Robinson College, fellow, 1983-98, fellow emeritus, 1998-, dean; Cranmer Theological House, professor, through 1999, emeritus professor of reformation studies, 1999-2002, director of graduate studies, 1999-2002. Writer. **Publications:** Thomas Cranmer's Doctrine of the Eucharist: An Essay in Historical Development, 1965, 2nd ed., 1992; Cranmer in Context, 1989; Hymns as Homilies, 1997. EDITOR and CONTRIBUTOR: Christian Spirituality: Essays Presented to Gordon Rupp, 1975; Reformation Principle and Practice: Essays Presented to A.G. Dickens, 1980; Seven-Headed Luther: Essays in Commemoration of a Quincentenary, 1483-1983, 1983. Contributor to books. **Address:** Robinson College, Grange Rd., Cambridge, CB CB3 9AN, England.

BROOKS, Rodney (A.). (Rodney Allen Brooks). American/Australian (born Australia), b. 1954. **Genres:** Information Science/Computers. **Career:** Massachusetts Institute of Technology, professor of computer science, 1984-, Artificial Intelligence Laboratory, director, 1997-2007, professor of robotics, Computer Science and Artificial Intelligence Laboratory, director, 2003-07, Fujitsu professor of computer science, Panasonic professor of robotics, now Panasonic professor of robotics emeritus; Heartland Robotics Inc., co-founder, chief technical officer and chairman; iRobot Corp., founder, 1991-2008, chief technical officer. **Publications:** Model-based Computer Vision, 1984; Programming in Common LISP, 1985; Cambrian Intelligence: The Early History of the New AI, 1999; Flesh and Machines: How Robots Will Change Us, 2002; Robot: The Future of Flesh and Machines, 2002. EDITOR: (with P. Maes) Artificial Life IV: Proceedings of the Fourth International Workshop on the Synthesis and Simulation of Living Systems, 1994; (with L. Steels) The Artificial Life Route to Artificial Intelligence Building Embodied, Situated Agents, 1995; (with S. Thrun and H.F. Durrant-Whyte) Robotics Research, 2007. Contributor to periodicals. **Address:** The Stata Ctr., Massachusetts Institute of Technology, Rm. 32-G430, Cambridge, MA 02139, U.S.A. **Online address:** brooks@csail.mit.edu

BROOKS, Rodney Allen. *See* **BROOKS, Rodney (A.).**

BROOKS, Roy L(avon). American (born United States), b. 1950. **Genres:** Law, Politics/Government, Race Relations, Social Sciences. **Career:** Yale Law Journal, senior editor; University of San Diego, Warren Distinguished Professor of Law, 1979-; U.S. District Court, clerk. **Publications:** Winning in Law School: Questions and Answers: Civil Procedure, 1987; Rethinking the American Race Problem, 1990; Civil Procedure: Adaptable to Third Edition of Yeazell Casebook, 1993; (with G.P. Carrasco and G.A. Martin Jr.) Civil Rights Litigation: Cases and Perspectives, 1995, 3rd ed., 2005; Integration or Separation?: A Strategy for Racial Equality, 1996; Critical Procedure, 1998; (ed.) When Sorry Isn't Enough: The Controversy over Apologies and Reparations for Human Injustice, 1999; Structures of Judicial Decision Making from Legal Formalism to Critical Theory, 2002, 2nd ed., 2005; Atonement and Forgiveness: A New Model for Black Reparations, 2004; Legalines: Civil Procedure: Adaptable to 6th Edition of the Yeazell Casebook, 6th ed., 2005; Racial Justice in the Age of Obama, 2009; (with G.P. Carrasco and M. Selmi) Law of Discrimination, 2011. **Address:** School of Law, University of San Diego, 5998 Alcala Pk., San Diego, CA 92110-2492, U.S.A. **Online address:** rbrooks@sandiego.edu

BROOKS, Stephen G. American (born United States), b. 1971?. **Genres:** International Relations/Current Affairs, Economics, Social Sciences. **Career:** Naval Postgraduate School, Department of National Security Affairs, research analyst, 1991-94; University of California Regents fellow, 1992-93; National Science Foundation fellow, 1995-98; Princeton University Woodrow Wilson School, visiting predoctoral fellow, 1998-2000; Yale University, research assistant, 1998, Marion C. Sheridan fellow, 1999-2000; Dartmouth College, instructor, 2000-01, assistant professor of government, 2001-07, associate professor, 2007-; Harvard University, Belfer Center for Science and International Affairs fellow, 2002-03. Writer. **Publications:** Producing Security: Multinational Corporations, Globalization, and the Changing Calculus of Conflict, 2005; (with W.C. Wohlforth) World Out of Balance: International Relations and the Challenge of American Primacy, 2008. Contributor to journals. **Address:** Department of Government, Dartmouth College, 205 Silsby Hall, 6108 Hillcrest Bldg., Hanover, NH 03755, U.S.A. **Online address:** stephen.brooks@dartmouth.edu

BROOKS, Victor. (Victor D. Brooks). American (born United States) **Genres:** History, Social Sciences, Military/Defense/Arms Control. **Career:** Villanova University, Department of Education and Counseling, professor of education. Writer. **Publications:** GREAT CAMPAIGNS SERIES: The Boston Campaign: April 1775-March 1776, 1999; The Fredericksburg Campaign: October 1862-January 1863, 2000; The Normandy Campaign: From D-Day to the Liberation of Paris, 2002. UNTOLD HISTORY OF THE CIVIL WAR SERIES: Civil War Forts, 1999; African Americans in the Civil War, 1999; (with A.A. Nofi) Spies in the Civil War, 1999; Secret Weapons in the Civil War, 2000; Boomers: The Cold-War Generation Grows Up, 2009. MILITARY HISTORY: (with R. Hohwald) How America Fought Its Wars: Military Strategy from the American Revolution to the Civil War, 1999; Honor the Brave: America's Wars and Warriors, 2000; Marye's Heights, Fredericksburg, 2001; Hell Is upon Us: D-Day in the Pacific, June-August 1944, 2005. **Address:** Department of Education & Counseling, Villanova University, 302 St. Augustine Ctr., 800 Lancaster Ave., Villanova, PA 19085, U.S.A. **Online address:** victor.brooks@villanova.edu

BROOKS, Victor D. *See* **BROOKS, Victor.**

BROOKS-GUNN, Jeanne. Also writes as Brooke Gunn, Brooke Brooks, Brooke Brooks. American (born United States), b. 1946. **Genres:** Education, Psychology, Sociology. **Career:** Educational Testing Service, associate research scientist, 1974-77, associate director, 1977-82, research scientist, 1978-83, Adolescent Study Program, director, 1982-2001; University of Pennsylvania, Department of Pediatrics, adjunct faculty, 1975-84, 1985-90; Columbia University, adjunct faculty, 1975-84, College of Physicians and Surgeons, Department of Pediatrics, assistant professor, 1978-85, professor, 2000-, Adolescent Study Program, director, 1982-2001, Teachers College, Virginia and Leonard Marx professor in child development and education, 1991-, National Center for Children and Families, founding director and co-director, 1991-, Graduate School of Arts and Sciences, faculty, 1993-, Institute on Child and Family Policy, founding director and co-director, 1998-; Barnard College, adjunct faculty, 1975-84; Institute for the Study of Exceptional Children, associate director, 1977-82; St. Luke's-Roosevelt Hospital Center, associate director, 1977-82; Center for Research in Human Development, research scientist, 1978-83; Division of Education Policy Research, senior research scientist, 1983-93; Princeton University, Bendheim-Thoman Center for Research on Child Wellbeing, visiting research collaborator, 1997-; Harvard University Multi-disciplinary Training Program in Inequality and Social Policy, national fellow, 1998-2004; Society for Research in Child Development, associate editor, 1999-2009; Harvard University Press, editor, 2001-. Writer. **Publications:** (With W.S. Matthews) He and She: How Children Develop Their Sex-Role Identity, 1979; (with M. Lewis) Social Cognition and the Acquisition of Self, 1979; (with F.F. Furstenberg, Jr. and S.P. Morgan) Adolescent Mothers in Later Life, 1987; (with D.E. Kohen and C. Hertzman) Neighbourhood Influences on Children's School Readiness, 1998. EDITOR: (with A.C. Petersen) Girls at Puberty, 1983; (with G. Baruch) Women in

Midlife, 1984; Time of Maturation and Psychosocial Functioning in Adolescence, 2 vols., 1985; (with A.C. Petersen and R. Lerner) The Encyclopedia of Adolescence, 1991; The Emergence of Depression and Depressive Symptoms during Adolescence, 1991; (with P.L. Chase-Lansdale) Escape from Poverty, 1995; (with G.A. Graber and A.C. Petersen) Transitions through Adolescence, 1996; (with G.J. Duncan) Consequences of Growing up Poor, 1997; (with G.J. Duncan and J.L. Aber) Neighborhood Poverty, 2 vols., 1997; (with M.J. Cox) Conflict and Cohesion in Families, 1999; (with P.R. Britto) Role of Family Literacy Environments in Promoting Young Children's Emerging Literacy Skills, 2001; (with A.S. Fuligni and L.J. Berlin) Early Child Development in the 21st Century, 2003. **Address:** National Center for Children and Families, Columbia University, 525 W 120th St., PO Box 226, New York, NY 10027-6605, U.S.A. **Online address:** brooks-gunn@columbia.edu

BROOM, Neil D. New Zealander (born New Zealand), b. 1945?. **Genres:** Sciences, Theology/Religion. **Career:** Health Research Council of New Zealand, senior research fellow, 1975-; University of Auckland, Department of Chemical and Materials Engineering, associate professor, 1989-2009, professor and head, 2009-. Writer. **Publications:** How Blind Is the Watchmaker?: Theism or Atheism: Should Science Decide?, 1998, 2nd ed. as How Blind Is the Watchmaker?: Nature's Design and the Limits of Naturalistic Science, 2001; Life's X-Factor: The Missing Link in Materialism's Science of Living Things, 2010. Contributor to journals. **Address:** Department of Chemical and Materials Engineering, University of Auckland, Rm. 401.809, 20 Symonds St., Auckland, 1142, New Zealand. **Online address:** nd.broom@auckland.ac.nz

BROOMALL, Robert W(alter). Also writes as Hank Edwards. American (born United States), b. 1946. **Genres:** Westerns/Adventure, Mystery/Crime/Suspense, Romance/Historical, Young Adult Fiction, History. **Career:** Williams & Wilkins, copy editor, publisher, 1968; U.S. Army, Corps of Engineers, civilian budget analyst, 1972-74; U.S. Defense Contracts Supply Agency, property administrator, 1974-75; freelance writer, 1975; Community College of Baltimore County, adjunct faculty, 1995-; Science and Technology Corp., technical writer, 2010-; Harford Community College, faculty; Johns Hopkins University, faculty; Anne Arundel Community College, faculty; Howard Community College, faculty. **Publications:** The Bank Robber, 1985; Dead Man's Canyon, 1986; Dead Man's Crossing, 1987; Dead Man's Town, 1988; Texas Kingdoms, 1989; (as Hank Edwards) The Judge, 1990; Hank Edwards-Texas Feud, 1991; (as Hank Edwards) War Clouds, 1991; (as Hank Edwards) Steel Justice, 1991; Dale Colter-the Scalphunters, 1992; Pardise Mountain, 1992; Desert Pursuit, 1992; California Kingdoms, 1992; K Company, 1992; The Lawmen, 1993; Montana Showdown, 1993; Conroy's First Command, 1994; (as Hank Edwards) Lady Outlaw, 1994; (as Hank Edwards) Gray Warrior, 1995; (as Hank Edwards) Ride for Rimfire, 1995; (as Hank Edwards) Apache Sundown, 1996; Murder in the Seventh Cavalry, 2001; (as Hank Edwards) Fluffers Inc., 2002; The Dispatch Rider, forthcoming. **Address:** Ethan Ellenberg, 548 Broadway 5C, New York, NY 10012, U.S.A. **Online address:** robertbroomall@gmail.com

BROOME, Errol. Australian (born Australia), b. 1937. **Genres:** Children's Fiction, Children's Non-fiction, Animals/Pets. **Career:** The West Australian, journalist, 1958-60; Herald-Sun Television, journalist, 1961; writer, 1978-. **Publications:** Wrinkles, 1978; Bird Boy, 1986; Town and Country Ducks, 1986; The Smallest Koala, 1987; A Year of Pink Pieces, 1988; Have a Go!, 1988; Dear Mr. Sprouts, 1991; Garry Keeble's Kitchen: How One Boy Left Home and Survived with 28 Recipes That Anyone Can Cook and Everyone Will Eat, 1992; Tangles, 1994; Rockhopper, 1995; Nightwatch, 1995; Splashback: A Great Greasy Journey, 1996; Fly with Me, 1996; Pets (series of eight), 1996; What a Goat!, 1997; Quicksilver, 1997; Tough Luck, 1998; Magnus Maybe, 1998; Away with the Birds, 2000; Cry of the Karri, 2001; Gracie and the Emperor, 2003; The Judas Donkey, 2003; Missing Mem, 2004; My Grandad Knew Phar Lap, 2006; Song of the Dove, 2011. **Address:** PO Box 9241, Brighton, VI 3186, Australia. **Online address:** errolbroome@bigpond.com

BROPHY, Grace. American (born United States), b. 1941. **Genres:** Criminology/True Crime, Young Adult Fiction, Mystery/Crime/Suspense. **Career:** City University of New York, Queens College, faculty, Hunter College, faculty; Bell Labs, systems engineer; ATT, systems engineer; Verizon, systems engineer. Writer. **Publications:** MYSTERY NOVEL: The Last Enemy, 2007; A Deadly Paradise, 2008; The Absence of Death, 2012. **Address:** Soho Press Inc., 853 Broadway, New York, NY 10003, U.S.A. **Online address:** brophygrace@yahoo.com

BROPHY, James M. American (born United States), b. 1959. **Genres:** Politics/Government, History, Cultural/Ethnic Topics. **Career:** University of Delaware, associate professor of modern European history. Writer and historian. **Publications:** (Co-ed. and contrib.) Perspectives from the Past: Primary Sources in Western Civilizations, 2 vols., 1998, 4th ed., 2009; Capitalism, Politics, and Railroads in Prussia, 1830-1870, 1998; Popular Culture and the Public Sphere in the Rhineland, 1800-1850, 2007. Contributor to books and periodicals. **Address:** Department of History, University of Delaware, 236 John Munroe Hall, Newark, DE 19716, U.S.A. **Online address:** jbrophy@udel.edu

BROPHY, Sarah. Canadian (born Canada), b. 1972?. **Genres:** Literary Criticism And History, Romance/Historical, Young Adult Fiction. **Career:** University of California, postdoctoral fellow, 2001-02; McMaster University, Department of English and Cultural Studies, faculty, 2002, associate professor of English and cultural studies, 2006-. Writer. **Publications:** Witnessing AIDS: Writing, Testimony, and the Work of Mourning, 2004; Midnight Eyes, 2007; Dark Heart, 2008. Contributor to periodicals. **Address:** Department of English & Cultural Studies, McMaster University, Rm. 331, Chester New Hall, 1280 Main St. W, Hamilton, ON L8S 4L8, Canada. **Online address:** brophys@mcmaster.ca

BROSNAHAN, L(eonard) F(rancis). Fijian/New Zealander (born New Zealand), b. 1922. **Genres:** Language/Linguistics. **Career:** University of Ibadan, lecturer, 1951-59, senior lecturer in English, 1959-62; Victoria University of Wellington, professor of English language, 1963-69; University of South Pacific, professor, 1969-82, deputy vice-chancellor, 1972-79, vice-chancellor, 1982-83, professor emeritus, 2004-. Writer. **Publications:** Some Old English Sound Changes, 1953; Genes and Phonemes, 1957; The Sounds of Language, 1961; (with J.W. Spencer) Language and Society: Four Talks Given for the Nigerian Broadcasting Corporation in February 1962, 1962; The English Language in the World, 1963; (with B. Malmberg) Introduction to Phonetics, 1970; Grammar Usage and the Teacher, 1973. **Address:** The University of the South Pacific, Laucala Campus, Suva, 1168, Fiji.

BROSS, Donald G. American (born United States), b. 1932. **Genres:** Novels, Adult Non-fiction, Essays. **Career:** Southwestern Bell Telephone, line worker, telephone installer and supervisor, 1951-84. Writer. **Publications:** Surrogate Son (novel), 1992; Farewell Ma Bell: Look Who's Dancing on the Old Girl's Grave, 1996; (with J.D. Taylor) Mountain Madness: A Deadly Night, A Bloody Secret, A True Story, 1996 as Murder on Shadow Mountain, 2008. **Address:** Japanese American National Museum, 369 E 1st St., Los Angeles, CA 90012, U.S.A. **Online address:** donbross@donbross.com

BROTHERS, Joyce (Diane). American (born United States), b. 1927. **Genres:** Psychology, Sciences. **Career:** Hunter College (now Hunter College of the City University of New York), teaching fellow, 1948-50, instructor, 1950-52; writer, 1952-. **Publications:** An Investigation of Avoidance, Anxiety, and Escape Behaviour in Human Subjects as Measured by Action Potentials in Muscle, 1956; (with E.P.F. Eagan) 10 Days to a Successful Memory, 1957, rev. ed. as Ten Days to a Successful Memory, 1984; Woman, 1961; The Brothers System for Liberated Love and Marriage, 1972; Better Than Ever, 1975; How to Get Whatever You Want Out of Life, 1978; What Every Woman Should Know about Men, 1981; What Every Woman Ought to Know about Love and Marriage, 1984; The Successful Woman: How You Can Have a Career, a Husband, and a Family And Not Feel Guilty about It, 1988; Widowed, 1990; Positive Plus: The Practical Plan for Liking Yourself Better, 1994. Contributor to periodicals. **Address:** King Features Syndicate Inc., 300 W 57th St., 15th Fl., New York, NY 10019, U.S.A.

BROTHERSTON, Gordon. (James Gordon Brotherston). British (born England), b. 1939. **Genres:** Literary Criticism And History, Translations, Anthropology/Ethnology. **Career:** University of London, King's College, Department of Spanish, assistant lecturer, 1964-65; National Extension College, tutor and advisor, 1964-68; Pergamon Press, Latin American Series, editor, 1965-; University of Essex, M.A. Schemes in Theory and Practice of Literary Translation, director, 1960-, Department of Literature, lecturer, 1965-68, senior lecturer, 1968-73, reader, 1973-78, professor, 1978-, chair, 1972-75, School of Comparative Studies, dean, 1976-79, Native American Studies, director, 1979-, Department of Literature, Film and Theater Studies, now professor emeritus; University of Iowa, visiting professor, 1968-69; University of British Columbia, visiting professor, 1975; Stanford Humanities Center, external faculty fellow, 2000-01; University of Manchester, School of Languages, Linguistics and Cultures, honorary professor. **Publications:** Manuel Machado: A Revaluation, 1968; Spanish American Modernista Poets: A Critical Anthology, 1968; (trans. with E. Dorn) Our Word, 1968; (trans. with E. Dorn) Tree Between Two Walls, 1969; Origins and Presence of Latin American Poetry, 1975; The Emergence of the Latin American Novel, 1977; (comp.) Image of the New World, 1979; A Key to the Mesoamerican Reckoning of Time, 1982; Voices of the First America, 1985; Aesop in Mexico, 1987; Book of the Fourth World, 1992; Painted Books of Mexico, 1995; Footprints through Time: Mexican Pictorial Manuscripts, 1997; La Ame2ACUrica indigena en su literature, 1997; (trans. with E. Dorn) The Sun Unwound: Poems from Occupied America, 1999; Feather Crown, 2005. EDITOR: (and intro.) Ariel, 1967; (and intro. with M. Vargas Llosa) Seven Stories from Spanish America, 1968, 1973; (and co-trans. with E. Dorn) Cesar Vallejo: Selected Poems, 1976; (with P. Hulme) Ficciones, 1976. Contributor of articles to periodicals and journals. **Address:** School of Languages, Linguistics & Cultures, University of Manchester, Oxford Rd., Manchester, GM M13 9PL, England. **Online address:** jamesgordon.brotherston@manchester.ac.uk

BROTHERSTON, James Gordon. *See* **BROTHERSTON, Gordon.**

BROTHERTON, Michael Sean. *See* **BROTHERTON, Mike Sean.**

BROTHERTON, Mike Sean. (Michael Sean Brotherton). American (born United States), b. 1968. **Genres:** Novels. **Career:** University of Wyoming, assistant professor, associate professor, 2002-; Lawrence Livermore National Laboratory, postdoctoral fellow, 1996-99; Kitt Peak National Observatory, noao postdoctoral researcher & fuse science team associate, 1999-2002. Writer. **Publications:** Star Dragon (novel), 2003; Spider Star (novel), 2008. Contributor to periodicals. **Address:** Department of Physics & Astronomy, University of Wyoming, Department 3905, Laramie, WY 82071, U.S.A. **Online address:** mbrother@uwyo.edu

BROTTMAN, Mikita. American/British (born England), b. 1966. **Genres:** Film, Intellectual History, Literary Criticism And History. **Career:** Eastern Mediterranean University, assistant professor of English, 1993-95; University of East London, Communication and Education Studies, lecturer, 1995-98; Indiana University, Department of Comparative Literature, visiting assistant professor, 1998-2000, visiting professor; Shippensburg University, Department of English, visiting assistant professor, 2000-01; Maryland Institute College of Art, Department of Humanistic Studies, professor, 2001-08, 2010-; Pacifica Graduate Institute, M.A. Program in Engaged Humanities, chair, 2008-10. **Publications:** Offensive Films, 1997; Meat Is Murder!, 1998; Hollywood Hex, 1999; Funny Peculiar: Gershon Legman and the Psychopathology of Humor, 2004; High Theory, Low Culture, 2005; The Solitary Vice: Against Reading, 2009; Phantoms of the Clinic, 2011. EDITOR: Jack Nicholson, Movie Top Ten, 2000; Car Crash Culture, 2002. Contributor to periodicals. **Address:** Maryland Institute College of Art, 1300 W Mount Royal Ave., Ste. 431, Baltimore, MD 21217, U.S.A. **Online address:** mbrottma@mica.edu

BROUGHTON, Philip Delves. American/Bangladeshi (born Bangladesh), b. 1972?. **Genres:** Institutions/Organizations, Education. **Career:** Daily Telegraph, reporter, 1994-2002, New York correspondent, 1998-2002, Paris bureau chief, 2002-04; Financial Times Ltd., columnist. **Publications:** Ahead of the Curve: Two Years at Harvard Business School in UK as What They Teach You at Harvard Business School: My Two Years Inside the Cauldron of Capitalism, 2008; The Art of the Sale: Learning from the Masters About the Business of Life, 2012. **Address:** Penguin Group Inc., 375 Hudson St., New York, NY 10014-3657, U.S.A. **Online address:** philip@philipdelvesbroughton.com

BROUGHTON, R(obert) Peter. Canadian (born Canada), b. 1940. **Genres:** History, Astronomy. **Career:** Toronto Board of Education, teacher, 1964-97; Royal Astronomical Society of Canada, president. Writer. **Publications:** Looking Up: A History of the Royal Astronomical Society of Canada, 1994. Contributor to periodicals. **Address:** 31 Killdeer Cres., Toronto, ON M4G 2W7, Canada. **Online address:** peterb@torfree.net

BROUGHTON, T. Alan. American (born United States), b. 1936. **Genres:** Novels, Novellas/Short Stories, Poetry, Adult Non-fiction, Young Adult Fiction. **Career:** University of Washington, teacher, 1962-64; Sweet Briar College, instructor in English, 1964-66; University of Vermont, assistant professor, 1966-70, associate professor, 1970-74, professor of English, 1974-96, department chair, 1994-; Corse professor of English language and literature, 1996-2001, emeritus, 2001-. Writer. **Publications:** POETRY: The Skin and All, 1972; In the Face of Descent, 1975; Adam's Dream, 1975; The Man on the Moon, 1979; Far from Home, 1979; The Others We Are, 1979; Dreams Before Sleep, 1982; Preparing to be Happy, 1988; In the Country of Elegies, 1995; The Origin of Green, 2001; A World Remembered, 2010. NOVELS: A Family Gathering, 1977; Winter Journey, 1980; The Horsemaster, 1981; Hob's Daughter, 1984. SHORT STORIES: The Jesse Tree, 1988; Suicidal Tendencies, 2003. Works appear in anthologies. **Address:** 124 Spruce St., Burlington, VT 05401, U.S.A. **Online address:** t.broughton@uvm.edu

BROUMAS, Olga. Greek (born Greece), b. 1949. **Genres:** Poetry, Translations, Women's Studies And Issues, Gay And Lesbian Issues. **Career:** University of Oregon, instructor in English and women's studies, 1972-76; University of Idaho, visiting associate professor of English, 1978; Goddard College, poet-in-residence, 1979-81; Freehand (community of women writers and photographers), founder and associate faculty member, 1982-87; Boston University, visiting associate professor, 1988-90; Brandeis University, poet-in-residence, 1990-, director in creative writing, 1992-, professor of English. Writer. **Publications:** POETRY: Restlessness, 1967; Caritas, 1976; Beginning with O, 1977; From Caritas: Poem 3, 1978; Soie Sauvage, 1979; Pastoral Jazz, 1983; (with J. Miller) Black Holes, Black Stockings, 1985; Perpetua, 1989; (with T. Begley) Sappho's Gymnasium, 1994; Helen Groves, 1994; Ithaca: Little Summer in Winter, 1996; Rave: Poems, 1975-1999, 1999. TRANSLATIONS: What I Love: Selected Translations of Odysseas Elytis, 1986; The Little Mariner, 1988; (with T. Begley) Open Papers: Selected Essays of Odysseas Elytis, 1995; Eros, Eros, Eros: Odysseas Elytis: Poems, Selected and Last, 1998. Contributor to journals. **Address:** Department of English, Brandeis University, MS 023, 415 South St., Waltham, MA 02453-2728, U.S.A. **Online address:** broumas@brandeis.edu

BROUSSARD, Meredith. American (born United States), b. 1974?. **Genres:** Adult Non-fiction, Humor/Satire, Popular Culture, Women's Studies And Issues, Human Relations/Parenting, Popular Culture. **Career:** Speaking Tree, technical director, 1996; Cross Connect, contributing editor; University of Pennsylvania, faculty. Freelance journalist. **Publications:** (Ed.) The Dictionary of Failed Relationships: 26 Tales of Love Gone Wrong, 2003; (ed.) The Encyclopedia of Exes: 26 Stories by Men of Love Gone Wrong, 2005. Contributor to periodicals. **Address:** Rosalie Siegel International Literary Agent Inc., 1 Abey Dr., Pennington, NJ 08534-2902, U.S.A. **Online address:** mer@failedrelationships.com

BROUSSEAU, Francine. Canadian (born Canada), b. 1951. **Genres:** History. **Career:** PLURAM Inc., project officer, 1975-81; Centre psycho pédagogique de Quebéc Inc., teacher of French and geography, 1976-77; Parks Canada, historian, 1977-78, architectural analyst, 1982; National Assembly of Quebec, research officer, 1978-81, information officer, 1981; Société du Musée des Grandes Rivières, project director, 1981-83; National Postal Museum-ottawa, curator of works of art, 1984-88; National Postal Museum-Hull, curator of exhibitions, 1988-90, exhibition manager, director; Canadian Museum of Civilization Corp., Canadian Postal Museum, director, 1990-, director of exhibitions, 2000-, vice president development, 2006-, curator; International Association of Transport and Communications Museums, vice president, 1998-2004; Canadian Museums Association, president, 2000-02. Writer. **Publications:** Historique du nouvel emplacement du Musée national de l'homme à Hull, 1984; Architecture in Canadian illustrated news and L'Opinion publique: inventory of references, 1984; Jean Paul Lemieux: His Canada, 1998; (ed.) Special Delivery: Canada's Postal Heritage, 2001. Contributor to periodicals. **Address:** Canadian Postal Museum, Canadian Museum of Civilization, 100 Laurier St., PO Box 3100, Sta. B, Gatineau, QC K1A 0M8, Canada. **Online address:** francine_brousseau@sympatico.ca

BROUWER, Sigmund. American/Canadian (born Canada), b. 1959?. **Genres:** Children's Fiction, Young Adult Fiction, Children's Non-fiction, Young Adult Non-fiction. **Career:** National Racquetball Magazine, editor; The Young Writer's Institute, co-founder and lecturer, 1993-. Writer. **Publications:** NOVELS: Morning Star, 1994; Moon Basket, 1994; Double Helix, 1995; Magnus, 1995; Sun Dance, 1995; Thunder Voice, 1995; Blood Ties, 1996; Blazer Drive, 1996; Chief Honor, 1997; Knights Honor, 1997; Pharaoh's Tomb, 1997; Pirate's Cross, 1997; Outlaw's Gold, 1997; Soldier's Aim, 1997; Galilee Man, 1998; Dance of Darkness, 1997; The Canary List: A Novel, 2011. JUVENILE CHRISTIAN NOVELS ACCIDENTAL DETECTIVE SERIES: Indians in the Deep Woods: A Ricky and Joel Adventure, 1988; The Mystery Tribe of Camp Blackeagle, 1990; Phantom Outlaw at Wolf Creek, 1990; The Disappearing Jewel of Madagascar, 1990; Lost beneath Manhattan,

1990; Race for the Park Street Treasure, 1991; Creature of the Mists, 1991; The Missing Map of Pirate's Haven, 1991; The Downtown Desperadoes, 1991; Madness at Moonshiner's Bay, 1992; Sunrise at the Mayan Temple, 1992; Short Cuts, 1993; Terror on Kamikaze Run, 1994. LIGHTNING ON ICE SERIES: Rebel Glory, 1995; All-Star Pride, 1995; Thunderbird Spirit, 1996; Winter Hawk Star, 1996. WINDS OF LIGHT SERIES: Wings of an Angel, 1992; Barbarians from the Isle, 1992; Legend of Burning Water, 1992; The Forsaken Crusade, 1992; A City of Dreams, 1993; Merlin's Destiny, 1993; The Jester's Quest, 1994. DR. DRABBLE SERIES (with W. Davidson): Dr. Drabble's Astounding Musical Mesmerizer, 1991; Dr. Drabble's Incredible Identical Robot Innovation, 1991; Dr. Drabble's Phenomenal Antigravity Dust Machine, 1991; Dr. Drabble's Remarkable Underwater Breathing Pills, 1991; Dr. Drabble's Spectacular Shrinker-Enlarger, 1994; Dr. Drabble and the Dynamic Duplicator, 1994. NONFICTION: Snowboarding-To the Extreme-Rippin, 1996; Mountain Biking-To the Extreme-Cliff Dive, 1996; Scuba Diving-To the Extreme-Off the Wall, 1996; Sky Diving-To the Extreme-Chute Roll, 1997. OTHER: Carpenter's Cloth, 1997; Weeping Chamber, 1998; Titan Clash, 1998; Tiger Heat, 1998; Scarlet Thunder, 1998; Maverick Mania, 1998; Galilee Man, 1998; Cobra Threat, 1998; Wings of the Dawn: A Novel, 1999; Into His Arms, 1999; Hurricane Power, 1999; Sun Dance, 2000; Silver Moon, 2000; Pony Express Christmas, 2000; Evening Star, 2000; Cyber Quest, 2000; Can the Real Jesus Still be Found?, 2000; Mommy Ant, Eat Your Vegetables, 2001; Little Spider, 2001; Daddy Ant, You Never Listen!, 2001; Annie Ant, Don't Cry!, 2001; Out of the Shadows, 2001; Volcano of Doom, 2002; Unrandom Universe, 2002; Tyrant of the Badlands, 2002; Long Shot, 2002; Leper: Based on the Painting by Ron DiCianni, 2002; Legend of the Gilded Saber, 2002; Disappearing Jewel of Madagascar, 2002; Crown of Thorns: A Nick Barrett Mystery, 2002; Bad Bug Blues, 2002; Tyrone's Story, 2003; Strunk Soup, 2003; Shroud of the Lion, 2003; Mystery Tribe of Camp Blackeagle, 2003; Mystery Pennies, 2003; Madness at Moonshiner's Bay, 2003; Lies of Saints: A Nick Barrett Mystery, 2003; Great Adventures, 2003; Fly Trap, 2003; Creature of the Mists, 2003; Camp Craziness, 2003; (with H. Hanegraaff) Last Disciple, 2004; Terror on Kamikaze Run, 2004; Sunrise at the Mayan Temple, 2004; Race for the Park Street Treasure, 2004; Dear Teacher: I'll Aways Remember You were My Teacher, 2004; Missing Map of Pirate's Haven, 2004; Lost Beneath Manhattan, 2004; Downtown Desperadoes, 2004; (with H. Hanegraaff) Last Sacrifice, 2005; Wired, 2005; Short Cuts, 2005; Phantom Outlaw at Wolf Creek, 2005; Angel and the Sword, 2005; Angel and the Ring, 2005; Angel and the Cross, 2005; Sewer Rats, 2006; All-star Pride, 2006; Fuse of Armageddon, 2007; In Galileo's Footsteps: A Father Explores How Genesis and Science Agree, 2007; Who made the Moon?: A Father Explores How Faith and Science Agree, 2008; Broken Angel: A Novel, 2008; Timberwolf Tracks, 2008; Timberwolf Challenge, 2008; Timberwolf Rivals, 2009; Death Trap, 2009; Final Battle, 2009; Double Cross, 2009; Failure to Protect, 2009; Counterattack, 2009; Ambush, 2009; Flight of Shadows, 2010. MARS DIARIES SERIES: Mission 1, Oxygen Level Zero, 2000, Mission 2, Alien Pursuit, 2000, Mission 3, Time Bomb, 2000; Mission 4, Hammerhead, 2001; Mission 5, Sole survivor, 2001; Mission 6, Moon Racer, 2001; Mission 7, Countdown, 2001; Mission 8, Robot War, 2001; Baby Ant has Stinky Pants, 2001; Mission 9, Manchurian Sector, 2002; Mission 10, Last Stand, 2002. Contributor to periodicals. **Address:** c/o Chariot Victor Publishing, 4050 Lee Vance View, Colorado Springs, CO 80918, U.S.A. **Online address:** feedback@sigmundbrouwer.com

BROWDER, Laura. American (born United States), b. 1963. **Genres:** History. **Career:** Virginia Commonwealth University, professor of English. Writer. **Publications:** Rousing the Nation: Radical Culture in Depression America, 1998; Slippery Characters: Ethnic Impersonators and American Identities, 2000; Her Best Shot: Women and Guns in America, 2006; (ed. and intro.) With the Weathermen: The Personal Journal of a Revolutionary Woman, 2007. **Address:** Department of English, Virginia Commonwealth University, Rm. 413, 900 Park Ave., PO Box 842005, Richmond, VA 23284, U.S.A. **Online address:** laurabrowder@gmail.com

BROWER, Kenneth. American (born United States), b. 1944. **Genres:** Environmental Sciences/Ecology, Natural History, Sciences, Biography, Earth Sciences. **Career:** Sierra Club, editor, 1964-69; Friends of the Earth, editor, 1969-71; freelance writer, 1971-. **Publications:** Earth and the Great Weather: The Brooks Range, 1971; With Their Islands Around Them, 1974; Micronesia: Island Wilderness, 1975; The Starship and the Canoe, 1978; Wake of the Whale, 1979; Micronesia: The Land, the People and the Sea, 1981; A Song for Satawal, 1983; Yosemite, 1990; One Earth, 1990; Realms of the Sea, 1991; American Legacy: Our National Forests, 1997; The Winemaker's Marsh: Four Seasons in a Restored Wetland, 2001; Freeing Keiko: The Journey of a Killer Whale from Free Willy to the Wild, 2005. CO-AUTHOR AND EDITOR: Galapagos: The Flow of Wildness, 1967; Maui: The Last Hawaiian Place, 1970; Cry Crisis, 1974. EDITOR: Navajo Wildlands, 1967; Kauai and the Park Country of Hawaii, 1967; Baja California and the Geography of Hope, 1967; The Primal Alliance, 1971; Guale: The Golden Coast of Georgia, 1974; Primal Alliance: Earth and Ocean, 1974. **Address:** 2379 Humboldt Ave., Oakland, CA 94601, U.S.A.

BROWER, Steven. American (born United States), b. 1952?. **Genres:** Design, Art/Art History, Biography, Autobiography/Memoirs. **Career:** Pushpin Group, associate; Print Magazine, creative director; New York Times, art director; Nation, art director; Kean University, assistant professor, Design Studio, director; School of Visual Arts, design instructor. Writer and graphic designer. **Publications:** (With N. Guthrie) Woody Guthrie: Art Works, 2005; (with R. Landa and R. Gonnella) 2D: Visual Basics for Designers, 2007; Satchmo: The Wonderful World and Art of Louis Armstrong, 2009; Breathless Homicidal Slime Mutants: The Art of the Paperback, 2010. Contributor to books. **Address:** Kean University, 1000 Morris Ave., Union, NJ 07083, U.S.A. **Online address:** sbrower@kean.edu

BROWN, Alan. American (born United States), b. 1950. **Genres:** Literary Criticism And History, Mythology/Folklore, Horror, Mystery/Crime/Suspense. **Career:** Flora High School, teacher, 1974-76; Griffin High School, English teacher, 1976-86; University of West Alabama, faculty, 1986-, professor of composition and Writing Center, Department of Languages and Literature, professor of English, 1996, Writing Center and the Compensatory Writing Program, director. Writer. **Publications:** (Ed.) Dim Roads and Dark Nights: The Collected Folklore of Ruby Pickens Tartt, 1993; (with K. Friday) Mama 'n' 'em: An Oral History of Thomaston, Alabama, 1994; The Face in the Window and Other Alabama Ghostlore, 1996; (ed. with D. Taylor) Gabr'l Blow Sof': Ex-Slave Narratives, 1997; A Literary Tour Guide of New Orleans, 1998; Shadows and Cypress, 2000; Haunted Places in the American South, 2002; Literary Landmarks of Chicago, 2004; Stories form the Haunted South, 2004; Ghost Hunters of the South, 2006; Haunted Georgia: Ghosts and Strange Phenomena of the Peach State, 2008; Haunted Texas: Ghosts and Strange Phenomena of the Lone Star State, 2008; Ghost Hunters of New England, 2008; Haunted Kentucky: Ghosts and Strange Phenomena of the Bluegrass State, 2009; Haunted Tennessee: Ghosts and Strange Phenomena of the Volunteer State, 2009; Haunted South Carolina: Ghosts and Strange Phenomena of the Palmetto State, 2010; Haunted Vicksburg, 2010; Haunted Pensacola, 2010; Haunted Natchez, 2010; Haunted Meridian, Mississippi, 2011; Ghosts Along the Mississippi River, 2011. Contributor to books and journals. **Address:** Department of Languages & Literature, College of Liberal Arts, University of West Alabama, Rm. 301A and 307A, Wallace Hall, Sta. 22, Livingston, AL 35470, U.S.A. **Online address:** ab@uwa.edu

BROWN, Archibald Haworth. (Archie Brown). British/Scottish (born Scotland), b. 1938. **Genres:** Politics/Government, Intellectual History, Adult Non-fiction, History, Essays. **Career:** Oxford University, lecturer, 1971-89, professor of politics, 1989-, St. Antony's College, fellow, 1971-2005, sub-warden, 1995-97, Russian and East European Centre, director, 1991-94, 1998-2002, emeritus fellow, 2005-; Glasgow University, lecturer of politics, 1964-71; Yale University, visiting professor, 1980; Columbia University, visiting professor, 1985; University of Texas, visiting professor, 1990-91; Political Studies Section, chair, 1999-2002; Kellogg Institute of International Studies, University of Notre Dame, distinguished visiting fellow, 1998; American Academy of Arts and Sciences, foreign honorary fellow, 2003-. Writer. **Publications:** AS ARCHIE BROWN: Soviet Politics and Political Science, 1974; The Gorbachev Factor, 1996; Seven Years that Changed the World: Perestroika in Perspective, 2007; The Rise and Fall of Communism, 2009. EDITOR/CO-AUTHOR: (with M. Kaser) The Soviet Union since the Fall of Khrushchev, 1975; (with J. Gray) Political Culture and Political Change in Communist States, 1977; (with T.H. Rigby and P. Reddaway) Authority, Power and Policy in the USSR: Essays Dedicated to Leonard Schapiro, 1980; The Cambridge Encyclopedia of Russia and the Soviet Union, 1982; (with M. Kaser) Soviet Policy for the 1980s, 1982; Political Culture and Communist Studies, 1984; Political Leadership in the Soviet Union, 1989; The Soviet Union: A Biographical Dictionary, 1991; New Thinking in Soviet Politics, 1992; (with J. Hayward and B. Barry) The British Study of Politics in the Twentieth Century, 1999; Contemporary Russian Politics: A Reader, 2001; (with L. Shevstova) Gorbachev, Yeltsin, and Putin: Political Leadership in Russia's Transition, 2001; The Demise of Marxism-Leninism in Russia, 2004.

Address: St. Antony's College, Oxford University, 62 Woodstock Rd., Oxford, OX OX2 6JF, England. **Online address:** archie.brown@sant.ox.ac.uk

BROWN, Archie. *See* **BROWN, Archibald Haworth.**

BROWN, Augustus. *See* **JENKINS, Garry.**

BROWN, Brian A. (Brian Arthur Brown). Canadian (born Canada), b. 1942. **Genres:** International Relations/Current Affairs. **Career:** United Churches of Canada, minister, 1966-; Royal Commission on the Post-Secondary Educational Needs of Northern British Columbia, head, 1973-75. **Publications:** The Sacramental Ministry to the Sick, 1968; The Burning Bush: A Reformed Ethic for the North, 1976; Separatism, 1976; The New Confederation, 1977; The Canadian Challenge, 1978; Your Neighbor as Yourself: Race, Religion and Region: North America into the Twenty-First Century, 1997; Noah's Other Son: Bridging the Gap Between the Bible and the Qur'an, 2007; Forensic Scriptures: Critical Analysis of Scripture and What the Qur'an Reveals about the Bible, 2009. **Address:** Lansing United Church, 49 Bogert Ave., Toronto, ON M2N 1K4, Canada. **Online address:** brian@brianarthurbrown.com

BROWN, Brian Arthur. *See* **BROWN, Brian A.**

BROWN, Brooks. American (born United States), b. 1981?. **Genres:** Young Adult Fiction, Mystery/Crime/Suspense, Adult Non-fiction. **Career:** Writer. **Publications:** (With R. Merritt) No Easy Answers: The Truth behind Death at Columbine, 2002. Contributor to periodicals. **Address:** Lantern Books, 1 Union Sq. W, Ste. 201, New York, NY 10003-3303, U.S.A.

BROWN, Bryan T(urner). American (born United States), b. 1952. **Genres:** Natural History, Environmental Sciences/Ecology, History. **Career:** Grand Canyon National Park, biological technician, 1976-80; University of Arizona, Cooperative Park Studies Unit, research ecologist, 1983-87; research biologist, 1986-90, 1991-; Northern Arizona University, Cooperative Park Studies Unit, research associate, 1990-91; SWCA Environmental Consultants Inc., avian ecologist, 1993-. Writer. **Publications:** Birds of the Grand Canyon Region: An Annotated Checklist, 1978, 2nd ed., 1984; (with S.W. Carothers and R.R. Johnson) Grand Canyon Birds: Historical Notes, Natural History and Ecology, 1987; (with K.D. Groschupf and R.R. Johnson) Annotated Checklist of the Birds of Organ Pipe Cactus National Monument, Arizona, 1988; (with S.W. Carothers) The Colorado River through Grand Canyon: Natural History and Human Change, 1991; (ed.) Brown's Bulletin: Memoirs of a Louisiana Family on the Move, 1876-1973, 2008. Contributor to periodicals. **Address:** SWCA Environmental Consultants Inc., 257 East 200 South, Ste. 200, Salt Lake City, UT 84111, U.S.A. **Online address:** bbrown@swca.com

BROWN, Canter. American (born United States), b. 1948. **Genres:** History, Essays. **Career:** Fort Valley State University, interim executive vice president, chief legal officer, professor of history department, special assistant, counsel to the president; Florida A&M University, professor of history. Writer. **Publications:** Floridas Peace River Frontier, 1991; Fort Meade, 1849-1900, 1995; Ossian Bingley Hart: Floridas Loyalist Reconstruction Governor, 1997; (contrib.) Things Remembered: An Album of African Americans in Tampa, 1997; Floridas Black Public Officials, 1867-1924, 1998; Tampa Before the Civil War, 1999; (ed. with J.M. Denham) Cracker Times and Pioneer Lives: The Florida Reminiscences of George Gillett Keen and Sarah Pamela Williams, 2000; Tampa in Civil War and Reconstruction, 2000; (with L.E. Rivers) Laborers in the Vineyard of the Lord: The Beginnings of the AME Church in Florida, 1865-1895, 2001; In the Midst of All That Makes Life Worth Living: Polk County, Florida, to 1940, 2001; (ed. with L.E. Rivers and R. Mathews) John Willis Menard, Lays in Summer Lands, 2002; (with B.G. Brown) Family Records of the African American Pioneers of Tampa and Hillsborough County, 2003; (with L.E. Rivers) For a Great and Grand Purpose: The Beginnings of the AMEZ Church in Florida, 1864-1905, 2004; (ed. with D.H. Jackson) Go Sound the Trumpet! Selections in Floridas African American History, 2005; None Can Have Richer Memories: Polk County, Florida, 1940-2000, 2005; (with W.W. Manley, II) The Supreme Court of Florida, 1917-1972, 2006; (ed. with L.E. Rivers) The Varieties of Womens Experiences: Portraits of Southern Women in the Post-Civil War Century, 2009. Contributor to periodicals. **Address:** Fort Valley State University, 1005 State University Dr., Fort Valley, GA 31030, U.S.A. **Online address:** brownc@fvsu.edu

BROWN, Christopher Boyd. American (born United States), b. 1972. **Genres:** Music, Theology/Religion. **Career:** Immanuel Lutheran Church, vicar; Boston University School of Theology, assistant professor. Writer and theologian. **Publications:** Singing the Gospel: Lutheran Hymns and the Success of the Reformation, 2005. Contributor of articles to books and journals. **Address:** School of Theology, Boston University, 745 Commonwealth Ave., Boston, MA 02215-1401, U.S.A.

BROWN, Clair. American (born United States), b. 1946. **Genres:** Economics. **Career:** University of California, professor of economics, 1973-, Institute for Research on Labor and Employment, associate director, 1983-92, director, 1992-; Stiles Hall, board director, 1975-95; Labor Center Reporter, Institute of Industrial Relations, editor, 1979-91; Minimum Wage Study Commission, consultant, 1980-81; Industrial Relations, editor, 1983-86; National Center for the Workplace, Institute of Industrial Relations, director, 1993-96; Center for Working Families, board director, 1999-2002; Doshisha University, School of Management, advisory Board, 2002-04, visiting fellow, 2003. **Publications:** (Ed. with J.A. Pechman) Gender in the Workplace, 1987; Women in the Labor Force, 1989; American Standards of Living, 1918-1988, 1994; American Standards of Living, 1996; (co-author) Work and Pay in the United States and Japan, 1997; (with J. Haltiwanger and J. Lane) Economic Turbulence: Is a Volatile Economy Good for America?, 2006; (with G. Linden) Chips and Change, 2009; (ed. with B. Eichengreen and M. Reich) Labor in the Era of Globalization, 2010. **Address:** Department of Economics, University of California, 549 Evans Hall, Ste. 3880, Berkeley, CA 94720-3880, U.S.A. **Online address:** cbrown@econ.berkeley.edu

BROWN, Cynthia Stokes. American (born United States) **Genres:** Education, History, Biography. **Career:** Eastern High School, teacher, 1961-63; University Without Walls, co-director, 1972-75; Antioch College West, faculty, 1980-82; Dominican College, director of secondary credential program, 1982-94, associate professor, professor, adjunct professor in history program, 1994-2010, now professor emeritus. Writer and historian. **Publications:** Literacy in 30 Hours: Paulo Freire's Process in North East Brazil, 1975; Alexander Meiklejohn: Teacher of Freedom, 1981; (ed. and intro.) Septima Poinsette Clark, Ready from Within: Septima Clark and the Civil Rights Movement, 1986; Like It Was: A Complete Guide to Writing Oral History, 1988; (with K. Jorgensen) New Faces in Our Schools: Student-Generated Solutions to Ethnic Conflict, 1992; Connecting with the Past: History Workshop in Middle and High Schools, 1994; Refusing Racism: White Allies and the Struggle for Civil Rights, 2002; (contrib.) She Would Not Be Moved: How We Tell the Story of Rosa Parks and the Montgomery Bus Boycott, 2005; Big History: From the Big Bang to the Present, 2007. **Address:** Department of History, Dominican University of California, 50 Acacia Ave., San Rafael, CA 94901, U.S.A. **Online address:** cbcynthia@earthlink.net

BROWN, Dale W. (Dale Weaver Brown). American (born United States), b. 1926. **Genres:** Theology/Religion, History, Politics/Government, Social Sciences. **Career:** Bethany Biblical Seminary and Training School, field worker and part-time instructor, 1956-58; McPherson College, director of religious life, assistant professor of philosophy and religion, 1958-62; Bethany Theological Seminary, associate professor, 1962-70, professor of Christian theology, 1970-94, professor emeritus, 1994-; Berea College, visiting Lilly professor, 1977-78. Pastor and writer. **Publications:** In Christ Jesus: The Significance of Jesus as the Christ, 1965; Four Words for the World, 1968; So Send I You, 1969; Brethren and Pacifism, 1970; The Christian Revolutionary, 1971; Flamed by the Spirit: Biblical Definitions of the Holy Spirit: A Brethren Perspective, 1978; Understanding Pietism, 1978, rev. ed., 1996; (ed.) What about the Russians?: A Christian Approach to U.S.-Soviet Conflict, 1984; Biblical Pacifism: A Peace Church Perspective, 1986, 2nd ed., 2003; Another Way of Believing: A Brethren Theology, 2005. **Address:** Bethany Theological Seminary, Butterfield & Meyers Rd., PO Box 408, Oak Brook, IL 60521, U.S.A.

BROWN, Dale Weaver. *See* **BROWN, Dale W.**

BROWN, Dan. (Danielle Brown). American (born United States), b. 1964. **Genres:** Novels, Literary Criticism And History, Young Adult Fiction, Mystery/Crime/Suspense. **Career:** Phillips Exeter Academy, English teacher. Writer. **Publications:** (As Danielle Brown) 187 Men to Avoid: A Survival Guide for the Romantically Frustrated Woman, 1995; Digital Fortress, 1998, 2nd ed., 2004; Angels and Demons, 2000; Deception Point, 2001; The Da Vinci Code: A Novel, 2003; Lost Symbol: A Novel, 2009. Contributor to periodicals. **Address:** Phillips Exeter Academy, 20 Main St., 1745 Broadway, Exeter, NH 03833-2460, U.S.A.

BROWN, Daniel James. American (born United States), b. 1951. **Genres:** Natural History. **Career:** Microsoft Corp., technical editor; San Jose State University, faculty; Stanford University, faculty. **Publications:** (with B. Burnette) Connections: A Rhetoric/Short Prose Reader, 1984; Under a Flaming Sky: The Great Hinckley Firestorm of 1894, 2006. **Address:** Redmond, WA , U.S.A. **Online address:** danieljamesbrown@comcast.net

BROWN, Danielle. *See* **BROWN, Dan.**

BROWN, David. British (born England), b. 1968. **Genres:** Race Relations, History, Civil Liberties/Human Rights, Autobiography/Memoirs. **Career:** University of Sheffield, faculty; University of Manchester, senior lecturer in American studies, 2006-. Writer. **Publications:** Southern Outcast: Hinton Rowan Helper and The Impending Crisis of the South, 2006; (with C. Webb) Race in the American South: From Slavery to Civil Rights, 2007. Contributor to books and periodicals. **Address:** School of Arts, Histories and Cultures, The University of Manchester, N1.7 Samuel Alexander Bldg., Manchester, GM M13 9PL, England. **Online address:** brown.d@manchester.ac.uk

BROWN, David S. American (born United States), b. 1966. **Genres:** Adult Non-fiction. **Career:** Elizabethtown College, Department of History, associate professor of history, 1997-, professor, chair. Writer. **Publications:** NON-FICTION: Thomas Jefferson: A Biographical Companion, 1998; Richard Hofstadter: An Intellectual Biography, 2006, Beyond the Frontier: The Midwestern Voice in American Historical Writing, 2009. **Address:** Department of History, Elizabethtown College, Wenger Ctr., Rm. 202, 1 Alpha Dr., Elizabethtown, PA 17022-2298, U.S.A. **Online address:** brownds@etown.edu

BROWN, Deborah J. Australian (born Australia), b. 1963?. **Genres:** Novels. **Career:** University of Queensland, senior lecturer in philosophy, director of honors (HPRC), deputy head of school and director of undergraduate studies. Writer. **Publications:** Descartes and the Passionate Mind, 2006. **Address:** University of Queensland, Forgan Smith E338, Brisbane St Lucia, QL 4072, Australia. **Online address:** deborah.brown@uq.edu.au

BROWN, Don. American (born United States), b. 1949?. **Genres:** Children's Non-fiction, Children's Fiction. **Career:** Freelance illustrator and animator, 1980-. Writer. **Publications:** SELF-ILLUSTRATED: Ruth Law Thrills a Nation, 1993; Alice Ramsey's Grand Adventure, 1997; Rare Treasure: Mary Anning and Her Remarkable Discoveries, 1999; Uncommon Traveler: Mary Kingsley in Africa, 2000; A Voice from the Wilderness: The Story of Anna Howard Shaw, 2001; Far beyond the Garden Gate: Alexandra David-Neel's Journey to Lhasa, 2002; Across a Dark and Wild Sea, 2002; Our Time on the River, 2003; American Boy: The Adventures of Mark Twain, 2003; Mack Made Movies, 2003; (adaptor) Beryl Markham, The Good Lion, 2005; The Notorious Izzy Fink, 2006; Dolley Madison saves George Washington, 2007. OTHER: One Giant Leap: The Story of Neil Armstrong, 1998, 1998; Kid Blink Beats the World, 2004; The Notorious Izzy Fink, 2006; Bright Path: Young Jim Thorpe, 2006; Train Jumper, 2007; Let it Begin Here!: April 19, 1775, The Day the American Revolution Began, 2008; All Stations! Distress!: April 15, 1912, The Day the Titanic Sank, 2008; Teedie: The Story of Young Teddy Roosevelt, 2009; Wizard from the Start: The Incredible Boyhood & Amazing Inventions of Thomas Edison, 2010; Gold! Gold from the American River!, 2011; America is Under Attack: September 11, 2001: The Day the Towers Fell, 2011. **Address:** c/o Author Mail, Houghton Mifflin, 222 Berkeley St., Boston, MA 02116-3764, U.S.A. **Online address:** donaldbrown@optonline.net

BROWN, Dona. (Dona L. Brown). American (born United States), b. 1956. **Genres:** History. **Career:** Rensselaer Polytechnic Institute, visiting lecturer, 1988; University of New Hampshire, assistant professor of history, 1990-93; University of Vermont, assistant professor of history, 1994-99, associate professor, 2000-. Writer. **Publications:** Inventing New England: Regional Tourism in the Nineteenth Century, 1995; (ed.) A Tourist's New England: Travel Fiction, 1820-1920, 1999; Back to the Land: The Enduring Dream of Self-sufficiency in Modern America, 2011. Contributor to books. **Address:** Department of History, University of Vermont, 204 Wheeler House, 133 S Prospect St., Burlington, VT 05405-1714, U.S.A. **Online address:** dona.brown@uvm.edu

BROWN, Dona L. *See* **BROWN, Dona.**

BROWN, Douglas Robert. American (born United States), b. 1960?. **Genres:** Food And Wine, Medicine/Health, Business/Trade/Industry. **Career:** Writer. **Publications:** The Restaurant Manager's Handbook: How to Set Up, Operate, and Manage a Financially Successful Restaurant, 1982, 4th ed., 2007; Controlling Restaurant & Food Service Operating Costs, 2003; (with J.H. Taylor) Building Restaurant Profits: How to Ensure Maximum Results, 2003; Controlling Restaurant & Food Service Food Costs, 2003; (with E. Godsmark and L. Arduser) How to Open a Financially Successful Coffee, Espresso & Tea Shop: With Companion CD-ROM, 2004; (with S.L. Fullen) How to Open a Financially Successful Specialty Retail & Gourmet Foods Shop: With Companion CD-ROM, 2004; (with S.L. Fullen) How to Open a Financially Successful Bakery, 2004; The Encyclopedia of Restaurant Forms: A Complete Kit of Ready-to-Use Checklists, Worksheets and Training Aids for a Successful Food Service Operation, 2004; (with L. Arduser) HACCP & Sanitation in Restaurants and Food Service Operations: A Practical Guide Based on the FDA Food Code, with Companion CD-ROM, 2005; (with L. Arduser) The Encyclopedia of Restaurant Training: A Complete Ready-to-Use Training Program for All Positions in the Food Service Industry, 2005; (with L. Arduser) The Waiter & Waitress and Waitstaff Training Handbook, 2005; (with L. Arduser) The Professional Caterer's Handbook: How to Open and Operate a Financially Successful Catering Business, with CD-ROM, 2006; The Food Service Manager's Guide to Creative Cost Cutting: Over 2, 001 Innovative and Simple Ways to Save Your Food Service Operation Thousands by Reducing Expenses, 2006; (with A. Miron) Professional Bar & Beverage Manager's Handbook: How to Open and Operate a Financially Successful Bar, Tavern and Nightclub, 2006; (with S. Henkel) Non-Commercial Food Service Manager's Handbook: A Complete Guide for Hospitals, Nursing Homes, Military, Prisons, Schools and Churches, with Companion CD-ROM, 2007. **Address:** c/o Author Mail, Atlantic Publishing Group Inc., 1210 SW 23rd Pl., Ocala, FL 34471, U.S.A.

BROWN, Ethan. American (born United States), b. 1972. **Genres:** Social Work, Criminology/True Crime, History, Politics/Government. **Career:** New York magazine, music editor. Writer. **Publications:** Queens Reigns Supreme: Fat Cat, 50 Cent and the Rise of the Hip-Hop Hustler, 2005; Snitch: Informants, Cooperators abd the Corruption of Justice, 2007; Shake the Devil Off: A True Story of the Murder that Rocked New Orleans, 2009. Contributor to periodicals. **Address:** c/o Author Mail, Anchor Books, 1745 Broadway, New York, NY 10019, U.S.A. **Online address:** ethanbrown72@gmail.com

BROWN, Gita. American (born United States), b. 1958?. **Genres:** Novels, Young Adult Fiction. **Career:** Rhode Island College, News and Public Relations, staff writer and editor. **Publications:** Be I Whole, 1995. **Address:** Rhode Island College, E Campus, 10 Bldg., Joseph F. Kauffman Ctr., 600 Mt. Pleasant Ave., Providence, RI 02908-1991, U.S.A. **Online address:** gbrown01@ric.edu

BROWN, Gordon. British/Scottish (born Scotland), b. 1951. **Genres:** Politics/Government, History. **Career:** University of Edinburgh, rector, 1972-75, lecturer, 1976; Glasgow College of Technology, lecturer, 1976-80; Scottish Television, current affairs editor, 1980-83; British Labour Party, Scottish Council, chair, 1983-84, opposition chief secretary at the treasury, 1987-89, opposition trade and industry secretary, 1989-92, shadow treasury chancellor, 1992-97, chancellor of the exchequer, 1997-2007, party chair, 2007-10. Writer and politician. **Publications:** The Red Paper on Scotland, 1975; A Voter's Guide to the Scottish Assembly and Why You Should Support It, 1979; The Politics of Nationalism and Devolution, 1980; Scotland, the Real Divide: Poverty and Deprivation in Scotland, 1983; Maxton, 1986; Where There Is Greed: Margaret Thatcher and the Betrayal of Britain's Future, 1989; John Smith: Life and Soul of the Party, 1994; (ed. with T. Wright) Values, Visions, and Voices: An Anthology of Socialism, 1995; New Scotland, New Britain, 1999; Civic Society in Modern Britain, 2001; Global Europe: Full- Employment Europe, 2005; Stronger Together: The 21st Century Case for Scotland and Britain, 2006; Courage: Eight Portraits, 2007; Britain's Everyday Heroes: The Making of the Good Society, 2007; Beyond the Crash: Overcoming the First Crisis of Globalization, 2010; The Change We Choose: Speeches 2007-2009, 2010. **Address:** 10 Downing St., London, GL SW1A 2AA, England.

BROWN, Gregory N. American (born United States), b. 1953. **Genres:** Transportation, Young Adult Non-fiction, Business/Trade/Industry, Air/Space Topics. **Career:** Phoenix, Arizona, independent flight instructor. Writer and educator. **Publications:** (With M.J. Holt) The Turbine Pilot's Flight Manual, 1995, 2nd ed., 2001; Job Hunting for Pilots: Networking Your Way to a Flying

Job, 1995, 2nd ed., 2001; The Savvy Flight Instructor: Secrets of the Successful CFI, 1997; (as Greg Brown) Flying Carpet: The Soul of an Airplane, 2003; (as Greg Brown, with L. Lippert) You Can Fly!, 2004. Contributor to magazines. **Address:** PO Box 17592, Fountain Hills, AZ 85269, U.S.A. **Online address:** pj@paperjet.net

BROWN, Gregory S. American (born United States), b. 1968. **Genres:** Literary Criticism And History, History. **Career:** City University of New York, Hunter College, professor; George Mason University, professor; Columbia University, faculty; University of Nevada, associate professor. Writer. **Publications:** A Field of Honor: Writers, Court Culture and Public Theater in French Literary Life from Racine to the Revolution, 2002; Cultures in Conflict: The French Revolution, 2003; Literary Sociability and Literary Property in France, 1775-1793: Beaumarchais, the Société des auteurs dramatiques and the Comédie-francaise, 2006. Contributor of articles to periodicals and journals. **Address:** Department of History, University of Nevada, 4505 Maryland Pkwy., P O Box 455020, Las Vegas, NV 89154-5020, U.S.A. **Online address:** gbrown@unlv.nevada.edu

BROWN, Harriet N(ancy). American (born United States), b. 1958. **Genres:** Documentaries/Reportage, Food And Wine, Human Relations/Parenting, Young Adult Non-fiction. **Career:** Popular Science Magazine, staff, 1979-89; Wigwag Magazine, staff, 1989-91; American Girl Magazine, staff, 1992-2000; Wisconsin Trail Magazine, editor-in-chief, editorial director; Syracuse University, S.I. Newhouse School of Public Communications, assistant professor. **Publications:** The Good-bye Window: A Year in the Life of a Day-Care Center, 1998; The Babysitter's Handbook: The Care and Keeping of Kids, 1999; Kit's Railway Adventure, 2002; Welcome to Kit's World, 1934: Growing Up during America's Great Depression, 2002; (with J. Young) Madison Walks, 2003; The Promised Land, 2004; (ed.) Mr. Wrong: Real-life Stories about the Men We Used to Love, 2007; (ed.) Feed Me!: Writers Dish About Food, Eating, Weight, and Body Image, 2009; Brave Girl Eating: A Family's Struggle with Anorexia, 2010. **Address:** S.I. Newhouse School of Public Communications, Syracuse University, Rm. 338, 2 Newhouse, 215 University Pl., Syracuse, NY 13244-2100, U.S.A. **Online address:** hnbrown@syr.edu

BROWN, Harry Clifford. American (born United States), b. 1953. **Genres:** Novels, Essays. **Career:** Writer and consultant. **Publications:** Sundays in August: A Novel, 1997. **Address:** c/o Sunstone Press, 239 Johnson St., PO Box 2321, Santa Fe, NM 87501-1826, U.S.A.

BROWN, Helen Gurley. American (born United States), b. 1922. **Genres:** Human Relations/Parenting, Sex, Women's Studies And Issues. **Career:** Music Corporation of America, executive secretary, 1942-45; William Morris Agency, executive secretary, 1946-47; Foote Cone and Belding Advertising Agency, copywriter, 1948-58; Kenyon and Eckhardt Advertising Agency, advertising writer and account executive, 1958-62; Cosmopolitan Magazine, editor-in-chief, 1965-97, editorial director of foreign editor, 1972-; EYE Magazine, supervising editor, 1967-68. **Publications:** Sex and the Single Girl, 1962; Sex and the Office, 1964; The Outrageous Opinions, 1966; Helen Gurley Brown's Single Girl's Cookbook, 1969; Sex and the New Single Girl, 1970; Having It All: Love, Success, Sex, Money, Even if You're Starting with Nothing, 1982; The Late Show: A Semiwild but Practical Survival Plan for Women Over 50, 1993; The Writer's Rules, The Power of Positive Prose-How to Write It and Get It Published, 1998; I'm Wild Again, Snippets from My Life and a Few Brazen Thoughts, 2000; Dear Pussycat: Mash Notes and Missives from the Desk of Cosmopolitan's Legendary Editor, 2004. **Address:** Cosmopolitan, The Hearst Corp., 959 8th Ave., New York, NY 10019-3737, U.S.A.

BROWN, H. Jackson. American (born United States), b. 1940. **Genres:** Children's Non-fiction, Theology/Religion. **Career:** END Inc. (advertising and marketing firm), president and creative director, 1974-92. Writer. **Publications:** (Comp.) A Father's Book of Wisdom, 1988; (comp.) P.S. I Love You, 1990; Life's Little Instruction Book, 1991; Live and Learn and Pass It On, 1991; Life's Little Treasure Book, 1994; (with R. Brown and K. Peel) Little Book of Christmas Joys, 1994; On Marriage and Family, 1994; (comp.) Wit and Wisdom from the Peanut Butter Gang, 1994; When You Lick a Slug, Your Tongue Goes Numb: Kids Share Their Wit and Wisdom, 1994; (with R. Brown and K. Peel) Life's Little Treasure Book of Christmas Traditions, 1996; (comp.) Hero in Every Heart, 1996; Life's Little Treasure Book on Friendship, 1996; Life's Little Treasure Book on Hope, 1996; Complete Life's Little Instruction Book, 1997; (comp.) Kids' Little Treasure Book on Happy Families, 1997; (comp.) The Complete Live and learn and Pass it On, 1998; On Fathers, 1998; On Mothers, 1998; Life's Little Treasure Book on Simple Pleasures, 1999; Life's Little Treasure Book on Things that Really Matter, 1999; Life's Instructions on Wisdom, Success and Happiness, 2000; (with R.F. Spizman) Life's Little Instruction Book for Incurable Romatics, 2000; (with K. Shea) Mothers to Daughters, 2000; (with R.C. Brown) Life's Little Instructions from the Bible, 2000; (with R. Pennington) Highlighted in Yellow: A Short Course in Living Wisely and Choosing Well, 2001; (with P.Y. Flautt and K. Shea) A Book of Love for My Daughter, 2001. **Address:** 3307 Wimbledon Rd., Nashville, TN 37215, U.S.A.

BROWN, Irene Quenzler. American (born United States), b. 1938. **Genres:** History, Humanities, Women's Studies And Issues. **Career:** University of Hartford, lecturer, 1976-77, assistant professor of history, 1978; University of Connecticut, director of women's studies program, 1979-85, assistant professor of human development and family studies, 1979-86, associate professor of human development and family studies, 1987-2003, associate professor emeritus and researcher, 2003-, associate director of honors program, 1992-2002, School of Family Studies, historian, 2003-; American Association of Family and Consumer Sciences, researcher and historian. Writer. **Publications:** (With R.D. Brown) The Hanging of Ephraim Wheeler: A Story of Rape, Incest and Justice in Early America, 2003. Contributor of articles to journals. **Address:** Department of Human Development and Family Studies, School of Family Studies, University of Connecticut, 348 Mansfield Rd., Ste. 2058, Storrs, CT 06269-2058, U.S.A. **Online address:** irene.q.brown@uconn.edu

BROWN, Isobel. *See* **GRANT-ADAMSON, Lesley (Heycock).**

BROWN, Jackie. American (born United States) **Genres:** Novels, Children's Fiction. **Career:** Writer. **Publications:** Little Cricket, 2004. Contributor to periodicals. **Address:** c/o Author Mail, Hyperion Editorial Department, 77 W 66th St., 11th Fl., New York, NY 10023, U.S.A.

BROWN, Janelle. American (born United States), b. 1973. **Genres:** Novels. **Career:** Writer. **Publications:** (with B. Traub and B. Wieners) Burning Man, 1997; All We Ever Wanted Was Everything: A Novel, 2008; This is Where We Live, 2010. Contributor of articles to periodicals. **Address:** Susan Golomb, 875 Ave. of the Americas, Ste. 2302, New York, NY 10001-3507, U.S.A. **Online address:** awewwe@janellebrown.com

BROWN, Jared. American (born United States), b. 1936. **Genres:** Plays/Screenplays, History, Theatre, Biography, Novels, Mystery/Crime/Suspense, Autobiography/Memoirs. **Career:** Western Illinois University, assistant professor of speech and dramatic art, 1965-72, associate professor, 1972-78, Department of Theater, acting chair, 1977-78, professor of theater, 1978-89, academic director of study abroad in London program, 1979-80; Illinois Wesleyan University, professor of theatre, School of Theatre Arts, director, 1989-2002, now professor emeritus of theatre arts. Writer. **Publications:** BIOGRAPHIES: The Fabulous Lunts: A Biography of Alfred Lunt and Lynn Fontanne, 1986; Zero Mostel, 1989; The Theatre in America during the Revolution, 1995; Alan J. Pakula: His Films and His Life, 2005; Moss Hart: A Prince of Theater, 2006. NOVEL: Mind the Gap and 2 Other Mysteries, 2009. Contributor to periodicals. **Address:** School of Theatre Arts, Illinois Wesleyan University, 1312 Park St., Bloomington, IL 61701, U.S.A. **Online address:** jbrown@iwu.edu

BROWN, Jeffrey. American (born United States), b. 1975?. **Genres:** Graphic Novels, Cartoons. **Career:** Barnes & Noble, music section manager. Writer and cartoonist. **Publications:** COMICS AND GRAPHIC BOOKS: Clumsy, 2002; Unlikely, or, How I Lost My Virginity, 2003; Maybe We Could Just Lie Here Naked, 2003; I Am Going to Be Small, 2003; Bighead, 2004; Be a Man, 2004; aeIOU, or, Any Easy Intimacy, 2004 as aeIOU: Any Easy Intimacy, 2007; (contrib.) Drawn & Quarterly Showcase: Book Two, 2004; (with J. Kochalka) Conversation #2, 2005; Minisulk: More Sappy Comics!, 2005; Every Girl Is the End of the World for Me: December 26, 2003-January 15, 2004, 2005; Incredible Change-Bots, 2007; Feeble Attempts, 2007; Cat Getting Out of a Bag and Other Observations, 2007; Little Things: A Memoir in Slices, 2008; Sulk vol. I: Bighead & Friends, 2008, vol. II: Deadly Awesome, 2008. Works appear in anthologies. Contributor to periodicals. **Address:** PO Box 120, Deerfield, IL 60015-0120, U.S.A. **Online address:** jeffreybrownrq@hotmail.com

BROWN, Jennifer S. H. Canadian/American (born United States), b. 1940. **Genres:** Anthropology/Ethnology, Cultural/Ethnic Topics, History, Theology/Religion, Business/Trade/Industry, Young Adult Non-fiction. **Career:** Colby College, instructor in sociology, 1966-69; Northern Illinois University, assistant professor of anthropology and sociology, 1969-81; University of Winnipeg, Department of History, associate professor, 1983-88, professor of history, 1988-, Canada research chair, 2004-11; Centre for Rupert's Land Studies, publications editor, 1984-2010, director, 1996-2010; Tulane University, Middle American Research Institute, publications editor, 1976-82; Indiana University, visiting assistant professor of anthropology, 1978-79; University of Manitoba, Department of Anthropology, adjunct professor, 1998-2011. Writer. **Publications:** Strangers in Blood: Fur Trade Company Families in Indian Country, 1980; (ed.) Excavations at Dzibilchaltun, Yucatan, Mexico, 1980; (co-ed.) The Stucco Decoration and Architectural Assemblage of Structure 1-sub, Dzibilchaltun, Yucatan, Mexico, 1983; (ed. with J. Peterson and contrib.) The New Peoples: Being and Becoming Métis in North America, 1985; (with R. Brightman) The Orders of the Dreamed: George Nelson on Cree and Northern Ojibwa Religion and Myth, 1823, 1988; (ed., intro. and afterword) Ojibwa of Berens River, Manitoba: Ethnography into History, 1992; (ed. with W.J. Eccles and D.P. Heldman) The Fur Trade Revisited: Selected Papers of the Sixth North American Fur Trade Conference, Mackinac Island, Michigan, 1991, 1994; (ed. with E. Vibert) Reading beyond Words: Contexts for Native History, 1996, 2nd ed., 2003; The Wasitay Religion: Omushkego Cree Prophecy, Literacy and Great Bookson Hudson Bay, 2004; (ed. with P.W. DePasquale and M.F. Ruml) Telling Our Stories: Omushkego Legends and Histories from Hudson Bay, 2005; (forword) Harmon's Journal 1800-1819, 2006; (ed. and intro. with S.E. Gray) Memories, Myths, and Dreams of an Ojibwe Leader, 2009; (ed. and intro. with S.E. Gray) Contributions to Ojibwe Studies: Essays, 1934-1972, 2010. Contributor to books and periodicals. **Address:** Department of History, University of Winnipeg, 515 Portage Ave., Winnipeg, MB R3B 2E9, Canada. **Online address:** jennifer@professorsbrown.com

BROWN, John. American (born United States), b. 1966. **Genres:** Young Adult Fiction. **Career:** Author. Arthur Andersen L.L.P., business consultant, 2000-02. Writer. **Publications:** Servant of a Dark God, 2009. **Address:** c/o Caitlin Blasdell, Liza Dawson Associates, 350 7th Ave., Ste. 2003, New York, NY 10001, U.S.A.

BROWN, John Gregory. American (born United States), b. 1960. **Genres:** Novels. **Career:** North Carolina State University, lecturer in English, 1984-87; Patuxent Publishing Co., staff writer, news editor, 1989-93; Johns Hopkins University, instructor in writing, 1993-94; Sweet Briar College, Julia Jackson Nichols professor of English, director of creative writing, 1994-. **Publications:** NOVELS: Decorations in a Ruined Cemetery, 1994; The Wrecked, Blessed Body of Shelton Lafleur, 1996; Audubon's Watch, 2001; The Ganesha Hotel, forthcoming. Contributor of stories to periodicals. **Address:** Department of English, Sweet Briar College, PO Box 1104, Sweet Briar, VA 24595, U.S.A. **Online address:** brown@sbc.edu

BROWN, Jonathan (Mayer). American (born United States), b. 1939. **Genres:** Art/Art History, Picture/Board Books. **Career:** Princeton University, staff, 1965-73; New York University, Institute of Fine Arts, director, 1973-78, Carroll and Milton Petrie Professor of Fine Arts, 1973-, professor of art history, 1977, chair. Writer. **Publications:** (With R. Enggass) Italy and Spain, 1600-1750: Sources and Documents, 1970; Jusepe de Ribera: Prints and Drawings, 1973; Francisco de Zurbarán, 1973; Murillo & His Drawings, 1976; Images and Ideas in Seventeenth-Century Spanish Painting, 1978; (with J.H. Elliott) A Palace for a King: The Buen Retiro and the Court of Philip IV, 1980, rev. ed., 2003; (ed.) Figures of Thought, El Greco as Interpreter of History, Tradition and Ideas, 1982; (contrib.) El Greco of Toledo, 1982; (ed. with J.M. Andrade) Greco: Italy and Spain, 1984; Velázquez, Painter and Courtier, 1986; (contrib.) Art and History: Images and Their Meaning, 1988; (with R.G. Mann) Spanish Paintings of the Fifteenth through Nineteenth Centuries: The Collections of the National Gallery of Art, 1990; The Golden Age of Painting in Spain, 1991; Arte de los Bayeu, 1992; Kings and Connoisseurs: Collecting Art in Seventeenth-Century Europe, 1995; (ed. and contrib.) Picasso and the Spanish Tradition, 1996; Painting in Spain: 1500-1700, 1998; Sala de Batallas de El Escorial: la obra dearte como artefacto Cultural, 1998; Velázquez: The Technique of Genius, 1998; Velázquez, Rubens y Van Dyck: pintores cortesanos delsiglo XVII, 1999; (ed. with J. Elliott) Sale of the Century: Artistic Relations Between Spain and Great Britain, 1604-1655, 2002; (with S.G. Galassi) Goya's Last Works, 2006; Collected Writings on Velazquez, 2008; The Spanish Manner: Drawings from Ribera to Goya, 2010; Murillo: Virtuoso Draftsman, 2011. **Address:** Institute of Fine Arts, New York University, 315 Duke House, 1 E 78th St., PO Box 9801, New York, NY 10075, U.S.A. **Online address:** jb5@nyu.edu

BROWN, J(oseph) P(aul) S(ummers). American (born United States), b. 1930. **Genres:** Westerns/Adventure, Literary Criticism And History, Young Adult Fiction. **Career:** El Paso Herald Post, reporter, 1953-54; actor; professional boxer, 1956-58, 1963-64; U.S. Marine Corps, mountain climbing instructor, 1954-58, Cold Weather Training Center, instructor guide, 1956; Cattleman, 1958; U.S. Forest Service, mountain climbing instructor, 1974. Writer. **Publications:** Jim Kane, 1970 in UK as Pocket Money, 1972; The Outfit: A Cowboy's Primer, 1971; The Forests of the Night, 1974; Steeldust, 1986, 2nd ed., 1997; Steeldust II: The Flight, 1987; Blooded Stock, 1990; Outfit, 1990; The Horseman, 1991; Jim Kane, 1991; Ladino, 1991; The Cinnamon Colt and Other Stories, 1991; Native Born, 1992; Keep the Devil Waiting, 1992; The Forests of the Night, 1992; The Cinnamon Colt, 1992; The World in Pancho's Eye, 2007; Wolves at Our Door, 2008. **Address:** PO Box 972, Patagonia, AZ 85624-0972, U.S.A. **Online address:** horsemn1020@cs.com

BROWN, Kathleen. American (born United States), b. 1960. **Genres:** History, Social Sciences. **Career:** St. Agnes School, high school teacher, 1981-83; Princeton University, assistant professor, 1990-93; Rutgers University, assistant professor, 1993-96; University of Pennsylvania, assistant professor, 1996-98, associate professor, 1998-2008, professor of American history, 2008-. Writer and historian. **Publications:** Good Wives, Nasty Wenches, and Anxious Patriarchs: Gender, Race, and Power in Colonial Virginia, 1996; Foul Bodies: Cleanliness in Early America, 2009. Contributor to books, periodicals and journals. **Address:** Department of History, School of Arts & Sciences, University of Pennsylvania, 208 College Hall, Philadelphia, PA 19104-6379, U.S.A. **Online address:** kabrown@sas.upenn.edu

BROWN, Kevin. American (born United States), b. 1960. **Genres:** Art/Art History, Bibliography, Biography, Autobiography/Memoirs, Children's Fiction. **Career:** Ross & Hardies, scrivener, 1994. Book reviewer, contributing editor, literary journalist, essayist, biographer, 1978-. **Publications:** Romare Bearden (Black Americans of Achievement), 1995; Malcolm X: His Life and Legacy, 1995; (ed.) New York Public Library African-American Desk Reference, 1999. Contributor to magazines and newspapers. Works appear in anthologies. **Address:** 65-60 Booth St., Apt. 2E, Rego Park, NY 11374, U.S.A. **Online address:** kevinbrown@aol.com

BROWN, Lee Ann. American/Japanese (born Japan), b. 1964?. **Genres:** Film, Poetry. **Career:** St. John's University, St. John's College of Liberal Arts and Sciences, Department of English, assistant professor of English, associate professor; Tender Buttons Press, founder and editor; Naropa Institute, Writing and Poetics Program, faculty. Poet and filmmaker. **Publications:** Polyverse (poems), 1999; (with A. Slacik) Dia/gnostic, 2000; (with B. Mayer, J. Hofer and D. Dinsmore) The 3:15 Experiment, 2001; The Sleep That Changed Everything (poems), 2003. Contributor to periodicals. **Address:** St. John's College of Liberal Arts and Sciences, St. John's University, Rm. B40-13, St. John Hall, 8000 Utopia Pkwy., Queens, NY 11439, U.S.A. **Online address:** brownl@stjohns.edu

BROWN, Lester R(ussell). American (born United States), b. 1934. **Genres:** Agriculture/Forestry, Demography, Economics, Environmental Sciences/Ecology, Transportation. **Career:** U.S. Department of Agriculture, international agricultural economist, 1959-64, policy advisory secretary of agriculture, 1964-66; International Agricultural Development Service, administrator, 1966-69; Worldwatch Institute, president, 1974-2000, founder and senior researcher, 1974-2001, chairman, 2000-01; Earth Policy Institute, president and founder, 2001-. Writer. **Publications:** Man, Land, and Food, 1963; Increasing World Food Output, 1965; Seeds of Change, 1970; World Without Borders, 1972; (with G.W. Finsterbusch) Man and His Environment, 1972; In the Human Interest, 1974; (with E.P. Eckholm) By Bread Alone, 1974; The Twenty-ninth Day, 1978; (with C. Flavin and C. Norman) Running on Empty, 1979; Building a Sustainable Society, 1981; (with C. Flavin and S. Postel) Saving the Planet, 1991; (ed.) The World Watch Reader, 1991, rev. ed., 1998; (with H. Kane) Full House, 1994; Who Will Feed China?, 1995; Tough Choices, 1996; Eko Kezai Kakume: Environmental Trends Reshaping The Global Economy, 1998; Beyond Malthus, 1999; Eco-Economy: Building an Economy for the Earth, 2001; (with J. Larsen and B. Fischlowitz-Roberts) The Earth Policy Reader, 2002; Plan B: Rescuing a Planet under Stress and a Civilization in

Trouble, 2003; Outgrowing the Earth, 2005; Plan B 2.0: Rescuing a Planet Under Stress and a Civilization in Trouble, 2006; Plan B 3.0: Mobilizing to Save Civilization, 2008; Plan B 4.0: Mobilizing to Save Civilization, 2009; World on the Edge: How to Prevent Environmental and Economic Collapse, 2011. Contributor to journals. **Address:** Earth Policy Institute, 1350 Connecticut Ave. NW, Ste. 403, Washington, DC 20036, U.S.A. **Online address:** lesterbrown@earthpolicy.org

BROWN, Lyn Mikel. American (born United States), b. 1956. **Genres:** Psychiatry, Psychology, Women's Studies And Issues, Human Relations/Parenting. **Career:** CETA Program, preschool teacher and coordinator, 1979-81; Connection Inc., substance abuse counselor, 1981-83; Harvard University, Graduate School of Education, teaching fellow, 1984-85, head teaching fellow, 1985-89, Laurel-Harvard Project, director, 1986-89, Project on Women's Psychology and Girls' Development, founding member, 1986-98, lecturer in education, 1989-90, research associate in education, human development, and psychology, 1989-92; Colby College, assistant professor and co-chair of education and human development program, 1991-98, associate professor of education and human development, 1998-2005, professor of education and human development, 2005-; Hardy Girls Healthy Women, co-creator, board director and senior researcher, 2000-. Writer. **Publications:** (With C. Gilligan) Meeting at the Crossroads: Women's Psychology and Girls' Development, 1992; Raising Their Voices: The Politics of Girls' Anger, 1998; Girlfighting: Betrayal and Rejection Among Girls, 2003; (with S. Lamb) Packaging Girlhood: Rescuing Our Daughters from Marketers' Schemes, 2006; (with S. Lamb and M. Tappan) Packaging Boyhood: Saving Our Sons from Superheroes, Slackers, and Other Media Stereotypes, 2009. Contributor to periodicals. Works appear in anthologies. **Address:** Program in Education and Human Development, Colby College, 105 Diamond, 4422 Mayflower Hill, Waterville, ME 04901-8844, U.S.A. **Online address:** lmbrown@colby.edu

BROWN, Lynne P. American (born United States), b. 1952. **Genres:** Education, Politics/Government. **Career:** U.S. House of Representatives, Office of the Majority Whip, staff, 1978-82; American University, adjunct professor, 1980-81; New York University, director of university relations and adjunct professor of politics, 1982-, senior vice president of university relations and public affairs, 2003-. Writer. **Publications:** (With J. Brademas) The Politics of Education: Conflict and Consensus on Capitol Hill, 1987. Contributor to periodicals. Works appear in anthologies. **Address:** University Relations and Public Affairs, New York University, 70 Washington Sq. S, 12th Fl., New York, NY 10012, U.S.A. **Online address:** lynne.brown@nyu.edu

BROWN, Margaret Lynn. American (born United States), b. 1958. **Genres:** Local History/Rural Topics, Biography, History, Travel/Exploration. **Career:** Brevard College, associate professor of history, 1996-, IWIL Program, coordinator; Stanford University, Knight Program, journalist. Writer and historian. **Publications:** (Co-author) Historic Buildings of the Smokies, 1995; The Wild East: A Biography of the Great Smoky Mountains, 2000. Contributor to books and periodicals. **Address:** Brevard College, MG-211, 1 Brevard College Dr., Brevard, NC 28712-4283, U.S.A. **Online address:** mbrown@brevard.edu

BROWN, Mary Ward. American (born United States), b. 1917. **Genres:** Novellas/Short Stories, Autobiography/Memoirs, Young Adult Fiction. **Career:** Judson College, publicity director, 1938-39; Marion Military Institute, Office of Guidance and Counseling, affiliated. Writer. **Publications:** Tongues of Flame (short story collection), 1986; It Wasn't All Dancing and Other Stories, 2002; Fanning The Spark: A Memoir, 2009. Contributor of articles to periodicals. Works appear in anthologies. **Address:** c/o Amanda Urban, International Creative Management, 730 5th Ave., New York, NY 10019, U.S.A.

BROWN, Michael F(obes). American (born United States), b. 1950?. **Genres:** Anthropology/Ethnology, Theology/Religion. **Career:** Williams College, professor of anthropology, James N. Lambert '39 professor of anthropology and Latin American studies, Oakley Center for the Humanities and Social Sciences, director. Writer. **Publications:** Una Paz Incierta: Historia y Cultura de las Comunidades Aguarunas Frente al Impacto de la Carretera Marginal, 1984; Tsewa's Gift: Magic and Meaning in an Amazonian Society, 1986; (with E. Fernández) War of Shadows: The Struggle for Utopia in the Peruvian Amazon, 1991, trans. as Guerra de sombras, 2001; The Channeling Zone: American Spirituality in an Anxious Age, 1997; Who Owns Native Culture?, 2003; Upriver: An Amazonian Chronicle and Meditation, forthcoming. **Address:** Department of Anthropology & Sociology, Williams College, Hollander Hall, 85 Mission Park Dr., Williamstown, MA 01267-2606, U.S.A. **Online address:** michael.f.brown@williams.edu

BROWN, Michael P. American (born United States), b. 1966. **Genres:** Genealogy/Heraldry, Geography, Politics/Government, Adult Non-fiction. **Career:** University of British Columbia, editorial assistant for society and space, 1993-95; University of Canterbury, lecturer in geography, 1995-97; University of Washington, acting assistant professor, 1998, assistant professor, 1998-2001, associate professor of geography, 2001-, professor. Writer. **Publications:** Replacing Citizenship: AIDS Activism and Radical Democracy, 1997; Closet Space: Geographies of Metaphor from the Body to the Globe, 2000; (ed. with R. Morrill) Seattle Geographies, 2011. Contributor to books and periodicals. **Address:** Department of Geography, University of Washington, Rm. 431 GEOG, 4518 University Way, PO Box 353550, Seattle, WA 98105-4530, U.S.A. **Online address:** michaelb@u.washington.edu

BROWN, Michelle P(atricia). British (born England), b. 1959. **Genres:** Archaeology/Antiquities, Art/Art History, History, Librarianship, Theology/Religion, Essays. **Career:** University of London, Courtauld Institute of Art, information officer, 1982-83, School of Advanced Study, part-time professor, 2006-; Birkbeck College and King's College, part-time lecturer in history and aleography, 1983-86, extramural lecturer, 1983-, senior tutor; British Library, curator of manuscripts, 1986-2004, part-time project officer, 2004-08; School of Advanced Study, Institute of English Studies, senior research fellow, 2000-, professor of medieval manuscript studies and course tutor to the History of the Book, 2005-. Writer. **Publications:** A Guide to Western Historical Scripts: From Antiquity to 1600, 1990, rev. ed., 1999; Lambeth Apocalypse, Manuscript 209 in Lambeth Palace Library: A Critical Study, 1990; Anglo-Saxon Manuscripts, 1991; (with J. Bately and J. Roberts) A Palaeographer's View: The Selected Papers of Julian Brown, 1993; Understanding Illuminated Manuscripts: A Glossary of Technical Terms, 1994; The Book of Cerne: Prayer, Patronage and Power in 9th Century England, 1996; (with L. Webster) The Transformation of the Roman World AD 400-900, 1997; The British Library Guide to Writing and Scripts: History and Techniques, 1998; (ed. with S. McKendrick) Illuminating the Book: Makers & Interpreters: Essays in Honor of Janet Backhouse, 1998; (with P. Lovett)The British Library Historical Source-Book for Scribes, 1999; (with P. Lovett) The Historical Source book for Scribes, 1999; In the Beginning Was the Word: Books and Faith in the Age of Bede, 2000; (with C. Farr) Mercia: An Anglo-Saxon Kingdom in Europe, 2001; Buch Von Lindisfarne: Cotton Ms Nero D.iv Der British Library, London, 2002; The Lindisfarne Gospels: Society, Spirituality and the Scribe, 2003; Painted Labyrinth: The World of the Lindisfarne Gospels, 2003; (ed. with R.J. Kelly) You're History!: How People Make the Difference, 2005; How Christianity Came to Britain and Ireland, 2006; St. Paul 's Cathedral, 2006; (ed.) In the Beginning: Bibles Before the Year 1000, Exhibition Cat., 2006; The Luttrell Psalter, 2006; The World of the Luttrell Psalter, 2006; Lion Hudson Companion to Christian Art, 2007; Manuscripts from the Anglo-Saxon Age, 2008; The Holkham Bible Picture-Book, 2008; (ed. with R. Palmer) Lambeth Palace Library, forthcoming; Catalogue of the Latin Manuscripts of the Holy Monastery of St Catherine's, Sinai, forthcoming. Contributor of articles to journals. **Address:** Institute of English Studies, School of Advanced Study, University of London, Rm. 252, Senate House, Malet St., London, GL WC1E 7HU, England. **Online address:** michelle.brown@as.ac.uk

BROWN, Mick. British (born England), b. 1950?. **Genres:** Travel/Exploration, Biography, Music. **Career:** London Sunday Times, staff writer and columnist, 1985-89; Sunday Correspondent, senior editor, 1989-90; Telegraph magazine, senior writer. Journalist. **Publications:** Richard Branson: The Inside Story, 1988; American Heartbeat: Travels from Woodstock to San Jose by Song Title, 1994; The Spiritual Tourist: A Personal Odyssey Through the Outer Reaches of Belief, 1998; The Dance of 17 Lives: The Incredible True Story of Tibets 17th Karmapa, 2004; Tearing Down the Wall of Sound: The Rise and Fall of Phil Spector, 2007. Contributor to periodicals. **Address:** Telegraph Weekley, Victory House, Meeting House Ln., Chatham, KT ME4 4TT, England.

BROWN, Montague. American (born United States), b. 1952. **Genres:** Ethics, Intellectual History, Philosophy. **Career:** Saint Anselm College, professor of philosophy, 1986-. Writer. **Publications:** The Romance of Reason: An Adventure in the Thought of Thomas Aquinas, 1993; The Quest for Moral Foundations: An Introduction to Ethics, 1996; One-Minute Philosopher: Quick Answers to Help You Banish Confusion, Resolve Controversies and Explain Yourself Better to Others, 2001; The One-Minute Philosopher, 2001; Half-Truths: What's Right (and What's Wrong) With the Clichés You and I

Live By, 2003; Restoration of Reason: The Eclipse and Recovery of Truth, Goodness and Beauty, 2006; Freedom, Philosophy, and Faith: The Transformative Role of Judeo-Christian Freedom in Western Thought, 2011. **Address:** Department of Philosophy, St. Anselm College, 100 St., Anselm Dr., Manchester, NH 03102-1310, U.S.A. **Online address:** mbrown@anselm.edu

BROWN, Murray. American (born United States), b. 1929. **Genres:** Economics, History, Novellas/Short Stories. **Career:** National Bureau of Economic Research, research assistant, 1955-56; City University of New York, City College, lecturer, 1955-56; George Washington University, Patent and Trademark Foundation, consultant, 1958-60, professor of econometrics, 1964-67; University of Pennsylvania, Wharton School of Finance and Commerce, assistant professor of economics, 1956-62; United States Department of Commerce, Office of Business Economics, consultant, 1962-65; Organization of American States, consultant, 1965-; United States Department of Justice, consultant, 1965-; Center of Economic Studies and Plans, research associate, 1966; State University of New York, professor of economics, 1967-72, Goodyear professor of economics, 1972-92, professor emeritus of economics, 1992-. Writer. **Publications:** On the Theory and Measurement of Technological Change, 1966; Tripartite Income Employment Contracts, Rand Journal of Economics, 1989; Uniqueness of Equilibrium, Games and Economic Behavior, 1991; Unsystematic Risk and Coalition Formation, 2002; (with S.H. Chiang) Coalitions in Oligopolies: An Introduction to the Sequential Procedure, 2003. EDITOR: (and intro.) The Theory and Empirical Analysis of Production, 1967; (with K. Sato and P. Zarembka) Essays in Modern Capital Theory, 1976; (with M.D. Palma and B. Ferrara) Regional National Econometric Modeling with an Application to the Italian Economy, 1978. Contributor to journals. **Address:** 80 Fairlawn Dr., Amherst, NY 14226, U.S.A. **Online address:** mbrown@buffalo.edu

BROWN, Nancy Marie. American (born United States) **Genres:** Women's Studies And Issues, Travel/Exploration, History. **Career:** Penn State University, director of research publications, 1981-2003, Research/Penn State Magazine, science writer and editor, 1981-2003; writer, 2003-. **Publications:** A Good Horse Has No Color: Searching Iceland for the Perfect Horse, 2001; (with N.V. Fedoroff) Mendel in the Kitchen: A Scientist's View of Genetically Modified Foods, 2004; The Far Traveler: Voyages of a Viking Woman, 2007; Abacus and The Cross: The Story of the Pope Who Brought the Light of Science to the Dark Ages, 2010. Contributor to periodicals. **Address:** c/o Michelle Tessler, Tessler Literary Agency, 27 W 20th St., Ste. 1003, New York, NY 10011, U.S.A. **Online address:** nmb1@psu.edu

BROWN, Nicholas. American (born United States), b. 1971. **Genres:** Literary Criticism And History, Politics/Government, Education. **Career:** University of Illinois, International Studies, advisor, 2000-, Department of English, associate professor and director of graduate studies, 2007-, Department of African American Studies, head, 2009-; Mediations, Editorial Board, chair, 2007-. Writer. **Publications:** (Ed. and intro. with I. Szeman) Pierre Bourdieu: Fieldwork in Culture, 2000; Utopian Generations: The Political Horizon of Twentieth-Century Literature, 2006. Contributor to books and periodicals. **Address:** Department of English, College of Liberal Arts and Sciences, University of Illinois, MC 162, 2027 University Hall, 601 S Morgan St., Chicago, IL 60607, U.S.A. **Online address:** cola@uic.edu

BROWN, Nickole. American (born United States), b. 1976?. **Genres:** Essays, Novels. **Career:** Hunter S. Thompson, editorial assistant, 1997; Vermont College of Fine Arts, program coordinator; Murray State University, faculty; Bellarmine University, lecturer; University of Louisville, lecturer; White Pine Press, editor; Arktoi Books, publicity consultant; Sarabande Books, staff. **Publications:** (Ed. with J. Taylor) Air Fare: Stories, Poems & Essays on Flight, 2004; Sister: A-Novel-in- Poems, 2007. Contributor to periodicals. **Address:** Louisville, KY , U.S.A. **Online address:** nikolebrown@yahoo.com

BROWN, Parry Ann. (Parry EbonySatin Brown). American (born United States), b. 1952?. **Genres:** Novels. **Career:** Shankrys Publishing, founder and general manager, 1999-; AB Positive Corp., co-founder and general manager; ANE Productions, partner; Ebony People Online, founder and chairperson. Writer. **Publications:** AS PARRY EBONYSATIN BROWN: The Shirt Off His Back, 1998; Sexy Doesn't Have a Dress Size: Lessons in Love, 2000; Sittin' In The Front Pew, 2002; Fannin' The Flames, 2004; (with P. Simmons and L. Watson) Love Is Blind, 2004; (with G. Forster and D. Hill) Destiny's Daughters, 2006; What Goes Around: A Novel, 2006. Works appear in anthologies. **Address:** The Shan Krys Group, 433 N Camden Dr., Ste. 600, Beverly Hills, CA 90210-4416, U.S.A. **Online address:** pbrown@parryabrown.com

BROWN, Parry EbonySatin. *See* **BROWN, Parry Ann.**

BROWN, Patricia Fortini. American (born United States), b. 1936. **Genres:** Art/Art History, History, Architecture. **Career:** State of California, Department of Employment, employment and claims specialist, 1960-65; Falkirk Community Cultural Center, Municipal Art Gallery, co-founder and curator, 1976-77; University of California, Department of History of Art, teaching assistant and associate, 1978-80; Mills College, Department of Art, lecturer in Italian Renaissance art, 1983; Princeton University, Department of Art and Archaeology, assistant professor, 1983-89, associate professor, 1989-97, professor of art and archaeology, 1997-2010, professor emeritus, 2010-, department chair, 1999-2005; University of Cambridge, Slade Professor of Fine Arts, 2000-01, St. John's College, Commoner Fellow; Venice International University, lecturer, 2003, 2004. Writer. **Publications:** Venetian Narrative Painting in the Age of Carpaccio, 1988; La pittura nell' eta di Carpaccio: i grandi cicli narrativi, 1992; Venice & Antiquity: The Venetian Sense of the Past, 1996; Art and Life in Renaissance Venice in UK as Renaissance in Venice: A World Apart, 1997; Private Lives in Renaissance Venice: Art, Architecture, and the Family, 2004; Venice Outside Venice, forthcoming. Contributor to books and journals. **Address:** Department of Art & Archaeology, Princeton University, 309 McCormick Hall, Princeton, NJ 08544-1018, U.S.A. **Online address:** pbrown@princeton.edu

BROWN, Peter A. American (born United States), b. 1949. **Genres:** Politics/Government. **Career:** United Press Intl., political reporter, 1974-81; Scripps Howard News Service, chief political writer, 1981-96, political editor; Orlando Sentinel, editor, 1996-; Harvard University, Neiman fellow; Quinnipiac University Polling Institute, assistant director, 2006-. **Publications:** Minority Party: Why Democrats Face Defeat in 1992 and Beyond, 1991; Mosby's Fighting Parson: The Life and Times of Sam Chapman, 2001; (ed.) Take Sides with the Truth: The Postwar Letters of John Singleton Mosby to Samuel F. Chapman, 2007. **Address:** Quinnipiac University Polling Institute, 275 Mount Carmel Ave., Hamden, CT 06518-1908, U.S.A. **Online address:** peter.brown@quinnipiac.edu

BROWN, Peter G. American/Canadian (born Canada), b. 1940. **Genres:** Politics/Government. **Career:** University of Maryland, professor of public affairs, environmental policy programs, director, Institute for Philosophy and Public Policy, founder, School of Public Policy, founder, International Institute of Environmental Policy and Management, founder; Urban Institute, assistant vice president for research operations; Battelle Seattle Research Center, visiting fellow; Aspen Institute for Humanistic Studies, consultant; McGill University, School of Environment, Department of Geography, professor, director; Hastings Center, fellow. Consultant and writer. **Publications:** American Law Institute Model land Development Code, the taking Issue and Private Property Rights, 1975; Personal Liability of Public Officials, Sovereign Immunity and Compensation for Loss, 1977; Restoring the Public Trust: A Fresh Vision for Progressive Government in America, 1994; Commonwealth of Life: A Treatise on Stewardship Economics, 2001; Ethics, Economics and International Relations: Transparent Sovereignty in the Commonwealth of Life, 2nd ed., 2008; (co-author) Right Relationship: Building a Whole Earth Economy, 2009; (with J.J. Schmidt) Water Ethics: Foundational Readings for Students and Professionals, 2010; Reverence for Life: A Philosophy for Civilization, forthcoming. EDITOR: (and intro. with H. Shue) Food Policy: The Responsibility of the United States in the Life and Death Choices, 1977; (with G. Dworkin and G. Bermant) Markets and Morals, 1977; (with D. MacLean) Human Rights and U.S. Foreign Policy: Principles and Applications, 1979; (with H. Shue) Boundaries: National Autonomy and Its Limits, 1981; (with C. Johnson and P. Vernier) Income Support: Conceptual and Policy, 1981; (with H. Shue) The Border That Joins: Mexican Migrants and U.S. Responsibility, 1983; (with D. MacLean) Energy and the Future, 1983. Contributor to books and periodicals. **Address:** Department of Geography, McGill University, 805 Sherbrooke St. W, Montreal, QC H3A 2K6, Canada. **Online address:** peter.g.brown@mcgill.ca

BROWN, Rajeswary Ampalavanar. British/Malaysian (born Malaysia) **Genres:** Business/Trade/Industry. **Career:** University of Malaya, lecturer, 1966-76; Hatfield Polytechnic, part-time faculty, 1976-86; University of Cambridge, Department of Economics, part-time faculty, 1976-86; Open University, part-time faculty, 1976-86; University of London, Royal Holloway College, London School of Economics and Political Science, lecturer in economic History, 1986-88, Business History Unit, research officer and part-time lecturer in the economic History department, 1988-90; School of Oriental and African Studies, research fellow and part-time lecturer, 1990-96, School of Management, lecturer in Asia-Pacific business and management, 1996-2002, reader in international comparative business, 2002-08, professor in international business, 2008-, now professor emeritus of international business. Writer. **Publications:** The Indian Minority and Political Change in Malaya, 1945-1957, 1981; (with I. Brown) Malaysia, 1986; Franchising at Work, 1993; Capital and Entrepreneurship in South-East Asia, 1994; (ed.) Chinese Business Enterprise in Asia, 1995; (ed.) Chinese Business Enterprise, 1996; Chinese Big Business and the Wealth of Asian Nations, 2000; The Rise of the Corporate Economy in Southeast Asia, 2006. **Address:** School of Management, Royal Holloway, University of London, Egham Hill, Egham, SR TW20 0EX, England. **Online address:** r.brown@rhul.ac.uk

BROWN, Richard E. American (born United States), b. 1946. **Genres:** Novels, Novellas/Short Stories, Plays/Screenplays, Young Adult Fiction. **Career:** University of Nevada, assistant professor, 1972-77, associate professor, 1977-89, professor of English, 1989-, now professor emeritus, vice-chair of faculty senate, 1989-90, chairman of faculty senate, 1990-91. Writer. **Publications:** Chester's Last Stand: A Novel, 1988; Fishing for Ghosts: Twelve Short Stories, 1994. **Address:** Department of English, University of Nevada, MS 098, 1664 N Virginia St., Reno, NV 89557-0098, U.S.A. **Online address:** rebrown@unr.nevada.edu

BROWN, Richard E(arl). Canadian (born Canada), b. 1948. **Genres:** Psychology, Zoology, Sciences, Politics/Government. **Career:** University of Oxford, Animal Behaviour Research Group, post-doctoral fellow, 1975-77; Dalhousie University, professor of psychology and neuroscience, 1978-, Department of Psychology, chair, 1989-96, 2002-08, Killam professor, 2002-, university research professor, Richard Brown's Laboratory, director, Neuroscience Institute, director, 1996-99. Writer. **Publications:** Review of Employee Evaluation Systems, 1961; (ed.) Effectiveness of Legislative Program Review, 1979; (with M.C. Williams and T.P. Gallagher) Auditing Performance in Government: Concepts and Cases, 1982; (ed. with D.W. Macdonald) Social Odors in Mammals, 2 vols., 1985; An Introduction to Neuroendocrinology, 1994; Hormones and Behavior, 1995. Contributor to periodicals. **Address:** Department of Psychology, Dalhousie University, Life Sciences Ctr., Halifax, NS B3H 4R2, Canada. **Online address:** rebrown@dal.ca

BROWN, Rita Mae. American (born United States), b. 1944. **Genres:** Novels, Plays/Screenplays, Poetry, Gay And Lesbian Issues, Translations, Animals/Pets, Picture/Board Books, Young Adult Non-fiction, Young Adult Non-fiction. **Career:** Sterling Publishing, photo editor, 1969-70; Federal City College, lecturer in sociology, 1970-71; Institute for Policy Studies, research fellow, 1971-73; Goddard College, visiting faculty in feminist studies, 1973-; American Artists Inc., president, 1980-. **Publications:** NOVELS: Rubyfruit Jungle, 1973; In Her Day, 1976; Six of One, 1978; Southern Discomfort, 1982; Sudden Death, 1983; High Hearts, 1986; Bingo, 1988; Venus Envy, 1993; Dolley: A Novel of Dolley Madison in Land War, 1994; Riding Shotgun, 1996; Loose Lips, 1999; Alma Mater, 2001; (with S.P. Brown) The Purrfect Murder, 2008; Fox Tracks, 2012. POETRY: The Hand That Cradles the Rock, 1971; Songs to a Handsome Woman, 1973; The Poems of Rita Mae Brown, 1987. THE SISTER JANE FOX HUNTING MYSTERIES: Outfoxed, 2000; (with S.P. Brown) Pawing Through the Past, 2000; Hotspur, 2002; Full Cry, 2003; The Hunt Ball, 2005; Hounds and the Fury, 2006; The Tell-Tale Horse: A Novel, 2008; Hounded to Death: A Novel, 2008. THE MRS. MURPHY BOOKS: (with S.P. Brown) Wish You Were Here, 1990; (with S.P. Brown) Rest in Pieces, 1992; (with S.P. Brown) Murder at Monticello, or, Old Sins, 1994; (with S.P. Brown) Pay Dirt, or, Adventures at Ash Lawn, 1995; (with S.P. Brown) Murder, She Meowed, 1996; Murder on the Prowl, 1998; (with S.P. Brown) Cat on the Scent, 1999, 3rd ed., 2003; Sneaky Pie's Cookbook for Mystery Lovers, 1999; Pawing through the Past, 2000; Claws and Effect, 2001; (with S.P. Brown) Catch as Cat Can, 2002; The Tail of the Tip-Off, 2003; Whisker of Evil, 2004; Cat's Eyewitness, 2005; (with S.P. Brown) Sour Puss: A Mrs. Murphy Mystery, 2006; Puss 'n Cahoots: A Mrs. Murphy Mystery, 2007; The Perfect Murder, 2008; (with S.P. Brown) Santa Clawed: A Mrs. Murphy Mystery, 2008. OTHERS: (trans.) Hrotsvitha: Six Medieval Latin Plays, 1971; A Plain Brown Rapper (essays), 1976; Starting from Scratch: A Different Kind of Writer's Manual, 1988; Rita Will: Memoir of a Literary Rabble-Rouser, 1997; Sneaky Pie's Cookbook for Mystery Lovers, 1999; (co-author) I'd Kill for That, 2004; Hunt Ball, 2005; Six of One, 2008; The Sand Castle, 2008; Animal Magnetism: My Life with Creatures Great and Small, 2009; (with S.P. Brown) Cat of the Century, 2010; A Nose for Justice, 2010; Soooo Cute!!!! Sticker Book: Puppies, 2010; (with S.P. Brown) Hiss of Death: A Mrs. Murphy Mystery, 2011; Murder Unleashed, 2011; Adorable You!, 2011; The Big Cat Nap, 2012; (with S.P. Brown) Sneaky Pie for President, 2012. Contributor to periodicals. **Address:** Sharon Propson, Random House Inc., 1745 Broadway, New York, NY 10019, U.S.A.

BROWN, Roberta Simpson. American (born United States), b. 1939. **Genres:** Novellas/Short Stories, Horror, Writing/Journalism, Young Adult Fiction. **Career:** Jefferson County Board of Education, teacher of language arts, 1963-99, retired, 1999; freelance writer, 1991-. **Publications:** JUVENILE HORROR: The Walking Trees and Other Scary Stories, 1991; Queen of the Cold-Blooded Tales, 1993; Scared in School, 1997, (with F.S. Atchley) Strains of Music, 2004; Lamplight Tales, 2005; (with L.E Brown) Spooky, Kooky Poems for Kids, 2006; (with L.E. Brown) Spookiest Stories Ever: Four Seasons of Kentucky Ghosts, 2010. Contributor to periodicals. **Address:** 11906 Lilac Way, Louisville, KY 40243-1409, U.S.A. **Online address:** robertasbrown@aol.com

BROWN, Robert G(oodell). American (born United States), b. 1923. **Genres:** Administration/Management, Information Science/Computers, History, Theology/Religion, Business/Trade/Industry, Engineering. **Career:** Northeastern University, visiting professor, 1960; Dartmouth College, visiting professor, 1963; Boston University, visiting professor, 1967; Materials Management Systems Inc., president, 1970-; Lehigh University, visiting professor, 1971. Writer. **Publications:** Statistical Forecasting for Inventory Control, 1959; Smoothing, Forecasting and Prediction of Discrete Time Series, 1963; Decision Rules for Inventory Management, 1967; Management Decisions for Production Operations, 1971; (comp.) Source Book in Production Management, 1971; APL-Plus 747 Forecasting Users Guide, 1973; Materials Management Systems, 1977; Advanced Service Parts Inventory Control, 1982; Shirley He Hath Born, 1984; LOGOL Systems Manual, 1985, rev. ed., 1994; Twigs Systems Manual, 1988; Consultantmanship, 1993; The Tall Boy Scout Playing Tennis, 1994; The People of the Old Testament, 1994; My Psalter, 1994. **Address:** PO Box 239, Thetford Center, VT 05075, U.S.A.

BROWN, Rosellen. American (born United States), b. 1939. **Genres:** Novels, Novellas/Short Stories, Plays/Screenplays, Poetry, Essays. **Career:** Tougaloo College, instructor in American and English literature, 1965-67; National Endowment for the Arts, fellow, 1973, 1982; Bunting Institute, fellow, 1973-75; Guggenheim, fellow 1976-77; Goddard College, instructor in creative writing, 1976; Boston University, visiting professor of creative writing, 1977-78; University of Houston, instructor of creative writing, professor of creative writing, 1982-85, 1989-95; School of the Art Institute of Chicago, MFA in Writing, professor, 1996-; Northwestern University, Center for the Writing Arts, writer-in-residence, 2000. **Publications:** POETRY: Some Deaths in Delta and Other Poems, 1970; Cora Fry, 1977; Cora Fry's Pillow Book, 1994. NOVELS: The Autobiography of My Mother, 1976; Tender Mercies, 1978; Civil Wars, 1984; Before and After, 1992; Half a Heart, 2000. OTHER: Street Games (short stories), 1974, rev. ed., 2001; Body my House, 1978; A Rosellen Brown Reader, 1992; (intro.) God of Nightmares, 2002. EDITOR: The Whole World Catalog, 1972; Ploughshares: Men Portray Women, Women Portray Men, 1978; Banquet, 1978; Intimate Exile (personal essays), 1994. **Address:** 5421 S Cornell Ave., Apt. 16, Apt. 16, Chicago, IL 60615, U.S.A. **Online address:** rosellen@rosellenbrown.com

BROWN, Ruth. British (born England), b. 1941. **Genres:** Children's Fiction, Animals/Pets, Illustrations. **Career:** Author and illustrator, 1979-. **Publications:** SELF-ILLUSTRATED: A Dark, Dark Tale, 1981. FOR CHILDREN: Crazy Charlie, 1979; If at First You Do Not See, 1982; The Grizzly Revenge, 1983; The Big Sneeze, 1985; Our Cat Flossie, 1986; Our Puppy's Holiday, 1987 in US as Our Puppy's Vacation, 1987; Ladybird, Ladybird, 1988 in the U.S. as Ladybug, Ladybug, 1988; I Don't Like It!, 1989; The World That Jack Built, 1990; The Four-Tongued Alphabet: An Alphabet Book in Four Languages, 1991 in US as Alphabet Times Four: An International ABC, 1991; The Picnic, 1992; One Stormy Night, 1992; Copycat, 1994; The Tale of the Monstrous Toad, 1996 in US as Toad, 1997; Baba, 1997 in US as Cry Baby, 1997; Mad Summer Night's Dream, 1998; The Shy Little Angel, 1998; Holly: The True Story of a Cat, 2000; Snail Trail, 2001; Ten Seeds, 2001; Night-time Tale, 2007; Old Tree, 2007; Gracie: The Lighthouse Cat, 2011. Illustrator of books by others. **Address:** Andersen Press Ltd., 20 Vauxhall Bridge Rd., London, GL SW1V 2SA, England.

BROWN, Ryan. American (born United States), b. 1975. **Genres:** Novels. **Career:** Writer and actor. **Publications:** Play Dead (novel), 2010. Contributor to books. Works appear in anthologies. **Address:** c/o Laurie Bernstein, Side by Side Literary Productions Inc., 15 W 26th St., 2nd Fl., New York, NY 10010, U.S.A. **Online address:** ryanbrownauthor@gmail.com

BROWN, Sandra. Also writes as Rachel Ryan, Erin St. Claire, Laura Jordan. American (born United States), b. 1948. **Genres:** Novels, Mystery/Crime/Suspense, Romance/Historical, Young Adult Fiction. **Career:** Merle Norman Cosmetics Studios, manager, 1971-73; KLTV-TV, weather reporter, 1972-75; WFAA-TV, weather reporter, 1976-79; Dallas Apparel Mart, model, 1976-87. Writer. **Publications:** ROMANCE/SUSPENSE NOVELS: Relentless Desire, 1983; Tempest in Eden, 1983; Temptation's Kiss, 1983; Tomorrow's Promise, 1983; A Secret Splendor, 1983; Breakfast in Bed, 1983; Heaven's Price, 1983; In a Class by Itself, 1984; Send No Flowers, 1984; Sunset Embrace, 1984; Riley in the Morning, 1985; Another Dawn, 1985; Thursday's Child, 1985; 22 Indigo Place, 1986; The Rana Look, 1986; Demon Rumm, 1987; Fanta C, 1987; Sunny Chandler's Return, 1987; Adam's Fall, 1988; Hawk's O'Toole's Hostage, 1988; Tidings of Great Joy, 1988; Slow Heat in Heaven, 1988; Long Time Coming, 1989; Temperatures Rising, 1989; Best Kept Secrets, 1989; A Whole New Light, 1989; Mirror Image, 1990; Breath of Scandal, 1991; Three Complete Novels, 1992; French Silk, 1992; Honor Bound, 1992; Shadows of Yesterday, 1992; Where There's Smoke, 1993; Charade, 1994; The Witness, 1995; Exclusive, 1996; Fat Tuesday, 1997; Unspeakable, 1998; The Alibi, 1999; Standoff, 2000; The Switch, 2000; Envy, 2001; The Crush, 2002; Hello, Darkness, 2003; White Hot, 2004; Chill Factor, 2005; Ricochet, 2006; Play Dirty, 2007; Smoke Screen, 2008; Smash Cut, 2009; Rainwater, 2009; Tough Customer, 2010; Lethal, 2011. TEXAS! SERIES: Texas! Lucky, 1989; Texas! Chase, 1989; Texas! Sage, 1989; Texas! Trilogy, 1992. ROMANCE NOVELS AS LAURA JORDAN: Hidden Fires, 1982; The Silken Web, 1982. NOVELS AS RACHEL RYAN: Love beyond Reason, 1981; Love's Encore, 1981; Eloquent Silence, 1982; A Treasure Worth Seeking, 1982; Prime Time, 1983. NOVELS AS ERIN ST. CLAIRE: Not Even for Love, 1982; A Kiss Remembered, 1983; A Secret Splendor, 1983; Seduction by Design, 1983; Bittersweet Rain, 1984; Words of Silk, 1984; Led Astray, 1985; A Sweet Anger, 1985; Tiger Prince, 1985; Above and Beyond, 1986; Honor Bound, 1986; The Devil's Own, 1987; Two Alone, 1987; Thrill of Victory, 1989. **Address:** c/o Tracey Guest, Simon & Schuster, 1230 Ave. of the Americas, New York, NY 10020, U.S.A. **Online address:** sandrab@sandrabrown.net

BROWN, Scott G. Canadian (born Canada), b. 1966. **Genres:** Literary Criticism And History, Humanities. **Career:** University of Toronto, sessional lecturer, 1989-. Writer. **Publications:** Mark's Other Gospel: Rethinking Morton Smith's Controversial Discovery, 2005; A Guide to Writing Academic Essays in Religious Studies, 2008. **Address:** University of Toronto, Toronto, ON M5S 3B1, Canada. **Online address:** scottg.brown@utoronto.ca

BROWN, Steve. American (born United States), b. 1944. **Genres:** Mystery/Crime/Suspense, Young Adult Fiction, History, Military/Defense/Arms Control, Novels. **Career:** Writer. **Publications:** Black Fire, 1999; Of Love and War, 1999; Color Her Dead, 1999; Dead Kids Tell No Tales, 2000; Stripped to Kill, 2000; Radio Secrets, 2000; America Strikes Back, 2001; Woman against Herself, 2001; Fallen Stars, 2001; When Dead Is Not Enough, 2001; Hurricane Party, 2002; Rescue!, 2002; River of Diamonds, 2002; Sanctuary of Evil, 2003; The Belles of Charleston, 2005; Carolina Girls, 2006; The Charleston Ripper, 2007; The Pirate and the Belle, 2008; The Charleston Vampire, 2009; The Old Maids' Club, 2010. **Address:** c/o Author Mail, Chick Springs Publishing, PO Box 1130, Taylors, SC 29687, U.S.A. **Online address:** chicksprgs@aol.com

BROWN, Steven Preston. American (born United States), b. 1964?. **Genres:** Politics/Government, Theology/Religion. **Career:** Auburn University, Department of Political Science, faculty, 1998-, Jane Dickerson Lanier Associate Professor, 1998-, Election Center, instructor. Writer. **Publications:** Trumping Religion: The New Christian Right, The Free Speech Clause, and The Courts, 2002. **Address:** Department of Political Science, Auburn University, 7006 Haley Ctr., Auburn, AL 36849-5208, U.S.A. **Online address:** brown32@auburn.edu

BROWN, Stewart. British (born England), b. 1951. **Genres:** Novellas/Short Stories, Poetry, Literary Criticism And History, Art/Art History, History, Essays. **Career:** High school teacher, 1972-74; Bayero University, lecturer in English, 1980-83; University of Birmingham, lecturer in African and Caribbean literature, 1988-, reader in African and Caribbean literatures. Writer. **Publications:** Beasts, 1975; Specimens, 1979; Writers from Africa: A Reader's Guide, 1989; Caribbean Stories Now, 1991; (with K. Ramchand and J. Stone) West Indian Literature: A Literary History, 1992; The Art of Edward Kamau Brathwaite: A Collection of Critical Essays, 1992; Kiss to Quarrel: Yoruba/English, Strategies of Mediation, 2000. POETRY: Mekin Foolishness, 1981; Zinder, 1986; Lugard's Bridge, 1989; Elsewhere: New & Selected Poems, 1999; Tourist, Traveller, Troublemaker: Essays on Poetry, 2007. EDITOR: Caribbean Poetry Now, 1986, 2nd. ed., 1992; (with M. Morris and G. Rohler) Voiceprint: An Anthology of Oral and Related Poetry from the Caribbean, 1989; Caribbean New Wave: Contemporary Short Stories, 1990; The Art of Derek Walcott: A Collection of Critical Essays, 1991; (with I. McDonald) The Heinemann Book of Caribbean Poetry, 1992; The Art of Kamau Brathwaite: A Collection of Critical Essays, 1995; The Pressures of the Text: Orality, Texts and the Telling of Tales, 1995; Caribbean New Voices, 1995; African New Voices, 1997; (with J. Wickham) The Oxford Book of Caribbean Short Stories, 1999; All Are Involved: The Art of Martin Carter, 2000; (with M. McWatt) The Oxford Book of Caribbean Verse, 2005; (with I. McDonald) Poems by Martin Carter, 2006; (with I. McDonald) The Bowling was Superfine: The Literature of West Indian Cricket, 2009; (with P. Nanton) Henry Swanzy, Frank Collymore and Caribbean Voices, 2010. **Address:** Centre of West African Studies, University of Birmingham, Arts Bldg., Edgbaston, Birmingham, WM B15 2TT, England. **Online address:** s.brown@bham.ac.uk

BROWN, Thomas J. American (born United States), b. 1960?. **Genres:** History. **Career:** Harvard University, lecturer on history, 1995-96; University of South Carolina, Department of History, assistant professor, 1996-2002, associate professor, 2002-, professor, Institute for Southern Studies, assistant director, 1996-2002, associate director, 2002-07. Writer. **Publications:** Dorothea Dix: New England Reformer, 1998. EDITOR: American Eras: Civil War and Reconstruction, 1850-1877, 1997; (with M.H. Blatt and D. Yacovone) Hope and Glory: Essays on the Legacy of the 54th Massachusetts Regiment, 2001; The Public Art of Civil War Commemoration: A Brief History with Documents, 2004; Reconstructions: New Perspectives on the Postbellum United States, 2006; City of the Silent: The Charlestonians of Magnolia Cemetery, 2010; (ed.) Remixing the Civil War: Meditations on the Sesquicentennial, 2011. **Address:** Department of History, University of South Carolina, Rm. 118, Gambrell Hall, 817 Henderson St., Columbia, SC 29208, U.S.A. **Online address:** browntj@gwm.sc.edu

BROWN, Tony. American (born United States), b. 1933. **Genres:** Plays/Screenplays, Adult Non-fiction. **Career:** Central Washington University, faculty; Federal City College, faculty; Detroit Courier, drama critic, editor; WTVS-TV, writer, producer, host; WNET-TV, host, 1970-77; Howard University, School of Communications, professor, founding dean, 1971-74; Tony Brown Productions Inc., president, 1977-; Hampton University, Scripps Howard School of Journalism and Communications, dean, 2004-09; The National Black College Alumni Hall of Fame Foundation Inc., chair; Harvard Foundation for Intercultural and Race Relations, advisor; Association for the Study of African American Life and History, board director; WHUR-FM Radio, chair. **Publications:** Black Lies, White Lies: The Truth According to Tony Brown (nonfiction), 1995; Empower the People: Overthrow The Conspiracy That Is Stealing Your Money And Freedom, 1999; What Mama Taught Me: The Seven Core Values of Life, 2003. **Address:** Tony Brown Productions Inc., 2214 Frederick Douglass Blvd., Ste. 124, New York, NY 10036, U.S.A. **Online address:** mail@tbol.net

BROWN, Tracy. American (born United States), b. 1974?. **Genres:** Novels, Criminology/True Crime. **Career:** Writer. **Publications:** NOVELS: Black: A Street Tale, 2003; Dime Piece, 2004; Criminal Minded, 2005; White Lines, 2007; Twisted, 2008; (with K'wan and A. Mitchell) Flirt, 2009; Snapped, 2010; Aftermath: A Snapped Novel, 2011; White Lines II: Sunny: A White Lines Novel, 2012. **Address:** St. Martin's Press, 175 5th Ave., New York, NY 10010, U.S.A.

BROWN, V(ictor) I(vy). American (born United States), b. 1949. **Genres:** Law. **Career:** Writer. **Publications:** Veteran Preference Employment Statutes: A State-by-State and Federal Government Handbook, 2000. **Address:** McFarland & Company Inc., 960 NC Hwy. 88 W, PO Box 611, Jefferson, NC 28640-8813, U.S.A. **Online address:** vbrown1845@aol.com

BROWNE, Anthony (Edward Tudor). British (born England), b. 1946. **Genres:** Children's Fiction, Illustrations, Animals/Pets, Picture/Board Books.

Career: Victoria University, Royal Infirmary, medical artist, 1968-70; Gordon Fraser Greeting Cards, designer, 1971-87; Tate Britain Gallery, writer, illustrator-in-residence, 2001-02; author, 1975-. **Publications:** SELF-ILLUSTRATED BEAR SERIES: Bear Hunt, 1980; Bear Goes to Town, 1982; Willy the Wimp, 1984; Willy the Champ, 1985; The Little Bear Book, 1989; A Bear-y Tale, 1989; Willy and Hugh, 1991; Willy the Wizard, 1995; Willy the Dreamer, 1997, 2nd ed., 2002; Willy's Pictures, 2000. OTHERS: Through the Magic Mirror, 1977; A Walk in the Park, 1977; Look What I've Got!, 1980; Gorilla, 1983, rev. ed., 1991; Piggy Book, 1986; I Like Books, 1988; Things I Like, 1989; The Tunnel, 1989; Changes, 1990; Zoo, 1992; The Big Baby: A Little Joke, 1993; King Kong, 1994; The Topiary Garden, 1995; Voices in the Park, 1998; My Dad, 2000; The Animal Fair: A Spectacular Pop-Up, 2002; The Shape Game, 2003; Into the Forest, 2004; I Like Books, 2004; My Mom, 2005; Silly Billy, 2006; My Brother, 2007; Little Beauty, 2008; How do You Feel?, 2012. Illustrator of books by others. **Address:** Walker Books Ltd., 87 Vauxhall Walk, London, GL SE11 5HJ, England. **Online address:** aetb@btinternet.com

BROWNE, Cameron Bolitho. Australian/British (born England), b. 1966. **Genres:** Technology. **Career:** La Trobe University, Department of Computing, tutor, 1994; Queensland University of Technology, tutor, 1995; International Computer Science Institute, visiting researcher, 1996; Canon Information Systems Research, developer, 1997, 1999, researcher, 1999, senior software engineer, 2000-02; Microsoft Corp., developer, 1998; Swishzone.com, software engineer, 2003; University of Edinburgh, research associate, 2008; AI & Games Network, administrator, 2009-; Imperial College London, Computational Creativity Group, postdoctoral research fellow, 2010-. Writer. **Publications:** Hex Strategy: Making the Right Connections, 2000; Connection Games: Variations on a Theme, 2005; Evolutionary Game Design, 2011. Contributor to books, journals and periodicals. **Address:** Computational Creativity Group, Imperial College London, Rm. 407, Huxley Bldg., Exhibition Rd., South Kensington Campus, London, GL SW7 2AZ, England. **Online address:** cameron.browne@btinternet.com

BROWNE, David. American (born United States), b. 1960. **Genres:** Biography, Music. **Career:** Music & Sound Output Magazine, staff; High Fidelity, staff, 1988; New York Daily News, staff reporter and music critic, 1988-89, columnist; Entertainment Weekly Magazine, music critic, 1990-2006; Rolling Stone Magazine, contributing editor, 2008-. **Publications:** Dream Brother: The Lives and Music of Jeff and Tim Buckley, 2001; Amped: How Big Air, Big Dollars, and a New Generation Took Sports to the Extreme, 2004; Goodbye 20th Century: A Biography of Sonic Youth, 2008; Fire and Rain: The Beatles, Simon & Garfunkel, James Taylor, CSNY and the Lost Story of 1970, 2011. Contributor to magazines. **Address:** New York, NY , U.S.A. **Online address:** david@david-browne.com

BROWNE, Gerald A(ustin). American (born United States), b. 1924?. **Genres:** Novels, Young Adult Fiction, Mystery/Crime/Suspense, Criminology/True Crime. **Career:** Grey Advertising, vice president. Fashion photographer and writer. **Publications:** It's All Zoo, 1968; 11 Harrowhouse, 1972; Hazard, 1973; Slide, 1976; Green Ice, 1978; Nineteen Purchase Street, 1982; Stone 588, 1986; Hot Siberian, 1989; The Arousers, 1989; The Ravishers, 1989; Eighteen Millimeter Blues, 1993; Blue Pearls, 1994; West Forty Seventh, 1996; Rush 929, 1998. **Address:** Warner Books Inc., Time Life Bldg., 1271 Ave. of the Americas, 9th Fl., New York, NY 10020, U.S.A. **Online address:** geraldabrowne@earthlink.net

BROWNE, Hester. British (born England) **Genres:** Young Adult Fiction, Novels, Humor/Satire. **Career:** Journalist. **Publications:** LITTLE LADY AGENCY SERIES: The Little Lady Agency, 2006; Little Lady, Big Apple, 2006; What the Lady Wants, 2007 in US as Little Lady Agency and the Prince, 2008. NOVELS: The Finishing Touches, 2009; Swept off Her Feet, 2011. **Address:** c/o Lizzy Kremer, David Higham Associates Ltd., 5-8 Lower John St., Golden Sq., London, GL W1F 9HA, England.

BROWNE, Michael Dennis. American/British (born England), b. 1940. **Genres:** Poetry, Songs/Lyrics And Libretti, Social Sciences. **Career:** University of Iowa, visiting lecturer in creative writing, 1967-68; Columbia University, adjunct assistant professor, 1968-69; University of Minnesota, visiting assistant professor, 1971-72, assistant professor, 1972-75, associate professor, 1975-83, professor of English, 1983-, Program in Creative Writing, director, 1989-92, Morse-Alumni distinguished teaching professor, professor emeritus. Writer. **Publications:** (With D. Lord) How the Stars Were Made, 1968; The Wife of Winter, 1970; (with D. Lord) Sea Journey, 1970; (with D. Lord) Non Songs, 1974; Sun Exercises, 1976; (with S. Paulus) Canticles, 1977; (with S. Paulus) Fountain of My Friends, 1977; (with S. Paulus) Mad Book, 1977; (with S. Paulus) North Shore, 1978; The Sun Fetcher, 1978; (with S. Paulus) A Village Singer, 1979; (with S. Paulus) All My Pretty Ones, 1981; Smoke from the Fires, 1985; (with J. Foley) Able to Fall, 1988; (with S. Paulus) Harmoonia, 1991; You Won't Remember This, 1992; Selected Poems 1965-1995, 1997; (with S. Paulus) The Three Hermits, 1997; Give Her the River: A Father's Wish for His Daughter, 2004; Things I Can't Tell You, 2005; Panthers, 2008; What the Poem Wants, 2009. Contributor to periodicals. **Address:** Department of English, University of Minnesota, 330A Lind Hall, 207 Church St. SE, Minneapolis, MN 55455, U.S.A. **Online address:** mdb@umn.edu

BROWNE, Nicky Matthews. British (born England) **Genres:** Novels, Children's Fiction, Science Fiction/Fantasy. **Career:** Writer and educator. **Publications:** Warriors of Alavna, 2000; Hunted, 2002; Warriors of Camlann, 2003; Basilisk, 2004; The Story of Stone, 2005; Silver Boy, 2007; The Spellgrinder's Apprentice, 2007; Shadow Web, 2008; Warriors of Ethandun, 2009; Wolf Blood, 2011. **Address:** Bloomsbury Children's Books, 36 Soho Sq., London, GL W1D 3QY, England. **Online address:** nicky.matthews@btinternet.com

BROWNELL, Charles E(dward). American (born United States), b. 1943. **Genres:** Art/Art History, Architecture, History. **Career:** University of Virginia, associate professor of architectural history; Virginia Commonwealth University, Department of Art History, professor of art history. Writer. **Publications:** (With E.C. Carter II and J.C. Van) HorneLatrobe's View of America, 1795-1820: Selections from the Watercolors and Sketches, 1985; (co-author) The Making of Virginia Architecture, 1992; (with J.A. Cohen) The Architectural Drawings of Benjamin Henry Latrobe, 1994. Contributor to periodicals. **Address:** Department of Art History, Virginia Commonwealth University, 922 W Franklin St., PO Box 843046, Richmond, VA 23284-3046, U.S.A. **Online address:** cbrownel@mail2.vcu.edu

BROWNELL, Susan. American (born United States), b. 1960. **Genres:** Anthropology/Ethnology, Sports/Fitness, Women's Studies And Issues, Social Sciences. **Career:** University of Washington, Middlebury College, lecturer; Yale University, lecturer; University of Missouri, assistant professor, 1994-98, associate professor of anthropology, 1998-, professor, Center for International Studies, fellow, 2006-07; Beijing Sport University, Fulbright senior researcher, 2007-08. Writer. **Publications:** Training the Body for China: Sports in the Moral Order of the People's Republic, 1995; (contrib.) Body Cultures: Essays on Sport, Space, and Identity, 1998; (ed. with J.N. Wasserstrom) Chinese Femininities/Chinese Masculinities: A Reader, 2002; (ed.) 1904 Anthropology Days and Olympic Games: Sport, Race and American Imperialism, 2008; Beijing's Games: What the Olympics Mean to China, 2008. **Address:** Department of Anthropology, Sociology & Languages, University of Missouri, 1 University Blvd., 507 Clark Hall, St. Louis, MO 63121-4400, U.S.A. **Online address:** sbrownell@umsl.edu

BROWNE-MILLER, Angela. American (born United States), b. 1952. **Genres:** Novels, Autobiography/Memoirs, Self Help, Social Commentary, Social Sciences, Theology/Religion, Writing/Journalism, Autobiography/Memoirs, Autobiography/Memoirs. **Career:** School District, substitute teacher, 1978-79; Metaterra Corporation Services, founder, 1982-98; Cokenders Alcohol and Drug Program, research director, 1983-89, treatment director; University of California, Schools of Social Welfare, Business and Public Policy, lecturer, 1983-92; Parkside Medical Services, executive consultant, 1989-90; Parkside Medical Services Corp., executive consultant, 1990-91; Whole Care Institute, director; Institute for Applied Meta-Sciences, director, 1998; Metaterra Inc., chief executive officer, 1998; FSA Domestic Violence and Anger Management Program, director; Californians for Drug-Free Youth, public relations director; Addiction Stoppers, founder; Metaxis Institute, director. Writer. **Publications:** The Day Care Dilemma: Critical Concerns for American Families, 1990; Working Dazed: Why Drugs Pervade the Workplace and What Can Be Done about It, 1991; Transcending Addiction and Other Afflictions: Lifehealing, 1993; Gestalting Addiction: The Addiction-Focused Group Therapy of Dr. Richard Louis Miller, 1993; Learning to Learn: Ways to Nuture your Child's Intelligence, 1994; Shameful Admissions: The Losing Battle to Serve Everyone in our Universities, 1995; Intelligence Policy: Its Impact on College Admissions and Other Social Policies, 1995; Omega Point, 1996; Adventures in Death, 1996; Embracing Death: Riding Life's Transitions into Power and Freedom, 1996; How to Die and Survive: The Interdimensional Travel Manual, 1997; How to Die and Survive

Addictions, Crises, and Transitions, 1999; To Have and to Hurt: Recognizing and Changing, or Escaping, Patterns of Abuse in Intimate Relationships, 2007; Domestic Violence Prevention Through the Lens of Cost Effectiveness, 2003; Rushing Water, 2003; (ed.) Praeger International Collection on Addictions, 2009; Raising Thinking Children and Teens, 2009; (ed.) Violence and Abuse In Society Set, 2009; Will You Still Need Me?: Finding Friends, Love and Meaning as We Age, 2010; Rewiring Your Self to Break Addictions and Habits: Overcoming Problem Patterns, 2010; Human Intelligence Is A Resource: Tools For Our Learning, 2011; Drugs In The Workplace, 2011; Alcohol, Drugs And Stress In The Workplace, forthcoming; Developing Human Intelligence: Overlooked and Neglected Abilities, forthcoming. **Address:** Browne & Associates, 1 Blackfield Dr., Ste. 343, Tiburon, CA 94920, U.S.A. **Online address:** drangela@drangela.com

BROWNER, Jesse. American (born United States), b. 1961?. **Genres:** Novels, Translations, Biography, Autobiography/Memoirs, Food And Wine, Young Adult Non-fiction. **Career:** Writer and translator. **Publications:** Conglomeros, 1992; Turnaway, 1996; The Duchess Who Wouldn't Sit Down: An Informal History of Hospitality, 2003; (contrib.) Landscapes of Long Island's North Fork, 2006; The Uncertain Hour, 2007; Everything Happens Today, 2011; (contrib.) Portrait of Long Island, 2011. TRANSLATOR: J. Cocteau, Diary of an Unknown, 1988; R.M. Rilke, Letters to Merline, 1989; P. Eluard, Letters to Gala, 1989; J. Cocteau, S. Portraits, 1990; F. Vitoux, Céline: A Biography, 1992; M. Ricard, Happiness, 2006; F. Mitterrand, The Bad Life: A Memoir of High Society, Sexual Politics, and the Nouvelle Vague, 2010. **Address:** c/o Gail Hochman, Brandt & Hochman Literary Agents, 1501 Broadway, Ste. 2310, New York, NY 10036, U.S.A. **Online address:** jesse@jessebrowner.com

BROWN-FLEMING, Suzanne. American (born United States), b. 1969?. **Genres:** History. **Career:** University of Maryland, teaching assistant, 1994-98; United States Holocaust Memorial Museum, University Programs Division, Center for Advanced Holocaust Studies, program officer, 2001-05, senior program officer, 2005-. Scholar and writer. **Publications:** The Holocaust and Catholic Conscience: Cardinal Aloisius Muench and the Guilt Question in Germany, 2006. Contributor to books and journals. **Address:** United States Holocaust Memorial Museum, Center for Advanced Holocaust Studies, University Programs Division, 100 Raoul Wallenberg Pl. SW, Washington, DC 20024-2126, U.S.A. **Online address:** sbrown-fleming@ushmm.org

BROWNING, Christopher R(obert). American (born United States), b. 1944. **Genres:** History, Cultural/Ethnic Topics, Race Relations, Adult Nonfiction, Literary Criticism And History. **Career:** Allegheny College, instructor in history, 1969-71; Pacific Lutheran University, assistant professor, 1974-79, associate professor, 1979-84, professor of history, 1984-97, distinguished university professor, 1997-99; Institute for Advanced Studies, fellow, 1995; U.S. Holocaust Memorial Museum, fellow; University of North Carolina, Frank Porter Graham professor of history, 1999-; Cambridge University, George Macaulay Trevelyan lecturer, 1999. Writer. **Publications:** The Final Solution and the German Foreign Office: A Study of Referat D III of Abteilung Deutschland, 1940-43, 1978; Fateful Months: Essays on the Emergence of the Final Solution, 1941-42, 1984, rev. ed., 1991; Ordinary Men: Reserve Police Battalion 101 and the Final Solution in Poland, 1992; The Path to Genocide: Essays on Launching the Final Solution, 1992; (with D.J. Goldhagen and L. Wieseltier) The Willing Executioners Ordinary Men Debate, 1996; DerWeg zur Englösung: Entscheidungen und Täter, 1998; Nazi Policy, Jewish Workers, German Killers, 2000; Collected Memories: Holocaust History and Postwar Testimony, 2003; Initiating the Final Solution: The Fateful Months of September-October 1941, 2003; (ed.) History of the Third Reich, 2003; The Origins of the Final Solution: The Evolution of Nazi Jewish Policy, September 1939-March 1942, 2004; (co-author) Ghettos 1939-1945: New Research and Perspectives on Definition, Daily Life, and Survival, 2005; (intro. and ed. with R.S. Hollander and N. Tec) Every Day Lasts A Year: A Jewish Family's Correspondence from Poland, 2007; Remembering Survival: Inside a Nazi Slave-labor Camp, 2010. **Address:** Department of History, University of North Carolina, 511 Hamilton Hall, PO Box 3195, Chapel Hill, NC 27599-3195, U.S.A. **Online address:** cbrownin@email.unc.edu

BROWNING, Dixie Burrus. Also writes as Bronwyn Williams, Zoe Dozier, Zoe Dozier. American (born United States), b. 1930. **Genres:** Romance/Historical, Adult Non-fiction. **Career:** Arts and Crafts Association, teacher, 1967-73; Art Gallery Originals, founder and co-director, 1968-73; Watercolor Society of North Carolina, co-founder and president, 1972-73; Art V Gallery, co-director, 1974-75; Browning Artworks, president and co-owner, 1984-99; Browning Studios of Hatteras Island, co-owner. Writer. **Publications:** Warm Side of the Island, 1977; Tumbled Wall, 1980; Unreasonable Summer, 1980; Chance Tomorrow, 1981; East of Today, 1981; Journey to Quiet Waters, 1981; Winter Blossom, 1981; Wren of Paradise 1981; Finders Keepers, 1982; Island on the Hill, 1982; Logic of the Heart, 1982; The Loving Rescue, 1982; Renegade Player, 1982; Practical Dreamer, 1983; Reach Out to Cherish, 1983; A Secret Valentine, 1983; Shadow of Yesterday, 1983; First Things Last, 1984; The Hawk and the Honey, 1984; Image of Love, 1984; Just Desserts, 1984; Late Rising Moon, 1984; The Love Thing, 1984; Stormwatch, 1984; Time and Tide, 1984; Visible Heart, 1984; A Bird in Hand, 1985; By Any Other Name, 1985; Matchmaker's Moon, 1985; Something for Herself, 1985; The Tender Barbarian, 1985; Reluctant Dreamer, 1986; The Security Man, 1986; In the Palm of Her Hand, 1986; A Winter Woman, 1986; Belonging, 1987; Henry the Ninth, 1987; A Matter of Timing, 1987; There Once Was a Lover, 1987; Along Came Jones, 1988; Fate Takes a Holiday, 1988; Thin Ice, 1989; Beginner's Luck, 1989; Ships in the Night, 1990; Twice in a Blue Moon, 1990; The Homing Instinct, 1990; Just Say Yes, 1991; Not A Marrying Man, 1991; Gus And The Night Lady, 1992; Best Man For The Job, 1992; Hazards Of The Heart, 1993; Kane's Way, 1993; Keegan's Hunt, 1993; Grace and the Law, 1994; Lucy and the Stone, 1994; Two Hearts, Shlightly Used, 1994; Alex and the Angel, 1995; Single Female (reluctantly) Seeks, 1995; The Beast, the Beauty and the Baby, 1996; The Baby Notion, 1996; Stryker's Wife, 1996; Look What the Stork Brought, 1997; The Passionate G-Man, 1998; His Business, Her Baby, 1998; A Knight in Rusty Armor, 1999; The Texas Millionaire, 1999; The Bride-in-Law, 1999; A Bride f or Jackson Powers, 2000; Cinderella's Midnight Kiss, 2000; The Virgin and the Vengeful Groom, 2000; Long Shadow's Woman, 2001; More to Love, 2001; Rocky and the Senator's Daughter, 2001; The Millionaire's Pregnant Bride, 2002; The Marrying Millionaire, 2002; Beckett's Cinderella, 2002; The Quiet Seduction, 2002; Beckett's Convenient Bride, 2002; Ann Elise, 2003; Social Graces, 2003; (with L. Banks and K. DeNosky) Home for the Holidays, 2003; Undertow, 2003; Driven to Distraction, 2004; Quinto marido, 2005; Her Passionate Plan B, 2005; Her Fifth Husband?, 2005; First Time Home, 2005; Her Man Upstairs, 2005. AS ZOE DOZIER: Warm Side of the Island, 1977; Home Again My Love, 1977; (intro.) Artists/U.S.A.: 1979-80, 1979. AS BRONWYN WILLIAMS (with M. Williams): White Witch, 1988; Dandelion, 1989; Stormwalker, 1990; Gideon's Fall, 1991; Mariner's Bride, 1991; A Promise Kept, 1992; The Warfield Bride, 1994; Bedeviled, 1995; Slow Surrender, 1995; Halfway Home, 1996; Seaspell, 1997; Sunshine, 1997; Entwined, 1998; Beholden, 1998; The Paper Marriage, 2000; Longshadow's Woman, 2001; Good As Gold, 2001; The Mail-Order Brides, 2001; Beckett's Birthright, 2002; Blackstone's Pride, 2003. **Address:** Browning Studios of Hatteras Island, PO Box 275, Frisco, NC 27936, U.S.A. **Online address:** dixiebb@mindspring.com

BROWNING, Guy. British/American (born United States), b. 1964?. **Genres:** Humor/Satire, Essays. **Career:** Daily Telegraph, columnist; The Guardian, columnist, 1999-2009; Radio 4, host; Smokehouse Consultant Agency, founder and creative director. Writer, consultant and speaker. **Publications:** Innervation: Redesign Yourself for a Smarter Future, 2001; Never Hit a Jellyfish with a Spade: How to Survive Life's Smaller Challenges (essays), 2004; (with J. Brown) The Pocket Guru: Priceless Nuggets of Business Wisdom, 2011. **Address:** c/o Author Mail, Gotham Books, Penguin Group Inc., 375 Hudson St., New York, NY 10014-3658, U.S.A. **Online address:** guy.browning@sfb.com

BROWNING, Pamela. (Melanie Rowe). American (born United States) **Genres:** Adult Non-fiction, Novels, Romance/Historical, Young Adult Fiction. **Career:** Coker College, public relations representative, 1992-94; The US-China Review, editor; NINK, editor, Novelists Inc., board director; The Marquis Corp., president; Ketter Corp., president. **Publications:** 1 On 1, 198. AS MELANIE ROWE: Sands of Xanadu, 1982; Wish for Tomorrow, 1983; Sea of Gold, 1984; Stardust Summer, 1984; Touch of Gold, 1984; Through the Eyes of Love, 1985; Handyman Special, 1985; Interior Designs, 1985; Cherished Beginnings, 1985; To Touch the Stars, 1986; Forever Is a Long Time, 1986; Ever Since Eve, 1986; The Flutter by Princess, 1987; Kisses in the Rain, 1987; Ice Crystals, 1987; Simple Gifts, 1988; Harvest Home, 1988; Fly Away, 1988; Until Spring, 1989; Feathers in the Wind, 1989; Humble Pie, 1990; RSVP Baby, 1999; For Auld Lang Syne, 1991; A Man Worth Loving, 1991; Sunshine and Shadows, 1992; Morgans Child, 1992; Merry Christmas Baby, 1993; The Worlds Last Bachelor, 1995; Angels Baby, 1995; Lovers Leap, 1996; Thats Our Baby!, 2000; Baby Christmas, 2000; Cowboy with a Secret, 2001; Pregnant and Incognito, 2002; Ranchers Double Dilemma, 2002; A Real-Thing Fling, 2003; Life Is a Beach, 2003; Cowboy Enchantment, 2003; Baby Enchantment, 2003; Heard It through the Grapevine, 2004; The Mommy Wish, 2005; Breakfast With Santa, 2005; The Treasure Man, 2006; Snapshots, 2007; Down Home Carolina Christmas, 2007; Down Home Dixie, 2008. OMNIBUS: (with D. Browning and R. Clay) Visible Heart/Handyman Special/Wanderer's Dream, 1992; (with B. Kaye and N. Martin) Forgotten Past, 1993; (with S. James and K. Young) Making Babies, 1995; (with J. McBride and R.Winters) Daddy For Christmas, 1998; (with J. Arnold) All They Want for Christmas: Comfort And Joy/Merry Christmas, Baby, 2001; Life Is a Beach/A Real Thing Fling, 2003. Contributor to journals. **Address:** c/o Ellen Levine, Trident Media, 41 Madison Ave., 36th Fl., New York, NY 10010, U.S.A. **Online address:** pamela@pamelabrowning.com

BROWNING, Wilfrid (Robert Francis). (W. R. F. Browning). British (born England), b. 1918. **Genres:** Theology/Religion, Reference. **Career:** Church of England, clergyman; St. Deiniol's Library, chaplain, 1946-48; St. Richard's Church, vicar, 1948-51; Cuddesdon College, New Testament Studies, lecturer, 1951-59; Blackburn Cathedral, canon residentiary, 1959-65; University of London, chief examiner in religious knowledge, 1959-65; Anglican Church, director, 1961-; Central Council for Women's Ministry, assessor, 1961-; Christ Church Cathedral, canon residentiary, 1965-88; University of Leeds, external examiner, 1965-. Writer. **Publications:** (Co-trans.) Vocabulary of the Bible, 1958; The Gospel According to St. Luke, 1960, 2nd ed., 1965; (ed.) The Anglican Synthesis, 1964; Meet the New Testament, 1964; Saint Luke's Gospel, 6th ed., 1981; Handbook of the Ministry: A Guide to Ordination in the Anglican Communion, 1985; (as W.R.F. Browning) Dictionary of the Bible, 1996,2nd ed., 2009. Contributor to journals. **Address:** 42 Alexandra Rd., Oxford, CW OX2 0DB, England.

BROWNING, W. R. F. *See* **BROWNING, Wilfrid (Robert Francis).**

BROWNJOHN, Alan (Charles). (John Berrington). British (born England), b. 1931. **Genres:** Novels, Poetry, Literary Criticism And History, Translations, Young Adult Non-fiction, Children's Fiction. **Career:** Beckenham and Penge Boys' Grammar School, teacher, 1957-65; Wandsworth Borough Councillor, 1962-65; University of the South Bank, Battersea College of Education, lecturer, senior lecturer in English, 1965-79; writer, 1979-; New Statesman, poetry critic, 1968-76; Greater London Arts Association, Literature Panel, chairman, 1973-77; Encounter, poetry critic, 1977-81; Poetry Society, deputy chair, 1979-82, chair, 1982-88, deputy president, 1988-92; Sunday Times, poetry critic, 1989-. **Publications:** POETRY: Travellers Alone, 1954; The Railings: Poems, 1961; The Lions' Mouths: Poems, 1967; Sandgrains on a Tray: Poems, 1969; Being a Garoon: A Poem, 1969; (with M. Hamburger and C. Tomlinson) Penguin Modern Poets 14, 1969; Woman Reading Aloud, 1969; A Day By Indirections, 1969; Brownjohn's Beasts, 1970; Warrior's Career, 1972; Tribute to Wystan Hugh Auden, 1973; A Song of Good Life, 1975; A Night in the Gazebo, 1980; Collected Poems 1952-1983, 1983; The Old Flea-Pit, 1987; Collected Poems 1952-88, 1988; The Observation Car, 1990; Inertia Reel, 1992; In The Cruel Arcade, 1994; The Cat without E-mail, 2001; The Men around Her Bed, 2004; Ludbrooke and Others, 2010. NOVELS: (as John Berrington) To Clear the River, 1964; The Way You Tell Them, 1990; The Long Shadows, 1997; A Funny Old Year, 2001; Windows On the Moon, 2009. OTHERS: Synopsis, 1970; An Equivalent, 1971; The Little Red Bus Book, 1972; She Made of It: A Draft, 1974; Philip Larkin, 1975; The Old Flea Pit, 1987; Ludbrooke, 2009. TRANSLATIONS: J.W. von Goethe, Torquato Tasso, 1985; P. Corneille, Horace, 1996. EDITOR: First I Say This (poems): A Selection of Poems for Reading Aloud, 1969; (with S. Heaney and J. Stallworthy) New Poems 1970-71: A P.E.N. Anthology of Contemporary Poetry, 1971; (with M. Duffy) New Poetry 3, 1977; New Year Poetry Supplement, 1982; (with S. Brownjohn) Meet and Write, I, II and III, 1985-87; (with K.W. Gransden) The Gregory Anthology, 1987-1990, 1990. **Address:** 2 Belsize Pk., London, GL NW3 4ET, England.

BROWNLEE, Andrea Barnwell. (Andrea D. Barnwell). American (born United States) **Genres:** Biography, Autobiography/Memoirs, Art/Art History, Social Sciences, Photography, Film. **Career:** Spelman College Museum of Fine Art, director, 2001-. Writer and educator. **Publications:** The Walter O. Evans Collection of African American Art, 1999; (as Andrea D. Barnwell) Charles White, 2002; (as Andrea D. Barnwell with I. Brielmaier) Engaging the Camera: African Women, Portraits and the Photography of Hector Acebes, 2004; Rozeal Brown: A 3... Black on Bothsides, 2004; (ed. and contrib. with G.W. Gayles and L. King-Hammond) Amalia Amaki: Boxes, Buttons and the Blues, 2005; (with A.K. Amaki) Hale Woodruff, Nancy Elizabeth Prophet and the Academy, 2007; (with V.C. Oliver) Cinema Remixed & Reloaded: Black Women Artists and the Moving Image since 1970, 2008. **Address:** Museum of Fine Art, Spelman College, 350 Spelman Ln., PO Box 1526, Atlanta, GA 30314-4399, U.S.A. **Online address:** museum@spelman.edu

BROWNLEE, David B(ruce). American (born United States), b. 1951. **Genres:** Architecture, History, Law. **Career:** Harvard University, Department of Fine Arts, teaching fellow, tutor and grader, 1975-80; University of Pennsylvania, Department of the History of Art, assistant professor, 1980-85, associate professor, 1985-93, professor, 1993-2003, Frances Shapiro-Weitzenhoffer professor of nineteenth-century European art, 2003-, department chair, Department of Architecture, adjunct professor, 1984-85. Writer. **Publications:** George Edmund Street and the Royal Courts of Justice, 1980; The Law Courts: The Architecture of George Edmund Street, 1984; The University of Pennsylvania: A Guide, 1985; Friedrich Weinbrenner, Architect of Karlsruhe, 1986; Building the City Beautiful: The Benjamin Franklin Parkway and the Philadelphia Museum of Art, 1989; (with D.G. DeLong) Louis I. Kahn: In the Realm of Architecture, 1991; (with D.G. DeLong) The Architecture of Louis I. Kahn, 1991; Making a Modern Classic: The Architecture of the Philadelphia Museum of Art, 1997; (with G.E. Thomas) Building America's First University: An Historical and Architectural Guide to the University of Pennsylvania, 2000; (with D.G. DeLong and K. Hiesinger) Out of the Ordinary: Robert Venturi, Denise Scott Brown and Associates: Architecture, Urbanism, Design, 2001; Modern Means and Modern Meanings: An Intellectual and Social History of Nineteenth-century Architecture, forthcoming. Contributor to journals. **Address:** Department of the History of Art, University of Pennsylvania, 202 Elliot and Roslyn Jaffe History of Art Bldg., 3405 Woodland Walk, Philadelphia, PA 19104-6208, U.S.A. **Online address:** dbrownle@sas.upenn.edu

BROWNLEE, Donald. *See* **BROWNLEE, Donald E(ugene).**

BROWNLEE, Donald E(ugene). (Donald Brownlee). American (born United States), b. 1943. **Genres:** Astronomy, Earth Sciences. **Career:** University of Washington, associate professor of astronomy, 1970-77, professor of astronomy, 1989-; National Aeronautics and Space Administration (NASA), consultant, 1976-, principal investigator; California Institute of Technology, associate professor of geochemistry, 1977-82; University of Chicago, Enrico Fermi Institute, distinguished visiting professor. Writer. **Publications:** WITH P.D. WARD: Rare Earth: Why Complex Life Is Uncommon in the Universe, 2000; The Life and Death of Planet Earth: How the New Science of Astrobiology Charts the Ultimate Fate of Our World, 2003. Contributor to journals. **Address:** Department of Astronomy, University of Washington, Rm. C331, Physics-Astronomy Bldg., 4060 George Washington Ln. NE, PO Box 351580, Seattle, WA 98195-1580, U.S.A. **Online address:** brownlee@astro.washington.edu

BROWNLEE, Nick. British (born England), b. 1967?. **Genres:** History. **Career:** Newcastle Evening Chronicle, reporter; Sunday People, feature writer; freelance journalist and writer, 2000-. **Publications:** NONFICTION, EXCEPT AS NOTED: Coronation St: Real Soap, 1999; The One Hundred Greatest Cricketers, 1999; This Is Cannabis, 2002; This Is Alcohol, 2002; The History of Plastic Pop, 2003; The Complete Illustrated Guide to Cannabis, 2003; Everything You Didn't Need to Know about the UK, 2003; The Little Box of Drugs: Unbiased and Unadulterated Commentary on the Drugs Debate, 2003; (with J. Motson) Motson's World Cup Extravaganza: Football's Greatest Drama 1930- 2006, 2006; Vive Le Tour! Amazing Tales of the Tour De France, 2007. JAKE AND JOUMA SERIES: Bait, 2009; Burn, 2009; Blood and Fire, 2010 as Machete, 2010. Contributor to periodicals. **Address:** Cumbria, England. **Online address:** mail@nickbrownlee.com

BROWNLEE, Shannon. American (born United States) **Genres:** Medicine/Health. **Career:** New America Foundation, senior fellow; Discover magazine, staff writer; U.S. News & World Report, senior writer. Writer and journalist. **Publications:** Overtreated: Why Too Much Medicine Is Making Us Sicker and Poorer, 2007. Works appear in anthologies. Contributor to journals. **Address:** New America Foundation, 1630 Connecticut Ave. NW, 7th Fl., Washington, DC 20009, U.S.A. **Online address:** brownlee@newamerica.net

BROWNLEY, James. British (born England), b. 1960. **Genres:** Mystery/Crime/Suspense, Young Adult Fiction. **Career:** Writer. **Publications:** ALISON GLASBY MYSTERY SERIES: A Picture of Guilt, 2007; The Sins of the Children, 2008. **Address:** Blake Friedmann Literary, Film & TV Agency, 122 Arlington Rd., London, GL NW1 7HP, England.

BROWNMILLER, Susan. American (born United States), b. 1935. **Genres:** Human Relations/Parenting, Women's Studies And Issues, Young Adult Nonfiction. **Career:** Actress, 1955-59; Coronet Magazine, assistant editor, 1959-60; Albany Report, editor, 1961-62; Newsweek, national affairs researcher, 1963-64; Village Voice, staff writer, 1965; National Broadcasting Corp., reporter, 1965; American Broadcasting Corp., network news writer, 1966-68; freelance journalist, 1968-70; Pace University, adjunct professor of women's and gender studies. **Publications:** Shirley Chisholm, 1970; Against Our Will: Men, Women and Rape, 1975; Femininity, 1984; Waverly Place, 1989; Seeing Vietnam: Encounters of the Road and Heart, 1994; In Our Time: Memoir of a Revolution, 1999. Contributor to periodicals and magazines. **Address:** Department of Women's and Gender Studies, Pace University, 41 Park Row, 15th Fl., New York, NY 10038, U.S.A. **Online address:** sbrownmiller@pace.edu

BROWNRIDGE, William R(oy). Canadian (born Canada), b. 1932. **Genres:** Children's Fiction, Sports/Fitness, Literary Criticism And History. **Career:** KB Graphic Design, partner; Francis, Williams & Johnson, associate creative director. Writer and artist. **Publications:** SELF-ILLUSTRATED: The Moccasin Goalie, 1995; Victory at Paradise Hill, 2002. OTHERS: The Final Game, 1997; Tracking the Iron Horse, 2006. Contributor to periodicals. **Address:** 705 145 Point Dr. NW, Calgary, AB T3B 4W1, Canada. **Online address:** info@heartofhockey.com

BROWNSTEIN, Gabriel. American (born United States), b. 1966. **Genres:** Novellas/Short Stories. **Career:** Barnard College, adjunct professor; Parsons School of Design, adjunct professor; Long Island University, adjunct professor; State University of New York-Stony Brook, Department of English, lecturer in English; St. John's University, Department of English, faculty, 2005, assistant professor, associate professor. Writer. **Publications:** The Curious Case of Benjamin Button, Apt. 3W, 2002; The Man From Beyond: A Novel, 2005. Contributor of short stories to periodicals. **Address:** Department of English, St. Johns University, Rm. B40-10, St. John Hall, 8000 Utopia Pkwy., Queens, NY 11439, U.S.A. **Online address:** brownstg@stjohns.edu

BROX, Jane (Martha). American (born United States), b. 1956. **Genres:** Poetry, Adult Non-fiction, Essays, History. **Career:** Freelance writer and poet, 1985-; Harvard Extension School, teaching assistant, 1995-96, instructor, 1997-2001, 2003; Harvard Summer School, instructor, 1996-2000; Harvard University, visiting Briggs-Copeland lecturer in English, 2002-03, visiting lecturer in English, 2003-04; Lesley University, MFA Nonfiction, faculty, 2005-; Bowdoin College, adjunct lecturer in English, 2008-09. **Publications:** EDITOR: (with K. Aponick and P. Marion) Merrimack: A Poetry Anthology, 1992. NONFICTION: Here and Nowhere Else: Late Seasons of a Farm and Its Family, 1995; Five Thousand Days Like This One: An American Family History, 1999; Clearing Land: Legacies of the American Farm, 2004; Brilliant: The Evolution of Artificial Light, 2010. CONTRIBUTOR: The Ucross Foundation Poetry Anthology, 1992; The Party Train: An Anthology of North American Prose Poetry, 1996; In Short (essays), 1996; Best American Essays, 1996, 1996; Pushcart Prize XXV, 2000; Sorrow's Company, 2001; Norton Book of Nature Writing, 2002. Contributor to periodicals. **Address:** Department of Creative Writing, Lesley University, 29 Everett St., Cambridge, MA 02138-2702, U.S.A.

BROYLES, Anne. American (born United States), b. 1953?. **Genres:** Theology/Religion, Children's Fiction, Children's Non-fiction. **Career:** Malibu United Methodist Church, co-pastor, through 1999. Writer. **Publications:** Meeting God through Worship, 1992; Growing Together in Love: God Known through Family Life, 1993; Journaling: A Spiritual Journey, 1999; At Home with God: Family Devotions for the School Year, 2002; (co-author) The Wisdom of Jesus, 2009. FOR CHILDREN: Shy Mama's Halloween, 2000; Priscilla and the Hollyhocks, 2008. Contributor to books. **Address:** Abingdon Press, 201 8th Ave. S, PO Box 801, Nashville, TN 37202-0801, U.S.A. **Online address:** annebroyles@annebroyles.com

BROYLES, Michael. American (born United States), b. 1939. **Genres:** Music, History, Adult Non-fiction. **Career:** University of Maryland, assistant professor, 1967-71, associate professor, 1971-87, professor of music, 1987-93, director of honors program in music, 1980-94, presidential research professor, 1993-94; Johns Hopkins University, lecturer, 1990-; American Antiquarian Society, research associate, 1990; Pennsylvania State University, State College, distinguished professor of music and professor of American history, 1994-, now professor emeritus; John F. Kennedy Center for the Performing Arts, lecturer, 1994; Florida State University, professor of music, 2008-. Writer. **Publications:** Beethoven: The Emergence and Evolution of Beethoven's Heroic Style, 1987; (ed. and intro.) A Yankee Musician in Europe: The 1837 Journals of Lowell Mason, 1990; Music of the Highest Class: Elitism and Populism in Antebellum Boston, 1992; Mavericks and Other Traditions in American Music, 2004; (ed. with D.V. Glahn) Quintette for Piano and Strings, op. 92, 2005; (with D.V. Glahn) Leo Ornstein: Modernist Dilemmas, Personal Choices, 2007; Beethoven in America, 2011. Works appear in anthologies. Contributor of articles to journals. **Address:** College of Music, Florida State University, Housewright Music Bldg., Tallahassee, FL 32306, U.S.A. **Online address:** meb11@psu.edu

BROZ, J. Lawrence. American (born United States), b. 1956. **Genres:** Politics/Government. **Career:** University of California, teaching fellow, 1985-89, instructor in political science, 1992; Harvard University, Department of Government, assistant professor, 1992-95, associate professor, 1995-2000, Weatherhead Center for International Affairs, faculty associate, 1992-2000, visiting associate professor, 2006-07; New York University, Department of Politics, associate professor, 2000-01; University of California-San Diego, Department of Political Science, associate professor, 2001-, director of graduate studies, 2005-. Writer. **Publications:** The International Origins of the Federal Reserve System, 1997; (ed. with W. Bernhard and W.B. Clark) The political Economy of Monetary Institutions, 2003; (with J.A. Frieden and D.A. Lake) International Political Economy: Perspectives on Global Power and Wealth, 5th ed., 2010. Contributor to periodicals. **Address:** Department of Political Science, University of California, 9500 Gilman Dr., M/C 0521, La Jolla, CA 92093-0521, U.S.A. **Online address:** jlbroz@ucsd.edu

BRUCE, Colin John. British/Scottish (born Scotland), b. 1960. **Genres:** Military/Defense/Arms Control, History. **Career:** Elmwood College, librarian, 1984-85; Imperial War Museum, map curator, 1985. Writer. **Publications:** (With E. Smithies) War at Sea, 1992; War on the Ground, 1995; Invaders: British and American Experience of Seaborne Landings, 1939-1945, 1999. **Address:** Imperial War Museum, Lambeth Rd., London, GL SE1 6HZ, England. **Online address:** books@iwm.org.uk

BRUCE, Dickson Davies. American (born United States), b. 1946. **Genres:** History. **Career:** University of California, professor of comparative culture, 1971-92, professor of history, 1992-2008, professor emeritus of history, 2008-; Attila Jozsef University, visiting professor, 1987-88. Writer. **Publications:** And They All Sang Hallelujah: Plain-Folk Camp-Meeting Religion, 1800-1845, 1974; Violence and Culture in the Antebellum South, 1979; The Rhetoric of Conservatism: The Virginia Convention of 1829-30 and the Conservative Tradition in the South, 1982; (with A. Binder and G. Geis) Juvenile Delinquency: Historical, Cultural, Legal Perspectives, 1988, 3rd ed., 2001; Black American Writing from the Nadir: The Evolution of a Literary Tradition 1877-1915, 1989; Archibald Grimké: Portrait of a Black Independent, 1993; The Origins of African American Literature, 1680-1865, 2001; The Kentucky Tragedy: A Story of Conflict and Change in Antebellum America, 2006. Contributor to periodicals. **Address:** Department of History, University of California, 224 Murray Krieger Hall, PO Box 3275, Irvine, CA 92697-3275, U.S.A. **Online address:** ddbruce@uci.edu

BRUCE, Robert S. Australian/British (born England), b. 1955. **Genres:** Paranormal, Poetry, Psychology, Medicine/Health. **Career:** Writer. **Publications:** M1 Does My Talking!: The U.S. M1 Garand Rifle in Pictures: World War Two and the Korean War, also Origin, Development, and Postwar Experimentation from World War One to the M14, 1992; Machine Guns of World War I, 1997; Astral Dynamics: A New Approach to Out-of-Body Experience, 1999, rev. ed. as Astral Dynamics: The Complete Book of Out-of-Body Experiences, 2009; Practical Psychic Self-Defense: Understanding and Surviving Unseen Influences, 2002, 2nd ed. as The Practical Psychic Self-Defense Handbook: A Survival Guide: Combat Psychic Attacks, Evil Spirits & Possession, 2011; (with C.E. Lindgren) Capturing the Aura, 2002; (with B. Mercer) Mastering Astral Projection: 90-day Guide To Out-of-Body Experience, 2004; (with B. Mercer) Mastering Astral Projection: Instruction Guide, 2007; Energy Work: The Secret of Healing and Spiritual Development, 2007. **Address:** c/o Author Mail, Hampton Roads Publishing Co., 65 Parker St., Ste. 7, Newburyport, MA 01950, U.S.A. **Online address:** robert@astralpulse.com

BRUCE, Steve. Scottish/British (born England), b. 1954. **Genres:** Theology/Religion, Politics/Government. **Career:** Queen's University, instructor, 1978-91; University of Aberdeen, School of Social Science, professor, 1991-, chair of sociology. Writer and sociologist. **Publications:** Firm in the Faith, 1984; No Pope of Rome: Anti-Catholicism in Modern Scotland, 1985; God Save Ulster: The Religion and Politics of Paisleyism, 1986; The Rise and Fall of the New Christian Right: Conservative Protestant Politics in America, 1978-1988, 1988; Pray TV: Televangelism in America, 1990; A House Divided: Protestantism, Schism, and Secularization, 1990; (ed.) Religion and Modernization: Sociologists and Historians Debate the Secularization Thesis, 1992; The Red Hand: Protestant Paramilitaries in Northern Ireland, 1992; The Edge of the Union: The Ulster Loyalist Political Vision, 1994; (ed. with P. Kivisto and W.H. Swatos, Jr.) The Rapture of Politics: The Christian Right as the United States Approaches the Year 2000, 1995; (ed.) The Sociology of Religion, 1995; Religion in Modern Britain, 1995; Religion in the Modern World: From Cathedrals to Cults, 1996; Conservative Protestant Politics, 1998; Sociology: A Very Short Introduction, 1999; Choice and Religion: A Critique of Rational Choice Theory, 1999; Fundamentalism, 2000, 2nd ed., 2008; God Is Dead: Secularization in the West, 2002; Politics and Religion, 2003; (co-author) Sectarianism in Scotland, 2004; (with S. Yearley) The Sage Dictionary of Sociology, 2006; Paisley: Religion and Politics in Northern Ireland, 2007. Contributor of articles to books and journals. **Address:** School of Social Science, University of Aberdeen, Edward Wright Bldg., Aberdeen, AB24 3QY, Scotland. **Online address:** s.bruce@abdn.ac.uk

BRUCE, Victoria. American (born United States) **Genres:** Documentaries/Reportage. **Career:** National Aeronautics and Space Administration, science writer; Portland Oregonian, science reporter; freelance writer and documentary film producer. **Publications:** Promises from the Past, 1995; Windmills in Time, 1998; No Apparent Danger: The True Story of Volcanic Disaster at Galeras and Nevado del Ruiz, 2001; (with K. Hayes and J.E. Botero) Hostage Nation: Colombia's Guerrilla Army and the Failed War on Drugs, 2010. **Address:** PO Box 551, Riva, MD 21140, U.S.A. **Online address:** vbruce@victoriabruce.com

BRUCE, (William) Harry. Canadian (born Canada), b. 1934. **Genres:** Area Studies, Young Adult Non-fiction, Art/Art History. **Career:** Ottawa Journal, reporter, 1955-59; Globe and Mail, reporter, 1959-61; Maclean's, assistant editor, 1961-64; Saturday Night, managing editor, 1964-65; Canadian Magazine, managing editor, 1965-66; Star Weekly, associate editor and featured columnist, 1967-68; Toronto Daily Star, columnist, 1968-69; Maclean's, columnist, reports and reviews editor, 1970-71; Nova Scotia Light and Power Company Ltd., executive editor, 1971; freelance writer, 1973-79; Atlantic Insight, editor, 1979-80, executive editor, 1981; Atlantic Salmon Journal, editor, 1991; Atlantic Salmon Federation, editor-in-chief. **Publications:** NON-FICTION FOR ADULTS: Short, Happy Walks of Max MacPherson, 1968; Nova Scotia, 1975; Lifeline, 1977; R.A.: The Story of R.A. Jodrey, Entrepreneur, 1979; A Basket of Apples: Recollections of Historic Nova Scotia, 1982; The Gulf of St. Lawrence, 1984; Each Moment as It Flies, 1984; Movin' East: The Further Writings of Harry Bruce, 1985; Frank Sobey: The Man and the Empire, 1985; Down Home: Notes of a Maritime Son, 1988; Atlantic Canada, 1991; An Illustrated History of Nova Scotia, 1997; The Pig that Flew: The Battle to Privatize Canadian National, 1997; Tall Ships: An Odyssey, 2000. NON-FICTION FOR YOUNG ADULTS: Maud: The Life of L.M. Montgomery, 1992; An Illustrated History of Nova Scotia, 1997; Never Content: How Mavericks and Outsiders Made a Surprise Winner of Maritime Life, 2002; Maud: The Early Years of L.M. Montgomery, 2003; Mr. Lawyer: Frank Covert, forthcoming; The Beginner's Encyclopedia of Fly-Fishing, forthcoming. OTHERS: Page Fright: Foibles and Fetishes of Famous Writers, 2009. Contributor of articles to periodicals. Works appear in anthologies. **Address:** Atlantic Salmon Federation, PO Box 429, St. Andrews, NB E5B 3S8, Canada. **Online address:** hbruce@auracom.com

BRUCE LOCKHART, Robin. (Robin Norman Bruce Lockhart). British (born England), b. 1920. **Genres:** Biography, Theology/Religion, History, Military/Defense/Arms Control, Criminology/True Crime, Recreation. **Career:** Financial Times, foreign manager, 1946-52; Beaverbrook Newspapers, senior executive, 1953-61; Central Wagon Co., deputy chairman, 1965-69; Moorgill Properties, chairman, 1967-72. Writer. **Publications:** Ace of Spies: Biography of Sidney Reilly, 1967; Reilly: Ace of Spies, 1984; Halfway to Heaven: The Hidden Life of the Sublime Carthusians, 1985; Reilly: The First Man, 1987; Listening to Silence, 1997; O Bonitos, Hushed to Silence, 2000. **Address:** Darton, Longman & Todd, 1 Spencer Ct., 140-142 Wandsworth High St., London, GL SW18 4JJ, England.

BRUCE LOCKHART, Robin Norman. *See* **BRUCE LOCKHART, Robin.**

BRUCHAC, Joseph. American (born United States), b. 1942. **Genres:** Novellas/Short Stories, Children's Fiction, Young Adult Fiction, Plays/Screenplays, Children's Non-fiction, History, Literary Criticism And History, Mythology/Folklore, Mythology/Folklore, Young Adult Non-fiction, Poetry. **Career:** Teacher, 1966-69; Greenfield Review Literary Center, co-founder and co-director, Greenfield Review Press, co-founder and co-director, 1969-; Skidmore College, English instructor, 1969-73, director of college program; Great Meadow Correctional Facility, instructor and coordinator for the writing program, 1974-81; Hamilton College, faculty, 1983, 1985, 1987; State University of New York, adjunct faculty, 1987-88; CRC Institute for Arts in Education, story-teller, 1989-90. Writer. **Publications:** FOR YOUNG ADULTS FICTION: Turtle Meat and Other Stories, 1992; Dawn Land: A Novel, 1993; Long River: A Novel, 1995; Dog People: Native Dog Stories, 1995; Children of the Longhouse, 1996; Eagle Song, 1997; The Arrow over the Door, 1998; The Waters Between: A Novel of the Dawn Land, 1998; The Heart of a Chief: A Novel, 1998; The Heart of a Chief: With Connections, 1998; Sacajawea: The Story of Bird Woman and the Lewis and Clark Expedition, 2000; Skeleton Man, 2001; The Journal of Jesse Smoke: A Cherokee Boy, 2001; Pocahontas, 2003; Hidden Roots, 2004. FOLK STORIES: Turkey Brother and Other Tales: Iroquois Folk Stories, 1975; Stone Giants & Flying Heads: Adventure Stories of the Iroquois, 1979; Iroquois Stories: Heroes and Heroines, Monsters and Magic, 1985; The Wind Eagle, 1985; The Faithful Hunter: Abenaki Stories, 1988; The Return of the Sun: Native American Tales from the Northeast Woodlands, 1989; Hoop Snakes, Hide-Behinds and Side-hill Winders: Tall Tales from the Adirondacks, 1991; Native American Stories, 1991; Native American Animal Stories, 1992; Flying with the Eagle, Racing the Great Bear: Stories from Native North America, 1993; (reteller with G. Ross) The Girl Who Married the Moon: Tales from Native North America, 1994; The Boy Who Lived with the Bears: And Other Iroquois Stories, 1995; Native Plant Stories, 1995; (reteller) Four Ancestors: Stories, Songs, and Poems from Native North America, 1996; (with J. Bruchac) When the Chenoo Howls: Native American Tales of Terror, 1998. NON-FICTION: Survival This Way: Interviews with American Indian Poets, 1987; (with M.J. Caduto) Keepers of the Animals: Native American Stories and Wildlife Activities for Children, 1991; The Native American Sweat Lodge, History and Legends, 1993; (with M.J. Caduto) Keepers of Life: Discovering Plants through Native American Stories and Earth Activities for Children, 1994; (with M.J. Caduto) Keepers of the Night: Native American Stories and Nocturnal Activities for Children, 1994; A Boy Called Slow: The True Story of Sitting Bull, 1994; (ed.) Native Wisdom, 1995; Roots of Survival, 1996; Roots of Survival: Native American Storytelling and the Sacred, 1996; (with M.J. Caduto) Native American Gardening: Stories, Projects, and Recipes for Families, 1996; Tell Me a Tale: A Book about Storytelling, 1997; Lasting Echoes: An Oral History of Native American People, 1997; Bowman's Store: A Journey to Myself (autobiography), 1997; Trail of Tears, 1999; Trails of Tears, Paths of Beauty, 2000; Navajo Long Walk: The Tragic Story of a Proud People's Forced March from Their Homeland, 2002; Our Stories Remember: American Indian History, Culture, & Values through Storytelling, 2003. PLAY: Pushing up the Sky: Seven Native American Plays for Children, 2000; FOR CHILDREN: FOLK STORIES: The First Strawberries: A Cherokee Story, 1993; The Great Ball Game, 1994; Gluskabe and the Four Wishes, 1995; (with G. Ross) The Story of the Milky Way: A Cherokee Tale, 1995; Between Earth and Sky: Legends of Native American Sacred Places, 1996; The Maple Thanksgiving, 1996; (with M.J. Fawcett) Makiawisug, 1997. PICTURE BOOKS: (with J. London) Thirteen Moons on Turtle's Back: A Native American Year of Moons (poetry), 1992; Fox Song, 1993; The Earth under Sky Bear's Feet: Native American Poems of the Land, 1995; The Circle of Thanks (songs and poetry), 1996; Many Nations: An Alphabet of Native America, 1997; Crazy Horse's Vision, 2000; Squanto's Journey: The Story of the First Thanksgiving, 2000; (with J. Bruchac) How Chipmunk Got His Stripes: A Tale of Bragging and Teasing, 2001; (reteller with J. Bruchac) Turtle's Race with Beaver: A Traditional Seneca Story, 2003; Jim Thorpe's Bright Path, 2004; My Father is Taller than a Tree, 2010. FOR ADULTS: POETRY: Indian Mountain and Other Poems, 1971; The Buffalo in the Syracuse Zoo, 1972; Great Meadow: Words of Hearsay and Heresy, 1973; Poetry of Pop, 1973; The Manabozho Poems, 1974; Flow, 1975; This Earth Is a Drum, 1976; Entering Onondaga, 1978; There Are No Trees inside the Prison, 1978; Mu'ndu Wi-' Go: Poems from Mohegan Stories and the Mohegan Diary of Flying Bird (Mrs. Fidelia A.H.

Fielding), 1978; The Good Message of Handsome Lake, 1979; Translator's Son, 1980; Ancestry, 1981; Remembering the Dawn, 1983; Tracking, 1985; Walking with My Sons, 1985; Near the Mountains, 1987; Langes Gedachtnis/Long Memory, 1988; Long Memory and Other Poems, 1989; No Borders: New Poems, 1999; Ndakinna: Our Land, 2003; Above the Line, 2003. STORIES: Foot of the Mountain and Other Stories, 2003. EDITOR: (with W. Witherup) Words from the House of the Dead: An Anthology of Prison Writings from Soledad, 1971, 2nd ed., 1974; The Last Stop: Writings from Comstock Prison, 1974; (with R. Weaver) Aftermath: An Anthology of Poems in English from Africa, Asia, and the Caribbean, 1977; The Next World: Poems, 1978; Songs from This Earth on Turtle's Back: Contemporary American Indian Poetry, 1983; Breaking Silence: An Anthology of Contemporary Asian American Poets, 1984; The Light from Another Country: Poetry from American Prisons, 1984; North Country: An Anthology of Contemporary Writing from the Adirondacks and the Upper Hudson Valley, 1985; New Voices from the Longhouse: An Anthology of Contemporary Iroquois Writing, 1989; Raven Tells Stories: An Anthology of Alaskan Native Writing, 1991; Singing of Earth, 1993; Returning the Gift: Poetry and Prose from the First North American Native Writers' Festival, 1994; Aniyunwiya/Real Human Beings: An Anthology of Contemporary Cherokee Prose, 1995; Smoke Rising: The Native North American Literary Companion, 1995; (with M.J. Caduto) Keepers of the Earth: Native American Stories and Environmental Activities for Children, 1997. OTHERS: Garter Snakes, 1976; The Road to Black Mountain: A Novel, 1976; The Dreams of Jesse Brown, 1978; How to Start and Sustain a Literary Magazine: Practical Strategies for Publications of Lasting Value, 1980; (contrib.) The Ghost & I: Scary Stories for Paticipatory Telling, 1992; (intro.) Native American Literature: A Catalog, 1996; Buffalo Boy, 1998; Seeing the Circle, 1999; (with J. Bruchac) Native American Games and Stories, 2000; Seasons of the Circle: A Native American Year, 2002; Winter People, 2002; Warriors, 2003; Dark Pond, 2004; Raccoon's Last Race: A Traditional Abenaki Story, 2004; (with T. Locker) Rachel Carson: Oreserving a Sense of Wonder, 2004; At the End of Ridge Road, 2005; (co-author) Sports Shorts: An Anthology of Short Stories, 2005; Code Talker: A Novel about the Navajo Marines of World War Two, 2005; Whisper in the Dark, 2005; Geronimo, 2006; (with G. Ross) Girl who Married the Moon: Tales from Native North America, 2006; Jim Thorpe: Original All-American, 2006; Return of Skeleton Man, 2006; Wabi: A Hero's Tale, 2006; Bearwalker, 2007; (reteller with J. Bruchac) Girl Who Helped Thunder and Other Native American Folktales, 2008; (co-author) Lay-ups and Long Shots, 2008; Buffalo Song, 2008; March toward the Thunder, 2008; Night Wings, 2009; Dragon Castle, 2011; Wolf Mark, 2011. **Address:** PO Box 308, Greenfield Center, NY 12833-0308, U.S.A. **Online address:** nudatlog@earthlink.net

BRUCHAC, Margaret M. *See* **BRUCHAC, Marge M.**

BRUCHAC, Marge M. (Margaret M. Bruchac). American/Indian (born India) **Genres:** Children's Non-fiction, Anthropology/Ethnology. **Career:** University of Connecticut, assistant professor of anthropology, Native American and Indigenous Studies, coordinator; University of Massachusetts, artist-in-residence, adjunct faculty; State University of New York, artist-in-residence; Amherst College, adjunct faculty; Keene State College, adjunct faculty; The State University of New York, adjunct faculty; Smith College, adjunct faculty; Tufts University, adjunct faculty; museum consultant, 1997-; Plimoth Plantation, Wampanoag Indigenous Program, advisor, 1998-2007. Writer. **Publications:** (With C.O. Grace) 1621: A New Look at Thanksgiving, 2001; (with F. Apffel-Marglin) Exorcising Anthropology's Demons, 2004; Malian's Song, 2006; (ed. with S.M. Hart and H.M. Wobst) Indigenous Archaeologies: A Reader on Decolonization, 2010. Contributor to books and anthologies. **Address:** Vermont Folklife Center, 88 Main St., Middlebury, VT 05753-1425, U.S.A. **Online address:** maligeet@earthlink.net

BRUCK, Connie. (Connie Jane Bruck). American (born United States), b. 1946. **Genres:** Documentaries/Reportage, Business/Trade/Industry, Politics/Government. **Career:** Freelance journalist, 1970-79; The American Lawyer (magazine), staff writer, 1979-89; The New Yorker, staff writer, 1989-. **Publications:** The Predators' Ball: The Junk Bond Raiders and the Man Who Staked Them, 1988; The Predators' Ball: The Inside Story of Drexel Burnham and the Rise of the Junk Bond Raiders, 1989; Master of the Game: Steve Ross and the Creation of Time Warner, 1994; When Hollywood had a King: The Reign of Lew Wasserman, Who Leveraged Talent into Power and Influence, 2003. Contributor to periodicals. **Address:** The New Yorker, 4 Times Sq., New York, NY 10036, U.S.A.

BRUCK, Connie Jane. *See* **BRUCK, Connie.**

BRUCKHEIMER, Linda. American (born United States), b. 1946?. **Genres:** Novels, Adult Non-fiction. **Career:** Mirabella Magazine, West Coast editor; Public Broadcasting Service, writer/producer; National Trust for Historic Preservation, trustee. Preservation activist. **Publications:** Dreaming Southern, 1999; The Southern Belles of Honeysuckle Way, 2004. **Address:** Hilsinger-Mendelson Inc., 8916 Ashcroft Ave., Los Angeles, CA 90048-2404, U.S.A.

BRÜCKNER, Martin. (Martin Christof Brückner). American/German (born Germany), b. 1963. **Genres:** Literary Criticism And History, Geography. **Career:** University of Delaware, associate professor. Writer. **Publications:** The Geographic Revolution in Early America: Maps, Literacy, and National Identity, 2006; (ed. with H.L. Hsu) American Literary Geographies: Spatial Practice and Cultural Production, 1500-1900, 2007. Contributor to journals. **Address:** Department of English, University of Delaware, 212 Memorial Hall, Newark, DE 19716, U.S.A. **Online address:** mcb@udel.edu

BRÜCKNER, Martin Christof. *See* **BRUCKNER, Martin.**

BRUCKNER, Pascal. French (born France), b. 1948. **Genres:** Novels, Adult Non-fiction, Children's Fiction, Essays, Young Adult Non-fiction, Young Adult Fiction, Children's Non-fiction. **Career:** Writer. **Publications:** NOVELS: Monsieur Tac, 1976; Allez jouer ailleurs, 1977; Lunes de fiel, 1981; Parias, 1985; Le divin enfant, 1992. NONFICTION: Fourier, 1975; Le nouveau desordre amoureux, 1977; Au coin de la rue, l'aventure, 1979; Le sanglotde l'homme blanc: Tiers-monde culpabilite, 1983; La mélancolie democratique, 1990; La tentation de l'innocence, 1995, trans. as The Temptation of Innocence Living in the Age of Entitlement, 2000; L'euphorieperpétuelle: essai sur le devoir de bonheur, 2000. OTHERS: Nouveaudésordre amoureux, 1977; Nostalgie express: le voyage dans leTranssibérien, 1978; Le palais des claques (children's fiction), 1986; Qui de nous deux inventa l'autre?: Roman, 1988; (co-author) Histoires d'Enfance, 1998; Les Ogres Anonymes: Suivi de, L'Effaceur: Deux Contes, 1998; Misère de la prospérité: la religion marchande et sesennemis, 2002; L'amour du prochain: roman, 2004; La tyrannie de lapénitence: Essai sur le masochisme occidental, 2006; Mon petit mari: roman, 2007; Le Paradoxe Amoureux, 2009; Le mariage d'amour, a-t-il échoué?: essai, 2010; Le fanatisme de l'apocalypse, 2011. Contributor to periodicals. **Address:** c/o Agence FMS, 7 rue Lincoln, Paris, 75008, France. **Online address:** bruckner@wanadoo.fr

BRUEMMER, Fred. Canadian (born Canada), b. 1929. **Genres:** Anthropology/Ethnology, Natural History, Photography, History, Animals/Pets. **Career:** Freelance photographer and writer, 1950-. **Publications:** The Long Hunt, 1969; (contrib.) Seasons of the Eskimo, 1971; (contrib.) Encounters with Arctic Animals, 1972; (contrib.) The Arctic, 1974; Saisons de l'Esquimau, 1974; (contrib.) The Life of the Harp Seal, 1977; Children of the North, 1979; Summer at Bear River, 1980; The Arctic World, 1985; Arctic Animals, 1987; Seasons of the Seal, 1988; World of the Polar Bear, 1989; The Narwhal, 1993; (with A. Delaunois) Les Animaux du Grand Nord, 1993; (with K. Pandell) Land of Dark, Land of Light, 1993; Arctic Memories: Living with the Inuit, 1993; (with A. Delaunois) Nanook and Nauja: The Polar Bear Cubs, 1995; (with A. Delaunois) Kotik: The Baby Seal, 1995; (with T. Mangelsen) Polar Dance: Born of the North Wind, 1997; Seals in the Wild, 1998; Glimpses of Paradise: The Marvel of Massed Animals, 2002; Survival: A Refugee Life, 2005; Islands of Fate, 2006; Arctic Visions: Pictures from a Vanished World, 2008. Contributor to magazines and newspapers. **Address:** 2 Strathearn S, Montreal, QC H4Z 1X4, Canada.

BRUER, John T. American (born United States), b. 1949?. **Genres:** Education, Sciences, Biology, Reference. **Career:** Rockefeller Foundation, Health Science Division, visiting research fellow and associate director, 1978-81; Josiah Macy, Jr. Foundation, program administrator, 1981-86; James S. McDonnell Foundation, president, 1986-; Washington University, adjunct professor of philosophy; St. Louis University Club Fund for Education, director. Writer. **Publications:** (Ed. with W. Goffman and K.S. Warren) Research on Selective Information Systems: A Bellagio Conference, October 23-27, 1979, 1980; (contrib.) Cognitive Science in Medicine, 1988; (ed. with H. Zuckerman and J.R. Cole) The Outer Circle: Women in the Scientific Community, 1991; Schools for Thought: A Science of Learning in the Classroom, 1993; The Myth of the First Three Years: A New Understanding of Early Brain Development and Lifelong Learning, 1999; (ed. with S.M. Fitzpatrick) Carving

Our Destiny: Scientific Research Faces a New Millennium, 2001. Contributor to books. **Address:** The James S. McDonnell Foundation, 1034 S Brentwood Blvd., Ste. 1850, Saint Louis, MO 63117-1284, U.S.A. **Online address:** bruer@jsmf.org

BRUGGER, E. Christian. American (born United States), b. 1964. **Genres:** Ethics, Philosophy, Psychology, Social Commentary, Biology, Popular Culture. **Career:** Rutgers University, campus ministry staff, 1987-92; Loyola University New Orleans, Department of Religious Studies, assistant professor of ethics, 2000-04, Yamauchi lecturer in religion, 2001; Westchester Institute for Ethics and the Human Person, senior fellow, 2002-; Institute for the Psychological Sciences, assistant professor of theology, 2004-06, director of integrative research, 2004-08, associate professor, 2006-08; Saint John Vianney Theological Seminary, associate professor of moral theology, 2008-. Writer. **Publications:** Capital Punishment and Roman Catholic Moral Tradition, 2003. Contributor to journals and periodicals. **Address:** Saint John Vianney Theological Seminary, Rm. 1010 Basement, 1300 S Steele St., Denver, CO 80210, U.S.A. **Online address:** christian.brugger@archden.org

BRUGIONI, Dino A. American (born United States), b. 1921. **Genres:** Air/Space Topics, Earth Sciences, History, Military/Defense/Arms Control, Photography, Politics/Government, Technology, Writing/Journalism, Illustrations. **Career:** Tennessee Valley Authority, part-time liaison officer, 1945-48; National Photographic Interpretation Center, Central Intelligence Agency, founding officer, expert on aerial reconnaissance and photographic interpretation, 1948-82, senior officer, 1963, chief, now retired; freelance writer and consultant, 1982-; U.S. Holocaust Museum, adviser; Smithsonian Air and Space Museum, adviser; Cold War Museum, advisor; Polytechnic Institute of New York, Institute of Imaging Sciences, distinguished lecturer; Federal Emergency Management Agency and Defense Intelligence College, National Emergency Training Center, adjunct faculty, 1990; National War College, lecturer; Defense Intelligence College, lecturer. **Publications:** (With R.G. Poirier) The Holocaust Revisited: A Retrospective Analysis of the Auschwitz-Birkenau Extermination Complex, 1979; The Civil War in Missouri: As Seen from the Capital City, 1987; Eyeball to Eyeball: The Inside Story of the Cuban Missile Crisis, 1991; From Balloons to Blackbirds: Reconnaissance, Surveillance, and Imagery Intelligence: How it Evolved, 1993; Photo Fakery: The History and Techniques of Photographic Deception and Manipulation, 1999; Eyes in the Sky: Eisenhower, the CIA, and Cold War Aerial Espionage, 2010. Contributor to journals, magazines and newspapers. **Address:** 301 Storck Rd., Hartwood, Fredericksburg, VA 22406-4731, U.S.A. **Online address:** dabrugioni@aol.com

BRUGMAN, Alyssa (F.). Australian (born Australia), b. 1974. **Genres:** Children's Fiction, Novels, Young Adult Fiction, Animals/Pets. **Career:** Aboriginal children tutor. Writer. **Publications:** Finding Grace, 2001; Walking Naked, 2002; Being Bindy, 2004; For Sale or Swap 2004; Beginner's Luck, 2005; Hot Potato, 2006; Hide and Seek, 2007; Solo, 2007; Greener Pastures, 2008; The Equen Queen, 2008; Girl Next Door, 2009. **Address:** c/o Sue Russell, Nexus Arts, PO Box 1009, Elsternwick, VI 3185, Australia. **Online address:** alyssa@alyssabrugman.com.au

BRUHNS, Karen Olsen. American (born United States), b. 1941. **Genres:** Anthropology/Ethnology. **Career:** University of California, acting assistant professor of anthropology, 1967-68; University of Calgary, assistant professor of anthropology, 1968-70; San Jose State University, assistant professor of anthropology, 1970-72; San Francisco State University, faculty, 1972-80, professor of anthropology, 1980-, now emeritus professor; Institute of Andean Studies, board director, 1977-91, secretary, 1991-94; California Academy of Sciences, research associate in anthropology, 1984-; Museo del Banco Central de Ecuador, research associate in archaeology, 1986-93; FUNDAR, founder, 1996-. Writer. **Publications:** (With T.W. Weller) A Coloring Album of Ancient Mexico and Peru, 1971; (with J. Dotta and G.R. Zelaya-Hidalgo) Monumental Art of Chontales: A Description of the Sculpture Style of the Department of Chontales, Nicaragua, 1974; Cihuatan, an Early Postclassic Town of El Salvador: The 1977-1978 Excavations, 1980; Ancient South America, 1994; Archaeological Investigations in Central Colombia, 1995; (with K.E. Stothert) Women in Ancient America, 1999; (with N.L. Kelker) Faking Ancient Mesoamerica, 2010; (with N.L. Kelker) Faking the Ancient Andes, 2010. Contributor of articles and reviews to periodicals. **Address:** Department of Anthropology, San Francisco State University, 1600 Holloway Ave., San Francisco, CA 94132, U.S.A. **Online address:** kbruhns@sfsu.edu

BRUINIUS, Harry. American (born United States) **Genres:** History. **Career:** Newmedia magazine, freelance writer, 1999-2001; City University of New York, Hunter College, Department of Film and Media Studies, adjunct assistant professor, 2001-, adjunct associate professor, 2010-; Village Quill (work space for writers), founder and executive director, 2005-. Writer. **Publications:** Better for All the World: The Secret History of Forced Sterilization and America's Quest for Racial Purity, 2006. Contributor to periodicals. **Address:** Department of Film & Media Studies, City University of New York, Hunter College, Rm. 1241 W, 695 Park Ave., New York, NY 10065, U.S.A. **Online address:** harryb@brown-bear.com

BRULOTTE, Gaetan. American/Canadian (born Canada), b. 1945. **Genres:** Novels, Novellas/Short Stories, Plays/Screenplays, Humanities, Literary Criticism And History, Sex, Essays. **Career:** Trois-Rivieres College, Department of French, assistant professor, 1970-72, associate professor, 1972-83, professor, 1970-83; Brevard Community College, visiting professor, 1983-84; University of South Florida, College of Arts and Sciences, French and Francophone literature, visiting professor, 1984-88, professor, 1988-2005, director of graduate studies in French, 1985-90, distinguished university professor, 2005-; I Harmattan, co-director of series, 1989-94. Writer and consultant. **Publications:** L'Emprise (novel: The Ascendancy), 1979, rev. ed., 1988; Le Surveillant (short stories), 1982, rev. ed., 1995. OTHER FICTION: Ce qui nous tient (short stories: What Holds Us), 1988; L'univers de Jean Paul Lemieux, 1996; oeuvres de chair of figures du discours erotique, 1998; Les Cahiers de Limentinus: Lectures fin de siècle, 1998; Epreuves (short stories), 1999; Le Client, 2001; La Vie de Biais (short stories), 2002. ESSAYS: L'Imaginaireet l'ecriture: Ghelderode (Writing and the Configuration of Imagination: Ghelderode), 1972; Aspects du texte erotique (Aspects of the Erotic Text), 1978; La Chambre des Lucidites, 2003; La Nouvelle quebecoise, 2010. OTHER: Dictionnaire bio-bibliographique, critique et anthologique/ Ecrivains de la Mauricie (Bio-bibliographical Dictionary of the Writers of the Mauricie Region, Quebec), 1981; (ed. with J. Phillips) Encyclopedia of Erotic Literature, 2006. Works appear on anthologies. Contributor to periodicals. **Address:** Department of World Languages, University of South Florida, CPR 424, 4202 E Fowler Ave., Tampa, FL 33620, U.S.A. **Online address:** brulotte@usf.edu

BRUMFIELD, William Craft. American (born United States), b. 1944. **Genres:** Architecture, Literary Criticism And History, Photography, Urban Studies. **Career:** University of Wisconsin, visiting lecturer in Russian literature, 1973-74; Harvard University, assistant professor of Russian literature, 1974-79; American Council of Teachers of Russian, Pushkin Institute, resident director, 1979-80; Russian Research Center, fellow, 1980-81; Tulane University, assistant professor to associate professor, 1981-91, professor of Slavic studies, 1992-, professor of Russian studies; University of Virginia, visiting associate professor, 1985-86; Kennan Institute for Advanced Russian Studies, fellow, 1989; National Humanities Center, fellow, 1992-93; NEH Summer Institute, co-director, 1994. Writer. **Publications:** Ukrainian Churches, 1980; Gold in Azure: One Thousand Years of Russian Architecture, 1983; William C. Brumfield Photograph Collection, 1987; (with B.A. Ruble and A. Kopp) Architecture and the New Urban Environment: Western Influences on Modernism in Russia and the U.S.S.R, 1988; The Origins of Modernism in Russian Architecture, 1991; A History of Russian Architecture, 1993; An Architectural Survey of St. Petersburg, 1840-1916: Building Inventory, 1994; Lost Russia: Photographing the Ruins of Russian Architecture, 1995; Life on the Russian Country Estate: A Social and Cultural History, 1995; Landmarks of Russian Architecture: A Photographic Survey, 1997; Russkii Sever: svidetelstvo Uiliama Brumfilda, 2001; Sviatyni Russkogo Severa: Dokumentalno-khudozhestvennye fotografi, 2001; Vologodskii albom: Arkhitekturnye pamiatniki Vologodskoi oblasti: svidetelstvo v fotografiiakh, 2005; Totma: Arkhitekturnoe Nasledie vFotografiiakh, 2005; Irkutsk: Arkhitekturnoe Nasledie v Fotografiiakh, 2006; Tobolsk: Arkhitekturnoe Nasledie v Fotografiiakh, 2006; Solikamsk: Arkhitekturnoe Nasledie v Fotografiiakh, 2007; Cherdyn: Arkhitekturnoe Nasledie v Fotografiiak, 2007; Velikii Ustiug, 2007; Kargopol: Arkhitekturnoe Nasledie v Fotografiiakh, 2007; Chita: Arkhitekturnoe Nasledie v Fotografiiakh, 2008; Buriatiia: Arkhitekturnoe Nasledie v Fotografiiakh, 2008; Solovki: Arkhitekturnoe Nasledie v Fotografiiakh, 2008; Kirillov. Ferapontovo, 2009; Sotsialnyi proekt v russkoi literature XIX veka, 2009; Kolomna: Arkhitekturnoe Nasledie v Fotografiiakh, 2009; Suzdal: Arkhitekturnoe Nasledie v Fotografiiakh, 2009; Torzhok: Arkhitekturnoe Nasledie v Fotografiiakh, 2010; Ustiuzhna, 2010; Belozersk, 2011. EDITOR: (contrib.) Reshaping Russian Architecture: Western Technology, Utopian Dreams, 1990; (with M. Velimirovich) Christianity and the Arts in Russia,

1991; (with B. Ruble) Russian Housing in the Modern Age: Design and Social History, 1993; (with B. Ruble) Zhilishche v Rossii: vek XX: Arkhitektura i sotsialnaia istoriia, 2001; (with B. Ananich and Y. Petrov) Commerce in Russian Urban Culture, 1861-1914, 2001; (with B. Ananich and Y. Petrov) Predprinimatelstvo i gorodskaia kultura v Rossii, 2002. **Address:** Department of Germanic and Slavic Studies, Tulane University, 305 Newcomb Hall, New Orleans, LA 70118, U.S.A. **Online address:** brumfiel@tulane.edu

BRUNDAGE, James A. American (born United States), b. 1929. **Genres:** Anthropology/Ethnology, Natural History, Photography, History, Animals/Pets. **Career:** Fordham University, instructor, 1953-57; University of Wisconsin, assistant professor, 1957-60, associate professor, 1960-65, professor of history, 1965-88, chairman, 1972-76; Journal of Medieval History, associate editor, 1974-; Cambridge University, Clare Hall, visiting fellow, 1977-78; University of Kansas, Ahmanson-Murphy distinguished professor of history and courtesy professor of law, 1989-, now distinguished professor emeritus of history and law. **Publications:** The Long Hunt, 1969; Seasons of the Eskimo, 1971; Encounters with Arctic Animals, 1972; The Arctic, 1974; The Life of the Harp Seal, 1977; Children of the North, 1979; Summer at Bear River, 1980; The Arctic World, 1985; Arctic Animals, 1987; Seasons of the Seal, 1988; World of the Polar Bear, 1989; Seals (with E.S. Grace), 1991; The Narwhal, 1993; (with K. Pandell) Land of Dark, Land of Light, 1993; (with A. Delaunois) Les Animaux du Grand Nord, 1993; Arctic Memories: Living with the Inuit, 1993; (with A. Delaunois) Nanook and Nauja: The Polar Bear Cubs, 1995; (with A. Delaunois) Kotik: The Baby Seal, 1995; (with T. Mangelsen) Polar Dance: Born of the North Wind, 1997; Seals in the Wild, 1998; Glimpses of Paradise: The Marvel of Massed Animals, 2002; Survival-A Refugee Life, 2005; Islands of Fate, 2006; Arctic Visions: Pictures from a Vanished World, 2008. **Address:** Department of History, University of Kansas, 3650 Wescoe Hall, 1445 Jayhawk Blvd., Lawrence, KS 66045-2130, U.S.A. **Online address:** jabrun@ku.edu

BRUNDIGE, Donald G. American (born United States), b. 1940. **Genres:** Travel/Exploration, Recreation, Sports/Fitness. **Career:** Aerospace Corp., senior project engineer, 1979-96, consultant, 1996-; writer, 1996-. **Publications:** (WITH S. BRUNDIGE): Bicycle Rides: Los Angeles and Orange Counties, 1987; Bicycle Rides: San Fernando Valley and Ventura County, 1988; Bicycle Rides: Orange County, 1988, 5th ed., 2000; Bicycle Rides: Los Angeles County, 1989, 4th ed., 2000; Bicycle Rides: Inland Empire, 1990; Bicycle Rides: San Diego County and Imperial County, 1992; Bicycle Rides: Santa Barbara and Ventura Counties, 1994; Mountain Biking L.A. County: Southern Section: 66 Selected Best Trips, 100 Rides, 1996; Outdoor Recreation Checklists, Outdoor Recreation Equipment, 1998; Bicycle Rides, Los Angeles County: 83 Rides with Detailed Maps and Elevation Contours, 2000; Cycling Orange County, 2006; Cycling Los Angeles, 2007. **Address:** 122 Mirabeau Ave., San Pedro, CA 90732, U.S.A. **Online address:** bnyduk@aol.com

BRUNDIGE, Sharron L(ea). American (born United States), b. 1943. **Genres:** Travel/Exploration, Recreation, Sports/Fitness, Westerns/Adventure. **Career:** Rockwell International Corp., technical staff, 1965-89; writer, 1989-. **Publications:** WITH D.G. BRUNDIGE: Bicycle Rides: Los Angeles and Orange Counties, 1987; Bicycle Rides: San Fernando Valley and Ventura County, 1988; Bicycle Rides: Orange County, 1988, 5th ed., 2001; Bicycle Rides: Los Angeles County, 1989, 4th ed. as Bicycle Rides: Los Angeles County: 83 Rides with Detailed Maps & Elevation Contours, 2000; Bicycle Rides: Inland Empire, 1990; Bicycle Rides: San Diego County and Imperial County, 1992; Bicycle Rides: Santa Barbara and Ventura Counties, 1994; Mountain Biking L.A. County: Southern Section: 66 Selected Best Trips, 100 Rides, 1996; Outdoor Recreation Checklists, 1998; Bicycle Rides: Orange County: 58 Rides with Detailed Maps & Elevation Contours, 5th ed., 2000; Cycling Orange County, 2006; Cycling Los Angeles, 2007. **Address:** 122 Mirabeau Ave., San Pedro, CA 90732, U.S.A. **Online address:** bnyduk@aol.com

BRUNELLE, Dorval. Canadian (born Canada), b. 1941?. **Genres:** History, Business/Trade/Industry, Marketing. **Career:** Province of Quebec, Minister of Municipal Affairs, chief of staff, 1964-66; Société Radio-Canada, journalist, 1967-68; University of Quebec, Department of Sociology, professor, 1970-, Centre International Studies and Global Studies, director of the Americas, 2004-08, Research Group on Continental Integration, co-founder and director, Institute of International Studies Montreal, director. Writer. **Publications:** Le code civil et les rapports de classes suivi d'une analyse sociologique de la loi Canadienne de l'assurance-chômage, 1975; La désillusion tranquille, 1978; La raison du capital: essais sur la dialectique, 1980; L'etat solide: sociologie du fédéralisme au Canada et au Québec, 1982; Socialisme, étatisme et démocratie, 1983; Les trois colombes: essai, 1985; (co-author) L'ere des libéraux: le pouvoir fédéral de 1963 à 1984, 1988; (with C. Deblock) Le Libre-échange par défaut, 1989; (ed. with C. Deblock) L'Amérique du nord et l'Europe communautaire: intégration économique, intégration sociale?, 1994; Dérive globale, 2003; (ed.) Main basse sur l'état: les partenariats public-privé au Québec et en amérique du nord, 2005. **Address:** Institute of International Studies Montreal, University of Quebec, Rue Sainte-Catherine St. E, Ste. A-1540, PO 8888, Sta. Centre-Ville, Montreal, QC H2L 3C5, Canada. **Online address:** brunelle.dorval@uqam.ca

BRUNELLI, Jean. American (born United States), b. 1934. **Genres:** Medicine/Health, Young Adult Non-fiction. **Career:** ABC Unified School District, school nurse and program director, 1975-; Southeast Council Serving Young Children with Special Needs and Their Families, chair. Writer. **Publications:** Your Pregnancy and Newborn Journey: How to Take Care of Yourself and Your Newborn if You're a Pregnant Teen, 1991; (with J.W. Lindsay) Teens Parenting: Your Pregnancy and Newborn Journey, Morning Glory, 1991; (with J.W. Lindsay) Nurturing Your Newborn: Young Parents Huide to Baby's First Month, 1999, 2nd ed., 2006; (with J.W. Lindsay) Your Pregnancy and Newborn Journey: A Guide for Pregnant Teens, rev. ed., 2000, 3rd ed., 2004. **Address:** 16800 Norwalk Blvd., Cerritos, CA 90701, U.S.A.

BRUNER, Jerome S(eymour). American (born United States), b. 1915. **Genres:** History. **Career:** Harvard University, lecturer, 1945-48, associate professor, 1948-52, professor of psychology, 1957-72, Center for Cognitive Studies, director, 1961-72; Oxford University, Watts Professor of Psychology, 1972-80; G.H. Mead University, New School for Social Research, professor, 1981-88; New York University, research professor of psychology, senior research fellow in law, 1984-94, professor, 1994-2004, university professor, 2004-. Writer. **Publications:** Public Thinking on Post-War Problems, 1943; Mandate from the People, 1944; (with J.J. Goodnow and G.A. Austin) A Study of Thinking, 1956; (co-author) Opinions and Personality, 1956; (co-author) Contemporary Approaches to Cognition, 1957; Logique et perception, 1958; The Process of Education, 1960; On Knowing: Essays for the Left Hand, 1962; Man: A Course of Study, 1965; (co-author) Studies in Cognitive Growth, 1966; Toward a Theory of Instruction, 1966; Processes of Cognitive Growth: Infancy, 1968; The Relevance of Education, 1971; Beyond the Information Given: Studies in the Psychology of Knowing, 1973; Patterns of Growth, 1974; Under Five in Britain, 1980; In Search of Mind: Essays in Autobiography, 1983; (with R. Watson) Child's Talk, 1983; Actual Minds, Possible Worlds, 1986; Acts of Meaning, 1990; (afterword) The Social Foundations of Language and Thought: Essays in Honor of Jerome S. Bruner, 1990; The Culture of Education, 1996; (foreword) Constructing Panic: The Discourse of Agoraphobia, 1999; (with A.G. Amsterdam) Minding the Law: How Courts Rely on Storytelling, and How Their Stories Change the Way We Understand Law and Ourselves, 2000; Making Stories: Law, Literature, Life, Farrar, 2002. EDITOR: Perception and Personality: A Symposium, 1950; Learning about Learning: A Conference Report, 1966; The Growth of Competence, 1974; Play: Its Role in Development and Evolution, 1976; (with A. Garton) Human Growth and Development, 1978; (with H. Hastle) Making Sense: The Child's Construction of the World, 1987; (with M.H. Bornstien) Interaction in Human Development, 1989. **Address:** University Professor, New York University, 200 Mercer St., New York, NY 10012, U.S.A. **Online address:** jerome.bruner@nyu.edu

BRUNKHORST, Alex. American (born United States) **Genres:** Novels. **Career:** Coldwell Banker, REO broker; United Talent Agency, writers agent. Writer. **Publications:** The Mating Season, 2004. **Address:** Coldwell Banker, 301 N Canon Dr., Beverly Hills, CA 90210, U.S.A. **Online address:** alex@alexbrunkhorst.com

BRUNKHORST, Hauke. German (born Germany), b. 1945. **Genres:** Adult Non-fiction, Economics. **Career:** University of Göttingen, research assistant, 1974-78; University of Frankfurt, research assistant, 1974-78, visiting professor, 1979-80, 1993-94; University of Konstanz, research assistant, 1974-78; University of Osnabrück, professor of sociology, 1982-83; University of Mainz, professor of educational sciences, 1982-84; Institute for Advanced Studies, visiting professor, 1985; Frankfurt University, professor of sociology, 1985-86, professor of philosophy, 1987-89, 1994-95, visiting professor, 1986-89; Inter University Center, course director, 1989-; Free University of Berlin, visiting professor, 1989-91, professor of political theory, 1990-92; University of Duisburg, visiting professor, 1992-93, professor of political theory,

1992-94; Kulturwissenschaftliches Institut des Wissenschaftszentrums NRW, research fellow, 1995-96; University of Flensburg, professor of sociology, Institute of Sociology, head, 1997-, managing director, managing director of European studies, master's program in European studies, head of studies, 2006-; University of Aarhus, Institute for Cultural Studies, visiting professor, 1998; University of Vienna, Institute for Political Science, visiting professor, 2002; Maison des Sciences de l'Homme, research fellow, 2005. Writer. **Publications:** Praxisbezug und theoriebildung: E. Kritik D. Modells entsubjektivierter Wiss, 1978; (with J. Ritsert) Theorie, Interesse, Forschungsstrategien: Probleme krit. Sozialforschung, 1978; Herbert Marcuse zur Einführung, 1987; Der Intellektuelle im Land der Mandarine, 1987; Der entzauberte Intellektuelle: Uber die neue Beliebigkeit des Denkens, 1990; Theodor W. Adorno: Dialektik Der Moderne, 1990; (ed. with M. Brumlik) Gemeinschaft und Gerechtigkeit, 1993; Demokratie und Differenz: egalitarer Individualismus, 1994; Solidarität unter Fremden, 1997; (ed.) Demokratischer Experimentalismus: Politik in der komplexen Gesellschaft, 1998; (ed. with W.R. Kohler and M.L. Bachmann) Recht auf Menschenrechte: Menschenrechte, 1999; (ed. with P. Niesen) Das Recht der Republik, 1999; Adorno and Critical Theory, 1999; Hannah Arendt, 1999; (ed.) Globalisierung und Demokratie: Wirtschaft, Recht, Medien, 2000; Solidarität: von der Bürgerfreundschaft zur globalen Rechtsgenossenschaft, 2002; (ed. with G. Grotzinger and W. Matiaske) Peripherie und Zentrum in der Weltgesellschaft, 2004; (ed. with S. Costa) Jenseits von Zentrum und Peripherie: Zur Verfassung der fragmentierten Weltgesellschaft, 2005; Habermas, 2006; (with G. Beestermöller) Rückkehr der Folter, 2006; (ed. with G. Beestermoller) Folter: Sicherheit zum Preis der Freiheit, 2006; Karl Marx: Der achtzehnte Brumaire des Louis Bonaparte-Kommentar, 2007; (ed. with W. Matiaske, G. Grozinger and M. Neves) The European Union as a Model for the Development of Mercosur? Transnational Order between Economic Efficiency and Political Legitimacy, 2007; (ed. with R. Voigt) Rechts-Staat: Hans Kelsens Rechts-und Staatsverstandnis, 2008; (with R. Kreide and C. Lafont) Habermas-Handbuch, 2009; La rivoluzione giuridica di Hans Kelsen e altri saggi, 2010. **Address:** Institute of Sociology, University of Flensburg, Rm. 358, Auf dem Campus 1, Flensburg, 24943, Germany. **Online address:** brunk@uni-flensburg.de

BRUNNER, Jose. Israeli/Swiss (born Switzerland), b. 1954. **Genres:** Politics/Government, History, Humanities, Philosophy, Economics. **Career:** Hebrew University of Jerusalem, Department of Political Science, instructor, 1983-85; Tel Aviv University, Department of Political Science, instructor, 1984-88, lecturer, 1988-95, adjunct lecturer, 1992-95, Buchmann Faculty of Law, visiting senior lecturer, 1995-96, senior lecturer, 1996-2003, Department of Philosophy of Science and History of Ideas, professor, 2002-, Cohn Institute of the History and Philosophy of Science and Ideas, visiting senior lecturer, 1995-96, senior lecturer, 1996-2003, Department of History and Philosophy of Science and Ideas, professor, 2002-, Minerva Institute for German History, director, 2005-; McGill University, visiting Hannah foundation professor, 1998-99; Friedrich Schiller University, distinguished visiting professor, 2008. Writer. **Publications:** Freud and the Politics of Psychoanalysis, 2001; (ed. with N. Frei and C. Goschler) Die Praxis der Wiedergutmachung, 2009. **Address:** Buchmann Faculty of Law, Tel Aviv University, Rm. 433, Minkoff Law Bldg., Ramat Aviv, 69978, Israel. **Online address:** joseb@post.tau.ac.il

BRUNO, Richard L(ouis). American (born United States), b. 1954. **Genres:** Medicine/Health, Psychology. **Career:** New York State Psychiatric Institute, clinical research scientist, 1978-81; Columbia University, College of Physicians and Surgeons, Department of Physical Medicine and Rehabilitation, fellow, 1981-84, clinical research coordinator, faculty of medicine, 1984-88; Kessler Institute for Rehabilitation, director of post-polio rehabilitation and research service; New Jersey Medical School, associate professor, International Post-Polio Task Force, chair, 1984-; Mount Sinai School of Medicine, associate professor; Post-Polio Institute, director, International Centre for Polio Education and Research, director. Writer. **Publications:** The Polio Paradox: What You Need to Know: Uncovering the Hidden History of Polio to Understand and Treat Post-Polio Syndrome and Chronic Fatigue, 2002; Crocodile Tears, 2007; Blue Moon, 2010. Contributor to magazines and journals. **Address:** Post-Polio Institute, 151 Prospect Ave., Ste. 17A, Hackensack, NJ 07601-2228, U.S.A. **Online address:** postpolioinfo@aol.com

BRUNS, Don. American (born United States), b. 1947. **Genres:** Mystery/Crime/Suspense, Novels. **Career:** Advertising executive; Bookends Used and Rare Books, founder and owner. Writer. **Publications:** Jamaica Blue, 2002; Barbados Heat, 2003; South Beach Shakedown: A Novel, 2006; Stuff to Die For: A Novel, 2007; Stuff Dreams Are Made Of, 2008; St. Barts Breakdown, 2008; Bahama Burnout, 2009; Stuff to Spy For, 2009; Don't Sweat the Small Stuff, 2010. Contributor to periodicals. **Address:** c/o Jane Chelius, Jane Chelius Agency, 548 Second St., Brooklyn, NY 11215, U.S.A. **Online address:** don@donbrunsbooks.com

BRUNS, Roger A. American (born United States), b. 1941. **Genres:** History, Young Adult Non-fiction, Biography, Humor/Satire. **Career:** National Historical Publications and Records Commission, National Archives, archivist, 1967-69, supervisory archivist, 1969-77, director of publications program, 1977-88, acting executive director, 1988, 1997, deputy executive director, 1989; NARA, policy and communications staff; National Archives and Records Administration, deputy director. Writer. **Publications:** (Ed. with A. Schlesinger, Jr.) Congress Investigates: A Documented History, 1792-1974, 1975, rev. ed. as (ed. with D.L. Hostetter, R.W. Smock and R.C. Byrd) Congress Investigates: A Critical and Documentary History, 2011; (ed.) Am I Not a Man and a Brother: The Antislavery Crusade of Revolutionary America, 1688-1787, 1977; Knights of the Road: A Hobo History, 1980; (with G. Vogt) Your Government In Action: Or, In God We'd Better Trust (humor), 1980; The Damndest Radical: The Life and World of Dr. Ben Reitman, Chicagos Celebrated Social Reformer, Hobo King, and Whorehouse Physician (biography), 1986; (with H. Richardson) Bermuda, 1986; Preacher: Billy Sunday and Big-Time American Evangelism (biography), 1992; The Bandit Kings: From Jesse to Pretty Boy, 1995; John Wesley Powell: Explorer of the Grand Canyon, 1997; Jesse James: Legendary Outlaw, 1998; Almost History: Close Calls, Plan Bs, and Twists of Fate in American History, 2000; Billy the Kid: Outlaw of the Wild West, 2000; Desert Honkytonk: The Story of Tombstones Bird Cage Theatre, 2000; Icons of Latino America: Latino Contributions to American Culture, 2008; Cesar Chavez and the United Farm Workers Movement, 2011; Negro Leagues Baseball, 2012. YOUNG ADULT BIOGRAPHY: Abraham Lincoln, 1986; Thomas Jefferson, 1986; George Washington, 1987; Julius Caesar, 1987; Billy Graham: A Biography, 2004; Cesar Chavez: A Biography, 2005; Jesse Jackson: A Biography, 2005; Martin Luther King, Jr.: A Biography, 2006. Contributor of articles to periodicals. **Address:** National Archives, 700 Pennsylvania Ave. NW, Washington, DC 20408-0001, U.S.A. **Online address:** roger.bruns@nara.gov

BRUNS, William John. American (born United States), b. 1935. **Genres:** Administration/Management, Economics, Business/Trade/Industry, Social Sciences. **Career:** Yale University, assistant professor of economics and industrial administration, 1962-66; University of Washington, associate professor, 1966-71, professor of accounting, 1971-72; Addison-Wesley Publishing Co., advisory editor, 1967-; Harvard University, visiting associate professor, 1969-70, Graduate School of Business Adminstration, professor of accounting, 1971-72, professor of business administration, 1972-93, Henry R. Byers professor of business administration, 1993-, now Henry R. Byers professor emeritus of business administration; Northeastern University, visiting professor of accounting, 2001-. **Publications:** Accounting for Decisions: Business Game, 1966; (ed. with D.T. DeCoster) Accounting and Its Behavioral Implications, 1969; Introduction to Accounting: Economic Measurement for Decisions, 1971; (with R.F. Vancil) Accounting for Inflation: Replacement Costs and Values, 1976; (ed. with M.E. Barrett) Case Problems in Management Accounting, 1982, 2nd ed., 1985; (ed. with R.S. Kaplan) Accounting and Management: Field Study Perspectives, 1987; (with S.M. McKinnon) The Information Mosaic, 1992; (ed.) Performance Measurement, Evaluation, and Incentives, 1992; Accounting for Managers: Text and Cases, 1994, 3rd ed., 2005. **Address:** Business School, Harvard University, Soldiers Field, Boston, MA 02163, U.S.A. **Online address:** wbruns@hbs.edu

BRUNSKILL, Ronald William. (R. W. Brunskill). British (born England), b. 1929. **Genres:** Architecture. **Career:** Massachusetts Institute of Technology, visiting fellow, 1956-57; William Deacon's Bank Ltd., architect, 1957-60; Victoria University of Manchester, lecturer, 1960-73, senior lecturer in architecture, 1973-83, reader, 1984-89; Carter, Brunskill & Associates, partner, 1965-73; University of Florida, visiting professor, 1969-70; Historic Buildings and Monuments Commission (English Heritage), commissioner, 1989-95, Vernacular Architecture Group, president, 1974-77; Ancient Monuments Society, chairman, 1990-2000; De Montfort University, visiting professor, lecturer, 1994-2001, professor, now professor emeritus. Writer. **Publications:** (With A. Clifton-Taylor) English Brickwork, 1977. AS R.W. BRUNSKILL: Illustrated Handbook of Vernacular Architecture, 1971, 4th ed. as Vernacular Architecture: An Illustrated Handbook, 2000; Vernacular Architecture of the Lake Counties: A Field Handbook, 1974; Traditional Buildings of Britain: An introduction to Vernacular Architecture, 1981, 3rd ed., 1999; Houses,

1982; Traditional Farm Buildings of Britain, 1982, 3rd ed. as Traditional Farm Buildings of Britain and Their Conservation, 1999; Timber Building in Britain, 1985, new ed., 1994; Brick Building in Britain, 1990; Houses and Cottages of Britain, 1997; Traditional Buildings of Cumbria, the County of the Lakes, 2002; Brick and Clay Building in Britain, 2009. Contributor to journals. **Address:** De Montfort University, Richmond St., Leicester, LE LE2 7BQ, England.

BRUNSKILL, R. W. *See* **BRUNSKILL, Ronald William.**

BRUNT, Stephen. Canadian (born Canada), b. 1959. **Genres:** Sports/Fitness. **Career:** The Globe and Mail, arts intern, 1982-, sportswriter, 1985-, sports columnist, 1989-; Prime Time Sports, co-host. **Publications:** Mean Business: The Creation of Shawn O'Sullivan, 1987; Second to None: The Roberto Alomar Story, 1993; Power Plays!: Hockey Tips and Trivia, 1993; Diamond Dreams: Twenty Years of Blue Jays Baseball, 1996; The New Ice Age: A Year in the Life of the NHL, 1999; Facing Ali: The Opposition Weighs In, 2003; The Italian Stallions: Heroes of Boxing's Glory Days, 2003; (ed. and intro.) The Way It Looks from Here: Contemporary Canadian Writing on Sports, 2004; Searching For Bobby Orr, 2007; Gretzky's Tears, 2009. **Address:** Globe & Mail, 444 Front St. W, Toronto, ON M5V 2S9, Canada.

BRUSATTE, Stephen Louis. *See* **BRUSATTE, Steve.**

BRUSATTE, Steve. (Stephen Louis Brusatte). American (born United States), b. 1984. **Genres:** Children's Fiction. **Career:** American Museum of Natural History, Division of Paleontology, researcher. Paleontologist and writer. **Publications:** (As Stephen Brusatte) Stately Fossils: A Comprehensive Look at the State Fossils and Other Official Fossils, 2002; Dinosaurs (for children), 2008; Field Guide to Dinosaurs: A Time Traveller's Survival Guide (for children), 2009. Contributor to books and periodicals. **Address:** Division of Paleontology, American Museum of Natural History, Central Pk. W, 79th St., New York, NY 10024, U.S.A. **Online address:** sbrusatte@amnh.org

BRUSETH, James E. American (born United States), b. 1952. **Genres:** Education, Young Adult Non-fiction. **Career:** Texas Historical Commission, director of archaeology division. Writer. **Publications:** NONFICTION: (with T.K. Perttula) Prehistoric Settlement Patterns at Lake Fork Reservoir, 1981; (contrib.) Settlement of the Prairie Margin: Archaeology of the Richland Creek Reservoir, Navarro and Freestone Counties, Texas, 1980-81: A Research Synopsis, 1982; (with T.S. Turner) From a Watery Grave: The Discovery and Excavation of La Salle's Shipwreck, La Belle, 2005; La Salle in Texas: A Teacher's Guide for the Age of Discovery and Exploration, 2007. **Address:** PO Box 12276, Austin, TX 78711-2276, U.S.A.

BRUSH, Kathleen (E.). American (born United States), b. 1956. **Genres:** Administration/Management, Technology, Business/Trade/Industry. **Career:** Siemens, computer analyst, 1979-85; Boole and Babbage, marketing management, 1985-91; Intek Management, consultant, 1992-; Rogue Wave Software, chief executive officer; Fornova.com, vice president of marketing. Writer. **Publications:** (With W. Davies) High Tech Industry Marketing: The Elements of a Sophisticated Global Strategy, 1997; (with W. Davies) Managing Product Development in the High-Tech Industry, 1997; (with W. Davies and S. Dill) Managing Unsatisfactory Employee Performance, 1997; Export Management, 1999; High-Tech Strategies in the Internet Era, 2000. **Address:** 612 Jefferson Ave., Cape Canaveral, FL 32920, U.S.A. **Online address:** intek_management@msn.com

BRUSH, Lisa D. American (born United States), b. 1963. **Genres:** Politics/Government, Gay And Lesbian Issues. **Career:** University of Pittsburgh, assistant professor, 1994-2000, associate professor, 2000-, Women's Studies Program, staff, Cultural Studies Program, staff, University Center for Social and Urban Research, staff; National Institute of Justice Research, consultant, 2002-; Evaluation Technical Assistance, consultant, 2002-. Writer. **Publications:** Gender and Governance, 2003. **Address:** University of Pittsburgh, 2425 Wesley W. Posvar Hall, 230 Bouquet St., Pittsburgh, PA 15260, U.S.A. **Online address:** lbrush@pitt.edu

BRUSSAT, Frederic. American (born United States) **Genres:** inspirational/Motivational Literature, Psychology. **Career:** Cultural Information Service, co-founder and co-director; Values & Visions Circles, co-director; Spirituality and Practice.com, co-director; Spirituality & Health Magazine, media editor, 1996-2007; Spirituality Health.com, web editor, 2001-05; CIStems Inc., founder and co-director. Writer. **Publications:** EDITOR WITH M.A. BRUSSAT: 100 Ways to Keep Your Soul Alive: Living Deeply and Fully Every Day, 1994; 100 More Ways to Keep Your Soul Alive, 1997. OTHERS WITH M.A. BRUSSAT: Spiritual Literacy: Reading the Sacred in Everyday Life, 1996; Spiritual Rx: Prescriptions for Living a Meaningful Life, 2000. Contributor to periodicals. **Address:** CIStems Inc., 15 W 24th St., 10th Fl., New York, NY 10010-3214, U.S.A. **Online address:** brussat@spiritualityandpractice.com

BRUSSAT, Mary Ann. American (born United States) **Genres:** inspirational/Motivational Literature, Psychology, Theology/Religion. **Career:** Spirituality & Health Magazine, media editor, 1996-2007; SpiritualityHealth.com, web editor, 2001-05; Cultural Information Service, co-founder and director; Values & Visions Circles, co-director. **Publications:** WITH F. BRUSSAT: (ed.) 100 Ways to Keep Your Soul Alive: Living Deeply and Fully Every Day, 1994; Spiritual Literacy: Reading the Sacred in Everyday Life, 1996; (ed.) 100 More Ways to Keep Your Soul Alive, 1997; Spiritual Rx: Prescriptions for Living a Meaningful Life, 2000. **Address:** Department SL, CIS/Values & Visions Circles, Madison Square Sta., PO Box 786, New York, NY 10159, U.S.A. **Online address:** brussat@spiritualrx.com

BRUSTEIN, Robert. (Robert Sanford Brustein). American (born United States), b. 1927. **Genres:** Theatre, Humanities. **Career:** Cornell University, instructor in English, 1955-56; Vassar College, instructor in drama, 1956-57; Columbia University, Columbia Drama School, instructor in drama, 1957-58, professor of English and comparative literature, 1958-66, National Arts Journalism Program, fellow, 2001-02; New Republic, drama critic, 1959-67, 1979-; WNET Opposition Theatre, host and writer, 1966-; Yale University, professor of English, Drama School, dean, Yale Repertory Theatre, founding artistic director, 1966-79; New York Times, contributor, 1967-; Yale/Theatre, founder and publisher, 1967-; Harvard University, professor of English, 1979-2002, senior research fellow, 2002-; American Repertory Theatre, founding artistic director, 1980-2001. Writer. **Publications:** The Theatre of Revolt, 1963; Introduction to the Plays of Chekhov, 1964; (ed.) The Plays of Strindberg, 1964; Season of Discontent, 1965; The Third Theatre, 1969; Revolution as Theatre, 1971; The Culture Watch, 1975; Critical Moments, 1979; Making Scenes: A Personal History of the Turbulent Years at Yale, 1966-1979 (memoir), 1981; Who Needs Theatre, 1987; Reimagining American Theatre, 1991; Dumbocracy in America: Studies in the Theatre of Guilt, 1994; Cultural Calisthenics: Writings on Race, Politics, and Theatre, 1998; The Siege of the Arts, 2001; Letters to a Young Actor, 2005; Millennial Stages: Essays and Reviews, 2001-2005, 2006; English Channel (play), 2008; The Tainted Muse: Prejudice and Presumption in Shakespeare and His Times, 2010; Rants and Raves, 2011. **Address:** Department of Theatre, Suffolk University, Boston, MA 02114, U.S.A. **Online address:** brustein@fas.harvard.edu

BRUSTEIN, Robert Sanford. *See* **BRUSTEIN, Robert.**

BRUSTEIN, William I. American (born United States), b. 1947. **Genres:** History, Sociology, Politics/Government. **Career:** University of Washington, instructor, 1979-81, Stewart Carter Dodd instructor in sociology, 1979-80; University of Utah, assistant professor, 1981-87, associate professor of sociology, 1987-88; University of Minnesota, assistant professor, 1988-89, associate professor, 1989-94, Center for European Studies, director, 1992-95, professor of sociology and adjunct professor of political science, 1994-2000, Morse Alumni distinguished teaching professor of sociology, 1994-2000, department head, 1995-98, McKnight distinguished university professor, 2000; Ecole Normale Superieure, lecturer, 1989; University of California, lecturer, 1990; Jewish Family Service, board director, 1991-96; University of Arizona, lecturer, 1992, 1996; University of Strathclyde, lecturer, 1992; North Dakota State University, lecturer, 1993; University of Iowa, lecturer, 1993; University of Colorado, lecturer, 1994; Purdue University, lecturer, 1994; Eotvos Lorand University, lecturer, 1996; Louisiana State University, lecturer, 1996; Georgia Institute of Technology, lecturer, 1996; Emory University, lecturer, 1996; U.S. Holocaust Memorial Museum, lecturer, 1997; University of Helsinki, lecturer, 1997; University of Pittsburgh, professor of sociology, political science and history, 2001-, University Center for International Studies, director, 2001-, professor, 2001-. Writer. **Publications:** The Social Origins of Political Regionalism: France, 1849 to 1981, 1988; The Logic of Evil: The Social Origins of the Nazi Party, 1925-1933, 1996; Roots of Hate: Anti-Semitism in Europe before the Holocaust, 2003. Contributor to books. Contributor of articles to periodicals. **Address:** University Center for International Studies, University of Pittsburgh, 4408 Posvar Hall, Pittsburgh, PA 15260, U.S.A. **Online address:** brustein@ucis.pitt.edu

BRYAN, Lynne. British (born England), b. 1961. **Genres:** Novels, Novellas/Short Stories. **Career:** Theatre Royal, deputy box office manager, 1989-90; Women's Support Project, information worker, 1990-94; Harpies and Quines (feminist magazine), founding director, 1992-93; Archway Housing Project (hostel), relief worker, 1994-95. Writer. **Publications:** Envy at the Cheese Handout (stories), 1995; Gorgeous (novel), 1999; Like Rabbits (novel), 2002; Long Lost, forthcoming. Works appear in anthologies. Contributor to periodicals. **Address:** c/o Judith Murray, Greene & Heaton Ltd., 37 Goldhawk Rd., London, GL W12 8QQ, England. **Online address:** lbryan@sitella.co.uk

BRYANT, Chris. (Christopher Bryant). Welsh (born Wales), b. 1962. **Genres:** Politics/Government, Novels, History, Social Sciences. **Career:** Church of England, ordained priest, 1986; All Saints, curate; Diocese of Peterborough, youth chaplain; Labour Party, government development officer, 1993; Christian Socialist Movement chair and Hackney councillor, 1993-98; Common Purpose (educational nonprofit), manager, 1994-96; British Broadcasting Corp. (BBC), head of European affairs, 1998-2000; National Youth Theatre of Great Britain, associate. Writer and politician. **Publications:** (Ed.) Reclaiming the Ground, 1993; Possible Dreams: A Personal History of British Christian Socialists, 1996; Stafford Cripps: The First Modern Chancellor, 1997. Contributor to periodicals. **Address:** House of Commons, London, GL SW1A 0AA, England. **Online address:** bryantc@parliament.uk

BRYANT, Christopher. *See* **BRYANT, Chris.**

BRYANT, Christopher G. A. British (born England), b. 1944. **Genres:** Sociology, Politics/Government. **Career:** University of Salford, College of Arts and Social Sciences, emeritus professor of sociology. Writer and sociologist. **Publications:** NONFICTION; Sociology in Action: A Critique of Selected Conceptions of the Social Role of a Sociologist, 1976; Positivism in Social Theory and Research, 1985; Practical Sociology: Post-Empiricism and the Reconstruction of Theory and Application, 1995; Nations of Britain, 2006. EDITOR: (with H.A. Becker) What Has Sociology Achieved?, 1990; (with D. Jary) Giddens' Theory of Structuration: A Critical Appreciation, 1991; (with E. Mokrzycki) The New Great Transformation? Change and Continuity in East-Central Europe, 1994; (with E. Mokrzycki) Democracy, Civil Society and Pluralism in Comparative Perspective: Poland, Great Britain and the Netherlands, 1995; (with D. Jary) Anthony Giddens: Critical Assessments, 4 vols., 1997; (with D. Jary) The Contemporary Giddens: Social Theory in a Globalizing Age, 2001. **Address:** College of Arts and Social Sciences, University of Salford, Salford, GM M5 4WT, England. **Online address:** c.g.a.bryant@salford.ac.uk

BRYANT, Dorothy (Calvetti). American (born United States), b. 1930. **Genres:** Novels, Plays/Screenplays, Literary Criticism And History, Speech/Rhetoric, Young Adult Non-fiction, Mystery/Crime/Suspense. **Career:** San Francisco Public Schools, English teacher, 1953-56; Teacher of music, 1953-76; Lick-Wilmerding High School, English teacher, 1956-61; San Francisco State University, instructor in English, 1962; Golden Gate College, instructor in English, 1963; Contra Costa College, instructor in English and creative writing, 1964-76; Ata Books, founder, president and publisher, 1978-. Writer. **Publications:** The Comforter, 1971 as The Kin of Ata Are Waiting for You, 1976; Ella Price's Journal: A Novel, 1972; Miss Giardino: A Novel, 1978; Writing a Novel: Some Hints for Beginners (nonfiction), 1978; The Garden of Eros: A Novel, 1979; Prisoners: A Novel, 1980; Killing Wonder: A Mystery Novel, 1981; A Day in San Francisco: A Novel, 1983; Myths to Lie By: Short Pieces, 1984; Confessions of Madame Psyche: Memoirs and Letters of Mei-li Murrow, 1986; The Test: A Novel, 1991; Anita, Anita: Garibaldi of the New World: A Novel, 1993; The Berkeley Pit: An Historical Novel, 2007. Works appear in anthologies. Contributor to periodicals. **Address:** Ata Books, 1928 Stuart St., Berkeley, CA 94703-2215, U.S.A. **Online address:** dorbob@sbcglobal.net

BRYANT, Edward (Arnot). Australian/American/Canadian (born Canada), b. 1948. **Genres:** Geography, Earth Sciences, Sciences. **Career:** Macquarie University, computer operator, 1976-77; Technical and Field Surveys, minerals researcher, 1978-79; Wollongong University, associate professor of geography, 1979-, supervisor of meteorological station, 1983-, head of department, 1990-92, School of Geosciences, head, 1999-, Science Faculty, associate dean; writer, 1987-. **Publications:** Natural Hazards, 1991, 2nd ed., 2005; (ed. with G.D. Calvert, C.E. Ewan and J.A. Garrick and contrib.) Health in the Greenhouse: The Medical and Environmental Health Effects of Global Climate Change, 1993; Climate Process and Change, 1997; Tsunami: The Underrated Hazard, 2001, 2nd ed., 2008. Works appear in anthologies. Contributor to journals. **Address:** School of Earth and Environmental Science, University of Wollongong, Northfields Ave., Wollongong, NW 2522, Australia. **Online address:** ebryant@uow.edu.au

BRYANT, Howard. American (born United States), b. 1968?. **Genres:** Sports/Fitness. **Career:** San Jose Mercury News, sports writer, 1995-2001; North Jersey Media Group, sports writer, 2001-; The Washington Post, staff; Boston Herald, staff; The Bergen Record, staff; The San Jose Mercury News, staff; The Oakland Tribune, staff; National Public Radio, Weekend Edition Saturday, sports correspondent, 2006-; ESPN.com, senior writer, 2007-, ESPN Magazine, senior writer, 2007-, columnist. Journalist. **Publications:** Shut Out: A Story of Race and Baseball in Boston, 2002; Juicing the Game: Drugs, Power, and the Fight for the Soul of Major League Baseball, 2005; The Last Hero: A Life of Henry Aaron, 2010. Contributor to books. **Address:** National Public Radio, 635 Massachusetts Ave. NW, Washington, DC 20001, U.S.A. **Online address:** sports@northjersey.com

BRYANT, Jen. *See* **BRYANT, Jennifer F(isher).**

BRYANT, Jennifer F(isher). (Jen Bryant). American (born United States), b. 1960. **Genres:** Science Fiction/Fantasy, Children's Fiction, Poetry, Children's Non-fiction, Biography. **Career:** Pennsylvania Council on the Arts, artist-in-residence; West Chester University, Writing and English Department, professor; writer, 1989-. **Publications:** WORKING MOMS SERIES: Anne Abrams, Engineering Drafter, 1991; Ubel Velez, Lawyer, 1991; Sharon Oehler, Pediatrician, 1991; Zoe McCully, Park Ranger, 1991; Jane Sayler, Veterinarian, 1991; Carol Thomas-Weaver, Music Teacher, 1991. EARTH KEEPERS SERIES: Marjory Stoneman Douglas: Voice of the Everglades, 1991; Margaret Murie: A Wilderness Life, 1993. PHYSICALLY CHALLENGED SERIES: Louis Braille: Inventor, 1993; Henri de Toulouse-Lautrec: The Artist Who was Crippled, 1994. GREAT ACHIEVERS SERIES: Lucretia Mott: A Guiding Light, 1996; Thomas Merton: Poet, Prophet, Priest, 1997. OTHER: Birds of a Feather (adult nature anthology), 1993; Hand-Crafted (poetry chapbook), 2001; The Whole Measure (poetry chapbook), 2005; Pieces of Georgia, 2006; Call Me Marianne, 2006; River of Words: The Story of William Carlos Williams, 2008; Ringside, 1925: Views from the Scopes Trial: A Novel, 2008; Kaleidoscope Eyes, 2009; Abe's Fish: A Boyhood Tale of Abraham Lincoln, 2009. PICTURE BOOKS: Into Enchanted Woods, 2001; Georgia's Bones, 2005; Music for the End of Time, 2005; Abe's Fish: A Boyhood Tale of Abraham Lincoln, 2009. NOVELS: The Trial, 2004; A River of Words, 2008; Kaleidoscope Eyes, 2009; The Fortune of Carmen Navarro, 2010; Fortune of Carmen Navarro, 2010. Contributor to literary magazines and periodicals. **Address:** Dayton Bookings, 2753 E Pedigo Bay Dr., Bloomington, IN 47401, U.S.A. **Online address:** jean@daytonbookings.com

BRYANT, John. British (born England), b. 1944?. **Genres:** Sports/Fitness, History, Biography, Autobiography/Memoirs. **Career:** Times, deputy editor; Daily Mail, consultant editor. **Publications:** 3: 59.4: The Quest to Break the 4 Minute Mile, 2004; The London Marathon: The Greatest Race on Earth, 2005. **Address:** Random House, 20 Vauxhall Bridge Rd., London, GL SW1V 2SA, England.

BRYANT, Jonathan M. American (born United States), b. 1957. **Genres:** History, Local History/Rural Topics, Social Sciences. **Career:** Emory University, Mellon Fellow in Southern Studies, 1992-93; University of Baltimore, director of jurisprudence program, 1993-96; Georgia Southern University, assistant professor of history, 1996-, associate professor of history and graduate program coordinator, 2002-, Zach S. Henderson Library, director of special collections, Graduate Studies, director. Writer. **Publications:** How Curious a Land: Conflict and Change in Greene County, Georgia, 1850-1885, 1996; Savannah: A City of the Old South and the New, forthcoming. **Address:** Deparment of History, Georgia Southern University, 1204 Forest Bldg., PO Box 8054, Statesboro, GA 30460-8054, U.S.A. **Online address:** jbryant@georgiasouthern.edu

BRYANT, Mark. British (born England), b. 1953. **Genres:** History, Reference, Cartoons, Art/Art History, Humor/Satire, Trivia/Facts, Military/Defense/Arms Control, Social Commentary, Social Commentary, Ghost Writer, Biography, Autobiography/Memoirs. **Career:** Freelance editor, 1987-; London Press Club, director and secretary, 2000-08. **Publications:** Riddles Ancient and Modern, 1983; Dictionary of Riddles, 1990; (ed.) The Complete Colonel Blimp, 1991; (ed.) The Comic Cruikshank, 1992; (with

S. Heneage) Dictionary of British Cartoonists and Caricaturists, 1730-1980, 1994; (ed.) Sins of the Fathers: An Anthology of Clerical Crime, 1996; (ed.) 25 Years of MAC, 1996; Private Lives: Curious Facts about the Famous and Infamous, 1996; (ed.) Vicky's Supermac: Harold Macmillan in Cartoons by Victor Weisz of the Evening Standard, 1996; God in Cartoons, 1997; Dictionary of Twentieth-Century British Cartoonists and Caricaturists, 2000; Casanova's Parrot and Other Tales of the Famous and Their Pets, 2002; (ed.) H.M.Bateman, 2002; (ed.) Nicolas Bentley, 2002; World War II in Cartoons, 2005; World War I in Cartoons, 2006; Wars of Empire in Cartoons, 2008; Napoleonic Wars in Cartoons, 2009; Illingworth's War in Cartoons: One Hundred of His Greatest Drawings from the Daily Mail, 1939-1945, 2009; (ed.) The Best of MAC, 2000-2009, 2009; (ed.) The Best of MAC 2000-2010: The Political Years, 2010; Constable: A Brief History of Britain's Oldest Independent Publisher, 2010; (ed.) Mac's Tee Time, 2011. Contributor to journals. **Address:** PO Box 6026, London, GL SW2 5XT, England. **Online address:** mark.bryant@virgin.net

BRYANT, Robert Harry. American (born United States), b. 1925. **Genres:** Theology/Religion. **Career:** Hamden Hall Country Day School, teacher, 1947-48; William Jewell College, associate professor of philosophy, 1952-53; Vanderbilt University, School of Religion, visiting assistant professor of theology, 1953-54; Mt. Holyoke College, assistant professor of religion, 1956-58; Centre College of Kentucky, associate professor of philosophy and religion, 1958-61; United Theological Seminary of the Twin Cities, professor of systematic theology, 1961-71, professor of constructive theology, 1971-91, professor emeritus of constructive theology, 1991-; St. John's University, visiting professor, 1971-72; Adams United College, visiting professor, 1973-74; East West Center, staff, 1993; United Church of Christ, Clergyman. Writer. **Publications:** The Bible's Authority Today, 1968. **Address:** United Theological Seminary of the Twin Cities, 3000 5th St. NW, New Brighton, MN 55112, U.S.A.

BRYANT, Sharon. American (born United States), b. 1954?. **Genres:** Novels, Young Adult Fiction, History. **Career:** Writer. **Publications:** The Earth Kitchen, 2002. Contributor to periodicals. **Address:** c/o Author Mail, HarperCollins Publishers, 10 E 53rd St., 7th Fl., New York, NY 10022-5244, U.S.A.

BRYCE, Robert. American (born United States) **Genres:** Adult Non-fiction, Business/Trade/Industry. **Career:** Austin Chronicle, journalist, 1989-2001; Energy Tribune, managing editor, 2006-10; Manhattan Institute, senior fellow, 2010-; Texas Observer, contributing writer. **Publications:** The Colchicine Factor, 1978; Pipe Dreams: Greed, Ego, and the Death of Enron, 2002; Cronies: Oil, the Bushes, and the Rise of Texas, America's Superstate, 2004; Gusher of Lies: The Dangerous Delusions of Energy Independence, 2008; Power Hungry: The Myths of Green Energy, and the Real Fuels of the Future, 2010. **Address:** c/o Author Mail, PublicAffairs, 387 Pk. Ave. S, New York, NY 10016, U.S.A. **Online address:** robert@robertbryce.com

BRYDEN, John (Herbert). Canadian (born Canada), b. 1943. **Genres:** History, Military/Defense/Arms Control, Social Sciences. **Career:** Hamilton Spectator, reporter, feature writer and city editor, 1969-77; Globe and Mail, copy editor and science editor, 1977-79; Toronto Star, feature editor, senior news editor, business editor and magazine editor, 1979-89. Politician and historian. **Publications:** Deadly Allies: Canada's Secret War, 1937-1947, 1989; Best Kept Secret: Canadian Secret Intelligence in the Second World War, 1993. Contributor to periodicals. **Address:** 83 Lynden Rd., Lynden, ON L0R 1T0, Canada.

BRYSK, Alison. American (born United States), b. 1960. **Genres:** International Relations/Current Affairs, Politics/Government. **Career:** Centro De Estudios Del Estado Y Sociedad, visiting researcher, 1988; University of New Mexico, assistant professor, 1990-92; Pomona College, assistant professor, 1992-95; Stanford University, Latin American Studies, visiting assistant professor, 1996-97; University of California, professor of political science and international studies, 1997-2010, Global and International Studies, Mellichamp chair in global governance, 2010-. Writer. **Publications:** The Politics of Human Rights in Argentina: Protest, Change, and Democratization, 1994; From Tribal Village to Global Village: Indian Rights and International Relations in Latin America, 2000; (ed.) Globalization and Human Rights, 2002; (ed. with G. Shafir) People Out of Place: Globalization, Human Rights, and the Citizenship Gap, 2004; Human Rights and Private Wrongs: Constructing Global Civil Society, 2005; (ed. with G. Shafir) National Insecurity and Human Rights: Democracies Debate Counterterrorism, 2007; Global Good Samaritans: Human Rights as Foreign Policy, 2009; (ed. with A.C. Fitzpatrick) From Human Trafficking to Human Rights: Reframing Contemporary Slavery, 2012. Contributor to periodicals. **Address:** Global and International Studies, University of California, 2221 Social Sciences Bldg., Santa Barbara, CA 93106, U.S.A. **Online address:** alison.brysk@gmail.com

BRYSON, Ellen. American (born United States), b. 1949. **Genres:** Novels. **Career:** Writer. **Publications:** The Transformation of Bartholomew Fortuno (novel), 2010. **Address:** San Diego, CA , U.S.A. **Online address:** info@ellenbryson.com

BRYSON, Norman. American/Scottish (born Scotland), b. 1949. **Genres:** Art/Art History. **Career:** King's College, fellow and director in English studies, 1976-; University of Rochester, professor of comparative arts, 1988-90, PhD program in Visual and Cultural Studies, director; Harvard University, professor of art history, 1990-98; University College, Slade School of Art, professor of art history and theory, 1999-; University of California, faculty, 2003-, professor of art history. Writer. **Publications:** Swimmer, & Other Poems, 1969; Word and Image: French Painting of the Ancien Régime, 1981; Vision and Painting: The Logic of the Gaze, 1983; Tradition and Desire: From David to Delacroix, 1984; Looking at the Overlooked: Four Essays on Still Life Painting, 1990; (with B. Barryte) In Medusa's Gaze: Still Life Paintings from Upstate New York Museums, 1991; (with R. Krauss) Cindy Sherman, 1979-1993, (essay, other text by Krauss), 1993; Thomas Struth, Portraits, 1997; (contrib.) Inside/out, 1998; (contrib.) Sharon Lockhart, 2001; (contrib.) Victor Burgin, 2001; Robert Therrien, 2008. EDITOR: (with S. Kappeler) Teaching the Text, 1983; Calligram: Essays in New Art History from France, 1988; (with M.A. Holly and K. Moxey) Visual Theory, 1991; (with M.A. Holly and K. Moxey) Visual Culture: Images and Interpretations, 1994; (with J.S. Mostow and M. Graybill) Gender and Power in the Japanese Visual Field, 2003; Complicity and the Daily Draw: Susan Turcot Drawings 2003-2005, 2004. Contributor to periodicals. **Address:** Department of Visual Arts, University of California, 9500 Gilman Dr., Ste. 0084, La Jolla, CA 92093-0327, U.S.A. **Online address:** wnbryson@ucsd.edu

BRZEZINSKI, Matthew. Canadian (born Canada), b. 1965. **Genres:** Autobiography/Memoirs, Literary Criticism And History, Young Adult Fiction. **Career:** New York Times, office assistant, bureau, 1991-; Wall Street Journal, foreign correspondent, 1996-98; New York Times Magazine, contributing writer. **Publications:** Casino Moscow: A Tale of Greed and Adventure on Capitalisms Wildest Frontier, 2001; Fortress America: On the Front Lines of Homeland Security an Inside Look at the Coming Surveillance State, 2004; Red Moon Rising: Sputnik and the Hidden Rivalries That Ignited the Space Age, 2007. Contributor to periodicals. **Address:** Bantam Books, 1745 Broadway, New York, NY 10019, U.S.A.

BRZEZINSKI, Zbigniew (Kasimierz). American/Polish (born Poland), b. 1928. **Genres:** International Relations/Current Affairs, Politics/Government, Adult Non-fiction, Public/Social Administration, Cultural/Ethnic Topics. **Career:** Harvard University, Russian Research Center, Center for International Affairs, instructor and research fellow, 1953-56, assistant professor of government and research associate, 1956-60; Columbia University, associate professor, 1960-62, Research Institute on International Change (formerly, Research Institute on Communist Affairs), Herbert Lehman professor of government and director, 1962-77, 1981-89; Policy Planning Council of the Department of State, staff, 1966-68; Humphrey Foreign Policy Task Force, chairman of Presidential campaign, 1968; Trilateral Commission, director, 1973-76; Center for Strategic and International Studies, counselor, 1981-; Johns Hopkins University, Robert E. Osgood professor of American foreign policy, 1989-; RAND Corp., consultant. Writer. **Publications:** (Ed. and contrib.) Political Controls in the Soviet Army, 1954; The Permanent Purge: Politics in Soviet Totalitarianism, 1956; (with C.J. Friedrich) Totalitarian Dictatorship and Autocracy, 1956; The Soviet Bloc: Unity and Conflict, 1960, rev. ed., 1967; Ideology and Power in Soviet Politics, 1962, rev. ed., 1967; (ed. and contrib.) Africa and the Communist World, 1963; (with S.P. Huntington) Political Power: USA/USSR, 1964; Alternative to Partition: For A Broader Conception of America's Rolein Europe, 1965; The Implications of Change for United States Foreign Policy, 1967; Dilemmi Internazionali in Un'Epoca Tecnetronica, 1969; (ed.and comp.) Dilemmas of Change in Soviet Politics, 1969; Between Two Ages: America's Role in the Technetronic Era, 1970; International Politics in the Technetronic Era, 1971; The Fragile Blossom: Crisis and Change in Japan, 1972; System Miedzynarodowy Napiecia i Przemiany, 1976; Power and Principle: Memoirs of the National Security Adviser

1977-1981, 1983; (co-author) Democracy Must Work: A Trilateral Agenda for the Decade: A Task Force Report to the Trilateral Commission, 1984; (co-author) The International Implications of the Papal Assassination Attempt: A Case of State-Sponsored Terrorism: A Report of the CSIS Steering Committee on Terrorism, 1985; Power and Principle: Memoirs of the National Security Adviser, 1977-1981, 1985; (co-ed.) Promise or Peril, the Strategic Defense Initiative: Thirty-Five Essays by Statesmen, Scholars, and Strategic Analysts, 1986; Game Plan: How to Conduct the U.S.-Soviet Contest, 1986; American Security in an Interdependent World: A Collection of Papers Presented at the Atlantic Council's 1987 Annual Conference, 1988; Mysl i dzialanie w olityce Miedzynarodowej, 1988; The Grand Failure: The Birth and Death of Communismin the 20th Century, 1989; (co-author) Wielkie Bankructwo: Narodziny iSmierc Komunizmu w XX Wieku, 1990; Out of Control: Global Turmoil on the Eve of the Twenty-First Century, 1993; The Grand Chessboard: American Primacy and Its Geostrategic Imperatives, 1997; (co-ed.) Russia and the Commonwealth of Independent States: Documents, Data and Analysis, 1997; In Quest of National Security, 1988; (contrib.) Fulfilling the Promise, 1999; The Geostrategic Triad: Living with China, Europe and Russia, 2001; (contrib.) Masaryk's Day in Washington, 2003; The Choice: Global Domination or Global Leadership, 2004; Da jue ze: Meiguo Zhan Zai Shi Zi Lu Kou, 2005; Second Chance: Three Presidents and the Crisis of American Superpower, 2007; (with B. Scowcroft and D. Ignatius) America and the World: Conversations on the Future of American Foreign Policy, 2008; Strategic Vision, 2012. **Address:** Johns Hopkins University, Rm. 735, Nitze Bldg., 1740 Massachusetts Ave. NW, Washington, DC 20036, U.S.A.

BUARQUE, Chico. Brazilian (born Brazil), b. 1944. **Genres:** Novels, Poetry, Plays/Screenplays, Romance/Historical, Songs/Lyrics And Libretti. **Career:** Writer and composer. **Publications:** (Ed.) Roda-viva (musical comedy), 1968; o elogio da traição (play), 1973; Fazenda Modelo: novela pecuária, 1974; (with P. Pontes) Gota d'água (play), 1975; Opera do malandro, 1978; Chapeuzinho amarelo (juvenile), 1979; Chico Buarque de Hollanda, 1980; (trans.) L. Enriquez and S. Bardotti, Escalada apresenta Os saltimbancos: fábula musical inspirada no conto dos Irmãos Grimm Os músicos de Bremen, 1980; (with V. Keating) A Bordo do Rui Barbosa, 1981; (with R. Guerra) Calabar: o elogio da traição, 1983; (with A. Boal and E. Lôbo) O Corsério do rei (play), 1985; Chico Buarque, 1989; (with N. Alves de Souza) Suburbano corcçaño: um apeça, 1989; Estorvo (novel); Turbulence, 1992; Chico Buarque: letra e música; incluindo Carta ao Chico de Tom Jobim e Gol de letras de Humberto Werneck, 1994; edição gráfica Holio de Almeida, 1994; Benjamim, 1995; (contrib.) Terra: Struggle of the Landless, 1997; Chico Buarque (printed music), 1999; A Imagem do som de Chico Buarque: 80 composições de Chico Buarque interpretadas por 80 artistas contemporaneous, 1999; Budapeste: Romance, 2003; O grande circo místico, 2004; Leite derramado, 2009. **Address:** c/o Author Mail, Grove/Atlantic Inc., 841 Broadway, 4th Fl., New York, NY 10003, U.S.A.

BUBE, Richard Howard. American (born United States), b. 1927. **Genres:** Engineering, Physics, Theology/Religion, Autobiography/Memoirs. **Career:** Radio Corporation of America Laboratories, research staff, senior scientist, 1948-62; Stanford University, Materials Science and Engineering, associate professor, 1962-64, professor, 1964-92, chairman, 1975-86, associate Chairman, 1990-91, professor emeritus, 1992-. Writer. **Publications:** To Every Man an Answer, 1955; A Textbook of Christian Doctrine, 1955; Photoconductivity of Solids, 1960; (ed.) The Encounter Between Christianity and Science, 1968; The Human Quest: A New Look at Science and Christian Faith, 1971; Electronic Properties of Crystalline Solids, 1974; Electrons in Solids: An Introductory Survey, 1981, 3rd ed., 1992; Fundamentals of Solar Cells, 1983; Science and the Whole Person, 1985; Photoelectronic Properties of Semiconductors, 1992; One Whole Life: Personal Memoirs, 1994; Putting It All Together: Seven Patterns for Relating Science and Christian Faith, 1995; Photo-Induced Defects in Semiconductors, 1995; (with D. Redfield) Photoinduced Defects in Semiconductors, 1996; Photovoltaic Materials, 1998. **Address:** Department of Materials Science & Engineering, Stanford University, Rm. 553 B, Stanford, CA 94305-2205, U.S.A. **Online address:** bube@stanford.edu

BUCCIERI, Lisa Rojany. (Adriana Gabriel). American (born United States), b. 1964. **Genres:** Children's Fiction, Young Adult Fiction, Children's Non-fiction, Young Adult Non-fiction, Ghost Writer, Self Help, Psychology, Women's Studies And Issues, Biography, Novels, E-books, Picture/Board Books, Novellas/Short Stories. **Career:** Triangle Publications, writer and editor for TV Guide, 1987-88; Brown Daily Herald Newspaper Services, staff editor, 1989; Ligature Inc., textbook editor, 1989-90; Intervisual Books Inc., senior editor, 1991-93; Price Stern Sloan Inc., editorial director, 1993-97; Gateway Learning Corp. (Hooked on Phonics), editorial director, 1997; Golden Books, West Coast Publishing, director, 1997-2000; Americhip Books, founding vice president and publisher, 2002-06; Editorial Services of Los Angeles, founder and owner, 1988-; NY Journal of Books, publisher, 2010. **Publications:** The Hands-On Book of Big Machines, 1992; (with S. Strong) Exploring the Human Body, 1992; (comp.) King Arthur's Camelot, 1993; The Story of Hanukkah: A Lift-the-Flap Rebus Book, 1993; Where's That Pig?: A Lift Up & Look Book, 1993; Santa's New Suit!: A Dress-Up and Fold-Out Santa, 1993; Jake and Jenny on the Town: A Finger Puppet Lift-the-Flap Book, 1993; Mr. Bump, 1993; Mr. Funny, 1993; Mr. Silly, 1993; Walt Disney's Alice in Wonderland: Down the Rabbit Hole, 1994; Token of Love, 1994; Spring Gardens, 1994; Mickey Mouse: Where's the Picnic?, 1994; Winnie the Pooh: The Surprise Party, 1994; (with C. Walker) Make Your Own Valentines, 1994; (comp.) Birthday Celebrations, 1994; (comp.) Cats: Those Wonderful Creatures, 1994; (comp.) Flowers for My Friend, 1994; (comp.) Friendship: What You Mean to Me, 1994; (comp.) Thoughts for a Sunny Day, 1994; (comp.) Wedding Sentiments, 1994; Melvin Martian, 1995; Dena Dinosaur, 1995; Gold Diggers: The Secret of Bear Mountain, 1995; Morty Monster, 1995; Wanda Witch, 1995; Hanukkah Candles, 1995; Casper: The Novelization, 1995; Dumbo's Circus Train: A Rolling Wheels Book, 1995; Cinderella's Coach: A Rolling Wheels Book, 1995; Kangaroo and Company, 1995; Hippo and Pals, 1995; (comp.) The Magic Feather: A Jamaican Legend, 1995; Pandora's Box and Over in the Meadow, 1995; Tell Me about When I Was a Baby: A Truly Interactive Pop-Up Book, 1996; (as Adriana Gabriel) Dragonheart: The Junior Novelization, 1996; Code Blue: In the Emergency Room, 1996; Giant Big Trucks and Bigger Diggers, 1996; Giant Giants and Magic Mermaids, 1996; In the Emergency Room, 1996; Leave It to Beaver: The Novelization, 1997; Making the Grade, 1997; (with D. Weizmann) Diary of a Rotten Stinking Liar, 1998; (with J. Stav) Fund Your Future: Winning Strategies for Managing Your Mutual Funds and 401 (k), 2001; (with P. Economy) Writing Children's Books for Dummies, 2005; Santa's Workshop, 2007; Sammy's Suitcase, 2008; (with E.M. Kor) Surviving the Angel of Death: The Story of a Mengele Twin in Auschwitz, 2009. EDITOR: Barbie: I Got So Mad, 1999; Barbie: I Love Kittens, 1999; Barbie: I Love Puppies, 1999; Barbie, My First Pony, 1999; Barbie World Traveler Scrapbook: A Trip to Mexico, 1999; The Ultimate Pink Touch & Feel Book, 1999. **Address:** Editorial Services of Los Angeles, 1543 Sycamore Canyon Dr., Westlake Village, CA 91361, U.S.A. **Online address:** editorialservicesofla@gmail.com

BUCCINI, Stefania. American/Italian (born Italy), b. 1959. **Genres:** Literary Criticism And History, History, Language/Linguistics. **Career:** University of Wisconsin, Department of French and Italian, associate professor, 1988-, professor and associate chair. Writer. **Publications:** Il Dilemma della Grande Atlantide: Le Americhe nella Letteratura Italiana del Sette Ottocento, 1990, trans. as The Americas in Italian Literature and Culture, 1700-1825, 1997; Sentimento della morte dal barocco aldeclino dei lumi, 2000; Alfieri beyond Italy: Atti del Convegno Internazionale di Studi, Madison, Wisconsin, 27-28 Settembre 2002, 2004; The Representation of Death in Italian Literature, 1600-1820, forthcoming; I piaceri della solitudine: intimi itinerari tra Sette e Ottocento, forthcoming; Le ragioni filantropiche di Lodovico Antonio Muratori, forthcoming; (ed.) Vittorio Alfieri beyond Italy, forthcoming. **Address:** Department of French and Italian, University of Wisconsin-Madison, 668 Van Hise Hall, 1220 Linden Dr., Madison, WI 53706, U.S.A. **Online address:** sbuccini@wisc.edu

BUCCOLA, Regina M. American (born United States), b. 1969. **Genres:** Poetry, Literary Criticism And History, Women's Studies And Issues, Cultural/Ethnic Topics. **Career:** Roosevelt University, associate professor. Writer. **Publications:** Fairies, Fractious Women, and the Old Faith: Fairy Lore in Early Modern British Drama and Culture, 2006; (ed. with L. Hopkins) Marian Moments in Early Modern British Drama, 2007; Conjuring (poems), 2009. Works appear in anthologies. Contributor to journals and periodicals. **Address:** Department of English, Roosevelt University, 430 S Michigan Ave., Chicago, IL 60605-1315, U.S.A. **Online address:** rbuccola@roosevelt.edu

BUCHANAN, Colin (Ogilvie). British (born England), b. 1934. **Genres:** Theology/Religion. **Career:** Cheadle Parish Church, assistant curator, 1961-64; St. John's College, lecturer, 1964-, librarian, 1964-69, registrar, 1969-74, director of studies, 1974-75, vice principal, 1975-78, principal, 1979-85; Grove Books, proprietor, 1970-; Group for Renewal Of Worship, chair, 1970-2003; Diocese of Rochester, honorary assistant bishop, 1989-96. Writer.

Publications: New Communion Service-Reasons for Dissent, 1966; A Guide to the New Communion Service, 1966; A Guide to 2nd Series Communion Service, 1968; (with P.S. Dawes) Proportional Representation in Church Elections, 1969 as Election by Preference, 1970; Evangelical Structures for the Seventies, 1969; (co-author) Growing into Union, 1970; (co-author) Growing into Union and Six Methodist Leaders, 1970; The Clarified Scheme Examined, 1971; Baptismal Discipline, 1972; The Job Prospects of the Anglican Clergy, 1972; Patterns of Sunday Worship, 1972; Recent Liturgical Revision in the Church of England, 1973; A Case for Infant Baptism, 1973; (with J.D. Pawson) Infant Baptism under Cross-Examination, 1974; Liturgy for Infant Baptism: Series 3, 1975; What Did Cranmer Think He was Doing?, 1976; Inflation, Deployment and the Job Prospects of the Clergy, 1976; Encountering Charismatic Worship, 1977; The End of the Offertory, 1978; Supplement for 1976-78, 1978; One Baptism Once, 1978; Liturgy for Initiation: The Series 3 Services, 1979; Liturgy for Communion: The Revised Series 3 Service, 1979; (comp.) The Development of the New Eucharistic Prayers of the Church of England, 1979; The Role and Calling of an Evangelical Theological College in the 1980's, 1980; Leading Worship, 1981; The Kiss of Peace, 1982; (with D. Wheaton) Liturgy for the Sick, 1983; ACIC and Lima on Baptism and Eucharist, 1983; The Christian Conscience and Justice in Representation, 1983; Latest Liturgical Revision in the Church of England 1978-1984, 1984; Evangelical Anglicans and Liturgy, 1984; Adult Baptisms, 1985; Anglican Eucharistic Liturgy 1975-1985, 1985; Anglican Confirmation, 1986; Policies for Infant Baptism, 1987; Anglicans and Worship in Local Ecumenical Projects, 1987; Lambeth and Liturgy 1988, 1989; Revising the ASB, 1989; Children in Communion, 1990; Open to Others, 1992; Infant Baptism in Church of England, 1992; The Heart of Sunday Worship, 1992; The Renewal of Baptismal Vows, 1993; Infant Baptism and the Gospel, 1993; Cut the Connection, 1994; The Lord's Prayer in the Church of England, 1995; Eucharistic Prayer H: An Unauthorized Account, 2000; Services of Wholeness and Healing, 2000; Infant Baptism in Common Worship, 2001; Mission in South East London, 2002; Is Papal Authority a Gift to Us?, 2003; Ordinations Rites in Common Worship, 2006; Historical Dictionary of Anglicanism, 2006; Taking the Long View: Three and a Half Decades of General Synod, 2006. (with D. Holeton) A History of the International Anglican Liturgical Consultations: 1983-2007, 2007; Justin Martyr on Baptism and Eucharist, 2007; An Evangelical among the Anglican Liturgists, 2009. EDITOR: Prospects for Reconciliation, 1967; Modern Anglican Liturgies 1958-68, 1968; Evangelical Essays on Church and Sacraments, 1972; Unity on the Ground, 1972; Further Anglican Liturgies 1968-1975, 1975; Anglican Worship Today, 1980; Anglo-Catholic Worship, 1983; Eucharistic Liturgies of Edward VI, 1983; Background Documents to Liturgical Revision 1547-1549, 1983; Essays on Eucharistic Sacrifice in the Early Church, 1984; Latest Anglican Liturgies 1976-1984, 1985; Liturgies of the Spanish and Portuguese Reformed Episcopal Churches, 1985; Nurturing Children in Communion: Essays from the Boston Consultation, 1985; Bishop Hugh-With Affection, 1987; Modern Anglican Ordination Rites, 1987; The Bishop in Liturgy, 1988; (co-ed.) Six Eucharistic Prayers as Proposed in 1996, 1996; (co-ed.) The New Initiation Rites, 1998; Eucharistic Consecration, 1998; Is the Church of England Biblical?, 1998; Michael Vasey-Liturgist and Friend, 1999; (co-ed.) The Eucharistic Prayers of Order One, 2000; Common Worship Today, 2001; The Savoy Conference Revisited, 2002; (with C. Hefling and C.L. Shattuck) The Oxford Guide to the Book of Common Prayer, 2006; The Hampton Court Conference and the 1604 Book of Common Prayer with Related Documents, Introduction and Annotation, 2009. Contributor to journals. **Address:** St. John's College, Chilwell Ln., Bramcote, NT NG9 3DS, England. **Online address:** colinbuchanan101@btinternet.com

BUCHANAN, Edna. American (born United States), b. 1949?. **Genres:** Novels, Novellas/Short Stories, Mystery/Crime/Suspense, Criminology/True Crime, Autobiography/Memoirs, Writing/Journalism. **Career:** Western Electric Co., switchboard wirer; Miami Beach Daily Sun, affiliate, 1965-70; Miami Herald, general assignment and criminal court reporter, 1970-73, police beat reporter, 1973-88. Writer. **Publications:** NONFICTION: Carr: Five Years of Rape and Murder, 1979; The Corpse Had a Familiar Face: Covering Miami, America's Hottest Beat, 1987; Vice: Life and Death on the Streets of Miami, 1992; Never Let Them See You Cry, 1992. NOVELS: Nobody Lives Forever, 1990; Contents Under Pressure, 1992; Miami, It's Murder, 1994; Suitable for Framing, 1995; Act of Betrayal, 1996; Margin of Error, 1997; Pulse, 1998; Garden of Evil, 1999; You Only Die Twice, 2001; The Ice Maiden, 2002; Cold Case Squad, 2004; Shadows, 2005; Love Kills: A Brit Montero Novel, 2007; Legally Dead, 2008; A Dark and Lonely Place, 2011. **Address:** c/o Michael Congdon, Don Congdon Associates, 156 5th Ave., Ste. 625, New York, NY 10010, U.S.A.

BUCHANAN, Mark. American (born United States), b. 1961. **Genres:** Physics, Sciences. **Career:** University of Virginia, research assistant professor of nuclear engineering/engineering physics and radiology, 1993-94; Nature, assistant editor, 1995-97; New Scientist, features editor, 1997-98; freelance writer, 1998; New York Times, columnist, 2007-; Nature Physics, writer; Complexus, associate editor. **Publications:** Ubiquity: The Science of History, or Why the World Is Simpler Than We Think, 2000; Small World: Uncovering Natures Hidden Networks, 2002; Nexus: Small Worlds and the Groundbreaking Science of Networks, 2002; The Social Atom: Why the Rich Get Richer, Cheaters Get Caught, and Your Neighbor Usually Looks Like You, 2007; Simplexity: Our Thinking Instincts and the Hidden Simplicity of Human Affairs, 2007; (ed.) Networks in Cell Biology, 2010; The Physics of Finance, forthcoming. **Address:** La Vignerie, Notre Dame de Courson, Livarot, 14140, France. **Online address:** mark.buchanan@wanadoo.fr

BUCHANAN, Oni. American (born United States), b. 1975. **Genres:** Poetry, Literary Criticism And History. **Career:** Writer and concert pianist. **Publications:** POETRY: What Animal: Poems, 2003; Spring: Poems, 2008; Must a Violence, forthcoming. Works appear in anthologies. Contributor to journals. **Address:** ARIEL ARTISTS, 12 Baldwin Pl., Apt. 2, Brighton, MA 02135, U.S.A. **Online address:** general@onibuchanan.com

BUCHANAN, Paul G. New Zealander/American (born United States), b. 1954. **Genres:** Social Sciences, Politics/Government, Essays, Young Adult Non-fiction, Business/Trade/Industry. **Career:** Naval Postgraduate School, assistant professor, 1985-87; University of Arizona, assistant professor, 1987-95; U.S. Department of Defense, regional policy analyst, 1993-94; New College, assistant professor of social sciences, 1995-; University of Auckland, strategic analyst, lecturer, Working Group On Alternative Security Perspectives, director; Auckland University, political scientist, political studies lecturer, senior lecturer in politics; National University of Singapore, visiting associate professor of political science. Writer. **Publications:** State, Labor, Capital: Democratizing Class Relations in the Southern Cone, 1995; (co-author) Globalizacion Y Regionalismo en las Relaciones Internacionales de Estados Unidos, 1996; (with K. Nicholls) Labour Politics in Small open Democracies: Australia, Chile, Ireland, New Zealand, and Uruguay, 2003; With Distance Comes Perspective: Essays on Politics, Security and International Affairs, 2005. **Address:** Department of Political Studies, University of Auckland, PO Box 92019, Auckland, 1, New Zealand. **Online address:** pa.buchanan@auckland.ac.nz

BUCHANAN, Roberta. Canadian/South African (born South Africa), b. 1937. **Genres:** Poetry, Biography, Autobiography/Memoirs, Young Adult Fiction. **Career:** University of Birmingham, Shakespeare Institute, research assistant, 1962-64; Memorial University of Newfoundland, lecturer, 1964-70, assistant professor, 1970-76, associate professor, 1976-86, professor of English, 1986-2005, Women's Studies Programme, supervisor, 1988-91, professor emeritus, 2005-. **Publications:** (Ed.) Ars Adulandi, or, The Art of Flattery, 1984; I Moved All My Women Upstairs, 1998; (ed. with B. Greene) The Woman Who Mapped Labrador: The Life and Expedition Diary of Mina Hubbard, 2005; (ed. with G.O. Queller and G.C. Rubia) A Charm against the Pain: An Anthology of All New Writing from Newfoundland, 2006. **Address:** Department of English, Memorial University of Newfoundland, PO Box 4200, St. John's, NL A1C 5S7, Canada. **Online address:** rbuchana@mun.ca

BUCHANAN, Robert Angus. British (born England), b. 1930. **Genres:** Archaeology/Antiquities, History, Engineering, Social Sciences. **Career:** University of Bath, professor of the history of technology, and director, Centre for the History of Technology, Science and Society, lecturer in social and technological history, 1960-95, professor, 1990-95, professor emeritus, 1995-, Centre for the History of Technology, honorary director; Annual Journal of the Bristol Industrial Archaeological Society, editor, 1968-74; Technology and Society, editor, 1971-74; Chalmers University of Technology, visiting professor, 1984-85; National Cataloguing Unit for the Archives of Contemporary Scientists, 2008. **Publications:** Technology and Social Progress, 1965; (with N. Cossons) Industrial Archaeology of Bristol, 1967; (ed.) Theory and Practice of Industrial Archaeology: The Bath Conference on Industrial Archaeology, 3-5 November 1967, 1968; (with N. Cossons) Industrial Archaeology of the Bristol Region, 1969; The Industrial Archaeology of Bath, 1969; (with N. Cossons) Industrial History in Pictures: Bristol, 1970; Industrial Archaeology in Britain, 1972, new ed., 1980; (with G. Watkins) Man and the Steam Engine, 1975; (with G. Watkins) The Industrial Archaeology of the Stationary Steam Engine, 1976; History and Industrial Civilization, 1979; (with C.A.

Buchanan) Industrial Archaeology of Central Southern England, 1980; (with C.A. Buchanan) The Batsford Guide to the Industrial Archaeology of Central Southern England: Avon County, Gloucestershire, Somerset, Wiltshire, 1980; (with M. Williams) Brunel's Bristol, 1982; The Engineers: A History of the Engineering Profession in Britain 1750-1914, 1989; The Power of the Machine: The Impact of Technology from 1700 to the Present Day, 1994; (ed.) Engineers and Engineering: Papers of the Rolt Fellows, 1996; (with E.E. Stansbury) Fundamentals Electromechanical Corrosion, 2000; (with E.E. Stansbury) Fundamentals of Electrochemical Corrosion, 2000; Brunel: The Life and Times of Isambard Kingdom Brunel, 2001; (ed.) Materials Lifetime Science & Engineering, 2003. **Address:** Centre for the History, of Technology, Science, and Society, University of Bath, Claverton Down, Bath, SM BA2 7AY, England. **Online address:** hssraab@bath.ac.uk

BUCHANAN, Thomas C. Australian/American (born United States), b. 1967. **Genres:** Adult Non-fiction, Civil Liberties/Human Rights. **Career:** University of Nebraska, assistant professor; University of Adelaide, lecturer in history, 2005-. Writer. **Publications:** Black Life on the Mississippi: Slaves, Free Blacks, and the Western Steamboat World, 2004. Contributor to journals. **Address:** School of History, University of Adelaide, Rm. 5 22, Napier 518 Bldg., North Terr., Adelaide, SA 5005, Australia. **Online address:** thomas.buchanan@adelaide.edu.au

BUCHEISTER, Patt. (Patt Parrish). American (born United States), b. 1942. **Genres:** Novels, Novellas/Short Stories, Romance/Historical, Young Adult Fiction. **Career:** Chamber of Commerce, secretary, 1959-60. Writer. **Publications:** AS PATT PARRISH: Make the Angel Weep, 1979 in US as His Fierce Angel, 1983; Summer of Silence, 1980 in US as A Gift to Cherish, 1985; Feather in the Wind, 1981; The Sheltered Haven, 1982; The Amberley Affair, 1983; Lifetime Affair, 1985; Escape the Past, 1985, rev. ed., 1999. AS PATT BUCHEISTER: Night and Day, 1986; The Dragon Slayer, 1987; Touch the Stars, 1987; Two Roads, 1987; The Luck of the Irish, 1988; Flynn's Fate, 1988; Time Out, 1988; Near the Edge, 1989; Fire and Ice, 1989; Elusive Gypsy, 1989; Once Burned, Twice as Hot, 1990; The Rogue, 1990; Relentless, 1990; Tropical Heat, 1990; Tropical Storm, 1991; Hot Pursuit, 1991; Island Lover, 1992; Mischief and Magic, 1992; Struck by Lightning, 1992; Tilt at Windmills, 1992; Stroke by Stroke, 1993; Tame a Wildcat, 1993; Strange Bedfellows, 1994; Unpredictable, 1994; Hot Southern Nights, 1995; Instant Family, 1995; Wild in the Night, 1995; Gypsy Dance, 1997; Below the Salt: A Gentlewoman's Commonplace Book, 1999. Contributor of articles and stories to magazines. **Address:** Joyce A. Flaherty, 816 Lynda Ct., St. Louis, MO 63122, U.S.A. **Online address:** raypatt@mindspring.com

BUCHELI, Marcelo. American (born United States) **Genres:** Business/Trade/Industry, Adult Non-fiction, Politics/Government. **Career:** University of Cambridge, summer school international fellow, 1993; Stanford University, Center for Latin American Studies, Ayacucho fellow, 1995-96, Department of History, fellow, 1996-98, instructor, 2001-03; University of San Francisco, instructor, 2002; California State University, instructor, 2003; Universidad de los Andes, assistant professor in economic history, 2004; Harvard Business School, Newcomen fellow in business history, 2004-05; University of Illinois, assistant professor of business administration, 2005-, Center for Advanced Study, fellow, 2009-10. Writer. **Publications:** Empresas Multinacionales y Enclaves Agricolas: El Caso de United Fruit en Magdalena y UrabA, Colombia 1948-1968, 1994; Bananas and Business: The United Fruit Company in Colombia, 1899-2000, 2005. Contributor to journals and periodicals. **Address:** Department of Business Administration, University of Illinois, 198 Wohlers Hall, Champaign, IL 61820, U.S.A. **Online address:** mbucheli@uiuc.edu

BUCHHOLZ, Todd G. American (born United States), b. 1961. **Genres:** Business/Trade/Industry, Economics, Adult Non-fiction, Social Sciences. **Career:** Harvard University, Department of Economics, teaching fellow, 1984-87; Breed, Abbott and Morgan, attorney, 1987-89; White House, director of economic policy, 1989-92; G7 Group Inc., president, 1993-96; Tiger Management L.L.C., managing director, 1996-98; Victoria Capital L.L.C., chairman, 1998-; Cambridge University, fellow, 2009. Worth magazine, contributing editor; Wall Street Journal, columnist; The New York Times, writer; Two Oceans Management L.L.C., co-founder and managing director. **Publications:** New Ideas from Dead Economists: An Introduction to Modern Economic Thought, 1989, rev. ed., 2007; From Here to Economy: A Shortcut to Economic Literacy, 1995; Market Shock: 9 Economic and Social Upheavals that Will Shake Your Financial Future and What to do About Them, 1999; Bringing the Jobs Home: How the Left Created the Outsourcing Crisis-and How We Can Fix It, 2004; New Ideas From Dead CEOs: Lasting Lessons from the Corner Office, 2007; The Castro Gene, 2007; Lasting Lessons from the Corner Office: Essential Wisdom from the Twentieth Century's Greatest Entrepreneurs, 2009; Rush: Why you Need and Love the Rat Race, 2011. Contributor to journals. **Address:** Victoria Capital L.L.C., Bethesda Metro Ctr., Ste. 530, Bethesda, MD 20814, U.S.A.

BUCHIGNANI, Walter. Canadian (born Canada), b. 1965. **Genres:** Young Adult Non-fiction, Novels. **Career:** The Gazette, reporter, 1987-, feature writer, copy editor. **Publications:** Tell No One Who You Are: The Hidden Childhood of Régine Miller (juvenile nonfiction), 1994. Contributor to periodicals. **Address:** The Gazette, 1010 Ste-Catherine St. W, Ste. 200, Montreal, QC H3B 5L1, Canada. **Online address:** walterb@thegazette.southam.ca

BUCHMANN, Stephen L. American (born United States), b. 1955?. **Genres:** Zoology, Natural History, Sciences. **Career:** Carl Hayden Bee Research Center, research associate, 1979-; The Bee Works L.L.C., founder, 1999-; University of Arizona, Department of Ecology and Evolutionary Biology, research associate, Department of Entomology, adjunct associate professor; Arizona-Sonora Desert Museum, research associate; American Museum of Natural History, research associate. Writer and entomologist. **Publications:** (Ed. with A. Matheson and C. O'Toole) The Conservation of Bees, 1996; (with G.P. Nabhan) The Forgotten Pollinators, 1996; How to Keep Stingless Bees in Mayan and Spanish, 2004; (with B. Repplier) Letters from the Hive: An Intimate History of Bees, Honey, and Humankind, 2005; Pollinators of the Sonoran Desert, 2005; (with D. Cohn) The Bee Tree, 2007; Honey Bees: Letters from the Hive, 2010; (with B. Moissett) Bee Basics: An Introduction to Our Native Bees, 2010. Contributor to books and periodicals. **Address:** The Bee Works L.L.C., 1870 W Prince Rd., Ste. 16, Tucson, AZ 85705, U.S.A. **Online address:** steve@thebeeworks.com

BUCHOLZ, Arden. American (born United States), b. 1936. **Genres:** History, Military/Defense/Arms Control, Politics/Government. **Career:** Amerikan Orta Okulu, teacher of English, 1958-60; Latin School of Chicago, teacher of history, 1965-70; State University of New York College, board of trustees distinguished teaching professor, 1970-2010; Brunel University, professor of history and co-director of program, 1987-88. Writer. **Publications:** Hans Delbruck and the German Military Establishment: War Images in Conflict, 1985; Moltke, Schlieffen, and Prussian War Planning, 1991; Delbrueck's Modern Military History, 1997; Moltke and the German Wars, 1864-1871, 2001; Helmuth von Moltke, 1800-1891, forthcoming; A Modern Biography, forthcoming. **Address:** Department of History, State University of New York College, 130 Albert W Brown Bldg., 350 New Campus Dr., Brockport, NY 14420-2914, U.S.A. **Online address:** abucholz@brockport.edu

BUCHWALTER, Andrew. American (born United States), b. 1949. **Genres:** Philosophy, Adult Non-fiction. **Career:** University of Massachusetts, lecturer in management and professional studies, 1980-81; Bentley College, adjunct professor of philosophy, 1985-86; University of North Florida, visiting assistant professor, 1987-89, assistant professor, 1989-94, associate professor of philosophy, 1994-95, chairperson, 1999-2007, professor of philosophy, 2009-11, John A Delaney Presidential Professor, 2011-, Center for the Humanities, director, 1990-92, director of humanities council, 1991-95, chairperson of humanities council, 1993-, Blue Cross and Blue Shield of Florida Center for Ethics, Public Policy and the Professions, director, 1999-2003, Graduate Program in Practical Philosophy and Applied Ethics, coordinator, 2008-; Yale University, visiting assistant professor, 1991-92; School for Social Research, visiting research fellow, 1995-96. Writer. **Publications:** (Trans. and intro.) Observations on The Spiritual Situation of the Age: Contemporary German Perspectives, 1984; (ed.) Culture and Democracy: Social and Ethical Issues in Public Support for the Arts and Humanities, 1992; Dialectics, Politics, and the Contemporary Value of Hegel's Practical Philosophy, 2011; The Doctrine of Objective Spirit: Hegel, Reason and the Politics of Modernity, forthcoming. Works appear in anthologies. Contributor of articles to periodicals. **Address:** Department of Philosophy, University of North Florida, 4567 St., Johns Bluff Rd. S, Jacksonville, FL 32224, U.S.A. **Online address:** abuchwal@unf.edu

BUCK, Christopher. (Christopher George Buck). American/Canadian (born Canada), b. 1950. **Genres:** Theology/Religion, History. **Career:** Carleton University, sessional lecturer, 1994-96; Millikin University, assistant professor, 1997-99; Quincy University, visiting assistant professor, 1999-2000; Michigan State University, visiting assistant professor, 2000-04; Pribanic &

Pribanic, attorney-at-law, 2007-. Attorney and writer. **Publications:** Symbol and Secret: Qur'an Commentary in Bahá'u'lláh's Kitáb-i íqán, 1995, 2nd ed., 2004; Paradise and Paradigm: Key Symbols in Persian Christianity and the Bahá'í Faith, 1999; (ed. with D.W. Stowe and S.L. Martin) Generation Y Speaks Out: A Policy Guide, 2002; Alain Locke: Faith and Philosophy, 2005; Religious Myths and Visions of America: How Minority Faiths Redefined America's World Role, 2009. Works appear in anthologies. Contributor of articles to journals. **Address:** 1735 Lincoln Way, White Oak, PA 15131-1715, U.S.A. **Online address:** buckc@msu.edu

BUCK, Christopher George. *See* **BUCK, Christopher.**

BUCK, Craig. American (born United States), b. 1952. **Genres:** Self Help, Adult Non-fiction, Human Relations/Parenting, Social Sciences. **Career:** Writer and television producer. **Publications:** (Contrib.) Traveler's Almanac, 3rd ed., 1977. WITH S. FORWARD: Betrayal of Innocence: Incest and Its Devastation, 1978, rev. ed., 1988; Toxic Parents: Overcoming Their Hurtful Legacy and Reclaiming Your Life, 1989; Obsessive Love: When Passion Holds You Prisoner, 1991; Money Demons: Keep Them from Sabotaging Your Relationships and Your Life, 1994 in Spain as Los Demonios Del Dinero, 2000. **Address:** 15183 Encanto Dr., Sherman Oaks, CA 91403, U.S.A.

BUCK, Rinker. American (born United States), b. 1951?. **Genres:** Air/Space Topics, Autobiography/Memoirs, Biography, History, Travel/Exploration. **Career:** Berkshire Eagle, reporter; Hartford Courant, editor; New York, Life, journalist; Adweek, journalist. **Publications:** Flight of Passage, 1997; If We Had Wings: The Enduring Dream of Flight, 2001; First Job: A Memoir of Growing up at Work, 2002; Shane Comes Home, 2005. Contributor of articles. **Address:** c/o Author Mail, Hyperion, 114 5th Ave., New York, NY 10011, U.S.A.

BUCK, Susan J. American (born United States), b. 1947. **Genres:** Law, Politics/Government, Public/Social Administration, Environmental Sciences/Ecology. **Career:** Virginia Institute of Marine Science, Wetlands Research Laboratory, laboratory specialist, 1976-79; Virginia Polytechnic Institute and State University, computer systems analyst, 1980, Department of English, instructor, 1981-83; Virginia Water Resources Research Center, graduate research assistant, 1980-81; Northern Arizona University, assistant professor, 1984-88; University of North Carolina, Department of Political Science, assistant professor, 1988-93, associate professor, 1993-, Environmental Studies, director, 1999-. Writer. **Publications:** Understanding Environmental Administration and Law, 1990, 3rd ed., 2006; (with R.W. Cox and B.N. Morgan) Public Administration in Theory and Practice, 1993, 2nd ed., 2011; Global Commons: An Introduction, 1998. **Address:** Department of Political Science, University of North Carolina, Greensboro, NC 27402, U.S.A. **Online address:** sjbuck@uncg.edu

BUCKELEW, Albert R. American (born United States), b. 1942. **Genres:** Zoology, Sciences. **Career:** Bethany College, professor of biology and chair, 1969-. Writer. **Publications:** Endangered and Threatened Species in West Virginia, 1990; (with G.A. Hall) The West Virginia Breeding Bird Atlas, 1994. **Address:** Department of Biology, Bethany College, Bethany, WV 26032, U.S.A. **Online address:** jbuckelew@bethanywv.edu

BUCKELL, Tobias S. American (born United States), b. 1979?. **Genres:** Novels, Science Fiction/Fantasy. **Career:** Bluffton University, Technology Center, manager, 1996-2006; SF Novelists Web Site, founder; author, 2006-. **Publications:** Crystal Rain, 2006; Ragamuffin, 2007; Sly Mongoose, 2008; The Cole Protocol, 2008; Tides From the New Worlds, 2009; (contrib.) Year's Best SF 14, 2009; (ed.) Halo Encyclopedia: The Definitive Guide to the Halo Universe, 2010. Contributor to periodicals. **Address:** c/o Author Mail, Tor Books, 175 5th Ave., New York, NY 10010-7703, U.S.A. **Online address:** tobias@tobiasbuckell.com

BUCKEY, Sarah Masters. American (born United States), b. 1955?. **Genres:** Mystery/Crime/Suspense, Novels, Children's Fiction. **Career:** Parkland Memorial Hospital, medical writer. Educator and researcher. **Publications:** The Smugglers Treasure, 1999; Enemy in the Fort, 2001; Samantha's Special Talent, 2003; Gangsters at the Grand Atlantic, 2003; The Curse of Ravenscourt: A Samantha Mystery, 2005; Stolen Sapphire: A Samantha Mystery, 2006; (with V. Tripp) Samantha's Short Story Collection, 2006; The Light in the Cellar: A Molly Mystery, 2007; Thief in the Theater, 2008; Clue in the Castle Tower, 2011. **Address:** c/o Author Mail, Pleasant Company Publications, PO Box 620991, Middleton, WI 53562-0991, U.S.A.

BUCKHANON, Kalisha. American (born United States), b. 1977. **Genres:** Novellas/Short Stories, Novels, Literary Criticism And History, Romance/Historical. **Career:** PEN America Center, Prison Writing Program, mentor; ETA Creative Arts Foundation, faculty in writing. Freelance writer. **Publications:** NOVELS: Upstate, 2005; Conception, 2008. COLLECTION: (with G.A. Haywood) Brown Sugar 4: Secret Desires, 2005. Contributor to periodicals. **Address:** c/o Lisa LaPointe, St. Martin's Press, 175 5th Ave., New York, NY 10010-7703, U.S.A. **Online address:** info@kalisha.com

BUCKINGHAM, Royce Scott. American (born United States), b. 1966?. **Genres:** Novels. **Career:** Whatcom County Prosecutor's Office, attorney, 1993-2006; writer, 1993-. **Publications:** Demonkeeper (novel), 2007; Goblins! An Under Earth Adventure (novel), 2008. **Address:** Bellingham, WA , U.S.A. **Online address:** royce@demonkeeper.com

BUCKLEY, Christopher Howard. American (born United States), b. 1948?. **Genres:** Poetry, History. **Career:** Ucross Foundation, artist-in-residence, 1990; University of California, Department of Creative Writing, professor and chair, Guggenheim fellow in poetry, 2007-08. Writer. **Publications:** Pentimento, 1980; Last Rites, 1980; Blue Hooks in Weather, 1983; Five Small Meditations on Summer and Birds, 1984; Other Lives, 1985; Dust Light, Leaves, 1986; Blossoms & Bones: On the Life and Work of Georgia O'Keeffe, 1988; Blue Autumn: Poems, 1990; (ed.) On the Poetry of Philip Levine: Stranger to Nothing, 1991; Dark Matter: Poems, 1993; Cruising State: Growing Up in Southern California, 1994; (ed. with C. Merrill) What Will Suffice: Contemporary American Poets on the Art of Poetry, 1995; Camino Cielo, 1997; Fall from Grace, 1998; (ed. with G. Young) The Geography of Home: California's Poetry of Place, 1999; (ed. with D. Oliveira and M.L. Williams) How Much Earth: The Fresno Poets, 2001; Star Apocrypha, 2001; (ed. with A. Long) A Condition of the Spirit: The Life and Work of Larry Levis, 2004; Sky, 2004; And the Sea: Poems, 2006; Sleepwalk: California Dreamin' and a Last Dance with the '60s, 2006; (ed.) Homage to Vallejo, 2008; (with G. Young) Bear Flag Republic: Prose Poems & Poetics from California, 2008; Modern History: Prose Poems 1987-2007, 2008; Rolling the Bones: Poems, 2010; White Shirt: Poems, 2011. Contributor to journals. **Address:** Department of Creative Writing, University of California, 900 University Ave., Riverside, CA 92521, U.S.A. **Online address:** christopher.buckley@ucr.edu

BUCKLEY, Cornelius M(ichael). American (born United States), b. 1925. **Genres:** History, Theology/Religion, Translations, Military/Defense/Arms Control. **Career:** Saint Ignatius College Preparatory High School, teacher, 1956-59, rector and president, 1970-73; University of San Francisco, trustee, 1970-83, professor of history, 1973-, dean, Saint Ignatius Institute, faculty; Santa Clara University, trustee, 1971-78; St. Patrick's College, trustee, 1972-74; Fellowship of Catholic Scholars, trustee, 1992-; Thomas Aquinas College, faculty, 2004; University of California, Hastings College of Law, Thomas More Society, chaplain; University of Santa Clara, faculty; Gonzaga University, faculty. Writer. **Publications:** (Ed. and trans.) Frenchman, a Chaplain, a Rebel: The War Letters of Pere Louis-Hippolyte Gache, S.J, 1980; Your Word, O Lord: Meditations for College Students and Anyone Else, 1987; Nicolas Point, S.J.: His Life and Northwest Indian Chronicles, 1989; When Jesuits Were Giants: Louis-Marie Ruellan, S.J., 1846-1885 and His Contemporaries, 1999. TRANSLATOR: S. Decloux, The Ignatian Way, 1991; A. Ravier, A Do-It-at-Home Retreat, 1991; C. de Dalmases, Francis Borgia, 1991; (ed.) J.I.T. Idigoras, Ignatius of Loyola: The Pilgrim Saint, 1993; A. Ravier, Like a Child, 1997. **Address:** Thomas Aquinas College, 10000 N Ojai Rd., Santa Paula, CA 93060, U.S.A.

BUCKLEY, Francis Joseph. American (born United States), b. 1928. **Genres:** Theology/Religion, Psychology, Sociology. **Career:** Bellarmine College Preparatory, instructor in classics and religion, 1952-55; University of San Francisco, instructor, 1960-61, assistant professor, 1963-68, associate professor, 1968-72, Department of Theology, chairman, 1971-73, 1978-79, 1988-92, professor of dogmatic and pastoral theology, 1972-2002, Department of Religious Education and Pastoral Ministries, director, 1974-75, 1979-82, 1986-87, 1992-96, professor emeritus of theology, 2002-; College Theology Society, president. Writer. **Publications:** Christ and the Church According to Gregory of Elvira, 1964; (with M. de la Cruz Aymes) On Our Way (series), 1966-70; (with J. Hofinger) The Good News and Its Proclamation, 1968; Children and God: Communion, Confession, Confirmation, 1970, rev. ed.,

1973; (with M. de la Cruz Aymes) New Life (series), 1971-74; (ed. with C. Miller) Faith and Life (series), 1971-72; I Confess-The Sacrament of Penance Today, 1972; (with M. de la Cruz Aymes) Jesus Forgives, 1974; (with M. de la Cruz Aymes) Lord of Life (series), 1978-80; Reconciling, 1981; (with M. de la Cruz Aymes) We Share Forgiveness, 1981; (with M. de la Cruz Aymes) We Share Reconciliation, 1981; (with M. de la Cruz Aymes and T.H. Groome) God with Us (series), 1982-85; (with M. de la Cruz Aymes) Fe y Cultura, 1985; Come Worship with Us, 1987; (with D.B. Sharp) Deepening Christian Life: Integrating Faith and Maturity, 1987; (with M. de la Cruz Aymes) Familia de Dios (series), 1990-96; Team Teaching: What, Why, How, 2000; Growing in the Church: From Birth to Death, 2000; The Church in Dialogue: Culture and Tradition, 2000. **Address:** Department of Theology, University of San Francisco, 2600 Turk Blvd., San Francisco, CA 94117, U.S.A. **Online address:** buckleyf@usfca.edu

BUCKLEY, Gail Lumet. American (born United States), b. 1937. **Genres:** Autobiography/Memoirs, Young Adult Fiction, History, Social Sciences. **Career:** Marie-Claire, journalist, 1959-63; Life, journalist, 1959-62, reporter, 1962-63; National Scholarship Service and Fund for Negro Students, student counselor, 1961-62. **Publications:** The Hornes: An American Family, 1986; American Patriots: The Story of Blacks in the Military from the Revolution to Desert Storm, 2001; (contrib. with W. Saroyan) Hirschfeld's Harlem, 2004. Contributor to periodicals. **Address:** c/o Lynn Nesbit, International Creative Management, 40 W 57th St., New York, NY 10128, U.S.A.

BUCKLEY, Geri. *See* **BORCZ, Geri.**

BUCKLEY, Jay H. American (born United States), b. 1969. **Genres:** Mystery/Crime/Suspense. **Career:** University of Nebraska, instructor, 2000; Nebraska Wesleyan University, adjunct instructor, 2000-01; Brigham Young University, assistant professor, 2001-08, associate professor of history, 2008-; Lewis and Clark Trail Heritage Foundation, board director, 2007-. Writer, historian, biographer, public speaker and consultant. **Publications:** (With V.L. Talbot and D.E. Jackson) Field Captain of the Rocky Mountain Fur Trade, 1996. (with John D.W. Guice and J.J. Holmberg) By His Own Hand?: The Mysterious Death of Meriwether Lewis, 2006; William Clark: Indian Diplomat, 2008; (with C. Arnold) Orem (Images of America series), 2010. Contributor to books, journals and periodicals. **Address:** Department of History, Brigham Young University, 2141 JFSB, Provo, UT 84602-6707, U.S.A. **Online address:** jay_buckley@byu.edu

BUCKLEY, John (F.). American (born United States), b. 1961. **Genres:** Law, Reference. **Career:** National Legal Research Group, senior attorney, 1987-. Writer. **Publications:** (With M. Lindsay) Defense of Equal Employment Claims, 1995; State by State Guide to Human Resources Law, 1995; Multistate Payroll Guide, 1996; Multistate Guide to Benefits Law, 1998, rev. ed., 2006; 2000 Multistate Guide to Benefits Law, 1999; Equal Employment Opportunity 2000 Compliance Guide, 1999, rev. ed., 2005; ERISA Law Answer Book, 2003, 6th ed., 2008; (with N.E. Roddy) Plan Correction Answer Book, 3rd ed., 2009. **Address:** 2421 Ivy Rd., Charlottesville, VA 22901, U.S.A. **Online address:** jbuckley@nlrg.com

BUCKLEY, Julia. American (born United States), b. 1964. **Genres:** Novels, Mystery/Crime/Suspense, Humor/Satire. **Career:** High school English teacher. Writer. **Publications:** MYSTERY NOVELS: The Dark Backward, 2006. MADELINE MANN SERIES: Madeline Mann, 2007; Lovely, Dark, and Deep, 2008. **Address:** Chicago, IL , U.S.A. **Online address:** julishka@sbcglobal.net

BUCKLEY, Mary (Elizabeth Anne). British (born England), b. 1951. **Genres:** Adult Non-fiction, Women's Studies And Issues, Military/Defense/Arms Control. **Career:** Edinburgh University, lecturer, 1983-91, senior lecturer, 1991-94, reader in politics, 1994-2000; University of London, Royal Holloway College, professor of politics, 2000-02; Cambridge University, Centre for Research in the Arts, Social Sciences and Humanities, visiting fellow, 2004, Hughes Hall College, fellow and director of studies in politics, psychology and sociology tripos; University of Michigan, Centre for Soviet and East European Studies, visiting faculty; St. Antony's College, visiting faculty; Oxford University, Centre for Research in the Arts, Social Sciences and Humanities, visiting faculty. Writer. **Publications:** (Ed.) Soviet Social Scientists Talking: An Official Debate about Women, 1986; (ed. with M. Anderson) Women, Equality, and Europe, 1988; Women and Ideology in the Soviet Union, 1989; (ed.) Perestroika and Soviet Women, 1992; Redefining Russian Society and Polity, 1993; (ed.) Post-Soviet Women: From the Baltic to Central Asia, 1997; (ed. with S.N. Cummings) Kosovo: Perceptions of War and Its Aftermath, 2001; (ed. with R. Fawn) Global Responses to Terrorism: 9/11, Afghanistan and Beyond, 2003; Mobilizing Soviet Peasants: Heroines and Heroes of Stalin's Fields, 2006; (ed. with R. Singh) The Bush Doctrine and the War on Terrorism: Global Responses, Global Consequences, 2006. Contributor to journals and periodicals. **Address:** c/o Author Mail, Taylor & Francis Group Ltd., 2 Park Sq., Milton Pk., Abingdon, OX OX14 4RN, England. **Online address:** meab2@cam.ac.uk

BUCKLEY, Thomas. (Thomas H. Buckley). American (born United States), b. 1932. **Genres:** History, Biography. **Career:** University of South Dakota, instructor, 1960-61, assistant professor, 1961-64, associate professor, 1964-68, professor of history, 1968-69; Indiana University, visiting professor of history, 1969-71; University of Tulsa, Department of History, professor and chairman, 1971-81, chairman of division of humanistic studies, 1974-, Jay P. Walker Professor of American History, 2007-, now Jay P. Walker Professor Emeritus of American History, Graduate School, associate dean, 1995-99. Writer. **Publications:** AS THOMAS H. BUCKLEY: The United States and the Washington Conference, 1921-1922, 1970; (ed. with E. Bennett and R. Burns) Diplomats in Crisis, 1975; (with E.B. Strong, jr.) American Foreign and National Security Policies 1914-1945, 1987. Contributor of articles to journals. **Address:** Department of History, University of Tulsa, 600 S College Ave., 229 Chapman Hall, Tulsa, OK 74104, U.S.A. **Online address:** thomas-buckley@utulsa.edu

BUCKLEY, Thomas H. *See* **BUCKLEY, Thomas.**

BUCKNALL, Barbara Jane. Canadian/British (born England), b. 1933. **Genres:** Children's Fiction, Poetry, Literary Criticism And History, Young Adult Fiction, Photography. **Career:** University of Illinois, Department of French, instructor, 1962-66, assistant professor, 1966-69; Brock University, Department of French, Italian and Spanish, assistant professor, 1969-71, associate professor, 1971-94, now retired; Canada Council, fellow, 1974-75. Librarian and writer. **Publications:** The Religion of Art in Proust, 1969; Ursula K. Le Guin, 1981; (ed.) Critical Essays on Marcel Proust, 1987; Marcel Proust Revisited, 1992; The Witch Poems, 1995; Barbara Bucknall's Fairy Tales for the Young at Heart, 2000, vol. II, 2000, vol. III, 2002. **Address:** 160 Highland Ave., St. Catharines, ON L2R 4J6, Canada.

BUCKNER, Rheuben. *See* **MCCOY, Max.**

BUCKSER, Andrew (S.). American (born United States), b. 1964. **Genres:** Anthropology/Ethnology. **Career:** Research and Planning Inc., researcher, 1986; High School Whitinsville, teacher, 1987; Hartwick College, assistant professor of anthropology, 1993-95; Purdue University, assistant professor of anthropology, 1995-2001, associate professor of anthropology, 2001-09, professor, 2009-. Writer. **Publications:** Communities of Faith: Sectarianism, Identity and Social Change on a Danish Island, 1996; (ed. with S.D. Glazier) Anthropology of Religious Conversion, 2003; After the Rescue: Jewish Identity and Community in Contemporary Denmark, 2003. Contributor to periodicals. **Address:** Department of Sociology and Anthropology, Purdue University, 314 STON,, 700 W State St., Ste. 219, West Lafayette, IN 47907-1365, U.S.A. **Online address:** buckser@purdue.edu

BUCUVALAS, Tina. American (born United States), b. 1951. **Genres:** Mythology/Folklore, Local History/Rural Topics, Art/Art History, Young Adult Fiction. **Career:** Historical Museum of Southern Florida, curator, 1986-91; freelance folklorist, 1991-; Florida Department of State, Florida Folklife Program, director, 1996-2009, folklorist, 1996-2009; Maine Indian Basketmakers Alliance and Portland Performing Arts, consultant; Division of Historical Resources, program coordinator; City of Tarpon Springs, curator of arts and historical resources, 2009-. Writer. **Publications:** Resource Guide for Arkansas Folk Artists, 1984; (with S. Frangos) Techne: Traditional Greek Arts in the Calumet Region, 1985; (with S. Poyser) Introduction to Arkansas Folklore: A Teacher-Student Guide, 1986; Native American Foodways and Recipes: Hopi, Navajo, Hualapai, Laguna, 1986; Traditions: South Florida Folk Life, 1987; South Florida Folk Arts: A Teacher Guide, 1988; (with P.A. Bulger and S. Kennedy) South Florida Folklife, 1994; (contrib.) Florida Folklife: Traditional Arts in Contemporary Communities, 1998; (with K.G. Congdon) Just Above the Water: Florida Folk Art, 2006; (ed.) The Florida Folklife Reader, 2012. Contributor to periodicals. **Address:** City of Tarpon Springs, City

Hall, 324 E Pine St., Tarpon Springs, FL 34689, U.S.A. **Online address:** tbucuvalas@mail.dos.state.fl.us

BUDBILL, David. American (born United States), b. 1940. **Genres:** Novels, Novellas/Short Stories, Children's Fiction, Film, Poetry, Music, Technology. **Career:** Writer. **Publications:** PLAYS: Mannequins Demise, 1964; A Pulp Cutters' Nativity, 1981; Judevine, 1990. POETRY: Barking Dog, 1968; The Chain Saw Dance, 1977; From Down to the Village, 1981; Why I Came to Judevine, 1987; Judevine: The Complete Poems, 1970-1990, 1991, rev. ed., 1999; Moment to Moment, 1999; While We've Still Got Feet, 2005; Drink a Cup of Loneliness, 2006; Nine Taoist Poems, 2007; Happy Life, 2010. OTHER: Christmas Tree Farm (for children), 1974; The Bones on Black Spruce Mountain (novel), 1978. SHORT STORIES: Snowshoe Trek to Otter River, 1976; (ed.) Rowland Robinson, Danvis Tales, 1995. EDITOR: Danvis Tales: Selected Stories by Rowland E. Robinson, 1995; (intro.) Dr. Norton's Wife, 1996; (intro.) The Brewers' Big Horses, 1996. ESSAY: A Little Introduction to Ancient Chinese Poetry; Shell Game; An End to the Age of Impunity; In and Out and Both At Once; What Confucius Said; Deep in the Neighbourhood of History and Influence; Hiding Out in Honky Heaven; Reading Ai Quing; Sympathy: A Talk about Race, Blacks, Whites and the Impeachments Process; Put on Your Scarlet Letter; The Hermit and the Activist; William Parker, David Budbill and Act 60. **Address:** c/o Susan Schulma, A Literary Agency, 454 W 44th St., New York, NY 10036, U.S.A. **Online address:** david@davidbudbill.com

BUDD, E. S. *See* **SIRIMARCO, Elizabeth.**

BUDD, Holly. *See* **JUDD, Alan.**

BUDDE, Michael L(eo). American (born United States), b. 1958. **Genres:** Theology/Religion. **Career:** Golden Gate University, instructor, 1988; DePaul University, Department of Political Science, instructor, 1989-90, assistant professor, 1993-96, associate professor, 1996-2001, professor, 2001-, chair, 2005-08; Northwestern University, Department of Political Science, instructor, 1988-90; Auburn University, Department of Political Science, assistant professor, 1990-93. Writer. **Publications:** The Two Churches: Catholicism and Capitalism in the World System, 1992; The (Magic) Kingdom of God: Christianity and Global Culture Industries, 1997; (ed. with R.W. Brimlow) Paths That Lead to Life: The Church as Counterculture, 2000; (with R.W. Brimlow) Christianity Incorporated: How Big Business is Buying the Church, 2002; (ed. with J. Wright) Conflicting Allegiances: The Church-Based University in a Liberal Democratic Society, 2004; (ed. with K. Scott) Witness of the Body: The Past, Present and Future of Christian Martyrdom, 2011; A World for All?, 2011. Contributor to journals. **Address:** Department of Political Science, DePaul University, Rm. 2201, 990 W Fullerton, Chicago, IL 60614, U.S.A. **Online address:** mbudde@depaul.edu

BUDDENSIEG, Tilmann. German (born Germany), b. 1928. **Genres:** Architecture, Art/Art History, Business/Trade/Industry, International Relations/Current Affairs, Translations. **Career:** Freie University, Art History Institute, assistant, 1962-65, professor, 1968-, affiliate, 1965-78; Rheinische Friedrich Wilhelms-University, professor, 1978-; Harvard University, visiting professor, 1967; Slade professor of fine arts, 1974; Humboldt University, honorary professor, 1995-, now professor emeritus; University of Bonn, Art History Program, director; Stanford University, visiting professor; University of California-Berkeley, visiting professor. Writer. **Publications:** (Ed. with M. Winner) Munuscula discipulorum: kunsthistorische Studien, 1968; (co-author) Industriekultur: Peter Behrens und die AEG, 1979, trans. as Industriekultur: Peter Behrens and the AEG, 1907-1914, 1984; Die Nuetzlichen Kuenste: Gestaltende Technik und Bildende Kunst seitder Industriellen Revolution, 1981; Ceramiche della Repubblica di Weimar, 1984; Villa Hugel: Das Wohnhaus Krupp in Essen, 1984; Keramik in der Weimarer Republik, 1919-1933: die Sammlung Tilmann Buddensieg im Germanischen Nationalmuseum, 1985; (co-ed.) Wien und die Architektur des 20, Jahrhunderts, 1986; (co-author) Berlin, 1900-1933: Architecture and Design, 1987; (co-ed.) Wissenschaften in Berlin, 1987; Ein Mann vieler Eigenschaften: Walther Rathenau und die Kultur der Moderne, 1990; Peter Behrens: umbautes Licht: das Verwaltungsgebäude der Hoechst AG, 1990; (contrib.) The Reichstag and Urban Projects, 1993; Berliner Labyrinth: preussische Rastervom Lustgarten zum Alexanderplatz, vom Reichstag ins Reichssportfeld, von Moabit nach Britz, vom Kemperplatz zum Waldsangerpfad, 1993; (contrib.) Hentrich-Petschnigg & Partner: Buildings and Projects, 1988-98, 1997; Berliner Labyrinth, Berlin, 1993, rev. ed., 1999; Hülle und Fülle: Festschrift fur Tilmann Buddensieg, 1993; Berliner Labyrinth: Preussische Raster Vom Lustgarten zum Alexanderplatz, vom Reichstag ins Reichssportfeld, 1993; Bauten und Pläne: Mit einer Einleitung vonAdolf Behne, 1995; Elektrische Hausgeräte 1910-1970: Sammlung Angelika Jensen, Hamburg: eine Schenkung an das Museum für Kunst und Kulturgeschichte der Hansestadt Lübeck im memoriam Gerhard Gerkens, 1999; Nietzsches Italien: Städte, Gärten und Paläste, 2002. **Address:** Kunstgeschichtliches Seminar, Humboldt Universityersitaet Berlin, Unter den Linden 6, Berlin, 10099, Germany.

BUDERI, Robert. American (born United States), b. 1954. **Genres:** Technology, Engineering, Information Science/Computers, Business/Trade/Industry. **Career:** Daily Republic, reporter of police news, 1977-79; Time Life News Service, contributing reporter, 1980-88; Massachusetts Institute of Technology, Vannevar Bush fellow, 1986-87, Technology Review, contributing editor, 1998, editor-at-large, 2000-02, editor-in-chief, 2002-04, Center for International Studies, research fellow, 2005-07; Business Week, technology editor, 1990-92; Upside, columnist, 1998-2000. **Publications:** The Invention That Changed the World: How a Small Group of Radar Pioneers Won the Second World War and Launched a Technological Revolution, 1996; Invention that Changed the World: The Story of Radar from War to Peace, 1998; Engines of Tomorrow: How the World's Best Companies Are Using Their Research Labs to Win the Future, 2000; (with G.T. Huang) Guanxi (The Art of Relationships): Microsoft, China, and Bill Gates's Plan to Win the Road Ahead, 2006. Contributor to periodicals. **Address:** c/o Raphael Sagalyn, The Sagalyn Literary Agency, 4922 Fairmont Ave., Ste. 200, Bethesda, MD 20814-6020, U.S.A. **Online address:** bob@guanxithebook.com

BUDGE, Ian. British (born England), b. 1936. **Genres:** Philosophy, Politics/Government, Social Sciences, Speech/Rhetoric, Law. **Career:** University of Edinburgh, assistant lecturer, 1962-64; University of Strathclyde, assistant lecturer, 1963-64, lecturer, 1964-66; University of Essex, lecturer, 1966-68, senior lecturer, 1968-71, reader, 1971-75, chairman of department, 1974-77, professor of government, 1975-2001, research professor, 2001-, head of department, graduate director, now professor emeritus, Essex Summer School on quantitative social research, founder, visiting professor; Summer School of European Consortium for Political Research, director, 1971-73, executive director, 1979-83; European University, Summer School on West European Politics Institute, director, 1984; Intl. Manifesto Research Project, founder. Writer. **Publications:** (With D.W. Urwin) Scottish Political Behaviour: A Case Study in British Homogeneity, 1966; Agreement and the Stability of Democracy, 1970; (with C. O'Leary) Belfast: Approach to Crisis: A Study of Belfast Politics 1613-1970, 1973; (ed. with I. Crewe and D.J. Farlie) Party Identification and Beyond: Representations of Voting And Party Competition, 1976; (with Farlie) Voting and Party Competition: A Theoretical Critique and Synthesis Applied To Surveys From Ten Democracies, 1977; (with D.J. Farlie) Explaining and Predicting Elections: Issue Effects and Party Strategies in Twenty-three Democracies, 1983; Ideology, Strategy and Party Change: Spatial Analyses of Post-War Election Programmes in Nineteen Democracies, 1987; (co-author) The Changing British Political System: Into the 1990s, 2nd ed., 1988; (with H.E. Keman) Parties and Democracy: Coalition Formation and Government Functioning in Twenty Countries, 1990; (ed. with M.J. Laver) Party Policy and Government Coalitions, 1992; The Developing British Political System: The 1990s, 1993; (ed. with J. Woldenddorp and H. Keman) Handbook of Democratic Government: Party Government in Twenty Democracies, 1945-1990, 1993; (ed. with D. McKay) Developing Democracy: Comparative Research in Honour of J.F.P. Blondel, 1994; Parties, Policies and Democracy, 1994; The New Challenge of Direct Democracy, 1996; The New British Politics, 1998, 4th ed., 2007; New British Politics, 2004; (co-author) New British Politics Election 2005 Update, 2005; (with M.D. McDonald) Elections, Parties, Democracy: Conferring the Median Mandate, 2005; Mapping Policy Preferences II: Estimates for Parties Governments and Electors in the OECD, EU and Central and Eastern Europe 1990-2003, 2006; Party Politics, 2006; (with M. McDonald) Election and Party System Effects on Policy Representation: Bringing Time into a Comparative Perspective, 2007; Do They Work? Validating Computerized Word Frequency Approaches Against Long Policy Series, 2007; New British Politics, 2007. CO-AUTHOR: Political Stratification and Democracy, 1972; The New British Political System: Government and Society in the 1980s, 1983, rev. ed., 1993; Parties, Policies and Democracy, 1994; The Politics of the New Europe: Atlantic to Urals, 1997; Party Government in 48 Democracies 1945-1998: Composition, Duration, Personnel, 2000; Mapping Policy Preferences: Estimates for Parties, Electors and Governments, 1945-1998, 2001. **Address:** Department of Government, University of Essex, Rm. 5B.016, Wivenhoe Pk., Colchester, EX CO4 3SQ, England. **Online address:** budgi@essex.ac.uk

BUDIANSKY, Stephen (Philip). American (born United States), b. 1957. **Genres:** Environmental Sciences/Ecology, Animals/Pets, History, Military/Defense/Arms Control. **Career:** American Chemical Society, writer, 1979-82; Nature, editor, 1982-85; U.S. Congress, Office of Technology Assessment, congressional fellow, 1985-86; U.S. News & World Report, national security correspondent, foreign editor, deputy editor, senior writer, 1986-; Atlantic Monthly, correspondent. **Publications:** The Covenant of the Wild, 1992; Nature's Keepers, 1995; The Nature of Horses, 1997; If a Lion Could Talk: Animal Intelligence and the Evolution of Consciousness, 1998; The World According to Horses, 2000; Battle of Wits, 2000; The Truth about Dogs: An Inquiry Into the Ancestry, Social Conventions, Mental Habits and Moral Fiber of Canis Familiaris, 2000; The Character of Cats, 2002; Air Power: The Men, Machines and Ideas That Revolutionized War, from Kitty Hawk to Gulf War II, 2004; Her Majestey's Spymaster: Elizabeth I, Sir Francis Walsingham and the Birth of Modern Espionage, 2005; The Bloody Shirt: Terror after Appomattox, 2008; Murder, by the Book, 2008; Perilous Fight: America's Intrepid War with Britain on the High Seas, 1812-1815, 2010. Contributor to periodicals. **Address:** U.S. News & World Report, 2400 N St. NW, Washington, DC 20037-1177, U.S.A. **Online address:** spb@budiansky.com

BUDMAN, Mark. American/Russian (born Russia), b. 1950?. **Genres:** Novels. **Career:** International Business Machines Corp., engineer; Vestal Review, founder, publisher and editor, 2000-; Web Del Sol (on-line literary journal), interview editor. **Publications:** (Ed. with T. Hazuka) You Have Time for This: Contemporary American Short-Short Stories, 2006; My Life at First Try: A Novel, 2008; (ed. with T. Hazuka and C. Perkins-Hazuka) Sudden Flash Youth, 2011; Mister Lenin, forthcoming; The Shifter Prince and the Time Traveler, forthcoming. Contributor to books. **Address:** Waxman Literary Agency, 80 5th Ave., Ste. 1101, New York, NY 10011, U.S.A.

BUDNITZ, Judy. American (born United States), b. 1973. **Genres:** Novellas/Short Stories, Novels. **Career:** Village Voice, cartoonist, 1996-; Provincetown Fine Arts Work Center, fellow; Princeton University, Council of the Humanities, fellow, 2005. Writer. **Publications:** Flying Leap (short stories), 1998; Hershel, 1998; If I Told You Once: A Novel, 1999; Nice Big American Baby, 2005. Contributor to periodicals, magazines and journals. Works appear in anthologies. **Address:** c/o Leigh Feldman, Darhansoff, Verrill & Feldman Agency, 236 W 26th St., Ste. 802, New York, NY 10001-6736, U.S.A.

BUDNY, Mildred. American (born United States) **Genres:** Essays, Biography, History, Adult Non-fiction, Art/Art History. **Career:** Research Group on Manuscript Evidence, senior research associate, executive director and editor-in-chief of publications; University of Cambridge, Downing College, Graham Robertson senior research fellow, Corpus Christi College, senior research associate. Medieval historian, author, educator. **Publications:** BOOKS: Minotaur, 1981; Requiem for Na'aman, 1982; Insular and Anglo-Saxon Illuminated Manuscripts, 1986; Matthew Parker and His Books: Sandars Lectures in Bibliography Delivered on 14, 16, and 18 May 1990 at the University of Cambridge, 1993; Insular, Anglo-Saxon and Early Anglo-Norman Manuscript Art at Corpus Christi College, Cambridge: An Illustrated Catalogue, 1997. **Address:** Research Group on Manuscript Evidence, 46 Snowdon Ln., Princeton, NJ 08542-3916, U.S.A. **Online address:** director@manuscriptevidence.org

BUDZ, Mark. American (born United States), b. 1960. **Genres:** Novels. **Career:** Writer, 1991-. **Publications:** NOVELS: Clade, 2003; Crache, 2004; Idolon, 2006; Till Human Voices Wake Us, 2007. **Address:** c/o Matt Bialer, Sanford J. Greenburger Associates Inc., 55 5th Ave., New York, NY 10003-4301, U.S.A. **Online address:** mark@markbudz.com

BUECHNER, (Carl) Frederick. American (born United States), b. 1926. **Genres:** Novels, Theology/Religion, Autobiography/Memoirs, Philosophy, Young Adult Non-fiction, Biography, Young Adult Fiction, Essays, Essays, Literary Criticism And History. **Career:** Lawrenceville School, teacher of English, 1948-53; New York University, instructor in creative writing, 1953-54; East Harlem Protestant Parish, head of employment clinic, 1954-58; United Presbyterian Church, ordained minister, 1958; Phillips Exeter Academy, Department of Religion, chair, 1958-60, school minister, 1960-67; writer, 1967-; Harvard University, William Belden Noble Lecturer, 1969; Tufts University, Russell Lecturer, 1971; Yale University, Divinity School, Lyman Beecher lecturer, 1976; Trinity Institute, lecturer, 1990. **Publications:** A Long Day's Dying, 1950; The Season's Difference, 1951; The Return of Ansel Gibbs, 1958; The Final Beast, 1965; The Magnificent Defeat (meditations), 1966; Morte di un Lungo Giorno, 1967; The Hungering Dark (meditations), 1968; The Entrance to Porlock, 1970; The Alphabet of Grace (autobiography), 1970; Lion Country, 1971; Open Heart, 1972; Wishful Thinking: A Theological ABC, 1973, rev. ed., 1993; Love Feast, 1974; (contrib.) The Faces of Jesus, 1974; Telling the Truth: The Gospel as Tragedy, Comedy and Fairy Tale, 1977; Treasure Hunt: A Novel, 1977; Peculiar Treasures: A Biblical Who's Who, 1979; The Book of Bebb, 1979; Godric, 1980; The Sacred Journey: A Memoir of Early Days (autobiography), 1982; Now and Then: A Memoir of Vocation (autobiography), 1983; A Room Called Remember (essays and sermons), 1984; Brendan: A Novel, 1987; Whistling in the Dark: A Doubter's Dictionary, 1988; The Wizard's Tide: A Story, 1990; Telling Secrets (autobiography), 1991; The Clown in the Belfry: Writings on Faith and Fiction, 1992; Listening to Your Life: Daily Meditations with Frederick Buechner, 1992; The Son of Laughter, 1993; The Longing for Home: Recollections and Reflections, 1996; On the Road with the Archangel (novel), 1997; The Storm (novel), 1998; The Eyes of the Heart: A Memoir of the Lost and Found, 1999; Speak What We Feel (Not What We Ought To Say): Reflections On Literature And Faith, 2001; Beyond Words: Daily Readings in the ABC's of Faith, 2004; Secrets in the Dark: A Life in Sermons, 2006; The Yellow Leaves: A Miscellany, 2008. **Address:** Lucy Kroll Agency, 390 W End Ave., New York, NY 10024, U.S.A.

BUEHLER, Evelyn Judy. American (born United States), b. 1953. **Genres:** Novellas/Short Stories, Poetry, Photography. **Career:** Writer and photographer. **Publications:** Tales of Summer (poems), 1998. Works appear in anthologies. **Address:** 5658 S Normal Blvd., Chicago, IL 60621-2966, U.S.A. **Online address:** evelyn_judy_buehler@yahoo.com

BUEHNER, Caralyn M. American (born United States), b. 1963. **Genres:** Picture/Board Books, Children's Fiction. **Career:** Writer. **Publications:** PICTURE BOOKS: The Escape of Marvin the Ape, 1992; A Job for Wittilda, 1993; It's a Spoon, Not a Shovel, 1995; Fanny's Dream, 1996; I Did It, I'm Sorry, 1998; I Want to Say I Love You, 2001; Snowmen at Night, 2002; Superdog, the Heart of a Hero, 2004; Snowmen at Christmas, 2005; Goldilocks and the Three Bears, 2007; In the Garden, 2007; Would I Ever Lie to You?, 2007; Queen of Style, 2008; Snowmen All Year, 2010. **Address:** c/o Lisa Sandick, Dial Press, 375 Hudson St., New York, NY 10014, U.S.A. **Online address:** m.buehner@comcast.net

BUELL, Frederick (Henderson). American (born United States), b. 1942. **Genres:** Poetry, Literary Criticism And History, Natural History, Environmental Sciences/Ecology. **Career:** City University of New York, Queens College, instructor, 1970-71, assistant professor, 1971-73, associate professor, 1973-79, professor of English, 1980-, director of American studies. Writer. **Publications:** Theseus and Other Poems, 1971; W. H. Auden as a Social Poet, 1973; Full Summer, 1979; National Culture and the New Global System, 1994; From Apocalypse to Way of Life: Four Decades of Environmental Crisis in the US, 2003. Contributor to periodicals. **Address:** Department of English, Queens College, City University of New York, Rm. 631, Klapper Hall, 65-30 Kissena Blvd., Flushing, NY 11367, U.S.A. **Online address:** buell@warwick.net

BUETTNER, Dan. American (born United States), b. 1960?. **Genres:** Travel/Exploration, History, Social Sciences. **Career:** Quest Network Inc., founder; Writer and educator. **Publications:** Sovietrek: A Journey by Bicycle across Russia, 1994; Maya Quest: The Interactive Expedition, 1996; Africa Trek: A Journey by Bicycle through Africa, 1996; Inside Grand Bahama: Africa Quest, 1998; Asia Quest, 1999; The Blue Zone: Lessons for Living Longer from The People Who've Lived the Longest, 2008; Thrive: Finding Happiness the Blue Zones Way, 2010. Contributor to periodicals. **Address:** Classroom Connect, 8000 Marina Blvd., Brisbane, CA 94005, U.S.A. **Online address:** dan_buettner@mecc.com

BUFFETT, James William. *See* **BUFFETT, Jimmy.**

BUFFETT, Jimmy. (James William Buffett). American (born United States), b. 1946. **Genres:** Young Adult Fiction, Songs/Lyrics And Libretti, Autobiography/Memoirs, Novels, Novellas/Short Stories. **Career:** Songwriter and performer, 1960-; Billboard Publications, writer, 1971-73. **Publications:** (With S.J. Buffett) The Jolly Mon (juvenile), 1988; Tales from Margaritaville: Fictional Facts and Factual Fictions (short story and autobiographical sketch collection), 1989; (with S.J. Buffett) Trouble Dolls (juvenile), 1991; Where is Joe Merchant?: A Novel Tale (novel), 1992; Daybreak On the Equator, 1997; A Pirate Looks at Fifty (autobiography), 1998; Meet Me in Margaritaville: The Ultimate Collection, 2003; Salty Piece of Land, 2004; License to Chill, 2004; Swine Not?, 2008. **Address:** c/o Cindy Thompson, Margaritaville Inc., 424-A Fleming St., Key West, FL 33040, U.S.A. **Online address:** info@margaritaville.com

BUFFIE, Margaret. Canadian (born Canada), b. 1945. **Genres:** Children's Fiction, Young Adult Fiction, Ghost Writer, Novels. **Career:** Hudson's Bay Co., fashion illustrator, 1968-70; Winnipeg Art Gallery, painting instructor, 1974-75; River East School Division, high school art teacher, 1976-77; writer, 1985-; University of Winnipeg, writing instructor, 1992-97. **Publications:** CHILDREN'S FICTION: Who Is Frances Rain?, 1987 in US as The Haunting of Frances Rain, 1989; The Guardian Circle, 1989 in US as The Warnings, 1991; My Mother's Ghost, 1992 in US as Someone Else's Ghost, 1995; The Dark Garden, 1995; Angels Turn Their Backs, 1998; The Watcher, 2000; The Seeker, 2002; The Finder, 2004; Out of Focus, 2006; Winter Shadows, 2010. **Address:** Kids Can Press Ltd., 25 Dockside Dr., Toronto, ON M5A 0B5, Canada. **Online address:** mabuffie@yahoo.ca

BUFORD, Bill. (William Holmes Buford). American (born United States), b. 1954. **Genres:** Travel/Exploration, Literary Criticism And History, Biography, Social Commentary. **Career:** Granta Magazine, editor and chairman, 1979-95, publisher, 1989; New Yorker, fiction editor, 1995-2002, European correspondent, 2003-. **Publications:** NONFICTION: Among the Thugs: 1991; (ed.) Granta Book of Travel, 1992; Granta Book of Reportage, 1993; Granta Book of the Family, 1995; Heat: An Amateur's Adventures as Kitchen Slave, Line Cook, Pasta Maker, and Apprentice to a Dante-Quoting Butcher in Tuscany, 2006. OTHER: (ed. with intro.) The Best American Travel Writing 2010, 2010. **Address:** The New Yorker, 4 Times Sq., New York, NY 10036-7440, U.S.A.

BUFORD, William Holmes. *See* **BUFORD, Bill.**

BUGAJSKI, Janusz. American/British (born England), b. 1954. **Genres:** International Relations/Current Affairs. **Career:** BBC-TV, consultant, 1981-83; Radio Free Europe, senior research analyst, 1984-85; Center for Strategic and International Studies, Lavrentis Lavrentiadis chair and New European Democracies program, director, 1986-, Europe Program, senior fellow; U.S. State Department Foreign Service Institute, South-Central Europe Area Studies Program, chair 2000-; American University, adjunct lecturer, 1991; Smithsonian Institution, Foreign Service Institute, Woodrow Wilson Center, lecturer; International Republican Institute, consultant; International Research and Exchanges Board, consultant; Institute for Democracy in Eastern Europe, consultant. Writer. **Publications:** Czechoslovakia: Charter 77's Decade of Dissent, 1987; (with M. Pollack) East European Fault Lines, 1989; Sandinista Communism and Rural Nicaragua, 1990; Fourth World Conflicts: Communism and Rural Societies, 1991; Nations in Turmoil: Conflict and Cooperation in Eastern Europe, 1993, 2nd ed., 1995; Ethnic Politics in Eastern Europe, 1994; Political Parties of Eastern Europe: A Guide to Politics in the Post-Communist Era, 2002; (ed.) Toward an Understanding of Russia, 2002; Cold Peace: Russia's New Imperialism, 2004; (with I. Teleki) America's New Allies: Central-Eastern Europe and the Transatlantic Link, 2006; (with M. Staneve) Economic Development and Investment Promotion in Southeast Europe, 2006; (with I. Teleki) Atlantic Bridges: America's New European Allies, 2007; Eastern Dimension of America's New European Allies, 2007; (co-author) Ukraine: A Net Assessment of 16 Years of Independence, 2008; Expanding Eurasia: Russia's European Ambitions, 2008; America's New European Allies, 2009. Dismantling the West: Russia's Atlantic Agenda, 2009; Western Balkans policy review 2010, 2010; Georgian Lessons, 2010. Contributor to periodicals. **Address:** Center for Strategic and International Studies, 1800 K St. NW, Washington, DC 20006, U.S.A. **Online address:** jbugajsk@csis.org

BUGAN, Carmen. British/Romanian (born Romania), b. 1970?. **Genres:** Poetry. **Career:** Oxford University, tutor in creative writing. Poet. **Publications:** At the Borders: Poems, 1995; Crossing the Carpathians (poems), 2005. Contributor to journals and periodicals. **Online address:** carmen.bugan@wolfson.ox.ac.uk

BUGEJA, Michael J. American (born United States), b. 1952. **Genres:** Poetry, Novels, Novellas/Short Stories, Adult Non-fiction. **Career:** United Press Intl., reporter, correspondent and state editor, 1976-79; Oklahoma State University, School of Journalism and Broadcasting, associate professor of journalism, 1979-86; Ohio University, E.W. Scripps School of Journalism, professor of journalism, 1986-2003, associate director, 2001-03, special assistant and ethics advisor to President Robert Glidden, 1996-2001; Iowa State University, Greenlee School of Journalism and Communication, professor, director, 2003-; Oklahoma State University, Daily O'Collegian, newspaper advisor. **Publications:** What We Do for Music (poetry chapbook), 1990; Platonic Love: Poems, 1991; Culture's Sleeping Beauty: Essays on Poetry, Prejudice and Belief, 1992; After Oz, 1993; Flight from Valhalla: Poems, 1993; The Art and Craft of Poetry, 1994; Academic Socialism: Merit and Morale in Higher Education, 1994; Poet's Guide: How to Publish and Perform Your Work, 1995; The Visionary, 1995; Living Ethics: Developing Values in Mass Communication, 1996; Little Dragons (story), 1996; Talk, 1997; Family Values (novel), 1997; Guide to Writing Magazine Nonfiction, 1998; Millennium's End: Poems, 1999; (with T.E. Wagner) Living without Fear: Understanding Cancer and the New Therapies, 2001; Crown and Garland, 2001; Greatest Hits 1981-2001, 2002; How-to News Writer: 25 Ways to Develop Reporting and Writing Skills, 2004; Interpersonal Divide: The Search for Community in a Technological Age, 2005; Living Ethics: Across Media Platforms, 2008; (with D.V. Dimitrova) Vanishing Act: The Erosion of Online Footnotes and Implications for Scholarship in the Digital Age, 2010. Contributor to periodicals. **Address:** Greenlee School of Journalism and Communication, Iowa State University, 101A Hamilton Hall, Ames, IA 50011-1180, U.S.A. **Online address:** bugeja@iastate.edu

BUGOS, Glenn E. American (born United States), b. 1961. **Genres:** Air/Space Topics, Engineering. **Career:** California Institute of Technology, faculty, 1988-90; University of California, faculty, 1990-91; Wissenschaftzentrum Berlin für Sozialforschung, faculty, 1991-93; Moment L.L.C. (now The Prologue Group), founder, 1993-; National Air and Space Museum, faculty; NASA Ames Research Center, historian. Writer. **Publications:** Engineering the F-4 Phantom II: Parts into Systems, 1996; Atmosphere of Freedom: Sixty Years at the NASA Ames Research Center, 2000. Contributor to journals. **Address:** Moment L.L.C., 188 King St., Redwood City, CA 94062-1940, U.S.A. **Online address:** glenn@prologuegroup.com

BUGUL, Ken. *See* **MBAYE, Marietou (Bileoma).**

BUHNER, Stephen Harrod. American (born United States), b. 1952. **Genres:** Poetry, Cultural/Ethnic Topics, Environmental Sciences/Ecology, Medicine/Health, Self Help, How-to Books, Language/Linguistics, Literary Criticism And History, Writing/Journalism, Adult Non-fiction, Theology/Religion. **Career:** Foundation for Gaian Studies, senior researcher, 1990-; Healer's Review, editor, 1990-95; Colorado Association of Holistic Healing Professionals, president, 1990-95; Rocky Mountain Center for Botanic Studies, faculty, 1992-94, adjunct faculty, 1994-97; writer, 1996-; Sage Mountain Herbal School, adjunct faculty, 1998-2001; Dreamtime Center for Herbal Studies, adjunct faculty, 2001-03. **Publications:** Sacred Plant Medicine: Explorations in the Practice of Indigenous Herbalism, 1996; One Spirit, Many Peoples: A Manifesto for Earth Spirituality, 1997; Sacred and Herbal Healing Beers: The Secrets of Ancient Fermentation, 1998; Herbal Antibiotics: Natural Alternatives for Drug-Resistant Bacteria, 1999, 2nd ed., 2012; Herbs for Hepatitis C and the Liver, 2000; The Lost Language of Plants: The Ecological Importance of Plant Medicines to Life on Earth, 2002; The Taste of Wild Water: Poems and Stories Found While Walking in Woods, 2002; Vital Man: Natural Health Care for Men at Midlife, 2003; The Fasting Path: The Way to Spiritual, Physical, and Emotional Enlightenment, 2003; The Secret Teachings of Plants: The Intelligence of the Heart in the Direct Perception of Nature, 2004; Healing Lyme: Natural Healing and Prevention of Lyme Borreliosis and Its Related Co-Infections, 2005; Sacred Plant Medicine: The Wisdom in Native American Herbalism, 2006; The Natural Testosterone Plan: For Sexual Health and Energy, 2007; The Taste of Wild Water: Poems and Stories Found While Walking in Woods, 2009; Ensouling Language: On the Art of Nonfiction and the Writers Life, 2010; The Transformational Power of Fasting: The Way to Spiritual, Physical, and Emotional Rejuvenation, 2nd ed., 2012; Natural Healing for the Coinfections of Lyme: Bartonella and Mycoplasma, 2012. **Address:** Foundation for Gaian Studies, 8 Pioneer Rd., Silver City, NM 88061, U.S.A. **Online address:** stephen@gaianstudies.org

BUHS, Joshua Blu. American (born United States), b. 1973?. **Genres:** Sciences. **Career:** Writer. **Publications:** The Fire Ant Wars: Nature, Science, and Public Policy in Twentieth-Century America, 2004; Bigfoot: The Life and Times of a Legend, 2009. Contributor to periodicals. **Address:** Folsom, CA , U.S.A. **Online address:** joshuabbuhs@yahoo.com

BUIDA, Yuri. Russian (born Russia), b. 1954?. **Genres:** Science Fiction/Fantasy, Novels. **Career:** Journalist. **Publications:** Don Domino, 1993, trans. as The Zero Train, 2001; Ermo, 1996; Boris and Gleb, 1997; Prusskaya Nevesta, 1998, trans. as The Prussian Bride, 2002; Gorod Palachei (title means: 'City of Executioners'), 2003. Contributor to periodicals. **Address:** c/o Author Mail, Dedalus Ltd., Langford Lodge, St. Judiths Ln., Sawtry, CB PE28 5XE, England.

BUJOLD, Lois McMaster. American (born United States), b. 1949. **Genres:** Science Fiction/Fantasy, Novels, Adult Non-fiction, Novellas/Short Stories, Young Adult Fiction. **Career:** Ohio State University Hospitals, pharmacy technician, 1972-78; writer, 1982-. **Publications:** SCIENCE FICTION: Shards of Honor, 1986; Ethan of Athos, 1986; The Warrior's Apprentice, 1986; Falling Free, 1988; Brothers in Arms, 1989; Borders of Infinity, 1989; The Vor Game, 1990; Vorkosigan's Game, 1990; Barrayar, 1991; Mirror Dance, 1994; Cetaganda, 1996; Memory, 1996; Komarr, 1998; A Civil Campaign, 1999; Miles, Mystery and Mayhem, 2001; Diplomatic Immunity: A Comedy of Terrors, 2002; Winterfair Gifts, 2008; Cryoburn, 2010. OTHERS: (with O.S. Card and D. Drake) Free Lancers, 1987; The Spirit Ring (fantasy), 1992; (ed. with R.J. Green) Women at War, 1995; The Curse of Chalion, 2001; Paladin of Souls, 2003; The Hallowed Hunt, 2005; Miles in Love, 2006; The Mountains of Mourning (novella). SHARING KNIFE SERIES: Beguilement, 2006; Legacy, 2007; Passage, 2008; Horizon, 2009. Contributor to periodicals. **Address:** Spectrum Literary Agency, 320 Central Pk. W, Ste. 1-D, New York, NY 10025, U.S.A. **Online address:** lmbujold@mu.uswest.net

BUJOR, Flavia. French/Romanian (born Romania), b. 1988. **Genres:** Novels, Children's Fiction, Young Adult Fiction. **Career:** Writer. **Publications:** La Prophétie des Pierres, 2002. Contributor to periodicals. **Address:** c/o Author Mail, Hyperion Editorial Department, 77 W 66th St., New York, NY 10023, U.S.A.

BUKEY, Evan Burr. American (born United States), b. 1940. **Genres:** History. **Career:** University of Arkansas, assistant professor, 1969-75, associate professor, 1975-86, professor of history, 1986-, now professor emeritus. Writer. **Publications:** Hitler's Hometown: Linz, Austria, 1908-1945, 1986; Hitler's Austria: Popular Sentiment in the Nazi Era, 1938-1945, 2000; Jews and Intermarriage in Nazi Vienna, 2011. Contributor of articles and journals. **Address:** Departmetn of History, University of Arkansas, 416 Old Main, Fayetteville, AR 72701, U.S.A. **Online address:** ebukey@uark.edu

BUKIET, Melvin Jules. American (born United States) **Genres:** Novellas/Short Stories, Young Adult Fiction, History. **Career:** Mt. Vernon Public Library, writing teacher, 1983; The Writer's Voice, writing teacher, 1988-93; Tikkun Magazine, fiction editor, 1992-96; Sarah Lawrence College, visiting professor, 1993-; KGB, owner, 1994-; Columbia University, visiting professor, 1996. **Publications:** Sandman's Dust, 1985; Signs and Wonders, 1999; Strange Fire, 2001. STORIES: Stories of an Imaginary Childhood, 1992; While the Messiah Tarries, 1995; After, 1996; A Faker's Dozen, 2003. EDITOR: Neurotica: Jewish Writers on Sex, 1999; Nothing Makes you Free: Writings by Descendants of Jewish Holocaust Survivors, 2002; (with D.G. Roskies) Scribblers on the Roof: Contemporary American Jewish Fiction, 2006. Contributor of short stories, essays, reviews and editorials to periodicals. **Address:** c/o Jennifer Lyons, Writers House, 21 W 26th St., New York, NY 10010, U.S.A.

BUKOSKI, Anthony. American (born United States), b. 1945. **Genres:** Novellas/Short Stories. **Career:** University of Wisconsin, professor of English. Writer. **Publications:** SHORT STORIES: Twelve below Zero, 1986; Children of Strangers, 1993; Polonaise, 1999; Time between Trains, 2003; North of the Port, 2008. **Address:** Department of English, University of Wisconsin, 230 Sundquist Hall, Belknap and Catlin, PO Box 2000, Superior, WI 54880, U.S.A. **Online address:** abukoski@uwsuper.edu

BUK-SWIENTY, Tom. Danish (born Denmark), b. 1966?. **Genres:** Biography. **Career:** University of Southern Denmark, instructor. Journalist and historian. **Publications:** Den Ideelle Amerikaner: En Biografi om Journalisten, Reformisten og Fotografen Jacob A. Riis (biography), 2005. **Address:** Faculty of Social Sciences, University of Southern Denmark, Campusvej 55, Odense, DK-5230, Denmark. **Online address:** tbu@journalism.sdu.dk

BULBECK, Chilla. Australian (born Australia), b. 1951. **Genres:** Women's Studies And Issues, Race Relations. **Career:** Australian Public Service, officer, 1972-75; Murdoch University, tutor, 1980, senior tutor in social and political theory, 1981-83; Griffith University, lecturer, 1983-87, senior lecturer, 1988-93, associate professor of humanities, 1993-96; Australian Institute for Women's Research and Policy, director, 1992-94; University of Adelaide, professor of women's studies, 1998-, chair of women's studies, through 2008, now professor emeritus; University of Tokyo, Centre for Pacific and American Studies, visiting professor of Australian Studies, 2002-03; University of Western Australia, honorary professorial research associate, 2006-10. Writer. **Publications:** (With C. Heath) Shadow of the Hill, 1985; Staying in Line or Getting Out of Place: The Experiences of Expatriate Women in Papua New Guinea, 1920-1960: Issues of Race and Gender, 1988; One World Women's Movement, 1988; Social Sciences in Australia, 1992, rev. ed., 1998; Australian Women in Papua New Guinea: Colonial Passages, 1920-1960, 1992; Living Feminism: The Impact of the Women's Movement on Three Generations of Australian Women, 1997; Re-orienting Western Feminism: Women's Diversity in a Postcolonial World, 1998; (ed.) Proceedings of the Australian Women's Studies Association Seventh Conference, 1998; Facing the Wild: Ecotourism, Conservation, and Animal Encounters, 2005; Sex, Love and Feminism in the Asia Pacific: A Cross-Cultural Study of Young People's Attitudes, 2009. Contributor to periodicals. **Address:** Gender Work & Social Inquiry, University of Adelaide, N Terrace Campus, 5 04a Ligertwood Bldg., Adelaide, SA 5005, Australia. **Online address:** chilla.bulbeck@adelaide.edu.au

BULGER, Peggy A. American (born United States), b. 1949. **Genres:** Music, Mythology/Folklore. **Career:** Bureau of Cultural Affairs, oral historian, 1975; Appalachian Museum, Traditional Folklife Project, research and participants co-ordinator, 1975-76; Florida Department of State, Florida Folk Arts Program, state folk arts coordinator, 1976-79, Bureau of Florida Folklife Programs, administrator, 1979-89; Southern Arts Federation, Regional Folk Arts Program, coordinator, 1989-92, folk arts director and senior program officer, 1992-99; Library of Congress, American Folklife Center, director, 1999-. Writer. **Publications:** (Ed.) Musical Roots of the South, 1991; (with T. Bucuvalas and S. Kennedy) South Florida Folklife, 1994. Contributor to books and journals. **Address:** American Folklife Center, Library of Congress, 101 Independence Ave. SE, Washington, DC 20540-4610, U.S.A. **Online address:** mbul@loc.gov

BULKELEY, Kelly. American (born United States), b. 1962. **Genres:** Psychology, Theology/Religion, Education. **Career:** University of Chicago, faculty, 1990-93; Graduate Theological Union, faculty, 1995-; University of Santa Clara, lecturer, 1996-2000; John F. Kennedy University, faculty, 1999-2009, Dream Studies Program, director; University of Philosophical Research, faculty, 2002-; Pastoral Psychology, editorial advisor; Dream Time Magazine, contributing editor; International Association for the Study of Dreams, president, Dreaming Journal, senior editor; The American Academy of Religion, Religion and the Social Sciences Section, co-chair, Culture and Religion Group, secretary and treasurer. **Publications:** The Wilderness of Dreams, 1994; Spiritual Dreaming, 1995; (ed.) Among All These Dreamers, 1996; An Introduction to the Psychology of Dreaming, 1997; (with A. Siegel) Dreamcatching, 1998; Visions of the Night, 1999; Transforming Dreams: Learning Spiritual Lessons from the Dreams You Never Forget, 2000; (ed.) Dreams: A Reader on Religious, Cultural, and Psychological Dimensions of Dreaming, 2001; Dreams of Healing: Transforming Nightmares into Visions of Hope, 2003; The Wondering Brain: Thinking about Religion with and beyond Cognitive Neuroscience, 2005; (with P. Bulkley) Dreaming beyond Death: A Guide to Pre-Death Dreams and Visions, 2005; (ed.) Soul, Psyche, Brain: New Directions in the Study of Religion and Brain-Mind Science, 2005; American Dreamers: What Dreams Tell Us about the Political Psychology of Conservatives, Liberals, and Everyone Else, 2008; Dreaming in the World's Religions: A Comparative History, 2008; (ed. with K. Adams and P.M. Davis) Dreaming in Christianity and Islam: Culture, Conflict, and Creativity, 2009; (with P. King and B. Welt) Dreaming in the Classroom: Practices, Methods, and Resources in Dream Education, 2011; (ed. with C. Weldon) Teaching Jung, 2011. **Address:** University of Philosophical Research, 3910 Los Feliz Blvd., Los Angeles, CA 90027, U.S.A. **Online address:** kellybulkeley@earthlink.net

BULKOWSKI, Thomas N. American (born United States), b. 1957?. **Genres:** Business/Trade/Industry, Economics. **Career:** Raytheon, Missile Systems Division, hardware design engineer, 1979-81; Tracor Westronics, software manager for process monitoring systems, 1981-82; Tandy Corp., senior software engineer, 1982-93; Keep Keller Beautiful, president, 1990-92; Friends of the Keller Library, vice president, 1990; IMI Systems (consulting service), consultant, 1993; freelance writer, 1993-; Keller Chamber of Commerce, vice president, 1994, treasurer, 1995. **Publications:** Encyclopedia of Chart Patterns, 2000, 2nd ed., 2005; Trading Classic Chart Patterns, 2002; Getting Started in Chart Patterns, 2006; Encyclopedia of Candlestick Charts, 2008. FORTHCOMING: Head's Law; Burning Desire; Pinion's Search. Contributor to periodicals. **Address:** c/o Author Mail, John Wiley & Sons Inc., 111 River St., Hoboken, NJ 07030-5774, U.S.A. **Online address:** tbul@hotmail.com

BULL, Angela (Mary). British (born England), b. 1936. **Genres:** Children's Fiction, Literary Criticism And History, Novellas/Short Stories, Children's Non-fiction, Biography. **Career:** Casterton School, teacher of English, 1961-62; Oxford University, Bodleian Library, assistant keeper, 1962-63. Writer. **Publications:** The Friend with a Secret, 1965; (with G. Avery) Nineteenth Century Children: Heroes and Heroines in English Children's Stories, 1780-1900, 1965; Wayland's Keep, 1966; Child of Ebenezer, 1974; Treasure in the Fog, 1976; Griselda, 1977; The Doll in the Wall, 1978; The Machine Breakers, 1980; The Bicycle Parcel, 1980; The Accidental Twins, 1982; Noel Streatfeild, 1984; Anne Frank, 1984; Florence Nightingale, 1985; Marie Curie, 1986; The Visitors, 1986; A Hat for Emily, 1986; Elizabeth Fry, 1987; A Wish at the Baby's Grave, 1988; Up the Attic Stairs, 1989; The Jiggery-Pokery Cup, 1990; Pink Socks, 1990; The Shadows of Owlsnap, 1992; The Winter Phantoms, 1993; The Kitchen Maid, 1994; Yellow Wellies, 1994; Blue Shoes, 1996; Purple Buttons, 1996; A Patchwork of Ghosts, 1996; The Terrible Birthday Present, 1998; Ghost Hunting, 1998; Time Traveler, Children Through Time, 1999; Flying Ace: The Story of Amelia Earhart, 2000; A Saint in Armor: The Story of Joan of Arc, 2000; Free at Last!: The Story of Martin Luther King, Jr., 2000; Robin Hood: The Tale of the Great Outlaw Hero, 2000. **Address:** c/o Murray Pollinger, Pollinger Ltd., 9 Staple Inn, London, GL WC1V 7QH, England.

BULL, Barry L. American (born United States), b. 1947. **Genres:** Education, Philosophy. **Career:** Teacher, 1972-74; Idaho State Department of Education, statistician and planner, 1974-76; Wellesley College, faculty, 1979-84, assistant professor, 1984-86; Washington State, Council for Postsecondary Education, policy associate, 1984-86; Office of the Superintendent of Public Instruction, program specialist, 1985-86; University of Hawaii, assistant professor, associate professor of education, 1986-89; University of Minnesota, associate professor of education, 1989-90; Indiana University, associate professor, 1990-96, professor of education, 1996-, Indiana Education Policy Center, co-director and director, 1992-97, Department of Educational Leadership and Policy Studies, chair, 1996-98, 2000-06, executive associate dean, 1998-2000, School of Education, executive associate dean, 1998-2000, Policy Council, secretary, Ethics in Teaching Project, director; Indiana Department of Education, Indiana School Funding Issues Group, researcher. Writer. **Publications:** A Study of Initial Teacher Preparation in Washington, 1985; (with R. Fruehling and V. Chatterby) The Ethics of Multicultural and Bilingual Education, 1992; Education in Indiana: An Overview, 1994; (with M. Buechler) Learning Together: Professional Development for Better Schools, 1996; (with M. Buechler) Planning Together: Professional Development for Teachers of All Students, 1997; Social Justice in Education: An Introduction, 2008. **Address:** School of Education, Indiana University, Rm. 4240 W.W. Wright Education Bldg., 201 N Rose Ave., Bloomington, IN 47405-1006, U.S.A. **Online address:** bbull@indiana.edu

BULL, Bartle. American/British (born England), b. 1939. **Genres:** Novels, Travel/Exploration. **Career:** Cadwalader, Wickersham and Taft (law firm), associate, 1967-70; Village Voice, president and publisher, 1970-76, director, 1976-80; New York Magazine, director; Citizens for McGovern/Shriver Campaign, executive director, 1972; Citizens for Hugh Carey for Governor, executive director, 1974; Democratic National Convention, alternate delegate, 1976; New West Magazine, director, 1976-80; St. Bernard's School, vice-president and trustee, 1977-2001; Firehouse Magazine, president and co-founder, 1977-80; Jones Hirsch Connors & Bull P.C., attorney and partner, 1980-. Writer. **Publications:** TRAVEL: Safari: A Chronicle of Adventure, 1988; Around the Sacred Sea: Mongolia and Lake Baikal on Horseback, 1999. NOVELS: The White Rhino Hotel, 1992; A Café on the Nile, 1998; The Devil's Oasis, 2001; Shanghai Station., 2005; China Star, 2006. Contributor to periodicals. **Address:** Jones Hirsch Connors & Bull P.C., 1 Battery Park Plz., 28th Fl., New York, NY 10004, U.S.A. **Online address:** bbull@jhcb.com

BULL, Malcolm. British (born England) **Genres:** History, Theology/Religion. **Career:** University of Oxford, Ruskin School of Drawing and Fine Art, university lecturer, 1992-, head of art history and theory, St. Edmund Hall, fellow; Courtauld Institute, teacher, 2009-10, Clark Fellow, Andrew W. Mellon visiting professor. Historian and writer. **Publications:** (With K. Lockhart) Seeking a Sanctuary: Seventh-Day Adventism and the American Dream, 1989, 2nd ed., 2007; (ed.) Apocalypse Theory and the Ends of the World, 1995; Seeing Things Hidden: Apocalypse, Vision and Totality, 1999; The Mirror of the Gods: How the Renaissance Artists Rediscovered the Pagan Gods, 2005; (with J. Cascardi and T.J. Clark) Nietzsche's Negative Ecologies, 2009. **Address:** The Ruskin School of Drawing & Fine Art, University of Oxford, 74 High St., Oxford, OX OX1 4BG, England. **Online address:** malcolm.bull@ruskin-school.oxford.ac.uk

BULL, Schuyler M. (Minckler). American (born United States), b. 1974. **Genres:** Travel/Exploration, Children's Fiction. **Career:** Soundprints, editorial assistant, 1996-97; Grosset and Dunlap, editorial assistant, 1997-98; Office of Paul Hastings, associate attorney, 2001-03; Friends of the Lawrence Library, president, 2004-07. **Publications:** Through Tsavo: A Story of an East African Savanna, 1998; Along the Luangwa: A Story of an African Floodplain, 1999. **Address:** 1055 Washington Blvd., 10th Fl., Stamford, CT 06901-2216, U.S.A. **Online address:** sky@minckler.org

BULLER, David J. American (born United States), b. 1959?. **Genres:** Psychology, Medicine/Health. **Career:** Northern Illinois University, professor of philosophy, distinguished research professor. Writer. **Publications:** (Ed.) Function, Selection and Design, 1999; Adapting Minds: Evolutionary Psychology and the Persistent Quest for Human Nature, 2005. Contributor of articles to books and journals. **Address:** Department of Philosophy, Northern Illinois University, Zulauf 902, DeKalb, IL 60115, U.S.A. **Online address:** buller@niu.edu

BULLINS, Ed. American (born United States), b. 1935. **Genres:** Novels, Novellas/Short Stories, Plays/Screenplays, Music, Social Sciences. **Career:** Black Arts/West, co-founder and producer, 1965-67; Black Arts Alliance, co-founder, Black House, cultural director, through 1967; New Lafayette Theater, staff, 1967, playwright-in-residence, 1968, associate director, 1971-73; American Place Theater, playwright-in-residence, 1973; The Surviving Theater, producing director, 1974; New York Shakespeare Festival, writers unit coordinator, 1975-83; New York University, School for Continuing Education, instructor, 1979, Department of Dramatic Writing, instructor, 1981; Hofstra University, Summer Playwrights Conference, instructor, 1982; Berkeley Black Repertory, public relations director, 1982; Magic Theater, public relations director, 1982-83; Julian Theatre, group sales coordinator, 1983; People's School of Dramatic Arts, playwriting teacher, 1983; Bay Area Playwrights Festival, summer drama workshop leader, 1983; City College of San Francisco, instructor in dramatic performance, play directing and playwriting, 1984-88; Antioch University, instructor in playwriting and administrative assistant in public information and recruitment, 1986-87; Antioch University, student instructor in playwriting, 1986-87; Bullins Memorial Theater, producer and playwright, 1988; Sonoma State University, Department of American Multicultural Studies, lecturer, 1988-; University of California, Department of Afro-American Studies, lecturer, 1988-; African American Humanities/Afro-American Theater, Contra Costa College, instructor, 1989-94; Northeastern University, Department of Theatre, professor of theater, 1995-; distinguished artist-in-residence, 2006-; Black Theater Magazine, editor; Fordham University, faculty; San Francisco State University, faculty. **Publications:** How Do You Do? A Nonsense Drama (one-act), 1965; Five Plays, 1969 in UK as The Electronic Nigger and Other Plays, 1970; Black Arts, 1969; A Black Quartet, 1970; The Duplex: A Black Love Fable in Four Movements, 1971; The Hungered One: Early Writings (short stories), 1971; Four Dynamite Plays, 1972; The Theme Is Blackness: The Corner and Other Plays, 1972; The Reluctant Rapist (novel), 1973; The House Party Suite, 1973; Famous American Plays of the 1970s, 1981; New/Lost Plays: An Anthology, 1993; Ed Bullins: Twelve Plays & Selected Writings, 2006; Story Ville: A Jazzy Musical of Old New Orleans, 2006. EDITOR AND CONTRIBUTOR: New Plays from tWriters as Teachers, Teachers as Writershe Black Theater, 1969; The New Lafayette Theater Presents: Plays with Aesthetic Comments by Six Black Playwrights, 1974. **Address:** Department of Theatre, Northeastern University, Rm. 180, Ryder Hall, 360 Huntington Ave., Boston, MA 02115, U.S.A. **Online address:** e.bullins@neu.edu

BULLITT, Dorothy. American (born United States), b. 1955. **Genres:** Adult Non-fiction, Autobiography/Memoirs. **Career:** Office of the Washington

State Attorneys General, assistant attorney general, 1980-85; Harbor Properties Inc., chief operating officer, 1985-92; Management consultant and arbitrator, 1993-; University of Washington, Evans School of Public Affairs, distinguished practitioner-in-residence, 2009-. Lawyer and writer. **Publications:** Filling the Void: Six Steps from Loss to Fulfillment, 1996; (with J. Wickwire) Addicted to Danger: A Memoir about Affirming Life in the Face of Death, 1998. Contributor to periodicals. **Address:** Evans School of Public Affairs, University of Washington, Rm. 328, Parrington Hall, PO Box 353055, Seattle, WA 98195-3055, U.S.A. **Online address:** bullid@u.washington.edu

BULLOUGH, Robert V. American (born United States), b. 1949. **Genres:** Education. **Career:** East High School, teacher, 1971-73; Ohio State University, Academic Faculty of Curriculum and Foundations, teaching associate, 1973-75, Graduate School, university fellow, 1975-76; University of Utah, Department of Education, visiting assistant professor, 1976-79, Department of Educational Studies, assistant professor, 1979-83, associate professor, 1983-89, professor of educational studies, 1989-99, emeritus professor, 1999-; Brigham Young University, David O. McKay School of Education, professor of teacher education, 1999-, Center for the Improvement of Teacher Education and Schooling, associate director of research, 2000. Writer. **Publications:** Democracy in Education: Boyd H. Bode, 1981; (with S.L. Goldstein and L. Holt) Human Interests in the Curriculum: Teaching and Learning in a Technological Society, 1984; The Forgotten Dream of American Public Education, 1988; First-Year Teacher: A Case Study, 1989; (with J.G. Knowles and N.A. Crow) Emerging as a Teacher, 1992; (with A.D. Gitlin) Becoming a Student of Teaching: Methodologies for Exploring Self and School Context, 1995, 2nd ed. as Becoming a Student of Teaching: Linking Knowledge Production and Practice, 2001; (ed. with C. Kridel and P. Shaker) Teachers and Mentors: Profiles of Distinguished Twentieth-Century Professors of Education, 1996; (with K. Baughman) First-Year Teacher Eight Years Later: An Inquiry into Teacher Development, 1997; Uncertain Lives: Children of Promise, Teachers of Hope, 2001; (with C. Kridel) Stories of the Eight-Year Study: Reexamining Secondary Education in America, 2007; Counternarratives: Studies of Teacher Education and Becoming and Being a Teacher, 2008; Adam's Fall: Traumatic Brain Injury: The First 365 Days, 2011. **Address:** David O. McKay School of Education, Brigham Young University, 149F MCKB, Provo, UT 84602, U.S.A. **Online address:** bob_bullough@byu.edu

BULOCK, Lynn. American (born United States) **Genres:** Mystery/Crime/Suspense, Romance/Historical, Young Adult Fiction. **Career:** Evangelical Lutheran Church, diaconal minister. Writer. **Publications:** Roses for Caroline, 1989; Tallies Song, 1989; Leave Yesterday Behind, 1990; Kisses Worth Waiting For, 1990; Promise of Summer, 1990; Heart Games, 1991; Sweet Dreams, Serena, 1991; In Your Dreams, 1992; Surprise Package (Under the Mistletoe), 1994; And Mommy Makes Three, 1996; Surrender, 1997; Dalton's Dilemma, 1998; Island Breeze, 1999; Gifts of Grace, 1999; Half the Battle, 1999; Looking for Miracles, 2000; Walls of Jericho, 2001; Prodigals Return, 2001; Change of the Heart, 2002; (with I. Hannon and L. Worth) The Three Gifts, 2002; Harbor of His Arms, 2003; Protecting Holly: Faith on the Line, 2004; Where Truth Lies, 2007; To Trust a Stranger, 2007; To Trust a Friend, 2008. GRACIE LEE HARRIS MYSTERY SERIES: Love the Sinner, 2005; Less Than Frank, 2006; No Love Lost, 2007. **Address:** Harlequin.com, PO Box 5190, Buffalo, NY 14240-5190, U.S.A. **Online address:** lbulock@hotmail.com

BULSON, Eric. American (born United States) **Genres:** Literary Criticism And History, Reference. **Career:** Columbia University, lecturer in English and comparative literature, professor Yale University, faculty. Writer. **Publications:** The Cambridge Introduction to James Joyce, 2006; Novels, Maps, Modernity: The Spatial Imagination, 1850-2000, 2007. **Address:** Yale University, 451 College St., Rm. 102, PO Box 208299, New Haven, CT 06520-8299, U.S.A. **Online address:** eric.bulson@yale.edu

BUMILLER, Elisabeth. Danish (born Denmark), b. 1956. **Genres:** Biography, Documentaries/Reportage. **Career:** The Miami Herald, Gulf Coast Bureau, writer, 1977; Washington Post, Style Section, social and political writer, 1979-84, reporter, 1979-87, New Delhi correspondent, 1985-87, Tokyo correspondent, 1989-91; New York Times, metro staff, 1995-, White House correspondent, 2001-07, Washington Bureau, domestic correspondent. **Publications:** May You Be the Mother of a Hundred Sons: A Journey Among the Women of India, 1990; The Secrets of Mariko: A Year in the Life of a Japanese Woman and Her Family, 1995; (with J. Berman and L. Berman) For Women Only: A Revolutionary Guide to Overcoming Sexual Dysfunction and Reclaiming Your Sex Life, 2001, 2nd ed., 2005; Condoleezza Rice: An American Life: A Biography, 2007. **Address:** New York Times, 229 W 43rd St., New York, NY 10019, U.S.A. **Online address:** bumiller@nytimes.com

BUMSTED, J(ohn) M(ichael). Canadian/American (born United States), b. 1938. **Genres:** History, Education, Biography, Autobiography/Memoirs. **Career:** Tufts University, instructor, 1965-67; McMaster University, assistant professor, 1967-69; Simon Fraser University, associate professor, 1969-75, professor of history, 1975-80; University of Manitoba, professor of history, 1980-, senior fellow. Writer. **Publications:** (Ed.) Documentary Problems in Canadian History, 2 vols., 1969; (ed.) The Great Awakening in Colonial America: The Beginnings of Evangelical Pietism, 1970; Henry Alline 1748-1784, 1971; (ed.) Canadian History before Confederation: Essays and Interpretations, 1972, 2nd ed., 1979; (with J. Van de Wetering) What Must I Do to be Saved?: The Great Awakening in Colonial America, 1976; The People's Clearance: Highland Emigration to British North America, 1770-1815, 1982; (ed. with R. Fisher) An Account of a Voyage to the North West Coast of America in 1785 and 1786, 1982; (ed. and intro.) Writings and Papers of Thomas Douglas, Fifth Earl of Selkirk, 1982; (ed. with R. Fisher) The Journal of Alexander Walker, 1982; (ed.) The Collected Writings of Lord Selkirk 1799-1809, 1984; (ed. with L. Kuffert) Interpreting Canada's Past, 1986, 3rd ed., 2005; Understanding the Loyalists, 1986; Land, Settlement and Politics in 18th Century Prince Edward Island, 1987; The Collected Writings of Lord Selkirk 1810-1820, 1988; The Pilgrim's Progress: The Ecclesiastical History of the Old Colony, 1620-1775, 1989; The Peoples of Canada: A Pre-Confederation History, 1992, 2nd ed., 2003; The Red River Rebellion, 1996; Floods of the Centuries: A History of Flood Disasters in the Red River Valley, 1776-1997, 1997; A History of the Canadian Peoples, 1998, 3rd ed., 2007; The Fur Trade Wars: The Founding of Western Canada, 1999; The Dictionary of Manitoba Biography, 1999; Louis Riel v. Canada: The Making of a Rebel, 2001; Canada's Diverse Peoples: A Reference Source Book, 2003; Trials and Tribulations: The Red River Settlement and the Emergence of Manitoba, 1811-1870, 2003; (with K. Branigan) From Clan to Clearance: History and Archaeology on the Isle of Barra, 850-1850 AD, 2005; St. John's College: Faith and Education in Western Canada, 2006; Lord Selkirk: A Life, 2009. **Address:** Department of History, University of Manitoba, 315 St. John's College, 403 Fletcher Argue Bldg., Winnipeg, MB R3T 5V5, Canada. **Online address:** bumsted@cc.umanitoba.ca

BUNCK, Julie Marie. American (born United States), b. 1960. **Genres:** Politics/Government. **Career:** Colgate University, Department of Political Science, assistant professor, 1987-88; Tufts University, visiting assistant professor, 1988-89; University of Virginia, visiting assistant professor, 1990-92; University of Pennsylvania, visiting assistant professor, 1993-94; University of Louisville, Department of Political Science, professor, 1994-. **Publications:** Fidel Castro and the Quest for a Revolutionary Culture in Cuba, 1994; (with M.R. Fowler) Law, Power, and the Sovereign State: The Evolution and Application of the Concept of Sovereignty, 1995; (with M.R. Fowler) Bribes, Bullets, and Intimidation: Drug Trafficking and the Law in Central America, 2010. **Address:** Department of Political Science, University of Louisville, Rm. 302, Ford Hall, 3rd Fl., Belknap Campus, Louisville, KY 40292, U.S.A. **Online address:** julie@louisville.edu

BUNDESEN, Lynne. American/Norwegian (born Norway), b. 1938. **Genres:** Information Science/Computers, Theology/Religion, Women's Studies And Issues, inspirational/Motivational Literature, Writing/Journalism. **Career:** Hearst Syndicated Newspaper, religion columnist, 1982-87; Isaiah Co., web site consultant and online content manager, 1993-2000; Microsoft Network Religion Communities, manager, 1995-2000; Boston Theological Institute, adjunct professor, 2003; DrWeil.com, communities director and spiritual expert. Journalist, speaker and consultant. **Publications:** SPIRITUAL WRITINGS: God Dependency: Finding Freedom from Codependency and Discovering Spiritual Self-Reliance, 1989; The Woman's Guide to the Bible, 1993; So the Woman Went Her Way: A Personal Journey, 1993; One Prayer at a Time: A Day-to-Day Path to Spiritual Growth, 1995; The Feminine Spirit: Recapturing the Heart of Scripture, 2007. OTHERS: Us, People of Washington, D.C.: A Photostory, 1976; Dear Miss Liberty: Letters to the Statue of Liberty, 1986; Click! 101 Computer Activities and Art Projects for Kids and Grown-Ups, 1997. **Address:** 3101 Old Pecos Trl., Ste. 156, Santa Fe, NM 87505, U.S.A. **Online address:** lynnebundesen@hotmail.com

BUNDEY, Nikki. *See* **STEELE, Philip.**

BUNDLES, A'Lelia Perry. American (born United States), b. 1952. **Genres:** Biography, Autobiography/Memoirs. **Career:** Du Pont Co., staff assistant, 1974-75; NBC News, producer, 1976-89; Radcliffe College, trustee, 1985-89; ABC News, producer for World News Tonight, 1989-96, deputy bureau chief, 1996-99, director of talent development, 2000-; Madam Walker Theatre Center, board director, 1997-; Poynter Institute for Media Studies, visiting faculty. Journalist. **Publications:** Madame C.J. Walker: Cosmetics Tycoon, 1983; Madam C.J. Walker: Entrepreneur, 1991; (foreword) Why Are Black Women Losing Their Hair?: The First Complete Guide to Healthy Hair, 2000; (foreword) Black Hair: Art, Style, and Culture, 2001; On Her Own Ground: The Life and Times of Madam C.J. Walker, 2001; The Walker Women, forthcoming. Contributor to books and periodicals. **Address:** ABC News, 1717 DeSales St. NW, Washington, DC 20036, U.S.A. **Online address:** alelia.bundles@abc.com

BUNDY, Carol. American (born United States), b. 1958?. **Genres:** Biography, History. **Career:** Script writer and biographer. **Publications:** The Nature of Sacrifice: A Biography of Charles Russell Lowell, Jr., 1835-64, 2005. **Address:** c/o Geri Thoma, Markson Thoma Literary Agency, 44 Greenwich Ave., New York, NY 10011-8347, U.S.A. **Online address:** clbundy@verizon.net

BUNGERT, D. Edward. Also writes as Edward Hess, Zach Adams. American (born United States), b. 1957. **Genres:** Novels. **Career:** World-Wide Business Centres, staff, 1977-, vice-president, 1988-. Writer. **Publications:** Deep Cover, 1993; Stranglehold, 1994; (as Zach Adams) Pursuit, 1996; (as Zach Adams) By Any Means Necessary, 2000. **Address:** World-Wide Business Ctr.s, 575 Madison Ave., 10th Fl., New York, NY 10022-2511, U.S.A.

BUNGEY, J. H. *See* **BUNGEY, John Henry.**

BUNGEY, John Henry. (J. H. Bungey). British (born England), b. 1944?. **Genres:** Engineering. **Career:** Scott, Wilson, Kirkpatrick and Partners, assistant, 1966-68; North West Road Construction Unit, Cheshire Sub-Unit, assistant engineer, 1969-71; University of Liverpool, lecturer, 1971-81, senior lecturer, 1981-93, reader, 1993-94, professor in civil engineering, 1994-, now emeritus; Structures and Materials Research Group, department head, 1997-2002; NDT-Titans, British Standards committee, chair. Writer. **Publications:** (With W.H. Mosley) Reinforced Concrete Design, 1976, 4th ed., 1990; The Testing of Concrete in Structures, 1982, (with S.G. Millard and M.G. Grantham) 4th ed., 2006; (with B. Mosley and R. Hulse as John Bungey) Reinforced Concrete Design to Eurocode 2, 2007. **Address:** Department of Civil Engineering, University of Liverpool, Brownlow St., Liverpool, MS L69 3GQ, England. **Online address:** bungey@liv.ac.uk

BUNKERS, Suzanne L. American (born United States), b. 1950. **Genres:** Children's Non-fiction, Education, History, Humanities, Literary Criticism And History, Women's Studies And Issues, Young Adult Non-fiction, Autobiography/Memoirs, Humor/Satire, Biography. **Career:** Minnesota State University, assistant professor, 1980-84, associate professor, 1984-89, professor of English, 1989-, director of university honors program, 1999-2002. Writer. **Publications:** Katherine Anne Porter: A Reassessment, 1980; (with F.W. Klein) Good Earth, Black Soil, 1981; (ed.) Guidebook for Teaching Assistants in English, 1989; In Search of Susanna: An Autobiography, 1996; A Midwestern Farm Girl's Diary, 2000. EDITOR: (and intro.) The Diary of Caroline Seabury, 1954-1863, 1991; All Will Yet Be Well: The Diary of Sarah Gillespie Huftalen, 1873-1952, 1993; (with C.A. Huff) Inscribing the Daily: Critical Essays on Women's Diaries, 1996; (with A. Hodgson) Pioneer Farm Girl: The Diary of Sarah Gillespie, 1877-1878, 2000; Diaries of Girls and Women: A Midwestern American Sampler, 2001; Out of Chaos: Reflections of a University President and His Contemporaries on Vietnam-era Unrest in Mankato and Its Relevance Today, 2006. Works appear in anthologies. **Address:** Department of English, Minnesota State University, 207G Armstrong Hall, 228 Wiecking Ctr., Mankato, MN 56001-6062, U.S.A. **Online address:** suzanne.bunkers@mnsu.edu

BUNT, Gary R. Welsh/British (born England) **Genres:** Theology/Religion, Cultural/Ethnic Topics. **Career:** University of Wales, lecturer in Islamic studies, senior lecturer, 1996-, School of Theology, Religious Studies and Islamic Studies, reader in Islamic studies, programme director of MA Islamic studies and academic coordinator. Writer. **Publications:** Virtually Islamic: Computer-Mediated Communication and Cyber Islamic Environments, 2000; The Good Web Guide to World Religions, 2001; Islam in the Digital Age, 2003; iMuslims: Rewiring The House Of Islam, 2009. Contributor to periodicals and journals. **Address:** School of Theology, Religious Studies and Islamic, Studies, University of Wales, 27 College St., Lampeter, SA48 7ED, Wales. **Online address:** g.bunt@trinitysaintdavid.ac.uk

BUNTING, (Anne) Eve(lyn Bolton). (Evelyn Bolton). American/Irish (born Ireland), b. 1928. **Genres:** Children's Fiction, Young Adult Fiction, Novels, Young Adult Non-fiction, Picture/Board Books. **Career:** Freelance writer, 1969-; University of California, teacher of writing, 1978-79. **Publications:** FICTION: (reteller) The Two Giants, 1971; A Gift for Lonny, 1973; Box, Fox, Ox and the Peacock, 1974; The Wild One, 1974; We Need a Bigger Zoo, 1974; The Once-a-Year Day, 1974; Barney the Beard, 1975; (as A.E. Bunting) High Tide for Labrador, 1975; Josefina Finds the Prince, 1976; Blacksmith at Blue ridge, 1976; Skateboard Saturday, 1976; One More Flight, 1976; Skateboard Four, 1976; Winter's Coming, 1977; The Big Cheese, 1977; Cop Camp, 1977; Ghost of Summer, 1977; The Big Find, 1978; For Always, 1978; Magic and the Night River, 1978; Going against Cool Calvin, 1978; The Haunting of Kildoran Abbey, 1978; The Big Red Barn, 1979; The Cloverdale Switch, 1979 as Strange Things Happen in the Woods, 1984; The Sea World Book of Sharks, 1979; The Sea World Book of Whales, 1979; Yesterday's Island, 1979; Mr. Pride's Umbrella, 1980; The Robot Birthday, 1980; Demetrius and the Golden Goblet, 1980; Terrible Things, 1980, rev. ed. as Terrible Things: An Allegory of the Holocaust, 1989; St. Patrick's Day in the Morning, 1980; Blackbird Singing, 1980; The Empty Window, 1980; The Skate Patrol, 1980; The Giant Squid, 1981; Goose Dinner, 1981; Jane Martin and the Case of the Ice Cream Dog, 1981; Rosie and Mr. William Star, 1981; The Waiting Game, 1981; The Spook Birds, 1981; The Skate Patrol Rides Again, 1982; The Skate Patrol Mystery Writer, 1982; The Happy Funeral, 1982; The Ghosts of Departure Point, 1982; The Great White Shark, 1982; The Traveling Men of Ballycoo, 1983; The Valentine Bears, 1983; Karen Kepplewhite is the World's Best Kisser, 1983; Clancy's Coat, 1984; The Ghost behind Me, 1984; The Man Who Could Call Down Owls, 1984; Monkey in the Middle, 1984; Someone is Hiding on Alcatraz Island, 1984; Mohammed's Monkey, 1984; Jane Martin, Dog Detective, 1984; Surrogate Sister, 1985 in US as Mother, How Could You!, 1987; Face at the Edge of the World, 1985; Janet Hamm Needs a Date for the Dance, 1985; The Mother's Day Mice, 1986; Scary, Scary Halloween, 1986; Sixth-Grade Sleepover, 1986; Ghost's Hour, Spook's Hour, 1987; Will You Be My Posslq?, 1987; Happy Birthday, Dear Duck, 1988; How Many Days to America, 1988; Is Anybody There, 1988; A Sudden Silence, 1988; The Wednesday Surprise, 1989; The Ghost Children, 1989; No Nap, 1989; In the Haunted House, 1990; The Wall, 1990; Such Nice Kids, 1990; Our Sixth Grade Sugar Babies, 1990; Fly Away Home, 1991; A Perfect Father's Day, 1991; The Hideout, 1991; Jumping the Nail, 1991; Night Tree, 1991; Sharing Susan, 1991; A Turkey for Thanksgiving, 1991; The Bicycle Man, 1992; Day before Christmas, 1992; Our Teacher's Having a Baby, 1992; Summer Wheels, 1992; Coffin on a Case, 1992; Just Like Everyone Else, 1992; Nobody Knows but Me, 1992; Eve Bunting Signature Library, 1992; Survival Camp, 1992; Red Fox Running, 1993; Someday a Tree, 1993; A Day's Work, 1994; Flower Garden, 1994; The In-Between Days; 1994; If I Asked, Would You Stay, 1994; Nasty Stinky Sneakers, 1994; Night of the Gargoyles; 1994; Smoky Night, 1994; Sunshine Home, 1994; Spying on Miss Muller, 1995; Cheyenne Again, 1995; Dandelions, 1995; Once Upon a Time, 1995; Market Day, 1996; Sunflower House, 1996; Going Home, 1996; The Blue and the Gray, 1996; Secret Place, 1996; SOS Titanic, 1996; I Don't Want to Go to Camp, 1996; Train to Somewhere, 1996; I am the Mummy Heb-Nefert, 1997; December, 1997; Ducky, 1997; My Backpack, 1997; On Call Back Mountain, 1997; The Christmas House, 1997; Moonstick: The Seasons of the Sioux, 1997; Your Move, 1997; Trouble on the T-Ball Team, 1997; Twinnies, 1997; Some Frog, 1997; The Pumpkin Fair, 1997; The Day the Whale Came, 1998; So Far from the Sea, 1998; Your Move, 1998; Blackwater, 1999; Butterfly House, 1999; Can You Do This, Old Badger?, 1999; Dreaming of America: An Ellis Island Story, 1999; I Have an Olive Tree, 1999; Rudi's Pond, 1999; Dear Wish Fairy, 2000; Doll Baby, 2000; The Memory String, 2000; I Like the Way You are, 2000; Wanna Buy an Alien?, 2000; (with L. Gore) Who Was Born this Special Day?, 2000; Swan in Love, 2000; Peepers, 2000; The Days of Summer, 2001; Too Many Monsters, 2001; Riding the Tiger, 2001; The Summer of Riley, 2001; Jin Woo, 2001; Gleam and Glow, 2001; Little Badger, Terror of the Seven Seas, 2001; We Were There: A Nativity Story, 2001; Little Badger's Just-about Birthday, 2002; Sing a Song of Piglets, 2002; One Candle, 2002; The Bones of Fred McFee, 2002; Christmas Cricket, 2002; Girls: A-Z, 2002; Little Bear's Little Boat, 2003; Whales Passing, 2003; Ana's Table, 2003; My Big Boy Bed, 2003; The Presence, 2003; Snowboarding on Monster Mountain, 2003; The Wedding, 2003; I Love You, Too!, 2004;

My Special Day at Third Street School, 2004; The Lambkins, 2005; My Red Balloon, 2005; That's What Leprechauns Do, 2005; My Mom's Wedding, 2006; My Robot, 2006; One Green Apple, 2006; Our Library, 2006; Pop's Bridge, 2006; Reggie, 2006; Baby Can, 2007; The Baby Shower, 2007; Emma's Turtle, 2007; Hurry! Hurry!, 2007; The Man with the Red Bag, 2007; S is for Shamrock: An Ireland Alphabet, 2007; Walking to School, 2008; I Loved You Before You Were Born, 2008; (with K. Barbour) You were Loved before You were Born, 2008; Mouse Island, 2008; The Banshee, 2009; Will it be a Baby Brother?, 2010; Finn McCool and the Great Fish, 2010; Green Shamrocks, 2011; My Dog Jack is Fat, 2011. AS EVELYN BOLTON: EVELYN BOLTON HORSE BOOK SERIES: Stable of Fear, 1974; Lady's Girl, 1974; Goodbye Charlie, 1974; Ride When You're Ready, 1974; The Wild Horses, 1974; Dream Dancer, 1974. AS A.E. BUNTING: HIGHPOINT SERIES: Pitcher to Center Field, 1974; Surfing Country, 1975; Springboard to Summer, 1975. DINOSAUR MACHINE SERIES: The Day of the Dinosaurs, 1975; Death of a Dinosaur, 1975; The Dinosaur Trap, 1975; Escape from Tyrannosaurus, 1975. NO SUCH THINGS SERIES: The Creature of Cranberry Cove, 1976; The Demon, 1976; The Ghost, 1976; The Tongue of the Ocean, 1976. EVE BUNTING SCIENCE FICTION SERIES: The Day of the Earthlings, 1978; The Followers, 1978; The Island of One, 1978; The Mask, 1978; The Mirror Planet, 1978; The Robot People, 1978; The Space People, 1978; The Undersea People, 1978. EVE BUNTING YOUNG ROMANCE SERIES: Fifteen, 1978; The Girl in the Painting, 1978; Just Like Everyone Else, 1978; Maggie the Freak, 1978; Nobody Knows but Me, 1978; Oh, Rick, 1978; A Part of the Dream, 1978; Survival Camp!, 1978; Two Different Girls, 1978. OTHERS: Seriously Stinky Trainers, 2003; Frog and Friends, 2011; Party at the Pond, 2011; Hey Diddle Diddle, 2011; Pirate Boy, 2011; The Pirate Captain's Daughter, 2011; Tweak Tweak, 2011; The Best Summer Ever, 2012; Ballywhinney Girl: An Irish Mummy, 2012; Voyage of the Sea Wolf, 2012; Big Bear's Big Boat, 2013. **Address:** 1512 Rose Villa St., Pasadena, CA 91106-3525, U.S.A.

BURACK, Elmer H(oward). American (born United States), b. 1927. **Genres:** Administration/Management, Civil Liberties/Human Rights, Social Sciences. **Career:** Booz, Allen and Hamilton, consultant, 1959-60; Illinois Institute of Technology, lecturer, 1960-64, associate professor, 1964-68, professor of management, 1966-77, head of department, 1969-71; National Academy of Management, Personnel and Human Resource Division, chairman, 1975, Health Care Division, chairman, 1977; Illinois Management Training Institute, president, co-founder, 1977-78; University of Illinois, Department of Management, professor, 1977-, head, 1978-83, College of Business Administration, director of doctoral studies, 1990-96, now professor emeritus; Midwest Human Resources Group, co-founder and director, 1981-95. Writer. **Publications:** Strategies for Manpower Planning and Programming, 1972; (ed. with J.W. Walker) Manpower planning and programming, 1972; (co-author) Human Resource Planning: Technology, Policy, Change, 1973; Organization Design, 1973; Organization Analysis, 1975; (with R.D. Smith) Personnel Management, 1977; (ed. with A.R. Negandhi)Organizational Design: Theoretical Perspectives and Empirical Findings, 1977; The Manager's Guide to Change, 1979; (with N.J. Mathys) Human Resource Planning, 1980, 4th ed., 2001; Career Management in Organizations, 1980; (with M. Albrecht and H. Seitler) Growing: A Woman's Guide to Career Satisfaction, 1980; (ed. with E.L. Miller and M.H. Albrecht) Management of Human Resources, 1980; Personnel Management, 1982; Introduction to Management, 1983; Creative Human Resource Planning, 1988; Corporate Resurgence and the New Employment Relationships, 1993; Retiring Retirement, 2002. **Address:** College of Business Administration, University of Illinois, 1118 University Hall, 601 S Morgan St., Chicago, IL 60607, U.S.A. **Online address:** elmerbur@uic.edu

BURAK, Carl S. American (born United States), b. 1942. **Genres:** Medicine/Health, Biography, Autobiography/Memoirs, Psychology. **Career:** American College of Legal Medicine, fellow; American Psychiatric Association, fellow; University of Florida, College of Medicine, clinical faculty; Indian Hospital, chief of medicine; Burak Inc., staff. Writer and psychiatrist. **Publications:** (With M.G. Remington) The Cradle Will Fall, 1994; When I Became a Psychiatrist, People Stopped Waving on Main Street: A Medical Conversation, 2006; Assholistic Healthcare, 2010. **Address:** 482 Jacksonville Dr., Jacksonville Beach, FL 32250, U.S.A.

BURAYIDI, Michael A. American/Ghanaian (born Ghana), b. 1958. **Genres:** Race Relations, Anthropology/Ethnology. **Career:** University of Science and Technology, instructor; University of Louisville, instructor; University of Wisconsin, professor, 1994-2009; Ball State University, Department of Urban Planning, professor and chairperson. Writer. **Publications:** Multiculturalism in a Cross-National Perspective, 1997; (with A.T. Kisubi) Race and Ethnic Relations in the First Person, 1998. EDITOR: Urban Planning in a Multicultural Society, 2000; Downtowns: Revitalizing the Centers of Small Urban Communities, 2001. **Address:** College of Architecture and Planning, Ball State University, Rm. 104, Architecture Bldg. (AB), Muncie, IN 47306, U.S.A. **Online address:** maburayidi@bsu.edu

BURCH, Geoff. British (born England), b. 1951. **Genres:** Administration/Management, Business/Trade/Industry. **Career:** Sales Coach, founder; ADT Security, consultant; Sears, consultant; Tandem Computers, consultant; Lloyds Bank, consultant; Barclays Bank, consultant; Prudential, consultant; Toshiba, consultant. Writer. **Publications:** Resistance Is Useless, 1994 in US as The Art and Science of Business Persuasion: Mastering the Power of Getting What You Want, 1996; Writing on the Wall: A Campaign for Commonsense Business, 2002; Go It Alone: Streetwise Secrets of Self Employment, 2003; The Way of the Dog, 2005; Irresistible Persuasion-the Secret Way to Get to Yes Every Time, 2010. Contributor to periodicals. **Address:** Hampton Garden Cottage, 94A Leckhampton Rd., Cheltenham, GC GL53 0BN, England. **Online address:** geoff@geoffburch.com

BURCH, Joann J(ohansen). American (born United States) **Genres:** Children's Non-fiction, Travel/Exploration, Biography, History, Autobiography/Memoirs. **Career:** Writer and educator. **Publications:** Fine Print: A Story about Johann Gutenberg, 1991; Isabella of Castile: Queen on Horseback, 1991; Kenya: Africa's Tamed Wilderness, 1992, 2nd ed., 1997; A Fairy-tale Life: A Story about Hans Christian Andersen, 1994; Marian Wright Edelman: Children's Champion, 1994; Chico Mendes: Defender of the Rain Forest, 1994; Jefferson Davis: President of the Confederacy, 1998. Contributor of articles to periodicals, newspapers and magazines. **Address:** 1301 Delresto Dr., Beverly Hills, CA 90210-2100, U.S.A. **Online address:** joannburch@msn.com

BURCHARD, Brendon. American (born United States) **Genres:** Education, Novels. **Career:** Accenture, business consultant. Writer and motivational speaker. **Publications:** The Student Leadership Guide, 2nd ed., 2003; Life's Golden Ticket: An Inspirational Novel, 2007; The Millionaire Messenger: Make a Difference and a Fortune Sharing your Advice, 2011. Contributor to periodicals. **Address:** The Burchard Group, PO Box 5368, Portland, OR 97228, U.S.A. **Online address:** author@lifesgoldenticket.com

BURCHARDT, Jeremy. British (born England), b. 1969. **Genres:** History, Politics/Government. **Career:** University of Reading, lecturer in rural history and coordinator, 1997-; Interwar Rural History Research Group, creator and chair, 2000. Writer. **Publications:** The Allotment Movement in England, 1793-1873, 2002; Paradise Lost: Rural Idyll and Social Change in England since 1800, 2002; (ed. with P. Brassley and L. Thompson) The English Countryside between the Wars: Regeneration or Decline?, 2006; (ed. with P. Conford) The Contested Countryside: Rural Politics and Land Controversy in Modern Britain, 2008. Contributor to journals. **Address:** Department of History, University of Reading, PO Box 217, Whiteknights, Reading, BR RG6 6AH, England. **Online address:** j.f.s.burchardt@rdg.ac.uk

BURCHELL, R(obert) A(rthur). British (born England), b. 1941?. **Genres:** History, Social Sciences, Autobiography/Memoirs. **Career:** Victoria University of Manchester, assistant lecturer, 1965-68, lecturer, 1968-80, senior lecturer in American history and institutions, 1980-91, head of department, 1989-93, professor of American studies, 1991-96; The Eccles Centre for American Studies, director, editor of the ASE Newsletter, 1991-. Writer. **Publications:** (Ed.) Westward Expansion, 1974; The San Francisco Irish 1848-80, 1980; (ed.) The End of Anglo-America: Historical Essays in the Study of Cultural Divergence, 1991; Harriet Martineau and America, 1995. **Address:** Eccles Centre for American Studies, The British Library, 96 Euston Rd., London, GL NW1 2DB, England. **Online address:** bob.burchell@bl.uk

BURCHILL, Julie. British (born England), b. 1959. **Genres:** Novels, Plays/Screenplays, Young Adult Non-fiction. **Career:** New Musical Express, journalist, 1976-81; London Daily Mail, journalist; The Guardian, journalist, 1998-2003; Sunday Times, film critic, 1984-86; The Modern Review, founding co-editor, 1991; Punch Magazine, staff; Spectator, staff; The Independent, columnist. **Publications:** (With T. Parsons) The Boy Looked at Johnny: The Obituary of Rock and Roll, 1978; Love It or Shove It, 1985; Damaged Gods: Cults and Heroes Reappraised, 1986; Girls on Film, 1986; Ambition (novel),

1989; Sex and Sensibility, 1992; No Exit (novel) 1993; Diana, 1998; I Knew I was Right, 1998; Married Alive (novel), 1999; The Guardian Columns, 1998-2000, 2001; On Beckham, 2001; Sugar Rush, 2004; (with D. Raven) Made in Brighton: From the Grand to the Gutter: Modern Britain as Seen from Beside the Sea, 2007; (with C. Newkey-Burden) Not In My Name: A Compendium of Modern Hypocrisy, 2008. Contributor to periodicals. **Address:** Capel & Land Ltd., 29 Wardour St., London, GL W1D 6PS, England. **Online address:** mail@julieburchill.org.uk

BURDEKIN, Richard C.K. American/British (born England), b. 1958. **Genres:** Economics. **Career:** University of Miami, assistant professor of economics, 1986-89; Claremont McKenna College, assistant professor, 1989-92, associate professor, 1992-99, professor, 1999-2003, department chair, 2002-05, Jonathan B. Lovelace professor of economics, 2003-. Writer and economist. **Publications:** (With F.K. Langdana) Budget Deficits and Economic Performance, 1992; (with F.K. Langdana) Confidence, Credibility, and Macroeconomic Policy: Past, Present, Future, 1995; (With T.D. Willett, R.J. Sweeney and C. Wihlborg) Establishing Monetary Stability in Emerging Market Economies, 1995; (with P. Burkett) Distributional Conflict and Inflation: Theoretical and Historical Perspectives, 1996; (ed. with P.L. Skilos) Deflation: Current and Historical Perspectives, 2004; Volatility in an Era of Reduced Uncertainty: Lessons from Pax Britannica, 2005; China's Monetary Challenges: Past Experiences and Future Prospects, 2008. Contributor to journals. **Address:** Robert Day School of Economics and Finance, Claremont McKenna College, 500 E 9th St., Claremont, CA 91711, U.S.A. **Online address:** richard.burdekin@claremontmckenna.edu

BURDEN, Barry C. American (born United States), b. 1971. **Genres:** Politics/Government. **Career:** Louisiana State University, assistant professor of political science, 1998-99; Institute for Quantitative Social Science, faculty associate, 1999-2006; Harvard University, Department of Government, assistant professor, 1999-2003, associate professor, 2003-06; Center for Basic Research in the Social Sciences, faculty associate, 2003-; Program on US-Japan Relations, faculty affiliate, 2004-06; Weatherhead Center for International Affairs, faculty associate, 2005-06; University Wisconsin, professor of political science, 2006-, associate chair and director of graduate studies, 2007-12, College of Letters and Science, Hamel Family faculty fellow, 2008-13, Graduate School, H. I. Romnes faculty fellow, 2010-15; La Follette School of Public Affairs, faculty associate, 2007-; Election Administration Project, co-founder, 2008-. Writer. **Publications:** (With D.C. Kimball) Why Americans Split Their Tickets: Campaigns, Competition and Divided Government, 2002; (ed.) Uncertainty in American Politics, 2003; Personal Roots of Representation, 2007. Contributor to periodicals. **Address:** Department of Political Science, University Wisconsin, 301 North Hall, 1050 Bascom Mall, Madison, WI 53706-1316, U.S.A. **Online address:** bcburden@wisc.edu

BURDEN, Matthew Currier. American (born United States), b. 1967?. **Genres:** Military/Defense/Arms Control. **Career:** Defense Intelligence Agency, intelligence officer. Writer. **Publications:** The Blog of War: Front-Line Dispatches from Soldiers in Iraq and Afghanistan, 2006. **Address:** Simon & Schuster Inc., 1230 Ave. of the Americas, 11th Fl., New York, NY 10020-1513, U.S.A. **Online address:** matt.burden@gmail.com

BURDEN, Wendy. American (born United States), b. 1955. **Genres:** Autobiography/Memoirs. **Career:** Chez Wendy, owner and chef. Writer. **Publications:** Dead End Gene Pool: A Memoir, 2010. Contributor to periodicals. **Address:** c/o Kimberly Witherspoon, InkWell Management, 521 5th Ave., New York, NY 10175, U.S.A.

BURDETT, John. British (born England), b. 1951. **Genres:** Novels, Literary Criticism And History, Young Adult Fiction. **Career:** Barrister at law; Government of Hong Kong, Attorney General's Department, barrister; Johnson, Stokes and Master, partner. Writer. **Publications:** NOVELS: A Personal History of Thirst, 1996; The Last Six Million Seconds, 1997; Bangkok 8, 2003; Bangkok Tattoo, 2005; Bangkok Haunts, 2007; The Godfather of Kathmandu, 2010. Contributor to periodicals. **Address:** 2 Old Brompton Rd., Ste. 241, London, GL SW7 3DQ, England.

BURFIELD, Eva. *See* **EBBETT, Eve.**

BURG, Shana. American (born United States), b. 1968. **Genres:** Novels. **Career:** Author and educator. **Publications:** A Thousand Never Evers (novel), 2008; Laugh with the Moon (novel), 2012. **Address:** Austin, TX , U.S.A. **Online address:** shana@shanaburg.com

BURG, Steven L. American (born United States), b. 1950. **Genres:** Politics/Government, Adult Non-fiction, History, Social Commentary. **Career:** Brandeis University, Department of Politics, lecturer, 1979-80, assistant professor, 1980-86, associate professor of political science, 1986-, Adlai Stevenson professor of international politics, Research Circle on Democracy and Cultural Pluralism Program, director, College of Arts and Sciences, dean, 1990-92; Harvard University, fellow, 1984. Writer. **Publications:** Conflict and Cohesion in Socialist Yugoslavia: Political Decision Making since 1966, 1978; The Political Integration of Yugoslavia's Muslims: Determinants of Success and Failure, 1983; (with R.C. Macridis) Introduction to Comparative Politics: Regimes and Change, 1991; War or Peace?: Nationalism, Democracy, and American Foreign Policy in Post-Communist Europe, 1996; The New York Roundtable: Toward Peaceful Accommodation in Kosovo: April 7-9, 1997, 1997; (with P.S. Shoup) The War in Bosnia-Herzegovina: Ethnic Conflict and International Intervention, 1999; State Policies Toward the Roma in Macedonia, 2001; Albanians and Their Neighbors: Moving Toward Real Communication, 2004; Macedonia: On the Road to Brussels, Mavrovo, Macedonia, June 10-11, 2005, 2005. Contributor to journals. **Address:** Department of Politics, Brandeis University, 108 Olin-Sang, 415 South St., PO Box 058, Waltham, MA 02453-2728, U.S.A. **Online address:** burg@brandeis.edu

BURGER, Joanna. American (born United States), b. 1941. **Genres:** Biology, Environmental Sciences/Ecology, Marine Sciences/Oceanography, Natural History, Zoology, Animals/Pets. **Career:** State University of New York College, instructor in biology, ecology and comparative anatomy, 1964-68; University of Minnesota, Department of Ecology and Behavior Biology, teaching assistant, 1968-72; Rutgers University-Newark, Institute of Animal Behavior, postdoctoral research fellow and research associate, 1972-73; Rutgers University-Piscataway, assistant professor, 1973-76, associate professor, 1976-81, professor of biological sciences, 1981-, distinguished professor of biology, ecology and evolution, Ecology Graduate Program, director, 1978-92, Department of Biological Sciences, associate chair for research, 1983-88, associate chair of biological sciences for graduate affairs, 1994-96; Cornell University, Shoals Marine Laboratory, associate professor, 1979; University of Medicine and Dentistry of New Jersey, School of Public Health, faculty, 2001-. Writer. **Publications:** SELF-ILLUSTRATED: A Naturalist along the Jersey Shore, 1996; Animals in Towns and Cities, 1999; Whispers in the Pines: A Naturalist in the Northeast, 2006. OTHERS: Pattern, Mechanism, and Adaptive Significance of Territoriality in Herring Gulls (Larus argentatus) (monograph), 1984; (with M. Gochfeld) The Black Skimmer: Social Dynamics of a Colonial Species, 1990; (with M. Gochfeld) The Common Tern: Its Breeding Biology and Social Behavior, 1991; Oil Spills, 1997; (with M. Gochfeld) Butterflies of New Jersey, 1997; (with M. Gochfeld) Twenty-Five Nature Spectacles in New Jersey, 2000; The Parrot Who Owns Me, 2001; Birds: A Visual Guide, 2006; (with R.T. Zappalorti) The Northern Pine Snake (Pituophis Melanoleucus), 2011; Stakeholders and Scientists, 2011; (with L. Niles and A. Dey) Life along the Delaware Bay, 2012. EDITOR: (with B.L. Olla) Behavior of Marine Animals: Perspectives in Research, 1972, (and H. Winn) vol. IV: Marine Birds, 1980, vol. V: Breeding Behavior and Populations, 1984, vol. VI: Migration and Foraging Behavior, 1984; Seabirds and Other Marine Vertebrates: Competition, Predation, and Other Interactions, 1988; Anatomy of an Oil Spill: The Arthur Kill, 1990; (with D.N. Nettleship and M. Gochfeld) Seabirds on Islands: Threats, Case Studies and Action Plans, 1994; Before and After an Oil Spill: The Arthur Kill, 1994; (co-ed.) Protecting the Commons: A Framework for Resource Management in the Americas, 2001; (with E.A. Schreiber) Biology of Marine Birds, 2002. Contributor to journals and magazines. **Address:** Department of Cell Biology & Neuroscience, Rutgers University, Rm. B218, Nelson Bio Lab Bldg., 604 Allison Rd., Piscataway, NJ 08854-6999, U.S.A. **Online address:** burger@biology.rutgers.edu

BURGER, Michael. American (born United States), b. 1962. **Genres:** History. **Career:** University of California, teaching assistant, 1984-91, associate in history, 1989, lecturer in history, 1991-92; Mississippi University for Women, assistant professor of history, 1992-97, associate professor of history, 1997-2000, professor of history, 2000-, History Program, coordinator, 2003-05, Department of History, Political Science, Geography and Paralegal Studies, chair, 2005-08, Department of History, Political Science and Geography, chair, 2008; Auburn University, dean of liberal arts, 2009-. Writer. **Publications:** Commentaries on Sources for the History of Western Civilization, With Questions for Students, 2003; (ed.) Sources for the History of Western Civilization, 2003; The Shaping of the West: From Antiquity to the Enlightenment,

2008. **Address:** Dept. of History, Poli. Science & Geography, Mississippi University for Women, Rm. MUW-1634, 1100 College St., Columbus, MS 39701-5800, U.S.A. **Online address:** mburger@muw.edu

BÜRGER, Peter. German (born Germany), b. 1936. **Genres:** Literary Criticism And History, Translations. **Career:** University of Lyon, lecturer in German language and literature, 1961-63; University of Bonn, assistant in French literature, 1964-70; University of Erlangen, assistant professor, 1970-71; University of Bremen, professor of French and comparative literature, 1971-. Writer. **Publications:** Der Französische Surrealismus, 1971, 2nd ed., 1995; Theorie der Avantgarde, 1974, 9th ed., 1993, trans. as Theory of the Avant-Garde, 1984; Vom ästhetizismus zum Nouveau Roman: Versuche Kritischer Literaturwissenschaft, 1975; Aktualität und Geschichtlichkeit: Studienzum Gesellschaftl, Funktionswandel d. Literatur, 1977; Seminar Literatur-und Kunstsoziologie, 1978; Vermittlung, Rezeption, Funktion: ästhetische Theorie u. Methodologie d. Literaturwissenschaft, 1979; (ed. with C. Bürger and J.S. Sasse) Naturalismus, ästhetizismus, 1979; (co-author) Zur Dichotomisierung Von Hoher und Niederer Literatur, 1982; (contrib.) Surrealismus, 1982; Zum Funktionswandel Der Literatur, 1983; Zur Kritikder Idealistischen ästhetik, 1983; Theory of the Avant-garde, 1984; The Decline of Modernism, 1992; (with C. Bürger) The Institutions of Art, 1992. IN GERMAN: Zur Kritik der Idealistischen Aesthetik, 1983; (with C. Bürger) Postmoderne: Alltag, Allegorie, und Avantgarde, 1987; (with C. Bürger) Prosa der Moderne, 1988, 2nd ed., 1992; Das Denken des Herrn: Bataille Zwischen Hegel und Dem Surrealismus: Essays, 1992; Thinking of the Master: Bataille between Hegel and Surrealism, 1992, rev. ed., 2002; Träenen des Odysseus (title means: 'The Tears of Ulysses'), 1993; (co-author) Rolf Iseli, 1993; (co-author) Kunst Ohne Geschichte?: Ansichten zu Kunst und Kunstgeschichte Heute, 1995; DasVerschwinden des Subjekts: Eine Geschichte der Subjektivitat Von Montaignebis Barthes, 1998; Ursprung des postmodernen Denkens, 2000; (co-author) Das Ich ist Etwas Anderes: Kunst am Ende des 20, 2000; Francis Bacon: Die Gewalt Des Faktischen, 2006; Joseph Beuys: Die Materialien und Ihre Botschaft, 2006. **Address:** University of Bremen, Bibliothekstrabe 1, Bremen, 28359, Germany.

BURGES, Dennis. American (born United States) **Genres:** Mystery/Crime/Suspense, Novels. **Career:** Longwood University, lecturer, professor of English. Writer. **Publications:** Graves Gate, 2003; Unspeakable, forthcoming. **Address:** c/o Jeff Gerecke, Gina Maccoby Literary Agency, PO Box 60, Chappaqua, NY 10514-0060, U.S.A. **Online address:** dennis@dennisburges.com

BURGESS, Charles. American (born United States), b. 1932. **Genres:** History, Biography. **Career:** University of California, assistant professor of history of education, 1962-64; University of Washington, assistant professor, 1964-66, associate professor, 1966-70, chairman of educational policy studies and professor of history of education, 1970-; Harvard University, National post-doctoral fellow, 1967-68; History of Education Society, president, 1971-72; American Educational Research Association, Division F, president, 1977-79; People's Republic of China, foreign expert, 1984-85. Writer. **Publications:** Nettie Fowler McCormick: Profile of an American Philanthropist, 1962; (ed., intro. and contrib. with C. Strickland) Health, Growth and Heredity: G. Stanley Hall on Natural Education, 1965; (with M.L. Borrowman) What Doctrines to Embrace: Studies in the History of American Education, 1969; Drama, 1969; Western Ideas and the Shaping of America, 1985. **Address:** 2111 SW 174th St., Seattle, WA 98166-3529, U.S.A.

BURGESS, Colin. Australian (born Australia), b. 1947?. **Genres:** Young Adult Fiction, Adult Non-fiction, Children's Fiction, Technology, Astronomy, Physics. **Career:** Qantas Airways, customer service manager, flight service director, 1970-, now retired. Writer. **Publications:** More Laughter in the Air: Further Tales from the Qantas Era, 1992; (with H.V. Clarke) Barbed Wire and Bamboo: Australian POWs in Europe, 1992; Freedom or Death: Australia's Greatest Escape Stories from Two World Wars, 1994; Destination Buchenwald, 1995; Oceans to Orbit: The Story of Australia's First Man in Space: Dr. Paul Scully-Power, 1995; (with J. Champ) The Diggers of Colditz: The Classic Australian POW Escape Story Now Completely Revised and Expanded, 1997; Australia's Astronauts: Three Men and a Spaceflight Dream, 1999; Teacher in Space: Christa McAuliffe and the Challenger Legacy, 2000; (with K. Doolan and B. Vis) Fallen Astronauts: Heroes Who Died Reaching for the Moon, 2003; Australia's Dambusters: The Men and Missions of 617 Squadron, 2003; (with C. Baker) How Wickie Saved the World (for children), 2006; (with F. French) Into That Silent Sea: Trailblazers of the Space Era, 1961-1965, 2007; (with F. French) In the Shadow of the Moon: A Challenging Journey to Tranquility, 1965-1969, 2007; (with D.J. Shayler) NASA's Scientist-Astronauts, 2007; Bush Parker: An Australian Battle of Britain Pilot in Colditz, 2007; (with C. Dubbs) Animals in Space: From Research Rockets to the Space Shuttle, 2007; (with R. Hall) First Soviet Cosmonaut Team: Their Lives, Legacy, and Historical Impact, 2009; (ed.) Footprints in the Dust, 2010; Selecting the Mercury Seven, 2011. **Address:** University of Nebraska Press, 1111 Lincoln Mall, Lincoln, NE 68588-0630, U.S.A.

BURGESS, Dean. American (born United States), b. 1937. **Genres:** Novels, History. **Career:** Portsmouth Public Library, clerk, 1963-65, assistant director, 1965-74, director, 1974-96; National Library Week for the American Library Association, chairman. Writer. **Publications:** Getting It Passed: Lobbying for Libraries, 1984; An Unclean Act, 2002; A History of Portsmouth, Virginia, 2007. FORTHCOMING: Death of a Drowned Man; Smoke On Water; All Problems Resolved Through Creative Reasoning. **Address:** Red Lion Square Studios, PO Box 126, Portsmouth, VA 23705-0126, U.S.A. **Online address:** redlion3@juno.com

BURGESS, Granville Wyche. American (born United States), b. 1947. **Genres:** Plays/Screenplays, Songs/Lyrics And Libretti, Children's Fiction. **Career:** Central State University, artist-in-residence, 1985-87; Walnut Street Theatre, director of theatre school, 1988-95; Columbia Broadcasting System, staff writer; Capitol (soap opera), staff writer. **Publications:** The Freak (three-act play), 1983; Dusky Sally (play), 1987; Conrack (musical), 1992; Te Death of Dracula, 1997; A Country Carol (musical), 1998; Play It as It Lies (play), 2004. Contributor to periodicals. **Address:** GB Productions Inc., 983 N St., Greenwich, CT 06831, U.S.A. **Online address:** gbprodinc@optonline.net

BURGESS, Melvin. British (born England), b. 1954. **Genres:** Novels, Mystery/Crime/Suspense. **Career:** Writer. **Publications:** The Cry of the Wolf, 1990; Burning Issy, 1992; An Angel for May, 1992; The Baby and Fly Pie, 1993; Loving April, 1995; The Earth Giant, 1995; Junk, 1996; Tiger, Tiger, 1996; Kite, 1997; Smack, 1998; Bloodtide, 1999; Old Bag, 1999; Copper Treasure, 2000; Ghost Behind the Wall, 2001; Billy Elliot: A Novel, 2001; Lady: My Life as a Bitch, 2001; Doing It, 2003; Bloodsong, 2005; (co-author) Shining On, 2006; Sara's Face, 2007; Nicholas Dane, 2010; Kill All Enemies, 2011. **Address:** 4 Hartley St., Garby, BB8 GNL, England. **Online address:** melvin.burgess@ntlworld.com

BURGESS, Michael. *See* **REGINALD, Robert.**

BURGESS, Patricia. American (born United States), b. 1947. **Genres:** Regional/Urban Planning, Business/Trade/Industry, Sciences. **Career:** Journal of the American Planning Association, managing editor, 1978-83; Illinois State University, assistant professor of history, 1988-89; University of Texas, assistant professor of urban and public affairs, 1989-91; Iowa State University, assistant professor, 1991-94, associate professor of community and regional planning, 1994-95; Cleveland State University, Urban Center Maxine Goodman Levin College of Urban Affairs, director planning and urban design services. Writer. **Publications:** Planning for the Private Interest: Land Use Controls and Residential Patterns in Columbus, Ohio, 1900-70, 1994. Contributor of articles to books and journals. **Address:** Cleveland State University, 2121 Euclid Ave., UR 335, Cleveland, OH 44115-2214, U.S.A.

BURGESS, Robert J(ohn). American (born United States), b. 1961. **Genres:** Business/Trade/Industry, Biography. **Career:** United Bank of Colorado, analyst, 1984-85; Coors Brewing, senior analyst, 1985-88; U.S. West Telecommunications, marketing analyst, 1988-91; Marketing Advocates Inc., founder, 1990, president, 1991-; University of Denver, adjunct faculty, 1991-; University of Colorado-Denver, adjunct faculty, 1991-; Denver Entrepreneurship Academy, board director, small business counselor, 1992-. Writer. **Publications:** Silver Bullets: A Soldier's Story of How Coors Bombed the Beer Wars, 1993. Contributor to journals. **Address:** Marketing Advocates Inc., 6901 S Pierce St., Ste. 370, Littleton, CO 80128, U.S.A. **Online address:** rburgess@marketingadvocates.com

BURGESS, Stephen F(ranklin). American (born United States), b. 1952. **Genres:** International Relations/Current Affairs, Politics/Government. **Career:** University of Zambia, lecturer in development studies, 1980-82; Vanderbilt University, instructor in political science, 1991-92; Hofstra University, assistant professor of political science, 1992-99; United States Air Force's Air University, Air War College, Department of International Security, assistant professor, 1999-, associate professor, professor, chair; U.S. Air Force

Counter-Proliferation Center, associate director; University of Zimbabwe, faculty. Writer. **Publications:** Smallholders and Political Voice in Zimbabwe, 1997; The United Nations under Boutros Boutros-Ghali, 1992-1997, 2001; (with H. Purkitt) The Rollback of South Africa's Chemical and Biological Warfare Program, 2001; India's Emerging Security Strategy, Missile Defense, and Arms Control, 2004; (with H.E. Purkitt) South Africa's Weapons of Mass Destruction, 2005. **Address:** Department of International Security, Air War College, United States Air Force's Air University, 325 Chennault Cir., Maxwell AFB, AL 36112-6006, U.S.A. **Online address:** stvburgess@aol.com

BURGH, Anita Lorna. British (born England), b. 1937. **Genres:** Novels, Mystery/Crime/Suspense, Young Adult Fiction, Romance/Historical. **Career:** Novelist, 1987-. **Publications:** Distinctions of Class, 1987; Love: The Bright Foreigner, 1988; The Azure Bowl, 1989; The Golden Butterfly, 1990; Hectors Hobbies, 1991; Mollys Flashings, 1991; The Stone Mistress, 1991; Advances, 1992; Tales fron Sarson Magna: Molley's Flashings, 1992; Overtures, 1993; Avarice, 1994; The Cult, 1997; Lottery, 1998; On Call, 1998; Breeders, 1999; Clare's War, 2000; The Family, 2000; Exiles, 2001; The House at Harcourt, 2002; The Visitor, 2003; The Broken Gate, 2004; The Heart's Citadel, 2005; The Breached Wall, 2007. **Address:** Mic Cheetham Agency, 50 Albemarle St., London, GL W1S 4BD, England.

BURGHARDT, Linda. American (born United States) **Genres:** Travel/Exploration, Humor/Satire, Reference, Social Sciences. **Career:** Burghardt Communications, founder. Journalist. **Publications:** Jewish Holiday Traditions, 2001; The Happy Empty Nest: Rediscovering Love and Success after Your Kids Leave Home, 2002; The Bar and Bat Mitzvah Book: Joyful Ceremonies and Celebrations for Today's Families, 2004. Contributor to periodicals. **Address:** c/o Author Mail, Kensington Publishing Corp., 850 3rd Ave., New York, NY 10022, U.S.A.

BURGOS, Adrian. American (born United States), b. 1969. **Genres:** History. **Career:** University of Illinois, assistant professor, 2001-07, associate professor of history, 2007-. Writer. **Publications:** Playing America's Game: Baseball, Latinos, and the Color Line, 2004. Contributor of articles to periodicals. **Address:** University of Illinois, 309 Gregory Hall, 810 S Wright St., PO Box 466, Urbana, IL 61801, U.S.A. **Online address:** burgosjr@illinois.edu

BURK, Frank. American (born United States), b. 1942. **Genres:** Mathematics/Statistics, Sciences. **Career:** California State University, mathematics faculty, now retired. Writer. **Publications:** Lebesgue Measure and Integration: An Introduction, 1998; A Garden of Integrals, 2007. **Address:** Department of Mathematics, California State University, Chico, CA 95929, U.S.A. **Online address:** fburk@csuchico.edu

BURK, Josh D. American (born United States), b. 1985. **Genres:** Education. **Career:** Maven of Memory Publishing, director of marketing and development, 2007-; Delph Town Productions, executive director; Sky Ranches Inc., marketing coordinator; 94.9 FM KLTY, promotions intern. Writer. **Publications:** The Summer of Saint Nick, 2007; I. M. for Murder, 2008. **Address:** Maven of Memory Publishing, 400 Woodland Ct., Hurst, TX 76053, U.S.A. **Online address:** josh@vocabcafe.com

BURK, Kathleen. British/American (born United States), b. 1946. **Genres:** History, International Relations/Current Affairs, Money/Finance, Politics/Government, Biography, Food And Wine. **Career:** University of Dundee, tutorial assistant in modern history, 1976-77; University of London, Imperial College of Science and Technology, lecturer in history and politics, 1980-90; University College London, lecturer in history, 1990-93, reader in modern and contemporary history, 1993-95, professor of modern and contemporary history, 1995-; Historians Press, chairman; Galleant Investments Ltd., chairman; Long Wittenham Local History Group, chairman. Writer. **Publications:** Britain, America and the Sinews of War, 1914-1918, 1985; The First Privatisation: The Politicians, the City, and the Denationalisation of Steel, 1988; Morgan Grenfell, 1838-1988: The Biography of a Merchant Bank, 1989; (with A. Cairncross) Goodbye, Great Britain: The 1976 IMF Crisis, 1992; (with M. Pohl) Deutsche Bank in London 1873-1998, 1998; Troublemaker: The Life and History of A.J.P. Taylor, 2000; Old World, New World: The Story of Britain and America, 2007; (with M. Bywater) Is This Bottle Corked? The Secret Life of Wine, 2008. EDITOR: War and the State: The Transformation of British Government, 1914-1919, 1982; (with M. Stokes) The United States and the European Alliance since 1945, 1999; The British Isles since 1945, 2003. Contributor to journals. **Address:** Department of History, University College London, Rm. 106, 24 Gordon Sq., Gower St., London, GL WC1E 6BT, England. **Online address:** k.burk@ucl.ac.uk

BURK, Robert F(rederick). American (born United States), b. 1955. **Genres:** Politics/Government, Sports/Fitness, Biography, Recreation, Young Adult Non-fiction, History, Social Sciences. **Career:** University of Wisconsin, lecturer in history, 1983; University of Cincinnati, visiting assistant professor of history, 1983-84; Muskingum College, assistant professor, 1984-89, associate professor of history, 1989-95, chairman of history department, 1992-2003, professor of history, 1995-, college archivist, 1988-94, Cole distinguished professor of American history, 2005-. Writer. **Publications:** The Eisenhower Administration and Black Civil Rights, 1984; Dwight D. Eisenhower: Hero and Politician, 1986; The Corporate State and the Broker State: The Du Ponts and American National Politics, 1925-40, 1990; Never Just a Game: Players, Owners, and American Baseball to 1920, 1994; Much More Than a Game: Players, Owners, and American Baseball Since 1921, 2001. Contributor to periodicals. **Address:** Department of History, Muskingum College, 163 Stormont, New Concord, OH 43762, U.S.A. **Online address:** burk@muskingum.edu

BURKE, Carolyn. Australian (born Australia) **Genres:** Literary Criticism And History, Biography. **Career:** University of California, research associate in humanities, 1998-; art critic; University of Western Sydney, teacher; University of New South Wales, teacher; University of Lille, teacher. Translator and writer. **Publications:** (Trans. with G.C. Gill) L. Irigaray, An Ethics of Sexual Difference (philosophy), 1993; (ed. with N. Schor and M. Whitford) Engaging with Irigaray: Feminist Philosophy and Modern European Thought (philosophy), 1994; Becoming Modern: The Life of Mina Loy, 1996; Lee Miller: A Life, 2005; No Regrets: The Life of Edith Piaf, 2011. Contributor to art journals. **Address:** c/o Agent, 2120 Berkeley Way, New York, NY 10022, U.S.A. **Online address:** carolynb@cruzio.com

BURKE, James. Irish (born Ireland), b. 1936. **Genres:** History, Sciences, Humanities, Technology. **Career:** Science historian, author and television producer. **Publications:** (With R. Baxter) Tomorrow's World, 1970; Connections: An Alternate View of Change, 1978 in US as Connections, 1979, rev. ed., 1995; The Impact of Science on Society, 1985; The Day the Universe Changed, 1985, rev. ed., 1995; (with R. Ornstein) The Axemaker's Gift: A Double-Edged History of Human Culture, 1995; The Pinball Effect: How Renaissance Water Gardens Made the Carburetor Possible and Other Journeys through Knowledge, 1996; The Knowledge Web: From Electronic Agents to Stonehenge and Back-and Other Journeys through Knowledge, 1999; Circles: 50 Round Trips Through History, Technology, Science, Culture, 2000; Twin Tracks: The Unexpected Origins of the Modern World, 2003; American Connections: The Founding Fathers, Networked, 2007. Contributor to books and periodicals. **Address:** Royce Carlton Inc., 866 UN Plz., New York, NY 10017-1880, U.S.A.

BURKE, Martyn. Canadian (born Canada), b. 1947?. **Genres:** Novels, Plays/Screenplays, Documentaries/Reportage, Young Adult Fiction. **Career:** Canadian Broadcasting Corp. (CBC-TV), director; Information Advisory Newsletter, founder and editor. **Publications:** Laughing War, 1980; The Commissar's Report, 1984; Ivory Joe, 1991. NOVELS: Tiara, 1995; The Shelling of Beverly Hills, 2000; The Truth About the Night, 2006. **Address:** 175 Howland Ave., Toronto, ON M5R 3B7, Canada. **Online address:** martyn@martynburke.com

BURKE, Richard E. American (born United States), b. 1953. **Genres:** Politics/Government. **Career:** U.S. Senator Edward Kennedy, administrative assistant and chief of staff, 1971-81; American Electro Products (electronics), senior vice president for marketing and director of human resources; Congress Video Group, chair and CEO; National Entertainment Group (producer and distributor of video cassettes), president. **Publications:** (With W. Hoffer and M. Hoffer) The Senator: My Ten Years with Ted Kennedy, 1992. **Address:** John Hawkins & Associates Inc., 71 W 23rd St., Ste. 1600, New York, NY 10010-4185, U.S.A.

BURKE, Sean. Welsh (born Wales), b. 1961. **Genres:** Plays/Screenplays, Literary Criticism And History, Novels, Education. **Career:** Freelance journalist, 1989-92; University of Durham, reader in English, lecturer in English, 1992-. Writer. **Publications:** The Revolutionist (play), 1987; Meet the Professor: Essays in Philosophy, 1989; The Death and Return of the Author: Criticism and Subjectivity in Barthes, Foucault and Derrida (literary theory),

1992, 2nd ed., 1998; Authorship: From Plato to the Postmodern (literary theory), 1995; Deadwater (novel), 2002 in France as Au bout des docks, 2007; The Ethics of Writing: Authorship and Legacy in Plato and Nietzsche, 2008. Contributor to journals. Works appear in anthologies. **Address:** Department of English Studies, University of Durham, Hallgarth House, 77 Hallgarth St., Durham, DU DH1 3AY, England. **Online address:** j.m.burke@durham.ac.uk

BURKE, Shannon. American (born United States), b. 1966. **Genres:** Novels, Young Adult Fiction, Mystery/Crime/Suspense. **Career:** Writer. **Publications:** Safelight: A Novel, 2004; Black Flies: A Novel, 2008. **Address:** Random House, 1745 Broadway, Fl. 3, New York, NY 10019, U.S.A.

BURKE, Timothy M. American (born United States) **Genres:** Mystery/Crime/Suspense, History. **Career:** District attorney's office, homicide prosecutor. Writer and attorney. **Publications:** The Paradiso Files: Boston's Unknown Serial Killer, 2008. Contributor to periodicals. **Address:** Law Office of Timothy M. Burke, Needham Corporate Center, 160 Gould St., Ste. 111, Needham, MA 02494-2300, U.S.A.

BURKE, W. *See* **BRAUN, Matt(hew).**

BURKEY, Stan. Ugandan/American (born United States), b. 1938. **Genres:** Third World, Economics, Business/Trade/Industry, Sociology. **Career:** Redd Barna, program coordinator, 1977-81; Uganda Change Agent Association, executive secretary, 1997-. Writer. **Publications:** People First: A Guide to Self-Reliant Participatory Rural Development, 1993; Bookkeeping for Development Groups, Quaker Service of Norway, 1993. **Address:** Uganda Change Agent Association, Rashid Khamis Rd., Plot 30, PO Box 2922, Kampala, 256, Uganda. **Online address:** ucaa@infocom.co.ug

BURKHARDT, Joanna M. American (born United States), b. 1954. **Genres:** Language/Linguistics, Art/Art History, Education. **Career:** University of Connecticut, library assistant, 1981-82, 1983-92, library director, 1987-92; University of Rhode Island, College of Continuing Education Library, director, 1992-, professor, librarian, CCE Library, head. Writer. **Publications:** (With M.C. MacDonald and A.J. Rathemacher) Teaching Information Literacy: Thirty-five Practical, Standards-Based Exercises for College Students, 2003, 2nd ed. as Teaching Information Literacy: 50 Standards-Based Exercises for College Students, 2010; (with M.C. MacDonald and A.J. Rathemacher) Creating a Comprehensive Information Literacy Plan: A How-to-Do-It Manual and CD-ROM for Librarians, 2005. **Address:** College of Continuing Education Library, University of Rhode Island, Providence Campus, 80 Washington St., Providence, RI 02903, U.S.A. **Online address:** jburkhardt@uri.edu

BURKITT, Ian. British (born England), b. 1956. **Genres:** Psychology, Sociology. **Career:** Leeds Area Health Authority, office clerk, 1975-78; University of Leeds, teaching fellow in sociology, 1989-90; University of Bradford, British Academy Post-Doctoral research fellow, 1990-92, lecturer, senior lecturer in sociology, 1992-2002, reader in social science, 2002-; University of Barcelona, Social Psychology Unit, visiting research professor, 2001. Writer. **Publications:** Social Selves: Theories of the Social Formation of Personality, 1991, 2nd ed. as Social Selves: Theories of Self and Society, 2008; Bodies of Thought: Embodiment, Identity, and Modernity, 1999. Contributor to journals. **Address:** Department of Social Sciences & Humanities, University of Bradford, Richmond Rd., Bradford, WY BD7 1DP, England. **Online address:** i.burkitt@bradford.ac.uk

BURKMAN, Thomas W. American (born United States), b. 1944. **Genres:** History. **Career:** Colby College, instructor, 1975-76; Old Dominion University, associate professor, 1976-91; Hamilton College, visiting associate professor, 1992-93; State University of New York, research professor of history and director of Asian studies, 1994-; University of Tokyo, visiting research professor; Kwansei Gakuin University, faculty; University of California, visiting professor; Virginia Consortium for Asian Studies, president. Writer. **Publications:** (Ed.) The Occupation of Japan: Educational and Social Reform: The Proceedings of a Symposium Sponsored by the MacArthur Memorial, Old Dominion University, and the MacArthur Memorial Foundation, October 16-18, 1980, 1982; (ed.) The Occupation of Japan: The International Context: The Proceedings of the Fifth Symposium Sponsored by the MacArthur Memorial, Old Dominion University, the MacArthur Memorial Foundation, 21-22 October 1982, 1984; (ed.) The Occupation of Japan: Arts and Culture: The Proceedings of the Sixth Symposium, 1988; Japan and the League of Nations: Empire and World Order, 1914-1938, 2008. Contributor to books and periodicals. **Address:** Asian Studies Program, State University of New York, 715 Clemens Hall, Buffalo, NY 14260-4610, U.S.A. **Online address:** burkman@buffalo.edu

BURKS, Brian. American (born United States), b. 1955. **Genres:** Westerns/Adventure, Young Adult Fiction, History. **Career:** Writer. **Publications:** Runs with Horses, 1995; Soldier Boy, 1997; Walks Alone, 1998; Wrango, 1999. MURPHY SERIES (with G. Paulsen): Murphy's Stand, 1993; Murphy's Ambush, 1995; Murphy's Trail, 1996. **Address:** 18 Burks Rd., Tularosa, NM 88352, U.S.A.

BURKS, Jean M. (Jean Maier Burks). American (born United States), b. 1949. **Genres:** Antiques/Furnishings, Art/Art History, Architecture. **Career:** Cooper-Hewitt Museum, research assistant to curator of decorative arts, 1983-84, Parsons School of Design, adjunct professor, 1986-87, 2003, 2005; Philadelphia Museum of Art, assistant curator of American decorative arts, 1984-86; Henry Francis du Pont Winterthur Museum, research assistant, 1987; Shaker Village Inc., curator, 1987-90; Strong Museum, curator of recreational artifacts, 1991-93; Bard Graduate Center for Studies in the Decorative Arts, adjunct professor, 1993-95; Shelbourne Museum, curator of decorative arts, 1995-, senior curator; lecturer on furniture and design; John Paul Getty Art and Architecture Thesaurus, consultant; Canterbury Shaker Village, consultant. Writer. **Publications:** Birmingham Brass Candlesticks, 1986; Documented Furniture: An Introduction to the Collections, 1989; (with T.D. Rieman) The Complete Book of Shaker Furniture, 1993; (with T.D. Rieman) The Encyclopedia of Shaker Furniture, 2003; The Dolls of Shelburne Museum, 2004; (with T.D. Rieman) The Shaker Furniture Handbook, 2005; Shaker Design: Out of this World, 2008. Contributor to periodicals. **Address:** Shelburne Museum, 6000 Shelburne Rd., PO Box 10, Shelburne, VT 05482, U.S.A. **Online address:** curators@shelburnemuseum.org

BURKS, Jean Maier. *See* **BURKS, Jean M.**

BURLEW, A(nn) Kathleen. American (born United States), b. 1948. **Genres:** Psychology, Biography. **Career:** University of Cincinnati, Department of Psychology, professor, 1993-. Writer. **Publications:** (With W.P. Smith, M. Mosely and W.M. Whitney) Minority Issues in Mental Health, 1978; (with W.P. Smith, M. Mosely and W.M. Whitney) Reflections on Black Psychology, 1979; (with W.C. Banks, H.M. McAdoo and D. Azibo) African American Psychology: Theory, Research, and Practice, 1992; Handbook of Racial, Ethnic Minority Psychology, 2003. **Address:** Department of Psychology, University of Cincinnati, 4130D EDWARDS 1 Edwards Ctr., Cincinnati, OH 45221-0376, U.S.A. **Online address:** burlewak@email.uc.edu

BURLINGAME, Michael. American (born United States), b. 1941. **Genres:** History, Biography. **Career:** Connecticut College, professor of history, 1968-2001, May Buckley Sadowski professor of history emeritus, 2001-; University of Illinois, chancellor Naomi B. Lynn distinguished chair in Lincoln studies, 2009-. Writer. **Publications:** The Inner World of Abraham Lincoln, 1994; Honest Abe, dishonest Mary, 1994; (ed.) An Oral History of Lincoln, 1996; (ed. with J.R.T. Ettlinger) Inside Lincoln's White House, 1997; Lincoln Observed, 1998; (ed.) Lincoln's Journalist: John Hay's Anonymous Writings for the Press, 1860-1864, 1998; (ed.) A Reporter's Lincoln, 1998; (ed.) At Lincoln's Side, 2000; (ed.) Inside the White House in War Times: Memoirs and Reports of Lincoln's Secretary, 2000; (ed.) With Lincoln in the White House: Letters, Memoranda, and Other Writings of John G. Nicolay, 1860-1865, 2000; (ed.) The Real Lincoln: A Portrait, 2002; (ed.) Lincoln's Humor and Other Essays, 2002; (ed.) Dispatches from Lincoln's White House: The Anonymous Civil War Journalism of Presidential Secretary William O. Stoddard, 2002; (ed.) Abraham Lincoln: The Observations of John G. Nicolay and John Hay, 2007; Abraham Lincoln: A Life, 2008; Lincoln and the Civil War, 2011. **Address:** Department of History, Connecticut College, 270 Mohegan Ave., New London, CT 06320-4196, U.S.A. **Online address:** burlingame@snet.net

BURLINGHAM, Bo. American (born United States), b. 1946. **Genres:** Business/Trade/Industry. **Career:** Inc. Magazine, senior editor, executive editor, 1983-90, editor-at-large, 1990-; Ramparts Magazine, managing editor; Fidelity Investments, writer; PAC World (international networking group), co-founder. **Publications:** (With J. Stack) The Great Game of Business, 1992; (with J. Stack) A Stake in the Outcome: Building a Culture of Ownership for the Long-Term Success of Your Business, 2002; Small Giants: Companies

That Choose to Be Great Instead of Big, 2005; (with N. Brodsky) The Knack: How Street-Smart Entrepreneurs Learn to Handle Whatever Comes Up, 2008. **Address:** c/o Les Tuerk, The BrightSight Group, 268 Wall St., Princeton, NJ 08540, U.S.A. **Online address:** bo@smallgiantsbook.com

BURMAN, Carina. Swedish (born Sweden), b. 1960. **Genres:** Young Adult Fiction, Biography, Novels. **Career:** Uppsala University, Department of Literature, assistant professor, associate professor. Writer. **Publications:** NONFICTION IN SWEDISH: Valtalaren Johan Henric Kellgren, 1988; Min salig Bror Jean Hendrich: En roman, 1993; Gustaf Wasa och andra pjäser frAn svenskt 1700-tal, Studentlitteratur Förlag, 1994; Livet i gamla Världen: Palestina, 1995; Skrifter, 1995; Brev: Ny följd: Tidigare ej samlade och tryckta brev, 1996; Den tionde sÅnggudinnan: Roman, 1996; Cromwells huvud: Antropologisk komedi, 1998; Dikter, 1999; Grannarne, 2000; Islandet: Roman, 2001; Bremer: En biografi, 2001; Den finländska Sapfo: Catharina Charlotta Swedenmarcks Liv Och Verk, 2004; Vit som marmor: Ett romerskt mysterium, 2006; K.J.: En biografi över Klara Johanson, 2007. OTHERS: The Streets of Babylon: A London Mystery (fiction), 2008; Kärleksroman, 2009; Djävulspakten: Gösta Ekmans liv och konstnärskap, 2011. **Address:** Department of Literature, Uppsala University, Thunbergsvagen 3 P, PO Box 632, Uppsala, S-751 26, Sweden. **Online address:** carina.burman@littvet.uu.se

BURMAN, Edward. Italian/British (born England), b. 1947. **Genres:** Novels, History, Politics/Government. **Career:** University of Rome, lecturer, 1972-74; Government of Iran, editor, 1974-79; University of L'Aquila, lecturer, 1979-84; writer, 1988-. **Publications:** Silvestro Aquilano, 1981; The Inquisition: The Hammer of Heresy, 1984; The Templars: Knights of God, 1986; The Assassins: Holy Killers of Islam, 1987; Italian Dynasties: The Great Families of Italy from the Renaissance to the Present Day, 1989; The World before Columbus: 1100-1492, 1989; (ed.) Logan Pearsall Smith: An Anthology, 1989; The Image of Our Lord (fiction), 1990; Emperor to Emperor: Italy before the Renaissance, 1991; Supremely Abominable Crimes: The Trial of the Knights Templar, 1994; Internet Nuovo Leviatano: Verso il futuro paradigma di pensiero e di business, 2002; Shift!: The Unfolding Internet: Hype, Hope and History, 2003; China and Iran: Parallel History, Future Threat?, 2009. Contributor to periodicals. **Address:** A.M. Heath & Company Ltd., 6 Warwick Ct., London, GL WC1R 5DJ, England.

BURNETT, Alan. Australian/New Zealander (born New Zealand), b. 1932. **Genres:** Economics, Ethics, Business/Trade/Industry. **Career:** New Zealand Foreign Service, staff, 1956-69; Australian National University, senior research fellow, 1970-92. Writer. **Publications:** (With R. Burnett) The Australia and New Zealand Nexus, 1978; The Australian and New Zealand Nexus: Annotated Documents, 1980; (ed.) Australia-New Zealand Economic Relations Issues for the 1980s, 1981; Australia and the European Communities in the 1980s, 1983; The A-NZ-US Triangle, 1988; (co-ed.) The ANZUS Documents, 1991; The Western Pacific: The Challenge of Sustainable Growth, 1992. **Address:** 13 Coles Pl., Torrens, Canberra, AC 2607, Australia.

BURNETT, Alfred David. British/Scottish (born Scotland), b. 1937. **Genres:** Poetry, Intellectual History, Librarianship, Literary Criticism And History, Translations, Young Adult Non-fiction, Essays, Adult Non-fiction, Animals/Pets. **Career:** Glasgow University Library, library assistant, 1959-64; Durham University Library, assistant librarian, 1964-90. Writer. **Publications:** NONFICTION: Cataloguing Policy Objectives and the Computer, 1966; Report of the North-East Libraries and Computers Group Working Party on the Operational Data Requirements of Different Kinds of Library, 1968; (with S. Simsova and R.K. Gupta) Studies in Comparative Librarianship: Three Essays Presented for the Sevensma Prize 1971, 1973; Wood and Type: An Exhibition of Books, 1977; Five Hundred Years of Science: Descriptive Catalogue of an Exhibition in the University Library, Palace Green, Durham, 1978; (ed. with E.E. Cumming) International Library and Information Programmes: Proceedings of the Tenth Anniversary Conference of the International and Comparative Librarianship Group of the Library Association, 1979; (ed. and intro. with D.F.C. Surman) Henri Gaudier-Brzeska and Ezra Pound: A Display of Printed Material and Related Items Arranged to Accompany the Fourth International Ezra Pound Conference, 1979; (ed. with S.P. Green) The British Commitment Overseas: A Transcript of Seminar Discussions Held at the Library Association Study School and National Conference, 1979; (ed. with H.A. Whatley) Language and Literacy: The Public Library Role: Proceedings of the Third Conference of the International and Comparative Librarianship, 1981; (ed.) Arabic Resources: Acquisition and Management in British Libraries, 1986; (ed.) Technology for Information in Development: Proceedings of the Sixth Conference of the International and Comparative Librarianship Group of the Library Association, 1988; Pharos: Two Essays upon Thais, 1989; The Presence of Japan: Lafcadio Hearn, 1890-1990, 1991. POETRY: Mandala, 1967; Diversities, 1968; A Ballad upon a Wedding, 1969; Columbaria, 1971; Shimabara, 1972; Thirty Snow Poems, 1973; Fescennines, 1973; The True Vine, 1974; Hero and Leander: A Poem, 1975; He and She, 1976; The Heart's Undesign, 1977; Figures and Spaces, 1978; Jackdaw, 1980; Thais, 1981; Romans, 1983; Vines: Poems, 1984; Kantharos, 1989; Lesbos, 1990; Root and Flower, 1990; 9 Poets, 1993; 12 Poems, 1994; The Island: A Poem, 1994, 2nd ed., 1996; 6 Poems, 1995; Transfusions: Poems from the French, 1995; Chesil Beach: A Poem, 1997. OTHERS: The Abbott Collection of Literary Manuscripts: An Introduction with the Catalogue of an Exhibition, 1975; Autolycus, 1987; Crystal and Flint, 1991; (trans. with J. Cayley) Mirror & Pool: Translations from the Chinese, 1992; Temenos, 1993; The Olive of Odysseus, 1993; Something of Myself, 1994; Transfusions: An Introduction, 1995; Hokusai, 1996; Marina Tsvetaeva, 1996; Moschatel and Morning Star, 1997; Akhmatova, 1998; The Engraved Title-Page of Bacon's Instauratio Magna, 1998; A Thinker for All Seasons, 2000; Butterflies, 2000; Cinara, 2001; Evergreens, 2002; Sister Margaret Tournour, 2003; Quoins for the Chase, 2003. Contributor to magazines and journals. **Address:** 33 Hastings Ave., Merry Oaks, DU DH1 3QG, England.

BURNETT, Amy Nelson. American (born United States), b. 1957. **Genres:** Theology/Religion, History. **Career:** University of Nebraska, Department of History, professor, 1989-. Writer and historian. **Publications:** The Yoke of Christ: Martin Bucer and Christian Discipline, 1994; Teaching the Reformation: Ministers and Their Message in Basel, 1529-1629, 2006; (with D. Bernstein and A. Goodburn) Making Teaching and Learning Visible: Course Portfolios and the Peer Review of Teaching, 2006; (with P. Savory and A. Goodburn) Inquiry into the College Classroom: A Journey toward Scholarly Teaching, 2007; (ed.) John Calvin, Myth and Reality: Images and Impact of Geneva's Reformer, 2011; (trans. and ed.) Eucharistic Pamphlets of Andreas Bodenstein Von Karlstadt, 2011. **Address:** Department of History, University of Nebraska, 626 Oldfather Hall, 1400 R St., Lincoln, NE 68588-0327, U.S.A. **Online address:** aburnett1@unl.edu

BURNETT, Gail Lemley. American (born United States), b. 1953. **Genres:** Medicine/Health, Children's Fiction. **Career:** Journal Tribune, news reporter, 1981-82, wire editor and copy editor, 1982-89, feature writer, 1989-94, editor of editorial page, 1994-; York County Parent Awareness, board directors, 1989-91. **Publications:** Muscular Dystrophy, 1996, (with S.D. Rioux and B. Wong) rev. ed., 2000. **Address:** Journal Tribune, PO Box 627, Biddeford, ME 04005-0627, U.S.A. **Online address:** burnett@gwi.net

BURNETT, Ron. Canadian/British (born England), b. 1949. **Genres:** Communications/Media, Cultural/Ethnic Topics, Film, Popular Culture, Design, Humanities, Intellectual History, Photography, Photography. **Career:** McGill University, Instructional Communications Centre, television cameraman, 1968-69, professor of communications, 1970-82, associate professor of cultural studies, 1988-96, director of graduate program in communications, 1990-96; Vanier College, founder and chair of media, fine arts, photography, 1972-75, 1977-80, Department of Theatre, founder and chair, 1972-75, 1977-80; Film Studies in Canada, co-founder; Ciné-Tracts Magazine, founder and editor-in-chief, 1976-83; La Trobe University, professor of film studies, 1983-88; Emily Carr Institute of Art and Design, president and vice-chancellor, 1996-; York University, Graduate Film Program, adjunct professor; New Media Innovation Centre, designer-in-residence. **Publications:** (Ed.) Explorations in Film Theory: Selected Essays from Ciné-tracts, 1991; Cultures of Vision: Images, Media and the Imaginary, 1995; How Images Think, 2004. Contributor to books and periodicals. **Address:** Emily Carr University of Art and Design, 1399 Johnston St., Granville Island, Vancouver, BC V6H 3R9, Canada. **Online address:** rburnett@ecuad.ca

BURNEY, Claudia Mair. American (born United States), b. 1964?. **Genres:** Young Adult Fiction, Novels. **Career:** Writer. **Publications:** Murder, Mayhem and a Fine Man, 2006; Death, Deceit and Some Smooth Jazz, 2006; Zora and Nicky: A Novel in Black and White (romance novel), 2008; Wounded: A Love Story, 2008; Exorsistah, 2008; Deadly Charm: An Amanda Bell Brown Mystery, 2009; God Alone is Enough: A Spirited Journey with St. Teresa of Avila, 2010; Exorsistah: X Returns, 2010. Contributor to periodicals. **Address:** PO Box 35002, Colorado Springs, CO 80935, U.S.A. **Online address:** claudia.mair.burney@gmail.com

BURNHAM, Terence (Charles). American (born United States) **Genres:** Psychology, Sciences. **Career:** Progenics Pharmaceuticals Inc., chief financial officer, 1987-89, co-chief executive officer, president and chief financial officer, 1989-92; University of Michigan, visiting assistant professor, 2001-; Harvard University, economics professor, 1997-2005; Acadian Asset Management, portfolio manager, senior vice president, director of economics, 2005. Writer. **Publications:** (With J. Phelan) Mean Genes: From Sex to Money to Food, Taming Our Primal Instincts, 2000; Mean Markets and Lizard Brains: How to Profit from the New Science of Irrationality, 2005, rev. ed., 2008. Contributor to journals and periodicals. **Address:** Acadian Asset Management Headquarters, 1 Post Office Sq., Boston, MA 02109, U.S.A. **Online address:** terry@post.harvard.edu

BURNINGHAM, Bruce R. American (born United States), b. 1964?. **Genres:** Young Adult Non-fiction, History, Humor/Satire, Art/Art History. **Career:** Illinois State University, Department of Languages, Literatures, and Cultures, chair, Hispanic Studies and Theatre, professor, associate professor of Spanish and comparative literature. Writer. **Publications:** Radical Theatricality: Jongleuresque Performance on the Early Spanish Stage, 2007; Tilting Cervantes: Baroque Reflections on Postmodern Culture, 2008. **Address:** Department of Languages, Literatures and Cultures, Illinois State University, PO Box 4300, Normal, IL 61790-4300, U.S.A. **Online address:** brburni@ilstu.edu

BURNINGHAM, John (Mackintosh). British (born England), b. 1936. **Genres:** Children's Fiction, Cultural/Ethnic Topics, Illustrations, Humor/Satire, Young Adult Fiction, Children's Fiction. **Career:** Illustrator of children's books, 1963-. Freelance designer and writer. **Publications:** SELF-ILLUSTRATED: Borka: The Adventures of a Goose with No Feathers, 1963; (with L. Taylor) ABC, 1964; Trubloff: The Mouse Who Wanted to Play the Balalaika, 1964; Cannonball Simp: The Story of a Dog Who Joins a Circus, 1966, 2nd ed. 1994; Humbert, Mister Firkin, and the Lord Mayor of London, 1967; Harquin: The Fox Who Went Down to the Valley, 1967; Seasons, 1969; Mr. Gumpy's Outing, 1970; Mr. Gumpy's Motor Car, 1973; Come Away from the Water, 1977; Time to Get out of the Bath, 1978; Would You Rather, 1978; The Shopping Basket, 1980, 2nd ed., 1996; Avocado Baby, 1982; Granpa, 1984; Where's Julius?, 1986; John Patrick Norman McHennessey: The Boy Who Was Always Late, 1987; Oi! Get off Our Train in US as Hey! Get off Our Train, 1989; Aldo, 1991; Harvey Slumfenburger's Christmas Present, 1993; Courtney, 1994; First Steps: Letters, Numbers, Colors, Opposites, 1994; Cloudland, 1996; Whaddayamean, 1999; Hushabye, 2000; The Magic Bed, 2003. SELF-ILLUSTRATED LITTLE BOOK SERIES: The Rabbit, 1975; The School, 1975; The Snow, 1975; The Baby, 1975, 2nd ed., 1994; The Blanket, 1975, 2nd ed. 1994; The Cupboard, 1975; The Dog, 1975, 2nd ed. 1993; The Friend, 1975. SELF-ILLUSTRATED NUMBER PLAY SERIES: Count Up: Learning Sets, 1983; Five Down: Numbers as Signs, 1983; Just Cats: Learning Groups, 1983; Pigs Plus: Learning Addition, 1983; Read One: Numbers as Words, 1983; Ride Off: Learning Subtraction, 1983; First Steps: Letters, Numbers, Colors, Opposites, 1994. SELF-ILLUSTRATED FIRST WORDSERIES: Sniff Shout, 1984; Skip Trip, 1984; Wobble Pop, 1984; Slam Bang, 1985; Cluck Baa, 1985; Jangle Twang, 1985. SELF-ILLUSTRATED PLAY AND LEARN SERIES: John Burningham's ABC, 1985 as Alphabet Book, 1987; John Burningham's Colors, 1985; John Burningham's 1 2 3, 1985; John Burningham's Opposites, 1985; Letters, 2003; Numbers, 2003. OTHERS: Birdland, 1966; Storyland, 1966; Lionland, 1966; Jungleland, 1968; Wonderland, 1968; Around the World in Eighty Days, 1972; (contrib.) Chitty Chitty Bang Bang, 1989; England, 1992; John Burningham's France, 1998; Colors, 2003; Opposites, 2003; (comp.) When We Were Young: A Compendium of Childhood, 2005; Edwardo: The Horriblest Boy in the Whole Wide World, 2006; John Burningham, 2009; It's a Secret!, 2009; There's Going to Be a Baby, 2010. **Address:** Conville & Walsh Ltd., 2 Ganton St., London, GL W1F 7QL, England.

BURNS, Ailsa (Milligan). Australian (born Australia), b. 1930. **Genres:** Human Relations/Parenting, Psychology, Self Help, Women's Studies And Issues. **Career:** Macquarie University, Department of Psychology, Children and Families Research Centre, lecturer, associate professor, now emeritus professor, honorary associate. Writer. **Publications:** Breaking Up: Separation and Divorce in Australia, 1980; (with J.J. Goodnow) Children and Families in Australia: Contemporary Issues and Problems, 2nd ed., 1985; (with J.J. Goodnow) Home and School, 1985; (with R. Dunlop) Don't Feel the World is Caving In, 1988; (with C. Scott) Mother-Headed Families and Why They Have Increased, 1994. EDITOR: (with G. Bottomley and P. Jools) The Family in the Modern World, 1983; (with N. Grieve) Australian Women: New Feminist Perspectives, 1986; (with N. Grieve) Australian Women: Contemporary Feminist Thought, 1994. Contributor of books to journals. **Address:** Department of Psychology, Macquarie University, North Ryde, NW 2109, Australia. **Online address:** aburns@psy.mq.edu.au

BURNS, Alan. British (born England), b. 1929. **Genres:** Novels, Plays/Screenplays, Young Adult Non-fiction. **Career:** Barrister, 1954-58; University of London, London School of Economics, research assistant, 1959; Daily Express, libel lawyer, 1959-62; Beaverbrook Newspapers, assistant legal manager, 1959-62; freelance writer, 1962-77; University of East Anglia, Henfield Fellow, 1971; Western Australian Institute of Technology, lecturer in creative writing, 1975; University of Minnesota, professor, 1977-91; Lancaster University, Creative Writing Department, lecturer, 1990-96. **Publications:** Buster, 1961; Europe after the Rain, 1965; Celebrations, 1967; Babel, 1969; Dreamerika!: A Surrealist Fantasy, 1972; The Angry Brigade, 1973; The Day Daddy Died, 1981; (ed. with C. Sugnet) The Imagination on Trial (non-fiction), 1981; Revolutions of the Night, 1986; (with W. Harris) The Review of Contemporary Fiction, 1997. **Address:** c/o Diana Tyler, MBA Literary Agents Ltd., 45 Fitzroy St., London, GL W1P 5HR, England.

BURNS, Anna. British/Irish (born Ireland), b. 1962?. **Genres:** Novels, Women's Studies And Issues, Young Adult Fiction. **Career:** Writer. **Publications:** No Bones, 2001; Little Constructions, 2007. Contributor to periodicals. **Address:** c/o Author Mail, W. W. Norton Co., 500 5th Ave., New York, NY 10110, U.S.A.

BURNS, Carol. British (born England), b. 1934. **Genres:** Novels, Art/Art History, Romance/Historical. **Career:** City Literary Institute, lecturer in creative writing, 1972-76; Resurgence, Limestone, and Christian Action, graphics designer. Writer. **Publications:** (Contrib.) New Writers, vol. IV, 1967; The Narcissist: A Novel, 1967; Infatuation, 1967; Stumato (novel), forthcoming. **Address:** Rogers, Coleridge & White Ltd., 20 Powis Mews, London, GL W11 1JN, England. **Online address:** caburns90@hotmail.com

BURNS, Diane L. American (born United States), b. 1950. **Genres:** Children's Fiction, Children's Non-fiction, Humor/Satire, Animals/Pets. **Career:** Elementary school teacher, 1972-74; Institute of Children's Literature, instructor by correspondence, 1989-2003; Story Cottage (writing workshops for children), founder and director. Writer. **Publications:** FOR YOUNG PEOPLE: Elephants Never Forget!: A Book of Elephant Jokes, 1987; Snakes Alive!: Jokes about Snakes, 1988; Hail to the Chief!: Jokes about the Presidents, 1988; Arbor Day, 1989; Sugaring Season: Making Maple Syrup, 1990; (with D. Scholten) Here's to Ewe: Riddles about Sheep, 1990; Rocky Mountain Seasons: From Valley To Mountaintop, 1993; (with A. Burns) Home on the Range: Ranch-Style Riddles, 1994; Cranberries: Fruit of the Bogs, 1994; Trees, Leaves, and Bark, 1995; Snakes, Salamanders, and Lizards, 1995; Berries, Nuts, and Seeds, 1996; Frogs, Toads, and Turtles, 1997; Wildflowers, Blooms, and Blossoms, 1998; (with J.A. Burns) Plant a Garden in Your Sneaker!, 1998; (with M. Boring and L. Dendy) Fun With Nature, 1999; (with P. Roop and C. Roop) Backyard Beasties: Jokes To Snake You Smile, 2004; (co-author) Horsing Around: Jokes To Make Ewe Smile, 2005. Works appear in anthologies. Contributor of articles to magazines. **Address:** 4099 N Shore Dr., Rhinelander, WI 54501-8346, U.S.A. **Online address:** highmountain@gza.net

BURNS, Edward. American (born United States), b. 1946?. **Genres:** Documentaries/Reportage, Plays/Screenplays, Politics/Government. **Career:** Public school teacher; Baltimore Police Department, patrol officer, detective. Writer. **Publications:** (With D. Simon) The Corner: A Year in the Life of an Inner-City Neighborhood (nonfiction), 1997; Three Screenplays, 1998. Contributor to periodicals. **Address:** Broadway Books, 1540 Broadway, New York, NY 10036-4039, U.S.A.

BURNS, Edward. British (born England), b. 1955?. **Genres:** Theatre, Plays/Screenplays, Literary Criticism And History, Humanities. **Career:** University of Liverpool, Department of English Language and Literature, senior lecturer. Writer. **Publications:** The Chester Mystery Cycle: A New Staging Text, 1987; Restoration Comedy: Crises of Desire and Identity, 1987; Character: Acting and Being on the Pre-Modern Stage, 1990; (ed.) Reading Rochester, 1995; (co-ed.) Five Romantic Plays, 1768-1821, 2000; Richard III, 2006. **Address:** Department of English Language and Literature, The School of English, University of Liverpool, Cypress Bldg., Chatham St., PO Box 147, Liverpool, MS L69 7ZR, England. **Online address:** edburns@liverpool.ac.uk

BURNS, Eric. American (born United States), b. 1945. **Genres:** History, Reference, Writing/Journalism, Autobiography/Memoirs. **Career:** Public Broadcasting Service, host; National Broadcasting Co., national correspondent, 1976-; Fox News Channel, KMSP-TV, staff, Fox News Watch, host, 1998-. **Publications:** Broadcast Blues (memoir), 1993; The Joy of Books, 1995; The Autograph (fable), 1997; The Spirits of America: A Social History of Alcohol, 2003; Infamous Scribblers: The Founding Fathers and the Rowdy Beginnings of American Journalism, 2006; Virtue, Valor, & Vanity: The Founding Fathers and the Pursuit of Fame, 2007; Smoke of the Gods: A Social History of Tobacco, 2007; All the News Unfit to Print: A History of How Things Were and How They Were Reported, 2009; Invasion of the Mind Snatchers: Television's Conquest of America in the Fifties, 2010. **Address:** Temple University Press, 1852 N 10th St., Philadelphia, PA 19122, U.S.A. **Online address:** ericburns@optonline.net

BURNS, James MacGregor. American (born United States), b. 1918. **Genres:** Administration/Management, History, Politics/Government, Biography, Autobiography/Memoirs. **Career:** Williams College, assistant professor of political science, 1947-50, associate professor, 1950-53, professor of political science, 1953-86, Woodrow Wilson professor of government, 1962-86, professor emeritus, 1986-; Salzburg Seminar in American Studies, staff, 1954, 1961; Institute of History of the Soviet Academy of Sciences, lecturer, 1963; University of Maryland, interdisciplinary study of constitution during bicentennial era, co-chairman, 1976-87. Writer. **Publications:** Congress on Trial: The Legislative Process and the Administrative State, 1949; Government by the People, 1952, (co-author) 20th ed., 2004; (with J.W. Peltason) Government by the People: The Dynamics of American National Government, 1952, 12th. ed., 1985; (with Peltason) Government by the People: The Dynamics of American State and Local Government, 1952, 12th. ed., 1985; (with Peltason) Government by the People: The Dynamics of American National State and Local Government, 1954, (with Peltason, Cronin and D.B. Magleby) 16th ed., 1994; Roosevelt: The Lion and the Fox, 1956; (ed. with Peltason) Functions and Policies of American Government, 1958, 3rd ed., 1967; John Kennedy: A Political Profile, 1960; The Deadlock of Democracy: 4-Party Politics in America, 1963; (contrib.) Dialogues in Americanism, 1964; Presidential Government: The Crucible of Leadership, 1966; (contrib.) Our American Government Today, 1966; (ed.) To Heal and to Build: The Programs of Lyndon B. Johnson, 1968; Roosevelt: The Soldier of Freedom, 1970; Uncommon Sense, 1973; Edward Kennedy and the Camelot Legacy, 1976; State and Local Politics: Government by the People, 1976, (co-author) 11th ed., 2004; Leadership, 1978; (with P. Bonomi and A. Ranney) The American Constitutional System under Strong and Weak Parties, 1981; The American Experiment, vol. I: The Vineyard of Liberty, 1982, vol. II: The Workshop of Democracy, 1985, vol. III: The Crosswinds of Freedom, 1989; The Power to Lead, 1984; Essays in Honor of James MacGregor Burns, 1989; (with L.M. Overby) Cobblestone Leadership: Majority Rule, Minority Power, 1990; (with S. Burns) A People's Charter: The Pursuit of Rights in America, 1991; (co-author) The Democrats Must Lead, 1992; (co-author) Dead Center: Clinton-Gore Leadership and the Perils of Moderation, 1999; (with S. Dunn) The Three Roosevelts, 2001; Transforming Leadership: A New Pursuit of Happiness, 2003; (ed. with G.R. Goethals and G.J. Sorenson) Encyclopedia of Leadership, 2004; (with S. Dunn) George Washington, 2004; Roosevelt, the Soldier of Freedom: 1940-1945, 2006; Running Alone: Presidential Leadership from JFK to Bush II: Why it has Failed and How We Can Fix it, 2007; Packing the Court: The Rise of Judicial Power and the Coming Crisis of the Supreme Court, 2009. **Address:** Department of Political Science, Williams College, 223 Schapiro Hall, Williamstown, MA 01267, U.S.A. **Online address:** james.macgregor.burns@williams.edu

BURNS, Jennifer L. American (born United States), b. 1975. **Genres:** Young Adult Non-fiction, Social Sciences. **Career:** University of Virginia, assistant professor of history, 2007-. Writer and historian. **Publications:** Goddess of the Market: Ayn Rand and the American Right, 2009. **Address:** Department of History, University of Virginia, PO Box 400180, Charlottesville, VA 22904-4180, U.S.A. **Online address:** jenniferburns@virginia.edu

BURNS, Jim. British (born England), b. 1936. **Genres:** Novellas/Short Stories, Poetry, Literary Criticism And History, Young Adult Fiction. **Career:** Tribune, contributor; writer and editor, 1964-; Ambit, contributor, 1964-; Move Magazine, editor, 1964-68; Palantir, editor, 1976-83; Beat Scene, jazz editor, 1990-. **Publications:** Some Poems, 1965; Some More Poems, 1966; My Sad Story and Other Poems, 1967; Cells: Prose Pieces, 1967; Saloon Bar: 3 Jim Burns Stories, 1967; The Store of Things, 1969; Types: Prose Pieces and Poems, 1970; A Single Flower, 1972; Leben in Preston, 1973; Easter in Stockport, 1976; Fred Engels in Woolworths, 1975; Playing It Cool, 1976; The Goldfish Speaks from Beyond the Grave, 1976; Catullus in Preston, 1979; Aristotle's Grill, 1979; Notes from a Greasy Spoon, 1980; Internal Memorandum, 1982; The Real World, 1986; Out of the Past: Selected Poems 1961-1986, 1987; Poems for Tribune, 1988; The Gift, 1989; Confessions of an Old Believer, 1996; As Good a Reason as Any, 1999; Beats, Bohemians, Intellectuals: Selected Essays, 2000; Take It Easy, 2003. Works appear in anthologies. **Address:** Beat Scene Press, 27 Court Leet, Binley Woods, Coventry, WW CV3 2JQ, England.

BURNS, Kathryn (Jane). American (born United States), b. 1959?. **Genres:** History, Social Sciences. **Career:** Ford Foundation, researcher, 1984-85, assistant program officer, 1985-87; Harvard University, teaching fellow, 1989-90; University of Florida, assistant professor, 1993-2000, associate professor of history, 2000; University of North Carolina, assistant professor, 2000-02, associate professor of history, 2002-. Writer. **Publications:** Colonial Habits: Convents and the Spiritual Economy of Cuzco, 1999; Into the Archive: Writing and Power in Colonial Peru, 2010. Contributor to periodicals. **Address:** Department of History, University of North Carolina, CB Ste. 3195, 465 Hamilton Hall, Chapel Hill, NC 27599, U.S.A. **Online address:** kjburns@email.unc.edu

BURNS, Ken(neth Lauren). American (born United States), b. 1953. **Genres:** History, Military/Defense/Arms Control, Sports/Fitness, Documentaries/Reportage. **Career:** MacDowell Colony, board director; Hampshire College, trustee; Florentine Films, co-founder. Producer and writer. **Publications:** BOOKS: (with G.C. Ward and R. Burns) The Civil War, 1990; (with G.C. Ward and P.R. Walker) Who Invented the Game?, 1994; (with G.C. Ward) Baseball: An Illustrated History, 1994; (with G.C. Ward and J. O'Connor) Shadow Ball: The History of the Negro Leagues, 1994; (with G.C. Ward and S.A. Kramer) 25 Great Moments, 1994; (intro.) The People, Yes, 1995; (intro.) Mark Twain: An Illustrated Biography, 2001; (with G.C. Ward and L. Novick) War: An Intimate History, 1941-1945, 2007; (foreword) Walpole, 2009; (intro.) The National Parks: America's Best Idea, 2009; (foreword) Jim Tully, 2011. Contributor to books. **Address:** Florentine Films, PO Box 613, Walpole, NH 03608, U.S.A.

BURNS, Khephra. American (born United States), b. 1950. **Genres:** Plays/Screenplays, Biography, Sciences, Children's Fiction, Travel/Exploration. **Career:** Golden State Mutual Life Insurance, salesman, 1974-76; PBS TV, staff, 1978; freelance writer, 1978-; WNET-13, writer and associate producer, 1978-80; RTP Inc., speech writer and publicist, 1980-81; freelance editor, 1981-. **Publications:** (With W. Miles) Black Stars in Orbit: NASA's African-American Astronauts, 1995; (ed. with S.L. Taylor) Confirmation: The Spiritual Wisdom That Has Shaped Our Lives, 1997; Mansa Musa: The Lion of Mali, 2001. Contributor to books and periodicals. **Address:** Faith Childs Literary Agency Inc., 915 Broadway, Ste. 1009, New York, NY 10010-7108, U.S.A.

BURNS, Marilyn. American (born United States), b. 1941?. **Genres:** Children's Fiction, Children's Non-fiction, Education, Mathematics/Statistics, Young Adult Fiction. **Career:** Marilyn Burns Education Associates Inc., principal and creator of Math Solutions training program for teachers and administrators, Math Solutions Professional Development, founder, 1984-; Math Activities for Hello Math Reader Series, sesigner, 1997-. Writer and educator. **Publications:** BROWNPAPER SCHOOL SERIES: The I Hate Mathematics! Book, 1975; The Book of Think: Or, How to Solve a Problem Twice Your Size, 1976; I Am Not a Short Adult! Getting Good at Being a Kid, 1977; Good for Me! All about Food in 32 Bites, 1978; This Book Is about Time, 1978; Math for Smarty Pants: Or, Who Says Mathematicians Have Little Pig Eyes, 1982. CHILDREN'S NONFICTION: The Hanukkah Book, 1981; The Hink Pink Book: Or, What Do You Call a Magician's Extra Bunny?, 1981; The $1.00 Word Riddle Book, 1990; How Many Feet? How Many Tails? A Book of Math Riddles, 1996. ADULT'S NONFICTION: A Collection of Math Lessons: Grades 3-6, 1987; (with B. Tank) A Collection of Math Lessons: Grades 1-3, 1988; (with C. Humphreys) A Collection of Math Lessons: Grades 6-8, 1990; Math by All Means: Multiplication, Grade 3, 1991; About Teaching Mathematics: A K-8 Resource, 1992, 3rd ed., 2007; Math and Literature: K-3, 1992; Writing in Math Class: A Resource for Grades 2-8, 1995; Fifty Problem-solving Lessons, 1995; Math: Facing an American Phobia, 1998; (ed.) Leading the Way: Principals and Superintendents Look at Math Instruction, 1999; (with R. Silbey) So You Have to Teach Math: Sound Advice for K-6

Teachers, 2000; Lessons for Introducing Fractions: Grades 4-5, 2001; Lessons for Introducing Multiplication: Grade 3, 2001; (with M. Wickett) Lessons for Extending Multiplication: Grades 4-5, 2001; (with M. Wickett and S. Ohanian) Lessons for Introducing Division: Grades 3-4, 2002; (with C.D. Francisco) Teaching Arithmetic: Lessons for Decimals and Percents, Grades 5-6, 2002; (with M. Wickett) Lessons for Introducing Place Value: Grade 2, 2002; (with L.V. Rotz) Lessons for Algebraic Thinking: Grades K-2, 2002; (with K. Kharas and M. Wickett) Lessons for Algebraic Thinking: Grades 3-5, 2002; (with C.D. Francisco) Lessons for Decimals and Percents: Grades 5-6, 2002; (with S. Sheffield) Lessons for Extending Fractions: Grade 5, 2003; Lessons for Multiplying and Dividing Fractions: Grades 5-6, 2003; (with M. Wickett) Lessons for Extending Division, 2003; (with S. Sheffield) Math and Literature: Grades 2-3, 2004; (with S. Sheffield) Math and Literature: Grades K-1, 2004; (with M. Wickett) Lessons for Extending Place Value: Grade 3, 2005. FICTION: The Greedy Triangle, 1994; Spaghetti and Meatballs for All! A Mathematical Story, 1997. OTHERS: The Fraction Kit Guide: Grades 4-6, 2003. **Address:** Math Solutions Professional Development, Marilyn Burns Education Associates Inc., 150 Gate 5 Rd., Sausalito, CA 94965, U.S.A.

BURNS, Ralph. American (born United States), b. 1949. **Genres:** Poetry, Young Adult Fiction. **Career:** University of Arkansas, professor, 1985-, co-director of creative writing; Crazyhorse, editor, 1985-2001. **Publications:** POETRY: US, 1983; Windy Tuesday Nights, 1984; Any Given Day, 1985; Mozart's Starling, 1990; Swamp Candles, 1996; Ghost Notes, 2000. Contributor to periodicals. **Address:** Department of English, University of Arkansas, 501-T Stabler Hall, 2801 S University Ave., Little Rock, AR 72204, U.S.A. **Online address:** rmburns@ualr.edu

BURNS, Ric. American (born United States), b. 1955?. **Genres:** History, Novels, Film. **Career:** Steeplechase Films Inc., founder, 1989. Writer and filmmaker. **Publications:** (Contrib.) The Statue of Liberty, 1985; (with K. Burns and G.C. Ward) The Civil War: An Illustrated History, 1990; (with J. Sanders and L. Ades) New York: An Illustrated History, 1999; (with A. Feuer) Still New York, 2005. **Address:** Steeplechase Films, 2095 Broadway, Rm. 503, New York, NY 10023, U.S.A.

BURNS, Richard Gordon. (Dick B.). American (born United States), b. 1925. **Genres:** History, inspirational/Motivational Literature, Medicine/Health, Psychology, Self Help, Theology/Religion, Biography, Bibliography, Reference. **Career:** Clausen & Burns, attorney, 1951-61; Almonte District Sanitary Board, director, 1952-60; Wyoming Pacific Oil Co., consultant, 1955-; Corte Madera Chamber of Commerce, president; Stanford Law Review, case editor; Merchants' Council, president; church retirement center, president; Freedom Ranch Maui Inc., executive director, 2006-; International Christian Recovery Coalition, executive director, 2009-. **Publications:** NON-FICTION AS DICK B: Doctor Bob's Library, 1992, 3rd ed. as Dr. Bob and His Library: A Major A.A. Spiritual Source, 1998; The Oxford Group and Alcoholics Anonymous: An A.A. Good Book Connection, 1992, 2nd rev. ed. as The Oxford Group & Alcoholics Anonymous: A Design for Living That Works, 1998; The Akron Genesis of Alcoholics Anonymous, 1992, 2nd ed., 1997; Anne Smith's Spiritual Workshop, 1992, rev. ed. as Anne Smith's Journal, 1933-1939: A.A.'s Principles of Success, 1994, 3rd ed., 1998; The Books Early A.A.s Read for Spiritual Growth, 1993, 7th ed., 1998; (ed.) How It Worked: The Story of Clarence S. Snyder and Early Cleveland Alcoholics Anonymous, 1993; (ed. and comp. with B. Pittman) Courage to Change: The Christian Roots of the 12-step Movement, 1994; Quiet Time: The Morning Watch Daily Meditation, 1994, rev. ed. as Good Morning!: Quiet Time, Morning Watch, Meditation and Early A.A., 1998; New Light on Alcoholism: The A.A. Legacy from Sam Shoemaker, 1994, rev. ed. as New Light on Alcoholism: God, Sam Shoemaker, and A.A., 1999; Shoemaker!: A Vital Key to Success in A.A., 1994; The Good Book and the Big Book: A.A.'s Roots in the Bible, 1994; That Amazing Grace: The Role of Clarence and Grace S. in Alcoholics Anonymous, 1996; Turning Point: A History of Early A.A.'s Spiritual Roots and Successes, 1997; Utilizing Early A.A.'s Spiritual Roots for Recovery Today, 1999; The Golden Text of A.A.: God, the Pioneers and Real Spirituality, 1999; (co-author) Women Pioneers in Twelve-step Recovery, 1999; By the Power of God: A Guide to Early A.A. Groups & Forming Similar Groups Today, 2000; Why Early A.A. Succeeded: The Good Book in Alcoholics Anonymous Yesterday and Today (a Bible Study Primer for A As and Other Twelve-steppers), 2001; Making Known the Biblical History and Roots of Alcoholics Anonymous: An Eleven-year Research, Writing, Publishing and Fact Dissemination Project, 2001; God and Alcoholism: Our Growing Opportunity in the 21st Century, 2002; Hope! The Story of Geraldine Owen Delaney, Alina Lodge & Recovery, 2002; Twelve Steps for You: Let Our Creator, A History, and the Big Book Be Your Guide, 2003; Cured!: Proven Help for Alcoholics and Addicts, 2003; Comments in Seven Lectures by Dick B. on God, Alcoholism and A.A., 2003; When Early A.A.s Were Cured and Why, 2003; Henrietta B. Seiberling: Ohio's Lady with a Cause, 2003; The James Club: The Original A.A. Program's Absolute Essentials, 2005; A New Way In, 2006; A New Way Out, 2006. **Address:** PO Box 837, Kihei, HI 96753-0837, U.S.A. **Online address:** dickb@dickb.com

BURNS, Shirley Stewart. American (born United States), b. 1971?. **Genres:** Natural History. **Career:** Journalist and historian. **Publications:** Bringing Down the Mountains: The Impact of Mountaintop Removal Surface Coal Mining on Southern West Virginia Communities, 1970-2004, 2007; (ed. with M. Evans and S. House) Coal Country: Rising Up against Mountaintop Removal Mining, 2009. Contributor of articles to books, periodicals and journals. **Address:** Charleston, WV , U.S.A. **Online address:** shirley@shirleystewartburns.com

BURNSTEIN, Daniel Eli. American (born United States), b. 1952. **Genres:** History. **Career:** Seattle University, associate professor of history. Writer. **Publications:** Next to Godliness: Confronting Dirt and Despair in Progressive Era New York City, 2006. **Address:** College of Arts and Sciences, Seattle University, 901 12th Ave., PO Box 222000, Seattle, WA 98122-4411, U.S.A. **Online address:** danielbu@seattleu.edu

BURR, David (Dwight). American (born United States), b. 1934. **Genres:** History, Translations, Theology/Religion, Reference, Social Sciences. **Career:** Virginia Polytechnic Institute and State University, Department of History, assistant professor, 1966-77, professor of history, 1977-2001, professor emeritus, 2001-; Cambridge University, Clare Hall, visiting fellow, 1988-89. Writer and historian. **Publications:** The Persecution of Peter Olivi, 1976; Eucharistic Presence and Conversion in Late Thirteenth-Century Franciscan Thought, 1984; Olivi and Franciscan Poverty: The Origins of the Usus Pauper Controversy, 1989; Petrus Ioannis Olivi's Quaestio de Usu Paupere and Tractatus de Usu Paupere, 1992; Olivi's Peaceable Kingdom: A Reading of the Apocalypse Commentary, 1993; Pierre de Jean Olieu: Franciscain Persécuté, 1997; The Spiritual Franciscans: From Protest to Persecution in The Century after Saint Francis, 2001; (trans. with E.R. Daniel) Angelo Clareno: A Chronicle or History of the Seven Tribulations of the Order of Brothers Minor, 2005. Contributor to books and journals. **Address:** Department of History, Virginia Polytechnic Institute and State, University, 431 Major Williams Hall, Blacksburg, VA 24061-0117, U.S.A. **Online address:** olivi@vt.edu

BURRELL, Brian. American (born United States), b. 1955?. **Genres:** Novels, Business/Trade/Industry. **Career:** University of Massachusetts, professor of mathematics, senior lecturer. Writer. **Publications:** Merriam-Webster's Pocket Guide to Business and Everyday Math, 1996; The Words We Live By: The Creeds, Mottoes and Pledges That Have Shaped America, 1997; Merriam-Webster's Guide to Everyday Math: A Home and Business Reference, 1998; Damn the Torpedoes!: Fighting Words Rallying Cries and the Hidden History of Warfare, 1999; Postcards from the Brain Museum: The Improbable Search for Meaning in the Matter of Famous Minds, 2004. Contributor to periodicals. **Address:** Department of Mathematics and Science, University of Massachusetts, 1244 Lederle Graduate Research Twr., PO Box 34515, Amherst, MA 01003-9305, U.S.A. **Online address:** burrell@math.umass.edu

BURRESON, Jay. American (born United States), b. 1943?. **Genres:** Chemistry, Humanities. **Career:** Mega Tech of Oregon, general manager; industrial chemist. Writer. **Publications:** (With P. Le Couteur) Napoleon's Buttons: How 17 Molecules Changed History, 2003. Contributor to periodicals. **Address:** Mega Tech of Oregon, 33866 SE Eastgate Cir., Corvallis, OR 97333, U.S.A.

BURRIDGE, Trevor David. Canadian/Welsh/Welsh (born Wales), b. 1932. **Genres:** History, Biography, Politics/Government, Education, Military/Defense/Arms Control, Autobiography/Memoirs. **Career:** School teacher, 1954-65; McGill University, assistant professor of history and philosophy of education, 1966-70; Universite de Montreal, associate professor, 1974-86, professor of British history, 1986-, now professor emeritus. Writer. **Publications:** What Happened in Education, 1970; British Labour and Hitler's War, 1976; Clement Attlee: A Political Biography, 1985. Contributor of articles to journals and periodicals. **Address:** Department of History, Universite de Montreal, PO Box 6128, Sta. Downtown, Montreal, QC H3C 3J7, Canada.

BURROUGH, Bryan. American (born United States), b. 1961. **Genres:** Documentaries/Reportage, Business/Trade/Industry, History, Biography, Autobiography/Memoirs. **Career:** Wall Street Journal, reporter, 1983-92; Columbia Missourian, reporter; Waco Tribune-Herald, reporter; Vanity Fair Magazine, staff, 1992-, special correspondent, 1995-. **Publications:** (With J. Helyar) Barbarians at the Gate: The Fall of RJR Nabisco, 1990; Vendetta: American Express and the Smearing of Edmond Safra, 1992; Dragonfly: NASA and the Crisis Aboard MIR, 1998; Public Enemies: America's Greatest Crime Wave and the Birth of the FBI, 1933-34, 2004; The Big Rich: The Rise and Fall of the Greatest Texas Oil Fortunes, 2009. Contributor to periodicals. **Address:** Vanity Fair Magazine, 4 Times Sq., New York, NY 10036, U.S.A.

BURROUGHS, Franklin (Gorham). American (born United States), b. 1942. **Genres:** Essays, Natural History. **Career:** Bowdoin College, instructor, assistant professor, associate professor, 1968-2002, Harrison King McCann research professor of the English language emeritus, 2002-. Writer. **Publications:** Billy Watson's Croker Sack: Essays, 1991; Horry and the Waccamaw, 1992; Confluence: Merrymeeting Bay, 2006. **Address:** Department of English, Bowdoin College, Massachusetts Hall, 8300 College Sta., Brunswick, ME 04011-8483, U.S.A. **Online address:** fburroug@bowdoin.edu

BURROUGHS, John. American (born United States), b. 1953?. **Genres:** Law, Business/Trade/Industry. **Career:** Lawyers' Committee on Nuclear Policy (LCNP), executive director; Rutgers Law School, adjunct professor of international law; Western States Legal Foundation, attorney. Writer. **Publications:** (ed. and contrib. with N. Deller and A. Makhijani) Rule of Power or Rule of Law? An Assessment of U.S. Policies and Actions Regarding Security-Related Treaties, 2003; (ed. and contrib. with M. Spies) Nuclear Disorder or Cooperative Security? U.S. Weapons of Terror, the Global Proliferation Crisis and Paths to Peace: An Assessment of the Final Report of the Weapons of Mass Destruction Commission and Its Implications for U.S. Policy, 2007. Contributor of articles to journal. **Address:** Lawyers' Committee on Nuclear Policy, 866 UN Plz., Ste. 4050, New York, NY 10017-1830, U.S.A. **Online address:** johnburroughs@lcnp.org

BURROW, J(ohn) A(nthony). British (born England), b. 1932?. **Genres:** Literary Criticism And History, Poetry, Essays, History. **Career:** University of Bristol, Winterstoke Professor of English, 1976-98, senior research fellow and emeritus professor, 1998-. Writer. **Publications:** A Reading of Sir Gawain and the Green Knight, 1966; Ricardian Poetry: Chaucer, Gower, Langland, and the Gawain Poet, 1971; Medieval Writers and Their Work: Middle English Literature and Its Background 1100-1500, 1982, 2nd ed. as Medieval Writers and Their Work: Middle English Literature 1100-1500, 2008; Essays on Medieval Literature, 1984; The Ages of Man: A Study in Medieval Writing and Thought, 1986; (with T. Turville-Petre) A Book of Middle English, 1992, 3rd ed., 2005; Langland's Fictions, 1993; Thomas Hoccleve, 1994; (contrib.) Essays on Ricardian Literature in Honour of J.A. Burrow, 1997; The Gawain-Poet, 2001; Gestures and Looks in Medieval Narrative, 2002; (intro. with A.I. Doyle) Thomas Hoccleve: A Facsimile of the Autograph Verse Manuscripts, 2002; Poetry of Praise, 2008. EDITOR: Geoffrey Chaucer: A Critical Anthology, 1969; Sir Gawain and the Green Knight, 1972; English Verse, 1300-1500, 1977; (and intro.) Middle English Literature: British Academy Gollancz Lectures, 1989; Thomas Hoccleve's Complaint and Dialogue, 1999; (with I.P. Wei) Medieval Futures: Attitudes to the Future in the Middle Ages, 2000; (with H.N. Duggan) Medieval Alliterative Poetry: Essays in Honour of Thorlac Turville-Petre, 2010. Contributor to journals. **Address:** Department of English, University of Bristol, 3-5 Woodland Rd., Bristol, GL BS8 1TB, England.

BURROWAY, Janet (Gay). American (born United States), b. 1936. **Genres:** Novels, Children's Fiction, Plays/Screenplays, Poetry, Autobiography/Memoirs, Essays, Young Adult Non-fiction, Picture/Board Books, Picture/Board Books. **Career:** Teacher, 1961-63; New York State Expansion Program for Young Audiences Inc., regional director, 1962-63; University of Sussex, School of English and American Studies, assistant lecturer, lecturer, 1965-70; New Statesman, reviewer, 1970-75; University of Illinois, Writing Laboratory, special assistant, 1971; Florida State University, associate professor, 1971-77, professor, 1977-2002, McKenzie professor of English literature and writing, 1986-95, Robert O. Lawton distinguished professor, 1995-2002, Robert O. Lawton distinguished professor emeritus of literature and writing, 2002-; New York Times Book Review, reviewer, 1989-. Writer. **Publications:** Descend Again, 1960; But to the Season (poetry), 1961; The Dancer from the Dance, 1965; Eyes, 1966; The Buzzards, 1969; The Truck on the Track, 1970; (with J.V. Lord) The Giant Jam Sandwich, 1972; Raw Silk, 1977; Material Goods (poetry), 1980; Writing Fiction, 1982, (with E. Stuckey-French and N. Stuckey-French) 8th ed., 2011; Opening Nights, 1985; Cutting Stone (novel), 1992; Embalming Mom (essays), 2002; Imaginative Writing, 2003, 3rd ed., 2011; (ed. and intro.) From Where You Dream (lectures), 2004; Bridge of Sand, 2009. Contributor to journals. **Address:** Emma Sweeney Agency L.L.C., 245 E 80th St., Ste. 7E, New York, NY 10065-0506, U.S.A. **Online address:** jburroway@fsu.edu

BURROWS, Edwin G(wynne). American (born United States), b. 1943. **Genres:** History, Politics/Government. **Career:** Marymount College, instructor in history, 1970-71; City University of New York, Lehman College, adjunct lecturer in history, 1971-72, Brooklyn College, instructor and assistant professor, 1972-79, associate professor, 1980-86, professor, 1986-, Claire and Leonard Tow professor of history, 1999-, Broeklundian professor of history, 2001-03, distinguished professor of history, 2003-; Society of American Historians, fellow, 2000; Hofstra University, visiting distinguished professor of history, 2002-03; Dyckman House Museum, director; Organization of American Historians, distinguished lecturer; Fraunces Tavern Museum, consultant; St. John's University, consultant; Brooklyn Arts and Culture Association, consultant. Writer. **Publications:** Albert Gallatin and the Political Economy of Republicanism, 1761-1800, 1986; (with M. Wallace) Gotham: A History of NYC to 1898, 1999; (intro.) In Old New York, 2000; Forgotten Patriots: The Untold Story of American Prisoners during the Revolutionary War, 2008. Contributor to books and periodicals. **Address:** Department of History, Brooklyn College, City University of New York, 503s Whitehead Hall, 2900 Bedford Ave., Brooklyn, NY 11210-2850, U.S.A. **Online address:** eburrows@brooklyn.cuny.edu

BURRS, Mick. (Steven Michael Berzensky). Canadian/American (born United States), b. 1940. **Genres:** Poetry, Plays/Screenplays, Literary Criticism And History. **Career:** CKUA-Radio, host of radio programs, 1971; Waking Image Press, founder, 1971; Warm Poets for Cold Nights, founder, 1975, organizer, 1975-77; Parkland Writers Alliance, co-founder, 1985; Grain literary magazine, editor, 1988-90. Poet, playwright and songwriter. **Publications:** CHAPBOOKS: In the Dark the Journeyman Landed, 1971; Adventures of the Midnight Janitor, 1972; Game Farm: Poems for Intereflection, 1975; Sockpan, 1976; Walls, 1977; Pages Torn from Trees: Some Poems Recently Rediscovered, Written Originally in Vancouver, Edmonton, and Regina between 1969 and 1976, 1981; Word Crumbs: Poems, 1981; Listening to the Crows: Poems and Collages, 1983; From My Box of Dreams: Poems, 1986; Lit like Gold: Poems, 1988; How the World Travels, 1999. POETRY: Moving in from Paradise, 1976; Children on the Edge of Space, 1977; Seeds of Light, 1978; Aurora: Poems, 1980; The Blue Pools of Paradise, 1983; Ghostwriters and Bookworms, 1984; Sleeping Among the Pumpkins, 1990; Junkyard of Dreams: Poetry, 1992; Dark Halo, 1993; Breathing in the Bees, 1994; The Silence of Horizons, 1996; (as Steven Michael Berzensky) Variations on the Birth of Jacob, 1997; Rainbows in the Dark, 1998; The Anti-Cola Man, 2000; The Names Leave the Stones: Poems New and Selected, 2001. EDITOR: Poems, in their Own Voices: Going to War, World War One, World War Two: Metis Series, 1975; Going to War: Found Poems of the Metis People, 1975; Sonnet's End and Other Lyrical Catastrophes: An Anthology of Poems, 1981; The Waking Image Bedside Companion, 1982; Grain Literary and Visual Arts: November 1988, vol. XVI, 1988; (with A. Briesmaster) Crossing Lines: Poets Who Came to Canada in the Vietnam War Era, 2008. OTHERS: (co-author) Video Verses: Yorkton TV's Poem of the Month Contest Winners, 1986; Dream Stories, forthcoming. Contributor to periodicals. **Address:** 1938 Bloor St. W, PO Box 30003, Toronto, ON M6P 4J2, Canada.

BURSTEIN, Andrew. American (born United States), b. 1952. **Genres:** History, Politics/Government. **Career:** University of Northern Iowa, assistant professor of history, associate professor of history, 1996-2000; University of Tulsa, Mary F. Barnard professor of history, 2000-08; Louisiana State University, Charles P. Manship professor of history, 2008-, Louisiana State University Press, editor. **Publications:** The Inner Jefferson: Portrait of a Grieving Optimist, 1995; Sentimental Democracy: The Evolution of America's Romantic Self-Image, 1999; America's Jubilee: How in 1826 a Generation Remembered Fifty Years of Independence, 2001; Letters from the Head and Heart: Writings of Thomas Jefferson, 2002; The Passions of Andrew Jackson, 2003; (ed. with N. Isenberg) Mortal Remains: Death in Early America, 2003; Jefferson's Secrets: Death and Desire at Monticello, 2005; The Original Knickerbocker: The Life of Washington Irving, 2007; (with N. Isenberg) Madison and Jefferson, 2010. Contributor to periodicals. **Address:** Department of History, Louisiana State University, 220 Himes Hall, Baton Rouge, LA 70803, U.S.A. **Online address:** aburstein@lsu.edu

BURSTEIN, Fred. American (born United States), b. 1950. **Genres:** Children's Fiction. **Career:** Rondout Valley Middle School, reading specialist, 1993-. Writer. **Publications:** Rebecca's Nap, 1988; Anna's Rain, 1990; Whispering in the Park, 1992; The Dancer, 1993. **Address:** Rondout Valley Middle School, PO Box 7, Accord, NY 12404, U.S.A. **Online address:** fburstein@rondout.k12.ny.us

BURSTON, Daniel. Canadian/American/Israeli (born Israel), b. 1954. **Genres:** Psychology, Biography, Autobiography/Memoirs. **Career:** Cornell University Medical Center, Eric T. Carlson fellow, 1986-88; York University, associate professor, 1989; Duquesne University, assistant professor of psychology, 1992-97, associate professor of psychology, 1998-, chair; University of Pittsburgh, Center for Philosophy of Science, associate; C.G. Jung Analyst Training Program, adjunct faculty, 1994-98. **Publications:** The Legacy of Erich Fromm, 1991; The Wing of Madness: The Life and Work of R.D. Laing, 1996; The Crucible of Experience: R.D. Laing and the Crisis of Psychotherapy, 2000; (with R. Frie) Psychotherapy as a Human Science, 2006; Erik Erikson and the American Psyche: Ego, Ethics, and Evolution, 2007. Contributor of articles to journals. **Address:** Psychology Department, Duquesne University, 544 College Hall, 600 Forbes Ave., Pittsburgh, PA 15282, U.S.A. **Online address:** burston@duq.edu

BURSTOW, Bonnie. Canadian (born Canada), b. 1945?. **Genres:** Psychiatry, Novels. **Career:** Memorial University, lecturer in English, 1968-69; Brock University, lecturer in English, 1968-69, lecturer in drama, 1973-76; Queen Street Mental Health Centre, AIS Local Initiatives Project, community worker, 1973-74; Therapist Support Group, founder, 1983, chairperson, 1983-84; My Brother's Place, executive director, 1984-85, co-director and supervisor, 1985-87; Ontario Coalition to Stop Electroshock, founding member, 1984, chairperson, through 1989; University of Manitoba, assistant professor of social work, 1987-88; Carleton University, assistant professor, 1988-89, faculty liaison for social work placement students, 1989-; private practice of feminist therapy, 1978-87, 1988-; social service training, 1980-; The Ontario Institute for Studies in Education, Adult Education and Counseling Psychology Programs, senior lecturer. Writer. **Publications:** (Ed. with D. Weitz) Shrink Resistant: The Struggle against Psychiatry in Canada, 1988; Radical Feminist Therapy: Working in the Context of Violence, 1992; The House on Lippincott: A Novel, 2006. Contributor to books and journals. **Address:** Department of Adult Education, The Ontario Institute for Studies in Education, 252 Bloor St. W, 7th Fl., Toronto, ON M5S 1V6, Canada. **Online address:** bburstow@oise.utoronto.ca

BURT, Austin. British (born England) **Genres:** Biology, Sciences. **Career:** University of California, researcher, 1990-92; University of California, Taylor Lab, staff, 1993-95; University of London, Imperial College of Science, Technology and Medicine, professor of evolutionary genetics, 1995-. Writer. **Publications:** (With R. Trivers) Genes in Conflict: The Biology of Selfish Genetic Elements, 2006. Contributor to periodicals. **Address:** Department of Biology, Imperial College of Science, University of London, South Kensington Campus, London, GL SW7 2AZ, England. **Online address:** a.burt@imperial.ac.uk

BURT, Christopher Clinton. American (born United States), b. 1954. **Genres:** Natural History, Environmental Sciences/Ecology, Geography. **Career:** Pacific Rim Press Inc., publisher and managing director, 1985; Compass American Guides Inc., co-founder and publisher, 1990-92, executive editor and creative director, 1990-. **Publications:** Extreme Weather: A Guide and Record Book, 2004, rev. ed., 2007. Contributor to periodicals. **Address:** c/o Author Mail, W.W. Norton & Co., 500 5th Ave., New York, NY 10110, U.S.A.

BURT, William. American (born United States), b. 1948?. **Genres:** Natural History, Environmental Sciences/Ecology, Animals/Pets, Photography, Biology. **Career:** Writer, naturalist and photographer. **Publications:** Shadowbirds: A Quest for Rails, 1994; Rare and Elusive Birds of North America, 2001; Marshes: The Disappearing Edens, 2007. **Address:** 35 Lyme St., Old Lyme, CT 06371, U.S.A. **Online address:** wburt48@yahoo.com

BURTCH, Brian. Canadian (born Canada), b. 1949. **Genres:** Law, Education. **Career:** Researcher for the attorney general of British Columbia, 1977-80; Simon Fraser University, School of Criminology, instructor, 1985-87, assistant professor, 1987-92, associate professor, 1992-98, professor of criminology, 1998-; University of Regina, Department of Justice Studies, adjunct faculty. Writer. **Publications:** (With R.V. Ericson) The Silent System: An Inquiry into Prisoners who Suicide, 1979; (with A. Wachtel) Excuses, An Analysis of Court Interaction in Show Cause Enforcement of Maintenance Orders, 1981; The Sociology of Law: Critical Approaches to Social Control, 1992, 2nd ed., 2003; Trials of Labour: The Re-Emergence of Midwifery, 1994; (ed. with N. Larsen) Law in Society: Canadian Readings, 1999, 3rd ed., 2010; (with R. Haskell) Get that Freak: Homophobia and Transphobia in High Schools, 2010. **Address:** School of Criminology, Simon Fraser University, 10209 Saywell Hall, Arts & Soc Sci Complex 1, 8888 University Dr., Burnaby, BC V5A 1S6, Canada. **Online address:** burtch@sfu.ca

BURTCHAELL, James Tunstead. American (born United States), b. 1934. **Genres:** Education, History, Theology/Religion, Law, Essays. **Career:** Congregation of Holy Cross, Ordained Catholic priest, 1960; University of Notre Dame, Department of Theology, assistant professor, 1966-69, associate professor, 1966-75, chairman, 1968-70, professor of theology, 1975-91, provost, fellow, 1970-77; Cambridge University, Gonville and Caius College, S.A. Cook bye fellow, 1965-66; St. Edmund's House, visiting fellow, 1965-66; Princeton University, visiting fellow, 1980-81, 1990-93. Writer. **Publications:** Catholic Theories of Biblical Inspiration since 1810: A Review and Critique, 1969; Philemon's Problem: The Daily Dilemma of the Christian, 1973; (co-author) Marriage among Christians: A Curious Tradition, 1977; (ed.) Abortion Parley: Papers Delivered at the National Conference on Abortion held at the University of Notre Dame in October 1979, 1980; Rachel Weeping and Other Essays on Abortion, 1982; Rachel Weeping: The Case Against Abortion, 1984; For Better, For Worse: Sober Thoughts on Passionate Promises, 1985; Major Decisions: How to Pick Your Major in College, 1986; Limits of the Law: Reflections on the Abortion Debate, 1987; (ed. and trans.) A Just War No Longer Exists: The Teaching and Trial of Don Lorenzo Milani, 1988; The Giving and Taking of Life: Essays Ethical, 1989; From Synagogue to Church: Public Services and Offices in the Earliest Christian Communities, 1992; The Dying of the Light: The Disengagement of Colleges and Universities from their Christian Churches, 1998; Philemon's Problem: A Theology of Grace, 1998. Contributor of articles to journals. **Address:** Casa Santa Cruz Holy Cross Church Organizations, 7126 N 7th Ave., Phoenix, AZ 85021-8608, U.S.A. **Online address:** jtbcsc@aol.com

BURTINSHAW, Julie. Canadian (born Canada), b. 1958. **Genres:** Novels, Young Adult Fiction, Local History/Rural Topics, inspirational/Motivational Literature. **Career:** Suite101.com, editor, senior editor and writer. **Publications:** Dead Reckoning, 2000; Adrift, 2002; Romantic Ghost Stories, 2004; The Freedom of Jenny, 2006; The Perfect Cut, 2008; How To Achieve A Heaven On Earth, 2009; The Darkness Between the Star, 2010. Contributor of articles to magazines. **Address:** 4605 Dunbar St., Vancouver, BC V6S 2G9, Canada. **Online address:** jburtinshaw@gmail.com

BURTLESS, Gary. American (born United States), b. 1950. **Genres:** Economics, Sciences, Social Sciences, Business/Trade/Industry. **Career:** U.S. Department of Health, Education and Welfare, economist, 1977-79; U.S. Department of Labor, economist, 1979-81; Brookings Institution, The John C. and Nancy D. Whitehead chair, 1981-, senior fellow, 1982-2001; Journal of Human Resources, co-editor, 1988-96; University of Maryland, School of Public Affairs, visiting professor, 1993; consultant. **Publications:** (With R. Haveman) Policy Lessons from Three Labor Market Experiments, 1984; (ed. with H.J. Aaron) Retirement and Economic Behavior, 1984; (with R. Haveman) Taxes, Transfers, and Labor Supply: The Evolving Views of U.S. Economists, 1985; (ed.) Work, Health, and Income among the Elderly, 1987; (with H.J. Aaron and B. Bosworth) Can America Afford to Grow Old?, 1989; (ed.) A Future of Lousy Jobs?: The Changing Structure of U.S. Wages, 1990; (with M. Baily and R. Litan) Growth with Equity: Economic Policymaking for the Next Century, 1993; (with D. Friedlander) Five Years After: The Long-Term Effects of Welfare to Work Programs, 1995; (ed.) Does Money Matter?: The Effect of School Resources on Student Achievement and Adult Success, 1996; (with B. Bosworth) Aging Societies: The Global Dimension, 1998; (with R. Lawrence and R. Litan) Globaphobia: Confronting Fears about Open Trade, 1998. **Address:** Brookings Institution, 1775 Massachusetts Ave. NW, Washington, DC 20036, U.S.A.

BURTON, Anthony. (Tony Burton). British (born England), b. 1934. **Genres:** Novels, History, Transportation, Travel/Exploration, Biography, Social Sciences. **Career:** Weidenfeld and Nicolson, editor, 1963-67; Penguin

Books, publicity manager, 1967-68. Broadcaster. **Publications:** Programmed Guide to Office Warfare (humour), 1969; The Jones Report (humour), 1970; The Canal Builders, 1972, 3rd ed., 1993; The Reluctant Musketeer (novel), 1973; (with A. Schiano) Solo: Self-portrait of an Undercover Cop, 1973; Canals in Colour, 1974; Remains of a Revolution, 1974; The Master Idol (novel), 1975; The Navigators (novel), 1976; Canal, 1976; Josiah Wedgwood: A Biography, 1976; The Miners, 1976; The Coventry Option, 1976; A Place to Stand (novel), 1977; Back Door Britain, 1977; Industrial Archaeological Sites of Britain, 1977; (with P. Burton) The Green Bag Travellers, 1978; The Past at Work, 1980; The Rainhill Story: The Great Locomotive Trial, 1980; The Changing River, 1982; Embrace of the Butcher, 1982; The Past Afloat, 1982; The Shell Book of Curious Britain, 1982; (contrib.) Rural France, 1983; The National Trust Guide to Our Industrial Past, 1983; The Waterways of Britain: A Guide to the Canals and Rivers of England, Scotland, and Wales, 1983; The Rise & Fall of King Cotton, 1984; (co-ed.) Canals: A New Look: Studies in Honour of Charles Hadfield, 1984; Walking the Line, 1985; Wilderness Britain, 1985; (with J. Morgan) Britain's Light Railways, 1985; The Shell Book of Undiscovered Britain and Ireland, 1986; (with J. May) Landscape Detective, 1986; Britain Revisited: One Man's Journeys in the Steps of the Travellers, 1986; Opening Time, 1987; Steaming Through Britain, 1987; Walk the South Downs, 1988; Walking through History, 1988; The Yorkshire Dales and York, 1989; The Great Days of the Canals, 1989; Cityscapes: A Tour Around the Great British Cities, 1990; Astonishing Britain, 1990; Slow Roads, 1991; The Railway Builders, 1992; Canal Mania, 1993; (with N. Curtis) The Grand Union Canal Walk, 1993; The Railway Empire, 1994; The Rise & Fall of British Shipbuilding, 1994; The Coswold Way, 1995; The Dales Way, 1995; The West Highland Way, 1996; The Southern Upland Way, 1997; The Wye Valley Walk, 1997; William Cobbett Englishman, 1997; The Caledonian Canal, 1998; Best Foot Forward, 1998; The Department of Correction, 1998; The Cumbria Way, 1999; The Wessex Ridgeway, 1999; Thomas Telford, 1999; Weekend Walks: Dartmoor and Exmoor, 2000, The Yorkshire Dales, 2000, Traction Engines, 2000; Richard Trevithick: Giant of Steam, 2000; The Peak District, 2001; The Orient Express, 2001; The Anatomy of Canals: The Early Years, 2001; Guide to Britain's Working Past, 2001; The Nania Years, 2002; Decline and Renewal, 2003; Hadrian's Wall Path, 2003; The Daily Telegraph Guide to Britain's Maritime Past, 2003; On the Rails, 2004; The Ridgeway, 2005; Tracing Your Shipbuilding Ancestors, 2010; Canal 250, 2011. Contributor to magazines. **Address:** c/o Sara Menguc, 4 Hatch Pl., Kingston upon Thames, SR KT2 SNB, England. **Online address:** contact@anthonygburton.co.uk

BURTON, Betsy. American (born United States) **Genres:** Biography, Autobiography/Memoirs, Language/Linguistics, History. **Career:** The King's English Bookstore, co-owner and co-founder, 1977-. Writer and entrepreneur. **Publications:** The King's English: Adventures of an Independent Bookseller, 2005. **Address:** The King's English Bookshop, 1511 South 1500 East, Salt Lake City, UT 84105-2809, U.S.A. **Online address:** books@kingsenglish.com

BURTON, Bonnie. American (born United States), b. 1972. **Genres:** Women's Studies And Issues, Children's Fiction. **Career:** EWorld/Apple Electronic Media Lab, web editor, 1995-96; Excite@Home, senior content editor, 1996-2001; AOL Music/Winamp.com, senior editor, 2001; Lucasfilm Ltd., senior editor and online content developer, 2003-; Virtual Corral L.L.C., Jitterfingers.com, editor, 2006-; Backwash.com, contributing editor. **Publications:** (Ed. with A. Graham) Never Threaten to Eat Your Co-workers: Best of Blogs, 2004; You Can Draw Star Wars, 2007; Girls against Girls: Why We Are Mean to Each Other and How We Can Change, 2009; (co-ed.) Draw Star Wars: The Clone Wars, 2009; Star Wars Craft Book, 2011. Contributor to periodicals. **Address:** Del Rey/Ballantine Books, Random House, Inc., 1745 Broadway, New York, NY 10019, U.S.A. **Online address:** bonnie@grrl.com

BURTON, Georganne B. American (born United States), b. 1946?. **Genres:** Novels. **Career:** Writer and community activist. **Publications:** (Ed. and intro. with O.V. Burton) The Free Flag of Cuba: The Lost Novel of Lucy Holcombe Pickens, 2002. **Address:** 107 Baywood Cir., Ninety Six, SC 29666-8755, U.S.A. **Online address:** georg@ncsa.uiuc.edu

BURTON, Humphrey (McGuire). British (born England), b. 1931. **Genres:** Music. **Career:** British Broadcasting Corp., BBC-Radio, trainee studio manager, 1955, sound studio manager, 1955-58, BBC-Television, production assistant of monitor series, associate producer, director, programme editor of Monitor, 1958-62, executive producer of music programs, 1963-64, head of music and arts programming, 1965-67, 1975-81, editor of Omnibus, 1967-, program host, 1975-89, staff, 1981; London Weekend TV, co-founder, 1967-, head of drama, arts and music, 1967-69, editor and presenter of Aquarius (program), 1970-75; Barbican Centre, artistic director of Tender Is the North, 1989-92. **Publications:** Leonard Bernstein, 1994; Yehudi Menuhin: A Life, 2001; (with M. Murray) William Walton: The Romantic Loner: A Centenary Portrait Album, 2002. **Address:** 17 Wendell Rd., London, GL W12 9RS, England.

BURTON, Ivor (Flower). British (born England), b. 1923. **Genres:** History, Politics/Government, Biography. **Career:** University of London, Bedford College, assistant lecturer, 1950-53, lecturer, 1953-64, senior lecturer, 1964-82, head of sociology, 1977-, reader in social administration, 1982-, professor, 1983-88, professor emeritus, 1988-. Writer. **Publications:** The Captain General: The Career of John Churchill, 1st Duke of Marlborough, 1702-11, 1968; (with G. Drewry) Legislation and Public Policy: Public Bills in the 1970-74 Parliament, 1981; (ed. with W.E. Minchinton) British Army Lists, 1740-1784, 1984. Contributor to periodicals. **Address:** Bedford College, University of London, Regent's Pk., London, GL NW1 4NS, England.

BURTON, John Andrew. British (born England), b. 1944. **Genres:** Animals/Pets, Natural History, Zoology, Travel/Exploration, Biology, Sciences. **Career:** British Museum of Natural History, assistant information officer, 1963-69; Natural History Museum, exhibition secretary, 1963-69; Birds of the World, assistant editor, 1969-71; Animals, assistant editor, 1971-72; Friends of the Earth, founder, natural history consultant, 1971-75; New Scientist, regular contributor, 1974-85; Fauna and Flora Preservation Society, executive secretary, 1975-88, director, 1982-89, chief executive officer; Birds Intl., editor, 1974-76; World Land Trust (World Wide Land Conservation Trust), chief executive and co-founder, 1989-; Wildlife Works Ltd., director, 1990-; IUCN, Species Survival Commission, member emeritus, 1990-, World Conservation Union, TRAFFIC Unit, chairman; Authors and Artists for Conservation, founder, 1995; Wyld Court Rainforest Ltd., director, 1996-; Bat Conservation Trust, founding chairman. **Publications:** Extinct Animals, 1972; Birds of the Tropics, 1973; Fossils, 1974; The Naturalist in London, 1974; (with D.H.S. Risdon) Love of Birds, 1975; Worlds Apart, 1976; Nature in the City, 1976; (with E.N. Arnold) A Field Guide to the Reptiles and Amphibians of Europe, 1978; Rare Animals, 1978; Gem Guide to Wild Animals, 1980; The Guinness Book of Mammals, 1982; Guinness Book of Mammals, 1982; Gem Guide to Zoo Animals, 1984; Collins' Guide to Rare Mammals of the World, 1987; Close to Extinction, 1988; (with V.G. Burton) Collins Guide to the Rare Mammals of the World, 1988; Mammals of America, 1989; The Book of Snakes, 1991; Mammals of North America, 1995; Jungles & Rainforests, 1996; Collins' Wild Guide to Wild Animals, 1998; Eye Witness 3D Reptile, 1998; Reptile, 1998; The Pocket Guide to Mammals of North America, 1999; Reptiles, 2001; (with G.A. Bertrand and P. Sterry) HarperCollins Complete North American Wildlife: A Photo Field Guide, 2003; The Ultimate Bird Feeder Handbook, 2005; Attracting Wildlife to Your Garden, 2006. EDITOR: Owls of the World, 1973, 3rd ed., 1992; National Trust Book of Wild Animals, 1984; The National Trust Book of British Wild Animals, 1984; The Atlas of Endangered Species, 1991, 2nd ed., 1999; (with B. Sherwood and D. Cutler) Wildlife and Roads: The Ecological Impact, 2002. **Address:** Kingfisher Publications P.L.C., New Penderel House, 283-288 High Holborn, London, GL WC1V 7HZ, England. **Online address:** john.a.burton@lineone.net

BURTON, L(awrence) DeVere. American (born United States), b. 1943. **Genres:** Agriculture/Forestry, Environmental Sciences/Ecology, Sciences. **Career:** Church of Jesus Christ of Latter-day Saints, missionary, 1962-64; agriculture teacher, 1967-70, 1972-84; Iowa State University, instructor in agricultural engineering, 1984-87; Idaho State Division of Vocational Education, area coordinator for vocational education, 1987-88; University of Idaho, affiliate assistant professor, 1987-97; Idaho State University, affiliate assistant professor, 1987-88; Idaho State Future Farmers of America Foundation, chair, 1988-97; State of Idaho, state supervisor of agricultural education, 1989-. Writer. **Publications:** Agriscience and Technology, 1992, 5th ed., 2009; Ecology of Fish and Wildlife, 1996, 3rd ed., Introduction to Forestry Science, 1998, 2nd ed., 2007; Fish and Wildlife: Principles of Zoology and Ecology, 2nd ed., 2001, 3rd ed., 2009; (with E.L. Cooper) Agriscience: Fundamentals and Applications, 3rd ed., 2002, 5th ed., 2010; Environmental Science: Fundamentals and Applications, 2008. Contributor to journals and periodicals. **Address:** College of Southern Idaho, 315 Falls Ave., PO Box 1238, Twin Falls, ID 83303, U.S.A. **Online address:** dburton@csi.edu

BURTON, Rebecca B(rown). (Rebecca Winters). American (born United

States), b. 1940. **Genres:** Romance/Historical, Novels. **Career:** Granite School District, French teacher, 1987-99. Novelist. **Publications:** By Love Divided, 1979; The Loving Season, 1979; To Love Again, 1987. AS REBECCA WINTERS; Blind to Love, 1989; Fully Involved, 1990; The Story Princess, 1990; Rites of Love, 1991; Rescued Heart, 1991; Blackie's Woman, 1991; The Marriage Bracelet, 1992; Meant for Each Other, 1992; Both of Them, 1992; Hero on the Loose, 1993; Bride of My Heart, 1994; The Mermaid Wife, 1994; The Rancher and the Redhead, 1993; The Nutcracker Prince, 1994; A Man for All Time, 1995; The Baby Business, 1995; The Wrong Twin, 1995; Return to Sender, 1995; For Better, for Worse, 1996; Kit and the Cowboy, 1996; The Badlands Bride, 1996; Three Little Miracles, 1996; Second-best Wife, 1996; Not without My Child, 1996; Strangers When We Meet, 1997; No Wife Required, 1997; Laura's Baby, 1997; Undercover Husband, 1997; Bride by Day, 1997; Deborah's Son, 1998; Until There Was You, 1998; Baby in a Million, 1998; A Daddy for Christmas, 1998; Undercover Baby, 1999; Undercover Bachelor, 1999; Undercover Fiancee, 1999; If He Could See Me Now, 1999; The Family Way, 1999; Husband Potential, 1999; The Faithful Bride, 2000; The Unknown Sister, 2000; Brides and Grooms, 2000; Sarah's First Christmas (anthology), 2000; The Billionaire and the Baby, 2000; His Very Own Baby, 2001; The Baby Discovery, 2000; Accidentally Yours, 2001; The Toddler's Tale, 2001; My Private Detective, 2001; Forbidden marriage, 2001; Husband for a Year, 2001; Claiming His Baby, 2001; Beneath a Texas Sky, 2002; The Bridegroom's Vow, 2001; Italian Weddings, 2001; The Prince's Choice, 2002; She's My Mom, 2002; The Baby Dilemma: Philippe's Story 2002; The Tycoon's Proposition, 2002; Another Man's Wife, 2003; Bride Fit for a Prince, 2002; Rush to the Altar, 2003; Manhattan Merger, 2003; Home to Copper Mountain, 2003; Frenchman's Bride, 2003; Rafael's Convenient Proposal, 2004; The Baby Proposal, 2004; Woman in Hiding, 2004; Woman in History, 2004; To Catch a Groom, 2004; To Win His Heart, 2004; To be a Mother, 2004; o Marry for Duty, 2004; Somebody's Daughter, 2005; Daughter's Return, 2005; Husband by Request, 2005; Their New-Found Family, 2005; Father by Choice, 2005; Bride of Montefalco, 2006; Having the Frenchman's Baby, 2006; Meant-to-Be Marriage, 2006; Matrimony with His Majesty, 2007; The Lazaridis Marriage, 2007; The Duke's Baby, 2007; Vow, 2008; Crazy About Her Spanish Boss, 2008; The Italian Tycoon and the Nanny, 2008; The Italian Playboy's Secret Son, 2008; The Royal Marriage Arrangement, 2008; (with L. Handeland and A. DeStefano) Mothers of the Year, 2008; Leaving Jetty Road, 2008; Italian Groom, Princess Bride, 2009; The Brooding Frenchman's Proposal, 2009; The Ranger's Secret, 2009; Cinderella on His Doorstep, 2009; The Chief Ranger, 2009; The Greek's Long-Lost Son, 2009; Miracle for the Girl Next Door, 2010; Santa in a Stetson, 2010; Beyond Evie, 2010; Doorstep Twins, 2010; (with D. Burton) A Mother's Wedding Day, 2010; The Bachelor Ranger, 2011; The Nanny and the CEO, 2011. **Address:** c/o Author Mail, Harlequin Enterprises Ltd., 300 E 42nd St., 6th Fl., New York, NY 10017, U.S.A. **Online address:** becky485@earthlink.net

BURTON, Robert A. (Robert Alan Burton). American (born United States), b. 1941?. **Genres:** Novels. **Career:** Mt. Zion-University of California at San Francisco Hospital, chief of the division of neurology, 1974-, associate chief of the department of neurosciences. Writer. **Publications:** (with others) Key Issues in Health, 1978; On Being Certain: Believing You Are Right Even When You're Not, 2008; NOVELS: Doc-in-a-Box, 1991; Final Therapy, 1994; Cellmates, 1997. **Address:** San Francisco, CA 94108, U.S.A. **Online address:** raburton@aya.yale.edu

BURTON, Robert Alan. *See* **BURTON, Robert A.**

BURTON, Thomas G(len). American (born United States), b. 1935. **Genres:** Mythology/Folklore, Theology/Religion, Essays, Music, Autobiography/Memoirs, Anthropology/Ethnology, Criminology/True Crime, Politics/Government, Politics/Government. **Career:** East Tennessee State University, Department of Literature and Language, faculty, 1958-95, professor of English, 1967-95, acting chair of English, 1981, director of Appalachian-Scottish studies program, 1988-95, professor emeritus, 1996-. Writer. **Publications:** EDITOR: (with A.N. Manning) A Collection of Folklore by Undergraduate Students of East Tennessee State University, 1966, rev. ed., 1970; (with Manning) The East Tennessee State University Collection of Folklore: Folksongs, 1967, rev. ed., 1970; (with Manning) The East Tennessee State University Collection of Folklore: Folksongs II, 1969; Essays in Memory of Christine Burleson: In Language and Literature by Former Colleagues and Students, 1969; Tom Ashley, Sam McGee, Bukka White: Tennessee Traditional Singers, 1981. OTHER: Some Ballad Folks, 1978; Serpent-Handling Believers, 1993; The Serpent and the Spirit: Glenn Summerford's Story, 2004; Beech Mountain Man: The Memoirs of Ronda Lee Hicks, 2009. **Address:** Department of Literature and Language, East Tennessee State University, PO Box 70683, Johnson City, TN 37614-1700, U.S.A. **Online address:** i22burt@etsu.edu

BURTON, Tony. *See* **BURTON, Anthony.**

BURTON, Wendy. American (born United States), b. 1951?. **Genres:** Novels, Medicine/Health. **Career:** Viking Penguin, sales representative, 1977-79; Simon and Schuster, sales representative, national accounts manager, publishing manager, through 1992; Stewart, Tabori Chang, vice president, director of sales and marketing and associate publisher, 1997; For A Small Fee Inc., photographer, designer and freelance literary agent and co-founder. **Publications:** Joy is a Plum-colored Acrobat: 46 Life-affirming Visualizations for Breast Cancer Treatment and Recovery, 2004. **Address:** c/o Author Mail, Harmony Books, 1745 Broadway, New York, NY 10019, U.S.A. **Online address:** wbrouws1@optonline.net

BURWELL, Jennifer. Canadian (born Canada), b. 1962?. **Genres:** Sociology, Essays. **Career:** Northwestern University, instructor in English and writing, 1989-93; Ryerson Polytechnic University, instructor in continuing education program, 1994-95, Department of English, assistant professor, 1997-, associate professor, Graduate Program in Communication and Culture, faculty; Council Fire Native Centre and Women's Native Resource Centre, literacy instructor, 1994-95; Wesleyan University, visiting assistant professor of English, 1996-97. Writer. **Publications:** Notes on Nowhere: Utopian Logic, and Social Transformation, 1997; (ed. with M. Tschofen) Image and Territory: Essays on Atom Egoyan, 2007. Contributor to periodicals. **Address:** Department of English, Ryerson Polytechnic University, 1010 Jorgenson Hall, 350 Victoria St., Toronto, ON M5B 2K3, Canada. **Online address:** jburwell@ryerson.ca

BUSBEE, Shirlee (Elaine). American (born United States), b. 1941. **Genres:** Romance/Historical, Young Adult Non-fiction, Novels. **Career:** Marin Country Title and Abstract Co., receptionist and typist, 1962-63; Fairfield Title Co., plant supervisor, 1963-66; Solano County Assessor's Office, clerk and drafting technician, 1966-; County Parks Department, drafting technician and secretary, 1974-. Writer. **Publications:** GYPSY LADY SERIES: Gypsy Lady, 1977; Lady Vixen, 1980; While Passion Sleeps, 1983; Deceive Not My Heart, 1984; The Tiger Lily, 1985; Midnight Masquerade, 1988; Whisper to Me of Love, 1991; Each Time We Love, 1993. NOVELS: This Spanish Rose, 1986; Love a Dark Rider, 1994; Lovers Forever, 1996; A Heart for the Taking, 1997; Love Be Mine, 1998; At Long Last, 2000; For Love Alone, 2000; Swear by the Moon, 2001. BALLINGER FAMILY SERIES: Return to Oak Valley, 2002; Coming Home, 2003. BECOMES HER: Scandal Becomes Her, 2007; Seduction Becomes Her, 2008; Surrender Becomes Her, 2009; Passion Becomes Her, 2010; Rapture Becomes Her, 2011; Desire Becomes Her, 2012. Contributor to periodicals. **Address:** Warner Books, Time-Life Bldg., 1271 Ave. of the Americas, New York, NY 10020, U.S.A. **Online address:** shirlee@shirlee-busbee.com

BUSBY, Brian. Also writes as Brian John Busby, Edward Humphreys. Canadian (born Canada), b. 1962. **Genres:** Language/Linguistics. **Career:** Federation of BC Writers, president. Writer. **Publications:** (Ed. with P. Brock) Classics Canada, 1994; (ed. with P. Brock) Coming to Canada, 1996; (ed. with P. Brock) Contemporary Canada, 1997; Question and Answer Encyclopedia: Canada, 2003; Character Parts: Who's Really Who in Canlit, 2003; (ed.) In Flanders Field and Other Poems of the First World War, 2005; A Gentleman of Pleasure, 2011. **Address:** Kathryn Mulders Literary Agency, 185-911 Yates St., Victoria, BC V8V 4Y9, Canada.

BUSBY, Brian John. *See* **BUSBY, Brian.**

BUSBY, Mark. American (born United States), b. 1945. **Genres:** Novels, Literary Criticism And History. **Career:** Indiana-Purdue University, associate faculty instructor, 1970-72; University of Colorado, instructor in English and black education, 1972-76; Texas A&M University, College Station, assistant professor, 1977-83, associate professor, 1983-91; Brazos Valley Soccer League, coach, 1978-81; College Station Little League, coach, 1979-80; StageCenter, director, 1980-83, director, 1980-84; Brazos County Art Council, director, 1981-82; Brazos Civil Liberties Union, director, 1982-83; East

Texas State University, Paul Barrus annual lecturer, 1988; San Antonio College, lecturer, 1991; Southwest Texas State University, associate professor, 1991-93, professor of English, Center for the Study of the Southwest, director, 1993-; Southwestern American Literature, co-editor, 1992-; American Culture Association, chairperson, 1993-; U.S. Information Agency, lecturer in Slovakia, 1995. **Publications:** Preston Jones, 1983; Lanford Wilson, 1987; Ralph Ellison, 1991; Larry McMurtry and the West: An Ambivalent Relationship, 1995; Fort Benning Blues (novel), 2001. EDITOR AND CONTRIBUTOR: The Frontier Experience and the American Dream: Essays on American Literature, 1989; New Growth/2: Contemporary Short Stories by Texas Writers, 1993; From Texas to the World and Back: The Journeys of Katherine Anne Porter, 2001; The Greenwood Encyclopedia of American Regional Cultures: The Southwest, 2004; (with T. Dixon) John Graves, Writer, 2007. Contributor of articles. **Address:** Center for the Study of the Southwest, Southwest Texas State University, 601 University Dr., San Marcos, TX 78666, U.S.A. **Online address:** mb13@swt.edu

BUSCALL, Jon. British (born England), b. 1970. **Genres:** Novels, Poetry, Young Adult Fiction, Marketing. **Career:** Stockholm University, instructor in creative writing, through 2004; Jontus Media HB, founder, 2004-. Writer and novelist. **Publications:** College.com, 1999; Reel People, 2001. **Address:** Jontus Media HB, Lindvägen 24, Stockholm, 18735, Sweden. **Online address:** jon@jontusmedia.com

BUSCH, Charles. American (born United States), b. 1954. **Genres:** Novels, Plays/Screenplays, Novellas/Short Stories, Music, Documentaries/Reportage. **Career:** Playwright and actor. **Publications:** Times Square Angel: A Hair-Boiled Christmas Fantasy, 1986; Psycho Beach Party, 1988; The Lady in Question (2-act), 1990; Four Plays by Charles Busch (contains Vampire Lesbians of Sodom, Sleeping Beauty or Coma, Psycho Beach Party, The Lady in Question), 1990; Red Scare on Sunset, 1991; Three Plays by Charles Busch (contains Theodora, She-Bitch of Byzantium, Times Square Angel, Pardon My Inquisition, or Kiss the Blood off My Castanets), 1992; Whores of Lost Atlantis (novel), 1993; You Should Be So Lucky: A New Comedy, 1995; (with L.T. Bond and W. Repicci) Swingtime Canteen, 1998; Queen Amarantha, 1998; The Green Heart (libretto), 1999; Shanghai Moon, 2000; The Tale of the Allergist's Wife and Other Plays (contains title play, Vampire Lesbians of Sodom, Psycho Beach Party, The Lady in Question, Red Scare on Sunset), 2001; Die, Mommy, Die!: A Comic Thriller, 2005; Our Leading Lady, 2007. Contributor to magazines. **Address:** c/o Marc Glick, Glick & Weintraub, 1501 Broadway, Ste. 2401, New York, NY 10036-5601, U.S.A.

BUSCH, Lawrence (Michael). American (born United States), b. 1945. **Genres:** Sociology, Ethics, Bibliography. **Career:** Volunteers in Service to America (VISTA), Community Action Council, supervisor, 1968-70; Cornell University, Department of Rural Sociology, teaching assistant, 1970-71, 1972-74, research associate, 1971-72; University of Kentucky, assistant professor, 1974-79, associate professor, 1979-84, professor of sociology, 1984-89; International Grain Sorghum/Pearl Millet Collaborative Research Support Program, vice chair, 1980-81; French Institute of Scientific Research for Development and Cooperation (ORSTOM), director of research, 1988-89; Council for Agricultural Science and Technology, director, 1990-93; Michigan State University, Department of Sociology, professor of sociology, 1990-96, university distinguished professor, 1997-, Institute for Food and Agricultural Standards, director, 1998-, Center for the Study of Standards in Society, founder and director, Partnerships for Food Industry Development-Fruits and Vegetables, director, 2001-04; University of Trondheim, visiting professor, 1994, 1995, 1996; Lancaster University, Centre for Science Studies, ESRC Centre for Economic and Social Aspects of Genomics (CESAGen), Cesagen professor of standards and society, 2008-10. Writer. **Publications:** Guinea, Ivory Coast, and Senegal: A Bibliography on Development, 1973; (with W.B. Lacy) Science, Agriculture, and the Politics of Research, 1983; (co-author) Making Nature, Shaping Culture: Plant Biodiversity in Global Context, 1995; The Eclipse of Morality, 2000; (co-author) Universities in the Age of Corporate Science, 2007. EDITOR: Science and Agricultural Development, 1981; (with W.B. Lacy) Food Security in the United States, 1984; (with W.B. Lacy) The Agricultural Scientific Enterprise: A System in Transition, 1986; (co-ed.) Toward a New Political Economy of Agriculture, 1991; (co-ed.) Plants, Power, and Profit, 1991; (co-ed.) From Columbus to Conagra: The Globalization of Agriculture, 1994; (with J. Bingen) Agricultural Standards, 2006. Contributor to books and journals. **Address:** Department of Sociology, Michigan State University, 429A Berkey Hall, East Lansing, MI 48824-1111, U.S.A. **Online address:** lbusch@msu.edu

BUSE, D(ieter) K(urt). Canadian (born Canada), b. 1941. **Genres:** History, Politics/Government, Bibliography. **Career:** University of Saskatchewan, faculty, 1966-67; Laurentian University, lecturer, 1969-71, assistant professor, 1971-75, associate professor, 1975-85, professor of history, 1985-, now professor emeritus; Kommission fuer die Geschichte des Parlamentarismus und der politischen Parteien, researcher, 1975-76; Sudbury Community Legal Clinic, chair, 1982-83, board director, 1984-88, president, 1988-89; University of Adelaide, visiting lecturer, 1983-84; Northern Lights/Festival Boreal, board director, 1987-88. Writer. **Publications:** (Trans. with J.L. Black and contrib.) G.F. Mueller and Siberia, 1733-43, 1988; (with J. Doerr) The German Century and Beyond, 2002; Regions of Germany: A Reference Guide to History and Culture, 2005; Come on Over!: Northeastern Ontario A to Z, 2011. EDITOR: Parteiagitation und Wahlkreisvertretung: Eine Dokumentation ueber Friedrich Ebert und seinen Wahlkreis Elberfeld-Barmen, 1910-1918, 1975; (with J. Doerr and contrib.) German Nationalisms: A Bibliographic Approach, 1985; (with J.L. Black) G.F. Müller and Siberia, 1733-1743, 1989; (with M. Steedman and P. Suschnigg) Hard Lessons: The Mine Mill Union in the Canadian Labour Movement, 1995; (with J.C. Doerr) Modern Germany: An Encyclopedia of History, People and Culture, 1871-1990, 2 vols., 1998; (with G. Kinsman and M. Steedman) Whose National Security: Canadian State Surveillance and the Creation of Enemies, 2000. Works appeared in anthologies. Contributor of articles to books and periodicals. **Address:** Department of History, Laurentian University, 935 Ramsey Lake Rd., Sudbury, ON P3E 2C6, Canada. **Online address:** dbuse@latsaurentian.ca

BUSER, Pierre. (Pierre A. Buser). French (born France), b. 1921. **Genres:** Psychology, Sciences, Medicine/Health. **Career:** Université Pierre et Marie Curie, assistant professor, 1944-50, associate professor, 1950-55, professor of neurosciences, 1955-91, professor emeritus, 1991-. Writer. **Publications:** (With M. Imbert) Neurophysiologie fonctionnelle: Centres Nerveux, Motricité et Régulation végétatives Autonomes, 1975; Neurophysiologie, 1975; Psychophysiologie, 1982; (ed. with W.A. Cobb and T. Okum as P.A. Buser) Kyoto symposia, 1982; Neurobiologie, 1993; Regulations Neurovegetatives, 1994; Cerveau de Soi, Cerveau de láutre, 1998; (with R. Lestienne) Cerveau, Information, Connaissance, 2001; Inconscient Aux Mille Visages, 2005; (ed. with C. Debru and A. Kleinert) Imagination et l'intuition dans les sciences, 2009; (with C. Debru) Temps, instant et durée, 2011. **Address:** Université Pierre et Marie Curie, 4 place Jussieu, Paris, 75005, France. **Online address:** pierre.buser@snv.jussieu.fr

BUSER, Pierre A. *See* **BUSER, Pierre.**

BUSEY-HUNT, Brook. (Diablo Cody). American (born United States), b. 1978. **Genres:** Plays/Screenplays, Humor/Satire, Biography, Autobiography/Memoirs. **Career:** City Pages (alternative weekly), associate arts editor. Screenwriter. **Publications:** (As Diablo Cody) Candy Girl: A Year in the Life of an Unlikely Stripper (memoir), 2005; Juno: The Shooting Script, 2007. **Address:** c/o Author Mail, Gotham Publicity, Penguin Group, 375 Hudson St., New York, NY 10014, U.S.A.

BUSFIELD, Andrea. Austrian/British (born England), b. 1970?. **Genres:** Novels. **Career:** Western Gazette, journalist; News Team Intl., journalist; Sun, reporter, 1997-2000; News of the World, reporter, 2000-, features editor, 2003-, television critic, through 2005; Sada-e Azadi, print editor, 2005-; Afghan Scene, staff, 2007; Gulf Times, deputy editor, through 2009. **Publications:** Born under a Million Shadows (novel), 2009; Aphrodite's War (novel), 2010. Contributor to periodicals. **Address:** c/o Charlie Campbell, Ed Victor Ltd., 6 Bayley St., Bedford Sq., London, GL WC1B 3HB, England. **Online address:** info@andreabusfield.com

BUSH, Anne Kelleher. (Kelleher Anne). American (born United States), b. 1959. **Genres:** Science Fiction/Fantasy, Romance/Historical, Literary Criticism And History. **Career:** Writer. **Publications:** SCIENCE FICTION/FANTASY NOVELS: Daughter of Prophecy, 1995; Children of Enchantment, 1996; The Misbegotten King, 1996; (as Anne Kelleher) A Once and Future Love, 1998; The Knight, the Harp and the Maiden, 1999; (as Anne Kelleher) The Ghost and Katie Coyle, 1999; Love's Labyrinth, 2000; The Highwayman, 2001; (as Anne Kelleher) Silver's Edge, 2004; Silver's Bane, 2005. OTHERS: (as Anne Kelleher) Sex Within Reason, 1987; (as Anne Kelleher) Future of Directory Assistance & White Pages, 1991-92 Update, 1991. **Address:** c/o Donald Maass, Donald Maass Literary Agency, 160 W 95th St., Ste. 1B, New York, NY 10025, U.S.A. **Online address:** ahay72a@prodigy.com

BUSH, Barney (Furman). American (born United States), b. 1946. **Genres:** Novels, Poetry, Songs/Lyrics And Libretti. **Career:** University of Wisconsin, Native American specialist, 1973-74; National Indian Youth Council, educational specialist, 1974-75; Institute of the Southern Plains, educational specialist, 1974-75; Milwaukee Area Technical College, instructor in American Indian literature and history, 1976-78; poet-in-residence, 1980-88; Council of Redwinds College, spokesman, 1996-; Institute of American Indian and Alaska Native Arts, faculty, professor; College of the Redwinds, president. **Publications:** My Horse and a Jukebox, 1979; Petroglyphs, 1982; Inherit the Blood: Poetry and Fiction, 1985. Works appear in anthologies. Contributor to periodicals. **Address:** PO Box 22779, Santa Fe, NM 87502-2779, U.S.A.

BUSH, Barry (Michael). British (born England), b. 1938. **Genres:** Animals/Pets, Medicine/Health. **Career:** Hounslow Borough College, lecturer and course adviser, 1962-90; University of London, Royal Veterinary College, lecturer, 1964-80, senior lecturer, 1980-90; College for the Distributive Trades, lecturer, 1967-88; Hill's Pet Nutrition, senior veterinary adviser, 1990-. Writer. **Publications:** Veterinary Laboratory Manual, 1975; First Aid for Pet Animals, 1980, rev. ed. as First Aid for Pets, 1984; The Cat Care Question and Answer Book, 1981; The Dog Care Question and Answer Book, 1982; Interpretation of Laboratory Results for Small Animal Clinicians, 1991. Contributor of articles to journals. **Address:** John Wiley & Sons Inc., 111 River St., Hoboken, NJ 07030-5774, U.S.A.

BUSH, Catherine. Canadian (born Canada), b. 1961. **Genres:** Novels, Young Adult Non-fiction. **Career:** Concordia University, assistant professor of creative writing, 1997-99; University of Florida, visiting professor of creative writing, 2001; University of British Columbia, low-residency creative writing, adjunct professor; University of Guelph, coordinator of creative writing MFA. Writer. **Publications:** FOR CHILDREN: Elizabeth I, 1985; Gandhi, 1985. NOVELS: Minus Time, 1993; Rules of Engagement, 2000; Claire's Head, 2004. Contributor to books. **Address:** c/o Bukowski Agency, 14 Prince Arthur Ave., Ste. 202, Toronto, ON M5R 1A9, Canada. **Online address:** info@catherinebush.com

BUSH, Duncan. Welsh (born Wales), b. 1946. **Genres:** Novels, Plays/Screenplays, Poetry, Literary Criticism And History. **Career:** Luxemburger Wort, reviewer; The Amsterdam Review, co-editor. **Publications:** POETRY: Aquarium, 1983; Salt, 1985; Black Faces, Red Mouths, 1986; Masks, 1994; Midway, 1998; The Hook, 1998; (trans.) C. Pavese, The Poems of Cesane Pavese, forthcoming. NOVELS: The Genre of Silence, 1988; Glass Shot, 1991; Now All the Rage, 2008; The Last Coming, forthcoming. Contributor to periodicals. **Address:** Godre Waun Oleu, Brecon Rd., Ynyswen, Penycae, Powys, PW SA9 1YY, Wales.

BUSH, M(ichael) L(accohee). British (born England), b. 1938. **Genres:** History, Social Commentary, Social Sciences, Local History/Rural Topics, Philosophy, Theology/Religion. **Career:** Victoria University of Manchester, lecturer in history, 1962-76, senior lecturer, 1976-88, reader, 1987-94; Manchester Metropolitan University, research professor in history, 1999-2003. Writer. **Publications:** Renaissance, Reformation and the Outer World: 1450-1660, 1966; The Government Policy of Protector Somerset, 1975; The European Nobility, vol. I: Noble Privilege, vol. II: Rich Noble, Poor Noble, vol. III: Noble Power, 1983; The English Aristocracy: A Comparative Synthesis, 1984; (ed.) Social Orders and Social Classes in Europe since 1500: Studies in Social Stratification, 1992; Pilgrimage of Grace: A Study of the Rebel Armies of October 1536, 1996; (ed.) Serfdom and Slavery: Studies in Legal Bondage, 1996; What Is Love?: Richard Carlile's Philosophy of Sex, 1998; (with D. Bownes) Defeat of the Pilgrimage of Grace: A Study of the Postpardon Revolts of December 1536 to March 1537 and Their Effect, 1999; Durham and the Pilgrimage of Grace, 2000; Servitude in Modern Times, 2000; The Casualties Of Peterloo, 2005; The Pilgrims' Complaint: A Study of Popular Thought in the Early Tudor North, 2009. Contributor to periodicals and journals. **Address:** 7 Hesketh Ave., Didsbury, Manchester, GM M20 2QN, England.

BUSH, Ronald. American (born United States), b. 1946. **Genres:** Literary Criticism And History. **Career:** Harvard University, assistant professor, 1974-79, associate professor of English, 1979-82; California Institute of Technology, associate professor, 1982-85, professor of literature, 1985-97; Oxford University, St. John's College, Department of English Language and Literature, Drue Heinz professor of American literature, 1997-. Writer. **Publications:** The Genesis of Ezra Pound's Cantos, 1976; T.S. Eliot: A Study in Character and Style, 1983; (ed.) T.S. Eliot: The Modernist in History, 1991; (ed. with E. Barkan) Prehistories of the Future: The Primitivist Project and the Culture of Modernism, 1995; American Voice/American Voices: An Inaugural Lecture Delivered Before the University of Oxford on 27 May 1999, 1999; (ed. with E. Barkan) Claiming the Stones/Naming the Bones: Cultural Property and the Negotiation of National and Ethnic Identity, 2002. FORTHCOMING: The Composition of The Pisan Cantos; The Pisan Cantos of Ezra Pound: A Critical Edition; Ezra Pound and the Ideologies of Modernism: Essays on the Major Poetry; James Joyce: A Critical Biography. Contributor to periodicals. **Address:** Department of English, St. John's College, University of Oxford, St. Giles, Oxford, OX OX1 3JP, England. **Online address:** ron.bush@ell.ox.ac.uk

BUSHELL, Agnes. (Agnes (Barr) Bushell). American (born United States), b. 1949. **Genres:** Novels, Mystery/Crime/Suspense, Young Adult Fiction. **Career:** Portland School of Art, instructor in liberal arts, 1983-92; San Francisco Art Institute, instructor in liberal arts, 1993; Maine College of Art, faculty, 1985-, associate professor, 1996-; University of Southern Maine, faculty. Editor. **Publications:** (Ed.) Balancing Act, 1975. NOVELS: Shadowdance, 1989; Local Deities, 1990; Death by Crystal, 1993; Days of the Dead, 1995; The Enumerator, 1997; Asian Vespers, 2000; In the Garden of Nicholas Treeson, 2003; Mothers and Sons, 2004; After Mistra, 2004; Fabrice in Flight, 2010. **Address:** Edite Kroll, 12 Grayhurst Pk., Portland, ME 04102, U.S.A. **Online address:** agnes.bushell@gmail.com

BUSHELL, Agnes (Barr). *See* **BUSHELL, Agnes.**

BUSHELL, Anne. *See* **CRAVEN, Sara.**

BUSHEY, Jeanne. Canadian/American (born United States), b. 1944. **Genres:** Children's Fiction, Young Adult Fiction, Adult Non-fiction, Young Adult Non-fiction, Children's Non-fiction, Education. **Career:** Beal Business College, English teacher, 1967-70; elementary school teacher, 1974-78; American Community School, teacher, 1978-80; N.J. Macpherson School, elementary teacher, 1980-; Stanton Regular Hospital Auxiliary, president, 1990-95; Mildred Hall Festival of Drama, co-founder. Writer. **Publications:** Reading Tips For Teachers, 1993; A Sled Dog for Moshi (fiction), 1994; Holiday Hang-ups!: A Step-by-Step Guide to Making 3-D Arts and Crafts, 1995; The Polar Bear's Gift, 2000; The Boy Who Became A Caribou, 2002; Orphans in the Sky, 2004; Wild Horses Couldn't Keep Me Away, 2006; Inuit Still (non-fiction), 2006. Contributor to magazines. **Address:** Houghton Mifflin Harcourt, 222 Berkeley St., Boston, MA 02116, U.S.A. **Online address:** jeannebushey@yahoo.ca

BUSHMAN, Richard Lyman. American (born United States), b. 1931. **Genres:** History, Young Adult Non-fiction. **Career:** Brigham Young University, assistant professor, 1960-63, 1965-66, associate professor of history, 1966-68, associate director of honors program, 1965-68; Brown University, interdisciplinary fellow in history and psychology, 1963-65; Boston University, professor of history, 1968-77; University of Delaware, professor of history, 1977-89; Columbia University, professor, 1989-2001, Gouverneur Morris professor emeritus of history, 2001-; Claremont Graduate University, Howard W. Hunter visiting professor in Mormon studies, 2007-08. Writer. **Publications:** From Puritan to Yankee: Character and the Social Order in Connecticut 1690-1765, 1967; (ed.) The Great Awakening: Documents on the Revival of Religion, 1740-1745, 1970; (with J.P. Greene and M. Kammen) Society, Freedom and Conscience: The American Revolution in Virginia, Massachusetts and New York, 1976; (co-ed.) Uprooted Americans: Essays to Honor Oscar Handlin, 1979; Joseph Smith and the Beginnings of Mormonism, 1984; King and People in Provincial Massachusetts, 1985; The Refinement of America: Persons, Houses, Cities, 1992; (with C.L. Bushman) Mormons in America, 1999; (with C.L. Bushman) Building the Kingdom: A History of Mormons in America, 2001; Believing History: Latter-Day Saint Essays, 2004; (with J. Woodworth) Joseph Smith: Rough Stone Rolling, 2005; On the Road with Joseph Smith: An Author's Diary, 2007; Mormonism: A Very Short Introduction, 2008; (contrib.) Revelations and translations, 2009; (ed. with A.S. Howe) Parallels and Convergences, 2011. **Address:** Departmentt of History, Columbia University, MC 2527, 1180 Amsterdam Ave., New York, NY 10027, U.S.A. **Online address:** rlb7@columbia.edu

BUSHNELL, Candace. American (born United States), b. 1959. **Genres:** Autobiography/Memoirs. **Career:** New York Observer, writer, 1993, columnist, 1994-98; Sirius Satellite Radio, host, 2006-08. Producer. **Publications:**

Sex and the City, 1996; Four Blondes, 2000; Trading Up, 2003; Lipstick Jungle, 2005; One Fifth Avenue, 2008; The Carrie Diaries, 2010; Summer and the City, 2011; The Two Mrs. Stones, 2012. **Address:** c/o Author Mail, Atlantic Monthly Press, 841 Broadway, 4th Fl., New York, NY 10003, U.S.A. **Online address:** candace@candacebushnell.com

BUSHNELL, Jack. American (born United States), b. 1952. **Genres:** Children's Fiction, Literary Criticism And History, Essays, Young Adult Fiction. **Career:** Rutgers University, assistant professor and lecturer, 1974-84; DMB&B Advertising, senior account planner, 1984-88; Geer, DuBois Advertising, vice president, 1988-92; Nabisco Foods, associate manager of business information, 1992-93; full-time writer, 1993-; University of Wisconsin, adjunct assistant professor, 1994-95, adjunct professor, 1995-2005, professor, 2005-07, chair, 2007-. **Publications:** FOR CHILDREN: Circus of the Wolves, 1994; Sky Dancer, 1996. LITERARY ESSAYS: Where is the Lamb for a Burnt Offering? in The Wordsworth Circle, 1981; Maggie Tulliver's Stored Up Force in Studies in the Novel, 1984; The Daughter's Dilemma in Configuration, 1994. OTHERS: Farm Crossing, 2004; Night of the White Deer, 2012; Midnight Run; Bayou Song; Great Grandfather's Farm; White Deer; The World According to Jumping Spiders; Exploring the Aurora Borealis; A Baseball Boy Turns Fifty, forthcoming. Contributor to periodicals. **Address:** Department of English, University of Wisconsin, Rm. 405, Hibbard Hall, 105 Garfield Ave., Eau Claire, WI 54702-4004, U.S.A. **Online address:** bushnejp@uwec.edu

BUSHNELL, Rebecca W. American (born United States), b. 1952?. **Genres:** Cultural/Ethnic Topics, History, Literary Criticism And History, Politics/Government. **Career:** University of Pennsylvania, Department of English, lecturer, 1982-84, assistant professor, 1984-90, associate professor, 1990-95, professor, 1995-, Thomas S. Gates, Jr. professor, 2005-, School of Arts and Sciences, associate dean of arts and letters, 1998-2003, dean of college of arts and sciences, 2003-04, dean, 2005-, Graduate Group in English, chair, 1991-94, Presidential Commission on Strengthening the Community, director, 1993-94. Writer. **Publications:** Prophesying Tragedy: Sign and Voice in Sophocles' Theban Plays, 1988; Tragedies of Tyrants: Political Thought and Theater in the English Renaissance, 1990; A Culture of Teaching: Early Modern Humanism in Theory and Practice, 1996; King Lear and Macbeth, 1674-1995: An Annotated Bibliography of Shakespeare Studies, 1996; Green Desire: Imagining Early Modern English Gardens, 2003; (ed.) A Companion to Tragedy, 2005; Tragedy: A Short Introduction, 2008. **Address:** School of Arts and Sciences, University of Pennsylvania, 249 S 36th St., Rm. 120, Logan Hall, Philadelphia, PA 19104-6219, U.S.A. **Online address:** bushnell@sas.upenn.edu

BUSHONG, Carolyn Nordin. American (born United States), b. 1947. **Genres:** Human Relations/Parenting, Psychology, Self Help, Social Sciences. **Career:** Kindergarten teacher, 1969-73; school counselor, 1973-75; Aspen Counseling and Tutoring, founder and operator, 1977-84; Carolyn Bushong Psychotherapy Associates Inc., private practice of psychotherapy, 1984-. Writer. **Publications:** Loving Him Without Losing You: Eight Steps to Emotional Intimacy Without Addiction, 1991; The Seven Dumbest Relationship Mistakes Smart People Make, 1997; Bring Back the Man You Fell in Love With, 2003. **Address:** Carolyn Bushong Psychotherapy Associates Inc., 360 S Monroe St., Ste. 290, Denver, CO 80209, U.S.A. **Online address:** carolyn@carolynsays.com

BUSIA, Akosua. American/Ghanaian (born Ghana), b. 1966. **Genres:** Novels, Plays/Screenplays, Children's Fiction. **Career:** Actress and writer. **Publications:** Color Purple, 1985; The Seasons of Beento Blackbird: A Novel, 1996. Contributor to periodicals. **Address:** Little Brown & Co., Time and Life Bldg., 1271 Ave. of the Americas, New York, NY 10020, U.S.A.

BUSIEK, Kurt. American (born United States), b. 1960. **Genres:** Children's Non-fiction, Novels, Humor/Satire. **Career:** Writer. **Publications:** COMIC-BOOK COLLECTIONS AND GRAPHIC NOVELS: Vampirella: The Dracula War!, 1993; Kurt Busiek's Astro City, vol. I: Life in the Big City, 1997; Kurt Busiek's Astro City, vol. II: Confession, 1997; Kurt Busiek's Astro City: Family Album, 1997; (ed. with S. Lee) Untold Tales of Spider-Man, 1997; (with D. Wenzel) The Wizard's Tale, 1998; (with N. Archer) Spider-Man: Goblin Moon, 1999; The Morgan Conquest: The Avengers, 2000; Kurt Busiek's Astro City: The Tarnished Angel, 2000; Marvels, 2001; Thunderbolts: Justice Like Lightning, 2001; The Avengers, Earth's Mightiest Heroes: Supreme Justice, 2001; Avengers: Ultron Unlimited, 2001; The Avengers: Clear and Present Dangers, 2001; The Liberty Project, 2003; Kurt Busiek's Astro City: Local Heroes, 2004; Superman: Secret Identity, 2004; (co-author) Arrowsmith: So Smart in Their Fine Uniforms, 2004; Local Heroes, 2005; JLA: Syndicate Rules, 2005; Avengers: Living Legends, 2004; Conan, vol. I: The Frost Giant's Daughter and Other Stories, 2005, vol. II: The God in the Bowl and Other Stories, 2005, vol. III: The Tower of the Elephant and Other Stories, 2006; (with F. Nicieza) Trinity, 2009; Astro City: The Dark Age, 2010; Astro City: Shinging Stars, 2012. Works appear in anthologies. **Address:** c/o Author Mail, Marvel Enterprises Inc., 417 5th Ave., Ste. 2, New York, NY 10016, U.S.A.

BUSKIN, Richard. American/British (born England), b. 1959?. **Genres:** Biography, Autobiography/Memoirs, Music, Film, History, Popular Culture, Adult Non-fiction, Documentaries/Reportage, Documentaries/Reportage, Art/Art History. **Career:** Full-time freelance journalist. **Publications:** John Lennon: His Life and Legend, 1991; The Films of Marilyn Monroe, 1992; Princess Diana: Her Life Story, 1997; The Complete Idiot's Guide to British Royalty, 1997; The Complete Idiot's Guide to the Beatles, 1998; Prince William: Born to be King, 1998; Inside Tracks: A First-Hand History of Popular Music from the World's Greatest Record Producers and Engineers, 1999; Blonde Heat: The Sizzling Screen Career of Marilyn Monroe, 2001; Sheryl Crow: No Fool to This Game, 2002; (with P. Diller) Like a Lampshade in a Whorehouse: My Life in Comedy, 2005; (with J. Ambrose) Effortless Style, 2006; (with L.L. Sánchez) Dream in Color: How the Sánchez Sisters are Making History in Congress, 2008; (with B. Parfet) Die Trying: One Man's Quest to Conquer the Seven Summits, 2009; (with S. Powers) One From the Hart, 2010; (with T. Coffey) It's Not Really About the Hair, 2011. Contributor to newspapers and magazines. **Address:** Simon & Schuster Inc., 1230 Ave. of the Americas, New York, NY 10020, U.S.A. **Online address:** rb@richardbuskin.com

BUSLIK, Gary. (Rex Harlan). American (born United States), b. 1946. **Genres:** Novels, Humor/Satire. **Career:** Lloyds Security, president, 1969-97; private detective, 1970-; freelance travel writer, 1990-; University of Illinois, Gary and Janice Buslik Caribbean Studies Program, founder. **Publications:** NOVELS: (as Rex Harlan) Black Blood, 1989; The Missionary's Position, 1999; A Rotten Person Travels the Caribbean, 2008. Contributor to magazines. **Address:** c/o Marcia Amsterdam, Amsterdam Literary Agency, 41 W 82nd St., New York, NY 10024, U.S.A. **Online address:** arottenperson@earthlink.net

BUSS, David M. American (born United States), b. 1953. **Genres:** Psychology, Mystery/Crime/Suspense, History. **Career:** Harvard University, assistant professor of psychology, 1981-85; University of Michigan, Department of Psychology, associate professor, 1985-91, professor, 1991-96, Evolution and Human Behavior Group, director, 1992-93; Center for Advanced Study, leader, 1989-90; International Consortium of Social and Personality Psychologists, director, 1990-; Human Behavior and Evolution Society, executive council, 1994-98, president, 2003-09, organizer, 2005; International Society for the Study of Individual Differences, board director, 1995-2001; American Psychologist, editor, 2002-03; University of Texas, professor, 1996-, Individual Differences and Evolutionary Psychology, head, 1996-; Society for the Scientific Study of Sex, president, 1998-99; la Ciudad de las Ideas, board advisor, 2008-10. Writer. **Publications:** (Ed. with N. Cantor) Personality Psychology: Recent Trends and Emerging Directions, 1989; The Evolution of Desire: Strategies of Human Mating, 1994, rev. ed., 2003; (ed. with N.M. Malamuth) Sex, Power, Conflict: Evolutionary and Feminist Perspectives, 1996; Evolutionary Psychology: The New Science of the Mind, 1999, 4th ed., 2012; The Dangerous Passion: Why Jealousy Is as Necessary as Love and Sex, 2000; (with R.J. Larsen) Personality Psychology: Domains of Knowledge about Human Nature, 2002, 4th ed., 2009; (ed.) The Handbook of Evolutionary Psychology, 2005; Murderer Next Door: Why the Mind is Designed to Kill, 2005; (with C.M. Meston) Why Women Have Sex, 2009; (ed. with P.H. Hawley) Evolution of Personality and Individual Differences, 2010. Contributor to journals. **Address:** Department of Psychology, University of Texas, Rm. SEA 3.228, 1 University Sta., Austin, TX 78712-0187, U.S.A. **Online address:** dbuss@gspsy.utexas.edu

BUSS, Helen M. *See* **CLARKE, Margaret.**

BUTALA, Sharon (Annette). Canadian (born Canada), b. 1940. **Genres:** Novels, Novellas/Short Stories, Environmental Sciences/Ecology, Essays. **Career:** Teacher, 1963-83; writer and artist, 1983-. **Publications:** NOVELS: Country of the Heart, 1984; The Gates of the Sun, 1985; Luna, 1988;

Upstream, 1991; The Fourth Archangel, 1992; The Garden of Eden, 1998. SHORT STORY COLLECTIONS: Queen of the Headaches, 1985; Fever, 1990; Real Life, 2002. OTHERS: Harvest, 1992; The Perfection of the Morning: An Apprenticeship in Nature, 1994; Coyote's Morning Cry: Meditations and Dreams from a Life in Nature, 1995; Perfection of the Morning: A Woman's Awakening in Nature, 1997; Wild Stone Heart, 2000; Old Man on His Back, 2002; Lilac Moon: Dreaming of the Real West, 2005; (contrib.) Saskatchewan, 2005; The Sweetest Face on Earth, 2007; The Girl in Saskatoon, 2008. Contributor to magazines and periodicals. **Address:** Westwood Creative Artists, 94 Harbord St., Toronto, ON M5S 1G6, Canada. **Online address:** sharon@sharonbutala.com

BUTCHER, Kristin. Canadian (born Canada), b. 1951. **Genres:** Children's Non-fiction, Young Adult Fiction, Mystery/Crime/Suspense, Biography, Children's Fiction. **Career:** Teacher in Manitoba and British Columbia, 1972-96; Education Intl., technical writer, 1996-97, author, 1997-. **Publications:** The Runaways, 1998; The Tomorrow Tunnel, 1999; The Gramma War, 2001; Cairo Kelly and the Mann, 2002; The Hemingway Tradition, 2002; The Trouble with Liberty, 2003; Zee's Way, 2004; Sylvia Stark: A Biography, 2005; Marie Rollet Hebert: A Biography, 2005; Chat Room, 2006; Zach & Zoe and the Bank Robber, 2008; Zach & Zoe: Bully and the Beagle, 2009; Return to Bone Tree Hill, 2009; Pharaohs and Foot Soldiers: One Hundred Ancient Egyptian Jobs You Might Have Desired or Dreaded, 2009; The Last Superhero, 2010; Cheat, 2010; Zack & Zoe and the River Rescue, 2011. Contributor to periodicals. **Address:** 752 Kalmar Rd., Campbell River, BC V9W 5S4, Canada. **Online address:** kristin@kristinbutcher.com

BUTLER, Anthea D. American (born United States), b. 1960. **Genres:** Theology/Religion. **Career:** Loyola Marymount University, assistant professor of theological studies, 1999-2005, University Honors Program, associate director, 2004-05; Princeton University, Center for the Study of Religion, postdoctoral fellow in race, religion and gender, 2001-02; University of Pennsylvania, assistant professor of religious studies, 2005-, graduate chair; Harvard Divinity School, research associate, 2008-09; North Star Journal, editor. Historian. **Publications:** Women in the Church of God in Christ: Making a Sanctified World, 2007. Contributor to journals. **Address:** U.S.A. **Online address:** antheadbutler@gmail.com

BUTLER, Daniel Allen. American (born United States), b. 1957. **Genres:** History, Military/Defense/Arms Control. **Career:** Author, historian and playwright. **Publications:** Unsinkable: The Full Story of RMS Titanic, 1998; The Lusitania: The Life, Loss, and Legacy of an Ocean Legend, 2000; Warrior Queens: The Queen Mary and Queen Elizabeth in World War II, 2002; The Age of Cunard: A Transatlantic History 1839-2003, 2004; Distant Victory: The Battle of Jutland and the Allied Triumph in the First World War, 2006; The First Jihad: The Battle for Khartoum, and the Dawn of Militant Islam, 2007; The Other Side of the Night: The Carpathia, the Californian and the Night the Titanic was Lost, 2009; The Burden of Guilt: How Germany Shattered the Last Days of Peace, Summer 1914, 2010; Shadow of the Sultan's Realm: The Destruction of the Ottoman Empire and the Making of the Modern Middle East, 2011. **Address:** 8643 Hayden Pl., Culver City, CA 90232, U.S.A. **Online address:** danielallenbutler@gmail.com

BUTLER, David (Edgeworth). British (born England), b. 1924. **Genres:** Politics/Government, History, Essays. **Career:** Princeton University, visiting fellow, 1947-48; University of Oxford, Nuffield College, fellow, 1951-, dean and senior tutor, 1956-64, researcher and academic, now emeritus fellow. Writer. **Publications:** The British General Election of 1951, 1952; The Electoral System in Britain since 1918, 1953; The British General Election of 1955, 1955; The Study of Political Behaviour, 1959; (ed.) Elections Abroad, 1958; (with R. Rose) The British General Election of 1959, 1960; Electoral System in Britain, since 1918, 1963; (with J. Freeman) British Political Facts, 1963, (with G. Butler) 8th ed. as Twentieth-Century British Political Facts, 1900-2000, 2000; (with A.S. King) The British General Election of 1964, 1965; (with A.S. King) The British General Election of 1966, 1966; (with D. Stokes) Political Change in Britain: Forces Shaping Electoral Choice, 1969, 2nd ed. as Political Change in Britain: The Evolution of Electoral Choice, 1974; (with M. Pinto-Duschinsky) British General Election of 1970, 1971; The Canberra Model: Essays on Australian Government, 1973; (with D. Kavanagh) The British General Election of February, 1974, 1974; (with D. Kavanagh) The British General Election of October 1974, 1975; (with U. Kitzinger) The 1975 Referendum, 1976, 2nd ed., 1996; (ed. with A.H. Halsey) Policy and Politics: Essays in Honour of Norman Chester, 1978; (ed.) Coalitions in British Politics, 1978; (ed. with A. Ranney) Referendums: A Comparative Study of Practice and Theory, 1978; (with D. Kavanagh) The British General Election of 1979, 1980; (with D. Marquand) European Elections and British Politics, 1981; (ed. with A. Ranney and H.R. Penniman) Democracy at the Polls: A Comparative Study of Competitive National Elections, 1981; (ed. with V. Bogdanor) Democracy and Elections: Electoral Systems and Their Political Consequences, 1983; Governing without a Majority: Dilemmas for Hung Parliaments in Britain, 1983; (with D. Kavanagh) The British General Election of 1983, 1984; (with A. Lahiri and P. Roy) A Compendium of Indian Elections, 1984; (with P. Jowett) Party Strategies in Britain: A Study of the 1984 European Elections, 1985; (with D. Kavanagh) The British General Election of 1987, 1988; British General Elections since 1945, 1989, 2nd ed., 1995; (with A. Lahiri and P. Roy) India Decides: Elections 1952-1989, 1989, 3rd ed. as India Decides: Elections 1952-1995, 1995; (ed. with D.A. Low) Sovereigns and Surrogates: Constitutional Heads of State in the Commonwealth, 1991; (with B. Cain) Congressional Redistricting: Comparative and Theoretical Perspectives, 1992; (ed. with A. Ranney) Electioneering: A Comparative Study of Continuity and Change, 1992; (ed.) Electoral Politics, 1992; (with D. Kavanagh) The British General Election of 1992, 1992; (with A. Adonis and T. Travers) Failure in British Government: The Politics of the Poll Tax, 1994; (ed. with A. Ranney) Referendums around the World: The Growing Use of Direct Democracy, 1994; (with M. Westlake) British Politics and European Elections, 1994, 1995; (ed. with I. McLean) Fixing the Boundaries: Defining and Redefining Single-Member Electoral Districts, 1996; (with D. Kavanagh) The British General Election of 1997, 1997; (ed. with V. Bogdanor and R. Summers) Law, Politics, and the Constitution: Essays in Honour of Geoffrey Marshall, 1999; (with M. Westlake) British Politics and European Elections 1999, 2000; (with D. Kavanagh) British General Election of 2001, 2002; (with M. Westlake) British Politics and European Elections, 2004, 2005; (with D. Kavanagh) British General Election of 2005, 2005; (with G. Butler) British Political Facts since 1979, 2006; British Political Facts, 2010. **Address:** Nuffield College, University of Oxford, New Rd., Oxford, OX OX1 1NF, England. **Online address:** david.butler@nuffield.ox.ac.uk

BUTLER, Dori Hillestad. American (born United States), b. 1965. **Genres:** Novels, Picture/Board Books, Children's Fiction. **Career:** Friends of the Coralville Public Library, teen writing-group facilitator. Writer. **Publications:** The Great Tooth Fairy Rip-Off, 1997; M Is for Minnesota, 1998; W Is for Wisconsin, 1998; ABC's of Wisconsin, 2000; H Is for Hoosier, 2001; Trading Places with Tank Talbott, 2003; Sliding into Home, 2003; Whodunit: How the Police Solve Crimes, 2004; My Moms Having a Baby!, 2005; Do You Know the Monkey Man?, 2005; Alexandra Hopewell Labor Coach, 2005; Zoe's Potty, 2005; Tank Talbotts Guide to Girls, 2006; Christmas: Season of Peace and Joy, 2007; My Grandpa Had a Stroke, 2007; F Is for Firefighting, 2007; The Truth about Truman School, 2008; Yes, I Know the Monkey Man, 2009; P is for Police, 2009; Buddy Files: the Case of the Missing Family, 2010; Buddy Files: the Case of the Mixed-up Mutts, 2010; Buddy Files: the Case of the Lost Boy, 2010; Buddy Files: the Case of the Fire Alarm, 2010; Buddy Files: the Case of the Library Monster, 2011; The Buddy Files: The Case of the School Ghost, 2012. **Address:** Albert Whitman, 6340 Oakton St., Morton Grove, IL 60053-2723, U.S.A. **Online address:** dori@dorihillestadbutler.com

BUTLER, Dorothy. New Zealander (born New Zealand), b. 1925. **Genres:** Children's Fiction, Novellas/Short Stories, Children's Non-fiction, Education, Literary Criticism And History, Autobiography/Memoirs. **Career:** Auckland Technical Institute, teacher of night classes, 1946-65; Dorothy Butler Children's Bookshop Ltd., owner and managing director, 1965-90; Dorothy Butler Reading Centre, owner, 1978-84; Reed Methuen, children's editor, 1984. **Publications:** (With M. Clay) Reading Begins at Home: Preparing Children for Reading Before They go to School, 1979; Cushla and Her Books, 1980; Babies Need Books: Sharing the Joy of Books with Children from Birth to Six, 1980, rev. Ed., 1998; The Dorothy Butler Pre-Reading Kit, 1980; I Will Build You a House: Poems for Cushla, 1984; Five to Eight, 1986; Come Back, Ginger, 1987; A Bundle of Birds, 1987; My Brown Bear Barney, 1989; Bears, Bears, Bears, 1989; Lulu, 1989; A Happy Tale, 1990; Higgledy Piggledy Hobbledy Hoy, 1991; Another Happy Tale, 1991; Good Morning, Mrs. Martin, 1992; The Little, Little Man, 1992; Farmyard Fiasco, 1992; By Jingo!, 1992; Where's Isabella?, 1992; My Brown Bear, Barney in Trouble, 1993; Birthday Rain, 1993; The Breakdown Day, 1993; My Brown Bear Barney at School, 1994; Farm Boy, City Girl, 1994; What Peculiar People, 1994; My Monkey Martha, 1995; Behave Yourself, Martha, 1995; Just a Dog, 1995; Hector: An

Old Bear, 1995; Children, Books & Families, 1995; What a Birthday!, 1996; There Was a Time: Remembering a Warm and Affectionate Childhood, 1999; My Brown Bear, Barney at the Party, 2000; O'Reilly and the Real Bears, 2002; Seadog: A Tale of Old New Zealand, 2007; All this and a Bookshop Too, 2009. EDITOR: The Magpies Said: Stories and Poems from New Zealand, 1980; For Me, Me, Me: Poems for the Very Young, 1983. **Address:** The Old House, Kare Kare, Auckland, 1002, New Zealand.

BUTLER, Geoff. Canadian (born Canada), b. 1945. **Genres:** Children's Fiction, Art/Art History, Military/Defense/Arms Control, Humor/Satire, Illustrations, Young Adult Non-fiction, Poetry, History, Sports/Fitness, Travel/Exploration, Novellas/Short Stories. **Career:** Artist and writer. **Publications:** SELF-ILLUSTRATED: The Killick: A Newfoundland Story, 1995. OTHERS: Art of War: Painting It Out of the Picture, 1990; The Hangashore, 1998; Ode to Newfoundland, 2003; Look of Angels: Angels in Art, 2004; With Every Breath We Take: A Modern Fable in Which a Snowflake Helps Put an End to War, 2007. Illustrator of books by A. Walsh and P. Wyman. **Address:** 5318 Granville Rd., PO Box 29, Granville Ferry, NS B0S 1K0, Canada. **Online address:** geoffbutler@ns.sympatico.ca

BUTLER, Gregory S. American (born United States), b. 1961. **Genres:** Politics/Government, History. **Career:** Catholic University of America, assistant professor of political science, 1989-90; New Mexico State University, Department of Government, associate professor, 1990-, Center for Latin American Studies, Central American peace scholarship program trainer, 1993, interim department head, 1998-2004; Washington Center for Internships and Academic Seminars, internship coordinator, 1991-, Intercollegiate Studies Institute, faculty associate. Writer. **Publications:** In Search of the American Spirit: The Political Thought of Orestes Brownson, 1992; (with J.D. Slack) U.S. Educational Groups: Institutional Profiles, 1994. Contributor to periodicals. **Address:** Department of Government, New Mexico State University, Rm. 342, Breland Hall, Las Cruces, NM 88003-0001, U.S.A. **Online address:** gbutler@nmsu.edu

BUTLER, Gwendoline (Williams). (Jennie Melville). British (born England), b. 1922. **Genres:** Mystery/Crime/Suspense, Romance/Historical, Literary Criticism And History, Horror, Criminology/True Crime. **Career:** Crime Time Magazine, historical crime fiction critic, 1998-. Writer. **Publications:** Receipt for Murder, 1956; Dead in a Row, 1957; The Dull Dead, 1958; The Murdering Kind, 1958; The Interloper, 1959; Death Lives Next Door in US as Dine and Be Dead, 1960; Make Me a Murderer, 1961; Coffin in Oxford, 1962; Coffin for Baby, 1963; Coffin Waiting, 1963; Coffin in Malta, 1964; A Nameless Coffin, 1966; Coffin Following, 1968; Coffin's Dark Number, 1969; A Coffin from the Past, 1970; A Coffin for Pandora, 1973 in US as Olivia, 1974; A Coffin for the Canary in US as Sarsen Place, 1974; The Vesey Inheritance, 1975; Brides of Friedberg in US as Meadowsweet, 1977; The Red Staircase, 1979; Albion Walk, 1982 as Cavalcade, 1984; Coffin in the Water, 1986; Coffin in Fashion, 1987; Coffin Underground, 1988; Coffin in the Museum of Crime, 1989 as Coffin in the Black Museum, 1989; Coffin and the Paper Man, 1990; Coffin on Murder Street, 1991; Cracking Open a Coffin, 1992; A Coffin for Charley, 1993; The Coffin Tree, 1994; A Dark Coffin, 1995; Butterfly, 1996; Let There Be Love, 1997; A Double Coffin, 1998; Coffin's Game: A John Coffin Mystery, 1999; A Grave Coffin: A Commander John Coffin Mystery, 2000; A Coffin for Christmas, 2000; Coffin's Ghost, 2001; Coffin Knows the Answer, 2002; Dread Murder, 2007. AS JENNIE MELVILLE: Come Home and Be Killed, 1962; Burning Is a Substitute for Loving, 1963; Murderers' Houses, 1964; There Lies Your Love, 1965; Nell Alone, 1966; A Different Kind of Summer, 1967; The Hunter in the Shadows, 1969; A New Kind of Killer, an Old Kind of Death, 1970 in US as A New Kind of Killer, 1971; The Summer Assassin, 1971; Ironwood, 1972; Nun's Castle, 1973; Raven's Forge, 1975; Dragon's Eye, 1976; Axwater in US as Tarot's Tower, 1978; Murder Has a Pretty Face, 1981; The Painted Castle, 1982; The Hand of Glass, 1983; Listen to the Children, 1986; Death in the Garden, 1987 as Murder in the Garden, 1990; Windsor Red, 1988; A Cure for Dying in US as Making Good Blood, 1989; Witching Murder, 1990; Footsteps in the Blood, 1990; Dead Set, 1992; Whoever Has the Heart, 1993; Baby Drop, 1994 in US as A Death in the Family, 1995; The Morbid Kitchen, 1995; The Woman Who Was Not There, 1996; Revengeful Death, 1997; Stone Dead, 1998; Dead Again, 1999; Complicity, 2000; Loving Murder, 2001. Works appear in anthologies. **Address:** St. Martin's Press, 175 5th Ave., New York, NY 10010, U.S.A.

BUTLER, Jack. American (born United States), b. 1944. **Genres:** Novels, Poetry, Novellas/Short Stories, Food And Wine, Young Adult Fiction. **Career:** Joint Educational Consortium, writer-in-residence, 1974-77; University of Arkansas, instructor in English, 1977-79; Cancer Cooperative Group of Northwest Arkansas, science writer and director of public relations, 1979-80; Blue Cross, actuarial analyst, 1980-83; Arkansas Public Service Commission, supervisor for capital recovery, 1985-88; Hendrix College, assistant dean, 1988-93; College of Santa Fe, co-director and associate professor of creative writing, 1993-2004, now retired. Consultant. **Publications:** West of Hollywood: Poems from a Hermitage, 1980; Hawk Gumbo and Other Stories, 1982; The Kid Who Wanted to be a Spaceman and Other Poems, 1984; Jujitsu for Christ (novel), 1986; Nightshade (novel), 1989; Living in Little Rock with Miss Little Rock (novel), 1993; Jack's Skillet: Plain Talk and Some Recipes from a Guy in the Kitchen, 1997; Dreamer (novel), 1998. **Address:** 2566 Camino Chueco, Santa Fe, NM 87505, U.S.A. **Online address:** silverqbuz@aol.com

BUTLER, Jon. American (born United States), b. 1940. **Genres:** History, Theology/Religion. **Career:** California State College, assistant professor of history, 1971-75; University of Illinois, instructor, 1975-85; Yale University, assistant professor, professor of history, 1985-2004, senior faculty fellow, 1987-88, chair of the American studies program, 1988-93, Howard R. Lamar professor of American studies, history and religious studies, 2004-, Department of History, chair, 1999-2004, Graduate School of Arts and Sciences, dean, 2004-10. Writer. **Publications:** Religion and Witch Craft in Early American Society, 1974; Power, Authority and the Origins of American Denominational Order: The English Churches in the Delaware Valley, 1680-1730, 1978; The Huguenots in America: A Refugee People in New World Society, 1983; Awash in a Sea of Faith: Christianizing the American People, 1990; (ed. with H.S. Stout) Religion in American History: A Reader, 1998; Becoming America: The Revolution Before 1776, 2000; Religion in Colonial America, 2000; (ed. with H.S. Stout) Women and American Religion, 2000; (ed.) Protestants in America, 2000; (contrib.) Myer Myers: Jewish Silversmith in Colonial New York, 2001; (with G. Wacker and R. Balmer) Religion in American Life: A Short History, 2003, 2nd ed., 2011; (contrib.) Life, Liberty and the Pursuit of Happiness, 2008; New World Faiths: Religion in Colonial America, 2008. Contributor to journals. **Address:** Graduate School of Arts and Sciences, Yale University, Hall of Graduate Studies, 300-D York St., PO Box 208236, New Haven, CT 06520-8236, U.S.A. **Online address:** jon.butler@yale.edu

BUTLER, Joseph T(homas). American (born United States), b. 1932. **Genres:** Antiques/Furnishings, Architecture, Art/Art History. **Career:** Historic Hudson Valley, Museum Operations, senior director, 1957-94, curator emeritus, 1994-, senior museum director emeritus; Columbia University, adjunct associate professor of architecture, 1970-80; Fashion Institute of Technology, professor of museum studies, 1987-97; The Connoisseur, American editor, 1967-77. **Publications:** Washington Irving's Sunnyside, 1962, 1974; American Antiques 1800-1900: A Collector's History and Guide, 1965; (co-author) World Furniture, 1965; Candleholders in America 1650-1900, 1967; The Family Collections at Van Cortlandt Manor, 1967; (co-author) The Arts in America: The 19th Century, 1969; American Furniture, 1973; (co-author) The Collector's Encyclopedia of Antiques, 1973; The Story of Boscobel and Its Builder: States Morris Dyckman, 1974; Van Cortlandt Manor, 1978; Sleepy Hollow Restorations. A Cross Section of the Collection, 1983; A Field Guide to American Antique Furniture, 1985; (contrib.) The Prendergasts & the Arts & Crafts Movement: The Art of American Decoration & Design, 1890-1920, 1989. **Address:** 222 Martling Ave., Tarrytown, NY 10591, U.S.A.

BUTLER, Judith P. American (born United States), b. 1956. **Genres:** Philosophy, Humanities, Theology/Religion. **Career:** Wesleyan University, assistant professor, 1983-86; George Washington University, assistant professor of philosophy, 1986-89; Johns Hopkins University, professor of humanities, 1989-93; University of California, Maxine Elliot professor of rhetoric and comparative literature, 1993-, Program of Critical Theory, co-director; Pembroke Center for Research and Teaching, English Institute, advisor, 1994; European Graduate School, Hannah Arendt professor of philosophy, 2003, 2005-, Hannah Arendt chair; Cornell University, Andrew D. White professor-at-large, 2003-07, School of Criticism & Theory, senior fellow; Goldsmiths College, professor-at-large, 2007-; Ecole normale superieure and Ecole des hautes etudes, visiting professor, 2008. Writer. **Publications:** Subjects of Desire: Hegelian Reflections in Twentieth-Century France, 1987; Gender Trouble: Feminism and the Subversion of Identity, 1990; (ed. with J.W. Scott) Feminists Theorize the Political, 1992; Bodies That Matter: On the Discursive Limits of Sex, 1993; (ed. and intro. with M. MacGrogan) Erotic Welfare: Sexual Theory and Politics in the Age of Epidemic, 1993; (co-ed.) Feminist Contentions: A Philosophical Exchange, 1994; Excitable Speech: A Politics of the Performative, 1997; The Psychic Life of Power: Theories in Subjection, 1997; (co-author) Das Undarstellbare der Politik: Zur Hegemonie Theorie Erneso Laclaus, 1998; Antigone's Claim: Kinship Between Life and Death, 2000; (with E. Laclau and S. Zizek) Contingency, Hegemony, Universality: Contemporary Dialogues on the Left, 2000; (ed. with J. Guillory and K. Thomas) What's Left of Theory?: New Work on the Politics of Literary Theory, 2000; (co-author) Women & Social Transformation, 2003; Precarious Life: Powers of Violence and Mourning, 2003; (ed. with S. Salih) The Judith Butler Reader, 2003; Undoing Gender, 2004; Giving an Account of Oneself, 2005; (with G.C. Spivak) Who Sings the Nation-State?, 2007; Judith Butler in Conversation: Analyzing the Texts and Talk of Everyday Life, 2007; (contrib.) Reification: A New Look at an Old Idea, 2008; Frames of War: When is Life Grievable?, 2009; (contrib.) Mixed Signals, 2009; Pourquoi des théories?, 2009; (contrib.) What does a Jew Want?, 2011; (ed. with E. Weed) Question of Gender, 2011; (co-author) Power of Religion in the Public Sphere, 2011; Parting Ways, 2012. Contributor to periodicals. **Address:** Department of Rhetoric, University of California, 7408 Dwinelle Hall, Ste. 2670, Berkeley, CA 94720-2670, U.S.A. **Online address:** jb_crittheory@berkeley.edu

BUTLER, Lance St. John. British (born England), b. 1947. **Genres:** Literary Criticism And History, Essays, Adult Non-fiction, Biography, History, Children's Non-fiction, Social Sciences. **Career:** University of Stirling, lecturer, senior lecturer in English studies, 1972-. Writer. **Publications:** (Ed.) Thomas Hardy after Fifty Years, 1977; Thomas Hardy, 1978; D.H. Lawrence's Sons and Lovers, 1980; Henry Fielding's Tom Jones, 1981; Daniel Defoe's Moll Flanders, 1982; Samuel Beckett and the Meaning of Being: A Study in Ontological Parable, 1984; Studying Thomas Hardy, 1986; (ed. with R. Davis) Make Sense Who May: Essays on Samuel Beckett's Later Works, 1988; (ed. and intro.) Alternative Hardy, 1989; (ed. with P.J. Wordie) The Royal Game, 1989; Victorian Doubt: Literary and Cultural Discourses, 1990; (ed. with R. Davis) Rethinking Beckett, 1990; (ed.) Critical Essays on Samuel Beckett, 1993; Registering the Difference: Reading Literature through Register, 1999. Works appear in anthologies. **Address:** Department of English Studies, University of Stirling, Stirling, FF FK9 4LA, Scotland. **Online address:** l.s.j.butler@stir.ac.uk

BUTLER, Leslie Ann. American (born United States), b. 1969. **Genres:** History. **Career:** Yale University, graduate instructor and Newhouse writing fellow, 1995-97; Reed College, visiting assistant professor of history, 1997-98; Michigan State University, James Madison College, assistant professor in humanities, 1998-2003; Dartmouth College, assistant professor of history, associate professor of history, 2003-. Historian and writer. **Publications:** Critical Americans: Victorian Intellectuals and Transatlantic Liberal Reform, 2007. Contributor to books and journals. **Address:** Department of History, Dartmouth College, 6107 Carson Hall, Hanover, NH 03755, U.S.A. **Online address:** leslie.butler@dartmouth.edu

BUTLER, Linda. American (born United States), b. 1947?. **Genres:** Photography, History, Travel/Exploration. **Career:** Writer and photographer. **Publications:** Inner Light: The Shaker Legacy, 1985; (with B. Bahbah) Israel and Latin America, 1986; Rural Japan: Radiance of the Ordinary, 1992; Presidio Gateways: Views of a National Landmark at San Francisco's Golden Gate, 1994; Italy: In the Shadow of Time, 1998; Yangtze Remembered: The River beneath the Lake, 2004. **Address:** c/o Author Mail, Stanford University Press, 1450 Page Mill Rd., Palo Alto, CA 94304-1124, U.S.A. **Online address:** lbphoto@aol.com

BUTLER, Marilyn (Speers). British (born England), b. 1937. **Genres:** Literary Criticism And History. **Career:** BBC, current affairs producer, 1960-63; St. Hilda's College, research fellow, 1970-73; St. Hugh's College, fellow and tutor, 1976-; Oxford University, lecturer in English literature, 1976-86; Cambridge University, King Edward VII professor of English literature, 1986-93; Exeter College, rector, 1993-2004. Writer. **Publications:** Maria Edgeworth: A Literary Biography, 1972; Jane Austen and the War of Ideas, 1975; Peacock Displayed: A Satirist in His Context, 1979; Romantics, Rebels, and Reactionaries: English Literature and Its Background 1760-1830, 1982; Literature as a Heritage, or, Reading Other Ways: Inaugural Lecture, Delivered 10 November 1987, 1988; Jane Austen, 2007. EDITOR: Burke, Paine, Godwin and the Revolution Controversy, 1984; (with J. Todd) The Works of Mary Wollstonecraft, 1989; Castle Rackrent and Ennui, 1992; Frankenstein, 1994; (and intro.) Austen's Northanger Abbey, 1995; (and intro.) Frankenstein, or, The Modern Prometheus, 1998; Works of Maria Edgeworth, 1999-2000; (with M. Myers) Selected Short Fiction, 1997; (with M. Myers and W.J. McCormack) Novels and Selected Works of Maria Edgeworth, 1999; (with M. Butler) Essay on Irish Bulls, 2006. **Address:** Oxford University Press, 198 Madison Ave., New York, NY 10016, U.S.A. **Online address:** rector@exeter.ox.ac.uk

BUTLER, Pierce A. Irish (born Ireland), b. 1952. **Genres:** Novels, Literary Criticism And History, History. **Career:** National University of Ireland, assistant lecturer in engineering design, 1976-79; University of Massachusetts, lecturer in English, 1982-83; Harvard University, instructor in creative writing, 1983; Bentley College, adjunct assistant professor of communication, 1983-84, writer-in-residence, 1988-, lecturer of English, Buddhist Community, coordinator, Literary Society, faculty adviser; Babson College, preceptor in English, 1984-88. Writer. **Publications:** A Malady (novel), 1982; Sean O'Faolain: A Study of the Short Fiction, 1993; Riddle of Stars: A Novel, 1999. Works appear in anthologies. Contributor to periodicals. **Address:** Department of English and Media Studies, Bently University, 175 Forest St., Waltham, MA 02452-4713, U.S.A. **Online address:** pbutler@bentley.edu

BUTLER, Rachel. *See* **PAPPANO, Marilyn.**

BUTLER, Rex D. American (born United States), b. 1952. **Genres:** Theology/Religion, History, Biography. **Career:** First Baptist Church, youth pastor, 1975-76; Trinity Baptist Church, deacon, 1977-79, 1984-95; Southcrest Baptist Church, deacon, 1995-98; Wayland Baptist University, adjunct professor, 1997-98, 2006; Waterford Retirement Center Chapel, Mission of Southcliff Baptist Church, ministry coordinator, music director, 2000-07; Tarrant County College, adjunct professor, 2001; Southwestern Baptist Theological Seminary, adjunct professor, 2003-05; New Orleans Baptist Theological Seminary, adjunct professor, 2004-07, associate professor of church history and patristics, 2007-. Writer. **Publications:** The New Prophecy & New Visions: Evidence of Montanism in the Passion of Perpetua and Felicitas, 2006. **Address:** New Orleans Baptist Theological Seminary, Rm. 105, Dodd bldg., 3939 Gentilly Blvd., New Orleans, LA 70126-4858, U.S.A. **Online address:** rbutler@nobts.edu

BUTLER, Robert Olen. American (born United States), b. 1945. **Genres:** Novels, Novellas/Short Stories, Young Adult Non-fiction. **Career:** Electronic News, editor and reporter, 1972-73; teacher, 1973-74; Energy User News, editor-in-chief, 1975-85; McNeese State University, assistant professor, 1985-93, professor of fiction writing, 1993-; Florida State University, Department of English, Michael Shaara chair in creative writing, Francis Eppes professor, Francis Eppes distinguished professor. **Publications:** NOVELS: The Alleys of Eden, 1981; Sun Dogs, 1982; Countrymen of Bones, 1983; On Distant Ground, 1985; Wabash, 1987; The Deuce, 1989; They Whisper, 1994; Fragments, 1997; The Deep Green Sea, 1998; Mr. Spaceman, 2000; Fair Warning, 2002; Hell, 2009; A Small Hotel, 2011. NONFICTION: From Where You Dream: The Process of Writing Fiction, 2005; Intercourse: Stories, 2008. SHORT STORY COLLECTIONS: A Good Scent from a Strange Mountain: Stories, 1992; Tabloid Dreams, 1996; Had a Good Time: Stories from American Postcards, 2004; Severance: Stories, 2006. Contributor to periodicals. **Address:** Department of English, Florida State University, 411 Williams Bldg., Tallahassee, FL 32306-1580, U.S.A. **Online address:** rbutler@fsu.edu

BUTLER, Ruth (Ann). American (born United States), b. 1931. **Genres:** Art/Art History. **Career:** University of Maryland, assistant professor of art history, 1969-72; University of Massachusetts, associate professor, 1973-76, chair of art department, 1976-80, professor of art history, 1976-94, professor emeritus, 1994-, Research Center for Urban Cultural History (RCUCH), fellow; University of Massachusetts Foundation, board director. Writer. **Publications:** (Ed. with J.V. Nimmen) Nineteenth Century French Sculpture: Monuments for the Middle Class, 1971; Western Sculpture: Definitions of Man, 1975; (ed.) Rodin in Perspective, 1980; Rodin: The Shape of Genius, 1993; (with J.M. Hunisak) Carvings, Casts & Replicas: Nineteenth-century Sculpture from Europe & America in New England Collections, 1994; (with J.P. Plottel and J.M. Roos) Rodin's Monument to Victor Hugo, 1998; (co-author) European Sculpture of the Nineteenth Century, 2000; Hidden in the Shadow of the Master: The Model-wives of Cézanne, Monet, and Rodin, 2008. Contributor to books and periodicals. **Address:** Department of Art History, University of Massachusetts, 100 Morrissey Blvd., Boston, MA 02125-3393, U.S.A.

BUTLIN, Martin (Richard Fletcher). British (born England), b. 1929.

Genres: Art/Art History, Photography. **Career:** Tate Gallery, Historic British Collection, assistant keeper, 1955-67, keeper, 1967-89; British Academy, fellow. Writer. **Publications:** Catalogue of the Works of William Blake in the Tate Gallery, 1957, 3rd ed., 1990; Samuel Palmer's Sketch Book of 1824, 1962; Turner Watercolors, 1962; (with J. Rothenstein) J.M.W. Turner, 1965; (co-author) Tate Gallery Catalogues: Modern British Paintings, Drawings and Sculpture, 1964; The Later Works of J.M.W. Turner, 1965; William Blake, 1966, 3rd ed., 1990; Watercolors from the Turner Bequest, 1819-1845, 1968; The Blake-Varley Sketchbook of 1819, 1969; (with E. Joll) The Paintings of J.M.W. Turner, 1977, 2nd ed., 1984; (intro.) Turner at the Tate: Ninety-Two Oil Paintings, 1980; The Paintings and Drawings of William Blake, 1981; (intro.) L'opera completa di Turner, 1830-1851, 1982; The Later Works of J.M.W. Turner, 1985; Aspects of British Painting, 1550-1800: From the Collection of the Sarah Campbell Blaffer Foundation, 1988; (with M. Luther and I. Warrell) Turner and Petworth: Painter & Patron, 1989; (with T. Gott) William Blake in the Collection of the National Gallery of Victoria, 1989; (ed. with E. Joll and L. Herrmann) The Oxford Companion to J.M.W. Turner, 2001; (co-author) Poets in the Landscape: The Romantic Spirit in British Art, 2007. Author of articles and reviews. Contributor to periodicals. **Address:** 74C Eccelston Sq., London, GL SW1V 1PJ, England.

BUTLIN, Ron. Scottish (born Scotland), b. 1949. **Genres:** Novels, Novellas/Short Stories, Plays/Screenplays, Poetry, Songs/Lyrics And Libretti, Translations, Young Adult Fiction. **Career:** University of Edinburgh, writer-in-residence, 1982, 1985, honorary writing fellow, 2009; University of New Brunswick, Scottish/Canadian exchange writing fellow, 1984-85; Stirling University, writing fellow, 1993; Craigmillar Literacy Trust, writer-in-residence, 1997-98; University of St. Andrews, novelist-in-residence, 1998-99; National Galleries of Scotland, poet-in-residence. **Publications:** NOVELS: The Sound of My Voice, 1987; Night Visits, 1997; Belonging, 2006. EDITOR: First Lines: Writing in Midlothian, 1991; Mauritian Voices, 1997; When We Jump We Jump High!, 1998. POETRY: Stretto, 1976; Creatures Tamed by Cruelty, 1979; The Exquisite Instrument: Imitations from the Chinese, 1982; Ragtime in Unfamiliar Bars, 1985; Histories of Desire, 1995; Selected Poems, 2002; Without a Backward Glance: New And Selected Poems, 2005. STORIES: The Tilting Room, 1983; Vivaldi and the Number 3, 2004; No More Angels, 2007. OTHERS: (contrib.) Shouting It Out: Stories from Contemporary Scotland, 1995; The Invisible Woman, forthcoming. Contributor to books and periodicals. **Address:** Serpent's Tail, 3A Exmouth House, Pine St., Exmouth Market, London, GL EC1R 0JH, England. **Online address:** ronbutlin@blueyonder.co.uk

BUTMAN, John. American (born United States), b. 1951. **Genres:** Business/Trade/Industry, Social Commentary, Biography, Humor/Satire, Women's Studies And Issues, Economics, Reference. **Career:** Friends of the Performing Arts, manager, 1972-76; Silver and Light Productions, director, 1976-80; Envision Corp., creative director, 1980-86; Spectrum Communications Ltd., creative director, 1986-88; Butman Co., president, 1988, principal, 1989-. Writer. **Publications:** Car Wars, 1991; Flying Fox: A Business Adventure in Teams and Teamwork, 1993; Introduction to Managerial Breakthrough, 1994; Juran: A Lifetime of Influence, 1997; The Book That's Sweeping America!: Or Why I Love Business!, 1997; Townie, 2002; (with M.J. Silverstein and N. Fiske) Trading Up: The New American Luxury, 2003, rev. ed. as Trading Up: Why Consumers Want New Luxury Goods. And How Companies Create Them, 2005; (with G. Stalk and R. Lachenauer) Hardball: Are You Playing to Play or Playing to Win?, 2004; (co-author) Sparkly Perfect, 2005; (with D. Balter) Grapevine: The New Art of Word-of-Mouth Marketing, 2005; (with J.P. Andrew and H.L. Sirkin) Payback: Reaping the Rewards of Innovation, 2006; (with M.J. Silverstein) Treasure Hunt: Inside the Mind of the New Global Consumer, 2006; (with G. Stalk) Five Future Strategies You Need Right Now, 2008; (with A.K. Bhattacharya, J.W. Hemerling and H.L. Sirkin) Globality: Competing with Everyone from Everywhere for Everything, 2008; WOM II: The Word of Mouth Marketing Manual, vol. II, 2008; (with M.J. Silverstein and K. Sayre) Women Want More: How to Capture Your Share of the World's Largest, Fastest-Growing Market, 2009. **Address:** The Butman Co., 37 Main St., Ste. 4, Concord, MA 01742, U.S.A. **Online address:** john@butman.us

BUTOW, Robert J. C. (Robert Joseph Charles Butow). American/Japanese (born Japan), b. 1924. **Genres:** Area Studies, International Relations/Current Affairs, History, Military/Defense/Arms Control. **Career:** Princeton University, instructor in history, 1954-59, assistant professor, 1959-60; University of Washington, Jackson School of International Studies, associate professor, 1960-66, professor, 1966-90, professor emeritus, 1990-. Writer. **Publications:** Japan's Decision to Surrender, 1954; Tojo and the Coming of the War, 1961; The John Doe Associates: Backdoor Diplomacy for Peace 1941, 1974. Contributor to professional periodicals. **Address:** Department of History, University of Washington, SMI 10, 315 Smith, PO Box 353560, Seattle, WA 98195-3650, U.S.A.

BUTSCH, Richard (J.). American (born United States), b. 1943?. **Genres:** Communications/Media, Sociology, Popular Culture, Humanities. **Career:** Rider University, professor of sociology, American studies and film and media studies, 1976-. Writer. **Publications:** (Ed.) For Fun and Profit: The Transformation of Leisure into Consumption, 1990; The Making of American Audiences: From Stage to Television, 1750-1990, 2000; (ed.) Media and Public Spheres, 2007; The Citizen Audience: Crowds, Publics, and Individuals, 2008. Contributor of articles to periodicals. **Address:** Depatment of Sociology, American & Film/Media, Studies, Rider University, Fine Arts 220, 2083 Lawrence Rd., Lawrenceville, NJ 08648-3001, U.S.A. **Online address:** butsch@rider.edu

BUTTERWORTH, Jeremy. (Jez Butterworth). British (born England), b. 1969?. **Genres:** Young Adult Fiction, Plays/Screenplays. **Career:** Playwright and screenwriter. **Publications:** AS JEZ BUTTERWORTH: I Believe in Love, 1992; Mojo, 1995, new ed., 1997; Mojo and a Film-Maker's Diary, 1998; Birthday Girl, 2001; Royal Court Theatre Presents The Night Heron, 2002; Night Heron, 2004; The Winterling, 2006; Parlour Song, 2009; Jerusalem, 2009. **Address:** Curtis Brown Group Ltd., Haymarket House, 28/29 Haymarket, London, GL SW1Y 4RX, England.

BUTTERWORTH, Jez. *See* **BUTTERWORTH, Jeremy.**

BUTTERWORTH, Nick. British (born England), b. 1946. **Genres:** Children's Fiction. **Career:** Snapper Productions, founding partner. Writer. **Publications:** SELF-ILLUSTRATED: B.B. Blacksheep and Company: A Collection of Favourite Nursery Rhymes, 1981; My Mom Is Excellent, 1989; My Dad Is Awesome, 1989; Nick Butterworth's Book of Nursery Rhymes, 1990; My Grandma is Wonderful, 1991; My Grandpa Is Amazing, 1991; Amanda's Butterfly, 1991; Jack the Carpenter and His Friends, 1991; Jill the Farmer and Her Friends, 1991; Busy People, 1992; Making Faces, 1993; When It's Time for Bed, 1994; When There's Work to Do, 1994; When We Go Shopping, 1994; When We Play Together, 1994; All Together Now!, 1994; Thud!, 1997; 1-2-3-London, 1998; A-B-C-London, 1998; Jingle Bells, 1998; QPootle5, 2000; Albert Le Blanc, 2002 in US as Albert the Bear, 2003; Q Pootle 5 in Space, 2003; Whisperer, 2004; Percy the Park Keeper: A Classic Treasury, 2007; Tiger in the Snow, 2008; Tiger, 2008; (with M. Evans) Present for Freddie Small, 2007; Albert the Bear to the rescue, 2014. UPNEY JUNCTION SERIES: Treasure Trove at Upney Junction, 1983; A Windy Day at Upney Junction, 1983; Invasion at Upney Junction, 1983; A Monster at Upney Junction, 1983. PERCY THE PARK KEEPER SERIES: One Snowy Night, 1989; After the Storm, 1992 in US as One Blowy Night; The Rescue Party, 1993; The Secret Path, 1993; A Year in Percy's Park, 1995; The Cross Rabbit, 1995; Percy the Park Keeper Press-Out Book, 1995; The Fox's Hiccups, 1995; The Treasure Hunt, 1996; The Hedgehog's Balloon, 1996; The Badger's Bath, 1996; Tales from Percy's Park, 1996; Percy the Park Keeper Activity Book, 1996; Percy Helps Out: Sticker Book, 1996; The Owl's Flying Lesson, 1997; One Warm Fox, 1997; Four Feathers in Percy's Park, 1998; Percy the Park Keeper A-B-C, 1998; Percy in the Park 1-2-3; Percy in the Percy the Park Keeper: A Classic Treasury, 2007. WITH M. INKPEN: The Nativity Play, 1985; The House on the Rock, 1986; The Precious Pearl, 1986; The Lost Sheep, 1986; The Two Sons, 1986; Nice and Nasty: A Book of Opposites in US as Nice or Nasty: A Book of Opposites; I Wonder at the Zoo, 1987; I Wonder in the Garden, 1987; I Wonder in the Country, 1987; I Wonder at the Farm in US as I Wonder on the Farm, 1987; Who Made... In the Country, 1987; Who Made 1987; Who Made...At the Zoo, 1987; Who Made and Zacchaeus, 1988; The Mouse's Story: Jesus and the Storm, 1988; The Cat's Tale: Jesus at the Wedding, 1988; The Fox's Tale: Jesus Is Born, 1988; The Good Stranger, 1989; Just Like Jasper!, 1989; The Little Gate, 1989; The Rich Farmer, 1989; The Ten Silver Coins, 1989; The School Trip, 1990; Wonderful Earth!, 1990; Field Day, 1991; Jasper's Beanstalk, 1992; Stories Jesus Told, 1994; Opposites, 1997; Animal Tales, 2002. OTHER: Q Pootle 5, 2001. Illustrator of books by others. **Address:** HarperCollins Publishers, 77-85 Fulham Palace Rd., Hammersmith, London, GL W6 8JB, England.

BUTTON, Kenneth J(ohn). American/British (born England), b. 1948.

Genres: Economics, Transportation. Career: University of Leeds, Leeds, researcher, teaching postgraduate, 1971-73; Loughborough University, reader in economics, 1973-, 1984-89, lecturer, 1973-81, senior lecturer, 1981-84, professor of applied economics and transport, 1989-96, deputy director of studies, 1979-81, 1982-83, director of graduate studies, 1984-89, director of studies, 1992-93, Centre for Research in European Economics and Finance, director, 1993-96; University of British Columbia, visiting professor, 1982; University of California, visiting fellow, 1982; Applied Micro-Economics Research Group, executive director, 1985-93; OECD, advisor, 1990, counselor, 1994; Tinbergen Institute, VSB Visiting Professor of Transport and the Environment, 1992-96; Transportation Research D: Transport and the Environment, editor-in-chief, 1996-; George Mason University, Institute of Public Policy, distinguished visiting professor, 1996-97, professor, 1996-2005, university professor of public policy, 1997-, Center for Transportation Policy, Operations and Logistics, director, 1998-, 2001-, Aerospace Policy Research Center, director, 2003-, TPOL Masters Program, director, 2005-06; Journal of Air Transport Management, editor-in-chief, 1997; University of Bologna, Applied Economics, visiting professor, 2003-08; University of Sydney, Institute of Transport and Logistics Studies, board director, 2003-; University of Porto, professor in transport engineering, 2004-; Boston University, Center for Transportation Studies, board director, 2004-; Annals of Tourism Research, associate editor, 2005-; Transportation Research Forum, president, 2008-09; University of Bergamo, visiting professor in applied economics, 2009-; Inha University, visiting professor in transportation economics, 2010-; Chartered Institute of Logistics and Transport, fellow; Chartered Institution of Highways and Transportation, fellow; Pearce, Sharp and Associates, director. Publications: (With P.J. Barker) Case Studies in Cost Benefit Analysis, 1975; Urban Economics, 1976; (with D. Gillingwater) Case Studies in Regional Economics, 1976; The Economics of Urban Transport, 1977; (with A.D. Pearman) The Economics of Urban Freight Transport, 1981; (with A.D. Pearman and A.S. Fowkes) Car Ownership Modelling and Forecasting, 1982; Transport Economics, 1982, 3rd ed., 2010; (with A.D. Pearman) The Practice of Transport Investment Appraisal, 1983; Transport Policy, Economics and the Environment, 1983; Road Haulage Licensing and EC Transport Policy, 1984; (with A.D. Pearman) Applied Transport Economics, 1985; (with D. Gillingwater) Future Transport Policy, 1986; (with A.J. Westaway) The Economic Impact of Aid Policy on Donor Country's Economies, 1989; Market and Intervention Failures in Transport Policy, 1992; (co-author) Academic Links and Communications, 1993; Transport, the Environment and Economic Policy, 1993; (co-author) Transport Policy, 1994; (co-author) Missing Transport Networks in Europe, 1994; (co-author) The Future of International Air Transport Policy, 1997; (co-author) Meta-Analysis in Environmental Economics, 1997; (with K. Haynes and R. Stough) Flying into the Future, 1998; (with E. Pentecost) Economic Convergence in Europe, 1999; (with E. Elgar) The Economics and Political Economy of Transportation Security, forthcoming. EDITOR: Transport Location and Spatial Policy, 1983; International Railway Economics, 1985; The Collected Essays of Harvey Leibenstein, 2 vols., 1989; The Age of Regulatory Reform, 1989; (with J.P. Barde) Transport Policy and the Environment, 1990; Airline Deregulation: An International Perspective, 1990; Transport in a Free Market Economy, 1991; Transport, the Environment and Sustainable Development, 1992; Location Theory, 2 vols., 1996; Regional Dynamics, 2 vols., 1996; Analytical Urban Economics, 1996; Regional Labour and Housing Markets, 1996; Regional Policy and Regional Integration, 1996; Transport and Land Use, 1996; Transport Networks in Europe, 1993; (with E.T. Verhoef) Road Pricing, Traffic Congestion and the Environment, 1998; Transport Policy, 1998; (with Y. Hayashi and P. Nijkamp) Environment and Transport, 1999; (with J.B. Opschoor and P. Nijkamp) Environmental Economics and Development, 1999; Global Aspects of the Environment, 2 vols., 1999; (with R.K. Turner and P. Nijkamp) Ecosystems and Nature, 1999; (with D. Banister and P. Nijkamp) Environment, Land Use and Urban Policy, 1999; (with J.B. Opschoor and P. Nijkamp) Environment Economics and Development, 1999; (with T. Tietenberg and P. Nijkamp) Environmental Instruments and Institutions, 1999; (with K.G. Willis and P. Nijkamp) Environmental Valuation, 2 vols., 1999; (with R. Stough) Air Transport Networks, 2000; (with D.A. Hensher) Handbook of Transport Modelling, 2000; (with A.M. Brewer and D.A. Hensher) Handbook of Logistics and Supply Chain Management, 2001; (with D.A. Hensher) Handbook of Transport Systems and Traffic Control, 2001; (with M.R. Brooks and P. Nijkamp) Maritime Transport, 2002; (with P. Forsyth and P. Nijkamp) Air Transport, 2002; Railways, 2002; Transport Infrastructure, 2002; (with P. Rietveld and P. Nijkamp) Urban Transport, 2003; (with A. McKinnon and P. Nijkamp) Transport Logistics, 2003; Recent Developments in Transport Economics, 2003; (with D.A. Hensher) Handbook of Transport and the Environment, 2003; (with L. Lundqvist and P. Nijkamp) The Automobile, 2003; Wings Across Europe: Towards and Efficient European Air Transport System, 2004; (with J. Lammersen-Baum and R. Stough) Defining Aerospace Policy: Essays In Honor of Francis T. Hoban, 2004; (with R. Stough, M. Bragg and S. Taylor) Telecommunications, Transportation and Location, 2006; (with J.P.H. Poon and P. Nijkamp) Social Planning, 2006; (with L. Kiminami and P. Nijkamp) Public Facilities Planning, 2006; (with J.C.J.M.V.D. Bergh and P. Nijkamp) Environmental Planning, 2007; (with H. Vega and P. Nijkamp) A Dictionary of Transport Analysis, 2010; (with A. Riggiani) Transportation and Economic Development Challenges, 2011; (with H. Vega) Globalization and Transport, forthcoming. Address: School of Public Policy, George Mason University, MS 3B1, 3351 Fairfax Dr., Fairfax, VA 22030, U.S.A. Online address: kbutton@gmu.edu

BUTTS, Anthony. American (born United States), b. 1969. **Genres:** Adult Non-fiction, Poetry, Literary Criticism And History. **Career:** Paper Street, poetry editor, 2006-; University of Dayton, professor; Carnegie Mellon University, assistant professor, associate professor of creative writing; Carnegie Mellon University Press, associate poetry editor. **Publications:** Fifth Season, 1997; Evolution, 1998; Little Low Heaven, 2003; Male Hysteria, 2007; Golden Underground: Poems, 2009. Contributor to periodicals. Works appear in anthologies. **Address:** Department of English, Carnegie Mellon University, Baker Hall 259, 5000 Forbes Ave., Pittsburgh, PA 15213-3890, U.S.A. **Online address:** ab25@andrew.cmu.edu

BUTTS, Dennis. British (born England), b. 1932. **Genres:** Literary Criticism And History, Bibliography, History, Essays. **Career:** University of Reading, lecturer in children's literature, head of English. Writer. **Publications:** R.L. Stevenson: A Monograph, 1966; (with J. Merrick) Living Words, 1966; (ed.) Good Writers for Young Readers: Critical Essays, 1977; (ed. and intro.) Secret Garden, 1987; (ed. and intro.) King Solomon's Mines, 1989; (ed. and intro.) Children of the New Forest, 1991; (ed. and intro.) Railway Children, 1991; (ed.) Stories and Society, 1992; Mistress of Our Tears: A Literary and Bibliographical Study of Barbara Hofland, 1992; (ed. and intro.) Little Lord Fauntleroy, 1993; (ed. and intro.) Allan Quatermain, 1995; (co-ed.) Children's Literature: An Illustrated History, 1995; (with J. Briggs and M.O. Grenby) Popular Children's Literature in Britain, 2007; From the Abbey to the Office, 2008; Children's Literature and Social Change: Some Case Studies from Barbara Hofland to Philip Pullman, 2010. **Address:** University of Reading, Redlands Rd., PO Box 218, Reading, BR RG1 5EX, England.

BUTTURINI, Paula. French/American (born United States), b. 1951?. **Genres:** Autobiography/Memoirs, Food And Wine. **Career:** Chicago Tribune, correspondent; United Press Intl., correspondent. Journalist. **Publications:** Keeping the Feast: One Couple's Story of Love, Food and Healing in Italy, 2010. Contributor to newspapers. **Address:** Paris, France. **Online address:** paulab.author@gmail.com

BÜTZ, Jeffrey J. American (born United States), b. 1957?. **Genres:** Theology/Religion. **Career:** Grace Lutheran Church, pastor, 1996-; Pennsylvania State University, adjunct professor of philosophy and world religions, 2002-. Author. **Publications:** The Brother of Jesus and the Lost Teachings of Christianity, 2005; The Secret Legacy of Jesus: The Judaic Teachings That Passed from James the Just to the Founding Fathers, 2010. **Online address:** revjeff2000@juno.com

BUTZER, C. M. American (born United States), b. 1974?. **Genres:** Graphic Novels, Illustrations. **Career:** Wizards of the Coast, illustrator and designer; Studio Galante, illustrator, 1997-2003; Rabid Rabbit, founder, 2005-; St. John's University, lecturer; School of Visual Arts, lecturer, 2009-. Cartoonist, illustrator and publisher. **Publications:** SELF-ILLUSTRATED: Gettysburg: The Graphic Novel, 2009. Works appear in anthologies. Illustrator of books by others. **Address:** HarperCollins Publishers, 10 E 53rd St., New York, NY 10022, U.S.A. **Online address:** chris@cmbutzer.com

BUXBAUM, Julie. British/American (born United States), b. 1977?. **Genres:** Novels, Literary Criticism And History. **Career:** Gibson, Dunn & Crutcher, lawyer; Hennigan, Bennett & Dorman, lawyer. Writer. **Publications:** The Opposite of Love, 2008; After You: A Novel, 2009. **Address:** London, GL , England. **Online address:** juliebux@gmail.com

BUXTON, Jayne. British (born England) **Genres:** Novels, Social Sciences, Business/Trade/Industry. **Career:** Flametree, co-founder and co-director;

writer. **Publications:** Ending the Mother War: Starting the Workplace Revolution, 1998; Lessons in Duck Hunting: A Novel, 2006; Take Someone Like Me, 2007. Contributor to periodicals. **Address:** Flametree, Plumtree Ct., London, GL EC4A 4HT, England.

BUZZELL, Colby. American (born United States), b. 1976. **Genres:** Autobiography/Memoirs. **Career:** Writer. **Publications:** My War: Killing Time in Iraq (memoir), 2005; Lost in America: A Dead-End Journey, 2011. **Address:** c/o Author Mail, G.P. Putnam's Sons, Penguin Group Inc., 375 Hudson St., New York, NY 10014-3657, U.S.A. **Online address:** mywarcbftw@gmail.com

BUZZELLI, Elizabeth Kane. American (born United States), b. 1946?. **Genres:** Young Adult Fiction, Natural History. **Career:** Traverse City Record-Eagle, book reviewer; The Northern Express, book reviewer; Northern Michigan College, writing instructor. Writer. **Publications:** A History of the Romeo Community School District, 1824-1976, 1976; A Gift of Evil, 1983. EMILY KINCAID MYSTERY SERIES: Dead Dancing Women, 2007; Dead Floating Lovers, 2009; Dead Sleeping Shaman, 2010; Dead Dogs and Englishmen, 2011. Contributor of articles to periodicals. **Address:** Michigan Humanities Council, 8453 Gedman Rd., Mancelona, MI 49659, U.S.A. **Online address:** ebuzzelli@aol.com

BUZZEO, Toni. American (born United States), b. 1951. **Genres:** Children's Fiction, Education, Librarianship, Bibliography, Picture/Board Books. **Career:** Baxter Memorial Library, children's librarian, 1987-88; Congin School, library media specialist, 1988-90; Margaret Chase Smith School, library media specialist, 1990-93; Longfellow Elementary School, library media specialist, 1993-2004; writer, 1995-. **Publications:** (With J. Kurtz) Terrific Connections with Authors, Illustrators, and Storytellers: Real Space and Virtual Links, 1999; (with J. Kurtz) 35 Best Books for Teaching U.S. Regions: Using Fiction to Help Students Explore the Geography, History, and Cultures of the Seven U.S. Regions, 2002; Collaborating to Meet Standards, Teacher/Librarian Partnerships for K-6, 2002, 2nd ed., 2007; Collaborating to Meet Standards, Teacher/LibrarianPartnerships for 7-12, 2002; Toni Buzzeo and YOU, 2005; Read! Perform! Learn! Ten Reader's Theater Projects for Literacy Enhancement, 2006; Collaborating to Meet Literacy Standards: Teacher/Librarian Partnerships for K-2, 2007; Read! Perform! Learn! Two: Ten More Reader's Theater Projects for Literacy Enhancement, 2007; The Collaboration Handbook, 2008; ABC, Read to Me: Teaching Letter of the Week in the Library and the Classroom, 2009. JUVENILE: The Sea Chest, 2002; Dawdle Duckling, 2003; Little Loon and Papa, 2004; Ready or Not, Dawdle Duckling, 2005; Our Librarian Won't Tell Us Aanything!, 2006; Fire Up with Reading, 2007; The Library Doors, 2008; R is for Research, 2008; The Great Dewey Hunt, 2009; Adventure Annie Goes to Work, 2009; No T. Rex in the Library, 2010; Adventure Annie Goes to Kindergarten, 2010; Lighthouse Christmas, 2010; One Cool Friend, 2012; Stay Close to Mama, 2012; Inside the Books, 2012; But I Read It on the Internet, 2012; Just Like My Papa, 2013. **Address:** U.S.A. **Online address:** tonibuzzeo@tonibuzzeo.com

BYALICK, Marcia. American (born United States), b. 1947. **Genres:** Children's Fiction, Young Adult Fiction, Self Help, Essays, Humor/Satire, Psychology. **Career:** Women's Record, editor-in-chief, 1985-93; Hofstra University, writing teacher, 1993-; Long Island University and C.W. Post Campus, faculty, 1995-; Spotlight, columnist and feature writer, 1996; Distinction, columnist and feature writer, 1996-; New York Times, journalist; BeingGirl.com, content editor. **Publications:** (With L. Saslow) Three-Career Couple: Mastering the Art of Juggling Work, Home and Family (humorous self-help), 1993; (with L. Saslow) How Come I Feel so Disconnected...If This is Such a User Friendly World?, 1995; (with R.A. Ruden) The Craving Brain: The Biobalance Approach to Controlling Addiction, 1997; (with R.A. Ruden) Craving Brain: A Bold New Approach to Breaking Free from Drug Addiction, Overeating, Alcoholism, Gambling, 2000. YOUNG ADULT NOVELS: Reel Life, 1993; You Don't Have to Be Perfect to Be Excellent, 1993; It's a Matter of Trust, 1995; Quit It, 2002. Contributor to magazines and newspapers. **Address:** 22 Lydia Ct., Albertson, NY 11507, U.S.A.

BYARS, Betsy (Cromer). American (born United States), b. 1928. **Genres:** Children's Fiction, Novellas/Short Stories, Science Fiction/Fantasy, Self Help, Social Sciences, Picture/Board Books, Young Adult Non-fiction. **Career:** Writer. **Publications:** Clementine, 1962; The Dancing Camel, 1965; Rama, the Gypsy Cat, 1966; The Midnight Fox, 1968; Trouble River, 1969; The Summer of the Swans, 1970; Go and Hush the Baby, 1971; The House of Wings, 1972; The 18th Emergency, 1973, 3rd ed., 1988; The Winged Colt of Casa Mia, 1973; After the Goat Man, 1974; The TV Kid, 1976; The Pinballs, 1977, 2nd ed., 1988; The Cartoonist, 1978; Good-bye, Chicken Little, 1979; The Night Swimmers, 1980; The Cybil War, 1981; The Animal, the Vegetable and John D. Jones, 1982; The Two-Thousand-Pound Goldfish, 1982; The Glory Girl, 1983; The Computer Nut, 1984; Cracker Jackson, 1985; (afterword) The Five Little Peppers and How They Grew, 1985; The Golly Sisters Go West, 1985, 2nd ed., 1994; The Not-Just-Anybody Family, 1986; The Blossoms Meet the Vulture Lady, 1986; The Blossoms and the Green Phantom, 1987; A Blossom Promise, 1987; (intro.) For Reading out Loud, 1987; Beans on the Roof, 1988; The Burning Questions of Bingo Brown, 1988, 2nd ed., 1989; Bingo Brown and the Language of Love, 1988; Hooray for the Golly Sisters, 1990; Bingo Brown, Gypsy Lover, 1990, 2nd ed., 1992; The Seven Treasure Hunts, 1991; Wanted... Mud Blossom, 1991; The Moon and I, 1991; Bingo Brown's Guide to Romance, 1992; Coast to Coast, 1992; McMummy, 1993; The Golly Sisters Ride Again, 1994; The Dark Stairs: A Herculeah Jones Mystery, 1994; (comp.) Growing up Stories, 1995; Tarot Says Beware, 1995; (intro.) A Newbery Zoo: A Dozen Animal Stories by Newbery Award-winning Authors, 1995; My Brother, Ant, 1996; The Joy Boys, 1996; Tornado, 1996; Dead Letter, 1996; Ant Plays Bear, 1997; Death's Door, 1997; Disappearing Acts, 1998; Me Tarzan, 2000; (with B. Duffey and L. Myers) My Dog, My Hero, 2000; Little Horse, 2001; The Keeper of the Doves, 2002; (comp.) Top Teen Stories, 2004; Little Horse on His Own, 2004; (with B. Duffey and L. Myers) The SOS File, 2004; Summer of the Swans, 2004; The Black Tower, 2006; Boo's Dinosaur, 2006; Death's Door, 2006; King of Murder, 2006; (with B. Duffey and L. Myers) Dog Diaries: Secret Writings of the WOOF Society, 2007; Domino, 2008; Not-Just-Anybody Family, 2008; Boo's Surprise, 2009; (with B. Duffey and L. Myers) Cat Diaries: Secret Writings of The MEOW Society, 2010. SELF-ILLUSTRATED: The Groober, 1967; The Lace Snail, 1975. **Address:** 401 Rudder Ridge, Seneca, SC 29678, U.S.A.

BYATT, A(ntonia) S(usan). British (born England), b. 1936. **Genres:** Novels, Novellas/Short Stories, Literary Criticism And History, Young Adult Nonfiction. **Career:** University of London, extra-mural lecturer, 1962-71; Central School of Art and Design, lecturer in literature, 1965-69; University College London, lecturer, 1972-81, senior lecturer in English, 1981-83, admissions tutor in English, 1980-83, fellow, 2004; University of Cambridge, Newnham College, associate, 1977-82, honorable fellow, 1999; writer, 1983-; University of the Arts London, honorable fellow, 2004. **Publications:** The Shadow of the Sun, A Novel, 1964; Degrees of Freedom: The Novels of Iris Murdoch, 1965 in UK as Degrees of Freedom: The Early Novels of Iris Murdoch, 1994; The Game, A Novel, 1967; Wordsworth and Coleridge in Their Time, 1970 as Unruly Times: Wordsworth and Coleridge in Their Time, 1989; Iris Murdoch, 1976; The Virgin in the Garden, 1978; (ed. and intro.) The Mill on the Floss, 1979; Still Life, 1985; Sugar and Other Stories, 1987; (ed.) Selected Essays, Poems and Other Writings, 1989; Possession: A Romance, 1990; (ed.) Dramatic Monologues, 1990; Passions of the Mind: Selected Writings, 1991; Angels and Insects: Two Novellas, 1992; (co-author) Deadly Sins, 1993; The Matisse Stories, 1993; The Djinn in the Nightingale's Eye: Five Fairy Tales, 1994; (ed. with A. Hollinghurst) New Writing 4, 1995; (with I. Sodre) Imagining Characters: Six Conversations about Women Writers, 1995; Babel Tower, 1996; (co-ed.) New Writing 6, 1997; Elementals: Stories of Fire and Ice, 1998; (ed.) The Oxford Book of English Short Stories, 1998; (contrib.) Patrick Heron(essay), 1998; Collected Stories, 1999; The Biographer's Tale, 2000; On Histories and Stories: Selected Essays, 2000; Portraits in Fiction, 2001; A Whistling Woman, 2001; The Little Black Book of Stories, 2003; Vintage Byatt, 2004; (contrib.) Julie Heffernan: Everything that Rises (essay), 2006; The Children's Book: A Novel, 2009; (contrib.) Butchers, Dragons, Gods & Skeletons: Film Installations by Philip Haas, 2009; (intro.) Grimm Reader: The Classic Tales of the Brothers Grimm, 2010; (intro.) Fifth Queen, 2011; Ragnarok: The End of the Gods, 2011. **Address:** c/o Deborah Rogers, Rogers, Coleridge & White Ltd., 20 Powis Mews, London, GL W11 1JN, England.

BYE, Beryl (Joyce Rayment). British (born England), b. 1926. **Genres:** Children's Fiction, Children's Non-fiction, Theology/Religion, Novels, Young Adult Fiction. **Career:** Freelance writer, 1960-. **Publications:** Three's Company, 1961; Wharf Street, 1962; Prayers at Breakfast, 1964; Teaching Our Children the Christian Faith, 1965; Please God, 1966; About God, 1967; Nobody's Pony, 1967; Looking into Life, 1967; Jesus Said, 1968; Pony for Sale, 1969; Learning from Life, 1969, Jesus at Work, 1969; Start the Day Well, 1970; Prayers for All Seasons, 1971; People Like Us, 1971; More People Like Us, 1972; To Be Continued, 1972; Belles Bridle, 1973; Following Jesus, 1974; Family Prayers, 1975; What about Lifestyle?, 1977; Time for Jesus, 1980; Hear a Minute, 1990; Hello God! It's Me!, 1992. **Address:** Cotswold, Priory Ln., Bishops Cleeve, GC GL52 8AN, England.

BYER, Heather. American (born United States) **Genres:** Natural History, Autobiography/Memoirs. **Career:** Franklin & Siegal Associates, film and television scout, 1992-95; Contentville, executive editor; Johns Hopkins University, fiction and poetry writing instructor, adjunct faculty, 1995-97; Kopelson Entertainment, vice president of literary acquisitions, 1998-2000; Towson University, English composition instructor; Brill Media, executive editor, 2000-01; writer and editor, 2001-; McKinsey & Co., senior copy editor, 2002-. **Publications:** Sweet: An Eight-Ball Odyssey (memoir), 2007. Contributor to books and periodicals. **Address:** Solow Literary Enterprises Inc., 862 Sir Francis Drake Blvd., Ste. 252, San Anselmo, CA 94960-1914, U.S.A. **Online address:** heather@heatherbyer.com

BYER, Kathryn Stripling. American (born United States), b. 1944. **Genres:** Poetry. **Career:** Western Carolina University, instructor in English, 1968-70, Cataloguing Department of Hunter Library, library clerk, 1976-78, Department of English, part-time faculty, 1980-85, poet-in-residence, 1990-98; University of North Carolina, M.F.A. Writing Program, faculty; Converse College, Sara Lura Mathews self distinguished writer-in-residence, 2004. **Publications:** POETRY: Search Party, 1979; Alma: Poems, 1983; The Girl in the Midst of the Harvest, 1986; Wildwood Flower, 1992; Black Shawl, 1998; (intro.) Late Mowing: Poems and Essays, 2000; Catching Light, 2002; Wake, 2003; Coming to Rest: Poems, 2006. (ed. with M. Kallet) The Movable Nest: A Mother/Daughter Companion, 2007; Descent: Poems, 2012. Contributor to periodicals. **Address:** Department of English, Western Carolina University, 565 H.F. Robinson Administration Bldg., Cullowhee, NC 28723, U.S.A. **Online address:** ksbyer@aol.com

BYERS, John A. American (born United States), b. 1948. **Genres:** Animals/Pets, Sciences, Zoology, Natural History. **Career:** Brookfield Zoo. research associate, 1977; University of Idaho, faculty, 1980-, professor of zoology, 1993-, department of biological sciences, professor; Tulane University, lecturer; University of Alberta, lecturer; Monash University, lecturer; City University of New York, lecturer; University of California, lecturer; University of Colorado, lecturer. Writer and consultant. **Publications:** (Contrib.) The Individual and Society, 1986; American Pronghorn: Social Adaptations and the Ghosts of Predators Past, 1997; (ed. with M. Bekoff) Animal Play: Evolutionary, Comparative and Ecological Perspectives, 1998; Built for Speed: A Year in the Life of Pronghorn, 2003. Contributor of articles to journals. **Address:** Department of Biological Sciences, University of Colorado, Life Sciences S Rm. 345, Moscow, ID 83844-3051, U.S.A. **Online address:** jbyers@uidaho.edu

BYERS, Michael. Canadian (born Canada), b. 1966?. **Genres:** Adult Nonfiction, Law, Politics/Government, Social Commentary, Translations. **Career:** Oxford University, Jesus College, research fellow, 1996-99, Keble College, Center for Socio-Legal Studies, Peter North visiting fellow, 2001-02; Max Planck Institute for Comparative Law and International Law, visiting fellow, 1996-99; Duke University, School of Law, associate professor, 1999-2003, professor of law, 2003-04, Center for Canadian Studies, director, JD/LLM Program, co-director in international and comparative law; Bucerius Law School, Commerzbank visiting professor, 2003; University of British Columbia, professor of political science, 2004-, Canada Research Chair in Global Politics and International Law; University of Tel Aviv, Buchmann Faculty of Law, visiting professor, 2004; University of Cape Town, Faculty of Law, visiting professor, 2005. Writer. **Publications:** Custom, Power, and the Power of Rules: International Relations and Customary International Law, 1999; (trans.) W.G. Grewe, The Epochs of International Law, 2000; (ed.) The Role of Law in International Politics: Essays in International Relations and International Law, 2000; (ed. with G. Nolte) United States Hegemony and the Foundations of International Law, 2003; War Law: Understanding International Law and Armed Conflict, 2006; Intent for a Nation: What is Canada For?, 2007. **Address:** Department of Political Science, University of British Columbia, C417 Buchanan Bldg., C425-1866 Main Mall, Vancouver, BC V6T 1Z1, Canada. **Online address:** michael.byers@ubc.ca

BYERS, William. Canadian (born Canada), b. 1943. **Genres:** Mathematics/Statistics, Education. **Career:** Concordia University, professor of mathematics, 1972-, professor emeritus of mathematics and statistics; Lonergan University College, acting principal, 1994-95, principal, 1995-2003. Writer. **Publications:** How Mathematicians Think: Using Ambiguity, Contradiction, and Paradox to Create Mathematics, 2007. Contributor to journals. **Address:** Department of Mathematics and Statistics, Concordia University, S-LB 677, 1455 de Maisonneuve Blvd. W, Montreal, QC H3G 1M8, Canada. **Online address:** wpbyers@mathstat.concordia.ca

BYLES, Jeff. American (born United States) **Genres:** Novels, History, Sociology, Art/Art History. **Career:** The Architect's Newspaper, managing editor, associate editor; Van Alen Institute, special projects manager, director of research. **Publications:** Rubble: Unearthing the History of Demolition, 2005; (co-ed.) The New York 2030 Notebook, 2008; (with A. Ferebee) A History of Design from the Victorian Era to the Present, 2nd ed., 2011. Contributor to periodicals. **Address:** c/o Author Mail, Harmony Books, 1745 Broadway, New York, NY 10019, U.S.A. **Online address:** info@jeffbyles.com

BYMAN, Daniel L. American (born United States), b. 1967. **Genres:** History, Politics/Government, Military/Defense/Arms Control. **Career:** Central Intelligence Agency, political analyst, 1990-93; RAND Corp., policy analyst and director for research at the Center for Middle East Public Policy, 1997-2002; U.S. House and Senate Intelligence Committees, staff of the Joint 9/11 Inquiry, 2001-02; 9/11 Commission, staff, 2003-04; Georgetown University, Department of Government, assistant professor, 2003-05, associate professor, 2005-, Edmund A. Walsh School of Foreign Service, associate professor, 2005-, Center for Peace and Security Studies, director, 2005-, Security Studies Program, director, 2005-; Brookings Institution, Saban Center for Middle East Policy, senior fellow of foreign policy, 2003-. Political scientist and writer. **Publications:** (with Z. Khalilzad and D.A. Shlapak) The Implications of the Possible End of the Arab- Israeli Conflict for Gulf Security, 1997; (with R. Cliff) China's Arms Sales: Motivations and Implications, 1999; (with M.C. Waxman and E. Larson) Air Power as a Coercive Instrument, 1999; (with J.D. Green) Political Violence and Stability in the States of the Northern Persian Gulf, 1999; (with M.C. Waxman) Confronting Iraq: U.S. Policy and the Use of Force since the Gulf War, 2000; (co-author) Strengthening the Partnership: Improving Military Coordination with Relief Agencies and Allies in Humanitarian Operations, 2000; (with M. Waxman) The Dynamics of Coercion: American Foreign Policy and the Limits of Military Might, 2001; (co-author) Trends in Outside Support for Insurgent Movements, 2001; (with S. Chubin, A. Ehteshami and J. Green) Iran's Security Policy in the PostRevolutionary Era, 2001; Keeping the Peace: Lasting Solutions to Ethnic Conflicts, 2002; (with J.R. Wise) The Persian Gulf in the Coming Decade: Trends, Threats, and Opportunities, 2002; (ed. with N. Bensahel) The Future Security Environment in the Middle East: Conflict, Stability, and Political Change, 2003; Deadly Connections: States That Sponsor Terrorism, 2005; (with K.M. Pollack) Things Fall Apart: Containing the Spillover from an Iraqi Civil War, 2007; Understanding Proto-Insurgencies, 2007; The Five Front War: The Better Way to Fight Global Jihad, 2008. Contributor to books, journals and periodicals. **Address:** Brookings Institution, 1775 Massachusetts Ave. NW, Washington, DC 20036-2103, U.S.A. **Online address:** dbyman@brookings.edu

BYNUM, Caroline Walker. American (born United States), b. 1941. **Genres:** Theology/Religion, History. **Career:** Harvard University, assistant professor, 1969-74, associate professor, 1974-76; University of Washington, associate professor, professor, 1976-88; Columbia University, professor, 1988-2003, Morris A. and Alma Schapiro Chair in History, 1990-98, university professor, 1999-2003, professor emeritus, 2003-, School of General Studies, dean and associate vice president for undergraduate education, 1993-94; Institute for Advanced Study, professor, 2003-. Writer. **Publications:** Docere Verbo et Exemplo: An Aspect of Twelfth-Century Spirituality, 1979; Jesus as Mother: Studies in the Spirituality of the High Middle Ages, 1982; (ed. with S. Harrell and P. Richman) Gender and Religion: On the Complexity of Symbols, 1986; Holy Feast and Holy Fast: The Religious Significance of Food to Medieval Women, 1987; Fragmentation and Redemption: Essays on Gender and the Human Body in Medieval Religion, 1991; The Resurrection of the Body in Western Christianity, 200-1336, 1995; (ed. with P. Freedman) Last Things: Death and the Apocalypse in the Middle Ages, 2000; Metamorphosis and Identity, 2001; Wonderful Blood: Theology and Practice in Late Medieval Northern Germany and Beyond, 2007. Contributor of articles to journals. **Address:** School of Historical Studies, Institute for Advanced Study, Einstein Dr., Princeton, NJ 08540-4907, U.S.A. **Online address:** cwbynum@ias.edu

BYNUM, Laura. American (born United States), b. 1968. **Genres:** Novels. **Career:** Writer. **Publications:** Veracity, 2010. **Address:** VA , U.S.A. **Online address:** laura@laurabynum.com

BYNUM, Sarah Shun-lien. American (born United States), b. 1972. **Genres:** Novels. **Career:** University of California, professor of writing, MFA Writing Program, director; Otis College of Art and Design, assistant chair of graduate writing. Writer. **Publications:** Madeleine Is Sleeping, 2004; Ms. Hempel Chronicles, 2008. Works appear in anthologies. Contributor to periodicals. **Address:** Otis College of Art and Design, 9045 Lincoln Blvd., Los Angeles, CA 90045, U.S.A. **Online address:** sbynum@otis.edu

BYNUM, Victoria E. American (born United States), b. 1947. **Genres:** History, Politics/Government, Humanities. **Career:** Texas State University at San Marcos (formerly Southwest Texas State University), associate professor, professor of history, 1986-, now professor emeritus of history. Writer. **Publications:** Unruly Women: The Politics of Social and Sexual Control in the Old South, 1992; Free State of Jones: Mississippi's Longest Civil War, 2001; Long Shadow of the Civil War: Southern Dissent and its Legacies, 2010; Communities at War: Southern Dissent During the Civil War, forthcoming. **Address:** Department of History, Texas State University at San Marcos, 210 Taylor-Murphy History, San Marcos, TX 78666, U.S.A. **Online address:** vb03@txstate.edu

BYRD, Adrianne. American (born United States) **Genres:** Romance/Historical, Novels, Sex. **Career:** Writer. **Publications:** Defenseless, 1997; Forget Me Not, 1998; (with D. Johnson and F. Mason) Man of the House, 1998; I Promise, 1999; Love's Deception, 2000; Say You Love Me, 2000; All I've Ever Wanted, 2001; Surrender to Love, 2002; My Destiny, 2003; Comfort of a Man, 2003; If You Dare, 2004; Unforgettable, 2004; Measure of a Man, 2005; Deadly Double, 2005; The Beautiful Ones, 2005; When You Were Mine, 2006; (with M. Jackson and D. Hill) Takin' Chances for the Holidays, 2006; She's My Baby, 2006; When Valentines Collide, 2007; Blue Skies, 2007; Feel the Fire, 2007; To Love a Stranger, 2007; Two Grooms And A Wedding, 2008; Controversy, 2008; Her Lover's Legacy, 2008; De'nesha Diamond, 2008; Sinful Chocolate, 2009; Love Takes Time, 2009; Queen Of His Heart, 2009; Tender to His Touch, 2009; Chasing Romeo, 2009; Body Heat, 2010; Lovers Premiere, 2010; Heart's Secret, 2010; My Only Desire, 2011; King's Passion, 2011; King's Pleasure, 2011; King's Promise, 2011; A Christmas Affair, 2011. **Address:** c/o Author Mail, Harper Collins Publishers, 10 E 53rd St., 7th Fl., New York, NY 10022, U.S.A. **Online address:** adriannebyrd@aol.com

BYRD, James P. American (born United States), b. 1965. **Genres:** Theology/Religion, History. **Career:** Vanderbilt University, Divinity School and Graduate Department of Religion, Department of American Religious History, lecturer, 1999-2003, senior lecturer, 2003-06, assistant professor, 2007-, assistant dean and director of graduate studies, 2003-07, associate dean of graduate education and research, 2007-. Writer. **Publications:** The Challenges of Roger Williams: Religious Liberty, Violent Persecution, and the Bible, 2002; Jonathan Edwards for Armchair Theologians, 2008. Works appear in anthologies. **Address:** The Divinity School, Vanderbilt University, 202 A, 411 21st Avenue S., Nashville, TN 37240-1121, U.S.A. **Online address:** james.p.byrd@vanderbilt.edu

BYRD, Max W. *See* **BYRD, William Max.**

BYRD, William Max. (Max W. Byrd). American (born United States), b. 1942. **Genres:** Mystery/Crime/Suspense, Literary Criticism And History, Romance/Historical, Novels. **Career:** Yale University, assistant professor of English, 1970-75, associate professor, 1975-76; University of California, associate professor, 1976-81, professor, 1981-, now professor emeritus; Eighteenth-Century Studies, editor, 1977-88; Stanford University, visiting professor; University of California-Berkeley, lecturer; University of California-Irvine, lecturer; University of Warwick, lecturer; University of Southern California, lecturer. **Publications:** MYSTERY NOVELS: California Thriller, 1981; Fly Away, Jill, 1981; Finders Weepers, 1983; Target of Opportunity, 1988; Fuse Time, 1991. HISTORICAL NOVELS: Jefferson, 1993; Jackson, 1997; Grant, 2000; Shooting the Sun, 2004. OTHER: Visits to Bedlam: Madness and Literature in the Eighteenth Century, 1974; (ed.) Daniel Defoe: A Collection of Critical Essays, 1976; London Transformed: Images of the City in the 18th Century, 1978; Tristram Shandy, 1985. **Address:** Department of English, University of California, Voorhies Hall, 1 Shields Ave., Davis, CA 95616-5224, U.S.A. **Online address:** max@maxbyrdbooks.com

BYRNE, Donn. American (born United States), b. 1931. **Genres:** Psychology, Social Sciences. **Career:** San Francisco State University, instructor, 1957-59; University of Texas, assistant professor, 1959-62, associate professor, 1962-66, professor of psychology, 1966-69, assistant professor, 1964-66; Stanford University, visiting professor, 1966-67; University of Hawaii, visiting professor, 1968; Purdue University, professor of psychology, 1969-79, Social-Personality Program, head, chair, 1972-78; State University New York, University at Albany, Department of Psychology, professor of psychology, 1979-91, distinguished professor of psychology, 1991-2001, distinguished professor emeritus, 2001-, Social-Personality Program, head, chair, 1980-84, Department of Psychology, chairman, 1984-89. Writer. **Publications:** (With H.C. Lindgren) Psychology: An Introduction to the Study of Human Behavior, 1961, 4th ed. as Psychology: An Introduction to a Behavioral Science, 1975; Progress in Experimental Personality Research, 1964; An Introduction to Personality, 1966, (with K. Kelley) 3rd ed., 1981; Handbook of Social Psychology, 1968; Advances in Experimental Social Psychology, 1969; The Attraction Paradigm, 1971; (with R.A. Baron and W. Griffitt) Social Psychology: Understanding Human Interaction, 1974, (with R.A. Baron, N.R. Branscombe) 12th ed., 2008; (with R. Baron and B. Kantowitz) Psychology: Understanding Behavior, 1977, 2nd ed., 1981; (with R.A. Baron) Exploring Social Psychology, 1979, (with R.A. Baron and B.T. Johnson) 4th ed., 1998; (with W.A. Fisher) Adolescence, Sex, and Contraception, 1983; (with K. Kelley) Alternative Approaches to the Study of Sexuality, 1986; (with H.C. Lindgren and L. Petrinovich) Hsin li hsueh: Hsing wei ko hseuth tao yin, 1986; (with Baron) Social Psychology: Understanding Human Interaction, 1987, 9th ed., 2000; (with R.A. Baron and N.R. Branscombe) Mastering Social Psychology, 2007; Getting Rich (or, at least richer) Slowly: Why, When, and How to Invest, forthcoming. EDITOR: (contrib.) Personality Change, 1964; (with M.L. Hamilton) Personality Research: A Book of Readings, 1966; (with H. Lindgren and G. Lindgren) Current Research in Psychology, 1971; (with L. Byrne) Exploring Human Sexuality, 1977; (with W.A. Fisher) Adolescents, Sex, and Contraception, 1983; (with K. Kelley) Alternative Approaches to the Study of Sexual Behavior, 1986. Contributor to journals. **Address:** Department of Psychology, University at Albany, State University of New York, 1400 Washington Ave., Albany, NY 12222-0100, U.S.A. **Online address:** vyaduckdb@aol.com

BYRNE, Frank J. American (born United States), b. 1968. **Genres:** Business/Trade/Industry. **Career:** State University of New York, associate professor of history, 2001-. Writer. **Publications:** Becoming Bourgeois: Merchant Culture in the South, 1820-1865, 2006. **Address:** Department of History, State University of New York, 433 Mahar Hall, Oswego, NY 13126-3599, U.S.A. **Online address:** fbyrne@oswego.edu

BYRNE, Paula. British (born England), b. 1967?. **Genres:** Biography, Literary Criticism And History. **Career:** Wirral Grammar School for Boys, teacher; Wirral Metropolitan College, faculty; University of Liverpool, research fellow; University of Warwick, royal literary fund fellow. Writer. **Publications:** Jane Austen and the Theatre, 2002; (ed.) Jane Austen's Emma: A Sourcebook, 2004; Perdita: The Literary, Theatrical, Scandalous Life of Mary Robinson in UK as Perdita: The Life of Mary Robinson, 2004; Mad World: Evelyn Waugh and the Secrets of Brideshead, 2009. Contributor to periodicals. **Address:** Wylie Agency, 250 W 57th St., Ste. 2114, New York, NY 10107, U.S.A. **Online address:** paula@bardbiz.com

BYRNE, Robert. American (born United States), b. 1930. **Genres:** Novels, Language/Linguistics, Recreation, Writing/Journalism. **Career:** Writer. **Publications:** Writing Rackets, 1969; McGoorty: The Story of a Billiard Bum, 1972; (ed. and intro.) Mrs. Byrne's Dictionary of Unusual, Obscure And Preposterous Words, 1974, new ed., 1994; Byrne's Standard Book of Pool and Billiards, 1978; Byrne's Treasury of Trick Shots in Pool and Billiards, 1982; The 637 Best Things Anybody Ever Said, 1982; (comp. and ed. with T. Skelton) Cat Scan: All the Best from the Literature of Cats, 1983 in UK as The Quotable Cat, 1985; McGoorty: A Billiard Hustler's Life, 1984; The Other 637 Best Things Anybody Ever Said, 1984; The Third 637 Best Things Anybody Ever Said, 1986; (comp.) 1911 Best Things Anybody Ever Said: Many Amusingly Illuminated By Antique Etchings and Line Cuts, 1988; Every Day Is Father's Day, 1989; The Fourth-and By Far the Most Recent 637 Best Things Anybody Ever Said, 1990; Byrne's Advanced Technique in Pool and Billiards, 1990; The Fifth and Far Finer than the First Four 637 Best

Things Anybody Ever Said: Presented With a Special Bonus Quote, 1993; Byrne's Book of Great Pool Stories, 1995; Byrne's Wonderful World of Pool and Billiards, 1996; Byrne's New Standard Book of Pool and Billiards, 1998; McGoorty: A Pool Room Hustler, 2000; (ed.) My Old Dubuque: Collected Writings On Dubuque Area History, 2000; (comp.) The 2548 Best Things Anybody Ever Said, 2003; Byrne's Complete Book of Pool Shots: 350 Moves Every Player Should Know, 2003; Behold My Shorts, 2009; The 2,548 Wittiest Things Anybody Ever Said, 2012. NOVELS: Memories of a Non-Jewish Childhood, 1971; The Tunnel, 1977; The Dam, 1981; Always Catholic, 1981; Skyscraper, 1984; Mannequin in UK as Death Train, 1988; Thrill, 1995. Contributor of articles to periodicals. **Address:** 198 Main St., Dubuque, IA 52001-3114, U.S.A. **Online address:** bob@byrne.org

BYRNES, Giselle. New Zealander (born New Zealand), b. 1967. **Genres:** Intellectual History, Essays. **Career:** Victoria University of Wellington, senior lecturer, 1997-2007; Georgetown University, Center for Australian and New Zealand Studies, Fulbright visiting Professor in New Zealand studies, 2006; University of Waikato, Department of History, chairperson, 2007-, professor, pro vice-chancellor, 2008-; New Zealand Department of Justice, Waitangi Tribunal, senior research officer. Writer and historian. **Publications:** Boundary Markers: Land Surveying and the Colonisation of New Zealand, 2001; The Waitangi Tribunal and New Zealand History, 2004; (ed.) The New Oxford History of New Zealand, 2009. CONTRIBUTOR: Essays in New Zealand Social and Cultural History, 2000; Going Public: The Changing Face of New Zealand History, 2001; Prospects and Retrospects: Law in History, Proceedings of the 20th Annual Conference of the Australia and New Zealand Law and History Society 2001, 2002; Literature of Travel and Exploration: An Encyclopedia, 2003. Contributor to periodicals. **Address:** Department of History, School of Social Sciences, University of Waikato, Rm. J3.24, PO Box 3105, Hamilton, 3240, New Zealand. **Online address:** giselle@waikato.ac.nz

BYRNES, Michael J. American (born United States) **Genres:** Novels, Mystery/Crime/Suspense. **Career:** X-Ell Employee Benefits L.L.C., co-owner. Writer. **Publications:** The Sacred Bones (novel), 2007; The Sacred Blood: A Novel, 2009; The Genesis Plague, 2010. **Address:** Simon & Schuster Ltd., 222 Gray's Inn Rd., London, GL WC1X8HB, England.

BYRT, Edwin Andrew. Australian (born Australia), b. 1932. **Genres:** Mathematics/Statistics, Education. **Career:** Education Department of Victoria, teacher, 1954-66; Suva Grammar School, teacher, 1967-68; University of the South Pacific, lecturer, 1969; Victoria College, senior lecturer, 1970-88; Royal Children's Hospital, research assistant, 1989-98. Writer. **Publications:** Contemporary Mathematics, 4 vols., 1969-72; Relationships Between Mathematical Experience, Spatial Ability and Conservation of Volume for Form 1 Pupils, 1976. **Address:** 60 Rolling Hills Rd., Chirnside Park, VI 3116, Australia.

C

CABOT, Francis H. American (born United States), b. 1925?. **Genres:** Horticulture, Architecture. **Career:** The Garden Conservancy, founder and president, 1989; New York Botanical Gardens, chairman, 1973-76. Writer and horticulturist. **Publications:** The Greater Perfection: The Story of the Gardens at Les Quatre Vents, 2001. **Address:** c/o Author Mail, W. W. Norton & Co. Inc., 500 5th Ave., New York, NY 10110-0002, U.S.A.

CABOT, Meg(gin Patricia). Also writes as Jenny Carroll, Patricia Cabot. American (born United States), b. 1967. **Genres:** Novels, Romance/Historical, Young Adult Fiction, Paranormal, Children's Fiction. **Career:** New York University, assistant residence hall director. Writer. **Publications:** FOR YOUNG ADULTS: PRINCESS DIARY SERIES: The Princess Diaries, 2000, vol. II: Princess in the Spotlight, 2001, vol. III: Princess in Love, 2002, vol. IV: Princess in Waiting, 2003, vol. IV: Project Princess, 2003, vol. V: Princess in Pink, 2004, vol. VI: Princess in Training, 2005; vol. VI: The Princess Present, 2004, vol. VII: Party Princess, 2006, vol. VII: Sweet Sixteen Princess, 2006, vol. VII: Valentine Princess, 2006, vol. VIII: Princess on the Brink, 2007, vol. IX: Princess Mia, 2008, vol. X: Forever Princess, 2009; Princess Lessons, 2003; Perfect Princess, 2004; The Princess Diaries 2, Royal Engagement: Movie Scrapbook, 2004; Mia Tells it like it is, 2004; The Highs and Lows of Being Mia, 2004; Holiday Princess, 2005. OTHER NOVELS: The Boy Next Door, 2002; She Went All the Way, 2002; Nicola and the Viscount, 2002; Victoria and the Rogue, 2003; All American Girl, 2003; Boy Meets Girl, 2004; Teen Idol, 2004; Ready or Not: An All-American Girl Novel, 2005; Every Boy's Got One, 2005; Avalon High, 2006; How to be Popular, 2006; Queen of the Babble, 2006; Size 12 is Not Fat Either: A Heather Wells Mystery, 2006; Size 14 is Not Fat Either: A Heather Wells Mystery, 2006; Pants on Fire, 2007; Prom Nights From Hell, 2007; Big Boned: A Heather Wells Mystery, 2007; Code Name Cassandra, 2007; Jinx, 2007; Merlin Prophency, 2007; Missing You, 2007; Queen of Babble in the Big City, 2007; Airhead, 2008; Homecoming, 2008; Moving Cat, 2008; Queen of Babble Gets Hitched, 2008; Hunter's Moon, 2009; (intro.) Ransom My Heart, 2009; Being Nikki: An Airhead Novel, 2009; Runaway, 2010; Insatiable, 2010. AS PATRICIA CABOT, ROMANCE NOVELS: Where Roses Grow Wild, 1998; An Improper Proposal, 1999; Portrait of My Heart, 1999; A Little Scandal, 2000; A Season in the Highlands, 2000; Educating Caroline, 2001; Lady of Skye, 2000; Kiss the Bride, 2002. THE MEDIATOR SERIES: (as Jenny Carroll) Shadowlands, 2000; (as Jenny Carroll) Ninth Key, 2001; (as Jenny Carroll) Reunion, 2001; (as Jenny Carroll) Darkest Hour, 2001; Haunted: A Tale of the Mediator, 2003; Twilight, 2005. 1-800-WHERE-R-YOU SERIES: (as Jenny Carroll) When Lightning Strikes, 2007; (as Jenny Carroll) Codename Cassandra, 2001, 2nd ed., 2004. ALLIE FINKLE SERIES: Moving Day, 2008; The New Girl, 2008; Best Friends and Drama Queens, 2009; Stage Fright, 2009; Glitter Girls and the Great Fake Out, 2010. OTHERS: (as Jenny Carroll) Safe House, 2002; (as Jenny Carroll) Sanctuary, 2002; (contrib.) Shelf Discovery, 2009; Vanished Books One and Two, 2010; Blast from the Past, 2010; Vanished Books Three and Four, 2011; Overbite, 2011; Abandon, 2011. Contributor to periodicals. **Address:** PO Box 4904, Key West, FL 33041-4904, U.S.A. **Online address:** meg@megcabot.com

CABOT, Patricia. *See* **CABOT, Meg(gin Patricia).**

CABRERA, Jane. British (born England), b. 1968. **Genres:** Children's Fiction, Children's Non-fiction, Picture/Board Books. **Career:** Apollo Arts and Antiques (magazine), art director, 1989-91; freelance graphic designer, 1991-98; illustrator, 1997-. Writer. **Publications:** SELF-ILLUSTRATED FICTION FOR CHILDREN: Cat's Colours, 1997; Dog's Day, 1998; Panda Big and Panda Small, 1998; Rory and the Lion, 1999; Dog's Day, 2000; Over in the Meadow, 2000; Old Mother Hubbard, 2001; Monkey's Play Time, 2002; The Lonesome Polar Bear, 2002; Bear's Good Night, 2002; If You're Happy and You Know It, 2003; Mummy, Carry Me Please!, 2004; Ten in the Bed, 2006; Cat's Cuddles, 2007; Old MacDonald had a Farm, 2008; One, Two, Buckle My Shoe, 2009; Here We Go Round the Mulberry Bush, 2010; The wheels on the Bus, 2011. Illustrator of books by J. Dunbar. Contributor to magazines. **Address:** The Drawing Rm., Panther House, 38 Mount Pleasant, London, GL WCIX 40P, England. **Online address:** jane.ecabrera@googlemail.com

CACACI, Joe. American (born United States) **Genres:** Horror, Plays/Screenplays, Film. **Career:** Provincetown Playhouse, producing director; American Premiere Stage, producing director; East Coast Arts (theater Co.), producing director, 1983-; The Trials of Rosie O'Neill, (television series), creator, 1990-92; John Grisham's The Client, executive consultant, 1995; Wildcliff Theatre, producing director; Jewish Repertory Theater, pianist, 1997; The Hoop Life, executive producer, 1999; The Education of Max Bickford, executive producer, 2001; Columbia University Film School, faculty, 2007-. Writer. **Publications:** L.A. Law: Divorce with Extreme Prejudice, 1987; The Trials of Rosie O'Neill, 1990. Contributor to periodicals. **Address:** The Alpern Group, 15645 Royal Oak Rd., Encino, CA 91436, U.S.A. **Online address:** joescript@verizon.net

CACHIA, Pierre (Jacques Elie). British (born England), b. 1921. **Genres:** Language/Linguistics, Literary Criticism And History. **Career:** Edinburgh University, assistant lecturer, 1949-50, lecturer, 1950-65, senior lecturer, 1965-69, reader in Arabic, 1969-76; Columbia University, professor of Arabic language and literature, 1975-91, professor emeritus, 1991-, Department of Middle Eastern Languages and Cultures, chairman, 1980-83. Writer. **Publications:** Taha Husayn: His Place in the Egyptian Literary Renaissance, 1956; (with W. Watt) A History of Islamic Spain, 1965; The Monitor: A Dictionary of Arabic Grammatical Terms: Arabic-English English/Arabic, 1973; Popular Narrative Ballads of Modern Egypt, 1989; An Overview of Modern Arabic Literature, 1990; (with A. Cachia) Landlocked Islands: Two Alien Lives in Egypt, 1999; Arabic Literature: An Overview, 2002. EDITOR: Eutychius of Alexandria, Kitab al-Burhan, vol. I, 1960, vol. II, 1961; Islam: Past Influence and Present Challenge, 1979; The Arch Rhetorician or the Schemer's Skimmer: A Handbook of Late Arabic Badi, 1998. TRANSLATOR: T. Al-Hakim, The Prison of Life, 1992; Y. Haqqi, Blood and Mud, 1999. **Address:** 456 Riverside Dr., Apt. 8A, New York, NY 10027-6811, U.S.A. **Online address:** pjc1@columbia.edu

CACIOPPO, John T. American (born United States), b. 1951. **Genres:** Sciences, Psychology, Social Sciences. **Career:** University of Notre Dame, assistant professor of psychology, 1977-79; University of Iowa, Department of Psychology, assistant professor, 1979-81, associate professor, 1981-85, professor, 1985-89; Yale University, Department of Psychology, visiting fellow, 1986; Ohio State University, Department of Psychiatry, professor of psychology, 1989-98, interim chairperson, 1997-98, faculty, 1997-99, university chair professor, 1998-99, Center for Cognitive Science, faculty, 1989-99, Institute for Behavioral Medicine Research, faculty, 1995-98, Medical Scientist Program, faculty, 1996-99, School of Public Health, faculty, 1997-99; University of Chicago, Department of Psychology, visiting professor, 1998, Tiffany and Margaret Blake distinguished service professor, 1999-, Institute for Mind and Biology, co-director, 1999-2004, Social Psychology Program, director, 1999-2005, 2007-08, 2010-, Graduate Program in Medicine, Arts and the Social Sciences, faculty, 2000-, Center for Cognitive and Social Neuroscience, founding director, 2004-, Center for Integrative Neuroscience and Neuroengineering, faculty, 2005-, Center for Health and the Social Sciences, faculty, 2005-, Department of Psychiatry and Behavioral Neuroscience, faculty, 2006-, Office of the Vice President for Research, founding faculty director, 2007-, National Laboratories, founding faculty director, 2007-10; Free University Amsterdam, external professor chair in social neurosciences, 2003-07; Stanford University, Department of Psychology, Hilgard visiting professor, 2008. Writer. **Publications:** (With R.E. Petty) Attitudes and Persuasion-Classic and Contemporary Approaches, 1981; (with R.E. Petty) Communication and Persuasion: Central and Peripheral Routes to Attitude Change, 1986; (with E. Hatfield and R.L. Rapson) Emotional Contagion, 1994; (with W. Patrick) Loneliness: Human Nature and the Need for Social Connection, 2008; (with L.A. Freberg) Discovering Psychology: The Science of Mind, 2012. EDITOR: (with R.E. Petty) Perspectives in Cardiovascular Psychophysiology, 1982; (with R.E. Petty) Social Psychophysiology: A Sourcebook, 1983; (with L.G. Tassinary) Principles of Psychophysiology: Physical, Social, and Inferential Elements, 1990; (with L.G. Tassinary and G.G. Berntson) Handbook of Psychophysiology, 2nd ed., 2000, 3rd ed., 2007; (co-ed.) Foundations in Social Neuroscience, 2002; (with G.G. Berntson) Essays in Social Neuroscience, 2004; (with G.G. Berntson) Social Neuroscience: Key Readings, 2004; (with P.S. Visser and C.L. Pickett) Social Neuroscience: People Thinking about Thinking People, 2006; (with G.G. Berntson) Handbook of Neuroscience for the Behavioral Sciences, 2009; (with J. Decety) Oxford Handbook of Social Neuroscience, 2011. Contributor to books. **Address:** Department of Psychology, University of Chicago, 406 Kelly Hall, 5848 S University Ave., Chicago, IL 60637, U.S.A. **Online address:** cacioppo@uchicago.edu

CADBURY, Deborah. British (born England), b. 1955?. **Genres:** Sciences, Technology, Animals/Pets, History. **Career:** British Broadcasting Corp-TV, trainee researcher, 1978-, producer, through 1982; writer, 1983-. **Publications:** The Feminisation of Nature: Our Future at Risk, 1997; Altering Eden: The Feminization of Nature, 1999; The Dinosaur Hunters: A True Story of Scientific Rivalry and the Discovery of the Prehistoric World, 2000; The Estrogen Effect: How Chemical Pollution is Threatening Our Survival, 2001; Terrible Lizard: The First Dinosaur Hunters and the Birth of a New Science, 2001; The Lost King of France: A True Story of Revolution, Revenge and DNA, 2002; The Lost King of France: How DNA Solved the Mystery of the Murdered Son of Louis XVI and Marie Antoinette, 2002; Seven Wonders of the Industrial World, 2003; Dreams of Iron and Steel: Seven Wonders of the Nineteenth Century, from the Building of the London Sewers to the Panama Canal, 2004; Space Race: The Epic Battle between America and the Soviet Union for Dominion of Space, 2006; Chocolate Wars: The 150-year Rivalry between the World's Greatest Chocolate Makers, 2010. **Address:** c/o Author Mail, HarperCollins Publishers Inc., 10 E 53rd St., 7th Fl., New York, NY 10022-5244, U.S.A.

CADDY, Caroline. Australian (born Australia), b. 1944. **Genres:** Poetry, Young Adult Fiction. **Career:** Dental nurse, 1960-65. Writer. **Publications:** POETRY: Singing at Night, 1981; Letters from the North, 1984; Beach Plastic, 1989; Conquistadors, 1991; Antarctica, 1996; Working Temple, 1997; Editing the Moon, 1998; Esperance: New and Selected Poems, 2007; Burning Bright, 2010. Works appear in anthologies. Contributor to magazines. **Address:** 7 Tregenna St., Gooseberry Hill, WA 6076, Australia.

CADDY, (Michael) Douglas. American (born United States), b. 1938. **Genres:** Business/Trade/Industry, Politics/Government. **Career:** New York State Government, assistant, 1962-65; Non Aligned Movement, assistant, 1966-67; General Foods Corp., Washington liaison, 1968-70; Gall, Lane, Powell & Kilcullen, associate, 1970-74; National Association of Realtors, legislative counsel, 1975-76; Office of the Texas Secretary of State, attorney, 1980-81; attorney-at-law, 1982-; Young Americans for Freedom, cofounder and executive director. **Publications:** The Hundred Million Dollar Payoff, 1974; How They Rig Our Elections: The Coming Dictatorship of Big Labor and the Radicals, 1975; Understanding Texas Insurance, 1984; (with H.C. Dethloff) Insurance Is Everybody's Business, 1985; Legislative Trends in Insurance Regulation, 1986; Exploring America's Future, 1987; Watergate Exposed: A Confidential Informant Reveals How the President of the United States and the Watergate Burglars Were Set-up, 2011. **Address:** 7941 Katy Fwy., Ste. 296, Houston, TX 77024, U.S.A. **Online address:** douglascaddy@justice.com

CADLE, Farris W(illiam). American (born United States), b. 1952. **Genres:** Geography, History, Law. **Career:** Delta Engineers and Surveyors, land surveyor's assistant, 1976-78; Donaldson Surveys, land surveyor's assistant, 1979-82; Helmly and Associates, land surveyor, 1982-84, 1986-89; registered land surveyor, 1986-; Belford Land Title Co., title abstractor, 1989-91, 1996-2002; Farris Cadle Inc., president, 2002-; Middle Georgia College, adjunct professor of surveying law, 2011-. Writer. **Publications:** Georgia Land Surveying History and Law, 1991. **Address:** 5228 Augusta Rd., Ste. 8, Garden City, GA 31408, U.S.A. **Online address:** fcadle@bellsouth.net

CADNUM, Michael. American (born United States), b. 1949. **Genres:** Novels, Novellas/Short Stories, Mystery/Crime/Suspense, Horror, Romance/Historical, Children's Fiction, Young Adult Fiction, Plays/Screenplays, Poetry. **Career:** Photographer and writer. **Publications:** NOVELS: Nightlight, 1990; Sleepwalker, 1991; Saint Peter's Wolf, 1991; Calling Home, 1991; Breaking the Fall, 1992; Ghostwright, 1993; The Horses of the Night, 1993; Skyscape, 1994; Taking It, 1995; The Judas Glass, 1996; Zero at the Bone, 1996; Edge, 1997; In a Dark Wood, 1998; Heat, 1998; Rundown, 1999; The Book of the Lion, 2000; Redhanded, 2000; Raven of the Waves, 2001; The Leopard Sword, 2002; Forbidden Forest, 2002; Daughter of the Wind, 2003; Ship of Fine, 2003; Blood Gold, 2004; Star Fall, 2004; The Dragon Throne, 2005; Nightsong, 2006; The King's Arrow, 2008; Peril on the Sea, 2009; Flash, 2010; Seize the Storm, 2012. POETRY: The Morning of the Massacre (chapbook), 1981; Invisible Mirror (chapbook), 1984; Foreign Springs (chapbook), 1985; Long Afternoon (chapbook), 1986; By Evening, 1992; The Cities We Will Never See, 1993; The Woman Who Discovered Math, 2001; Illicit, 2001. FOR CHILDREN: The Lost and Found House, 1997. SHORT FICTION: Ella and the Canary Prince, 1999; Together Again, 2001; Can't Catch Me, 2006. Works appear in anthologies. Contributor to periodicals. **Address:** A M Heath & Company Ltd., 6 Warwick Ct., Holborn, NY WC1R 5DJ, England.

CADUTO, Michael J. American (born United States), b. 1955. **Genres:** Children's Fiction, Songs/Lyrics And Libretti, Adult Non-fiction, Cultural/Ethnic Topics, Education, Environmental Sciences/Ecology, Mythology/Folklore, Natural History, Natural History. **Career:** Audubon Society of Rhode Island, land management planner, 1975-78, teacher, 1976-78; W. Alton Jones Environmental Education Center, teacher and naturalist, 1979; Pocono Lake Preserve, curator of exhibits and program director, 1979; Living Rivers Environmental Education Program, senior instructor, 1980; VINS management, land management, 1982-85, environmental education, 1982-83; Programs for Environmental Awareness and Cultural Exchange, founder, 1984-, director, 1984-; Vermont Council on the Arts, touring artist; New Hampshire Council on the Arts, artist-in-residence; Vermont Council on the Humanities, speaker and performer. Writer. **Publications:** Ann Arbor Alive, 1981; A Guide on Environmental Values Education, 1985; Pond and Brook: A Guide to Nature Study in Freshwater Environments, 1985; (with J. Bruchac) Keepers of the Earth: Native American Stories and Environmental Activities for Children, 1988; (with J. Bruchac) Keepers of the Animals: Native American Stories and Wildlife Activities for Children, 1991; (with J. Bruchac) Keepers of the Night: Native American Stories and Nocturnal Activities for Children, 1994; (with J. Bruchac) Keepers of the Life: Discovering Plants Through Native American Stories and Earth Activities for Children, 1994; All One Earth: Songs for the Generations, 1994; (with J. Bruchac) Native American Gardening: Stories, Projects, and Recipes for Families, 1996; The Crimson Elf: Italian Tales of Wisdom, 1997; Earth Tales from around the World, 1997; Remains Unknown: The Final Journey of a Human Spirit, 1999; All One Earth: Songs for the Generations, 2000; Long River Waltzes, 2000; A Time Before New Hampshire: The Story of a Land and Native Peoples, 2003; In the Beginning: The Story of Genesis and Earth Activities for Children, 2004; Child of God: Stories of Jesus and Stewardship Activities for Children, 2005; Abraham's Bind & Other Bible Tales of Trickery, Folly, Mercy and Love, 2006; Catch the Wind, Harness the Sun, 2011. SELF-ILLUSTRATED: Everyday Herbs in Spiritual Life: A Guide to Many Practices, 2007. Contributor to books and articles. **Address:** P.E.A.C.E., PO Box 1052, Norwich, VT 05055, U.S.A. **Online address:** michaelcaduto@p-e-a-c-e.net

CAFERRO, William. American (born United States), b. 1959?. **Genres:**

History, Business/Trade/Industry. **Career:** Vanderbilt University, professor, Gertrude Conaway Vanderbilt professor of history and director of undergraduate studies. Writer and historian. **Publications:** (Ed. with D.G. Fisher) The Unbounded Community: Papers in Christian Ecumenism in Honor of Jaroslav Pelikan, 1996; Mercenary Companies and the Decline of Siena, 1998; (with P. Jacks) The Spinelli of Florence: Fortunes of a Renaissance Merchant Family, 2001; John Hawkwood: An English Mercenary in Fourteenth-Century Italy, 2006; Contesting the Renaissance, 2008. **Address:** Department of History, Vanderbilt University, 219 Benson Hall, 2301 Vanderbilt Pl., Ste. 351802, Sta. B, Nashville, TN 37235-1802, U.S.A. **Online address:** william.p.caferro@vanderbilt.edu

CAFFREY, Margaret M. American (born United States), b. 1947. **Genres:** Women's Studies And Issues, History. **Career:** University of Memphis, assistant professor, 1988-93, associate professor of American history and women's history, 1993-, Writer. **Publications:** Ruth Benedict: Stranger in This Land, 1989; (ed. with P. Francis) To Cherish the Life of the World: Selected Letters of Margaret Mead, 2006. Contributor to books and periodicals. **Address:** Department of History, University of Memphis, 127 Mitchell Hall, 3705 Alumni Dr., Memphis, TN 38152-3450, U.S.A. **Online address:** mcaffrey@memphis.edu

CAFRUNY, Alan W(eston). American (born United States), b. 1951. **Genres:** Economics, Politics/Government, History, Social Sciences. **Career:** University of Virginia, Department of Government and Foreign Affairs, assistant professor, 1982-88; Hamilton College, Department of Government, assistant professor, 1988-91, associate professor, 1991-96, Henry Platt Bristol endowed chair, 1991, professor, 1996-, chair, 1996-2004, Henry Platt Bristol professor of international affairs; European University Institute, Department of Political and Social Sciences, visiting professor, 1993-94, external professor, 1994-2000. Writer. **Publications:** Ruling the Waves: The Political Economy of International Shipping, 1987; (with J.M. Ryner) Europe at Bay: In the Shadow of U.S. Hegemony, 2007. EDITOR AND CONTRIBUTOR: (with G.G. Rosenthal) The State of the European Community, vol. II: The Maastricht Debates and Beyond, 1993; (with C. Lankowski) Europe's Ambiguous Unity: Conflict and Consensus in the Post-Maastricht Era, 1995; (with P. Peters) Union and the World: The Political Economy of a Common European Foreign Policy, 1998; (with M. Ryner) Ruined Fortress?: Neoliberal Hegemony and Transformation in Europe, 2003. **Address:** Department of Government, Hamilton College, 198 College Hill Rd., Clinton, NY 13323-1218, U.S.A. **Online address:** acafruny@hamilton.edu

CAHALAN, James Michael. American (born United States), b. 1953. **Genres:** Literary Criticism And History, Education, History, Novels, Cultural/Ethnic Topics, Young Adult Fiction. **Career:** University of Cincinnati, Department of English, teaching assistant, 1977-79; University of Massachusetts-Boston, part-time instructor in English, 1979-81, lecturer in English, 1982-84, Irish Studies Program, director, 1983-84; Northeastern University, instructor in English, 1981-82; Indiana University of Pennsylvania, Department of English, assistant professor, 1984-88, associate professor, 1988-92, professor, 1992-, director of graduate studies in literature, 1987-91; Pennsylvania Consortium for International Education, founder and director, 1985-88. Writer. **Publications:** Great Hatred, Little Room: The Irish Historical Novel, 1983; The Irish Novel: A Critical History, 1988; Liam O'Flaherty: A Study of the Short Fiction, 1991; (ed. with D. Downing and contrib.) Practicing Theory in Introductory College Literature Courses, 1991; Modern Irish Literature and Culture: A Chronology, 1993; Double Visions: Women and Men in Modern and Contemporary Irish Fiction, 1999; Edward Abbey: A Life, 2001. Contributor to books and journals. **Address:** Department of English, Indiana University of Pennsylvania, Rm. 110, Leonard Hall, 421 North Walk, Indiana, PA 15705-1094, U.S.A. **Online address:** jim.cahalan@iup.edu

CAHILL, Lisa Sowle. American (born United States), b. 1948. **Genres:** Theology/Religion, History, Adult Non-fiction. **Career:** Concordia College, instructor, 1976; Boston College, Department of Theology, assistant professor, 1976-82, associate professor, 1982-89, J. Donald Monan professor, 1989-; Religious Studies Review, associate editor, 1981-; Journal of Religious Ethics, associate editor, 1981-; College of Theology Society, associate editor, 1983-; Journal of Medicine and Philosophy, associate editor, 1989-; Concilium, associate editor, 1989; Yale University, visiting professor of Catholic theology, 1997. **Publications:** Between the Sexes: Foundations for a Christian Ethics of Sexuality, 1985; (with T.A. Shannon) Religion and Artificial Reproduction: An Inquiry into the Vatican Instruction on Respect for Human Life in Its Origin and on the Dignity of Human Reproduction, 1988; (ed. with D. Mieth) Aging, 1991; Women and Sexuality, 1992; (ed. with D. Mieth) Migrants and Refugees, 1993; Love Your Enemies: Discipleship, Pacifism, and Just War Theory, 1994; (ed. with M.A. Farley) Embodiment, Morality, and Medicine, 1995; (ed. with D. Mieth) The Family, 1995; Sex, Gender, and Christian Ethics, 1996; (ed. with J.F. Childress) Christian Ethics: Problems and Prospects, 1996; (ed. with M. Junker-Kenny) The Ethics of Genetic Engineering, 1998; Family: A Christian Social Perspective, 2000; (co-ed.) Catholic Ethicists on HIV/AIDS Prevention, 2000; Bioethics and the Common Good, 2004; (co-ed.) Modern Catholic Social Teaching: Commentaries and Interpretations, 2005; Theological Bioethics: Participation, Justice, and Change, 2005; (ed.) Genetics, Theology, and Ethics: An Interdisciplinary Conversation, 2005; (ed. with J. Garvey and T.F. Kennedy) Sexuality and the U.S. Catholic Church: Crisis and Renewal, 2006. Works appear in anthologies. Contributor to periodicals. **Address:** Department of Theology, Boston College, Rm. 321, 21 Campanella Way, Chestnut Hill, MA 02467, U.S.A. **Online address:** lisa.cahill@bc.edu

CAHILL, Nicholas D. American (born United States) **Genres:** Air/Space Topics, Homes/Gardens, Art/Art History, Humanities. **Career:** Harvard University, project curator for art and archaeology for Perseus project, 1991-93, department of fine arts, visiting lecturer, 1993; University of Wisconsin in Madison, assistant professor of art history, 1993-2000, affiliate professor in classics, 2000-, associate professor of art history, 2000-05, professor of art history, 2005-; Harvard Art Museum, research manager, 2007; Sardis Expedition, senior archaeologist, 1994-, field director, 2008-. Writer. **Publications:** Olynthus and Greek Town Planning, 2000; Household and City Organization at Olynthus, 2002; Lydian Houses, Domestic Assemblages and Household Size, 2002; (co-author) The City of Sardis: Approaches in Graphic Recording, 2003; (ed.) Love for Lydia. A Sardis Anniversary Volume Presented to Crawford H. Greenewalt, Jr, 2008. Contributor to periodicals. **Address:** Department of Art History, University of Wisconsin, 202 Elvehjem Bldg., 800 University Ave., Madison, WI 53706, U.S.A. **Online address:** ndcahill@wisc.edu

CAHILL, Tim. American (born United States), b. 1944?. **Genres:** Travel/Exploration, Essays, Biography. **Career:** Rolling Stone, associate editor and staff writer, 1971-; Outside Magazine, founding editor, 1976-77. **Publications:** Buried Dreams: Inside the Mind of a Serial Killer, 1986; Jaguars Ripped My Flesh: Adventure is a Risky Business, 1987; A Wolverine Is Eating My Leg, 1989; Road Fever: A High-Speed Travelogue, 1991; Packed to Death by Ducks, 1993; (ed. and contrib.) Wild Places: Twenty Journeys into the North American Outdoors, 1996; Pass the Butterworms: Remote Journeys Oddly Rendered, 1997; (ed.) Not So Funny When It Happened: The Best of Travel Humor and Misadventure, 2000; Dolphins, 2000; Hold the Enlightenment, 2002; Lost in My Own Backyard: A Walk in Yellowstone National Park, 2004. Contributor to books and periodicals. **Address:** Villard Books, 201 E 50th St., New York, NY 10022-7703, U.S.A.

CAIL, Carol. (Kara Galloway). American (born United States), b. 1937. **Genres:** Mystery/Crime/Suspense, Romance/Historical, Novels, Children's Fiction. **Career:** Teacher, 1965-67, 1991-98; Daily Office Supply, co-owner and operator, 1978-89; full-time writer, 1989-; Writer's Digest School, faculty, 1994-2001. **Publications:** (As Kara Galloway) Sleight of Heart, 1990; (as Kara Galloway) Love at Second Sight, 1991; Ivory Lies, 1992; Private Lies, 1993; Unsafe Keeping, 1995; If Two of Them Are Dead, 1996; Who Was Sylvia?, 2000; The Seeds of Time, 2001; Death Kindly Stopped, 2003; His Horror the Mayor, 2003; Cupid's Ghost, 2003; It's a Zoo Around Here (children's picture book), 2012. Works appear in anthologies. Contributor of articles to magazines and newspapers. **Address:** 4 Colgate Ct., Longmont, CO 80503-2253, U.S.A. **Online address:** carol@carolcail.com

CAIN, Peter J. *See* **CAIN, P. J.**

CAIN, P. J. (Peter J. Cain). British (born England), b. 1941. **Genres:** History. **Career:** Birmingham University, faculty; Sheffield Hallam University, research professor in history, 1995-, now professor emeritus in history; Yale University, visiting professor. Writer. **Publications:** Economic Foundations of British Overseas Expansion, 1815-1914, 1980; (ed. and intro.) Writings on Imperialism and Internationalism, 1992; (with A.G. Hopkins) British Imperialism: Innovation and Expansion, 1688-1914, 1993; (with A.G. Hopkins) British Imperialism: Crisis and Deconstruction, 1914-1990, 1993; (ed.) Empire and Imperialism: The Debate of the 1870s, 1999; (with A.G. Hopkins)

British Imperialism, 1688-2000, 2001; (ed. with M. Harrison) Imperialism: Critical Concepts in Historical Studies, 2001; Hobson and Imperialism: Radicalism, New Liberalism and Finance, 1887-1938, 2002. **Address:** Development & Society, Sheffield Hallam University, City Campus, Howard St., Sheffield, SY S1 1WB, England. **Online address:** p.j.cain@shu.ac.uk

CAIN, Robert. *See* **KEITH, William H(enry).**

CAINE, Barbara. Australian/South African (born South Africa), b. 1948. **Genres:** Women's Studies And Issues, History, Biography. **Career:** University of Sydney, assistant professor of history and director of centre for women's studies, 1989-95, School of Philosophical and Historical Inquiry, head, 2011-; Monash University, professor of history and ARC professorial fellow, 1995-2010. Writer. **Publications:** Destined to Be Wives: The Sisters of Beatrice Webb, 1986; (ed. with E.A. Grosz and M. de Lepervanche) Crossing Boundaries: Feminisms and the Critique of Knowledges, 1988; Victorian Feminists, 1992; (co-ed.) History at Sydney, 1891-1991: Centenary Reflections, 1992; (ed.) The Woman Question in England and Australia, 1994; (ed. with R. Pringle) Transitions: A New Australian Feminism, 1995; English Feminism, 1780-1980, 1997; (co-ed.) Australian Feminism: A Companion, 1998; (with G. Sluga) Gendering European History, 2000; (ed. with M. Spongberg and A. Curthoys) Companion to Women's Historical Writing, 2005; Bombay to Bloomsbury: A Biography of the Strachey Family, 2005; (ed.) Friendship: A History, 2009; Biography and History, 2010. Contributor to periodicals. **Address:** School of Philosophical and Historical Inquiry,, University of Sydney, Rm. 608, A18 Brennan MacCallum Bldg., Sydney, NW 2006, Australia. **Online address:** barbara.caine@sydney.edu.au

CAINE, Michael. (Maurice Joseph Micklewhite). British (born England), b. 1933. **Genres:** Film, Trivia/Facts, Autobiography/Memoirs. **Career:** British Army, 1951-53; Westminster Repertory, assistant stage manager, 1953; Lowestoft Repertory, actor, 1953-55; Theatre Workshop, actor, 1955; South Beach Brasserie, restaurant owner, 1996-. Writer. **Publications:** Not Many People Know That!: Michael Caine's Almanac of Amazing Information, 1984 in US as Michael Caine's Almanac of Amazing Information, 1986; Not Many People Know It's This Either, 1988; Michael Caine's Moving Picture Show (film trivia), 1988; And Not Many People Know This Either!, 1988; Acting in Film: An Actor's Take on Moviemaking, 1990; What's It All About? (autobiography), 1992; Spies and Sleuths, 1997; (with M. White) Canteen Cuisine: In the Kitchen with Michael Caine, 1997; Elephant to Hollywood, 2010. Contributor to periodicals. **Address:** Gwyn Foxx Talent Agency, 4401 Wilshire Blvd., Los Angeles, CA 90010-3728, U.S.A.

CAIRNS, Kathleen A. American (born United States), b. 1946. **Genres:** Women's Studies And Issues, Young Adult Fiction. **Career:** California Polytechnic State University, Department of History, lecturer in history, Department of Women's and Gender Studies, faculty. Writer and historian. **Publications:** Front-Page Women Journalists, 1920-1950, 2003; The Enigma Woman: The Death Sentence of Nellie May Madison, 2007; Hard Time at Tehachapi: California's First Women's Prison, 2009. Contributor to journals. **Address:** Department of History, California Polytechnic State University, 25D, Bldg. 47, 1 Grand Ave., San Luis Obispo, CA 93407, U.S.A. **Online address:** kcairns@calpoly.edu

CAIRNS, Scott. American (born United States), b. 1954. **Genres:** Humanities, Intellectual History, Theology/Religion, Language/Linguistics, Writing/Journalism, Biography, Autobiography/Memoirs. **Career:** Bowling Green State University, teaching fellow, 1979-81; Kansas State University, instructor, 1981-84; University of Utah, teaching fellow, 1984-87; Westminster College, assistant professor, 1987-90; University of North Texas, assistant professor of English and director of creative writing, 1990-94; Old Dominion University, associate professor of English and director of creative writing, 1994-99; University of Missouri, professor of English, 1999-, director creative writing program. Writer. **Publications:** The Theology of Doubt, 1985; The Translation of Babel, 1990; Figures for the Ghost, 1994; The Sacred Place: Witnessing the Holy in the Physical World, 1996; Recovered Body, 1998, 2nd ed., 2003; Philokalia: New and Selected Poems, 2002; Compass of Affection: Poems New and Selected, 2006; (trans.) Love's Immensity: Mystics on the Endless Life, 2007; God with Us: Rediscovering the Meaning of Christmas, 2007; (memoir) Short Trip to the Edge: Where Earth Meets Heaven, a Pilgrimage, 2007; (nonfiction) The End of Suffering: Finding Purpose in Pain, 2009. **Address:** Department of English, University of Missouri, Tate Hall, Columbia, MO 65211-1500, U.S.A. **Online address:** cairnss@missouri.edu

CAISTOR *See* **Hopkinson, Amanda.**

CALABRO, Marian. American (born United States), b. 1954. **Genres:** Business/Trade/Industry, Communications/Media, History, Writing/Journalism, Young Adult Non-fiction, Institutions/Organizations, Autobiography/Memoirs, Documentaries/Reportage, Documentaries/Reportage. **Career:** Dell Publishing, staff promotion writer, manager, senior copywriter, 1977-81; New American Library, staff; Warren Gorham Lamont, staff promotion writer and manager; Learning Corporation of America, staff promotion writer, promotion manager, 1981-84, editor, promotion director; freelance writer, 1984-; Media and Methods, contributing editor; CorporateHistory.net L.L.C., founder, president and publisher, 2004-. **Publications:** Operation Grizzly Bear, 1989; ZAP!: A Brief History of Television, 1992; Great Courtroom Lawyers, 1996; The Perilous Journey of the Donner Party, 1999; A Wealth of History, 2001; Making Things Work: PSEG'S First Century, 2003; The Pep Boys: A Company History, 2005; A. W. Hastings: An Illustrated History, 2006; Melwood: A Story of Empowerment, 2007; Flying High Again: PARC's Redevelopment of Plattsburgh Air Force Base, 2008; Clinton County ARC-Past & Present, 2009; (contrib.) Dominion's First Century: A Legacy of Service, 2010. **Address:** CorporateHistory.net L.L.C., 327 Cleveland Ave., Hasbrouck Heights, NJ 07604, U.S.A. **Online address:** info@mariancalabro.com

CALASSO, Roberto. Italian (born Italy), b. 1941. **Genres:** Novels, Autobiography/Memoirs, Literary Criticism And History. **Career:** Adelphi Edizioni (publishing house), staff, 1962-, editorial director, 1968-, chairman, 1999-. **Publications:** Note Senza Testo, 1970; L'Impuro Folle, 1974; Le Fou Impur, 1976; La Rovina di Kasch, 1983; (ed.) Ecce Homo: Come si Diventa cio Che si e (autobiography), 1985; Le Nozze di Cadmo e Armonia, 1988; Quarantanove Gradini, 1991; Ruin of Kasch, 1993; The Marriage of Cadmus and Harmony, 1994; Ka, 1996; Sentieri Tortuosi: Bruce Chatwin Fotografo, 1998; Letteratura e gli Dèi, 2001; K, 2002; (ed.) Scritti, 2002; Cento Lettere a uno Sconosciuto, 2003; Follia che Viene Dalle Ninfe, 2005; Rosa Tiepolo, 2006; La Folie Baudelaire, 2008; Tiepolo Pink, 2009; L'ardore, 2010. Contributor of articles to professional journals. **Address:** Adelphi Edizioni SpA, Via S. Giovanni sul Muro 14, Milan, 20121, Italy.

CALAVITA, Kitty. American (born United States), b. 1944. **Genres:** Social Sciences, Law. **Career:** University of California, Department of Criminology, Law and Society, professor of sociology, chancellor's professor, 2008-, now professor emeritus. Writer. **Publications:** California's Employer Sanctions: The Case of the Disappearing Law, 1982; U.S. Immigration Law and the Control of Labor, 1820-1924, 1984; Inside the State: The Bracero Program, Immigration, and the I.N.S., 1992; (with H.N. Pontell and R.H. Tillman) Big Money Crime: Fraud and Politics in the Savings and Loan Crisis, 1997; Immigrants at the Margins: Law, Race, and Exclusion in Southern Europe, 2005; Invitation to Law & Society: An Introduction to the Study of Real Law, 2010. **Address:** Department of Criminology, Law and Society, School of Social Ecology, University of California, 2379 Social Ecology II, Irvine, CA 92697-7080, U.S.A. **Online address:** kccalavi@uci.edu

CALBERT, Cathleen. American (born United States), b. 1955. **Genres:** Poetry, Young Adult Fiction. **Career:** University of Houston, teaching fellow, 1984-89, visiting lecturer, 1989-90; Rhode Island College, Department of English, assistant professor, 1990-95; associate professor, 1995-2000, professor, 2000-. Writer. **Publications:** POETRY: My Summer as a Bride: Poems, 1995; Lessons in Space, 1997; Bad Judgment: Poems, 1999. FICTION: The Ten Worst Human Fears, 1999; Modifications, 2001; My Argentine, 2004; Sleeping with a Famous Poet, 2007. Contributor of articles to books. **Address:** Department of English, Rhode Island College, 365 Craig-Lee Hall, 600 Mt. Pleasant Ave., Providence, RI 02908-1991, U.S.A. **Online address:** ccalbert@ric.edu

CALDER, Andrew. British (born England), b. 1942?. **Genres:** Novels, Literary Criticism And History, Art/Art History, History, Young Adult Fiction. **Career:** University College London, reader in French. Writer. **Publications:** Molière: The Theory and Practice of Comedy, 1993; The Fables of La Fontaine: Wisdom Brought Down to Earth, 2001; (ed. with D. Bradby) The Cambridge Companion to Molièr, 2006. **Address:** c/o Author Mail, Librairie Droz S. A., 11 rue Firmin Massot, PO Box 389, Geneva, 1211, Switzerland. **Online address:** a.calder@ucl.ac.uk

CALDER, Jason. *See* **DUNMORE, John.**

CALDER, John (Mackenzie). British (born England), b. 1927. **Genres:** Literary Criticism And History, Poetry. **Career:** John Calder Publishers Ltd., founder and managing director, 1950-; Calder and Boyars Ltd., managing director, 1961-; Ledlanet Nights, founder, 1963; Federation of Scottish Theatres, chair, 1972-74; European Parliament for Mid Scotland and Fife, 1979; University of Nanterre, lecturer in history, Ecole Active Bilingue Professor of English Literature, 1994-95; Operabout Ltd., director; Calders Ltd., director; Riverrun Press Inc., director; Canadian International Library Ltd., director; Godot Co., administrator. Journalist and columnist. **Publications:** The Garden of Eros, The Philosophy of Samuel Beckett, 1996; What's Right, What's Wrong, 1999; Pursuit, 2001; Solo: Collected Poems, 1997-2007, 2008. EDITOR: A Henry Miller Reader, 1983; A Samuel Beckett Reader, 1984; (with M. Esslin, B. Whitelaw and D. Warrilow) As No Other Dare Fail: Festschrift for Samuel Beckett's Eightieth Birthday, 1986; (with J. Fletcher) Nouveau Roman Reader, 1986. **Address:** Calder Publications Ltd., 51 The Cut, London, GL SE1 8LF, England. **Online address:** info@calderpublications.com

CALDER, Marie D(onais). Canadian (born Canada), b. 1948. **Genres:** Young Adult Fiction, History, Novels, Young Adult Fiction, Children's Fiction, Documentaries/Reportage, Biography, Military/Defense/Arms Control, Military/Defense/Arms Control. **Career:** Teacher, 1971-74, 1976-80; Estevan Rural Schools, teacher, 1980-2001; writer, 2002-. **Publications:** Humpty Dumpty is a Friend of Mine, 1997; The Other Side of War, 2010; The Other Side of Fear, 2010; The Other Side of Pain, 2010; The Other Side of Trauma, 2011; The Other Side of Torn, 2011. **Address:** 413 Maple Bay, Estevan, SK S4A 2E6, Canada. **Online address:** mdcalder@sasktel.net

CALDER, Martin. British (born England), b. 1967. **Genres:** Literary Criticism And History, Travel/Exploration. **Career:** University of Bristol, Department of French, lecturer, senior lecturer, 1999-. Writer. **Publications:** Encounters with the Other: A Journey to the Limits of Language through Works by Rousseau, Defoe, Prevost and Graffigny, 2003; (ed.) Experiencing the Garden in the Eighteenth Century, 2006; A Summer in Gascony: Discovering the Other South of France, 2008. **Address:** Department of French, University of Bristol, 17 Woodland Rd., Bristol, BS8 1TE, England. **Online address:** martin@asummeringascony.com

CALDER, Nigel (David Ritchie). British (born England), b. 1931. **Genres:** Sciences, Technology, Astronomy, Physics, Earth Sciences, Environmental Sciences/Ecology, Meteorology/Atmospheric Sciences, Psychology, Social Sciences, Military/Defense/Arms Control, Marine Sciences/Oceanography, History, Intellectual History, Documentaries/Reportage, Language/Linguistics, Travel/Exploration, Sociology. **Career:** Mullard Research Laboratories, research physicist, 1954-56; New Scientist, staff writer, 1956-60, science editor, 1960-62, editor, 1962-66; freelance author, scriptwriter, 1966-. **Publications:** Robots, 1957; Electricity Grows Up, 1958; Radio Astronomy, 1959; What They Read and Why: The Use of Technical Literature in the Electrical and Electronics Industries, 1959; Spin-off, a Selection of Cartoons from New Scientist, 1965; The Environment Game, 1967 in US as Eden was No Garden: An Inquiry Into the Environment of Man, 1968; Technopolis: Social Control of the Uses of Science, 1969; Violent Universe: An Eye-Witness Account of the Commotion in Astronomy 1968-69, 1969; The Mind of Man: An Investigation into Current Research on the Brain and Human Nature, 1970; Living Tomorrow, 1970; Restless Earth: A Report on the New Geology, 1972; The Life Game: Evolution and the New Biology, 1973; The Weather Machine, 1974; The Human Conspiracy: The New Science of Social Behavior, 1975; The Key to the Universe: A Report on the New Physics, 1977; Spaceships of the Mind, 1978; Einstein's Universe, 1979, rev. ed., 2005; The Comet is Coming!: The Feverish Legacy of Mr. Halley, 1979; Nuclear Nightmares: An Investigation into Possible Wars, 1980; Timescale: An Atlas of the Fourth Dimension, 1983; The English Channel, 1986; The Green Machines: Life and Liberty in the Era of High Biotechnology, 1986; Spaceship Earth, 1991; Giotto to the Comets, 1992; Hubble Space Telescope: The Harvest So Far, 1993; Beyond this World: Scientific Missions of the European Space Agency, 1995; The Manic Sun: Weather Theories Confounded, 1997; Magic Universe: The Oxford Guide to Modern Science, 2003; (intro.) Relativity: The Special and the General Theory, 2006; (with H. Svensmark) The Chilling Stars: A New Theory of Climate Change, 2007, rev. ed., 2008. EDITOR: The World in 1984: The Complete New Scientist Series, 1965; Unless Peace Comes: A Scientific Forecast of New Weapons, 1968; Nature in the Round: A Guide to Environmental Science, 1973; (ed. with J. Newell) Future Earth: Exploring the Frontiers of Science, 1988 in US as On the Frontiers of Science: How Scientists See Our Future, 1989; Scientific Europe: Research and Technology in 20 Countries, 1990; Success Story: 30 Discoveries, 1999. Contributor to newspapers, magazines and journals. **Address:** 26 Boundary Rd., Northgate, Crawley, WS RH10 8BT, England. **Online address:** nc@windstream.demon.co.uk

CALDERONE, Melissa A. *See* **MAC.**

CALDERWOOD, James Lee. American (born United States), b. 1930. **Genres:** History, Essays, Reference. **Career:** Michigan State University, instructor, 1961-63; University of California, assistant professor of English, 1963-66, associate professor, professor of English, 1966-94, associate dean of humanities, 1974, now professor emeritus. Writer. **Publications:** (Ed. with J.L. Barroll) William Shakespear, Love's Labour's Lost, 1970; Shakespearean Metadrama: The Argument of the Play in Titus Andronicus, Love's Labour's Lost, Romeo and Juliet, A Midsummer Night's Dream and Richard II, 1971; Metadrama in Shakespeare's Henriad: RichardII to Henry V, 1979; If It Were Done: Macbeth and Tragic Action, 1986; Shakespeare & the Denial of Death, 1987; Properties of Othello, 1989; A Midsummer Night's Dream, 1992. EDITOR WITH H.E. TOLIVER: Forms of Poetry, 1968; Perspectives on Drama, 1968; Perspectives on Poetry, 1968; Perspectives on Fiction, 1968; Forms of Drama, 1969; Essays in Shakespearen Criticism, 1970; Forms of Tragedy, 1972; Forms of Prose Fiction, 1972; To Be and Not to Be: Negation and Metadrama in Hamlet, 1983. Contributor of articles to journals. **Address:** Department of English and Comparative Literature, University of California, Irvine, 435 Humanities Instructional Bldg., Irvine, CA 92697, U.S.A. **Online address:** jlcalder@uci.edu

CALDWELL, David H(epburn). Scottish (born Scotland), b. 1951. **Genres:** Art/Art History, Technology, Engineering, Military/Defense/Arms Control, Young Adult Fiction. **Career:** National Museums Scotland, deputy keeper, keeper; Finlaggan Archaeological Project, director. Writer. **Publications:** The Scottish Armoury, 1979; Scotland's Wars and Warriors: Winning Against the Odds, 1998; Islay, Jura and Colonsay: A Historical Guide, 2001; Islay: The Land of the Lordship, 2008. EDITOR: Scottish Weapons and Fortifications, 1100-1800, 1981; Angels, Nobles and Unicorns: Art and Patronage in Medieval Scotland, 1982. Contributor to learned journals. **Address:** National Museums of Scotland, Chambers St., Edinburgh, EH1 1JF, Scotland. **Online address:** d.caldwell@nms.ac.uk

CALDWELL, Grant. Australian (born Australia), b. 1947. **Genres:** Poetry, Novellas/Short Stories, Biography, Autobiography/Memoirs, Young Adult Fiction. **Career:** SCOPP (literary magazine), editorial reader, 1977-79; freelance writer, 1979-; MEUSE (art and literature magazine), editor and publisher, 1980-82; Angus and Robertson Publishers, editorial reader, 1982-84; Darlinghurst Non-School of Writing, teacher and director, 1984-87; Victoria College of the Arts, writer and teacher, 1995-97; University of Melbourne, School of Culture and Communication, lecturer of creative writing. **Publications:** POETRY: The Screaming Frog That Ralph Ate, 1979; The Bells of Mr. Whippy, 1982; The Nun Wore Sunglasses, 1984; The Life of a Pet Dog, 1993; You Know What I Mean, 1996; Dreaming of Robert De Niro, 2003. OTHER: The Revolt of the Coats (short stories), 1988; Malabata (autobiography), 1991. Contributor to periodicals. **Address:** School of Culture and Communication, The University of Melbourne, Rm. 227, John Medley Bldg., Parkville, VI 3010, Australia. **Online address:** cal@unimelb.edu.au

CALDWELL, Laura. American (born United States), b. 1967. **Genres:** Novels. **Career:** Loyola University of Chicago, School of Law, adjunct professor; Lake Magazine, contributing editor and writer. **Publications:** NOVELS: Burning the Map, 2002; A Clean Slate, 2003; The Year of Living Famously, 2004; The Night I Got Lucky, 2005; Look Closely, 2005; The Rome Affair, 2006; The Good Liar, 2008. IZZY MCNEIL MYSTERIES SERIES: Red Hot Lies, 2009; Red Blooded Murder, 2009; Red, White & Dead, 2009. Works appear in anthologies. Contributor of articles to magazines. **Address:** 2506 N Clark St., PO Box 436, Chicago, IL 60614, U.S.A.

CALETTI, Deb. American (born United States), b. 1963. **Genres:** Young Adult Fiction, Novels. **Career:** Writer. **Publications:** The Queen of Everything, 2002; Honey, Baby, Sweetheart, 2004; Wild Roses, 2005; The Nature of Jade, 2007; The Fortunes of Indigo Skye, 2008; The Secret Life of Prince Charming, 2009; The Six Rules of Maybe, 2010; Stay, 2011. Contributor to books. **Address:** c/o Author Mail, Simon Schuster, 1230 Ave. of the Americas, New York, NY 10020, U.S.A. **Online address:** deb@debcaletti.com

CALHOUN, B. B. (L. E. Blair). American (born United States), b. 1961.

Genres: Young Adult Fiction, Young Adult Non-fiction, Children's Fiction. **Career:** Writer and teacher. **Publications:** AS L.E. BLAIR: Peer Pressure, 1990; Mixed Feelings, 1990; Drummer Girl, 1990; Face-off!, 1990; Welcome To Junior High, 1990; Falling In Like, 1990; The New You, 1990; The Ghost of Eagle Mountain, 1990; It's all in the Stars, 1990; Stealing the Show, 1990; Perfect Match, 1991; Baby Talk, 1991; Beauty Queens, 1991; Center Stage, 1991; Earth Alert!, 1991; Rockin' Class Trip, 1991; Family Rules, 1991; Horse Fever, 1991; Family Affair, 1991; Problem Dad, 1991; House Party, 1991; Cousins, 1992; Katie's Beverly Hills Friend, 1992; Katie And Sabrina's Big Competition, 1992; The Bookshop Mystery, 1992; Allison, Shape Up!, 1992; Allison to the Rescue!, 1992; Katie's Close Call, 1992; Randy and the Great Canoe Race, 1992; It's a Scream!, 1992; Randy and the Perfect Boy, 1992; Randy's Big Chance, 1992; Randy's Big Dream, 1992; Sabrina and the Calf-Raising Disaster, 1992; Sabrina and Too Many Boys, 1992; Sabrina Wins Big!, 1992; Katie and the Impossible Cousins, 1992; Allison's Baby-sitting Adventure, 1993. GIRL TALK SERIES: Odd Couple, 1990. PINK PARROTS SERIES: All That Jazz, 1990; Fielder's Choice, 1991. DINOSAUR DETECTIVE SERIES: On the Right Track, 1994; Fair Play, 1994; Bite Makes Right, 1994; Out of Place, 1994; Scrambled Eggs, 1995; Night of the Carnotaurus, 1995; The Competition, 1995; The Raptor's Claw, 1995. FORD SUPERMODELS OF THE WORLDSERIES: The New Me, 1994; Party Girl, 1994; Having It All, 1994; Making Waves, 1994; Stepping Out, 1995; High Style, 1995; Model Sister, 1995; Cover Girl, 1995; Diamond Dreams No. 11, 1995; Starring Me No. 10, 1995. SILVER BLADES SERIES: Center Ice, 1995; The Big Audition, 1995; Nutcrackeron Ice, 1995; A New Move, 1996; Wedding Secrets, 1996; Rival Roommates, 1997. HIS AND HERS SERIES: New in Town, 1997; Summer Dreams, 1998. OTHERS: H & H 1: New in Town, 1997. **Address:** c/o Fran Lebowitz, Writers House, 21 W 26th St., New York, NY 10010, U.S.A. **Online address:** bbcalhoun@earthlink.net

CALHOUN, Craig (Jackson). American (born United States), b. 1952. **Genres:** Anthropology/Ethnology, History, Sociology. **Career:** University of Southern California, Department of Sociology and Anthropology, course assistant, 1970-71; Columbia University, Teachers College, program coordinator, 1972-73, Horace Mann-Lincoln Institute, research associate, 1973-74, Bureau of Applied Social Research, research assistant, 1974-75, professor of sociology, 2006-07; University of North Carolina, instructor, 1977-80, assistant professor, 1980-85, associate professor, 1985-89, professor of sociology and history, 1989-96, Program in Social Theory and Cross-Cultural Studies, director, 1989-96, Office of International Programs, director and chair of curriculum in international studies, 1990-93, University Center for International Studies, director, 1993-96, Graduate School, dean, 1994-96, Department of Anthropology, adjunct professor, Department of Communication Studies, adjunct professor; University of Khartoum, Development Studies and Research Centre, visiting research associate, 1983; Center for Psychosocial Studies, research fellow, 1983; Comparative Social Research, editor, 1988-93; Beijing Foreign Studies University, Center for Comparative Cultural Studies, visiting professor, 1989; McGraw-Hill Publishers, consulting editor, 1990-2000; University of Oslo Center for Psychosocial Studies, Department of Sociology, visiting lecturer, 1991, professor, 1993-98; Social Science Research Council, president, 1996-; New York University, professor of sociology and history, 1996-, Center for Applied Social Science Research, director, 1996-, Department of Sociology, chair, 1996-99, university professor, 2004-, Institute for Public Knowledge, director, 2007-, professor of media, culture and communications, 2007-. Writer. **Publications:** The Question of Class Struggle: Social Foundations of Popular Radicalism During the Industrial Revolution, 1982; Neither Gods Nor Emperors: Students and the Struggle for Democracy in China, 1994; Critical Social Theory: Culture, History and the Challenge of Difference, 1995; (with D. Light and S. Keller) Sociology, 7th ed., 1997; Nationalism, 1997; Nations Matter: Citizenship, Solidarity, and the Cosmopolitan Dream, 2007; Cosmopolitanism and Belonging: From European Integration to Global Hopes and Fears, 2007; Roots of Radicalism: Tradition, the Public Sphere, and Early 19th Century Social Movements, 2012. EDITOR: (with F.A.J. Ianni) The Anthropological Study of Education, 1976; (with W.R. Scott and M. Meyer) Structures of Power and Constraint: Essays in Honor of Peter M. Blau, 1990; Habermas and the Public Sphere, 1992; (with E. LiPuma and M. Postone) Bourdieu: Critical Perspectives, 1993; Social Theory and the Politics of Identity, 1994; (with J. McGowan) Hannah Arendt and the Meaning of Politics, 1997; The Dictionary of the Social Sciences, 2002; (co-ed.) The Classical Social Theory Reader, 2002; (co-ed.) The Contemporary Social Theory Reader, 2002; (with P. Price and A. Timmer) Understanding September 11, 2002; (with C. Rojek and B. Turner) The Sage Handbook of Sociology, 2005; (with F. Cooper and K. Moore) Lessons of Empire, 2006; Sociology in America: A History, 2007; (with R. Sennett) Practicing Culture, 2007; (with M. Warner and J. Van Antwerpen) Varieties of Secularism: Charles Taylor and A Secular Age, 2010; Robert K. Merton: Sociology of Science, Sociology as Science, 2010; (with D. Rhoten) Knowledge Matters: The Public Mission of the Research University, 2010; (with G. Derluguian) Aftermath: A New Global Economic Order?, 2011; (with G. Derluguian) Business As Usual: The Roots of the Global Financial Meltdown, 2011; (with G. Derluguian) The Deepening Crisis: Governance Challenges After Neoliberalism, 2011; (with M. Juergensmeyer and J. Van Antwerpen) Rethinking Secularism, 2011; (co-ed.) Classical Sociological Theory, 2012; (with R. Sennett) Creating Authority, forthcoming; Contributor to books and periodicals. **Address:** Social Science Research Council, 300 Cadman Plz. W, 15th Fl., Brooklyn, NY 11201, U.S.A. **Online address:** calhoun@ssrc.org

CALIAN, Carnegie Samuel. American (born United States), b. 1933?. **Genres:** Theology/Religion. **Career:** Calvary Presbyterian Church, assistant pastor, 1958-60; University of Dubuque Theological Seminary, visiting professor of theology, 1963-67, associate professor, 1967-72, professor, 1972-81; Pontificio Instituto Orientale, research fellow, 1969-70; Juniata College, J. Omar Good visiting professor of evangelical Christianity, 1975-77; Pittsburgh Theological Seminary, president, 1981-2006, professor of theology, president emeritus and professor emeritus of theology, 2006-; University of Neuchatel, lecturer; University of Pittsburgh, Joseph M. Katz Graduate School of Business, visiting professor, 2007-10. Writer. **Publications:** The Significance of Eschatology in the Thoughts of Nicolas Berdyaev, 1965, rev. ed. as Berdyaev's Philosophy of Hope: A Contribution to Marxist-Christian Dialogue, 1969; Icon and Pulpit: The Protestant-Orthodox Encounter, 1968; Grace, Guts and Goods: How to Stay Christian in an Affluent Society, 1971; The Gospel According to The Wall Street Journal, 1975; Today's Pastor in Tomorrow's World, 1977, rev. ed., 1982; For All Your Seasons: Biblical Direction Through Life's Passages, 1979; Where's the Passion for Excellence in the Church?: Shaping Discipleship Through Ministry and Theological Education, 1989; Theology without Boundaries: Encounters of Eastern Orthodoxy and Western Tradition, 1992; Survival or Revival: Ten Keys to Church Vitality, 1998; The Ideal Seminary: Pursuing Excellence in Theological Education, 2002; The Spirit-Driven Leader: Seven Keys to Succeeding under Pressure, 2010. Contributor to journals. **Address:** Pittsburgh Theological Seminary, 616 N Highland Ave., Pittsburgh, PA 15206-2596, U.S.A. **Online address:** calian@pts.edu

CALIMANI, Riccardo. Italian (born Italy), b. 1946. **Genres:** Intellectual History, Sciences. **Career:** Radiotelevisione Italiana (RAI), manager, 1977-2000; Jewish Community of Venice, vice president; Honorary Swiss Consul, vice president. Writer. **Publications:** Una di Maggio, 1974; Energia: Piu dubbi meno certezze, 1981; La polenta e la mercanzia: un viaggio nel Veneto, 1984; Di ebrei, di cose ebraiche e del resto, 1984; Storia del ghetto di Venezia, 1985; Energia e informazione, 1987; The ghetto of Venice, 1987; Storia dell'ebreo errante, 1987; Gesù ebreo, 1990; (with A. Lepschy) Feedback, 1990; Storie di marrani a Venezia, 1991; Stella gialla, Ebrei e pregiudizio, 1993; Presenze ebraico-cristiane nelle Venezie, 1993; I Destini e le avventure dell'intellettuale ebreo, 1650-1933, 1996; Capitali europee dell'ebraismo, 1998; Paolo, l'ebreo che fondo il Cristianesimo, 1999; Ebrei e pregiudizio, 2000; (with G.S. Reinisch and C. Vivante) Venice: Guide to the Synagogues, Museum And Cemetery, 2001; L'Inquisizione a Venezia, 2002; L'Europa degli ebrei, 2003; Non e facile essere ebreo, 2004; (ed. with V. Pierobon) Le radici del futuro: 1985-2005: i protagonisti del Veneto, 2005; (with A.V. Sullam) The Venetian Ghetto, 2005; Passione e tragedia: la storia degli ebrei russi, 2006; Storia del pregiudizio contro gli ebrei: antigiudaismo, antisemitismo, antisionismo, 2007; Ebrei eterni inquieti, 2007; Il mercante di Venezia, 2008. Contributor to periodicals. **Address:** Cannaregio, S-Felice 3830, Venice, 30131, Italy.

CALKINS, Robert G. American (born United States), b. 1932. **Genres:** Art/Art History, Adult Non-fiction, Architecture. **Career:** Cornell University, Department of History of Art, associate professor, 1966-80, chairman, 1976-81, professor of medieval art and architecture, 1980-2002, professor emeritus, 2002-; International Center of Medieval Art, vice-president and board director, 1980-81, president, 1981-84. Writer. **Publications:** Medieval Treasury; An Exhibition of Medieval Art from the Third to the Sixteenth Century, 1968; Distribution of Labor: The Illuminators of the Hours of Catherine of Cleves and Their Workshop, 1979; Monuments of Medieval Art, 1979, 2nd ed., 1985; Illuminated Books of the Middle Ages, 1983; Programs of Medieval Illumination, 1984; Medieval Architecture in Western Europe: From A.D. 300 to 1500,

1998. **Address:** 4 Indigo Run Dr., Apt. 2720, Hilton Head, SC 29926, U.S.A. **Online address:** rgc1@cornell.edu

CALLAGHAN, Barry. Canadian (born Canada), b. 1937. **Genres:** Novels, Novellas/Short Stories, Poetry, Translations, Adult Non-fiction. **Career:** Universities of Rome, writer-in-residence; University of Toronto, teaching fellow, 1960-64; York University, professor, 1965-2003, professor emeritus; Toronto Telegram, literary editor, 1966-71; war correspondent, 1969-71; Villon Films, co-owner, 1972-76; Exile Magazine, founder and publisher, 1972-; Exile Editions, publisher, 1976-; CTV Network, critic of contemporary affairs, 1976-82; Toronto Life Magazine, contributing editor, 1978-85; Exile Quarterly, editor-in-chief. **Publications:** The Hogg Poems and Drawings, 1978; The Black Queen Stories, 1982; The Way the Angel Spreads Her Wings (novel), 1989; When Things Get Worst (novel), 1993; A Kiss Is Still A Kiss (stories), 1995; Barrelhouse Kings (memoir), 1998; Between Trains, 2007; Raise You Twenty: Essays and Encounters, 2011. POETRY: As Close as We Came, 1982; Stone Blind Love, 1988; Hogg: The Seven Last Words, 2001; Beside Still Waters, 2009. TRANSLATOR: R. Marteau, Atlante, 1979; R. Marteau, Treatise on White and Tincture, 1979; Interlude, 1982; M. Pavlovic, Singing at the Whirlpool and Other Poems, 1983; M. Pavlovic, A Voice Locked in Stone, 1985: J. Brault, Fragile Moments, 1986; Flowers of Ice, 1987; R. Marteau, Eidolon, 1991. EDITOR: Lord of Winter and of Love: A Book of Canadian Love Poems in English and French, 1983; Canadian Travellers in Italy, 1989; Exile: The First Fifteen Years, 2 vols., 1992; Exile's Exiles, 1992; (with D. Lampe) Occasion of Sin: Stories, 1992; (with M. Atwood) Gwendolyn MacEwen, 1993; Lords of Winter and of Love: A Book of Canadian Love Poems in English and French, 1993; Austin Clarke Reader, 1996; This Ain't No Healing Town, 1996; (with B. Meyer) We Wasn't Pals: Canadian Poetry and Prose of the First World War, 2001; Young Bloods: Stories from Exile 1972-2001, 2001. NON FICTION: Raise You, vol. I, 2005, vol. II, 2006, vol. III, 2011. Contributor to periodicals. **Address:** c/o Nancy Colbert, 303 Davenport Rd., Toronto, ON M5R 1K5, Canada. **Online address:** exile2@sympatico.ca

CALLAGHAN, Sheila. American (born United States), b. 1973. **Genres:** Plays/Screenplays. **Career:** University of California, playwriting faculty, teaching assistant, 1997; College of New Jersey, adjunct professor, 2003-; Brooklyn College, adjunct professor, 2004; LaGuardia Community College, adjunct professor, 2004; University of Rochester, adjunct professor, 2005; Spalding University, M.F.A. program in creative writing, faculty member, 2005-; William Inge Center for the Arts, guest teaching artist, 2007. Playwright and educator. **Publications:** Scab, 2002; Kate Crackernuts, 2004; Star-crossed Lovers, 2004; Dead City, 2006. **Address:** Mark Christian Subias Agency, 331 W 57th St., Ste. 462, New York, NY 10019, U.S.A. **Online address:** sheilacallaghan@gmail.com

CALLAHAN, Bob. American (born United States), b. 1942. **Genres:** Cultural/Ethnic Topics, Social Sciences, History. **Career:** Turtle Island Foundation, executive director, 1969-91; Kollected Krazy Kat, editor, 1989-; Bob Callahan Studios, proprietor, 1991-. **Publications:** Idols, 1970; Algonquin Woods, 1978; (ed. and intro.) A Jaime de Angulo Reader, 1979; (ed.) Select Essays: 1963-1975, 1981; (ed.) The Big Book of American Irish Culture, 1987; (ed.) The New Comics Anthology, 1991; Who Shot JFK: A Guide to the Major Conspiracy Theories, 1993; Fireside, 1993; Barry Gifford's Perdita Durango, 1995; (with B. Gifford) Perdita Durango, 1999; (ed.) The New Smithsonian Book of Comic-book Stories: From Crumb to Clowes, 2004; (contrib.) Krazy & Ignatz 1919-1921: A Kind, Benevolent and Amiable Brick, 2010. **Address:** c/o Norman Kurz, Lowenstein & Associates, 121 W 27th St., Ste. 601, New York, NY 10001, U.S.A.

CALLAHAN, Daniel (J.). American (born United States), b. 1930. **Genres:** Education, Ethics, Humanities, Law, Medicine/Health, Politics/Government, Theology/Religion. **Career:** Harvard University, Divinity School, teaching fellow of Roman Catholic studies, 1959-61, Harvard Center for Population and Development Studies, visiting assistant professor, 1996, Harvard Medical School, Friends of Ethics, chairman, 1997, Division of Medical Ethics, senior fellow, 1998-; Commonweal, executive editor, 1961-68; Temple University, visiting assistant professor, 1963; Brown University, visiting assistant professor, 1965; The Population Council, staff associate, 1969-70; Hasting Center, co-founder and president, 1969-96, president emeritus, 1996-, International Programs, director, 1997-; Council for International Organizations of Medical Sciences, consultant, 1992; Yale University, Department of Philosophy, senior research fellow, 2004-, Institution for Social and Policy Studies, fellow, 2004-, Yale-Hastings Program in Ethics and Health Policy, co-director. Writer. **Publications:** The Mind of the Catholic Layman, 1963; Honesty in the Church, 1965; The New Church, 1966; (co-author) The Role of Theology in the University, 1967; Abortion; Law, Choice and Morality, 1970; Ethics and Population Limitation, 1971; The American Population Debate, 1972; The Tyranny of Survival: And Other Pathologies of Civilized Life, 1973; (co-author) The Teaching of Ethics in the Military, 1982; (co-author) Congress and the Media: The Ethical Connection, 1985; Setting Limits; Medical Goals in an Aging Society, 1987, 2nd ed., 1995; What Kind of Life?: The Limits of Medical Progress, 1990, 2nd ed., 1995; The Troubled Dream of Life: Living with Mortality, 1993, rev. ed. as In Search of Peaceful Death, 1994; False Hopes: Why Americas Quest for Perfect Health Is a Recipe for Failure, 1998, rev. ed. as False Hopes: Overcoming the Obstacles to an Affordable, Sustainable Medicine, 1999; What Price Better Health?: Hazards of the Research Imperative, 2003; Medicine and the Market: Equity v. Choice, 2006; Taming the Beloved Beast, 2009. EDITOR: (with D. O'Hanlon and H. Oberman) Christianity Divided, 1961; Federal Aid and Catholic Schools, 1964; Generation of the Third Eye, 1965; The Secular City Debate, 1966; God, Jesus and Spirit, 1969; The Catholic Case for Contraception, 1969; (with H.T. Engelhardt, Jr.) Science, Ethics and Medicine, 1976; (with H.T. Engelhardt, Jr.) Knowledge, Value and Belief, 1977; (with H.T. Engelhardt, Jr.) Morals, Science and Sociality, 1978; (with H.T. Engelhardt, Jr.) Knowing and Valuing; The Search for Coinmon Roots, 1980; (with S. Bok) Ethics Teaching in Higher Education, 1980; (with P.G. Clark) Ethical Issues of Population Aid: Culture, Economics and International Assistance, 1981; (with A.L. Caplan) Ethics in Hard Times, 1981; (with H.T. Engelhardt, Jr.) The Roots of Ethics; Science, Religion and Values, 1981; (with B. Jennings) Ethics, the Social Sciences and Policy Analysis, 1983; (with S. Callahan) Abortion: Understanding Differences, 1984; (with A.L. Caplan and B. Jennings) Applying the Humanities, 1985; (with B. Jennings) Representation and Responsibility: Exploring Legislative Ethics, 1985; (with G.R. Dunstan) Biomedical Ethics: An Anglo-American Dialogue, 1988; (with P.J. Boyle) What Price Mental Health?: The Ethics and Politics of Setting Priorities, 1995; (with R.H.J. ter Meulen and E. Topinková) A World Growing Old: The Coming Health Care Challenges, 1995; (with M.J. Hanson) The Goals of Medicine: The Forgotten Issue in Health Care Reform, 1999; Promoting Healthy Behavior: How Much Freedom?: Whose Responsibility?, 2000; The Role of Complementary and Alternate Medicine: Accommodating Pluralism, 2002. Contributor to books. **Address:** Hastings Center, 21 Malcolm Gordon Rd., Garrison, NY 10524-5555, U.S.A. **Online address:** callahan@thehastingscenter.org

CALLAHAN, Nelson J. American (born United States), b. 1927. **Genres:** Theology/Religion, History. **Career:** St. Patrick West Park Parish, assistant pastor, 1953-58; St. Agatha Parish, assistant pastor, 1958-63, Church of the Conversion of St. Paul, assistant pastor, 1963-65; St. Peter High School, director of guidance, 1965-67; St. John College, part-time instructor, 1965-66, chaplain and assistant professor of theology, 1967-74; St. Raphael Parish, pastor, 1968-2002, pastor emeritus, 2002-. Writer. **Publications:** A Case for Due Process in the Church: Father Eugene O'Callaghan American Pioneer of Dissent, 1971; The Role of an Ethnic Pastor in a Cleveland Parish, 1972; (ed.) A Catholic Journey Through Ohio, 1976; (with W.F. Hickey) The Irish Americans and Their Communities of Cleveland, 1978; (ed.) The Diary of Richard L. Burtsell, Priest of New York: The Early Years, 1865-1868, 1978; (with J. Toman) Years in Passing: St. Ignatius High School, an Anecdotal History, 1986. **Address:** St. Raphael Parish, 525 Dover Ctr., Bay Village, OH 44140, U.S.A.

CALLAHAN, Sadie. *See* **MCCLANAHAN, Jeffery.**

CALLANAN, Frank. Irish (born Ireland), b. 1956. **Genres:** Politics/Government, Biography. **Career:** Barrister, 1980-; senior counsel, 1998-. Writer. **Publications:** (Ed.) Edward Byrne, Parnell: A Memoir, 1991; The Parnell Split, 1890-91, 1992; T.M. Healy, 1996; (ed) The Literary and Historical Society 1985-2005, 2005; James Joyce and the United Irishman, Paris 1902-3, 2010. **Address:** Law Library, 145-151 Church St., Dublin, DU 7, Ireland. **Online address:** fcallanan@lawlibrary.ie

CALLAWAY, Barbara J. American (born United States), b. 1940. **Genres:** Biography, History, Women's Studies And Issues, Social Commentary. **Career:** California State University, Mount St. Mary's College, assistant professor, 1966-72; University of California, assistant professor, 1966-72; Rutgers University, professor of political science, 1972-, now professor emeritus of political science, College of Nursing, acting dean, 1976-77, associate provost of the university, 1987-95, Graduate School, dean, 1990-92. Writer. **Publications:** (Ed. with A. Stone) Turmoil and Consensus: The World of Politics, 1975; Muslim Hausa Women in Nigeria: Tradition and Change, 1987; (with L. Creevey) The Heritage of Islam: Women Religion and Politics in West Africa, 1994; Hildegard Peplau: Psychiatric Nurse of the Century, 2002; Islamic Feminism And Fundamentalism In West Africa, forthcoming. **Address:** Department of Political Science, Rutgers University, 303 Hickman Hall, 89 George St., New Brunswick, NJ 08901, U.S.A. **Online address:** callaway@rci.rutgers.edu

CALLAWAY, C. Wayne. American/British (born England), b. 1941. **Genres:** Medicine/Health, Sciences, Food And Wine. **Career:** Northwestern University Medical School, rotating intern, 1967-68, resident in internal medicine, 1968-69; Mayo Graduate School of Medicine, resident in internal medicine, 1971-73, advanced clinical resident in endocrinology and metabolism, 1973-75, Graduate School, instructor in medicine, Mayo Medical School, instructor, 1974-78, assistant professor of medicine and instructor in the history of medicine, 1978-86, Nutrition Clinic and Nutrition Consulting Services, director, 1980-86, Lipid Clinic, director, 1982-86; American Medical Association, Joseph Goldberger Visiting Professor of Clinical Nutrition, 1974-78; Harvard Medical School, Elliot P. Joslin Research Laboratory, instructor and research associate, 1976-78; National Institute of Arthritis, Metabolism and Digestive Diseases, medical officer in nutrition program, 1979-80; National Dairy Council, visiting professor, 1980-; National Research Council and National Academy of Sciences, Food and Nutrition Board, senior science consultant, 1987-88; George Washington University, associate professor of medicine and director of center for clinical nutrition at university medical center, 1986-88, associate clinical professor, 1988-; University of Maryland at College Park, adjunct associate professor, 1987-; private practice of internal medicine, endocrinology and metabolism and clinical nutrition, 1988-; University of Florida, Pew Charitable Trust visiting professor, 1988; South Dakota State University, Ethel Austin Martin visiting professor of nutrition, 1989; Mayo Clinic, director. Writer. **Publications:** (With C. Whitney) The Callaway Diet: Successful Permanent Weight Control for Starvers, Stuffers and Skippers, 1990; (with C. Whitney) Surviving with AIDS: A Comprehensive Program of Nutritional Co-therapy, 1991; (with M.B. Albert) Clinical Nutrition for the House Officer, 1992; (co-author) American Medical Association Family Health Cookbook: Good Food That's Good for You, 1997. Works appear in anthologies. Contributor of articles to journals. **Address:** 2311 M St. NW, Ste. 301, Washington, DC 20037, U.S.A. **Online address:** cwcallaway@doctorcallaway.com

CALLAWAY, Trey. American (born United States) **Genres:** Mystery/Crime/Suspense, Plays/Screenplays, Young Adult Fiction. **Career:** University of Southern California, School of Cinematic Arts, professor in Cinematic Arts. Screenwriter, producer and actor. **Publications:** I Still Know What You Did Last Summer, 1998; Mercy Point, 1998; Lost in Oz, 2000; Phobia, 2001; Utopia, 2003; Tahoe Search and Rescue, 2003; The Branch, 2003; Quantum Leap: A Bold Leap Forward, 2004; Witch, 2004. **Address:** The Walt Disney Co., 500 S Buena Vista St., Burbank, CA 91521-4551, U.S.A.

CALLE, Carlos I. American (born United States), b. 1945. **Genres:** Sciences. **Career:** Sweet Briar College, Department of Physics, instructor, 1981-84, assistant professor, 1984-86, chair, 1984-87, associate professor, 1986-91, professor of physics, 1991-99; National Aeronautics and Space Administration, Kennedy Space Center, Electrostatics and Surface Physics Lab, founder, director and senior research scientist, 1999-. Writer, scientist, researcher and physicist. **Publications:** Superstrings and Other Things: A Guide to Physics, 2001, 2nd ed., 2010; Einstein for Dummies, 2005; Coffee with Einstein, 2008; The Universe: Order without Design, 2009. **Address:** Electrostatics and Surface Physics Lab, Kennedy Space Center, National Aeronautics and Space Administration, PO Box KT-B-1, Merritt Island, FL 32899, U.S.A. **Online address:** carlos.i.calle@nasa.gov

CALLENBACH, Ernest. American (born United States), b. 1929. **Genres:** Science Fiction/Fantasy, Environmental Sciences/Ecology, Film, Human Relations/Parenting, Social Commentary, Animals/Pets. **Career:** University of California Press, publicity writer and assistant editor, 1955-58, Film Quarterly, editor, 1958-91, film book editor, 1958-91; Banyan Tree Books, founder, 1975. **Publications:** FICTION: Ecotopia: The Notebooks and Reports of William Weston, 1975; Ecotopia Emerging, 1981. OTHERS: Our Modern Art: The Movies, 1955; Living Poor with Style, 1971; (with C. Leefeldt) The Art of Friendship, 1979; The Ecotopian Encyclopedia for the 80's, 1980; (with M. Phillips) A Citizen Legislature, 1985; (with C. Leefeldt) Humphrey the Wayward Whale, 1986; Publisher's Lunch, 1989; (co-author) EcoManagement: The Elmwood Guide to Ecological Auditing and Sustainable Business, 1993; Living Cheaply with Style: Live Better and Spend Less, 1993, 2nd ed., 2000; Bring Back the Buffalo! A Sustainable Future for America's Great Plains, 1996; Ecology: A Pocket Guide, 1998, rev. ed., 2008. **Address:** Banyan Tree Books, 1963 El Dorado Ave., Berkeley, CA 94707-2441, U.S.A. **Online address:** ec2@berkeley.edu

CALLICOTT, J(ohn) Baird. American (born United States), b. 1941. **Genres:** Philosophy, Literary Criticism And History, Environmental Sciences/Ecology, Humanities, Young Adult Non-fiction. **Career:** Syracuse University, lecturer in philosophy, 1965-66; University of Memphis, instructor in philosophy, 1966-69; University of Wisconsin, assistant professor, 1969-74, associate professor, 1974-82, director of environmental studies program, 1980-86, professor of philosophy, 1982-95, joint professor of natural resources, 1984-95; University of Florida, visiting professor of philosophy, 1983; University of California, research associate, 1987-90; International Society for Environmental Ethics, vice-president, 1994-97, president, 1997-2000; James Cook University, visiting professor fellow, 1995; University of North Texas, Department of Philosophy and Religion Studies, professor of philosophy, 1995-2006, regents professor of philosophy, 2006-10, chair, 2008-10, distinguished research professor, 2010-; Yale University, visiting professor, 2004-05; Suny Press, editor. **Publications:** (With T.W. Overholt) Clothed-in-Fur and Other Tales, 1982; In Defense of the Land Ethic (essays), 1989; Earth's Insights: A Multicultural Survey of Ecological Ethics, 1994; Beyond the Land Ethic: More Essays in Environmental Philosophy, 1999; (with M.P. Nelson) American Indian Environmental Ethics: An Ojibwa Case Study, 2004. EDITOR: (and contrib.) Companion to A Sand County Almanac (essays), 1987; (with R.T. Ames and contrib.) Nature in Asian Traditions of Thought (essays), 1989; (with S.L. Flader and intro.) The River of the Mother of God and Other Essays, 1991; (co-ed.) Environmental Philosophy, 1993, 4th ed., 2004; (with F.J.R. da Rocha) Earth Summit Ethics, 1996; (with M.P. Nelson) The Great New Wilderness Debate, 1998; (with E.T. Freyfogle) For the Health of the Land: Previously Unpublished Essays and Other Writings, 1999; (with C. Palmer) Environmental Philosophy: Critical Concepts in the Environment, 2004; (with M.P. Nelson) Wilderness Debate Rages On: Continuing the Great New Wilderness Debate, 2008; (with R. Frodeman) Encyclopedia of Environmental Ethics and Philosophy, 2009. Contributor to professional journals and magazines. **Address:** Department of Philosophy and Religion Studies, College of Arts and Sciences, University of North Texas, 1155 Union Cir., Ste. 310920, Denton, TX 76203-5017, U.S.A. **Online address:** callicott@unt.edu

CALLOW, Simon. British (born England), b. 1949. **Genres:** Autobiography/Memoirs, Biography, Literary Criticism And History, Autobiography/Memoirs, Adult Non-fiction. **Career:** Old Vic, theater box office assistant; Order of the British Empire, commander, 1999. Writer, actor and director. **Publications:** Being an Actor (memoir), 1984; Charles Laughton: A Difficult Actor (biography), 1987; (with D. Makavejev) Shooting the Actor; Or, The Choreography of Confusion (nonfiction), 1990; Acting in Restoration Comedy (nonfiction), 1991; Charles Laughton, a Difficult Actor, 1995; Orson Welles, the Road to Xanadu, 1996; Snowdon on Stage: A Personal View of the British Theatre, 1997; The National, 1997; Love is Where It Falls: The Story of a Passionate Friendship, 1999; Oscar Wilde and His Circle, 2000; Shakespeare on Love, 2000; Night of the Hunter, 2000; Henry IV, vol. I, 2002, vol. II, 2003; Dickens' Christmas: A Victorian Celebration, 2003; Shooting the Actor, 2003; Orson Welles: Hello Americans, 2006; My Life in Pieces: An Alternative Autobiography, 2010. **Address:** c/o Maggie Hanbury, 27 Walcot St., London, GL SE11 4UB, England.

CALLOWAY, Colin G(ordon). British (born England), b. 1953. **Genres:** History, Writing/Journalism, Bibliography. **Career:** Wakefield College of Technology and Arts, part-time lecturer, 1978-79; College of Ripon and York, lecturer in history and American studies, 1979-82; Keene State College, adjunct lecturer in history, 1982-83; Newberry Library, assistant director, D'Arcy McNickle Center for the History of the American Indian, editor, 1985-87; University of Wyoming, assistant professor, 1987-91, associate professor of history, 1991-; Dartmouth College, visiting assistant professor, 1990-91, professor of history and Native American studies, 1995-, John Kimball, Jr. 1943 professor of history. Consultant and writer. **Publications:** Crown and Calumet: British-Indian Relations, 1783-1815, 1987; (ed.) New Directions in American Indian History, 1988; The Abenaki (young adult), 1989; The

Western Abenakis of Vermont, 1600-1800: War, Migration and the Survival of an Indian People, 1990; The Indians of the Northeast (young adult), 1991; New Country Captives: Selected Narratives of Indian Captivity from Vermont and New Hampshire, 1992; (comp. and intro.) North Country Captives: Selected Narratives of Indian Captivity from Vermont and New Hampshire, 1992; The American Revolution in Indian Country: Crisis and Diversity in Native American Communities, 1995; (comp. with J. Miller and R.A. Sattler) Writings in Indian History, 1985-1990, 1995; New Worlds for All: Indians, Europeans and the Remaking of Early America, 1997; First Peoples: A Documentary Survey of American Indian History, 1999, 4th ed., 2011; One Vast Winter Court: The Native American West before Lewis and Clark, 2003; The Scratch of a Pen: 1763 and the Transformation of North America, 2006; The Shawnees and the War for America, 2007; White People, Indians and Highlanders: Tribal Peoples and Colonial Encounters in Scotland and America, 2008; (contrib.) The Hovey Murals at Dartmouth College, 2011. EDITOR: New Directions in Indian History: A Bibliography of Recent Writings in American Indian History, 1988; (comp. and intro.) Dawnland Encounters: Indians and Europeans in Northern New England, 1991; (and intro.) The World Turned Upside Down: Indian Voices from Early America, 1994; (intro.) Our Hearts Fell to the Ground: Plains Indian Views of How the West was Lost, 1996; (and intro.) After King Philip's War: Presence and Persistence in Indian New England, 1997; Germans and Indians: Fantasies, Encounters, Projections, 2002; (with N. Salisbury) Reinterpreting New England Indians and the Colonial Experience, 2003; Indian History of an American Institution: Native Americans and Dartmouth, 2010. **Address:** History/Native American Studies, Dartmouth College, 204 Sherman House, Hanover, NH 03755, U.S.A. **Online address:** colin.calloway@dartmouth.edu

CALNE, Donald B. Canadian/British (born England), b. 1936. **Genres:** Psychology. **Career:** University of British Columbia, professor of neurology, 1981-, distinguished medical research lecturer, 1989; Vancouver Hospital, Neurodegenerative Disorders Centre, director, 1990-2001. Writer. **Publications:** Parkinsonism: Physiology, Pharmacology and Treatment, 1970; (ed.) Progress in the Treatment of Parkinsonism, 1973; Therapeutics in Neurology, 1975; (ed. with T.N. Chase and A. Barbeau) Dopaminergic Mechanisms, 1975; (with M.O. Thorner and E. Fluckiger) Bromocriptine, a Clinical and Pharmacological Review, 1980; (ed. with S. Fahn and I. Shoulson) Experimental Therapeutics of Movement Disorders, 1983; (co-ed.) Lisuride and Other Dopamine Agonists, 1983; (ed. with S. Fahn and C.D. Marsden) Dystonia 2, 1988; Drugs for the Treatment of Parkinson's Disease, 1989; (co-ed.) Parkinsonism and Aging, 1989; (with Y. Mizuno) Advances in Research on Neurodegeneration, 1994; Within Reason: Rationality and Human Behavior, 1999. Contributor of articles to journals. **Address:** University of British Columbia Hospital, 2221 Westbrook Mall Rm. M31, Vancouver, BC V6T 2B5, Canada.

CALOMIRIS, Charles William. American (born United States), b. 1957. **Genres:** Economics, Business/Trade/Industry, Money/Finance. **Career:** Northwestern University, assistant professor of economics, 1984-91; University of Pennsylvania, Wharton School of Business, visiting associate professor, 1991-92; University of Illinois, associate professor, 1992-96; Columbia University, Paul M. Montrone professor of finance and economics, 1996-2003, Henry Kaufman professor of financial institutions, 2003-, Jerome Chazen Institute of International Business, academic director, 2004-, Center for International Business and Education Research, director, 2005-07; National Bureau of Economic Research, research associate, 1991, 1996-; American Enterprise Institute, co-director, 1997-; Gauss Fund, managing partner. Writer. **Publications:** Universal Banking and the Financing of Industrial Development, 1995; (with C.P. Himmelberg) Government Credit Policy and Industrial Performance: Japanese Machine Tool Producers, 1963-1991, 1995; The Postmodern Bank Safety Net: Lessons from Developed and Developing Economies, 1997; (with J. Karceski) Is the Bank Merger Wave of the 1990s Efficient? Lessons from Nine Case Studies, 1998; (with J.R. Mason) High Loan-to-Value Mortgage Lending: Problem or Cure?, 1999; (with A. Powell) Can Emerging Market Bank Regulators Establish Credible Discipline? The Case of Argentina, 1992-1999, 2000; U.S. Bank Deregulation in Historical Perspective, 2000; (with D.O. Beim) Emerging Financial Markets, 2001; A Global Manifesto for Public Policy, 2002; (with J.R. Mason) Resolving the Puzzle of the Underissuance of National Bank Notes, 2004; (with D. Klingebiel and L. Laeven) A Taxonomy of Financial Crisis Resolution Mechanisms: Cross- country Experience, 2004; (with D.M. Hitscherich) Banker Fees and Acquisition Premia for Targets in Cash Tender Offers: Challenges to the Popular Wisdom on Banker Conflicts, 2005; (with T. Pornrojnangkool) Monopoly-Creating Bank Consolidation? The Merger of Fleet and Bank Boston, 2005; (with A.G. de Carvalho and J.A. de Matos) Venture Capital as Human Resource Management, 2005; U.S. Bank Deregulation in Historical Perspective, 2006; (with D. Nissim) Activity-based Valuation of Bank Holding Companies, 2007; (ed.) China's Financial Transition at a Crossroads, 2007; (ed. with J.N. Bhagwati) Sustaining India's Growth Miracle, 2008; (with J. Mason and D. Wheelock) Did Doubling Reserve Requirements Cause the Recession of 1937-1938? A Microeconomic Approach, 2011; (with S.D. Longhofer and W. Miles) Housing Wealth Effect: The Crucial Roles of Demographics, Wealth Distribution and Wealth Shares, 2012. Contributor to books and journals. **Address:** Columbia Business School, 3022 Broadway, Uris Hall 601, New York, NY 10027, U.S.A. **Online address:** cc374@columbia.edu

CALVERT, Pam. American (born United States), b. 1966?. **Genres:** Children's Fiction. **Career:** Teacher, 1990-92, 2003-06. Writer. **Publications:** Flying Saucer, 2002; Mystery of the Stolen Spider Stone, 2003; Case of the Bunsen Burner Frame Up, 2004; The Mat Maker, 2004; Multiplying Menace: The Revenge of Rumpelstiltskin, 2006; Mystery at the Ballpark, 2007; Princess Peepers, 2008; Multiplying Menace Divides!, 2010; Princess Peepers Picks a Pet, 2011. Contributor to books and periodicals. **Address:** Heacock Literary Agency Inc., Grand Blvd., PO Box 226, Cloudcroft, NM 88317-0226, U.S.A. **Online address:** pam@pamcalvert.com

CALVERT, Patricia. American (born United States), b. 1931. **Genres:** Young Adult Fiction, History, Biography, Novels, Autobiography/Memoirs. **Career:** St. Mary's Hospital, laboratory clerk, 1948-49; General Motors Acceptance Corp., clerk typist, 1950-51; Mayo Clinic, cardiac laboratory technician, 1961-64, enzyme laboratory technician, 1964-70, senior editorial assistant in publications, 1970-92; Institute of Children's Literature, instructor, 1987-. **Publications:** FICTION FOR YOUNG ADULTS: The Snowbird, 1980; The Money Creek Mare, 1981; The Stone Pony, 1982; The Hour of the Wolf, 1983; Hadder MacColl, 1985; Yesterday's Daughter, 1986; Stranger, You and I, 1987; When Morning Comes, 1989; Picking Up the Pieces, 1993; Bigger, 1994; Writing to Richie, 1994; Glennis, Before and After, 1996; Great Lives: The American West, 1997; American Frontier, 1997; Sooner, 1998; Michael, Wait for Me, 2000; Stand Off at Standing Rock: The Story of Sitting Bull and James McLaughlin, 2001; Betrayed!, 2002; Daniel Boone: Beyond the Mountains, 2002; Robert E. Peary: To the Top of the World, 2002; Sir Ernest Shackleton: By Endurance We Conquer, 2003; Hernando Cortés: Fortune Favored the Bold, 2003; The Ancient Inca, 2004; Vasco Da Gama: So Strong a Spirit, 2005; Zebulon Pike: Lost in the Rockies, 2005; The Ancient Celts, 2005; Kit Carson: He Led the Way, 2007. Contributor to periodicals. **Address:** The Millbrook Press Inc., 2 Old New Milford Rd., Brookfield, CT 06804, U.S.A.

CALVERT, Peter (Anthony Richard). British (born England), b. 1936. **Genres:** History, International Relations/Current Affairs, Politics/Government. **Career:** University of Michigan, teaching fellow, 1960-61; University of Southampton, lecturer, 1964-71, senior lecturer, 1971-74, reader, 1974-83, professor of comparative and international politics, 1984-2002, emeritus professor; University of California, visiting lecturer, 1966; Harvard University, research fellow, 1969-70; Birkbeck College, visiting lecturer, 1983-84; Democratization, co-editor, 1996-2007. **Publications:** The Mexican Revolution 1910-1914: The Diplomacy of Anglo-American Conflict, 1968, 2nd ed. 2008; Latin America: Internal Conflict and International Peace, 1969; Revolution, 1970; A Study of Revolution, 1970; Mexico, 1973; The Mexicans: How They Live and Work, 1975; Emiliano Zapata, 1979; The Concept of Class: An Historical Introduction, 1982; The Falklands Crisis: The Rights and the Wrongs, 1982; Politics, Power, and Revolution: An Introduction to Comparative Politics, 1983; Boundary Disputes in Latin America, 1983; Revolution and International Politics, 1984, 2nd ed., 1996; Guatemala, a Nation in Turmoil, 1985; Britain's Place in the World, 1986; The Foreign Policy of New States, 1986; (with S. Calvert) Argentina: Political Culture and Instability, 1989; Revolution and Counter-Revolution, 1990; (with S. Calvert) Latin America in the Twentieth Century, 1990; (with S. Calvert) Sociology Today, 1992; An Introduction to Comparative Politics, 1993; The International Politics of Latin America, 1994; (with S. Calvert) Politics and Society in the Third World, 1996; The Democratic Transition in Central America, 1998; (with S. Calvert) The South, the North and the Environment, 1999; Comparative Politics, 2002; A Political and Economic Dictionary of Latin America, 2004; (with S. Calvert) Politics and Society in the Developing World, 2007; Terrorism, Civil War, and Revolution, 2010. EDITOR: The Process of Political Succession, 1987; The Central American Security System: North-South or East-West, 1988, 2nd ed. 2008; Political and Economic Encyclopedia of South America and the Caribbean, 1991; (with P. Burnell) The Resilience of Democracy: Persistent Practice, Durable Idea, 1999; (with P. Burnell) Civil Society in Democratization, 2003; Border and Territorial Disputes, 4th ed., 2004; Civil Society in Democratization: Idea and Practice, 2004. **Address:** School of Social Sciences, Politics and International Relations, University of Southampton, Highfield, Southampton, HM S017 1BJ, England. **Online address:** pcpol@soton.ac.uk

CALVIN, William H(oward). American (born United States), b. 1939. **Genres:** Medicine/Health, Earth Sciences, Anthropology/Ethnology, Psychology, Sciences, Adult Non-fiction, History. **Career:** University of Washington School of Medicine, faculty, 1966, instructor, 1967-69, assistant professor, 1969-73, associate professor of neurological surgery, 1974-86, affiliate associate professor of biology, 1986-92, affiliate professor of psychiatry and behavioral sciences, 1998-2004, affiliate professor emeritus, 2004-; Hebrew University of Jerusalem, visiting professor, 1978-79. Writer. **Publications:** (With G.A. Ojemann) Inside the Brain, 1980; The Throwing Madonna: From Nervous Cells to Hominid Brains, 1983; The River That Flows Uphill: A Journey from the Big Bang to the Big Brain, 1987; The Cerebral Symphony: Seashore Reflections on the Structure of Consciousness, 1989; The Ascent of Mind: Ice Age Climates and the Evolution of Intelligence, 1990; How the Shaman Stole the Moon: In Search of Ancient Prophet-Scientists: From Stonehenge to the Grand Canyon, 1991; (with G.A. Ojemann) Conversations with Neil Brain: The Neural Nature of Thought and Language, 1994; How Brains Think: Evolving Intelligence, Then and Now, 1996; The Cerebral Code: Thinking a Thought in the Mosaics of the Mind, 1996; (with D. Bickerton) Lingua Ex Machina: Reconciling Darwin and Chomsky with the Human Brain, 2000; A Brain for All Seasons: Human Evolution and Abrupt Climate Change, 2002; A Brief History of the Mind: From Apes To Intellect and Beyond, 2004; Almost Us, 2005; Global Fever: How to Treat Climate Change, 2008. Contributor to books and periodicals. **Address:** Department of Psychiatry & Behavioral Sciences, University of Washington, Rm. BB1644, 1959 NE Pacific St., PO Box 356560, Seattle, WA 98195-6560, U.S.A. **Online address:** mail@williamcalvin.com

CAMBIE, R(ichard) C(onrad). New Zealander (born New Zealand), b. 1931. **Genres:** Chemistry, Sciences. **Career:** University of Auckland, junior lecturer, 1957-58, lecturer, 1958-60, senior lecturer, 1961-63, associate professor, 1964-69, professor of organic chemistry, 1970-96, head of department, 1984-91, professor emeritus, 1996-; Oxford University, Pressed Steel fellow, 1961-62; Australian National University, visiting professor, 1981; Chinese University of Hong Kong, visiting professor, 1981; University of the South Pacific, visiting professor, 1982-83; University of Melbourne, Wilsmore visiting professor, 1986, Writer. **Publications:** (With S.G. Brooker and R.C. Cooper) New Zealand Medicinal Plants, 1981, 3rd ed., 1991; (with S.G. Brooker and R.C. Cooper) Economic Native Plants of New Zealand, 1988; (with R.C. Cooper) New Zealand's Economic Native Plants, 1991; (with J. Ash) Fijian Medicinal Plants, 1994; (with A.A. Brewis) Anti-fertility Plants of the Pacific, 1997. Contributor to periodicals. **Address:** The University of Auckland, Victoria St. W, PO Box 92019, Auckland, 1142, New Zealand.

CAMBOR, Kate. American (born United States), b. 1975. **Genres:** Biography, History. **Career:** Writer and historian. **Publications:** Gilded Youth: Three Lives in France's Belle Époque, 2009. Contributor to magazines and periodicals. **Address:** New York, NY , U.S.A. **Online address:** kdcambor@gmail.com

CAMERON, Averil Millicent. British (born England), b. 1940. **Genres:** History, Translations. **Career:** King's College London, assistant lecturer, 1965-70, reader in ancient history, 1970-78, professor of ancient history, 1978-89, professor of late antique and Byzantine studies and director of the center for Hellenic studies, 1989-94; Columbia University, visiting professor, 1967-68; Institute for Advanced Studies, visiting professor, 1977-78; University of California, Sather professor of classical literature, 1986; College de France, faculty, 1987; University of Oxford, Keble College, warden and professor of late antique and Byzantine history, 1994-. Writer and historian. **Publications:** Agathias, 1970; (ed. and trans.) F.C. Corippus, In laudem Iustini Augusti minoris, 1976; Continuity and Change in Sixth-Century Byzantium, 1981; (ed. with A. Kuhr) Images of Women in Antiquity, 1983; (ed. with J. Herrin) Constantinople in the Early Eighth Century: The Parastaseis Syntomoi Chronikai; Introduction, Translation, and Commentary, 1984; Procopius and the Sixth Century, 1985; (ed.) History as Text: The Writing of Ancient History, 1989; (ed. with S. Walker) The Greek Renaissance in the Roman Empire: Papers from the Tenth British Museum Classical Colloquium, 1989; Christianity and the Rhetoric of Empire: The Development of Christian Discourse, 1991; (ed. with L.I. Conrad) The Byzantine and Early Islamic Near East, vol. I: Problems in the Literary Source Material, 1992, (ed. with G. King) vol. II: Land Use and Settlement Patterns, 1994, vol. III: States, Resources and Armies, 1995; The Mediterranean World in Late Antiquity, AD 395-600, 1993; The Church in the Byzantine Dark Ages, 1993; The Later Roman Empire, AD 284-430, 1993; Changing Cultures in Early Byzantium, 1996; (contrib.) Morfologie sociali e culturali in Europa fra tarda antichita e alto Medioevo: 3-9 aprile 1997, 1998; (co-ed.) Cambridge Ancient History, XIII: The Late Empire, AD 337-425, 1998; (co-ed.) Cambridge Ancient History, XIV: Late Antiquity, Empire and Successors, AD 425- 600, 1998; (trans. with S.G. Hall) Eusebius, Life of Constantine, 1999; (ed.) Fifty Years of Prosopography: The Later Roman Empire, Byzantium and Beyond, 2003; (co-ed.) Cambridge Ancient History, XII: The Crisis of Empire, AD 193-337, 2005; The Byzantines, 2006; (with J. Pettifer) The Enigma of Montenegrin History: The Example of Svac, 2008. Contributor of articles to journals. **Address:** Ioannou Centre for Classical and Byzantine Studies, Faculty of Classics, University of Oxford, 66 St. Giles, Oxford, OX OX1 3LU, England. **Online address:** averil.cameron@keble.ox.ac.uk

CAMERON, Bill. American (born United States), b. 1963. **Genres:** Mystery/Crime/Suspense, Literary Criticism And History. **Career:** Writer. **Publications:** Lost Dog, 2007; Chasing Smoke, 2008; Day One, 2010; County Line, 2011. Works appear in anthologies. **Address:** c/o Janet Reid, FinePrint Literary Management, 240 W 35th St., Ste. 500, New York, NY 10001, U.S.A. **Online address:** bc@billcameronmysteries.com

CAMERON, Catherine M(ary). American (born United States), b. 1946?. **Genres:** Sociology, Art/Art History, Social Sciences. **Career:** Eastern New Mexico University, San Juan Valley Archaeological Project, lithic analyst, 1974-75; National Park Service Chaco Center, archaeologist, 1975-82; Black Mesa Archaeological Project, lithic analyst, 1982-85; Cedar Crest College, associate professor of anthropology, professor, 1983-, Department of Social Sciences, professor; Coronado National Forest, archaeologist, 1987-90; Laboratory of Tree-Ring Research, graduate assistant, 1988-90; School of American Research, archaeological consultant conducting research and writing, 1991-92; University of Colorado, University Museum, Department of Anthropology and Associate Curator Anthropology Section, assistant professor, 1996-2000, associate professor, 2001-; Camwood Research Associates, partner; Federation of Small Anthropology Programs, co-president. Writer. **Publications:** (Contrib.) Prehistoric Stone Technology on Northern Black Mesa, Arizona, 1987; (contrib. with J.D. Beal) Architecture of Arroyo Hondo Pueblo, New Mexico, 1993; (ed. with S.A. Tomka) Abandonment of Settlements and Regions: Ethnoarchaeological and Archaeological Approaches, 1993; Dialectics in the Arts: The Rise of Experimentalism in American Music, 1996; Hopi Dwellings: Architecture at Orayvi, 1999; (ed.) Invisible Citizens: Captives and Their Consequences, 2008; Chaco and After in the Northern San Juan: Excavations at the Bluff Great House, 2009. Contributor to journals. **Address:** Department of Anthropology, University of Colorado, 1350 Pleasant St., PO Box 233, Boulder, CO 80309-0233, U.S.A. **Online address:** catherine.cameron@colorado.edu

CAMERON, Charla. *See* **SKINNER, Gloria Dale.**

CAMERON, Christian. (Gordon Kent). Canadian/American (born United States), b. 1962. **Genres:** Military/Defense/Arms Control, Mystery/Crime/Suspense. **Career:** U.S. Navy, military historian, 1987-99, intelligence officer, pilot; writer, 1999-. **Publications:** MILITARY SUSPENSE NOVELS WITH KENNETH M. CAMERON AS GORDON KENT: Night Trap, 1998; Peacemaker, 2001; Rules of Engagement, 2001; Top Hook, 2002; Hostile Contact, 2003; Washington and Caesar, 2004; Force Protection, 2004; Damage Control, 2006; Tyrant, 2008; The Spoils of War, 2008; The Falconer's Tale, 2008; Storm of Arrows, 2009; Killer of Men, 2010; Marathon, 2011; King of the Bosporus, 2011; God of War, 2012; Destroyer of Cities, 2013; Beyond the Pale, forthcoming. Contributor to periodicals. **Address:** c/o Author Mail, Random House, 1745 Broadway, New York, NY 10019-4368, U.S.A.

CAMERON, Hope. *See* **MORRITT, Hope.**

CAMERON, Ian. *See* **PAYNE, Donald Gordon.**

CAMERON, Julia. American (born United States), b. 1948. **Genres:** inspirational/Motivational Literature, Plays/Screenplays, Poetry, Novels, Young Adult Non-fiction. **Career:** Chicago Tribune, special correspondent. Novelist. **Publications:** ADULT NONFICTION: (with M. Bryan) The Money Drunk: Ninety Days to Financial Sobriety, 1992; (with M. Bryan) The Artist's Way: A Spiritual Path to Higher Creativity, 1992; (with M. Bryan) The Artist's Way Morning Pages Journal: A Companion Volume to The Artist's Way, 1995; The Vein of Gold: A Journey to Your Creative Heart, 1996; Heart Steps: Prayers and Exercises for a Creative Life, 1997; (with M. Toms) The Well of Creativity, 1997; (with M. Bryan and C. Allen) The Artist's Way at Work: Riding the Dragon, 1998; Blessings: Prayers and Declarations for a Heartful Life, 1998; The Right to Write: An Invitation and Initiation into the Writing Life, 1998; The Artist's Date Book: A Companion Volume to The Artist's Way, 1999; The Church that Went Under, 1999; Transitions: Prayers and Declarations for a Changing Life, 1999; God Is No Laughing Matter: Observations and Objections on the Spiritual Path, 2000; The Artist's Way Creativity Kit, 2000; God Is Dog Spelled Backwards, 2000; Supplies: A Pilot's Guide to Creative Flight, 2000 as Supplies: A Troubleshooting Guide for Creative Difficulties, 2003; Inspirations: Meditations from The Artist's Way, 2001; The Writer's Life: Insights from the Right to Write, 2001; Walking in This World: The Practical Art of Creativity, 2002; Prayers from a Nonbeliever: A Story of Faith, 2003; The Sound of Paper: Starting from Scratch, 2004; Answered Prayers: Love Letters from the Divine, 2004; How to Avoid Making Art, 2005; Letters to a Young Artist: Building a Life in Art, 2005; The Artist's Way Workbook, 2006; Finding Water: The Art of Perseverance, 2006; Floor Sample: A Creative Memoir, 2006; Complete Artist's Way: Creativity as a Spiritual Practice, 2007; Writing Diet: Write Yourself Right-Size, 2007; Mozart's Ghost, 2008; Prayers to the Great Creator: Prayers and Declarations for a Meaningful Life, 2008; Faith and Will: Weathering the Storms in Our Spiritual Lives, 2009; The Artist's Way Every Day: A Year of Creative Living, 2009; The Creative Life: True Tales of Inspiration, 2010; The Prosperous Heart, 2011; The Artist's Way Starter Kit, 2011; The Artist's Way: Creative Kingdom Collection, 2011. FOR CHILDREN: Prayers for the Little Ones, 1999; Prayers to the Nature Spirits, 1999. FICTION: The Dark Room (crime), 1998; Popcorn: Hollywood Stories, 2000. POEMS: This Earth, 1997; The Quiet Animal. Works appear in anthologies. Contributor to periodicals. **Address:** c/o Author Mail, Penguin Group Inc., 375 Hudson St., New York, NY 10014-3658, U.S.A.

CAMERON, Lorna. *See* **FRASER, Anthea.**

CAMERON, M(alcolm) L(aurence). Canadian (born Canada), b. 1918. **Genres:** Medicine/Health. **Career:** University of New Brunswick, research associate, 1953-55; University of Saskatchewan, assistant professor, associate professor of biology, 1955-65; Dalhousie University, assistant professor, professor, 1965-79, Campbell professor of biology, 1979-84; Nova Scotia Institute of Science, president, 1969-70. Writer. **Publications:** Anglo-Saxon Medicine, 1993. Contributor to journals. **Address:** 6306 Jubilee Rd., Halifax, NS B3H 2G7, Canada.

CAMERON, Maxwell A(lan). American (born United States), b. 1961. **Genres:** Economics, Politics/Government, Adult Non-fiction, Business/Trade/Industry. **Career:** Carleton University, assistant professor, 1989-95, associate professor, 1995-99; University of British Columbia, associate professor, 1999-2002, professor of political science, 2002-. Writer. **Publications:** Democracy and Authoritarianism in Peru, 1994; El estado de la democracia en la region andina, 2010. EDITOR: (with A.R.M. Ritter and D.H. Pollock) Latin America to the Year 2000: Reactivating Growth, Improving Equity, Sustaining Democracy, 1992; (with R. Grinspun) The Political Economy of North American Free Trade, 1993; (with P. Mauceri) The Peruvian Labyrinth: Polity, Society, Economy, 1997; (with R.J. Lawson and B.W. Tomlin) To Walk Without Fear: The Global Movement to Ban Landmines, 1998; (with B.W. Tomlin) The Making of NAFTA: How the Deal Was Done, 2000; (ed. with E. Hershberg) Latin America's Left Turns: Politics, Policies, and Trajectories of Change, 2010; El estado de la democracia en la region andina, forthcoming. **Address:** Department of Political Science, University of British Columbia, 1866 Main Mall, Buchanan C472, Buchanan C419, Vancouver, BC V6T 1Z1, Canada. **Online address:** cameron@politics.ubc.ca

CAMERON, Stella. Also writes as Alicia Brandon. American (born United States), b. 1943. **Genres:** Novels. **Career:** Writer. **Publications:** Moontide, 1985; All that Sparkles, 1986; Shadows, 1986; No Stranger, 1987; Second to None, 1987; Party of Two, 1988; Some Die Telling, 1988; Death in the House, 1989; Friends, 1989; Late Gentleman, 1989; Angel in Time, 1991; Undercurrents, 1991; Mirror, Mirror, 1991; Snow Angels, 1991; (co-author) Christmas Collection, 1992; Fascination, 1993; His Magic Touch, 1993; Pure Delights, 1995; Sheer Pleasures, 1995; Charmed, 1995; Bride, 1995; Beloved, 1996; True Bliss, 1996; Guilty Pleasures 1997; Dear Stranger, 1997; Wait for Me, 1997; The Best Revenge, 1998; The Wish Club, 1998; French Quarter, 1998; More and More, 1999; Key West, 1999; Glass Houses, 2000; All Smiles, 2000; Finding Ian, 2001; Tell Me Why, 2001; 7B, 2001; The Orphan, 2002; Cold Day in July, 2002; About Adam, 2003; Kiss Them Goodbye, 2003; (with J.K. Johnson) Wrong Turn, 2003; Useful Affair, 2004; Now You See Him, 2004; Testing Miss Toogood, 2005; Grave Mistake, 2005; Marked Man, 2006; Body of Evidence, 2006; Target, 2007; Cold Day in Hell, 2007; Cypress Nights, 2008; Tails of Love, 2009; Out of body, 2010; Out of Sight, 2010; Out of Mind: A Court of Angels Novel, 2010. Contributor to books and periodicals. **Address:** Steven Axelrod Agency, 49 Main St., PO Box 357, Chatham, NY 12037, U.S.A. **Online address:** pushpen@aol.com

CAMERON, Sue. American (born United States), b. 1944?. **Genres:** Romance/Historical, Food And Wine, Young Adult Non-fiction, Novels, Young Adult Fiction, Literary Criticism And History. **Career:** The Hollywood Reporter, daily columnist; American Broadcasting Corp., executive; Beverly Hills 213, columnist. Writer. **Publications:** NOVELS: Honey Dust, 1993; Love, Sex, and Murder, 1996; The Cheating Classes, 2002. NONFICTION: The Bible Cookbook: Nourishment for the Body and Soul, 1996. Contributor to periodicals. **Address:** c/o Warner Books, 1271 Ave. of the Americas, New York, NY 10020, U.S.A.

CAMINALS *See* **Caminals-Heath, Roser.**

CAMINALS-HEATH, Roser. (Caminals). American (born United States), b. 1956. **Genres:** Novels, Translations, Novels. **Career:** Tutor, 1978-79; teacher, 1979-81; Mount St. Mary's College, instructor, 1981; Hood College, instructor, 1981-86, assistant professor, 1986-92, associate professor of Spanish language and literature, 1992-97, professor of Spanish language and literature, 1997-. Writer. **Publications:** TRANSLATIONS: Emilia Pardo Bazan's The House of Ulloa, 1992; (co-trans.) Carme Riera, A Matter of Self-Esteem and Other Stories, 2001. FICTION: Once Remembered, Twice Lived, 1993; Un segle de prodigis, 1995; Les herbes secretes, 1998; El Carrer dels Tres Llits, 2002; Amores oscuros, 2003; La petita mort, 2004; La pequena muerte, 2005; La dona de mercuri, 2005; La mujer de mercurio, 2006; The Street of the Three Beds, 2010; Cinc-cents bars i una llibreria, 2010. NONFICTION: La seduccio americana, 2009. Contributor to periodicals. **Address:** Department of Foreign Languages & Literatures, Hood College, 401 Rosemont Ave., Frederick, MD 21701, U.S.A. **Online address:** rheath@hood.edu

CAMLOT, Jason. Canadian (born Canada), b. 1967. **Genres:** Poetry, History. **Career:** Concordia University, associate professor and chair of English, 1999-. Writer and educator. **Publications:** The Animal Library, 2000; Attention All Typewriters, 2005; (ed. with T. Swift) Language Acts: Anglo-Québec Poetry, 1976 to the 21st Century, 2007; Style and the Nineteenth-Century British Critic: Sincere Mannerisms, 2008; The Debaucher (poems), 2008. Contributor to periodicals. **Address:** Department of English, Concordia University, LB 641, 1455 de Maisonneuve Blvd. W, Montreal, QC H3G 1M8, Canada. **Online address:** camlot@alcor.concordia.ca

CAMMERMEYER, Margarethe. Norwegian/American (born United States), b. 1942. **Genres:** Gay And Lesbian Issues, Medicine/Health, Military/Defense/Arms Control, Women's Studies And Issues. **Career:** Veteran's Hospital, staff nurse, 1970-73, clinical nurse specialist in neurology and epilepsy, 1976-81; Veteran's Medical Center, clinical nurse specialist in neuro-oncology, 1981-86, clinical nurse specialist in neuroscience and nurse researcher, 1986-96; Army Reserve Hospital, assistant chief nurse and supervisor, 1985-88; Washington Army National Guard and National Guard Hospital, chief nurse, 1988-96; Washington National Guard, Chief nurse, nurse. Writer. **Publications:** (Co-author) Neurological Assessment for Nursing Practice, 1984; (ed. with C. Appeldorn) Core Curriculum for Neuroscience Nursing, 1990; (with C. Fisher) Serving in Silence (memoir), 1994. Contributor to periodicals. **Address:** 4632 S Tompkins Rd., Langley, WA 98260-9695, U.S.A. **Online address:** grethe@cammermeyer.com

CAMMISA, Anne Marie. American (born United States) **Genres:** Politics/Government, Young Adult Non-fiction. **Career:** The Urban Institute, consultant and research associate in human resources policy and health policy, 1987-93; University of New Hampshire, assistant professor in political science,

1992-94; Suffolk University, assistant professor of government, 1994-99, associate professor, 1999-2005, professor of government, 2005-07; Saint Anselm College, professor of politics, 2007-08, New Hampshire Institute of Politics, Center for the Study of New Hampshire Politics and Civic Life, director, 2007-08; The Washington Center, associate faculty, 2008-11; Georgetown University, Government Affairs Institute, senior fellow, 2010-11, Georgetown Public Policy Institute, visiting professor, 2011-; Harvard University, Radcliffe Institute for Advanced Studies, fellow. Writer. **Publications:** Governments As Interest Groups: Intergovernmental Lobbying and the Federal System, 1995; From Rhetoric to Reform?: Welfare Policy in American Politics, 1998; (with P.C. Manuel) Checks & Balances?: How a Parliamentary System Could Change American Politics, 1999. **Address:** Georgetown Public Policy Institute, Georgetown University, 408 Old N, 37th and O Streets NW, Washington, DC 20057, U.S.A. **Online address:** amc38@georgetown.edu

CAMNITZER, Luis. Uraguayian/American/German (born Germany), b. 1937. **Genres:** Art/Art History. **Career:** Escuela de bellas artes, instructor, 1961-64; Fairleigh Dickinson University, instructor in art, 1968-69; State University of New York College, professor of art, 1969-2000; Studio Camnitzer, Valdottavo, director; State University of New York, professor emeritus; The Drawing Center, viewing program curator, 2000-07; Fundacion Cisneros, pedagogical adviser, 2009-. **Publications:** Arte y Ensenanza: La etica del poder, 2000; Por América: La Obra De Juan Francisco Elso, 2000; New Art of Cuba, 2003; Conceptualism in Latin American Art: Didactics of Liberation, 2007; Negatec, 2007; Didática de la liberación: arte conceptualista latinoamericano, 2008; On Art, Artists, Latin America, and Other Utopias, 2009; De la Coca-cola al arte boludo, 2009. **Address:** University of Texas Press, PO Box 7819, Austin, TX 78713-7819, U.S.A. **Online address:** camnitzerl@aol.com

CAMON, Ferdinando. Italian (born Italy), b. 1935. **Genres:** Novels, Poetry. **Career:** Writer. **Publications:** Il mestiere di poeta, 1965; Fuori storia, 1967; La moglie del tiranno, 1969; Il quinto stato, 1970; La vita eterna, 1972; Liberare l'animale, 1973; Mestiere di scrittore, 1973; Letteratura e classi subalterne, 1974; Occidente, 1975; Avanti popolo, 1977; Un altare per la madre, 1978, trans. as Memorial, 1996; La chiamata uomo, 1981, trans. as The Sickness Called Man, 1992; Mestiere di poeta, 1982; Storia di Sirio: parabola per la muova generazione, 1984, trans. as, The Story of Sirio: A Parable, 1985; La donna dei fili, 1986; Autoritratto di Primo Levi, 1987; I miei personaggi mi scrivono, 1987; Romanzi della pianura, 1988; Alberto Moravia: Io e il mio tempo: conversazioni critiche con Ferdinando Camon, 1988; Il canto delle balene, 1989; Il Super-Baby, 1991; Il santo assassino: dichiarazioni apocrife, 1991; Mai visti sole e luna, 1994; La terra é di tutti, 1996; Dal silenzio delle campagne: tori mucche diavoli contadini drogati mercanti di donne e serial-killer: scene e raccontini in versi, 1998; La cavallina la ragazza e il diavolo: racconto campestre, 2004; Tenebre su tenebre, 2006; Figli perduti, la droga discussa con i ragazzi, 2009; La mia stirpe, 2011. **Address:** Garzanti Libri, Via Giuseppe Parini 14, Milan, 20121, Italy. **Online address:** fercamon@alice.it

CAMP, Helen C(ollier). American (born United States), b. 1939. **Genres:** History, Politics/Government, Adult Non-fiction, Autobiography/Memoirs, Biography. **Career:** Manhattan College, adjunct professor, 1973-78; Brooklyn College, teacher, 1981; Bernard M. Baruch College, teacher, 1981; University of New York, Herbert H. Lehman College, instructor, 1982-83, 1985; State University of New York, Empire State College, adjunct professor, 1984-85; Pace University, adjunct professor of American history, 1985-86, 1987-, instructor, 1998-2000; New York University, instructor, 1987. Writer. **Publications:** (Ed. with B. Blumberg and K. Centola) From World War to Cold War: Readings in Foreign and Domestic Policy, 1988; Iron in Her Soul: Elizabeth Gurley Flynn and the American Left, 1995. Contributor to books and periodicals. **Address:** 8818 Dolphin Ln., PO Box 118, Gulf Shores, AL 36542, U.S.A. **Online address:** hacamp@gulftel.com

CAMP, John (Roswell). *See* **SANDFORD, John.**

CAMP, Robert C. New Zealander/American (born United States), b. 1935. **Genres:** Administration/Management, Business/Trade/Industry, Economics, Education. **Career:** Rochester Institute of Technology, adjunct professor, 1972-85; Xerox Corporation's United States Customer Operations (USCO), benchmarking competency, manager, 1990, logistics and distribution division, manager for planning, Xerox Business Services, manager of business analysis; Quality Network Inc., president; Global Benchmarking Network, chairperson; Best Practice Institute, principal; Mobil Oil and DuPont Co., staff; Centre for Organisational Excellence Research, conference keynote speaker and facilitator. **Publications:** Benchmarking: The Search for Industry Best Practices That Lead to Superior Performance, 1989; Business Process Benchmarking: Finding and Implementing Best Practices, 1995; Benchmarking Case Studies, 1996; Leadership of Benchmarking, 1996; (ed.) Global Cases in Benchmarking: Best Practices from Organizations around the World, 1998. **Address:** Centre for Organisational Excellence Research, Massey University, Riddet Bldg., PO Box 11 222, Palmerston North, 14850-2418, New Zealand. **Online address:** rcampbpi@att.net

CAMP, Stephanie M. H. American (born United States) **Genres:** Social Sciences, Gay And Lesbian Issues, History, Politics/Government. **Career:** University of Pennsylvania, instructor, 1997; University of Washington, faculty, 2002-, associate professor of history, 2004-, Dio Richardson endowed professor. Writer. **Publications:** Closer to Freedom: Enslaved Women and Everyday Resistance in the Plantation South, 2004; (ed. with E.E. Baptist) New Studies in the History of American Slavery, 2006. (contrib.) The Encyclopedia of Slavery in the Americas, 2008. Contributor to journals. **Address:** Department of History, University of Washington, SMI 103D, 315 Smith Hall, PO Box 353560, Seattle, WA 98195-3560, U.S.A. **Online address:** stcamp@u.washington.edu

CAMPAGNA, Palmiro. Canadian (born Canada), b. 1954. **Genres:** Military/Defense/Arms Control, History, Transportation. **Career:** Department of National Defense, engineer and internal auditor, 1981-. Writer. **Publications:** Storms of Controversy: The Secret Avro Arrow Files Revealed, 1992, 4th ed., 2010; The UFO Files: The Canadian Connection Exposed, 1997; Requiem for a Giant: A.V. Roe Canada and the Avro Arrow, 2003. Contributor to periodicals. **Address:** Department of National Defence, 101 Colonel By Dr., Ottawa, ON K1A 0K2, Canada. **Online address:** maxcam@storm.ca

CAMPBELL, Alexandra. British (born England), b. 1954?. **Genres:** Novels, Homes/Gardens, Architecture. **Career:** Harpers & Queen, associate and beauty editor; She Magazine, health and beauty editor; Good Housekeeping, managing editor. Journalist. **Publications:** NOVELS: The Office Party, 1998; The Ex-Girlfriend, 2000; The Daisy Chain, 2001; That Dangerous Age, 2002; Remember This, 2005. INTERIOR DESIGN GUIDES: East Meets West: Global Design for Contemporary Interiors, 1997; (with L. Bauwens) Spaces for Living: How to Create Multifunctional Rooms for Today's Homes, 1999; (with L. Bauwens) Country Chic: Country Style for Modern Living, 2001; (contrib.) Nina Campbell's Decorating Notebook: Insider Secrets and Decorating Ideas for Your Home, 2004. Contributor to magazines. **Address:** c/o Author Mail, Penguin Books Ltd., 80 Strand, London, GL WC2R 0RL, England. **Online address:** niniacampb@aol.com

CAMPBELL, Beatrix. British/Canadian (born Canada), b. 1947. **Genres:** Civil Liberties/Human Rights, Criminology/True Crime, Psychology, Sociology, Women's Studies And Issues, Social Sciences, Humanities. **Career:** Morning Star, journalist, 1967-76; Time Out, reporter, journalist, 1979-81; City Limits, co-owner, journalist, 1981-87; Marxism Today, columnist; University of Newcastle, professor and visiting professor of women's studies. **Publications:** (With A. Coote) Sweet Freedom: The Struggle for Women's Liberation, 1982, 2nd ed., 1987; Wigan Pier Revisited: Poverty and Politics in the Eighties, 1984; The Iron Ladies: Why Do Women Vote Tory?, 1987; Unofficial Secrets: Child Sexual Abuse, the Cleveland Case, 1988, rev. ed., 1998; Goliath: Britain's Dangerous Places, 1993; Diana, Princess of Wales: How Sexual Politics Shook the Monarchy, 1998; (with J. Jones and A. Castledine) And All the Children Cried, 2002; Agreement!, 2008. Works appear in anthologies. Contributor to periodicals. **Address:** Lawrence & Wishart Ltd., PO Box 7701, Latchingdon, Chelmsford, EX CM3 6WL, England. **Online address:** beatrix.campbell@ncl.ac.uk

CAMPBELL, Broos. American (born United States), b. 1957. **Genres:** Novels. **Career:** Metro Newspapers, staff, 1986-2000; Broos Campbell, editor, 2000-; Village Voice Media, copy editor, 2001-02; Cherbo Publishing Group, feature editor, 2003-09; Hispanic Business, copy editor and staff writer, 2011-. Writer. **Publications:** MATTY GRAVES NAVAL ADVENTURE SERIES: No Quarter, 2006; The War of Knives, 2007; Peter Wicked, 2008. Contributor of articles to magazines. **Address:** Hispanic Business Inc., 475 Pine Ave., Santa Barbara, CA 93117-3709, U.S.A. **Online address:** broos.campbell@yahoo.com

CAMPBELL, Christopher. (Christy Campbell). American (born United

States), b. 1951?. **Genres:** Novels, History, Social Sciences. **Career:** Sunday Telegraph, journalist, 1990-. **Publications:** (Ed.) Naval Aircraft, 1977; Aces and Aircraft of World War I, 1981; War Facts Now, 1982; Weapons of War, 1983; Nuclear Weapons Fact Book, 1984; Air Warfare: The Fourth Generation, 1984; Airland Battle 2000, 1986; The World War II Fact Book, 1939-1945, 1987; (ed.) War in Peace, 1987; The VW Beetle, 1990; Air War Pacific, 1991; Commercial Aircraft Markings and Profiles, 1991; The Hamlyn Guide to Commercial Aircraft and Airline Markings, 1992; The Maharajah's Box: An Imperial Story of Conspiracy, Love and a Guru's Prophecy, 2002; Fenian Fire: The British Government Plot to Assassinate Queen Victoria, 2002; Phylloxera: How Wine Was Saved for the World, 2004; The Botanist and the Vintner: How Wine Was Saved for the World, 2005. **Address:** c/o Author Mail, HarperCollins Publishers, 77-85 Fulham Palace Rd., London, GL W6 8JB, England.

CAMPBELL, Christy. *See* **CAMPBELL, Christopher.**

CAMPBELL, Colin. British/Jamaican (born Jamaica), b. 1949. **Genres:** Biography, Autobiography/Memoirs, History, Self Help. **Career:** Writer. **Publications:** Guide to Being a Modern Lady, 1986; Diana in Private: The Princess Nobody Knows, 1992; The Royal Marriages: What Really Goes on in the Private World of the Queen and Her Family, 1993; A Life Worth Living, 1997; The Real Diana, 1998; Empress Bianca, 2006; Daughter of Narcissus: A Family's Struggle to Survive Their Mother's Narcissistic Personality Disorder, 2009. **Address:** 45 Bourne St., London, GL SW1W 8JA, England.

CAMPBELL, Colleen Carroll. American (born United States), b. 1974. **Genres:** Social Commentary, Theology/Religion, Women's Studies And Issues, Politics/Government. **Career:** St. Louis Post-Dispatch, op-ed columnist. Journalist and radio host. **Publications:** The New Faithful: Why Young Adults Are Embracing Christian Orthodoxy, 2002; Take Heart: Catholic Writers on Hope in Our Time, 2007. Contributor of articles to newspapers, magazines and journals. **Address:** U.S.A. **Online address:** info@colleen-carroll.com

CAMPBELL, David G. American (born United States) **Genres:** Natural History, Agriculture/Forestry, Social Sciences. **Career:** Nanjing University, adjunct professor; Bahamas National Trust for the Conservation of Wildlife, director; International Union for the Conservation of Nature, consultant; New York Botanical Garden, scientific staff; Grinnell College, Henry R. Luce professor of nations and the global environment, 1991-, professor of biology. Writer. **Publications:** The Ephemeral Islands: A Natural History of the Bahamas, 1978; (ed. with H.D. Hammond) Floristic Inventory of Tropical Countries: The Status of Plant Systematics, Collections, and Vegetation, Plus Recommendations for the Future, 1989; The Crystal Desert: Summers in Antarctica, 1992; Islands in Space and Time, 1996; A Land of Ghosts: The Braided Lives of People and the Forest in Far Western Amazonia, 2005. **Address:** Department of Biology, Grinnell College, Rm. 1824, Robert N. Noyce '49 Science Ctr., 1116 8th Ave., PO Box 805, Grinnell, IA 50112-1690, U.S.A. **Online address:** campbell@grinnell.edu

CAMPBELL, Donald E. New Zealander (born New Zealand), b. 1943. **Genres:** Economics. **Career:** University of Toronto, Scarborough College, Division of Social Sciences, assistant professor, 1970-74, assistant chair, 1972-74, 1986-87, associate professor, 1975-80, professor, 1980-92; College of William and Mary, CSX professor of economics and public policy, 1990-. Writer. **Publications:** Resource Allocation Mechanisms, 1987; Equity, Efficiency, and Social Choice, 1992; Incentives: Motivation and the Economics of Information, 1995, 2nd ed., 2006. **Address:** Department of Economics, The College of William & Mary, Morton Hall 114, PO Box 8795, Williamsburg, VA 23187-8795, U.S.A. **Online address:** decamp@wm.edu

CAMPBELL, Drusilla. American (born United States) **Genres:** Business/Trade/Industry, Novels, Economics. **Career:** Writer. **Publications:** The Frost and the Flame, 1980; A Dream Come True, 1981; A Dream of Fire, 1982; Silent Dreams, 1982; Stolen Passions, 1982; Broken Promises, 1982; Tomorrow's Journey, 1982; Autumntide, 1984; Men Like Gods, 1984; Reunion, 1985; (with M. Graham) Drugs and Alcohol in the Workplace: A Guide for Managers, 1988; Wildwood, 2003; The Edge of the Sky, 2004; Blood Orange: A Novel, 2005; Bone Lake, 2007; The Good Sister, 2010; Little Girl Gone, 2012. **Address:** c/o Author Mail, Kensington Publishing Corp., 850 3rd Ave., New York, NY 10022, U.S.A. **Online address:** dnc2@aol.com

CAMPBELL, Duncan Andrew. American (born United States), b. 1968. **Genres:** Military/Defense/Arms Control, Politics/Government. **Career:** University of Wales, Department of American Studies, lecturer, 1998-; University of Maryland, faculty. Writer and historian. **Publications:** (Ed. with J. Roper) The American Civil War, 2000; English Public Opinion and the American Civil War, 2003; Unlikely Allies: Britain, America, and the Victorian Origins of the Special Relationship, 2007. **Address:** University of Maryland, 1000 Hilltop Cir., Baltimore, MD 21250-0001, U.S.A. **Online address:** d.a.campbell@swan.ac.uk

CAMPBELL, Eddie. Australian/Scottish (born Scotland), b. 1955. **Genres:** Graphic Novels, Cartoons, Illustrations, Biography. **Career:** Illustrator and author of comic-book series and graphic novels, 1981-; Escape Magazine, founder; Harrier New Wave Comics, co-founder; Eddie Campbell Comics, co-founder, publisher, 1995-. **Publications:** (With E. Hillyer) Deadface: Immortality Isn't Forever, 1990; The Complete Alec, 1990; (with P. Ford) Catalyst: Agents of Change, 1994; (with A. Moore) From Hell, 1995; Bacchus, 10 vols., 1995-2001; (with A. Moore) The Birth Caul, 1999; Alce: The King Canute Crowd, 2000; Alec: How to Be an Artist, 2001; After the Snooter, 2002; Egomania 1-2, 2002; (with D. White) Batman, the Order of Beasts, 2004; The Fate of the Artist: An Autobiographical Novel, with Typographical Anomalies, in which the Author Does Not Appear as Himself, 2006; The Black Diamond Detective Agency, 2007; (with D. Best) The Amazing Remarkable Monsieur Leotard: A Novel with Typographical Acrobatics and Illustrational Feats in an Ideal Production of Entirely New Tricks, Statuesque Acts and Performances, 2008; Alec: The Years Have Pants, 2009; (with A. Moore) A Disease of Language, 2008; (with D. White) The Playwright, 2010; (ed.) PS Magazine: The Best of the Preventive Maintenance Monthly, 2011. Contributor to anthologies. **Address:** Eddie Campbell Comics, PO Box 230, Paddington, QL 4064, Australia.

CAMPBELL, Eric. British (born England), b. 1941. **Genres:** Novels, Animals/Pets, Literary Criticism And History. **Career:** Writer and educator. **Publications:** NOVELS: The Place of Lions, 1991; The Year of the Leopard Song, 1992; The Shark Callers, 1994; Elephant Gold, 1997 in U..S as Papa Tembo, 1998; Gorilla Dawn, 2003. **Address:** c/o Author Mail, Harcourt Trade Publishers, 525 B St., Ste. 1900, San Diego, CA 92101-4495, U.S.A.

CAMPBELL, G(aylon) S(anford). American (born United States), b. 1940. **Genres:** Environmental Sciences/Ecology, Biology. **Career:** Washington State University, Department of Crop and Soil Sciences, assistant professor, 1971-75, associate professor, 1975-79, professor of soils and soil scientist, 1979-. Writer. **Publications:** An Introduction to Environmental Biophysics, 1977; Soil Physics with BASIC, 1985; Biophysical Measurements and Instrumentation, 1990. **Address:** Department of Crop & Soil Sciences, Washington State University, PO Box 646420, Pullman, WA 99164-6420, U.S.A.

CAMPBELL, Gordon. American (born United States), b. 1942. **Genres:** Novels. **Career:** Parsons Behle & Latimer, Litigation Department, lawyer. Writer. **Publications:** Missing Witness (novel), 2007. **Address:** Parsons Behle & Latimer, Salt Lake City Headquarters, 201 S Main St., Ste. 1800, Salt Lake City, UT 84111, U.S.A. **Online address:** gcampbell@parsonsbehle.com

CAMPBELL, Gwyn. Welsh/British (born England), b. 1952. **Genres:** History. **Career:** South African Government, academic consultant, 1997; McGill University, professor, research chair for Indian Ocean world history; Indian Ocean World Centre, director. Writer. **Publications:** An Economic History of Imperial Madagascar, 1750-1895: The Rise and Fall of an Island Empire, 2005; (with E. Alpers and M. Salman) Resisting Bondage in Indian Ocean Africa and Asia, 2006. EDITOR: The Indian Ocean Rim: Southern Africa and Regional Co-Operation, 2003; The Structure of Slavery in Indian Ocean Africa and Asia, 2004; Abolition and Its Aftermath in Indian Ocean Africa and Asia, 2005; Abolition and its Aftermath in Indian Ocean Africa and Asia, 2005; (with S. Miers and J.C. Miller) Women and Slavery, 2007; (with N. Guibert) Wine, Society, and Globalization: Multidisciplinary Perspectives on the Wine Industry, 2007; (with S. Miers and J.C. Miller) Children in Slavery through the Ages, 2009. **Address:** Indian Ocean World Ctr., Peterson Hall, Rm. 100, 3460 McTavish St., Montreal, QC H3A 1X9, Canada. **Online address:** gwyn.campbell@mcgill.ca

CAMPBELL, Ian Barclay. New Zealander (born New Zealand), b. 1916?. **Genres:** Law, History, Medicine/Health, Social Sciences. **Career:** Massey University, teaching fellow; Accident Compensation Commission, safety director; Workers' Compensation Board, secretary. Writer. **Publications:** Handbook to the Workers' Compensation Act 1956, 1958; Workers' Compensation Law in New Zealand, 2nd ed., 1964; The Accident Compensation Act 1972, 1973; Safety Legislation in Great Britain: Its Significance for New Zealand, 1975; Accident Statistics and Significance: Their Practical Application in New Zealand, 1980; Safety Legislation and the Work Place, 1982; Legislating for Workplace Hazards in New Zealand, 1987; Compensation for Personal Injury in New Zealand: Its Rise and Fall, 1996; Health and Safety in Employment Act: An Overview, 1998. **Address:** 30 Field Way, Waikanae, 5036, New Zealand. **Online address:** iancampbell1@compuserve.com

CAMPBELL, James. American (born United States) **Genres:** Novels, Travel/Exploration, Biography, History. **Career:** National Geographic Adventure, journalist and freelance writer; Mens Journal, writer; Audubon, writer. **Publications:** Senior Guide, Day-hikes in the Southwestern National Parks and Monuments, 1986; (with P. Werres and P. Beicken) Doctor Faustus: Archetypal Subtext at the Millenium, 1999; The Final Frontiersman: Heimo Korth and His Family Alone in Alaskas Arctic Wilderness, 2004; Little Box of Jokes, 2006; The Ghost Mountain Boys: Their Epic March and the Terrifying Battle for New Guinea-The Forgotten War of the South Pacific, 2007; Color of War: How One Battle Broke Japan and Another Changed America, 2012. **Address:** Atria Books, 1230 Ave. of the Americas, 13th Fl., New York, NY 10020, U.S.A. **Online address:** jim@jamesmcampbell.net

CAMPBELL, James B. American (born United States), b. 1944. **Genres:** Geography, Area Studies. **Career:** University of Kansas, Remote Sensing Laboratory, faculty, 1970-72; Kansas Geological Survey, staff, 1972-76; Virginia Polytechnic Institute and State University, assistant professor, 1976-81, associate professor, 1981-88, professor of geography, 1988-, department head, 1993-2002. Writer. **Publications:** Mapping the Land: Aerial Imagery for Land Use Information, 1983; (with F.D. Hole) Soil Landscape Analysis, 1985; Introduction to Remote Sensing, 1987, 4th ed., 2008; (ed.) Manual of Geospatial Science and Technology, 2010. Contributor to journals. **Address:** Department of Geography, College of Natural Resources, Virginia Polytech Institute & State University, 115 Major Williams Hall, Blacksburg, VA 24061, U.S.A. **Online address:** jayhawk@vt.edu

CAMPBELL, James T. American (born United States), b. 1958. **Genres:** Theology/Religion, Travel/Exploration, Humanities. **Career:** University of the Witwatersrand, Department of History, junior lecturer, 1986-87, Institute for Advanced Social Research, senior research officer, 1996-98; Stanford University, Department of History, instructor, 1988-89, Edgar E. Robinson professor in United States history, 2008-; Northwestern University, assistant professor, 1989-96; Brown University, associate professor, 1999-2007, professor of American civilization and Africana studies, 2007-08. Writer. **Publications:** Songs of Zion: The African Methodist Episcopal Church in the United States and South Africa, 1995; Middle Passages: African American Journeys to Africa, 1787-2005, 2006; (ed. with M.P. Guterl and R.G. Lee) Race, Nation, and Empire in American History, 2007. Contributor of articles to books, journals and periodicals. **Address:** Department of History, Stanford University, 450 Serra Mall, Bldg. 200, Stanford, CA 94305-2024, U.S.A. **Online address:** jtcampb@stanford.edu

CAMPBELL, Jodi. American (born United States), b. 1968. **Genres:** History, Cultural/Ethnic Topics, Politics/Government, Literary Criticism And History. **Career:** University of Minnesota, Department of History, instructor and teaching assistant, 1993-98; Centenary College of Louisiana, Department of History, assistant professor, 1999-2002; Texas Christian University, Department of History, assistant professor, 2002-05, associate professor, 2005-. Writer. **Publications:** Monarchy, Political Culture, and Drama in Seventeenth-Century Madrid: Theater of Negotiation, 2006. Contributor of articles to journals. **Address:** Department of History, Texas Christian University, Reed Hall 306, PO Box 297260, Fort Worth, TX 76129, U.S.A. **Online address:** j.campbell@tcu.edu

CAMPBELL, John. American/Scottish (born Scotland), b. 1956. **Genres:** Philosophy, Adult Non-fiction. **Career:** Christ Church, research lecturer, 1983-86; New College, fellow and tutor in philosophy, 1986-2001; British Academy, research reader 1995-97; University of Oxford, reader in philosophy, 1997-2001, Wilde professor of mental philosophy, 2001-04, Corpus Christi College, professorial fellow, 2001-04; Center for Advanced Study in the Behavioral Sciences, fellow, 2003-04; European Society for Philosophy and Psychology, president, 2003-06; University of California, Department of Philosophy, Willis S. and Marion Slusser professor, 2004-. Writer. **Publications:** Past, Space and Self, 1994; Reference and Consciousness, 2002. **Address:** Department of Philosophy, University of California, 140 Moses Hall, Ste. 2390, Berkeley, CA 94720-2390, U.S.A. **Online address:** jjcampbell@berkeley.edu

CAMPBELL, Judith. Also writes as Anthony Grant. British (born England), b. 1914. **Genres:** Animals/Pets, Biography, Adult Non-fiction. **Career:** Writer and broadcaster. **Publications:** NONFICTION: Family Pony, 1961; Queen Rides, 1965; Horses in the Sun, 1966; Police Horses, 1967; The World of Horses, 1969; Pony Events, 1969; The World of Ponies, 1970; Anne: Portrait of a Princess, 1970; Horses and Ponies, 1971; (with N. Toyne) Family on Horseback, 1972; Princess Anne and Her Horses, 1972; Elizabeth & Philip: A Royal Love Story, 1972; The Champions: Great Racehorses and Show Jumpers of Our Time, 1973; Royalty on Horseback, 1974, 2nd ed., 1975; The Horseman's World, 1975; The World of the Horse, 1975; Eventing, 1976; Anne and Mark, 1976; Your Own Pony Club, 1979; Queen Elizabeth II, 1980; (as Anthony Grant) The Mutant, 1980; Charles: A Prince of Our Time, 1981; The Royal Partners: The Queen's Thirty-Five Years of Marriage, 1982; Royal Horses, 1983; Ponies, People and Palaces, forthcoming. **Address:** A. M. Heath & Company Ltd., 79 St. Martin's Ln., London, GL WC2N 4AA, England.

CAMPBELL, Karen. *See* **BEATY, Betty (Smith).**

CAMPBELL, Kellyna K. American (born United States), b. 1959. **Genres:** Sports/Fitness, Self Help. **Career:** Lehua Center for Well-Being, co-founder and healer. Writer. **Publications:** 9 Inner Jewels: Life-changing Meditations For Finding Your Soul's Purpose, 2004. **Address:** c/o Author Mail, Lehua Publishing, 708 Gravenstein Hwy. N, Ste. 40, Sebastopol, CA 95472-2808, U.S.A.

CAMPBELL, Malcolm. New Zealander (born New Zealand), b. 1963?. **Genres:** Politics/Government, History. **Career:** Charles Sturt University, lecturer, 1989-90; University of Missouri, Fulbright postdoctoral fellow, 1990-91; University of Auckland, Department of History, lecturer in history, 1992-98, senior lecturer in history, 1999-2005, associate professor of history, 2006-, head; University of Liverpool, Institute of Irish Studies, honorary visiting senior fellow, 2005-; University of Washington, Giovanni Costigan Lecturer, 2007. Writer and historian. **Publications:** The Kingdom of the Ryans: The Irish in Southwest New South Wales, 1816-1890, 1997; Ireland's New Worlds: Immigrants, Politics and Society in the United States and Australia, 1815-1922, 2008. Contributor to books and periodicals. **Address:** New Zealand. **Online address:** mc.campbell@auckland.ac.nz

CAMPBELL, Mary B(aine). American (born United States), b. 1954. **Genres:** Literary Criticism And History, Poetry, Young Adult Fiction. **Career:** Columbia University, research fellow, 1985-87; Harvard University, lecturer in literature, 1987-88; Brandeis University, assistant professor of English, 1988-94, chair of creative writing committee, 1990-, associate professor of English, 1994-, professor; American Council of Learned Societies, fellow. Writer. **Publications:** The Witness and the Other World: Exotic European Travel Writing, 400-1600, 1988; (ed. with M. Rollins) Begetting Images: Studies in the Art and Science of Symbol Production, 1989; The World, the Flesh, and Angels (poems), 1989; Wonder and Science: Imagining Worlds in Early Modern Europe, 1999; Trouble (poetry), 2003. Contributor to periodicals. **Address:** Department of English, Brandeis University, Rabb 263, 415 South St., PO Box 9110, Waltham, MA 02453, U.S.A. **Online address:** campbell@brandeis.edu

CAMPBELL, Mavis C. (Mavis Christine Campbell). American/Jamaican (born Jamaica) **Genres:** History, Business/Trade/Industry, Economics, Humanities. **Career:** City University of New York, Hunter College, faculty, 1971-77; Amherst College, Department of History, professor, 1977-, now professor emeritus; University of Guyana, visiting professor and director of Caribbean studies, 1979-80; University of Edinburgh, visiting fellow, 1985-86. Writer. **Publications:** The Dynamics of Change in a Slave Society: A Sociopolitical History of the Free Coloreds of Jamaica, 1800-1865, 1975; The Maroons of Jamaica, 1655-1796: A History of Resistance, Collaboration and Betrayal, 1988; Nova Scotia and the Fighting Maroons: A Documentary History, 1990; Back to Africa: George Ross and the Maroons: From Nova Scotia to Sierra Leone, 1993; Black Women of Amherst College, 1999. Contributor to books and journals. **Address:** Department of History, Amherst College, AC Ste. 2254, PO Box 5000, Amherst, MA 01002-5000, U.S.A. **Online address:** mccampbell@amherst.edu

CAMPBELL, Mavis Christine. *See* **CAMPBELL, Mavis C.**

CAMPBELL, Peter A. American (born United States), b. 1948. **Genres:** Picture/Board Books, Reference, Education. **Career:** Writer and artist. **Publications:** SELF ILLUSTRATED: Launch Day, 1995; Alien Encounters, 2000; Old-Time Base Ball and the First Modern World Series, 2002; Boston Pilgrims vs. Pittsburgh Pirates: The First Modern World Series, 2003. Contributor to periodicals. **Address:** Stauch-Vetromile & Mitchell, 2 Charles St., 3rd Fl., North Providence, RI 02904, U.S.A. **Online address:** pcampbellspace@yahoo.com

CAMPBELL, Ramsey. British (born England), b. 1946. **Genres:** Novels, Novellas/Short Stories, Mystery/Crime/Suspense, Horror. **Career:** Inland Revenue, tax officer, 1962-66; Liverpool Public Libraries, library assistant, 1966-71, acting librarian in charge, 1971-73; British Fantasy Society, president, 1976-; Society of Fantastic Films, president, 1990-; BBC Radio, film critic. Writer. **Publications:** The Inhabitant of the Lake and Less Welcome Tenants, 1964; Demons by Daylight, 1973; The Height of the Scream, 1976; The Doll Who Ate His Mother: A Novel of Modern Terror, 1976; The Face That Must Die, 1979; Parasite, 1980; The Nameless, 1981; Dark Companions, 1982; Night of the Claw, 1983; Incarnate, 1983; Obsession, 1985; Cold Print, 1985; The Hungry Moon, 1986; Scared Stiff, 1986; (with L. Tuttle and C. Barker) Night Visions 111, 1987; Dark Feasts, 1987; Fine Frights: Stories that Scared Me, 1988; The Influence, 1988; Ancient Images, 1989; Needing Ghosts, 1990; Midnight Sun, 1991; Waking Nightmares, 1991; The Count of Eleven, 1992; Alone with the Horrors: The Great Short Fiction of Ramsey Campbell, 1961-1991, 1993; Two Obscure Tales, 1993; Strange Things and Stranger Places, 1993; The Long Lost, 1994; The One Safe Place, 1996; Far Away and Never, 1996; Nazareth Hill, 1997; The Last Voice They Hear, 1998; Ghosts and Grisly Things, 2000; Silent Children, 2000; Meddling with Ghosts: Stories in the Tradition of M.R. James, 2001; Pact of the Fathers, 2001; Scared Stiff: Tales of Sex and Death, 2002; The Darkest Part of the Woods, 2002; (with S.T. Joshi) Probably, 2002; Told by the Dead, 2003; The Overnight, 2004; Secret Story, 2005; The Grin of the Dark, 2007; (with R. McGough, B. Patten and M. Murphy) The Book of Liverpool: A City in Short Fiction, 2007; Thieving Fear, 2008; Inconsequential Tales, 2008; Just Behind You, 2009; Creatures of the Pool, 2009; The Seven Days of Cain, 2010; Solomon Kane: Official Movie Novelisation, 2010; (intro.) Mammoth Book of the Best of Best New Horror: A Twenty-Year Celebration, 2010. EDITOR/CO-EDITOR: Superhorror, 1976; New Terrors, 2 vols., 1980; New Tales of the Cthulhu Mythos, 1980; The Gruesome Book, 1983; Stories That Scared Me, 1987; Best New Horror, 1990; Meddling with Ghosts, 2002; (with D. Etchison and J. Dann) Gathering the Bones: Original Stories from the World's Masters of Horror, 2003. **Address:** The Pimlico Agency, PO Box 20447, Cherokee Sta., New York, NY 10021, U.S.A. **Online address:** ramseycampbell99@gmail.com

CAMPBELL, Rhonda. (Denise Turney). American (born United States), b. 1962. **Genres:** Novels, Children's Fiction. **Career:** U.S. Navy, staff writer, 1984-88; The College of New Jersey, administrative assistant; Merrill Lynch, human resources senior specialist, administrative assistant; Chistell Publishing, executive director. Freelance writer. **Publications:** Portia (novel), 1997; Love Has Many Faces (novel), 2000. (as Denise Turney) Spiral (novel), 2003; (as Denise Turney) Long Walk Up, 2007. Contributor of articles to periodicals. **Address:** Chistell Publishing, 2500 Knights Rd., Ste. 19-01, Bensalem, PA 19020, U.S.A. **Online address:** rcampb3422@aol.com

CAMPBELL, R(obert) Wayne. Canadian (born Canada), b. 1942. **Genres:** Animals/Pets, Environmental Sciences/Ecology, Natural History, Bibliography, Zoology. **Career:** British Columbia Ministry of Recreation and Conservation, park naturalist, 1964-68; University of British Columbia, Cowan Vertebrate Museum, curator of vertebrates, 1969-72; Royal British Columbia Museum, curator of ornithology, 1973-92; British Columbia Ministry of Environment, Lands and Parks, senior research scientist, 1993-2000, now retired; North American Breeding Bird Survey, British Columbia coordinator, 1976-; Wild Bird Trust of British Columbia, WBT Wildlife Data Center, director, 2000-. Writer. **Publications:** (With M.G. Shepard and W.C. Weber) Vancouver Birds in 1971, 1972; Ornithology, 1973; (with D.F. Hatler and A. Dorst) Birds of Pacific Rim National Park, 1978; (with H. Hosford) Attracting and Feeding Birds in British Columbia, 1979; (co-author) A Bibliography of British Columbia Ornithology, 1979; (with E.D. Forsman and B.M.V.D. Raay) Annotated Bibliography of Literature on the Spotted Owl, 1984; (with D.M. Green) The Amphibians of British Columbia, 1984; (with P.T. Gregory) The Reptiles of British Columbia, 1984; (with R.W. Butler) Birds of the Fraser River Delta: Populations, Ecology and International Significance, 1987; (with R. Bovey) The Birds of Vancouver and the Lower Mainland, 1989; (with W.G. Turnbull) Illustrated Keys to the Identification of the Birds of Prey of British Columbia, 1989; (co-author) The Birds of British Columbia, 1990; (with H. Thommasen, K. Hutchings and M. Hume) Birds of the Raincoast: Habits and Habitat, 2004. **Address:** WBT Wildlife Data Centre, Wild Bird Trust of British Columbia, 124-1489 Marine Dr., West Vancouver, BC V7T 1B8, Canada. **Online address:** rwcampbell@shaw.ca

CAMPBELL, Robin. *See* **STRACHAN, Ian.**

CAMPBELL, Rod. Scottish (born Scotland), b. 1945. **Genres:** Children's Fiction. **Career:** Freelance artist, 1981-. Illustrator and writer. **Publications:** SELF-ILLUSTRATED CHILDREN'S BOOKS: An ABC, 1980; Dressing Up, 1980; A Grand Parade Counting Book, 1980; Great, Greater, Greatest, 1980; Eddie Enginedriver, 1981; Freddie Fireman, 1981; Charlie Clown, 1981; Nigel Knight, 1981; Gertie Gardener, 1981; Nancy Nurse, 1981; Dear Zoo, 1982; Rod Campbell's Book of Board Games, 1982; Wheels!, 1982; Look Inside! All Kinds of Places, 1983; Look Inside! Land, Sea, Air, 1983; Oh, Dear!, 1983; My Farm, 1983; My Zoo, 1983; My Pets, 1983; My Garden, 1983; Rod Campbell's Noisy Book, 1983; Rod Campbell's Magic Circus, 1983; Rod Campbell's Magic Fairground, 1983; Henry's Busy Day, 1984; Take the Wheel, 1984; Look Up at the Sky, 1984; How Many Hats?, 1984; What Color Is That?, 1984; Lots of Animals, 1984; Buster's Morning, 1984; Buster's Afternoon, 1984; From Gran, 1984; Toy Soldiers, 1984; Baby Animals, 1984; Pet Shop, 1984; Circus Monkeys, 1984; Buster's Bedtime, 1985; Playwheels with Moving Parts!, 1985; Funwheels with Moving Parts!, 1985; Big and Strong, 1985; Cars and Trucks, 1985; Road Builders, 1985; Speed!, 1985; Misty's Mischief, 1986; I'm a Mechanic, 1986; I'm a Nurse, 1986; My Bath, 1986; My Favorite Things, 1986; My Teatime, 1986; My Toys, 1986; My Day, 1986; It's Mine, 1987; Lift-the-Flap ABC, 1987; Lift-the-Flap 123, 1987; Make a Word, 1987; Numbers, 1988; Shapes, 1988; Alphabet, 1988; Buster Gets Dressed, 1988; Buster Keeps Warm, 1988; My Presents, 1989; The Pop-Up Pet Shop, 1990; We Have a Pet, 1990; We Have a Rabbit, 1990; We Have a Dog, 1990; We Have a Guinea Pig, 1990; Look, Touch and Feel with Buster, 1991; My Stand Up Baby Animals, 1991; My Stand Up Farm Animals, 1991; My Stand Up Wild Animals, 1991; Naughty Henry, 1991; Henry in the Park, 1991; Noisy Farm, 1991; A Simple Rhyming ABC, 1991; Rod Campbell's Lift-the-Flap Animal Book, 1991; Misty, 1993; My Lift-the-Flap Nursery Book, 1993; I Won't Bite, 1993; My Pop-Up Garden Friends, 1993; Oh Dear!, 1994; Creepy Things, 1996; Fishy Things, 1996; Flying Things, 1996; Scary Things, 1996; Farm 123, 1996; Dear Zoo: A Lift-the-flap Book, 1999; Toddler Time Casepack, 2003; Dear Santa, 2004; I'm Hungry: A Touch-and-feel Book, 2004; Dear Zoo: A Pop-Up Book, 2005. **Address:** London, GL , England. **Online address:** rod@rodcampbell.co.uk

CAMPBELL, Scott. American (born United States), b. 1945. **Genres:** Novels, Human Relations/Parenting, Gerontology/Senior Issues. **Career:** Provandie, Eastwood & Lombardi, broadcast director, 1969-74; freelance writer, 1974-; Massachusetts Institute of Technology, writer and editor, 1979-2004, lecturer in writing, 1984-85, director of communications, School of Architecture + Planning, 2004-; Emerson College, lecturer in fiction, 2001-05. **Publications:** (With P. Silverman) Widower: When Men Are Left Alone (oral histories), 1987; Touched (novel), 1996; Aftermath (novel), 2008. Works appear in anthologies. Contributor of articles to periodicals. **Address:** Richard Parks Agency, PO Box 693, Salem, NY 12865-0693, U.S.A. **Online address:** scott@scottcampbellbooks.com

CAMPBELL, Siobhán. British/American/Irish (born Ireland), b. 1962. **Genres:** Poetry, Young Adult Fiction, Literary Criticism And History. **Career:** Butler Sims Ltd., manager, 1983-85; Wolfhound Press Ltd., publishing manager, 1985-90, director and publishing manager, 1990-98, director, 1998-2002; Wolfhound Press Ltd.-Dublin Office, director, 1999-2002; The Airfield Writers, founder and head of creative writing department, 2002-04; writer, lecturer and editor, 2004-05; Kingston University, senior lecturer in creative writing, 2005-, principal lecturer in creative writing. **Publications:** The Permanent Wave, 1996; That Other Walking Stick, 1999; The Cold That Burns, 2000; Cross-Talk, 2009. Contributor to magazines and newspapers.

Works appear in anthologies. **Address:** Faculty of Arts and Social Sciences, Kingston University, HH25, Penrhyn Rd., Kingston upon Thames, SR KT1 2EE, England. **Online address:** s.campbell@kingston.ac.uk

CAMPBELL, Stephen J. (Stephen John Campbell). Irish (born Ireland), b. 1963?. **Genres:** Novels. **Career:** Case Western Reserve University, faculty member, 1993-94; University of Michigan, faculty member, 1995-99; University of Pennsylvania, faculty member, 1999-2002; Metropolitan Museum of Art, doctoral fellowships, 1994-95; Johns Hopkins University, department of the History of Art, faculty member in the, 2002-. Writer. **Publications:** The Great Irish Famine: Words and Images from the Famine Museum, 1994; Cosme Tura of Ferrara: Style, Politics, and the Renaissance City, 1450-1495, 1997; (ed. and author of intro. with Stephen J. Milner) Artistic Exchange and Cultural Translation in the Italian Renaissance City, 2004; (ed. and author of intro.) Artists at Court: Image-making and Identity, 1300- 1550, 2004; (as S. Campbell) The Cabinet of Eros: Renaissance Mythological Painting and the Studiolo of Isabella D'Este, 2006. **Address:** Department of the History of Art, Johns Hopkins University, 257 Mergenthaler Hall, 3400 N Charles St., Baltimore, MD 21218, U.S.A. **Online address:** stephen.campbell@jhu.edu

CAMPBELL, Stephen John. *See* **CAMPBELL, Stephen J.**

CAMPBELL, Susan. American (born United States), b. 1959. **Genres:** Autobiography/Memoirs. **Career:** Hartford Courant, columnist. Writer. **Publications:** (With B. Heald) Connecticut Curiosities: Quirky Characters, Roadside Oddities & Other Offbeat Stuff, 2002; (with B. Gellerman) The Big Book of New England Curiosities: From Orange, CT, to Blue Hill, ME: A Guide to the Quirkiest, Oddest and Most Unbelievable Stuff You'll See, 2009; Dating Jesus: A Story of Fundamentalism, Feminism, and the American Girl, 2009. Contributor to journalism. **Online address:** susan@datingjesus.net

CAMPBELL, Tracy (A.). American (born United States), b. 1962. **Genres:** History, Politics/Government, inspirational/Motivational Literature. **Career:** Union College, assistant professor of history and director of Appalachian Semester Program, 1989-91; Mars Hill College, assistant professor to associate professor of history, 1991-99; University of Kentucky, Mellon fellow in the humanities, 1994-95, associate professor of history, 1999-2006, Wendell H. Ford Public Policy Research Center, co-director, 2005-, Department of History, Undergraduate Studies, director; Dakota Wesleyan University, George McGovern visiting professor of public leadership, 2008. Writer. **Publications:** The Politics of Despair: Power and Resistance in the Tobacco Wars, 1993; Short of the Glory: The Fall and Redemption of Edward F. Prichard, Jr., 1998; Deliver the Vote: A History of Election Fraud, an American Political Tradition, 1742-2004, 2005. Contributor to history journals. **Address:** Department of History, University of Kentucky, 1715 Patterson Office Twr., Lexington, KY 40506-0027, U.S.A. **Online address:** tracamp@uky.edu

CAMPBELL, Walter E. American (born United States), b. 1952. **Genres:** Biography, History. **Career:** Moses Cone Hospital, computer clerk, 1978-80; Memory Lane Productions Inc., president and chief executive officer, 1996-; Duke University, Medical Center, historian, 2003-06. Writer. **Publications:** Across Fortune's Tracks: A Biography of William Rand Kenan, Jr., 1996; Foundations for Excellence: 75 Years of Duke Medicine, 2006. Contributor of articles to books. **Address:** Memory Lane Productions Inc., 5212 Memory Ln., Durham, NC 27712-2126, U.S.A. **Online address:** cmpbll@acpub.duke.edu

CAMPBELL-CULVER, Maggie. French/British (born England) **Genres:** Horticulture, Biography, Sciences. **Career:** Ballet Rambert, dancer; Fishbourne Roman Palace, garden conservationist; British Broadcasting Corp., Radio 4, contributor. Writer. **Publications:** The Origin of Plants: The People and Plants That Have Shaped Britain's Garden History since the Year 1000, 2001; (co-ed.) The Oxford Companion to the Garden, 2006; A Passion for Trees: The Legacy of John Evelyn, 2006. Contributor to books and periodicals. **Address:** c/o Author Mail, Hodder Headline, 338 Euston Rd., London, GL NW1 3BH, England.

CAMPBELL-KELLY, Martin. British (born England), b. 1945. **Genres:** Information Science/Computers, History. **Career:** Leicester Polytechnic, reader in computer science, 1963-73; Sunderland Polytechnic, senior lecturer, 1973-80; University of Warwick, Department of Computer Science, lecturer, 1980-89, senior lecturer, 1989-94, reader in computer science, 1994-2004, professor, 2004-, now professor emeritus; University of Calgary, research fellow, 1983; Smithsonian Institute, research fellow, 1988; University of Manchester, National Archive for the History of Computing, senior research fellow, 1993-94; Massachusetts Institute of Technology, Dibner Institute for the History of Science and Technology, senior research fellow, 1995; London School of Economics, visiting fellow, 1996-99; Portsmouth University, History of Computing Group, visiting professor; International Business Machine, consultant; University College, consultant; Manchester Business School, consultant. Educator and author. **Publications:** An Introduction to Macros, 1973; The Computer Age, 1978; ICL: A Business and Technical History, 1989; (with W. Aspray) Computer: A History of the Information Machine, 1996, 2nd ed., 2004; (contrib.) The Modern Worlds of Business and Industry: Cultures, Technology, Labor, 1998; From Airline Reservations to Sonic the Hedgehog: A History of the Software Industry, 2003. EDITOR: (with M.R. Williams) The Moore School Lectures: Theory and Techniques for Design of Electronic Digital Computers, 1985; (and intro. with M.R. Williams) The Early British Computer Conferences, 1989; The Works of Charles Babbage, 1989; (and intro.) Passages from the Life of a Philosopher, 1994; (co-ed.) The History of Mathematical Tables: From Sumer to Spreadsheets, 2003. Contributor to books and periodicals. **Address:** Department of Computer Science, University of Warwick, Rm. CS326, Kirby Corner Rd., Coventry, WM CV4 7AL, England. **Online address:** m.campbell-kelly@warwick.ac.uk

CAMPBELL-SLAN, Joanna. *See* **SLAN, Joanna Campbell.**

CAMPER, Carol. Canadian (born Canada), b. 1954. **Genres:** Novellas/Short Stories, Poetry, Plays/Screenplays. **Career:** Hassle Free Clinic, counselor, 1990-; Black Coalition for AIDS Prevention, board director; Come As You Are, staff. Writer. **Publications:** (Ed.) Miscegenation Blues: Voices of Mixed Race Women, 1994; (intro.) Hippolytus Temporizes & Ion: Adaptations of Two Plays by Euripides, 2003. Works appear in anthologies. Contributor to periodicals. **Address:** 253 Strathmore Blvd., Toronto, ON M4J 1P7, Canada.

CAMPION, Christopher John. American (born United States), b. 1965?. **Genres:** Autobiography/Memoirs. **Career:** Knockout Drops, lead singer. Author. **Publications:** Escape from Bellevue: A Dive Bar Odyssey (short stories) as Escape from Bellevue: A Memoir of Rock N Roll, Recovery and Redemption, 2009. **Online address:** chris@knockoutdrops.com

CAMPION, Dan(iel Ray). American (born United States), b. 1949. **Genres:** Poetry, Literary Criticism And History. **Career:** Encyclopaedia Britannica Inc., production editor, 1972-74; Follett Publishing Co., children's book editor, 1977-78; University of Iowa, teaching and research assistant, 1978-84, visiting assistant professor of English, 1990-95; ACT Inc., test specialist and senior test editor, 1984-, manager of editorial quality assurance. **Publications:** (Ed. with J. Perlman and E. Folsom) Walt Whitman: The Measure of His Song (criticism), 1981, 2nd ed., 1998; Calypso (poetry), 1981; Peter De Vries and Surrealism (criticism), 1995. Contributor of articles to periodicals. **Address:** ACT Inc., 500 ACT Dr., PO Box 168, Iowa City, IA 52245, U.S.A. **Online address:** dan.campion@act.org

CAMPION, Jane. Australian/New Zealander (born New Zealand), b. 1954. **Genres:** Film. **Career:** Writer and director. **Publications:** Jane Campion: Interviews, 1999; Piano: A Novel, 1999. **Address:** HLA Management Pty Ltd., PO Box 1536, Strawberry Hills, NW 2012, Australia. **Online address:** hla@hlamgt.com.au

CAMPION, Nicholas. British (born England), b. 1953. **Genres:** Astronomy, Psychology. **Career:** Bath Spa University, School of Historical and Cultural Studies, director of Sophia Centre; University of Wales, Cultural Astronomy and Astrology, senior lecturer, Department of Archaeology and Anthropology, editor. **Publications:** (With M. Baigent and C. Harvey) Mundane Astrology, 1984; The Practical Astrologer, 1987; The Book of World Horoscopes, 1988; (co-author) The Astrology of the Macrocosm: New Directions in Mundane Astrology, 1990; The Great Year: Astrology, Millenarianism, and the History in the Western Tradition, 1994; (with S. Eddy) The New Astrology: The Art and Science of the Stars, 1999; Zodiac, 2000; The Ultimate Astrologer: A Simple Guide to Calculating and Interpreting Birth Charts for Effective Application in Daily Life, 2002; The Encyclopedia of the History of Astrology and Cultural Astronomy, 2005; Cosmos: A Cultural History of Astrology, 2005; What Do Astrologers Believe?, 2005; Astrology, History and Apocalypse, 2006; (ed. with P. Curry) Sky and Psyche: The Relationship Between Cosmos and Consciousness, 2006; Dawn of Astrology: A Cultural History of Western Astrology, vol. I: The Ancient & Classical Worlds, 2008, History of Western Astrology, vol. II: The Medieval and Modern Worlds, 2009; Astrology and Popular Religion: Prophecy, Cosmology, and the New Age Movement, 2012; Astrology and Public Attitudes to Science, forthcoming. **Address:** Trafalgar Square Books, 388 Howe Hill Rd., North Pomfret, VT 05053, U.S.A. **Online address:** n.campion@lamp.ac.uk

CAMPLING, Christopher Russell. British/Australian (born Australia), b. 1925. **Genres:** Music, Theology/Religion, Autobiography/Memoirs, Photography. **Career:** Church of England, ordained priest, 1951; Basingstoke, assistant curate, 1952-55; King's School, chaplain, 1955-60; Lancing College, chaplain, 1961-67; Pershore and Canon of Worcester Cathedral, vicar and rural dean, 1968-76; Worcestershire Diocese of Church of England, director for religious education, 1976-; archdeacon, 1976-84; Open Synod Group, chairman, 1983; Ripon Cathedral, dean, 1984-95, dean emeritus of Ripon, 1995-. Writer. **Publications:** (Co-author) Guide to Divinity Teaching, 1960: The Way, the Truth and the Life (series), 1965; (co-ed.) Words for Worship, 1970; (ed.) The Fourth Lesson, vol. I, 1973, vol. II, 1974; Music for Rite A Eucharist, 1988; The Food of Love: Reflections on Music and Faith, 1997; I Was Glad: The Memoirs of Christopher Campling, Dean Emeritus of Ripon Cathederal, 2005. **Address:** Ripon Cathedral, Liberty Court House, Minster Rd., Ripon, NY HG4 1QS, England.

CAMPO, Rafael. American (born United States), b. 1964. **Genres:** Poetry, Essays, Literary Criticism And History. **Career:** Beth Israel Deaconess Medical Center in Boston, physician; Harvard Medical School, physician general internal medicine, Beth Israel Deaconess Medical Center, director, Office of Multicultural Affairs, director; Lesley University, Low Residency Creative Writing Program, faculty. Writer, poet and practicing physician. **Publications:** The Other Man Was Me: A Voyage to the New World, 1994; What the Body Told, 1996; The Poetry of Healing: A Doctor's Education in Empathy, Identity and Desire, 1997; Diva, 1999; Landscape with Human Figure, 2002; The Healing Art: A Doctor's Black Bag of Poetry, 2003; The Enemy, 2007. Contributor to periodicals. **Address:** Beth Israel Deaconess Medical Center, 330 Brookline Ave., Boston, MA 02215, U.S.A. **Online address:** rcampo@bidmc.harvard.edu

CAMPOS, Paul F. American (born United States), b. 1959. **Genres:** Law, History. **Career:** The Sports Periodical Index, editor, 1985-86; Michigan Law Review, associate editor, 1987-88, editor; Latham and Watkins, attorney, 1989-90; University of Colorado, School of Law, associate professor, 1990-97, professor, 1997-; Byron R. White Center for American Constitutional Study, director, 1995-99. **Publications:** (With P. Schlag and S.D. Smith) Against the Law, 1996; Jurismania: The Madness of American Law, 1998; The Obesity Myth: Why America's Obsession with Weight is Hazardous to Your Health, 2004. Contributor to periodicals. **Address:** University of Colorado Law School, 466 Wolf Law Bldg., 401 UCB, PO Box 401, Boulder, CO 80309-0401, U.S.A. **Online address:** paul.campos@colorado.edu

CANADA, Geoffrey. American (born United States), b. 1952. **Genres:** Psychology, Social Sciences, Education. **Career:** Robert White School, teacher and counselor, 1975-76, associate director, 1976-77, director, 1977-81; Health Care Inc., executive director, 1981-83; Chang Moo Kwan Martial Arts School, founder and chief instructor, 1983; Robert White School, director; Harlem Children's Zone Inc., director of Truancy Prevention Program and Center 54, 1983-90, president and chief executive officer, 1990-. Writer. **Publications:** Fist, Stick, Knife, Gun: A Personal History of Violence in America, 1995, rev. ed., 2010; Reaching Up for Manhood: Transforming the Lives of Boys in America, 1998. Contributor to magazines and newspapers. **Address:** Harlem Children's Zone Inc., 35 E 125th St., New York, NY 10035, U.S.A. **Online address:** rheelen@rheelen.org

CANAVAGGIO, Jean. French (born France), b. 1936. **Genres:** Literary Criticism And History, Theatre. **Career:** Sorbonne University, assistant, 1966-69; University of Caen, assistant lecturer, 1969-75, professor, 1975-91; University of Virginia, visiting professor, 1983; University of Paris X Nanterre, professor, 1991-96, Casa de Velazquez, director, 1996-2001, professor, 2001-06; emeritus, 2006-. Writer. **Publications:** L'Espagne au temps de Philippe II, 1965; (ed.) Comedia de los amores y locuras del Conde loco, 1969; Cervantes dramaturge: un theatre a naitre, 1977; (ed.) Entremeses, 1981; Theatre espagnol du XVIe siecle, 1983; Cervantes, Mazarine, 1986; (intro.) Theatre espagnol du XVIIe siecle, 1992; (ed.) Miguel de Cervantes Saavedra, Los Banos de Argel; Pedro de Urdemalas, 1992; Histoire de la litterature espagnole, 1993-94; (ed. with I. Arellano) Rostros y máscaras, 1999; Un mundo abreviado, 2000; Cervantes entre vida y creacion, 2000; (ed.) Cervantes, Oeuvres romanesques completes, 2001; Don Quichotte, du livre au mythe, 2005; (contrib.) Un Quijote y cien ediciones de locura, 2005. **Address:** Universite de Paris X Nanterre, 200 Ave. Republique, Nantere Cedex, 92001, France. **Online address:** jean.f.canavaggio@wanadoo.fr

CANAVAN, Trudi. Australian (born Australia), b. 1969. **Genres:** Science Fiction/Fantasy. **Career:** Lonely Planet Publishers, designer, illustrator and cartographer; Oxford University Press Australia, promotional designer, 1993-95; Aurealis magazine, art director and designer, 1995-2004; The Telltale Art, Ferntree Gully, Australia, 1995-. Writer. **Publications:** BLACK MAGICIAN TRILOGY: The Magician's Guild, 2001; The Novice, 2002; The High Lord, 2003; The Magician's Apprentice, 2009. AGE OF THE FIVE TRILOGY: Priestess of the White, 2006; Last of the Wilds, 2006; Voice of the Gods, 2007. THE TRAITOR SPY TRILOGY: Ambassador's Mission, 2010; Rogue, 2011; The Traitor Queen, 2012. Contributor to books. **Address:** Orbit, Level 17, 207 Kent St., Sydney, NW 2000, Australia. **Online address:** trudi@spin.net.au

CANBY, C. C. *See* **JACKSON, Sid J.**

CANDILIS, Wray O. American/British (born England), b. 1927. **Genres:** Economics, Geography, Social Sciences. **Career:** National Association of Real Estate Board, Department of Research, assistant director, 1960-64; Institute of Life Insurance, Division of Statistics and Research, senior economics associate, 1964-66; American Bankers Association, Department of Research and Planning, economist, 1966-70, research project director, 1970-71; U.S. Department of Commerce, special assistant for financial affairs, 1971-73, Office of Service Industries, International Trade Administration, Information Industries Division, director, 1971-; Business Economics, associate editor, 1976-. Writer. **Publications:** The Economy of Greece 1944-66, Efforts for Stability and Development, 1968; Long-Range Planning in Banking, 1968; Financing America's States and Cities, Policy Statement of the American Bankers Association Together with Staff Study of the A.B.A. Department of Economic Research, 1970; Variable Rate Mortgage Plans, 1971; Consumer Credit: Factors Influencing Its Availability and Costs, 1976. EDITOR: The Future of Commercial Banking, 1975; Changing Minority Markets, 1978; (and co-author) Franchising in the Economy 1976-1978, 1978; Market Center Shifts, 1978; The Motor Vehicle Leasing and Rental Industry: Trends and Prospects, 1979; Measuring Markets: Guide to the Use of Federal and State Statistical Data, 1979; United States Service Industries Handbook, 1988; (and trans.) The Flowergarden, 2001. **Address:** Service Industries Division, Office of Consumer Goods and Service Industries, U.S. Department of Commerce, Washington, DC 20230, U.S.A.

CANDISKY, Catherine A. American (born United States), b. 1961. **Genres:** Mystery/Crime/Suspense, Criminology/True Crime, Young Adult Non-fiction. **Career:** Columbus Dispatch, reporter, 1984-. **Publications:** (With R. Yocum) Insured for Murder, 1993. **Address:** Columbus Dispatch, 34 S 3rd St., Columbus, OH 43215, U.S.A.

CANDLAND, Douglas Keith. American (born United States), b. 1934. **Genres:** Psychology, Medicine/Health. **Career:** United States Public Health Service, postdoctoral research fellow in psychology, 1959-60; National Science Foundation, postdoctoral fellow, 1967-68; Tulane University, research fellow, 1967-68; Pennsylvania State University, research fellow, 1968-69; National Institute of Health, special research fellow, 1968-69; Bucknell University, assistant professor, 1960-64, associate professor, 1964-67, professor of psychology, 1967-, Program in Animal Behavior, director, 1967-2002, coordinator of graduate study, 1962-64, presidential professor of animal behavior, 1973-80, professor of psychology and animal behavior, 1985-2002, Homer P. Rainey professor of psychology and animal behavior emeritus, 2002-; University of Stirling, research fellow, 1972-73; Review of General Psychology, editor, 2002-. **Publications:** (With J.F. Campbell) Exploring Behavior: An Introduction to Psychology, 1961; (contrib.) Sensory Deprivation, 1961; (ed.) Emotion: Bodily Change, 1962; (contrib.) Conformity and Deviation, 1962; (with S.A. Manning) Studying Learning Patterns in Mental Retardates, 1967; Psychology: The Experimental Approach, 1968, (with R.S. Moyer) 2nd ed., 1978; (contrib.) Classical Psychophysics and Scaling, 1968; (contrib.) The Development of Vertebrate Behavior, 1971; (contrib.) The Limbic and Autonomic Nervous Systems, 1974; (co-author) Emotion, 1977; Feral Children and Clever Animals: Reflections on Human Nature 1993; Archeopsychology and the Modern Mind, 2011. **Address:** Department of Psychology, Bucknell University, Lewisburg, PA 17837, U.S.A. **Online address:** dcandlan@bucknell.edu

CANES-WRONE, Brandice. American (born United States), b. 1971. **Genres:** Politics/Government, Social Sciences. **Career:** Massachusetts Institute of Technology, assistant professor, 1998-2002; California Institute of Technology, visiting assistant professor, 2001-02; Northwestern University, associate professor, 2002-04; Princeton University, Department of Politics and Woodrow Wilson School, associate professor of politics and public affairs, 2004-08, professor of politics and public affairs, 2008-. **Publications:** (Contrib.) Continuity and Change in House Elections, 2000; Who Leads Whom? Presidents, Policy, and the Public, 2006; (contrib.) The Macropolitics of Congress, 2006. Contributor of articles to journals. Writer. **Address:** Department of Politics and Woodrow Wilson School, Princeton University, 34 Corwin, 214 Robertson Hall, Princeton, NJ 08544-1013, U.S.A. **Online address:** bcwrone@princeton.edu

CANFIELD, Jack. American (born United States), b. 1944. **Genres:** Education, How-to Books, inspirational/Motivational Literature, Philosophy, Self Help, Cartoons, Travel/Exploration. **Career:** Teacher, 1967-68; Clinton Job Corps Center, director of teacher program, 1968-69; New England Center for Personal and Organizational Development, founder and director, 1971-77; Institute for Wholistic Education, founder and director, 1978-80; Insight Training Seminars, director of educational services, 1981-83; Foundation for Self-Esteem, founder and chairperson, 1986-; National Council for Self-Esteem, co-founder, 1986-96; Maui Writers Conference and Retreat School, faculty, 1996-; Chicken Soup for the Soul Enterprises, founder, chief executive officer, 1998-, Chicken Soup for the Soul Magazine, executive editor and contributor, 2005-; Canfield Training Group, founder, chairman. Writer. **Publications:** (With H.C. Wells) About Me: A Curriculum for a Developing Self, 1971; (with H.C. Wells) 100 Ways to Enhance Self-Concept in the Classroom: A Handbook for Teachers and Parents, 1976, 2nd ed., 1994; Personalized Learning: Confluent Processes in the Classroom, 1976 as Loving to Learn, 1997; (co-author) Self-Esteem in the Classroom: A Curriculum Guide, 1986; Self-Esteem and Peak Performance: A Transcript, 1991; (with F. Siccone) 101 Ways to Develop Student Self-Esteem and Responsibility in the Classroom, vol. I: The Teacher as Coach, 1992, vol. II: The Power to Succeed in School and Beyond, 1992; Los Angeles Dodgers Team Esteem Program: A Self-Esteem Curriculum Guide, 1992; (comp. with M.V. Hansen) Chicken Soup for the Soul: 101 Stories to Open the Heart and Rekindle the Spirit, 1993; (with M.V. Hansen) Dare to Win, 1994; (with K. Goldberg) Follow Your Dreams: A Goals Setting Workbook, 1994; (comp. with M.V. Hansen) A 2nd Helping of Chicken Soup for the Soul: 101 More Stories to Open the Heart and Rekindle the Spirit, 1995; (with M.V. Hansen) The Aladdin Factor: How to Ask for and Get Everything You Want in Life, 1995; (comp. with M.V. Hansen and D.W. Wentworth) Chicken Soup for the Soul Cookbook: 101 Stories and Recipes from the Heart, 1995; (comp. with M.V. Hansen) A 3rd Serving of Chicken Soup for the Soul: 101 More Stories to Open the Heart and Rekindle the Spirit, 1996; (with J. Miller) Heart at Work: Stories and Strategies for Building Self-Esteem and Reawakening the Soul at Work, 1996; (comp.) Chicken Soup for the Surviving Soul: 101 Stories of Courage and Inspiration from Those Who Have Survived Cancer, 1996; (with M.V. Hansen and B. Spilchuk) A Cup of Chicken Soup for the Soul: Stories to Open the Heart and Rekindle the Spirit, 1996; (comp. with M.V. Hansen and P. Hansen) Condensed Chicken Soup for the Soul, 1996; (comp.) Chicken Soup for the Woman's Soul: 101 Stories to Open and Hearts and Rekindle the Spirits of Women, 1996; (comp.) Chicken Soup for the Soul at Work: 101 Stories of Courage, Compassion, and Creativity in the Workplace, 1996; (comp. with M.V. Hansen, H. McCarty and M. McCarty) A 4th Course of Chicken Soup for the Soul: 101 Stories to Open the Heart and Rekindle the Spirit, 1997; (comp. with M.V. Hansen and K. Kirberger) Chicken Soup for the Teenage Soul: 101 Stories about Life, Love, and Learning, 1997; (comp. with M.V. Hansen, P. Aubery and N. Mitchell) Chicken Soup for the Christian Soul: 101 Stories to Open the Heart and Rekindle the Spirit, 1997; (comp. with M.V. Hansen, M. Shimoff and J. Hawthorne) Chicken Soup for the Mother's Soul: 101 Stories to Open the Hearts and Rekindle the Spirits of Mothers, 1997; A Little Sip of Chicken Soup for The Soul: Inspiring Stories of Self-Affirmation, 1997; (comp. with M.V. Hansen and K. Kirberger) Chicken Soup for the Teenage Soul: Journal, 1998; (comp.) A Second Chicken Soup for the Woman's Soul: 101 More Stories to Open the Hearts and Rekindle the Spirits of Women, 1998; (comp. with M.V. Hansen) A Spirited Sip of Chicken Soup for the Soul: In Celebration of Women, 1998; (comp. with M.V. Hansen) A 5th Portion of Chicken Soup for the Soul: 101 More Stories to Open the Heart and Rekindle the Spirit, 1998; (comp. with M.V. Hansen and R. Camacho) Chicken Soup for the Country Soul: Stories Served Up Country-Style and Straight from the Heart, 1998; (comp. with M.V. Hansen, P. Hansen and I. Dunlap) Chicken Soup for the Kid's Soul: 101 Stories of Courage, Hope, and Laughter, 1998; (comp.) Chicken Soup for the Pet Lover's Soul: Stories about Pets as Teachers, Healers, Heroes, and Friends, 1998; (comp.) Chicken Soup for the Teenage Soul II: 101 More Stories of Life, Love, and Learning, 1998; Chicken Soup for the Soul Family Storybook Collection, 1998; (comp. with M.V. Hansen) A Stirring Sip of Chicken Soup for the Soul: Uplifting Moments from Everyday Heros, 1998; (comp.) Chicken Soup for the Couple's Soul: Inspirational Stories about Love and Relationships, 1999; (comp.) Chicken Soup for the College Soul: Inspiring and Humorous Stories about College, 1999; (comp. with M.V. Hansen) A 6th Bowl of Chicken Soup for the Soul: 101 More Stories to Open the Heart and Rekindle the Spirit, 1999; (comp.) Chicken Soup for the Cat & Dog Lover's Soul: Celebrating Pets as Family with Stories about Cats, Dogs, and Other Critters, 1999; (comp.) Chicken Soup for the Golden Soul: 101 Heartwarming Stories of People 50and Over, 1999; (comp.) Chicken Soup for the Golfer's Soul: 101 Stories of Insights, Inspiration, and Laughter on the Links, 1999; (comp.) Chicken Soup for the Single's Soul: Stories of Love and Inspiration for the Single, Divorced, and Widowed, 1999; (comp. with M.V. Hansen) Soup for the Soul: In Celebration of Women, 1999; (comp. with M.V. Hansen) Chicken Soup for the Soul at Christmas, 1999; (comp. with M.V. Hansen) Chicken Soup for the Soul: Stories to Warm a Mother's Heart, 1999; (comp. with M.V. Hansen and H. McNamara) Chicken Soup for the Unsinkable Soul: 101 Inspirational Stories of Overcoming Life's Challenges, 1999; (comp. with M.V. Hansen) Chicken Soup for the Soul: Stories to Uplift the Spirits, 1999; Chicken Soup for the Soul: Heartwarming Stories to Renew Your Faith, 1999; Chicken Soup for Little Souls: Della Splatnuk Birthday Girl, 1999; (comp.) Chicken Soup for the Christian Family Soul: Stories to Open the Heart and Rekindle the Spirit, 2000; (co-author) Chicken Soup for the Sports Fan's Soul: 101 Stories of Insight, Inspiration and Laughter from the World of Sports, 2000; (comp.) Chicken Soup for the Expectant Mother's Soul: 101 Stories to Inspire and Warm the Hearts of Soon-to-Be Mothers, 2000; (comp. with M.V. Hansen, P. Hansen and I. Dunlap) Chicken Soup for the Preteen Soul: 101 Stories of Changes, Choices, and Growing up for Kids Ages 9-13, 2000; (comp. with M.V. Hansen and T. Lagana) Chicken Soup for the Prisoner's Soul: 101 Stories to Open the Heart and Rekindle the Spirit of Hope, Healing and Forgiveness, 2000; (with M.V. Hansen and L. Hewitt) The Power of Focus, 2000; (comp. with M.V. Hansen) A Little Sip of Chicken Soup for the Golfer's Soul, 2000; (comp. with M.V. Hansen) A Pet Lover's Collection of Chicken Soup for the Soul, 2000; (comp. with M.V. Hansen and B. Gardner) Chicken Soup for the Writer's Soul: Stories to Open the Heart and Rekindle the Spirit of Writers, 2000; (comp.) Chicken Soup for the Teenage Soul III: More Stories of Life, Love, and Learning, 2000; (comp.) Chicken Soup for the Golden Soul: Heartwarming Stories of People 60 and Over, 2000; (co-ed.) Chicken Soup for the Gardener's Soul: 101 Stories to Sow Seeds of Love, Hope, and Laughter, 2000; (comp.) Chicken Soup for the Mother's Soul 2: More Stories to Open the Hearts and Rekindle the Spirits of Mothers, 2001; (comp.) Chicken Soup for the Father's Soul: Stories to Open the Hearts and Rekindle the Spirits of Fathers, 2001; (comp.) Chicken Soup for the Gardener's Soul: 101 Stories to Tend to the Souls and Nurture the Spirits of Gardeners, 2001; (comp.) Chicken Soup for the Nurse's Soul: 101 Stories to Celebrate, Honor, and Inspire the Nursing Profession, 2001; (comp. with M.V. Hansen and S.R. Slagter) Chicken Soup for the Veteran's Soul: Stories to Stir the Pride and Honor the Courage of Our Veterans, 2001; (comp. with M.V. Hansen and K. Kirberger) Chicken Soup for the Teenage Soul on Tough Stuff: Stories of Tough Times and Lessons Learned, 2001; (comp. with M.V. Hansen) Chicken Soup for the Soul Christmas Treasury: Holiday Stories to Warm the Heart, 2001; (comp. with M.V. Hansen and D.P. Elkins) Chicken Soup for the Jewish Soul: Stories to Open the Heart and Rekindle the Spirit, 2001; (comp.) Chicken Soup for the Baseball Fan's Soul: Inspirational Stories of Baseball, Big-League Dreams and the Game of Life, 2001; Chicken Soup for the Teenage Soul Letters: Letters of Life, Love, and Learning, 2001; (comp.) Chicken Soup for the Volunteer's Soul: Stories to Celebrate the Spirit of Courage, Caring and Community, 2002; (comp. with M.V. Hansen and S. Zikman) Chicken Soup for the Traveler's Soul: Stories of Adventure, Inspiration, and Insight to Celebrate the Spirit of Travel, 2002; (comp. with M.V. Hansen) Chicken Soup for the Teacher's Soul: Stories to Open the Hearts and Rekindle the Spirits of Educators, 2002; (comp.) Chicken Soup for the Grandparent's Soul: Stories to Open the Hearts and Rekindle the Spirits of Grandparents, 2002; (comp. with M.V. Hansen and M.E. Adams) Chicken Soup for the Soul of America: Stories to Heal the Heart of Our Nation, 2002; Chicken Soup for the Golfer's Soul: The 2nd Round: More Stories of Insight, Inspiration and Laughter on the Links, 2002; Chicken Soup for the Christian Woman's Soul: Stories to Open the Heart and Rekindle the Spirit, 2002; Chicken Soup for the Canadian Soul: Stories to Inspire and Uplift the Hearts of Canadians, 2002; (comp.) Chicken Soup for the Romantic Soul: Inspirational Stories About Love and Romance, 2002; Chicken Soup for the Sister's Soul, 2002; Chicken Soup for the Soul Christmas Treasury for Kids: A Story a Day from December 1st Through Christmas for Kids and their Families, 2002; (comp.) Chicken Soup for the Teenage Soul on Love & Friendship, 2002; (comp.) Chicken Soup for the Soul: Cartoons for Moms, 2003; (comp.) Chicken Soup for the Soul: Cartoons for Dads, 2003; You've GOT to Read This Book!, 2006; The Key to Living the Law of Attraction, 2007; Chicken Soup for the Soul: Teens Talk High School, 2008; (with M.V. Hansen and A. Newmark) Chicken Soup for the Soul: Teens Talk Relationships, 2008; (with K. Healy) Success Principles for Teens, 2008; (co-author) Chicken Soup for the Cancer Survivor's Soul, 2008; (co-author) Chicken Soup for the Father & Son Soul, 2008; (comp.) Chicken Soup for the Soul: A Tribute to Moms, 2008; (comp.) Chicken Soup for the Soul: Christian Kids, 2008; (comp.) Chicken Soup for the Soul: Moms Know Best, 2008; (comp.) Chicken Soup for the Soul: My Resolution, 2008; (co-author) Life Lessons for Mastering the Law of Attraction, 2008; (with M.V. Hansen and L. Thieman) Chicken Soup for the Adopted Soul, 2008; (with M.V. Hansen and M. Adler) Chicken Soup for the Soul and Golf Digest Present the Golf Book, 2009; (co-author) Chicken Soup for the Soul Count your Blessings, 2009; (with M.V. Hansen and S.M. Heim) Chicken Soup for the Soul: Twins and More, 2009; (co-author) Chicken Soup for the Soul: Family Matters, 2010; (ed. with V. Hansen and A. Newmark) Chicken Soup for the Soul: Teacher Tales, 2010; (with M. V. Hansen and A. Newmark) Chicken Soup for the Soul: Think Positive, 2010; Golden Motorcycle Gang, 2011; (comp.) Chicken Soup for the Soul: Country Music, 2011; (with W. Gladstone) The Golden Motorcycle Gang, 2011; (with P. Bruner) Tapping into Ultimate Success, 2012; (with M.V. Hansen and L. Hewitt) The Power of Focus, 2012. **Address:** The Canfield Training Group, PO Box 30880, Santa Barbara, CA 93130-0880, U.S.A. **Online address:** jcanfield@chickensoupforthesoul.com

CANFIELD, Oran. American (born United States), b. 1974?. **Genres:** Autobiography/Memoirs, Biography. **Career:** Writer and musician. **Publications:** Long Past Stopping: A Memoir, 2009. **Address:** Loretta Barrett Books Inc., 220 E 23rd St., 11th Fl., New York, NY 10010, U.S.A. **Online address:** longpaststopping@gmail.com

CANHAM, Elizabeth. (Elizabeth J. Canham). American/British (born England), b. 1939?. **Genres:** Novels, Theology/Religion. **Career:** Stillpoint Ministries, founder and executive director; Hospites Mundi (pilgrimage program), founder and director. Writer. **Publications:** Pilgrimage to Priesthood, 1985; Praying the Bible: A Parish Life Sourcebook, 1987; Journaling with Jeremiah, 1992; Heart Whispers: Benedictine Wisdom for Today, 1999. AS ELIZABETH J. CANHAM: A Table of Delight: Feasting with God in the Wilderness, 2005; Ask the Animals: Spiritual Wisdom from All God's Creatures, 2006. **Address:** Hospites Mundi, 51 Laurel Ln., Black Mountain, NC 28711-8788, U.S.A.

CANHAM, Elizabeth J. *See* **CANHAM, Elizabeth.**

CANHAM, Marsha. Canadian (born Canada), b. 1984. **Genres:** Romance/Historical, Novels, Children's Fiction, Young Adult Fiction, Westerns/Adventure, Literary Criticism And History. **Career:** Writer. **Publications:** China Rose, 1984; Bound by the Heart, 1984; The Wind and the Sea, 1986; The Pride of Lions, 1988; The Blood of Roses, 1989; Through a Dark Mist, 1991; Under the Desert Moon, 1992; Dark and Dangerous, 1992; In the Shadow of Midnight, 1994; Straight for the Heart, 1995; Across a Moonlit Sea, 1996; The Last Arrow, 1997; Pale Moon Rider, 1998; Swept Away, 1999; Midnight Honor, 2001; Iron Rose, 2003; My Forever Love, 2004. **Address:** Author Mail, Dell Publishing Co., 1540 Broadway, New York, NY 10036-4040, U.S.A. **Online address:** marsha.canham@sympatico.ca

CANIN, Ethan. American (born United States), b. 1960. **Genres:** Novels, Novellas/Short Stories, Medicine/Health, Travel/Exploration. **Career:** Writers' Grotto, co-founder; physician private practice, through 1998; University Iowa, Iowa Writers Workshop, faculty, 1998-, F. Wendell Miller professor of English. Writer. **Publications:** Emperor of the Air (short stories), 1988; Blue River, 1991; The Palace Thief (novellas), 1994, 2nd ed., 2002; (ed.) Writers Harvest 2, 1996; For Kings and Planets, 1998; Carry Me Across the Water, 2001; America America, 2008. Works appear in anthologies. Contributor of articles. **Address:** Maxine Groffsky Literary Agency, 2 5th Ave., New York, NY 10001, U.S.A. **Online address:** ecanin@ethancanian.com

CANN, Kate. British (born England), b. 1954. **Genres:** Young Adult Fiction. **Career:** Time Life Books, copyeditor, 1979-83. Freelance writer. **Publications:** FOR YOUNG ADULTS. FICTION: Diving In, 1996; In the Deep End, 1997; Sink or Swim, 1998; Footloose, 1999; Breaking Up, 2000; Hard Cash, 2000; Shacked Up, 2001; Fiesta, 2001; Speeding, 2002; Grecian Holiday; or, How I Turned Down the Best Possible Thing Only to Have the Time of My Life, 2002; Escape, 2003; Spanish Holiday; or, How I Transformed the Worst Vacation Ever into the Best Summer of My Life, 2004. OTHERS: Living in the World, 1997; Sex, 2001; Go!, 2001; Ready, 2001; California Holiday: Or, How the World's Worst Summer Job Gave Me a Great New Life, 2003; Crow Girl, 2005; Crow Girl Returns, 2006; Mediterranean Holiday: Or, How I Moved to a Tiny Island and Found The Love Of My Life, 2007; A' chaileag starraig, 2007; Possessed, 2010; Consumed, 2011; Fire and Rayne, 2011. NOVELS: Too Hot to Handle, 1997; Caught in the Act, 1997; Breaking Up, 2001; Shop Dead, 2001; Text Game, 2004; Leaving Poppy, 2006; Sea Change, 2007; Leader of the Pack, 2008; Possessing Rayne, 2008. **Address:** 34 Denton Rd., Twickenham, Middlesex, TWI 2HQ, England. **Online address:** katescann@aol.com

CANNATO, Vincent J. American (born United States), b. 1967. **Genres:** History, Politics/Government. **Career:** Columbia University, Department of History, teaching assistant, 1993-96; Jersey City Mayor's Office, director of policy development, 1998-99; University of Maryland, Department of History, adjunct professor, 2000; U.S. Department of Housing and Urban Development, speech writer, 2001; University of Massachusetts, Department of History, assistant professor, 2002-08, associate professor, 2008-. **Publications:** The Ungovernable City: John Lindsay and His Struggle to Save New York, 2002; (ed. with G. Troy) Living in the Eighties, 2009; American Passage: The History of Ellis Island, 2009. Contributor of articles to periodicals. **Address:** Department of History, University of Massachusetts, 4-635 McCormack Hall, 100 Morrissey Blvd., Boston, MA 02125-3393, U.S.A. **Online address:** vincent.cannato@umb.edu

CANNELL, Dorothy. American/British (born England), b. 1943?. **Genres:** Mystery/Crime/Suspense, Criminology/True Crime, Novels, Novellas/Short Stories. **Career:** Writer. **Publications:** MYSTERY NOVELS: The Thin Woman: An Epicurean Mystery, 1984; Down the Garden Path: A Pastoral Mystery, 1985; The Widows Club, 1988; Mum's the Word, 1990; Femmes Fatal, 1992; How to Murder Your Mother-in-Law, 1994; How to Murder the Man of Your Dreams, 1995; God Save the Queen, 1997; The Spring Cleaning Murders, 1998; (co-author) Naked Came the Farmer, 1998; The Trouble With Harriet, 1999; Bridesmaids Revisited, 2000; The Family Jewels and Other Stories, 2001; The Importance of Being Ernestine, 2002; (co-author) The Sunken Sailor, 2004; Withering Heights, 2007; Goodbye, Ms. Chips, 2008; She Shoots to Conquer, 2009. **Address:** Bantam Books, 1540 Broadway, New York, NY 10036, U.S.A.

CANNELL, Fenella. British (born England), b. 1962. **Genres:** Anthropology/Ethnology, Theology/Religion. **Career:** London School of Economics and Political Science, lecturer in social anthropology. Writer and educator. **Publications:** Power and Intimacy in the Christian Philippines, 1999; (ed.) The Anthropology of Christianity, 2006. Contributor to journals. **Address:** London School of Economics and Political Science, Houghton St., London, GL WC2A 2AE, England. **Online address:** f.cannell@lse.ac.uk

CANNEY, Donald L. American (born United States), b. 1947. **Genres:** Military/Defense/Arms Control, Transportation. **Career:** Maranatha Christian High School, teacher, 1974-84; Blue and Grey, editorial staff, 1984-87; U.S. Coast Guard, Museum System, registrar, 1991-. **Publications:** The Old Steam Navy, vol. I: Frigates, Sloops and Gunboats, 1989, vol. II: The Ironclads, 1842-1885, 1993; U.S. Coast Guard and Revenue Cutters, 1790-1935, 1995; Lincoln's Navy: The Ships, Men and Organization, 1861-65, 1998; Sailing Warships of the U.S. Navy, 2001; Africa Squadron: The U.S. Navy and the Slave Trade, 1842-1861, 2006; In Katrina's Wake: the U.S. Coast Guard and the Gulf Coast Hurricanes of 2005, 2010. **Address:** 12618 Kornett Ln., Bowie, MD 20715, U.S.A.

CANNING, Peter. American (born United States), b. 1937. **Genres:** Biography, Autobiography/Memoirs. **Career:** Reader's Digest (magazine), staff, 1965-88, managing editor, 1980-88. **Publications:** American Dreamers: The

Wallaces and Reader's Digest: An Insider's Story, 1996. **Address:** 1103 Horseneck Rd., Westport, MA 02790-1324, U.S.A.

CANNON, A. E. (Ann Edwards Cannon). American (born United States), b. 1956?. **Genres:** Novels, Poetry, Children's Fiction, Young Adult Fiction. **Career:** Deseret News, columnist; King's English Bookshop, bookseller. **Publications:** Cal Cameron by Day, Spider-Man by Night, 1988; The Shadow Brothers, 1990; Amazing Gracie, 1991; Great-Granny Rose and the Family Christmas Tree, 1996; I Know What You Do When I Go to School, 1996; Sam's Gift, 1996; What's a Mother to Do?, 1997; On the Go with Pirate Pete and Pirate Joe!, 2002; Charlotte's Rose, 2002; Let the Good Times Roll with Pirate Pete and Pirate Joe, 2004; Way Out West with Pirate Pete and Pirate Joe, 2006; Loser's Guide to Life and Love, 2008; The Chihuahua Chase in US as The Chihuahua Races, 2010; Sophie's Fish, 2012. **Address:** 295 Greenwich St., Ste. 260, New York, NY 10007, U.S.A. **Online address:** annlouisecannon@gmail.com

CANNON, Ann Edwards. *See* **CANNON, A. E.**

CANNON, Carl M. American (born United States), b. 1953. **Genres:** Politics/Government, Military/Defense/Arms Control. **Career:** Knight-Ridder Newspapers, Washington bureau reporter, 1982-93; Baltimore Sun, White House correspondent, 1993-98; National Journal, White House correspondent, 1998-2007, contributing editor, 2007-; Reader's Digest, Washington bureau chief; San Jose Mercury News, reporter, 1989; Harvard University, John F. Kennedy School Government, Institute of Politics, fellow-in-residence, 2007; National Public Radio, contributor; George Magazine, columnist; AmericanPresident.org, contributing editor. Journalist. **Publications:** (with L. Dubose and J. Reid) Boy Genius: Karl Rove, the Brains behind the Remarkable Political Triumph of George W. Bush, 2003, rev. ed. as Boy Genius: Karl Rove, the Architect of George W. Bush's Remarkable Political Triumphs, 2005; The Pursuit of Happiness in Times of War, 2004; (with L. Cannon) Reagan's Disciple: George W. Bush's Troubled Quest for a Presidential Legacy, 2008. Contributor to books and periodicals. **Address:** National Journal, 600 New Hampshire Ave. NW, Washington, DC 20037-2403, U.S.A. **Online address:** ccannon@nationaljournal.com

CANNON, Dolores Eilene. American (born United States), b. 1931. **Genres:** Paranormal, Theology/Religion, History, Young Adult Non-fiction. **Career:** Ozark Mountain Publishing Inc., owner and publisher. Regressive hypnotist and writer. **Publications:** Jesus and the Essenes: Fresh Insights into Christ's Ministry and the Dead Sea Scrolls, 1985; Conversations with Nostradamus, vol. I, 1989, vol. II, 1990, vol. III: His Prophecies Explained, 1992; Conversations with a Spirit: Between Death and Life, 1993; A Soul Remembers Hiroshima, 1993; Keepers of the Garden, 1993; The Legend of Starcrash, 1994; They Walked with Jesus, 1994; Legacy from the Stars, 1996; The Custodians: Beyond Abduction, 1998; The Convoluted Universe, 2001; They Walked with Jesus: Past Life Experiences with Christ, 2001; Convoluted Universe Book Two, 2005, rev. ed. 2007; Convoluted Universe Book Three, 2008; Five Lives Remembered, 2009. Contributor to journals and periodicals. **Address:** Ozark Mountain Publishing Inc., PO Box 754, Huntsville, AR 72740, U.S.A. **Online address:** decannon@msn.com

CANNON, Eileen E(mily). Also writes as Emily Toll, Taffy Cannon. American (born United States), b. 1948. **Genres:** Mystery/Crime/Suspense, Plays/Screenplays, Young Adult Fiction, Children's Fiction, Novels, Horror, Criminology/True Crime, Travel/Exploration, Travel/Exploration. **Career:** Writer. **Publications:** (Co-ed.) How Gorious is Youth, 1968; The Summer of My Content, 1976; Putting Life in Your Life Story, 1977; (with E.J. Pinegar) The Mighty Change, 1977; The Seasoning, 1981; Life, One to a Customer, 1981; The Girl's Book, 1982; Baptized and Confirmed: Your Lifeline to Heaven, 1986; Adversity, 1987; Bedtime Stories for Grownups, 1988; Merry, Merry Christmases, 1988; Be a Bell Ringer, 1989; Boy of the Land, Man of the Lord, 1989; Turning Twelve or More: Living by the Articles of Faith, 1990; Elaine Cannon's As a Woman Thinketh, 1990; Not Just Ordinary Young Men & Young Women, 1991; (with E.J. Pinegar) Called to Serve Him: Preparing Missionaries to Bring People to Christ, 1991; (comp.) Notable Quotables: From Women to Women, 1992; Mothering, 1993; Beyond Baptism: A Guide for New Converts, 1994; Sunshine, 1994; Count Your Many Blessings, 1995; The Truth about Angels, 1996; Mississippi Treasure Hunt, 1996; Mary's Child, 1997; (with S.A. Teichert) Minerva!: The Story of an Artist with a Mission, 1997; Women Testify of Jesus Christ, 1998; Christmas Crèche, 1998; The Little Book of Big Ideas about Hope, 2000; Adversity, 2000; Gatherings: Favorite Writings, 2000; The Little Book of Big Ideas about Joy, 2000; The Little Book of Big Ideas about Love, 2001; Five-Star Recipes from Well-Known Latter-Day Saints, 2002. AS TAFFY CANNON: Convictions: A Novel of the Sixties, 1985; A Pocketful of Karma, 1993; Tangled Roots, 1995; Class Reunions are Murder, 1996; Guns and Roses: An Irish Eyes Travel Mystery Set in Colonial Williamsburg, 2000; (with R. Rothenberg) The Tumbleweed Murders: A Claire Sharples Botanical Mystery, 2001; Open Season on Lawyers: A Novel of Suspense, 2002; Paradise Lost: A Novel of Suspense, 2005; Blood Matters: A Roxanne Prescott Mystery, 2007. AS EMILY TOLL: Murder Will Travel, 2002; Murder Pans Out, 2003; Fall Into Death, 2004; Keys to Death, 2005. **Address:** Jane Chelius Literary Agency Inc., 548 2nd St., Brooklyn, NY 11215, U.S.A. **Online address:** feedback@taffycannon.com

CANNON, Frank. *See* **MAYHAR, Ardath (Hurst).**

CANNON, Garland. American (born United States), b. 1924. **Genres:** Language/Linguistics, Bibliography, Biography, History, Autobiography/Memoirs. **Career:** University of Hawaii, instructor, 1949-52; University of Texas, instructor, 1952-54; University of Michigan, instructor, 1954-55; University of California, assistant professor of speech, 1955-56; American University Language Center, academic director, 1956-57; University of Florida, assistant professor, 1957-58; Columbia University, Teachers College, assistant professor, 1959-62, English Language Program in Afghanistan, director, 1960-62; Northeastern Illinois State College (now Northeastern Illinois University), associate professor, 1962-63; Queens College of the City University of New York, associate professor of English, 1963-66; Texas A&M University, associate professor, 1966-68, professor of English, 1968-95, founder and director of linguistics program, 1970-94, professor emeritus of English, 1995-. Writer. **Publications:** Sir William Jones, Orientalist: A Anotated Bibliography, 1952; Oriental Jones: A Biography of Sir William Jones, 1746-1794, 1964; A History of the English Language, 1972; Teacher's Manual to a History of the English Language, 1972; An Integrated Transformational Grammar of English Language, 1978; Sir William Jones: A Bibliography of Primary and Secondary Sources, 1979; Historical Change and English Word-Formation: Recent Vocabulary, 1987; The Life and Mind of Oriental Jones: Sir William Jones, The Father of Modern Linguistics, 1990; (with J.A. Pfeffer) German Loanwords in English: An Historical Dictionary, 1994; Arabic Loanwords in English: An Historical Dictionary, 1994; Arabic Contributions to the English Language: An Historical Dictionary, 1994; Japanese Contributions to the English Language: An Historical Dictionary, 1996; (with A.S. Kaye) The Persian Contributions to the English Language: An Historical Dictionary, 2001. EDITOR: The Letters of Sir William Jones, 2 vols., 1970; (co-author and contrib.) Language and Communication, 1980; (intro.) The Collected Works of Sir William Jones, 13 vols., 1993; (with K. Brine) Objects of Enquiry: The Life, Contributions, and Influences of Sir William Jones, 1746-1794, 1995. **Address:** Department of English, Texas A&M University, 227 Blocker Bldg., PO Box 4227, College Station, TX 77843-4227, U.S.A.

CANNON, Michael. Scottish/Australian (born Australia), b. 1929. **Genres:** Area Studies, Novels. **Career:** Historical Records of Victoria, chief editor, 1981-91; Strathclyde University, contracts manager. **Publications:** The Land Boomers, 1966, 2nd ed. as Land Boom and Bust, 1972; Who's Master? Who's Man?, 1971, 2nd ed., 1982; Australia in the Victorian Age, 1971, 2nd ed., 1982; Life in the Country, 1973; An Australian Camera, 1851-1914, 1973; Lola Montes, 1973; Life in the Cities, 1975; That Damned Democrat: John Norton, An Australian Populist, 1858-1916, 1981; The Long Last Summer: Australia's Upper Class Before the Great War, 1985; The Exploration of Australia, 1987; Who Killed the Koories?, 1990; Melbourne After the Gold Rush, 1993; The Woman as Murderer: Five Who Paid with Their Lives, 1994; The Borough, 1995; Perilous Voyages to the New Land, 1995; A Conspiracy of Hope, 1996; The Human Face of the Great Depression, 1997; That Disreputable Firm: The Inside Story of Slater & Gordon, 1998; (with M. Pace and L. Wingard) Selling Machine, 2006; Lachlan's War, 2006. EDITOR: (intro.) The Vagabond Papers, 1969, 2nd ed., 1983; (intro.) Our Beautiful Homes, N.S.W., 1977; (intro.) Vagabond Country: Australian Bush and Town Life in the Victorian Age, 1981; (intro.) The Victorian Gold Fields, 1852-53: An Original Album, 1982; (ed.) The Aborigines of Port Phillip, 1835-1839, 1982; (ed.) Aborigines and Protectors, 1838-1839, 1983; (with I. MacFarlane) The Early Development of Melbourne, 1984; (intro.) Forty Years in the Wilderness, 1990; (with I. MacFarlane) The Crown, the Land and the Squatter, 1835-1840, 1991; (intro.) Hold Page One: Memoirs of Monty Grover, 1993; (ed. with P. Jones) Historical Records of Victoria: Beginnings of Permanent Government; (with I. MacFarlane) Communications, Trade, and Transport, 2002.

Address: University of Strathclyde, 16 Richmond St., Glasgow, G1 1XQ, Scotland. **Online address:** michael.cannon@strath.ac.uk

CANNON, Michael F. American (born United States) **Genres:** How-to Books, Medicine/Health, Adult Non-fiction. **Career:** U.S. Senate Republican Policy Committee, domestic policy analyst; Cato Institute, director of health policy studies; Kaiser Health News, columnist. **Publications:** (With M.D. Tanner) Healthy Competition: What's Holding Back Health Care and How to Free It, 2005. Contributor to periodicals. **Address:** Cato Institute, 1000 Massachusetts Ave. NW, Washington, DC 20001-5403, U.S.A. **Online address:** mcannon@cato.org

CANNON, Taffy. *See* **CANNON, Eileen E(mily).**

CANO, Daniel. American (born United States), b. 1947?. **Genres:** Novels, History. **Career:** University of California-San Francisco, staff; California State University, staff; University of California-Davis, staff; University of California-San Diego, visiting lecturer; Santa Monica College, associate professor of English, professor of English. Writer. **Publications:** Pepe Ríos, 1991; Shifting Loyalties (novel), 1995; (contrib.) Unnatural Disasters: Recent Writings from the Golden State, 1996; Death and the American Dream, 2009. Contributor to periodicals. **Address:** Department of English, Santa Monica College, Drescher Hall, 310 Office B, 1900 Pico Blvd., Santa Monica, CA 90405, U.S.A. **Online address:** dcano@smc.edu

CANOVAN, Margaret Evelyn Leslie. British (born England), b. 1939. **Genres:** Politics/Government, Philosophy. **Career:** University of Lancaster, lecturer in politics, 1965-71; Lancaster University, Department of Politics, professor; Keele University, lecturer, 1971-, professor of political thought, 1974-2002, professor emeritus, 2002-. Writer. **Publications:** The Political Thought of Hannah Arendt, 1974, rev. ed., 1977; G.K. Chesterton: Radical Populist, 1977; Populism, 1981; Hannah Arendt: A Reinterpretation of Her Political Thought, 1992; Nationhood and Political Theory, 1996; The People, 2005. Contributor to journals. **Address:** School of Politics, International Relations and Philosophy, University of Keele, Keele, ST ST5 5BG, England.

CANTER, Mark. American (born United States), b. 1952. **Genres:** Novels. **Career:** Men's Health, editor; Blue Heron Zen Center, founder; Cloud Forest Zen Center, founder; Feature writer. **Publications:** Ember From the Sun (novel), 1996. Contributor to periodicals. **Address:** 5012 Crestwood Ct., Tallahassee, FL 32311-8756, U.S.A.

CANTON, Katia. Brazilian (born Brazil), b. 1962. **Genres:** Literary Criticism And History, Art/Art History. **Career:** University of Sao Paulo, curator, professor of contemporary art history; Art in America, journalist; Artforum, journalist; jornal da Tarde, journalist; vogue Magazine, journalist; Elle magazine, journalist; O Estado de S. Paulo, journalist; Museum of Contemporary Art, curator; Museum of Modern Art, staff. Writer. **Publications:** The Fairy Tale Revisited: A Survey of the Evolution of the Tales, from Classical Literary Interpretations to Innovative Contemporary Dance Theatre Productions, 1994; Maria Martins: Mistério Das Formas, 1997; Novíssima Arte Brasileira: Um Guia De Tendeencias, 2001; Salas Da Memória, 2002; Alex Flemming, Uma Poética, 2002; Pele, Alma: Centro Cultural Banco do Brasil, São Paulo, 25 de janeiro a 16 demarço de 2003, trans. as Skin, Soul: January 25th through March 16th, 2003, 2003; Natureza-morta, 2003, trans. as Still Life, 2004; Moda: Uma História Para Crianças, 2004; Brincadeiras, 2006; (with F. Pessoa) Sentidos e arte contemporânea, 2007; (with A. Farias) Luiz Hermano, 2008; (with A. Farias) Nair Kremer, 2009. **Address:** Universidade de Sao Paulo, Musem de Arte Contemporanian, Cidade Universitaria, Rua da Reitoria 160, Sao Paulo, SP 05508-900, Brazil. **Online address:** katiacanton@uol.com.br

CANTRELL, Lisa W. American (born United States), b. 1945?. **Genres:** Horror, Mystery/Crime/Suspense, Young Adult Fiction, Science Fiction/Fantasy. **Career:** Novelist. **Publications:** The Manse, 1987; The Ridge, 1989; Torments, 1990; Boneman, 1992. Works appears in anthologies. **Address:** Tor Books, 175 5th Ave., 14th Fl., New York, NY 10010, U.S.A.

CANTU, Norma Elia. American (born United States), b. 1947. **Genres:** Novels, Poetry, Women's Studies And Issues, Documentaries/Reportage, Education, Autobiography/Memoirs. **Career:** Texas A&M International University, professor of English, 1980-2000; Georgetown University, School for Continuing Education, visiting professor, 1994-95; University of Texas, professor of English and U.S. Latino Studies, 2000-; University of Nebraska, instructor and teaching assistant. Writer. **Publications:** Canícula: Snapshots of a Girlhood en la Frontera, 1995; Telling to Live: Latina Feminist Testimonios, 2001; Canícula: Imágenes de una Niñez Fronteriza, 2001; (ed. with O. Nájera-Ramírez) Chicana Traditions: Continuity and Change, 2002; (ed.) Paths to Discovery: Autobiographies from Chicanas with Careers in Science, Mathematics, and Engineering, 2008; (ed. with O. Nájera-Ramírez and B.M. Romero) Dancing Across Borders: Danzas y Bailes Mexicanos, 2009; (ed. with M. Fránquiz) Inside the Latino Experience: A Latino Studies Reader, 2010; (ed.) La Mesa de Moctezuma: Rolando Briseño's Chicano and Mexican Tablescapes, 2010. Contributor of articles to books and periodicals. **Address:** Department of English, University of Texas, 1 UTSA Cir., San Antonio, TX 78249, U.S.A. **Online address:** norma.cantu@utsa.edu

CAN XUE *See* **Deng Xiao hua.**

CAO, Lan. American/Vietnamese (born Vietnam), b. 1961. **Genres:** Novels, Law, International Relations/Current Affairs, History. **Career:** Paul, Weiss, Rifkind, Wharton and Garrison (law firm), Litigation Department, associate, 1987-88, 1990-91, Corporate Law Department, associate, 1992-93; U.S. District Court (Southern District), Judge Constance Motley, law clerk, 1988-89; Brooklyn Law School, assistant professor, 1993-, professor, 1994-2000; William & Mary Law School, Cabell professor, 2002-03, Boyd fellow, professor. **Publications:** (With H. Novas) Everything You Need to Know about Asian American History, 1996; Monkey Bridge (novel), 1997. Contributor to journals. **Address:** William & Mary Law School, Rm. 261, PO Box 8795, Williamsburg, VA 23187-8795, U.S.A. **Online address:** lxcaox@wm.edu

CAPACCHIONE, Lucia. American (born United States) **Genres:** Medicine/Health, Psychology, Adult Non-fiction, inspirational/Motivational Literature, Self Help, Children's Fiction. **Career:** Catholic Archdiocese of Los Angeles, child development supervisor, 1960-; Creative Journal Expressive Arts Training Program, director. Writer. **Publications:** The Creative Journal: The Art of Finding Yourself, 1979, 2nd ed., 2002; (with R. Young and L. Young) Reincarnation Handbook, 1980; The Power of Your Other Hand: A Course in Channeling the Inner Wisdom of the Right Brain, 1988; The Creative Journal for Children: A Guide for Parents, Teachers and Counselors, 1989; The Well-Being Journal: Drawing upon Your Inner Power to Heal Yourself, 1989; The Picture of Health: Healing Your Life through Art, 1990; Recovery of Your Inner Child, 1991; The Creative Journal for Teens, 1992, 2nd ed. as The Creative Journal for Teens: Making Friends with Yourself, 2002; (with S. Bardsley) Creating a Joyful Birth Experience, 1994; (with P. Van Pelt) Putting Your Talent to Work: Identifying, Cultivating and Marketing Your Natural Talents, 1996; The Creative Journal for Parents: An Inner Guide to Parenthood: Preparation, Pregnancy, Birth, Adoption and Parenting, 2000; Visioning: Ten Steps to Designing the Life of Your Dreams, 2000; Living with Feeling: The Art of Emotional Expression, 2001; The Art of Emotional Healing, 2006. **Address:** PO Box 1355, Cambria, CA 93428, U.S.A. **Online address:** lucia@luciac.com

CAPECI, Anne. American (born United States) **Genres:** Children's Fiction, Young Adult Fiction, Animals/Pets, Natural History. **Career:** Writer. **Publications:** Meet Jacqueline Kennedy Onassis, 1995; The Maltese Dog, 1998; Forgotten Heroes, 1998; Key to the Golden Dog, 1998; The Halloween Joker, 1998; The Case of the Cyber-hacker, 1999; The Giant Germ, 2000; (with C. Jablonski and B. Strickland) The Wishbone Halloween Adventure, 2000; Feed Me!, 2001; Insect Invaders, 2001; Forest Fire, 2002; Dee Dee's Amazing Bones, 2002; Watch Out!: The Daring Disasters of Ethan Flask and Professor von Offel, 2002; Mixed-up Magnetism, 2002; Now You See It...: The Incredible Illusions of Ethan Flask and Professor von Offel, 2002; Electric Storm, 2002; Flash Flood, 2003; Food Chain Frenzy, 2003; Danger! Dynamite!, 2003; What's the Matter with Dee Dee?, 2003; Little Lab or Horrors, 2003; Ghost Train, 2004; Daredevils, 2004; Missing!, 2005. MAGIC SCHOOL BUS SERIES: FlashFlood: To The Rescue, 1949; Has a Heart, 2005; Rides the Wind, 2006; Builds the Statue of Liberty, 2007; Bus Gets Recycled, 2007; Flies With The Dinosaurs, 2008. **Address:** c/o Author Mail, Peachtree Publishers Ltd., 1700 Chattahoochee Ave., Atlanta, GA 30318-2112, U.S.A.

CAPEK, Michael. American (born United States), b. 1947. **Genres:** Young Adult Fiction, Plays/Screenplays, Art/Art History, Children's Non-fiction, History. **Career:** Walton-Verona High School, teacher of English, 1969-96, retired, 1996. Writer, 1996-. **Publications:** Artistic Trickery: The Trompe L'Oeil Tradition, 1995; Murals: Cave, Cathedral, to Street, 1996; A Ticket to Jamaica, 1999; Jamaica, 1999; Globetrotter's Club: Jamaica, 1999; A Personal Tour of a Shaker Village, 2001; How Rivers Shape the Earth, 2001; Old Mr. Muddy, 2001; The Spider is Watching!, 2001; Avalanche!, 2001; Lively Stones: A Narrative History of Belleview Baptist Church, 1803-2003, 2002; Putting Jesus First, Yesterday, Today & Tomorrow, 2003; Church at the Crossroads: The Story of Florence Baptist Church, 1855-2005, 2005; Emperor Qin's Terra Cotta Army, 2008; Easter Island, 2009. Contributor to periodicals. **Address:** 5965 Tipp Dr., Taylor Mill, KY 41015, U.S.A. **Online address:** mcapek@goodnews.net

CAPITAN, William H(arry). American (born United States), b. 1933. **Genres:** Art/Art History, Philosophy, Theology/Religion, Ethics, History. **Career:** University of Minnesota, instructor in philosophy, 1959-60; University of Maryland, instructor in philosophy, 1960-62; Oberlin College, Department of Philosophy, assistant professor, 1962-65, associate professor of philosophy, 1965-70, chairman, 1968-70; State University of New York, visiting professor, 1967-; Saginaw Valley College, director of fine arts, 1970-72, vice-president of academic affairs, 1972-74, acting president, 1974-79; West Virginia Wesleyan College, vice-president for academic affairs and dean, 1975-; Georgia Southwestern State University, president, 1979-96; University of Georgia, president emeritus, adjunct professor of philosophy; World Publishing Co., editorial consultant. **Publications:** Introduction to The Philosophy of Religion (textbook), 1972; Speak for Yourself, 1989; The Ethical Navigator, 2000. EDITOR: (with D.D. Merrill) Metaphysics and Explanation, 1966; (with D.D. Merrill) Art, Religion and Mind, 1967. Works appear in anthologies. **Address:** Educational Resources Corp., 128 E 74th St., New York, NY 10021, U.S.A.

CAPLAN, Arthur L(eonard). American (born United States), b. 1950. **Genres:** Humanities, Medicine/Health, Administration/Management. **Career:** Columbia University, associate for social medicine, 1978-81, School of Public Health, instructor, 1977-78, Hastings Center, associate for the humanities, 1976-85, associate director, 1985-87; City University of New York, adjunct associate professor, 1981-; University of Pittsburgh, visiting associate professor, 1986; University of Minnesota, Center for Biomedical Ethics, professor of philosophy, professor of surgery, director, 1987-94; University of Pennsylvania, Center for Bioethics, trustee professor of bioethics, director, Department of Medical Ethics, chairman, 1994-, Emanuel and Robert Hart professor of bioethics, Sydney D Caplan professor, Emmanuel and Robert Hart director; National Endowment for the Humanities, consultant; National Science Foundation, consultant; Exxon Foundation, consultant. Writer. **Publications:** (With B. Rosen) Ethics in the Undergraduate Curriculum, 1980; Beyond Baby M, 1990; Everyday Ethics: Resolving Dilemmas in Nursing Home Life, 1990; If I Were a Rich Man Could I Buy a Pancreas?: And Other Essays on Medical Ethics, 1992; Moral Matters: Ethical Issues in Medicine and the Life Sciences, 1995; Due Consideration: Controversy in an Age of Medical Miracles, 1998; Am I My Brother's Keeper?, 1998; Finding Common Ground, 2001; Smart Mice, Not-So-Smart People: An Interesting and Amusing Guide to Bioethics, 2007; (intro. and contrib. with M.D. West and R.A. Freitas, Jr.) Timeship: The Architecture of Immortality, 2009; (with D.M. Bartels and B.S. LeRoy) Genetic Counseling: Ethical Challenges and Consequences, 2010. EDITOR: The Sociobiology Debate: Readings on Ethical and Scientific Issues, 1978; (with J.J. McCartney and H.T. Engelhardt, Jr.) Concepts of Health and Disease: Interdisciplinary Perspectives, 1980; (with D. Callahan) Ethics in Hard Times, 1981; (with N. Daniels and R. Bayer) In Search of Equity, 1983; (with B. Jennings) Darwin, Marx and Freud: Their Influence on Moral Theory, 1983; (with D. Callahan and B. Jennings) Applying the Humanities, 1985; (with T.H. Murray) Which Babies Shall Live?: Humanistic Dimensions of the Care of Imperiled Newborns, 1985; (with H.T. Engelhardt. Jr.) Scientific Controversies: Case Studies in the Resolution and Closure of Disputes in Science and Technology, 1987; (with R.A. Kane) Resolving Dilemmas in Nursing Home Life, 1989; (with R.H. Blank and J.C. Merrick) Compelled Compassion: Government Intervention in the Treatment of Critically Ill Newborns, 1992; When Medicine Went Mad: Bioethics and the Holocaust, 1992; (with D.M. Bartels and B.S. LeRoy) Prescribing Our Future, 1993; (with R.A. Kane) Ethical Conflicts in the Management of Home Care: The Case Manager's Dilemma, 1993; (with D.H. Coelho) The Ethics of Organ Transplants: The Current Debate, 1999; (with D. Magnus and G. McGee) Who Owns Life?, 2002; (with L. Snyder) Assisted Suicide: Finding Common Ground, 2002; (with G. McGhee) Human Cloning Debate, 2004; (with James J. McCartney, Dominic A. Sisti) Health, Disease and Illness: Concepts in Medicine, 2004; (with J.J. McCartney and D.A. Sisti) Case of Terri Schiavo: Ethics at the End of Life, 2006; Smart Mice Not So Smart People, 2006; (with V. Ravitsky and A. Fiester) Penn Center Guide to Bioethics, 2009. Contributor to journals. **Address:** Center for Bioethics, University of Pennsylvania Medical Ctr., 3401 Market St., Ste. 320, Philadelphia, PA 19104-3308, U.S.A. **Online address:** caplan@mail.med.upenn.edu

CAPLAN, Bryan D. (Bryan Douglas Caplan). American (born United States), b. 1971. **Genres:** Economics. **Career:** George Mason University, assistant professor, 1997-2003, associate professor of economics, 2003-. Writer. **Publications:** The Myth of the Rational Voter: Why Democracies Choose Bad Policies, 2007. Contributor to periodicals. **Address:** Department of Economics, Center for Study of Public Choice, George Mason University, Fairfax, VA 22030, U.S.A. **Online address:** bcaplan@gmu.edu

CAPLAN, Bryan Douglas. *See* **CAPLAN, Bryan D.**

CAPLAN, Lincoln. American (born United States), b. 1950. **Genres:** Law, Adult Non-fiction. **Career:** New Republic, staff writer, 1975-76; Connecticut Supreme Court, law clerk, 1976-77; Boston Consulting Group, management consultant, 1977-79; United States Department of Energy, assistant, 1979-80; New Yorker, contributor, 1980-88, staff writer, 1980-92; Newsweek, contributing editor, 1993-95; U.S. News & World Report, editor of special projects, 1996-; Yale Law School, Knight senior journalist and lecturer in law and English, 1998-; Legal Affairs, editor and president, 2000-. **Publications:** NON-FICTION: The Insanity Defense and the Trial of John W. Hinckley, Jr., 1984; The Tenth Justice: The Solicitor General and the Rule of Law, 1987; An Open Adoption, 1990; Skadden: Power, Money, and the Rise of a Legal Empire, 1993; Up against the Law: Affirmative Action and the Supreme Court, 1997. Contributor to books and periodicals. **Address:** Legal Affairs, 254 Elm St., New Haven, CT 06511, U.S.A.

CAPLAN, Mariana. American (born United States), b. 1969. **Genres:** Human Relations/Parenting, Self Help, Theology/Religion. **Career:** Reproductive health counselor, 1991-93; Battered Women's Shelter, bilingual groups counselor, 1992-93; Center for World Spirituality, co-founder; California Institute of Integral Studies, adjunct professor; Naropa University, adjunct professor. Writer. **Publications:** When Sons and Daughters Choose Alternative Lifestyles, 1996; When Holidays Are Hell...!: A Guide to Surviving Family Gatherings, 1997; Untouched: The Need for Genuine Affection in an Impersonal World, 1998, rev. ed. as To Touch Is to Live: The Need for Genuine Affection in an Impersonal World, 2002; Half Way up the Mountain: The Error of Premature Claims to Enlightenment, 1999; The Way of Failure: Winning through Losing, 2001; Do You Need a Guru?: Understanding the Student-Teacher Relationship in an Era of False Prophets, 2002; Eyes Wide Open: Cultivating Discernment on the Spiritual Path, 2009; Guru Question: The Perils and Rewards of Choosing A Spiritual Teacher, 2011. **Address:** Narpo University, 2130 Arapahoe Ave., Boulder, CO 80302, U.S.A. **Online address:** mariana@realspirituality.com

CAPLAN, Suzanne H. American (born United States), b. 1943. **Genres:** Business/Trade/Industry, Economics. **Career:** PGM Group, principal, 1998-2001; Crossroads Associates, partner, 2001. Writer. **Publications:** Saving Your Business: How to Survive Chapter 11 Bankruptcy and Successfully Reorganize Your Company, 1992; A Piece of the Action: How Women and Minorities Can Launch Their Own Successful Business, 1994; Turn Your Business Around, 1994; (with T.M. Nunnally) Small Business Insiders Guide to Bankers, 1997; (with M.M. Cronin) Everyone Remembers the Elephant in the Pink Tutu, 1998; High Profit Financial Management for Your Small Business, 1999; Streetwise Finance and Accounting, 2000; Streetwise Small Business Success Kit, 2001; Second Wind: Turnaround Strategies for Business Revival, 2003; (with W. Timmerson) Building Big Profits in Real Estate: A Guide for the New Investor, 2004; Streetwise Finance & Accounting for Entrepreneurs, 2006; Streetwise Credit and Collections: Maximize Your Collections Process to Improve Profitability, 2007; Start Your Own Business and Hire Yourself: Insider Tips for Successful Self-employment in Any Economy, 2010. **Address:** c/o Laurie Harper, Sebastion Literary Agency, 172 E 6th St., St. Paul, PA 55101, U.S.A. **Online address:** suzcaplan@aol.com

CAPOBIANCO, Michael. American (born United States), b. 1950. **Genres:** Science Fiction/Fantasy, Astronomy, Young Adult Fiction, Air/Space Topics. **Career:** Science Fiction and Fantasy Writers of America Inc., president, 1996-98, 2007-08. Writer. **Publications:** SCIENCE FICTION: Burster, 1990; (with W. Barton) Iris, 1990; (with W. Barton) Fellow Traveler: Sputnik Mira, 1991; (with W. Barton) Alpha Centauri, 1997; (with W. Barton) White Light,

1998. Contributor of articles to periodicals. **Address:** PO Box 827, Bryantown, MD 20617, U.S.A. **Online address:** michaelcapo@verizon.net

CAPON, Robert Farrar. American/South African (born South Africa), b. 1925. **Genres:** Novels, Human Relations/Parenting, Theology/Religion, Film, Law, Humor/Satire. **Career:** Ordained episcopal priest, 1949; All Soul's Church, vicar, 1949-58; Christ Church, vicar, 1949-77; George Mercer Jr. Memorial School of Theology, dean, professor of dogmatic theology, instructor in Greek, 1957-77. Writer. **Publications:** Bed and Board: Plain Talk about Marriage, 1965; An Offering of Uncles: The Priesthood of Adam and the Shape of the World, 1967; The Supper of the Lamb: A Culinary Reflection, 1969, 2nd ed., 1989 in UK as Angels Must Eat: A Culinary Entertainment, 1969; The Third Peacock: The Goodness of God and the Badness of the World, 1971, rev. ed. as The Third Peacock: The Problem of God and Evil, 1986; Hunting the Divine Fox: Images and Mystery in Christian Faith, 1974; Exit 36: A Fictional Chronicle, 1975; Food for Thought: Resurrecting the Art of Eating, 1978; Supper of the Lamb: A Culinary Reflection, 1979; Party Spirit: Some Entertaining Principles, 1979; A Second Day: Reflections on Remarriage, 1980; Between Noon and Three: A Parable of Romance, Law, and the Outrage of Grace (novel), 1982; Capon on Cooking, 1983; The Youngest Day: Shelter Island's Seasons in the Light of Grace, 1983; The Parables of the Kingdom, 1985; Hunting the Divine Fox: An Introduction to the Language of Theology, 1985; The Parables of Grace, 1988; The Parables of Judgment, 1989; Health, Money, and Love-and Why We Don't Enjoy Them, 1990; The Man Who Met God in a Bar: The Gospel According to Marvin (novel), 1990; The Mystery of Christ, 1993; The Romance of the Word: One Man's Love Affair with Theology, 1995; The Astonished Heart: Reclaiming the Good News from the Lost-and-Found of Church History, 1996; Between Noon and Three: Romance, Law, and the Outrage of Grace, 1997; The Foolishness of Preaching: Proclaiming the Gospel againt Wisdom of the World, 1998; The Fingerprints of God: Tracking the Divine Suspect through a History of Images, 2000; Kingdom, Grace, Judgment: Paradox, Outrage, and Vindication in the Parables of Jesus, 2002; Genesis: The Movie, 2003; Light Theology & Heavy Cream: The Culinary Adventures of Pietro & Madeleine, 2004. Contributor of articles to periodicals. **Address:** Publicity Department, Eerdmans Publishing Co., 2140 Oak Industrial Dr. NE, Grand Rapids, MI 49505-6014, U.S.A.

CAPONIGRO, Jeffrey R. American (born United States), b. 1957. **Genres:** Administration/Management, Human Relations/Parenting, Business/Trade/Industry, Economics. **Career:** Casey Communications Management Inc., president and chief executive officer, 1984-95; Caponigro Public Relations Inc., founder, president and chief executive officer, 1995-, vice chair, 2005-. Writer. **Publications:** The Crisis Counselor: The Executive's Guide to Avoiding, Managing, and Thriving on Crises That Occur in All Businesses, 1998; The Crisis Counselor: A Step-by-Step Guide to Managing a Business Crisis, 2000; On Your Own: Advice for Young Adults Leaving Home for the First Time, 2002. Works appear in anthologies. **Address:** Caponigro Public Relations Inc., 24725 W. 12 Mile Rd., Ste. 120, Southfield, MI 48075, U.S.A. **Online address:** jcap@caponigro.com

CAPOTORTO, Carl. American (born United States), b. 1959. **Genres:** Autobiography/Memoirs. **Career:** Edward F. Albee Foundation, foundation secretary, 1984-89; Manhattan Theatre Club, teaching artist. Actor, playwright and screenwriter. **Publications:** Twisted Head: An Italian-American Memoir, 2008. **Address:** New York, NY , U.S.A. **Online address:** carl@twistedhead.com

CAPOUYA, John. American (born United States), b. 1956?. **Genres:** Autobiography/Memoirs, Biography, Medicine/Health, Humor/Satire. **Career:** Sport Magazine, journalist; Newsweek, editor; New York Times, editor; SmartMoney Magazine, editor; New York Newsday, editor; New York University, faculty; University of Tampa, professor of journalism, 2008-. **Publications:** Real Men Do Yoga: 21 Star Athletes Reveal Their Secrets for Strength, Flexibility, and Peak Performance, 2003; Gorgeous George: The Outrageous Bad-Boy Wrestler Who Created American Pop Culture, 2008. Contributor to periodicals. **Address:** University of Tampa, 401 W. Kennedy Blvd., Tampa, FL 33606, U.S.A. **Online address:** johnc@realmendoyoga.com

CAPP, Bernard (Stuart). (B. S. Capp). British (born England), b. 1943. **Genres:** History, Literary Criticism And History, Women's Studies And Issues, Biography. **Career:** University of Warwick, Department of History, assistant lecturer, 1968-70, lecturer, 1970-80, senior lecturer in history, 1980-90, reader in history, 1990-94, chairman, 1992-95, professor of history, 1994-2010, professor emeritus, 2010-; New DNB (17th century naval/maritime), associate editor, 1996-. Writer. **Publications:** (Contrib. as B.S. Capp) Puritans, the Millennium and the Future of Israel: Puritan Eschatology, 1600 to 1660: A Collection of Essays, 1970; (as B.S. Capp) The Fifth Monarchy Men: A Study in Seventeenth-Century English Millenarianism, 1972; English Almanacs, 1500-1800: Astrology and the Popular Press in UK as Astrology and the Popular Press: English Almanacs, 1500-1800, 1979; Cromwell's Navy: The Fleet and the English Revolution, 1648-1660, 1989; The World of John Taylor, the Water-poet, 1578-1653, 1994; When Gossips Meet: Women, Family, and Neighbourhood in Early Modern England, 2003; England's Culture Wars: Puritan Reformation and its Enemies in the Interregnum, 1649-1660, 2012. **Address:** Department of History, University of Warwick, Rm. 318, Humanities Bldg., University Rd., Coventry, WW CV4 7AL, England. **Online address:** b.s.capp@warwick.ac.uk

CAPP, B. S. *See* **CAPP, Bernard (Stuart).**

CAPPELLANI, Ottavio. Italian (born Italy), b. 1969. **Genres:** Novels. **Career:** Journalist, songwriter and musician. **Publications:** Chi ha incastrato Lou Sciortino?: Una storia vintage, 2009. Contributor to newspapers. **Address:** The Susijn Agency Ltd., 64 Great Titchfield St., 3rd Fl., London, GL W1W 7QH, England.

CAPPELLI, Peter. American (born United States), b. 1956. **Genres:** Business/Trade/Industry. **Career:** Massachusetts Institute of Technology, Sloan School of Management, research associate, 1982; University of Illinois, Institute of Labor and Industrial Relations, assistant professor, 1983; University of Pennsylvania, professor of management, 1985-, George W. Taylor professor of management, 1999-; U.S. Secretary of Labor's Commission, staff, 1988-90; Haas School of Business, acting associate professor, 1989; U.S. Department of Education's National Center, co-director, 1990-; Universitia Luigi Bocconi, visiting professor, 1993; The Wharton School, Department of Management, chair, 1995-98, Center for Human Resources, director, 1998-; Stanford Graduate School of Education, board director, 1996-; National Bureau of Economic Research, research associate, 2000-; National Academy of Human Resources, fellow, 2003; Government of Bahrain, senior advisor for employment policy, 2003-04; Academy of Management Executive, editor, 2005-08. **Publications:** (Ed.) Training and Development in Public and Private Policy, 1994; (ed.) Airline Labor Relations in the Global Era: The New Frontier, 1995; Change at Work: Trends That Are Transforming the Business of Business, 1997; The New Deal at Work: Managing the Market Driven Workforce, 1999; (ed.) Employment Practices and Business Strategy, 1999; Talent on Demand: Managing Talent in an Age of Uncertainty, 2008; Employment Relationships: New Models of White-Collar Work, 2008; (with B. Novelli) Managing the Older Worker: How to Prepare for the new Organizational Order, 2010; The India Way: How India's Top Business Leaders are Revolutionizing Management, 2010. **Address:** Department of Managment, Wharton School, University of Pennsylvania, 2205 Steinberg Hall-Dietrich Hall, 3620 Locust Walk, Philadelphia, PA 19104-6370, U.S.A. **Online address:** cappelli@wharton.upenn.edu

CAPPELLO, Mary C. American (born United States), b. 1960?. **Genres:** Novels, Biography, Autobiography/Memoirs, Adult Non-fiction. **Career:** University of Rochester, faculty; University of Rhode Island, associate professor of English, professor of English, affiliated professor of women's studies; Gorky Literary Institute, Fulbright lecturer. Writer. **Publications:** Night Bloom: A Memoir, 1998; Awkward: A Detour, 2007; Called Back: My Reply to Cancer, My Return to Life, 2009; Swallow: Foreign Bodies, Their Ingestion, Aspiration and Extraction in the Age of Chevalier Jackson, 2011. FORTHCOMING: My Commie Sweetheart: Scenes from a Queer Friendship; The Awkward Moment. **Address:** Department of English, University of Rhode Island, 308A Swan Hall, 60 Upper College Rd., Kingston, RI 02881, U.S.A. **Online address:** mcapp@uri.edu

CAPRIOLO, Paola. Italian (born Italy), b. 1962. **Genres:** Novels, Travel/Exploration, Literary Criticism And History. **Career:** Writer. **Publications:** La grande Eulalia, 1988, 2nd ed., 1990; Il nocchiero, 1989; La ragazza dalla stella d'oro e altri racconti, 1991; Il doppio regno, 1991, 2nd ed., 1995; Vissi d'amore, 1992; Il premio Berto: 1988-1993, 1994; La spettatrice, 1995; Un uomo di carattere, 1996; Floria Tosca, 1997; Con i miei mille occhi, 1997; Barbara, 1998; Il sogno dell'agnello, 1999; The Woman Watching, 1999; A

Man of Character, 2000; Una di loro, 2001; Unaluce nerissima: romanzo, 2005; Rilke: biografia di uno sguardo, 2006; Ancilla, 2008; Il pianista muto, 2009. **Address:** c/o Author Mail, Bompiani, Libreria Ambrosiana, 20122, Italy.

CAPSHEW, James H. American (born United States), b. 1954. **Genres:** History, Psychology, Design, Architecture. **Career:** University of Maryland, research associate in history, 1986-89; Indiana University, Department of History and Philosophy of Science, assistant professor, 1990-96, associate professor, 1996-, director of graduate studies, 1998-2005, 2009-10, School of Education, adjunct associate professor, American Studies Program, adjunct associate professor, Department of History, adjunct associate professor; History of Psychology, editor, 2006-09. **Publications:** (Ed. with E. Hearst) Psychology at Indiana University: A Centennial Review and Compendium, 1988; Psychologists on the March: Science, Practice, and Professional Identity in America, 1929-1969, 1999; (ed. with P.C. Bantin) The Wells Archive: Exploring the World of Higher Education, 2000; Herman B Wells: The Promise of the American University, 2012. **Address:** Department of History and Philosophy of Science, Indiana University, Goodbody Hall 130, 1011 E 3rd St., Bloomington, IN 47405-7005, U.S.A. **Online address:** jcapshew@indiana.edu

CAPUTO, Philip. American (born United States), b. 1941. **Genres:** Novels, Novellas/Short Stories, Adult Non-fiction, Autobiography/Memoirs, Mystery/Crime/Suspense, Ghost Writer. **Career:** 3-M Corp., promotional writer, 1968-69; Chicago Tribune, local correspondent, 1969-72; Mercury-Douglas Productions, freelance writer, 1987-; Paramont Pictures, screenwriter. **Publications:** A Rumor of War (memoir), 1977; Horn of Africa: A Novel, 1980; DelCorso's Gallery (novel), 1983; Indian Country, 1987; Means of Escape: An Imagined Memoir, 1991; Equation for Evil: A Novel, 1996; Rumor of War: With a Twentieth Anniversary Postscript by the Author, 1996; Exiles: Three Short Novels, 1997; The Voyage, 1999; Del Corso's Gallery, 2001; Ghosts of Tsavo: Stalking the Mystery Lions of East Africa (nonfiction), 2002; In the Shadows of the Morning: Essays on Wild Lands, Wild Waters, and a Few Untamed People, 2002; Horn of Africa, 2002; Indian Country, 2004; Acts of Faith (novel), 2005; Ten Thousand Days of Thunder: A History of the Vietnam War, 2005; Acts of Faith (novel), 2005; 13 Seconds: A Look Back at the Kent State Shootings, 2005; Crossers: A Novel, 2009; Means of Escape: A War Correspondent's Memoir of Life and Death in Afghanistan, the Middle East, and Vietnam, 2009. Contributor to books and periodicals. **Address:** Aaron Priest Literary Agency, 708 3rd Ave., Ste. 2301, New York, NY 10017, U.S.A.

CARABELLI, Giancarlo. Italian (born Italy), b. 1939. **Genres:** Philosophy, Bibliography, Art/Art History, History. **Career:** University of Ferrara, lecturer, 1973-82, professor of the history of philosophy, 1983-. Writer. **Publications:** Hume e la retorica dell'ideologia: Uno studio dei Dialoghi sulla religionenaturale, 1972; Tolandiana: Materiali bibliografici per lo studiodell'opera e della fortuna di John Toland, 1670-1722, 1975; (contrib.) Scienza e filosofia scozzese nell'età di Hume, 1976; Intorno a Hume, 1992; In the Image of Priapus, 1996; Veneri epriapi: culti di fertilita e mitologie falliche tra napoli e londranell'eta dell'Illuminismo, 1996; Gentleman Filosofo: Nuovi Saggi Su Shaftesbury, 2003; (ed. with P. Zanardi) Pan Among Philosophers: Essays on Spinoza's Pantheism of the New Age: Proceedings of the International Conference "Pantheism and Enlightenment", Ferrara, 7-8 June 2007, 2008. **Address:** University of Ferrara, Istituto di discipline filosofiche, 9, Via Savonarola, Ferrara, 44121, Italy. **Online address:** giancarlo.carabelli@unife.it

CARAFANO, James Jay. American (born United States), b. 1955. **Genres:** Military/Defense/Arms Control. **Career:** U.S. Military Academy, assistant professor; U.S. Army Center of Military History, director of military studies; Heritage Foundation, Douglas and Sarah Allison Center for Foreign Policy Studies, senior research fellow, 2003-, Kathryn and Shelby Cullom Davis Institute for International Studies, assistant director, 2006-; Mount Saint Mary College, lecturer; U.S. Army Field Artillery School, lecturer; U.S. Naval War College, fleet professor; National Defense University, visiting professor; Georgetown University, visiting professor; George Washington University's Homeland Security Policy Institute, senior fellow; U.S. Army, staff. Writer. **Publications:** (Ed.) Dennis J. Reimer, Soldiers Are Our Credentials: The Collected Works and Selected Papers of the Thirty-third Chief of Staff, United States Army, 2000; After D-Day: Operation Cobra and the Normandy Breakout, 2000; Waltzing into the Cold War: The Struggle for Occupied Austria, 2002; (with P. Rosenzweig) Winning the Long War: Lessons from the Cold War for Defeating Terrorism and Preserving Freedom, 2005; (with M.A. Sauter) Homeland Security: A Complete Guide to Understanding, Preventing and Surviving Terrorism, 2005; GI Ingenuity: Improvisation, Technology and Winning World War II, 2006; Private Sector, Public Wars: Contractors in Combat'Afghanistan, Iraq and Future Conflicts, 2008; (ed. with R. Weitz) Mismanaging Mayhem: How Washington Responds to Crisis, 2008; Wiki at War: Conflict in a Socially Networked World, 2012. Contributor to periodicals. **Address:** Heritage Foundation, 214 Massachusetts Ave. NE, Washington, DC 20002, U.S.A. **Online address:** staff@heritage.org

CARAVANTES, Peggy. American (born United States), b. 1935. **Genres:** Biography, Children's Non-fiction. **Career:** East Central Independent School District, assistant principal, principal, curriculum director, deputy superintendent for instruction and personnel, 1982-99. Writer. **Publications:** Petticoat Spies: Six Women Spies of the Civil War, 2002; Marcus Garvey: Black Nationalist, 2003; An American in Texas: The Story of Sam Houston, 2004; American Hero: The Audie Murphy Story, 2004; Waging Peace: The Story of Jane Addams, 2004; Best of Times: The Story of Charles Dickens, 2005; Writing is My Business: The Story of O. Henry, 2006; Deep Woods: The Story of Robert Frost, 2006; Great and Sublime Fool: The Story of Mark Twain, 2009; Self-Reliance: The Story of Ralph Waldo Emerson, 2011; The De Leon Family of Texas, 2011. Contributor to books and periodicals. **Address:** 131 Da Vinci, San Antonio, TX 78258-4301, U.S.A. **Online address:** pcaravantes@att.net

CARBERRY, Ann. *See* **CHILD, Maureen.**

CARBIN, Debbie. British (born England), b. 1968. **Genres:** Young Adult Fiction, Romance/Historical, Novels. **Career:** Writer. **Publications:** Thanks for Nothing, Nick Maxwell, 2008; Three Men and a Maybe, 2009. **Address:** St. Martin's Press, 175 5th Ave., New York, NY 10010, U.S.A. **Online address:** debbiecarbin@yahoo.com

CARBO, Nick. American/Filipino (born Philippines), b. 1964?. **Genres:** Poetry, Cultural/Ethnic Topics, Essays, Literary Criticism And History, Race Relations, Sex, Third World. **Career:** Educator and writer. **Publications:** El Grupo McDonald's (poems), 1995; (ed. and intro.) Returning A Borrowed Tongue: An Anthology of Contemporary Filipino and Filipino-American Poetry, 1995; (ed. with D. Duhamel) Sweet Jesus: Poems About the Ultimate Icon, 2000; (ed. with E. Tabios) Babaylan: An Anthology of Filipina and Filipina American Writing, 2000; Andalusian Dawn (poems), 2004; Secret Asian Man (poems), 2004; (ed.) Pinoy Poetics: Autobiographical and Critical Essays by Filipino and Filipino American Poets, 2004. **Address:** 2201 S Ocean Dr., Hollywood, FL 33019, U.S.A. **Online address:** ncarbo@gmail.com

CARBONE, Elisa Lynn. American (born United States), b. 1954. **Genres:** Children's Fiction, Young Adult Fiction, Education. **Career:** Independent consultant and trainer of teaching and communication skills, 1973-; University of Maryland, lecturer, 1985-98. Full-time writer and consultant. **Publications:** My Dad's Definitely Not a Drunk!, 1992, rev. ed. as Corey's Story: Her Family's Secret, 1997; Teaching Large Classes: Tools and Strategies, 1998; Starting School with an Enemy, 1998; Stealing Freedom: With Related Readings, 1998; Sarah and the Naked Truth, 2000; Storm Warriors, 2001; The Pack, 2003; Last Dance on Holladay Street, 2005; Blood on the River: James Town 1607, 2006; (with R. Khan and U. Krishnaswami) Many Windows, 2008; Night Running: How James Escaped with the Help of his Faithful Dog, 2008; Jump, 2010; Heroes of the Surf, 2012. **Address:** c/o Author Mail, Knopf Delacorte Dell Young Readers Group, 1745 Broadway, 9th Fl., New York, NY 10019, U.S.A. **Online address:** elcarbone@earthlink.net

CARCATERRA, Lorenzo. American (born United States), b. 1954. **Genres:** Novels, Plays/Screenplays, Adult Non-fiction, Novellas/Short Stories, Biography. **Career:** Norwegian Lutheran School of Theology, assistant professor, 1980-90, professor of church history, 1990-; Caspari Center, curriculum writer, 1983. **Publications:** NONFICTION: A Safe Place: The True Story of a Father, a Son, a Murder, 1992; Sleepers, 1995. NOVELS: Apaches, 1997; Gangster, 2001; Street Boys, 2002; Paradise City, 2004; Chasers: A Novel, 2007; Midnight Angels: A Novel, 2010. **Address:** Villard Books, 1540 Broadway, New York, NY 10036-4039, U.S.A. **Online address:** lgc41@aol.com

CARD, Orson Scott. (Scott Richards). American (born United States), b. 1951. **Genres:** Novels, Science Fiction/Fantasy, Plays/Screenplays, Novellas/Short Stories, Young Adult Non-fiction, Graphic Novels. **Career:** Brigham Young University Press, proofreader, 1974, editor, 1974-76; freelance writer and editor, 1978-; Ensign Magazine, assistant editor, 1976-78; University of Utah, instructor, 1979-80, 1981; Brigham Young University, instructor, 1981; University of Notre Dame, instructor, 1981-82; Compute Books, senior editor, 1983; Appalachian State University, instructor, 1987-, part-time teacher, 1989-; Lucasfilm Games, game design consultant, 1989-92; Southern Virginia University, distinguished professor of English, 2005-, professor of writing and literature. **Publications:** Listen, Mom and Dad, 1978; Capitol (short stories), 1978; (ed.) Dragons of Light, 1980; Unaccompanied Sonata and Other Stories, 1981; (ed.) Dragons of Darkness, 1981; Saintspeak: The Mormon Dictionary, 1981; Ainge, 1982; How to Write Science Fiction and Fantasy, 1984; Saints (A Woman of Destiny) (novel), 1984; Cardography, 1987; Seventh Son (novel), 1987; Character and Viewpoint, 1988, rev. ed., 2010; Prentice Alvin (novel), 1989; Maps in the Mirror (stories), 1990; Eye for Eye, 1990; The Changed Man, 1992; Flux, 1992; Cruel Miracles, 1992; The Memory of Earth, 1992; The Call of Earth, 1992; Lost Boys, 1992; Monkey Sonatas, 1993; A Storyteller in Zion: Essays and Speeches, 1993; Earthfall, 1994; Lovelock, 1994; The Ships of Earth, 1994; Turning Hearts: Short Stories on Family Life, 1994; Earthborn, 1995; (with M. Ridpath, A. Dibell and L. Turco) How to Write a Million, 1995; Alvin Journeyman, 1995; Pastwatch, 1996; Children of the Mind, 1996; Treasure Box, 1996; Stone Tables, 1997; Homebody, 1998; Heart Fire, 1998; Enchantment, 1999; Sarah, 1999; Ender's Shadow, 1999; Magic Mirror, 1999; Shadow of the Hegemon, 2000; Rebekah, 2001; The Elephants of Posnan, 2001; Shadow Puppets, 2002; The Crystal City, 2003; (with D. Chiang) Robota, 2003; Rachel and Leah, 2004; An Open Book, 2004; Shadow of the Giant, 2005; Posing as People, 2005; Magic Street, 2005; Lies to Live By, 2005; Empire, 2006; (ed.) Getting Lost, 2006; The Space Boy, 2007; A War of Gifts, 2007; (with J. Millman and A. Berner) The Great Snape Debate, 2007; (with A. Johnston) Invasive Procedures, 2007; Stonefather, 2008; Ender in Exile, 2008; Keeper of Dreams, 2008; (as Scott Richards) Zanna's Gift: A Life in Christmases, 2008; Hidden Empire, 2009; (with J. Blake) The Authorized Ender Companion, 2009; (co-author) The Writer's Digest Guide to Science Fiction & Fantasy, 2010; Pathfinder, 2010; The Lost Gate: A Novel of the Mither Mages, 2011; Hamlet's Father, 2011; Shadows in Flight, 2012; Ruins, 2012. SCIENCE FICTION: Hot Sleep, 1978; A Planet Called Treason, 1979; Songmaster, 1980; Hart's Hope, 1983; The Worthing Chronicle, 1983; Ender's Game, 1985; Speaker for the Dead, 1986; Wyrms, 1987; Folk of the Fringe, 1989; The Abyss, 1989; Worthing Saga, 1990; Xenocide, 1991. GRAPHIC NOVELS SERIES: Ultimate Iron Man, 2006, vol. II, 2008; Wyrms Graphic Novel, 2006; Red Prophet: The Tales Of Alvin Maker, vol. I, 2007, vol. II, 2008; (with E.J. Card) Laddertop, vol. I, 2011; Formic Wars: Burning Earth, 2012. Works appear in anthologies. **Address:** Barbara Bova Literary Agency, 3951 Gulf Shore Blvd. N, Ste. PH 1-B, PO Box 770365, Naples, FL 34103, U.S.A. **Online address:** oscard@southernvirginia.edu

CARDIERI, Anthony J. American (born United States), b. 1965. **Genres:** Novels. **Career:** New York Department of Sanitation, district superintendent. Writer. **Publications:** NOVELS: Our Own Worst Enemy, 2004; Luck of the Draw, 2009. **Address:** New York, NY , U.S.A. **Online address:** anthonycardieri@aol.com

CARDINAL, Roger. British (born England), b. 1940. **Genres:** Art/Art History, Literary Criticism And History, Education, Politics/Government. **Career:** University of Manitoba, assistant professor of French, 1965-67; University of Warwick, lecturer in French, 1967-68; University of Kent, Keynes College, lecturer, 1968-76, senior lecturer in French, 1976-81, reader in comparative literary studies, 1981-87, professor of literary and visual studies, 1987-, now professor emeritus, Centre for Comparative Literary Studies, director; University of Toronto, visiting associate professor, 1976-77; Australian National University, research fellow, 1988. Writer. **Publications:** (With R.S. Short) Surrealism: Permanent Revelation, 1970; Outsider Art, 1972, 2nd ed., 1973; German Romantics in Context, 1975; (ed.) Sensibility and Creation: Studies in Twentieth Century French Poetry, 1977; Primitive Painters, 1978, 2nd ed., 1979; Figures of Reality: A Perspective on the Poetic Imagination, 1981; Expressionism, 1984; Andre Breton: Nadja, 1986; The Landscape Vision of Paul Nash, 1989; (ed. with J. Elsner) The Cultures of Collecting, 1994; (ed. with M.D. Hall and E.W. Metcalf, Jr.) The Artist Outsider: Creativity and the Boundaries of Culture, 1994; (contrib.) Pictured in My Mind: Contemporary American Self-Taught Art from the Collection of Kurt Gitter and Alice Rae Yelen, 1995; (with J.F. Hernandez and J. Beardsley) A.G. Rizzoli: Architect of Magnificent Visions, 1997; (with J. Beardsley) Private Worlds, 1998; (ed. with M. Lusardy) Messages dOutre-Monde, 1999; Henry Moore: In the Light of Greece, 2000; (contrib.) Grandma Moses in the Twenty-First Century, 2001; (with A. van Berkum, J. ten Berge and C. Rhodes) Marginalia, 2001; (contrib.) Create and Be Recognized: Photography on the Edge, 2004; (with F. Kaiser and B. Vouilloux) Arnulf Rainer et sa Collection dart brut, 2005; (with R. Grayson and C. Carolin) A Secret Service: Art, Compulsion, Concealment, 2006; (foreword) Art and Disability: The Social and Political Struggles Facing Education, 2009. Contributor to periodicals. **Address:** Keynes College, University of Kent, Canterbury, KT CT2 7NX, England. **Online address:** r.cardinal@ukc.ac.uk

CARDONA, Manuel. German/Spanish/American (born United States), b. 1934. **Genres:** Sciences, Physics. **Career:** RCA Laboratories, physicist, 1959-64; Brown University, associate professor of physics, 1964-66, professor, 1966-71; Max Planck Institute of Solid State Research, founding director, 1971-2000, founding director emeritus, 2000-. Writer. **Publications:** Modulation Spectroscopy, 1965; (with P.Y. Yu) The Physics of Semiconductors, 1994; (with P.Y. Yu) Fundamentals of Semiconductors: Physics and Materials Properties, 1996, 4rd ed., 2005. EDITOR: Light Scattering in Solids, vol. I-IX, 1975-2007; (and contrib. with L. Ley) Photoemission in Solids, 1978; (with G.R. Castro) Lectures on Surface Science, 1987; (co-ed.) International Conference on Modulation Spectroscopy, The International Society for Optical Engineering, 1990; (with F.A. Ponce) Surface Science: Lectures on Basic Concepts and Applications, 1991. Contributions to journals and periodicals. **Address:** Max Planck Institute for Solid State Research, Heisenbergstr 1, Stuttgart, 70569, Germany. **Online address:** m.cardona@fkf.mpg.de

CARENS, Timothy L. American (born United States), b. 1965. **Genres:** Literary Criticism And History, Novels, History. **Career:** New York University, writing instructor, teaching assistant and lecturer in English, 1993-98; College of Charleston, assistant professor, 1998-2004, associate professor of English, 2004-. Writer. **Publications:** Outlandish English Subjects in the Victorian Domestic Novel, 2005. **Address:** Department of English, College of Charleston, 26 Glebe St., Ste. 302, Charleston, SC 29424-1409, U.S.A. **Online address:** carenst@cofc.edu

CAREW, Jan (Rynveld). American/Guyanese (born Guyana), b. 1920. **Genres:** Novels, Novellas/Short Stories, Children's Fiction, Plays/Screenplays, Poetry, History. **Career:** British Colonial Civil Service, customs officer, 1940-43; British Broadcasting Corp., Overseas Service, broadcaster, writer and editor, 1952-65; University of London, Extra-Mural Department, lecturer in race relations, 1953-57, program director; London Observer, Latin American correspondent, 1962; African Review, editor, 1965-66; CBC Broadcaster, staff, 1966-69; Princeton University, Department of Afro-American Studies, lecturer, 1969-72, Council of Humanities, senior fellow, 1969-72, program director; Northwestern University, Department of African-American Studies, professor, 1972-87, professor emeritus, 1987-, chairman; Third World Energy Institute, co-chairman, 1978-; Linear Alpha Inc., board director, 1978-; Hampshire College, visiting professor, 1986-87, program director; George Mason University, visiting Clarence J. Robinson professor, 1989-91, program director; Lincoln University, Center for the Humanities, director, 1993-95, program director; Rutgers University, program director; University of Namibia, advisor; St. Petersburg University, advisor. **Publications:** Streets of Eternity (poetry), 1952; Black Midas, 1958 in US as A Touch of Midas, 1958; The Wild Coast. 1958; The Last Barbarian, 1961; Moscow is Not My Mecca, 1964; Green Winter, 1965; Cry Black Power, 1970; Sons of the Flying Wing, 1970; Rope the Sun, 1973; The Third Gift (children's fiction), 1974; (ed.) Out of Time, 1975; Stranger than Tomorrow: Three Stories of the Future, 1976; Save the Last Dance for Me, and Other Stories, 1976; The Twins of Ilora, 1977; The Lost Love, and Other Stories, 1978; The Origins of Racism and Resistance in the Americas, 1978; The Man Who Came Back, 1979; The Cat People, 1979; Children of the Sun, 1980; Dark Night, 1981; Dead Man's Creek: Two Stories, 1981; Sea Drums in My Blood (poetry), 1981; House of Fear: Two Stories, 1981; Don't Go Near the Water, 1982; Time Loop, 1982; Death Comes to the Circus, 1983; Indian and African Presence in the Americas, 1984; (contrib.) Expressions of Power in Education, 1994; Grenada: The Hour Will Strike Again (history), 1985; The Riverman, 1987; The Sisters, 1987; Fulcrums of Change (essays), 1988, Rape of Paradise, 1994; Ghosts in Our Blood: With Malcolm X in Africa, England and the Caribbean, 1994; The Guyanese Wanderer, 2007. **Address:** Department of African American Studies, Northwestern University, 633 Clark St., Evanston, IL 60208, U.S.A.

CAREW, Rivers (Verain). British (born England), b. 1935. **Genres:** Poetry. **Career:** Irish Tourist Board, production assistant, 1962-67; Ireland of the Welcomes Magazine, assistant editor, 1964-77; The Dublin Magazine, joint editor, 1964-69; Irish National Broadcasting Organization, sub-editor, 1967-77, deputy chief sub-editor, 1977-82, chief sub-editor, 1982-87; Radio Telefis Eireann, sub-editor, 1967-87; BBC World Service, chief sub-editor, 1987-93. **Publications:** (With T. Brownlow) Figures out of Mist, 1966. **Address:** Cherry Bounds, 37 Hicks Ln., Girton, CB CB3 OJS, England. **Online address:** rivers.carew@btopenworld.com

CAREY, Benedict. American (born United States), b. 1960?. **Genres:** Mystery/Crime/Suspense. **Career:** American Shipper Magazine, reporter; Health Magazine, reporter, 1987-97; Los Angeles Times, health reporter, through 2004; New York Times, science reporter, 2004-. **Publications:** The Unknowns: A Mystery, 2009. **Address:** New York Times, 620 8th Ave., New York, NY 10018, U.S.A. **Online address:** b.carey50@yahoo.com

CAREY, Charles W. American (born United States), b. 1951. **Genres:** Politics/Government, Adult Non-fiction. **Career:** Central Virginia Community College, adjunct history instructor, 1995-2004; freelance writer, 1996-2008; Lynchburg College, adjunct history instructor, 1997-2001; Virginia Tech, adjunct history instructor, 2003-08; Roanoke College, adjunct history instructor, 2003-08, lecturer; Radford University, adjunct history instructor, 2004. **Publications:** George Washington Carver, 1999; The Emancipation Proclamation, 2000; The Mexican War: Mr. Polk's War, 2002; American Inventors, Entrepreneurs and Business Visionaries, 2002; Eugene V. Debs: Outspoken Labor Leaders and Socialist, 2003; (ed.) Life under Soviet Communism, 2003; (ed.) The American Revolution, 2004; African-American Political Leaders, 2004; (ed.) The Kennedy Assassination, 2004; (ed.) Castro's Cuba, 2004; American Scientists, 2006; (ed.) Living through the Korean War, 2006; African Americans in Science: An Encyclopedia of People and Progress, 2008. Contributor to periodicals. **Address:** 1102 Biltmore Ave., Lynchburg, VA 24502, U.S.A. **Online address:** wahokie@gmail.com

CAREY, George (Leonard). British (born England), b. 1935. **Genres:** inspirational/Motivational Literature, Theology/Religion, Autobiography/Memoirs. **Career:** St. Mary's Islington, assistant curate, 1962-66; Oak Hill Theological College, lecturer, 1966-70; St. John's Theological College, lecturer and chaplain, 1970-75; St. Nicholas' Church, vicar, 1975-82; Trinity College, principal, 1982-87; Bath and Wells, bishop, 1987-91; archbishop of Canterbury, 1991-2002; life peer, 2002; University of Gloucestershire, chancellor, through 2010; London College of Theology, president. Writer. **Publications:** NONFICTION: I Believe in Man, 1977; God Incarnate, 1977 in US as God Incarnate: Meeting the Contemporary Challenges to a Classic Christian Doctrine, 1978; (co-author) The Great Acquittal, 1980; Tale of Two Churches: Can Protestants and Catholics Get Together?, 1985; The Meeting of the Waters, 1985; The Gate of Glory, 1986; (ed.) The Message of the Bible, 1986 in US as The Bible for Everyday Life, 1996; The Great God Robbery, 1989; The Church in the Market Place, 1991; I Believe, 1991; Why I Believe in a Personal God: The Credibility of Faith in a Doubting Culture, 1991; (contrib.) Year with the Bible, 1991; Encounter with Canterbury, 1992; The Charter for the Church: Sharing a Vision for the 21st Century in UK as Sharing a Vision, 1993; Spiritual Journey: 1,000 Young Adults Share the Reconciling Experience of Taizé with the Archbishop of Canterbury, 1994; My Journey, Your Journey, 1996; Canterbury Letters to the Future, 1998; Know the Truth: A Memoir, 2004. Contributor of articles to periodicals. **Address:** HarperCollins, 77-85 Fulham Palace Rd., Hammersmith, London, GL W6 8JB, England.

CAREY, George Wescott. American (born United States), b. 1933. **Genres:** Politics/Government. **Career:** Georgetown University, professor of government; The Political Science Reviewer, editor, 1973-2005. **Publications:** (With W. Kendall) The Basic Symbols of the American Political Tradition, 1970, 2nd ed., 1995; In Defense of the Constitution, 1989, rev. ed., 1995; The Federalist: Design for a Constitutional Republic, 1989; A Student's Guide to American Political Thought, 2004. EDITOR: (with C.S. Hyneman) A Second Federalist: Congress Creates a Government, 1967; (with G.J. Graham) The Post-Behavioral Era: Perspectives on Political Science, 1972; (with J.V. Schall) Essays on Christianity and Political Philosophy, 1984; Freedom and Virtue: The Conservative/Libertarian Debate, 1984, rev. ed., 1998; Order, Freedom and the Polity: Critical Essays on the Open Society, 1986; (with J. McClellan) The Federalist, 1990; (with B. Frohnen) Community and Tradition: Conservative Perspectives on the American Experience, 1998; The Political Writings of John Adams, 2000. Contributor to books. **Address:** Department of Government, Georgetown University, 668 ICC, PO Box 571034, Washington, DC 20057-1034, U.S.A. **Online address:** careygw@georgetown.edu

CAREY, Jacqueline. American (born United States), b. 1964?. **Genres:** Science Fiction/Fantasy, Novels, Adult Non-fiction, Young Adult Non-fiction. **Career:** Writer. **Publications:** KUSHIEL'S LEGACY TRILOGY: Kushiel's Dart, 2001; Kushiel's Chosen, 2002; Kushiel's Avatar, 2003, Kushiel's Scion, 2005; Kushiel's Justice, 2007; Kushiel's Mercy, 2008; Naamah's Kiss, 2009; Naamah's Curse, 2010; Naamah's Blessing, 2011. SUNDERING SERIES: Banewreaker, 2004; Godslayer, 2005. NON-FICTION: Angels: Celestial Spirits in Art & Legend, 1997. SANTA OLIVIA SERIES: Santa Olivia, 2009; Saints Astray, 2011. OTHERS: (contrib.) Songs of Love & Death, 2010; Dark Currents, 2012. NOVEL: Elegy for Darkness, forthcoming. Contributor to periodicals. **Address:** Dystel & Goderich Literary Management, 1 Union Sq. W, Ste. 904, New York, NY 10003-3313, U.S.A. **Online address:** contact@jacquelinecarey.com

CAREY, Jacqueline. American (born United States), b. 1954. **Genres:** Novels, Novellas/Short Stories, Mystery/Crime/Suspense, Young Adult Fiction. **Career:** Writer. **Publications:** Good Gossip (stories), 1992; The Other Family (novel), 1996; Wedding Pictures: A Novel, 1997; The Crossley Baby (novel), 2002; It's A Crime: A Novel, 2008; Saints Astray, 2011; Hurricane Zeta, forthcoming. Contributor to periodicals. **Address:** c/o Andrew Wylie, Wylie, Aitken & Stone Inc., 250 W 57th St., Ste. 2114, New York, NY 10107, U.S.A. **Online address:** jaycarey@aol.com

CAREY, John. British (born England), b. 1934. **Genres:** Literary Criticism And History. **Career:** Oxford University, Christ Church, lecturer, 1958-59, Balliol College, Andrew Bradley research fellow, 1959, Keble College, tutorial fellow, 1960-64, St. John's College, lecturer in English literature and fellow, 1964-75, Merton College, Merton professor of English literature, 1976-2001, chair, through 2002, professor emeritus, 2002-; Liverpool University, honorary professor. Writer. **Publications:** (Comp.) Andrew Marvell: A Critical Anthology, 1969; Milton, 1969, 2nd ed., 1972; (contrib.) The Sphere History of Literature, vol. II, 1970; The Violent Effigy: A Study of Dickens Imagination, 1973, 2nd ed., 1991; (trans.) Milton, Christian Doctrine, 1973; Here Comes Dickens: The Imagination of a Novelist, 1974; Thackeray: Prodigal Genius, 1977; Wording and Rewording: Paraphrase in Literary Criticism, 1977; John Donne: Life, Mind, and Art, 1981, 2nd ed., 1990; Original Copy: Selected Reviews and Journalism, 1969-1986, 1987; The Intellectuals and the Masses: Pride and Prejudice Among the Literary Intelligentsia, 1880-1939, 1993; Pure Pleasure: A Guide to the Twentieth Centurys Most Enjoyable Books, 2000; What Good are the Arts?, 2006; Ireland and the Grail, 2007; William Golding: The Man Who Wrote Lord of the Flies, 2009; (into.) Believe in People: The Essential Karel Capek, Previously Unstranslated Journalism and Letters, 2010. EDITOR: (with A. Fowler) The Poems of John Milton, 1968, 2nd ed., 1997; James Hogg, The Private Memoirs and Confessions of a Justified Sinner, 1969; Complete Shorter Poems, 1972, 2nd ed. as Milton: Complete Shorter Poems, 2006; English Renaissance Studies Presented to Dame Helen Gardner in Honour of Her Seventieth Birthday, 1980; William Golding: The Man and His Books: A Tribute on his 75th Birthday, 1987; Eyewitness to History, 1987; The Faber Book of Reportage, 1987; (and intro.) A Critical Edition of the Major Works, 1990, rev. ed. as Major Works, 2000; (and intro.) Short Stories and The Unbearable Bassington, 1994; The Faber Book of Science, 1995; (and intro.) Selected Poetry, 1996; The Faber Book of Utopias, 1999; (and intro.) Vanity Fair: A Novel Without a Hero, 2001. **Address:** 57 Stapleton Rd., Headington, Oxford, OX OX4 1RE, England. **Online address:** john.carey123@btinternet.com

CAREY, Lisa. American (born United States), b. 1970?. **Genres:** Novels, Young Adult Fiction, Literary Criticism And History. **Career:** Brookline Booksmith, sales clerk. Writer. **Publications:** The Mermaids Singing, 1998; In the Country of the Young, 2000; Love in the Asylum: A Novel, 2004; Every Visible Thing, 2006. Contributor to periodicals. **Address:** c/o Avon Books, 1350 Ave. of the Americas, New York, NY 10019, U.S.A.

CAREY, Patrick W. American (born United States), b. 1940. **Genres:** Theology/Religion, History, Adult Non-fiction, Biography. **Career:** St. Peter's College, assistant professor of theology, 1975-76; Elizabeth Seton College, assistant professor, 1976; Carleton College, assistant professor of theology, 1976-77; Gustavus Adolphus College, assistant professor of theology, 1977-78; Marquette University, assistant professor, 1978-84, associate professor of religious studies, 1984-99, department head, 1991-, professor, 1999-. Writer. **Publications:** Altogether: A Parish Family, 1974; An Immigrant Bishop: John England's Adaptation of Irish Catholicism to American Republicanism, 1982; People, Priests and Prelates: Ecclesiastical Democracy and the Tensions of

Trusteeism, 1987; (ed.) American Catholic Religious Thought, 1987; (ed.) Orestes A. Brownson: Selected Writings, 1991; The Roman Catholics, 1993, rev. ed. as The Roman Catholics in America, 1996; Orestes A. Brownson: A Bibliography, 1826-1876, 1997; (ed. with E.C. Muller) Theological Education in the Catholic Tradition: Contemporary Challenges, 1997; (ed. and intro.) The Pastoral Letters of the United States Catholic Bishops, vol. VI: 1989-1997, 1998; (ed. with J.T. Lienhard) Biographical Dictionary of Christian Theologians, 2000; The Early Works of Orestes A. Brownson, vol. I: The Universalist Years, 1826-29, 2000, vol. II: The Free Thought and Unitarian Years, 1826-29, 2001, vol. III: The Transcendentalist Years, 1837-38, 2002; vol. IV: The Transcendentalist Years, 1838-39, 2003, vol. V: The Transcendentalist Years, 1840-41, 2004, vol. VI: Life by Communion, 1842, 2005, vol. VII: Life by Communion Years, 1843-44, 2007; Orestes A. Brownson: American Religious Weather vane in Library of Religious Biography, 2004; (ed.) American Catholic Religious Thought: The Shaping of a Theological and Social Tradition, 2004; Catholics in America: A History, 2004, rev. ed., 2007; Avery Cardinal Dulles, SJ: A Model Theologian, 1918-2008, 2010. Contributor to books and periodicals. **Address:** Department of Theology, Marquette University, 100 Coughlin Hall, Milwaukee, WI 53216, U.S.A. **Online address:** patrick.carey@marquette.edu

CAREY, Peter. British/Australian (born Australia), b. 1943. **Genres:** Novels, Novellas/Short Stories, Young Adult Non-fiction, History. **Career:** Grey's Advertising Agency, staff, 1974-; McSpedden Carey Advertising Consultants, co-founder, 1980-90; New York University, writing instructor; Princeton University, writing instructor; City University of New York, Hunter College, Master of Fine Arts in Creative Writing Program, executive director, 2003-. Writer. **Publications:** STORIES: The Fat Man in History, 1974 in UK as Exotic Pleasures, 1981; War Crimes, 1979; The Fat Man in History and Other Stories, 1980; Collected Stories, 1994. NOVELS: Bliss, 1981; Illywhacker, 1985; Oscar and Lucinda, 1988; The Tax Inspector, 1991; A Letter to Our Son, 1994; The Unusual Life of Tristan Smith, 1994; The Big Bazoohley, 1995; Jack Maggs, 1997; True History of the Kelly Gang, 2000; My Life as a Fake, 2003; Wrong about Japan: A Father's Journey with His Son, 2005; Theft: A Love Story, 2006; His Illegal Self, 2008. OTHERS: 30 Days in Sydney: A Wildly Distorted Account, 2001; Parrot and Olivier in America, 2009. Contributor to periodicals. **Address:** Rogers, Coleridge & White Ltd., 20 Powis Mews, London, GL W11 1JN, England.

CARGILL, Linda B. American (born United States), b. 1955. **Genres:** Novels, Mystery/Crime/Suspense. **Career:** Writer. **Publications:** To Follow the Goddess, 1991; The Witch of Pungo, 1993; The Seawitch, 1995; The Surfer, 1995; Hang Loose, 1996; Pool Party, 1996; The Girl in Blue, 1996; Up from the Grave, 1997; The Graveyard at Midnight Beach, 1997; The Tree of Dead Spirits, 1997; Siren Song, 1998; Bloody Thorns, 1999; Still Waters Run Deep, 1999; Mirror, Mirror, 2000; Gold Hair, 2000; River of No Return, 2000; Sink or Swim, 2000; Grizzly!, 2001; Heart of Stone, 2001; Lullaby and Good-Night, 2001; Horror in Hilton Head, 2001; One Perfect Rose, 2002; Are You Scared of the Dark?, 2002; The Opium Cave, 2002; Note in a Bottle, 2002; Vampire on Board!, 2002; Fire Lake, 2002; Curse of Fire, 2002; Horror House, 2002; Shadow Plays, 2003; The Dark Lake, 2003; Fire! Fire!, 2003; The Fatal Shore, 2003; The Tenant, 2003; The Dark 1, 2003; The Dark 2, 2004; The Spiral Staircase, 2004; Never Kiss a Vampire, 2004; Date with the Dead, 2004; The Mysterious Surfer, 2004; Volcano, 2004; Who Hates You So Much, Shawna?, 2004; The Double, 2004; The Raven, 2005; Face in the Falls, 2005; Murder on the Mountain, 2005; Snow Ghost, 2005; Eyes of the Dragon, 2006; The Louvered Window, 2006; Murder in Yellowstone, 2006; She Who Watches, 2006; The Black Stone, 2008; The Minotaur, 2008; Burning Waters, 2008; Light at Sea, 2008; Mirror Lake, 2008; Those Who Dream by Day, 2009; (with G. Cargill) The Seven-Pillared House, 2009; Witch of the White Rose, 2009; Spirit Island, 2009; Lights! Action! Camera!, 2009; Mystery Gift, 2009; Murder in the Backyard, 2009; The Lost, 2009; Spirit Island, 2009; The Third Coming, 2009; The Totem Pole, 2009; White Rose, Red Rose, 2009; The Oldest House, 2009; (with G. Cargill) In the Shadow of the Sphinx, 2010; (with G. Cargill) Captive at the Berghof, 2010; (with G. Cargill) King Abdullah's Tomb, 2010; Boardwalk to Nowhere, 2010; Dead Man's Rock, 2010; Eyes, 2010; The Eyes of the Dragon, 2010; The Hood, 2010; I Can Never Die, 2010; Ice, 2010; The Island, 2010; Louvred Window, 2010; Lozen, 2010; Maid of the Mists, 2010; Never Kiss a Vampire, 2010; No Man's Rapids, 2010; Note in a Bottle, 2010; River of No Return, 2010; Sink or Swim, 2010; The Skull, 2010; Sleepwalker, 2010; Spiral Staircase, 2010; Stepsisters, 2010; Through a Glass Darkly, 2010; Undine, 2010; Vampire on Board, 2010; Yonder Crow's Nest, 2010; Zombie Master, 2010; Echoes, 2010; Whispers, 2010; Voodoo, 2010; Vampire Blues, 2010; Drop Dead, 2010; The Burning, 2010; The Book of the Dead, 2010; War and Peace, 2011; The Cleopatra Stone Mystery, 2011; Vampire Gals, 2011; Vampires At Sea, 2011; Saint Simons Island, 2011; Queen of Kings, 2011; For Love of Julia, 2011; Vampire Gals, 2011; The Cleopatra Stone Mystery, 2011; Arizona to California, 2011. Contributor to periodicals. **Address:** c/o Pema Browne, Pema Browne Ltd., 11 Tena Pl., Valley Cottage, NY 10989-2215, U.S.A. **Online address:** lindabcargill@cox.net

CARHEDEN, Göorel Kristina. *See* **NAASLUND, Göorel Kristina.**

CARIN, Michael. Canadian (born Canada), b. 1951. **Genres:** Novels, Adult Non-fiction. **Career:** Montreal Business Magazine, editor-in-chief, 1994-2005; corporate communications and investor relations specialist, 2005-; Maison Brison Inc., senior writer. **Publications:** NOVELS: Five Hundred Keys, 1980; The Neutron Picasso, 1989. NON-FICTION: The Future Jew, 2001. **Address:** Michael Carin Communications, 2500 Pierre-Dupuy Ave., Ste. 403, Montreal, QC H3C 4L1, Canada. **Online address:** info@thefuturejew.com

CARKEET, David. American (born United States), b. 1946. **Genres:** Novels, Young Adult Fiction, Autobiography/Memoirs, Mystery/Crime/Suspense. **Career:** University of Missouri, Department of English, faculty, 1973-2002. Writer. **Publications:** Double Negative, 1980; The Greatest Slump of All Time, 1984; I Been There Before, 1985; The Silent Treatment, 1988; The Full Catastrophe, 1990; Quiver River, 1991; The Error of Our Ways, 1997; Campus Sexpot: A Memoir, 2005; From Away, 2010. Contributor to periodicals. **Address:** 418 Macey Rd., North Middlesex, VT 05682, U.S.A. **Online address:** davidcarkeet@hotmail.com

CARL, JoAnna. *See* **SANDSTROM, Eve K.**

CARLE, Eric. American (born United States), b. 1929. **Genres:** Children's Fiction, Children's Non-fiction, Autobiography/Memoirs, Essays, Illustrations, Picture/Board Books. **Career:** U.S. Information Center, poster designer, 1950-52; New York Times, graphic designer, 1952-56; L.W. Frohlich and Co., art director, 1956-63; freelance writer, illustrator, designer, 1963-. **Publications:** SELF-ILLUSTRATED: VERY AND VERY FIRST SERIES: The Very Hungry Caterpillar, 1969; My Very First Book of Colors, 1974; My Very First Book of Numbers, 1974; My Very First Book of Shapes, 1974; My Very First Book of Words, 1974; The Very Busy Spider, 1984; My Very First Book of Heads and Tails, 1986; My Very First Book of Sounds, 1986; My Very First Book of Food, 1986; My Very First Book of Tools, 1986; My Very First Book of Touch, 1986; My Very First Book of Motion, 1986; My Very First Book of Growth, 1986; My Very First Book of Homes, 1986; My Very First Book of Heads, 1986; The Very Quiet Cricket, 1990; The Very Lonely Firefly, 1995; The Very Clumsy Click Beetle, 1999. CATCH THE BALL SERIES: Catch the Ball!, 1982; Lets Paint A Rainbow, 1982; What's For Lunch?, 1982. BILINGUAL BOOKS: Animals/Animals, 1989; Colors/Colores, 1991. PICTURE BOOKS: 1, 2, 3 to the Zoo, 1968; Tiny Seed, 1970; Pancakes, Pancakes!, 1970, 2nd ed., 2005; Do You Want to Be My Friend?, 1971; Walter the Baker, 1972; The Secret Birthday Message, 1972; Rooster's Off to See the World, 1972; I See a Song, 1973; Have You Seen My Cat?, 1973; Animals and Their Babies, 1974; All About Arthur (An Absolutely Absurd Ape), 1974; The Mixed-Up Chameleon, 1975; The Grouchy Ladybug, 1977 in UK as The Bad-Tempered Ladybird, 1978; Watch Out! A Giant!, 1978; The Honeybee and the Robber, 1981; Papa, Please Get the Moon for Me, 1986; All Around Us, 1986; A House for Hermit Crab, 1987; Draw Me a Star, 1992; Today Is Monday, 1993; My Apron, 1994; Little Cloud, 1996; From Head to Toe, 1997; Hello, Red Fox, 1998; Dream Snow, 2000; Does A Kangaroo Have A Mother, Too?, 2000; A Journal for Baby's First Year, 2002; Slowly, Slowly, Slowly, Said the Sloth, 2002; (with K. Iwamura) Where Are You Going? To See My Friend!, 2003; Mister Seahorse, 2004; 10 Little Rubber Ducks, 2005; Quack Said Billy Goat, 2005; Eric Carle's Very Special Baby Journal, 2006; Eric Carle's The Rabbit and the Turtle & Other Aesop's Fables, 2008. OTHERS: The Say-with-Me ABC Book, 1967; Geheimnis der acht Zeichen, 1971; Wil je Mijn Vriendje Zijn?, 1971; The Very Long Tail, 1972; The Very Long Train, 1972; Ich hab die Geige KlingenSehn, 1973; La Mariquita Malhumorada, 1992; Art of Eric Carle, 1996; Flora and Tiger: 19 Very Short Stories from My Life, 1997; The Magical Papers of Eric Carle, 1997; Stories for All Seasons, 1998; You Can Make a Collage, 1998; (intro.) The One and Only Shrek!: Plus 5 Other Stories, 2007; The Artist Who Painted a Blue Horse, 2011; (reteller) Tom Thumb: Grimms' Tales, 2011. **Address:** PO Box 485, Northampton, MA 01060, U.S.A. **Online address:** fanclub@eric-carle.com

CARLEBACH, Michael L(loyd). American (born United States), b. 1945. **Genres:** Photography. **Career:** University of Miami, School of Communication, faculty, 1973-98, Department of Art and Art History, faculty, 1998-2004; U.S. Environmental Protection Agency, freelance photographer, 1973; U.S. Department of State, Cuban-Haitian Task Force, photographer, 1980. Writer. **Publications:** The Origins of Photojournalism in America, 1992; (with E. Provenzo) Farm Security Administration Photographs of Florida, 1993; American Photojournalism Comes of Age, 1997; Working Stiffs: Occupational Portraits in the Age of the Tintype, 2002; Sunny Land: Pictures from Paradise, 2010; Bain's New York: The City in News Pictures, 1900-1925, 2012. **Address:** Deparment of Art and Art History, University of Miami, PO Box 248106, Coral Gables, FL 33124-2618, U.S.A. **Online address:** michael.carlebach@gmail.com

CARLEON, A. *See* **O'GRADY, Rohan.**

CARLESS, Jennifer. American (born United States), b. 1960. **Genres:** Environmental Sciences/Ecology, Earth Sciences, Business/Trade/Industry, Technology, Sciences. **Career:** Manager of research support, 1983-85; U.S. Online Information Service, manager of European agents, 1986-87; freelance technical writer of software users manuals, 1987-88; office manager and attorney's assistant, 1992-. **Publications:** Taking out the Trash: A No-Nonsense Guide to Recycling, 1992; Renewable Energy: A Concise Guide to Green Alternatives, 1993. **Address:** PO Box 7616, Santa Cruz, CA 95061-7616, U.S.A.

CARLEY, James P. Canadian (born Canada), b. 1946?. **Genres:** History, Biography. **Career:** York University, professor of English and distinguished research professor. Writer. **Publications:** John of Glastonbury, Cronica, Sive, Antiquitates Glastoniensis Ecclesie: Text with Introduction, Notes, and Commentary, 1978; The Chronicle of Glastonbury Abbey: An Edition, Translation and Study of John of Glastonbury's Cronica, Sive, Antiquitates Glastoniensis Ecclesie, 1985; Glastonbury Abbey: The Holy House at the Head of the Moors Adventurous, 1988; (intro.) Edwin Arlington Robinson (poems), 1990; (intro.) Matthew Arnold and William Morris, 1990; (intro.) Algernon Charles Swinburne, 1990; (ed. with L. Abrams) The Archaeology and History of Glastonbury Abbey: Essays in Honour of the Ninetieth Birthday of C.A. Ralegh Radford, 1991; (ed. with M.B. Shichtman) Culture and the King: The Social Implications of the Arthurian Legend: Essays in Honor of Valerie M. Lagorio, 1994; (ed. with C.G.C. Tite) Books and Collectors, 1200-1700: Essays Presented to Andrew Watson, 1997; (ed.) The Libraries of King Henry VIII, 2000; (ed. with M. Axton) Triumphs of English: Henry Parker, 2000; (ed.) Glastonbury Abbey and the Arthurian Tradition, 2001; The Books of King Henry VIII and His Wives, 2004; De Uiris Illustribus=On Famous Men, 2010. **Address:** Department of English, York University, Rm. 130, Founders College, 4700 Keele St., Toronto, ON M3J 1P3, Canada. **Online address:** jcarley@yorku.ca

CARLEY, Lionel (Kenneth). British (born England), b. 1936. **Genres:** Poetry, Music, Biography, Plays/Screenplays. **Career:** Teacher, 1962-63. Writer. **Publications:** Delius and America: An Exhibition of Photographs, Scores, Letters and Other Material Relating to Delius's Visits to America and Illustrating the American Background to Koanga and Other Works, 1972; Delius: The Paris Years, 1975; Night Watch (poems), 1976; (contrib.) A Delius Companion, 1976; (with R. Threlfall) Delius: A Life in Pictures, 1977; (contrib.) The Percy Grainger Companion, 1981; (trans.) Gunnar Heiberg, Folkeraadet (title means: People's Parliament), 1982; Delius: A Life in Letters, 1862-1908, 1984; Delius: A Life in Letters, 1909-1934, 1988; (comp. and trans.) Grieg and Delius: A Chronicle of Their Friendship in Letters, 1993; Frederick Delius: Music, Art and Literature, 1998; Edvard Grieg in England, 2006. Contributor to books and periodicals. **Address:** c/o Andrew Best, Curtis Brown, 162-168 Regent St., London, GL W1R 5TA, England.

CARLIN, Martha. American (born United States) **Genres:** Food And Wine, History, Technology, Reference. **Career:** University of Wisconsin, Department of History, assistant professor, 1990-95, associate professor, 1995-, professor, director of graduate studies, 1996-. Writer and historian. **Publications:** Medieval Southwark, 1996; London and Southwark Inventories 1316-1650: A Handlist of Extents for Debts (reference), 1997; (ed. with J.T. Rosenthal) Food and Eating in Medieval Europe, 1998; (ed. and trans. with D. Crouch) English Society, 1200-1250: Letters from a Lost World, 2012. **Address:** Department of History, University of Wisconsin, 328 Holton Hall, 2442 E Hartford Ave., PO Box 413, Milwaukee, WI 53211-3159, U.S.A. **Online address:** carlin@uwm.edu

CARLIN, Vivian F. American (born United States), b. 1919. **Genres:** Gerontology/Senior Issues, Social Sciences, Medicine/Health, Psychology. **Career:** Clinical psychologist, 1940-45; vocational counselor, 1945-52; New Jersey State Division on Aging, supervisor, 1969-84; White House Conference on Aging, staff coordinator, 1981; consultant in gerontology, 1984-. Writer. **Publications:** (With R. Mansberg) If I Live to Be 100: Congregate Housing for Later Life, 1984, 2nd ed., 1989; (with Mansberg) Where Can Mom Live? A Family Guide to Living Arrangements for Older Parents, 1987; Can Mom Live Alone? A Family Guide to Helping Older People Stay in Their Own Homes, 1991; (with V.E. Greenberg) Should Mom Live with Us? And is Happiness Possible if She Does, 1992. **Address:** 41 Quince Ct., Lawrenceville, NJ 08648, U.S.A.

CARLING, Alan H(ugh). British (born England), b. 1949. **Genres:** Social Sciences, Humanities. **Career:** University of Bradford, Department of Sociology, lecturer, senior lecturer 1978-2002, retired, 2002, Association of University Teachers, officer, 1982-, local president, 1992-94, School of Social and International Studies, honorary senior research fellow in sociology, PPC Research Hub, coordinator. Freelance academic research worker. Writer. **Publications:** Social Division, 1991; (ed. with S. Duncan and R. Edwards) Analysing Families: Morality and Rationality in Policy and Practice, 2002; (ed.) Globalization and Identity: Development and Integration in a Changing World, 2006. Contributor to periodicals. **Address:** Department of Social Sciences and Humanities, University of Bradford, Richmond Rd., Bradford, WY BD7 1DP, England. **Online address:** a.h.carling@bradford.ac.uk

CARLING, Paul J. American (born United States), b. 1945. **Genres:** Medicine/Health, Psychology, Public/Social Administration, Self Help, Theology/Religion, Literary Criticism And History. **Career:** Fellowship House Farm, farm manager, 1968-69; Carling & Keitt, partner, contractor and carpenter, 1970-72; St. Joseph's College, psychology intern at Counseling Center, 1973-74; Horizon House, director of program development, director of residential services and intern, 1974-78; New Jersey Division of Mental Health and Hospitals, Bureau of Housing Policy and Development, chief, 1978-79, Bureau of Transitional Services, acting chief, 1978-79; National Institute of Mental Health, special assistant, 1979-81; Vermont Department of Mental Health, deputy commissioner, 1981-83; University of Vermont, Burlington, research and clinical associate professor of psychology, 1982-, Behavior Therapy and Psychotherapy Center, consultant; Trinity College of Vermont, Graduate Program in Community Mental Health, professor, and director, 1993-; University of Pennsylvania, lecturer, 1972-75; Boston University, research associate professor and director of community residential rehabilitation project at Center for Psychiatric Rehabilitation, 1984-87; Center for Community Change through Housing and Support, executive director, 1987-; episcopal priest, 2000; St. Michael's, associate rector; Saint Luke's Parish, associate rector for Pastoral Care & Outreach. Writer. **Publications:** (Ed. with J.W. Jacobson and S.N. Burchard) Community Living for People with Developmental and Psychiatric Disabilities, 1992; Return to Community: Building Support Systems for People with Psychiatric Disabilities, 1995. Contributor to books and journals. **Address:** St. Luke's Parish, 1864 Post Rd., Darien, CT 06820, U.S.A. **Online address:** paul.carling@saintlukesdarien.org

CARLISE, Carris. *See* **PEMBERTON, Margaret.**

CARLISLE, Donna. *See* **BALL, Donna Rochelle.**

CARLISLE, Elizabeth Pendergast. American (born United States) **Genres:** Biography, History, Women's Studies And Issues. **Career:** Author and educator. **Publications:** Earthbound and Heavenbent: The Life of Elizabeth Porter Phelps and Life at Forty Acres, (1747-1817), 2004. Contributor to periodicals. **Address:** Victoria Sanders & Associates L.L.C., 241 Ave. of the Americas, Ste. 11-H, New York, NY 10014-7522, U.S.A.

CARLOMAGNO, Mary. American (born United States) **Genres:** Self Help. **Career:** Order, owner and founder. Author and speaker. **Publications:** Give It Up!: My Year of Learning to Live Better with Less, 2005; Secrets of Simplicity: Learn to Live Better with Less, 2008; Live More, Want Less: 52 Ways to Find Order in Your Life, 2011. Contributor to magazines and newspapers. **Address:** 920 Jefferson St., Apt. 305, Hoboken, NJ 07030-9203, U.S.A. **Online address:** mary@orderperiod.com

CARLS, Stephen D(ouglas). American (born United States), b. 1944. **Genres:** History, Young Adult Non-fiction. **Career:** University of Minnesota, teaching assistant, 1970-71; Sterling College, assistant professor, 1971-81, associate professor, 1981-83; Union University, associate professor, 1983-90, professor, 1990-2000, Department of History, chair, 1990-, university professor of history, 2000-. Writer. **Publications:** Louis Loucheur and the Shaping of Modern France, 1916-1931, 1993; Louis Loucheur: Ingénieur, homme d'état, modernisateur de la France, 1872-1931, 2000. Contributor to books. **Address:** Department of History, Union University, PAC CB5, 1050 Union University Dr., PO Box 1882, Jackson, TN 38305-3697, U.S.A. **Online address:** scarls@uu.edu

CARLSEN, Spike. American (born United States), b. 1952. **Genres:** History. **Career:** Family Handyman Magazine, executive editor. **Publications:** A Splintered History of Wood: Belt Sander Races, Blind Woodworkers, and Baseball Bats, 2008. Contributor to periodicals. **Address:** Stillwater, MN , U.S.A. **Online address:** carlsen@usinternet.com

CARLSON, Allen R. American (born United States), b. 1968. **Genres:** Social Sciences. **Career:** Cornell University, Department of Government, associate professor, director of the undergraduate studies program; National Science Foundation fellow, 1992-95; Cheng Lee language fellow, 1993, 1995; Volker fellow, 1995; Columbia University, Expanding East Asian Studies fellow, 2003-04; Fulbright-Hays faculty research abroad fellow, 2004-05; Peking University, visiting scholar. Academic and writer. **Publications:** (ed. with J.J. Suh and P.J. Katzenstein) Rethinking Security in East Asia: Identity, Power and Efficiency, 2004; Beijing's Tibet Policy: Securing Sovereignty and Legitimacy, 2004; Unifying China, Integrating with the World: Securing Chinese Sovereignty in the Reform Era, 2005. Contributor to journals. **Address:** Cornell University, Department of Government, 310 White Hall, Ithaca, NY 14853, U.S.A. **Online address:** arc26@cornell.edu

CARLSON, David J. American (born United States), b. 1970. **Genres:** Autobiography/Memoirs, Law. **Career:** California State University, professor. Writer. **Publications:** Sovereign Selves: American Indian Autobiography and the Law, 2006. Contributor to journals. **Address:** Department of English, California State University, 5500 University Pkwy., San Bernardino, CA 92407-2393, U.S.A. **Online address:** dajcarls@csusb.edu

CARLSON, Joan. *See* **CHAPMAN, J. Dudley.**

CARLSON, John V. American (born United States), b. 1947. **Genres:** Theology/Religion, Humanities. **Career:** First Presbyterian Church, assistant pastor, 1973-75; Hyattsville Presbyterian Church, pastor, 1975-86; Pastoral Counseling and Consultation Centers of Greater Baltimore, pastoral counselor, 1985-88; Pastoral Counseling and Consultation Center of Greater Washington, pastoral counselor and regional director; clinical professional counselor, 1991-; Counseling Ministry at Oaklands, pastoral counselor, 1995-; Highland Presbyterian Church, pastor, 2003-. Writer. **Publications:** The Spiritual Dimensions of Self-Esteem, 2001; The Spiritual Power of Communication, forthcoming; The Disciple's Song (poem), forthcoming. **Address:** Highland Presbyterian Church, 701 Highland Rd., Street, MD 21154, U.S.A. **Online address:** jvcarlson@hotmail.com

CARLSON, Keith Thor. Canadian (born Canada), b. 1966. **Genres:** Cultural/Ethnic Topics, History. **Career:** Freelance historical research consultant, 1992-2001; Sto:lo Nation, historian, 1992-2001; University of Saskatchewan, professor of history, 2001-, director of the ICCC. Writer. **Publications:** Twisted Road to Freedom, 1995; You are Asked to Witness, 1997; I am Stó: Lo (juvenile nonfiction), 1998; A Stó: Lo-Coast Salish Historical Atlas, 2001; (ed. with K. Fagan) Call Me Hank, 2006; The Power of Place, the Problem of Time: Aboriginal Identity and Historical Consciousness in the Cauldron of Colonialism, 2010; Orality and literacy, 2010. FORTHCOMING: The Crown's Promise in BC Native-Newcomer Relations and Historical Consciousness; Oblate-Salish Relations: Reports of the Oblates of Mary Immaculate from the Salish Pacific Coast 1862-1904; (ed. with K. Fagon and N. Shostak) Talking About Writing, Writing About Talking: Orality-Literacy Dynamics and Tensions; (ed.) An Historical Atlas of the Metis of N.W. Saskatchewan; The Lynching of Louie Sam; The Ancestors Put Us Here: The Life Story of Sonny McHalsie; Huk Supremo: The Collective Writings and Reflections of Luis Taruc. **Address:** Department of History, University of Saskatchewan, Rm. 1023, 9 Campus Dr., 721 Arts Bldg., Saskatoon, SK S7N 5A5, Canada. **Online address:** keith.carlson@usask.ca

CARLSON, Laurie. American (born United States), b. 1952. **Genres:** Children's Non-fiction, History, Novels, Medicine/Health. **Career:** Teacher, 1976-77, 1988-92; artist and sculptor, 1977-86; Eastern Washington University, faculty, 1998-2001. Writer. **Publications:** Home Study Opportunities: A Complete Guide to Going to School by Mail, 1989; Kids Create!, 1990; Eco Art! Earth-Friendly Art and Craft Experiences for Three-to-Nine-Year-Olds, 1993; More Than Moccasins, 1994; Huzzah! Means Hooray!, 1994; Green Thumbs, 1995; (with J. Dammel) Kids Camp!, 1995; Westward Ho!, 1996; Colonial Kids!, 1997; Boss of the Plains: The Story of the Cowboy Hat, 1998; Days of Knights and Damsels: An Activity Guide, 1998; Classical Kids: An Activity Guide to Ancient Greece and Rome, 1998; On Sidesaddles to Heaven: The Women of the Rocky Mountain Mission, 1998; Fever in Salem: A New Interpretation of the New England Witch Trials, 1999; Fits and Fevers: Salem's Witches and the Forgotten Epidemic, 1999; Cattle: An Informal Social History, 2001; (with M.K. Green) Washington in the Pacific Northwest, 2002; Seduced by the West: Jefferson's America and the Lure of the Spanish West, 2003; Queen of Inventions: How the Sewing Machine Changed the World, 2003; 1952- William J. Spillman and the Birth of Agricultural Economics, 2005; Thomas Edison for Kids: His Life and Ideas: 21 Activities, 2006; Harry Houdini for Kids: His Life and Adventures with 21 Magic Tricks and Illusions, 2009; Sunlight Solution: Why more Sun Exposure is Essential to Your Health, 2009. Contributor to periodicals. **Address:** 16502 W Stoughton Rd., Cheney, WA 99004, U.S.A. **Online address:** laucarlson@aol.com

CARLSON, Lori Marie. American (born United States), b. 1957. **Genres:** Picture/Board Books, Novels. **Career:** Writer. **Publications:** PICTURE BOOKS: Sol a Sol, 1998; Hurray for Three Kings Day!, 1999. NOVELS: The Sunday Tertulia, 2000; The Flamboyant, 2002; Moon When All Things Ripen, 2003. EDITOR: (co-ed.) Where Angels Glide at Dawn: New Stories from Latin America (young adult), 1990; (co-ed.) Return Trip Tango and Other Stories from Abroad, 1992; Cool Salsa: Bilingual Poems on Growing up Latino in the U.S. (young adult), 1994; American Eyes: New Asian American Short Stories for Young Adults, 1994; (and author of intro.) Barrio Streets, Carnival Dreams: Three Generations of Latino Artistry (young adult), 1996; You're On!: Seven Bilingual Plays (juvenile), 1999; Red Hot Salsa: Bilingual Poems on Being Young and Latino in the United States, 2005; Moccasin Thunder: American Indian Stories for Today, 2005; (with O. Hijuelos) Burnt Sugar, 2006; Voices in First Person: Reflections on Latino Identity, 2008; Light of Desire La luz del deseo, 2009. Contributor to periodicals. **Address:** c/o Jennifer Lyons, Writers House Inc., 21 W 26th St., New York, NY 10010, U.S.A. **Online address:** contact@lorimariecarlson.com

CARLSON, Paul H. American (born United States), b. 1940. **Genres:** History, Biography. **Career:** Texas Lutheran College, professor of history; Texas Tech University, professor of history, through 2009, emeritus professor of history, 2009-, Center for the Southwest, director. Writer and historian. **Publications:** (Comp. with K.D. Yeilding) Ah That Voice: The Fireside Chats of Franklin Delano Roosevelt, 1974; Texas Woollybacks: The Range Sheep and Goat Industry, 1982; (with D. Abbe and D.J. Murrah) Lubbock and the South Plains: An Illustrated History, 1989; Pecos Bill: A Military Biography of William R. Shafter, 1989; Empire Builder in the Texas Panhandle: William Henry Bush, 1996; The Plains Indians, 1998; (ed.) The Cowboy Way: An Exploration of History and Culture, 2000; The Buffalo Soldier Tragedy of 1877, 2003; Deep Time and the Texas High Plains: History and Geology, 2005; Amarillo: The Story of a Western Town, 2006; (ed. with B.A. Glasrud and T.D. Kreidler) Slavery to Integration: Black Americans in West Texas, 2007; (with D.R. Abbe) Historic Lubbock County: An Illustrated History, 2008; The Centennial History of Lubbock: Hub City of the Plains, 2008; (with T. Crum) Myth, Memory and Massacre, 2010. **Address:** Department of History, Texas Tech University, 2500 Broadway, Lubbock, TX 79409, U.S.A. **Online address:** paul.carlson@ttu.edu

CARLSON, Richard A. American (born United States), b. 1956. **Genres:** Psychology. **Career:** University of Illinois-Urbana-Champaign, research assistant, 1981-82, 1983-84, instructor in cognitive psychology, 1982, 1983, Human Attention Research Laboratory, associate director, 1984-85; Pennsylvania State University, assistant professor, 1985-91, associate professor, 1991-97, professor of psychology, 1997-, chair of cognitive studies, 1988-93, Graduate Program in Cognitive Psychology, coordinator, 1989-95, 2007-08, Penn State Behavioral IRB, chair, 1992-97, director of undergraduate studies in psychology, 1995-, associate head. Writer. **Publications:** Experienced Cognition, 1997. Contributor to journals. **Address:** Department of Psychology, Pennsylvania State University, 613 Moore Bldg., University Park, PA 16802-3106, U.S.A. **Online address:** racarlson@psu.edu

CARLSON, Richard C. American (born United States), b. 1942. **Genres:** Politics/Government, Social Commentary. **Career:** Public Health Service, management analyst, 1964; Executive Office of the President of the United States, Office of Management and the Budget, budget analyst, 1965-69; U.S. Office of Education, Office for Renewal, director of planning, 1971-73; State of Illinois, Bureau of the Budget, Office of the Governor, assistant director, 1973-75; SRI Intl., senior regional economist, 1976-84; QED Research Inc., vice president and principal, 1984-88; Spectrum Economics Inc., president, 1988-92, chairperson, 1992-. Writer. **Publications:** (Co-author) Energy Future: Human Values and Lifestyles: A New Look at Energy Crisis (future studies), 1982; (with R.L. Thomas) West, Harbinger of Change?, 1984; (with D.C. Henton and G.M. Morse) Managing the Changing Work Force: Work Force Implications of Economic Restructuring, 1984; 2020 Visions: Long View of a Changing World (future studies), 1991; I'll Surely Pay You Tuesday: Issues and Candidates in the 1992 Election (politics), 1992; (with B. Goldman) Fast Forward: Where Technology, Demographics and History will Take America and the World in the Next Thirty Years (future studies), 1994. **Address:** Spectrum Economics Inc., 201 San Antonio Cir., Ste. A105, Mountain View, CA 94040-1252, U.S.A. **Online address:** rccarl@sjm.inti.net

CARLSON, Ron. American (born United States), b. 1947. **Genres:** Novels, Novellas/Short Stories. **Career:** Hotchkiss School, English teacher, 1971-81; Bread Loaf fellow, 1983; National Endowment for the Arts, fellow, 1985; Arizona State University, writer-in-residence, 1986-87, assistant professor, 1987-89, associate professor, 1989-94, professor of English, 1994-, director of creative writing, 1989-96, 2003-, foundation professor, 2003, regents professor of English, 2004-06; University of Hawaii, visiting writer, 1997; Beloit College, Mackey distinguished professor of creative writing, 2000; University of California, professor of English, director of MFA writing program, 2006-. **Publications:** NOVELS: Betrayed by F. Scott Fitzgerald, 1977; Truants, 1981; The Speed of Light, 2003; Five Skies, 2007; The Signal, 2009. STORIES: The News of the World, 1987, 2nd ed., 1988; Plan B for the Middle Class, 1992; The Hotel Eden, 1997; At the Jim Bridger, 2002, 2nd ed., 2003; A Kind of Flying, 2003; Ron Carlson Writes a Story, 2007. OTHERS: Room Service: Poems, Meditations, Outcries & Remarks, 2012. Works appear in anthologies. **Address:** Department of English, University of California, Creative Writing Program, 312 Humanities Instructional Bldg., PO Box 2650, Irvine, CA 92697-2650, U.S.A. **Online address:** ron.carlson@asu.edu

CARLSON, Ron. (Ronald L. Carlson). American (born United States), b. 1934. **Genres:** Criminology/True Crime, Law. **Career:** U.S. commissioner, 1964-65; University of Iowa, assistant professor, 1965-67, associate professor, 1967-69, professor of law, 1969-73; Iowa Legislature, Criminal Code Review Study Committee, consultant, 1969-73; Washington University, professor of law, 1973-84; University of Georgia, Fuller E. Callaway professor of law, 1984-2001, Fuller E. Callaway chair of law emeritus, 2001-. Writer. **Publications:** Criminal Justice Procedure, 1970, 7th ed., 2005; Criminal Law and Procedure, 1979; Criminal Law Advocacy, 1982; (with E.J. Imwinkelried and E.J. Kionka) Materials for the Study of Evidence, 1983, 2nd ed., 1986; Successful Techniques for Civil Trials, 1983, 2nd ed., 1992; Adjudication of Criminal Justice: Problems and References, 1986, 2nd ed., 2007; (with E.J. Imwinkelried) Dynamics of Trial Practice, 1989, 4th ed., 2010; (with M. Bright) Objections at Trial: A Concise Guide, 1990, 5th ed., 2008; (with M. Bright) Maine Objections at Trial, 1991; (with R.H. Aronson and M.H. Bright) Washington Objections at Trial, 1991; (with E.J. Imwinkelried and E.J. Kionka) Evidence in the Nineties, 3rd ed., 1991; (with E.J. Imwinkelried and M.H. Bright) California Objections at Trial, 1992; (with M.H. Bright) New Hampshire Objections at Trial, 1992; (with A.D. Montgomery and M.H. Bright) Minnesota Objections at Trial, 1992, 5th ed., 2008; (with M.H. Bright) Oregon Objections at Trial, 1992; (with W. Eleazer and M.H. Bright) Florida Objections at Trial, 1992; (with S. Crump and M.H. Bright) Texas Objections at Trial, 1992; Successful Techniques for Civil Trials, 1992; Trial Handbook for Georgia Lawyers, 1993, 3rd ed., 2003; (with J.C. O'Brien and M.H. Bright) Missouri Objections at Trial, 1993; (with J.H. Young and M.H. Bright) Virginia Objections at Trial, 1993; Pocket Proof of Facts, 1993; Evidence: Teaching Materials for an Age of Science and Statutes, 1997, 6th ed., 2007. **Address:** School of Law, University of Georgia, 219 Hirsch Hall, 225 Herty Dr., Athens, GA 30602, U.S.A. **Online address:** mlfield@uga.edu

CARLSON, Ronald L. *See* **CARLSON, Ron.**

CARLTON, David. British (born England), b. 1938. **Genres:** History, International Relations/Current Affairs, Military/Defense/Arms Control. **Career:** Polytechnic of North London, assistant lecturer, 1967-68, lecturer, 1968-70, senior lecturer in diplomatic history, 1970-; University of Warwick, Department of Politics and International Studies, lecturer, senior lecturer, professor, 1986-. Writer. **Publications:** MacDonald versus Henderson: The Foreign Policy of the Second Labour Government, 1970; Anthony Eden: A Biography, 1981; Britain and the Suez Crisis, 1988; Churchill and the Soviet Union, 2000; West's Road to 9/11: Resisting, Appeasing, and Encouraging Terrorism Since 1970, 2005; (co-author) Theatre Censorship: From Walpole to Wilson, 2007. CO-EDITOR: The Dynamics of the Arms Race, 1975; International Terrorism and World Security, 1975; Arms Control and Technological Innovation, 1977; Terrorism: Theory and Practice, 1979; Contemporary Terror: Essays in Sub-State Violence, 1981; The Hazards of the International Energy Crisis, 1982; The Arms Race in the 1980s, 1982; South-Eastern Europe after Tito, 1983; Reassessing Arms Control, 1984; The Nuclear Arms Race Debated, 1986; The Cold War Debated, 1988; The Arms Race in the Era of Star Wars, 1988; New Technologies and the Arms Race, 1989; Perspectives on the Arms Race, 1989; The Arms Race in an Era of Negotiations, 1991; Reducing Nuclear Arsenals, 1991; Space and Nuclear Weaponry, 1992; Controlling the International Transfer of Weaponry and Related Technology, 1995; Rising Tension in Eastern Europe and the Former Soviet Union, 1996; Racism, Xenophobia and Ethnic Conflict, 1996; The Search for Stability in Russia and the Former Soviet Bloc, 1997. **Address:** The Global Policy Institute, London Metropolitan University, 31 Jewry St., London, GL EC3N 2EY, England. **Online address:** d.carlton@global-policy.com

CARLTON, Jim. American (born United States), b. 1955?. **Genres:** Documentaries/Reportage, Biography. **Career:** Wall Street Journal, reporter. **Publications:** Apple: The Inside Story of Intrigue, Egomania, and Business Blunders, 1997. **Address:** Random House Inc., 1745 Broadway, 18th Fl., New York, NY 10019-4368, U.S.A.

CARLTON, Susan. American (born United States), b. 1960?. **Genres:** Novels, Children's Fiction. **Career:** Magazine writer and editor. **Publications:** (With C. Myers) The Nanny Book: The Smart Parent's Guide to Hiring, Firing, and Every Sticky Situation in Between, 1999; Lobsterland (novel), 2007. Contributor to periodicals. **Address:** St. Martin's Press, 175 5th Ave., New York, NY 10010, U.S.A. **Online address:** susan@susancarlton.com

CARLYLE, Liz. *See* **WOODHOUSE, S(usan) T.**

CARLYON, David. American (born United States), b. 1949?. **Genres:** Novels, History. **Career:** University of Michigan, assistant professor, 1993-96. Writer. **Publications:** Dan Rice: The Most Famous Man Youve Never Heard Of, 2001; (contrib.) The Amazing American Circus Poster: The Strobridge Lithographing Company, 2011. Contributor to periodicals. **Address:** c/o. Author Mail, Public Affairs, 250 W 57th St., Ste. 1321, New York, NY 10107-1307, U.S.A.

CARMAN, Patrick. American (born United States), b. 1966. **Genres:** Novels. **Career:** Ran Advertising Agency, founder, 1989-98; MyWebPal, (Web site providing online newspaper publishing), founder; Amped Radio (syndicator of radio shows), founder. Childrens novelist. **Publications:** LAND OF ELYON: The Dark Hills Divide, 2003; Beyond the Valley of Thorns, 2005; The Tenth City, 2006; Into The Mist, 2007; Land of Elyon-Boxed Set, 2007; Stargazer, 2008. ATHERTON: The House of Power, 2007; Rivers of Fire, 2008; The Dark Planet, 2009. ELLIOT'S PARK: Saving Mister Nibbles, 2008; Haunted Hike, 2008; Walnut Cup, 2009. OTHERS: Skeleton Creek, 2009; The Black Circle, 2009; Ghost in the Machine, 2009; Trackers, 2010; Thirteen Days To Midnight, 2010; The Crossbones, 2010; Dark Eden, 2011; Floors, 2011; Shantorian, 2011. **Address:** Scholastic Inc., 557 Broadway, New York, NY 10012, U.S.A. **Online address:** fanmail@patrickcarman.com

CARMICHAEL, Clair. *See* **MCNAB, Claire.**

CARMICHAEL, E. D. H. *See* **CARMICHAEL, Liz.**

CARMICHAEL, Liz. (E. D. H. Carmichael). British (born England) **Genres:** Theology/Religion. **Career:** St. John's College, chaplain and tutor in theology, emeritus research fellow. Writer. **Publications:** AS E.D.H. CARMICHAEL: Friendship: Interpreting Christian Love, 2004. Contributor to books and periodicals. **Address:** Theology Faculty Ctr., 41 St. Giles, Oxford, OX OX1 3LW, England. **Online address:** liz.carmichael@sjc.ox.ac.uk

CARNAHAN, Burrus M. American (born United States), b. 1944?. **Genres:** Law. **Career:** U.S. Department of State Bureau of International Security and Nonproliferation, foreign affairs officer; George Washington University, Law School, professional lecturer in law; U.S. Air Force, lawyer. Consultant and writer. **Publications:** Act of Justice: Lincoln's Emancipation Proclamation and the Law of War, 2007; Lincoln on Trial: Southern Civilians and the Law of War, 2010. Contributor to periodicals. **Address:** Law School, The George Washington University, 2000 H St. NW, Washington, DC 20052, U.S.A. **Online address:** bcarnahan@law.gwu.edu

CARNALL, Geoffrey Douglas. British (born England), b. 1927. **Genres:** Literary Criticism And History, Biography, Art/Art History, Essays. **Career:** Baring Union Christian College, lecturer in English, 1949; The Queen's University of Belfast, lecturer in English, 1952-60; University of Edinburgh, lecturer in English literature, 1960-65, senior lecturer, 1965-69, reader, 1969-, School of Literatures, Languages and Cultures, honorary fellow, 2003-; Edinburgh Council for Nuclear Disarmament, vice-chairman, 1962-65, chairman, 1965-71. Writer. **Publications:** Robert Southey and His Age: The Development of a Conservative Mind, 1960; Robert Southey, 1964; To Keep the Peace: The United Nations Peace Force, 1965; Gandhi's Interpreter: A Life of Horace Alexander, 2010. EDITOR: Pope, Dickens and Others: Essays and Addresses, 1969; The Mid-Eighteenth Century, vol. VIII, 1979, rev. ed. as The Age of Johnson, 1990; (with C. Nicholson) The Impeachment of Warren Hastings: Papers from a Bicentenary Commemoration, 1989; (with M. Barefoot) Dr. Joseph Priestley: A Scottish Perspective-Catalogue of an Exhibition of Books and Manuscripts in Edinburgh University Library, 1992; (ed.) An Indian Tapestry: Quaker Threads in the History of India, Pakistan and Bangladesh: From the Seventeenth Century to Independence, 1997. Contributor of articles to journals. **Address:** Edinburgh University Press, 22 George Sq., Edinburgh, EH8 9LF, Scotland. **Online address:** g.d.carnall@ed.ac.uk

CARNECI, Magda. French/Romanian (born Romania), b. 1955?. **Genres:** Novels, Novellas/Short Stories, Poetry, Essays, Anthropology/Ethnology. **Career:** Institute of Art History, senior researcher; National Institute of Oriental Languages and Civilizations (INALCO), visiting professor; Romanian Cultural Institute, deputy director, 2005-, director; International Center for Contemporary Art, chairman, president; AICA-Romania, co-director. Writer. **Publications:** Lon Tuculescu, 1984; Experiment: In arta romaneasca dupa 1960, 1997; Poeme, 1999; Poetrix: Texte despre poezie soi alte eseuri, 2002; Perspectives roumaines: Du postcommunisme à l'intégration Européenne, 2004; Chaosmos, 2006; Art et pouvoir en roumanie, 1945-1989, 2007. **Address:** Romanian Cultural Institute, 1 Rue de l'Exposition, Paris, 75007, France. **Online address:** magda.carneci@wanadoo.fr

CARNEY, Judith A(nn). American (born United States) **Genres:** Anthropology/Ethnology, Biography, History. **Career:** University of California, Department of Geography, associate professor, professor. Writer. **Publications:** Triticale Production in the Central Mexican Highlands: Smallholders' Experiences and Lessons for Research, 1990; Black Rice: The African Origins of Rice Cultivation in the Americas, 2001; (with R.N. Rosomoff) In the Shadow of Slavery: Africa's Botanical Legacy in the Atlantic World, 2009. **Address:** Department of Geography, University of California, 1255 Bunche Hall, Los Angeles, CA 90095-1524, U.S.A. **Online address:** carney@geog.ucla.edu

CARNEY, Pat. Canadian/Chinese (born China), b. 1935. **Genres:** Autobiography/Memoirs. **Career:** Canadian House of Commons, secretary of state, 1980-84, minister of energy, mines and resources, 1984-88, minister of international trade, 1984-88, Treasury Board, president, 1984-88; Canadian Senate, staff, 1990-, conservative senator, 2004-08, senator emeritus, 2008-; University of British Columbia, School of Community and Regional Planning, adjunct professor, 1990-99; Asia Pacific Initiative, minister. Journalist and economic consultant. **Publications:** Tiara & Atigi; Northwest Territories 1970 Centennial, the Royal Tour, 1971; Trade Secrets: A Memoir, 2000. Contributor to newspapers and magazines. **Address:** c/o Perry Goldsmith, Contemporary Communications Ltd., 1663 W 7th Ave., Vancouver, BC V6J 1S4, Canada. **Online address:** carnep@sen.parl.gc.ca

CARNEY, Raymond. American (born United States), b. 1950. **Genres:** Film, Art/Art History, Social Sciences. **Career:** Middlebury College, assistant professor of literature and film, 1978-; Stanford University, assistant professor, Humanities Center, William Rice Kimball fellow; Boston University, professor of film studies, 1990-, director of the graduate and undergraduate film studies programs and chair of graduate admissions in film studies, 1995-2005; Whitney Museum of American Art, consultant; The Museum of Modern Art, consultant; University of Texas, associate professor in the humanities program. Writer. **Publications:** (Ed. and intro.) The Spoils of Poynton and What Maisie Knew, 1985; (ed. and intro.) Kim, 1985; American Dreaming: The Films of John Cassavetes and the American Experience, 1985; American Vision: The Films of Frank Capra and the Transcendental Impulse, 1986; (intro.) Mont Saint Michel and Chartres, 1986; Speaking the Language of Desire: The Films of Carl Dreyer, 1989; (ed.) The Cambridge Film Classics, 25 vols., 1989-93. OTHERS: Films of John Cassavetes: Pragmatism, Modernism, and the Movies, 1994; American Vision: The Films of Frank Capra, 1996; Why Art Matters, 1999; Films of Mike Leigh: Embracing the World, 2000; (ed.) Cassavetes on Cassavetes, 2001; Shadows, 2001; Necessary Experiences, 2002; What's Wrong with Film Books, Film Courses, and Film Reviewing, 2004; (and ed.) John Cassavetes in Person, 2009; The Real Independent Movement-Beyond the Hype, forthcoming; Henry James, forthcoming. Works appear in anthologies. Contributor to periodicals. **Address:** Department of Film and Television, College of Communication, Boston University, 223B, 640 Commonwealth Ave., Boston, MA 02215, U.S.A. **Online address:** rcarney@bu.edu

CARNLEY, Peter Frederick. Australian (born Australia), b. 1937. **Genres:** Theology/Religion, Humanities. **Career:** Diocese of Bath, deacon, 1962, priest, 1964; Diocese of Ely, deacon, 1966-69; Mitchell College of Advanced Education, chaplain, 1970-72; St. John's College, research fellow, 1971-72, fellow, 2000-; St. John's Cathedral, residentiary canon, 1975-81; Anglican Church of Australia, primate, 2000-; University of Melbourne, Trinity College, fellow, 2000-; University of Queensland, lecturer in theology. Writer. **Publications:** The Structure of Resurrection Belief, 1987; Faithfulness in Fellowship: Reflections on Homosexuality and the Church, 2001; The Yellow Wallpaper and Other Sermons, 2001; Reflections in Glass: Trends and Tensions in the Contemporary Anglican Church, 2004. **Address:** PO Box W2067, Perth, WA 6846, Australia.

CARNOCHAN, W. B. American (born United States), b. 1930. **Genres:** Literary Criticism And History, Autobiography/Memoirs. **Career:** Stanford University, Department of English, instructor, 1960-62, assistant professor, 1962-68, associate professor, 1968-73, professor, 1973-92, Richard W. Lyman professor of humanities, 1993-94, Richard W. Lyman professor emeritus of humanities, 1994-, dean of grad studies, 1975-80, vice-provost, 1976-80, Stanford Humanities Center, director, 1985-91. Writer. **Publications:** (Ed.) The Man of Mode, 1966; Lemuel Gulliver's Mirror for Man, 1968; Confinement and Flight: An Essay on English Literature of the Eighteenth Century, 1977; (with P.M. Spacks) A Distant Prospect, 1982; Gibbon's Solitude: The Inward World of the Historian, 1987; (contrib.) Cultural Landscapes, 1989; The Battleground of the Curriculum: Liberal Education and American Experience, 1993; Nataka kuwa hura kabisa!, 1997; Momentary Bliss: An American Memoir, 1999; The Sad Story of Burton, Speke, and the Nile, 2006; Golden Legends: Images of Abyssinia, Samuel Johnson to Bob Marley, 2008; Confessions of a Dodger Fan, 2010. **Address:** Department of English, Stanford University, 460 Bldg., Margaret Jacks Hall, Stanford, CA 94305, U.S.A. **Online address:** carnochan@stanford.edu

CARO, Robert A. American (born United States), b. 1935. **Genres:** Biography, History, Adult Non-fiction. **Career:** Daily Princetonian, managing editor; Columbia University, Carnegie Fellow; Harvard University, Nieman Fellow; New Brunswick Daily Home News, reporter; Newsday, investigative reporter. **Publications:** The Power Broker: Robert Moses and the Fall of New York, 1974; The Years of Lyndon Johnson, 1982; The Path to Power, 1982; (co-author) Extraordinary Lives, 1986; Means of Ascent, 1990; Master of the Senate, 2002; The Theofore H. White Lecture with Robert A. Caro, 2003. **Address:** 250 W 57th St., Ste. 2215, New York, NY 10107-2207, U.S.A. **Online address:** randaltracy@aol.com

CARON, Brane Mozetic. (Brane Mozetič). Slovenian/Yugoslav (born Slovenia), b. 1958. **Genres:** Poetry. **Career:** Poet and translator. **Publications:** AS BRANE MOZETIC: Sneguljcica je sedem palckov, 1976; Soledadesi, 1978; Skucev literarni zbornik, 1981; Modrina dotika, 1986; Zaklinjanja, 1987; Obsedenost, 1991; Pasijon, 1993; Pesmi za umrlimi sanjami, 1995; Angeli, 1996; (co-author) The Imagination of Terra Incognita: Slovenian Writing, 1945-1995, 1997; Cinco Autores Eslovenos, 2000; Quatro Escritores Eslovenos, 2000; Metulji, 2000; Zgubljena Zgodba, 2001; Obsession, 2002; Parole Che Bruciano=Besede, Ki Zgejo, 2002; Banalije, 2003; Poemas para los Sueños Muertos, 2004; Se Banalije, 2005; Metulji=Mariposas, 2006. Contributor to periodicals. **Address:** Center for Slovenian literature, Metelkova 6, Ljubljana, 1000, Slovenia. **Online address:** brane.mozetic@guest.arnes.si

CARONE, Gabriela Roxana. American (born United States) **Genres:** Philosophy, History. **Career:** University of Colorado, assistant professor, 1995-2005; Princeton University, Center for Human Values, fellow, 2003-04; Harvard University, Center for Hellenic Studies, fellow, 2004-05; school founder and director. Writer. **Publications:** Mind as the Foundation of Cosmic Order in Plato's Late Dialogues, 1995; (contrib.) Oxford Studies in Ancient Philosophy, vol. XXVI, 2004; Plato's Cosmology and Its Ethical Dimensions, 2005. Contributor to periodicals. **Address:** Philosophy Department, University of Colorado, UCB 232, Boulder, CO 80309-0232, U.S.A. **Online address:** gabrielacarone@colorado.edu

CAROTHERS, Thomas. American (born United States), b. 1956?. **Genres:** Politics/Government, Business/Trade/Industry. **Career:** U.S. Department of State, attorney-adviser, 1980; Arnold and Porter (law firm), attorney, 1990-93; Carnegie Endowment for International Peace, director of research, vice president for studies, 1997-2002, senior associate, Democracy and Rule of Law Project, co-director; Central European University, recurrent visiting professor, 2002-04; University of Oxford, Nuffield College, senior research fellow; Johns Hopkins School of Advanced International Studies, faculty. Writer. **Publications:** In the Name of Democracy: U.S. Policy toward Latin America in the Reagan Years, 1991; (co-author) Moldovan Parliamentary Elections: February 27, 1994, 1994; Assessing Democracy Assistance: The Case of Romania, 1996; Aiding Democracy Abroad: The Learning Curve, 1999; (ed. with M. Ottaway) Funding Virtue: Civil Society Aid and Democracy Promotion, 2000; Critical Mission: Essays on Democracy Promotion, 2004; (ed. with M. Ottaway) Uncharted Journey: Promoting Democracy in the Middle East, 2005; Confronting the Weakest Link: Aiding Political Parties in New Democracies, 2006; (ed.) Promoting the Rule of Law Abroad: In Search of Knowledge, 2006. Contributor of articles to periodicals and books. **Address:** Carnegie Endowment for International Peace, 1779 Massachusetts Ave. NW, Washington, DC 20036, U.S.A. **Online address:** tcarothers@carnegieendowment.org

CARPENTER, Bogdana. American/Polish (born Poland), b. 1941. **Genres:** Literary Criticism And History, Translations, Essays. **Career:** University of Washington, assistant professor of Polish, 1974-83; University of Michigan, associate professor, 1983-91, professor of Polish and comparative literature, 1991-, Slavic Languages and Literatures, professor emeritus; Cross Currents, associate editor, 1987-; World Literature Today, staff reviewer. **Publications:** The Poetic Avant-Garde in Poland, 1918-1939, 1983; Monumenta Polonica: The First Four Centuries of Polish Poetry, 1989; (intro. and ed. with M.G. Levine) To Begin Where I Am: Selected Essays, 2001; (trans. with C. Leach and M.G. Levine) C. Miłosz, Proud to be a Mammal, 2010. TRANSLATOR: WITH J. CARPENTER, WORKS BY Z. HERBERT: Selected Poems of Zbigniew Herbert, 1977; Report from the Besieged City and Other Poems, 1985; Still Life with a Bridle, 1991; Mr. Cogito, 1993; The King of the Ants: Mythological Essays, 1999; Elegy for the Departure and Other Poems, 1999; J. Hartwig, In Praise of the Unfinished: Selected Poems, 2008; J. Hartwig, It will Return: Poems, 2010; Between Dada and Conctructivism: Polish Poetic Avant-garde, forthcoming. **Address:** Department of Slavic Languages and Literature, University of Michigan, 3040 Modern Languages Bldg., 812 E Washington, Ann Arbor, MI 48109, U.S.A. **Online address:** bogdana@umich.edu

CARPENTER, Jeanne. *See* **BANAZEK, Jeanne M. (Carpenter).**

CARPENTER, Kenneth E(dward). American (born United States), b. 1936. **Genres:** Librarianship, Literary Criticism And History, History. **Career:** Harvard University, Houghton Library, assistant in reading room, 1959-61, assistant to the librarian, 1961-62, Bibliography of American Literature, Houghton Library, assistant to the editor, 1963-67, Kress Library, associate, 1967-68, curator, 1968-80, research and publications librarian, 1980-84, assistant director for research resources, 1984-, Widener Library, staff, 1993, Harvard Library Bulletin, editor; Bowdoin College, reference librarian, 1962-63; Simmons College, staff, 1963. Writer. **Publications:** (With C.E. Vose) Municipal Charters in Maine: The Case of Brunswick, 1958; (comp.) Russian Revolutionary Literature Collection, 1976; Dialogue in Political Economy: Translations from and into German in the 18th Century: Issued on the Occasion of an Exhibition in the Kress Library, 1977; (comp. with P. Barucci, R.R. Rogers and A.C. Abrami) Italian Economic Literature in the Kress Library, 1985; The First 350 Years of the Harvard University Library: Description of an Exhibition, 1986; (contrib.) The Legacy of James Bowdoin III, 1994; Readers and Libraries: Toward a History of Libraries and Culture in America, 1996; Dissemination of The Wealth of Nations in French and in France, 1776-1843, 2002. EDITOR: British Labour Struggles: Contemporary Pamphlets, 1727-1850, 32 vols., 1975; Books and Society in History: Papers of the Association of College and Research Libraries Rare Books and Manuscripts Preconference, 24-28 June, 1980, Boston, Massachusetts, 1983; Harvard University Library: A Documentary History: Bibliographic Guide, 1990; (with T. Augst) Institutions of Reading: The Social Life of Libraries in the United States, 2007. **Address:** Library, Wadsworth House, Harvard University, 1341 Massachusetts Ave., Cambridge, MA 02138, U.S.A.

CARPENTER, Lynette. Also writes as Della Borton, D. B. Borton. American (born United States), b. 1951. **Genres:** Mystery/Crime/Suspense, Literary Criticism And History, Bibliography. **Career:** University of Cincinnati, assistant professor of English, associate director, acting director of women's studies, 1980-89; Ohio Wesleyan University, Department of English, assistant professor, 1989-96, associate professor, 1996-2001, professor of English, 2001-, chairperson. Writer. **Publications:** (Ed. with W.K. Kolmar) Haunting the House of Fiction: Feminist Perspectives on Ghost Stories by American Women, 1991; (with W. Kolmar) Ghost Stories by British and American Women: A Selected, Annotated Bibliography, 1998; Eight Miles High, forthcoming. AS D.B. BORTON: One for the Money, 1993; Two Points for Murder, 1993; Three Is a Crowd, 1994; Four Elements of Murder, 1995; Five Alarm Fire, 1996; Six Feet Under, 1997; Two-Shot Foul, 2005. AS DELLA BORTON: Fade to Black, 1999; Freeze Frame, 2000; Slow Dissolve, 2001; Seventh Deadly Sin, 2004. **Address:** Department of English, Ohio Wesleyan University, 311 Sturges, 61 S Sandusky St., Delaware, OH 43015, U.S.A. **Online address:** llcarpen@owu.edu

CARPENTER, Mary Wilson. Canadian (born Canada), b. 1937. **Genres:** History, Theology/Religion. **Career:** Queen's University, professor of English, professor emerita; Harvard University, lecturer in history and literature. Educator and writer. **Publications:** George Eliot and the Landscape of Time: Narrative Form and Protestant Apocalyptic History, 1986; Imperial Bibles, Domestic Bodies: Women, Sexuality and Religion in the Victorian Market, 2003. Contributor to books and journals. **Address:** Department of English, Queen's University, Kingston, ON K7L 3N6, Canada. **Online address:** carpentm@post.queensu.ca

CARPENTER, Novella. American (born United States), b. 1972. **Genres:** Humor/Satire. **Career:** Sasquatch Books, editorial assistant, 1998-2001. Writer. **Publications:** (With T. Vogel) Don't Jump! The Northwest Winter Blues Survival Guide, 2000; Farm City: The Education of an Urban Farmer, 2009. **Address:** Oakland, CA , U.S.A. **Online address:** novella@novellacarpenter.com

CARPENTER, Sue. American (born United States), b. 1966?. **Genres:** Young Adult Non-fiction. **Career:** UHF magazine, editor, 1996; freelance writer, 1997-, staff writer; Los Angeles Times, feature writer, 1998-; Jane magazine, senior contributor. **Publications:** Forty Watts from Nowhere: A Journey into Pirate Radio, 2004. Contributor to periodicals. **Address:** Los Angeles Times, 202 W 1st St., Los Angeles, CA 90012, U.S.A. **Online address:** sue.carpenter@latimes.com

CARR, Alex. *See* **SILER, Jenny.**

CARR, Caleb. American (born United States), b. 1955. **Genres:** Novels, Biography, Military/Defense/Arms Control, History, Novellas/Short Stories. **Career:** Bard College, visiting professor of history, 2005, James Clarke Chace professor in foreign affairs and the humanities; MHQ: The Quarterly Journal of Military History, co-founder, 2005-, contributing editor, 2005-08. Historian. **Publications:** Casing the Promised Land, 1980; (with J. Chace) America Invulnerable: The Quest for Absolute Security from 1812 to Star Wars, 1988; Bad Attitudes, 1991; The Devil Soldier: The Story of Frederick Townsend Ward, 1991; Devil Soldier: The American Soldier of Fortune Who Became God in China, 1992; The Alienist, 1994; The Angel of Darkness, 1997; Killing Time: A Novel of the Future, 2000; Lessons of Terror: A History of Warfare Against Civilians: Why It Has Always Failed and Why It Will Fail Again, 2002; Lessons of Terror: A History of Warfare Against Civilians, 2003; (contrib. with W. Wisher) Exorcist, The Beginning: A Novelization,

2004; The Italian Secretary: A Further Adventure of Sherlock Holmes, 2005; (with S.E. Ambrose, T. Fleming and V. Hanson) The Cold War: A Military History, 2006. Contributor to periodicals. **Address:** Bard College, PO Box 5000, Annandale-On-Hudson, NY 12504-5000, U.S.A. **Online address:** carr@bard.edu

CARR, David. (David Michael Carr). American (born United States), b. 1956. **Genres:** Young Adult Non-fiction, Biography, Autobiography/Memoirs. **Career:** Twin Cities Reader, writer, 1981-84, editor, 1993-95; Corporate Report Minnesota, editor, 1986-87; Minnesota Lawyer, editor, 1990-93; Washington City Paper, editor, 1995-2000; Insider.com, media writer, 2000; New York Times, reporter and columnist, 2002-. **Publications:** Rewriting the Odds: The Law Firm of Robins, Kaplan, Miller & Ciresi L.L.P. (nonfiction), 2005; The Night of the Gun: A Reporter Investigates the Darkest Story of His Life, His Own (memoir), 2008. Contributor of articles to periodicals. **Address:** New York Times, 620 8th Ave., New York, NY 10018, U.S.A.

CARR, David McLain. American (born United States), b. 1961?. **Genres:** Theology/Religion. **Career:** Methodist Theological School, from assistant to professor, 1988-99; Biblical Interpretation, Williams Chair, 1998; Union Theological Seminary, professor of the Old Testament, 1999. Writer. **Publications:** From D to Q: A Study of Early Jewish Interpretations of Solomon's Dream at Gibeon, 1991; (ed. with R.D. Weis) A Gift of God in Due Season: Essays on Scripture and Community in Honor of James A. Sanders, 1996; Reading the Fractures of Genesis: Historical and Literary Approaches, 1996; The Erotic Word: Sexuality, Spirituality and the Bible, 2003; Writing on the Tablet of the Heart: Origins of Scripture and Literature, 2005. **Address:** Union Theological Seminary, 3041 Broadway, 121st St., New York, NY 10027, U.S.A. **Online address:** dcarr@uts.columbia.edu

CARR, David Michael. *See* **CARR, David.**

CARR, Duane. American (born United States), b. 1934. **Genres:** Novels, Poetry, Literary Criticism And History, Adult Non-fiction. **Career:** University of Texas, instructor, 1974, 1979; University of Arkansas, instructor, 1983, 1986-87; University of New Orleans, instructor, 1987-88; Western Kentucky University, instructor, 1988-95. Writer. **Publications:** The Bough of Summer, 1976; A Question of Class: The Redneck Stereotype in Southern Fiction, 1996. Contributor of articles to magazines. Works appear in anthologies. **Address:** c/o Barbara Kouts, Barbara S Kouts Literary Agency, PO Box 560, Bellport, NY 11713-0560, U.S.A. **Online address:** duanekalidasa@yahoo.com

CARR, Howie Louis. American (born United States), b. 1952. **Genres:** Young Adult Non-fiction. **Career:** Boston Herald American (now Boston Herald), Boston city hall bureau chief, 1980-81, State House bureau chief, columnist; Winston-Salem Journal, assistant city editor; WNEV, political reporter. **Publications:** The Brothers Bulger: How They Terrorized and Corrupted Boston for a Quarter Century, 2006; Hitman: The Untold Story of Johnny Martorano: Whitey Bulger's Enforcer and the Most Feared Gangster in the Underworld, 2011; Hard Knocks, 2012. Contributor to periodicals. **Address:** WRKO, 20 Guest St., 3rd Fl., Boston, MA 02135, U.S.A. **Online address:** howiecarr@wrko.com

CARR, Jacqueline Barbara. American/British (born England), b. 1954. **Genres:** History, Social Sciences. **Career:** Sacramento City College, adjunct, 1992-98; California State University, lecturer, 1998-2000, assistant professor, 2000-04; University of Vermont, Department of History, assistant professor, 2004-08, associate professor, 2008-. Writer. **Publications:** After the Siege: A Social History of Boston, 1775-1800, 2005. **Address:** Department of History, University of Vermont, 201 Wheeler House, 133 S Prospect St., Burlington, VT 05405-1714, U.S.A. **Online address:** jacqueline.carr@uvm.edu

CARR, J(ames) Revell. American (born United States), b. 1939. **Genres:** Travel/Exploration, History, Military/Defense/Arms Control. **Career:** Mystic Seaport (maritime museum), president and director; Council of American Maritime Museums, president; International Congress of Maritime Museums, president. Writer. **Publications:** All Brave Sailors: The Sinking of the Anglo-Saxon, August 21, 1940, 2004; Seeds of Discontent: The Deep Roots of the American Revolution, 1650-1750, 2008. Contributor to periodicals. **Address:** c/o Author Mail, Simon and Schuster, 1230 Ave. of the Americas, New York, NY 10020, U.S.A.

CARR, Julie. American (born United States), b. 1966?. **Genres:** Poetry, Literary Criticism And History, Translations. **Career:** University of Colorado, assistant professor of English; Counterpath Press, co-publisher. Writer. **Publications:** Mead: An Epithalamion, 2004; Equivocal, 2007; Sarah-of Fragments and Lines: Poems, 2010; 100 Notes on Violence, 2010. **Address:** Department of English, University of Colorado, 127 Hellems, 226 UCB, Boulder, CO 80309-0226, U.S.A. **Online address:** julie.carr@colorado.edu

CARR, Lauren. American (born United States) **Genres:** Novels, Mystery/Crime/Suspense. **Career:** Writer. **Publications:** A Small Case of Murder, 2004; A Reunion to Die For: A Joshua Thornton Mystery, 2007. MAC FARADAY MYSTERY SERIES: It's Murder, My Son, 2010; Old Loves Die Hard, 2011. **Address:** 415 Moonridge Ln., Harpers Ferry, WV 25425-5598, U.S.A. **Online address:** laurencarr@laurencarr.com

CARR, Margaret. Also writes as Carole Kerr, Belle Jackson, Martin Carroll. British (born England), b. 1935. **Genres:** Novels, Mystery/Crime/Suspense, Romance/Historical, Education, Young Adult Fiction. **Career:** Writer. **Publications:** NOVELS: Spring into Love, 1967. MYSTERY NOVELS: Tread Warily at Midnight, 1971; Sitting Duck, 1972; Who's The Target, 1974; Wait for the Wake, 1974; Too Close for Comfort, 1974; Blood Will Out, 1975; Blindman's Bluff, 1976; Dare the Devil, 1976; Sharendel, 1976; Out of the Past, 1976; Twin Tragedy, 1977; The Witch of Wykham, 1978; Daggers Drawn, 1980; Deadly Pursuit, 1991; Dark Intruder, 1991. MYSTERY NOVELS AS MARTIN CARROLL: Begotten Murder, 1967; Blood Vengeance, 1968; Dead Trouble, 1968; Goodbye Is Forever, 1968; Too Beautiful to Die, 1969; Bait, 1970; Miranda Said Murder, 1970; Hear No Evil, 1971. AS BELLE JACKSON: In the Dark of the Day, 1988; Valdez's Lady, 1989. NOVELS AS CAROLE KERR: Not for Sale, 1975; Shadow of the Hunter, 1975; A Time to Surrender, 1975; Love All Start, 1977; Lamb to the Slaughter, 1978; An Innocent Abroad, 1979; When Dreams Come True, 1980; Stolen Heart, 1981. **Address:** Waverley, Wavering Ln., Gillingham, DS SP8 4NR, England.

CARR, Marvin N. American (born United States), b. 1927. **Genres:** Novels, Mystery/Crime/Suspense, Young Adult Fiction. **Career:** Carr's One of a Kind in the World Museum, proprietor and curator. Writer. **Publications:** Positively Negative (novel), 1994; Men Are Cruel but Women Are Dangerous, 1996; The Deliquescent Lights, 1997. **Address:** Trom Publishing, 5225 N Freya St., Spokane, WA 99217, U.S.A.

CARR, Nicholas. American (born United States), b. 1959. **Genres:** Social Sciences. **Career:** Mercer Management Consulting, principal; Harvard Business Review, executive editor. **Publications:** (Ed. and intro.) The Digital Enterprise: How to Reshape Your Business for a Connected World, 2001; Does IT Matter? Information Technology and the Corrosion of Competitive Advantage, 2004; The Big Switch: Rewiring the World, from Edison to Google, 2008; The Shallows: What the Internet Is Doing to Our Brains, 2010. Contributor to periodicals. **Online address:** ncarr@mac.com

CARR, Patrick J. American/Irish (born Ireland), b. 1966. **Genres:** Law. **Career:** Rutgers University, assistant professor of sociology. Sociologist and writer. **Publications:** (Ed. with C.M. Renzetti and D.J. Curran) Theories of Crime: A Text Reader, 2003; Clean Streets: Controlling Crime, Maintaining Order, and Building Community Activism, 2005; (with M.J. Kefalas) Hollowing Out the Middle: The Rural Brain Drain and What It Means for America, 2009. Contributor to journals. **Address:** Department of Sociology, Rutgers, The State University of New Jersey, 54 Joyce Kilmer Ave., Piscataway, NJ 08854, U.S.A. **Online address:** pcarr@sociology.rutgers.edu

CARR, Roger Vaughan. Australian (born Australia), b. 1937. **Genres:** Children's Fiction. **Career:** EKIDna eBooks, publisher. Journalist. **Publications:** CHILDREN'S NOVELS: Surfie, 1966; Dead Man's Float, 1973; Old Cranky Jack, 1973; Surfboard, 1975; Noose over the Valley, 1977; Rollin' Through, 1979; Firestorm!, 1985; The Split Creek Kids, 1988; The Nearly-Always-Come-Home-Again Hat, 1989; The Clinker, 1989; Piano Bay, 1991; Nipper and the Gold Turkey, 1991; The Imprint, 1994; The Butterfly, 1996; (with K. Knapsey) Awesome Adventures, 2001; The Frog Who Thought He Was a Horse, 2001; Crossing the Divide, 2001; How to Discover the World, 2007; Climb, 2007. **Address:** c/o Barbara Mobbs, PO Box 126, Edgecliff, NW 2027, Australia. **Online address:** ekidna@onaustralia.com.au

CARRADICE, Ian A. Colombian/British (born England), b. 1953. **Genres:**

Archaeology/Antiquities, Antiques/Furnishings, History. **Career:** British Museum, Department of Coins and Medals, curator, 1977-89; University of St. Andrews, senior lecturer, professor of art history and course director in museum and gallery studies, 1989-, keeper of university collections and museums, 1990-, University Museum Collections, director; Scottish Museums Council, university director, 1994-2001; University Museums in Scotland, convener, 1999-2005; Marc Garneau Collegiate Institute, director. Writer. **Publications:** Ancient Greek Portrait Coins, 1978; Coinage and Finances in the Reign of Domitian, 1983; (ed.) Coinage and Administration in the Athenian and Persian Empires: The Ninth Oxford Symposium on Coinage and Monetary History, 1987; Coinage in the Greek World, 1988; (with J. Cribb and B. Cook) Coin Atlas: The World of Coinage From its Origins to the Present Day, 1990; Greek Coins, 1995; Roman Provincial Coinage, vol. II, 1999; (with T.V. Buttrey) Roman Imperial Coinage, 2007; Les Monedes de Vespasia de la Provincia Tarraconensis, 2010. **Address:** School of Art History, University of St. Andrews, 79 North St., Saint Andrews, FF KY16 9AJ, Scotland. **Online address:** iac@st-andrews.ac.uk

CARRAHER, Charles E. American (born United States), b. 1941. **Genres:** Chemistry. **Career:** University of South Dakota, instructor, 1967-68, assistant professor, 1968-70, associate professor, 1970-73, professor of chemistry, 1973-76, Science Division, chairman, 1971-74; Sigma Xi, president, 1972-73; ACS Polymer Laboratory Exercises, editor, 1974-; Wright State University, professor of chemistry, 1976-85, chairman, 1976-84; American Institute of Chemists, fellow; University-Industry/Community Cooperation, chair; Florida Atlantic University, College of Science, dean, 1985-95, professor of chemistry, Florida Center for Environmental Studies, associate director, 1995-; Journal of Polymer Materials, associate editor, 1988-. **Publications:** Chemistry Applied, 1970; Chemistry in Everyday Life, 1972, rev. ed., 1976; Chemistry in Our World, 1974; (ed.) Interfacial Synthesis, (with F. Millich) vol. I: Fundamentals, 1977, (with F. Millich) vol. II: Polymer Applications and Technology, 1977, (with J. Preston) vol. III: Recent Advances, 1982; (with J. Sheats and C. Pittman) Organometallic Polymers, 1978; (with M. Tsuda) Modification of Polymers, 1979, rev. ed., 1980; (with R. Seymour) Polymer Chemistry, 1981, 8th ed., 2011; (with Sheats and Pittman) Metallo-Organic Polymers, 1981; (with Sheats and Pittman) Advances in Organometallic Polymer Science, 1982; (with C. Gebelein) Polymeric Drugs, 1982; (with L. Sperling) Polymer Applications of Renewable-Resource Materials, 1983; (with J. Moore) Chemical Modification of Polymers, 1983; (with L. Mathias) Crown Ethers and Phase Transfer Agents for Polymer Applications, 1984; (with Sheats and Pittman) Metal-Containing Polymeric Systems, 1985; (with Gebelein) Bioactive Polymeric Systems, 1985; (with Gebelein) Polymeric Materials in Medication, 1985; (with Sperling) Renewable Resource Materials, 1986; (with Gebelein and V. Foster) Applied Bioactive Polymeric Systems, 1989; (with Seymour) Giant Molecules, 1990; (co-author) Inorganic and Metal-Containing Polymeric Materials, 1990; (with Gebelein) Biotechnology, 1994; (with Gebelein) Industrial Biotechnological Polymers, 1995; (co-author) Metal-Containing Polymers Materials, 1996; (with Swift and Bowman) Polymer Modification, 1997; (with Craver) Applied Polymer Science, 2000; (co-author) Bonding, 2001; (with Swift) Functional Condensation Polymers, 2002; (co-author) A Half Century of Metal and Metalloid Containing Polymers, 2003; (co-author) Organoiron Polymers, 2004; (co-author) Biomedical Applications, 2004; (co-author) Group IVA Polymers, 2005; (co-author) Metal Coordination Polymers, 2005; Introduction to Polymer Chemistry Solutions Manual, 2006; (co-author) Transition Metal-Containing Polymers, 2006; (co-author) Nancoscale Interactions of Metal-Containing Polymers, 2006; Self Discovery Labs, 2007; Introduction to Polymer Chemistry, 2007, 2nd ed., 2010; Non-Science Chemistry, 2007; (co-author) Boron-Containing Polymers, 2008; (co-author) Inorganic and Organometallic Macromolecules: Design and Application, 2008; Photophysics and Photochemistry of Metal-Containing Polymers, 2010. **Address:** Department of Chemistry & Biochemistry, Florida Atlantic University, SC 148, PH 229, Boca Raton, FL 33431, U.S.A. **Online address:** carraher@fau.edu

CARRANZA, Andreu. (Andreu Carranza Font). Spanish (born Spain), b. 1957. **Genres:** Translations, Novels, Novellas/Short Stories, Poetry. **Career:** Writer. **Publications:** (As Andreu Carranza Font) La Tinta de la Immortalitat (novel), 1991; (as Andreu Carranza Font) Aigua de València (short-story collection), 1993; El Desert de l'Oblit (novel), 1993; Trilogia del Deliri (poetry), 1993; Riu Avall (short-story collection), 1996; Llibre de les set Xibeques (novel), 1997; Anjub: Confessions d'un Bandoler (novel), 2000; A Mumpare (poetry), 2000; La Filla de la Memòria (novel), 2001; El que l'Herbolària Sap (novel), 2002; L'Hivern del Tigre (novel), 2004; Invierno del tigre, 2006; (with E. Martín) La Clave Gaudí (novel), 2007; Imprenta Babel (novel), 2009. Works appear in anthologies. Contributor to periodicals. **Address:** HarperCollins Publishers, 10 E 53rd St., New York, NY 10022, U.S.A. **Online address:** acarranza@gencat.net

CARREL, Annette Felder. American (born United States), b. 1929. **Genres:** Young Adult Non-fiction, Law. **Career:** Educator and writer. **Publications:** It's the Law: A Young Person's Guide to Our Legal System, 1994. **Address:** 2010 Garden St., Santa Barbara, CA 93105-3615, U.S.A.

CARRERA, Magali M. (Magali Marie Carrera). American (born United States), b. 1950. **Genres:** Art/Art History. **Career:** Columbus Quincentenary, Smithsonian Institution, coordinator of planning and research; University of Massachusetts, professor of art history, chancellor professor; Writer. **Publications:** Imagining Identity in New Spain: Race, Lineage and the Colonial Body in Portraiture and Casta Paintings, 2003; Traveling from New Spain to Mexico: Mapping Practices of Nineteenth-century Mexico, 2011. **Address:** University of Massachusetts, Rm. 313, CVPA, 285 Old Westport Rd., North Dartmouth, MA 02747, U.S.A. **Online address:** mcarrera@umassd.edu

CARRERA, Magali Marie. *See* **CARRERA, Magali M.**

CARRETTA, Vincent (Albert). American (born United States), b. 1945. **Genres:** Literary Criticism And History, Politics/Government, Biography. **Career:** Newberry Library, fellow, 1975; Folger Shakespeare Library, fellow, 1976; Mount Mercy College, instructor in English, 1977; University of Iowa, visiting lecturer, 1977; William Andrews Clark Memorial Library, fellow, 1978; University of Wisconsin, Institute for Research in the Humanities, visiting fellow, 1978-79; University of Maryland, Department of English, assistant professor, 1978-83, associate professor, 1983-90, professor of English, 1990-, associate chair, 2005-07; Huntington Library, fellow, 1983; National Humanities Center, fellow, 1983-84; John Carter Brown Library, fellow, 1984; Yale University, Center for British Art and British Studies, fellow, 1985. Writer. **Publications:** The Snarling Muse: Verbal and Visual Political Satire from Pope to Churchill, 1983; George III and the Satirists from Hogarth to Byron, 1990; (ed.) Unchained Voices: An Anthology of Black Authors in the English-Speaking World of the Eighteenth Century, 1996; (with P. Gould) Genius in Bondage: Literature of the Early Black Atlantic, 2001; Equiano, the African: Biography of a Self-Made Man, 2005; (ed. with T.M. Reese) Life and Letters of Philip Quaque, the First African Anglican Missionary, 2010; Phillis Wheatley: Biography of a Genius in Bondage, 2011. EDITOR AND AUTHOR OF INTRODUCTION: The Satires of Mr. (Paul) Whitehead, 1984; The Interesting Narrative and Other Writings, 1995, rev. ed., 2003; Letters of the Late Ignatius Sancho, an African, 1998; Thoughts and Sentiments on the Evil of Slavery and Other Writings, 1999; Complete Writings, 2001. Contributor of articles to books and journals. **Address:** Department of English, University of Maryland, 3242 Tawes Hall, College Park, MD 20742, U.S.A. **Online address:** vac@umd.edu

CARR-HILL, Roy. British (born England), b. 1943. **Genres:** Criminology/True Crime, Education, Mathematics/Statistics, Medicine/Health, Public/Social Administration, Social Sciences, Politics/Government. **Career:** University of Sussex, lecturer, 1971-74; Organization for Economic Cooperation and Development, administrator, 1974-77; Universdade Eduardo Mondlane, professor, 1978-81; University of York, Centre for Health Economics, senior research fellow, 1983-90, reader, 1990-95, professor in health and social statistics, 1996-; University of Hull, School of Social and Political Sciences, research coordinator, 1991-93; University of London, Institute of Education, professor, 1992-, visiting professor of education; University of Liverpool, Liverpool School of Tropical Medicine, professor of health economics, 2010-. Writer. **Publications:** (With O. Magnusson) Indicators of Performance of Educational Systems, 1973; (with N.H. Stern) Crime, the Police and Criminal Statistics: An Analysis of Official for England and Wales using Econometric Methods, 1979; (with C. Pritchard) The Development and Exploitation of Empirical Birthweight Standards, 1985; (ed. with A. Bhat) Britain's Black Population: A New Perspective, 2nd ed., 1988; Social Conditions in Sub-Saharan Africa, 1990; The Functioning and Effects of the Tanzanian Literacy Programme, 1991; Method for Future Revenue Allocation: Report, 1991; (with K. King) International Aid to Basic Education: Flows, Policies, Modalities, 1992; (co-author) Skill Mix and the Effectiveness of Nursing Care, 1992; (with C.W. Pritchard) Women's Social Standing: The Empirical Problem of Female Social Class, 1992; (co-author) Les inegalities de sante en France et en Grande Borlagne, 1991; (with G. Carron) Non-formal Education, 1992;

(co-ed.) Adult Literacy Programs in Uganda, 2001; (with J. Lintott) Consumption, Jobs and the Environment: A Fourth Way?, 2002; (with E. Peart) The Education of Nomadic Peoples in East Africa: Djibouti, Eritrea, Ethiopia, Kenya, Tanzania and Uganda, 2005. **Address:** Centre for Health Economics, University of York, Alcuin 'A' Block, Heslington, York, NY YO10 5DD, England. **Online address:** roy.carrhill@york.ac.uk

CARRICK, Malcolm. British/Welsh (born Wales), b. 1945. **Genres:** Children's Fiction, Novellas/Short Stories. **Career:** Malcolm Carrick Productions, owner, 1985-. Writer. **Publications:** All Sorts of Everything, 1973; The Wise Men of Gotham, 1973; The Extraordinary Hat-Maker, 1974; Mr. Pedagouge's Sneeze, 1974; The Extraordinary Hatmaker, 1974; The Fairy Tale Book, 1974; Once There Was a Boy and Other Stories, 1974; The Little Pilgrim, 1975; The Farmer's Wish, 1975; Make and Do, 1975; Once There Was a Boy and Other Stories, 1975; Splodges, 1976; Making Magic, 1976; See You Later Alligator, 1976; Tramp, 1977; Today Is Shrew's Day, 1978; Science Experiments, 1978; I Can Squash Elephants: A Masai Tale about Monsters, 1978; Horror Costumes and Makeup, 1978; The Year of Mr. Nobody, 1978; Happy Jack, 1979; Making Devil and Demon Masks, 1979; I'll Get You, 1979; Making Masks, 1980; Mr. Tod's Trap, 1980; You'll Be Sorry, You'll Be Sorry When I'm Dead, 1980; Butterfingers!, 1985; Skem, 1994; Oddjob Is the Sandman, 1999; Oddjob's Lunch Box, 2002. **Address:** Flat 4 Vicarage Ct., 215 Church Rd., London, GL SE19 2QQ, England. **Online address:** mickcarrick_2@hotmail.com

CARRIER, James G(olden). British/American (born United States), b. 1947. **Genres:** Anthropology/Ethnology. **Career:** University of Papua New Guinea, lecturer, 1980-84, senior lecturer in anthropology and sociology, 1985-86, department head, 1984-86; University of Virginia, lecturer in sociology, 1987-94; University of Durham, lecturer in anthropology, 1994-99; University of Edinburgh, reader in anthropology, 1999-2000; Oxford Brookes University, senior research associate in anthropology, 2002-; Indiana University, adjunct professor of anthropology. Writer. **Publications:** Education and Society in a Manus village, 1984; Learning Disability: Social Class and the Construction of Inequality in American Education, 1986; Ponam Fish Freezer: Analysis of the Failure of a Small-Scale Development Project in Manus Province, 1988; (with A. Carrier) Wage, Trade, and Exchange in Melanesia: A Manus Society in the Modern State, 1989; (with A. Carrier) Structure and Process in a Melanesian Society: Ponam's Progress in the Twentieth Century, 1991; Gifts and Commodities: Exchange and Western Capitalism Since 1700, 1994, 2nd ed., 1995. EDITOR AND CONTRIBUTOR: History and Tradition in Melanesian Anthropology, 1992; Occidentalism: Images of the West, 1995; (with J. Friedman) Melanesian Modernities, 1996; Meanings of the Market: The Free Market in Western Culture, 1997; (with D. Miller) Virtualism: A New Political Economy, 1998; Confronting Environments, 2004; A Handbook of Economic Anthropology, 2005, 2nd ed., 2012; (with P. West) Virtualism, Governance and Practice: Vision and Execution in Environmental Conservation, 2009; (with D. Macleod) Tourism, Power and Culture: Anthropological Insights, 2010; (with P. Luetchford) Ethical Consumption: Social Value and Economic Practice, 2012. Contributor to books and journals. **Address:** Oxford Brookes University, Gipsy Ln., Oxford, OX OX3 0BP, England. **Online address:** jcarrier@brookes.ac.uk

CARRIER, Roch. Canadian (born Canada), b. 1937. **Genres:** Novels, Children's Fiction, Poetry, Young Adult Fiction, Novellas/Short Stories, Translations, Biography, Autobiography/Memoirs, Autobiography/Memoirs. **Career:** Collège militaire royal de Saint-Jean, Department of French, teacher, 1964-70, director of department and coordinator of the undergraduate program in Canadian studies, 1973-80; Université de Montréal, faculty, 1970-71; Theatre du Nouveau Monde, secretary-general, 1971-; Canada Council, director, 1994-97; Order of Canada, officer, 1991; National Librarian of Canada, staff, 1999-2004; Salon du Livre, chairman. Writer. **Publications:** Les Jeux Incompris (poems), 1956; Cherche Tesmots, Cherche Tes Pas, 1958; Jolis Deuils: Petites Tragedies Pour Adultes (stories), 1964; La Guerre, Yes Sir! (novel), 1968; Floralie, où es-tu? (novel), 1969; Il Est Par Là, Le Soleil (novel), 1970; L'Aube D'acier (poem), 1971; Le Deux-millième étage (novel), 1973; Floralie, 1974; Le Jardin Des Délices: Roman (novel), 1975; Il N'ya Pas De Pays Sans Grand-père (novel), 1977; Les Enfants Du Bonhomme Dans La Lune (stories), 1979; La Céleste Bicyclette, 1980; Les Fleurs Viventellesailleurs Que Sur La Terre?, 1980; Les Voyageurs De L'arc-en-ciel, 1980; La Dame Qui Avaitdes Chaines Aux Chevilles (novel), 1981; Le Cirque Noir, 1982; (with L. Moser) Québec à l'été 1950, 1982; De L'amour Dans La Feraille (novel), 1984; Nefaites Pas Mal a L'avenin (juvenile), 1984; La Fleur Et Autres Personnages (short stories), 1984; L'ours Et Le Kangourou, 1986; Canada: La Belle Aventure, 1986; L'Ours Et Le Kangourou, 1986; Prières D'un Enfant Très Très Sage, 1988; Un Chameau En Jordanie, 1988; Enfants De La Planete (short stories), 1989; L'Eau De Polguk SA (short stories), 1989; Une Bonne Et Heureuse Annee, 1991; A Happy New Year's Day, 1991; Le Canot Dans Les Nuages, 1991; Un Champion, 1991; Le Martien De Noël, 1991; L'Homme Dans Le Placard (novel), 1991; Fin (novel), 1992; (contrib.) Le Plus Long Circuit, 1993; Basketball Player, 1996; Petit Homme Tornade (novel), 1996; Une chaise: roman, 1999; Le Rocket, 2000; La Chasse-galerie, 2004; Les Moines Dans La Tour: Roman, 2004; 626 by 9: A Goal-by-Goal Timeline of Maurice The Rocket Richard's Scoring Career in Pictures, Stats and Stories, 2004; (reteller) The Flying Canoe, 2004. **Address:** c/o Author Mail, Tundra Books of Northern New York, 75 Sherbourne St., 5th Fl., Toronto, ON M5A 2P9, Canada.

CARRIER, Thomas J. American (born United States), b. 1956. **Genres:** Travel/Exploration, History, Politics/Government. **Career:** Writer. **Publications:** The Small Meetings Handbook, 1993; Historic Walking Tour of Alexandria, 1749: Alexandria As It Was Originally Laid Out by the General Assembly of Virginia in 1749, 1996; Washington D.C.: A Historical Walking Tour, 1999; Historic Georgetown: A Walking Tour, 1999; The White House, the Capitol, and the Supreme Court: Historic Self-Guided Tours, 2000; Complete Small Meetings Planner, 2003. Contributor to periodicals. **Address:** c/o Author Mail, Arcadia Publishing, 420 Wando Park Blvd., Mount Pleasant, SC 29464-7845, U.S.A. **Online address:** tcines@aol.com

CARRIKER, S. David. American (born United States), b. 1951. **Genres:** History, Local History/Rural Topics, Transportation. **Career:** Third Creek Presbyterian Church, minister, 1998-; Heritage Publishing Co., publisher. Writer. **Publications:** The Carriker Family, 1977; The Geology of Richmond County, North Carolina, 1982; The Eighteenth-Century Churches of Richmond County, North Carolina, 1984; Railroading in the Carolina Sandhills, vol. I: The Nineteenth Century (1825-1900), 1985, vol. II: The Twentieth Century (1900-1985), 1987, vol. III, 1992, vol. IV, 1991, vol. V, 1996; North Carolina Railroads: The Common Carrier Railroads of North Carolina, 1988; (ed.) N & W RY Number 1218: Through the Loops to Asheville, 1989; (comp.) The Third Creek Presbyterian Church Cemetery Index, 1761-2000: A Exact Rendering, Expended Reference and Genealogical Work of Those Buried at Third Creek, 2001. EDITOR: The North Carolina Railroad Map, 1990. **Address:** Heritage Publishing Co., 207 Kimrod Ln., Charlotte, NC 28270-2751, U.S.A.

CARRILLO, H. G. American/Cuban (born Cuba), b. 1960?. **Genres:** Novels, Young Adult Fiction. **Career:** George Washington University, Department of English, assistant professor; Cornell University, Department of English, instructor. Writer. **Publications:** Loosing My Espanish, 2004. Contributor to periodicals. **Address:** Department of English, George Washington University, Rm. 768, Rome Hall, 801 22nd St. NW, Washington, DC 20052, U.S.A. **Online address:** hgc@gwu.edu

CARRINGTON, Paul D(ewitt). American (born United States), b. 1931. **Genres:** Law. **Career:** University of Wyoming, assistant professor, 1958-60; Indiana University, assistant professor, 1960-62; Ohio State University, associate professor, 1962-64, professor, 1964-65; University of Michigan, Law School, professor of law, 1965-78; Duke University, School of Law, professor, 1978-, dean, 1978-88. Writer. **Publications:** Accommodating the Workload of the United States Courts of Appeal, 1968; (ed.) Civil Procedure: Cases with Comment on the Process of Adjudication, 1969, 3rd ed., 1983; (with D.J. Meador and M. Rosenberg) Justice on Appeal, 1976; (with D.J. Meador and M. Rosenberg) Appellate Courts, 1995; (with D.J. Meador and M. Rosenberg) Stewards of Democracy, 1999; Spreading America's Word: Stories of Its Lawyer-Missionaries, 2005; (ed. with R.C. Cramton) Reforming the Court: Term Limits for Justices, 2006; (ed. with T. Jones) Law and Class in America: Trends Since the End of the Cold War, 2006. **Address:** School of Law, Duke University, Science Dr. & Towerview Rd., Durham, NC 27708-0362, U.S.A. **Online address:** pdc@law.duke.edu

CARRINGTON, Roslyn. (Simona Taylor). Trinidadian (born Trinidad and Tobago) **Genres:** Novels, Young Adult Fiction. **Career:** Writer. **Publications:** A Thirst for Rain, 1999; Every Bitter Thing Sweet, 2001; Candy Don't Come in Gray, 2002. AS SIMONA TAYLOR: Night Heat, 1999; Mesmerized,

2000; Soul's Desire, 2000; Love Me All the Way, 2003; Wonderful and Wild, 2003; Then I Found You, 2005; May Summer Never End, 2006; Dear Rita, 2008; Meet Me in Paris, 2009; Intimate Exposure, 2011; Everything to Me, 2012. **Address:** PO Box 528, Maloney, 1, Trinidad and Tobago. **Online address:** roslyn@scribble-scribble.com

CARRINGTON, Ruth. *See* **HARTLAND, Michael.**

CARRINGTON, Tori. *See* **KARAYIANNI, Lori.**

CARRINGTON, Tori. *See* **KARAYIANNI, Tony.**

CARROL, Kathleen. *See* **CREIGHTON, Kathleen.**

CARROLL, Brendan G. British (born England), b. 1952. **Genres:** Biography. **Career:** International Korngold Society (now Erich Wolfgang Korngold Society), co-founder, 1983-, president; Royal Liverpool Philharmonic Orchestra, board director, 1988-92. Writer, independent marketing consultant and music critic. **Publications:** Erich Wolfgang Korngold: His Life and Works, 1983; The Last Prodigy: A Biography of Erich Wolfgang Korngold, 1997; (ed.) Lieder aus dem Nachlass, 2006. **Address:** 2 S Bank Rd., Liverpool, LC L19 9AR, England. **Online address:** brendan_carroll@compuserve.com

CARROLL, Cathryn. American (born United States) **Genres:** Adult Nonfiction, Biography. **Career:** Gallaudet University, National Deaf Education Network and Clearinghouse, Laurent Clerc National Deaf Education Center, managing editor. **Publications:** (With S.M. Mather) Movers and Shakers: Deaf People Who Changed the World; Twenty-six Tales of Genius, Struggle, Perseverance and Heroism, 1997. (with C.H. Fisher) Orchid of the Bayou: A Deaf Woman Faces Blindness, 2001; (ed.) History through Deaf Eyes, 2002. Contributor to periodicals. **Address:** Laurent Clerc National Deaf Education Center, Gallaudet University, 800 Florida Ave. NE, Washington, DC 20002, U.S.A. **Online address:** cathryn.carroll@gallaudet.edu

CARROLL, Francis M(artin). American (born United States), b. 1938. **Genres:** History, Politics/Government. **Career:** South Dakota State University, faculty, 1962-64, F.O. Butler lecturer, 1988; Kalamazoo College, faculty, 1967-68; University of Manitoba, history faculty, 1969-98, professor emeritus, 2002-, St. John's College, dean of studies, 1976-78, acting warden, 1985-86, chair of assembly, 1989-90; National University of Ireland, University College, Mary Ball Washington professor of American history, 1984-85; University of London, Institute of United States Studies, John Adams fellow, 1994-95; University of St. Thomas, visiting Irish historian, 2000; Royal Military College of Canada, Division of Continuing Studies, visiting professor, 2002-03. Writer. **Publications:** (Comp.) Guide to Documents on International Relations in the University of Manitoba, Provincial and University of Winnipeg Libraries, 1972; American Opinion and the Irish Question, 1910-23: A Study in Opinion and Policy, 1978; (ed.) The American Commission on Irish Independence, 1919: The Diary, Correspondence and Report, 1985; Crossroads in Time: A History of Carlton County, Minnesota, 1987; (with F.R. Raiter) Fires of Autumn: The Cloquet-Moose Lake Disaster of 1918, 1990; (with M. Wisuri) Reflections of Our Past: A Pictorial History of Carlton County, 1997; A Good and Wise Measure: The Search for the Canadian-American Boundary, 1783-1842, 2001; Money for Ireland: Finance, Diplomacy, Politics and the First Dáil Éireann Loans, 1919-1936, 2002; American Presence in Ulster: A Diplomatic History, 1796-1996, 2005; (with M. Wisuri) Carlton Chronicles, 2006. Contributor to journals. **Address:** Department of History, University of Manitoba, 403 Fletcher Argue Bldg., 315 St. John's College, Winnipeg, MB R3T 2N2, Canada. **Online address:** fcarrol@cc.umanitoba.ca

CARROLL, Glenn R. American (born United States), b. 1953. **Genres:** Economics, Institutions/Organizations. **Career:** Brown University, Department of Sociology, assistant professor, 1981-82; University of California, Haas School of Business, assistant professor, 1982-86, associate professor, 1986-89, professor of management, 1989-, Paul Cortese distinguished professor of management, through 2000; Stanford University, Graduate School of Business, professor, 2000-, Laurence W. Lane professor of organizations, senior associate dean for academic affairs, School of Humanities and Sciences, professor of sociology, Executive Program in International Management, co-director; Columbia University, Business School, professor, 2004-06. Writer. **Publications:** NONFICTION: (ed. with D. Vogel) Strategy and Organization: A West Coast Perspective, 1984; Publish and Perish: The Organizational Ecology of Newspaper Industries, 1987; (ed. with D. Vogel) Organizational Approaches to Strategy, 1987; (ed.) Ecological Models of Organizations, 1988; (with M.T. Hannan) Dynamics of Organizational Populations: Density, Legitimation, and Competition, 1992; (ed. with M.T. Hannan) Organizations in Industry: Strategy, Structure, and Selection, 1995; (ed. with D.J. Teece) Firms, Markets, and Hierarchies: The Transaction Cost Economics Perspective, 1999; (with M.T. Hannan) The Demography of Corporations and Industries, 2000; (with J.R. Harrison) Culture and Demography in Organizations, 2006; (with M.T. Hannan and L. Pólos) Logics of Organization Theory: Audiences, Codes, and Ecologies, 2007. **Address:** Graduate School of Business, Stanford University, 518 Memorial Way, Stanford, CA 94305-5015, U.S.A. **Online address:** carroll_glenn@gsb.stanford.edu

CARROLL, Jaye. *See* **CARROLL, Michael.**

CARROLL, Jenny. *See* **CABOT, Meg(gin Patricia).**

CARROLL, Linda. American (born United States), b. 1944?. **Genres:** Novels, Self Help. **Career:** Writer. **Publications:** Her Mother's Daughter: A Memoir of the Mother I Never Knew and of My Daughter, 2005; Remember Who You Are: Seven Stages on a Woman's Journey of Spirit, 2008; Return to Essence: Seven Stages of a Woman's Spiritual Journey, forthcoming; Love's Four Journeys, forthcoming. **Address:** Master Pairs Teachers, 1242 NW Hillcrest Dr., Corvallis, OR 97330, U.S.A. **Online address:** lindacarroll44@gmail.com

CARROLL, Martin. *See* **CARR, Margaret.**

CARROLL, Matthew S. American (born United States), b. 1955. **Genres:** Environmental Sciences/Ecology. **Career:** Black Hills National Forest, seasonal forestry aide, 1975; U.S. Forest Service, Northeast Forest Experiment Station, research technician at forest insect and disease laboratory, 1976-77; University of Washington, instructor in forest resources, 1982, Resources for the Future, fellow in forest economics and policy, 1982-83, College of Forest Resources, Cooperative Park Studies Unit, research analyst, 1983-85; Pennsylvania State University, postdoctoral research associate, 1985-87; Washington State University, assistant professor, associate professor of natural resource sciences, 1987-, professor, assistant resource sociologist, 1991-. Writer. **Publications:** Community and the Northwestern Logger: Continuities and Change in the Era of the Spotted Owl, 1995; (co-author) Social Assessment for the Wenatchee National Forest Wildfires of 1994: Targeted Analysis for the Leavenworth, Entiat, and Chelan Ranger Districts, 2000; (with A.J. Findley and K.A. Blatner) Social Assessment for the Colville National Forest CROP Program, 2000; (co-ed.) People, Fire, and Forests: A Synthesis of Wildfire Social Science, 2007. Contributor of articles to periodicals. **Address:** Department of Natural Resource Sciences, Washington State University, 183 Johnson Hall, PO Box 646410, Pullman, WA 99164-6410, U.S.A. **Online address:** carroll@wsu.edu

CARROLL, Michael. (Jaye Carroll). Irish (born Ireland), b. 1966. **Genres:** Novels. **Career:** Postman, 1982-85; computer programmer, 1985-99; PFJ, co-founder, 1991-; writer, 1999-; FT, editor. **Publications:** Moonlight, 1993; She Fades Away, 1996; The Throwback, 2001; Renegade, 2001. PELICOS SERIES: Last Starship, 1993; Reclaiming the Earth, 2001; The Dead Colony, 2001. NEW HEROES SERIES: Quantum Prophecy, 2006; Sakkara, 2006; Absolute Power, 2007. AS JAYE CARROLL: If the Shoe Fits, 2000; Sweetest Feeling, 2001; Loving the Stars, 2002; Looking for Mr. Wrong, 2004; Awakening, 2007; Gathering, 2008; Reckoning, 2009. OTHERS: Super Human, 2010; Ascension, 2011; Stronger, 2012. **Address:** Poolbeg, 123 Grange Hill, Baldoyle Industrial Estate, Baldoyle, DU 13, Ireland. **Online address:** quantumprophecy@gmail.com

CARROLL, Michael P. Canadian (born Canada), b. 1944. **Genres:** Psychology, Social Sciences. **Career:** University of Western Ontario, professor of sociology. Sociologist, educator and writer. **Publications:** The Cult of the Virgin Mary: Psychological Origins, 1986; Catholic Cults and Devotions: A Psychological Inquiry, 1989; Madonnas That Maim: Popular Catholicism in Italy since the Fifteenth Century, 1992; Veiled Threats: The Logic of Popular Catholicism in Italy, 1996; Irish Pilgrimage: Holy Wells and Popular Catholic Devotion, 1999; The Penitente Brotherhood: Patriarchy and Hispano-Catholicism in New Mexico, 2002; American Catholics in the Protestant Imagination: Rethinking the Academic Study of Religion, 2007. Contributor to books and journals. **Address:** Social Science Ctr., Ste. 5306, University of Western Ontario, London, ON N6A 5C2, Canada. **Online address:** mcarroll@uwo.ca

CARROLL, Noel. American (born United States), b. 1947. **Genres:** Film, Philosophy, Essays. **Career:** Temple University, Andrew W. Mellon professor in the humanities; New York University, faculty; Cornell University, faculty; Columbia University, faculty; City University New York, The Graduate Center, Philosophy Program, distinguished professor of philosophy. Writer. **Publications:** Mystifying Movies: Fads & Fallacies in Contemporary Film Theory, 1988; Philosophical Problems of Classical Film Theory, 1988; The Philosophy of Horror: Or, Paradoxes of the Heart, 1990; (ed. with D. Bordwell) Post-Theory, 1996; Theorizing the Moving Image, 1996; Interpreting the Moving Image, 1998; A Philosophy of Mass Art, 1998; Philosophy of Art: A Contemporary Introduction, 1999; Theories of Art Today, 2000; Beyond Aesthetics: Philosophical Essays, 2001; Engaging the Moving Image, 2003; (ed. with J. Choi) Philosophy of Film and Motion Pictures: An Anthology, 2006; Comedy Incarnate: Buster Keaton, Physical Humor and Bodily Coping, 2007; The Philosophy of Motion Pictures, 2008; On criticism, 2008; (ed.) The Poetics, Aesthetics and Philosophy of Narrative, 2009; (ed. with L. Hunt) Philosophy in the Twilight Zone, 2009; Art in Three Dimensions, 2010; Narrative, Emotion, and Insight, 2011. Contributor to periodicals. **Address:** The Graduate Center, City University of New York, 365 5th Ave., New York, NY 10016-4309, U.S.A. **Online address:** knollcarroll@gmail.com

CARROLL, Noel. *See* **MUNSON, Carol Barr Swayze.**

CARROLL, Noel. *See* **MUNSON, Noel J.**

CARROLL, Rebecca. American (born United States), b. 1969. **Genres:** Cultural/Ethnic Topics. **Career:** Blackside Inc., research assistant, 1992-93; Harvard University, Department of Afro-American Studies, editorial and administrative assistant, 1993-94; Elle, assistant editor, 1994-; Huffington Post Media Group, culture editor. **Publications:** I Know What the Red Clay Looks Like: The Voice and Vision of Black Women Writers, 1994; Swing Low: Black Men Writing, 1995; (ed.) Sugar in the Raw: A Nonfiction Profile of Young Black Girls in America, 1997; Melody's Incredible Adventure, 1998; Saving the Race: Conversations on Du Bois from A Collective Memoir of Souls, 2004; (ed.) Uncle Tom or New Negro?: African Americans Reflect on Booker T. Washington and Up from Slavery One Hundred Years Later, 2006. **Address:** c/o Meredith G. Bernstein, 2112 Broadway, Ste. 503A, New York, NY 10023, U.S.A.

CARROLL, Richard J. American (born United States), b. 1957. **Genres:** Economics. **Career:** World Bank, researcher, 1981-86; independent economic and financial consultant, 1988-; Bethesda Toastmasters, president. Writer. **Publications:** (Ed. with G.M. Meier and W.F. Steel) Industrial Adjustment in Sub-Saharan Africa, 1989; An Economic Record of Presidential Performance from Truman to Bush, 1995; Congressional Quarterly's Desk Reference on the Economy, 2000; Desk Reference on the Economy: More Than 600 Answers to Questions That Will Help You Understand News, Trends and Issues; News Guides Series on Controversial Issues, 2004. **Address:** PO Box 363, Glen Echo, MD 20812, U.S.A. **Online address:** rcarroll@uspolicy.com

CARROLL, Rodney (James). American (born United States), b. 1957. **Genres:** Novels, Business/Trade/Industry. **Career:** United Parcel Service, manager, 1983, division manager; Welfare to Work Partnership (now Business Interface L.L.C.), founder, executive, 1998, chief executive officer and president, 2000-. Writer. **Publications:** (With G. Karton) No Free Lunch: One Man's Journey from Welfare to the American Dream, 2002. **Address:** Business Interface L.L.C., 1501 East Fayette St., 1st Fl., Baltimore, MD 21231, U.S.A. **Online address:** rcarroll@welfaretowork.org

CARROLL, Stuart M. British (born England), b. 1965. **Genres:** History. **Career:** University of York, Vanbrugh College, professor of history. Writer. **Publications:** Noble Power during the French Wars of Religion: The Guise Affinity and the Catholic Cause in Normandy, 1998; Blood and Violence in Early Modern France, 2006; Cultures of Violence: Interpersonal Violence in Historical Perspective, 2007. **Address:** Department of History, Vanbrugh College, University of York, Heslington, YO10 5DD, England. **Online address:** smc4@york.ac.uk

CARROLL, Susan. Also writes as Serena Richards, Susan Coppula. American (born United States), b. 1952?. **Genres:** Novels, Young Adult Fiction. **Career:** Freelance writer. **Publications:** ST. LEGER SERIES: (as Susan Coppula) Winterbourne, 1987; (as Susan Coppula) Shades of Winter, 1988; The Bride Finder, 1998; The Night Drifter, 1999; Midnight Bride, 2001. NOVELS: The Lady Who Hated Shakespeare, 1986; The Sugar Rose, 1987; Brighton Road, 1988; (as Serena Richards) Masquerade, 1989; The Bishop's Daughter, 1990; (as Serena Richards) Rendezvous, 1991; The Wooing of Miss Masters, 1991; (as Serena Richards) Escapade, 1991; (as Susan Coppula) Avenging Angel, 1991; The Mistress Mischief: The Lady Who Hated Shakespeare, 1992; Christmas Belles, 1992; Miss Prentiss and the Yankee, 1993; The Valentine's Day Ball, 1994; Black Lace and Linen, 1994; Love Power, 1994; The Painted Veil, 1995; Parker and the Gypsy, 1997; The Courtesan: A Novel, 2005; The Dark Queen: A Novel, 2005; The Silver Rose: A Novel, 2006; The Huntress: A Novel, 2007; Twilight of a Queen: A Novel, 2008. **Address:** c/o Author Mail, Ballantine Books, 1745 Broadway, New York, NY 10019, U.S.A.

CARSON, Anne. Canadian (born Canada), b. 1950. **Genres:** Poetry, Essays, Novels, inspirational/Motivational Literature. **Career:** Princeton University, instructor; Emory University, instructor; University of Michigan, professor of classics and comparative literature; McGill University, John MacNaughton professor of classics, 2000-. Poet and essayist. **Publications:** Eros the Bittersweet: An Essay, 1986; Short Talks, 1992; Plainwater: Essays and Poetry, 1995; Glass, Irony, and God, 1995; Autobiography of Red: A Novel in Verse, 1998; Economy of the Unlost: Reading Simonides of Keos with Paul Celan, 1999; Men in the Off Hours, 2000; (trans.) Electra, 2001; The Beauty of the Husband: A Fictional Essay in 29 Tangos (poetry), 2001; (trans.) If Not, Winter: Fragments of Sappho, 2002; Decreation: Opera, Essays, Poetry, 2005. (trans.) Euripides, Grief Lessons: Four Plays by Euripides, 2006; (intro.) It, 2006; (contrib.) Troyjam, 2008; (trans.) Oresteia, 2009; Nox, 2010; (trans.) Antigonick, 2012. Works appear in anthologies. Contributor to periodicals. **Address:** Department of History, McGill University, Rm. 608, Leacock Bldg., 855 Sherbrooke St. W, Montreal, QC H3A 2T7, Canada. **Online address:** decreation@hotmail.com

CARSON, Anne (Regina). American (born United States), b. 1950. **Genres:** Literary Criticism And History, Women's Studies And Issues, Novellas/Short Stories, Theology/Religion, Bibliography. **Career:** University of Pittsburgh, library assistant, 1976-80; Brown University, rare book cataloger, 1980-82; Cornell University, reference librarian and selector for philosophy and religion, 1983-95, 1997-; freelance researcher and editor, 1993-. **Publications:** Feminist Spirituality and the Feminine Divine: An Annotated Bibliography, 1986; (ed.) Spiritual Parenting in the New Age, 1989; Goddesses and Wise Women: The Literature of Feminist Spirituality, 1980-1992: An Annotated Bibliography, 1992; (ed.) Caretaking a New Soul: Writing on Parenting from Thich Nhat Hanh to Z. Budapest, 1999. **Address:** Kroch Library, Division of Asia Collections, Cornell University, Rm. 2B59, Kroch,Carl A Library, Ithaca, NY 14850, U.S.A. **Online address:** arc3@cornell.edu

CARSON, Barbara Harrell. American (born United States), b. 1943. **Genres:** Literary Criticism And History, Young Adult Fiction. **Career:** Towson State College, assistant professor of English, 1968-71; University of Massachusetts, assistant professor of English, 1971-72; Florida Technological University, adjunct instructor, 1973-79; Valencia Community College, adjunct instructor, 1973-79; Rollins College, adjunct instructor, 1973-79, assistant professor, 1979-81, associate professor, 1981-88, professor of English, 1988-94, Theodore Bruce and Barbara Lawrence Alfond professor of English, 1994-2007, Alfond emeritus professor of English, 2007-. Writer. **Publications:** Eudora Welty: Two Pictures at Once in Her Frame, 1992; ISLE: Interdisciplinary Studies in Literature and Environment, forthcoming. Contributor to periodicals. **Address:** Department of English, Rollins College, 1000 Holt Ave., Ste. 2666, Winter Park, FL 32789-4499, U.S.A. **Online address:** bcarson@rollins.edu

CARSON, Benjamin S(olomon). American (born United States), b. 1951. **Genres:** Medicine/Health, Autobiography/Memoirs, Theology/Religion. **Career:** Johns Hopkins University, surgical intern, 1977-78, neurosurgical resident, 1978-82, chief resident neurosurgery, 1982-83, assistant professor of neurosurgery, 1984-, assistant professor of oncology, 1984-, assistant professor of pediatrics, 1987-, associate professor, 1991-, director of pediatric neurosurgery, 1985-91, professor of neurosurgery, The Johns Hopkins Craniofacial Center, co-director; Queen Elizabeth II Medical Center, senior registrar of neurosurgery, 1983-84. Writer. **Publications:** (With C. Murphey) Gifted Hands, The Ben Carson Story, 1990; (with C. Murphey) Think Big: Unleashing Your Potential for Excellence, 1992; (ed. with C.R. Dufresne and S.J. Zinreich) Complex Craniofacial Problems: A Guide to Analysis and Treatment, 1992; (with G. Lewis) The Big Picture: Getting Perspective on What's Really

Important in Life, 1999; (with G. Lewis) Take the Risk: Learning to Identify, Choose and Live with Acceptable Risk, 2008. Contributor to periodicals. **Address:** The Johns Hopkins Hospital, Department of Neurosurgery, Harvey 811, 600 N Wolfe St., Baltimore, MD 21287, U.S.A.

CARSON, Ciaran. Irish (born Ireland), b. 1948. **Genres:** Poetry, Music, Translations. **Career:** Teacher, 1974-75; Northern Ireland Arts Council, traditional arts officer, 1975-92, literature officer, 1992-98; Queen's University Belfast, Seamus Heaney Centre for Poetry, professor and center director. Writer. **Publications:** The New Estate, 1976; The Lost Explorer, 1978; Pocket Guide to Irish Traditional Music, 1986; The Irish for No (poetry), 1987; The New Estate and Other Poems, 1988; Belfast Confetti (poetry), 1989; First Language (poetry), 1993; Letters from the Alphabet, 1995; Opera Et Cetera (poetry), 1996; Last Night's Fun: In and Out of Time with Irish Music (prose), 1996; Star Factory, 1997; The Twelfth of Never (poetry), 1998; Alexandrine Plan: Versions of Sonnets by Baudelaire, Mallarmé and Rimbaud, 1998; The Ballad of HMS Belfast: A Compendium of Belfast Poems (poetry), 1999; Fishing for Amber: A Long Story (prose), 2000; Shamrock Tea (prose), 2001; Ciaran Carson: Selected Poems, 2001; Shamrock Tea, 2001; (trans.) Inferno of Dante Alighieri: A New Translation, 2002; Breaking News, 2003; (trans.) B. Merriman, Midnight Court: A New Translation of Cúirt an mheán oíche, 2005; For All We Know, 2008; (trans. and ed.) Táin, 2007; Collected Poems, 2008; On the Night Watch, 2009; Pen Friend, 2009; Until Before After, 2010. **Address:** Seamus Heaney Centre for Poetry, School of English, Queen's University Belfast, Belfast, BF BT7 1NN, Northern Ireland. **Online address:** c.carson@qub.ac.uk

CARSON, D(onald) A(rthur). American/Canadian (born Canada), b. 1946. **Genres:** Theology/Religion, inspirational/Motivational Literature, Songs/Lyrics And Libretti. **Career:** Central Baptist Seminary, lecturer in French, 1967-70; Richmond Baptist Church, pastor, 1970-72; Richmond College, lecturer, 1969-70; Northwest Baptist Theological College, lecturer, 1971-72, associate professor of New Testament, 1975-76, academic dean of Seminary, 1976-78; Trinity Evangelical Divinity School, associate professor, 1978-82, professor, 1982-91, research professor of New Testament, 1991-; Moore College, lecturer, 1985; Ontario Bible College, lecturer, 1991; Wycliffe Hall, Griffith Thomas lecturer, 1993; GRAMCORD Institute, founding chairperson, vice-chairperson. Writer. **Publications:** (Contrib.) New Testament Commentary Survey, 1977, 6th ed., 2007; The Sermon on the Mount: An Exposition of Matthew 5-7, 1978; The King James Version Debate: A Plea for Realism, 1979; The Farewell Discourse and Final Prayer of Jesus: An Exposition of John 14-17, 1980 in UK as Jesus and His Friends: His Farewell Message and Prayer in John 14 to 17, 1986; Divine Sovereignty and Human Responsibility: Biblical Themes in Tension, 1981; (ed. and intro.) From Sabbath to Lord's Day: A Biblical, Historical and Theological Investigation, 1982; (ed. with J.D. Woodbridge and contrib.) Scripture and Truth, 1983; Matthew, 1984; Exegetical Fallacies, 1984, 2nd ed., 1996; From Triumphalism to Maturity: An Exposition of 2 Corinthians 10-13, 1984; (ed. and contrib.) Biblical Interpretation and the Church: Text and Context, Paternoster, 1984; Biblical Interpretation and the Church: The Problem of Contextualization, 1985; God with Us: Themes from Matthew, 1985; Greek Accents: A Student's Manual, 1985; Red action Criticism: The Nature of an Interpretative Tool, 1985; (ed. with J.D. Woodbridge and contrib.) Hermeneutics, Authority and Canon, 1986; Showing the Spirit: A Theological Exposition of 1 Corinthians 12-14, 1987; (ed. and contrib.) The Church in the Bible and the World: An International Study, 1987; When Jesus Confronts the World: An Exposition of Matthew 8-10, 1987; (ed. with H.G.M. Williamson and contrib.) It Is Written: Scripture Citing Scripture; Essays in Honour of Barnabas Lindars, S.S.F., 1988; How Long, O Lord? Reflections on Suffering and Evil, 1990, 2nd ed., 2006; (ed. and contrib.) Teach Us to Pray: Prayer in the Bible and the World, 1990; The Gospel According to John, 1991; (with L. Morris and D.J. Moo) An Introduction to the New Testament, 1991, 2nd ed., 2005; A Call to Spiritual Reformation: Priorities From Paul and His Prayers, 1992; (co-author) An Evangelical Response to Baptism, Eucharist and Ministry, 1992; (ed.) Right With God: Justification in the Bible and the World, 1992; The Cross & Christian Ministry, 1993; (ed.) Worship: Adoration and Action, 1993; (ed. with J.D. Woodbridge and contrib.) God and Culture: Essays in Honor of Carl F.H. Henry, 1993; (ed. with S.E. Porter) Biblical Greek Language and Linguistics: Open Quest, Current Research, 1993; (with J.D. Woodbridge) Letters Along the Way: A Novel of the Christian Life, 1993; Holy Sonnets of the Twentieth Century, 1994; (co-ed.) New Bible Commentary Revised, 1994; (ed. with S.E. Porter) On Discourse and Other Topics, 1995; The Gagging of God: Christianity Confronts Pluralism, 1996; Basics for Believers: An Exposition of Philippians, 1996; Inclusive-Language Debate: A Plea for Realism, 1998; For the Love of God: A Daily Companion for Discovering the Riches of God's Word, 1998; (ed. with S.E. Porter) Linguistics and the New Testament: Critical Junctures, 1999; The Difficult Doctrine of the Love of God, 2000; Telling the Truth: Evangelizing Postmoderns, 2000; (co-ed.) Justification and Variegated Nomism, 2001; (ed.) Worship by the Book, 2002; Love in Hard Places, 2002; Becoming Conversant with the Emerging Church: Understanding a Movement and Its Implications, 2005; (with D.J. Moo) Introduction to the New Testament, 2005; A Model of Christian Maturity: An Exposition of 2 Corinthians 10-13, 2007; (ed. with G.K. Beale) Commentary on the New Testament Use of the Old Testament, 2007; Christ and Culture Revisited, 2007; Memoirs of an Ordinary Pastor: The Life and Reflections of Tom Carson, 2008; Christ and Culture Revisited, 2008; (ed.) Letter to the Hebrews, 2008; Collected Writings on Scripture, 2010; The God Who is There: Finding Your Place in God's Story Leaders's Guide, 2010; (ed.) Entrusted with the Gospel: Pastoral Expositions of 2 Timothy, 2010; Scandalous: The Cross and Resurrection of Jesus, 2010; (with D.J. Moo) Introducing the New Testament: A Short Guide to Its History and Message, 2010; (with J. Piper) The Pastor as Scholar and the Scholar as Pastor: Reflections on Life and Ministry, 2011; The Intolerance of Tolerance, 2011; (ed. with T. Keller) The Gospel as Center, 2012. Works appear in anthologies. Contributor of articles to periodicals. **Address:** Trinity Evangelical Divinity School, 2065 Half Day Rd., Deerfield, IL 60015, U.S.A.

CARSON, Donald W. American (born United States), b. 1933?. **Genres:** Biography, Novels. **Career:** Arizona Daily Star, reporter and writer, 1957-61, associate editor, 1967-68; Associated Press, newsman, assistant bureau chief, 1961-66; University of Arizona, School of Journalism, assistant professor, professor of journalism, head of department, 1966-67, 1968-97, professor emeritus of journalism, 1997-; Goals for Tucson Tabloid, editor, 1982. **Publications:** (With J.W. Johnson) Mo: The Life & Times of Morris K. Udall, 2001. Contributor of articles to newspapers. **Address:** School of Journalism, University of Arizona, Rm. 334, Marshall Bldg., 845 N Park Ave., PO Box 210158B, Tucson, AZ 85721-0158, U.S.A. **Online address:** dcarson@email.arizona.edu

CARSON, Herbert L. American (born United States), b. 1929. **Genres:** Literary Criticism And History, Philosophy, Cultural/Ethnic Topics. **Career:** Teacher, 1953-55; University of Minnesota, instructor in English, 1956-59, Independent Study Department, instructor in creative writing, 1957-59; University of Nebraska, instructor in speech and drama, 1959-60; Ferris State University, assistant professor, 1960-64, associate professor, 1964-68, professor of humanities and literature, 1968-94, professor emeritus of humanities, 1994-; Youngstown University, visiting professor, 1966; Institute on Blacks in Movies, National Endowment for Humanities, director, 1969; Ford Foundation, director, 1969; Grand Rapids Press, book reviewer, 1973-94. Writer. **Publications:** Steps in Successful Speaking, 1967; (contrib.) Great American Speeches, 1970; (comp. with A.L. Carson) The Impact of Fiction: An Anthology of Short Stories, 1970; (with A.L. Carson) Royall Tyler, 1979; (with A.L. Carson) Domestic Tragedy in England, 1982; (with A.L. Carson) The Image of the West: A Brief Survey of Classical Civilization, 1989. Contributor of articles to journals. **Address:** Ferris State University, 1201 S State St., Big Rapids, MI 49307, U.S.A.

CARSON, Mary Kay. American (born United States), b. 1964. **Genres:** Children's Non-fiction, Young Adult Non-fiction. **Career:** National Marine Fisheries Service, observer, 1990; Super Science, associate editor and writer, 1991-94; Don Bosco Center, teacher of English, 1993-96; Delta School, teacher of English, 1993-96; Science World Scholastic Inc., freelance writer, 1994-. **Publications:** Epilepsy, 1998; The Creepiest, Scariest, Weirdest Creatures Ever!, 2002; The Wright Brothers for Kids: How They Invented the Airplane, 2003; Mars, 2003; In the Deep, 2003; The Underground Railroad for Kids, 2005; Exploring the Solar System, 2006; Weather Projects for Young Scientists, 2007; Alexander Graham Bell: Giving Voice to the World, 2007; Emi and the Rhino Scientist, 2007; Extreme Planets!, 2008; The Bat Scientists, 2010; Inside Hurricanes, 2010; Inside Tornadoes, 2010; Inside Weather, 2011. LEVELED READERS: The Rockies, 2003; Fair Day USA; Cool Science Jobs, 2003; Gross Body Facts, 2003; Driving on Mars, 2004; The Bald Eagle Is Back, 2004; The Greatest Electrician in the World, 2004; The Return of Wild Whoopers, 2004; Native American Homes, 2005; The Mighty Mississippi, 2005; Don't Sweat It, 2006; Diamonds!, 2006; Amazing Stuff, 2007; How Airplanes Fly, 2007; The Lost City: Machu Picchu and the Incas, 2008. PROFESSIONAL TITLES FOR TEACHERS: Space: Hands-On Activities, the Latest Information and a Colorful Learning Poster, 1996; Colonial America: A Complete Theme Unit Developed in Cooperation with the Colonial Williamsburg Foundation, 1999; The Wow's and Why's of Weather, 2000; Great Weather Activities: All the Background Info and How To's You Need for Teaching about the Wonders of Weather, 2000; Space: Quick and Easy Internet Activities for the One-Computer Classroom, 2001; Weather: Quick and Easy Activities for the One-Computer Classroom, 2002; Easy Science Activity Journals, 2003. **Address:** 4308 Leeper St., Cincinnati, OH 45223, U.S.A. **Online address:** mkc@fuse.net

CARSON, Paul. Irish (born Ireland), b. 1949?. **Genres:** Novels, Medicine/Health. **Career:** Allergy & Asthma Clinic, pediatrician. Physician and novelist. **Publications:** NOVELS: Scalpel, 1997; Cold Steel, 1998; Final Duty, 2000; Betrayal, 2007; Ambush, 2008. CHILDREN'S NOVELS: Norbett Bear MD, 1994; Norbett's Bistro, 1995. MEDICAL ADVICE BOOKS: How to Cope with Your Child's Allergies, 1987; Coping Successfully with Your Child's Asthma, 1987; Coping Successfully with Your Hyperactive Child, 1987; Coping Successfully with Your Child's Skin Problems, 1987. Contributor of articles to periodicals and journals. **Address:** Darley Anderson Literary, TV & Film Agency, Estelle House, 11 Eustace Rd., London, GL SW6 1JB, England.

CARSTAIRS, Catherine. Canadian (born Canada), b. 1969?. **Genres:** Criminology/True Crime, History. **Career:** Stockholm University, postdoctoral fellow, 2001; University of Waterloo, postdoctoral fellow, 2002; University of British Columbia, assistant professor, 2002-04; University of Guelph, assistant professor, 2004-. Writer. **Publications:** Jailed for Possession: Illegal Drug Use, Regulation, and Power in Canada, 1920-1961, 2006. Contributor of articles to journals. **Address:** Department of History, University of Guelph, 50 Stone Rd. E, Guelph, ON N1G 2W1, Canada. **Online address:** ccarstai@uoguelph.ca

CARSTENS, Catherine Mansell. *See* **MAYO, C(atherine) M(ansell).**

CARSWELL, Grace. British (born England), b. 1969. **Genres:** Economics. **Career:** University of Sussex, faculty, 2000-, lecturer in geography. Writer. **Publications:** (Ed. with S. Jones) The Earthscan Reader in Environment, Development and Rural Livelihoods, 2004; Cultivating Success in Uganda: Kigezi Farmers and Colonial Policies, 2007. Contributor to books and journals. **Address:** University of Sussex, Sussex House, Brighton, ES BN1 9RH, England.

CARSWELL, Sue. American (born United States), b. 1962?. **Genres:** Autobiography/Memoirs, Politics/Government. **Career:** American Broadcasting System, Good Morning America, senior story editor; Oprah Magazine, executive editor; People magazine, correspondent; Vanity Fair, researcher and reporter. Editor and writer. **Publications:** Faded Pictures from My Backyard: A Memoir, 2005. **Address:** Ballantine Books, 1745 Broadway, New York, NY 10019, U.S.A.

CARTARESCU, Mircea. Romanian (born Romania), b. 1956. **Genres:** Poetry. **Career:** General School, professor of Romanian language and literature, 1980-89; Caiete Critice Magazine, editor, 1989-90; Romanian Writers Union, writer-in-residence, 1991-; University of Bucharest, Faculty of Letters, lecturer and chairman of Romanian literature history, 1991-, associate professor, professor; University of Amsterdam, visiting lecturer, 1994-95; New Europe College, fellow, 1995. **Publications:** Faruri, vitrine, fotografii, 1980; (contrib.) Aer cu diamante, 1982; Poeme de amor, 1983; (contrib.) Desant 83, 1983; Totul, 1985; Visul, 1989; Levantul, 1990; Visul chimeric, 1992; Nostalgia, 1993; Dragostea, 1994; Travesti, 1994, 2nd ed., 2002; (contrib.) Antologia poeziei generat□iei '80, 1995; Orbitor, 1996; Dublu CD: Antologie de poezie, 1998; Postmodernismul românesc, 1999; (contrib.) Generatia '80 în proza scurta, 1999; Jurnal, 2001; Enciclopedia zmeilor, 2002; Pururi tinăr, infăș urat in pixeli: din periodice, 2003; Cincizeci de sonete de Mircea Cărtărescu cu cincizeci de desene originale de Tudor Jebeleanu, 2003; Plurivers: Volum Antologic, 2003; De ce iubim femeile, 2004; Baroane!, 2005; Rem: Roman, 2006; Gemenii: Roman, 2006; Mendebilul: Povestiri, 2007; Frumoasele străine, 2010. Contributor to periodicals. **Address:** Faculty of Letters, University of Bucharest, Str. Edgar Quinet nr. 5-7, Sector 1, Bucharest, 1, Romania.

CARTER, Abigail. American (born United States), b. 1965. **Genres:** Autobiography/Memoirs. **Career:** Writer. **Publications:** The Alchemy of Loss: A Young Widow's Transformation (memoir), 2008. Contributor to magazine. **Address:** Seattle, WA , U.S.A. **Online address:** abigail@abigailcarter.com

CARTER, Alden R(ichardson). American (born United States), b. 1947. **Genres:** Novels, Young Adult Fiction, Children's Non-fiction, History, Young Adult Non-fiction, Novellas/Short Stories, Adult Non-fiction. **Career:** Writer and educator. **Publications:** YOUNG ADULT NONFICTION: (with W.J. LeBlanc) Supercomputers, 1985; Modern China, 1986; (with W.J. LeBlanc) Modern Electronics, 1986; Radio: From Marconi to the Space Age, 1987; Illinois, 1987; The Shoshoni, 1989; Last Stand at the Alamo, 1990; The Battle of Gettysburg, 1990; The Colonial Wars: Clashes in the Wilderness, 1992; The American Revolution: War for Independence, 1992; The War of 1812: Second Fight for Independence, 1992; The Mexican War: Manifest Destiny, 1992; The Civil War: American Tragedy, 1992; The Spanish-American War: Imperial Ambitions, 1992; Battle of the Ironclads: The Monitor and the Merrimack, 1993; China Past, China Future, 1994; China: From the First Chinese to the Olympics, 2008. THE AMERICAN REVOLUTION SERIES: Colonies in Revolt, 1988; Darkest Hours, 1988; At the Forge of Liberty, 1988; Birth of the Republic, 1988. YOUNG ADULT FICTION: Growing Season, 1984; Wart, Son of Toad, 1985; Sheila's Dying, 1987; Up Country, 1989; Robo Dad, 1990, as Dancing on Dark Water, 1994; Dogwolf, 1994; Between a Rock and a Hard Place, 1995; Bull Catcher, 1996; Crescent Moon, 1999; Brothers Keeper, 2003; Love, Football and Other Contact Sports, 2006; Walkaway, 2008. FOR CHILDREN: (with S.M. Carter) I'm Tougher Than Asthma!, 1996; Big Brother Dustin, 1997; Seeing Things My Way, 1998; Dustin's Big School Day, 1999; Stretching Ourselves: Kids with Cerebral Palsy, 2000; I'm Tougher Than Diabetes, 2001. ADULT FICTION: Bright Starry Banner: A Novel of the Civil War, 2004. ADULT NONFICTION: (ed.) Auschwitz Veterinarian: Five Years in the Death Camps, 2003; (ed.) Brother to the Eagle: Civil War Journal of Sgt. Ambrose Armitage, 8th Wisconsin Infantry, 2006; The Sea Eagle: The Civil War Memoir of Lt. Cdr. William Barker Cushing USN, 2009; (with D.W. Chang) The Scholar and the Tiger: A Memoir of Famine and War in Revolutionary China, 2009. OTHERS: Robodad, 1990. Contributor to books. Works appear in anthologies. **Address:** 1113 W Onstad Dr., Marshfield, WI 54449, U.S.A. **Online address:** acarterwriter@tznet.com

CARTER, Ally. American (born United States), b. 1974. **Genres:** Poetry, Young Adult Fiction, Novels. **Career:** Writer. **Publications:** Cheating at Solitaire: A Novel, 2005; Learning to Play Gin, 2006; I'd Tell You I Love You, but Then I'd Have to Kill You, 2006; Cross My Heart and Hope to Spy, 2007; Don't Judge a Girl by Her Cover, 2009; Heist Society, 2010; Only the Good Spy Young, 2011. **Address:** c/o Kristin Nelson, Nelson Literary Agency L.L.C., 1732 Wazee St., Ste. 207, Denver, CO 80202-2312, U.S.A. **Online address:** ally@allycarter.com

CARTER, Ashton B. American (born United States), b. 1954. **Genres:** Military/Defense/Arms Control. **Career:** Fermi National Accelerator Laboratory, experimental research associate, 1975; Brookhaven National Laboratory, experimental research associate, 1976; Oxford University, physics instructor, 1977-79; Rockefeller University, research associate theoretical physics, 1979-80; Office of the Secretary of Defense The Pentagon, Program Analysis and Evaluation, staff, 1981-82; Massachusetts Institute of Technology, Center for International Studies, research fellow, 1982-84; Harvard University, assistant professor, 1984-86, associate professor, 1986-88, professor and associate director for center for science and international studies, 1988-90, John F. Kennedy School of Government, Center For Science and International Studies, director, 1990-93, Ford Foundation professor of science and international studies International and Global Affairs Faculty, chair, Preventive Defense Project, co-director; MITRE Corp., Los Alamos Scientific Laboratory, consultant; Brookings Institution, Los Alamos Scientific Laboratory, consultant; U.S. Department of Defense, International Security Policy, assistant secretary of defense, 1993-96, under secretary of defense for acquisition, technology and logistics, 2009-; U.S. Department of State, senior advisor to the North Korea policy review, 1998-2000; State Condoleezza Rices International Security Advisory Board, secretary, 2006-08; Stanford University, Preventive Defense Project, co-director. Writer. **Publications:** (Ed. with D.N. Schwartz and contrib.) Ballistic Missile Defense, 1984; Directed Energy Missile Defense in Space, 1984; (ed. with J.D. Steinbruner and C.A. Zraket and contrib.) Managing Nuclear Operations, 1987; (ed. with J.S. Nye, Jr. and J.A. Schear and contrib.) Seeking Stability in Space: Anti-Satellite Weapons and the Evolving Space Regime, 1987; (ed. with K.W. Thompson) Ashton B. Carter on Arms Control, 1990; (W.J. Perry) New Thinking and American Defense Technology, 1990, 2nd ed., 1993; (with K. Campbell and others) Soviet Nuclear Fission: Control of the Nuclear Arsenal in a Disintegrating Soviet Union, 1991; (with W.J. Perry and J.D. Steinbruner) A New Concept of Cooperative Security, 1992; (co-author) Beyond Spinoff: Military and Commercial Technologies in a Changing World, 1992; (with W.J. Perry) Preventive Defense: A New Strategy for America, 1999; (with S.E. Miller and E. Sherwood-Randall) Fulfilling the Promise: Building an Enduring Security Partnership Between Ukraine and NATO, 1999; (ed. with J.P. White) Keeping the Edge: Managing Defense for the Future, 2001. Contributor to journals. Works appear in anthologies. **Address:** Belter Center for Science and Int Affairs, John F. Kennedy School of Government, Littauer 374, 79 John F. Kennedy St., PO Box 53, Cambridge, MA 02138, U.S.A. **Online address:** ashton_carter@harvard.edu

CARTER, Betty. American (born United States), b. 1944?. **Genres:** Bibliography, Adult Non-fiction. **Career:** Librarian, educator and writer. **Publications:** (With R.F. Abrahamson) Books for You: A Booklist for Senior High Students, 1988; (with R.F. Abrahamson) Nonfiction for Young Adults: From Delight to Wisdom, 1990; Best Books for Young Adults: The Selections, the History, the Romance, 1994, (co-author) 2nd ed., 2000; (co-author) Best Books for Young Adults, 2000, (foreword) 3rd ed., 2007. **Address:** American Library Association, 50 E Huron St., Chicago, IL 60611, U.S.A.

CARTER, Betty Smartt. American (born United States), b. 1965. **Genres:** Children's Fiction, Novels, Autobiography/Memoirs, Cartoons. **Career:** Books and Culture, contributing editor. Novelist and educator. **Publications:** I Read It in the Wordless Book, 1996; The Tower, the Mask and the Grave, 1997; Home is Always the Place You Just Left, 2003; While Rachel Weeps, forthcoming. Contributor of articles to periodicals. **Address:** Paraclete Press Inc., 36 Southern Eagle Cartway, PO Box 1568, Brewster, MA 02631, U.S.A. **Online address:** bettycart@juno.com

CARTER, C. Barry. American (born United States) **Genres:** Sciences, Engineering, Chemistry. **Career:** Cornell University, assistant professor, 1979-83, assistant professor, 1983-88, professor of material science and engineering, through 1988-91; Bristol University, visiting professor and Guggenheim fellow, 1985-86; University of Minnesota, professor and 3M endowed chair of chemical engineering and materials science, 1991-2007; University of Connecticut, School of Engineering, Department of Chemical, Materials & Biomolecular Engineering, department head and professor. Writer. **Publications:** (With D.B. Williams) Transmission Electron Microscopy: A Textbook for Materials Science, 1996; (co-ed.) Interfacial Engineering for Optimized Properties: Symposium Held December 2-5, 1996, 1997; (co-ed.) Interfacial Engineering for Optimized Properties II: Symposium Held December 1- 2, 1999, 2000; (co-ed.) Structure-Property Relationships of Oxide Surfaces and Interfaces: Symposium Held November 27-29, 2000, 2001; (with M.G. Norton) Ceramic Materials: Science and Engineering, 2007. **Address:** Department of Chemical, Materials & Biomolecular, Engineering, University of Connecticut, 191 Auditorium Rd., Ste. 3222, Storrs, CT 06269-3222, U.S.A. **Online address:** carter@cems.umn.edu

CARTER, Charlotte. American (born United States), b. 1943?. **Genres:** Mystery/Crime/Suspense, Novels. **Career:** Writer. **Publications:** NANETTE HAYES SERIES: Rhode Island Red, 1997; Coq Au Vin, 1999; Drumsticks, 2000; Rooster's Riff, 2001. COOK COUNTY SERIES: Jackson Park, 2003; Trip Wire, 2005. NOVELS: Personal Effects, 1991; Walking Bones, 2002; A Mysterious History, 2005; A Light in the Dark, 2006; The Mystery of Daisy Doe, 2006; Out of the Ashes, 2007; Plundered Treasure, 2008; Strength in Numbers, 2010; Christmas Miracles, 2010. Contributor to periodicals. **Address:** Mysterious Press, Warner Books, 1271 Ave. of the Americas, New York, NY 10020, U.S.A.

CARTER, Christine Jacobson. American (born United States), b. 1968. **Genres:** History, Biography, Autobiography/Memoirs. **Career:** Emory University, assistant professor of history. Writer. **Publications:** The Diary of Dolly Lunt Burge, 1848-1879, 1997; Southern Single Blessedness: Unmarried Women in the Urban South, 1800-1865, 2006. **Address:** Department of History, Emory University, 221 Bowden Hall, 561 S Kilgo Cir., Atlanta, GA 30322-3651, U.S.A.

CARTER, David. American (born United States), b. 1954?. **Genres:** Novels, Technology. **Career:** Writer and director. **Publications:** Build it Underground: A Guide for the Self-Builder & Building Professional, 1982; Cheap Shelter, 1984; George Santayana, 1992; Salvador Dali, 1995; Teach Yourself How to Write a Play, 1999; (ed.) Spontaneous Mind: Selected Interviews 1958-1996, 2001; (with N. Carter) Little Mouse and Daddy: A Touch and Feel Book, 2003; Stonewall: The Riots That Sparked the Gay Revolution, 2004. Contributor to periodicals. **Address:** c/o Author Mail, St. Martins Press, 175 5th Ave., New York, NY 10010, U.S.A. **Online address:** info@davidcarter-author.com

CARTER, Dean Vincent. British (born England), b. 1976. **Genres:** Novels, Horror. **Career:** Transworld Publishers, temporary mail sorter, 1999, mail sorter, 2002-; Hammicks Bookshop, staff. Writer. **Publications:** The Hand of the Devil (young adult horror novel), 2006; The Hunting Season (young adult horror novel), 2007; Blood Water, 2009. **Address:** Corgi Childrens Publishers, The Random House Group Ltd., 20 Vauxhall Bridge Rd., London, GL SW1V 2SA, England. **Online address:** info@deanvincentcarter.com

CARTER, (Elizabeth) Susanne. American (born United States), b. 1950. **Genres:** Education, Women's Studies And Issues, Literary Criticism And History, Bibliography, Humanities. **Career:** Springfield Daily News, news reporter, 1973-74; Missouri State Auditor's Office and Missouri Department of Natural Resources, staff writer, 1974-77; Southwest Missouri State University, microforms supervisor, 1980-92; University of Oregon, Western Regional Resource Center, research assistant and information specialist, 1992-95; University of Missouri, Center for Innovations in Special Education, library coordinator, 1995-99, College of Education, grant writer, 1999-. **Publications:** War and Peace through Women's Eyes: A Selected Bibliography of Twentieth-Century American Women's Fiction, 1992; (comp.) Mothers and Daughters in American Short Fiction: An Annotated Bibliography of Twentieth-Century Women's Literature, 1993. Contributor to magazines and newspapers. **Address:** University of Missouri, 911 Sunset Ln., Columbia, MO 65203, U.S.A. **Online address:** cartere@missouri.edu

CARTER, Emily. American (born United States), b. 1960. **Genres:** Poetry, Young Adult Fiction, Novellas/Short Stories. **Career:** Pulse (newspaper), columnist; Loft Literary Center, teacher; Speakeasy Magazine, columnist; Star Tribune, staff. **Publications:** Glory Goes and Gets Some, 2000. Works appear in anthologies. Contributor to periodicals. **Address:** Coffee House Press, 79 13th Ave. NE, Ste. 110, Minneapolis, MN 55413, U.S.A.

CARTER, Frances Monet. (Frances Monet Carter Evans). American (born United States), b. 1923. **Genres:** Medicine/Health. **Career:** University of San Francisco, instructor, associate professor, 1957-70, professor, 1970-88, Psychiatric Nursing, professor emeritus, 1988-; Gustavus Adolphus College, consultant; Indiana University, consultant. Writer. **Publications:** AS FRANCES MONET CARTER EVANS: The Role of the Nurse in Community Mental Health, 1968; Psychosocial Nursing: Theory and Practice in Hospital and Community Mental Health, 1971, 3rd ed., 1981. Contributor to journals. **Address:** University of San Francisco, 2130 Fulton St., San Francisco, CA 94117-1080, U.S.A.

CARTER, Harold. Welsh (born Wales), b. 1925. **Genres:** Geography, Urban Studies, Language/Linguistics, Adult Non-fiction, Literary Criticism And History, Essays. **Career:** Aberystwyth University, lecturer, 1952-68, Gregynog professor of human geography, 1968-86, professor emeritus, 1986-, Welsh Medium Studies, dean, vice principal. Writer. **Publications:** The Towns of Wales: A Study in Urban Geography, 1965; (ed. with E.G. Bowen and J.A. Taylor) Geography at Aberystwyth: Essays Written on the Occasion of the Departmental Jubilee 1917-18-1967-68, 1968; The Growth of the Welsh City System: An Inaugural Lecture Delivered at the University College of Wales, Aberystwyth, on 12 February 1969, 1969; (with W.K.D. Davies) Urban Essays: Studies in the Geography of Wales, 1970; The Study of Urban Geography, 1972, 4th ed., 1995; (co-author) Advanced Geography of The British Isles, 1974; (ed. and intro.) Geography, Culture and Habitat: Selected Essays of E.G. Bowen, 1976; (ed. with H.M. Griffiths) National Atlas of Wales, 1980, 2nd ed., 1989; (with S. Wheatley) Merthyr Tydfil in 1851: A Study of the Spatial Structure of a Welsh Industrial Town, 1982; An Introduction to Urban Historical Geography, 1983; (with J.W. Aitchison) Welsh Language, 1961-1981: An Interpretative Atlas, 1985; An Urban Geography of England and Wales in the Nineteenth Century, 1990; Urban and Rural Settlements, 1990; A Geography of the Welsh Language, 1961-1991, 1994; (with J. Aitchison) Language, Economy and Society: The Changing Fortunes of the Welsh Language in the Twentieth Century, 2000. **Address:** Aberystwyth University, Old College, King St., Aberystwyth, DY SY23 2AX, Wales. **Online address:** 101571.3476@compuserve.com

CARTER, Jared. American (born United States), b. 1939. **Genres:** Poetry, History, Photography, Young Adult Fiction. **Career:** Bobbs-Merrill Co., editor and interior designer; Hackett Publishing Co., staff. **Publications:** POETRY: Early Warning, 1979; Work, for the Night Is Coming, 1981; Fugue State, 1984; Pincushion's Strawberry (poems and photographs), 1984; Indiana, 1984; Millennial Harbinger, 1986; The Shriving, 1990; Situation Normal, 1991; Blues Project, 1991; After the Rain, 1993; Les Barricades Mystérieuses: Thirty-Two Villanelles, 1999; Cross this Bridge at a Walk, 2006; A Dance in the Street, 2011. Contributor to periodicals. **Address:** 1220 N State Ave., Indianapolis, IN 46201-1162, U.S.A.

CARTER, Jean Wilmot. *See* **WILMOT, Jeanne.**

CARTER, Jimmy. American (born United States), b. 1924. **Genres:** Politics/Government, Autobiography/Memoirs, inspirational/Motivational Literature. **Career:** State Government, state senator, 1963-67, governor of Georgia, 1971-75; United States Government, thirty-ninth president of the United States, 1977-81; Carter Center, founder, 1982; Emory University, distinguished professor, 1982-; The Carter-Menil Human Rights Foundation, founder, 1986; writer, 1981-. **Publications:** Why Not the Best?, 1975, as Why Not the Best?: The First Fifty Years, 1996; Addresses of Jimmy Carter, Governor of Georgia, 1971-75, 1975; I'll Never Lie to You: Jimmy Carter in His Own Words, 1976; The Wit and Wisdom of Jimmy Carter, 1977; A Government as Good as Its People, 1977; Carter on the Arts, 1977; Letters to the Honorable William Prescott, 1977; The Spiritual Journey of Jimmy Carter, in His Own Words, 1978; (co-author) Amerika gaikō no kichō, 1979; (contrib.) Carter vs. Ford: The Counterfeit Debates of 1976, 1980; Keeping Faith: Memoirs of a President, 1982; Negotiation: The Alternative to Hostility, 1984; The Blood of Abraham: Insights into the Middle East, 1985, 3rd ed. 2007; (with R. Carter) Everything to Gain: Making the Most of the Rest of Your Life, 1987, rev. ed., 1995; An Outdoor Journal: Adventures and Reflections, 1988; The 1900 General Elections in Haiti, 1991; (with G.O. Barney) Global 2000: The Report to the President: Entering the Twenty-first Century, 1991; Turning Point: A Candidate and a State and a Nation Come of Age, 1992; Jimmy Carter, National Historic Site and Preservation District, Georgia: General Management Plan, Development Concept Plan, 1993; Observing Guyana's Electoral Process, 1990-92, 1993; Talking Peace: A Vision for the Next Generation, 1993, rev. ed., 1995; U.S.: President Clinton's First 100 Days, 1995; Always a Reckoning and Other Poems, 1995; Living Faith, 1996; Lessons for Life, 1996; (with A. Carter) The Little Baby Snoogle-Fleejer, 1996; Sources of Strength: Meditations on Scripture for Daily Living, 1997; Conversations with Carter, 1998; The Virtues of Aging, 1998; Family of Wiley Carter: 1798-1998, 1998; Atlanta: The Right Kind of Courage, 2000; (contrib.) Empower Zone: Youth Photography from the Empowerment Zone/Enterprise Community Initiative, 2000; An Hour before Daylight: Memories of a Rural Boyhood, 2001; Christmas in Plains: Memories, 2001; As Time Goes By: Memories of the Past, A Legacy for the Future, 2001; U.S. Law Affecting Americans Living and Working Abroad, 2001; Personal Beliefs of Jimmy Carter, 2002; The Hornet's Nest: A Novel of the Revolutionary War, 2003; Seasons of Life and Land: Wildling Art Museum, America's Wilderness in Art, 2004; Our Endangered Values: America's Moral Crisis, 2005, 2nd ed., 2006; Sharing Good Times, 2005; (with M.J.T. Stepanek) Just Peace: A Message of Hope, 2006; Palestine: Peace Not Apartheid, 2006; Civil Rights During the Carter Administration, 1977-1981, 2007; (foreword) For the Common Good: The Ethics of Leadership in the 21st Century, 2007; Beyond the White House: Waging Peace, Fighting Disease, Building Hope, 2007; Remarkable Mother, 2008; (intro.) American Revolution, 2008; We Can Have Peace in the Holy Land: A Plan That Will Work, 2009; (forword) Field Guide to Environmental Engineering for Development Workers: Water, Sanitation, and Indoor Air, 2009; White House Diary, 2010; (with S. Halliday) Through the Year with Jimmy Carter, 2011; Lessons from Life Bible, 2012. **Address:** The Carter Center, 1 Copenhill, 453 Freedom Pkwy., Atlanta, GA 30307-1498, U.S.A. **Online address:** carter.library@nara.gov

CARTER, J. Kameron. American (born United States), b. 1967. **Genres:** Theology/Religion. **Career:** Duke University, Divinity School, associate professor of theology and black church studies. Writer. **Publications:** Race: A Theological Account, 2008. **Address:** Divinity School, Duke University, PO Box 90968, Durham, NC 27708-0968, U.S.A. **Online address:** jcarter@div.duke.edu

CARTER, John T(homas). American (born United States), b. 1921. **Genres:** Children's Fiction, Children's Non-fiction, Archaeology/Antiquities. **Career:** Wood Junior College, professor of agriculture, 1947-48; Clarke Memorial College, professor of agriculture, 1948-56; Samford University, professor of education, 1956-, associate dean of education. Writer. **Publications:** Mike and His Four-Star Goal, 1960; East Is West, 1964; Witness in Israel: The Story of Paul Rowden, 1969; (with F. Carter) Sharing Times Seven, 1971; (contrib.) The Archaeology of Kentucky: Past Accomplishments and Future Directions, 1990. **Address:** Samford University, PO Box 292305, Birmingham, AL 35229, U.S.A. **Online address:** j-fcarter@juno.com

CARTER, Joseph H(enry). American (born United States), b. 1932. **Genres:** Biography, Autobiography/Memoirs. **Career:** United Press International (UPI), correspondent, 1959-64; Honolulu Advertiser, reporter, 1964-65; Oklahoma Journal, associate editor, 1964-68; White House Council on Wage and Price Stability, deputy assistant director, 1979-80; H/CA Inc., president, 1980-85; Cameron University, vice president, 1985-89; Will Rogers Memorial Museums, director, 1989-91; Oklahoma State Chamber of Commerce, director, 1990. **Publications:** Never Met a Man I Didn't Like: The Life and Writings of Will Rogers, 1991; 1991 Avon Book, 1991; Quotable Will Rogers, 2005. **Address:** c/o Gibbs Smith, PO Box 667, Layton, UT 84041, U.S.A. **Online address:** joecarter@willrogers.com

CARTER, Julian B. American (born United States), b. 1967. **Genres:** Young Adult Non-fiction. **Career:** Stanford University, faculty; New York University, faculty; California College of the Arts, associate professor of visual and critical studies, 2006-. Writer and historian. **Publications:** The Heart of Whiteness: Normal Sexuality and Race in America, 1880-1940 (nonfiction), 2007. **Address:** U.S.A. **Online address:** juliancarter@cca.edu

CARTER, Marie. American/British/Scottish (born Scotland), b. 1978. **Genres:** Young Adult Fiction. **Career:** Hanging Loose Press, editor, 2000-. **Publications:** (Ed.) Word Jig: New Fiction from Scotland, 2003; The Trapeze Diaries, 2008. Works appear in anthologies. Contributor to periodicals. **Address:** Hanging Loose Press, 231 Wyckoff St., Brooklyn, NY 11217, U.S.A. **Online address:** mariecarter@ymail.com

CARTER, Martin R(oger). Canadian/British (born England), b. 1946. **Genres:** Agriculture/Forestry, Environmental Sciences/Ecology, Sciences, Engineering, Earth Sciences, Mathematics/Statistics. **Career:** Agriculture Canada, Investigation Section at PFRA Tree Nursery, assistant head, Indian head, 1977-80, officer in charge of soils and crops substation, 1981-83; Agriculture and Agri-Food Canada, research scientist, 1983-; Nova Scotia Agricultural College, adjunct professor, 1983-99; Rutherglen Research Institute, visiting scientist, 1990-91; Ballarat University, visiting fellow, 1995-96; Agriculture, Ecosystems and Environment, editor-in-chief, 1997-; Soil and Tillage Research, editor-in-chief, 1998-; University of Prince Edward Island, adjunct professor, 2000-. **Publications:** (Ed. with E.G. Gregorich) Soil Sampling and Methods of Analysis, 1993, 2nd ed., 2008; (ed.) Conservation Tillage in Temperate Agroecosystems, 1994; (ed. with B.A. Stewart) Structure and Organic Matter Storage in Agricultural Soils, 1996; (ed. with E.G. Gregorich) Soil Quality for Crop Production and Ecosystem Health, 1997; (co-ed.) Soil and Environmental Science Dictionary, 2001. **Address:** Research Centre, Research Br., Agriculture and Agri-Food Canada, PO Box 1210, Charlottetown, PE C1A 7M8, Canada. **Online address:** carterm@em.agr.ca

CARTER, Maureen. British (born England) **Genres:** Novels, Mystery/Crime/Suspense. **Career:** BRMB radio, news reader; British Broadcasting Corp. (BBC), broadcast journalist, assistant editor. **Publications:** BEV MORRISS CRIME SERIES: Working Girls, 2004; Dead Old, 2005; Baby Love, 2006; Hard Time, 2007; Bad Press, 2008; Blood Money, 2009; Criminal Tendencies (short stories), 2009; Death Line, 2010. DI SARAH QUINN CRIME SERIES: A Question of Despair, 2011; Mother Love, 2011. **Online address:** maureencarter@gmail.com

CARTER, Melanie. *See* **LANAGAN, Margo.**

CARTER, Mike. British (born England), b. 1936?. **Genres:** Novels, Young Adult Fiction, Sciences. **Career:** Teacher, 1961-89; writer, 1989-. **Publications:** Biggest Pool of All, 1995; Space Games, 2001. YOUNG ADULT NOVELS: Jessie, 2003; Access to the Universe, 2004. Contributor of articles to periodicals. **Address:** Te Kohanga Rd., Onewhero, R.D. 2 Tuakau, Auckland, 1007, New Zealand. **Online address:** diannacarter@clear.net.nz

CARTER, Miranda. British (born England), b. 1965?. **Genres:** Biography,

History. **Career:** Journalist and publisher. **Publications:** Anthony Blunt: His Lives, 2001; The Three Emperors: Three Cousins, Three Empires and the Road to World War One, 2009; George, Nicholas and Wilhelm: Three Royal Cousins and The Road to World War I, 2010. **Address:** Farrar, Straus & Giroux, 19 Union Sq. W, New York, NY 10003-3304, U.S.A.

CARTER, Nick. *See* **CRIDER, (Allen) Bill(y).**

CARTER, Nick. *See* **SMITH, Martin Cruz.**

CARTER, Raphael. American (born United States) **Genres:** Science Fiction/Fantasy, Novels, Novellas/Short Stories. **Career:** Writer. **Publications:** The Fortunate Fall, 1996; Congenital Agenesis of Gender Ideation by K.N. Sirsi and Sandra Botkin (short story), 1998. **Address:** Tor Books, 175 5th Ave., 14th Fl., New York, NY 10010-7703, U.S.A. **Online address:** raphael@wavefront.com

CARTER, Rosalynn (Smith). American (born United States), b. 1927. **Genres:** Self Help, Autobiography/Memoirs, Medicine/Health, Psychology. **Career:** Agnes Scott College, distinguished centennial lecturer, 1988-92; Southwestern State University, Rosalynn Carter Institute for Caregiving of Georgia, president, founder. Writer. **Publications:** First Lady from Plains, 1984; (with J. Carter) Everything to Gain: Making the Most of the Rest of Your Life, 1987, rev. ed., 1995; (with S.K. Golant) Helping Yourself Help Others: A Book for Caregivers, 1994; (with S.K. Golant) Helping Someone with Mental Illness: A Compassionate Guide for Family, Friends and Caregivers, 1998; (with S.K. Golant and K.E. Cade) Within our Reach: Ending the Mental Health Crisis, 2010. **Address:** The Carter Ctr., 1 Copenhill, Atlanta, GA 30307, U.S.A.

CARTER, Stephen L(isle). American (born United States), b. 1954. **Genres:** Law. **Career:** U.S. Court of Appeals, District of Columbia Circuit, law clerk, 1979-80; U.S. Supreme Court, law clerk for Justice Thurgood Marshall, 1980-81; Shea and Gardner (law firm), associate, 1981-82; Yale University Law School, assistant professor, 1982-84, associate professor, 1984-85, professor, 1985-, William Nelson Cromwell professor of law. Writer. **Publications:** Reflections of an Affirmative Action Baby, 1991; The Culture of Disbelief: How American Law and Politics Trivialize Religious Devotion, 1993; Confirmation Mess: Cleaning up the Federal Appointments Process, 1994; Integrity, 1996; Dissent of the Governed: A Meditation on Law, Religion, and Loyalty, 1998; Civility: Manners, Morals, and the Etiquette of Democracy, 1998; God's Name in Vain: How Religion Should and Should Not Be Involved in Politics, 2000; The Emperor of Ocean Park (novel), 2002; New England White, 2007; Palace Council, 2008; Jericho's Fall, 2009; The Violence of Peace: America's Wars in the Age of Obama, 2011. **Address:** Yale University Law School, 127 Wall St., Rm. 324, PO Box 208215, New Haven, CT 06520, U.S.A. **Online address:** stephen.carter@yale.edu

CARTER, Steven. American (born United States), b. 1959. **Genres:** Psychology, Self Help, Human Relations/Parenting, Sex, How-to Books, Social Commentary, Humor/Satire. **Career:** Yo San University of Traditional Chinese Medicine, dean of administration, professor. Author. **Publications:** What Every Man Should Know About the New Woman: A Survival Guide, 1984; (with J. Levine) How to Make Love to a Computer, 1984; (with H. Levinson) Phobia-Free: A Medical Breakthrough Linking Ninety Percent of All Phobia and Panic Attacks to a Hidden Physical Problem, 1985; (with J. Sokol) Men Who Can't Love: When a Man's Fear Makes Him Run from Commitment, 1987; (with J. Sokol) What Really Happens in Bed: A Demystification of Sex, 1988; (with J. Sokol) What Smart Women Know, 1990; (with J. Sokol) Lives without Balance: When You're Giving Everything You've Got and Still Not Getting What You Hoped For, 1992; (with J. Sokol) He's Scared, She's Scared, 1993; (with J. Sokol) Men Like Women Who Like Themselves, 1996; Getting to Commitment, 1998; This is How Love Works, 2001; (with J. Sokol) Help! I'm In Love With A Narcissist, 2005; (with B. Keesling) Seven titles between 1994 and 2000; (with J. Sokol) Os Segredos da Muljeres Inteligentes, 2010. **Address:** Lowenstein Associates, 121 W 27th St., Ste. 601, New York, NY 10001, U.S.A. **Online address:** caspublic@aol.com

CARTER, Steven R(ay). American (born United States), b. 1942. **Genres:** Mystery/Crime/Suspense, Literary Criticism And History, Theatre, Graphic Novels. **Career:** Youngstown State University, instructor in English, 1968-70, 1972-73; University of Akron, instructor, 1975-76; University of Sassari, lecturer, 1976-77; University of North Carolina, assistant professor of English, 1977-82; University of Puerto Rico, assistant professor of English, 1982-87, associate professor, 1988-96; Trenton State College, visiting professor, 1991-92; Salem State College, associate professor, 1996-98, professor, 1998-, Department of English, chairperson, 2004-07. Writer. **Publications:** (Ed. with M. Curran) Questioning: A Thematic and Rhetorical Reader, 1971; Hansberry's Drama: Commitment amid Complexity, 1991; James Jones: An American Literary Orientatlist Master, 1998. Contributor to periodicals. Works appear in anthologies. **Address:** Department of English, Salem State College, Meier Hall, 352 Lafayette St., Salem, MA 01970, U.S.A. **Online address:** scarter@salemstate.edu

CARTER, Thomas Earl. *See* **CARTER, Tom.**

CARTER, Timothy. Canadian/British (born England), b. 1972. **Genres:** Social Sciences. **Career:** Novelist and screenwriter. **Publications:** Attack of the Intergalactic Soul Hunters, 2005; Closets, 2006; Epoch, 2007; Section K, 2008; Evil?, 2009; Cupid War, 2011. **Address:** Toronto, ON , Canada. **Online address:** tim@timothycarterworld.com

CARTER, Tom. (Thomas Earl Carter). American (born United States), b. 1947. **Genres:** Biography, Autobiography/Memoirs. **Career:** Tulsa World, columnist and general assignment writer, 1971-75, director of suburban news bureau, 1975-78, entertainment reporter and columnist, 1978-82, human interest columnist, 1982-88; Time Magazine, writer, 1976-78; People Magazine, writer, 1984-88; RCC Publications Inc., president. **Publications:** (With R. Milsap) Almost Like a Song, 1990; (with R. Emery) Memories: The Autobiography of Ralph Emery: The Moving True Story of a Country Legend, 1991; (with R. Emery) More Memories, 1993; (with B. Killen) By the Seat of My Pants: My Life in Country Music, 1993; (with G. Campbell) Rhinestone Cowboy: An Autobiography, 1994; (with R. McEntire) Reba: My Story, 1994; (with G. Jones) I Lived to Tell It All, 1996; (with L. Rhimes) Holiday in Your Heart, 1997; (with N. Jones) Nashville Wives: Country Music's Celebrity Wives Reveal the Truth about Their Husbands and Marriages, 1998; (with M. Haggard) Merle Haggard's My House of Memories: For the Record, 1999; (with J. Daly) Tammy Wynette: A Daughter Recalls Her Mother's Tragic Life and Death, 2000; First Lady of Tennis: Hazel Hotchkiss Wightman, 2001. **Address:** RCC Publications Inc., PO Box 210783, Nashville, TN 37221, U.S.A. **Online address:** tecarter@bellsouth.net

CARTER, Walter. American (born United States), b. 1950. **Genres:** Music, History. **Career:** Tennessean, music reporter, 1978-82; Gruhn Guitars, writer and researcher, 1988-92; Gibson Guitar Corp., historian, 1993-98. **Publications:** (With E. Widner) The Oak Ridge Boys: Our Story, 1987; The Songwriter's Guide to Collaboration, 1988, rev. ed., 1997; (with G. Gruhn) Gruhn's Guide to Vintage Guitars, 1991, 3rd ed., 2010; (with G. Gruhn) Acoustic Guitars and Other Fretted Instruments: A Photographic History, 1993; (with G. Gruhn) Electric Guitars and Basses: A Photographic History, 1993; Gibson Guitars: One Hundred Years of an American Icon, 1994; The Martin Book, 1995; Epiphone: The Complete History, 1995; The Ovation Story, 1995; The History of the Ovation Guitar, 1996. **Address:** 1907 Cedar Ln., Nashville, TN 37212, U.S.A. **Online address:** walter.carter@gibson.com

CARTER, Warren. American/New Zealander (born New Zealand), b. 1955. **Genres:** Theology/Religion, Politics/Government, History. **Career:** Saint Paul School of Theology, instructor, 1990-91, assistant professor, 1991-95, associate professor, 1995-2000, professor of New Testament, Lindsey P. Pherigo professor of New Testament, 2000-; Brite Divinity School, professor of New Testament. Writer. **Publications:** What are They Saying about Matthew's Sermon on the Mount?, 1994; Households and Discipleship: A Study of Matthew 19-20, 1994; Matthew: Storyteller, Interpreter, Evangelist, 1996, rev. ed., 2004; (with J.P. Heil) Matthew's Parables: Audience-Oriented Perspectives, 1998; Matthew and the Margins: A Sociopolitical and Religious Reading, 2000; Matthew and Empire: Initial Explorations, 2001; (with D. Jacobson, C.J. Dempsey and J.P. Heil) New Proclamation: Year A, 2001-2002, 2002; Pontius Pilate: Portraits of a Roman Governor, 2003; (contrib.) Westminster Discipleship Study Bible, 2003; (contrib.) New Interpreter's Study Bible, 2003; Got Life? John: Storyteller, Interpreter, Evangelist, 2006; Roman Empire and the New Testament: An Essential Guide, 2006; John and Empire: Initial Explorations, 2008; What Does Revelation Reveal?, 2011. Contributor to journals and magazines. **Address:** Brite Divinity School, 2925 Princeton St., Fort Worth, TX 76129, U.S.A. **Online address:** warren.carter@tcu.edu

CARTER, W. Hodding. *See* **CARTER, W(illiam).**

CARTER, W(illiam). (W. Hodding Carter). American (born United States), b. 1963?. **Genres:** Travel/Exploration, History, Social Sciences. **Career:** Penobscot Bay YMCA, assistant aquatics director. Writer. **Publications:** AS W. HODDING CARTER: Westward Whoa: In the Wake of Lewis and Clark, 1994; Illustrated Viking Voyage: Retracing Leif Eriksson's Journey in an Authentic Viking Knarr, 2000; A Viking Voyage: In Which an Unlikely Crew of Adventurers Attempts an Epic Journey to the New World, 2000; Stolen Water: Saving the Everglades from Its Friends, Foes and Florida, 2004; Flushed: How the Plumber Saved Civilization, 2006; Off the Deep End: The Probably Insane Idea that I Could Swim My Way through a Midlife Crisis-and Qualify for the Olympics, 2008. **Address:** c/o Author Mail, Atria Books, 1230 Ave. of the Americas, New York, NY 10020, U.S.A.

CARTER, William E. American (born United States), b. 1939. **Genres:** Astronomy, Earth Sciences, History, Biography. **Career:** University of Hawaii, research geodesist, 1972-76; National Oceanic and Atmospheric Administration, staff, 1976-96, Geodetic Research and Development Laboratory, chief, 1992-96; University of Florida, Department of Civil and Coastal Engineering, researcher, adjunct professor, 1996-; University of Houston, research professor, 2010-. Writer. **Publications:** (With M.S. Carter) Latitude: How American Astronomers Solved the Mystery of Variation, 2002; Simon Newcomb, America's Unofficial Astronomer Royal, 2006. Contributor to journals and periodicals. **Address:** Department of Civil & Environmental Engineering, University of Houston, Rm. 2011, 3605 Cullen Blvd., Houston, TX 77204-5059, U.S.A. **Online address:** wecarter@uh.edu

CARTLEDGE, Mark J. British (born England), b. 1962. **Genres:** Theology/Religion, History, Essays. **Career:** University of Wales, lecturer in Christian theology; University of Durham, St. John's College, chaplain and tutor; University of Birmingham, Department of Theology and Religion, senior lecturer in pentecostal and charismatic theology, Centre for Pentecostal and Charismatic Studies, director; PentecoStudies: An Interdisciplinary Journal for Research on the Pentecostal and Charismatic Movements, general editor. **Publications:** (Ed. with D. Mills) Covenant Theology: Contemporary Approaches, 2002; Testimony: Its Importance, Place and Potential, 2002; Charismatic Glossolalia: An Empirical-Theological Study, 2002; Practical Theology: Charismatic and Empirical Perspectives, 2003; The Gift of Speaking in Tongues: The Holy Spirit, the Human Spirit and the Gift of Holy Speech, 2005; (ed.) Speaking in Tongues: Multidisciplinary Perspectives, 2006; Encountering the Spirit: The Charismatic Tradition, 2007; (contrib.) Anglicanism: Essays in History, Belief and Practice, 2007; (contrib.) Theology and Religious Studies: A Study of Disciplinary Boundaries, 2008; Testimony in the Spirit: Rescripting Ordinary Pentecostal Theology, 2010; (ed. with D. Cheetham) Intercultural Theology: Approaches and Themes, 2011. Contributor to periodicals. **Address:** Department of Theology and Religion, University of Birmingham, ERI Bldg., Edgbaston, Birmingham, WM B15 2TT, England. **Online address:** m.j.cartledge@bham.ac.uk

CARTMILL, Matt. American (born United States), b. 1943. **Genres:** Anthropology/Ethnology, Medicine/Health, Social Sciences. **Career:** Chadwick School, teacher, 1963; Pomona College, teaching assistant, 1964; University of Chicago, teaching assistant, 1967-69; University of Chicago, teaching assistant, 1967-69; Duke University, Department of Anatomy, assistant professor, 1970-74, associate professor, 1974-81, professor, 1981-2008, Department of Anthropology (now Department of Evolutionary Anthropology), assistant professor, 1972-74, associate professor, 1974-83, professor, 1983-, Department of Biological Anthropology, professor, 1988-2008; Boston University, Department of Anthropology, professor, 2008-. Writer. **Publications:** Primate Origins, 1975; (with W.L. Hylander and J. Shafland) Human Structure, 1987; A View to a Death in the Morning: Hunting and Nature through History, 1993; Do Horses Gallop in Their Sleep?: Consciousness, Evolution and the Problem of Animal Minds, 1996; (with C. Oxnard and K.B. Brown) The Human Body: Developmental, Functional and Evolutionary Bases, 2008; (with F. Smith) The Human Lineage, 2009; (with K.A. Korey and K.B. Brown) Human Population Genetics, 2009. **Address:** Department of Anthropology, Boston University, 232 Bay State Rd., Ste. 101A, Boston, MA 02215, U.S.A. **Online address:** cartmill@bu.edu

CARTON, Bernice. American (born United States), b. 1922. **Genres:** Novels, Travel/Exploration, Autobiography/Memoirs, History. **Career:** Travel writer and photographer, 1971-. **Publications:** Beyond the Brooklyn Bridge, 1998. Contributor to magazines and newspapers. **Address:** 880 5th Ave., Apt. 7G, New York, NY 10021-4951, U.S.A.

CARTWRIGHT, Anthony. British (born England), b. 1973?. **Genres:** Novels, Literary Criticism And History. **Career:** Royal Docks Community School, teacher. Writer. **Publications:** The Afterglow, 2004; Heartland, 2009. Contributor to periodicals. **Address:** c/o Luke Brown, Tindal Street Press, 217 Custard Factory, Gibb St., Birmingham, B9 4AA, United Kingdom.

CARTWRIGHT, Justin. British (born England), b. 1945?. **Genres:** Novels, Adult Non-fiction. **Career:** Writer. **Publications:** Deep Six, 1972; New Avenger Series: Fighting Men, 1977; The Revenge, 1978; The Horse of Darius, 1980; Freedom for the Wolves, 1983; Interior, 1988; Look at It This Way, 1990; Masai Dreaming, 1995; In Every Face I Meet, 1995; Not Yet Home: A South African Journey, 1996; Leading the Cheers, 1998; Half in Love, 2001; White Lightning, 2002; Promise of Happiness, 2006; The Song Before It is Sung, 2007; This Secret Garden: Writer & the City, 2008; Oxford Revisited, 2009; To Heaven by Water, 2009; Other People's Money, 2011. **Address:** c/o James Gill, United Agents, 12-26 Lexington St., London, GL W1F 0LE, England.

CARUSONE, Al. American (born United States), b. 1949. **Genres:** Children's Fiction, Children's Non-fiction, Natural History, Humor/Satire. **Career:** AccuWeather, educational sales representative, 1989-; Restek Corp., technical services representative; Keystone Scientific Inc., technical sales and service staff. Writer. **Publications:** Don't Open the Door After the Sun Goes Down: Tales of the Real and Unreal, 1994; The Boy with Dinosaur Hands, 1998. Contributor to periodicals. **Address:** 1961 Old 220 Rd., Howard, PA 16841, U.S.A.

CARVELL, Marlene. American (born United States) **Genres:** Adult Non-fiction. **Career:** Cazenovia College, faculty, through 1986; Writer. **Publications:** Who Will Tell My Brother?, 2002; Sweetgrass Basket, 2005; Caught between the Pages, 2008. **Address:** c/o Author Mail, Dutton Publicity, 375 Hudson St., New York, NY 10014, U.S.A. **Online address:** marlenecarvell@gmail.com

CARVER, Martin. British/Scottish (born Scotland), b. 1941. **Genres:** Archaeology/Antiquities, History, Urban Studies. **Career:** Freelance archaeologist, 1972-76; Birmingham University Field Archaeology Unit, director, 1977-86; Sutton Hoo Research Trust, director, 1983-2005; University of York, head of department of archaeology, 1986-96, Tarbat Discovery Programme, 1994-, Centre for Medieval Studies, director, 2001-02, professor, 1986-2008, professor emeritus, 2008-; Field Archaeology Specialists Ltd., director, 1992-, chairman, 1999-; Antiquity, editor, 2003-. **Publications:** AS M. O. H. CARVER: Underneath English Towns: Interpreting Urban Archaeology, 1987; Arguments in Stone: Archaeological Research and the European Town in the First Millennium, 1993; Sutton Hoo Burial Ground of Kings?, 1998; Surviving in Symbols: A Visit to the Pictish Nation, 1999; Archaeological Value and Evaluation, 2003; Sutton Hoo: A Seventh-century Princely Burial Ground and Its Context, 2005; (with J. Scheschkewitz) A Frontier Cemetery in Early Medieval Britain: Wasperton on the Warwickshire Avon, 2007; Post-Pictish Problems: The Moray Firthlands in the 9-11th Centuries, 2008; Portmahomack: Monastery of the Picts, 2008; Pictish Monastery at Portmahomack, 2008; Archaeological Investigation, 2009. EDITOR: Medieval Worcester, 1980; Two Town Houses in Medieval Shrewsbury: The Excavation and Analysis of Two Medieval and Later Houses Built on the Town Wall at Shrewsbury, 1983; The Age of Sutton Hoo: The Seventh Century in North-Western Europe, 1992; In Search of Cult: Archaeological Investigations in Honour of Philip Rahtz, 1993; The Cross Goes North: Processes of Conversion in Northern Europe, AD 300-1300, 2003; (with C. Hills and J. Scheschkewitz) Wasperton: A Roman, Roman, British and Anglo-saxon Community in Central England, 2009; (with A. Sanmark and S. Semple) Signals of Belief in Early England: Anglo-Saxon Paganism Revisited, 2010; Making Archaeology Happen: Design Versus Dogma, 2011. **Address:** Department of Archaeology, University of York, King's Manor, York, NY YO1 7EP, England. **Online address:** martincarver@yahoo.co.uk

CARVER, Norman Francis. American (born United States), b. 1928. **Genres:** Architecture, Travel/Exploration, History. **Career:** Kalamazoo Institute of Arts, teacher of advanced photography, 1970-. Writer. **Publications:** Form and Space of Japanese Architecture, 1955, 2nd ed., 1993; Silent Cities: Mexico and the Maya, 1966; Italian Hilltowns, 1979, 2nd ed., 1995; Iberian Villages, 1980; Japanese Folkhouses, 1984; North African Villages, 1989; Greek Island Villages, 2001. Contributor of articles to journals. **Address:** Kalamazoo Institute of Arts, 314 S Park St., Kalamazoo, MI 49007-5102, U.S.A. **Online address:** nfcarver@iserv.net

CARVER, Terrell. American (born United States), b. 1946. **Genres:** History, Politics/Government, Biography, Philosophy. **Career:** University of Liverpool, lecturer in politics, 1975-79; University of Bristol, School of Sociology, Politics and International Studies, lecturer, 1980-89, reader in politics, 1990-94, professor of political theory, 1995-, research fellow, 1995-96, 2004-05; Virginia Commonwealth University, visiting professor, 1985-86; Seikei University, Centre for Asian and Pacific Studies, visiting fellow, 1991; Marx-Engels Gesamtausgabe, editorial commission, 1995-; Claremont Colleges, Pitzer College, visiting professor, 2003; Senshu University, visiting professor, 2006; Australian Research Quality Framework, Politics and Social Sciences Panel, assessor, 2008; Australian National University, Research School of Social Sciences, visiting fellow. Writer. **Publications:** Engels, 1981; Marx's Social Theory, 1982; Marx and Engels: The Intellectual Relationship, 1983; A Marx Dictionary, 1987; Friedrich Engels: His Life and Thought, 1990; Marx, 1991; (contrib.) Atlas of Communism, 1991; Gender Is Not a Synonym for Women, 1996; The Postmodern Marx, 1998; Men in Political Theory, 2004; (with S.A. Chambers) Judith Butler and Political Theory: Troubling Politics, 2008. EDITOR: (and trans.) Texts on Method/Karl Marx, 1975; (and trans.) The Logic of Marx, 1980; Marx's Grundrisse and Hegel's Logic, 1988; The Cambridge Companion to Marx, 1991; (and trans.) Marx: Later Political Writings, 1991, rev. ed., 1996; (with P. Thomas) Rational Choice Marxism, 1995; Interpreting the Political: New Methodologies, 1997; Politics of Sexuality: Identity, Gender, Citizenship, 1998; (with M.B. Steger) Engels after Marx, 1999; (with J. Martin) Palgrave Advances in Continental Political Thought, 2006; (with S.A. Chambers) William E. Connolly: Democracy, Pluralism and Political Theory, 2007; (with S.A. Chambers) Judith Butler's Precarious Politics: Critical Encounters, 2008; (with J. Pikalo) Political Language and Metaphor: Interpreting and Changing the World, 2008; (with J. Bartelson) Globality, Democracy and Civil Society, 2010; (with S.A. Chambers) Carole Pateman: Democracy, Feminism, Welfare, 2011; (with S. A. Chambers)Michael J. Shapiro: Discourse, Culture, Violence, 2012. **Address:** Department of Politics, University of Bristol, 1.3 10 Priory Rd., Bristol, GL BS8 1TU, England. **Online address:** t.carver@bristol.ac.uk

CARVILLE, (Chester) James. American (born United States), b. 1944. **Genres:** Politics/Government, Military/Defense/Arms Control. **Career:** Teacher, 1969-70; McKernnan, Beychok, Screen and Pierson, attorney, 1973-79; Gus Weill and Raymond Strother (political consulting firm), director of campaigns, 1979-80; administrative assistant, 1980-81; Carville & Begala (a consulting firm), founding partner, 1989-; CNN, commentator; Tulane University, Department of Political Science, professor, 2009-. Political consultant and writer. **Publications:** (With M. Matalin and P. Knobler) All's Fair: Love, War and Running for President, 1994; We're Right, They're Wrong: A Handbook for Spirited Progressives, 1996; And the Horse He Rode in On, 1998; Stickin': The Case for Loyalty, 2000; (with P. Begala) Buck Up, Suck Up-and Come Back When You Foul Up: 12 Winning Secrets from the War Room, 2002; Had Enough?: A Handbook for Fighting Back, 2003; (with P.C. McKissack) Lu and the Swamp Ghost, 2004; (with P. Begala) Take It Back: Our Party, Our Country, Our Future, 2006; (with R. Buckwalter-Poza) 40 More Years: How the Democrats Will Rule the Next Generation, 2009. **Address:** Washington Speakers Bureau, 1663 Prince St., Alexandria, VA 22314-2818, U.S.A.

CARWARDINE, Richard J(ohn). British (born England), b. 1947. **Genres:** History, Theology/Religion. **Career:** University of Sheffield, lecturer, 1971-90, senior lecturer, 1990-94, professor of American history, 1994-2002, dean, 1999-2001; Syracuse University, visiting professor, 1974-75; University of North Carolina, research fellow, 1989; Sheffield Hallam Liberal Democrats, chairperson, 1992-94; St Catherine's College, fellow; University of Oxford, Rhodes Professor of American History, 2002-09, Corpus Christi College, president, 2010-. Writer. **Publications:** Transatlantic Revivalism: Popular Evangelicalism in Britain and America, 1790-1865, 1978; Evangelicals and Politics in Antebellum America, 1993; Lincoln, 2003, rev. ed. as Lincoln: A Life of Purpose and Power, 2006; Accepting the Prize: Two Historians Speak, 2005; (ed. with J. Sexton) Global Lincoln, 2011; Building a Righteous Nation: Religion and the Construction of the United States, 1776-1865, forthcoming. **Address:** Corpus Christi College, University of Oxford, Wellington Sq., Oxford, OX OX1 2JD, England. **Online address:** richard.carwardine@history.ox.ac.uk

CARWELL, L'Ann. *See* **MCKISSACK, Patricia C(arwell).**

CARY, Lorene. American (born United States), b. 1956. **Genres:** Novels, Autobiography/Memoirs, Biography. **Career:** St. Paul's School, teacher; TV Guide, associate editor; Newsweek, contributing editor, 1993; Art Sanctuary, founder and executive director, 1998-; University of Pennsylvania, senior lecturer in creative writing. **Publications:** Black Ice (memoir), 1991; The Price of a Child: A Novel, 1995; Pride: A Novel, 1998; Free!: Great Escapes from Slavery on the Underground Railroad: Based on True Stories, 2005; If Sons, Then Heirs, 2011. **Address:** Department of English, University of Pennsylvania, 333 Fisher-Bennett Hall, 3340 Walnut St., Philadelphia, PA 19104-6273, U.S.A. **Online address:** lcary@artsanctuary.org

CARY, Margaret. American (born United States) **Genres:** Medicine/Health. **Career:** Community Hospital of Sonoma County, intern, 1978-81; Mammoth Hospital, Emergency Department, co-director, 1982-83; Rose Medical Center, medical director, 1983-86; Cary Communications Intl., president, 1989-94; University of Colorado, assistant clinical professor of family medicine, 1991-, Graduate School of Business, lecturer; U.S. Department of Health and Human Services, regional director, 1994-2000; Military Health Services, specialist advisor, 1996-2000; Acueity, vice president, 2000; Vox Medica (health care communications group), medical director, chief medical officer and senior vice president, 2001-; KBDI-TV, co-anchor and researcher; Colorado Business Group on Health, chief medical officer; Boundroids Inc., president. Writer. **Publications:** (With A.W. Darkins) Telemedicine and Telehealth: Principles, Policies, Performance, and Pitfalls, 2000. Contributor to books and periodicals. **Address:** Vox Medica Inc., 601 Walnut St., Ste. 250-S, Philadelphia, PA 19106, U.S.A. **Online address:** mcary@voxmedica.com

CASAGRANDE, June M. American (born United States), b. 1966. **Genres:** Language/Linguistics, Education, Writing/Journalism. **Career:** Business Wire, editor and proofreader, 1994-2001; Los Angeles Times, Times Community News, editor, staff writer, columnist, and reporter, 1996-2004. **Publications:** Grammar Snobs Are Great Big Meanies: A Guide to Language for Fun and Spite, 2006; Mortal Syntax: 101 Language Choices that Will get You Clobbered by the Grammar Snobs-Even if You're Right, 2008; It was the Best of Sentences, It was the Worst of Sentences: A Writer's Guide to Crafting Killer Sentences, 2010. **Address:** c/o Laurie Abkemeier, DeFiore and Co., 72 Spring St., Ste. 304, New York, NY 10012, U.S.A. **Online address:** june@grammarsnobs.com

CASANOVA, Mary. American (born United States), b. 1957. **Genres:** Children's Fiction, Young Adult Fiction, Picture/Board Books, Autobiography/Memoirs, Adult Non-fiction, Novels, Novellas/Short Stories. **Career:** Author, lecturer and writing instructor. **Publications:** MIDDLE GRADE NOVELS: Moose Tracks, 1995, 2nd ed., 2010; Riot, 1996; Wolf Shadows, 1997, 2nd ed., 2009; Stealing Thunder, 1998; Curse of a Winter Moon, 2000; When Eagles Fall, 2002; Cécile: Gates of Gold, 2002; Danger at Snow Hill, 2006; Trouble in Pembrook, 2006; Dog-Napped, 2006; Klipfish Code, 2007; Extreme Stunt Dogs, 2007; Some Dog!, 2007; To Catch a Burglar, 2007; Mary Casanova and You, 2007; (with O. Rayyan) Turtle-Hatching Mystery, 2008. PICTURE BOOKS: (reteller) The Hunter, 2000; One-Dog Canoe, 2003; Utterly Otterly Day, 2008; The Day Dirk Yeller Came to Town, 2011; Some Cat!, 2012. OTHER: The Golden Retriever (nonfiction), 1990; Jess, 2006; Chrissa Stands Strong, 2008; Chrissa, 2008; Utterly Otterly Night, 2011. **Address:** PO Box 141, Ranier, MN 56668-0141, U.S.A. **Online address:** casanova@marycasanova.com

CASATI, Roberto. Italian (born Italy), b. 1961. **Genres:** Translations, Philosophy. **Career:** University of Geneva, Swiss National Foundation for Scientific Research, researcher, 1988-90, research fellow, 1991-93; Ecole Polytechnique, Centre de Recherche en Epistemologie Appliquee, research associate, 1993-; University of Neuchatel, assistant professor, 1991-94; University of Aix, Centre National de la Recherche Scientifique, research fellow, 1993-2002, Research Group on Epistemology, researcher, 1994-, tenured senior researcher, 2002-; Ecole Normale Supérieure-Paris, teacher, 2001-03; Istituto Universitario di Arti Visive-Venezia, visiting research professor, 2004-08; University of Turin, visiting professor, 2008-09. Writer. **Publications:** L'immagine, 1991; (with A. Varzi) Holes and Other Superficialities, 1994; (with J. Dokic) La Philosophie du Son, 1994; (with Varzi) Events: An Annotated Bibliography, 1994; (with A. Varzi) 50 Years of Events: An Annotated Bibliography, 1947 to 1997, 1997; (with A.C. Varzi) Parts and Places: The Structures of Spatial Representation, 1999; La Scoperta Dell'ombra:

Da Platone a Galileo: La Storia di un Enigma che ha Affascinato le Grandi Menti Dell'umanità, 2000; (contrib.) Das Geheimnis des Schattens, 2002; The Shadow Club, 2003; (with A. Varzi) Semplicità Insormontabili: 39 Storie Filosofiche, 2004; (with A. Varzi) Insurmountable Simplicities: Thirty-Nine Philosophical Stories, 2006; Il caso Wassermann e Altri Incidenti Metafisici, 2006; Prima lezione di filosofia, 2011. TRANSLATOR: G. Frege, Logische Untersuchungen/Ricerche Logiche, 1989; A.J. Ayer, Russell, 1992. EDITOR: (with G. White) Philosophy and the Cognitive Sciences, 1993; (with White and B. Smith) Philosophy and the Cognitive Sciences, 1994; (with A.C. Varzi) Events, 1995; (co-editor) De la perception à l'action. Contributor to books and periodicals. **Address:** Department of Philosophy, Centre National de la Recherche Scientifique, University of Aix-Marseille, 29 Ave. Robert Schuman, Aix-en-Provence, 13621, France. **Online address:** casati@ehess.fr

CASCONE, A. G. *See* **CASCONE, Annette.**

CASCONE, Annette. (A. G. Cascone). American (born United States), b. 1960. **Genres:** Children's Fiction, Young Adult Fiction, Plays/Screenplays, Novels, Humor/Satire. **Career:** Writer. **Publications:** WITH G. CASCONE AS A.G. CASCONE: FOR CHILDREN: The Attack of the Aqua Apes, 1995; Eye of the Fortuneteller, 1996. DEADTIME STORIES SERIES: Terror in Tiny Town, 1996; Invasion of the Appleheads, 1996; Along Came a Spider, 1996; Ghost Knight, 1996; Revenge of the Goblins, 1996; Little Magic Shop of Horrors, 1996; It Came from the Deep, 1997; Grave Secrets, 1997; Mirror, Mirror, 1997; Grandpa's Monster Movies, 1997; Nightmare on Planet X, 1997; Welcome to the Terror-Go-Round, 1997; The Beast of Baskerville, 1997; Trapped in Tiny Town, 1997; Cyber Scare, 1997; Night of the Pet Zombies, 1997; Faerie Tale, 1997. FOR YOUNG ADULTS: In a Crooked Little House, 1994; If He Hollers, 1995; I Was a Ninety-Eight Pound Duckling, 1996; There's No Place Like Home, 1997; Grave Secrets, 2012; The Witching Game, 2012. **Address:** New England Publishing Associates Inc., PO Box 66066, Lawrence, NJ 08648, U.S.A. **Online address:** agcascone@bookwire.com

CASE, Chris. American (born United States), b. 1976?. **Genres:** Children's Fiction, Illustrations. **Career:** Writer and illustrator. **Publications:** SELF-ILLUSTRATED: Sophie and the Next-Door Monsters, 2008. Contributor to magazines and newspapers. **Address:** c/o Ronnie Anne Herman, Herman Agency, 350 Central Pk. W, New York, NY 10025, U.S.A. **Online address:** chris@christophercase.com

CASE, George (Andrew Thomas). Canadian (born Canada), b. 1967. **Genres:** Novels, Communications/Media, Social Commentary, Essays, Music, Intellectual History, Autobiography/Memoirs, Biography, Biography. **Career:** Writer. **Publications:** Silence Descends: The End of the Information Age, 2000-2500 (fiction), 1997; Jimmy Page: Magus, Musician, Man: An Unauthorized Biography, 2007; Arcadia Borealis: Childhood and Youth in Northern Ontario (memoir), 2008; Out of Our Heads: Rock 'n' Roll Before the Drugs Wore Off (history), 2010; Led Zeppelin FAQ: All That's Left to Know About the Greatest Hard Rock Band of All Time, 2011. **Address:** Robert Lecker Agency, 4055 Melrose Ave., Montreal, QC H4A 2S5, Canada. **Online address:** george_case@shaw.ca

CASEY, Barbara. American (born United States), b. 1944. **Genres:** Children's Non-fiction, History, inspirational/Motivational Literature, How-to Books, Novels, Medicine/Health, Paranormal, Photography, Young Adult Non-fiction, Mystery/Crime/Suspense, Romance/Historical, Science Fiction/Fantasy, Young Adult Fiction, Criminology/True Crime. **Career:** North Carolina Wesleyan College, director of alumni and public relations, 1975-77; North Carolina State University, Department of Athletics, faculty, 1977-79; writer and literary agent, 1979-; Barbara Casey Literary Agency, president. **Publications:** NOVELS: Leilani Zan, 1992; Grandma Jock and Christabelle, 1994; Shyla's Initiative, 2002; The Coach's Wife, 2003; The House of Kane, 2007; Just Like Family, 2009; The Cadence of Gypsies, 2011. Contributor to periodicals. Works appears in anthologies. **Address:** GA , U.S.A. **Online address:** barcafer@aol.com

CASEY, Don. American (born United States) **Genres:** How-to Books, Industrial Relations, Young Adult Non-fiction. **Career:** Banker, through 1983. Writer. **Publications:** Sensible Cruising: The Thoreau Approach, 1988; This Old Boat, 1991, 2nd ed., 2009; Sailboat Refinishing, 1996; Sailboat Hull & Deck Repair, 1996; Canvaswork & Sail Repair, 1996; Inspecting the Aging Sailboat, 1997; 100 Fast & Easy Boat Improvements, 1998; Dragged Aboard: A Cruising Guide for the Reluctant Mate, 1998; Sailboat Electrics Simplified, 1999; Don Casey's Complete Illustrated Sailboat Maintenance Manual, 2006. **Address:** c/o Author Mail, International Marine Publishing Co., Rte. 1, PO Box 220, Camden, ME 04843, U.S.A.

CASEY, Eavan. *See* **BOLAND, Eavan (Aisling).**

CASEY, James. British (born England), b. 1944?. **Genres:** History, Anthropology/Ethnology. **Career:** University of East Anglia, emeritus reader. Writer. **Publications:** SPANISH HISTORY: The Kingdom of Valencia in the Seventeenth Century, 1979; Early Modern Spain: A Social History, 1999. FAMILY HISTORY: (co-author) La Familia En La Espanìa Mediterranea (siglos XV-XIX), 1987; The History of the Family, 1989; Family and Community in Early Modern Spain: The Citizens of Granada, 1570-1739, 2007; The Kingdom of Valencia in the Seventeenth Century, 2008; Familia Y Sociedad en el Reino de Granada Durante el Antiguo Regimen, 2008. Works appear in anthologies. Contributor of books. **Address:** University of East Anglia, Norwich Research Park, Norwich, NF NR4 7TJ, England. **Online address:** j.casey@uea.ac.uk

CASEY, John (Dudley). American (born United States), b. 1939. **Genres:** Novels, Novellas/Short Stories, Literary Criticism And History, Essays, Translations, Poetry. **Career:** University of Iowa, College of Law, instructor, 1965-67; University of Rhode Island, instructor, 1969-71; University of Virginia, assistant professor, 1972-93, associate professor, professor of English, through 1992, associate professor of creative writing, 1998-, Henry Hoyns professor of English, 1998-; Strauss living fellow, 1992-97; Iowa Writers' Workshop, professor, 1998. Writer. **Publications:** NOVELS: An American Romance, 1977; Spartina, 1989; Supper at the Black Pearl, 1995; The Half-Life of Happiness, 1998, Compass Rose, 2010. TRANSLATION: (with M. Santminiatelli) A. Boffa, You're an Animal, Viskovitz!, 2002. OTHER: Testimony and Demeanor (short stories), 1979; (afterword) Stories of Breece D'J Pancake, 2002. Contributor to magazines and newspapers. **Address:** Department of English, University of Virginia, 405 Bryan Hall, PO Box 400121, Charlottesville, VA 22904-4121, U.S.A. **Online address:** jdc@virginia.edu

CASEY, Maud. American (born United States) **Genres:** Novellas/Short Stories, Novels, Human Relations/Parenting, Literary Criticism And History. **Career:** Illinois Wesleyan University, writing instructor; H.E.L.P. Haven shelter, writing instructor; Lee Strasberg Theatre Institute, staff; University of Maryland, writing instructor, lecturer, assistant professor of English, associate professor of English, associate director of the program in creative writing; Goddard College, writing instructor, lecturer. Writer. **Publications:** The Shape of Things to Come (novel), 2001; Drastic: Stories, 2002; The Art of Reading Barbara Comyns: Gather Your Hats While You May, 2002; Genealogy: A Novel, 2006. Contributor to newspapers and periodicals. **Address:** c/o Alice Tasman, Jean V. Naggar Literary Agency, 216 E 75th St., Ste. 1E, New York, NY 10021, U.S.A. **Online address:** maud.casey@verizon.net

CASEY, Shaun Allen. American (born United States), b. 1957. **Genres:** History, Young Adult Non-fiction. **Career:** Wesley Theological Seminary, associate professor of Christian ethics and director of the National Capital Semester for Seminarians (NCSS); Center for American Progress, visiting fellow; Center for Strategic and International Studies, Project on Religion and Post Conflict Reconstruction, consultant. Writer. **Publications:** NON-FICTION: (co-author) Love for the Poor: God's Love for the Poor and the Church's Witness to It, 2005; The Making of a Catholic President: Kennedy vs. Nixon 1960, 2009. **Address:** Fairfax, VA , U.S.A. **Online address:** scasey@wesleyseminary.edu

CASEY, Steven. (Steven Michael Casey). American (born United States), b. 1952?. **Genres:** Sciences, Adult Non-fiction. **Career:** Ergonomic Systems Design Inc., president and principal scientist. Writer. **Publications:** (With H. Simpson as Steven M. Casey) Developing Effective User Documentation: A Human Factors Approach, 1988; Set Phasers on Stun: And Other True Tales of Design, Technology, and Human Error, 1993, 2nd ed., 1998; The Atomic Chef: And Other True Tales of Design, Technology, and Human Error, 2006. **Address:** Ergonomic Systems Design Inc., 5290 Overpass Rd., Ste. 105, Santa Barbara, CA 93111, U.S.A. **Online address:** scasey@ergonomicsystemsdesign.com

CASEY, Steven Michael. *See* **CASEY, Steven.**

CASH, Anthony. (Tony Cash). British (born England), b. 1933. **Genres:** Communications/Media, History, Music, Translations. **Career:** Teacher of Russian, 1958-63; British Broadcasting Corp., television program assistant, 1963-68, television program director and assistant, 1968-77; London Weekend Television, producer and director, 1977-; Lilyville Screen Entertainment, owner, 1983-. Writer. **Publications:** Great Neighbors: U.S.S.R., 1965; (trans.) A.V. Gorbatov, Years off My Life, 1966; The Russian Revolution, 1967; Russian Revolution: A Collection of Contemporary Documents, 1968; (ed. as Tony Cash) Anatomy of Pop, 1970; Lenin, 1972. **Address:** Lilyville Screen Entertainment, 7 Lilyville Rd., London, GL SW6 5DP, England. **Online address:** tony.cash@btclick.com

CASH, Dixie. *See* **CUMBIE, Pamela.**

CASH, Dixie. *See* **MCCLANAHAN, Jeffery.**

CASH, Jean W(ampler). American (born United States), b. 1938. **Genres:** Biography. **Career:** Teacher, 1959-80; University of Mississippi, instructor, 1976-77; James Madison University, associate professor, 1986-96, professor of English, 1996-2009, professor emerita, 2009-. Writer. **Publications:** Flannery O'Connor: A Life, 2002; (ed. with K. Perry) Larry Brown and the Blue-Collar South, 2008; Larry Brown, A Writer's Life, 2012. **Address:** Department of English, James Madison University, Keezell 410, MSC 1801, 800 S Main St., Harrisonburg, VA 22807, U.S.A. **Online address:** cashjw@jmu.edu

CASH, Steve. American (born United States), b. 1946. **Genres:** Children's Fiction, Science Fiction/Fantasy. **Career:** Novelist and musician. **Publications:** The Meq, 2005; Time Dancers, 2006; The Remembering, 2011. **Address:** Del Rey Manga, 1745 Broadway, New York, NY 10019, U.S.A.

CASH, Tony. *See* **CASH, Anthony.**

CASHDAN, Linda. American (born United States), b. 1942. **Genres:** Novels, Ghost Writer, Young Adult Fiction. **Career:** Voice of America, broadcaster, reporter, feature writer, 1967-83, economics correspondent, 1983-. Ghostwriter. **Publications:** Special Interests (novel), 1990; It's Only Love (novel), 1992; (with M. Benoliel) Done Deal: Insights from Interviews with the World's Best Negotiators, 2005; (with M. Benoliel) Upper Hand: Winning Strategies from World-Class Negotiators, 2006. Contributor to magazines. **Address:** c/o Elaine Markson, Elaine Markson Literary Agency Inc., 44 Greenwich Ave., New York, NY 10011, U.S.A.

CASHILL, Jack. American (born United States), b. 1947. **Genres:** Local History/Rural Topics, Adult Non-fiction, Novels, Social Sciences. **Career:** Ingram's Magazine, executive editor; WorldNetDaily, columnist; KMBZ-AM Radio, talk-show host; Catholic Family Radio Network, talk-show host; Purdue University, faculty for media and literature. **Publications:** Snake Handling in Mid- America: An Incite-ful Look at American Life and Work in the 90s (essays), 1991; 2006: The Chautauqua Rising (novel), 2000; (with J. Sanders) First Strike: TWA Flight 800 and the Attack on America, 2003; Ron Brown's Body: How One Man's Death Saved the Clinton Presidency and Hillary's Future, 2004; Hoodwinked: How Intellectual Hucksters Have Hijacked American Culture, 2005; Helping America Help Itself, 2005; Sucker Punch: The Hard Left Hook That Dazed Ali and Killed King's Dream, 2006; What's the Matter with California? Cultural Rumbles from the Golden State and Why the Rest of Us Should Be Shaking, 2007; Reconsidering the Region: Wyandotte County REBORN, 2008; Popes & Bankers, 2010; Deconstructing Obama, 2011. Contributor to periodicals. **Address:** Simon & Schuster Inc., 5666 La Jolla Blvd., Ste. 154, La Jolla, CA 92037-7523, U.S.A. **Online address:** jcashill@aol.com

CASHIN, Joan E. American (born United States) **Genres:** History, Civil Liberties/Human Rights. **Career:** Ohio State University, professor of history. Writer. **Publications:** A Family Venture: Men and Women on the Southern Frontier, 1991; (ed.) Our Common Affairs: Texts from Women in the Old South, 1996; (intro.) Clotel, or, The president's Daughter, 1996; (ed. and contrib.) The War Was You and Me: Civilians in the American Civil War, 2002; Never at Peace: Varina Howell Davis And the Civil War, 2005; First Lady of the Confederacy: Varina Davis's Civil War, 2006. Contributor to periodicals. **Address:** Department of History, Ohio State University, 106 Dulles Hall, 230 W 17th Ave., Columbus, OH 43210, U.S.A. **Online address:** cashin.2@osu.edu

CASHORE, Kristin. American (born United States), b. 1976?. **Genres:** Novels, Women's Studies And Issues, History. **Career:** Writer. **Publications:** YOUNG-ADULT NOVELS: Graceling, 2008; Fire, 2009. OTHERS: A Time of Change: Women in the Early Twentieth Century, 2005; Bitterblue, 2012. **Address:** Faye Bender Literary Agency, 19 Cheever Pl., Brooklyn, NY 11231, U.S.A.

CASIL, Amy Sterling. American (born United States), b. 1962. **Genres:** Science Fiction/Fantasy, Young Adult Fiction, Novellas/Short Stories, Poetry. **Career:** Chapman University, instructor in English, 1997-00; Saddleback College, instructor in English, 2000-05; Pierce College, faculty; Beyond Shelter, director, 2005-, vice president of development. Writer. **Publications:** Without Absolution (short stories and poetry), 2000; Imago (science fiction novel), 2002; Choosing a Career in Aircraft Maintenance (textbook), 2002; Shakespeare in Hell, 2002; B-1 Lancer (non-fiction), 2003; Coping with Terrorism (young adult non-fiction), 2004; Buzz Aldrin, 2004; Trinity (science fiction novel), 2004; Lois Duncan, 2005; Hantavirus, 2005; John Dewey: The Founder of American Liberalism, 2005; Department of Labor, 2006; Tony Hawk: Skateboard Mogul, 2009; Pancreatic Cancer: Current and Emerging Trends in Detection and Treatment, 2009; Bomb Scares, 2009; Creation of Canyons, 2010; Why Banks Fail, 2011; Mississippi: Past and Present, 2011. Contributor to periodicals. **Address:** Saddleback College, 20800 Marguerite Pkwy., Mission Viejo, CA 92692, U.S.A. **Online address:** asterling@aol.com

CASKIE, Kathryn. American (born United States) **Genres:** Romance/Historical, Novels. **Career:** Writer. **Publications:** FEATHERTON SERIES: Rules of Engagement, 2004; A Lady's Guide to Rakes, 2005; Lady in Waiting, 2005; Love is in the Heir, 2006. ROYLE SISTER SERIES: How to Seduce a Duke, 2006; How to Engage an Earl, 2007; How to Propose to a Prince, 2008. OTHERS: To Sin with a Stranger, 2008; The Most Wicked of Sins, 2009; The Duke's Night of Sin, 2010; A Sin in White, 2011; The Seven Deadly Sins, forthcoming. Contributor to periodicals. **Address:** Avon Books, 10 E 53rd St., New York, NY 10022, U.S.A. **Online address:** kathryn@kathryncaskie.com

CASPER, Claudia. Canadian (born Canada), b. 1957?. **Genres:** Novels, Young Adult Fiction, Mystery/Crime/Suspense. **Career:** Writer. **Publications:** NOVELS: The Reconstruction, 1996; The Continuation of Love by Other Means, 2003. OTHERS: (ed. with M. Anderson) Dropped Threads, 2001. **Address:** Penguin Books Canada Ltd., 10 Alcorn Ave., Ste. 300, Toronto, ON M4V 3B2, Canada. **Online address:** claudia@claudiacasper.com

CASPER, Leonard (Ralph). American (born United States), b. 1923. **Genres:** Novels, Novellas/Short Stories, Literary Criticism And History. **Career:** Cornell University, instructor, 1952-53; University of the Philippines, visiting professor, 1953-56; Panorama, contributing editor, 1954-61; Boston College, professor of English, 1956-99, now emeritus; University of Rhode Island, director of summer writing program, 1958; University of the Philippines, Fulbright lecturer, 1962-63; Solidarity, drama critique, 1966-68; Literature East and West, drama critique, 1969-77; Ateneo University, Fulbright lecturer, 1973; Pilipinas, drama critique, 1987-2002. **Publications:** Robert Penn Warren: The Dark and Bloody Ground, 1960; Wayward Horizon: Essays on Modern Philippine Literature, 1961; The Wounded Diamond: Studies in Modern Philippine Literature, 1964; New Writing from the Philippines: A Critique and Anthology, 1966; A Lion Unannounced: 12 Stories and a Fable, 1971; Firewalkers, 1987; In Burning Ambush, 1991; The Opposing Thumb, 1995; Sunsurfers Seen from Afar: Critical Essays 1991-96, 1996; The Blood-Marriage of Earth and Sky, 1997; The Circular Firing Squad, 1999; Green Circuits of the Sun, 2002. EDITOR: Six Filipino Poets, 1955; (with T.A. Gullason) The World of Short Fiction: An International Collection, 1962; Modern Philippine Short Stories, 1962. **Address:** Department of English, Boston College, 140 Commonwealth Ave., Chestnut Hill, MA 02467, U.S.A.

CASPER, Monica J. American (born United States), b. 1966. **Genres:** Medicine/Health. **Career:** University of Chicago Library, fundraising staff; University of California-San Francisco, research assistant, 1990-93, project assistant, 1992, instructor in social and behavioral sciences, 1993-95, research associate, 1995; Stanford University, research consultant, 1993-95, Center for Biomedical Ethics, fellow in genomics, ethics and society, 1995-96; San Francisco State University, lecturer, 1994; University of California-Davis, lecturer in sociology, 1996; University of California-Santa Cruz, assistant professor of sociology, 1996-2000, associate professor, 2000-04; Intersex Society of North America, executive director, 2003; University of Washington, adjunct faculty in women studies, 2003-04; Vanderbilt University, associate professor, 2004-08, Women's and Gender Studies Program, director, 2004-08; Arizona State University, New College, Division of Humanities, Arts and Cultural Studies, director, 2008-. Writer. **Publications:** (Co-author) The Long Term Care Crisis: Elders Trapped in the No-Care Zone, 1992; The Making of the Unborn Patient: A Social Anatomy of Fetal Surgery, 1998; (ed.) Synthetic Planet: Chemical Politics and the Hazards of Modern Life, 2003; (with L.J. Moore) Missing Bodies: The Politics of Visibility, 2009; Corpus: An Interdisciplinary Reader on Bodies and Knowledge, 2011. Contributor to books and periodicals. **Address:** Division of Humanities, Arts and Cultural Studies, Arizona State University, MC 2151, PO Box 37100, Phoenix, AZ 85069-7100, U.S.A. **Online address:** monica.casper@asu.edu

CASPER, Scott E. American (born United States), b. 1964. **Genres:** History. **Career:** Wesleyan University, visiting lecturer in history, 1991; University of Nevada, assistant professor, 1992-97, associate professor of history, 1997-2007, foundation professor of history, 2007-, chair, 2003-05, 2007-, director of graduate studies in history, 1999-2003; National Humanities Center, fellow, 2005-06; Virginia Foundation for the Humanities, fellow, 2006; William and Mary Quarterly, visiting editor, 2008-09; Journal of American History, contributing editor. **Publications:** Constructing American Lives: Biography and Culture in Nineteenth-Century America, 1999; Sarah Johnson's Mount Vernon: The Forgotten History of an American Shrine, 2008. EDITOR: (with R.O. Davies) Five Hundred Years: Exploring American Traditions, 1995, 3rd ed., 2000; (with Davies) Of Sagebrush and Slot Machines: This Curious Place Called Nevada, 1997; (with J.D. Groves and J.D. Chaison) Perspectives on American Book History: Artifacts and Commentary, 2001; (ed. with L.M. Long) Moving Stories: Migration and the American West, 1850-2000, 2001; (ed. with J.D. Groves, S. Nissenbaum and M. Winship) A History of the Book in America, vol. III: The Industrial Book, 1840-1880, 2007. Contributor to books and periodicals. **Address:** Department of History, University of Nevada, 201 Mack Social Sciences Bldg., 1664 N Virginia St., PO Box 0308, Reno, NV 89557-0037, U.S.A. **Online address:** casper@unr.edu

CASPERS, Nona. American (born United States) **Genres:** Novels, Literary Criticism And History. **Career:** San Francisco State University, assistant professor, associate professor of creative writing. Writer. **Publications:** (With J. Blackwomon) Lesbian Short Fiction, 1990; (with J. Blackwoman) Voyages Out 2, 1990; The Blessed, 1991; Heavier Than Air, 2006; Little Book of Days, 2009. Contributor to journals. **Address:** Department of Creative Writing, San Francisco State University, 380 HUM, 1600 Holloway Ave., San Francisco, CA 94112-2224, U.S.A. **Online address:** info@nonacaspers.com

CASS, Dennis. American (born United States), b. 1968?. **Genres:** Psychology, Sciences, Sports/Fitness, Medicine/Health. **Career:** Journalist, educator and public speaker. **Publications:** (Comp. with P.M. Smith) Cass Chronicles 2000: An Updating of The Chronicles of the Descendants of John Cass, 2000; Head Case: How I Almost Lost My Mind Trying to Understand My Brain, 2007. Contributor to periodicals. **Address:** HarperCollins Publishers, 10 E 53rd St., New York, NY 10022, U.S.A. **Online address:** dennis.cass@gmail.com

CASSADY, Marsh. American (born United States), b. 1936. **Genres:** Theatre, Novels, How-to Books, Plays/Screenplays, Poetry, Science Fiction/Fantasy, Novellas/Short Stories, Biography, Biography, Music. **Career:** Daily Reporter, staff reporter, 1960-63; Kent State University, teacher of theater; Montclair State College, teacher of theater; San Diego State University, part-time teacher, 1985-92; Long Island University, part-time teacher, 1985-92; University of California, part-time teacher, 1985-92; Los Hombres Press, editor and publisher, 1987-97; Long Ridge Writers Group, instructor, 1991-93. **Publications:** (With P. Cassady) An Introduction to Theatre & Drama, 1975; (with P. Cassady) Theatre: A View of Life, 1982; Characters in Action: A Guide to Playwriting, 1984; Playwriting Step-by-Step, 1984, rev. ed., 1992; The Book of Scenes for Acting Practice, 1985; Melinda: A Survivor (biography), 1987; Acting Step by Step, 1989; The Book of Cuttings for Acting and Directing, 1989; Love Theme with Variations (novel), 1989; Storytelling Step-by-Step, 1990; (with J. Sturkie) Acting It Out: 74 Short Dramas for Conversations with Teenagers, 1990; Alternate Casts, 1990; (with R.L. Stone and S.R. Smith) Triple Fiction (stories), 1990; (ed.) Introduction to Modern One-Act Plays, 1991; Creating Stories for Storytelling, 1991; Perverted Proverbs, 1992; Mind Swap, 1992; The Theatre and You: A Beginning, 1992; (with J. Sturkie) Acting It Out Junior, 1992; The Music of Tree Limbs (poems), 1993; Short Plays for Small Casts, 1993; Acting Games: Improvisations and Exercises, 1993; The Art of Storytelling: Creative Ideas for Preparation and Performance, 1994; Light (novel), 1994; The Times of the Double Star, 1994; Perverted Proverbs/Sudden Drama, 1994; Characters in Action: Playwriting the Easy Way, 1995; The Book of Scenes for Aspiring Actors, 1995; Great Scenes from Women Playwrights: Classic and Contemporary Selections for One to Six Actors, 1995; The Book of Monologues for Aspiring Actors, 1995; To Ride a Wild Pony, 1996; Tongues of Men and Angels, 1996; Funny Business: An Introduction to Comedy with Royalty-Free Plays and Sketches, 1996; Theatre: An Introduction, 1997; (ed.) Great Scenes from Minority Playwrights: Seventy-Four Scenes of Cultural Diversity, 1997; Vampire Wedding, 1998; (with J. Anderson) Newhall Incident: America's Worst Uninformed Cop Massacre, 1999; Spontaneous Performance: Acting through Improv, 2000; An Introduction to the Art of Theatre: A Comprehensive Text, Past, Present and Future, 2007. **Address:** c/o Helen McGrath, Helen McGrath & Associates Agency, 1406 Idaho Ct., Concord, CA 94521, U.S.A. **Online address:** marsh@tis.cetys.mx

CASSEL, Susie Lan. American/South African (born South Africa), b. 1966. **Genres:** History, Literary Criticism And History. **Career:** City Colleges of Chicago, faculty, 1988-90; University of Maryland, teacher at extension, 1989-90; California State University, Asian Pacific Faculty and Staff Association, vice president, 1994-96, Department of Literature and Writing Studies, associate professor, 1996-, professor, coordinator of ethnic studies program, 1998-2002, department chair, 2002-, professor; University of California, lecturer in comparative cultures, 1995; Lely Hayslip Global Village Foundation, director, 1999-2001. Writer. **Publications:** Nation Language Culture: A Collection of Oral Histories, 2000; (ed.) The Chinese in America: A History from Gold Mountain to the New Millennium, 2002; (with K. Moore) Techniques for College Writing: The Thesis Statement and Beyond, 2011. **Address:** Department of Literature & Writing, California State University, Markstein Hall 134, 333 Twin Oaks Blvd., San Marcos, CA 92096-0001, U.S.A. **Online address:** scassel@csusm.edu

CASSELL, Eric J. American (born United States), b. 1928. **Genres:** Medicine/Health, Philosophy, Essays, Medicine/Health. **Career:** Bellevue Hospital, intern, 1954-55, assistant resident, 1955-56, 1958-59, assistant visiting physician, 1965-66; Cornell University, Medical College, U.S. Public Health Service, trainee, 1959-63, clinical instructor, 1961-65, clinical assistant professor, 1964-65, clinical professor of public health, 1971, now professor emeritus, director of program for study of ethics and values in medicine, 1981-86; New York Hospital, physician to outpatients, 1961-65, assistant attending physician to inpatients, 1971-77, associate attending physician, 1977-84, attending physician, 1984-; French Hospital, assistant attending physician, 1961-63, associate attending physician, 1963-65, attending physician, 1965-74; New York University Hospital, associate attending physician, 1965-66; New York University, lecturer and associate professor, 1965-66; Mount Sinai School of Medicine, associate clinical professor, 1966, 1968, associate professor, 1967-71, lecturer, 1971-73; Mount Sinai Hospital, associate attending physician and assistant attending physician, 1966-71, associate director of ambulatory care, 1966-68; New York Hospital/Cornell Medical Center, attending physician to inpatients, 1984-. Writer. **Publications:** Healer's Art: A New Perspective on the Doctor-Patient Relationship, 1976, rev. ed., 1985; Place of the Humanities in Medicine, 1984; Talking with Patients, vol. I: The Theory of Doctor-Patient Communication, vol. II: Clinical Technique, 1985; (ed. with M. Siegler and contrib.) Changing Values in Medicine, 1985; Nature of Suffering, 1991, rev. ed., 2004; Doctoring: Nature of Primary Care Medicine, 1997. Works appear in anthologies. **Address:** 28 Old Fulton St., Brooklyn, NY 11201-0001, U.S.A. **Online address:** eric@ericcassell.com

CASSELL, Joan. American (born United States), b. 1929. **Genres:** Women's Studies And Issues, Anthropology/Ethnology, Medicine/Health, Politics/Government. **Career:** Institute for Scientific Analysis, research associate, 1975-77; Princeton University, visiting fellow in anthropology, 1976-78; Center for Policy Research, senior research associate, 1977-83; Institute for the Study of Human Issues, senior research associate, 1983-86; Research Institute for the Study of Man, research fellow, 1986-87; Washington University, research associate in anthropology and sociology, 1987-; Macy's, Daniel & Charles Agency, Media Promotion Agency, advertising copywriter. **Publications:** A Group Called Women: Sisterhood and Symbolism in the Feminist Movement, 1977; A Fieldwork Manual for Studying Desegregated Schools, 1978; (ed. with M.L. Wax) Federal Regulations: Ethical Issues and Social Research, 1979; (ed. with S. Jacobs) Handbook of Ethical Issues in Anthropology, 1987; (ed.) Children in the Field: Anthropological Experiences, 1987; Expected Miracles: Surgeons at Work, 1991; The Woman in the Surgeon's Body,

1998; Life and Death in Intensive Care, 2005. Contributor to journals and magazines. **Address:** Department of Anthropology, Washington University, 1 Brookings Dr., PO Box 1114, St. Louis, MO 63130, U.S.A.

CASSELLA, Carol Wiley. American (born United States), b. 1957. **Genres:** Novels. **Career:** Simon & Schuster Inc., novelist; Virginia Mason Medical Center, anesthesiologist; Bill & Melinda Gates Foundation, freelance medical writer. **Publications:** Oxygen (novel), 2008; Healer (novel), 2010. **Address:** Bainbridge Island, WA , U.S.A. **Online address:** carol@carolcassella.com

CASSELS, Alan. Canadian/British (born England), b. 1929. **Genres:** History, International Relations/Current Affairs. **Career:** Sweet Briar College, visiting lecturer, 1956-57; Trinity College, instructor in History, 1959-62; University of Pennsylvania, assistant professor of history, 1962-67; Haverford College, visiting assistant professor, 1963-64; McMaster University, associate professor of history, 1967-71, professor of history, 1971-94, emeritus professor of history, 1994-; Royal Historical Society, fellow.; Society for Italian Historical Studies, vice-president, 1978-80, president, 1980-82. Writer. **Publications:** Fascist Italy, 1968, 2nd ed., 1985; Mussolini's Early Diplomacy, 1970; Fascism, 1975; (ed.) Italian Foreign Policy 1918-1945: A Guide to Research and Research Materials, 1981, rev. ed., 1991; Ideology and International Relations in the Modern World, 1996. Contributor to books and periodicals. **Address:** Department of History, McMaster University, 1280 Main St. W, Hamilton, ON L8S 4L8, Canada. **Online address:** cassels@mcmaster.ca

CASSELS, J(ohn) W(illiam) S(cott). British (born England), b. 1922. **Genres:** Mathematics/Statistics, Sciences. **Career:** Manchester University, lecturer, 1949-50; Cambridge University, Trinity College, fellow, 1949-, Department of Pure Mathematics and Mathematical Statistics, lecturer, 1950-63, reader in arithmetic, 1963-67, Sadleirian professor of pure mathematics, 1967-84, head, 1969-84, emeritus professor, 1984-. Writer. **Publications:** An Introduction to Diophantine Approximation, 1957; An Introduction to the Geometry of Numbers, 1959, rev. ed., 1997; (ed. with A. Fröhlich) Algebraic Number Theory: Proceedings of an Instructional Conference, 1967, 2nd ed., 2010; Rational Quadratic Forms, 1978; Economics for Mathematicians, 1981, rev. ed., 1985; Local Fields, 1986; Lectures on Elliptic Curves, 1991, rev. ed., 1993; (with E.V. Flynn) Prolegomena to a Middlebrow Arithmetic of Curves of Genus 2, 1996. **Address:** University of Cambridge, Rm. C2.08, Ctr. for Mathematical Sciences, Wilberforce Rd., Cambridge, CB CB3 0WB, England. **Online address:** j.w.s.cassels@dpmms.cam.ac.uk

CASSIDY, Anne. British (born England), b. 1952. **Genres:** Novels, Picture/Board Books, Young Adult Fiction. **Career:** Writer and educator. **Publications:** Big Girls' Shoes, 1990; Good Days, Bad Days, 1993; In Real Life, 1993; Talking to Strangers, 1994; Driven to Death, 1994; A Family Affair, 1995; Spider Pie, 1995; Accidental Death, 1996; End of the Line, 1996; No Through Road, 1996; Temples, 1996; Optical Illusions, 1996; Brotherly Love, 1997; The Hidden Child, 1997; Parents Who Think Too Much: Why We Do it, How to Stop, 1998; Death by Drowning, 1998; Killing Time, 1999; Cheeky Monkey, 2000; Pippa and Poppa, 2000; The Crying Princess, 2000; Dead Quiet, 2000; Jasper and Jess, 2001; Tough Love, 2001; Missing Judy, 2002; Naughty Nancy, 2002; The Queen's Dragon, 2002; Cleo and Leo, 2002; Freddie's Fears, 2002; The Sassy Monkey, 2002; Blood Money, 2003; Love Letters, 2003; The Best Den Ever, 2004; A Bunch of Balloons, 2004; Jumping Josie, 2004; Toby's Trousers, 2004; Looking for JJ, 2004; Birthday Blues, 2005; Snow White, 2005; Witness, 2005; Puss in Boots, 2005; Sammy and the Starman, 2005; El mono malcriado, 2006; The Story of My Life, 2006; Innocent, 2006; The Bone Room, 2007; Careless, 2007; The Nightingale, 2007; Forget Me Not, 2008; The Dead House, 2009; Just Jealous, 2009; Wizard Balloon, 2009; Wizard Woof, 2009; Wizard Wig, 2009; Getting Away With It, 2009; Guilt Trip, 2010; Cheeky Monkey's Treasure Hunt, 2010; Heart Burn, 2011; Wizard Prince, 2011; Murder Notebooks, 2012. **Address:** Scholastic Ltd., Euston House, 24 Eversholt St., London, GL NW1 1DB, England.

CASSIDY, Cathy. British (born England), b. 1962. **Genres:** Novels, Young Adult Fiction, Children's Fiction, Young Adult Non-fiction. **Career:** Jackie Magazine, fiction editor. Educator. **Publications:** Dizzy, 2004; Indigo Blue, 2005; Driftwood, 2005; Scarlett, 2006; Sundae Girl, 2007; Love, Peace and Chocolate, 2007; Lucky Star, 2007; Ginger Snaps, 2008; The Cathy Cassidy Dreams and Doodles Daybook, 2008; (co-author) Our City, 2008; Shine On, Daizy Star, 2009; Angel Cake, 2009; Cupcakes & Kisses, 2009; Letters to Cathy, 2009; Daizy Star and the Pink Guitar, 2010; Cherry Crush, 2010; Strike a Pose, Daizy Star, 2011; Marshmallow Skye, 2011; Summer's Dream, 2012; Sweet Honey, 2013. **Address:** c/o Darley Anderson, Darley Anderson Literary, TV and Film Agency, Estelle House, 11 Eustace Rd., London, GL SW6 1JB, England. **Online address:** cathy.cassidy1@virgin.net

CASSIDY, David C(harles). American (born United States), b. 1945. **Genres:** Physics, History. **Career:** University of California, postdoctoral research fellow, 1976-77; University of Stuttgart, Alexander von Humboldt fellow, 1977-80; University of Regensburg, assistant professor, 1980-83; Einstein Papers Project, associate editor, 1983-90; Hofstra University, professor of natural science, 1990-. Writer and historian. **Publications:** Werner Heisenberg and the Crisis in Quantum Theory, 1920-1925, 1976; Werner Heisenberg: A Bibliography of His Writings, 1984, 2nd ed., 2001; (ed.) The Collected Papers of Albert Einstein, vol. I, 1987, vol. II, 1989; Uncertainty: The Life and Science of Werner Heisenberg, 1992; Einstein and Our World, 1995; (with G. Holton and J. Rutherford) Understanding Physics, 2002; J. Robert Oppenheimer and the American Century, 2005; Beyond Uncertainty: Heisenberg, Quantum Physics, and the Bomb, 2009; Short History of Physics in the American Century, 2011. Contributor to journals. **Address:** Natural Science Program, Hofstra University, 106 Berliner Hall, Hempstead, NY 11549, U.S.A. **Online address:** chmdcc@hofstra.edu

CASSIDY, Michael. South African (born South Africa), b. 1936. **Genres:** Human Relations/Parenting, Theology/Religion, Social Sciences. **Career:** African Enterprise, founder and international team leader, 1961-; The Natal Witness, religious columnist, 1968-2004; Johannesburg Star, religious columnist, 1968-73; South African Congress on Mission and Evangelism, co-convener, 1973; National Initiative for Reconciliation, chairman, 1985-88; Pan African Christian Leadership Assembly, co-convener, 1976, 1994; South African Christian Leadership Assembly, co-covenor, 1979, 2003. **Publications:** Decade of Decisions in US as Where Are You Taking the World Anyway?, 1970; Relationship Tangle, 1974; Prisoners of Hope, 1974; (with G. Osei-Mensah) Together in One Place: The Story of PACLA, December 9-19, 1976, Nairobi, 1978; Christianity for the Open Minded, 1978; Bursting the Wineskins: The Holy Spirit's Transforming Work in a Peacemaker and His World, 1983; Chasing the Wind: Man's Search for Life's Answers, 1988; The Passing Summer: A South African's Response to White Fear, Black Anger, and the Politics of Love, 1990; The Politics of Love, 1991; A Witness For Ever, 1995; Michael Cassidy's Window on the Word, 1997; Getting to the Heart of Things, 2005; What On Earth Are You Thinking for Heaven's Sake?, 2006; A Passion for Preaching, 2006; Making an Impact, 2006. EDITOR: I Will Heal Their Land, 1974; (co-ed.) Facing the New Challenges, 1978; (intro.) Light on the Way, 2006. **Address:** African Enterprise, 128 E Palm Ave., Ste. 100, Monrovia, CA 91016, U.S.A. **Online address:** mcassidy@pobox.com

CASSIDY, Robert M. American (born United States) **Genres:** History, Military/Defense/Arms Control. **Career:** United States Military Academy, assistant professor of international relations; U.S. Army, 4th Infantry Division, brigade operations officer during Operation Iraqi Freedom, squadron executive officer of the 1-10 Cavalry, 82nd Airborne Division, troop commander in the 1-17 Cavalry, lieutenant colonel. U.S. Army forces in Europe, battalion commander & special assistant to Commanding General. Writer. **Publications:** Russia in Afghanistan and Chechnya: Military Strategic Culture and the Paradoxes of Asymmetric Conflict, 2003; Peacekeeping in the Abyss: British and American Peacekeeping Doctrine and Practice after the Cold War, 2004; Counterinsurgency and the Global War on Terror: Military Culture and Irregular War, 2006. Contributor to periodicals. **Address:** Ctr. for Advanced Defense Studies, 10 G St. NE, Ste. 610, Washington, DC 20002, U.S.A.

CASSON, Mark (Christopher). British (born England), b. 1945. **Genres:** Economics, Business/Trade/Industry, Humanities. **Career:** University of Reading, Department of Economics, lecturer, 1969-76, reader, 1976-81, professor of economics, 1981-, head of department, 1987-94, Centre for Institutional Performance, director; World Bank, consultant; Commission of the European Communities, consultant; International Labor Office, consultant; DTI (Central Evaluation Team), Trade Partners UK, consultant; New Zealand Treasury, consultant; UNCTAD (Transnational Corporations), consultant; University of Leeds, visiting professor of international business, 1995-; University of Lancaster, Centre for Entrepreneurship, associate, 2003-; University of York, visiting professor of management, 2010-. Writer. **Publications:** Introduction to Mathematical Economics, 1973; (with P.J. Buckley) The Future of the Multinational Enterprise, 1976; Alternatives to the Multinational Enterprise, 1979; Youth Unemployment, 1979; Unemployment: A Disequilibrium Approach, 1981; The Entrepreneur: An Economic Theory,

1982, 2nd ed., 2003; Economics of Unemployment: An Historical Perspective, 1983; Unemployment Theory before Keynes, 1983; (with P.J. Buckley) The Economic Theory of the Multinational Enterprise: Selected Papers, 1985; (co-author) Multinationals and World Trade: Vertical Integration and the Division of Labour in World Industries, 1986; The Firm and the Market: Studies in Multinational Enterprise and the Scope of the Firm, 1987; Enterprise and Competitiveness: A Systems View of International Business, 1990; The Economics of Business Culture: Game Theory, Transaction Costs, and Economic Welfare, 1991; Entrepreneurship and Business Culture, 1995; Organization of International Business, 1995; Information and Organization: A New Perspective on the Theory of the Firm, 1996; (with M.B. Rose) Institutions and the Evolution of Modern Business, 1997; Economics of International Business: A New Research Guide, 2000; Enterprise and Leadership: Studies on Firms, Markets and Networks, 2000; (comp. and intro.) The Hegemony of International Business, 1945-1970, 2000; The World's First Railway System, 2009; (with P.J. Buckley) Multinational Enterprise Revisited: The Essential Buckley and Casson, 2010; (co-author) Entrepreneurship: Theory, Networks, History, 2010. EDITOR: The Growth of International Business, 1983; Entrepreneurship, 1990; Multinational Corporations, 1990; Global Research Strategy and International Competitiveness, 1991; International Business and Global Integration, 1992; (with P.J. Buckley) Multinational Enterprises in the World Economy: Essays in Honour of John Dunning, 1992; (with J. Creedy) Industrial Concentration and Economic Inequality: Essays in Honour of Peter Hart, 1993; The Theory of the Firm, 1996; Culture, Social Norms, and Economics, 1997; (with M. Carter and V. Suneja) The Economics of Marketing, 1998; (with A.C. Godley) Cultural Factors in Economic Growth, 2000; (co-ed.) Oxford Handbook of Entrepreneurship, 2006; (with M.D. Giusta) Economics of Networks, 2008; Markets and Market Institutions: Their Origin and Evolution, 2011. Contributor to journals. **Address:** Department of Economics, University of Reading, 313 HUMMS, Whiteknights, PO Box 218, Reading, BR RG6 2AA, England. **Online address:** m.c.casson@reading.ac.uk

CASSTEVENS, Thomas William. American (born United States), b. 1937. **Genres:** Politics/Government, Social Sciences. **Career:** University of California, lecturer in political science, 1963-64, Institute of Governmental Studies, assistant research political scientist, 1963-66; Oakland University, assistant professor, 1966-6. Writer. **Publications:** Politics, Housing and Race Relations: The Defeat of Berkeley's Fair Housing Ordinance, 1965; Politics, Housing and Race Relations: The Rumford Act and Proposition 14, 1967; (co-ed.) The Politics of Fair Housing Legislation, 1968; (ed. with B.K. Shrivastava) American Government and Politics, 1980. **Address:** Department of Political Science, Oakland University, 418 Varner Hall, Rochester, MI 48309-4488, U.S.A. **Online address:** cass@oakland.edu

CASSUTT, Michael (Joseph). American (born United States), b. 1954. **Genres:** Science Fiction/Fantasy, Autobiography/Memoirs, Air/Space Topics, Biography, Reference, Novels. **Career:** KHYT Radio, disc jockey and operations manager, 1975-78; CBS Television, children's programming executive, 1979-85; freelance writer and television producer, 1985-; Scifi.com, columnist, 2000-09; University of Southern California, adjunct faculty, 2007-. **Publications:** The Star Country (science fiction), 1986; Who's Who in Space: The First 25 Years, 1987; (intro.) Valentin Lebedev, Diary of a Cosmonaut: 211 Days in Space, 1988; Dragon Season (fantasy), 1991; (ed. with A. Greeley) Sacred Visions (science fiction anthology), 1991; (with D.K. Slayton) Deke! U.S. Manned Space: Mercury to the Shuttle, 1994; Missing Man (novel), 1998; Red Moon (novel), 2001; (with T.P. Stafford) We Have Capture: Tom Stafford and the Space Race, 2002; Tango Midnight (novel), 2003; (with D.S. Goyer) Heaven's Shadow (novel), 2011. Contributor to periodicals. Works appear in anthologies. **Address:** School of Cinematic Arts, University of Southern California, SCA 335, University Pk., Los Angeles, CA 90089-2211, U.S.A. **Online address:** cass54@aol.com

CASTALDO, Nancy Fusco. British/American (born United States), b. 1962. **Genres:** Children's Fiction, Children's Non-fiction. **Career:** New York State Department of Environmental Conservation and National Audubon Society, environmental educator; The Historical Novel Society, secretary. Writer. **Publications:** FOR CHILDREN: Sunny Days and Starry Nights, 1996; Rainy Day Play!, 1996; The Little Hands Nature Book, 1996; Winter Day Play!, 2001; Oceans: An Activity Guide for Ages 6-9, 2002; Rainforests: An Activity Guide for Ages 6-9, 2003; Deserts: An Activity Guide for Ages 6-9, 2004; Pizza for the Queen, 2005; River Wild: An Activity Guide to North American Rivers, 2006; Leap Into Space, 2008; Keeping Our Earth Green: Over 100 Hands-on Ways to help Save the Earth, 2008. Contributor to magazines. **Address:** Historical Novel Society, Marine Cottage, The Strand, Starcross, EX6 8NY, England. **Online address:** ntcastaldo@taconic.net

CASTANEDA, Christopher James. American (born United States), b. 1959. **Genres:** History, Environmental Sciences/Ecology, Anthropology/Ethnology, Sciences, Business/Trade/Industry, Earth Sciences, Science Fiction/Fantasy. **Career:** Houston Community College, lecturer in history, 1989-90; University of Houston, director, oral history of the houston economy, 1990-92, adjunct professor, 1991-92; California State University, department of history, assistant professor, 1994-97, director, history internship program, 1994-, director, oral history program, 1994-, associate professor of history, 1997-, public history program, associate director, 1997-2000, director, public history program, 2000-. Writer. **Publications:** Regulated Enterprise: Natural Gas Pipelines and Northeastern Markets, 1938-1954, 1993; (with J.A. Pratt) From Texas to the East: A Strategic History of Texas Eastern Corporation, 1993; (with C.M. Smith) Gas Pipelines and the Emergence of America's Regulatory State: A History of Panhandle Eastern Corporation, 1928-1993, 1996; (with J.A. Pratt and T. Priest) Offshore Pioneers: Brown & Root and the History of Offshore Oil and Gas, 1997; Invisible Fuel: Manufactured and Natural Gas in America, 1800-2000, 1999; (with J.A. Pratt) Builders: Herman and George R. Brown, 1999; (co-author) The Public Historian, 2007. Contributor of articles to journals. **Address:** Department of History, California State University, 6000 J St., Sacramento, CA 95819-6059, U.S.A. **Online address:** cjc@csus.edu

CASTANEDA, Jorge G. American/Mexican (born Mexico), b. 1953. **Genres:** Politics/Government, International Relations/Current Affairs, Social Sciences. **Career:** National Autonomous University of Mexico, professor of economics and international affairs, 1978-82, professor of political science, 1982-; advisor to Mexican government, 1980-82; Carnegie Endowment for International Peace, senior associate, 1985-87; University of California, visiting professor, 1990-92; Princeton University, visiting professor, 1990-94; foreign minister of Mexico, 2000-03; secretary of foreign affairs, 2000-03; University of Cambridge, faculty; New York University, global distinguished professor of politics and Latin American and Caribbean studies; Los Angeles Times, columnist; Newsweek, columnist; Reforma, columnist. **Publications:** (With E. Hett) El Economismo Dependentista, 1978; Nicaragua: Contradicciones en la Revolucion, 1980; (with E. Semo and P. Lopez) La Renovacion del PCM, 1981; Los Últimos Capitalismos, 1981; México: El Futuro en Juego, 1987; (with R.A. Pastor) Limits to Friendship: The United States and Mexico, 1988; La Casa por la Ventana, 1993; Utopia Unarmed: The Latin American Left after the Cold War, 1993, 2nd ed., 1995; Sorpresas te da la Vida, 1994, 2nd ed., 1995; The Mexican Shock, 1995; The Estados Unidos Affair. Cinco Ensayos Sobre un amor Oblicuo, 1996; La Vida en Rojo: Una Biografía del Ché Guevara, 1997; La Herencia: Arqueología de la Sucesión Presidencial en México, 1999; Respuestas al Neoliberalismo, 1999; Somos Muchos: Ideas para el Mañana, 2004; Ex Mex: From Migrants to Immigrants, 2007; (with R. Aguilar) La Diferencia: Radiografía de un Sexenio, 2007; (ed. with M.A. Morales) Leftovers: Tales of the Latin American Left, 2008; (with M.W. Rodríguez) Y México por Qué no?, 2008; (with H.A. Camín) Futuro Para México, 2009; (with R.V. Aguilar) El Narco: La Guerra Fallida, 2009; Mañana Forever?: Mexico and the Mexicans, 2011. Contributor to books and periodicals. **Address:** New York University, 5 Washington Sq. N, 1st Fl., New York, NY 10003, U.S.A.

CASTEEL, Sarah Phillips. Canadian (born Canada), b. 1974. **Genres:** History. **Career:** Carleton University, associate professor of English, Centre for Transnational Cultural Analysis, co-founder. Writer. **Publications:** Second Arrivals: Landscape and Belonging in Contemporary Writing of the Americas, 2007; (ed. with W. Siemerling) Canada and Its Americas: Transnational Navigations, 2010. Contributor to books and journals. **Address:** Carleton University, 1125 Colonel By Dr., Ottawa, ON K1S 5B6, Canada. **Online address:** sarah_casteel@carleton.ca

CASTEL-BLOOM, Orly. (Orli Kastel-Blum). Israeli (born Israel), b. 1960?. **Genres:** Novels, Young Adult Fiction, Children's Fiction. **Career:** Tel Aviv University, teacher of creative writing. Writer. **Publications:** Lo raḥoḳ mimerkaz ha-ir, 1987; Sevivah 'oyenet, 1989; Hekhan ani nimtset, 1990; Doli siṭti, 1992; Sipurim bilti-retsoniyim, 1993; Ha-Minah Lizah, 1995; Shenenu nitnaheg yafeh: sihot im beni, 1997; Ha-Sefer he-ḥadash, 1998; Radiḳalim ḥofshiyim, 2000; ḥalaḳim enoshiyim, 2002; Human Parts, 2003; Im orez lo mityakḥim: mivḥar sipurim, 1987-2004, 2004; Teḳsṭil: roman, 2006; Doli siṭi,

2007. Contributor to periodicals. **Address:** The Department of Literature, Tel Aviv University, Gilman 358, PO Box 39040, Tel-Aviv, 69978, Israel.

CASTELL, Megan. *See* **WILLIAMS, Jeanne.**

CASTELLI, Elizabeth A. (Elizabeth Anne Castelli). American (born United States), b. 1958. **Genres:** Women's Studies And Issues, Theology/Religion, Cultural/Ethnic Topics, History. **Career:** College of Wooster, assistant professor, 1987-94; University of California, visiting assistant professor, 1993; Occidental College, assistant professor, 1994-95; Columbia University, Barnard College, assistant professor, 1995-2003, associate professor, 2003-07, professor and department chair, 2007-, Centennial Scholars Program, co-director, 2004-. Writer. **Publications:** Imitating Paul: A Discourse of Power, 1991; (ed. with H. Taussig) Reimagining Christian Origins: A Colloquium Honoring Burton L. Mack, 1996; (ed. with R.C. Rodman) Women, Gender, Religion: A Reader, 2001; (ed. with J.R. Jakobsen) Interventions: Activists and Academics Respond to Violence, 2004; Martyrdom and Memory: Early Christian Culture Making, 2004. Contributor of articles to books and journals. **Address:** Department of Religion, Barnard College, 219 Milbank Hall, 3009 Broadway, New York, NY 10027-6909, U.S.A. **Online address:** ec225@columbia.edu

CASTELLI, Elizabeth Anne. *See* **CASTELLI, Elizabeth A.**

CASTELLUCCI, Cecil. (Cecil Seaskull). American (born United States), b. 1969. **Genres:** Novels, Graphic Novels. **Career:** Alpha 60 Film Club, founding member; MTV Big Urban Myth Show, field producer; Museum of Television and Radio, director of recreating radio; indie rock musician, film writer, entertainer and performance artist. **Publications:** Boy Proof, 2005; The Queen of Cool, 2006; Beige, 2007; (with J. Rugg) The Plain Janes, 2007; (with J. Rugg) Janes in Love (Minx), 2008; (ed. with H. Black) Geektastic: Stories from the Nerd Herd, 2009; Rose Sees Red, 2010; Grandma's Gloves, 2010; First Day on Earth, 2012; Odd Duck, 2013; The Tin Star, 2013. **Address:** PO Box 29095, Los Angeles, CA 90039, U.S.A. **Online address:** misscecil@earthlink.com

CASTER, Andrew I. American (born United States), b. 1954. **Genres:** Medicine/Health, Sciences. **Career:** Caster Eye Center, medical director, 1984-. Writer. **Publications:** The Eye Laser Miracle: The Complete Guide to Better Vision, 1997, rev. ed., 2001; Lasik: The Eye Laser Miracle: The Complete Guide to Better Vision, 2008. **Address:** Caster Eye Center, 9100 Wilshire Blvd., Ste. 265E, Beverly Hills, CA 90212-3440, U.S.A. **Online address:** acaster@castervision.com

CASTIGLIONE, Caroline. American (born United States), b. 1962. **Genres:** History, Politics/Government, Social Sciences. **Career:** University of Texas, assistant professor of history, 1995-2005; Brown University, Department of Italian Studies and history, assistant professor, 2005-08, associate professor, 2008-. Writer. **Publications:** Patrons and Adversaries: Nobles and Villagers in Italian Politics, 1640-1760, 2005. Contributor to periodicals. **Address:** Department Italian Studies and History, Brown University, 190 Hope St., PO Box 1942, Providence, RI 02912, U.S.A. **Online address:** caroline_castiglione@brown.edu

CASTILE, George Pierre. American (born United States), b. 1939. **Genres:** Cultural/Ethnic Topics, History. **Career:** Whitman College, professor, 1971-2006, professor emeritus, 2006-. Writer and anthropologist. **Publications:** North American Indians: An Introduction to the Chichimeca, 1979; Persistent Peoples: Cultural Enclaves in Perspective, 1981; The Indians of Puget Sound: The Notebooks of Myron Eells, 1985; (ed. with R.L. Bee) State and Reservation: New Perspectives on Federal Indian Policy, 1992; To Show Heart: Native American Self-Determination and Federal Indian Policy, 1960-1975, 1998; Taking Charge: Native American Self-Determination and Federal Indian Policy, 1975-1993, 2006. **Address:** Department of Anthropology, Whitman College, Maxey Hall, 345 Boyer St., Walla Walla, WA 99362, U.S.A.

CASTILE, Rand. American/British (born England), b. 1938. **Genres:** Art/Art History, Social Sciences. **Career:** Freelance writer and critic, 1963-67; Japan Society Inc., education director, 1967-70; Japan Society Gallery, founding director, 1970-85; Asian Art Museum of San Francisco, director, 1985-94, director emeritus, 1995-; National Endowment for the Humanities, consultant; National Endowment for the Arts, consultant. Writer. **Publications:** The Way of Tea, 1971, 2nd ed., 1979; Ikeda & Ida: Two New Japanese Printmakers, 1974; Japanese Art Now: Tadaaki Kuwayama and Rikuro Okamoto, 1980; Shinohara, 1982; Shikō Munakata, 1903-1975: Works on Paper, 1983; (foreword) Exquisite Pursuits: Japanese Art in the Harry G.C. Packard Collection, 1994; (foreword) The Asian Art Museum of San Francisco: Selected Works, 1994. Contributor to journals and magazines. **Address:** Asian Art Museum, 200 Larkin St., San Francisco, CA 94102, U.S.A. **Online address:** rcastile3@aol.com

CASTILLO, Debra A(nn Garsow). American/Egyptian (born Egypt), b. 1953. **Genres:** Literary Criticism And History, Women's Studies And Issues. **Career:** University of Maryland, instructor in English composition, 1981-82; University of Wisconsin, instructor in Spanish, 1983; University of Tulsa, visiting assistant professor of English composition and Spanish, 1984-85; Cornell University, Stephen H. Weiss presidential fellow and professor of comparative literature, 1985-, Emerson Hinchliff professor of Hispanic studies, Latin American Studies Program, director. Writer. **Publications:** The Translated World: A Postmodern Tour of Libraries in Literature, 1984; Talking Back: Toward a Latin American Feminist Literary Criticism, 1992; (trans. and intro.) F. Campbell, Tijuana: Stories on the Border, 1995; Easy Women: Sex and Gender in Modern Mexican Fiction, 1998; (ed. with M.J. Dudley) Transforming Cultures in the Americas, 2000; (ed. with J.E.P. Soldán) Beyond the Lettered City: Latin American Literature and Mass Media, 2000; (ed. with M.J. Dudley and B. Mendoza) Rethinking Feminisms in the Americas, 2000; (with M.S.T. Córdoba) Border Women: Writing from La Frontera, 2002; (with J. López-Arias) España: Lecturas Interculturales, 2003; Redreaming America: Toward a Bilingual American Culture, 2005; (ed.) Sirena Selena vestida de pena, 2008; (co-ed.) Cartographies of Affect: Across Borders in South Asia and the Americas, 2010. FORTHCOMING: (with M.G.R. Gómez, A.R. SolíS and C. Castillo-Chavez) Este ambiente denoche: La prostitución femenina en Tijuana; (with E. Paz-Soldán and J. Durán) Umbilical Object; (with M.G.R. Gómez, A.R. Solís and C. Castillo-Chavez) Este ambiente de noche: La prostitución femenina en Tijuana. Works appear in anthologies. Contributor to periodicals. **Address:** Department of Comparative Literature, Cornell University, 240 Goldwin Smith Hall, Ithaca, NY 14853-3201, U.S.A. **Online address:** dac9@cornell.edu

CASTILLO, Mary. American (born United States), b. 1974?. **Genres:** Young Adult Fiction, Romance/Historical, Novels. **Career:** Los Angeles Times, reporter. Full-time writer. **Publications:** (With S. Quintero, B. Platas, C. Piñeiro) Friday Night Chicas: Sexy Stories from La Noche, 2005; Hot Tamara, 2005; In Between Men, 2006; (with S. Quintero, B. Platas and L. Sandoval) Names I Call My Sister, 2007; Switchcraft, 2007; (contrib.) Orange County Noir, 2010. **Address:** c/o Author Mail, Avon Books, 10 E 53rd St., New York, NY 10022, U.S.A. **Online address:** mary@marycastillo.com

CASTLE, Alfred L. American (born United States), b. 1948. **Genres:** History, Literary Criticism And History, Philosophy, Social Commentary, Theology/Religion, Essays, Politics/Government, Social Sciences, Autobiography/Memoirs. **Career:** New Mexico Military Institute, professor of history, 1976-83, vice president, 1983-87; Hawaii Pacific University, vice president, 1987-95; California State University, vice president, 1995-98; Samuel N. and Mary Castle Foundation, executive director and treasurer, 1998-. Writer. **Publications:** A Century of Philanthropy: A History of the Samuel N. and Mary Castle Foundation, 1992; Diplomatic Realism: William R. Castle, Jr., and American Foreign Policy, 1919-1953, 1998. Contributor to books. Works appear in anthologies. **Address:** Samuel N. and Mary Castle Foundation, Pacific Guardian Ctr., Makai Twr., 733 Bishop St., Ste. 1275, Honolulu, HI 96813, U.S.A. **Online address:** acastle@aloha.net

CASTLE, Gregory. American (born United States) **Genres:** History, Literary Criticism And History. **Career:** Arizona State University, College of Liberal Arts and Sciences, Department of English, assistant professor, 1992-98, associate professor, 1998-2007, professor of English, 2007-, M.A. Literature Program, director, 1997-2002, interim director of undergraduate studies, 2007-08, director of undergraduate studies, 2009-. Writer. **Publications:** (Contrib.) Quare Joyce, 1998; (contrib.) Joyce: Feminism/Post/Colonialism (European Joyce Studies series), 1998; (ed.) Postcolonial Discourses: An Anthology, 2001; Modernism and the Celtic Revival, 2001; (contrib.) Dracula (Case Studies in Contemporary Criticism series), 2002; (contrib.) Reading Irish History: Text, Contexts, and Memory in Modern Ireland, 2003; Reading the Modernist Bildungsroman, 2006; The Blackwell Guide to Literary Theory, 2007; (contrib.) James Joyce in Context, 2008; (contrib.) The Encyclopedia of Literary and Cultural Theory, 2011; Inventing Souls: Pedagogies of Irish Revivalism, forthcoming. Contributor to journals and periodicals. **Ad-**

dress: Department of English, College of Liberal Arts and Sciences, Arizona State University, Rm. 542, 851 S Cady Mall, PO Box 870302, Tempe, AZ 85287-0302, U.S.A. **Online address:** dedalus@asu.edu

CASTLE, Kathryn. British/American (born United States), b. 1946?. **Genres:** History, Humanities, Social Sciences. **Career:** London Metropolitan University (formerly University of North London), programme director for history and women's studies, 1982-, principal lecturer in history, 1992-, academic leader for humanities. Writer. **Publications:** (Contrib.) The Imperial Curriculum, 1993; Britannia's Children: Reading Colonialism Through Children's Books and Magazines, 1996. Contributor to periodicals. **Address:** Department of Humanities, Arts, Languages and, Education, London Metropolitan University, 166-220 Holloway Rd., London, GL N7 8DB, England. **Online address:** k.castle@londonmet.ac.uk

CASTLE, Linda. (Linda Lea Castle). American (born United States), b. 1952. **Genres:** Mystery/Crime/Suspense, Romance/Historical, Westerns/Adventure, Language/Linguistics, Paranormal, Novels. **Career:** Writer. **Publications:** ROMANCE NOVELS: Fearless Hearts, 1995; Abbie's Child, 1996; Lightening Lexicon, 1998; Territorial Bride, 1998; Gideon's Angel, 1999; Heart of the Lawman, 1999; By King's Command, 2000; Addie and the Laird, 2000; Mattie and the Blacksmith, 2001; Lottie and the Rustler, 2001. OTHER NOVELS: The Return of Chase Cordell (historical), 1996; Temple's Prize (western), 1997; Promise the Moon, 2002; Surrender the Stars, 2002; Embrace the Sun, 2002; Stained Glass Window, 2006; The Templar's Treasure, 2007; Taos Chill, 2009. **Address:** c/o Pattie Steele-Perkins, Steele-Perkins Literary Agency, 38 Eastview Mall Dr., Victor, NY 14564, U.S.A. **Online address:** lindacrockett@hotmail.com

CASTLE, Linda Lea. *See* **CASTLE, Linda.**

CASTLEDEN, Rodney. British (born England), b. 1945. **Genres:** Songs/Lyrics And Libretti, Archaeology/Antiquities, Area Studies, Earth Sciences, Geography, History, Music, Mythology/Folklore, Theatre, Reference. **Career:** Teacher, 1968-79; Roedean School, Department of Geography, head, 1979-90, head of humanities faculty, 1990-2001, head of social science faculty, 2001-04. Writer. **Publications:** SELF-ILLUSTRATED: The Wilmington Giant, 1983; The Stonehenge People: An Exploration of Life in Neolithic Britain, 4700-2000 B.C, 1987; The Knossos Labyrinth, 1990; Minoans: Life in Bronze Age Crete, 1990; Neolithic Britain, 1992; The Making of Stonehenge, 1993; King Arthur: The Truth behind the Legend, 2000. OTHERS: Classic Landforms of the Sussex Coast, 1982, rev. ed., 1996; (co-ed.) Classic Landform Guides Series, 1983-98; The Book of British Dates, 1991; World History: A Chronological Dictionary of Dates, 1994, rev. ed., 2003; The Cerne Giant, 1996; Knossos, Temple of the Goddess, 1997; Out in the Cold: Ideas on Glaciation, 1998; Atlantis Destroyed, 1998; The English Lake District, 1998; The Search for King Arthur, 1999; The Little Book of Kings and Queens of Britain, 1999; Ancient British Hill Figures, 2000; Winfrith: A Music Drama, 2000, rev. ed., 2001; The History of World Events, 2003; Britain 3000 BC, 2003; Infamous Murderers, 2004; Serial Killers, 2004; The World's Most Evil People, 2005; Mycenaeans, 2005; People who Changed the World, 2005; Events that Changed the World, 2005; English Castles, 2006; Castles of the Celtic Lands, 2006; The Book of Saints, 2006; The Attack on Troy, 2006; Assassinations and Conspiracies, 2006; Natural Disasters that Changed the World, 2007; Inventions that Changed the World, 2007; Conflicts that Changed the World, 2008; Encounters that Changed the World, 2009; Spree Killers: The Enigma of Mass Murder, 2011. Contributor to journals and periodicals. **Address:** 15 Knepp Close, Bevendean, Brighton, ES BN2 4LD, England. **Online address:** rodney@castleden.fsnet.co.uk

CASTO, William R. American (born United States), b. 1946. **Genres:** Law. **Career:** University of Alabama, distinguished visiting professor; University of Connecticut, distinguished visiting professor; University of South Carolina, distinguished visiting professor; University of Tennessee, distinguished visiting professor; Texas Tech University, School of Law, Paul Whitfield Horn professor of law. Writer and lawyer. **Publications:** The Supreme Court in the Early Republic: The Chief Justiceships of John Jay and Oliver Ellsworth, 1995; Oliver Ellsworth and the Creation of the Federal Republic, 1997; Foreign Affairs and the Constitution in the Age of Fighting Sail, 2006. **Address:** School of Law, Texas Tech University, 1802 Hartford Ave., Lubbock, TX 79409, U.S.A.

CASTOR, Helen. (Helen R. Castor). British (born England), b. 1968?. **Genres:** Language/Linguistics, History, Politics/Government. **Career:** Cambridge University, Sidney Sussex College, fellow in history, director of studies in history. Writer. **Publications:** The King, the Crown, and the Duchy of Lancaster: Public Authority and Private Power, 1399-1461, 2000; Blood and Roses: The Paston Family in the Fifteenth Century, 2004 in US as Blood and Roses: One Family's Struggle and Triumph during England's Tumultuous Civil War, 2006; She-Wolves: The Women Who Ruled England Before Elizabeth, 2010. **Address:** Sidney Sussex College, Cambridge University, Sidney St., Cambridge, CB2 3HU, England. **Online address:** hrc12@cam.ac.uk

CASTOR, Helen R. *See* **CASTOR, Helen.**

CASTRO, Brian (Albert). Australian (born Australia), b. 1950. **Genres:** Novels, Essays, Literary Criticism And History. **Career:** Mt. Druitt High School, teacher, 1972-76; Lycee Technique, assistant in languages, 1976-77; St. Joseph's College, French master, 1978-79; Asiaweek magazine, literary journalist, 1983-87; Mitchell College, writer-in-residence, 1985; Nepean College, visiting fellow, 1988; All-Asia Review of Books, literary journalist, 1989-; University of Western Sydney, tutor in literary studies, 1989-90; University of Hong Kong, writer-in-residence, 1994; Cite des Arts, writer-in-residence, 2000; The University of Melbourne, Macgeorge fellow, 2006, professorial research fellow (creative writing), 2007-08; University of Adelaide, chair creative writing, J.M. Coetzee centre for Creative Practice, co-director. Writer. **Publications:** NOVELS: Birds of Passage, 1982; Pomeroy, 1991; Double-Wolf, 1991; After China, 1992; Drift, 1994; Writing Asia: Two Lectures, 1995; Stepper, 1997; Shanghai Dancing, 2003; The Garden Book, 2005. OTHER: Looking for Estrellita (essays), 1999; The Bath Fuges, 2009. **Address:** University of Adelaide, Napier Bldg., Rm. 6 05, North Terrace Campus, Adelaide, SA 5005, Australia. **Online address:** brian.castro@adelaide.edu.au

CASTRO, Daniel. American (born United States), b. 1945. **Genres:** Social Sciences. **Career:** Loyola University, Spanish instructor, 1988-89; Tulane University, Latin American studies instructor, 1989-92, adjunct professor of Latin American history, 1993-94, program director of summer program in Mexico, 1990; Hartwick College, assistant professor of history and coordinator of Latin American and Caribbean studies program, 1994-96; Southwestern University, Department of History, assistant professor, 1996-2001, associate professor, 2002-06, chair, 2003-06, professor, 2006-, chair of Latin studies program, 2007-; Loyola University, Institute of Politics, affiliate. Writer and historian. **Publications:** (Ed.) Revolution and Revolutionaries: Guerrilla Movements in Latin America, 1999; Another Face of Empire: Bartolomé de Las Casas, Indigenous Rights, and Ecclesiastical Imperialism, 2007. Contributor to books and journals. **Address:** Southwestern University, 1001 E University Ave, Georgetown, TX 78626, U.S.A. **Online address:** castrod@southwestern.edu

CASTRO, Efren D. American (born United States), b. 1947. **Genres:** Young Adult Fiction, Romance/Historical, Literary Criticism And History. **Career:** University of Texas of the Permian Basin, PASS Office (assistance programs), director, 1993-. Writer. **Publications:** Lost in West Texas (adult fiction), 2006; El Midnighter (adult fiction), 2007; Malosa: A Graduate School Romance, 2008. Contributor to books. **Address:** University of Texas of the Permian Basin, 1160 Mesa Bldg., 4901 E University, Odessa, TX 79762, U.S.A. **Online address:** castro_e@utpb.edu

CASTRO, Michael. American (born United States), b. 1945. **Genres:** Poetry, Literary Criticism And History, Translations. **Career:** KDNA-Radio, coordinator, 1963-73; River Styx, co-founder; University of Missouri, instructor in English, 1971; Lindenwood University, Southwestern Illinois College, professor of communications, director of communications programs, 1980-, faculty advisor in the LCIE; College of Individualized Education, faculty administrator. Writer. **Publications:** The Kokopilau Cycle (poem), 1975; Ghost Hiways & Other Homes (poems), 1976; Cracks, 1977; Interpreting the Indian: Twentieth-Century Poets and the Native American, 1983; The Man Who Looked into Coltrane's Horn, 1997; Human Rites, 2002; (ed. and trans. with G.G. Gyukics) Swimming in the Ground: Contemporary Hungarian Poetry, 2003. **Address:** Lindenwood University, LUCC 309, 209 S Kings Hwy., St. Charles, MO 63301, U.S.A. **Online address:** mcastro@lindenwood.edu

CASTRONOVA, Edward. *See* **BIRD, Edward J.**

CASWAY, Jerrold. (Jerrold I. Casway). American (born United States) **Genres:** History, Biography, Young Adult Non-fiction, Sports/Fitness. **Ca-**

reer: Howard Community College, professor of history, 1971-, division chair, Rouse Scholars Program, director. Writer. **Publications:** NONFICTION: Owen Roe O'Neill and the Struggle for Catholic Ireland, 1984; Ed Delahanty in the Emerald Age of Baseball, 2004. Contributor to periodicals. **Address:** Social Sciences/Teacher Education Division, Howard Community College, ST 149, 10901 Little Patuxent Pkwy., Columbia, MD 21044-3197, U.S.A. **Online address:** jcasway@howardcc.edu

CASWAY, Jerrold I. *See* **CASWAY, Jerrold.**

CASWELL, Brian. Australian/Welsh (born Wales), b. 1954. **Genres:** Children's Fiction, Young Adult Fiction, Novels, Science Fiction/Fantasy, Young Adult Fiction. **Career:** New South Wales Department of Education, high school teacher of English and history, 1976-91. University of Western Sydney, writer-in-residence. **Publications:** FOR YOUNG ADULTS: Merryll of the Stones, 1989; A Dream of Stars, 1991; A Cage of Butterflies, 1992; Dreamslip, 1994; Deucalion, 1995; Asturias, 1996; (with D. Phu An Chiem) Only the Heart, 1997; The View from Ararat, 1999; (with D. Chiem) The Full Story, 2002. BOUNDARY PARK TRILOGY: Mike, 1993; Lisdalia, 1994; Maddie, 1995. ALIEN ZONES SERIES: Tee Dee and the Collectors or How it all Began, 1998; Messengers of the Great Orff, 1998; Gladiators in the Holo-Colosseum, 1998; Gargantua, 1998; What Were the Gremnholzs' Dimensions Again?, 1998; Whispers from the Shibboleth, 1998. OTHERS: (contrib.) The Written World: Youth and Literature, 1994; Relax Max!, 1997; Double Exposure, 2005; Loop, 2006. Contributor to periodicals. **Address:** Rick Raftos Management, PO Box 445, Paddington, NW 2021, Australia. **Online address:** brian@alienzones.com

CATALANO, Nick. American (born United States), b. 1939. **Genres:** Biography, Music. **Career:** Pace University, professor of music and literature, 1976-, director of performing arts. Writer. **Publications:** Clifford Brown: The Life and Art of the Legendary Jazz Trumpeter, 2000; New York Nights, 2008; A New Yorker at Sea, 2012. Contributor of articles to journals. **Address:** Department of Performing Arts, Dyson College of Arts and Sciences, Pace University, 78 N Broadway, Pleasantville, NY 10570-1702, U.S.A. **Online address:** ncatalano@pace.edu

CATALANOTTO, Peter. American (born United States), b. 1959. **Genres:** Children's Fiction, Children's Non-fiction, Cartoons. **Career:** Freelance illustrator, 1982-87; Freelance writer and illustrator of children's books, 1987-. **Publications:** WROTE and ILLUSTRATED: Dylan's Day Out, 1989; Mr. Mumble, 1990; Christmas Always-, 1991; The Painter, 1995; Dad and Me, 1999; Emily's Art, 2001; Matthew A.B.C., 2002; Daisy 1,2,3, 2003; Kitten Red, Yellow, Blue, 2005; (with P. Schembri) The Secret Lunch Special, 2006; (with P. Schembri) No More Pumpkins, 2007; Ivan the Terrier, 2007; (with P. Schembri) The Veteran's Day Visitor, 2008; Question Boy Meets Little Miss Know-it-All, 2012. Illustrator of books by others. **Address:** Simonand Schuster, 1230 Ave. of the Americas, New York, NY 10020, U.S.A. **Online address:** leftcat3@aol.com

CATANOSO, Justin. American (born United States), b. 1959. **Genres:** Biography, Autobiography/Memoirs. **Career:** Centre Daily Times, staff, 1982; Knoxville Journal, Knoxville, reporter; News & Record, reporter; Wake Forest University, lecturer, 1993-, senior lecturer, program director of journalism; Business Journal, founding executive editor, 1998. **Publications:** My Cousin the Saint: A Search for Faith, Family and Miracles, 2008. Contributor to periodicals. **Address:** Department of English, Wake Forest University, C106 Tribble Hall, PO Box 7387, Winston-Salem, NC 27109, U.S.A. **Online address:** catanojj@wfu.edu

CATHCART, Brian. British/Irish (born Ireland), b. 1956. **Genres:** Young Adult Fiction, Criminology/True Crime, Biography. **Career:** Reuters News Agency, foreign correspondent, 1978-86; The Independent, foreign staff and assistant foreign editor, 1986-90; The Independent on Sunday, foreign editor, 1990-94, deputy editor, 1995-2003; Kingston University, senior lecturer in journalism, 2003-06, professor in journalism, 2006-; freelance journalist, 2003-; New Statesman, assistant editor, contributing editor and media columnist, 2005-. **Publications:** Test of Greatness: Britain's Struggle for the Atom Bomb, 1994; Were You Still Up for Portillo?, 1997; The Case of Stephen Lawrence, 1999; Jill Dando: Her Life and Death, 2001; Rain, 2002; The The Fly in the Cathedral: How a Group of Cambridge Scientists Won the International Race to Split the Atom, 2005. Contributor to newspapers and magazines. **Address:** Kingston University, Rm. 2, River House, Kingston upon Thames, SR KT1 1LQ, England. **Online address:** b.cathcart@kingston.ac.uk

CATHCART, Jim. American (born United States), b. 1946. **Genres:** Business/Trade/Industry, Economics, Self Help, Psychology, Marketing. **Career:** Professional Speaking Institute, chief operating officer and co-founder; personal development speaker, 1977-; Cathcart Institute Inc., founder and president, 1977-. Writer. **Publications:** Communication Dynamics, 1976; Executive Stress: How to Avoid Falling Face Down on the Bottom Line, 1983; (with A.J. Alessandra) The Business of Selling, 1984; Winning with People through Service and Customer Relationships, 1986; (with T. Alessandra and P. Wexler) Selling by Objectives, 1988; (with A.J. Alessandra and J. Monoky) Be Your Own Sales Manager: Strategies and Tactics for Managing Your Accounts, Your Territory, and Yourself, 1990; Relationship Selling: The Key to Getting and Keeping Customers, 1990; (with A.J. Alessandra and G. Baron) The Sales Professional's Idea-a-Day Guide: Two Hundred Fifty Ways to Increase Your Top and Bottom Lines-Every Selling Day of the Year, 1997; The Acorn Principle: Know Yourself-Grow Yourself: Discover, Explore, and Grow the Seeds of Your Greatest Potential, 1998; (with A.J. Alessandra) The Business of Selling: How to Be Your Own Sales Manager, 1998; Eight Competencies of Relationship Selling: How to Reach the Top 1 Percent in Just 15 Extra Minutes a Day, 2002; (with D. Ryback and D. Nour) ConnectAbility: 8 Keys to Building Strong Partnerships with your Colleagues and Your Customers, 2010. **Address:** Cathcart Institute Inc., 5927 Balfour Ct., Ste. 103, Carlsbad, CA 92008, U.S.A. **Online address:** jim@cathcart.com

CATHERWOOD, Christopher. British (born England), b. 1955. **Genres:** Theology/Religion, History. **Career:** University of Cambridge, Institute of Economic and Political Studies, tutor, Institute of Continuing Education, faculty; University of Richmond, School of Continuing Studies, instructor, writer-in-residence; Institute of Economic and Political Studies (INSTEP), instructor; University of Virginia, Rockefeller Fellow, 2001; Fulton College, Crosby Kemper memorial lecturer, 2008; Churchill College, SCR Associate, 2008-, Archives Bye fellow, 2008; Westminster College, Churchill Memorial and Library, Crosby Kemper Memorial lecturer, 2008; Virginia Military Institute, George C. Marshall Center, George C. Marshall lecturer, 2009. Writer and consultant. **Publications:** Joy Unspeakable: Power & Renewal in the Holy Spirit, 1985; (ed.) Prove All Things: The Sovereign Work of the Holy Spirit, 1985; (ed.) The Sovereign Spirit: Discerning His Gifts, 1985; Five Evangelical Leaders, 1985; (ed.) I Am Not Ashamed: Advice to Timothy, 1986; (ed.) Saved in Eternity: The Assurance of Our Salvation, 1988; (ed.) Safe in the World: The Assurance of Our Salvation, 1988; (ed.) Growing in the Spirit: The Assurance of Our Salvation, 1989; (ed.) Sanctified through the Truth: The Assurance of Our Salvation, 1989; (ed.) The Heart of the Gospel, 1991; The Kingdom of God, 1992; (ed.) Enjoying the Presence of God, 1992; Martyn Lloyd-Jones: A Family Portrait, 1995; Why the Nations Rage, 1997, rev. ed. as Why the Nations Rage: Killing in the Name of God, 1997; Crash Course on Church History, 1998, rev. ed., 2007; From Wales to Westminster: The Story of Dr. Martyn Lloyd-Jones, 1999; Whose Side is God On? Nationalism and Christianity, 2003; Christians, Muslims, and Islamic Rage: What is Going on and Why It Happened, 2003; The Balkans in World War Two: Britain's Balkan Dilemma, 2003; Churchill's Folly: How Winston Churchill Created Modern Iraq, 2004; Seeking the Face of God: Nine Reflections on the Psalms, 2005; (with L.A. Horvitz) Encyclopedia of War Crimes and Genocide, 2006, rev. ed., 2011; A Brief History of the Middle East, 2006; Making War in the Name of God, 2007; A God Divided: Understanding the Differences between Islam, Christianity, and Judaism, 2007; (with J. DiVanna) Merchants of Fear, 2008; Winston Churchill, 2009; Evangelicals, 2010; His Finest Hours, 2010. **Address:** INSTEP Cambridge, Warkworth House, Warkworth Terr., Cambridge, CB CB1 1EE, England.

CATHERWOOD, (Henry) Frederick (Ross). British/Irish (born Ireland), b. 1925. **Genres:** Social Commentary, Theology/Religion, Economics. **Career:** Law Stores Ltd., secretary, 1952-54; Richard Costain Ltd., secretary and controller, 1954-55, chief executive, 1955-60; British Aluminum Co., assistant managing director, 1960-62, managing director, 1962-64; Department of Economic Affairs, chief industrial adviser, 1964-66; National Economic Development Council, director general, 1966-71; John Laing & Sons Ltd., managing director and chief executive, 1971-74, director, 1975-; British Institute of Management, fellow, vice-chairman, 1972-74, chairman, 1974-76; vice-president, 1976-; Wittenborg Automat Ltd., chairman; Royal Institute of Chartered Accountants, fellow; Machine Tool Industry Research Association, president, 1977-; Association of Colleges of Further Education, presdient, 1979. Goodyear Great Britain Ltd., director, 1975-86; British Overseas Trade Board, chairman, 1975-79; Goodyear Tyre & Rubber Company Ltd., director, 1975-; Mallinson-Denny Ltd., chairman, 1976-79; European Parliament, vice president, 1989-92; Evangelical Alliance, president, 1992-. Writer. **Publications:** The Christian in Industrial Society, 1966, 3rd ed., 1980 in US as Nine to Five, 1983; Britain with the Brakes Off, 1966; The High Risks of Low Growth, 1968; The Christian Citizen, 1969; The Christian College, 1969; Christian Duty in Ulster Today, 1970; Government Industry Dialogue: An Aspect of Economic Strategy, 1972; Making Knowledge Useful, 1975; A Better Way, 1975; The Difference Between a Reformer and a Progressive, 1977; First Things First, 1979; (with E. Catherwood) Martyn Lloyd-Jones: The Man and His Books, 1982; On the Job, 1983; God's Time, God's Money, 1987; Pro Europe?, 1991; David: Poet, Warrior, King, 1993; At the Cutting Edge, 1995; Jobs and Justice, 1997; It Can Be Done: The Real Heroes of the Inner City, 2000; The Creation of Wealth, 2002. **Address:** Sutton Hall, Balsham, Balsham, CB1 6DX, England.

CATO, Heather. New Zealander (born New Zealand) **Genres:** Young Adult Fiction, Novels, Animals/Pets, Children's Fiction, Literary Criticism And History. **Career:** Writer. **Publications:** Dark Horses (novel), 1997; In Full Cry, forthcoming. Contributor to periodicals. **Address:** 5 Arney Cres., Remuera, Auckland, 5, New Zealand.

CATROW, David J. American (born United States) **Genres:** Children's Fiction, Illustrations. **Career:** Springfield News-Sun, editorial cartoonist, 1984-, now retired; Copley News Service, syndicated cartoonist, 1988-. Writer and illustrator. **Publications:** (Foreword) We the Kids: The Preamble to the Constitution of the United States, 2002; (with K. Ireland) Don't Take Your Snake for a Stroll, 2003; (with A. Katz) Where did They Hide My Presents?: Silly Dilly Christmas Songs, 2005; (with A. Katz) Are You Quite Polite?: Silly Dilly Manners Songs, 2006; Dinosaur Hunt, 2009; Max Spaniel: Funny Lunch, 2010; Max Spaniel: Best in Show, 2011; Fly Flew In, 2012; Monster Mash, 2012. Illustrator of books by others. **Address:** Holiday House, 425 Madison Ave., New York, NY 10017, U.S.A. **Online address:** dcatrow@coxohio.com

CATT, Louis. *See* **FRENCH, Vivian.**

CATTERALL, Lee. American (born United States), b. 1944. **Genres:** Art/Art History. **Career:** Omaha World-Herald, general assignment reporter, 1969-70; Montgomery County Sentinel, general assignment reporter, 1971-; Service Employees International Union, writer, 1971-72; Mountain States News Service, owner and writer, 1973-77; Associated Press, news writer, 1977-80; Honolulu Star-Bulletin, legal affairs reporter, 1980-; KTWO Radio, stringer; Harriscope Broadcasting Corp., stringer. **Publications:** The Great Dali Art Fraud and Other Deceptions, 1992. Contributor to periodicals. **Address:** Honolulu Star-Bulletin, 500 Ala Moana Blvd., Ste. 7-210, Honolulu, HI 96813, U.S.A. **Online address:** hicatt@pixi.com

CATTERALL, Peter. British (born England), b. 1961. **Genres:** History, Bibliography, Young Adult Non-fiction. **Career:** University of London, Queen Mary College, School of History, visiting lecturer in modern British history, 1987-, lecturer in history, London School of Economics and Political Science, British Political Archives Project, consultant, Institute of Contemporary British History, research fellow, 1988-89, director, 1989-2000; Westfield College, visiting lecturer in modern British history, 1987-; Westminster College, Fulbright Robertson professor of British history, 1999-2000; Institute of Historical Research, senior research fellow, 2000-; Modern History Review, editor; Contemporary Record, co-editor. **Publications:** British History, 1945-1987: An Annotated Bibliography, 1991; (ed.) Contemporary Britain: An Annual Review 1991, 1991; (ed. with C.J. Morris) Britain and the Threat to Stability in Europe, 1918-45, 1993; History of Electrex 1950-1993, 1993; (ed. with J. Obelkevich) Understanding Post-War British Society, 1994; (ed. with S. McDougall) The Northern Ireland Question in British Politics, 1996; (ed.) The Making of Channel 4, 1999; (ed. with C. Seymour-Ure and A. Smith) Northcliffe's Legacy: Aspects of the British Popular Press, 1896-1996, 2000; (ed. with W. Kaiser and U. Walton-Jordan) Reforming the Constitution: Debates in Twentieth-Century Britain, 2000; (ed. and intro.) The Macmillan Diaries: The Cabinet Years, 1950-1957, 2003. Contributor to journals and periodicals. **Address:** Department of History, Queen Mary College, University of London, 4.11 Arts Two Bldg., Mile End Rd., London, GL E1 4NS, England. **Online address:** p.p.catterall@qmul.ac.uk

CAUDILL, (Charles) Edward. American (born United States), b. 1953. **Genres:** Writing/Journalism. **Career:** Columbus Citizen-Journal, copy editor, 1977-83; Franklin Chronicle, reporter and photographer, 1975-77; Dayton Daily News, stringer, 1975; Columbus Citizen Journal, editor, 1977-83; University of North Carolina, writing course faculty, 1983-84; University of Tennessee, professor of journalism, 1985-, Graduate Studies and Research, associate dean, 1999-2005, NACEL Exchange Program, Program director, 1993, 1994, 1995, UT Graduate Deans Group, chair, 2001-04. **Publications:** Darwinism in the Press: The Evolution of an Idea, 1989; Darwinian Myths: The Legends and Misuses of a Theory, 1997; (intro.) Scopes Trial: A Photographic History, 2000; (with P. Ashdown) Mosby Myth: A Confederate Hero in Life and Legend, 2002; (with P. Ashdown) Myth of Nathan Bedford Forrest, 2005; (with P. Ashdown) Sherman's March in Myth and Memory, 2008; (co-author) Voices of a Nation: A History of Mass Media in the United States, 2009. Contributor to books and periodicals. **Address:** School of Journalism & Electronic Media, University of Tennessee, 431 Communications Bldg., Knoxville, TN 37996-0347, U.S.A. **Online address:** ccaudill@utk.edu

CAUFIELD, Catherine. American (born United States) **Genres:** Environmental Sciences/Ecology, Economics, Adult Non-fiction, Business/Trade/Industry. **Career:** The New Yorker, reporter, reporter-at-large. **Publications:** NONFICTION: The Emperor of the United States of America and Other Magnificent British Eccentrics, 1981; Tropical Moist Forests: The Resource, The People, The Threat, 1982; (with V.P. Zambrano) Bosquestropicales húmedos: La situación Mundial y la Amazonia Peruana, 1985; In the Rainforest, 1985; Multiple Exposures: Chronicles of the Radiation Age, 1989; Masters of Illusion: The World Bank and the Poverty of Nations, 1996. Contributor to periodicals. **Address:** Henry Holt & Company Inc., 175 5th Ave., New York, NY 10010, U.S.A.

CAUGHFIELD, Adrienne. American (born United States), b. 1971. **Genres:** Women's Studies And Issues, Adult Non-fiction, History. **Career:** Heritage Farmstead Museum, director of academic programs, 2004-08. Writer. **Publications:** True Women and Westward Expansion, 2005. Contributor to journals. **Address:** Texas A&M University Press, Lewis St., College Station, TX 77843-0001, U.S.A. **Online address:** ahcaughfield@yahoo.com

CAUGHIE, Pamela L. American (born United States), b. 1953?. **Genres:** Social Sciences, Literary Criticism And History, History. **Career:** Blue Ridge Community College, learning lab instructor in English and mathematics, 1977-78; James Madison University, instructor, 1978-80; University of Virginia, graduate instructor, 1981-85; Mary Baldwin College, instructor, 1986-87; Loyola University Chicago, Department of English, faculty, 1987-, professor, 1999-, graduate program director; Modernist Studies Association, president, 2010-. Writer. **Publications:** Virginia Woolf and Postmodernism: Literature in Quest and Question of Itself, 1991; Passing and Pedagogy: The Dynamics of Responsibility, 1999; (ed.) Virginia Woolf in the Age of Mechanical Reproduction, 2000; (ed.) Disciplining Modernism, 2009; Class Acts, forthcoming. **Address:** Department of English, Loyola University Chicago, 1032 W Sheridan Rd., Chicago, IL 60660, U.S.A. **Online address:** pcaughi@luc.edu

CAULFIELD, Carlota. American (born United States), b. 1953. **Genres:** Poetry, Literary Criticism And History. **Career:** Cuban Ministry of Culture, book editor and researcher, 1975-80; Ediciones el gato tuerto, editor and publisher, 1984; El gato tuerto (literary journal), founding editor, 1984-90; San Francisco State University, teaching assistant, 1984-85, lecturer, 1985-87; Tulane University, teaching assistant, 1988-92; Mills College, Department of Hispanic Studies, assistant professor, 1992-98, associate professor, 1998-2006, professor of Spanish and Spanish American Studies, 2005-, Graduate Liberal Studies Program, co-director, 1998-99, director, 2000, Spanish and Spanish American Studies Program, chair, 2009-; Corner (on-line journal), founding editor, 1998-2002. **Publications:** POETRY: Palabra Solar, 1982; (trans. with C. Allen) Fanaim, 1984; Oscuridad divina, 1985; (trans. with C. Allen) Sometimes I Call Myself Childhood, 1985; El tiempo es una mujer que espera, 1986; 34th Street and Other Poems, 1987; Oscuridad divina, 1987; Angel Dust, 1990; Visual Games for Words and Sounds (hyperpoems), 1993; Libro de los XXXIX escalones, 39 vols., 1995; Estrofas de papel, barro y tinta (plaquette), 1995; Book of the XXXIX Steps (hyperbook), 1995; A las puertas del papel con amoroso fuego, 1996, trans. as At the Gates of the Paper with Burning Desire, 2001; Autorretrato en ojo ajeno, 2001; The Book of Giulio Camillo, 2003; Movimientos metlicos para juguetes abandonados, 2003; Quincunce/Quincunx, 2004; Ticket to Ride (essays and poems), 2005; A Mapmaker's Diary: Selected Poems, 2007. EDITOR: Rosa Luxemburgo, 1977; Los socialistas anteriores a Marx, 3 vols., 1978; Pablo Lafargue, 1979; (with M. Zapata) Literary and Cultural Journeys: Selected Letters to Arturo

Torres-Rioseco, 1995; Web of Memories: Interviews with 5 Cuban Poets, 1997; Voces viajeras, 2002; From the Forbidden Garden: Letters from Alejandra Pizarnik to Antonio Beneyto, 2003; (with J. Parra) The Other Poetry of Barcelona: Spanish and Spanish-American Women Poets, 2004; (with D. Davies) A Companion to U.S. Latino Literatures, 2007; No soy tu musa. Antologfa de poetas irlandesas contemporneas, 2008. Contributor to periodicals. **Address:** Mills College, 5000 MacArthur Blvd., Oakland, CA 94613, U.S.A. **Online address:** amach@mills.edu

CAUSEY, Toni McGee. *See* **MCGEE, Toni.**

CAUTE, (John) David. (John Salisbury). British/Egyptian (born Egypt), b. 1936. **Genres:** Novels, Plays/Screenplays, History, Politics/Government, Literary Criticism And History. **Career:** Oxford University, All Souls College, fellow, 1959-65; Harvard University, Henry fellow, 1960-61; New York University, visiting professor, 1966-67; Columbia University, visiting professor, 1966-67; Brunel University, reader in social and political theory, 1967-70; University of California, regents lecturer, 1974; New Statesman, literary and arts editor, 1979-80; Writers Guild of Great Britain, deputy chair, 1979-80, co-chair, 1981-82; University of Bristol, visiting professor, 1985. **Publications:** Communism and the French Intellectuals 1914-1960, 1964; The Left in Europe since 1789, 1966; Linke in Europa, 1966; (ed. and intro.) Essential Writings of Karl Marx, 1967; The Demonstration (play), 1970; Fanon, 1970; Frantz Fanon, 1970; The Illusion, 1971; The Fellow-Travellers, 1973; Collisions: Essays and Review, 1974; Cuba, Yes?, 1974; The Great Fear: The Anti-Communist Campaign under Truman and Eisenhower, 1978; Under the Skin: The Death of White Rhodesia, 1983; The Espionage of the Saints, 1986; Sixty-Eight: The Year of the Barricades, 1988; Joseph Losey: A Revenge on Life, 1994; The Dancer Defects: The Struggle for Cultural Supremacy during the Cold War, 2003; Politics and the Novel during the Cold War, 2010. NOVELS: At Fever Pitch (novel), 1959; Comrade Jacob, 1961; The Decline of the West, 1966; The Occupation, 1971; The K Factor, 1983; News from Nowhere, 1986; Veronica or the Two Nations, 1989; The Woman's Hour, 1991; Dr. Orwell and Mr. Blair, 1994; Fatima's Scarf, 1998. AS JOHN SALISBURY: The Baby Sitters, 1978; Moscow Gold, 1980. Contributor to periodicals. **Address:** 41 Westcroft Sq., London, GL W6 0TA, England.

CAUTHEN, (W.) Kenneth. American (born United States), b. 1930. **Genres:** Theology/Religion. **Career:** First Baptist Church of Locust Grove, pastor, 1953-55; Mercer University, assistant professor, 1957-60, associate professor of Christian ethics, 1960-61; Crozer Theological Seminary, associate professor, 1961-63, professor of theology, 1963-70; Colgate-Rochester/Crozer Theological Seminary, professor of Christian theology, 1961-70, John Price Crozer Griffith professor of theology, 1970-92, John Price Crozer Griffith professor of theology emeritus, 1992-. Writer. **Publications:** The Impact of American Religious Liberalism, 1962; The Triumph of Suffering Love, 1966; Science, Secularization and God, 1969; (ed. and contrib.) Shailer Mathews: Jesus on Social Institutions, 1971; Christian Biopolitics, 1971; The Ethics of Enjoyment, 1975; Process Ethics, 1984; Systematic Theology, 1986; The Passion for Equality, 1987; Theological Biology, 1991; Toward a New Modernism, 1997; The Many Faces of Evil, 1997; Evil Has Many Faces, 1997; The Ethics of Assisted Death, 1999; The Ethics of Belief, 2001; Rejoicing in Life's Melissa Moments, 2003; I Don't Care What the Bible Says, 2003; Born into the Wrong World, 2004. **Address:** 46 Azalea Rd., Rochester, NY 14620, U.S.A. **Online address:** kenc@frontiernet.net

CAVALLARO, Michael J. American (born United States), b. 1975?. **Genres:** Novels, Science Fiction/Fantasy, Business/Trade/Industry. **Career:** HarperCollins Publishers, editor, 2000-03; freelance writer, 2003-; Polis, editor. **Publications:** Cybernetica, 2006; How to Open & Operate a Financially Successful Private Investigation Business: With Companion CD-ROM, 2010; How to get Your Amazing Invention on Store Shelves, 2011. **Address:** 27 W 20th St., Ste. 1102, New York, NY 10011-3723, U.S.A. **Online address:** author@cybernetica-book.com

CAVANAGH, Thomas B. American (born United States) **Genres:** Novels, Mystery/Crime/Suspense, Young Adult Fiction. **Career:** Embry-Riddle Aeronautical University, Online Course Design and Production, director; Valencia Community College, screen writer; Full Sail University, Full Sail Media School, teacher; University of Central Florida, Center for Distributed Learning, assistant vice president. Writer. **Publications:** NOVEL: Murderland, 2005. MIKE GARRITY MYSTERY SERIES: Head Games, 2007; Prodigal Son, 2008. Contributor of articles to magazines. **Address:** Daniel Lazar, Writers House, 21 W 26th St., New York, NY 10010-1003, U.S.A. **Online address:** tbcavana@bellsouth.net

CAVAZOS-GAITHER, Alma E(lisa). American (born United States), b. 1955. **Genres:** Sciences, Reference, History. **Career:** CARMA, president; freelance writer, 1995-. **Publications:** WITH C.C. GAITHER: Statistically Speaking: A Dictionary of Quotations, 1996; Physically Speaking: A Dictionary of Quotations, 1997; Mathematically Speaking: A Dictionary of Quotations, 1998; Practically Speaking: A Dictionary of Quotations, 1998; Medically Speaking: A Dictionary of Quotations, 1998; Scientifically Speaking: A Dictionary of Quotations, 2000; Naturally Speaking: A Dictionary of Quotations, 2001; Chemically Speaking: A Dictionary of Quotations, 2002; Astronomically Speaking: A Dictionary of Quotations, 2003; The Gaither's Dictionary of Scientific Quotations, 2007. **Address:** 502 Weiss, Killeen, TX 76542, U.S.A. **Online address:** cgaither6281@earthlink.net

CAVE, Emma. (Caroline Lassalle). British (born England) **Genres:** Novels, Romance/Historical. **Career:** Picador Books, editor, 1972-77. **Publications:** Little Angie, 1977; The Blood Bond, 1979; Cousin Henrietta, 1981; (as Caroline Lassalle) Breaking the Rules, 1987; (as Caroline Lassalle) Going Too Far, 1989; The Inferno Corridor, 1991; Bluebeard's Room, 1995; The Lair, 1997. **Address:** Random House Group Ltd., Random House, 20 Vauxhall Bridge Rd., London, GL SW1V 2SA, England.

CAVE, Eric M. American/Swedish (born Sweden), b. 1965. **Genres:** Philosophy, Humanities. **Career:** Union College, visiting assistant professor of humanities, 1994-95; Arkansas State University, Department of English and Philosophy, assistant professor, 1995-2000, associate professor, 2000-. Writer. **Publications:** Preferring Justice: Rationality, Self-Transformation, and the Sense of Justice, 1998. Contributor to periodicals. **Address:** Department of English and Philosophy, Arkansas State University, 205A Wilson Hall, PO Box 1890, State University, AR 72467, U.S.A. **Online address:** ecave@astate.edu

CAVE, Kathryn. British (born England), b. 1948. **Genres:** Young Adult Fiction, Novels, Picture/Board Books, Young Adult Non-fiction. **Career:** Penguin Publishing, editor, 1970-71; Blackwell (publishers), editor, 1971-72; Metier (publishers), technical editor, 1987-88; Frances Lincoln Ltd., editorial director for children's nonfiction, 1990-92. **Publications:** (Ed. with A. Macintyre) Diary of Joseph Farington, 1978; Dragonrise, 1984; Many Happy Returns, 1987; Just My Luck! and Other Stories, 1987; Poor Little Mary, 1988; (with T. McKenna) Just in Time, 1989; Henry Hobbs, Alien, 1990; Jumble, 1990; William and the Wolves, 1991; Out for the Count, 1991; Running Battles, 1992; Best Friends for Ever, 1994; Andrew Takes the Plunge, 1994; My Journey Through Art: Create Your Own Masterpiece, 1994; The Emperor's Gruckle Hound, 1996; Similon: The Chronicles of Theromantia, 1996; Horatio Happened, 1998; Something Else, 1998; W is For World, 1998; The Boy Who Became an Eagle, 2000; Septimus Similon, Practising Wizard, 2000; Henry's Song, 2000; Henry Hobbs, Space Voyager, 2001; Henry Hobbs and the Lost Planet, 2002; The Brave Little Grork, 2002; You've Got Dragons, 2003; One Child, One Seed: A South African Counting Book, 2003; That's What Friends Do, 2004; Friends, 2005. Contributor to periodicals. **Address:** c/o Gina Pollinger, 222 Old Brompton Rd., London, GL SW5 OBZ, England.

CAVE, Peter. British (born England), b. 1965. **Genres:** Education. **Career:** University of Manchester, School of Languages, Linguistics and Cultures, lecturer in Japanese studies. Writer. **Publications:** Primary School in Japan: Self, Individuality and Learning in Elementary Education, 2007. Contributor to books and journals. **Address:** School of Languages, Linguistics and Cultures, University of Manchester, Oxford Rd., Manchester, GM M13 9PL, England. **Online address:** peter.cave@manchester.ac.uk

CAVELL, Benjamin. American (born United States) **Genres:** Adult Nonfiction, Novellas/Short Stories. **Career:** Writer. **Publications:** Rumble, Young Man, Rumble (short stories), 2003. **Address:** c/o Author Mail, Alfred A. Knopf Inc., International Division, Random House Inc., 1745 Broadway, New York, NY 10019, U.S.A.

CAVELL, Marcia. American (born United States), b. 1931. **Genres:** Psychology, Biography, Adult Non-fiction. **Career:** State University of New York, associate professor of philosophy, 1972-84, Purchase College, associate professor of philosophy, now associate professor emeritus of philosophy; University of California-Berkeley, visiting associate professor of philosophy,

1986-89; New York University, visiting associate professor of philosophy, 1994; Bard College, faculty, 2006-07. Writer. **Publications:** The Psychoanalytic Mind: From Freud to Philosophy, 1993; Becoming a Subject: Reflections in Philosophy and Psychoanalysis, 2006. Contributor to journals. **Address:** Department of Philosophy, Purchase College, 735 Anderson Hill Rd., Purchase, NY 10577-1402, U.S.A. **Online address:** cavell@bard.edu

CAVELL, Richard. Canadian (born Canada), b. 1949?. **Genres:** Geography, Military/Defense/Arms Control. **Career:** University of Padua, faculty, 1979; University of British Columbia, Department of English, assistant professor, 1989, professor, International Canadian Studies Centre, director, chair of curriculum development, Program in Canadian Studies, chair; University of Bologna, visiting professor; University of Urbino, visiting professor; University of Pisa, visiting professor; Canadian Association for Cultural Studies, co-founder. Writer. **Publications:** McLuhan in Space: A Cultural Geography, 2002; (ed.) Love, Hate, and Fear in Canada's Cold War, 2004; (ed. with P. Dickinson) Sexing The Maple: A Canadian Sourcebook, 2006. Contributor to periodicals. **Address:** Department of English, University of British Columbia, 397-1873 E Mall, Vancouver, BC V6T 1Z1, Canada. **Online address:** r.cavell@ubc.ca

CAVENDER, Chris. *See* **MYERS, Tim.**

CAVENEY, Graham. British (born England) **Genres:** Literary Criticism And History, Biography, History. **Career:** University of East Anglia, lecturer in American literature. Writer. **Publications:** NONFICTION: (with E. Young) Shopping in Space: Essays on America's Blank Generation Fiction, 1994; The Priest, They Called Him: The Life and Legacy of William S. Burroughs, 1997 in US as Gentleman Junkie: The Life and Legacy of William S. Burroughs, 1998; Screaming with Joy: The Life of Allen Ginsberg, 1999. **Address:** Department of American Literature, University of East Anglia, Earlham Rd., Norwich, NF NR4 7TJ, England.

CAVES, Richard Earl. American (born United States), b. 1931. **Genres:** Economics. **Career:** Harvard University, teaching fellow, 1955-57, assistant professor, 1957-59, associate professor, 1959-62, professor of economics, 1962-, department chairman, 1966-69, 1984-97, George Gund professor of economics and business administration, 1986-97, Ropes professor, 1997-2003, Nathaniel Ropes research professor of political economy, 2003-; University of California, assistant professor, associate professor, 1957-62; Council of Economic Advisers, U.S. Treasury Department, consultant, 1960-61; Review of Economics and Statistics, editor, 1992-96. Writer. **Publications:** (With R.H. Holton) The Canadian Economy, 1959; Trade and Economic Structure, 1960; Air Transport and Its Regulators, 1962; American Industry, 1964, 7th ed., 1992; (with J.S. Bain and J. Margolis) Northern California's Water Industry, 1966; (with G.L. Reuber) Canadian Economic Policy and the Impact of International Capital Flows, 1969; (co-author) Capital Transfers and Economic Policy, 1971; (with R.W. Jones) World Trade and Payments, 1973, 10th ed., 2007; International Trade, International Investment and Imperfect Markets, 1974; Diversification, Foreign Investment and Scale in North American Manufacturing Industries, 1975; Political Economy of Tariff Structures, 1975; (with M. Uekusa) Industrial Organization in Japan, 1976; (co-author) Studies in Canadian Industrial Organization, 1977; (with M.E. Porter and A.M. Spence) Competition in the Open Economy, 1980; (with T.A. Pugel) Intraindustry Differences in Conduct and Performance: Viable Strategies in U.S. Manufacturing Industries, 1980; Multinational Enterprise and Economic Analysis, 1982, 3rd ed., 2007; (with S.W. Davies) Britain's Productivity Gap, 1987; (with D.R. Barton) Efficiency in U.S. Manufacturing Industries, 1990; Adjustment to International Competition, 1990; Creative Industries: Contracts between Art and Commerce, 2000. EDITOR AND CONTRIBUTOR: (with H.G. Johnson and P.B. Kenen) Trade, Growth and the Balance of Payments, 1965; (with H.G. Johnson) Readings in International Economics, 1967; Britain's Economic Prospects, 1968; (with M.J. Roberts) Regulating the Product, 1975; (with L.B. Krause) Britain's Economic Performance, 1980; (with L.B. Krause) The Australian Economy, 1984; Industrial Efficiency in Six Nations, 1992; Creative Industries, 2000; Switching Channels, 2005. **Address:** Department of Economics, Harvard University, Littauer 311, Cambridge, MA 02138, U.S.A. **Online address:** rcaves@harvard.edu

CAVOUKIAN, Raffi. *See* **RAFFI.**

CAWS, Mary Ann. American (born United States), b. 1933. **Genres:** Art/Art History, Literary Criticism And History, Essays, Translations, Autobiography/Memoirs, Biography, Food And Wine, Film, Film. **Career:** Columbia University, Barnard College, lecturer in French, 1962-63; University of Kansas, visiting assistant professor in French, 1963; City University of New York, Hunter College, lecturer, 1964-65, assistant professor of French, 1966-67, Hunter College and Graduate School and University Center, associate professor, 1970-74, professor of romance languages and comparative literature, 1974-, distinguished professor of French and comparative literature, 1983-, distinguished professor of French, English and comparative literature, 1987-; Sarah Lawrence College, visiting professor in French, 1965-66; Association for Study of Dada and Surrealism, president, 1971-75; Princeton University, visiting professor, 1974, School of Visual Arts, visiting professor, 1994; Henri Peyre Institute for the Humanities, co-director, 1981-2002; Modern Language Association of America, president, 1983; Academy of Literary Studies, president, 1984-85; American Comparative Literature Association, president, 1989-91; Phi Beta Kappa, visiting lecturer; University of Iowa, Dada/Surrealism, co-editor; Le Siecle eclate, director; University of London, Institute of Germanic and Romance Studies, honorary senior fellow; New York Institute for the Humanities, fellow; American Academy of Arts, fellow. **Publications:** Surrealism and the Literary Imagination, 1966; The Poetry of Dada and Surrealism, 1970; Andre Breton, 1971; The Inner Theatre of Recent French Poetry, 1972; The Presence of Rene Char, 1976; (trans.) Poems of Rene Char, 1976; The Surrealist Voice of Robert Desnos, 1977; Rene Char, 1977; La Main de Pierre Reverdy, 1979 L'Oeuvre Filante de Rene Char, 1981; A Metapoetics of the Passage, 1981; The Eye in the Text, 1981; Yves Bonnefoy, 1984; Reading Frames in Modern Fiction, 1985; (trans.) A. Breton, Mad Love, 1988; Edmond Jabes, 1988; The Art of Interference, 1989; Women of Bloomsbury, 1990; (co-trans.) A. Breton, Communicating Vessels, 1990; Robert Motherwell: What Art Holds, 1996; Surrealist Look: An Erotics of Encounter, 1997; (with S.B. Wright) Bloomsbury and France, 2000; Picasso's Weeping Woman, 2000; Dora Maar With and Without Picasso: A Biography, 2000; Virginia Woolf: Illustrated Lives, 2001; Robert Motherwell: With Pen and Brush, 2003; To the Boathouse: A Memoir, 2004; Glorious Eccentrics: Modernist Women Painting and Writing, 2006; Henry James, 2006; (intro. and trans. with P. Terry and N. Kline) Capital of Pain, 2006; Surprised in Translation, 2006; Provencal Cooking: Savoring the Simple Life in France, 2007; (co-author) Wilhelm Freddie, 2009; (contrib.) The Surreal House, 2010. EDITOR: (trans.) Approximate Man and Other Writings of Tristan Tzara, 1974; About French Poetry from Dada to Tel Quel, 1974; (trans.) Selected Poems of Rene Char, 1976; (trans. with P. Terry) Roof Slates and Other Poems of Pierre Reverdy, 1981; Stephane Mallarme: Selected Poetry and Prose, 1981; St. John Perse, Selected Poems, 1982; Selected Poetry and Prose, 1982; Selected Poems, 1982; (with H. Riffaterre) Prose Poem in France: Theory and Practice, 1983; Writing in a Modern Temper, 1984; Reading Frames in Modern Fiction, 1985; Textual Analysis: Some Readers Reading, 1986; Perception in Philosophy, Art and Literature, 1989; Reading Proust Now, 1989; Selected Poems of Rene Char, 1991; (with R.E. Kuenzli and G. Raaberg) Surrealism and Women, 1991; City Images, 1991; (intro.) Joseph Cornell, Theater of the Mind; Selected Diaries, Letters and Files, 1993; (chief ed.) HarperCollins World Reader, 1994; Contre-courants: les femmes s'ecrivent a travers les siecles, 1995; Manifesto, 2001; Mallarme in Prose, 2001; Surrealist Painters and Poets, 2001; Vita Sackville-West: Selected Writings, 2002; (with N. Luckhurst) Reception of Virginia Woolf in Europe, 2002; Robert Motherwell with Pen and Brush, 2002; Surrealist Love Poems, 2002; Mallarme in Prose, 2002; Marcel Proust, 2003; Surrealism, 2004; Yale Anthology of Twentieth-Century French Poetry, 2004; Maria Jolas: Woman of Action: A Memoir and other Writings, 2004; (intro.) Essential Poems and Writings of Robert Desnos, 2007; (co-ed.) Picasso and the Allure of Language, 2009. Contributor to periodicals. **Address:** English Ph.D. Program, The Graduate Center, City University of New York, 365 5th Ave., New York, NY 10016, U.S.A. **Online address:** cawsma@aol.com

CAWS, Peter (James). American/British (born England), b. 1931. **Genres:** Education, Philosophy, Sciences, Translations, Humanities, Politics/Government. **Career:** Michigan State University, instructor in natural science, 1956-57; Wilmington College, visiting professor and lecturer, 1956; University of Kansas, assistant professor of philosophy, 1957-60, associate professor, 1960-62, department chair, 1961-62, Rose Morgan Visiting Professor, 1963; University of Costa Rica, visiting professor and lecturer, 1961; Carnegie Corp., executive associate, 1962-65; City University of New York, Hunter College, professor of philosophy, 1965-82, department chair, 1965-67, Graduate Center, executive officer of doctoral program in philosophy, 1967-70, 1981-82; New York University, visiting professor, 1982; George Washington University, university professor of philosophy, 1982-, Ph.D. Program in the Human Sciences, director, 1991-93, professor of human sciences; University of Maryland, visiting professor of comparative literature, 1985. Writer. **Publications:** The Philosophy of Science: A Systematic Account, 1965; (trans.) J.M. Bochenski, The Methods of Contemporary Thought, 1965; Science and the Theory of Value, 1967; (with S.D. Ripley) The Bankruptcy of Academic Policy, 1972; Sartre, 1979; (ed. and intro.) Two Centuries of Philosophy in America, 1980; Structuralism: The Art of the Intelligible, 1988; (ed.) The Causes of Quarrel: Essays on Peace, War, and Thomas Hobbes, 1989; Yorick's World: Science and the Knowing Subject, 1993; The Capital Connection: Business, Science, and Government, 1993; Ethics from Experience, 1996; (ed. with S. Jones) Religious Upbringing and the Costs of Freedom: Personal and Philosophical Essays, 2010; The Astrocats, 2011. CONTRIBUTOR: Measurement: Definition and Theories, 1959; Six Studies in Nineteenth-Century Literature and Thought, 1962; The Little Magazine and Contemporary Literature, 1966; The Concept of Order, 1968; The Arts on Campus, 1970; The Enlightened University, 1970; Philosophy and Political Action, 1972; The History and Philosophy of Technology, 1979. **Address:** Department of Philosophy, Columbian College of Arts & Sciences, George Washington University, Phillips Hall T-525, 801 22nd St. NW, Washington, DC 20052, U.S.A. **Online address:** pcaws@gwu.edu

CAWTHORNE, Nigel. British (born England), b. 1951. **Genres:** Novels, Science Fiction/Fantasy, Children's Fiction, Young Adult Fiction, Sex, Art/Art History, Astronomy, Criminology/True Crime, Ghost Writer, History, Human Relations/Parenting, Intellectual History, Military/Defense/Arms Control, Sciences. **Career:** IPC Business Press, Electrical and Electronic Trader, reporter, 1975-76; Club Intl., writer, 1976-77; Hi-Fi Weekly, writer, 1977; Haymarket Publishing, writer, 1977; New York Tribune, reviewer and features writer, 1977-78; Davis Publications, editorial staff, 1978; Financial Times, World Business Weekly, writer and sub-editor, 1978-79; freelance writer, 1979-. **Publications:** The Loving Touch, 1987; How to Assess Mortgages and Loans, 1988; How to Build an Airliner as Airliners (juvenile), 1988; The Sixties Source Book, 1989; The Bamboo Cage, 1991; Great Record Labels, 1992; The Iron Cage, 1993; Spree Killers, 1993; Sex Killers, 1994; Killers, 1994; The Winning System, 1994; The Universe Explained, 1994; Sex Lives of the Kings and Queens of England, 1994; Satanic Murder, 1995; Sex Lives of the Popes, 1996; The New Look, 1996; Sex Lives of the U.S. Presidents, 1996; The Art of Japanese Prints, 1997; The Art of India, 1997; The Art of Native North America, 1997; A Century of Shoes, 1997; Sex Lives of the Hollywood Idols, 1997; The Secrets of Love: The Erotic Arts Through the Ages, 1997; Sex Lives of the Hollywood Goddesses, 1997, vol. II, 2004; Sex Lives of the Great Artists, 1998; Sex Lives of the Great Composers, 1998; (co-author) Key Moments in Fashion: From Haute Couture to Streetwear, Key Collections, Major Figures and Crucial Moments that Changed the Course of Fashion History from 1890 to the 1990s, 1999; The Art of the Aztecs, 1999; 911 Exposed, 1999; Steps, 1999; Another Level, 1999; Five Take Five, 1999; B*Witched, 1999; Images of the Cat, 1999; (with I. Turner) Takin' Back My Name: The Confessions of Ike Turner, 1999; The World's Greatest Alien Abductions, 1999; The World's Greatest Serial Killers, 1999; The World's Greatest Serial Cults, 1999; The World's Greatest Serial Royal Scandals, 1999; The World's Greatest Political Scandals, 1999; The World's Worst Atrocities, 1999; The Art of Icon, 2000; The Art of Frescoes, 2000; The Vulva, 2000; Magical Mythery Tour, 2000; The History of the SS Cricket Team, 2000; The Alien Who Thought He Was Elvis, 2000; The World's Greatest UFO and Alien Encounters, 2000; The World's Greatest Alien Encounters, 2002; The World's Greatest UFO Sightings, 2002; The World's Greatest Alien Conspiracy Theories, 2002; A Life as History, 2002; Million Dollar Trivia, 2002; Turning the Tide, 2002; Fighting Them on the Beaches, 2002; Steel Fist, 2003; A History of Pirates, 2003; Witch Hunt, 2003; The Empress of South America, 2003; Vietnam: A War Lost and Won, 2003; Victory 100 Great Military Commanders, 2004; 100 Great Disasters, 2004; Alexander the Great, 2004; 100 Tyrants and Despots, 2004; The Strange Laws of Old England, 2005; Pirates an Illustrated History, 2005; Sexual Lives of Famous Gays, 2005; Julius Ceaser, 2005; Sex Lives of Great Dictators, 2005; The Curious Cures of Old England, 2005; Sex Lives of Roman Emperors, 2005; Doomsday, 2005; Shipwrecks, 2005; Victory in World War II, 2005; The Who and Making of Tommy, 2005; Witches: History of a Persecution, 2005; Public Executions, 2006; The Amorous Antics of Old England, 2006; Killers: The Most Barbaric Murderers of Our Time, 2006; Vinyl Frontier, 2006; 100 Catastrophic Disasters, 2006; History's Greatest Battles: Masterstrokes of War, 2006; Reaping the Whirlwind: The German and Japanese Experiences of WWII, 2007; Daughter of Heaven: The True Story of The Only Woman to Become Emperor of China, 2007; Heroes: The True Stories Behind Every VC Winner Since World War Two, 2007; Sex Lives of Famous Lesbians, 2007; Serial Killers and Mass Murderers: Profiles of the World's Most Barbaric Criminals, 2007; Mammoth Book of Killers at Large, 2007; The Mammoth Book of Inside the Elite Forces, 2008; Killers, 2008; House of Horrors, 2008; On The Frontline, 2008; The Mammoth Book of Inside the Elite Forces: Training, Equipment, and Endeavours of British and American Elite Combat Units, 2008; (ed. with C. Cawthorne) Mammoth Book of the Mafia, 2009; The Immortals, 2009; Fighting Elites, 2009; Pirates of the 21st Century, 2009; The World's Most Evil Gangsters, 2009; Australian True Crime, 2009; Spitfire, 2009; Special Forces War on Terror, 2009; Spree Killers, 2009; The Battle of Britain; 2010; Sordid Sex Lives, 2010; Jack the Ripper's Secret Confession: The Hidden Testimony of the World's First Serial Killer, 2010; A Brief History of Robin Hood, 2010; Vigilantes, 2010; The Kings and Queens of England, 2010; Stalin's Crimes, 2010; The Story of the SS, 2010; A History of the Mafia, 2010; Lancaster Bomber, 2010; Warrior Elite, 2011; Confirmed Kill, 2011; A Brief History of Sherlock Holmes, 2011; Amazing Guitars, 2011; Beastly Battles of Old England, 2011. FORTHCOMING: A Mammoth Book of New CS!; A Brief Guide to James Bond; A Brief Guide to Jeeves and Wooster; A Mammoth Book of Sex Scandals; Canine Commandos; Against Their Will. Contributor to magazines and newspapers. **Address:** Bevan House, Flat D, Boswell St., London, GL WC1N 3BT, England. **Online address:** nigelcawthorne@compuserve.com

CAYER, D. M. *See* **DUFFY, Maureen (Patricia).**

CAYLEFF, Susan Evelyn. American (born United States), b. 1954. **Genres:** Women's Studies And Issues. **Career:** University of Texas Medical Branch, assistant professor of medical humanities, 1983-87, Women's History Seminar Series, humanities faculty founder, 1984-87, clinical adjunct in nursing, 1986-87, Institute for the Medical Humanities, adjunct faculty, 1987-95, assistant professor; San Diego State University, American Indian Studies and Chicano/Chicana Studies, adjunct faculty, associate professor of women's studies, 1987-92, professor of women's studies, 1993-, department chair, 1997-2005, Master's Program, director. Writer. **Publications:** Wash and Be Healed: The Water-Cure Movement and Women's Health, 1987; (ed. with Bair) Wings of Gauze: Women of Color and the Experience of Health and Illness, 1993; Babe: The Life and Legend of Babe Didrikson Zaharias, 1995; Babe Didrikson: The Greatest All-Sport Athlete of all time, 2000. Contributor of articles to journals. **Address:** Department of Women's Studies, San Diego State University, 5500 Campanile Dr., San Diego, CA 92182, U.S.A. **Online address:** cayleff@mail.sdsu.edu

CAZDEN, Courtney B(orden). American (born United States), b. 1925. **Genres:** Education, Essays, Adult Non-fiction, Language/Linguistics, Politics/Government. **Career:** Elementary school teacher in public schools, 1947-49, 1954-61, 1974-75; Harvard University, assistant professor, 1965-68, associate professor, 1968-71, professor, 1971, Charles William Eliot professor of education, now professor emeritus. Writer. **Publications:** Environmental Assistance to the Child's Acquisition of Grammar, 1965; Child Language and Education, 1972; (ed. with V.P. John and D. Hymes) Functions of Language in the Classroom, 1972; (ed.) Language in Early Childhood Education, 1972; Classroom Discourse: The Language of Teaching and Learning, 1988, 2nd ed., 2001; (ed.) Review of Research in Education, vol. XVI, 1990; (co-ed.) English Plus: Issues in Bilingual Education, 1990; (co-author) Whole Language Plus: Essays on Literacy in the United States and New Zealand, 1992. Contributor to periodicals. **Address:** Harvard Graduate School of Education, Harvard University, 205 Longfellow Hall, Appian Way, Cambridge, MA 02138, U.S.A. **Online address:** courtney_cazden@gse.harvard.edu

CAZET, Denys. American (born United States), b. 1938. **Genres:** Children's Fiction, Illustrations. **Career:** Corcoran and St. Helena, teacher, 1960-75; Parhelion and Co., founder, 1972-73; St. Helena, Elementary School, librarian and media specialist, 1975-85; University of California, faculty member and teacher of extension classes, 1976-78; St. Helena Elementary Media Centers, director, 1979-81; California College of Arts and Crafts, instructor, 1985-86. Writer. **Publications:** SELF-ILLUSTRATED FOR CHILDREN: Requiem for a Frog, 1971; The Non-Coloring Book: A Drawing Book for Mind Stretching and Fantasy Building, 1973; The Duck with Squeaky Feet, 1980; Mud Baths for Everyone, 1981; You Make the Angels Cry: Story and Pictures, 1983; Lucky Me, 1983; Big Shoe, Little Shoe, 1984; Christmas Moon, 1984; Saturday, 1985; December 24th, 1986; Frosted Glass, 1987; A Fish in His Pocket, 1987; Sunday, 1988; Great-Uncle Felix, 1988; Mother Night, 1989; Good Morning Maxine!, 1989; Never Spit on Your Shoes, 1990; Daydreams, 1990; I'm Not Sleepy, 1992; Are There Any Questions?, 1992; Born in the

Gravy, 1993; Nothing at All!, 1994; Dancing, 1995; Night Lights: 24 Poems to Sleep On, 1997; Minnie and Moo Go to the Moon, 1998; Minnie and Moo Go Dancing, 1998; Minnie and Moo Save the Earth, 1999; Minnie and Moo Go to Paris, 1999; Minnie and Moo and the Musk of Zorro, 2000; Never Poke a Squid, 2000; Minnie and Moo and the Thanksgiving Tree, 2000; Minnie and Moo Meet Frankenswine, 2001; Minnie and Moo: The Night Before Christmas, 2002; Minnie and Moo and the Potato from Planet X, 2002; Minnie and Moo: Will You be My Valentine?, 2003; Minnie and Moo: The Night of the Living Bed, 2003; Minnie & Moo and the Seven Wonders of the World, 2003; Elvis the Rooster almost Goes to Heaven, 2003; Minnie and Moo: The Attack of the Easter Bunnies, 2004; Elvis the Rooster and the Magic Words, 2004; Perfect Pumpkin Pie, 2005; Octopus, 2005; Minnie and Moo: The Case of the Missing Jelly Donut, 2005; Snout for Chocolate, 2006; Minnie and Moo, Wanted Dead or Alive, 2006; Will You Read to Me?, 2007; Shrunken Head, 2007; Minnie and Moo and the Haunted Sweater, 2007; I Can Read Books, forthcoming. Contributor to newspapers. **Address:** 1300 Ink Grade Rd., Pope Valley, CA 94567-9434, U.S.A.

CEBULASH, Mel. Also writes as Jared Jansen. American (born United States), b. 1937. **Genres:** Novels, Novellas/Short Stories, Children's Fiction, Young Adult Fiction, Sports/Fitness, Humor/Satire, Young Adult Non-fiction, Autobiography/Memoirs, Humor/Satire. **Career:** Teacher, 1962-64; Fairleigh Dickinson University, instructor in reading clinic, 1965-67; Scholastic Magazines Inc., editor for language arts, 1966-76; Bowmar/Noble Publishing Co., editor-in-chief, 1976-80; Cebulash Associates, publisher, 1980-83, executive, 1986-; Fearon Educational, publisher, 1983-86. **Publications:** Through Basic Training with Walter Young, 1968; Man in a Green Beret and Other Medal of Honor Winners, 1969; The Ball That Wouldn't Bounce, 1972; Benny's Nose, 1972; The See-Saw, 1972; Nancy and Jeff, 1972; Penny the Poodle, 1972; Petey the Pup, 1972; Baseball Players Do Amazing Things, 1973; Dic-tion-ary Skilz, 1974; Football Players Do Amazing Things, 1975; Basketball Players Do Amazing Things, 1976; The Grossest Book of World Records, 1977; The Grossest Book of World Records II, 1978; Math Zingo, 1978; Reading Zingo, 1978; The Champion's Jacket, 1978; Blackouts, 1979; Big League Baseball Reading Kit, 1979; Crosswinds Reading Program, 1979; Crosswinds Reading Program, 1979; Spanish Math Zingo, 1979; The 1, 000 Point Pro Sports Quiz Book: Football, 1979; The 1, 000 Point Pro Sports Quiz Book: Basketball, 1979; The 1, 000 Point Pro Sports Quiz Book: Baseball, 1980; The Spring Street Boys Team Up, 1981; I'm an Expert: Motivating Independent Study Projects for Grades 4-6, 1982; The Spring Street Boys Settle a Score, 1982; The Spring Street Boys Hit the Road, 1982; The Spring Street Boys Go for Broke, 1982; Ruth Marini of the Dodgers, 1983; Ruth Marini, Dodger Ace, 1983; The Face That Stopped Time, 1984; Ruth Marini, World Series Star, 1985; Hot Like the Sun: A Terry Tyndale Mystery, 1986; Terry Tyndale in Hot like the Sun, 1986; Campground Caper, 1990; Carly & Co, 1990; Part-Time Shadow, 1990; Carly and Company, 1990; (as Jared Jansen) Showtimes, 1991; Das Saves the Day, 1991; Bat Boy, 1993; Catnapper, 1993; Flipper's Boy, 1993; Muscle Bound, 1993; Rattler, 1993; Snooperman, 1993; Willie's Wonderful Pet, 1993; Bases Loaded: Great Baseball of the 20th Century, 1993; Fast Break: Great Basketball of the 20th Century, 1993; Lights Out: Great Fights of the 20th Century, 1993; 3rd and Goal: Great Football of the 20th Century, 1993; Dirty Money, 1993; Knockout Punch, 1993; Set to Explode, 1993; A Sucker for Redheads, 1993; Scared Silly, 1995; My Family Band, 1996; Let's Visit the Moon, 1996; One More Time, 1996; What a Shower!, 1996; Play Ball!, 1996; Kid With the Left Hook, 1999. Contributor to periodicals. **Address:** 11820 N 112th St., Scottsdale, AZ 85259, U.S.A. **Online address:** cebulash@att.net

CEDERLUND, Johan. Swedish (born Sweden), b. 1963?. **Genres:** History, Architecture. **Career:** Uppsala University, Gustavianum Museum, chief curator, senior curator of art; Zorn Museum, director. Writer. **Publications:** Ritmästarna vid Lunds Universitet, 1990; Thureholm under Frihetstiden: Återuppbyggnad och Nyinredning, 1994; Skulptören Pierre Hubert L'Archevêque, 1721-1778, 2003; Classical Swedish Architecture and Interiors: 1650-1840, 2006; (ed.) Zorn Masterpieces, 2010. **Address:** Museum Gustavianum, Akademigatan 3, Uppsala, 753 10, Sweden.

CELENZA, Anna Harwell. American (born United States) **Genres:** Music. **Career:** Michigan State University, visiting assistant professor in musicology, 1997-99, assistant professor in musicology, 1999-2003, associate professor in musicology, 2003-05, chair of musicology and ethnomusicology area, 2004, 2005; National Public Radio, Performance Today, staff writer, 2005-07; Georgetown University, Department of Performing Arts, Thomas E. Caestecker Associate Professor of Music, 2006-10, chair, 2007-10, Thomas E. Caestecker Professor of Music, 2010-; Michigan Public Radio, writer. Musicologist. **Publications:** The Farewell Symphony, 2000; The Early Works of Niels W. Gade: In Search of the Poetic, 2001; (ed.) St. Hans' Evening Play Overture, 2001; Pictures at an Exhibition, 2003; Heroic Symphony, 2004; Bach's Goldberg Variations, 2005; Hans Christian Andersen and Music: The Nightingale Revealed, 2005; Gershwin's Rhapsody in Blue, 2006; Duke Ellington's Nutcracker Suite, 2011; Vivaldi's Four Seasons, 2012. Contributor of articles to periodicals. **Address:** Department of Performing Arts, Georgetown University, 112B Poulton, 108 Davis Performing Arts Ctr., 37th & O St. NW, PO Box 571063, Washington, DC 20057, U.S.A. **Online address:** ahc27@georgetown.edu

CELL, Edward Charles. American (born United States), b. 1928. **Genres:** Theology/Religion, inspirational/Motivational Literature, Business/Trade/Industry, Economics, Self Help. **Career:** Pastor of Congregational church, 1953-55; Danvers State Hospital, occupational therapist, 1954-55; Simpson College, assistant professor, 1959-64, associate professor of philosophy and religion, 1964-66; Albion College, associate professor of philosophy, 1966-72; National Endowment for the Humanities, program officer, 1971-72; United States International University, professor of philosophy, 1972-74; University of Illinois, professor of philosophy, 1974-. Writer. **Publications:** (Ed.) Religion and Contemporary Western Culture, 1967; Language, Existence and God, 1971; Learning to Learn from Experience, 1984; Daily Readings from Quaker Spirituality, 1987; Organizational Life: Learning to Be Self-Directed, 1998. **Address:** Department of Philosophy, University of Illinois, 1 University Plz., Springfield, IL 62703, U.S.A. **Online address:** ecell1@uis.edu

CENTER, Katherine Pannill. American (born United States), b. 1972. **Genres:** Novels. **Career:** University of Houston, faculty, Gulf Coast, coeditor. **Publications:** The Bright Side of Disaster (novel), 2007; Everyone is Beautiful: A Novel, 2009; Get Lucky: A Novel, 2010. **Address:** Ballantine Books, 1745 Broadway, New York, NY 10019, U.S.A. **Online address:** katherine@katherinecenter.com

CENTER-SHABAZZ, Lois. American (born United States), b. 1954. **Genres:** Money/Finance, Business/Trade/Industry, Economics. **Career:** Dentist, 1980-98; MsFinancialSavvy.com (Internet Web site), founder, senior investments host, editor in-chief and graphic designer. **Publications:** Let's Get Financial Savvy!: From Debt-free to Investing with Ease, 2003. **Address:** c/o Author Mail, CenNet Systems Publishing, PO Box 1385, Chesapeake, VA 23327-1385, U.S.A. **Online address:** msfy29@yahoo.com

CEPERO, Helen. American (born United States), b. 1951?. **Genres:** Writing/Journalism, Theology/Religion. **Career:** North Park Theological Seminary, professor and director of spiritual formation. Writer. **Publications:** Journaling as a Spiritual Practice: Encountering God through Attentive Writing, 2008. **Address:** North Park Theological Seminary, 3225 W Foster Ave., PO Box 14, Chicago, IL 60625, U.S.A.

CERAMI, Charles A. American (born United States), b. 1927. **Genres:** Adult Non-fiction, Self Help, Business/Trade/Industry, Economics, Politics/Government. **Career:** Research Institute of America, senior editor; Kiplinger Washington Publications, foreign affairs editor; Atlantic Council of the United States, senior fellow, councilor. Economist. **Publications:** Successful Leadership in Business, 1955; How to Solve Management Problems, 1957; Living the Business Life: Putting New Meaning and Purpose in Your Career, 1958; Stop Hiding from Success, 1959; Alliance Born of Danger, 1963; Crisis, the Loss of Europe, 1975; More Profit, Less Risk: Your New Financial Strategy, 1982; More Profit, Less Risk: An Investment Guide to the '80s, 1984; (ed.) A Marshall Plan for the 1990s: An International Roundtable on World Economic Development, 1989; Real Estate for Profit: New Trends & Strategies for the '90s, 1990; Benjamin Banneker: Surveyor, Astronomer, Publisher, Patriot, 2002; Jefferson's Great Gamble: The Remarkable Story of Jefferson, Napoleon and the Men Behind the Louisiana Purchase, 2003; Young Patriots: The Remarkable Story of Two Men, their Impossible Plan, and the Revolution that Created the Constitution, 2005; Dinner at Mr. Jefferson's: Three Men, Five Great Wines, and the Evening that Changed America, 2008. Contributor of articles to periodicals. **Address:** c/o Author Mail, Sourcebooks Inc., 1935 Brookdale Rd., Ste. 139, Naperville, IL 60563, U.S.A.

CERCAS, Javier. Spanish (born Spain), b. 1962?. **Genres:** Novels, Novellas/Short Stories, Essays. **Career:** University of Illinois, faculty; Universitat de Girona, lecturer in Spanish literature, 1989-2006, professor of Spanish literature; El Pais, columnist. Writer. **Publications:** El Móvil, 1987; El Inquilino, 1989; La Obra Literaria de Gonzalo Suarez, 1993; El Vientre de la Ballena, 1997; Una Buena Temporada, 1998; Relato Reales, 2000; Soldados de Salamina, 2001; Diálogos de Salamina: Un Paseo por el Cine y la Literatura, 2003; Soldiers of Salamis, 2004; La Velocidad de la Luz, 2005; La Verdad de Agamenón: Crónicas, Arti'culos y un Cuento, 2006; The Speed of Light, 2006; Anatomía de un Instante, 2009; The Anatomy of a Moment: Thirty-Five Minutes in History and Imagination, 2011. Contributor to periodicals. **Address:** Universitat de Girona, 3 Sant Domnec Pl., Girona, 17071, Spain.

CERF, Muriel. French (born France), b. 1950?. **Genres:** Young Adult Fiction, Novels, Literary Criticism And History, Humanities. **Career:** Writer. **Publications:** L'Antivoyage, 1974; Le diable vert, 1975; Les rois et les Voleurs, 1975; Hiéroglyphes de nos Fins Dernières, 1977; Le Lignage du Serpent, 1978; Les Seigneurs du Ponant, 1979; Amérindiennes, 1979; Une Passion, 1981; Maria Tiefenthaler, 1982; Une Pâle beauté, 1984; Dramma per Musica, 1986; Doux Oiseaux de Galileé, 1988; Street Girl, 1988; Primavera Toscana: Détail de la Légended'une Florentine, 1989; La Nativité à L'étoile, 1989; Julia M, ou, Le Premier Regard, 1991; Le Verrou, 1997; Ogres, Et Autres Contes, 1997; Une Vie Sans Secret, 1998; Servantes de L'oeil, 1999; Ils Ont Tué Vénus Ladouceur, 2000; Triomphe de L' Agneau, 2000; La Lumière de l'île, 2001; La Femme au Chat, 2001; Le Bandit Manchot, 2002; L' Homme du Souterrain, 2003; L' étoile de Carthage, 2004; La Petite Culotte, 2005; Bertrand Cantat; ou, Le Chant des Automates, 2006. **Address:** c/o Author Mail, Editions du Rocher, 6 Pl. St.-Sulpice, Paris, 75006, France. **Online address:** mc.site@murielcerf.com

CERNADA, George P. American (born United States) **Genres:** Demography, Medicine/Health, Social Sciences. **Career:** Population Council, Taiwan resident representative, 1965-76, senior associate and director of Asian operations research, 1990-95; United Service Organizations, Taiwan vice chair, 1970-72; University of Massachusetts, School of Public Health and Health Sciences, Department of Public Health, professor of community health education, 1976-90, 1995-2002, professor emeritus of public health, 2002-. Writer and consultant. **Publications:** (Ed.) Taiwan Family Planning Reader, 1970, 3rd ed., 1994; Basic Beliefs about Human Life Relating to Ethical Judgements Family-Planning Field Workers Make about Induced Abortion, Taiwan, 1973, 1975; Knowledge into Action: Taiwan's Research Utilization, 1980; Knowledge into Action: A Guide to Research Utilization, 1982; (ed. with M.E. Khan) Spacing as an Alternative Strategy: India's Family Welfare Programme, 1996; (ed. with D. Buchanan) Progress in Preventing AIDS?, 1998; (ed. with M.I. Torres) Sexual and Reproductive Health Promotion in Latino Populations, 2003. Contributor to periodicals. **Address:** Department of Public Health, School of Public Health and Health Sciences, University of Massachusetts, 330 Arnold House, 715 N Pleasant St., Amherst, MA 01003-9304, U.S.A. **Online address:** gcernada@schoolph.umass.edu

CERNY, Frank J. American (born United States), b. 1946. **Genres:** Medicine/Health, Sports/Fitness. **Career:** University of Windsor, instructor, 1974-76; Children's Hospital, Children's Lung Center, co-founder and associate director, 1976-85; State University of New York, University at Buffalo, School of Public Health and Health Professions, associate professor, 1985, Department of Exercise and Nutrition Sciences, professor and chair, now professor emeritus; Eden United Methodist Church, assistant pastor. Writer. **Publications:** (With H.W. Burton) Exercise Physiology for Health Care Professionals, 2001. Contributor to journals. **Address:** School of Public Health and Health Professions, University at Buffalo, State University of New York, 401 Kimball Twr., 3435 Main St., Buffalo, NY 14214-3079, U.S.A. **Online address:** cerny@acsu.buffalo.edu

CERULLO, Mary M. American (born United States), b. 1949. **Genres:** Zoology, Children's Fiction. **Career:** RISE (Resources in Science Education), owner, schools and environmental organizations, consultant, 1988-; Friends of Casco Bay, associate director; Maine Mathematics and Science Alliance, communications coordinator. Writer. **Publications:** Sharks: Challengers of the Deep, 1993; Lobsters: Gangsters of the Sea, 1994; Coral Reef: A City That Never Sleeps, 1996; Reading the Environment: Children's Literature in the Science Classroom, 1997; Octopus: Phantom of the Sea, 1997; Dolphins: What They can Teach Us, 1998; Sea Soup: Phytoplankton, 1999; Hop Jump, 1999; Ocean Detectives: Solving the Mysteries of the Sea, 2000; Truth about Great White Sharks, 2000; Sea Soup: Zooplankton, 2001; Truth about Dangerous Sea Creatures, 2003; Life Under Ice, 2003; Sea Turtles: Ocean Nomads, 2003; Shipwrecks: Exploring Sunken Cities Beneath the Sea, 2009; City Fish, Country Fish, 2012; Giant Squid, 2012. **Address:** c/o Author Mail, Dutton Children's Books, 345 Hudson St., New York, NY 10014, U.S.A. **Online address:** mcerullo@cascobay.org

CERUZZI, Paul Edward. American (born United States), b. 1949. **Genres:** Information Science/Computers, Technology, History, Business/Trade/Industry. **Career:** Clemson University, assistant professor of history of technology, 1981-; Smithsonian National Air and Space Museum, curator of aerospace engineering and computing. Writer. **Publications:** Reckoners: The Prehistory of the Digital Computer, from Relays to the Stored Program Concept, 1935-1945, 1983; Beyond the Limits: Flight Enters the Computer Age, 1989; (with P.A. Kidwell) Landmarks in Digital Computing: A Smithsonian Pictorial History, 1994; A History of Modern Computing, 1998, 2nd ed., 2003; Internet Alley: High Technology in Tysons Corner, 1945-2005, 2008; (ed. with W. Aspray) The Internet and American Business, 2008. Contributor to books. **Address:** Division of Space History, National Air and Space Museum, Smithsonian Institution, PO Box 37012, Washington, DC 20013-7012, U.S.A. **Online address:** ceruzzip@si.edu

CERVENKA, Jarda. American/Czech (born Czech Republic), b. 1933. **Genres:** Novels, Novellas/Short Stories, Children's Fiction, Young Adult Fiction, Westerns/Adventure. **Career:** University of Minnesota, visiting professor of medical genetics, 1965-68, professor of medical genetics, 1968-2000, School of Dentistry, Dental research Institute, Department or Oral Sciences, professor, 2000-; American College of Medical Genetics, founding fellow, 1993. Writer. **Publications:** Mal d'Afrique: And Stories from Other Places (short stories), 1995; Revenge of Underwater Man and Other Stories, 2000. Contributor of articles to periodicals. Works appear in anthologies. **Address:** School of Dentistry, University of Minnesota, Moos Health Sciences Twr., 515 Delaware St., SE, Minneapolis, MN 55455-0357, U.S.A.

CESPEDES, Frank V. American (born United States), b. 1950. **Genres:** Administration/Management, Business/Trade/Industry, Marketing, Economics. **Career:** Bain & Co., staff, 1995-2007; Harvard University, research associate, Harvard Business School, professor of business administration, Strategic Marketing Management Program, leader, 1978-95, Entrepreneurial Management Unit, senior lecturer of business administration; Center for Executive Development, managing partner. Consultant and writer. **Publications:** (Co-author) Managerial Communications, 1984; (with E.R. Corey and V.K. Rangan) Going to Market: Case Studies in Industrial Distribution, 1989; (with E.R. Corey and V.K. Rangan) Going to Market: Distribution Systems for Industrial Products, 1989; Organizing and Implementing the Marketing Effort: Text and Cases, 1991; Concurrent Marketing: Integrating Product, Sales and Service, 1995; Managing Marketing Linkages: Text, Cases and Readings, 1996; Sales Management, 1998. Contributor of articles to periodicals. **Address:** Harvard Business School, Harvard University, Rock Ctr. 216, Soldiers Field, Boston, MA 02163, U.S.A. **Online address:** fcespedes@hbs.edu

CESSARIO, Romanus. American (born United States), b. 1944. **Genres:** Theology/Religion, Law. **Career:** Dominican Order, ordained Catholic priest, 1971; Providence College, instructor, 1972-76, administrative assistant, 1974-76; Roman Catholic Community, priest, 1976-79; Pontifical Faculty of the Immaculate Conception, vice president, academic dean, 1980-87, professor, 1980-95; The Thomist, associate editor, 1980-; Saint John's Seminary, theology professor, 1995-; Université de Fribourg, visiting professor, 1989-90; Fordham University Press, editor, 1993-2010; Pierre d'angle, Rédacteur, 1994-; National Catholic Register, contributing editor, 1995-98, senior writer, 1998-2000; Pastoral Provision, chairman, 1997-2006; senior editor, 1998-; John Paul II Institute for Marriage and Family, visiting professor. **Publications:** Christian Satisfaction in Aquinas: Towards a Personalist Understanding, 1982; The Godly Image: Christ & Salvation in Catholic Thought from St. Anselm to Aquinas, 1990; The Moral Virtues and Theological Ethics, 1991, 2nd ed., 2009; (with C.E. O'Neill) Meeting Christ in the Sacraments, 1991; Le Virtu, 1994; Perpetual Angelus: As the Saints Pray the Rosary, 1995; Christian Faith and the Theological Life, 1996; Les Thomisme et les Thomistes, 1999 in US as A Short History of Thomism, 2005; Introduction to Moral Theology, 2001; (trans. with K. White) J. Capreolus, On the Virtues, 2001; The Virtues, or, the Examined Life, 2002; (ed.) Boston's Cardinal: Bernard Law, the Man and His Witness, 2002. Contributor of books to journals and periodicals. **Address:** Saint John's Seminary, 127 Lake St., Brighton, MA 02135, U.S.A.

CEVASCO, G(eorge) A(nthony). Also writes as Serge O. Cogcave. American (born United States), b. 1924. **Genres:** Art/Art History, Environmental Sciences/Ecology, Language/Linguistics, Literary Criticism And History, Biography, Philosophy. **Career:** Brooklyn Public Library, research librarian, 1950-51; Gannon College, instructor in English, 1951-52; Notre Dame College, associate professor of English, 1952-55; Fordham University, lecturer in English, 1954-63; St. John's University, assistant professor of English, 1955-65, associate professor of English, professor of English, 1955-, assistant dean, 1965-. Writer. **Publications:** J.K. Huysmans in England and America: A Bibliographical Study, 1960; (with J. Fee) Wordcraft, 1962; Grammar Self-Taught, 1963; (co-author) Functional English, 1963; Salvador Dali: Master of Surrealism and Modern Art, 1971; Oscar Wilde, 1972; The Population Problem, 1973; New Words for You, 1977; J.K. Huysmans: A Reference Guide, 1980; John Gray, 1982; The Sitwells: Edith, Osbert, Sacheverell, 1987; Three Decadent Poets: Ernest Dowson, John Gray and Lionel Johnson: An Annotated Bibliography, 1990; (ed.) The 1890s: An Encyclopedia of British Literature, Art and Culture, 1993; (co-author) Biographical Dictionary of American and Canadian Naturalists and Environmentalists, 1997; The Breviary of the Decadence: J.K. Huysmans's A Rebours and English Literature, 2001; (ed. with R.P. Harmond) Modern American Environmentalists: A Biographical Encyclopedia, 2009. **Address:** Department of English, St. John's University, 8000 Utopia Pkwy., Queens, NY 11439, U.S.A.

CHABRIS, Christopher F. American (born United States), b. 1966?. **Genres:** Information Science/Computers. **Career:** Harvard University, lecturer, 2002, research associate in psychology, 2002-07; Union College, assistant professor of psychology; Albany Medical College, adjunct assistant professor of neurology; American Chess Journal, founder; Chess Horizons, editor. **Publications:** Artificial Intelligence and Turbo Pascal, 1987; Artificial Intelligence and Turbo C, 1989; (with T. Hoechst and N. Melander) Guide to ORACLE, 1990; (contrib.) The Complete Idiot's Guide to Chess, 1997; (with D.J. Simons) The Invisible Gorilla: And Other Ways Our Intuitions Deceive Us, 2010. Contributor to books and periodicals. **Address:** Department of Psychology, Union College, 807 Union St., Schenectady, NY 12308, U.S.A. **Online address:** chabrisc@union.edu

CHADBOURN, Mark. British (born England), b. 1960. **Genres:** Novels. **Career:** Writer. **Publications:** AGE OF MISRULE SERIES: World's End, 2009; Darkest Hour, 2009; Always Forever, 2009. DARK AGE SERIES: The Devil in Green, 2010; The Queen of Sinister, 2010; The Hounds of Avalon, 2010. KINGDOM OF THE SERPENT SERIES: Jack of Ravens, 2006; The Burning Man, 2008; Destroyer of Worlds, 2009. NOVELS: The Underground, 1993; Nocturne, 1994: Eternal, 1996; Testimony, 1996; Scissorman, 1997; The Fairy Feller's Master Stroke, 2002; Lord of Silence, 2009; The Silver Skull (Swords of Albion Series), 2009; The Scar-crow Men (Swords of Albion Series), 2011. OTHERS: Doctor Who: Wonderland, 2003. (With M. Mignola) Hellboy: The Ice Wolves, 2009. Contributor to periodicals. **Address:** London, GL , England. **Online address:** webcontact@markchadbourn.net

CHADWICK, Alex. *See* **ZOSS, Joel.**

CHADWICK, Cydney. American (born United States), b. 1959. **Genres:** Novels, Novellas/Short Stories. **Career:** Chadwick Marketing, regional sales manager, 1984-92; Syntax Projects for the Arts, executive director, 1988-; Avec Books, founder, 1992-, director and editor. **Publications:** STORIES: Enemy Clothing, 1993; Persistent Disturbances, 1995; Oeuvres, 1995; Interims, 1997. FICTION: Dracontic Nodes, 1993; The Gift Horse's Mouth, 1994; Inside the Hours, 1998; Benched (novella), 2000; Flesh and Bone, 2001; Under the Sun, 2003; Cut and Run, 2005. **Address:** Avec Books, PO Box 1059, Penngrove, CA 94951-1059, U.S.A. **Online address:** aveclivres@yahoo.com

CHADWICK, Elizabeth. *See* **HERNDON, Nancy.**

CHADWICK, Elizabeth E. British (born England) **Genres:** Young Adult Fiction. **Career:** Author. **Publications:** NOVELS: Wanton Angel, 1989; The Wild Hunt, 1991; Virgin Fire, 1991; The Running Vixen, 1992; Bride Fire, 1992; Children of Destiny, 1993; Reluctant Lovers, 1993; The Leopard Unleashed, 1993; Elusive Lovers, 1994; Shields of Pride, 1994; Daughters of the Grail, 1995; First Knight (novelization of the film), 1995; The Conquest, 1997; The Champion, 1998; The Love Knot, 1999; The Marsh Kings Daughter, 2000; Lords of the White Castle, 2002; The Winter Mantle, 2002; The Falcons of Montabard, 2004; The Greatest Knight: The Story of William Marshall, 2005; Shadows and Strongholds: A Novel, 2005; A Place Beyond Courage, 2007; The Time of Singing, 2008; The Greatest Knight: The Unsung Story of the Queen's Champion, 2009; For the King's Favor, 2010; The Scarlet Lion, 2010; To Defy a King, 2011; Lady of the English, 2011; Eleanor of Aquitaine Trilogy, forthcoming. **Address:** c/o Author Mail, St. Martin's Press, 175 5th Ave., New York, NY 10010, U.S.A. **Online address:** elizabethchadwick@live.co.uk

CHADWICK, Owen. British (born England), b. 1916. **Genres:** History, Intellectual History, Theology/Religion. **Career:** Cambridge University, dean of Trinity Hall, 1949-56, Selwyn College, master, 1956-83, Regius professor emeritus of modern history, 1956-83, Dixie professor of ecclesiastical history, 1958-68, vice-chancellor, 1969-71; Archbishops Commission on Church and State, chairman, 1966-70; University of East Anglia, chancellor, 1984-94. Writer. **Publications:** John Cassian: A Study in Primitive Monasticism, 1950; The Founding of Cuddesdon, 1954; From Bossuet to Newman, 1957, 2nd ed., 1987; (trans. and ed.) Western Asceticism, 1958; Mackenzie's Grave, 1959; Creighton on Luther, 1959; Victorian Miniature, 1960; (ed.) The Mind of the Oxford Movement, 1960; Westcott and the University, 1962; (ed. with G.F. Nuttall) From Uniformity to Unity, 1662-1962, 1962; The Reformation, 1964, 15th ed., 1984; History of the Church: A Select Bibliography, 1966, 3rd ed., 1976; The Victorian Church, vol. I, 1966, 3rd ed., 1972, vol. II, 1970, 3rd ed., 1979; John Cassian, 1968; Freedom and the Historian: An Inaugural Lecture, 1969; Acton and Gladstone, 1976; The Secularization of the European Mind, 1976; Catholicism and History, 1978; The Popes and European Revolution, 1981; Newman, 1983; Hensley Henson: A Study in the Friction between Church and State, 1983; History, Society and the Churches, 1985; Britain and the Vatican in the Second World War, 1986; A History of Christian Missions, 2nd ed., 1986; Michael Ramsey: A Life, 1990; Secularization of the European Mind in the Nineteenth Century, 1990; The Spirit of the Oxford Movement, 1990; Victorian Miniature, 1991; Edward King: Bishop of Lincoln, 1885-1910, 1991; The Christian Church in the Cold War, 1992; A History of Christianity, 1995; Prince Albert and the university, 1997; A History of the Popes, 1830-1914, 1998; Acton and History, 1998; The Early Reformation on the Continent, 2001. **Address:** Oxford University Press, 198 Madison Ave., New York, NY 10016, U.S.A. **Online address:** OC207@cam.ac.uk

CHADWICK, Whitney. American (born United States), b. 1943. **Genres:** Novels, Art/Art History, Photography, Literary Criticism And History. **Career:** Massachusetts Institute of Technology, lecturer, 1972-, associate professor of art history, through 1978; University of California, visiting professor of art history, 1977; San Francisco State University, Department of art history, professor, 1978-, now professor emeritus; Williams College, Clark professorship, 2003. Writer. **Publications:** Myth in Surrealist Painting, 1929-1939, 1980; Women Artists and the Surrealist Movement, 1985; Women, Art, and Society, 1990, 5th ed., 2012; (ed. with I. de Courtivron) Significant Others: Creativity and Intimate Partnership, 1993; Leonora Carrington: La Realidad de Imaginacion, 1994; (contrib.) More Than Minimal, 1996; Framed (novel), 1998; (ed.) Mirror Images, 1998; (contrib.) American Dreamer, 1999; Amazons in the Drawing Room: The Art of Romaine Brooks, 2000; (contrib.) Mirror, Mirror, 2002; (ed. with T.T. Latimer) Modern Woman Revisited: Paris Between the Wars, 2003; (contrib.) Sheila Hicks: 50 Years, 2010; Contemporary Feminist Studies and Its Relation to Art History and Visual Studies, 2010. Contributor of articles to periodicals. **Address:** Department of Art, San Francisco State University, 1600 Holloway Ave., San Francisco, CA 94132, U.S.A. **Online address:** wchad@sfsu.edu

CHAFE, Wallace. American (born United States), b. 1927. **Genres:** Language/Linguistics. **Career:** University of Buffalo (now State University of New York at Buffalo), assistant professor of modern languages, 1958-59; Smithsonian Institute, linguist, 1959-62; University of California-Berkeley, professor of linguistics, 1962-86, chairman of department, 1969-74, 1977-78; University of California-Los Angeles, Linguistic Institute, visiting professor, 1966; Cornell University, visiting professor, 1967-68; Sydney University, visiting professor, 1975; Center for Advanced Study in the Behavioral Sciences, visiting professor, 1976-77; Wellesley College, Henry R. Luce Professor, 1979; State University of New York, visiting professor, 1981-85; Georgetown University, Linguistic Institute, visiting professor, 1985; University of California-Santa Barbara, professor of linguistics, 1986-91, professor emeritus, 1991-, Linguistic Institute, visiting professor, 2001, research professor, 2002-, Constantine Panunzio Distinguished Professor Emeritus, 2007-08; University of New Mexico, Linguistic Institute, visiting professor, 1995; University of Queensland, Australian Linguistic Institute, visiting professor, 1998; Rice University, visiting professor, 1999. **Publications:** Seneca Thanksgiving Rituals, 1961; Handbook of the Seneca Language, 1963; (co-ed.) Proceedings of the 1962 Annual Spring Meeting of the American Ethnological Society, 1963; Seneca Morphology and Dictionary, 1967; Meaning and the Structure of Language, 1970; Semantically Based Sketch of Onondaga, 1970; Discussing language, 1974; The Caddoan, Iroquoian and Siouan Languages, 1976; (ed.) American Indian Languages and American Linguistics: Papers of the Second Golden Anniversary Symposium of the Linguistic Society of America, Held at the University of California, Berkeley, on November 8 and 9, 1974, 1976; (ed.) The Pear Stories: Cognitive, Cultural, and Linguistic Aspects of Narrative Production, 1980; (ed. with J. Nichols) Evidentiality: The Linguistic Coding of Epistemology, 1986; Discourse, Consciousness, and Time: The Flow and Displacement of Conscious Experience in Speaking and Writing, 1994; (ed.) Symposium on Language and Culture: Proceedings of the 1962 Annual Spring Meeting of the American Ethnological Society, 1994; Importance of Not Bearnest: The Feeling Behind Laughter and Humor, 2007. **Address:** Department of Linguistics, University of California, Santa Barbara, CA 93106, U.S.A. **Online address:** chafe@linguistics.ucsb.edu

CHAFEE, Lincoln D. (Lincoln Davenport Chafee). American (born United States), b. 1953. **Genres:** Autobiography/Memoirs. **Career:** General Dynamics, planner; Northeast Corridor Initiative, executive director; Rhode Island Constitutional Convention, delegate, 1985; City of Warwick, mayor, 1993-99; State of Rhode Island, U.S. senator, 1999-2007; Brown University, Thomas J. Watson, Jr., Institute of International Studies, distinguished visiting fellow, 2007. Writer. **Publications:** Against the Tide: How a Compliant Congress Empowered a Reckless President (memoir), 2008. **Address:** Watson Institute for International Studies, 111 Thayer St., Box 1970, Providence, RI 02912-9043, U.S.A.

CHAFEE, Lincoln Davenport. *See* **CHAFEE, Lincoln D.**

CHAFEL, Judith A. American (born United States), b. 1945. **Genres:** Education, Sciences, History. **Career:** Boston Redevelopment Authority, relocation worker, 1968; John F. Kennedy Family Service Center, assistant director of youth services, 1968-69; Sodus Primary School, teacher, 1974-76; University of Texas, visiting assistant professor of curriculum and instruction, 1979-80; Indiana University-Bloomington, Curriculum and Instruction, assistant professor, 1980-86, associate professor, 1986-2001, professor, 2001-, Early Childhood Program, coordinator, 1988, 1992-93, co-coordinator, 1993-; U.S. House of Representatives, Committee on Ways and Means, professional staff, 1989-90; Indiana University-Purdue University, Center on Philanthropy, associate professor of philanthropic studies, 1991-2001. Writer. **Publications:** (Ed. and contrib.) Child Poverty and Public Policy, 1993; (with S. Reifel) Advances in Early Education and Day Care, 1997. Contributor of articles to journals and books. **Address:** School of Education, Indiana University, Rm. 3214, W. W. Wright Education Education Bldg., 201 N Rose Ave., Bloomington, IN 47405-1006, U.S.A. **Online address:** chafel@indiana.edu

CHAFFEY, Will. American (born United States), b. 1969?. **Genres:** Animals/Pets. **Career:** Apple Computer Inc., staff. Writer. **Publications:** Swimming with Crocodiles: A True Story of Adventure and Survival, 2008. **Address:** c/o Margaret Gee, PO Box 221, Double Bay, NW 1360, Australia.

CHAI, Arlene J. American (born United States), b. 1955. **Genres:** Novels, Social Sciences, Literary Criticism And History, Young Adult Fiction. **Career:** George Patterson's advertising agency, advertising copywriter, 1972; advertising copywriter, 1976-. Writer. **Publications:** NOVELS: The Last Time I Saw Mother, 1995: Eating Fire and Drinking Water, 1996; On the Goddess Rock, 1998; Black Hearts, 2000. Work appears in anthologies. **Address:** c/o Sally Wofford Girand, Elaine Markson Literary Agency Inc., 44 Greenwich Ave., New York, NY 10011, U.S.A.

CHAI, May-lee. American (born United States) **Genres:** Area Studies, Novels, History, Travel/Exploration. **Career:** Associated Press, reporter; University of California, research associate; Amherst College, visiting writer, 2004-06; San Francisco State University, faculty; University of Wyoming, faculty; University of Colorado, faculty. Writer. **Publications:** (Ed. with W. Chai) Chinese: Mainland and Taiwan: A Study of Historical, Cultural, Economic and Political Relations with Documents, 1996; My Lucky Face (novel), 1997; (with W. Chai) The Girl from Purple Mountain: Love, Honor, War, and One Family's Journey from China to America (biography), 2001; Glamorous Asians: Short Stories & Essays, 2004; Hapa Girl: A Memoir, 2007; (with W. Chai) China A to Z: Everything You Need to Know to Understand Chinese Customs and Culture, 2007; Dragon Chica: A Novel, 2010. Contributor to periodicals. **Address:** c/o Author Mail, Thomas Dunne Books, 175 5th Ave., New York, NY 10010, U.S.A. **Online address:** mayleechai@aol.com

CHAITIN, Gregory J. American (born United States), b. 1947. **Genres:** Mathematics/Statistics, Adult Non-fiction, Education. **Career:** IBM Watson Research Center, mathematician, emeritus researcher; University of Buenos Aires, visiting professor; University of Auckland, visiting professor. Writer and researcher. **Publications:** Computational Complexity and GOdel's Incompleteness Theorem, 1970; Information, Randomness & Incompleteness: Papers on Algorithmic Information Theory, 1987, 2nd ed., 1990; Algorithmic Information Theory, 1987; Information-Theoretic Incompleteness, 1992; The Limits of Mathematics: A Course on Information Theory and Limits of Formal Reasoning, 1998; The Unknowable, 1999; Exploring Randomness, 2001; Conversations with a Mathematician: Math, Art, Science, and the Limits of Reason: A Collection of His Most Wide-Ranging and Non-technical Lectures and Interviews, 2002; Meta Math! The Quest for Omega, 2005; Thinking about Godel and Turing: Essays on Complexity 1970-2007, 2007; Randomness and Complexity: From Leibniz to Chaitin, 2007. **Address:** IBM Research Division, Thomas J. Watson Research Ctr., PO Box 218, Yorktown Heights, NY 10598, U.S.A. **Online address:** chaitin@us.ibm.com

CHAKRAVARTY, Sumita S(inha). American/Indian (born India), b. 1951. **Genres:** Film, Theatre. **Career:** Lucknow University, research fellow, 1971-74, lecturer in English, 1974-77; University of Illinois, Department of English, teaching assistant, 1977-80; The New School for Social Research, faculty, 1988-91, Media Studies and Films, core faculty, 1990-; Graduate Faculty of Political and Social Science, faculty, 1993-99; New York University, SCPS, 1999-2000; The New School, Eugene Lang College, Culture and Media, chair, 2000-08, associate professor of media studies, 2005-, associate dean; New School for Social Research, editor of interstices. **Publications:** National Identity in Indian Popular Cinema, 1947-1987, 1993, 3rd ed., 1998; (ed.) The Enemy Within: The Films of Mrinal Sen, 2000. **Address:** Department of Media Studies and Film, Rm. 1214, 2 W 13th St., 12th Fl., The New School for Social Research, New York, NY 10011, U.S.A. **Online address:** chakravs@newschool.edu

CHALEFF, Ira. American (born United States), b. 1945. **Genres:** Poetry, Politics/Government, Administration/Management, inspirational/Motivational Literature, Business/Trade/Industry. **Career:** Congressional Management Foundation, executive director, 1982-89; Institute for Business Technology U.S. Inc., president, 1989-97; Executive Coaching & Consulting Associates, founder and president, 1998-; Georgetown University, Center for Professional Development, adjunct faculty. Writer. **Publications:** (Ed. with G.D. Serota) Politicians and their Spouses' Careers, 1985; Setting Course: A Congressional Management Guide, 1986; (ed. with G.D. Serota) Cutback Management for Congressional Offices, 1986; Secret Winds: Poems of a Spiritual Journey, 1990; The Courageous Follower: Standing Up to and For Our Leaders, 1995, 3rd ed., 2009; (ed. with R.E. Riggio and J. Lipman-Blumen) Art of Followership: How Great Followers Create Great Leaders And Organizations, 2008. **Address:** Executive Coaching & Consulting Associates, 9621 Hillridge Dr., Kensington, DC 20895-3121, U.S.A. **Online address:** ira.chaleff@exe-coach.com

CHALFONT. Also writes as Arthur Gwynne Jones Chalfont, Arthur Gwynne Jones Baron Chalfont, Alun Arthur Gwynne Jones. British/Welsh (born Wales), b. 1919. **Genres:** History, Military/Defense/Arms Control, Biography. **Career:** Times, defense correspondent, 1961-64; British Foreign and Commonwealth Office, minister of state, 1964-70, Western European Union, representative, 1969-70; British Broadcasting Corp., broadcaster on defense and foreign affairs, 1961-64; Twentieth Century Bank, deputy chair, 1971-72, General Investments. chair, 1971-72; International Business Machines U.K. Ltd., director, 1973; International Business Machines U.K. (Holdings) Ltd., director, 1973; Welsh Institute, Hispanic Council and Luso Brazilian Council, president, 1973-79; Royal National Institute for the Deaf, faculty, 1980-; House of Lords, All Party Defense Group, chair, 1980-; Nottingham Building Society, president, 1983-; European Atlantic Committee and United Kingdom Committee for UNICEF, vice-president. **Publications:** The Sword and the Spirit, 1963; Disarmament, 1965; The Great Commanders, 1973; (as Alun Chalfont) Montgomery of Alamein, 1976; (ed. as Lord Chalfont) Waterloo, 1979; (as Alun Chalfont) Star Wars: Suicide or Survival, 1985; (as Alun Chalfont) Defence of the Realm, 1987; By God's Will: A Portrait of the Sultan of Brunei, 1989; The Shadow of My Hand, 2000. **Address:** House of Lords, London, GL SW1A 0PW, England.

CHALKER, Dennis. (Dennis C. Chalker). American (born United States), b. 1954. **Genres:** Military/Defense/Arms Control, History, Young Adult Non-fiction, Young Adult Fiction, Mystery/Crime/Suspense. **Career:** DSC Inc., chief executive officer; Global Studies Group Inc., director of operations. Writer. **Publications:** WITH K. DOCKERY: The United States Navy SEALs Workout Guide: The Exercise and Fitness Programs Based on the U.S. Navy SEALs and BUD/S Training, 1998; One Perfect Op: An Insider's Account of the Navy SEAL Special Warfare Teams, 2002; Hell Week: SEALS in Training, 2002; The Home Team: Undeclared War, 2004; The Home Team: Hostile Borders, 2005, Home Team: Weapons Grade, 2006. **Address:** c/o Author Mail, Avon Books/HarperCollins, 10 E 53rd St., 7th Fl., New York, NY 10022, U.S.A.

CHALKER, Dennis C. *See* **CHALKER, Dennis.**

CHALKER, Sylvia. British (born England) **Genres:** Travel/Exploration, Language/Linguistics, Reference, Art/Art History. **Career:** Teacher of English as a foreign language; Oxford Companion, contributor. Journalist and public relations representative. **Publications:** Going It Alone, 1978; Let's See Great Britain, 1979; Advanced English Course: Study Programmes, 1979; Police!, 1981; Fire!, 1981; Current English Grammar, 1984; Intermediate Grammar Workbooks, vol. I-III, 1987; (with M. Geddes) Fast Forward 3 Resource Book, 1988, abridged ed., 1990; English Grammar Word by Word, 1991; A Student's English Grammar Workbook, 1992; (with E. Weiner) The Oxford Dictionary of English Grammar, 1994; The Little Oxford Dictionary of English Grammar, 1995; Collins COBUILD English Guides: Linking Words, 1996 Contributor to books, articles and reviews to periodicals. **Address:** Oxford University Press, 200 Madison Ave., New York, NY 10016, U.S.A.

CHALLIS, Sarah. British (born England) **Genres:** Young Adult Fiction, Women's Studies And Issues. **Career:** Writer and educator. **Publications:** Killing Helen, 2000; Turning for Home, 2001; Blackthorn Winter, 2003; On Dancing Hill, 2004; Jumping to Conclusions, 2005; Footprints in the Sand, 2006; That Summer Affair, 2007; Love and Other Secrets, 2009; The Garden Party, 2011. **Address:** c/o Author Mail, St. Martin's Press, 175 5th Ave., New York, NY 10010, U.S.A.

CHALMERS, Alan D(ouglas). British (born England), b. 1957. **Genres:** Literary Criticism And History. **Career:** University of Southern California, assistant lecturer, 1981-90, assistant professor, 1991-96, associate professor of English, 1996-; University of Oregon, visiting assistant professor of English, 1990-91; Wofford College, professor of English. Writer. **Publications:** Jonathan Swift and the Burden of the Future, 1995. **Address:** Department of English, Wofford College, 429 N Church St., Spartanburg, SC 29303-3663, U.S.A. **Online address:** achalmers@gw.uscs.edu

CHALMERS, Penny. *See* **KEMP, Penn.**

CHALMERS, Robert. British (born England) **Genres:** Novels, Young Adult Fiction, Romance/Historical, Mystery/Crime/Suspense. **Career:** Writer. **Publications:** Who's Who in Hell, 2002; Fortune's Bastard, 2004. **Address:** c/o Author Mail, Grove/Atlantic Inc., 841 Broadway, 4th Fl., New York, NY 10003, U.S.A.

CHAMBERLAIN, Lesley. British (born England), b. 1951. **Genres:** Food And Wine, Travel/Exploration, Autobiography/Memoirs, Literary Criticism And History, Novellas/Short Stories, Psychology, Philosophy. **Career:** Portsmouth Polytechnic, lecturer in Russian and German, 1976-77; Reuters Agency, journalist, 1977-86; freelance writer, critic and teacher, 1986-. **Publications:** The Food and Cooking of Russia, 1982; The Food and Cooking of Eastern Europe, 1989; (ed. and intro.) Marinetti La Cucina Futurista, 1989; In the Communist Mirror: Journeys in Eastern Europe, 1990; Volga, Volga: A Journey down Russia's Great River, 1995; Nietzsche in Turin: The End of the Future, 1996; In a Place Like That (fiction), 1998; The Secret Artist: A Close Reading of Sigmund Freud, 2000; Girl in a Garden, 2003; Motherland: A Philosophical History of Russia, 2004; Philosophy Steamer: Lenin and the Exile of the Intelligentsia, 2006 in US as Lenin's Private War: The Voyage of the Philosophy Steamer and The Exile of the Intelligentsia, 2007; The Losers, forthcoming. Contributor to periodicals. **Address:** c/o Author Mail, Atlantic Books, Ormond House, 26-27 Boswell St., London, GL WC1N 3JZ, England. **Online address:** lvc@lesleychamberlain.co.uk

CHAMBERLAIN, Lisa. American (born United States), b. 1968?. **Genres:** Economics, Money/Finance. **Career:** Cleveland Free Times, reporter and news editor, through 1996, editor-in-chief, 1999-2002. Journalist. **Publications:** Slackonomics: Generation X in the Age of Creative Destruction, 2008. Contributor to periodicals. **Address:** New York, NY , U.S.A. **Online address:** lisacchamberlain@gmail.com

CHAMBERLAIN, Lorna M(arie). *See* Obituaries.

CHAMBERLAIN, Marisha. American (born United States), b. 1952. **Genres:** Poetry, Novels, Plays/Screenplays. **Career:** Circle in the Field, Director of Development, Seneca Falls Project, project director; Ceridian/St. Paul Central High School Partnership, project manager; Cricket Theater, playwright-in-residence; Victory Gardens Theater, playwright-in-residence; The Playwrights' Center, working resident writer; MacDowell Colony, artist-in-residence; Anderson Center, artist-in-residence; Rockefeller Foundation, The Bellagio Center, artist-in-residence. **Publications:** FICTION: The Rose Variations (novel), 2009. PLAYS: Scheherazade: A Full-Length Play without Intermission, 1985; Evergreen: A Christmas Story, 2003; Young Jane Eyre: A Drama, 2003; Little Women: A Drama, 2003; Rebecca of Sunnybrook Farm, 2004; The Canterville Ghost, 2004; Hope for Breakfast: A Drama, 2005. POETRY: Powers (poetry collection), 1979. **Address:** Hastings, MN , U.S.A. **Online address:** marisha@marishachamberlain.com

CHAMBERLAIN, Mary (Christina). British (born England), b. 1947. **Genres:** Area Studies, History, Women's Studies And Issues. **Career:** Arms Control and Disarmament Research Unit, Foreign and Commonwealth Office, research officer, 1970-71; Richardson Institute for Peace and Conflict Research, research officer, 1972; Social Science Research Council, administrative officer, 1972; Norfolk College of Art and Technology, lecturer in liberal studies, 1973-74; London College of Fashion, lecturer in liberal studies, 1974-75; Ipswich Civic College, lecturer in liberal studies, 1977-87; London College of Printing, senior lecturer in cultural studies, 1977-87; University of the West Indies, part-time lecturer, 1988-91; University of Essex, fellow, 1991-93; National Life Story Collection of the British Library National Sound Archive, trustee, 1991-; International Yearbook of Oral History and Life Stories, associate reviews editor, 1992-; Oxford Brookes University, School of Arts and Humanities, senior lecturer, 1993, professor of modern history, 1995-, now professor emeritus; Routledge Studies in Memory and Narrative, founder and principal editor, 1997-; Barbados Government's National Oral History Project, consultant, 1999-. **Publications:** Fenwomen: A Portrait of Women in an English Village, 1975, 3rd ed., 2010; Old Wives' Tales: Their History, Remedies, and Spells, 1981, 2nd ed., 2006; Growing Up in Lambeth, 1989; Narratives of Exile and Return, 1997; Family Love in the Diaspora: Migration and the Anglo-Caribbean Experience, 2006; Empire and Nation-building in the Caribbean: Barbados, 1937-1966, 2010; New Perspectives on Caribbean Families, forthcoming. EDITOR: Writing Lives: Conversations Between Women Writers, 1988; Caribbean Migration: Globalised Identities, 1998; (with P. Thompson) Narrative and Genre, 1998; (with H. Goulbourne) Caribbean Families in Britain and the Trans-Atlantic World, 2001; (with N. Adler, L. Neyzi and S. Leydesdorff) Memories of Mass Repression, 2009. **Address:** School of Arts and Humanities, Oxford Brookes University, Headington Campus, Gipsy Ln., Oxford, OX OX3 0BP, England. **Online address:** mchamberlain@brookes.ac.uk

CHAMBERLIN, Ann. American (born United States), b. 1954. **Genres:** Novels, Plays/Screenplays, Young Adult Non-fiction. **Career:** Writer. **Publications:** NOVELS: The Virgin and the Tower, 1979; Tamar, 1994; Sofia, 1996; The Sultan's Daughter, 1997; The Reign of the Favored Women, 1998; Leaving Eden, 1999; The Merlin of St. Gilles' Well, 1999; The Merlin of the Oak Wood, 2001; Gloria: The Merlin and the Saint, 2005; A History of Women's Seclusion in the Middle East: The Veil in the Looking Glass, 2006; Snakesleeper, 2007; The Woman at the Well, 2011. **Address:** PO Box 711114, Salt Lake City, UT 84171-1114, U.S.A. **Online address:** ann@annchmberlin.com

CHAMBERLIN, Kate. American (born United States), b. 1945. **Genres:** Children's Fiction. **Career:** Teacher, 1967-69; Rochester Institute of Technology, National Technical Institute for the Deaf, departmental secretary, 1971-73; Wayne Central School District, substitute teacher and tutor, 1973-97; Rochester Museum and Science Center, instructor in youth program, 1976-82; Teddy Bear Trail Nursery School, teacher, 1984-86; Community Partners: The Homework Place, director, 1993-95. Writer. **Publications:** The Night Search, 1997; Charles and David, 2010. Contributor to magazines and newspapers. **Address:** 3877 Orchard St., Walworth, NY 14568-9548, U.S.A. **Online address:** kathryngc@juno.com

CHAMBERS, Aidan. American (born United States), b. 1934. **Genres:** Politics/Government, Autobiography/Memoirs, inspirational/Motivational Literature, Novellas/Short Stories, Novels. **Career:** Teacher of English and drama, 1957-68; writer, 1968-; Thimble Press, publisher and proprietor, 1969; University of Bristol, Further Professional Studies Department, tutor, 1970-82; Westminster College, visiting lecturer, 1982-92; University of Kansas, May Hill Arbuthnot lecturer, 1986; Turton & Chambers, co-founder and editorial publisher, 1989-. **Publications:** Cycle Smash, 1967; Marle, 1968; The Reluctant Reader, 1969; Mag and Lugs, 1971; Haunted Houses, 1971; Don't Forget Charlie and the Vase, 1971; Ghosts 2, 1972; More Haunted Houses, 1973; Book of Ghosts and Hauntings, 1973; Introducing Books to Children, 1973, 2nd ed., 1983; Great British Ghosts, 1974; Great Ghosts of the World, 1974; Snake River, 1975; Book of Flyers and Flying, 1976; Book of Cops and Robbers, 1977; Ghost Carnival: Stories of Ghosts in Their Haunts, 1977; Breaktime, 1978; Seal Secret, 1980; Fox Tricks, 1980; Axes for Frozen Seas, 1981; Dream Cage: A Comic Drama in Nine Dreams, 1982; Dance on My Grave, 1982; The Present Takers, 1983; Booktalk: Occasional Writing on Children and Literature, 1985; NIK: Now I Know in UK as Now I Know, 1987; The Reading Environment: How Adults Help Children Enjoy Books, 1990; The Toll Bridge, 1992; Tell Me: Children, Reading and Talk, 1993; Postcards from No Man's Land, 1998; (with S. Gates and M. Watts) More Cool School Stories, 1999; Reading Talk, 2001; This Is All: The Pillow Book of Cordelia Kenn, 2006; Driving Down to Galilee, 2008; The Kissing Game: Flash Fictions and Stories of Defiance, 2011; Dying to Know You, 2012. PLAYS: Johnny Salter, 1966; The Car, 1967; The Chicken Run, 1968; The Dram Cage: A Comic Drama in Nine Dreams, 1982; Only Once: A Play for Young Actors, 1998. EDITOR: (with N. Chambers) Ghosts, 1969; (with N. Chambers) World Zero Minus: An SF Anthology, 1971; I Want to Get Out: Stories and Poems by Young Writers, 1971; (with N. Chambers) Hi-Ran-Ho: A Picture Book of Verse, 1971; (with N. Chambers) In Times to Come: An SF Anthology, 1973; (comp.) Fighters in the Sky, 1976; Funny Folk: A Book of Comic Tales, 1976; Men at War, 1977; Escapers, 1978; (comp.) War at Sea, 1978; (as Malcolm Blacklin) Ghosts 4, 1978; Animal Fair, 1979; Ghosts That Haunt You, 1980; Loving You Loving Me, 1980; Ghost after Ghost, 1982; Plays for Young People to Read and Perform, 1982; (comp.) Out of Time: Stories of the Future, 1984; (comp.) Shades of Dark, 1984; (with J. Bennett) Poetry for Children: A Signal, 1984; A Sporting Chance: Stories of Winning and Losing, 1985; A Quiver of Ghosts, 1987; (and contrib.) A Haunt of Ghosts, 1987; Love All, 1988; On the Edge, 1990; Favourite Ghost Stories, 2002; Favorite Ghost Stories, 2002; More Ghost Stories, 2004. Contributor to books. **Address:** Thimble Press, Lockwood, Station Rd., Woodchester, Stroud, GL GL5 5EQ, England.

CHAMBERS, Chris. Canadian (born Canada) **Genres:** Poetry. **Career:** This Magazine, literary editor. Poet. **Publications:** (With D. McCormack) Wild Mouse, 1998; Lake Where No One Swims, 1999; Patience, forthcoming. Contributor to periodicals. **Address:** Pedlar Press, PO Box 26, Sta. P, Toronto, ON M5S 2S6, Canada.

CHAMBERS, Christopher. American (born United States), b. 1963?. **Genres:** Horror, Mystery/Crime/Suspense. **Career:** Queens College, adjunct professor in communications, 2000-01; Central Piedmont Community College, adjunct professor; University of Maryland, lecturer in writing; Georgetown University, professor. Writer. **Publications:** Sympathy for the Devil: An Angela Bivens Thriller, 2001; A Prayer for Deliverance: An Angela Bivens Thriller, 2003; Voices From The Other Side: Dark Dreams II, 2006; Whispers in the Night: Dark Dreams III, 2007; (ed. with G. Phillips) Darker Mask, 2008; Yella Patsy's Boys, 2009; Calypso's Song, forthcoming; Carolina Pancakes, forthcoming. Works appear in anthologies. Contributor to periodicals. **Address:** Randy Duke, Literary Group International, 270 Lafayette St., Ste. 1505, New York, NY 10012, U.S.A.

CHAMBERS, Diane. American (born United States), b. 1953. **Genres:** Novels. **Career:** American Red Cross, swimming instructor, 1973-91; Asbury Elementary School, diagnostic aide, 1976-77; Baker Junior High School, sign language tutor and interpreter, 1977-80; University of Colorado, sign-language interpreter, 1979-81; Gove Community School, director, 1979-91; West Jefferson Elementary School, sign-language instructor, 1982; Ellexa Press L.L.C., publisher, 2004-; National League of American Pen Women, Denver Branch, president; Jefferson County Adult Education, sign-language instructor/interpreter; Community College of Denver, sign-language instructor/interpreter. Writer. **Publications:** Words in My Hands: A Teacher, a Deaf-Blind Man, an Unforgettable Journey, 2005. **Address:** Ellexa Press L.L.C., 32262 Steven Way, Conifer, CO 80433, U.S.A. **Online address:** dianelane@direcway.com

CHAMBERS, John Whiteclay. American (born United States), b. 1936. **Genres:** History, Essays, Military/Defense/Arms Control, Politics/Government, Documentaries/Reportage. **Career:** Independent, Star-News, news reporter, 1958-60; Independent-Journal, news reporter, 1960-61; KRON-TV, news writer and producer, 1961-65; Columbia University, Barnard College, assistant professor of history, 1972-82; Rutgers University, Department of History, assistant professor, 1982-87, associate professor, 1987-93, professor, 1993-2000, distinguished professor, 2002-, department chair, 1997-98. **Publications:** Draftees or Volunteers: A Documentary History of the Debate Over Military Conscription in the United States, 1787-1973, 1975; Tyranny of Change: America in the Progressive Era, 1900-1917, 1980, 2nd ed. as Tyranny of Change: America in the Progressive Era, 1890-1920, 2000; To Raise an Army: The Draft Comes to Modern America, 1987, George Washington in Cranbury: The Road to the Battle of Monmouth, 2003; (with A.L. Gardner) Conflict Resolution and United States History, 2007; Cranbury: A New Jersey Town from the Colonial Era to the Present, 2012. EDITOR: Eagle and the Dove: The American Peace Movement and United States Foreign Policy, 1900-1922, 1976, 2nd ed., 1991; (with J. Chambers) American History, 1983, 3rd ed., 1990; (with C.C. Moskos) The New Conscientious Objection: From Sacred to Secular Resistance, 1993; (with D. Culbert) World War II, Film and History, 1996; (with G.K. Piehler) Major Problems in American Military History: Documents and Essays, 1998; The Oxford Companion to American Military History, 2000; George Washington in Cranbury: The Road to the Battle of Monmouth, Cranbury Historical and Preservation Society, 2003. **Address:** Department of History, Rutgers University, 210 Van Dyck Hall, 16 Seminary Pl., 83 Somerset St., New Brunswick, NJ 08901, U.S.A. **Online address:** chamber@rci.rutgers.edu

CHAMBERS, Veronica. American (born United States), b. 1970?. **Genres:** Film, Novels, Literary Criticism And History. **Career:** Glamour magazine, contributing editor; Newsweek, culture writer; Premiere, senior associate editor; New York Times Magazine, senior editor; Simon's Rock College literary magazine, editor; Savoy, executive editor; Sassy, staff; Seventeen, staff; Essence, staff; Life, staff; MTV, staff; Campus Lecture Series, founder. **Publications:** (With J.Singleton) Poetic Justice: Film making South Central Style, 1993; Mama's Girl, 1996; Harlem Renaissance, 1997; Amistad Rising: A Story of Freedom, 1998; Marisol and Magdalena: The Sound of Our Sisterhood, 1998; Quinceañera Means Sweet Fifteen, 2001; Double Dutch: A Celebration of Jump Rope, Rhyme, and Sisterhood, 2002; Having It All?: Black Women and Success, 2003; When Did You Stop Loving Me?: A Novel, 2004; Celia Cruz, Queen of Salsa, 2005; Miss Black America, 2005; Joy of Doing Things Badly: A Girl's Guide to Love, Life, and Foolish Bravery, 2006; Kickboxing Geishas: How Modern Japanese Women are Changing Their Nation, 2007; Plus, 2009; Amigas: Lights, Camera, Quince!, 2010; Amigas: She's Got Game, 2010; Fifteen Candles, 2011. Contributor of articles to magazines. **Address:** c/o Sandra Dijkstra, Sandra Dijkstra Literary Agency, 1155 Carmino del Mar, Ste. 515, Del Mar, CA 92014, U.S.A. **Online address:** veronica@veronicachambers.com

CHAMOISEAU, Patrick. French (born France), b. 1953. **Genres:** Novels, Literary Criticism And History, Autobiography/Memoirs, Young Adult Fiction, Translations. **Career:** Writer. **Publications:** Manman Dlo contre la fée Carabosse: Théâtre contaé, 1982; Chronique des sept misères (novel), 1986, trans. as Chronicle of the Seven Sorrows, 1999; Solibo Magnifique (novel), 1988, trans. as Solibo Magnificent, 1997; (contrib.) Martinique, 1988; (with J. Bernabe and R. Confiant) Eloge de la créolité (literary criticism), 1989; (with R. Confiant) Lettres créoles: Tracees antillaises et continentales de la litterature-Haiti, Guadeloupe, Martinique, Guyane 1635-1975 (literary criticism), 1991; Texaco (novel), 1992; Antan d'enfance (memoir), 1993; Au temps de l'antan (folktales), 1994; Guyane: Traces-mémoires du bagne, 1994; Chemin-d'école (memoir), 1994; Creole folktales, 1994; Une enfance crole, 1996; To Write in a Dominated Country, 1997; Ecrire en pays dominé, 1997; School Days=Chemin-d'école, 1997; Esclave vieil homme et le molosse: Roman, 1997; Elmire des sept bonheurs: Confidences d'un vieux travailleur de la distillerie Saint-Etienne, 1998; Strange Words, 1998; Seven Dreams of Elmira: A Tale of Martinique: Being the Confessions of an Old Worker at the Saint-Etienne Distillery, 1999; Childhood=Antan Denfance, 1999; Biblique des derniers gestes: Roman, 2001; Cases en pays-mêlés, 2001; (with Dominique Berthet) Les bois sacrés d'Hélénon, 2002; A bout denfance, 2005; Dimanche au cachot: Roman, 2007; Neuf consciences du malfini: Roman, 2009; (with E. Glissant) Lintraitable Beaut du monde: Adresse à Barack Obama, 2009. **Address:** 31 Favorite, Larentin, 97232, Martinique.

CHAMPAGNE, Duane (Willard). American (born United States), b. 1951. **Genres:** Sociology, History, International Relations/Current Affairs, Social Commentary, Politics/Government, Cultural/Ethnic Topics. **Career:** Cultural Survival Inc., intern, 1982-83; University of Wisconsin, assistant professor, 1983-84; University of California, assistant professor, 1984-91, associate professor, 1991-97, professor of sociology, 1997-, American Indian Studies Center, director, 1991-2002, associate director, 2011-; Washington University, distinguished visiting professor, 2006; University of South Dakota, visiting professor, 2006; Indian Country Today, senior editor, 2006-; Banff Centre, Aboriginal Leadership Program, academic leader, 2006-; Champagne & Goldberg Consultants, partner. **Publications:** American Indian Societies: Strategies and Conditions of Political and Cultural Survival, 2nd ed., 1989; Social Order and Political Change: Constitutional Governments among the Cherokee, the Choctaw, the Chickasaw and the Creek, 1992; Social Change and Cultural Continuity among Native Nations, 2007; Notes from the Center of Turtle Island, 2010. EDITOR: Native America: Portrait of the Peoples, 1994; (and contrib.) Native North American Almanac, 2 vols., 1994; (and intro.) Chronology of Native Norath American History, 1994; Reference Library of Native North America, vol. I-IV, 1996; (with T. Johnson and J. Nagel and contrib.) American Indian Activism: Alcatraz to the Longest Walk, 1997; (and contrib.) Contemporary Native American Cultural Issues, 1999; Native American Studies in Higher Education, 2002; (with I.A. Saad and contrib.) The Future of Indigenous Studies: Strategies for Survival and Development, 2003; (co-ed.) Indigenous People and the Modern State, 2005; (with I.A. Saad and contrib.) Indigenous Education and Empowerment: International Perspectives, 2006; (with I.A. Saad and contrib.) Education, Social Development and Empowerment among Indigenous Peoples: International Perspectives, 2006; (co-ed.) Encyclopedia of American Indian History, 2007; (co-ed. and contrib.) American Indian Nations: Yesterday, Today and Tomorrow, vol. I, 2007; Captured Justice: Native Nations Under Public Law 280, forthcoming. Contributor to books and journals. **Address:** Department of Sociology, University of California, 264 Haines Hall, PO Box 951551, Los Angeles, CA 90095-1551, U.S.A. **Online address:** duanechampagne@me.com

CHAMPION, Craige B. (Craige Brian Champion). American (born United States), b. 1956. **Genres:** History, Cultural/Ethnic Topics. **Career:** Princeton University, lecturer in classics, 1990, 1992; College of New Jersey, adjunct professor of history, 1991-92; The Lewis School and Diagnostic Center of Princeton, instructor, 1992-93; Rutgers University, lecturer in classics, 1993; Reed College, visiting assistant professor of classics and humanities, 1993-95; Allegheny College, assistant professor of ancient history and classical languages, 1995-2001; Syracuse University, Maxwell School of Citizenship and Public Affairs, assistant professor of ancient professor, 2001-03, associate professor of ancient history, 2003-, department chair, 2006-09. Writer. **Publications:** (Ed.) Roman Imperialism: Readings and Sources, 2004; Cultural Politics in Polybius's Histories, 2004. Contributor of articles to journals. **Address:** Department of History, Maxwell School of Citizenship and Public Affairs, Syracuse University, 145 Eggers Hall, 310 B Maxwell Hall, Syracuse, NY 13244-1020, U.S.A. **Online address:** cbchamp@maxwell.syr.edu

CHAMPION, Craige Brian. *See* **CHAMPION, Craige B.**

CHAMPION, J(ustin) A. I. British (born England), b. 1960. **Genres:** History, Intellectual History, Medicine/Health, Social Sciences. **Career:** University of London, Royal Holloway College, faculty, 1990-, senior lecturer in early modern history, 1992-, professor of the history of early modern ideas, head of department. Writer. **Publications:** The Pillars of Priestcraft Shaken: The Church of England and Its Enemies, 1660-1730, 1992; London's Dreaded Visitation: The Social Geography of the Great Plague in 1665, 1995; Republican Learning: John Toland and the Crisis of Christian Culture, 1680-1730, 2003. EDITOR: Early Modern History, 1992; Epidemic Disease in London, 1993; John Toland's Nazarenus 1718, 1999. **Address:** Department of History, Royal Holloway College, University of London, McCrea 312, Egham Hill, Egham, SR TW20 0EX, England. **Online address:** j.champion@rhul.ac.uk

CHAMPION, Larry S. American (born United States), b. 1932. **Genres:** Novellas/Short Stories, Literary Criticism And History, Bibliography, History. **Career:** Davidson College, instructor in English, 1955-56; University of North Carolina, Department of English, teaching fellow, 1959-60; North Carolina State University, instructor, 1960-61, assistant professor, 1961-65, associate professor, 1965-68, professor of English, 1968-94, associate head, 1968-71, head of department, 1971-94, professor emeritus of English, 1994-; Prentice-Hall Inc., Canada Council, editorial consultant; University of Georgia Press, editorial consultant; University of Kentucky Press, editorial consultant; Pennsylvania State Press, editorial consultant; Princeton University Press, editorial consultant. **Publications:** Ben Jonson's Dotages: A Reconsideration of the Late Plays, 1967; The Evolution of Shakespeare's Comedy: A Study in Dramatic Perspective, 1970; Shakespeare's Tragic Perspective: The Development of His Dramatic Technique, 1976; Tragic Patterns in Jacobean and Caroline Drama, 1977; Perspective in Shakespeare's English Histories, 1980; (comp.) King Lear, An Annotated Bibliography, 1980; Thomas Dekker and the Traditions of English Drama, 1985; The Essential Shakespeare: An Annotated Bibliography of Major Modern Studies, 1986, 2nd ed., 1993; The Noise of Threatening Drum: Dramatic Strategy and Political Ideology in Shakespeare and the English Chronicle Plays, 1990. EDITOR: Quick Springs of Sense: Studies in the Eighteenth Century, 1974. Contributor to journals. **Address:** Department of English, College of Humanities and Social Sciences, lNorth Carolina State University, 221 Tompkins Hal, PO Box 8105, Raleigh, NC 27695-8105, U.S.A. **Online address:** larrychampion@webtv.net

CHAMPLIN, Margaret Derby. *See* **CHAMPLIN, Peggy.**

CHAMPLIN, Peggy. (Margaret Derby Champlin). American (born United States), b. 1925. **Genres:** History, Biography. **Career:** Sterling-Winthrop Research Institute, assistant librarian, 1947-49; Chicago Public Library, librarian, 1949-50; California State University, science reference librarian and coordinator of computerized reference services, 1972-96; Autry Museum of Western Heritage, assistant librarian, 1990-91. Writer. **Publications:** Raphael Pumpelly: Gentleman Geologist of the Gilded Age, 1994. Contributor to books. **Address:** 2169 Linda Flora Dr., Los Angeles, CA 90077, U.S.A. **Online address:** champc@aol.com

CHAMPLIN, Tim. American (born United States), b. 1937. **Genres:** Westerns/Adventure, Young Adult Fiction, Novels, Romance/Historical. **Career:** Youth Organization, youth director, 1965-67; U.S. Department of the Interior, Bureau of Outdoor Recreation, recreation resource specialist, 1967-68, Department of Veterans' Affairs, veterans' benefits counselor, 1970-77, supervisor, 1977-94; Stewart Air Force Base, Smyrna, youth director, 1968-70. Writer. **Publications:** Summer of the Sioux, 1982; Dakota Gold, 1982; Staghorn, 1984; Shadow Catcher, 1985; Great Timber Race, 1986; Iron Trail, 1987; Colt Lightning, 1989; King of the Highbinders, 1989; Flying Eagle, 1990; The Last Campaign: A Western Story, 1996; The Survivor: A Western Story, 1996; Deadly Season: A Western Story, 1997; Swift Thunder: A Western Story, 1998; The Tombstone Conspiracy: A Western Story, 1999; Lincoln's Ransom: A Western Story, 1999; Treasure of the Templars: A Western Story, 2000; Wayfaring Strangers: A Frontier Story, 2000; A Trail to Wounded Knee: A Frontier Story, 2001; By Flare of Northern Lights: A North-Western Story, 2001; Raiders of the Western and Alantic: A Western Story, 2002; White Lights Roar: A Western Story, 2003; Fire Bell in the Night: A Western Story, 2004; Territorial Rough Rider: A Western Story, 2004; Devils' Domain: Far from the Eye of God, 2005; Blaze Of Noon: A Western Story, 2006; Cold Cache: A Western Story, 2007; West of Washoe: A Western Story, 2009; Beecher Island: A Western Story, 2010. Contributor of articles to magazines. **Address:** Dorchester Publishing Company Inc., 11 West Ave., Ste. 103, PO Box 6640, Wayne, PA 19087, U.S.A.

CHAN, Gerald. New Zealander (born New Zealand) **Genres:** Politics/Government, History. **Career:** National University of Singapore, East Asian Institute, visiting fellow, 1998; Victoria University of Wellington, School of Political Science and International Relations, senior lecturer; Durham University, professor of East Asian politics, Centre for Contemporary Chinese Studies, director; University of Auckland, Department of Political Studies, professor of political studies, head of department, 2009-; New Zealand Journal of East Asian Studies; co-editor. **Publications:** China and International Organizations: Participation in Non-Governmental Organizations since 1971, 1989; International Studies in China: An Annotated Bibliography, 1998; Chinese Perspectives on International Relations: A Framework for Analysis, 1999; China's International Relations in the 21st Century Dynamics of Paradigm Shifts, 2000; China's Compliance in Global Affairs: Trade, Arms Control, Environmental Protection, Human Rights, 2006; (ed. with L. Chan and F. Kwan)

China At 60: Global-Local Interactions, 2011; (with P.K. Lee and L. Chan) China Engages Global Governance: A New World Order in the Making?, 2011. Contributor to periodicals. **Address:** Department of Political Studies, University of Auckland, Rm. G02, 12 Symonds St., PO Box 92019, Auckland, 1142, New Zealand. **Online address:** gerald.chan@auckland.ac.nz

CHAN, Gillian. Canadian/British (born England), b. 1954. **Genres:** Novellas/Short Stories, Young Adult Fiction, Children's Fiction. **Career:** Teacher and librarian, 1980-90; Writer, 1994-. **Publications:** Golden Girl and Other Stories, 1994; Glory Days and Other Stories, 1996; The Carved Box, 2001; A Foreign Field, 2002; An Ocean Apart: The Gold Mountain Diary of Chin Mei-Ling, 2004; The Turning, 2005. **Address:** 41 Thornton Trl., Dundas, ON L9H 6Y2, Canada. **Online address:** gillian@gillianchan.com

CHANCE, Megan. American (born United States), b. 1959. **Genres:** Novels, Romance/Historical. **Career:** Television news photographer, 1983-86; special events coordinator, 1987-89; commercial studio manager, 1988-95; full-time fiction writer, 1995-. **Publications:** A Candle in the Dark, 1993; After the Frost, 1994; The Portrait, 1995; A Heart Divided, 1996; Fall from Grace, 1997; The Way Home, 1997; The Gentleman Caller, A Season in Eden, 1999; Susannah Morrow, 2002; An Inconvenient Wife, 2004; The Spiritualist, 2008; Prima Donna, 2009; City of Ash, 2011. **Address:** c/o Kim Witherspoon, Inkwell Management, 521 5th Ave., Ste. 2600, New York, NY 10175, U.S.A. **Online address:** meganchance@meganchance.com

CHANCER, Lynn S. American (born United States), b. 1954?. **Genres:** Sociology, Social Commentary, Sex, Psychiatry. **Career:** Columbia University, Barnard College, assistant professor, 1989; Fordham University, associate professor of sociology and anthropology, associate chair of graduate studies; City University of New York, Hunter College, Sociology Department, professor. Writer. **Publications:** Sadomasochism in Everyday Life: The Dynamics of Power and Powerlessness, 1992; Reconcilable Differences: Confronting Beauty, Pornography, and the Future of the Feminism, 1998; High-Profile Crimes: When Legal Cases become Social Causes, 2005; (with B.X. Watkins) Gender, Race and Class: A Theortical and Practical Overview, 2006. **Address:** Sociology Department, Hunter College, City University of New York, 1602 Hunter W, 695 Park Ave., New York, NY 10065, U.S.A. **Online address:** lchancer@hunter.cuny.edu

CHANCY, Myriam J(osephe) A(imee). American/Haitian (born United States), b. 1970. **Genres:** Literary Criticism And History, History. **Career:** Vanderbilt University, assistant professor of English, 1994-97; Arizona State University, associate professor of English, 1997-; University of California, Journal of Haitian Studies, editorial board, 2000-; Louisiana State University, professor, 2003-; University of Cincinnati, Department of English and Comparative Literature, professor. Writer. **Publications:** Searching for Safe Spaces: Afro-Caribbean Women Writers in Exile, 1997; Framing Silence: Revolutionary Novels by Haitian Women, 1997; Spirit of Haiti, 2003; The Scorpion's Claw, 2005; The Loneliness of Angels: Fractured, 2009; From Sugar to Revolution: Women's Visions of Haiti, Cuba and the Dominican Republic, 2012; Floating Islands: Cosmopolitanism, Transnationalism and Racial Identity Formation, forthcoming. Contributor of articles to journals. Works appear in anthologies. **Address:** Department of English and Comparative Literature, University of Cincinnati, 214B McMicken Hall, 2700 Campus Way, PO Box 210069, Cincinnati, OH 45221-0069, U.S.A. **Online address:** myriam.chancy@uc.edu

CHANDA, Nayan. American/Indian (born India), b. 1946?. **Genres:** Military/Defense/Arms Control, History, Business/Trade/Industry. **Career:** Far Eastern Economic Review, correspondent, editor, editor-at-large, 1974-2001; Carnegie Endowment for International Peace, senior fellow, 1989-90; Asian Wall Street Journal Weekly, editor, 1990-92; Yale Center for the Study of Globalization, director of publications, YaleGlobal Online Magazine, editor, 2001-; Business World and Singapore Straits Times, columnist. Writer. **Publications:** (co-ed.) Ho- tschi-minh-stadt: die stunde null: reportagen vom ende e. 30jaehrigen krieges, 1975; Brother Enemy: The War after the War, 1986; Cambodia's Future: The View from Vietnam, 1987; (ed. with S. Talbott) The Age of Terror: America and the World after September 11, 2001; (co-ed.) The Paradox of a Global USA, 2007; Bound Together: How Traders, Preachers, Adventurers and Warriors Shaped Globalization, 2007. Contributor of articles to journals. **Address:** Yale Center for the Study of Globalization, Betts House, 393 Prospect St., New Haven, CT 06511, U.S.A.

CHANDLER, Daniel Ross. American (born United States), b. 1937. **Genres:** Theology/Religion, History, Biography, Reference. **Career:** Augustana College, instructor, associate debate coach, 1965-66; Central Michigan University, assistant professor of communication, 1969-70; State University of New York College-New Paltz, assistant professor of communication, 1970-71; City University of New York, assistant professor of communication, 1971-75, adjunct assistant professor, adjunct associate professor, 1983-90; Yale University, research fellow, 1974-78; Princeton Theological Seminary, visiting fellow, 1974-84; Northeastern Illinois University, adjunct professor, 1974-75, 1994-95; Rutgers University, assistant professor of communication, 1976-83; New Brunswick Theological Seminary, adjunct professor, 1978-79; New York Institute of Technology, adjunct professor, 1985-89; Hofstra University, adjunct professor, 1985, 1990; State University of New York-Garden City, adjunct professor, 1986-90; Loyola University-Chicago, lecturer, 1991-93; Harold Washington College, lecturer, 2002-03; United Methodist Church, ordained minister. Writer. **Publications:** The Official, Authorized Biography of the Reverend Dr. Preston Bradley, 1971; The Rhetorical Tradition: Principles and Practice, 1978; The History of Rhetoric, 1990; The 1993 Parliament of the World's Religions, 1995; Toward Universal Religion: Voices of American and Indian Spirituality, 1996; Outsiders: Speakers and Writers Who Influenced American Religion, forthcoming; Universal Religion: Some Exponents, forthcoming; The Human Quest for Spiritual Unity: A Life of Henry Steel Olcott, forthcoming. Contributor of articles to books and periodicals. **Address:** 1929 Sherman Ave., Apt. W1, PO Box 953, Evanston, IL 60201-3231, U.S.A. **Online address:** dchandler@nccumc.org

CHANDLER, Glenn. British/Scottish (born Scotland), b. 1949?. **Genres:** Young Adult Non-fiction, Novels. **Career:** Writer. **Publications:** The Sanctuary, 1981; The Tribe, 1981; Killer, 1983; Taggart's Glasgow, 1989; Burning Poison, 2000; Savage Tide, 2003; Dead Sight, 2004. **Address:** c/o Diana Tyler, MBA Literary Agents Ltd., 62 Grafton Way, London, GL W1T 5DW, England. **Online address:** leavalleypress@yahoo.com

CHANDLER, James K. American (born United States), b. 1948. **Genres:** Literary Criticism And History, Romance/Historical. **Career:** University of Chicago, professor of English, 1978-, Department of English Language and Literature, George M. Pullman professor, Barbara E. & Richard J. Franke professor, Franke Institute for the Humanities, director, 2001-. Writer. **Publications:** Wordsworth's Second Nature: A Study of the Poetry and Politics, 1984; (ed. with A.I. Davidson and H. Harootunian) Questions of Evidence: Proof, Practice, and Persuasion Across the Disciplines, 1994; England in 1819: The Politics of Literary Culture and the Case of Romantic Historicism, 1998; (ed. with K. Gilmartin) Romantic Metropolis: The Urban Scene of British Culture, 1780-1840, 2005; (ed. with M.N. McLane) The Cambridge Companion to Romantic Poetry, 2008; (ed.) Cambridge History of English Romantic Literature, 2009. **Address:** The Franke Institute for the Humanities, University of Chicago, S102 Joseph Regenstein Library, 1100 E 57th St., Chicago, IL 60637, U.S.A. **Online address:** docj@uchicago.edu

CHANDLER, Laurel. *See* **HOLDER, Nancy L.**

CHANDLER, Marc. American (born United States), b. 1961. **Genres:** Economics. **Career:** Brown Brothers Harriman (a bank), chief foreign exchange strategist, 2005-; HSBC Bank USA, chief currency strategist; Mellon Bank, chief currency strategist; New York University, Center for Continuing and Professional Studies, associate professor. Writer, economic consultant, public speaker and investment expert. **Publications:** Making Sense of the Dollar: Exposing Dangerous Myths about Trade and Foreign Exchange, 2009. Contributor to magazines and newspapers. **Address:** New York University SCPS, Woolworth Bldg., 145 4th Ave., 15 Barclay, New York, NY 10003, U.S.A.

CHANDLER, Marilyn R(uth). *See* **MCENTYRE, Marilyn Chandler.**

CHANDRA, Vikram. American/Indian (born India), b. 1961. **Genres:** Novels, Novellas/Short Stories. **Career:** University of Houston, adjunct professor, 1987-93; Letters and Light, owner, 1987-94; George Washington University, visiting writer, 1994-95, assistant professor, 1995-96; University of California, Department of English, instructor of creative writing, senior lecturer, John Hopkins University, faculty. **Publications:** Red Earth and Pouring Rain (novel), 1995; Love and Longing in Bombay: Stories, 1997; City of Gold (television series), 1996; Sacred Games, 2006. Contributor to periodicals. **Address:** Department of English, University of California, 322 Wheeler Hall, Berkeley, CA 94720-1030, U.S.A. **Online address:** vikramchandra@berkeley.edu

CHANEY, Edward (Paul de Gruyter). British (born England), b. 1951. **Genres:** History, Area Studies, Travel/Exploration, Art/Art History, Humanities. **Career:** European University Institute, ricercatore, 1978-85; University of Pisa, lecturer in English, 1979-85; Oxford University, Lincoln College, Shuffrey research fellow in architectural history, 1985-90; Charles A. Strong Center, Georgetown University Florence Program, adjunct assistant professor, 1982-83; Oxford Brookes University, part-time lecturer art history, 1991-96; London Region of English Heritage, historian, 1991-93; Southampton Solent University, professor of fine and decorative arts, senior lecturer in visual arts, History of Collecting Research Centre, chair. Writer. **Publications:** (Intro.) Southern Italy, 1982; (ed. with N. Ritchie) Oxford, China and Italy: Writings in Honour of Sir Harold Acton on His Eightieth Birthday, 1984; The Grand Tour and the Great Rebellion: Richard Lassels and the Voyage of Italy in the Seventeenth Century, 1985; (ed. and intro. with H. Acton) Florence: A Travellers' Companion, 1986; (intro.) Sicily, 1988, rev. ed., 1990; (ed. with P. Mack) England and the Continental Renaissance, 1990; (ed. with J. Bold) English Architecture, Public and Private: Essays for Kerry Downes, 1993; The Evolution of the Grand Tour: Anglo-Italian Cultural Relations Since the Renaissance, 1998; (ed. and intro.) The Evolution of English Collecting: Receptions of Italian Art in the Tudor and Stuart Periods, 2003; (with C. Clearkin) Richard Eurich, 1903-1992: Visionary Artist, 2003. Contributor of articles to periodicals. **Address:** Southampton Solent University, East Park Terr., Southampton, HB SO14 0YN, England.

CHANEY, Jill. British (born England), b. 1932. **Genres:** Children's Fiction, Romance/Historical, Young Adult Fiction, Literary Criticism And History. **Career:** Chorleywood Bookshop, director, 1971-88. Writer. **Publications:** On Primrose Hill, 1961; Half a Candle, 1969; A Penny for the Guy, 1970; Mottram Park, 1971; Christopher's Dig, 1972; Taking the Woffle to Pebblecombe on Sea, 1974; Return to Mottram Park, 1974; Christopher's Find, 1975; The Buttercup Field, 1976; Woffle, R.A., 1976; Canary Yellow, 1977; Angel Face, 1977; Vectis Diary, 1979; Leaving Mottram Park, 1989; Three Weeks in August, 1995. **Address:** Glen Rosa, Colleyland, Chorleywood, HF WD3 5LL, England.

CHANG, Gordon G. American (born United States) **Genres:** Politics/Government, Public/Social Administration, History, Business/Trade/Industry, Economics, Money/Finance. **Career:** Baker & McKenzie (law firm), law partner; Paul Weiss (law firm), counsel; Cornell University, trustee; Forbes.com, columnist. Attorney and speaker. **Publications:** The Coming Collapse of China, 2001; Nuclear Showdown: North Korea Takes on the World, 2006. Contributor to periodicals. **Address:** c/o Author Mail, Random House, 1745 Broadway, 18th Fl., New York, NY 10019, U.S.A. **Online address:** info@gordonchang.com

CHANG, Ha-Joon. British/Korean (born Korea (South)), b. 1963. **Genres:** Economics, Politics/Government, Business/Trade/Industry, Money/Finance, History. **Career:** University of Cambridge, assistant director of development studies, 1990-2004, lecturer, 2004-05, reader, 2005-, Cambridge Advanced Programme on Rethinking Development Economics, director, 2001-08; Institute of Developing Economies Advanced School, visiting professor, 1998; Korea Development Institute (KDI) School of International Development and Management, visiting professor, 1999; Korea University, visiting professor, 2003-04; World Bank, consultant; Asian Development Bank, consultant; European Investment Bank, consultant. Writer. **Publications:** The Political Economy of Industrial Policy, 1994; (ed. with P. Nolan) The Transformation of the Communist Economies: Against the Mainstream, 1995; (ed. with R. Rowthorn) The Role of the State in Economic Change, 1995; (co-ed.) Institutions and the Role of the State, 2000; Who Benefits from the New International Intellectual Property Rights Regime? And What Should Africa Do?, 2001; (ed.) The Rebel Within: Joseph Stiglitz and the World Bank, 2001; Breaking the Mould: An Institutionalist Political Economy Alternative to the Neoliberal Theory of the Market and the State, 2001; (co-ed.) Financial Liberalization and the Asian Crisis, 2001; Kicking Away the Ladder: Development Strategy in Historical Perspective, 2002; (ed.) Rethinking Development Economics, 2003; Globalisation, Economic Development, and the Role of the State, 2003; (with J. Shin) Restructuring Korea Inc., 2003; (co-ed.) The Politics of Trade and Industrial Policy in Africa: Forced Consensus?, 2004; (with I. Grabel) Reclaiming Development: An Alternative Manual for Economic Policy, 2004; What Danger Lies in the WTO-Nama Negotiations for Africa?, 2005; The East Asian Development Experience: The Miracle, the Crisis, and the Future (essays), 2006; Bad Samaritans: Rich Nations, Poor Policies, and the Threat to the Developing World, 2007 in US as Bad Samaritans: The Myth of Free Trade and the Secret History of Capitalism, 2008; (ed.) Institutional Change and Economic Development, 2007; 23 Things They Don't Tell You About Capitalism, 2010; (ed.) Public Policy and Agricultural Development, 2011; (with B. Turok and J.C. Ferraz) Development in a Divided Country, 2011. Contributor of articles to books and journals. **Address:** Faculty of Economics, Cambridge University, Austin Robinson Bldg., Sidgwick Ave., Cambridge, CB CB3 9DD, England. **Online address:** ha-joon.chang@econ.cam.ac.uk

CHANG, Joan Chiung-huei. Taiwanese (born Taiwan), b. 1962. **Genres:** Literary Criticism And History. **Career:** Soochow University, Department of English, chair, 2000-01, associate professor of English, 1997-. Writer. **Publications:** Transforming Chinese American Literature: A Study of History, Sexuality, and Ethnicity, 2000; (ed.) The Globalization of Comparative Literature: Asian Initiatives, 2004. Contributor to periodicals. **Address:** Department of English, Soochow University, Rm. H107, 70 Linhsi Rd., Shihlin, Taipei, 111, Taiwan. **Online address:** eugene@mail.scu.edu.tw

CHANG, Kang-i Sun. American (born United States), b. 1944. **Genres:** Literary Criticism And History. **Career:** Tufts University, visiting assistant professor of Chinese Literature, 1979-80; Princeton University, Gest Oriental Library and East Asian Collections, curator, 1980-81; Yale University, assistant professor of Chinese literature, 1982-86, associate professor of Chinese literature, 1986-90, professor of Chinese, 1990-2009, director of graduate studies, 1984-91, 1998-2000, 2003, 2008-09, Women's and Gender Studies Program, associated faculty, 1990-, Department of East Asian Languages and Literatures, chair, 1991-97, Department of Comparative Literature, associated faculty, 2001-, inaugural Malcolm G. Chace 56 professor of East Asian languages and literature, 2009-. Writer. **Publications:** The Evolution of Chinese Tz'u Poetry, 1980; Six Dynasties Poetry, 1986; The Late-Ming Poet Ch'en Tzu-lung, 1991; Writing Women in Late Imperial China, 1997; (co-ed.) Women Writers of Traditional China, 1999; Journey Through the White Terror: A Daughter's Memoir, 2006; (co-ed.) Tradition and Modernity: Comparative Perspectices, 2007; (co-ed.) The Cambridge History of Chinese Literature, 2010. **Address:** Department of East Asian Languages & Literatures, Yale University, 306 Hall of Graduate Studies, PO Box 208236, New Haven, CT 06520, U.S.A. **Online address:** kang-i.chang@yale.edu

CHANG, Kevin O'Brien. Jamaican (born Jamaica), b. 1958. **Genres:** Music. **Career:** Fontana Pharmacy, managing director, 1989-. Writer. **Publications:** (With W. Chen) Reggae Routes: The Story of Jamaican Music, 1998. Contributor to periodicals. **Address:** Fontana Pharmacy, Mobay Shopping Ctr., Montego Bay, 872, Jamaica. **Online address:** superv@cwjamaica.com

CHANG, Leonard. American (born United States), b. 1978. **Genres:** Novels. **Career:** Antioch University, Master of Fine Arts Program, mentor faculty, 1998-2011; Mills College, distinguished visiting writer, 2001-03. Novelist. **Publications:** The Fruit 'N Food, 1996; Dispatches from the Cold, 1998; Over the Shoulder, 2001; Underkill, 2003; Fade to Clear, 2004; Crossings, 2009; Triplines, 2013. **Address:** Black Heron Press, PO Box 13396, Mill Creek, WA 98082-1396, U.S.A. **Online address:** len@leonardchang.com

CHANG, Leslie. (Leslie T. Chang). American/Chinese (born China) **Genres:** Novels. **Career:** Wall Street Journal, correspondent. Writer. **Publications:** Beyond the Narrow Gate: The Journey of Four Chinese Women from the Middle Kingdom to Middle America, 1999; Factory Girls: From Village to City in a Changing China, 2008, new ed., 2009. **Address:** c/o Author Mail, Penguin Putnam/Dutton, 375 Hudson St., New York, NY 10014, U.S.A. **Online address:** leslie.chang@wsj.com

CHANG, Leslie T. *See* **CHANG, Leslie.**

CHANG, Margaret. American (born United States), b. 1941. **Genres:** Novels. **Career:** Joseph Estabrook School, librarian, 1965-67; New York Public Library, children's librarian, 1967-68; Mount Greylock Regional High School, librarian, 1968-72; Williams College, part-time reference librarian, 1979-89; Buxton School, librarian, 1985-; Massachusetts College of Liberal Arts, instructor in literature for children and young adults, 1989-2006, Department of Education, adjunct instructor. Writer. **Publications:** Discovering Your Library, 1976. WITH R. CHANG: Speaking of Chinese, 1978, rev. ed., 2001; In the Eye of War, 1990; The Cricket Warrior: A Chinese Tale, 1994; The Beggar's Magic: A Chinese Tale, 1997; How To Grasp The Bird's Tail: If You Don't Speak Chinese, 1997; Da Wei's Treasure: A Chinese Tale, 1999; Celia's Robot, 2009. **Address:** Department of Education, Massachusetts College of Liberal Arts, 375 Church St., North Adams, MA 01247, U.S.A.

CHANG, Maria Hsia. American/Hong Kong (born Hong Kong), b. 1950. **Genres:** Area Studies, International Relations/Current Affairs, Politics/Government, Theology/Religion. **Career:** San Francisco State University, lecturer in international relations, 1979-80; Washington State University, visiting assistant professor of political science, 1980-82; University of California, Institute of International Studies, associate research specialist, 1982-83; University of Puget Sound, assistant professor of political science, 1983-89; University of Nevada, professor of political science, 1989-, now professor emeritus; U.S. Marine Corps, War College, lecturer on China, 2003-; American Association for Chinese Studies, board director. Writer and consultant. **Publications:** (With E.K. Snyder and A.J. Gregor) The Taiwan Relations Act and the Defense of the Republic of China, 1980; (with A.J. Gregor and A.B. Zimmerman) Ideology and Development: Sun Yat-sen and the Economic History of Taiwan, 1981; (with A.J. Gregor) The Republic of China and U.S. Policy, 1983; (with A.J. Gregor) Essays on Sun Yat-sen and the Economic Development of Taiwan, 1983; (with A.J. Gregor) The Iron Triangle: A U.S. Security Policy for Northeast Asia, 1984; The Chinese Blue Shirt Society, 1985; (co-ed.) Human Rights in the People's Republic of China, 1985; (co-ed.) The Aftermath of the 1989 Tiananmen Crisis in Mainland China, 1992; The Labors of Sisyphus: The Economic Development of Communist China, 1998; Return of the Dragon: China's Wounded Nationalism, 2001; Falun Gong: The End of Days, 2004. Contributor to periodicals. **Address:** Department of Political Science, University of Nevada, Rm. 236, Mack Social Science Bdg., 1664 N Virginia St., PO Box 0302, Reno, NV 89557-0302, U.S.A. **Online address:** mariac@scs.unr.edu

CHANIOTIS, Angelos. British/Greek (born Greece), b. 1959?. **Genres:** History. **Career:** University of Heidelberg, Department of Ancient History, research fellow, 1986-87, assistant professor, 1987-92, associate professor, 1992-94, professor and department chair, 1998-2006, Faculty of Oriental and Ancient Studies, associate dean, 2000-01, vice rector for international relations, 2001-06, Collaborative Research Project, associate director, 2002-06, Priority Research Project, director, 2004-06; New York University, Department of Classics, visiting professor, 1993, associate professor, 1994-98, acting chair, 1996, professor of Greek history, 1997-98, director of graduate studies, 1997-98; Oxford University, senior research fellow, 2006-10, visiting professor of ancient history, 2010-; Institute for Advanced Study, professor, 2010-. Writer. **Publications:** Historie und historiker in den griechischen inschriften: Epigraphische beitrage zur griechischen historiographie, 1988; Franz Steiner Verlag (Wiesbaden, Germany), Die vertrage zwischen kretischen poleis in der hellenistischen zeit, 1996; (ed.) From Minoan Farmers to Roman Traders: Sidelights on the Economy of Ancient Crete, 1999; (ed. with P. Ducrey) Army and Power in the Ancient World, 2002; War in the Hellenistic World: A Social and Cultural History, 2005; Theatrikoteta kai demosios vios ston Hellenistiko kosmo, 2009; Applied Classics: Comparisons, Constructs, Controversies, 2009. **Address:** All Souls College, Oxford University, Oxford, OX OX1 4AL, England. **Online address:** angelos.chaniotis@urz.uni-heidelberg.de

CHANOFF, David. American (born United States), b. 1943. **Genres:** Biography, International Relations/Current Affairs, History, Medicine/Health, Reference, Autobiography/Memoirs. **Career:** Sudbury Valley School, founding teacher and administrator, 1968-; Tufts University, English instructor, 1977-80; Harvard University, English instructor, 1977-83. Writer. **Publications:** (With T.N. Tang and D.V. Toai) A Vietcong Memoir, 1985; (with D.V. Toai) The Vietnamese Gulag, 1986; (with D.V. Toai) Portrait of the Enemy, 1986; (with B. Diem) In the Jaws of History, 1987; (with A. Sharon) Warrior: The Autobiography of Ariel Sharon, 1989; (with O. DeForest) Slow Burn: The Rise and Bitter Fall of American Intelligence in Vietnam, 1990; (with K. Good) Into the Heart: One Man's Pursuit of Love and Knowledge among the Yanomama in UK as Into the Heart: An Amazonian Love Story, 1991; (with W.J. Crowe, Jr.) The Line of Fire: From Washington to the Gulf, the Politics and Battles of the New Military, 1993; (with F. Zandman) Never the Last Journey, 1995; (with J. Elders) Joycelyn Elders, M.D.: From Sharecropper's Daughter to Surgeon General of the United States of America, 1996; (with D.V. Toai) Vietnam: A Portrait of Its People at War, 1996; (with W. Ungar) Destined to Live, 2000; (with E. Nuwere) Hacker Cracker: A Journey from the Mean Streets of Brooklyn to the Frontiers of Cyberspace, 2002; (with W. Ungar) Only in America: From Holocaust to National Industry Leadership, 2005; (with V. Damone) Singing was the Easy Part, 2009; (with A.A. White III) Seeing Patients: Unconscious Bias in Health Care, 2011. Contributor to periodicals. **Address:** c/o Owen Laster, William Morris Agency Inc., 1325 Ave. of the Americas, 15th Fl., New York, NY 10019-6067, U.S.A.

CHAO, Patricia. American (born United States), b. 1955. **Genres:** Novels, Children's Fiction. **Career:** Sarah Lawrence College, undergraduate writing workshop teacher; Global Rhythm Magazine, reviewer. Writer. **Publications:** Monkey King (novel), 1997; Mambo Peligroso, 2005. Contributor to periodicals. Works appear in anthologies. **Address:** New York, NY , U.S.A. **Online address:** patricia@patriciachao.com

CHAPIN, F. Stuart. American (born United States), b. 1916. **Genres:** Regional/Urban Planning, Adult Non-fiction, Social Sciences. **Career:** Tennessee Valley Authority, regional planner, 1940-42, 1946-47; City of Greensboro, director of planning, 1947-49; University of North Carolina, Department of City and Regional Planning, associate professor, 1949-54, professor of planning, 1954-78, alumni distinguished professor emeritus of planning, 1978-, Center for Urban and Regional Studies, director, 1957-70. Writer. **Publications:** (With S. Schiller) Communities for Living, Prepared for the Advisory Panel on Regional Materials of Instruction for the Tennessee Valley, 1941; Urban Land Use Planning, 1957, (with E.J. Kaiser and D.R. Godschalk) 4th ed., 1995; (with G.C. Hemmens, S.F. Weiss and T.G. Donnelly) Land Development Patterns in the Piedmont Industrial Crescent, 1960; (with S.F. Weiss and T.G. Donnelly) Factors Influencing Land Development: Evaluation of Inputs for a Forecast Model, 1962; Evaluation Of Inputs For A Forecast Model, 1962; (co-ed. and contrib.) Urban Growth Dynamics, 1962; (with S.F. Weiss and T.G. Donnelly) Some Input Refinements for a Residential Model, 1965; (with H.C. Hightower) Household Activity Systems, a Pilot Investigation, 1966; Urban Growth Dynamics in a Regional Cluster of Cities, 1966; (with P.G. Hammer, Jr.) Human Time Allocation: A Case Study of Washington, D.C.: A Technical Monograph, 1972; (with R.B. Zehner and J.T. Howell) Across the City Line: A White Community in Transition, 1974; Human Activity Patterns in the City, Things People Do in Time and in Space, 1974. CONTRIBUTOR: The Urban South, 1955; Readings in Urban Geography, 1959; Hirsch, 1963; Introduction to Urban Planning and Urbanism, 1966; Urban Development Models, 1968; The Quality of the Urban Environment, 1969; Encyclopedia of Urban Planning, 1974; Timing Space and Spacing Time, 1978. **Address:** Department of City and Regional Planning, University of North Carolina, New E Bldg., PO Box 3140, Chapel Hill, NC 27599-3140, U.S.A. **Online address:** planning@unc.edu

CHAPIN, Miles. American (born United States), b. 1954. **Genres:** Autobiography/Memoirs, Art/Art History, Music, Reference. **Career:** Professional actor, 1964-; Steinway Piano, officer. Writer. **Publications:** (Ed. with D.R. Katz) Tales from the Jungle: A Rainforest Reader, 1995; 88 Keys: The Making of a Steinway Piano, 1997. **Address:** c/o Kristine Dahl, International Creative Management, 40 W 57th St., New York, NY 10019, U.S.A. **Online address:** blueelver@aol.com

CHAPIN, Sarah. American (born United States), b. 1931. **Genres:** History, Novels, Young Adult Fiction. **Career:** Independent Broadcast Associates, National Public Radio, Series, research adviser, 1986. Writer. **Publications:** The Tin Box Collection: Letters of Roger Sessions, His Family and Friends, 1992; (ed.) Traditions and Reminiscences of Concord, Massachusetts, 1779-1878, 1993; A Wreath of Joy: Selected Holdings from the Special Collections of the Concord Free Public Library, 1996; Images of Concord, 1997; Concord, Massachusetts, Aracadia, 1997; (co-author) Concord: Then and Now, 2001; Entering Concord, 2005; History of Concord, forthcoming. Contributor to journals. **Address:** 261 Sudbury Rd., Concord, MA 01742, U.S.A.

CHAPMAN, Herb. American (born United States), b. 1951. **Genres:** Novels, Mystery/Crime/Suspense, Young Adult Fiction, Literary Criticism And History. **Career:** South Carolina Department of Mental Health, psychologist, 1976-80; Midlands Technical College, adjunct faculty, 1980-86; South Carolina Department of Juvenile Justice, psychologist, 1986-87; Baptist Medical Center, Center for Pain Management, coordinator and manager, 1987-98; writer, 1998-. **Publications:** The Book of Cain: A Novel of Suspense, 2001. Contributor to periodicals. **Address:** Stephanie von Hirschberg Literary Agency, 1385 Baptist Church Rd., Yorktown Heights, NY 10598, U.S.A.

CHAPMAN, J. Dudley. Also writes as Joan Carlson, Joseph Dudley. American (born United States), b. 1928. **Genres:** Psychology, Sex, Human Relations/Parenting. **Career:** College of Osteopathic Medicine and Surgery, Still Osteopathic Hospital, associate professor of obstetrics and gynecology, 1956-58, chairman of department, 1957-58; Brentwood Hospital, chief of obstetrics and gynecology, 1958-61; Private practice of obstetrics and gynecology, 1958-; Bayview Hospital, senior obstetrician and gynecologist, 1961-63, consultant, 1963-; American College of Osteopathic Obstetricians and Gynecologists, president, 1966-67; Northeastern Ohio General Hospital, staff, 1967-; Osteopathic Physician, ed-in-chief, 1968-; Ohio University College of Osteopathic Medicine, clinical professor, 1979-; The Institute for the Advanced Study of Human Sexuality, faculty, 1979-; Penthouse FORUM, The Journal American Osteopathic Association, editorial consultant. **Publications:** The Feminine Mind and Body: The Psychosexual and Psychosomatic Reactions of Women, 1967; The Sexual Equation: Woman, Man, Socially, Sexually, 1977. Contributor of articles to journals. **Address:** PO Box 340, North Madison, OH 44057-0340, U.S.A.

CHAPMAN, Lynne F(erguson). Welsh/American (born United States), b. 1963. **Genres:** Biography, History, Architecture. **Career:** Mayfield Publishing, editorial assistant, 1985-87; Windsor Publications, photography editor, 1987-88; Dushkin Publishing, annual editions editor, 1988-89; freelance editor and writer, 1989-. **Publications:** Sylvia Plath, 1994; Leo Tolstoy, 1997; Medieval Castles, 2000; Egyptian Pyramids, 2000; Cathedrals, 2000. **Address:** Creative Education Inc., 123 S Broad St., Mankato, MN 56001, U.S.A.

CHAPMAN, Melvin. *See* **CHIPMAN, Donald.**

CHAPMAN, Myriam. American (born United States), b. 1936?. **Genres:** Novels, Translations, Romance/Historical. **Career:** Dover Publications, publicity director; Bank Street School for Children, instructor in French, 1975-. Writer and translator. **Publications:** (Trans. and adapter) V. Antoine, Double Vision: Artists Face to Face, 1996; Why She Married Him, 2005. Contributor to journals. **Address:** Bank Street School for Children, 610 W 112th St., New York, NY 10025-1898, U.S.A.

CHAPMAN, Paul K. American (born United States), b. 1931. **Genres:** Business/Trade/Industry. **Career:** Packard Manse Retreat Center, director, 1957-75; Center for Seafarer's Rights, director, 1981-90; North American Maritime Ministry Association, executive secretary, 1991-; The Employment Project, director, 1994-2004; American Baptist Home Mission Societies, representative of priority areas. Writer. **Publications:** Trouble on Board: The Plight of International Seafarers, 1992. **Address:** American Baptist Home Mission Societies, 588 N Gulph Rd., PO Box 696, King of Prussia, PA 19406, U.S.A. **Online address:** p.chapman@mindspring.com

CHAPMAN, Peter. British (born England), b. 1948?. **Genres:** Novellas/Short Stories, History. **Career:** Financial Times, sport and feature editor; Independent Television (ITV), researcher & producer, 1986-90; British Broadcasting Corp., correspondent, 1980; London Guardian in Central America, correspondent, 1980. Journalist. **Publications:** The Goalkeeper's History of Britain, 2000; Jungle Capitalists: A Story of Globalisation, Greed and Revolution, 2007 in US as Bananas! How the United Fruit Company Shaped the World, 2008. **Address:** Felicity Bryan Literary Agency, 2a N Parade Ave., Oxford, OX OX2 6LX, England. **Online address:** peter.chapman@ft.com

CHAPMAN, Samuel Greeley. American (born United States), b. 1929. **Genres:** Criminology/True Crime, Social Sciences. **Career:** Berkeley Department of Police, undercover agent, 1950-51, patrolman, 1951-56; Public Administration Service, police consultant, 1956-59; Michigan State University, School of Police Administration, assistant professor, 1959-63; Multnomah County Sheriff's Police Department, police chief, 1963-65; President's Commission on Law Enforcement and Administration of Justice, assistant director, 1965-67; University of Oklahoma, professor of political science, 1967-91, Law Enforcement Administration Program, director, now retired; Norman City Council, councilman, 1972-76, vice-mayor, 1976, 1978, 1982-84; Oklahoma University Athletics Council, chairman, 1970-72, 1979-80. Writer. **Publications:** Dogs in Police Work: A Summary of Experience in Great Britain and the United States, 1960; (with E. St. Johnston) The Police Heritage in England and America, 1962; (ed.) Police Patrol Readings, 1964, 2nd ed., 1970; (with D. Clark) A Forward Step: Educational Backgrounds for Police, 1966; (with C.K. Meyer and C.G. Swanson) A Descriptive Profile of the Assault Incident, 1974; (co-author) Perspectives on Police Assaults in the South Central United States, 1974; (with C.K. Meyer and C.G. Swanson) Introduction and Methodology to the Study of Police Assailants in the South Central United States, 1974; (with G. Eastman) Short of Merger: Countywide Police Resource Pooling, 1976; Police Murders and Effective Countermeasures, 1976; Police Dogs in America, 1979; (contrib.) Police Patrol, Operations and Management, 1981; Cops, Killers and Staying Alive, 1986; Police Dogs in North America, 1990; Murdered on Duty: The Killing of Police Officers in America, 1999. **Address:** 2421 Hollywood, Norman, OK 73069, U.S.A. **Online address:** sgchapman@renonevada.net

CHAPNICK, Adam. Canadian (born Canada), b. 1976?. **Genres:** Area Studies. **Career:** Canadian Stage Co., sales and marketing, consultant, 2000-03; Ryerson University, faculty; University of Toronto, instructor in history, 2003, lecturer in history, 2004-06; Royal Military College, assistant professor of defense studies, 2006; Canadian Forces College, Department of Command, Leadership and Management, deputy chair, 2006-07, deputy director of education and research, 2007, deputy director of education, 2007-. Writer. **Publications:** (Ed.) Through Our Eyes: An Alumni History of the University of Toronto Schools, 1960-2000, 2004; The Middle Power Project: Canada and the Founding of the United Nations, 2005; (ed. with N. Hillmer) Canada's of the Mind: The Making and Unmaking of Canadian Nationalisms in the Twentieth Century, 2007; Canada's Voice: The Public Life of John Wendell Holmes, 2009. **Address:** Canadian Forces College, 215 Yonge Blvd., Toronto, ON M5M 3H9, Canada. **Online address:** chapnick@cfc.dnd.ca

CHAPPELL, Audrey. British (born England), b. 1954. **Genres:** Children's Fiction, Children's Non-fiction, Literary Criticism And History. **Career:** Islington School, preschool teacher, 1976-83; Haringey School, preschool teacher, 1984-91. Writer. **Publications:** A Surprise for Oliver, 1989; An Outing for Oliver, 1990. **Address:** The Old Forge, Berghapton, Mill Rd., Norwich, NF NR15 1BQ, England. **Online address:** aud-chap@dircon.co.uk

CHAPPELL, Booie. *See* **CHAPPELL, Ruth Paterson.**

CHAPPELL, Fred(erick Davis). American (born United States), b. 1936. **Genres:** Novels, Novellas/Short Stories, Poetry, Literary Criticism And History, Writing/Journalism, Young Adult Fiction. **Career:** Brown Supply Co., general manager, 1957-59; Candler Furniture Co., credit manager, 1959-60; Duke University Press, proofreader, 1961; University of North Carolina, professor of English, 1964-2004, now emeritus professor of English. Writer. **Publications:** NOVELS: It Is Time, Lord, 1963; The Inkling, 1965; Dagon, 1968; The Gaudy Place, 1973; I Am One of You Forever: A Novel, 1985; Brighten the Corner Where You Are, 1989; More Shapes Than One, 1991; Farewell, I'm Bound to Leave You, 1996; Look Back All the Green Valley, 1999. POETRY: The World between the Eyes, 1971; River: A Poem, 1975; The Man Twice Married to Fire, 1977; Bloodfire: A Poem, 1978; Awakening to Music, 1979; Wind Mountain: A Poem, 1979; Earthsleep: A Poem, 1980; Driftlake: A Lieder Cycle, 1981; Midquest: A Poem, 1981; Castle Tzingal: A Poem, 1984; Source: A Poem, 1985; First and Last Words: A Poems, 1989; C: A Poems, 1993; Spring Garden: New and Selected Poems, 1995; Way of Happening: Observations of Contemporary Poetry, 1998; (co-author) New Pléiade: Selected Poems, 1998; Family Gathering: A Poems, 2000; Backsass: A Poems, 2004; Ancestors and others, 2009; Shadow Box, 2009. STORIES: Moments of Light, 1980. OTHER: The Fred Chappell Reader, 1987; More Shapes than One, 1991; Plow Naked: Selected Writings on Poetry, 1993; A Way of Happening: Observations of Contemporary Poetry, 1998; Dagon, 2002; (ed.) Locales: Poems from the Fellowship of Southern Writers, 2003. **Address:** The University of North Carolina, 1400 Spring Garden St., PO Box 26170, Greensboro, NC 27402, U.S.A.

CHAPPELL, Ruth Paterson. (Booie Chappell). American (born United States), b. 1928?. **Genres:** Children's Non-fiction, Young Adult Fiction. **Career:** Educator and writer. **Publications:** AS BOOIE CHAPPELL: (with B.P. Shipe) The Mysterious Tail of a Charleston Cat (juvenile), 1995; All 'bout Charleston (juvenile), 1998; Counting the Ways to Love Charleston (juvenile), 2001; Turtle Named Caretta, 2008. **Address:** Drayton Hall Plantation, 3380 Ashley River Rd., Charleston, SC 29414, U.S.A.

CHAPPLE, John Alfred Victor. British (born England), b. 1928. **Genres:** History, Literary Criticism And History, Women's Studies And Issues, Humanities. **Career:** Yale University, research assistant, 1955-58; University of Aberdeen, assistant lecturer in English, 1958-59; University of Manchester, assistant lecturer, 1959-67, senior lecturer in English, 1967-71; University of Hull, professor of English, 1971-92, emeritus professor of English literature, 1992-; Gaskell Society, president, 1998-2005. Writer. **Publications:** (Ed.) Samuel Johnson's Proposals for Printing the History of the Council of Trent, 1963; (ed. with A. Pollard) The Letters of Mrs. Gaskell, 1967; Documentary and Imaginative Literature 1880-1920, 1970; Dryden's Earl of Shaftesbury, 1973; (with J.G. Sharps) Elizabeth Gaskell: A Portrait in Letters, 1980; Science and Literature in the Nineteenth Century, 1986; (ed. with A. Wilson)

Private Voices: The Diaries of Elizabeth Gaskell and Sophia Holland, 1996; Elizabeth Gaskell: The Early Years, 1997; (ed. with A. Shelston) Further Letters of Mrs. Gaskell, 2000. Contributor to journals. **Address:** Department of English, University of Hull, Cottingham Rd., Hull, HU6 7RX, England.

CHAQUÉRI, Cosroe. *See* **SHAKERI, Khosrow.**

CHARAN, Ram. American/Indian (born India), b. 1939. **Genres:** Business/Trade/Industry, inspirational/Motivational Literature, Economics. **Career:** Harvard University, assistant professor, 1967-73; Northwestern University, associate professor, 1973-76; Boston University, professor, 1976-78. Writer and consultant. **Publications:** (With N.M. Tichy) Every Business Is a Growth Business: How Your Company Can Prosper Year after Year, 1998; Boards at Work: How Corporate Boards Create Competitive Advantage, 1998; Action, Urgency, Excellence: Seizing Leadership in the Digital Economy, 2000; (with S. Drotter and J. Noel) The Leadership Pipeline: How to Build the Leadership-powered Company, 2001, 2nd ed., 2011; What the CEO Wants You to Know: How Your Company Really Works, 2001; (with L. Bossidy and C. Burck) Execution: The Discipline of Getting Things Done, 2002; (with L. Bossidy and C. Burck) Confronting Reality: Doing What Matters to Get Things Right, 2004; Profitable Growth Is Everyone's Business: 10 Tools You Can Use Monday Morning, 2004; Boards That Deliver: Advancing Corporate Governance from Compliance to Creating Competitive Advantage, 2005; (with G. Willigan) Know- How: The 8 Skills That Separate People Who Perform from Those Who Don't, 2007; What the Customer Wants You to Know: How Everybody Needs to Think Differently about Sales, 2007; (with A.G. Lafley) The Game-Changer: How You Can Drive Revenue and Profit Growth with Innovation, 2008; Leaders at All Levels: Deepening Your Talent Pool to Solve the Succession Crisis, 2008; Owning Up: The 14 Questions Every Board Member Needs to Ask, 2009; Leadership in the Era of Economic Uncertainty: The New Rules for Getting the Right Things Done in Difficult Times, 2009; (with B. Conaty) The Talent Masters: Why Smart Leaders Put People Before Numbers, 2010. Contributor of articles to periodicals. **Address:** 12655 N Central Expy., Ste. 103, Dallas, TX 75243-1763, U.S.A.

CHARBONNEAU, Eileen. American (born United States), b. 1951. **Genres:** Mystery/Crime/Suspense, Romance/Historical, Young Adult Fiction, Plays/Screenplays, Novels, Romance/Historical. **Career:** The New York Times, staff; Lady's Circle, staff; Romantic Interludes, staff; Mothering Magazine, staff; freelance writer, 1974-; La Leche League, leader and district advisor. **Publications:** The Ghosts of Stony Clove, 1988; In the Time of the Wolves, 1994; Honor to the Hills, 1996. Z-FAVE YOU-SOLVE-IT MYSTERY SERIES: The Mound Builders' Secret, 1994; Disappearance at Harmony Festival, 1994; The Conner Emerald, 1995; Waltzing in Ragtime, 1996; The Randolph Legacy, 1997; Rachel Le Moyne, 1998. Contributor to periodicals. **Address:** c/o Susan Yuen, Susan Herner Rights Agency, PO Box 303, Scarsdale, NY 10583, U.S.A. **Online address:** eileenc@theromanceclub.com

CHARBONNET, Gabrielle. American (born United States), b. 1961. **Genres:** Children's Fiction, Novels, Picture/Board Books, Young Adult Fiction. **Career:** Random House, production assistant, 1987-88; Daniel Weiss Associates Inc., associate editor, 1988-89, managing editor, 1989-93. **Publications:** NOVELS: Snakes Are Nothing to Sneeze At, 1990; Else-Marie and Her Seven Little Daddies, 1991; Boodil, My Dog, 1992; Tutu Much Ballet, 1994; Escape from De Vil Mansion: 101 Dalmatians, 1996; I Made Herc a Hero, 1997; Disney's the Lion King: Just Can't Wait to Be King, 1998; (reteller) Disney's Once Upon a Time with Mary-Kate & Ashley, 1998; (with J. Patterson) Sundays at Tiffany's, 2008; (with J. Patterson) Witch and Wizard, 2009. PRINCESS SERIES: Molly's Heart, 1995; A Room in the Attic, 1995; Home at Last, 1995. AMERICAN GOLD GYMNASTS SERIES: Competition Fever, 1996; Balancing Act, 1996; Split Decision, 1996; The Bully Coach, 1996. DISNEY GIRLS SERIES: One of Us, 1998; Attack of the Beast, 1998; And Sleepy Makes Seven, 1998; A Fish Out of Water, 1998; Cinderella's Castle, 1998; One Pet Too Many, 1999; Adventure at Walt Disney World, 1999; Beastly Visitor, 1999; Beauty's Revenge, 1999; Good-Bye, Jasmine?, 1999; Princess of Power, 1999; The Gum Race, 1999; The Divine Miss Ariel, 1999; Magic Treasury, 4 vols., 2002. AS CATE TIERNAN: WICCA: SWEEP SERIES: Book of Shadows, 2001; The Coven, 2001; Blood Witch, 2001; Dark Magick, 2001; Awakening, 2001; Spellbound, 2001; The Calling, 2001; Changeling, 2001; Strife, 2002; Seeker, 2002; Origins, 2002; Eclipse, 2002; Reckoning, 2002; Full Circle, 2002; Night's Child, 2003. BALEFIRE: A Chalice of Wind, 2005; A Circle of Ashes, 2005; A Feather of Stone, 2005; A Necklace of Water, 2005. IMMORTAL BELOVED: Everlasting Life, 2010; Darkness Falls, 2011; Everlasting Dark, 2011; Everlasting War, 2012. **Address:** Henry Holt and Company Inc., 175 5th Ave., 6th Fl., New York, NY 10010, U.S.A.

CHARBONNIER, Rita. Italian (born Italy), b. 1966?. **Genres:** History, Literary Criticism And History. **Career:** Writer. **Publications:** La Sorella di Mozart: Romanzo, 2007. Contributor to periodicals. **Address:** Luigi Bernabo Associates s.r.l., Via Cernaia, 4, Milan, 20121, Italy.

CHARD, Judy (Gordon). (Lyndon Chase). British (born England), b. 1916. **Genres:** Novellas/Short Stories, Mystery/Crime/Suspense, Romance/Historical, Travel/Exploration, Novels, Horror, Young Adult Non-fiction. **Career:** David & Charles (publishers), director of studies for Writers College, 1988-96; British Broadcasting Corp., broadcaster. Writer and lecturer. **Publications:** NOVELS: Through the Green Woods, 1974; The Weeping and the Laughter, 1975; Encounter in Berlin, 1976; The Uncertain Heart, 1976; The Other Side of Sorrow, 1977; In the Heart of Love, 1978; Out of the Shadows, 1978; All Passion Spent, 1979; Seven Lonely Years, 1980; The Darkening Skies, 1981; When the Journey's Over, 1981; Haunted by the Past, 1982; Sweet Love Remembered, 1982; Where the Dream Begins, 1982; Hold Me in Your Heart, 1983; Rendezvous with Love, 1984; (as Lyndon Chase) Tormentil, 1984; To Live with Fear, 1984; Wings of the Morning, 1985; A Time to Love, 1987; Wild Justice, 1987; For Love's Sake Only, 1988; Person Unknown, 1988; To Be So Loved, 1988; Enchantment, 1989; Appointment With Danger, 1990; Betrayed, 1990; Encounter in Spain, 1994; The Survivors, 2001. NONFICTION: Along the Lemon: The Life Story of a Devon River, 1978; Along the Dart, 1979; About Widecombe, 1979; Devon Mysteries, 1979; The South Hams, 1980; Along the Teign, 1981; (ed.) Traditional Devonshire Recipes, 1985; Tales of the Unexplained in Devon, 1986; Devon Air Book of Haunted Happenings, 1987; Burgh Island and Bigbury Bay, 1988; (with C. Barber) Tales of the Teign, 1990; Haunted Happenings, Burgh Island, Traditional Cookery, Devon Companion, 1993; The Mysterious Lady of the Moor-The Story of Beatrice Chase, 1994; Haunted Happenings in Devon, 1994; Murder and Mystery in Devon, 1994; A Guide to the South Hams: Devon Tales of Mystery and Murder, 2001; Devon Stories of the Supernatural, 2003; Mayhem, Murder and Mystery in Devon, 2008. Contributor of articles to periodicals. **Address:** Morley Farm, Highweek, Newton Abbey, DN TQ12 6NA, England. **Online address:** d.chard1@btopenworld.com

CHAREF, Mehdi. French (born France), b. 1952. **Genres:** Novels, Reference. **Career:** Writer and director. **Publications:** Le thé au harem d'Archi Ahmed, 1983; Le Harki de Meriem, 1989; La Maison d'Alexina: A Roman, 1999; Á bras-le-coeur: roman, 2006. **Address:** Livre de Poche, Hachette Livre, 43, quai de Grenelle, Paris, 75905, France.

CHARIANDY, David. Canadian (born Canada), b. 1969?. **Genres:** Novels. **Career:** Simon Fraser University, Department of English, assistant professor, associate professor; Commodore Books, co-founder. Writer. **Publications:** Soucouyant (novel), 2007; Brother, 2013. Contributor to journals. **Address:** Department of English, Simon Fraser University, 6105 Academic Quadrangle, 8888 University Dr., Burnaby, BC V5A 1S6, Canada. **Online address:** chariand@sfu.ca

CHARLEBOIS, Lucile C. American (born United States), b. 1950. **Genres:** Literary Criticism And History, Bibliography, Adult Non-fiction. **Career:** Department of Public Welfare, social worker, 1968-69; College of Our Lady of the Elms, instructor in Spanish, 1970-76, 1977-78, head of modern language department, 1975-76; Volunteers for Educational and Social Services, teacher of Spanish, 1976-77; Residencia Buendia, instructor in English, 1981; University of Nebraska, visiting assistant professor, 1982-83, assistant professor of Spanish and coordinator of basic language, 1983-88; University of South Carolina, Spanish Tutorial Center, director, 1988-92, assistant professor, 1988-94, associate professor of Spanish, 1994-, graduate director, 1995-98. Writer. **Publications:** Understanding Camilo José Cela, 1998; (intro.) Christ Versus Arizona, 2007; La Cuentistica de Camilo Jose Cela, forthcoming. Contributor to books and periodicals. **Address:** Department of Arts and Sciences, Languages, Literatures and Cultures, University of South Carolina, Rm. HUO 710, 713 Welsh Humanities, Columbia, SC 29208, U.S.A. **Online address:** charlelc@mailbox.sc.edu

CHARLES, Douglas M. American (born United States), b. 1971?. **Genres:** History. **Career:** The Pennsylvania State University, Greater Allegheny Campus (known as Penn State Greater Allegheny), assistant professor of history;

University of Edinburgh, tutor of history; Marietta College, visiting professor; Behrend College, Penn State Erie, lecturer in history. Historian and writer. **Publications:** J. Edgar Hoover and the Anti-interventionists: FBI Political Surveillance and the Rise of the Domestic Security State, 1939-1945, 2007. Contributor to books and journals. **Address:** Penn State Greater Alleghen, 4000 University Dr., McKeesport, PA 15132, U.S.A. **Online address:** dmc166@psu.edu

CHARLES, Hampton. *See* **MARTIN, (Roy) Peter.**

CHARLES, Henry. *See* **HARRIS, Marion (Rose).**

CHARLES, John. Canadian/American (born United States), b. 1965. **Genres:** Film, History. **Career:** Video Watchdog, associate editor and reviewer, 1992-; Hong Kong Digital Web site, host and reviewer, 2000-. **Publications:** The Hong Kong Filmography 1977-1997: A Complete Reference to 1, 100 Films Produced by British Hong Kong Studios, 2000. **Address:** Video Watchdog, PO Box 5283, Cincinnati, OH 45205-0283, U.S.A. **Online address:** dosun892@hotmail.com

CHARLES, Kate. British/American (born United States), b. 1950. **Genres:** Mystery/Crime/Suspense. **Career:** WGUC Radio, promotion assistant and record librarian, 1981-85; St. Paul's Church, parish administrator, 1988-91. Writer. **Publications:** A Drink of Deadly Wine, 1991; The Snares of Death, 1992; Appointed to Die, 1993; A Dead Man Out of Mind, 1994; Evil Angels among Them, 1995; Unruly Passions, 1998; Strange Children, 1999; Cruel Habitations, 2000; Evil Intent, 2005; Secret Sins, 2007; Deep Waters, 2009. **Address:** Dorian Literary Agency, 27 Church Rd., St. Marychurch, Torquay, Torbay, DN TQ1 4QY, England. **Online address:** kate@katecharles.com

CHARLES, Keith. *See* **WRIGHT, Keith.**

CHARLES, Sara C. *See* **CHARLES, Sara C(onnor).**

CHARLES, Sara C(onnor). (Sara C. Charles). American (born United States), b. 1934. **Genres:** Medicine/Health, Biography, Sciences. **Career:** St. Vincent's Hospital and Medical Center, intern, 1964-65; Seton Institute, resident in psychiatry, 1965-68; University of Notre Dame, psychiatrist, 1968-72; University of Illinois, assistant professor, 1972-79, associate professor, 1979-88, professor of clinical psychiatry, 1988-, now emerita. Writer. **Publications:** WITH E. KENNEDY: Defendant, a Psychiatrist on Trial for Medical Malpractice: An Episode in America's Hidden Health Care Crisis, 1985; On Becoming a Counselor: A Basic Guide for Non-Professional Counselors, 1990, rev. 3rd ed., 2001; Authority: The Most Misunderstood Idea in America, 1997. (with P.R. Frisch) Adverse Events, Stress and Litigation: A Physician's Guide, 2005. **Address:** Department of Psychiatry, University of Illinois, 912 S Wood St., Chicago, IL 60612, U.S.A. **Online address:** scharlesmd@compuserve.com

CHARLES BUTOW, Robert Joseph. *See* **BUTOW, Robert J. C.**

CHARLESWORTH, James H(amilton). American (born United States), b. 1940. **Genres:** Theology/Religion. **Career:** Ordained United Methodist minister, deacon, 1963; American Schools of Oriental Research, Thayer fellow, 1968-69; Duke University, assistant professor, 1969-74, associate professor of religion, 1974-84, International Center on Christian Origins, director, 1975-84; University of Tuebingen, Alexander von Humboldt fellow, 1983-84; Princeton Theological Seminary, George L. Collord professor of New Testament language and literature, 1984-; Hebrew University of Jerusalem, Lady Davis visiting professor, 1988; Albright Institute-Jerusalem, professor, 1998-99. Writer. **Publications:** Tools for the Study of the Apocrypha, Pseudepigrapha, and Cognate Works, 1970; The Pseudepigrapha and Modern Research, 1976, rev. ed., 1981; Papyri and Leather Manuscripts of the Odes of Solomon, 1981; (with G.T. Zervos) The New Discoveries in St. Catharine's Monastery, 1981; The History of the Rechabites, vol. I: The Greek Recension, 1982; The Old Testament Pseudepigrapha and the New Testament, 1985; The Discovery of a Dead Sea Scroll (4Q Therapeia), 1985; (with H. Lichtenberger) Pseudepigraphen des Alten Testaments, 1986; The New Testament Apocrypha and Pseudepigrapha, 1987; Jesus within Judaism, 1988; Graphic Concordance to the Dead Sea Scrolls, 1991; (co-author) Miscellaneous Texts from the Judaean Desert, 1991; (co-author) Jesus and the Dead Sea Scrolls, 1992; (co-author) The Dead Sea Scrolls: Hebrew, Aramaic, and Greek Texts with English Translations, 1994; (with W.P. Weaver) Images of Jesus Today, 1994; The Beloved Disciple: Whose Witness Validates the Gospel of John?, 1995; Authentic Apocrypha: False and Genuine Christian Apocrypha, 1998; The Odes of Solomon, 1998; How Barisat Bellowed, 1998; The Old Testament Pseudepigrapha and the New Testament, 1998; The Millennium Guide for Pilgrims to the Holy Land, 2000; The Pesharim and Qumran History, 2002; Resurrection: The Origin and Future of a Biblical Doctrine, 2006; Historical Jesus: An Essential Guide, 2008; Good and Evil Serpent: How a Universal Symbol became Christianized, 2009. EDITOR: (and contrib.) John and Qumran, 1972; (and trans.) The Odes of Solomon, 1973, rev. ed., 1978; (and contrib.) The Old Testament Pseudepigrapha, vol. I: Apocalyptic Literature and Testaments, 1983, vol. II: Expansions of the Old Testament and Legends, 1985; Jews and Christians, 1990; (with J.M. O'Connor) Paul and the Dead Sea Scrolls, 1990; John and the Dead Sea Scrolls, 1990; (with J.J. Collins) Mysteries and Revelations, 1991; Jesus's Jewishness, 1991; The Messiah, 1992; Overcoming Fear between Jews and Christians, 1992; (with W.P. Weaver) What has Archaeology to Do with Faith?, 1992; The Message of the Scrolls, 1992; (with K. Stendahl) The Scrolls and the New Testament, 1992; The Rule of the Community and Related Documents, 1993; (with W.P. Weaver) The Old and New Testaments, 1993; (with C.A. Evans) The Pseudepigrapha and Early Biblical Interpretation, 1993; (with W.P. Weaver) Images of Jesus Today, 1994; (with M. Harding and M. Kiley) The Lord's Prayer and Other Prayer Texts form the Greco-Roman Era, 1994; (with W.P. Weaver) Earthing Christologies, 1995; Damascus Document, War Scroll and Related Documents, 1995; Qumran Questions, 1995; The Faith of Qumran: Theology of the Dead Sea Scrolls, 1995; The Dead Sea Scrolls, 1996; Pseudepigrapha and Non-Masoretic Psalms, Daily Prayers, and Related Documents, 1997; (with L. Johns) Hillel and Jesus, 1997; (with W.P. Weaver) The Dead Sea Scrolls and Christian Faith, 1998; Qumran-Messianism: Studies on the Messianic Expectations in the Dead Sea Scrolls, 1998; Caves of Enlightenment, 1998; Angelic Liturgy, 1999; (with W.P. Weaver) Jesus Two Thousand Years Later, 2000; The Hebrew Bible and Qumran, 2000; (with M.A. Daise) Light in a Spotless Mirror: Reflections on Wisdom Traditions in Judaism and Early Christianity, 2003; The Bible and the Dead Sea Scrolls: The Second Princeton Symposium on Judaism and Christian Origins, 2006; Jesus and Archaeology, 2006; (with G.S. Oegema) Pseudepigrapha and Christian Origins: Essays from the Studiorum Novi Testamenti Societas, 2008. **Address:** Department of Biblical, Princeton Theological Seminary, PO Box 821, Princeton, NJ 08542-0803, U.S.A. **Online address:** james.charlesworth@ptsem.edu

CHARLESWORTH, Monique. British (born England), b. 1951?. **Genres:** Novels, Young Adult Fiction, Science Fiction/Fantasy, Plays/Screenplays, Writing/Journalism. **Career:** Saville Charlesworth Films, co-founder; IPC, trade and technical feature writer and screenwriter. **Publications:** The Glass House, 1986; Life Class, 1988; The Shadowy Third, 1991; Foreign Exchange, 1995; Three Miles Up, 1995; The Children's War, 2004. Contributor to periodicals. **Address:** c/o Charles Walker, United Agents Ltd., 12-26 Lexington St., London, GL W1F 0LE, England. **Online address:** me@moniquecharlesworth.co.uk

CHARLIER, Roger Henri. (Henri Rochard). American/Belgian (born Belgium), b. 1921. **Genres:** Novels, Poetry, Earth Sciences, Travel/Exploration, Environmental Sciences/Ecology, Marine Sciences/Oceanography, Engineering, Sciences, Sciences. **Career:** Teacher at secondary school, 1941-42; newspaper correspondent, 1945-50; United Nations Relief and Rehabilitation Administration, deputy director, 1946-48; University Travel Inc., travel project director, 1948-71, Division of Educational Travel, director, 1963-67; Polycultural University, associate professor of geography and chairman of department, 1950-52; Berlitz School, teacher, 1951-52; Finch College, professor of physical sciences, chairman of department and professor of mathematics, 1952-55; Hofstra University, professor of geology and geography and chairman of department, 1955-58; University of Paris, faculty of sciences adjunct professor of geology, 1958-59; University of Minnesota, visiting professor of education, 1959-60; Parsons College, professor of earth sciences, 1960-61; Northeastern Illinois University, professor of geology, geography and oceanography, 1961-86, coordinator of earth sciences, 1961-65; DePaul University, visiting professor, 1965-67; Academy of Romania, exchange senior scientist, 1968, 1978-79; University of Bordeaux, visiting professor, 1970-73, 1983-84, honorary professor, 1987-; U.S. Information Service, lecturer, 1971-84; Free University of Brussels, visiting professor, 1971-88; Academy of Sciences of Bulgaria, exchange senior scientist, 1979; University of Bordeaux, honorary professor, 1987-; Lovania Publishers, staff, 1988-95; University of Brussels, professor emeritus, 1989-; University of Maryland, visiting professor. Writer. **Publications:** Cours d'analyse infinitesimale, 5 vols., 1940; Analysemathematique, 1941; The Belgians and the Flemings, 1953; Antwerpen: die Bedeutung der belgischen Handelsmetropole im westeuropaeischen Raum, 1958; The Gifted: A National Resource, 1960; Introductory Earth Science, 1960; Introduction to Oceanography, 1964; (co-author) Discovering Hawaii: A Series of Seminars, 1965; The Physical Environment: A Brief Outline, 1966; (ed.) Geography of the USSR, 1967; Harnessing the Energies of the Ocean, 1970; (ed. with P.S. Charlier and J.J. Karpeck) The World around Us: A Book of Readings, 1971; The Study of Rocks, 1971; The Study of Oceans, 1971; (ed.) A Digest of Master's Theses in Geography at Northeastern Illinois University, 1972; (contrib.) Marine Resources, 1972; Esquisse d'un cours d'oceanographie regionale, 1973; (contrib.) The Oceans and Man, 1975; Economic Oceanography, 1977; (contrib.) Energy from the Sea, 1977; Ocean Resources: An Introduction to Economic Oceanography, 1978; (contrib.) Ocean Yearbook, vol. I, 1978, vol. IV, 1984; vol. IX, 1989; Marine Science and Technology: An Introduction to Oceanography, 1980; Our Physical Environment, 1980; Marine Geology, 1980; Tidal Energy, 1982; (contrib.) Small Energy Resources, 1987; (contrib.) Seaweeds of Europe, 1992; (with J.R. Justus) Ocean Energies: Environmental, Economic and Technological Aspects of Alternative Power Sources, 1993; (contrib.) Benthic Marine Plants and Eutrophicasion, 1996; (with C.F. De Meyer) Coastal Erosion: Response and Management, 1998; (with J. Gordon and B. Gordon) Ocean Sciences, Resources and Technology: A Guide to the Sea, 1998; Using Today's Knowledge for Black Sea Area's Tomorrow, 2000; 2nd Leadership Conference of International Ocean Institute: The Proceedings, 2003; Oceans Bridging the Millenium, 2004. AS HENRI ROCHARD: I Was a Male War Bride (novel), 1947; For the Love of Kate (novel), 1963; Pensees (poetry), 1964. **Address:** Universite Libre de Bruxelles, Franklin D. Roosevelt 50 Ave., Bruxelles, B-1050, Belgium. **Online address:** roger.charlier@pophost.eunet.be

CHARLIP, Remy. American (born United States), b. 1929. **Genres:** Plays/Screenplays, Poetry, Children's Fiction, Humor/Satire, Illustrations, Literary Criticism And History, Social Commentary. **Career:** London Contemporary Dance Theatre, choreographer, 1972-76; Scottish Theatre Ballet, choreographer, 1973; Welsh Dance Theatre, choreographer, 1974; International All-Star Dance Co., director, 1977-. Educator, writer and illustrator of children's books. **Publications:** SELF-ILLUSTRATED: Dress Up and Let's Have a Party, 1956; Where is Everybody?, 1957; Fortunately, 1964; (with B. Supree) Mother, Mother, I Feel Sick, Send for the Doctor, Quick, Quick, Quick, 1966, 3rd ed., 2001; I Love You, 1967, 2nd ed., 1999; Arm in Arm: A Collection of Connections, Endless Tales, Reiterations, and Other Echolalia, 1969; What Good Luck! What Bad Luck!, 1969; (with B. Supree) Harlequin and the Gift of Many Colors, 1973; (with G. Ancona and M.B. Miller) Handtalk: An ABC of Finger Spelling and Sign Language, 1974; (with L. Moore) Hooray for Me!, 1975; (with J. Joyner) Thirteen, 1975; First Remy Charlip Reader, 1986; (with M. Beth and G. Ancona) Handtalk Birthday: A Number and Story Book in Sign Language, 1987; Amaterasu, 1988; Ideas for Teaching Arts to Children, 1995; Peanut Butter Party: Including the History, Uses, and Future of Peanut Butter, 1999; Sleepytime Rhyme, 1999; Why I Will Never Ever Ever Ever Have Enough Time to Read This Book, 2000; Baby Hearts and Baby Flowers, 2002; Little Old Big Beard and Big Young Little Beard: A Short & Tall Tale, 2002; Perfect Day, 2007. **Address:** 521 Precita Ave., San Francisco, CA 94110-4719, U.S.A.

CHARLOT, Anita M. American (born United States), b. 1965. **Genres:** Gay And Lesbian Issues. **Career:** Six Sigma Center of Excellence for Allstate Insurance, diversity trainer and operations analyst; BSE, operations manager, 1999-; Anita Charlot International L.L.C., president and chief executive officer, Purrfect Harmony Unlimited, founder and executive director, 1999-. Writer. **Publications:** Poetic Growing Pains, 2000; The Reality of Loving a Lesbian/Bisexual Mother, 2001; The 5 Phases of Dating...Without Losing Sight of Your Purrfectly Authentic Self, 2005; At Least My Mom's Not Gay, forthcoming. **Address:** Anita Charlot International L.L.C., 159 N Marion St., Ste. 329, Oak Park, IL 60301-1032, U.S.A. **Online address:** purrfectharmonyunlimited@onebox.com

CHARLTON-TRUJILLO, E. E. American (born United States) **Genres:** Novels. **Career:** Ohio University, School of Film, teaching assistant, 2000-01; Pinata Productions, company creator. Film director, actor, film producer and writer. **Publications:** Prizefighter en Mi Casa, 2006; Feels Like Home, 2007; Fat Angie, forthcoming; Wooden Spoon Fishbowl, forthcoming. **Address:** Pinata Productions, PO Box 23263, Cincinnati, OH 45223, U.S.A. **Online address:** writertx@bigdreamswrite.com

CHARLWOOD, Don. *See* **CHARLWOOD, D(onald) E(rnest Cameron).**

CHARLWOOD, D(onald) E(rnest Cameron). (Don Charlwood). Australian (born Australia), b. 1915. **Genres:** Novels, Novellas/Short Stories, History, Autobiography/Memoirs, Military/Defense/Arms Control, Travel/Exploration. **Career:** Australian Department of Civil Aviation, Air Traffic Control, senior supervisor, 1945-75; Central Training College, instructor, 1952. Writer. **Publications:** No Moon Tonight (memoirs), 1956; All the Green Year (novel), 1965; An Afternoon of Time (short stories), 1966; Take-Off to Touchdown: The Story of Air Traffic Control, 1967; The Wreck of the Loch Ard: End of A Ship, End of An Era, 1971; (co-author) Autumn Anthology: Geelong and District Autumn Festival 1976, 1976; Flight and Time (short stories), 1979. AS DON CHARLWOOD: Wrecks and Reputations: The Loss of the Schomberg and Loch Ard, 1977; Settlers under Sail, 1978; The Long Farewell, 1981; Marching as to War, (autobiography), 1990; Journeys into Night (autobiography), 1991. Contributor to magazines. **Address:** Yarra Gardens, 7/2 Everard Dr., Warrandyte, VI 3113, Australia.

CHARMÉ, Stuart Zane. American (born United States), b. 1951. **Genres:** Philosophy, Theology/Religion. **Career:** University of Chicago Divinity School, research assistant, 1977-78; State University of New Jersey, Rutgers University, Department of Philosophy and Religion, visiting lecturer, 1978-80, assistant professor, 1980-86, associate professor, 1986-98, department chairperson, 1986-91, 2001-07, professor, 1998-, Rutgers Study Abroad Program in Israel, director, 1993-94, Graduate Program in Liberal Studies, director, 2006-. Writer. **Publications:** Meaning and Myth in the Study of Lives: A Sartrean Perspective, 1984; Vulgarity and Authenticity: Dimensions of Otherness in the World of Jean-Paul Sartre, 1991. **Address:** Department of Philosophy and Religion, Rutgers University, State University of New Jersey, Armitage Hall, 311 N 5th St., Camden, NJ 08102-1405, U.S.A. **Online address:** scharme@crab.rutgers.edu

CHARMING, Prince. *See* **THOMAS, Rosanne Daryl.**

CHARMLEY, John. British (born England), b. 1955. **Genres:** Politics/Government, History, Biography. **Career:** University of East Anglia, lecturer, 1979-, professor of modern British history, School of History, head, 2001-, Faculty for Research, associate dean; Westminster College, Churchill memorial professor, 1993-. Writer. **Publications:** Duff Cooper: The Authorized Biography, 1986; (ed.) E. Shuckburgh, Descentto Suez: Foreign Office Diaries, 1951-56, 1987; Lord Lloyd and the Decline of the British Empire (biography), 1987; (ed. with E. Homberger) The Troubled Face of Biography, 1988; Chamberlain and the Lost Peace (biography), 1989; Churchill, The End of Glory: A Political Biography, 1993; Churchill's Grand Alliance: The Anglo-American Special Relationship, 1940-57, 1995; A History of Conservative Politics, 1900-1996, 1996, 2nd ed. as History of Conservative Politics since 1830, 2008; Splendid Isolation?: Britain and the Balance of Power, 1874-1914, 1999; Splendid Isolation?: Britain, the Balance of Power, and the Origins of the First World War, 1999; The Princess and the Politicians: Sex, Intrigue and Diplomacy, 1812-40, 2005. **Address:** School of History, University of East Anglia, 4.09 Arts Bldg., Norwich Research Pk., Norwich, NF NR4 7TJ, England. **Online address:** j.charmley@uea.ac.uk

CHARNAS, Suzy McKee. (Rebecca Brand). American (born United States), b. 1939. **Genres:** Novellas/Short Stories, Horror, Science Fiction/Fantasy, Young Adult Fiction, Songs/Lyrics And Libretti, Essays, Novels. **Career:** University of Ife, lecturer in economic history, 1961-63; teacher, 1965-67; Flower Fifth Avenue Hospital, Division of Community Mental Health, curriculum development worker, 1967-69. Writer, 1969-. **Publications:** Walk to the End of the World, 1974; Motherlines, 1978; Listening to Brahms (novella), 1978; The Vampire Tapestry, 1980; Radical Utopias, 1985; The Bronze King, 1985; Dorothea Dreams, 1986; The Silver Glove, 1988; The Golden Thread (juvenile), 1989; Vampire Dreams (play), 1990; Moonstone and Tiger Eye, 1992; The Kingdom of Kevin Malone, 1993; The Furies, 1994; Beauty and the Opera, or the Phantom Beast (novella), 1996; (as Rebecca Brand) The Ruby Tear (science fiction), 1997; The Conqueror's Child (science fiction), 1999; Strange Seas, 2001; My Father's Ghost: The Return of My Old Man and Other Second Chances (memoir), 2002; Stagestruck Vampires: And Other Phantasms, 2004. **Address:** 212 High St. NE, Albuquerque, NM 87102-3625, U.S.A. **Online address:** smc@suzymckeecharnas.com

CHARNEY, Mark J. American (born United States), b. 1956. **Genres:** Theatre, Plays/Screenplays, Film, Literary Criticism And History. **Career:**

Clemson University, instructor, 1980-82, assistant professor, 1987-91, associate professor of English, 1991-, professor of theatre, film and screenwriting, Department of English, chair, 2003-06, Department of Performing Arts, director of theatre and professor of playwriting, 2006-; Kennedy Center American Theatre Festival, national coordinator of criticism and dramaturgy; O'Neill National Critics Institute, associate administrator; THE LOOP, features editor. **Publications:** Barry Hannah, 1992. **Address:** Department of Performing Arts, Brooks Center, Clemson University, Clemson, SC 29634-0525, U.S.A. **Online address:** cmark@clemson.edu

CHARNEY, Noah. American (born United States), b. 1979. **Genres:** Novels. **Career:** The Jump Into, Punk rock band, songwriter, 1999-2002. Singer and guitarist. **Publications:** The Art Thief: A Novel, 2007. **Address:** c/o Lois Wallace, Wallace Literary Agency Inc., 301 E 79th St., Ste. 14J, New York, NY 10021, U.S.A. **Online address:** theartthief@gmail.com

CHARNON-DEUTSCH, Lou. American (born United States), b. 1946. **Genres:** Language/Linguistics, Literary Criticism And History. **Career:** Purdue University, Department of Romance Languages, teaching assistant, 1969-71; University of Chicago, Department of Romance Languages, lecturer, 1976; State University of New York, Department of Hispanic Languages and Literature, assistant professor, 1980-88, associate professor, 1988-96, professor of Hispanic languages and literature and women's studies, 1996-, director of undergraduate studies, 1982-84, 1987-88, 1994-96, chairperson, 1989-91, 1999-2000, 2003-04, director of graduate studies, 2005-08, Women's Studies Program, affiliate faculty, 1990-, Department of Comparative Studies, affiliate faculty, 1999-. Writer. **Publications:** (Comp.) A checklist of Serials Pertaining to Romance Languages and Literatures at the University of Chicago Library, 1976; The Nineteenth-Century Spanish Short Story: Textual Strategies of a Genre in Evolution, 1985; Gender and Representation: Women in Spanish Realist Fiction, 1990; Narratives of Desire: Nineteenth-Century Spanish Fiction by Women, 1994; Fictions of the Feminine in the Nineteenth-Century Spanish Press, 2000; The Spanish Gypsy: The History of a European Obsession, 2004; Hold that Pose: Visual Culture in the Late-Nineteenth-Century Spanish Periodical, 2008. EDITOR: (and intro.) Estudios Sobre Escritoras hispánicas en Honor de Georgina Sabat-Rivers, 1992; (and comp.) An Annotated Bibliography of Hispanic Feminist Criticism, 1994; (with J. Labanyi) Culture and Gender in Nineteenth-Century Spain, 1995. Contributor to journals. **Address:** Department of Hispanic Languages and Literature, State University of New York, N3018 Frank Melville, Jr. Memorial Library, Stony Brook, NY 11794-3371, U.S.A. **Online address:** ldeutsch@notes.cc.sunysb.edu

CHARNY, Israel Wolf. American/Israeli (born Israel), b. 1931. **Genres:** Human Relations/Parenting, International Relations/Current Affairs, Psychology, Theology/Religion, Essays. **Career:** Board of Education, clinical psychologist, 1956-58; Oakbourne Hospital, chief psychologist, 1958-62; Guidance Consultants Psychological Group Practice, director, 1962-73; Reconstructionist Rabbinical College, professor of psychology, counseling consultant, 1971-73; Szold National Institute for Research in Behavioral Sciences, senior researcher, 1973-; Ribbutz Family Clinic, senior consultant, 1973-; Tel-Aviv University, Bob Shapell School of Social Work, associate professor, 1973-93, associate professor of psychology, 1974-, now retired; Institute on the Holocaust and Genocide, executive director, 1979-; Hebrew University of Jerusalem, Martin Buber Center and Department of Psychology, professor of psychology and family therapy, 1993-97, Program for Advanced Studies in Integrative Psychotherapy, founder, director, 1993-. Writer. **Publications:** Individual and Family Developmental Review, 1969; Marital Love and Hate, 1972; (intro.) War and Its Causes, 1972; (ed.) Strategies Against Violence: Design for Nonviolent Change, 1978; (with C. Rapaport) How Can We Commit the Unthinkable?: Genocide, the Human Cancer, 1982; (ed.) Toward the Understanding and Prevention of Genocide, 1984; (ed.) Genocide: A Critical Bibliographical Review, 1991; (ed. with D. Fromer) Holding on to Humanity-the Message of Holocaust Survivors: The Shamai Davidson Papers, 1992; Existential/Dialectual Marital Therapy: Breaking the Secret Code of Marriage, 1992; (ed. with A.L. Berger) Genocide: A Critical Bibliographic Review, vol. III: The Widening Circle of Genocide, 1994, vol. IV: Medical and Psychological Effects of Concentration Camps on Holocaust Survivors, 1997; (with S. Totten and W. Parsons) Genocide in the Twentieth Century: Critical Essays and Eyewitness Accounts, 1995 as Century of Genocide: Eyewitness Accounts and Critical Views, 1997, 2nd ed., 2004; (ed.) Encyclopedia of Genocide, 2 vols., 1999; Century of Genocide: Critical Essays and Eyewitness Accounts, 2004; Fascism and Democracy in the Human Mind: A Bridge Between Mind and Society, 2006; Fighting Suicide Bombing: A Worldwide Campaign for Life, 2007. **Address:** Institute on the Holocaust and Genocide, PO Box 10311, Jerusalem, 91102, Israel. **Online address:** encygeno@mail.com

CHARRETTE, Robert N. (Richard Fawkes). American (born United States), b. 1953?. **Genres:** Novels, Science Fiction/Fantasy, Adult Non-fiction, Mystery/Crime/Suspense. **Career:** Freelance writer, 1975-; freelance graphic artist, 1975-81; Fantasy Games Unlimited, art director, 1981-82; freelance sculptor, 1982-84, 1986-; Ral Partha Enterprises, staff sculptor, 1984-86. **Publications:** NOVELS: Never Trust An Elf, 1992; A Prince Among Men, 1994; Just Compensation, 1996; A King Beneath the Mountain, 1995; A Knight Among Knaves, 1995; Chretien De Troyes, 1998; Initiation to War, 2001. BATTLETECH SERIES: Wolves on the Border, 1989; Heir to the Dragon, 1989; Wolf Pack, 1991. SECRETS OF POWER TRILOGY (SHADOWRUN): Never Deal with a Dragon, 1990; Choose Your Enemies Carefully, 1991; Find Your Own Truth, 1991. CHRONICLES OF AELWYN SERIES: Timespell, 1996; The Eye of the Serpent, 1996; Wizard of Bones, 1996. ROLE-PLAYING GAMES: (with P. Hume) Bushido, 1975; (with P. Hume) Aftermath!, 1981; (with P. Hume) Daredevils, 1982; Land of Ninja, 1986. OTHER: Fiore dei liberi's armizare, 2011. AS RICHARD FAWKES: Dion Boucicault, 1981; (with M. Langdon) Notes from a Low Singer, 1982; Face of the Enemy, 1999; Nature of the Beast, 2004. **Address:** c/o Donald Maass, Donald Maass Literary Agency, 121 W 27th St., Ste. 801, New York, NY 10001, U.S.A. **Online address:** bob@parroom.net

CHARTERS, Ann. American (born United States), b. 1936. **Genres:** Literary Criticism And History, Biography, Young Adult Fiction, Novellas/Short Stories. **Career:** Colby Junior College, instructor, 1961-63; Random House-Knopf, assistant editor, 1965; Columbia University, instructor in literature, 1965-66; New York City Community College of Applied Arts and Sciences of the City University of New York, assistant professor of English, 1967-70; University of Connecticut, associate professor, 1974-77, professor of English, 1978-2005, professor emeritus, 2005-; Uppsala University, Fulbright professor, 1980. Writer. **Publications:** The Ragtime Songbook, 1965; Bibliography of Works by Jack Kerouac, 1967, rev. ed., 1975; Olson/Melville: A Study in Affinity, 1968; (comp.) Scenes Along the Road, 1970; Nobody: The Life of Bert Williams, 1970; Kerouac: A Biography, 1973; (with S. Charters) I Love: The Story of Vladimir Mayakovsky and Lili Brik, 1979; Beats & Company, 1986; (intro.) Three Lives, 1990, rev. ed., 2005; (intro.) On the Road, 1991; Beat Poetry, 1993; (intro.) Speed and Kentucky, 1993; Resources for Teaching Major Writers of Short Fiction, 1993; (intro.) Big Sur, 1995; (afterword) Women of the Beat Generation, 1997; (foreword) Kerouac's Crooked Road, 1997; (with S. Charters) Blues Faces: A Portrait of the Blues, 2000; (intro.) Encyclopedia of Beat Literature, 2007; (with S. Charters) Brother-Souls: John Clellon Holmes, Jack Kerouac and the Beat Generation, 2010; The Story and its Writer Compact: An Introduction to Short Fiction, 8th ed., 2010. EDITOR: The Special View of History, 1969, rev. ed., 2006; Scattered Poems, 1970; The Story and Its Writer, 1983, 8th ed., 2011; The Beats: Literary Bohemians in Post-War America, 1983; The Portable Beat Reader in UK as The Penguin Book of the Beats, 1992; Major Writers of Short Fiction, 1993; The Kerouac Reader, 1995; The Portable Jack Kerouac, 1995; (and intro.) Selected Letters of Jack Kerouac, 1940-1956, 1995; (with S. Charters) Literature and Its Writers, 1998, 5th ed., 2010; Selected Letters of Jack Kerouac, 1957-1969, 2000; (comp.) The American Short Story and Its Writer, 2000; (and intro.) Beat Down to Your Soul: What Was the Beat Generation?, 2001; The Portable Sixties Reader, 2003. **Address:** Department of English, University of Connecticut, Class Rm. 129,, 215 Glenbrook Rd., Ste. 4025, Storrs Mansfield, CT 06269-4025, U.S.A. **Online address:** ann.charters@uconn.edu

CHARTERS, Samuel. (Samuel (Barclay) Charters). American (born United States), b. 1929. **Genres:** Novels, Poetry, Music, Translations. **Career:** Folkways Records, recording director, 1956-63; writer, 1959-; Prestige Records, recording editor, 1963-65; Vanguard Recording Society, producer, 1965-70, 1984-; Sonet Grammofon AB, producer, 1970-84; Gazell Productions/Records, owner, 1984-; Country Joe And The Fish, producer, 1966-70. **Publications:** Jazz: New Orleans, 1958; The Country Blues, 1959; Eight Poems in the Imagist Manner, 1960; (with L. Kunstadt) Jazz: The New York Scene, 1962; Heroes of the Prize Ring (poetry), 1963; The Poetry of the Blues, 1963; Jazz New Orleans (1885-1963): An Index to the Negro Musicians of New Orleans, 1963; The Bluesmen, 1967; Looking for Michael McClure at the Corner of Haight and Ashbury, 1967; Days (poetry), 1967; To This Place, 1967; Days:

Or, Days as Thoughts in a Season's Uncertainties, 1967; Some Poems against the War, 1968; To This Place (poetry), 1969; As I Stand at This Window, 1970; Some Poems/Poets (literary criticism), 1971; From a London Notebook (poetry), 1973; From a Swedish Notebook, 1973; Robert Johnson, 1973; (trans.) Baltics, by Tomas Transtruomer, 1975; The Legacy of the Blues, 1975; In Lagos (poetry), 1976; (trans.) We Women, by Edith Suodergran, 1977; Sweet as the Showers of Rain (poetry), 1977; Spelmännen, 1979; of Those Who Died: A Poem of Spring of 1945, 1980; (with A. Charters) I Love (biography), 1980; (with A. Charters) I love: The Story of Vladimir Mayakovsky and Lili Brik, 1979; Planes, 1980; The Roots of the Blues: An African Search, 1981; (trans.) The Courtyard, by Bo Carpelan, 1982; After the Rain, 1983; Mr. Jabi and Mr. Smythe: A Novel, 1983; Jelly Roll Morton's Last Night at the Jungle Inn: An Imaginary Memoir, 1984; Louisiana Black: A Novel, 1986; Blues Makers, 1991; A Country Year: A Chronicle, 1992; Elvis Presley Calls His Mother after the Ed Sullivan Show (novel), 1992; (trans.) Two Poems, 1996; (ed. with A. Charters) Literature and its Writers: An Introduction to Fiction, Poetry and Drama, 1997, (with A. Charters) 5th ed., 2010; The Day Is So Long and the Wages So Small: Music on a Summer Island, 1999; (with A. Charters and intro.) Blues Faces: A Portrait of the Blues, 2000; Mambo Time, the Story of Bebo Valdes, 2001; Walking a Blues Road: A Blues Reader, 1965-2004, 2004; New Orleans: Playing a Jazz Chorus, 2006; A Trumpet Around the Corner: The Story of New Orleans Jazz, 2008; Language of Song: Journeys in the Musical World of the African Diaspora, 2009; Brother-Souls: John Clellon Holmes, Jack Kerouac and the Beat Generation, 2010; Summer Soldiers, forthcoming. **Address:** Marion Boyars Publishers, 24 Lacy Rd., London, GL SW15 1NL, England.

CHARTERS, Samuel (Barclay). *See* **CHARTERS, Samuel.**

CHARTRAND, Lili. Canadian (born Canada), b. 1963. **Genres:** Art/Art History. **Career:** Writer and graphic designer. **Publications:** Malédiction, farces et attrapes!, 2000; Vent de folie sur Craquemou (novel), 2002; Le fou du rouge, 2003; L'affaire Von Bretzel, 2004; Le gros monstre qui aimait trop lire, 2005; Rouge-Babine, vampire détective, 2006; Taming Horrible Harry, 2006; Pagaille à Couzudor, 2007; Les maléfices de Mimi Réglisse, 2007; Mission royale pour Rouge-Babine, 2008; L'histoire parfumée d'Henriette la belette, 2008; The Smelly Story of Hazel the Weasel, 2009; L'arbre à saucisses de Mimi Réglisse, 2009; Mimi Rglisse et la Terrible crevisse, 2009; Bonne idée!, 2009; Le chevalier triple crème, 2009; Les jujubes-robots, 2009; Le mystère du rouge cabriole, 2010; Le mystère des bonbons sopranos, 2010; Rouge-Babine et l'opération Jade, 2010; La Craie Rose, 2010; Le Parapluie Jaune, 2011; Mimi Réglisse et la Terrible écrevisse, 2011; Ding!, 2011; Le Grain de Sable, 2011. FORTHCOMING: Le Gratte-ciel en Caramel; Pas de Moutons Pour Pépita!; Pas de Perruque Pour Pépita!; Les Brocolis Zombis; Fanfan joue à cache-cache; Fanfan et le fabuleux trésor, Lapinokio. **Address:** Montreal, QC , Canada. **Online address:** lili@lilichartrand.com

CHARYN, Jerome. American/French (born France), b. 1937. **Genres:** Novels, Novellas/Short Stories, Plays/Screenplays, Literary Criticism And History, Adult Non-fiction. **Career:** High School English teacher, 1962-64; City University of New York, lecturer in English, 1965, Herbert H. Lehman College, assistant professor, 1968-72, associate professor, 1972-78, professor of English, 1978-80; Stanford University, assistant professor of English, 1965-68; Rice University, Mellon visiting professor, 1979; Princeton University, lecturer in creative writing, 1981-85; American University of Paris, professor of film studies, 1995, distinguished professor emeritus; Dutton Review, editor; Cahiers du cinema, critic. **Publications:** Once upon a Droshky, 1964; On the Darkening Green, 1965; The Man Who Grew Younger and Other Stories, 1967; Going to Jerusalem: A Novel, 1967; American Scrapbook, 1969; The Single Voice: An Anthology of Contemporary Fiction, 1969; Eisenhower, My Eisenhower, 1971; The Troubled Vision: An Anthology of Contemporary Short Novels and Passages, 1970; The Tar Baby, 1973; Blue Eyes, 1975; The Education of Patrick Silver, 1976; Marilyn the Wild, 1976; The Franklin Scare, 1977; Secret Isaac: A Novel, 1978; The Seventh Babe: A Novel, 1979; The Catfish Man, 1980; Darlin' Bill: A Love Story of the Wild West, 1980; Panna Maria: A novel, 1982; Pinocchio's Nose, 1983; The Isaac Quartet, 1984; War Cries over Avenue C, 1985; Metropolis: New York as Myth, Marketplace and Magical Land, 1986; La Femme du Magician, 1986; Paradise Man, 1987; The Magician's Wife, 1987; Movieland: Hollywood and the Great American Dream Culture, 1989; The Good Policeman, 1990; Elsinore, 1991; (with M. Frezzato) Margot in Badtown, 1991; Maria's Girls, 1992; Back to Bataan, 1993; Montezuma's Man, 1993; Little Angel Street, 1994; Family Man, 1995; El Bronx, 1997; The Dark Lady from Belorusse: A Memoir, 1997; Death of a Tango King, 1998; Citizen Sidel, 1999; Captain Kidd, 1999; The Black Swan: A Memoir, 2000; Sizzling Chops and Devilish Spins: Ping-pong and the Art of Staying Alive, 2001; Hurricane Lady, 2001; Bronx Boy: A Memoir, 2002; Gangsters and Gold Diggers: Old New York, the Jazz Age and the Birth of Broadway, 2003; The Green Lantern: A Romance of Stalinist Russia, 2004; Savage Shorthand: The Life and Death of Isaac Babel, 2005; New York Sketchbook, 2005; Raised by Wolves: The Turbulent Art and Times of Quentin Tarantino, 2006; Johnny One-Eye: A Tale of the American Revolution, 2008; Discoveries, Marilyn: The Last Goddess, 2008; Secret Life of Emily Dickinson: A Novel, 2010; Joe DiMaggio: The Long Vigil, 2011. EDITOR: The New Mystery: The International Association of Crime Writers Essential Crime Writing of the Late Twentieth Century, 1993; Inside the Hornet's Head: An Anthology of Jewish American Writing, 2005. Contributor of articles to periodicals. **Address:** c/o Georges Borchardt Inc., 136 East 57th St., New York, NY 10022, U.S.A. **Online address:** jeromecharyn@aol.com

CHASE, Alyssa. Also writes as Alyssa Chase Rebein, Alyssa Ann Chase. American (born United States), b. 1965. **Genres:** Children's Fiction, Animals/Pets. **Career:** Dial Books for Young Readers, assistant editor, 1989-90; Holiday House, associate editor, 1990-92; freelance copy writer, proofreader and researcher, 1990-; Buffalo Spree (magazine), associate editor, 1992-95; Riverfront Times (newspaper), copy editor/writer, 1995-; St. Louis Magazine, copy editor/writer, 1995-. **Publications:** Jomo and Mata, 1993; Tessa on Her Own, 1994; (as Alyssa Chase Rebein) Stanleys This is the Life!, 2009. Contributor to periodicals. **Address:** 306 N Ridgeview Dr., Indianapolis, IN 46219, U.S.A.

CHASE, Alyssa Ann. *See* **CHASE, Alyssa.**

CHASE, Elaine Raco. American/Italian (born Italy), b. 1949. **Genres:** Mystery/Crime/Suspense, Romance/Historical, Criminology/True Crime, How-to Books, Young Adult Fiction. **Career:** New York State Narcotic Addiction Control Commission, secretary, 1967-68; WGY/WRGB-TV, audio visual librarian, 1968-70; Beckman Advertising, copywriter and producer, 1970-71; John D. Rockefeller Cultural Center, teacher of creative writing, 1980; Fairfax County Public Schools, teacher of creative writing, 1988-2009; Anne Arundel Community College, teacher of creative writing, 1998; Miami-Dade University, teacher of creative writing, 2009-10. Writer. **Publications:** ROMANCE NOVELS: Rules of the Game, 1980, 2nd ed., 2003; Tender Yearnings, 1981; A Dream Come True, 1982; Double Occupancy, 1982; Designing Woman, 1982; Calculated Risk, 1983; No Easy Way Out, 1983; Video Vixen, 1983; Best Laid Plans, 1983; Lady Be Bad, 1984; Special Delivery, 1984; Dare the Devil, 1987; In Care and After: A Positive Perspective, 2006. MYSTERY FICTION: Dangerous Places, 1987; Dark Corners, 1988; The Best of Elaine Raco Chase, vol. I, 1990, vol. II, 1991, vol. III, 1992; Partners in Crime, 1994; (with A. Wingate) Amateur Detectives: A Writer's Guide to How Private Citizens Solve Criminal Cases, 1996. CONTRIBUTOR: How to Write a Romance and Get It Published: With Intimate Advice from the World's Most Popular Romance Writers, 1983; Lovelines, 1983; The Fine Art of Murder, 1993. **Address:** 22575 Leanne Terr., Ste. 213, Ashburn, VA 20148, U.S.A. **Online address:** elainerc@juno.com

CHASE, Emily. *See* **GARWOOD, Julie.**

CHASE, Joan. American (born United States) **Genres:** Novels, Novellas/Short Stories. **Career:** Ragdale Foundation, assistant director, 1980-84; Iowa Writers Workshop, teacher, 1988; Princeton University, teacher, 1990. Writer. **Publications:** During the Reign of the Queen of Persia (novel), 1983; The Evening Wolves (novel), 1989; Bonneville Blue (short stories), 1991. **Address:** Ellen Levine Literary Agency Inc., 15 E 26th St., Ste. 1801, New York, NY 10010-1505, U.S.A.

CHASE, Karen. American (born United States), b. 1943?. **Genres:** Poetry, Children's Non-fiction, Young Adult Non-fiction. **Career:** Robert Frost Place, resident faculty; Camel River Writing Center, founder, 1991-2004; New York Hospital-Cornell Medical Center, poet-in-residence, through 2007. **Publications:** Kazimierz Square (poetry), 2000; Land of Stone: Breaking Silence Through Poetry, 2007; Bear: Poetry, 2008; Jamali-Kamali, 2011. Contributor to periodicals. **Address:** c/o Jonathan Matson, Harold Matson Company Inc., 276 5th Ave., New York, NY 10001, U.S.A. **Online address:** karenchase2@verizon.net

CHASE, Karen Susan. American (born United States), b. 1952. **Genres:**

Literary Criticism And History. **Career:** University of Virginia, assistant professor, 1979-85, associate professor, 1985-91, professor of English, 1992-, Linden Kent Memorial professor; University Press of Virginia, Virginia Victorian Studies Series, co-editor, 1990-2000. Writer. **Publications:** Eros & Psyche: The Representation of Personality in Charlotte Brontë, Charles Dickens and George Eliot, 1984; George Eliot, Middlemarch, 1991; (with M. Levenson) The Spectacle of Intimacy: A Public Life for the Victorian Family, 2000; (ed.) Middlemarch in the Twenty-first Century, 2006; The Victorians and Old Age, 2009. Contributor to periodicals. **Address:** Department of English, University of Virginia, 219 Bryan Hall, PO Box 400121, Charlottesville, VA 22904-4121, U.S.A. **Online address:** ksc3j@virginia.edu

CHASE, Kerry A. American (born United States), b. 1969. **Genres:** Novels. **Career:** University of California, Department of Political Science, visiting assistant professor, 1998-99; Tufts University, Department of Political Science, assistant professor, 1999-2007, Fletcher School of Law and Diplomacy, adjunct assistant professor, 2000-01, 2002-06, assistant professor of political science, 1999-2007; Brandeis University, Department of Politics, assistant professor, 2007-. Writer. **Publications:** Trading Blocs: States, Firms and Regions in the World Economy, 2005; Theater of Conflict: Commerce, Culture, and Competition in the Global Entertainment Industry, forthcoming. Contributor to academic journals. **Address:** Department of Politics, Brandeis University, 120 Golding, 415 South St., PO Box 058, Waltham, MA 02453, U.S.A. **Online address:** chase@brandeis.edu

CHASE, Loretta Lynda. American (born United States), b. 1949?. **Genres:** Romance/Historical, Young Adult Fiction. **Career:** Writer. **Publications:** TREVELYAN FAMILY: Isabella, 1987; The English Witch, 1988. REGENCY NOBLEMEN: Viscount Vagabond, 1988; The Devil's Delilah, 1989, 2nd ed., 1990. SCOUNDRELS: The Lion's Daughter, 1992; Captives of the Night, 1994; Lord of Scoundrels, 1995; The Last Hellion, 1998. CARSINGTON: Miss Wonderful, 2004; Mr. Impossible, 2005; Lord Perfect, 2006; Not Quite a Lady, 2007; Last Night's Scandal, 2010. NOVELS: Knaves' Wager, 1990; The Sandalwood Princess, 1990; Your Scandalous Ways, 2008; Don't Tempt Me, 2009. OTHERS: Falling Star: A Christmas Collection, 1992; Falling Star: A Christmas Present, 1994; The Mad Earl's Bride: Three Weddings and a Kiss (short stories), 1995; (with C. Anderson and S. James) Three Times a Bride, 2010. DRESS MAKERS: Silk is for Seduction, 2011. **Address:** c/o Author Mail, HarperCollins Publishers, 10 E 53rd St., New York, NY 10022, U.S.A. **Online address:** author@lorettachase.com

CHASE, Lyndon. *See* **CHARD, Judy (Gordon).**

CHASE, Nicholas. *See* **HYDE, Christopher.**

CHASE, Nicholas. *See* **HYDE, Anthony.**

CHASE, Steven. American (born United States) **Genres:** Theology/Religion, Humanities. **Career:** Jesuit School of Theology, adjunct professor; Western Theological Seminary, resident associate professor of Christian spirituality; Institute of Spirituality, Dominican Center, associate director, spiritual director, 1992-; Christian Spirituality Group, American Academy of Religion, founder, co-chair; John Hopkins University, Society for the Study of Christian Spirituality, Collegeville Institute, president, 2010-11. Writer. **Publications:** NONFICTION: Angelic Wisdom: The Cherubim and the Grace of Contemplation in Richard of St. Victor, 1995; (ed.) Doors of Understanding: Conversations in Global Spirituality in Honor of Ewert Cousins, 1997; (trans. and intro.) Angelic Spirituality: Medieval Perspectives on the Ways of Angels, 2002; Contemplation and Compassion: The Victorine Tradition, 2003; The Tree of Life: Models of Christian Prayer, 2005; Field Guide to Nature as Spiritual Practice, 2011; Nature as Spiritual Practice, 2011. **Address:** Western Theological Seminary, 101 E 13th St., Holland, MI 49423, U.S.A. **Online address:** steven.chase@westernsem.edu

CHASNOFF, Joel. American (born United States), b. 1973. **Genres:** Autobiography/Memoirs. **Career:** Writer and comedian. **Publications:** The 188th Crybaby Brigade: A Skinny Jewish Kid from Chicago Fights Hezbollah: A Memoir, 2010. Contributor to books. **Address:** New York, NY , U.S.A. **Online address:** joel@joelchasnoff.com

CHAST, Roz. American (born United States), b. 1954. **Genres:** Cartoons, Illustrations. **Career:** New Yorker, cartoonist, 1979-. Freelance illustrator. **Publications:** SELF-ILLUSTRATED: (co-author) Sex and Sensibility: Ten Women Examine the Lunacy of Modern Love- In 200 Cartoons, 2008; Rco Goes to School, 2012. OTHERS: Unscientific Americans, 1982; Parallel Universes: An Assortment of Cartoons, 1984; Mondo Boxo: Cartoon Stories, 1987; Proof of Life on Earth, 1991; Childproof: Cartoons About Parents and Children, 1997; The Party, After You Left, 2004; Theories of Everything: Selected, Collected, and Health-Inspected Cartoons, 1978-2006, 2006; (with S. Martin) The Alphabet From A To Y With Bonus Letter, Z!, 2007; Too Busy Marco, 2010; What I Hate: From A to Z, 2011. Contributor to periodicals. **Address:** Steven Barclay Agency, 12 Western Ave., Petaluma, CA 94952, U.S.A. **Online address:** roz@rozchast.com

CHATAWAY, Carol. Australian/British (born England), b. 1955. **Genres:** Children's Fiction, Animals/Pets. **Career:** Birdwood, school treasurer, 1983-88; Crafers Primary School, staff. Writer. **Publications:** The Perfect Pet, 2001; Wings 2005; Edwina Sparrow: Girl of Destiny, 2007; (with D. Snell) You Are My Special Baby, 2011. **Address:** Crafers Primary School, 55 Piccadilly Rd., Crafers, SA 5152, Australia. **Online address:** carol.chataway@bigpond.com

CHÂTEAUREYNAUD, Georges-Olivier. French (born France), b. 1947?. **Genres:** Autobiography/Memoirs, Young Adult Fiction, Novellas/Short Stories. **Career:** Writer. **Publications:** Le Fou Dans la Chaloupe, 1973; Les Messagers, 1974, rev. ed., 1990; Labelle charbonnière, 1976; Mathieu Chain, 1978; Le Verger, 1978; La Faculté Des Songes, 1982; Le Congrès de Fantomologie, 1985; (with D. Thompson) Le Tiroir Secret, 1986; La Fortune: Et Autres Textes, 1987; Le Héros Blessé au Bras, 1987; Le jardin dans l'île (short stories), 1989; Le Jardin d'éden: La Seule Mortelle, 1992; Le Kiosque et le Tilleul, 1993; Nouvelles, 1972-1988, 1993; Le Château de Verre, 1994; Monsieur d'Orsay, 1995; Le Styx Et Autres Nouvelles, 1995; Les Ormeaux, 1996; Le Goût de l'ombre, 1997; Le démon à lacrécelle, 1999; Le Conquête du Pérou: récit, 1999; Les Chevaliers Sans Nom, 2001; Civils de plomb, 2002; Au Fond Du Paradis, 2002; (with H. Haddad and F. Tristan) Petite suite cherbourgeoise, 2004; Les Intermittences D'Icare, 2006; Mécomptes cruels, 2006; Singe savant tabassé par deux clowns, 2005; Autre Rive, 2007; Le Corps de l'autre: Roman, 2010; Vie nous regarde passer, 2011; Résidence dernière, 2011. **Address:** c/o Author Mail, Zulma, 122, Bd. Haussmann, Paris, 75008, France.

CHATELLIER, Louis. French (born France), b. 1935. **Genres:** Theology/Religion. **Career:** Centre Nationale Recherche Scientifique, research assistant, 1966-70; Universite de Strasbourg, assistant principal, 1970-80; Universite Lyon, professor, 1980-81; Universite Nancy II, professor, 1981-2003, professor emeritus, 2003-; Institut Universitaire de France, professor, 1996-2003; Ecole pratiques des Hautes Etudes, section des sciences religieuses, 1998-2003. Writer. **Publications:** Tradition christienne et renouveau catholique dans l'ancien diocese de Strasbourg (title means: 'Christian Tradition and Catholic Renewal in the Old Diocese of Strasbourg'), 1981; L'Europe de devots, 1987, trans. as The Europe of the Devout: The Catholic Reformation and the Formation of a New Society, 1989; La religion des pauvres: les missions rurales en Europe et la formation du catholicisme moderne, XVIe-XIXe siècle, 1993; The Religion of the Poor: Rural Missions in Europe and the Formation of Modern Catholicism, c. 1500-1800, 1993; (ed.) Religions en transition dans la seconde moitie du XVIII siecle, 2000; Les espaces infinis et le silence de Dieu: science et religion, XVI-XIXe siècle, 2003; écriture du croyant, 2005; Lumiéres, religions et laicité: rencontres historiques de Nancy, novembre 2005, 2009. **Address:** Faculty of Historical and Geographical Sciences, Universite Nancy II, 23 Blvd. Albert I, Nancy, 54015, France. **Online address:** louis.chatellier@gmail.com

CHATFIELD, Cheryl A. American (born United States) **Genres:** How-to Books, Money/Finance. **Career:** National Association of Securities Dealers, registered representative, 1980, financial principal, 1984; Chatfield, Dean and Company Inc., founder, partner and chief executive officer; Women Securities International Inc., founder and owner; Center for Entrepreneurship and Economic Development, instructor; University of Arizona, adjunct professor; University of New Mexico, adjunct professor; State Penitentiary of New Mexico, Alice King Family Center, executive director; Nottingham Institute, founder and president; Central Connecticut State University, assistant professor; Campfire, supervisor and curriculum specialist. Writer. **Publications:** Low-Priced Riches: Investing in the OTC Market, 1985; Selling Low-Priced Riches: Being a Successful OTC Stock Broker, 1986; The Trust Factor: The Art of Doing Business in the 21st Century, 1996; Don't Fall off the Bicycle:

Balancing Chaos and Order in Our Lives, 2002; The Lost Principles, 2010; Do It Yourself Guide to Spirituality: Seven Simple Steps, 2011. **Address:** The Nottingham Institute, 85 Jerome Ave., PO Box 1204, Burlington, CT 06013-2407, U.S.A. **Online address:** chatfield@nottinstitute.org

CHATFIELD, E. Charles. American (born United States), b. 1934. **Genres:** History, Institutions/Organizations, Intellectual History, International Relations/Current Affairs, Biography. **Career:** Wittenberg University, instructor, 1961-65, assistant professor, 1965-69, associate professor, 1969-74, professor of history, 1974-99, H. Orth Hirt chair in history, 1998-, H. Orth Hirt professor emeritus of history, 1999-, director of international education, 1975-; Peace and Change, co-editor, 1980-83. **Publications:** For Peace and Justice: Pacifism in America, 1914-1941, 1971; The Life and Writings of Devere Allen, 1976; (with C. DeBenedetti) Kirby Page and the Social Gospel, 1977; (with C. DeBenedetti) An American Ordeal: The Antiwar Movement of the Vietnam Era, 1990; (with R. Kleidman) The American Peace Movement: Ideals and Activism, 1992. EDITOR: Ethics of War: Bertrand Russell and Ralph Barton Perry on World War I, 1972; (contrib.) The Garland Library of War and Peace, 1974-78, 1972; American Peace Movements, 1973; (and intro.) Peace Movements in America, 1973; The Radical No: The Correspondence and Writings of Evan Thomas on War, 1974; International War Resistance through World War II, 1975; (and intro.) The Americanization of Gandhi: Images of the Mahatma, 1976; (with P. van den Dungen) Peace Movements and Political Cultures, 1988; (with R. Ilukhina) Peace/Mir: An Anthology of Historic Alternatives to War, 1994; (ed. with J. Smith and R. Pagnucco) Transnational Social Movements and Global Politics: Solidarity Beyond the State, 1997. **Address:** Department of History, Wittenberg University, 200 W Ward St., PO Box 720, Springfield, OH 45501, U.S.A. **Online address:** echatfield@wittenberg.edu

CHATMAN, Seymour. American (born United States), b. 1928. **Genres:** Literary Criticism And History, Film, Speech/Rhetoric, History, Biography. **Career:** Cornell University, research associate, 1951-52; Wayne State University, instructor in English, 1954-56; University of Pennsylvania, assistant professor of English, 1956-60; University of California, assistant professor of speech, 1960-61, professor of rhetoric, 1961-93, professor emeritus of rhetoric, 1993-; Systems Development Corp., consultant, 1962. Writer. **Publications:** A Theory of Meter, 1965; An Introduction to the Language of Poetry, 1968; Later Style of Henry James, 1972; Story and Discourse: Narrative Structure in Fiction and Film, 1978; Antonioni, or, the Surface of the World, 1985; Coming to Terms: The Rhetoric of Narrative in Fiction and Film, 1990; Michelangelo Antonioni: The Complete Films, 2004. EDITOR: (with M. Peckham) Word, Meaning, Poem, 1961; (with S.R. Levin) Essays on the Language of Literature, 1967; (and trans.) Literary Style: A Symposium, 1971; (and foreword) Approaches to Poetics: Selected Papers from the English Institute, 1973; (with U. Eco) A Semiotic Landscape, 1979; (ed. with G. Fink) L'Avventura: Michelangelo Antonioni, Director, 1989; Reading Narrative Fiction, 1992; (and intro.) Benjamin Graham: Memoirs of the Dean of Wall Street, 1996; (ed. with W. van Peer) New Perspectives on Narrative Perspective, 2001. **Address:** Department of Rhetoric, University of California, 7408 Dwinelle Hall, Ste. 2670, Berkeley, CA 94720-2670, U.S.A. **Online address:** seymour.chatman4@gmail.com

CHATTAM, Maxim. French (born France), b. 1976. **Genres:** Young Adult Fiction, Mystery/Crime/Suspense, Adult Non-fiction. **Career:** Writer. **Publications:** (As Maxime Williams) Le 5éme règne, 2003; L'Ame du mal, 2004; Intenebris, 2004; Maléfice, 2005; Le sang du temps, 2005; Les arcanes duchaos, 2006; Prédateurs, 2007; (as Maxime Williams) The Cairo Diary, 2007; La Thèorie Gaïa, 2008; Autre-Monde, 2008, vol. II: Malronce, 2009; La Promesse des Ténèbres, 2009; (as Maxime Williams) Léviatemps, 2010. **Address:** R. de l'enclos 75, Bte 7, Etalle, 6740, Belgium. **Online address:** max@maximechattam.com

CHATTARJI, Sampurna. Indian/Ethiopian (born Ethiopia), b. 1970. **Genres:** Poetry, Novels. **Career:** J. Walter Thompson Agency, copywriter. Poet. **Publications:** POETRY: The Greatest Stories Ever Told, 2004; (trans.) S. Ray, Abol Tabol: The Nonsense World of Sukumar Ray, 2004 as Wordygurdyboom! The Nonsense World of Sukumar Ray, 2008; Sight May Strike You Blind, 2007; Mulla Nasruddin, 2008; The Panchatantra: Three Brothers and the Flower of Gold, 2008; The Fried Frog and Other Funny Freaky Foodie Feisty Poems, 2009; Rupture (novel), 2009. Works appear in anthologies. Contributor to periodicals. **Address:** Mumbai, MH , India. **Online address:** sampurna_c@yahoo.co.uk

CHATTERJEE, Debjani. British/Indian (born India), b. 1952. **Genres:** Children's Fiction, Mythology/Folklore, Local History/Rural Topics, Adult Non-fiction, Poetry, Translations, Food And Wine. **Career:** Sheffield Racial Equality Council, director, 1984-94; Oxfordshire Racial Equality Council, director, 1994-; York St. John University, fellow, 2006-09; Sahitya Press, founder; Tadeeb Intl., associate editor; Pratibha India, associate editor; The Colour of Heath, literary editor. **Publications:** FOR CHILDREN: (reteller) The Elephant-Headed God and Other Hindu Tales, 1989, rev. ed., 1993; The Monkey God and Other Hindu Tales, 1993; (trans.) The Parrot's Training, 1993; Nyamia and the Bag of Gold, 1994; Sufi Stories from Around the World, 1994; The Most Beautiful Child, 1996; (ed. with R. Choudhury) The Snake Prince & Other Folk Tales from Bengal, 1999; Animal Antics, 2000; Nazrul Islam Poster-Poems+ Teachers Notes, 2001; (ed. with B.F. Hodder) Rainbow World: Poems From Many Cultures, 2003. OTHERS: The Role of Religion in A Passage to India, 1984; (ed. with C. Searle) Peaces: Poems for Peace, 1987; (ed. and contrib.) I Was That Woman, 1989; (ed. with R. Islam) Barbed Lines (bilingual anthology), 1990; (ed. with W. Scammell) Northern Poetry: vol. II, 1991; (co-ed.) The Sun Rises in the North, 1992; (co.ed.) Sweet and Sour (bilingual anthology), 1993; (trans.) Album, 1997; The Message Of Thunder & Other Plays, 1999; Who Cares? Reminiscences of Yemeni Carers in Sheffield, 2001; (ed. with A. Sen) Daughters Of A Riverine Land, 2003; Namaskar, 2004; Sixties Press Anthology of Gregory Fellows' Poetry, 2004; The Song of the Scythe, 2005; Masala: Poems from India, Bangladesh, Pakistan and Sri Lanka, 2005; A Special Assembly, 2006; (ed.) Mango Shake, 2006; The Heart's Echoes, 2006. **Address:** Oxfordshire Racial Equality Council, Macclesfield House, Tidmarsh Ln., Oxford, OX OX1 1NA, England. **Online address:** debjani@chatterjee.freeserve.co.uk

CHATTERJEE, Upamanyu. Indian (born India), b. 1959?. **Genres:** Novellas/Short Stories, Humor/Satire, Novels, Literary Criticism And History. **Career:** Indian Administrative Service, officer, 1983-; Bombay Slum Improvement Board, chief officer, 1983-; freelance writer, 1986-; University of Kent, writer-in-residence, 1990; Government of India, Ministry of Human Resource Development, director (languages), 1998. **Publications:** FICTION: English, August: An Indian Story, 1988, rev. ed. as The Mammaries of the Welfare State, 2000; The Last Burden, 1993; Weight Loss, 2006; Way to Go, 2010. Contributor of articles to periodicals. **Address:** Faber and Faber Ltd., 3 Queen Sq., London, GL WC1N 3AU, England.

CHATTERJI, Joya. British/Indian (born India), b. 1964. **Genres:** History. **Career:** University of Cambridge, Trinity college, fellow, 1989-94, Centre for South Asian Studies, senior research fellow, 1995-, lecturer, reader in modern south asian history; London School of Economics and Political Science, Department of International History, lecturer, 2001-, senior visiting fellow. Writer. **Publications:** Bengal Divided: Hindu Communalism and Partition, 1932-1947, 1994; Spoils of Partition: Bengal and India, 1947-1967, 2007; (with C. Alexander and A. Jalais) Bengal Diaspora: Muslim Migrants in Britain, India and Bangladesh, forthcoming. **Address:** University of Cambridge, Trinity College, Trinity St., Cambridge, CB2 1TQ, United Kingdom. **Online address:** j.chatterji@lse.ac.uk

CHATTO, James. Canadian/British (born England), b. 1955. **Genres:** Novellas/Short Stories, Food And Wine. **Career:** Toronto Life Gardens, editor, 1996-97; Gardening Life, editor, 1997-2002; Harry magazine, editor; LCBO's Food & Drink magazine, consultant and senior editor. **Publications:** SHORT STORIES: The Atheist, 1985; Tricky Customers, 1986. NONFICTION: The Seducer's Cookbook, 1981; (with W.L. Martin) A Kitchen in Corfu, 1987; The Man Who Ate Toronto: Memoirs of a Restaurant Lover, 1998, new ed., 2011; (with L. Waverman) A Matter of Taste, 2004; The Greek for Love: A Memoir of Corfu, 2005. Contributor of articles to books and periodicals. **Address:** Toronto Life, 111 Queen St. E, Ste. 320, Toronto, ON M5C 1S2, Canada.

CHATZKY, Jean. (Jean Sherman Chatzky). American (born United States), b. 1964?. **Genres:** Money/Finance. **Career:** Working Woman Magazine, editorial assistant, assistant editor, 1986-87; Business Traveler International Magazine, staff member, 1988; Dean Witter, associate editor, 1989-91; Forbes Magazine, reporter and researcher, 1991-98; Money Magazine, editor-at-large, 1998; National Broadcasting Co., Today Show, financial editor; America Online, money coach, 2003; More Magazine, contributing editor; Daily News, columnist. **Publications:** (As Jean Sherman Chatzky) The Rich and Famous Money Book: Investment Strategies of Leading Celebrities, 1997; Talking Money: Everything You Need to Know about Finances and Your Future, 2001; You Don't Have to Be Rich: Comfort Happiness and Financial Security on Your Own Terms, 2003; Pay It Down!: From Debt to Wealth on $10 a Day, 2004, rev. ed. 2009; Make Money, Not Excuses: Wake Up, Take Charge, and Overcome Your Financial Fears Forever, 2006; Difference, 2009; Not Your Parent's Money Book: Making, Saving, and Spending Your Own Money, 2010; (with A. McGowen) Money 911: Your Most Pressing Money Questions Answered, Your Money Emergencies Solved, 2010. Contributor to periodicals. **Address:** The Robert E. Shepard Agency, 1608 Dwight Way, Berkeley, CA 94703-1804, U.S.A.

CHATZKY, Jean Sherman. *See* **CHATZKY, Jean.**

CHAUDHURI, Amit. British/Indian (born India), b. 1962. **Genres:** Novels, Novellas/Short Stories, Young Adult Non-fiction. **Career:** Wolfson College, creative arts fellow, 1992-95; Cambridge University, faculty of English, through 1999, Leverhulme Special Research Fellow; Columbia University, School of Arts, faculty, 2002, visiting professor; University of East Anglia, professor in contemporary literature. Writer. **Publications:** A Strange and Sublime Address, 1991; Afternoon Raag, 1993; Freedom Song: Three Novels, 1999; A New World, 2000; (ed.) Picador Book of Modern Indian Literature, 2001; Real Time: Stories and a Reminiscence, 2002; Small Orange Flags: On Living During a State of Emergency, 2003; D.H. Lawrence and 'Difference', 2003; (ed.) Vintage Book of Modern Indian Literature, 2004; St. Cyril Road and Other Poems, 2005; (ed.) Memory's Gold: Writings on Calcutta, 2008; Clearing a Space: Reflections on India, Literature and Culture, 2008; The Immortals, 2009. Contributor to periodicals and anthologies. **Address:** School of Literature and Creative Writing, University of East Anglia, Arts Bldg. 1.28, 20 John St., Norwich, GL NR4 7TJ, England. **Online address:** a.chaudhuri@uea.ac.uk

CHAUNCEY, George. American (born United States), b. 1953?. **Genres:** Gay And Lesbian Issues, History, Young Adult Non-fiction. **Career:** University of Chicago, assistant professor to professor of history, 1991-2006; Yale University, professor of history, 2006-, Research Initiative on the History of Sexualities, co-director. Writer. **Publications:** (Ed. with M.B. Duberman and M. Vicinus) Hidden from History: Reclaiming the Gay and Lesbian Past, 1989; Gay New York: Gender, Urban Culture and the Making of the Gay Male World, 1890-1940, 1994; Why Marriage?: The History Shaping Today's Debate over Gay Equality, 2004. **Address:** Department of History, Yale University, 2684 Hall of Graduate Studies, PO Box 208324, New Haven, CT 06520-8324, U.S.A. **Online address:** george.chauncey@yale.edu

CHAURETTE, Normand. Canadian (born Canada), b. 1954. **Genres:** Plays/Screenplays, History, Humor/Satire. **Career:** Quebec publisher Leméac, editor, 1984-88. **Publications:** Rêve d'une Nuit D'hôpital, 1980; Provincetown Playhouse, Juillet 1919, J'avais 19 ans, 1981; Fetes d'Automne, 1982; La Société De Métis, 1983; Fragments D'une Lettre D'adieu lus Par Des Geologies, 1986; Scènes D'enfants: Récit, 1988; Les Reines, 1991; The Queens, 1992; Je Vous Ecris Du Caire, 1996; Le Passage de l'Indiana, 1996; Stabat Mater I, 1997; Fragments of a Farewell Letter Read by Geologists, 1998; Stabat Mater II, 1999; Le Petit Köchel, 2000; All the Verdis of Venice, 2000. Works appear in anthologies. **Address:** Union des écrivains québécois, 3492, Ave. Laval, Montreal, QC H2X 3C8, Canada.

CHAVE, Anna C. American (born United States), b. 1953?. **Genres:** Art/Art History, Literary Criticism And History. **Career:** Hunter College, instructor; Harvard University, associate professor of fine arts; City University of New York, Queens College and the Graduate Center, professor of art history, professor of contemporary art and theory. Writer. **Publications:** ART CRITICISM: Mark Rothko: Subjects: October 15-February 26, 1983; Mark Rothko: Subjects in Abstraction, 1989; (contrib.) Power: Its Myths and Mores in American Art, 1961-1991, 1991; (contrib.) Agnes Martin, 1992; Constantin Brancusi: Shifting the Bases of Art, 1993; (intro.) Valerie Jaudon, 1996. Contributor to books. **Address:** The Graduate Center, City University of New York, 365 5th Ave., New York, NY 10016-4309, U.S.A. **Online address:** annachave@aol.com

CHAVES, Mark (Alan). American (born United States), b. 1960?. **Genres:** Theology/Religion, Women's Studies And Issues, Social Sciences, Politics/Government. **Career:** Harvard University, instructor in sociology, 1989-90; Loyola University, instructor and assistant professor of sociology, 1990-92; University of Notre Dame, assistant professor, associate professor of sociology, 1992-96; American Journal of Sociology, consulting editor, 1993-95; University of Illinois, visiting associate professor of sociology, 1997-98; University of Chicago, National Opinion Research Center, research associate, 1997-98; University of Arizona, Department of Sociology, associate professor, 1998-2001, professor and head, 2001-07; Duke University, professor of sociology, religion, and divinity, 2007-. Writer. **Publications:** Ordaining Women: Culture and Conflict in Religious Organizations, 1997; (ed. with S.L. Miller) Financing American Religion, 1999; How Do We Worship?, 1999; Religious Congregations and Welfare Reform: Who Will Take Advantage of Charitable Choice?, 1999; Congregations in America, 2004. Contributor to periodicals. **Address:** Department of Sociology, Duke University, 248 Soc/Psych Bldg., PO Box 90088, Durham, NC 27708-0088, U.S.A. **Online address:** mac58@soc.duke.edu

CHÁVEZ-GARCÍA, Miroslava. American/Mexican (born Mexico), b. 1968. **Genres:** History. **Career:** University of California, Chicana/o Studies Program, assistant professor, associate professor; California Hispanic Commission on Alcohol, staff; Drug Abuse Inc., staff. Historian and writer. **Publications:** Negotiating Conquest: Gender and Power in California, 1770s to 1880s, 2004; (intro. and comp.) The Child Savers: The Invention of Delinquency, 2009. Contributor to periodicals. **Address:** Department of Chicana/o Studies, University of California, 2102 Hart Hall, 1 Shields Ave., Davis, CA 95616, U.S.A. **Online address:** chavezgarcia@ucdavis.edu

CHAVIARAS, Strates. *See* **HAVIARAS, Stratis.**

CHAYAT, Roko Sherry. *See* **CHAYAT, Sherry.**

CHAYAT, Sherry. (Roko Sherry Chayat). American (born United States), b. 1943. **Genres:** Theology/Religion, Art/Art History. **Career:** Zen Center of Syracuse, abbot, 1978; teacher, 1992. Zen instructor, art critic, editor and art consultant. **Publications:** Life Lessons: The Art of Jerome Witkin, 1994, 2nd ed., 2006; (trans. with K. Tanahashi) Endless Vow: The Zen Path of Soen Nakagawa, 1996; (ed. and intro.) Subtle Sound: The Zen Teachings of Maurine Stuart, 1996; (intro. and ed.) Eloquent Silence: Nyogen Senzaki's Gateless Gate and Other Previously Unpublished Teachings and Letters, 2008. Contributor to periodicals. **Address:** Zen Center of Syracuse, 266 W Seneca Tpke., Syracuse, NY 13207, U.S.A.

CHAZAN, Robert. American (born United States), b. 1936. **Genres:** Theology/Religion. **Career:** New York University, Department of Hebrew and Judaic Studies, S.H. and Helen R. Scheuer professor, Morse Academic Plan, director. Academic and writer. **Publications:** Medieval Jewry in Northern France: A Political and Social History, 1973; (ed. with M.L. Raphael) Modern Jewish History: A Source Reader, 1974; (ed. and intro.) Church, State and Jew in the Middle Ages, 1980; European Jewry and the First Crusade, 1987; Daggers of Faith: Thirteenth-Century Christian Missionizing and Jewish Response, 1989; Barcelona and Beyond: The Disputation of 1263 and Its Aftermath, 1992; In the Year 1096: The First Crusade and the Jews, 1996; Medieval Stereotypes and Modern Antisemitism, 1997; (ed. with W.W. Hallo and L.H. Schiffman) Ki Baruch Hu: Ancient Near Eastern, Biblical and Judaic Studies in Honor of Baruch A. Levine, 1999; God, Humanity and History: The Hebrew First Crusade Narratives, 2000; Fashioning Jewish Identity in Medieval Western Christendom, 2004; The Jews of Medieval Western Christendom, 1000-1500, 2006. **Address:** Hebrew & Judaic Studies, New York University, Heyman Hall, 51 Washington S, New York, NY 10012-1075, U.S.A. **Online address:** rc2@nyu.edu

CHEANEY, J. B. American (born United States), b. 1950?. **Genres:** Novels, Humor/Satire, Young Adult Fiction. **Career:** Writer. **Publications:** Wordsmith: A Creative Writing Course for Young People, 1992, 2nd ed., 2003; The Room, 1992; Wordsmith Apprentice, 1995, 2nd ed., 2003; Wordsmith Craftsman, 1996, 2nd ed., 2003; The Playmaker, 2000; The True Prince, 2002; My Friend the Enemy, 2005; The Middle of Somewhere, 2007. Contributor to magazines. **Address:** PO Box 634, Bolivar, MO 65613, U.S.A.

CHEATHEM, Mark R. American (born United States), b. 1973. **Genres:** History, Biography, Autobiography/Memoirs. **Career:** Southern New Hampshire University, assistant professor of history, 2004-08; Cumberland University, associate professor of history, 2008-; Mississippi State University, faculty; Mississippi University for Women, faculty. Historian and writer. **Publications:** Old Hickory's Nephew: The Political and Private Struggles of Andrew Jackson Donelson, 2007; (ed.) Jacksonian and Antebellum Age: People and Perspectives, 2008. Contributor to books. **Address:** Cumberland University, 1 Cumberland Sq., Lebanon, TN 37087-3408, U.S.A. **Online address:** mcheathem@cumberland.edu

CHECKEL, Jeffrey T(aylor). Canadian/American (born United States), b. 1959. **Genres:** Politics/Government. **Career:** Cornell University, Wilson Particle Accelerator Laboratory, synchrotron operator, 1981-83; University of Pittsburgh, Department of Political Science, assistant professor, 1991-96, Graduate School of Public and International Affairs, assistant professor, 1991-96; University of Konstanz, Department of Administrative Sciences, Humboldt fellow, 1996-98; University of Oslo, Arena Centre for European Studies, senior researcher, 1998-99, research professor of international politics, 2000-01, Department of Political Science, professor, 2002-08; International Peace Research Institute, Centre for the Study of Civil War, adjunct research professor, 2008-, working group leader; Simon Fraser University, School for International Studies, professor and Simons chair in international law and human security, 2008-, undergraduate chair. Writer. **Publications:** Ideas and International Political Change: Soviet/Russian Behavior and the End of the Cold War, 1997; (ed.) International Institutions and Socialization in Europe, 2007; (ed. with P.J. Katzenstein) European Identity, 2009. **Address:** School for International Studies, Simon Fraser University, 7248 Harbour Ctr., 515 W Hastings St., Ste. 7200, Vancouver, BC V6B 5K3, Canada. **Online address:** jtcheckel@sfu.ca

CHECKOWAY, Julie. American (born United States), b. 1963. **Genres:** Autobiography/Memoirs, Writing/Journalism. **Career:** University of Iowa, Iowa Writer's Workshop, instructor, 1987; Johns Hopkins University, instructor for writing seminars, 1988-95; Gilman School, Writing Center, director, 1989-95; University of Georgia, assistant professor of English, 1995-, Creative Writing Program, director, 1996-; Associated Writing Programs, president, 1998-99; Hebei Teachers University, visiting professor. Writer. **Publications:** Little Sister: Searching for the Shadow World of Chinese Women (memoir), 1996; (ed.) Creating Fiction: Instruction and Insights from Teachers of Associated Writing Programs, 1999. Works appear in anthologies. Contributor to magazines. **Address:** Creative Writing Program, University of Georgia, 329A Park Hall, Athens, GA 30602, U.S.A. **Online address:** jcheckow@arches.uga.edu

CHEERS, D. Michael. American (born United States) **Genres:** Autobiography/Memoirs, History, Photography. **Career:** Auburn University, teacher; Wayne State College, teacher; Ebony Magazine, editor; University of Mississippi, assistant professor, professor; San Jose State University, Photojournalism Program, head. **Publications:** (Ed. with E. Easter and D.M. Brooks) Songs of My People: African-Americans, a Self-Portrait, 1992; (with H. Masekela) Still Grazing: The Musical Journey of Hugh Masekela, 2004. Contributor of articles to newspapers and magazines. **Address:** Meek School of Journalism & New Media, University of Mississippi, 331 Farley Hall, University, MS 38677, U.S.A. **Online address:** dcheers@olemiss.edu

CHEEVER, Susan. American (born United States), b. 1943. **Genres:** Novels, Biography. **Career:** Colorado Rocky Mountain School, teacher, 1966-70; Scarborough School, teacher, 1968-69; Tarrytown Daily News, reporter, 1971-72; Westchester Rockland Newspapers, reporter, 1972; Newsweek Magazine, general editor and writer, 1974-79; Newsday, columnist; Marymount Manhattan, teacher, 1994-96; Hunter College, faculty, 1995; Bennington College, M.F.A. Program, professor, 1995-; The New School, M.F.A. program, professor, 2004-. **Publications:** Looking for Work, 1979; A Handsome Man, 1981; The Cage, 1982; Home before Dark: A Biographical Memoir of John Cheever, 1984; Doctors and Women, 1987; Elizabeth Cole, 1989; Treetops: A Family Memoir, 1991; A Woman's Life: The Story of an Ordinary American and Her Extraordinary Generation, 1994; Note Found in a Bottle: My Life as a Drinker (memoir), 1999; As Good as I Could Be, 2001; My Name is Bill: Bill Wilson: His Life and the Creation of Alcoholics Anonymous, 2004; American Bloomsbury: Louisa May Alcott, Ralph Waldo Emerson, Margaret Fuller, Nathaniel Hawthorne, and Henry David Thoreau: Their Lives, Their Loves, Their Work, 2006; (afterword) Addiction: Why Can't They Just Stop?, 2007; Desire: Where Sex Meets Addiction, 2008; Louisa May Alcott, 2010. **Address:** The New School, 66 W 12th St., New York, NY 10011, U.S.A. **Online address:** susancheever@yahoo.com

CHEHAK, Susan Taylor. American (born United States), b. 1951. **Genres:** Novels, Young Adult Fiction, Biography. **Career:** Kirkwood Community College, teacher of fiction writing, 1975-76; Antioch University, MFA Program, teacher of fiction writing; University of Iowa, teacher of fiction writing; University of California, teacher of fiction writing, 1992-95; University of Southern California, visiting lecturer, 1993-96. Writer. **Publications:** NOVELS: The Story of Annie D., 1989; Harmony, 1990; Dancing on Glass, 1993; Smithereens, 1995; Rampage, 1998. SHORT STORIES: End of the World Dreams, 1989; Coulda Been You, 1992. NONFICTION: Don Quixote Meets the Mob: The Craft of Fictions the Art of Life, 2001. **Address:** c/o Betsy Lerner, Gernert Co., 136 E 57th St., New York, NY 10022, U.S.A. **Online address:** susantaylorchehak@zinkville.com

CHEN, Calvin. American (born United States), b. 1968. **Genres:** Politics/Government. **Career:** Mount Holyoke College, associate professor of politics, 2002-. Writer and scientist. **Publications:** Some Assembly Required: Work, Community, and Politics in China's Rural Enterprises, 2008. Contributor to periodicals. **Address:** U.S.A. **Online address:** cchen@mtholyoke.edu

CHEN, Joseph T(ao). American/Chinese (born China), b. 1925. **Genres:** History, Social Sciences. **Career:** University of California, Center for Chinese Studies, head librarian, 1963-64; California State University, assistant professor, 1964-68, associate professor, 1968-71, professor of history, 1971-2001. Writer. **Publications:** The May Fourth Movement in Shanghai: The Making of a Social Movement in Modern China, 1971. **Address:** Department of History, California State University, 401 Golden Shore, Long Beach, CA 90802-4210, U.S.A.

CHEN, Ken. American (born United States), b. 1979. **Genres:** Poetry. **Career:** Hughes, Hubbard & Reed L.L.P., attorney, 2005-; Asian American Writers' Workshop, executive director, 2008-. Writer. **Publications:** Juvenilia, 2010. Contributor of articles to periodicals. **Address:** Brooklyn, NY , U.S.A. **Online address:** kensanwaychen@gmail.com

CHEN, Patrizia. American/Italian (born Italy), b. 1948?. **Genres:** Autobiography/Memoirs, Literary Criticism And History, Travel/Exploration, Biography, Novels. **Career:** Writer. **Publications:** Rosemary and Bitter Oranges: Growing up in a Tuscan Kitchen (memoir), 2003; It Takes Two: A Novel, 2009. **Address:** c/o Author Mail, Simon and Schuster Inc., 1230 Ave. of the Americas, New York, NY 10020, U.S.A.

CHEN, Ran. American/Chinese (born China), b. 1962?. **Genres:** Novels, Novellas/Short Stories. **Career:** Writer. **Publications:** Wu Chu Gao Bie, 1993; Fan Qiang Dou Shi Men, 1996; Chen Ran Zuo Pin Zi Xuan Ji, 1996; Mi Huan Hua Yuan: Nü Xing Xin Li Ti Yan Xiao Shuo, 1997; Nü Xing Ti Yan Xiao Shuo, 1999; Sha Lou Jie De Bu Yu, 2001; Sui Yin, 2002; Si ren sheng huo, 2004, trans. as A Private Life, 2004; Wu chu gao bie, 2005. **Address:** c/o Author Mail, Columbia University Press, 61 W 62nd St., New York, NY 10023, U.S.A.

CHEN, Victor Tan. American (born United States), b. 1976. **Genres:** Social Sciences. **Career:** Researcher and journalist. **Publications:** (Contrib.) Chutes and Ladders: Navigating the Low-Wage Labor Market, 2006; (with K.S. Newman) The Missing Class: Portraits of the Near Poor in America, 2007. Contributor to journals and periodicals. **Address:** 33 Kirkland St., Cambridge, MA 02138, U.S.A. **Online address:** vchen@wjh.harvard.edu

CHEN, Xiaoming. American (born United States), b. 1956. **Genres:** Art/Art History. **Career:** Ohio Wesleyan University, associate professor of history. Historian and writer. **Publications:** From the May Fourth Movement to Communist Revolution: Guo Moruo and the Chinese Path to Communism, 2007. Contributor to journals. **Address:** Ohio Wesleyan University, 61 S Sandusky St., Delaware, OH 43015, U.S.A. **Online address:** xmchen@owu.edu

CHEN, Ying. Canadian/Chinese (born China), b. 1961?. **Genres:** Novels. **Career:** Writer. **Publications:** Ying wen wen fa jing jie, 1977; Shuang feng dou long: Dong zu min jian gu shi ji, 1984; Zhongguo lun li si xiang shi, 1985; Nian qing jun ren di qi zi, 1987; Chu ci jing hua, 1987; Zhongguo lun li da ci dian, 1989; Li di ben fang, mei di re lian: Zhongguo gu dai lü you shuo sou, 1990; Zhi wu ti xi bao yi chuan yu zuo wu gai liang, 1990; Xian dai lun li xue, 1990; La mémoire de l'eau, 1992; Les lettres chinoises, 1993; Zhong Ri shi jian lun li xue tao lun hui shi lu, 1993; Zhongguo chuan tong dao de, 1995; Jing shen zi you yu min zu wen hua: Zhang Junmai xin ru xue lun zhu ji yao, 1995; L'ingratitude, 1995; Zhang Junmai si xiang yan jiu: xin ru xue, 1996; Immobile, 1998; Le champ dans la mer: roman, 2002; Querelle d'un squelette avec son double, 2003; Su Shi zuo pin liang ci yan jiu, 2003; Quatre mille marches, 2004; Mangeur: roman, 2006; Enfant Àma Porte: Roman, 2008; Espèces, 2010. **Address:** c/o Author Mail, Farrar, Straus and Giroux, 19 Union Sq. W, New York, NY 10003, U.S.A.

CHÉNETIER, Marc. French (born France), b. 1946. **Genres:** Translations, Literary Criticism And History, History, Young Adult Fiction. **Career:** Centre Pedagogique Regional de Tours, teacher of English in training, 1969-70; Stanford University, lecturer in French, 1970-72, visiting professor, 1981; University of Paris III-Sorbonne Nouvelle, assistant professor, 1972-79; University of East Anglia, visiting professor, 1979-80; University of Orleans, professor, 1980-91; University of Virginia, visiting professor, 1983-84; Princeton University, visiting professor, 1987; Ecole Normale Superieure, professor of American literature, 1991-; University of Paris VII-Denis Diderot, professor of American literature, head of the observatoire de littérature américaine; University of California, faculty. Writer and translator. **Publications:** TRANSLATOR: (with O. Chenetier) Vers un modele conceptuel deducation permanente, 1973; Un Prive a Babylone (title means: Dreaming of Babylon), 1981; Ce soir, on joue mes reves (title means: Reruns), 1983; Memoires Sauves du vent (title means: So The Wind Wont Blow It All Away), 1983; Cervantes, 1984; Lea et Lazare (title means: Lea and Lazar), 1984; Le Mortet e Archevque (title means: Death Comes for the Archbishop), 1986; Monennemi mortal (title means: My Mortal Enemy), 1986; Frog, 1988; Pionniers, Une Dame Perdue, and Un des notres, 1988; Fiskadoro, 1988; Au coeur ducoeur de ce pays, 1989; Un Bon Flic, 1990; Le Nez de Pinocchio (title means: Pinocchios Nose), 1990; Elseneur, 1991; Demandez le programme, 1991; Les Filles de Maria, 1994; La Maison du Professeur, 1993; Romans, 1994; Star Café, 1994; Continents à la Dérive: Livres: Russell Banks, 2000; Three Frogs, forthcoming. EDITOR: Letters of Vachel Lindsay, 1978; (with R. Kroes) Impressions of a Gilded Age: The American fin desiecle, 1983; Critical Angles: European Views of Contemporary American Literature, 1986; (with V. Béghain) The Cultural Shuttle: The United States in/of Europe, 2004. OTHERS: (with J. Barson) Textuellement, 1974; LObsession des signes: LEsthétique de Vachel Lindsay 1879-1931: Prose, Poèmes et dessins, 1979; By Signs Obsessed: The Aesthetics of Vachel Lindsay, 1981; Richard Brautigan, 1983; Au-delà du soupcon: Lanouvelle fiction américaine de 1960 à nos jours, 1989; Au-dela du soupcon: La Nouvelle Fiction Americaine de 1960 a nos Jours, 1989; Brautigan Sauve duVent, 1992; Sgraffites, encres & Sanguines: Neuf études sur lesfigures de lécriture dans la fiction américaine contemporaine, 1994; Américônes: Etudes sur limage aux Etats-Unis, 1997; De la Caverne a la Pyramide, 2000; La Perte de lAmérique: Archéologiedun amour, 2000; Steven Millhauser: La précision du limpossible, 2003; La Fiction Americaine de 1960 a 1985. Works appear in anthologies. Contributor to journals and periodicals. **Address:** Observatoire de Littérature Américaine, Université Paris 7-Denis Diderot, 5, rue Thomas Mann, Paris, 75205, France. **Online address:** marche@paris7.jussieu.fr

CHENEY, Martha. American (born United States), b. 1953. **Genres:** Education, Children's Fiction, Animals/Pets. **Career:** Preschool teacher, 1986-88; Los Angeles Unified School District, teacher, 1988-94; Ninemile Community Center, board director, 1995-97; writer, 1995-. **Publications:** (With E. Pesiri) Word Book: A Reference Workbook for Ages 4-6, 1994; How to Develop Your Child's Gifts and Talents in Reading, 1996; How to Develop Your Child's Gifts and Talents in Vocabulary, 1997; How to Develop Your Child's Gifts and Talents in Writing, 1997; Animal Almanac, 1999; (contrib.) Glacier National Park: Legends and Lore along Going-to-the-Sun Road, 2002; Moving West, 2003. **Address:** 32150 Ranch Ln., Huson, MT 59846, U.S.A.

CHENEY, Patrick Gerard. American (born United States), b. 1949. **Genres:** Literary Criticism And History, Poetry. **Career:** Pennsylvania State University, assistant professor of English, 1980-, distinguished professor of English and comparative literature, Institute for the Arts and Humanities, research fellow, 1987, 1995, 1996, 1997, fellow, 1999-2001; Oxford University, Merton College, visiting research fellow, 2001; University of Texas, Harry Ransom Center, Mellon fellow, 2005. Writer. **Publications:** Spenser's Famous Flight: A Renaissance Idea of a Literary Career, 1993; Marlowe's Counterfeit Profession: Ovid, Spenser, Counter-Nationhood, 1997; (with A.L. Prescott) Approaches to Teaching Shorter Elizabethan Poetry, 2000; (ed. with L. Silberman) Worldmaking Spenser: Explorations in the Early Modern Age, 2000; (ed. with F.A. de Armas) European Literary Careers: The Author from Antiquity to the Renaissance, 2002; (ed. with J. Bellamy and M. Schoenfeldt) Imagining Death in Spenser and Milton, 2003; Shakespeare, National Poet-Playwright, 2004; The Cambridge Companion to Christopher Marlowe, 2004; (ed. with G.A. Sullivan, Jr. and A. Hadfield) Early Modern English Drama: A Critical Companion, 2006; (ed. with B.J. Striar) The Collected Poems of Christopher Marlowe, 2006; (ed.) The Cambridge Companion to Shakespeare's Poetry, 2007; (ed. with G.A. Sullivan, Jr. and A. Hadfield) Early Modern English Poetry: A Critical Companion, 2007; Shakespeare's Literary Authorship, 2008; Marlowe's Republican Authorship: Lucan, Liberty, and the Sublime, 2009. Contributor to periodicals and journals. **Address:** Department of English, Pennsylvania State University, 117 Burrowes Bldg., University Park, PA 16802, U.S.A. **Online address:** pgc2@psu.edu

CHENEY, Terri. American (born United States), b. 1959. **Genres:** Autobiography/Memoirs. **Career:** Manatt, Phelps & Phillips, attorney; University of California, Mood Disorders Research Program, member of the community advisory board. Writer and attorney. **Publications:** Manic: A Memoir, 2008. **Address:** c/o Lydia Wills, Paradigm, 360 Park Ave. S, 16th Fl., New York, NY 10010, U.S.A. **Online address:** terri@terricheney.com

CHENG, Andrea. American (born United States), b. 1957. **Genres:** Children's Fiction, Children's Non-fiction, Literary Criticism And History. **Career:** Cincinnati State Technical and Community College, instructor in English as a second language and director of English as a second language, 1996-. Writer. **Publications:** When the Bees Fly Home, 2002; Marika, 2002; Goldfish and Chrysanthemums, 2003; Grandfather Counts, 2003; The Key Collection, 2003; Anna the Bookbinder, 2003; Honeysuckle House, 2004; The Lace Dowry, 2005; Shanghai Messenger, 2005; Eclipse, 2006; The Lemon Sisters, 2006; Tire Mountain, 2007; Bear Makers, 2008; Where the Steps Were, 2008; Brushing Mom's Hair, 2009; Only One Year, 2010. **Address:** Cincinnati State Technical & Community College, 3520 Central Pkwy., Cincinnati, OH 45223, U.S.A. **Online address:** cheng@frontstreetbooks.com

CHENG, Christopher. Australian (born Australia), b. 1959. **Genres:** Children's Non-fiction, Animals/Pets. **Career:** Taronga Zoo, public relations assistant, 1981-84; Bourke Public School, teacher, 1984-86; North Sydney Demonstration School, teacher, 1987; Taronga Zoo Education Centre, education officer, 1987-93; Dymocks Booksellers, national children's development manager, 1994-98; Dulwich Hill Public School, teacher, 1994; Purdue University, author and education consultant, 1998-. **Publications:** (With L. Hathorn) Stuntumble Monday, 1990; The Eyespy Book of Night Creatures, 1990; The Eyespy Book of Endangered Animals, 1991; Bancks' Ginger Meggs and Friends Pet Care Book, 1992; The Eyespy Book of Rainforest Animals, 1994; The Eyespy Book of Party Animals, 1995; One Child, 1997; Rainforests, 1998; Alpine Regions, 1998; ZOO You Later, 2000; New Gold Mountain, 2005; Seams of Gold, 2007; 30 Amazing Australian Animals, 2007; William's Backyard, 2007; Locally Wild, 2007; The Melting Pot, 2007; 60 Classic Australian Poems, 2009. Contributor to books and journals. **Address:** PO Box 279, Newtown, NW 2042, Australia. **Online address:** chris@chrischeng.com

CHENIER, Elise. Canadian (born Canada), b. 1967?. **Genres:** History. **Career:** McGill University, faculty; Simon Fraser University, faculty, 2004-, associate professor and chair of graduate studies program in history; University of Toronto, Mark S. Bonham Centre for Sexual Diversity Studies, SDS fellow. Writer. **Publications:** Strangers in Our Midst: Sexual Deviancy in Postwar Ontario, 2008. Contributor to books and journals. **Address:** Department of History, Simon Fraser University, University Dr., Burnaby, BC V5A 1S6, Canada. **Online address:** echenier@sfu.ca

CHENUT, Helen Harden. American (born United States), b. 1939. **Genres:** Adult Non-fiction, Social Commentary, Civil Liberties/Human Rights, History, Translations. **Career:** University of California, lecturer in history, visiting researcher. Writer. **Publications:** (Contrib.) Gender and Class in Modern Europe, 1996; (contrib.) L'histoire sans les femmes est-elle possible?, 1998; The Fabric of Gender: Working-Class Culture in Third Republic France, 2005; (trans. and intro.) Fadela Amara and Sylvia Zappi, Breaking the Silence: French Women's Voices from the Ghetto, 2006; (contrib.) The Human Tradition in Modern Europe, 2008. Contributor to periodicals. **Address:** Department of History, University of California, 200 Murray Krieger Hall, Irvine, CA 92697-3275, U.S.A. **Online address:** hchenut@uci.edu

CHER, Ming. New Zealander (born New Zealand), b. 1947. **Genres:** Novels, Young Adult Non-fiction. **Career:** Writer. **Publications:** Spider Boys,

1995. **Address:** c/o Michael Gifkins & Associates, Wellesley St., PO Box 6496, Auckland, 1000, New Zealand.

CHERCHI-USAI, Paolo. American (born United States), b. 1957. **Genres:** Film, Adult Non-fiction. **Career:** Film curator and historian; Lavoro, editor of arts section, 1982-88; Cineteca del Friuli, deputy curator, 1986-88; George Eastman House, assistant curator, 1989-92, International Museum of Photography and Film, Motion Picture Department, senior curator, 1994-2004; Royal Film Archive, head of preservation projects, 1993-94; Selznick School of Film Preservation, director, 1996-; University of Liege and International School for Film Preservation, teacher; University of Rochester, adjunct professor of English; National Film and Sound Archive, director, now curator emeritus; Pordenone Silent Film Festival, co-founder and co-director; Haghefilm Foundation, director; L. Jeffrey Selznick School of Film Preservation, co-founder and co-director; Telluride Film Festival, resident curator. Writer. **Publications:** Georges Méliès, 1983; Giovanni Pastrone: Gli anni d'oro del cinema a Torino, 1986; Schiave Bianche Allo Specchio: Le Origini del Cinema in Scandinavia (1896-1918), 1986; Vitagraph Co. of America: il Cinema Prima di Hollywood, 1987; The Vitagraph Company of America (1897-1916), 1987; (with L. Codelli) Sulla via di Hollywood, 1911-1920, 1988; Testimoni Silenziosi: Film Russi, 1908-1919, 1989; Prima di Caligari: Cinema Tedesco, 1895-1920, 1990; Schermo Incantato: Georges Méliès (1861-1938), 1991; (with L. Codelli) Eredità DeMille, 1991; Passione Infiammabile: Guida allo studio del Cinema Muto, 1991; Burning Passions: An Introduction to the Study of Silent Cinema, 1994; Silent Cinema: An Introduction, 2000; The Death of Cinema: History, Cultural Memory, and the Digital Dark Age, 2001; David Wark Griffith, 2008. EDITOR: Silent Witnesses: Russian Films, 1908-1917, 1989; (with S. Chabria) Light of Asia: Indian Silent Cinema, 1912-1934, 1994; (with C. Rowell) The Griffith Project, vol. I: Films Produced 1907-1908, 2000, vol. II: Films Produced in January-June 1909, 2000, vol. III: Films Produced in July-December 1909, 2000, vol. IV: Films Produced in 1910, 2001, vol. V: Films Produced in1911, 2002; (co-ed.) Film Curatorship: Archives, Museums, and the Digital Marketplace, 2008. Contributor to journals. **Address:** George Eastman House, 900 E Ave., Rochester, NY 14607-2298, U.S.A. **Online address:** usai@mail.rochester.edu

CHERCOVER, Sean. Canadian (born Canada), b. 1966. **Genres:** Horror, Mystery/Crime/Suspense, Novels, Young Adult Fiction. **Career:** AvidProNet.com, columnist. **Publications:** Big City Bad Blood, 2007; Trigger City, 2008. Contributor to periodicals. **Address:** c/o Danielle Bartlett, HarperCollins Publishers, 10 E 53rd St., New York, NY 10022-5308, U.S.A. **Online address:** sean@chercover.com

CHERIPKO, Jan. American (born United States), b. 1951. **Genres:** Children's Fiction, Education, Animals/Pets, Literary Criticism And History, Theology/Religion. **Career:** Sullivan County Democrat, reporter and editor, 1979-86; The Family School, English teacher, 1986-; Times Herald-Record, correspondent, 1989-92; Boyds Mills Press, institutional promotion specialist, 1990-. **Publications:** Voices of the River: Adventures on the Delaware, 1993; Imitate the Tiger, 1996; Get Ready to Play Tee Ball, 1999; Rat, 2002; Caesar Rodney's Ride: The Story of a Patriot, 2004; Brother Bartholomew and the Apple Grove, 2004; Sun, Moon, Stars, Rain 2006. **Address:** Boyds Mills Press, 815 Church St., Honesdale, PA 18431, U.S.A. **Online address:** cheripko@frontstreetbooks.com

CHERLIN, Andrew J. American (born United States), b. 1948. **Genres:** Human Relations/Parenting, Social Sciences. **Career:** Johns Hopkins University, assistant professor, 1976-82, associate professor, 1982-86, professor of sociology, 1986-, Benjamin H. Griswold III professor of public policy, 1998-, Institute for Policy Studies, associate director, 2003-04, interim director, 2004-05, Hopkins Population Center, director, 2006-; University of Michigan, National Poverty Center, senior research affiliate, 2003-. Writer. **Publications:** Marriage, Divorce, Remarriage, 1981, rev. ed., 1992; (with F.F. Furstenberg, Jr.) The New American Grandparent: A Place in the Family, a Life Apart, 1986; (ed.) The Changing American Family and Public Policy, 1988; (with F.F. Furstenberg, Jr.) Divided Families: What Happens to Children When Parents Part, 1991; Public and Private Families: An Introduction, 1996, 5th ed., 2008; (ed.) Public and Private Families: A Reader, 1998, 4th ed., 2005; The Marriage-Go-Round: The State of Marriage and the Family in America Today, 2009. Contributor to books and periodicals. **Address:** Department of Sociology, Johns Hopkins University, Baltimore, MD 21218, U.S.A. **Online address:** cherlin@jhu.edu

CHERNAIK, Warren L(ewis). British/American (born United States), b. 1931. **Genres:** Literary Criticism And History. **Career:** Queen Mary and Westfield College, University of London, lecturer, professor, Center for English Studies, program director, now professor emeritus; Yale University, teacher; Ohio State University, teacher; City College of New York, teacher; Boston University, teacher; University of Massachusetts, teacher; University College of North Wales, teacher; Kings College, visiting professor. Writer. **Publications:** The Poetry of Limitation: A Study of Edmund Waller, 1968; The Poet's Time: Politics and Religion in the Work of Andrew Marvell, 1983; (with C. Davis and M. Deegan) The Politics of the Electronic Text, 1993; Sexual Freedom in Restoration Literature, 1995; (with M. Deegan and A. Gibson) Beyond the Book: Theory, Culture and the Politics of Cyberspace, 1996; (ed. with I. Willison and W. Gould) Modernist Writers and the Marketplace, 1996; (with P. Parrinder) Textual Monopolies: Literary Copyright and the Public Domain, 1997; (ed. with M. Dzelzainis) Marvell and Liberty, 1999; (ed. with M. Swales and R. Vilain) The Art of Detective Fiction, 2000; The Merchant of Venice, 2005; The Cambridge Introduction to Shakespeare's History Plays, 2007; The Myth of Rome in Shakespeare and His Contemporaries, 2011. **Address:** Cambridge University Press, 32 Ave. of the Americas, New York, NY 10013-2473, U.S.A. **Online address:** warren.chernaik@kcl.ac.uk

CHERNENKO, Dan. *See* **TURTLEDOVE, Harry (Norman).**

CHERNENKO, Eric. *See* **TURTLEDOVE, Harry (Norman).**

CHERNOFF, Maxine. American (born United States), b. 1952. **Genres:** Novels, Novellas/Short Stories, Poetry. **Career:** University of Illinois-Chicago Circle, lecturer in English, 1977-80; Columbia College, instructor, 1978-85; Truman College, associate professor of English, 1980-94; Poetry Center, president and board directors, 1982-87; School of the Art Institute of Chicago, visiting lecturer, 1988-94; San Francisco State University, professor of creative writing, 1994. **Publications:** POETRY: A Vegetable Emergency, 1976; Utopia TV Store, 1979; New Faces of 1952, 1985; Japan, 1988; Leap Year Day: New and Selected Poems, 1990; Next Song (poetry), 1998; World, 2001; Evolution of the Bridge, 2004; Among the Names, 2005; The Turning, 2008; (trans. with P. Hoover) Selected Poems of Friederich Hoelderlin, 2009; To Be Read in the Dark, 2011; Without, 2012. FICTION: Bop, 1987; Signs of Devotion, 1993; Some of Her Friends That Year, 2002. NOVELS: Plain Grief, 1991; American Heaven, 1996; A Boy in Winter, 1999. EDITOR: New American Writing, 1986. **Address:** Department of Creative Writing, San Francisco State University, 1600 Holloway Ave., San Francisco, CA 94132, U.S.A. **Online address:** maxpaul@sfsu.edu

CHERNOW, Barbara A. (Barbara Ann Chernow). American (born United States), b. 1948. **Genres:** Communications/Media, Biography, Reference, Architecture, Biography, Autobiography/Memoirs. **Career:** Macmillan Publishing, associate editor of reference books, 1977-82; Chernow Editorial Services Inc., president, 1982-; New York University, Center for Publishing, lecturer, 2000-. **Publications:** Robert Morris: Land Speculator, 1790-1801, 1979; Guide to the Research Collections of the Columbia University Libraries, 1984; (with S. Lindner) Retail Profitability, 2004. EDITOR: International Encyclopedia of the Social Sciences Biographical Supplement, 1979; Macmillan Encyclopedia of Architects, 1982; (with G.A. Vallasi) The Reader's Adviser, 6 vols., 1986-88; (with G.A. Vallasi) The Concise Columbia Encyclopedia, 2nd ed., 1989; (with G.A. Vallasi) The Columbia Encyclopedia, 5th ed., 1993. **Address:** Chernow Editorial Services Inc., 1133 Broadway, New York, NY 10010, U.S.A.

CHERNOW, Barbara Ann. *See* **CHERNOW, Barbara A.**

CHERNY, Andrei. American (born United States), b. 1975?. **Genres:** Adult Non-fiction, History. **Career:** State of Arizona, assistant attorney general, U.S. Government, speechwriter, senior speechwriter; Democratic Party, platform director, 2000, Democratic Party Platform, lead negotiator and chief drafter, 2000; California State Assembly, policy adviser; New Democrat, contributing editor; Harvard University, Kennedy School of Government, Belfer Center for Science and International Affairs, senior fellow, 2004; Democracy: A Journal of Ideas, co-founder, co-editor and president; Arizona Democratic Party, chair, 2011-. **Publications:** The Next Deal: The Future of Public Life in the Information Age, 2000; Candy Bombers: The Untold Story of the Berlin Airlift and America's Finest Hour, 2008. **Address:** c/o Author Mail, Basic Books, 387 Park Ave. S, New York, NY 10016-8810, U.S.A. **Online address:** andreicherny@yahoo.com

CHERNY, Robert W(allace). American (born United States), b. 1943. **Genres:** History, Biography. **Career:** San Francisco State University, Department of History, instructor, 1971-72, assistant professor, 1972-77, associate professor, 1977-81, professor of American history, 1981-, chair, 1987-92, School of Behavioral and Social Sciences, acting dean, 1984-85, dean of undergraduate studies, 2005-08; University of Nebraska, visiting associate professor, 1980, visiting professor, 1982; Moscow State University, distinguished Fulbright lecturer, 1996; University of Heidelberg, senior Fulbright lecturer, 2009. Writer. **Publications:** (Contrib.) The Study of American History, 1974; (comp.) Populism and the Election of 1896, 1974; Populism, Progressivism and the Transformation of Nebraska Politics, 1885-1915, 1981; (with W. Issel) San Francisco: Presidio, Port and Pacific Metropolis, 1981; A Righteous Cause: The Life of William Jennings Bryan, 1985; (with W. Issel) San Francisco, 1865-1932: Power, Politics and Urban Development, 1986; (with C. Berkin and A. Brinkley) American Voices: A History of the United States, 1992; (with C. Berkin, C. Miller and J. Gormley) Making America: A History of the United States, 1995, 6th ed., 2011; (intro.) The Cross of Gold: Speech Delivered Before the National Democratic Convention at Chicago, July 9, 1896, 1996; American Politics in the Gilded Age: 1868-1900, 1997; (ed. with W. Issel and K. Taylor) American Labor and the Cold War: Grassroots Politics and Postwar Political Culture, 2004; (co-author) Competing Visions: A History of California, 2005; (ed. with M.A. Irwin and A.M. Wilson) California Women and Politics from Gold Rush to the Great Depression, 2011. **Address:** Department of History, San Francisco State University, 1600 Holloway Ave., San Francisco, CA 94132-4155, U.S.A. **Online address:** cherny@sfsu.edu

CHERNYKH, E(vgenij) N(ikolaevich). Russian (born Russia), b. 1935. **Genres:** Archaeology/Antiquities, Engineering, History. **Career:** Russian Academy of Sciences, Institute of Archaeology, scientist, 1958-72, professor of archaeology, head of the laboratory nature sciences in archaeology, 1972-. **Publications:** History of Ancient Metallurgy in Eastern Europe (in Russian), 1966; Gornoe Delo I Metallurgia v Drevneĭsheĭ Bolgarii, 1978; Ancient Mining and Metallurgy in Bulgaria (in Russian), 1978; (ed.) Metallurgiia Volgo-Kam'ia v rannem zheleznom veke, 1983; (ed. with K.N. Pitskhelauri) Kavkaz v sisteme paleometallicheskikh kul'tur Evrazii, 1987; (ed.) Estestvennonauchnye metody v arkheologii, 1989; (with S.V. Kuz'minykh) Drevniaia Metallurgiia Severnoĭ Evrazii: Seĭminsko-Turbinskiĭ Fenomen, 1989; Kargaly-Zabytyĭ Mir, 1997; (with L.I. Avilova and L.B. Orlovskaia) Metallurgical Provinces and Radiocarbon Chronology, 2000; (ed.) Kargaly, 2002; Stepnoĭ Poias Evrazii: Fenomen Kochevykh Kul'tur, 2009. Contributor to journals and magazines. **Address:** Institute of Archaeology, Russian Academy of Sciences, 19, Dm. Ulyanova str., Moscow, 117036, Russia. **Online address:** chernykh.e@g23.relcom.ru

CHERRY, Bridget (Katherine). British (born England), b. 1941. **Genres:** Architecture, History, Bibliography. **Career:** Courtauld Institute, assistant librarian, 1964-68; Penguin, Buildings of England Series, research assistant, 1968-83, editor, 1983-; English Heritage, commissioner, 1991-; Royal Institute of British Architecture, honorary fellow, 1993; Sir John Soane's Museum, life trustee, 1995-. **Publications:** The Buildings of England, Ireland, Scotland, and Wales: A Short History and Bibliography (pamphlet), 1998; (contrib.) Bristol, 2004. EDITOR: BUILDINGS OF ENGLAND SERIES: Surrey, 2nd ed., 1971; London 1: The Cities of London and Westminister, 1973; Wiltshire, 2nd ed., 1975; Hertfordshire, 2nd ed., 1977; London 2: South, 1983; London, 1983; (with J. Newman) The Best Buildings of England, 1983; Devon, 1986; London 3: North West, rev. ed., 1991; Northamptonshire, rev. ed., 1999; London 4: North, rev. ed., 1999; London 5, East, 2005; (ed. with A. Robey) Rediscovered Utopias: Saving London's Suburbs, 2010. Contributor to periodicals and books. **Address:** Penguin Books Ltd., 80 Strand, London, GL WC2R 0RL, England.

CHERRY, Charles Conrad. (Conrad Cherry). American (born United States), b. 1937. **Genres:** Theology/Religion, Social Sciences. **Career:** Pennsylvania State University, assistant professor to professor of religious studies, 1964-81; Scholars Press, director, 1981-88; Indiana University, Department of Religious Studies, distinguished professor of religious studies, 1988-2001, distinguished professor emeritus, 2001-. Writer. **Publications:** AS CONRAD CHERRY: Theology of Jonathan Edwards: A Reappraisal, 1966; God's New Israel: Religious Interpretations of American Destiny, 1971, rev. ed., 1988; Nature and Religious Imagination: From Edwards to Bushnell, 1980; Hurrying toward Zion: Universities, Divinity Schools and American Protestantism, 1995; (B.A. Deberg and A. Porterfield) Religion on Campus, 2001. EDITOR: (with J.Y. Fenton) Religion in the Public Domain: Proceedings of the Consultation at University Park, Pennsylvania, May 1-3, 1966, 1966; Horace Bushnell, Sermons, 1985; (with R.A. Sherrill) Religion, the Independent Sector and American Culture, 1992. **Address:** Department of Religious Studies, Indiana University, 230 Sycamore Hall, Bloomington, IN 47405, U.S.A. **Online address:** ibdd100@iupui.edu

CHERRY, Conrad. *See* **CHERRY, Charles Conrad.**

CHERRY, Kelly. American (born United States), b. 1940. **Genres:** Novels, Novellas/Short Stories, Poetry, Philosophy, Autobiography/Memoirs, Essays, Translations, Literary Criticism And History, Women's Studies And Issues. **Career:** University of Wisconsin, professor of English and writer-in-residence, 1977-99, Romnes professor of English, 1983-88, Evjue-Bascom professor in the humanities, 1993-99, Eudora Welty professor of English, 1997-99, Eudora Welty professor emerita of English and Evjue-Bascom professor emerita in the humanities, 1999-; Western Washington University, distinguished visiting full professor and writer-in-residence, 1981; Rhodes College, distinguished visiting professor, 1985; Associated Writing Programs, board director, 1990-93; Hollins University, Wyndham Thompson visiting writer, 2000; Colgate University, NEH visiting professor in English, 2005; Mercer University, Ferrol A. Sams, Jr. distinguished chair in English, 2006; Atlantic Center for the Arts, master artist, 2008; Hollins University, Louis D. Rubin writer-in-residence, 2009; Appalachian State University, Rivers-Coffey distinguished chair, 2010; Hollins Critic, contributing editor. **Publications:** (Ed. and co-author) Lessons from Our Living Past, 1972, Teacher's Guide, 1972; Sick and Full of Burning, 1974; Lovers and Agnostics, 1975, rev. ed., 1995; Relativity, 1977, rev. ed., 2000; Augusta Played, 1979; Conversion, 1979; Songs for a Soviet Composer, 1980; In the Wink of an Eye, 1983, 2004; The Lost Traveller's Dream, 1984; Natural Theology, 1988; My Life and Dr. Joyce Brothers, 1990; The Exiled Heart, 1991; Benjamin John, 1993; God's Loud Hand, 1993; Time out of Mind, 1994; Writing the World, 1995; Death and Transfiguration, 1997; The Society of Friends, 1999; The Poem, 1999; An Other Woman, 2000; Rising Venus, 2002; We Can Still Be Friends, 2003; Welsh Table Talk, 2004; History, Passion, Freedom, Death and Hope: Prose about Poetry, 2005; The Globe and the Brain: On Place in Fiction, 2006; Hazard and Prospect: New and Selected Poems, 2007; Girl in a Library: On Women Writers & the Writing Life, 2009; The Retreats of Thought: Poems, 2009; The Woman Who, 2010. Contributor to books and periodicals. **Address:** University of Wisconsin, Madison, WI 53706, U.S.A. **Online address:** kcherry@wisc.edu

CHERRY, Kittredge. American (born United States), b. 1957. **Genres:** Gay And Lesbian Issues, Theology/Religion, inspirational/Motivational Literature, Art/Art History, Women's Studies And Issues, Novels, Adult Non-fiction, Cultural/Ethnic Topics, Cultural/Ethnic Topics. **Career:** Metropolitan Community Churches, priest, 1987-. Writer. **Publications:** Womansword: What Japanese Words Say about Women, 1987, rev. ed., 2007; Hide and Speak: How to Free Ourselves from Our Secrets, 1991, rev. ed., 2006; (ed. with Z. Sherwood) Equal Rites: Lesbian and Gay Worship, Ceremonies, and Celebrations, 1995; Jesus in Love: A Novel, 2006; Art That Dares: Gay Jesus, Woman Christ, and More, 2007; Jesus in Love: At the Cross, 2008. Contributor to periodicals. **Address:** PO Box 31133, Los Angeles, CA 90031, U.S.A. **Online address:** kitt@jesusinlove.org

CHERRY, Mark J. American (born United States), b. 1969?. **Genres:** Medicine/Health, Theology/Religion, Humanities. **Career:** St. Edward's University, associate professor; Journal of Medicine and Philosophy, senior associate editor; Christian Bioethics, senior associate editor. **Publications:** (Ed.) Persons and Their Bodies: Rights, Responsibilities, Relationships, 1999; (ed. with H.T. Engelhardt, Jr.) Allocating Scarce Medical Resources: Roman Catholic Perspectives, 2002; (ed. with J.F. Peppin) Regional Perspectives in Bioethics, 2003; Natural Law and the Possibility of a Global Ethics, 2004; (ed. with J.F. Peppin) Religious Perspectives in Bioethics, 2004; Kidney for Sale by Owner: Human Organs, Transplantation, and the Market, 2005; (ed.) The Death of Metaphysics, the Death of Culture: Epistemology, Metaphysics, and Morality, 2006; Normativity of the Natural: Human Goods, Human Virtues, and Human Flourishing, 2009; (ed. with A.S. Iltis) At the Roots of Christian Bioethics: Critical Essays on the Thought of H. Tristram Engelhardt, Jr., 2010. **Address:** Department of Philosophy, St. Edward's University, 3001 S Congress Ave., PO Box 844, Austin, TX 78704-6425, U.S.A. **Online address:** markc@stedwards.edu

CHERRYH, C. J. American (born United States), b. 1942. **Genres:** Science Fiction/Fantasy, Young Adult Fiction, Novels, Novellas/Short Stories. **Career:** Oklahoma City Public Schools, teacher of Latin and ancient history, 1965-77; freelance writer, 1977-; Central State University, artist-in-residence and teacher, 1980-81. Writer. **Publications:** SCIENCE FICTION: Brothers of Earth, 1976; Gates of Ivrel, 1976; Hunter of Worlds, 1977; Well of Shiuan, 1978; The Fires of Azeroth, 1979; Hestia, 1979; The Book of Morgaine, 1979; Serpent's Reach, 1980; Downbelow Station, 1981; Sunfall, 1981; Wave Without a Shore, 1981; Ealdwood, 1981; Merchanter's Luck, 1982; Port Eternity, 1982, rev. ed., 2001; The Dreamstone, 1983; Chanur's Venture, 1984; Angel with the Sword, 1985; (with J. Haldeman and T. Zahn) Alien Stars, 1985; Visible Light, 1986; (with J. Morris) The Gates of Hell, 1986; The Pride of Chanur, 1987; Cyteen, 1988; Rimrunners, 1989; Rusalka, 1989; Chernevog, 1990; Heavy Time, 1991; Yvgenie, 1991; Chanur's Legacy: A Novel of Compact Space, 1992; Hellburner, 1992; The Goblin Mirror, 1992; Tripoint, 1994; Fortress in the Eye of Time, 1995; Rider at the Gate, 1995; (co-author) The Sword of Knowledge, 1995; Cloud's Rider, 1996; Lois and Clark: A Superman Novel, 1996; Finity's End, 1997; The Dreaming Tree, 1997; Fortress of Eagles, 1998; Fortress of Owls, 1999; Devil to the Belt, 2000; The Morgaine Saga, 2000; Hammerfall, 2001; At the Edge of Space, 2003; The Collected Short Fiction of C.J. Cherryh, 2004; Forge of Heaven, 2004; Fortress of Ice, 2006; Deliverer, 2007. THE FADED SUN TRILOGY: The Faded Sun: Kesrith, 1977; The Faded Sun: Shon Jir, 1978; The Faded Sun: Kutath, 1979; The Faded Sun Trilogy, 2000. FOREIGNER UNIVERSE SERIES: Foreigner: A Novel of First Contact, 1994; Invader, 1995; Inheritor, 1996; Precursor, 1999; Defender, 2001; Explorer, 2002; Destroyer, 2005; Pretender, 2005; Deliverer, 2007; Conspirator, 2009; Deceiver, 2010; Betrayer, 2011; Intruder, 2012. CONTRIBUTOR: The Year's Best Fantasy No. 3, 1977; The 1979 Annual World's Best SF, 1979; Amazons!, 1979; The Best Science Fiction of the Year, 1980; Flashing Swords No. 5, 1981; Hecate's Children, 1981; Elsewhere, 1981; Shadows of Sanctuary, 1982; The Year's Best Fantasy, 1982. OTHER: The Tree of Swords and Jewels, 1983; Voyager in Night, 1984; Forty Thousand in Gehenna, 1984; Cuckoo's Egg, 1985; The Kif Strikes Back, 1985; Chanur's Homecoming, 1986; (with J. Morris and L. Abbey) Soul of the City, 1986; (with J. Morris) Kings in Hell, 1986; (ed.) Fever Season, 1987; (ed.) Festival Moon, 1987; The Faded Sun Trilogy, 1987; Glass and Amber, 1987; Legions of Hell, 1987; The Paladin, 1988; Exile's Gate, 1988; (ed.) Troubled Waters, 1988; (ed.) Smuggler's Gold, 1988; (ed.) Divine Right, 1989; (ed.) O Flood Tide, 1990; Endgame, 1991; Faery in Shadow, 1993; (co-author) The Sword of Contact, 1995; Alternate Realities, 2000; The Chanur Saga, 2000; The Faded Sun, 2000; Fortress of Dragons, 2000; Regenesis, 2010; Conspirator, 2010. Contributor to periodicals. **Address:** Daw Books, 375 Hudson St., 3rd Fl., New York, NY 10014-3658, U.S.A. **Online address:** fancher@cherryh.com

CHERTOW, Marian R. American (born United States), b. 1955. **Genres:** Environmental Sciences/Ecology. **Career:** Resource Recovery Systems Inc., director of marketing and development, 1978-79; U.S. Government-San Francisco, financial manager and assistant to the chief administrative officer, 1981-83; Town of Windsor, assistant to the assistant town manager, 1983-86; Connecticut Resources Recovery Authority (bonding authority), president, 1986-88; U.S. Conference of Mayors, senior fellow, 1988-89; Yale University, Institution for Social and Policy Studies, visiting fellow, 1989-90, Program on Solid Waste Policy, director, 1990-, School of Forestry and Environmental Studies, director of industrial environmental management program, 1991-, assistant professor of industrial environmental management, 2002-07, associate professor of industrial environmental management, 2007-, Corporate Environmental Leadership Seminar, chair and founder, 1992-2002, Center for Environmental Law and Policy, director, 1995-99, School of Management, associate professor, 2009; National University of Singapore, School of Design and Environment, MSc in Environmental Management Programme, visiting associate professor, 2001-; Nankai University, National Center for Innovation Research on Circular Economy, visiting professor, 2006-. Writer. **Publications:** Garbage Solutions: A Public Official's Guide to Recycling and Alternative Solid Waste Management Technologies, 1989; (ed. with D. Esty) Thinking Ecologically: The Next Generation of Environmental Policy, 1997. **Address:** School of Forestry & Environmental Studies, Yale University, Rm. 205, Sage Hall, 380 Edwards St., 195 Prospect St., New Haven, CT 06511, U.S.A. **Online address:** marian.chertow@yale.edu

CHESHIRE, Simon. British (born England) **Genres:** Novels, Children's Fiction. **Career:** Writer. **Publications:** Jeremy Brown of the Secret Service, 1997; Jeremy Brown and the Mummy's Curse, 1998; Jeremy Brown on Mars, 1999; They Melted His Brain!, 1999; Totally Unsuitable for Children, 2000; Dirty Rotten Tricks, 2001; Me and My Big Mouse, 2002; Kissing Vanessa, 2004; Plastic Fantastic, 2006; The Prince and the Snowgirl, 2007; Treasure of Dead Man's Lane, 2009; Pants On Fire, 2010; Bottomby, 2010; Jeremy Brown: Spy, 2010. SAXBY SMART: PRIVATE DETECTIVE SERIES: (with R.W. Alley) The Curse of the Ancient Mask and Other Casefiles, 2009; The Fangs of the Dragon and Other Casefiles, 2008; The Pirate's Blood, 2008; The Hangman's Lair, 2008; The Eye Of The Serpent, 2009; Pirate's Blood and Other Case Files, 2011. **Address:** The Agency Ltd., 24 Pottery Ln., London, GL W11 4LZ, England. **Online address:** simon.cheshire@ukonline.co.uk

CHESLER, Ellen. American (born United States), b. 1947. **Genres:** Women's Studies And Issues, Biography, Adult Non-fiction. **Career:** New York City Council President, campaign manager and chief of staff, 1977-83; Open Society Institute, senior fellow, 1997-2006, Program on Reproductive Health and Rights, director; City University of New York, Hunter College, director and distinguished lecturer, 2006-, Eleanor Roosevelt Initiative, distinguished lecturer and director; Barnard College, adjunct assistant professor; Planned Parenthood Federation, director; Roosevelt Institute, senior fellow. Writer. **Publications:** Woman of Valor: Margaret Sanger and the Birth Control Movement in America, 1992; (ed. with W. Chavkin) Where Human Rights Begin: Health, Sexuality and Women in the New Millennium, 2005. Contributor to periodicals. **Address:** Hunter College, 140 N Bldg., 695 Park Ave., New York, NY 10065, U.S.A. **Online address:** ellen.chesler@hunter.cuny.edu

CHESMAN, Andrea. American (born United States), b. 1952?. **Genres:** Food And Wine, Medicine/Health. **Career:** Writer. **Publications:** (With P. Joan) Guide to Women's Publishing, 1978; Pickles & Relishes: One-Hundred-Fifty Recipes from Apples to Zucchini, 1983; (with J. Ballantyne and D. Rankin) Garden Way's Joy of Gardening Cookbook, 1984; Summer in a Jar: Making Pickles, Jams and More, 1985; Salsas!, 1985; (ed.) Fruit Desserts!, 1987; (ed.) Salad Dressings!, 1987; (ed.) Good for You Cookies!, 1987; (with K. Trabant) Sauces for Pasta!, 1990; Sun-Dried Tomatoes!, 1990; (with F. Raboff) The Great American Dessert Cookbook, 1990; Simply Healthful Pasta Salads, 1993; Simply Healthful Skillet Suppers: Delicious New Low-Fat Recipes, 1993; (ed.) Yankee Magazine's Church Suppers & Potluck Dinners Cookbook, 1996; Salad Suppers: Fresh Inspirations for Satisfying One-Dish Meals, 1997; 366 Delicious Ways to Cook Rice, Beans and Grains, 1998; Vegetarian Grill: 200 Recipes for Inspired Flame-Kissed Meals, 1998; The Roasted Vegetable, 2002; (with N.C. Ralston and M. Jordan) The Classic Zucchini Cookbook: 225 Recipes for All Kinds of Squash, 2002; (with F. Raboff) Mom's Best Desserts: 100 Classic Treats that Taste as Good Now as They Did Then, 2002; Mom's Best One-Dish Suppers: 101 Easy Homemade Favorites as Comforting Now as They were Then, 2005; The Garden-Fresh Vegetable Cookbook, 2005; Mom's Best Crowd-Pleasers: 101 Home Style Recipes for Family Gatherings, Casual Get-Togethers & Surprise Company, 2006; Serving Up the Harvest, 2007; New Vegetarian Grill: 250 Flame-Kissed Recipes for Fresh, Inspired Meals, 2008; (with F. Raboff) 250 Treasured Country Desserts, 2009; Recipes from the Root Cellar, 2010; (ed.) Back to Basics, 2010. **Address:** PO Box 185, Ripton, VT 05766, U.S.A. **Online address:** andreachesman@gmail.com

CHESNEY, Elizabeth Anne. *See* **ZEGURA, Elizabeth Chesney.**

CHESS, Richard. American (born United States), b. 1953. **Genres:** Poetry, Theology/Religion. **Career:** University of North Carolina-Charlotte, lecturer, 1988-89; University of North Carolina-Asheville, assistant professor of literature and language, 1989-, Roy Carroll professor of honors arts and sciences and professor of literature and language, Creative Writing Program, director, 1989-, Center for Jewish Studies, director, 1989-; Brandeis Bardin Institute, writer-in-residence; Isabella Freedman Retreat Center, Jewish Arts Institute at Elat Chayyim, assistant director; Zeek: A Jewish Journal of Thought and Culture, poetry editor. **Publications:** Tekiah: Poems, 1994, new ed., 2002; Chair in the Desert: Poems, 2000; Third Temple: Poems, 2007. Contributor of articles to periodicals. **Address:** Department of Literature and Language, University of North Carolina, 223 Karpen Hall, 1 University Heights, PO Box 2130, Asheville, NC 28804-3251, U.S.A. **Online address:** rchess@bulldog.unca.edu

CHESTER, Jeff. American (born United States) **Genres:** Politics/Government. **Career:** Center for Media Education, co-founder; Center for Digital Democracy, executive director. Writer. **Publications:** Digital Destiny: New Media and the Future of Democracy, 2007. Contributor to periodicals. **Ad-**

dress: Center for Digital Democracy, 1220 L St. NW, Ste. 300, Washington, DC 20005-4053, U.S.A. **Online address:** jeff@democraticmedia.org

CHESTER, Mark (S.). American (born United States), b. 1945. **Genres:** Photography, Writing/Journalism, Art/Art History. **Career:** American Society of Composers, Authors, and Publishers, director of photography and assistant director of public relations, 1970-72; freelance photographer and writer, 1972-. **Publications:** (Contrib.) Dateline America, 1979; (contrib.) No in America, 1986; (contrib.) Shanghai: In Black and White, 1987; Diary of a Thought Criminal, 1996; Twosomes and Then Some: Photographs, 1999; Newspapers and Magazines, 2002; Twosomes, 2004. Contributor to books and periodicals. **Address:** Mark Chester Photography, PO Box 545, Woods Hole, MA 02543-2543, U.S.A. **Online address:** info@markchesterphotography.com

CHESTER, Tessa Rose. British (born England), b. 1950. **Genres:** Poetry, Illustrations, Bibliography, Art/Art History. **Career:** Cambridge Central Library, assistant, 1975-77; Bethnal Green Museum of Childhood, part-time employee, 1982-84, Children's Book Collections, curator, 1984-2001. Writer and healer. **Publications:** (With J.I. Whalley) A History of Children's Book Illustration, 1988; Children's Books Research: A Practical Guide to Techniques and Sources, 1989; Sources of Information about Children's Books, 1989; (as Tessa Rose Chester) Provisions of Light (poetry), 1996. Contributor of articles to newspapers and periodicals. **Address:** Pencarreg, Sarnau, Llandysul SW, Ceredigion, PW SA44 6QA, Wales. **Online address:** rosiandkeith@gmail.com

CHESTERS, Graham. British (born England), b. 1944. **Genres:** Literary Criticism And History, Education. **Career:** University College, tutor in French, 1969-70; Queen's University, lecturer in French, 1970-72; University of Hull, lecturer, 1972-80, senior lecturer, 1980-88, head of department, 1983, professor of French, 1988-, now professor emeritus, School of Euro Languages and Cultures, dean, 1988-91, pro-vice-chancellor, 1991-96, Computers in Teaching Initiative Centre for Modern Languages, director, 1989-2000, Institute for Learning, director, 1997-2005, university advisor, 2005; French Studies Bull, founder and editor, 1982. Writer. **Publications:** Some Functions of Sound Repetition in Les Fleurs du Mal, 1975; (with P. Broome) The Appreciation of Modern French Poetry 1850-1950, 1976; Baudelaire and the Poetics of Craft, 1988; Baudelaire: Les Fleurs du Mal, 1995. EDITOR: (with P. Broome) An Anthology of Modern French Poetry 1850-1950, 1976; (with N. Gardner) The Use of Computers in the Teaching of Language and Languages, 1987; (with J. Thompson) Emancipation through Learning Technology, 1994. **Address:** Institute for Learning, University of Hull, Cottingham Rd., Hull, HU6 7RX, England.

CHETHIK, Neil. American (born United States), b. 1957?. **Genres:** Self Help, Social Sciences, Business/Trade/Industry. **Career:** Tallahassee Democrat, staff reporter; San Jose Mercury News, staff reporter; freelance writer and public speaker, 1991-; Carnegie Center for Literacy and Learning, writer-in-residence, executive director. **Publications:** NONFICTION: Fatherloss: How Sons of All Ages Come to Terms with the Deaths of Their Dads, 2001; VoiceMale: What Husbands Really Think about Their Marriages, Their Wives, Sex, Housework, and Commitment, 2006. **Address:** 121 Arcadia Pk., Lexington, KY 40503, U.S.A. **Online address:** neil@neilchethik.com

CHETKOVICH, Carol A. American (born United States), b. 1948. **Genres:** Public/Social Administration, Race Relations, Sociology, Women's Studies And Issues, Politics/Government. **Career:** Family Planning Alternatives, vice-president and program director, 1972-85; Berkeley Planning Associates, senior analyst and project director, 1987-89; University of California, instructor in public policy and in education, 1994-96; Mills College, visiting assistant professor of public policymaking and administration, 1996-97, associate professor and director of public policy program, 2005-08, professor and director of public policy program, 2008-; Harvard University, John F. Kennedy School of Government, assistant professor, associate professor of public policy, 1997-2005. Writer. **Publications:** (Ed. with S.L. Radl) And the Pursuit of Happiness, 1978; Real Heat: Gender and Race in the Urban Fire Service, 1997; (with F. Kunreuther) From the Ground Up: Grassroots Organizations Making Social Change, 2006. Contributor to periodicals. **Address:** Mills College, Vera Long 123, 5000 MacArthur Blvd., Oakland, CA 94613-1301, U.S.A. **Online address:** cchetkov@mills.edu

CHETWIN, Grace. American/British (born England), b. 1964?. **Genres:** Humor/Satire, Horror, Science Fiction/Fantasy, Children's Fiction, Novels, Picture/Board Books, Young Adult Fiction. **Career:** Educator and writer. **Publications:** On All Hallow's Eve, 1984; Out of the Dark World, 1985; Mr. Meredith and the Truly Remarkable Stone, 1989; Collidescope, 1990; Box and Cox, 1990; Child of the Air, 1991; Friends in Time, 1992; Jason's Seven Magical Night Rides, 1994; Jason's Wonderful Week of Fabulous Night Rides 2003 Rufus, 1996; Briony's ABC of Abominable Children, 1997; Emily and the Twelve Days of Christmas, 1997; Beauty and the Beast: A Modern Retelling, 1998; Deathwindow, 1999; The Burning Tower, 2000. 9-BOOK GOM SERIES: Gom on Windy Mountain, 1986; The Riddle and the Rune, 1987; The Crystal Stair, 1988; The Starstone, 1989; Gerrad's Quest, 1998; The Fall of Aelyth-Kintalyn 2002; The Foundling of Snawbyr Crygg, 2003; Wycan 2004; The Stargate of Lantyn 2008; The Last Legacy Quartet, vol. I: The Atheling, 1988, vol II: The Orborgon, 2000, vol. III: The Hesta; The Chimes of Alyafaleyn, 2nd ed., 2006. **Address:** c/o Feral Press Inc., 304 Strawberry Field Rd., Flat Rock, NC 28731, U.S.A. **Online address:** gchet@feralpressinc.com

CHEUSE, Alan. American (born United States), b. 1940. **Genres:** Novels, Literary Criticism And History, Autobiography/Memoirs, Biography, Novellas/Short Stories. **Career:** Fairchild Publications, reporter, 1962-63; Kirkus Reviews Service, staff, 1963-64; Butler Institute, teacher of history and English, 1965-66; Bennington College, Division of Literature and Languages, faculty, 1970-78; National Public Radio, All Things Considered, book commentator, 1982-; University of the South, writer-in-residence, 1984; University of Michigan, writer-in-residence, 1984-86; Bennington College, acting director of writing workshops, 1986-87; George Mason University, writing faculty, 1987-; University of Virginia, visiting writer, 1987. **Publications:** (Ed. with R. Koffler) The Rarer Action: Essays in Honor of Francis Fergusson, 1970; Memories of the Future: A Critical Biography of Alejo Carpentier, 1974; Candace & Other Stories, 1980; The Bohemians: John Reed & His Friends Who Shook the World (novel), 1982; The Grandmother's Club (novel), 1986, rev. ed., 1994; Fall Out of Heaven: An Autobiographical Journey, 1987; The Tennessee Waltz and Other Stories, 1990; Light Possessed, 1990, rev. ed. as The Light Possessed: A Novel, 1998; (ed. with C. Marshall) The Sound of Writing, 1991; (ed. with C. Marshall) Listening to Ourselves: More Stories from The Sound of Writing, 1993; (ed. with N. Delbanco) Talking Horse: Bernard Malamud on Life and Work, 1996; Lost and Old Rivers: Stories, 1998; Listening to the Page: Adventures in Reading and Writing, 2001; (ed. with L. Alvarez) Writers Workshop in a Book: The Squaw Valley Community of Writers on the Art of Fiction, 2007; Fires, 2007; To Catch the Lightning (novel), 2008: A Trance After Breakfast (travel essays), 2009; (ed. with N. Delbanco) Literature, Craft and Voice (Fiction, Poetry, Drama), 2009, 2nd ed., 2012; Song of Slaves in the Desert (novel), 2011. Contributor to periodicals. **Address:** Department of English, George Mason University, A 487 Robinson, Rm. 208, 1 Science & Tech 1, 4400 University Dr., Fairfax, VA 22030, U.S.A. **Online address:** acheuse@gmu.edu

CHEVALIER, Tracy. British/American (born United States), b. 1962. **Genres:** Novels, History, Young Adult Fiction, Novellas/Short Stories, Reference, Essays. **Career:** Writer. **Publications:** NOVELS: The Virgin Blue, 1997; Girl with a Pearl Earring, 1999; Falling Angels, 2001; The Lady and the Unicorn, 2003; Burning Bright, 2007; Remarkable Creatures, 2009. EDITOR: Twentieth-Century Children's Writers, 1989; Contemporary Poets, 5th ed., 1991; Contemporary World Writers, 1993; Encyclopedia of the Essay, 1997. OTHERS: (with C. Wiggins) Tom Hunter: Living in Hell and Other Stories, 2006. Contributor to periodicals. **Address:** c/o Jonny Geller, Curtis Brown, Haymarket House, 28/29 Haymarket, London, GL SWIY 4SP, England. **Online address:** hello@tchevalier.com

CHEYETTE, Bryan (Henry). British (born England), b. 1959. **Genres:** Race Relations, Literary Criticism And History, Theology/Religion. **Career:** Spiro Institute, adult education lecturer, 1983-85; Hebrew University of Jerusalem, research fellow, 1985-86; University of Leeds, Montague Burton research fellow, 1986-89, British academy fellow, 1989-92; University of London, Queen Mary and Westfield College, lecturer in English, 1992-99, reader in English and Judaic studies, 1992-99; University of Michigan, Department of English, Padnos visiting professor in Judaic studies and associate professor, 1997; University of Southampton, professor of English, 1999-2005, Twentieth Century Literature, chair, 1999-2005; Dartmouth College, Rownstone visiting professor in English and Jewish studies, 2004; University of Pennsylvania, Center for Advanced Judaic Studies, visiting research fellow, 2005; The University of Reading, Department of English Language and Literature, professor, 2005-. Writer. **Publications:** (Ed. with L.I. Yudkin) Modern Hebrew Literature in English Translation, 1987; Constructions of The Jew in English Literature and Society: Racial Representations, 1875-1945, 1993; (ed.) Between Race and Culture: Representations of The Jew in English and American Literature, 1995; (ed. and intro.) Tono-Bungay, 1997; (ed.) Contemporary Jewish Writing in Britain and Ireland: An Anthology, 1998; (ed. with L. Marcus) Modernity, Culture and the Jew, 1998; Muriel Spark: Writers and Their Work, 2000; (ed. with N. Valman) The Image of the Jew in European Liberal Culture, 1789-1914, 2004; Diasporas of the Mind: Literature and Race after the Holocaust, 2007; (ed. with P. Boxall) Oxford History of the Novel in English: British and Irish Fiction, 1940-2000, forthcoming. Contributor of articles to journals, books and newspapers. **Address:** The School of English and American Literature, Faculty of Arts and Humanities, The University of Reading, PO Box 218, Reading, BR RG6 6AA, England. **Online address:** b.h.cheyette@reading.ac.uk

CHIA, Mantak. Thai (born Thailand), b. 1944. **Genres:** Sex, Medicine/Health, Psychology. **Career:** Natural Healing Center, founder; Universal Healing Tao Center (originally named Taoist Esoteric Yoga Center), founder and director, 1979-; Tao Garden Health Spa & Resort, founding director; Gestetner Co. (office equipment manufacturer), manager. Writer. **Publications:** Awaken Healing Energy through the Tao: The Taoist Secret of Circulating Internal Power, 1983; (with M. Winn) Taoist Secrets of Love: Cultivating the Male Sexual Energy, 1984; Taoist Ways to Transform Stress into Vitality: The Inner Smile, Six Healing Sounds, 1985; (with M. Chia) Healing Love through the Tao: Cultivating Female Sexual Energy, 1986; Chi Self-Massage: The Taoist Way of Rejuvenation, 1986, 2nd ed., 2006; Iron Shirt Chi Kung I: Once a Martial Art, Now the Practice that Strengthens the Internal Organs, Roots Oneself Solidly and Unifies Physical, Mental and Spiritual Health, 1986; Fusion of the Five Elements I: Basic and Advanced Meditations for Transforming Negative Emotions, 1989; (with M. Chia) Chi Nei Tsang: Internal Organ Chi Massage, 1990; Awaken Healing Light of the Tao, 1993; The Inner Structure of Tai Chi: Tai Chi Chi Kung I, 1996; (with D.A. Arava) The Multi-Orgasmic Man: Sexual Secrets Every Man Should Know, 1996; Chi Nei Tsang II: Internal Organ Chi Massage Chasing the Winds, 2000; The Multi-Orgasmic Couple: Sexual Secrets Every Couple Should Know, 2000; (with W.U. Wei) Sexual Reflexology: Activating the Taoist Points of Love, 2003; Taoist Cosmic Healing: Chi Kung Color Healing Principles for Detoxification and Rejuvination, 2003; Tan Tien Chi Kung: Empty Force, Perineum Power and the Second Brain, 2002; Tan Tien Chi Kung: Foundational Exercises for Empty Force and Perineum Power, 2004; (with D. Oellibrandt) Taoist Astral Healing: Chi Kung Healing Practices Using Star and Planet Energies, 2004; Energy Balance Through the Tao: Exercises for Cultivating Yin Energy, 2005; Golden Elixir Chi Kung, 2005; (with T. Huang) Secret Teachings of the Tao Te Ching: Mantak Chia and Tao Huang, 2005; (with R.C. Abrams) The Multi-Orgasmic Woman: Discover Your Full Desire, Pleasure, and Vitality, 2005; (with J. Li) The Inner Structure of Tai Chi: Mastering the Classic Forms of Tai Chi Chi Kung, 2005; Iron Shirt Chi Kung, 2006; Bone Marrow Nei Kung: Taoist Techniques for Rejuvenating the Blood and Bone, 2006; Chi Nei Tsang: Chi Massage for the Vital Organs, 2007; Fusion of the Five Elements: Meditations for Transforming Negative Emotions, 2007; Cosmic Fusion: The Inner Alchemy of the Eight Forces, 2007; The Taoist Soul Body: Harnessing the Power of Kan and Li, 2007; Healing Light of the Tao: Foundational Practices to Awaken Chi Energy, 2008; Fusion of the Eight Psychic Channels: Opening and Sealing the Energy Body, 2008; Healing Light of the Tao: Foundational Practices to Awaken Chi Energy, 2008; The Inner Smile: Increasing Chi through the Cultivation of Joy, 2008; Wisdom Chi Kung: Practices for Enlivening the Brain with Chi Energy, 2008; (with D. Saxer) Emotional Wisdom: Daily Tools for Transforming Anger, Depression, and Fear, 2009; The Six Healing Sounds: Taoist Techniques for Balancing Chi, 2009; Tendon Nei Kung: Building Strength, Power, and Flexibility in the Joints, 2009; (with W.U. Wei) Living in the Tao: The Effortless Path of Self-discovery, 2009; Advanced Chi Nei Tsang: Enhancing Chi Energy in the Vital Organs, 2009; Alchemy of Sexual Energy: Connecting to the Universe from Within, 2009; (with R.T. Lewanski) Art of Cosmic Vision: Practices for Improving Your Eyesight, 2010; (with K.D. North) Taoist Shaman: Practices from the Wheel of Life, 2010; (with K.D. North) Taoist Foreplay: Love Meridians and Pressure Points, 2010; Healing Energy of Shared Consciousness: A Taoist Approach to Entering the Universal Mind, 2011; (with W.U. Wei) Cosmic Detox, 2011; Karsai nei tsang, 2011; (with L. Holden) Simple chi kung, 2011; (with W.U. Wei) Cosmic Nutrition, 2012; (with A. Jan) Tai chi fa jin, 2012. **Address:** Tao Garden Health Spa & Resort, 274 Moo 7, Luang Nua, Doi Saket, 50220, Thailand. **Online address:** info@tao-garden.com

CHIANG, Lynette. Australian (born Australia), b. 1962. **Genres:** Novels, History. **Career:** Writer. **Publications:** The Handsomest Man in Cuba: An Escapade, 2007. Contributor to periodicals. **Address:** Globe Pequot Press, 246 Goose Ln., PO Box 480, Guilford, CT 06437, U.S.A. **Online address:** galfromdownunder@gmail.com

CHIAPPE, Luis M. American (born United States), b. 1962. **Genres:** Sciences, Children's Non-fiction, Animals/Pets, Children's Fiction. **Career:** American Museum of Natural History, research associate; Natural History Museum of Los Angeles County, Dinosaur Institute, director, Department of Vertebrate Paleontology, associate curator, curator, chairman; University of Southern California, adjunct professor. Writer. **Publications:** (With L. Dingus) The Tiniest Giants: Discovering Dinosaur Eggs, 1999; (with L. Dingus) Walking on Eggs: The Astonishing Discovery of Thousands of Dinosaur Eggs in the Badlands of Patagonia, 2001; (ed. with L.M. Witmer) Mesozoic Birds: Above the Heads of Dinosaurs, 2002; Glorified Dinosaurs: The Origin and Early Evolution of Birds, 2007; (with L. Dingus and R. Coria) Dinosaur Eggs Discovered!: Unscrambling the Clues, 2008. Contributor to periodicals. **Address:** Department of Vertebrae Paleontology, Natural History Museum of Los Angeles County, 900 Exposition Blvd., Los Angeles, CA 90007, U.S.A. **Online address:** chiappe@nhm.org

CHIARELLA, Tom. American/Italian (born Italy), b. 1961. **Genres:** Novellas/Short Stories, Writing/Journalism. **Career:** DePauw University, professor of English and head of department, 1988-, visiting professor of creative writing; Children's Center, president; Esquire Magazine, writer-at-large and fiction editor. **Publications:** Foley's Luck: Stories, 1992; Writing Dialogue (nonfiction), 1998; Thursday's Game: Notes from a Golfer with Far to Go, 2004. Contributor to periodicals. **Address:** Department of English, DePauw University, Rm. 229, Harrison Hall, PO Box 37, Greencastle, IN 46135-0037, U.S.A. **Online address:** tchiarel@depauw.edu

CHIARELLO, Michael. American (born United States), b. 1962. **Genres:** Food And Wine. **Career:** Tra Vigne, executive chef, 1986-2001; Napa Valley Kitchens, chair person and culinary director, 1992-2001; Caffe Museo, owner, 1994-; Ajax Tavern, owner, 1995-2001; NapaStyle Inc., founder. Writer. **Publications:** (With P. Wisner) Flavored Oils: 50 Recipes for Cooking with Infused Oils, 1995; (with P. Wisner) Flavored Vinegars: 50 Recipes for Cooking with Infused Vinegars, 1996; (with P. Wisner) The Tra Vigne Cookbook: Seasons in the California Wine Country, 1999; (with J. Fletcher) Napa Stories: Profiles, Reflections and Recipes from the Napa Valley, 2001; Recipes from Michael Chiarello's Napa, 2001; Michael Chiarello's Casual Cooking: Wine Country Recipes for Family and Friends-A Napastyle Cookbook, 2002; At Home with Michael Chiarello: Easy Entertaining, Recipes, Ideas, Inspiration, 2005; Michael Chiarello's Flavored Oils and vinegars: 100 Recipes for Cooking with Infused Oils and Vinegars, 2006; (with A.K. Spivack and C. Sansone) Bottega: Bold Italian Flavors from the Heart of California's Wine Country, 2010. **Address:** NapaStyle Inc., 360 Industrial Ct., Ste. A, Benicia, CA 94510, U.S.A. **Online address:** chefmc@napa.net

CHIBNALL, Marjorie McCallum. (Marjorie Morgan). British (born England), b. 1915. **Genres:** History, Theology/Religion. **Career:** University of Southampton, faculty; University of Aberdeen, lecturer in history, 1943-47; University of Cambridge, lecturer in history, 1947-65, Girton College, fellow, 1947-65, honorary fellow, 1988-, Clare Hall, research fellow, 1969-75, fellow, 1975-, Department of Medieval History and Historiography, now emeritus fellow; Lady Margaret Hall, research fellow. Writer. **Publications:** (As Marjorie Morgan) The English Lands of the Abbey of Bec, 1946; (trans. and intro.) Memoirs of the Papal Court, 1956; (with A.T. Gaydon) Victoria County History of Shropshire, 1973; The World of Orderic Vitalis, 1984; Anglo-Norman England, 1066-1166, 1987; The Empress Matilda: Queen Consort, Queen Mother and Lady of the English, 1992; The Debate on the Norman Conquest, 1999; Piety, Power, and History in Medieval England and Normandy, 2000; The Normans, 2002. EDITOR: (and trans.) Historia Pontificalis of John of Salisbury, 1956; (and trans. and intro.) The Ecclesiastical History of Orderic Vitalis, 6 vols., 1969-80; (with J. Walmsley) Chartersand Custumals of the Abbey of Holy Trinity Caen, 2 vols., 1982-94; Anglo-Norman Studies, vol. XIII-XVII, 1990-94; (with L. Watkiss) The Waltham Chronicle: An Account of the Discovery of Our Holy Cross at Montacute and Its Conveyance to Waltham, 1994; (and trans. with R.H.C. Davis) The Gesta Guillelmi of William of Poitiers, 1998. **Address:** Clare Hall, University of Cambridge, Herschel Rd., 1 Brookside Cambridge, Cambridge, CB CB2 1JE, England.

CHIDESTER, David. South African/American (born United States), b. 1952. **Genres:** Theology/Religion, History, Politics/Government. **Career:** University of Cape Town, Department of Religious Studies, professor, 1994-, chair of religious studies comparative religion, head; Institute for Comparative Religion in Southern Africa, director. Writer. **Publications:** Patterns of Action: Religion and Ethics in a Comparative Perspective, 1987; Salvation and Suicide: An Interpretation of Jim Jones, the Peoples Temple and Jonestown, 1988, rev. ed., 2003; Patterns of Power: Religion and Politics in American Culture, 1988; Patterns of Transcendence: Religion, Death and Dying, 1990, 2nd ed., 2002; Shots in the Streets: Violence and Religion in South Africa, 1991; Religions of South Africa, 1992; Word and Light: Seeing, Hearing and Religious Discourse, 1992; (co-author) Religion in Public Education: Options for a New South Africa, rev. ed., 1994; (ed. with E.T. Linenthal) American Sacred Space, 1995; Savage Systems: Colonialism and Comparative Religion in Southern Africa, 1996; (co-author) African Traditional Religion in South Africa: An Annotated Bibliography, 1997; Islam, Hinduism and Judaism in South Africa: An Annotated Bibliography, 1997; (with J. Tobler and D. Wratten) Christianity in South Africa: An Annotated Bibliography, 1997; (ed. with J. Stonier and J. Tobler) Diversity as Ethos: Challenges for Interreligious and Intercultural Education, 1999; Christianity: A Global History, 2000; (with K. Asmal and W. James) In His Own Words, 2003; (ed. with K. Asmal and W. James) Nelson Mandela: From Freedom to the Future: Tributes and Speeches, 2003; (ed. with K. Asmal and W. James) South Africa's Nobel Laureates: Peace, Literature and Science, 2004; (ed. with A. Tayob and W. Weisse) Religion, Politics and Identity in a Changing South Africa, 2004; (ed. with P. Dexter and W. James) What Holds Us Together: Social Cohesion in South Africa, 2004; (ed. with K. Asmal and C. Lubisi) Legacy of Freedom: The ANC's Human Rights Tradition: Africans' Claims in South Africa, the Freedom Charter, the Women's Charter and Other Human Rights Landmarks of the African National Congress, 2005; Authentic Fakes: Religion and American Popular Culture, 2005; Wild Religion: Tracking the Sacred in South Africa, 2012. **Address:** Department of Religious Studies, University of Cape Town, Rm. 5.40, Leslie Social Science Bldg., Private Bag, Rondebosch, Cape Town, 7701, South Africa. **Online address:** david.chidester@uct.ac.za

CHIENG, Chieh. American/Chinese (born China), b. 1975?. **Genres:** Novels, Young Adult Fiction, Literary Criticism And History. **Career:** Novelist. **Publications:** A Long Stay in a Distant Land, 2005. Contributor of periodicals. **Address:** c/o Dorian Karchmar, Lowenstein-Yost Associates, 121 W 27th St., Ste. 601, New York, NY 10001, U.S.A.

CHIERICHETTI, David. American (born United States) **Genres:** Biography, Adult Non-fiction, Fash Ion/Costume. **Career:** Fashion Institute of Design and Merchandising, teacher and part-time faculty; Otis College of Art and Design, teacher, 1998-, continuing education faculty. Writer and freelance costume designer. **Publications:** NONFICTION: Hollywood Director: The Career of Mitchell Leisen, reprinted as Mitchell Leisen: Hollywood Director, 1973; Hollywood Costume Design, 1976; (with S. Shapiro) The Movie Poster Book, 1979; Edith Head: The Life and Times of Hollywood's Celebrated Costume Designer, 2003. **Address:** Otis College of Art and Design, 9045 Lincoln Blvd., Los Angeles, CA 90045, U.S.A. **Online address:** dchierichetti@otis.edu

CHIFFOLO, Anthony F. American (born United States), b. 1959?. **Genres:** inspirational/Motivational Literature, Theology/Religion. **Career:** Praeger Publishers, managing editor and acquisitions editor. **Publications:** (Comp.) At Prayer with the Saints, 1998; Be Mindful of Us: Prayers to the Saints, 2000; One Hundred Names of Mary: Stories and Prayers, 2002; (with R.W. Hesse, Jr.) We Thank You, God for These, 2003; (with R.W. Hesse, Jr.) Cooking with the Bible: Biblical Food, Feasts, and Lore, 2006; (with R.W. Hesse) Cooking with the Bible: Recipes for Biblical Meals, 2009; (with R.W. Heese, Jr.) Cooking with the Movies: Meals on Reels, 2010. EDITOR: (comp.) In My Own Words: Pope John Paul II, 1998; In My Own Words: Pope John XXIII, 1999; Padre Pio: In My Own Words, 2000; Advent and Christmas with the Saints, 2003. **Address:** c/o Author Mail, St. Anthony Messenger Press, 28 W Liberty St., Cincinnati, OH 45202, U.S.A. **Online address:** anthonychiffolo@yahoo.com

CHIGNON, Niles. *See* **LINGEMAN, Richard.**

CHILCOTE, Ronald H. American (born United States), b. 1935. **Genres:** Economics, Politics/Government. **Career:** Stanford University, instructor, 1961-63, Institute of Hispanic American and Luso-Brazilian Studies, assistant director, 1961-63; University of California-Riverside, assistant professor, 1963-69, associate professor, 1969-75, professor of political science, 1975-94, professor emeritus, 1994-, Latin American Research Program, coordinator, 1965-70, Program on Latin American Studies, director, 1986-90, Education Abroad Program, Brazil Study Center, director, 1992-94; Latin American Perspectives, managing editor, 1974-; Temple Hills Community Association, president and coordinator, 1974-85, 1987-; Laguna Greenbelt Inc., director, 1975-; Westview Press, series editor, 1980-2000; Laguna Wilderness Press, director, 2000-. **Publications:** Press in Latin America, Spain, and Portugal: A Summary of Recent Developments, 1963; (ed.) Portuguese Africa, 1967; Spain's Iron and Steel Industry, 1968; Emerging Nationalism in Portuguese Africa: A Bibliography of Documentary Ephemera through 1965, 1969; Revolution and Structural Change in Latin America: A Bibliography on Ideology, Development, and the Radical Left (1930-1965), 1970; (ed.) Protest and Resistance in Angola and Brazil: Comparative Studies, 1972; The Brazilian Communist Party: Conflict and Integration, 1922-1972, 1974; (with J. Edelstein) Latin America: The Struggle with Dependency and Beyond, 1974; (ed. and comp.) Brazil and its Radical Left, 1980; Theories of Comparative Politics: The Search for a Paradigm, 1981, 2nd ed., 1994; (ed.) Dependency and Marxism: Toward a Resolution of the Debate, 1982; (ed. with D.L. Johnson) Theories of Development: Mode of Production or Dependency?, 1983; Theories of Development and Underdevelopment, 1984; (with J. Edelstein) Latin America: Capitalist and Socialist Perspectives of Development and Underdevelopment, 1986; (ed. and comp. with S. Lutjens) Cuba, 1953-1978, 1986; (comp. and ed.) The Portuguese Revolution of 25 April 1974, 1987; Power and the Ruling Classes in Northeast Brazil, 1990; (co-author) Transitions from Dictatorship to Democracy: Comparative Studies of Spain, Portugal, and Greece, 1990; Amílcar Cabral's Revolutionary Theory and Practice: A Critical Guide, 1991; Theories of Comparative Politics: The Search for a Paradigm Reconsidered, 1994; (ed.) Political Economy of Imperialism: Critical Appraisals, 1999; Theories of Comparative Political Economy, 2000; (ed.) Imperialism: Theoretical Directions, 2000; Comparative Inquiry in Politics and Political Economy: Theories and Issues, 2000; Nature's Laguna Wilderness, 2003; (ed.) Development in Theory and Practice: Latin American Perspectives, 2003; (ed.) Alternatives to Neoliberalism in Latin America, 2004; (ed.) Wind River Wilderness, 2006; The Portuguese Revolution, 2010. Contributor to books. **Address:** Department of Economics, University of California, 107 Highlander Hall, Bldg. B, 900 University Ave., Riverside, CA 92521, U.S.A. **Online address:** ronald.chilcote@ucr.edu

CHILD, Lincoln B. American (born United States), b. 1957. **Genres:** Novels, Young Adult Fiction. **Career:** St. Martin's Press, editorial assistant, assistant editor, associate editor, 1979-84, editor, 1984-88; Metropolitan Life Insurance Co., analyst, 1988-95; freelance writer, 1995-. **Publications:** NOVELS WITH DOUGLAS PRESTON: Relic, 1995; Mount Dragon, 1996; Reliquary, 1997; Riptide, 1998; Thunderhead, 1999; Land of Fire, 2000; The Ice Limit, 2000; The Cabinet of Curiosities, 2002; Still Life with Crows, 2003; Brimstone, 2004; Dance of Death, 2005; The Book of the Dead, 2006; The Wheel of Darkness, 2007; Cemetery Dance, 2009; Fever Dream, 2010; Cold Vengeance, 2011; Gideon's Sword, 2011; Gideon's Corpse, 2012. NOVELS: Utopia, 2002; Death Match, 2004; Deep Storm, 2007; Terminal Freeze: A Novel, 2009. EDITOR: Dark Company: The Ten Greatest Ghost Stories, 1984; Dark Banquet: A Feast of Twelve Great Ghost Stories, 1985; Tales of the Dark, 1987; Tales of the Dark Two, 1987; Tales of the Dark Three, 1988. OTHER: Third Gate, 2012. **Address:** PO Box 162, Convent Station, NJ 07961, U.S.A. **Online address:** lchild@prestonchild.com

CHILD, Maureen. Also writes as Kathleen Kane, Emilie Rose, Ann Carberry. American (born United States), b. 1951. **Genres:** Novels, Children's Fiction. **Career:** Writer. **Publications:** NOVELS: The Bandits Lady, 1995; Have Bride, Need Groom, 1997; The Surprise Christmas Bride, 1997; The Littlest Marine, 1998; The Non-Commissioned Baby, 1998; The Oldest Living Married Virgin, 1998; Maternity Bride, 1998; Simply Magic, 1999; Colonel Daddy, 1999; Marine Under the Mistletoe, 1999; Mom in Waiting, 1999; The Daddy Salute, 2000; The Last Santini Virgin, 2000; The Next Santini Bride, 2000; Marooned with a Marine, 2000; Did You Say Twins?, 2001; His Baby!, 2001; The Last Virgin in California, 2001; Prince Charming in Dress Blues, 2001; The Marine and the Debutante, 2002; The Royal Treatment, 2002; The Seals Surrender, 2002; Beauty and the Blue Angel, 2003; Loving You, 2003; Finding You; Knowing You, 2003; Kiss Me, Cowboy!, 2003; Sleeping with the Boss, 2003; And Then Came You: Sams Story, 2004; Forever-Again,

2004; Man Beneath the Uniform, 2004; Some Kind of Wonderful, 2004; Lost in Sensation, 2004; (with P. Webb) Summer Surrender, 2004; A Crazy Kind of Love: Mikes Story, 2005; The Last Reilly Standing, 2005; Whatever Reilly Wants, 2005; Turn My World Upside Down: Jos Story, 2005; The Tempting Mrs. Reilly, 2005; Expecting Lonergans Baby, 2005; The Part-time Wife, 2005; Satisfying Lonergans Honor, 2006; Eternally, 2006; Thirty Day Affair, 2007; More Than Fiends, 2007; Nevermore, 2007; Holiday With a Vampire: Christmas Cravings, 2007; The Surprise Christmas Bride, 2007; Captured by the Billionaire, 2007; Seduced by the Rich Man, 2007; Fiend in Need, 2008; Bargaining For Kings Baby, 2008; Falling For Kings Fortune, 2008; Marrying For Kings Millions, 2008; (Emilie Rose) Bargained into Her Bosss Bed, 2009; An Officer And A Millionaire, 2009; Vanished, 2009; Claiming Kings Baby, 2009; Conquering Kings Heart, 2009; Wedding at Kings Convenience, 2009; Bedeviled, 2009; Beguiled, 2009; Desiring the Reilly Brothers, 2010; Cinderella & the CEO, 2010; (contrib.) The Best is Yet to Come, 2010; Last Lone Wolf, 2010; King's Million-Dollar Secret, 2011; (with J. Miller) At Her Service, 2011; Ready for King's Seduction, 2011; The Temporary Mrs. King, 2011; To Kiss a King, 2012; Gilded Secrets, 2012. NOVELS: AS KATHLEEN KANE: Mountain Dawn, 1992; Small Treasures, 1993; Coming Home, 1994; Keeping Faith, 1994; Charms, 1995; Wishes, 1995; A Pocketful of Paradise, 1997; Still Close to Heaven, 1997; Dream weaver, 1998; This Time for Keeps, 1998; The Soul Collector, 1999; Catch a Fallen Angel, 2000; Wish upon a Cowboy, 2000; Just West of Heaven, 2001; When the Halo Falls, 2002. NOVELS: AS ANN CARBERRY: Maggie and the Gambler, 1995; Alice and the Gunfighter, 1996; Frannie and the Charmer, 1996. Contributor to periodicals. **Address:** c/o Author Mail, St. Martins Press, 175 5th Ave., New York, NY 10010, U.S.A. **Online address:** maureen@maureenchild.com

CHILDRESS, Mark. American (born United States), b. 1957. **Genres:** Novels, Children's Fiction. **Career:** The Birmingham News, staff writer, 1977-80; Southern Living magazine, features editor, 1980-84; The Atlanta Journal-Constitution, regional editor, 1984-85; Community of Writers, staff and director; full-time writer, 1985-. **Publications:** NOVELS: A World Made of Fire, 1984; V for Victor, 1984; Tender, 1990; Crazy in Alabama, 1993; Gone for Good, 1998; One Mississippi, 2006; Georgia Bottoms, 2011. JUVENILE: Joshua and Bigtooth, 1992; Joshua and the Big Bad Blue Crabs, 1996; Henry Bobbity is Missing and It is All Billy Bobbity's Fault!, 1996. Contributor to periodicals. **Address:** c/o Henry Dunow, Dunow, Carlson & Lerner, 27 W 20th St., Ste. 1107, New York, NY 10011, U.S.A. **Online address:** markchildress123@aol.com

CHILDS, Christopher. American (born United States), b. 1949. **Genres:** Environmental Sciences/Ecology, inspirational/Motivational Literature. **Career:** Middlesex School, English teacher and coach, 1970-73; actor, director and designer, 1972-; Massachusetts Council on the Arts and Humanities, chair, 1981; American Premiere Stage, board director, 1980-82; Environmental Testing Service, technician, 1987; Greenpeace, campaigner, 1987-88, national speaker, 1988-96; New Eden Foundation, director, 1996-98; Ken Pentel for Governor, media relations coordinator 2002; Sierra Club-North Star Chapter, Clean Air and Renewable Energy, chair, 2004-08, conservation chair, 2006-08; Elizabeth Dickinson for Mayor, communications director, 2005; Minnesota Renewable Energy Society, board director, 2007-10. Writer. **Publications:** (Ed.) Clear Sky, Pure Light: Encounters with Henry David Thoreau, 1978; The Spirit's Terrain: Creativity, Activism, and Transformation, 1998; Green Days, White Knights: A Greenpeace Decade, forthcoming. **Address:** 384 Hall Ave., St. Paul, MN 55107, U.S.A. **Online address:** worldgarden@igc.org

CHILDS, Craig. American (born United States), b. 1967. **Genres:** Literary Criticism And History, Archaeology/Antiquities, History, Animals/Pets. **Career:** River Guide, staff, 1986-. Writer. **Publications:** Stone Desert: A Naturalist's Exploration of Canyonlands National Park, 1995; Crossing Paths: Uncommon Encounters with Animals in the Wild, 1997; Grand Canyon: Time below the Rim, 1999; (with L.W. Banks) Grand Canyon Stories: Then & Now, 1999; The Secret Knowledge of Water: Discovering the Essence of the American Desert, 2000; (contrib.) Colorado, 2000; The Southwest's Contrary Land: Forever Changing Between Four Corners and the Sea of Cortes, 2001; The Southwest's Contrary Land: Forever Changing Between Four Corners and the Sea of Cortes, 2001; Desert Cries: A Season of Flash Floods in a Dry Land, 2002; Soul of Nowhere: Traversing Grace in a Rugged Land, 2002; Way Out: A True Story of Ruin and Survival, 2004; (contrib.) The Elements: Earth, Air, Fire, Water, 2004; House of Rain: Tracking a Vanished Civilization Across the American Southwest, 2007; The Animal Dialogues: Uncommon Encounters in the Wild, 2007; Finders Keepers: A Tale of Archaeological Plunder and Obsession, 2010. **Address:** c/o Author Mail, Little, Brown Book Group, 100 Victoria Embankment, London, GL EC4Y 0DY, England.

CHILDS, David (Haslam). British (born England), b. 1933. **Genres:** Area Studies, History, International Relations/Current Affairs, Politics/Government, Reference. **Career:** University of Nottingham, lecturer, 1966-71, senior lecturer, 1971-76, reader, 1976-89, Institute of German, Austrian and Swiss Affairs, director, 1986-92, professor of German politics, 1989-, now retired. Writer. **Publications:** From Schumacher to Brandt, 1966; East Germany, 1969; Germany since 1918, 1971, 2nd ed., 1980; Marx and the Marxists, 1973; Britain since 1945, 1979, 6th ed., 2006; (with J. Johnson) West Germany: Politics and Society, 1981; The GDR: Moscow's German Ally, 1983, rev. ed., 1988; East Germany to the 1990s, 1987; Germany on the Road to Unity, 1990; Germany in the 20th Century, 1991; Britain since 1939: Progress and Decline, 1995, 2nd ed., 2002; (with R. Popplewell) The Stasi: The East German Intelligence and Security System, 1996, 2nd ed., 2000; The Two Red Flags: European Social Democracy and Soviet Communism, 2000; The Fall of the GDR: Germany's Road to Unity, 2001; We Were No Heroes, 2009. EDITOR/CO-EDITOR: The Changing Face of Western Communism, 1980; Honecker's Germany, 1985; East Germany in Comparative Perspective, 1989; Children in War, 1990. Contributor to books. **Address:** 1 Grange Pk., W Bridgford, Nottingham, NT NG2 6HW, England. **Online address:** david@jcit.co.uk

CHILDS, Elizabeth C(atharine). American (born United States), b. 1954. **Genres:** Art/Art History, Cartoons, Theology/Religion, Photography. **Career:** Metropolitan Museum of Art, lecturer and program assistant in museum education, 1976-81; National Gallery of Scotland, educational consultant, 1977-78; Museum of Modern Art, museum lecturer, 1979; Solomon R. Guggenheim Museum, curatorial consultant, 1984-85, research associate, 1987-91; State University of New York College-Purchase, lecturer, 1987-89, assistant professor of art history, 1989-92; Princeton University, Gould fellow in art and archaeology, 1992-93; Washington University, Department of Art History and Archaeology, assistant professor, 1992-98, associate professor of art history and archaeology, 1998-, chair; Middlebury College, lecturer; University of Chicago, lecturer; Vassar College, lecturer; University of Bielefeld, lecturer; Fashion Institute of Technology, lecturer; Wake Forest University, lecturer; Mount Holyoke College, lecturer. Writer. **Publications:** (With L. Flint) The Handbook to the Peggy Guggenheim Collection, 1986; (ed. and intro.) Honoré Daumier: A Thematic Guide to the Oeuvre, 1989; (ed. with K. Powell) Femmes D'esprit: Women in Daumier's Caricature, 1990; (ed.) Suspended License: Censorship and the Visual Arts, 1997; (contrib.) Vincent Van Gogh and the Painters of the Petit Boulevard, 2001; Daumier and Exoticism: Satirizing the French and the Foreign, 2004; Catholicism and the Modern Mind: The Painter as Writer in Late Career, 2004; (contrib.) John La Farge's Second Paradise, 2010. Contributor to journals. **Address:** Department of Art History and Archaeology, Washington University, 213 Kemper, 1 Brookings Dr., PO Box 1189, St. Louis, MO 63130-4862, U.S.A. **Online address:** ecchilds@artsci.wustl.edu

CHILDS, John Charles Roger. British (born England), b. 1949. **Genres:** History. **Career:** University of Leeds, faculty, 1976, professor emeritus of military history, 2009. Writer. **Publications:** The Army of Charles II, 1976; The Army, James II, and the Glorious Revolution, 1980; Armies and Warfare in Europe, 1648-1789, 1982; The British Army of William III, 1689-1702, 1987; The Nine Years' War and the British Army, 1688-1697: The Operations in the Low Countries, 1991; (ed.) A Dictionary of Military History and the Art of War, rev. ed., 1994; The Military Use of Land: A History of the Defence Estate, 1998; Warfare in the Seventeenth Century, 2004; The Williamite Wars in Ireland, 1688-91, 2007. Contributor to books. **Address:** School of History, University of Leeds, Leeds, WY LS2 9JT, England. **Online address:** j.c.r.childs@leeds.ac.uk

CHILDS, Matt D. American (born United States), b. 1970. **Genres:** History, Social Sciences. **Career:** University of Texas, instructor, 1995-97, Donald Harrington fellow, 2008-09; Florida State University, Department of History, assistant professor, 2001-07, associate professor, 2007-08; University of South Carolina, College of Arts and Sciences, Department of History, associate professor, 2009-, History Center, director, 2011-. Writer and historian. **Publications:** (Ed. with T. Falola) The Yoruba Diaspora in the Atlantic World, 2004; The 1812 Aponte Rebellion in Cuba and the Struggle against

Atlantic Slavery, 2006; (ed. with T. Falola) The Changing Worlds of Atlantic Africa: Essays in Honor of Robin Law, 2009. Contributor to periodicals. **Address:** Department of History, University of South Carolina, 121 Gambrell Hall, 817 Henderson St., Columbia, SC 29208, U.S.A. **Online address:** childsmd@mailbox.sc.edu

CHILDS, Michael J. Canadian (born Canada), b. 1956. **Genres:** History. **Career:** University of Lethbridge, assistant professor of history, 1987-88; Bishop's University, assistant professor, 1988-92, associate professor of history, 1992-, vice-principal academic. Writer. **Publications:** Labour's Apprentices: Working-Class Lads in Late Victorian and Edwardian England, 1992. **Address:** Department of History, Bishop's University, MCG 216, 2600 College St., PO Box 22, Sherbrooke, QC J1M 1Z7, Canada. **Online address:** mchilds@ubishops.ca

CHILDS, Tera Lynn. American (born United States), b. 1976?. **Genres:** Children's Fiction, Children's Non-fiction. **Career:** Writer and educator. **Publications:** Oh. My. Gods, 2008; Oh. My. Gods: Goddess Bootcamp, 2009. **Address:** c/o Jenny Bent, Trident Media Group, 41 Madison Ave., 36th Fl., New York, NY 10010-2257, U.S.A. **Online address:** tlc@teralynnchilds.com

CHILDS, William R. American (born United States), b. 1951. **Genres:** History, Business/Trade/Industry, Law, Communications/Media. **Career:** University of Texas, instructor; University of Georgia, instructor; Ohio State University, Department of History, professor, 1984-; Contemporary American Theatre Co. (CATCO), historical consultant and president, 1998-2000. Writer and historian. **Publications:** Trucking and the Public Interest: The Emergence of Federal Regulation, 1914-1940, 1985; (contrib.) The Encyclopedia of the United States in the Twentieth Century, 1996; (ed. with S.B. Martin and W.S. Gohdes) Business and Industry, 2003; The Texas Railroad Commission: Understanding Regulation in America to the Mid-Twentieth Century, 2005. **Address:** Department of History, Ohio State University, 204 Dulles Hall, 230 W 17th Ave., Columbus, OH 43210, U.S.A. **Online address:** childs.1@osu.edu

CHILES, James R. American (born United States), b. 1955?. **Genres:** Transportation, Technology. **Career:** Writer, educator and commentator. **Publications:** (With J.R. Gilkeson) Problem Materials Plan I, 1992; (and contrib. with T. Osdoba) Internalizing Waste Management Costs: Presented to the Legislative Commission on Waste Management, January, 1992, 1992; Loosefill Comparison Study, 1993; (with C. Leavitt and R. Swenson) MMSW LandFill Liability Report: Methods to Address Landfill Liabilities at Mixed Municipal Solid Waste Landfills, 1998; Inviting Disaster: Lessons from the Edge of Technology: An Inside Look at Catastrophes and Why They Happen, 2001; The God Machine: From Boomerangs to Black Hawks, the Story of the Helicopter, 2007. Contributor to periodicals. **Address:** Bantam Books, 1745 Broadway, New York, NY 10019, U.S.A. **Online address:** chiles@invitingdisaster.com

CHILSON, Peter. American (born United States), b. 1961. **Genres:** Education, History. **Career:** High Country News, associate editor, 1997-98; Washington State University, assistant professor of English, 1998-, associate professor of English, Undergraduate Creative Writing, director, 1998-; Associated Press, freelance reporter. **Publications:** BOOKS: Riding the Demon (nonfiction), 1999; Disturbance-Loving Species, 2007. CREATIVE NONFICTION: How to Live It and Write It, 1996. OTHER: We Never Knew Exactly Where: Stories from an African Borderland, forthcoming. **Address:** Department of English, Washington State University, 367 Avery Hall, PO Box 645020, Pullman, WA 99164-5020, U.S.A. **Online address:** pchilson@mail.wsu.edu

CHILSON, Rob(ert) (Dean). American (born United States), b. 1945. **Genres:** Science Fiction/Fantasy, Novellas/Short Stories, Military/Defense/Arms Control, Young Adult Fiction. **Career:** Writer, 1967-. **Publications:** As the Curtain Falls, 1974; The Star-Crowned Kings, 1975; The Shores of Kansas, 1976. (with W.F. Wu) Cyborg, 1987; Refuge, 1988; Men Like Rats, 1989; Rounded with Sleep, 1990; Black as Blood, 1998. SHORT STORIES: Truck Driver, 1972; People Reviews, 1977; Slowly, Slowly in the Wind, 1984; (with W.F. Wu) Flash to Darkness, 1985; (with W.F. Wu) The Ungood Earth, 1985; This Side of Independence, 1998. ANTHOLOGIES: Universe 7, 1977; Terrorists of Tomorrow, 1985; The Year's Best Science Fiction Sixteenth Annual Collection, 1999; Year's Best SF 4, 1999. Contributor to magazines. **Address:** PO Box 12583, Kansas City, KS 66112-0583, U.S.A. **Online address:** info@robchilson.com

CHILTON, Bruce. American (born United States), b. 1949. **Genres:** Theology/Religion. **Career:** Sheffield University, lecturer in biblical studies, 1976-85; Yale University, Lillian Claus professor of the New Testament, 1985-87; Bard College, professor, Bernard Iddings Bell professor of religion, 1987-, Asher Edelman fellow, chaplain of the college, Institute of Advanced Theology, founder and executive director, 2000-; Church of Saint John the Evangelist, rector, 1987-; College of Emmanuel, Bishop Henry Martin memorial lecturer; St Chad's College, Bishop Henry Martin memorial lecturer; Institute for Biblical Research, Bulletin for Biblical Research, editor-in-chief; Journal for the Study of the New Testament, founding editor; University of Münster, faculty; Universities of Cambridge, faculty. **Publications:** The Glory of Israel: The Theology and Provenience of the Isaiah Targum, 1983; A Galilean Rabbi and His Bible: Jesus Own Interpretation of Isaiah, 1984; Targumic Approaches to the Gospels (essays): Essays in the Mutual Definition of Judaism and Christianity, 1986; Beginning New Testament Study, 1986; (trans. and intro.) The Isaiah Targum, 1987; (with J.I.H. McDonald) Jesus and the Ethics of the Kingdom, 1988; Profiles of a Rabbi: Synoptic Opportunities in Reading about Jesus, 1989; The Temple of Jesus: His Sacrificial Program Within a Cultural History of Sacrifice, 1992; A Feast of Meanings: Eucharistic Theologies from Jesus through Johannine Circles, 1994; Judaic Approaches to the Gospel, 1994; (with J. Neusner) Judaism in the New Testament: Practices and Beliefs, 1995; (with J. Neusner) Revelation: The Torah and the Bible, 1995; Pure Kingdom: Jesus' Vision of God, 1996; (with J. Neusner) The Body of Faith: Israel and the Church, 1996; (with J. Neusner) Trading Places: The Intersecting Histories of Judaism and Christianity, 1996; (with J. Neusner) The Intellectual Foundations of Christian and Jewish Discourse: The Philosophy of Religious Argument, 1997; Jesus' Prayer and Jesus' Eucharist: His Personal Practiceof Spirituality, 1997; (with J. Neusner) God in the World, 1997; (with C.A. Evans) Jesus in Context: Temple, Purity, and Restoration, 1997; Jesus' Baptism and Jesus' Healing: His Personal Practice of Spirituality, 1998; (with J. Neusner) Jewish-Christian Debates: God, Kingdom, Messiah, 1998; (with J. Neusner) Types of Authority in Formative Christianity and Judaism, 1999; (with J. Neusner) Comparing Spiritualities: Formative Christianity and Judaism on Finding Life and Meeting Death, 2000; (with J. Neusner) Jewish and Christian Doctrines: The Classics Compared, 2000; Rabbi Jesus: An Intimate Biography, 2000; (contrib.) Making an Honest Living: What Do We Owe the Community?, 2001; (contrib.) Life of Virtue: What Do We Owe Ourselves?, 2001; (contrib.) Ethics of Family Life: What Do We Owe One Another?, 2001; Redeeming Time: The Wisdom of Ancient Jewish and Christian Festal Calendars, 2002; (with J. Neusner and B.A. Chilton) Missing Jesus: Rabbinic Judaism and the New Testament, 2002; (with J. Neusner and W. Graham) Three Faiths, One God: The Formative Faith and Practice of Judaism, Christianity, and Islam, 2003; Rabbi Paul: An Intellectual Biography, 2004; (with J. Neusner) Classical Christianity and Rabbinic Judaism: Comparing Theologies, 2004; Mary Magdalene: A Biography, 2005; Abraham's Curse: Child Sacrifice in the Legacies of the West, 2008; (with J. Neusner and B.A. Levine) Torah Revealed, Torah Fulfilled: Scriptural Laws in Formative Judaism and Earliest Christianity, 2008; Way of Jesus: to Repair and Renew the World, 2010; (with D.J. Good) Studying the New Testament: A Fortress Introduction, 2011; (with P.V.M. Flesher) The Targums, 2011; (foreword) The Pope's War, 2011. EDITOR: (and intro.) The Kingdom of God in the Teaching of Jesus, 1984; (with C.A. Evans) Studying the Historical Jesus: Evaluations of the State of Current Research, 1994; (with Neusner) Trading Places Sourcebook, 1997; Judaism in Late Antiquity, 1995; (with C.A. Evans) Authenticating the words of Jesus, 1999; (with C.A. Evans) James the Just and Christian Origins, 1999; (with J. Neusner) Brother of Jesus: James the Just and his Mission, 2001; (with J. Neusner) Altruism in World Religions, 2005; (with C. Evans) Missions of James, Peter, and Paul: Tensions in Early Christianity, 2005; (with J. Neusner) In Quest of the Historical Pharisees, 2007; Cambridge Companion to the Bible, 2008; (with J. Neusner) Religious Tolerance in World Religions, 2008; (with J. Neusner) Golden Rule: The Ethics of Reciprocity in World Religions, 2008; (with D. Bock and D.M. Gurtner) Comparative Handbook to the Gospel of Mark, 2010. **Address:** Religion Program, Bard College, PO Box 5000, Annandale-on-Hudson, NY 12504-5000, U.S.A. **Online address:** chilton@bard.edu

CHIMA, Cinda Williams. American (born United States), b. 1952?. **Genres:** Novels. **Career:** University of Akron, instructor, assistant professor of nutrition, 2004-09. Writer. **Publications:** The Warrior Heir, 2006; The Wizard Heir, 2007; The Dragon Heir, 2008; Demon King: A Seven Realms Novel, 2009; Exiled Queen, 2010; Gray Wolf Throne, 2011; The Crimson Crown,

2012. Contributor to books. **Address:** c/o Christopher Schelling, Selectric Artists, 56 Planetarium Sta., New York, NY 10024, U.S.A. **Online address:** cinda@cindachima.com

CHIN, Justin. American/Malaysian (born Malaysia), b. 1969?. **Genres:** Poetry, Essays, Writing/Journalism, Education, Biography. **Career:** Writer and artist. **Publications:** Bite Hard, 1997; Mongrel: Essays, Diatribe and Pranks, 1999; Harmless Medicine (poetry), 2001; Burden of Ashes, 2002; Attack of the Man-Eating Lotus Blossoms, 2005; Gutted, 2006; 98 Wounds, 2011. Contributor to periodicals and journals. **Address:** c/o Author Mail, Manic D Press, PO Box 410804, San Francisco, CA 94141, U.S.A. **Online address:** jchin69@yahoo.com

CHIN, Rita. American (born United States), b. 1970. **Genres:** Social Sciences. **Career:** Oberlin College, assistant professor of history, 1999-2003; University of Michigan, assistant professor of history, associate professor of history, 2003-; Institute for Advanced Study, School of Social Sciences, faculty, 2010-11. Historian and writer. **Publications:** The Guest Worker Question in Postwar Germany, 2007; (with H. Fehrenbach, G. Eley and A. Grossmann) After the Nazi Racial State: Difference and Democracy in Germany and Europe, 2009. Contributor to journals. **Address:** Department of History, University of Michigan, 1029 Tisch Hall, 435 S State St., Ann Arbor, MI 48109-1003, U.S.A. **Online address:** rchin@umich.edu

CHIN, Staceyann. Jamaican (born Jamaica), b. 1972. **Genres:** Autobiography/Memoirs. **Career:** Writer and artist. **Publications:** The Other Side of Paradise: A Memoir, 2009. Contributor to periodicals. **Address:** Brooklyn, NY , U.S.A. **Online address:** chinpoet@gmail.com

CHINEN, Nate. American (born United States) **Genres:** Autobiography/Memoirs, Music. **Career:** City Paper, music reporter; Billboard Online, co-founder; JazzTimes, columnist, 2004-. Writer and musician. **Publications:** (With G. Wein) Myself Among Others: A Life in Music, 2004. Contributor to magazines and periodicals. **Address:** c/o Author Mail, Da Capo Press, 387 Park Ave. S, 12th Fl., New York, NY 10016, U.S.A.

CHINERY, Michael. British (born England), b. 1938. **Genres:** Biology, Natural History, Zoology, Animals/Pets, Photography, Adult Non-fiction. **Career:** Freelance writer, 1965-. **Publications:** NONFICTION: Breeding and Growing: Foundations of Genetics, Anthropology and Agriculture, 1966; (with D. Larkin) Patterns of Living: Foundations of Ecology, 1966; A Pictorial Dictionary of the Animal World: An Illustrated Demonstration of Terms Used in Animal Biology, With Over 500 Colour Pictures, 1966, rev. ed. as A Science Dictionary of the Animal World: An Illustrated Demonstration of Terms Used in Animal Biology, with Over 500 Colour Pictures, 1969; (with M.H. Gabb) Human Kind: Foundations of Human Biology, 1966; (with M.H. Gabb) The Life of Animals with Backbones: Foundations of Invertebrate Zoology, 1966; (with M.H. Gabb) The Life of Animals without Backbones: Foundations of Invertebrate Zoology, 1966; (with M.H. Gabb) The World of Plants: Foundations of Botany, 1966; A Pictorial Dictionary of the Plant World: An Illustrated Demonstration of Terms Used in Plant Biology; with Over 400 Colour Pictures, 1967, rev. ed. as A Science Dictionary of the Plant World: An Illustrated Demonstration of Terms Used in Plant Biology, with Over 400 Colour Pictures, 1969; Visual Biology, 1968; Animal Communities, 1972; Concise Color Encyclopedia of Nature, 1972; (co-author) Field Guide to the Insects of Britain and Northern Europe, 1973; Animals in the Zoo, 1973; Life in the Zoo, 1976; Discovering Nature, 1977; Enjoying Nature with Your Family: Look, Learn, Collect, Conserve, Explore the Wildlife of Town and Country in Fascinating Projects and Experiments, 1977; The Natural History of the Garden, 1977; The Family Naturalist, 1977; (ed.) The World of Animals, 1978; Discovering Animals, 1978; Pictorial Atlas of Animals, 1978; Purnell's Find out about Natural Wonders of the World, 1978; Purnell's Nature All Around, 1978; Guide to Wild Flowers, 1979; Killers of the Wild, 1979; Pouched Mammals, 1979; (contrib.) Insects: An Illustrated Survey of the Most Successful Animals on Earth, 1979; (ed.) Woods & Forests, 1979; (ed.) Lakes & Rivers, 1979; Rand McNally's Picture Atlas of Animals, 1980; (ed.) Animals of the African Plains, 1980; (ed.) Birds of Prey, 1980; (ed.) Mountain Animals, 1980; (ed.) Prehistoric Life, 1980; (ed.) The Frozen North, 1981; (ed.) Animals of the Seashore, 1981; (with M. Atkinson) Child's Book of Birds and Flowers, 1981; (with M. Atkinson) Child's Book of Butterflies and Flowers, 1981; (with B. Hargreaves) Collins Gem Guide to Butterflies and Moths, 1981; Natural History of Britain and Europe, 1982; (with L. Butler) The Seasons, 1982; Mushrooms, 1983; Garden Birds of the World, 1983; Concise Pocket Dictionary of Nature, 1984; (ed.) Dictionary of Animals, 1984; Exploring the Countryside, vol. I: Parks and Gardens, vol. II: Woodlands, vol. III: Seashore, Ponds and Streams, vol. IV: Fields and Hedgerows, 1985; (with W.G. Teagle) The Country Life Guide to the Wildlife in Towns and Cities, 1986; The Living Garden, 1986; The Collins Guide to the Insects of Britain and Western Europe, 1986; Collins Gem Guide to Insects, 1986; Garden Creepy Crawlies, 1986; (ed.) Kingfisher Field Guide to the Plant Life of Britain and Europe, 1987; (ed.) Kingfisher Field Guide to the Wildlife of Britain and Europe, 1987; Collins New Generation Guide to the Butterflies and Day-Flying Moths of Britain and Europe, 1989; Countryside Handbook, 1990; All About Baby Animals, 1990; Frog, 1991; Shark, 1991; Snake, 1991; Spider, 1991; Ant, 1991; Butterfly, 1991; Desert Animals, 1992; Grassland Animals, 1992; Ocean Animals, 1992; Rainforest Animals, 1992; (ed.) The Kingfisher Illustrated Encyclopedia of Animals: From Aardvark to Zorille: And 2, 000 Other Animals, 1992; All Kinds of Animals, 1993; Questions and Answers About Forest Animals, 1994; Questions and Answers About Freshwater Animals, 1994; Questions and Answers About Polar Animals, 1994; Questions and Answers About Seashore Animals, 1994; Baby Animals, 1994; Creepy Crawlies, 1994; How Bees Make Honey, 1997; (with P. Leraut) Photo-Guide des Papillons d'Europe, 1998; Plants and Planteaters, 2000; Poisoners and Pretenders, 2000; Predators and Prey, 2000; Partners and Parents, 2000; People and Places, 2001; Resources and Conservation, 2001; Butterflies, 2004; The World Encyclopedia, 2004; Attracting Wildlife to Your Garden, 2004; Creating a Wildlife-Friendly Garden, 2004; Complete British Insects, 2007; Domino Guide to the Insects of Britain and Western Europe, 2007; Creating a Bird-Friendly Garden, 2007; Amazing Insects: Images of Fascinating Creatures, 2008. STEP INTO NATURE SERIES: Around a Tree, 1984; By Ponds and Streams, 1984; By the Roadside, 1984; By the Sea, 1984; In Fields and Meadows, 1984; In the Garden, 1984; In the Woods, 1984; On Heath and Moor, 1984. **Address:** Mousehole, Mill Rd., Hundon, SU CO10 8EG, England.

CHIN-LEE, Cynthia D. American/Chinese (born China), b. 1958. **Genres:** Business/Trade/Industry, Children's Non-fiction, How-to Books, Children's Fiction, Young Adult Fiction, Gay And Lesbian Issues, Geography, Human Relations/Parenting, Self Help, inspirational/Motivational Literature, Picture/Board Books. **Career:** Freelance writer and consultant, 1983-; De Anza College, instructor, 1985-89; Santa Clara University, adjunct lecturer, 1989-93; professional speaker, 1991-; Palo Alto Adult School, teacher, 1996-97; Oracle Corp., documentation manager, 1999-2000, 2010-; i2 Technologies, documentation manager, 2000-02; Remedy-BMC Software Co., staff technical writer, 2003; Sun Microsystems, documentation manager, 2003-10. **Publications:** FOR CHILDREN: Almond Cookies and Dragon Well Tea, 1993; A Is for Asia, 1997; (with T. de la Pena) A Is for the Americas, 1999; Amelia to Zora: Twenty-Six Women Who Changed the World, 2005; Akira to Zoltan: Twenty-six Men Who Changed the World, 2006; Operation Marriage, 2011. FOR ADULTS: It's Who You Know: Career Strategies for Making Effective Personal Contacts, 1991; It's Who You Know: The Magic of Networking, in Person and on the Internet, 1998. **Address:** Oracle Corp., Rm. 1802, 4170 Network Cir., Santa Clara, CA 95054, U.S.A. **Online address:** cynthia_chin-lee@post.harvard.edu

CHINN, Carl. British (born England), b. 1956. **Genres:** History, Local History/Rural Topics, Politics/Government. **Career:** Bookmaker, 1980-84; University of Birmingham, lecturer in modern history and community historian, 1991-, professor of Birmingham community history, Birmingham Lives project, director. Writer. **Publications:** They Worked All Their Lives: Women of the Urban Poor in England, 1880-1939, 1988; Better Betting with a Decent Feller: Bookmaking, Betting and the British Working Class, 1750-1900, 1991; Homes for People: 100 Years of Council Housing in Birmingham, 1991; Birmingham: The Great Working City, 1994; Poverty Amidst Prosperity: The Urban Poor in England, 1834-1914, 1995; The Cadbury Story: A Short History, 1998; From Little Acorns Grow: 150 Years of West Bromwich Building Society, 1999: (with S. Thorne) Proper Brummie: A Dictionary of Birmingham Words and Sayings, 2001; Birmingham Irish: Making Our Mark, 2003; Brum and Brummies, vol. II, 2001, vol. III, 2003; Birmingham: Bibliography of a City, 2003; The Streets of Brum, 2003. Contributor to books and periodicals. **Address:** 10 Hollybank Rd., Kings Heath, Birmingham, B13 0RJ, England. **Online address:** carl@brummagem.fsnet.co.uk

CHINODYA, Shimmer. (B. S. Chiraska). Zimbabwean (born Zimbabwe), b. 1957. **Genres:** Novels, Novellas/Short Stories, Children's Fiction, Plays/Screenplays, Poetry, Young Adult Fiction. **Career:** Teacher, 1957; Curriculum Development Unit, editor-in-chief, 1983-; editor, publisher, 1988-94; St. Lawrence University, visiting professor of creative writing, 1995-96, distinguished visiting professor in creative writing, 1996-97; Zimbabwe Book Development Council, board director. Writer. **Publications:** Dew in the Morning, 1982; Farai's Girls, 1984; (ed.) Classroom Plays for Primary Schools, 1986; (as B. S.Chiraska) Child of War, 1986; Harvest of Thorns, 1989; Traditional Tales of Zimbabwe, Books 1-6, 1989; (ed.) Poems for Primary Schools, 1990; Everyone's Child, 1996; Can We Talk and Other Stories, 1998; Tale of Tamari, 2004; Chairman of Fools, 2005; Strife, 2006; Tindo's Quest, 2011. **Address:** Curriculum Development Unit, PO Box 133, Harare, 1, Zimbabwe.

CHINOSOLE. American (born United States), b. 1942. **Genres:** Autobiography/Memoirs. **Career:** San Francisco State University, dean, 1970-, professor of black studies and women's studies, 1970-2003, professor emerita, 2003-, Department of Women and Gender Studies, chair, 1989. Writer. **Publications:** (Ed.) Schooling the Generations in the Politics of Prison, 1996; The African Diaspora & Autobiographics: Skeins of Self and Skin, 2001. Contributor to periodicals. **Address:** Department of Women and Gender Studies, San Francisco State University, HUM 315, 1600 Holloway Ave., San Francisco, CA 94132, U.S.A.

CHINOY, Mike. American (born United States), b. 1952. **Genres:** Communications/Media, History. **Career:** CNN, reporter, 1983-87, Beijing bureau chief, 1987-95, Hong Kong bureau chief, 1996-2000, senior Asia correspondent, 2000-06; University of Southern California, Annenberg Center for Communication, visiting professor, senior fellow, 2006-; Pacific Council on International Policy, Edgerton Fellow in Korean Security, 2006-. Journalist and researcher. **Publications:** China Live: Two Decades in the Heart of the Dragon, 1997, rev. ed. as China Live: People Power and the Television Revolution, 1999; Meltdown: The Inside Story of the North Korean Nuclear Crisis, 2008. **Address:** Annenberg School for Communication & Journalism, University of Southern California, 3502 Watt Way, Los Angeles, CA 90089-0281, U.S.A. **Online address:** mchinoy@pacificcouncil.org

CHIOCCA, Olindo Romeo. Canadian (born Canada), b. 1959. **Genres:** Food And Wine, Young Adult Non-fiction, Biography, Novels, History, Humor/Satire, Autobiography/Memoirs. **Career:** Writer, engineer and photographer. **Publications:** Dinner Wit Da Dons (cookbook), 1999; Mobsters and Thugs: Quotes From the Underworld (nonfiction), 2000; College Street, 2005. **Address:** 4323 Stanley St., Nelson, BC V1L 1P9, Canada. **Online address:** mata_hari@uniserve.com

CHIPMAN, Bruce Lewis. American (born United States), b. 1946. **Genres:** Film, Social Commentary, Adult Non-fiction, Literary Criticism And History, Novellas/Short Stories. **Career:** Tufts University, instructor in American literature, 1969-73, faculty adviser, 1970-73; Tatnall School, head of English department and teacher of literature and creative writing, 1973-, now emeritus head of English; University of Delaware, part-time lecturer, lecturer in English, 1977-, adjunct associate professor of English; University of Khartoum, Fulbright lectureship, 1983. Writer. **Publications:** (Ed. and intro.) Hardening Rock: An Organic Anthology of the Adolescence of Rock'n Roll, 1972; Into America's Dream-Dump: A Postmodern Study of the Hollywood Novel, 1999. Contributor to magazines and periodicals. **Address:** Department of English, Tatnall School, 1501 Barley Mill Rd., Wilmington, DE 19807, U.S.A. **Online address:** chipman@tatnall.org

CHIPMAN, Donald. (Melvin Chapman). American (born United States), b. 1928. **Genres:** History. **Career:** Teacher, 1955-57; University of Washington, visiting professor of history, 1962; Fort Hays Kansas State College, assistant professor of history, 1962-64; University of North Texas, associate professor, 1964-67, professor of history, 1967-2002, professor emeritus, 2002-; University of San Francisco, visiting professor, 1970. Writer. **Publications:** Nuño de Guzmán and the Province of Pánuco in New Spain 1518-1533, 1967; (with R. Campbell and R. Calvert) Dallas Cowboys and the NFL, 1970; Spanish Texas, 1519-1821, 1992, (with H.D. Joseph) rev. ed., 2010; Texas en la Época Colonial, 1992; (with H.D. Joseph) Notable Men and Women of Spanish Texas, 1999; (with H.D. Joseph) Explorers and Settlers of Spanish Texas, 2001; Moctezuma's Children: Aztec Royalty Under Spanish Rule, 1520-1700, 2005. Contributor of articles and journals. **Address:** Department of History, University of North Texas, 1155 Union Cir., Ste. 310650, Denton, TX 76203, U.S.A. **Online address:** dchipman@unt.edu

CHIPPENDALE, Lisa A. American (born United States) **Genres:** Young Adult Fiction, Novels, Children's Non-fiction, Biography, Autobiography/Memoirs. **Career:** TV Guide Magazine, editorial assistant, 1992-93; American Association for Cancer Research, staff editor, 1993-96, senior staff editor, 1996; Chelsea House Publishers, senior production editor, 1996-99; freelance writer and editor, 1998-; Dream Chaser Enterprises, senior editor, 1999-2000; Strategic Communications & Planning, editorial manager, 2000-. **Publications:** The San Francisco Earthquake of 1906, 2001; Triumph of the Imagination: The Story of Writer J.K. Rowling, 2002; Yo-Yo Ma: A Cello Superstar Brings Music to the World, 2004. **Address:** c/o Author Mail, Enslow Publishers, 40 Industrial Rd., PO Box 398, Berkeley Heights, NJ 07922-0398, U.S.A. **Online address:** fiddlechip@yahoo.com

CHIRA, Susan. American (born United States) **Genres:** Women's Studies And Issues. **Career:** New York Times, staff, 1981-82, reporter, 1982-, bureau chief in Tokyo, 1984-89, deputy foreign editor, 1997-99, The Week in Review, editor, 1999-, Foreign Desk, deputy editor, national education correspondent, Albany Bureau, metropolitan reporter, Stamford Bureau, metropolitan reporter, editorial director of book development, 2002-04, foreign editor, 2004-. **Publications:** Cautious Revolutionaries: Occupation Planners and Japan's Post-War Land Reform, 1982; A Mother's Place: Taking the Debate About Working Mothers Beyond Guilt and Blame, 1998; A Mother's Place: Choosing Work and Family without Guilt or Blame, 1998. **Address:** HarperCollins Publishers, 10 E 53rd St., New York, NY 10022, U.S.A.

CHIRAS, Daniel D. American (born United States), b. 1950. **Genres:** Environmental Sciences/Ecology, Sciences, Biology, Earth Sciences. **Career:** Colorado Environmental Coalition, director, 1987-90, Environmental Health Committee, head, 1988-93, president, 1990-92; Center for Environmental Solutions, director, 1993-; Sustainable Futures Society, co-founder, 1993, president and director of sustainable development and policy analysis, 1993-; University of Colorado, adjunct professor; University of Denver, adjunct professor; University of Washington, visiting professor. Writer. **Publications:** Environmental Science: A Framework for Decision Making, 1985, 8th ed., 2010; (with O.S. Owen) Natural Resource Conservation: An Ecological Approach, 5th ed., 1990, (with J.P. Reganold) 10th ed., 2010; Beyond the Fray: Reshaping America's Environmental Response, 1990; Human Biology: Health, Homeostasis, and the Environment, 1991, 7th ed., 2012; Lessons from Nature: Learning to Live Sustainably on the Earth, 1992; Biology: The Web of Life, 1993; Study Skills for Science Students, 1994; (ed.) Regional Issues: Supplement to Environmental Science, 1994; (ed.) Voices for the Earth: Vital Ideas from America's Best Environmental Books, 1995; The Natural House: A Complete Guide to Healthy, Energy-Efficient, Environmental Homes, 2000; Essential Study Skills for Science Students, 2000; Solar House: Passive Heating and Cooling, 2002; (with D. Wann) Superbia!: 31 Ways to Create Sustainable Neighborhoods, 2003; (with C.R. Guelberth) The Natural Plaster Book: Earth, Lime and Gypsum Plasters for Natural Home, 2003; Human Body Systems: Structure, Function, and Environment, 2003; New Ecological Home: The Complete Guide to Green Building Options, 2004; EcoKids: Raising Children Who Care for The Earth, 2005; Homeowner's Guide to Renewable Energy: Achieving Energy Independence Through Solar, Wind, Biomass And Hydropower, 2006; Green Home Improvement: 65 Projects That Will Cut Utility Bills, Protect Your Health, Help the The Environment, 2008; (with R. Aram and K. Nelson) Power from the Sun, 2009; Power from the Wind, 2009; Solar Electricity Basics, 2010; (with M. Sagrillo and I. Woofenden) Wind Power Basics, 2010. Contributor to journals and newspapers. **Address:** 9124 S Armadillo Trl., Evergreen, CO 80439-6210, U.S.A. **Online address:** danchiras@msn.com

CHIRASKA, B. S. *See* **CHINODYA, Shimmer.**

CHIREAU, Yvonne P. (Yvonne Patricia Chireau). American (born United States), b. 1961. **Genres:** Theology/Religion. **Career:** Princeton University, teaching assistant & preceptor in religion department, 1989-91; Swarthmore College, assistant professor, 1993-99, associate professor, 1999-2007, professor of religion, 2007-, department of religion, chair, 2002-06, Asian American, Latino, Native American and African Heritage Concerns Committee, chair, 1999-. **Publications:** (ed. with N. Deutsch) Black Zion: African American Religious Encounters with Judaism, 2000; Black Magic: Religion and the African American Conjuring Tradition, 2003. **Address:** Department of Religion, Swarthmore College, 500 College Ave., Pearson 211, Swarthmore, PA 19081-1397, U.S.A. **Online address:** ychirea1@swarthmore.edu

CHIREAU, Yvonne Patricia. *See* **CHIREAU, Yvonne P.**

CHIROT, Daniel. American/French (born France), b. 1942. **Genres:** History, Politics/Government, Sociology. **Career:** Columbia University, lecturer in sociology, 1969; University of North Carolina, instructor, assistant professor of sociology, 1971-74; University of Washington, Henry M. Jackson School of International Studies, assistant professor, professor of sociology, 1975-80, professor of International studies and professor of sociology, 1980-, Job and Gertrud Tamaki professor of international studies; University of Texas, visiting professor, 2007. Writer. **Publications:** Social Change in a Peripheral Society: The Creation of a Balkan Colony, 1976; Social Change in the Twentieth Century, 1977; Social Change in the Modern Era, 1986; National Liberations and Nationalist Nightmares: The Consequences of the End of Empires in Eastern Europe in the 20th Century, 1993; How Societies Change, 1994; Modern Tyrants: The Power and Prevalence of Evil in Our Age, 1994; (with C. McCauley) Why Not Kill Them All?: The Logic and Prevention of Mass Political Murder, 2006, 2nd ed., 2010; Contentious Identities: Ethnic, Religious, and Nationalist Conflicts in Today's World, 2011. EDITOR: The Origins of Backwardness in Eastern Europe: Economics and Politics from the Middle Ages Until the Early Twentieth Century, 1989; The Crisis of Leninism and the Decline of the Left: The Revolutions of 1989, 1991; (with A. Reid) Essential Outsiders: Chinese and Jews in the Modern Transformation of Southeast Asia and Central Europe, 1997; (with M.E.P. Seligman) Ethnopolitical Warfare: Causes, Consequences, and Possible Solutions, 2001. **Address:** Henry M. Jackson School of International Studies, University of Washington, Thompson 201, PO Box 353650, Seattle, WA 98195-3650, U.S.A. **Online address:** chirot@u.washington.edu

CHISHOLM, Michael. British (born England), b. 1931. **Genres:** Economics, Geography, Politics/Government, Essays, Social Sciences. **Career:** Oxford University, departmental demonstrator in agricultural economics, 1954-59; University of London, Bedford College, assistant lecturer geography, 1960-62, lecturer in geography, 1962-64; University of Ibadan, visiting senior lecturer in geography, 1964-65; University of Bristol, lecturer in geography, 1965-67, reader in economic geography, 1967-72, professor of economic and social geography, 1972-76; Cambridge University, Department of Geography, professor, 1976-96, professor emeritus, 1996-, head of the department, 1976-84, St. Catharine's College, now emeritus fellow. Writer. **Publications:** Geography and Economics, 1966, rev. ed., 1970; Rural Settlement and Land Use: An Essay in Location, 1967, 3rd ed., 1979; Research in Human Geography, 1971; (contrib.) Applied Coastal Geomorphology, 1971; (with P.O Sullivan) Freight Flows and Spatial Aspects of the British Economy, 1973; (with J. Oeppen) The Changing Pattern of Employment: Regional Specialisation and Industrial Localisation in Britain, 1973; Human Geography: Evolution or Revolution?, 1975; Games Investors Play, 1981; Modern World Development: A Geographical Perspective, 1982; Regions in Recession and Resurgence, 1990; Britain on the Edge of Europe, 1995; Structural Reform of British Local Government: Rhetoric and Reality, 2000. EDITOR: The Future of the City Region: Report of the SSRC/CES Joint Conference Held on 6/7 July 1968, 1968; (with A.E. Frey and P. Haggett) Regional Forecasting: Proceedings of the Twenty Second Symposium of the Colston Research Society held in the University of Bristol, April 6th to 10th, 1970, 1971; (with G. Manners) Spatial Policy Problems of the British Economy, 1971; Resources for Britain's Future: A Series from the Geographical Magazine, 1972; (with B. Rodgers) Studies in Human Geography, 1973; (with R. Peel and Huggett) Processes in Physical and Human Geography: Bristol Essays, 1975; (ed. with D.M. Smith) Shared Space, Divided Space: Essays on Conflict and Territorial Organization, 1990. Contributor to journals. **Address:** Department of Geography, University of Cambridge, 5 Clerndon Rd., Downing Pl., Cambridge, CB CB2 2BH, England.

CHITHAM, Edward (Harry Gordon). British (born England), b. 1932. **Genres:** Children's Fiction, History, Literary Criticism And History, Biography, Education, Autobiography/Memoirs, Humanities. **Career:** Rowley Regis Grammar School, master in charge of Latin, 1956-61, head of library department, 1961-67; The Open University, part-time tutor, 1970-, assistant staff tutor, 1991-, associate tutor; Dudley College of Education, senior lecturer in English, 1973-77; The Polytechnic, faculty of education, senior lecturer, 1977-88; National Association for Gifted Children, education consultant, 1988-. Writer. **Publications:** The Black Country, 1972; Ghost in the Water, 1973; The Poems of Anne Brontë, 1979; (with T. Winnifrith) Brontë Facts and Brontë Problems, 1984; (with T. Winnifrith) Selected Bronte Poems, 1985; The Brontës' Irish Background, 1985; A Life of Emily Brontë, 1987; (with T. Winnifrith) Literary Lives: Charlotte and Emily Brontë, 1989; A Life of Anne Brontë, 1990; A Bright Start, 1995; (with D. Roper) The Poems of Emily Brontë, 1996; Birth of Wuthering Heights: Emily Brontë at Work, 1998; Brontë Family Chronology, 2003; Harborne: A History, 2004; Rowley Regis, 2006; West Bromwich: A History, 2009. **Address:** Educational Consultant, National Association for Gifted Children, Park Campus, Boughton Green Rd., Northampton, WM NN2 7AL, England.

CHITWOOD, Michael. American (born United States), b. 1958. **Genres:** Poetry, Documentaries/Reportage. **Career:** Independent Weekly, columnist, 1995-98; WUNC radio, commentator, 1995-; Universities of North Carolina, visiting lecturer, lecturer, freelance writer, fellow, 1989, faculty of English and comparative literature. **Publications:** Salt Works: Poems, 1992; Whet: Poems, 1995; The Weave Room, 1998; Hitting Below the Bible Belt: Baptist Voodoo, Blood Kin, Grandma's Teeth, and Other Stories from the South, 1998; Finishing Touches, 2006; From Whence: Poems, 2007; Spill: Poems, 2007; Poor-mouth Jubilee: Poems, 2010. Contributor to publications. **Address:** Down Home Press, PO Box 4126, Asheboro, NC 27204, U.S.A. **Online address:** mchitwoo@email.unc.edu

CHIVIAN, Eric. American (born United States), b. 1942. **Genres:** Medicine/Health. **Career:** Massachusetts Institute of Technology, staff psychiatrist, 1980-2000; Harvard Medical School, Center for Health and the Global Environment, founder and director, 1996, assistant clinical professor, 1988-; International Physicians for the Prevention of Nuclear War, co-founder, 1980, treasurer, director, Writer. **Publications:** Last Aid: The Medical Dimensions of Nuclear War, 1982; (ed.) Critical Condition: Human Health and the Environment, 1993; (ed. with A. Bernstein) Sustaining Life: How Human Health Depends on Biodiversity, 2008. **Address:** Center for Health and the Global Environment, 401 Park Dr., 2nd Fl. E, Boston, MA 02115, U.S.A. **Online address:** eric_chivian@harvard.edu

CHIZMAR, Richard T(homas). American (born United States), b. 1965?. **Genres:** Adult Non-fiction, Mystery/Crime/Suspense. **Career:** Cemetery Dance Magazine, founder, editor, editor-in-chief, publisher, 1988-, Cemetery Dance Publications, owner, 1992-; Chesapeake Films, co-founder. Producer. **Publications:** Midnight Promises, 1996; Blood Brothers, 1997. EDITOR: Cold Blood, 1991; The Earth Strikes Back: New Tales of Ecological Horror, 1994; Thrillers, 1994; Screamplays, 1997; Monsters and Other Stories, 1998; (with W. Schafer) Subterranean Gallery, 1999; (with R. Morrish) October Dreams: A Celebration of Halloween, 2000; The Best of Cemetery Dance, 2001; Night Visions 10, 2001; Trick or Treat: A Collection of Halloween Novellas, 2001; Shivers, 2002; Shivers II, 2003; (with M. Schwartz) Shocklines: Fresh Voices in Terror, 2004; Cemetery Dance-A Fifteen Year Celebration, 2004; Shivers III, 2004; Legacies, 2006; Shivers IV, 2006; Shivers V, 2009; Shivers VI, 2010; Smoke and Mirrors, 2011; (with K. Laymon and S. Gerlach) In Laymon's Terms, 2011. Contributor to periodicals. **Address:** c/o Author Mail, Cemetery Dance Publications, 132-B Industry Ln., Ste. 7, Forest Hill, MD 21050, U.S.A. **Online address:** info@cemeterydance.com

CHMIELEWSKI, Wendy E. American/British (born England), b. 1955. **Genres:** Women's Studies And Issues, History. **Career:** Swarthmore College, Peace Collection, project editor, 1986-87, archivist, 1987-88, George R. Cooley Curator, 1988-, curator, lecturer in peace studies, 1991-96; Greater Philadelphia Women's Medical Fund, director, 1992-94. Consultant and writer. **Publications:** EDITOR: Guide to Sources on Women in the Swarthmore College Peace Collection, 1988; (with M. Klee-Hartzell and L. Kern and contrib.) Women in Spiritual and Communitarian Societies in the United States, 1993; (with M. Fischer, C. Nackenoff) Jane Addams and the Practice of Democracy, 2009; Women's Experiences Shaping Theory: Essays on Jane Addams, forthcoming. Works appear in anthologies. Contributor to journals. **Address:** Swarthmore College, 500 College Ave., Swarthmore, PA 19081, U.S.A. **Online address:** wchmiel1@swarthmore.edu

CHO, Margaret. (Moran Cho). Korean/American (born United States), b. 1968. **Genres:** Humor/Satire, Autobiography/Memoirs. **Career:** Writer, actor, comedian, producer and director. **Publications:** I'm the One that I Want (comedy special), 2001; I Have Chosen to Stay and Fight, 2005; I Hate Girls, forthcoming. **Address:** c/o Author Mail, Penguin Group, Riverhead Books Publicity, 375 Hudson St., New York, NY 10014, U.S.A. **Online address:** margaretcho@margaretcho.com

CHO, Moran. *See* **CHO, Margaret.**

CHOATE, Jean. *See* **CHOATE, Jean (Marie).**

CHOATE, Jean (Marie). (Jean Choate). American (born United States), b. 1935. **Genres:** History, Military/Defense/Arms Control. **Career:** Northern Michigan University, assistant professor, 1992-99; Coastal Georgia Community College, associate professor of general studies and history, professor of history, 1999-, now professor emeritus of history. Writer. **Publications:** Disputed Ground: Farm Groups That Opposed the New Deal Agricultural Program, 2002; Eliza Johnson, Unknown First Lady, 2004; Eliza Johnson in Perspective, 2006; At Sea Under Impressment: Accounts of Involuntary Service Aboard Navy and Pirate Vessels 1700-1820, 2010. **Address:** Department of General Studies, College of Coastal Georgia, 3700 Altama Ave., Brunswick, GA 31520-3632, U.S.A. **Online address:** jchoate@cgcc.edu

CHOCIOLKO, Christina. Canadian (born Canada), b. 1958. **Genres:** Ethics, Technology, Sciences, Earth Sciences. **Career:** Transport Canada, radio operator, 1977-78; Arctic Exploration Services Ltd., senior radio operator, 1979-83; MacDonald Dettwiler & Associates Ltd., hardward technologist for electro-optical products, 1984-85; British Columbia Institute of Technology, assistant instructor in microelectronics, 1985-86; University of British Columbia, research assistant in international relations, 1989; Simon Fraser University, Centre for Policy Research on Science and Technology, research director, 1990-94; Queen's University, research associate in environmental policies, 1994-, instructor in policy studies, 1995. Writer. **Publications:** (With W. Leiss) Risk and Responsibility, 1994. Contributor to periodicals. **Address:** Department of Microbiology & Immunology, University of British Columbia, Rm. 300, Wesbrook Bldg., 6174 University Blvd., Vancouver, BC V6T 1Z3, Canada. **Online address:** chociolk@interchange.ubc.ca

CHOCOLATE, Debbi. (Deborah M. Newton Chocolate). American (born United States), b. 1954. **Genres:** Children's Fiction, Children's Non-fiction, Picture/Board Books, Novels. **Career:** Riverside Publishing Co., editor, 1978-90; Oak Park Public Schools, Youth Authors Conference, writing workshop leader, 1985-95; Triton College, English instructor, 1990-92; Columbia College, faculty. **Publications:** NEATE to the Rescue!, 1992; Elizabeth's Wish, 1994; On the Day I Was Born, 1995; A Very Special Kwanzaa, 1996; Kente Colors, 1996; The Piano Man, 1998; Pigs Can Fly!: The Adventures of Harriet Pig and Friends, 2004; El Barrio!, 2009. AS DEBORAH M. NEWTON CHOCOLATE: Kwanzaa, 1990; My First Kwanzaa Book, 1992; (reteller) Spider and the Sky God: An Akan Legend, 1993; (reteller) Talk, Talk: An Ashanti Legend, 1993; Imani in the Belly, 1994; Biddy Mason: The Open Hand, 2000; Keesha and the Family Party, forthcoming. **Address:** Henry Holt & Co., 175 5th Ave., New York, NY 10010, U.S.A. **Online address:** debbichocolate@hotmail.com

CHOCOLATE, Deborah M. Newton. *See* **CHOCOLATE, Debbi.**

CHODOROW, Nancy Julia. American (born United States), b. 1944. **Genres:** Essays, Psychology, Women's Studies And Issues, Sociology. **Career:** Wellesley College, instructor in women's studies, 1973-74; University of California-Santa Cruz, lecturer, 1974-76, assistant professor, 1976-79, associate professor of sociology, 1979-86; University of California-Berkeley, Institute for Personality Assessment and Research, associate research sociologist, 1981-83, associate professor, 1986-89, professor of sociology, 1989-, clinical faculty in psychology, 1999-2005, professor emeritus, 2005-; San Francisco Psychoanalytic Institute and Society, graduate psychoanalyst, 1994-; Boston Psychoanalytic Society and Institute, training and supervising analyst, 2006-; Harvard Medical School, lecturer on psychiatry, 2007-; Russell Sage Foundation, fellow. Writer. **Publications:** The Reproduction of Mothering, 1978; Feminism and Psychoanalytic Theory, 1989; Femininities, Masculinities, Sexualities: Freud and Beyond, 1994; The Power of Feelings: Personal Meaning in Psychoanalysis, Gender and Culture, 1999; Individualizing Gender and Sexuality: Theory and Practice, 2011. Contributor to periodicals and anthologies. **Address:** Department of Sociology, University of California-Berkeley, 410 Barrows Hall, Berkeley, CA 94720-1980, U.S.A.

CHODOS, Robert. Canadian (born Canada), b. 1947. **Genres:** Social Commentary, Theology/Religion, Translations, Novels, Local History/Rural Topics. **Career:** Last Post, parliamentary correspondent, news editor and editorial board, 1969-80; This Magazine, briefings editor, 1986-94; Temple Shalom Religious School, principal, 1986-96; Compass: A Jesuit Journal, editor, 1987-97; Canadian Forum, editor, 1998-2000; Voices across Boundaries, managing editor, 2002-; Inroads, managing editor, 2002-. Freelance book editor and translator. **Publications:** Right-of-Way: Passenger Trains for Canada's Future, 1971; The CPR: A Century of Corporate Welfare, 1973; (with P. Brown and R. Murphy) Winners, Losers: The 1976 Tory Leadership Convention, 1976; The Caribbean Connection: The Double-Edged Canadian Presence in the West Indies, 1977; (with P. MacFadden and R. Murphy) Your Place or Mine? (novel), 1978; (with R. Murphy and N. Auf der Maur) Brian Mulroney: The Boy From Baie-Comeau, 1984; (with A. Leis) Write All about It: A Basic Writing Workbook for Adults, 1986; (with E. Hamovitch) Quebec and the American Dream, 1991; (trans.) M. Venne, ed., Vive Quebec!: New Thinking and New Approaches to the Quebec Nation, 2001; (with J. Swift) Faith and Freedom, 2002; (trans.) S. Larocque, Gay Marriage: The Story of a Canadian Social Revolution, 2006. EDITOR: (with N. Auf der Maur) Quebec: A Chronicle 1968-1972; A Last Post Special, 1972; (with R. Murphy) Let Us Prey, 1974; Compass Points: Navigating the 20th Century, 1999. WITH R. MURPHY AND E. HAMOVITCH: Selling Out: Four Years of the Mulroney Government, 1988; The Unmaking of Canada: The Hidden Theme in Canadian History Since 1945, 1991; Canada and the Global Economy: Alternatives to the Corporate Strategy for Globalization, 1993; Lost in Cyberspace?, 1997; Paul Martin: A Political Biography, 1998. Contributor to periodicals. **Address:** Inroads, 280 Huron St., New Hamburg, ON N3A 1J5, Canada. **Online address:** leischod@rogers.com

CHODOS-IRVINE, Margaret. American (born United States) **Genres:** Illustrations, Picture/Board Books. **Career:** Writer and artist. **Publications:** SELF-ILLUSTRATED: Ella Sarah Gets Dressed, 2003; Best Best Friends, 2006. Illustrator of books by others. **Address:** Sheldon Fogelman Agency Inc., 10 E 40th St., Ste. 3205, New York, NY 10016, U.S.A. **Online address:** margaret@chodos-irvine.com

CHÖDRÖN, Pema. American/Canadian (born Canada), b. 1936. **Genres:** Self Help, Theology/Religion. **Career:** Karma Dzong, director, through 1984; Gampo Abbey, director, 1984-; The Pema Chödrön Foundation, chairperson. Writer and educator. **Publications:** The Wisdom of No Escape: And the Path of Loving-kindness, 1991; Start Where You Are: A Guide to Compassionate Living, 1994; Awakening Loving-Kindness, 1996; When Things Fall Apart: Heart Advice for Difficult Times, 1997; The Places that Scare You: A Guide to Fearlessness in Difficult Times, 2001; Comfortable with Uncertainty: 108 Teachings, 2002; No Time to Lose: A Timely Guide to the Way of the Bodhisattva, 2005; Practicing Peace in Times of War, 2006; (intro.) Always Maintain a Joyful Mind: And Other Lojong Teachings on Awakening Compassion and Fearlessness, 2007; The Pocket Pema Chödrön, 2008; Taking the Leap: Freeing Ourselves from Old Habits and Fears, 2009. **Address:** The Pema Chödrön Foundation, PO Box 770630, Steamboat Springs, CO 80477, U.S.A.

CHOI, Annie. American (born United States), b. 1976?. **Genres:** Human Relations/Parenting, Biography. **Career:** Writer. **Publications:** Happy Birthday or Whatever: Track Suits, Kim Chee and Other Family Disasters, 2007. Contributor to periodicals. **Address:** New York, NY , U.S.A. **Online address:** annie@annietown.com

CHOI, Frederick D. S. American (born United States), b. 1942. **Genres:** Business/Trade/Industry, Economics. **Career:** Bank of Hawaii, management trainee, 1965, 1966; Federal Deposit Insurance Corp., assistant bank examiner, 1967; University of Hawaii, assistant professor, 1972-76, associate professor, 1976-79, professor of accounting, 1979, head of department, 1980-81; University of Washington, visiting assistant professor, 1974-75; Japan-America Institute, lecturer, 1974, 1976-79; Oregon State University, distinguished visiting lecturer, 1978; ACL Intl., principal, 1978-; University of Connecticut, Health, Education and Welfare, distinguished visiting professor, 1980; National Center for Industrial Science and Technology Management Development, founding professor, 1980; New York University, professor of accounting and international business, 1981-87, research professor, 1988-95, Japan-American Business and Cultural Studies Program, director, 1981-83, Ross Institute of Accounting Research, director, 1983-85, chairperson of international business area, 1994-, Department of Accounting, Taxation and Business Law, head, 1983-86, International Business Department, head, 1994-95, Stern School of Business, vice dean, dean, 1995-2004, interim vice dean, distinguished service professor of business and chair of the department of accounting, Abraham L. Gitlow professor of accounting and international business, 2002-04, dean emeritus, 2005-, Department of Accounting and Taxation, chair, 2006-10, Undergraduate College, interim dean, 2010-11; Center for Japan-U.S. Business and Economic Studies, research associate, 1988-; Journal of International Financial Management and Accounting, founding editor. **Publications:** (With G.G. Mueller) An Introduction to Multinational Accounting, 1978; (co-author) Analyzing the Financial Ratios of the World's One-Thousand Leading Industrial Companies, 1981; Accounting and Control, 1982; (with J. Czechowicz) Assessing Foreign Subsidiary Performance: Systems and Practices of Leading Multinational Companies, 1982; (with G.G. Mueller) International Accounting, 1984, (with G.K. Meek) 7th ed., 2011; (with R.M. Levich) The Capital Market Effects of International Accounting Diversity, 1990; (contrib.) Interest Rate Swaps, 1990; (contrib.) Global Investing, 1992; (contrib.) Restructuring Japan's Financial Markets, 1993; (with Mueller) Globalization of Financial Accounting and Reporting, 1994; (co-author) Barriers to Business in the Single European Equity Market, 1996. EDITOR: (with G.G. Mueller) Essentials of Multinational Accounting: An Anthology, 1979; Multinational Accounting: A Research Framework for the Eighties, 1981; (with G.G. Mueller) Frontiers of International Accounting: An Anthology, 1985; (co-ed. and contrib.) Essays on the American Economy, Business and Finance for Japanese Executives, 1987; (with K. Hiramatsu) Accounting and Financial Reporting in Japan, 1987; Handbook of International Accounting, 1991, 3rd ed. as International Finance and Accounting Handbook, 2003; (with R.M. Levich) International Capital Markets in a World of Accounting Differences, 1994; International Accounting and Finance Handbook, 2nd ed., 1997. Contributor to journals. **Address:** Leonard N. Stern School of Business, New York University, Kaufman Management Ctr., Rm. 10-88, 44 W 4th St., New York, NY 10012, U.S.A. **Online address:** fchoi@stern.nyu.edu

CHOI, Hyaeweol. Korean (born Korea (South)), b. 1962. **Genres:** Adult Non-fiction, Bibliography, History, Young Adult Non-fiction. **Career:** Research Institute of Korean History, research fellow, 1987-89; Yonsei University, Korean Language Institute, instructor, 1988; Sangmyung Women's University, lecturer, 1988-89; State University of New York, Korean Language and Culture Program at World Languages Institute, assistant director, 1994; University of Kansas, East Asian Languages and Cultures, visiting assistant professor, 1994-98; Arizona State University, College of Liberal Arts and Sciences, assistant professor, 1998-2002, associate professor, 2002-; Frontiers: A Journal of Women Studies, associate editor, 2008-09; Western Conference of the Association for Asian Studies, president, 2008-09; The Journal of Asian Studies, Korean book review editor, 2009-. Writer. **Publications:** (With P.G. Altbach) Publishing and Book Development in the Third World, 1980-1993: Bibliography and Analysis, 1993; An International Scientific Community: Asian Scholars in the United States, 1995; Gender And Mission Encounters in Korea: New Women, Old Ways, 2009. Contributor to journals. **Address:** School of International Letters & Cultures, Arizona State University, LL 448C, University Dr., Mill Ave., PO Box 870202, Tempe, AZ 85287-0202, U.S.A. **Online address:** hyaeweol.choi@asu.edu

CHOLDENKO, Gennifer. American (born United States), b. 1957. **Genres:** Humor/Satire, Literary Criticism And History. **Career:** Writer. **Publications:** Moonstruck: The True Story of the Cow Who Jumped Over the Moon, 1997; Notes from a Liar and Her Dog, 2001; Al Capone Does My Shirts, 2004; How to Make Friends With a Giant, 2006; Louder, Lili, 2007; If a Tree Falls at Lunch Period, 2007; Al Capone Shines My Shoes, 2009; A Giant Crush, 2011; No Passengers Beyond This Point, 2011; Al Capone Does My Homework, 2013; Putting the Monkeys to Bed, forthcoming. **Address:** c/o Author Mail, Putnam Publicity, 345 Hudson St., New York, NY 10014, U.S.A. **Online address:** choldenko@earthlink.net

CHOLODENKO, Marc. French (born France), b. 1950. **Genres:** Novels, Young Adult Fiction, Translations, Autobiography/Memoirs. **Career:** Poet, screenwriter and translator. **Publications:** Parcs, 1971; Le Prince: Portrait de L'artiste En Enfant, 1974; Le Roi Des Fées, 1974; Cent Chants à L'adresse De Ses Frères, 1975; Les états Du Désert, 1976; Dem Folgt Deutscher Gesang: Tombeau De Hölderlin, 1979; Les Pleurs: Ou, Le Grand oeuvre d'Andrea Bajarsky, 1979; Le Tentation du Trajet Rimbaud, 1980; 2 Odes, 1981; Meurtre, 1982; Mordechai Schamz, 1982; Histoire de Vivant Lanon, 1985; (trans.) W. Gaddis, Gothique Charpentier, 1988; Bela jai, 1989; 1983 M'eloignant m'en Revenant 1986, 1990; Métamorphoses: Autobiographie d'un Autre, 1992; (trans.) W. Gaddis, J.R., 1993; Le Poésie La Vie, 1994; (trans.) V.S. Naipul, La Traversée du Milieu, 1994; Quasi una fantasia, 1996; Quelques Petits Portraits de Ce Monde, 1997; (trans.) E. White, Ecorché vif, 1997; Un Rêve Ou Un Rêve, 1999; Mon Héros: Je Ne Sais Pas, 2000; Imitation, 2002; NYC, 2004; Thierry, 2006; Glossaire, 2007; Filet, 2009; Deux cents et quelques commencements ou exercices d'écriture ou de lecture amusants, 2011. **Address:** c/o Author Mail, Editions P.O.L., 33, rue Saint-André-des-Arts, Paris, 75006, France.

CHOMSKY, Aviva. American (born United States), b. 1957. **Genres:** Economics, History, Politics/Government. **Career:** University of California, Department of Spanish, teaching assistant, 1985-87, Department of History, teaching assistant, 1987-90; Bates College, assistant professor of history, 1990-97; Institute for Health and Social Justice, faculty research associate, 1995-96; Salem State College, associate professor of history, 1997-99, Latin American Studies, associate professor of history and coordinator, 1999-2002, professor of history and coordinator, 2002-. Writer. **Publications:** West Indian Workers and the United Fruit Company in Costa Rica, 1870-1940, 1996; (ed. with A. Lauria-Santiago) Identity and Struggle at the Margins of the Nation-State: The Laboring Peoples of Central America and the Hispanic Caribbean, 1998; (ed. with B. Carr and P. Smorkaloff) The Cuba Reader: History, Culture, Politics, 2003; They Take Our Jobs!? And Twenty Other Myths about Immigration, 2007; (ed. with G. Leech and S. Striffler) The People Behind Colombian Coal: Mining, Multinationals and Human Rights/Bajo el manto del carbón: Pueblos y multinacionales en las minas del Cerrejón, Colombia, 2007; Linked Labor Histories: New England, Colombia, and the Making of a Global Working Class. 2008; A History of the Cuban Revolution, 2011. Contributor of articles to books and periodicals. **Address:** Department of History, Salem State College, Rm. 102F, Sullivan Bldg., 352 Lafayette St., Salem, MA 01970-5348, U.S.A. **Online address:** aviva.chomsky@salemstate.edu

CHOMSKY, (Avram) Noam. American (born United States), b. 1928. **Genres:** International Relations/Current Affairs, Language/Linguistics, Philosophy, Politics/Government, Essays. **Career:** Massachusetts Institute of Technology, Department of Linguistics and Philosophy, assistant professor, 1955-58, associate professor, 1958-61, professor, 1961-66, Ferrari P. Ward professor, 1966-76, institute professor, 1976-, emeritus professor of linguistics; Columbia University, visiting professor of linguistics, 1957-58; University of California, visiting professor of linguistics, 1966-67; Oxford University, John Locke lecturer, 1969; Cambridge University, Bertrand Russell Memorial lecturer, 1971; University of New Delhi, Nehru Memorial lecturer, 1972; University of Leiden, Huizinga lecturer, 1977; Stanford University, Kant lecturer, 1979. Syracuse University, visiting professor of linguistics, 1982. Writer. **Publications:** Syntactic Structures, 1957; Current Issues in Linguistic Theory, 1964; Aspects of the Theory of Syntax, 1965; Cartesian Linguistics: A Chapter in the History of Rationalist Thought, 1966, 3rd ed., 2009; Topics in the Theory of Generative Grammar, 1966; (with M. Halle) Sound Patterns of English, 1968; Language and Mind, 1968; Sobre la responsabilidad de los intelectuales, 1968; American Power and the New Mandarins, 1969; Amérique et sesnouveaux mandarins, 1969; (contrib.) Trials of the Resistance, 1970; At War with Asia, 1970; Two Essays on Cambodia, 1970; Problems of Knowledge and Freedom, 1971; Studies on Semantics in Generative Grammar, 1972; The Backroom Boys, 1973; (with E.S. Herman) Counter-revolutionary Violence, 1973; For Reasons of State, 1973; (with M. Halle) Principes de phonologie générative, 1973; Peace in the Middle East?: Reflections on Justice and Nationhood, 1974; The Logical Structure of Linguistic Theory, 1975; Reflections on Language, 1975; Essays on Form and Interpretation, 1977; (co-author) Chomsky o Skinner?: la genesis del lenguaje, 1977; (co-author) Langue: Théorie générative étendue, 1977; Lingwistyka i filozofia: wspólczesny spór o filozoficzne zalozeniateorii je'zyka, 1977; Cuestiones de forma y de interpretación, 1977; Human Rights and American Foreign Policy, 1978; (ed.) Carter y lalógica del imperialismo, 1978; Intellectuals and the State, 1978; Lashon ya-ruah?, 1978; De intellectuelen en de staat, 1978; (with E.S. Herman) Political Economy of Human Rights, 2 vols., 1979; (with E.S. Herman) After the Cataclysm, Postwar Indochina and the Reconstruction of Imperial Ideology, 1979; Language and Responsibility: Based on Conversations with Mitsou Ronat, 1979; The Washington Connection and Third World Fascism, 1979; Morphophonemics of Modern Hebrew, 1979; Rules and Representations, 1980; Lectures on Government and Binding, 1981, 7th ed., 1993; Radical Priorities, 1981, 3rd ed., 2003; Towards a New Cold War: Essays on the Current Crisis and How We Got There, 1982; Some Concepts and Consequences of the Theory of Government and Binding, 1982; (with J. Steele and J. Gittings) Superpowers in Collision: The Cold War Now, 1982; Fateful Triangle: The U.S., Israel and the Palestinians, 1983, rev. ed., 1999; Réponses inédites: à mes détracteurs parisiens, 1984; Turning the Tide: U.S. Intervention in Central America and the Struggle for Peace, 1985; Knowledge of Language: Its Nature, Origin, and

Use, 1986; Barriers, 1986; Pirates and Emperors: International Terrorism in the Real World, 1986; On Power and Ideology, 1987; Quinta libertad: lapolítica internacional y de seguridad de Estados Unidos, 1987; Language in a Psychological Setting, 1987; Language and Problems of Knowledge, 1987; The Chomsky Reader, 1987; The Culture of Terrorism, 1988; Language and Politics, 1988; Nuestra pequeña región de poraquí: política de seguridad de los Estados Unidos, 1988; Manufacturing Consent: The Political Economy of the Mass Media, 1988; Necessary Illusions: Thought Control in Democratic Societies, 1989; Terrorizing the Neighborhood: American Foreign Policy in the Post Cold War Era, 1991; Deterring Democracy, 1991; Chronicles of Dissent, 1992; What Uncle Sam Really Wants, 1992; Year 501: The Conquest Continues, 1993; Rethinking Camelot: JFK, the Vietnam War, and U.S. Political Culture, 1993; Prosperous Few and the Restless Many, 1993; Letters from Lexington: Reflections on Propaganda, 1993; World Order and Its Rules: Variations on Some Themes, 1993; Language and Thought, 1994; Keeping the Rabble in Line: Interviews with David Barsamian, 1994; Secrets, Lies, and Democracy, 1994; World Orders, Old and New, 1994, rev. ed., 1996; The Minimalist Program, 1995; Prospects for Democracy, 1995; Powers and Prospects: Reflections on Human Nature and the Social Order, 1996; Perspectives on Power: Reflections on Human Nature and the Social Order, 1996; Class Warfare: Interviews with David Barsamian, 1996; (with H. Dieterich) Sociedadglobal: educación, mercado y democracia, 1996; Cold War & the University: Toward an Intellectual History of the Postwar Years, 1997; Media Control: The Spectacular Achievements of Propaganda, 1997; Objectivity and Liberal Scholarship, 1997; Common Good, 1998; On Language: Chomsky's Classic Works Language and Responsibility and Reflections on Language, 1998; (with E. Said and R. Clark) Acts of Aggression: Policing Rogue States, 1999; Profit Over People: Neoliberalism and Global Order, 1999; The New Military Humanism: Lessons from Kosovo, 1999; Umbrella of U.S. Power: The Universal Declaration of Human Rights and the Contradictions of U.S. Policy, 1999; New Horizons in the Study of Language and Mind, 2000; Architecture of Language, 2000; A New Generation Draws the Line: Kosovo, East Timor, and the Standards of the West, 2000; Rogue States: The Rule of Force in World Affairs, 2000; Chomsky on Miseducation, 2000; (contrib.) Gambito de torres: dos caras del terrorismo, 2001; Amerika Serikat dan dunia ketiga pasca perang dingin, 2001; (with D.Barsamian) Propaganda and the Public Mind, 2001; 9-11, 2002; Nature and Language, with an Essay on The Secular Priesthood and the Perils of Democracy, 2002; On Nature and Language, 2002; Understanding Power: The Indispensable Chomsky, 2002; Peering into the Abyss of the Future, 2002; Hegemony or Survival: America's Quest for Global Dominance, 2003; Chomsky on Democracy & Education, 2003; Middle East Illusions: Including Peace in the Middle East?: Reflections on Justice and Nationhood, 2003; Power and Terror: Post-9/11 Talks and Interviews, 2003; Towards a New Cold War: U.S. Foreign Policy from Vietnam to Reagan, 2003; Howard Zinn: A Radical American Vision, 2003; (with P. Farmer and A. Goodman) Getting Haiti Right this Time: The U.S. and the Coup, 2004; Chomsky on Anarchism, 2005; Government in the Future, 2005; Hated Political Enemy: Allen Bell Interviews, 2005; Imperial Ambitions: Conversations on the Post-9/11 World, 2005; (with M. Foucault) Chomsky-Foucault Debate: On Human Nature, 2006; Failed States: The Abuse of Power and the Assault on Democracy, 2006; Interventions, 2007; (with G. Achcar) Perilous Power: The Middle East and U.S. Foreign Policy: Dialogues on Terror, Democracy, War, and Justice, 2007; What We Say Goes: Conversations on U.S. Power in a Changing World: Interviews with David Barsamian, 2007; (with D. Barsamian)Targeting Iran, 2007; Essential Chomsky, 2008; (foreword) The European Union and Turkish Acccession, 2008; Sobre el anarquismo, 2009; Of Minds and Language: A Dialogue with Noam Chomsky in the Basque Country, 2009; (with J. Bricmont) Raison contre pouvoir, 2009; Selected Readings on Transformational Theory, 2009; Hopes and Prospects, 2009; (contrib.) Of Minds and Language, 2009; (contrib.) Chomsky Notebook, 2010; (co-author) La tendencia militarista del imperio, 2010; (with I. Pappé) Gaza in Crisis, 2010; (contrib.) Rethinking Race, Class, Language, and Gender: A Dialogue With Noam Chomsky and Other Leading Scholars, 2011; Power and Terror: Conflict, Hegemony, and the Rule of Force, 2011; L'université selon Chomsky, 2011; Permanence et mutations de l'université, 2011; Science of Language, 2012; Making the Future: Occupations, Interventions, Empire and Resistance, 2012; Occupy, 2012. Contributor to journals. **Address:** Department of Linguistics & Philosophy, Massachusetts Institute of Technology, 77 Massachusetts Ave., Bldg. 32-D808, Cambridge, MA 02139, U.S.A. **Online address:** chomsky@mit.edu

CHOPRA, Deepak (K.). American/Indian (born India), b. 1946. **Genres:** How-to Books, Medicine/Health, Self Help, Sports/Fitness, Novels, Young Adult Non-fiction. **Career:** Muhlenbert Hospital, intern, 1970-71; Boston Regional Medical Center, chief of staff, 1981-85; Maharishi Ayur-Veda Products International Inc., co-founder, 1985, sole stockholder, 1985-87, president, treasurer and clerk, 1985-88; Maharishi Ayur-Veda Health Center for Behavioral Medicine and Stress Management, director, 1985-93; Sharp Institute for Human Potential and Mind/Body Medicine, executive director, 1993-; Center for Mind/Body Medicine at L'Auberge, director, 1993-95; The Chopra Center for Wellbeing, co-founder, 1996-, director and co-chairman; The Chopra Foundation, founder; American College of Physicians, fellow; Kellogg School of Management, adjunct professor, academic director; The Gallup Organization, senior scientist. Physician, lecturer and writer. **Publications:** Creating Health: The Psychophysiological Connection, 1985, 2nd ed. as Creating Health: Beyond Prevention, toward Perfection, 1987, rev. ed. as Creating Health: How to Wake Up the Body's Intelligence, 1991; Return of the Rishi: A Doctor's Search for the Ultimate Healer (autobiography), 1988, rev. ed. as Return of the Rishi: A Doctor's Story of Spiritual Transformation and Ayurvedic Healing, 1991; Quantum Healing: Exploring the Frontiers of Mind/Body Medicine, 1989; (with R. Averbach and S. Rothenberg) Perfect Health: Maharishi Ayurveda, the Mind/Body Program for Total Well-Being, 1990; Perfect Health: The Complete Mind Body Guide, 1991, rev. ed., 2000; La perfecta salud: la guía completa del mente ycuerpo, 1991; Unconditional Life: Mastering the Forces That Shape Personal Reality, 1991, rev. ed. as Unconditional Life: Discovering the Power to Fulfill Your Dreams, 1992; Creating Affluence: Wealth Consciousness in the Field of All Possibilities, 1993, rev. ed. as The Seven Spiritual Laws of Success: A Pocketbook Guide to the Fulfilling of Your Dreams, 2007; Ageless Body, Timeless Mind: The Quantum Alternative to Growing Old, 1993, rev. ed. as The Essential Ageless Body, Timeless Mind: The Essence of the Quantum Alternative to Growing Old, 2007; The A-to-Z Steps to a Richer Life, 1994; Restful Sleep: The Complete Mind/Body Program for Overcoming Insomnia, 1994; Perfect Weight: The Complete Mind/Body Program for Achieving and Maintaining Your Ideal Weight, 1994; Journey into Healing: Awakening the Wisdom within You, 1994, rev. ed. as Journey into Healing: A Step-by-Step Personal Guide Compiled from the Timeless Wisdom of Deepak Chopra, M.D., 1994; Body, Mind, and Soul: The Mystery and the Magic, 1995; Perfect Digestion: The Key to Balanced Living, 1995; The Return of Merlin (novel), 1995; Living without Limits, 1995; Boundless Energy: The Complete Mind/Body Program for Overcoming Chronic Fatigue, 1995; The Way of the Wizard: Twenty Spiritual Lessons for Creating the Life You Want, 1995; The Path to Love: Renewing the Power of Spirit in Your Life, 1997, rev. ed. as The Path to Love: Spiritual Strategies for Healing, 1998; The Seven Spiritual Laws for Parents: Guiding Your Children to Success and Fulfillment, 1997; Overcoming Addictions: The Spiritual Solution, 1997; (ed. and trans. with F. Kia) The Love Poems of Rumi, 1998; Healing the Heart: A Spiritual Approach to Reversing Coronary Artery Disease, 1998; World of Infinite Possibilities, 1998, rev. ed. as A Deepak Chopra Companion: Illuminations on Health and Human Consciousness, 1999; Everyday Immortality: A Concise Course in Spiritual Transformation, 1999; (with M. Greenberg) Deepak Chopra's Lords of Light (adventure novel), 1999; On the Shores of Eternity: Poems from Tagore on Death and Immortality, 1999; (with R. Parks) Secrets of Inner Power: A Profile in Courage, 1999; (foreword) Hot Chocolate for the Mystical Lover: 101 True Stories of Soul Mates Brought Together by Divine Intervention, 2000; How to Know God: The Soul's Journey into the Mystery of Mysteries, 2000; (with M. Greenberg) Deepak Chopra's The Angel is Near (novel), 2000; (with D. Simon) The Chopra Center Herbal Handbook: Natural Prescriptions for Perfect Health, 2000; (ed.) The Soul in Love: Classic Poems of Ecstasy and Exaltation, 2001; (with D. Simon) Grow Younger, Live Longer: Ten Steps to Reversing Aging, 2001; The Deeper Wound: Recovering the Soul from Fear and Suffering, 2001; Soulmate (novel), 2001; Chopra Center Cookbook: Nourishing Body and Soul, 2002; The Daughters of Joy: An Adventure of the Heart (novel), 2002; Golf for Enlightenment: The Seven Lessons for the Game of Life, 2003; The Spontaneous Fulfillment of Desire: Harnessing the Infinite Power of Coincidence, 2003; The Book of Secrets: Unlocking the Hidden Dimensions of Your Life, 2004; Fire in the Heart: A Spiritual Guide for Teens, 2004; (with D. Simon) The Seven Spiritual Laws of Yoga: A Practical Guide to Healing Body, Mind, and Spirit, 2004; (with D. Simon and V. Abrams) Magical Beginnings, Enchanted Lives: A Holistic Guide to Pregnancy and Childbirth, 2005; Peace is the Way: Bringing War and Violence to an End, 2005; Life after Death: The Burden of Proof, 2006; Power, Freedom, and Grace: Living from the Source of Lasting Happiness, 2006; Teens Ask Deepak: All the Right Questions, 2006; (with D. Simon) Freedom from Addiction: The Chopra Center Method for Overcoming Destructive Habits, 2007; Buddha: A Story of Enlightenment, 2007; The Essential How to Know

God: The Soul's Journey into the Mystery of Mysteries, 2007; The Essential Spontaneous Fulfillment of Desire: The Essence of Harnessing the Infinite Power of Coincidence, 2007; The Third Jesus: The Christ we Cannot Ignore, 2008; Tercer Jesús, 2008; Why is God Laughing?: The Path to Joy and Spiritual Optimism, 2008; Jesus: A Story of Enlightenment, 2008; Ultimate Happiness Prescription: 7 Keys to Joy and Enlightenment, 2009; Reinventing the Body, Resurrecting the Soul: How to Create a New You, 2009; (with G. Chopra) Walking Wisdom, 2010; (with K. Tracy) 7 Spiritual Laws of Success for Kids, 2010; You with the Stars in Your Eyes, 2010; Soul of Leadership, 2010; (with D. Ford and M. Williamson) The Shadow Effect, 2010; Muhammad, 2010; Receta de la felicidad, 2011; (with L. Mlodinow) War of the Worldviews: Science vs. Spirituality, 2011; Conocer a Dios: el viaje del alma hacia el misterio de los misterios, 2011; Yasassaptasutri: saphalyasya sapta adhyatmikasiddhantah bhavatam svapnanam purtaye vyahariki margadarsika sampattisarjanadharita, 2011. Contributor to periodicals. **Address:** The Chopra Center for Wellbeing, 2013 Costa del Mar Rd., Carlsbad, CA 92009-6801, U.S.A. **Online address:** learn@chopra.com

CHORAFAS, Dimitris N. Greek (born Greece), b. 1926. **Genres:** Administration/Management, Business/Trade/Industry, Communications/Media, Engineering, Information Science/Computers, Money/Finance. **Career:** University of California, affiliate, 1953-56; Catholic University of America, School of Engineering and Architecture, faculty, 1956-63; IBM World Trade Europe Corp., affiliate, 1957-60; Booz, Allen & Hamilton International Inc., director of management information systems, 1960-61; Washington State University, Program in Information Science and School of Business Administration, visiting professor, 1965-67; Georgia Institute of Technology, visiting professor, 1968-69; University of Florida, visiting professor, 1980; University of Alberta, visiting professor, 1982; University of Vermont, visiting professor, 1982. Writer. **Publications:** Operations Research for Industrial Management, 1958; Statistical Processes and Reliability Engineering, 1960; The Functions of Research in the Enterprise, 1960; Computer Theory, 1960; Computer Applications in Industry and Commerce, 1961; Programming Systems for Electronic Computers, 1962; Industrial Strategy, 1962; New Methods of Economic Analysis, 1963; The Influence of the Computer on the Organization, 1964; Systems and Simulation, 1965; Control Systems Functions and Programming Approaches, vol. II, 1966; Simulation mathématique et ses applications, 1966; La Direction des Produits Nouveaux, 1967; An Introduction to Product Planning and Reliability Management, 1967; Sales Engineering: The Marketing of Technological Products, 1967; Managing Industrial Research for Profits: With Case Studies, 1967; Selecting the Computer System, 1967; Developing the International Executive, 1967; The Knowledge Revolution: An Analysis of the International Brain Market and the Challenge to Europe, 1968; How to Manage Computers for Results, 1969; The Communication Barrier in International Management, 1969; Management Development, 1971; Formation permanente des cadres; problèmes et solutions, 1971; Information Systems Design, 1972; Computers in Medicine, 1972; Management Planning, 1973; Die Kranke Geselschaft, 1974; Warehousing: Planning, Organising and Controlling the Storage and Distribution of Goods, 1974; Microform and Computer Output to Microfilm, 1976; Computer Networks for Distributed Information Systems, 1980; Data Communication for Distributed Information Systems, 1980; Interactive Videotex: The Domesticated Computer, 1981; Office Automation, the Productivity Challenge, 1982; Microprocessors for Management, CAD, CAM and Robotics, 1982; Money: The Banks of the 1980's, 1982; Information Systems in Financial Institutions: A Guide to Strategic Planning, Based on the Japanese Experience, 1983; DBMS for Distributed Computers and Networks, 1983; Local Area Networks, 1984; Interactive Message Services: Planning, Designing and Implementing Videotex, 1984; Designing and Implementing Local Area Networks, 1984; Telephony: Today and Tomorrow, 1984; Software Handbook, 1984; Handbook of Data Communications and Computer Networks, 1985; Management Workstations for Greater Productivity, 1985; Fourth and Fifth Generation Languages, 2 vols., 1986; Personal Workstations for Greater Productivity, 1986; Interactive Workstations, 1986; Personal Computers & Data Communications, 1986; Engineering Productivity through CAD/CAM, 1987; The New Communications Disciplines, 1987; Applying Expert Systems in Business, 1987; (with S.J. Legg) Engineering Databases, 1988; Membership of the Board of Directors: The Job Top Executives Want No More, 1988; Electronic Document Handling: The New Communications Architecture, 1988; Electronic Funds Transfer, 1988; (with H. Steinmann) High Technology at UBS, 1988; Implementing Networks for Banks and Financial Institutions, 1988; Handbook of Database Management and Distributed Relational Databases, 1989; Handbook of Relational Databases and DBMS, 1989; Bank Profitability, 1989; Local Area Network Reference, 1989; System Architecture and System Design, 1989; New Technology: A Survival Guide to New Materials, Supercomputers & Global Communications for the 1990s, 1990; Knowledge Engineering: Knowledge Acquisition, Knowledge Representation, the Role of the Knowledge Engineer and Domains Fertile to AI Implementation, 1990; Handbook of Management for Scientific and Technical Personnel, 1990; (with H. Steinmann) Intelligent Networks: Telecommunications Solutions for the 1990s, 1990; Supercomputers, 1990; The Handbook of Management, 1990; Risk Management in Financial Institutions, 1990; (with H. Steinmann) Expert Systems in Banking: A Guide for Senior Managers, 1990; New Technology of Financial Management, 1992; Expert Systems in Manufacturing, 1992; Using High Technology in Foreign Exchange and the Treasury Business, 1992; Treasury Operations and the Foreign Exchange Challenge: A Guide to Risk Management Strategies for the New World Markets, 1992; Simulation, Optimization and Expert Systems in Securities Trading, 1992; The Globalization of Money and Securities, 1992; The New Information Technologies: A Practitioner's Guide, 1992; (with E.M. Binder) Technoculture and Change, 1992; (with H. Steinmann) Object-Oriented Databases, 1993; Manufacturing Databases and Computer Integrated Systems, 1993; Measuring Return on Technology Investments, 1993; (with H. Steinmann) Solutions for Networked Databases: How to Move from Heterogeneous Structures to Federated Concepts, 1993; Chaos Theory in the Financial Markets: Applying Fractals, Fuzzy Logic, Genetic Algorithms, Swarm Simulation & the Monte Carlo Method to Manage Market Chaos & Volatility, 1994; Beyond LANs: Client/Server Computing, 1994; (with H. Steinmann) Off-Balance Sheet Financial Instruments: Maximizing Profitability and Managing Risk in Financial Services, 1994; Intelligent Multimedia Databases: From Object Orientation and Fuzzy Engineering to Intentional Database Structures, 1994; Financial Models and Simulation, 1995; (with H. Steinmann) Virtual Reality: Practical Applications in Business and Industry, 1995; Derivative Financial Instruments, 1995; Managing Derivatives Risk: Establishing Internal Systems and Controls, 1995; How to Understand and Use Mathematics for Derivatives: Establishing Internal Systems and Controls, vol., 1, 1995, vol. II, 1996; Rocket Scientists in Banking, 1996; (with H. Steinmann) An Introduction to Communications Networks and the Information Superhighway, 1996; The Money Magnet, 1996; Protocols, Servers and Projects, 1997; High Performance Networks, Mobile Computing and Personal Communications, 1997; Visual Programming Technology, 1997; Network Computers versus High Performance Computers, 1997; Internet Financial Services, 1998; Transaction Management: Managing Complex Transactions and Sharing Distributed Databases, 1998; Agent Technology Handbook, 1998; Cost-Effective IT Solutions for Financial Services, 1998; The Market Risk Amendment: Understanding the Marking-to-Model and Value-at-Risk, 1998; Understanding Volatility and Liquidity in Financial Markets, 1998; Commercial Banking Handbook, 1999; Setting Limits for Market Risk, 1999; Credit Derivatives and the Management of Risk, 2000; Managing Credit Risk, vol. II, 2000; New Regulation of the Financial Industry, 2000; Reliable Financial Reporting and Internal Control: A Global Implementation Guide, 2000; Enterprise Architecture: For New Generation Information Systems, 2001; Implementing and Auditing the Internal Control System, 2001; Integrating ERP, CRM, Supply Chain Management, and Smart Materials, 2001; Internet Supply Chain: Impact on Accounting and Logistics, 2001; Managing Operational Risk: Risk Reduction Strategies for Investment and Commercial Banks, 2001; Managing Risk in the New Economy, 2001; Liabilities, Liquidity and Cash Management: Balancing Financial Risks, 2002; Modelling the Survival of Financial and Industrial Enterprises: Advantages, Challenges and Problems with the Internal Ratings-Based (IRB) Method, 2002; Alternative Investments and the Mismanagement of Risk, 2003; Outsourcing, Insourcing and I.T. for Enterprise Management, 2003; Corporate Accountability: With Case Studies in Pension Funds and in the Banking Industry, 2004; Economic Capital Allocation with Basel II: Cost, Benefit and Implementation Procedures, 2004; Management Risk: The Bottleneck is at the Top of the Bottle, 2004; Rating Management's Effectiveness: With Case Studies in Telecommunications, 2004; Management of Bond Investments and Trading of Debt, 2005; Real-Time Enterprise, 2005; IFRS, Fair Value and Corporate Governance: The Impact on Budgets, Balance Sheets and Management Accounts, 2006; Strategic Business Planning for Accountants: Methods, Tools and Case Studies, 2006; Wealth Management: Private Banking, Investment Decisions and Structured Financial Products, 2006; Introduction to Derivative Financial Instruments: Options, Futures, Forwards, Swaps and Hedging, 2008; Risk Accounting and Risk Management for Accountants, 2008; IT Auditing and Sarbanes-Oxley Compliance: Key Strategies for Business Improvement, 2009; Globalization's Limits: Conflicting National Interests in Trade and Finance, 2009; Financial Boom and Gloom: the Credit and Banking Crisis of 2007-2009 and Beyond, 2009; Capitalism Without Capital, 2009; Education and Employment in the European Union: the Social Cost of Business, 2010; Energy, Environment, Natural Resources and Business Competitiveness: The Fragility of Interdependence, 2010; Business of Europe is Politics: Business Opportunity, Economic Nationalism and the Decaying Atlantic Alliance, 2010; Cloud Computing Strategies, 2011; Sovereign Debt Crisis: The New Normal and the Newly Poor, 2011. **Address:** Villa Romantic, Vitznau, 6354, Switzerland.

CHORBAJIAN, Levon. American (born United States), b. 1942. **Genres:** History, Organized Labor, Sociology, Sports/Fitness, Politics/Government, Translations, Humanities. **Career:** University of Massachusetts, Department of Sociology, professor of sociology, 1970-; Journal of Sport and Social Issues, office managing editor, 1982-86; ARENA Review, office managing editor, 1982-86; Zoryan Institute, director. **Publications:** (With P. Donabedian and C. Mutafian) The Caucasian Knot: The History and Geopolitics of Nagorno-Karabagh, 1994; (trans.) P. Verluise, Armenia in Crisis: The 1988 Earthquake, 1995; Conflict and Struggle, 2004. EDITOR: Readings in Critical Sociology, 1989; The Hand in Your Pocket May Not Be Your Own, 1991; (with G. Shirinian) Studies in Comparative Genocide, 1999; The Making of Nagorno-Karabagh: From Secession to Republic, 2001; (with D. Egan) Power: A Critical Reader, 2005; (with R. Grantham) Urban Society: The Shame of Governance, 2011. **Address:** Department of Sociology, University of Massachusetts, 101C Olney Hall, 1 University Ave., Lowell, MA 01854, U.S.A. **Online address:** levon_chorbajian@uml.edu

CHORLTON, David. British/Austrian (born Austria), b. 1948. **Genres:** Poetry, Essays, Translations, Novellas/Short Stories. **Career:** Arizona Composers Forum, board directors, 1987-89; Arizona Center to Reverse the Arms Race, board directors, 1990-92. Freelance writer and artist. **Publications:** Corn Dance, 1978; No Man's Land, 1983; Without Shoes, 1987; Village Painters, 1990; Outposts, 1994; (trans.) H. Raimund, Viennese Ventriloquies, 1998; Assimilation, 2000; Common Sightings, 2001; A Normal Day Amazes Us, 2003; Return to Waking Life, 2004; The Porous Desert, 2007; The Lost River, 2008; From the Age of Miracles, 2009, The Taste of Fog (novel) 2011. **Address:** 118 W Palm Ln., Phoenix, AZ 85003, U.S.A. **Online address:** rdchorlton@netzero.com

CHOTJEWITZ, David. German (born Germany), b. 1964. **Genres:** Young Adult Non-fiction. **Career:** Burgtheater, assistant director; Deutsche Schauspielhaus, assistant director. Writer. **Publications:** (Ed. and co-author) Precocious, 1984; Das Abenteuer des Denkens, Roman über Albert Einstein, 1994; Tödliche Safari, Roman, 1995; Roman aus dem Leben eines jungen Philosophen, 1996; Daniel Halber Mensch, 2000; Daniel Half Human: And the Good Nazi, 2004; Crazy Diamond, 2006. **Address:** c/o Author Mail, Simon Schuster Inc., 1230 Ave. of the Americas, New York, NY 10020, U.S.A. **Online address:** theaterplaystation@yahoo.de

CHOTZINOFF, Robin. American (born United States), b. 1958. **Genres:** Homes/Gardens, Autobiography/Memoirs, Social Sciences. **Career:** Westword, staff writer, 1985-. Journalist. **Publications:** People with Dirty Hands: The Passion for Gardening, 1996; People Who Sweat: Ordinary People, Extraordinary Pursuits, 1999; Holy Unexpected: My New Life as a Jew, 2006. **Address:** c/o Jaime Leifer, PublicAffairs, 1094 Flex Dr., Jackson, TN 38301, U.S.A. **Online address:** robin@robinchotzinoff.com

CHOU, Tsu Wei. American/Chinese (born China), b. 1940. **Genres:** Engineering, Technology, Education. **Career:** University of Delaware, Department of Mechanical Engineering, faculty, 1969-, Materials and Metallurgy Faculty chairman, 1976-78, Center for Composite Materials, associate director, 1977-78, National Science Foundation-Engineering Research Center, program director, 1985-90, University Research Initiative Program/Army Research Office, Co-PI, 1986-98, Jerzy L. Nowinski professor of mechanical engineering, 1989-2002, Department of Mechanical Engineering, acting chair, 1999-2000, chair, 2000-04, Pierre S. du Pont chair of engineering, 2003-; Argonne National Laboratory, visiting scientist, 1975-76; British Science Research Council, senior visiting research fellow, 1976; The University of the Witerwatersrand, visiting professor, 1977; National Commission for the Investigation of Space, visiting professor, 1981; DFVLR-Germany Aerospace Research Establishment, visiting professor, 1983; U.S. Office of Naval Research, liaison scientist, 1983; Tongji University, visiting professor, 1990; Tokyo Science University, visiting professor, 1990; Industrial Research Institute, visiting professor, 1997. Writer. **Publications:** (With J.R. Vinson) Composite Materials and Their Use in Structures, 1975; Microstructural Design of Fiber Composites, 1992. EDITOR: (with F.K. Ko) Textile Structural Composites, 1988; (with S.B. Biggers) Use of Composite Materials in Transportation Systems, 1991; Structure and Properties of Composites, 1993; (with J.R. Vinson) Proceedings of the American Society for Composites 9th Technical Conference, 1994; (co.ed.) Innovative Processing and Characterization of Composite Materials, 1995; (with W. Tzuchiang) Progress in Advanced Materials and Mechanics, 1996; Comprehensive Composite Materials, vol. I: Fiber Reinforcements and General Theory of Composites, 2000. **Address:** Department of Mechanical Engineering, University of Delaware, 126 Spencer Laboratory, Newark, DE 19716-3140, U.S.A. **Online address:** chou@udel.edu

CHOUAKI, Aziz. French/South African (born South Africa), b. 1955?. **Genres:** Novels, Literary Criticism And History. **Career:** Guitarist and writer. **Publications:** Argo, 1982; Baya, 1988; L'étoile d'Alger: roman, 1998; Passez àl'orange! tentatives d'écritures, 1999; Les Oranges, 1999; Aigle, 2000; El Maestro: tapuscrit du texte, 2000; El maestro suivi de lesoranges, 2001; (with B. Hadjih) Avoir 20 ans à Alger, 2001; Arobase: Roman, 2004; Nadia Ferroukhi: photographe, 2005; Star of Algiers: A Novel, 2005. **Address:** Graywolf Press, 250 3rd Ave. N, Ste. 600, Minneapolis, MN 55401, U.S.A. **Online address:** aziz.chouaki@mac.com

CHOUDHURY, Ashok. (Ashok Kumar Choudhury). American/Indian (born India), b. 1957. **Genres:** Engineering, Sciences, Art/Art History, Cultural/Ethnic Topics. **Career:** Oak Ridge National Laboratory, Metals and Ceramics Division, staff, 1989-92, Technology Transfer and Economic Development, commercialization manager, 1992-. Writer. **Publications:** Vacuum Metallurgy, 1990; (with C.R. Brooks) Metallurgical Failure Analysis, 1993; (with B. Sinha as Ashok K. Choudhury) All India Directory of Art, Culture and Allied Centres, 1995; (with B. Sinha as Ashok K. Choudhury) Encyclopaedia of Indian Writers: Akademi Laurels, 1996; (with B. Sinha as Ashok K. Choudhury) Bhasa, 2000; (with B. Sinha as Ashok K. Choudhury) International Guide to Art Research Materials, 2001; (with C.R. Brooks) Failure Analysis of Engineering Materials, 2002; (with B. Parida as Ashok K. Choudhury) Art and Art Libraries of India, 2006; (as Ashok K. Choudhury) Nurslings of Immortality: A Panorama of Modern Indian Writers, 2008. **Address:** Oak Ridge National Laboratory, 1 Bethel Valley Rd., PO Box 2008, Oak Ridge, TN 37830-8050, U.S.A. **Online address:** choudhurya@ornl.gov

CHOUDHURY, Ashok Kumar. *See* **CHOUDHURY, Ashok.**

CHOUDHURY, Masudul Alam. Indonesian/Canadian/Indian (born India), b. 1948. **Genres:** Area Studies, Economics, Third World, Money/Finance. **Career:** University of Chittagong, assistant professor of statistics, 1969-72; Ontario Ministry of Labour, research economist, Saskatchewan Department of Labour, manpower economist, 1977-79, manpower planning officer, 1978-79; University of Regina, adjunct lecturer, 1978-79; King Abdulaziz University, assistant professor of economics, 1979-83; Islamic Development Bank, Economics and Policy Planning Department, senior economist, 1983-84; University of Toronto, Ontario Institute for Studies in Education, visiting professor, 1984-85; Cape Breton University, professor of economics, 1985-, Centre of Humanomics, director; Oxford University, Saint Cross College, Centre for Islamic Studies, visiting fellow, 1990-91; Trent University, visiting professor, 1991; King Fahd University of Petroleum and Minerals, College of Industrial Management, professor of finance and economics, 1999-2001; Sultan Qaboos University, professor of economics and finance, through 2004; National University of Malaysia, visiting professor; Trisakti University, PPIEF, international chair. Writer. **Publications:** Manpower Planning and Policies for Saudi Arabia, 1982; From Growth to Development Manifesto for the South, 1984; Contributions to Islamic Economic Theory: A Study in Social Economics, 1986; Islamic Economic Cooperation, 1989; Paradigm of Humanomics, 1989; (with U.A. Malik) The Foundations of Islamic Political Economy, 1992; The Unicity Precept and the Socio-Scientific Order, 1993; The Principles of Islamic Political Economy, 1993; Theory and Practice of Islamic Development Cooperation, 1993; Comparative Development Studies: In Search of the World View, 1993; Economic Theory and Social Institutions: A Critique with Special Reference to Canada, 1994; Epistemological Foundations of the Islamic Economic, Social, and Scientific Order, 1995; (ed.) Alternative Perspectives in Third-World Development: The Case of Malaysia, 1996; Money in Islam, 1997; (co-ed.) Islamic Political Economy in Capitalist-Globalization: An Agenda for Change, 1997; Studies in Islamic Social Sciences, 1998; Studies in Islamic Science and Polity, 1998; Reforming the Muslim World,

1998; Comparative Economic Theory, 1999; The Islamic World View, 2000; A Dynamic Analysis of Trade and Development in Islamic Countries: Selected Case Studies, 2003; Explaining the Qur'an: A Socio-Scientific Inquiry, 2003; (with M.Z. Haque) An Advanced Exposition of Islamic Economics and Finance, 2004; Islamic World-System: A Study in Polity-Market Interaction, 2004; Science and Epistemology in the Koran, 2006; (with S.H. Hossain) Development Planning in the Sultanate of Oman, 2006; Universal Paradigm and the Islamic World-System: Economy, Society, Ethics and Science, 2007. Contributor to periodicals. **Address:** Islamic Economics & Finance, Trisakti University, Jl. Kyai Tapa Ste. 1, Grogol, Jakarta, 11440, Indonesia. **Online address:** masud_choudhury@capebretonu.ca

CHOUNG, James. American (born United States), b. 1973. **Genres:** Theology/Religion. **Career:** InterVarsity Christian Fellowship, divisional director; Onnuri Community Church, pastor; Asian American Ministries with Inter Varsity Christian Fellowship, national director, 2009. Writer. **Publications:** True Story: A Christianity Worth Believing In, 2008; Based on a True Story, 2008. **Address:** La Jolla, CA , U.S.A. **Online address:** james.choung@gmail.com

CHOW, Claire S. American (born United States), b. 1952. **Genres:** Psychology, Women's Studies And Issues, Children's Fiction. **Career:** John F. Kennedy University, adjunct faculty, 1994-; Pleasanton Counseling and Training, clinical supervisor of interns, 1997-; University California Berkeley Extension, faculty, 1999-; Grief Healing and Resource Center, founder. Writer. **Publications:** Leaving Deep Water: The Lives of Asian American Women at the Crossroads of Two Cultures, 1998. Contributor to periodicals. **Address:** c/o Barbara Lowenstein, Lowenstein-Morel Associates, 121 W 27th St., New York, NY 10001, U.S.A. **Online address:** clairechow@aol.com

CHOW, Kai-wing. American/Hong Kong (born Hong Kong), b. 1951. **Genres:** History, Cultural/Ethnic Topics, Reference. **Career:** University of Illinois, Department of East Asian Languages and Cultures, assistant professor, associate professor, 1988-, professor, Spurlock Museum, curator. Writer. **Publications:** The Rise of Confucian Ritualism in Late Imperial China: Ethics, Classics, and Lineage Discourse, 1994; (ed. with O. Ng and J.B. Henderson) Imagining Boundaries: Changing Confucian Doctrines, Texts, and Hermeneutics, 1999; (ed. with K.M. Doak and P. Fu) Constructing Nationhood in Modern East Asia, 2001; Publishing, Culture, and Power in Early Modern China, 2004; (ed. with C.J. Brokaw) Printing and Book Culture in Late Imperial China, 2005; (co-ed.) Beyond the May Fourth Paradigm: In Search of Chinese Modernity, 2008. **Address:** Department of East Asian Languages and Cultures, University of Illinois, 424 Greg Hall, 2090A Foreign Languages Bldg., 707 S Mathews Ave., Urbana, IL 61801-3625, U.S.A. **Online address:** kchow1@uiuc.edu

CHOW, Rey. American/Hong Kong (born Hong Kong), b. 1957?. **Genres:** Literary Criticism And History. **Career:** Brown University, postdoctoral fellow, 1986-87; University of Minnesota, assistant professor, 1987-91, associate professor, 1991-92; University of California, associate professor, 1992-95, professor of English and comparative literature, 1995-99; Brown University, Andrew W. Mellon professor of the humanities, 2000-. Writer. **Publications:** FILM: Primitive Passions: Visuality, Sexuality, Ethnography and Contemporary Chinese Cinema, 1995; Ethics after Idealism: Theory, Culture, Ethnicity, Reading, 1998; Sentimental Fabulations, Contemporary Chinese Films: Attachment in the Age of Global Visibility, 2008. CULTURAL CRITICISM: Woman and Chinese Modernity: The Politics of Reading between West and East, 1991; Writing Diaspora: Tactics of Intervention in Contemporary Cultural Studies, 1993; (ed.) Modern Chinese Literary and Cultural Studies in the Age of Theory: Reimagining a Field, 2000; The Protestant Ethnic and the Spirit of Capitalism, 2000; The Age of the World Target: Self-Referentiality in War, Theory and Comparative Work, 2006; The Rey Chow Reader, 2010. Contributed of articles to journals. Works appear in anthologies. **Address:** Department of Comparative Literature, Brown University, Marston Hall, PO Box E, Providence, RI 02912, U.S.A. **Online address:** rey_chow@brown.edu

CHOWDHURY, Bernie. American/British (born England), b. 1959. **Genres:** Documentaries/Reportage, Biography, Young Adult Non-fiction. **Career:** Columbia University, data communications technician, 1982-87, senior data communications technician, 1987-89; Goldman, Sachs and Co., telecommunications analyst, 1989-94, senior staff analyst, 1994-95; Immersed (magazine), founder, co-publisher and executive editor, 1995-; Divers Alert Network, diving instructor; National Association of Underwater Instructors, diving instructor; Professional Association of Diving Instructors, diving instructor; TDI, diving instructor. Writer. **Publications:** The Last Dive: A Father and Son's Fatal Descent into the Ocean's Depths (nonfiction), 2000. **Address:** PO Box 638, Chester, NY 10918-0638, U.S.A. **Online address:** bernie@immersed.com

CHOWDHURY, Subir. American/Bangladeshi (born Bangladesh), b. 1967. **Genres:** Administration/Management, Engineering. **Career:** Ciproco Computers Ltd., software and systems manager, 1989-91; Silocon magazine, founding editor, 1990; General Motors Corp., quality management consultant, 1993-97; author, 1996-; American Supplier Institute, executive vice president, 1997-; Automotive Excellence, editor-in-chief, 1997-99; ASI Consulting Group L.L.C., chairman and chief executive officer; Society of Manufacturing Engineers, fellow; Society of Automotive Engineers, fellow; American Society for Quality, chairman, 1999-2000; Engineering Society of Detroit, fellow; Royal Statistical Society, fellow; Quality Society Australia, fellow. **Publications:** (With K. Zimmer) QS-9000 Pioneers: Registered Companies Share Their Strategies for Success, 1996; (with G. Taguchi and S. Taguchi) Robust Engineering, 2000; Management 21C: Someday We'll All Manage This Way, 2000; The Power of Six Sigma: An Inspiring Tale of How Six Sigma Is Transforming the Way We Work, 2001; (with G. Taguchi and Y. Wu) The Mahalanobis-Taguchi System, 2001; The Talent Era: Achieving a High Return on Talent, 2002; Design for Six Sigma: The Revolutionary Process for Achieving Extraordinary Profits, 2002; Organization 21C: Someday All Organizations Will Lead This Way, 2003; The Power of Design for Six Sigma, 2003; Next Generation Business Handbook, 2004; The Ice Cream Maker: An Inspiring Tale About Making Quality a Key Ingredient in Everything You Do, 2005; (with G. Taguchi and Y. Wu) Taguchi's Quality Engineering Handbook, 2005. Contributor to periodicals. **Address:** ASI Consulting Group L.L.C., 30200 Telegraph Rd., Ste. 100, Bingham Farms, MI 48025, U.S.A. **Online address:** subir.chowdhury@asiusa.com

CHOYCE, Lesley. Canadian/American (born United States), b. 1951. **Genres:** Novels, Novellas/Short Stories, Mystery/Crime/Suspense, Science Fiction/Fantasy, Young Adult Fiction, Literary Criticism And History, Local History/Rural Topics, Natural History, Travel/Exploration, Autobiography/Memoirs, Essays, Humor/Satire, Children's Fiction. **Career:** Freelance broadcaster, 1972-; Referrals Workshop, rehabilitation counselor, 1973-74; Bloomfield College, coordinator, 1974; Montclair State College, instructor, 1974-78; City of Halifax, Continuing Education Program, creative writing instructor, 1978-83; St. Mary's University, instructor, 1978-82; Alternate Energy Consultants, writer and consultant, 1979-80; Dalhousie University, part-time instructor, instructor in English, 1981-, senior instructor of English, professor; Nova Scotia College of Art and Design, instructor, 1981; Mount St. Vincent University, instructor, 1982; Pottersfield Press, founding director; Canadian Writers' Foundation, board director. **Publications:** NON-FICTION: Edible Wild Plants of the Maritimes, 1977; An Avalanche of Ocean (autobiography), 1987; December Six/The Halifax Solution, 1988; Transcendental Anarchy (autobiography), 1993; Nova Scotia: Shaped by the Sea: A Living History, 1996, rev. ed., 2007; The Coasts of Canada, 2002; Famous At Last, 2002; Carrie Loses Her Nerve, 2003; Smoke and Mirrors, 2004; Sudden Impact, 2005; Deconstructing Dylan, 2006; Skunks for Breakfast: Based on a True Story, 2006; Driving Minnie's Piano: Memoirs of a Surfing Life in Nova Scotia, 2006; Peggy's Cove: The Amazing History of a Coastal Village, 2008; Seven Ravens: Two Summers in a Life by the Sea, 2009. EDITOR: Alternating Currents, 1977; (with P. Thompson) Atlantic Canada Community Energy Strategy Sourcebook, 1979; The Cape Breton Collection, 1984; Ark of Ice, 1992; (with R. Joe) The Mi'kmaq Anthology, 1997; Atlantica, 2001; Pottersfield Nation, 2004; Nova Scotia: A Traveller's Companion: Over 300 Years of Travel Writing, 2005; Nova Scotia: Visions of the Future, 2009. POETRY: (ed.) Chezzetcook (and stories), 1977; Re-Inventing the Wheel, 1980; Fast Living, 1982; The End of Ice, 1985; The Top of the Heart, 1986; The Man Who Borrowed the Bay of Fundy, 1988; The Coastline of Forgetting, 1995; Beautiful Sadness, 1998; Caution to the Wind, 2000; Typographical Eras, 2003; Revenge of the Optimist, 2004. FICTION: Eastern Sure, 1981; Downwind, 1984; Billy Botzweiler's Last Dance, 1984; Conventional Emotions, 1985; Coming Up for Air, 1988; The Second Season of Jonas MacPherson, 1989; Magnificent Obsessions, 1991; Ecstasy Conspiracy, 1992; Margin of Error, 1992; The Republic of Nothing, 1994; Dance the Rocks Ashore, 1997; World Enough, 1998; The Summer of Apartment X, 1999; Cold Clear Morning, 2001; Shoulder the Sky, 2002; Sea of Tranquility, 2003; The End Of The World As We Know It, 2007; The Book of Michael, 2008; Skate Freak, 2008; Book of Michael, 2008; Hell's Hotel, 2008; The Discipline of Ice, 2008; Running the Risk, 2009; Last Chance, 2009; Reaction, 2010; Reckless, 2010; Living Outside the Lines, 2010; Raising Orion, 2010; Random, 2010. SCIENCE FICTION: (ed. with J. Bell) Visions from the Edge (anthology), 1981; The Dream Auditor (stories), 1986; Trap Door to Heaven, 1996. YOUNG ADULT FICTION: Skateboard Shakedown, 1989; Hungry Lizards, 1990; Wavewatch, 1990; Some Kind of Hero, 1991; Wrong Time, Wrong Place, 1991; Clear-cut Danger, 1993; Full Tilt, 1993; Good Idea Gone Bad, 1993; Dark End of Dream Street, 1994; Big Burn, 1995; Falling through the Cracks, 1996; Couleurs Troubles, 1997; Roid Rage, 1999; Far Enough Island, 2000; Refuge Cove, 2002; Thunderbowl, 2004. FOR CHILDREN: Go for It Carrie, 1997; Carrie's Crowd, 1998; Carrie's Camping Adventure, 2001. **Address:** Pottersfield Press, 83 Leslie Rd., East Lawrencetown, NS B2Z 1P8, Canada. **Online address:** lesley@lesleychoyce.com

CHRIS, Cynthia. American (born United States), b. 1961. **Genres:** Adult Non-fiction, Natural History, Women's Studies And Issues, Medicine/Health, Social Sciences. **Career:** City University of New York, College of Staten Island, Department of Media Culture, assistant professor, 2004-, associate professor. Writer. **Publications:** (Contrib.) Women, AIDS, and Activism, 1990; Watching Wildlife, 2006; (ed. with S. Banet-Weiser and A. Freitas) Cable Visions: Television beyond Broadcasting, 2007. Contributor to periodicals. **Address:** Department of Media Culture, College of Staten Island, City University of New York, Rm. 224F, Bldg. 1P, 2800 Victory Blvd., Staten Island, NY 10314-6609, U.S.A. **Online address:** cynthia.chris@csi.cuny.edu

CHRIST, Carol P(atrice). American (born United States), b. 1945. **Genres:** Theology/Religion, Women's Studies And Issues, Social Sciences. **Career:** Columbia University, assistant professor of religion, 1972-77; San Jose State University, professor of religious studies and women's studies, 1977-88; Harvard Divinity School, visiting lecturer and research associate, 1986-87; Pomona College, distinguished visiting professor of religion, 1988; California Institute of Integral Studies, Rockefeller distinguished professor, 1994; Ariadne Institute for the Study of Myth and Ritual, director, 1995-; Journal of Feminist Studies in Religion, contributing editor. **Publications:** Diving Deep and Surfacing: Women Writers on Spiritual Quest, 1980; Laughter of Aphrodite: Reflections on a Journey to the Goddess, 1987; Odyssey with the Goddess: A Spiritual Quest in Crete, 1995; Rebirth of the Goddess: Finding Meaning in Feminist Spirituality, 1997; She Who Changes: Re-imagining the Divine in the World, 2003. EDITOR WITH J. PLASKOW: Womanspirit Rising: A Feminist Reader in Religion, 1979; Weaving the Visions: New Patterns in Feminist Spirituality, 1989. Contributor to periodicals. **Address:** Ariadne Institute, PO Box 5053, Eugene, OR 97405, U.S.A.

CHRIST, Henry I(rvine). American (born United States), b. 1915. **Genres:** Language/Linguistics, Literary Criticism And History, Sports/Fitness, Biography, Education. **Career:** Teacher, 1936-46; Andrew Jackson High School, Department of English, head, 1946-70; New York City Board of Examiners, assistant, 1946-70; Brightwaters Recreation Council, president, 1950-51. Writer. **Publications:** (With J. Carlin) English on the Job, 1944, (with J. Carlin and G. Older) 2nd ed., 1962; Winning Words, 1948, 3rd ed., 1967; (ed. with J. Shostak) Short Stories, 1948; (adaptor) Odyssey of Homer, 1948; (ed.) A Courageous Conquest, 1951; (with J.C. Tressler) Practice in English Usage, 1952; (with J.C. Tressler) English in Action, 1955; Grammar in Action, 4th ed., 1962; Modern English in Action 7-12, 1965; (with H. Potell) Adventures in Living, 1968; Adventures for Today, 3rd ed., 1968; Myths and Folklore, 1968; Modern Short Biographies, 1970, 3rd ed., 1979; Language and Literature, 1972; Short World Biographies, 1973; The World of Sports, 2 vols., 1975-77; The Challenge of Sports, 1978; The World of Careers, 1979; Going Places, 1980; (with M.E. Christ) World Biographies, 1987; (with M.E. Christ) American Biographies, 1987; Globe World Biographies, 1987; English for the College Boards, 1987; Greek Tragedies, 1992; English for the College Boards, 1994-95; Heroes and Villains, 1995; Themes in American and World Literature, 1997; Shakespeare for the Modern Reader, 2001; Lexicon for Lovers of Language, 2003. **Address:** PO Box 361062, Melbourne, FL 32936-1062, U.S.A.

CHRIST, Ronald. American (born United States), b. 1936. **Genres:** Architecture, Literary Criticism And History, Translations. **Career:** Manhattan College, assistant professor of English, 1961-69; Rutgers University, Livingston College, professor of English, 1969-96, professor emeritus, 1996-; Richmond College of the City University of New York, instructor, 1971, New School for Social Research, staff fellow, 1975-77; Indiana University, Full Responsibility/Faculty of Record, associate instructor, 1972-74; Center for Inter-American Relations, literature program, director, 1973-78; Halifax Community College, North Carolina Visiting Artist Program, visiting artist in visual arts, 1975-76; Wichita State University, instructor of painting and drawing, 1976-78, assistant professor of painting and drawing, 1978-85, associate professor of painting and drawing, 1985-97, professor of painting and drawing, 1997-, graduate coordinator; psychotherapist, 1978-; Lumen Books, co-publisher, 1983-; Lumen Inc., chairman; PEN New Mexico, president, 2002-. Writer and consultant. **Publications:** Narrow Act: Borges' Art of Allusion, 1969; Julio Alpuy, 1971; (contrib.) The Cardinal Points of Borges, 1971; (contrib.) Prose for Borges, 1972; (contrib.) Focus on Hitchcock, 1972; (contrib.) Writers at Work, 1976; (foreword) The Boom in Spanish American Literature: A Personal History, 1977; (with D.L. Dollens) Barcelona Pavilion, 1988; (with D. Dollens) New York: Nomadic Design, 1993; (ed.) The Brotherhood, 1998; (co-ed.) Bonevardi: Chasing Shadows, Constructing Art, 2007. TRANSLATOR: Tri-Quarterly Anthology of Contemporary Latin American Literature, 1969; Pippa Subway Can't Laugh, 1973; (with G. Kolovakos) Captain Pantoja and the Special Service, 1978; (with G. Kolovakos) The Cubs and Other Stories, 1979; (with Kolovakos and A. Wipfler) Chile: A Report to the Freedom-to-Write Committee, 1980; Under a Mantle of Stars, 1985; Augusto Torres, 1986; (with G. Waldman) Borges in/and/on Film, 1988; The Architecture of Jujol, 1997; E. Luminata, 1997; Soul's Infarct, 2009. **Address:** School of Art and Design, Wichita State University, Ctr. 306, 1845 Fairmount St., PO Box 67, Wichita, KS 67260-0067, U.S.A. **Online address:** ronaldchrist@wichita.edu

CHRISTAKIS, Nicholas A. American (born United States), b. 1962?. **Genres:** Medicine/Health. **Career:** University of Chicago, professor of medicine and sociology; Harvard Medical School, Department of Health Care Policy, professor, Department of Medicine, professor; Harvard University Faculty of Arts and Sciences, Department of Sociology, professor. Writer, physician and social scientist. **Publications:** Death Foretold: Prophecy and Prognosis in Medical Care, 1999; (ed. with P. Glare) Prognosis in Advanced Cancer, 2008; (with J. H. Fowler) Connected: The Surprising Power of Our Social Networks and How They Shape Our Lives, 2009 as Connected: Amazing Power of Our Social Networks and How They Shape Our Lives, 2010. Contributor of articles to periodicals. **Address:** Department of Health Care Policy, Harvard Medical School, 180 Longwood Ave., Boston, MA 02115-5899, U.S.A. **Online address:** christak@hcp.med.harvard.edu

CHRISTE, Ian. American/Swiss (born Switzerland) **Genres:** Adult Non-fiction, History, Music. **Career:** Bazillion Points, publisher, 2007-. Musician and writer. **Publications:** (With J. Cooper) Voter Registration and the States: Effective Policy Approaches to Increasing Participation, 1991; Sound of the Beast: The Complete Headbanging History of Heavy Metal, 2003; Everybody Wants Some: The Van Halen Saga, 2007. Contributor to magazines. **Address:** Bazillion Points Publishing, 61 Greenpoint Ave., Ste. 504, Brooklyn, NY 11222, U.S.A. **Online address:** ian@soundofthebeast.com

CHRISTENSEN, Allan Conrad. Italian/American (born United States), b. 1940. **Genres:** Literary Criticism And History. **Career:** Fulbright fellow, 1960-63; University of California, assistant professor of English, 1967-73; Nineteenth-Century Fiction, assistant editor, 1970-73; New School, lecturer, 1973-81; John Cabot University, adjunct professor of English, 1981-2005, professor emeritus, 2005-, chairman. Writer. **Publications:** Edward Bulwer-Lytton: The Fiction of New Regions, 1976; A European Version of Victorian Fiction: The Novels of Giovanni Ruffini, 1996; (co-author) The Challenge of Keats: Bicentenary Essays, 2001; (ed. and intro.) The Subverting Vision of Bulwer Lytton: Bicentenary Reflections, 2004; Nineteenth-Century Narratives of Contagion: Our Feverish Contact, 2005. Contributor to journals. **Address:** Department of English Language and Literature, John Cabot University, 233 Via della Lungara, Rome, 00165, Italy. **Online address:** allan.christensen@tin.it

CHRISTENSEN, Damascene. (Hieromonk Damascene). American (born United States), b. 1961. **Genres:** Theology/Religion, History, Biography, Autobiography/Memoirs, Theology/Religion. **Career:** Priest, monk and writer. **Publications:** Not of This World: The Life and Teaching of Fr. Seraphim Rose: Pathfinder to the Heart of Ancient Christianity, 1993; (as Hieromonk Damascene) Christ the Eternal Tao, 1999; (as Hieromonk Damascene) Father Seraphim Rose: His Life and Works, 2003. Contributor to periodicals. **Address:** St. Herman Monastery, PO Box 70, Platina, CA 96076, U.S.A.

CHRISTENSEN, Kate. American (born United States), b. 1962. **Genres:** Novels, Humanities. **Career:** Writer and educator. **Publications:** In the

Drink, 1999; Jeremy Thrane, 2001; The Epicure's Lament: A Novel, 2004; The Great Man: A Novel, 2007; Trouble: A Novel, 2008; The Astral, 2010. **Address:** c/o Nick Dewey, Doubleday, Random House, 1745 Broadway, New York, NY 10019, U.S.A.

CHRISTENSEN, Kathleen E(lizabeth). American (born United States), b. 1951. **Genres:** Psychology. **Career:** Urban Institute, policy analyst, 1973-75; City University of New York, assistant professor, associate professor, professor of psychology, 1981-99; Alfred P. Sloan Foundation, director of family-work research program, 1995-. Writer. **Publications:** (Co-author)State-required Impact Evaluation of Land Developments: An Initial Look at Current Practices and Key Issues, 1974; Social Impacts of Land Development: An Initial Approach for Estimating Impacts on Neighborhood Usages and Perceptions, 1976; The New Era of Home-based Work: Directions and Policies, 1988; Women and Home-based Work: The Unspoken Contract, 1988; Flexible Staffing and Scheduling in U.S. Corporations, 1989; (ed. with I. Altman) Environment and Behavior Studies: Emergence of Intellectual Traditions, 1990; Turbulence in the American Workplace, 1990; (co-author) Perspectives on Employment Stability, 1996; (ed. with K. Barker) Contingent Work: American Employment Relations in Transition, 1998; (ed. with B. Schneider) Workplace Flexibility: Realigning 20th-century Jobs for a 21st-century Workforce, 2010. **Address:** Alfred P. Sloan Foundation, 630 5th Ave., Ste. 2550, New York, NY 10111, U.S.A. **Online address:** christensen@sloan.org

CHRISTENSEN, Kit Richard. American (born United States), b. 1953. **Genres:** Philosophy, Social Sciences. **Career:** Indiana University-Purdue University, teacher of philosophy, 1980; Moorhead State University, teacher of philosophy, 1980-81; Bemidji State University, professor of philosophy, 1981-. Writer. **Publications:** The Politics of Character Development: A Marxist Reappraisal of the Moral Life, 1994; (ed.) Philosophy and Choice: Selected Readings from Around the World, 1999, 2nd ed., 2001; Nonviolence, Peace, and Justice: A Philosophical Introduction, 2010. Contributor to books and periodicals. **Address:** Department of Philosophy, Bemidji State University, Hagg-Sauer 310, 1500 Birchmont Dr. NE, Bemidji, MN 56601, U.S.A. **Online address:** kchristensen@bemidjistate.edu

CHRISTENSEN, Lars Saabye. Norwegian (born Norway), b. 1953. **Genres:** Novels, Poetry, Plays/Screenplays, Young Adult Fiction. **Career:** Writer. **Publications:** Historien om Gly: Dikt-Prosa, 1976; Amatoren, 1977; Ordbok, 1977; Kameleni mitt hjerte: dikt, 1978; Jaktmarker: Dikt, 1979; Billettene: roman, 1980; Jokeren, 1981; (ed.) Sa stor du er blitt: 11 norske fortellere, 1981; Paraply: Dikt, 1982; (ed. with A. Sandberg) Nar det tause far og paseg: student noveller, 1983; Graffiti, 1984; Beatles, 1984; Blodets band, 1985; Columbus' ankomst, 1986; Asteder, 1986; Sneglene, 1987; Amatøren, 1988; Herman, 1988; Stempler: Dikt, 1989; (with A. Oxem and O. Aalo) Vesterålen: lyset, livet, landskapet, 1989; Bly, 1990; Hvor er det blitt av alle gutta: dikt i utvalg 1973-1990, 1991; Ingens: noveller, 1992; Den misunnelige frisøren, 1992; Gutten som ville vare en av gutta, 1992; Nordmarka, 1993; Den Akustiskeskyggen: Dikt, 1993; Mekka: skuespill, 1994; Jubel, 1994; Andre siden avblatt: et bilde-dikt fra Lofoten og Vesteralen, 1996; Pasninger: dikt, 1998; Falleferdig himmel: Dikt, 1998; Under en sort paraply: dikt iutvalg, 1998; Noen som elsker hverandre: noveller, 1999; Kongen som villeha mer enn en krone, 1999; Pinnsvinsol: dikt, 2000; Mann for sin katt, 2000; Dracula, 2000; Halvbroren: roman, 2001; Halvbroren, 2001; (ed. with A. Gjeitanger) Bauers bok, 2002; Maskeblomstfamilien, 2003; (with T. Myrann) Sanger & Steiner, 2003; The Half Brother, 2003; Oscar Wildes heis, 2004; Modellen, 2005; (with B. Løken) Norske omveier-i blues og bilder, 2005; Saabyes circus, 2006; Stille lengde, 2006; (with T.I. Bergsmo) Den Arktiskedrømmen, 2007; Bisettelsen, 2008; Visning, 2009; Bernhard Hvals forsnakkelser, 2010. Contributor to periodicals. **Address:** c/o Author Mail, Arcadia Books, 15-16 Nassau St., London, GL W1W 7AB, England.

CHRISTENSEN, Mark. American (born United States) **Genres:** Novels, Young Adult Non-fiction, Young Adult Fiction, Business/Trade/Industry. **Career:** Rolling Stone Magazine, media columnist, 1984-89. Journalist. **Publications:** (With C. Stauth) The Sweeps: Behind the Scenes in Network TV, 1984; Mortal Belladaywic, 1987; Aloha: A Novel, 1994; (ed.) Wild Life, 1997; Journey to Nowhere: A Child's Story of Abuse, 1998; Build the Perfect Beast: The Quest to Design the Coolest Car Ever Made, 2001; Super Car: The Story of the Xeno, 2003; So-Cal Speed Shop: The Fast Tale of the California Racers Who Made Hot Rod History, 2005; Acid Christ: Ken Kesey, LSD and the Politics of Ecstasy, 2010. Contributor to periodicals. **Address:** Schaffner Press, PO Box 41567, Tucson, AZ 85717, U.S.A.

CHRISTENSEN, Paul. American (born United States), b. 1943. **Genres:** Poetry, Literary Criticism And History, Photography, Essays, Intellectual History, Social Commentary. **Career:** Eastern Publishing Co., associate editor, 1967-68; Texas A&M University, instructor, 1974-76, assistant professor, 1976-80, associate professor, 1980-83, professor of English, 1983-; Quartet Magazine, poetry editor, 1975-77; Cedarshouse Press, editor and publisher, 1977-. **Publications:** (Co-author) Good Writer: A Freshman English Manual, 1976; Charles Olson: Call Him Ishmael (criticism), 1979; Gulfsongs, 1982; Signs of the Whelming, 1983; (ed. and intro.) In Love, In Sorrow: The Complete Correspondence of Charles Olson and Edward Dahlberg, 1990; Minding the Underworld: Clayton Eshleman and Late Postmodernism, 1991; West of the American Dream: An Encounter with Texas, 2001; Like Thunder: American Poets Respond to Violence, 2002; The Mottled Air, 2003; (ed. with R. Bass) Falling from Grace in Texas: A Literary Response to the Demise of Paradise, 2004; Strangers in Paradise: An American Family in Provence, 2006; Strangers in Paradise: A Memoir of Provence, 2007. POETRY: (co-author) Seven Poets, 1977; Old and Lost Rivers, 1977; The Vectory, 1982; Weights and Measures: Selected Poems, 1985; (with J. Campion and J. Herndon) Where Three Roads Meet, 1996; Blue Alleys: Prose Poetry, 2001; Hard Country, 2005; The Human Condition, 2011. Contributor to books. **Address:** Department of English, Texas A&M University, 201C Blocker Bldg., MS 4227, College Station, TX 77843-4227, U.S.A. **Online address:** p-christensen@tamu.edu

CHRISTENSON, James A. American (born United States), b. 1944. **Genres:** Adult Non-fiction. **Career:** North Carolina State University, assistant professor, 1972-75, associate professor, 1975-76, extension community development specialist, 1972-76; University of Kentucky, associate professor, 1976, Survey Research Center, founder and director, 1979-82, professor of sociology, 1981-89, head of department, 1982-89; University of Arizona, College of Agriculture and Life Sciences, Cooperative Extension, associate dean, director and associate vice president for outreach, 1989-, professor, 1989-; International Research Group in Extension, co-founder, 1988. Writer. **Publications:** (Ed. with J.W. Robinson, Jr.) Community Development in America, 1980; (with P.D. Warner) The Cooperative Extension Service: A National Assessment, 1984; (ed. with J.W. Robinson, Jr.) Community Development in Perspective, 1989; (ed. with C.B. Flora) Rural Policies for the 1990s, 1991; (ed. with R.C. Maurer and N.L. Strang) Rural Data, People, and Policy: Information Systems for the 21st Century, 1994; Zion in Our Neighborhood: The Story of Harvest Hills, 1970-1995, 1997. Works appear in anthologies. Contributor to periodicals. **Address:** Cooperative Extension, College of Agriculture and Life Sciences, University of Arizona, Rm. 301, Forbes, 1140 SE Campus Dr., PO Box 210036, Tucson, AZ 85721-0036, U.S.A. **Online address:** jimc@cals.arizona.edu

CHRISTIAN, Carol Cathay Tuttle. British/American/Chinese (born China), b. 1923. **Genres:** Novels, Children's Fiction, Human Relations/Parenting, Biography, Theology/Religion, Women's Studies And Issues. **Career:** Writer. **Publications:** Into Strange Country, 1958; (with G. Plummer) God and One Redhead: Mary Slessor of Calabar, 1970; Tales of the Cross River, 1972; Great People of Our Time, 1973; Proverbs and Rhymes, 1974; Johnny Ring, 1975; The Girl Who Laughed, 1975; More People of Our Time, 1978; (with D. Christian) Famous Women of the 20th Century, 1982; (ed.) In the Spirit of Truth: Reader in the Work of Frank Lake, 1991. **Address:** 20 Pitfold Ave., Shottermill, Haslemere, SR GU27 1PN, England. **Online address:** ccarol@fish.co.uk

CHRISTIAN, David Gilbert. American (born United States), b. 1946. **Genres:** Economics, History. **Career:** Macquarie University, lecturer, 1975-81, senior lecturer, 1982-91, associate professor, 1991-2001; San Diego State University, Department of History, associate professor, 2001-02, professor, 2002-. Writer. **Publications:** (with R.E.F. Smith) Bread and Salt: A Social and Economic History of Food and Drink in Russia, 1984; Living Water: Vodka and Russian Society on the Eve of Emancipation, 1990; Imperial and Soviet Russia: Power, Privilege, and the Challenge of Modernity, 1997; A History of Russia, Central Asia, and Mongolia, vol. I: Inner Eurasia from Prehistory to the Mongol Empire, 1998; (co-ed.) Worlds of the Silk Roads, Ancient and Modern: Proceedings from the Second Conference of the Australasian Society for Inner Asian Studies (A.S.I.A.S.), Macquarie University, September 21-22, 1996, 1998; (co-ed.) Realms of the Silk Roads, Ancient and Modern: Proceedings from the Third Conference of the Australasian Society for Inner Asian Studies (ASIAS), Macquarie University, September 18-20, 1998, 2000; Maps of Time: An Introduction to Big History, 2004; This Fleeting World:

A Short History of Humanity, 2008. **Address:** Department of History, San Diego State University, 5500 Campanile Dr., San Diego, CA 92182-6050, U.S.A.

CHRISTIAN, Garna L. American (born United States), b. 1935. **Genres:** Architecture, History, Music. **Career:** South Texas Junior College, instructor, 1962-74; University of Houston, Department of Social Science, professor of history, 1974-; Texas State Historical Association, fellow. Writer. **Publications:** Stay a Little Longer: The First Generation of Houston Country Music, 1985; 40,000 Window Panes: The Story of the Merchants and Manufacturers Building, 1983; Black Soldiers in Jim Crow Texas, 1899-1917, 1995; George Sessions Perry: The Man and His Words, 2009. **Address:** Department of Social Sciences, University of Houston, N-1029, 1 Main St., Houston, TX 77002, U.S.A. **Online address:** christiang@uhd.edu

CHRISTIAN, Jeffrey E. American (born United States), b. 1956?. **Genres:** Business/Trade/Industry, Economics, Human Relations/Parenting. **Career:** Christian & Timbers (now CT Partners), founder, 1980-, chairman and chief executive officer, through 1980. Writer. **Publications:** Headhunter Confidential: How to Get the Best Jobs and the Best People-Exclusive Tips from One of the Top Headhunters in the Business, 2002; Talent: Secrets for Finding, Hiring, and Keeping the Best Managers in the World, 2002; The Headhunter's Edge, 2002. **Address:** CTPartners, 28601 Chagrin Blvd., Ste. 600, Cleveland, OH 44122, U.S.A. **Online address:** jchristian@ctnet.com

CHRISTIAN, William. Canadian (born Canada), b. 1945. **Genres:** Philosophy, Politics/Government, Biography, Young Adult Non-fiction. **Career:** Mount Allison University, assistant professor of political science, 1970, associate professor of political studies, 1978; London School of Economics, academic visitor, 1976-77, 1984-85, 1989; University of Guelph, professor of political science, 1978-2008; University of Toronto, visiting professor, 1987-90; Waterloo Region Record, freelance journalist, 1989-; McMaster University, faculty, 1990; University of Edinburgh, International Social Sciences Institute, visiting associate, 1996. Writer. **Publications:** (With C. Campbell) Political Parties and Ideologies in Canada, 1974, 3rd ed., 1990; George Grant: A Biography, 1993; (with C. Campbell) Parties, Leaders and Ideologies in Canada, 1996; Political Ideologies and the Democratic Ideal, 2006; Parkin: Canada's Most Famous Forgotten Man, 2008. EDITOR: The Idea File of Harold Adams Innis, 1980; Innis on Russia, 1981; Time as History, 1995; Philosophy in the Mass Age, 1996; Selected Letters of George Grant, 1996; The George Grant Reader, 1998. **Address:** 4 Wolseley Rd., Guelph, ON N1E 1J5, Canada.

CHRISTIANSEN, Rupert. British (born England), b. 1954. **Genres:** History, Music, Writing/Journalism, Young Adult Non-fiction, Biography. **Career:** Associated with Oxford University Press, 1979-82; freelance writer and editor, 1982-; Harpers & Queen, arts editor, 1988-95; Contemporary Review, editor, 1989; The Spectator, opera critic, 1989-96; Observer, deputy arts editor, 1990-93; Gates Theatre, director, 1995-; The Daily Telegraph, opera critic, 1996-; Mail on Sunday, dance critic, 1996-; Harper's and Queen, arts editor; The Observer, arts editor. **Publications:** Prima Donna: A History, 1984; Romantic Affinities: Portraits from an Age, 1780-1830, 1988; (ed.) The Grand Obsession: Anthology of Opera, 1988; Tales of the New Babylon: Paris, 1869-1875 in US as Paris Babylon: The Story of the Paris Commune, 1994; (ed.) Cambridge Arts Theatre, 1997; The Visitors: Culture Shock in Nineteenth-Century Britain, 2000 in US as The Victorian Visitors: Culture Shock in Nineteenth-Century Britain, 2000; The Voice of Victorian Sex: Arthur Hugh Clough, 1819-1861, 2001; A Pocket Guide to Opera, 2002; William Shakespeare: The Mystery of the World's Greatest Playwright, 2003; Paris Babylon: Grandeur, Decadence and Revolution 1869-1875, 2003; (with B. Brophy) The Complete Book of Aunts, 2006; (ed.) Once More, with Feeling!: A Book of Classic Hymns, 2007; Complete Book of Aunts, 2007. **Address:** c/o Caroline Dawnay, PFD, Drury House, 34-43 Russell St., London, GL WC2B 5HA, England. **Online address:** rupec@dircon.co.uk

CHRISTIANSON, Paul. Canadian/American (born United States), b. 1937. **Genres:** History. **Career:** Queen's University, professor of history, 1964-, now professor emeritus. Writer. **Publications:** Reformers and Babylon: English Apocalyptic Visions from the Reformation to the Eve of the Civil War, 1978; Discourse on History, Law, and Governance in the Public Career of John Selden, 1610-1635, 1996. **Address:** Department of History, Queens University, 303 Watson Hall, Kingston, ON K7L 3N6, Canada. **Online address:** christia@queensu.ca

CHRISTIANSON, Sven-Åke. Swedish (born Sweden), b. 1954. **Genres:** Psychology, Mystery/Crime/Suspense. **Career:** Umea University Hospital, consultant, 1981-; Linkoping University Hospital, consultant, 1981-; Swedish National Police College, consultant, 1983-; University of Umea, assistant professor, 1984-89, associate professor of psychology, 1989-90; Montreal Neurological Institute and Hospital, research fellow, 1984; University of Washington and University Hospital, visiting scientist, 1988-89; University of Stockholm, associate professor, 1990-99, professor of psychology, 1999-. Writer. **Publications:** Amnesia and Emotional Arousal, 1984; (ed.) The Handbook of Emotion and Memory: Research and Theory, 1992; Traumatic Memories, 1994; Forensic Psychology, 1996; (with G. Wentz) Crime and Memory, 1996; (ed.) Rättspsykologi: Den Forensiska Psykologin i Sverige: en kunskapsöversikt, 1996; (with E. Engelberg and U. Holmberg) Advanced Interrogation and Interviewing Technique, 1998; (ed. with P.A. Granhag) Police Psychology, 2004; (ed.) Offender's Memories of Violent Crimes, 2007; (ed. with P.A. Granhag) Handbook in Legal Psychology, 2008; In the Mind of a Serial Killer, 2010; Psychological Myths in the Legal System, 2011. **Address:** Department of Psychology, Stockholm University, Rm. B212, Frescati Hagvag 8, Stockholm, SE-106 91, Sweden. **Online address:** scn@psychology.su.se

CHRISTIE, Ian. British (born England), b. 1956. **Genres:** Business/Trade/Industry, Politics/Government, Economics. **Career:** British Film Institute, staff, 1976-96; Policy Studies Institute, senior research fellow, 1986-; New Economics Foundation, associate; Surrey University, visiting professor; Oxford University, visiting lecturer, 1995-98; University of Kent, professor of film studies, 1997-99; Birkbeck, University of University of London, Department of History of Art and Screen Media, anniversary professor of film and media history, 1999-, AHRB Centre for British Film and Television Studies, director, 2003-05, London Project, director, London Screen Study Collection, director. Writer and consultant. **Publications:** (With M. Trevor) Manufacturers and Suppliers in Britain and Japan: Competitiveness and the Growth of Small Firms, 1988; (with J. Northcott and A. Walling) The Employment Effects of New Technology, 1990; (with M. Fogarty) Companies and Communities, 1991; (with M. Carley, R. Legard and M. Fogarty) Profitable Partnerships: A Report on Business Investment in the Community: Case Studies from Three British Cities, 1991; (ed. with N. Ritchie) Energy Efficiency: The Policy Agenda for the 1990s, 1992; (with M. Carley) Managing Sustainable Development, 1993, 2nd ed., 2000; (with H. Rolfe and R. Legard) Cleaner Production in Industry: Integrating Business Goals and Environmental Management, 1995; (with K. Hughes) UK and European Science Policy: The Role of Collaborative Research, 1995; (ed. with I. Hargreaves) Tomorrow's Politics: The Third Way and Beyond, 1998; (with D. Warburton) From Here to Sustainability: Politics in the Real World, 2000; (contrib.) Transforming Britain: Labour's Second Term, 2001. Contributor to periodicals. **Address:** Department of History of Art and Screen Media, School of Arts, Birkbeck, University of London, 43 Gordon Sq., London, GL WC1H 0PD, England. **Online address:** i.christie@bbk.ac.uk

CHRISTIE, Stuart. British/Scottish (born Scotland), b. 1946. **Genres:** Politics/Government. **Career:** Writer. **Publications:** (With A. Meltzer) The Floodgates of Anarchy, 1970; The Christie File, 1980; Stefano Delle Chiaie: Portrait of a Black Terrorist, 1984; We, the Anarchists! A Study of the Iberian Anarchist Federation (FAI), 1927-1937, 2000; General Franco Made Me a Terrorist: The Interesting Years Abroad of a West of Scotland Baby-boomer, 2003; Granny Made Me an Anarchist: General Franco, the Angry Brigade and Me, 2007; The Story of King Bomba-Emidio Recchioni, 1864-1934, 2012. **Address:** ChristieBooks, PO Box 35, Hastings, ES TN34 2UX, England. **Online address:** christie@btclick.com

CHRISTMAN, Jill. American (born United States), b. 1969. **Genres:** Autobiography/Memoirs. **Career:** University of Minnesota, coordinator of creative writing program; Ball State University, assistant professor of English and assistant chair of programs. Writer. **Publications:** Darkroom: A Family Exposure (memoir), 2002. **Address:** Department of English, Ball State University, Rm. 297, Robert Bell Bldg., 2000 W University Ave., Muncie, IN 47306, U.S.A. **Online address:** jcchristman@bsu.edu

CHRISTMAS, Joyce. (Christmas Peterson). American (born United States), b. 1939. **Genres:** Mystery/Crime/Suspense, Novels, Young Adult Non-fiction. **Career:** The Writer Magazine, editorial assistant, 1963-68, associate editor, 1973-76; Plays Magazine, associate editor; Chervenak, Keane and Co. (hotel consultants), hotel computer consultant and managing editor, 1981-. **Publications:** Blood Child, 1982; Dark Tide, 1983; Suddenly in Her Sorbet,

1988; Simply to Die For, 1989; A Fete Worse than Death, 1990; A Stunning Way to Die, 1991; Friend or Faux, 1991; It's Her Funeral, 1992; This Business Is Murder, 1993; A Perfect Day for Dying, 1994; Old Westbury Gardens, 1994; Death at Face Value, 1995; Mourning Gloria, 1996; Downsized to Death, 1997; Going Out in Style, 1998; Mood to Murder, 1999; Dying Well, 2000; A Better Class of Murder, 2000; Forged in Blood, 2002. Works appear in anthologies. **Address:** Chervenak, Keane & Co., Rm. 1311, 307 E 44th St., New York, NY 10017, U.S.A. **Online address:** christmasj@aol.com

CHRISTMAS, Linda (Irene). British (born England), b. 1943. **Genres:** Travel/Exploration, Social Sciences. **Career:** Swindon Evening Advertiser, journalist, 1966-68; Times Educational Supplement, journalist, 1969-70; Guardian, journalist, 1971-82, feature writer; freelance writer, 1982-; City University, senior lecturer in journalism, 1989-, programme director in newspaper journalism, 2004-05, now emeritus fellow; Newspaper Journalism, director of the PG Dip, through 2005; BBC Newsnight, reporter. **Publications:** The Ribbon and the Ragged Square: An Australian Journey, 1986; Chopping Down the Cherry Trees: A Portrait of Britain in the Eighties, 1989. Contributor to periodicals. **Address:** Department of Journalism, City University London, Northampton Sq., London, GL EC1V 0HB, England. **Online address:** l.christmas@city.ac.uk

CHRISTODOULOU, Demetrios. Cypriot/American (born United States), b. 1919. **Genres:** Agriculture/Forestry, Economics, Politics/Government, Sociology, Mathematics/Statistics. **Career:** Government of Cyprus, teacher, 1940-45, Teachers Training College, lecturer in geography and teaching methods, 1949-53, inspector of secondary schools, 1955-56, land consolidation officer, 1956-60, agricultural development officer, 1958-60, minister of agriculture and natural resources, 1982-85; Food and Agriculture Organization of the UN, senior officer and policy advisor, 1960-81, International Agencies on Missions, staff, 1961-80. Writer. **Publications:** Physical Geography, 1954; The Evolution of the Rural Land Use Pattern in Cyprus, 1959; The Unpromised Land: Agrarian Reform and Conflict Worldwide, 1990; Inside the Cyprus Miracle: The Labors of an Embattled Mini-Economy, 1992; (with S. Klainerman) The Global Nonlinear Stability of the Minkowski Space, 1993; Where the Cyprus Miracle Fell Short (in Greek), 1995; Ekei pou to kypriako thauma den ephtase: domikes kai thesmikes aneparkeies kai politikokoinōnika elleimmata, 1995; The Action Principle and Partial Differential Equations, 2000. **Address:** Flat 201, Anemomylos Bldg., 6 Michael Karaolis St., Nicosia, 162, Cyprus.

CHRISTOFFERSON, April. American (born United States) **Genres:** Novels, Literary Criticism And History, Mystery/Crime/Suspense. **Career:** North Idaho College, faculty of business law, adjunct instructor; University of Montana, College of Technology, faculty, 2005, Department of Continuing Education, writer. **Publications:** After the Dance, 1994; Edgewater, 1998; The Protocol, 1999; Clinical Trial, 2000; Patent to Kill, 2003; Buffalo Medicine, 2004; Alpha Female, 2009. **Address:** c/o Author Mail, Tom Doherty Associates L.L.C., 175 5th Ave., 14th Fl., New York, NY 10010, U.S.A. **Online address:** aprilchristoff@msn.com

CHRISTOPH, Peter R(ichard). American (born United States), b. 1938. **Genres:** Genealogy/Heraldry, History, Adult Non-fiction, Biography, Local History/Rural Topics, Politics/Government, Reference. **Career:** New York State Library, assistant cataloging librarian, 1965-68, senior librarian for manuscripts and history, 1968-72, associate librarian for manuscripts and special collections, 1972-88, New York Historical Manuscripts, editor, 1974-86, senior editor, 1986-, Project to Translate and Edit the Archives of New Netherland, director, 1974-87, New Netherland Project, associate librarian, 1988-91. **Publications:** Albert Andriessen Bradt: A Norwegian Settler in Rensselaerswyck, 1987. EDITOR: (with K. Scott and K. Stryker-Rodda) The Kingston Papers, 1661-1675, 2 vols., 1976; Administrative Papers of Governors Richard Nicolls and Francis Lovelace, 1664-1673, 1980; (with F.A. Christoph) Books of General Entries of the Colony of New York, 1664-1688, 2 vols., 1982; (with F.A. Christoph) Records of the People of the Town of Bethlehem, 1690-1880, 1982; (with F. Christoph) Records of the Court of Assizes for the Colony of New York, 1665-1682, 1983; (with F.A. Christopher) The Andros Papers: Files of the Provincial Secretary of New York during the Administration of Governor Sir Edmund Andros, 1674-1680, 3 vols., 1989-91; The Dongan Papers, 1683-1688, 2 vols., 1993-96; The Diary of Henry Edgar Whittelsey, Catskill Mountains Storekeeper, 1835-1836, 1999; The Leisler Papers, 1689-1691, 2002. Work appear in anthologies. Contributor to journals and books. **Address:** New York Historical Manuscripts, 181 Maple Ave., Selkirk, NY 12158-1711, U.S.A. **Online address:** pchrist1@nycap.rr.com

CHRISTOPHER, Paul. *See* **HYDE, Christopher.**

CHRISTOPHER, Renny (Teresa). American (born United States), b. 1957. **Genres:** Poetry, Literary Criticism And History, Military/Defense/Arms Control, Reference. **Career:** Horse Lovers' National, features editor, 1976-79; Literature of Liberty, production editor, 1982; Gilroy Dispatch, graphic arts editor, 1983-84; teacher, 1984-85; San Jose State University, lecturer in English, 1986-87, 1993-94; Cabrillo Community College, instructor in English, 1988-95; California State University-Stanislaus, assistant professor, 1995-98, associate professor of English, 1998-; University of California, lecturer, 1992-95; University of Barcelona, visiting professor, 2000; California State University-Channel Islands, associate professor of English, professor of English, associate vice president for faculty affairs. **Publications:** The Viet Nam War/The American War: Images and Representations in Euro-American and Vietnamese Exile Narratives, 1995; A Carpenter's Daughter: A Working-Class Woman in Higher Education, 1995; My Name Is Medea (poems), 1996; Viet Nam and California (poems), 1998; Longing Fervently for Revolution (poems), 1998; Love That Is a Commitment to the World, 1998. FORTHCOMING: American Nightmares: U.S. Working-Class Literature; A Different Sort of Heroism. Works appear in anthologies. Contributor of articles to books and periodicals. **Address:** Department of English, California State University, W Wing, Bell Twr., 1 University Dr., Camarillo, CA 93012-8599, U.S.A. **Online address:** renny.christopher@csuci.edu

CHRYSSAVGIS, John. American/Australian (born Australia), b. 1958. **Genres:** Education, Theology/Religion, Human Relations/Parenting. **Career:** Greek Orthodox Church in Australia, protodeacon, 1984-94; St. Andrew's Theological College, co-founder, 1985, subdean, 1985-95; Divinity School, lecturer, 1986-90; Sydney University, School of Studies in Religion, lecturer, 1986-95; Institute for Theology and the Arts, advisor, 1990-95; Holy Cross School of Theology, professor, 1995-, acting dean, 1997-98, Hellenic College, Religious Studies Program, director, 1995-2002, Environment Office, founder, 2001; Greek Orthodox Archdiocese of America, deacon, 1995-; Balamand University, professor of patristics. Writer. **Publications:** Persons and Events: Historical Moments in the Development of Orthodox Christianity, 1985; Fire and Light: Aspects of the Eastern Orthodox Tradition, 1987; Fire and Light: The Theology of the Human Person, 1989; Ascent to Heaven: The Theology of the Human Person according to Saint John of the Ladder, 1989; (with S. Chryssavgis) The World, My Church, 1990, rev. ed., 1998; The Desert is Alive: Dimensions of Australian Spirituality, 1990; Repentance and Confession in the Orthodox Church, 1990; Love, Sexuality, and the Sacrament of Marriage, 1996; The Way of the Fathers: Exploring the Patristic Mind, 1998; Beyond the Shattered Image, 1999, 2nd ed., 2007; Soul Mending: The Art of Spiritual Direction, 2000; In the Footsteps of Christ: The Ascetic Teaching of Abba Isaiah of Scetis, 2001; (trans. and intro. with P. Penkett) Abba Isaiah of Scetis Ascetic Discourses, 2002; In the Heart of the Desert: The Spirituality of the Desert Fathers and Mothers, 2003, rev. ed., 2008; (trans. and intro.) Barsanuphius and John, Letters from the Desert: A Selection of Questions and Responses, 2003; (ed.) Cosmic Grace and Humble Prayer: The Ecological Vision of the Green Patriarch Bartholomew I, 2003; John Climacus: From the Egyptian Desert to the Sinaite Mountain, 2004; Light through Darkness: The Orthodox Tradition, 2004; Ecumenical Patriarchate: A Brief Guide, 2006; (trans.) Letters, 2006; Remembering and Reclaiming Diakonia, 2009; (ed. and intro.) In the World, Yet Not of the World, 2010; (ed. with D. Trakatellis) In the Footsteps of St. Paul, 2010; (ed. and intro.) Speaking the Truth in Love, 2011; (ed. and intro.) On Earth as in Heaven, 2012. Contributor to books. **Address:** Hellenic College, 50 Goddard Ave., Brookline, MA 02445-7415, U.S.A.

CHU, Miyoko. American (born United States) **Genres:** Natural History, Travel/Exploration, Environmental Sciences/Ecology. **Career:** Cornell University, Cornell Lab of Ornithology, ornithologist, staff writer, senior director of communications, BirdScope, editor; Living Bird Magazine, assistant editor. Ornithologist. **Publications:** Songbird Journeys: Four Seasons in the Lives of Migratory Birds, 2006. **Address:** Cornell Lab of Ornithology, 159 Sapsucker Woods Rd., Ithaca, NY 14850-1923, U.S.A. **Online address:** mcc37@cornell.edu

CHU, Petra ten-Doesschate. Dutch (born Netherlands), b. 1942. **Genres:** Art/Art History, Literary Criticism And History. **Career:** Institut Neerlandais, researcher, 1965-72; Seton Hall University, Department of Communication and the Arts, assistant professor, 1972-77, associate professor, 1977-80, professor, 1980-, Department of Art and Music, chairperson, 1980-2001, MA Program Museum Professions, academic director, 2002-, Graduate Studies Art Center, director; Princeton University, visiting professor, 1990-92; Nineteenth-Century Art Worldwide, managing editor, founding editor. **Publications:** French Realism and the Dutch Masters: The Influence of Dutch Seventeenth-Century Painting on the Development of French Painting between 1830 and 1870, 1975; (ed.) Courbet in Perspective, 1977; Dominique Vivant Denon. French Masters of the Nineteenth Century, 1985; Im Lichte Hollands: Holländische Malerei: des 17. Jahrhunderts aus den Sammlungen des Fürsten von Liechtenstein und aus Schweizer Besitz, 1987; (with R. Hollenstein) Frank Buchser 1828-1890, 1990; Redefining Genre: French and American Painting 1850-1900, 1995; Gustave Courbet: en revoltör lanserar sitt verk, 1999; Nineteenth-Century European Art, 2002, 2nd ed., 2006; (with J.S. Johnson, Jr.) Beyond the Frame: Impressionism Revisited, 2003; Most Arrogant Man in France: Gustave Courbet and the Nineteenth-Century Media Culture, 2007; (with G.P. Weisberg) The Orient Expressed: Japan's Influence on Western Art, 1854-1918, 2011. EDITOR: (trans.) Letters of Gustave Courbet, 1992; (with G. Weisberg) The Popularization of Images: Visual Culture under the July Monarchy, 1994; Correspondance de Courbet, 1996; (with J. Zutter) Courbet: Artiste et promoteur de son oeuvre, 1998; (with L.S. Dixon) Twenty-First-Century Perspectives on Nineteenth-Century Art: Essays in Honor of Gabriel P. Weisberg, 2008; Work appear in anthologies. Contributor to journals. **Address:** Department of Art and Music, Seton Hall University, Art Center 205, 400 S Orange Ave., South Orange, NJ 07079-2697, U.S.A. **Online address:** chupetra@shu.edu

CHU, Tien-wen. Also writes as Tianwen Zhu. Taiwanese (born Taiwan), b. 1956. **Genres:** Essays, Novels, Novellas/Short Stories. **Career:** Novelist and screenwriter. **Publications:** Xiao Bi dig u shi, 1983; Chuan shuo, 1983; Zui xiang nian di ji jie, 1984; (with Z. Tianxin and Z.T. Zhu) San zi mei, 1985; Tong nian wang shi dian ying zhuan ji, 1985; (with M. Xi) San wen ji duan pian, 1985; Bei qing chengshi, 1989; (with L. Yaode) Fei xiang meng huan di guo du, 1992; Huang jen shou chi, 1994; Hua yi qian shen, 1996; Hai shang hua, 1998; Qianxi manbo, 2001. **Address:** Columbia University Press, 61 W 62nd St., New York, NY 10023, U.S.A.

CHU, Wai C. American/Chinese (born China), b. 1967. **Genres:** Engineering, Sciences. **Career:** NGE Electronica, design engineer, 1989-90; Texas Instruments Hong Kong, field applications engineer, 1993-94; Digital Video Express, research and development engineer, 1998-99; Intervideo Inc., technical staff, 1999-2001; DoCoMo USA Labs, senior research engineer, 2001-. Writer. **Publications:** Speech Coding Algorithms: Foundation and Evolution of Standardized Coders, 2003. Contributor to engineering journals. **Address:** DoCoMo USA Labs, 181 Metro Dr., Ste. 300, San Jose, CA 95110, U.S.A. **Online address:** wcc2@ieee.org

CHUDE-SOKEI, Louis Onuorah. American/Nigerian (born Nigeria), b. 1967. **Genres:** Literary Criticism And History, Natural History. **Career:** Bowdoin College, assistant professor; University of the West Indies, lecturer, 1997; University of California, associate professor of literature, 1998-. Writer. **Publications:** The Incomprehensible Rain of Stars: Black Modernism, Black Diaspora, 1995; The Last Darky: Bert Williams, Black-on-Black Minstrelsy, and the African Diaspora, 2006. **Address:** Department of Literature, University of California, Rm. 303, Humanities 1, Santa Cruz, CA 95064, U.S.A. **Online address:** locsokei@ucsc.edu

CHUPACK, Cindy. American (born United States), b. 1973?. **Genres:** Advertising/Public Relations, Essays. **Career:** Columbia Broadcasting System Inc., television series scriptwriter, 1996-98; Home Box Office, scriptwriter and executive producer, 1998-2004. **Publications:** The Between Boyfriends Book: A Collection of Cautiously Hopeful Essays, 2003; Dispatches from the Dating Front Lines, 2011. Contributor to periodicals. **Address:** Home Box Office, 1100 Ave. of the Americas, New York, NY 10036-6712, U.S.A.

CHURCH, Audrey P. American (born United States), b. 1957. **Genres:** Librarianship, Education. **Career:** Lunenburg Board of Education, school librarian, 1980-2000; Longwood University, lecturer, 2000-02, instructor, 2002-07, assistant professor, 2007-09, associate professor, 2009-. Writer. **Publications:** Leverage Your Library Program to Help Raise Test Scores: A Guide for Library Media Specialists, Principals, Teachers, and Parents, 2003; Your Library Goes Virtual, 2007. **Address:** School Library Media Program, Longwood University, 201 High St., Farmville, VA 23909, U.S.A. **Online address:** churchap@longwood.edu

CHURCHETT, Stephen. British (born England), b. 1947. **Genres:** Plays/Screenplays, Young Adult Fiction. **Career:** Writer. **Publications:** PLAYS: Tom & Clem, 1997; Heritage, 1997. **Address:** The Agency Ltd., 24 Pottery Ln., Holland Pk., London, GL W11 4LZ, England.

CHURCHILL, Caryl. British (born England), b. 1938. **Genres:** Plays/Screenplays, Music, Young Adult Fiction. **Career:** Royal Court Theatre, resident dramatist, 1974-75; Joint Stock Theatre Co., writer; Monstrous Regiment Theatre Co., writer. **Publications:** Owners, 1973; Light Shining in Buckinghamshire, 1978; Vinegar Tom, 1978; Traps, 1978; Cloud Nine: A Play, 1979, 4th ed., 1984; Top Girls, 1982; Fen: A Drama, 1984; Softcops, 1984; Collected Plays, vol. I, 1985, vol. II, 1988; Softcops & Fen, 1986; (with D. Lan) A Mouthful of Birds, 1986; Serious Money: A City Comedy, 1987; Icecream, 1989; Ice Cream: With Hot Fudge, 1990; Churchill Shorts: Short Plays, 1990; Mad Forest: A Play from Romania, 1991; (contrib.) Lives of the Great Poisoners: A Production Dossier, 1993; The Skriker, 1994; (trans. and intro.) L.A. Seneca, Thyestes, 1995; Hotel: In a Room Anything Can Happen, 1997; Blue Heart, 1997; Churchill: Plays Three, 1998; This is a Chair, 1999; Far Away, 2001; A Number, 2002; A Dream Play, 2005; Drunk Enough to Say I Love You?, 2006; (trans.) O. Choiniére, Félicité (title means: 'Bliss'), 2008; (and intro.) Plays: Four, 2008. **Address:** Casarotto Ramsay & Associates Ltd., Waverley House, 7-12 Noel St., London, GL W1F 8GQ, England.

CHURCHILL, E. Richard. (Cora Verlag). American (born United States), b. 1937. **Genres:** Novellas/Short Stories, Education, History, Recreation, Novels, Horror, Travel/Exploration. **Career:** Park Elementary School, teacher, 1959-80; Maplewood Middle School, librarian, 1974-; Timberline Books, co-owner, 1971-. Writer and librarian. **Publications:** The McCartys, 1972; Colorado Quiz Bag, 1973; Doc Holliday, Bat Masterson and Wyatt Earp: Their Colorado Careers, 1974; Hidden Word Puzzles, 1975; Shaggy Dog Stories, 1975; Six-Million Dollar Cucumber, 1976; Hidden Word Puzzles 2, 1977; New Puzzles, 1980; Classroom Activity Program, 1980; I Bet I Can!, 1981; Devilish Bets to Trick Your Friends, 1985; Sneaky Tricks to Fool Your Friends, 1986; Instant Paper Toys, 1986; Quick and Easy Paper Toys, 1988; Instant Paper Airplanes, 1988; Paper Toys that Fly, Soar, Zoom, and Whistle, 1989; Optical Illusion Tricks and Toys, 1989; Fast and Funny Paper Toys You Can Make, 1989; Building with Paper, 1990; Science Paper Toys, 1990; Dartmoor Danger, 1990; Paper Science Toys, 1990; Visions of Terror, 1990; Terrific Paper Toys, 1991; Amazing Science Experiments with Everyday Materials, 1991; Fabulous Paper Airplanes, 1991; Paper Tricks and Toys, 1992; Who I Am and Who I Want to Be, 1992; Holiday Paper Projects, 1992; Fantastic Paper Flying Machines, 1993; Paper Action Toys, 1993; No Fair Standing Still, 1994; Where Is It?, 1995; A Haunted Mine Is a Terrible Thing to Waste (juvenile novel), 1998; You and the Law, 1998; Understanding Our Economy, 1998; Short Lessons in U.S. History, 1999; American History Jeopardy, 2002; Little Giant Book of Tricks & Pranks, 2005; Amazing Science Experiments, 2005. CO-AUTHOR: (with E.H. Blair) Games and Puzzles for Family Leisure, 1965; (with L.R. Churchill and E.H. Blair) Fun with American History, 1966; Fun with American Literature, 1968; Short Lessons in World History, 1971; (with L.R. Churchill) How Our Nation Became Great, 1971; Puzzle It Out, 1971; Everybody Came to Leadville, 1971; Community Civic Case Book, 1973; (with L.R. Churchill) Enriched Social Studies Teaching through the Use of Games and Activities, 1973; Puzzles and Quizzes, 1974; American History Activity Reader, 1974; World History Activity Reader, 1974; (with E. Churchill and S. Churchill) Holiday Hullabaloo!, 1977; (with L.R. Churchill) Bionic Banana, 1979; (with L.R. Churchill) 45 Profiles in Modern Music, 1996; 365 Simple Science Experiments with Everyday Materials, 1997; (with N. Schmidt) Paper Airplanes on the Flip Side: 77 Fold-and-Fly Projects for Your Inner Aviator, 2006. YOUNG ADULT NOVELS: Secret Fear, 1992; Fear the Fog, 1992; Images of Evil, 1993; Destination Horror, 1993; Fearful Shadows, 1998; Devil's Deep, 1998. **Address:** 25890 County Rd. 53, Kersey, CO 80644-8802, U.S.A.

CHURCHLAND, Paul M. American/Canadian (born Canada), b. 1942. **Genres:** Philosophy, Essays, History. **Career:** University of Toronto, lecturer, 1967-69; University of Pittsburgh, instructor, 1969; University of Manitoba, assistant professor, 1969-74, associate professor, 1974-79, professor, 1979-84; Institute for Advanced Study, faculty, 1982-83; University of California, professor of philosophy, 1984-, department chair, 1986-90, Valtz chair of philosophy, 2003-; Philosophy of Science, associate editor, 1994-98.

Publications: Scientific Realism and the Plasticity of the Mind, 1979; Matter and Consciousness: A Contemporary Introduction to the Philosophy of the Mind, 1984, rev. ed., 1988; (ed. with C.A. Hooker) Images of Science: Essays on Realism and Empiricism, with a Reply from Bas C. van Fraassen, 1985; A Neurocomputational Perspective: The Nature of the Mind and the Structure of Science, 1989; The Engine of Reason, the Seat of the Soul: A Philosophical Journey into the Brain, 1995; The Churchlands and Their Critics, 1996; (with P.S. Churchland) On the Contrary: Critical Essays, 1987-1997, 1998; (foreword with P.S. Churchland) The Computer and the Brain, 2000; Neurophilosophy At Work, 2007; Plato's Camera: How the Physical Brain Captures a Landscape of Abstract Universals, 2012; Inner Spaces and Outer Spaces: The New Epistemology, forthcoming. Contributor to periodicals. **Address:** Department of Philosophy, University of California, San Diego, HSS 8016, 9500 Gilman Dr., 9500 Gilman Dr., La Jolla, CA 92093-0119, U.S.A. **Online address:** pchurchland@ucsd.edu

CHWAST, Seymour. American (born United States), b. 1931. **Genres:** Children's Fiction, Illustrations, Adult Non-fiction. **Career:** Graphic artist, designer and illustrator, 1956-; New York Times, junior designer; Push Pin Studios, co-founder, partner, originator and director of studio publication, 1956-80, studio director, 1975-82; Cooper Union Art School, instructor of design and illustration, 1975-81; Pushpin, Lubalin, Peckolick Inc., partner, 1982-86; Pushpin Group, president and director, 1982-; Parsons School of Design, visiting lecturer; Esquire, staff; House and Garden Magazine, staff; Glamour Magazine, staff; American Institute of Graphic Arts, vice president and board director; New York Art Directors Guild, board director. Writer. **Publications:** FOR CHILDREN: (with M.S. Moskof) Still Another Alphabet Book, 1969; (with Moskof) Still Another Number Book, 1971; Still Another Children's Book, 1972; (with Moskof) Flip-Flap Limerickricks, 1972; Flip Flap Mother Gooooose, 1972; Bushy Bride: Norwegian Fairy Tale, 1983; Tall City, Wide Country: A Book to Read Forward and Backward, 1983; The Left-Handed Designer, 1985; Happy Birthday Bach, 1985; The Alphabet Parade, 1991; Paper Pets: Make Your Own Three Dogs, Two Cats, One Parrot, One Rabbit, One Monkey, 1993; The Twelve Circus Rings, 1993; Bra Fashions by Stephanie, 1994; Mr. Merlin and the Turtle, Books, 1996; Traffic Jam, 1999; (with H. Ziefert) Moonride, 2000; (with S. Heller) Graphic Style: From Victorian to Digital, 2000, (S. Heller) 3rd ed. as Graphic Style: From Victorian to New Century, 2011; Harry, I Need You!, 2002; Push Pin Graphic: A Quarter Century of Innovative Design and Illustration, 2004; (with S. Heller) Illustration: A Visual History, 2008; (intro.) Seymour: The Obsessive Images of Seymour Chwast, 2009; (adaptor) Dante's Divine Comedy, 2010. OTHERS: The Book of Battles, 1957; (with D.J.R. Bruckner and S. Heller) Art against War: 400 Years of Protest in Art, 1984; (with D. Barthelme) Sam's Bar, 1987; (with S. Heller) Graphic Style: From Victorian to Post-Modern, 1988; (with B. Cohen and S. Heller) Trylon and Perisphere: The 1939 New York World's Fair, 1989; (with V.G. Levi and S. Heller) You Must Have Been a Beautiful Baby: Baby Pictures of the Stars, 1992; (with S. Heller) Jackets Required: An Illustrated History of the American Book Jacket 1920-1950, 1995; (with J. Fraser and S. Heller) Japanese Modern: Graphic Design between the Wars, 1996. EDITOR: (with J-C Suares) The Literary Cat, 1977; (and comp. with S. Heller) The Art of New York, 1983; (and comp. with B. Cohen and S. Heller) New York Observed: Artists and Writers Look at the City, 1650 to the Present, 1987; (with S. Heller) Sourcebook of Visual Ideas, 1989. OTHERS: (adaptor) The Canterbury Tales, 2010; Bobo's Smile, 2012. Illustrator of books by others. **Address:** Pushpin Group Inc., 55 E 9th St., Ste. 1G, New York, NY 10003, U.S.A. **Online address:** seymour@pushpininc.com

CHWEDYK, Richard. American (born United States), b. 1955?. **Genres:** Novellas/Short Stories, Science Fiction/Fantasy. **Career:** Oakton Community College, creative writing instructor; Pioneer Press/Sun-Times Media, copy editor. **Publications:** A Man Makes a Machine (short story), 1990; Last One Close the Door (novelette), 1993; Surfaces (novelette), 1994; Auteur Theory (novelette), 1998; The Measure of All Things (novelette), 2001; The Cthulhu Orthodontist (short story), 2001; Bronte's Egg (novella), 2002; In Tibor's Cardboard Castle (novelette), 2004; The Button (short story), 2007; Where We Go (short story), 2007; The Ambiguities (short story), 2008; Orfy (novella), 2010. Contributor of articles to magazines. Works appear in anthologies. **Address:** 7538 N Bell Ave., Ste. 3A, Chicago, IL 60645-1962, U.S.A. **Online address:** rchwedyk@att.net

CHWIN, Stefan. (Max Lars). Polish (born Poland), b. 1949. **Genres:** Novels, Essays, Young Adult Fiction. **Career:** Gdansk University, professor of history and literature. Writer. **Publications:** (As Max Lars) Ludzie-Skorpiony, 1984; (as Max Lars) Czlowiek-Litera: Przygody Aleksandra Umwelta Podczas Akcji Specjalnej w Gorach Santa Cruz, 1989; Literatura i Zdrada: Od Konrada Wallenroda do Malej Apokalipsy, 1993; Hanemann, 1996; Esther, 1999; Krótka Historia Pewnego Zartu, 1999; Złoty Pelikan, 2002; Kartki z Dziennika, 2004; (co-author) Wszystkie dni lata, 2005; Żona prezydenta, 2005; Dolina radości, 2006; Dziennik dla dorosłych, 2008; Samobójstwo Jako Doświadczenie Wyobrazni, 2010; Panna Ferbelin, 2011. **Address:** Harcourt, 6277 Sea Harbor Dr., Orlando, FL 32887, U.S.A.

CHYNA. (Joanie Laurer). American (born United States), b. 1970. **Genres:** Autobiography/Memoirs. **Career:** World Wrestling Federation, wrestler, 1997-2001. Writer and actress. **Publications:** (With M. Angeli as Joanie Laurer) Chyna: If They Only Knew, 2001. **Address:** c/o Author Mail, HarperCollins Publishers, 10 E 53rd St., 7th Fl., New York, NY 10022-5244, U.S.A.

CIABATTARI, Jane. American (born United States) **Genres:** Writing/Journalism, Novellas/Short Stories, Literary Criticism And History. **Career:** Chautauqua Institution, Writers' Center, fiction writer-in-residence, 2003, 2005; Knox College, distinguished writer-in-residence, 2004; National Book Critics Circle, president, 2008-11, vice president, 2011-12; Parade Magazine, contributing editor; California Living, managing editor; Redbook, managing editor; Dial Magazine, editor-in-chief; McCall's, senior consulting editor in fiction; Montana Standard, reporter and columnist; Columbia University, Graduate School of Journalism, writing instructor; New York University, writing instructor; Squaw Valley Community of Writers, writing instructor; Borderlands Writing Workshop, writing instructor. **Publications:** Winning Moves: How to Come Out Ahead in a Corporate Shakeup, 1989; Stealing the Fire, 2002. **Address:** c/o Ellen Levine, Trident Media Group L.L.C., 41 Madison Ave., 36th Fl., New York, NY 10010-2257, U.S.A. **Online address:** janeciab@gmail.com

CIARAVINO, Helene. American (born United States), b. 1972. **Genres:** Adult Non-fiction, Poetry, Language/Linguistics, Theology/Religion, Self Help. **Career:** Our Lady of Mercy Academy, teacher of American literature and college writing. Writer. **Publications:** How to Pray: Tapping into the Power of Divine Communication, 2001; How to Publish Your Poetry: A Complete Guide to Finding the Right Publishers for Your Work, 2001. **Address:** c/o Author Mail, Square One Publishers, 6 Birch Hill Rd., Ballston Lake, NY 12019, U.S.A.

CIDDOR, Anna. Australian (born Australia), b. 1957?. **Genres:** Picture/Board Books, Science Fiction/Fantasy. **Career:** Teacher of mathematics, 1979-80; freelance writer and illustrator, 1989-. **Publications:** Take Me Back, 1988; Christmas in Australia, 1993; (with E. Ciddor and D. Ciddor) Going Places: The Kids' Own Travel Book, 1995; Have Kids, Will Travel, 1995; Unplugged! The Bare Facts on Toilets through the Ages, 1997; Australia in the Twentieth Century, 1998; Australian Houses and Buildings, 1999; Focus on Australia: Houses, 1999; Federation: Changing Australia, 2001; Prisoner of Quentaris, 2006; Night of the Fifth Moon, 2007. THROUGH CHILDREN'S EYES PICTURE-BOOK SERIES: SELF-ILLUSTRATED: Early Colonial Times, 1995; The Depression, 1995; Victorian Times, 1995; The Squatters, 1995; The First World War, 1995; The Goldfields, 1995. VIKING MAGIC TRILOGY: Runestone, 2002; Wolfspell, 2003; Stormriders, 2004. Works appear in anthologies. **Address:** Melbourne, VI , Australia. **Online address:** anna@annaciddor.com

CIEPIELA, Catherine. American (born United States) **Genres:** Biography, History. **Career:** Amherst College, Department of Russian Studies, associate professor of Russian, professor, Creative Writing Center, faculty, Department of European Studies, faculty. Writer. **Publications:** The Same Solitude: Boris Pasternak and Marina Tsvetaeva, 2006; (ed. with H. Moore) The Stray Dog Cabaret: A Book of Russian Poems, 2007. **Address:** Department of Russian Studies, Amherst College, 209 Webster Hall, 220 S Pleasant St., PO Box 2260, Amherst, MA 01002-2372, U.S.A. **Online address:** caciepiela@amherst.edu

CIMBALA, Stephen J. American (born United States), b. 1943. **Genres:** Military/Defense/Arms Control, Politics/Government. **Career:** State University of New York, assistant professor of political science, 1969-73; Pennsylvania State University, associate professor, 1973-86, chief academic officer, 1973-81, professor of political science, 1986-, distinguished professor, 2000-, Institute for the Study of Nonlethal Defense Technologies, associate; Ohio State University, visiting associate professor, 1976; U.S. Arms Control and Disarmament Agency, consultant, 1997-99; U.S. Department of State, consultant, 1999; Grace Lutheran Church, chairman; Armed Forces and Society, associate editor. Writer and speaker. **Publications:** Extended Deterrence: The U.S. and NATO Europe, 1987; Nuclear War and Nuclear Strategy, 1987; Rethinking Nuclear Strategy, 1988; Nuclear Strategizing: Deterrence and Reality, 1988; Nuclear Endings, 1989; NATO Strategy and Nuclear Escalation, 1989; Uncertainty and Control: Future Superpower Strategy, 1990; First Strike Stability, 1990; Conflict Termination in Europe, 1990; Strategy after Deterrence, 1991; Clausewitz and Escalation, 1991; Force and Diplomacy in the Future, 1992; U.S. Nuclear Strategy in the New World Order, 1993; U.S. Military Strategy and the Cold War Endgame, 1995; The Politics of Warfare, 1997; The Past and Future of Nuclear Deterrence, 1998; Clausewitz and Chaos: Friction in War and Military Policy, 2000; Nuclear Strategy in the 21st Century, 2000; Russia and Armed Persuasion, 2001; Through a Glass Darkly: Looking at Conflict Prevention, Management, and Termination, 2001; The Dead Volcano: The Background and Effects of Nuclear War Complacency, 2002; (with J. Scouras) A New Nuclear Century: Strategic Stability and Arms Control, 2002; Shield of Dreams: Missile Defenses and Nuclear Strategy, 2002; (with S.C. Sarkesian and J.A. Williams) U.S. National Security: Policymakers, Processes, and Politics, 2002. Military Persuasion in War and Policy: The Power of Soft, 2002; (with P.K. Forster) US, NATO and Military Burden-Sharing, 2005; Nuclear Weapons and Strategy: U.S. Nuclear Policy for the Twenty-First Century, 2006; (with P. Rainow) Russia and Postmodern Deterrence: Military Power and Its Challenges for Security, 2007; (with S.C. Sarkesian and J.A. Williams) U.S. national Security: Policymakers, Processes, and Politics, 2008; Shield of Dreams: Missile Defense and U.S.-Russian Nuclear Strategy, 2008; Nuclear Weapons and Cooperative Security in the 21st Century: The New Disorder, 2010; (with P.K. Forster) Multinational Military Intervention: NATO Policy, Strategy and Burden Sharing, 2010; George W. Bush Defense Program: Policy, Strategy, & War, 2010; Nuclear Weapons in the Information Age, 2012. EDITOR AND CONTRIBUTOR: National Security Strategy, 1984; Strategic War Termination, 1986; The Reagan Defense Program, 1986; Soviet Command, Control, and Communications, 1987; Challenges to Deterrence, 1987; Intelligence and Intelligence Policy in a Democratic Society, 1987; The Technology, Strategy, and Politics of SDI, 1987; (with K. Dunn) Conflict Termination and Military Strategy, 1987; Artificial Intelligence and National Security, 1987; (with J. Douglass, Jr.) Ending a Nuclear War, 1988; The Soviet Challenge in the 1990s, 1989; Strategic Arms Control after SALT, 1989; Strategic Air Defense, 1989; (with S.R. Waldman) Controlling and Ending Conflict, 1992; Clinton and Post-Cold War Defense, 1996; Coercive Military Strategy, 1998; Mysteries of the Cold War, 1999; Deterrence and Nuclear Proliferation in the Twenty-First Century, 2001; The Russian Military into the Twenty-First Century, 2001; Civil-Military Relations in Perspective: Strategy, Structure and Policy, 2012. Works appear in anthologies. Contributor to professional journals. **Address:** Department of Political Science, Pennsylvania State University, 118 Vairo Library, 25 Yearsley Mill Rd., Media, PA 19063, U.S.A. **Online address:** sjc2@psu.edu

CIMENT, James D. American/Canadian (born Canada), b. 1958. **Genres:** Children's Non-fiction, Politics/Government, Cultural/Ethnic Topics, Economics, History. **Career:** City College of New York, lecturer, 1985-94; freelance writer and editor, 1992-2000; ABC-CLIO, acquisitions editor, 2000-01; East River Books, president, 2002-. **Publications:** Law and Order, 1995; The Kurds: State and Minority in Turkey, Iraq, and Iran, 1996; (with R. LaFrance) Scholastic Encyclopedia of the North American Indian, 1996; Algeria: The Fundamentalist Challenge, 1997; Angola and Mozambique: Postcolonial Wars in Southern Africa, 1997; Palestine/Israel: The Long Conflict, 1997; The Young People's History of the United States, 1998; (with I. Ness) Encyclopedia of Global Population and Demographics, 1999; Atlas of African-American History, 2001, rev. ed., 2007. EDITOR: Encyclopedia of Conflicts since World War II, 1999, 2nd ed., 2007; (with I. Ness) Encyclopedia of Third Parties in America, 2000; Encyclopedia of the Great Depression and New Deal, 2001; Encyclopedia of American Immigration, 2001; Colonial America: An Encyclopedia of Social, Political, Cultural, and Economic History; Social Issues in America: An Encyclopedia, 2006; Postwar America: An Encyclopedia of Social, Political, Cultural, and Economic History, 2007; (with T. Russell) Home Front Encyclopedia, 2007; Encyclopedia of the Jazz Age: From the End of World War I to the Great Crash, 2007; Booms and Busts, 2010; World Terrorism: An Encyclopedia of Political Violence From Ancient Times to the Post-9/11 Era, 2011. **Address:** East River Books, 2020 De La Vina, Ste. B, Santa Barbara, CA 93105-3814, U.S.A. **Online address:** james.ciment@verizon.net

CIMENT, Jill. American/Canadian (born Canada), b. 1953. **Genres:** Novels, Novellas/Short Stories, Autobiography/Memoirs. **Career:** University of Florida, professor of creative writing. Writer. **Publications:** Small Claims (short stories and novella), 1986; The Law of Falling Bodies (novel), 1993; Half a Life (autobiography), 1996; Teeth of the Dog: A Novel, 1999; The Tattoo Artist, 2005; Heroic Measures: A Novel, 2009. Contributor to periodicals. **Address:** Department of English, University of Florida, 4211G Turlington Hall, PO Box 117300, Gainesville, FL 32611-7310, U.S.A. **Online address:** jciment@ufl.edu

CIMINO, Richard P. American (born United States) **Genres:** Theology/Religion, Humanities. **Career:** Religion Watch, editor and publisher. **Publications:** Against the Stream: The Adoption of Traditional Christian Faiths by Young Adults, 1997; (with D. Lattin) Shopping for Faith: American Religion in the New Millennium, 1998; Trusting the Spirit: Renewal and Reform in American Religion, 2001; (ed.) Lutherans Today: American Lutheran Identity in the Twenty-First Century, 2003. Contributor to magazines and periodicals. **Address:** Religion Watch, PO Box 652, North Bellmore, NY 11710, U.S.A.

CIOCHON, Russell L. American (born United States), b. 1948. **Genres:** Anthropology/Ethnology, Archaeology/Antiquities, Earth Sciences, Essays, History, Environmental Sciences/Ecology. **Career:** University of North Carolina, lecturer in anthropology, 1978-81; University of California, teaching associate, 1978, research specialist in paleontology, 1982-83, Institute of Human Origins, research associate, 1983-85; State University of New York, research associate in anatomical sciences, 1985-86; University of Arizona, visiting lecturer in anthropology, 1987; University of Iowa, Department of Anthropology, assistant professor, 1987-89, associate professor, 1990-96, professor, 1996-, chairman, 1997-2000, Program in Ecology and Evolutionary Biology, researcher, 1987-92, College of Dentistry, Department of Pediatric Dentistry, assistant professor, 1989-90, associate professor, 1990-96, professor of anthropology and pediatric dentistry, 1996-; Subject of Television Documentaries, television scriptwriter and writer. **Publications:** (With J.W. Olsen and J. James) Other Origins: The Search for the Giant Ape in Human Prehistory, 1990; Warum musBte Giganto sterben: Auf der Suche nach dem Riesenaffen in Prahistorischer Zeit, 1992; Evolution of the Cercopithecoid Forelimb: Phylogenetic and Functional Implications from Morphometric Analyses, 1993; (with N. Boaz) Dragon Bone Hill: An Ice Age Saga of Homoerectus, 2004. EDITOR: (with A.B. Chiarelli and contrib.) Evolutionary Biology of the New World Monkeys and Continental Drift, 1980; (with R.S. Corruccini and contrib.) New Interpretations of Ape and Human Ancestry, 1983; (with J.G. Fleagle) Primate Evolution and Human Origins, 1985; Advances in Human Evolution Series, 1991; (with J.G. Fleagle) The Human Evolution Source Book, 1993, rev. ed., 2006; (with R.S. Corruccini and contrib.) Integrative Paths to the Past: Paleoanthropological Advances in Honor of F. Clark Howell, 1994; (with R. Nisbett) The Primate Anthology: Essays on Primate Behavior, Ecology and Conservation from Natural History, 1998; (with B. Wood) Human Evolution (series), 1998; (with H.V. Tan and Olsen) The Prehistory of Vietnam, forthcoming. Contributor to journals and magazines. **Address:** Department of Anthropology, University of Iowa, 129 Macbride Hall, Iowa City, IA 52242-1322, U.S.A. **Online address:** russell-ciochon@uiowa.edu

CIRESI, Rita. American (born United States), b. 1960. **Genres:** Novels, Novellas/Short Stories. **Career:** Pennsylvania State University, science writer, 1989-92, Department of Agriculture, editor, 1989-92; Hollins College, assistant professor of English, 1992-95; University of South Florida, assistant professor, 1995-, associate professor, professor of English and coordinator of creative writing, director of creative writing; American Academy in Rome, visiting writer. **Publications:** STORIES: Mother Rocket, 1993. NOVELS: Blue Italian, 1996; Pink Slip, 1999; Sometimes I Dream in Italian, 2000; Remind Me Again Why I Married You, 2003. Works appear in anthologies. Contributor to periodicals. **Address:** Department of English, University of South Florida, CPR 320, 4202 E Fowler Ave., Tampa, FL 33620-5550, U.S.A. **Online address:** rciresi@hotmail.com

CIRINCIONE, Joseph. American (born United States) **Genres:** International Relations/Current Affairs, Politics/Government, History, Social Sciences. **Career:** U.S. House of Representatives, Committee on Armed Services, professional staff, 1985-91, Government Operations Subcommittee on National Security Legislation, deputy staff director, 1991-93; Henry L. Stimson Center, senior associate, 1993-98; Carnegie Endowment for International peace, senior associate and director for nonproliferation, 1998-2006; Center for American Progress, senior vice president for national security, 2006-08; Ploughshares

Fund, president, 2008-; Georgetown University, School of Foreign Service, faculty. Writer. **Publications:** (Ed.) Central America and the Western Alliance, 1985; (ed.) Repairing the Regime: Preventing the Spread of Weapons of Mass Destruction, 2000; (with J.B. Wolfsthal and M. Rajkumar) Deadly Arsenals: Tracking Weapons of Mass Destruction, 2002, 2nd ed., 2005; (with J.T. Matthews and G. Perkovich) WMD in Iraq: Evidence and Implications, 2004; (co-author) Universal Compliance: A Strategy for Nuclear Security, 2005, 2nd ed., 2007; Bomb Scare: The History and Future of Nuclear Weapons, 2007. **Address:** Ploughshares Fund, 1430 K St. NW, Ste. 550, Washington, DC 20005, U.S.A. **Online address:** jcirincione@ploughshares.org

CITRO, Joseph A. American (born United States) **Genres:** Science Fiction/Fantasy, Young Adult Fiction, Young Adult Non-fiction, Novels, Mythology/Folklore, Local History/Rural Topics, Horror, Paranormal, Paranormal. **Career:** Writer and educator. **Publications:** NOVELS: Shadow Child, 1987; Guardian Angels, 1988; The Unseen, 1990; The Gore, 1990; Dark Twilight, 1991; Deus-X, 1994; Lake Monsters, 2001; Deus-X: The Reality Conspiracy, 2003. COLLECTION: Monsters: Three Tales, 1986; Joe Citro's Weird Vermont, 2003; Not Yet Dead, 2009. NON FICTION: Green Mountain Ghosts, Ghouls and Unsolved Mysteries, 1994; Passing Strange: True Tales of New England Hauntings and Horrors, 1996; Green Mountains, Dark Tales, 1999; The Vermont Ghost Guide, 2000; Curious New England: The Unconventional Traveler's Guide to Eccentric Destinations, 2003; Cursed in New England: Stories of Damned Yankees, 2004; Weird New England, 2005; Vermont Monster Guide, 2009; Vermont's Haunts, 2011. **Address:** Bat Books, 217 Saint Paul St., Burlington, VT 05401, U.S.A. **Online address:** jacitro@burlingtontelecom.net

CITRON, Stephen. American (born United States) **Genres:** Novels, Poetry, Art/Art History, Humor/Satire. **Career:** Writer. **Publications:** (With A. Edwards) The Inn and Us, 1976; Songwriting: A Complete Guide to the Craft, 1985; The Musical from the Inside Out, 1992; Noel and Cole: The Sophisticates, 1993; The Wordsmiths: Oscar Hammerstein 2nd and Alan Jay Lerner, 1995; Sondheim and Lloyd-Webber: The New Musical, 2001; Jerry Herman: Poet of the Showtune, 2004. **Address:** Yale University Press, PO Box 209040, New Haven, CT 06520-9040, U.S.A.

CIVIL-BROWN, Sue. *See* **LEE, Rachel.**

CLABOUGH, Casey Howard. American (born United States), b. 1974. **Genres:** Humanities, Literary Criticism And History, Local History/Rural Topics, Mythology/Folklore, Natural History, Paranormal, Philosophy, Sports/Fitness, Writing/Journalism, Horror, Ghost Writer, Novels, Novellas/Short Stories, Adult Non-fiction, Agriculture/Forestry, Classics, Horticulture, Travel/Exploration. **Career:** Lynchburg College, Department of English, assistant professor, 2001-06, associate professor of English, 2006-, English graduate director, 2007-11, department chair, 2008-11; Virginia Foundation for the Humanities, fellow, 2005; University of Virginia, Harrison Institute, Lillian Gary Taylor fellow, 2006; Encyclopedia Virginia, literature editor, 2006-; Road Rangers Project, archivist, 2006-; Lynchburg College, English graduate director, 2007-; University of South Carolina, Institute for Southern Studies, fellow, 2007; James Dickey Review, general editor, 2010-. **Publications:** Elements: The Novels of James Dickey, 2002; Experimentation and Versatility: The Early Novels and Short Fiction of Fred Chappell, 2005; The Warrior's Path: Reflections Along an Ancient Route, 2007; The Art of the Magic Striptease: The Literary Layers of George Garrett, 2008; Gayl Jones: The Language of Voice and Freedom in Her Writings, 2008; Confederado: A Novel of the Americas, 2011. **Address:** Department of English, Lynchburg College, 1501 Lakeside Dr., Lynchburg, VA 24501, U.S.A. **Online address:** c.clabough@yahoo.com

CLAGUE, Christopher K. American (born United States), b. 1938. **Genres:** Economics, Politics/Government, Social Sciences. **Career:** Harvard University, instructor in economics, 1965-67; President's Council of Economic Advisers, senior staff economist, 1967-68; University of Maryland, assistant professor, 1968-71, associate professor, 1971-79, professor of economics, 1979-, now professor emeritus, department head, 1980-82, Project on Institutional Reform and the Informal Sector, director of research, 1990-; Boston University, Center for Latin American Development Studies, visiting professor, 1974-75; University of California, visiting professor, 1983; University of Hawaii, visiting professor, 1990; University of Nottingham, visiting professor, 1990; World Bank consultant; Organization for Economic Cooperation and Development, consultant. Writer. **Publications:** (With R.I. Rotberg) Haiti: The Politics of Squalor, 1971; (with R.R. Betancourt) Capital Utilization: A Theoretical and Empirical Analysis, 1981; (ed. with G.C. Rausser) The Emergence of Market Economies in Eastern Europe, 1992; (ed.) Institutions and Economic Development: Growth and Governance in Less-Developed and Post-Socialist Countries, 1997; (ed. with S. Grossbard-Shechtman) Expansion of Economics: Toward a More Inclusive Social Science, 2002. Contributor to journals. **Address:** Department of Economics, University of Maryland, 3105 Tydings Hall, College Park, MD 20742-7211, U.S.A.

CLAIBORNE, Shane. American (born United States), b. 1975. **Genres:** inspirational/Motivational Literature, Social Sciences, Philosophy. **Career:** The Simple Way (faith community), founding partner; Writer, activist, evangelist, and public speaker. **Publications:** The Irresistible Revolution: Living As an Ordinary Radical, 2006; (with C. Haw) Jesus for President: Politics for Ordinary Radicals, 2008; (with J. Wilson-Hartgrove) Becoming the Answer to Our Prayers: Prayer for Ordinary Radicals, 2008; (with J.M. Perkins) Follow Me to Freedom, 2009; (with J. Wilson-Hartgrove and E. Okoro) Common Prayer: A Liturgy for Ordinary Radicals, 2010. Contributor to periodicals. **Address:** The Simple Way, PO Box 14751, Philadelphia, PA 19134, U.S.A.

CLAIRE, Cherie. (Cheré Dastugue Coen). American (born United States), b. 1960. **Genres:** Novels, Romance/Historical, Poetry, Young Adult Fiction, History. **Career:** The Advocate Magazine, features editor and writer, 1995-2000; Tulane University, instructor, 1997-98; Variety, copy editor, 2000-02; The Daily Advertiser, features editor, 2004-06; Louisiana Book News, editor, 2004-11; University of Louisiana, instructor of writing, 2005-; freelance journalist and travel writer, 2006-; The History Press, author, 2011-. **Publications:** A Cajun Dream, 1999; (with P. Conn and V. Dark) Snow Angels (anthology), 1999; Emilie, 2000; Rose, 2000; Gabrielle, 2001; Delphine, 2002. AS CHERé DASTUGUE COEN: (with K. Breaux) Cooking in Cajun Country, 2009; (with J. Bradley) Magic's in the Bag, 2010; Exploring Cajun Country, 2011. **Address:** The History Press, 635 Rutledge Ave., Ste. 107, Charleston, SC 29403, U.S.A. **Online address:** chere@louisianabooknews.com

CLAIRE, Rodger W(illiam). American (born United States) **Genres:** Writing/Journalism, Business/Trade/Industry, History, Young Adult Non-fiction. **Career:** Oui and Playboy Magazines, articles editor; Los Angeles Magazine, executive editor. **Publications:** (With A. Renetzky and H. Rudd) Directory of Career Training and Development Programs, 1979; Entertainment 101: An Industry Primer, 1999; Raid on the Sun: Inside Israel's Secret Campaign That Denied Saddam the Bomb, 2004. **Address:** c/o Author Mail, Random House, 1745 Broadway, New York, NY 10019-4368, U.S.A.

CLAMP, Cathy. Also writes as Cat Adams, Cathy L. Clamp. American (born United States), b. 1961?. **Genres:** Novels, Young Adult Fiction, Young Adult Non-fiction. **Career:** Writer. **Publications:** (With C.T. Adams as Cathy L. Clamp) Road to Riches: The Great Railroad Race to Aspen, 2003. TALES OF THE SAZI SERIES WITH C.T. ADAMS: Hunter's Moon, 2004; Moon's Web, 2005; Captive Moon, 2006; Howling Moon, 2007; Moon's Fury, 2007; Timeless Moon, 2008; Cold Moon Rising, 2009; Serpent Moon, 2010. THRALL SERIES WITH C.T. ADAMS: Touch of Evil, 2006; Touch of Madness, 2007; Touch of Darkness, 2008. OTHER: (co-author) Weirdly: A Collection of Strange Tales, 2007. AS CAT ADAMS WITH C.T. ADAMS: BLOOD SONG SERIES: Blood Song, 2010; Siren Song, 2010; Demon Song, 2011; The Isis Collar, 2012. NOVEL CAT ADAMS WITH C.T. ADAMS: Magic's Design, 2009. Works appear in anthologies. Contributor to periodicals. **Address:** Western Reflections Publishing Co., 951 N Hwy. 149, PO Box 1149, Lake City, CO 81235, U.S.A. **Online address:** catadamsfans@gmail.com

CLAMP, Cathy L. *See* **CLAMP, Cathy.**

CLANCY, Flora Simmons. American (born United States), b. 1942. **Genres:** Art/Art History, Archaeology/Antiquities. **Career:** Colgate University, lecturer, 1973-78; University of New Mexico, Department Art and Art History, associate professor, professor, 1979-2003, chair, 1985, 1997-2000, professor emeritus, 2003-. Writer. **Publications:** Maya: Treasures of an Ancient Civilization, 1985; (ed. with P.D. Harrison) Vision and Revision in Maya Studies, 1990; Pyramids, 1994; Sculpture in the Ancient Maya Plaza: The Early Classic Period, 1999; The Monuments of Piedras Negras an Ancient Maya City, 2009. Contributor of articles to periodicals. **Address:** Department of Art and Art History, University of New Mexico, 1 University of New Mexico, Albuquerque, NM 87131-0001, U.S.A. **Online address:** flora@unm.edu

CLANCY, Tom. American (born United States), b. 1947. **Genres:** Novels, Novellas/Short Stories, Military/Defense/Arms Control, Biography, History. **Career:** O.F. Bowen Agency, agent, 1973-, owner, 1980-. Writer. **Publications:** FICTION: The Hunt for Red October, 1984; (with L. Bond) Red Storm Rising, 1986; Patriot Games, 1987; The Cardinal of the Kremlin, 1988; Clear and Present Danger, 1989; The Sum of All Fears, 1991; Red Storm Rising: The Cardinal of the Kremlin: Two Complete Novels, 1993; Without Remorse, 1993; Debt of Honor, 1994; Executive Orders, 1996; (with M.H. Greenberg) SSN: Strategies of Submarine Warfare, 1996; Rainbow Six, 1997; (with C. Horner) Every Man a Tiger, 1999; The Bear and the Dragon, 2000; Tom Clancy's Net Force, 2000; Red Rabbit, 2002; The Teeth of the Tiger, 2003. TOM CLANCY'S OP-CENTER SERIES WITH S. PIECZENIK: Mirror Image, 1995; Game of State, 1997; Acts of War, 1997; Sea of Fire, 2003. OTHERS: (intro.) North SAR, 1991; Submarine: A Guided Tour inside a Nuclear Warship, 1993, (with J. Gresham) rev. ed., 2003; Armored Cav: A Guided Tour of an Armored Cavalry Regiment, 1994; Fighter Wing: A Guided Tour of an Air Force Combat Wing, 1995; Reality Check: What's Going On out There?, 1995; Marine: A Guided Tour of a Marine Expeditionary Unit, 1996; (with F. Franks, Jr.) Into the Storm: A Study in Command, 1997; Airborne: A Guided Tour of an Airborne Task Force, 1997; (contrib.) Fighting Chance: Journeys Through Childhood Cancer, 1998; (with C. Horner) Every Man A Tiger, 1999; Carrier: A Guided Tour of an Aircraft Carrier, 1999; (with S. Piecznik) Cyberspy, 1999; Special Ops, 2000; Divide and Conquer, 2000; (with J. Gresham) Special Forces: A Guided Tour of U.S. Army Special Forces, 2001; (with C. Stiner and T. Koltz) Shadow Warriors: Inside the Special Forces, 2002; (with T. Zinni and T. Kolz) Battle Ready, 2004; (with W.J. Rude) War in the Boats: My World War II Submarine Battles, 2004; Tom Clancy Companion, 2005; Operation Baracuda, 2005; (with D. Michaels) Tom Clancy's Endwar, 2008; (with D. Michaels) Tom Clancy's Ghost Recon, 2008; (with D. Michaels) Tom Clancy's H.A.W.X., 2009; (with G. Blackwood) Dead or Alive, 2010; (with P. Telep) Against All Enemies, 2011; (with M. Greaney) Locked On, 2011; (with P. Telep) Search and Destroy, 2012. TOM CLANCY'S SPLINTER CELL SERIES WITH D. MICHAELS: Tom Clancy's Splinter Cell, 2004; Operation Barracuda, 2005; Checkmate, 2006; Fallout, 2007; Conviction, 2009; (with S. Pieczenik) End Game, 2009. **Address:** Red Storm Entertainment, 2000 Centre Green Way, Ste. 300, Cary, NC 27513, U.S.A.

CLAPHAM, Christopher S. British (born England), b. 1941. **Genres:** International Relations/Current Affairs, Politics/Government, Economics, History, Social Sciences. **Career:** Lancaster University, lecturer, 1971-74, senior lecturer in politics, 1974-89, professor of politics and international relations, 1989-2002; Cambridge University, Centre of African Studies, professor, 2002-. Writer. **Publications:** (With J.C.N. Paul) Ethiopian Constitutional Development: A Sourcebook, 1967; The Caves of Sof Omar, 1967; Haile-Selassie's Government, 1969; Liberia and Sierra Leone: An Essay in Comparative Politics, 1976; (ed.) Foreign Policy Making in Developing States: A Comparative Approach, 1977; (ed.) Private Patronage and Public Power: Political Clientelism in the Modern State, 1982; (ed. with G. Philip) The Political Dilemmas of Military Regimes, 1984; Third World Politics: An Introduction, 1985; Transformation and Continuity in Revolutionary Ethiopia, 1988; Africa and the International System: The Politics of State Survival, 1996; (ed.) African Guerrillas, 1998; (co-ed.) Regional Integration in Southern Africa: Comparative International Perspectives, 1999; War and State Formation in Ethiopia and Eritrea, 2000; (ed. with J. Herbst and G. Mills) Big African States, 2006. **Address:** Centre of African Studies, Cambridge University, Free School Ln., Cambridge, CM CB2 3RQ, England. **Online address:** csc34@cam.ac.uk

CLAPP, Jennifer. Canadian (born Canada), b. 1963. **Genres:** Adult Nonfiction, Politics/Government, Social Commentary. **Career:** Alternatives Journal, contributing editor, 1998-; Trent University, associate professor of environmental and resource studies, International Development Studies Program, chair; University of Waterloo, The Balsillie School of International Affairs, Department of Environment and Resource Studies, professor, Centre for International Governance, innovation chair, Global Environmental Governance, CIGI Chair; faculty of environmental studies. Writer. **Publications:** Adjustment and Agriculture in Africa: Farmers, the State, and the World Bank in Guinea, 1997; Toxic Exports: The Transfer of Hazardous Wastes from Rich to Poor Countries, 2001; (with P. Dauvergne) Paths to a Green World: The Political Economy of the Global Environment, 2005. (ed. with P. Utting) Corporate Accountability and Sustainable Development, 2008; (ed. with J. Clapp) Corporate Power in Global Agrifood Governance, 2009; (ed. with R. Wilkinson) Global Governance, Poverty and Inequality, 2010; (with P. Dauvergne) Paths to a Green World: The Political Economy of the Global Environment, 2011; Hunger in the Balance: The New Politics of international Food Aid, 2012. Contributor to periodicals and journals. **Address:** Department of Environment and Resource Studies, University of Waterloo, 2016 Environment Bldg. 2, 200 University Ave. W, Waterloo, ON N2L 3G1, Canada. **Online address:** jclapp@uwaterloo.ca

CLAPP, Nicholas. American (born United States), b. 1936. **Genres:** Documentaries/Reportage, Mystery/Crime/Suspense, History, Social Sciences. **Career:** Documentary filmmaker, host and writer. **Publications:** The Road to Ubar: Finding the Atlantis of the Sands, 1998; Sheba: Through the Desert in Search of the Legendary Queen, 2001; Who Killed Chester Pray?: A Death Valley Mystery, 2007. **Address:** 1551 S Robertson Blvd., Los Angeles, CA 90035, U.S.A.

CLAPP, Rodney. American (born United States) **Genres:** Theology/Religion, History, Social Sciences. **Career:** Christianity Today, associate editor, through 1999; InterVarsity Press, senior editor; Brazos Press, editor, executive editor and editorial director. Theologian. **Publications:** (With R.E. Webber) People of the Truth: The Power of the Worshiping Community in the Modern World, 1988; (with R.E. Webber) People of the Truth: A Christian Challenge to Contemporary Culture, 1993; Families at the Crossroads: Beyond Traditional and Modern Options, 1993; A Peculiar People: The Church as Culture in a Post-Christian Society, 1996; (ed.) The Consuming Passion: Christianity and the Culture of Consumption, 1998; Border Crossings: Christian Trespasses on Popular Culture and Public Affairs, 2000; Tortured Wonders: Christian Spirituality for People, Not Angels, 2004; Johnny Cash and The Great American Contradiction: Christianity and the Battle for the Soul of a Nation, 2008. **Address:** Baker Publishing Group, 6030 E Fulton Rd., PO Box 6287, Grand Rapids, MI 49516-6287, U.S.A. **Online address:** rclapp@brazospress.com

CLAPPER, Gregory S(cott). American (born United States), b. 1951. **Genres:** inspirational/Motivational Literature, Theology/Religion, History. **Career:** Emory University, Candler School of Theology, graduate assistant, 1979-83; Westmar College (now Teikyo Westmar University), assistant professor, 1985-89, associate professor of religion and philosophy, 1989-91; Metodistkirkens Studiesenter, visiting professor, 1988; United Methodist Church, senior minister, 1991-94; Huntingdon College, associate professor in Chapman-Benson chair of Christian faith and philosophy, 1994-98; University of Indianapolis, associate professor and associate director of the Lantz center for Christian vocations, 1998-, professor. Writer. **Publications:** John Wesley on Religious Affections: His Views on Experience and Emotion and Their Role in the Christian Life and Theology, 1989; As if the Heart Mattered: A Wesleyan Spirituality, 1997; When the World Breaks Your Heart: Spiritual Ways to Live with Tragedy, 1999; Living Your Heart's Desire: God's Call and Your Vocation, 2005; Renewal of the Heart is the Mission of the Church: Wesley's Heart Religion in the Twenty-First Century, 2010. Contributor of articles to periodicals. **Address:** Department of Philosophy and Religion, University of Indianapolis, Esch 044H, 1400 E Hanna Ave., Indianapolis, IN 46227, U.S.A. **Online address:** gclapper@uindy.edu

CLARE, Alys. (Elizabeth Harris). British (born England), b. 1944?. **Genres:** Mystery/Crime/Suspense. **Career:** Writer. **Publications:** AELF FEN MYSTERIES: Out of the Dawn Light, 2009; Mist Over the Water, 2009; Music of the Distant Stars, 2010. HAWKENLYE HISTORICAL MYSTERY SERIES: Fortune Like the Moon, 1999; Ashes of the Elements, 2000; The Tavern in the Morning, 2000; The Chatter of the Maidens, 2001; The Faithful Dead, 2002; A Dark Night Hidden, 2003; Whiter Than the Lily, 2004; Girl in a Red Tunic, 2005; Heart of Ice, 2006; The Enchanter's Forest, 2007; The Paths of the Air, 2008; The Joys of My Life, 2008; The Rose of the World, 2011. AS ELIZABETH HARRIS: The Herb Gatherers, 1991; The Egyptian Years, 1992; The Sun Worshippers, 1993; Prologue and the Gospel: The Theology of the Fourth Evangelist, 1994; Prologue and Gospel, 1994; Shadows in the Sand, 1994; Time of the Wolf, 1994; The Quiet Earth, 1995; The Sacrifice Stone, 1996; A Good Man's Love, 1996; Singing in the Wilderness, 1997; The Twilight Child, 1997; (with D. Nutbeam and M. Wise) Theory in a Nutshell, 2004. **Address:** Merric Davidson Literary Agency, 12 Priors Heath, Goudhurst, KT TN17 2RE, England. **Online address:** alys@alysclare.com

CLARE, Ellen. *See* **SINCLAIR, Olga (Ellen).**

CLARK, A(ilsa) M. (Ailsa McGown Clark). British (born England), b. 1926. **Genres:** Zoology, Natural History, Marine Sciences/Oceanography, Sciences. **Career:** British Museum-National History (now Natural History Museum), curator of echinoderms, 1948-86. Writer. **Publications:** (With A.H. Clark) A Revision of the Sea-stars of the Genus Tethyaster, 1954; Starfishes and Related Echinoderms, 1962, 3rd ed. 1977; Notes of Asteroids in the British Museum, 1967; Notes on Some Tropical Indo-Pacific Ophiotrichids and Ophiodermatids, 1968; Echinodermata Crinoidea, 1970; (with F.W.E. Rowe) Indo-Pacific Echinoderms, 1971; Monograph of Shallow-water Indo-West Pacific Echinoderms, 1971; Some Crinoids from the Indian Ocean, 1972; Some New Taxa of Recent Stalked Crinoidea, 1973; Notes on Some Echinoderms from Southern Africa, 1974; The Swain Reefs Expedition: Crinoidea, 1975; (with J. Courtman-Stock) Echinoderms of Southern Africa, 1976; (P.E. Gibbs and C.M. Clark) Echinoderms from the Northern Region of the Great Barrier Reef, Australia, 1976; Notes on Deep-water Atlantic Crinoidea, 1977; (with N.A. Sloan and J.D. Taylor) Echinoderms of Aldabra and Their Habitats, 1979; Notes on Atlantic and Other Asteroidea: 1. Family Benthopectinidae, 1981; (with M.E. Downey) Starfishes of the Atlantic, 1991; (with Y. Liao) Echinoderms of Southern China, 1995. **Address:** Gyllyngdune, South Rd., Wivelsfield Green, Haywards Heath, Sussex, RH17 7QS, England.

CLARK, Ailsa McGown. *See* **CLARK, A(ilsa) M.**

CLARK, Andrew. Canadian (born Canada), b. 1966?. **Genres:** Mystery/Crime/Suspense, Social Sciences, Law. **Career:** Eye Weekly, comedy critic; Toronto Star, comedy critic; Humber College, professor, Humber School of Comedy, director; Maclean's magazine, senior writer. Journalist and documentary filmmaker. **Publications:** Stand and Deliver: Inside Canadian Comedy, 1997; A Keen Soldier: The Execution of Second World War Private Harold John Pringle, 2002; The Next Big Thing, 2003. **Address:** c/o Dean Cooke, The Cooke Agency Inc., 278 Bloor St. E, Ste. 305, Toronto, ON M4W 3M4, Canada. **Online address:** andrew@andrewclark.ca

CLARK, Andrew F. American (born United States), b. 1954. **Genres:** History, Area Studies, Third World, Travel/Exploration, International Relations/Current Affairs. **Career:** University of North Carolina Wilmington, assistant professor, professor of African and global history, 1990-. Writer. **Publications:** (With L.C. Phillips) Historical Dictionary of Senegal, 2nd ed., 1994; From Frontier to Backwater: Economy and Society in the Upper Senegal Valley, 1850-1920, 1999; Lost and Found in West Africa: An American in Senegal, forthcoming. **Address:** Department of History, University of North Carolina, Morton Hall 227, Wilmington, NC 28403, U.S.A. **Online address:** clarka@uncw.edu

CLARK, Andy. British (born England), b. 1957. **Genres:** Medicine/Health, Psychology, Sciences, Information Science/Computers, Technology, Psychology. **Career:** University of Glasgow, temporary lecturer in philosophy, 1984-85; University of Sussex, lecturer, 1985-93, reader in philosophy, 1992-93, faculty, 2000-02; Washington University, professor of philosophy and director of philosophy, neuroscience and psychology program, 1993-2000; Indiana University, professor of philosophy and director; University of Edinburgh, chair in logic and metaphysics, 2004-, professor of philosophy. Writer. **Publications:** Microcognition: Philosophy, Cognitive Science, and Parallel Distributed Processing, 1989; Associative Engines: Connectionism, Concepts, and Representational Change, 1993; Being There: Putting Brain, Body and World Together Again, 1997; Mindware: An Introduction to the Philosophy of Cognitive Science, 2001; Natural-Born Cyborgs: Minds, Technologies and the Future of Human Intelligence, 2003; Supersizing the Mind: Embodiment, Action and Cognitive Extension, 2008. EDITOR: (with R. Lutz) Connectionism in Context, 1992; (with L. May and M. Friedman) Mind and Morals: Essays on Cognitive Science and Ethics, 1996; (with P. Millican) Essays in Honour of Alan Turing, vol. I: The Theory of Computation, vol. II: Connectionism, Concepts and Folk Psychology, 1996; (with J. Ezquerro and J. Larrazabal) Philosophy and Cognitive Science: Categories, Consciousness and Reasoning, 1996; (and intro. with J. Toribio) Congnitive Architectures in Artificial Intelligence: The Evolution of Research Programs, 1998; (and intro. with J. Toribio) Consciousness and Emotion in Cognitive Science: Conceptual and Empirical Issues, 1998; (and intro. with J. Toribio) Language and Meaning in Cognitive Science: Cognitive Issues and Semantic Theory, 1998; (and intro. with J. Toribio) Machine Intelligence: Perspectives on the Computational Model, 1998. Contributor to books and periodicals. **Address:** Department of Philosophy, University of Edinburgh, Dugald Stewart Bldg., 3 Charles St., George Sq., Edinburgh, BR EH8 9AD, Scotland. **Online address:** andy.clark@ed.ac.uk

CLARK, Anna (K.). (Anna Kirsten Clark). American (born United States) **Genres:** History, Women's Studies And Issues, Politics/Government, Law. **Career:** University of North Carolina, Department of History, assistant professor, 1988-94, associate professor, 1994-99; Kingston University, resident faculty director, 1997-98, University of Minnesota, Department of History, associate professor, 1999-2001, professor, 2001-, Samuel Russell chair in the humanities, 2005-11; Journal of British Studies, editor, 2005-10. **Publications:** Women's Silence, Men's Violence: Sexual Assault in England, 1770-1845, 1987; The Struggle for the Breeches: Gender and the Making of the British Working Class, 1995; (intro. with S. Richardson) History of Suffrage, 1760-1867, 2000; Scandal: The Sexual Politics of the British Constitution, 2004; (ed. with T. Brotherstone and K. Whelan) These Fissured Isles: Ireland, Scotland and the Making of Modern Britain 1798-1848, 2005; (ed. with S. Dudink and K. Hagemann) Representing Masculinity: Male Citizenship in Modern Western Culture, 2007; Desire: A History of European Sexuality, 2008; (co-author) Greening Your Company, 2009; (ed.) The History of Sexuality in Europe: A Sourcebook and Reader, 2010. **Address:** Department of History, University of Minnesota, 1051 HellerH, 614 Social Science Twr., 267 19th Ave. S, Minneapolis, MN 55455-0499, U.S.A. **Online address:** clark106@umn.edu

CLARK, Anna Kirsten. *See* **CLARK, Anna (K.).**

CLARK, Beverly Lyon. American (born United States), b. 1948. **Genres:** Literary Criticism And History, Women's Studies And Issues, Cultural/Ethnic Topics, Essays, Education. **Career:** Wheaton College, lecturer, assistant professor, associate professor, professor of English, 1977-. Writer. **Publications:** Talking about Writing: A Guide for Tutor and Teacher Conferences, 1985; (ed. with M.J. Friedman) Critical Essays on Flannery O'Connor, 1985; Reflections of Fantasy: The Mirror-Worlds of Carroll, Nabokov and Pynchon, 1986; Lewis Carroll, 1990; Regendering the School Story: Sassy Sissies and Tattling Tomboys, 1996; (ed. with M.J. Friedman) Critical Essays on Carson McCullers, 1996; (ed. with J.M. Alberghene) Little Women and the Feminist Imagination: Criticism, Controversy, Personal Essays, 1999; (ed. with M.R. Higonnet) Girls, Boys, Books, Toys: Gender in Children's Literature and Culture, 1999; Kiddie Lit: The Cultural Construction of Children's Literature in America, 2003; (ed.) Louisa May Alcott: The Contemporary Reviews, 2004; Oxford Encyclopedia of Children's Literature, 2006; (ed.) Adventures of Tom Sawyer, 2007. **Address:** Department of English, Wheaton College, 311 Meneely, 26 E Main St., Norton, MA 02766-2322, U.S.A. **Online address:** bclark@wheatoncollege.edu

CLARK, Carol Higgins. American (born United States), b. 1956?. **Genres:** Mystery/Crime/Suspense, Novels. **Career:** Actress and novelist. **Publications:** REGAN REILLY SERIES: Decked, 1992; Snagged, 1993; Iced, 1995; Twanged, 1998; Fleeced, 2001; Jinxed, 2002; Popped, 2003; Burned, 2005; Hitched, 2006; Laced, 2007; Zapped, 2008; Cursed, 2009; Wrecked, 2010; Mobbed, 2011. WITH M.H. CLARK: Deck the Halls, 2000; He Sees You When You're Sleeping, 2001; The Christmas Thief, 2004; Santa Cruise: A Holiday Mystery at Sea, 2006; Dashing Through the Snow, 2008. **Address:** Simon & Schuster Inc., 1230 Ave. of the Americas, New York, NY 10020, U.S.A. **Online address:** chc4rr@aol.com

CLARK, (Carter) Blue. American (born United States), b. 1946. **Genres:** Law, History. **Career:** University of Utah, program director, 1976-77; Morningside College, assistant professor, 1977-79; California State University, associate professor and professor, 1979-92; Oklahoma City University, university administrator, executive vice-president, 1991-98, instructor of law, professor, 1998-; Oakerhater Guild, president; Red Earth Festival, adviser. Writer. **Publications:** (Ed.) Chiang Kai-Shek and the United States, 1986; Lone Wolf v. Hitchcock: Treaty Rights and Indian Law at the End of the Nineteenth Century, 1994; Indian Tribes of Oklahoma: A Guide, 2009. Contributor to books and periodicals. **Address:** School of Law, Oklahoma City University, Native Law Ctr., 2501 N Blackwelder, Oklahoma City, OK 73106-1402, U.S.A. **Online address:** bclark@okcu.edu

CLARK, Catherine. Also writes as Caitlyn Davis, Kathy Clark. American (born United States), b. 1962. **Genres:** Novels. **Career:** Novelist and bookseller. **Publications:** YOUNG ADULT NOVELS: What's So Funny about Ninth Grade?, 1992; Girl of the Year, 1993; Truth or Dairy, 2000 as Banana Splitsville, 2008; Wurst Case Scenario, 2001; Star-Crossed, 2001; Frozen Rodeo, 2003 as Better Latte Than Never, 2008; The Alison Rules, 2004; Maine Squeeze, 2004; Icing on the Lake, 2006; So Inn Love, 2007; (as Caitlyn Davis) What's Hot, 2007; Picture Perfect, 2008; Wish You Were Here, 2008; Rocky

Road Trip, 2008. NOVELIZATIONS BASED ON TELEVISION SERIES: YOUNG ADULT NOVELS: My So-Called Life, 1995; Bailey's Journal: Party of Five, 1998; My So-Called Life Goes On, 1999; 7th Heaven: Middle Sister, 2000; (adapter) I Do, Don't I?, 2002; (adapter) Like Mother, Like Daughter, 2002. FULL HOUSE: CLUB STEPHANIE SERIES: NOVELIZATIONS OF THE TELEVISION SERIES AS KATHY CLARK: Forget It, Flamingoes!, 1999; Flamingoes Forever?, 1999; Five Flamingo Summer, 1999; Summertime Secrets, 2000; Truth or Dare, 2000; The Real Thing, 2000; Rumor Has It, 2001; He's the One!, 2001; Three's a Crowd, 2001. **Address:** Minneapolis, MN , U.S.A. **Online address:** frozen_rodeo@catherineclark.com

CLARK, Charles E. American (born United States), b. 1929. **Genres:** History, Social Sciences, Communications/Media, Adult Non-fiction. **Career:** Valley News, reporter, 1952; Providence Journal and Evening Bulletin, reporter, 1956-61; Southeastern Massachusetts Technological Institute, assistant professor of history, 1965-67; University of New Hampshire, assistant professor of history, 1967-70, associate professor of history, 1970-75, professor of history, 1975-97, chairman of the department, 1977-80, James H. Hayes and Claire Short Hayes chair in the humanities, 1993-97, professor emeritus of history, 1998-. **Publications:** The Eastern Frontier: The Settlement of Northern New England, 1610-1763, 1970; (comp.) Maine During the Colonial Period: A Bibliographical Guide, 1974; (comp. and ed. with C.W. Eastman, Jr.) The Portsmouth Project: An Exercise in Inductive Historical Scholarship, 1974; Printers, The People and Politics: The New Hampshire Press and Ratification, 1989; Maine: A Bicentennial History, 1977, 1990; The Public Prints: The Newspaper in Anglo-American Culture, 1665-1740, 1993; The Meetinghouse Tragedy: An Episode in the Life of a New England own, 1998; Bates Through the Years: An Illustrated History, 2005. EDITOR: (with J.S. Leamon and K. Bowden) Maine in the Early Republic: From Revolution to Statehood, 1988; (with E.C. Nordbeck) Granite and Grace: Essays Celebrating the Two Hundredth Anniversary of the New Hampshire Conference, United Church of Christ, 2001. **Address:** Department of History, College of Liberal Arts, University of New Hampshire, 20 Academic Way, Durham, NH 03824-2616, U.S.A. **Online address:** charles.clark@unh.edu

CLARK, Charles Michael Andres. American (born United States), b. 1960. **Genres:** Economics, Essays, Adult Non-fiction. **Career:** St. John's University, Peter J. Tobin College of Business, instructor, 1984-90, assistant professor, 1990-91, associate professor of economics, 1991-96, professor of economics, 1996-, associate dean for faculty affairs, Vincentian Center for Church and Society, senior fellow; University College Cork, visiting professor of economics; Pontifical University, visiting professor of economics. Writer and consultant. **Publications:** Economic Theory and Natural Philosophy: The Search for the Natural Laws of the Economy, 1992; (ed.) History and Historians of Political Economy, 1994; (ed.) Institutional Economics and the Theory of Social Value: Essays in Honor of Marc R. Tool, 1995; (with J. Healy) Pathways to a Basic Income, 1997; (ed. with C. Kavanagh) Unemployment in Ireland: Alternative Perspectives, 1998; (with S. Lerner and W.R. Needham) Basic Income: Economic Security for All Canadians, 1999; (ed.) Economic Tradition in Historical Perspective: Lessons from the History of Economics, 2001; Basic Income Guarantee: Ensuring Progress and Prosperity in the 21st Century, 2002; (ed. with H. Alford, S. Cortright and M. Naughton) Rediscovering Abundance: Interdisciplinary Essays on Wealth, Income and their Distribution in the Catholic Social Tradition, 2006; (with H. Alford) Rich and Poor, 2010. **Address:** Peter J. Tobin College of Business, St. John's University, Rm. 111C, Bent Hall, 8000 Utopia Pkwy., Queens, NY 11439, U.S.A. **Online address:** clarkc@stjohns.edu

CLARK, Christopher M. British/Australian (born Australia), b. 1960?. **Genres:** Politics/Government, History. **Career:** University of Cambridge, St. Catherine's College, professor. Freelance writer. **Publications:** The Politics of Conversion: Missionary Protestantism and the Jews in Prussia, 1728-1941, 1995; Kaiser Wilhelm II, 2000; (ed. with W. Kaiser) Culture Wars: Secular-Catholic Conflict in Nineteenth-Century Europe, 2003; Iron Kingdom: The Rise and Downfall of Prussia, 1600-1947, 2006. Works appear in anthologies. Contributor of articles to journals. **Address:** St. Catherine's College, Cambridge University, Cambridge, CB CB2 1RL, England. **Online address:** cmc11@cam.ac.uk

CLARK, David. *See* **HARDCASTLE, Michael.**

CLARK, David Lindsey. British (born England), b. 1926. **Genres:** Music, Reference, Art/Art History, Humanities. **Career:** Central Music Library, assistant, 1952-59; Blackwell's Music Shop, assistant, 1959-62; Oxford University, Bodleian Library, assistant, 1962-65; Exeter City Library, music librarian, 1965-72; Oxford County Library, music librarian, 1972-91. Writer. **Publications:** Music for Wind Instruments: A Survey of Anthologies in Print, 1970; (comp.) Music for Guitar and Lute, 1972; (with M. Stoneham and J.A. Gillespie) Wind Ensemble Sourcebook and Biographical Guide, 1997; (with M. Stoneham and J.A. Gillespie) The Wind Ensemble Catalog, 1998; Appraisals of Original Wind Music: A Survey and Guide, 1999; Settings for Shakespeare Plays in Music of His Time: A Bibliographical Survey and Discography, forthcoming. **Address:** 19 Lower King's Ave., Exeter, Devon, EX EX4 6JT, England.

CLARK, Dick. American (born United States), b. 1929. **Genres:** History, Music. **Career:** Bandstand, host, 1956-89; Dick Clark productions, chairman and chief executive officer, 1956-; United Stations Radio Network, co-founder and principal owner. Writer. **Publications:** Your Happiest Years, 1959; To Goof or not to Goof, 1963; (with R. Robinson) Rock, Roll & Remember, 1976; Dick Clark's Program for Success in Your Business and Personal Life, 1980; (with B. Libby) Looking Great, Staying Young, 1981; (with B. Solomon) Dick Clark's the First 25 years of Rock & Roll, 1981; (with M. Shore) The History of American Bandstand: It's Got a Great Beat and You Can Dance to It, 1985; Dick Clark's Easygoing Guide to Good Grooming, 1986; Murder on Tour: A Rock 'n' Roll Mystery, 1989; Dick Clark's American Bandstand, 1997. **Address:** Dick Clark Productions Inc., 2900 Olympic Blvd., Santa Monica, CA 90404, U.S.A. **Online address:** hello@dickclark.com

CLARK, Emily. American (born United States), b. 1954?. **Genres:** History. **Career:** Tulane University, associate professor, Clement Chambers Benenson professor in American colonial history; Lewis & Clark College, adjunct professor; University of Southern Mississippi, assistant professor. Writer. **Publications:** Masterless Mistresses: The New Orleans Ursulines and the Development of a New World Society, 1727- 1834, 2007; (ed. and trans.) Voices from an Early American Convent: Marie Madeleine Hachard and the New Orleans Ursulines, 1727-1760, 2007. Contributor of articles to journals. **Address:** Department of History, Tulane University, 6823 St. Charles Ave., 115 Hebert Hall, New Orleans, LA 70118, U.S.A. **Online address:** eclark@tulane.edu

CLARK, Emma Chichester. British (born England), b. 1955. **Genres:** Children's Fiction, Illustrations, Picture/Board Books, Poetry. **Career:** Middlesex Polytechnic, visiting lecturer, 1984-86; City and Guilds School of Art, visiting lecturer, 1984-86; Thumb Gallery, exhibitor, 1984, 1987. Writer. **Publications:** SELF-ILLUSTRATED FOR CHILDREN: Myrtle, Tertle and Gertle, 1989; Tea with Aunt Augusta, 1991 in US as Lunch with Aunt Augusta, 1992; Miss Bilberry's New House in US as Across the Blue Mountains, 1993; (co-author) Tom's Pirate Ship and Other Stories, 1996; Little Miss Muffet Counts to Ten in US as Little Miss Muffet's Count-Along Surprise, 1997; (co-author) Mostly Animal Poetry, 1997; I'll Show You Blue Kangaroo!, 2003; My First Ballet Stories, 2004; No More Teasing, 2005; We Are Not Fond of Rat, 2006; Eliza and the Moonchild, 2007; Melrose and Croc: A Hero's Birthday, 2008; Minty and Tink, 2008. OTHERS: The Story of Horrible Hilda and Henry, 1988; (with P. Lockwood) Cissy Lavender, 1989; The Bouncing Dinosaur, 1990; Catch That Hat!, 1990; I Never Saw a Purple Cow and Other Nonsense Rhymes, 1990; Follow My Leader!, 1999; I Love You, Blue Kangaroo!, 1999; More!, 1999; Where Are You, Blue Kangaroo?, 2000; It Was You, Blue Kangaroo!, 2001; No More Kissing!, 2002; Mimi's Book of Opposites, 2002; Follow the Leader!, 2003; Mimi's Book of Counting, 2003; What Shall We Do, Blue Kangaroo?, 2003; Merry Christmas to You, Blue Kangaroo!, 2004; Up in Heaven, 2004; Happy birthday to you, Blue Kangaroo!, 2006; Melrose and Croc: A Christmas to Remember, 2006; Melrose and Croc: Friends for Life, 2006; Will and Squill, 2006; Amazing Mr. Zooty, 2007; Melrose and Croc: Beside the Sea, 2007; Melrose and Croc: Go To Town, 2007; Piper, 2007; Melrose and Croc: An Adventure to Remember, 2008; Goldilocks and the Three Bears, 2010. Contributor to periodicals. **Address:** c/o Laura Cecil, 17 Alwyne Villas, London, GL N1 2HG, England.

CLARK, Eric. British (born England), b. 1937. **Genres:** Novels, International Relations/Current Affairs, Advertising/Public Relations, Business/Trade/Industry. **Career:** Daily Mail, reporter, 1961-63; The Guardian, staff writer, 1963-64; The Observer, staff writer, 1964-72; freelance writer, 1972-. **Publications:** (Co-author) Len Deighton's London Dossier, 1967; Everybody's Guide to Survival, 1969; Corps Diplomatique, 1973; Diplomat; The World of International Diplomacy, 1974; Black Gambit: A Novel, 1978; The Sleeper,

1980; Send in the Lions, 1981; Chinese Burn, 1984; China Run, 1984; The Want Makers: Lifting the Lid off the World Advertising Industry: How They Make You Buy, 1988; The Want Makers: Inside the World of Advertising, 1989; Hide and Seek, 1995; The Secret Enemy, 2002; The Real Toy Story: Inside the Ruthless Battle for America's Youngest Consumers, 2007. Contributor to periodicals. **Address:** Jonathan Clowes Ltd., 10 Iron Bridge House, Bridge Approach, London, GL NW1 8BD, England.

CLARK, Francesco. American (born United States), b. 1978?. **Genres:** Autobiography/Memoirs. **Career:** Clark's Botanicals, founder. Writer and entrepreneur. **Publications:** Walking Papers (memoir), 2010. Contributor to periodicals. **Address:** Clark's Botanicals, 81 Pondfield Rd., Ste. 263, Bronxville, NY 10708, U.S.A. **Online address:** info@clarksbotanicals.com

CLARK, Geoffrey (D.). American (born United States), b. 1940. **Genres:** Novellas/Short Stories. **Career:** Roger Williams University, teacher of creative writing, 1971-99; Ampersand Press, co-founder, 1980; University of Wisconsin, superior. Writer. **Publications:** STORIES: (with R. Crotty and R.L. McRoberts) Workshop: A Spontaneous Approach to Literature, 1971; What the Moon Said, 1983; Ruffian on the Stair, 1988; Schooling the Spirit, 1993; All the Way Home, 1997; Rabbit Fever, 2000; Necessary Deaths, 2007. NOVELS: Jackdog Summer, 1996; Wedding in October, 2002. EDITOR: The Best I Can Wish You (anthology), 1985; How the Weather Was (anthology), 1990. Works appear in anthologies. **Address:** School of Fine & Performing Arts, Roger Williams University, 1 Ferry Rd., Bristol, RI 02809, U.S.A. **Online address:** waypamgeof@aol.com

CLARK, George. Canadian/Irish (born Ireland), b. 1932. **Genres:** Literary Criticism And History. **Career:** University of Wisconsin, instructor in English, 1961-63; University of Texas, assistant professor of English, 1963-65; Queen's University, assistant professor, 1965-68, associate professor, 1968-74, professor of English, 1974-, now professor emeritus; University of Helsinki, lecturer, 1966-67. Writer. **Publications:** (Ed.) Reign of George III, 1760-1815, 1960; Beowulf, 1990; (ed. with D. Timmons) J.R.R. Tolkien and His Literary Resonances: views of Middle-earth, 2000; Maldon and the Viking Tide, forthcoming. Contributor to journals. **Address:** Department of English, Queen's University, 99 University Ave., Kingston, ON K7L 3N6, Canada. **Online address:** geoclark@kingston.net

CLARK, Gillian. American (born United States), b. 1963. **Genres:** Autobiography/Memoirs, Biography, Food And Wine. **Career:** Colorado Kitchen, chef and owner, 2000-. Writer. **Publications:** Out of the Frying Pan: A Chef's Memoir of Hot Kitchens, Single Motherhood and the Family Meal, 2007. **Address:** Colorado Kitchen, 5515 Colorado Ave. NW, Washington, DC 20011-7801, U.S.A.

CLARK, Gordon L. Australian/British (born England), b. 1950. **Genres:** Law, Business/Trade/Industry, Economics. **Career:** Harvard University, assistant professor, 1978-83; University of Chicago, associate professor, 1983-85; Carnegie-Mellon University, professor, 1985-91; Monash University, professor, 1989-95, Faculty of Business and Economics, Sir Louis Matheson distinguished visiting professor; University of Oxford, School of Geography and the Environment, Halford Mackinder professor of geography, 1995-, head, Transformations: Economy, Society and Place, coordinator, Centre for the Environment, director, St Peter's College, fellow. Writer. **Publications:** Interregional Migration, National Policy, and Social Justice, 1983; (with M. Dear) State Apparatus, 1984; Judges and the Cities, 1985; (with M.S. Gertler and J.E.M. Whiteman) Regional Dynamics, 1986; Unions and Communities Under Siege, 1989; Pensions and Corporate Restructuring in American Industry, 1993; (ed. with D. Forbes and R. Francis) Multiculturalism, Difference and Postmodernism, 1993; (with P. Marden) Regulation of Private Pensions (superannuation) and Strategic Unionism in Australia, 1994; (ed. with W.B. Kim) Asian NIEs and the Global Economy, 1995; Britain and Europe, 1996; (ed. with E.P. Jonson and W. Caldow) Accountability and Corruption: Public Sector Ethics, 1997; (ed. with M.P. Feldman, M.S. Gertler and K. Williams) The Oxford Handbook of Economic Geography, 2000; Pension Fund Capitalism, 2000; European Pensions & Global Finance, 2003; (ed. with N. Whiteside) Pension Security in the 21st Century: Redrawing the Public-Private Debate, 2003; (with P. Tracey) Global Competitiveness and Innovation: An Agent-centred Perspective, 2004; Unions and Communities under Siege: American Communities and the Crisis of Organized Labor, 2006; (ed. with A.H. Munnell and J.M. Orszag) Oxford Handbook of Pensions and Retirement Income, 2006; (with D. Wójcik) The Geography of Finance, 2007; (ed. with A.D. Dixon and A.H.B. Monk) Managing Financial Risks: From Global to Local, 2009. **Address:** School of Geography and the Environment, University of Oxford, South Parks Rd., Oxford, OX OX1 3QY, England. **Online address:** gordon.clark@ouce.ox.ac.uk

CLARK, Gregory. American/Scottish (born Scotland), b. 1957. **Genres:** Economics, History. **Career:** Stanford University, assistant professor, 1984-89; University of Michigan, assistant professor, 1989-90; University of California, associate professor, 1990-96, professor, 1996-, Economy, Justice and Society Program, director, 2002-05, department chair, 2007-10; Brown University, distinguished visiting professor, 2003; Wissenschaftskolleg zu, fellow, 2005-06. Writer. **Publications:** A Farewell to Alms: A Brief Economic History of the World, 2007; (with K.H. O'Rourke and A.M. Taylor) Made in America? The New World, the Old and the Industrial Revolution, 2008. Contributor of articles to journals. **Address:** Department of Economics, University of California, 1 Shields Ave., Davis, CA 95616, U.S.A. **Online address:** gclark@ucdavis.edu

CLARK, J. C. D. British (born England), b. 1951. **Genres:** History, Intellectual History, Theology/Religion. **Career:** London Stock Exchange, staff, 1972-73; Cambridge University, fellow, 1977-81; Eton College, assistant master, 1981; Oxford University, All Souls College, fellow, 1986-; University of Kansas, Hall Distinguished Professor of British History, 1995-, Joyce and Elizabeth Hall Distinguished Professor of British History, Hall Center, chaired professor; University of Northumbria, visiting professor, 2001-; Oxford Brookes University, Centre for Methodism and Church History, visiting professor, 2008-13; University of Manitoba, distinguished visiting lecturer. Writer. **Publications:** The Dynamics of Change: The Crisis of the 1750s and English Party Systems, 1982; English Society 1688-1832: Ideology, Social Structure and Political Practice during the Ancien Regime, 1985; Revolution and Rebellion: State and Society in England in the Seventeenth and Eighteenth Centuries, 1986; The Language of Liberty, 1660-1832: Political Discourse and Social Dynamics in The Anglo-American World, 1994; Samuel Johnson: Literature, Religion and English Cultural Politics from the Restoration to Romanticism, 1994; English Society, 1660-1832: Religion, Ideology and Politics During the Ancient Regime, 2000; Our Shadowed Present: Modernism, Postmodernism and History, 2003; The Enlightenment, forthcoming. EDITOR: The Memoirs and Speeches of James, 2nd Earl Waldegrave, 1742-1763, 1988; Ideas and Politics in Modern Britain, 1990; Reflections on the Revolution in France, 2001; (with H. Erskine-Hill) Samuel Johnson in Historical Context, 2001; World by Itself: A History of the British Isles, 2010. **Address:** University of Kansas, Rm. 3024, 3164 Wescoe Hall, 1445 Jayhawk Blvd., Lawrence, KS 66045-7590, U.S.A. **Online address:** jcdclark@ku.edu

CLARK, Jerome. American (born United States), b. 1946. **Genres:** Songs/Lyrics And Libretti, Biology, History, Paranormal, Sciences, Theology/Religion. **Career:** Fate, associate editor, 1976-87, senior editor, 1987-89, consulting editor, 1989-93; songwriter, 1978-; writer, 1989-; J. Allen Hynek Center for UFO Studies, vice president, 1987-, director. **Publications:** (With L. Coleman) The Unidentified: Notes toward Solving the UFO Mystery, 1975; (with L. Coleman) Creatures of the Outer Edge, 1978; (with D.S. Rogo) Earth's Secret Inhabitants, 1979; (with J.G. Melton and A.A. Kelly) New Age Encyclopedia, 1990 as New Age Almanac, 1991; The UFO Encyclopedia, 1990, 2nd ed. as UFO Encyclopedia: The Phenomenon from the Beginning, 1998; UFOs in the 1980s, 1990; The Emergence of a Phenomenon: UFOs from the Beginning through 1959, 1992; UFO Encounters: Sightings, Visitations, and Investigations, 1992; Encyclopedia of Strange and Unexplained Physical Phenomena, 1993; Unexplained!: 347 Strange Sightings, Incredible Occurrences, and Puzzling Physical Phenomena, 1993, 2nd ed., 1999; (ed. with N. Pear) Strange and Unexplained Happenings: When Nature Breaks the Rules of Science, 3 vols. 1995; High Strangeness: UFOs from 1960 through 1979, 1996; The UFO Book, 1998; (with L. Coleman) Cryptozoology A to Z, 1999; Extraordinary Encounters, 2000; Strange Skies: Pilot Encounters with UFOs, 2003; Unnatural Phenomena: A Guide to the Bizarre Wonders of North America, 2005; Hidden Realms, Lost Civilizations, and Beings from Other Worlds, 2010. Contributor to periodicals. **Address:** LT Mead & Associates, 379 Burning Tree Ct., Half Moon Bay, CA 94019, U.S.A. **Online address:** jkclark@frontiernet.net

CLARK, Joshua. American (born United States), b. 1975?. **Genres:** Young Adult Non-fiction, Young Adult Fiction, Sports/Fitness. **Career:** Light of

New Orleans Publishing, president, editor and founder; Scat Magazine, associate editor; Katrina Arts Relief and Emergency Support fund, director. **Publications:** (Ed.) French Quarter Fiction: The Newest Stories of America's Oldest Bohemia, 2003; (ed.) Louisiana in Words, 2007; Heart Like Water: Surviving Katrina and Life in Its Disaster Zone, 2007; (with M. Lauren) You are Your Own Gym: The Bible of Bodyweight Exercises for Men and Women, 2010. Contributor to periodicals. **Address:** Light of New Orleans Publishing, 828 Royal St., Ste. 307, New Orleans, LA 70116, U.S.A. **Online address:** jclark@frenchquarterfiction.com

CLARK, Kathleen Ann. American (born United States) **Genres:** History, Sociology, Social Sciences. **Career:** University of Georgia, Department of History, assistant professor, 1999-2005, associate professor, 2006-; Yale University, faculty. Writer and historian. **Publications:** Defining Moments: African American Commemoration & Political Culture in the South, 1863- 1913, 2005. **Address:** Department of History, University of Georgia, Rm. 310, LaConte Hall, Athens, GA 30602, U.S.A. **Online address:** katclark@uga.edu

CLARK, Kathy. *See* **CLARK, Catherine.**

CLARK, Kelly James. American (born United States), b. 1956. **Genres:** Philosophy, Humanities, Theology/Religion. **Career:** University of Notre Dame, teaching assistant, 1982-83, 1984-85; Gordon College, assistant professor of philosophy, 1985-89; Calvin College, Department of Philosophy, professor, 1989-; Society of Christian Philosophers, secretary and treasurer, 1994-; University of St. Andrews, visiting professor, 1995-96; Fudan University, visiting professor, 2007-. Writer. **Publications:** Return to Reason: A Critique of Enlightenment Evidentialism, and a Defense of Reason and Belief in God, 1990; (ed.) Our Knowledge of God: Essays on Natural and Philosophical Theology, 1992; (ed.) Philosophers Who Believe: The Spiritual Journeys of 11 Leading Thinkers, 1993; When Faith is Not Enough, 1997; (co-author) Five Views on Apologetics, 2000; (ed.) Readings in the Philosophy of Religion, 2000, 2nd ed., 2008; (with A. Poortenga) The Story of Ethics: Fulfilling Our Human Nature, 2003; (ed.) A Dialogue Between Science and Religion, 2004; (with R. Lints and J.K.A. Smith) 101 Key Terms in Philosophy and Their Importance for Theology, 2004; (ed.) Human Nature in Chinese and Western Culture, 2005; (ed.) Ethics, Religion and Society, 2007; (ed. with X. Taotao) Faith, Knowledge and Naturalism, 2007; (ed. with M. Rea) Reason, Metaphysics, and Mind, 2012. Contributor of articles to periodicals. **Address:** Department of Philosophy, Calvin College, 353 Hiemenga Hall, 3201 Burton St. SE, Grand Rapids, MI 49546, U.S.A. **Online address:** kclark@calvin.edu

CLARK, Martin. *See* **Clark, Martin Fillmore.**

CLARK, Martin Fillmore. (Martin Clark). American (born United States), b. 1959. **Genres:** Novels, Young Adult Fiction, Humor/Satire. **Career:** Twenty-first Judicial Circuit, juvenile and domestic relations district court judge, 1992-95, Patrick circuit court judge, 1995-. Writer. **Publications:** NOVELS: The Many Aspects of Mobile Home Living: A Novel, 2000; Plain Heathen Mischief: A Novel, 2004; Legal Limit, 2008. **Address:** c/o Joe Regal, Regal Literary Inc., 1140 Broadway, Penthouse, New York, NY 10001, U.S.A. **Online address:** mischief@martinclark.com

CLARK, Mary Ann. American (born United States), b. 1949?. **Genres:** Young Adult Non-fiction, Theology/Religion. **Career:** Credit Bureau of Greater Houston, personnel assistant, 1973-74; Scientific Products, customer service representative, 1974-77; Redact Corp., president, 1977-96; Rice University, teaching assistant, 1995-99, Fondren Library, user services associate, 1999-; Southwest Commission on Religious Studies, secretary, 1996-99, 2000-05; Kingwood College, lecturer, 2000-01; University of Houston, lecturer, 2001-; Council of Societies for the Study of Religion, coordinator. Writer. **Publications:** Where Men Are Wives and Mothers Rule: Santerla Ritual Practices and Their Gender Implications, 2005; Santeria: Correcting the Myths and Uncovering the Realities of a Growing Religion, 2007. Contributor to books and periodicals. **Address:** A.D. Bruce Religion Center, University of Houston, 4800 Calhoun Rd., Houston, TX 77204, U.S.A.

CLARK, Mary Higgins. American (born United States), b. 1929. **Genres:** Mystery/Crime/Suspense, Novels, Young Adult Fiction, Young Adult Nonfiction, Picture/Board Books. **Career:** Remington Rand, advertising assistant, 1946; Pan American Airlines, stewardess, 1949-50; Robert G. Jennings, radio scriptwriter and producer, 1965-70; Aerial Communications, partner and vice president, creative director and producer of radio programming, 1970-80; D.J. Clark Enterprises, creative director and chairman, 1980-; International Crime Writers Congress, chair, 1988. Writer. **Publications:** NOVELS: Aspire to the Heavens: A Biography of George Washington, 1969; Where Are the Children?, 1975; A Stranger Is Watching, 1978; The Cradle Will Fall, 1980; A Cry in the Night, 1982; Stillwatch, 1984; Weep No More, My Lady, 1987, 2nd ed., 1988; Caribbean Blues, 1988; Death at the Cape, 1989; While My Pretty One Sleeps, 1989, new ed., 2009; Mary Higgins Clark, 3 vols., 1990; Loves Music, Loves to Dance, 1991; All Around the Town, 1992; (ed.) Missing in Manhattan: The Adams Round Table, 1992; Mists from Beyond: Twenty-two Ghost Stories and Tales from the Other Side, 1993; I'll Be Seeing You, 1993; Remember Me, 1994; Let Me Call You Sweetheart, 1995; Silent Night, 1995; Moonlight Becomes You, 1996; Pretend You Don't See Her, 1997; You Belong to Me, 1998; All through the Night, 1998; We'll Meet Again, 1999; Before I Say Good-bye, 2000; (with C.H. Clark) Deck the Halls, 2000; On the Street Where You Live, 2001; (with C.H. Clark) He Sees You When You're Sleeping, 2001; Daddy's Little Girl, 2002; Kitchen Privileges, 2002; Mount Vernon Love Story, 2002; The Second Time Around, 2003; (with C.H. Clark) The Christmas Thief, 2004; Nighttime is My Time, 2004; No Place Like Home, 2005; Two Little Girls in Blue, 2006; (with C.H. Clark) Santa Cruise: A Holiday Mystery at Sea, 2006; I Heard That Song Before, 2007; Ghost Ship: A Cape Cod Story, 2007; (with C.H. Clark) Dashing Through the Snow, 2008; Where Are You Now?: A Novel, 2008; Just Take My Heart, 2009; The Shadow of Your Smile, 2010; Christmas Ornament, 2011; The Lost Years, 2012. STORIES: The Anastasia Syndrome and Other Stories, 1989; Stow Away and Milk Run, 1993; The Lottery Winner: Alvirah and Will Stories, 1994; My Gal Sunday, 1996. EDITOR: Murder on the Aisle: The 1987 Mystery Writers of America Anthology, 1987; (and intro.) The International Association of Crime Writers Presents Bad Behavior, 1995; The Plot Thickens, 1997; Night Awakens: A, Mystery Writers of America Anthology, 2000. OTHERS: Death on the Cape and Other Stories, 1993; Stowaway and Milk Run, 1993; Snagged, 1993; (with M. Angelou and A. Tan) Mother, 1996; On a Raven's Wing, 2009; (co-author) By Hook or By Crook: And 27 More of the Best Crime and Mystery Stories of the Year, 2010; I'll Walk Alone, 2011; The Magical Christmas Horse, 2011. Contributor to books and periodicals. **Address:** c/o Eugene H. Winick, McIntosh & Otis Inc., 353 Lexington Ave., New York, NY 10016, U.S.A.

CLARK, Mary Jane Behrends. American (born United States) **Genres:** Cultural/Ethnic Topics, Mystery/Crime/Suspense, Novels, Young Adult Fiction. **Career:** Columbia Broadcasting System Inc., desk assistant, news writer and producer. **Publications:** The Commonwealth of Independent States, 1992; Do You Want to Know a Secret?, 1998; Do You Promise Not to Tell?, 1999; Let Me Whisper in Your Ear, 2000; Close to You, 2001; Nobody Knows, 2002; Nowhere to Run, 2003; Hide Yourself Away, 2004; Dancing in the Dark, 2005; Lights Out Tonight, 2006; When Day Breaks, 2007; It Only Takes a Moment, 2008; Dying for Mercy: A Novel of Suspense, 2009; To Have and to Kill, 2010. **Address:** c/o Sharyn Rosenblum, William Morrow Publishers, 10 E 53rd St., New York, NY 10022-5299, U.S.A. **Online address:** mjc@maryjaneclark.com

CLARK, Mary T. American (born United States), b. 1913?. **Genres:** Philosophy, Theology/Religion, Biography, Translations. **Career:** Teacher, 1945-53; Manhattanville College, instructor, 1951-52, assistant professor, 1953-57, associate professor, 1957-61, professor of philosophy, 1961-, chair of philosophy department, 1962-64, 1966-68, 1972-79, now professor emeritus; University of San Francisco, visiting professor, 1967-71; Villanova University, visiting professor, 1980; Fordham University, visiting professor, 1981, 1991, 1993; Saint John Neuman Seminary, visiting professor, 1982-; University of Santa Clara, visiting professor, 1983; State University of New York, visiting professor, 1989-91; New York University, visiting professor, 1991; Fairfield University, visiting professor, 1992; Marquette University, visiting professor, 1993; University of San Francisco, visiting professor. Writer. **Publications:** Augustine, Philosopher of Freedom: A Study in Comparative Philosophy, 1958; (with Casey) Logic, a Practical Approach, 1963; Discrimination Today: Guidelines For Civic Action, 1966; Augustinian Personalism, 1970; (ed. and intro.) An Aquinas Reader, 1973, rev. ed., 2000; (comp.) The Problem of Freedom, 1973; (trans.) M. Victorinus, Theological Treatises on the Trinity, 1981; Augustine of Hippo: Selected Writings, 1984; The Spirituality of St. Augustine, 1984; Augustine, 1994. Contributor to journals. **Address:** Department of Philosophy, Manhattanville College, 2900 Purchase St., Purchase, NY 10577, U.S.A. **Online address:** clarkm@mville.edu

CLARK, Merle. *See* **GESSNER, Lynne.**

CLARK, Paul F. American (born United States), b. 1954. **Genres:** Politics/Government, Industrial Relations, Organized Labor, Social Sciences. **Career:** United Mine Workers of America, research assistant, 1975; Cornell University, School of Industrial and Labor Relations, labor extension associate, 1979; Pennsylvania State University, instructor, 1979-82, assistant professor, 1982-87, associate professor of labor studies and industrial relations, 1987-, Department of Labor Studies and Employment Relations, professor and head, Department of Health Policy and Administration, professor, Center for Work and Family Research, faculty associate, Center for Health Care and Policy Research, faculty associate; Alfred P. Sloan Foundation Industry Studies Program, affiliate; Royal Roads University, adjunct professor. Writer. **Publications:** The Miner's Fight for Democracy, 1981; A Union Member's Guide to the New Right, 1983; Industrial Relations: A Correspondence Study Course, 1985, 3rd ed., 1992; (ed. with P. Gottlieb and D. Kennedy) Forging a Union of Steel, 1987; Changing Labor's Image: A Union Member's Guide, 1989; Building More Effective Unions, 2000, 2nd ed., 2009; (ed. with A.C. Frost and J.T. Delaney) Collective Bargaining in the Private Sector, 2002. Contributor to periodicals. **Address:** Department of Labor and Industrial Relations, Pennsylvania State University, 127 Willard Bldg., University Park, PA 16802, U.S.A. **Online address:** pfc2@psu.edu

CLARK, Paul John Abott. New Zealander (born New Zealand), b. 1949?. **Genres:** Film, History. **Career:** East-West Center, 1983-93; University of Auckland, professor of Chinese, 1993-; Peking University, New Zealand Centre, academic director, 2008; New Zealand Journal of Asian Studies, editor, 2009. **Publications:** Hauhau: The Pai Marire Search for Maori Identity, 1975; Chinese Cinema: Culture and Politics since 1949, 1987; (ed. with J. Kember) China and New Zealand: A Thriving Relationship Thirty Years On, 2003; Reinventing China: A Generation and Its Films, 2005; (ed.) Ten Shipwrecks of the Northern Territory, 2008; The Chinese Cultural Revolution: A History, 2008. Contributor to books and journals. **Address:** New Zealand. **Online address:** paul.clark@auckland.ac.nz

CLARK, Roger Y. Canadian (born Canada), b. 1960. **Genres:** Novels. **Career:** University of British Columbia, instructor, 1996-2000; Douglas College, Department of English, instructor, 2000-04, faculty. Writer. **Publications:** Stranger Gods: Salman Rushdie's Other Worlds, 2001. **Address:** Department of English, Douglas College, 700 Royal Ave., PO Box 2503, New Westminster, BC V3M 5Z5, Canada. **Online address:** ryoclark@gmail.com

CLARK, Sally. Canadian (born Canada), b. 1953. **Genres:** Plays/Screenplays. **Career:** Playwright and filmmaker, 1983-. director and writer. **Publications:** Moo, 1989; (co-author) Canadian Brash: New Voices in Fiction, Drama and Poetry, 1990; Trial of Judith K, 1991; Big Time Women From Way Back When, 1993; Life Without Instruction, 1994; Saint Frances of Hollywood, 1996; Trial of a Ladies Man, 1997; Wasps: A Drawing Room Comedy for Distempered Times, 1998; Lost Souls and Missing Persons, 1998; Wanted, 2004; Waiting for the Revolution, 2010. **Address:** c/o Shain Jaffe, Great North Artists Management, 350 Dupont St., Toronto, ON M5R 1V9, Canada. **Online address:** info@sallyclark.ca

CLARK, Suzanne. American (born United States) **Genres:** Literary Criticism And History. **Career:** Dickinson State College, assistant professor, 1980-85; Western Washington University, visiting associate professor, 1985-86; Oregon State University, assistant professor, 1986-89, associate professor, 1989-90; University of Oregon, associate professor, 1990-97, director of graduate studies, 1991-94, professor of English, 1997-2010. Writer. **Publications:** Sentimental Modernism: Women Writers and the Revolution of the Word, 1991; Cold Warriors: Manliness on Trial in the Rhetoric of the West, 2000. **Address:** Department of English, University of Oregon, 1286 University of Oregon, Eugene, OR 97403, U.S.A. **Online address:** sclark@uoregon.edu

CLARK, Terry N(ichols). American (born United States), b. 1940. **Genres:** Sociology, Politics/Government, Environmental Sciences/Ecology. **Career:** Columbia University, instructor in sociology, 1965-66; University of Chicago, assistant professor, 1966-71, associate professor, 1972-85, professor of sociology, 1985-, College Sociology Program, chairman, 1989-94; National Opinion Research Center, research associate, 1974-, senior study director, 1974-, Comparative Study of Community Decision-Making, director, 1967-; Urban Institute, visiting researcher, 1970; Yale University, visiting associate professor, 1972; Harvard University, visiting associate professor, 1972; University of Paris, visiting associate professor, 1973; Fiscal Austerity and Urban Innovation Project, coordinator of U.S. and international; UER de Sciences Sociales, visiting associate professor, visiting professor. Writer. **Publications:** (With I.P. Leif) Community Power and Decision-Making: A Trend Report and Bibliography, 1970; Prophets and Patrons: The French University and the Emergence of the Social Sciences, 1973; Community Power and Policy Outputs, 1973; (with I. Leif) Community Power and Decision-Making, 1974; Leadership in American Cities, 1974; (with Schumaker and Getter) Policy Responsiveness and the Fiscal Strain in 51 American Communities, 1979; (with L.C. Ferguson) City Money: Political Processes, Fiscal Strain and Retrenchment, 1983; (with G.E. DeSeve and J.C. Johnson) Financial Handbook for Mayors and City Managers, 2nd ed., 1985; New Political Culture, 1998. EDITOR: (contrib.) Community Structure and Decision-Making, 1968; (and intro.) On Communication and Social Influence, 1969; (co-ed.) Comparative Research on Community Decision-Making, 1970; (with C.M. Bonjean and R.L. Lineberry) Community Politics: A Behavioral Approach, 1971; Comparative Community Politics, 1974; Citizen Preferences and Urban Public Policy: Models, Measures, Uses, 1976; (with J. Ben-David) Culture and Its Creators: Essays in Honor of Edward Shils, 1977; Urban Policy Analysis: Directions for Future Research, 1981; Research in Urban Policy (annual), 1985; Monitoring Local Governments: How Personal Computers Can Help Systematize Municipal Fiscal Analysis, 1990; Urban Innovation: Creative Strategies for Turbulent Times, 1994; (with M. Rempel) Citizen Politics in Post-Industrial Societies, 1997; (with V. Hoffmann-Martinot) The New Political Culture, 1998; (with K. Hoggart) Citizen Responsive Government, 2000; (with S.M. Lipset) The Breakdown of Class Politics: A Debate on Post-Industrial Stratification, 2001; The City as an Entertainment Machine, 2004; (with A.M. McCright) Community and Ecology: Dynamics of Place, Sustainability and Politics, 2006. Contributor of articles to journals. **Address:** Department of Sociology, University of Chicago, 322 Social Sciences Bldg., 1126 E 59th St., Chicago, IL 60637, U.S.A. **Online address:** tnclark@uchicago.edu

CLARK, T(imothy) J(ames). American/British (born England), b. 1943. **Genres:** Art/Art History. **Career:** Essex University, lecturer, 1967-69; Camberwell School of Art, senior lecturer, 1970-74; University of California-Los Angeles, visiting professor, 1974-75, associate professor, 1975-76; Leeds University, chair of fine art, 1976-80; Harvard University, professor, 1980-88; University California-Berkeley, professor, 1988-2010, George C. and Helen N. Pardee chair, retired 2010, professor emeritus, 2010-; Getty Research Institute, fellow, 2000, professor emeritus. Art historian and writer. **Publications:** The Absolute Bourgeois: Artists and Politics in France, 1848-1851, 1973; Image of the People: Gustave Courbet and the Second French Republic, 1848-1851, 1973; The Painting of Modern Life: Paris in the Art of Manet and His Followers, 1985, rev. ed., 1999; Farewell to an Idea: Episodes from a History of Modernism, 1999; (Contrib.) Self Portrait, 2005; Sight of Death: An Experiment in Art Writing, 2006; (with M. Bull and A.J. Cascardi) Nietzsche's Negative Ecologies, 2009. **Address:** Department of History of Art, University of California, 416 Doe Library, Ste. 6020, Berkeley, CA 94720, U.S.A. **Online address:** travesty@berkeley.edu

CLARK, Tom. American (born United States), b. 1941. **Genres:** Novels, Plays/Screenplays, Poetry, Literary Criticism And History. **Career:** Paris Review, poetry editor, 1963-73; Los Angeles Times, editor; University of Essex, instructor in American poetry, 1966-67; Boulder Monthly, senior writer, 1978-79; New College of California, instructor in poetics, 1987-. **Publications:** Airplanes, 1966; The Sand Burg: Poems, 1966; The Emperor of the Animals (play), 1967; (with R. Padgett) Bun, 1968; Stones, 1969; Air, 1970; Green, 1971; John's Heart, 1972; (ed.) All Stars, 1972; (with T. Berrigan and R. Padgett) Back in Boston Again, 1972; Smack, 1972; Blue, 1974; Suite, 1974; Chicago, 1974; At Malibu, 1975; Baseball, 1976; Champagne and Baloney, 1976; Fan Poems, 1976; 35, 1977; (with M. Fidrych) No Big Deal, 1977; How I Broke in Six Modern Masters, 1978; The World of Damon Runyon, 1978; When Things Get Tough on Easy Street: Selected Poems, 1978; Kerouac's Last Word: Jack Kerouac in Escapade, 1978; One Last Round for the Shuffler, 1979; Who is Sylvia? (novel), 1979; The Master (novel), 1979; The Great Naropa Poetry Wars, 1980; The Last Gas Station and Other Stories, 1980; The End of the Line, 1980; A Short Guide to the High Plains, 1981; Nine Songs, 1981; Heartbreak Hotel, 1981; Under the Fortune Palms, 1982; Jack Kerouac, 1984; The Exile of Celine, 1987; Easter Sunday, 1987; Disordered Ideas, 1987; Fractured Karma, 1990; Charles Olson: The Allegory of a Poet's Life, 1991; Sleepwalker's Fate: New and Selected Poems 1965-1991, 1992; Robert Creeley and the Genius of the American Common Place, 1993; Junkets on a Sad Planet: Scenes from the Life of John Keats, 1994; Like Real People, 1995; White Thought, 1997; Empire of Skin, 1997; The Spell: A Romance, 2000; Cold Spring: A Diary, 2000; Charles Olson: The Allegory of a Poet's Life, 2000; (with T. Leach) Things Happen for a Reason: The True Story of an Itinerant Life in Baseball, 2000; Edward Dorn: A World of Difference, 2002; Light & Shade, 2006. Contributor to periodicals. **Address:** 1740 Marin Ave., Berkeley, CA 94707, U.S.A.

CLARK, Wesley K. American (born United States), b. 1944. **Genres:** Military/Defense/Arms Control. **Career:** Center for Strategic and International Studies, distinguished senior adviser; Stephens Inc., consultant, 2000, managing director of merchant banking, 2001-03; University of California Los Angeles, Burkle Center for International Relations, senior fellow, 2006-; President's Commission, White House fellow, 2009-. Writer. **Publications:** Waging Modern War: Bosnia, Kosovo, and the Future of Combat, 2001; Winning Modern Wars: Iraq, Terrorism, and the American Empire, 2003; (with T. Carhart) Time To Lead: For Duty, Honor, and Country, 2007. Contributor to periodicals. **Address:** Center for Strategic and International Studies, 1800 K St. NW, Ste. 400, Washington, DC 20006-2230, U.S.A.

CLARK, Will. American (born United States), b. 1939. **Genres:** Administration/Management, Novels, Mystery/Crime/Suspense. **Career:** ADT Security Systems, distribution manager, 1980-90; management and motivation consultant, 1990-. Writer. **Publications:** Simply Success, 1989; The Leadership Handbook, 1991; The Power of Positive Education, 1993; Who's Blaming Who? 1993; School Bells and Broken Tales: Exploring with Jack and Jill, 1998; Behold Leviathan, 1999. **Address:** 467 Gordon Rd., Union, MS 39365-8468, U.S.A. **Online address:** will01@aol.com

CLARK, William R. American (born United States), b. 1938. **Genres:** Medicine/Health, Sciences, Social Sciences. **Career:** Weizmann Institute of Science, trainee in cellular immunology, 1968-70; University of California, Department of Molecular, Cell and Developmental Biology, assistant professor of cell biology, 1970-74, associate professor, 1974-78, professor of immunology, 1978-, chair, 1989-96, professor and chair emeritus, 1996-; Parvin Cancer Research Laboratories, head, 1975-. Writer. **Publications:** The Experimental Foundations of Modern Immunology (textbook), 1980, 4th ed., 1991; (ed. with P. Golstein) Mechanisms of Cell-Mediated Cytotoxicity, 1982; At War Within: The Double-Edged Sword of the Immunity, 1995; Sex and the Origins of Death, 1996; The New Healers: The Promise and Problems of Molecular Medicine in the Twenty-First Century, 1997; A Means to an End: The Biological Basis of Aging and Death, 1999; (with M.Grunstein) Are We Hardwired?: The Role of Genes in Human Behavior, 2000; (with G. Berke) Killer Lymphocytes, 2005; Petrodollar Warfare: Oil, Iraq and the Future of the Dollar, 2005; In Defense of Self: How the Immune System Really Works in Managing Health and Disease, 2007; Bracing for Armageddon?: The Science and Politics of Bio terrorism in America, 2008. Contributer to periodicals. **Address:** Department of Molecular, Cell and Developmental, Biology, University of California, 10833 Le Conte Ave., Ste. 12-138, Los Angeles, CA 90095-1606, U.S.A. **Online address:** wclark2@compuserve.com

CLARKE, Alison (Jane). Austrian/British (born England) **Genres:** Adult Non-fiction. **Career:** University of Southampton, Winchester School of Art, senior lecturer; University of Brighton, senior lecturer; Royal College of Art, School of Humanities, senior tutor; University of Applied Arts, visiting professor in design history and theory, professor, 2003-, Department Design History and Theory, chair; Victor J. Papanek Foundation, research director. Writer. **Publications:** Tupperware: The Promise of Plastic in 1950s America, 1999; (ed. with V. Buchli and D. Upton) Home Cultures, 2007; Design Anthropology: Object Culture in the 21st Century, 2010. **Address:** Department of Design History and Theory, University of Applied Arts, Postgasse 2 St., Vienna, 1010, Austria. **Online address:** alison.clarke@uni-ak.ac.at

CLARKE, Boden. *See* **REGINALD, Robert.**

CLARKE, Brenda. Also writes as Brenda Honeyman, Kate Sedley. British (born England), b. 1926. **Genres:** Romance/Historical, Novellas/Short Stories. **Career:** British Civil Service, Ministry of Labour, clerical officer, 1943-55; Writer, 1968-. **Publications:** The Glass Island, 1978; The Lofty Banners, 1980; The Far Morning, 1982; All Through the Day, 1983; A Rose in May, 1984; Three Women, 1985; Winter Landscape, 1986; Under Heaven, 1988; An Equal Chance, 1989; Sisters and Lovers, 1990; Beyond the World, 1991; Riches of the Heart, 1991; A Durable Fire, 1993; Sweet Auburn, 1995; Richard Plantagenet, 1997; Last of the Barons, 1998; A Royal Alliance, 1999. AS BRENDA HONEYMAN: Richard by Grace of God, 1968; The Kingmaker, 1969; Richmond and Elizabeth, 1971; Harry the King, 1971 in US as The Warrior King, 1972; Brother Bedford, 1972; Good Duke Humphrey, 1973; The King's Minions, 1974; The Queen and Mortimer, 1974; Edward the Warrior, 1975; All the King's Sons, 1976; The Golden Griffin, 1976; At the King's Court, 1977; The King's Tale, 1977; Macbeth, King of Scots, 1977; Emma the Queen, 1978; Harold of the English, 1979. AS KATE SEDLEY: Death and the Chapman, 1992; The Plymouth Cloak: The Second Tale of Roger the Chapman, 1993; The Hanged Man, 1993; The Weaver's Tale, 1994; The Holy Innocents, 1994; The Wicked Winter, 1995; The Eve of Saint Hyacinth, 1996; The Brothers of Glastonbury, 1997; The Weaver's Inheritance, 1998; Saint John's Fern, 1999; The Goldsmith's Daughter, 2001; Saint John's Fern: A Roger the Chapman Medieval Mystery, 2002; The Lammas Feast, 2002; Nine Men Dancing, 2003; The Midsummer Rose, 2004; The Burgundian's Tale, 2005; Prodigal Son, 2006; For King and Country, 2006; The Three Kings of Cologne, 2007; The Green Man, 2008; The Dance of Death, 2009; Wheel of Fate, 2010; The Midsummer Crown, 2011. **Address:** 25 Torridge Rd., Keynsham, Bristol, BS31 1QQ, England.

CLARKE, Brock. American (born United States), b. 1968. **Genres:** Novels, Young Adult Fiction. **Career:** Cornell University, lecturer in English, 1997-98; Clemson University, assistant professor of English, 1998-2001; University of Cincinnati, assistant professor of English, 2001-, associate professor of English; Bowdoin College, associate professor of English. Writer. **Publications:** The Ordinary White Boy, 2001; What We Won't Do, 2002; Carrying the Torch, 2004; Arsonist's Guide to Writers' Homes in New England, 2007; Exley: A Novel, 2010. **Address:** c/o Elizabeth Sheinkman, Curtis Brown Group Ltd., Haymarket House, 28-29 Haymarket, London, GL SW1Y 4SP, England. **Online address:** brock@arsonistsguide.com

CLARKE, Erskine. American (born United States), b. 1941. **Genres:** History, Theology/Religion. **Career:** Belton Presbyterian Church, pastor, 1970-73; Columbia Theological Seminary, professor of American religious history, 1973-2008, now professor emeritus, 2008-, Program in Presbyterian and Reformed History and Theology, director; Wesley Theological Seminary, consultant; McCormick Theological Seminary, consultant; Garrett Theological Seminary, consultant; United Theological College of the West Indies, consultant; University of Debrecen, consultant; Nanjing Theological Seminary, consultant; University of Stellenbosch, consultant; Yale University, consultant; University of London, consultant; University of Virginia, consultant; Journal for Preachers, publisher and editor. **Publications:** Wrestlin' Jacob: A Portrait of Religion in the Old South, 1979; Our Southern Zion: A History of Calvinism in the South Carolina Low Country, 1690-1990, 1996; (ed.) Exilic Preaching: Testimony for Christian Exiles in an Increasingly Hostile Culture, 1998; (contrib.) American National Biography, 1998; Dwelling Place: A Plantation Epic, 2005. **Address:** Columbia Theological Seminary, 701 S Columbia Dr., PO Box 520, Decatur, GA 30031, U.S.A. **Online address:** clarkee@ctsnet.edu

CLARKE, Gillian. Welsh (born Wales), b. 1937. **Genres:** Children's Fiction, Plays/Screenplays, Poetry. **Career:** British Broadcasting Corp., researcher, 1958-60; Taliesin Trust, president for life; Gwent College of Art and Design, lecturer in art history, 1975-84; Anglo-Welsh Review, editor, 1976-84; Anglo-Welsh Review, editor, 1976-; St. David's University College, writing fellow, 1984-85; freelance writer, 1985-; Welsh Academy, chair, 1988-93; Ty Newydd, president, co-founder, 1990. **Publications:** POETRY: Snow on the Mountain, 1971; The Sundial, 1978; Letter from a Far Country, 1982; Selected Poems, 1985; (ed.) Poetry Book Society Anthology, 1987-88, 1987; Letting in the Rumour, 1989; The King of Britain's Daughter, 1993; (ed.) The Whispering Room (for children): Haunted Poems, 1996; (ed.) I Can Move the Sea (for children), 1996; Cell Angel, 1996; Collected Poems, 1997; Five Fields, 1998; The Animal Wall (for children), 1999; Nine Green Gardens, 2000; Owain Glyn Dwr, 2000; Making the Beds for the Dead, 2004. OTHER: Sheila na gig: A Song Cycle for Soprano and Piano, 1985; One Moonlit Night, 1991; (ed.) Trying the Line: A Volume of Tribute to Gillian Clarke, 1997; (trans.) One Bright Morning, 2008; At the Source: A Writer's Year, 2008; A Recipe for Water, 2009. **Address:** Blaen Cwrt, Talgarreg Landysul, Ceredigion, SA44 4EU, Wales. **Online address:** enquirer@gillianclarke.co.uk

CLARKE, Gus. (Sam Clarke). British (born England), b. 1948?. **Genres:** Children's Fiction, Illustrations, Animals/Pets, Young Adult Fiction. **Career:** Writer. **Publications:** SELF-ILLUSTRATED FOR CHILDREN: Eddie and Teddy, 1990; Along Came Eric, 1991; How Many Days to My Birthday?, 1992; Betty's Not Well Today, 1993; Ten Green Monsters, 1993; Pat, the Dog, 1994; Too Many Teddies, 1995; Helping Hector, 1995; Cheeky Monkey,

1995; Michael's Monsters, 1996; Naughty Monkey: A Mix-and-Fix Book, 1996; Scratch 'n' Sniff, 1996; Nothing But Trouble, 1997; Lucy's Bedtime Book, 1998 in US as Goodnight Lucy, 1998; Sammy's Waggy Tail, 1998; Can We Keep It Dad?, 1999; What Would We Do without Missus Mac?, 1999; The Sun Robbers, 2000; Let's Go Driving!, 2001; Nervous Norris, 2002; Max and the Rainbow Rain Hat, 2002; Lucky, 2005. Illustrator of books by others. **Address:** Anderson Press Ltd., 20 Vauxhall Bridge Rd., London, GL SW1V 2SA, England.

CLARKE, John R. American (born United States), b. 1945. **Genres:** Art/Art History, Architecture. **Career:** Vassar College, instructor in history of art, 1972-73; University of Michigan, visiting assistant professor, 1973-74; University of California, assistant professor, 1974-75; Yale University, assistant professor, 1975-80; University of Texas, College of Fine Arts, Department of Art & Art History, assistant professor, 1980-82, associate professor, 1982-87, professor of history of art, 1987-, E.W. Doty professor, 1989-90, Annie Laurie Howard regents professor of fine arts, 1991-. Writer and public speaker. **Publications:** Roman Black-and-White Figural Mosaics, 1979; (contrib.) IL 60: Essays Honoring Irving Lavin on His Sixtieth Birthday, 1990; The Houses of Roman Italy, 100 B.C.-A.D. 250: Ritual, Space, and Decoration, 1991; (contrib.) Roman Art in The Private Sphere: New Perspectives on the Architecture and Decor of the Domus, Vill, and Insula, 1991; Looking at Lovemaking: Constructions of Sexuality in Roman Art, 100 B.C.-A.D. 250, 1998, rev. ed., 2001; Art in the Lives of Ordinary Romans: Visual Representation and Non-Elite Viewers in Italy, 100 B.C.-A.D. 315, 2003; Roman Sex: 100 B.C. to A.D. 250, 2003; Looking at Laughter: Humor, Power, and Transgression In Roman Visual Culture, 100 B.C.-A.D. 250, 2007; Roman Life: 100 B.C. to A.D. 200, 2007. Contributor to books and periodicals. **Address:** Department of Art & Art History, University of Texas, 2.114 Doty Fine Art Bldg., 1 University Sta., Ste. D1300, Austin, TX 78712-0337, U.S.A. **Online address:** j.clarke@mail.utexas.edu

CLARKE, Judith. Australian (born Australia), b. 1943. **Genres:** Novels, Novellas/Short Stories, Children's Non-fiction, Picture/Board Books. **Career:** Writer, educator and librarian. **Publications:** The Boy on the Lake: Stories Of The Supernatural, 1989; The Torment of Mr. Gully: Stories of the Supernatural, 1990; Teddy B. Zoot, 1990; Luna Park at Night, 1991; Riffraff, 1992; Friend of My Heart, 1994; Big Night Out, 1995; Panic Stations, 1995; The Lost Day, 1997; Night Train, 1998; Angels Passing By, 1999; (co-author) The Moral of the Story: Stories for Children, 1999; Wolf on the Fold, 2001; Mother Tough Wrote the Book, 2001; Starry Nights, 2001; Kalpana's Dream, 2004; One Whole And Perfect Day, 2006; That's All She Wrote, 2007; The Winds of Heaven, 2009. AL CAPSELLA SERIES: The Heroic Life of Al Capsella, 1988; Al Capsella and the Watchdogs, 1990; Al Capsella on Holidays, 1992 in US as Al Capsella Takes a Vacation, 1993. Contributor to periodicals. **Address:** 31 Alice St., Mt. Waverley, Melbourne, VI 3149, Australia.

CLARKE, Kenneth L. American (born United States), b. 1957. **Genres:** Mystery/Crime/Suspense, Novels, Literary Criticism And History. **Career:** Sprint Corp., customer service associate and departmental assistant, 1987-2001. Writer. **Publications:** (With R. Barnhorst and S. Barnhorst) Criminal Law and the Canadian Criminal Code, 1977; (with N.C. Bala) The Child and the Law, 1981; The Case of the Magnolia Murders (mystery novel), 1998; Deadly Justice (mystery novel), 2002; And Then You Die, 2002. **Address:** Final Cut Press, 13141 Hadley St., Apt. 2114, Overland Park, KS 66213-5161, U.S.A. **Online address:** kclarke5@juno.com

CLARKE, Lee. (Lee B. Clarke). American (born United States), b. 1946?. **Genres:** Adult Non-fiction, Humanities. **Career:** University of California, fellow and adjunct assistant professor, 1985-87; Rutgers University, Department of Sociology, assistant professor, 1988-93, associate professor, 1993-2010, professor, 2010-, Center for Social Research and Instruction, co-director, 1996-98, Teaching Excellence Center, fellow, 1999-2000, Center for the Critical Analysis of Contemporary Culture, fellow, 2004-05; American Sociological Association, editor, 1995-96; American Association for the Advancement of Science, fellow, 2009; sociologist. Writer. **Publications:** Acceptable Risk? Making Decisions in a Toxic Environment, 1989; (ed. with J.F. Short) Organizations, Uncertainties, and Risk, 1992; MissionImprobable: Using Fantasy Documents to Tame Disaster, 1999; (ed. with W.R. Freudenburg and T.I.K. Youn) Terrorism and Disaster: New Threats, 2003; Worst Cases: Terror and Catastrophe in the Popular Imagination, 2005; (ed.) Twenty-First Century Disasters: Why Should We Care About Worst Cases, 2008. Contributor to periodicals. **Address:** Department of Sociology, Rutgers University, 113 Davison Hall, 26 Nichol Ave., New Brunswick, NJ 08901-2882, U.S.A. **Online address:** lee@leeclarke.com

CLARKE, Lee B. *See* **CLARKE, Lee.**

CLARKE, Liz. American (born United States), b. 1960. **Genres:** Young Adult Non-fiction. **Career:** Writer and reporter. **Publications:** One Helluva Ride: How NASCAR Swept the Nation, 2008. **Address:** Washington Post, PO Box 17370, Arlington, VA 22216, U.S.A.

CLARKE, Margaret. (Helen M. Buss). Canadian (born Canada), b. 1941. **Genres:** Novels, Literary Criticism And History, Women's Studies And Issues, Autobiography/Memoirs. **Career:** Dryden High School Board, teacher, 1966-72; River East School Division, teacher, 1972-83; University of Calgary, assistant professor, 1991-93, associate professor, 1993-96, professor of English, 1996-2003, professor emeritus, 2004-. Writer. **Publications:** The Cutting Season (novel), 1984; Healing Song (novel), 1988; Memoirs from Away: A New Found Land Girlhood, 1999; Repossessing the World: Reading Memoirs by Contemporary Women, 2002. AS HELEN M. BUSS: Mother and Daughter Relationships in the Manawaka Works of Margaret Laurence, 1985; Mapping Our Selves: Canadian Women's Autobiography, 1993; (ed. with J.H. Beattie) Undelivered Letters to Hudson's Bay Company Men on the Northwest Coast of America, 1830-57, 2003. **Address:** Department of English, University of Calgary, 2500 University Dr. NW, Calgary, AB T2N 1N4, Canada. **Online address:** hbuss@ucalgary.ca

CLARKE, Mary. British (born England), b. 1923. **Genres:** Dance/Ballet, Novellas/Short Stories, Art/Art History. **Career:** Dance Magazine, correspondent, 1943-55; Ballet Annual, assistant editor, 1952-63; Dancing Times, assistant editor, 1954-63, editor and co-director, 1963-, editor emeritus; Dance News of New York, correspondent, 1955-70. **Publications:** (With R. Wood) Shakespeare at the Old Vic, 1954; The Sadler's Wells Ballet, 1955; Six Great Dancers, 1957; Presenting People Who Dance, 1961; Dancers of Mercury: The Story of Ballet Rambert, 1962; Margot Fonteyn, 1976; (ed. with D. Vaughan) An Encyclopedia of Dance and Ballet, 1977; (intro.) Classics of the Royal Ballet, 1978; Antoinette Sibley, 1981. WITH C. CRISP: Ballet: An Illustrated History, 2nd ed., 1973; Making a Ballet, 1974; Understanding Ballet, 1976; Introducing Ballet, 1976; Ballet in Art: From the Renaissance to the Present, 1978; Design for Ballet, 1978; The History of Dance, 1981; Ballet Goer's Guide, 1981; How to Enjoy Ballet, 1983; Men in Dance, 1985; Ballerina: The Art of Women in Classical Ballet, 1987; London Contemporary Dance Theatre: The First 21 Years, 1989. **Address:** Dancing Times, Clerkenwell House, 45-47 Clerkenwell Green, London, GL EC1R 0EB, England. **Online address:** maryat@dancing-times.co.uk

CLARKE, Michael Tavel. Canadian (born Canada), b. 1967. **Genres:** History. **Career:** The University of Calgary, associate professor. Writer. **Publications:** These Days of Large Things: The Culture of Size in America, 1865-1930, 2007. **Address:** Department of English, The University of Calgary, 2500 University Dr. NW, Calgary, AB T2N 1N4, Canada. **Online address:** michael.t.clarke@ucalgary.ca

CLARKE, Norma. British (born England), b. 1948?. **Genres:** Children's Fiction, Adult Non-fiction, Literary Criticism And History. **Career:** City and Islington College, lecturer, 1990-94; London Guildhall University, lecturer, 1997-98; Kingston University, senior lecturer, professor in English literature and creative writing. Writer. **Publications:** Ambitious Heights: Writing, Friendship, Love: The Jewsbury Sisters, Felicia Hemans and Jane Welsh Carlyle (history and criticism), 1990; Queen of the Wits: A Life of Laetitia Pilkington, 2008. JUVENILE FICTION: Patrick in Person, 1991; Patrick and the Rotten Roman Rubbish, 1993; (with P. Kavanagh) Trouble on the Day, 1995; The Doctor's Daughter, 1996; (with H. Weinstein) Spinning with the Brian: Women's Writing in Seventeenth Century England, 1996; Dr. Johnson's Women (biography), 2000; The Rise and Fall of the Woman of Letters (history and criticism), 2004. Contributor to books. **Address:** Kingston University, HH32, John Galsworthy Bldg., Penrhyn Rd., Kingston upon Thames, SR KT1 2EE, England. **Online address:** n.clarke@kingston.ac.uk

CLARKE, Patricia. Australian (born Australia), b. 1926. **Genres:** History, Women's Studies And Issues, Biography, Writing/Journalism. **Career:** Australian News and Information Bureau, journalist; ABC, journalist; M. Newton Publications, editor and journalist; National Capital Development Commission, editor and journalist; Canberra Historical Journal, editor, 1987-2000. **Publications:** The Governesses: Letters from the Colonies, 1862-1882, 1985; Colonial Woman: The Life and Times of Mary Braidwood Mowle, 1827-1857, 1986; Pen Portraits: Women Writers and Journalists in Nineteenth Century Australia, 1988; Pioneer Writer: The Life of Louisa Atkinson, Novelist, Journalist, Naturalist, 1990; Tasma: The Life of Jessie Couvreur, 1994; Rosa! Rosa! A Life of Rosa Praed, Novelist and Spiritualist, 1999. EDITOR: (with D. Spender) Life Lines: Australian Women's Letters and Diaries, 1788-1840, 1992; Tasma's Diaries: The Diaries of Jessie Couvreur with Another by Her Young Sister Edith Huybers, 1995; Half a Lifetime, 1999; Steps to Federation: Lectures marking the Centenary of Federation, 2001; (with M. McKinney) Equal Heart and Mind: Letters Between Judith Wright and Jack McKinney, 2004; (with M. McKinney) With Love & Fury: Selected Letters of Judith Wright, 2006; (and comp.) Wartime letters of Daniel J. Clarke, 414467 RAAF, 1941-43, 2007. **Address:** 14 Chermside St., Deakin, Canberra, AC 2600, Australia. **Online address:** clarke.patricia@netspeed.com.au

CLARKE, Peter Frederick. British/Canadian (born Canada), b. 1942. **Genres:** Economics, Politics/Government, History. **Career:** University College, lecturer and reader, 1966-80, review editor of history, 1967-73; Cambridge University, professor of modern British history, lecturer and reader, 1980-2004, professor emeritus of modern British history, 2004-, Trinity Hall, master, 2000-04. **Publications:** Lancashire and the New Liberalism, 1971; (ed. and intro.) Democracy and Reaction, 1972; (ed. and intro.) The Crisis of Liberalism, 1974; Liberals and Social Democrats, 1978; (with D. Graham) New Enlightenment, 1986; Keynesian Revolution in the Making, 1924-1936, 1988; A Question of Leadership: From Gladstone to Thatcher, 1991; Hope and Glory: Britain, 1900-1990, 1997, 2nd ed. as Hope and Glory: Britain, 1900-2000, 2004; (ed. with C. Trebilcock) Understanding Decline: Perceptions and Realities of British Economic Performance, 1997; Keynesian Revolution and Its Economic Consequences: Selected Essays, 1998; Cripps Version: The Life of Sir Stafford Cripps, 1889-1952, 2002; The Last Thousand Days of the British Empire, 2007 in US as Last Thousand Days of the British Empire: Churchill, Roosevelt, and the Birth of the Pax Americana, 2008; Keynes: The Twentieth Century's Most Influential Economist, 2009; Keynes: The Rise, Fall, and Return of the 20th Century's Most Influential Economist, 2009; Mr. Churchill's Profession: The Statesman as Author and the Book that Defined the Special Relationship, 2012. **Address:** Faculty of History, Cambridge University, West Rd., Cambridge, CB CB3 9EF, England. **Online address:** pfc1000@cam.ac.uk

CLARKE, Sally H. American (born United States), b. 1971. **Genres:** Business/Trade/Industry. **Career:** University of Texas, professor. Writer. **Publications:** Regulation and the Revolution in United States Farm Productivity, 1994; Trust and Power: Consumers, the Modern Corporation, and the Making of the United States Automobile Market, 2007; The Challenge of Remaining Innovative: Insights from Twentieth-Century American Business, 2009. **Address:** Department of History, University of Texas, 1 University Sta., PO Box B7000, Austin, TX 78712-0220, U.S.A. **Online address:** sclarke@mail.utexas.edu

CLARKE, Sam. *See* **CLARKE, Gus.**

CLARKE, (Victor) Lindsay. British (born England), b. 1939. **Genres:** Novels, Mythology/Folklore, History, Young Adult Fiction, Military/Defense/Arms Control. **Career:** Senior master, 1962-65; College of Further Education, lecturer in English, 1965-67; Norwich City College, coordinator of liberal studies, 1967-70; Friends World College, European Center, co-director, 1970-78; freelance teacher, counselor and writer, 1978-; University of Wales, writer-in-residence, 1996, associate lecturer in creative writing, 1997-. **Publications:** Sunday Whiteman, 1987; The Chymical Wedding, 1989; Alice's Masque, 1994; Cathal of the Woods, 1994; (ed.) Essential Celtic Mythology, 1997 as Lindsay Clarke's Traditional Celtic Stories, 1999; Parzival and the Stone from Heaven: A Grail Romance Retold for Our Time, 2001; The War at Troy, 2004; The Return from Troy, 2005; The Water Theatre, 2010. **Address:** c/o Sarah Ballard, United Agents, 12-26 Lexington St., London, GL W1F OLE, England.

CLARKE-RICH, Elizabeth L. American (born United States), b. 1934. **Genres:** Children's Fiction, Poetry, Adult Non-fiction. **Career:** Teacher, 1950-55; librarian, 1953-55; Prince George's County Public Schools, librarian, 1960-66, resource teacher, 1967-69, high school, librarian, 1970-89. Writer. **Publications:** We Ain't Arrived Yet (poems), 1991; The Big Mistake, 1995; And the Winner Is, 1998. **Address:** 11611 Tyre St., Upper Marlboro, MD 20772, U.S.A.

CLARKSON, Wensley. British (born England), b. 1956. **Genres:** Plays/Screenplays, Documentaries/Reportage, Biography, Photography. **Career:** Wimbledon News, reporter, 1977-79; Sunday Mirror, reporter, 1979-81; Mail on Sunday, reporter, 1981-82; Sunday Mirror, reporter, 1982-87; freelance writer, 1987-. **Publications:** Dog Eat Dog: Confessions of a Tabloid Journalist (autobiography), 1990; Hell Hath No Fury (true crime), 1990; Like a Woman Scorned (true crime), 1991; Love You to Death, Darling (true crime), 1991; Doctors of Death (true crime), 1992; Year in La La Land (autobiography), 1992; Mel: The Inside Story (biography), 1993; Tom Cruise Unauthorized (biography), 1994; Whatever Mother Says: An Incredible True Story of Death and Destruction Inside One Ordinary Family (true crime), 1994; Deadly Seduction (true crime), 1995; Quentin Tarantino: Shooting from the Hip (biography), 1995; John Travolta: Back in Character (biography), 1996; Sting (biography), 1996, rev. ed. as Sting: The Secret Life of Gordon Sumner, 1999; Slave Girls (true crime), 1996; True Patriot (military/espionage), 1996; Caged Heat (true crime), 1997; Death at Every Stop, 1997; Harvey Keitel: Prince of Darkness, 1997; In the Name of Satan, 1998; The Valkyrie Operation, 1998; Deadlier than the Male, 1999; Mel Gibson: Living Dangerously, 1999; The Railroad Killer, 1999; Women in Chains, 2000; Female of the Species, 2000; The Mother's Day Murder, 2000; Doctors Who Kill, 2000; Killer on the Road, 2000; The Mother's Day Murder, 2000; Killer Women, 2001; Hitman, 2001; Sisters in Blood, 2002; The Good Doctor, 2002; Hit 'em Hard: Jack Spot, King of the Underworld, 2002; Kenny Noye, 2002; The Boss, 2002; Murder in Room 1406, 2002; Born to Kill: The Twisted Life and Bizarre Death of the Man Who Murdered Gianni Versace, 2004; Killing Charlie: The Bloody, Bullet-Riddled Hunt for the Most Powerful Great Train Robber of All, 2004; Costa del Crime, 2004; Driven to Kill. 2004; Moody: The Life and Crimes of Britain's Most Notorious Hitman, 2004; Evil Beyond Belief, 2005; The Predator, 2007; Bindon: Fighter, Gangster, Actor, Lover: The True Story of John Bindon, a Modern Legend, 2007; Wolf Man: The True Story of Francisco Arce Montes the First Global Serial Killer Maps, 2008; Gangs of Britain: The Gripping True Stories of the Faces Who Run Britains Organised Crime, 2008; Gang Wars of London, 2008; Gang Wars on the Costa, 2009; Hell Hath No Fury Like A Woman Scorned: True Stories of Women Who Kill, 2009; Billy Hill: Godfather of London, 2009; John Travolta: King of Cool, 2010. Contributor to periodicals. **Address:** c/o Author Mail, Overlook Press, 149 Wooster St., New York, NY 10012, U.S.A. **Online address:** wensleyclarkson@yahoo.com

CLARVOE, Jennifer. American (born United States) **Genres:** Poetry. **Career:** Kenyon College, faculty, 1990-, associate professor of English, professor of English; Harvard Summer School, instructor; Wellesley College, instructor; Boston University, instructor; University of California-Irvine, MFA Program, faculty. Poet. **Publications:** Invisible Tender (poetry), 2000; Day of Needs, 2002; On the Stairmaster, 2003; Pelt of Un-want, 2003; Counter-Amores, 2011. **Address:** Department of English, Kenyon College, 210 Lentz House and Sunset Cottage, 102 College Dr., Gambier, OH 43022, U.S.A. **Online address:** clarvoe@kenyon.edu

CLARY, David A. American (born United States), b. 1946. **Genres:** History, Military/Defense/Arms Control, Biography. **Career:** University of Texas, National Park Service, Fort Davis National Historical Site, historian, 1968-76; Office of Archaeology and Historical Preservation, coordinator of environmental and protection activities, 1972-74; U.S. Forest Service, chief historian, 1976-; David A. Clary and Associates, principal, 1979-. Writer. **Publications:** The Place Where Hell Bubbled Up: A History of the First National Park, 1972; (with W.J. Miller and R.B. Hartzer) River Raisin Battlefield and Massacre Site, Monroe County, Michigan: A Feasibility Study of Alternatives for Acquisition, Development, Management, and Interpretation, 1981; These Relics of Barbarism: A History of Furniture in Barracks and Guardhouses of the United States Army, 1800-1880, 1981; (with R.B. Hartzer) Half a Century in Forest Conservation: A Biography and Oral History of Edward P. Cliff, 1981; Timber and the Forest Service, 1986; (with J.W.A. Whitehorne) The Inspectors General of the United States Army, 1777-1903, 1987; Fortress America: The Corps of Engineers, Hampton Roads, and United States Coastal Defense, 1990; Before and After Roswell: The Flying Saucer in America, 1947-1999, 2000; Rocket Man: Robert H. Goddard and the Birth of the Space Age, 2003; Adopted Son: Washington, Lafayette, and the Friendship That Saved the Revolution, 2007; Eagles and Empire: The United States, Mexico, and the Struggle for a Continent, 2009; George Washington's First

War: His Early Military Adventures, 2011. Contributor to periodicals. **Address:** Simon & Schuster Inc., 1230 Ave. of the Americas, New York, NY 10020-1513, U.S.A.

CLARY, Killarney. American (born United States), b. 1953. **Genres:** Poetry, Young Adult Fiction. **Career:** University of California, faculty; University of Iowa, faculty. Poet. **Publications:** By Me, by Any, Can or Can't Be Done: Poems, 1980; Who Whispered Near Me, 1989; Shine Empty in Daylight, 1992; By Common Salt, 1996; Potential Stranger, 2003. **Address:** 6224 Rockcliff Dr., Los Angeles, CA 90068-1652, U.S.A.

CLASON, Marmy A. American (born United States), b. 1965. **Genres:** inspirational/Motivational Literature, Business/Trade/Industry, Reference, Education. **Career:** Concordia University, teacher of communication; Sam Houston State University, teacher of communication; University of Wisconsin, teacher of communication; Mount Mary College, teacher of communication; Trinity International University, visiting assistant professor of communication, 2005. Writer. **Publications:** (With J.A. Beck) On the Edge of Success, 2003; (with J.A. Beck) Light on the Path: A Christian Perspective on College Success, 2005, 3rd ed., 2011. **Address:** Department of Communication, Trinity International University, 2065 Half Day Rd., Deerfield, IL 60015, U.S.A. **Online address:** mclason@tiu.edu

CLAUDE-PIERRE, Peggy. Canadian (born Canada) **Genres:** Psychology, Medicine/Health, Self Help. **Career:** Outpatient and residential therapist, 1988-; Montreux Counselling Centre, founder, 1988-; Montreux Clinic, founder, 1993-. Writer. **Publications:** The Secret Language of Eating Disorders: The Revolutionary New Approach to Understanding and Curing Anorexia and Bulimia, 1997. Contributor to periodicals. **Address:** Random House of Canada Ltd., 2775 Matheson Blvd. E, Mississauga, ON L4W 4P7, Canada.

CLAUSEN, Andy. Belgian (born Belgium), b. 1943. **Genres:** Poetry, Novels, Music, Literary Criticism And History. **Career:** Naropa Institute (now Naropa University), teacher, 1980; Renegade, publisher. Writer. **Publications:** Extreme Unction, 1974; Austin, Texas, 1981; The Iron Curtain of Love, 1985; Without Doubt, 1991; Trek to the Top of the World, 1996; 40th Century Man: Selected Verse, 1996-1966, 1997; Songs of Bo Baba, 2004. EDITOR WITH A. GINSBERG AND E. KATZ: Poems for the Nation: A Collection of Contemporary Political Poems, 1999. **Address:** c/o Author Mail, Seven Stories Press, 140 Watts St., New York, NY 10013, U.S.A.

CLAUSEN, Christopher (John). American (born United States), b. 1942. **Genres:** Literary Criticism And History, Intellectual History, Politics/Government, Social Commentary, Essays, Young Adult Fiction, History. **Career:** University of Hawaii, instructor in English, 1965-66; Concord College, assistant professor of English, 1966-68; Canada Council, fellow, 1970-72; Virginia Polytechnic Institute and State University, visiting assistant professor, 1972, assistant professor, 1973-79, associate professor, 1979-84, professor of English, 1984-85; Pennsylvania State University, professor of English, 1985-2006, now retired. Writer. **Publications:** The Place of Poetry: Two Centuries of an Art in Crisis, 1981; The Moral Imagination: Essays on Literature and Ethics, 1986; My Life with President Kennedy, 1994; Faded Mosaic: The Emergence of Post-Cultural America, 2000. Contributor of articles to periodicals and journals. Works appear in anthologies. **Address:** Ivan R. Dee, 4501 Forbes Blvd., Ste. 200, Lanham, MD 20706, U.S.A. **Online address:** cqc1@psu.edu

CLAUSEN, Lowen. American (born United States) **Genres:** Mystery/Crime/Suspense, Novels, Young Adult Fiction. **Career:** Seattle Police Department, police officer. Writer. **Publications:** First Avenue, 1999; Second Watch: A Novel, 2003; Third & Forever, 2004; River, 2008. **Address:** Silo Press, PO Box 326, St. Paul, NE 68873-0326, U.S.A.

CLAUSEN, Meredith L(eslie). American (born United States), b. 1942. **Genres:** Architecture, Art/Art History. **Career:** University of Santa Clara, teacher, 1976; Colorado College, teacher, 1976-77; Stanford University, acting assistant professor, 1977-78, visiting assistant professor, 1985-86; University of Washington, assistant professor, 1979-85, associate professor, 1985-93, professor of art history, 1993-, professor of architecture, adjunct professor of romance languages and literature, graduate program adviser of art history, 1996-. Writer. **Publications:** Frantz Jourdain and the Samaritaine: Art Nouveau Theory and Criticism, 1987; Spiritual Space: The Religious Architecture of Pietro Belluschi, 1992; Pietro Belluschi: Modern American Architect, 1994; Pan Am Building and the Shattering of the Modernist Dream, 2005. Contributor of articles to books and journals. **Address:** School of Art, University of Washington, Rm. 222, Art Bldg., PO Box 353440, Seattle, WA 98195-3440, U.S.A. **Online address:** mlc@u.washington.edu

CLAUSEN, Tammy Hennigh. American (born United States) **Genres:** Librarianship, Young Adult Fiction. **Career:** Cicero Public Library, young adult and adult services librarian; Berwyn Public Library (BPL), public librarian, Department of Readers Advisory, manager, director, 2009-. Writer. **Publications:** (With B.S. Spratford) The Horror Readers' Advisory: The Librarian's Guide to Vampires, Killer Tomatoes, and Haunted Houses, 2004. Contributor to periodicals. **Address:** Berwyn Public Library, 2701 S Harlem Ave., Berwyn, IL 60402, U.S.A. **Online address:** tammyclausen@berwynlibrary.net

CLAVEL, Pierre. American (born United States), b. 1935?. **Genres:** Regional/Urban Planning, Politics/Government, Institutions/Organizations. **Career:** Blair Associates, city planner, 1960-62; University of Puerto Rico, assistant professor of planning, 1965-67; Cornell University, Department of City and Regional Planning, assistant professor, associate professor, 1967-82, professor of city and regional planning, 1982-2010, professor emeritus, 2010-, chair, 2001-04, director of progressive planning summer program, 1979-83. Writer. **Publications:** (With W.W. Goldsmith and D. Roth) Bibliography on Public Planning in Puerto Rico, 1975; (with K.C. Parsons) National Growth Policy: An Institutional Perspective, 1977; Planning in Wales and Appalachia: Case Studies, 1979; Opposition Planning in Wales and Appalachia, 1983; The Progressive City: Planning and Participation, 1969-1984, 1986; (with N. Krumholz) Reinventing Cities: Equity Planners Tell Their Stories, 1994; Activists in City Hall: The Progressive Response to the Reagan Era in Boston and Chicago, 2010. EDITOR: (with W.W. Goldsmith) Urban and Regional Planning in an Age of Austerity, 1980; (with W. Wiewel) Harold Washington and the Neighborhoods: Progressive City Government in Chicago, 1983-1987, 1991. **Address:** Department of City and Regional Planning, Cornell University, 219 W Sibley Hall, Ithaca, NY 14853, U.S.A. **Online address:** pc29@cornell.edu

CLAWSON, Calvin C. American (born United States), b. 1941. **Genres:** Mathematics/Statistics, Novels, Education, How-to Books. **Career:** Seattle Police Department, systems analyst and planner, 1969-83; freelance writer, 1983-; South Seattle Community College, instructor in mathematics, 1994-. **Publications:** Conquering Math Phobia, 1991; The Mathematical Traveler: Exploring the Grand History of Numbers, 1994; Mathematical Mysteries: The Beauty and Magic of Numbers, 1996; Mathematical Sorcery: Revealing the Secrets of Numbers, 2001; Buffalo Man, 2009. Contributor of short stories and articles to periodicals. **Address:** 27106 SE 146th St., Issaquah, WA 98027, U.S.A. **Online address:** ccclawson@comcast.net

CLAWSON, James G. American (born United States), b. 1947. **Genres:** Business/Trade/Industry, Administration/Management. **Career:** Wells Fargo Bank, international credit officer, 1973-75; Massachusetts College of Art, instructor, 1975-76; Harvard University, Business School, assistant professor, 1979-81; University of Virginia, Darden School of Business, associate professor, 1981-, professor of business administration, Johnson & Higgins professor of business administration, 1981-, chair; International University of Japan, visiting faculty, 1991; Career Next Step Inc., chairman, 2004-10; European School of Management and Technology, visiting professor, 2006-. Consultant and writer. **Publications:** Self-Assessment and Career Development, 1986, (co-author) 3rd ed., 1992; (with D.D. Ward) An MBA's Guide to Self-Assessment and Career Development, 1987; Level Three Leadership: Getting Below the Surface, 1999, 5th ed., 2012; Practical Problems in Organizations: Cases in Leadership, Organizational Behavior and Human Resources, 2003; (M.L. Conner) Creating a Learning Culture: Strategy, Technology and Practice, 2004; (with M.E. Haskins) Teaching Management: A Field Guide for Professors, Corporate Trainers and Consultants, 2006; (with D.S. Newburg) Powered by Feel: How Individuals, Teams and Companies Excel, 2008; Balancing Your Life: Executive Lessons for Work, Family and Self, 2010. **Address:** The Darden Graduate School of Business, University of Virginia, PO Box 6550, Charlottesville, VA 22906, U.S.A. **Online address:** jimclawson@virginia.edu

CLAWSON, Rosalee A. American (born United States), b. 1968. **Genres:** Law, Politics/Government. **Career:** Purdue University, visiting assistant professor, 1996-97, assistant professor, 1997-2003, associate professor, 2003-10, professor of political science, 2010-, Center for Instructional Excellence, faculty consultant, 2009-. Writer and political scientist. **Publications:** (With Z.M. Oxley) Public Opinion: Democratic Ideals, Democratic Practice, 2008; (with E.N. Walternburg) Legacy and Legitimacy: Black Americans and the Supreme Court, 2009. Contributor to books and periodicals. **Address:** U.S.A. **Online address:** clawsonr@purdue.edu

CLAXTON, Melvin. American (born United States), b. 1960?. **Genres:** Novels, History. **Career:** Virgin Islands Daily News, intern, 1983-85, reporter, 1985-88, 1994-97; freelance writer, 1988-94; Chicago Tribune, reporter, 1997; Detroit News, reporter, 1998-. Writer. **Publications:** (With M. Puls) Uncommon Valor: A Story of Race, Patriotism and Glory in the Final Battles of the Civil War, 2006. Contributor to periodicals. **Address:** c/o Author Mail, John Wiley & Sons, 111 River St., Ste. 2000, Hoboken, NJ 07030, U.S.A.

CLAY, Rita. *See* **ESTRADA, Rita Clay.**

CLAY, Rosamund. *See* **OAKLEY, Ann.**

CLAYDEN, Andy. British (born England) **Genres:** Environmental Sciences/Ecology, Earth Sciences. **Career:** GIS and Landscape Planning, research assistant; Manchester Metropolitan University, undergraduate programme; University of Sheffield, Department of Landscape, lecturer, 1994, senior lecturer, environmental consultant. Writer. **Publications:** (With N. Dunnett) Rain Gardens: Managing Water Sustainably in the Garden and Designed Landscape, 2007; (with N. Dunnett and C. Smith) Residential Landscape Sustainability: A Checklist Tool, 2007. **Address:** Department of Landscape, The University of Sheffield, Rm. 3.19, Crookesmoor Bldg., Conduit Rd., Sheffield, S10 1FL, England. **Online address:** a.clayden@sheffield.ac.uk

CLAYSON, Alan. British (born England), b. 1951. **Genres:** Music, History, Biography, Literary Criticism And History. **Career:** Portsmouth Sinfonia, viola player, 1974-75. Writer. **Publications:** Call Up the Groups!: The Golden Age of British Beat, 1962-1967, 1985; Back in the High Life: A Biography of Steve Winwood, 1988; Only the Lonely: Roy Orbison's Life and Legacy, 1989; The Quiet One: A Life of George Harrison, 1990; Ringo Starr: Straight Man or Joker?, 1992; Death Discs, 1992; (with P. Sutcliffe) Backbeat: Stuart Sutcliffe, the Lost Beatle (movie tie-in), 1994; (ed. with S. Leigh) Aspects of Elvis: Tryin' to Get to You, 1994; Beat Merchants: The Origins, History, Impact, and Rock Legacy of the 1960's British Pop Groups, 1995; (with J. Ryan) The Troggs Files: Rock's Wild Things, 2000; The Yardbids, 2002; Edgard Varese, 2003; Sunset on a Legend: John Lennon, 2003; Paul McCartney, 2003; The Little Box of Beatles, 2003; Brain Jones, 2004; Charlie Watts, 2004; Woman: The Incredible Life of Yoko Ono, 2004; Keith Richards, 2005; Serge Gainsbourg: A View from the Exterior, 2005; Led Zeppelin, 2006; The Rolling Stones Complete Discography, 2006; Legendary Sessions: The Rolling Stones: Beggars Banquet, 2008. Contributor of articles to books. **Address:** Carol Boyer, 894 Monterey Dr., Shoreview, MN 55126-5872, U.S.A.

CLAYSON, (S.) Hollis. American (born United States), b. 1946. **Genres:** Art/Art History. **Career:** Pierce College, adviser on student affairs, 1968-69; University of California, Department of Art History, slide librarian, 1970-72; California Institute of the Arts, instructor in complementary studies, 1974-76; Schiller College, instructor in English and art history, 1977-78; Wichita State University, assistant professor of art history, 1978-82; University of Illinois, assistant professor of the history of architecture and art, 1984-85; Northwestern University, visiting assistant professor of art history, 1982-84, assistant professor, 1985-91, associate professor, 1991-2001, Chapin Humanities Residential College, faculty associate, 1985-87, 1989-91; Andrew W. Mellon Program in the History of Art Objects, director, 1989-90, 1992-93, Charles Deering McCormick professor of teaching excellence, 1993-95, 1996-97, Graduate School, associate dean, 1995-98, special assistant, 1998-99, department chair, 2000-03, professor of art history, 2001-, Mary and Leich Block Museam of Art, vice-chair, 2002-06, Martin J. and Patricia Koldyke outstanding teaching professor, 2004-06; Office of the Provost, special project manager, 2005-06; Bergen Evans professor in the humanities, 2006-; Alice Kaplan Institute for the Humanities, director, 2006-, professor of art history and history. Writer. **Publications:** Painted Love: Prostitution in French Art of the Impressionist Era, 1991; Understanding Paintings: Themes in Art Explored and Explained, 2000; Paris in Despair: Art and Everyday Life under Siege (1870-71), 2002; (with C. Hertel and N. Penny) Darker Side of Light: Arts of Privacy, 1850-1900, 2009. Contributor to journals. **Address:** Department of Art History, Northwestern University, 3-400 Kresge Hall, 1880 Campus Dr., Evanston, IL 60208-2208, U.S.A. **Online address:** shc@northwestern.edu

CLAYTON, Anthony. British (born England), b. 1928. **Genres:** Military/Defense/Arms Control. **Career:** Royal Military Academy, senior lecturer, 1965-93; Conflict Studies Research Centre, librarian, 1994-99; University of Surrey, tutor, 1994-. Writer. **Publications:** (With D.C. Savage) Government and Labour in Kenya, 1895-1963, 1973; 1948 Zanzibar General Strike, 1976; Communication for New Loyalties: African Soldiers' Songs (monograph), 1978; The Zanzibar Revolution and Its Aftermath, 1981; Counter-Insurgency in Kenya, 1952-56 (monograph), 1985; The British Empire as a Superpower, 1919-39, 1986; France, Soldiers, and Africa, 1988; (with D. Killingray) Khaki and Blue: The Military and Police in Colonial Africa, 1989; Three Marshals of France, 1992; Forearmed: A History of the Intelligence Corps, 1993; The Wars of French Decolonization, 1994; The End of Empire: The Experience of Britain and France and the Soviet Union/Russia Compared (monograph), 1996; (ed. with A. Russell and contrib.) Dresden: A City Reborn, 1998; Frontiersmen: Warfare in Africa since 1950, 1999; Paths of Glory: The French Army, 191418, 2003; The British Officer: Leaders of the Army from 1660 to the Present, 2006; The Killing Fields of Kenya, 1952-1960: British Military Operations against the Mau Mau, 2006; Warfare in Woods and Forests, 2011. **Address:** April Cottage, 43 Ford Ln., Lower Bourne, Farnham, SR GU10 3NB, England.

CLAYTON, David J. American (born United States) **Genres:** Medicine/Health. **Career:** Physician; Mount Sinai School of Medicine, clinical instructor in medicine. Writer. **Publications:** (With L. Vanderkam) The Healthy Guide to Unhealthy Living: How to Survive Your Bad Habits, 2006. Contributor to periodicals. **Address:** Division of General Internal Medicine, Mount Sinai School of Medicine, 1 Gustave L Levy Pl., New York, NY 10029, U.S.A.

CLAYTON, Elaine. American (born United States), b. 1961. **Genres:** Children's Fiction, Illustrations, inspirational/Motivational Literature. **Career:** Cesar Chavez Migrant Camp, Head Start teacher, 1980; High Museum of Art, gallery instructor, 1980-85; Woodruff Memorial Arts Center Gallery, gallery manager, 1984; Paideia School, assistant teacher and artist-in-residence, 1985-89; Mary Lin Elementary School, artist-in-residence, 1985; Atrium School, elementary teacher, 1990-94. Illustrator and author. **Publications:** SELF-ILLUSTRATED FOR CHILDREN: Pup in School, 1993; Ella's Trip to the Museum, 1996; (ed.) Puzzle Gallery Books, 1997; The Yeoman's Daring Daughter and the Princes in the Tower, 1999; Blue Ribbon for Sugar, 2006; Illuminara Intuitive Journal With Cards, 2011. **Address:** CT , U.S.A. **Online address:** elaineclayton@mac.com

CLAYTON, Lawrence (Otto). American (born United States), b. 1945. **Genres:** Psychology, Self Help, Medicine/Health, Sciences. **Career:** Diversa Inc., mobile home sales representative, 1969-72; United Methodist Church, Central Texas Conference, pastor, 1973-81; Johnson County Mental Health Clinic, director, 1981-83; United Methodist Counseling Services, administrator, 1983-88; Central Oklahoma Medical Group, mental health consultant, 1987-88; Clayton Clinic, owner and president, 1988-90; Fountainview, clinical director, 1990; Oklahoma Family Institute, executive director, 1990-95; Gospel Celebration Fellowship, associate pastor, 1996-98, now retired. Writer and publisher. **Publications:** Assessment and Management of the Suicidal Adolescent, 1990; (with S. Carter) Coping with Depression, 1990; Coping with a Drug Abusing Parent, 1991; (with S. Carter) Coping with Being Gifted, 1992; (with J. Morrison) Coping with a Learning Disability, 1992, rev. ed., 1999; Careers in Psychology, 1992; (with B.S. Smith) Coping with Sports Injuries, 1992; (with R. Van Norstrand) The Professional Drug and Alcohol Counselor Supervisor's Handbook, 1993; Designer Drugs, 1994; Barbiturates and Other Depressants, 1994, rev. ed., 2001; Amphetamines and Other Stimulants, 1994, rev. ed., 2001; Everything you Need to Know about Sports Injuries, 1994; Steroids, 1995; Working Together against Drug Addiction, 1996; Drugs, Drug Testing, and You, 1997; Tranquilizers, 1997; Alcohol Drug Dangers, 1999; Diet Pill Drug Dangers, 1999; Drug Testing, 2000; Delayed Gratification, 2001; Careers in Behavioral Science, 2001; Managing Suicidal Individuals and Their Families, 2002; Introduction to Alcohol and Drug Abuse Counseling, 2002; Behavioral Science Research, 2002; Personality Development, 2002; Stress Management, 2002; Lifespan Human Development, 2002; Small Groups, 2002; Biblical Concepts of Mental Health, 2002; Abnormal Psychology, 2002; Marriage and Family Development, 2002. Contributor to books and periodicals. **Address:** PO Box 485, Piedmont, OK 73078-0485, U.S.A. **Online address:** firegreen15@aol.com

CLAYTON, Martin. British (born England), b. 1967. **Genres:** Art/Art History, Biography, Photography. **Career:** Royal Library, Print Room, assistant curator, 1990-. Writer. **Publications:** (With R. Philo) Leonardo da Vinci: The Anatomy of Man, 1992; Seven Florentine Heads, 1993; Poussin: Works on Paper, 1995; Leonardo da Vinci: A Curious Vision, 1996; Raphael and his Circle, 1999; Leonardo da Vinci: The Divine and the Grotesque, 2002; (ed.) Fungi, 2005; (with S. Owens, M. Clayton and R. Alexandratos) Amazing Rare Things: The Art of Natural History in the Age of Discovery, 2007; (ed. with B. Elliott) Flora: The Erbario Miniato and other Drawings, 2007; (with L. Whitaker) The Art of Italy in the Royal Collection: Renaissance & Baroque, 2007; (with L. Guerrini and A. de Ávila) Flora: The Aztec Herbal, 2009. **Address:** Royal Library, Windsor Castle, London, GL SL4 1NY, England.

CLAYTON, Mary. Irish/American (born United States), b. 1954. **Genres:** Theology/Religion, Literary Criticism And History. **Career:** University College Dublin, School of English, Drama & Film, professor, 1982-, now chair of old and middle English language and literature; Harvard University, Fulbright visiting professor, 1988-89; University of California, Fulbright visiting professor, 1996. Writer. **Publications:** The Cult of the Virgin Mary in Anglo-Saxon England, 1990; (with H. Magennis) The Old English Lives of St. Margaret, 1994; The Apocryphal Gospels of Mary in Anglo-Saxon England, 1998. Contributor to periodicals. **Address:** School of English, Drama and Film, University College Dublin, Newman Bldg., Belfield, DU 4, Ireland. **Online address:** mary.clayton@ucd.ie

CLAYTON, Mary. *See* **LIDE, Mary.**

CLAYTON, Michael. British (born England), b. 1934. **Genres:** Sports/Fitness, Biography. **Career:** Evening Standard, deputy news editor, 1961-64; The New Zealand Herald, reporter and deputy news editor, 1962-65; Southern Television, news editor, 1964-65; British Broadcasting Corp., news and current affairs staff correspondent, 1965-73; Horse and Hound, editor, 1973-95; IPC Magazines, director, 1994-97; Horse and Hound, editor-in-chief, 1994-97; Country Life, editor-in-chief, 1994-97; The Field, editor-in-chief, 1994-97. **Publications:** A-Hunting We Will Go, 1967; Hickstead: The First Twelve Years, 1972; My Pony, 1973; (ed. with W. Steinkraus) Complete Book of Show Jumping, 1975; (ed.) Cross Country Riding, 1977; The Hunter: Horse, Cob and Pony, 1980; The Golden Thread: Foxhunting Today, 1984; Prince Charles: Horseman, 1987; The Chase: A Modern Guide to Foxhunting, 1987; Your Pony, 1991; Foxhunting in Paradise, 1993; (ed. and intro.) Ronnie Wallace: A Manual of Foxhunting, 2003; Endangered Species: Foxhunting - The History, the Passion, and the Fight for Survival, 2004; The Glorious Chase, 2005; Peterborough Royal Foxhound Show, 2006; The Belvoir: The Duke of Rutland's Hounds, 2011. **Address:** King's Reach Twr., Stamford St., London, GL SE1 9LS, England.

CLAYTON, Paul. American (born United States), b. 1948?. **Genres:** Novels, Literary Criticism And History. **Career:** Writer. **Publications:** Calling Crow, 1995; Calling Crow Nation, 1997; Flight of the Crow, 1998; Carl Melcher Goes to Vietnam, 2001; White Seed, 2009. Contributor to periodicals. **Address:** c/o Author Mail, Thomas Dunne Books, 175 5th Ave., New York, NY 10010, U.S.A. **Online address:** paulclayton@carlmelcher.com

CLAYTON, Peter A(rthur). British (born England), b. 1937. **Genres:** Archaeology/Antiquities, Classics. **Career:** Islington Public Libraries, chartered librarian, 1954-58; St. Marylebone Public Libraries, chartered librarian, 1958-63; Thames & Hudson Ltd., archeology editor, 1963-74; University of Leiden, visiting lecturer, 1970; Longman Group Ltd., humanities publisher, 1974; British Museum Publications, managing editor, 1974-79; University of Padua, visiting professor, 1978; B.A. Seaby Ltd., publications director, 1980-2009, head of the antiquities department. Writer. **Publications:** Guide to the Archaeological Sites of Britain, 1976, 2nd ed., 1985; (ed.) Manfred Lurker, The Gods and Symbols of Ancient Egypt: An Illustrated Dictionary, rev. ed., 1980; (ed.) Companion to Roman Britain, 1980; The Rediscovery of Ancient Egypt: Artists and Travellers in the Nineteenth Century, 1982; David Roberts' Egypt, 1985; David Roberts' Holy Land, 1986; The Treasures of Ancient Rome, 1986; (with M.J. Price) The Seven Wonders of the Ancient World, 1988; (trans. and ed.) Coinage and Economy in the Late Roman Empire, 1989; Great Figures of Mythology, 1990; Chronicle of the Pharaohs: The Reign-by-Reign Record of the Rulers and Dynasties of Ancient Egypt, 1994; Family Life in Ancient Egypt, 1995; The Valley of the Kings, 1996. Contributor to journals and periodicals. **Address:** B A Seaby Ltd., 8 Cavendish Sq., London, GL W1M 0AJ, England.

CLAYTON, Philip. American (born United States), b. 1956. **Genres:** Theology/Religion, History, Essays. **Career:** Haverford College, visiting assistant professor, 1986; Williams College, assistant professor, 1986-91; University of Munich, Fulbright senior research fellow, 1990-91; Ludwig-Maximilians-Universität, Alexander von Humboldt Professor, 1994-95; California State University, professor of philosophy, 1991-2003, department chair, 1998-2001; Claremont Graduate University, professor, 2003-; St. Edmund's College, visiting fellow, 2006; University of Cambridge, senior research associate and visiting professor, 2006; Harvard Divinity School, visiting professor, 2006-07. Writer. **Publications:** GOD AND PHILOSOPHY: Das Gottesproblem, 1996 in US as The Problem of God in Modern Thought, 2000; Adventures in the Spirit: God, World, Divine Action, 2008. GOD AND SCIENCE: Explanation from Physics to Theology: An Essay in Rationality and Religion, 1989; God and Contemporary Science, 1997; Mind and Emergence: From Quantum to Consciousness, 2004. EDITOR: (with C.E. Braaten) The Theology of Wolfhart Pannenberg: Twelve American Critiques, with an Autobiographical Essay and Response, 1988; (with W.M. Richardson, R.J. Russell and K. Wegter-McNelly) Science and the Spiritual Quest: New Essays by Leading Scientists, 2002; (with A. Peacocke) In Whom We Live and Move and Have Our Being: Panentheistic Reflections on God's Presence in a Scientific World, 2004; (with J. Schloss) Evolution and Ethics: Human Morality in Biological and Religious Perspective, 2004; (with P. Davies) The Re- emergence of Emergence: The Emergentist Hypothesis from Science to Religion, 2006; (with Z. Simpson) The Oxford Handbook of Religion and Science, 2006; All That Is: A Naturalistic Faith for the Twenty-first Century: A Theological Proposal with Responses from Leading Thinkers in the Religion-Science Dialogue, 2007. Works appear in anthologies. Contributor of articles to books and journals. **Address:** Claremont Graduate University, 160 E 10th St., Claremont, CA 91711-5909, U.S.A. **Online address:** pclayton@cst.edu

CLEALL, Charles. British (born England), b. 1927. **Genres:** Literary Criticism And History, Music, Theology/Religion. **Career:** Trinity College of Music, professor of solo singing and voice production, 1949-52; Morley College Orchestra, conductor, 1950-52; Wesley's Chapel, organist and choirmaster, 1950-52; Glasgow Choral Union, conductor, 1952-54; British Broadcasting Corp., music assistant, 1954-55; Glyn Grammar School for Boys, music master, 1955-66; The Aldeburgh Festival Choir, conductor, 1957-60; Musical Opinion, columnist, 1957-60; St. Paul's Church, organist and choirmaster, 1957-61; Holy Trinity Church, organist and choirmaster, 1961-65; Church of England Newspaper, music critic, 1963-; The Froebel Institute, lecturer in music, 1967-68; London Borough of Harrow, music adviser, 1968-72; Northern Division of Her Majesty's Inspectorate of Schools, Scottish Education Department, music specialist, 1972-87; Journal of the Ernest George White Society, editor, 1983-88. **Publications:** Voice Production in Choral Technique, 1955, rev. ed., 1969; The Selection and Training of Mixed Choirs in Churches, 1960; (ed.) Sixty Songs from Sankey, 1960, rev. ed., 1966; (ed.) John Merbecke's Music for the Congregation at Holy Communion, 1963; Music and Holiness, 1964; Authentic Chanting, 1969; (ed.) Plainsong for Pleasure, 1969; (with F.B. Westbrook) Reading Hymn-Tunes and Singing Psalms, 1969; A Guide to Vanity Fair, 1982; Walking Round the Church of St. James the Great Stonehaven, 1993; A Jewel of a Church, 2000. Contributor to journals. **Address:** 14 Heathfields Way, Shaftesbury, Dorset, DS SP7 9JZ, England.

CLEAR, Caitriona. Irish (born Ireland), b. 1960. **Genres:** History, Autobiography/Memoirs. **Career:** National University of Ireland, lecturer in modern Irish and European history. Writer and historian. **Publications:** Nuns in Nineteenth-Century Ireland, 1988; Growing Up Poor, 1993; Women of the House: Women's Household Work in Ireland, 1926-1961: Discourses, Experiences, Memories, 2000; Social Change and Everyday Life in Ireland 1850-1922, 2007. **Address:** Department of History, National University of Ireland, University Rd., Ste. 414, Galway, GL 1, Ireland. **Online address:** caitriona.clear@nuigalway.ie

CLEARE, John S. British (born England), b. 1936. **Genres:** Photography, Travel/Exploration, History. **Career:** Queen Magazine, photographer, 1960-61; Sargent/Gamma Ltd., Gamma Group, co-founder and director, 1962-69; Alpina Technica Productions, director, 1969-73; Mountain Life, co-editor, 1973-75; Mountain Camera Photo Library and Consultancy, proprietor, 1976. **Publications:** (With T. Smythe) Rock-Climbers in Action in Snowdonia, 1966; (with R. Collomb) Sea-Cliff Climbing in Britain, 1973; Mountains, 1975; World Guide to Mountains and Mountaineering, 1979; Mountaineering in Colour, 1980; (ed.) Whymper's Scrambles amongst the Alps, 7th ed., 1986;

John Cleare's Fifty Best 100 Hill Walks in Britain, 1988; Trekking: Great Walks of the World, 1988; (with R. Smith) Walking the Great Views, 1991; (with M. Andrew) Discovering the English Lowlands, 1991; (with K. Sngden) Walking the Pilgrim Ways, 1991; (with R. Smith) On Foot in the Pennines, 1993; (with R. Smith) On Foot in the Yorkshire Dales, 1996; Mountains of the World, 1997; Distant Mountains, 1998; (with P. Ziegler and F.F. Archive) Britain Then and Now, 1999; (with R. Sale) On Top of the World, 2000; (with R. Sale) Climbing the World's 14 Highest Mountains: The History of the 8,000-Meter Parks, 2000; (with A. Alderson) Pembrokeshire: National Park, 2001; (with R.A. Dale) Tao Te Ching-A New Translation, 2002; Moods of Pembrokshire, 2004; Portrait of Bath, 2004; (with S. Banoobhai) Book of Songs, 2004; The Tao, 2005; Teachings of the Buddha: The Wisdom of the Dharma, from the Pali Canon to the Sutras, 2009; Confucian & Taoist Wisdom: Philosophical Insights from Confucius, Mencius, Laozi, Zhuangzi, and other Masters, 2010. Contributor to periodicals. **Address:** Mountain Camera Picture Library, Fonthill Gifford, Salisbury, WT SP3 6QW, England. **Online address:** cleare@btinternet.com

CLEARY, Beverly. American (born United States), b. 1916. **Genres:** Children's Fiction, Novels, Humor/Satire, Literary Criticism And History, Young Adult Fiction. **Career:** Librarian, 1939-40; U.S. Army Hospital, post librarian, 1942-45; writer, 1950-. **Publications:** HENRY HUGGINS SERIES: Henry Huggins, 1950; Henry and Beezus, 1952; Henry and Ribsy, 1954; Henry and the Paper Route, 1957; Henry and the Clubhouse, 1962; Ribsy, 1964. BEEZUS AND RAMONA SERIES: Beezus and Ramona, 1955; Ramona the Pest, 1968; Ramona the Brave, 1975; Ramona and Her Father, 1977; Ramona and Her Mother, 1979; Ramona Quimby, Age 8, 1981; Cutting Up with Ramona! Paper Cutout Fun for Boys and Girls, 1983; Ramona Forever, 1984; The Ramona Quimby Diary, 1984; The Beezus and Ramona Diary, 1986; Meet Ramona Quimby, 1989; Ramona's World, 1999. RALPH S. MOUSE SERIES: The Mouse and the Motorcycle, 1965; Runaway Ralph, 1970; Ralph S. Mouse, 1982. JANET AND JIMMY SERIES: The Real Hole, 1960; Two Dog Biscuits, 1961; The Growing-up Feet, 1987; Janet's Thingamajigs, 1987. FOR CHILDREN: Ellen Tebbits, 1951; Otis Spofford, 1953; Leave It to Beaver, 1960; The Hullabaloo ABC, 1960, rev. ed., 1998; Beaver and Wally, 1961; Emily's Runaway Imagination, 1961; Mitch and Amy, 1967; Socks, 1973; Dear Mr. Henshaw, 1983; Lucky Chuck, 1984; Muggie Maggie, 1990; Strider, 1991; Petey's Bedtime Story, 1993. NOVELS: Fifteen, 1956; The Luckiest Girl, 1958; Jean and Johnny, 1959; Sister of the Bride, 1963. OTHERS: The Sausage at the End of the Nose (play), 1974; A Girl from Yamhill: A Memoir, 1988; My Own Two Feet: A Memoir, 1995; (foreword) Heidi, 2002; Raoncito de la moto, 2003; El ratoncito de la moto, 2003; Two Times the Fun, 2005. Contributor to periodicals. **Address:** HarperCollins Children, 1350 6th Ave., New York, NY 10019, U.S.A.

CLEARY, Brian P. American (born United States), b. 1959. **Genres:** Poetry, Children's Non-fiction, Humor/Satire. **Career:** American Greetings, senior editor. Humor writer and freelance copywriter. **Publications:** Jamaica Sandwich?, 1995; It Looks a Lot Like Reindeer, 1995; Give Me Bach My Schubert, 1996; You Never Sausage Love, 1996; A Mink, a Fink, a Skating Rink: What is a Noun?, 1999; Hairy, Scary, Ordinary: What is an Adjective?, 2000; To Root, to Toot, to Parachute: What is a Verb?, 2000; Under, Over, by the Clover: What Is a Preposition?, 2001; Dearly, Nearly, Insincerely: What Is an Adverb?, 2003; I and You and Don't Forget Who: What is a Pronoun?, 2004; Rainbow Soup: Adventures in Poetry, 2004; How Much Can a Bare Bear Bear?: What Are Homonyms and Homophones?, 2005; The Mission of Addition, 2005; Pitch and Throw, Grasp and Know: What is a Synonym?, 2005; Rhyme and Punishment: Adventures in Wordplay, 2006; Eight Wild Nights: A Family Hanukkah Tale, 2006; The Action of Subtraction, 2006; Stop and Go, Yes and No: What is an Antonym?, 2006; A Lime, a Mime, a Pool of Slime: More About Nouns, 2006; How Long or How Wide?: A Measuring Guide, 2007; Quirky, Jerky, Extra-Perky: More About Adjectives, 2007; Slide and Slurp, Scratch and Burp: More About Verbs, 2007; Peanut Butter and Jellyfishes: A Very Silly Alphabet Book, 2007; Stroll and Walk, Babble and Talk: More About Synonyms, 2008; On the Scale: A Weighty Tale, 2008; Lazily, Crazily, Just a Bit Nasally: More About Adverbs, 2008; The Laugh Stand: Adventures in Humor, 2008; Mrs. Riley bought Five Itchy Aardvarks and Other Painless Tricks for Memorizing Science Facts, 2008; Whose Shoes would You Choose?: A Long Vowel Sounds Book with Consonant Digraphs, 2008; Peaches on the Beaches: A Book about Inflectional Endings By, 2009; Stop, Drop and Flop in the Slop: A Short Vowel Sounds Book with Consonant Blends, 2009; Skin like Milk, Hair of Silk: What are Similes and Metaphors?, 2009; Frail Snail on the Trail: Long Vowel Sounds with Consonant Blends, 2009; Thing on the Wing can Sing: Short Vowel Sounds and Consonant Digraphs, 2009; Clown in the Gown Drives the Car with the Star: A Book about Diphthongs and R-Controlled Vowels, 2009; Nice Mice in the Rice: A Long Vowel Sound Book, 2009; Bug in the Jug Wants a Hug: A Short Vowel Sounds Book, 2009; Straight and Curvy, Meek and Nervy: More about Antonyms, 2009; Windows, Rings and Grapes: A Look at Different Shapes, 2009; Super-Hungry Mice Eat Onions and other Painless Tricks for Memorizing Geography Facts, 2010; A-B-A-B-A: A Book of Pattern Play, 2010; But and For, Yet and Nor: What is a Conjunction?, 2010; I'm and Won't, They're and Don't: What's a Contraction?, 2010; Punctuation Station, 2010; Macaroni and Rice and Bread by the Slice: What is in the Grains Group?, 2010; Social Studies and other Painless Tricks for Memorizing Social Studies Facts, 2011; A Fraction's Goal: Parts of a Whole, 2011; You Oughta Know By Now, 2010; Cool! Whoa! Ah! and Oh!: What is an Interjection?, 2011; Black Beans and Lamb, Poached Eggs and Ham: What is in the Meat and Beans Group?, 2011; Apples, Cherries, Red Raspberries: What is in the Fruits Group?, 2011; Yogurt and Cheeses and Ice Cream that Pleases: What is the Milk Group?, 2011; Washing Adam's Jeans and other Painless Tricks for Memorizing Social Studies Facts, 2011; Run and Hike, Play and Bike: What is Physical Activity?, 2011; Six Sheep Sip Thick Shakes: And Other Tricky Tongue Twisters, 2011; Green Beans, Potatoes and Even Tomatoes: What is in the Vegetable Group?, 2011; Oils (just a bit) to Keep your Body Fit: What are Oils?, 2011; Thumbtacks, Earwax, Lipstick, Dipstick, 2011; Feet And Puppies, Thieves And Guppies, 2011; Do You Know Dewey?, 2012; Dollar, A Penny, How Much And How Many?, 2012; Madam And Nun And 1001, 2012; Miss Pell would never Misspell and Other Painless Tricks for Memorizing how to Spell and Use Wily Words, 2012; Butterfly, Flea, Beetle, And Bee, 2013; Catfish, Cod, Salmon, And Scrod, 2013; Dolphin, Fox, Hippo And Ox, 2013; Salamander, Frog, And Polliwog, 2013; Sparrow, Eagle, Penguin, And Seagull, 2013; Tortoise, Tree Snake, Gator, and Sea Snake, 2013. Contributor of articles to magazines. **Address:** 16505 Southland Ave., Cleveland, OH 44111, U.S.A. **Online address:** baberuth60@aol.com

CLEARY, Christopher. American (born United States), b. 1974. **Genres:** Young Adult Fiction, Novels. **Career:** Writer. **Publications:** Writing on the Wall, 2007. Contributor to Periodicals. **Address:** Immortality Press, 18 Cumming St., Alpharetta, GA 30004, U.S.A. **Online address:** chriscleary@immortalitypress.com

CLEARY, Edward L. *See* Obituaries.

CLEARY, Matthew R. American (born United States) **Genres:** History, Politics/Government, Law, International Relations/Current Affairs. **Career:** Princeton University, Woodrow Wilson School of Public and International Affairs, Center for the Study of Democratic Politics, postdoctoral fellow, 2004-05; Syracuse University, Maxwell School of Citizenship and Public Affairs, assistant professor of political science, 2004-10, associate professor of political science, 2010-, Political Science Research Workshop, coordinator. Writer. **Publications:** (With S.C. Stokes) Democracy and the Culture of Skepticism: Political Trust in Argentina and Mexico, 2006; Sources of Democratic Responsiveness in Mexico, 2010. **Address:** Department of Political Science, Maxwell School of Citizenship and Public Affairs, Syracuse University, 100B Eggers Hall, Syracuse, NY 13244, U.S.A. **Online address:** macleary@maxwell.syr.edu

CLEARY, Melissa. American (born United States) **Genres:** Mystery/Crime/Suspense, Animals/Pets, Literary Criticism And History. **Career:** Writer. **Publications:** (With J. Burger) Snarlz, 2000; MYSTERY NOVELS. JACKIE WALSH AND JAKE SERIES: A Tail of Two Murders, 1992; Hounded to Death, 1993; Dog Collar Crime, 1993; Dead and Buried, 1994; First Pedigree Murder, 1994; Skull and Dog Bones, 1994; The Maltese Puppy, 1995; Murder Most Beastly, 1996; Old Dogs, 1997; And Your Little Dog, Too, 1998; In the Dog House, 2000. Contributor to periodicals. **Address:** c/o Author Mail, Berkley Publishing Group, 200 Madison Ave., New York, NY 10016, U.S.A.

CLEAVER, Jerry. American (born United States) **Genres:** Novels, Writing/Journalism. **Career:** Northwestern University, writing instructor, teacher of professional fiction; The Writers Loft, founder, teacher, writing coach. Writer. **Publications:** Immediate Fiction: A Complete Writing Course, 2002. Contributor to periodicals. **Address:** Writers Loft, 1450 W Waveland Ave., Chicago, IL 60613-3728, U.S.A. **Online address:** jerry@immediatefiction.com

CLEEK, Richard K. American (born United States), b. 1945. **Genres:** Architecture, Homes/Gardens. **Career:** University of Wisconsin Colleges, chief information officer, University of Wisconsin Center, professor of geography and computer science, 1970-. Writer. **Publications:** (With A.G. Noble) The Old Barn Book: A Field Guide to North American Barns and Other Farm Structures, 1995. **Address:** Department of Information Technology, University of Wisconsin, 780 Regent St., Ste. 130, Madison, WI 53708, U.S.A. **Online address:** dcleek@pharos.uwc.edu

CLEESE, John (Marwood). British (born England), b. 1939. **Genres:** Self Help, Humor/Satire, Plays/Screenplays, Sciences, Young Adult Non-fiction. **Career:** Clifton College, teacher, 1959; University of St Andrews, rector, 1970-73; Video Arts Ltd., founder, 1972-; British Broadcasting Corp., Radio, writer; The Frost Report, scriptwriter and performer; Cornell University, Andrew D. White Professor-at-Large, 1999-2006, provost's visiting professor. **Publications:** (Co-author) The Magic Christian, 1970; (with J. Hobbs and J. McGrath) The Strange Case of the End of Civilization As We Know It, 1977; (with C. Booth) Fawlty Towers, vol. I, 1977, vol. II, 1979, 2nd ed. as The Complete Fawlty Towers, 1989; (with R. Skynner) Families and How to Survive Them, 1983; (co-author) The Golden Skits of Wing Commander Muriel Volestrangler, FRHS and Bar, 1984; A Fish Called Wanda, 1988; (with R. Skynner) Life and How to Survive It, 1994; (with I. Johnstone) Fierce Creatures: A Novel, 1997; Pocket Full of Pythons, vol. II, 2000; (with B. Bates) The Human Face (nonfiction), 2001; (contrib.) Superman: True Brit, 2004. Contributor to periodicals. **Address:** David Wilkinson Associates, 115 Hazlebury Rd., London, GL SW6 2LX, England.

CLEGG, Douglas. (Andrew Harper). American (born United States), b. 1958?. **Genres:** Novels, Horror, Literary Criticism And History. **Career:** Writer and educator. **Publications:** Goat Dance, 1989; Breeder, 1990; Neverland, 1991; Dark of the Eye, 1994; The Childrens Hour, 1995; (as Andrew Harper) Bad Karma, 1997; The Halloween Man, 1998; The Nightmare Chronicles, 1999; Purity, 1999; You Come When I Call You, 2000; Mischief, 2000; The Infinite, 2001; Naomi, 2001; The Hour before Dark, 2002; The Necromancer, 2002; Red Angel, 2003; Afterlife, 2004; Nightmare House, 2004; Night Cage, 2004; The Attraction, 2004; The Machinery of Night, 2005; The Priest of Blood, 2005; The Abandoned, 2005; Wild Things: Four Tales, 2006; The Lady of Serpents, 2006; The Queen of Wolves, 2007; Mordred, Bastard Son, 2007; Isis, 2009. Contributor to periodicals. **Address:** 200 Madison Ave., Ste. 2000, New York, NY 10016, U.S.A. **Online address:** dclegg@douglasclegg.com

CLEGG, Holly Berkowitz. American (born United States), b. 1955. **Genres:** Food And Wine, Medicine/Health. **Career:** Petroleum Club, menu planner and coordinator of social functions; Sherwood Forest Country Club, party planner; Bocage Racquet Club, food service manager; Mercantile (department store chain), houseware spokesperson, 1995-; Cooking Light Magazine, contributing editor, 1997-99; Healthy Cooking Magazine, bimonthly columnist. **Publications:** From a Louisiana Kitchen, 1983; A Trim & Terrific Louisiana Kitchen, 1993; Trim & Terrific American Favorites: Over 250 Fast and Easy Low-Fat Recipes, 1996; Trim & Terrific One-Dish Favorites: Over 200 Fast & Easy Low-Fat Recipes, 1997; The Devils Food: A Dessert Cookbook, 1998; Meals on the Move: Rush Hour Recipes, 1999; Holly Clegg's Trim & Terrific Too Hot in the Kitchen, 2000; (with G. Miletello) Eating Well through Cancer: Easy Recipes and Recommendations During and After Treatment, 2001; The Holly Clegg Trim and Terrific Cookbook: More Than 500 Fast, Easy, and Healthy Recipes, 2002; Holly Clegg Trim & Terrific Cookbook, 2002; Holly Clegg's Trim & Terrific Home Entertaining the Easy Way: Fast and Delicious Recipes for Every Occasion, 2003; Holly Clegg Trim & Terrific Freezer Friendly Meals: Quick and Healthy Recipes You Can Make in Advance, 2006; The New Holly Clegg Trim & Terrific Cookbook, 2006; Holly Clegg's Trim & Terrific Diabetic Cooking: Over 250 Recipes that Can Be on Your Table in 30 Minutes or Less, 2007; Holly Clegg's Trim & Terrific Gulf Coast Favorites, 2008. **Address:** 13431 Woodmont Ct., Baton Rouge, LA 70810-5334, U.S.A. **Online address:** info@hollyclegg.com

CLELAND, Max. American (born United States), b. 1942. **Genres:** Autobiography/Memoirs, Biography. **Career:** Georgia State Senate, state senator, 1971-75; U.S. Senate, Commission on Veterans Affairs, professional staff, 1975-77; Veterans Administration, administrator, 1977-81; State of Georgia, secretary of state, 1982-95, United States senator, 1997-2003; American University, Washington Semester Program, distinguished adjunct professor, 2003, Center for Congressional & Presidential Studies, fellow; Export-Import Bank of the United States, board director, 2003-07; American Battle Monuments Commission, secretary, 2009-; Carmen Group, strategic consultant. Writer. **Publications:** Strong at the Broken Places: A Personal Story, 1980, rev. ed., 2000; Going for the Max! 12 Principles for Living Life to the Fullest, 1999; (with B. Raines) Heart of a Patriot: How I Found the Courage to Survive Vietnam, Walter Reed and Karl Rove, 2009. **Address:** American Battle Monuments Commission, Courthouse Plz. II, 2300 Clarendon Blvd., Ste. 500, Arlington, VA 22201, U.S.A.

CLEM, Alan L(eland). American (born United States), b. 1929. **Genres:** Politics/Government. **Career:** Ayres Advertising Agency, copywriter, 1950-52; U.S. House of Representative, press secretary, 1953-59; Foreign Agricultural Service, information specialist, 1959-60; University of South Dakota, assistant professor, 1960-62, associate professor, 1962-64, professor of government, 1964-76, professor of political science, 1978-, Governmental Research Bureau, assistant director, 1960-64, associate director, 1964-76, Department of Political Science, chairman, 1976-78, now professor emeritus. Writer. **Publications:** U.S. Agricultural Attache: His History and his Work, 1960; South Dakota Political Almanac, 1962, 2nd ed., 1969; The Nomination of Joe Bottum, 1963; Precinct Voting: The Vote in Eastern South Dakota, 1940-1960, 1963; (comp. with G.M. Platt) A Bibliography of South Dakota Government and Politics, 1965; Prairie State Politics: Popular Democracy in South Dakota, 1967; The Agricultural attaché, rev. ed., 1970; (ed.) Contemporary Approaches to State Constitutional Revision, 1970; (comp.) Precinct-Level Voting Returns for Major Races in the 1972 Primary Election in South Dakota, 1972; A Curious Profession, 1974; (comp.) Precinct-Level Voting Returns for Major Races in the 1974 Primary Election in South Dakota, 1975; Making of Congressmen: Seven Campaigns of 1974, 1976; American Electoral Politics: Strategies for Renewal, 1981; (with J. Rumbolz) Law Enforcement: The South Dakota Experience, 1982; The Government We Deserve: Principles, Institutions and Politics of American National Government, 1985, 5th ed., 1995; Congress: Powers, Processes and Politics, 1989; Government by the People?: South Dakota Politics in the Last Third of the Twentieth Century, 2002. **Address:** Department of Political Science, University of South Dakota, 414 E Clark St., Vermillion, SD 57069, U.S.A.

CLEM, Margaret H(ollingsworth). American (born United States), b. 1923. **Genres:** Children's Fiction, Poetry, Novellas/Short Stories, Young Adult Fiction. **Career:** Women's Department, weekly column writer, 1962-86. **Publications:** Elbert Ein Swine, Genius Pig, 1993; Elbert Ein Swine, Genius Pig, Learns Line Dancing, 1995; Little Candles: A Collection of Poems and Stories, 1995; Children Choices, 1997; Who Shot the Spatzies? A True-life Story of the Great Depression, 2010. FORTHCOMING: Plant Zoo; Elbert Ein Swine Teaches Pig Latin; Elbert Ein Swine Saves Pigdom Park; Little Buffalo; Champagne Velvet or Bottles. **Address:** 140 S 26th St., Terre Haute, IN 47803, U.S.A. **Online address:** clemsgems@aol.com

CLEMENS, Brian (Horace). British (born England), b. 1931. **Genres:** Plays/Screenplays, Horror, Mystery/Crime/Suspense, Art/Art History. **Career:** Super Sound Vision Ltd., co-founder and executive producer; Avengers Enterprises Ltd., co-founder and executive producer; Crumel Productions Ltd., co-founder and executive producer; Order of the British Empire, officer, 2010. Writer. **Publications:** Thriller, 1974; The Edge of Darkness: A Play, 1978; Shock!: A Thriller, 1979; (with D. Spooner) A Sting in the Tail: A Thrilling Comedy in Two Acts, 1988; (with D. Spooner) Anybody for Murder?: A Play, 1990; (with D. Spooner) Will You Still Love Me in the Morning?: A Farce, 1992; Inside Job: A Thriller, 1993. PLAYS: Rabbit Pie, 1990. **Address:** Samuel French Inc., 45 W 25th St., New York, NY 10010, U.S.A.

CLEMENS, Walter C. American (born United States), b. 1933. **Genres:** International Relations/Current Affairs, Military/Defense/Arms Control, History. **Career:** Iolani School, Department of Language, chairman, 1960-61; University of California, assistant professor of political science, 1961-63; Massachusetts Institute of Technology, assistant professor of political science, 1963-66, Center for International Studies, research associate, 1963-66; Harvard University, Davis Center for Russian and Eurasian Studies, associate, 1963-78; Salzburg Seminar on American Studies, faculty, 1965; Boston University, associate professor, 1966-69, professor of political science, 1969-, Soviet and East European Program, acting director, 1968-69; United States Department of State Specialist Program, Asia-lecturer, 1970, Europe and Latin America-lecturer, 1976-78; University of the West Indies, Institute of International Relations, Fulbright Hays lecturer, 1977-78. Writer. **Publications:** Soviet Disarmament Policy, 1917-1963: An Annotated Bibliography of Soviet and Western Sources, 1965; (ed. and intro.) World Perspectives on

International Politics, 1965; Soviet Interests in Arms Control and Disarmament: The Decade Under Khrushchev, 1954-1964, 1965; (ed. and contrib.) Toward a Strategy of Peace, 1965; (with L.P. Bloomfield and F. Griffiths) Khrushchev and the Arms Race, 1966; Outer Space and Arms Control, 1966; The Arms Race and Sino-Soviet Relations, 1968; Die Tschechoslowakei unter Husak, 1970; (co-author) The Soviet Union and Arms Control: A Superpower Dilemma, 1970; The Superpowers and Arms Control: From Cold War to Interdependence, 1973; The USSR and Global Interdependence: Alternative Futures, 1978; National Security and U.S.-Soviet Relations, 1981; Can Russia Change?: The USSR Confronts Global Interdependence, 1990; Baltic Independence and Russian Empire, 1991; Dynamics of International Relations: Conflict and Mutual Gain in an Era of Global Interdependence, 1998, 2nd ed., 2004; America and the World, 1898-2025: Achievements, Failures, Alternative Futures, 2000; The Baltic Transformed: Complexity Theory and European Security, 2001; (with J. Morin) Ambushed!: A Cartoon History of the George W. Bush Administration, 2008; Getting to Yes in Korea, 2010; Complexity Theory as a Way to Understand Our World, forthcoming; Three Revolutions That Shape Our World, forthcoming. **Address:** Department of Political Science, Boston University, PLS 221-222, 232 Bay State Rd., Boston, MA 02215, U.S.A. **Online address:** wclemens@bu.edu

CLÉMENT, Dominique. Canadian (born Canada), b. 1975?. **Genres:** History, Politics/Government. **Career:** University of Birmingham, postdoctoral fellow; University of Victoria, assistant professor and postdoctoral fellow; University of Alberta, assistant professor of sociology and adjunct professor of history; Clément Consulting, owner, web site designer, consultant, historical researcher and preservationist. Writer and entrepreneur. **Publications:** Canada's Rights Revolution: Social Movements and Social Change, 1937-82, 2008. Contributor to periodicals. **Address:** Department of Sociology, University of Alberta, 4-12 Tory Bldg., Edmonton, AB T6G 2H4, Canada.

CLEMENT, Mary. *See* **CLEMENT, Mary H.**

CLEMENT, Mary H. (Mary Clement). American (born United States), b. 1943?. **Genres:** Law, Politics/Government. **Career:** Virginia Commonwealth University, professor of criminal justice and coordinator of dual-degree M.A. program in criminal justice and divinity; Gentle Closure Inc., president. Writer and attorney. **Publications:** The Juvenile Justice System: Law and Process, 1997, 2nd ed., 2002; (with D. Humphry) Freedom to Die: People, Politics, and the Right-to-Die Movement, 1998; How to Die without a Lawyer: A Practical Guide to Creating an Estate Plan without Paying Legal Fees, 2000. Contributor to periodicals. **Address:** c/o Author Mail, St. Martin's Press, 175 5th Ave., New York, NY 10010-7703, U.S.A.

CLEMENT, Priscilla Ferguson. American (born United States), b. 1942. **Genres:** History, Civil Liberties/Human Rights, Adult Non-fiction, Social Sciences. **Career:** Pennsylvania State University, professor of history, 1967-2006, director of academic affairs, now professor emeritus of history and women's studies. Writer. **Publications:** NONFICTION: Welfare and the Poor in the Nineteenth- Century City: Philadelphia, 1800-1854, 1985; (ed. with A.G. Hess) History of Juvenile Delinquency: A Collection of Essays on Crime Committed by Young Offenders, in History and in Selected Countries, 1990; (ed. with J.S. Reinier) Growing Pains: Children in the Industrial Age, 1850-1890, 1997; (ed. with J.S. Reinier) Boyhood in America: An Encyclopedia, 2 vols., 2001; Blood on the Path, 2010; Mama Cat, forthcoming. **Address:** Department of History, Pennsylvania State University, Delaware County, 25 Yearsley Mill Rd., Media, PA 19063, U.S.A. **Online address:** p4c@psu.edu

CLEMENT-MOORE, Rosemary. American (born United States) **Genres:** Young Adult Fiction. **Career:** Educator and writer. **Publications:** Prom Dates from Hell, 2007; Hell Week, 2008; Highway to Hell, 2009; The Splendor Falls, 2009; Texas Gothic, 2011. **Address:** The Knight Agency, 570 East Ave., PO Box 550648, Madison, GA 30650, U.S.A. **Online address:** rosemary@readrosemary.com

CLEMENTS, Alan. British (born England), b. 1948. **Genres:** Information Science/Computers. **Career:** Loughborough University, Department of Electronic Engineering, research fellow, 1974-77; University of Teesside, Teesside Polytechnic, lecturer, senior lecturer in computer science 1977-87, School of Computing and Mathematics, reader in applied computing, 1987-92, Motorola professor, 1992-, teaching fellow, 2002-; Microprocessors and Microsystems, associate editor, 1986-; Technical Institute of Crete, visiting professor, 1989-90; Manchester Metropolitan University, external examiner for computer science degree, 1990-94; South Bank University, external examiner, 1991-95; International Institute for Computer Studies, external examiner, 1992-94; University of Massachusetts, adjunct professor, 1996-97; Colorado State University, visiting professor, 2001. **Publications:** Microcomputer Design and Construction: Building Your Own System with the Motorola 6800, 1982; The Principles of Computer Hardware, 1985, 4th ed., 2006; Microprocessor Systems Design: 68000 Software, Hardware, and Interfacing, 1987, 3rd ed., 1997; Microprocessor Interfacing and the 68000: Peripherals and Systems, 1989; Microprocessor Support Chip Sourcebook, 1991; 68000 Family Assemblage Language, 1994. EDITOR: 68000 Sourcebook, 1990; Analog Interface and the DSP Sourcebook, 1993. **Address:** University of Teesside, Borough Rd., Middlesbrough, TS1 3BA, England. **Online address:** a.clements@asttees.ac.uk

CLEMENTS, Alan. American (born United States), b. 1951?. **Genres:** Area Studies, Theology/Religion, History, Self Help. **Career:** Lecturer and spokesperson, 1983-. Writer. **Publications:** Burma: The Next Killing Fields?, 1992; Dossier noir Birmanie: autour d'uneenquête d'Alan Clements, 1994; (with L. Kean) Burma's Revolution of the Spirit: The Struggle for Democratic Freedom and Dignity, 1995; (with K. Wark and Kenny) Restless Nation, 1996; (with A.S. Suu Kyi) The Voice of Hope: Conversations with Alan Clements, 1997, rev. ed., 2008; Instinct for Freedom: Finding Liberation Through Living, 2002. Contributor to periodicals. **Address:** Seven Stories Press, 140 Watts St., New York, NY 10013, U.S.A.

CLEMENTS, Andrew. (Andrew Elborn). American (born United States), b. 1949. **Genres:** Children's Fiction, Young Adult Fiction, Novels, Picture/Board Books. **Career:** Sunset Ridge School, fourth grade teacher, 1972-74; Wilmette Junior High School, eighth grade teacher, 1974-77; New Trier High School, English teacher, 1977-79; Allen D. Bragdon Publishers, editor, 1980-82; Alphabet Press, sales and marketing manager and editor, 1982-85; Keller Graduate School of Management, director, 1985-87; Picture Book Studio Ltd., vice-president and editorial director, 1987-93; Houghton Mifflin, School Division, editor, 1994-95; Christian Science Publishing Society, editor, 1997-98. **Publications:** FOR CHILDREN: Bird Adalbert, 1985; Big Al, 1988; (trans.) E. Tharlet, Little Pig, Big Trouble, 1989; Santa's Secret Helper, 1990; Good Morning, Good Night, 1991; (as Andrew Elborn) Noah and the Ark and the Animals, 1991; Temple Cat, 1991; Mother Earth's Counting Book, 1992; Billy and the Bad Teacher, 1992; Midnight Play, 1994; Who Owns the Cow?, 1995; Bright Christmas: An Angel Remembers, 1996; Christmas Won't Wait, 1996; Frindle, 1996; (adaptor) Philipp's Birthday Book, 1996; Riff's BeBop Book, 1996; Real Monsters Go for the Mold!, 1997; Things That Go EEK on Halloween, 1997; Real Monsters Stage Fright, 1997; Music Time, Any Time!, 1997; Double Trouble in Walla Walla, 1997; Gromble's Haunted Halloween, 1998; (trans.) I. Gantschev, Where the Moon Lives, 1998; Workshop, 1998; The Landry News, 1999; Look Who's in the Thanksgiving Play!, 1999; Hey Dad, Could I Borrow Your Hammer?, 1999; The Christmas Kitten, 2000; The Mouse Family, 2000; Circus Family Dog, 2000; The Janitor's Boy, 2000; Circus Family, 2000; The School Story, 2001; Brave Norman: A True Story, 2001; Ringo Saves the Day!: A True Story, 2001; Dolores and the Big Fire: A True Story, 2002; The Jacket, 2002; Things Not Seen, 2002; Tara and Tiree, Fearless Friends: A True Story, 2002; Big Al and Shrimpy, 2002; A Week in the Woods, 2002; The Report Card, 2004; The Last Holiday Concert, 2004; Slippers at Home, 2004; Because Your Daddy Loves You, 2005; Lunch Money, 2005; Naptime for Slippers, 2005; Slippers at School, 2005; Million Dots, 2006; Room One: A Mystery or Two, 2006; Slippers Loves to Run, 2006; Things Hoped For, 2006; Dogku, 2007; No Talking, 2007; Lost and Found, 2008; Things That Are, 2008; Extra Credit, 2009; We the Children, 2010; The Handiest Things in the World, 2010; Fear Itself, 2011; Troublemaker, 2011; Whites of Their Eyes, 2012. JAKE DRAKE SERIES: Bully Buster, 2001; Know-It-All, 2001; Teacher's Pet, 2002; Class Clown, 2002. READING PROGRAM BOOKS FOR SCHOOLS: Karen's Island, 1995; Three Wishes for Buster, 1995; Bill Picket, 1996; Hurricane Andrew, 1998; Ham and Eggs for Jack, 1998; Life in the Desert, 1998; Krumm's Halloween Treat, 1998; Desert Treasure, 1998; Inventors: Making Things Better, 1998; Milo's Great Invention, 1998; The Big Gust, 2001; RoboCat, 2001; Once upon a Box, 2001; Ruthie's Perfect Poem, 2001; The Mummy Moved, 2001. ADAPTOR: Where Is Mr. Mole?, 1989; The Christmas Teddy Bear, 1994; The Beast and the Boy, 1995; A Dog's Best Friend, 1995; Brave as a Tiger, 1995. **Address:** 23 Old Nourse St., Westborough, MA 01581-3542, U.S.A.

CLEMENTS, Bruce. American (born United States), b. 1931. **Genres:** Children's Fiction, History, Adult Non-fiction, Romance/Historical. **Career:** Pastor, 1957-64; Union College, instructor, 1964-67; Eastern Connecticut State University, Department of English, professor and chair, 1967-, now retired. Writer. **Publications:** FICTION: Two Against the Tide, 1967; The Face of Abraham Candle, 1969; I Tell a Lie Every So Often, 1974; Prison Window, Jerusalem Blue, 1977; Anywhere Else But Here, 1980; Coming About, 1984; The Treasure of Plunderell Manor, 1986; Tom Loves Anna Loves Tom, 1990; Chapel of Thieves, 2002; What Erika Wants, 2005. OTHER: From Ice Set Free: The Story of Otto Kiep, 1972; (with H. Clements) Coming Home to a Place You've Never Been Before, 1975. **Address:** c/o Author Mail, Farrar, Straus & Giroux, 19 Union Sq. W, New York, NY 10003, U.S.A.

CLEMENTS, Jonathan. American (born United States), b. 1963. **Genres:** Money/Finance. **Career:** Euromoney, writer and researcher, 1985-86; Forbes, staff writer, 1986-90; Wall Street Journal, columnist, senior special writer, 1990-2008; myFi, director of financial guidance, 2008-09; Citi Personal Wealth Management, director of financial education, 2009-. **Publications:** (Ed.) Stock Answers: A Guide to the International Equities Market, 1988; Funding Your Future: The Only Guide To Mutual Funds You'll Ever Need, 1993; 25 Myths You've Got to Avoid-If You Want to Manage Your Money Right, 1998; You've Lost It, Now What?: How To Beat The Bear Market And Still Retire On Time, 2003; Little Book Of Main Street Money: 21 Simple Truths That Help Real People Make Real Money, 2009. **Address:** 1 Court Sq., Long Island City, NY 11101-4302, U.S.A. **Online address:** jonathan.clements@citi.com

CLEMMER, Richard O. (Richard Clemmer-Smith). American (born United States), b. 1945. **Genres:** Anthropology/Ethnology, History, Biography, Social Sciences. **Career:** University of California, reader, 1967; University of Illinois, teaching assistant, 1969-70; State University of New York, Department of Anthropology, visiting assistant professor, 1972-73; City University of New York, Brooklyn College, Department of Anthropology, assistant professor, 1973-76; University of British Columbia, Department of Anthropology and Sociology, visiting extrasessional faculty, 1976-78; College of New Rochelle, School of New Resources, adjunct faculty, 1976; California State University, Department of Anthropology, visiting lecturer, 1977-78, associate professor of anthropology and American Indian studies, 1978-79, adjunct associate professor, 1979-81; Community and Social Development Strategy Project, Southern Ute Indian Tribe, 1981-83, head, social and economic development specialist, 1983; University of Denver, Pinon Canyon Archaeological Project, seasonal staff, 1984, Department of Anthropology, senior lecturer, 1983-86, associate professor, 1986-87, Denver University Museum of Anthropology, associate professor and curator of ethnology, 1999-2002, Iliff School of Theology, graduate faculty in religion, 1999-, professor and curator of ethnology, 2002-11, assistant director, 2010-11. Writer. **Publications:** Continuities of Hopi Culture Change, 1978; (co-author) Selected Papers from the 14th Great Basin Anthropological Conference, 1978; Roads in the Sky: The Hopi Indians in a Century of Change, 1995; (ed. with L.D. Myers and M.E. Rudden) Julian Steward and the Great Basin: The Making of an Anthropologist, 1999. Contributor of articles to books and periodicals. **Address:** Department of Anthropology, University of Denver, 146 Sturm Hall, 2000 E Asbury, PO Box 100796, Denver, CO 80208-2360, U.S.A. **Online address:** rclemmer@du.edu

CLEMMER-SMITH, Richard. *See* **CLEMMER, Richard O.**

CLENDENEN, Avis. American (born United States) **Genres:** Theology/Religion, Essays. **Career:** Saint Xavier University, Catholic Theological Union, adjunct professor of pastoral theology, chair of religious studies, professor, Pastoral Ministry Institute, academic director. Writer. **Publications:** (Ed.) Spirituality in Depth: Essays in Honor of Sister Irene Dugan R.C., 2002; (with T.W. Martin) Forgiveness: Finding Freedom Through Reconciliation, 2002; (with I. Dugan) Love Is All around in Disguise: Meditations for Spiritual Seekers, 2004; Experiencing Hildegard: Jungian Perspectives, 2009. **Address:** Department of Religious Studies, St. Xavier University, Rm. N304, Warde Academic Ctr., 3700 W 103rd St., Chicago, IL 60655, U.S.A. **Online address:** clendenen@sxu.edu

CLENDENIN, Daniel B. American (born United States) **Genres:** Theology/Religion. **Career:** Midlands State Home for the Mentally Retarded, student director, 1975-76; Bethany EFCA, youth pastor, 1982-83; Drew University, teaching fellow in systematic theology, 1984-85; William Tyndale College, visiting professor, 1985-91; Moscow State University, Department of Scientific Atheism, visiting professor, 1991-95; Stanford University, faculty, 1995-2003; The Journey with Jesus Foundation, founder, 2004-. Writer. **Publications:** Theological Method in Jacques Ellul, 1987; (intro.) J. Ellul, The Presence of the Kingdom, 1989; From the Coup to the Commonwealth: An Inside Look at Life in Contemporary Russia, 1992; Many Gods, Many Lords: Christianity Encounters World Religions, 1995. EDITOR: (with W.D. Buschart) Scholarship, Sacraments and Service: Historical Studies in Protestant Tradition: Essays in Honor of Bard Thompson, 1990; Eastern Orthodox Theology: A Contemporary Reader, 1995, 2nd ed., 2003. Contributor to periodicals. **Address:** The Journey with Jesus Foundation, PO Box 60781, Palo Alto, CA 94306, U.S.A. **Online address:** dan@journeywithjesus.net

CLENDINEN, Dudley. American (born United States), b. 1944. **Genres:** Politics/Government, History, Cultural/Ethnic Topics. **Career:** Atlanta Journal-Constitution, features editor, through 1988, assistant managing editor; St. Petersburg Times, reporter; New York Times, editorial writer and national correspondent; Johns Hopkins University, Writing Program, visiting writer, 2009-. **Publications:** (Ed.) The Prevailing South: Life and Politics in a Changing Culture, 1988; Homeless in America, 1988; (with A. Nagourney) Out for Good: The Struggle to Build a Gay Rights Movement in America, 1999; A Place Called Canterbury: Tales of the New Old Age in America, 2008. **Address:** Johns Hopkins University, Wyman Park Bldg., 3400 N Charles St., Ste. S740, Baltimore, MD 21218-2685, U.S.A.

CLENDINNEN, Inga. Australian (born Australia), b. 1934. **Genres:** Novellas/Short Stories, History, Anthropology/Ethnology, Archaeology/Antiquities, Essays. **Career:** University of Melbourne, tutor, 1956-57, senior tutor in history, 1958-65, 1968; La Trobe University, lecturer, 1969-82, senior lecturer, 1982-89, reader in history, 1989-91; Princeton University, Shelby Cullom Davis Center for Historical Research, fellow, 1983-84; Institute for Advanced Study, School for Historical Studies, fellow, 1987; University of Michigan, Arthur H. Aiton memorial lecturer, 1987; Australian Broadcasting Co., Boyer lecturer, 1999. Writer. **Publications:** Ambivalent Conquests: Maya and Spaniard in Yucatan, 1517-1571, 1987, 2nd ed., 2003; Aztecs: An Interpretation, 1991; Reading the Holocaust, 1999; True Stories: Boyer Lectures, 1999; Tiger's Eye: A Memoir, 2001; Dancing with Strangers, 2003; Dancing with Strangers: Europeans and Australians at First Contact, 2005; Agamemnon's Kiss: Selected Essays, 2006; Cost of Courage in Aztec Society, 2010. Works appear in anthologies. Contributor to journals. **Address:** Faculty of Humanities and Social Sciences, School of Historical and European Studies, La Trobe University, Bundoora, VI 3083, Australia.

CLEVELAND, Ceil. American (born United States), b. 1940. **Genres:** Mystery/Crime/Suspense, Literary Criticism And History, Autobiography/Memoirs, Reference, Novels. **Career:** Cincinnati Arts and Humanities Consortium, director of curriculum, 1972-74; University of Cincinnati, lecturer, 1972-74; Xavier University, lecturer, 1972-74; University of Cincinnati, University Press, associate editor, 1974-76; Columbia University, Columbia Magazine, founder and editor-in-chief, 1976-86; Syzygy: A Journal of Short Fiction, co-founder, 1976; Cleveland Communications Inc., founder and president, 1986-; City University of New York, Queens College, vice president for university relations, 1991-95, vice president for communications; State University of New York, vice president for university affairs and associate professor of English and women's studies, 1995-98, adjunct professor; Cincinnati Women's Press, founder, 1996; Brook, founder, 1996; New York University, adjunct professor of English, 1998-, professor; Washington College, lecturer; Rhodes College, lecturer; Goucher College, lecturer; Austin College, lecturer. **Publications:** NONFICTION: Who, What, When, Where, Why: In the World of Literature, 1991; Whatever Happened to Jacy Farrow?, 1997; Better Punctuation in 30 Minutes a Day, 2002; For Better and for Words, 2005; 1500 Words in 15 Minutes a Day: A Year-Long Plan to Learn 28 Words a Week, 2005. NOVELS: The Bluebook Solution, 2001; Against the Setting Sun, 2005; The Blue Pig Solution, 2007; Peterson's Short Stories Unzipped, 2007. EDITOR: English Musical Culture, 1776-1976, 1977; Managing with Power, 1979. Contributor to periodicals and journals. **Address:** 11 Prospect Rd., Centerport, NY 11721, U.S.A. **Online address:** ceilc@nc.rr.com

CLEVELAND, Les. *See* **CLEVELAND, Leslie.**

CLEVELAND, Leslie. (Les Cleveland). New Zealander/Australian (born Australia), b. 1921. **Genres:** Poetry, Communications/Media, Film, Mythology/Folklore, Photography, Social Sciences. **Career:** Christchurch Press, journalist, 1946-48; Wellington Evening Post, journalist, 1948-50; Truth, journalist, 1955-62; Technical Publications Ltd., assistant editor, 1962-63; freelance journalist, 1963-66; Victoria University of Wellington, lecturer in politics, 1969-70, senior lecturer, 1970-79, reader, 1979-; Political Science Journal, editor, 1969-75; Smithsonian Institution, senior fellow, 1988-89; University of Wellington, research associate, 1992, lecturer in political science. **Publications:** The Songs We Sang, 1959; The Silent Land, 1966; The Anatomy of Influence, 1972; (with A.D. Robinson) Readings in New Zealand Government, 1972; (with R.J. Campbell) Daily Newspaper journalists in New Zealand, 1J72; The Iron Hand, 1979; The Politics of Utopia, 1979; The Great New Zealand Songbook, 1991; Dark Laughter, 1994; Six Decades, 1998; (ed.) Facts Concerning the Consumption and Production of Electric Power in Iowa, 2000. **Address:** 38 Havelock St., Wellington, MB 027, New Zealand. **Online address:** lesandmary@hotmail.com

CLEVELAND, Ray L. American (born United States), b. 1929. **Genres:** History, Classics, Archaeology/Antiquities. **Career:** American Schools of Oriental Research, Jerusalem, fellow, 1955-56; Johns Hopkins University, research associate in Arabian archaeology, 1956-64; University of Saskatchewan, visiting associate professor of history, 1966-67, associate professor, 1967-71, professor of history, 1971-74; University of Regina, professor of history, 1974-94, professor emeritus, 1994-. Writer. **Publications:** An Ancient South Arabian Necropolis, 1965; The Middle East and South Asia, 1967, 9th ed., 1975; (ed.) Readings on the History of the Holy Land from Earliest Times to the Nineteenth Century, 1979; (ed. with K.B. Leyton-Brown) Alexander the Great: An Exercise in the Study of History, 1992. Contributor of articles and book reviews. **Address:** Department of History, University of Regina, 2201 College Ave., Regina, SK S4S 0A2, Canada. **Online address:** ray.cleveland@uregina.ca

CLEVELAND-PECK, Patricia. British (born England) **Genres:** Children's Fiction, Plays/Screenplays, Homes/Gardens, Travel/Exploration, Writing/Journalism, Autobiography/Memoirs, Biography. **Career:** Journalist. **Publications:** FOR CHILDREN: The String Family, 1979; William the Wizard, 1980; The Birthday Cake, 1981; The String Family in Summer, 1983; Community Magic, 1984; The String Family Move House, 1986; Bus from Beyond, 1990; Shepherd Boy, 1990; The Wandering Wizard, 1990; Ark Angel, 1991; Much Too Much, 1991; City Cat, Country Cat in UK as Freckle and Clyde, 1992; The Saturday Pony, 1996; Tim's Bedtime, 1996; (contrib.) Read Me a Story Please, 1998. OTHERS: Your Own Dairy Cow: Essential Guidelines for the Management of a Single Cow, 1979; Making Cheeses, Butters, Cream and Yogurt at Home: How to Make the Most of Your Milk Supply, 1980; (ed.) The Cello and the Nightingale: The Autobiography of Beatrice Harrison, 1985. Contributor to magazines. **Address:** Harelands, Ashurst Woods, E Grinstead, Sussex, ES RH19 3SL, England. **Online address:** patriciacp@mistral.co.uk

CLEWELL, David. American (born United States), b. 1955. **Genres:** Poetry. **Career:** Webster University, professor of English, 1985-, director of creative writing. Writer. **Publications:** Room to Breathe, 1977; The Blood Knows to Keep Moving, 1980; As Far as the Eye Can See, 1988; Blessings in Disguise, 1991; Lost in the Fire, 1993; Now We're Getting Somewhere, 1994; The Conspiracy Quartet, 1997; Jack Ruby's America, 2000; The Low End of Higher Things, 2003; A Pocket Guide to Trouble, 2009; Taken Somehow By Surprise, 2011. Contributor to magazines. **Address:** Department of English, Webster University, 470 E Lockwood, Webster Groves, MO 63119, U.S.A. **Online address:** cleweldw@webster.edu

CLIFFORD, Christine. American (born United States), b. 1954. **Genres:** inspirational/Motivational Literature, Self Help, Adult Non-fiction, Cartoons, Business/Trade/Industry, Women's Studies And Issues, Humor/Satire, Biography, Biography. **Career:** The Cancer Club (firm marketing humorous and helpful products to cancer-affected individuals), president and chief executive officer; Christine Clifford Enterprises, president and chief executive officer; Divorcing Divas, president and chief executive officer. Writer. **Publications:** Not Now, I'm Having a No Hair Day, 1996; Our Family Has Cancer, Too! 1997; Inspiring Breakthrough Secrets to Live Your Dreams, 2001; Cancer Has Its Privileges: Stories of Hope & Laughter, 2002; Your Guardian Angel's Gift, 2005; (with H. Beckwith) You, Inc.: The Art of Selling Yourself, 2007; The Clue Phone's Ringing... It's for You! Healing Humor for Women Divorcing, 2011; Laugh ' Til It Heals: Notes from the World's Funniest Cancer Mailbox, 2011. **Address:** The Cancer Club, PO Box 24747, Edina, MN 55424-0747, U.S.A. **Online address:** christine@christineclifford.com

CLIFFORD, Mary Louise. American (born United States), b. 1926. **Genres:** Children's Fiction, Children's Non-fiction, History, Technology, Adult Non-fiction, Social Commentary, Local History/Rural Topics, Third World, Women's Studies And Issues, Essays, Anthropology/Ethnology, Area Studies, Young Adult Fiction. **Career:** American Legation, staff fellow, 1949-51; National Center for State Courts, staff associate, 1977-87. **Publications:** The Land and People of Afghanistan, 1962, rev. ed., 1973, 1994; The Land and People of Malaysia, 1968; The Noble and Noble African Studies Program, 1971; The African Environment: Portrait of a Continent, 1971; The Voices of Africa: The People, Creeds and Cultures in Modern Africa: Belief, Tradition, and Change, 1971; Echoes from the African Past: Hunting and Fishing Peoples, 1971; The Creative Africans: Artists and Craftsmen, 1971; Challenge of the City: The Urban African, 1971; Stone and Steel: The Builders of Africa, 1971; Africa: The Beginning of Tomorrow-Government, Statesmen, and African Unity, 1971; The Land and People of Liberia, 1971; (co-author) Bisha of Burundi (children's fiction), 1973; The Land and People of Sierra Leone, 1974; Salah of Sierra Leone (children's fiction), 1975; The Land and People of the Arabian Peninsula, 1977; State Court Model Statistical Dictionary, 1989; Computer-Aided Transcription in the Courts, 1981; (with L.A. Jensen) Court Case Management Information Systems Manual: With Model Data Elements, Reporting Forms, and Management Reports, 1983; 1984 State Trial Court Jurisdiction Guide for Statistical Reporting: Summary Tables, 1985; (with R.T. Roper) When the Great Canoes Came (children's fiction), 1993; Women Who Kept the Lights: An Illustrated History of Female Lighthouse Keepers, 1993, 2nd ed., 2001; From Slavery to Freetown: Black Loyalists after the American Revolution, 1999; (co-author) Nineteenth Century Lights: Historic Images of American Lighthouses, 2000; Maine Lighthouses: Documentation of their Past, 2005; (co-author) Mind the Light, Katie, 2005; Lonesome Road, 2005; The Shalamar Code, 2006; (co-author) Lighthouses Short and Tall, 2008; Timeless Search: The Pastoral People of Africa; Master of the Soil: The Farming People of Africa. **Address:** 31 E Rosemont Ave., Alexandria, VA 22301, U.S.A. **Online address:** mlclifford@earthlink.net

CLIFTON, Chas S. American (born United States), b. 1951. **Genres:** Paranormal, Theology/Religion. **Career:** Mountain States Collector, publisher and editor, 1977-79; Colorado Springs Sun, reporter, 1979-82; Colorado College, staff writer, 1983-84; Johnson Books, marketing director, 1984-85; Colorado Outdoor Journal, managing editor, 1986-87; Canon City Daily Record, reporter and photographer, 1987-90; Pueblo Community College, adjunct instructor, 1988-92; Colorado State University, lecturer in English, 1992-. **Publications:** Ghost Tales of Cripple Creek, 1983; Encyclopedia of Heresies and Heretics, 1992; (with E.J. Jones) Sacred Mask, Sacred Dance, 1996; Her Hidden Children: The Rise of Wicca and Paganism in America, 2006. EDITOR: The Modern Craft Movement, 1992; Modern Rites of Passage, 1993; Shamanism and witchcraft, 1994, Living Between Two Worlds: Challenges of the Modern Witch, 1996; (with J. Harvey) The Paganism Reader, 2004. **Address:** Departmentof English and Foreign Languages, Colorado State University, 2200 Bonforte Blvd., Pueblo, CO 81001-4901, U.S.A. **Online address:** chas.clifton@colostate-pueblo.edu

CLIMO, Shirley. American (born United States), b. 1928. **Genres:** Children's Fiction, Children's Non-fiction, Mythology/Folklore, Young Adult Fiction, inspirational/Motivational Literature, Animals/Pets. **Career:** WGAR-Radio, scriptwriter; Fairytale Theatre (weekly juvenile series), scriptwriter, 1949-53; Los Altos Morning Forum, president, 1971-73. Freelance writer, 1976-. Writer. **Publications:** CHILDREN'S FICTION: The Cobweb Christmas, 1982; Gopher, Tanker, and the Admiral, 1984; Someone Saw a Spider, 1985; A Month of Seven Days, 1987; King of the Birds, 1988; T.J.'s Ghost, 1988; The Egyptian Cinderella, 1989; The Korean Cinderella, 1993; The Little Red Ant and the Great Big Crumb, 1995; The Irish Cinderlad, 1996. OTHERS FOR CHILDREN: (reteller) Piskies, Spriggans, and Other Magical Beings: Tales from the Droll-Teller, 1981; (contrib.) Writing and Selling Fillers, 1982; City! New York, 1990; City! San Francisco, 1990; City! Washington, DC, 1991; The Match between the Winds, 1991; (reteller) Stolen Thunder: A Norse Myth, 1994; Atalanta's Race: A Greek Myth, 1995; (reteller) A Treasury of Princesses: Princess Tales from around the World, 1996; (reteller) A Treasury of Mermaids: Mermaid Tales from around the World, 1997; (comp. and reteller) Magic & Mischief, 1999; The Persian Cinderella, 1999; Monkey Business, 2004; Tuko And The Birds: A Tale from the Philippines, 2008. Works appear in anthologies. **Address:** 24821 Prospect Ave., Los Altos Hills, CA 94022, U.S.A. **Online address:** sbclimo@aol.com

CLINCH, Jon. American (born United States) **Genres:** Novels, Young Adult Fiction. **Career:** Advertising executive and writer. **Publications:** Finn (novel), 2007; Kings of the Earth, 2010. **Address:** Random House Inc., 1745 Broadway, 17th Fl., New York, NY 10019, U.S.A. **Online address:** jonclinch@gmail.com

CLINE, Foster W. American (born United States), b. 1940. **Genres:** Human Relations/Parenting. **Career:** Evergreen Psychotherapy Center, Consultants, child psychiatrist, 1970-92; Colorado Christian Home, psychiatric consultant, 1970-90; Bethesda Hospital, psychiatric staff, 1973-85; Bureau of Indian Health, special child psychiatric consultant, 1979-83; Denver Public Schools, T.L.C. Program, psychiatric consultant, 1983; Alabama Family Practice Unit, psychiatric consultant, 1983; Travencore Child Care Centre, special psychiatric consultant, 1984; Shadow Mountain Institute, psychiatric consultant, 1989-92; Crittenden Center, psychiatric consultant, 1984-87; Cline-Fay Institute, co-founder and partner; Colorado State University, instructor; The Love and Logic Institute, co-founder; University of Washington, Child Psychiatry, chief resident. Writer. **Publications:** (With J. Fay) Parenting with Love and Logic: Teaching Children Responsibility, 1990; (with Fay) Parenting Teens with Love and Logic: Preparing Adolescents for Responsible Adulthood, 1992; (with Fay) Grandparenting with Love and Logic: Practical Solutions to Today's Grandparenting Challenges, 1994; Conscienceless Acts, Societal Mayhem: Ucontrollable, Unreachable Youth and Today's Desensitized World, 1994; (with J.Fay) Love and Logic Journal: Tenth Anniversary Collection, 1995; (with C. Helding) Can this Child be Saved?: Solutions for Adoptive and Foster Families, 1999; (with J.Fay, B. Sornson) Meeting the Challenge: Using Love and Logic to Help Children Develop Attention and Behavior Skills, 2000; (with J. Fay) Pearls of Love and Logic for Parents and Teachers, 2000; Uncontrollable Kids: From Heartbreak to Hope, 2001; (with J. Fay and C. Fay) Taking the Stress Out of Raising Great Kids, 2005; (with J.Fay and C.Fay) More Ideas about Parenting with Less Stress, 2005; (with H. Cline) Marriage, Love, and Logic, 2005; (with L.C. Greene) Parenting Children with Health Issues, 2007; (with L.C. Greene) Parenting Children with Health Issues and Special Needs, 2009. **Address:** Love and Logic Institute, 2207 Jackson St., Ste. 102, Golden, CO 80401-2300, U.S.A. **Online address:** drfcline@netw.com

CLINE, Lynn Hunter. American/Swedish (born Sweden), b. 1961. **Genres:** Travel/Exploration. **Career:** Writer, 1993-; Santa Fe Community College, teacher of writing courses; SantaFe.com, owner; Writer's Ink, president. **Publications:** Romantic Days and Nights in Santa Fe: Intimate Escapes in the City Different (travel book), 1998, 2nd ed., Romantic Days and Nights in Santa Fe: Romantic Diversions In and Around the City, 2001; Literary Pilgrims: The Santa Fe and Taos Writers' Colonies, 1917-1950, 2007. Contributor of articles to periodicals. **Address:** SantaFe.com, 2502 Camino Entrada, Ste. C, Santa Fe, NM 87505, U.S.A. **Online address:** lyncli@aol.com

CLINE, Wayne. American (born United States), b. 1945. **Genres:** Transportation. **Career:** Teacher, 1968-77; Bishop Kenny HS, mathematics instructor, 1969-70; Public Schools in Alabama and Georgia, mathematics instructor, 1971-77; AG Edwards and Sons, stockbroker, 1978-82; Calhoun County Commission, license inspector, 1982-83; United States Department of Defense, technical editor, technical training instructor, quality assurance specialist, 1983-; author, 1997-. **Publications:** Alabama Railroads, 1997. **Address:** University of Alabama Press, PO Box 870380, Tuscaloosa, AL 35487, U.S.A.

CLINE, William R. American (born United States), b. 1941. **Genres:** Economics, Money/Finance. **Career:** Princeton University, lecturer, assistant professor of economics, 1967-70; Ford Foundation, visiting professor, 1970-71; U.S. Treasury, deputy director of trade, development and research, 1971-73; Brookings Institution, senior fellow, 1973-81; Peter G. Peterson Institute for International Economics, Center for Global Development, senior research fellow, 1981-; Institute of International Finance, deputy managing director and chief economist, 1996-2001. Writer. **Publications:** Prediction of a Land Reform's Effect on Agricultural Production: The Brazilian Case, 1969; The Economic Consequences of a Land Reform in Brazil, 1970; Potential Effects of Income Redistribution on Economic Growth: Latin American Cases, 1972; International Monetary Reform and the Developing Countries, 1976; (co-author) Trade Negotiations in the Tokyo Round: A Quantitative Assessment, 1978; (ed. with E. Delgado) Economic Integration in Central America: A Study, 1978; (ed.) Policy Alternatives for a New International Economic Order: An Economic Analysis, 1979; (with R. A. Berry) Agrarian Structure and Productivity in Developing Countries: A Study Prepared for the International Labour Office within the Framework of the World Employment Programme, 1979; (ed. with S. Weintraub) Economic Stabilization in Developing Countries, 1981; (co-author) World Inflation and the Developing Countries, 1981; Reciprocity: A New Approach to World Trade Policy?, 1982; (ed. with C.F. Bergsten) Trade Policy in the 1980s, 1982; An International Debt and the Stability of the World Economy, 1983; International Debt: Systemic Risk and Policy Response, 1984; Exports of Manufactures from Developing Countries: Performance and Prospects for Market Access, 1984; (with C.F. Bergsten) United States-Japan Economic Problem, 1985; (with C.F. Bergsten and J. Williamson) Bank Lending to Developing Countries: The Policy Alternatives, 1985; The Future of World Trade in Textiles and Apparel, 1987, rev. ed., 1989; Informatics and Development: Trade and Industrial Policy in Argentina, Brazil, and Mexico, 1987; Mobilizing Bank Lending to Debtor Countries, 1987; American Trade Adjustment: The Global Impact, 1989; United States External Adjustment and the World Economy, 1989; Baker Plan: Progress, Shortcomings, and Future, 1989; The Economics of Global Warming, 1992; Global Warming: The Economic Stakes, 1992; Global Warming: The Benefits of Emission Abatement, 1992; Third World Debt: A Reappraisal, 1992; International Economic Policy in the 1990s, 1994; Serials-ly Speaking: Essays on Cliffhangers, 1994; Predicting External Imbalances for the United States and Japan, 1995; International Debt Reexamined, 1995; Trade and Income Distribution, 1997; Restoring Economic Growth in Argentina, 2003; Trade Policy and Global Poverty, 2004; United States as a Debtor Nation, 2005; Global Warming and Agriculture: Impact Estimates by Country, 2007; Financial Globalization, Economic Growth, and the Crisis of 2007-09, 2010; Carbon Abatement Costs and Climate Change Finance, 2011; (ed. with G. Wolff) Resolving the European Debt Crisis, 2012. **Address:** Peterson Inst for Intl Economics, 1750 Massachusetts Ave. NW, Washington, DC 20036-1903, U.S.A. **Online address:** wcline@piie.com

CLINTON, Catherine. American (born United States), b. 1952. **Genres:** History, Women's Studies And Issues. **Career:** University of Benghazi, lecturer in history, 1974; Union College, assistant professor of history, 1979-83; Brandeis University, visiting professor of history, 1988-90; Harvard University, assistant professor of history, 1983-88, Department of Afro-American Studies, visiting professor, 1990-93, W.E.B. Du Bois Institute, fellow, 1993-97, Charles Warren Center, affiliate, 1998-99; University of Richmond, Douglas Southall Freeman distinguished visiting chair of history, 1997-98; Wofford College, Lewis Jones distinguished visiting chair of history, 1998-99; City University of New York, Baruch College, Weissman visiting chair of history, 1999-2001; Yale University, Gilder Lehrman Center, affiliate, 1999-2006; The Citadel, Mark Clark chair of history, 2001-02; Wesleyan University, visiting professor, 2003-04; Queen's University, professor of U.S. history and chair, 2006-. Writer. **Publications:** The Plantation Mistress, 1982; The Other Civil War, 1984; (comp. with G.J. Barker-Benfield) Portraits of American Women, 1991; Tara Revisited, 1995; (contrib.) Life in Civil War America, 1996; We the People (textbook series), 1997; Civil War Stories, 1998; Public Women and the Confederacy, 1999; The Scholastic Encyclopedia of the Civil War, 1999; The Black Soldier: 1492 to the Present, 2000; (with C. Lunardini) The Columbia Guide to American Women in the Nineteenth Century, 2000; Fanny Kemble's Civil Wars, 2000; The African-American Experience, 1565-1877, 2004; Harriet Tubman: The Road to Freedom, 2004; Hold the Flag High, 2005; Reminiscences of My Life in Camp: An African-American Woman's Civil War Memoir, 2006; When Harriet Met Sojourner, 2007; Phillis's Big Test, 2008; Mrs. Lincoln: A Life, 2009; (intro.) Mary Chesnut's Diary, 2011. EDITOR: (with N. Silber) Divided Houses: Gender and the Civil War, 1992; Half-Sisters of History: Southern Women and the American Past, 1994; (with M. Gillespie) The Devil's Lane: Sex and Race in the Early South, 1997; (with M. Gillespie) Taking off the White Gloves: Southern Women and Women Historians, 1998; Sing America: Three Centuries of African American Poetry, 1998; Southern Families at War: Loyalty and Conflict in the Civil War South, 2000; (and intro.) Fanny Kemble's Journals, 2000; A Poem of Her Own: Voices of American Women Yesterday and Today, 2003; (with N. Silber) Battle Scars: Gender and Sexuality in the Civil War, 2006; Susie King Taylor's Reminiscences of My Life in Camp: An African-American Woman's Civil War Memoir, 2006. **Address:** c/o Kris Dahl, International Creative Management, 730 5th Ave., New York, NY 10019, U.S.A. **Online address:** c.clinton@qub.ac.uk

CLINTON, Hillary Rodham. American (born United States), b. 1947. **Genres:** Human Relations/Parenting, Law, Politics/Government. **Career:** Children's Defense Fund, attorney, 1973-74; Carnegie Council on Children, legal consultant, 1973-74; U.S. House of Representatives, counsel for the impeachment inquiry staff, 1974; University of Arkansas, assistant professor of law, 1974-77, lecturer at law school, 1979-80; U.S. District Court of Arkansas, reporter for federal court speedy trial planning group, 1975-79; Rose Law Firm, partner, 1977-92; Legal Services Corp., head, 1978-83; Committee on Health Care, committee head, 1993-; New York senator, 1993-2001, 2001-09; State of the United States, secretary, 2001-08, 2009-. Writer. **Publications:** NONFICTION: It Takes a Village: And Other Lessons Children Teach Us, 1996; The Unique Voice of Hillary Rodham Clinton: A Portrait in Her Own Words, 1997; (comp. and foreword) Dear Socks, Dear Buddy: Kids' Letters to the First Pets, 1998; An Invitation to the White House: At Home with History, 2000; Living History (memoir), 2003; Handbook on Legal Rights for Arkansas Women. **Address:** United States Senate, 476 Russell Senate Office Bldg., Washington, DC 20510, U.S.A.

CLINTON, James H(armon). American (born United States), b. 1946. **Genres:** Poetry, Literary Criticism And History. **Career:** Louisiana Division of Administration, assistant commissioner, 1973-80; Gulf South Research Institute, director of administration, president, 1980-88; Louisiana Partnership for Technology and Innovation, president, 1988-97; Mercatus L.L.C., president, 1997-98; Journey of Hope Institute, chairperson, 1997-98. Writer. **Publications:** What is Fair, 1997. **Address:** 375 Wesley Ct., Chapel Hill, NC 27516, U.S.A. **Online address:** jhc1@concentric.net

CLINTON, James W(illiam). American (born United States), b. 1929. **Genres:** Politics/Government, Autobiography/Memoirs, History. **Career:** Department of the Air Force, navigator, operations analyst and project officer, 1951-55, 1959-77; Procter and Gamble, staff assistant in advertising, 1955; Brown & Haley, assistant to sales manager, 1955-56; U.S. Civil Service Commission, field investigator, 1956-59; University of Missouri, associate professor of aerospace studies, 1972-75; University of Wisconsin, assistant professor of management, 1977-80; University of Northern Colorado, professor of management, 1980-99. Writer. **Publications:** The Loyal Opposition: Americans in North Vietnam, 1965-1972, 1995. Contributor to periodicals. **Address:** University Press of Colorado, 5589 Arapahoe Ave., Ste. 206C, Boulder, CO 80303, U.S.A. **Online address:** jclinton@coba1.univnortco.edu

CLINTON, Kate. American (born United States), b. 1951?. **Genres:** Humor/Satire, Gay And Lesbian Issues, Young Adult Non-fiction. **Career:** Teacher, 1973-81; comedian and writer, 1981-; Fine Arts Work Center, faculty. **Publications:** Don't Get Me Started, 1998; What the L?, 2005; I Told You So, 2009. **Address:** Michele Karlsberg Marketing and Management, 101 Lexington Ave., Staten Island, NY 10302-2025, U.S.A. **Online address:** kate@kateclinton.com

CLIPPER SETHI, Robbie. American (born United States), b. 1951. **Genres:** Novels, Novellas/Short Stories, Poetry. **Career:** Rider University, professor of English, 1985-, department chair. Writer. **Publications:** The Bride Wore Red: Tales of a Cross-Cultural Family, 1996; Fifty-Fifty: A Novel in Many Voices, 2003; Heat, 2005; Dry Land Sailors, forthcoming; The music of the Spheres, forthcoming. Contributor to periodicals. **Address:** Department of English, Rider University, Fine Arts 326, 2083 Lawrenceville Rd., Lawrenceville, NJ 08648, U.S.A. **Online address:** herself@robertclippersethi.com

CLIPPINGER, Carol. American (born United States) **Genres:** Young Adult Fiction, Sports/Fitness. **Career:** Writer. **Publications:** Open Court, 2007. **Address:** Chudney Agency, 72 N State Rd., Ste. 501, Briarcliff Manor, NY 10510, U.S.A.

CLIPPINGER, John Henry. American (born United States), b. 1943. **Genres:** Adult Non-fiction. **Career:** Harvard University, Law Lab, co-director, Harvard Law School, Berkman Center for Internet and Society, director of Open Identity metasystem, senior fellow; Coopers and Lybrand, director of intellectual capital; Open Identity Exchange Advisory Board, co-chair; Stanford University, visiting faculty member; Brandeis University, research associate; Boston University, School of Management, Institute for Leading a Dynamic Economy, senior fellow; Context Media L.L.C., chief executive officer; Azigo Inc., founder and chief executive officer; Brattle Research Corp., chief executive officer and founder. Writer. **Publications:** (Ed.) The Biology of Business: Decoding the Natural Laws of Enterprise, 1999; Operating at the Edge: Meeting Current and Future Security Challenges, 2004; A Crowd of One: The Future of Individual Identity, 2007. **Address:** Berkman Center for Internet and Society, Harvard Law School, 23 Everett St., 2nd Fl., Cambridge, MA 02138, U.S.A. **Online address:** jclippinger@cyber.law.harvard.edu

CLOAKE, John (Cecil). British (born England), b. 1924. **Genres:** History, Local History/Rural Topics, Biography, Novels. **Career:** British Diplomatic Service, third secretary at embassy in Baghdad, 1949-51, second secretary at legation in Saigon, 1951-54, private secretary to permanent under-secretary, 1956-57, parliamentary under-secretary, 1957-58, commercial consult, 1958-62, first secretary at embassy in Moscow, 1962-63, commercial counselor at embassy in Tehran, 1968-72, Department at Foreign and Commonwealth Office, head of trade relations and exports, 1973-76, ambassador to Bulgaria, 1976-80. Writer. **Publications:** Templer: Tiger of Malaya (biography), 1985; (ed.) Richmond in Old Photographs, 1990; Richmond Past, 1991; Royal Bounty: The Richmond Parish Lands Charity 1786-1991, 1992; Palaces and Parks of Richmond and Kew, vol. II, 1995; Richmond Past and Present, 1999; Cottages and Common Fields of Richmond and Kew, 2001; (co-author) Early Modern Industry and Settlement: Excavations at George Street, Richmond, and High Street, Mortlake, in the London Borough of Richmond upon Thames, 2003. **Address:** 4 Terr., 140 Richmond Hill, Richmond, SR TW10 6RN, England.

CLOS, Charles. *See* **STOKOE, E(dward) G(eorge).**

CLOSE, Ajay. Scottish/British (born England) **Genres:** Novels, Autobiography/Memoirs. **Career:** Scotsman, news reporter. Journalist. **Publications:** Official and Doubtful, 1996; Forspoken, 1998; The Morality of Slaves, forthcoming; Faking Good, forthcoming. **Address:** Judy Moir Agency, 5 Gayfield Sq., Edinburgh, EH1 3NW, Scotland. **Online address:** ajay@ajayclose.orangehome.co.uk

CLOTFELTER, Beryl E(dward). American (born United States), b. 1926. **Genres:** Astronomy, Physics. **Career:** Phillips Petroleum Co., research physicist, 1953-55; University of Idaho, assistant professor of physics, 1955-56; Oklahoma Baptist University, assistant professor, 1956-58, associate professor, 1958-61, professor of physics, 1961-63; Grinnell College, faculty, 1963-96, professor emeritus of physics, 1996-. Writer. **Publications:** Reference Systems and Inertia, 1970; The Universe and Its Structure, 1976. Contributor to journals. **Address:** Department of Physics, Grinnell College, Rm. 1232, Noyce Science Bldg,, 1116 8th Ave., PO Box 805, Grinnell, IA 50112-1690, U.S.A. **Online address:** clotfelt@grinnell.edu

CLOTFELTER, Charles T. American (born United States), b. 1947. **Genres:** Economics, Politics/Government, Education, Reference. **Career:** University of Maryland, Department of Economics, assistant professor, 1974-79; Duke University, Sanford Institute of Public Policy, associate professor, 1979-84, Institute of Policy Sciences and Public Affairs, director of graduate studies, 1979-81, 1989-90, vice provost for academic policy and planning, 1983-85, professor of public policy studies and economics, 1984-95, vice chancellor of university, 1985-88, Center for the Study of Philanthropy and Voluntarism, director, 1986-, vice provost for academic programs, 1993-94, Z. Smith Reynolds professor Of public policy, 1995-, professor of economics and law, 1996-; National Bureau of Economic Research, research associate, 1982-. Writer. **Publications:** (With L.M. Salamon) Federal Government and the Nonprofit Sector: The Impact of the 1981 Tax Act on Individual Charitable Giving: A Study for the Independent Sector, 1981; Federal Tax Policy and Charitable Giving, 1985; (with P.J. Cook) Selling Hope: State Lotteries in America, 1989; (with R. Ehrenderg, M. Getz and J. Siegfried) Economic Challenges in Higher Education, 1991; (ed.) Who Benefits from the Nonprofit Sector?, 1992; (ed. with M. Rothschild) Studies of Supply and Demand in Higher Education, 1993; Buying the Best: Cost Escalation in Elite Higher Education, 1996; (ed. with T. Ehrlich) Philanthropy and the Nonprofit Sector in a Changing America, 1999; After Brown: The Rise and Retreat of School Desegregation, 2004; (co-author) Would Higher Salaries Keep Teachers in High-Poverty Schools?, 2006; (ed.) American Universities in a Global Market, 2010; Big-Time Sports in American Universities, 2011. **Address:** Sanford Institute of Public Policy, Duke University, 221 Sanford Bldg., PO Box 90245, Durham, NC 27708-0360, U.S.A. **Online address:** charles.clotfelter@duke.edu

CLOUD, Darrah. American (born United States), b. 1955. **Genres:** Film, Romance/Historical, Literary Criticism And History. **Career:** Denver Center Theatre, playwright-in-residence, 1992; Goddard College, MFA in Creative Writing Program, faculty advisor. Writer and executive producer. **Publications:** The Stick Wife, 1987; O Pioneers!, 1991. Contributor to periodicals. **Address:** Peregrine Whittlesey Agency, 345 E 80th St., New York, NY 10021, U.S.A. **Online address:** darrah.cloud@goddard.edu

CLOUDSLEY-THOMPSON, John (Leonard). British/Pakistani (born Pakistan), b. 1921. **Genres:** Novels, Biology, Children's Non-fiction, Environmental Sciences/Ecology, Natural History, Zoology, Animals/Pets, Sciences, Sciences. **Career:** University of London, King's College, lecturer in zoology, 1950-60, Birkbeck College, professor of zoology, 1972-85, University College, professor emeritus of zoology, 1985-; University of Khartoum, Sudan Natural History Museum, professor of zoology and keeper, 1960-71; Linnean Society, vice-president, 1975-76, 1977-78; Journal of Arid Environments, editor-in-chief, 1978-97; University of Kuwait, visiting professor, 1978, 1983; University of Nigeria, visiting professor, 1981; British Society for Chronobiology, chairman, 1985-87; University of Qatar, visiting professor, 1986; Australian National University, visiting professor, 1987. **Publications:** (Ed.) Biology of Deserts, 1954; Spiders, Scorpions, Centipedes, and Mites, 1958; Animal Behaviour, 1960; (with J. Sankey) Land Invertebrates, 1961; Rhythmic Activity in Animal Physiology and Behaviour, 1961; (with M.J. Chadwick) Life in Deserts, 1964; Desert Life, 1965; Animal Conflict and Adaptation, 1965; Animal Twilight: Man and Game in Eastern Africa, 1967; Microecology, 1967; The Zoology of Tropical Africa, 1969; Animals of the Desert, 1969; (with F.T. Abushama) A Guide to the Physiology of Terrestrial Arthropods, 1970; The Temperature and Water Relations of Reptiles, 1971; Spiders and Scorpions, 1973; Bees and Wasps, 1974; The Ecology of Oases, 1974; Crocodiles and Alligators, 1975; Terrestrial Environments, 1975; Insects and History, 1976; Man and the Biology of Arid Zones, 1976; (ed. with J. Bligh and A.G. Macdonald) Environmental Physiology of Animals, 1976; The Size of Animals, 1976; (contrib.) Deserts and Grasslands, 1976; Dietary Adaptations of Animals, 1976; Evolutionary Trends in the Mating of Arthropods, 1976; The Water and Temperature Relations of Woodlice, 1976; Tortoises and Turtles, 1976; The Desert, 1977; Form and Function in Animals, 1978; Animal Migration, 1978; Why the Dinosaurs Became Extinct, 1978; Wildlife of the Deserts, 1979; Camels, 1980; Biological Clocks, 1980; Tooth and Claw, 1980; Seals and Sea Lions, 1981; Vultures, 1981; (with D.G. Applin) Biological Periodicities: A New Interpretation, 1982; (contrib.) Nightwatch, 1983; (ed.) Sahara Desert, 1984; Guide to Woodlands, 1985; Living in the Desert, 1985; Evolution and Adaptation of Terrestrial Arthropods, 1988; Adaptations of Desert Organisms Series, 1989-2000; Ecophysiology of Desert: Arthropods and Reptiles, 1991; Invertebrate Animals, 1992; The Diversity of Desert Life, 1993; The Nile Quest (novel), 1994; Predation and Defence amongst Reptiles, 1994; Biotic Interactions in Arid Lands, 1996; Teach Yourself Ecology, 1998; The Diversity of Amphibians and Reptiles, 1999; Ecology and Behaviour of Mesozoic Reptiles, 2005. Contributor to journals. **Address:** Department of Zoology, University College, University of London, Gower St., London, GL WC1E 6BT, England.

CLOUGH, David L. British (born England), b. 1968. **Genres:** Theology/Religion, Ethics. **Career:** University of Durham, St. Chad's College, F.D. Maurice postdoctoral research fellow, 1999-2000, St. John's College, director of studies and tutor in ethics and systematic theology, 2000-07; University of Chester, senior lecturer in theology, 2007-, professor of theological ethics. Writer and academic. **Publications:** Ethics in Crisis: Interpreting Barth's Ethics, 2005; (with B. Stiltner) Faith and Force: A Christian Debate about War, 2007; (with C. Deane-Drummond) Creaturely Theology: On God, Humans and Other Animals, 2009. **Address:** Department of Theology and Religious Studies, University of Chester, Parkgate Rd., Chester, CH CH1 4BJ, England. **Online address:** d.clough@chester.ac.uk

CLOUSE, Robert Gordon. American (born United States), b. 1931. **Genres:** History, Theology/Religion, Politics/Government. **Career:** First Brethren Church, pastor, 1957-60; Indiana State University, associate professor, 1963-70, professor of history, 1970-, now professor emeritus of history; Indiana University, visiting professor, 1964-65, 1968-69; University of Illinois, visiting professor; Juniata College, visiting professor. Writer. **Publications:** (Ed. with R.D. Linder and R.V. Pierard) Protest and Politics; Christianity and Contemporary Affairs, 1968; (co-author) Puritans, the Millennium and the Future of Israel, 1970; (ed. with R.V. Pierard) The Cross and the Flag (social criticism), 1972; (co-author) Christ and the Modern Mind, 1972; (contrib.) Streams of Civilization: Ancient History to 1600 A.D., 1976; (ed.) The Meaning of the Millennium: Four Views, 1977; The Church in the Age of Orthodoxy and the Enlightenment: Consolidation and Challenge from 1600 to 1800, 1980; (with R.V. Pierard) Streams of Civilization: The Modern World to the Nuclear Age, 1980; (ed.) War: 4 Christian Views, 1981, new ed., 1991; (ed.) Wealth and Poverty, Four Christian Views of Economics, 1984; (ed. with B. Clouse) Women in Ministry: Four Views, 1989; (co-ed.) New 20th-century Encyclopedia of Religious Knowledge, 1991; (with R.V. Pierard and E.M. Yamauchi) Two Kingdoms: The Church and Culture through the Ages, 1993; (with R.N. Hosak and R.V. Pierard) The New Millennium Manual: A Once and Future Guide, 1999; (with R.V. Pierard and E.M. Yamauchi) The Story of the Church, 2002; (contrib.) The End of Days, 2007; (co-author) The Church From Age to Age, 2011. Contributor to journals. **Address:** Department of History, Indiana State University, 621 Chestnut St., Terre Haute, IN 47809-1911, U.S.A. **Online address:** hiclous@ruby.indstate.edu

CLOUSER, Roy A. American (born United States), b. 1937. **Genres:** Theology/Religion, Philosophy. **Career:** Rutgers University, instructor in symbolic logic, 1965-66; La Salle College, instructor in philosophy, 1966-68; Trenton State College, professor of philosophy and religion, 1968-; College of New Jersey, adjunct associate professor of philosophy, 1969-85, professor of philosophy and religion, 1968-2002, department head, 1979-82, 1985-86, 1996-98, professor emeritus, 2002-. Writer. **Publications:** The Myth of Religious Neutrality: An Essay on the Hidden Role of Religious Belief in Theories, 1991, rev. ed., 2005; Knowing With the Heart: Religious Experience and Belief in God, 1999; Comparative Religion for Christians, forthcoming. Contributor to books and journals. **Address:** Department of Philosophy and Religion, College of New Jersey, PO Box 7718, Ewing, NJ 08628-0718, U.S.A. **Online address:** roy.a.clouser@gmail.com

CLOUTIER, Cécile. Canadian (born Canada), b. 1930. **Genres:** Poetry, History, Social Sciences. **Career:** University of Ottawa, assistant professor of French literature and aesthetics, 1958-64; Laval University, faculty; University of Toronto, associate professor, 1964-, professor of French and Quebec literatures and aesthetics, professor emeritus; Royal Ontario Museum, lecturer, 1966; New York University, lecturer, 1966; Canadian Council of the Arts and Canadian Humanities Council, consultant. Poet, essayist and playwright. **Publications:** Mains de Sable, 1960; Cuivre et Soies, Suivi de Mains de Sable, 1964; Cannelles et Craies, 1969; Paupières, 1970; Cablogrammes, 1972; Chaleuils, 1979; Springtime of Spoken Words, 1979; Près, 1983; (ed. with C. Seerveld) Opuscula Aesthetica Nostra, 1984; L'échangeur, 1985; L'écouté: Poèmes 1960-1983, 1986; Lampées, 1990; Périhélies, 1990; Ancres D'encre: Poesie, 1993; Ostraka: Poésie, 1994; Le Poaimier: Poèmes, 1996; Bagues, 1996; (ed. with B. Shek) Miron, ou, La Marche à L'amour, 2002. Contributor to books and periodicals. **Address:** 44 Farm Greenway, Don Mills, Toronto, ON M3A 3M2, Canada.

CLOVER, Peter. British (born England), b. 1952?. **Genres:** Children's Fiction, Animals/Pets, Science Fiction/Fantasy. **Career:** Writer and illustrator. **Publications:** SHELTIE THE SHETLAND PONY SERIES: Sheltie the Shetland Pony, 1996; Sheltie Saves the Day!, 1996; Sheltie and the Runaway, 1996; Sheltie in Danger, 1997; Sheltie to the Rescue, 1997; Sheltie Rides to Win, 1998; Sheltie in Trouble, 1998; Sheltie and the Saddle Mystery, 1998; Sheltie Leads the Way, 1998; Sheltie on Parade, 1999; Sheltie the Snow Pony, 1999; The Big Adventure, 1999; Sheltie on Patrol, 1999; Sheltie Goes to School, 1999; Sheltie Gallops Ahead, 1999; The Big Show, 1999; Sheltie: The Big Surprise, 1999; Sheltie in Double Trouble, 1999; Sheltie Forever, 1999; The Big Present, 1999; Sheltie in Peril, 2000; Sheltie and the Foal, 2000; Sheltie: The Big Wish, 2000; Sheltie by the Sea, 2000; Sheltie Races On, 2000; Sheltie Finds a Friend, 2000; Sheltie at the Funfair, 2001; Sheltie the Hero, 2004; Sheltie and the Stray, 2005; The Big Discovery, forthcoming. RESCUE RIDERS SERIES: Race against Time, 1998; Fire Alert, 1998; Ghost Pony, 1998. HERCULES SERIES: New Pup on the Block, 2000; Operation Snowsearch, 2000; Treasure Hound, 2000. DONKEY DIARIES SERIES: Donkey Danger, 2001; Donkey Disaster, 2001; Donkey Drama, 2001; Donkey in Distress, 2002. LITTLE BRIDGE FARM SERIES: Oscars New Friends, 2007; Smudge Finds The Trail, 2007; Tiger's Great Adventure, 2007; Dilly Saves The Day, 2007; Socks Cleans Up, 2007. OTHERS: Drawing Horses and Ponies, 1994; The Best Pony for Me!, 1995; The Phantom Pony, 1999; The Storm Pony, 2000; Hercules: New Pup on the Block, 2001; Dead Cool, 2007; Dead Cooler, 2007; The Tale of Black-Eye Jack, 2009. **Address:** c/o Aladdin, Simon & Schuster, 1230 Ave. of the Americas, New York, NY 10020, U.S.A.

CLOW, Barbara Hand. American (born United States), b. 1943. **Genres:** Self Help, Sex, Medicine/Health, Natural History. **Career:** Bear and Company Inc., executive vice-president, 1983-2000. Writer. **Publications:** Stained Glass: A Basic Manual, 1976; Eye of the Centaur: A Visionary Guide Into

Past Lives, 1986; Chiron: Rainbow Bridge Between The Inner And Outer Planets, 1987; Heart of the Christos: Starseeding From The Pleiades, 1989; Liquid Light of Sex: Understanding Your Key Life Passages, 1991 as Liquid Light of Sex: Kundalini, Astrology, and the Key Life Transitions, 2001; Signet of Atlantis: War in Heaven Bypass, 1992; The Pleiadian Agenda: A New Cosmology for the Age of Light, 1995; (intro.) Pleiadian Perspectives on Human Evolution, 1996; Catastrophobia: The Truth Behind Earth Changes in the Coming Age of Light, 2001; (with G. Clow) Alchemy of Nine Dimensions: Decoding The Vertical Axis, Crop Circles, And The Mayan Calendar, 2004, rev. ed. as Alchemy of Nine Dimensions: The 2011/2012 Prophecies and Nine Dimensions of Consciousness, 2010; The Mind Chronicles: A Visionary Guide Into Past Lives, 2007; The Mayan Code: Time Acceleration And Awakening The World Mind, 2007; Awakening the Planetary Mind: Beyond the Trauma of the Past to a New Era of Creativity, rev. ed., 2011. Contributor to books. **Address:** c/o Author Mail, Hampton Roads Publishing Co., 65 Parker St., Ste. 7, Newburyport, MA 01950-4600, U.S.A.

CLUBBE, John L(ouis) E(dwin). American (born United States), b. 1938. **Genres:** Architecture, Art/Art History, Literary Criticism And History, Essays, Urban Studies, Biography, Humanities. **Career:** Columbia University, part-time lecturer in English, 1962-63; City University of New York, part-time lecturer in English, 1963-65; University of Munster, lecturer in English, 1965-66; Duke University, Department of English, assistant professor, 1966-70, associate professor, 1970-75; University of Kentucky, professor of English, 1975-99, professor emeritus, 1999-. Writer. **Publications:** Victorian Forerunner: The Later Career of Thomas Hood, 1968; (ed. and intro.) Selected Poems of Thomas Hood, 1970; Two Reminiscences of Thomas Carlyle, 1974; Nineteenth-Century Literary Perspectives, 1974; (ed.) Carlyle and His Contemporaries: Essays in Honor of Charles Richard Sanders, 1976, rev. ed. as Carlyle's Friendship and Other Studies: Essays in Honour of Charles Richard Sanders, 1977; (ed.) Froude's Life of Carlyle, 1979; Byron's Natural Man: Daniel Boone & Kentucky, 1980; The Collected Letters of Thomas and Jane Welsh Carlyle, 9 vols., 1970, 1977, 1981; (with E. Giddey) Byron et la Suisse, 1982; (with E.J. Lovell, Jr.) English Romanticism: The Grounds of Belief, 1983; (co-author) The English Romantic Poets: A Review of Research and Criticism, 1985; (ed. with J. Meckier) Victorian Perspectives: Six Essays, 1989; Cincinnati Observed: Architecture and History, 1992; Byron, Sully and the Power of Portraiture, 2005. **Address:** Department of English, College of Arts & Science, University of Kentucky, 213 Patterson Office Twr., Lexington, KY 40506-0027, U.S.A. **Online address:** jclubbe@newmexico.com

CLUNIS, D. Merilee. American (born United States) **Genres:** Gay And Lesbian Issues, Social Sciences, History. **Career:** Psychotherapist and writer. **Publications:** WITH G.D. GREEN: Lesbian Couples, 1988, rev. ed. as Lesbian Couples: Creating Healthy Relationships for the 90s, 1993; The Lesbian Parenting Book: A Guide to Creating Families and Raising Children, 1995, 2nd. ed., 2003; Lives of Lesbian Elders: Looking Back, Looking Forward, 2005. **Address:** Seal Press, 3131 Western Ave., Ste. 410, Seattle, WA 98121, U.S.A.

CLUYSENAAR, Anne (Alice Andrée). Welsh/Belgian (born Belgium), b. 1936. **Genres:** Poetry, Songs/Lyrics And Libretti, inspirational/Motivational Literature, Literary Criticism And History, Natural History, Autobiography/Memoirs, Biography. **Career:** Manchester University, assistant lecturer, 1957-58; Trinity College, assistant lecturer, 1961-62; Aberdeen University, Kings College, lecturer in English literature, 1963-65; Lancaster University, lecturer in linguistics and literature, 1965-71; Huddersfield Polytechnic, senior lecturer in language and literature, 1972-73; Birmingham University, lecturer in linguistics and literature, 1973-76; Sheffield City Polytechnic, senior lecturer in communication studies, 1976-89. Writer. **Publications:** A Fan of Shadows, 1967; Nodes, 1969; An Introduction to Literary Stylistics: A Discussion of Dominant Structure in Verse and Prose, 1976 in US as Aspects of Literary Stylistics, 1976; (with S. Hewat) Double Helix, 1982; Timeslips: New and Selected Poems, 1997. EDITOR/CO-EDITOR: Selected Poems of James Burns Singer, 1977; (with N. Schwenk) The Hare That Hides Within, 2004; Henry Vaughan, Selected Poems, 2004. Contributor to books. **Address:** Little Wentwood Farm, Llantrisant, Usk, GW NP15 1ND, Wales. **Online address:** anne.cluysenaar@virgin.net

CLYDESDALE, Tim. American (born United States), b. 1965. **Genres:** Young Adult Non-fiction, Sociology, Education. **Career:** Gordon College, assistant professor of sociology, 1994-96; College of New Jersey, professor of sociology, 1996-. Writer. **Publications:** The First Year Out: Understanding American Teens after High School, 2007. Contributor of articles to periodicals. **Address:** College of New Jersey, 2000 Pennington Rd., Social Science Bldg. 338, PO Box 7718, Ewing, NJ 08628-0718, U.S.A. **Online address:** clydesda@tcnj.edu

COAN, Richard W. American (born United States), b. 1928. **Genres:** Novels, Psychology. **Career:** University of Illinois, research associate in psychology, 1955-57; University of Arizona, assistant professor, 1957-60, associate professor, 1960-64, professor, 1964-89, professor emeritus of psychology, 1989-. Writer. **Publications:** Perceptual Aspects of Attributed Movement, 1956; The Optimal Personality: An Empirical and Theoretical Analysis, 1974; Hero, Artist, Sage or Saint?: A Survey of Views on What Is Variously Called Mental Health, Normality, Maturity, Self-Actualization and Human Fulfillment, 1977; Psychologists: Personal and Theoretical Pathways, 1979; Psychology of Adjustment: Personal Experience and Development, 1983; Human Consciousness and Its Evolution: A Multidimensional View, 1987; A Princess for Larkin, 2001; Shaul of Tarsos: The Man Who Came to Be Known as Saint Paul, 2005; Horatio: The Loyal Friend of Prince Hamlet, 2006; Masculine, Feminine, and Fully Human: Developmental Paths through the Adult Years, 2008. **Address:** Department of Psychology, University of Arizona, Tucson, AZ 85721, U.S.A. **Online address:** rwcoan@cox.net

COARELLI, Filippo. Italian (born Italy), b. 1936?. **Genres:** History, Sociology, Archaeology/Antiquities. **Career:** University of Perugia, professor of Greek and Roman antiquities. Writer. **Publications:** Arte Nel Mezzogiorno, 1966; Loreficeria Nellarte Classica, 1966; Roma, 1971, rev. ed., 2008; (ed.) Il Sepolcro degli Scipioni, 1972; Tesori Dell'oreficeria, 1973; Arena di Verona, 1973; (with L. Usai) Guida Archeologica di Roma, 1974; (with F. Boitani, M. Cataldi and M. Pasquinucci) Etruscan Cities, 1975; (ed. with A. Rossi and R. Schezen) Templi Dell 'Italia Antica, 1980; (ed. with L.F. Dell Orto) La Pittura Antica, 1980; Dintorni di Roma, 1981; Lazio, 1982; Il foro Romano, 1983; (with M. Torelli) Sicilia, 1984; (with A. La Regina) Abruzzo, Molise, 1984; Italia Centrale, 1985; (co-author) Dictionnaire méthodique de larchitecture grecque et romaine, 1985; (ed. with P.G. Monti) Fregellae, 1986; Roma Repubblicana Dal 270 A.C.alletá Augustea, 1987; I Santuari Del Lazio in etá Repubblicana, 1987; Il Sepolcro degli Scipioni a Roma, 1988; Il Foro Boario: Dalleorigini Alla fine della Repubblica, 1988; (ed.) Minturnae, 1989; (with A. Corcella and P. Rossi) Un angolo di mondo: i luoghi oraziani, 1993; Da Pergamo a Roma: i Galati nella cittá degli Attalidi, 1995; (ed. with G. Bonamente) Assisi e gli Umbri nell'antichitá: Atti Del Convengo Internazionale, Assisi, 18-21 Dicembre 1991, 1996; (ed. with V. Casale and B. Toscano) Scritti di Archeologia e Storia Dellarte in Onore di Carlo Pietrangeli, 1996; Revixit Ars: Arte e Ideologia a Roma, Dai Modelliellenistici Alla Tradizione Repubblicana, 1996; Il Campo Marzio: Dalleorigini Alla Fine Della Repubblica, 1997; (co-author) Il Colosseo, 1999; La Colonna Traiana, 1999; Belli e lantico, 2000; (ed. with C. Fratini) Archeologia e Arte in Umbria e Nei Suoi Musei, 2001; (ed.) Pompei: La Vita Ritrovata, 2002; Via Cavour: Una Strada Della Nuova Roma, 2003; Lexicon Topographicum Urbis Romae, Supplementum II, 2004; (ed. with F. Pesando) Rileggere Pompei, 2005; Rome and Environs: An Archaeological Guide, 2007; (ed. with H. Patterson) Mercator Placidissimus: The Tiber Valley in Antiquity: New Research in the Upper and Middle River Valley: Rome, 27-28 February 2004, 2008; (ed. with S. Sisani) Museo Comunale di Terni: Raccolta Archeologica, Sezione Romana, 2008; (ed. with J. Uroz and J.M. Noguera) Iberia e Italia: modelos romanos de integración territorial, 2008; Colonna di Marco Aurelio, 2008; (ed.) Divus Vespasianus: Il Bimillenario Dei Flavi, 2009; Le origini di Roma, 2011. **Address:** Riverside Book Co., 250 W 57th St., New York, NY 10107, U.S.A.

COATES, Carrol F(ranklin). American (born United States), b. 1930. **Genres:** Literary Criticism And History, Translations, Novellas/Short Stories, Biography. **Career:** Ohio University, instructor, 1960-62; Lycoming College, assistant professor, 1962-63; State University of New York, Binghamton University, assistant professor, professor of French and comparative literature, 1963-; Universite D'Aix-Marseille I, exchange lecturer, 1980, 1983-84. Writer. **Publications:** (Ed.) Repression and Expression: Literary and Social Coding in Nineteenth-century France, 1996; TRANSLATOR: The Festival of the Greasy Pole (novel), 1990; Of Rice and Blood (novel), 1994; (and afterword) Dignity, 1996; (and intro.) General Sun, My Brother (novel), 1999; (afterword) Waiting for the Vote of the Wild Animals (novel), 2001; (and afterword with E. Danticat) J.S. Alexis, In the Flicker of an Eyelid, 2002; Little Peul, 2010. **Address:** Department of Romance Languages and Literatures, Binghamton University-State University of New York, 4400 Vestal Pkwy. E, PO Box 6000, Binghamton, NY 13902-6000, U.S.A. **Online address:** ccoates@binghamton.edu

COATES, Charles (K.). American (born United States), b. 1929. **Genres:** Communications/Media, Politics/Government, Writing/Journalism, Business/Trade/Industry. **Career:** Nashville Tennessean, reporter and editor, 1956-61; National Broadcasting Co., writer, editor, producer of news, 1961-72, 1975, 1980-81; University of New Mexico, associate professor, 1972-96, professor emeritus, 1996-. **Publications:** Professional's TV News Handbook, 1994; The Total Manager: Break Out of Your Department and Manage the Whole Business, 1995. **Address:** Department of Communication & Journalism, University of New Mexico, MSC03 2240, Albuquerque, NM 87131, U.S.A. **Online address:** chascoates@msn.com

COATES, Robert Crawford. American/South African (born South Africa), b. 1937. **Genres:** Food And Wine, Social Commentary, Poetry, Young Adult Fiction, Social Sciences, Literary Criticism And History. **Career:** City of San Diego, civil engineer and administrative analyst in city manager's office, 1959-63; Coates and Miller (attorneys), partner, 1971-82; San Diego Superior Court, judge; University of San Diego, adjunct professor, 1981-; Western State University College of Law of San Diego, adjunct professor, 1981-; San Diego Ecology Center, president, 1985-86; San Diego Natural History Museum, vice-president, 1989-90; Seven Seas Exploration Inc., treasurer, 1990-; San Diego County Law Library, president, 1992. Writer. **Publications:** Ships Crossing at the Dead of Night (poems), 1984; A Street Is Not a Home: Solving America's Homeless Dilemma, 1990; The Guys Who Can't Cook Cookbook, 1992. Contributor to law journals and local newspapers. **Address:** San Diego Superior Ct., Rm. 2004, 220 W Broadway, San Diego, CA 92101-3814, U.S.A.

COATES, Ta-Nehisi. American (born United States), b. 1975?. **Genres:** Autobiography/Memoirs, Biography, Human Relations/Parenting. **Career:** The Atlantic, senior editor; Village Voice, staff writer; Time Magazine, staff writer. **Publications:** The Beautiful Struggle: A Father, Two Sons, and an Unlikely Road to Manhood (memoir), 2008. Contributor to books, periodicals and magazines. **Address:** Random House Inc., 1745 Broadway, New York, NY 10019, U.S.A. **Online address:** tcoates@theatlantic.com

COATS, Wendell John. American (born United States), b. 1947. **Genres:** Politics/Government. **Career:** U.S. House of Representatives, legislative assistant, 1979; Connecticut College, professor of government and department chair, 1984-. Writer. **Publications:** The Activity of Politics and Related Essays, 1989; A Theory of Republican Character and Related Essays, 1994; Statesmanship: Six Modern Illustrations of a Modified Ancient Ideal, 1995; Oakeshott and His Contemporaries, 2000; Political Theory and Practice: Eight Essays on a Theme, 2003; Montaigne's Essais, 2004; Armed Force and Moderate Political Life, 2008. Contributor to periodicals. **Address:** Department of Government and International Relatio, Connecticut College, PO Box 5425, New London, CT 06320, U.S.A. **Online address:** wjcoa@conncoll.edu

COATSWORTH, John H(enry). American (born United States), b. 1940. **Genres:** Economics, History. **Career:** El Colegio de Mexico, visiting professor, 1968, 1974-75; University of Chicago, assistant professor, 1969-77, associate professor, 1977-80, professor of history, 1980-92; Harvard University, professor of history and Monroe Gutman professor of Latin American affairs, 1992-2006, David Rockefeller Center for Latin American Studies, director, 1994-2006; Universidad Nacional de Buenos Aires, senior Fulbright lecturer, 1985; Instituto Torcuato di Tella, senior Fulbright lecturer, 1989; Instituto Tecnologico Autonoma de Mexico, senior Fulbright lecturer, 1992; Instituto Universitario Ortega y Gassett, visiting professor, 1993; Columbia University, Columbia School of International and Public Affairs, visiting professor, 2006-07, interim dean, 2007-08, dean, 2008-, professor of history and international and public affairs, interim provost, 2011-. Writer. **Publications:** Growth against Development: The Economic Impact of Railroads in Porfirian Mexico, 1981; Los origenes del atraso: Nueve ensayos de historia economicade Mexico, siglos XVIII y XIX, 1990; Central America and the United States: The Clients and the Colossus, 1994; Culturas Encontradas: Cuba y Los Estados Unidos, 2001. EDITOR AND CONTRIBUTOR: (with C.M. Rico) Images of Mexico in the United States, 1989; (with A.M. Taylor) Latin America and the World Economy since 1800, 1998; (with V. Bulmer-Thomas and R.C. Connde) Cambridge Economic History of Latin America, 2006. **Address:** School of International and Public Affairs, Columbia University, Rm. 1414, International Affairs Bldg., 420 W 118th St., New York, NY 10027, U.S.A. **Online address:** john.coatsworth@sipa.columbia.edu

COBB, Cathy. American (born United States) **Genres:** Novels, Sciences, Chemistry, Physics. **Career:** Aiken Preparatory School, physics and calculus instructor, 2001-; University of South Carolina, adjunct professor of chemistry; California State University, faculty; Augusta State University, faculty; Westinghouse Savannah River Co., staff. Writer. **Publications:** (With H. Goldwhite) Creations of Fire: Chemistry's Lively History from Alchemy to the Atomic Age, 1995; Magick, Mayhem, and Mavericks: The Spirited History of Physical Chemistry, 2002; (with M.L. Fetterolf) The Joy of Chemistry: The Amazing Science of Familiar Things, 2005; (with M.L. Fetterolf and J. Goldsmith) Crime Scene Chemistry for the Armchair Sleuth, 2007. **Address:** c/o Author Mail, Prometheus Books, 59 John Glenn Dr., Amherst, NY 14228-2197, U.S.A. **Online address:** ccobb@aikenprep.org

COBB, Clifford W(illiam). American (born United States), b. 1951. **Genres:** Education, Economics, Business/Trade/Industry. **Career:** National Association of Counties, research associate, 1976-78; Palmore Institute, English teacher, 1979-81; Claremont School District, substitute teacher, 1984-89; Institute for Educational Choice, executive director, 1991-93; California Futures, researcher, 1991-93; Redefining Progress, staff, 1994-; Robert Schalkenbach Foundation, interim executive director, program director, president; Henry George School, director. Writer. **Publications:** (Contrib.) For the Common Good: Redirecting the Economy Toward Community, the Environment, and a Sustainable Future, 1989, 2nd ed., 1994; Responsive Schools, Renewed Communities, 1992; (with J.B. Cobb, Jr.) The Green National Product: A Proposed Index of Sustainable Economic Welfare, 1994; (ed. with J.A. Giacalone) Path to Justice: Following in the Footsteps of Henry George, 2001; (intro.) Studies in Economic Reform and Social Justice: After the Crash: Designing a Depression-free Economy, 2009; (with P. Diaz) Why Global Poverty?, 2009. Contributor to books and periodicals. **Address:** Redefining Progress, 1904 Franklin St., 6th Fl., Oakland, CA 94612, U.S.A.

COBB, James H(arvey). American (born United States), b. 1953. **Genres:** Mystery/Crime/Suspense, Novels, Young Adult Fiction. **Career:** Writer. **Publications:** Choosers of the Slain (suspense novel), 1996; Storm Dragon in US as Sea Strike, 1997; West on 66: A Novel, 1999; Sea Fighter, 1999; Target Lock, 2001; Cibola, 2004; (with R. Ludlum) The Arctic Event, 2007; (with R. Ludlum) The Infinity Affair, 2009. Works appear in anthologies. **Address:** Henry Morrison Inc., PO Box 235, Bedford Hills, NY 10507-0235, U.S.A.

COBB, Kelton. American (born United States), b. 1958. **Genres:** Theology/Religion, Cultural/Ethnic Topics, Sociology, Social Sciences. **Career:** University of Iowa, School of Religion, research assistant, 1986-87; St. Joseph's University, Department of Theology, adjunct instructor, 1991-92; Hartford Seminary, professor of theology, 1995-; Wesleyan University, visiting assistant professor of religion, 2002-03; Conversations in Religion and Theology, associate editor, 2002-. **Publications:** The Blackwell Guide to Theology and Popular Culture, 2005. Contributor of articles to periodicals. **Address:** Center for Faith in Practice, Hartford Seminary, 77 Sherman St., Hartford, CT 06105-6203, U.S.A. **Online address:** kcobb@hartsem.edu

COBB, Nancy (Howard). American (born United States), b. 1949. **Genres:** Adult Non-fiction, Children's Non-fiction, Self Help. **Career:** Primary school teacher, 1970-71; actress and documentary film producer, 1975-82; writer, 1982-; Pilobolus Dance Co., director, 1989-91. **Publications:** How They Met, 1992; Letter Writer Book for Kids, 1994; In Lieu of Flowers: A Conversation for the Living, 2000; (with C. Grigsby) Is There a Moose in Your Marriage?, 2000; The Best Thing I Ever Did for My Marriage: 50 Real Life Stories, 2003; The Politically Incorrect Wife: God's Plan for Marriage Still Works Today, 2003; (with C. Grigsby) How to Get Your Husband to Talk to You, 2006; (with C. Grigsby) How to Get Your Husband to Listen to You, 2008. **Address:** c/o Jonathan Dolger, Jonathan Dolger Agency, 49 E 96th St., New York, NY 10128, U.S.A.

COBB, Thomas. American (born United States), b. 1947. **Genres:** Novels, Novellas/Short Stories, Young Adult Fiction, Poetry. **Career:** Rhode Island College, professor of English, 1987-2011. Writer. **Publications:** We Shall Curse the Dead (poems), 1976; Crazy Heart (novel), 1987; Acts of Contrition (stories), 2003; Shavetail (novel), 2008. **Address:** 198 Plainfield Pke., Foster, RI 02825, U.S.A. **Online address:** tc@thomascobb.net

COBB, Vicki. American (born United States), b. 1938. **Genres:** Children's Non-fiction, Sciences, Education. **Career:** Sloan-Kettering Institute, scientific researcher, 1958-61; Pfizer & Co., scientific researcher, 1958-61; teacher,

1961-64; Scott Publishing Co., public relations director, 1978-83; Pinwheel Publishers, vice-president; Ink Think Tank L.L.C., president. Writer. **Publications:** Logic, 1969; (ed.) Biology Study Prints, 1970; Cells: The Basic Structure of Life, 1970; Gases, 1970; Making Sense of Money, 1971; Sense of Direction: Up, Down and All Around, 1972; Science Experiments You Can Eat, 1972, rev. ed., 1994; Heat, 1973; The Long and Short of Measurement, 1973; How the Doctor Knows You're Fine, 1973; Arts and Crafts You Can Eat, 1974; Supersuits, 1975; Magic... Naturally!: Science Entertainments and Amusements, 1976, rev. ed., 1993; More Science Experiments You Can Eat, 1979; Truth on Trial: The Story of Galileo Galilei, 1979; (with K. Darling) Bet You Can't!: Science Impossibilities to Fool You, 1980; How to Really Fool Yourself: Illusions for All Your Senses, 1981; Lots of Rot, 1981; The Secret Life of School Supplies, 1981; The Secret Life of Hardware: A Science Experiment Book, 1982; Fuzz Does It!, 1982; Gobs of Goo, 1983; The Monsters Who Died: A Mystery about Dinosaurs, 1983; (with K. Darling) Bet You Can!: Science Possibilities To Fool You, 1983, 2nd ed., 1990; Brave in the Attempt: The Special Olympics Experience, 1983; Chemically Active!: Experiments You Can Do at Home, 1985; The Secret Life of Cosmetics: A Science Experiment Book, 1985; The Scoop on Ice Cream, 1985; Sneakers Meet Your Feet, 1985; More Power to You, 1986; The Trip of a Drip, 1986; Inspector Bodyguard Patrols the Land of U, 1986; Skyscraper Going Up!: A Pop-up Book, 1987; Scraps of Wraps, 1988; Why Doesn't the Earth Fall Up?: And Other Not Such Dumb Questions about Motion, 1988; This Place Is Cold, 1989; This Place Is Dry, 1989; This Place Is High, 1989; This Place Is Wet, 1989; Feeding Yourself, 1989; For Your Own Protection: Stories Science Photos Tell, 1989; Getting Dressed, 1989; Keeping Clean, 1989; Writing It Down, 1989; Natural Wonders: Stories Science Photos Tell, 1990; Why Doesn't the Sun Burn Out?: And Other Not Such Dumb Questions about Matter, 1990; Why Can't You Unscramble an Egg?: And Other Not Such Dumb Questions About Matter, 1990; Fun and Games: Stories Science Photos Tell, 1991; This Place Is Lonely, 1991; This Place is Crowded, 1992; (with K. Darling) Wanna Bet?: Science Challenges to Fool You, 1993; (with J. Cobb) Light Action!: Amazing Experiments with Optics, 1993; On The Tip Of Your Tongue, 1996; Why Can't I Live Forever?: And Other Not Such Dumb Questions about Life, 1997; Blood and Gore, Like You've Never Seen, 1997; Dirt and Grime, Like You've Never Seen, 1998; (with K. Darling) Don't Try This at Home!: Science Fun for Kids on the Go, 1998; This Place Is Wild: East Africa, 1998; You Gotta Try This: Absolutely Irresistible Science, 1999; Your Tongue Can Tell: Discover Your Sense of Taste, 2000; Bangs and Twangs: Science Fun with Sound, 2000; Squirts and Spurts: Science Fun with Water, 2000; Follow Your Nose: Discover Your Sense of Smell, 2000; See for Yourself: More than One Hundred Experiments for Science Fairs and Projects, 2001; Feeling Your Way: Discover Your Sense of Touch, 2001; Perk Up Your Ears: Discover Your Sense of Hearing, 2001; See for Yourself: More than 100 Experiments for Science Fairs and Projects, 2001; Whirlers and Twirlers: Science Fun with Spinning, 2001; Open Your Eyes: Discover Your Sense of Sight, 2002; Sources of Forces: Science Fun With Force Fields, 2002; I See Myself, 2002; I Get Wet, 2002; I Face the Wind, 2003; I Fall Down, 2004; Harry Houdini, 2005; Fireworks, 2006; Junk Food, 2006; Sneakers, 2006; On Stage, 2006; (with K. Darling) We Dare You!: Hundreds of Science Bets, Challenges and Experiments You can Do at Home, 2008; Marie Curie, 2008; Your Body Battles an Earache, 2009; Your Body Battles a Stomachache, 2009; Your Body Battles a Skinned Knee, 2009; Your Body Battles a Cold, 2009; Your Body Battles a Cavity, 2009; Your Body Battles a Broken Bone, 2009; What's the Big Idea?: Amazing Science Questions for Curious Kids, 2010; See for Yourself: More Than 100 Amazing Experiments for Science Fairs and School Projects, 2010. Contributor to periodicals. **Address:** 302 Pondside Dr., White Plains, NY 10607, U.S.A. **Online address:** email@vickicobb.com

COBBS, Elizabeth Anne. *See* **HOFFMAN, Elizabeth Cobbs.**

COBEN, Harlan. American (born United States), b. 1962. **Genres:** Mystery/Crime/Suspense, Novels. **Career:** Writer. **Publications:** MYSTERY NOVELS: Play Dead, 1990; Miracle Cure, 1991; Tell No One, 2001; Gone for Good, 2002; No Second Chance, 2003; Just One Look, 2004; The Innocent, 2005; The Woods, 2007; Hold Tight, 2008; Caught, 2010; Stay Close, 2012. MYRON BOLITAR SERIES: Deal Breaker, 1995; Drop Shot, 1996; Fade Away, 1996; Back Spin, 1997; One False Move, 1998; The Final Detail, 1999; Darkest Fear, 2000; Promise Me, 2006; Long Lost, 2009; Live Wire, 2011. MICKEY BOLITAR SERIES: Shelter, 2011. OTHER: (ed. and contrib.) Mystery Writers of America Presents Death Do Us Part: New Stories about Love, Lust, and Murder, 2006. **Address:** The Aaron M. Priest Literary Agency Inc., 708 3rd Ave., 23rd Fl., New York, NY 10017-4201, U.S.A. **Online address:** me@harlancoben.com

COBLE, Colleen. (Colleen Rhoads). American (born United States), b. 1952. **Genres:** Novels, Novellas/Short Stories, Young Adult Fiction, Romance/Historical. **Career:** Romantic suspense novelist. **Publications:** NOVELS: Where Leads the Heart, 1998; Plains of Promise, 1999; The Heart Answers, 1999; To Love a Stranger, 2000; From Russia with Love, 2000; Love Ahoy, 2001; The Cattle Barons Bride, 2001; Red River Bride, 2002; Maggies Mistake, 2002; (co-author) Aloha, 2002; Without a Trace (romantic suspense), 2003; (co-author) Gold Rush Christmas, 2003; Beyond a Doubt (romantic suspense), 2004; Into the Deep (romantic suspense), 2004; Distant Echoes, 2005; (as Colleen Rhoads) Shadow Bones, 2005; (as Colleen Rhoads) Windigo Twilight, 2005; Black Sands, 2005; Dangerous Depths, 2006; (as Colleen Rhoads) Stormcatcher, 2006; Alaska Twilight, 2006; Fire Dancer, 2006; Midnight Sea, 2007; Abomination, 2007; Lonestar Sanctuary, 2007; Anathema, 2008; Lonestar Secrets, 2008; Cry in the Night, 2009; The Lightkeeper's Daughter: A Mercy Falls Novel, 2009; Lonestar Homecoming, 2009; The Lightkeeper's Bride, 2010; Lonestar Angel, 2011; Smitten, 2011; The Lightkeeper's Ball, 2011; Blue Moon Promise, 2012. OTHERS: (co-author) Home for Christmas, 2001; (contrib.) Blind Dates, 2003. Contributor to periodicals. **Address:** c/o Karen Solem, Spencerhill Associates, 24 Park Row 1935, PO Box 374, Chatham, NY 12037, U.S.A. **Online address:** colleen@colleencoble.com

COBURN, Andrew. American (born United States), b. 1932. **Genres:** Novels, Mystery/Crime/Suspense, Writing/Journalism. **Career:** Suburban Ed, feature writer and police reporter, 1963-73; Boston Globe, book reviewer and part-time copy editor, 1973-78. Political columnist. **Publications:** The Trespassers, 1974; The Babysitter, 1979; Off Duty, 1980; Company Secrets, 1982; Widow's Walk, 1984; Sweetheart: A Novel of Revenge, 1985; Love Nest, 1987; Goldilocks, 1989; No Way Home, 1992; Voices in the Dark, 1994; Birthright, 1997; On the Loose, 2006; My Father's Daughter, 2007; Updike of Ipswich, 2009. Contributor to magazines. **Address:** Smith/Skolnik Literary Management, 23 E 10th St., Ste. 712, New York, NY 10003, U.S.A. **Online address:** andrew1coburn@aol.com

COBURN, Ann. British (born England) **Genres:** Young Adult Fiction, Children's Fiction, Novels, Plays/Screenplays. **Career:** Writer, 1991-. Educator and library assistant. **Publications:** JUVENILE NOVELS: The Granite Beast, 1991; The Secret Club, 1992; Welcome to the Real World, 1992; The Domino Effect, 1994; Glint, 2005. BORDERLANDS SERIES: Worm Songs, 1996; Web Weaver, 1996; Dark Water, 1998; Blind Side, 2001. DREAM TEAM: Flying Solo, 2006; Showtime, 2006; The Daydream Shift, 2007; Speed Challenge, 2007. OTHER: Get Up and Tie Your Fingers, 2001; Three Plays: Get Up And Tie Your Fingers/Safe/Devil's Ground, 2004; Alex and the Warrior, 2004; Alex and The Winter Star, 2009. **Address:** The Peters Fraser and Dunlop Group Ltd., Drury House, 34-43 Russell St., London, GL WC2B 5HA, England.

COBURN, Pip. American (born United States) **Genres:** Business/Trade/Industry, Engineering, Communications/Media. **Career:** Lynch and Mayer Inc., senior vice president; UBS Investment Research, managing director and global technology strategist, 1999-2005; Coburn Ventures L.L.C., co-founder, 2005-. Writer. **Publications:** The Change Function: Why Some Technologies Take Off and Others Crash and Burn, 2006. **Address:** Coburn Ventures L.L.C., 10 Chestnut St., Pleasantville, NY 10570, U.S.A. **Online address:** pip@coburnventures.com

COCHRAN, Gregory. American (born United States), b. 1953?. **Genres:** Humanities, Sciences, History. **Career:** University of Utah, adjunct professor of human evolutionary genetics. Writer, consultant, physicist and anthropologist. **Publications:** (With H. Harpending) The 10, 000 Year Explosion: How Civilization Accelerated Human Evolution, 2009. Contributor to journals. **Address:** Department of Anthropology, University of Utah, Rm. 102, 270 South 1400 East, Salt Lake City, UT 84112, U.S.A.

COCHRAN, Heather. American (born United States) **Genres:** Young Adult Fiction, Human Relations/Parenting, Romance/Historical. **Career:** Writer. **Publications:** Mean Season, 2004; The Return of Jonah Gray, 2007. Contributor to periodicals. **Address:** c/o Katherine Fausset, Curtis Brown Ltd., 10 Astor Pl., New York, NY 10003-6935, U.S.A. **Online address:** hkcochran@yahoo.com

COCHRAN, Robert B(rady). American (born United States), b. 1943. **Genres:** Novels, Poetry, Literary Criticism And History, Local History/Rural Topics, Bibliography, Music, Songs/Lyrics And Libretti. **Career:** Ball State University, instructor, 1969-70; University of Southern Mississippi, assistant professor, 1970-71; National Endowment for the Humanities, lecturer/performer, 1971-72, Summer Seminar for School Teachers, project director, 1993, 1995; University of Indiana, assistant professor, 1973-76; University of Arkansas, assistant professor, 1976-79, associate professor, 1979-87, professor, 1987-, Center for Arkansas and Regional Studies, director, 1989-, chair of American studies, J. William Fulbright College of Arts and Sciences, faculty. Writer. **Publications:** (With M. Luster) For Love and for Money: Vance Randolph, An Annotated Bibliography, 1979; Vance Randolph: An Ozark Life, 1985; Samuel Beckett: A Study of the Short Fiction, 1991; Our Own Sweet Sounds: A Celebration of Popular Music in Arkansas, 1996, 2nd ed., 2005; Singing in Zion: Music and Song in the Life of an Arkansas Family, 1999; A Photographer of Note: Arkansas Artist Geleve Grice, 2003; Louise Pound: Scholar, Athlete, Feminist Pioneer, 2009. Contributor of articles to periodicals and books. **Address:** Department of English, University of Arkansas, 333 Kimp Hall, KIMP 334, Fayetteville, AR 72701, U.S.A. **Online address:** rcochran@uark.edu

COCHRANE, Peggy. American (born United States), b. 1923. **Genres:** Plays/Screenplays, Architecture, Medicine/Health, Psychology, Social Sciences, Translations. **Career:** Daniel, Mann, Johnson and Mendenhall, architectural designer, 1956-59; architect, 1960-; Association of Women in Architecture, president, 1970-72. Writer. **Publications:** (And trans.) Moscow, Sketches on the Russian Capital, 1947; Mayaland (musical), 1967; Witch Doctor's Cookbook, 1984; Witch Doctor's Manual, 1984; Cable Car (musical), 1986; Harry, Go Home! (play), 1990; Winning from Rejection, 1991; How to Con a Con Artist, 1991; The Sorcerer's Guide to Health, 1993; Finding Your Dream Home, forthcoming. **Address:** 3888 Sherview Dr., Sherman Oaks, CA 91403-5035, U.S.A.

COCKAYNE, Emily. British (born England), b. 1973?. **Genres:** Adult Nonfiction, History. **Career:** Magdalen College, Prize fellow in modern history, 1999; Open University in the East Midlands, research associate, associate lecturer, 2003-. Writer. **Publications:** Hubbub: Filth, Noise, & Stench in England 1600-1770, 2007. Contributor to Journals. **Address:** c/o Clare Alexander, Aitken Alexander Associates, 18-21 Cavaye Pl., London, GL SW10 9PT, England.

COCKBURN, Patrick. British/Irish (born Ireland), b. 1950. **Genres:** International Relations/Current Affairs, Autobiography/Memoirs, Business/Trade/Industry, History. **Career:** Financial Times, Middle East correspondent, 1979-90, Moscow correspondent, 1984-88; Independent, staff, 1990-, Moscow correspondent, through 2002, Middle East correspondent. **Publications:** Getting Russia Wrong: The End of Kremlinology, 1990; (with A. Cockburn) Out of the Ashes: The Resurrection of Saddam Hussein, 1999; The Broken Boy, 2006; The Occupation, 2006; The Occupation: War and Resistance in Iraq, 2007; Muqtada: Muqtada al-Sadr, the Shia Revival and the Struggle for Iraq, 2008; Muqtada Al Sadr and the Fall of Iraq, 2009; (with H. Cockburn) Henry's Demons: Living with Schizophrenia, a Father and Son's Story, 2011. **Address:** Independent, Independent House, 191 Marsh Wall, London, GL E14 9RS, England.

COCKER, Mark. British (born England), b. 1959?. **Genres:** Biography, Animals/Pets, Natural History. **Career:** The Daily Telegraph, writer; The Times, writer; The Independent, writer; BBC Wildlife, writer; RSPB, environmentalist, 1985; English Nature, environmentalist, 1985-60; BirdLife Intl., environmentalist, 1988-90; The Guardian, columnist, 1988-, Guardian Weekly, staff, 1996-2002. **Publications:** (With C. Inskipp) A Himalayan Ornithologist: The Life and Work of Brian Houghton Hodgson, 1988; Richard Meinertzhagen: Soldier, Scientist and Spy, 1989; Loneliness and Time: British Travel Writing in the Twentieth Century, 1992; Rivers of Blood, Rivers of Gold: Europe's Conflict with Tribal Peoples, 1998; Rivers of Blood, Rivers of Gold: Europe's Conquest of Indigenous Peoples, 2000; Birders: Tales of a Tribe, 2001; (with R. Mabey) Birds Britannica, 2005; A Tiger in the Sand, 2006; Crow Country, 2008. Contributor to periodicals. **Address:** c/o Author Mail, Random House United Kingdom, Vintage Publicity, 20 Vauxhall Bridge Rd., London, GL SW1V 2SA, England. **Online address:** markcocker@btinternet.com

COCKERILL, A(rthur) W(illiam). British (born England), b. 1929. **Genres:** Plays/Screenplays, History, Writing/Journalism, Biography, Engineering, Information Science/Computers, Local History/Rural Topics, Public/Social Administration, Public/Social Administration, Environmental Sciences/Ecology, Engineering, Education. **Career:** Metropolitan-Vickers Electrical Co., contracts engineer, 1951-54; British Timkin Ltd., applications engineer, 1954-57; Iron Ore Co., operating manager, 1957-60; Twin Falls Power Corp., operations manager, 1960-64; Mathews Conveyer Co., contracts international installation engineer, 1964-79; Spectrum Engineering Corp., consultant, 1979-85; Delta Tech Systems Inc., partner, consulting engineer and technical publisher, 1984-93. Writer. **Publications:** That's the Style (musical review) 1958; The Yukon Trail (musical review), 1962; Sir Percy Sillitoe (biography), 1975; Airport Baggage-Handling, 1978; Sons of the Brave, 1984; Energy Management Handbook, 1985; Handbook of Technical Writing, 1986; (with J. Nissen) Winning the Radar War, 1987; Operating Manual, Ontario Hydro Bruce Nuclear Generating Station 'A', 1988; Handbook of A-C Maintenance, 1990; Handbook of Airport Baggage-Handling Systems, 1990; Maintenance Manual for Air-conditioning Systems, 1994; The Slobourg Journal, 1995; Emma on Albert Street, 1997; Handbook of Technical Writing, 1998; Anatomy of the Materials Regulation Division, 1999; Kitchen Ventilation Systems, 2000; Manual of Compliance Inspection (Nuclear Materials), 2000; Guide to the Preparation of Documents for (Nuclear) Commission Hearings, 2001; Short History of the Royal Hiberninan Military School, 2001; Chronicles of the Lodge, 2001; Chronicles of the Lodge, 2001; The Charity of Mars, 2002; Out of the Boroughs, 2008; Descent into the Abyss, 2010. Contributor to magazines and newspapers. **Address:** 98 Maria's Quay, Cobourg, ON K9A 5R6, Canada. **Online address:** achart@sympatico.ca

COCKEY, Tim. *See* **HAWKE, Richard.**

COCKRELL, Alan. American (born United States), b. 1949. **Genres:** Autobiography/Memoirs, History. **Career:** United Airlines, pilot; U.S. Air Force, air pilot; Air National Guard, air pilot. Writer. **Publications:** Tail of the Storm (memoir), 1995; Drilling Ahead: The Quest for Oil in the Deep South, 1945-2005, 2005. Contributor of articles to periodicals. **Address:** U.S.A. **Online address:** yakpilot@bellsouth.net

COCKRELL, Thomas D(errell). American (born United States), b. 1949. **Genres:** History, Biography. **Career:** Louisville Police Department, police officer, 1971-78; social studies teacher, 1974-75; Mississippi Farm Bureau Insurance Co., salesperson, 1978-79; Louisville Fire Department, firefighter, 1979-89; East Mississippi Community College, instructor, 1983-87; Louisiana State University, librarian, archivist and assistant professor of history and political science, 1989-90; Mississippi State University, lecturer in history, 1990-92; Blue Mountain College, professor of history and head of social science, 1992-; Mississippi Historical Society, director, 2001-04. Writer. **Publications:** The Descendants of William Jasper Cockrell and Martha Ann Crowson, 1982; (ed. with M.B. Ballard) A Mississippi Rebel in the Army of Northern Virginia: The Civil War Memoirs of Private David Holt, 1995; (ed. with M.B. Ballard) Chickasaw, A Mississippi Scout for the Union, 2005. Contributor to books and journals. **Address:** Department of Social Sciences, Blue Mountain College, Administration Bldg., Blue Mountain, MS 38610, U.S.A. **Online address:** tdc@bmc.edu

COCKS, Nancy L. Canadian (born Canada) **Genres:** Design, Theology/Religion, Children's Fiction, Animals/Pets. **Career:** Isle of Iona, presbyterian minister; Atlantic School of Theology, professor. Writer. **Publications:** ADVENTURES OF FERGIE THE FROG SERIES: Fearless Fergie, 1996; Fergie Feels Left Out, 1996; Fergie Goes Moose Hunting, 1996; Fergie Hogs the Lily Pad, 1996; Fergie Fails a Test, 1997; Fergie, Frog Scout, 1997; Fergie Loses a Friend, 1997; Welcome Home, Fergie, 1997; Where, Oh Where, Is Fergie?, 2002; Fergie Tries to Fly, 2002; Nobody Loves Fergie, 2002; You Can Count on Fergie, 2002; Fergie Counts His Blessings, 2003; Fergie Has a Birthday Party, 2003; Fergie Goes to Grandma's, 2003; Fergie Cleans Up, 2003. OTHER: Growing Up with God: Using Stories to Explore a Child's Faith and Life, 2003. Contributor to periodicals. **Address:** Atlantic School of Theology, 660 Francklyn St., Halifax, NS B3H 3B5, Canada.

COCQUYT, Kathryn Marie. American (born United States), b. 1960. **Genres:** Novels, Children's Fiction, Young Adult Fiction, Literary Criticism And History. **Career:** MI Publishing, editor; Silver Fox Racing Stables, staff. **Publications:** Little Freddie at the Kentucky Derby, 1992; Little Freddie's Legacy, 1994; The Celtic Heart, 1994; A Pony for Luke, 1998; Perihelion, forthcoming. **Address:** 2392 Torrance, Simi Valley, CA 93065, U.S.A.

CODINA, Carles. (Carles Codina i Armengol). Spanish (born Spain), b. 1961?. **Genres:** Adult Non-fiction. **Career:** Massana School, professor of jewelry-making, 1980. Writer. **Publications:** NONFICTION: La joyeria, 1999; The Complete Book of Jewelry Making: A Full-Color Introduction To The Jeweler's Art, 2000; (as Carles Codina i Armengol) Orfebreria, 2001, Goldsmithing and Silver Work: Jewelry, Vessels and Ornaments, 2003; Nueva joyeria, 2003; The New Jewelry: Contemporary Materials and Techniques, 2005; Color, Texture and Casting for Jewelers: Hands-On Demonstrations and Practical Applications, 2010. **Address:** Lark Books, A Division of Sterling Publishing Company Inc., 67 Broadway, Asheville, NC 28801, U.S.A. **Online address:** carles@codinaorfebres.com

CODINA I ARMENGOL, Carles. *See* **CODINA, Carles.**

CODRESCU, Andrei. American/Romanian (born Romania), b. 1946. **Genres:** Novels, Poetry, Autobiography/Memoirs, Novellas/Short Stories, Young Adult Fiction, Essays. **Career:** Institute for Paleo-Cybernetic Research, director, 1967-73; Louisiana State University, professor of English, MacCurdy distinguished professor, 1984-2009, MacCurdy distinguished professor emeritus of English, 2009-; National Public Radio, columnist, commentator; Exquisite Corpse, editor; Johns Hopkins University, faculty; University of Baltimore, faculty. **Publications:** ESSAYS: Secret Training, 1973; Raised by Puppets Only to be Killed by Research, 1987; Craving for Swan, 1988; The Disappearance of the Outside, 1990; The Hole in the Flag: A Romanian Exile's Story of Return and Revolution, 1991; Road Scholar: Coast to Coast Late in the Century, 1993; Zombification: Stories from National Public Radio, 1994; The Muse is Always Half-Dressed in New Orleans, 1995; The Dog With the Chip in His Neck, 1996; Hail Babylon!, 1998; The Devil Never Sleeps and Other Essays, 2000; (co-author); New Orleans, Mon Amour: Twenty Years of Writings From the City, 2006; Posthuman Dada Guide: Tzara and Lenin Play Chess, 2009; The Poetry Lesson, 2010; Whatever Gets You Through the Night: A Story of Sheherezade & The Arabian Entertainments, 2011. POETRY: License to Carry a Gun, 1970; The Here What Where, 1971; Grammar and Money, 1972; A Serious Morning, 1973; The History of the Growth of Heaven, 1973; A Mote Suite for Jan and Anselm, 1976; For the Love of a Coat, 1978; The Lady Painter, 1979; Diapers on the Snow, 1981; Necrocorrida, 1980; Selected Poems 1970-1980, 1983; Comrade Past and Mister Present, 1991; Belligerence, 1993; Alien Candor: Selected Poems, 1970-1995, 1996; Candoare străină: poeme alese, 1970-1996, 1997; It Was Today: New Poems, 2003; Instrumentul Negru: Poezii 1965-1968, 2004; (with R. Cesereanu) Submarinul Iertat, 2007; Jealous Witness, 2008. MEMOIRS/REPORTAGE/FANCIES: In the Most Beautiful Life, 2002; Why I Can't Talk on the Telephone (short stories), 1972; (with A. Saroyan) San Francisco, 1973; The Life and Times of an Involuntary Genius (autobiography), 1974, rev. ed., 2001; Involuntary Genius in America's Shoes, 2001; Travels of a Vigilante, 1975; For Max Jacob, 1975; In America's Shoes, 1983; Ectoplasm is My Hobby: Blackouts and Dramatic Objects 1971 and 1986, 1987; Monsieur Teste in America and Other Instances of Realism, 1987; Land of the Free, 1999; Ay, Cuba! A Socio-Erotic Journey, 2001. FICTION: The Repentance of Lorraine, 1994; The Blood Countess, 1995; Messiah, 1999; A Bar in Brooklyn: Novellas & Stories, 1970-1978, 1999; Casanova in Bohemia, 2002; Wakefield, 2004. EDITOR: American Poetry Since 1970: Up Late, 1987; The Stiffest of the Corpse: An Exquisite Corpse Reader, 1988; Reframing America: Alexander All and Otto Hagel & Hansel Mieth, John Gutmann, Lisette Model, Marion Palfi, Robert Frank, 1995; Thus Spake the Corpse, 1999; (and intro. with L. Rosenthal) American Poets Say Goodbye to the Twentieth Century, 1996; Thus Spake the Corpse: An Exquisite Corpse Reader 1988-1998, vol. I: Poetry and Essays, 1999, vol. II: Fictions, Travels and Translations, 2000. OTHERS: (intro.) Obituary Cocktail, 1999; (with L.E. Herman) Thomas Mann, 2001; (contrib.) Walker Evans, 2001; (contrib.) States of Mind, 2007. Works appear in anthologies. Contributor of articles to periodicals. **Address:** Department of English, Louisiana State University, 260 Allen Hall, Baton Rouge, LA 70803, U.S.A. **Online address:** acodrescu@gmail.com

CODY, Diablo. *See* **BUSEY-HUNT, Brook.**

CODY, Jeffrey W. American (born United States), b. 1950. **Genres:** Architecture, History. **Career:** Cornell University, visiting assistant professor, 1989-95; Chinese University of Hong Kong, architecture faculty, associate professor, 1995-2004; The Getty Conservation Institute, faculty, 2004-, senior project specialist. **Publications:** Building in China, 2001; Exporting American Architecture, 1870-2000, 2002; (ed. with N.S. Steinhardt and T. Atkin) Chinese Architecture and the Beaux-Arts, 2011; (ed. with F. Terpak) Brush & Shutter: Early Photography in China, 2011. **Address:** The Getty Conservation Institute, 1200 Getty Center Dr., Los Angeles, CA 90049-1679, U.S.A. **Online address:** jwcody@cuhk.edu.hk

CODY, Lisa Forman. American (born United States), b. 1964. **Genres:** Adult Non-fiction. **Career:** University of California, instructor in history, women's studies and interdisciplinary studies, 1989-93; Stanford University, Andrew W. Mellon postdoctoral fellow, 1993-95, visiting assistant professor in history, 1993-95; Denison University, assistant professor of history, 1995-96; Claremont McKenna College, assistant professor, 1996-2003, associate professor of history, 2003-, department chair, 2004-06, associate dean of faculty, 2008-11. Writer. **Publications:** (Ed. and intro.) Writings on Medicine, 1660-1700, 2001; (contrib.) The Streets of London, 1660-1870, 2003; (contrib.) History of Childhood, 2004; (contrib.) The Oxford Dictionary of National Biography, 2004; Birthing the Nation: Sex, Science, and the Conception of Eighteenth-Century Britons, 2005. Contributor to periodicals. **Address:** Department of History, Claremont McKenna College, B-1 Center Ct., North Mills Ave., Claremont, CA 91711, U.S.A. **Online address:** lisa.cody@claremontmckenna.edu

CODY, Liza. British (born England), b. 1944. **Genres:** Mystery/Crime/Suspense, Novels. **Career:** Writer and graphic designer. **Publications:** MYSTERY NOVELS: Dupe, 1980; Bad Company, 1982; Stalker, 1984; Headcase, 1985; Under Contract, 1986; Rift, 1988; Backhand, 1991; Bucket Nut, 1992; Monkey Wrench, 1994; Musclebound, 1997; Gimme More, 2000. OTHERS: Head Case, 1986; (ed. with M.Z. Lewin) 1st Culprit: An Annual of Crime Stories, 1992; (ed. with M.Z. Lewin) 2nd Culprit: An Annual of Crime Stories, 1994; (ed. with M.Z. Lewin and P. Lovesey) Third Culprit, 1996; Lucky Dip and Other Stories, 2003; Mr. Bo, 2009. **Address:** c/o Felicity Bryan, Felicity Bryan Associates, 2A N Parade Ave., Oxford, OX OX2 6PE, England.

CODY, Paul. American (born United States), b. 1953. **Genres:** Novels, Young Adult Fiction. **Career:** Freelance writer, 1976-; Perkins School for the Blind, child-care worker, 1983-85; Cornell University, lecturer in English, 1987-89, visiting professor of writing, 1997-, fiction writer; Cornell Magazine, associate editor and staff writer, 1991-96; Ithaca College, assistant professor of writing, 2004-, professor. **Publications:** NOVELS: The Stolen Child, 1995; Eyes Like Mine, 1996; So Far Gone, 1998; Shooting the Heart, 2004; The Thing He Did, forthcoming. Contributor to periodicals. **Address:** Department of Writing, Ithaca College, 430 Smiddy Hall, 953 Danby Rd., Ithaca, NY 14850-7002, U.S.A. **Online address:** pcody@ithaca.edu

CODY, Robin. American (born United States), b. 1943. **Genres:** Local History/Rural Topics, Travel/Exploration, Young Adult Non-fiction, Natural History. **Career:** Writer. **Publications:** Umbrella Guide to Bicycling the Oregon Coast (travel guide), 1990; Ricochet River (fiction), 1992; Voyage of a Summer Sun: Canoeing the Columbia River (travelogue), 1995; (intro.) Reach of Tide, Ring of History: A Columbia River Voyage, 2000; Another Way the River Has: Taut True Tales of the Northwest, 2010. **Address:** 5003 SE 34th Ave., Portland, OR 97202-4105, U.S.A. **Online address:** robin@robincody.net

COE, Jonathan. (Jonathan Roger Coe). British (born England), b. 1961. **Genres:** Novels, Biography, Young Adult Non-fiction. **Career:** University of Warwick, tutor in English poetry, 1984-85; semi-professional musician, 1985-87; freelance writer and journalist, 1988-. **Publications:** NOVELS: The Accidental Woman, 1987; A Touch of Love, 1989; The Dwarves of Death, 1990; What a Carve Up!, 1994 in US as The Winshaw Legacy, 1995; The House of Sleep, 1997; The Rotters' Club, 2001; The Closed Circle, 2004; The Terrible Privacy of Maxwell Sim, 2010. NON-FICTION: Like a Fiery Elephant: The Story of B.S. Johnson, 2004; 9th and 13th, 2005; The Rain Before It Falls, 2007; (co-author) Ox-Tales: Earth, 2009. BIOGRAPHIES: Humphrey Bogart: Take It and Like It, 1991; James Stewart: Leading Man, 1994. **Address:** c/o Tony Peake, Peake Associates, 14 Grafton Cres., London, GL NW1 8SL, England.

COE, Jonathan Roger. *See* **COE, Jonathan.**

COE, Michael (Douglas). American (born United States), b. 1929. **Genres:** Anthropology/Ethnology, Food And Wine, History, Archaeology/Antiquities. **Career:** University of Tennessee, assistant professor of anthropology, 1958-60; Yale University, instructor, 1960-62, assistant professor, 1962-63, Charles J. MacCurdy Professor of Anthropology, 1963-94, emeritus professor of anthropology, 1994-, Peabody Museum of Natural History, curator, 1968-94, curator emeritus, 1994-; Harvard University, Robert Woods Bliss Collection of Pre-Columbian Art, advisor, 1963-80. Writer. **Publications:** La Victoria: An Early Site on the Pacific Coast of Guatemala, 1961; Mexico, 1962, (with R. Koontz) 6th ed. as Mexico: From the Olmecs to the Aztecs, 2008; The Jaguar's Children: Preclassic Central Mexico, 1965; The Maya, 1966, 7th ed., 2005; An Early Stone Pectoral from Southeastern Mexico, 1966; (with E.P. Benson) Three Maya Relief Panels at Dumbarton Oaks, 1966; (with K.V. Flannery) Early Cultures and Human Ecology in South Coastal Guatemala, 1967; America's First Civilization: Discovering the Olmec, 1968; Map of San Lorenzo, An Olmec Site in Veracruz, Mexico, 1968; (intro.) Pre-Columbian Mexican Miniatures: The Josef and Anni Albers Collection, 1970; The Maya Scribe and His World, 1973; Classic Maya Pottery at Dumbarton Oaks, 1975; The Lords of the Underworld: Masterpieces of Classic Maya Ceramics, 1978; (with R.A. Diehl) In the Land of the Olmec, 1980; Olmec & Their Neighbors: Essays in Memory of Matthew W. Stirling, 1981; Old Gods and Young Heroes: The Pearlman Collection of Maya Ceramics, 1982; (with G. Whittaker) Aztec Sorcerers in Seventeenth Century Mexico: The Treatise on Superstitions by Hernando Ruiz de Alarcon, 1982; (with D. Snow and E. Benson) Atlas of Ancient America, 1986; (with R. Sieber and D. Newton) African, Pacific, and Pre-Columbian Art in the Indiana University Art Museum, 1986; (contrib.) Swords and Hilt Weapons, 1989; Messico fino alla conquista spagnola, 1989; Breaking the Maya Code, 1992, rev. ed., 1999; (with S.D. Coe) The True History of Chocolate, 1996, rev. ed., 2007; (ed.) The Olmec World: Ritual and Rulership, 1996; (with J. Kerr) The Art of the Maya Scribe, 1998; (with M.V. Stone) Reading the Maya Glyphs, 2001; Angkor and the Khmer Civilization, 2003; Final Report: An Archaeologist Excavates his Past, 2006; Line of Forts: Historical Archaeology on the Colonial Frontier of Massachusetts, 2006; (with J. Stubbs) Preah Khan Monastic Complex, Angkor, Cambodia, 2011. **Address:** Department of Anthropology, Yale University, 10 Sachem St., New Haven, CT 06511, U.S.A. **Online address:** olmecc@aol.com

COELHO, Ivo. Indian (born India), b. 1958. **Genres:** Novels, Essays, Philosophy. **Career:** Salesian Institute of Philosophy, teacher, 1981-83, 1988-90, 1994-2002, principal, 1988-90, rector, 1994-2002, lecturer and chair of gnoseology and metaphysics, 2000-, librarian, 2008-, reader, 2009-; Province of St. Francis Xavier of the Salesians, provincial, 2002-08; Society of St. Francis de Sales, Roman Catholic priest. Writer. **Publications:** Hermeneutics and Method: The Universal Viewpoint in Bernard Lonergan, 2001; (ed. with J. Kuttianimattathil) In One Salutation to Thee: A Collection of Prayers and Readings from the Various Religious Traditions, 2002; (ed.) Brahman and Person: Essays, 2009. Contributor to books and periodicals. **Address:** Salesian Institute of Philosophy, Don Bosco Marg, Nashik, MH 422 005, India. **Online address:** provincialoffice@vsnl.com

COEN, Cheré Dastugue. *See* **CLAIRE, Cherie.**

COERS, Donald V. American (born United States), b. 1941. **Genres:** Literary Criticism And History, Essays, Military/Defense/Arms Control, History, Young Adult Fiction. **Career:** Sam Houston State University, professor of English, 1969-92, coordinator of graduate studies, 1992-95, associate vice president for academic affairs, 1995-2000; Angelo State University, vice president for academic affairs, 2000-, provost and vice president of academic and student affairs. Writer. **Publications:** John Steinbeck as Propagandist: The Moon Is Down Goes to War, 1991; (ed. with R.J. Demott and P.D. Ruffin) After The Grapes of Wrath: Essays on John Steinbeck in Honor of Tetsumaro Hayashi, 1995; John Steinbeck Goes to War: The Moon is Down as Propaganda, 2006. **Address:** Angelo State University, A 039B, San Angelo, TX 76909-0001, U.S.A. **Online address:** don.coers@angelo.edu

COETZEE, J(ohn) M(ichael). Australian/South African (born South Africa), b. 1940. **Genres:** Novels, Novellas/Short Stories, Translations, Young Adult Fiction, Young Adult Non-fiction, Essays. **Career:** International Business Machine Corp., applications programmer, 1962-63; International Computers Ltd., systems programmer, 1964-65; State University of New York, assistant professor, 1968-71, Butler professor of English, 1984, 1986; University of Cape Town, lecturer in English, 1972-83, professor of general literature, 1983-99, distinguished professor of literature, 1999-2001, professor emeritus, 2002-; Johns Hopkins University, Hinkley professor of English, 1986, 1989; Harvard University, visiting professor of English, 1991; University of Chicago, professor of social thought, 1998-2003; Stanford University, faculty; University of Adelaide, Department of English, honorary research fellow. Writer. **Publications:** Dusklands, 1974; (trans. and intro.) M. Emants, A Posthumous Confession, 1976; In the Heart of the Country in US as From the Heart of the Country, 1977; Waiting for the Barbarians, 1980; (trans.) W. Stockenstrom, The Expedition to the Baobab Tree, 1983; The Life and Times of Michael K, 1983; Foe, 1986; (ed. with A. Brink) A Land Apart: A Contemporary South African Reader, 1987; White Writing: On the Culture of Letters in South Africa, 1988; Age of Iron, 1990; Doubling the Point: Essays and Interviews, 1992; The Master of Petersburg, 1994; (with G. Swift, J. Lanchester and I. Jack) Food: The Vital Stuff, 1995; Giving Offense: Essays on Censorship, 1996; Boyhood: Scenes from Provincial Life, 1997; (with B. Reichblum) What Is Realism?, 1997; Politics, Leadership, and Justice, 1998; Disgrace, 1999; (co-author) The Lives of Animals, 1999; (with D. Cameron and C. Christov-Bakargiev) William Kentridge, 1999; Stranger Shores: Literary Essays, 1986-1999, 2001; The Humanities in Africa/Die Geisteswissenschaften in Afrika, 2001; (contrib.) Fifty-One Years, 2001; (intro.) The Confusions of Young Törless, 2001; Youth: Scenes from Provincial Life, 2002; Letter of Elizabeth, Lady Chandos, to Francis Bacon, 2002; Elizabeth Costello, 2003; (trans. and intro.) Landscape with Rowers: Poetry from the Netherlands, 2004; African Compass: New Writing from Southern Africa, 2005; Slow Man, 2005; African Road: New Writing from Southern Africa 2006, 2006; African Pens: New Writing from Southern Africa 2007, 2007; Diary of a Bad Year, 2007; Inner Workings: Literary Essays, 2000-2005, 2007; Dance of the Freaky Green Gold, 2009; Summertime: Fiction, 2009; (contrib.) African Pens 2011: New Writing from southern Africa, 2011. **Address:** David Higham Associates Ltd., 5-8 Lower John St., Golden Sq., London, GL W1F 9HA, England.

COFER, Judith Ortiz. American/Puerto Rican (born Puerto Rico), b. 1952. **Genres:** Novels, Poetry, Autobiography/Memoirs, Young Adult Fiction, Novellas/Short Stories. **Career:** Broward Community College, adjunct instructor in English, 1978-80, instructor in Spanish, 1979; Palm Beach Junior College, adjunct instructor, 1978-80; University of Miami, instructor in Spanish, 1979, lecturer in English, 1980-84; University of Georgia, instructor in English, 1984-87, Georgia Center for Continuing Education, instructor in English, 1987-88, associate professor of creative writing, 1992-97, professor of English and creative writing, 1997-99, Franklin professor of English and creative writing, 1999-2006, Regents' and Franklin professor of English and creative writing, 2006-; Macon College, instructor in English, 1988-89; Mercer University College, special programs coordinator, 1990; University of Michigan, visiting professor; University of Minnesota, visiting professor, Arizona University, visiting professor. Writer. **Publications:** Reaching for the Mainland (poetry), 1984; Peregrina, 1986; Terms of Survival: Poems, 1987; (co-author) Triple Crown: Chicano, Puerto Rican and Cuban-American Poetry, 1987; The Line of the Sun: A Novel, 1989; Silent Dancing: A Partial Remembrance of a Puerto Rican Childhood, 1990; The Latin Deli (prose and poetry), 1993; An Island Like You: Stories of the Barrio, 1995; Reaching for the Mainland & Selected New Poems, 1995; Year of Our Revolution, 1998; (ed. with M. Kallet) Sleeping With One Eye Open, 1999; Woman in Front of the Sun, 2000; (ed. and intro.) Riding Low on the Streets of Gold, 2003; Meaning of Consuelo, 2003; Call Me Maria: A Novel, 2004; Love Story Beginning in Spanish, 2005; If I Could Fly, 2011; A bailar!, 2011; Lessons from a Writer's Life, 2011. **Address:** Department of English, Franklin College, The University of Georgia, Park Hall 130, Athens, GA 30602, U.S.A. **Online address:** jocofer@uga.edu

COFFEY, Brian. *See* **KOONTZ, Dean R(ay).**

COFFEY, John Robert David. British (born England), b. 1969. **Genres:** Politics/Government, Social Sciences, Humanities. **Career:** University of Leicester, School of Historical Studies, professor of early modern history. Writer. **Publications:** Politics, Religion and the British Revolutions: The Mind of Samuel Rutherford, 1997; Persecution and Toleration in Protestant England, 1558-1689, 2000; John Goodwin and the Puritan Revolution: Religion and Intellectual Change in Seventeenth-Century England, 2006; (ed. and intro. with P.C.H. Lim) The Cambridge Companion to Puritanism, 2008; (ed. with A. Chapman and B.S. Gregory) Seeing Things Their Way: Intellectual History and The Return of Religion, 2009. Contributor to books and periodicals. **Address:** School of Historical Studies, University of Leicester, 713 Attenborough, University Rd., Leicester, LE1 7RH, England. **Online address:** jrdc1@le.ac.uk

COFFEY, Michael. British (born England), b. 1926. **Genres:** Classics, Language/Linguistics, Reference. **Career:** University College London, assistant lecturer, 1951-54, lecturer, 1954-66, senior lecturer, 1966-76, reader in Greek and Latin, 1977-91, research fellow, 1991-, emeritus reader. Writer. **Publications:** Roman Satire, 1976, 2nd ed., 1989; (ed. with R. Mayer) Seneca: Phaedra, 1990. **Address:** Department of Greek and Latin, University College London, Gower St., London, GL WC1E 6BT, England.

COFFIN, Tristram Potter. *See* Obituaries.

COFFMAN, Edward M. American (born United States), b. 1929. **Genres:** History, Military/Defense/Arms Control. **Career:** Memphis State University, instructor, 1957-58, assistant professor of history, 1959-60; G.C. Marshall Research Foundation, research associate, 1960-61; University of Wisconsin, Department of History, assistant professor, 1961-66, associate professor, 1966-68, professor of history, 1968-92, professor emeritus, 1992-; Kansas State University, visiting professor, 1969-70; U.S. Military Academy, visiting professor, 1977-78; U.S. Air Force Academy, visiting professor, 1982-83; U.S. Army Military History Institute, visiting professor, 1986-87; U.S. Army Command and General Staff College, visiting professor, 1990-91; U.S. Army War College, visiting professor. Writer. **Publications:** The Hilt of the Sword: The Career of Peyton C. March, 1966; The War to End All Wars: The American Military Experience in World War I, 1968, 3rd ed., 1998; Lincoln as Military Strategist, 1968; The Young Officer in the Old Army, 1976; The Old Army: A Portrait of the American Army in Peacetime, 1784-1898, 1986; (contrib.) Cantigny at Seventy-five, 1994; The Regulars: The American Army, 1898-1941, 2004. **Address:** Department of History, University of Wisconsin, 3211 Mosse Humanities Bldg., 455 N Park St., Madison, WI 53706-1483, U.S.A. **Online address:** maccoffman@aol.com

COGAN, Brian A. American (born United States), b. 1967. **Genres:** Politics/Government, Music. **Career:** Ferco-Video Rental Co., assistant video manager, 1989-91; BIC Productions, freelance producer, 1989; New York University, School of Education, teaching fellow and instructor, 1991, Arthur L. Carter Journalism Institute, faculty; Radiant Multimedia, executive producer, 1993-96; Puddle Cruiser, line producer, 1996; City University of New York, College of Staten Island, adjunct faculty, 1998-; Molloy College, assistant professor of communication arts, associate professor of communication arts and sciences. Writer and musician. **Publications:** The Encyclopedia of Punk Music and Culture, 2006; (ed. with T. Kelso) Mosh the Polls: Youth Voters, Popular Culture, and Democratic Engagement, 2008; (with T. Kelso) Encyclopedia of Politics, the Media, and Popular Culture, 2008; (with W. Phillips) Encyclopedia of Heavy Metal Music, 2009; (ed.) Deconstructing South Park, 2012. Contributor of articles to books and periodicals. Works appear in anthologies. **Address:** Department of Communication Arts and Sciences, Molloy College, 1000 Hempstead Ave., Rockville Centre, NY 11571-5002, U.S.A.

COGAN, Marc. American (born United States) **Genres:** Adult Non-fiction, History. **Career:** Wayne State University, College of Liberal Arts, Department of Humanities, associate professor, professor. Writer. **Publications:** The Human Thing: The Speeches and Principles of Thucydides History, 1981; The Design in the Wax: The Structure of the Divine Comedy and Its Meaning, 1999. Contributor to periodicals. **Address:** Department of Humanities, College of Liberal Arts, Wayne State University, 5057 Woodward Ave., Ste. 11205, Detroit, MI 48202, U.S.A. **Online address:** aa4771@wayne.edu

COGCAVE, Serge O. *See* **CEVASCO, G(eorge) A(nthony).**

COGGESHALL, Nancy. American (born United States), b. 1941. **Genres:** Biography. **Career:** Harrowsmith magazine, contributing editor. **Publications:** Gila Country Legend: The Life and Times of Quentin Hulse (biography), 2009. Works appear in anthologies. Contributor to periodicals. **Address:** c/o Will Lippincott, Lippincott Massie McQuilkin, 27 W 20th St., Ste. 305, New York, NY 10011, U.S.A. **Online address:** gilacountrylegend@gmail.com

COGLIANO, Francis D. Scottish/American (born United States), b. 1964. **Genres:** History, Politics/Government, Humanities. **Career:** La Sainte Union College, senior lecturer, 1992; University of Edinburgh, lecturer, 1997-2001, senior lecturer, 2001-03, reader, 2003-07, professor, 2007-. Writer. **Publications:** No King, No Popery: Anti- Catholicism in Revolutionary New England, 1995; Revolutionary America, 1763-1815: A Political History, 1999, 2nd ed., 2009; American Maritime Prisoners in the Revolutionary War: The Captivity of William Russell, 2001; Thomas Jefferson: Reputation and Legacy, 2006; (ed. with S. Manning) The Atlantic Enlightenment, 2008. Contributor of articles to journals. **Address:** School of History, Classics, and Archaeology, University of Edinburgh, William Robertson Bldg., 50 George Sq., Edinburgh, EH8 9JY, Scotland. **Online address:** f.cogliano@ed.ac.uk

COHEN, Aaron. American/Canadian (born Canada), b. 1976. **Genres:** Autobiography/Memoirs. **Career:** Israeli Defense Forces, staff, 1995-98; Security 360/IMS Counter-Terror School, founder and managing director, 2001-. Writer, counterterrorism and security consultant, entrepreneur and trainer. **Publications:** Brotherhood of Warriors (memoir), 2008. **Address:** Security 360/IMS Counter-Terror School, 269 S Beverly Dr., Ste. 987, Beverly Hills, CA 90212-3851, U.S.A. **Online address:** info@ims-security.com

COHEN, Allan R(ay). American (born United States), b. 1938. **Genres:** Business/Trade/Industry. **Career:** Harvard University, Harvard Business School, Ford Foundation, Philippines research associate, 1961-62, India consultant, 1963-65; University of New Hampshire, Whittemore School of Business and Economics, assistant professor, J.R. Carter professor of management, 1966-82, MBA Program, director, 1974-79; Babson College, professor of management, W. Carpenter professor of management, 1982-91, vice president of academic affairs and dean of faculty 1991-98, Edward A Madden pistinguished Professor of global leadership, 1998-, interim graduate dean, 2007-09; Institute of Social Studies, visiting professor. Writer. **Publications:** Tradition, Change, and Conflict in Indian Family Business, 1974; (co-author) Effective Behavior in Organizations: Learning from the Interplay of Cases, Concepts, and Student Experiences, 1976, 7th ed. (with S.L. Fink), 2001; (with H. Gadon) Alternative Work Schedules: Integrating Individual and Organizational Needs, 1978; (with D.L. Bradford) Managing for Excellence: The Leadership Guide to Developing High Performance in Contemporary Organizations, 1984; (with D.L. Bradford) Influence without Authority, 1990, 2nd ed., 2005; (ed.) The Portable MBA in Management, 1993, 2nd ed., 2002; (with D.L. Bradford) Power Up: Transforming Organizations through Shared Leadership, 1998. **Address:** Babson College, 231 Forest St., Babson Park, MA 02457-0310, U.S.A. **Online address:** cohen@babson.edu

COHEN, Alvin. American (born United States), b. 1931. **Genres:** Economics, Money/Finance. **Career:** Universidad Nacional de San Marcos, Fulbright professor, 1961-62; Lehigh University, assistant professor, 1962-65, associate professor, 1965-71, professor of economics, 1971-, now professor emeritus; University Nacional de El Salvador, visiting professor, 1962; Universidad Catolica de Cordoba, Fulbright professor, 1971; Universidad Francisco Marroquin, visiting professor, 1980; Middle Atlantic Council for Latin American Studies, managing editor, 1991-94, secretary and treasurer; Writer. **Publications:** Economic Change in Chile, 1929-1959, 1960; Ensayos sobre la teoria del desarrollo economico, 1965; Desarrollo economico, 1971; (ed. with F.R. Gunter) The Colombian Economy: Issues of Trade and Development, 1992. Contributor to books and journals. **Address:** Lehigh University, 37 Rauch Business Ctr., 621 Taylor St., Bethlehem, PA 18015, U.S.A.

COHEN, Amy. American (born United States), b. 1966?. **Genres:** Biography. **Career:** New York Observer, dating columnist; New York Central, dating correspondent. Script writer and television shows producer. **Publications:** The Late Bloomer's Revolution: A Memoir, 2007. **Address:** Hyperion Books, 114 5th Ave., New York, NY 10011-5604, U.S.A. **Online address:** thelatebloomersrevolution@gmail.com

COHEN, Andrew (Z.). Canadian (born Canada), b. 1955. **Genres:** Documentaries/Reportage, History, Social Sciences, Young Adult Fiction. **Career:** Ottawa Citizen, staff writer, 1977-80; United Press Intl., parliamentary correspondent, 1980-84, editor, foreign desk, 1983; Financial Post, political writer, 1984-87, foreign editor, 1987-90, foreign affairs columnist, 1989-93, senior editor and columnist 1990-91, national affairs columnist, 1993-94; Saturday Night Magazine, national political correspondent, 1993-94; The Editorial Board, national correspondent; The Globe and Mail, national correspondent, 1994-; University of Cambridge, Centre of International Studies, visiting fellow; Carleton University, associate professor. **Publications:** (Ed.) Patrick Gossage, Close to the Charisma, 1986; A Deal Undone: The Making and Breaking of the Meech Lake Accord, 1990; (ed. with J.L. Granatstein) Trudeau's Shadow: The Life and Legacy of Pierre Elliott Trudea, 1998; While Canada Slept: How We Lost Our Place in the World, 2003; Unfinished Canadian: The People We Are, 2007. Contributor of articles to periodicals. **Address:** Carleton University, 1125 Colonel By Dr., Ottawa, ON K1S 5B6, Canada. **Online address:** andrew_cohen@carleton.ca

COHEN, Avner. American/Israeli (born Israel), b. 1951?. **Genres:** Military/

Defense/Arms Control, Humanities, History, Social Sciences, Philosophy. **Career:** Tel Aviv University, philosophy instructor, 1983-91; Harvard University, Kennedy School of Government, research fellow, 1987-88; Massachusetts Institute of Technology, Middle East at the Security Studies Program, Project on Nuclear Arms Control, co-director, 1990-95; United States Institute of Peace, senior fellow, 1997-98, 2007-08; Hebrew University, Forchheimer visiting professor, 2005; George Washington University, National Security Archive, senior research fellow; Monterey Institute of International Studies, James Martin Center for Nonproliferation Studies, senior fellow, 2010-. Writer, philosopher and historian. **Publications:** (Ed. with S. Lee) Nuclear Weapons and the Future of Humanity: The Fundamental Questions, 1986; Enoshut be-tsel ha-aṭom, 1987; (ed. with M. Dascal) The Institution of Philosophy: A Discipline in Crisis?, 1989; (with M. Miller) Nuclear Shadows in the Middle East: Prospects for Arms Control in the Wake of the Gulf Crisis, 1990; Sugyah ha-garinit ṿe-tahalikh ha-shalom, 1995; Israel and the Bomb, 1998; Ha-ṭabu ha-aḥaron: sod ha-matsav ha-garini shel Yiśrael u-mah she-tsarikh la-aśot ito, 2005; Worst-kept Secret: Israel's Bargain with the Bomb, 2010. Contributor to journals. **Address:** James Martin Center for Nonproliferation Studies, Monterey Institute of International Studies, 1400 K St. NW, Ste. 450, Washington, DC 20005-2423, U.S.A. **Online address:** avner.cohen@miis.edu

COHEN, Benyamin. American (born United States), b. 1975. **Genres:** Theology/Religion. **Career:** Torah from Dixie, founder and writer, 1994; Atlanta Jewish Times, writer and editor; Fulton County Daily Report, special sections editor; Jewsweek.com, founder and editor, 2001-05; Atlanta Jewish Life, editor, 2004; Jewishcontent.com, founder and editor; Mother Nature Network, content director. Writer. **Publications:** Torah from Dixie: Intriguing Thoughts on the Weekly Torah Portion and Jewish Festivals, 1997; My Jesus Year: A Rabbi's Son Wanders the Bible Belt in Search of His Own Faith, 2008. **Online address:** theauthor@myjesusyear.com

COHEN, Bernard. Australian/American (born United States), b. 1963?. **Genres:** Novels, Children's Fiction, Social Sciences, Self Help. **Career:** Peckham Library, writer-in-residence; Sir John Soane's Museum, writer-in-residence; The Writing Workshop, founder, 2006-. **Publications:** Tourism, 1992; The Blindman's Hat, 1997; Snowdome, 1998; Hardly Beach Weather, 2002; Paul Needs Specs, 2003. **Address:** The Writing Workshop, PO Box 223, Annandale, NW 2038, Australia. **Online address:** bernard@hermes.net.au

COHEN, Cary. American (born United States), b. 1935. **Genres:** Administration/Management, Business/Trade/Industry, Economics, Industrial Relations, Law, Money/Finance. **Career:** Burns & Roe Inc., corporate director of contracts, 1968-75; Virginia Power, director of contracts, 1975-84; Caldwell Consulting Associates, senior partner, 1984-; Veterans Radio and Television Guild, director of Virginia operation, 1990-2002; University of Virginia, adjunct faculty. Writer. **Publications:** The Manual of Financial Policies and Procedures, 1985; The Manual of Personnel Policies and Procedures, 1986; The Manual of Sales and Marketing Policies and Procedures, 1987; (co-author) Federal Contract Management, 1989; Effective Communication in Contract Administration: Course Manual, 1990; Complete Company Policies and Procedures Manual, 1992; Effective Contract Administration: The Complete Handbook and Guide, 1997; The World's Biggest Government Contracting Dictionary, forthcoming; Who Murdered Thomas Jefferson?, forthcoming. **Address:** Caldwell Consulting Associates, PO Box 29143, Richmond, VA 23242-0143, U.S.A. **Online address:** cary@fedmedia.com

COHEN, Daniel A. American (born United States), b. 1957. **Genres:** History, Literary Criticism And History, Social Sciences, Popular Culture, Sociology, Women's Studies And Issues. **Career:** The College of William and Mary, Commonwealth Center for the Study of American Culture, visiting assistant professor of history and postdoctoral fellow, 1988-90; Florida International University, assistant professor of history, 1990-94, associate professor of history, 1994-2004; Case Western Reserve University, associate professor of history, 2004-. Writer. **Publications:** Pillars of Salt, Monuments of Grace: New England Crime Literature and the Origins of American Popular Culture, 1674-1860, 1993; (ed. and intro.) The Female Marine and Related Works: Narratives of Cross-Dressing and Urban Vice in America's Early Republic, 1997. Contributor to journals. **Address:** Department of History, Case Western Reserve University, 11201 Euclid Ave., Cleveland, OH 44106-7068, U.S.A. **Online address:** dac37@case.edu

COHEN, Daniel J. American (born United States), b. 1968?. **Genres:** History, Theology/Religion, Information Science/Computers. **Career:** George Mason University, postdoctoral fellow, 2001-03, assistant professor, 2003-07, associate professor, 2008-, Center for History and New Media, director of research projects, 2001-, ECHO, co-managing director. Writer. **Publications:** (With R. Rosenzweig) Digital History: A Guide to Gathering, Preserving and Presenting the Past on the Web, 2006; Equations from God: Pure Mathematics and Victorian Faith, 2007. Contributor to books, periodicals and journals. **Address:** Department of History and Art History, George Mason University, MSN 3G1, 4400 University Dr., Fairfax, VA 22030, U.S.A. **Online address:** dcohen@gmu.edu

COHEN, David William. American (born United States), b. 1943?. **Genres:** History, Politics/Government, Social Sciences. **Career:** Johns Hopkins University, assistant professor of history, 1968-71, associate professor of history, 1971-76; professor of anthropology and history, 1976-77, 1987-89; Northwestern University, professor of anthropology and history, 1989-93, Program on International Cooperation in Africa, director, 1989-93, Program of African Studies, director, 1989-93, Institute for Advanced Study and Research in the African Humanities, founder and secretary, 1990-93, Program of African Studies, director, 1990-93; University of Michigan, Department of History, professor of history, 1993-, Lemuel A. Johnson collegiate professor of history, associate chair, 2002-, now professor emeritus, Department of Anthropology, professor of anthropology, 1993-, Lemuel A. Johnson Collegiate professor of African anthropology, now professor emeritus, International Institute, director and founder, 1993-99. Writer. **Publications:** The Historical Tradition of Busoga, Mukama and Kintu, 1972; (ed. and intro. with J.P. Greene) Neither Slave nor Free: The Freedman of African Descent in the Slave Societies of the New World, 1972; Womunafu's Bunafu: A Study of Authority in a Nineteenth-Century African Community, 1977; (contrib.) Reliving the Past: The Worlds of Social History, 1985; (with E.S.A. Odhiambo) Siaya: The Historical Anthropology of an African Landscape, 1989; (with E.S.A. Odhiambo) Burying SM: The Politics of Knowledge and the Sociology of Power in Africa, 1992; The Combing of History, 1994; (ed. with L. White and S.F. Miescher) African Words, African Voices: Critical Practices in Oral History, 2001; (with E.S.A. Odhiambo) The Risks of Knowledge: Investigations into the Death of the Hon. Minister John Robert Ouko in Kenya, 1990, 2004; (ed. with M.D. Kennedy) Responsibility in Crisis: Knowledge Politics and Global Publics, 2005. **Address:** Department of History, University of Michigan, 1029 Tisch Hall, 435 S State St., Ann Arbor, MI 48109-1003, U.S.A. **Online address:** dwcohen@umich.edu

COHEN, Debra Nussbaum. American (born United States), b. 1964?. **Genres:** Human Relations/Parenting, Marketing, Popular Culture, Theology/Religion, Women's Studies And Issues. **Career:** Jewish Telegraphic Agency, staff writer, 1990-2000; New York Jewish Week, staff writer, 2000-08; Drisha Institute for Jewish Education, arts fellow, 2008-09; The Forward, contributing editor, 2009-. **Publications:** Celebrating Your New Jewish Daughter: Creating Jewish Ways to Welcome Baby Girls into the Covenant-New and Traditional Ceremonies, 2001. Contributor to periodicals. **Address:** 221 Prospect Pl., Brooklyn, NY 11238, U.S.A. **Online address:** dncnews@optonline.net

COHEN, Elizabeth S. (Elizabeth Storr Cohen). Canadian (born Canada), b. 1946?. **Genres:** Social Sciences. **Career:** York University, associate professor of history and humanities, chair of history. Writer. **Publications:** (co-author) Rinascimento Al Femminile, 1991; (with T.V. Cohen) Words and Deeds in Renaissance Rome: Trials before the Papal Magistrates, 1993; (with T.V. Cohen) Daily Life in Renaissance Italy, 1993. Contributor to books and journals. **Address:** York University, 262 Vanier College, 4700 Keele St., Toronto, ON M3J 1P3, Canada.

COHEN, Elizabeth Storr. *See* **COHEN, Elizabeth S.**

COHEN, Elliot D. American (born United States), b. 1951. **Genres:** Philosophy. **Career:** Providence College, lecturer in philosophy of law, 1974-77; University of Florida, Humanities Perspectives on the Professions, fellow, 1977-78, instructor in behavioral studies, 1978-79; Florida Atlantic University, assistant professor of philosophy, 1979-80; Indian River Community College (now Indian River State College), Department of Humanities, assistant professor, 1980-82, associate professor, 1983-88, professor of philosophy, 1989-, chair, 1999-, School of Nursing, faculty of medical ethics for nurses, 1981-; Barry University, adjunct professor of philosophy, 1986-92; Institute of Critical Thinking, director, 1990-; Indian River Memorial Hospital, medical ethics consultant, 1993-; Port St. Lucie Medical Center, medical ethics consultant, 1994-. Writer. **Publications:** Making Value Judgements: Principles of Sound Reasoning, 1985; Improving Your Thinking and Decision Making Skills: A Handbook of Fallacies, 1990; Caution: Faulty Thinking Can Be Harmful to Your Happiness: Logic for Everyday Living, 1991, 2nd ed., 1994; (with G.S. Cohen) The Virtuous Therapist: Ethical Practice of Counseling and Psychotherapy, 1999; What Would Aristotle Do?: Self-Control through the Power of Reason, 2003; The New Rational Therapy: Thinking Your Way to Serenity, Success, and Profound Happiness, 2007; (with B.W. Fraser) The Last Days of Democracy: How Big Media and Power-Hungry Government are Turning America into a Dictatorship, 2007; Critical Thinking Unleashed, 2009; Mass Surveillance and State Control: The Total Information Awareness Project, 2010; Dutiful Worrier: How to Stop Compulsive Worry Without Feeling Guilty, 2011. EDITOR: Philosophers at Work: An Introduction to the Issues and Practical Uses of Philosophy, 1989, 2nd ed. as Philosophers at Work: Issues and Practice of Philosophy, 2000; Philosophical Issues in Journalism, 1992; (with M. Davis) AIDS: Crisis in Professional Ethics, 1994; (with D. Elliott) Journalism Ethics: A Reference Handbook, 1997; News Incorporated: Corporate Media Ownership and Its Threat to Democracy, 2005; (with M. Davis and F.A. Elliston) Ethics and the Legal Profession, 2009. Works appear in anthologies. Contributor to journals. **Address:** Department of Humanities, Indian River State College, Rm. R204, 3209 Virginia Ave., Fort Pierce, FL 34981, U.S.A. **Online address:** ecohen@irsc.edu

COHEN, Gary P. American (born United States), b. 1952. **Genres:** Theatre, Film. **Career:** Cranford High School, theater director, 1987-; Plays in the Park, Middlesex County Department of Parks and Recreation, producing director; Celebration Playhouse, co-founder; Bickford Theatre, staff; Forum Theatre, staff. Writer. **Publications:** Community Theater Handbook: A Complete Guide to Organizing and Running a Community Theater, 2003; The Theater Director's Primer, 2005. **Address:** Middlesex County Department of Parks and, Recreation, Plays in the Park, 1 Pine Dr., PO Box 661, Edison, NJ 08837, U.S.A. **Online address:** gary@playsinthepark.com

COHEN, Getzel M. American (born United States), b. 1942. **Genres:** History. **Career:** University of Cincinnati, professor of classics, 1971-; University of Leuven, visiting professor, 1981; École Pratique des Hautes Études, visiting professor, 2000; École Normale SupÉrieure, visiting professor, 2003. Writer. **Publications:** The Seleucid Colonies: Studies in Founding, Administration and Organization, 1978; The Hellenistic Settlements in Europe, the Islands and Asia Minor, 1995; Breaking Ground: Pioneering Women Archaeologists, 2004; The Hellenistic Settlements in Syria, the Red Sea Basin and North Africa, 2006. Contributor of essays, articles to periodicals. **Address:** Department of Classics, University of Cincinnati, PO Box 210226, Cincinnati, OH 45221-0226, U.S.A. **Online address:** getzel.cohen@uc.edu

COHEN, Henry. American (born United States), b. 1933. **Genres:** Criminology/True Crime, Demography, Economics, Humanities, History, Psychology, Politics/Government, Biography, Biography. **Career:** Ohio State University, instructor in history, 1962-64; California State University, assistant professor of history, 1964-69; Loyola University, assistant professor, 1969-71, associate professor, 1971-80, professor, 1980-93. Writer. **Publications:** (Contrib.) The Frontier in American Development: Essays in Honor of Paul Wallace Gates, 1969; Business and Politics in America from the Age of Jackson to the Civil War, the Career Biography of W.W. Corcoran, 1971; Brutal Justice: Ordeal of an American City, 1980. EDITOR: Criminal Justice History: An International Annual, 1980-83; (and intro.) The Public Enemy, 1981. **Address:** 491 Utah St., San Francisco, CA 94110-1434, U.S.A.

COHEN, Hubert I. American (born United States), b. 1930. **Genres:** Film, Biography, Art/Art History. **Career:** University of Michigan, College of Engineering, instructor in English, 1965-70, Department of Humanities, assistant professor, 1970-75, associate professor, 1975-85, professor, 1995-, film and video program director, 1978-80, Residential College, professor of screen arts and cultures, 1985-. Writer. **Publications:** Ingmar Bergman: The Art of Confession, 1993. Contributor of articles to periodicals. **Address:** Residential College, University of Michigan, RC-229 Tyler, E Quadrangle, 701 E University, Ann Arbor, MI 48109-1245, U.S.A. **Online address:** hicohen@umich.edu

COHEN, Jared. American (born United States), b. 1981. **Genres:** Civil Liberties/Human Rights, Military/Defense/Arms Control, Adult Non-fiction, Children's Fiction. **Career:** U.S. Department of State, Policy Planning, staff, 2006-; Google Ideas, director. Writer. **Publications:** Children of Jihad: A Young American's Travels among the Youth of the Middle East, 2007; One Hundred Days of Silence: America and the Rwanda Genocide, 2007. Contributor to periodicals. **Address:** Rowman & Littlefield Publishers Inc., 4501 Forbes Blvd., Ste. 200, Lanham, MD 20706, U.S.A.

COHEN, Jason. American (born United States), b. 1967. **Genres:** Humor/Satire, Social Sciences. **Career:** WNUR Radio, music director, 1987-89; Fire Records, co-manager, 1989-90; journalist, 1990-. **Publications:** (With M. Krugman) Generation Ecch!: The Backlash Starts Here, 1994. Contributor to periodicals. **Address:** Abigail Rose, International Creative Management, 40 W 57th St., New York, NY 10019, U.S.A.

COHEN, Jean-Louis. American/French (born France), b. 1949. **Genres:** Architecture. **Career:** French Institute of Architecture, director 1998-; New York University Institute of Fine Arts, Sheldon H. Solow professor in the history of architecture, professor, Sheldon H. Solow chair in the history of architecture. Historian and writer. **Publications:** (With M. De Michelis and M. Tafuri) URSS, 1917-1978: La ville, l'architecture, 1979; (ed. with O. Seyler and B. Fortier) Architecture et politiques Sociales 1900-1940: Les principes architecturaux à leage du réformisme, 1981; La recherche en architecture: un bilan international: Actes du colloque rencontres, recherche, architecture, Marseille, Nancy, Nantes, Paris, 12-13-14 Juin 1984, 1986; Le Corbusier et la mystique de l'URSS: Théories et projets pour Moscou, 1928-1936, 1987; (ed. with B. Fortier) Paris: La ville et ses projets: Ouvrage publié à l'occasion de l'exposition permanente Paris, la ville et ses projets, Inaugurée le 13 Décembre 1988 au pavillon de l'arsenal, 1988; (with A. Lortie) Des fortifs au périf: Paris, les seuils de la ville, 1991; (ed. with H. Damisch) Américanisme et Modernité: L'Idéal Américain Dans L'Architecture, 1993; André Lurcat: 1894-1970: Autocritique d'un moderne, 1995; Scenes of the World to Come: European Architecture and the American Challenge, 1893-1960, 1995; (ed.) Les Années 30: L'Architecture et les arts de l'éspace entre industrie et nostalgie, 1997; (with M. Eleb) Casablanca: Mythes et figures d'une aventure urbaine, 1998; (with M. Eleb) Paris Architecture, 1900-2000, 2000; (with M. Eleb) Une cité à Chaillot: Avant-première: La cité de l'architecture et du patrimoine, 2001; (with M. Eleb) Casablanca: Colonial Myths and Architectural Ventures, 2002; (ed. with J. Abram and G. Lambert) Encyclopédie Perret, 2002; (ed. with N. Oulebsir and Y. Kanoun) Alger: Paysage urbain et architectures, 1800-2000, 2003; Le Corbusier, 1887-1965: The Lyricism of Architecture in the Machine Age, 2004; Le Corbusier, La planéte comme Chantier, 2005; Urban Structures: Yves Lion, 2005; Above Paris: The Aerial Survey of Roger Henrard, 2006; Le tour de Paris: Les promenades aériennes de Roger Henrard, 2006; (ed. with G.M. Moeller) Liquid Stone: New Architecture in Concrete, 2006; (ed. with G.M. Moeller) Architectures du Béton: Nouvelles Vagues, Nouvelles Recherches, 2006; Ludwig Mies van der Rohe, 2007; Mies van der Rohe, 2007; (intro.) Toward an architecture, 2007; Between Earth and Heaven: the Architecture of John Lautner, 2008; France ou Allemagne?: un livre inédit de Le Corbusier, 2009; New York, 2010; Architecture en Uniforme: Projeter et Construire Pour la Seconde Guerre mondiale, 2011. **Address:** New York University, Duke House, 1 E 78 St., 325, New York, NY 10075-0119, U.S.A. **Online address:** jlc2@nyu.edu

COHEN, Jeffrey A. American (born United States), b. 1952. **Genres:** Architecture, Art/Art History. **Career:** Drexel University, lecturer in architecture, 1977-80; Philadelphia Historic Sites Survey, researcher and surveyor, 1977-80; University Museum Expedition, architectural draftsman and surveyor, 1978, 1979; Muhlenberg College, instructor, 1979; Maryland Historical Society, assistant editor for architectural history, 1981-86, associate editor, 1986-91; Society of Architectural Historians, lecturer; Pennsylvania Academy of Fine Arts, lecturer; Bryn Mawr College, Growth and Structure of Cities Department, lecturer, 1995-2002, senior lecturer, 2002-, chair, Digital Media and Resource Center, director; University of Pennsylvania, School of Design, Graduate Program in Historic Preservation, instructor, 1999-2005. Writer. **Publications:** (Co-ed.) The Correspondence and Miscellaneous Papers of Benjamin Henry Latrobe: vol. I, 1784-1804, 1984, vol. II, 1805-10, 1986, vol. III, 1811-20, 1988; (co-author) Drawing Toward Building: Philadelphia Architectural Graphics, 1732-1986, 1986; (with G.E. Thomas and M.J. Lewis) Frank Furness: The Complete Works, 1991, rev. ed., 1996; (with C.E. Brownell) The Architectural Drawings of Benjamin Henry Latrobe, 1994; (with N. Johnston and K. Finkel) Eastern State Penitentiary: Crucible of Good Intentions, 1994; American Immigration: A Practical Guide to United States Visa and Immigration Applications, 1995. Contributor to journals. **Address:** Growth and Structure of Cities Program, Bryn Mawr College, 248 Thomas Hall, 101 N Merion Ave., Bryn Mawr, PA 19010-2899, U.S.A. **Online address:** jcohen@brynmawr.edu

COHEN, Jeffrey E. American (born United States), b. 1951. **Genres:** Politics/Government. **Career:** Colgate University, instructor, 1979-80; University of Alabama, assistant professor, 1980-84; University of New Orleans, associate professor, 1984-87; University of Illinois, associate professor, 1987-91; University of Houston, associate professor, 1991-92; University of Kansas, associate professor, 1992-97; Fordham University, professor of political science and department chair of American politics/presidency, 1997-. Writer. **Publications:** (Ed. with S.A. Shull) Economics and Politics of Industrial Policy: The United States and Western Europe, 1986; The Politics of the U.S. Cabinet: Representation in the Executive Branch, 1789-1984, 1988; The Politics of Telecommunications Regulation: The States and the Divestiture of AT&T, 1992; Politics and Economic Policy in the United States, 1997; Presidential Responsiveness and Public Policy-Making: The Public and the Policies that Presidents Choose, 1997; Politics and Economic Policy in the United States, 2000; (ed. with R. Fleisher and P. Kanntor) American Political Parties: Decline or Resurgence?, 2001; (ed.) Public Opinion in State Politics, 2006; The Presidency in the Era of 24-Hour News, 2008; Going Local: Presidential Leadership in the Post-Broadcast Age, 2010. Contributor to journals and periodicals. **Address:** Department of Political Science, Fordham University, 667 Faber Hall, 441 E Fordham Rd., Bronx, NY 20458, U.S.A. **Online address:** cohen@fordham.edu

COHEN, Jeremy. Israeli/American (born United States), b. 1953. **Genres:** Cultural/Ethnic Topics, Theology/Religion, History. **Career:** Cornell University, Department of Near Eastern Studies, instructor, 1977-78, assistant professor of Jewish history and coordinator of program of Jewish studies, 1978-81, Society for the Humanities, fellow, 1980-81; Ohio State University, Department of History, associate professor, 1982-89, professor of Jewish history, 1989-97, Samuel and Esther Melton chair in Jewish history, Melton Center for Jewish Studies, acting director, 1988; Methodist Theological School, adjunct associate professor, 1983-89, adjunct professor of church history, 1989-91; Tel Aviv University, Department of Jewish History, senior lecturer, 1989, associate professor, 1989-98, professor in Jewish history, 1998-, Abraham and Edita Spiegel Family Foundation professor of European Jewish history, Abraham and Edita Spiegel Family Foundation chair for European Jewish history, 2004-, Goldstein-Goren Diaspora Research Center, director, 2002-05; College of William and Mary, Department of Religion, Bronfman visiting distinguished professor in Judaic studies, 1995, 2000, 2005, 2010; University of Oxford, Oxford Centre for Hebrew and Jewish Studies, Louis Jacobs lecturer, 1996; University of Chicago, Divinity School, Regenstein visiting professor of Jewish studies, 1999; Johns Hopkins University, Department of History, Crane Foundation distinguished visiting professor of Jewish studies, 2005. Writer. **Publications:** The Friars and the Jews: The Evolution of Medieval Anti-Judaism, 1982; Be Fertile and Increase, Fill the Earth and Master It: The Ancient and Medieval Career of a Biblical Text, 1989; (ed.) Essential Papers on Judaism and Christianity in Conflict: From Late Antiquity to the Reformation, 1991; (ed.) From Witness to Witchcraft: Jews and Judaism in Medieval Christian Thought, 1996; Living Letters of the Law: Ideas of the Jew in Medieval Christianity, 1999; (ed. with M. Goodman and D. Sorkin) Oxford Handbook of Jewish Studies, 2002; Sanctifying the Name of God: Jewish Martyrs and Jewish Memories of the First Crusade, 2004; Christ Killers: The Jews and the Passion from the Bible to the Big Screen, 2007; (ed. with R.I. Cohen) The Jewish Contribution to Civilization: Reassessing An Idea, 2008; (ed. with M. Rosman) Rethinking European Jewish History, 2008; (ed. with A. Baumgarten and E. Mendelsohn) Remembering and Forgetting: Israeli Historians Look at the Jewish Past, 2009. **Address:** Department of Jewish History, Tel Aviv University, Rm. 206, Carter Bldg., 2nd Fl., PO Box 39040, Ramat Aviv, 69978, Israel. **Online address:** jecohen@post.tau.ac.il

COHEN, Judith Love. American (born United States), b. 1933. **Genres:** Children's Non-fiction, Self Help, Young Adult Non-fiction, Plays/Screenplays, Sciences, Women's Studies And Issues, Sports/Fitness, Young Adult Fiction, Young Adult Fiction. **Career:** TRW-Aerospace, project manager, 1959-90; Command Systems Group-Aerospace, project manager, 1990-92; freelance consulting engineer, 1993-. Writer. **Publications:** A Passover to Remember (play), 1985; (with F. McAlary) You Can Be a Woman Marine Biologist, 1993, rev. ed., 2001; (with D.L. Gabriel) You Can Be a Woman Paleontologist, 1993; (with V. Thompson) You Can Be a Woman Zoologist, 1993, rev. ed., 2001; (with S.R. Franks) You Can Be a Woman Oceanographer, 1994; (with A.M. Ghez) You Can Be A Woman Astronomer, 1995; You Can Be a Woman Engineer, 1995; (with R.F. Redberg) You Can Be a Woman Cardiologist, 1996; (with M. Siegel) You Can Be a Woman Architect, 1998; You Can Be... Science Career Activities, 1998; (with K.R. Bozak) You Can Be a Woman Botanist, 1999; (with T. Dixon) You Can Be a Woman Basketball Player, 1999; (with B.M. Bryan) You Can Be a Woman Egyptologist, 1999; (with S.C. Douty) You Can Be a Woman Softball Player, 2000; (with T.L. Venturini) You Can Be a Woman Soccer Player, 2000; (with D.A. Katz) Lessons in Love: A Guide to Making Your Loving Relationship for a Lifetime, 2001; (with K. Perez) You Can Be a Woman Meteorologist, 2002; (with D.L.A. Underwood) You Can Be a Woman Entomologist, 2002; (co-author) You Can Be a Woman Movie Maker, 2003; You Can be A Woman Animator, 2004; You Can be a Woman Video Game Producer, 2005; (with R.C. Friend) You Can be a Woman Makeup Artist or Costume Designer, 2005; (with P. Moore) You Can be a Woman Chemist, 2005; The Women of Apollo: The Stories of Judith Cohen, Ann Dickson, Ann Maybury and Bobbie Johnson, Four Remarkable Women Who Helped Put the First Man on the Moon, 2006; (with R.C. Friend) A Clean Sky: The Global Warming Story, 2007; (with R.C. Friend) Clean City: The Green Construction Story, 2008; (with R.C. Friend) Clean Planet: The Solar Energy Story, 2009; (with R.C. Friend) A Clean Earth: The Geothermal Story, 2010; A Cleaner Port, A Brighter Future: The Greening of the Port of Los Angeles, 2011. Contributor to journals. **Address:** Cascade Pass, 4223 Glencoe Ave., Ste. C-105, Marina Del Rey, CA 90292-8801, U.S.A. **Online address:** jlc@cascadepass.com

COHEN, Karl F. American (born United States), b. 1940. **Genres:** Film. **Career:** San Francisco State University, lecturer, assistant professor of cinema studies. Writer. **Publications:** Forbidden Animation: Censored Cartoons and Blacklisted Animators, 1997. **Address:** Department of Cinema, College of Creative Arts, San Francisco State University, 1600 Holloway Ave., San Francisco, CA 94132, U.S.A. **Online address:** karlcohen@earthlink.net

COHEN, Kerry. (Kerry Cohen Hoffman). American (born United States), b. 1970. **Genres:** Novels, Autobiography/Memoirs, Romance/Historical. **Career:** Writer, psychotherapist, consultant and memoirist. **Publications:** (As Kerry Cohen Hoffman) Easy (young adult novel), 2006; Loose Girl: A Memoir of Promiscuity, 2008; Good Girl, 2008; It's Not You, It's Me, 2009. Contributor to periodicals. **Address:** Delacorte press, 1745 Broadway, New York, NY 10019, U.S.A. **Online address:** kerry@kerrycohen.com

COHEN, Leah Hager. American (born United States), b. 1967?. **Genres:** Adult Non-fiction, Novels, Young Adult Fiction, Social Sciences. **Career:** Lesley University, faculty of creative writing; Boston University, faculty freshman writing; Emerson College, professor; College of the Holy Cross, W.H. Jenks chair in contemporary American letters, visiting professor of English. Writer. **Publications:** Train Go Sorry: Inside a Deaf World (nonfiction), 1994; Glass, Paper, Beans: Revelations on the Nature and Value of Ordinary Things (nonfiction), 1997; Heat Lightning (novel), 1997; Stuff of Dreams: Behind the Scenes of an American Community Theater, 2001; Heart, You Bully, You Punk, 2003; Without Apology: Girls, Women, and the Desire to Fight, 2005; House Lights, 2007; The Grief of Others, 2011. **Address:** c/o Barney Karpfinger, The Karpfinger Agency, 357 W 20th St., New York, NY 10011, U.S.A.

COHEN, Lenard J. Canadian (born Canada) **Genres:** International Relations/Current Affairs, Area Studies, Politics/Government. **Career:** Simon Fraser University, School for International Studies, co-founder, professor of international studies, now professor emeritus of international studies, 2009-, Centre for International Studies, director. Writer. **Publications:** (With P. Warwick) Political Cohesion in a Fragile Mosaic: The Yugoslav Experience, 1983; (with P. Warwick and P. Smith) The Vision and the Game: Making the Canadian Constitution, 1987; The Socialist Pyramid: Elites and Power in Yugoslavia, 1989; Regime Transition in a Disintegrating Yugoslavia: The Law-of-Rule vs. The Rule-of-Law, 1992; Broken Bonds: The Disintegration of Yugoslavia, 1993, 2nd ed., 1995; The Politics of Despair, 1998; Serpent in the Bosom: The Rise and Fall of Slobodan Milošević, 2001, 2nd ed., 2002; (with J.R. Lampe) Embracing Democracy in the Western Balkans, 2011. EDITOR: (with J.P. Shapiro) Communist Systems in Comparative Perspective, 1974; (with A. Moens and A.G. Sens) NATO and European Security: Alliance Politics from the End of the Cold War to the Age of Terrorism, 2003; (with J. Dragović-Soso) State Collapse in South-Eastern Europe: New Perspectives on Yugoslavia's Disintegration, 2008. **Address:** School for International Studies, Simon Fraser University, 515 W Hastings St., Ste. 7200, Vancouver, BC V6B 5K3, Canada. **Online address:** cohen@sfu.ca

COHEN, Leonard. Canadian (born Canada), b. 1934. **Genres:** Novels, Plays/Screenplays, Poetry, Songs/Lyrics And Libretti, Young Adult Fiction,

Young Adult Non-fiction, Music, Photography, Photography. **Career:** Writer. **Publications:** POETRY: Let Us Compare Mythologies, 1956; Flowers for Hitler, 1964; The Spice-Box of Earth, 1965; Parasites of Heaven, 1966; Selected Poems, 1956-68, 1968; The Energy of Slaves, 1972; (with J. Jaensch) Credo/22 Federzeichn, 1977; Death of a Lady's Man, 1978; Two Views (poetry), 1980; Light and Splendour: Song for High Voice with Flute and Clarinet, 1981; Book of Mercy, 1984; Leonard Cohen Anthology (songs), 1991; Stranger Music: Selected Poems and Songs, 1993; Dance Me to the End of Love, 1995; God is Alive, Magic is Afoot, 2000; Mój Cohen, 2002; Book of Longing, 2006; The Lyrics of Leonard Cohen, 2009; Soul Feathers, 2011; Leonard Cohen Poems, 2011. OTHERS: The Favorite Game: A Novel, 1963; Beautiful Losers (novel), 1966; You Do Not Have to Love Me, 1996; The Little Black Songbook, 2010. Contributor to periodicals. **Address:** Stranger Management, 5042 Wilshire Blvd., Ste. 585, Los Angeles, CA 90036-4305, U.S.A.

COHEN, Lisa R. American (born United States), b. 1958. **Genres:** Social Sciences. **Career:** Columbia Broadcasting System Inc. (CBS), producer; American Broadcasting Companies Inc. (ABC), producer; Columbia University, Graduate School of Journalism, adjunct professor; Princeton University, adjunct professor. Writer and media consultant. **Publications:** After Etan: The Missing Child Case That Held America Captive, 2009. **Address:** New York, NY , U.S.A. **Online address:** lisa@lisarcohen.com

COHEN, Lizabeth (Ann). American (born United States), b. 1952. **Genres:** Design, History, Regional/Urban Planning. **Career:** Fine Arts Museum, assistant curator, 1975-77; Camron-Stanford House Museum, director, 1976-78; Carnegie-Mellon University, Department of History, faculty, 1986-92; New York University, faculty, 1992-97; American University of Beirut, American Studies Center, advisor, 2004, 2010; Russian State Humanities University, Russian-American Center for American Studies, advisor, 2006; Oxford University, Vyvyan Harmsworth professor of American history, 2007-08; Harvard University, Howard Mumford Jones professor of American studies, Department of History, chair. Writer. **Publications:** Making a New Deal: Industrial Workers in Chicago, 1919-1939, 1990, 2nd ed., 2008; (with T.A. Bailey and D.M. Kennedy) The American Pageant: A History of the Republic, 1998, 14th ed., 2010; A Consumers' Republic: The Politics of Mass Consumption in Postwar America, 2003. Contributor to journals. **Address:** Department of History, Harvard University, Rm. 111, Robinson Hall, 35 Quincy St., Cambridge, MA 02138, U.S.A. **Online address:** cohen3@fas.harvard.edu

COHEN, Lynne. Canadian (born Canada), b. 1944. **Genres:** Art/Art History. **Career:** Eastern Michigan University, faculty, 1968-73; Algonquin College, faculty, 1973-75; University of Ottawa, faculty, 1974-2005; Carleton University, adjunct professor, 2003-; Virginia Commonwealth University, distinguished graduate adjunct faculty, 2003-. Writer and photographer. **Publications:** Occupied Territory, 1987; L'endroit du décor/Lost and Found, 1992; No Man's Land, 2001; Camouflage, 2005; Cover, 2009. Contributor to periodicals. **Address:** c/o Author Mail, Thames & Hudson Inc., 500 5th Ave., New York, NY 10110, U.S.A. **Online address:** lynne.cohen@sympatico.ca

COHEN, Marcel. French (born France), b. 1937. **Genres:** Novels, Young Adult Fiction. **Career:** Journalist, 1958-. **Publications:** Galpa: Roman, 1969; Malestroit: Chroniques du silence, 1973; Voyage àWaïzata, 1976; Murs: Anamnèses, 1979; Miroirs, 1980; (contrib.) Camps en Provence: Exil, Internement, Déportation, 1933-1944, 1984; Letras a un pintor ke kreya azerretratos imaginarios por un sefardi de Turkia, ke se akodra perfektamentede kada uno de sus modeles, 1985; Je ne sais pas le nom, 1986; Le grandpaon-de-nuit, 1990; Lettre à Antonio Saura: Traduit de judéo-espagol, 1997; Assassinat d'un garde, 1998; Quelques faces visibles du silence: Antonio Saura, 2000; Faits: Lecture courante à l'usage des grands débutants, 2002; (contrib.) Ombre nue, 2008. Contributor to books. **Address:** 197 rue de Grenelle, Paris, 75007, France.

COHEN, Mark. American (born United States), b. 1958?. **Genres:** Mystery/Crime/Suspense, Adult Non-fiction. **Career:** Dwyer, Pohren, Wood, Heavy & Grimm, attorney, 1987-90; Cohen, Vacanti, Higgins & Shattuck, partner, 1990-95; City of Westminster, municipal prosecutor, 1996-2003; DART Inc., board director, 2001-; City of Boulder, interim municipal judge, 2001-02; Town of Lochbuie, municipal judge, 2004-; Cohen Horner, LLP, partner, 2005-07; The Cohen Law Group PC, attorney, 2008-; The Colorado Lawyer, editor, 2009-; Muddy Gap Press, founder. **Publications:** The Fractal Murders: A Pepper Keane Mystery, 2002; Bluetick Revenge, 2005. Contributor of articles to periodicals. **Address:** Bond Literary Agency, 1430 E Bates Ave., Englewood, CO 80113-3004, U.S.A. **Online address:** mark@cohenslaw.com

COHEN, Michael A. American (born United States), b. 1971. **Genres:** History, Politics/Government, International Relations/Current Affairs. **Career:** Robinson, Lerer and Montgomery, senior vice president; U.S. Department of State, speechwriter; Senator Chris Dodd, speechwriter; Columbia University, School of International and Public Affairs, instructor; New America Foundation, senior research fellow, 2006-09; Foreign Policy Magazine, staff. **Publications:** Live from the Campaign Trail: The Greatest Presidential Campaign Speeches of the 20th Century and How They Shaped Modern America, 2008. Contributor of articles to periodicals. **Address:** Walker & Co., 175 5th Ave., New York, NY 10010, U.S.A. **Online address:** michael@livefromthetrail.com

COHEN, Milton A. American (born United States), b. 1946. **Genres:** Art/Art History. **Career:** Wayne State University, adjunct professor, 1971-74; University of Texas, assistant professor, professor, 1980-. Writer. **Publications:** NONFICTION: E.E. Cummings Paintings: The Hidden Career: The University of Texas at Dallas, September 8- October 12, 1982: The Dallas Public Library, October 18-November 27, 1982, 1982; Poet and Painter: The aesthetics of E.E. Cummings's Early Work, 1987; Movement, Manifesto, Melee: The Modernist Group, 1910-1914, 2004; Hemingway's Laboratory: The Paris in Our Time, 2005. **Address:** University of Texas, PO Box 830688, Richardson, TX 75083-0688, U.S.A. **Online address:** mcohen@utdallas.edu

COHEN, Morton N(orton). (John Moreton). American/Canadian (born Canada), b. 1921. **Genres:** Children's Fiction, Literary Criticism And History, Travel/Exploration, Biography, Autobiography/Memoirs. **Career:** West Virginia University, instructor, 1950-51; City University of New York, City College, tutor, 1952-53, lecturer, 1953-59, instructor, 1959-62, assistant professor, 1963-65, associate professor, 1966-70, professor of English, 1971-81, Ph.D. Program in English, deputy executive officer, 1976-81, professor emeritus, 1981-, Graduate Center, faculty; Syracuse University, visiting professor, 1965-66, 1967-68; Oxford University, senior fulbright research fellow, 1974-75; Royal Society of Literature, fellow, 1996-; Rutgers University, faculty. Writer. **Publications:** (With R.C. Dickson) Brief Guide to Better Writing, 1960; Rider Haggard: His Life and Works, 1960, 2nd ed., 1968; (as John Moreton) Punky: Mouse for a Day, 1962; Search for Rudyard Kipling, 1966; (reteller as John Moreton) The Love for Three Oranges, 1966; Lewis Carroll, Photographer of Children: Four Nude Studies, 1979; Lewis Carroll and Alice 1832-1982, 1982; Lewis Carroll: A Biography, 1995; Reflections in a Looking Glass: A Centennial Celebration of Lewis Carroll, 1998. EDITOR: Rudyard Kipling to Rider Haggard: The Record of a Friendship, 1965; (with R.L. Green) The Letters of Lewis Carroll, 2 vols., 1979; (and intro.) The Russian Journal-II: A Record Kept by Henry Parry Liddon of a Tour Taken with C.L. Dodgson in the Summer of 1867, 1979; (and intro.) Lewis Carroll and the Kitchins: Containing Twenty-Five Letters not Previously Published and Nineteen of his Photographs, 1980; Selected Letters of Lewis Carroll, 1982; (with A. Gandolfo) Lewis Carroll and the House of Macmillan, 1987; Lewis Carroll: Interviews and Recollection, 1989; (with E. Wakeling) Lewis Carroll & His Illustrators: Collaborations and Correspondence, 1865-1898, 2003. **Address:** AP Watt Ltd., 20 John St., London, GL WC1N 2DR, England.

COHEN, Norman J. American (born United States), b. 1943. **Genres:** Information Science/Computers, Theology/Religion, Social Sciences, Reference. **Career:** Hebrew Union-Jewish Institute of Religion, professor of medrash, 1975-, provost, 1996-; Rabbinic School in New York, director, 1986-; New York School, dean, 1988-96. Writer. **Publications:** Self, Struggle and Change: Family Conflict Stories in Genesis and Their Healing Insights for Our Lives, 1995; Voices from Genesis: Guiding Us Through the Stages of Life, 1998; The Way into Torah, 2000; (with L. Kruger and P. Karmel) Thirty Pieces/Thirty Years: Sculpture by Ann Sperry, 2003; Hineini in Our Lives: Learning How to Respond to Others Through 14 Biblical Texts and Personal Stories, 2003; Moses and the Journey to Leadership: Timeless Lessons of Effective Management from the Bible and Today's Leaders, 2007. EDITOR: The Fundamentalist Phenomenon: A View from Within; A Response from Without, 1990; (with R.M. Seltzer) The Americanization of the Jews, 1995. **Address:** Hebrew Union College, 1 W 4th St., New York, NY 10012, U.S.A. **Online address:** ncohen@huc.edu

COHEN, Paul (M.). American (born United States), b. 1955?. **Genres:** History, Film, Intellectual History. **Career:** The American College, instructor,

1982-83; University of Chicago, lecturer in western civilization, 1983-85; Lawrence University, assistant professor, 1985-90, associate professor, 1990-99, professor of history, 1999-, department chair, 2000-05, Patricia Hamar Boldt professor of liberal studies, 2003-, Freshman Studies, director, 1996-98; Newberry Library Program in the Humanities, director, 1991-92. **Publications:** Piety and Politics: Catholic Revival and the Generation of 1905-1914 in France, 1987; Freedom's Moment: An Essay on the French Idea of Liberty from Rousseau to Foucault, 1997. **Address:** Department of History, Lawrence University, 711 E Boldt Way, PO Box 599, Appleton, WI 54911, U.S.A. **Online address:** paul.m.cohen@lawrence.edu

COHEN, Peter Zachary. American (born United States), b. 1931. **Genres:** Children's Fiction, Plays/Screenplays, Animals/Pets, Young Adult Fiction. **Career:** Kansas State University of Agriculture and Applied Science, associate professor of English, 1961-. Writer. **Publications:** The Muskie Hook, 1969; The Bull in the Forest, 1969; Morena, 1970; Foal Creek, 1972; The Authorized Autumn Charts of the Upper Red Canoe River Country, 1972; Bee, 1975; Deadly Game at Stony Creek, 1978; Calm Horse, Wild Night, 1982; The Great Red River Raft, 1984; Heyday Squares II, 1993. Contributor to periodicals. **Address:** 38382 Sycamore Creek Rd., Alta Vista, KS 66834, U.S.A.

COHEN, Rachel. American (born United States) **Genres:** Novels. **Career:** Sarah Lawrence College, nonfiction instructor, faculty. Writer. **Publications:** (With J. Meyer) éducation sans frontières, école européenne, écoles internationales, par Geneviève Guéron, 1967; L'apprentissage précoce de la lecture: á six ans est-il déjà trop tard?, 1977; Plaidoyer pour les apprentissages précoces: stratégies éducatives pour la réalisation des potentialités humaines, 1982; (with H. Gilabert) Découverte et apprentissage du langage écrit avant six ans: un pari pour la réussite au cours préparatoire, 1986; (ed. with M. Barriere) Les Jeunes enfants, la découverte de l'écrit et l'ordinateur, 1987; Mr Pin's, ou-, Les pin's de A-à Z, 1991; Mr Pin's ou les pin's de A à Z: nouvelles cotes 1992, 1992; (ed.) La Communication télématique internationale: des expériences à travers l'Europe: une mutation dans l'éducation, 1995; A Chance Meeting: Intertwined Lives of American Writers and Artists, 1854-1967, 2004. Contributor to periodicals. **Address:** Sarah Lawrence College, 1 Mead Way, Bronxville, NY 10708, U.S.A.

COHEN, Ralph. American (born United States), b. 1917. **Genres:** Literary Criticism And History. **Career:** University of Virginia, Kenan Professor of English, 1978-, Commonwealth Center for Literary and Cultural Change, director, 1988-94, now William R. Kenan, Jr. professor emeritus; New Literary History, editor; University of Toronto, distinguished professor of comparative literature, 1979; Academy of Literary Studies, president, 1980; William Andrew Clark Memorial Library, research professor, 1980-81; Conference of Editors of Learned Journals, president, 1980-82; Society for Critical Exchange, president, 1983-86; Indiana University, Institute for Advanced Study, fellow, 1984; British Academy, fellow, 1986; University of California, Humanities Research Institute, fellow, 1988. **Publications:** The Art of Discrimination, 1964; The Unfolding of the Seasons, 1970. EDITOR: (and intro.) Essential Works, 1965; New Directions in Literary History, 1974; (with M. Krieger) Literature and History: Papers Read at a Clark Library Seminar, March 3, 1973, 1974; Studies in Eighteenth-Century British Art and Aesthetics, 1985; New Literary History International Bibliography of Literary Theory and Criticism, 1988; The Future of Literary Theory, 1989; (and intro.) Studies in Historical Change, 1992; (with M.S. Roth) History and-: Histories within the Human Sciences, 1995. **Address:** Department of English, University of Virginia, 102C Bryan Hall, PO Box 400121, Charlottesville, VA 22904-4121, U.S.A. **Online address:** rc@virginia.edu

COHEN, Raymond. Israeli (born Israel), b. 1947. **Genres:** Art/Art History, Cultural/Ethnic Topics, International Relations/Current Affairs, Young Adult Non-fiction. **Career:** Hebrew University of Jerusalem, faculty, 1976-, Chaim Weizmann chair of international relations; Boston College, Center for Christian-Jewish Learning, Corcoran visiting professor; Georgetown University, visiting professor; Brown University, Watson Institute, research fellow. Writer. **Publications:** NONFICTION: (with S. Cohen) Peace Conferences'the Formal Aspects, 1974; Threat Perception in International Crisis, 1979; International Politics: The Rules of the Game, 1981; Theatre of Power: The Art of Diplomatic Signalling, 1987; Culture and Conflict in Egyptian-Israeli Relations: A Dialogue of the Deaf, 1990; Negotiating across Cultures: Communication Obstacles in International Diplomacy, 1991, rev. ed., 1997; (ed. with R. Westbrook) Amarna Diplomacy: The Beginnings of International Relations, 2000; (ed.) Mediniyut ha-huts shel Artsot ha-Berit likrat kehunato ha-sheniyah shel ha-nasi Bush, 2005; Saving the Holy Sepulchre: How Rival Christians Came Together to Rescue Their Holiest Shrine, 2008; Isaiah's Vision of Peace in Biblical and Modern International Relations: Swords into Plowshares, 2008. **Address:** Department of International Relations, Hebrew University of Jerusalem, Jerusalem, 91905, Israel. **Online address:** msrcohen@mscc.huji.ac.il

COHEN, Rich. American (born United States), b. 1968. **Genres:** Documentaries/Reportage, Novels, Literary Criticism And History, Autobiography/Memoirs, Biography. **Career:** New York Observer, reporter; Rolling Stone magazine, contributing editor, 1994-; Vanity Fair, contributing editor, 2007-. **Publications:** Tough Jews, 1998; The Avengers, 2000; Lake Effect, 2002; The Record Men: The Chess Brothers and the Birth of Rock & Roll, 2004; Sweet and Low: A Family Story, 2006; Israel is Real, 2009; (with J. Weintraub) When I Stop Talking, You'll Know I'm Dead: Useful Stories from a Persuasive Man, 2010. Contributor to periodicals and magazine. **Address:** Rolling Stone Magazine, 1290 Ave., of the Americas, New York, NY 10104-0101, U.S.A.

COHEN, Richard. American (born United States), b. 1952. **Genres:** Novels, Novellas/Short Stories, Writing/Journalism, Natural History. **Career:** Hutchinson and Hodder & Stoughton, publishing director; Richard Cohen Books, founder; manuscript reader, 1973-76, 1977-79; freelance writer, 1987-; University of Wisconsin, lecturer in creative writing, 1988. **Publications:** Seduction of Joe Tynan, 1979; Domestic Tranquility, 1980; Don't Mention the Moon, 1983; Say You Want Me, 1988; Writer's Mind: Crafting Fiction, 1994; Pronoun Music: Stories, 2001. Contributor to periodicals. **Address:** Trident Media Group L.L.C., 41 Madison Ave., 36th Fl., New York, NY 10010-2257, U.S.A.

COHEN, Richard M(artin). American (born United States), b. 1941. **Genres:** Documentaries/Reportage, Biography, Autobiography/Memoirs, Medicine/Health. **Career:** United Press Intl., reporter, 1967-68; Washington Post, general assignment reporter, 1968-76, syndicated columnist, 1976-. Author. **Publications:** (With J. Witcover) A Heartbeat Away: The Investigation and Resignation of Vice President Spiro T. Agnew, 1974; Blindsided: Lifting a Life Above Illness: A Reluctant Memoir, 2004; Strong at the Broken Places: Voices of Illness, a Chorus of Hope, 2008. **Address:** Washington Post, 1150 15th St. NW, Washington, DC 20071, U.S.A.

COHEN, Robert. American (born United States), b. 1957. **Genres:** Novels, Novellas/Short Stories. **Career:** State University of New York, adjunct professor of English, 1984-88; University of Houston, visiting professor, 1989-90; Harvard University, Briggs Copeland professor, 1993-; Rice University, faculty; Middlebury College, professor of English and American literatures. Writer. **Publications:** NOVELS: The Organ Builder, 1988; The Here and Now, 1996; Inspired Sleep, 2001; Amateur Barbarians, 2009. STORIES: The Varieties of Romantic Experience, 2002. Contributor to magazines and periodicals. **Address:** Department of English & American Literatures, Middlebury College, Rm. 205, Axinn Ctr. at Starr Library, 15 Old Chapel Rd., Middlebury, VT 05753-2001, U.S.A. **Online address:** cohen@middlebury.edu

COHEN, Robin. Canadian (born Canada), b. 1944. **Genres:** Politics/Government, Race Relations, Sociology, Third World, History, Military/Defense/Arms Control. **Career:** University of Ibadan, lecturer in politics, 1967-69; University of Birmingham, research fellow, 1969-71, lecturer, 1971-75, senior lecturer in sociology, 1975-77; University of Mauritius, moderator, 1976; University of the West Indies, professor of sociology, 1977-79; University of Warwick, professor of sociology, 1979-2007, Centre for Research in Ethnic Relations, executive director, 1985-89, honorary professor; University of Cape Town, dean of humanities, 2001-03; University of Oxford, professor of development studies, International Migration Institute, director, professorial research fellow, 2007-, now professor emeritus. Writer and consultant. **Publications:** Greater South: Or What Might Have Happened in the Nigerian Civil War, 1971; (with A. Hughes) Towards the Emergence of a Nigerian Working Class, 1971; Labour and Politics in Nigeria, 1945-71, 1974; (with R. May) Interaction between Race and Colonialism, 1974; Marxism and Africa: Old, New, and Projected, 1975; Making of a West African Working Class, 1975; Hidden Forms of Labour Protest in Africa, 1976; (with R. Poulton) Contemporary Communes, A Bibliographical and Interpretative Essay, 1977; (with S. Amin) Classes and Class Struggle in Africa, 1977; (with M. Minogue and J. Craig) Small Island Economies, 1983; Endgame in South Africa?, 1986; The New Helots: Migrants in the International Division of Labour, 1987; Contested Domains: Debates in International Labour Studies, 1991; Frontiers of Identity: The British and the Others, 1994; Global Diasporas: An Introduction, 1997; (with P. Kennedy) Global Sociology, 2001, 2nd ed., 2007; Migration and Its Enemies: Global Capital, Migrant Labour, and the Nation-State, 2006. EDITOR: (with R. Sandbrook) The Development of an African Working Class, 1975; (with P.C.W. Gutkind and J. Copans) African Labor History, 1978; (with P.C.W. Gutkind and P. Brazier) Peasants and Proletarians, 1979; (and intro.) Forced Labour in Colonial Africa, 1979; African Islands and Enclaves, 1983; (with F. Ambursley) Crisis in the Caribbean, 1983; (with R.E. Boyd and P.C.W. Gutkind) International Labour and the Third World, 1987; (with W. Cobbett) Popular Struggles in South Africa, 1988; (with D. Joly) Reluctant Hosts: Europe and Its Refugees, 1989; (with Y.G. Muthien and A. Zegeye) Repression and Resistance: Insider Accounts of Apartheid, 1990; (with H. Goulbourne) Democracy and Socialism in Africa, 1991; The Cambridge Survey of World Migration, 1995; (with J.F. Van Nostrand and R. Suzman) Trends in the Health of Older Americans: United States, 1994, 1995; The Sociology of Migration, 1996; Theories of Migration, 1996; (with Z. Layton-Henry) The Politics of Migration, 1997; (with S. Vertovec) Migration, Diasporas, and Transnationalism, 1999; (with S. Rai) Global Social Movements, 2000; (with S. Vertovec) Conceiving Cosmopolitanism, 2003; (and intro. with P. Toninato) Creolization Reader: Studies in Mixed Identities and Cultures, 2009. **Address:** Department of International Development, University of Oxford, Queen Elizabeth House, 3 Mansfield Rd., Oxford, OX OX1 3TB, England. **Online address:** robin.cohen@qeh.ox.ac.uk

COHEN, Shaye J. D. American (born United States), b. 1948. **Genres:** Theology/Religion, History. **Career:** Jewish Theological Seminary, Department of History, instructor, assistant professor, associate professor of Jewish history, 1974-86, chair, 1981-85, acting librarian, 1984-85, professor of Jewish history and Jack and Miriam Shenkman professor of the post-biblical foundations of western civilization, 1986-91, Graduate School, dean, 1987-91; Columbia University, visiting associate professor of history, 1982; Brown University, professor of religious studies and Ungerleider professor of Judaic studies, 1991-2001, Program in Judaic Studies, director, 1995-98; Hebrew University, Lady Davis visiting professor of Jewish history, 1998-99; Harvard University, Department of Near Eastern Languages and Civilizations, professor of Hebrew literature and philosophy, 2001-, Nathan Littauer professor of Hebrew literature and philosophy. Writer. **Publications:** NONFICTION: Josephus in Galilee and Rome: His Vita and Development as a Historian, 1979; From the Maccabees to the Mishnah, 1987, 2nd ed., 2006; (ed. with E.L. Greenstein) The State of Jewish Studies, 1990; (ed.) The Jewish Family in Antiquity, 1993; (ed. with E.S. Frerichs) Diasporas in Antiquity, 1993; (ed.) Studies in the Cult of Yahweh, 1996; The Beginnings of Jewishness: Boundaries, Varieties, Uncertainties, 1999; (ed.) The Synoptic Problem in Rabbinic Literature, 2000; Why Aren't Jewish Women Circumcised?: Gender and Covenant in Judaism, 2005; (ed. with J.J. Schwartz) Studies in Josephus and the Varieties of Ancient Judaism: Louis H. Feldman Jubilee Volume, 2007. Contributor of articles to periodicals. **Address:** Department of Near Eastern Languages and, Civilizations, Harvard University, Rm. 105, Semitic Museum, 6 Divinity Ave., Cambridge, MA 02138-2020, U.S.A. **Online address:** scohen@fas.harvard.edu

COHEN, Sholom. American (born United States), b. 1951. **Genres:** Children's Fiction, Humor/Satire, Children's Non-fiction. **Career:** University of Western Ontario, music librarian, 1974-78; Columbia University, systems librarian, 1979-81; McDonnell Douglas Corp., software engineer, 1982-88; Carnegie-Mellon University, software consultant, 1988-, Software Engineering Institute, senior technical staff; University of Pittsburgh, Department of Computer Engineering, instructor, 2000-02. Writer. **Publications:** YITZ BERG FROM PITTSBURGH SERIES: Yitzy and the G.O.L.E.M., 1992; The Lopsided Yarmulke, 1995. **Address:** Software Engineering Institute, Carnegie-Mellon University, 4500 5th Ave., Pittsburgh, PA 15213-2612, U.S.A. **Online address:** sgc@sei.cmu.edu

COHEN, Stanley I. American (born United States), b. 1928. **Genres:** Novels, Novellas/Short Stories, Mystery/Crime/Suspense, Literary Criticism And History, Young Adult Fiction. **Career:** May Hosiery Mills, process development, 1950-52; Oak Ridge National Laboratory, nuclear research engineer, 1952-57; Olin Corp., Packaging Division, supervisor of product development, 1958-64, market development manager, 1964-73, technical service manager, 1973-86. Writer. **Publications:** NOVELS: Taking Gary Feldman in UK as The Abduction, 1970; Tell Us Jerry Silver, 1973; The Diane Game, 1973; 330 Park, 1977; Angel Face, 1982. SHORT STORY COLLECTION: A Night in the Manchester Store, 2002. Contributor to books. **Address:** Five Star Publications Inc., PO Box 6698, Chandler, AZ 85246, U.S.A.

COHEN, Stephanie. American (born United States), b. 1937?. **Genres:** Homes/Gardens, Horticulture. **Career:** Temple University-Ambler, faculty, 1980-; Landscape Arboretum, founding director, teacher of advanced perennial design, Center for Sustainable Communities, associated faculty; Perennial-Plant-of-the-Year Program, co-chair; Country Living Gardener, contributing editor. **Publications:** (With N.J. Ondra) The Perennial Gardener's Design Primer, 2005; (with N.J. Ondra) Fallscaping: Extending Your Garden Season into Autumn, 2007; (with J. Benner) The Nonstop Garden: Easy Designs and Smart Plant Choices for Four-season Landscapes, 2010. Contributor to magazines and periodicals. **Address:** Center for Sustainable Communities, Temple University Ambler, 580 Meetinghouse Rd., Ambler, PA 19002-3923, U.S.A.

COHEN, Stephen F(rand). American (born United States), b. 1938. **Genres:** History, Politics/Government, Adult Non-fiction, Social Sciences. **Career:** Princeton University, assistant professor, 1968-72, associate professor, 1973-79, professor of politics, 1979-98, professor emeritus, 1998-, director of Russian studies, 1973-80, 1986-; Columbia University, Russian Institute, senior fellow, 1972-73, Research Institute on Communist Affairs, senior fellow, 1972-, visiting professor of history, 1973-74, 1974-75; Nation, columnist, 1982-87, contributing editor, 1994-; New York University, professor of Russian studies and history, 1998-; Slavic Review, associate editor; CBS News, consultant. **Publications:** Bukharin and the Bolshevik Revolution: A Political Biography 1888-1938, 1973; (co-author) Common Sense in U.S.-Soviet Relations, 1978; (foreword) Selected Writings on the State and the Transition to Socialism, 1982; Rethinking the Soviet Experience: Politics and History since 1917, 1985; Sovieticus: American Perceptions and Soviet Realities, 1985; Bukharin: Politicheskai a biografii a, 1888-1938, 1988; (with K. vanden Heuvel) Voices of Glasnost: Interviews with Gorbachevs Reformers, 1989; (intro.) This I Cannot Forget, 1993; (intro.) Inside Gorbachevs Kremlin, 1993; (contrib.) Tiuremnye rukopisi N.I. Bukharina: v 2-khknigakh, 1996; (intro.) The Commissar Vanishes: The Falsification of Photographs and Art in Stalins Russia, 1997; (intro.) How It All Began, 1998; Failed Crusade: America and the Tragedy of Post-Communist Russia, 2000; Soviet Fates and Lost Alternatives: From Stalinism to the New Cold War, 2009; The Victims Return: Survivors of the Gulag after Stalin, 2010. EDITOR: (with R.C. Tucker) The Great Purge Trial, 1965; (with A. Rabinowitch and R. Sharlet) The Soviet Union since Stalin, 1980; (and intro.) An End to Silence: Uncensored Opinion in the Soviet Union from Roy Medvedevs Underground Magazine Political Diary, 1982. Contributor to periodicals. **Address:** Department of Russian and Slavic Studies, New York University, 19 University Pl., 2nd Fl., New York, NY 10003-4556, U.S.A. **Online address:** stephen.cohen@nyu.edu

COHEN, Stuart. (Stuart Archer Cohen). American (born United States), b. 1958?. **Genres:** Novels, Young Adult Fiction, Mystery/Crime/Suspense. **Career:** Paititi Woolens Co., owner, 1985-96; Invisible World, owner, 2002-. Novelist. **Publications:** Invisible World (novel), 1998; The Stone Angels, 2003; Army of the Republic, 2008. **Address:** HarperCollins Inc., 10 E 53rd St., New York, NY 10022, U.S.A. **Online address:** invworld@alaska.net

COHEN, Stuart. Israeli/British (born England), b. 1946?. **Genres:** Theology/Religion, History, Young Adult Non-fiction. **Career:** Bar-Ilan University, faculty, 1972-, professor of political studies. Writer. **Publications:** NONFICTION: (with R. Cohen) Peace Conferences: The Formal Aspects, 1974; British Policy in Mesopotamia, 1903-1914, 1976; (with D.J. Elazar) A Gazetteer of Jewish Political Organization, 1981; The Concept of the Three Ketarim: Its Place in Jewish Political Thought and Its Implications for a Study of Jewish Constitutional History, 1982; English Zionists and British Jews: The Communal Politics of Anglo-Jewry, 1895-1920, 1982; (with D.J. Elazar) The Jewish Political Tradition and Its Contemporary Uses: A Program for Investigation, Interpretation, and Application, 1982; (with D.J. Elazar) The Jewish Polity: Jewish Political Organization from Biblical Times to the Present, 1985; Zionism and the Reconstitution of Jewish Political Society, 1986; Muśag sheloshet ha-ketarim: mekomo ba-mahshavah ha-medinit ha-Yehudit ve-hashlakhotav 'al heker ha-historyah ha-hukatit ha-Yehudit, 1988; The Bible and Intra-Jewish Politics: Early Rabbinic Portraits of King David, 1989; The Three Crowns: Structures of Communal Politics in Early Rabbinic Jewry, 1990; Mista'arvim-Masqueraders in the Israel Defense Forces, 1991-1992: The Military Unit and the Public Debate, 1994; (with E. Kanovsky and E. Inbar) Military, Economic and Strategic Aspects of the Middle East Peace Process, 1995; Studying the Israel Defense Forces: A Changing Contract with Israeli

Society, 1995; The Scroll or the Sword? Dilemmas of Religion and Military Service in Israel, 1997; Adat bene Yiśra'el: ha-hit'argenut ha-medinit ha-Yehudit mi-tekufat ha-Mikra ve-'ad yamenu, 1997; (ed.) Democratic Societies and Their Armed Forces: Israel in Comparative Context, 2000; (ed. with M. Shain) Israel: Culture, Religion, and Society 1948-1998, 2000; Tsahal vehahevrah ha-Yiśre'elit: behinah me-hadash, 2001; Kefifut Yeter Shel Tsahal: Shinui Be-ma'arkhot Ha-yehasim Ben Ha-dereg Ha-ezrahi Le-ven Ha-tsava Be-Yiśrael, 2006; Israel and Its Army: From Cohesion to Confusion, 2008; (ed.) The New Citizen Armies: Israel's Armed Forces in Comparative Perspective, 2010. **Address:** Bar-Ilan University, Ramat Gan, 52900, Israel. **Online address:** cohenst@mail.biu.ac.il

COHEN, Stuart Archer. *See* **COHEN, Stuart.**

COHEN, Susan. American (born United States), b. 1948. **Genres:** Poetry, Young Adult Non-fiction. **Career:** San Jose Mercury News, reporter; University of California, Graduate School of Journalism, professor. Journalist. **Publications:** Backstroking (poetry), 2005; (with C. Cosgrove) Normal at Any Cost: Tall Girls, Short Boys, and the Medical Industry's Quest to Manipulate Height, 2009; Finding the Sweet Spot (poetry), 2009. Contributor of articles to periodicals. **Address:** U.S.A. **Online address:** cohenyoungs@sbcglobal.net

COHEN, Thomas V. Canadian/American (born United States), b. 1942. **Genres:** History, Language/Linguistics, Urban Studies. **Career:** York University, lecturer, 1969-72, assistant professor, 1972-76, associate professor, 1976-2004, professor of history and humanities, 2004-. Writer. **Publications:** (Contrib.) Prophetic Rome in the High Renaissance Period, 1992; (contrib.) Essays on Life Writing, 1992; (with E.S. Cohen) Words and Deeds in Renaissance Rome: Trials before the Papal Magistrates, 1993; (contrib. with E.S. Cohen) A Global Encyclopedia of Historical Writing, 1998; (with E.S. Cohen) Daily Life in Renaissance Italy, 2001; (trans.) Court and Politics in Papal Rome, 1492-1700, 2002; Love and Death in Renaissance Italy, 2004; (contrib. with E.S. Cohen) Shell Games, 2004; (trans.) Court Culture in Rome, 2006; (ed. with R. Laitinen) The Cultural History of the Early Modern European Street, 2009; (trans.) Fosi, The Pope's Justice, 2011. Contributor to journals. **Address:** Department of History, York University, Vari Hall 2156, 100 York Blvd., Toronto, ON M3J 1P3, Canada. **Online address:** tcohen@yorku.ca

COHEN, Tish. Canadian (born Canada), b. 1963. **Genres:** Novels. **Career:** Writer. **Publications:** Town House (novel), 2007; The Invisible Rules of the Zoë Lama, 2007; The One and Only Zoë Lama, 2008; Inside Out Girl, 2008; Little Black Lies, 2009; The Truth About Delilah Blue, 2010; Switch, 2011. **Address:** c/o Daniel Lazar, Writers House, 21 W 26th St., New York, NY 10010, U.S.A. **Online address:** tish@tishcohen.com

COHEN, Youssef. American/Egyptian (born Egypt), b. 1947. **Genres:** Politics/Government, Area Studies. **Career:** University of Michigan, Inter-University Consortium for Political and Social Research, instructor, 1977-81, lecturer in political science, 1979-82; University of Pennsylvania, assistant professor of political science, 1982-88; New York University, Department of Politics, associate professor, 1988-, director of graduate studies, 1994-95, 1989-90, director of undergraduate studies, 2004-. Writer. **Publications:** (Co-author) Births, Deaths and Taxes: The Demographic and Political Transitions, 1984; The Manipulation of Consent: The State and Working-Class Consciousness in Brazil, 1989; Radicals, Reformers and Reactionaries: The Prisoner's Dilemma and the Collapse of Democracy in Latin America, 1994. Contributor to journals. **Address:** Department of Politics, New York University, Rm. 223, 19 W 4th St., New York, NY 10003, U.S.A. **Online address:** youssef.cohen@nyu.edu

COHEN-SHALEV, Amir. Israeli (born Israel), b. 1951. **Genres:** History. **Career:** University of Haifa, adjunct professor, 1985-, Department of Gerontology, lecturer; Jordan Valley College, senior lecturer, 2000-; Kinneret College, senior lecturer, 2000. Writer. **Publications:** Two Worlds at Once: Art in Old Age, 2002; Visions of Aging: Images of the Elderly in Film, 2009. **Address:** Department of Gerontology, University of Haifa, Rm. 1012, Eshkol Bldg., 10th Fl., Mount Carmel, 31905, Israel. **Online address:** cohenshalev@gmail.com

COHN, David. American (born United States), b. 1954?. **Genres:** Architecture, Novels, History. **Career:** Expansion (Spanish newspaper), architecture critic. Writer. **Publications:** Manuel Gallego, 1998; Young Spanish Architects, 2000. Contributor of articles to periodicals. **Address:** Tres Peles, 14 Estudio, Madrid, E-28012, Spain.

COHN, Henry S. American (born United States), b. 1945. **Genres:** History, Law, Biography. **Career:** District of Connecticut, law clerk for U.S. District Judge T. Emmet Clarie, 1970-71; University of Connecticut, School of Law, lecturer and adjunct professor, 1970-; assistant U.S. attorney, 1971-75; Office of the Secretary of the State, elections attorney, 1975-78, deputy secretary of state, 1978-79, secretary of state, 1978-79; Fleischmann, Sherbacow, McWeeny and Cohn, partner, 1979-82; Siegel, O'Connor and Kainen, Hartford, associate, 1982-83; Connecticut Attorney General's Office, assistant attorney general, 1983-; Connecticut Consortium for Law and Citizenship Education, assistant attorney general and president, 1990-. Writer. **Publications:** (With D. Bollier) The Great Hartford Circus Fire: Creative Settlement of Mass Disasters, 1991; Remembrances of Judge Clarie by His Clerks, 1993. Contributor to periodicals. **Address:** School of Law, University of Connecticut, 65 Elizabeth St., Hartford, CT 06105, U.S.A. **Online address:** cpilj@law.uconn.edu

COHN, Jonathan. American (born United States), b. 1969?. **Genres:** Medicine/Health. **Career:** American Prospect, writer, 1991-97, executive editor, contributing editor; New Republic, executive editor, senior editor, 1997-; Henry J. Kaiser Family Foundation, media fellow, 2002-04; Demos, senior fellow. **Publications:** Sick: The Untold Story of America's Health Care Crisis--and the People Who Pay the Price, 2007. Contributor to periodicals. **Address:** New Republic, 1331 H St. NW, Ste. 700, Washington, DC 20005, U.S.A.

COHN, Rachel. American (born United States), b. 1968. **Genres:** Novels, Romance/Historical, Literary Criticism And History. **Career:** Writer. **Publications:** Gingerbread, 2002; The Steps, 2003; Pop Princess, 2004; Shrimp, 2005; Two Steps Forward, 2006; (with D. Levithan) Nick and Norah's Infinite Playlist, 2006; Cupcake, 2007; (with D. Levithan) Naomi and Ely's No Kiss List: A Novel, 2007; You Know Where to Find Me, 2008; Very LeFreak, 2010; (with D. Levithan) Dash and Lily's Book of Dares, 2010; (with D. Levithan) The Twelve Days of Dash and Lily, 2010. **Address:** c/o Author Mail, Simon and Schuster Inc., 1230 Ave. of the Americas, 11th Fl., New York, NY 10020-1513, U.S.A. **Online address:** rachel@rachelcohn.com

COHN-SHERBOK, Dan. American (born United States), b. 1945. **Genres:** Theology/Religion, History, Adult Non-fiction, Biography. **Career:** University of Kent at Canterbury, lecturer in theology, 1975-97, Board of Theology and Religious Studies, chairman, 1980-82, Centre for the Study of Religion and Society, director, 1982-90, Canterbury Theological Network, convener, 1992-; University of Wales, School of Theology, Religious Studies and Islamic Studies, professor of Judaism, 1997-, visiting professor emeritus of Judaism, now professor emeritus of Judaism; University of Essex, visiting professor, 1993-94; Middlesex University, visiting professor, 1994; University of Aberystwyth, honorary professor; St Mary's University College, visiting professor; Charles University-Prague, visiting professor; Trinity University College, visiting professor; Durham University, visiting professor; Vilnius University, visiting professor; St. Andrews University, visiting professor. Writer. **Publications:** NONFICTION: The Jewish Community of Canterbury, 1984; On Earth as It Is in Heaven, 1987; The Jewish Heritage, 1988; Jewish Petitionary Prayer: A Theological Exploration, 1989; Holocaust Theology, 1989; Rabbinic Perspectives on the New Testament, 1990; Issues in Contemporary Judaism, 1991; A Dictionary of Judaism and Christianity, 1991; A Dictionary of Judaica, 1992; The Crucified Jew, 1992; Israel: The History of an Idea, 1992; Exodus: An Agenda for Jewish-Christian Dialogue, 1992; The Blackwell Dictionary of Judaica, 1992; The Jewish Faith, 1993; Judaism and Other Faiths, 1994; Atlas of Jewish History, 1994; The Future of Judaism, 1994; Jewish and Christian Mysticism, 1994; A Short History of Judaism, 1994; (with L. Cohn-Sherbok) A Popular Dictionary of Judaism, 1995; (with L. Cohn-Sherbok) The American Jew: Voices from an American Jewish Community, 1995; God and the Holocaust, 1996; Modern Jewish, 1996; (with A. Linzey) After Noah, 1996; Medieval Jewish Philosophy, 1996; The Hebrew Bible, 1996; 50 Key Jewish Thinkers, 1997; The Jewish Messiah, 1997; A Short Introduction to Judaism, 1997; Fifty Key Jewish Thinkers, 1997, 2nd ed., 2007; Judaism, 1998; Jews, Christians and Religious Pluralism, 1999; Jesus, Christians and Religious Pluralism, 1999; Understanding the Holocaust, 1999; Messianic Judaism, 2000; The Palestine-Israel Conflict, 2001, rev. ed., 2008; Interfaith Theology, 2001; The Wisdom of the Kabbalah, 2002; Anti-semitism: A History, 2002; Judaism: History Belief and Practice, 2003; The Vision of Judaism: Wrestling with God, 2004; The Dictionary of Jewish Biography, 2005; The Paradox of Anti-Semitism, 2006; Kabbalah and

Jewish Mysticism, 2006; Judaism Today, 2010; Introduction to Zionism and Israel: From Ideology to History, 2011. EDITOR/CO-EDITOR: (and contrib.) Exploring Reality, 1987; (and contrib.) The Canterbury Papers (essays), 1990; (and contrib.) The Salman Rushdie Controversy in Interreligious Perspective, 1990; (and contrib.) Tradition and Unity: Sermons in Honour of Robert Runcie, 1990; (and contrib.) A Traditional Quest: Essays in Honour of Louis Jacobs, 1991; The Sayings of Moses, 1991; Using the Bible Today, 1991; Problems in Contemporary Jewish Theology, 1991; (and contrib.) Islam in a World of Diverse Faiths, 1991; (and contrib.) The World's Religions and Human Liberation, 1992; Anti-Semitism in Our Time, 1992; (with D. McLellan) Religion in Public Life, 1992; Torah and Revelation, 1992; World Religions and Human Liberation, 1992; (with C. Lewis) Beyond Death: Theological and Philosphical Reflections on Life After Death, 1992; Many Mansions: Interfaith and Religious Intolerance, 1992; Glimpses of God, 1993; Divine Intervention and Miracles, 1996; (with M. Leahy) The Liberation Debate: Rights at Issue, 1996; (and comp. with L. Cohn-Sherbok) A Short Reader in Judaism, 1996; Biblical Hebrew for Beginners, 1996; Theodicy, 1997; (with C. Lamb) The Future of Religion: Postmodern Perspectives: Essays in Honour of Ninian Smart, 1999; The Future of Jewish Christian Dialogue, 1999; Voices of Messianic Judaism: Confronting Critical Issues Facing a Maturing Movement, 2001; (with J.M. Court) Religious Diversity in the Graeco-Roman World: A Survey of Recent Scholarship, 2001; (and comp.) Holocaust Theology, 2002. **Address:** Department of Theology & Religious Studies, University of Wales, Lampeter Campus, Lampeter, SA48 7ED, Wales. **Online address:** cohnsherbok@googlemail.com

COHRS, Patrick O. American (born United States), b. 1972. **Genres:** History, Military/Defense/Arms Control, International Relations/Current Affairs, Politics/Government. **Career:** Harvard University, fellow, 2002-03, Belfer Center for Science and International Affairs, post-doctoral fellow, 2005-06, International Security Program, research fellow, 2005-06; University of Oxford, St. Antony's College, senior associate, 2004, Alistair Horne Fellow, 2006-07; Humboldt University, Department of History, research fellow, 2004-05; Yale University, assistant professor of history, 2007-, International Security Studies, fellow; Jackson Institute, MacMillan Center for International and Area Studies, faculty. Writer. **Publications:** The Unfinished Peace after World War I: America, Britain and the Stabilisation of Europe, 1919- 1932, 2006. **Address:** Department of History, Hall of Graduate Studies, Yale University, 320 York St., Ste. 2688, New Haven, CT 06511, U.S.A. **Online address:** patrick.cohrs@yale.edu

COJOCARU, Steven. American/Canadian (born Canada), b. 1965. **Genres:** Autobiography/Memoirs, Art/Art History, Medicine/Health. **Career:** Flare, correspondent, 1989-91, staff, 1991-; People Magazine, stringer, style editor, west coast fashion editor, columnist, 1994-, fashion correspondent; Today Show, style correspondent, 2000-05; Entertainment Tonight, fashion correspondent, 2003-; American Idol, staff, 2003-04; E! and Access Hollywood, staff. **Publications:** Red Carpet Diaries: Confessions of a Glamour Boy, 2003; Glamour, Interrupted: How I Became the Best-dressed Patient in Hollywood, 2007. **Address:** c/o Author Mail, Random House, 1745 Broadway, New York, NY 10019, U.S.A.

COKAL, Susann. American (born United States), b. 1965?. **Genres:** Novellas/Short Stories, Novels. **Career:** California Polytechnic State University, Department of Creative Writing and Modern Literature, assistant professor, 2001-04; Virginia Commonwealth University, Department of English, assistant professor, 2004-, associate professor, director of creative writing. Writer. **Publications:** Mirabilis, 2001; Breath and Bones, 2005. Works appear in anthologies. Contributor to journals. **Address:** Department of English, Virginia Commonwealth University, 302B Anderson House, Rm. 306, Hibbs Hall, 900 Park Ave., PO Box 842005, Richmond, VA 23284-2005, U.S.A. **Online address:** correspondence@susanncokal.com

COKER, Christopher. British (born England), b. 1953. **Genres:** Economics, Politics/Government, Military/Defense/Arms Control, Young Adult Nonfiction, History. **Career:** London School of Economics and Political Science, Department of International Relations, lecturer, 1982-, professor and department head; The Atlantic Quarterly, editor; The European Security Analyst, editor; Norwegian Staff College, adjunct professor; Centre for Media and Communications of a Democratic Romania, president; Royal College of Defence Studies, lecturer; NATO Defence College, lecturer; Centre for International Security, lecturer; National Institute for Defence Studies, lecturer. **Publications:** NONFICTION: U.S. Military Power in the 1980s, 1983; The Future of the Atlantic Alliance, 1984; The Soviet Union, Eastern Europe, and the New International Economic Order, 1984; NATO, the Warsaw Pact, and Africa, 1985; A Nation in Retreat?: Britain's Defence Commitment, 1986; The United States and South Africa, 1968-1985: Constructive Engagement and Its Critics, 1986; British Defence Policy in the 1990s: A Guide to the Defence Debate, 1987; South Africa's Security Dilemmas, 1987; Less Important than Opulence: The Conservatives and Defence, 1988; Reflections on American Foreign Policy since 1945, 1989; War and the 20th Century: A Study of War and Modern Consciousness, 1994; Twilight of the West, 1998; War and the Illiberal Conscience, 1998; Humane Warfare, 2001; Globalisation and Insecurity in the Twenty-First Century: NATO and the Management of Risk, 2002; Waging War without Warriors?: The Changing Culture of Military Conflict, 2002; Empires in Conflict: The Growing Rift between Europe and the United States, 2003; Future of War: The Re-Enchantment of War in the Twenty-First Century, 2004; Warrior Ethos: Military Culture and the War on Terror, 2007; Ethics and War in the Twenty-First Century, 2008; War in an Age of Risk, 2009; Barbarous Philosophers: Reflections on the Nature of War From Heraclitus to Heisenberg, 2010. JUVENILE NONFICTION: Terrorism, 1986; Terrorism and Civil Strife, 1987. EDITOR: The United States, Western Europe, and Military Intervention Overseas, 1988; Drifting Apart?: The Superpowers and Their European Allies, 1989; Shifting into Neutral?: Burden Sharing in the Western Alliance in the 1990s, 1990; (ed. with C. Holmqvist-Jonsaater) Character of War in the 21st Century, 2010. **Address:** Department International Relations, London School of Economics & Political Science, Houghton St., London, GL WC2A 2AE, England. **Online address:** c.coker@lse.ac.uk

COKER, Joe L. American (born United States), b. 1969?. **Genres:** History. **Career:** Baylor University, lecturer in religion, 2008-; Samford University, faculty. Writer. **Publications:** Liquor in the Land of the Lost Cause: Southern White Evangelicals and the Prohibition Movement, 2007. Contributor to journals. **Address:** Department of Religion, Baylor University, 1 Bear Pl., Ste. 97284, Waco, TX 76798-7284, U.S.A. **Online address:** joe_coker@baylor.edu

COLALILLO-KATES, Isabella. Canadian/Italian (born Italy), b. 1948. **Genres:** Poetry, Children's Fiction, Education, Novellas/Short Stories, Psychology, Science Fiction/Fantasy, Humanities, Translations, Translations. **Career:** Writer, psychotherapist, educator, consultant and translator. **Publications:** (As Isabella Colalillo-Katz) Tasting Fire, 1999; (co-ed.) Holistic Learning and Spirituality in Education, 2005; (as Isabella Colalillo-Katz) And Light Remains, 2006; Awakening Creativity and Spiritual Intelligence, 2009; (ed. with C.L. Harvey) The Wheels of Soul in Education, 2010. **Address:** 431 Whitmore Ave., Toronto, ON M6E 2N6, Canada. **Online address:** isa@axxent.ca

COLANTUONI, Joe. American (born United States), b. 1948. **Genres:** Novels, Theology/Religion. **Career:** Writer. **Publications:** The Surfmaster: A Tale of Love and Hope, 2006; The Melody of the Soul, 2007. **Address:** Outskirts Press Inc., 10940 S Parker Rd., Ste. 515, Parker, CO 80134-4901, U.S.A. **Online address:** bch4joe@comcast.net

COLASANTI, Susane. American (born United States), b. 1973?. **Genres:** Young Adult Fiction, Romance/Historical. **Career:** New York City Department of Education, teacher, 1998-2007; full-time writer, 2007-. **Publications:** NOVELS: When It Happens, 2006; Take Me There, 2008; Waiting for You, 2009; Something Like Fate, 2010. Contributor to periodicals. **Address:** New York, NY , U.S.A. **Online address:** friendly.neighbor@hotmail.com

COLDEN, Kevin. American (born United States), b. 1978. **Genres:** Graphic Novels. **Career:** House of Twelve, writer and illustrator, 2003-; Asylum Press, writer and illustrator, 2003-; Media-Blasters, writer and illustrator, 2003-; Chemistry Set (webcomics collective), co-founder, 2006; Heads Up Display, drummer. Graphic artist and cartoonist. **Publications:** Fishtown (graphic novel), 2008. Works appear in anthologies. **Address:** New York, NY , U.S.A. **Online address:** kevin@kevincolden.com

COLE, Allan. American (born United States), b. 1943. **Genres:** Science Fiction/Fantasy, Romance/Historical, Mystery/Crime/Suspense, Adult Non-fiction, Novels. **Career:** Writer. **Publications:** SCIENCE FICTION NOVELS WITH CHRIS BUNCH: Sten, 1982; The Wolf Worlds, 1984; The Court of a Thousand Suns, 1985; A Reckoning for Kings: A Novel of the Tet Offensive, 1987; Fleet of the Damned, 1988; Revenge of the Damned, 1989; The Return of the Emperor, 1990; Vortex, 1992; Empire's End, 1993. FANTASY NOVELS: The Far Kingdoms, 1993; The Warrior's Tale, 1994; (with C. Bunch) Kingdoms of the Night, 1995; The Warrior Returns, 1996; When the Gods Slept, 1997; Wizard of the Winds, 1998; Wolves of the Gods, 1998; The God's Awaken, 1999. HISTORICAL NOVELS: (with C. Bunch) A Daughter of Liberty, 1993; The Blacksmith's Daughter, 2005; Lord of Terror, 2006; (with C. Bunch) Freedom Bird, 2009; (with C. Bunch) The Wars of the Shannons, 2009; A Cop's Life, 2009; MacGregor, 2010; (with N. Perumov) The Hate Parallax, 2011; Drowned Hopes: The Novel & Screenplay, 2011. OTHER: (with N. Perumov) Armageddon, 2000. Contributor to periodicals. **Address:** c/o Russell Galen, Scovil Galen Ghosh Literary Agency Inc., 276 5th Ave., Ste. 708, New York, NY 10001, U.S.A. **Online address:** sten3001@aol.com

COLE, Barry. British (born England), b. 1936. **Genres:** Novels, Poetry, Travel/Exploration, Young Adult Fiction, Mystery/Crime/Suspense, Adult Non-fiction. **Career:** Reuters news agency, clerk, writer, 1958; Central Office of Information, reporter, 1965-70, senior editor, 1974-94; University of Durham, northern arts fellow in literature, 1970-72; University of Newcastle-upon-Tyne, northern arts fellow, 1970-72; freelance writer, 1972-74; Central Office of Information, staff, senior editor, 1974-94. **Publications:** POETRY: Blood Ties, 1967; Ulysses in the Town of Coloured Glass, 1968; Moon Search, 1968; The Visitors, 1970; Vanessa in the City, 1971; Pathetic Fallacies, 1973; Dedications, 1974; The Rehousing of Scaffardi, 1976; Inside Outside: New and Selected Poems, 1998; Ghosts Are People Too, 2003. NOVELS: A Run across the Island, 1968; Joseph Winter's Patronage, 1969; The Search for Rita, 1970; The Giver, 1971; Doctor Fielder's Common Sense, 1972; The Edge of the Common, 1989. Contributor to periodicals. **Address:** 68 Myddelton Sq., London, GL EC1R 1XP, England. **Online address:** barryh.cole@virgin.net

COLE, Betsy. American (born United States), b. 1940. **Genres:** Animals/Pets, Children's Fiction. **Career:** Teacher, 1962-65, 1971-72, 1975-76; Martinsville Piedmont Arts Association, board director, 1989-92; Druid Hills Elementary Parent Teacher Association, president. **Publications:** Green Creatures Ten to One, 1988; Is Aetosaur a Dinosaur?, 1992. **Address:** 1510 White Oak Ct., Martinsville, VA 24112-5520, U.S.A. **Online address:** ecc@kimbanet.com

COLE, Bruce. American (born United States), b. 1938. **Genres:** Art/Art History. **Career:** University of Rochester, assistant professor, 1969-73; Indiana University, associate professor, 1973-77, professor of art history, 1977-88, distinguished professor of fine arts, 1988-, now distinguished professor emeritus of fine arts and professor emeritus of comparative literature; National Endowment for the Humanities, chairman, 2001-09; The American Revolution Center, president and chief executive officer, 2009-11, advisor, 2011-; Kunsthistorisches Institut-Florence, William E. Suida Fellow; Association for Art History, founder, co-president. Writer. **Publications:** Giotto and Florentine Painting, 1280-1375, 1976; Agnolo Gaddi, 1977; Sienese Painting, from Its Origins to the Fifteenth Century, 1980; Masaccio and the Art of Early Renaissance Florence, 1980; The Renaissance Artist at Work: From Pisano to Titian, 1983; Sienese Painting in the Age of the Renaissance, 1985; Italian Art, 1250-1550: The Relation of Renaissance Art to Life and Society, 1987; (with A. Gealt) Art of the Western World: From Ancient Greece to Post-modernism, 1989; Piero della Francesca: Tradition and Innovation in Renaissance Art, 1991; (contrib.) Venetian Paintings of The Renaissance, 1991; Giotto: The Scrovegni Chapel, Padua, 1993; Studies in the History of Italian Art, 1250-1550, 1996; Titian and Venetian Painting, 1450-1590, 1999; Informed Eye: Understanding Masterpieces of Western Art, 1999; (with P.L. Roberts and H.B.J. Maginnis) Sacred Treasures: Early Italian Paintings from Southern Collections, 2002; Fearless and Free: Celebrating the 40th Anniversary of the National Endowment For the Humanities, 2005. **Address:** Indiana University, 107 S Indiana Ave., Bloomington, IN 47405-7000, U.S.A. **Online address:** bcole@neh.gov

COLE, David. American (born United States), b. 1958?. **Genres:** Young Adult Non-fiction. **Career:** United States Court of Appeals for the Third Circuit, law clerk, 1984-85; Center for Constitutional Rights, staff attorney, 1985-90; Georgetown University, Law Center, associate professor, 1990-94, professor of law, 1994-; Nation, legal affairs correspondent, 1998-; National Public Radio, commentator. **Publications:** (With J.X. Dempsey) Terrorism and the Constitution: Sacrificing Civil Liberties in the Name of National Security, 1999, 3rd ed., 2006; No Equal Justice: Race and Class in the American Criminal Justice System, 1999; Enemy Aliens: Double Standards and Constitutional Freedoms in the War on Terrorism, 2003; (with J. Lobel) Less Safe, Less Free: Why America Is Losing the War on Terror, 2007; Justice At War: The Men and Ideas that Shaped America's War on Terror, 2008; (ed. and intro.) Torture Memos: Rationalizing the Unthinkable, 2009; (ed.) Securing Liberty: Debating Issues of Terrorism and Democratic Values in the Post-9/11 United States, 2011. **Address:** Law Center, Georgetown University, 600 New Jersey Ave. NW, Washington, DC 20001, U.S.A. **Online address:** cole@law.georgetown.edu

COLE, Diane. (Diane Joyce Cole). American (born United States), b. 1952. **Genres:** Adult Non-fiction, Biography, Women's Studies And Issues, How-to Books, Business/Trade/Industry. **Career:** National Jewish Monthly, assistant editor, 1976-77; University of Pennsylvania Almanac, editor, 1978-79; freelance writer, 1979-; Savvy Magazine, contributing editor, 1983-87; Psychology Today, contributing editor, 1988-90; In Touch, book editor, 1999-. **Publications:** Hunting the Headhunters: A Woman's Guide, 1988; After Great Pain: A New Life Emerges, 1992; (with S. Wetzler) Is It You Or Is It Me?: How We Turn Our Emotions Inside Out and Blame Each Other, 1998. Works appear in anthologies. Contributor to periodicals. **Address:** Susan Lee Cohen, 2673 Broadway, New York, NY 10025, U.S.A. **Online address:** cole@winedalebooks.com

COLE, Diane Joyce. *See* **COLE, Diane.**

COLE, Edmund Keith. (Keith Cole). Australian (born Australia), b. 1919. **Genres:** Anthropology/Ethnology, History, Biography, Novellas/Short Stories. **Career:** Moore Theological College, lecturer, 1944-50; Kahuhia Normal School, staff, 1950-52; Saint Paul's United Theological College, principal, 1954-60; Archdeacon of Central Kenya, 1961-63; University of Melbourne, Ridley College, vice-principal, 1964-73; Church Missionary Society, historian, 1968-; Nungalinya College, principal, 1973-78; Theological Education, director, 1978-84; Diocese of Bendigo, director of theological education, 1978; Australian College of Theology, fellow. Writer. **Publications:** Mau Mau Mission, 1954; After Mau Mau, 1956; Kenya, Hanging in the Middle Way, 1959; Roper River Mission, 1968; Commissioned to Care: The Golden Jubilee History of the Mission of St. James and St. John 1919-1969, 1969; Short History of the C.M.S. Roper River Mission, 1908-1969, 1969; Cross Over Mount Kenya: A Short History of the Anglican Church in the Diocese of Mount Kenya (1900-1970), 1970; Sincerity My Guide: A Biography of the Right Reverend P. W. Stephenson (1888-1962), 1970; Groote Eylandt Pioneer: A Biography of the Reverend Hubert Ernest de Mey Warren, Pioneer Missionary and Explorer among the Aborigines of Arnhem Land, 1971; Groote Eylandt Mission: A Short History of the C.M.S. Groote Eylandt Mission, 1921-1971, 1971; History of Church Missionary Society of Australia, 1971; Oenpelli Stories, 1972; Oenpelli Pioneer: A Biography of the Reverend Alfred John Dyer; Pioneer Missionary among the Aborigines in Arnhem Land and Founder of the Oenpelli Mission, 1972; Perriman in Arnhem Land: A Biography of Harry Leslie Perriman, Pioneer Missionary among the Aborigines at Roper River, Groote Eylandt and Oenpelli in Arnhem Land, 1973; Totems and Tamarinds: Aborigines and Macassans in Eastern Arnhem Land, 1973; Groote Eylandt: Changing Aboriginal Life Styles, 1975, rev. ed., 1992; History of Oenpelli, 1975; Oenpelli Jubilee, 1975; Outlines of Christian Doctrine, 1976; Life of Christ, 1976; Winds of Fury, 1977; Worship, 1978; Introducing the Old Testament, 1978; The Aborigines of Arnhem Land, 1979; Cole Family History: (Including the Families of) Cole, Brookes, Descor, Goodwin, Gough, Hume, Johnston, Pretty, Maiden, Newell, Shipley, Truscott, 1979; Arnhem Land: Places and People, 1980; Dick Harris: Missionary to the Aborigines: A Biography of the Reverend Canon George Richmond Harris, M.B.E., Pioneer Missionary to the Aborigines of Arnhem Land, 1980; Seafarers of the Groote Archipelago, 1980; Aborigines: Towards Dignity and Identity, 1981; Aborigines and Mining on Groote Eylandt, 1981; A History of Numbulwar, 1982; The Aborigines of Victoria, 1982; Through Hardship to the Stars, 1984; The Lake Condah Mission, 1984; Fred Gray of Umbakumba: The Story of Frederick Harold Gray, the Founder of the Umbakumba Aboriginal Settlement on Groote Eylandt, 1984; The Aborigines of Western Australia, 1985; From Mission to Church: The CMS Mission to the Aborigines of Arnhem Land, 1908-1985, 1985; Pethy, Lee and Mary: Three CMS Missionaries in East Africa, 1986; Crusade Hymns: Their Stories and Their Meanings, 1987; Beneath the Southern Cross: Sacred Hymns, Poetry and Readings, 1988; Letters from China, 1893-1895: The Story of the Sister Martyrs of Ku Cheng, 1988; Groote Eylandt Aborigines and Mining: A Study in Cross-Cultural Relationships, 1988; Robert Harkness: The Bendigo Hymnwriter, 1988; But I Will Be with You: An Autobiography, 1988; Men of Faith and Vision: Archdeacon A. Crawford and Dean J.C. MacCullagh, 1989; A History of All Saints

Church, Bendigo: The Rise and Demise of a Cathedral, 1990; A History of Holy Trinity Church, Bendigo, 1990; A History of Christ Church, Echuca, 1990; A History of Christ Church, East Bendigo, 1990; The Bendigo Crusade Choir, 1990; A History of the Diocese of Bendigo: an Anglican Diocese in Rural Victoria, 1991; Sharing in Mission: The Centenary History of the Victorian Branch of the Church Missionary Society, 1892-1992, 1992; Servants for Jesus' Sake: Long-serving Victorian CMS Missionaries, 1993. EDITOR: Groote Eylandt Stories, 1972; A Taste of Salt: A Selection of Sermons and Articles by Bishop Oliver Heyward, 1991. **Address:** 28 Woodbury St., Bendigo, VI 3550, Australia.

COLE, Johnnetta B(etsch). American (born United States), b. 1936. **Genres:** Anthropology/Ethnology. **Career:** University of California, faculty, 1964; Washington State University, assistant professor of anthropology and director of black studies, 1967-70; University of Massachusetts, professor of anthropology and Afro-American studies, 1970-83, provost of undergraduate education, 1981-83; City University of New York, Hunter College, Russell Sage visiting professor of anthropology, 1983, professor of anthropology, 1983-87, director of Latin American and Caribbean studies, 1984-87; Spelman College, president, 1987-97, president emeritus; Emory University, faculty, 1998, Presidential distinguished professor, 1999-2002, Presidential distinguished professor emeritus; Bennett College, president, 2002-07, Johnnetta B. Cole Global Diversity & Inclusion Institute, founder; Smithsonian Institution, National Museum of African Art, director. Writer. **Publications:** Race Toward Equality, 1986; Conversations: Straight Talk with America's Sister President, 1993; Dream the Boldest Dreams: And Other Lessons of Life, 1997; (with B.G. Sheftall) Gender Talk: The Struggle for Women's Equality in African American Communities, 2003. EDITOR: Anthropology for the Eighties: Introductory Readings, 1982; All-American Women: Lines that Divide, Ties that Bind, 1986; (and intro.) Anthropology for the Nineties: Introductory Readings, 1988. OTHERS: (intro.) Student Culture and Activism in Black South African Universities: The Roots of Resistance, 1984; (with M. Berger) Race and Representation: Art/Film/Video, January 26-March 6, 1987, 1987; (intro.) Art by Metamorphosis: Selections of African Art from the Spelman College Collection, 1988; (with R.P. Byrd and B. Guy-Sheftall) I am Your Sister: Collected and Unpublished Writings of Audre Lorde, 2009; (with B. Guy-Sheftall) Who Should be First?: Feminists Speak Out on the 2008 Presidential Campaign, 2010. Contributor to journals. **Address:** Emory University, 201 Dowman Dr., Atlanta, GA 30322, U.S.A.

COLE, Keith. *See* **COLE, Edmund Keith.**

COLE, Peter. Israeli/American (born United States), b. 1957. **Genres:** Translations. **Career:** Ibis Editions, co-founder and co-editor, 1998-; Yale University, visiting writer and professor; Middlebury College, visiting writer and professor; Wesleyan University, visiting writer and professor; Whitney Center for Humanities, Franke visiting fellow, 2006. **Publications:** POEMS, EXCEPT WHERE NOTED: Rift, 1986; Hymns & Qualms, 1998; What Is Doubled: Poems 1981-1998, 2005; (ed.) Hebrew Writers on Writing (essays), 2008; Things on Which I've Stumbled, 2008. TRANSLATOR: Shmuel HaNagid, Selected Poems of Shmuel Ha-Nagid, 1996; Aharon Shabtai, Love & Selected Poems, 1997; Harold Schimmel, From Island to Island, 1997; Harold Schimmel, Qasida, 1997; (co-author) Taha Muhammad Ali, Never Mind: Twenty Poems and a Story, 2000; Yoel Hoffmann, The Heart Is Katmandu, 2001; Solomon Ibn Gabirol, Selected Poems of Solomon Ibn Gabirol, 2001; Avraham Ben Yitzhak, Collected Poems, 2003; Aharon Shabtai, J'accuse, 2003; Yoel Hoffman, The Shunra and the Schmetterling, 2004; (with Y. Hijazi and G. Levin) Taha Muhammad Ali, So What: New & Selected Poems (with a Story), 1971-2005, 2006; (and ed. and intro.) The Dream of the Poem: Hebrew Poetry from Muslim & Christian Spain, 950-1492, 2007; Yoel Hoffmann, Curriculum Vitae, 2009. **Address:** Ibis Editions, PO Box 8074, German Colony, Jerusalem, 91080, Israel. **Online address:** colehoff@netvision.net.il

COLE, Phyllis (Blum). American (born United States), b. 1944. **Genres:** Literary Criticism And History. **Career:** Wellesley College, assistant professor of English, 1973-78, part-time assistant professor of English, 1978-83; Harvard University, Divinity School, visiting lecturer in women's studies and history of Christianity and research associate, 1984-85, Extension Division, lecturer, 1987-88; Pennsylvania State University, associate professor of English and women's studies, 1989-2000, professor of English, American studies and women's studies, 2000-, American Studies Program, director. Writer. **Publications:** The American Writer and the Condition of England, 1815-1860, 1987; (with S. Striefel) Providing Psychological and Related Services to Children and Adolescents: A Comprehensive Guidebook, 1987; Mary Moody Emerson and the Origins of Transcendentalism: A Family History, 1998. Contributor of articles to books and periodicals. **Address:** Department of English, Pennsylvania State University, 312 F Main Bldg., 25 Yearsley Mill Rd., Media, PA 19063-5596, U.S.A. **Online address:** pbc2@psu.edu

COLE, Robert. American (born United States), b. 1939. **Genres:** History, Travel/Exploration, Bibliography. **Career:** Whittier College, instructor in summer school, 1967-68; Pomona College, instructor, 1967-69; Utah State University, assistant professor, 1970-76, associate professor, 1976-90, professor, 1990-; University of North London, visiting senior lecturer, 1982-83. Writer. **Publications:** (Ed. with M. Moody) The Dissenting Tradition, 1975; A Traveller's History of France, 1988, 7th ed., 2005; Britain and the War of Words in Neutral Europe, 1939-45, 1990; A.J.P. Taylor: The Traitor within the Gates, 1993; A Traveller's History of Paris, 1994; Twentieth-Century Political and War Propaganda: An Annotated Bibliography, 1996; (ed.) The Encyclopedia of Propaganda, 3 vols., 1998; A Traveller's History of Germany, 2004; Propaganda, Censorship and Irish Neutrality in the Second World War, 2006; Propaganda and War, 1939-1945, forthcoming. **Address:** Department of History, Utah State University, Main 321-K, Logan, UT 84322-0710, U.S.A. **Online address:** robert.cole@usu.edu

COLE, Sheila R. American/Canadian (born Canada), b. 1939. **Genres:** Novels, Children's Fiction, History, Psychology, Sociology, Young Adult Fiction, Children's Non-fiction. **Career:** Sunnyvale Daily Standard, reporter, 1963-64; Community Progress Inc., public information officer, 1965-66; Newport Beach Pilot, reporter, 1966-67; New York Times Sunday Book Review, reviewer; University of California, research assistant, 1968-69; freelance writer, 1969-; Deutsch, Shea & Evans Inc., director of communications, 1977. **Publications:** Meaning Well, 1974; (ed. with M. Cole) The Making of Mind: A Personal Account of Soviet Psychology, 1979; Working Kids on Working, 1980; When the Tide is Low, 1985; (with M. Cole) The Development of Children, 1989, 6th ed., 2009; The Dragon in the Cliff: A Novel Based on the Life of Mary Anning, 1991; When the Rain Stops, 1991; The Hen That Crowed, 1993; What Kind of Love? The Diary of a Pregnant Teenager, 1995; The Canyon (middle-grade novel), 2002; To Be Young in America: Growing Up with the Country, 1776-1940, 2005. Contributor to periodicals. **Address:** 522 Glencrest Dr., Solana Beach, CA 92075, U.S.A. **Online address:** sheila_cole@yahoo.com

COLE, Simon A. American (born United States), b. 1967?. **Genres:** History, Social Sciences, Criminology/True Crime, Sociology, Social Sciences. **Career:** Cornell University, Department of Science and Technology Studies, instructor, 1995, consultant, 2001, visiting scientist, 2001-02; Rutgers University, Institute for Health, Health Care Policy and Aging Research, postdoctoral fellow, 1997-99; City University of New York, Borough of Manhattan Community College, adjunct lecturer, 1997, John Jay College of Criminal Justice, visiting scientist, 2001-02; Visual Networks Inc., visualization architect, 2000; University of California, School of Social Ecology, Department of Criminology, Law & Society, assistant professor, 2002-06, associate professor, 2006-09, chair, 2009-; Harvard University, Kennedy School of Government, instructor; Theoretical Criminology, U.S. book review editor, 2005-07, co-editor, 2008-. **Publications:** Suspect Identities: A History of Fingerprinting and Criminal Identification, 2001. Contributor to periodicals. **Address:** Department of Criminology, Law & Society, School of Social Ecology, University of California, 2357 Social Ecology II, Irvine, CA 92697-7080, U.S.A. **Online address:** scole@uci.edu

COLE, Stephanie. British (born England), b. 1941. **Genres:** Autobiography/Memoirs, Music. **Career:** Order of the British Empire, officer, 2005-. Writer. **Publications:** A Passionate Life, 1998. Contributor to periodicals. **Address:** c/o Author Mail, Hodder Stoughton Ltd., 338 Euston Rd., London, GL NW1 3BH, England.

COLE, Stephen A. American (born United States), b. 1955. **Genres:** Local History/Rural Topics, Sports/Fitness, Transportation, Agriculture/Forestry, Technology, Photography. **Career:** Maine State Planning Office, senior planner, 1991-98; Coastal Enterprises Inc., project manager, 1998-, director of natural resources and sustainable communities. Writer. **Publications:** (With C.N. Chatterley and A.J. Rouverol) I Was Content and Not Content, 2000; The Rangeley and Its Region: The Famous Boat and Lakes of Western Maine, 2007; (with L. Gifford) Cranberry: Hard Work and Holiday Sauce, 2009. Contributor to periodicals. **Address:** Coastal Enterprises Inc.,

36 Water St., PO Box 268, Wiscasset, ME 04578, U.S.A. **Online address:** scole@celmaine.org

COLE, Susan Letzler. American (born United States), b. 1940. **Genres:** Theatre, Social Sciences. **Career:** University of Virginia, instructor, 1964, 1966; Cleveland State University, assistant professor of English, 1968-69; Southern Connecticut State College, lecturer in English, 1969; Yale University, tutor in English, 1969-70; Quinnipiac College, assistant professor of English, 1970-71; Albertus Magnus College, assistant professor, 1971-76, associate professor and department head, 1977-83, professor of English and academic director of concentration in creative writing and drama concentration in English, 1983-, dramaturg for college plays, 1988-. Writer. **Publications:** The Absent One: Mourning Ritual, Tragedy, and The Performance of Ambivalence, 1985; Directors in Rehearsal: A Hidden World, 1992; Playwrights In Rehearsal: The Seduction of Company, 2001; Missing Alice: In Search of a Mother's Voice, 2007. Contributor to books and journals. **Address:** Department of English, Albertus Magnus College, Rm. 318, Aquinas Hall, 700 Prospect St., New Haven, CT 06511-1224, U.S.A. **Online address:** scole@albertus.edu

COLE, Terrence (Michael). American (born United States), b. 1953. **Genres:** History, Local History/Rural Topics, Military/Defense/Arms Control, Autobiography/Memoirs. **Career:** State of Alaska, research analyst, 1975, historian, 1979, historical consultant, 1980-82; Alaska Northwest Publishing Co., research editor, 1981-83, Alaska Journal, editor, 1983-86; National Bank of Alaska, corporate historian, 1986-88; University of Alaska, Department of History, assistant professor, 1988-91, associate professor, 1991-, professor, affiliate professor, chair, 1992-98, Office of Public History, director. **Publications:** Ghost of the Gold Rush: A Historical Walking Tour of Fairbanks (monograph), 1977, rev. ed., 1987; E.T. Barnette: The Strange Story of the Man Who Founded Fairbanks, 1981, rev. ed. as Crooked Past: The History of Frontier Mining Camp, Fairbanks, Alaska, 1991; Nome: City of the Golden Beaches, 1984; The Cornerstone on College Hill: A History of the University of Alaska Fairbanks, 1994; (with E.E. Rasmuson) Banking on Alaska: A History of the National Bank of Alaska, 2000; Blinded by Riches: The Permanent Funding Problem and the Prudhoe Bay Effect, 2004; Fighting for the Forty-Ninth Star: C.W. Snedden and the Crusade for Alaska Statehood, 2010. EDITOR: Along Alaska's Great, 1983; Nome Nugget, 1983; Gold Hunting in Alaska, 1983; The Alaskan Gold Fields, 1984; The Capture of Attu: Tales of World War II in Alaska, 1984; The Sourdough Expedition: Stories of the Pioneer Alaskans Who Climbed Mount McKinley in 1910, 1985; Wheels on Ice: Bicycling in Alaska, 1898-1908, 1985; Old Yukon: Tales, Trails and Trials, 2009. Contributor to books. **Address:** Department of History, University of Alaska, 613-C Gruening, Gruening Bldg., Ste. 605, PO Box 756460, Fairbanks, AK 99775-6460, U.S.A. **Online address:** fftmc@uaf.edu

COLE, Thomas R(ichard). American (born United States), b. 1949. **Genres:** Gerontology/Senior Issues, Biography, Humanities, History, Medicine/Health. **Career:** University of Texas, Medical Branch-Galveston, Institute for the Medical Humanities, professor, 1982-, director of medical humanities graduate program, 1983-93; University of Texas-Houston, School of Medicine, McGovern Center for Humanities and Ethics, McGovern chair and founding director, 2004-. Writer and filmmaker. **Publications:** The Journey of Life: A Cultural History of Aging America, 1992; No Color Is My Kind: The Life of Eldrewey Stearns and the Integration of Houston, 1997; (with N. Carlin and R. Carson) Introduction to Medical Humanities, 2013. EDITOR: (with S.A. Gadow) What Does It Mean to Grow Old?: Reflections from the Humanities, 1986; (with D.D. Van Tassel and R. Kastenbaum) Handbook of the Humanities and Aging, 1992, 2nd ed., 2000; (co-ed.) Voices and Visions of Aging: A Critical Gerontology, 1993; (with M.G. Winkler) The Oxford Book of Aging, 1995; (with R.A. Carson and C.R. Burns) Practicing the Medical Humanities: Engaging Physicians and Patients, 2003; (with T.J. Goodrich and E.R. Gritz) Faculty Health in Academic Medicine: Physicians, Scientists, and the Pressures of Success, 2009; (with R.E. Ray and R. Kastenbaum) A Guide to Humanistic Studies in Aging?, 2010. **Address:** McGovern Center for Humanities and Ethics, School of Medicine, University of Texas, JJL 400, 6431 Fannin St., Houston, TX 77030, U.S.A. **Online address:** thomas.cole@uth.tmc.edu

COLE, Wayne S. American (born United States), b. 1922. **Genres:** History, International Relations/Current Affairs, Biography, Autobiography/Memoirs. **Career:** University of Arkansas, instructor, 1950-52, assistant professor, 1952-54; Iowa State University, assistant professor, 1954-56, associate professor, 1956-60, professor of history, 1960-65; University of Keele, Fulbright lecturer, 1962-63; University of Maryland, professor of history, 1965-92, distinguished school teacher, Stanley professor emeritus. Writer. **Publications:** America First: The Battle Against Intervention, 1940-1941, 1953; Senator Gerald P. Nye and American Foreign Relations, 1962; Interpretive History of American Foreign Relations, 1968, rev. ed., 1974; Charles A. Lindbergh and the Battle against American Intervention in World War II, 1974; (contrib.) Charles A. Lindbergh: An American Life, 1977; Roosevelt & the Isolationists 1932-1945, 1983; Norway and the United States, 1905-1955: Two Democracies in Peace and War, 1989; Determinism and American Foreign Relations during the Franklin D. Roosevelt Era, 1995; Life in Twentieth Century America: From Small Town Iowa to Suburban Maryland, 2002. **Address:** Department of History, University of Maryland, 2115 Francis Scott Key Hall, College Park, MD 20742, U.S.A. **Online address:** wcole5@verizon.net

COLEBANK, Susan. British/American (born United States), b. 1976. **Genres:** Novels, Young Adult Fiction. **Career:** Writer. **Publications:** Black Tuesday, 2007; Cashing in, 2009. **Address:** NH , U.S.A. **Online address:** susancolebank@gmail.com

COLEGATE, Isabel. British (born England), b. 1931. **Genres:** Novels, Young Adult Non-fiction, inspirational/Motivational Literature, Theology/Religion, Young Adult Fiction, Literary Criticism And History. **Career:** Anthony Blond Ltd., literary agent, 1952-57. Novelist and critic. **Publications:** The Blackmailer, 1958; A Man of Power, 1960; The Great Occasion, 1962; Statues in a Garden, 1964; Orlando King, 1968; Orlando at the Brazen Threshold, 1971; Agatha, 1973; News from the City of the Sun, 1979; The Shooting Party, 1980; Three Novels: The Blackmailer, A Man of Power and The Great Occasion, 1983; The Orlando Trilogy, 1984; A Glimpse of Sion's Glory, 1985; Deceits of Time, 1988; The Summer of the Royal Visit, 1992; Winter Journey, 1995; A Pelican in the Wilderness: Hermits, Solitaires and Recluses, 2002. Contributor to magazines, journals and newspapers. **Address:** Peters Fraser & Dunlop, Drury House, 34-43 Russell St., London, GL WC2B 5HA, England.

COLEMAN, A(llan) D(ouglass). American (born United States), b. 1943. **Genres:** Communications/Media, Photography, Art/Art History. **Career:** Da Capo Press Inc., assistant editor, 1967-68; The Village Voice, photography critic, 1968-73; New York Times, photography critic, 1970-74; New School for Social Research, instructor in photography, 1970-71, faculty, 1979-; Pratt Institute, instructor in photography, 1971-72; Maryland Institute College of Art, visiting lecturer, 1971-73; Camera 35, contributing editor, 1975-82; Center for Photographic Studies, critic-in-residence, 1977; Photography Media Institute Inc., vice-president, 1977-; New York University, Tisch School of Arts, Department of Photography, assistant professor, associate professor, 1978-93; A New England Journal of Photography, editor emeritus, 1982-; New York Observer, photography critic, 1988-; Photo Metro, columnist, 1989-; Camera & Darkroom, senior contributing editor, 1990-95; Photography In New York, columnist, 1992-; The Nearby Café, founder, 1995-, executive director. Freelance photography critic and lecturer. **Publications:** (Contrib.) The Grotesque in Photography, 1977; Light Readings: A Photography Critic's Writings 1968-1978, 1979, 2nd ed., 1998; Lee/Model/Parks/Samaras/Turner: Five Interviews Before the Fact, 1979; (ed. with P. Grantz and D. Sheer) The Photography A-V Program Directory, 1980; (contrib.) Light Work: Photography Over the 70's and 80's: A Retrospective Exhibition at the Everson Museum of Art, Syracuse, New York, September 13-October 20, 1985, 1985; (contrib.) Manuel Alvarez Bravo, 1987; Animals, 1995; Tarnisched Silver, 1996; Available Light, 1997; Depth of Field: Essays on Photography, Mass Media and Lens Culture, 1998; (contrib.) One Hundred Flowers, 2000; (contrib.) Hank O'Neal: Portraits, 1971-2000, 2000; (contrib.) Screen Tests, Portraits, Nudes, 1964-1996, 2000; (contrib.) Saga: The Journey of Arno Rafael Minkkinen, 2005. **Address:** 465 Van Duzer St., Staten Island, NY 10304-2029, U.S.A. **Online address:** adcoleman@photocriticism.com

COLEMAN, Carter. American (born United States) **Genres:** Novels, Young Adult Fiction, Humor/Satire. **Career:** Time Magazine, reporter; Tanzania Wildlife Fund, vice president. **Publications:** The Volunteer, 1998; Cages Bend, 2005. Contributor to periodicals. **Address:** c/o Author Mail, Warner Books Inc., 1271 Ave. of the Americas, New York, NY 10020, U.S.A.

COLEMAN, Clare. *See* **EASTON, Malcolm Coleman.**

COLEMAN, C. Norman. American (born United States), b. 1945. **Genres:** Medicine/Health, Sports/Fitness. **Career:** National Cancer Institute, clinical associate in oncology, 1972-74, Radiation Oncology Sciences Program, director, 1999-, Radiation Oncology Branch, chief, 1999-2004, Radiation Research Program, associate director, Office of Mass Casualty Planning Preparedness and Emergency Operations (OPEO), senior medical advisor and chief of the CBRN team, 2004-, Radiation Oncology Branch, Experimental Therapeutics Section, head, senior investigator; Stanford University School of Medicine, teacher of medical and radiation oncology, 1975-85, Department of Radiation and Medical Oncology, associate professor, 1978-85; Harvard University, Joint Center for Radiation Therapy, Fuller-American Cancer Society Professor and chairperson, 1985-99. Writer. **Publications:** (Ed. with R.E. Wittes) Conference on the Interaction of Radiation Therapy and Chemotherapy: Williamsburg, 1998; Understanding Cancer: A Patient's Guide to Diagnosis, Prognosis, and Treatment, 1998, 2nd ed., 2006. **Address:** National Cancer Institute, Radiation Oncology Br., NIH, Rm. B2-3561, Bldg. 10/CRC,, MSC 1682, 10 Center Dr.,, Bethesda, MD 20892-1007, U.S.A. **Online address:** ccoleman@mail.nih.gov

COLEMAN, David G. Australian (born Australia) **Genres:** History. **Career:** University of Queensland, Department of History, guest lecturer, 1997-99; University of Virginia, Miller Center of Public Affairs, assistant professor, 1999-, Presidential Recordings Program, deputy director, director, 2004-. Historian and writer. **Publications:** (with J.M. Siracusa) Depression to Cold War: A History of America from Herbert Hoover to Ronald Reagan, 2002; (with J.M. Siracusa) Real-World Nuclear Deterrence: The Making of International Strategy, 2006. Contributor to books, journals and encyclopedias. **Address:** Miller Ctr. of Public Affairs, University of Virginia, 2201 Old Ivy Rd., PO Box 400406, Charlottesville, VA 22904-4406, U.S.A. **Online address:** dgcoleman@virginia.edu

COLEMAN, Deirdre. Australian (born Australia), b. 1954. **Genres:** Writing/Journalism. **Career:** University of Wollongong, faculty; University of Adelaide, faculty; University of Sydney, faculty; University of Melbourne, School of Culture and Communication, Robert Wallace chair of English, 2006-, professor and deputy dean of the faculty of arts. Writer. **Publications:** Coleridge and the Friend (1809-1810), 1988; (ed.) Reporting Home: Her Writings as a Journalist, 1990; (ed. with P. Otto) Imagining Romanticism: Essays on English and Australian Romanticisms, 1992; (comp. with R. Ward) Gender Awareness: A List of Selected Resources, 1992; (ed.) Maiden Voyages and Infant Colonies: Two Women's Travel Narratives of the 1790s, 1999; Romantic Colonization and British Anti-Slavery, 2004; (ed. with H. Fraser) Minds, Bodies, Machines, 1770-1930, 2011; (with S. Douglas) The Flycatcher: Science, Slavery and Empire in the Age of Reason, forthcoming. Contributor to books and journals. **Address:** School of Culture and Communication, University of Melbourne, Rm. 207, John Medley Bldg., West Twr., Parkville, Melbourne, VI 3010, Australia. **Online address:** colemand@unimelb.edu.au

COLEMAN, Emmett. *See* **REED, Ishmael.**

COLEMAN, James A. British/American (born United States), b. 1921. **Genres:** Physics, Astronomy, inspirational/Motivational Literature, Humanities. **Career:** Johns Hopkins University, Applied Physics Laboratory, associate physicist, 1947-50; Connecticut College for Women, instructor in physics and astronomy, 1950-57; American International College, Department of Physics, professor and chairman, 1957-; University of Portsmouth, School of Languages and Area Studies, professor. Writer. **Publications:** SELF-ILLUSTRATED: Relativity for the Layman: A Simplified Account of the History, Theory and Proofs of Relativity, 1954; Modern Theories of the Universe, 1963; Early Theories of the Universe, 1967; (ed.) Rabelais in Glascow: Proceedings of the Colloquium held at the University of Glascow in December 1983, 1984; (ed.) Medee, 1985; (ed.) Poesies Completes, 1992; (co-ed.) Television in Europe, 1997. **Address:** School of Languages and Area Studies, University of Portsmouth, Portsmouth, MS PO1 2UP, England. **Online address:** jim@hum.potr.ac.uk

COLEMAN, James W. American (born United States), b. 1946?. **Genres:** Theology/Religion, Literary Criticism And History. **Career:** University of North Carolina, Department of English and Comparative Literature, professor. Writer. **Publications:** Blackness and Modernism: The Literary Career of John Edgar Wideman, 1989; Black Male Fiction and the Legacy of Caliban, 2001; Faithful Vision: Treatments of the Sacred, Spiritual, and Supernatural in Twentieth-Century African American Fiction, 2006; Writing Blackness: John Edgar Wideman's Art and Experimentation, 2010. **Address:** Department of English and Comparative Literature, University of North Carolina, Greenlaw Hall, PO Box 3520, Chapel Hill, NC 27599-3520, U.S.A. **Online address:** coleman3@email.unc.edu

COLEMAN, Jane Candia. American (born United States), b. 1939. **Genres:** Novels, Novellas/Short Stories, Poetry, Essays, Young Adult Fiction. **Career:** University of Pittsburgh, technical writer for medical school, 1960-65; Carlow College, Women's Creative Writing Center, co-founder and director, 1980-85; writer, 1985-. **Publications:** No Roof but Sky: Poetry of the American West, 1990; Deep in His Heart J.R. Is Laughing at Us (poems), 1991; Stories from Mesa Country, 1991; Discovering Eve (stories), 1993; Shadows in My Hands (essays), 1993; Doc Holliday's Woman, 1995; The Red Drum (poetry), 1994; Moving On (stories), 1997; I, Pearl Hart, 1998; The O'Keefe Empire, 1999; Doc Holliday's Gone, 1999; Borderlands, 2000; The Italian Quartet, 2001; Desperate Acts, 2001; Mountain Time, 2001; Wives and Lovers, 2002; Country Music, 2002; Matchless (novel), 2003; Lost River: A Western Story, 2003; Tombstone Travesty: Allie Earp Remembers (novel), 2004; White Dove, 2007; Tumbleweed, 2008; The Silver Queen, 2008; Range Queen, 2010. Contributor to periodicals. **Address:** 1702 E Lind Rd., Tucson, AZ 85719, U.S.A. **Online address:** elcisco@candiasystems.com

COLEMAN, Janet Wyman. American (born United States) **Genres:** Children's Non-fiction, Children's Fiction, Picture/Board Books, Picture/Board Books. **Career:** Janet Wyman Coleman Productions (multimedia Co.), founder. Writer and photographer. **Publications:** Fast Eddie, 1993; Famous Bears & Friends: One Hundred Years of Teddy Bear Stories, Poems, Songs, and Heroics, 2002; (with E.V. Warren) Baseball for Everyone: Stories from the Great Game, 2003; Secrets, Lies, Gizmos, and Spies: A History of Spies and Espionage, 2006. **Address:** 104 Plain Rd., Wayland, MA 01778, U.S.A. **Online address:** janet.coleman@gmail.com

COLEMAN, Jon. American (born United States), b. 1970?. **Genres:** History, Biography. **Career:** University of Colorado, teaching assistant, 1994-97; Yale University, teaching fellow, 1997-98; Indiana University-Purdue University Indianapolis, lecturer, 2000-02, visiting assistant professor, 2003-04; University of Notre Dame, assistant professor of history, 2004-08, associate professor of history, 2008-. Writer. **Publications:** Vicious: Wolves and Men in America, 2004; Here Lies Hugh Glass, 2012. **Address:** Department of History, University of Notre Dame, 219 O'Shaughnessy Hall, Notre Dame, IN 46556, U.S.A. **Online address:** jcolema2@nd.edu

COLEMAN, Jonathan (Mark). American (born United States), b. 1951. **Genres:** Adult Non-fiction, Documentaries/Reportage, Social Commentary. **Career:** New Review (magazine), editorial assistant, 1974, U.S. representative, 1975; Alfred A. Knopf Inc., publicity writer, 1975-77; Simon & Schuster Inc., associate editor, 1977-78, senior editor, 1978-81, staff, 1980-81; Columbia Broadcasting System Inc., associate producer of network news, 1981-83; University of Virginia, lecturer in advanced nonfiction writing, 1986-93; President Clinton's Race Initiative, advisor, 1997. Writer, 1983-. **Publications:** At Mother's Request: A True Story of Money, Murder and Betrayal, 1985; Exit the Rainmaker, 1989; Long Way to Go: Black and White in America, 1997; (with J. West) West by West: My Charmed, Tormented Life, 2011. Contributor to periodicals. **Address:** Atheneum Books, PO Box 70660, Chicago, IL 60673, U.S.A. **Online address:** jonacoles@aol.com

COLEMAN, Loren (Elwood). American (born United States), b. 1947. **Genres:** Paranormal, Adult Non-fiction, Animals/Pets, Communications/Media, Psychology, Film, Social Sciences, Mythology/Folklore, Mythology/Folklore, Natural History, Social Work, Anthropology/Ethnology, Zoology, Biography, Sports/Fitness. **Career:** Little Grassy Outdoor Laboratory, counselor and activity therapist, 1967-70; Paid, professional author, 1969-; TARGET Program Youth Home, supervisor, 1971-74; Behavioral Foundation for Children, treatment team leader and group counselor, 1974-75; Walker School for Children, Weekend Program, assistant intake coordinator, 1975-78; Framingham Youth Guidance Clinic, group program coordinator and psychiatric social worker, 1978-80; Department of Social Services, supervisor and administrator, 1980-83; University of Southern Maine, Muskie Institute, research associate, 1983-96; Youth Alternatives, program director, 1996-97; University of New England, visiting professor, 1997-98; Youth Suicide Prevention Program, consultant, 1998-; Boston University, instructor and associate professor in social work, sociology and anthropology, 1981-83; Bunker Hill Community College, instructor and associate professor in social work, sociology and anthropology, 1981-83; University of Southern Maine, instructor, associate professor of cryptozoology, documentary film and social science, 1990-2003. **Publications:** (With J. Clark) The Unidentified: Notes Toward Solving the UFO Mystery, 1975; (with J. Clark) Creatures of the Outer Edge, 1978 as Creatures of the Goblin World, 1984; Mysterious America, 1983, rev. ed., 2004; (with B. Sparks) Working Together: Community Involvement in Maineûs Foster Care Case Review: A Training Curriculum, 1984; Working Together: Community Involvement in Foster Care Case Review, 1984; Adolescent Stabilization, 1984; Curious Encounters: Phantoms, Trains, Spooky Spots, and other Mysterious Wonders, 1985; (co-author) Teen Suicide in Foster Care: Coded Cries for Help, 1987; Suicide Clusters, 1987; (co-author) Unattended Children, 1987; (co-ed.) Working with Older Adoptees: A Sourcebook of Innovative Models, 1988; Tom Slick and the Search for the Yeti, 1989; (with K. Buxton) Elder Fire Safety for the 90s, 1991; (with D. Porter) Working With Rural Youth, 1994; (with S.K. Roszia and A. Baran) Creating Kinship, 1996; (with K. Sahanhik) Child Maltreatment and Abuse Investigations for Law Enforcement Officers, 1998; (with P. Huyghe) The Field Guide to Bigfoot, Yeti, and Other Mystery Primates Worldwide, 1999; Bloodlines, 1999; (with J. Clark) Cryptozoology A to Z: The Encyclopedia of Loch Monsters, Sasquatch, Chupacabras, and Other Authentic Mysteries of Nature, 1999; Mothman and Other Curious Encounters, 2002; Tom Slick: True Life Encounters in Cryptozoology, 2002; Bigfoot! The True Story of Apes in America, 2003; (with P. Huyghe) The Field Guide to Lake Monsters and Sea Serpents, 2003; (with S.O. Halloran) Preventing Youth Suicide Through Gatekeeper Training, 1998, 8th ed., 2004; Copycat Effect: How the Media and Popular Culture Trigger the Mayhem in Tomorrow's Headlines, 2004; (with J. Willis and A. Henderson) Weird Ohio, 2005; The Unidentified/ Creatures of the Outer Edge: The Early Works of Jerome Clark and Loren Coleman, 2006; (with P. Huyghe) The Field Guide to Bigfoot, 2006; (foreword) Bigfoot Casebook Updated: Sightings and Encounters from 1818 to 2004, 2006; Monsters of New Jersey: Mysterious Creatures in the Garden State, 2010; So You Want to Be A Cryptozoologist?, forthcoming. Contributor to periodicals. **Address:** PO Box 360, Portland, ME 04112, U.S.A. **Online address:** lcoleman@maine.rr.com

COLEMAN, Mary DeLorse. American (born United States), b. 1954. **Genres:** Law, Public/Social Administration, Politics/Government, Social Sciences. **Career:** Jackson State University, Department of Political Science, professor and chair; Blackside Inc., consultant. Writer. **Publications:** Legislators, Law and Public Policy: Political Change in Mississippi and the South, 1993. Works appear in anthologies. **Address:** Department of Political Science, Jackson State University, PO Box 18420, Jackson, MS 39217, U.S.A. **Online address:** mary.delorse.coleman@ccaix.jsums.edu

COLEMAN, Michael. (Fiona Kelly). British (born England), b. 1946. **Genres:** Novels, Novellas/Short Stories, Picture/Board Books, Young Adult Non-fiction, Children's Fiction, Sports/Fitness. **Career:** Portsmouth University, lecturer, 1969-88; IBM United Kingdom Laboratories, quality assurer and consultant, 1988-93; writer, 1988-. **Publications:** PICTURE BOOKS: The Mum Who Was Made of Money, 1993; Ozzie Owl, 1994; Hank the Clank, 1994; Lazy Ozzie, 1994; Hank Clanks Again, 1995; Hank Clanks Back, 1996; Ridiculous!, 1996; One, Two, Three, Oops!, 1998; George and Sylvia: A Tale of True Love, 2000. FICTION FOR CHILDREN AND YOUNG ADULTS: Triv in Pursuit, 1992; Double Trouble, 1992; Tutankhamun Is a Bit of a Mummy's Boy ... and Fifty Other Unpublished School Reports, 1992; Gizmo Lewis, Fairly Secret Agent, 1993; Fizzy Hits the Headlines, 1993; Fizzy Steals the Show, 1994; Redville Rockets, 1994; Shoot, Dad!, 1994; Grounds for Suspicion/Race against Time, 1994; Lexy Boyd and the Spadewell Sparklers, 1994; Fizzy TV Star!, 1995; The Magic Sponge, 1996; Weirdo's War, 1996; Fizzy in the Spotlight, 1997; Madame Retsmah Predicts, 1998; Tag, 1998; The Snog Log, 2001; Going Straight, 2003 as On the Run, 2004; The Cure, 2007; Danger Signs, 2010; The Mermaid of Zennor, 2012. AS FIONA KELLY: MYSTERY KIDS SERIES: Treasure Hunt, 1995; Funny Money, 1995; Wrong Number, 1996. INTERNET DETECTIVES SERIES: Net Bandits, 1996; Escape Key, 1996; Speed Surf, 1996; (with J. Levy) Cyber Feud, 1996; (with J. Levy) System Crash, 1996; Web Trap, 1996; (with A.F. Jones) Virus Attack, 1997; (with A.F. Jones) Access Denied, 1997. ANGELS F.C. SERIES: Touchline Terror, 1997; Dirty Defending, 1997; Handball Horror!, 1997; Gruesome Goalkeeping!, 1997; Goal Greedy!, 1998; Midfield Madness, 1998; Frightful Fouls!, 1998; Dazzling Dribbling!, 1999; Awful Attacking!, 1999; Fearsome Free-Kicks!, 1999; Awesome Attacking!, 1999; Suffering Substitutes!, 2000; Shocking Shooting!, 2000; Squabbling Squads!, 2000; Wicked Wingers!, 2000; Crafty Coaching!, 2000; Hat Trick!, 2000; Squabbling Squads, and Other Stories, 2004; Shocking Shooting, and Other Stories, 2004; Dazzling Dribbling, and Other Stories, 2004; Awesome Attacking, and Other Stories, 2004; Touchline Terror, and Other Stories, 2004. FOUL FOOTBALL SERIES: Foul Football, 1997; Furious Euro's: The European Championships, 1960-2000, 2000; Legendary Leagues, 2001; Triumphant Teams, 2001; Phenomenal F.A. Cup, 2001; World Cup Quiz Book, 2002; The Ultimate Fan's Handbook, 2002; Prize Players, 2003; Even Fouler Football, 2004; England: All the Foul Facts, 2006; Famously Foul Football Book, 2009; Wicked World Cup 2010, 2010. BEAR KINGDOM TRILOGY: The Howling Tower, 2006; The Fighting Pit, 2006; The Hunting Forest, 2007. FABULOUS FACT BOOKS SERIES: NONFICTION: Flaming Olympics, 1996, 2nd ed., 2000; Wicked World Cup, 1998, 3rd ed., 2006; Top Ten Bible Stories, 1998 as Bible Stories, 2004; Top Ten Fairy Stories, 1999; Crashing Computers, 1999; Great Big Quiz Book, 2001; Flaming Olympics Quiz Book, 2004. OTHERS: (with T. Manns) Software Quality Assurance (nonfiction for adults), 1988; (co-author) Risk Management for Software Projects (nonfiction for adults), 1994. **Address:** Laurence Pollinger Ltd., 18 Maddox St., London, GL W1R 0EU, England.

COLEMAN, Michael. *See* **JONES, Allan Frewin.**

COLEMAN, Reed Farrel. (Tony Spinosa). American (born United States), b. 1956. **Genres:** Mystery/Crime/Suspense. **Career:** Writer. **Publications:** DYLAN KLEIN DETECTIVE SERIES: Life Goes Sleeping, 1991; Little Easter, 1993; They Don't Play Stickball in Milwaukee, 1997. MOE PRAGER MYSTERY SERIES: Walking the Perfect Square, 2001; Redemption Street, 2004; The James Deans: A Moe Prager Mystery, 2005; Soul Patch, 2007; Empty Ever After, 2008; Innocent Monster, 2010. STAND-ALONE NOVEL: (with K. Bruen) Tower, 2009. JOE SERPE SERIES AS TONY SPINOSA: Hose Monkey, 2005; The Fourth Victim, 2008. **Address:** DHS Literary Agency, 10711 Preston Rd., Ste. 100, Dallas, TX 75230, U.S.A. **Online address:** reed@reedcoleman.com

COLEMAN, Terry. British (born England), b. 1931. **Genres:** Novels, History, Politics/Government, Transportation, Biography, Documentaries/ Reportage, Autobiography/Memoirs. **Career:** University College, Lyon lecturer in medieval law, 1959; The Guardian Newspaper, arts correspondent, chief feature writer and reporter, 1961-74, chief feature writer and political interviewer, 1976-79, New York correspondent, 1981-82, roving special correspondent, 1982-89; Daily Mail Newspaper, special writer, 1974-76; The Independent, associate editor, 1989-91; Savoir Faire, editor. **Publications:** The Railway Navvies: A History of the Men Who Made the Railways, 1965; Girl for the Afternoons, 1965; (with L. Deacon) Providence and Mr. Hardy, 1966; The Only True History, 1969; Passage to America: A History of Emigrants from Great Britain and Ireland to America in the Mid-Nineteenth Century, 1972; Going to America, 1972; The Pantheretti (poems), 1973; (ed.) The Poor Man and the Lady, 1974; The Liners: A History of the North Atlantic Crossing, 1976; The Scented Brawl, 1978; Movers and Shakers: Collected Interviews, 1987; Thatcher's Britain, 1987; Nelson: The Man and the Legend, 2001; Nelson Touch: The Life and Legend of Horatio Nelson, 2002; Olivier: The Authorised Biography, 2005. NOVELS: A Girl for the Afternoons, 1965; Southern Cross, 1979; Thanksgiving: A Novel in Celebration of America, 1981; Empire, 1994. **Address:** Peters Fraser and Dunlop, 34-43 Russell St., London, GL WC2B 5HA, England.

COLEMAN, Verna (Scott). Australian (born Australia) **Genres:** Literary Criticism And History, Biography, Autobiography/Memoirs. **Career:** Mitchell Library, librarian. Writer. **Publications:** Miles Franklin in America: Her Unknown Brilliant Career, 1981; The Last Exquisite: A Portrait of Frederic Manning, 1990; Adela Pankhurst: The Wayward Suffragette, 1885-1961, 1996. Contributor to books. **Address:** 4/311 B Edgecliff Rd., Woollahra, NW 2025, Australia.

COLEMAN, William Oliver. Australian (born Australia), b. 1959. **Genres:** Economics. **Career:** University of Sydney, part-time tutor, 1981; Reserve Bank of Australia, Research Department, research officer, 1982, 1984; London School of Economics, Economics Department, part-time tutorial fellow, 1986-87; University of Exeter, Economics Department, tutorial fellow, 1987-88; Victoria University of Wellington, Economics Department, lecturer, 1988-91; University of Tasmania, Economics Department, lecturer, 1991-93, senior lecturer, 1993-2002; Australian National University, Department of Economic History, visiting professor, 1995, College of Business and Economics, reader, 2006-, Centre for Applied Macroeconomic Analysis, research associate; Duke University, Department of Economics, visiting professor, 1999; University of Cambridge, faculty of economics and politics, lecturer, 2003; University of Bristol, Department of Economics, visiting professor, 2003. Writer. **Publications:** (With B. Felmingham) Money and Finance in the Australian Economy, 1994; Rationalism and Anti-Rationalism in the Origins of Economics: The Philosophical Roots of 18th Century Economic Thought, 1995; (with A. Hagger) Exasperating Calculators: The Rage Against Economic Rationalism And The Campaign Against Australian Economists, 2001; Economics and Its Enemies: Two Centuries of Anti-Economics, 2002; Giblin's Platoon: The Trials and Triumph of the Economist in Australian Public Life, 2006; The Causes, Costs and Compensations of Inflation: An Investigation of Three Problems in Monetary Theory, 2007; Political Economy of Wages and Unemployment, 2010. **Address:** School of Economics, Australian National University, Rm. 1021, HW Arndt Bldg. 25a, Hobart, Tasmania, AC 0200, Australia. **Online address:** william.coleman@anu.edu.au

COLERIDGE, Nicholas (David). British (born England), b. 1957. **Genres:** Novels, Documentaries/Reportage. **Career:** Tatler, associate editor, 1979-82; London Evening Standard, columnist, 1982-86; Harpers and Queen, features editor, 1985-86, editor, 1986-89; Condé Nast Publications, editorial director, 1989-91, managing director, 1992-; Condé Nast Intl., vice president, 1999-; Condé Nast India, staff, 2005-. **Publications:** Tunnel Vision (collection of journalism), 1981; (with N. Miles) The Long Weekend Book, 1983; Shooting Stars (novel), 1984; Around the World in Seventy-eight Days, 1985; (ed. with S. Quinn) The Sixties in Queen, 1987; The Fashion Conspiracy: A Remarkable Journey through the Empires of Fashion, 1988; How I Met My Wife and Other Stories, 1991; Paper Tigers: The Latest, Greatest Newspaper Tycoons and How They Won the World, 1993; With Friends Like These, 1997; Street Smart, 1999; Godchildren, 2002; Much Married Man, 2007; Deadly Sins, 2009; Pride and Avarice, 2010. Contributor to periodicals. **Address:** Conde Nast Publications, Vogue House, 1-2 Hanover Sq., London, GL W1S 1JU, England.

COLES, Don. Canadian (born Canada), b. 1928. **Genres:** Novels, Poetry, Translations, Biography, Adult Non-fiction. **Career:** York University, Vanier College, instructor, 1965-66, lecturer, 1966-68, assistant professor, 1968-71, associate professor, 1971-81, professor of humanities and creative writing, 1981-, director of Programme in Creative Writing, 1981-86. Writer. **Publications:** Sometimes All Over, 1975; Anniversaries, 1979; The Prinzhorn Collection, 1982; Landslides: Selected Poems, 1975-1985, 1986; K. in Love, 1989; Little Bird, 1991; Forests of the Medieval World, 1993; Someone Has Stayed in Stockholm: New & Selected Poems, 1994; (trans.) T. Transtromer, For the Living and the Dead, 1996; Kurgan, 2000; Doctor Bloom's Story (novel), 2004; How We all Swiftly: The First Six Books, 2005; Dropped Glove in Regent Street: An Autobiography by Other Means, 2007; Essential Don Coles, 2009; Where We Might have Been, 2010. **Address:** Vanier College, York University, 4700 Keele St., North York, ON M3J 1P3, Canada. **Online address:** dcoles@yorku.ca

COLES, John Morton. British/Canadian (born Canada), b. 1930. **Genres:** Archaeology/Antiquities. **Career:** Cambridge University, Fitzwilliam College, lecturer in archaeology and anthropology, 1960-75, reader, 1976-79, professor of European prehistory, 1980-86, founding fellow and life fellow, 1986-; University of Exeter, professor. Writer. **Publications:** (With E.S. Higgs) Archaeology of Early Man, 1969; Field Archaeology in Britain, 1972; Archaeology by Experiment, 1973; (with A.F. Harding) The Bronze Age in Europe, 1979; Experimental Archaeology, 1979; (with B. Orme) Prehistory of the Somerset Levels, 1980; The Archaeology of Wetlands, 1984; (with B. Coles) Sweet Track to Glastonbury, 1986; Meare Village East: The Excavation of A. Bulleid and H.S.G. Gray 1932-1956, 1987; (with B. Coles) People of the Wetlands, 1989; (with L. Bengtsson) Images of the Past, 1990; Waterlogged Wood, 1990; From the Waters of Oblivion, 1991; (with A. Goodall and S. Minnitt) Arthur Bulleid and the Glastonbury Lake Village 1892-1992, 1992; (with D. Hall) Fenland Survey, 1994; The Rock Carvings of Uppland, 1994; (with S. Minnitt) Industrious and Fairly Civilized: The Glastonbury Lake Village, 1995; (with B. Coles) Enlarging the Past, 1996; (with S. Minnitt) The Lake Villages of Somerset, 1996; (with D. Hall) Changing Landscapes: The Ancient Fenland, 1998; Patterns in a Rocky Land: Rock Carvings in South-West Uppland, 2000; Shadows of a Northern Past: Rock Carvings of Bohuslän and Østfold, 2005. EDITOR: (with D.D.A. Simpson) Studies in Ancient Europe, 1968; (with A.J. Lawson) European Wetlands in Prehistory, 1987; (with V. Fenwick and G. Hutchinson) A Spirit of Enquiry, 1993; (with R. Bewley and P. Mellars) World Prehistory, 1999; (with B. Coles and M. Jorgensen) Bog Bodies, Sacred Sites and Wetland Archaeology, 1999; (with T. Lane) Through Wet and Dry, 2002; (with A. Marciniak) Grahame Clark and His Legacy, 2010. **Address:** Fitzwilliam College, Cambridge University, Cambridge, CB CB3 0DG, England. **Online address:** johnmcoles@aol.com

COLES, Robert. American (born United States), b. 1929. **Genres:** Poetry, Paranormal, Psychiatry, Psychology, Social Commentary, Sociology, Biography, Novellas/Short Stories, Education, Reference. **Career:** University of Chicago, intern at university clinics, 1954-55; Massachusetts General Hospital, resident in psychiatry, 1955-56; McLean Hospital, resident in psychiatry, 1956-57; Judge Baker Guidance Center-Children's Hospital, resident, 1957-58; Massachusetts General Hospital, alcoholism clinic staff, 1957-58; Metropolitan State Hospital, supervisor in children unit, 1957-58; Judge Baker Guidance Center-Children's Hospital, fellow in child psychiatry, 1960-61; Lancaster Industrial School for Girls, psychiatric consultant, 1960-62; Massachusetts General Hospital, psychiatric staff, 1960-62; Harvard University, clinical assistant in psychiatry at Medical School, 1960-62, research psychiatrist, 1963, lecturer in general education, 1966, professor of psychiatry and medical humanities, 1978, James Agee professor of social ethics, now professor emeritus; Southern Regional Council, research psychiatrist, 1961-63; University of Pittsburgh, Horace Mann lecturer, 1969; Duke University, visiting professor of history. Writer. **Publications:** Children of Crisis: vol. I: A Study in Courage and Fear, 1967, vol. II: Migrants, Sharecroppers, Mountaineers, 1972, vol. III: The South Goes North, 1972, vol. IV: Eskimos, Chicanos, Indians, 1978, vol. V: Privileged Ones: The Well Off and Rich in America, 1978; Dead End School, 1968; Still Hungry in America, 1968; The Grass Pipe, 1969; The Image Is You, 1969; (with M.W. Piers) The Wages of Neglect, 1969; Uprooted Children: The Early Lives of Migrant Farmers, 1970; (with J.H. Brenner and D. Meagher) Drugs and Youth: Medical, Psychiatric and Legal Facts, 1970; Erik H. Erikson: The Growth of His Work, 1970; The Middle Americans, 1971; (with D. Berrigan) The Geography of Faith, 1971, rev. ed. as The Geography of Faith: Underground Conversations on Religious, Political, and Social Change, 2001; Saving Face, 1972; (co-ed.) Twelve to Sixteen: Early Adolescence (essays), 1972; Farewell to the South, 1972; A Spectacle unto the World, 1973; Riding Free, 1973; Doris Ulmann: The Darkness and the Light, 1974; The Buses Roll, 1974; Irony in the Mind's Life: Essays on Novels by James Agee, Elizabeth Bowen and George Eliot, 1974; Headsparks, 1975; William Carlos Williams, 1975; The Mind's Fate: Ways of Seeing Psychiatry and Psychoanalysis, 1975; A Festering Sweetness (poetry), 1978; (with J.H. Coles) Women of Crisis: vol. I: Lives of Struggle and Hope, 1978, vol. II: Lives of Work and Dreams, 1980; The Last and First Eskimos, 1978; Walker Percy: An American Search, 1978; Flannery O'Connor's South, 1980; Dorothea Lange: Photographs of a Lifetime, 1982; The Old Ones of New Mexico, 1984; (ed.) The Doctor Stories, 1984; (with R. Spears) Agee, 1985; (with G. Stokes) Sex and the American Teenager, 1985; The Moral Life of Children, 1986; The Political Life of Children, 1986; (with H. Levitt) In the Streets, 1987; Simone Weil: A Modern Pilgrimage, 1987; Dorothy Day: A Radical Devotion, 1987; Harvard Diary: Reflection on the Sacred and the Secular, 1988; The Red Wheelbarrow: Selected Literary Essays, 1988; Times of Surrender: Selected Essays, 1988; Learning by Example: Stories and the Moral Imagination, 1989; The Call of Stories: Teaching and the Moral Imagination, 1989; Rumors of Separate Worlds, 1989; The Spiritual Life of Children, 1990; Their Eyes Meeting the World: The Drawings and Paintings of Children, 1992; Anna Freud: The Dream of Psychoanalysis, 1992; Conversations with Robert Coles, 1992; A Robert Coles Omnibus, 1993; The Call of Service: A Witness to Idealism, 1993; The Story of Ruby Bridges, 1995; The Ongoing Journey: Awakening Spiritual Life in At-Risk Youth, 1995; The Mind's Fate: A Psychiatrist Looks at His Profession, 1995; (comp. and foreword) In God's House: Children's Drawings, 1996; Doing Documentary Work, 1997; (co-author) The Youngest Parents: Teenage Pregnancy As It Shapes Lives, 1997; Old and on Their Own, 1997; The Moral Intelligence of Children, 1997; (with N. Nixon) School, 1998; The Secular Mind, 1999; Lives of Moral Leadership, 2000; (ed. with R. Testa and M. Coles) Growing Up Poor: A Literary Anthology, 2000; (ed.) The Erik Erikson Reader, 2000; (ed. with R. Testa) A Life in Medicine: A Literary Anthology, 2002; When They Were Young: A Photographic Retrospective of Childhood from the Library of Congress, 2002; Bruce Springsteen's America: The People Listening, A Poet Singing, 2003; Teaching Stories: An Anthology On The Power Of Learning And Literature, 2004; (with R. Smerek) Political Leadership: Stories of Power and Politics from Literature and Life, 2005; (contrib.) Earth's

Elders, 2005; (contrib.) Chekhov the Immigrant: Translating a Cultural Icon, 2007; (with T. Roma) House Calls with William Carlos Williams, 2008; (ed. with A. LaFarge) Minding the Store: Great Writing About Business, from Tolstoy to Now, 2008; Handing One Another Along: Literature and Social Reflection, 2010; Lives We Carry With Us: Profiles of Moral Courage, 2010. Contributor to books. **Address:** Kennedy School of Government, Harvard Medical School, Taubman Bldg., 15 Eliot St., Cambridge, MA 02138, U.S.A. **Online address:** robert_coles@hms.harvard.edu

COLES, Roberta L. American (born United States), b. 1952?. **Genres:** Human Relations/Parenting, Social Sciences. **Career:** University of Missouri, Freedom of Information Center, Department of Journalism, publications editor, 1979-82; freelance writer, 1983-85; Marquette University, assistant professor, 1995-2003, associate professor, 2003-10, professor of social and cultural sciences, 2010-; University of Wisconsin, faculty. Sociologist. **Publications:** Race & Family: A Structural Approach, 2006; The Best Kept Secret: Single Black Fathers, 2009; (ed. with C. Green) The Myth of the Missing Black Father, 2009. Contributor to journals. **Address:** Department of Social and Cultural Sciences, Marquette University, 2474 N 68th St., Milwaukee, WI 53201, U.S.A. **Online address:** roberta.coles@mu.edu

COLFAX, David (John). (J. David Colfax). American (born United States), b. 1936. **Genres:** Education, Politics/Government, Urban Studies, History. **Career:** London School of Economics and Political Science, research fellow, 1960-61; University of Connecticut, associate professor, 1963-69; Washington University, associate professor, 1969-72; Colfax Associates, partner, 1972-; National Center for Appropriate Technology (NCAT), regional director, 1977-81; Policy Research Group, senior consultant, 1979-81; Mendocino County, Arts Council, vice president, 1983-87; Mendocino County Board of Education, president, 1986-; Mountain House Press, publisher and editor, 1988-; Mountain School, board director; Black Fox Productions, board director; Northern California Homeschooling Association, vice president and director. **Publications:** AS J. DAVID COLFAX: The Big City Voter: A Study of Political Participation in Chicago, 1964; (with I.L. Allen and H.G. Stetler) Metropolitan Connecticut: A Demographic Profile, 1965; (with Allen) Urban Sample Survey Field Procedures: Materials and Strategies, 1967; (with Allen) The Inner City in Crisis: The Case of Connecticut, 1968; (with Allen) Urban Problems and Public Opinion in Four Connecticut Cities, 1968; (with A.K. Cohen and M.L. Farber) A Panel Discussion of Urban Demonstrations, 1968; (ed. with J.L. Roach) Radical Sociology, 1971. OTHERS: (with M. Colfax) Homeschooling for Excellence, 1987; (ed. with M. Colfax) J. Crepin, La Chèvre, 1990; (with M. Colfax) Hard Times in Paradise: An American Family's Struggle to Carve Out a Homestead in California's Redwood Mountains, 1992; 101 Ways to Enhance Your Child's Education, 1993. **Address:** 246 Redwood Ridge Rd., Boonville, CA 95415, U.S.A. **Online address:** dcolfax@pacific.net

COLFAX, J. David. *See* **COLFAX, David (John).**

COLGAN, Jenny. British/Scottish (born Scotland), b. 1971?. **Genres:** Novels. **Career:** British National Health Service, administrator. Novelist and cartoonist. **Publications:** Amanda's Wedding, 2000; Talking to Addison, 2001; Looking For Andrew McCarthy, 2002; Working Wonders, 2003; Scottish Girls About Town, 2003; Do You Remember the First Time?, 2004; The Boy I Loved Before, 2005; Where Have All The Boys Gone?, 2005; Postcards From the Hedge, 2005; West End Girls, 2007; Operation: Sunshine!, 2008; Diamonds Are a Girl's Best Friend, 2009; The Good, The Bad and the Dumped, 2010; Cover Image Meet Me at the Cupcake Café, 2011; Welcome to Rosie Hopkins' Sweetshop of Dreams, 2012; Christmas at the Cupcake Cafe, 2012. **Address:** c/o Author Mail, HarperCollins Publishers, 77-85 Fulham Palace Rd., Hammersmith, W6 8JB, England.

COLICCHIO, Joseph. American (born United States), b. 1952?. **Genres:** Novels, Humor/Satire, Young Adult Fiction. **Career:** Hudson County Community College, associate professor of English. Writer. **Publications:** NOVELS: High Gate Health and Beauty, 2000; The Trouble with Mental Wellness, 2004. **Address:** c/o Author Mail, Rowman & Littlefield Publishing Group, 4501 Forbes Blvd., Ste. 200, Lanham, MD 20706-4346, U.S.A. **Online address:** jcolicchio@hccc.edu

COLIN, Beatrice. British/Scottish (born Scotland), b. 1963?. **Genres:** Novels, Literary Criticism And History, Young Adult Fiction. **Career:** Scotsman Newspaper, reporter; Sunday Herald Glasgow, reporter; Guardian, reporter; Strathclyde University, creative writing teacher; Glasgow University, creative writing teacher. **Publications:** NOVELS: Nude Untitled, 2000; Disappearing Act, 2002; The Glimmer Palace in UK as The Luminous Life of Lilly Aphrodite, 2008; (with S. Pinto) My Invisible Sister, 2010; The Songwriter, 2010. Contributor to magazines. **Address:** c/o Simon Trewin, United Agents, 130 Shaftesbury Ave., London, GL W1D 5EU, England. **Online address:** beatricecolin@hotmail.com

COLIN, Chris. American (born United States), b. 1975?. **Genres:** Novels, Humanities. **Career:** Salon.com, editor and feature writer, 1999-2002, Life and People Sections, associate editor. Journalist. **Publications:** What Really Happened to the Class of '93: Start-Ups, Dropouts, and Other Navigations through an Untidy Decade, 2004; Changing Face of Help: The American Red Cross Turns 125, 2006. Contributor of articles to books and periodicals. **Address:** Salon Media Group Inc., 101 Spear St., Ste. 203, San Francisco, CA 94105-1517, U.S.A. **Online address:** chris@chriscolin.com

COLINAS, Antonio. Spanish (born Spain), b. 1946. **Genres:** Poetry, Romance/Historical, Translations, Essays. **Career:** Universities of Milan and Bergamo, lecturer in Spanish, 1970-74. Writer. **Publications:** Poémas de la tierra y de la sangre, 1969; Poemas de la tierra y la sangre, 1969; Preludios a una noche total, 1969; Truenos y flautas en un templo, 1972; Leopardi, 1974; Las cenizas de Gramsci, 1975; Wirrwarr, 1975; Sepulcro en Tarquinia, 1975; Viaje a los monasteries de España, 1976; Conocer Vicente Aleixandre y su obra, 1977; Poetas italianos contemporáneos, 1978; Astrolabio, 1979; Canti (bilingue), 1979; Diario del primer amor, 1979; Poesía y prosa, 1979; Diálogos, 1979; Cristo se paró en eboli, 1980; Orillas del Orbigo, 1980; Los tigres de mompracen, 1981; Poesía 1967-1981, 1982; La montaña de luz, 1982; Aleixandre, 1982; Noche más allá de la noche, 1982; La viña salvaje, 1984; Un año en el sur (para una educación estética), 1985; Larga carta a Francesca, 1986; Jardín de Orfeo, 1988; La llamada de los árboles, 1988; Hacia el infinito naufragio (una biografia de Giacomo Leopardi), 1988; Libro de las noches abiertas, 1989; Stendhal, 1989; El sentido primero de la palabra poética, 1989; Pere Alemany y la música de los signos, 1989; Elegies i paisatges (1933-1943), 1990; Caminos y dias: antología poética, 1990; Tratado de armonía, 1991; Los silencios de fuego, 1992; Días en Petavonium, 1994; (with J. Lledo) Mitología clásica, 1994; Rafael Alberti en Ibiza: seis semanas del verano de 1936, 1995; (with J. Lledó) Grand tour, 1995; Sobre la vida nueva, 1996; El viaje hacia el centro: la poesia de Antonio Colinas, 1997; El crujido de la luz, 1999; Río de sombra: treinta años de poesía, 1967-1997, 1999; Nuevo tratado de armonía, 1999; Del pensamiento inspirado, 2001; Tierra de silencio: doce relatos de Castilla y León, 2001; La hora interior: Antología poética 1967-2001, 2002; Tiempo y abismo: Poesia, 2002; Viaje a los monasterios de España, 2003; Huellas, 2003; En la luz respirada, 2004; Noche más allá de la noche 1980-1981, 2004; Los días en la isla, 2004; La simiente enterrada: un viaje a China, 2005; Leyendo en las piedras, 2006; Cerca de la montaña Kumgang, 2007; Desiertos de la luz, 2008; Nuestra poesía en el tiempo: una antología, 2009; Tres tratados de armonía, 2010; Obra poètica completa: (1967-2010), 2011. **Address:** c/o Edicions Catedra, Juan Ignacio Luc da Tena, Ste. 15, Madrid, 28027, Spain.

COLISH, Marcia L(illian). American (born United States), b. 1937. **Genres:** History, Philosophy, Language/Linguistics, Social Sciences. **Career:** Skidmore College, instructor in history, 1962-63; Oberlin College, instructor, 1963-65, assistant professor, 1965-69, associate professor, 1969-75, department head, 1973-74, 1978-81, 1985-86, professor, 1975-2001, Frederick B. Artz professor of history, 1985-2001, now retired; Case Western Reserve University, lecturer, 1966-67; Ohio State University, Center for Medieval and Renaissance Studies, affiliate, 1996-; Yale University, visiting fellow, 2001-, visiting professor of history and religious studies, 2002-03, lecturer in history, 2004-05. Writer. **Publications:** The Mirror of Language: A Study in the Medieval Theory of Knowledge, 1968, rev. ed., 1983; The Stoic Tradition from Antiquity to the Early Middle Ages, vol. I: Stoicism in Classical Latin Literature, 1985, vol. II: Stoicism in Latin Christian Thought through the Sixth Century, 1990; Peter Lombard, 2 vols., 1994; Medieval Foundations of the Western Intellectual Tradition, 400-1400, 1997; Ambrose's Patriarchs: Ethics for the Common Man, 2005; Studies in Scholasticism, 2006; Fathers and Beyond: Church Fathers Between Ancient and Medieval Thought, 2008; (ed. with C.J. Nederman, N.V. Deusen and E.A. Matter) Mind Matters: Studies of Medieval and Early Modern Intellectual History in Honour of Marcia Colish, 2009. Contributor to books and periodicals. **Address:** Yale University, 310 Whitney Humanities Ctr., 53 Wall St.., PO Box 208313, New Haven, CT 06520-8313, U.S.A. **Online address:** marcia.colish@yale.edu

COLL, Steve. American (born United States), b. 1958. **Genres:** Documentaries/Reportage, Adult Non-fiction. **Career:** California Magazine, journalist, contributing editor 1983-84; KCET-TV, Community Information Project, staff reporter, 1982-83; Washington Post Magazine, Paper's Style Section, general assignment feature writer, 1985-, foreign correspondent, staff writer, chief of New York financial bureau, 1987-89, South Asia bureau chief, 1989-92, editor, 1995-98, publisher, 1996-, managing editor, 1998-2005, associate editor, 2004-05, senior editor, International investigative correspondent, 1992-; The New Yorker Magazine, staff writer, 2005; New America Foundation, president and chief executive officer, 2007-. **Publications:** The Deal of the Century: The Breakup of AT&T, 1986; The Taking of Getty Oil: The Full Story of the most Spectacular & Catastrophic Takeover of All Time, 1987; (with D.A. Vise) Eagle on the Street: Based on the Pulitzer Prize-Winning Account of the SEC's Battle with Wall Street, 1991; On The Grand Trunk Road: A Journey into South Asia, 1994; Ghost Wars: The Secret History of the CIA, Afghanistan, and bin Laden, from the Soviet Invasion to September 10, 2001, 2004; The Bin Ladens: An Arabian Family in the American Century, 2008; On the Grand Trunk Road: A Journey Into South Asia, 2009. Contributor to periodicals. **Address:** The New America Foundation, 1899 L St. NW, Ste. 400, Washington, DC 20036, U.S.A. **Online address:** coll@newamerica.net

COLL, Susan. American (born United States) **Genres:** Novels, Young Adult Fiction. **Career:** Bethesda Writer's Center, teacher; Politics and Prose Bookstore, editorial and programming director. Writer. **Publications:** Karlmarx.com: A Love Story, 2001; Rockville Pike: A Suburban Comedy of Manners, 2005; Acceptance: A Novel, 2007; Beach Week, 2010. **Address:** Melanie Jackson Agency, 250 W 57th St., Ste. 1119, New York, NY 10019, U.S.A. **Online address:** susancoll@susancoll.com

COLLARD, Sneed B. American (born United States), b. 1959. **Genres:** Children's Fiction, Young Adult Fiction, Children's Non-fiction, Mystery/Crime/Suspense, History, Natural History, Sciences, Environmental Sciences/Ecology, Environmental Sciences/Ecology. **Career:** California Department of Agriculture, Dutch Elm Disease Project, agricultural aide, 1980; University of California, lab assistant, 1981, Neuroscience Research Institute, Computer Laboratory, director, 1986-92; University of California, Zoology Department, research assistant, Research Diving Program, assistant instructor, 1982-83; California Department of Fish and Game, Wild Trout Program, seasonal aide, 1983; writer, 1983-; Woodward-Clyde Consultants, environmental consultant, 1984; Bucking Horse Books, publisher, 2010-. **Publications:** CHILDREN'S NONFICTION: Sea Snakes, 1993; Do They Scare You? Creepy Creatures, 1993 as Creepy Creatures, 1997; Green Giants, 1994; Tough Terminators, 1994; Smart Survivors, 1994; Where Do We Live?, 1996; Where Do They Live?, 1996; Our Natural Homes, 1996; Alien Invaders: The Continuing Threat of Exotic Species Invasions, 1996; Animal Dads, 1997; Monteverde: Science and Scientists in a Costa Rican Cloud Forest, 1997; Our Wet World: Discovering Earth's Aquatic Ecosystems, 1998; Animal Dazzlers, 1998; Birds of Prey, 1999; 1, 000 Years Ago on Planet Earth, 1999; Acting for Nature, 2000; Amazing Animals: Nature's Most Incredible Creatures, 2000; Making Animal Babies, 2000; Forest in the Clouds, 2000; A Whale Biologist at Work, 2000; Lizard Island, 2000; A Firefly Biologist at Work, 2001; Leaving Home, 2002; Beaks!, 2002; The Deep-Sea Floor, 2003; Animals Asleep, 2004; A Platypus Probably, 2005; One Night in the Coral Sea, 2005; The Prairie Builders, 2005; Science Adventures series (4 books), 2005; Wings!, 2006; Teeth!, 2006; Shep: Our Most Loyal Dog, 2006; The Prairie Builders: Reconstructing America's Lost Grasslands, 2006; Pocket Babies and Other Amazing Marsupials, 2007; Reign of the Sea Dragons, 2008; Teeth!, 2008; Wings, 2008; Science Warriors, 2008. WORLD OF DISCOVERY SERIES: Green Giants-Twelve of the Earth's Tallest Trees, 1994; Tough Terminators-Twelve of the Earth's Most Fascinating Predators, 1994; Smart Survivors-Twelve of the Earth's Most Remarkable Living Things, 1994. SCIENCE ADVENTURES SERIES: In the Deep Sea, 2006; On the Coral Reefs, 2006; In the Wild, 2006; In the Rain Forest Canopy, 2006. AMERICAN HEROES SERIES: Benjamin Franklin: The Man Who Could Do Just about Anything, 2007; John Adams: Our Second President, 2007; Rosa Parks: The Courage to Make a Difference, 2007; Sacagawea: Brave Shoshone Girl, 2007; David Crockett: Fearless Frontiersman, 2007; Abraham Lincoln: A Courageous Leader, 2007; Thomas Jefferson, 2008; Eleanor Roosevelt, 2008; John Glenn, 2008; Lady Bird Johnson: Keeping America Green, 2009; John Glenn: Hooked on Flying, 2009; Jacob Lawrence: A Painter's Story, 2009; George Washington, Our First President, 2009; Eleanor Roosevelt: Making the World a Better Place, 2009; Thomas Jefferson: Let Freedom Ring!, 2009; Tatanka-Iyotake: Sitting Bull, 2009; Phillis Wheatley: She Loved Words, 2009; Many Biomes, One Earth, 2009; Cesar Chavez: The Farm Workers' Best Friend, 2009. OTHER: The World Famous Miles City Bucking Horse Sale, 2010; Global Warming: A Personal Guide to Causes and Solutions, 2011; Sneed B. Collard III's Most Fun Book Ever about Lizards, 2012. CHILDREN'S FICTION: California Fire, 1999; The Polar Bear and the Jaguar, 2000; Butterfly Count, 2002; Dog Sense (novel), 2005; Flash Point (novel), 2006; Double Eagle (novel), 2009; The Governor's Dog is Missing (novel), 2011. Contributor to periodicals. **Address:** Bucking Horse Books, PO Box 8507, Missoula, MT 59807, U.S.A. **Online address:** collard@bigsky.net

COLLECTOR, Stephen. American (born United States), b. 1951. **Genres:** Photography, Art/Art History. **Career:** Freelance photographer, 1975-. **Publications:** Law of the Range: Portraits of Old-Time Brand Inspectors, 1991. Contributor to periodicals. **Address:** 4209 26th St., Boulder, CO 80304-0907, U.S.A. **Online address:** stephenc@indra.com

COLLEE, John (Gerald). British (born England), b. 1955. **Genres:** Novels, Plays/Screenplays, Literary Criticism And History. **Career:** Medical doctor, 1979-82; radio scriptwriter, 1983-84; writer, 1983-; Amoco Corp., doctor. **Publications:** NOVELS: Kingsley's Touch, 1984; A Paper Mask, 1987; The Rig, 1991. Contributor to periodicals. **Address:** 31 Linden Gardens, London, GL W2, England.

COLLETTA, Lisa. American (born United States) **Genres:** Novels, Social Sciences. **Career:** Boston University, Scripps College, instructor; Claremont McKenna College, visiting professor of literature; Babson College, associate professor of English; Women's Studies: An Interdisciplinary Journal, associate editor; The American University of Rome, Department of Communication and English, associate professor of English, English and Writing Program, director; Getty Museum, writer; Bon Appetit Magazine, writer. **Publications:** Dark Humor and Social Satire in the Modern British Novel, 2003; (ed.) Kathleen and Christopher: Christopher Isherwood's Letters to His Mother, 2005; (ed. with M. O'Connor) Wild Colonial Girl: Essays on Edna O'Brien, 2006. Contributor to journals. **Address:** Department of Communication and English, The American University of Rome, Via Pietro Roselli 4, Rome, 00153, Italy. **Online address:** lcolletta@babson.edu

COLLETTE, Christine. French/British (born England), b. 1947. **Genres:** History, Women's Studies And Issues, Politics/Government. **Career:** Swindon College, lecturer in politics and sociology, 1986-; Edge Hill University, College of Higher Education, faculty, reader in class and gender studies, 1994-2002. Writer. **Publications:** (With J. Laureillard) Comprendre la Fiscalité du Profit, 1976; (with J. Bertrandon) Gestion Fiscale et Finances de l'entreprise, 1987; For Labour and for Women: The Women's Labour League, 1906-1918, 1989; The International Faith: British Labour Attitudes to Europe 1918-1939, 1998; (with J. Richard) Les Systemes Comptables Francais et Anglo-saxons: Normes IAS, 6th ed., 2002; The Newer Eve: Femnism, Women and the Labour Party, 2009. EDITOR: (with F. Montgomery) Into the Melting Pot: Teaching Women's Studies in the New Millennium, 1997; (with S. Bird) Jews, Labour and the Left 1918-1948, 2000; (with F. Montgomery) The European Women's History Reader, 2001; (with K. Laybourn) Modern Britain since 1979, 2003. Contributor to journals. Works appear in anthologies. **Address:** Chez Jean de Beaulieu, Chassiecq, 16350, France. **Online address:** christine.collette@wanadoo.fr

COLLEY, Barbara. (Anne Logan). American (born United States), b. 1947. **Genres:** Mystery/Crime/Suspense, Romance/Historical, Novels. **Career:** Minden Press and Herald, classified advertisement receptionist, 1966-67; Sperry Rand Corp., line dispatcher, 1967-68; Ebasco Services, receptionist and filing and dispatch clerk, 1977-78; temporary clerical worker, 1984-85; Ormond Country Club, secretary and receptionist, 1985-87, 1989-91; writer, 1991-. **Publications:** MYSTERIES: Maid for Murder: A Squeaky Clean Charlotte LaRue Mystery, 2002; Death Tidies Up, 2003; Polished Off, 2004; Wiped Out, 2005; Married to the Mop, 2006; Scrub-a-Dub Dead, 2007; Wash and Die, 2008; Dusted to Death: A Charlotte LaRue Mystery, 2010. ROMANCE NOVELS: Dangerous Memories, 2004; Rachel's War, 2007. ROMANCE NOVELS AS ANNE LOGAN: Gulf Breezes, 1992; Twin Oaks, 1993; Dial D for Destiny, 1994; That Old Devil Moon, 1996; Finding Kendall, 1997; A Dance with the Devil, 1997. **Address:** Evan Marshall Agency, 6 Tristam Pl., Pinebrook, NJ 07058-9445, U.S.A. **Online address:** BarbaraColley@eclectics.com

COLLEY, David P. American (born United States) **Genres:** Military/Defense/Arms Control, History. **Career:** Trentonian, reporter and assistant city editor; Baltimore Evening Sun, reporter. **Publications:** Sound Waves, 1985; The Road to Victory: The Untold Story of World War II's Red Ball Express, 2000; Blood for Dignity: The Story of the First Integrated Combat Unit in the U.S. Army, 2003; Safely Rest, 2004; Decision at Strasbourg: Ike's Strategic Mistake to Halt the Sixth Army Group at the Rhine in 1944, 2008. Contributor to books and periodicals. **Address:** St. Martins Press, 175 5th Ave., New York, NY 10010, U.S.A. **Online address:** david.colley@verizon.net

COLLEY, Linda. British (born England), b. 1949. **Genres:** History, Politics/Government, Biography. **Career:** Cambridge University, research fellow and lecturer in history, 1975-82; King's College and Newnham College, joint lecturer, 1978-79; Christ's College, fellow and lecturer in history, 1979-82; Yale University, Department of History, assistant professor, 1982-85, associate professor, 1985-90, senior faculty fellow, 1987, director of graduate studies, 1988-90, Lewis Walpole Library, director, 1988-96, professor of history, 1990-92, Richard M. Colgate professor of history, 1992-98; London university, London School of Economics, Leverhulme research professor in history, 1998-2003; McMaster University, Hooker distinguished visiting professor, 1999; Princeton University, Shelby M.C. Davis professor of history, 2003-. Historian and Writer. **Publications:** In Defiance of Oligarchy: The Tory Party, 1714-1760, 1982; Lewis Namier, 1989; Crown Pictorial: Art and the British Monarchy, 1990; Britons: Forging the Nation, 1707-1837, 1992; Captives: Britain, Empire and the World 1600-1850, 2002; The Ordeal of Elizabeth Marsh: A Woman in World History, 2007; Taking Stock of Taking Liberties, 2008. Contributor of articles. **Address:** Department of History, Princeton University, 123 Dickinson Hall, Princeton, NJ 08544-1017, U.S.A. **Online address:** lcolley@princeton.edu

COLLICOTT, Sharleen. American (born United States), b. 1937. **Genres:** Children's Fiction. **Career:** Duntog Foundation, artist-in-residence, 1983; Otis/Parson Design Institute, teacher, 1983; California State University, teacher, 1983-84; National Endowment for the Arts, panelist, 1985; India Ink Galleries, staff, 1985-86; Every Picture Tells a Story, staff, 1991-95. Writer, illustrator, ceramist and sculptor. **Publications:** SELF-ILLUSTRATED: Seeing Stars, 1996; Toestomper and the Bad Butterflies, 2003. OTHERS: Teardrop Baby, 1994; (contrib.) The Chicken Sisters, 1997; Toestomper and the Caterpillars, 1999; Mildred and Sam, 2003; Mildred and Sam and Their Babies, 2005; Mildred and Sam go to School, 2008. Illustrator of books by others. Contributor to periodicals. **Address:** 2960 Bel Air Dr., Las Vegas, NV 89109-1581, U.S.A. **Online address:** rubincolli@cox.net

COLLIER, Christopher. American (born United States), b. 1930. **Genres:** Young Adult Fiction, Children's Non-fiction, History, Local History/Rural Topics, Education, Reference. **Career:** Julian Curtis School, teacher, 1955-58; Columbia University, Teachers College, instructor, 1958-59; New Canaan High School, teacher, 1959-61, Seminar on Early American history, chairman, 1978-79; University of Bridgeport, instructor, 1961-64, assistant professor, 1964-67, associate professor, 1967-71, professor of history, 1971-78, David S. Day professor of history, 1978-84, chairman of department, 1978-81, professor of American history; New York University, visiting professor, 1974; Yale University, visiting lecturer, 1977, 1981; Connecticut state historian, 1984-2004; University of Connecticut, professor, 1984-2000, professor of history emeritus, 2000-; National Endowment for the Humanities, Summer Institute for College Teachers, director, 1989. Writer and consultant. **Publications:** NON FICTION FOR ADULTS: (ed.) The Public Records of the State of Connecticut, 1802-03, vol. II, 1967; Roger Sherman's Connecticut: Yankee Politics and the American Revolution, 1971; Connecticut in the Continental Congress, 1973; Roger Sherman: Puritan Politician, 1976; (with B.B. Collier) The Literature of Connecticut History, 1983; The American Revolution, 1763-1783, 1998; All Politics Is Local: Family and Provincial Interests in the Creation of the Constitution, 2003. HISTORICAL NOVELS FOR YOUNG ADULTS (with J.L. Collier): My Brother Sam Is Dead, 1974, rev. ed., 1988; (with J.L. Collier) The Bloody Country, 1976; (with J.L. Collier) The Winter Hero, 1978; Jump Ship to Freedom, 1981; War Comes to Willy Freeman, 1983; (with J.L. Collier) Who Is Carrie?, 1984; The Clock, 1992; (with J.L. Collier) With Every Drop of Blood, 1994. NON-FICTION FOR YOUNG ADULTS: (with J.L. Collier) The Drama of American History Series (middle school), 23 vols., 1996-2001. WITH JAMES LINCOLN COLLIER: Building a New Nation, 1789-1803, 1998; Civil War, 1860-1865, 1998; The Cotton South and the Mexican War, 1835-1850, 1998; French and Indian War, 1660-1763, 1998; Pilgrims and Puritans, 1620-1676, 1998; Paradox of Jamestown, 1585-1700, 1998; The Jeffersonian Republicans, 1800-1823: The Louisiana Purchase and the War of 1812, 1999; Creating the Constitution, 1787, 1999; Century of Immigration: 1820-1924, 1999; Brother Sam and All That: Historical Context and Literary Analysis of the Novels of James and Christopher Collier, 1999; Andrew Jackson's America, 1824-1850, 1999; Rise of Industry: 1860-1900, 2000; Slavery and the Coming of the Civil War, 1831-1861, 2000; Reconstruction and the Rise of Jim Crow, 1864-1896, 2000; United States in World War II, 1941-1945, 2001; Progressivism, the Great Depression and the New Deal, 1901 to 1941, 2001; The Rise of the Cities, 1820-1920, 2001; Indians, Cowboys and Farmers and the Battle for the Great Plains, 1865-1910, 2001; The United States Enters the World Stage: From Alaska Purchase Through World War I, 1867-1919, 2001; The Changing Face of American Society, 1945-2000, 2001; The Middle Road: American Politics, 1945 to 2000, 2002; The United States in the Cold War: 1945-1989, 2002; Decision in Philadelphia: The Constitutional Convention of 1787, 2007. OTHERS: (with B.B. Collier) Essay Toward a Bibliography of Connecticut History for Teachers, 1980; Clash of Cultures: Prehistory-1638, 1998. Contributor to books and journals. **Address:** Department of History, College of Liberal Arts and Sciences, University of Connecticut, 241 Glenbrook Rd., Storrs, CT 06269-2103, U.S.A.

COLLIER, Gary. Canadian/American (born United States), b. 1947. **Genres:** Psychology, Sciences, Psychology. **Career:** University of Alberta, research associate in psychiatry, 1977-78; St. Mary's University, assistant professor of psychology, 1978-79; University College of Cape Breton, assistant professor, professor of psychology, 1978-, chair of the department of psychology, 1989-90, 1991-92; Universite de Paris (VII), Laboratoire de Psychologie Sociale, chercheur invite, 1984-85. Writer. **Publications:** Emotional Expression, 1985; (with Henry L. Minton and G. Reynolds) Currents of Thought in American Social Psychology, 1991; Social Origins of Mental Ability, 1994. **Address:** Department of Behavioural & Life Science, University College of Cape Breton, PO Box 5300, Sydney, NS B1P 6L2, Canada.

COLLIER, Graham. British (born England), b. 1937. **Genres:** Music, Education. **Career:** Composer and musician; writer, 1963-; Royal Academy of Music, director of jazz studies. **Publications:** Inside Jazz, 1973; Compositional Devices, 1975; Jazz: A Guide for Teachers and Students, 1975; (comp. and ed.) Cleo and John: A Biography of the Dankworth, 1976; Jazz Workshop: The Blues, 1988; Interaction, Opening Up the Jazz Ensemble, 1995; The Jazz Composer, Moving Music Off the Paper, 2009. **Address:** c/o Julian Burton, Laurence Pollinger Ltd., 18 Maddox St., London, GL W1R 0EU, England. **Online address:** graham@jazzcontinuum.com

COLLIER, James Lincoln. American (born United States), b. 1928. **Genres:** Novels, Children's Fiction, Children's Non-fiction, History, Biography, Social Sciences, Essays, Sex, Sex, Science Fiction/Fantasy. **Career:** Magazine editor, 1952-58. **Publications:** The Hypocritical American: An Essay on Sex Attitudes in America, 1964; Battleground: The United States Army in World War II, 1965; (co-author) The Fine Art of Swindling, 1966; A Visit to the Firehouse, 1967; The Teddy Bear Habit, 1967; Sex Education U.S.A: A Community Approach, 1968; Which Musical Instrument Shall I Play?, 1969; Rock Star, 1970; Practical Music Theory: How Music is Put Together From Bach to Rock, 1970; Danny Goes to the Hospital, 1970; Why Does Everybody Think I'm Nutty?, 1971; Its' Murder at St. Baskets', 1972; The Hard Life of the Teenager, 1972; Jug Bands and Handmade Music: A Creative Approach To Music Theory and The Instruments, 1973; Inside Jazz, 1973; (with C. Collier) My Brother Sam is Dead, 1974; The Making of Man: The Story of Our Ancient Ancestors, 1974; Rich and Famous: The Further Adventures of George Stable, 1975; Making Music for Money, 1976; Give Dad My Best, 1976; (with C. Collier) The Bloody Country, 1976; The Great Jazz Artists, 1977; CB, 1977; (with C. Collier) The Winter Hero, 1978; The Making of Jazz: A Comprehensive History, 1978; (with C. Collier) Jump Ship to Freedom, 1981; (with C. Collier) War Comes to Willy Freeman, 1983; Planet Out of the Past, 1983; Louis Armstrong, an American Genius, 1983; (with C. Collier) Who is Carrie?, 1984; Louis Armstrong: An American Success Story, 1985; When the Stars Begin to Fall, 1986; (with C. Collier) Decision in Philadelphia: The Constitutional Convention of 1787, 1986; Outside Looking in, 1987; Duke Ellington, 1987; The Winchesters, 1988; The Reception of Jazz in America: A New View, 1988; Benny Goodman and the Swing Era, 1989; The Rise of Selfishness in America, 1991; My Crooked Family, 1991; (with C. Collier) The Clock, 1992; Jazz: The American Theme Song, 1993; (with C. Collier) With Every Drop of Blood, 1994; The Jazz Kid, 1994; Jazz:

An American Saga, 1997; (with C. Collier) Pilgrims and Puritans, 1620-1676, 1998; (with C. Collier) The Paradox of Jamestown, 1585-1700, 1998; (with C. Collier) The French and Indian War, 1660-1763, 1998; (with C. Collier) The Cotton South and the Mexican War, 1835-1850, 1998; (with C. Collier) Clash of Cultures: Prehistory, 1638, 1998; (with C. Collier) The Civil War, 1860-1865, 1998; (with C. Collier) Building a New Nation, 1789-1803, 1998; (with C. Collier) The American Revolution, 1763-1783, 1998; (with C. Collier) The Jeffersonian Republicans, 1800-1823: The Louisiana Purchase and the War of 1812, 1999; (with C. Collier) Creating the Constitution, 1787, 1999; (with C. Collier) A Century of Immigration: 1820-1924, 1999; (with C. Collier) Andrew Jackson's America, 1824-1850, 1999; The Worst of Times, 2000; The Corn Raid, 2000; (with C. Collier) Slavery and the Coming of the Civil War, 1831-1861, 2000; (with C. Collier) The Rise of the Cities, 1820-1920, 2000; (with C. Collier) The Rise of Industry: 1860-1900, 2000; (with C. Collier) Reconstruction and the Rise of Jim Crow, 1864-1896, 2000; Chipper, 2001; (with C. Collier) The United States in World War II, 1941-1945, 2001; (with C. Collier) The United States Enters the World Stage: From Alaska Purchase Through World War I, 1867-1919, 2001; (with C. Collier) Progressivism, the Great Depression, and the New Deal, 1901 to 1941, 2001; (with C. Collier) Indians, Cowboys, and Farmers and the Battle for the Great Plains, 1865-1910, 2001; Wild Boy, 2002; (with C. Collier) The United States in the Cold War: 1945-1989, 2002; (with C. Collier) The Middle Road: American Politics, 1945 to 2000, 2002; (with C. Collier) The Changing Face of American Society, 1945-2000, 2002; The Sitting Bull You Never Knew, 2003; The George Washington You Never Knew, 2003; The Frederick Douglass You Never Knew, 2003; The Clara Barton You Never Knew, 2003; The Alexander Hamilton You Never Knew, 2003; The Abraham Lincoln You Never Knew, 2003; Vaccines, 2004; The Tecumseh You Never Knew, 2004; The Susan B. Anthony You Never Knew, 2004; Me and Billy, 2004; The Mark Twain You Never Knew, 2004; The Louis Armstrong You Never Knew, 2004; Gunpowder and Weaponry, 2004; The Empty Mirror, 2004; The Eleanor Roosevelt You Never Knew, 2004; Clocks, 2004; The Benjamin Franklin You Never Knew, 2004; Steam Engines, 2006; Electricity and the Light Bulb, 2006; The Automobile, 2006; Christopher Columbus: To the New World, 2007; Dreadful Revenge of Ernest Gallen, 2008. **Address:** c/o William Deiss, John Hawkins & Associates, 71 W 23rd St., Ste. 1600, New York, NY 10010-4185, U.S.A.

COLLIER, Jane. *See* **JACKSON, Jane.**

COLLIER, Jane. *See* **COLLIER, Zena.**

COLLIER, Michael. American (born United States), b. 1953. **Genres:** Literary Criticism And History, Poetry. **Career:** Folger Shakespeare Library, director of poetry programs, 1983-84; University of Maryland, professor, 1984-, Creative Writing Program, faculty, 1989-94; Johns Hopkins University, visiting lecturer, 1985-89; Yale University, visiting lecturer, 1990, Warren Wilson College, instructor 1991-; Middlebury College, Bread Loaf Writers' Conference, director, 1994-, visiting professor of English, 2006; University of Michigan, Zell distinguished professor in creative writing, 2009. **Publications:** The Clasp and Other Poems, 1986; The Folded Heart, 1989; The Wesleyan Tradition: Four Decades of American Poetry, 1993; The Neighbor, 1995; (with S. Plumly) The New Bread Loaf Anthology of Contemporary American Poetry, 1999; The Ledge, 2000; The New American Poets: A Bread Loaf Anthology, 2000; (with C. Baxter and E. Hirsch) A William Maxwell Portrait: Memories and Appreciations, 2004; Dark Wild Realm, 2006; (trans. with G. Machemer) Euripides, Medea, 2006; Make Us Wave Back: Essays on Poetry and Influence, 2007. Contributor of poems and reviews to periodicals. **Address:** Department of English, University of Maryland, 3103 Tawes, College Park, MD 20742, U.S.A. **Online address:** collierm@umd.edu

COLLIER, Paul. British (born England), b. 1949. **Genres:** Military/Defense/Arms Control, Politics/Government, History. **Career:** World Bank, Development Research Group, director, 1998-2003; Oxford University, professor, Centre for the Study of African Economies, director, St. Antony's College, fellow, 2003-; Prime Minister Tony Blair's Commission on Africa, senior advisor. Writer and economist. **Publications:** (with D. Lal) Poverty and Growth in Kenya, 1980; (co-author) Labour and Poverty in Rural Tanzania: Ujamaa and Rural Development in the United Republic of Tanzania, 1986; (with D. Lal) Labour and Poverty in Kenya, 1900-1980, 1986; (co-author) Consequences of a Commodity Boom in a Controlled Economy: Accumulation and Redistribution in Kenya, 1975-83, 1986; (with M. Lockwood) Maternal Education and the Vicious Cycle of High Fertility and Malnutrition: An Analytic Survey, 1988; Women in Development: Defining the Issues, 1988; (with J.C. Jackson) Incomes, Poverty, and Food Security in the Communal Lands of Zimbabwe, 1988; (co-author) Peasants and Governments: An Economic Analysis, 1989; (co-author) Gender, Education, and Employment in Cote d'Ivoire, 1990; (co-author) Controlled Open Economies: A Neoclassical Approach to Structuralism, 1990; (co-author) Nigeria, Policy Responses to Shocks, 1970-1990, 1992; (with J.W. Gunning) The Macroeconomics of the Transition to Peace in Ethiopia, 1992; (co-author) Agriculture and the Policy Environment: Tanzania and Kenya, 1993; (with J.W. Gunning) Trade Shocks: Consequences and Policy Responses in Developing Countries, 1994; Trade Policy and Regional Integration: Implications for the Relations between Europe and Africa, 1994; Explaining Economic Performance, 1997; (with C. Pattillo) Private Investment, Risk, and the Policy Environment in Africa, 1997; Regional Integration and Trade Liberalization in Sub-Saharan Africa, 1997; Explaining African Economic Performance, 1998; The Political Economy of Ethnicity, 1998; (with J.W. Gunning) The IMF's Role in Structural Adjustment, 1999; (co-author) Nigeria and Indonesia, 1999; (co-ed.) Trade Shocks in Developing Countries, 1999; (co-author) Flight Capital as a Portfolio Choice, 1999; Greed and Grievance in Civil War, 2000; (with A. Bigsten and S. Dercon) Exports and Firm-Level Efficiency in African Manufacturing, 2000; (with A. Bigsten and S. Dercon) Credit Constraints in Manufacturing Enterprises in Africa, 2000; (ed. with C. Pattillo) Investment and Risk in Africa, 2000; (with J. MacKinnon and S. Dercon) Density versus Quality in Health Care Provision: Using Household Data to Make Budgetary Choices in Ethiopia, 2000; (co-author) On the Duration of Civil War, 2001; (ed. with R. Reinikka) Uganda's Recovery: The Role of Farms, Firms, and Government, 2001; (with J. Dehn) Aid, Shocks, and Growth, 2001; The Macroeconomic Repercussions of Agricultural Shocks and Their Implications for Insurance, 2002; Globalization, Growth, and Poverty: Building an Inclusive World Economy, 2002; (with A. Hoeffler) Military Expenditure: Threats, Aid, and Arms Races, 2002; (with A. Hoeffler) Aid, Policy, and Growth in Post-conflict Societies, 2002; (co-author) Breaking the Conflict Trap: Civil War and Development Policy, 2003; (ed. with I. Bannon) Natural Resources and Violent Conflict: Options and Actions, 2003; (co-ed.) Post-Conflict Economies in Africa, 2004; (ed. with N. Sambanis) Understanding Civil War: Evidence and Analysis, 2005; The Bottom Billion: Why the Poorest Countries Are Failing and What Can Be Done about It, 2007; (with A.J. Venables) Rethinking Trade Preferences: How Africa Can Diversify Its Exports, 2007; (ed. with J.W. Gunning) Globalization and Poverty, vol. I: What Has Happened?, vol. II: What Are the Channels of Transmission?, vol. III: Policy Responses, 2008; (co-ed.) Economic Policy Options for a Prosperous Nigeria, 2008; (with B. Goderis) Does Aid Mitigate External Shocks?, 2008; Wars, Guns, and Votes: Democracy in Dangerous Places, 2009. **Address:** St. Antony's College, 62 Woodstock Rd., Oxford, OX OX2 6JF, England. **Online address:** paul.collier@economics.ox.ac.uk

COLLIER, Zena. Also writes as Jane Collier, Zena Shumsky. American/British (born England), b. 1926. **Genres:** Novels, Novellas/Short Stories, Young Adult Fiction, Young Adult Non-fiction, Literary Criticism And History. **Career:** Nazareth College, Writer's Workshop, teacher, 1984-; Aesthetic Education Institute, Eastman School of Music, artist-teacher, 1987; Chautauqua Institute, Writer's Workshop, staff, 1992. Full-time writer. **Publications:** ADULT NOVELS: A Cooler Climate, 1990; Ghost Note, 1992; After Long Silence, forthcoming. YOUNG ADULT FICTION: (as Zena Shumsky with L. Shumsky) First Flight, 1962; (as Jane Collier) The Year of the Dream, 1962; (as Zena Shumsky with L. Shumsky) Shutterbug, 1963; (as Jane Collier) A Tangled Web, 1967; (as Jane Collier) Sweet and Gentle Word, 1969; (as Zena Collier) Next Time I'll Know, 1981. YOUNG ADULT NON-FICTION: Seven for the People: Public Interest Groups at Work, 1979. CONTRIBUTOR: Alfred Hitchcock Presents Stories to be Read with the Lights On, 1963; Best Detective Stories, 1969; Three-Way Mirror: Reflections in Fiction and Nonfiction, 1989; Shaking Eve's Tree: Short Stories of Jewish Women, 1990; A Sound of Thunder: A Green Anthology, 1993. Contributor of articles to journals and magazines. **Address:** c/o Harvey Klinger, 300 W 55th St., Ste. 11V, New York, NY 10019-5766, U.S.A. **Online address:** zcollier@earthlink.net

COLLIER-THOMAS, Bettye. American (born United States), b. 1941. **Genres:** Women's Studies And Issues, History. **Career:** W.A. Perry Jr. High School, instructor, 1963-65; Howard University, instructor, 1966-69, College of Liberal Arts, director of honors program, 1969-71, professor, 1969-76; Washington Technical Institute, assistant professor, 1969-71; William & Mary College, associate professor, 1969-70; University of Maryland, lecturer in history, 1971; National Endowment for the Humanities, consultant, 1977-81; Bethune Museum of Archives Inc., founder and executive director, 1977-89; Temple University, associate history professor, 1989-97, professor of history, 1998-, Center African-American History and Culture, director, 1989-97. Writer. **Publications:** Freedom and Community: 19th Century Black Pennsylvania, 1992; (with J. Turner) Race, Class, Nationality and Color: The African American Search for Identity, 1992; (ed.) A Treasury of African-American Christmas Stories, 2 vols., 1997; (ed. with A.D. Gordon) African American Women and the Vote, 1837-1965, 1997; Daughters of Thunder: Black Women Preachers and Their Sermons, 1850-1979, 1998; (with V.P. Franklin) My Soul Is a Witness: A Chronology of the Civil Rights Era in the United States, 1954-1965, 2000; (ed. with V.P. Franklin) Sisters in the Struggle: African American Women in the Civil Rights-Black Power Movement, 2001; Jesus, Jobs and Justice: African American Women and Religion, 2010. **Address:** Department of History, Temple University, Philadelphia, PA 19122, U.S.A. **Online address:** bcollier@temple.edu

COLLIGNON, Jeff. American (born United States), b. 1953. **Genres:** Novels, Mystery/Crime/Suspense, Young Adult Fiction. **Career:** Probation officer, educator and writer. **Publications:** Her Monster, 1992; A.S. (After Sarah), 2006; Revelations, 2007. Contributor to books and journals. **Address:** Soho Press Inc., 853 Broadway, New York, NY 10003, U.S.A.

COLLIGNON, Rick. American (born United States), b. 1948?. **Genres:** Novels, Young Adult Fiction, Literary Criticism And History. **Career:** Writer. **Publications:** NOVELS: The Journal of Antonio Montoya, 1996; Perdido, 1997; A Santo in the Image of Cristóbal García, 2002; Madewell Brown, 2009. **Address:** Mac Adam-Cage Publishing Inc., 820 16th St., Ste. 331, Denver, CO 80202-3251, U.S.A.

COLLIN, Marion (Cripps). British (born England), b. 1928. **Genres:** Romance/Historical, Literary Criticism And History, Medicine/Health, Young Adult Fiction, Adult Non-fiction, Novels. **Career:** Student nurse, 1945-48; medical secretary, 1948-52; Woman's Own Magazine, fiction editor, 1952-56; West Kent College of Further Education, Department of Office Arts, lecturer, 1972-89. **Publications:** NOVELS: (with A. Britton) Romantic Fiction, 1960; Nurse Maria, 1963; Nurse at the Top, 1964; Doctors Three, 1964; Nurse in the Dark, 1965; The Shadow of the Court, 1967; The Doctor's Delusion, 1968; The Man on the Island, 1968; Sun on the Mountain, 1970; Nurse on an Island, 1970; Calling Doctor Savage, 1970; House of Dreams, 1971; Sawdust and Spangles, 1972; Nurses in the House, 1989. NON-FICTION: Hospital Office Practice, 1981; (with M. Drury) The Medical Secretary's and Receptionist's Handbook, 1986. **Address:** Elaine Greene Ltd., 2 Caxton St., London, GL TN4 8HJ, England.

COLLIN, Matthew. American/British (born England), b. 1955?. **Genres:** Sociology, History. **Career:** British Broadcasting Corp., producer, presenter, 1989-95, Caucasus, correspondent; Style Magazine, writer; Big Issue, editor; Time Out, editor; I-D Magazine, editor. **Publications:** (With J. Godfrey) Altered State: The Story of Ecstasy Culture and Acid House, 1997; Blimey!: The British Art Scene from Francis Bacon to Damien Hirst, 1998; This is Serbia Calling, 2001; Guerrilla Radio: Rock 'n' Roll Radio and Serbia's Underground Resistance, 2001; This Is Serbia Calling: Rock 'n' Roll Radio and Belgrade's Underground Resistance, 2004; The Time of the Rebels: Youth Resistance Movements and 21st Century Revolutions, 2007. **Address:** c/o Pete Aryton, Serpent's Tail Publishing, 3A Exmouth House, Pine St., London, GL EC1R 0JH, England.

COLLINGE, Alan Michael. American (born United States), b. 1970. **Genres:** Young Adult Non-fiction, Business/Trade/Industry. **Career:** StudentLoanJustice.org, founder, 2005-; California Institute of Technology, associate scientist of aeronautics; U.S. Department of Transportation, regional project director for a government loan program. Writer and engineer. **Publications:** The Student Loan Scam: The Most Oppressive Debt in U.S. History-and How We Can Fight Back, 2009. **Address:** StudentLoanJustice.org, 2123 Mt. View, University Place, WA 98466, U.S.A.

COLLINGE, William (B.). American (born United States), b. 1949. **Genres:** Medicine/Health, Psychology, How-to Books. **Career:** Pittsburg State University, Department of Social Science, assistant professor, 1975-78; Shawnee Community Mental Health Center, clinical social worker, 1978-79; University of Kansas, School of Social Welfare, instructor, 1979-81; University of California, research assistant, research associate and teaching associate, 1981-83; University of Alaska, Department of Social and Behavioral Sciences, assistant professor, 1984; Fairbanks Community Mental Health Center, Child Sexual Abuse Treatment Program, consultant, 1984; University of Nevada, Department of Social and Health Resources, assistant professor, 1984-85; Northern Nevada Cancer Council, Washoe Medical Center, consultant, 1986-87; The Cancer Support and Education Center, clinical supervisor and principal investigator, 1987-96; The Flowing River Institute, principal investigator, 1994-96; Counseling Services Inc., consultant, 2001-05; The Natural Standard Research Collaboration, senior editor, 2001-05; National Institutes of Health, Center for Scientific Review, scientific review panelist, 2001-, principal investigator, 2006-09; Collinge and Associates, president, 2001-; Constella Health Sciences, scientific review panelist, 2002-07; National Cancer Institute, principal investigator, 2003-04; National Institute on Aging, principal investigator, 2004-05; National Institute of Mental Health, principal investigator, 2006-07, 2010-11; American Institute for BiologicalSciences, part-time executive secretary, 2008-09; SRA Intl., scientific review officer, 2008; National Institute of Arthritis and Musculoskeletal and Skin Diseases, principal investigator, 2008-10. **Publications:** Recovering from Chronic Fatigue Syndrome: A Guide to Self-Empowerment, 1993; The American Holistic Health Association Complete Guide to Alternative Medicine, 1996; Subtle Energy: Awakening to the Unseen Forces in Our Lives, 1998; Partners in Healing: Simple Ways to Offer Support, Comfort, and Care to a Loved One Facing Illness, 2008. **Address:** Collinge and Associates, PO Box 309, Kittery, ME 03904, U.S.A. **Online address:** william@collinge.org

COLLINGHAM, E. M. Also writes as Lizzie Collingham. British (born England) **Genres:** Food And Wine, History. **Career:** University of Warwick, Department of History, faculty; Cambridge University, Jesus College, research fellow. Writer. **Publications:** Imperial Bodies: The Physical Experience of the Raj, c. 1800-1947, 2001; (as Lizzie Collingham) Curry: A Tale of Cooks and Conquerors, 2006; (as Lizzie Collingham) The Taste of War: World War Two and the Battle for Food, 2011. Contributor to periodicals. **Address:** Gillon Aitken Associates, 18-21 Cavaye Pl., London, GL SW10 9PT, England.

COLLINGHAM, Lizzie. *See* **COLLINGHAM, E. M.**

COLLINGS, Gillian. (Frances Gilbert). British/American (born United States), b. 1939. **Genres:** Education, Children's Fiction, Mystery/Crime/Suspense, Children's Non-fiction. **Career:** Trumbull Board of Education, special education teacher and chairperson of special education, 1980-. Writer. **Publications:** (Co-author) Language Chain, Language Connection, 1989; Teaching Guide (teacher's companion to Turtle on a Summer's Day and Celeste and Regine in the Rain Forest), 1997; To Know the Sea, 2000. CHILDREN'S BOOKS (as Frances Gilbert): Turtle on a Summer's Day, 1994; Celeste and Regine in the Rain Forest, 1997. **Address:** Greene Bark Press, PO Box 1108, Bridgeport, CT 06601-1108, U.S.A. **Online address:** author@francesgilbert.com

COLLINGS, I. J. (Jillie Collings). British/Australian (born Australia) **Genres:** Novels, Environmental Sciences/Ecology, Paranormal, Medicine/Health. **Career:** Woman, feature writer, 1969-70, deputy features editor, 1970; The Guardian, health/ecology columnist, 1987-90. Television broadcaster and public speaker. **Publications:** The Malevolent Despot, 1968. AS JILLIE COLLINGS: Astrology and Your Child, 1980; Around the Next Corner, 1990; Life Forces: Guidelines for a Healthy Life on a Polluted Planet, 1991; The Ordinary Person's Guide to Extraordinary Health, 1993; Beat Heart Disease without Surgery, 1995; Colonic Irrigation, 1995. **Address:** 14 Highbourne House, 13-15 Marylebone High St., London, GL W1U 4NS, England.

COLLINGS, Jillie. *See* **COLLINGS, I. J.**

COLLINGS, Matthew. British (born England), b. 1955?. **Genres:** Art/Art History, Picture/Board Books. **Career:** British Broadcasting Corp., art critic, 1988-97; Artscribe Magazine, editor; Channel 4 TV, staff. **Publications:** (Co-author) Georg Herold: X. Baracke, 1986, 1986; Blimey! From Bohemia to Britpop: The London Artworld from Francis Bacon to Damien Hirst, 1997, 3rd ed., 1997; It Hurts: New York Art from Warhol to Now, 1998; (with N. Brown and S. Kent) Tracey Emin. I Need Art Like I Need God, 1998; This Is Modern Art, 2000; (intro.) British Abstract Painting 2001, 2001; Art Crazy Nation: The Post-Blimey! Art World, 2001; SL: Sarah Lucas, 2002; Ron Arad Talks to Matthew Collings., 2004; This is Civilisation, 2008. **Address:** c/o Author Mail, Harry N. Abrams Inc., 100 5th Ave., New York, NY 10011, U.S.A.

COLLINGS, Michael R(obert). American (born United States), b. 1947. **Genres:** Horror, Science Fiction/Fantasy, Plays/Screenplays, Poetry, Literary Criticism And History, Novels, Young Adult Non-fiction. **Career:** University of California-Riverside, associate in English, 1973-78; San Bernardino Community College, instructor in English, 1976-78; University of California-Los Angeles, instructor, 1978-79; Pepperdine University, Seaver College, assistant professor, 1979-81, associate professor of English, 1981-85, professor of English, 1985-, now professor emeritus, Creative Writing Program, director, poet-in-residence, 1997-2000; Rockefeller Foundation, consultant. Writer. **Publications:** (With J. Collings) Whole Wheat Harvest, 1981; A Reader's Guide, 1983; Piers Anthony: A Reader's Guide, 1983; Stephen King as Richard Bachman, 1985; (with D. Engebretson) The Shorter Works of Stephen King, 1985; The Many Facets of Stephen King, 1985; The Films of Stephen King, 1986; The Annotated Guide to Stephen King, 1986; The Stephen King Phenomenon, 1987; In the Image of God: Theme, Characterization and Landscape in the Fiction of Orson Scott Card, 1990; The Work of Stephen King: An Annotated Bibliography and Guide, 1996; The Art and Craft of Poetry, 1996; He's Scaring Us to Death, 1997; (with B. Clarke) The Work of Orson Scott Card: An Annotated Bibliography and Guide, 1997; Storyteller: The Official Guide to the Works of Orson Scott Card, 2001; Horror Plum'D: An International Stephen King Bibliography and Guide, 1960-2000, 2003; Hauntings: The Official Peter Straub Bibliography, 2003; Stephen King Is Richard Bachman, 2007; Gem Lore: An Introduction to Precious and Semi-Precious Stones, 2nd ed., 2009; In Endless Morn of Light: Moral Freedom in Milton's Universe, 2010; Toward Other Worlds: Perspectives on John Milton, C.S. Lewis, Stephen King, Orson Scott Card, and Others, 2010. NOVELS: The House beyond the Hill, 1997; Singer of Lies: A Science Fantasy Novel, 2009; The Slab, forthcoming. WORDSMITH SERIES: The Veil of Heaven, 2009; The Thousand Eyes of Flame, 2009. OTHER: (ed.) Reflections on the Fantastic, 1986. POETRY: A Season of Calm Weather, 1974; Naked to the Sun: Dark Visions of Apocalypse, 1985; Dark Transformations (poetry), 1990; All Calm, All Bright: Christmas Offerings, 1995; (ed. with S.E. Gratner) Retooling for the Renaissance in the 3rd Millennium, 1995; Haiku, 1995; Matrix, 1995; Epyllion in Anamnesis: Remembery/Taliesin: Two Cycles of Poems, 1996; Nestlings of a Dark God, 1996, 2nd ed., 1999; Tales through Time, 1996; Still Secrecies of Love, 1996; Poetry, Especially for Children, 1996; The Nephiad, 1996; Potpourri: A Medley of Poems, 1996; The Art and Craft of Poetry: Twenty Exercises Toward Mastery, 1996; Som Certaine Sonets, 1998; Compositae: Chapbooks and Poems, 1999; Elementals: Auto-Reductive Sonets in Major and Minor Modes, 1999; In the Void, 2009. Works appear in anthologies. **Address:** Seaver College, Pepperdine University, 24255 Pacific Coast Hwy., Malibu, CA 90263-3999, U.S.A. **Online address:** mcolling@pepperdine.edu

COLLINI, Stefan. British (born England), b. 1947. **Genres:** History, Literary Criticism And History, Politics/Government, Economics, Young Adult Non-fiction. **Career:** Cambridge University, Faculty of English, professor of intellectual history and English literature, Clare Hall, fellow. Writer. **Publications:** Liberalism and Sociology: L.T. Hobhouse and Political Argument in England, 1880-1914, 1979; (with D. Winch and J. Burrow) That Noble Science of Politics: A Study in Nineteenth-Century Intellectual History, 1983; Arnold, 1988; (ed.) On Liberty, with the Subjection of Women, 1989; Public Moralists: Political Thought and Intellectual Life in Britain, 1850-1930, 1991; (ed.) Interpretation and Overinterpretation, 1992; (ed.) Culture and Anarchy and Other Writings, 1993; English Pasts: Essays in Culture and History, 1999; (ed. with R. Whatmore and B. Young) History, Religion, and Culture: British Intellectual History, 1750-1950, 2000; (ed. with R. Whatmore and B. Young) Economy, Polity, and Society: British Intellectual History, 1750-1950, 2000; Absent Minds: Intellectuals in Britain, 2006; Matthew Arnold: A Critical Portrait, 2008; Common Reading: Critics, Historians, Publics, 2008. Contributor to periodicals. **Address:** Faculty of English, Cambridge University, 9 West Rd., Cambridge, CB CB3 9DP, England. **Online address:** sc107@cam.ac.uk

COLLINS, Ace. American (born United States), b. 1953. **Genres:** Novels, Adult Non-fiction, Children's Non-fiction, Theology/Religion. **Career:** Freelance writer. **Publications:** ADULT NONFICTION: (with Mandrell) The Mandrell Family Album, 1983; The Christian Executive, 1984 (with L. Chapin as Andrew Collins) Father Does Know Best, 1989; Bette Midler, 1989; Sigourney Weaver, 1989; After the Storm, 1992; I Saw Him In Your Eyes, vol. I, 1993, vol. II, 1995, vol. III, 1995; Lassie, A Dog's Life: The First Fifty Years, 1993, Tanya Tucker: A Biography, 1994; The Stories Behind Country Music's All-Time Greatest 100 Songs, 1996; Pam Tillis: Out of Her Father's Shadow, 1997; Country Music The Book of Lists, 1998; Disco Duck and Other Adventures in Novelty Music, 1998; Lassie's Guide to a Family's Best Friend: Building the Bond of Love Between Dog and Family, 1998; Lorrie Morgan, 1998 (co-author) The Cathedrals: The Story of America's Best-Loved Gospel Quartet, 1998; All About the Dixie Chicks, 1999 (with J. Hillman) Blackball Superstars: Legendary Players of the Negro Baseball Leagues, 1999; Evel Knievel: An American Hero, 1999; Turn Your Radio On: The Stories Behind Gospel Music's All-Time Greatest Songs 1999, Stories Behind the Best-Loved Songs of Christmas, 2001; Songs Sung Red, White and Blue: The Stories Behind America's Best -Loved Patriotic Songs, 2003; Tragedies of American History: 13 Stories of Human Error and Natural Disaster, 2003; Stories Behind The Hymns That Inspire America: Songs That Unite Our Nation, 2003; Stories Behind The Great Traditions of Christmas, 2003; Untold Gold: The Stories Behind Elvis Presley's No. 1 Hits, 2005; I Saw Him in Your Eyes: Everyday People Making Extraordinary Impact in the Lives of Karen Kingsbury, Terri Blackstock, Bobby Bowden, Dale Evans, Charlie Daniels, S. Truett Cathy and More, 2006; More Stories Behind the Best-Loved Songs of Christmas, 2006; Stories Behind The Traditions and Songs of Easter, 2007; Stories Behind Women of Extraordinary Faith, 2008; Farraday Road, 2008; Sticks and Stones: Using Your Words as a Positive Force, 2009; 25 days, 26 Ways to Make this your Best Christmas Ever, 2009; Stories Behind Men of Faith, 2009; Swope's Ridge, 2009; Words of the Father, 2010; Gratitudes, 2010; The Stories Behind Christmas's Top 40 Hit Records, 2010. HOLIDAY ADVENTURE SERIES FOR CHILDREN (with L. Mandrell): Runaway Thanksgiving, 1992, Jonathan's Gifts, 1992; Peril in Evans Woods, 1993; All in a Day's Work, 1993; Eddie Finds a Hero, 1993; Best Man for the Job, 1993; A Mission for Jenny, 1993; Sunrise over the Harbor, 1993; Bond of Trust; Kimi's American Dream, Candy's Frog Prince; Abe's Hard Lesson; The End of the Rainbow; Twin Disasters, The Eyes of an Eagle; The Parade. YOU CAN DO IT SERIES FOR CHILDREN: You Can Do It Running, 1993; You Can Do It Dog Training, 1993; You Can Do It Juggling, 1993; You Can Do It Sidewalk Art and Games, 1993; You Can Do It Balloon Shapes and Animals, 1993. ADULT FICTION: Darkness Before Dawn, 1994; The Cutting Edge, 1994; Saving Grace, 1995; The Image of Truth, 1995. OTHERS: The Country Music Book of Lists, 1998; Stories behind the Greatest Hits of Christmas, 2010; Grattitude: Practicing Contagious Optimism for Positive Change, 2010; Reich of Passage, 2011; Jefferson Burke and the Secret of the Lost Scroll, 2011. **Address:** 18 Timber Ridge Cir., Arkadelphia, AR 71923, U.S.A. **Online address:** ace@acecollins.com

COLLINS, Barbara. (Barbara Allan). American (born United States), b. 1948. **Genres:** Young Adult Fiction, Mystery/Crime/Suspense. **Career:** M.A.C. Productions, production manager. Writer. **Publications:** FICTION: (ed. with R.J. Randisi) Lethal Ladies, 1996; Landscaping Herbs, 1998; Becoming a Trans-Cultural Woman, 1999; Too Many Tomcats and Other Feline Tales of Suspense, 2000; How to Be a Wedding Planner, 2010. FICTION WITH MAX ALLAN COLLINS: Regeneration, 1999; Murder-His and Hers (short stories), 2001; Bombshell (novel), 2004; (as Barbara Allan) Antiques Roadkill, 2006; (as Barbara Allan) Antiques Maul, 2007. **Address:** Kensington Publishing Corp., 119 West 40th St., New York, NY 10018, U.S.A.

COLLINS, Billy. (William Collins). American (born United States), b. 1941. **Genres:** Poetry. **Career:** City University of New York, Lehman College, professor of English, 1968-, distinguished professor; Sarah Lawrence College, writer-in-residence; Rollins College, chair; Winter Park Institute, senior distinguished fellow; U.S. Poet Laureate, staff, 2001-03; New York State Poet Laureate, staff, 2004-06. Writer. **Publications:** POETRY: Pokerface, 1977; Video Poems, 1980; The Apple That Astonished Paris: Poems, 1988; Questions About Angels: Poems, 1991; The Art of Drowning, 1995; Picnic, Lightning, 1998; Taking off Emily Dickinson's Clothes, 2000; The Eye of the Poet: Six Views of the Art and Craft of Poetry, 2001; Sailing Alone around the Room: New and Selected Poems, 2001; Nine Horses: Poems, 2002; (ed. and intro.) Poetry 180: A Turning Back to Poetry, 2003; Daddy's Little Boy, 2004; (foreword) Leaves of Grass, 2005; (ed. and intro.) 180 More: Extraordinary Poems For Every Day, 2005; The Trouble With Poetry And Other Poems, 2005; Design=Diseño, 2005; She Was Just Seventeen, 2006; Ballistics: Poems, 2008; (ed.) Bright Wings: An Illustrated Anthology of Poems About Birds, 2009; Horoscopes for the Dead: Poems, 2011. Contributor to periodicals. **Address:** City University of New York, Lehman College, 250 Bedford Pk. Blvd. W, Bronx, NY 10468-1589, U.S.A.

COLLINS, Bud. American (born United States), b. 1929. **Genres:** Sports/Fitness, Biography. **Career:** Boston Herald, sports writer, 1955-63; freelance writer, 1955-; Brandeis University, varsity tennis coach, 1959-63; Boston

Globe, sports and general columnist, 1963-; Public Broadcasting Service, sportscaster, 1963-84; CBS Sports, sportscaster, 1968-72; National Broadcasting Co., sportscaster, 1964-; ESPN, staff, 2007-. **Publications:** (With R. Laver) The Education of a Tennis Player, 1971; (with E. Goolagong) Evonne! On the Move, 1975; My Life with the Pros, 1989; U.S. Open: Unmatched, 2002. EDITOR: (with R. Laver) Rod Laver's Tennis Digest, 1973; (with Z. Hollander) Bud Collins' Modern Encyclopedia of Tennis, 1980, 3rd ed., 1997; Total Tennis: The Ultimate Tennis Encyclopedia, 2003. Contributor to periodicals. **Address:** Sharf Marketing Group Inc., 822 Boylston St., Ste. 203, Chestnut Hill, MA 02467, U.S.A.

COLLINS, Catherine Fisher. American (born United States) **Genres:** Medicine/Health, Women's Studies And Issues. **Career:** Model City Agency, component manager, 1971-73; Human Resource Department, component manager, 1971-73; Comprehensive Health Planning Council of Western New York Inc., coordinator of federal funds, 1973-76; Health Systems Agency, director of quality assurance, 1976-86; Medaille College, professor, 1980-82; State University of New York, assistant professor, 1984-90, chair and professor, Empire State College, associate professor of community health and human services, 1992-, adjunct assistant professor, 1998-, University at Buffalo, Women's Studies Department, adjunct professor; Erie County Medical Center, director of ambulatory care, 1986-89; Erie Community College, adjunct assistant professor, 1988-90, professor and department head, 1990-92; Jack and Jill of America Inc., eastern regional director, 1993-95, national editor, 1998-2000, national vice president, 2000-02. Writer. **Publications:** (Ed.) African American Women's Health and Social Issues, 1996, 2nd ed., 2006; The Imprisonment of African American Women: Causes, Conditions, and Future Implications, 1997, 2nd ed. as The Imprisonment of African American Women: Causes, Experiences and Effects, 2010; Sources of Stress and Relief for African American Women, 2003; Handbook for African American Women's Health and Social Issues, 2003; South Africa Women Prisoners, 2005; Prisoner African American Women, 2006. **Address:** Department of Community Health and Human Services, State University of New York, Empire State College, 617 Main St., 3rd Fl., Buffalo, NY 14203-1498, U.S.A. **Online address:** catherine.collins@esc.edu

COLLINS, Floyd G. American (born United States), b. 1951. **Genres:** Novels, Poetry, Literary Criticism And History, History. **Career:** Quincy University, visiting assistant professor, 1999-2000; Wabash College, visiting assistant professor, 2000-01. Writer. **Publications:** Scarecrow, 1980; The Wedding Guest, 1987; Forecast: Poems, 1993; Seamus Heaney: The Crisis of Identity (literary criticism), 2003; What Harvest, forthcoming. Contributor to journals. **Address:** 200 Southland Dr., Apt. H-1, Barnesville, GA 30204, U.S.A. **Online address:** floydcolli659@bellsouth.net

COLLINS, Gail. American (born United States), b. 1945. **Genres:** Politics/Government, Women's Studies And Issues. **Career:** Connecticut State News Bureau, founder, 1972-77; freelance writer, 1977-79; Southern Connecticut State University, journalism instructor, 1977-79; Connecticut Public Television, public affairs program host, 1977-79; Connecticut Business Journal, columnist, 1977-79; Connecticut Magazine, senior editor, 1977-79; Columbia University, Bagehot Fellow, 1981-82; United Press Intl., financial reporter, 1982-85; New York Daily News, columnist, 1985-91; New York Newsday, columnist, 1991-95; This Week Close-Up, cable news program host, 1997; New York Times, op-ed columnist, 2000-01, 2007-, editorial page editor, 2001-07; Columbia University, Graduate School of Journalism, opinion writing instructor, 2009-. **Publications:** (With D. Collins) The Millennium Book: Your Essential All-Purpose Guide to the Year 2000, 1991; Scorpion Tongues: Gossip, Celebrity, and American Politics, 1998, rev. ed. as Scorpion Tongues: The Irresistible History of Gossip in American Politics, 1999, new ed., 2007; America's Women: Four Hundred Years of Dolls, Drudges, Helpmates, and Heroines, 2003; When Everything Changed: The Amazing Journey of American Women from 1960 to the Present, 2009. Contributor to periodicals. **Address:** New York Times, 229 W 43rd St., New York, NY 10036, U.S.A.

COLLINS, Helen (Frances). American (born United States), b. 1937?. **Genres:** Novels, Science Fiction/Fantasy, Mystery/Crime/Suspense. **Career:** Nassau Community College, professor of English, 1967-; Brooklyn College, faculty of English. Writer. **Publications:** Mutagenesis (science fiction), 1993, 2nd ed., 2011; Egret (novel), 2001; NeuroGenesis, 2008, 2nd ed., 2011. Contributor to periodicals. **Address:** 22 Fairhaven Rd., Niantic, CT 06357-1702, U.S.A. **Online address:** info@helencollins.net

COLLINS, Hugh. British (born England), b. 1953?. **Genres:** Law, Business/Trade/Industry, Economics, Social Sciences. **Career:** University of Oxford, Brasenose College, fellow and tutor in law; University of London, London School of Economics and Political Science, Department of Law, chair of English Law, 1991-2006, professor of English law, 2006-; Boston University, visiting professor. Writer. **Publications:** Marxism and Law, 1982; The Law of Contract, 1986, 4th ed., 2003; Justice in Dismissal: The Law of Termination of Employment, 1992; Regulating Contracts, 1999; (with K.D. Ewing and A. McColgan) Labour Law: Text and Materials, 2001, 2nd ed., 2005; Employment Law, 2003, 2nd ed., 2010; European Civil Code: The Way Forward, 2008. EDITOR: (with D. Campbell and J. Wightman) Implicit Dimensions of Contract: Discrete, Relational, and Network Contracts, 2003; Forthcoming EC Directive on Unfair Commercial Practices, 2004; Standard Contract Terms in Europe: A Basis for and a Challenge to European Contract Law, 2008; (and intro.) Networks as Connected Contracts, 2011. **Address:** Department of Law, London School of Economics and Political Science, University of London, 7.10 New Academic Bldg., Houghton St., London, GL WC2A 2AE, England. **Online address:** h.collins@lse.ac.uk

COLLINS, Irene. British (born England), b. 1925. **Genres:** History, Social Sciences. **Career:** University of Liverpool, lecturer, reader, 1947-86, School of History, honorary senior fellow, 1986-. Writer. **Publications:** Liberalism in Nineteenth-Century Europe, 1957; The Government and the Newspaper Press in France, 1814-81, 1959; The Age of Progress: Europe, 1789-1870, 1970; (ed.) Government and Society in France, 1814-1848, 1970; Revolutionaries in Europe, 1815-1848, 1974; Napoleon and His Parliaments, 1800-1815, 1979; Jane Austen and the Clergy, 1993; Jane Austen, The Parson's Daughter, 1998. **Address:** School of History, University of Liverpool, 9 Abercromby Sq., Liverpool, L69 3BX, England.

COLLINS, Jackie. British (born England), b. 1941. **Genres:** Novels, Novellas/Short Stories, Mystery/Crime/Suspense, Romance/Historical. **Career:** Writer. **Publications:** The World Is Full of Married Men, 1968; The Stud, 1969; Sunday Simmons and Charlie Brick, as Sinners, 1971; Lovehead, 1974; The World Is Full of Divorced Women, 1975; The Hollywood Zoo, 1975; The Love Killers, 1977; Lovers and Gamblers, 1977; The Bitch, 1979; Chances, 1981; Hollywood Wives, 1983; Lucky, 1985; Hollywood Husbands, 1986; Rock Star, 1988; Lady Boss: A Novel, 1990; American Star: A Love Story, 1993; Hollywood Kids: A Novel, 1994; Vendetta: Lucky's Revenge, 1997; Revenge, 1998; Thrill!, 1998; Murder, 1998; Power, 1998; Obsession, 1998; L.A. Connections, 1999; Dangerous Kiss: A Novel, 1999; Lethal Seduction, 2000; Hollywood Wives: The New Generation, 2001; Deadly Embrace, 2002; Hollywood Divorces, 2003; Lovers and Players, 2006; Drop Dead Beautiful, 2007; Married Lovers, 2008; Poor Little Bitch Girl, 2010; Goddess of Vengeance, 2011. **Address:** c/o John Murphy, St. Martins Press, 175 5th Ave., 15th Fl., New York, NY 10010, U.S.A.

COLLINS, Joan. British (born England), b. 1933. **Genres:** Novels, Fash Ion/Costume, Biography, Young Adult Fiction, Medicine/Health. **Career:** Actress and writer. **Publications:** Past Imperfect: An Autobiography, 1978; The Joan Collins Beauty Book, 1980; (intro.) Joan Collins: Portraits of a Star, 1987; My Secrets, 1994; Health, Youth and Happiness: My Secrets, 1995; Second Act, 1996; My Friends' Secrets, 1999; (co-author) Big Night Out, 2002; Joan's Way: Looking Good, Feeling Great, 2004; The Art of Living Well: Looking Good, Feeling Great, 2007; The World According to Joan, 2011. NOVELS: Prime Time, 1988; Love and Desire and Hate, 1990; Infamous, 1996; Star Quality, 2002; Misfortune's Daughters, 2005. **Address:** Peter Charlesworth & Associates, 67 Holland Pk. Mews, London, GL W11 3SS, England.

COLLINS, Josie. *See* **BENTLEY, Joyce.**

COLLINS, Julie (Hubbard). American (born United States), b. 1959. **Genres:** Travel/Exploration, Illustrations, Sports/Fitness, Biography, Autobiography/Memoirs. **Career:** Writer and photographer, 1979-. **Publications:** NONFICTION WITH M. COLLINS: Trapline Twins, 1989, 2nd ed., 2010; Dog Driver: A Guide for the Serious Musher, 1991, rev. ed., 2009; Riding the Wild Side of Denali: Alaska Adventures with Horses and Huskies, 1998. Contributor to journals. **Address:** Alpine Publications Inc., 38262 Linman Rd., Crawford, CO 81415, U.S.A.

COLLINS, Kathleen. American (born United States), b. 1965. **Genres:** Food And Wine, Communications/Media. **Career:** City University of New York, John Jay College of Criminal Justice, librarian. Writer and researcher.

Publications: Watching What We Eat: The Evolution of Television Cooking Shows, 2009. Contributor to books and journals. **Address:** New York, NY , U.S.A. **Online address:** kcollins@jjay.cuny.edu

COLLINS, Martha. American/British (born England), b. 1940. **Genres:** Poetry, Translations. **Career:** Northeast Missouri State College, assistant professor, 1965-66; University of Massachusetts, instructor, professor of English, 1966-2002, founder and co-director of creative writing, 1979-2000; Oberlin College, Pauline Delaney chair, Pauline Delaney professor of creative writing and co-director of creative writing, 1997-2007, Oberlin College Press, editor-at-large; FIELD Magazine, editor-at-large. **Publications:** (Ed.) Critical Essays on Louise Bogan, 1984; The Catastrophe of Rainbows (poetry), 1985, 2nd ed., 1998; The Arrangement of Space (poetry), 1991; A History of Small Life on a Windy Planet: Poems, 1993; (ed. and trans.) N.Q. Thieu, The Women Carry River Water: Poems, 1997; Some Things Words Can Do (poetry), 1998; (trans. with T. Dinh) L.T.M. Da, Green Rice: Poems, 2005; Blue Front, 2006; Sheer, 2008. Contributor to periodicals. **Address:** Oberlin College Press, 50 N Professor St., Oberlin, OH 44074-1095, U.S.A. **Online address:** martha.collins@oberlin.edu

COLLINS, Max Allan. Also writes as Patrick Culhane, Peter Brackett, Mickey Spillane. American (born United States), b. 1948. **Genres:** Mystery/Crime/Suspense, Graphic Novels. **Career:** Musician, 1966-72, 1976-79, 1986-; Daybreakers group, musician, 1966-71; Tree Intl., songwriter, 1967-71; Muscatine Journal, reporter, 1968-70; Muscatine Community College, instructor in English, 1971-77; writer, 1972-; Mississippi Valley Writers Conference, instructor, 1973-; Cruisin group, musician, 1976-79; The International Association of Media Tie-in Writers, co-founder; film producer/director/screenwriter, 1994-. **Publications:** MYSTERY NOVELS: Bait Money, 1973; Blood Money, 1973; The Broker, 1976; The Broker's Wife, 1976; The Dealer, 1976; The Slasher, 1977; Fly Paper, 1981; Hush Money, 1981; Hard Cash, 1981; Scratch Fever, 1982; The Baby Blue Rip-Off, 1983; No Cure for Death, 1983; True Detective, 1983; Kill Your Darlings, 1984; True Crime, 1984; A Shroud for Aquarius, 1985; The Million Dollar Wound, 1986; Nice Weekend for a Murder, 1986; Midnight Haul, 1986; Spree, 1987; Primary Target, 1987; Neon Mirage, 1988; Stolen Away, 1991; Carnal Hours, 1994; Blood and Thunder, 1995; Damned in Paradise, 1996; Flying Blind, 1999; Majic Man, 1999; Mourn the Living, 1999; Kisses of Death, 2001; Angel in Black, 2001; Chicago Confidential, 2002; The Lusitania Mysteries, 2002; The Last Quarry, 2006; Criminal Minds: Jump Cut, 2007; Criminal Minds: Finishing School, 2008; Criminal Minds: Killer Profile, 2008; The First Quarry, 2008; Quarry In The Middle, 2009; Quarry's Ex, 2010; Bye Bye, Baby, 2011. NOVELIZATIONS OF FILMS: Dick Tracy and the Nightmare Machine, 1991; In the Line of Fire, 1994; (as Peter Brackett) I Love Trouble, 1994; Waterworld, 1995; Daylight, 1996; Air Force One, 1997; U.S. Marshals, 1998; Saving Private Ryan, 1998; The Mummy, 1999; U-571, 2000; Pink Panther, 2005. The Rise of Cobra, 2009. AS PATRICK CULHANE: Black Hats: a Novel of Wyatt Earp & Al Capone, 2007; Red Sky in Morning, 2008. CSI SERIES: CSI: Double Dealer, 2001; CSI: Sin City, 2002; CSI: Body of Evidence, 2003; CSI: Miami: Florida Getaway, 2003; CSI: Cold Burn, 2003; CSI: Grave Matters, 2004; CSI: Miami: Heat Wave, 2004; CSI: Killing Game, 2005; CSI: Binding Ties, 2005; CSI: Snake Eyes, 2006. EDITOR: (with M. Spillane) Tomorrow I Die, 1984; (with D. Locher) The Dick Tracy Casebook, 1990; (with D. Locher) Dick Tracy: The Secret Files, 1990; (with D. Locher) Dick Tracy's Fiendish Foes, 1991; (with M. Spillane) Murder Is My Business, 1994; (and intro. with B. Collins) Too Many Tomcats and Other Feline Tales of Suspense, 2000; (with J. Gelb) Flesh and Blood, 2001; (and intro. with M. Spillane) Together We Kill, 2001; (with M. Spillane) A Century of Noir, 2002; (with L.F. Myers, Jr.) Byline, 2004. OTHERS: Quarry's Deal, 1976; Quarry's Cut, 1977; Dick Tracy Meets Angeltop, 1980; Dick Tracy Meets the Punks, 1980; The Mike Mist Minute Mist-eries, 1981; (co-ed.) Mike Hammer: The Comic Strip, vol. I, 1982, vol. II, 1985; (with E. Gorman) The Killers inside Him, 1983; (with J.L. Traylor) One Lonely Knight: Mickey Spillane's Mike Hammer, 1984; (with T. Beatty) The Files of Ms. Tree, 3 vols., 1984-86; (with D. Locher) Dick Tracy: Tracy's Wartime Memories, 1986; The Dark City, 1987; Butcher's Dozen, 1988; (with J. Javna) The Best of Crime and Detective TV, 1988; Bullet Proof, 1989; Dick Tracy Goes to War, 1991; Dying in the Post-war World (short stories), 1991; Tough Tender, 1991; Dick Tracy Meets His Match, 1992; Murder by the Numbers, 1993; Maverick (adventure), 1994; NYPD Blue: Blue Beginning, 1995; The Mystery Scene Movie Guide, 1996; Earl MacPherson, 1997; NYPD Blue: Blue Blood, 1997; Mommy, 1997; Gil Elvgren, 1997; Pin-up Poster Book, 1997; Road to Perdition (graphic novel), 1998; Mommy's Day, 1998; (with D. Elvgren) Elvgren, 1998; Swimsuit Sweeties, 1999; Varga Girls I and II, 1999; Elvgren Girls I and II, 1999; Exotic Ladies, 1999; The Titanic Murders, 1999; (with B. Collins) Regeneration, 1999; For the Boys!, 2000; The Hindenburg Murders, 2000; The Mummy Returns, 2001; Indian Maidens, 2001; Pirate and Gypsy Girls, 2001; The Pearl Harbor Murders, 2001; Pin-up Nudes, 2001, vol. II, 2002; Seaside Sweethearts, 2001; Windtalkers, 2001; Blue Christmas and Other Holiday Homicides, 2001; (with B. Collins) Murder: His and Hers (short stories), 2001; The History of Mystery, 2001; Patriotic Pin-ups, 2002; The Scorpion King: A Novel, 2002; The Lusitania Murders, 2002; Cowgirl Pin-ups, 2002; Playful Pinups, 2002; I Spy, 2002; Before the Dawn, 2002; Dick Tracy, 2003; Skin Game, 2003; After the Dark, 2003; Oasis, 2003; Sanctuary, 2003; CSI: Crime Scene Investigation, 2003; Johnny Dynamite, 2003; On the Road to Perdition, 2003; Road to Perdition 2, 2004; Detour, 2004; Road To Purgatory, 2004; (with B. Collins) Bombshell, 2004; Two for the Money, 2004; The London Blitz Murders, 2004; Road to Paradise, 2005; The War of the Worlds Murder, 2005; (with B. Collins) Antiques Roadkill, 2006; Bones: Buried Deep, 2006; (with B. Collins) Antiques Maul, 2007; A Killing in Comics, 2007; Jump Cut, 2007; American Gangster, 2007; Deadly Beloved, 2007; Mortal Wounds, 2007; Finishing School, 2008; Strip For Murder, 2008; Killer Profile, 2008; (contrib.) Men's Adventure Magazines in Postwar America, 2008; (with B. Collins) Antiques Flee Market, 2008; The Mummy: Tomb of the Dragon Emperor, 2008; (with M. Spillane) Dead Street, 2007; (with M. Spillane) The Goliath Bone, 2008; The X Files: I Want to Believe, 2008; The New Adventures of Mickey Spillane's Mike Hammer, vol. II: The Little Death, 2009, vol. III: Encore for Murder, 2011; (with M. Spillane) Big Bang, 2010; (with B. Collins) Antiques Bizarre, 2010; (with M. Clemens) You Can't Stop Me, 2010; (intro.) Blood, Guts & Whiskey, 2010; (with M. Spillane) Kiss Her Goodbye: A Mike Hammer Novel, 2011; (with B. Collins) Antiques Knock-Off, 2011; No One Will Hear You, 2011; (with M. Spillane) The Consummata, 2011; Return to Perdition, 2011. **Address:** 301 Fairview Ave., Muscatine, IA 52761, U.S.A. **Online address:** macphilms@hotmail.com

COLLINS, Merle. American (born United States), b. 1950. **Genres:** Novels, Novellas/Short Stories, Poetry. **Career:** Teacher, 1974; McDonald College, teacher; Government of Grenada, Research on Latin America and the Caribbean, coordinator; University of North London, faculty, 1984-95; University of Maryland, professor of comparative literature and English, 1995-, Study Abroad Program, director; Poet and educator, 1985-; St. George's University, School of Arts and Sciences, visiting professor. **Publications:** POETRY: Because the Dawn Breaks! Poems Dedicated to the Grenadian People, 1985; Rotten Pomerack, 1992; Lady in a Boat, 2003. NOVELS: Angel, 1987; The Color of Forgetting, 1995. SHORT STORIES: Rain Darling: Stories, 1990. EDITOR: (with R. Cobham) Watchers and Seekers: Creative Writing by Black Women in Britain, 1987; Jump-Up-and-Kiss Me: Two Stories of Grenadian Childhood, 1990. OTHERS: The Colour of Forgetting, 1995. Contributor to anthologies and periodicals. **Address:** Department of Comparative Literature, University of Maryland, 3104 Tawes Hall, College Park, MD 20742, U.S.A. **Online address:** mc188@umail.umd.edu

COLLINS, Michael. Irish (born Ireland), b. 1964. **Genres:** Novels, Novellas/Short Stories, Biography. **Career:** Northwestern University, head of computer lab and creative writing teacher; Microsoft, programmer. Writer. **Publications:** The Meat Eaters, 1992 in US as The Man Who Dreamt of Lobsters, 1993; The Life and Times of a Teaboy, 1994; The Feminists Go Swimming, 1996; The Emerald Underground, 1998; The Keepers of Truth: A Novel, 2001; The Resurrectionists: A Novel, 2002; Lost Souls, 2003; The Secret Life of E. Robert Pendleton in US as Death of a Writer, 2006; Midnight in a Perfect Life, 2010. **Address:** c/o Author Mail, Simon & Schuster, 1230 Ave. of the Americas, New York, NY 10020, U.S.A.

COLLINS, Miki (Dickey). American (born United States), b. 1959. **Genres:** Adult Non-fiction, Animals/Pets, Sports/Fitness. **Career:** Writer, 1974-; handcrafter, 1975-; trapper, 1976-. **Publications:** NONFICTION WITH J. COLLINS: Trapline Twins, 1989, 2nd ed., 2010; Dog Driver: A Guide for the Serious Musher, 1991, rev. ed., 2009; Riding the Wild Side of Denali: Alaska Adventures with Horses and Huskies, 1998. Contributor to magazines. **Address:** Alpine Publications, PO Box 7027, Loveland, CO 80537, U.S.A.

COLLINS, Nancy A. (Nanzi Regalia). American (born United States), b. 1959. **Genres:** Novels, Mystery/Crime/Suspense, Horror, Graphic Novels,

Young Adult Fiction, Humor/Satire, Adult Non-fiction. **Career:** The International Horror Guild, founder. Writer. **Publications:** FICTION: Sunglasses after Dark (novel), 1989; Tempter, 1990, rev. ed., 2001; (as Nanzi Regalia) Love Throbbing Bob, 1990; The Tortuga Hill Gang's Last Ride: The True Story, 1991; In the Blood, 1992; Cold Turkey, 1992; Wild Blood, 1993; Paint It Black, 1995; Nameless Sins, 1994; Midnight Blue: The Sonja Blue Collection, 1995; Walking Wolf, 1995; The Fantastic Four: To Free Atlantis, 1995; A Dozen Black Roses, 1996; Dark Destiny: Proprietors of Fate, 1996; Dhampire: Stillborn, 1996; The Big Book of Losers, 1996; Kiches and Tales, 1997; Lynch: A Gothik Western, 1998; Angels on Fire, 1998; Avenue X and Other Dark Streets, 2000; Voodoo Chile, 2001; Person(s) Unknown, 2002; Darkest Heart, 2002; Dead Roses for a Blue Lady, 2002; Knuckles and Tales, 2003; Dead Man's Hand: Five Tales of the Weird Wes, 2004; In the Blood: A Sonya Blue Novel, 2004; (with N. Rhodes) Final Destination II: The Movie, 2006; Looks Could Kill, 2006; Vamps, 2008; After Dark, 2009; Night Life, 2009; Right Hand Magic, 2010. EDITOR: (with M.H. Greenberg and E.E. Kramer) Dark Love, 1995; Forbidden Acts, 1995; (with G. Wilson) Gahan Wilson's the Ultimate Haunted House, 1996; Absalom's Wake (novel), forthcoming. OTHERS: Hard to Get: Fast Talk and Rude Questions along the Interview Trail, 1990; The Big Book of Hoaxes, 2000; Left Hand Magic, 2011. Contributor to books and periodicals. Works appear in anthologies. **Address:** Donald Maas Literary Agency, 121 W 27th St., New York, NY 10001, U.S.A.

COLLINS, Patricia Hill. American (born United States), b. 1948. **Genres:** Women's Studies And Issues, Race Relations. **Career:** Harvard University, teacher, 1970-73; Design Programs Inc., educational consultant, 1972-73; Saint Joseph Community School, curriculum specialist, 1973-76; Tufts University, African American Center, director, 1976-80; University of Cincinnati, assistant professor, associate professor, 1987-94, acting chair, 1987-88, chair, 1999-2002, professor of African American studies, 1994-2005, Charles Phelps Taft professor of sociology, 1996-2005, Charles Phelps Taft distinguished emeritus professor of sociology, 2005-; PHC Educational Services, founder and president, 2002-; University of Maryland, Wilson Elkins professor of sociology, 2005-06, distinguished university professor, 2006-; American Sociological Association, president. Writer. **Publications:** Black Feminist Thought: Knowledge, Consciousness and the Politics of Empowerment, 1990, rev. ed., 2000; (comp. with M.L. Andersen) Race, Class and Gender: An Anthology, 1992, 8th ed., 2010; Fighting Words: Black Women and the Search for Justice, 1998; Black Sexual Politics: African Americans, Gender and the New Racism, 2004; From Black Power to Hip Hop: Racism, Nationalism and Feminism, 2006; Another Kind of Public Education, 2009; (ed. with J. Solomos) SAGE Handbook of Race and Ethnic Studies, 2010. Contributor of books to periodicals. **Address:** Department of Sociology, University of Maryland, 4105 Art-Sociology Bldg., 2112 Art-Sociology Bldg., College Park, MD 20742, U.S.A. **Online address:** pcollins@socy.umd.edu

COLLINS, Paul. American (born United States), b. 1969. **Genres:** History, Novels. **Career:** Portland State University, assistant professor of literature, associate professor; McSweeney's Books, Collins Library Imprint, founder and editor; National Public Radio, literary detective on weekend edition. **Publications:** Community Writing: Researching Social Issues Through Composition, 2001; Banvard's Folly: Thirteen Tales of Renowned Obscurity, Famous Anonymity, and Rotten Luck, 2001; Sixpence House: Lost in a Town of Books, 2003; Not Even Wrong: Adventures in Autism, 2004; (ed.) Lady into Fox, 2004; Trouble with Tom: The Strange Afterlife and Times of Thomas Paine, 2005; Book of William: How Shakespeare's First Folio Conquered the World, 2009; Nack and Thorn: A Murderous Love Story, forthcoming. EDITOR: English as She is Spoke, 2002; To Ruhleben and Back, 2003; Lady Into Fox, 2004; The Riddle of the Traveling Skull, 2005; The Lunatic at Large, 2007; Curious Men, 2008. **Address:** Department of English, Portland State University, 409 Neuberger Hall, 724 SW Harrison St., PO Box 751, Portland, OR 97201, U.S.A. **Online address:** pcollins@pdx.edu

COLLINS, Richard (Wayne). American (born United States), b. 1952. **Genres:** Novels. **Career:** Louisiana State University, instructor in English, 1982-84; University of Wales, University College, Leverhulme lecturer in American studies, 1984-85; Louisiana State University, assistant professor of English, 1985-92; Southern University, visiting assistant professor, 1988; University of Bucharest, Fulbright senior lecturer in American literature, 1992-93; University of Timisoara, Fulbright senior lecturer in American literature, 1993-94; American University, associate professor of English, 1995-97; Center for Independent Journalism, visiting lecturer, 1995; Xavier University, faculty, 1997-, Rosa Mary endowed professor of English. Writer. **Publications:** Foolscape, 1983; This Degradation, 1992; (trans. with C. Poenaru) C.R. Constantinescu, Ilfoveanu, 1992; (trans.) Bucharest in the 1920s-1940s: Between Avant-Garde and Modernism, 1994; (trans. with A. Banta) I. Flora, Cincizeci de romane i alte utopii/Fifty Novels and Other Utopias, 1996; John Fante: A Literary Portrait, 2000; (ed. with T. Bonner, Jr. and R. Skinner) Silver Threads: 25 Years of Fiction from Xavier Review, 2009. Contributor to books and periodicals. Works appear in anthologies. **Address:** Xavier Review Press, 1 Drexel Dr., New Orleans, LA 70125, U.S.A. **Online address:** rcollins@xula.edu

COLLINS, Robert. American (born United States), b. 1965. **Genres:** Science Fiction/Fantasy, Humor/Satire. **Career:** Writer. **Publications:** Ghost Railroads of Kansas, 1977, rev. ed., 2009. Kansas Railroad Attractions, 2004; General James G. Blunt: Tarnished Glory, 2005; Jim Lane: Scoundrel, Statesman, Kansan, 2007; Expert Assistance, 2007. **Address:** Pelican Publishning Co., 1000 Burmaster St., Gretna, LA 70053-2246, U.S.A. **Online address:** rlckansas@cox.net

COLLINS, Roger. Scottish (born Scotland), b. 1949. **Genres:** History. **Career:** University of Liverpool, professor; University of Bristol, professor; University of Edinburgh, professor, 1994-98; honorary fellow in history, 1998-. Writer. **Publications:** Early Medieval Spain: Unity in Diversity, 400-1000, 1983, 2nd ed., 1995; The Basques, 1987; The Arab Conquest of Spain, 710-797, 1989; Early Medieval Europe, 300-1000, 1991, 2nd ed., 1999; Law, Culture, and Regionalism in Early Medieval Spain, 1992; Charlemagne, 1998; Spain: An Oxford Archaeological Guide, 1998; Cronica, 2002; Visigothic Spain, 409711, 2004; Keepers of the Keys of Heaven: A History of the Papacy, 2009. EDITOR: (with P. Wormald and D. Bullough) Ideal and Reality in Frankish and Anglo-Saxon Society: Studies Presented to J.M. Wallace-Hadrill, 1983; (with P. Godman) Charlemagne's Heir: New Perspectives on the Reign of Louis the Pious (814- 840), 1990; (with J. McClure) The Ecclesiastical History of the English People; The Greater Chronicle; Bede's Letter to Egbert, 1994, new ed., 2008; (with A. Goodman) Medieval Spain: Culture, Conflict, and Coexistence: Studies in Honour of Angus MacKay, 2002. **Address:** University of Edinburgh, School of History, Classics and Archaeology, Teviot Pl., William Robertson Wing, Old Medical School, Edinburgh, EH8 9AG, Scotland. **Online address:** r.collins@ed.ac.uk

COLLINS, Ronald K. L. American (born United States), b. 1949. **Genres:** Law, Biography, Social Commentary. **Career:** Stanford Law School, teaching fellow; Center for the Study of Commercialism, co-founder; Temple University, visiting associate professor, professor of law, 1988-90; George Washington University, visiting professor, professor of law, 1992-95; Seattle University, professor of law, 1995-; The First Amendment Center, fellow, 2002-09; Oregon Supreme Court, law clerk; The Center for Science in the Public Interest, staff; Syracuse University, visiting associate professor; University of Washington, School of Law, visiting professor. Writer. **Publications:** (Ed.) Constitutional Government in America: Essays and Proceedings from Southwestern University Law Review's First West Coast Conference on Constitutional Law, 1980; (ed.) The Death of Contract, 1995; (with D.M. Skover) The Death of Discourse, 1996, 2nd ed., 2005; The Trials of Lenny Bruce: The Fall and Rise of an American Icon, 2002; (with S. Chaltain) We Must Not Be Afraid to be Free: Stories of Free Expression in America, 2005; (forward) Top Secret: When Our Government Keeps Us in the Dark, 2007; (forward) The Interpretive Game, 2008; (ed.) Fundamental Holmes: A Free Speech Chronicle and Reader-Selections from the Opinions, Books, Articles, Speeches, Letters and Other Writings by and about Oliver Wendell Holmes, Jr., 2010; (with D. Skover) Mania: The Madcap Stories of the Lives that Launched a Generation, 2010; (forward) Make No Law: Exceptions to the First Amendment, 2010; (co-author) Dissent in America, 2012; Contributor to books and periodicals. **Address:** School of Law, University of Washington, 310 William H. Gates Hall, PO Box 353020, Seattle, WA 98195-3020, U.S.A. **Online address:** collins@seattleu.edu

COLLINS, Stephen. American (born United States), b. 1947. **Genres:** Novels, Plays/Screenplays. **Career:** The Creative Coalition, board director, 1989-; American Clean Water Foundation, board director, 1990-. Writer. **Publications:** Eye Contact (novel), 1994; Double Exposure (novel), 1998. **Address:** The WB Network, 3701 Oak St., Bldg. 34R, Burbank, CA 91505-3404, U.S.A. **Online address:** stephencollins3@earthlink.net

COLLINS, Stephen L. American/British (born England), b. 1949. **Genres:** Intellectual History, History. **Career:** Shimer College, humanities faculty,

1975-78; Boston University, assistant professor of social science, 1978-83; Babson College, assistant professor, 1983-88, associate professor of history, 1988-, William R. Dill Term Chair in History and Society, 1992-, professor of history; Emory University, teacher. Writer. **Publications:** From Divine Cosmos to Sovereign State: An Intellectual History of Consciousness and the Idea of Order in Renaissance England, 1989. **Address:** Department of History, Babson College, Hollister Hall, 231 Forest St., Babson Park, MA 02457-0310, U.S.A. **Online address:** collins@babson.edu

COLLINS, Tess. American (born United States) **Genres:** Plays/Screenplays, Novels, Young Adult Fiction, Literary Criticism And History. **Career:** Curran Theatre, manager; Freelance writer, 1997-. **Publications:** The Law of Revenge (novel), 1997; The Law of the Dead, 1999; How Theater Managers Manage, 2003; The Law of Betrayal, 2003. **Address:** Curran Theatre, 445 Geary St., San Francisco, CA 94102-1222, U.S.A. **Online address:** tessala@pacbell.net

COLLINS, William. *See* **COLLINS, Billy.**

COLLINSON, Alan S. (Stan Freedman). British (born England), b. 1934?. **Genres:** Biology, Botany, Geography, Novels, Social Sciences, Sciences, Engineering. **Career:** Trent Park College, lecturer, 1967-72; Middlesex Polytechnic, lecturer, 1967-72; Sunderland Polytechnic, principal lecturer in fine art, 1972-88. Writer. **Publications:** Introduction to World Vegetation, 1978, 2nd ed., 1988; Working with Oceans, Polar Lands and Space, 1990; Choosing Health, 1991; Renewable Energy, 1991; Mountains, 1991; Grasslands, 1992; Pollution, 1992; He Fell Among Artists, 1995. **Address:** 54 Bolton Ave., Richmond, NY DL10 4BA, England.

COLLINSON, Roger (Alfred). American/British (born England), b. 1936. **Genres:** Children's Fiction, Children's Non-fiction, Humor/Satire, Literary Criticism And History. **Career:** Teacher, 1975-97; Church of England, priest, 1997. Writer. **Publications:** A Boat and Bax, 1967; Butch and Bax, 1970; Four Eyes, 1976; Get Lavinia Goodbody!, 1983; Paper Flags and Penny Ices, 1984; Hanky Panky, 1986; Willy and the Semolina Pudding and Other Stories, 1994; Willy and the UFO, 1995; Sticky Fingers, 1996; Butterfingers, 1997; Grisel and the Tooth Fairy, 1998; Las Cosas De Berta, 2005. Contributor to periodicals. **Address:** c/o Author Mail, Anderson Press Ltd., Random Century House, 20 Vauxhall Bridge Rd., London, GL SW1V 2SA, England.

COLLINSON, Sarah. British (born England), b. 1965?. **Genres:** International Relations/Current Affairs, Politics/Government, Social Sciences, History. **Career:** European Commission, trainee and researcher, 1990-91; University of Reading, visiting research fellow, 1992-97; Overseas Development Institute, team leader. Writer. **Publications:** Europe and International Migration, 1993, rev. ed., 1994; (with H. Miall and A. Michalski) A Wider European Union? Integration and Cooperation in the New Europe, 1993; Beyond Borders: West European Migration Policy Towards the Twenty-First Century, 1994; Migration, Visa and Asylum Policies in Europe, 1995; Shore to Shore: The Politics of Migration in Euro-Maghreb Relations, 1996; Politically Informed Humanitarian Programming: Using a Political Economy Approach, 2002; (ed.) Power, Livelihoods and Conflict, 2003. **Address:** Overseas Development Institute, 111 Westminster Bridge Rd., London, GL SE1 7JD, England. **Online address:** s.collinson@odi.org.uk

COLLIS, Louise (Edith). British/Myanmar (born Myanmar), b. 1925. **Genres:** Novels, Art/Art History, History, Biography, Women's Studies And Issues, Music, Adult Non-fiction. **Career:** Art critic and writer. **Publications:** Without a Voice, 1951; A Year Passed, 1952; After the Holiday, 1954; The Angel's Name, 1955; Seven in the Tower, 1958; The Apprentice Saint, 1960; Memoirs of a Medieval Woman: The Life and Times of Margery Kempe, 1964; Soldier in Paradise: The Life of Captain John Stedman, 1744-1797, 1965; The Great Flood, 1966; A Private View of Stanley Spencer, 1972; Maurice Collis Diaries, 1978; Impetuous Heart: The Story of Ethel Smyth, 1984. Contributor to periodicals. **Address:** 65 Cornwall Gardens, London, GL SW7 4BD, England.

COLLIS, Rose. British (born England), b. 1959?. **Genres:** Gay And Lesbian Issues, Biography. **Career:** Brighton Museum and Art Gallery, writer and principal researcher, 2005-06. Journalist. **Publications:** Portraits to the Wall: Historic Lesbian Lives Unveiled, 1994; A Trouser-Wearing Character: The Life and Times of Nancy Spain, 1995; (ed.) Lesbian Pillow Book, 1995; K.D. Lang, 1999; (ed.) Mammoth Book of Lesbian Erotica, 2000; Colonel Barker's Monstrous Regiment: A Tale of Female Husbandry, 2001; Brighton Boozers: A History of the City's Pub Culture, 2005; Coral Browne: This Effing Lady, 2007; The New Encyclopedia of Brighton, 2010; Wanting the Moon: The Biography of Clemence Dane, forthcoming. Contributor to periodicals. **Address:** c/o Author Mail, Carroll & Graf Publishers, 245 W 17th St., 11th Fl., New York, NY 10011-5300, U.S.A. **Online address:** rose@rosecollis.com

COLLISON, Kerry B(oyd). Australian (born Australia), b. 1944. **Genres:** Novels, Poetry, History, International Relations/Current Affairs, Social Commentary, Third World, Autobiography/Memoirs, Film, Film. **Career:** Topaz Satellite Broadcasting Co., founder, 1990-95; Sid Harta Publishers, chief executive officer, 1995-; novelist, 1995-; Defense & Foreign Affairs, Strategic Policy, Asia correspondent. Entrepreneur. **Publications:** HISTORY-BASED NOVELS: The Fifth Season, 1998; Indonesian Gold, 2002; Crescent Moon: Rising-The Bali Bombings, 2005. ASIAN TRILOGY SERIES: The Tim-Tim Man, 1996 as The Timor Man, 1999; Merdeka Square, 1997, 2nd ed. as Freedom Square, 1999; Jakarta, 1998; The Happy Warrior, 2001. OTHER: Biography, In Search of Recognition: The Leo Stach Story, 2000. **Address:** Toorak Rd., PO Box 1102, Hartwell, VI 3124, Australia. **Online address:** author@sidharta.com.au

COLLUM, Danny Duncan. American (born United States), b. 1954. **Genres:** History, Race Relations, Biography, Autobiography/Memoirs. **Career:** Sojourners Magazine, associate editor, 1980-88, contributing editor, 1988-, contributing writer; Abraham Lincoln Brigade Archives, executive director, 1988-93; Rust College, assistant professor of English, 1999-; Kentucky State University, assistant professor of English and journalism, 2005-. **Publications:** (Ed.) African Americans in the Spanish Civil War: This Ain't Ethiopia, But It'll Do, 1992; Black and White Together: The Search for Common Ground, 1996; Beyond Black & White: An Invitation toward Racial Reconciliation and Forging Bonds of Interracial Cooperation, 1999; Black and Catholic in the Jim Crow South: The Stuff That Makes Community, 2006; Rising to Common Ground: Overcoming America's Color Lines, 2006. Works appear in anthologies. **Address:** Kentucky State University, 400 E Main St., Frankfort, KY 40601-2334, U.S.A. **Online address:** pdcollum@dixie-net.com

COLLURA, Mary-Ellen Lang. Canadian (born Canada), b. 1949. **Genres:** Young Adult Fiction, Literary Criticism And History, Young Adult Fiction. **Career:** District 72, school teacher, 1972-; North Island Wildlife Rehabilitation Association, director, 1990-92; Transition House, director, 1994-96. Writer. **Publications:** NOVELS: Winners, 1985 in UK as Jordy, 1988; Sunny, 1988; Dreamers, 1995. Contributor to periodicals. **Address:** 4068 Barclay Rd., Campbell River, BC V9N 4Y6, Canada.

COLLVER, Michael. American (born United States), b. 1953. **Genres:** Music. **Career:** Longy School of Music, faculty; Massachusetts Institute of Technology, Department of Mathematics, editorial assistant and reading room staff. Writer. **Publications:** Musik für Zink-Ein Quellenkatalog, Baseler Jahrbuch Für Historische Musikpraxis V, 1982; (with B. Dickey) A Catalog of Music for the Cornett, 1996. **Address:** Department of Mathematics, Massachusetts Institute of Technology, Rm. 2-382, 2 Bldg., 77 Massachusetts Ave., Cambridge, MA 02139-4307, U.S.A. **Online address:** collver@math.mit.edu

COLMAN, Andrew. *See* **PINE, Nicholas.**

COLMAN, Carol. American (born United States) **Genres:** Adult Non-fiction, Medicine/Health, Women's Studies And Issues. **Career:** Writer. **Publications:** Love and Money: What Your Finances Say about Your Personal Relationships and How to Improve Them, 1983; (with M.A. Perelman) Late Bloomers: How to Achieve Your Potential at Any Age, 1985; (with S. Semchyshyn) How to Prevent Miscarriage and Other Crises of Pregnancy, 1989; (with M.J. Legato) The Female Heart: The Truth about Women and Coronary Artery Disease, 1991; (with C.J. Eagle) All That She Can Be: Helping Your Daughter Achieve Her Full Potential and Maintain Her Self-Esteem duringthe Critical Years of Adolescence, 1993. (with R. Dibner) The Lupus Handbook for Women: Up-to-Date Information on Understanding and Managingthe Disease Which Affects One in 500 Women, 1994; (with W. Pierpaoli and W. Regelson) The Melatonin Miracle: Nature's Age-reversing, Disease-fighting, Sex-enhancing Hormone, 1995; (with W.N. Scott) Dr. Scott's Knee Book: Symptoms, Diagnosis, and Treatment of Knee Problems, Including Torn Cartilage, Ligament Damage, Arthritis, Tendinitis, Arthroscopic Surgery, and Total Knee Replacement, 1996; (with W. Regelson) The Superhormone

Promise: Nature's Antidote to Aging, 1996; (with M. Legato) What Women Need to Know: From Headaches to Heart Disease and Everything in Between, 1997; (with J. Whitaker) Shed Ten Years in Ten Weeks, 1997; (with E. Schwartz) Natural Energy: From Tired to Terrific in Ten Days, 1998; (with R. Brown and T. Bottiglieri) Stop Depression Now: SAM-e, the Breakthrough Supplement That Works as Well as Prescription Drugs in Half the Time, with No Side Effects, 1999; (with L. Packer) The Antioxidant Miracle: Put Lipoic Acid, Pycnogenol, and Vitamins E and C to Work forYou, 1999; (with L. Packer) The Antioxidant Miracle: Your Complete Plan for Total Health and Healing, 1999; (with R. Rountree) Immunotics: A Revolutionary Way to Fight Infection, Beat Chronic Illness, and Stay Well, 2000; (with A.S. Connelly) Body Rx, 2001; (with R. Kellman) Gut Reactions: Aradical New Four-Step Program for Treating Chronic Stomach Distres and Unlocking the Secret to Total Body Wellness, 2002; (with G. Hevin) Curves: Permanent Results without Permanent Dieting, 2003; (with D. Perlmutter) The Better Brain Book: The Best Tools for Improving Memory, Sharpness, and Preventing Aging of the Brain, 2004; (with G. Heavin) Curves on the Go, 2004; (with R. Rosedale) Rosedale Diet, 2004; (with D. Perlmutter) Raise a Smarter Child by Kindergarten: Build a Better Brain and Increase IQ up to 30 Points, 2006; (with R. Felder) Bonus Years Diet: 7 Miracle Foods Including Chocolate, Red Wine, and Nuts that Can Add 6.4 Years on Average to Your Life, 2007; Great Life Makeover: A Mid-Life Couples' Guide to Sex, Weight and Mood for the Best Years of your Life and Your Relationship, 2008. **Address:** c/o Author Mail, Putnam, 375 Hudson St., New York, NY 10014, U.S.A.

COLMAN, E. Adrian M. (Ernest Adrian Mackenzie Colman). Australian/ Scottish (born Scotland), b. 1930. **Genres:** Literary Criticism And History, Novels, History, Poetry. **Career:** Fibre Building Board Development Organization, industrial journalist, 1954-62; University of New South Wales, lecturer in English, 1962-71; University of Birmingham, The Shakespeare Institute, research associate, 1968-69; University of Sydney, senior lecturer, 1971-74, associate professor, 1975-78; Australian Theatre for Young People, chairman, 1974-75; University of Tasmania, professor of English, 1978-90, professor emeritus of English, 1990-. **Publications:** Shakespeare's Julius Caesar, 1965; The Structure of Shakespeare's Antony and Cleopatra, 1971; The Dramatic Use of Bawdy in Shakespeare, 1974; Horizon Study of Shakespeare's Henry IV, vol. I, 1990. EDITOR: Poems of Sir Walter Raleigh, 1977; King Lear, 1982; Henry IV, vol. I, 1987; Romeo and Juliet, 1993. Contributor to journals. **Address:** c/o Word Wise, 250 Churchill Ave., Sandy Bay, TA 7005, Australia. **Online address:** words@word-wise.com.au

COLMAN, Ernest Adrian Mackenzie. *See* **COLMAN, E. Adrian M.**

COLMAN, Penny (Morgan). American (born United States), b. 1944. **Genres:** Young Adult Fiction, Young Adult Non-fiction, Biography, Adult Non-fiction. **Career:** Freelance writer and editor, 1975-; United Presbyterian Church, program developer, 1977-81; Granger Galleries, founder and president, 1981-85; Center for Food Action, executive director, 1986-87; New Jersey Commission on Hunger, staff, 1986; New Jersey State Women Infant Children Advisory Council, staff, 1987; Columbia University, Teachers College, teacher, 2001-; The City University of New York, Queens College, distinguished lecturer, 2003-10; Ohio State University, faculty. **Publications:** ADULT NONFICTION: (ed.) Spiritual Disciplines for Everyday Living, 1982; Grand Canyon Magic, 1987; This Is Bergen County Where People Make a Difference, 1989; (with S. Chess and A. Thomas) Fifty Years Together: Researchers, Psychiatrists, Professors and Parents, 1993; Equal Rights Amendment: A Curriculum Guide, 1993. JUVENILE FICTION: I Never Do Anything Bad, 1988; Dark Closets and Noises in the Night, 1991. JUVENILE NONFICTION: Breaking the Chains: The Crusade of Dorothea Lynde Dix, 1992; Spies! Women and the Civil War, 1992; Fannie Lou Hamer and the Fight for the Vote, 1993; A Woman Unafraid: The Achievements of Frances Perkins, 1993; 101 Ways to Do Better in School, 1994; Madame C.J. Walker: Building a Business Empire, 1994; Mother Jones and the Children's Crusade, 1994; Toilets, Bathtubs, Sinks and Sewers: The History of the Bathroom, 1994; Rosie the Riveter, 1995; Corpse, Coffins and Crypts, 1997; Girls: A History of Growing Up Female in America, 2000; Where the Action Was, 2002. OTHERS: Mother Jones and the March of the Mill Children, 1994; Women in Society. United States, 1994; Strike!, 1995; Corpses, Coffins, and Crypts, 1997; Adventurous Women: Eight True Stories About Women Who Made a Difference, 2006; Thanksgiving: The True Story, 2008. Elizabeth Cady Stanton and Susan B. Anthony: A Friendship that Changed the World, 2011. Contributor to periodicals. **Address:** 138 Knickerbocker Rd., Englewood, NJ 07631, U.S.A. **Online address:** pennycolman@pennycolman.com

COLODNY, Len. (Leonard Colodny). American (born United States), b. 1938. **Genres:** Politics/Government, Adult Non-fiction, History, Autobiography/Memoirs. **Career:** Colodny's Inc., vice president, 1960-73, president, 1973-75; Colodny's of Maryland Inc., president, 1973-79, political analyst and lecturer, 1991-. Writer. **Publications:** (With R. Gettlin) Silent Coup: The Removal of a President in UK as Silent Coup: The Removal of Richard Nixon, 1991; (with T. Shachtman) THE FORTY YEARS WAR: The Rise and Fall of the Neocons, from Nixon to Obama, 2009. **Address:** 6909 Lake Place Ct., Tampa, FL 33634-1046, U.S.A. **Online address:** len@colodny.com

COLODNY, Leonard. *See* **COLODNY, Len.**

COLOGNE-BROOKES, Gavin (John). British (born England), b. 1961. **Genres:** Literary Criticism And History, Women's Studies And Issues. **Career:** University of Evansville, Harlaxton College, assistant professor of English, 1988-92; Bath Spa University College, School of Humanities and Cultural Industries, Department of English and creative studies, lecturer, 1993-, senior lecturer, 1993-, professor. Writer. **Publications:** The Novels of William Styron: From Harmony to History, 1995; (ed. with N. Sammells and D. Timms) Writing and America, 1996; Dark Eyes on America: The Novels of Joyce Carol Oates, 2005. **Address:** Department of English, Bath Spa University College, NP.NE. 207, Newton Pk., Bath, BA2 9BN, England. **Online address:** gcologne-brookes@bathspa.ac.uk

COLOMBO, John Robert. Canadian (born Canada), b. 1936. **Genres:** Poetry, Literary Criticism And History, Local History/Rural Topics, Paranormal, Social Commentary, Bibliography. **Career:** University of Toronto Press, editorial assistant, 1957-59; Ryerson Press, assistant editor, 1960-63; York University, occasional instructor, 1963-66; McClelland Stewart, advisory editor and editor-at-large, 1964-70; Ontario Arts Council, adviser, 1965-69; Mohawk College, writer-in-residence, 1978; CBC-TV, host, 1979; Macmillan, general editor, 1991-; Atkinson College, faculty; Glendon College, faculty; Montrealer, editor; Exchange, editor; Ghosts and Hauntings Research Society, adviser; Ontario Skeptics Society for Critical Inquiry, consultant. Compiler, translator and anthologist. **Publications:** (With W.L. Mackenzie) The Mackenzie poems, 1966; Abracadabra, 1967; (with J. Godbout) La grande muraille de Chine, 1969; Mostly Monsters, 1977; Variable Cloudiness, 1977; Private Parts, 1978; Colombo's Book of Canada, 1978; The Poets of Canada, 1978; (co-author) CDNSF and F: A Bibliography of Canadian Science Fiction and Fantasy, 1979; Blackwood's Books, 1981; (with M. Richardson) Not to Be Taken at Night, 1981; Poems of the Inuit, 1981; Friendly Aliens, 1981; Years of Light, 1982; Selected Poems, 1982; Colombo's Canadian Quiz Book, 1983; Rene Levesque Buys Canada Savings Bonds and Other Great Canadian Graffiti, 1983; Colombo's 101 Canadian Places, 1983; The Toronto Puzzle Book, 1984; Canadian Literary Landmarks, 1984; Great Moments in Canadian History, 1984; (with M. Richardson) We Stand on Guard, 1985; 1001 Questions about Canada, 1986; Colombo's New Canadian Quotations, 1987; Off Earth (poetry), 1987; Mysterious Canada, 1988; 999 Questions about Canada, 1989; Extraordinary Experiences, 1989; Songs of the Great Land, 1989; Mysterious Encounters, 1990; Quotations from Chairman Lamport, 1990; Mackenzie's Ghost, 1991; The Dictionary of Canadian Quotations, 1991; Walt Whitman's Canada, 1992; The Canadian Global Almanac, 1993, 1992; The Little Blue Book of Canadian UFOs, 1993; The Mystery of the Shaking Tent, 1993; Haunted Toronto, 1996; Shapely Places, 1996; Mysteries of Ontario, 1998; Ghost Stories of Canada, 2000; Colombo's Famous Lasting Words, 2000; Yet More Iron Curtains, 2000; Canadian Capers, 2000; Ghosts in Our Past, 2000; Half a World Away, 2000; Impromptus: 1, 000 Poems, 2000; Incredible Canadiana, 2000; Open Secrets, 2000; Small Wonders, 2000; Three Mysteries of Nova Scotia, 2000; Weird Stories from 19th-Century Canadian Newspapers, 2000; Briefs, 2001; Far Star, 2001; The Humor of Us, 2001; Many Mysteries, 2001; 1000 Questions about Canada, 2001; The Penguin Book of Canadian Jokes, 2001; Half Life, 2002; Foundlings, 2002; Only in Canada, 2002; The Ukrainian and the Tractor and Other Canadian Jokes and Anecdotes, 2002; The Penguin Treasury of Popular Canadian Poems and Songs, 2002; Making Light, 2002; Say It Again, Sam, 2003; More or Less, 2003; True Canadian Ghost Stories, 2003; 100 Poems, 2003; O Rare Denis Saurat, 2003; The Denis Saurat Reader, 2004; The Native Series, 2004; The Monster Book of Canadian Monsters, 2004; To Take from Life: Poems and Effects, 2005; Terrors of the Night: Canadian Accounts of Eerie Events and Weird Experiences, 2005; Autumn in August: Poems and Effects, 2006; All the Poems of John Robert Colombo, 2006; A is for Aphorism: A New Collection, 2006; Parts of the World, 2007; End Notes, 2008; The Big Book of Canadian Ghost Stories, 2008; Footloose: A Commentary on the Books of Gordon Sinclair, 2008; Whistle While You Work: A Chrestomathy, 2008; The Big Book of Canadian Hauntings, 2009. EDITOR: Rubato: New Poems by Young Canadian Poets, 1958; The Varsity Chapbook, 1959; (with J. Godbout) Poesis 64/Poetry 64, 1963; (with R. Souster) Shapes and Sounds: Poems of W.W.E. Ross, 1968; How Do I Love Thee: Sixty Poets of Canada (and Quebec) Select and Discuss Their Favorite Poems from Their Own Work, 1970; (with R. Bentley) Rhymes and Reasons: Nine Canadian Poets Discuss Their Work, 1971; New Direction in Canadian Poetry, 1971; An Alphabet of Annotations, 1972; Colombo's Canadian Quotations, 1974; Colombo's Little Book of Canadian Proverbs, Graffiti, Limericks, and Other Vital Matters, 1975; Colombo's Canadian References, 1976; East and West: Selected Poems by George Faludy, 1978; Colombo's Book of Canada, 1978; The Poets of Canada, 1978; Colombo's Names and Nicknames, 1978; The Great Cities of Antiquity, 1979; Other Canada's: An Anthology of Science Fiction and Fantasy, 1979; Colombo's Hollywood, 1979; Colombo's Book of Marvels, 1979; The Canada Coloring Book, 1980; 222 Canadian Jokes, 1981; Colombo's Last Words, 1982; Colombo's Laws, 1982; Windigo, 1982; Songs of the Indians, 1983; Great Moments in Canadian History, 1984; The Toronto Puzzle Book, 1984; Toronto's Fantastic Street Names, 1984; Canadian Literary Landmarks, 1984; (with M. Richardson) We Stand on Guard: Poems and Songs of Canadians in Battle, 1985; 1, 001 Questions about Canada, 1986; Off Earth, 1987; Mysterious Canada: Strange Sights, Extraordinary Events, and Peculiar Places, 1988; 999 Questions about Canada, 1989; Extraordinary Experiences: Personal Accounts of the Paranormal in Canada, 1989; Songs of the Great Land, 1989; Quotations from Chairman Lamport, 1990; Mysterious Encounters: Personal Accounts of the Supernatural in Canada, 1990; UFOs over Canada: Personal Accounts of Sightings and Close Encounters, 1991; Dark Visions: Personal Accounts of the Mysterious in Canada, 1991; Mackenzie King's Ghost: And Other Personal Accounts of Canadian Hauntings, 1991; The Dictionary of Canadian Quotations, 1991; Worlds in Small: An Anthology of Miniature Literary Compositions, 1992; Quotations on Sex and Love in Canada, 1992; The Little Blue Book of Canadian UFOs, 1992; (with C. Greenland) Walt Whitman's Canada, 1992; The Mystery of the Shaking Tent, 1993; Colombo's All-Time Great Canadian Quotations, 1994; Close Encounters of the Canadian Kind: Personal Accounts of UFOs in Canada, 1994; Penguin Dictionary of Popular Canadian Quotations, 2005. TRANSLATOR: R. Zend, From Zero to One, 1973; (with I. Currie) P. Eluard and B. Peret, 152 Proverbs Adapted to the Taste of the Day, 1975; (with N. Roussanoff) Under the Eaves of a Forgotten Village: 60 Poems from Contemporary Bulgaria, 1975; (with N. Roussanoff) The Balkan Range: A Bulgarian Reader, 1976; (with S. Wald and L. Zeller) When the Animal Rises from the Deep the Head Explodes, 1976; (with N. Roussanoff) The Left-Handed One: Poems by Lyubomir Levchev, 1977; (with N. Roussanoff) Remember Me Well: Poems by Andrei Germanov, 1978; (with N. Roussanoff) Depths: Poems by Dora Gabe, 1978; Dark Times: Poems of Waclaw Iwaniuk, 1979; Such Times: Poems of Ewa Lipska, 1981; Far from You: Poems of Pavel Javor, 1981; Selected Translations, 1982; Beyond Labels: Poems of Robert Zend, 1982; Symmetries: Poems of Marin Sorescu, 1982; Learn This Poem of Mine by Heart: Poems of George Faludy, 1983. Contributor to periodicals. **Address:** 42 Dell Park Ave., Toronto, ON M6B 2T6, Canada. **Online address:** jrc@ca.inter.net

COLOROSO, Barbara. American (born United States), b. 1948?. **Genres:** Psychology, Social Commentary, How-to Books, Human Relations/Parenting, Education. **Career:** Writer, educator and consultant. **Publications:** Media for Kids, 1982; Kids Are Worth It!: Giving Your Child the Gift of Inner Discipline, 1994, rev. ed., 2002; Parenting through Crisis: Helping Kids in Times of Loss, Grief, and Change, 2000; Parenting Wit & Wisdom, 2001; The Bully, the Bullied, and the Bystander: From Preschool to High School: How Parents and Teachers Can Help Break the Cycle of Violence, 2003; (contrib.) Who's in Charge Anyway?: How Parents Can Teach Children to Do, 2003; Extraordinary Evil: A Short Walk to Genocide, 2007; (contrib.) And Now I Know Why Tigers Eat Their Young: Surviving a New Generation of Teenagers, 2007; Just Because It's Not Wrong Doesn't Make It Right: Teaching Kids to Think and Act Ethically, 2008. **Address:** Kids Are Worth It! Inc., PO Box 621108, Littleton, CO 80162, U.S.A. **Online address:** info@kidsareworthit.com

COLQUHOUN, Glenn. New Zealander (born New Zealand), b. 1964?. **Genres:** Children's Fiction, Poetry. **Career:** Whangarei Hospital, doctor; Waikato Hospital, doctor. Writer. **Publications:** Uncle Glenn and Me, 1999; The Art of Walking Upright, 1999; An Explanation of Poetry to My Father, 2001; Playing God, 2002; Jumping Ship, 2004; Uncle Glenn and Me Too, 2004; Mr. Short Mr. Thin Mr. Bald and Mr. Dog, 2005; How We Fell: A Love Story, 2006. **Address:** c/o Author Mail, Steele Roberts Publishing, PO Box 9321, Wellington, 6021, New Zealand.

COLQUHOUN, Kate. British (born England), b. 1964. **Genres:** History, Social Sciences. **Career:** Faber and Faber, staff; Random House Publishers, staff; Oxford University Press, marketing director; Bloomsbury, staff; Prospect magazine, publisher. Writer. **Publications:** A Thing in Disguise: The Visionary Life of Joseph Paxton, 2003; Taste: The Story of Britain through Its Cooking, 2007; The Thrifty Cookbook: 476 Ways to Eat Well with Leftovers, 2009; Mr Briggs' Hat: A Sensational Account of Britain's First Railway Murder, 2011. **Address:** c/o Caroline Dawnay, Drury House, 34-43 Russell St., London, GL WC2B 5HA, England. **Online address:** katec@f2s.com

COLSON, Charles W(endell). American (born United States), b. 1931. **Genres:** Theology/Religion, Autobiography/Memoirs, History. **Career:** United States Marine Corps, staff, 1953-55; Assistant Secretary of the U.S. Navy, assistant, 1955-56; U.S. Senator Leverett Saltonstall, administration assistant, 1956-61; Gadsby and Hannah, senior partner, 1961-69; Richard Nixon, special counsel to the president of the United States, 1969-73; Colson and Shapiro, partner, 1973-74; Fellowship House, associate, 1975-76; Prison Fellowship Ministries, founder and president, 1976-84, chairman of the board, 1984-; Prison Fellowship Intl., chair of the board, 1979-; Voice of Calvary and Ligonier Valley Study Center, director, 1980-; Justice Fellowship, chair of the board, 1983-84, vice chair of the board, 1984-; BreakPoint, radio commentator; Wilberforce Forum, chairman. Writer. **Publications:** Born Again, 1976; Life Sentence, 1979; Loving God, 1983; Who Speaks for God: Confronting the World with Real Christianity, 1985; Dare to Be Different, Dare to Be Christian, 1986; (with W. Coleman) Being Good Isn't Easy, 1986; Presenting Belief in an Age of Unbelief, 1986; (with W. Coleman) Guess Who's at My Party, 1986; The Role of Church in Society, 1986; (with W. Coleman) Watch Out for Becky, 1986; (with W. Coleman) Trouble in the School Yard, 1986; The Struggle for Men's Hearts and Minds, 1986; (co-author) Christianity in Conflict: The Struggle for Christian Integrity and Freedom in Secular Culture, 1986; Loving God, 1987; (with E.S. Vaughn) Kingdoms in Conflict, 1987; (with E.S. Vaughn) Against the Night: Living in the New Dark Ages, 1989; (with D. Van Ness) Convicted: New Hope for Ending America's Crime Crisis, 1989; Christ in Easter: A Family Celebration of Holy Week, 1990; Freedom Behind Bars, 1990; (with E.S. Vaughn) God of Stones and Spiders: Letters to a Church in Exile, 1990; (with J. Eckerd) Why America Doesn't Work, 1991; Power Religion: The Selling Out of the Evangelical Church?, 1992; (with E.S. Vaughn) The Body, 1992; (with N. Pearcey) A Dance with Deception: Revealing the Truth behind the Headlines, 1993; (with N. Pearcey) A Dangerous Grace: Daily Readings, 1994; Faith on the Line, 1994; (with E.S. Vaughn) Gideon's Torch, 1995; (with J. Neuhaus) Evangelicals and Catholics Together: Toward a Common Mission, 1995; (with J. Trent) Go the Distance: The Making of a Promise Keeper, 1996; Enduring Revolution: A Battle to Change the Human Heart, 1996; (with C. Swindoll and M. Lucado) Glory of Christmas, 1996; Burden of Truth: Defending Truth in an Age of Unbelief, 1997; Line between Right and Wrong: Developing a Personal Code of Ethics, 1997; (with E.S. Vaughn) Against the Night: Living in the New Dark Ages, 1999; Life Sentence, 1999; (with N. Pearcey) How Now Shall We Live, 1999; Answers to Your Kids' Questions, 2000; (with N. Pearcey) Developing a Christian Worldview of Science and Evolution, 2001; (with N. Pearcey) Developing a Christian Worldview of the Christian in Today's Culture, 2001; (with N. Pearcey) Developing a Christian Worldview of the Problem of Evil, 2001; Justice that Restores, 2001; (ed. with R.J. Neuhaus) Your Word is Truth: A Project of Evangelicals and Catholics Together, 2002; (ed. with M. Earley) Six Million Angels: Stories from 20 Years of Angel Tree's Ministry to the Children of Prisoners, 2003; (with E.S. Vaughn) Being the Body, 2003; (with N.M.S. Cameron) Human Dignity in the Biotech Century: A Christian Vision for Public Policy, 2004; (with H. Fickett) Good Life, 2005; Lies that Go Unchallenged in Media and Government, 2005; Lies that Go Unchallenged in Popular Culture, 2005; Tough Questions about God, Faith and Life, 2006; Good Life Charles Colson, 2006; God and Government: An Insider's View on the Boundaries BFaithetween Faith & Politics, 2007; (with H. Fickett) Faith: What Christians Believe, Why They Believe It, and Why It Matters, 2008; (ed.) God and Governing: Reflecting on Ethics, Virtue, and Statesmanship, 2009; (ed.) Dancing with Max: A Mother and Son who Broke Free, 2010. Contributor to newspapers. **Address:** Prison Fellowship, 44180 Riverside Pkwy., Lansdowne, VA 20176, U.S.A.

COLSON, Elizabeth. American (born United States), b. 1917. **Genres:** Anthropology/Ethnology. **Career:** War Relocation Authority, assistant social science analyst, 1942-43; Harvard University, research assistant, 1944-45; Rhodes-Livingstone Institute, senior research officer, 1946-47, 1956-57, 1962-63, director, 1947-51; Manchester University, senior lecturer, 1951-53; Goucher College, associate professor of anthropology, 1954-55; Boston University, associate professor and research associate in African studies program, 1955-59; Brandeis University, professor, 1959-63; Northwestern University, visiting professor, 1963-64; University of California, professor of anthropology, 1964-84, professor emeritus, 1984-; University of Rochester, Morgan lecturer, 1973; California Institute of Technology, Fairchild Fellow, 1975-76; University of Zambia, visiting professor, 1987; Refugee Studies Programme, visiting senior research fellow, 1988-89. Writer. **Publications:** Life Among the Cattle-Owning Plateau Tonga: The Material Culture of a Northern Rhodesia Native Tribe, 1949; (ed. with M. Gluckman) Seven Tribes of British Central Africa, 1951; The Makah, 1953; The Makah Indians: A Study of an Indian Tribe in Modern American Society, 1953; Marriage and the Family Among the Plateau Tonga of Northern Rhodesia, 1958; Seven Tribes of British Central Africa, 1959; The Social Organization of Gwembe Tongo, 1960; The Plateau Tonga of Northern Rhodesia, Social and Religious Studies, 1962; The Social Consequences of Resettlement: The Impact of the Kariba Resettlement Upon the Gwembe Tongo, 1971; Tradition and Contract: The Problem of Order, 1974; Three Pomo Life Histories, 1974; (with T. Scudder) Secondary Education and the Formation of an Elite: The Impact of Education on Gwembe District, Zambia, 1980; (with T. Scudder and M.E.D. Scudder) An Evaluation of the Gwembe South Development Project, Zambia, 1982; (with L. Ralston and J. Anderson) Voluntary Efforts in Decentralized Management: Opportunities and Constraints in Rural Development, 1983; (ed. with S. Morgan) People in Upheaval, 1987; (with T. Scudder) For Prayer and Profit: The Ritual, Economic and Social Importance of Beer in Gwembe District, Zambia, 1950-1982, 1988; History of Nampeyo, 1991; Tonga Religious Life in the Twentieth Century, 2006; (contrib.) The Tonga-speaking Peoples of Zambia and Zimbabwe: Essays in Honor of Elizabeth Colson, 2007. Contributor to journals. **Address:** Department of Anthropology, University of California, 232 Kroeber Hall, Berkeley, CA 94720-3710, U.S.A. **Online address:** gwembe@uclink.berkeley.edu

COLT, George Howe. American (born United States), b. 1954?. **Genres:** Autobiography/Memoirs, Mystery/Crime/Suspense, Psychology. **Career:** Life, staff writer. **Publications:** The Enigma of Suicide, 1991; The Big House: A Century in the Life of an American Summer Home, 2003; November of the Soul: The Enigma of Suicide, 2006. Contributor to periodicals. **Address:** 160 Chestnut Plain Rd., PO Box 244, Whately, MA 01093, U.S.A.

COLTEN, Craig E. American (born United States), b. 1952. **Genres:** Public/Social Administration, Social Sciences, History. **Career:** Louisiana State University, Department of Geography and Anthropology, Carl O. Sauer professor; Illinois State Government, private consultant; Community and Regional Resilience Institute (CARRI), research associate; Historical Geography, co-editor, 1999-. **Publications:** Industrial Waste Management Practices, 1890-1950: A Bibliography, 1986; (with G.E. Breen) Historical Industrial Waste Disposal Practices in Winnebago County, Illinois, 1870-1980, 1986; (with D. Friel) Guidelines and Methods for Conducting Property Transfer Site Histories, 1990; (with D. Friel and D. Moore) Environmental Liability, Property Transfers, and Historical Hazardous Materials: A Bibliography, 1990; (ed. with L.M. Dilsaver) The American Environment: Interpretations of Past Geographies, 1992; Derelict Properties: Scale and Scope of an Urban Environmental Problem, 1995; (with P.N. Skinner) The Road to Love Canal: Managing Industrial Waste before EPA, 1996; (ed.) Transforming New Orleans and Its Environs: Centuries of Change, 2000; (ed. with L.M. Brosseau) Respiratory Protection: A Manual and Guideline, 3rd ed., 2001; An Unnatural Metropolis: Wresting New Orleans from Nature, 2005; (co-author) Southern United States: An Environmental History, 2006; Perilous Place, Powerful Storms, 2009; (contrib.) City of Memory, 2009. Contributor to periodicals and journals. **Address:** Department of Geography & Anthropology, Louisiana State University, 259 Howe-Russell Geoscience Complex, Baton Rouge, LA 70803-4105, U.S.A. **Online address:** ccolten@lsu.edu

COLVILE, Georgiana M. M. French (born France) **Genres:** Literary Criticism And History, Biography, Women's Studies And Issues. **Career:** University of California, professor of French, film and comparative literature; University of Colorado, associate professor of French, film and comparative literature; University of Tours, professor of English, professor emeritus of Anglophone studies. Writer and researcher. **Publications:** Vers un Langage des Arts Autour des Années Vingt, 1977; Beyond and Beneath the Mantle: On Thomas Pynchon's The Crying of Lot 49, 1988; Blaise Cendrars Ecrivain Proteiforme, 1994; Scandaleusement D'elles: Trente-Quatre Femmes Surréalistes, 1999; (intro.) Ecrits d'une femme surréaliste, 2001. EDITOR: Contemporary Women Writing in the Other Americas, 1996; (with K. Conley) Femme s'entête, 1998; Lettres à Denise Lévy, 1919-1929: Et Autres Textes, 1924-1975, 2005. **Address:** Edwin Mellen Press, 415 Ridge St., PO Box 450, Lewiston, NY 14092-1205, U.S.A. **Online address:** silhol@paris7.jussieu.fr

COLVIN, James. *See* **MOORCOCK, Michael (John).**

COMAROFF, Jean. American/Scottish (born Scotland), b. 1946. **Genres:** Anthropology/Ethnology, Sociology. **Career:** University of Wales, University College of Swansea, research fellow in sociology and anthropology, 1971-73; Victoria University of Manchester, Bolton Institute of Technology, lecturer in anthropology, 1973-74, senior research fellow in medical sociology and anthropology, 1976-78, honorary senior fellow, 1994-95; University of Chicago, assistant professor, 1978-84, associate professor, 1984-87, professor of anthropology and social sciences, 1987-96, professor of sociology, 1987-94, Divinity School, Nuveen lecturer 1989, Woodward Court, Wirzup lecturer, 1992, Department of Anthropology, chair, 1991-94, 1996-99, Harold H. Swift distinguished service professor of anthropology and social sciences, 1996-, Bernard E. & Ellen C. Sunny distinguished service professor, 1996, Chicago Center for Contemporary Theory, faculty fellow and co-founder, 2004-; Harvard University, fellow of Bunting Institute, 1981-82, Radcliffe Institute for Advanced Study, fellow, Martina Horner distinguished visiting professor, 2003; École des Hautes Études en Sciences Sociales, director of studies, 1988, 1995; Duke University, visiting professor, 1989; University of Washington, Olson Lecturer, 1989; Cornell University, messenger lecturer, 1991; American Bar Foundation, senior research fellow, 1991-; University of Helsinki, Westermarlk memorial lecturer, 1993; University of the North West, visiting research associate, 1999-2000; Tel Aviv University, visiting professor, 2000; University of Cape Town, honorary professor, 2004-; University of Basel, visiting professor, 2005. Writer. **Publications:** Body of Power, Spirit of Resistance: The Culture and History of a South African People, 1985; (with J.L. Comaroff) Of Revelation and Revolution: Christianity and Colonialism in South Africa, vol. I, 1991; (with J.L. Comaroff) Ethnography and the Historical Imagination: Selected Essays, 1992; (with J.L. Comaroff) Modernity and Its Malcontents: Ritual and Power in Postcolonial Africa, 1993; (ed. with J.L. Comaroff) Civil Society and the Political Imagination in Africa: Critical Perspectives, 1999; Millennial Capitalism and the Culture of Neoliberalism, 2001; (ed. with J.L. Comaroff) Law and Disorder in the Postcolony, 2006; (ed. with J.L. Comaroff and D. James) Picturing a Colonial Past: The African Photographs of Isaac Schapera, 2007; (ed. with J.L. Comaroff) Ethnicity Inc., 2009; (with J.L. Comaroff) Theory from the South, or, How Euro-America is Evolving Toward Africa, 2011. Contributor of articles to journals. **Address:** Department of Anthropology, University of Chicago, 1126 E 59th St., Chicago, IL 60637, U.S.A. **Online address:** jcomaro@uchicago.edu

COMERFORD, Kathleen M. (Kathleen Mary Comerford). American (born United States), b. 1966. **Genres:** History, Theology/Religion, Education. **Career:** University of Wisconsin, teaching assistant, 1991-93; Georgia Southern University, professor of history. Writer. **Publications:** Ordaining the Catholic Reformation: Priests and Seminary Pedagogy in Fiesole, 1575-1675, 2001; (ed. and contrib. with H.M. Pabel) Early Modern Catholicism: Essays in Honour of John W. O'Malley, 2001; Reforming Priests and Parishes: Tuscan Dioceses in the First Century of Seminary Education (Education and Society in the Middle Ages and Renaissance series), 2006. **Address:** Department of History, Georgia Southern University, Rm. 1105, Forest Dr. Bldg., PO Box 8054, Statesboro, GA 30460-8054, U.S.A. **Online address:** kcomerfo@georgiasouthern.edu

COMERFORD, Kathleen Mary. *See* **COMERFORD, Kathleen M.**

COMFORT, B(arbara). American (born United States), b. 1916. **Genres:** Mystery/Crime/Suspense, Novels, Literary Criticism And History. **Career:** Comfort Inc., designer of acrylics; Landgrove Press, director. Writer and artist. **Publications:** MYSTERY NOVELS: Vermont Village Murder, 1982; Green Mountain Murder, 1986; Phoebe's Knee, 1986; Grave Consequences, 1989; The Cashmere Kid, 1993; Elusive Quarry, 1995; A Pair for the Queen, 1998. Illustrator of the book by M. De Jong. Contributor to periodicals. **Address:** 39 Charlton St., New York, NY 10014, U.S.A.

COMFORT, Philip W(esley). American (born United States), b. 1950.

Genres: Poetry, Theology/Religion, Language/Linguistics. **Career:** Ohio State University, instructor in English, 1983-84; Tyndale House Publishers, New Living Translation, New Testament editor, Bible Reference Works, senior editor, 1984-2000; College of DuPage, New Testament Greek lecturer, 1984-86; Wheaton College, visiting professor of New Testament literature and interpretation, 1987-98; North Park College, visiting professor of Biblical studies, 1992-93; Trinity Episcopal Seminary, adjunct professor, 1997-2000; Coastal Carolina University, instructor, 1998-; Columbia International University, professor, 1999-. **Publications:** From Text to Translation: Studies in New Testament Translation, 1986; Portraits of Jesus in the Gospel of John, 1986; A Study Guide to Translating the Gospel of John: With the Greek Text of the Gospel of John Compiled from the Earliest Papyrus Manuscripts, 1986; Early Manuscripts and Modern Translations of the New Testament, 1990, 2nd ed., 1996; (trans. with R. Brown) The New Greek-English Interlinear New Testament, 1990; The Complete Guide to Bible Versions, 1991, rev. ed., 1996; The Quest for the Original Text of the New Testament, 1992; (with G. Comfort) Dying to Live, 1992; (with W. Hawley) Opening the Gospel of John, 1994; I Am the Way: A Spiritual Journey through the Gospel of John, 1994; The Books of the New Testament, 1999; Essential Guide to Bible Versions, 2000; English Bible Versions, 2000; Selected Poems, 2001; The Text of the Earliest New Testament Greek Manuscripts, 2001; (with E. Carpenter) Holman Treasury of Key Bible Words; (W.A. Elwell) The Complete Book of Who's Who in the Bible, 2004; Encountering the Manuscripts: An Introduction to New Testament Paleography & Textual Criticism, 2005; (with J. Driesbach) Many Gospels of Jesus: Sorting Out the Story of the Life of Jesus, 2007; New Testament Text and Translation Commentary: Commentary on the Variant Readings of the Ancient New Testament Manuscripts and How They Relate to the Major English Translations, 2008; (with W.C. Hawley) Opening John's Gospel and Epistles, 2009. POETRY WITH WIPF AND STOCK: Oceanic, 2004; Spirit Journey, 2004; Jesus Speaks, 2004. EDITOR: Philippians, Colossians, Philemon, 1995; (New Testament) New Living Translation, 1996; Ephesians, 1996; Hebrews, 1997; (with D. Barrett) The Complete Text of the Earliest New Testament Manuscripts, 1999, rev. ed., 2001; Christian Classics, 1999; Life Application New Testament Commentary, 2001; Cornerstone Biblical Commentary, 2005; Ezekiel, 2010. EDITOR AND CONTRIBUTOR: A New Commentary on the Whole Bible, 1990; The Origin of the Bible, 1992; (with J.D. Douglas) Who's Who in Christian History, 1992; (with D. Partner) The One Year Book of Poetry, 1999; (with W. Elwell) Tyndale Bible Dictionary, 2001. Contributor to reference books and periodicals. **Address:** Columbia International University, 7435 Monticello Rd., Columbia, SC 29203, U.S.A. **Online address:** philcomfort@verizon.net

COMFORT, Ray. American/New Zealander (born New Zealand), b. 1949. **Genres:** Novels, How-to Books, Philosophy, Theology/Religion, Autobiography/Memoirs, Humor/Satire. **Career:** Living Waters Publications, founder, president, director and chief executive officer; Hosanna Chapel, pastor; The Way of the Master Television, co-founder. Writer. **Publications:** My Friends are Dying, 1977; Words of Comfort Living Waters, 1983; Poured Out for a Thirsty World, 1986; In Search of New Jawbones: Aggressive Evangelism, 1986; Springboards for Budding Preachers Inspiring Illustrations, Stimulating Thoughts, Quoates and Aids for Street Preaching and Personal Witnessing. Living Waters, 1987; Hell's Best Kept Secret, 1989; You've Got to Be Choking, 1990; Russia Will Attack Israel, 1991; The Key to Heaven, 1993; God Doesn't Believe in Atheists, 1993; Revival's Golden Key, 1993; The Devils Nightmare, 1993; The Undertaker's Nightmare, 1994; America, America: The Healing of a Nation, 1994; Militant Evangelism, 1994; Everyday Evangelism, 1995; Comfort, the Feeble-minded, 1995; The Secrets of Nostradamus Exposed, 1996; Bride of Heaven, Pride of Hell, 1997; 101 Things Men Do to Annoy Their Wives; 101 Things Kids Can Do to Annoy Their Parents, 1998; The Power of Darkness, 1999; How to Win Souls and Influence People, 1999; God Has a Wonderful Plan for Your Life, 2000; Evidence Bible-Romans: Irrefutable Evidence for the Thinking Mind, 2000; Evidence Bible: Irrefutable Evidence for the Thinking Mind, 2000; The Mystery, 2001; Untearable Bible for the Terrible Twos, 2001; Scientific Facts in the Bible: 100 Reasons to Believe the Bible is Supernatural in Origin, 2001; Evidence-for Kids: With Albert Brainstein, 2001; Nostradamus: Attack on America, 2001; Miracle in the Making, 2003; Who is the Lord of the Ring?, 2002; End Time Believer's Bible, 2002; Out of the Comfort Zone: The Authorized Autobiography, 2003; (with K. Cameron) World's Greatest Preachers, 2003; (with K. Cameron) Way of the Master: How to Share Your Faith Simply, Effectively, Biblically-The Way Jesus Did, 2004; What Hollywood Believes: An Intimate Look at the Faith of the Famous, 2004; Whitefield Gold, 2005; How to Bring Your Children to Christ ... and Keep Them There, 2005; What Did Jesus Do? A Call to Return to the Biblical Gospel, 2005; Overcoming Panic Attacks, 2005; Behind the Scenes: the Way of the Master, 2005; How to Live Forever . . . Without Being Religious, 2006; (with K. Cameron) Thanks a Million!: An Adventure in Biblical Evangelism, 2006; The Way of the Master Minute: a One-Minute, One Year Devotional for the Busy Christian, 2006; Scratch & Sniff, 2007; Way of The Master, 2006; Intelligent Design vs. Evolution: Letters to an Atheist, 2006; What Your Nose Shows, 2007; (with K. Cameron) Evidence Bible, 2007; Overcoming Insomnia: Practical Help for those Who Suffer from Sleep Deprivation, 2007; 101 Annoying Things About Air Travel, 2007; 101 Annoying Things About Other Drivers, 2007; (comp.) Wesley Gold, 2007; Hollywood be Thy Name: The Idol Makers, 2007; 101 of the Dumbest Things People Have Done, 2008; How to Know God Exists: Scientific Proof of God, 2008; Evolution: A Fairy Tale for Grown Ups, 2008; World Religions in a Nutshell, 2008; (with K. Cameron) School of Biblical Evangelism, 2004; Comfort Food: Delectable Devotions to Satisfy the Soul, 2008; (comp.) Spurgeon Gold, 2008; You Can Lead an Atheist to Evidence, But You Can't Make him Think: Answers to Questions Asked by Angry Atheists, 2009; The Atheist Bible, 2009; Luther Gold, 2009; Moody Gold, 2009; The Charles Darwin Bible, 2009; (with K. Cameron) Conquer your Fear, Share your Faith, 2009; (with A. Jackson) Jake's Fortune, 2009; Nothing Created Everything: The Scientific Impossibility of Atheistic Evolution, 2009; The Defender's Guide for Life's Toughest Questions, 2011; Edwards Gold, 2011. **Address:** Living Water Publications, 9818 Arkansas St., PO Box 1172, Bellflower, CA 90706, U.S.A. **Online address:** ray@raycomfort.com

COMINI, Alessandra. American (born United States), b. 1934. **Genres:** Art/Art History, History, Autobiography/Memoirs, Biography. **Career:** Columbia University, assistant professor, 1969-74; Princeton University, Alfred Hodder resident humanist, 1972-73; Yale University, faculty, 1973; Southern Methodist University, Department of Art History, university distinguished professor of art history, 1974-, now professor emeritus; Oxford University, European Humanities Research Centre, distinguished visiting lecturer, 1996; University of California, faculty. Writer. **Publications:** Schiele in Prison, 1973; Egon Schiele's Portraits, 1974; Gustav Klimt, 1975; Egon Schiele, 1976; The Fantastic Art of Vienna, 1978; The Changing Image of Beethoven: A Study in Mythmaking, 1987, rev. ed., 2008; (contrib.) Käthe Kollwitz, 1992; (contrib.) Nudes, Egon Schiele, 1994; In Passionate Pursuit: A Memoir, 2004; (contrib.) Egon Schiele: The Ronald S. Lauder and Serge Sabarsky Collections, 2005. Contributor to books. **Address:** Department of Art History, Southern Methodist University, Owen Arts Ctr., 6101 Bishop Blvd., PO Box 750356, Dallas, TX 75205, U.S.A. **Online address:** acomini@smu.edu

COMISKEY, Michael. American (born United States) **Genres:** Law, Adult Non-fiction, Politics/Government. **Career:** Oberlin College, Department of Government, teaching assistant, 1978; North Dame University, Department of Economics, teaching assistant, 1980-81; Princeton University, lecturer and teaching assistant, 1984-88; Pennsylvania State University, assistant professor, 1988-95, associate professor of political science, 1955-. Writer. **Publications:** Seeking Justices: The Judging of Supreme Court Nominees, 2004. **Address:** Pennsylvania State University, Fayette Campus, Rm. 206 D, Rte. 119 N, Eberly Bldg., PO Box 519, Uniontown, PA 15401-0519, U.S.A. **Online address:** cmc2@psu.edu

COMMINS, David Dean. American (born United States), b. 1954. **Genres:** Theology/Religion, Politics/Government, History. **Career:** University of Michigan, visiting lecturer, 1985-86; Illinois State University, assistant professor, 1986-87; Dickinson College, professor, 1987-, Clarke Center for the Interdisciplinary Study of Contemporary Issues, executive director, 2003-06, Benjamin Rush Distinguished Chair in Liberal Arts and Sciences, 2007-. Writer. **Publications:** Islamic Reform: Politics and Social Change in Late Ottoman Syria, 1990; Historical Dictionary of Syria, 1996, 2nd ed., 2004; The Wahhabi Mission and Saudi Arabia, 2006. Contributor of articles to journals and periodicals. **Address:** Department of History, Dickinson College, Carlisle, PA 17013, U.S.A. **Online address:** commins@dickinson.edu

COMMONER, Barry. American (born United States), b. 1917. **Genres:** Environmental Sciences/Ecology, Sciences, Social Commentary, Economics, Natural History, Politics/Government, Engineering. **Career:** Harvard University, assistant biology, 1938-40; Queens College (now of the City University of New York), instructor in biology, 1940-42, professor of geology, 1981, Center for the Biology of Natural Systems, director, 1981-2000, director emeritus, 2000-, professor of earth and environmental science, 1981-87, professor emeritus, 1987-, senior scientist; Science Illustrated Magazine, associate editor, 1946-47; Washington University, associate professor, 1947-53, professor of plant physiology, 1953-76, professor of environmental science, 1976-81, Department of Botany, chairman, 1965-69, Center for the Biology of Natural Systems, director, 1965-81; Albert Einstein College of Medicine, visiting professor of community health, 1981-87; University of Massachusetts, visiting distinguished professor of industrial policy, 1992. **Publications:** Scientific Statesmanship in Air Pollution Control, 1964; Science and Survival, 1966; (co-author) Balance and Biosphere: A Radio Symposium on the Environmental Crisis, 1971; The Closing Circle: Nature, Man, and Technology, 1971 in UK as The Closing Circle: Confronting the Environmental Crisis, 1972; (ed.) Air Pollution, 1973; Ecology and Social Action, 1973; (co-author) The Effect of Recent Energy Price Increases on Field Crop Production Costs, 1974; (ed.) Water Pollution, 1974; (ed.) The Social Costs of Power Production, 1975; (ed.) Human Welfare: The End Use for Power, 1975; (ed.) Alternative Technologies for Power Production, 1975; (ed. with H. Boksenbaum and M. Corr) Energy and Human Welfare, vol. I: The Social Costs of Power Production, vol. II: Alternative Technologies for Power Production, vol. III: Human Welfare: The End Use for Power, 1976; The Poverty of Power: Energy and the Economic Crisis, 1976; (with V. Bettini) Ecologia e Lotte Sociali: Ambiente, Popolazione, Inquinamento, 1976; Tekhnologiia Pribyli, 1976; Energy, 1976; Reliability of Bacterial Mutagenesis Techniques to Distinguish Carcinogenic and Noncarcinogenic Chemicals, 1976; The Politics of Energy, 1979; Global Resources, 1980; Making Peace with the Planet, 1990. Contributor to journals. **Address:** Center for the Biology of Natural Systems, Queens College, City University of New York, 163-03 Horace Harding Expy., 4th Fl., Flushing, NY 11367-0904, U.S.A. **Online address:** commoner@cbns.qc.edu

COMO, David R. American (born United States), b. 1970. **Genres:** History, Military/Defense/Arms Control. **Career:** Stanford University, associate professor of history, 2002-. Writer. **Publications:** Blown by the Spirit: Puritanism and the Emergence of an Antinomian Underground in Pre-Civil-War England, 2004. Contributor to books and periodicals. **Address:** Department of History, Stanford University, 450 Serra Mall, Bldg. 200, Stanford, CA 94305-2024, U.S.A. **Online address:** dcomo@stanford.edu

COMPESTINE, Ying Chang. Chinese (born China), b. 1963. **Genres:** Food And Wine, Children's Fiction. **Career:** Author. **Publications:** Secrets of Fat-Free Chinese Cooking: Over 120 Low-Free and Fat-Free, Traditional Chinese Recipes, from Egg Rolls to Almond Cookies, 1997; Cooking with Green Tea, 2000; The Runaway Rice Cake, 2001; The Story of Chopsticks, 2001; The Story of Noodles, 2002; Secrets from a Healthy Asian Kitchen, 2002; The Story of Kites, 2003; The Story of Paper, 2003; D Is for Dragon Dance, 2006; Revolution is not a Dinner Party, 2007; The Real Story of Stone Soup, 2007; Boy Dumplings, 2007; The Singing Wok, 2009; Cooking with an Asian Accent, 2009; Banquet for Hungry Ghosts, 2009; Crouching Tiger, 2011; Runaway Wok: A Chinese New Year Tale, 2011; Ying's Best One-Dish Meals, 2011; Menu For Hungry Ghosts, forthcoming. Contributor to periodicals. **Address:** Sheldon Fogelman Agency Inc., 10 E 40th St., New York, NY 10016, U.S.A. **Online address:** yingc@yingc.com

COMPTON, D(avid) G(uy). Also writes as Frances Lynch, Guy Compton. British (born England), b. 1930. **Genres:** Mystery/Crime/Suspense, Romance/Historical, Science Fiction/Fantasy, Young Adult Fiction. **Career:** Writer, 1960-; Reader's Digest Condensed Books, editor, 1969-81. **Publications:** The Quality of Mercy, 1965, rev. ed., 1970; Farewell, Earth's Bliss, 1966; The Silent Multitude, 1966; Synthajoy, 1968; The Palace, 1969; The Electric Crocodile in US as The Steel Crocodile, 1970; Chronocules, 1970 in UK as Hot Wireless Sets, Aspirin Tablets, The Sandpaper Sides of Used Matchboxes and Something That Might Have Been Castor Oil, 1971; The Missionaries, 1972; The Unsleeping Eye, 1973 in UK as The Continuous Katherine Mortenhoe, 1974; A Usual Lunacy, 1978; Windows, 1979; Ascendancies, 1980; Deathwatch, 1981; Scudder's Game, 1988; Ragnarok, 1991; Nomansland, 1993; Stammering: Its Nature, History, Causes & Cures (nonfiction), 1993; Justice City, 1994; Back of Town Blues, 1995. MYSTERY NOVELS AS GUY COMPTON: Too Many Murderers, 1962; Medium for Murder, 1963; Dead on Cue, 1964; Disguise for a Dead Gentleman, 1964; High Tide for a Hanging, 1965; And Murder Came Too, 1966. ROMANCE NOVELS AS FRANCES LYNCH: Twice Ten Thousand Miles, 1974 as Candle at Midnight, 1977; The Fine and Handsome Captain, 1975; Stranger at the Wedding, 1977; A Dangerous Magic, 1978; In the House of Dark Music, 1979. Works appear in anthologies. **Address:** Virginia Kidd, PO Box 278, Milford, PA 18337-0278, U.S.A.

COMPTON, Guy. *See* **COMPTON, D(avid) G(uy).**

COMPTON, James V(incent). American (born United States), b. 1928. **Genres:** History, International Relations/Current Affairs, Social Sciences. **Career:** University of Maryland, lecturer in history and government, 1956-64; University of London, Department of Extramural, lecturer in history and international relations, 1961-63; University of Edinburgh, Program of North American Studies, lecturer in history, 1963-69, chairman, 1964-68; Trinity College, assistant professor of history, 1968-69; San Francisco State University, associate professor, 1969-72, professor of history, 1972-95, professor emeritus, 1995-; Doshisha University, visiting professor; British Broadcasting Co., consultant; Southwest German Radio, consultant. Writer. **Publications:** The Swastika and the Eagle: Hitler, the United States, and the Origins of World War II, 1967; (ed.) America and the Origins of the Cold War, 1972; (contrib. and ed. with O. Bullitt) For the President: Personal and Secret Correspondence between Ambassador William C. Bullitt and President Franklin D. Roosevelt, 1973; Anticommunism in American Life since World War II, 1973; (comp.) The New Deal, 1973. Contributor to periodicals. **Address:** Department of History, San Francisco State University, 1600 Holloway Ave., San Francisco, CA 94132, U.S.A. **Online address:** jvcompton@aol.com

COMPTON, Patricia A. American (born United States), b. 1936. **Genres:** Novels, Social Sciences, Children's Fiction. **Career:** Laguna Salada School District, art teacher, 1969-75; Pyramid Alternatives, art therapist, 1974-76; Laguna Salada Union School District, Alternative School, director and teacher, 1975-76; Golden Gate University, lecturer, 1976; J.F. Kennedy University, lecturer, 1977-78; City of Walnut Creek Civic Arts, supervisor of arts education, 1977-79; Montalvo Center for the Arts, executive director, 1979-82; Greenbelt Alliance, board director, 1986-91; The Art Scene, columnist, 1997; Commonwealth Club-Silicon Valley, executive director, 1997-. **Publications:** The Terrible Eek: A Japanese Tale, 1991. Contributor to periodicals. **Address:** 15040 Oriole Rd., Saratoga, CA 95070, U.S.A.

COMSTOCK, Gary D(avid). (Glen David Comstock). American (born United States), b. 1945. **Genres:** Gay And Lesbian Issues, Sociology, Theology/Religion, Sex. **Career:** Wesleyan University, university protestant chaplain and visiting professor of sociology, 1990-. Writer. **Publications:** Violence Against Lesbians and Gay Men, 1991; Religion, homosexuality and literature, 1992; Gay Theology without Apology, 1993; A Rainbow of Religious Studies, 1996; Unrepentant, Self-Affirming, Practicing: Lesbian/Bisexual/Gay People within Organized Religion, 1996; (co-ed.) Que(e)rying Religion: A Critical Anthology, 1997; A Whosoever Church: Welcoming Lesbians and Gay Men into African-American Congregations, 2001; The Work of a Gay College Chaplain: Becoming Ourselves in the Company of Others, 2001. **Address:** Wesleyan University, 70 Wyllys Ave., Wesleyan Sta., Middletown, CT 06459, U.S.A. **Online address:** gcomstock@wesleyan.edu

COMSTOCK, Glen David. *See* **COMSTOCK, Gary D(avid).**

COMTE-SPONVILLE, Andre. French (born France), b. 1952. **Genres:** Translations. **Career:** University of Paris I, lecturer. Writer and philosopher. **Publications:** IN ENGLISH: Petit Traité des Grandes Vertus, 1995; L'esprit de l'Athéisme: Introduction à une Spiritualité sans Dieu, 2006. IN FRENCH: Le Mythe D'Icare: Traité du désespoir et de la béatitude, 1984; Une éducation Philosophique: Et Autres Articles, 1989; Pourquoi Nous Ne Sommes Pas Nietzschéens, 1991; L'amour la Solitude, 1992, new ed., 2000; Je Ne Suis Pas Philosophe: Montaigne Et La Philosophie, 1993; (with L. Bove and P. Renou) Camus: De L'absurde à L'amour: Lettres Inédites D'Albert Camus, 1995; Valeur et Vérité: études Cyniques, 1995; Impromptus, 1996; Arséne Lupin, Gentilhomme-Philosopheur, 1996; De l'Autre Côt du Désespoir: Introduction à la Pensée de Svâmi Prajnânpad, 1997; Intimes Convictions: Entretiens Avec André Compte-Sponville, Sylvie Bonnet, Véronique Chica, Charles Juliet, Fran oise Bon, Gilles Derome, 1997; (with L. Ferry) La Sagesse Des Modernes: Dix Questions Pour Notre Temps, 1998; (with M. de Solemne, E. Klein and J. Leloup) Aimer Désespérément, 1998; Chardin ou la Matière Heureuse, 1999; L'être-temps: Quelques Réflexions Sur Le Temps De La Conscience, 1999; Une Fin De Siècle Philosophique: Entretiens Avec André Comte-Sponville, Marcel Conche, Luc Ferry, Gilles Lipovetsky, Michel Onfray, Clément Rosset, 1999; Le Donheur, Désespérément, 2000; Présentations de la Philosophie, 2000; Lucrèce: Poète Et Philosophe, 2001; (with G. Perrault and J. Mougenot) Marie Laurence Gaudrat, 2001; Dictionnaire Philosophique, 2001; Confession D'un Philosophe, 2003; Le Capitalisme Est-il Moral? Sur Quelques Ridicules Et Tyrannies De Notre Temps, 2004; (with J.

Delumeau and A. Farge) La Plus Belle Histoire Du Bonheur, 2004; La Philosophie, 2005; (with S. Thybert) La Vie Humaine, 2005; (with P. Capelle) Dieu Existe-t-il Encore?, 2005; Le Miel et l'Absinthe: Poésie et Philosophie Chez Lucrèce, 2008; Du Corps, 2009. Contributor of articles to periodicals. **Online address:** ac-s@orange.fr

CONANT, Michael. American (born United States), b. 1924. **Genres:** Economics, Law. **Career:** University of California, Haas School of Business, professor, 1954-91, professor emeritus, 1991-; University of Singapore, visiting professor, 1964-65; Antitrust Litigation, consultant economist. Writer. **Publications:** Antitrust in the Motion Picture Industry: Economic and Legal Analysis, 1960; Railroad Mergers and Abandonments, 1964; The Constitution and Capitalism, 1974; The Constitution and the Economy: Objective Theory and Critical Commentary, 1991; Constitutional Structure and Purposes: Critical Commentary, 2001; The Constitution and Economic Regulation: Objective Theory and Critical Commentary, 2008. Contributor to journals. **Address:** Haas School of Business, University of California, 545 Student Services, Ste. 1900, Berkeley, CA 94720-1900, U.S.A. **Online address:** conant@haas.berkeley.edu

CONARD, Rebecca. American (born United States), b. 1946. **Genres:** History, Intellectual History, Institutions/Organizations, Biography. **Career:** American River College, English faculty, 1976-78; Wichita State University, assistant professor of history and director of public history program, 1992-98; Middle Tennessee State University, associate professor, 1998-2003, co-director of public history program, 1998-, professor of history, 2003-; Tallgrass Historians, co-founder, 1993, principal, 1993-. Writer. **Publications:** (Contrib.) Santa Barbara by the Sea, 1982; The Conservation of Local Autonomy: California's Agricultural Land Policies, 1900-1966, 1984; (with C. Nelson) Santa Barbara: El Pueblo Viejo, 1986, 2nd ed., 1989; Places of Quiet Beauty: Parks, Preserves and Environmentalism, 1997; (with S. Hess) Tallgrass Prairie National Preserve Legislative History, 1920-1996, 1998; Benjamin Shambaugh and the Intellectual Foundations of Public History, 2002; Women's Rights National Historical Park: Administrative History, 2010; (with P.M. Melvin, P.V. Scarpino and N. Stowe) Public History: A Critical Perspective on the Field, forthcoming. Contributor to journals and periodicals. **Address:** Department of History, Middle Tennessee State University, KOM 301E, 1301 E Main St., PO Box 23, Murfreesboro, TN 37132-0001, U.S.A. **Online address:** rconard@mtsu.edu

CONATI, Marcello. Italian (born Italy), b. 1928. **Genres:** Music, Reference. **Career:** Centro Internazionale di Ricerca sui Periodici Musicali, director; Conservatorio A. Boito, music teacher; Istituto di Studi Verdiani, researcher and librarian, 1971-; University of Macerata, contract faculty, 1991-94; Società Italiana di Musicologia, counselor and director, 1992-. Writer. **Publications:** (Contrib.) Giuseppe Verdi, autobiografia dalle lettere, 1951; Canti-popolari della Val d'Enza e Val Cedra Palatina, 1976; (ed. with M. Medici) Carteggio Verdi-Boito, 1978; (ed.) Interviste e incontri con Verdi, 1980, Correspondências italianas, 1982; Labottega della musica: Verdi e La Fenice, 1983; Rigoletto di GiuseppeVerdi: guida all'opera, 1983; (intro.) Amleto, 1984; (ed. and intro.) Encounters With Verdi, 1984; Interviews and Encounters With Verdi, 1984; La Musica, 1855, La Musica, 1857-1859, 1989; La Musica, 1876-1878, 1883-1885, 1989. La Musica, 1883-1885, 1989; Strenna teatrale europea, 1838-1848, 1989; L'Italia musicale, 1847-1859, 1992; Rigoletto: Un'analisi drammatico-musicale, 1992; (with N. Grilli) Simon Boccanegra di Giuseppe Verdi, 1993; (ed. with P. Colombo) La Musica Popolare, 1882-1885, 1993; (ed. with F.M. Noguera) Paganini, 1887-1891, 1993; (with M. Medici and intro.) The Verdi-Boito Correspondence, 1994; Vita e opere narrate ai giovani, 1999; Piaacente Estate Di San Martino: Studi e Ricerche Per Marcello Conati, 2000; Verdi: Interviste e incontri, 2000; Canti veronesi di tradizione orale: da unaricerca in Valpolicella e in Lessinia, 1969-1982, 2005; Musica d'oggi, 1919-1942, 2006; Rassegna Dorica, 1929-1942, 2008; Gazzetta Musicale Di Milano: 1866-1902, 2008. Contributor to periodicals. **Address:** CIRPM, via Conservatorio 31/B, Parma, 43100, Italy. **Online address:** mconati@netvalley.it

CONDEE, William Faricy. American (born United States), b. 1954. **Genres:** Architecture, Theatre, Social Sciences. **Career:** Stage manager, 1976-78; New York, director of stage plays, 1983; Vassar College, visiting lecturer, 1983-84; Ohio University, professor of theater and director of studies for honors tutorial program, 1986-, associate director of School of Theater, 1988-2001, Ohio Leipzig European Center, faculty director, 2001, School of Interdisciplinary Arts, director, 2001-, J. Richard Hamilton/Baker and Hostetler professor of humanities; University of Wales, honorary visiting lecturer, 1990; University of Leipzig, Institute for American Studies, visiting lecturer, 1995; lighting designer and dramaturg. Writer. **Publications:** Theatrical Space: A Guide for Directors and Designers, 1995; Crossroads of a Community: Stuarts Opera House and Nelsonville Ohio, 1998; Coal and Culture: Opera Houses in Appalachia, 2004. Contributor to books and periodicals. **Address:** School of Interdisciplinary Arts, Ohio University, Rm. 102, Lindley Hall, 1 Park Pl., Athens, OH 45701-2979, U.S.A. **Online address:** condee@ohio.edu

CONDRAY, B. *See* **HUMPHRYS, Leslie George.**

CONDRELL, Ken. *See* **CONDRELL, Kenneth N.**

CONDRELL, Kenneth N. (Ken Condrell). American (born United States), b. 1937?. **Genres:** Psychology, Psychiatry. **Career:** State University of New York, Department of Psychiatry, clinical assistant professor; The Condrell Center, founder. Writer and clinical psychologist. **Publications:** How to Raise a Brat, 1985; (with L.L. Small) Wimpy Parents: From Toddler to Teen-How Not to Raise a Brat, 1998; (with L.L. Small) Be a Great Divorced Dad, 1998; The Unhappy Child: What Every Parent Needs to Know, 2006. **Address:** Stonegate Office Pk., 8201 Main St., Ste. 2, Williamsville, NY 14221, U.S.A. **Online address:** info@drcondrell.com

CONDRY, Ian Richard. American (born United States), b. 1965. **Genres:** Social Sciences. **Career:** Yomiuri Shimbun, researcher, 1992; Union College, assistant professor, 1999-2001; Harvard University, Reischauer Institute of Japanese Studies, fellow, 2001-02; Massachusetts Institute of Technology, assistant professor, 2002-. Cultural anthropologist, academic and writer. **Publications:** Hip-Hop Japan: Rap and the Paths of Cultural Globalization, 2006. Contributor to books and periodicals. **Address:** Foreign Languages & Literature, Massachusetts Institute of Technology, 77 Massachusetts Ave., Cambridge, MA 02139, U.S.A. **Online address:** condry@mit.edu

CONES, John W. American (born United States), b. 1945. **Genres:** Film, Philosophy, Law, Money/Finance, Industrial Relations, Young Adult Nonfiction. **Career:** Radio and television news reporter, 1968-74; securities lawyer, 1981-86; attorney, writer, and lecturer, 1987-; University of California, adjunct professor of film and television. **Publications:** Film Finance & Distribution: A Dictionary of Terms, 1992; 43 Ways to Finance Your Feature Film: A Comprehensive Analysis of Film Finance, 1995, 3rd ed., 2008; Film Industry Contracts, 1996; Hollywood Corruption, 1996; How the Movie Wars Were Won, 1996; Legacy of the Hollywood Empire, 1996; Movie Picture Biographies: The Hollywood Spin on Historical Figures, 1996; Motion Picture Industry Reform, 1996; Patterns of Bias in Motion Picture Content, 1996; Politics, Movies and the Role of Government, 1996; A Study in Motion Picture Propaganda: Hollywood's Preferred Movie Messages, 1996; Who Really Controls Hollywood?, 1996; What's Really Going on in Hollywood, 1997; The Feature Film Distribution Deal: A Critical Analysis of the Single Most Important Film Industry Agreement, 1997; The Book of Secular Wisdom, 2003; Hollywood Wars: How Insiders Gained and Maintain Illegitimate Control Over The Film Industry, 2007; Dictionary of Film Finance and Distribution: A Guide For Independent Filmmakers, 2008; Introduction to the Motion Picture Industry: A Guide for Students, Filmmakers and Scholars, 2008; Business Plans for Filmmakers, 2010. **Address:** 794 Via Colinas, Westlake Village, CA 91362, U.S.A. **Online address:** jwc6774@roadrunner.com

CONEY, Sandra. New Zealander (born New Zealand), b. 1944. **Genres:** History, Area Studies, Women's Studies And Issues, Sciences, Biography, Autobiography/Memoirs. **Career:** Broadsheet (feminist magazine), founder, 1972, editor, 1972-85; Auckland Medical Aid Centre, counselor, 1974-84; freelance writer, 1985-; Auckland Fertility Action, staff, 1985; Women's Health Action Trust, director, 1986-, consultant; Sunday Star-Times, columnist, 1986-; Auckland Women's Health Clinic, staff, 1988. **Publications:** (Ed.) United Womens Convention, 1973; Every Girl: A Social History of Women and the YWCA in Auckland, 1885-1985, 1986; The Unfortunate Experiment, 1988; (ed.) Salute to New Zealand, 1989; Out of the Frying Pan: Inflammatory Writings, 1972-1989, 1990; (with L. Potter) Hysterectomy, 1990 The Great New Zealand Diary, 1992; (ed.) Unfinished Business: What Happened to the Cartwright Report?, 1993; Standing in the Sunshine: A History of New Zealand Women since They Won the Vote, 1993; Menopause Industry: How the Medical Establishment Exploits Women, 1994; I Do: 125 Years of Weddings in New Zealand, 1995; Into the Fire: Writings on Women, Politics, and New Zealand in the Era of the New Right, 1997; Stroppy Sheilas and Gutsy Girls: New Zealand Women of Dash and Daring, 1998. Contributor to books and periodicals. **Address:** Women's Health Action Trust, 27 Gillies Ave., Level 2, PO Box 9947, Newmarket, 1149, New Zealand.

CONFER, Dennis W. American (born United States), b. 1941. **Genres:** How-to Books, Recreation, Travel/Exploration, Autobiography/Memoirs, Sports/Fitness, Recreation, History. **Career:** Wily Ventures, owner and manager, 1981-2003; Alyeska Pipeline, budget analyst, 1981-82; Municipality of Anchorage, controller, management analyst and executive, 1982-88; Wily Ventures Inc., owner, publisher, hunting and business consultant, 1995-. Writer. **Publications:** Wily Ventures Equipment List, 1982; Hunt Alaska Now: Self-Guiding for Trophy Moose and Caribou: How to Plan Affordable, Successful Hunts You Do Yourself, 1997, 2nd rev. ed., 2000; Adventures of an Alaskan-You Can Do, 2003. Contributor to periodicals. **Address:** Wily Ventures Inc., 2509 Kilkenny Cir., Anchorage, AK 99504-3422, U.S.A. **Online address:** wilyv@gci.net

CONFIANT, Raphaël. Guyanese (born Guyana), b. 1951. **Genres:** Poetry, Novels, Language/Linguistics, Plays/Screenplays. **Career:** Teacher, 1977-96; Central Trade Union of Martiniquais Workers, secretary, 1982-85; University of Antilles and Guyana, lecturer in languages and regional cultures, 1997-; University of Santo Domingo, honorary professor. Writer. **Publications:** Jou Bare (poems), 1979; Jik Deye do Bondye, 1979; Bitako-a, 1985; Kod Yanm, 1986; Marisosè, 1987; Le Nègre et Lamiral: Roman, 1988; (with J. Bernabé and P. Chamoiseau) Eloge de la Créolité, 1989; Eau Decafé: A Roman, 1991; Aimé Césaire: Une Traverséeparadoxale du Siècle, 1993; Barrancos del Alba: Literature Francocaribeña Novela, 1993; Ravines du Devant-jour: Récit, 1993; (trans.) J. Berry, A Robber in the Village, 1993; LAllée des Soupirs: Roman, 1994; Mamzelle Libellule: Roman, 1994; Bassin des Ouragans, 1994; Commandeur du Sucre: Récit, 1994; Contes Créoles des Amériques, 1995; Les Maîtres de la Parole Créole, 1995; Le Gouverneur des Dés, 1995; La Savane des Petrifications, 1995; La Vièrge du Grande Rétour: Roman, 1996; Le Meurtre du Samedi-Gloria: Roman, 1997; (trans.) E. Jones, Adventure on the Knos Plant, 1998; Larchetdu Colonel: Roman, 1998; (ed.) Dictionnaire des Titim et Sirandes, 1998; Régisseur du Rhum: Récit, 1999; (with P. Chamoiseau) LettresCréoles: Tracées Antillaise et Continentales de Lalittérature: Haïti, Guadeloupe, Martinique, Guyane, 1635-1975, 1999; La Dernière Java de Mama Josépha, 1999; Le Cahier Deromances, 2000; La Lessive du Diable: Roman, 2000; (with D. Damoison) Le Galion, 2000; (intro.) L. Hearn, Two Years in the French West Indies, 2000; (ed.) Dictionnaire des Nelogismes Creoles, 2001; Brin dAmour: Roman, 2001; Morne-Pichevin: Roman, 2002; Nuée Ardente: Roman, 2002; La Dissidence: Récit, 2002; Le Barbare Enchanté: Roman, 2003; Lapanse du Chacal: Roman, 2004; Adèle et la Pacotilleuse: Roman, 2005; Trilogie Tropicale, 2006; Nègre Marron: Récit, 2006; Case à Chine: Roman, 2007; (with L. Boutrin) Chronique dun Empoisonnement Annoncé: Le Scandale du Chlordécone aux Antilles Françaises, 1972-2002, 2007; Dictionnaire Créole Martiniquais-français, 2007; Black is Black: Récit, 2008; Ténèbres extérieures: Récit, 2008; LHôtel du Bon Plaisir, 2009; Le gouverneur des dés, 2009; Citoyens au-dessus de tout soupçon, 2010; Jarre d'or: roman, 2010; émerveillable chute de Louis Augustin et autres nouvelles, 2010; (co-author) Elogio de la creolidad, 2011. Contributor to periodicals. **Address:** University of Antilles and Guyana, Campus Fouillole, Pointe a Pitre, BP25097157, Guyana. **Online address:** raphael.confiant@martinique.univag.fr

CONFINO, Alon. American (born United States), b. 1959. **Genres:** History, Cultural/Ethnic Topics, Theology/Religion. **Career:** University of Virginia, assistant professor, 1992-98, associate professor, 1998-2006, professor, 2006-; École des Hautes Études en Sciences Sociales, visiting professor, 1999; Hebrew University, visiting professor, 2006, 2007; Tel Aviv University, visiting professor, 2006; European University, Department of History and Civilization, visiting fellow, 2009-10. Writer. **Publications:** The Nation as a Local Metaphor: Württemberg, Imperial Germany and National Memory, 1871-1918, 1997; (ed. with P. Fritzsche) The Work of Memory: New Directions in the Study of German Society and Culture, 2002; Germany as a Culture of Remembrance: Promises and Limits of Writing History, 2006; (ed. with P. Betts and D. Schumann) Between Mass Death and Individual Loss: The Place of the Dead in Twentieth-Century Germany, 2008; Foundational Pasts: The Holocaust As Historical Understanding, 2012. Contributor to books and journals. **Address:** Department of History, University of Virginia, Nau Hall, PO Box 400180, Charlottesville, VA 22903, U.S.A. **Online address:** confino@virginia.edu

CONFORD, Ellen. American (born United States), b. 1942. **Genres:** Children's Fiction, Novels, Humor/Satire, Picture/Board Books. **Career:** University of Minnesota, instructor in English composition; University of Wisconsin, instructor in philosophy, through 1975; writer and illustrator, 1975-. **Publications:** FICTION: Impossible, Possum, 1971; Why Can't I Be William?, 1972; Dreams of Victory, 1973; Felicia the Critic, 1973; Just the Thing for Geraldine, 1974; Me and the Terrible Two, 1974; The Luck of Pokey Bloom, 1975; Dear Lovey Hart, I Am Desperate, 1975; Alfred G. Graebner Memorial High School Handbook of Rules and Regulations: A Novel, 1976; And This Is Laura, 1977; Eugene the Brave, 1978; Hail, Hail Camp Timberwood, 1978; Anything for a Friend, 1979; We Interrupt This Semester for an Important Bulletin, 1979; The Revenge of the Incredible Dr. Rancid and His Youthful Assistant, Jeffrey, 1980; Seven Days to a Brand-New Me, 1981; To All My Fans, with Love, from Sylvie, 1982; Lenny Kandell, Smart Aleck, 1983; If This Is Love, I'll Take Spaghetti (short stories), 1983; You Never Can Tell, 1984; Why Me?, 1985; Strictly for Laughs, 1985; A Royal Pain, 1986; The Things I Did for Love, 1987; Genie with the Light Blue Hair, 1989; Loving Someone Else, 1991; Dear Mom, Get Me out of Here!, 1992; I Love You, I Hate You, Get Lost, 1994; My Sister the Witch, 1995; (with D.A. Adler) Birthday Surprises, 1995; Norman Newman and the Werewolf of Walnut Street, 1995; (with E. Leroe, J. McFann and J. Thesman) A Night to Remember, 1995; The Frog Princess of Pelham, 1997; Crush, 1997; Diary of a Monster's Son, 1999; Loathe at First Sight, 2000. JENNY ARCHER SERIES: BEGINNING READERS: A Job for Jenny Archer, 1988; A Case for Jenny Archer, 1988; Jenny Archer, Author, 1989; What's Cooking, Jenny Archer?, 1989; Jenny Archer to the Rescue, 1990; Can Do, Jenny Archer, 1991; Nibble, Nibble, Jenny Archer, 1993; Get the Picture, Jenny Archer?, 1994. ANNABEL THE ACTRESS SERIES: CHAPTER BOOKS: Starring in Gorilla My Dreams, 1999; Starring in Just a Little Extra, 2000; Starring in Hound of the Barkervilles, 2002; Starring in Camping It Up, 2004. **Address:** McIntosh & Otis Inc., 353 Lexington Ave., New York, NY 10016, U.S.A.

CONFORTI, Joseph A. American (born United States), b. 1945. **Genres:** Theology/Religion. **Career:** Brown University, teaching assistant, 1972-74; Rhode Island College, instructor of history, 1976-78, assistant professor of history, 1978-80, assistant professor, 1980-82, associate professor of English and history, 1982-87; University of Southern Maine, professor of American and New England studies, 1987-, American and New England studies, director, 1987-97. Writer. **Publications:** Samuel Hopkins and the New Divinity Movement: Calvinism, the Congregational Ministry and Reform in New England between the Great Awakenings, 1981; Jonathan Edwards, Religious Tradition and American Culture, 1995; Imagining New England: Explorations of Regional Identity from the Pilgrims to the Mid-Twentieth Century, 2001; (ed.) Creating Portland: History and Place in Northern New England, 2005; Saints and Strangers: New England in British North America, 2006. **Address:** American and New England Studies Program, University of Southern Maine, 11 Granite St., PO Box 9300, Portland, ME 04104-9300, U.S.A. **Online address:** conforti@usm.maine.edu

CONGDON, Kristin G. American/Irish (born Ireland), b. 1948. **Genres:** Art/Art History, Education. **Career:** Booth Residential Treatment Center, education coordinator, 1978-79; Community Relations and Social Development Commission, coordinator, 1979; University of Oregon, instructor, 1981-83; Bowling Green State University, assistant professor of art education, 1984-87; University of Central Florida, professor of art, 1996-2000, professor of art and philosophy, 2000-, Cultural Heritage Alliance, director. Writer. **Publications:** Uncle Monday and Other Traditional Tales form Florida, 2001; Artists from Latin American Cultures, 2002; Community Art in Action, 2004; (with T. Bucuvalas) Just above the Water: Florida Folk Art, 2006; (with K.K. Hallmark) Twentieth Century United States Photographers, 2008. EDITOR: (with D. Blandy) Art in a Democracy, 1987; (with D. Blandy) Pluralistic Approaches to Art Education, 1991; (co-ed.) Women Art Educators III, 1993; Evaluating Art Education Programs in Community Centers, 1998. OTHERS: Making Invisible Histories of Art Education Visible, 2000; (with D. Blandy and P. Bolin) Histories of Community-based Art Education, 2001. **Address:** School of Film and Digital Media, University of Central Florida, OTC5, 4000 Central Florida Blvd., Orlando, FL 32816-3120, U.S.A. **Online address:** kcongdon@pegasus.cc.ucf.edu

CONGDON, Lee (Walter). American (born United States), b. 1939. **Genres:** History, Intellectual History. **Career:** Encyclopaedia Britannica, editorial assistant, 1965, writer, 1967-68; James Madison University, assistant professor, 1972-78, associate professor, 1978-83, professor of history, 1983-2005, professor emeritus, 2005-. **Publications:** The Young Lukacs, 1983; Exile and Social Thought: Hungarian Intellectuals in Germany and Austria, 1919-1933, 1991; Seeing Red: Hungarian Intellectuals in Exile and the Challenge of Communism, 2001; (ed. with B.K. Kiraly) Ideas of the Hungarian Revolution, Suppressed and Victorious, 1956-1999, 2003; (ed. with B.K. Kiraly and K. Nagy) 1956: The Hungarian Revolution and War for Independence, 2006; George Kennan: A Writing Life, 2008; Baseball and Memory: Winning, Losing, and the Remembrance of Things Past, 2011. Contributor to books and periodicals. **Address:** 46 Laurel St., Harrisonburg, VA 22801, U.S.A. **Online address:** congdolw@jmu.edu

CONGER, Jay A. American (born United States), b. 1952. **Genres:** Business/Trade/Industry, inspirational/Motivational Literature. **Career:** Attorney General's Office, assistant to the director, 1974-75; Solarex Corp., manager of international marketing, 1977-80; Georgetown University, adjunct professor of business administration in marketing, 1979-80; Harvard University, Graduate School of Business Administration, faculty, 1981-83, visiting associate professor, 1992-93; Harbridge House, associate consultant, 1982-85; Northeastern University, instructor in organizational behaviour, 1982; McGill University, assistant professor, 1985-90, associate professor of organizational behavior, 1990-95, chair of organizational behavior, 1993-95, professor of management in organizational behaviour, 1995; INSEAD (European Institute of Business Administration), visiting associate professor, 1991-92; University of Southern California, The Leadership Institute, executive director and chairman, 1995-99, School of Business, professor of management in organizational behaviour, 1995-99, Center for Effective Organizations, senior research scientist, 1999-; London Business School, professor of organizational behavior, 1999-2005; Claremont McKenna College, Henry Kravis Research professor of leadership studies, 2005-, Henry R. Kravis Research chair in leadership studies. Writer. **Publications:** (Contrib.) Charismatic Leadership: The Elusive Factor in Organizational Effectiveness, 1988; The Charismatic Leader: Behind the Mystique of Exceptional Leadership, 1989; Learning to Lead: The Art of Transforming Managers into Leaders, 1992; (contrib.) Spirit at Work: Discovering the Spirituality in Leadership, 1994; Winning 'Em Over: A New Model for Managing in the Age of Persuasion, 1998; (with R.N. Kanungo) Charismatic Leadership in Organizations, 1998; (ed. with G.M. Spreitzer and E.E. Lawler III) The Leader's Change Handbook: An Essential Guide to Setting Direction and Taking Action, 1999; (with B. Benjamin) Building Leaders: How Successful Companies Develop the Next Generation 1999; (with E.E. Lawler III and D.L. Finegold) Corporate Boards: Strategies for Adding Value at the Top, 2001; (ed. with C.L. Pearce) Shared Leadership: Reframing the Hows and Whys of Leadership, 2003; (with R.M. Fulmer) Growing Your Company's Leaders: How Great Organizations Use Succession Management to Sustain Competitive Advantage, 2004; (ed. with R.E. Riggio) Practice of Leadership: Developing the Next Generation of Leaders, 2007; Necessary Art of Persuasion, 2008; (ed.) Boardroom Realities: Building Leaders across Your Board, 2009. Contributor to journals and newspapers. **Address:** Kravis Leadership Institute, Claremont McKenna College, Rm. 226, Seaman Hall, 500 E 9th St., Claremont, CA 91711, U.S.A. **Online address:** jay.conger@cmc.edu

CONGER, Syndy McMillen. American (born United States), b. 1942. **Genres:** Literary Criticism And History, Young Adult Fiction. **Career:** Western Illinois University, professor of English and director of graduate studies in English, department chairperson, 1972-2002, professor emeritus, general editor of essays in literature, 1979-83, outstanding research professor, 1984. **Publications:** Matthew G. Lewis, Charles Robert Maturin, and the Germans: An Interpretative Study of the Influence of German Literature on Two Gothic Novels, 1977; (ed. with J.R. Welsch) Narrative Strategies: Original Essays in Film and Prose Fiction, 1980; (ed.) Sensibility in Transformation: Creative Resistance to Sentiment from the Augustans to the Romantics, 1990; Mary Wollstonecraft and the Language of Sensibility, 1994; (ed. with C.H. Hay) The Past as Prologue, 1994; (ed. with F.S. Frank, G. O'Dea and J. Yocum) Iconoclastic Departures: Mary Shelley after Frankenstein: Essays in Honor of the Bicentenary of Mary Shelley's Birth, 1997. **Address:** Department of English & Journalism, Western Illinois University, 1 University Cir., Macomb, IL 61455, U.S.A. **Online address:** syndy_conger@wiu.edu

CONGRESS, Richard. (Rick Congress). American (born United States), b. 1943. **Genres:** Novellas/Short Stories. **Career:** City University of New York System, teacher of English, 1988-93; Random Chance Records, owner, 1999-. Writer. **Publications:** (Ed.) Vernon Bellecourt: The Nicaraguan Revolution and Indian Rights, 1986; (comp.) The Afro-Nicaraguans: The Revolution and Autonomy, 1987; Blues Mandolin Man: The Life and Music of Yank Rachell, 2001. **Address:** Random Chance Records, 200 E 10th St., PO Box 208, New York, NY 10003, U.S.A. **Online address:** agnosticcat@yahoo.com

CONGRESS, Rick. *See* **CONGRESS, Richard.**

CONIGLIARO, Vincenzo. American/Italian (born Italy), b. 1928. **Genres:** Psychiatry, Psychology. **Career:** Fordham University, assistant professor, 1961-66, associate professor of psychiatry, 1967-86, professor, 1986-; Catholic Charities, senior psychiatrist and director of training at guidance clinics, 1961-63; St. Francis Monastery, co-founder, 1961-63, Institute of Pastoral Counseling, instructor, 1961-63; School of Theology for Laymen, lecturer, 1961-63; Postgraduate Center for Mental Health, lecturer and staff psychiatrist in community mental health and public education, 1963-66; Iona College, assistant professor, 1963-66, associate professor, 1966-68, Graduate School of Pastoral Counseling, co-founder, staff, 1963-68; Metropolitan Consultation Center, lecturer, 1963-68, medical director, 1966-; Training Institute for Mental Health Practitioners, co-founder, training analyst, senior supervisor, medical director, board director, 1968-, dean and president, 1978-, teacher, retired 2004; Aquinas College, lecturer; Rutgers University, lecturer; City University of New York, John Jay College of Criminal Justice, lecturer; Temple University, lecturer; Central Islip State Hospital, senior resident. Writer. **Publications:** American History for Children and Young Adults: An Annotated Bibliographic Index, 1990; World History for Children and Young Adults: An Annotated Bibliographic Index, 1991; Dreams as a Tool in Psychodynamic Psychotherapy: The Royal Road to the Unconscious, 1997; America in Historical Fiction: A Bibliographic Guide, 1997; The Internal Soliloquy, 2010. Contributor to journals and magazines. **Address:** Training Institute for Mental Health, 4th Fl., 115 W 27th St., New York, NY 10001-6217, U.S.A. **Online address:** mail@vincenzoconigliaro.com

CONKLIN, John E. American (born United States), b. 1943. **Genres:** Criminology/True Crime, Film, Art/Art History, Popular Culture, Sociology, Social Sciences. **Career:** Harvard University, Law School, Center for Criminal Justice, research associate, 1969-70; Tufts University, Department of Sociology, assistant professor, 1970-76, associate professor, 1976-81, professor of sociology, 1970-, chairman, 1981-86, 1990-91, 2011-. Writer. **Publications:** Robbery and the Criminal Justice System, 1972; The Impact of Crime, 1975; Illegal But Not Criminal: Business Crime in America, 1977; Criminology, 1981, 10th ed., 2010; Sociology: An Introduction, 1984, 2nd ed., 1987; Art Crime, 1994; Why Crime Rates Fell, 2003; Campus Life in the Movies: A Critical Survey from the Silent Era to the Present, 2008. EDITOR: The Crime Establishment: Organized Crime and American Society, 1973; New Perspectives in Criminology, 1996. **Address:** Department of Sociology, Tufts University, 115 Eaton Hall, 5 The Green, Medford, MA 02155, U.S.A. **Online address:** john.conklin@tufts.edu

CONLEY, Brenda Edgerton. American (born United States), b. 1948. **Genres:** Education. **Career:** Baltimore City Public School System, teacher, 1971-80, Division of Personnel, staff associate, 1980-83, Division of Human Resources and Labor Relations, acting divisional specialist, 1983-84, Division of Personnel, staff specialist, 1984-86, staff director of personnel administration, 1986-88, director of human resources, 1988-92, director of policy development and leadership support in Bureau of Management Services, 1992, Department of Professional Development, Organizational Development and Attitudinal Reform, director, 1992-93, assistant superintendent, 1993-98, project director for performance based teacher evaluation project, 1998-2000; Pritchett and Associates Inc., certified trainer, 1996; Johns Hopkins University, Project Site Support, project coordinator, 2000; University of Maryland, Graduate School, associate professor, chair of teacher education programs, 2000-05; Maryland Council of Staff Developers, board director, 2000-; Towson University, visiting assistant professor, Institute at Center for Leadership in Education, program developer for assistant principal's, 2002-03; Job Corp., staff. Writer. **Publications:** Alternative Schools: A Reference Handbook, 2002. Contributor to periodicals. **Address:** Department of Instructional Leadership and, Professional Development, Towson University, Rm. 431H, Hawkins Hall, 8000 York Rd., Towson, MD 21252-0001, U.S.A. **Online address:** bconley@towson.edu

CONLEY, Carolyn A. American (born United States), b. 1953. **Genres:** History, Criminology/True Crime, Psychology, Humanities. **Career:** University of Alabama, Department of History, assistant professor, 1985-92, associate professor, 1992-99, professor of history, 1999-, director of graduate studies, 1993-2002, department chair, 2008-. Writer. **Publications:** The Unwritten

Law: Criminal Justice in Victorian Kent, 1991; Melancholy Accidents: The Meaning of Violence in Post-Famine Ireland, 1999; Certain Other Countries: Homicide, Gender and National Identity in Late Nineteenth-Century England, Ireland, Scotland and Wales, 2007; Female Killers in London, 1671-1913, forthcoming; British Interactions With Non-European People, forthcoming. Contributor of articles to journals. **Address:** Department of History, University of Alabama, 360H1 Heritage Hall Bldg., 1401 University Blvd., Birmingham, AL 35294, U.S.A. **Online address:** cconley@uab.edu

CONLEY, Tom (Clark). American (born United States), b. 1943. **Genres:** Film, Literary Criticism And History, Translations, Sciences. **Career:** University of Minnesota, Department of French and Italian, assistant professor, 1971-75, associate professor, 1975-79, professor, 1979-95, head, 1983-88; University of Michigan, visiting instructor, 1978; University of California, visiting associate professor, 1978-79; Miami University, visiting professor, 1981, distinguished visiting professor, 1989-90; Harvard University, professor of romance languages, 1995-, Abbott Lawrence Lowell professor, 2005-; Case Western Reserve University, lecturer; University of Paris, lecturer; University of Iowa, lecturer; Johns Hopkins University, lecturer; University of Georgia, lecturer; Washington University, lecturer; University of Valencia, lecturer. Writer. **Publications:** Film Hieroglyphs: Ruptures in Classical Cinema, 1991; The Graphic Unconscious in Early Modern French Writing, 1992; Les Mistons and Undercurrents of French New Wave Cinema, 2003; The Self Made Map: Cartographic Writing in Early Modern France, 1996; Cartographic Cinema, 2007; The Vulnerable Country, 2009; Errant Eye, 2011. CO-EDITOR: Rethinking Technologies, 1993; French Culture, 1900-1975, 1995; (with S. Ungar) Identity Papers: Contested Nationhood in Twentieth-Century France, 1996. TRANSLATOR: M. de Certeau, The Writing of History, 1988; G. Deleuze, The Fold: Leibniz and the Baroque, 1993; J.L. Schefer, The Deluge, the Plague: Paolo Uccello, 1994; R. Bensmaia, A Year of Passages (novel), 1995; de Certeau, The Capture of Speech, 1997; de Certeau, Culture in the Plural, 1997; M. Augé, In the Metro, 2002; C. Jacob, The Sovereign Map, 2005; M. Augé, Casablanca, 2008; J. Derrida, Parages, 2011. Contributor to books and periodicals. **Address:** Department of Romance Languages, Harvard University, 509 Boylston Hall, Cambridge, MA 02138, U.S.A. **Online address:** tconley@fas.harvard.edu

CONLIN, Diane Atnally. American (born United States) **Genres:** History, Art/Art History. **Career:** University of Michigan, Department of Classical Studies and the History of Art, visiting assistant professor, 1994-96; University of Colorado, Department of Art and Art History and Classics, assistant professor, 1998-2006, associate professor, 2006-10, Undergraduate Studies of Classics, associate chair, 2005-06, 2008-, Undergraduate Studies of Art and Art History, associate chair, 2007-08, Department of Classics, associate professor, 2010-. Writer. **Publications:** The Artists of the Ara Pacis: The Process of Hellenization in Roman Relief Sculpture, 1997; Political Art in Flavian Rome, 2008; (with P. Jacobs) The Campus Martius in the Life of Ancient Rome, forthcoming. **Address:** Department of Art and Art History, University of Colorado, CB 248, 388 Eatons Humanities Bldg., Boulder, CO 80309-1000, U.S.A. **Online address:** conlind@colorado.edu

CONLON, Evelyn. Irish (born Ireland), b. 1952?. **Genres:** Novels, Novellas/Short Stories, History, Young Adult Fiction. **Career:** Dublin City Library, writer-in-residence; Dublin Rape Crisis Centre, founding member. **Publications:** SHORT STORIES: My Head is Opening, 1987; Taking Scarlet As a Real Colour, 1993; (intro.) Tales from Bective Bridge, 1996; Telling: New and Selected Stories, 2000. NOVELS: Stars in the Daytime, 1989; A Glassful of Letters, 1998. OTHER: Where Did I Come From? (for children), 1982; (ed. with Hans-Christian Oeser) Cutting the Night in Two: Short Stories by Irish Women Writers, 2001; Skin of Dreams, 2003; (ed.) Later On: The Monaghan Bombing Memorial Anthology, 2004; (co-ed.) Annaghmakerrig, 2006. **Address:** Blackstaff Press Ltd., 3 Galway Pk., Dundonald, Belfast, BT16 2AN, Northern Ireland. **Online address:** mail@evelynconlon.com

CONLON, Kathleen (Annie). (Kate North). British (born England), b. 1943. **Genres:** Novels, Romance/Historical. **Career:** Writer. **Publications:** Apollo's Summer Look, 1968; Tomorrow's Fortune, 1971; My Father's House, 1972; A Twisted Skein, 1975; A Move in the Game, 1979; A Forgotten Season, 1980; Consequences, 1981; Developments, 1982; The Best of Friends, 1984; Face Values, 1985; Distant Relations, 1989; Unfinished Business, 1990; (as Kate North) Land of My Dreams, 1997. Contributor to periodicals. **Address:** 26A Brighton Rd., Birkdale, Southport, PR8 4DD, England. **Online address:** kateconlon@easynet.co.uk

CONLON-MCKENNA, Marita. Irish (born Ireland), b. 1956. **Genres:** Children's Fiction, Picture/Board Books, Novels. **Career:** Writer. **Publications:** CHILDREN'S FICTION: My First Holy Communion, 1990; Under the Hawthorn Tree: Children of the Famine, 1990; Wildflower Girl, 1992; Little Star, 1993; The Very Last Unicorn, 1994; Fields of Home, 1996; Granny Macginty, 1997. NOVELS: The Blue Horse, 1992; No Goodbye, 1994; Safe Harbour, 1995; In Deep Dark Wood, 1999; Promised Land, 2000; Miracle Woman, 2002; The Magdalen, 2002; Im Drachenwald, 2002; A Girl Called Blue, 2003; The Stone House, 2004; The Hat Shop On The Corner, 2006; The Matchmaker, 2008; Chini ya Mti wa Matumaini, 2010; Mother of the Bride, 2010; School for Cooks, 2011; Taste for Love, 2011. **Address:** Homewood, 50 Stillorgan Grove, Blackrock, DU 51210, Ireland.

CONN, Andrew Lewis. American (born United States), b. 1973. **Genres:** Novels, Mystery/Crime/Suspense, Literary Criticism And History. **Career:** P&F Communications/The Berney Group, account executive; Robinson Lerer & Montgomery, vice president. Writer. **Publications:** P: A Novel, 2003. Contributor to periodicals. **Address:** 1345 Ave. of the Americas, New York, NY 10105, U.S.A. **Online address:** connandrew@aol.com

CONN, Didi. American (born United States), b. 1951. **Genres:** Film, Children's Fiction, Art/Art History. **Career:** Writer and actor. **Publications:** Frenchy's Grease Scrapbook: We'll Always Be Together!, 1998. **Address:** William Morris Agency, 151 S El Camino Dr., Beverly Hills, CA 90212-2775, U.S.A.

CONN, Stewart. Scottish (born Scotland), b. 1936. **Genres:** Plays/Screenplays, Poetry, Essays, Autobiography/Memoirs. **Career:** British Broadcasting Corp., senior radio drama producer and head of radio drama, 1972-92; freelance writer and reviewer, 1992-; Queen Margaret University College, visiting lecturer, 2001; Poet laureate of Edinburgh, 2002. **Publications:** POETRY: Thunder in the Air: Poems, 1967; The Chinese Tower, 1967; Stoats in the Sunlight: Poems, 1968 in US as Ambush and Other Poems, 1970; An Ear to the Ground, 1972; Under the Ice, 1978; In the Kibble Palace, 1987; The Luncheon of the Boating Party, 1992; In the Blood, 1995; At the Aviary, 1995; Stolen Light, 1999; L'anima del teixidor, 2000; Ghosts at Cockcrow, 2005. PLAYS: The Burning, 1973; Thistlewood, 1975; The Aquarium and Other Plays, 1976; Play Donkey, 1977; Hugh Miller, 2002. OTHERS: Distances: A Personal Evocation of People And Places, 2001; (ed.) Murdo: The Life and Works, 2001; (ed.) 100 Favourite Scottish Poems, 2006; Breakfast Room, 2010. Contributor to periodicals. **Address:** The Agency (London) Ltd., 24 Pottery Ln., London, GL W11 4LZ, England. **Online address:** stewart@jsconn.freeserve.co.uk

CONNELL, Evan S(helby). American (born United States), b. 1924. **Genres:** Novels, Novellas/Short Stories, Biography, inspirational/Motivational Literature, Young Adult Fiction, Literary Criticism And History. **Career:** Writer. **Publications:** The Anatomy Lesson and Other Stories, 1957; Mrs. Bridge, 1959; The Patriot, 1960; Notes from a Bottle Found on the Beach at Carmel, 1963; At the Crossroads: Stories, 1965; The Diary of a Rapist: A Novel, 1966; Mr. Bridge, 1969; Points for a Compass Rose, 1973; The Connoisseur, 1974; Double Honeymoon, 1976; A Long Desire, 1979; The White Lantern, 1980; St. Augustine's Pigeon, 1980; Son of the Morning Star: Custer and the Little Bighorn, 1984; The Alchymist's Journal, 1991 as Alchymic Journals, 2006; Mesa Verde, 1992; The Collected Stories of Evan S. Connell, 1995; Deus Lo Volt!: Chronicle of the Crusades, 2000; The Aztec Treasure House: Selected Essays, 2001; Francisco Goya, 2004; Lost in Uttar Pradesh: New and Selected Stories, 2008. EDITOR: I am a Lover, 1961; Woman by Three, 1969. Contributor of articles to periodicals. **Address:** Don Congdon Associates Inc., 156 5th Ave., Ste. 625, New York, NY 10010-7782, U.S.A.

CONNELL, George B(oyce). American (born United States), b. 1957. **Genres:** Philosophy, Ethics. **Career:** Mercer University, visiting instructor in philosophy, 1982; North Carolina State University, visiting associate professor of philosophy, 1984; North Carolina Wesleyan College, assistant professor of philosophy, 1984-86; Concordia College, assistant professor, 1986-90, associate professor of philosophy, 1990-, professor of philosophy, division chair for arts and humanities. Writer. **Publications:** To Be One Thing: Personal Unity in Kierkegaard's Thought, 1985; (ed. with C.S. Evans and contrib.) Foundations of Kierkegaard's Vision of Community: Religion, Ethics and Politics in Kierkegaard, 1992. Contributor of articles to journals and magazines. **Address:** Department of Philosophy, Concordia College, Rm. 150, Bishop Whipple Hall, 901 8th St. S, Moorhead, MN 56562, U.S.A. **Online address:** connell@cord.edu

CONNELL, John. Australian (born Australia), b. 1946?. **Genres:** Anthropology/Ethnology, Area Studies, Geography, Medicine/Health, Music. **Career:** Sydney University, associate professor of geography, professor of geography; South Pacific Commission, director. Writer and geographer. **Publications:** Rural Migration in Less Developed Countries: A Preliminary Bibliography, 1973; Evolution of Tanzanian Rural Development, 1974; (co-author) Migration from Rural Areas, 1976; (with M. Lipton) Assessing Village Labour Situations in Developing Countries, 1977; Hunting and Gathering: The Forage Economy of the Siwai of Bougainville, 1977; The End of Tradition, 1978; Taim Bilong Mani, 1978; Remittances and Rural Development, 1980; (with P. Roy) Greenhouse: The Impact of Sea Level Rise on Low Coral Islands in the South Pacific, 1989; (with R. Aldrich) France's Overseas Frontier: Départements et territoires d'outre-mer, 1992; (with J.P. Lea) Pacific 2010: Planning the Future: Melanesian Cities in 2010, 1993; (with J.P. Lea) Pacific 2010: Urbanisation in Polynesia, 1995; Papua New Guinea: The Struggle for Development, 1997; (with R. Aldrich) The Last Colonies, 1998; (wih J. Lea) Urbanisation in the Island Pacific, 2002; (with C. Gibson) Sound Tracks: Popular Music, Identity and Place, 2003; (with C. Gibson) Music and Tourism: On the Road Again, 2005; (with R.P.C. Brown) Remittances in the Pacific: An Overview, 2005; Global Health Care Chain: From the Pacific to the World, 2009; Medical Tourism, 2010; (with P. McManus) Rural Revival?: Place Marketing, Tree Change and Regional Migration in Australia, 2011. EDITOR: Local Government Councils in Bougainville, 1977; Traditional Medicine in Bougainville, 1980; (with M. Spencer and A. Ward) New Caledonia: Essays in Nationalism and Dependency, 1988; (with R. Aldrich) France in World Politics, 1989; Migration and Development in the South Pacific, 1990; (with R. Howitt) Mining and Indigenous Peoples in Australasia, 1991; (with G. McCall) World Perspective on Pacific Islander Migration: Australia, New Zealand, and the USA, 1993; (with R. King and P. White) Writing across Worlds, 1995; (with R. Howitt and P. Hirsch) Resources, Nations, and Indigenous Peoples, 1996; (with R. King) Small Worlds, Global Lives: Islands and Migration, 1999; Sydney, the Emergence of a World City, 2000; (with B. Rugendyke) Tourism at the Grassroots: Villagers and Visitors in the Asia Pacific, 2007; (with E. Waddell) Environment, Development and Change in Rural Asia-Pacific: Between Local and Global, 2007; International Migration of Health Workers, 2008; (with C. Gibson) Festival Places: Revitalising Rural Australia, 2011. Contributor to periodicals. **Address:** Division of Geography, School of Geosciences, University of Sydney, Rm. 476, Madsen Bldg. (F09), Sydney, NW 2006, Australia. **Online address:** john.connell@sydney.edu.au

CONNELLY, Donald B. American (born United States) **Genres:** Politics/Government. **Career:** U.S. Army Command and General Staff College, associate professor of joint and multinational operations; U.S. Army, intelligence officer. Writer and educator. **Publications:** John M. Schofield and the Politics of Generalship, 2006. **Address:** Command & General Staff College, 100 Stimson Ave., Fort Leavenworth, KS 66027-1352, U.S.A. **Online address:** dbconnelly@aol.com

CONNELLY, Frances S(usan). American (born United States), b. 1953?. **Genres:** Art/Art History, Social Sciences, Photography. **Career:** Ithaca College, assistant professor of art history, 1983-88; University of Missouri-Kansas City, assistant professor, 1988-94, associate professor of art history, 1994, head of department, 1995, professor of art history. Writer. **Publications:** The Sleep of Reason: Primitivism in Modern European Art and Aesthetics, 1725-1907, 1995; (ed.) Modern Art and the Grotesque, 2003; The Grotesque in Western Art and Culture: The Image at Play, 2012. Contributor to periodicals and journals. **Address:** Department of Art and Art History, University of Missouri-Kansas City, FA 215, 205C Fine Arts Bldg., 5100 Rockhill Rd., Kansas City, MO 64110, U.S.A. **Online address:** connellyf@umkc.edu

CONNELLY, Joan Breton. American (born United States), b. 1954. **Genres:** History, Women's Studies And Issues, Theology/Religion. **Career:** Bryn Mawr College, Undergraduate College, assistant dean and lecturer in classical archaeology, 1982-84; New York University, assistant professor of art history, 1986-92, associate professor of art history, 1992-2007, professor of art history, 2007-09, Institute of Fine Arts, institute lecturer for the conservation center, 1993-, Yeronisos Island Excavations, director, Lillian Vernon chair for teaching excellence, 2002-04, Department of Classics, professor of classics, 2007-. Writer. **Publications:** Votive Sculpture of Hellenistic Cyprus, 1988; Portrait of a Priestess: Women and Ritual in Ancient Greece, 2007. Contributor to books and journals. **Address:** Department of Classics, New York University, Rm. 503 Silver Center, 100 Washington Sq. E, New York, NY 10003, U.S.A. **Online address:** joan.connelly@nyu.edu

CONNELLY, Joe. American (born United States), b. 1963?. **Genres:** Novels, Young Adult Non-fiction, Young Adult Fiction, Literary Criticism And History. **Career:** Emergency medical technician and paramedic, 1986-96. Writer. **Publications:** (With J. Tiner and J.M. Conneely) Accounting for Treasury Products, 1996; Bringing Out the Dead, 1998; Crumbtown, 2003. **Address:** Alfred A. Knopf Inc., 201 E 50th St., New York, NY 10022-7703, U.S.A.

CONNELLY, Karen. Canadian (born Canada), b. 1969. **Genres:** Poetry, Travel/Exploration, Autobiography/Memoirs, Biography. **Career:** University of New Brunswick, writer-in-residence 1994-; York University, instructor of creative writing, 2008. Writer. **Publications:** The Small Words in My Body (poetry), 1990; Touch the Dragon: A Thai Journal, 1992; This Brighter Prison: A Book of Journeys, 1993; One Room in a Castle, 1995; The Disorder of Love, 1997; Dawn without Breaking, 1999; The Border Surrounds Us, 2000; Dream of a Thousand Lives: A Sojourn in Thailand, 2001; Grace and Poison, 2001; The Lizard Cage, 2005; Burmese Lessons: a True Love Story, 2010. FORTHCOMING: Group Portrait by Starlight. Works appear in anthologies. **Address:** c/o Westwood Creative Artists, 94 Harbord St., Toronto, ON M5S 1G6, Canada.

CONNELLY, Matthew. (Matthew James Connelly). American (born United States), b. 1967. **Genres:** History, Military/Defense/Arms Control. **Career:** University of Michigan, assistant professor, 1997-2001; Columbia University, associate professor of history, 2000-, Columbia University and London School of Economics M.A. Program in International and World History, director. Writer. **Publications:** A Diplomatic Revolution: Algeria's Fight for Independence and the Origins of the Post-Cold War Era, 2002; Fatal Misconception: The Struggle to Control World Population, 2008 . Contributor to journals and periodicals. **Address:** Department of History, Columbia University, 611 Fayerweather Hall, PO Box 2527, New York, NY 10027, U.S.A. **Online address:** mjc96@Columbia.edu

CONNELLY, Matthew James. *See* **CONNELLY, Matthew.**

CONNELLY, Michael. American (born United States), b. 1956. **Genres:** Novels, Novellas/Short Stories, Young Adult Non-fiction. **Career:** Mystery Writers of America, president, 2003-04. Writer, reporter and novelist. **Publications:** SHORT STORIES: Murderer's Row, 2001; The Best American Mystery Stories 2002, 2002; Measures of Poison, 2003; Men From Boys, 2003; Murder and All That Jazz, 2004; Dangerous Women, 2005; The Secret Society Of Demolition Writers, 2005; Plots With Guns, 2005; Hollywood and Crime, 2007; Los Angeles Noir, 2007; Dead Man's Hand, 2007; The Blue Religion, 2008, 1st ed., 2009; (ed.) Shadow of the Master, 2009. FICTION: NON-FICTION: Crime Beat: A Decade Of Covering Cops And Killers, 2006. NOVELS: The Black Echo, 1992; The Black Ice, 1993; The Concrete Blonde, 1994; The Last Coyote, 1995; The Poet, 1996; Trunk Music, 1997; Blood Work, 1998; Angels Flight, 1999; Void Moon, 2000, 1st ed., 2004; A Darkness More Than Night, 2001; City Of Bones, 2002; Chasing The Dime, 2002; Lost Light, 2003; The Narrows, 2004; The Closers, 2005; (ed. and intro.) Murder in Vegas, 2005; The Lincoln Lawyer, 2005; Echo Park, 2006; The Overlook, 2007; Suitcase City, 2008; Brass Verdict: A Novel, 2008; Scarecrow: A Novel, 2009; Nine Dragons: A Novel, 2009; Harry Bosch Novels 3: A Darkness More Than Night, City of Bones, Lost Light, 2010; The Reversal, 2010; The Fifth Witness, 2011. OTHERS: (foreword) Star, 2002; Drop, 2011; The Black Box, 2012. **Address:** Philip G. Spitzer Literary Agency, 50 Talmage Farm Ln., East Hampton, NY 11937, U.S.A. **Online address:** janed@michaelconnelly.com

CONNER, Patrick (Roy Mountifort). British (born England), b. 1947. **Genres:** Art/Art History, Social Sciences. **Career:** Teacher, 1969-70; The Royal Pavilion, Art Gallery and Museums, staff, 1975-86; Bucknell University, adjunct professor, 1978-; Martyn Gregory Gallary, director, 1986-. Writer. **Publications:** Savage Ruskin, 1979; Oriental Architecture in the West, 1979; People at Home, 1982; People at Work, 1982; (ed.) The Inspiration of Egypt, 1983; Michael Angelo Rooker 1746-1801, 1984; The China Trade, 1986; Hilda May Gordon: A Colourist Abroad, 1987; George Chinnery (1774-1852): The Artist of India and the China Coast, 1993; (contrib.) Hai Mao Liu Zhen, 2003; (contrib.) Dong Fang Yin Xiang, 2005; Hongs of Canton: Western Merchants in South China 1700-1900 as Seen in Chinese Export Paintings, 2009. **Address:** Martyn Gregory Gallery, 34 Bury St., St. James's, London, GL SW1Y 6AU, England. **Online address:** mgregory@dircon.co.uk

CONNERLY, Charles E. American (born United States), b. 1946?. **Genres:**

Civil Liberties/Human Rights, Sociology. **Career:** University of Michigan, Population Studies Center, research associate, 1976-78, Institute for Social Research, research investigator, 1978-79; U.S. Department of Housing and Urban Development, social science research analyst, 1979-81; Florida State University, assistant professor, 1981-87, associate professor, 1987-97, professor, 1997-2003, Department of Urban and Regional Planning, chair, 1998-, William G. and Budd Bell professor 2003-. Writer and educator. **Publications:** The Most Segregated City in America: City Planning and Civil Rights in Birmingham, 1920-1980, 2005; (ed. with T.S. Chapin and H.T. Higgins) Growth Management in Florida: Planning for Paradise, 2007. Contributor to books and periodicals. **Address:** Department of Urban & Regional Planning, Florida State University, Tallahassee, FL 32306-2280, U.S.A. **Online address:** cconnerl@fsu.edu

CONNERS, Peter. American (born United States), b. 1970. **Genres:** Autobiography/Memoirs. **Career:** Double Room (online journal) founder and co-editor; BOA Editions, fiction editor and marketing director. **Publications:** (Ed.) PP/FF: An Anthology, 2006; (ed.) Of Whiskey and Winter, 2007; (ed.) Emily Ate the Wind, 2008; Growing Up Dead: The Hallucinated Confessions of a Teenage Deadhead, 2009. Contributor of to journals. **Address:** Rochester, NY , U.S.A. **Online address:** phconners@hotmail.com

CONNOLLY, Harry J. American (born United States), b. 1952. **Genres:** Novels. **Career:** Writer. **Publications:** Child of Fire: A Twenty Palaces Novel, 2009; Game of Cages: A Twenty Palaces Novel, 2010. **Address:** Seattle, WA , U.S.A. **Online address:** harryconnolly@sff.net

CONNOLLY, John. Irish (born Ireland), b. 1968. **Genres:** Mystery/Crime/Suspense. **Career:** The Irish Times newspaper, freelance journalist. **Publications:** Every Dead Thing, 1999; Dark Hollow, 2001; The Killing Kind, 2001; The White Road, 2002; Bad Men: A Thriller, 2004; Nocturnes, 2005; Black Angel, 2005; Underbury Witches, 2006; The Book of Lost Things, 2007; Cailleacha Underbury, 2007; The Unquiet, 2007; The Reapers, 2008; The Lovers, 2009; The Gates: A Novel, 2009; Whisperers, 2010; The Burning Soul, 2011; Hell's Bells, 2011; Infernals, 2011; The Wrath of Angels, 2012. Contributor to periodicals. **Address:** c/o Author Mail, Hodder & Stoughton, 338 Euston Rd., London, GL NW1 3BH, England.

CONNOLLY, Joseph. British (born England), b. 1950. **Genres:** Novels, Bibliography, Design, Humor/Satire, Writing/Journalism, Bibliography, Humor/Satire. **Career:** Freelance writer, 1970-; Flask Bookshop, owner and manager, 1974-89. **Publications:** NON FICTION: Collecting Modern First Editions, 1977; P.G. Wodehouse: An Illustrated Biography, with Complete Bibliography and Collector's Guide, 1979, rev. ed., 1987; Jerome K. Jerome: A Critical Biography, 1982; Modern First Editions: Their Value to Collectors, 1984, 4th ed., 1993; The Penguin Book Quiz Book, 1985; Children's Modern First Editions: Their Value to Collectors, 1988; Beside the Seaside, 1999; All Shook Up: A Flash of the Fifties, 2000; Christmas and How to Survive It: Laughter Matters, 2003; Faber And Faber: Eighty Years Of Book Cover Design, 2009. NOVELS: Poor Souls, 1995; This Is It, 1996; Stuff, 1997; Summer Things, 1998; Winter Breaks, 1999; It Can't Go On, 2000; S.O.S., 2001; The Works, 2003; Love Is Strange, 2005; Jack The Lad And Bloody Mary, 2007; England's Lane, 2012. Contributor to periodicals. **Address:** c/o Jonathan Lloyd, Curtis Brown Group Ltd., Haymarket House, 28-29 Haymarket, London, GL SW1Y 4SP, England.

CONNOLLY, Kevin Michael. American (born United States), b. 1985. **Genres:** Autobiography/Memoirs. **Career:** Writer and photographer. **Publications:** Double Take: A Memoir, 2009. **Address:** c/o Erica Langston, 1880 Century Pk. E, Ste. 711, Los Angeles, CA 90067, U.S.A. **Online address:** connollyphotography@gmail.com

CONNOLLY, Peter. British (born England), b. 1935. **Genres:** History, Theology/Religion. **Career:** Writer and illustrator, 1974-; University College of London, Institute of Archaeology, honorary research fellow, 1985-. **Publications:** SELF-ILLUSTRATED: The Roman Army, 1976; The Greek Armies, 1977; Hannibal and the Enemies of Rome, 1978; Pompeii, 1979; Living in the Time of Jesus of Nazareth, 1983; A History of the Jewish People in the Time of Jesus: From Herod the Great to Masada, 1987; Tiberius Claudius Maximus, vol. II, 1988; The Roman Fort, 1991; Greek Legends, 1993. OTHERS: Greece and Rome at War, 1981; The Legend of Odysseus, 1986; (with H. Dodge) The Ancient City: Life in Classical Athens and Rome, 1998; Holy Land, 1998; The Ancient Greece of Odysseus, 1998; Ancient Greece, 2001; Ancient Rome, 2001. **Address:** Institute of Archaeology, University College of London, 31-34 Gordon Sq., London, GL WC1H 0PY, England.

CONNOLLY, Ray. British (born England), b. 1940. **Genres:** Novels, Plays/Screenplays, Biography, Young Adult Fiction. **Career:** Evening Standard, journalist, 1967-73; freelance writer, 1974-. **Publications:** A Girl Who Came to Stay, 1973; That'll Be the Day, 1973; Trick or Treat?, 1975; James Dean: The First American Teenager, 1975; Newsdeath, 1978; Sunday Kind of Woman, 1980; Honky Tonk Heroes, 1980; John Lennon, 1940-1980, 1981; The Sun Place, 1982; Stardust Memories: Talking About My Generation, 1983; Forever Young, 1984; Lytton's Diary, 1985-86; Defrosting the Fridge, 1989; Perfect Scoundrels, 1990; Sunday Morning, 1992; Shadows on a Wall, 1995; (ed.) In the Sixties, 1995; High Southern California, 1998; Love Out of Season, 2007. **Address:** United Agents, 12-26 Lexington St., London, GL W1F OLE, England. **Online address:** mail@rayconnolly.co.uk

CONNOLLY, S(ean) J. Irish (born Ireland), b. 1951. **Genres:** History. **Career:** Public Record Office of Ireland, archivist, 1977-80; St. Patrick's College, lecturer in history, 1980-81; University of Ulster, lecturer, 1981-89, reader in history, 1989-96; Queen's University of Belfast, professor of Irish history, 1996-, History Research Cluster, director of research; Irish Economic and Social History, editor, 1983-89, 2004-. **Publications:** (Comp.) Rebellion of 1798: Facsimile Document, 1979; (comp.) Public Record: Sources for Local Studies in the Public Record Office of Ireland, 1982; Priests and People in Pre-Famine Ireland, 1780-1845, 1982; Religion and Society in Nineteenth-Century Ireland, 1985; Religion, Law and Power: The Making of Protestant Ireland, 1660-1760, 1992; (ed. with R.A. Houston and R.J. Morris.) Conflict, Identity and Economic Development: Ireland and Scotland, 1600-1939, 1995; (ed.) The Oxford Companion to Irish History, 1998, 2nd ed., 2011; (ed.) Kingdoms United?: Great Britain and Ireland since 1500: Integration and Diversity, 1999; (ed.) Political Ideas in Eighteenth-Century Ireland, 2000; Refiguring Ireland: Essays in Honour of L.M. Cullen, 2003; (contrib.) Irish Economic and Social History, 2004; Contested Island: Ireland, 1460-1630, 2007; Divided Kingdom: Ireland, 1630-1800, 2008. **Address:** School of History and Anthropology, Queen's University, Rm. 17UQ.205, 15 University Sq., Belfast, AT BT7 1NN, Northern Ireland. **Online address:** s.connolly@qub.ac.uk

CONNOLLY, William E(ugene). American (born United States), b. 1938. **Genres:** Politics/Government. **Career:** Ohio University, assistant professor of political science, 1965-68; University of Massachusetts, assistant professor, professor, 1968-85; University of Michigan, assistant professor, 1968-71, associate professor, 1971-74, professor, 1974-85; Amherst College, visiting associate professor, 1972; Political Theory, editor, 1984-90; Johns Hopkins University, professor, 1985-, chair of political science department, 1996-2003, Krieger Eisenhower professor of political science, 2003-. **Publications:** Political Science and Ideology, 1967; (comp. with G. Gordon) Social Structure and Political Theory, 1974; The Terms of Political Discourse, 1974, 3rd ed., 1993; (with M.H. Best) The Politicized Economy, 1976, 2nd ed. 1982; Appearance and Reality in Politics, 1981; Politics and Ambiguity, 1987; Political Theory and Modernity, 1988; Identity, Difference: Democratic Negotiations of Political Paradox, 1991; The Augustine Imperative: A Reflection on the Politics of Morality, 1993; The Augustinian imperative: A Reflection on the Politics of Morality, 1993; The Ethos of Pluralization, 1995; Why I Am Not a Secularist, 1999; Neuropolitics: Thinking, Culture, Speed, 2002; Pluralism, 2005; Political Science and Ideology, 2006; William E. Connolly: Democracy, Pluralism and Political Theory, 2007; Capitalism and Christianity, American Style, 2008; World of Becoming, 2010. EDITOR: The Bias of Pluralism, 1969; Legitimacy and the State, 1984; (with A. Botwinick) Democracy and Vision: Sheldon Wolin and the Vicissitudes of the Political, 2001; Pluralism in Political Analysis, 2010. Contributor to journals. **Address:** Department of Political Science, Johns Hopkins University, 338 Mergenthaler Hall, 3400 N Charles St., Baltimore, MD 21218, U.S.A. **Online address:** pluma@jhu.edu

CONNOR, Carolyn L. American (born United States), b. 1943. **Genres:** Art/Art History, Young Adult Non-fiction, Theology/Religion. **Career:** University of North Carolina, Department of Classics, professor of Byzantine studies. Historian and writer. **Publications:** Art and Miracles in Medieval Byzantium: The Crypt at Hosios Loukas and Its Frescoes, 1991; (with W.R. Connor) The Life and Miracles of Saint Luke of Steiris: Text, Translation and Commentary, 1994; The Color of Ivory: Polychromy on Byzantine Ivories, 1998; Women of Byzantium, 2004. **Address:** Department of Classics, University of North Carolina, 212 Murphey Hall, CB 3145, Chapel Hill, NC 27599-3145, U.S.A. **Online address:** clconnor@email.unc.edu

CONNOR, Daniel. (Daniel F. Connor). American (born United States), b. 1953. **Genres:** Psychiatry, Medicine/Health. **Career:** Tufts University, New England Medical Center Hospitals, fellow in child psychiatry, 1985-87; University of Massachusetts, Medical School, assistant professor, 1987-97, associate professor of psychiatry, 1997-, Pediatric Psychopharmacology Clinic, founder and director, 1987-89, 1990-, director of pediatric psychopharmacology, 1994-, director of ambulatory child and adolescent psychiatry and co-director of research in child and adolescent psychiatry, 2002-; Westboro State Hospital, Acute Adolescent Unit, medical director, 1987-89; Wing Memorial Hospital, consulting psychiatrist, 1989-90; Devereux Foundation, consulting psychiatrist, 1990-2003; Worcester Youth Guidance Center, consulting psychiatrist, 1989-97; University of Connecticut, School of Medicine, Department of Psychiatry, professor, Lockean distinguished professor of psychiatry, 2005-, Lockean distinguished chair in mental health education, research, and clinical improvement, Health Center, division chief of child and adolescent psychiatry. Writer. **Publications:** AS DANIEL F. CONNOR: Aggression and Antisocial Behavior in Children and Adolescents: Research and Treatment, 2002; Pediatric Psychopharmacology: Fast Facts, 2006. Contributor to books and journals. **Address:** Department of Psychiatry, University of Connecticut, MC1410, 263 Farmington Ave., Farmington, CT 06030-1410, U.S.A. **Online address:** connor@psychiatry.uchc.edu

CONNOR, Daniel F. *See* **CONNOR, Daniel.**

CONNOR, Joan. American (born United States), b. 1954. **Genres:** Novellas/Short Stories, Novels. **Career:** Vermont Department of Public Health, representative of Women's Health Outreach Program, 1977-79; Mount Hermon School, English teacher, 1980-81; Vermont League of Writers, leader of fiction writing workshop, 1994-95; Ohio University, fiction writing, visiting assistant professor, 1995-96, assistant professor of English, 1996-2001, associate professor of English, 2001-05, professor of English, 2005-, director of creative writing, 2003-08. Writer. **Publications:** Here on Old Route 7, 1997; We Who Live Apart, 2000; History Lessons, 2003; The World Before Mirrors, 2006; How to Stop Loving Someone, 2011. Works appear in anthologies. Contributor of articles to magazines. **Address:** Department of English, Ohio University, 328 Carroll Rd., Athens, OH 45701, U.S.A. **Online address:** connor@ohio.edu

CONNOR, Patrick E. American (born United States), b. 1941. **Genres:** Business/Trade/Industry. **Career:** Boeing Co., scientific programmer, 1962-63; Control Data Corp., checkout engineer, 1964; General Dynamics Corp., Convair Division, engineering administrator, 1965-67; University of Washington, instructor in organization theory, 1968-70; Oregon State University, assistant professor, 1971-74, associate professor, 1974-80, professor of management, 1980-81; Willamette University, professor of organizational analysis, 1982-2006, emeritus professor of organizational analysis, 2007-; State Farm Insurance Companies, executive consultant, 1984-2004; University of British Columbia, visiting professor, 1990-91. Writer. **Publications:** Dimensions in Modern Management, 1974, 3rd ed. as Dimensions in Management, 1982; (with T. Haimann and W.G. Scott) Management, 5th ed., 1985; Organizations: Theory and Design, 1980; Organization Structure and Design, 1984; (with L.K. Lake and R.W. Stackman) Managing Organizational Change, 1988, 3rd ed., 2003; (with P. Cherry and K. Earner-Sparks) Questions that Get Results: Innovative Ideas Managers Can use to Improve Their Teams Performance, 2011. Contributor to books and periodicals. **Address:** Atkinson Graduate School of Management, Willamette University, 900 State St., Salem, OR 97301, U.S.A. **Online address:** pconnor@willamette.edu

CONNOR, Steven. British (born England), b. 1955. **Genres:** Literary Criticism And History, History. **Career:** University of London, Birkbeck College, lecturer, 1980-, professor of modern literature and theory, London Consortium, Graduate Programme in Humanities and Cultural Studies, director, 2002. Writer. **Publications:** Charles Dickens, 1985; Samuel Beckett: Repetition, Theory, and Text, 1988; Postmodernist Culture: An Introduction to Theories of the Contemporary, 1989, 2nd ed., 1997; Waiting for Godot and Endgame-Samuel Beckett, 1992; Theory and Cultural Value, 1992; The English Novel in History, 1950 to the Present, 1995; James Joyce, 1996; Dumbstruck: A Cultural History of Ventriloquism, 2000; The Cambridge Companion to Postmodernism, 2004; The Book of Skin, 2004; Fly, 2006; The Matter of Air, 2010; (ed.) Samuel Beckett: The Unnamable, 2010; Paraphernalia, 2011. **Address:** Department of English and Humanities, Birkbeck College, University of London, 43-46 Gordon Sq., Malet St., London, GL WC1E 7HX, England. **Online address:** s.connor@bbk.ac.uk

CONNOR, Tony. American/British (born England), b. 1930. **Genres:** Plays/Screenplays, Poetry, Translations. **Career:** Textile designer, 1944-60; Bolton Technical College, Liberal Studies, lecturer, 1961-64; Amherst College, visiting poet, 1965-68; Wesleyan University, visiting poet and lecturer, 1968-69, professor of English, 1971-99, professor emeritus of English, 1999-. Writer. **Publications:** POETRY: With Love Somehow: Poems, 1962; (with A. Clarke and C. Tomlinson) Poems: A Selection, 1964; Lodgers: Poems, 1965; 12 Secret Poems, 1965; Kon in Springtime: Poems, 1968; In the Happy Valley: Poems, 1971; The Memoirs of Uncle Harry, 1974; Seven Last Poems from the Memoirs of Uncle Harry, 1974; City of Strangers, 1975; New and Selected Poems, 1982; Metamorphic Adventures (poems), 1996. OTHER: (trans. with G. Gomori) Love of the Scorching Wind, 1973; To a Friend, Who Asked for a Poem, 1975; Twelve Villanelles, 1977; Spirits of the Place, 1986; Things Unsaid: Selected Poems 1960-2005, 2006. **Address:** Department of English, Wesleyan University, 294 High St., Middletown, CT 06459, U.S.A. **Online address:** jconnor@wesleyan.edu

CONNOR, William S. D. *See* **CONNOR, William S. P.**

CONNOR, William S. P. (William S. D. Connor). American (born United States), b. 1958. **Genres:** Essays, Romance/Historical. **Career:** WCSH-TV, reporter and news anchor, 1986-94; Hearst Television, White House correspondent, 1994-97; Evergreen Media Counselors, senior consultant, 1997-. Writer. **Publications:** (With C. Hacinli) Romantic Days and Nights in Washington, D.C.: Intimate Escapes in the Capital, 1998, 2nd ed., 2000. **Address:** Evergreen Media Counselors, 2000 L St. NW, Ste. 300, Washington, DC 20036, U.S.A. **Online address:** bconnor@mediatrainer.com

CONNORS, Bruton. British/Welsh (born Wales), b. 1931. **Genres:** Novels, Novellas/Short Stories, Poetry, Theology/Religion. **Career:** Ministry of Supply, machine gun inspector, 1954-56; Ladysmith Junior Senior High School, teacher, 1956-57; St. Bonaventure's School, art teacher and head of the art department, 1958-73; Ilford County High School for Boys, art teacher, 1973-82. Writer. **Publications:** Nightpriest, 1965; Bruised Concourse, 1973; Old Drunk Eyes Haiku, 1974; Scorpio Broadside 15, 1975; Poems/Poemas, 1976; 109 Haiku and One Seppuku for Maria, 1987; Sonnets for Maria Marriage, 1988; Sonnets: Second Sequence for Maria, 1989. Works appear in anthologies. Contributor to magazines. **Address:** 57 Kinfauns Rd., Goodmayes, Ilford, EX IG3 9QH, England.

CONOVER, Roger L(loyd). American (born United States), b. 1950. **Genres:** Poetry, Literary Criticism And History, Biography. **Career:** University of Minnesota, writing instructor, 1976; MIT Press, acquisition editor in art, writer, architecture, photography and design, 1977-93, senior editor, executive editor, curator; Jargon Society, director, 1984-89; Maine Crafts Association, director, 1988-. **Publications:** (Ed. and intro.) The Last Lunar Baedeker (poetry), 1982, new ed., 1996; Insel (novel), 1991; Arthur Cravan: Poète et Boxeur, 1992; Four Dada Suicides (criticism), 1995; Boxes: An Anthology of Writings on Boxing and Visual Culture (criticism), 1996; (with E. Cufer and P. Weibel) Call Me Istanbul ist mein Name: Kunst und urbane Visionen einer Metapolis, 2004. Contributor to periodicals. **Address:** The MIT Press, 55 Hayward St., Cambridge, MA 02142-1493, U.S.A. **Online address:** conover@mit.edu

CONQUEST, (George) Robert (Acworth). Also writes as Ted Pauker, Victor Gray, J. E. M. Arden. American/British (born England), b. 1917. **Genres:** Science Fiction/Fantasy, Poetry, History, International Relations/Current Affairs, Literary Criticism And History, Novels. **Career:** H.M. Foreign Service, secretary, 1946-56; London School of Economics and Political Science, Sydney and Beatrice Webb research fellow, 1956-58; University of Buffalo (now State University of New York), visiting poet and lecturer in English, 1959-60; The Spectator, literary editor, 1962-63; Columbia University, Russian Institute, senior fellow, 1964-65; Smithsonian Institution, Woodrow Wilson International Center for Scholars, fellow, 1976-77; Stanford University, Hoover Institution, research fellow, 1977-79, senior research fellow, 1981-; Harvard University, Ukrainian Research Institute, research associate, 1983-; Center for Strategic and International Studies, adjunct fellow. **Publications:** A World of Difference (novel), 1955; Poems, 1955; (as J.E.M. Arden) Where Do Marxists go from Here?, 1958; Common Sense About Russia, 1960; Soviet Deportation of Nationalities, 1960; Power and Politics in the U.S.S.R., 1960; Courage of Genius: The Pasternak Affair, 1961; Power and Policy in the U.S.S.R., 1961; Between Mars and Venus (poetry), 1962; Marxism To-Day, 1964; (with K. Amis) The Egyptologists (novel), 1965; Russia after

Khrushchev, 1965; The Great Terror, 1968; Religion in the U.S.S.R., 1968; Soviet Political System, 1968; Arias from a Love Opera (poetry), 1969; Where Marx Went Wrong, 1970; The Nation Killers: The Soviet Deportation of Nationalities, 1970; Lenin, 1970; V.I. Lenin, 1972; (co-author) Defending America, 1977; Kolyma: The Arctic Death Camps, 1978; Forays (poetry), 1979; Present Danger: Towards a Foreign Policy, 1979; The Abomination of Moab, 1979; We & They, 1980; (with J.M. White) What to Do When the Russians Come: A Survivor's Guide, 1984; (co-author) Man-Made Famine in Ukraine, 1984; Inside Stalin's Secret Police: NKVD Politics, 1936-1939, 1985; The Harvest of Sorrow: Soviet Collectivization and the Terror-Famine, 1986; New and Collected Poems, 1986; Stalin and the Kirov Murder, 1989; Tyrants and Typewriters: Communiqués from the Struggle for Truth, 1989; The Great Terror: A Reassessment, 1990; Stalin: Breaker of Nations, 1991; Zhnyva skorboty: Radianska kolektyvizatsiiai holodomor, 1993; History, Humanity, and Truth, 1993; Demons Don't (poetry), 1999; Reflections on a Ravaged Century, 1999; Dragons of Expectation: Reality and Delusion in the Course of History, 2005; Penultimata, 2009. EDITOR: New Lines, 1956; Back to Life, 1958; (with K. Amis) Spectrum: A Science Fiction Anthology, 5 vols., 1962-66; Politics of Ideas in the U.S.S.R., 1967; Industrial Workers in the U.S.S.R., 1967; Soviet Nationalities Policy in Practice, 1967; Justice and the Legal System in the U.S.S.R., 1968; Soviet Police System, 1968; Soviet Studies Series, 7 vols., 1968; Agricultural Workers in the U.S.S.R., 1968; (and intro.) Russian Tradition, 1974; The Last Empire: Nationality and the Soviet Future, 1986; (with D.J. Djordjevich) Political and Ideological Confrontations in Twentieth-Century Europe: Essays in Honor of Milorad M. Drachkovitch, 1996. **Address:** Hoover Institution, Stanford University, 434 Galvez Mall, Stanford, CA 94305-6010, U.S.A.

CONQUEST, Ned. American (born United States), b. 1931. **Genres:** Novels, Plays/Screenplays, Songs/Lyrics And Libretti, Poetry, Literary Criticism And History. **Career:** Milbank, Tweed, Hadley & McCloy, associate, 1960-64; Georgetown University, assistant professor of English literature, 1967-73. Writer. **Publications:** The Gun and Glory of Granite Hendley, 1969; Achilles and Company, 1988; Virginia, the Gray and the Green, 1990; The Way of the Eagle, 1994; The Widow's Might: Three Plays, 1997; Lays and Legends of Virginia and Otherwhere: Poems, 2004. Contributor to periodicals. **Address:** 1547 33rd St. NW, Washington, DC 20007-2750, U.S.A.

CONRAD, Christine. American (born United States), b. 1946?. **Genres:** Women's Studies And Issues, Biography, Novels. **Career:** New York City, film, television and theater office, commissioner, 1970-74; Bantam Books, editor, 1974-82; Warner Books, editor, 1974-82, screenwriter, 1982-; Natural Woman Institute, founder, 1997. Speaker. **Publications:** (With M. Laux) Natural Woman, Natural Menopause, 1997; Jerome Robbins: That Broadway Man, That Ballet Man (biography), 2000; A Woman's Guide to Natural Hormones, 2000; Mademoiselle Benoir, 2006. **Address:** c/o Taryn Roeder, Houghton Mifflin Co., 222 Berkeley St., Boston, MA 02116, U.S.A. **Online address:** chriscoprd@aol.com

CONRAD, James H. American (born United States), b. 1940?. **Genres:** Social Sciences, Bibliography. **Career:** East Texas State University (now Texas A&M University), lecturer in history, 1967-70, 1972-74, James G. Gee Library, university archivist, 1976-; Hunt County Historical Commission, chairman, 1987-89; TOHA, vice president, 1996-97, president, 1997-98. Writer. **Publications:** Texas Educational History: A Bibliography, 1979; Reference Sources in Social Work: An Annotated Bibliography, 1982; (ed. with T. Sitton) Every Sun That Rises: Wyatt Moore of Caddo Lake, Including Building the Last Caddo Bateau, 1985; (ed. with O.C. Spencer) John Black's Pictorial History: Honey Grove, Texas, 1880-1925, 1988; Developing Local History Programs in Community Libraries, 1989; (as Jim Conrad) Blacklands: Historical Sketches of Hunt County, Texas, 1992; (with T. Sitton) Nameless Towns: Texas Sawmill Communities, 1880-1942, 1998; (with T. Sitton) Freedom Colonies: Independent Black Texans in the Time of Jim Crow, 2005. Contributor to periodicals. **Address:** Texas A&M University-Commerce, PO Box 3011, Commerce, TX 75429, U.S.A. **Online address:** james_conrad@tamu-commerce.edu

CONRAD, Jean. *See* **MARTINEZ, Nancy C.**

CONRAD, Jessamyn. American (born United States), b. 1978?. **Genres:** Politics/Government, Social Sciences. **Career:** Writer. **Publications:** What You Should Know about Politics...But Don't: A Nonpartisan Guide to the Issues, 2008. **Address:** New York, NY , U.S.A. **Online address:** questions@jessamynconrad.com

CONRAD, Margaret R. Canadian (born Canada), b. 1946. **Genres:** History. **Career:** Clarke, Irwin Publishing Co., editor, 1968-69; Acadia University, faculty, 1969-87, professor of history, 1987-2002, department head, 1992-95; Dalhousie University, adjunct professor, 1992-2002; Mount Saint Vincent University, Nancy Rowell Jackman chair of women's studies, 1996-98; University of New Brunswick, Atlantic Canada Studies, research chair, 2002-09, professor emeritus, 2010-. **Publications:** (With J. Ricker) Twentieth-Century Canada, 1974; George Nowlan: Maritime Conservative in National Politics, 1986; (with T. Laidlaw and D. Smyth) No Place Like Home: The Diaries and Letters of Nova Scotia Women, 1771-1938, 1988; (co-author) History of the Canadian Peoples, 2 vols., 1993, 6th ed., 2009; (with J. Hiller) Atlantic Canada, 2001; Canada: A National History, 2nd ed., 2006; (with J. Hiller) Atlantic Canada: A History, 2010; History of Nova Scotia, forthcoming. EDITOR: They Planted Well: New England Planters in Maritime Canada, 1988; Making Adjustments: Change and Continuity in Planter Nova Scotia, 1759-1800, 1991; (contrib.) New England Planters in Maritime Canada, 1759-1800: Bibliography of Sources, 1993; Intimate Relations: Family and Community in Planter Nova Scotia, 1759-1800, 1995; Saturday's Child: The Memoirs of Ellen Louks Fairclough, 1995; Looking into Acadie: 3 Illustrated Lectures, 1999; (and contrib.) Active Engagements: A Collection of Lectures by the Holders of Nancy's Chair in Women's Studies, 1986-1998, 2001; (with B. Moody) Planter Links: Culture and Community in Colonial Nova Scotia, 2001. Contributor of articles to books and journals. **Address:** Department of History, University of New Brunswick, 120 Tilley Hall, 9 Macaulay Ln., Fredericton, NB E3B 5A3, Canada. **Online address:** mconrad@unb.ca

CONRAD, Peter. British/Australian (born Australia), b. 1948. **Genres:** Novels. **Career:** All Souls College, fellow, 1970-73; Christ Church, tutor in English literature, 1973-; Princeton University, visiting professor; Williams College, visiting professor; Observer, reviewer and feature writer. **Publications:** The Victorian Treasure- House, 1973; Romantic Opera and Literary Form, 1977; Shandyism: The Character of Romantic Irony, 1978; Imagining America, 1980; Television, the Medium and Its Manners, 1982; The Art of the City: Views and Versions of New York, 1984; The Everyman History of English Literature, 1985; The History of English Literature: One Indivisible, Unending Book, 1987, rev. ed. as Cassell's History of English Literature, 2003; A Song of Love and Death: The Meaning of Opera, 1987; Down Home: Revisiting Tasmania, 1988 in US as Behind the Mountain: Return to Tasmania, 1990; Where I Fell to Earth: A Life in Four Cities, 1990 in UK as Where I Fell to Earth: A Life in Four Places, 1990; Underworld (novel), 1992; To Be Continued: Four Stories and Their Survival, 1995; A Song of Love and Death: The Meaning of Opera, 1996; Modern Times, Modern Places, 1999; The Hitchcock Murders, 2002; Orson Welles: The Stories of His Life, 2003; At Home in Australia, 2003; Tales of Two Hemispheres, 2004; Creation: Artists, Gods and Origins, 2007. Contributor to periodicals. **Address:** Christ Church, Oxford, OX OX1 1DP, England.

CONRAD, Peter. American (born United States), b. 1945. **Genres:** Sociology, Psychology, Medicine/Health, Social Sciences. **Career:** Drake University, assistant professor of sociology, 1975-78; Brandeis University, Department of Sociology, professor of sociology, 1979-93, Harry Coplan professor of social sciences, 1993-; McMaster University, Hooker distinguished visiting professor, 1992. Writer. **Publications:** Identifying Hyperactive Children, 1976; (with J.W. Schneider) Deviance and Medicalization: From Badness to Sickness, 1980; (ed. with R. Kern) The Sociology of Health and Illness: Critical Perspectives, 1981, 7th ed., 2005; (with J.W. Schneider) Having Epilepsy, 1983; (co-author) Einwanderer: Zur Geschichte und Biologie eingeschleppter undeingewanderter Arten in Rheinland-Pfalz: Symposium am 20 Februar 1988, 1988; (ed. with E.B. Gallagher) Health and Health Care in Developing Countries, 1993; (ed. with J. Gabe) Sociological Perspectives on the New Genetics, 1999; (co-ed.) Handbook of Medical Sociology, 2000; (ed. with V. Leiter) Health and Health Care as Social Problems, 2003; Medicalization of Society: On the Transformation of Human Conditions into Treatable Disorders, 2007. **Address:** Department of Sociology, Brandeis University, 102 Pearlman Bldg., 415 South St., PO Box 071, Waltham, MA 02453, U.S.A. **Online address:** conrad@brandeis.edu

CONRADI, Peter J(ohn). British (born England), b. 1945. **Genres:** Literary Criticism And History, Theology/Religion. **Career:** University of Colorado, visiting professor of English, 1978-80; University of East Anglia, visiting lecturer, 1981; Kingston University, professor of English, 1981-97, professor emeritus, 1997-, writer-in-residence; Jagiellonian University, British Council professor in English, 1990-92; University College London, honorary research fellow, 1998-; Magdalen College, visiting fellow, 1999. Writer. **Publications:** John Fowles, 1982; Iris Murdoch: The Saint and the Artist, 1986; Fyodor Dostoevsky, 1988; Angus Wilson, 1997; Existentialists and Mystics: Writings on Philosophy and Literature, 1998; Iris Murdoch: A Life, 2001; Going Buddhist: Panic and Emptiness, the Buddha and Me, 2005; At the Bright Hem of God, 2009; (ed. and intro.) Iris Murdoch, Writer at War: The Letters and Diaries of Iris Murdoch: 1939-1945, 2009; A Writer at War: Letters & Diaries, 1938-46, 2010. Contributor to periodicals. **Address:** Kingston University, Rm. 105, Town House, Penrhyn Rd., Kingston Hill, Kingston upon Thames, SR KT2 7HG, England. **Online address:** p.conradi@kingston.ac.uk

CONRAN, Shirley (Ida). British (born England), b. 1932. **Genres:** Novels, Design, Women's Studies And Issues, Adult Non-fiction, Literary Criticism And History, Young Adult Fiction, Young Adult Non-fiction. **Career:** Conran Fabrics Ltd., founder, co-owner and fabric designer, 1957-62; British Council of Industrial Design, judge, 1961-69; Sidgwick and Jackson Ltd., editorial adviser; Daily Mail, home editor, 1962, women's editor, 1963-68; Westinghouse Kitchens, design and promotion consultant, 1969; Vanity Fair Magazine, columnist, 1970-71; Over 21 Magazine, life and styles editor, 1972-74; Work-Life Balance Trust, founder and president, 2001. **Publications:** Superwoman: Every Woman's Book of Household Management, 1975, 2nd ed., 1977 in US as Superwoman, 1978; Superwoman Yearbook, 1976; Superwoman 2, 1977 in US as Superwoman in Action, 1979; (with E. Sidney) Futures: How to Survive Life After Thirty, 1979, rev. ed. as Futurewoman: How to Survive Life After Thirty, 1981; Lace: A Novel, 1982; The Magic Garden, 1983; Lace 2, 1985; The Legend, 1985; Savages: A Novel, 1987; Down with Superwoman: For Everyone Who Hates Housework, 1990; (with Jasper and Sebastian) The Amazing Umbrella Shop, 1990; Crimson, 1992; Tiger Eyes, 1994; Three Complete Novels, 1994; Star Struck, 1998; Revenge, 1998. Contributor to periodicals. **Address:** Morton Janklow Associates, 598 Madison Ave., New York, NY 10022, U.S.A.

CONROY, (Donald) Pat(rick). American (born United States), b. 1945. **Genres:** Novels, Plays/Screenplays, Education, Autobiography/Memoirs, Biography, Food And Wine, Young Adult Fiction, Essays. **Career:** High school teacher, 1967-69; elementary school teacher, 1969. Writer. **Publications:** The Boo, 1970; The Water Is Wide, 1972; The Great Santini, 1976; The Lords of Discipline, 1980; The Prince of Tides, 1986; Beach Music, 1995; My Losing Season, 2002; (with S.W. Pollak) Pat Conroy Cookbook: Recipes of My Life, 2004; The Prince of Tides, 2005; (intro.) War and Peace, 2007; (with S.W. Pollak) The Pat Conroy Cookbook: Recipes and Stories of my Life, 2009; South of Broad: A Novel, 2009; My Reading Life, 2010. **Address:** c/o Nan A. Talese, Doubleday Publicity, 1745 Broadway, 10th Fl., New York, NY 10019-4368, U.S.A.

CONROY, John. American/Italian (born Italy), b. 1951. **Genres:** History, Politics/Government, Adult Non-fiction, Military/Defense/Arms Control, Biography. **Career:** Chicago Guide, senior editor, 1974-76; Chicago Reader, staff writer, 1978-2008. **Publications:** NON FICTION: Belfast Diary: War as a Way of Life, 1987; Unspeakable Acts, Ordinary People: The Dynamics of Torture, 2000. Contributor to periodicals. **Address:** Wendy Weil Agency Inc., 232 Madison Ave., Ste. 1300, New York, NY 10016-2901, U.S.A.

CONSER, Walter H. American (born United States), b. 1949. **Genres:** History, Theology/Religion, Architecture. **Career:** University of North Carolina, Department of Philosophy and Religion, professor, Department of History, professor. Writer. **Publications:** Church and Confession: Conservative Theologians in Germany, England, and America, 1815-1866, 1984; (with W.G. McLoughlin and V.D. McLoughlin) The Cherokee Ghost Dance: Essays on the Southeastern Indians, 1789-1861, 1984; God and the Natural World: Religion and Science in Antebellum America, 1993; Sacred Spaces: Architecture and Religion in Historic Wilmington, 1999; A Coat of Many Colors: Religion and Society along the Cape Fear River of North Carolina, 2006; (with R.J. Cain) Presbyterians in North Carolina: Race, Politics, and Religious Identity in Historical Perspective, 2012. EDITOR: (co-ed.) Resistance, Politics, and the American Struggle for Independence, 1765-1775, 1986; (with S.B. Twiss) Experience of the Sacred: Readings in the Phenomenology of Religion, 1992; The Cherokees and Christianity, 1794-1870: Essays on Acculturation and Cultural Persistence, 1994; (with S.B. Twiss) Religious Diversity and American Religious History: Studies in Traditions and Cultures, 1997; (with R.M. Payne) Southern Crossroads: Perspectives on Religion and Culture, 2008. **Address:** Department of History, University of North Carolina, 274 Bear Hall, 601 S College Rd., Wilmington, NC 28403-3297, U.S.A. **Online address:** conserw@uncw.edu

CONSTABLE, Giles. American/British (born England), b. 1929. **Genres:** History, Young Adult Fiction. **Career:** University of Iowa, instructor and assistant professor, 1955-58; Speculum, assistant editor, 1958-78; Harvard University, assistant professor, 1958-61, associate professor, 1961-66, H.C. Lea professor of Medieval history, 1966-77, professor of history, 1977-84; Center for Advanced Studies in Medieval Civilization, lecturer, 1961; St John's University, visiting professor, 1973; Dumbarton Oaks Research Library and Collection, director, 1977-84; Catholic University of America, visiting professor, 1978-84; Georgetown University, visiting professor, 1982, 1997; Institute for Advanced Study, professor, 1985-2003, professor emeritus, 2003-; Princeton University, visiting professor, 1989, 1995; Arizona State University, visiting professor, 1992, 2005. Writer. **Publications:** (Ed. with J. Kritzeck) Petrus Venerabilis, 1156-1956: Studies and Texts Commemorating the Eighth Centenary of His Death, 1956; Monastic Tithes from Their Origins to the Twelfth Century, 1964; (ed., intro. and contrib.) The Letters of Peter the Venerable, 2 vols., 1967; (trans. with B. Smith) Libellus De Diversis Ordinibus et Professionibus Qui Sunt in Aecclesia: Orders and Callings of the Church, 1972, rev. ed., 2003; (ed. with J. Martin) Peter the Venerable: Selected Letters, 1974; Consuetudines Benedictinae Variae: (Saec. XI-Saec. XIV), 1975; Medieval Monasticism: A Select Bibliography, 1976; Letters and Letter-Collections, 1976; Religious Life and Thought (11th-12th Centuries), 1979; Cluniac Studies, 1980; Attitudes Toward Self-Inflicted Suffering in the Middle Ages, 1982; (with A.P. Kazhdan) People and Power in Byzantium: An Introduction to Modern Byzantine Studies, 1982; (ed. with R.L. Benson and C.D. Lanham) Renaissance and Renewal in the Twelfth Century, 1982; (intro.) Apologiae Duae, 1985; Monks, Hermits and Crusaders in Medieval Europe, 1988; (ed. with T. Evergates) The Cartulary and Charters of Notre-Dame of Homblières, 1990; (ed. with E.H. Beatson and L. Dainelli) The Letters between Bernard Berenson and Charles Henry Coster, 1993; Three Studies in Medieval Religious and Social Thought, 1995; Reformation of the Twelfth Century, 1996; Culture and Spirituality in Medieval Europe, 1996; (with G. Melville and J. Oberste) Cluniazenser in Ihrem Politisch-Sozialen Umfeld, 1998; Cluny From the Tenth to the Twelfth Centuries: Further Studies, 2000; Byzantine Monastic Foundation Documents, 2000; (ed. with J. Thomas and A.C. Hero) Byzantine Monastic Foundation Documents: A Complete Translation of the Surviving Founders' Typika and Testaments, 2000; (ed.) Secolo XII: La Renovatio Dell'Europa Cristiana, 2003; (with W.J. Connell) Sacrilege and Redemption in Renaissance Florence: The Case of Antonio Rinaldeschi, 2005; (with Collectif and M. Rouche) Auctoritas: mélanges offerts à Olivier Guillot, 2006; (ed. and intro.) Three Treatises from Bec on the Nature of Monastic Life, 2008; Crusaders and Crusading in the Twelfth Century, 2008; Abbey of Cluny, 2010; (trans. and contrib.) How to Defeat the Saracens, 2012. Contributor to journals. **Address:** School of Historical Studies, Institute for Advanced Study, Einstein Dr., Princeton, NJ 08540-4907, U.S.A.

CONSTABLE, Kate. Australian (born Australia), b. 1966?. **Genres:** Novels, Children's Fiction, Young Adult Fiction. **Career:** Warner Music, administrative assistant. Writer. **Publications:** CHANTERS OF TREMARIS TRILOGY: The Singer of All Songs, 2002; The Waterless Sea, 2003; The Tenth Power, 2005; The Taste Of Lightning, 2007; Always Mackenzie, 2008; Winter of Grace, 2009; Cicada Summer, 2009; (with P. Russon) Dear Swoosie, 2010; Crow Country, 2011. **Address:** c/o Author Mail, Allen & Unwin, 83 Alexander St., Crows Nest, Sydney, NW 2065, Australia. **Online address:** kate@kateconstable.com

CONSTANT, Paule. French (born France), b. 1944. **Genres:** Novels, Young Adult Fiction. **Career:** University of Abidjan, assistant lecturer in French literature, 1968-75; University Paul Cézanne, instructor in French, 1975-90, professor, 1995-; Centre des écrivains du Sud-Jean Giono, founder, 2000, chair. Writer. **Publications:** Ouregano, 1980; Propriété privée, 1981; Balta, 1983; Un Monde à l'usage Des Demoiselles, 1987; White Spirit, 1989; Le grand Ghâpal, 1991; La Fille Du Gobernator, 1994; Confidence Pour Confidence, 1998; Sucre et secret, 2003; White Spirit, 2005; Bête à Chagrin, 2007. Contributor of articles to periodicals. **Address:** Inst d'Etudes Francaises pour Etudiants Etrangers, 23 rue Gaston de Saporta, Aix-en-Provence, 13265, France.

CONSTANT, Stephen. (Stephen Constantine Daneff). British (born England), b. 1931. **Genres:** Biography, Autobiography/Memoirs, History. **Ca-**

reer: Daily Telegraphy, special correspondent, 1953-55, 1961-73; United Press of America, staff, 1955-56; Daily Express, special correspondent, 1956-61; British Broadcasting Corp., broadcaster, 1973-. Writer. **Publications:** Foxy Ferdinand, 1861-1948, Tsar of Bulgaria, 1979. **Address:** 66 Earlsfield Rd., London, GL SW18, England.

CONSTANTELOS, Demetrios J. American/Greek (born Greece), b. 1927. **Genres:** History, Human Relations/Parenting, Humanities, Theology/Religion. **Career:** St. Demetrios Greek Orthodox Church, pastor, 1955-64; Dumbarton Oaks Research Library, junior fellow, 1964-65; Holy Cross Greek Orthodox Theological School, assistant professor, 1965-67, associate professor of history, 1967-71; Boston College, visiting lecturer, 1967-68; Richard Stockton College of New Jersey, professor, 1971-86, Charles Cooper Townsend senior distinguished professor of history and religious studies, 1986-96, Charles Cooper Townsend Sr. distinguished professor emeritus of history and religious studies, Hellenic Studies Program, chair; New York University, visiting lecturer, 1991; Rutgers University, visiting lecturer; Hellenic College, visiting lecturer; Greek Orthodox Archdiocese of North and South America at National and International Congresses, representative. Writer. **Publications:** An Old Faith for Modern Man: The Greek Orthodox Church, Its History and Teachings, 1964; The Greek Orthodox Church: History, Faith and Practice, 1967; Byzantine Philanthropy and Social Welfare, 1968, 2nd ed., 1991; Marriage, Sexuality and Celibacy: A Greek Orthodox Perspective, 1975; (ed.) Orthodox Theology and Diakonia: Trends and Prospects: Essays in Honor of His Eminence Archbishop Iakovos on the Occasion of His Seventieth Birthday, 1981; Understanding the Greek Orthodox Church, 1982, 3rd ed., 1998; Issues and Dialogues in the Orthodox Church since World War Two, 1986; Byzantine Kleronomia, 1990; Vizantine Kleronomia: Theologia, Historia, Paideia, 1990; Understanding the Greek Orthodox Church: Its Faith, History, and Practice, 1990; Poverty, Society, and Philanthropy in the Late Medieval Greek World, 1992; Ethnike Tautoteta kai Threskeutike Idiaiteroteta tou Hellenismou, 1993; The Greeks: Their Heritage and Its Value Today, 1996; Christian Hellenism: Essays and Studies in Continuity and Change, 1996; Christian Faith and Cultural Heritage: Essays From a Greek Orthodox Perspective, 2005; Renewing the Church: The Significance of the Council in Trullo, 2006; That They May be One: Position Papers, Essays, Homilies, and Prayers on Christian Unity, 2007; (with N.Tobais) Basil I, Founder of the Macedonian Dynasty: A Study of the Political and Military History of the Byzantine Empire in the Ninth Century, 2007. EDITOR: Encyclicals and Documents of the Greek Orthodox Archdiocese 1922-1972, 1975; (co-author) Greece: Today and Tomorrow, 1979; Orthodox Theology and Diakonia: Trends and Prospects, 1981; Visions and Expectations for a Living Church: Addresses to Clergy-Laity Congresses, 1960-1996, 1998; The Complete Works of His Eminence Archbishop Iakovos, Primate of North and South America 1959-1996, 1998; Anemizonta Rasa: Pastoral Encyclicals of Archbishop Iakovos, 2 vols., 1999; The Torch Bearer, vol. I, 1999, vol. II, 2001; Paterika meletemata Kai Ekklesiastika Themata, 1999; Phocus Angelatos: Paterika Meletemata kai Ekklesiastika Themata, 1999; Paideia: Addresses to Young People, 2002. Contributor to books. **Address:** Arts and Humanities, Richard Stockton College of New Jersey, Rm. K111, 101 Vera King Farris Dr., Galloway, NJ 08205, U.S.A. **Online address:** demetrios.constantelos@stockton.edu

CONSTANTINE, David (John). British (born England), b. 1944. **Genres:** Novels, Novellas/Short Stories, Poetry, Literary Criticism And History, Translations. **Career:** University of Durham, lecturer, senior lecturer in German, 1969-81; Queens College, tutor fellow in German, lecturer, 1981-2000. Writer. **Publications:** POETRY: A Brightness to Cast Shadows, 1980; Watching for Dolphins, 1983; (with R. Pybus) Talitha Cumi, 1983; Mappa Mundi, 1984; Madder, 1987; Selected Poems, 1992; Caspar Hauser (long poem), 1994; The Pelt of Wasps, 1998; Something for the Ghosts, 2002; A Poetry Primer, 2004; Collected Poems, 2004; Nine Fathom Deep, 2009. TRANSLATOR: (with H. Constantine) H. Michaux, Deplacements Degagements, 1990; (with M. Treharne) P. Jaccottet, Under Clouded Skies, 1994; J.W. von Goethe, Elective Affinities, 1994; F. Hölderlin, Selected Poems, 1996; Selected Writings of Heinrich von Kleist, 1997; Holderlin's Sophocles, 2001; H.M. Enzensberger, Lighter than Air, 2002; B. Brecht, Collected Plays, 2003; Faust, vol. I, 2005, vol. II, 2009. OTHERS: (ed.) German Short Stories 2, 1976; The Significance of Locality in the Poetry of Friederich Holderlin, 1979; Early Greek Travellers and the Hellenic Ideal, 1984; Davies (novel), 1985; Holderlin, 1988; Back at the Spike (short stories), 1994; (ed.) Oxford Poets, 2000; Fields of Fire (biography of Sir William Hamilton) 2001; A Living Language (essays), 2004; Under the Dam (short stories), 2005; The Shieling (short stories), 2009. **Address:** Queen's College, Oxford University, Oxford, OX OX1 4AW, England. **Online address:** david.constantine@queens.ox.ac.uk

CONSTANTINE, Storm. British (born England), b. 1956. **Genres:** Science Fiction/Fantasy, Novels. **Career:** Freelance writer, 1987-. **Publications:** WRAETHTHU TRILOGY I: The Enchantments of Flesh and Spirit: The First Book of Wraeththu, 1987; The Bewitchments of Love and Hate, 1988; The Fulfillments of Fate and Desire, 1989; (with W. Darling) Paragenesis: Stories of the Dawn of Wraeththu, 2010. WRAETHTHU TRILOGY II: The Wraiths of Will and Pleasure, 2003; The Shades of Time and Memory, 2004; The Ghosts of Blood and Innocence, 2005. MAGRAVANDIAS TRILOGY: Sea Dragon Heir, 1998; Crown of Silence, 2000; The Way of Light, 2001. OTHER NOVELS: The Monstrous Regiment, 1990; Hermetech, 1991; Aleph, 1991; Burying the Shadow, 1992; Sign for the Sacred, 1993; Calenture, 1994; Stalking Tender Prey, 1995; Scenting Hallowed Blood, 1996; Stealing Sacred Fire, 1997; (with G. Child) Thin Air, 1999; (with M. Moorcock) Silverheart, 2000; Stealing Sacred Fire, 2001; The Hienama: A Story of the Sulh, 2005; Grimoire Dehara: Kaimana, 2005. OTHERS: Colurastes, 1995; Three Heralds of the Storm, 1997; (with D. Benstead) The Inward Revolution, 1998; The Oracle Lips, 1999; The Thorn Boy, 1999; (with E. Coquio) Bast and Sekhmet: Eye of Ra, 1999; Egyptian Birth Signs: The Secrets of the Ancient Egyptian Horoscope, 2002; The Thorn Boy and Other Dreams of Dark Desire, 2002; (with T. Elwood) Pop Culture Magick: An Exploration Modern Magick, 2004; Mythanima: A Collection of Stories, 2006; Mythophidia: A Collection of Stories, 2008; Sekhem Heka, 2008; Student of Kyme, 2008; Mythangelus: A Collection of Stories, 2009; Mytholumina, 2010. **Address:** 8 Rowley Grove, Stafford, ST ST17 9BJ, England.

CONSTANTINE-SIMMS, Delroy. Jamaican/British (born England), b. 1964. **Genres:** Sex, Education, Reference. **Career:** Open University, tutor counselor, 1990-92; University of Stirling, tutor counselor, 1993-94; Barnet College of Further Education, lecturer, 1993-99; University of Kingston, research assistant, 1994-95; University of Hertfordshire, research fellow, 1995-96; University of North Carolina, Sonja Haynes Black Cultural Center, research associate, 1996; RHEMA Consulting, senior occupational psychologist, 1999-2002, 2002-05; Multi-cultural Media Foundation, news editor, 2000-; Network for Professional Managers, consulting occupational psychologist, 2006-; Reed Consulting, Talent Management Consultant, 2006-07; Lambeth College of Further Education, consultant and trainer; CEL, trainer; Barclays, consultant occupational psychologist; Family Housing Association, senior occupational psychologist; Southwark Local Authority, NCH, senior occupational psychologist; T-Mobile, senior occupational psychologist; Book Club Association, lead facilitator; Cable & Wireless, co-facilitator; Cable & Wireless and Orange Communications, senior occupational psychologist; Courts Furnishing, Jamaica, consultant occupational psychologist; Bank of Scotland, Lloyds TSB Royal, consultant occupational psychologist; University of East London, researcher; Birmingham Partnership for Change, organizational development consultant; Digicell, organizational development consultant; London Borough of Walthamstow, organizational development consultant; Boro Fashion, London, organizational development consultant. Writer. **Publications:** (Ed. with V. Showunmi and contrib.) Teachers for the Future, 1995; Hitler's Forgotten Black Victims, 1997; (ed.) The Greatest Taboo: Homosexuality in Black Communities, 2001. Contributor to periodicals. **Address:** Multi-cultural Media Foundation, PO Box 13258, London, GL E1 2RR, England. **Online address:** dthinkdoctor@aol.com

CONTEH-MORGAN, Earl. American (born United States), b. 1950. **Genres:** Politics/Government, International Relations/Current Affairs, Economics. **Career:** Northwestern University, instructor in political science, 1981-85; University of South Florida, Department of Government and International Affairs, visiting assistant professor, 1985-88, assistant professor, 1988-92, associate professor, 1993-98, professor of international studies, 1998-, senior research fellow, 1995-96, professor, 1996-; Oakton Community College, adjunct professor, 1985; Eckerd College, adjunct professor, 1989-90. Writer. **Publications:** American Foreign Aid and Global Power Projection: The Geopolitics of Resource Allocation, 1990; Japan and the United States: Global Dimensions of Economic Power, 1992; (contrib.) Internal Conflict and Governance, 1992; Democratization in Africa: The Theory and Dynamics of Political Transitions, 1997; (ed. with K.P. Magyar) Peacekeeping in Africa: ECOMOG in Liberia, 1998; (contrib.) Strategic Challenges to U.S. Foreign Policy in the Post-Cold War, 1998 (with M. Dixon-Fyle) Sierra Leone at the End of the Twentieth Century: History, Politics and Society, 1999;

(contrib.) U.S. Interests and Policies in Africa: Transition to a New Era, 1999; Collective Political Violence: An Introduction to the Theories and Cases of Violent Conflicts, 2004; Globalization and the Human Security Problematic: The Continuing Search for Order and Peace, 2004; The Military, Militarism, State Integrity in Africa: Issues, Solutions Contradictions and The State in Africa: Beyond False Starts, 2004. Contributor of articles to books and journals. **Address:** Department of Government and International Affairs, College of Arts & Sciences, University of South Florida, 107 SOC, 4202 E Fowler Ave., Tampa, FL 33620, U.S.A. **Online address:** conteh-m@cas.usf.edu

CONTI, Gregory. Italian (born Italy) **Genres:** Translations, History. **Career:** University of Perugia, professor of English; University of Rochester, faculty. Translator and writer. **Publications:** TRANSLATOR: E. Deaglio, The Banality of Goodness: The Story of Giorgio Perlasca, 1998; R. Loy, First Words: A Childhood in Fascist Italy, 2000; R. Loy, Cioccolata da Hanselmann (title means: 'Hot Chocolate at Hanselmann's'), 2003; R. Loy, Porta dell'acqua (title means: 'The Water Door'), 2006; T. Scarpa, Corpo, forthcoming. Contributor to periodicals. **Address:** Science, Ling, Fil, Area Anglo-German, Universita degli Studi de Perugia, Piazza Universita, Perugia, 06100, Italy. **Online address:** gregconti@fastwebnet.it

CONVERSE, Nathan. American (born United States), b. 1979. **Genres:** Politics/Government. **Career:** Center for Global Development, research assistant; International Institute of Finance, research assistant. Writer and economist. **Publications:** (With E.B. Kapstein) The Fate of Young Democracies, 2008. **Online address:** n.l.converse@lse.ac.uk

CONVERSE, Philip E. (Philip Ernest Converse). American (born United States), b. 1928. **Genres:** Politics/Government. **Career:** Horace H. Rackham fellow, 1955-56; Fulbright research fellow, 1959-60; University of Michigan, Survey Research Center, study director, 1960-65, program director, 1965-, Department of sociology and political science, assistant professor, 1960-63, associate professor, 1963-65, professor, 1965-75, chair, Robert Cooley Angell professor, 1975-, Robert Cooley Angell distinguished professor, 1975-89, Robert Cooley Angell distinguished professor emeritus, 1989-, Center for Political Studies, director, 1982-86, Institute for Social Research, director, 1986-89; Inter-university Consortium for Political Research, associate director, 1962-; National Science Foundation, postdoctoral fellow, 1967-68; Guggenheim fellow, 1975-76; Center for Advanced Study in the Behavioral Sciences, fellow, 1979, director, 1989-94. Writer. **Publications:** The American Voter, 1960; The Nature of Belief Systems in Mass Publics, 1964; (with T.M. Newcomb and R.H. Turner) Social Psychology, 1965; Elections and the Political Order, 1966; Some Priority Variables in Comparable Electoral Research, 1968; (with S.M.J. Rosenberg) Vietnam and the Silent Majority: The Dove's Guide, 1970; Verba and (ed. with A. Campbell) The Human Meaning of Social Change, 1972; Velgere og Politiske Frontlinjer. Stemmegivning og Stridsspørsmål 1957-1969, 1972; (with W.L. Rodgers and A. Campbell) The Quality of American Life, 1976, 2nd ed. (with A. Campbell) as Quality of American Life, 1978, 1984; The Dynamics of Party Support: Cohort-analyzing Party Identification, 1976; (co-author) American Social Attitudes Data Sourcebook, 1947-1978, 1980; Political Representation in France, 1986; (co-author) Assessing Progress Toward Democracy and Good Governance: Summary of a Workshop, 1992; (co-author) Democratization in the Middle East, 1993; (co-author) Civil-Military Relations and Democratization: Summary of a Workshop, 1993; (with W.H. Eaton) Eight-generation Genealogy of the Eatons of Salisbury and Haverhill, Massachusetts, 2004. Contributor of articles to journals. **Address:** Department of Political Science, University Michigan, 5700 Haven Hall, 505 S State St., Ann Arbor, MI 48109-1045, U.S.A. **Online address:** pconvers@umich.edu

CONVERSE, Philip Ernest. *See* **CONVERSE, Philip E.**

CONWAY, Alan. New Zealander/British (born England), b. 1920. **Genres:** History, Military/Defense/Arms Control, Social Sciences. **Career:** University of Wales, senior lecturer in American history, 1950-67; University of Canterbury, foundation professor of American history, 1967-85. Writer. **Publications:** The Welsh in America, 1961; Causes of American Civil War, 1961; (co-author) Hanes yr Unol Daleithiau, 1965; The Reconstruction of Georgia, 1966; History of the Negro in the United States, 1968; (with J.O. Baylen) Soldier-Surgeon: The Crimean War Letters of Douglas A. Reid 1855-56, 1968; Welsh Emigration to the United States, 1974. Contributor of periodicals. **Address:** 11 Clissold St., Christchurch, 8014, New Zealand.

CONWAY, Diana C(ohen). American (born United States), b. 1943. **Genres:** Children's Fiction, Social Sciences, Travel/Exploration. **Career:** Anchorage Community College, Spanish teacher, 1971-87; University of Alaska, professor of Spanish, 1987-89. Writer. **Publications:** Northern Lights: A Hanukkah Story, 1994; Darren's Work, 1998. Contributor to periodicals. **Address:** PO Box 6461, Halibut Cove, AK 99603-6461, U.S.A.

CONWAY, Erik M. American (born United States), b. 1965?. **Genres:** Sciences, History. **Career:** National Aeronautics and Space Administration (NASA), Langley Research Center, historian, California Institute of Technology, Jet Propulsion Laboratory, resident historian. Writer. **Publications:** NONFICTION: High-Speed Dreams: NASA and the Technopolitics of Supersonic Transportation, 1945-1999, 2005; Blind Landings: Low-Visibility Operations in American Aviation, 1918-1958, 2006; (with M.S. Reidy and G. Kroll) Exploration and Science: Social Impact and Interaction, 2007; Atmospheric Science at NASA: A History, 2008; (with N. Oreskes) Merchants of Doubt: How a Handful of Scientists Obscured the Truth on Issues from Tobacco Smoke to Global Warming, 2010. Contributor to books and journals. **Address:** Jet Propulsion Laboratory, National Aeronautics and Space Administration, 4800 Oak Grove Dr., Pasadena, CA 91109, U.S.A.

CONWAY, Jill Ker. American/Australian (born Australia), b. 1934. **Genres:** Women's Studies And Issues, Administration/Management, Humanities, Social Sciences, Autobiography/Memoirs, Education, History. **Career:** University of Sydney, lecturer in history, 1958-60; University of Toronto, lecturer, 1964-68, assistant professor, 1968-70, associate professor of history, 1970-75, vice president of internal affairs, 1973-75; Smith College, president, Sophia Smith professor of history, 1975-85, now professor emeritus; Massachusetts Institute of Technology, professor, visiting professor of history of women. Writer. **Publications:** Merchants and Merinos, 1960; Women Reformers and American Culture: 1870-1930, 1972; The Female Experience in Eighteenth and Nineteenth-Century America: A Guide to the History of American Women, 1982; The First Generation of American Women Graduates, 1987; Utopian Dream or Dystopian Nightmare? Nineteenth- Century Feminist Ideas about Equality, 1987; (ed. with S. Bourque and J.W. Scott) Learning About Women: Gender, Politics and Power, 1989; The Road From Coorain: An Autobiography, 1989; (ed. with S.C. Bourque) The Politics of Women's Education: Perspectives from Asia, Africa, and Latin America, 1993; True North: A Memoir, 1994; When Memory Speaks: Reflections on Autobiography, 1998; (ed. with K. Keniston and L. Marx) Earth, Air, Fire, Water: Humanistic Studies of the Environment, 1999; (ed. and intro.) In Her Own Words: Women's Memoirs from Australia, New Zealand, Canada and the United States, 1999; A Woman's Education, 2001; Felipe the Flamingo, 2006; Flamingo Felipe, 2009. Contributor to books. **Address:** Massachusetts Institute of Technology, Bldg. E51-185, 77 Massachusetts Ave., Cambridge, MA 02139-4307, U.S.A. **Online address:** kerconway@aol.com

CONWAY, Martha. American (born United States) **Genres:** Adult Nonfiction, Novels, Mystery/Crime/Suspense. **Career:** Author. **Publications:** 12 Bliss Street, 2003; All Her Favorite Fruit, forthcoming. Works appear in anthologies. **Address:** c/o Matt Williams, The Gernet Co., 136 E 57th St., New York, NY 10022-2707, U.S.A. **Online address:** conway@aimnet.com

CONWAY, Rosaleen D. New Zealander (born New Zealand), b. 1934?. **Genres:** Novels. **Career:** National Office of Catholic Communications, journalist; Marist Messenger, proofreader; freelance radio and print writer. **Publications:** Saints Alive, 1987; Purely Business, 1995; Feed My Revenge, 2003; The Seeking Feet 2007. **Address:** University of California Press, 2120 Berkeley Way, Berkeley, CA 94704-1012, U.S.A. **Online address:** rconway@paradise.net.nz

CONWAY, Simon. American (born United States), b. 1967?. **Genres:** Young Adult Fiction, Mystery/Crime/Suspense. **Career:** Writer. **Publications:** FICTION: Damaged, 1998; Rage, 2006; The Afghan Guides, 2009; A Loyal Spy, 2010. **Address:** Annette Green Authors Agency, 1 E Cliff Rd., Tunbridge Wells, KT TN4 9AD, England. **Online address:** info@simonconwaybooks.com

CONY, Carlos Heitor. Brazilian (born Brazil), b. 1926. **Genres:** Biography, Novels, Romance/Historical, Young Adult Fiction. **Career:** Jornal do Brazil, staff; Correio da Manhã newspaper, reporter, 1964, columnist, editor; Folha, columnist; Brazilian radio, commentator; CBN, radio commentator and Band News. **Publications:** O Ventre, 1958; Os dez mandamentos, 1959; Tijolode segurança: Romance, 1960; A verdade de cada dia: Romance, 1960; Informação ao crucificado, 1961; Matéria de memória, 1962; Da arte de falar mal crônicas, 1963; O at e o fato: Crônicas políticas, 1964; Posto 6: Crônicas, 1965; Balé branco: Romance, 1966; Antes, o verão: Romance, 1966; Chaplin: Ensaio-anologia, 1967; Pessach: A Travesia, 1967; 64 DC, 1967; Quem matou Vargas, 1968, as Quem matou Vargas: 1954, 1974; Sôbre tôdas as coisas, 1968; Pilatos: Romance, 1974; O casa Lou: Assim é se lhe parece, 1975; Luciano saudade, 1975; O Planeta Kalgar, 1976; Paranoía: A noite do massacre, 1976; Babilônia! Babilônia!: Contos, 1978; Marina Marina, 1978; O ato e o fato, 1979; Nos Pasos de João de Deus, 1980; JK, memorial do exilio, 1982; (with H.G. Mathias) Getúlio Vargas, 1983; Orlando Teruz, Painter, 1985; Antologia escolar de crônicas: 80 crônicas exemplars, 1992; A casa do poeta trágico, 1995; Quase memória: Quase- romance, 1995; O piano e a orquestra, 1996; Lagoa: História, morfologia e sintaxe, 1996; O burguês e o crime eoutros contos, 1997; O harém das bananeiras, 1997; Matéria dememória, 1998; Os anos mais antigos do passado: Crônicas, 1998; Romance sem palavras, 1999; O indigitado, 2000; O presidente que sabiajavanês, 2001; (with S. Lamarão) Wolff Klabin: A trajetória deum pioneiro, 2001; JK, como nasce uma estrela, 2002; (co-author) Ficções urbanas, 2003; (co-author) Liberdade de expressão, 2003; Tarde da sua ausência: Romance, 2003; (with A. Lee) Beijo da morte, 2003; Revolução doscaranguejos, 2004; Quem matou Vargas: 1954, uma traģdia brasileira, 2004; Adiantado da hora: romance, 2006; Morte e a vida: romance, 2007; Macá: a natureza revelada, 2008; (co-author) Aconteceu na Manchete: as histórias que ninguéa noite do massacrem contou, 2008; Eu, aos pedaços, 2010. Contributor to periodicals. **Address:** c/o Author Mail, Editoria Companhia das Letras, Editoria Schwarcs Ltda., Rua Bandeira Paulista 702, cj 72, Satildeo Paulo, 04532-002, Brazil.

CONYBEARE, Catherine. American (born United States) **Genres:** Theology/Religion. **Career:** Bryn Mawr College, Department of Greek, Latin and classical studies, associate professor. Writer. **Publications:** Paulinus Noster: Self and Symbols in the Letters of Paulinus of Nola, 2000; The Irrational Augustine, 2006. **Address:** Graduate Group in Archaeology, Classics & History of Art, Bryn Mawr College, 101 N Merion Ave., Bryn Mawr, PA 19010, U.S.A. **Online address:** cconybea@brynmawr.edu

COOGAN, Michael D(avid). American (born United States), b. 1942. **Genres:** Archaeology/Antiquities, Theology/Religion, Translations. **Career:** Tell el-Hesi, area supervisor, 1970-71, field supervisor, 1973-75; University of Waterloo, St. Jerome's College, assistant professor, 1971-74; Wilfrid Laurier University, adjunct assistant professor, 1972-74; W. F. Albright Institute of Archaeological Research, professor of archaeology, 1975-76; Harvard University, visiting lecturer, 1976-77, assistant professor, 1977-80, associate professor, 1980-85, visiting professor, 1989-90, 1994-95, 1997-98, Harvard Semitic Museum, director of publications, 1998-; Wadi Tumilat Project, associate director, 1977; Southeast Dead Sea Plain, field director, 1979-83; Stonehill College, associate professor, 1985-88, professor of religious studies, 1988-, now professor emeritus of religious studies; Wellesley College, visiting professor, 1986-89; Catholic Biblical Quarterly, associate editor, 1991-. Writer. **Publications:** West Semitic Personal Names in the Murašû Documents, 1976; The Old Testament: A Historical and Literary Introduction to the Hebrew Scriptures, 2006, 2nd ed., 2011; The Old Testament: A Very Short Introduction, 2008; Brief Introduction to the Old Testament: The Hebrew Bible in Its Context, 2009, 2nd ed., 2012; God and Sex: What the Bible Really Says, 2010. EDITOR: (and trans. with M.S. Smith) Stories from Ancient Canaan, 1978; (with B.M. Metzger) The Oxford Companion to the Bible, 1993; (with J.C. Exum) Scripture and Other Artifacts: Essays on the Bible and Archaeology in Honor of Philip J. King, 1994; The Oxford History of the Biblical World, 1998; The Illustrated Guide to World Religions, 1998; (with L.E. Stager and J.A. Greene) The Archaeology of Jordan and Beyond: Essays in Honor of James A. Sauer, 2000; (with M.Z. Brettler and C.A. Newsom) The New Oxford Annotated Bible with the Apocrypha, 3rd ed., 2001; (with B.M. Metzger) The Oxford Guide to Ideas and Issues of the Bible, 2001; (with B.M. Metzger) The Oxford Guide to People & Places of the Bible, 2001; Eastern Religions: Origins, Beliefs, Practices, Holy Texts, Sacred Places, 2005. Contributor to books and journals. **Address:** Stonehill College, 220-C, Duffy, 320 Washington St., Easton, MA 02357, U.S.A. **Online address:** mcoogan@stonehill.edu

COOGAN, Tim(othy) Pat(rick). Irish (born Ireland), b. 1935. **Genres:** Area Studies, History, Autobiography/Memoirs, Social Sciences, Politics/Government. **Career:** Freelance author, 1966-95; Irish Press, editor, 1968-87. **Publications:** Ireland since the Rising, 1966; The I.R.A., 1970, rev. ed., 2002; The Irish: A Personal View, 1975; On the Blanket: The H Block Story, 1980; (ed.) Ireland and the Arts, 1983; Disillusioned Decades: Ireland 1966-87, 1987; Michael Collins: A Biography, 1990 in US as The Man Who Made Ireland: The Life and Death of Michael Collins, 1992; Eamon De Valera: The Man Who Was Ireland, 1993; The Troubles: Ireland's Ordeal, 1966-1995, and the Search for Peace, 1995; (forward) The Path to Freedom, 1996; Irish Diaspora: Irish Communities Round the World and How They Work, 1997; (with G. Morrison) Irish Civil War, 1999; Wherever Green Is Worn: The Story of the Irish Diaspora, 2000; 1916: The Easter Rising, 2001; On the Blanket: The Inside Story of the IRA Prisoners' Dirty Protest, 2002; Ireland in the Twentieth Century, 2003; A Memoir, 2008. Contributor to journals and periodicals. **Address:** Palgrave Macmillan, St. Martin's Press, 175 5th Ave., New York, NY 10010-7703, U.S.A.

COOK, Bob. British (born England), b. 1961. **Genres:** Novels, Physics, Young Adult Fiction, Mystery/Crime/Suspense. **Career:** Writer. **Publications:** MICHAEL WYMAN SERIES: Disorderly Elements, 1985; Questions of Identity, 1987; Faceless Mortals, 1988. NOVELS: Paper Chase, 1989; Fire and Forget, 1990. **Address:** St. Martin's Press, 175 5th Ave., New York, NY 10010, U.S.A.

COOK, Chris(topher). British (born England), b. 1945. **Genres:** History, Politics/Government, Reference, Theology/Religion. **Career:** Oxford University, Magdalen College, lecturer in politics, 1969-70; University of London, London School of Economics and Political Science, senior research officer, 1970-80; University of North London, Department of History, head, 1980-89; British Library of Political and Economic Science, visiting research fellow, 1990-. Writer. **Publications:** (Ed. with D. McKie) The Decade of Disillusion, 1972; (ed. with J. Ramsden) By-Elections in British Politics, 1973; (ed.) Pears Cyclopaedia, 1974; (with J. Paxton) European Political Facts 1918-1973, 1975; (ed. with G. Peele) The Politics of Reappraisal 1918-1939, 1975; (with B. Keith) British Historical Facts 1830-1900, 1975; (with P. Jones) Sources in British Political History, 1975; The Age of Alignment: Electoral Politics in Britain 1922-1929, 1975; (ed. with A. Sked) Crisis and Controversy: Essays in Honour of A.J.P. Taylor, 1976; A Short History of the Liberal Party 1900-1976, 1976, 6th ed. as A Short History of the Liberal Party 1900-2001, 2002; (ed. with M. Barker) Pears Encyclopaedia of Myths and Legends, 1976; (with K. Powell) English Historical Facts 1485-1603, 1977; A History of the Great Trains, 1977; (with J. Stevenson) The Slump: Society and Politics During the Depression, 1977; Trends in British Politics since 1945, 1978; Atlas of Modern Warfare, 1978; (comp. with M. Phillips and D. McKie) The Guardian/Quartet Election Guide, 1978; Longman Atlas of Modern British History: A Visual Guide to British Society and Politics 1700-1970, 1978; (with J. Paxton) European Political Facts 1848-1918, 1978; (with A. Sked) Post-War Britain: A Political History, 1979, 3rd ed., 1990; (ed. with M. Zander) Pears Guide to the Law, 1979; (ed. with W. Awdry) A Guide to the Steam Railways of Great Britain, 1979; Commonwealth Political Facts, 1979; (with M. Francis) The First European Elections: A Handbook and Guide, 1979; (ed. with I. Taylor) The Labour Party: An Introduction to Its History, Structure, and Politics, 1980; (with J. Stevenson) Weapons of War, 1980; (with J. Stevenson) British Historical Facts, 1760-1830, 1980; (with J. Wroughton) English Historical Facts, 1603-1688, 1980; (with J. Paxton) European Political Facts, 1789-1848, 1981; (ed.) The Penguin Guide to the Railways of Britain, 1981; (ed. with B. Pimlott) Trade Unions in British Politics, 1982; (with J. Stevenson) Longman Handbook of Modern British History, 1714-1980, 1983, 4th ed. as Longman Handbook of Modern British History 1714-2001, 2001; (with D. Killingray) African Political Facts since 1945, 1983, 2nd ed., 1991; Dictionary of Historical Terms: A Guide to Names and Events of Over 1000 Years of World History, 1983; Short History of the Liberal Party, 1900-1984, 1984; (with G. Pugh) Sources in European Political History, vol. I: The European Left, 1987; Dictionary of Historical Terms, 1989; Facts on File World Political Almanac, 1989, 4th ed., 2001; (ed. with B. Pimlott) Trade Unions in British Politics: The First 250 Years, 1991; Longman Handbook of World History Since 1914, 1991; European Political Facts, 1918-90, 1992; Longman Guide to Sources in Contemporary British History, 2 vols., 1993-94; Facts on File Asia Political Almanac, 1994; (with D. Bewes) What Happen Where, 1997; (with J. Stevenson) Longman Handbook of the Modern World, 1998; (with J. Stevenson) Longman Companion to Britain Since 1945, 2000; Short History of the Liberal Party, 1900-2001, 2002; Routledge Companion to Britain in the Nineteenth Century, 1815-1914, 2005; (with J. Stevenson) Routledge Companion to Modern European History Since 1763, 2005; (with J. Stevenson) Routledge Companion to World History Since 1914, 2005; (with

P. Broadhead) Routledge Companion to Early Modern Europe, 1453-1763, 2006; (with J. Stevenson) Slump: Britain in the Great Depression, 2010; Short History of the Liberal Party: The Road to Power, 2010; Routledge Guide to European Political Archives: Sources Since 1945, 2012. **Address:** Modern Archives Survey, London School of Economics, British Library of Political and Economic Science, Houghton St., Aldwych, London, GL WC2A 2AE, England.

COOK, Claire. American (born United States), b. 1955. **Genres:** Novels. **Career:** Montessori Community School, teacher; Physical fitness teacher. Writer. **Publications:** Ready to Fall: A Novel, 2000; Must Love Dogs: A Novel, 2002; Multiple Choice: A Novel, 2004; Life's a Beach, 2007; Summer Blowout, 2008; Wildwater Walking Club: A Novel, 2009; Seven Year Switch, 2010; Best Staged Plans, 2011. **Address:** c/o Lisa Bankoff, International Creative Management Inc., 825 8th Ave., New York, NY 10019, U.S.A. **Online address:** claire@clairecook.com

COOK, David. British (born England), b. 1940. **Genres:** Novels, Young Adult Fiction, Literary Criticism And History. **Career:** Actor, 1961-; St. Martin's College, writer-in-residence, 1982-83. **Publications:** Albert's Memorial, 1972; Happy Endings, 1974; Walter, 1978; Winter Doves, 1979; Sunrising, 1986; Missing Persons, 1986; Crying Out Loud, 1988; Walter and June, 1989; Second Best, 1991. **Address:** Greene & Heaton Ltd., 37 Goldhawk Rd., London, GL W12 8QQ, England.

COOK, David Bryan. American (born United States), b. 1966. **Genres:** Literary Criticism And History, Theology/Religion. **Career:** Rice University, associate professor of religious studies. Writer. **Publications:** Studies in Muslim Apocalyptic, 2002; Contemporary Muslim Apocalyptic Literature, 2005; Understanding Jihad, 2005; Martyrdom in Islam, 2007; (with O. Allison) Understanding and Addressing Suicide Attacks: The Faith and Politics of Martyrdom Operations, 2007; (ed.) Jihad and Martyrdom, 2009. Contributor to books and journals. **Address:** Rice University, PO Box 1892, Houston, TX 77251-1892, U.S.A. **Online address:** dbcook@rice.edu

COOK, Dawn. (Kim Harrison). American (born United States), b. 1966?. **Genres:** Children's Fiction. **Career:** Writer. **Publications:** Hidden Truth, 2002; First Truth, 2002; Forgotten Truth, 2003; Dead Witch Walking, 2004; Lost Truth, 2004; The Decoy Princess, 2005; Princess at Sea, 2006; (contrib.) The Mammoth Book of Vampire Romance 2, 2009. AS KIM HARRISON: Dead Witch Walking, 2004; The Good, the Bad, and the Undead, 2005; Every Which Way But Dead, 2005; A Fistful of Charms, 2006; For a Few Demons More, 2007; The Outlaw Demon Wails, 2008; White Witch, Black Curse, 2009; Black Magic Sanction, 2010; Pale Demon, 2011; The Hollows Insider, 2011; Blood Work, 2011; A Perfect Blood, 2012. **Address:** Richard Curtis Associates Inc., 171 E 74th St., 2nd Fl., New York, NY 10021, U.S.A. **Online address:** dawncook@dawncook.com

COOK, Dawn. *See* **HARRISON, Kim.**

COOK, Deanna F. American (born United States), b. 1965. **Genres:** Food And Wine. **Career:** Scholastic Inc., associate editor, 1989-92; FamilyFun Magazine, senior editor, 1992-. **Publications:** Kids' Multicultural Cookbook: Food & Fun around the World, 1995; Disney's Family Cookbook, 1996; (co-author) FamilyFun's Parties, 1999; Kids' Pumpkin Projects: Planting & Harvest Fun, 1998; (co-author) FamilyFun Parties, 2002; (co-author) FamilyFun Home, 2003; FamilyFun Super Snacks: 125 Quick Snacks that are Fun to Make and to Eat, 2004. CO-EDITOR: Disney's FamilyFun Crafts, 1997; FamilyFun's Cookies for Christmas, 1998; FamilyFun Tricks and Treats, 2000; FamilyFun Boredom Busters, 2002; FamilyFun Homemade Holidays, 2002; FamilyFun Birthday Cakes, 2003; FamilyFun Cooking with Kids, 2006; FamilyFun Homemade Holidays: 150 Festive Crafts, Recipes, Gifts & Parties, 2009; FamilyFun Cookies For Christmas: 50 Cute & Quick Holiday Treats, 2009; FamilyFun Birthday Cakes: 50 Cute & Easy Party Treats, 2009. **Address:** FamilyFun Magazine, 114 5th Ave., New York, NY 10011-5604, U.S.A.

COOK, Eileen. Canadian (born Canada), b. 1969?. **Genres:** Novels. **Career:** Michigan State University, counselor. Writer. **Publications:** Unpredictable, 2008; What Would Emma Do? (young adult novel), 2009; Getting Revenge on Lauren Wood, 2010; Fourth Grade Fairy, 2011; Gnome Invasion, 2011; Education of Hailey Kendrick, 2011; Wishes for Beginners, 2011; Unraveling Isobel, 2012. Contributor to periodicals. **Address:** Simon & Schuster, 166 King St. E, Ste. 300, Toronto, ON M5A 1J3, Canada. **Online address:** eileen@eileencook.com

COOK, Ferris. American (born United States), b. 1950. **Genres:** Homes/Gardens, Poetry. **Career:** Gear, product designer, 1987; Fred C. Gloeckner Co. (horticultural brokerage), customer service representative, 1987-88; Smithsonian Guide to Historic America, assistant photographic editor, 1988-89; illustrator and writer, 1989-; American Museum of Natural History, assistant to the manager of special publications, 1991. **Publications:** EDITOR: Invitation to the Garden: A Literary and Photographic Celebration, 1992. EDITOR and ILLUSTRATOR: Garden Dreams, 1991; Remembered Gardens, 1993; Garden Trellis: Designs to Build and Vines to Cultivate, 1996; The Sonnets of Shakespeare, 1998; Gifts of Love: A Selection of Love Poetry, 2000; Contributor of articles to periodicals. **Address:** 2 Washington Sq. Village, Ste. 4B, New York, NY 10012, U.S.A. **Online address:** ferris@ferriscook.com

COOK, Glen (Charles). (Greg Stevens). American (born United States), b. 1944. **Genres:** Novels, Science Fiction/Fantasy. **Career:** General Motors Corp., auto assembler, 1965-67, Fisher Body Plant, auto assembler, 1965-67, Chevrolet Army Plant, munitions inspector, 1967-70, material controller, 1970-74, staff, 1974-98, retired, 1998. Writer. **Publications:** AS GREG STEVENS: The Swap Academy (novel), 1970. SCIENCE FICTION NOVELS: The Heirs of Babylon, 1972; A Shadow of All Night Failing, 1979; October's Baby, 1980; All Darkness Met, 1980; The Swordbearer, 1982; Shadowline, 1982; Starfishers, 1982, Stars' End, 1982; The Fire in His Hands, 1984; The Black Company, 1984; Shadows Linger, 1984; Passage at Arms, 1985; A Matter of Time, 1985; With Mercy toward None, 1985; The White Rose, 1985; Doomstalker, 1986; Warlock, 1986; Ceremony, 1986; Reap the East Wind, 1987; Sweet Silver Blues, 1987; Ill Fate Marshalling, 1988; Bitter Gold Hearts, 1988; Cold Copper Tears, 1988; The Dragon Never Sleeps, 1988; Shadow Games, 1989; Old Tin Sorrows, 1989; The Silver Spike, 1989; The Tower of Fear, 1989; Dread Brass Shadows, 1990; Dreams of Steel, 1990; Sung in Blood, 1990; Red Iron Nights, 1991; Deadly Quicksilver Lies, 1994; Petty Pewter Gods, 1995; Bleak Seasons, 1996; She is the Darkness, 1997; Water Sleeps, 1998; Faded Steel Heat, 1999; Soldiers Live, 2000; Angry Lead Skies, 2002; Whispering Nickel Idols, 2005; The Tyranny of the Night, 2005; Lord of the Silent Kingdom, 2007; Chronicles of the Black Company, 2007; A Fortress in Shadow, 2007; An Empire Unacquainted with Defeat, 2008; Cruel Zinc Melodies, 2008; Return of the Black Company, 2009; Surrender to the Will of the Night, 2010; An Empire Unacquainted with Defeat, 2010; Gilded Latten Bones, 2010; Darkwar, 2010. **Address:** c/o Russell Galen, Scovil Galen Ghosh Literary Agency, 276 5th Ave., Ste. 708, New York, NY 10001, U.S.A.

COOK, Hugh. Canadian (born Canada), b. 1942?. **Genres:** Novels, Sciences. **Career:** Dordt College, professor of English; Redeemer College, professor of English, now professor emeritus; Calvin College, Wiersma Memorial Lecturer, 2001. Writer. **Publications:** Cracked Wheat and Other Stories, 1984; The Homecoming Man, 1989; Home in Alfalfa: Stories, 1998; Heron River, 2011. Contributor of articles to journals. **Address:** Redeemer University College, 777 Garner Rd. E, Ancaster, Ontario, ON L9K 1J4, Canada. **Online address:** hcook@redeemer.ca

COOK, James L(ister). Scottish (born Scotland), b. 1932. **Genres:** Engineering, Money/Finance, Agriculture/Forestry. **Career:** Sybron/Balfour, senior design draftsman, 1965-69, research engineer, 1971-79; Munro & Millar, pipe design engineer, 1969-71; University of Salford, lecturer, 1977; Rank Strand Electric Ltd. (now Strand Lighting Ltd.), senior mechanical design engineer, 1979-81; C.E. Lummus Co., senior designer and checker in vessels department, 1981-82; Howard Doris Ltd., senior planning engineer, 1982; Cooxint Ltd., director, 1983-86; Prime Actuator Control Systems Ltd., chief engineer, 1986-88; Lewis C. Grant Ltd., product design engineer, 1988-89; Ardmel Auto Ltd., contract design engineer, 1989; Glenrothes College, adjunct lecturer, 1990-91. Writer. **Publications:** Conversion Factors, 1991; Property Loans, 1999. Contributor to magazines. **Address:** 21 Haig Ave., Kirkcaldy, St. Andrews, FF KY1 2JE, Scotland. **Online address:** james.lister.cook@tesco.net

COOK, Jean Thor. American (born United States), b. 1930. **Genres:** Children's Non-fiction, Children's Fiction, Novels, Young Adult Fiction. **Career:** St. Mary College, Inner-City Adult Baccalaureate Program, publicity director, 1978-80. Writer. **Publications:** Hugs for Our New Baby, 1987; Butterflies for Grandpa, 1990; Audrey and the Nighttime Skies, 1994; Sam, the Terror of Westbrook Elementary, 1994; Jesus Calms the Storm, 1994; Room for a Stepdaddy, 1995; Los Amiquitos' Fiesta: The Little Friends Fiesta, 2001. **Address:** 325 Jack Boot Rd., Monument, CO 80132, U.S.A. **Online address:** jthorcook1@aol.com

COOK, Kevin Graeme. American (born United States), b. 1953. **Genres:** Biography, Sports/Fitness, Autobiography/Memoirs. **Career:** Sports Illustrated, senior editor, beginning 1997; Travel and Leisure Golf, executive editor; Golf, editor-in-chief. **Publications:** Tommy's Honor: The Story of Old Tom Morris and Young Tom Morris, Golf's Founding Father and Son, 2007; Driven: Teen Phenoms, Mad Parents, Swing Science and the Future of Golf, 2008; (ed.) The Golf Book, 2009; Titanic Thompson: The Man Who Bet on Everything, 2011. **Address:** c/o James Gill, PFD, Drury House, 34-43 Russell St., London, GL WC2B 5HA, England.

COOK, Lorna J. American (born United States), b. 1962?. **Genres:** Novels, Mystery/Crime/Suspense. **Career:** Legislative assistant. Writer. **Publications:** Departures, 2004; Home Away From Home, 2005; Outside Wonderland, 2011. **Address:** St. Martins Press, 175 5th Ave., New York, NY 10010, U.S.A. **Online address:** info@lornacook.com

COOK, Mark. Welsh/British (born England), b. 1942. **Genres:** Human Relations/Parenting, Psychology, Sex, Romance/Historical. **Career:** University of Aberdeen, assistant lecturer in psychology, 1968-69; Oxford University, research officer, 1969-73; Swansea University, School of Human Sciences, lecturer in psychology, 1973-, honorary lecturer and emeritus; Psychological Consultancy Services Ltd., director of research, 1981-. Writer. **Publications:** Interpersonal Perception, 1971; (with M. Argyle) Gaze and Mutual Gaze, 1976; (with R. McHenry) Sexual Attraction, 1978; Perceiving Others: The Psychology of Interpersonal Perception, 1979; Levels of Personality, 1984, 2nd ed., 1993; Personnel Selection and Productivity, 1988, 5th ed. as Personnel Selection: Adding Value Through People, 2009; Personnel Selection: Adding Value through People, 1998, 5th ed., 2009; (with B. Cripps) Psychological Assessment in the Workplace: A Manager's Guide, 2005. EDITOR: (with G. Wilson) Love and Attraction: An International Conference, 1979; (with K. Howells) Adult Sexual Interest in Children, 1981; The Bases of Human Sexual Attraction, 1981; Issues in Person Perception, 1984. **Address:** Department of Psychology, School of Human Sciences, Swansea University, Singleton Pk., Swansea, SA2 8PP, Wales. **Online address:** m.cook@swansea.ac.uk

COOK, Marshall. (Marshall J. Cook). American (born United States), b. 1944. **Genres:** Novels, Mystery/Crime/Suspense, Young Adult Non-fiction, Young Adult Fiction. **Career:** University of Wisconsin, Department of Continuing Education, instructor. Writer. **Publications:** NONFICTION: How to Write with the Skill of a Master and the Genius of a Child, 1992; Freeing Your Creativity: A Writer's Guide, 1992; Slow Down-and Get More Done, 1993; Hometown Wisconsin, 1994; Leads & Conclusions, 1995; (with J. Walsh) Pack Your Bags: Baseball's Trade Secrets, 1998; Time Management: Proven Techniques for Making the Most of Your Valuable Time, 1998; How to Handle Worry: A Catholic Approach, 1999; Effective Coaching, 1999; Streetwise Time Management: Get More Done with Less Stress by Efficiently Managing Your Time, 1999; How to Be a Great Coach: 24 Lessons for Turning on the Productivity of Every Employee, 2004; The Great Wisconsin Manhunt of 1961, 2004; (with B. Camenson) Give 'em What They Want: The Right Way to Pitch Your Novel to Editors and Agents, 2005. FICTION: The Year of the Buffalo: A Novel of Love and Minor League Baseball, 1997; Off Season: A Novel of Love, Faith and Minor League Baseball, 2002. MONONA QUINN MYSTERY SERIES: Murder Over Easy, 2003; Murder at Midnight, 2005; Twin Killing, 2007; Obsessions, 2008. Contributor of articles to periodicals. **Address:** 3 Hanover Sq., New York, NY 10004, U.S.A. **Online address:** mcook@dcs.wisc.edu

COOK, Marshall J. *See* **COOK, Marshall.**

COOK, Noble David. American (born United States), b. 1941. **Genres:** Theology/Religion, History. **Career:** University of Florida, teaching assistant, 1964-64; University of Texas, teaching assistant, 1964-65; University of Bridgeport, from instructor to professor, 1969-92; Catholic University of Peru, Fulbright professor, 1974, 1984; Yale University, visiting professor, 1989-90; Florida International University, Department of History, professor, 1992-, chair, 1995-98, 2006-07. Writer and historian. **Publications:** (Intro.) Padrón De Los Índios De Lima En 1613, 1968; (with A.M. Medina and T. Bouysse-Cassagne) Tasa De La Visita General De Francisco De Toledo, 1975; Demographic Collapse, Indian Peru, 1520-1620, 1981; The People of the Colca Valley: A Population Study, 1982; (intro.) Numeracion General De Todas Las Personas De Ambos Sexos, Edades Y Calidades Q[ue] Se Hà Hecho En Esta Ciudad De Lima, Año De 1700, 1985; (ed. and contrib. with W.G. Lovell) Secret Judgments of God: Old World Disease in Colonial Spanish America, 1991; (with A.P. Cook) Good Faith and Truthful Ignorance: A Case of Transatlantic Bigamy, 1991; Born to Die: Disease and New World Conquest, 1492-1650, 1998; (intro.) Luis Geronimo de Ore, Relación De La Vida Y Milagros De San Francisco Solano, 1998; (with A.P. Cook) People of the Volcano: Andean Counterpoint in the Colca Valley of Peru, 2007; (with A.P. Cook) The Plague Files: Crisis Management in Sixteenth-Century Seville, 2009. Contributor to books and journals. **Address:** Department of History, Florida International University, Miami, FL 33199-0001, U.S.A. **Online address:** cookn@fiu.edu

COOK, Paul. American (born United States), b. 1950. **Genres:** Science Fiction/Fantasy, Poetry, Novels. **Career:** Arizona State University, College of Liberal Arts and Sciences, Department of English, lecturer, 1982-87, senior lecturer in English, 1987-. Writer. **Publications:** SCIENCE FICTION: Tintagel, 1981; The Alejandra Variations, 1984; Duende Meadow, 1985; Halo, 1986; On the Rim of the Mandala, 1987; Fortress on the Sun, 1997; Engines of Dawn, 1999; Thinking of You, 2000; Presidential Leadership by Example: A Presidential and First Ladies Report Card for the New Millennium, 2001; Karma Kommandos, 2008; Cooked in LA: I Shot for the Stars and Hit Bottom, 2009. POEMS: Inevitable Weather: Poems, 2003; (ed.) American Literature: From the Colonies to the Civil War, 2009. OTHERS: (contrib.) Lost World, 2009; (contrib.) Time Machine, 2009; (contrib.) Frankenstein: Or the Modern Prometheus, 2009; (contrib.) Moon Pool, 2010. OTHERS: (contrib.) A Princess of Mars, 2010. **Address:** Department of English, Arizona State University, Rm. 542, 851 S Cady Mall, 699 S Mill Ave., PO Box 870302, Tempe, AZ 85281, U.S.A. **Online address:** paul.cook@asu.edu

COOK, Philip J. American (born United States), b. 1946. **Genres:** Politics/Government, Social Commentary, Adult Non-fiction. **Career:** Duke University, assistant professor, 1973-79, associate professor, 1979-84, professor of public policy, 1984-, Institute of Policy Sciences, director, 1985-89, professor of public policy studies, economics and sociology, 1992-, Department of Public Policy Studies, chair, 1985-89, 1997-99, Fuqua School of Business, visiting professor, 1989-90, Center for Child and Family Policy, faculty affiliate; senior associate dean for faculty and research, Sanford Institute of Public Policy, Department of Policy, director and chair, 1997-99, ITT/Sanford professor of public policy and economics, 1994-; University of Maryland, Schelling visiting professor of public policy, 2008-09. Writer. **Publications:** (With F. Besag) Anatomy of a Riot: Buffalo, 1967, 1970; (ed.) Gun Control, 1981; (with C.T. Clotfelter) Selling Hope: State Lotteries in America, 1989; (with D.B. Slawson) The Costs of Processing Murder Cases in North Carolina, 1993; (with R.H. Frank) The Winner-Take-All Society: How More and More Americans Compete for Ever Fewer and Bigger Prizes, Encouraging Economic Waste, Income Inequality, and an Impoverished Cultural Life, 1995; (with J. Ludwig) Guns in America: Results of a Comprehensive National Survey on Firearms Ownership and Use, 1996; (with J. Ludwig) Gun Violence: The Real Costs, 2000; (ed. with Jens Ludwig) Evaluating Gun Policy: Effects on Crime and Violence, 2003; Paying the Tab: The Economics of Alcohol Policy, 2007; (ed. with J. Ludwig and J. McCrary) Controlling Crime: Strategies and Tradeoffs, 2012. **Address:** Sanford Institute of Public Policy, Duke University, 215 Sanford Bldg., PO Box 90245, Durham, NC 27708, U.S.A. **Online address:** pcook@duke.edu

COOK, Rebecca J. Canadian/American (born United States), b. 1946. **Genres:** Law, Medicine/Health, Ethics. **Career:** Lester Pearson Commission, World Bank, research associate, 1969; Woodrow Wilson International Center, Smithsonian Institute, research associate, 1970-71; Population Council, research associate, 1972; United Nations Population Fund, research associate, 1973; International Planned Parenthood Federation, Law Programme, director, 1973-78; United States Congress, research officer, 1978-80; Beveridge, Fairbanks and Diamond, associate, 1980; Columbia University, School of Public Health, Division of Population and Family Health, assistant professor of clinical public health, 1983-87; University of Toronto, faculty of law, faculty of medicine, School of Graduate Studies, assistant professor, 1987-90, associate professor, 1990-95, International Human Rights Law Programme, director, faculty of law, 1987-98, faculty of law professor in international human rights, 1995-, International Programme On Reproductive And Sexual Health Law, co-director, 1995-, Graduate Studies, associate dean, 1998. Writer.

Publications: (With B.M. Dickens) Abortion Laws in Commonwealth Countries, 1979; (with B.M. Dickens) Emerging Issues in Commonwealth Abortion Laws, 1982, 1983; (with B.M. Dickens) Women's Health and Human Rights: The Promotion and Protection of Women's Health through International Human Rights Law, 1994; (co-author) Reprodução e sexualidade: uma quesão dejustiça, 2002; Reproductive Health and Human Rights: Integrating Medicine, Ethics and Law, 2003; (with S. Cusack) Gender Stereotyping: Transnational Legal Perspectives, 2009. EDITOR: (with P. Senanayake) The Human Problem of Abortion: Medical and Legal Dimensions, 1979; Human Rights of Women: National and International Perspectives, 1994; (ed. with C.G. Ngwena) Health and Human Rights, 2007. Contributor to journals and periodicals. **Address:** Faculty of Law, University of Toronto, 84 Queen's Pk., Toronto, ON M5S 2C5, Canada. **Online address:** rebecca.cook@utoronto.ca

COOK, Robert. (Robert J. Cook). British (born England), b. 1958. **Genres:** History, Civil Liberties/Human Rights. **Career:** University of Sheffield, senior lecturer in American history, 1990-, professor, through 2007; University of Sussex, Department of American Studies, professor of American history, 2007-, head of American studies. Writer. **Publications:** Baptism of Fire: The Republican Party in Iowa, 1838-1878, 1994; Northampton, 1996; Sweet Land of Liberty?: The African-American Struggle for Civil Rights in the Twentieth-century, 1998; Civil War America: Making a Nation 1848-1877, 2003; Troubled Commemoration: The American Civil War Centennial, 1961-1965, 2007; Civil War Senator: William Pitt Fessenden and the Fight to Save the American Republic, 2011. **Address:** Department of American Studies, University of Sussex, Arts A A150, Sussex House, Brighton, ES BN1 9RH, England. **Online address:** r.cook@sussex.ac.uk

COOK, Robert J. *See* **COOK, Robert.**

COOK, Roger F. American (born United States), b. 1948. **Genres:** Literary Criticism And History. **Career:** University of Missouri, Department of German and Russian Studies, professor of German and chair, 1986-, director of film studies program. Writer. **Publications:** The Demise of the Author: Autonomy and the German Writer, 1770-1848, 1993; (ed. with G. Gemünden) The Cinema of Wim Wenders: Image, Narrative, and the Postmodern Condition, 1997; By the Rivers of Babylon: Heinrich Heine's Late Songs and Reflections, 1998; (ed.) A Companion to the Works of Heinrich Heine, 2002. **Address:** Department of German and Russian Studies, University of Missouri, 449 Strickland Hall, Columbia, MO 65211-4170, U.S.A. **Online address:** cookrf@missouri.edu

COOK, Stephen L(loyd). American (born United States), b. 1962. **Genres:** Theology/Religion, inspirational/Motivational Literature. **Career:** Yale Divinity School, teaching fellow, 1988-91, instructor, 1990, 1991; Columbia University, Union Theological Seminary, assistant professor of OldTestament, 1992-96; Virginia Theological Seminary, assistant professor of old testament, 1996-99, associate professor of Old Testament, 1999-2006, Catherine N. McBurney professor of Old Testament language and literature, 2006-. Writer. **Publications:** Prophecy and Apocalypticism: The Postexilic Social Setting, 1995; The Apocalyptic Literature, 2003; Social Roots of Biblical Yahwism, 2004; (co-author) New Proclamation Year B, 2008-2009, Advent Through Holy Week, 2008; Conversations with Scripture: 2 Isaiah, 2008. EDITOR: (with S.C. Winter) On the Way to Nineveh: Studies in Honor of George M. Landes, 1999; (with C.L. Patton and J.W. Watts) The Whirlwind: Essays on Job, Hermeneutics and Theology in Memory of Jane Morse, 2001; (with C.L. Patton) Ezekiel's Hierarchical World: Wrestling with a Tiered Reality, 2004; (ed. with J.J. Ahn) Thus Says the LORD: Essays on the Former and Latter Prophets in Honor of Robert R. Wilson, 2009. Contributor of articles to periodicals. **Address:** Virginia Theological Seminary, 3737 Seminary Rd., Alexandria, VA 22304, U.S.A. **Online address:** scook@vts.edu

COOK, William A. American (born United States), b. 1944. **Genres:** Sports/Fitness, Adult Non-fiction, History, Biography. **Career:** Writer. **Publications:** The 1919 World Series: What Really Happened?, 2001; The Summer of '64: A Pennant Lost, 2002; Pete Rose: Baseball's All-Time Hit King, 2004; Waite Hoyt: A Biography of the Yankees' Schoolboy Wonder, 2004; Louisville Grays Scandal of 1877: The Taint of Gambling at the Dawn of the National League, 2005. Contributor to periodicals. **Address:** 3 Claremont Dr., North Brunswick, NJ 08902, U.S.A.

COOKE, Bernard. (Bernard J. Cooke). American (born United States), b. 1922. **Genres:** Theology/Religion, Literary Criticism And History. **Career:** Marquette University, professor of theology, Department of Theology, chairman, 1957-69; North Central Association of Colleges and Schools, consultant, 1962-70; Yale Divinity School, fellow, 1969-70; University of Windsor, professor of religious studies, 1970-76; University of Santa Clara, visiting professor of theology, 1973-74; University of Calgary, professor of religious studies, 1976-80; College of the Holy Cross, professor of theology, 1980-92, now Loyola professor emeritus of religious studies; Incarnate Word College, professor of theology, 1992-98; University of San Diego, professor of theology, 1999-, now retired. Writer. **Publications:** Christian Sacraments and Christian Personality, 1965; Formation of Faith, 1965; New Dimensions in Catholic Life, 1967; Beyond Trinity, 1969; God of Space and Time, 1969; The Eucharist: Mystery of Friendship, 1969; (contrib.) Spirit and Power of Christian Secularity, 1969; Christian Community: Response to Reality, 1970; (contrib.) Toward a Future for Religious Education, 1970; Theology in an Age of Revolution, 1971; Rethinking the Faith, 1972; Ministry to Word and Sacraments, 1976; Sacraments and Sacramentality, 1983; Reconciled Sinners: Healing Human Brokeness, 1986; (ed.) The Papacy and the Church in the United States, 1989; The Distancing of God: The Ambiguity of Symbol in History and Theology, 1990; God's Beloved, 1992; Why Angels?: Are They Real...Really Needed?, 1996; The Future of Eucharist, 1997; Power and the Spirit of God: Toward an Experience-based Pneumatology, 2004; Christian Symbol and Ritual: An Introduction, 2004. **Address:** College of the Holy Cross, Worcester, MA 01610, U.S.A. **Online address:** turn53122@aol.com

COOKE, Bernard J. *See* **COOKE, Bernard.**

COOKE, Carolyn. American (born United States), b. 1959?. **Genres:** Novellas/Short Stories, Novels. **Career:** California Institute of Integral Studies, MFA Writing Program, core faculty; New College of California, MFA Writing Program, director, 2006-08. Writer. **Publications:** The Bostons (short stories), 2001; Daughters of the Revolution (novel), 2011. Works appear in anthologies. Contributor to periodicals. **Address:** California Institute of Integral Studies, 1453 Mission St., San Francisco, CA 94103-2557, U.S.A. **Online address:** redtag@mcn.org

COOKE, Deborah. *See* **DELACROIX, Claire.**

COOKE, Jacob Ernest. *See* Obituaries.

COOKE, John Peyton. British/American (born United States), b. 1967. **Genres:** Novels, Gay And Lesbian Issues, Travel/Exploration, Young Adult Fiction. **Career:** HP Publishing, editor, 1992-94; Scientific American Medicine (periodical), associate editor, 1994-. **Publications:** NOVELS: The Lake, 1989; Out for Blood, 1991; Torsos, 1993; The Chimney Sweeper, 1994; Haven, 1996; The Rape of Ganymede, 2008; The Fall of Lucifer, 2008. Contributor to periodicals. Works appear in anthologies. **Address:** Mysterious Press, Warner Books, 1271 Ave. of the Americas, New York, NY 10020, U.S.A. **Online address:** johnpeytoncooke@gmail.com

COOKE, Lynne. Spanish (born Spain) **Genres:** Young Adult Non-fiction. **Career:** University College, art history lecturer, 1979-89; Venice Biennale, joint curator, 1986; Syracuse University, teacher, 1987; Yale University, Graduate Sculpture School, teacher, 1990, 1992, 1998; Carnegie Intl., joint curator, 1991; Dia Art Foundation, curator, 1991-2009, artistic director, 1996; Whitechapel Art Gallery, curator of exhibitions; Hayward Gallery, curator of exhibitions; Third Eye Center; Institute of Contemporary Art; American Center; Museo Nacional Centro de Arte Reina Sofia, deputy director and chief curator, 2008-. Writer. **Publications:** (With A. Rorimer and S.K. Essink) Allan McCollum: Stedelijk Van Abbemuseum, 1989; (with H. Friedel) Ian McKeever: A History of Rocks, 1986-1988, 1990; (ed. with K. Kelly) Arena: Where Would I Have Got If I Had Been Intelligent!, 1994; (ed. with B. Schwabsky and L. Tillman) Jessica Stockholder, 1995; (with A. Magnin) Worlds Envisioned: Alighiero e Boetti and Frederic Bruly Bouabre, 1995; (contrib. with V. Combalia and A. Zweite) Sean Scully, Twenty Years, 1976-1995, 1995; (ed. with P. Wollen) Visual Display: Culture beyond Appearances, 1998; (ed. with K. Kelly) Joseph Beuys: Drawings after the Codices Madrid of Leonardo Da Vinci, 1998; (with I. Julien and S. Shepard) Tracey Moffatt: Free-Falling, 1998; (co-author) Thomas Schuette, 2001; (with J. Elderfeld) Bridget Riley: Reconnaissance, 2001; (ed. with K. Kelly) Diana Thater: Knots + Surfaces, 2002; (with M. Govan) Dia: Beacon, 2003; (ed. with K. Kelly and B. Funcke) Robert Whitman: Playback, 2003; (co-ed.) Robert Smithson: Spiral Jetty: True Fictions, False Realities, 2005; (with K. McShine) Richard Serra: Sculpture: Forty Years, 2007; (with K. Baker) Walter De Maria: The

Lightning Field, 2007; (ed. with K. Kelly and B. Schröder) Max Neuhaus: Times Square, Time Piece Beacon, 2009; (ed. with K. Kelly and B. Schröder) Palermo: To The People of New York City, 2009; (ed. with D. Crimp and K. Poor) Mixed Use, Manhattan: Photography and Related Practices, 1970s to the Present, 2010; (ed. with K. Kelly and B. Schroder) Zoe Leonard: You See I Am Here After All, 2010; (ed.) Blinky Palermo: Retrospective 1964-77, 2010; (ed. with M. Godfrey and C. Rattemeyer) Alighiero Boetti: Game Plan, 2011; (ed. with K. Kelly and B. Schroder) Agnes Martin, 2011. Contributor to periodicals. **Address:** Museo Nacional Centro de Arte Reina Sofia, 52 Santa Isabel, Madrid, 28012, Spain. **Online address:** lcooke@diaart.org

COOKE, Nathalie. Canadian/Indian (born India), b. 1960?. **Genres:** Literary Criticism And History. **Career:** McGill University, assistant professor, 1991-97, associate professor, 1997-2009, professor, 2009-, associate dean of arts, 2006-10; associate provost, 2010-, Press, editor, 1997-; CuiZine, editor. **Publications:** (Ed. with R. Brown and D. Bennett) An Anthology of Canadian Literature in English, 1990; Margaret Atwood: A Biography, 1998; Margaret Atwood: A Critical Companion, 2004; (ed. with S. Morton) The Torontonians, 2008; (ed. with S. Morton) Psyche, 2009; (ed.) What's to Eat? Entrées in Canadian Food History, 2009. Contributor to journals. **Address:** Office of the Provost, McGill University, Rm. 600, James Administration Bldg., 845 Peel St., Montreal, QC H3A 2T5, Canada. **Online address:** nathalie.cooke@mcgill.ca

COOKE, William. British (born England), b. 1942. **Genres:** Novellas/Short Stories, Poetry, Literary Criticism And History, Biography, Humor/Satire, Writing/Journalism. **Career:** Thistley Hough School, teacher, 1968-70; Stoke-on-Trent College, tutor of English literature, 1970-79, lecturer, 1979-95; Cauldon College of Further Education, faculty, 1979-. Writer. **Publications:** Edward Thomas: A Critical Biography, 1878-1917, 1970; Edward Thomas: A Portrait, 1978; Builder (poetry), 1980; Small Ads (poetry), 1980; Business English, 1990; The Miracles of the Lord Jesus Christ: Evidence of the Divine Authority of His Mission as the Savior of the World (1883), 2008; The Medallic History of Imperial Rome, 2010; The Way to the Temple of True Honor and Fame by the Paths of Heroic Virtue, 2010; (foreword with C. Bladey) Justice At Salem: Re-examining The Witch Trials, 2010; Pr Lectio ad Actum Publicum Habitum Cantabrigi, 8vo. ID. MART. MDCCLXXXVII. Auctore Gulielmo Cooke ., 2010. EDITOR: Anvil, 1979; Howlers, 1988; Edward Thomas: Everyman Poetry, 1997. **Address:** 17 Stuart Ave., Trentham, Stoke-on-Trent, ST ST4 8BG, England.

COOK-LYNN, Elizabeth. American (born United States), b. 1930. **Genres:** Novels, Novellas/Short Stories, Poetry, Cultural/Ethnic Topics, History, Literary Criticism And History, Young Adult Fiction, Young Adult Non-fiction, Young Adult Non-fiction. **Career:** University of California, visiting professor; Eastern Washington University, associate professor of Native American studies, 1971-, professor of English and native American studies, professor emeritus of English and native American studies, 1990-; Stanford University, National Endowment for the Humanities, fellow, 1976; Wicazo Sa Review, co-founder; Arizona State University, visiting professor. **Publications:** POETRY: Then Badger Said This, 1983; Seek the House of Relatives, 1985; I Remember the Fallen Trees: New and Selected Poems, 1998. STORIES: The Power of Horses and Other Stories, 1990; From the River's Edge (novella), 1991. ESSAYS: Why I Can't Read Wallace Stegner and Other Essays: A Tribal Voice, 1996; (with M. Gonzalez) The Politics of Hallowed Ground: Wounded Knee and the Struggle for Indian Sovereignty, 1999; Anti-Indianism in Modern America: A Voice from Tatekeya's Earth, 2001. OTHER: A Crow Creek Trilogy (fiction), 1999; Aurelia: A Crow Creek Trilogy, 1999; New Indians, Old Wars, 2007; Notebooks of Elizabeth Cook-Lynn, 2007; Separate Country, 2012. **Address:** Rte. 8, PO Box 510, Dakotah Meadows, Rapid City, SD 57702-4716, U.S.A. **Online address:** elizcoly@aol.com

COOL, Paul. American (born United States), b. 1950. **Genres:** History. **Career:** Writer, historian and government program administrator. **Publications:** Salt Warriors: Insurgency on the Rio Grande, 2008. Contributor to books and periodicals. **Address:** Eldersburg, MD , U.S.A. **Online address:** paul@paulcoolbooks.com

COOLEY, Alexander. (Alexander Anthony Cooley). American (born United States) **Genres:** Politics/Government, Business/Trade/Industry. **Career:** Columbia University, Barnard College, assistant professor, School of International and Public Affairs, adjunct professor, Department of Political Science, associate professor, Tow professor of political science, associate professor of international relations, 2008-, president's fellow, 1995-97; Harriman Institute, MosleyBacker fellow, 1998-99. Writer. **Publications:** Logics of Hierarchy: The Organization of Empires, States and Military Occupations, 2005; Base Politics: Democratic Change and the U.S. Military Overseas, 2008; Contracting States: Sovereign Transfers in International Relations, 2009; Great Games, Local Rules: the New Power Contest in Central Asia, 2012. Contributor to periodicals and journals. **Address:** Barnard College, Columbia University, 414 Lehman Hall, 3009 Broadway, New York, NY 10027-6598, U.S.A. **Online address:** acooley@barnard.edu

COOLEY, Alexander Anthony. *See* **COOLEY, Alexander.**

COOLEY, Martha S. American (born United States), b. 1955. **Genres:** Novels. **Career:** Adelphi University, assistant professor, associate professor; A Public Space, contributing editor; WP Writer's Chronicle, contributing editor. **Publications:** The Archivist, 1998; Thirty-three Swoons, 2005. **Address:** Department of English, Adelphi University, Rm. 210, Harvey Hall, 1 South Ave., PO Box 701, Garden City, NY 11530-0701, U.S.A. **Online address:** cooley@adelphi.edu

COOLEY, Nicole (Ruth). American (born United States), b. 1966. **Genres:** Poetry. **Career:** Emory University, instructor in English, 1992-95; Queens College, City University of New York, assistant professor and program director, 1995-, associate professor, professor of English and creative writing, MFA Program in Creative Writing and Literary Translation, director. Writer. **Publications:** Resurrection (poems), 1996; Judy Garland, Ginger Love, 1998; The Afflicted Girls: Poems, 2004; (ed. with P. Stone) Mother: Women's Studies Quarterly, 2009; Breach: Poems, 2010; Milk Dress, 2010; Artificial Curiosities, forthcoming. Works appear in anthologies. Contributor of stories, poems and articles to periodicals. **Address:** Department of English, Queens College, City University of New York, 702 Klapper Hall, 65-30 Kissena Blvd., Flushing, NY 11367, U.S.A. **Online address:** nicole.cooley@qc.cuny.edu

COOLEY, Ronald W. Canadian (born Canada) **Genres:** Social Sciences. **Career:** University of Saskatchewan, College of Arts and Science, Department of English, professor; Early-Modern Electronic Texts Project, supervising editor. **Publications:** Full of All Knowledg: George Herbert's Country Parson and Early Modern Social Discourse, 2004. Contributor to books. **Address:** Department of English, University of Saskatchewan, 322 Arts Bldg., 9 Campus Dr., Saskatoon, SK S7N 5A5, Canada. **Online address:** ron.cooley@usask.ca

COOLEY, Thomas (Winfield). American (born United States), b. 1942. **Genres:** Literary Criticism And History, History, Young Adult Fiction. **Career:** Ohio State University, assistant professor, 1970-79, associate professor, 1980-98, professor of English, 1999-2003, professor emeritus, 2003-. Writer. **Publications:** Educated Lives: The Rise of Modern Autobiography in America, 1976; The Norton Sampler: Short Essays for Composition, 1979, (ed.) 7th ed., 2010; The Norton Guide to Writing, 1992; (ed.) The Adventures of Huckleberry Finn: An Authoritative Text, Contexts and Sources, Criticism, 1998; The Ivory Leg in the Ebony Cabinet: Madness, Race and Gender in Victorian America, 2001; Back to the Lake: Readings for Writers, 2009, 2nd ed., 2012. **Address:** Department of English, Ohio State University, 421 Denney Hall, 164 W 17th Ave., Columbus, OH 43210, U.S.A. **Online address:** cooley.1@osu.edu

COOLING, Wendy. British (born England) **Genres:** Children's Fiction, Bibliography, History, Education, Reference. **Career:** Book House Training Centre, director of course on children's publishing, 1995-; Disney Consumer Products, director of course on children's publishing, 1997; Children's Book Foundation (now Book Trust), head. Writer and consultant. **Publications:** Finding Out... How to Find Out, 1989; Fame!: Who's Who in History at Madame Tussaud's, 1992; Sandy the Seal, 1994; (with P. Kropp) The Reading Solution, 1995; Books to Enjoy, 12-16, 1996; D Is for Dahl, 2005; A is Amazing, 2012. EDITOR: Thirteen! Unpredictable Tales from Paul Jennings, 1995; The Great Automatic Grammatizator and Other Stories, 1996; The Puffin Book of Stories for Eight-Year-Olds, 1996; The Puffin Book of Stories for Five Year-Olds, 1996; The Puffin Book of Stories for Seven-Year-Olds, 1996; The Puffin Book of Stories for Six-Year-Olds, 1996; It's Christmas, 1997; Simply Spooky, 1997; Surprise Surprise, 1997; Farmyard Tales from Far and Wide, 1998; Read Me a Story Please, 1998; Centuries of Stories, 1999; Skin and Other Stories, 1999; All the Colours of the Earth: Poems from Around the World, 2004; Come to the Great World: Poems from Around the

Globe, 2004; All the Wild Wonders: Poems of Our Earth, 2010. EDITOR: QUIDS FOR KIDS SERIES: Aliens to Earth, 1997; Animal Stories, 1997; Bad Dreams, 1997; Ghost Stories, 1997; Go for Goal, 1997; Horror Stories, 1997; On the Run, 1997; Soccer Stories, 1997; Spine Chillers, 1997; Stars in Your Eyes, 1997; Stories of Growing Up, 1997; Stories of Hopes and Dreams, 1997; Stories of Past and Future, 1997; Stories of Strange Visitors, 1997; Stories of the Unexpected, 1997; Stories to Keep You Guessing, 1997; Time Watch, 1997; Top Secret, 1997; Weird and Wonderful, 1997; Wild and Free, 1997. COMPILER: With Love: A Celebration of Words and Pictures for the Very Young, 2004. Contributor to periodicals. **Address:** Barefoot Books, 41 Schermerhorn St., Ste. 145, Brooklyn, NY 11201-4802, U.S.A. **Online address:** wendycooling@bookconsult.freeserve.co.uk

COOMBES, Annie E. British (born England), b. 1956. **Genres:** Theology/Religion, Cultural/Ethnic Topics, Politics/Government, History, Popular Culture. **Career:** University of London, Birkbeck College, professor of material and visual culture; University of Bayreuth, visiting professor; Brown University, visiting professor; Rochester University, visiting professor; Northwestern University, visiting professor; Australian National University, visiting professor; World Health Organization, research consultant; United States Center for Disease Control and Prevention, research consultant. Writer, educator and consultant. **Publications:** Reinventing Africa: Museums, Material Culture, and Popular Imagination in Late Victorian and Edwardian England, 1994; (ed. with A. Brah) Hybridity and Its Discontents: Politics, Science, Culture, 2000; History after Apartheid: Visual Culture and Public Memory in a Democratic South Africa, 2003; (ed.) Rethinking Settler Colonialism: History and Memory in Australia, Canada, New Zealand and South Africa, 2005. **Address:** Birkbeck College, University of London, Malet St., Bloomsbury, London, GL WC1E 7HX, England. **Online address:** a.coombes@bbk.ac.uk

COOMBS, Patricia. American (born United States), b. 1926. **Genres:** Children's Fiction, Children's Non-fiction, Illustrations, Literary Criticism And History, Science Fiction/Fantasy. **Career:** Writer. **Publications:** SELF-ILLUSTRATED: Dorrie's Magic, 1962; Dorrie and the Blue Witch, 1964; Dorrie's Play, 1965; Dorrie and the Haunted House, 1970; Lisa and the Grompet, 1970; Mouse Café, 1972; Dorrie and the Fortune Teller, 1973. OTHERS: The Lost Playground, 1963; Waddy and His Brother, 1963; Dorrie and the Weather-Box, 1966; Dorrie and the Witch Doctor, 1967; Dorrie and the Wizard's Spell, 1968; Dorrie and the Birthday Eggs, 1971; Dorrie and the Goblin, 1972; Dorrie and the Amazing Magic Elixir, 1974; Dorrie and the Witch's Imp, 1975; Molly Mullet, 1975; Dorrie and the Halloween Plot, 1976; The Magic Pot, 1977; Dorrie and the Dreamyard Monsters, 1977; Tilabel, 1978; Dorrie and the Screebit Ghost, 1979; Dorrie and the Witchville Fair, 1980; Dorrie and the Witches' Camp, 1983; The Magician and the McTree, 1984; Dorrie and the Museum Case, 1986; Dorrie and the Pin Witch, 1989; Dorrie and the Haunted Schoolhouse, 1992. Contributor of articles to periodicals. **Address:** c/o Dorothy Markinko, McIntosh & Otis Inc., 353 Lexington Ave., Ste. 1500, New York, NY 10016-0900, U.S.A.

COOMER, Joe. American (born United States), b. 1958. **Genres:** Novels, Adult Non-fiction, Young Adult Fiction, Literary Criticism And History. **Career:** Owner of antiques malls, 1986-. Writer. **Publications:** The Decatur Road, 1983; Kentucky Love, 1985; A Flatland Fable, 1986; Dream House: On Building a House By a Pond, 1992; The Loop, 1992; Beachcombing for a Shipwrecked God, 1995; Sailing in a Spoonfull of Water, 1997; Apologizing to Dogs, 1999; One Vacant Chair, 2003; Pocketful of Names, 2005. **Address:** c/o Elaine Markson, Elaine Markson Literary Agency Inc., 44 Greenwich Ave., New York, NY 10011, U.S.A.

COONEY, Doug. American (born United States) **Genres:** Novels, Plays/Screenplays. **Career:** Author and playwright. **Publications:** I Know Who Likes You, 2004; (with M. Matlin) Nobody's Perfect, 2006; (with M. Matlin) Leading Ladies, 2007; Mustardseed, 2008. FOR YOUNG ADULTS: The Beloved Dearly: A Play, 2000; Innocent Until, forthcoming. Contributor to periodicals. **Address:** Harden-Curtis Associates, 850 7th Ave., Ste. 903, New York, NY 10019-5438, U.S.A.

COONEY, Ellen. American (born United States), b. 1952. **Genres:** Novels, Novellas/Short Stories, Literary Criticism And History, Young Adult Fiction. **Career:** Massachusetts Institute of Technology, faculty; Boston College, faculty; University of Maine, faculty; Harvard University, faculty. Writer. **Publications:** Small-Town Girl, 1983; All the Way Home, 1984; The Old Ballerina, 1999; The White Palazzo, 2002; Gun Ball Hill, 2004; A Private Hotel for Gentle Ladies, 2005; Lambrusco, 2008; Ancestors The Trees, 2010. Contributor to periodicals. **Address:** c/o Author Mail, Pantheon/Random House, 1745 Broadway, New York, NY 10019, U.S.A. **Online address:** ellencooney@suscom-maine.net

COONEY, Ray(mond George Alfred). British (born England), b. 1932. **Genres:** Plays/Screenplays, Humor/Satire. **Career:** Actor, 1946-; theatre director and producer, 1965-; Ray Cooney Productions Ltd., director, 1966-; Theatre of Comedy, founding artistic director, 1983-. Writer. **Publications:** One for the Pot, 1963; Chase Me, Comrade! A Farce, 1966; (with J. Chapman) My Giddy Aunt: A Comedy-Thriller, 1970; (with J. Chapman) Not Now, Darling: A Comedy, 1970; Bang Bang Beirut, or Stand by Your Bedouin, 1971; Charlie Girl, 1972; (with J. Chapman) Move Over, Mrs. Markham: A Comedy, 1972; Why Not Stay for Breakfast?, 1974; (with J. Chapman) There Goes the Bride: A Comedy, 1975; Run for Your Wife: A Comedy, 1984; Two into One: A Comedy, 1985; (with A. Sultan and E. Barret) Wife Begins at Forty: A Comedy, 1986; It Runs in the Family: A Comedy, 1990; Run for Your Wife: A New Comedy, 1990; It Runs in the Family: A New Comedy, 1990; Out of Order: A Comedy, 1991; One Good Turn, 1994; Funny Money: A New Comedy, 1995; Caught in the Net, 2001; (with M. Cooney) Tom, Dick and Harry: A Comedy, 2006. **Address:** Ray Cooney Plays, Everglades, 29 Salmons Rd., Chessington, SR KT9 2JE, England.

COONTS, Stephen (Paul). (Eve Adams). American (born United States), b. 1946. **Genres:** Novels, Young Adult Fiction. **Career:** Attorney, 1980-81; Petro-Lewis Corp. (oil and gas company), counsel, 1981-86; West Virginia Wesleyan College, trustee; writer, 1986-. **Publications:** NOVELS: Flight of the Intruder, 1986; Final Flight, 1988; The Minotaur, 1989; Under Siege, 1990; The Red Horseman, 1993; The Intruders, 1994; Fortunes of War, 1998; Cuba, 1999; Hong Kong, 2000; America, 2001; Saucer, 2002; Liberty, 2003; Liars and Thieves, 2004; Saucer: The Conquest, 2004; The Traitor, 2006; The Assassin, 2008; The Disciple, 2009; (with W.H. Heith) Deep Black. Death Wave, 2011. OTHER: The Cannibal Queen, 1992; War in the Air, 1996; (ed. and intro.) Combat, 2001; (ed. and intro.) Victory, 2003; (ed. and intro.) On Glorious Wings, 2003; (with J. DeFelice) Stephen Coonts' Deep Black, 2003. AS EVE ADAMS: The Garden of Eden, 2005. Contributor to periodicals. **Address:** c/o Robert Gottlieb, William Morris Agency, 1350 Ave. of the Americas, New York, NY 10019, U.S.A. **Online address:** stevecoonts@aol.com

COONTZ, Stephanie. American (born United States), b. 1944. **Genres:** History, Social Sciences, Social Commentary. **Career:** Evergreen State College, Department of History and Women's Studies, faculty, 1975-; University of Washington, Department of Women's Studies, visiting faculty, 1976; Kobe University of Commerce, exchange professor, 1986; Washington Humanities Commission, lecturer, 1989-91; University of Hawaii, Social Sciences Division, exchange professor, 1992, visiting associate professor of sociology, 1994, associate professor of history, 1999-2000; Council on Contemporary Families, director of research and public education. Writer. **Publications:** (Ed. with P. Henderson) Women's Work, Men's Property: On the Origins of Gender and Class, 1986; The Social Origins of Private Life: A History of American Families, 1988; America's Families: Fables and Facts, 1991; The Way We Never Were: American Families and the Nostalgia Trap, 1992, rev. ed., 2000; The Way We Really Are: Coming to Terms with America's Changing Families, 1997; (ed. with M. Parson and G. Raley) American Families: A Multicultural Reader, 1999, 2nd ed., 2008; Marriage, a History: From Obedience to Intimacy or How Love Conquered Marriage, 2005; A Strange Stirring: The Feminine Mystique and American Women at the Dawn of the 1960s, 2011. Contributor to periodicals. **Address:** Department of History and Women's Studies, Evergreen State College, Olympia, WA 98505, U.S.A. **Online address:** coontzs@msn.com

COOPER, Adam G. Australian (born Australia) **Genres:** Philosophy, Theology/Religion, Humanities. **Career:** Lutheran Church of Australia, pastor; John Paul II Institute for Marriage and Family, senior lecturer. Writer. **Publications:** The Body in St. Maximus the Confessor: Holy Flesh, Wholly Deified, 2005; Life in the Flesh: An Anti-Gnostic Spiritual Philosophy, 2008. **Address:** John Paul II Institute, 278 Victoria Parade, East Melbourne, VI 3002, Australia. **Online address:** adam.cooper@lca.org.au

COOPER, Ann (Catharine). American/British (born England), b. 1939. **Genres:** Children's Non-fiction, Natural History, Animals/Pets, Sports/Fitness. **Career:** University of London, Bedford College, medical research, 1960-65; Prosound Music, computing, 1984-86; writer, 1988-. **Publications:**

FOR CHILDREN: (with A. Armstrong and C. Kampert) The Wildwatch Book: Ideas, Activities, and Projects for Exploring Colorado's Front Range, 1990; Eagles: Hunters of the Sky, 1992; Bats: Swift Shadows in the Twilight, 1994; Owls: On Silent Wings, 1994; Above the Treeline, 1996; In the Forest, 1996; Along the Seashore, 1997; In the Desert, 1997; Around the Pond, 1998; In the City, 2000. **Address:** 2839 3rd St., Boulder, CO 80304-3038, U.S.A. **Online address:** wordswild@att.net

COOPER, Barry (Anthony Raymond). British (born England), b. 1949. **Genres:** Music, Literary Criticism And History. **Career:** University of Saint Andrews, lecturer, 1973; University of Aberdeen, lecturer, 1974-90; University of Manchester, senior lecturer, 1990-2000, reader, 2000-03, professor of Music, 2003-, chairman of music faculty. Writer. **Publications:** English Solo Keyboard Music of the Middle and Late Baroque, 1989; Beethoven and the Creative Process, 1990, 2nd ed., 1992; (ed.) Three Bagatelles, 1991; (ed. and contrib.) The Beethoven Compendium, 1991, 2nd ed., 1996; Beethoven's Folksong Settings: Chronology, Sources, Style, 1994; (ed.) Complete Organ Music, 1996; Beethoven, 2000; Child Composers and Their Works: A Historical Survey, 2009. Contributor of articles to journals. **Address:** Martin Harris Centre for Music and Drama, School of Arts, Histories and Cultures, University of Manchester, Manchester, M13 9PL, England. **Online address:** barry.cooper@manchester.ac.uk

COOPER, Boden. *See* **REGINALD, Robert.**

COOPER, Brian (Newman). British (born England), b. 1919. **Genres:** Mystery/Crime/Suspense, History. **Career:** County Grammar School, history assistant, 1947-48; Selective Central School, senior history master, 1948-55; Bolsover School, senior history master, 1955-79; Moorfield School, senior history master, 1955-79, now retired; detective chief inspector, now retired. Writer. **Publications:** FICTION: Where the Fresh Grass Grows, 1955; Maria, 1956; A Path to the Bridge, 1958; Giselle, 1958; The Van Langeren Girl, 1960; A Touch of Thunder, 1962; A Time to Retreat, 1963; Genesis 38, 1965; The Murder of Mary Steers, 1966; A Mission for Betty Smith, 1967; Monsoon Murder, 1967; Messiter's Dream, 1991; The Cross of San Vincente, 1991; The Singing Stones, 1993; Covenant with Death, 1994; Shadows on the Sand, 1995; The Travelling Dead, 1997; The Blacknock Woman, 1999; The Norfolk Triangle, 2000; The Murder Column, 2003; Out with the Tide, 2006. NONFICTION: Transformation of a Valley: The Derbyshire Derwent, 1983. **Address:** 43 Parkland Close, Mansfield, NT NG18 4PP, England.

COOPER, Carolyn (Joy). Jamaican (born Jamaica), b. 1950. **Genres:** Literary Criticism And History. **Career:** Canadian International Development Agency, fellow, 1971-72; Atlantic Union College, assistant professor, 1975-80, associate professor of English, 1980, All-College Cultural Study of the Caribbean, director and coordinator of study-abroad research visit to Jamaica, 1977-78, director of program, 1980, Honors Core Curriculum Program, head, 1979-80; University of the West Indies, lecturer, 1980-90, senior lecturer in English, 1990-, professor in FHE-literatures in English, professor of literary and cultural studies, Reggae Studies Unit, coordinator; Ibadan University, commonwealth foundation fellow, 1982; University of Hull, visiting lecturer, 1982; Howard University, senior Fulbright fellow, 1985; Jamaica Telephone Company Ltd., course facilitator, 1988-; University of the South Pacific, fellow, 1992; Spelman College, visiting professor, 1993. Writer. **Publications:** Noises in the Blood: Orality, Gender and the Vulgar Body of Jamaican Popular Culture, 1993; (ed. with E. Wint) Bob Marley, 2003; Sound Clash: Jamaican Dancehall Culture from Lady Saw to Dancehall Queen, 2004. Contributor to books and periodicals. **Address:** Department of Literatures in English, University of the West Indies, Mona, Kingston, 7, Jamaica. **Online address:** carolyn.cooper@uwimona.edu.jm

COOPER, Cary L. American (born United States), b. 1940. **Genres:** Administration/Management, Business/Trade/Industry, Medicine/Health. **Career:** University of Manchester, Institute of Science and Technology, professor, 1974-2003, pro-vice-chancellor, 1995-2000, deputy vice-chancellor, 2000-03; Robertson Cooper Ltd., director, 1999-; Lancaster University, professor and pro-vice-chancellor, 2003-, distinguished professor of organisational psychology and health; Heriot-Watt University, visiting professor. Writer. **Publications:** (With I.L. Mangham) T-Groups, 1971; (with D. Bowles) Hurt or Helped?, 1977; (with J. Marshall) Understanding Executive Stress, 1978; (with J. Marshall) Executives under Pressure, 1979; The Executive Gypsy, 1979; Learning from Others in Groups, 1979; (with A. Jones) Combating Managerial Obsolescence, 1980; The Stress Check, 1981; Executive Families under Stress, 1982; (co-author) Introducing Organisational Behaviour, 1982; (with M. Davidson) High Pressure: Working Lives of Women Managers, 1982; Improving Interpersonal Relations: A Guide to Social Skill Development for Managers and Group Leaders, 1982; (with M. Davidson) Stress and the Woman Manager, 1983; (with I. Robertson) Human Behaviour in Organisations, 1983; (with L. Thompson) Public Faces, Private Lives, 1984; (with P. Hingley) The Changemakers, 1985; (with V. Sutherland) Man and Accidents Offshore, 1986; (with P. Hingley) Stress and the Nurse Manager, 1986; (with S. Sloan) Airline Pilots under Pressure, 1986; (with C. Cox) High Flyers, 1988; (with J. Wills) Pressure Sensitive, 1988; (with S. Sloan and S. Williams) Occupational Stress Indicator, 1988; (with R. Cooper and L. Eaker) Living with Stress, 1988; (with A. McGoldrick) Early Retirement, 1989; (with P. Makin and C. Cox) Managing People at Work, 1989; (with S. Lewis) Career Couples, 1989; (with V. Sutherland) Understanding Stress, 1990; (with J. Arnold and I. Robertson) Work Psychology, 1991, 3rd ed., 1998; (with V. Sutherland) Stress and Accidents in the Offshore Oil and Gas Industry, 1991; Cary Cooper on Stress, 1991; (with B. Dale) Total Quality and Human Resources, 1991; (with M. Davidson) The Stress Survivors, 1992; (with S. Cartwright) Mergers and Acquisitions, 1992; (with M. Davidson) Shattering the Glass Ceiling, 1992; (with M. Watts) Relax, 1992; (with B. White and C. Cox) Women's Career Development, 1992; (with H. Kahn) Stress in the Dealing Room, 1993; (with A. Straw) Successful Stress Management in a Week, 1993; (with S. Lewis) The Workplace Revolution, 1993; (with S. Cartwright) No Hassle!, 1994; (with R. Jennings and C. Cox) Business Elites, 1994; (with C. Travers) Teachers under Pressure, 1995; (with P. Makin and C. Cox) Organizations and the Psychological Contract, 1995; (with S. Cartwright) Managing Mergers, Acquisitions and Strategic Alliances, 1995; (with J. Earnshaw) Stress and Employer Liability, 1996; (with S. Cartwright) Mental Health and Stress in the Workplace, 1996; (with P. Liukkonen and S. Cartwright) Stress Prevention in the Workplace, 1996; (with J. Berridge and C. Highley) Employee Assistance Programmes, 1997; (with V. Sutherland) Dealing with Difficult People, 1997; (with B. Dale and A. Wilkinson) Managing Quality and Human Resources, 1997; (with M. Watts) Stop the World, 1997; (with N. Holden) Management Cultures in Collision, 1998; (with S. Lewis) Balancing Career, Family and Life, 1998; (with J. Quick) Stress and Strain, 1999; (with S. Palmer) Conquer Your Stress, 2000; (with V. Sutherland) Strategic Stress Management, 2000; (with S. Cartwright) HR Know-How in Mergers and Acquisitions, 2000; (with S. Cartwright) Organizational Stress, 2001; Organizational Health Psychology, 2001; (with C. Rayner and H. Hoel) Workplace Bullying, 2001; (with J. Quick) FT Guide to Executive Health, 2002; (with S. Palmer and K. Thomas) Creating a Balance, 2003; (with P. Sparrow) The Employment Relationship, 2003; (with S. Clarke) Managing the Risk of Workplace Stress, 2004; (with T. Theobold) Shut Up and Listen, 2004; (with P. Dewe) Stress: A Brief History, 2004; (with S. Lewis) Work-Life Integration, 2005; (with V. Kusstatscher) Managing Emotions in Mergers and Acquisitions, 2005; (with B. Hoag) Managing Value-Based Organizations: It's Not What You Think, 2006; (co-author) Happy-Performing Managers, 2006; (with S. Palmer) How to Deal with Stress, 2007; (with T. Theobald) Detox Your Desk: De-Clutter Your Life and Mind, 2007; (co-author) Employee Well-Being Support: A Workplace Resource, 2008; (with I. Rothman) Organizational and Work Psychology: Topics in Applied Psychology, 2008; (with L. Gadman) Open Source Leadership, 2009; (with J.P. Brun) Missing Pieces: 7 Ways to Improve Employee Well-being and Organizational Effectiveness, 2009; (with D. Bowles) Employee Morale: Driving Performance in Challenging Times, 2009; (with P. Dewe and M.P. O'Driscoll) Coping With Work Stress: a Review and Critique, 2010; (with U. Lundberg) Science of Occupational Health: Stress, Psychobiology and the New World of Work, 2011. EDITOR: Theories of Group Processes, 1975; Developing Social Skills in Managers, 1976; OD Organizational Development in the U.S.A. and the U.K., 1977; (with C. Alderfer) Advances in Experiential Social Processes, vol. I, 1978, vol. II, 1980; (with R. Payne) Stress at Work, 1978; Behavioural Problems in Organisations, 1979; (with E. Mumford) The Quality of Working Life in Western and Eastern Europe, 1979; Developing Managers for the '80s, 1980; (with R. Payne) Current Concerns in Occupational Stress, 1980; (with J. Marshall) White Collar and Professional Stress, 1980; (with R. Payne) Groups at Work, 1981; (with J. Marshall) Coping with Stress at Work: Case Studies from Industry, 1981; Psychology and Management, 1981; Improving Interpersonal Relations: Some Current Approaches to Social Skill Training, 1981; (with D. Torrington) After Forty: The Time for Achievement, 1982; (co-ed.) Management Education: Theory, Research and Practice, 1982; Stress Research: Issues for the Eighties, 1983; Practical Approaches to Women's Career Development, 1983; Group Training for Individual and Organisational Development, 1983; (with M. Davidson) Women in Management: Career Development for Managerial Success, 1984; (with P. Makin) Psychology for Managers, 1984; (with M. Davidson) Working Women: An International Survey, 1984; Psychosocial Stress and Cancer, 1984; (with M. Smith) Job Stress and Blue Collar Work, 1985; (with I.T. Robertson) Review of Industrial and Organisational Psychology, 1986; (with R. Kalimo) Psychosocial Factors at Work and Their Relation to Health, 1987; (with S. Kasl) Stress and Health: Issues in Research Methodology, 1987; (with K. Markides) Retirement in Industrialized Societies: Social, Psychological and Health Factors, 1987; (with M. Davidson) Women and Information Technology, 1987; (with R. Payne) Causes, Coping and Consequences of Stress at Work, 1988; (co-ed.) Occupational Stress: Issues and Developments in Research, 1988; Stress and Breast Cancer, 1988; (with S. Sauter and J. Hurrell) Job Control and Worker Health, 1989; (with K. Markides) Aging, Stress and Health, 1989; Industrial and Organizational Psychology, vol. I: Critical Writings in Psychology, 1991; (with S. Fisher) On the Move: The Psychology of Change and Transition, 1991; (with R. Payne) Personality and Stress: Individual Differences in the Stress Process, 1991; (with M. Watson) Cancer and Stress: Psychological, Biological and Coping Studies, 1991; (with P. Barrar) Managing Organisations in 1992: The Strategic Response, 1991; (with D. Rousseau) Trends in Organizational Behavior, 4 vols., 1991-97; (with M. Davidson) European Women in Business and Management, 1993; (with S. Williams) Creating Healthy Work Organizations, 1994; (with I.T. Robertson) Key Reviews in Managerial Psychology, 1994; (with S. Kasl) Research Method in Stress and Health Psychology, 1995; Handbook of Stress, Medicine and Health, 1996; (with M.J. Schabracq and A.M. Winnubst) Handbook of Work and Health Psychology, 1996; (with S. Jackson) Creating Tomorrow's Organisations: A Handbook for Future Research in Organizational Behavior, 1997; (with C. Argyris) Encyclopedia of Management, 1997; (with A. Roney) Professionals on Workplace Stress, 1997; (with L. Pervin) Personality: Critical Concepts in Psychology, 1998; (with C. Argyris) Concise Encyclopedia of Management, 1998; (with M. Kompier) Preventing Stress and Improving Production, 1999; (with E. Locke) Industrial and Organizational Psychology: Linking Theory with Practice, 2000; (with L. Baider and A.K. DeNour) Cancer and the Family, 2000; (with R. Burke) The Organization in Crisis, 2000; Who's Who in the Management Sciences, 2000; Classics in Management Thought, vols. 1-2, 2000; (with L. Murphy) Healthy and Productive Work, 2000; (with A. Gregory) Advances in Mergers and Acquisitions, 2000; Fundamentals of Organizational Behavior, 2002; (with R.J. Burke) New World of Work: Challenges and Opportunities, 2002; (with R.J. Burke) Leading in Turbulent Times: Managing in the New World of Work, 2004; Handbook of Stress Medicine and Health, 2005; Leadership and Management in the 21st Century: Business Challenges of the Future, 2005; (with R.J. Burke) Reinventing Human Resource Management: Challenges and New Directions, 2005; (with A. Antoniou) Research Companion to Organizational Health Psychology, 2005; (with W.H. Starbuck) Work: Contexts and Consequences, 2005; (co-ed.) Workplace Violence: Issues, Trends, Strategies, 2005; (with R.J. Burke) Inspiring Leaders, 2006; (with D.L. Nelson) Positive Organizational Behavior, 2007; (co-ed.) Research Companion to the Dysfunctional Workplace, 2007; (with R.J. Burke) Building More Effective Organizations, 2008; (with S. Cartwright) Oxford Handbook of Organizatonal Well-Being, 2008; (with S. Cartwright) Oxford Handbook of Personnel Psychology, 2008; (with R.J. Burke) Peak Performing Organization, 2008; (with N. Ashkanasy) Research Companion to Emotion in Organizations, 2008; (with J. Barling) SAGE Handbook of Organizational Behavior, 2008; New Directions in Organizational Behavior, 2008; (with R.J. Burke) International Terrorism and Threats to Security: Managerial and Organizational Challenges, 2008; (with R.J. Burke) Research Companion to Corruption in Organizations, 2009; (with J.C. Quick and M.J. Schabracq) International Handbook of Work and Health Psychology, 2009; (with A.S. Antoniou) New Directions in Organisational Psychology and Behavioural Medicine, 2010; Mental Capital and Wellbeing, 2010; (with R.J. Burke and E.C. Tomlinson) Crime and Corruption in Organizations: Why It Occurs and What To Do About It, 2010. **Address:** Vice-Chancellor's Office, Lancaster University, Rm. D17, Lancaster, LC LA1 4YW, England. **Online address:** c.cooper1@lancaster.ac.uk

COOPER, C. Everett. *See* **REGINALD, Robert.**

COOPER, Dave. (David Charles Cooper). Canadian (born Canada), b. 1967?. **Genres:** Graphic Novels. **Career:** Writer and graphic artist. **Publications:** GRAPHIC NOVELS: Suckle: The Status of Basil, 1996; Crumple, 2000; Dan and Larry In: Don't Do That!, 2001; Dave Cooper's Underbelly: Additional Observations on the Beauty/Ugliness of Mostly Pillowy Girls, 2004. **Address:** Canada. **Online address:** dave@davegraphics.com

COOPER, David A. American (born United States), b. 1939?. **Genres:** Theology/Religion, Business/Trade/Industry. **Career:** Heart of Stillness Hermitage, director. Lecturer, rabbi, meditation guide and writer. **Publications:** The Heart of Stillness: The Elements of Spiritual Practice, 1992; Silence, Simplicity and Solitude: A Guide for Spiritual Retreat, 1992; Entering the Sacred Mountain: A Mystical Odyssey, 1994; Renewing Your Soul: A Guided Retreat for the Sabbath and Other Days of Rest, 1995; God is a Verb: Kabbalah and the Practice of Mystical Judaism, 1997; Handbook of Jewish Meditation Practices: A Guide for Enriching the Sabbath and Other Days of Your Life, 2000; Three Gates to Meditation Practice: A Personal Journey into Sufism, Buddhism and Judaism, 2000; Ecstatic Kabbalah, 2005; Invoking Angels, 2006; Preaching Through the Year vol. II: 52 Impactful Messages, 2009; Leadership Risk: A Guide for Private Equity and Strategic Investors, 2010. **Address:** c/o Sounds True, PO Box 8010, Boulder, CO 80306, U.S.A. **Online address:** davidcoop99@yahoo.com

COOPER, David Charles. *See* **COOPER, Dave.**

COOPER, David D. American (born United States), b. 1948. **Genres:** Literary Criticism And History, Biography. **Career:** University of California, lecturer in English, 1978-88; Michigan State University, assistant professor, associate professor, professor, of American thought and language, 1988-; Berea College, Eli Lilly distinguished visiting professor of religion and American culture, 1991. Writer. **Publications:** Thomas Merton's Art of Denial: The Evolution of a Radical Humanist, 1989; (ed.) James Laughlin and Thomas Merton: Selected Letters, 1997; (ed.) Lives We Carry with Us: Profiles of Moral Courage, 2010. Work appears in anthologies. **Address:** Writing, Rhetoric & American Cultures, Michigan State University, 286 Bessey Hall, East Lansing, MI 48824, U.S.A. **Online address:** cooperd@msu.edu

COOPER, Derek (Macdonald). British (born England), b. 1925. **Genres:** Food And Wine, Transportation, Travel/Exploration, History. **Career:** Guild of Food Writers, founding member and chairman; Radio Malaya and Radio Singapore, producer, 1950-60; Independent Television News, producer, 1960-61; freelance writer and presenter for radio and television, 1961-. **Publications:** The Bad Food Guide, 1967; The Beverage Report, 1970; Skye, 1970; The Gullibility Gap, 1974; Hebridean Connection: A View of the Highlands and Islands, 1977; A Guide to the Whiskies of Scotland, 1978; Road to the Isles: Travellers in the Hebrides, 1770-1914, 1979; (with D. Pattullo) Enjoying Scotch, 1980; Wine with Food, 1980, 1986; The Whisky Roads of Scotland, 1981; Skye Remembered, 1983; The Century Companion to Whiskies, 1983; The World of Cooking, 1983; The Road to Mingulay: A View of the Western Isles, 1985; The Gunge File, 1986; A Taste of Scotch, 1989; The Little Book of Malt Whiskies, 1992; The Balvenie, 1993; Snail Eggs and Samphire: Dispatches from the Food Front, 2000. **Address:** 4 St., Helena Terr., Richmond, SR TW9 1NR, England.

COOPER, Dominic (Xavier). Scottish/British (born England), b. 1944. **Genres:** Novels, Novellas/Short Stories, Essays, Poetry, Young Adult Fiction. **Career:** Decca Record Co., promotional assistant, 1967-69; Fabbri & Partners, editor, 1969-70; Malaskolinn Mimir, teacher, 1970-71; freelance writer, 1972-74. **Publications:** The Dead of Winter, 1975; Sunrise, 1977, rev. ed., 1986; Jack Fletcher, 1978; Men at Axlir: A Fiction Concerning the Case of Sunnefa Jónsdóttir, 1978; Will Stringer, 1980; The Country of the Gull, 1981; The Horn Fellow, 1987; (ed.) Judgements of Value: Selected Writings on Music, 1988; (contrib.) Shadow of Heaven: Scotland from Above, 1989. **Address:** 9 Swordle Chorrach, Achateny, Acharacle, Argyll, HI PH36 4LG, Scotland. **Online address:** tiercel9@tiscali.co.uk

COOPER, Elisha. American (born United States), b. 1971. **Genres:** Children's Non-fiction, Documentaries/Reportage. **Career:** New Yorker Magazine, messenger, 1993-95; writer and artist, 1995-. **Publications:** FOR CHILDREN: Country Fair, 1997; Ballpark, 1998; Building, 1999; Dance!, 2001; Ice Cream, 2002; Magic Thinks Big, 2004; Ridiculous/Hilarious/Terrible/Cool: A Year in an American High School, 2008. OTHERS: A Year in New York, 1995; Off the Road: An American Sketchbook, 1996; A Day at Yale, 1998; Henry, 1999; California: A Sketchbook, 2000; Paris Night and Day: From the Marais to the Cafe, 2002; A Good Night Walk, 2005; Crawling: A Father's First Year, 2006; Bear Dreams, 2006; Beach, 2006; Beaver is Lost, 2010; Farm, 2010; Homer, 2012. **Address:** Darhansoff & Verrill, 236 W 26th St., Ste. 802, New York, NY 10001-6736, U.S.A. **Online address:** elicooper@aol.com

COOPER, Floyd. American (born United States), b. 1956. **Genres:** Biography, Illustrations. **Career:** Author and freelance illustrator, 1984-. **Publications:** SELF-ILLUSTRATED: Coming Home: From the Life of Langston Hughes, 1994; Mandela: From the Life of the South African Statesman, 1996; Cumbayah, 1998; Jump!: From the Life of Michael Jordan, 2004; Willie and the Barnstormin' All-Stars, 2008. Illustrator of books by others. **Address:** HarperCollins Children's Books, 1350 Ave. of the Americas, New York, NY 10019, U.S.A. **Online address:** fcooper4@msn.com

COOPER, Hannah. *See* **SPENCE, William John Duncan.**

COOPER, Helen. British (born England), b. 1963. **Genres:** Children's Fiction, Illustrations, Picture/Board Books, Literary Criticism And History. **Career:** Writer and illustrator. **Publications:** SELF-ILLUSTRATED: Kit and the Magic Kite, 1987; (with M. Miller) Lucy and the Egg Witch, 1989; Ella and the Rabbit, 1990; Chestnut Grey: A Folktale from Russia, 1993; The Bear under the Stairs, 1993; The House Cat, 1993; The Tale of Bear, 1994; The Tale of Duck, 1994; The Tale of Pig, 1994; The Tale of Frog (board books), 1994; Little Monster Did It!, 1995; The Baby Who Wouldn't Go to Bed, 1996 in US as The Boy Who Wouldn't Go to Bed, 1997; Pumpkin Soup, 1998; Toy Tales, 2000; Tatty Ratty, 2001; Sandmare, 2003; A Pipkin of Pepper, 2003; (ed.) Villette, 2005; Delicious!, 2006; Dog Biscuit, 2008. OTHERS: (ed.) Great Grandmother Goose, 1978. Illustrator of books by E. Johns, E. Lear and S. Pirotta. Contributor to periodicals. **Address:** c/o Hilary Delemere, The Agency, 24 Pottery Ln., Holland Pk., London, GL W11 4LZ, England.

COOPER, Helene. American (born United States), b. 1966?. **Genres:** Autobiography/Memoirs. **Career:** Providence Journal Bulletin, reporter, 1987-92; Wall Street Journal, Washington Bureau, reporter, 1992-97, assistant chief, 2002-04, Atlanta Bureau, reporter, 1992-97, London Bureau, reporter, 1997-99, international economics reporter, 1999-2002; New York Times, editorial writer and assistant editorial page editor, 2004, diplomatic correspondent. Journalist and memoirist. **Publications:** (ed.) At Home in the World: Collected Writings from the Wall Street Journal, 2002; The House at Sugar Beach: In Search of a Lost African Childhood (memoir), 2008. **Address:** Editorial Page Office, New York Times, 229 W 43rd St., New York, NY 10036-3913, U.S.A.

COOPER, Henry. *See* **KAYE, Barrington.**

COOPER, Ilene. American (born United States), b. 1948. **Genres:** Novels, Young Adult Fiction, Young Adult Non-fiction, Psychology, Education, Biography. **Career:** Winnetka Public Library, children's librarian, 1976-80; ABC-TV, consultant to ABC afterschool specials, 1976-82; Booklist, children's book editor, 1985-; WGN TV, editorial researcher. **Publications:** NOVELS: The Winning of Miss Lynn Ryan, 1987; Buddy Love-Now on Video, 1995; I'll See You in My Dreams, 1997; Sam I Am, 2004. KIDS FROM KENNEDY MIDDLE SCHOOL SERIES: Queen of the Sixth Grade, 1988; Choosing Sides, 1990; Mean Streak, 1991; The New, Improved Gretchen Hubbard, 1992. FRANCES IN THE FOURTH GRADE SERIES: Frances Takes a Chance, 1991; Frances Dances, 1991; Frances Four-Eyes, 1991; Frances and Friends, 1991. HOLLYWOOD WARS SERIES: Lights, Camera, Attitude, 1993; My Co-Star, My Enemy, 1993; Seeing Red, 1993; Trouble in Paradise, 1993. HOLIDAY FIVE SERIES: Trick or Trouble, 1994; The Worst Noel, 1994; Stupid Cupid, 1995; Star Spangled Summer, 1996; No-Thanks Thanksgiving, 1996. YOUNG ADULT NONFICTION: Jewish Holidays All Year 'Round, 2002; Jack: The Early Years of John F. Kennedy, 2003. OTHERS: Susan B. Anthony (biography), 1984; (ed. with D. Wilms) Guide to Non-Sexist Children's Books, vol. II: 1976-1985, 1987; The Dead Sea Scrolls, 1997; Absolutely Lucy, 2000; Lucy on the Loose, 2000; Annoying Team, 2002; Oprah Winfrey: A Twentieth-Century Life, 2007; Golden Rule, 2007; Jake's Best Thumb, 2008; Look at Lucy!, 2008; Lucy on the Ball, 2011; Angel in My Pocket, 2011; Little Lucy, 2011. **Address:** Booklist, American Library Association, 50 E Huron St., Chicago, IL 60611, U.S.A. **Online address:** icooper@ala.org

COOPER, Jilly (Sallitt). British (born England), b. 1937. **Genres:** Romance/Historical, Children's Fiction, Young Adult Fiction, Human Relations/Parenting, Humor/Satire, Novels. **Career:** Middlesex Independent Newspaper, reporter, 1957-59; Sunday Times, columnist, 1969-82; Mail On Sunday, writer, columnist, 1982-87. **Publications:** How to Stay Married, 1969; How to Survive from Nine to Five, 1970; Jolly Super, 1971; Men and Super Men, 1972; Jolly Super Too, 1973; Women and Super Women, 1974; Jolly Superlative, 1975; Super Men and Super Women (omnibus), 1976; Work and Wedlock (omnibus), 1977; Superjilly, 1977; Class: A View from Middle England, 1979; (ed.) The British in Love, 1979; Supercooper, 1980; Little Mabel series (juvenile), 4 vols., 1980-85; (ed. with T. Hartman) Violets and Vinegar: An Anthology of Women's Writings and Sayings, 1980; Love and Other Heartaches, 1981; Intelligent and Loyal, 1981; Jolly Marsupial: Down Under And Other Scenes, 1982; Animals in War, 1983; (ed. with T. Hartman) Beyond Bartlett: Quotations by and About Women, 1983; The Common Years, 1984; Leo and Jilly Cooper on Rugby, 1984; Riders: A Novel, 1985; Hotfoot to Zabriskie Point, 1985; Leo and Jilly Cooper on Cricket, 1985; Horse Mania!, 1986; How to Survive Christmas, 1986; Turn Right at the Spotted Dog, 1987; Rivals, 1988; Players, 1989; Angels Rush In: The Best of Jilly Cooper's Satire And Humour, 1990; Polo, 1991; Mongrel Magic, 1992; Turn Right at the Spotted Dog and Other Diversions, 1992; The Man Who Made Husbands Jealous, 1993; Appassionata, 1996; Score!, 1999; Pandora, 2002; Wicked!, 2006. ROMANCE NOVELS: Emily, 1975; Bella, 1976; Harriet, 1976; Octavia, 1977; Imogen, 1978; Prudence, 1980; Lisa and Co., 1982; Araminta's Wedding, or, A Fortune Secured: A Country House Extravaganza, 1993; Jump!, 2010. PICTURE BOOKS: Little Mabel, 1980; Little Mabel's Great Escape, 1981; Little Mabel Wins, 1982; Little Mabel Saves the Day, 1985. **Address:** c/o Vivienne Schuster, Curtis Brown, Haymarket House, 28/29 Haymarket, London, GL SW1Y 4SP, England.

COOPER, Kate. British (born England), b. 1960. **Genres:** History, Theology/Religion, Adult Non-fiction. **Career:** University of Manchester, senior lecturer, 1995-, Centre for Late Antiquity, director. Writer. **Publications:** The Virgin and the Bride: Idealized Womanhood in Late Antiquity, 1996; (ed. with J. Hillner) Religion, Dynasty and Patronage in Early Christian Rome, 300-900, 2007; The Fall of the Roman Household, 2007. STUDIES IN CHURCH HISTORY SERIES: (ed. with J. Gregory) Retribution, Repentance and Reconciliation: Papers Read at the 2002 Summer Meeting and the 2003 Winter Meeting of the Ecclesiastical History Society, 2004; (ed. with J. Gregory) Signs, Miracles, Wonders: Representations of Divine Power in the Life of the Church, 2005; (ed. with Jeremy Gregory) Elite and Popular Religion: Papers Read at the 2004 Summer Meeting and the 2005 Winter Meeting of the Ecclesiastical History Society, 2006; (ed. with J. Gregory) Discipline and Diversity: Papers Read at the 2005 Summer Meeting and the 2006 Winter Meeting of the Ecclesiastical History Society, 2007; (ed. with J. Gregory) Revival and Resurgence in Christian History: Papers Read at the 2006 Summer Meeting and the 2007 Winter Meeting of the Ecclesiastical History Society, 2008. Contributor to books, journals and periodicals. **Address:** University of Manchester, Oxford Rd., Manchester, GM M13 9PL, England. **Online address:** kate.cooper@manchester.ac.uk

COOPER, Kenneth H(ardy). American/Canadian (born Canada), b. 1931. **Genres:** Medicine/Health, Sports/Fitness, Biography. **Career:** Lackland Air Force Base, Aerospace Medical Laboratory Clinic, director, 1964-70, flight surgeon; Cooper Aerobics Center, founder. chairman, president and chief executive officer, 1970-; National Defense University, visiting lecturer, 1973-90; University of California, regent's lecturer, 1980; Mayo Clinic, visiting lecturer, 1981. Writer. **Publications:** Aerobics, 1968; The New Aerobics, 1970; (with M. Cooper) Aerobics for Women, 1972; The Aerobics Way: New Data on the World's Most Popular Exercise Program, 1977; The Aerobics Program for Total Well-Being: Exercise, Diet, Emotional Balance, 1982; Running without Fear: How to Reduce the Risk of Heart Attack and Sudden Death during Aerobic Exercise, 1985; Controlling Cholesterol: Dr. Kenneth H. Cooper's Preventive Medicine Program, 1988; (with M. Cooper) The New Aerobics for Women, 1988; Preventing Osteoporosis: Dr. Kenneth H. Cooper's Preventive Medicine Program, 1989; Overcoming Hypertension: Dr. Kenneth H. Cooper's Preventive Medicine Program, 1990; Kid Fitness: A Complete Shape-up Program from Birth Through High School, 1991, rev. ed., 1999; Dr. Kenneth H. Cooper's Antioxidant Revolution, 1994; It's Better to Believe, 1995; Advanced Nutritional Therapies, 1996; Can Stress Heal?, 1997; Regaining the Power of Youth at Any Age, 1998; Controlling Cholesterol the Natural Way: Eat Your Way to Better Health with New Breakthrough Food Discoveries, 1999; Managing Cholesterol in the 21st Century, 1999; (with T.C. Cooper and W. Proctor) Start Strong, Finish Strong: Prescriptions for a Lifetime of Great Health, 2007; Matters of the Heart: Adventures in Sports Medicine, 2007. Contributor to periodicals. **Address:** Cooper Aerobic Center, 12200 Preston Rd., Dallas, TX 75230, U.S.A.

COOPER, Lee Pelham. *See* **ROWE, Lee Pelham.**

COOPER, Leon N. American (born United States), b. 1930. **Genres:** Physics. **Career:** Institute for Advanced Study, National Science Foundation postdoctoral fellow, 1954-55; University of Illinois, research associate in physics, 1955-57; Ohio State University, assistant professor, 1957-58; Brown University, associate professor, 1958-62, professor of physics, 1962-66, Henry Ledyard Goddard University professor, 1966-74, Center for Neural Sciences, co-chair, 1973-, Thomas J. Watson senior professor of science, 1974-, Institute for Brain and Neural Systems, director; Alfred P. Sloan Foundation, research fellow, 1959-66; Nestor Inc., co-founder and co-chairman; John Simon Guggenheim Memorial Foundation, fellow, 1965-66; American Academy of Arts and Sciences, fellow. Writer. **Publications:** (With B.B. Schwartz) The Physics and Application of Superconductivity, 1968; An Introduction to the Meaning and Structure of Physics, 1968, rev. ed., 1970; Physics: Structure and Meaning, 1992; (ed.) How We Learn, How We Remember: Toward an Understanding of Brain and Neural Systems, 1995; (co-author) Theory of Cortical Plasticity, 2004; (with D. Feldman) BCS: 50 Years, 2011. Contributor to journals and periodicals. **Address:** Department of Physics, Brown University, Barus-Holley Bldg., 182 Hope St., PO Box 1843, Providence, RI 02912, U.S.A. **Online address:** leon_cooper@brown.edu

COOPER, Mark Garrett. American (born United States), b. 1967. **Genres:** Art/Art History, Romance/Historical, Film. **Career:** Florida State University, assistant professor of English, 1998-2007; University of South Carolina, Department of Film and Media Studies, associate professor, 2007-, Department of English Language and Literature, associate professor, 2007-, Moving Image Research Collections, interim director, Public History Program, Women's and Gender Studies, faculty. Writer. **Publications:** Love Rules: Silent Hollywood and the Rise of the Managerial Class, 2003; Universal Women: Filmmaking and Institutional Change in Early Hollywood, 2010. **Address:** Department of English, University of South Carolina, 212 Humanities Office Bldg., 728 Pickens St., Columbia, SC 29208, U.S.A. **Online address:** coopermg@sc.edu

COOPER, M. E. *See* **WAGNER, Sharon Blythe.**

COOPER, M. E. *See* **DAVIS, Maggie S.**

COOPER, Melrose. *See* **KROLL, Virginia L(ouise).**

COOPER, Michelle. Australian (born Australia), b. 1969?. **Genres:** History. **Career:** Author and speech pathologist. **Publications:** The Rage of Sheep, 2007. MONTMARAY JOURNALS SERIES: A Brief History of Montmaray, 2008; The FitzOsbornes in Exile, 2010. Contributor to periodicals. **Address:** Sydney, NW , Australia. **Online address:** michelle@michellecooper-writer.com

COOPER, Natasha. *See* **WRIGHT, Daphne.**

COOPER, N. J. *See* **WRIGHT, Daphne.**

COOPER, Paulette. American/Belgian (born Belgium), b. 1942. **Genres:** Animals/Pets, Travel/Exploration. **Career:** Writer. **Publications:** The Scandal of Scientology, 1971; (ed.) Growing up Puerto Rican, 1972; Let's Find Out about Halloween (juvenile), 1972; The Medical Detectives, 1973; (with R. Linn) Staying Thin: The Doctor's Guide to Permanent Weight Control, 1980; (with P. Noble) Reward!, 1994; 277 Secrets Your Dog Wants You to Know: A Doggie Bag of Unusual and Useful Information, 1995; 277 Secrets Your Cat Wants You to Know, 1997; 277 Secrets Your Snake and Lizard Wants You to Know: Unusual and Useful Information for Snake Owners and Snake Lovers, 1999; The Most Romantic Resorts for Destination Weddings, Marriage Renewals, and Honeymoons, 2002; Bargain Shopping in Palm Beach County, 2010; Bargain Shopping in Fort Lauderdale, 2011. Contributor to periodicals. **Address:** PO Box 621, Palm Beach, FL 33480-0621, U.S.A. **Online address:** southfloridatrav@aol.com

COOPER, Polly Wylly. American (born United States), b. 1940. **Genres:** History, Autobiography/Memoirs. **Career:** Crabettes (music group), founding member. Writer. **Publications:** (With E.K. Cooper) A Visitor's Guide to Savannah, 1995; Savannah Safari Walking Tour, 1998; Savannah Movie Memories, 2000; Isle of Hope, Wormsloe and Bethesda, 2002; (with B.W. Collins) Beaufort, 2003; (with E.L. Taber) Sand between Our Toes: The Tybee Island Family Photo Album, 2009; (with E.L. Taber) Tybee Days: One Hundred Years on Georgia's Playground Island, 2009. **Address:** 519 Parkersburg Rd., Savannah, GA 31406, U.S.A.

COOPER, Richard Newell. American (born United States), b. 1934. **Genres:** Economics, International Relations/Current Affairs. **Career:** Council of Economic Advisers, Executive Office of the President, senior staff economist, 1961-63; Yale University, senior staff, 1961-63, assistant professor of economics, 1963-65, Frank Altschul professor of international economics, 1966-77, provost, 1972-74; Council of Economic Advisers, consultant, 1963-69; RAND Corp., consultant, 1964-65; United Nations, consultant, 1964-67; U.S. Treasury Department, consultant, 1964-77; U.S. Department of State, deputy assistant secretary of state for international monetary affairs, 1965-66, consultant, 1966-77, under secretary of state for economic affairs, 1977-81; National Security Council, consultant, 1969-70; Harvard University, Maurits C. Boas professor of international economics, 1981-; Federal Reserve Bank of Boston, chairman, 1990-92; National Intelligence Council, chairman, 1995-97; Phoenix Mutual Life Insurance Co., director; Wards Co., director. Writer. **Publications:** Growth and Trade, 1964; The Economics of Interdependence, 1968; (co-author) Britain's Economic Prospects, 1968; Issues for Trade Policy in the Seventies, 1971; Currency Devaluation in Developing Countries, 1971; Sterling, European Monetary Unification, and the International Monetary System, 1972; (with M. Kaji and C. Segre) Towards a Renovated World Monetary System, 1973; Economic Mobility and National Economic Policy, 1974; (with K. Kaiser and M. Kosaka) Towards a Renovated International System, 1977; (with K. Kaiser and M. Kosaka) Wege zur Erneuerung des internationalen Systems, 1979; (contrib.) Global Dilemmas, 1985; Economic Policy in an Interdependent World, 1986; The International Monetary System: Essays in World Economics, 1987; (co-author) Can Nations Agree?, 1989; (with S. Ogata and H. Schulmann) International Financial Integration, 1989; Economic Stabilization in Developing Countries, 1991; Economic Stabilization and Debt in Developing Countries, 1992; (co-author) Boom, Crisis, and Adjustment, 1994, trans. as Auge, crisis y ajuste: la experiencia macroeconómica de los países en desarrollo, 1970-90: resumen, 1995; Environment and Resource Policies for the World Economy, 1994; (co-author) Macroeconomic Policy and Adjustment in Korea, 1994. EDITOR: International Finance, 1969; A Reordered World: Emerging International Economic Problems, 1973; (co-ed.) The International Monetary System under Flexible Exchange Rates, 1982; (ed. with A. Clesse and Y. Sakamoto) The International System after the Collapse of the East-West Order, 1994; (with R. Layard) What the Future Holds, 2002. Contributor to books, journals and periodicals. **Address:** Weatherhead Center for International Affairs, Harvard University, K217, 1737 Cambridge St., Cambridge, MA 02138, U.S.A. **Online address:** rcooper@harvard.edu

COOPER, Roger. British (born England), b. 1935?. **Genres:** Area Studies, Theology/Religion, Law, Politics/Government, Adult Non-fiction, History. **Career:** McDermott, agent, 1985; Tehran University, instructor of English; British Army Intelligence Corps, interpreter. Journalist. **Publications:** NON-FICTION: The Baha'is of Iran, 1982, rev. ed., 1985; Death Plus Ten Years (memoir), 1993; (co-author) Charlesworth & Percy on Negligence, 10th ed., 2001, 11th ed., 2006; (with J. Erickson) Impressions, 2002. **Address:** HarperCollins, 77-85 Fulham Palace Rd., Hammersmith, London, GL W6 8JB, England.

COOPER, Ron L. American (born United States), b. 1960. **Genres:** Philosophy, Novels, Literary Criticism And History. **Career:** Central Florida Community College, associate professor of philosophy, 1995-, professor of philosophy and humanities; Florida Humanities Council, Resource Center, director. Writer. **Publications:** Heidegger and Whitehead: A Phenomenological Examination into the Intelligibility of Experience, 1993; Hume's Fork, 2007; Purple Jesus, a novel, 2010. Contributor to journals. **Address:** Department of Humanities, College of Central Florida, 3001 SW College Rd., Ocala, FL 34478, U.S.A. **Online address:** ron@roncooper.org

COOPER, T. American (born United States), b. 1972?. **Genres:** Novels. **Career:** Writer. **Publications:** Some of the Parts, 2002; Lipshitz Six, or Two Angry Blondes, 2006; (ed. with A. Mansbach) A Fictional History of the United States with Huge Chunks Missing, 2006; The Beaufort Diaries, 2010. Works appear in anthologies. Contributor to periodicals. **Address:** c/o Author Mail, Akashic Books, 232 3rd St., Ste. B404, Brooklyn, NY 11215, U.S.A. **Online address:** goget@t-cooper.com

COOPER, Terry L. American (born United States), b. 1938. **Genres:** Administration/Management, Public/Social Administration. **Career:** University of Southern California, lecturer, 1971-72, instructor in religion, 1972-73, assistant professor of social ethics and urban affairs, 1973-75, assistant professor, 1975-82, associate professor, 1982-91, professor of public administration, 1991-, The Maria B. Crutcher professor in citizenship and democratic values, Neighborhood Participation Project, co-principal investigator; Yonsei University, visiting professor, 1983; University of Kansas, visiting professor, 1984; Chinese University of Hong Kong, Fulbright professor, 1988-89. Writer. **Publications:** The Responsible Administrator: An Approach to Ethics for the Administrative Role, 1982, 6th ed., 2012; An Ethic of Citizenship for Public Administration, 1991; (ed. with N.D. Wright) Exemplary Public Administrators: Character and Leadership in Government, 1992; (ed.) Handbook of Public Administrative Ethics, 1994, 2nd ed., 2001; (with P.C. Kathi and J.W. Meek) Role of the University as a Mediating Institution in Neighborhood Council-City Agency Collaboration, forthcoming; (with A. Bryer and J.W. Meek) Outcomes Achieved through Citizen-Centered Collaborative Public Management, forthcoming. Contributor to journals. **Address:** School of Policy, Planning, and Development, University of Southern California, 302 Ralph and Goldy Lewis Hall, Los Angeles, CA 90089-0626, U.S.A. **Online address:** tlcooper@usc.edu

COOPER, Wyn. American (born United States), b. 1957. **Genres:** Poetry. **Career:** Quarterly West, editor-in-chief, 1983-85; Bennington College, teacher and editor, 1989-94; North Bennington Independent Artist's Space, director, 1992-95; Marlboro College, professor, 1993-96; Wyn Cooper Music, founder and owner, 1995-; freelance writer, 1996-; Frost Place, teacher, 2000-03; Brattleboro Literary Festival/Marlboro College Writing Workshops, director, 2011-. **Publications:** POETRY: The Country of Here Below, 1987; The Way Back, 2000; Secret Address (chapbook), 2002; Postcards from the Interior, 2005; Chaos is the New Calm, 2010. Contributor to periodicals. Works appear in anthologies. **Address:** Halifax, VT , U.S.A. **Online address:** wyncooper@gmail.com

COOPERRIDER, Allen Y(ale). American (born United States), b. 1944. **Genres:** Environmental Sciences/Ecology, Sciences, Business/Trade/Industry. **Career:** U.S. Department of the Interior, Bureau of Land Management, wildlife biologist, 1974-90; Big River Associates, partner, 1991-94; U.S. Fish and Wildlife Service, Ecosystem Restoration Office, senior biologist, 1994-98; Ukiah Brewing Co., general manager, 1999-. Writer. **Publications:** (Ed. with R. Boyd and H. Stuart) The Inventory and Monitoring of Wildlife Habitats, 1967; (with R. Noss) Saving Nature's Legacy: Protecting and Restoring Biodiversity, 1994; (with D. Wilcove) Defending the Desert, 1995. **Address:** 18451 Orr Springs Rd., Ukiah, CA 95482, U.S.A.

COOTES, Jim E. Australian (born Australia), b. 1950. **Genres:** Horticulture, Homes/Gardens. **Career:** Australian Department of Defense, engraver, 1966-97; Australia Post, delivery officer, 2000-; Centre for Plant Biodiversity Research, research associate. Writer. **Publications:** The Orchids of the Philippines, 2001; Philippine Native Orchid Species, 2011. Contributor to magazines. **Address:** c/o Author Mail, Timber Press, 133 SW 2nd Ave., Ste. 450, Portland, OR 97204-3527, U.S.A. **Online address:** jecootes@ozemail.com.au

COOVER, Robert. American (born United States), b. 1932. **Genres:** Novels, Novellas/Short Stories, Plays/Screenplays, Poetry, Young Adult Fiction. **Career:** Bard College, instructor, 1966-67; University of Iowa, writer, 1967-69; Princeton University, writer, 1972-73; Columbia University, writer, 1972; Virginia Military Institute, instructor, 1976; Brandeis University, instructor, 1981; Brown University, writer-in-residence, distinguished professor, 1981-, T.B. Stowell adjunct professor of literary arts, visiting professor of literary arts. **Publications:** The Origin of the Brunists, 1966; The Universal Baseball Association, J. Henry Waugh, Prop., 1968; Pricksongs and Descants (short fictions), 1969; A Theological Position (plays), 1972; (ed. with K. Dixon) The Stone Wall Book of Short Fiction, 1973; (ed. with E. Anderson) Minute Stories, 1976; The Public Burning, 1977; Charlie in the House of Rue, 1980; A Political Fable, 1980; After Lazarus: A Filmscript, 1980; The Convention, 1981; Spanking the Maid, 1982; In Bed One Night and Other Brief Encounters, 1983; Aesop's Forest, 1986; Gerald's Party, 1987; A Night at the Movies, or You Must Remember This, 1987; Whatever Happened to Gloomy Gus of the Chicago Bears?, 1987; Pinocchio in Venice, 1991; John's Wife, 1996; Briar Rose, 1997; Ghost Town, 1998; The Grand Hotels (of Joseph Cornell), 2001; The Adventures of Lucky Pierre: Directors' Cut, 2002; Stepmother, 2004; A Child Again, 2005; Noir, 2010. Works appear in anthologies. Contributor of articles to periodicals. **Address:** Department of Literary Arts, Brown University, Rm. 308, 1923 Literary Arts, 68 1/2 Brown St., Providence, RI 02912-0001, U.S.A. **Online address:** robert_coover@brown.edu

COPE, David. American (born United States), b. 1948. **Genres:** Poetry. **Career:** Grand Rapids Community College, faculty, 1986-; Western Michigan University, adjunct faculty, 1997-2004. Poet. **Publications:** POEMS: Quiet Lives, 1983; On the Bridge, 1986; (ed.) Nada Poems, 1988; Fragments from the Stars, 1990; Coming Home, 1993; Silences for Love, 1998; Turn the Wheel, 2003; Masks of Six Decades, 2010; Moonlight Rose in Blue, forthcoming. **Address:** 2782 Dixie Ave. SW, Grandville, MI 49418, U.S.A. **Online address:** dcope@grcc.edu

COPE, Wendy. British (born England), b. 1945. **Genres:** Poetry. **Career:** Portway Junior School, teacher, 1967-69; Keyworth Junior School, teacher, 1969-73; Cobourg Junior School, teacher, 1973-81, deputy headmaster, 1980-81; ILEA Contact (teachers' newspaper), arts and reviews editor, 1982-84; Brindishe Primary School, music teacher, 1984-86; freelance writer, 1986-; The Spectator Magazine, television columnist, 1986-90. **Publications:** Across the City, 1980; Hope and the 42, 1984; Making Cocoa for Kingsley Amis, 1986; Poem from a Colour Chart of House Paints, 1986; Men and Their Boring Arguments, 1988; Does She Like Word-Games?, 1988; Twiddling Your Thumbs: Hand Rhymes (for children), 1988; (contrib.) Strugnell's Haiku, 1990; The River Girl (poem), 1991; Serious Concerns (poems), 1992; (contrib.) The Faber Book of Drink, Drinkers and Drinking, 1993; The Squirrel and the Crow, 1994; (contrib.) Poems 1, 1995; (co-author) Another Day on Your Foot and I Would Have Died, 1996; (co-author) Casting a Spell and Other Poems, 1996; (contrib.) Over the Moon: Championship Football Poems, 1996; (contrib.) A Draft of XXX Cantos, 1997; (contrib.) For All Occasions, 1997; (contrib.) Evergreen Verse, 1997; (contrib.) Dear Future: A Time Capsule of Poems, 1997; (contrib.) Funnybones, 1998; (contrib.) Silly Bones, 1998; (contrib.) The Epic Poise, 1999; If I Don't Know (poems), 2001; Two Cures for Love, 2008. EDITOR: Is That the New Moon?: Poems by Women Poets, 1989; The Orchard Book of Funny Poems, 1993; The Funny Side: 101 Humorous Poems, 1998; The Faber Book of Bedtime Stories, 1999; Big Orchard Book of Funny Poems, 2000; Heaven on Earth: 101 Happy Poems, 2001; (and intro.) George Herbert: Verse and Prose, 2002. Works appear in anthologies. Contributor to books and periodicals. **Address:** c/o Carol MacArthur, United Agents, 12-26 Lexington St., London, GL W1F OLE, England.

COPELAND, Anne P. American (born United States), b. 1951. **Genres:** Psychology, Travel/Exploration, Women's Studies And Issues, Anthropology/Ethnology, Area Studies, Cultural/Ethnic Topics, Education. **Career:** Kent State University, assistant professor, 1977-79; Boston University, associate professor, 1979-97, adjunct associate professor, through, 2007, Family Research Training Program, director, 1986-88, acting director of British programs, 1988-89, academic advisor for British programmes, Doctoral Program on Human Development in Context, head, 1990; The Interchange Institute, founder and executive director, 1997-, Newcomer's Almanac, editor. **Publications:** NONFICTION: (with K.M. White) Studying Families, 1991; (co-author) Separating Together: How Divorce Transforms Families, 1997; (with K. Rudnick and H. Wright) International Newcomer's Guide to Boston, 1997, 9th ed., 2010; (with G. Bennett) Understanding American Schools: The Answers to Newcomers' Most Frequently Asked Questions, 2001, 3rd ed., 2007; Global Baby: Tips to Keep You and Your Infant Smiling Before, During, and After Your International Move, 2004. Contributor of articles to books and periodicals. **Address:** The Interchange Institute, 11 Hawes St., Brookline, MA 02446-5412, U.S.A. **Online address:** copeland@interchangeinstitute.org

COPELAND, Gary A. American (born United States), b. 1952. **Genres:** Communications/Media, Language/Linguistics. **Career:** Public schools, Regional Occupational Program, teacher, 1974-77; Modesto Junior College, instructor, 1976-77; California State University, instructor in speech communication, 1977-79; Pennsylvania State University, instructor in continuing education, 1980-82; University of Alabama, assistant professor, 1982-89, associate professor of telecommunication and film, 1989-, graduate coordinator, 1989-, now professor emeritus, Institutional Review Board for the Protection of Human Subjects, chair, 1991-; General Electric News and Information Exchange, assistant system operator for Showbiz Roundtable, 1990-93; Impression Management Consulting, senior research associate; Alabama Radio Reading Service, reader; Universitat Klagenfurt, lecturer; University of Aruba, lecturer. Writer. **Publications:** (With J. Dominick and B.L. Sherman) Broadcasting/Cable and Beyond: An Introduction to Modern Electronic Media, 1990, 3rd ed., 1996; (with K.S. Johnson-Cartee) Negative Political Advertising: Coming of Age, 1991; (ed. with W.L. Nothstine and C. Blair) Critical Questions: Invention, Creativity, and the Criticism of Discourse and

Media, 1993; (with K.S. Johnson-Cartee) Inside Political Campaigns: Theory and Practice, 1997; (with K.S. Johnson-Cartee) Manipulation of the American Voter: Political Campaign Commercials, 1997; (with K.S. Johnson-Cartee) Strategic Political Communication: Rethinking Social Influence, Persuasion, and Propaganda, 2004. Works appear in anthologies. Contributor of articles to journals. **Address:** Department of Telecommunication and Film, University of Alabama, 484-C Reese Phifer Hall, PO Box 870152, Tuscaloosa, AL 35487, U.S.A. **Online address:** copeland@ua.edu

COPELAND, Gloria. American (born United States), b. 1942. **Genres:** Theology/Religion, Cultural/Ethnic Topics. **Career:** Kenneth Copeland Ministries, co-founder, 1967-. Pastor and writer. **Publications:** Walk with God, 1995; Living Contact: The Secret of the Overcoming Life, 1997; Hidden Treasures: Abundant Living in the Riches of Proverbs, 1998; Are You Listening? Hearing His Word, Doing His Will, 2000; Hearing from Heaven: Recognizing the Voice of God, 2001; Words That Heal, 2002; The Secret Place of God's Protection, 2002; To Know Him: Beyond Religion Waits a Relationship That Will Change Your Life, 2003, rev. ed., 2005; Blessed Beyond Measure: Experience the Extraordinary Goodness of God, 2004; God's Master Plan for Your Life: Ten Keys to Fulfilling Your Destiny, 2008. WITH KENNETH COPELAND: Family Promises, 1997; Generation Faith: The Teen Alternative, 1998; Pursuit of His Presence: Daily Devotions to Strengthen Your Walk with God, 1998; From Faith to Faith: Devotional: A Daily Guide to Victory, 1999; Protection Promises, 1999; (comp.) One Word from God Can Change Your Health, 1999; One Word from God Can Change Your Finances, 1999; One Word from God Can Change Your Destiny, 1999; One Word from God Can Change Your Family, 1999; One Word from God Can Change Your Relationships, 2000; One Word from God Can Change Your Formula for Success, 2000; Load Up: A Youth Devotional, 2002; Load Up for Graduates: 31 Devotions to Revolutionize Your Future: A Devotional, 2004; He Did It All for You, 2005. Contributor to magazine. **Address:** Kenneth Copeland Ministries, Fort Worth, TX 76192-0001, U.S.A.

COPELAND, Pala. Canadian (born Canada), b. 1950?. **Genres:** Fash Ion/Costume, Sex. **Career:** Writer and educator, 1997-; 4 Freedoms Relationship Tantra, co-founder. **Publications:** WITH A. LINK: Soul Sex: Tantra for Two, 2003; The Complete Idiot's Guide to Supercharged Kama Sutra Illustrated, 2007; 28 Days to Ecstasy for Couples: Tantra Step by Step, 2007; (and B. Dempsey) The Everything Tantric Sex Book: Learn Meditative, Spontaneous, and Intimate Lovemaking, 2007; Sensual Love Secrets for Couples: The Four Freedoms of Body, Mind, Heart and Soul, 2007. Contributor to newspapers and magazines. **Address:** 4 Freedoms Relationship Tantra, PO Box 144, Pembroke, ON K8A 6X1, Canada. **Online address:** 4freedoms@tantraloving.com

COPELAND, Peter. American (born United States), b. 1957. **Genres:** Autobiography/Memoirs, Biography, History, Communications/Media, Politics/Government, Writing/Journalism. **Career:** City News Bureau of Chicago, staff, 1980-81; El Paso Herald Post, reporter, 1982-83; Scripps Howard News Service, Latin America correspondent, 1984-89, Pentagon correspondent and defense and foreign affairs correspondent, 1989-94, assistant managing editor/news, managing editor, 1996-99, editor and general manager, 1999-; E.W. Scripps Co., Washington bureau chief. **Publications:** (With R. Cornum) She Went to War: The Rhonda Cornum Story, 1992; (with D. Hamer) The Science of Desire, 1994; The Heidi von Beltz Story, 1995; (with H.V. Beltz) My Soul Purpose: Living, Learning, and Healing, 1996; (with D. Hamer) Living With Our Genes, 1998. **Address:** Scripps Howard News Service, 1090 Vermont Ave. NW, 10th Fl., Ste. 1000, Washington, DC 20005, U.S.A. **Online address:** copelandp@shns.com

COPELAND, Rebecca L. American (born United States), b. 1956. **Genres:** Biography, Translations, Mystery/Crime/Suspense. **Career:** Washington University, Department of East Asian Languages and Cultures, assistant professor, 1991-98, director of East Asian studies, 1998-2002, associate professor of Japanese literature, 1998-2006, Visiting East Asian Professionals Program, director, 2002, professor of Japanese literature, 2006-; University College, associate dean, Summer School, director, 2006-. Writer. **Publications:** The Sound of the Wind: The Life and Work of Uno Chiyo (biography with translations) in UK as The Sound of the Wind: A Biography of Uno Chiyo with Three Novellas, 1992; Lost Leaves: Women Writers of Meiji Japan, 2000; (ed. with E. Ramirez-Christensen) The Father-Daughter Plot: Japanese Literary Women and the Law of the Father, 2001; (ed.) Woman Critiqued: Translated Essays on Japanese Women's Writing, 2006; (co-ed.) The Modern Murasaki: Selected Works by Women Writers of Meiji Japan, 1885-1912, 2006; (ed. with M. Ortabasi) The Modern Murasaki: Writing by Women of Meiji Japan, 2006. TRANSLATOR: Uno Chiyo, Aru hitori no onna no hanashi (title means: 'The Story of a Single Woman'), 1992; Grotesque, 2007. Works apppear in anthologies. Contributor of articles to books and periodicals. **Address:** Washington University, 222 Busch Hall, 1 Brookings Dr., PO Box 1111, St. Louis, MO 63130-4899, U.S.A. **Online address:** copeland@artsci.wustl.edu

COPEMAN, George Henry. British/Australian (born Australia), b. 1922. **Genres:** Administration/Management, Economics, Business/Trade/Industry. **Career:** Daily Telegraph, financial journalist, 1950-51; Director, assistant editor, 1951-53; Business, editor, 1953-58; Business Publications Ltd., editorial director, 1958-64; Copeman Paterson Ltd., managing director, 1964-69, chairman, 1969-74; Business Intelligence Services Ltd., chairman, 1974-96. Writer. **Publications:** Leaders of British Industry: A Study of The Careers of More Than A Thousand Public Company Directors, 1955; Promotion and Pay for Executives, 1957; The Challenge of Employee Shareholding: How to Close The Gap Between Capital and Labour, 1958; The Role of the Managing Director, 1960; (ed. with P. Marchand and B. Wilmot) A.D.P. handbook, 1962; Laws of Business Management and the Executive Way of Life, 1962, 2nd ed., 1963; (with H. Luijk and F. de P. Hanika) How the Executive Spends his Time, 1963; The Chief Executive and Business Growth: A Comparative Study in the United States, 1971; (with T. Rumble) Capital as an Incentive, 1972; What Every Director Wants to Know About the Business, 1973; Employee Share Participation in Nationalized-and Other-Enterprises, 1974; Employee Share Ownership and Industrial Stability, 1975; The Managing Director, 1978, 2nd ed., 1982; (ed. with N. Dewar-Gibb and I. Peacock) Planning Employee Share Schemes: Report of a Conference on Choosing the Right Incentives in a Recession, 1981; London: Business Books, 2nd ed., 1982; (with P. Moore and C. Arrowsmith) Shared Ownership: How to Use Capital Incentives to Sustain Business Growth, 1984; International Employee Share Ownership: Why? How? Where?, 1989; Employee Share Ownership, 1991; Employee Share Ownership Accountants Digest No. 325, 1994. **Address:** Moonraker, Batts Ln., Marehill, Pulborough, WS RH20 2ED, England.

COPENHAVER, John D. American (born United States), b. 1949. **Genres:** Theology/Religion. **Career:** Kings Canyon National Park, student pastor, 1975; James Madison University, Wesley Foundation, campus minister, 1981-83; Shenandoah University, professor of religion and philosophy, 1987-2011, Department of Religion, chair, 1987-2004; Shenandoah University, chaplain, 1987-89. **Publications:** Prayerful Responsibility: Prayer and Social Responsibility in the Religious Thought of Douglas Steere, 1992; Contemplative Practices that Animate the Study of Religion in Religion and the Classroom, 2011. **Address:** Department of Religion, Shenandoah University, 1460 University Dr., Winchester, VA 22601-1595, U.S.A. **Online address:** jcopenha@su.edu

COPLAN, David B. South African/American (born United States), b. 1948. **Genres:** Music, Cultural/Ethnic Topics. **Career:** Indiana University-Bloomington, associate instructor, 1979; Indiana University-Purdue University, Columbus Center, adjunct faculty, 1979-80; DePauw University, visiting professor of anthropology, 1980; Department of State, Foreign Service Institute, African Studies Program, occasional lecturer in African studies, 1981-92; State University of New York College, Program in Comparative Humanities, associate professor of anthropology and African humanities, 1981-92; New York University, Tisch School of the Arts, Department of Performance Studies, adjunct graduate faculty, 1990; University of the Western Cape, Fulbright lecturing and research professor, 1991; University of Cape Town, Fulbright lecturing and research professor, 1991, Department of Social Anthropology, associate professor of social anthropology, 1993-96; Rice University, Department of Anthropology, visiting professor, 1994-95; University of the Witwatersrand, professor and chair in social anthropology, 1997-, head of department, 1997-2001, 2003-06. Writer. **Publications:** In Township Tonight! South Africa's Black City Music and Theatre, 1985, 2nd ed., 2008; (contrib.) Sesotho Language and Culture, 1992; In the Time of Cannibals: The Word Music of South Africa's Basotho Migrants, 1994; (ed., intro. and trans. with S. Santho) Lyrics of Basotho Migrants: Translations of African Historical Documents, 1995; In Township Tonight!: Three Centuries of South African Black City Music and Theatre, 2007. Contributor to books and periodicals. **Address:** Department of Social Anthropology, University of the Witwatersrand, 2050 Wits, PO Box 3, Johannesburg, 2010, South Africa. **Online address:** david.coplan@wits.ac.za

COPLIN, Keith. American (born United States), b. 1942. **Genres:** Novels.

Career: Colby Community College, English teacher. Writer. **Publications:** Croftons Fire, 2004. Contributor of articles to magazines. **Address:** c/o Bobbe Siegel, Bobbe Siegel Literary Agency, 41 W 83rd St., New York, NY 10024, U.S.A. **Online address:** englshprof@yahoo.com

COPPA, Frank John. American (born United States), b. 1937. **Genres:** Communications/Media, History, Theology/Religion, Urban Studies, Biography. **Career:** St. John's University, instructor, 1965-66, assistant professor, 1966-71, associate professor, 1971-79, professor of history, 1979-, Doctoral Program in Modern World History, director. Writer. **Publications:** (Ed. with W. Griffin and B. Bast) From Vienna to Vietnam: War and Peace in the Modern World, 1969; Planning, Protectionism and Politics in Liberal Italy: Economics and Politics in the Giolittian Age, 1971; Camillo di Cavour, 1973; (ed. and intro.) Religion in the Making of Western Man, 1974; (ed. with P.C. Dolce) Cities in Transition: From the Ancient World to Urban America, 1974; (ed. with T.J. Curran) Immigrant Experience in America, 1976; Urban Government and Politics: A Bibliographical Overview, 1979; Transportation Policy: A Guide to Key Publications, 1979; (ed.) Screen and Society: The Impact of Television Upon Aspects of Contemporary Civilization, 1979; Pope Pius IX, Crusader in a Secular Age, 1979; New Jersey Government and Politics: A Bibliographical Guide to Selected Publications, 1979; Housing, A Bibliographical Overview, 1979; Energy Policy: A Bibliographical Overview, 1979; Public Finance, Intergovernmental Fiscal Relations: A Bibliographical Overview, 1979; (ed. with R. Harmond) Technology in the Twentieth Century, 1983; (ed.) Dictionary of Modern Italian History, 1985; Studies in Modern Italian History: From the Risorgimen to to the Republic, 1986; Cardinal Giacomo Antonelli and Papal Politics in European Affairs, 1990; (comp. with W. Roberts) Modern Italian History: An Annotated Bibliography, 1990; Origins of the Italian Wars of Independence, 1992; (ed. with M. Repetto-Alaia) Formation of the Italian Republic: Proceedings of the International Symposium on Postwar Italy, 1993; Modern Papacy Since 1789, 1998; (ed.) Encyclopedia of the Vatican and Papacy, 1999; (ed.) Controversial Concordats: The Vatican's Relations with Napoleon, Mussolini and Hitler, 1999; (ed.) Great Popes through History: An Encyclopedia, 2002; Papacy Confronts the Modern World, 2003; Papacy, The Jews, and the Holocaust, 2006; (ed.) Encyclopedia of Modern Dictators: From Napoleon to the Present, 2006; Politics and the Papacy in the Modern World, 2008; The Policies and Politics of Pope Pius XII: Between Diplomacy and Morality, 2012. Contributor to journals. **Address:** Department of History, St. John's University, 8000 Utopia Pkwy., Jamaica, NY 11439-9000, U.S.A. **Online address:** coppaf@stjohns.edu

COPPER, Basil. (Lee Falk). British (born England), b. 1924. **Genres:** Novels, Novellas/Short Stories, Mystery/Crime/Suspense, Romance/Historical, Science Fiction/Fantasy, Young Adult Fiction, Adult Non-fiction. **Career:** Freelance writer, 1970-; Crime Writers Association of Great Britain, chairman, 1981-82. **Publications:** MIKE FARADAY NOVELS: The Dark Mirror, 1966; Night Frost, 1966; No Flowers for the General, 1967; Scratch on the Dark, 1967; Die Now, Live Later, 1968; Don't Bleed on Me, 1968; The Marble Orchard, 1969; Dead File, 1970; No Letters from the Grave, 1971; Strong Arm, 1972; The Big Chill, 1972; (as Lee Falk) The Phantom, 1972; (as Lee Falk) The Phantom and the Scorpia Menace, 1972; (as Lee Falk) The Phantom and the Slave Market of Mucar, 1972; The Breaking Point, 1973; A Great Year for Dying, 1973; Shock Wave, 1973; A Voice from the Dead, 1974; Feedback, 1974; Ricochet, 1974; The High Wall, 1975; Impact, 1975; A Good Place to Die, 1975; The Lonely Place, 1976; Crack in the Sidewalk, 1976; Tight Corner, 1976; The Year of the Dragon, 1977; Death Squad, 1977; Murder One, 1978; A Quiet Room in Hell, 1978; The Big Rip-Off, 1979; The Caligari Complex, 1979; Flip-Side, 1980; The Long Rest, 1981; The Empty Silence, 1981; Dark Entry, 1981; Hang Loose, 1982; Shoot-Out, 1982; The Far Horizon, 1982; Trigger-Man, 1982; Pressure-Point, 1983; The Narrow Corner, 1983; Hard Contract, 1983; The Hook, 1984; You Only Die Once, 1984; Tuxedo Park, 1984; The Far Side of Fear, 1985; Jet-Lag, 1986; Blood on the Moon, 1986; Snow-Job, 1986; Heavy Iron, 1987; Turn Down an Empty Glass, 1987; Bad Scene, 1987; House-Dick, 1988; Print-Out, 1988; Cold Hand on My Shoulder, 2002. SHORT STORIES: Not after Nightfall, 1967; From Evil's Pillow, 1973; When Footsteps Echo, 1975; And Afterward, the Dark, 1977; Here Be Daemons, 1978; Voices of Doom, 1980; Whispers in the Night, 1999; Cold Hand on My Shoulder: Tales of Terror and Suspense, 2002. NONFICTION: The Vampire in Legend and Fact, 1971; The Vampire in Legend, Fact and Art, 1971; The Werewolf: In Legend, Fact and Art, 1977. GOTHIC: Necropolis, 1975; The Curse of the Fleers, 1976; The House of the Wolf, 1982; The Black Death, 1992. FANTASY: The Great White Space, 1975; The Horror on Planet X, 1975; Into the Silence, 1983. SOLAR PON NOVELS: The Dossier of Solar Pons, 1978; The Further Adventures of Solar Pons, 1979; The Secret Files of Solar Pons, 1979; Exploits of Solar Pons, 1993; The Recollections of Solar Pons, 1995; Solar Pons Versus the Devil's Claw, 2004; Solar Pons: The Final Cases, 2005. OTHERS: The Uncollected Cases of Solar Pons, 1980; The Solar Pons Omnibus, 1982; Darkness, Mist & Shadow, 2010. **Address:** Stockdoves, South Pk., Sevenoaks, KT TN13 1EN, England.

COPPOLARO-NOWELL, Annalisa. British/Italian (born Italy), b. 1966?. **Genres:** Humor/Satire. **Career:** Journalist, 1984-93; Tuscan Press Publications, writer, 1985-. Educator and translator. **Publications:** Giochi d'amore e d'infedelta, 2005; How to Live Like an Italian: A User's Guide to La Dolce Vita, 2008. Contributor to magazines and periodicals. **Address:** c/o Lorella Belli, Lorella Belli Literary Agency, 54 Hartford House, 35 Tavistock Cres., Notting Hill, London, GL W11 1AY, England. **Online address:** annalisa@nowell.me.uk

COPPULA, Susan. *See* **CARROLL, Susan.**

COPUS, Julia. British (born England), b. 1969. **Genres:** Poetry. **Career:** Tim Aston Design Ltd., copywriter, 1990-91; Libri (second-hand book store), co-owner, 1991-92; Pearson Young Ltd., editorial assistant, 1992-93; teacher of English, 1993-; University of Exeter, Department of English, Royal Literary Fund fellow, 2005-08, advisory fellow, 2008-11, honorary fellow; The Guardian, poet in residence, 2007; Arvon Foundation, faculty. **Publications:** Walking in the Shadows, 1995; The Shuttered Eye, 1995; In Defence of Adultery, 2003; Brilliant Writing Tips for Students, 2009; Essential Writing Tips, 2009; Twenty Three Skidoo, forthcoming. **Address:** Bloodaxe Books Ltd., Highgreen, Southampton, Tarset, NM NE48 1RP, England. **Online address:** j.c.copus@exeter.ac.uk

COQUERY-VIDROVITCH, Catherine. French (born France), b. 1935. **Genres:** Area Studies, Literary Criticism And History, History. **Career:** Universite Paris 7, professor of modern African history, 1972-2001, professor emeritus of modern African history, 2001-; State University of New York, adjunct professor, 1981-; New York University, Institute of French Studies, visiting professor. Writer. **Publications:** (Intro. and contrib.) Brazza et la prise de possession du Congo, 1969; (with S. Amin) Histoire économique du Congo, 1880-1968, du Congo francais à l'Union douanière et économique d'Afrique centrale, 1969; Le Congo au temps des grandes compagnies concessionnaires, 1898-1930, 1972; Actes du Colloque Entreprises et entrepreneurs en Afrique, XIXe et XXe siècles, 1983; Black Africa: Continuity and Ruptures, Payot, 1985, rev. ed., 1993; Les Africaines: Histoire des Femmes d'Afrique Noire of XIX eau Twentieth Century, 1994. OTHERS: The Discovery of Africa: Black Africa Atlantic des Origines the Eighteenth Century, 1965, 2nd ed., 1971; Brazza dispossession and the Prize of the Congo: The Mission of West Africa, 1883-1885, 1969; (co-author) History économique of Congo, 1880-1968, 1970; Congo rancais The Time of the Great Companies Dealerships, 1898-1930, 1972; (with H. Moniot) L'Afrique Noire de 1800 a Our Days, 1974, 3rd ed., 1993; (ed.) Africa and the Crisis of 1930: 1924-1938: Proceedings du Colloque, 1976; L'Afrique et la crise de 1930: 1924-1938, 1976; Knowledge of the Third World: Multidisciplinary Approach, 1977; Connaissance du Tiers Monde: approche pluridisciplinaire, 1977; (contrib.) Sociétés paysannes du Tiers-Monde, 1980; Peasant Societies in the Third World, 1980; Proceedings of Colloque Entreprises and Entrepreneurs in Africa, Nineteenth and Twentieth Centuries, 1983; Villeset Contemporary Urban Problems in Sub-Saharan Africa: Contemporary Research en Histoire: Information: Teaching Recherche 1982-1983, 1984; (ed. with P.E. Lovejoy) The Workers of African Trade, 1985; Story about Démographique Concept of Race: Various Research, 1985; (co-author) Décolonisations and New Dependencies: Models et Contre-Ideological and Cultural Models in the Third World: Texts, 1986; (co-author) Rébellions Révolution Zaire, 1963-1965, 1987; (co-author) For a History of Development: States, Societies, Development, 1988; (ed. with D. Hémery and J. Piel) Pour une histoire du développement: états, sociétés, développement /, 1988; (ed.) Processus d'urbanisation en Afrique, 1988; Afrique noire, 1988; (co-ed.) Third World: The Informal Question?, 1991; (co-author) History of Colonial France, 1991; Africa Occidentaleau time of the French Colonizers and Colonized, 1860-1960, 1992; (ed.) Histoire africaine du XXe siècle: sociétés, villes, cultures, 1993; History of African Cities Black Origins of Colonization, 1993; (ed.) History of the Twentieth Century Africa: Societies, Cities, Cultures, 1993; Histoire des villes d'Afrique noire: des origines à la colonisation, 1993; (co-ed.) African History in Africa: Census Analytic des Travaux University Inedits Supported in Universities Francophonesd 'Black

Africa, 1995; (ed. with C. Chanson-Jabeur) L'histoire africaine en Afrique: recensement analytique des travaux universitaires inédits soutenus dans les universités francophones d'Afrique noire, 1995; Urban-Campagnesen Africa: Mobility of People, Movement of Goods and Diffusion des Modeles Since Independence, 1996; (with H. Almeida-Topor and J. Sénéchal) Interdépendances villes-campagnes en Afrique: mobilité des hommes, circulation des biens et diffusion des modèles depuis les indépendances, 1996; (with O. Goerg) La ville européenne outre mers: un modèle conquérant? (XVe-XXe siècles), 1996; The Addition Ville Europeenne Seas: A Model Conqueror? (XV-XX centuries), 1996; African Women: A Modern History, 1997; (comp.) History of African Historians in Africa: The Story of Yesterday et d'Aujourd'hui: Logic and Pass the Current Dynamics, 1998; Histoireet Settlement: Ethnic Groups, Clans and Lineages in Rwanda Former et Contemporain: PhD Thesis, 1998; (contrib. with O. Goerg and H. Tenoux) Des historiens africains en Afrique: l'histoire d'hier et d'aujourd'hui: logiques du passé et dynamiques actuelle, 1998; Histoire et peuplement: ethnies, clans et lignages dans le Rwanda ancien et contemporain: thése de doctorat, 1998; Etre étranger et migrant en Afrique au XXe siècle: enjeux identitaires et modes d'insertion, 2003; La découverte de l'Afrique: l'Afrique noire atlantique des origines au XVIIIe siécle, 2003; (ed. with C. Chanson-Jabeur and O. Goerg) Politiques d'équipement et Services Urban Cities In The Country: étude Compare Acue, 2004; Mama Africa: Tribute to Catherine Coquery-Vidrovitch, 2005; The History of African Cities South of the Sahara: From the Origins to Colonization, 2005; The Forgotten Victims of Nazism: The Black and Germany in the Premíère Half of the Twentieth siècle, 2007; Des victimes oubliées du nazisme: les noirs et l'Allemagne dans la première moitié du XXe siècle, 2007; Enjeux politiques de l'histoire coloniale, 2009; History of 19th Century Africansau, forthcoming. Contributor to books and journals. **Address:** Universite Paris 7-Denis Diderot, Case 7017, 2 Place Jussieu, Paris, 75251, France. **Online address:** coqueryv@ext.jussieu.fr

CORBETT, Ben. American (born United States), b. 1969. **Genres:** Novels, History. **Career:** Writer and photographer, 1995-; Big World Magazine, associate editor; Boulder Weekly, senior writer. **Publications:** This is Cuba: An Outlaw Culture Survives, 2002; (intro. and contrib.) Gonzo, 2009. Contributor to newspapers, magazines and periodicals. **Address:** PO Box 546, Lafayette, CO 80026, U.S.A. **Online address:** mail@bencorbett.net

CORBETT, Holly C. American (born United States), b. 1978?. **Genres:** Autobiography/Memoirs, Travel/Exploration. **Career:** Writer. **Publications:** (With J. Baggett and A. Pressner) The Lost Girls: Three Friends, Four Continents, One Unconventional Detour around the World, 2010. Contributor to periodicals. **Address:** New York, NY , U.S.A. **Online address:** hollyc@lostgirlsworld.com

CORBETT, Patricia. American (born United States), b. 1951?. **Genres:** Art/Art History, Antiques/Furnishings, Biography, Theology/Religion. **Career:** The Connoisseur, editor. **Publications:** Roman Art, 1980; (with C. Eisler) Prayer Book of Michelino da Besozzo, 1981; (with C. Lebeau) Fabrics: The Decorative Art of Textiles, 1994; With Compliments: An Illustrated History of Visiting Cards, 1995; Verdura: The Life and Work of a Master Jeweler, 2002. Contributor to periodicals. **Address:** c/o Author Mail, Harry N Abrams Inc., 100 5th Ave., New York, NY 10011, U.S.A.

CORBETT, Richard (Graham). British (born England), b. 1955. **Genres:** Politics/Government. **Career:** Voluntary sector, 1977-81; civil servant, 1981-89; Socialist Group in the European Parliament, policy advisor, 1989-94, deputy secretary general, 1994-96; MEP 1996-2009: Committee on Constitutional Affairs, vice president, 1997-99, socialist coordinator, 1999-2009; NEC Task Force on Electoral Turnout, EPLP deputy leader, 2006-09; Labour Movement for Europe, chair, 2009-10; advisor to the President of the European Council, 2010-. Writer. **Publications:** (With R. Northawl) Electing Europe's First Parliament, 1977; (with F. Jacobs and M. Shackleton) The European Parliament, 1990, 8th ed., 2011; The Treaty of Maastricht, from Conception to Ratification, 1993; The European Parliament's Role in Closer EU Integration, 1998; The European Parliament and the European Constitution, 2005; The European Union-Who Makes the Decisions? A Guide to the Process and the U.K.'s Role, 2006. Contributor to periodicals. **Address:** President's Cabinet, European Council, 175 rue de la Loi, Brussels, 1048, Belgium. **Online address:** richard@richardcorbett.org.uk

CORBETT, William. American (born United States), b. 1942. **Genres:** Poetry, Literary Criticism And History, Adult Non-fiction, History. **Career:** Massachusetts Institute of Technology, lecturer, Student Writing Activities, director; Grand Street, poetry editor. **Publications:** POETRY: Three New Poets, 1966; Columbus Square Journal, 1976; St. Patrick's Day, 1976; Spoken in Sleep, 1979; Schedule Rhapsody, 1980; Runaway Pond, 1981; City Nature: Collected Poems, 1984; Remembrances, 1987; On Blue Note, 1989; Don't Think, Look, 1991; New and Selected Poems, 1995; John Raimondi Sculptor, 1999; Boston Vermont: Poems, 1999; (ed. with M. Gizzi and J. Torra) The Blind See Only This World: Poems for John Wieners, 2000; Just The Thing: Selected Letters of James Schuyler, 2004; The Letters of James Schuyler to Frank O'Hara, 2005; Poems on Occasion, 2008; Albert York, 2010; The Whalen Poem, 2011. NON-FICTION: Literary New England: A History and Guide, 1993; Philip Guston's Late Work: A Memoir, 1994; Furthering My Education, 1997; New York Literary Lights, 1998; (with S. Hunter) John Raimondi, 1999; All Prose: Selected Essays and Reviews, 2001; Opening Day, 2008. Contributor to periodicals. **Address:** Program in Writing and Humanistic Studies, Massachusetts Institute of Technology, Rm. 14E-303, 77 Massachusetts Ave., Cambridge, MA 02139-4307, U.S.A. **Online address:** bevcobett@aol.com

CORBIN, Alain. French (born France), b. 1936. **Genres:** History, Translations. **Career:** University of Limoges, assistant lecturer, 1968-69; University of Tours, senior lecturer, 1969-72, assistant professor, 1973-85, professor of history, 1985-86; Universite Paris I, Pantheon-Sorbonne, professor of history, 1987-, now professor emeritus; Institute Universitaire de France, professor of history, 1992-2002. Writer. **Publications:** Archaisme et modernité en Limousin au XIXe siècle, 1845-1880, 1975; Les filles de noce: misère sexuelle et prostitution: 19e et 20e siécles, 1978; Le miasme et la jonquille: l'odorat et l'imaginaire social XVIIIe-XIXe siécles, 1982; The Foul and the Fragrant: Odor and the French Social Imagination, 1986; Le territoire du vide: l'Occident et le désir du rivage, 1750-1840, 1988; (with M. Perrot) A History of Private Life, (ed. with G. Duby) vol. IV: From the Fires of Revolution to the Great War, 1990; Women for Hire: Prostitution and Sexuality in France after 1850, 1990; Le Village des Cannibales, 1990, trans. as The Village of Cannibals: Rage and Murder in France, 1870, 1991; Le temps, le désir et l'horreur: essais sur le dix-neuviéme siécle, 1991; Guerre fratricide: le guerre civili in età contemporanea, 1994; The Lure of the Sea: The Discovery of the Seaside in the Western World, 1750-1840, 1994; Time, Desire and Horror, 1996; Village Bells: Sound and Meaning in the 19th-Century Countryside, 1998; Le monde retrouvé de Louis-Francois Pinagot: sur les traces d'un inconnu, 1798-1876, 1998; Historien du sensible: entretiens avec Gilles Heure, 2000; The Life of an Unknown: The Rediscovered World of a Clog Maker in 19th Century France, 2001; (ed. with H. Richard) La mer, terreur et fascination, 2004; (intro.) Révolutions et républiques, 2005; (ed.) 1515 et les grandes dates de l'histoire de France revisitées par les grands historiens d'aujourd'hui, 2005; (ed. with J. Courtine and G. Vigarello) Histoire du corps, 2005; Minzokugaku to rekishigaku, 2007; (foreword) Hommes et masculinités de 1789 a nos jours, 2007; (ed.) Histoire du christianisme, 2007; L'harmonie des plaisirs, 2008; L'homme dans le paysage, 2001; L'harmonie des plaisirs: les manières de jouir du siécle des Lumières à l'avènement de la sexologie, 2008; Les héros de l'histoire de France expliqués a mon fils, 2011; Les conférences de Morterolles, hiver 1895-1896, 2011. Contributor to periodicals. **Address:** Universite Paris I, Pantheon-Sorbonne, 17 rue de la Sorbonne, Paris, 75005, France. **Online address:** crhxixe@univ-paris1.fr

CORBIN, Jane. British (born England), b. 1954. **Genres:** Documentaries/Reportage, History, Adult Non-fiction. **Career:** ITN-TV, Channel 4 News, foreign correspondent, 1983-88; British Broadcasting Corp., current affairs and investigative journalist, Panorama series, senior foreign correspondent, 1988-, Behind the Headlines, presenter, 1991-. **Publications:** The Norway Channel: The Secret Talks that Led to the Middle East Peace Accord, 1994; Al-Qaeda: In Search of the Terror Network that Threatens the World, 2002, rev. ed., 2003. Contributor to periodicals. **Address:** British Broadcasting Corp., 201 Wood Ln., London, GL W12, England.

CORCORAN, Neil (Cornelius). Irish (born Ireland), b. 1948. **Genres:** Literary Criticism And History, Poetry, Novels. **Career:** University of Sheffield, lecturer, 1974-, senior lecturer in English literature, 1991-; University of Wales, professor of English, 1994-96; University of Saint Andrews, professor of English, 1996-; University of Liverpool, King Alfred chair of English and professor, 2004-10; professor emeritus of English, 2010-. Writer. **Publications:** The Song of Deeds: A Study of The Anathemata of David Jones, 1982; Seamus Heaney, 1986; (ed.) The Chosen Ground: Essays on the Contemporary Poetry of Northern Ireland, 1992; English Poetry since 1940, 1993; After

Yeats and Joyce: Reading Modern Irish Literature, 1997; The Poetry of Seamus Heany: A Critical Study, 1999; Poets of Modern Ireland, 1999; Elizabeth Bowen: The Enforced Return, 2004; (ed.) Cambridge Companion to Twentieth-Century English Poetry, 2007; Shakespeare and the Modern Poet, 2010. **Address:** School of English, The University of Liverpool, Liverpool, MS L69 3BX, England. **Online address:** nc23@liverpool.ac.uk

CORDAIRE, Christina. *See* **KINGSTON, Christina.**

CORDEIRO, Pat. *See* **CORDEIRO, Patricia (A.).**

CORDEIRO, Patricia (A.). (Pat Cordeiro). British (born England), b. 1944?. **Genres:** Education, Language/Linguistics, Literary Criticism And History, Reference. **Career:** Elementary school teacher, 1965-66, 1968-72, 1974-90; Norwich University, Vermont College, field faculty adviser, 1987-92; Educational Developmental Corp., curriculum developer and evaluator, 1988-89; Whitman Institute, fellow, 1988; University of Massachusetts, adjunct faculty, 1988-94; Lucretia Crocker Academy, fellow, 1989-; Lesley College, adjunct faculty, 1990; French River Education Center, instructor, 1990; Rhode Island College, Feinstein School of Education and Human Development, Department of Elementary Education, assistant professor, 1990-93, associate professor of education and human development, 1993-, chair, 1995-2004, 2008-, professor; Learning Center, instructor, 1991; Harvard University Graduate School of Education, instructor, 1996-2002. Writer. **Publications:** (With C.B. Cazden) Whole Language Plus: Essays on Literacy in the United States and New Zealand, 1992; Whole Learning: Whole Language and Content in the Upper Elementary Grades, 1992; (ed. with J. Blatt) Endless Possibilities: Generating Curriculum in Social Studies and Literacy, 1995. Contributor to journals and books. **Address:** Feinstein School of Education and Human, Development, Rhode Island College, 217 Horace Mann Hall, 600 Mount Pleasant Ave., Providence, RI 02908-1991, U.S.A. **Online address:** pcordeiro@ric.edu

CORDELLI, Franco. Italian (born Italy), b. 1943. **Genres:** Novels, Literary Criticism And History, Translations. **Career:** RAI Radio3, staff. Novelist and playwright. **Publications:** Procida, 1973, rev. ed., 2006; (ed. with A. Berardinelli) Il Pubblicodella poesia, 1975; Fuoco celeste, 1976; Il poeta postumo: manie, pettegolezzi, rancori, 1978; Le forze in campo, 1979; Partenze eroiche, 1980; I puri spiriti, 1982; Proprietà perduta, 1983; (ed. with G. Raboni) I cento romanzi stranierie, 1900-1943, 1986; Pinkerton, 1986; (with G. Büchner) L'antipasqua, 1987; Guerre Lontane, 1990; L'Italia di mattina, 1990; Scipione l'italiano, 1991; (ed.) La mia America: antologia dellaletteratura Americana dal 1945 a oggi, 1991; Diderot dondero: [Quattrocommedie], 1993; Arancio, 1994; (intro.) Teatro moderno, 1995; La democrazia magica: il narratore, il-romanziere, lo scrittore (criticism), 1997; Un inchino a terra, 1999; Diario del disamore, 1999; Lontano dal romanzo, 2002; (ed. with A. Cortellessa) Pensa alla tua liberta: il cinema di Emidio Greco, 2002; Lareligione del romanzo: Franco Cordelli, a cura di Enzo Di Mauro, 2002; (with F. Cordelli) Il mondo di Francesco Savio: recensioni, 1973-1976, 2002; Il duca di Mantova, 2004; Marea umana, 2010; Ombra di Piovene, 2011. TRANSLATOR: (with M.M. Ricci) AndréGide, I nutrimenti terrestri, 1975; H. James, Principessa Casamassima, 1975; L. Carroll, Sylvie e Bruno, 1978; V. Woolf, Tra un atto e l'altro, 1979; M. Twain, Wilson lo svitato (title means: 'Pudd'nhead Wilson'), 1979; E. Zola, L'opera, 1981; Stendahl, Armance, o alcune scene di unsalotto parigino nel 1827, 1982; J. Cazotte, Il diavolo inamorato, 1992; Vacanze romane: set, protagonisti, film, 2008. **Address:** c/o Author Mail, RCS Rizzoli Libri SpA, Via Mecenate 91, Milan, 20138, Italy.

CORDEN, Warner Max. Australian/German (born Germany), b. 1927. **Genres:** Economics, Essays. **Career:** University of Melbourne, lecturer in economics, 1958-61; Australian National University, fellow in economics, 1962-67, professor, 1977-88, professorial fellow in economics, 2002-; Oxford University, Nuffield reader in international economics, 1967-76; International Monetary Fund, senior advisor, 1986-88; Johns Hopkins University, Paul H. Nitze School of Advanced International Studies, professor, 1989-2002, now professor emeritus. Writer. **Publications:** Tax on Advertising?, 1961; (ed. with H.W. Arndt) The Australian Economy: A Volume of Readings, 1963; Recent Developments in the Theory of International Trade, 1965; Australian Economic Policy Discussion: A Survey, 1968; The Theory of Protection, 1971; Monetary Integration, 1972; Trade Policy and Economic Welfare, 1974, 2nd ed., 1997; (with I.M.D. Little and M.FG. Scott) Import Controls Versus Devaluation and Britain's Economic Prospects, 1975; (ed. with G. Fels) Public Assistance to Industry: Protection and Subsidies in Britain and Germany, 1976; Monetary Union: Main Issues Facing the European Community, 1976; Inflation, Exchange Rates, and the World Economy: Lectures on International Monetary Economics, 1977, 3rd ed., 1985; (with M.FG. Scott and I.M.D. Little) The Case Against General Import Restrictions, 1980; The Revival of Protectionism, 1984; Protection, Growth, and Trade: Essays in International Economics, 1985; Protection and Liberalization: A Review of Analytical Issues, 1987; Exchange Rate Policy in Developing Countries, 1990; International Trade Theory and Policy: Selected Essays of W. Max Corden, 1992; Integration and Trade Policy in the Former Soviet Union, 1992; (with I.M.D. Little, R.N. Cooper and S. Rajapatirana) Boom, Crisis, and Adjustment: The Macroeconomic Experience of Developing Countries, 1993; Economic Policy, Exchange Rates, and the International System, 1994; Protection and Liberalization in Australia and Abroad, 1995; Pragmatic Orthodox: Macroeconomic Policies in Seven East Asia Economies, 1996; The Road to Reform: Essays on Australian Economic Policy, 1997; Asian Crisis: Is There a Way Out?, 1999; Too Sensational: On the Choice of Exchange Rate Regimes, 2002. Contributor to books and periodicals. **Address:** Department of Economics, University of Melbourne, Level 5, Arts West Bldg., Melbourne, VI 3010, Australia. **Online address:** m.corden@unimelb.edu.au

CORDEROY, Conor. British (born England), b. 1957. **Genres:** Novels, Science Fiction/Fantasy. **Career:** Author, decorator and barrister. **Publications:** Dark Rain (science fiction novel), 2006. **Address:** Pan Macmillan, 4 Crinan St., London, GL N1 9XW, England. **Online address:** speak@conorcorderoy.co.uk

CORDERY, Stacy A. American (born United States) **Genres:** History. **Career:** Monmouth College, faculty, 1994, professor of history, 2006-, department chair; University of Texas, Bess Heflin fellow, 1986; University of Arkansas, lecturer, 1988-90; University of Texas, Dora Bonham fellow, 1989; University of Texas, assistant instructor, 1990-91; East Carolina University, visiting assistant professor, 1992-94; Monmouth College Archives, curator; National First Ladies' Library, bibliographer. Academic and historian. Writer. **Publications:** Theodore Roosevelt: In the Vanguard of the Modern, 2003; Historic Photographs of Theodore Roosevelt, 2007; Alice: Alice Roosevelt Longworth, from White House Princess to Washington Power Broker, 2007. Contributor to periodicals and journals. **Address:** Monmouth College, Department of History, Monmouth, IL 61462-2433, U.S.A. **Online address:** stacy@monm.edu

CORDESMAN, Anthony H. American (born United States), b. 1939. **Genres:** Novels. **Career:** Georgetown University, professor of national security; Center for Strategic and International Studies, Arleigh A. Burke chair in strategy; ABC News, national security analyst. Writer. **Publications:** (With J.M. Collins) Imbalance of Power: An Analysis of Shifting U.S.-Soviet Military Strengths, 1978; Deterrence in the 1980s, 1982; Jordanian Arms and the Middle East Balance, 1985; The Gulf and the Search for Strategic Stability: Saudi Arabia, the Military Balance in the Gulf, and Trends in the Arab-Israeli Military Balance, 1984; The Arab-Israeli Military Balance and the Art of Operations: An Analysis of Military Lessons and Trends and Implications for Future Conflicts, 1987; The Iran-Iraq War and Western Security, 1984-87: Strategic Implications and Policy Options, 1987; Western Strategic Interests in Saudi Arabia, 1987; The Gulf and the West: Strategic Relations and Military Realities, 1988; NATO's Central Region Forces: Capabilities, Challenges, Concepts, 1988; (with A.R. Wagner) The Lessons of Modern War, 1990; Weapons of Mass Destruction in the Middle East, 1991; Strategy and Technology, 1992; After the Storm: The Changing Military Balance in the Middle East, 1993; Iran and Iraq: The Threat from the Northern Gulf, 1994; U.S. Defense Policy: Resources and Capabilities, 1994; Perilous Prospects: The Peace Process and the Arab-Israeli Military Balance, 1996; Bahrain, Oman, Qatar, and the UAE: Challenges of Security, 1997; (with A.S. Hashim) Iran: Dilemmas of Dual Containment, 1997; (with A.S. Hashim) Iraq: Sanctions and Beyond, 1997; Kuwait: Recovery and Security after the Gulf War, 1997; Saudi Arabia: Guarding the Desert Kingdom, 1997; U.S. Forces in the Middle East: Resources and Capabilities, 1997; Iran's Military Forces in Transition: Conventional Threats and Weapons of Mass Destruction, 1999; Iraq and the War of Sanctions: Conventional Threats and Weapons of Mass Destruction, 1999; Transnational Threats from the Middle East: Crying Wolf or Crying Havoc?, 1999; The Lessons and Non- lessons of the Air and Missile Campaign in Kosovo, 2001; A Tragedy of Arms: Military and Security Developments in the Maghreb, 2002; Cyber-Threats, Information Warfare, and Critical Infrastructure Protection: Defending the U.S. Homeland, 2002; Iraq's Military Capabilities in 2002: A Dynamic Net Assessment, 2002; The Lessons of Afghanistan: War Fighting, Intelligence, and Force Transformation, 2002; Peace and War: The Arab Israeli Military Balance Enters the Twenty-first Century, 2002; Strategic Threats and National Missile Defenses: Defending the U.S. Homeland, 2002; Terrorism, Asymmetric Warfare, and Weapons of Mass Destruction: Defending the U.S. Homeland, 2002; The Iraq War: Strategy, Tactics, and Military Lessons, 2003; Saudi Arabia Enters the Twenty-first Century: The Military and International Security Dimensions, 2003; Saudi Arabia Enters the Twenty-first Century: The Political, Foreign Policy, Economic, and Energy Dimensions, 2003; (with G.R. Faith) Weapons of Mass Destruction in the Middle East: Regional Trends, National Forces, Warfighting Capabilities, Delivery Options, and Weapons Effects, 2003; Energy Developments in the Middle East, 2004; The Military Balance in the Middle East, 2004; The War after the War: Strategic Lessons of Iraq and Afghanistan, 2004; The Challenge of Biological Terrorism, 2005; Iran's Developing Military Capabilities, 2005; (with P. Baetjer) Iraqi Security Forces: A Strategy for Success, 2005; (with J. Moravitz) The Israeli-Palestinian War: Escalating to Nowhere, 2005; (with N. Obaid) National Security in Saudi Arabia: Threats, Responses, and Challenges, 2005; Arab-Israeli Military Forces in an Era of Asymmetric Wars, 2006; (with K.R. Al-Rodhan) The Changing Dynamics of Energy in the Middle East, 2006; (with K.R. Al-Rodhan) The Global Oil Market: Risks and Uncertainties, 2006; (with K.R. Al-Rodhan) Iran's Weapons of Mass Destruction: The Real and Potential Threat, 2006; (with P.S. Fredericksen and W.D. Sullivan) Salvaging American Defense: The Challenge of Strategic Overstretch, 2007; (with M. Kleiber) Chinese Military Modernization: Force Development and Strategic Capabilities, 2007; (with K.R. Al-Rodhan) Gulf Military Forces in an Era of Asymmetric Wars, 2007; (with M. Kleiber) Iran's Military Forces and Warfighting Capabilities: The Threat in the Northern Gulf, 2007; (with A. Mausner) Iraqi Force Development: Conditions for Success, Consequences of Failure, 2007; (with G. Sullivan and W.D. Sullivan) Lessons of the 2006 Israeli-Hezbollah War, 2007; (with E.R. Davies) Iraq's Insurgency and the Road to Civil Conflict, 2008; (with A. Nerquizian and I.C. Popescu) Israel and Syria: The Military Balance and Prospects of War, 2008; (with A.C. Seitz) Iranian Weapons of Mass Destruction: The Birth of a Regional Nuclear Arms Race?, 2009; (with A. Nerguizian) North African Military Balance: Force Developments in the Maghreb, 2009; Saudi Arabia: National Security in a Troubled Region, 2009; Winning in Afghanistan: Creating Effective Afghan Security Forces, 2009; (with A. Mausner) Withdrawal from Iraq: Assessing the Readiness of Iraqi Security Forces, 2009; (with A. Mausner and J. Lemieux) Afghan National Security Forces: What it will Take to Implement the Isaf Strategy, 2010; (with A. Mausner and E. Derby) Iraq and the United States: Creating a Strategic Partnership, 2010; (co-author) Korean Military Balance: Comparative Korean Forces and the Forces of Key Neighboring States, 2011; (with V. Vira) Pakistan, Violence Versus Stability: A National Net Assessment: A Report of the Csis Burke Chair in Strategy, 2011. Contributor to books. **Address:** Center for Strategic & International Studies, 1800 K St. NW, Washington, DC 20006, U.S.A. **Online address:** amausner@csis.org

CORDING, Robert. American (born United States), b. 1949. **Genres:** Poetry. **Career:** Holy Cross College, professor of English, James N. and Sarah L. O'Reilly Barrett professor in creative writing, James N. and Sarah L. O'Reilly Barrett chair in creative writing. Writer. **Publications:** Mortage Loan Warehousing in the New York City and Long Island Area, 1973; Life-List, 1987; What Binds Us to This World, 1991; Heavy Grace: Poems, 1996; (ed. with S. Jankowski-Smith and E.J.M. Laino) In My Life: Encounters with the Beatles, 1998; Against Consolation, 2001; (ed. and intro.) The Actual Moon, the Actual Stars, 2003; Common Life: Poems, 2006; (comp.) The Lion and the Land of Narnia, 2008; Walking With Ruskin: Poems, 2010. **Address:** Department of English, College of the Holy Cross, 1 College St., Worcester, MA 01610, U.S.A. **Online address:** rcording@holycross.edu

CORDINGLY, David. British (born England), b. 1938. **Genres:** Art/Art History, History, Young Adult Non-fiction. **Career:** Peter Hatch Partnership, graphic designer, 1963-65; British Museum, exhibition designer, 1967-71; Art Gallery and Museum, keeper, 1971-78; Museum of London, assistant director, 1978-80; National Maritime Museum, keeper of pictures, head of exhibitions, 1980-93. Writer. **Publications:** Marine Painting in England 1700-1900, 1974; Painters of the Sea: A Survey of Dutch and English Marine Paintings from British Collections, 1979; The Art of the Van de Veldes, 1982; Nicholas Pocock, 1740-1821, 1986; Captain James Cook, Navigator, 1988; Pirates, Fact and Fiction, 1992; Under the Black Flag, the Romance and the Reality of Life among the Pirates, 1995; Life Among the Pirates, 1995; (ed.) Pirates: Terror on the High Seas, From the Caribbean to the South China Sea, 1996; Ships and Seascapes: An Introduction to Maritime Prints, Drawings and Watercolours, 1997; (intro.) Complete Book Of Maritime Design: A Compendium of Naval Art and Painting, 1998; Women Sailors and Sailors' Women: An Untold Maritime History, 2001; Heroines and Harlots: Women at Sea in the Great Age of Sail, 2002; Billy Ruffian: The Bellerophon and the Downfall of Napoleon, 2003; Cochrane the Dauntless: The Life and Adventures of Admiral Thomas Cochrane, 1775-1860, 2007; Cochrane: The Real Master and Commander, 2007; (intro.) A General History of the Robberies & Murders of the Most Notorious Pirates, 2010; Pirate Hunter of the Caribbean, 2011; Spanish Gold: Captain Woodes Rogers and the Pirates of the Caribbean, 2011. **Address:** c/o Suzanne Gluck, William Morris Agency Inc., 1325 Ave. of the Americas, New York, NY 10019, U.S.A. **Online address:** d.cordingly@btinternet.com

COREN, Stanley. Canadian/American (born United States), b. 1942. **Genres:** Psychology, Animals/Pets, Sciences, Medicine/Health, History, Mythology/Folklore, Psychiatry, Social Sciences, Zoology, Illustrations, Biology. **Career:** University of British Columbia, scientist and professor of psychology, 1973-, now professor emeritus, Human Neuropsychology and Perception Laboratory, director; SC Psychological Enterprises Ltd., director; New School for Social Research, assistant professor; Psychological Laboratories, chairperson. Writer. **Publications:** (With L.M. Ward, A. Gruft and J.B. Collins) The Behavioral Basis of Design, vol. I, 1976; (with J.S. Girgus) Seeing is Deceiving: The Psychology of Visual Illusions, 1978; (with C. Porac) Lateral Preferences and Human Behavior, 1981; (with L.M. Ward and C. Porac) Sensation and Perception, 1979, (with L.M. Ward and J.T. Enns), 6th ed., 2004; (ed.) Left-Handedness: Behavioral Implications and Anomalies, 1990; The Left-Hander Syndrome: The Causes and Consequences of Left-Handedness, 1992; Left Hander: Everything You Need to know About Left-Handedness, 1993; The Intelligence of Dogs: Canine Consciousness and Capabilities, 1994; Intelligence of Dogs: A Guide to the Thoughts, Emotions, and Inner Lives or Our Canine Companions, 1995; Sleep Thieves: An Eye-Opening Exploration into the Science and Mysteries of Sleep, 1996; (with J. Walker) What Do Dogs Know?, 1997; Why We Love the Dogs We Do: How to Find the Dog that Matches Your Personality, 1998; How to Speak Dog: Mastering the Art of Dog-Human Communication, 2000; The Pawprints of History: Dogs and the Course of Human Events, 2002; How Dogs Think: Understanding the Canine Mind, 2004; Why Does My Dog Act That Way?: A Complete Guide to Your Dog's Personality, 2006; (with S. Hodgson) Understanding Your Dog for Dummies, 2007; Modern Dog: A Joyful Exploration of How We Live with Dogs Today, 2008; (co-author) Dogs All-In-One for Dummies, 2010; Born to Bark, 2010. **Address:** Department of Psychology, University of British Columbia, 2136 West Mall, Vancouver, BC V6T 1Z4, Canada. **Online address:** drcoren@stanleycoren.com

COREY, Deborah Joy. American/Canadian (born Canada), b. 1958?. **Genres:** Novels, Young Adult Fiction. **Career:** Freelance writer, 1983-. **Publications:** NOVELS: Losing Eddie, 1993; The Skating Pond, 2003. Contributor to periodicals. **Address:** c/o Author Mail, Penguin Putnam Inc., 375 Hudson St., New York, NY 10014, U.S.A.

CORFIELD, Richard. British (born England), b. 1962?. **Genres:** Geography, Sciences, Natural History. **Career:** Jesus College Oxford, junior research fellow; Oxford University, Department of Earth Science, faculty; Hanborough Consultants, managing director and owner. Writer. **Publications:** Architects of Eternity: The New Science of Fossils, 2001; The Silent Landscape: The Scientific Voyage of HMS Challenger, 2003; Lives of the Planets: A Natural History of the Solar System, 2007. Contributor to periodicals. **Address:** c/o Peter Robinson, Rogers Coleridge & White Literary Agency, 20 Powis Mews, London, GL W11 1JN, England. **Online address:** contact@richardcorfield.com

CORGAN, Billy Patrick. American (born United States), b. 1967. **Genres:** Music, Poetry. **Career:** The Smashing Pumpkins, founder, vocalist and lead guitarist. Writer. **Publications:** Blinking with Fists, 2004. **Address:** Farrar, Straus and Giroux, 18 W 18th St., New York, NY 10011, U.S.A.

CORIN, Joshua. American (born United States), b. 1975. **Genres:** Novels. **Career:** Tiferes Academy, instructor, 2000-04; Richard Frankel Productions, management associate, 2000-01; Georgia Perimeter College, instructor, 2005-; Commuter College, instructor. Writer. **Publications:** Nuclear Winter Wonderland (novel), 2008; While Galileo Preys, 2010; Before Cain Strikes, 2011. **Address:** MIRA Books, 225 Duncan Mill Rd., Don Mills, ON M3B 3K9, Canada. **Online address:** joshua@joshuacorin.com

CORIO, David. American/British (born England), b. 1960?. **Genres:** Architecture, Photography, Design. **Career:** Photographer and photojournalist, 1978-. **Publications:** The Black Chord: Vision of the Groove: Connections between Afro-Beats, Rhythm & Blues, Hip-Hop and More, 1999; (with L.N. Corio) Stones: Megaliths of England and Wales and the Stories Behind Them, 2001; The Couture Accessory, 2002; (with B.L. Benes) Celebrity Relics, Historical Fossils, and Other Metamorphic Rubbish, 2002. **Address:** 16 Jane St., Ste. 1C, New York, NY 10014, U.S.A. **Online address:** davidcorio@davidcorio.com

CORIOLANUS *See* **McMillan, James.**

CORK, Richard (Graham). British (born England), b. 1947. **Genres:** Art/Art History, Essays. **Career:** Evening Standard, art critic, 1969-77, 1980-83; Studio Intl., editor, 1975-79; The Listener, art critic, 1984-90; Cambridge University, Slade professor of fine art, 1989-90; The Times, chief art critic, 1991-2001; Courtauld Institute, Henry Moore senior fellow, 1992-95; Arts Council of England, Visual Arts and Architecture Panel, chairperson, 1995-; The New Statesman, art critic, 2003-. **Publications:** Beyond Painting and Sculpture, 1973; Vorticism and Abstract Art in the First Machine Age, 1976; (contrib.) Art & Criticism: Proceedings of a Conference Held in London on 23rd and 24th April 1976, 1976; Social Role of Art: Essays in Criticism for a Newspaper Public, 1979; Henri Gaudier and Ezra Pound: A Friendship, 1982; Art Beyond the Gallery in Early 20th Century England, 1985; David Bomberg, 1987; (contrib. with P. Fuller) Henry Moore, 1988; (co-ed.) Phillip King, Skulpturen: Städtische Kunsthalle Mannheim, 28. November 1992-24, 1992; (with E. Rosenberg) Architect's Choice: Art in Architecture in Great Britain since 1945, 1992; A Place for Art, 1993; Painting and Sculpture in Europe, 1880-1940, 1993; A Bitter Truth: Avant-Garde Art and the Great War, 1994; Bottle of Notes: Claes Oldenburg/Coosje van Bruggen, 1997; Jacob Epstein, 1999; (contrib.) Young British Art: The Saatchi Decade, 1999; Everything Seemed Possible: Art in the 1970s, 2003; New Spirit, New Sculpture, New Money: Art in the 1980s, 2003; Breaking Down the Barriers: Art in the 1990s, 2003; Annus Mirabilis? Art in the Year 2000, 2003; (with S.D. McElroy) David Nash: Making and Placing Abstract Art: 1978-2004, 2004; Michael Craig-Martin, 2007; Wild Thing: Epstein, Gaudier-Brzeska, Gill, 2009; The Healing Presence of Art: A History of Western Art in Hospitals, 2012. Contributor to periodicals. **Address:** Yale University Press, 302 Temple St., PO Box 209040, New Haven, CT 06511-8909, U.S.A.

CORLETT, Mary Lee. American (born United States), b. 1957. **Genres:** Adult Non-fiction, Art/Art History. **Career:** Cleveland Museum of Art, assistant, 1985-88; Smithsonian Institution, Department of National Portrait Gallery, research assistant in print, 1988-89; National Gallery of Art, Department of Modern Prints and Drawings, research associate, 1989-2002, Department of Special Projects in Modern Art, research associate, 2002-. Writer. **Publications:** WITH R.E. FINE: Graphic Studio: Contemporary Art from the Collaborative Workshop at the University of South Florida, 1991; Prints of Roy Lichtenstein, 1994, rev. ed., 2002; (contrib.) Art of Romare Bearden, 2003; OTHERS: (contrib.) From Process to Print, 2009; Belle: The Amazing, Astonishingly Magical Journey of an Artfully Painted Lady, 2011. Works appear in anthologies. **Address:** Department of Modern Prints and Drawings, National Gallery of Art, 4th and Constitution Ave. NW, Washington, DC 20565, U.S.A.

CORLEY, Thomas Anthony Buchanan. British (born England), b. 1923. **Genres:** Business/Trade/Industry, Economics, History, Biography, Sciences, Autobiography/Memoirs. **Career:** Ministry of National Insurance, staff, 1949-50; Bank of England, clerk, 1950-53, 1955-56; Central Bank of Iraq, director of issue department, 1953-55; University of Cambridge, Department of Applied Economics, research officer, 1956-58; Queen's University, assistant lecturer and lecturer, 1958-63; University of Reading, lecturer, 1963-68, senior lecturer in economics, 1968-88, distinguished business historian. Writer. **Publications:** True Book about Napoleon, 1958; Democratic Despot: A Life of Napoleon III, 1961; (intro.) Otto Wolff: Ouvrard, Speculator of Genius, 1962; The True Story of Napoleon, Emperor of France, 1964; Domestic Electrical Appliances, 1966; Quaker Enterprise in Biscuits: Huntley and Palmers of Reading, 1822-1972, 1972; History of the Burmah Oil Company, vol. I, 1983, vol. II, 1988. Contributor of articles to journals. **Address:** Department of Management, Centre for International Business History, University of Reading, PO Box 218, Reading, BR RG6 6AA, England. **Online address:** t.a.b.corley@reading.ac.uk

CORLISS, Richard (Nelson). American (born United States), b. 1944. **Genres:** Film, Biography, Art/Art History. **Career:** National Review, film critic, 1966-70; Museum of Modern Art, Film Department, staff, 1968-70; Film Comment, editor, 1970-89; New Times, film critic, 1975-78; Soho Weekly News, film critic, 1980; Time Magazine, associate editor, 1980-85, senior writer, 1985-. **Publications:** The Hollywood Screenwriters (biography), 1972; Greta Garbo (biography), 1974; Talking Pictures: Screenwriters in the American Cinema, 1927-1973, 1974; Talking Pictures: Screenwriters of Hollywood, 1975; Lolita (monograph), 1994; (co-author) Crouching Tiger, Hidden Dragon: A Portrait of Ang Lee's Epic Film, 2001; (contrib.) Preston Sturges: un humorista Americano, 2003. Contributor of articles to periodicals. **Address:** Time Magazine, Time-Life Bldg., Rockefeller Ctr., New York, NY 10020, U.S.A.

CORMACK, Baron. *See* **CORMACK, Patrick (Thomas).**

CORMACK, Patrick (Thomas). (Baron Cormack). British (born England), b. 1939. **Genres:** Architecture, History, Politics/Government, Social Commentary. **Career:** Wrekin College, assistant house master, 1967-69; Brewood Grammar School, head of history, 1969-; Department of Health and Social Security, parliamentary private secretary, 1970-73; member of Parliament for Cannock, 1970-74; member of Parliament (Conservative), 1974-2010; St. James School, master, 1961-70; Ross Ltd., training and education officer, 1966; House Magazine, editor, 1983-; St. Antony's College, visiting fellow, 1994-95; First Magazine, international president, 1996-. **Publications:** Heritage in Danger, 1976, new ed., 1978; (ed.) Right Turn: Eight Men who Changed their Minds, 1978; Westminster: Palace and Parliament, 1981; Castles of Britain, 1982; Wilberforce: The Nation's Conscience, 1983; English Cathedrals, 1984. **Address:** House of Commons, London, GL SW1, England.

CORMACK, Robert J. Scottish (born Scotland), b. 1946. **Genres:** Education, Public/Social Administration. **Career:** Queen's University, lecturer, 1973-87, senior lecturer, 1987-92, reader in sociology, 1992-94, dean of the faculty of economics and social sciences, 1992-94, professor of sociology, 1994-2009, pro-vice-chancellor, 1995-2001; UHI Millennium Institute, Inverness, director and chief executive, 2001-03, principal, 2001-09, now professor emeritus; Belfast Citizens Advice Bureau, chairperson, 1989-92, Cape Breton University, professor; Pristina University, faculty; Royal Society of Edinburgh, fellow; Royal Society of Arts, fellow. Writer. **Publications:** (With R.D. Osborne and W.T. Thompson) Into Work?: Young School Leavers and the Structure of Opportunity in Belfast, 1980; (with R.D. Osborne) Religion, Education, and Employment, 1983; (with R.D. Osborne and R.L. Miller) Education and Policy in Northern Ireland, 1987. EDITOR (with R.D. Osborne) Discrimination and Public Policy in Northern Ireland, 1991; (with R.D. Osborn and A.M. Gallaher) After the Reforms: Education and Policy in Northern Ireland, 1993. **Address:** Department of Sociology, Queen's University, University Rd., Belfast, BT7 1NN, England. **Online address:** robert.cormack@uhi.ac.uk

CORN, Alfred. American (born United States), b. 1943. **Genres:** Novels, Poetry, Literary Criticism And History, Essays, Autobiography/Memoirs. **Career:** University Review, associate editor, 1970-71; Da Capo Press Inc., staff writer, 1971-72; freelance writer, 1972-76; Yale University, visiting lecturer in English, 1977-78; Connecticut College, visiting associate professor of English, 1978-81; Columbia University, visiting lecturer, 1983, 1985-87, Graduate Writing Division, instructor, 1991-95; City University of New York, visiting lecturer, 1983, 1985; University of Cincinnati, Elliston professor of poetry, 1989; University of California, visiting professor, 1990; Ohio State University, visiting professor, 1990; University of Tulsa, Bell professor, 1992; Washington University, Hurst resident in poetry, 1994; Poetry School, teacher, 2005-06; Oklahoma State University, faculty. **Publications:** All Roads at Once, 1976; A Call in the Midst of the Crowd: Poems, 1978; The Various Light, 1980; Tongues on Trees, 1981; New Life, 1983; Notes from a Child of Paradise, 1984; Navidad, St. Nicholas Avenue, 1984; The Metamorphoses of Metaphor: Essays in Poetry and Fiction, 1987; Xmas Murder, 1987; The West Door: Poems, 1988; (ed.) Incarnation: Contemporary Writers on the New Testament, 1990; Autobiographies: Poems, 1992; (trans.) M. Proust, L'Indifferent, 1992; Part of His Story, 1997; Present, 1997; The Poem's Heartbeat: A Manual of Prosody, 1997; Stake: Poems, 1972-1992, 1999; (contrib.) Aaron Rose, 2001; Contradictions: Poems, 2002; Atlas: Selected Essays, 1989-2007, 2008. **Address:** c/o Author Mail, Copper Canyon Press, 313 Bldg., Fort Worden State Pk., PO Box 271, Port Townsend, WA 98368-0271, U.S.A.

CORN, David. American (born United States), b. 1959. **Genres:** Documentaries/Reportage, Mystery/Crime/Suspense, History, Biography, Philosophy, Politics/Government. **Career:** The Nation, Washington editor, 1987-; Mother Jones' Washington, bureau chief, through 2007. **Publications:** Blond Ghost: Ted Shackley and the CIA's Crusades, 1994; Deep Background (political thriller), 1999; The Lies of George W. Bush: Mastering the Politics of Deception, 2003; (with M. Isikoff) Hubris: The Inside Story of Spin, Scandal, and the Selling of the Iraq War, 2006. Contributor to periodicals. **Address:** The Nation, 110 Maryland Ave. NE, Ste. 308, Washington, DC 20002, U.S.A.

CORNELL, Gary. American (born United States) **Genres:** Information Science/Computers, Education. **Career:** University of Connecticut, professor, Center for Professional Development, director of modern visual computing; Apress Inc., co-founder; International Business Management, Watson Laboratories, visiting scientist; United States's National Science Foundation, program director. Professional computer programmer and writer. **Publications:** (With W. Abikoff) The Basic Adam, 1984; (with W. Abikoff) The Basic Apple IIc: A Self-Teaching Guide, 1985; ProDOS and Beyond: Applesoft File Techniques, 1985; Basics for DOS, 1991; QuickBASIC 4.5, 1991; Visual Basic for Windows Inside and Out, 1992; Visual Basic 3 for Windows Handbook, 1993; Teach Yourself Word for Windows, 1994; (with T. Strain) Delphi Nuts and Bolts: For Experienced Programmers, 1995, 2nd ed., 1996; (with T. Strain) Visual Basic 4 Nuts and Bolts: For Experienced Programmers, 1995; The Visual Basic 4 for Windows 95 Handbook, 1996; (with C.S. Horstmann) Core Java, 1996, 8th ed., 2008; (with C.S. Horstmann and D. Jezak) Activex: Visual Basic 5 Control Creation Edition, 1997; (with C.S. Horstmann) Core Java 1.1: Advanced Features, 1997; (with C.S. Horstmann and D. Jezak) Core Visual Basic 5, 1997; Visual Basic 5 From the Ground Up, 1997; (with C.S. Horstmann and K. Abdali) Cgi Programming With Java, 1998; (with C.S. Horstmann and K. Topley) Core Java Foundation Classes, 1998; (with P. Patel) Core NT Web Server With CDROM, 1998; Visual Basic 6 From the Ground Up, 1998; (with C.S. Horstmann and J.L. Traub) Core Visual J, 1998; Learn Microsoft Visual Basic Scripting Edition Now, 1998; Learn Microsoft Visual Basic Scripting Editor Now, 1998; (with C.S. Horstmann) Core Java 1.2, 1999; (with C.S. Horstmann) Core Java 2, 2000, 7th ed., 2005. EDITOR: (with J.H. Silverman) Arithmetic Geometry, 1986, rev. ed., 1998; (with J.H. Silverman and G. Stevens) Modular Forms and Fermat's Last Theorem, 1997. **Address:** Apress Inc., 2855 Telegraph Ave., Ste. 600, Berkeley, CA 94705, U.S.A. **Online address:** gary_cornell@apress.com

CORNELL, Jennifer C. American (born United States), b. 1967?. **Genres:** Novellas/Short Stories, Young Adult Fiction. **Career:** Oregon State University, College of Liberal Arts, assistant professor of English, 1994-; liberal arts senator, 1996-; University Honors College, readers, 1999-. Writer. **Publications:** (Co-author) Wordsmiths: The Winners of the Guildhall Press Tenth Anniversary Short Story Competition, 1990; Departures (short stories) in Ireland as All There Is, 1995. Works appear in anthologies. **Address:** Department of English, Oregon State University, 238 Moreland Hall, Corvallis, OR 97331-5302, U.S.A.

CORNER, James. American/British (born England), b. 1961. **Genres:** Horticulture. **Career:** Robert Camlin Associates, drafter, 1980-82; Maurice Wrangell Associates, landscape architectural intern, 1982; William Gillespie and Partners, landscape architectural assistant, 1982-84; Robert Fleming and Associates, landscape architect, 1984-86; Wallace, Roberts and Todd, landscape architect, 1987; University of Pennsylvania, School of Design, studio critic, 1987, lecturer, 1987-90, assistant professor, 1990-96, associate professor of landscape architecture and regional planning, 1996-, Ian McHarg honorary lecturer, 1997, department chair, 2000-, professor of landscape architecture; University of Norway, visiting professor, 1993; Harvard University, Daniel Urban Kiley lecturer, 1993; University of Chicago, visiting lecturer, 1994; Landscape Forum, board director, 1995-; University of Illinois, Jens Jensen professor of landscape and urbanism, 1997; Royal Danish Academy of Art, visiting professor, 1997; Yale University, Timothy Egan memorial lecturer, 1997; KTH School of Architecture, visiting professor, 1999; Stan Allen Architect, principal; Field Operations, principal. Writer. **Publications:** SELF-ILLUSTRATED: (with A.S. MacLean) Taking Measures across the American Landscape, 1996. OTHERS: Landscape Architectural Theory: Anthology, 1960-1996, 1997; (ed.) Recovering Landscape: Essays in Contemporary Landscape Architecture, 1999; (ed. with L. Margulis and B. Hawthorne) Ian McHarg: Conversations with Students: Dwelling in Nature, 2007. Contributor of articles to books and journals. **Address:** Field Operations, 475 10th Ave., 10th Fl., New York, NY 10018, U.S.A. **Online address:** corner@design.upenn.edu

CORNGOLD, Stanley. American (born United States), b. 1934. **Genres:** Literary Criticism And History. **Career:** University of Maryland, European Division, instructor in English, 1959-62; Cornell University, teaching assistant in English, 1963-64, teaching assistant in French, 1964-65; Princeton University, assistant professor, 1966-72, associate professor of Germanic languages and literatures, 1972-79, associate professor of Germanic languages and literatures and comparative literature, 1979-81, professor of German and comparative literature, 1981-2009, professor emeritus, 2009-; National Endowment for the Humanities, junior fellow, 1973-74; Bryn Mawr University, visiting professor, 1983-84; Kafka Society of America, vice president, 1985-86, president, 1987-88; University of Freiburg, Fulbright research fellow, 1986-87; Institute for Advanced Study, visiting professor, 2003-04; Internationales Forschungszentrum, fellow, 2004; Columbia University, adjunct professor of law, 2006-07; University of Cambridge, King's College, visiting fellow, 2009; American Academy in Berlin, fellow, 2010; University of Wisconsin, Jay C. & Ruth Halls fellow, 2010; University of Pittsburgh, Humanities Center, fellow, 2011. Writer. **Publications:** The Commentators' Despair: The Interpretation of Kafka's Metamorphosis, 1973; The Fate of the Self: German Writers and French Theory, 1986, 2nd ed., 1994; Franz Kafka: The Necessity of Form, 1988; (with I. Giersing) Borrowed Lives, 1991; (trans.) Goethe's Elective Affinities, 1997; Complex Pleasure: Forms of Feeling in German Literature, 1998; (contrib.) Literary Paternity, Literary Friendship: Essays in Honor of Stanley Corngold, 2002; Lambent Traces: Franz Kafka, 2004; (with B. Wagner) The Ghosts in the Machine: Franz Kafka, 2011. EDITOR: Max Frisch, Ausgewaehlte Prosa, 1968; (trans. and intro.) The Metamorphosis, 1972; (with R. Ludwig) Thomas Mann, 1875-1975, 1975; (with M. Curschmann and T. Ziolkowski) Aspekte der Goethezeit, 1977; (and trans.) The Metamorphosis: Translation, Backgrounds and Contexts, Criticism, 1996; (and trans.) Kafka's Selected Stories: New Translations, Backgrounds and Contexts, Criticism, 2007; (with J. Greenberg and B. Wagner) Franz Kafka: The Office Writings, 2009; (with R. Gross) Kafka for the Twenty-First Century, 2010; (ed. and intro.) The Sufferings of Young Werther, 2012. Contributor to books and journals. **Address:** Department of German, Princeton University, 219 E Pyne Bldg., 28 W Dillon Ct., Princeton, NJ 08544-5210, U.S.A. **Online address:** corngold@princeton.edu

CORNIER, Nadia. (Nina Beck). American (born United States), b. 1980. **Genres:** Novels. **Career:** Creative Media Agency, young adult and speculative fiction agent, 2004-; Auden Media Corp., partner, 2006-; Cornier and Associates, founder and owner; Firebrand Literary subsidiary, founder. Writer. **Publications:** (With L. Barnholdt) Writing and Selling the Young Adult Novel, 2007; (as Nina Beck) This Book Isn't Fat, It's Fabulous, 2008; (as Nina Beck) This Girl Isn't Shy, She's Spectacular (young adult novel), 2009. **Address:** New York, NY , U.S.A. **Online address:** nadia@nadiacornier.com

CORNIS-POPE, Marcel (H.). American/Romanian (born Romania), b. 1946. **Genres:** Literary Criticism And History, Humanities, Intellectual History, Language/Linguistics, Translations, Film. **Career:** University of Timisoara, assistant professor, 1968-77, associate professor of English, 1977-83; University of Northern Iowa, senior Fulbright lecturer in English, 1983-85, adjunct professor of English, 1985-87; Virginia Commonwealth University, Department of English, associate professor, 1988-91, professor of English, 1991-, chair, 2000-06, co-chair, 2010-, PhD Program in Media, Arts and Text, director, 2006-10. Writer. **Publications:** Modern Fiction, 1981; Anatomia Balenei Albe: Poetica Romanului American Epopeic-Simbolic, 1982; Hermeneutic Desire and Critical Rewriting: Narrative Interpretation in the Wake of Post structuralism, 1992; The Unfinished Battles: Romanian Postmodernism before and after 1989, 1996; Narrative Innovation and Cultural Rewriting in the Cold War Era and After, 2001. TRANSLATOR: I. Brad, The Outlying Temple, 1975; T. Wolfe, Priveste, Inger catre casa, 1977; K. Vonnegut, Fii Binecuvintat, Domnule Rosewater, 1980; D. Thomas, Fiicele Rebecai, 1982; K. Kesey, Zbor deasupra unui cuib de cuci, 1983; D. Tudoran, Optional Future: Selected Poems, 1999; P. Iliesu, Romania: Post Scriptum, 1999. EDITOR: Caiet de Americanistica: De la William Carlos Williams la Charles Olson; Innoiri in lirica Americana contemporana, 1983; Anghel umbraveanu, Iarna Imperiala, 1986; Violence and Mediation in Contemporary Culture, 1996; Anghel Dumbraveanu, Lacrima timpului/The Tear of Time: Poeme/Poems, 1997; (with J. Neubauer) History of the Literary Cultures of East-Central Europe: Junctures and Disjunctures in the Nineteenth and Twentieth Centuries, vol. I, 2004, vol. II, 2006, vol. III, 2007, vol. IV, 2010. **Address:** Department of English, Virginia Commonwealth University, Rm. 306, 900 Park Ave., PO Box 842005, Richmond, VA 23284-2005, U.S.A. **Online address:** mcornis@vcu.edu

CORNWELL, Anita (R.). American (born United States), b. 1923. **Genres:** Women's Studies And Issues, Gay And Lesbian Issues, Children's Fiction. **Career:** Pennsylvania State Department of Public Welfare, staff. Freelance writer. **Publications:** Black Lesbian in White America, 1983; The Girls of Summer (juvenile), 1989. Contributor to periodicals. **Address:** New Seed Press, PO Box 9488, Berkeley, CA 94709-7556, U.S.A.

CORNWELL, Autumn. American (born United States) **Genres:** Young Adult Non-fiction, Novels. **Career:** Writer. **Publications:** Carpe Diem (young-adult novel), 2007. **Address:** c/o Rosemary Stimola, Stimola Literary Studio, 306 Chase Ct., Edgewater, NJ 07020, U.S.A. **Online address:** autumn@autumncornwell.com

CORNYETZ, Nina. American (born United States) **Genres:** Psychology, History, Social Commentary, Literary Criticism And History. **Career:** Rutgers University, assistant professor; New York University, Gallatin School of Individualized Study, associate professor. Writer. **Publications:** Dangerous Women, Deadly Words: Phallic Fantasy and Modernity in Three Japanese Writers, 1999; The Ethics of Aesthetics in Japanese Cinema and Literature: Polygraphic Desire, 2006; (ed. with J.K. Vincent) Perversion and Modern Japan: Psychoanalysis, Literature, Culture, 2010. **Address:** Gallatin School of Individualized Study, New York University, Rm. 606, 1 Wash Pl., 715 Broadway, New York, NY 10003, U.S.A. **Online address:** nina.cornyetz@nyu.edu

CORONA, Laurel. American (born United States), b. 1949?. **Genres:** Military/Defense/Arms Control, Novels, Travel/Exploration. **Career:** San Diego Community College, professor of English. Writer. **Publications:** Kenya, 2000; Poland, 2000; South Africa, 2000; Ethiopia, 2001; Life in Moscow, 2001; Norway, 2001; Peru, 2001; The Russian Federation, 2001; Ukraine, 2001; The World Trade Center, 2002; France, 2002; Afghanistan, 2002; Judaism, 2003; Israel, 2003; Hunting down the Terrorists: Declaring War and Policing Global Violations, 2004; Jewish Americans, 2004; War within a War: Vietnam and the Cold War, 2004; (with M. Bart) Until Our Last Breath: A Holocaust Story of Love and Partisan Resistance, 2008; The Four Seasons: A Novel of Vivaldi's Venice, 2008. **Address:** San Diego City College, 1313 Park Blvd., San Diego, CA 92101-4712, U.S.A. **Online address:** lcorona@sdccd.edu

CORP, Edward. French/British (born England), b. 1948?. **Genres:** History, Biography, Autobiography/Memoirs, History. **Career:** Universite de Paris VII, senior lecturer in British history; University of Toulouse, professor of British history. Writer. **Publications:** (With J. Sanson) La cour des Stuarts a Saint-Germain-en-Laye au temps de Louis XIV, 1992; (with S. Crowe) Our Ablest Public Servant: Sir Eyre Crowe, 1864-1925, 1993; L'autre exil: Les Jacobites en France au debut du XVIIIe siecle, 1993; (with E. Cruickshanks) The Stuart Court in Exile and the Jacobites, 1995; Lord Burlington: The Man and His Politics, 1998; The King over the Water, 2001; The Stuart Court in Rome: The Legacy of Exile, 2003; A Court in Exile: The Stuarts in France, 2004; Jacobites at Urbino: An Exiled Court in Transition, 2009. **Address:** 15 rue Des Arts, Toulouse, 31000, France. **Online address:** e.corp@wanadoo.fr

CORRADO, Anthony. American (born United States), b. 1957. **Genres:** Politics/Government, Social Sciences. **Career:** The White House, personnel officer for the office of presidential personnel, 1980-81; Capitol Services Inc., executive director, 1981-82; Colby College, Department of Government, instructor, 1986-89, assistant professor, 1989-94, associate professor, 1994-2001, professor of government, 2001-03, Charles A. Dana professor of government, 2003-; The Brookings Institution, non-resident senior fellow, governance studies, 1999-2009. Writer. **Publications:** Creative Campaigning: PACs and the Presidential Selection Process, 1992; Paying for Presidents, 1993; (contrib.) Let America Decide: The Report of the Twentieth Century Fund Task Force on Presidential Debates, 1995; (with H. Alexander) Financing the 1992 Election, 1996; (co-author)Campaign Finance Reform: A Sourcebook, 1997; Campaign Finance Reform, 2000; (comp.) Campaigns in Cyberspace: Toward a New Regulatory Approach, 2000; Inside the Campaign Finance Battle: Court Testimony on the New Reforms, 2003; The New Campaign Finance Sourcebook, 2005; (co-author) Financing the 2004 Election, 2006; (ed. with D.B. Magleby) Financing the 2008 Election: Assessing Reform, 2011. **Address:** Department of Government, Colby College, 5302 Mayflower Hill, Waterville, ME 04901-8853, U.S.A. **Online address:** ajcorrad@colby.edu

CORRAN, Mary. British (born England), b. 1953. **Genres:** Science Fiction/Fantasy, Young Adult Fiction, Literary Criticism And History. **Career:** Trainee system analyst, 1980-82; oil analyst, 1982-92. Writer. **Publications:** FANTASY NOVELS: Imperial Light, 1994; Fate, 1995; Darkfell, 1996; History of Medicine, forthcoming. Contributor to books and anthologies. **Address:** Millennium Publisher, 21 Bloomsbury Sq., London, GL WC1A 2NS, England.

CORRICK, James A. American (born United States), b. 1945. **Genres:** Young Adult Non-fiction, Air/Space Topics, Novellas/Short Stories, Sciences, Science Fiction/Fantasy, History. **Career:** Writer and editor, 1979-; University of Arizona, tutor, 1981-82; L5 Society, editor, 1985-87; National Space Society, editor, 1987; Muscular Dystrophy Association, science writer, 1991-92. **Publications:** The Human Brain: Mind and Matter, 1983; Recent Revolutions in Chemistry, 1986; Recent Revolutions in Biology, 1987; Career Preparation, 1988; Double Your Pleasure: The Ace SF Double, 1989; The World of Nature: Farm Animals, 1991; Mars, 1991; Muscular Dystrophy, 1992; Science People, Profiling the Men and Women of Science, 1993; The Early Middle Ages, 1995; The Late Middle Ages, 1995; The Battle of Gettysburg, 1996; The Byzantine Empire, 1997; The Industrial Revolution, 1998; The Renaissance, 1998; Life among the Soldiers and Cavalry, 2000; The Incas, 2001; Life of a Medieval Knight, 2001; The Louisiana Purchase, 2001; The Civil War, 2003; Life among the Inca, 2004; Uniquely Arizona, 2004; Ancient India, 2005; The Early Middle Ages, 2006; The Byzantine Empire, 2006; Civil War and Emancipation, 2008; Dwayne The Rock Johnson, 2009; Bloody, Rotten Roman Empire: The Disgusting Details About Life in Ancient Rome, 2011; The Rough, Stormy Age of Vikings, 2011; Gritty, Stinky Ancient Egypt: The Disgusting Details About Life in Ancient Egypt, 2011. Contributor to books and periodicals. **Address:** 4402 E Cooper Cir., Tucson, AZ 85711-4260, U.S.A.

CORRIGAN, Eireann. American (born United States), b. 1977?. **Genres:** Autobiography/Memoirs, Poetry, Horror. **Career:** Rutgers Preparatory School, teacher, 2000-. Writer. **Publications:** You Remind Me of You: A Poetry Memoir, 2002; Splintering, 2004; Ordinary Ghosts, 2007; Accomplice, 2010. **Address:** Rutgers Preparatory School, 1345 Easton Ave., Somerset, NJ 08873-1412, U.S.A. **Online address:** corrigan@rutgersprep.org

CORRIGAN, John R. American (born United States), b. 1970. **Genres:** Mystery/Crime/Suspense. **Career:** Pomfret School, English teacher; Golf Today Magazine, columnist, 2001-05, journalist. **Publications:** Cut Shot (mystery novel), 2001; Snap Hook (mystery novel), 2004; Center Cut, 2004; Bad Lie, 2005; Out of Bounds, 2006. **Address:** PO Box 128, Pomfret, CT 06258-0128, U.S.A. **Online address:** jcorrigan@pomfretschool.org

CORRIGAN, Kelly. American (born United States), b. 1967. **Genres:** Autobiography/Memoirs, Biography, Medicine/Health. **Career:** Writer. **Publications:** The Middle Place (memoir), 2007; Lift (memoir), 2009. Contributor to periodicals. **Address:** c/o Andrea Barzvi, International Creative Management, 10250 Constellation Blvd., Los Angeles, CA 90067, U.S.A.

CORRINGTON, Robert S. American (born United States), b. 1950?. **Genres:** Administration/Management, Theology/Religion, Philosophy, Natural History, Biography, Medicine/Health, Psychology. **Career:** Pennsylvania State University, professor; Drew University, Casperson School of Graduate Studies, professor of philosophical theology. Writer. **Publications:** (Ed. with C. Hausman and T.M. Seebohm) Pragmatism Considers Phenomenology, 1987; The Community of Interpreters: On the Hermeneutics of Nature and the Bible in the American Philosophical Tradition, 1987, 2nd ed., 1995; (ed. with K. Wallace and A. Marsoobian) Metaphysics of Natural Complexes, 1990; (ed. with A. Marsoobian and K. Wallace) Nature's Perspective: Prospects of Ordinal Metaphysics, 1991; Nature and Spirit: An Essay in Ecstatic Naturalism, 1992; An Introduction to C.S. Pierce: Philosopher, Semiotician and Ecstatic Naturalist, 1993; Ecstatic Naturalism: Signs of the World, 1994; Nature's Self: Our Journey from Origin to Spirit, 1996; Nature's Religion, 1997; A Semiotic Theory of Theology and Philosophy, 2000; Wilhelm Reich: Psychoanalyst and Radical Naturalist, 2003; Riding the Windhorse: Manic Depressive Disorder and the Quest for Wholeness, 2003. Contributor to journals and periodicals. **Address:** Caspersen School of Graduate Studies, Theological School, Drew University, 36 Madison Ave., 3rd Fl., Madison, NJ 07940, U.S.A. **Online address:** rcorring@drew.edu

CORSETTI, Emilio. American (born United States), b. 1957. **Genres:** Air/Space Topics. **Career:** Apollo Software, president, 1985-91; Odyssey Interactive, creative director and vice president, 1994. Writer and pilot. **Publications:** 35 Miles from Shore: The Ditching and Rescue of ALM Flight 980, 2008. Contributor of articles to periodicals. **Address:** Odyssey Publishing, 113980 Nahelenani St., Volcano, HI 96785, U.S.A. **Online address:** emilio@emiliocorsetti.com

CORSON, Trevor. American (born United States), b. 1969?. **Genres:** Marine Sciences/Oceanography, Environmental Sciences/Ecology, Natural History. **Career:** Harvard China Review, executive editor; Transition Magazine, managing editor; Atlantic Magazine, writer. **Publications:** The Secret Life of Lobsters: How Fishermen and Scientists Are Unraveling the Mysteries of Our Favorite Crustacean, 2004; The Zen of Fish: The Story of Sushi, From Samurai to Supermarket, 2007. Works appear in anthologies. Contributor to periodicals. **Address:** Stuart Krichevsky Literary Agency Inc., 381 Park Ave. S, Ste. 914, New York, NY 10016-8806, U.S.A. **Online address:** info@trevorcorson.com

CORTEN, Irina H. American/Russian (born Russia), b. 1941. **Genres:** Education, Language/Linguistics, Area Studies. **Career:** University of Wisconsin-Madison, instructor in Russian, 1973-74; University of Kansas, visiting assistant professor of Russian, 1974-75; University of Minnesota, associate professor of Russian, 1975-, professor, now professor emeritus. Writer. **Publications:** Vocabulary of Soviet Society and Culture: A Selected Guide to Russian Words, Idioms and Expressions of the Post-Stalin Era, 1992. **Address:** College of Liberal Arts, University of Minnesota, 205 Folwell Hall, 9 Pleasant St SE, Minneapolis, MN 55455, U.S.A. **Online address:** corte001@umn.edu

CORUM, James S(terling). Estonian/French (born France), b. 1953. **Genres:** History. **Career:** Oxford University, tutor, 1979-81, All Souls College, visiting fellow, 2004-05; St. Lawrence University, Department of Military Studies, assistant professor of military studies, 1983-86; Mater Dei College, instructor, 1986-87; Queen's University, instructor in history, 1988-91; U.S. Air Force School of Advanced Air and Space Studies; Maxwell Air Force Base, professor of comparative military studies, 1991-2004; U.S. Army Command and General Staff College, associate professor, 2005-08; Austin Peay State University, adjunct professor of military history, 2009-12; Baltic Defence College, dean, 2009-. Writer. **Publications:** The Roots of Blitzkrieg: Hans von Seeckt and German Military Reform, 1992; (with R. Muller) The Luftwaffe's Way of War, 1997; The Luftwaffe: Creating the Operational Air War 1918-1940, 1998; (with W. Johnson) Airpower in Small Wars: Fighting Insurgents and Terrorists, 2003; Training Indigenous Forces in Counterinsurgency: A Tale of Two Insurgencies, 2006; Fighting the War on Terror: A Counterinsurgency Strategy, 2007; Bad Strategies: How Major Powers Fail in Counterinsurgency, 2008; Wolfram von Richthofen: Master of the German Air War, 2008; (ed.) Air Power, Insurgency and the War on Terror, 2009; (ed.) Rearming Germany, 2011. Contributor to periodicals. **Address:** Baltic Defence College, Riia 12, Tartu, 51013, Estonia. **Online address:** james.corum@bdcol.ee

CORY, Charlotte. British (born England), b. 1956. **Genres:** Novels, Poetry, Young Adult Fiction. **Career:** Novelist and photographer. **Publications:** The Unforgiving, 1991; The Laughter of Fools, 1993; The Guest, 1996; Imperial Quadrille, 2003; The Visitors, 2007. **Address:** David Godwin Associates Ltd., 55 Monmouth St., London, GL WC2H 9DG, England. **Online address:** charlotte@charlottecory.com

CORYELL, Janet L(ee). American (born United States), b. 1955. **Genres:** History, Biography, Women's Studies And Issues, Politics/Government. **Career:** Butler County Community College, lecturer, 1980-82, special program coordinator, 1981-82; Christopher Newport College, adjunct lecturer, 1984; University of Dayton, assistant professor of history, 1986-89; Auburn University, assistant professor of history, 1989-91; Western Michigan University, Department of History, assistant professor, 1991-92, associate professor, 1992-, professor. Writer. **Publications:** Neither Heroine nor Fool: Anna Ella Carroll of Maryland, 1990; (ed. with J.M. Greiner and J.R. Smither) A Surgeon's Civil War: The Letters and Diary of Daniel M. Holt, M.D., 1994; (co-ed.) Beyond Image and Convention: Explorations in Southern Women's History, 1998; (ed. with R.C. Myers) Adeline and Julia: Growing up in Michigan and on the Kansas Frontier: Diaries from 19th-Century America, 2000; (co-ed.) Negotiating Boundaries of Southern Womanhood: Dealing with the Powers that Be, 2000; (with N. Faires) History of Women in America, 2012. Contributor to periodicals. **Address:** Department of History, Western Michigan University, 4406 Friedmann Hall, Kalamazoo, MI 49008-5334, U.S.A. **Online address:** janet.coryell@wmich.edu

COSBY, Bill. American (born United States), b. 1937. **Genres:** Children's Non-fiction, Human Relations/Parenting, Humor/Satire. **Career:** Writer and actor. **Publications:** The Wit and Wisdom of Fat Albert, 1973; Bill Cosby's Personal Guide to Tennis Power; or, Don't Lower the Lob, Raise the Net, 1975; Fat Albert's Survival Kit, 1975; You Are Somebody Special, 1978; Fatherhood, 1986; Time Files, 1987; Love and Marriage, 1989; Childhood, 1991; The Best Way to Play, 1997; The Meanest Thing to Say, 1997; Treasure Hunt, 1997; Kids Say the Darndest Things, 1998; Shipwreck Saturday, 1998; Money Troubles, 1998; Hooray for the Dandelion Warriors!, 1999; Congratulations! Now What?: A Book For Graduates, 1999; The Day I Was Rich, 1999; My Big Lie, 1999; One Dark and Scary Night, 1999; Worst Day of My Life, 1999; The Day I Saw My Father Cry, 2000; Cosbyology: Essays and Observations from the Doctor, 2001; Honeywood Street Fair, 2001; Presents for Everyone!, 2001; Let's Go to the Supermarket!, 2001; We're Going to the Zoo!, 2001; Adventure with Captain Brainstorm!, 2001; Who's Hiding, Little Bill?, 2001; Elephant on the Loose, 2001; Extra-thankful Thanksgiving, 2001; Visit to the Dentist, 2002; Cleanup Day!, 2002; Little Bill's Big Book of Words, 2002; Super Detective Little Bill: Spin the Wheel, Find the Answer!, 2002; Yay! A Snow Day!: With 17 Flaps to Lift, 2002; Big Storm, 2002; Little Bill's Birthday Party, 2003; I Am What I Ate And I'm Frightened: And Other Digressions from the Doctor of Comedy, 2003; Friends of a Feather: One of Life's Little Fables, 2003; Big Day at School, 2003; Hello, Santa!, 2003; Happy Easter, Everyone!, 2003; Thank You, Dr. King!, 2003; (with A.F. Poussaint) Come On, People!: On the Path from Victims to Victors, 2007; (intro.) The Black Book, 2009; I Didn't Ask to be Born (But I'm Glad I Was), 2011. **Address:** The Brokaw Co., 9255 Sunset Blvd., Ste. 804, Los Angeles, CA 90069, U.S.A. **Online address:** service@billcosby.com

COSCARELLI, Don. American/Lebanese (born Lebanon), b. 1954. **Genres:** Plays/Screenplays, Novels, Literary Criticism And History. **Career:** Writer, film director and producer. **Publications:** Jim the World's Greatest, 1976; Kenny & Company, 1976; Phantasm, 1978; The Beastmaster, 1982; Phantasm II, 1988; Survival Quest, 1989; Phantasm III: Lord of the Dead, 1994; Phantasm IV: Oblivion, 1998; Bubba Ho-tep, 2002; Incident On and Off a Mountain Road, 2005; John Dies at the End, 2009; Bubba Nosferatu, 2011. Contributor to periodicals. **Address:** Metro-Goldwyn-Mayer Pictures, 2450 Broadway, Santa Monica, CA 90404, U.S.A.

COSENTINO, Frank. Canadian (born Canada), b. 1937. **Genres:** History, Sports/Fitness. **Career:** Canadian Football League, professional football player, 1960-69; teacher, 1963-65; University of Western Ontario, assistant professor, 1970-74, associate professor of physical education, 1975-76, chair of department, 1975-76, head football coach, 1970-74; York University, professor of physical education, recreation and athletics, chair and director of department, 1976-81, head football coach, 1978-80, 1984-87, professor emeritus, 1997-, School of Kinesiology and Health Science, Stong fellow. Writer. **Publications:** Canadian Football: The Grey Cup Years, 1969; (with M.L. Howell) A History of Physical Education in Canada, 1971; (with G. Leyshon) Olympic Gold, 1975; Ned Hanlan, 1978; (with D. Morrow) Lionel Conacher, 1981; (with G. Leyshon) Winter Gold, 1983; (with M. Dinning, K. Jones and G. Malszecki) A History of Physical Education, 1985; (co-author) A Concise History of Sport in Canada, 1989; Not Bad, Eh? Prose and Poetry in Canadian Sport, 1990; Renfrew Millionaires: The Valley Boys of Winter, 1910, 1990; A Passing Game: A History of the CFL, 1995; Almonte's Brothers of the Wind: R. Tait McKenzie and James Naismith, 1996; Afros, Aboriginals and Amateur Sport in Pre WWI Canada, 1998; Almonte, 2000; Hail Mary Heaven Sent, 2006; Hockey Gods at the Summit, 2011. **Address:** York University, 4700 Keele St., Toronto, ON M3J 1P3, Canada. **Online address:** frankc@yorku.ca

COSGROVE, Brian. British/Irish (born Ireland), b. 1941?. **Genres:** Poetry, Autobiography/Memoirs. **Career:** University of Aberdeen, assistant lecturer, 1965-67; University College Dublin, lecturer, 1967-92; National University of Ireland, St. Patrick's College, professor of English and head of the department of English, 1992-2005, professor emeritus of English, 2005-; Jonathan Swift Seminar, academic director, 1994-96. Writer. **Publications:** Wordsworth and the Poetry of Self-Sufficiency: A Study of the Poetic Development, 1796-1814, 1982; (ed.) Literature and the Supernatural: Essays for the Maynooth Bicentenary, 1995; The Yew-Tree at the Head of the Strand (memoir), 2001; James Joyce's Negations: Irony, Indeterminacy and Nihilism in Ulysses and Other Writings, 2007. Contributor to periodicals. **Online address:** brian.cosgrove@nuim.ie

COSGROVE, Charles H. American (born United States), b. 1952. **Genres:** Theology/Religion, History. **Career:** Northern Seminary, professor of New Testament Studies and Christian ethics, 1984-. Writer, editor, educator and theologian. **Publications:** The Cross and the Spirit: A Study in the Argument and Theology of Galatians, 1988; (ed. with J.T. Carroll and E.E. Johnson) Faith and History: Essays in Honor of Paul W. Meyer, 1990; (with D.D. Hatfield) Church Conflict: The Hidden Systems behind the Fights, 1994; Elusive Israel: The Puzzle of Election in Romans, 1997; A History of the 134th New York Volunteer Infantry Regiment in the American Civil War, 1862-1865: Long Night's Journey into Day, 1997; Appealing to Scripture in Moral Debate: Five Hermeneutical Rules, 2002; (ed.) The Meanings We Choose: Hermeneutical Ethics, Indeterminacy, and the Conflict of Interpretations, 2004; (with H. Weiss and K.K. Yeo) Cross-Cultural Paul: Journeys to Others, Journeys to Ourselves, 2005; (with W.D. Edgerton) In Other Words: Incarnational Translation for Preaching, 2007. **Address:** Northern Seminary, 660 E Butterfield Rd., Lombard, IL 60148, U.S.A. **Online address:** cosgrove@seminary.edu

COSGROVE, Michael H. American (born United States), b. 1943?. **Genres:** Economics. **Career:** Gulf Oil, director of strategy development, 1977-87; The Econoclast Inc., founder and principal, 1979-; University of Dallas, College of Business, associate professor, 1987-, professor of economics. Writer and economist. **Publications:** The Cost of Winning: Global Development Policies and Broken Social Contracts, 1996. Contributor to journals. **Address:** The Econoclast Inc., 3419 Westminister Ave., Ste. 251, Dallas, TX 75205-1387, U.S.A. **Online address:** mcos@gsm.udallas.edu

COSIC, Dobrica. American (born United States), b. 1921. **Genres:** Novels, Essays. **Career:** Serbia to the Yugoslav Assembly, people's deputy, 1945-68; Marshal Tito's, courtly poet; Liubomin Tadic, founder; Federal Republic of Yugoslavia, president, 1992-93. Writer. **Publications:** Daleko je Sunce (novel), 1951; Koreni, 1954; Daleko je Sunce, 1955; Deobe, 1966; Koreni, 1966; Prilike, 1966; Bajka, 1966; Odgovornosti. Akcija 2, 1966; Vreme Smrti, 1972; Koreni, 1977; Daleko je Sunce, 1977; Time of Death, 1978; Into the Battle: Novel, 1983; This Land, this Time, 1983; South to Destiny, 1983; Reach to Eternity, 1983; Gresnik: Roman, 1985; Otpadnik: Roman, 1986; Mića Popović, Vreme, Prijatelji, 1988; Stvarno i Moguće: članci i ogledi, 1988; Vernik: Rroman, 1990; Srpsko Pitanje-Demokratsko Pitanje, 1992; Promene, 1992; Srbija u Vremenu Smrti, 1992; Yougoslavie et la Question Serbe, 1992; Vreme Vlasti, 1996; Otkriće, 1998; Za Preporod Srbije sa Novim Ljudima u Novom Društvu: rec u Srpskoj Akademiji Nauka I Umetnosti 13. Juna 1999, 1999; Pisci Moga Veka, 2002; Srpsko Pitanje, 2002; Na Têkom Putu, 2004; Pisci Moga Veka, 2004; Kosovo, 2004; On a Difficult Path, 2005; Vreme Zmija: Piščevi Zapisi 1999-2000, 2008; Piščevi Zapisi, 1993-1999, 2008; Lična istorija jednog doba, 2009.Works appear in anthologies. Contributor to periodicals. **Address:** c/o Harcourt Brace, 525 B St., Ste. 1900, San Diego, CA 92101-4495, U.S.A.

COSKRAN, Kathleen. American (born United States), b. 1943. **Genres:** Novellas/Short Stories. **Career:** University of Minnesota-Twin Cities, adjunct faculty, 1988-; Hamline University, adjunct faculty, 1989-; First Universalist Church, president, 1992-93; Lake Country School, head, now retired; Zhejiang College of Media and Communications, faculty. Writer. **Publications:** The High Price of Everything (stories), 1988; (ed. with C.W. Truesdale) Tanzania on Tuesday: Writing by American Women Abroad, 1997; (ed. with C.W. Truesdale) Inn Near Kyoto: Writing by American Women Abroad, 1998. Contributor to periodicals. Works appear in anthologies. **Address:** c/o Robin Rue, Anita Diamant Literary Agency, 310 Madison Ave., New York, NY 10017, U.S.A.

COSMAN, Mark. American (born United States), b. 1945. **Genres:** How-to Books, Human Relations/Parenting, Social Sciences. **Career:** Volunteers of America (VOA), Friends of Volunteers of America, president, 1984-; CCR Inc., president, founder and chief executive officer. Writer. **Publications:** In the Wake of Death: Surviving the Loss of a Child, 1996; A Father's Unraveling: When Tragedy Strikes, Will The Self You've Made Survive?, 2008; Lives of Pandora, 2009; We The Immortals, 2010. **Address:** CCR Inc., PO Box 56884, Albuquerque, NM 87187-6884, U.S.A. **Online address:** mark.cosman@gmail.com

COSPER, Darcy. American (born United States) **Genres:** Novels, Young Adult Fiction. **Career:** Writer. **Publications:** Wedding Season, 2004; (contrib.) Sex and Sensibility: 28 True Romances from the Lives of Single Women, 2005; (contrib.) 2033: The Future of Misbehavior, 2007. **Address:** c/o Author Mail, Random House Inc., 1745 Broadway, 3rd Fl., New York, NY 10019-4368, U.S.A.

COSSOLOTTO, Matthew. American (born United States), b. 1953. **Genres:** Plays/Screenplays, Advertising/Public Relations, Communications/Media, How-to Books, Politics/Government, Self Help, Technology, Ghost Writer, Ghost Writer, Young Adult Non-fiction. **Career:** U.S. House of Representatives, legislative assistant, 1977-81, special assistant to James C. Wright Jr., 1983-88; Peace Corps, staff, 1981-82; MCI Communications Corp., Corporate Communications Department, senior manager, 1988-92; PepsiCo Foods and Beverages Intl., director of communications, 1992-95; Center for Voting and Democracy, president, 1991-96; General Telephone and Electronics Corp., director of communications, 1995-96; Ovations International Inc., founder and president, 1996-. Writer. **Publications:** NONFICTION: Almanac of Transatlantic Politics, 1991; Almanac of European Politics, 1995; Habit Force! How to Kick the Habits of F.A.I.L.U.R.E and Adopt the Habits of S.U.C.C.E.S.S., 2004; All The World's A Podium, 2007; The Real F Word, 2009; The Power of Making a Promise; The Joy of Speaking, 2010. Contributor to periodicals. **Address:** 3481 Wildwood St., Yorktown Heights, NY 10598, U.S.A. **Online address:** matthew@ovations.com

COSTA, Manuel J(oseph). American (born United States), b. 1933. **Genres:** inspirational/Motivational Literature, Sports/Fitness. **Career:** Roman Catholic priest, 1961-75; Roman Catholic parish, pastor, 1968-74; College of Notre Dame, assistant professor of religious studies and director of campus ministry, 1974-75; Bridge Counseling Center, executive director, 1975-79; psychotherapist, 1978-; Miramonte Mental Health Services, executive director, 1979-88; Guild for Psychological Studies, seminar leader, 1981-. Writer. **Publications:** (With M. Eussen) Life and Love, 1969; Tackling Life Head On: Lessons for Kids' Lives with Ronnie Lott as Coach, 1997. **Address:** c/o John Williams, PO Box 231, Cannon Beach, OR 97110, U.S.A. **Online address:** mjmmc46987@aol.com

COSTELLO, Matthew J. American (born United States), b. 1948?. **Genres:** Novels, Children's Fiction, Young Adult Fiction. **Career:** British Broadcasting Corp., interactive and creative consultant; Public Broadcasting Service, interactive and creative consultant; The Disney Channel, interactive and creative consultant. Novelist, news script writer, games scriptwriter and television writer. **Publications:** Sleep Tight, 1987; Revolt on Majippor: A Crossroads Adventure in the World of Robert Silverbergs Majipoor, 1987; Fate's Trick, 1988; The Greatest Puzzles of All Time, 1988; Guardians of the Three Volume Three: The Wizard of Tizare, 1989; Beneath Still Waters, 1989; Childs Play Two, 1990; Midsummer, 1990; Time of the Fox, 1990; Wurm, 1991; The Greatest Games of All Time, 1991; Hour of the Scorpion, 1991; Childs Play Three, 1991; Day of the Snake, 1992; How to Write Science Fiction, 1992, 2nd. ed., 1995; Homecoming, 1992; Garden, 1993; Seaquest DSV: Fire Below: A Seaquest DSV Novel, 1994; See how She Runs, 1994; (with C.S. Gardner) The 7th Guest, 1995; (with F.P. Wilson) Mirage, 1996; (with F.P. Wilson) Masque, 1998; Magic Everywhere: How to Do Absolutely Incredible Magic with Totally Ordinary Things, 1999; Poltergeist the Legacy: Maelstrom, 2000; Unidentified, 2002; Missing Monday, 2004; (with L. Mlodinow) The Kids of Einstein Elementary: The Last Dinosaur, 2004; Island of the Skull: An Original Novel, 2005; The Titanic Cat, 2005; In Dreams, 2006; Nowhere: A Novel by Shane Christopher, 2007; Doom 3 Worlds on Fire, 2008; Maelstrom: Based on the Video Game Doom 3 from Id Software, 2009; Rage, 2011; Vacation, 2012. **Address:** Berkley Books, 375 Hudson St., New York, NY 10014, U.S.A. **Online address:** matt@mattcostello.com

COSTELLO, Matthew John. American (born United States), b. 1963. **Genres:** Literary Criticism And History. **Career:** University of North Carolina, graduate instructor, 1987-91; Duke University, visiting instructor, 1989; Saint Xavier University, professor of history and political science. Writer. **Publications:** Secret Identity Crisis: Comic Books and the Unmasking of Cold War America, 2009. **Address:** U.S.A. **Online address:** costello@sxu.edu

COSTER, Graham. British (born England), b. 1960?. **Genres:** Novels, Travel/Exploration, History. **Career:** Granta, assistant editor, 1983-87; Independent, writer; Daily Telegraph. **Publications:** Train, Train: A Novel, 1989; A Thousand Miles from Nowhere: Trucking Two Continents, 1995; (ed. and intro.) The Wild Blue Yonder: The Picador Book of Aviation, 1997; Corsairville: The Lost Domain of the Flying Boat, 2000. Contributor to periodicals. **Address:** c/o Author Mail, Viking, 27 Wrights Ln., London, GL W8 5TZ, England.

COSTIGAN, Lee. *See* **SEARLS, Hank.**

COSTLEY, Bill. American (born United States), b. 1942. **Genres:** Plays/Screenplays, Poetry, Advertising/Public Relations, Communications/Media, Writing/Journalism, Documentaries/Reportage. **Career:** Harvard University, Medical School, medical technician, 1966; Massachusetts Institute of Technology, engineering periodicals librarian, 1967; National Aeronautics and Space Administration, librarian and book acquisitioner, 1967; Boston College, associate editor, 1968; Grahm Junior College, instructor in English, 1968; City Demonstration Agency Inc., newspaper editor and public information officer for Model Cities program, 1968-73; high school English teacher, 1996-97; Silicon Graphics, project manager, 1997; Stone & Webster Corp., technical editor and writer, 1974-93; Sanders Associates, technical editor and writer, 1974-93; General Telephone and Electronics, technical editor and writer, 1974-93; GRI Computer, technical editor and writer, 1974-93; Data General Corp., technical editor and writer, 1974-93; Softbridge Microsystems, technical editor and writer, 1974-93; Installed Technology Intl., technical editor and writer, 1974-93; Digital Equipment Corp., marketing communications writer, 1984-88; Wellesley Townsman, journalist, 1987; Middlesex News, columnist, 1989-93; Wellesley Cable Television, co-producer, 1987; Wellesley Symphony Orchestra, poet-in-residence, 1987-88, president, 1990-91, public relations director, 1992; Sawyer Public Relations, assistant account executive, 1993-95; Instruction Set, senior marketing communications writer, 1995-97; Allan Public Relations, account executive, 1997-99; Peter Arnold Associates, senior associate, 1999-2001; MassBay Community College, adjunct faculty, 2002-03; San Francisco Call, columnist, 2004-. **Publications:** POETRY: Knosh I Cir, 1975; Rag(a)s, 1978; A(y)s(h)a, 1988; Terrazzo, 1993; Siliconia, 1995. Contributor to periodicals. Works appear in anthologies. **Address:** Arts End Books, PO Box 441, West Dover, VT 05356-0441, U.S.A. **Online address:** billcostley@yahoo.com

COTE, Nancy. (Nancy Marek). American/Austrian (born Austria) **Genres:** Children's Fiction, Poetry, Illustrations, Picture/Board Books. **Career:** Rhode Island School of Design, Continuing Education Certificate Program, instructor. Author and illustrator. **Publications:** SELF-ILLUSTRATED: Palm Trees, 1993; Flip-Flops, 1998; It Feels Like Snow, 2003; It's All About Me, 2005; Jackson's Blanket, 2008. **Address:** 31 Avon St., Somerset, MA 02726, U.S.A. **Online address:** nancycote@comcast.net

CÔTÉ, Richard N. American (born United States), b. 1945. **Genres:** Novels, History, Local History/Rural Topics, Genealogy/Heraldry, Biography, Adult Non-fiction, Young Adult Fiction, Sciences, Sciences. **Career:** Freelance writer, 1971-; freelance photographer and historical researcher, 1971-79; South Carolina Historical Society, project director, field archivist and historical writer, 1979-80; County of Charleston, director of micrographics, 1982-85; Corinthian Books, editor-in-chief. **Publications:** (With C.A. Coté) Genealogists' Guide to Sheboygan County, Wisconsin, 1977; (comp.) Genealogists' Guide to Manitowoc County, Wisconsin, 1977; Genealogists' Guide to Charleston County, S.C., 1978; (comp.) Local and Family History in South Carolina: A Bibliography, 1981; (ed.) Historic Goose Creek, South Carolina, 1670-1980, 1983; (ed. with P.H. Williams) The Dictionary of South Carolina Biography, 1985; Ports, Power and Trade: A History of the South Carolina State Ports Authority, 1991; Love by Mail: The International Guide to Personal Advertising, 1992; Jewel of the Cotton Fields: A History of Secessionville Manor, A Nineteenth-Century Raised Plantation Cottage on James Island, Charleston County, South Carolina, 1995; Safe House: The Compelling Memoirs of the Only CIA Spy to Seek Asylum in Russia, 1995; Rice and Ruin: The William Bull Pringles and the Death of the South Carolina Rice Culture, 1800-1884, 1995; Death by HMO: The Jennifer Gigliello Tragedy, 1998; (ed.) Patriot Dreams: The Murder of Lieutenant Colonel Rich Higgins, USMC, 1999; Mary's World: Love, War and Family Ties in Nineteenth-Century Charleston, 2000; (with E.B. Martin, Jr.) Stopping the Train: The Landmark Victory over Same-Sex Sexual Harassment in the Workplace, 2000; Beach Magic, 2001; Redneck Riviera, 2001; Theodosia Burr Alston: Portrait of a Prodigy, 2002; Strength and Honor: The Life of Dolley Madison, 2005; City of Heroes: The Great Charleston Earthquake of 1886, 2006. **Address:** Corinthian Books, 483 Old Carolina Ct., Mt. Pleasant, SC 29464, U.S.A. **Online address:** dickcote@corinthianbooks.com

COTHAM, Edward T. American (born United States), b. 1953. **Genres:** Military/Defense/Arms Control. **Career:** Houston Civil War Roundtable, president; Friends of Sabine Pass Battleground, president; Terry Foundation, president. Writer. **Publications:** Battle on the Bay: The Civil War Struggle for Galveston, 1998; Sabine Pass: The Confederacy's Thermopylae, 2004; (ed.) The Southern Journey of a Civil War Marine: The Illustrated Note-Book of Henry O. Gusley, 2006. Contributor of article to newspapers. **Address:** Terry Foundation, 3104 Edloe, Ste. 205, Houston, TX 77027, U.S.A. **Online address:** cotham1025@aol.com

COTHRAN, James R(obert). American (born United States), b. 1940. **Genres:** Homes/Gardens, Horticulture, Photography. **Career:** South Carolina State Highway Department, landscape designer, 1965; Lyles, Bissette, Carlisle & Wolfe, site planner, 1966; Robert and Marvin Associates, landscape architect, 1967; U.S. Department of Housing and Urban Development, site planner and landscape architect, 1968-70; Robert and Co., landscape architect and planner, 1970-78, head of planning and landscape architecture department, 1978-, assistant vice president, 1978-81, vice president, 1981-; Emory University, instructor, 1989-; Georgia State University, instructor, 1990-, adjunct professor; University of Georgia, visiting lecturer, 2002-, adjunct professor. Writer. **Publications:** Gardens of Historic Charleston, 1995; Gardens and Historic Plants of the Antebellum South, 2003; Charleston Gardens and the Landscape Legacy of Loutrel Briggs, 2010. **Address:** Robert and Co., 229 Peachtree St. NE, International Twr., Ste. 2000, Atlanta, GA 30303, U.S.A. **Online address:** j.cothran@robertco.com

COTMAN, John Walton. American (born United States), b. 1954. **Genres:** Area Studies, International Relations/Current Affairs, Politics/Government, Third World, Biography. **Career:** Howard University, instructor, 1990-91, assistant professor of political science, 1991-96, associate professor, 1996-2011, professor, 2011; American University, School of International Service, visiting assistant research professor, 1994-95. Writer. **Publications:** Birmingham, JFK, and the Civil Rights Act of 1963: Implications for Elite Theory, 1989; The Gorrion Tree: Cuba and the Grenada Revolution, 1993; (ed. with E. Linger) Cuban Transitions at the Millennium, 2000. Contributor to books and journals. **Address:** Department of Political Science, Howard University, Douglass Hall, Rm. 142, 2400 6th St. NW, Washington, DC 20059, U.S.A. **Online address:** jcotman@howard.edu

COTRONEO, Roberto. (Mamurio Lancillotto). Italian (born Italy), b. 1961. **Genres:** Young Adult Fiction, Plays/Screenplays, Novels. **Career:** L'Espresso, culture editor, 1994-; L'Unità, columnist; Panorama, columnist. **Publications:** All'indice: sulla cultura degli anni Ottanta, 1991; Se una mattinad'estate un bambino, 1994; Presto con fuoco, 1995; La diffidenza comesistema: saggio sulla narrativa di Umberto Eco, 1995; Otranto, 1997; (ed.) Giorgio Bassani, Opere, 1998; L'età perfetta, 1999; Eco: due otre cose che so di lui, 2001; Per un attimo immenso ho dimenticato il mionome, 2002; Chiedimi chi erano I Beatles: lettera a mio figlio sull'amoreper la musica, 2003; Questo Amore, 2006; Vento Dell'odio: Romanzo, 2008; Adagio Infinito E Altri Racconti Sospesi, 2009; E nemmeno un rimpianto: il segreto di Chet Baker: romanzo, 2011. **Address:** c/o Author Mail, Arnoldo Mondadori Editore SpA, Via Mondadori, 1, Segrate, Milan, 20090, Italy.

COTT, Nancy F(alik). American (born United States), b. 1945. **Genres:** History, Women's Studies And Issues. **Career:** Wheaton College, part-time instructor of history, 1971; Clark University, part-time instructor of history, 1972; Wellesley College, part-time instructor of history, 1973-74; Boston Public Library, NEH Learning Library Program, lecturer, 1975; Yale University, assistant professor, 1975-79, associate professor, 1979-86, professor, 1986-90, Stanley Woodward professor of history and American studies, 1990-2000, Sterling professor of history and American studies, 2001, Women's Studies Program, chair, 1980-87, 1992-93, American Studies Program, chair, 1994-97; Harvard University, Jonathan Trumbull professor of American history, 2002-, Radcliffe Institute for Advanced Study, Arthur and Elizabeth Schlesinger Library on the History of Women in America, Carl and Lily Pforzheimer Family Foundation Director, 2002-, Charles Warren Center, director. Writer. **Publications:** (Ed. and intro.) Root of Bitterness: Documents of the Social History of American Women, 1972, (co-ed. and intro.) 2nd ed., 1996; The Bonds of Womanhood: Woman's Sphere in New England, 1780-1835, 1977, 2nd ed., 1997; (ed. and intro. with E.H. Pleck) A Heritage of Her Own: Toward a New Social History of American Women, 1979; (co-author) What is Feminism?, 1986; The Grounding of Modern Feminism, 1987; (ed. and intro.)

A Woman Making History: Mary Ritter Beard Through Her Letters, 1991; (ed. and intro.) History of Women in the United States: Historical Articles on Women's Lives and Activities, 1992; (ed.) Women in U.S. History, 20 vols., 1994; (ed.) The Young Oxford History of Women in the United States, 1994; Public Vows: A History of Marriage and the Nation, 2000; (ed.) No Small Courage: A History of Women in the United States, 2000. Contributor of articles to journals. **Address:** Department of History, Harvard University, Rm. 211, Robinson Hall, 35 Quincy St., Cambridge, MA 02138-3834, U.S.A. **Online address:** ncott@fas.harvard.edu

COTTEN, Cynthia. American (born United States) **Genres:** Novels, Natural History, Children's Fiction. **Career:** Writer. **Publications:** Snow Ponies, 2001; At the Edge of the Woods: A Counting Book, 2002; Abbie in Stitches, 2006; This Is the Stable, 2006; Some Babies Sleep, 2007; Fair Has Nothing to Do with It, 2007; Rain Play, 2008. **Address:** Farrar, Straus and Giroux, 175 5th Ave., New York, NY 10010, U.S.A. **Online address:** cynthia@cynthiacotten.com

COTTER, James Finn. American (born United States), b. 1929. **Genres:** Literary Criticism And History, Poetry, Theology/Religion. **Career:** Fordham University, English Department, instructor, 1960-63, assistant professor of English, 1963; Mount Saint Mary College, associate professor, 1963-67, professor of English, 1967-; University of Oran, Fulbright lecturer, 1970-71; The Hudson Review, writer; America Magazine, contributor. **Publications:** Inscape: The Christology and Poetry of Gerard Manley Hopkins, 1972; (trans.) Divine Comedy, 1988; Beginnings, 1988. **Address:** Mount Saint Mary College, Rm. 201, Whittaker Hall, 330 Powell Ave., Newburgh, NY 12550, U.S.A. **Online address:** cotter@msmc.edu

COTTERRELL, Roger (B. M.). British (born England), b. 1946. **Genres:** Law, Music. **Career:** Music critic, 1965-; University of Leicester, lecturer-in-law, 1969-74; University of London, Queen Mary and Westfield College, Department of Law, lecturer, 1974-78, senior lecturer, 1978-85, acting head, 1989-90, head, 1990-91, 2004-, reader in legal theory, 1985-90, professor of legal theory, 1990-2005, Faculty of Laws, dean, 1993-96, anniversary professor of legal theory, 2005-; University of Hong Kong, Department of Extra-Mural, visiting lecturer, 1986, 1987-, 1988; University of Texas, School of Law, visiting professor and Jay H. Brown centennial faculty fellow in law, 1989; Katholiek University, visiting professor, 1996, 1997; Facultes universitaires Saint-Louis, visiting professor, 1996, 1997; Antigua Universidad, International Institute for the Sociology of Law, visiting professor, 2003, 2004. Writer. **Publications:** The Sociology of Law: An Introduction, 1984, rev. ed., 1992; The Politics of Jurisprudence: A Critical Introduction to Legal Philosophy, 1989, 2nd ed., 2003; Law's Community: Legal Theory in Sociological Perspective, 1995; Emile Durkheim: Law in a Moral Domain, 1999; (with C. Goode) Bass Lines: A Life in Jazz, 2002; Law, Culture and Society: Legal Ideas in the Mirror of Social Theory, 2006; Living law: Studies in Legal and Social Theory, 2008. EDITOR: (with B. Bercusson) Law, Democracy and Social Justice, 1988; Law and Society, 1994; Sociological Perspectives on Law, 2 vols., 2001; Law in Social Theory 2006; Émile Durkheim: Justice, Morals and Politics, 2010. **Address:** Department of Law, Queen Mary, University of London, Mile End Rd., London, GL E1 4NS, England. **Online address:** r.b.m.cotterrell@qmul.ac.uk

COTTINGHAM, John (Graham). British (born England), b. 1943. **Genres:** Philosophy, Social Sciences. **Career:** University of Washington, lecturer in philosophy, 1967-68; Oxford University, Exeter College, lecturer in philosophy, 1968-71, St. John's College, honorary fellow; University of Reading, lecturer, 1971-87, reader, 1987-90, professor of philosophy, 1990-, department head, 1989-93, now professor emeritus of philosophy; University of London, Heythrop College, professorial research fellow. Consultant and writer. **Publications:** Descartes' Conversation with Burman, 1976; Rationalism: A Selective Critical Survey of Rationalist Thought from Plato to the Present Day, 1984; Descartes, 1986; The Rationalists, 1988; A Descartes Dictionary, 1993; Philosophy and the Good Life: Reason and the Passions in Greek Cartesian and Psychoanalytic Ethics, 1998; On the Meaning of Life, 2003; Spiritual Dimension: Religion, Philosophy, and Human Value, 2005; Cartesian Reflections: Essays on Descartes's Philosophy, 2008; (contrib.) Moral Life, 2008; Why Believe?, 2009. EDITOR: The Cambridge Companion to Descartes, 1992; Reason, Will and Sensation: Studies in Cartesian Metaphysics, 1994; Western Philosophy (anthology), 1996, 2nd ed., 2008; Descartes, 1998; Meaning of Theism, 2007; (with J. Suikkanen) Essays on Derek Parfit's On What Matters, 2009; (with P. Hacker) Mind, Method, and Morality, 2010; Partiality and Impartiality, 2010. TRANSLATOR: (with Stoothoff and Murdoch) Descartes: Selected Philosophical Writings, 1988. EDITOR and TRANSLATOR: (with R. Stoothoff and D. Murdoch) The Philosophical Writings of Descartes, 2 vols., 1985, 3rd vols., (with R. Stoothoff, D. Murdoch and A. Kenny), 1991; Meditations on First Philosophy and Selections from the Objections and Replies, 1986; (with R. Ariew and T. Sorell) Descartes' Meditations, Background Source Materials, 1998. **Address:** Department of Philosophy, University of Reading, PO Box 217, Reading, BR RG6 6AA, England. **Online address:** j.g.cottingham@reading.ac.uk

COTTLE, Thomas J. American (born United States), b. 1937. **Genres:** Education, Psychology, Sociology, Novels. **Career:** Harvard University, assistant professor of social relations, 1965-69; University of Illinois, Center for Advanced Study, fellow, 1969-70; Massachusetts Institute of Technology, research sociologist, 1970-73; ABC-TV, consultant, 1972-; Boston University, professor of education. Writer and research sociologist. **Publications:** Time's Children: Impressions of Youth, 1971; The Prospect of Youth: Contexts for Sociological Inquiry, 1972; (with C. Eisendrath and L. Fink) Lighting a Fire in the University, 1972; (with C.R. Eisendrath) Out of Discontent: Visions of the Contemporary University, 1972; The Abandoners: Portraits of Loss, Separation and Neglect, 1973; The Voices of School, 1973; (with S.L. Klineberg) The Present of Things Future: Explorations of Time in Human Experience, 1974; Black Children, White Dreams, 1974; A Family Album: Portraits of Intimacy and Kinship, 1974; Perceiving Time: A Psychological Investigation with Men and Women, 1976; Busing, 1976; Barred from School: Two Million Children!, 1976; Readings in Adolescent Psychology: Contemporary Perspectives, 1977; Children in Jail: Seven Lessons in American Justice, 1977; College: Reward and Betrayal, 1977; Private Lives and Public Accounts, 1978; (ed. with P. Whitten) Readings in Personality and Adjustment, 1978; Psychotherapy: Current Perspectives, 1980; Black Testimony: The Voices of Britain's West Indians, 1980; Children's Secrets, 1980; Hidden Survivors: Portraits of Poor Jews in America, 1980; (with C.S. Greenblat) Getting Married, 1980; Divorce and the Jewish Child, 1981; Like Fathers, Like Sons: Portraits of Intimacy and Strain, 1981; Hardest Times: The Trauma of Long Term Unemployment, 2001; At Peril: Stories of Injustice, 2001; Mind Field: Adolescent Consciousness in a Culture of Distraction, 2001; Intimate Appraisals: The Social Writings of Thomas J. Cottle, 2002; A Sense of Self: The Work of Affirmation, 2003; Beyond Self-Esteem: Narratives of Self Knowledge and Devotion to Others, 2003; When the Music Stopped: Discovering My Mother, 2004. Contributor of articles to periodicals. **Address:** Faculty of Education, Boston University, 2 Silber Way, Boston, MA 02215, U.S.A. **Online address:** tcottle@bu.edu

COTTON, Ronald. American (born United States), b. 1962?. **Genres:** Autobiography/Memoirs, Biography. **Career:** Writer and public speaker. **Publications:** (With J. Thompson-Cannino and E. Torneo) Picking Cotton: Our Memoir of Injustice and Redemption, 2009. Contributor to periodicals. **Address:** c/o Tina Dubois Wexler, International Creative Management, 825 8th Ave., New York, NY 10019, U.S.A.

COTTONWOOD, Joe. American (born United States), b. 1947. **Genres:** Children's Fiction, Novels, Poetry, Young Adult Fiction, Songs/Lyrics And Libretti, Literary Criticism And History. **Career:** Writer. **Publications:** FOR CHILDREN: The Adventures of Boone Barnaby, 1990; Danny Ain't, 1992; Quake!, 1995; Babcock, 1996. FOR ADULTS: Famous Potatoes, 1976; Frank City(Goodbye), 1981, Clear Heart, 2008. POETRY: Son of a Poet, 1986. **Address:** PO Box 249, La Honda, CA 94020, U.S.A. **Online address:** joecot@coastside.net

COTTRELL, Alan (Howard). British (born England), b. 1919. **Genres:** Environmental Sciences/Ecology, Physics, Sciences. **Career:** University of Birmingham, lecturer, 1942-49, professor of physical metallurgy, 1949-55; Atomic Research Establishment, Metallurgy Division, deputy head, 1955-58; University of Cambridge, Goldsmiths' professor of metallurgy, 1958-65, Christ's College, fellow, 1958-70, honorary fellow, 1970, Jesus College, master, 1973-86, vice-chancellor of university, 1977-79, honorary fellow, 1980, now retired; Ministry of Defense, deputy chief adviser, 1965-67, chief adviser, 1967; H.M. Government, deputy chief scientific adviser, 1968-71, chief scientific adviser, 1971-74. Writer. **Publications:** Theoretical Structural Metallurgy, 1948, 2nd ed., 1955; Dislocations and Plastic Flow in Crystals, 1953; The Mechanical Properties of Matter, 1964; Superconductivity, 1964; Theory of Crystal Dislocations, 1964; An Introduction to Metallurgy, 1967;

Portrait of Nature: The World as seen by Modern Science, 1975; Environmental Economics: An Introduction for Students of the Resource and Environmental Sciences, 1978; How Safe is Nuclear Energy?, 1981; Introduction to the Modern Theory of Metals, 1988; Concepts in the Electron Theory of Alloys, 1998. **Address:** The Institute of Materials, Minerals and Mining, 1 Carlton House Terr., London, GL SW1Y 5DB, England. **Online address:** ah.cottrell@virgin.net

COTTRELL, David. (R. David Cottrell). American (born United States), b. 1953. **Genres:** Natural History, Photography, Communications/Media, How-to Books. **Career:** CornerStone Leadership Institute, founder and chief executive officer. Writer. **Publications:** (with A. Adams) Birdies, Pars and Bogies: Leadership Lessons from the Links, 1997; (with B. Dodge) Becoming the Obvious Choice, 2001; Listen Up, Leader!, 2002; (with S. Garcia) Listen Up, Teacher! You Are Making a Difference, 2002; (with T. Jeary) 136 Effective Presentation Tips, 2002; Listen Up, Sales and Customer Service: The Game Has Changed, 2002; The Manager's Coaching Handbook: A Practical Guide to Improving Employee Performance, 2002; (with A. Adams and J. Baldwin) Monday Morning Leadership: 8 Mentoring Sessions You Can't Afford to Miss, 2002; (with A. Lucia and E.L. Harvey) The Leadership Secrets of Santa Claus, 2003; (with K. Carnes and M.C. Layton) Management Insights, 2003; (with D. Reed) Monday Morning Customer Service, 2004; (with C. Novak) Conquering Adversity, 2004; Leadership: Biblically Speaking, 2005; (with A. Adams) The Next Level: Leading beyond the Status Quo, 2005; 12 Choices That Lead to Your Success, 2005; (with T. Jeary and G. Lowe) Monday Morning Communications, 2005; (with K. Carnes and S. Smith) Escape from Management Land: A Journey Every Team Wants Their Leader to Take, 2006; Monday Morning Mentoring: Ten Lessons to Guide You up the Ladder, 2006; David Cottrell's Collection of Favorite Quotations, 2006; Monday Morning Choices: 12 Powerful Ways to Go from Everyday to Extraordinary, 2007; Leadership Energy: A High Velocity Formula to Energize Your Team, 2008; (with L. Colan) The Nature of Excellence, photography by Tom Fox, 2008; (with I.J. Geller and J. Baldwin) The Manager's Conflict Resolution Handbook: A Practical Guide for Creating Positive Change, 2008; Monday Morning Motivation: 5 Steps to Energize Your Team, Customers and Profits, 2009; (with L.J. Colan) Winners Always Quit: Seven Pretty Good Habits You Can Swap for Really Great Results, 2009. WITH MARK C. LAYTON: 175 Ways to Get More Done in Less Time, 2000; The Manager's Coaching Handbook (A Walk the Walk Handbook), 2002; Listen Up, Customer Service: A Guide to Develop Customer Loyalty, 2006. WITH ERIC L. HARVEY: Memos to: Managers, 2002; The Manager's Communication Handbook, 2003; Leadership Courage, 2005. **Address:** CornerStone Leadership Institute, PO Box 764087, Dallas, TX 75376, U.S.A. **Online address:** info@cornerstoneleadership.com

COTTRELL, R. David. *See* **COTTRELL, David.**

COTTRELL, Robert C. American (born United States), b. 1950. **Genres:** Biography, Civil Liberties/Human Rights, History, Intellectual History, Politics/Government, Theology/Religion, Popular Culture. **Career:** South Oklahoma City Community College, adjunct professor, 1980-84; University of Oklahoma, instructor, 1983-84; California State University, assistant professor, 1984-89, associate professor, 1989-94; professor of history and American studies, 1994-. Writer. **Publications:** Izzy: A Biography of I.F. Stone, 1992; The Social Gospel of E. Nicholas Comfort: Founder of the Oklahoma School of Religion, 1997; Roger Nash Baldwin and American Civil Liberties, 2000; The Best Pitcher in Baseball: The Life of Rube Foster, Negro League Giant, 2001; Blackball, the Black Sox, and the Babe: Baseball's Crucial 1920 Season, 2002; (with B.T. Brown) Uncertain Order: The World in the Twentieth Century, 2003; Vietnam, The 17th Parallel, 2004; (with B.T. Browne) Lives and Legacies: Biographies in Western Civilization, 2004; The Czech Republic: The Velvet Revolution, 2005; The Green Line: The Division of Palestine, 2005; South Africa: A State of Apartheid, 2005; Northern Ireland and England: The Troubles, 2005; London: From the Walled City to New Towns, 2006; Smoke jumpers of the Civilian Public Service in World War II: Conscientious Objectors as Firefighters for the National Forest Service, 2006; Modern American Lives: Individuals and Issues in American History since 1945, 2008; Lives and Times: Individuals and Issues in American History, 2009; Icons of American Popular Culture: from P.T. Barnum to Jennifer Lopez, 2010. Contributor to books and periodicals. **Address:** College of Humanities and Fine Arts History, California State University, 201 Trinity Hall, 400 W 1st St., Chico, CA 95929-0740, U.S.A. **Online address:** bcottrell@csuchico.edu

COTTRET, Bernard. French (born France), b. 1951. **Genres:** History. **Career:** Oxford University, Merton College, lecturer in French, 1972-73; University of Paris IV, assistant professor, 1981-89; University of Lille III, professor of British studies, 1989-92; University of Versailles-Saint-Quentin-en-Yvelines, professor, 1992-, Humanities Department, chairman, 1992-96; College of Charleston, visiting professor, 1994; Institute of France, senior fellow. Writer. **Publications:** Terre d'exil, 1985; La Glorieuse Revolution, 1988; Le Christ des Lumieres, 1990; The Huguenots in England, 1991; Cromwell, 1992; Bolingbroke, 1992; Calvin, 1995; Histoire d'Angleterre, 1996; (with M. Cottret) Histoire politique de l'Europe, 1996; Bolingbroke's Political Writings, 1997; 1598. L'edit de Nantes, 1997; Henri VIII: le pouvoir par la force, 1999; La Renaissance, 1492-1598: Civilisation et barbarie, 2000; Histoire de la Reforme protestante: Luther, Clavin, Wesley, XVIe-XVIIIe siecle, 2001; Le Revolution Americaine, 2003; Jean-Jacques Rousseau en son temps, 2005; (ed.) Jardin: Figures et métamorphoses, 2005; (ed.) Cosmopolitismes, patriotismes, Europe et Amériques, 1773-1802, 2005; (ed.) Saintes ou sorcieres: l'heroisme chrétien au féminin, 2006; Histoire de l'Angleterre: de Guillaume le conquerant a nos jours, 2007; Republique et le royaume: XVIe-XVIIIe siecles, l'heritage protestant, 2008; Royaute au feminin: Elisabeth Ire, 2009; Karl Marx: une vie entre romantisme et révolution, 2010. Contributor to periodicals. **Address:** Department of Humanities, Universite de Versailles-Saint-Quentin-en-Yvelines, Vauban 510, 47 Blvd. Vauban, Guyancourt, 78280, France. **Online address:** bernard.cottret@wanadoo.fr

COTTRINGER, Anne. British/Canadian (born Canada), b. 1952. **Genres:** Children's Fiction, Literary Criticism And History, Education, Reference. **Career:** Director for films and television, 1980-; freelance producer, director and cinematographer. Writer. **Publications:** Ella and the Naughty Lion, 1996; GordonGordon, 1998; Movie Magic: A Star Is Born, 1999; Danny and the Great White Bear, 1999; Buster's Bark, 2001; Buster's Bone, 2002; Bruna, 2003; Rosa & Galileo, 2003; Hot Dog, 2004; Mary Is Scary, 2005; Singing It, 2007; Eliot Jones, Midnight Superhero, 2008. Contributor to magazines. **Address:** c/o Caroline Walsh, David Higham Associates, 5-8 Lower John St., Golden Sq., London, GL W1F 9HA, England. **Online address:** anne@cantilupe.demon.co.uk

COTTROL, Robert J. American (born United States), b. 1949. **Genres:** Social Sciences. **Career:** Connecticut College, instructor, 1974-77; Emory University, assistant professor of American studies, 1977-79; Georgetown University, lecturer, 1979-84, assistant dean, visiting professor of law and legal history, 1995-96, Harold Paul Green Research professor of law and history, 1996-, professor of law, of history, and of sociology; Bar of Pennsylvania State, staff, 1984; Boston College Law School, assistant professor, 1984-87, associate professor of law, 1987-90; Bar of the District of Columbia, staff, 1985; University of Charlottesville, visiting assistant professor of law, 1988-89; Rutgers School of Law, associate professor, 1990-91; National Rifle Association Civil Rights Defense Fund trustee. Lawyer and writer. **Publications:** The Afro-Yankees: Providence's Black Community in the Antebellum Era, 1982; (ed. and intro.) Gun Control and the Constitution: Sources and Explorations on the Second Amendment, vol. I: The Courts and Congress, 1993, vol. II: Partisans and Scholars: The Modern Debate, 1993, vol. III: Special Topics, 1993; (comp.) From African to Yankee: Narratives of Slavery and Freedom in Antebellum New England, 1998; (with R.T. Diamond and L.B. Ware) Brown v. Board of Education: Caste, Culture and the Constitution, 2003. Contributor to periodicals and journals. **Address:** George Washington University Law School, 2000 H St. NW, Washington, DC 20052, U.S.A. **Online address:** bcottrol@law.gwu.edu

COUCH, Dick. American (born United States), b. 1943?. **Genres:** Young Adult Fiction, Adult Non-fiction, Novels, Young Adult Non-fiction. **Career:** Central Intelligence Agency, maritime operations officer, 1972-; Naval Reserve, senior reserve SEAL officer, captain, retired, 1997; United States Naval Academy, lecturer; Fox TV, analyst; MS/NBC TV, analyst; Air Force Academy, lecturer; Naval Special Warfare Center, lecturer; John F. Kennedy Special Warfare Center and School, lecturer; FBI Academy, lecturer; Naval Postgraduate School, lecturer; Joint Special Operations University, lecturer. Writer. **Publications:** NONFICTION: The Warrior Elite: The Forging of SEAL Class 228, 2001; To Be a U.S. Navy SEAL, 2003; The Finishing School: Earning the Navy SEAL Trident, 2004; Down Range: Navy SEALs in the War on Terrorism, 2005; Chosen Soldier: The Making of a Special Forces Warrior, 2007; The Sheriff of Ramadi, 2008; A Tactical Ethic: Moral Conduct in the Insurgent Battlespace, 2010. NOVELS: Seal Team One, 1991; Pressure Point, 1992; Silent Descent, 1993; Rising Wind, 1996. GARRETT WALKER SE-

RIES: The Mercenary Option, 2003; Covert Action, 2005. **Address:** United States Naval Academy, 121 Blake Rd., Annapolis, MD 21402, U.S.A. **Online address:** dick@dickcouch.com

COULMAS, Florian. Japanese/German (born Germany), b. 1949. **Genres:** Language/Linguistics, Social Sciences, Documentaries/Reportage, Economics. **Career:** University of Duesseldorf, assistant professor, 1980-88, professor of linguistics, 1988; Chuo University, professor of Germanic linguistics, 1988-; professor of sociology of language, faculty of policy studies, 1992-; Institute of Advanced Study, fellow, 1994-95; Duisburg University, professor of Japanese studies; Deutsches Institut Für Japanstudien, German Institute for Japanese Studies, director; Georgetown University, visiting professor; International Journal of the Sociology of Language, associate editor. **Publications:** Rezeptives Sprachverhalten: E. Theoret. Studie über Faktoren d. Sprachl. Verstehens prozesses, 1977; (ed.) Soziolinguistik: Zur Ethnographie d. Kommunikation, 1979; (ed.) Festschrift for Native Speaker, 1980; (ed.) Conversational Routine: Explorations in Standardized Communication Situation and Prepatterned Speech, 1981; Routine Im Gespräch: Zur Pragmatischen Fundierung Der Idiomatik, 1981; über Schrift, 1981; (ed.) Writing in Focus, 1983; (ed.) Linguistic Minorities and Literacy: Language Policy Issues in Developing Countries, 1984; Sprache und Staat: Studien zu Sprachplanung und Sprachpolitik, 1985; (ed.) Direct and Indirect Speech, 1986; The Writing Systems of the World, 1989; (ed.) Language Adaptation, 1989; Language and Economy, 1992; (ed.) A Language Policy for the European Community: Prospects and Quandaries, 1991; Wirtschaft Mit Der Sprache: Eine Sprachsoziologische Studie, 1992; Das Land der rituellen Harmonie, 1993; The Blackwell Encyclopedia of Writing Systems, 1996; (co-ed.) Bibliography on Writing and Written Language, 1996; Gewahlte Worte: Uber Sprache als Wille und Bekenntnis, 1996; (ed.) Handbook of Sociolinguistics, 1996, 2nd ed., 1998; (with J. Staplers) Neue Asien: EinKontinent Findet Zu Sich Selbst, 1998; Japan Ausser Kontrolle, 1998; Japanische Zeiten: Eine Ethnographie der Vergçinglichkeit, 2000; Deutschen schreien: Beobachtungen voneinem, der aus dem Land des Lächelns kam, 2002; Writing Systems: An Introduction to Their Linguistic Analysis, 2003; Die Kultur Japans, 2003; Hiroshima: Geschichte und Nachgeschichte, 2005; Sociolinguistics: The Study of Speakers' Choices, 2005; Language Regimes in Transformation: Future Prospects For German and Japanese in Science, Economy and Politics, 2007; (with M. Koch and C. Harmer) Trilingual Glossary of Demographic Terminology: English-Japanese-German, Japanese-English-German, German-Japanese-English, 2007; Population Decline and Ageing in Japan: The Social Consequences, 2007; (co-ed.) Demographic Challenge: A Handbook About Japan, 2008; (ed.) International Journal of the Sociology of Language 189: Authenticity and Linguistic Heritage in the Age of Globalization, 2008; Die Illusion Vom Glück: Japan Und Der Westen, 2009; (ed. with P. Backhaus and H. Shōji) Nihon No Gengo Keikan, 2009; (ed. with R. Lützeler) Imploding Populations in Japan and Germany: A Comparison, 2011. Contributor to periodicals. **Address:** German Institute For Japanese Studies, DIJ Tokyo, Jochi Kioizaka Bldg. 2F, 7-1 Kioicho, Chiyoda-ku, Tokyo, 102-0094, Japan. **Online address:** dijtokyo@dijtokyo.org

COULOMBE, Charles A. American (born United States), b. 1960. **Genres:** History, Poetry, Military/Defense/Arms Control. **Career:** West Coast Review of Books, reviewer, 1982-95; National Catholic Register, contributing editor, 1989-96; L.A. Lay Mission, reporter, 1995. Poet, historian and journalist. **Publications:** Everyman Today Call Rome, 1987; The White Cockade (poems), 1990; (ed.) The Muse in the Bottle: Great Writers on the Joys of Drinking, 2002; Vicars of Christ: A History of the Popes, 2003; (ed.) Classic Horror Stories: Sixteen Legendary Stories of the Supernatural, 2003; Haunted Castles of the World: Ghostly Legends and Phenomena from Keeps and Fortresses around the Globe, 2004; Rum: The Epic Story of the Drink That Conquered the World, 2004; Haunted Places in America: A Guide to Spooked and Spooky Public Places in the United States, 2004; The Pope's Legion: The Multinational Fighting Force That Defended the Vatican, 2008; Puritan's Empire: A Catholic Perspective on American History, 2008. Contributor to books and periodicals. **Address:** PO Box 660771, Arcadia, CA 91066-0771, U.S.A.

COULOUMBIS, Audrey. American (born United States), b. 1947?. **Genres:** Children's Fiction, Novels, inspirational/Motivational Literature. **Career:** Writer. **Publications:** NOVELS: Just Before Daybreak, 1987; Getting Near to Baby, 1999; Say Yes, 2002; The Misadventures of Maude March, or, Trouble Rides a Fast Horse, 2005; Summer's End, 2005; Maude March on the Run!, or, Trouble Is Her Middle Name, 2007; Love Me Tender, 2008; (with A. Couloumbis) War Games, 2009; Jake, 2010; Lexie, 2011; Not Exactly a Love Story, 2012. **Address:** Jill Grinberg Literary Management L.L.C., 16 Court St., Ste. 3306, Brooklyn, NY 11241, U.S.A. **Online address:** audreycouloumbis@yahoo.com

COULSON, Juanita. American (born United States), b. 1933. **Genres:** Romance/Historical, Science Fiction/Fantasy, Westerns/Adventure, Novels, Mystery/Crime/Suspense, Literary Criticism And History. **Career:** Yandro, art editor and publisher, 1953-; elementary school teacher, 1954-55; Heckman's Bookbindery, collator, 1955-57; SFWA Forum, publisher; freelance writer, 1963-. **Publications:** KRANTIN SERIES: The Web of Wizardry, 1978; The Death God's Citadel, 1980. CHILDREN OF THE STARS SERIES: Tomorrow's Heritage, 1981; Outward Bound, 1982; Legacy of Earth, 1989; The Past of Forever, 1989. NOVELS: Crisis on Cheiron, 1967; The Singing Stones, 1968; Door into Terror, 1972; The Secret of Seven Oaks, 1972; Stone of Blood, 1975; Unto the Last Generation, 1975; Space Trap, 1976; Fear Stalks the Bayou, 1976; Dark Priestess, 1977; Fire of the Andes, 1979; Star Sister, 1990; Shadow over Scorpio, 2004. OTHERS: Intersection Point, 1976; Cold, Hard Silver, 1994; A Matter of Faith, 1995; Avenger, 2004. Works appear in anthologies. Contributor to books and periodicals. **Address:** 227 Toland St., London, OH 43140-1558, U.S.A.

COULTER, Catherine. American (born United States) **Genres:** Romance/Historical, Mystery/Crime/Suspense. **Career:** Writer. **Publications:** ROMANCE NOVELS: The Autumn Countess, 1978; The Rebel Bride, 1979; Lord Harry's Folly, 1980; Lord Deverill's Heir, 1980 as The Heir, 1996; An Honorable Offer, 1981 as The Offer, 1997; The Generous Earl, 1981 as The Duke, 1995; Devil's Embrace, 1982; An Intimate Deception, 1983 as The Deception, 1998; Chandra, 1984; Sweet Surrender, 1984; Devil's Daughter, 1985; Fire Song, 1985; Aftershocks, 1985; The Aristocrat, 1986; Midnight Star, 1986; Wild Star, 1986; Jade Star, 1987; Afterglow, 1987; Midsummer Magic, 1987; Moonspun Magic, 1988; Calypso Magic, 1988; False Pretenses, 1988; Night Shadow, 1989; Night Fire, 1989; Night Storm, 1990; Impulse, 1990; Earth Song, 1990; Secret Song, 1991; Season of the Sun, 1991; Beyond Eden, 1992; Sherbrooke Bride, 1992; Hellion Bride, 1992; The Heiress Bride, 1993; Lord of Hawkfell Island, 1993; Lord of Raven's Peak, 1994; The Wyndham Legacy, 1994; The Nightingale Legacy, 1994; Lord of Falcon Ridge, 1995; The Valentine Legacy, 1995; Rosehaven, 1996; The Wild Baron, 1997; Mad Jack, 1999; The Courtship, 2000; The Scottish Bride, 2001; Pendragon, 2002; The Sherbrooke Twins, 2004; Lyon's Gate, 2005; Born to be Wild, 2006; Wizard's Daughter, 2008; The Valcourt Heiress, 2010. SUSPENSE NOVELS: The Cove, 1996; The Maze, 1997; The Target, 1998; The Edge, 1999; Eleventh Hour, 2002; Blindside, 2003; Blowout, 2004; Point Blank, 2005; Double Take, 2007; Tail Spin, 2008; KnockOut, 2009; Whiplash, 2010. **Address:** PO Box 17, Mill Valley, CA 94942, U.S.A. **Online address:** readmoi@gmail.com

COUNIHAN, Carole. American (born United States), b. 1948. **Genres:** Food And Wine, Human Relations/Parenting. **Career:** Franklin & Marshall College, visiting assistant professor of anthropology, 1981-83; Boston University, assistant professor of social science, 1983-84; Stockton State College (now College of New Jersey), assistant professor of anthropology, 1984-87; Millersville University, Department of Anthropology, assistant professor, 1987-92, associate professor, 1992-99, professor, 1999-, acting department chair, 2007-08, director of women's studies, 1989-96, 1999-2002; University of Gastronomic Sciences, visiting professor, 2005-. Writer and speaker. **Publications:** (Ed. with P.V. Esterik) Food and Culture: A Reader, 1997, 2nd ed., 2008; The Anthropology of Food and Body: Gender, Meaning, and Power, 1999; (ed.) Food in the USA: A Reader, 2002; Around the Tuscan Table: Food, Family, and Gender in Twentieth Century Florence, 2004; Tortilla is Like Life: Food and Culture in the San Luis Valley of Colorado, 2009; Taking Food Public: Redefining Foodways in a Changing World, 2011. Contributor to books and periodicals. **Address:** Department of Sociology/Anthropology, Millersville University, 200 Susquehanna House, PO Box 1002, Millersville, PA 17551-0302, U.S.A. **Online address:** carole.counihan@millersville.edu

COUNSEL, June. British/South African (born South Africa), b. 1926. **Genres:** Children's Fiction, Young Adult Fiction, Novellas/Short Stories, Illustrations. **Career:** Teacher and writer, 1962-; Peterborough Arts Council, Celebration of Writing, lecturer, 1988; London University, Senate House, clerk. **Publications:** Mostly Timothy, 1971; A Dragon in Class 4, 1984; But Martin!, 1984; The Quest for the Golden Dragon, 1987; A Dragon in Spring Term, 1988; A Dragon in Summer, 1988; Now You See It, Now You Don't, 1991; Dragon in Top Class, 1994; The Secrets Tree, 1995; Steggie's Way,

1998; Once upon Our Time, 2000. **Address:** c/o Helen Connealy, Transworld Publishers Ltd., 61-63 Uxbridge Rd., London, GL W5 5SA, England.

COUPER, Stephen. *See* **GALLAGHER, Stephen.**

COUPLAND, Douglas. Canadian/German (born Germany), b. 1961. **Genres:** Novels, Essays, Young Adult Fiction, Adult Non-fiction. **Career:** Writer. **Publications:** NOVELS: Generation X: Tales for an Accelerated Culture, 1991; Shampoo Planet, 1992; Microserfs, 1995; Girlfriend in a Coma, 1998; Miss Wyoming, 1999; God Hates Japan, 2001; All Families Are Psychotic: A Novel, 2001; Hey Nostradamus!, 2003; Eleanor Rigby: A Novel, 2004; JPod, 2006; The Gum Thief, 2007; Marshall McLuhan, 2010. OTHER: (intro.) Slacker, 1992; Life after God Sound Recording, 1994; Polaroids from the Dead (essays and short fiction), 1996; (with K. Ward) Lara Book: Lara Croft and the Tomb Raider Phenomenon, 1998; (co-author) Disco 2000, 1998; City of Glass: Douglas Coupland Vancouver, 2000; Souvenir of Canada, 2002; School Spirit, 2002; Souvenir of Canada 2, 2004; Terry-The Life of Canadian Tery Fox, 2005; (foreword) Dictator Style: Lifestyles of the World's Most Colorful Despots, 2005; (intro.) The Vancouver Stories: West Coast Fiction from Canada Best Writers, 2005; Generation A, 2009; 2010 Massey Lectures, U.S. ed, 2010; Player One, 2010; (with G. Roumieu) Highly Inappropriate Tales for Young People, 2011. Contributor to periodicals. **Address:** c/o Author Mail, HarperCollins Publishers, 10 E 53rd St., 7th Fl., New York, NY 10022, U.S.A.

COURNOS, Francine. American (born United States), b. 1945. **Genres:** Medicine/Health, Psychiatry, Psychology, Social Sciences. **Career:** Montefiore Hospital, intern, 1971-72, resident, 1972-73; New York State Psychiatric Institute, psychiatric resident, 1973-76, interim director, 2003-04, deputy director, 2005-06, Washington Heights Community Service, director, 1978-; New York State Office of Mental Health, New York City Regional Office, chief medical officer and psychiatric consultant, 1982-89; Columbia University, College of Physicians and Surgeons, Department of Psychiatry, professor of clinical psychiatry, 1995-2010, New York/New Jersey AIDS Education and Training Center, principal investigator, 2006-, director, International Center for AIDS Care and Treatment Programs, faculty, Center for Psychoanalytic Training and Research, research faculty, Joseph L. Mailman School of Public Health, professor of clinical psychiatry and epidemiology, 2010-; New York Presbyterian Hospital, psychiatrist. Writer and psychiatrist. **Publications:** Frequently Asked Questions about HIV/AIDS and People with Mental Illness, 1998; City of One: A Memoir, 1999. EDITOR: (with N. Bakalar) AIDS and People with Severe Mental Illness: A Handbook for Mental Health Professionals, 1996; (with M. Forstein) What Mental Health Practitioners Need to Know about HIV and AIDS, 2000. Contributor to books and journals. **Address:** Joseph L. Mailman School of Public Health, Columbia University, Rm. 1030C, 722 W 168th St., 10th Fl., New York, NY 10032, U.S.A. **Online address:** fc15@columbia.edu

COURT, Wesli. *See* **TURCO, Lewis (Putnam).**

COURTENAY, Bryce. Australian/South African (born South Africa), b. 1933. **Genres:** Novels, Biography, Documentaries/Reportage, Essays. **Career:** McCann-Erickson (advertising agency), advertising writer, 1956-66, creative director and southeast Asia chair, 1960-66; J. Walter Thompson Advertising Agency, creative director and southeast Asia chair, 1966-71; Courtenay Beirnstein, partner, 1971-76; Harrison, Robinson and Courtenay Ltd. (advertising agency), founder, 1976-87. Writer. **Publications:** The Eleven Powers (documentary), 1986; The Power of One (novel), 1989; Tandia (novel), 1990; The Pitch (essays), 1992; April Fools' Day: A Modern Tragedy (biography), 1993; (co-author) Stranger Inside: An Erotic Adventure, 1994; Potato Factory, 1995; Family Frying Pan, 1997; Jessica, 1998; Night Country, 1998; Tommo and Hawk, 1998; A Recipe for Dreaming, 1998; Solomon's Song, 1999; Four Fires, 2001; Smoky Joe's Cafe, 2001; Matthew Flinders's Cat, 2002; (intro.) Anzac's Story, 2003; Brother Fish, 2004; White Thorn, 2005; Solomon's Song, 2006; Sylvia, 2006; The Persimmon Tree, 2008; Fishing for Stars, 2009; Story of Danny Dunn, 2010; Fortune Cookie, 2011. **Address:** 2/29 Benelong Cres., Bellevue Hill, NW 2023, Australia.

COURTER, Gay (Eleanor). American (born United States), b. 1944. **Genres:** Novels, Novellas/Short Stories, Adult Non-fiction, Civil Liberties/Human Rights, Young Adult Fiction. **Career:** Courter Films and Associates, secretary and treasurer, 1972-, producer/writer; Courter Media Corp., president, 1978-. **Publications:** The Beansprout Book (nonfiction), 1973; (with P. Courter) The Filmmaker's Craft (textbook), 1976; The Midwife (novel), 1981; River of Dreams (novel), 1984; Code Ezra (novel), 1986; Flowers in the Blood (novel), 1990; The Midwife's Advice (novel), 1992; I Speak for this Child: True Stories of a Child Advocate (non-fiction), 1995; (with P. Gaudette) How to Survive Your Husband's Midlife Crisis: Strategies and Stories from the Midlife Wives Club, 2003. Contributor to periodicals. **Address:** Courter Film & Associates, 121 NW Crystal St., Crystal River, FL 34428, U.S.A. **Online address:** gay@gaycourter.com

COURTNEY, Caroline. *See* **JORDAN, Penny.**

COURTNEY, Dayle. *See* **POSNER, Richard.**

COURTNEY, D. G. *See* **GURR, David.**

COURTRIGHT, Nicola. American (born United States), b. 1954. **Genres:** Theology/Religion, History. **Career:** Amherst College, associate professor, 1998-2004, professor of art and the history of art, 2004-, associate dean of the faculty, 2008-; Women's and Gender Studies, affiliate faculty; European Studies, affiliate faculty. Writer. **Publications:** The Papacy and the Art of Reform in Sixteenth-Century Rome: Gregory XIII's Tower of the Winds in the Vatican, 2003. **Address:** Amherst College, 206 Fayerweather Hall, AC Ste. 2249, Amherst, MA 01002-5000, U.S.A. **Online address:** nmcourtright@amherst.edu

COUSINEAU, Phil. American (born United States), b. 1952. **Genres:** Plays/Screenplays, History, Adult Non-fiction. **Career:** Shakespeare and Co., Bookstore, writer-in-residence, 1987; Holy Names University, visiting faculty. Film director and film producer. **Publications:** EDITOR: (intro.) The Hero's Journey: The World of Joseph Campbell: Joseph Campbell on His Life and Work, 1990; (with J. Densmore) Riders on the Storm: My Life with Jim Morrison, 1991; (intro.) The Soul of the World: A Modern Book of Hours, 1993; Design Outlaws: On the Ecological Frontier, 1994; Prayers at 3 A.M.: Poems, Songs, Chants, and Prayers for the Middle of the Night, 1995; (intro.) The Soul Aflame: A Modern Book of Hours, 2000; (intro.) The Way Things are: Conversations with Huston Smith on the Spiritual Life, 2003; (and preface) A Seat at the Table: Huston Smith in Conversation with Native Americans on Religious Freedom, 2006; Beyond Forgiveness: Reflections on Atonement, 2011. OTHER: Deadlines: A Rhapsody on a Theme of Famous Last Words, 1991; (comp.) Soul: An Archaeology: Readings from Socrates to Ray Charles, 1994; Burning the Midnight Oil, 1995; UFOs: A Manual for the Millenium, 1995; UFO Secrets Revealed, 1995; Soul Moments: Marvelous Stories of Synchronicity: Meaningful Coincidences from a Seemingly Random World, 1997, rev. ed. as Coincidence or Destiny, 2002; The Art of Pilgrimage: The Seeker's Guide to Making Travel Sacred, 1998; Riddle Me This: A World Treasury of Word Puzzles, Folk Wisdom, and Literary Conundrums, 1999; The Book of Roads, 2000; Once and Future Myths: The Power of Ancient Stories in Modern Times, 2001; The Olympic Odyssey: Rekindling the True Spirit of the Great Games, 2003; The Blue Museum, 2004; Stoking the Creative Fires: 9 Ways to Rekindle Passion and Imagination, 2008; The Oldest Story in the World: A Mosaic of Meditation on the Secret Strength of Stories, 2010; Wordcatcher: An Odyssey into the World of Weird and Wonderful Words, 2010. Contributor to periodicals and magazines. **Address:** HarperCollins Publications, 353 Sacramento St., San Francisco, CA 94111, U.S.A. **Online address:** cous@philcousineau.net

COUSSINS, Craig. Scottish/British (born England) **Genres:** Environmental Sciences/Ecology, Homes/Gardens, Dance/Ballet, How-to Books, Horticulture. **Career:** Writer, educator and artist. **Publications:** Stage Makeup 1975; Fitting Ballet, Pointe and Dance shoes 1987; Bonsai for Beginners, 2000; Totally Bonsai: The Practical Guide to Growing Bonsai: A Guide to Growing, Shaping and Caring for Miniature Trees and Shrubs, 2001; Bonsai School, 2003; Bonsai Master Class, 2008; Fitting Dance Shoes-Irish and Highland, 2011. **Address:** Hullachan Pro Ltd., 6 Milrig Rd., Glasgow, G73 2NH, Scotland. **Online address:** craig.coussins@btinternet.com

COUTO, Nancy Vieira. American (born United States), b. 1942. **Genres:** Poetry. **Career:** Teacher, 1964-65; National Academy of Sciences, staff assistant, 1967-68; General-American Life Insurance Co., claims representative, 1968-72; Sperry Univac, secretary, 1972-73; WTEV-6, executive secretary, 1975-78; Cornell University, lecturer in English, 1980-82; Cornell University Press, secondary rights assistant, 1981-82, subsidiary rights manager, 1982-94; The Laurel Review, associate editor, 1992-2000; Leatherstocking Literary Services, owner, 1994-2004; Epoch Magazine, poetry editor, 2000-. **Publica-**

tions: The Face in the Water, 1990; Carlisle & The Common Accident, 2011. Contributor to journals and periodicals. **Address:** 508 Turner Pl., Ithaca, NY 14850-5630, U.S.A. **Online address:** nvcouto@twcny.rr.com

COUVILLON, Jacques. American (born United States) **Genres:** Novels. **Career:** Writer. **Publications:** The Chicken Dance (novel), 2007. **Address:** Vermilion Parish, LA , U.S.A. **Online address:** cowgarcon@gmail.com

COVELL, Stephen G. American (born United States), b. 1965. **Genres:** Adult Non-fiction, Theology/Religion. **Career:** Western Michigan University, Department of Comparative Religion, Mary Meader professor of comparative religion; Taisho University, research associate; International Christian University, research associate. Writer and translator. **Publications:** Japanese Temple Buddhism: Worldliness in a Religion of Renunciation, 2005. **Address:** Michitoshi Soga Japan Center, Western Michigan University, 1903 W Michigan Ave., Kalamazoo, MI 49008-5245, U.S.A. **Online address:** s.covell@wmich.edu

COVENEY, Peter (Vivian). British (born England), b. 1958. **Genres:** Sciences. **Career:** Oxford University, junior research fellow, 1984-87; University of Wales, lecturer, 1987-90; Schlumberger Cambridge Research Laboratory, program leader, 1990-, senior scientist, through 1999; University College London, Department of Chemistry, professor, 1999-, chair, Center for Computational Science, director, honorary professor in computer science; American University of Beirut, Center for Advanced Mathematical Science, associate; Queen Mary and Westfield College, Interdisciplinary Research Centre on Biomedical Materials, associate; Institute of Physics, fellow; University of Oxford, Department of Theoretical Physics, visiting fellow; Yale University, Medical School, adjunct professor; Journal of Computational Science, founding editor. **Publications:** (With R. Highfield) The Arrow of Time: A Voyage through Science to Solve Time's Greatest Mystery, 1990; (with R. Highfield) Frontiers of Complexity: The Search for Order in a Chaotic World, 1995. **Address:** Department of Chemistry, University College London, 20 Gordon St., London, GL WC1H 0AJ, England. **Online address:** p.v.coveney@ucl.ac.uk

COVEY, Herbert C. American (born United States), b. 1949. **Genres:** Young Adult Non-fiction, Social Sciences. **Career:** Colorado State Juvenile Parole Board, vice chair, 1994-; Colorado Department of Human Services, field administrator, 1999-. Writer. **Publications:** NONFICTION: (with B. Mercer) Theoretical Frameworks in the Sociology of Education, 1980; Images of Older People in Western Art and Society, 1991; (with S. Menard and R.J. Franzese) Juvenile Gangs, 1997; Social Perceptions of People with Disabilities in History, 1998; Street Gangs throughout the World, 2003; (contrib. with S. Menard) Youth Gangs, 2006; (ed.) The Methamphetamine Crisis: Strategies to Save Addicts, Families, and Communities, 2007; African American Slave Medicine: Herbal and Non-herbal Treatments, 2007; (with N.T. Taylor) Helping People Addicted to Methamphetamine: A Creative New Approach for Families and Communities, 2008; (with D. Eisnach) What the Slaves Ate: Recollections of African American Foods and Foodways from the Slave Narratives, 2009. **Address:** U.S.A. **Online address:** herb.covey@dss.co.adams.co.us

COVIN, David L. American (born United States), b. 1940. **Genres:** Novels, Area Studies, Politics/Government. **Career:** California State University, assistant professor of government and ethnic studies, 1970-74, associate dean of general studies, 1972-74, associate professor of government and ethnic studies, 1975-79, professor of government and ethnic studies, 1979-, now professor emeritus, director of Pan African studies; Union Graduate School, adjunct professor, 1979, professor; National Conference of Black Political Scientists, president. Writer. **Publications:** Brown Sky, 1987; The Unified Black Movement in Brazil, 2006; Black Politics After the Civil Rights Movement: Activity and Beliefs in Sacramento, 1970-2000, 2009; Wimbey's Corner, 2011. Contributor of articles to periodicals. **Address:** The Black Group, 3555 3rd Ave., Sacramento, CA 95817, U.S.A. **Online address:** covindl@csus.edu

COVINGTON, Dennis. American (born United States), b. 1948. **Genres:** Novels. **Career:** El Salvador, freelance journalist, 1983-; New York Times, journalist; University of Alabama, professor and director of creative writing program, through 2004; Texas Tech University, Department of English, professor of creative writing, 2003-. **Publications:** Lizard, 1991; Lasso the Moon, 1995; Salvation on Sand Mountain: Snake Handling and Redemption in Southern Appalachia, 1995; (with V. Covington) Cleaving: The Story of a Marriage, 1999; Redneck Riviera: Armadillos, Outlaws, and the Demise of an American Dream, 2004. **Address:** Department of English, Texas Tech University, Rm. 431, PO Box 43091, Lubbock, TX 79409-3091, U.S.A. **Online address:** dennis.covington@ttu.edu

COVINGTON, James W. (James Warren Covington). American (born United States), b. 1917. **Genres:** History, Education. **Career:** University of Tampa, associate professor, 1950-53, professor, 1954-89, Evening Division, dean, 1961-64, Dana professor of history, emeritus Dana professor of history, 1989-; Apollo History, National Aeronautics and Space Administration, Kennedy Space Center, historian, 1968-70. Writer. **Publications:** (With C.H. Laub) Story of the University of Tampa, 1955; Story of Southwestern Florida, 1957; The British Meet the Seminoles, 1961; (ed.) Pirates, Indians and Spaniards, 1963; Under the Minarets: The University of Tampa Celebrates Fifty Years of Progress, 1931-1981, 1981; The Billy Bowlegs War, 1855-1858: The Final Stand of the Seminoles Against the Whites, 1982; Plant's Palace: Henry B. Plant and the Tampa Bay Hotel, 1990; Seminoles of Florida, 1993. **Address:** Department of History, University of Tampa, 401 W Kennedy Blvd., Tampa, FL 33606-1490, U.S.A.

COVINGTON, James Warren. *See* **COVINGTON, James W.**

COVINGTON, Linda. *See* **WINDSOR, Linda.**

COVINGTON, Vicki. American (born United States), b. 1952. **Genres:** Novellas/Short Stories, Essays, Women's Studies And Issues, Art/Art History, Young Adult Fiction. **Career:** University of Alabama, social worker in substance abuse programs, 1978-88; writer, 1988-. **Publications:** Gathering Home, 1988; Bird of Paradise, 1990; Night Ride Home, 1992; The Last Hotel for Women, 1996; (with D. Covington) Cleaving: The Story of a Marriage, 1999; Women in a Man's World, Crying: Essays, 2002. **Address:** c/o Amanda Urban, International Creative Management, 730 5th Ave., New York, NY 10019, U.S.A.

COWAN, Brian William. American/Canadian (born Canada), b. 1969?. **Genres:** Social Sciences, Sociology, History, Economics, Business/Trade/Industry. **Career:** University of Sussex, lecturer in history, 2000-01; Yale University, assistant professor of history, 2001-04; McGill University, Department of History, assistant professor, 2004-06, associate professor, 2006-, communications officer, 2005-06, Canada research chair in early modern British history, 2005-10. Writer and historian. **Publications:** The Social Life of Coffee: The Emergence of the British Coffeehouse, 2005. **Address:** Department of History, McGill University, Rm. 636, Leacock Bldg., 855 Sherbrooke W, Montreal, QC H3A 2T5, Canada. **Online address:** brian.cowan2@mcgill.ca

COWAN, Edward (James). Scottish/British (born England), b. 1944. **Genres:** History, Biography. **Career:** University of Edinburgh, lecturer in Scottish history, 1967-79; University of Guelph, associate professor, 1979-83, professor of history, 1983-93; University of Glasgow, Department of Scottish History, chair, 1993-, professor of Scottish history, through 2009, professor emeritus, 2009-, Crichton Campus, director, through 2009, Dumfries Campus, director, School of Interdisciplinary Studies, honorary research fellow. Writer. **Publications:** (Ed. and intro. with H. Pálsson) On the Character of the Old Northern Poetry: Icelandic Studies in Eighteenth and Nineteenth Century Scotland, 1972; Montrose: For Covenant and King, 1977; The Historical Highlands: A Guide to Reading, 1977; (ed.) The People's Past: Scottish Folk in Scottish History, 1980; (ed. with D. Gifford) The Polar Twins, 1999; (ed. with R.A. McDonald) Alba: Celtic Scotland in the Middle Ages, 2000; (ed.) The Ballad in Scottish History, 2000; (with R. Finlay and W. Paul) Scotland Since 1688: Struggle for a Nation, 2000; (with L. Henderson) Scottish Fairy Belief: A History, 2001; (ed. with R.J. Finlay) Scottish History: The Power of the Past, 2002; For Freedom Alone: The Declaration of Arbroath, 1320, 2003; (ed.) The Wallace Book, 2007; (ed. with M. Paterson) Folk in Print: Scotland's Chapbook Heritage, 2007; (ed. with A. Murdoch and R.J. Finlay) Scottish Nation, 2007. **Address:** School of Interdisciplinary Studies, University of Glasgow, Rutherford/McCowan Bldg., Dumfries, DG1 4ZL, Scotland. **Online address:** edward.cowan@glasgow.ac.uk

COWAN, Elizabeth. *See* **NEELD, Elizabeth Harper.**

COWAN, Gordon. British (born England), b. 1933. **Genres:** Education, Sports/Fitness, How-to Books. **Career:** Liverpool Secondary Schools, teacher, 1955-64; Edge Hill S.M. School, History and Geography Department, head, 1964-65; C.F. Mott College of Education, lecturer in education, 1965-

68, Education Department, head, 1968-72; Manchester College of Education, deputy acting principal, 1972-77, assistant principal, 1977-83; Manchester Metropolitan University, head of student services, 1983-95. Writer. **Publications:** Project Work in the Secondary School, 1967; A Centennial History of Sale Moor Cricket Club, 1987; Cricket Coaching Series, 1986; Step by Step Soccer Skills, 1994; Step by Step Cricket Skills, 1994. **Address:** 39 Barwell Rd., Sale, CH M33 5EE, England.

COWAN, Shannon. Canadian (born Canada), b. 1973. **Genres:** Young Adult Non-fiction, Young Adult Fiction, Novels. **Career:** Express Communications, creative director. Writer. **Publications:** NONFICTION: (with C. Wilson and B. Austin) Caring for Our Shores: A Handbook for Coastal Landowners in the Strait of Georgia, 1998; (with L. Cowan) Hiking Vancouver Island: A Guide to Vancouver Island's Greatest Hiking Adventures, 2003; (ed. with F.T. Lam and C. Stonehouse) Double Lives: Writing and Motherhood, 2008. FICTION: Leaving Winter, 2000; Tin Angel (young adult novel), 2007. Works appear in anthologies. Contributor to periodicals. **Address:** Express Communications, PO Box 445, Errington, BC V0R 1V0, Canada. **Online address:** shannon@youngpoets.ca

COWART, Jack. American (born United States), b. 1945. **Genres:** Art/Art History, Crafts, History. **Career:** National Gallery of Art, 20th Century Art Department, head and curator, 1983-92; Wadsworth Atheneum, assistant curator of paintings, 1972-74; St. Louis Museum, 19th and 20th century art curator, 1974-83; Corcoran Gallery of Art, deputy director and chief curator, 1992-99; Roy Lichtenstein Foundation, founding executive director, 1999-. Writer. **Publications:** (Co-author) Henri Matisse: Paper Cut-Outs, 1977; De Kooning, 1969-78, 1978; Roy Lichtenstein, 1970-1980, 1981; (ed.) Expressions: New Art from Germany: Georg Baselitz, Jörg Immendorff, Anselm Kiefer, Markus Lüpertz, A.R. Penck, 1983; (with D. Fourcade) Henri Matisse: The Early Years in Nice, 1916-1930, 1986; (with J. Hamilton) Georgia O'Keeffe, Art and Letters, 1987; (co-author) Matisse in Morocco: The Paintings and Drawings, 1912-1913, 1990; (with Y. Bois and A. Pacquement) Ellsworth Kelly: The Years in France, 1948-1954, 1992; (contrib.) Proof Positive: Forty Years of Contemporary American Printmaking at ULAE, 1957-1997, 1997; (co-author) Manuel Neri: Early Work 1953-1978, 1996; (with D. Chihuly and D. Kuspit) Chihuly, 1997; (ed.) Lichtenstein in Process, 2009. **Address:** Roy Lichtenstein Foundation, 745 Washington St., New York, NY 10014-2042, U.S.A.

COWASJEE, Saros. Canadian (born Canada), b. 1931. **Genres:** Novels, Novellas/Short Stories, Plays/Screenplays, Literary Criticism And History. **Career:** Times of India Press, assistant editor, 1961-63; University of Regina, professor of English, 1963-95, professor emeritus, 1995-; Wascana Review, managing editor, 1966-70; University of California, research associate, 1970-71; University of Aarhus, visiting commonwealth professor, 1974-75; Arnold Publishers, general editor, 1984-2000. **Publications:** Sean O'Casey: The Man behind the Plays, 1964; O'Casey, 1966; Stories and Sketches, 1970; Goodbye to Elsa (novel), 1974; Mulk Raj Anand: Coolie: An Assessment, 1976; So Many Freedoms: A Study of the Major Fiction of Mulk Raj Anand, 1977; Nude Therapy (short stories), 1978; Suffer Little Children (novel), 1982; Studies in Indian and Anglo-Indian Fiction(criticism), 1993; The Assistant Professor: A Novel, 1996. EDITOR: (and intro.) Author to Critic: The Letters of Mulk Raj Anand, 1973; (with V. Shahane) Modern Indian Fiction, 1981; Stories from the Raj, 1982; (with S.K. Kumar) Modern Indian Short Stories, 1982; The Raj and After (fiction anthology), 1986; More Stories from the Raj and After (anthology), 1986; (with K.S. Duggal) When the British Left: Stories on the Partitioning of India, 1947, 1987; Women Writers of the Raj: Short Fiction (anthology), 1990; (with K.S. Duggal) Orphans of the Storm: Stories on the Partition of India, 1995; The Best Short Stories of Flora Annie Steel, 1995; The Oxford Anthology of Raj Stories, 1998; (and intro.) The Mulk Raj Anand Omnibus, 2004; A Raj Collection, 2005; (and intro.) Mulk Raj Anand: Selected Short Stories, 2006; The Lasting Legacies of Mulk Raj Anand, 2008; (and intro.) Conversations in Bloomsbury, 2011. **Address:** Department of English, Regina University, Rm. 315, AH Bldg., 3737 Wascana Pkwy., Regina, SK S4S 0A2, Canada. **Online address:** saros.cowasjee@uregina.ca

COWDEN, Robert H. American (born United States), b. 1934. **Genres:** Music, Bibliography, Biography. **Career:** University of Rochester, instructor, 1961, 1964-65; Jacksonville University, assistant professor of music, Opera Workshop, director, 1966-68; Chautauqua Opera Co., Apprentice Artist Program, director and coordinator, 1968; Wayne State University, assistant professor, 1968-72, director of graduate program in lyric theater, 1968-72, Hilberry Classic Theatre, director, 1969-70, Lyric Theatre, director, 1970-71, adjunct professor of music, 1972-74, College of Lifelong Learning, director of fine and applied arts, 1972-74, executive producer of television adult education activities, 1972-74; Michigan Opera Theatre, director, 1969-70; Detroit Symphony Orchestra, director, 1969-72; Banff School of Fine Arts, director, 1971; University of Windsor, director, 1972; University of Nebraska, J.J. Isaacson professor of music, department head, 1974-76; San Jose State University, professor of music, 1976-, department head, 1976-82, emeritus, 2007-; California State Summer School for the Arts, faculty, Music Division, head, 1987-, Music Program, founding chair. Writer. **Publications:** The Chautauqua Opera Association, 1929-1958: An Interpretive History, 1974; (comp.) Concert and Opera Singers: A Bibliography of Biographical Materials, 1985; (comp.) Concert and Opera Conductors: A Bibliography of Biographical Materials, 1987; (comp.) Instrumental Virtuosi: A Bibliography of Biographical Materials, 1989; (ed.) Opera Companies of the World, 1992; Classical Singers of the Operatic and Recital Stages, 1994; Popular Singers of the 20th Century: A Bibliography of Biographical Materials, 1999. TRANSLATOR: G. Verdi, Un Ballo in Maschera, 1970; Lortzing, Der Wildschuetz; Brecht and Weill, Der Jasager; Pergolesi, La Serva Padrona. Contributor of articles to journals. **Address:** School of Music & Dance, San Jose State University, MUS 204, 1 Washington Sq., San Jose, CA 95192-0095, U.S.A. **Online address:** robert.cowden@sjsu.edu

COWELL, Alan S. American/British (born England), b. 1947. **Genres:** Novels, Mystery/Crime/Suspense. **Career:** Swiss Broadcasting Corp., reporter; Reuters News Agency, staff, 1972, reporter, correspondent; New York Times, London bureau, journalist and correspondent, 1981-, NYTimes.com, senior correspondent, 2008-. **Publications:** (Contrib.) Why Are They Weeping? South Africans under Apartheid, 1988; Killing the Wizards: Wars of Power and Freedom from Zaire to South Africa, 1992; A Walking Guide (novel), 2003; The Terminal Spy: A True Story of Espionage, Betrayal, and Murder, 2008; The Paris Correspondent, 2011. **Address:** New York Times, 229 W 43rd St., New York, NY 10036-3959, U.S.A.

COWELL, Cressida. British (born England), b. 1966. **Genres:** Children's Fiction. **Career:** Writer and illustrator. **Publications:** Little Bo Peep's Library Book, 1999; Don't Do That, Kitty Kilroy!, 2000; What Shall We Do with the Boo-Hoo Baby?, 2000; Hiccup, the Viking Who Was Seasick in US as Hiccup, the Seasick Viking, 2000; Claydon Was a Clingy Child, 2001; One Too Many Tigers, 2002; Super Sue, 2003; There's No Such Thing as A Ghostie, 2004; How to Train Your Dragon, 2004; How to be a Pirate, 2005; Super Sue at Super School, 2005; Daddy on the Moon, 2005; How to Train Your Viking, by Toothless, 2006; (trans.) H.H. Haddock, How to Speak Dragonese, 2006; That Rabbit Belongs to Emily Brown, 2007; Emily Brown and the Thing, 2007; How to Cheat a Dragon's Curse: The Heroic Misadventures of Hiccup Horrendous Haddock III, 2007; How To Twist a Dragon's Tale, 2007; Dragon Training and Sword Fighting Tips, 2008; A Hero's Guide to Deadly Dragons: The Heroic Misadventures of Hiccup the Viking as Told to Cressida Cowell, 2009; How to Break a Dragon's Heart, 2009; How to Ride a Dragon's Storm, 2010; How to Steal a Dragon's Sword, 2010; Cheer Up Your Teddy Bear, Emily Brown, 2011. The Queen and the Ghosties, forthcoming. Contributor to periodicals. **Address:** c/o Caroline Walsh, David Higham Associates Ltd., 5-8 Lower John St., Golden Sq., London, GL W1F 9HA, England. **Online address:** cressida@cressidacowell.co.uk

COWELL, Stephanie. American (born United States), b. 1943. **Genres:** History, Translations, Novels, Literary Criticism And History. **Career:** Singer, writer and historical educator. **Publications:** Nicholas Cooke: Actor, Soldier, Physician, Priest, 1993; The Physician of London, 1995; The Players, 1997; Marrying Mozart, 2004; Claude & Camille, 2010; In the Chambers of the King, forthcoming. Contributor to periodicals. **Address:** 585 W End Ave., New York, NY 10024-1715, U.S.A. **Online address:** stephaniecowell@nyc.rr.com

COWEN, Ron(ald). American (born United States), b. 1944. **Genres:** Plays/Screenplays, Young Adult Fiction. **Career:** New York University, instructor in theatre, 1969; University of Pennsylvania, associate trustee. Writer. **Publications:** PLAYS: Summertree, 1967, rev. ed., 2003; (with S. Glasse) Billy, 1969; Saturday Adoption, 1969; The Book of Murder, 1974. Contributor to periodicals. **Address:** William Morris Agency, 1 William Morris Pl., Beverly Hills, CA 90212, U.S.A.

COWEN, Zelman. Australian (born Australia), b. 1919. **Genres:** Law, Essays, Autobiography/Memoirs. **Career:** Oxford University, Oriel College, fellow, 1947-50, provost, 1982-90; University of Melbourne, professor of public law, dean of faculty of law, 1951-66, professor emeritus, 1967-; University of New England, vice chancellor, 1967-70; Hebrew University of Jerusalem, academic governor, 1969-77; Australian Opera, board director, 1969-77; University of Queensland, vice chancellor, 1970-77; Australian Institute of Urban Studies, president, 1973-77; Commonwealth of Australia, governor-general, 1977-82; British Press Council, chairman, 1983-88; John Fairfax Holdings Ltd., chairman, 1992-94; National Academy of Music, chairman, 1995-2000; University of Calcutta, Tagore professor of law; University of Chicago, visiting professor; University of Illinois, visiting professor; University of Washington, visiting professor. Writer. **Publications:** (Ed.) Dicey: Conflict of Laws, 6th ed., 1949; Australia and the United States: Some Legal Comparisons, 1954; (with P.B. Carter) Essays on the Law of Evidence, 1956; American-Australian Private International Law, 1957; Federal Jurisdiction in Australia, 1959, 3rd ed. (with L. Zines), 2002; (with D.M. da Costa) Matrimonial Causes Jurisdiction; Being the Law of Jurisdiction, Choice of Law, and Recognition of Foreign Decrees Under the Matrimonial Causes Act 1959, 1961; The British Commonwealth of Nations in a Changing World: Law, Politics & Prospects, 1965; (co-author) Fair Trial vs. a Free Press, 1965; Sir John Latham and Other Papers, 1965; Sir Isaac Isaacs, 1967; The Private Man, 1969; Some Thoughts on the Australian Universities, 1970; Individual Liberty and the Law, 1975; (with M. Goldsmith and R. Myers) Patterns of Change: The Fabric of Australian Society in the 80s, 1981; The Virginia Lectures, 1984; Press, the Law, and Beyond: A View from the Press Council: Esso Lecture Delivered in the Coombs Lecture Theatre at the Australian National University, Friday, 6 September 1985, 1985; Reflections on Medicine, Biotechnology and the Law, 1986; A Touch of Healing: Speeches by Sir Zelman Cowen, 1977-1982, 1986; Public Life: The Memoirs of Zelman Cowen, 2006. **Address:** University of Melbourne, 500 Yarra Blvd., Richmond, VI 3121, Australia.

COWIE, Colin. American/Zambian (born Zambia), b. 1962. **Genres:** Food And Wine, Design, Young Adult Fiction, Human Relations/Parenting. **Career:** Colin Cowie Lifestyle (an event planning, catering, and design company), founder, 1985-; InStyle and O, contributing editor; NetJets, creative director; The Oprah Magazine, contributing editor; CBS, lifestyle contributor; designer. **Publications:** Effortless Elegance: Menus, Tips, Strategies and More Than 200 Recipes for Easy Entertaining, 1996; Weddings, 1998; For the Bride, 1999; For the Groom, 1999; Dinner After Dark, 2002; Colin Cowie Weddings, 2003; Colin Cowie's Extraordinary Weddings, 2006; Colin Cowie Chic: The Guide to Life as It Should Be, 2007; Wedding Chic: 1, 2001 Ideas for Every Moment of Your Celebration, 2008. Contributor to periodicals. **Address:** Colin Cowie Lifestyle, 80 5th Ave., Ste. 1004, New York, NY 10011, U.S.A.

COWIE, Hamilton Russell. Australian/New Zealander (born New Zealand), b. 1931. **Genres:** History, International Relations/Current Affairs, Economics, Politics/Government, Children's Fiction. **Career:** University of Queensland, lecturer, 1972-75, senior lecturer in education, 1975-. Writer. **Publications:** (With J.H. Allsopp) Challenge and Response: A History of the Modern World, vol. I, 1969, vol. II, 1970, rev. ed., 1976; (ed.) Heritage, vol. I: The First Fifty Thousand Years, 1974, vol. II: Australia and the Modern World, 1975; Frankfurt to Fra Mauro: A Thematic History of the Modern World, 1975, rev. ed., 1981; (ed.) Foundations, 1976; A New Look at History Teaching: Ideas on the Theory and Practice of Teaching History in Secondary Schools, 1977; (ed.) Horizons, 1978; Revolutions in the Modern World, 1979; Crossroads, vol. I: Nationalism and Internationalism in the Modern World, 1979, vol. II: Economic Trends in the Modern World and Their Social Effects, 1980, vol. III: Asia and Australia in World Affairs, 1980, vol. IV: Historical Background to Problems of Contemporary Society, 1981; (with K. Cowie) Discovering Brisbane, 1980; Dictionary of Australian History, 1981; (co-author) Outcomes, 1981; Obedience or Choice: The Major Issues of the Modern World, 1987; Legacies: The Modern State, Nationalism and Internationalism, Australia and Asia, a Changing Relationship, Imperialism, Racism and Reassessments, 3 vols., 1992-94; The Essential Collection: Bastille to Sarajevo, Versailles to Bosnia, 2 vols., 1993-94; Modern Revolutions: Their Character and Influence, 1996. **Address:** PO Box 1588, Milton, QL 4064, Australia.

COWLEY, (Cassia) Joy. New Zealander (born New Zealand), b. 1936. **Genres:** Novels, Novellas/Short Stories, Children's Fiction, Children's Nonfiction, Theology/Religion, Picture/Board Books, Young Adult Non-fiction, Education, Autobiography/Memoirs, Young Adult Fiction. **Career:** Writer, 1967-. **Publications:** FOR CHILDREN FICTION: The Duck in the Gun, 1969; The Silent One, 1981; London, Methuen, 1982; The Terrible Taniwha of Timberditch, 1982; Two of a Kind: Stories, 1984; Salmagundi, 1985; Old Tuatara, 1985; Captain Felonius, 1986; Brith the Terrible, 1986; The Lucky Feather, 1986; The King's Pudding, 1986; Turnips for Dinner, 1986; Mrs. Grindy's Shoes, 1986; My Tiger (stories), 1986; The Train Ride Story, 1987; Giant on the Bus, 1987; Seventy Kilometers from Ice Cream, 1987; Far Out, 1988; Yukadoos, 1988; Train that Ran Away, 1988; The White Horse, 1988; Kangaroo from Wooloomooloo, 1988; My Bad Mood, 1988; Mouse Monster, 1989; Morning Dance, 1989; Magician's Lunch, 1989; Ten Loopy Caterpillars, 1989; Plants of my Aunt, 1989; Pawprints in the Butter: A Collection of Cats, 1991; Bow Down, Shadrach, 1991; Happy Birthday, Mrs. Felonius, 1992; Bow Down Shadrach, 1992; The Day of the Rain, 1993; Little Unicorn Library: The Park Street Playground, 1993; Stolen Food: A Maori Legend, 1993; Annabel, 1993; (with D. Cox) The Screaming Mean Machine, 1993; Beep and the Telephone, 1994; Beyond the River, 1994; The Day of the Snow, 1994; Gladly Here I Come, 1994; Song of the River, 1994; The Cheese Trap, 1995; Babysitter Bother, Chicken Dinners, and Croack-a-roo-roo-roo (The Happy Hens Series), 1995; The Day of the Wind, 1995; The Mouse Bride, 1995; Brave Mama Puss, Papa Puss to the Rescue, Mabel and the Marvellous Meow, and Oscar in Danger (Puss Quartet), 1995-96; The Sea Daughter, 1995; Tulevai and the Sea, 1995; Gracias the Thanksgiving Turkey, 1996; Snake and Lizard, 1996; Elephant Rhymes, 1997; The Great Bamboozle, 1997; A Haunting Tale, 1997; The Hitchhikers: Stories from Joy Cowley, 1997; Singing Down the Rain, 1997; Ticket to the Sky Dance, 1997; The Bump, 1997; Splishy-Sploshy, 1997; (contrib.) Time for Bed, Little Bear, 1997; Agapanthus Hum and the Eyeglasses, 1998; Starbright and the Dream Eater, 1998; Wild West Gang, 1998; Big Moon Tortilla, 1998; Dragon Slayer, 1999; The Day the Truck Got Stuck, 1999; The Rusty, Trusty Tractor, 1999; Nicketty-Nacketty-Noo-Noo-Noo, 1999; Red-eyed Tree Frog, 1999; More of the Wild Wests, 1999; (contrib.) The Video Shop Sparrow, 1999; Agapanthus Hum and Major Bark, 2000; Apple, Banana, Cherry, 2000; Cricket's Storm, 2000; Eating Plums in Bed, 2000; Pip the Penguin, 2000; Wild Wests and Pong Castle, 2000; Wild Wests and the Haunted Fridge, 2000; Shadrach Girl, 2000; Mrs. Goodstory, 2001; Tabby Tiger, Taxi Driver, 2001; Pudding, 2001; Brodie, 2001; JOY Chapter Books (30), 2001; Froghopper, 2002; Weta: A Knight in Shining Armour, 2002; Froghopper and the Paua Poachers, 2003; Mrs Wishy Washy Farm, 2003; The Wishing of Biddie Malone, 2003; A Nice Little Tractor, 2003; Agapanthus Hum and the Angel Hoot, 2003; Mr Wishy-Washy, 2003; Mrs Wishy Washy Makes a Splash, 2003; Where Horses Run Free: A Dream for the American Mustang, 2003; Hunter, 2004; (contrib.) Wishing of Biddy Malone, 2004; (contrib.) Chameleon, Chameleon, 2005; Mrs. Wishy-washy's Scrubbing Machine, 2005; Mrs. Wishy-Washy's Christmas, 2005; Mrs. Wishy-Washy's Splishy-Sploshy, 2005; Bedtime Train, 2008; Chicken Feathers, 2008. NONFICTION: Write On!, 1994 in US as A Guide for Young Authors, 1995; Joy Cowley Answers Kids' Questions, 1995. NOVELS: Nest in a Fallen Tree, 1967; Man of Straw, 1970; Of Men and Angels, 1972; The Mandrake Root, 1975; The Growing Season, 1978; Classical Music, 1999; Holy Days, 2001. SHORT STORIES: Heart Attack and Other Stories, 1985; The Complete Short Stories, 1997. OTHERS: (ed. with T. France) Women Writers of New Zealand 1932-1982, 1982; Aotearoa Psalms: Prayers of a New People, 1989; Whole Learning: Whole Child, 1994; Psalms Down-Under, 1996; Everything 'round Us Is Praise, 1997; Psalms for the Road, 2002; Friends: Snake and Lizard, 2009; Fierce Little Woman and the Wicked Pirate, 2010; Navigation: A Memoir, 2010; Writing from the Heart, 2011. Contributor to books and periodicals. **Address:** Te Mangawa, Fish Bay, Kenepuru, Rd. 2, Picton, 7372, New Zealand.

COWLEY, Marjorie. American (born United States), b. 1925. **Genres:** Children's Fiction, Young Adult Fiction, Mythology/Folklore. **Career:** University of California, International Student Center, Host Family Program, director, 1961-68, Museum of Cultural History, lecturer on prehistoric archaeology, 1973-87; graphic designer and calligrapher, 1973-93; teacher, 1975-88; Children's Museum of Los Angeles, instructor. Writer. **Publications:** FOR CHILDREN: Dar and the Spear-Thrower, 1994; Anooka's Answer, 1998; The Golden Bull, 2008. **Address:** 2544 Hutton Dr., Beverly Hills, CA 90210-1212, U.S.A. **Online address:** mhcowley@aol.com

COWSER, Bob. American (born United States), b. 1971?. **Genres:** Language/Linguistics, Poetry. **Career:** Marquette University, teaching assistant, 1992-94, Ott Memorial Writing Center, writing consultant, 1992-94; University of Nebraska, teaching assistant, 1994-98, writing assistance center, writing consultant, 1994-95; St. Lawrences Young Writers Conference, workshop leader; St. Lawrence University, Department of English, assistant professor, 1998-2003, associate professor, 2004, coordinator of creative-writing program, interim director of writing program, 2004-05, professor, 2010-; River Teeth, associate editor, 2008-; Ashland University, Low-Residency MFA Program, adjunct faculty, 2008-. Writer. **Publications:** Dream Season: A Professor Joins Americas Oldest Semi-Pro Football Team, 2004; Scorekeeping: Essays from Home, 2006; Green Fields: Crime, Punishment and A Boyhood Between, 2010; (ed.) Why Were Here: New York Essayists On Living Upstate, 2010. Contributor to books. Works appear in anthologies. **Address:** Department of English, St. Lawrence University, 309 Richardson Hall, 58 Riverside Dr., Canton, PA 13617, U.S.A. **Online address:** rcowser@stlawu.edu

COX, Alex. British (born England), b. 1954. **Genres:** Plays/Screenplays, Popular Culture. **Career:** Writer, actor, director and producer. **Publications:** Repo Man, 1984; (with A. Wool) Sid and Nancy: Love Kills, 1986; X-films, 2008; 10,000 Ways to Die: A Director's Take on the Spaghetti Western, 2009. Contributor of articles to periodicals. **Address:** Film Studies Program, University of Colorado, Rm. 349, ATLAS, PO Box 316, Boulder, CO 80309-0316, U.S.A. **Online address:** info@alexcox.com

COX, Ana Marie. (Ann O'Tate). American (born United States), b. 1972. **Genres:** Novels, Humor/Satire, Politics/Government, Literary Criticism And History. **Career:** Alfred A. Knopf, editorial assistant; Mother Jones, features editor; Suck.com, executive editor; Wonkette.com, author, 2003-06, editor emeritus, 2006-; Playboy, contributing editor; Time.com, editor, 2006-. **Publications:** (Ed. with J. Anuff) Suck: Worst-Case Scenarios in Media, Culture, Advertising, and the Internet, 1997; Dog Days, 2006. **Address:** Riverhead Books Publicity, Penguin Group, 375 Hudson St., New York, NY 10014, U.S.A. **Online address:** dogdaysgirl@gmail.com

COX, Anna-Lisa. American (born United States) **Genres:** Novels, History, Social Sciences. **Career:** Newberry Library, fellow, 2002-03. Writer. **Publications:** A Stronger Kinship: One Town's Extraordinary Story of Hope and Faith, 2006. Contributor to periodicals. **Address:** c/o Author Mail, Warner Books, 1271 Ave. of the Americas, New York, NY 10020, U.S.A. **Online address:** annalisa_cox@hotmail.com

COX, Caroline. American/Scottish (born Scotland), b. 1954. **Genres:** History. **Career:** University of the Pacific, assistant professor, 1998-2004, associate professor of history, 2004-. Writer. **Publications:** A Proper Sense of Honor: Service and Sacrifice in George Washington's Army, 2004; (with K. Albala) Opening Up North America, 1497-1800, 2005, rev. ed., 2010; The Fight to Survive: A Young Girl, Diabetes, and the Discovery of Insulin, 2009. Contributor to books and journals. **Address:** Department of History, University of the Pacific, Stockton, CA 95211, U.S.A. **Online address:** ccox@uop.edu

COX, C. B. *See* **COX, Christopher Barry.**

COX, C. Barry. *See* **COX, Christopher Barry.**

COX, Christopher Barry. Also writes as C. B. Cox, C. Barry Cox. British (born England), b. 1931. **Genres:** Botany, Earth Sciences, Geography, Marine Sciences/Oceanography, Zoology, Sciences. **Career:** University of London, King's College, lecturer, 1956-66, senior lecturer, 1966-69, reader, 1969-76, professor, 1976-96, Department of Biology, head, 1984-88, assistant principal, 1989-96; Epsom High School, vice chairman of governors. Writer. **Publications:** Two New Dicynodonts from the Triassic Ntawere Formation, Zambia, 1969; (as C. Barry Cox) The Problematic Permian Reptile Eunotosaurus, 1969; Prehistoric Animals, 1969; (with P.D. Moore and I.N. Healey) Biogeography: An Ecological and Evolutionary Approach, 1973, (with P.D. Moore) 7th ed., 2005; (ed. with A. Bellairs) Morphology and Biology of Reptiles, 1976; Prehistoric World, 1985; Macmillan Illustrated Encyclopedia of Dinosaurs and Prehistoric Animals, 1988; Atlas of the Living World, 1989; (with P.D. Moore and P. Whitfield) Biomes and Habitats, 2002. **Address:** Forge Cottage, 11 Blacksmith Close, Ashtead, ES KT21 2BD, England.

COX, Gary W(alter). American (born United States), b. 1955. **Genres:** Politics/Government, History. **Career:** University of Texas, Department of Government, assistant professor, 1982-84, associate professor, 1986-87; Washington University, Department of Political Science, visiting assistant professor, 1984-85, visiting associate professor, 1985-86; University of California, Department of Political Science, associate professor, professor, 1987-98, distinguished professor, 1998-, chair, 2004-, now professor emeritus. Writer. **Publications:** The Efficient Secret: The Cabinet and the Development of Political Parties in Victorian England, 1987; (ed. with S. Kernell) The Politics of Divided Government, 1991; (with M.D. McCubbins) Legislative Leviathan: Party Government in the House, 1993; Making Votes Count: Strategic Coordination in the World's Electoral Systems, 1997; (with J.N. Katz) Elbridge Gerry's Salamander: The Electoral Consequences of the Reapportionment Revolution, 2002; (with M.D. McCubbins) Setting the Agenda: Responsible Party Government in the U.S. House of Representatives, 2005. **Address:** Department of Political Science, University of California, Rm. 301, Social Sciences Bldg., 9500 Gilman Dr., La Jolla, CA 92093-0521, U.S.A. **Online address:** gcox@ucsd.edu

COX, Gordon. British/Welsh (born Wales), b. 1942. **Genres:** Music. **Career:** School teacher, 1964-80; University of Reading, lecturer in education, 1980-, senior lecturer, International Centre for Research in Music Education, program director. Writer. **Publications:** Folk Music in a Newfoundland Outport, 1980; A History of Music Education in England, 1872-1928, 1993; Living Music in Schools, 1923-1999: Studies in the History of Music Education in England, 2002; (ed.) Sir Arthur Somervell on Music Education: His Writings, Speeches and Letters, 2003; (ed. with R. Stevens) The Origins and Foundations of Music Education: Cross-cultural Historical Studies of Music in Compulsory Schooling, 2010. Contributor of articles to journals. **Address:** University of Reading, Whiteknights, PO Box 217, Reading, BR RG6 6AH, England. **Online address:** g.s.a.cox@reading.ac.uk

COX, Jeffrey. (Jeffrey L. Cox). American (born United States), b. 1947. **Genres:** History. **Career:** University of Iowa, College of Liberal Arts and Sciences, Department of History, professor, 1977-, chair, 1993-96, president of faculty senate, 2002-03, director of honors program. Writer. **Publications:** The English Churches in a Secular Society: Lambeth, 1870-1930, 1982; (ed. with S. Stromquist) Contesting the Master Narrative: Essays in Social History, 1998; Imperial Fault Lines: Christianity and Colonial Power in India, 1818-1940, 2002; The British Missionary Enterprise since 1700, 2008. Works appear in anthologies. Contributor to journals. **Address:** Department of History, College of Liberal Arts and Sciences, University of Iowa, 109 Schaeffer Hall, 20 E Washington St., Iowa City, IA 52242-1409, U.S.A. **Online address:** jeffrey-cox@uiowa.edu

COX, Jeffrey L. *See* **COX, Jeffrey.**

COX, Jim. American (born United States), b. 1939?. **Genres:** Classics, Photography. **Career:** McKendree College, professor, now retired. Writer. **Publications:** The Great Radio Soap Operas, 1999; The Great Radio Audience Participation Shows: Seventeen Programs from the 1940s and 1950s, 2001; Radio Crime Fighters: Over 300 Programs from the Golden Age, 2002; Say Goodnight, Gracie: The Last Years of Network Radio, 2002; Frank and Anne Hummert's Radio Factory: The Programs and Personalities of Broadcasting's Most Prolific Producers, 2003; Mr. Keen, Tracer of Lost Persons: A Complete History and Episode Log of Radio's most Durable Detective, 2004; Music Radio: The Great Performers and Programs of the 1920s Through Early 1960s, 2005; Historical Dictionary of American Radio Soap Operas, 2005; Daytime Serials of Television, 1946-1960, 2006; Great Radio Sitcoms, 2007; Radio Speakers: Narrators, News Junkies, Sports Jockeys, Tattletales, Tipsters, Toastmasters and Coffee Klatch Couples Who Verbalized the Jargon of the Aural Ether from the 1920s to the 1980s: A Biographical Dictionary, 2007; Sold on Radio: Advertisers in the Golden Age of Broadcasting, 2008; This Day in Network Radio: A Daily Calendar of Births, Deaths, Debuts, Cancellations and Other Events in Broadcasting History, 2008; American Radio Networks: A History, 2009; Rails Across Dixie, 2010. Contributor to periodicals. **Address:** McFarland & Company Inc., PO Box 611, Jefferson, NC 28640, U.S.A.

COX, Judy. American (born United States), b. 1954. **Genres:** Picture/Board Books, Children's Fiction. **Career:** Welches School District, teacher, 1985-92; West Linn-Wilsonville School District, teacher, 1996-2002; Ontario Public Schools, reading specialist, 2004-. Writer. **Publications:** Now We Can Have a Wedding!, 1998; The West Texas Chili Monster, 1998; Third Grade Pet, 1998; Rabbit Pirates: A Tale of the Spinach Main, 1999; Mean, Mean Maureen Green, 2000; Weird Stories from the Lonesome Café, 2000; Butterfly Buddies, 2001; Cool Cat, School Cat, 2002; My Family Plays Music, 2003; Go to Sleep, Groundhog!, 2004; That Crazy Eddie and the Science Project of Doom, 2005. Don't Be Silly, Mrs. Millie!, 2005; The Mystery of the Burmese Bandicoot, 2007; Mrs. Millie Goes to Philly!, 2008; Puppy

Power, 2008; One Is a Feast for Mouse: A Thanksgiving Tale, 2008; The Case of the Purloined Professor, 2009; Pick a Pumpkin, Mrs. Millie!, 2009; The Secret Chicken Society, forthcoming; Happy Birthday, Mrs. Millie, forthcoming. Contributor of articles to periodicals. **Address:** 99 White Plains Rd., Tarrytown, NY 10591, U.S.A. **Online address:** gtrmouse@aol.com

COX, Kevin Robert. American/British (born England), b. 1939. **Genres:** Geography, Politics/Government, Urban Studies, Social Sciences. **Career:** Ohio State University, assistant professor, 1965-68, associate professor, 1968-71, professor of geography, 1971-, distinguished university professor, 2003-, Center for African Studies, research fellow, 1990-; University of Reading, distinguished visiting professor, 1995-99. Writer. **Publications:** (Ed. with R.G. Golledge) Behavioral Problems in Geography: A Symposium, 1969; Man, Location and Behavior: An Introduction to Human Geography, 1972; Conflict, Power and Politics in the City: A Geographic View, 1973; (ed. with D.R. Reynolds and S. Rokkan) Locational Approaches to Power and Conflict, 1974; (with J.A. Agnew) Spatial Correspondence of Territorial Partitions, 1976; (ed.) Urbanization and Conflict in Market Societies, 1978; Location and Public Problems: A Political Geography of the Contemporary World, 1979; (ed. with R.G. Golledge) Behavioral Problems in Geography Revisited, 1981; (ed. with R.J. Johnston) Conflict, Politics and the Urban Scene, 1982; (ed.) Spaces of Globalization: Reasserting the Power of the Local, 1997; Political Geography: Territory, State and Society, 2002; (ed. with M. Low and J. Robinson) SAGE Handbook of Political Geography, 2007. **Address:** Department of Geography, Ohio State University, 1106 Derby Hall, 154 N Oval Mall, Columbus, OH 43235-5125, U.S.A. **Online address:** cox.13@osu.edu

COX, Lynne. American (born United States), b. 1957. **Genres:** Sports/Fitness. **Career:** Writer. **Publications:** Swimming to Antarctica: Tales of a Long-Distance Swimmer, 2004; Grayson, 2006; Elizabeth, Queen of the Seas, 2012. Contributor to magazines. **Address:** c/o Martha Kaplan, Martha Kaplan Agency, 115 W 29th St., 10th Fl., Ste. 3, New York, NY 10001, U.S.A.

COX, Madison. American (born United States), b. 1958. **Genres:** Homes/Gardens, Art/Art History, Horticulture. **Career:** Madison Cox Design Inc., owner, 1989-. Writer. **Publications:** Private Gardens of Paris, 1989; (co-author) Gardens of the World, 1991; Artist's Gardens: From Claude Monet to Jennifer Bartlett, 1993; (with P. Berge) Majorelle: A Moroccan Oasis, 1999. **Address:** Madison Cox Design Inc., 127 W 26th St., 9th Fl., New York, NY 10001, U.S.A. **Online address:** madisoncox@madisoncox.com

COX, Mike. American (born United States), b. 1948. **Genres:** History, Novellas/Short Stories. **Career:** Austin American-Statesman, reporter; Texas Department of Public Safety, chief of media relations; Texas Press Association, columnist; Texas Department of Transportation, communication manager, retired, 2007. Consultant and public speaker. **Publications:** Red Rooster Country: A Ragtag Collection of Stories about a Hunk of the Lone Star State Bigger Than Ohio, 1970; Fred Gipson, Texas Storyteller, 1980; (with J.B. Frantz) Lure of the Land: Texas County Maps and the History of Settlement, 1988; The Texas Rangers: Men of Valor and Action, 1991. O. Henry and the Lost San Saba Mine, 1995; Texas Ranger Tales: Stories That Need Telling, 1997; Historic Austin: An Illustrated History, 1998; Stand-Off in Texas: Just Call Me a Spokesman for the DPS, 1998; Texas Ranger Tales II, 1999; Historic Amarillo: An Illustrated History, 2000; Texas Disasters: True Stories of Tragedy and Survival, 2006; The Texas Rangers: Wearing the Cinco Peso, 1821-1900, 2008; Historic Photos of Texas Lawman, 2008. Contributor to periodicals. **Address:** Austin, TX , U.S.A. **Online address:** mikecoxtex@austin.rr.com

COX, Patsi Bale. *See* Obituaries.

COX, Paul(us). Dutch (born Netherlands), b. 1940. **Genres:** Plays/Screenplays, Photography, Film, Sciences, Young Adult Fiction. **Career:** Prahran College, teacher; Teacher of photography and cinematography, 1971-82; Illumination Films, co-founder, producer and director, 1975-. Photographer and screenwriter. **Publications:** (With U. Beier) Home of Man: The People of New Guinea, 1971; (contrib.) Mirka, 1980; Reflections: An Autobiographical Journey, 1998; 3 Screenplays, 1998; (with R.G. Driggers and T. Edwards) Introduction to Infrared and Electro-Optical Systems, 1999; (with D. Malcolm and S. Benegal) World Cinema, Power, Politics and Hegemony, 2005; The Last Scalp, 2005; The Eleventh Man, 2006. **Address:** S.T.E. Representation, 9301 Wilshire Blvd., Ste. 312, Beverly Hills, CA 90210, U.S.A.

COX, Richard. American (born United States), b. 1970. **Genres:** Novels, Mystery/Crime/Suspense. **Career:** Writer. **Publications:** Rift, 2004; The God Particle: A Novel, 2005. **Address:** c/o Author Mail, Random House, 1745 Broadway, 10th Fl., New York, NY 10019-4368, U.S.A. **Online address:** contact1@richardcox.net

COX, Richard (Hubert Francis). Also writes as R. Heber, R. Heber. British (born England), b. 1931. **Genres:** Novels, International Relations/Current Affairs, Travel/Exploration, How-to Books, Young Adult Fiction, Translations. **Career:** Colman, Prentis & Varley, advertising executive, 1957-59; Sunday Times, staff foreign correspondent, 1961-64, foreign office staff, 1964-66; Westinghouse Broadcasting Corp., Chelsea borough councillor, 1962-65; Daily Telegraph, defense correspondent, 1966-72; Thornton Cox Ltd., managing director, 1974-78; Brassey's Publishers, managing director, 1974-78; novelist, 1974-. **Publications:** Pan Africanism in Practice: An East African Study, PAFMECSA 1958-1964, 1964; Kenyatta's Country, 1965; Traveller's Guide to East Africa, 1966; Institute of Directors Guide to Europe: A Comprehensive Business Guide to Western Europe and Sacndinavia, 1970; (ed.) Travellers Guide to Majorca, Minorca, Ibiza & Formentera, 1973, 2nd ed., 1981; (ed.) Operation Sea Lion, 1974; Travellers' Guide to Malta: A Concise Guide to the Mediterranean Islands of Malta, 2nd ed., 1975; Sam 7, 1977; (ed. and trans.) Battleships of the U.S. Navy in World War II, 1977; Botticelli Madonna: A Novel, 1979; Auction, 1979; The Time It Takes, 1980; The KGB Directive, 1981; The Ice Raid, 1983; Ground Zero, 1985; The Columbus Option, 1986; An Agent of Influence, 1988; Hartman's Game, 1988; Park Plaza, 1991; Eclipse, 1996; Traveller's Guide to Kenya and Northern Tanzania, 1997; (as R. Heber) Murder at Wittenham Park, 1998; (with L. Fitzgerald) How to Meet a Puffin, 2004. **Address:** Curtis Brown Group Ltd., Haymarket House, 28-29 Haymarket, London, GL SW1 4SP, England.

COX, Robert H(enry). American (born United States), b. 1961. **Genres:** Politics/Government. **Career:** Indiana University, associate instructor in political science, 1984-86, 1988-89; Erasmus University, research assistant in public administration, 1987; University of Oklahoma, assistant professor of political science, 1989-95, associate professor with tenure, 1995-2008, professor with tenure, 2008-, European Area Studies, coordinator, 1994-2001, International and Area Studies, acting director, 1999, interim director, 2000-01, European Union Center, co-director, 2001-, School of International and Area Studies, director, 2001-09, European Studies and Russian and East European Studies, coordinator, 2008-; An International Journal of Policy, co-editor, 2005-; United Nations Association, president, 2006-10; Miami University Western College Program Alumni Association, president, 2009-10. Writer. **Publications:** The Development of the Dutch Welfare State: From Workers' Insurance to Universal Entitlement, 1993; (ed. with Daniel Béland) Ideas and Politics in Social Science Research, 2010. Contributor of articles to books and journals. **Address:** Department of Political Science, School of International & Area Studies, University of Oklahoma, Rm. 138, 729 Elm Ave., Norman, OK 73019, U.S.A. **Online address:** rhcox@ou.edu

COX, Roger (Kenneth). British (born England), b. 1936. **Genres:** Business/Trade/Industry, Marketing, Economics, Administration/Management, Law. **Career:** John Menzies, retail development manager, 1968-71; ADA Halifax, group marketing officer of development, 1973-75. Writer. **Publications:** Retail Site Assessment, 1968; Retail Development, 1972; Retailing, 1978, (with P. Brittain) 5th ed., 2004; Running Your Own Shop, 1985; (with J.P.R. Brittain) Retail Management, 1988. **Address:** 30 London Rd., Westerham, KT TN16 1BD, England.

COX, Ruth P. American (born United States), b. 1947. **Genres:** Medicine/Health. **Career:** University of Virginia Hospital, staff nurse, 1968-71; Watts Hospital, staff nurse, 1969; University of Virginia, Pediatric Diabetic Camp, member of instructional staff, 1970; Porlock Vale Equestrian Center, member of instructional staff, 1973-76; Craven County Hospital, Neuropsychiatric Unit, evening charge nurse, 1977; Fortune Center, teacher of riding for the handicapped, 1978; Craven County Hospital, quality care assurance coordinator, 1979-80, B.S.N. Degree Program, director and consultant, 1980-81, assistant director of nursing for quality assurance and infection control, 1980-81; Carteret Technical College, instructor, 1980; American Heart Association of North Carolina, instructor, 1980, instructor trainer, 1981; Brighton Rescue Squad, emergency medical technician, 1980-81; Atlantic Christian College, adjunct faculty member, 1981; Health Care Services, home health nurse, 1981-82; Valdosta State College, assistant professor of nursing, 1981-86; Greenleaf Center, nurse, 1986; Florida State University, Marriage and Family

Therapy Center, family therapy intern, 1987-90, student counselor, 1988-89; Florida Board of Nursing, support group facilitator, 1990-91; University of Alabama-Birmingham, assistant professor, 1991-2000, Wellness Center, marriage and family therapist, 1992-93, Center for Health Promotion, associate scientist, 1997-2004, associate professor of nursing, 2000-04, Family Place Pediatric Practice, family nurse practitioner, 1997-2004, Adult Inborn Errors of Metabolism Clinic, family nurse practitioner, 2000-01, Family Nurse Practitioner Program, coordinator, 2000-04; Samaritan Counseling Center, marriage and family therapist, 1992-2004, supervisor, 1993-2004; Special Equestrians, health consultant, 1995-2002; Birmingham Health Care, family nurse practitioner, 1996-2004; East Carolina University, clinical associate professor of nursing and director of family nurse practitioner program, 2004-. Writer. **Publications:** Health Related Counseling with Families of Diverse Cultures: Family, Health, and Cultural Competencies, 2003. Contributor to books. **Address:** School of Nursing, East Carolina University, E 5th St., Greenville, NC 27858-4353, U.S.A. **Online address:** ruthpcox@msn.com

COX, Stephen D. American (born United States), b. 1948. **Genres:** Literary Criticism And History, Economics. **Career:** University of California, professor; Liberty magazine, senior editor, editor-in-chief. **Publications:** The Stranger within Thee: Concepts of the Self in Late-Eighteenth-Century Literature, 1980; Love and Logic: The Evolution of Blake's Thought, 1992; The Titanic Story: Hard Choices, Dangerous Decisions, 1999; The Woman and the Dynamo: Isabel Paterson and the Idea of America, 2004; The New Testament and Literature: A Guide to Literary Patterns, 2006; The Big House: Image and Reality of the American Prison, 2009; (as Stephen Cox with P. Cantor) Literature and the Economics of Liberty: Spontaneous Order in Culture, 2010. Contributor to periodicals. **Address:** University of California, Humanities 0306, 9500 Gilman Dr., La Jolla, CA 92093, U.S.A. **Online address:** sdcox@ucsd.edu

COX, Stephen (LeRoy). American/Canadian (born Canada), b. 1966. **Genres:** Communications/Media, Film, Biography, Autobiography/Memoirs. **Career:** Comedy Magazine, writer, 1987-88; St. Louis Post-Dispatch, columnist, 1989-90. **Publications:** The Beverly Hillbillies, 1988; The Munchkins Remember the Wizard of Oz and Beyond, 1989; The Munsters: Television's First Family of Fright, 1989; (with J. Lofflin) The Official Abbott and Costello Scrapbook, 1990; The Addams Chronicles: Everything You Ever Wanted to Know About the Addams Family, 1991, rev. ed., 1998; Here's Johnny!: Thirty Years of America's Favorite Late - Night Entertainment, 1992; The Hooterville Handbook: A Viewer's Guide to Green Acres, 1993; (with R. Johnson) Here on Gilligan's Isle, 1993; The Munchkins of Oz, 1996; Dreaming of Jeannie: TV's Prime Time in a Bottle, 1997; (with E. Willingham) Cooking in Oz: Kitchen Wizardry and a Century of Marvels from America's Favorite Tale, 1999; The Addams Chronicles, 1998; It's a Wonderful Life: A Memory Book, 2003; The Munsters: A Trip Down Mockingbird Lane, 2006; (with J. Terry) One Fine Stooge: Larry Fine's Frizzy Life in Pictures: An Authorized Biography, 2006; (with K. Mahanka) The Incredible Mr. Don Knotts: An Eye-Popping Look at His Movies, 2008; (with J. Marren) Short and Sweet: The Life and Times of the Lollipop Munchkin, 2008. Contributor to periodicals. **Address:** 1918 Grismer Ave., Ste. B, Burbank, CA 91504, U.S.A.

COX, Steve. British (born England), b. 1962. **Genres:** History, Documentaries/Reportage, Photography. **Career:** Giles Smith Photography, advertising and industrial photographer, 1981-86; Steve Bicknell Photography, senior photographer, 1986-87; University of Birmingham, photographer, 1986, 1988. Public speaker and freelance photojournalist. **Publications:** (With P. Carey) Generations of Resistance: East Timor, 1995. Contributor to magazines and newspapers. **Address:** 30 Instow Rd., Earley, Reading, BR RG6 5QJ, England.

COX, Vic. American (born United States), b. 1942. **Genres:** Children's Non-fiction, Environmental Sciences/Ecology, Travel/Exploration, Young Adult Non-fiction. **Career:** Westways Magazine, writer and editor, 1971-75; freelance writer and editor, 1976-; California State University, Department of Journalism, instructor, 1977-78; Los Angeles Times, copy editor, 1979-83; Santa Barbara News-Press, copy editor, 1982-88; University of Southern California Sea Grant, consultant, 1982-83; University of California, public information representative, 1989, 1991-92, senior editor, 1996-2008; Santa Barbara City College, Journalism Department, assistant adviser, 1989-91. **Publications:** Whales and Dolphins, 1989; Ocean Life: Beneath the Crystal Seas, 1990; The Challenge of Immigration, 1995; Guns, Violence and Teens, 1997. Contributor to books. **Address:** 82 Warwick Pl., Goleta, CA 93117, U.S.A. **Online address:** vic.cox@cox.net

COX, Vicki. American (born United States), b. 1945. **Genres:** Novels, Young Adult Non-fiction, Children's Non-fiction, Biography, Education, Reference. **Career:** Teacher, 1998-2001; Drury University, instructor, 2001-03; Ozark Technical College, faculty. Writer. **Publications:** SELF-ILLUSTRATED: Rising Stars and Ozark Constellations, 2001. OTHERS: Diana, Princess of Wales, 2001; Marion Jones, 2001; Hosni Mubarak, 2003; Fidel Castro, 2004; Margaret Sanger, 2004; Anne Hutchinson, 2005; John F. Kennedy, 2005; Betsy Ross, 2006; Maya Angelou: Poet, 2006; Oscar Arias Sánchez: Bringing Peace to Central America, 2007; History of the Third Parties, 2007; Clarence Thomas, 2008. **Address:** c/o Author Mail, Chelsea House Publishers L.L.C., 2080 Cabot Blvd. W, Ste. 201, Langhorne, PA 19047-1813, U.S.A. **Online address:** vcox01@yahoo.com

COX-JOHNSON, Ann. *See* **SAUNDERS, Ann Loreille.**

COY, John. American (born United States), b. 1958. **Genres:** Novels, Young Adult Fiction, Children's Fiction, Young Adult Non-fiction. **Career:** Anderson Center for Interdisciplinary Studies, resident, 2000, 2002, 2004. Writer and educator. **Publications:** FOR CHILDREN: Night Driving, 1996; (ed.) A Special Stretch of Sky (anthology of student writing), 1997; Strong to the Hoop, 1999; Vroomaloom Zoom, 2000; Two Old Potatoes and Me, 2003; Around the World, 2005; Top of the Order, 2009; Eyes on the Goal, 2010; Love of the Game, 2011; Take Your Best Shot, 2012. OTHERS: Crackback (young-adult novel), 2005; Box Out, 2008; (contrib.) Libraries of Minnesota, 2011. **Address:** 225 Cecil St. SE, Minneapolis, MN 55414-3612, U.S.A. **Online address:** comments@johncoy.com

COYLE, Beverly (Jones). American (born United States), b. 1946. **Genres:** Novels, Plays/Screenplays. **Career:** University of Newcastle, instructor in English, 1974-77; Vassar College, assistant professor, 1977-85, associate professor of English, 1985-92, professor of English, 1993, Mary Augusta Scott chair of literature, 1999-2003, professor of literature, now professor emeritus; Organization Cross Currents, director; Yale University, lecturer in religion and literature and visiting professor emerita. Writer. **Publications:** A Thought to Be Rehearsed: Aphorism in Wallace Stevens' Poetry, 1983; (ed. with A. Filreis) Secretaries of the Moon: The Letters of Wallace Stevens and Jose Rodriguez Feo, 1986; The Kneeling Bus, 1990; In Troubled Waters, 1993; Taken In, 1998. Contributor to periodicals. **Address:** Yale University, 77 Bleecker St., Ste. 1211-1212, New York, NY 10012, U.S.A. **Online address:** bevcoyle1@gmail.com

COYLE, Bill. American (born United States), b. 1968?. **Genres:** Poetry, Theology/Religion. **Career:** Salem State College, Writing Center, co-coordinator. Writer. **Publications:** The God of This World to His Prophet: Poems, 2006. Works appear in anthologies. Contributor to magazines. **Address:** Salem State College, 352 Lafayette St., Salem, MA 01970, U.S.A. **Online address:** bcoyle@salemstate.edu

COYLE, William. *See* **KENEALLY, Thomas (Michael).**

COYNE, James K(itchenman). American (born United States), b. 1946. **Genres:** Politics/Government. **Career:** George S. Coyne Chemical Company Inc., president, 1971-79, director; University of Pennsylvania, Wharton School, lecturer, 1974-79; U.S. Congress, representative, 1980-82; White House, special assistant, 1983-85; American Consulting Engineers Council, chief executive officer, 1985-86; American Tort Reform Association, president, 1987-88; Roy F. Woston Inc., vice president and director, 1988-90; Americans to Limit Congressional Terms, president, 1991-92; First Washington Management Group, chair, 1992-94. Writer. **Publications:** (With J.H. Fund) Cleaning House: America's Campaign for Term Limits, 1992; Kick the Bums Out, 1992. **Address:** 1007 Turkey Run Rd., McLean, VA 22101-1707, U.S.A.

COYNE, Jerry. *See* **COYNE, Jerry A.**

COYNE, Jerry A. Also writes as Jerry Coyne. American (born United States), b. 1949. **Genres:** Sciences. **Career:** Cornell University Medical School, medical technician, 1971-72; Harvard University, Museum of Comparative Zoology, research associate, 1978-79; University of Maryland, assistant professor, 1982-86, associate professor, 1986; University of Chicago, associate professor, 1986-91, professor, 1991-; University of Paris-Sud, distinguished visiting professor, 1994; Université Pierre et Marie Curie, distinguished visiting professor, 1998; Université de Bourgogne, visiting professor, 2005-06. Writer, biologist, evolutionary geneticist and researcher. **Publications:** (With H.A. Orr) Speciation, 2004; Why Evolution Is True, 2009. Contributor to books. **Address:** Department of Ecology and Evolution, University of Chicago, 1101 E 57th St., Chicago, IL 60637, U.S.A. **Online address:** j-coyne@uchicago.edu

COYNE, Michael. American/Scottish (born Scotland), b. 1960. **Genres:** Film, Ethics, Humanities. **Career:** Historian and writer. **Publications:** The Crowded Prairie: American National Identity in the Hollywood Western, 1997. Contributor to periodicals. **Address:** I. B. Tauris & Company Ltd., 6 Salem Rd., London, GL W2 4BU, England.

COZZENS, Peter. American (born United States), b. 1957. **Genres:** History, Military/Defense/Arms Control, Social Sciences. **Career:** U.S. Department of State, foreign service officer, 1983-. Consultant and writer. **Publications:** No Better Place to Die: The Battle of Stones River, 1990; This Terrible Sound: The Battle of Chickamauga, 1992; The Shipwreck of Their Hopes: The Battles for Chattanooga, 1994; (with D.S. Hartwig) On Campaign: Te Civil War art of Keith Rocco, 1994; The Battle of Stones River, 1995; The Battles for Chattanooga, 1996; The Darkest Days of the War: The Battles of Iuka and Corinth, 1997; (ed. with R.I. Girardi) The Military Memoirs of General John Pope, 1998; General John Pope: A Life for the Nation, 2000; (ed.) Eyewitnesses to the Indian Wars, 1865-1890, 2001; (ed.) Battles and leaders of the Civil War, vol. V, 2002, vol. VI, 2004; (ed. with R.I. Girardi) The New Annals of the Civil War, 2004; Shenandoah 1862: Stonewall Jackson's Valley Campaign, 2008. Contributor to Journals. **Address:** University of Illinois Press, 1325 S Oak St., Champaign, IL 61820-6903, U.S.A. **Online address:** pecozzens@gmail.com

CRAATS, Rennay. Canadian (born Canada), b. 1973. **Genres:** Area Studies, History, Sports/Fitness, Travel/Exploration, Animals/Pets, Children's Non-fiction, Cultural/Ethnic Topics, Fash Ion/Costume, Homes/Gardens, Paranormal, Writing/Journalism, Young Adult Non-fiction. **Career:** Calgary Board of Education, freelance writer, editor; Calgary Catholic School Board, freelance writer, editor. **Publications:** Canada through the Decades: The 1940s, 1999; Canada through the Decades: The 1910s, 1999; Canada through the Decades: The 1970s, 2000; Living Science: The Science of Fire, 2000; Living Science: The Science of Sound, 2000; Great Canadian Prime Ministers, 2000; 20th Century USA: History of the 1900s, 2002; Canadian Provinces: Quebec, 2002; Canadian Cities: Toronto, 2002; Roald Dahl, 2002; Canadian History: Canada in the Global Age, 2003; American Cities: New Orleans, 2003; War and Peace: The American Civil War, 2003; United Way, 2003; Ranching, 2003; Gold Rush, 2003; Whooping Cranes, 2003; Black-footed Ferret, 2003; E.B. White, 2003; Ronald Dahl, 2003; Caring for your Gecko, 2004; Columbus Day, 2004; Natural Landmarks, 2004; Construction: Structures, Style and Building, 2004; Cherokee, 2004; Navajo, 2004; Caring for Your Frog, 2005; Caring for Your Snake, 2005; Exploration of North America, 2005; Maasai, 2005; Sports: USAPast, Present, Future, 2009; Fashion: USA-Past, Present, Future, 2009; Trends: USA-Past, Present, Future, 2009; Foreign Affairs: USA Past, Present, Future, 2009; Science and Technology: USA Past, Present, Future, 2009; Economy: USA Past, Present and Future, 2009; Construction, 2009; Gecko, 2010; My Pet Snake, 2011; Frog: My Pet, 2011; Columbus Day: American Celebrations, 2011. FOR THE LOVE OF SERIES: Baseball, 2001; Basketball, 2001; Karate, 2002; Judo, 2002; Skateboarding, 2002; Biking, 2002; Snowboarding, 2002; Cycling, 2002; In-line Skating, 2002. AMERICAN STATES SERIES: Indiana, 2001; Michigan, 2001; Arizona, 2002; Illinois, 2002; New Mexico, 2002; New Hampshire, 2002; Maryland, 2002. Contributor to periodicals. **Address:** Weigl Publishers Inc., 350-5th Ave., 59th Fl., New York, NY 10118, U.S.A. **Online address:** boomerang-com@shaw.ca

CRABTREE, Adam. Canadian/American (born United States), b. 1938. **Genres:** Psychology, Medicine/Health, Psychiatry, Adult Non-fiction. **Career:** St. John's Abbey, monk; Center for Training in Psychotherapy, co-founder, 1985, training psychotherapist and lecturer, 1986-; Open International University, clinical teacher, 1993-; Willow Workshops, founder and director; Stress Analysis Consultants, co-founder; St. John's University, Humber College, lecturer; McMaster University, lecturer. Writer. **Publications:** Multiple Man: Explorations in Possession and Multiple Personality, 1985; Animal Magnetism, Early Hypnotism and Psychical Research from 1766 to 1925: An Annotated Bibliography, 1988; From Mesmer to Freud: Magnetic Sleep and the Roots of Psychological Healing, 1993; Trance Zero: Breaking the Spell of Conformity, 1997 in US as Trance Zero: The Psychology of Maximum Experience, 1999; (with E.F. Kelly and E.W. Kelly) Irreducible Mind: Toward a Psychology for the 21st Century, 2006. Contributor to journals. **Address:** Psychotherapy Services, 344 Dupont St., Ste. 401, Toronto, ON M5R 1V9, Canada. **Online address:** adamcrabtree@rogers.com

CRABTREE, John. British (born England), b. 1950. **Genres:** Area Studies, History, Politics/Government, Social Sciences. **Career:** Oxford Analytica (consulting firm), Latin America editor, 1985-97; Oxford University, St. Antony's College, senior associate, 1987-90, 1994-95, 2000-04, Latin American Centre, research associate; Universidade de Sao Paulo, visiting professor, 1990; University of London, Institute of Latin American Studies, visiting fellow, 1997-99. **Publications:** El fraude electoral en Bolivia, 1978; (with G. Duffy and J. Pearce) The Great Tin Crash, 1987; Peru Under García: An Opportunity Lost, 1992; (ed. with J. Thomas) Fujimori's Peru: The Political Economy, 1998; Perú de Fujimori: 1990-1998, 1999; (with L. Whitehead) Towards Democratic Viability: The Bolivian Experience, 2001; Peru: The Background, 2002; Patterns of Protest: Politics and Social Movements in Bolivia, 2005, 2nd ed. as Perfiles De La Protesta: Política y movimientos sociales en Bolivia, 2005; Construir instituciones: democracia, desarrollo y desigualdad en el Perú desde 1980, 2006; (ed.) Making Institutions Work in Peru: Democracy, Development and Inequality since 1980, 2006; (co-ed.) Unresolved Tensions: Bolivia Past and Present, 2008. **Address:** 11 Walton St., Oxford, OX SW3 2JD, England. **Online address:** crabtree-condor@crabtree-condor.u-net.com

CRACE, Jim. British (born England), b. 1946. **Genres:** Novels. **Career:** Voluntary Service Overseas, television assistant, 1968-69; Kgosi Kgari Sechele Secondary School, teacher, 1969; BBC, writing educational programmes, 1970; freelance radio and feature journalist, 1970-86; Midlands Arts Centre, writer-in-residence, 1981-83; novelist, 1986-; University of Central England (Birmingham City University), visiting professor of creative writing, 2001-06; University of Texas, James Michener Center, distinguished writer-in-residence, 2008, visiting professor of creative writing, 2009. **Publications:** NOVELS: Continent, 1986; The Gift of Stones, 1988; Arcadia, 1991; Signals of Distress, 1995; Quarantine, 1997; Being Dead, 2000; The Devil's Larder, 2001; Six, 2003; Genesis, 2003; The Pesthouse, 2007; All that Follows, 2010; Archipelago, forthcoming. Contributor to periodicals. **Address:** David Godwin Associates, 55 Monmouth St., London, GL WC2H 9DG, England. **Online address:** jim@crace.fsnet.co.uk

CRACKEN, Jael. *See* **ALDISS, Brian (Wilson).**

CRAFT, Michael. American (born United States), b. 1950?. **Genres:** Young Adult Fiction. **Career:** Chicago Tribune, art director, 1976-87. Writer. **Publications:** MARK MANNING SERIES: Flight Dreams, 1997; Eye Contact, 1998; Body Language, 1999; Name Games, 2000; Boy Toy, 2001; Hot Spot, 2002; Bitch Slap, 2004; The MacGuffin, 2011. CLAIRE GRAY SERIES: Rehearsing, 1993; Desert Autumn, 2001; Desert Winter, 2003; Desert Spring, 2004; Desert Summer, 2005. Contributor to periodicals. **Address:** c/o Author Mail, St. Martin Press, 175 5th Ave., New York, NY 10010, U.S.A. **Online address:** michael@michaelcraft.com

CRAGG, (Albert) Kenneth. British (born England), b. 1913. **Genres:** Theology/Religion, Translations, Bibliography, Literary Criticism And History. **Career:** Church of England, ordained deacon, priest, 1936-37; curate, 1936-39; chaplain, 1939-47; American University of Beirut, assistant professor of philosophy, 1942-47; Hartford Seminary Foundation, professor and chair of Arabic and Islamics, 1951-56; Muslim World Quarterly, editor, 1952-60; St. George's Collegiate Church, canon, 1956-61; St. Augustine's College, fellow, 1959-60, warden, 1961-67; Union Theological Seminary, visiting professor, 1965-66; University of Ibadan, visiting professor, 1968; Cambridge University, Gonville and Caius College, Bye fellow, 1968-73; University of Sussex, reader in religious studies, 1973-78; Anglican Archdiocese of Jerusalem, assistant bishop; Diocese of Oxford, honorary assistant bishop. Writer. **Publications:** The Call of the Minaret, 1956, rev. ed., 1985; Sandals at the Mosque, 1959; The Dome and the Rock, 1964; Counsels in Contemporary Islam, 1965; Christianity in World Perspective, 1968; The Privilege of Man: A Theme in Judiasm, 1968; The House of Islam, 1969, (with R.M. Speight) 1988, 3rd ed.; (comp. and intro.) Alive to God: Muslim and Christian Prayer,

1970; The Event of the Qurān, 1971; The Mind of the Qurān, 1973; (comp.) Wisdom of the Sufis, 1976; The Christian and Other Religion: The Measure of Christ, 1977; (comp. with R.M. Speight) Islam from Within: Anthology of a Religion, 1980; This Year in Jerusalem: Israel in Experience, 1982; (contrib.) Cathedral on the Nile: A History of All Saints Cathedral, Cairo, 1984; Muhammad and the Christian: A Question of Response, 1984, rev. ed., 1999; The Pen and the Faith: Eight Modern Muslim Writers and the Qurān, 1985; Jesus and the Muslim: An Exploration, 1985; The Christ and the Faiths: Theology in Cross-reference, 1987; Readings in the Qurān, 1988; What Decided Christianity, 1989; The Arab Christian: A History in the Middle East, 1991; Troubled by Truth, 1992; To Meet and to Greet 1993; Faith and Life Negotiate, 1994; Returning to Mount Hira, 1994; The Lively Credentials of God, 1995; Palestine: The Prize and Price of Zion, 1997; The Secular Experience of God, 1998; With God in Human Trust: Christian Faith and Contemporary Humanism: A Meeting of Minds, 1999; The Weight in the Word: Prophethood, Biblical and Quaranic, 1999; The Education of Christian Faith: Critical and Literary Encounters with the New Testament, 2000; Faiths in Their Pronouns: Websites of Identity, 2002; Muhammad in-the-Qurān, 2002; The Christian Jesus: Faith in the Finding, 2003; Certain Sympathy of Scriptures: Biblical and Quarnic, 2004; Semitism: The Whence and Whither, How Dear are Your Counsels, 2005; Faith at Suicide: Lives Forfeit: Violent Religion, Human Despair, 2005; Qurān and the West, 2005; God's Wrong is Most of All: Divine Capacity-Per Necessitatem Christianus, 2006; Christian-Muslim Inter-text Now: From Anathemata to Theme, 2008; Mosque Sermons: A Listener for the Preacher, 2008; Trans Action in Biblical Society, 2009; Iron in the Soul: Joseph and the Undoing of Violence, 2009; Compass of the Globe: Shakespeare's Drama, Mind and Faith, 2009; Bent to Literary Event: Masters in Their Masterpieces, 2011. TRANSLATOR: K. Husain, City of Wrong, 1959; M. Abduh, The Theology of Unity, 1966; T. Husain, A Passage to France, 1976; M.K. Hussein, The Hallowed Valley, 1977; (with E.H. Paxton and H. Wayment) T. Hussein, The Days, 1997; Readings in the Qurān, 1999. **Address:** 3 Goring Lodge, White House Rd., Oxford, OX OX1 4QE, England.

CRAGGS, Stewart R. British (born England), b. 1943. **Genres:** Music, Biography, Bibliography, Autobiography/Memoirs. **Career:** University of Sunderland, technical services librarian, 1973-81, reader services librarian, 1981-92, development services librarian, 1992-95, professor of music bibliography, 1993, now retired; freelance researcher and bibliographer, 1995-. Writer. **Publications:** William Walton: A Thematic Catalogue of his Musical Works, 1977, rev. ed., 1990; (comp.) Theses on North East England, 1983; William Alwyn: A Catalogue, 1985; Arthur Bliss: A Bio-Bibliography, 1988; Richard Rodney Bennett: A Bio-Bibliography, 1989; John McCabe: A Bio-Bibliography, 1991; William Walton: A Source Book, 1993; Alun Hoddinott: A Bio-Bibliography, 1993; William Mathias: A Bio-Bibliography, 1995; (comp.) Edward Elgar: A Source Book, 1995; (comp.) Arthur Bliss: A Source Book, 1996; Soundtracks: An International Dictionary of Composers for Film, 1998; Malcolm Arnold: A Bio-Bibliography, 1998; (ed.) William Walton: Music and Literature, 1999; (comp.) Lennox Berkeley: A Source Book, 2000; Benjamin Britten: A Bio-Bibliography, 2001; (comp.) Peter Maxwell Davies: A Source Book, 2002; (ed.) Arthur Bliss: Music and Literature, 2002; Alun Hoddinott: A Source Book, 2007; (comp.) John Ireland: A Catalogue, Discography and Bibliography, 2007; (comp.) Alan Bush: A Source Book, 2007. **Address:** 106 Mount Rd., High Barnes, Sunderland, TW SR4 7NN, England. **Online address:** stewcraggs@aol.com

CRAIG, Amanda. British/South African (born South Africa), b. 1959. **Genres:** Novels, Young Adult Fiction. **Career:** J. Walter Thompson, executive, 1981-82; Terence Conran, press officer, 1982-83; freelance journalist, 1983-85; Tatler, assistant features editor, 1985-86; Sunday Express, features writer, 1986-88; freelance writer, 1988-; London Times, columnist; Sunday Times, columnist; New Statesman, columnist. **Publications:** Foreign Bodies, 1990; A Private Place, 1991; A Vicious Circle, 1996; In a Dark Wood: A Novel, 2000; Love in Idleness, 2003; Hearts and Minds, 2009. Contributor to periodicals. **Address:** c/o Giles Gordon, Curtis Brown Agency, 6 Ann St., Edinburgh, EH4 1PJ, Scotland.

CRAIG, Barry L. Canadian (born Canada), b. 1960. **Genres:** Theology/Religion, Biography, Autobiography/Memoirs. **Career:** Saint Thomas University, associate professor of philosophy, 1997-. Writer. **Publications:** Apostle to the Wilderness: Bishop John Medley and the Evolution of the Anglican Church, 2005. **Address:** Holy Cross House, St. Thomas University, 51 Dineen Dr., Ste. 206, Fredericton, NB E3B 5G3, Canada. **Online address:** craig@stu.ca

CRAIG, Brian. *See* **STABLEFORD, Brian M(ichael).**

CRAIG, Colleen. Canadian (born Canada), b. 1956?. **Genres:** How-to Books, Sports/Fitness, Medicine/Health, Novels, Young Adult Non-fiction. **Career:** Writer. **Publications:** Pilates on the Ball: The World's Most Popular Workout Using the Exercise Ball, 2001; Abs on the Ball: A Pilates Approach to Building Superb Abdominals, 2003; Strength Training on the Ball: A Pilates Approach to Optimal Strength and Balance, 2005; (with J. Aronovitch and M. Taylor) Get On It!: BOSU Balance Trainer Workouts for Core Strength and a Super Toned Body, 2008; Afrika, 2008. Contributer to periodicals. **Address:** Tundra Books, 75 Sherbourne St., 5th Fl., Toronto, ON M5A 2P9, Canada. **Online address:** info@pilatesontheball.com

CRAIG, Daniel Edward. Canadian (born Canada), b. 1966. **Genres:** Mystery/Crime/Suspense, Novels, Literary Criticism And History. **Career:** Opus Hotel, general manager and vice president, 2002-. Writer. **Publications:** FIVE-STAR MYSTERY SERIES: Murder at the Universe, 2007; Murder at Hotel Cinema, 2008; Murder at Graverly Manor, 2009. **Address:** 1273 Richards St., Vancouver, BC V6B 3G3, Canada. **Online address:** dcraig@telus.net

CRAIG, David. *See* **TUCKER, (Allan) James.**

CRAIG, G(illian) M(ary). British/Welsh (born Wales), b. 1949. **Genres:** Agriculture/Forestry, Technology, Engineering, Sciences. **Career:** Commonwealth Bureau of Pastures and Field Crops, information scientist, 1970-76; University of Reading, Agricultural Extension and Rural Development Centre, research officer, 1976-78, Centre for Agricultural Strategy, research fellow, 1985-93; freelance consultant for agricultural information, 1993-. Writer. **Publications:** Information Systems in United Kingdom Agriculture, 1979; Information Systems for the Communication of U.K. Agriculture and Rural Land Use Information, 1995. EDITOR: (with J.L. Jollans and A. Korbey) The Case for Agriculture: An Independent Assessment, 1986; The Agriculture of the Sudan, 1991; The Agriculture of Egypt, 1993. **Address:** Center for Agricultural Strategy, University of Reading, 1 Early Gate, Reading, BR RG6 2AT, England.

CRAIG, Jeff. *See* **CRAIG, J. Marshall.**

CRAIG, J. Marshall. (Jeff Craig). American/Canadian (born Canada) **Genres:** Novels, Autobiography/Memoirs, Business/Trade/Industry, Economics. **Career:** Writer and director. **Publications:** Eating My Words, 1998; (as Jeff Craig) Playing with My Food: A Very Personal Cookbook, 1998, rev. ed., 2007; (with E. Burdon) Don't Let Me Be Misunderstood, 2001; (contrib.) She's a Bad Motorcycle Writers on Riding, 2002; Eh Mail, 2003; You're Lucky if You're Killed, 2003; Fabulous Shiksa in Distress, 2003; My Secret Life, 2004; (with C. Leavell) Between Rock and a Home Place, 2004; (with D. Young) Guilty by Association, 2011; (with C. Leavell) Growing A Better America: Smart, Strong and Sustainable, 2011. Contributor to books. **Address:** c/o Author Mail, Mercer University Press, 368 Orange St., 1400 Coleman Ave., Macon, GA 31201, U.S.A. **Online address:** agent@jmarshallcraig.com

CRAIG, Joe Alexander. British (born England), b. 1979. **Genres:** Children's Non-fiction. **Career:** Writer and Musician. **Publications:** JIMMY COATES SERIES: Jimmy Coates: Killer, 2005; Jimmy Coates: Target, 2006; Jimmy Coates: Revenge, 2007; Jimmy Coates: Sabotage, 2007; Jimmy Coates: Survival, 2008; Jimmy Coates: Power, 2008. Forthcoming: Jimmy Coates: Blackout, Jimmy Coates: Genesis. OTHER: Lifters, 2011. **Address:** c/o Sarah Manson, 6 Totnes Walk, London, GL N2 0AD, England. **Online address:** joe@joecraig.co.uk

CRAIG, Lee A(llen). American (born United States), b. 1960?. **Genres:** Economics, Business/Trade/Industry, History. **Career:** Indiana University, Center for Econometric Model Research, research associate, 1985-89; North Carolina State University, assistant professor, 1989-94, associate professor of economics, 1994-99, professor of economics, 1999-2004, alumni distinguished undergraduate professor, 2004-; Duke University, postdoctoral fellow, 1991-94, visiting professor of economics, 2000-04, 2006-10; National Bureau of Economic Research, faculty research fellow, 1991-95, research economist, 1995-2004. Writer. **Publications:** To Sow One Acre More: Childbearing and Farm Productivity in the Antebellum North, 1993; (with D. Fisher) The Integration of the European Economy, 1850-1913, 1997; (with D. Fisher) The European Macroeconomy: Growth, Integration and Cycles 1500-1913, 2000; (with R.L.

Clark and J.W. Wilson) A History of Public Sector Pensions in the United States, 2003; (with R.L. Clark and J. Sabelhaus) State and Local Retirement Plans in the United states, 2011. Contributor to journals. **Address:** Department of Economics, North Carolina State University, 4102B Nelson Hall, PO Box 8110, Raleigh, NC 27695, U.S.A. **Online address:** lee_craig@ncsu.edu

CRAIG, Patricia. British/Irish (born Ireland), b. 1949. **Genres:** Novels, Novellas/Short Stories, Adult Non-fiction, History. **Career:** The Literary Review, children's books editor; teacher, 1972-73; freelance writer, 1976-. **Publications:** (With M. Cadogan) You're a Brick, Angela!: A New Look at Girls' Fiction 1839-1975, 1976; (with M. Cadogan) Women and Children First: The Fiction of Two World Wars, 1978; (with M. Cadogan) The Lady Investigates: Women Detectives and Spies in Fiction, 1981; (with M. Cadogan) You're a Brick, Angela!: The Girls' Fiction 1839-1975, 1986; Elizabeth Bowen, 1986; (ed.) The Oxford Book of English Detective Stories, 1990; The Penguin Book of British Comic Stories, 1990; The Penguin Book of British Comic Writing, 1992; The Rattle of the North: An Anthology of Ulster Prose, 1992; (ed.) The Oxford Book of Schooldays, 1994; (ed.) The Oxford Book of Modern Women's Stories, 1994; (with S. Kaplan and C.A. Petravage) Historic Furnishings Report: Building 34/35, Harpers Ferry National Historical Park, Harpers Ferry, West Virginia, 1995; (ed.) The Oxford Book of Travel Stories, 1996; (intro.) Twelve Irish Ghost Stories, 1998; (ed.) Oxford Book of Ireland, 1998; (ed.) Belfast Anthology, 1999; (ed.) Oxford Book of Detective Stories, 2000; (ed.) Oxford Book of English Detective Stories, 2002; Brian Moore: A Biography, 2002; (ed.) Ulster Anthology, 2006; Asking for Trouble: The Story of an Escapade with Disproportionate Consequences, 2007. **Address:** 2 Cresswell Pk., Blackheath, London, GL SE3 9RD, England.

CRAIG, Robert H. (Robert Hedborg Craig). American (born United States), b. 1942. **Genres:** History, Politics/Government, Theology/Religion, Ethics, Area Studies, Civil Liberties/Human Rights. **Career:** University of Maine, instructor in philosophy, 1971-74; Bucknell University, visiting assistant professor of religion, 1976-78, visiting associate professor of religion and political science, 1983-86; National University of Costa Rica, professor of religion, 1978-82; Latin American Biblical Seminary, professor, 1980-82; College of the Holy Cross, assistant professor of social ethics, 1986-90; Mount Union College, associate professor of religious studies, 1990-96; The College of St. Scholastica, director of general education, 1996-99, Department of History, professor of history and international studies, 1999, chair, through 2008; Unted International College, visiting professor of government and international studies, 2009-10. Writer. **Publications:** (With J.M. Bonino and C. Alvarez) Protestantismo y Liberalismo en America Latina, 1985; Religion and Radical Politics: An Alternative Christian Tradition in the United States, 1992; Religion and Civil Liberties in Times of War: Race, Citizenship, and the Internment of Japanese-Americans, forthcoming. **Address:** 1000 Cannon Valley Dr., Apt. 108, Northfield, MN 55057, U.S.A. **Online address:** rcraig@css.edu

CRAIG, Robert Hedborg. *See* **CRAIG, Robert H.**

CRAIG, Stephen C. American (born United States), b. 1948. **Genres:** Politics/Government. **Career:** Northwestern University Evening Division, instructor, 1976-77; Texas Tech University, visiting assistant professor, 1977-78; University of New Mexico, visiting assistant professor, 1978-79; University of Florida, assistant professor, 1979-85, associate professor, 1985-94, professor of political science, 1994-, director of graduate program, 1985-, department chair; Florida Campaign Associates, partner and political consultant. Writer. **Publications:** The Malevolent Leaders: Popular Discontent in America, 1993. EDITOR AND CONTRIBUTOR: Broken Contract?: Changing Relationships Between Americans and Their Government, 1995; After the Boom: The Politics of Generation X, 1997; (with M.D. Martinez) Ambivalence, Politics, and Public Policy, 2005; (with M.D. Martinez) Ambivalence and the Structure of Political Opinion, 2005; The Electoral Challenge: Theory Meets Practice, 2006. **Address:** Department of Political Science, University of Florida, 3324 Turlington Hall, PO Box 117325, Gainesville, FL 32611-7325, U.S.A. **Online address:** sccraig@ufl.edu

CRAIK, Elizabeth M(ary). Scottish (born Scotland), b. 1939. **Genres:** History, Classics. **Career:** University of Birmingham, research fellow in Greek, 1963-64; University of St. Andrews, assistant lecturer, senior lecturer in Greek, 1967-97, honorary professor, 1997-, associate; Kyoto University, Kyoto, professor of classics, 1997-2002; University of Newcastle upon Tyne, visiting professor. Writer. **Publications:** The Dorian Aegean, 1980; (ed. and trans.) Euripides, Phoenician Women, 1988; (ed.) Owls to Athens: Essays on Classical Subjects Presented to Sir Kenneth Dover, 1990; (ed.) Marriage and Property: Women and Marital Customs in History, 1991; (ed., trans. and intro.) Hippocrates: Places in Man, 1998; Stobaeus: The Seven Deadly Sins, 1998; (ed., trans. and intro.) Two Hippocratic Treatises on Sight and on Anatomy, 2006; (ed., trans. and intro.) Hippocratic Treatise on Glands, 2009. **Address:** School of Classics, University of St. Andrews, Swallowgate, The Scores, St. Andrews, FF KY16 9AL, Scotland. **Online address:** ec@st-andrews.ac.uk

CRAIK, T(homas) W(allace). British (born England), b. 1927. **Genres:** Literary Criticism And History, History, Theatre, Poetry, Young Adult Fiction. **Career:** University of Leicester, assistant lecturer, 1953-55, lecturer, 1955-65; City University of New York, visiting lecturer, 1958-59; University of Aberdeen, lecturer, 1965-67, senior lecturer, 1967-73; University of Dundee, professor of English, 1973-77; University of Durham, professor of English, 1977-89, professor emeritus, 1989-. Writer. **Publications:** The Tudor Interlude: Stage, Costume and Acting, 1958, 3rd ed., 1967; The Comic Tales of Chaucer, 1964; A Fly in Shakespeare's Amber, 1981. EDITOR: Massinger, A New Way to Pay Old Debts, 1964; Massinger, The City Madam, 1964; Selected Poetry and Prose of Sir Philip Sidney, 1965; Marlowe, The Jew of Malta, 1966; Minor Elizabethan Tragedies, 1974; (with J.M. Lothian) Shakespeare, Twelfth Night, 1975; (with C. Leech and L. Potter) The Revels History of Drama in English, 6 vols., 1975-83; (with R.J. Craik) John Donne: Selected Poetry and Prose, 1986; Beaumont and Fletcher, The Maid's Tragedy, 1988; Shakespeare, The Merry Wives of Windsor, 1989; Shakespeare, King Henry V, 1995. Contributor to periodicals. **Address:** Department of English Studies, University of Durham, Hallgarth House, 77 Hallgarth St., Durham, DU DH1 3AY, England.

CRAIS, Clifton C(harles). American (born United States), b. 1960. **Genres:** History, Race Relations. **Career:** University of London, London School of Oriental and African Studies, Institute of Commonwealth Studies, faculty, 1985-, Institute of Historical Research, faculty, 1985-86; Kenyon College, visiting instructor, 1987-88, assistant professor, 1988-93, associate professor of history, 1993-2001, founder and chairperson of Kenyon seminar, 1990-93, professor of history, 2001-04; University of Cape Town, visiting assistant professor, 1988-89, Center for African Studies, visiting associate, 1988-89, 1991-92, post-doctoral research fellow, 1989; Stanford University, Stanford Humanities Center, fellow, 1994-95; Emory University, professor of history, 2004-, Interdisciplinary Workshop in Colonial and Post-Colonial Studies, co-director, 2005-, Institute of African Studies, director, 2010-. Writer. **Publications:** White Supremacy and Black Resistance in Pre-Industrial South Africa: The Making of the Colonial Order in the Eastern Cape, 1770-1865, 1992; (ed. with N. Worden) Breaking the Chains: Slavery and Its Legacy in Nineteenth-Century South Africa, 1994; Politics of Evil: Magic, State Power and The Political Imagination in South Africa, 2002; (ed.) Culture of Power in Southern Africa: Essays on State Formation and the Political Imagination, 2003; (ed.) Oxford Encyclopedia of World History, 8 vols., 2008; (with P. Scully) Sara Baartman and the Hottentot Venus: A Ghost Story and a Biography, 2009; Poverty, War, and Violence in South Africa, 2011. FORTHCOMING: A Century of Sadness: Violence and Poverty in South Africa; The Memory Box; (with P. Scully) A South African Reader; History Lessons. Contributor of articles to periodicals. **Address:** Department of History, Emory University, 326 Bowden Hall, 561 S Kilgo Cir., Atlanta, GA 30322, U.S.A. **Online address:** ccrais@emory.edu

CRAMER, Clayton E. American (born United States), b. 1956. **Genres:** History, Military/Defense/Arms Control, Reference, Technology. **Career:** Telos Computing, technical staff, 1975-76, account executive and technical staff, 1979; Delta Management Systems, employment agent, 1976-79; Raytheon, Lexitron Division, engineer, 1979-80; Futuredata (now Kontron Electronics), software engineer III, 1980-82, software project leader, 1984-87; Harris Digital Telephone Systems, software engineer III, 1982-84; Optilink Corp., software engineer, 1987-96; Nokia Diamond Lane Communications, senior software engineer and manager of technical marketing, 1996-2000; American Communication Technologies Intl., software engineer, 2000-01; Hewlett-Packard Corp., research and development engineer, 2001-08; Paladin POS Systems, contractor, 2008-09. Writer. **Publications:** (Ed.) By the Dim and Flaring Lamps: The Civil War Diary of Samuel McIlvaine, 1990; For the Defense of Themselves and the State: The Original Intent and Judicial Interpretation of the Right to Keep and Bear Arms, 1994; Firing Back!: Defending Your Right to Keep and Bear Arms, 1994; Black Demographic Data, 1790-1860: A Sourcebook, 1997; Concealed Weapon Laws of the Early Republic:

Dueling, Southern Violence, and Moral Reform, 1999; Armed America: The Remarkable Story of How and Why Guns became as American as Apple Pie, 2006. Contributor to periodicals. **Address:** 36 Sunburst Rd., Horseshoe Bend, ID 83629-9007, U.S.A. **Online address:** clayton@claytoncramer.com

CRAMER, John G(leason). American (born United States), b. 1934. **Genres:** Physics. **Career:** Indiana University, postdoctoral fellow, 1961-63, assistant professor, 1963-64; University of Washington, assistant professor, 1964-68, associate professor, 1968-74, professor, 1974-, Nuclear Physics Laboratory, director, 1983-90; Lawrence Berkeley Laboratory, program advisor and consultant, 1979-82; Analog Magazine, columnist, 1983-; National Superconducting Cyclotron Laboratory, staff, 1983-87; University of British Columbia, staff, 1985-88. **Publications:** Twistor, 1989; Einstein's Bridge, 1997. Contributor to periodicals. **Address:** Department of Physics, University of Washington, PO Box 351560, Seattle, WA 98195-1560, U.S.A. **Online address:** cramer@phys.washington.edu

CRAMER, Richard Ben. American (born United States), b. 1950. **Genres:** Biography, Politics/Government, Theology/Religion, Sports/Fitness. **Career:** Sun, reporter, 1973-76; Philadelphia Inquirer, reporter, 1976-78, foreign correspondent 1978-; Esquire, contributing editor; Rolling Stone, journalist. **Publications:** Ted Williams: The Season of the Kid, 1991; What It Takes: The Way to the White House, 1992; Bob Dole, 1995; Joe DiMaggio: The Hero's Life, 1999; What Do You Think of Ted Williams Now?: A Remembrance, 2002; How Israel Lost: The Four Questions, 2004. Contributor to newspapers and periodicals. **Address:** Sterling Lord Literistic Inc., 65 Bleeker St., New York, NY 10012-2420, U.S.A.

CRAMER, Stanley H. American (born United States), b. 1933. **Genres:** Education, Psychology, How-to Books. **Career:** State University of New York, professor and associate provost, 1965-2001, professor emeritus, 2001-. Writer. **Publications:** (With E.L. Herr) Guidance of the College Bound: Problems, Practices and Perspectives, 1968; (with E.L. Herr, C.N. Morris and T.T. Frantz) Research and the School Counselor, 1970; (ed. with J.D. Hansen) Group Guidance and Counseling in the Schools, 1971; (with E.L. Herr) Vocational Guidance and Career Development in the Schools: Toward a Systems Approach, 1972; (with E.L. Herr) Career Guidance through the Lifespan: Systematic Approaches, 1979, (with E.L. Herr and S.G. Niles) 6th ed., 2004; Perspectives on Work and the Family, 1984; (with E.L. Herr) Controversies in the Mental Health Professions, 1987; (with J.C. Hansen and R.H. Rossberg) Counseling: Theory and Process, 1993. **Address:** Sarsota, FL , U.S.A. **Online address:** staroz1676@aol.com

CRAMER, W. American (born United States) **Genres:** Young Adult Fiction, Novels. **Career:** Novelist, electrician and part-time construction worker. **Publications:** Sutter's Cross, 2003; Bad Ground, 2004; Levi's Will: A Novel, 2005; Summer of Light: A Novel, 2007; Paradise Valley, 2011. Contributor to periodicals. **Address:** c/o Author Mail, Bethany House Publishers, 11400 Hampshire Ave. S, Minneapolis, MN 55438, U.S.A.

CRAMSIE, John. American (born United States), b. 1964?. **Genres:** History. **Career:** Drury University, visiting assistant professor, 1997-2000; Union College, associate professor of history, 2000-. Writer. **Publications:** Kingship and Crown Finance under James VI and I, 1603-1625, 2002; (contrib.) The Crisis of 1614 and the Addled Parliament: Literary and Historical Perspectives, 2003; (contrib.) James VI and I: Ideas, Authority and Government, 2007. Contributor to journals. **Address:** Department of History, Union College, 36 Union Ave., Ste. 101, Schenectady, NY 12308, U.S.A. **Online address:** cramsiej@union.edu

CRANDALL, Susan. American (born United States) **Genres:** Young Adult Fiction, Romance/Historical, Novels. **Career:** Writer. **Publications:** Back Roads, 2003; The Road Home, 2004; Magnolia Sky, 2004; Promises to Keep, 2005; On Blue Falls Pond, 2006; A Kiss in Winter, 2007; Pitch Black, 2008; Seeing Red, 2009; Sleep No More, 2010. Contributor to periodicals. **Address:** PO Box 1092, Noblesville, IN 46061, U.S.A. **Online address:** susan@susancrandall.net

CRANDELL, Doug. American (born United States) **Genres:** Novels. **Career:** Georgia Writers Association, writing instructor; Midwest Writers Workshop, writing instructor; Virginia Center for the Creative Arts, Sherwood Anderson fellow; Goldfarb fellow, 2005. Writer. **Publications:** Pig Boy's Wicked Bird (memoir), 2004; The All-American Industrial Motel (memoir), 2007; The Flawless Skin of Ugly People (novel), 2007; Hairdos of the Mildly Depressed (novel), 2008. Contributor to periodicals and journals. **Address:** c/o Robert Guinsler, Sterling Lord Literistic Inc., 65 Bleecker St., New York, NY 10012, U.S.A. **Online address:** pigboy@dougcrandell.com

CRANE, Caroline. (Carolyn Wesley). American (born United States), b. 1930. **Genres:** Mystery/Crime/Suspense, Young Adult Fiction, Romance/Historical. **Career:** Author. **Publications:** Lights Down the River, 1963; Pink Sky at Night, 1964; A Girl Like Tracy, 1966; Wedding Song, 1967; Don't Look at Me that Way, 1970; Stranger on the Road, 1971; Summer Girl, 1979; The Girls Are Missing, 1980; Coast of Fear, 1981; Wife Found Slain, 1981; The Foretelling, 1982; The Third Passenger, 1983; Trick or Treat, 1983; Woman Vanishes, 1984; Something Evil, 1984; Someone at the Door, 1985; Circus Day, 1986; Man in the Shadows, 1987; (as Carolyn Wesley) King's Castle, 1987; The People Next Door, 1988; Whispers from Oracle Falls, 1991; Night Memories, 1994; The Love Detective, 1994; Land of Glory, 2003; Murder and Mayhem in the Catskills, 2008. **Address:** 62 Herschel Dr., Wurtsboro, NY 12790-4502, U.S.A. **Online address:** caroline.crane48@gmail.com

CRANE, Conrad C(harles). American (born United States), b. 1952. **Genres:** History, Military/Defense/Arms Control. **Career:** United States Military Academy, assistant professor, 1983-86, associate professor, 1990-97, professor of American and military history, 1997-2000; United States Army Air Defense Artillery School, chief and military historian, 1986-88; 6th Air Defense Artillery, 2nd Battalion, battalion executive officer, 1988-90; United States Army War College, research professor of military strategy, 2000-03, United States Army Military History Institute, director, 2003-, Strategic Studies Institute, researcher, 2000-. Writer. **Publications:** Bombs, Cities, and Civilians: American Airpower Strategy in World War II, 1993; Civilians: American Airpower Strategy in World War II, 1993; (ed. with R. Doughty) West Point Atlas of American Wars: 1900-1918, rev. ed., 1997; American Airpower Strategy in Korea, 1950-1953, 2000; Alternative National Military Strategies for the United States, 2000; Landpower and Crises: Army Roles and Missions in Smaller-Scale Contingencies during the 1990s, 2001; (ed.) Transforming Defense, 2001; (with W.A. Terrill) Reconstructing Iraq: Insights, Challenges, and Missions for Military Forces in a Post-conflict Scenario, 2003; (with W.A. Terrill) Precedents, Variables, and Options in Planning a U.S. Military Disengagement Strategy from Iraq, 2005. Works appear in anthologies. Contributor to journals. **Address:** United States Army Military History Institute, United States Army War College, 632 Wright Ave., Carlisle, PA 17013-5244, U.S.A. **Online address:** conrad.crane@carlisle.army.mil

CRANE, Elizabeth. American (born United States), b. 1961. **Genres:** Novellas/Short Stories. **Career:** Northwestern University School of Continuing Studies, writing teacher; University of Chicago, writing teacher; University of California Riverside, faculty. Writer. **Publications:** SHORT-STORIES: When the Messenger Is Hot: Stories, 2003; All This Heavenly Glory: Stories, 2005; Feu Occulte, 2005; Bonté Divine, 2006; You Must Be This Happy to Enter: Stories, 2008; Banana Love, 2009; We Only Know So Much: A Novel, 2012. Contributor to periodicals. **Address:** Jean V. Naggar Literary Agency Inc., 216 E 75th St., Ste. 1E, New York, NY 10021, U.S.A. **Online address:** mabyers18@aol.com

CRANE, Hamilton. *See* **MASON, Sarah J.**

CRANE, Peter R(obert). American/British (born England), b. 1954. **Genres:** Natural History, Botany, Sciences. **Career:** University of Reading, lecturer in botany, 1978-81, School of Plant Sciences, visiting professor, 1999-2006; Indiana University, researcher in biology, 1981-82; Field Museum of Natural History, assistant curator of paleobotany, 1982-85, associate curator, 1985-90, curator, 1990-92, MacArthur curator, 1992-94, Department of Geology, chairperson, 1991-92, Center for Evolutionary and Environmental Biology, vice president, 1992-93, vice-president for academic affairs, 1994-, A. Watson Armour III curator, 1994-, director of the museum, 1995-99, research associate, 1999-; University of Chicago, lecturer, 1984-, research associate in geophysical sciences, 1989-92, professor, 1992-, John and Marion Sullivan university professor, 2006-; University of Zurich, visiting professor, 1987; University of Massachusetts, Department of Biology, adjunct professor, 1989-; Natural History Museum, visiting research fellow, 1990-93, Department of Botany, honorary research fellow, 2002-; Smithsonian Institution, senior Mellon fellow, 1993-95; Takamatsu University, senior fellow, 1997; The Royal Botanic Gardens, director and chief executive officer, 1999-2006, honorary research fellow, 2006-; Chinese Academy of Sciences, Xishuangbanna Tropical Botanical Garden, adjunct professor, 2004-; University of London, visiting professor, 2000-06; Imperial College of Science & Technology, Department of Biological Sciences, visiting professor, 2002-06. Writer. **Publications:** (With E.M. Friis and K.R. Pedersen) Reproductive Structures of Cretaceous Platanaceae, 1988; (with G.R. Upchurch, Jr. and A.N. Drinnan) The Megaflora from the Quantico Locality (Upper Albian), Lower Cretaceous Potomac Group of Virginia, 1994; (with P. Kenrick) The Origin and Early Diversification of Land Plants, 1997; (with E.M. Friis and K.R. Pedersen) Early Flowers and Angiosperm Evolution, 2011. EDITOR: (with E.M. Friis and W.G. Chaloner and contrib.) The Origins of Angiosperms and Their Biological Consequences, 1987; (with S. Blackmore and contrib.) The Evolution, Systematics, and Fossil History of the Hamamelidae, 2 vols., 1989; (with S. Lidgard) The Fifth North American Paleontological Convention: Abstracts and Program, 1992; (with P.S. Herendeen) The Origin of Modern Terrestrial Ecosystems: Fossils, Phylogeny and Biogeography, 1999. **Address:** Department of Geophysical Sciences, University of Chicago, Hinds 201, 5734 S Ellis Ave., Chicago, IL 60637, U.S.A. **Online address:** pcrane@geosci.uchicago.edu

CRANE, Richard (Arthur). British (born England), b. 1944. **Genres:** Plays/Screenplays, Songs/Lyrics And Libretti, Children's Fiction. **Career:** Actor, writer and director for theater, film and television, 1966-; University of Bradford, fellow in theatre, 1972-74; National Theatre, resident dramatist, 1974-75; University of Leicester, fellow in creative writing, 1976; Royal Court Theatre, literary manager, 1978-79; Brighton Theatre, associate director, 1980-85; Tron Theatre, dramaturg, 1983-84; University of East Anglia, fellow in creative writing, 1988; University of Maryland, lecturer in English, 1990; Birmingham Polytechnic, writer-in-residence, 1990-91; University of Birmingham, tutor in playwriting, 1990-91; University of Sussex, lecturer in creative writing and literature development, 1994-. **Publications:** Thunder: A Play of the Brontës, 1976; Gunslinger: A Wild West Show, 1979; Under the Stars: A Comedy, 1994. **Address:** Casarotto Ramsay & Associates Ltd., Waverley House, 7-12 Noel St., London, GL W1F 8GQ, England.

CRANFIELD, Charles Ernest Burland. British (born England), b. 1915. **Genres:** Theology/Religion, Reference, Young Adult Fiction. **Career:** University of Durham, lecturer in theology, 1950-62, senior lecturer, 1962-66, reader, 1966-78, professor of theology, 1978-80, emeritus professor, 1980-; International Critical Commentary, joint general editor, 1966-. **Publications:** The First Epistle of Peter, 1950; The Gospel According to Saint Mark, 1959; I and II Peter and Jude, 1960; A Commentary on Romans 12-13, 1965; (ed. with J.A. Emerton and G.N. Stanton) The International Critical Commentary on the Holy Scriptures of the Old and New Testaments, 1969; A Critical and Exegetical Commentary on the Epistle to the Romans, 1975, 3rd ed., 1983; Romans: A Shorter Commentary, 1985; The Bible and Christian Life (essays), 1985; If God Be For Us (sermons), 1985; The Apostles' Creed: A Faith to Live By, 1993; On Romans and Other New Testament Essays, 1998. **Address:** 30 Western Hill, Durham, DH1 4RL, England.

CRANFIELD, Ingrid. British (born England), b. 1945. **Genres:** Architecture, Art/Art History, Children's Non-fiction, Geography, Natural History, Recreation, Travel/Exploration, Language/Linguistics, Translations, Education, International Relations/Current Affairs, Politics/Government. **Career:** International Wool Secretariat, research assistant, 1966-68; Royal Geographical Society, senior assistant, 1968-72; writer, translator and teacher, 1972-; Map Productions Ltd., map project coordinator, 1972; Endeavour Training Ltd., board trustee, 1978-; London Borough of Barnet, Comprehensive Secondary School, governor, 1988-2003; London Borough of Enfield-Primary School, governor, 1999-, chairman of governors, 2004-; Dictionary of Art, senior desk editor, 1991-96; West Herts College, Professional Development Diploma in Publishing Course, lecturer, tutor and course leader, 2002-04; Southgate College, Literacy Learning Support, tutor, 2005-10, lecturer, 2008-; Editing and Proofreading Course, lecturer and course manager, 2005-10. **Publications:** The Challengers: British and Commonwealth Adventure since 1945, 1976; Skiing Down Everest and Other Crazy Adventures, 1983; Q Challenge Quiz Books, 4 vols., 1988; Animal World, 1991; 100 Greatest Natural Wonders, 1997; Georgian House Style: An Architectural and Interior Design Source Book, 1997; The Archaeology Kit: Science Action Book, 1998; Art Deco House Style: An Architectural and Interior Design Source Book, 2001; At Last Michael Reeves: An Investigative Memoir of the Acclaimed Filmmaker, 2007. TRANSLATOR: (with P. Adler) The Ships of the German Fleets, 1848-1945, 1974; Genghis Khan, 1990; Kosmogenese (Cosmogenesis), 2009. EDITOR: (with R. Harrington) Off the Beaten Track, 1977; (with R. Harrington) The Independent Traveller's Handbook, 1980; (with R. Harrington) The International Traveler's Handbook in UK as The Traveller's Handbook, 1982; The Age of the Dinosaurs, 12 vols., 2000; The Illustrated Directory of Dinosaurs and Other Prehistoric Creatures, 2000. Contributor of articles to periodicals. **Address:** 16 Myddelton Gardens, Winchmore Hill, London, GL N21 2PA, England. **Online address:** ingrid_cranfield@hotmail.com

CRANG, Jeremy A. British (born England) **Genres:** History. **Career:** University of Edinburgh, lecturer, 1993-2003, senior lecturer in history, 2003-, Centre for Second World War Studies, assistant director and deputy head of history. Writer. **Publications:** The British Army and the People's War, 1939-1945, 2000; (ed. with P. Addison) The Burning Blue: A New History of the Battle of Britain, 2000; (ed. with P. Addison) Firestorm: The Bombing of Dresden 1945, 2006; (ed. and intro. with P. Addison) Listening To Britain: Home Intelligence Reports on Britain's Finest Hour, May To September 1940, 2010. **Address:** School of History, Classics and Archaeology, University of Edinburgh, Rm. 2.34, Doorway 4, Teviot Pl., William Robertson Bldg., 50 George Sq., Edinburgh, EH8 9AG, Scotland. **Online address:** j.a.crang@ed.ac.uk

CRANSHAW, Whitney. American (born United States) **Genres:** Zoology, Horticulture, Environmental Sciences/Ecology, Homes/Gardens. **Career:** Colorado State University, professor of entomology and extension specialist. Writer and entomologist. **Publications:** Pests of the West: Prevention and Control for Today's Garden and Small Farm, 1992, rev. ed., 1998; (with B. Kondratieff) Bagging Big Bugs: How to Identify, Collect and Display the Largest and Most Colorful Insects of the Rocky Mountain Region, 1995; Garden Insects of North America: The Ultimate Guide to Backyard Bugs, 2004; (with B. Kondratieff) Guide to Colorado Insects, 2006. Contributor to periodicals and journals. **Address:** Department of Bioagricultural Science and, Pest Management, Colorado State University, C201 Plant Sciences Bldg., Ft. Collins, CO 80523-1177, U.S.A. **Online address:** whitney.cranshaw@colostate.edu

CRARY, Alice. *See* **CRARY, Alice Marguerite.**

CRARY, Alice Marguerite. (Alice Crary). American (born United States), b. 1967. **Genres:** Philosophy, Social Sciences. **Career:** Colegio Americano de Quito, teacher, 1990-91; Greater Pittsburgh Womens Center and Shelter, counselor and advocate, 1992-93, 1994-98; New School University, New School for Social Research, Department of philosophy, assistant professor, 2000-06, associate professor, 2006-. Writer. **Publications:** (Ed. with R. Read) The New Wittgenstein, 2000; (ed. with S. Shieh) Reading Cavell, 2006; (ed.) Wittgenstein and the Moral Life: Essays in Honor of Cora Diamond, 2007; Beyond Moral Judgment, 2007, Humans, Animals, Right and Wrong, forthcoming. **Address:** Department of Philosophy, New School for Social Research, Eugene Lang College of New School University, Rm. 1115, 6 E 16th St., 79 5th Ave., New York, NY 10003, U.S.A. **Online address:** crarya@newschool.edu

CRARY, Elizabeth (Ann). American (born United States), b. 1942. **Genres:** Human Relations/Parenting, Children's Non-fiction. **Career:** University of Wisconsin, Food Research Institute, research assistant, 1966-70, food science department, 1971-77; Parenthood Education Programs, founder and director, 1974-77; North Seattle Community College, instructor in parent education, 1977; Parenting Press, publisher, 1978; Parent Education Associates, co-director, 1980; STAR Parenting, founder, parent educator, speaker and author. **Publications:** NON-FICTION: Without Spanking or Spoiling: A Practical Approach to Toddler and Preschool Guidance, 1979, 2nd ed., 1993; Kids Can Cooperate: A Practical Guide to Teaching Problem Solving, 1984; Pick Up Your Socks and Other Skills Growing Children Need!, 1990; Love & Limits: Guidance Tools for Creative Parenting, 1994; Magic Tools for Raising Kids, 1995; 365 Wacky, Wonderful Ways to Get Your Children to Do What You Want, 1995. DEALING WITH FEELINGS SERIES: One Dozen Feeling Games, 1980; I'm Proud, 1992; I'm Frustrated, 1992; I'm Mad, 1992; I'm Excited, 1994; I'm Furious, 1994; I'm Scared, 1994; (with S. Steelsmith) When You're Happy and You Know It: Feelings for Little Children, 1996; (with S. Steelsmith) When You're Mad and You Know It, 1996; (with S. Steelsmith) When You're Silly and You Know It, 1996; Dealing with Disappointment: Helping Kids Cope When Things Don't Go Their Way, 2003; The Feeling Elf Cards and Games, 2003; Self-calming Cards and Games, 2004. CHILDREN'S PROBLEM SOLVING SERIES: I Can't Wait, 1982, 2nd ed., 1996; I Want It, 1982, 2nd ed., 1996; I Want to Play, 1982, 2nd ed., 1996; My Name is Not Dummy, 1983, 2nd ed., 1996; I'm Lost, 1985, 2nd ed., 1996; Mommy Don't Go, 1986, 2nd ed., 1996; Finders, Keepers?, 1987; Help! The Kids

Areat It Again: Using Kids' Quarrels to Teach People Skills, 1997; Amy's Disappearing Pickle, 2001; Willy's Noisy Sister, 2001; Heidi's Irresistible Hat, 2001. OTHERS: When You're Shy and You Know It, 1996; STAR Parenting Tales and Tools, 2011. **Address:** Parenting Press Inc., PO Box 75267, Seattle, WA 98175-0267, U.S.A. **Online address:** fam181@starparent.com

CRAVEN, Michael. American (born United States), b. 1970. **Genres:** Novels, Literary Criticism And History. **Career:** Grey Entertainment, advertising copywriter; Music Television Network (MTV), advertising copywriter; TBWA-Chiat-Day, advertising copywriter; Crispin Porter + Bogusky, associate creative director, 2007-. **Publications:** Body Copy, 2009. Contributor to periodicals. **Address:** Crispin Porter + Bogusky, 6450 Gunpark Dr., Boulder, CO 80301, U.S.A.

CRAVEN, Sara. (Anne Bushell). British (born England), b. 1938?. **Genres:** Romance/Historical, Novels. **Career:** Writer. **Publications:** Garden of Dreams, 1975; A Place of Storms, 1977; Temple of the Moon, 1977; Strange Adventure, 1977; Wild Melody, 1977; Gift for a Lion, 1977; Past All Forgetting, 1978; Dragon's Lair, 1978; The Devil at Archangel, 1978; High Tide at Midnight, 1978; Solitaire, 1979; Flame of Diablo, 1979; Moth to the Flame, 1979; Moon of Aphrodite, 1980; Fugitive Wife, 1980; Shadow of Desire, 1980; Summer of the Raven, 1981; Witching Hour, 1981; Dark Summer Dawn, 1981; Unguarded Moment, 1982; Counterfeit Bride, 1982; A Bad Enemy, 1983; Sup with the Devil, 1983; Pagan Adversary, 1983; Dark Paradise, 1984; Act of Betrayal, 1985; Alien Vengeance, 1985; Escape Me Never, 1985; Promise of the Unicorn, 1985; The Marriage Deal, 1986; A High Price to Pay, 1986; Witch's Harvest, 1987; Outsider, 1987; Night of the Condor, 1987; King of the Swords, 1988; Devil and the Deep Sea and King of Swords, 1988; Devil and the Deep Sea, 1988; Comparative Strangers, 1988; Storm Force, 1989; Flawless, 1989; Island of the Heart, 1989; The Sara Craven Collection, 1990; Desperate Measures, 1991; When the Devil Drives, 1991; Alien Vengeance and Dark Paradise, 1992; Dark Ransom, 1992; The Sara Craven Duet, 1993; Dawn Song, 1993; Tower of Shadows, 1993; Dark Apollo, 1994; Thunder on the Reef, 1994; (with L. Armstrong) Marriage of Convenience: Marrying Game; Marriage Deal, 1995; Deceived, 1996; Ultimate Temptation, 1997; A Nanny for Christmas, 1997; One Reckless Night, 1997; (with J. Baird and E. Darcy) Passion with a Vengeance, 1998; Marriage at a Distance, 1998; Marriage under Suspicion, 1998; Seduction Game, 1999; Irresistible Temptation, 1999; Bartaldi's Bride, 1999; The Tycoons Mistress, 2000; Mistress on Loan, 2000; Marriage by Deception, 2000; Smokescreen Marriage, 2001; Rome's Revenge, 2001; The Marriage Proposition, 2002; The Marriage Truce, 2002; His Convenient Marriage, 2002; The Forced Marriage, 2002; The Token Wife, 2003; (with M. Reid and S. Weston) Hot Latin Lovers, 2003; (with J. Baird and C. Williams) Passion in Paradise, 2004; (with P. Jordan and A. McAllister) Greek Millionaires, 2004; (with J. Matthews and M. Way) A Christmas Engagement, 2004; Mistress at a Price, 2004; His Forbidden Bride, 2004; The Bedroom Barter, 2004; The Marcheses Love Child, 2005; In the Millionaire's Possession, 2005; His Wedding Night Heir, 2005; The Count's Blackmail Bargain, 2005; (with R. Donald and A. Mather) Dark Seductions, 2005; (with M. Mayo) Escape to Greek Affairs, 2006; (with S. Field and S. Napier) His Virgin Lover, 2006; (with E. Darcy and K. Lawrence) Sweet Revenge, 2006; Bride of Desire, 2006; Wife Against Her Will, 2006; (with D. Hamilton and C. Marinelli) The Italian's Pleasure, 2006; Innocent On Her Wedding Night, 2007; The Forced Bride, 2007; (with E. Darcy and J. Hart) Blind-Date Grooms, 2007; Marriage Vows, 2008; The Virgin's Wedding Night, 2008; One Night with His Virgin Mistress, 2008; Ruthless Awakening, 2009; The Innocent's Surrender, 2009; Huerfana de Amor: Love Orphan, 2009; Santangeli Marriage, 2009; His Untamed Innocent, 2010; The Highest Stakes of All, 2011; Wife in the Shadows, 2011; The End of Her Innocence, 2012. **Address:** c/o Author Mail, Harlequin Enterprises Ltd., PO Box 5190, Buffalo, NY 14240-5190, U.S.A.

CRAVENS, Hamilton. American (born United States), b. 1938. **Genres:** History. **Career:** Iowa State University, fellow, 1964-65, instructor, 1968-73, associate professor, 1973-80, professor of history, 1980-; Goettingen University, George Bancroft professor of American history, distinguished Fulbright professorship in American history, 1988-89; University of Maryland, faculty; Ohio State University, faculty; University of Washington, faculty; University of California, faculty, Davis Humanities Center, fellow, 1990-92. **Publications:** The Triumph of Evolution: American Scientists and the Heredity-Environment Controversy, 1900-1941, 1978, rev. ed., 1988; (ed.) Ideas in America's Cultures from Republic to Mass Society, 1982; Before Head Start, 1993, rev. ed., 2002; Technical Knowledge in American Culture: Science, Technology and Medicine Since the Early 1800s, 1996; Health Care Policy in Modern America, 1997; (ed.) The Social Sciences Go to Washington: The Politics of Knowledge in the Postmodern Age, 2004; (ed. with P. Farber) Race and Science: Scientific Challenges to Racism in Modern America, 2009; (ed.) Great Depression: People and Perspectives, 2009; A History of Social Sciences in America, forthcoming. **Address:** Department of History, Iowa State University, 615 Ross Hall, Ames, IA 50011, U.S.A. **Online address:** hcravens@iastate.edu

CRAVEY, Pamela J. American (born United States), b. 1945. **Genres:** Librarianship, How-to Books, Adult Non-fiction. **Career:** Florida State University, instructor and librarian, 1968-69; University of Georgia, instructor and librarian, 1972-75; Georgia State University, associate professor and librarian, 1975-2000, associate professor emeritus, 2000-; consultant, 2000-. Writer. **Publications:** Protecting Library Staff, Users, Collections and Facilities: A How-to-Do-It Manual, 2001. Contributor to books and periodicals. **Address:** 2103 N Decatur Rd., Ste. 308, Decatur, GA 30033-5305, U.S.A. **Online address:** pcravey@sacscoc.org

CRAWFORD, Alan. British (born England), b. 1943?. **Genres:** Architecture, Crafts, Design, Art/Art History, Education. **Career:** University of Leicester, Victorian Studies Centre, research fellow, 1970-72; Birmingham Polytechnic, lecturer in history of design, 1972-78. Writer. **Publications:** (Co-author) Birmingham Pubs 1890-1939, 1975, 2nd ed., 1986; (ed.) By Hammer and Hand: The Arts and Crafts Movement in Birmingham, 1984; C.R. Ashbee: Architect, Designer and Romantic Socialist, 1985; Charles Rennie Mackintosh, 1995; (contrib.) Edward Burne-Jones, Victorian Artist-Dreamer, 1998; (with W. Kaplan) The Arts and Crafts Movement in Europe and America: Design for the Modern World 1880-1920, 2004; (co-author) Teaching and Learning Strategies for the Thinking Classroom, 2005. **Address:** 58 Cecile Pk., London, GL N8 9AU, England.

CRAWFORD, Craig. American (born United States), b. 1956. **Genres:** Politics/Government, Biography. **Career:** Attorney, 1981-84; Orlando Sentinel, political reporter and legal columnist, 1985-89, bureau chief, 1989-97; Hotline (online political publication), writer, editor-in-chief and publisher, 1997-2003; Congressional Quarterly, columnist and contributing editor, 2003-. **Publications:** Attack the Messenger: How Politicians Turn You Aagainst the Media, 2006; Politics of Life: 25 Rules for Survival in a Brutal and Manipulative World, 2007; (with H. Thomas) Listen Up, Mr. President: Everything You Always Wanted Your President to Know and Do, 2009. **Address:** Congressional Quarterly Inc., 1255 22nd St. NW, Washington, DC 20037-1217, U.S.A. **Online address:** ccrawford@cq.com

CRAWFORD, Gary W(illiam). American (born United States), b. 1953. **Genres:** Poetry, Reference, Mystery/Crime/Suspense, Horror. **Career:** Gothic Press, founder and editor, 1979-. **Publications:** Horror Literature: A Core Collection and Reference Guide, 1981; (comp.) The 1980 Bibliography of Gothic Studies, 1983; Ramsey Campbell, 1988; Poems of the Divided Self, 1992; J. Sheridan Le Fanu: A Bio-Bibliography, 1995; In Shadow Lands (poems), 1998; Gothic Fevers, 2000; Robert Aickman: An Introduction, 2003; Mysteries of Von Domarus, 2004; The Shadow City, 2005; The Phantom World, 2008. **Address:** Gothic Press, 2272 Quail Oak, Baton Rouge, LA 70808-9023, U.S.A. **Online address:** gothicpt12@aol.com

CRAWFORD, Gregory A. American (born United States), b. 1956. **Genres:** How-to Books, Adult Non-fiction, History, Medicine/Health, Librarianship, Bibliography, Archaeology/Antiquities. **Career:** University of North Carolina, School of Library Science, research assistant, 1982-84; Lafayette College, David Bishop Skillman Memorial Library, technical services librarian, 1984-85; Moravian College, Reeves Library, reference and public services librarian, 1985-90, Automation Project, director, 1986-90; Pennsylvania State University, Capital College, Penn State Harrisburg Library, assistant librarian, 1993-99, associate librarian, 1999-2005, head of public services, 1993-2005, librarian, 2005, director, 2005-. Writer. **Publications:** (Co-author) Using Microsoft PowerPoint: A How-to-Do-It Manual for Librarians, 1998; Petra and the Nabataeans: A Bibliography, 2003; The Medical Library Association Guide to Finding Out About Complementary and Alternative Medicine, 2010. Contributor of articles to periodicals. **Address:** Penn State Harrisburg Library, Capital College, Pennsylvania State University, 351 Olmsted Dr., Middletown, PA 17057, U.S.A. **Online address:** gac2@psu.edu

CRAWFORD, Katherine. American (born United States), b. 1966. **Genres:** History, Sex, Cultural/Ethnic Topics, Social Sciences. **Career:** University of Chicago, Harper postdoctoral fellow, 1997-99; Vanderbilt University, Department of History, assistant professor, associate professor, 1999-, professor of history, director of graduate studies; Robert Penn Warren Center for the Humanities, fellow, 2002-03, 2005-06; Folger Shakespeare Library, fellow, 2006-07. Writer. **Publications:** Perilous Performances: Gender and Regency in Early Modern France, 2004; European Sexualities, 1400-1800, 2007; Sexual Culture of the French Renaissance, 2010. Contributor to periodicals and journals. **Address:** Department of History, Vanderbilt University, 220 Benson Hall, 2201 W End Ave., Nashville, TN 37240-0002, U.S.A. **Online address:** katherine.b.crawford@vanderbilt.edu

CRAWFORD, Lynn. American (born United States), b. 1959?. **Genres:** Novels, Young Adult Fiction, Social Sciences, Literary Criticism And History. **Career:** Writer. **Publications:** Solow, 1994; Blow (novella), 1998; Simply Separate People, 2002. Works appear in anthologies. **Address:** c/o Author Mail, Hammer Books, 1200 Broadway, Apt. 3-C, New York, NY 10001-4316, U.S.A.

CRAWFORD, Mark. American (born United States), b. 1954. **Genres:** Earth Sciences, Environmental Sciences/Ecology, History, Marketing, Military/Defense/Arms Control, Sciences, Bibliography. **Career:** Mining geologist, 1977-95; professional geologist and science editor. Writer. **Publications:** Toxic Waste Sites, 1997; Physical Geology, 1998; Encyclopedia of the Mexican-American War, 1998; Courage on Lesser Fields, 1998; Endangered Habitats and Ecosystems, 1998; The Spanish-American War: Historical Overview and Select Bibliography, 1998; Habitats and Ecosystems: An Encyclopedia of Endangered America, 1999; Confederate Courage on Other Fields: Four Lesser Known Accounts of the War between the States, 2000. **Address:** 5101 Violet Ln., Madison, WI 53714, U.S.A. **Online address:** giltedge@chorus.net

CRAWFORD, Mary. (Mary E. Crawford). American (born United States), b. 1942. **Genres:** Psychology, Women's Studies And Issues. **Career:** University of Illinois, visiting instructor, 1973-74; Buena Vista College, assistant professor, 1974-78; West Chester University of Pennsylvania, assistant professor, 1978-81, associate professor, 1981-84, professor of psychology and women's studies, 1984-93; Hamilton College, visiting professor, 1981, Jane Watson Irwin visiting professor of psychology and women's studies, 1986-88, Jane W. Irwin chair in women's studies; Women's College Coalition, research director, 1991-94; University of South Carolina, Barnwell College, professor of psychology and graduate director of women's studies, 1993-; University of Connecticut, fellow, professor of psychology and director of the women's studies program, 1998-. Writer. **Publications:** (Ed. with M. Gentry) Gender and Thought: Psychological Perspectives, 1989; (with R. Unger) Women and Gender: A Feminist Psychology, 1992, 4th ed., 2004; Talking Difference: Gender and Conversational Style, 1995; (comp. with R. Unger) In Our Own Words: Readings on the Psychology of Women and Gender, 1997, 2nd ed. (ed. with R. Unger) as In Our Own Words: Writings From Women's Lives, 2001; (ed. with E.B. Kimmel) Innovations in Feminist Psychological Research, 1999; (ed. with S.N. Davis and J. Sebrechts) Coming into Her Own: Educational Success in Girls and Women, 1999; (with R. Chaffin and G. Imreh) Practicing Perfection: Memory and Piano Performance, 2002; Transformations: Women, Gender and Psychology, 2006, 2nd ed., 2011; Sex Trafficking in South Asia, 2010. Works appear in anthologies. Contributor of articles to journals and magazines. **Address:** College of Liberal Arts and Sciences, Humanities Institute, University of Connecticut, 215 Glenbrook Rd., Ste. 4234, Storrs, CT 06269, U.S.A.

CRAWFORD, Mary E. *See* **CRAWFORD, Mary.**

CRAWFORD, Robert. Scottish (born Scotland), b. 1959?. **Genres:** Poetry. **Career:** Verse Magazine, founder, 1984; Polygon (publisher), poetry editor, 1990; University of St. Andrews, professor of modern Scottish literature; Open University, associate lecturer. **Publications:** The Savage and the City in the Work of T.S. Eliot, 1987; Devolving English Literature, 1992; Identifying Poets: Self and Territory in Twentieth-Century Poetry, 1993; (co-author) Contraflow on the Super Highway: Poems, 1994; Literature in Twentieth-Century Scotland: A Select Bibliography, 1995; The God/Man/World/ Triangle: A Dialogue between Science and Religion, 1997; The Modern Poet: Poetry, Academia, and Knowledge since the 1750s, 2001; (intro.) Apollos of the North: Selected Poems of George Buchanan and Arthur Johnston, 2006; The New Penguin Book of Scottish Verse, 2006; Scotland's Books: The Penguin History of Scottish Literature, 2007; The Bard: Robert Burns, a Biography, 2009; Scotland's Books: A History of Scottish Literature, 2009; The Beginning and the End of the World: St Andrews, Scandal and the Birth of Photography, 2011. POETRY: A Scottish Assembly, 1990; (with W.N. Herbert) Sharawaggi: Poems in Scots, 1990; Talkies, 1992; Masculinity, 1996; Spirit Machines, 1999; The Tip of My Tongue, 2003; Selected Poems, 2005; Full Volume, 2008. EDITOR: (with H. Whyte) About Edwin Morgan, 1990; (with A. McSeveney) Other Tongues: Young Scottish Poets in English, Scots and Gaelic, 1990; (with T. Nairn) The Arts of Alasdair Gray, 1991; (with D. Kinloch) Reading Douglas Dunn, 1992; (with A. Varty) Liz Lochhead's Voices, 1993; (with H. Hart, D. Kinloch and R. Price) Talking Verse: Interviews with Poets, 1995; Robert Burns and Cultural Authority, 1997; Launch-Site for English Studies: Three Centuries of Literary Studies at the University of St Andrews, 1997; The Scottish Invention of English Literature, 1998; (with S. Armitage) The Penguin Book of Poetry from Britain and Ireland since 1945, 1998; (with M. Imlah) The New Penguin Book of Scottish Verse, 2000; (with M. Bateman and J. McGonigal) Scottish Religious Poetry: From the Sixth Century to the Present: An Anthology, 2000; Heaven-Taught Fergusson: Robert Burns's Favourite Scottish Poet: Poems and Essays, 2003; The Book of St Andrews, 2005; Contemporary Poetry and Contemporary Science, 2006; (with C. MacLachlan) The Best Laid Schemes: Selected Poetry and Prose of Robert Burns, 2009. Contributor to journals. Works appear in anthologies. **Address:** David Godwin Associates, 55 Monmouth St., London, GL WC2H 9DG, England.

CRAWFORD, Robert. *See* **RAE, Hugh C(rawford).**

CRAWFORD, Tad. American (born United States), b. 1946. **Genres:** Art/Art History, Law, Money/Finance, Mythology/Folklore, Psychology, Writing/Journalism. **Career:** Attorney, 1971-86; School of Visual Arts, instructor in humanities, 1973-98; Allworth Press, founder and publisher, 1989-; Communication Arts, columnist. **Publications:** The Writer's Legal Guide, 1977, (with K. Murray) 4th ed., 2002; Legal Guide for the Visual Artist, 1977, 5th ed., 2010; The Visual Artist's Guide to the New Copyright Law, 1978; (with A. Kopelman) Selling Your Photography, 1980; (with A. Kopelman) Selling Your Graphic Design and Illustration, 1981; (with S. Mellon) The Artist-Gallery Partnership: A Practical Guide to Consignment, 1981, rev. ed., 2008; Business and Legal Forms for Fine Artists, 1990, 4th ed., 2010; Business & Legal Forms for Authors & Self-Publishers, 1990, 3rd ed., 2004; Business and Legal Forms for Illustrators, 1990, 3rd ed., 2004; (with E.D. Bruck) Business and Legal Forms for Graphic Designers, 1990, 3rd ed., 2003; Business and Legal Forms for Photographers, 1991, 4th ed., 2010; The Secret Life of Money, 1995; Business and Legal Forms for Crafts, 1998, 2nd ed., 2005; (ed.) AIGA Professional Practices in Graphic Design, 1998, 2nd ed., 2008; The Money Mentor: A Tale of Finding Financial Freedom, 2001; (with E.D. Bruck) Business and Legal Forms for Interior Designers, 2001; (with K. Murray) The Writer's Legal Guide: An Authors Guild Desk Reference, 2002; Starting Your Career As a Freelance Photographer, 2003; (co-author) Business and Legal Forms for Industrial Designers, 2005; Graphic Design Business Book, 2005; (with S. Mellon) Artist-Gallery Partnership: A Practical Guide to Consigning Art, 1998, 3rd ed., 2008. **Address:** Allworth Press, 307 W 36th St., 11th Fl., New York, NY 10018, U.S.A. **Online address:** crawford@allworth.com

CRAWFORD, T. Hugh. American (born United States), b. 1956. **Genres:** Literary Criticism And History. **Career:** Virginia Military Institute, associate professor of English; Georgia Institute of Technology, Literature Communication and Culture, associate professor. Writer. **Publications:** Modernism, Medicine & William Carlos Williams, 1993. **Address:** Literature Communication & Culture, Georgia Institute of Technology, 686 Cherry St., Atlanta, GA 30332-0165, U.S.A. **Online address:** hugh.crawford@lcc.gatech.edu

CRAWLEY, Harriet. British (born England), b. 1948. **Genres:** Novels, Education, Romance/Historical, Young Adult Fiction. **Career:** Crawley & Asquith (art gallery), director. Writer. **Publications:** Degree of Defiance: Students in England and Europe Now, 1969. NOVELS: The Goddaughter, 1975; The Lovers and the Loved, 1990; Painted Lady, 1994. **Address:** Peters Fraser and Dunlop Group Ltd., Drury House, 34-43 Russell St., London, GL WC2B 5HA, England.

CRAY, David. *See* **SOLOMITA, Stephen.**

CRAY, Edward. American (born United States), b. 1933. **Genres:** Civil Liberties/Human Rights, Law, Mythology/Folklore, Social Commentary, Art/Art

History. **Career:** University of California, instructor in folklore and folksong, 1958-60; Frontier, associate editor and business manager, 1961-64; Frontier magazine, associate editor, 1962-64; freelance writer, 1964-65, 1971-; American Civil Liberties Union of Southern California, director of publications, 1965-70; Southern California Symphony, Hollywood Bowl Association, director of publicity, 1970-71; City News Service, editor, 1972-73; University of Southern California, School of Journalism, adjunct instructor, 1976, senior lecturer, 1976-82, associate professor, 1982-85, professor of journalism, 1985-, tenured professor; Holt, Rinehart and Winston, consultant, 1979; Los Angeles Times, Metro Training Programs, director, 1983-84; Jewish Federation Council, consultant, 1984-85; The Hollywood Reporter, consultant, 1985-88; McGraw-Hill, consultant, 1989; University of Illinois Press, consultant, 1990-; University of Chicago Press, consultant, 1990-; Aberdeen University Press, staff, 1990-. **Publications:** An Introductory Bibliography to American Folklore and Folksong, 1960; (ed.) The Anthology of Erotic Restoration Verse, 1965; The Pill Pushers, 1966; (ed.) The Fifteen Plagues of Maidenhead and Other Forbidden Verse, 1966; The Big Blue Line: Police Power versus Human Rights, 1967; (ed. and comp.) The Erotic Muse: American Bawdy Songs, 1967, (comp.) 2nd ed., 1992; (comp.) Bawdy Ballads, 1970; In Failing Health: The Medical Crisis and the A.M.A., 1971; The Enemy in the Streets: Police Malpractice in America, 1972; Burden of Proof: The Case of Juan Corona, 1973; Levi's: The History of Levi Strauss & Co., 1978; Chrome Colossus: General Motors and Its Times, 1980; General of the Army: George C. Marshall, Soldier and Statesman, 1990; (ed. with J. Kotler and M. Beller) American Datelines: An Anthology of 150 of the Most Important Pieces in American Journalism from 1700s to the Present, 1990; Chief Justice: A Biography of Earl Warren, 1997; Turning Points: War, Peace, and Other Crises in 20th-Century America, 1998; (ed. with J. Kotler and M. Beller) American Datelines: Major News Stories from Colonial Times to the Present, 2003; Ramblin' Man: The Life and Times of Woodie Guthrie, 2004. Contributor to periodicals. **Address:** Annenberg School for Communication, University of Southern California, ASC 307C, 3502 Watt Way, Los Angeles, CA 90089-0281, U.S.A. **Online address:** cray@usc.edu

CREADY, Gwyn. American (born United States), b. 1962. **Genres:** Romance/Historical. **Career:** Novelist. **Publications:** Tumbling through Time, 2008; Seducing Mr. Darcy, 2008. **Address:** Pittsburgh, PA , U.S.A. **Online address:** gwyn@cready.com

CREAGER, Clara. American (born United States), b. 1930?. **Genres:** Crafts. **Career:** Ohio State University, Department of Art, professor, now professor emeritus. Writer. **Publications:** Weaving: A Creative Approach for Beginners, 1974; All About Weaving: A Comprehensive Guide to the Craft, 1984. **Address:** Ohio State University, Enarson Hall, 154 W 12th Ave., Columbus, OH 43210-1302, U.S.A. **Online address:** creager.1@osu.edu

CREAMER, Robert W. American (born United States), b. 1922. **Genres:** Sports/Fitness, Biography, Autobiography/Memoirs, History. **Career:** Grey Advertising, junior copywriter, 1946-48; Bronxville Review-Press, advertising manager, 1948-49; Westchester Herald, advertising manager, 1949; William Weintraub (now Norman, Craig, & Kummel), junior account executive, 1949-50; P.F. Collier & Co., Collier's Encyclopedia, assistant editor, 1950-54; Sports Illustrated, staff writer, 1954-55, senior editor, 1955-84, now retired; New York Times, writer. **Publications:** The Quality of Courage, 1964; (with J. Conlan) Jocko, 1967; (with R. Barber) Rhubarb in the Catbird Seat, 1968; Babe: The Legend Comes to Life, 1974; (co-author) The Yankees, 1979; Stengel: His Life and Times, 1984; (with R. Houk) Season of Glory: The Amazing Saga of the 1961 New York Yankees, 1988; Baseball in '41: A Celebration of the Best Baseball Season Ever-In the Year America Went to War, 1991; Baseball and other Matters in 1941, 1991; (co-author) Mantle Remembered, 1995; (with M. Mantle) The Quality of Courage, 1999; Going, Going, Gone: The History, Lore and Mystique of the Home Run, 2000. CONTRIBUTOR: The Ultimate Baseball Book, 1979; Baseball Hall of Fame 50th Anniversary Book, 1988; The Birth of a Fan, 1993; Sports Illustrated Baseball, 1993; Baseball, an Illustrated History, 1994; Sports Illustrated Presents Mantle Remembered: Stories Excerpted from the Pages of Sports Illustrated, 1995. **Address:** Sterling Lord Literistic Inc., 65 Bleecker St., New York, NY 10012-2420, U.S.A.

CREAN, Susan M. Canadian (born Canada), b. 1945. **Genres:** Art/Art History, Communications/Media, Cultural/Ethnic Topics, History, Intellectual History, Organized Labor, Race Relations, Women's Studies And Issues, Autobiography/Memoirs, Biography. **Career:** Consultant and journalist, 1970-; Ryerson University, School of Journalism, instructor; Canadian Copyright Institute, delegate, 1973-76, vice chair, 1976-77; Mayor's Task Force on Cultural Policy, staff, 1973-74; National Youth Orchestra Association, board director, 1974-85, chair of development committee, 1976-77; University of British Columbia, Maclean-Hunter chair, 1989-90; Canadian Art, 1989-92; Ryerson Polytechnic, journalism teacher, 2000-01; Native Earth Performing Arts, board director, 2001-. **Publications:** NONFICTION: Who's Afraid of Canadian Culture?, 1976; (with M. Rioux) Deux Pays Pour Vivre: Un Plaidoyer, 1980; (with M. Rioux) Two Nations: An Essay on the Culture and Politics of Canada and Quebec in a World of American Pre-Eminence, 1983; Newsworthy: The Lives of Media Women, 1985; In the Name of the Fathers, 1989; Grace Hartman: A Woman for Her Time (biography), 1995; The Laughing One: A Journey to Emily Carr, 2001; (ed.) Opposite Contraries: The Unknown Journals of Emily Carr and Other Writings, 2003. Contributor of articles to periodicals. **Address:** 17 Coady Ave., Toronto, ON M4M 2Y9, Canada. **Online address:** smc@istar.ca

CRECELIUS, Daniel. American (born United States), b. 1937. **Genres:** Area Studies, History, Translations, Theology/Religion. **Career:** California State University, assistant professor, 1964-, professor of Middle East history, through 2001, professor emeritus, 2002-. Writer. **Publications:** The Roots of Modern Egypt: A Study of the Regimes of 'Ali Bey al-Kabir and Muhammad Bey Abu al-Dhahab, 1760-1775, 1981; Fihris Waqfiyyat al-'Asr al-'Uthmani al-Mahfuthah bi Wizarat al-Awqaf wa Dar al-Watha'iq al-Ta'rikhiyyah al-Qawmiyyah bi al-Qahirah, 1992; Abḥāth al-Mu'tamar al-Thālith lil-Dirāsāt al-Uthmānīyah fī Miṣ r, 2004. EDITOR: Eighteenth Century Egypt: The Arabic Manuscript Sources, 1990; (and trans. With A.A.W. Bakr) Al-Damurdashi's Chronicle of Egypt, 1688-1755, 1991; (with A.A.W. Bakr) Makhtutat al-Durrah al-Musanah fi Akhbar al-Kinanah, 1992; (and trans., with H. Badr) A Short Manuscript History of the Mamluk Amir Murad Bey; (with H. Badr and H.A.D. Ismail) Ta'rikh al-Wazir Muhammad Ali Basha li al-Shaykh Khalil ibn Ahmad al-Rajabi, 1997. Works appear in anthologies. Contributor of articles to journals. **Address:** Department of History, California State University, 5151 State University Dr., Los Angeles, CA 90032, U.S.A. **Online address:** dcrecel@calstatela.edu

CRECY, Jeanne. *See* **WILLIAMS, Jeanne.**

CREDARO, Amanda. Australian (born Australia) **Genres:** Adult Non-fiction, Librarianship. **Career:** Penarroya, administrative geologist, 1979-81; Australian Diatomite Mining, chief geologist, 1983-85; Riverstone High School, science teacher, 1985-91; Shoalhaven High School, science teacher, 1992-96; Rooty Hill High School, science teacher, 1997-98; Australian Casual and Relief School Library Staff Database, creator and administrator, 1999-; Parramatta Catholic Education Office, Christ Catholic College, teacher librarian, 2000; New South Wales Department of Education, teacher librarian, 2001-03; Pendle Hill High School, teacher librarian, 2007-. Writer. **Publications:** Biblia's Guide to Warrior Librarianship: Humor for Librarians Who Refuse to Be Classified, 2003. FORTHCOMING: Be Quiet, I'm Trying to Read; Random Thoughts from a Sick Mind; Warrior Librarian Weekly-The First Decade; The Road to Hell. Contributor to periodicals. **Address:** c/o Author Mail, Libraries Unlimited, PO Box 6926, Portsmouth, NH 03802-6926, U.S.A. **Online address:** abcredaro@ozemail.com.au

CREECH, Sharon. (Sharon Rigg). American (born United States), b. 1945. **Genres:** Young Adult Fiction, Novels, Children's Fiction, Picture/Board Books. **Career:** Federal Theater Project Archives, affiliater; Congressional Quarterly, editorial assistant; TASIS England American School, teacher of American and British literature, 1979-82, 1984-94; TASIS (The American School in Switzerland), teacher of American and British literature, 1983-85. **Publications:** FOR YOUNG PEOPLE: Absolutely Normal Chaos, 1990; Walk Two Moons, 1994; Pleasing the Ghost, 1996; Chasing Redbird, 1997; Bloomability, 1998; Fishing in the Air, 2000; The Wanderer, 2000; A Fine, Fine School, 2001; Love That Dog, 2001; Ruby Holler, 2002. OTHER: The Center of the Universe: Waiting for the Girl (play), 1992; Granny Torrelli Makes Soup, 2003; Heartbeat, 2004; Replay: A New Book, 2005; Who's That Baby?: New-Baby Songs, 2005; Castle Corona, 2007; Hate that Cat, 2008; The Unfinished Angel, 2009. AS SHARON RIGG: The Recital, 1990; Nickel Malley, 1991. **Address:** c/o Author Mail, HarperCollins Children's Books, 10 E 53rd St., New York, NY 10022, U.S.A.

CREED, John. *See* **MCNAMEE, Eoin.**

CREED, William S. American (born United States) **Genres:** Science Fiction/

Fantasy, Mystery/Crime/Suspense. **Career:** Writer. **Publications:** Comes the End: A Futuristic Thriller, 2003; The Gathering: The Christian Adventure Continues, 2007; The Promise, 2009; The Final Day, forthcoming; Faith: God's Gift, forthcoming. **Address:** House of Stuart, 8531 W 32 Mile Rd., Romeo, MI 48065, U.S.A. **Online address:** infocontact@williamcreed.com

CREEDEN, Sharon. American (born United States), b. 1938. **Genres:** Mythology/Folklore, Law, Young Adult Fiction, Children's Fiction. **Career:** Storyteller, 1983-95; deputy prosecuting attorney. Writer. **Publications:** Fair Is Fair: World Folktales of Justice, 1994; In Full Bloom: Tales of Women in Their Prime, 1999. **Address:** 2536 Alki SW, Ste. 201, Seattle, WA 98116-2270, U.S.A.

CREEGAN, Nicola Hoggard. New Zealander/American (born United States) **Genres:** Theology/Religion. **Career:** Bible College of New Zealand, lecturer, 2000-. Laidlaw College, School of Theology Mission and Ministry, lecturer in systematic theology, 2000, senior lecturer, Laidlaw-Carey Graduate School, dean; Colloquium, co-editor. **Publications:** (With C.D. Pohl) Living on the Boundaries: Evangelical Women, Feminism and the Theological Academy, 2005. **Address:** Bible College of New Zealand, 221 Lincoln Rd., PO Box 93104, Waitakere City, 0612, New Zealand. **Online address:** nhoggard-creegan@laidlaw.ac.nz

CREEKMORE, Marion V. American (born United States), b. 1939. **Genres:** History, Politics/Government. **Career:** U.S. Department of State, staff, 1965-93; U.S. Embassy, Pretoria, South Africa, junior officer, 1965-66; U.S. Embassy, Accra, Ghana, economic officer, 1966-68; Memphis State University, manager of family business and assistant professor, 1968-70; U.S. Embassy, Bonn, West Germany, economic officer, 1970-73; Bureau of Economic and Business Affairs, officer in charge of producer countries, 1975-77; Office of Development Finance, director, 1977-; Department of Energy, office director, 1978; Bureau of International Organizations Affairs, deputy assistant secretary of state, 1979-81; U.S. Embassy, New Delhi, India, deputy chief of mission, 1981-84; National Defense University, senior research fellow, 1984-85; deputy director of policy planning staff, 1985; deputy assistant secretary of state for Persian Gulf, 1985-87; George Washington University, diplomat-in-residence, 1987-88; Department of State in Washington, D.C., Afghan coordinator, 1988; Sri Lanka and Republic of Maldives, ambassador, 1989-92; Emory University, Carter Center, director, 1993-96, vice provost for international affairs, 1993-2000, Claus M. Halle Institute for Global Learning, director, 1996-2000, distinguished visiting professor of history and political science, 2000. Writer. **Publications:** A Moment of Crisis: Jimmy Carter, the Power of a Peacemaker and North Korea's Nuclear Ambitions, 2006. Contributor to periodicals. **Address:** Department of Political Science, Emory University, 113B Tarbutton Hall, 1555 Dickey Dr., Atlanta, GA 30322, U.S.A. **Online address:** mcreekm@emory.edu

CREEL, Ann Howard. American (born United States), b. 1953. **Genres:** Young Adult Fiction, History, Novels, Romance/Historical. **Career:** Nurse and writer. **Publications:** Water at the Blue Earth, 1998; A Ceiling of Stars, 1999; Nowhere, Now Here, 2000; The Magic of Ordinary Days (adult novel), 2001; Under a Stand Still Moon, 2005; Call Me the Canyon, 2006; Nicki, 2007; Thanks to Nicki, 2007. **Address:** Roberts Rinehart Publishing Inc., 4501 Forbes Blvd., Ste. 200, Lanham, MD 20706, U.S.A. **Online address:** contactme@annhowardcreel.com

CREGAN, David (Appleton Quartus). British (born England), b. 1931. **Genres:** Novels, Plays/Screenplays, Young Adult Fiction. **Career:** Palm Beach Private School, Department of English, head, 1955-57; Burnage Boys Grammar School, assistant English master, 1957; Hatfield School, assistant English master and head of drama department, 1958-62; New Theatre Workshops, Gulbenkian Foundation, co-founder and director, 1979-84. Writer. **Publications:** Ronald Rossiter (novel), 1959; Three Men for Colverton, 1967; Transcending: And the Dancers, 1967; The Houses by the Green, 1969; Miniatures, 1970; Land of Palms, 1973; (intro.) How We Held the Square: A Play for Children, 1973; Poor Tom & Tina: Two Plays, 1976; Sleeping Beauty: A Pantomime, 1984; Red Ridinghood: A Pantomime, 1986; Jack and the Beanstalk: A Pantomime, 1987; Beauty and the Beast, 1988; Cinderella, 1991; Aladdin, 1993; Three Plays, 2001. **Address:** Casarotto Ramsay Ltd., 7-12 Noel St., London, GL W1F 8GQ, England.

CREGAN, Sean. *See* **RICKARDS, John.**

CREIGHTON, Joan Scott. (J. S. Borthwick). American (born United States), b. 1923?. **Genres:** Novels, Mystery/Crime/Suspense, Young Adult Non-fiction, Young Adult Fiction. **Career:** State University of New York, faculty; Indiana University, lecturer in English; Coastal Senior College, teacher, 2002-; Maine High Schools, teacher. Writer. **Publications:** MYSTERY NOVELS AS J.S. BORTHWICK: The Case of the Hook-Billed Kites, 1982; The Down East Murders, 1985; The Student Body, 1986; Bodies of Water, 1990; Dude on Arrival, 1992; The Bridled Groom, 1994; Dolly Is Dead, 1995; The Garden Plot, 1997; My Body Lies over the Ocean, 1999; Coup de Grâce, 2000; Murder in the Rough, 2002; Intensive Scare Unit, 2004; Foiled Again, 2007. **Address:** c/o Author Mail, St. Martins Press, 175 5th Ave., New York, NY 10010, U.S.A.

CREIGHTON, Kathleen. (Kathleen Carrol). American (born United States), b. 1943. **Genres:** Romance/Historical, Novels, Mystery/Crime/Suspense, Young Adult Fiction. **Career:** Writer. **Publications:** NOVELS: Demon Lover, 1985; Delilah's Weakness, 1986; Double Dealings, 1986; Still Waters, 1986; Gypsy Dancer, 1987; In Defense of Love, 1987; Katie's Hero, 1987; The Prince and the Patriot, 1988; Winter's Daughter, 1988; The Sorcerer's Keeper, 1988; Rogue's Valley, 1988; Tiger Dawn, 1989; Love and Other Surprises, 1990; The Heart mender, 1990; In from the Cold, 1991; Wolf and the Angel, 1992; A Christmas Love, 1992; Eyewitness, 1995; Never Trust a Lady, 1997; One Christmas Knight, 1997; One More Knight, 1998. ROMANCE FICTION: A Wanted Man, 1994; One Good Man, 1995; Man of Steel, 1995; One Summer's Knight, 1999; Eve's Wedding Knight, 1999; The Cowboy's Hidden Agenda, 2000; The Awakening of Dr. Brown, 2001; The Seduction of Goody Two-Shoes, 2001; The Virgin Seduction, 2002; The Black Sheep's Baby, 2002; All I Want for Christmas, 2003; Shooting Starr, 2003; The Top Gun's Return, 2003; Starr's Quest, 2004; Order of Protection, 2004; Undercover Mistress, 2005; Secret Agent Sam, 2005; (with R. Thayne) Never Too Late and Secret Agent Sam, 2005; Sheriff of Heartbreak County, 2006; (with A.J. Fetzer) His Baby Surprise, 2006; Lazlo's Last Stand, 2007; Danger Signals, 2008; Daredevil's Run, 2008; Lady Killer, 2009; Kincaid's Dangerous Game, 2009; (with D. Fossen) Questioning the Heiress/Daredevils Run, 2009; Memory of Murder, 2010; Sheriff's Runaway Witness, 2011; The Pretender, 2012. AS KATHLEEN CARROL: Angel's Walk, 1986. Works appear in anthologies. Contributor to books. **Address:** c/o Patricia Teal, Patricia Teal Literary Agency, 2036 Vista Del Rosa, Fullerton, CA 92831, U.S.A. **Online address:** kat@kathleencreighton.com

CREIGHTON, Margaret S. American (born United States), b. 1949?. **Genres:** History, Humanities, Adult Non-fiction, Women's Studies And Issues, Cultural/Ethnic Topics, Race Relations. **Career:** Bates College, professor of history; Dartmouth College, visiting assistant professor of history. Writer. **Publications:** Dogwatch and Liberty Days: Seafaring Life in the Nineteenth Century, 1982; Rites and Passages: The Experience of American Whaling 1830-1870, 1995; (co-ed.) Iron Men Wooden Women: Gender and Seafaring in the Atlantic World 1700-1920, 1996; The Colors of Courage: Gettysburg's Forgotten History: Immigrants, Women and African Americans in the Civil War's Defining Battle, 2005. **Address:** Department of History, Bates College, Rm. 109, Pettengill Hall, Lewiston, ME 04240-6028, U.S.A. **Online address:** mcreight@bates.edu

CREIGHTON, Sarah Hammond. American (born United States) **Genres:** Education. **Career:** Tufts University, Tufts Climate Initiative, director of campus sustainability & project manager. Writer. **Publications:** Greening the Ivory Tower: Improving the Environmental Track Record of Universities, Colleges, and Other Institutions, 1998; (with A. Rappaport) Degrees That Matter: Climate Change and the University, 2007. **Address:** Tufts University Information Technology, 169 Holland St., Somerville, MA 02144, U.S.A. **Online address:** creighton@tufts.edu

CREMO, Michael (A.). (Drutakarma Dasa). American (born United States), b. 1948. **Genres:** Adult Non-fiction, Archaeology/Antiquities. **Career:** George Washington University, School of International Affairs, faculty, 1966-68; historian of archeology; Royal Institution in London, lecturer; Russian Academy of Sciences in Moscow, lecturer; International Society for Krishna Consciousness (ISKCON), teacher of Bhakti-yoga, 1973-; Bhaktivedanta Book Trust, writer and editor, 1980-86, 1995-; Bhaktivedanta Institute, research associate, 1984-95. **Publications:** (With R.L. Thompson) Forbidden Archeology: The Hidden History of the Human Race, 1993; (with R.L. Thompson) Hidden History of the Human Race, 1994; (with M. Goswami) Divine Nature: A Spiritual Perspective on the Environmental Crisis, 1995;

Forbidden Archaeology's Impact, 1998; Human Devolution: A Vedic Alternative to Darwin's Theory, 2003; Forbidden Archeologist: The Atlantis Rising Columns of Michael Cremo, 2010; Nature's IQ: How Extraordinary Animal Behaviors Defy Evolution, forthcoming. AS DRUTAKARMA DASA (co-author): Coming Back: The Science of Reincarnation, 1982; Chant and Be Happy: The Power of Mantra Meditation, 1982; The Higher Taste: A Guide to Gourmet Vegetarian Cooking and a Karma-Free Diet, 1983. Contributor to periodicals. **Address:** Bhaktivedanta Book Trust, PO Box 34074, Los Angeles, CA 90034, U.S.A. **Online address:** mail@mcremo.com

CRENSHAW, James L. American (born United States), b. 1934. **Genres:** Theology/Religion, Essays, Reference, Humanities. **Career:** Clergyman of Baptist Church, Atlantic Christian College, assistant professor of religion, 1964-65; Mercer University, associate professor, 1965-69; Vanderbilt University, Divinity School, associate professor, professor of Old Testament, 1969-87; Duke University, Divinity School, professor of Old Testament, 1987-2007, Robert L. Flowers professor of Old Testament, 1993-2007. Writer. **Publications:** Prophetic Conflict: Its Effect Upon Israelite Religion, 1971; (co-author) Old Testament Form Criticism, 1974; Hymnic Affirmation of Divine Justice, 1975; Studies in Ancient Israelite Wisdom, 1976; Gerhard von Rad, 1978; Samson: A Secret Betrayed, A Vow Ignored, 1978; Old Testament Wisdom, 1981, 3rd ed., 2010; Proverbs, Ecclesiastes, Song of Songs, vol. I-II, 1983; A Whirlpool of Torment, 1984; Story and Faith, 1986; Ecclesiastes: A Commentary, 1987; Old Testament Story and Faith: A Literary and Theological Introduction, 1992; Trembling at the Threshold of a Bibical Text, 1994; (trans. and intro.) Joel, 1995; Urgent Advice and Probing Questions, 1995; Sirach, 1997; Education in Ancient Israel, 1998; The Psalms: An Introduction, 2001, Defending God: Biblical Responses to the Problem of Evil, 2005; Prophets, Sages & Poets, 2006; Prophetic Conflict: Its Effect Upon Israelite Religion, 2007; Whirlpool of Torment: Israelite Traditions of God as an Oppressive Presence, 2008; Reading Job, 2011. EDITOR/CO-EDITOR: Essays in Old Testament Ethics, 1974; The Divine Helmsman, 1980; Theodicy in the Old Testament, 1983; Perspectives on the Hebrew Bible, 1988. **Address:** Duke University Divinity School, PO Box 90967, Durham, NC 27708-0967, U.S.A. **Online address:** jcrenshaw@div.duke.edu

CRENSON, Matthew A. American (born United States), b. 1943. **Genres:** History, Politics/Government. **Career:** Brookings Institution, research fellow, 1968; Massachusetts Institute of Technology, instructor in political science, 1969-69; Johns Hopkins University, Department of Political Science, assistant professor, 1969-73, associate professor, 1973-76, professor, David Bernstein professor of political science, 1976-, chairman, 1989, now professor emeritus, School of Arts and Sciences, associate dean, 1984-87. Writer. **Publications:** Non-issues in City Politics: The Case of Air Polution, 1969; Un-politics of Air Pollution: A Study of Non-Decisionmaking in the Cities, 1971; Federal Machine: Beginnings of Bureaucracy in Jacksonian America, 1975; (with M. Greenberger and B.L. Crissey) Models in the Policy Process: Public Decision Making in the Computer Era, 1976; Neighborhood Politics, 1983; Building the Invisible Orphanage: A Prehistory of the American Welfare System, 1998; (with B. Ginsberg) Downsizing Democracy: How America Sidelined its Citizens and Privatized its Public, 2002; (with B. Ginsberg) Presidential Power: Unchecked and Unbalanced, 2007. **Address:** Department of Political Science, Johns Hopkins University, 359 Mergenthaler Hall, 3400 N Charles St., Baltimore, MD 21218, U.S.A. **Online address:** crenson@jhu.edu

CRENSON, Victoria. American (born United States), b. 1952. **Genres:** Children's Non-fiction, Young Adult Non-fiction, Animals/Pets, Biography, Autobiography/Memoirs, Natural History, Children's Fiction. **Career:** Writer. **Publications:** FOR CHILDREN: Discovering Dinosaurs: All Up-to-Date Guide Including the Newest Theories, 1988; Butterflies and Moths, 1993; Bay Shore Park: The Death and Life of an Amusement Park, 1995; Horseshoe Crabs and Shorebirds: The Story of a Food Web, 2003. THE SENSES SERIES WITH K.B. SMITH: Hearing, 1988; Seeing, 1988; Smelling, 1988; Tasting, 1988; Thinking, 1988; Touching, 1988. HOW AND WHY SERIES: Prehistoric Life, 1988; Sea Creatures, 1988; Snakes, 1988; Wild Animals, 1988. FOR ADULTS: Norman Rockwell's Portrait of America, 1989. LEARNING FUNBOOK SERIES: Insects, 1990; Space, 1990; Strange Creatures, 1990. ADVENTURES IN COURAGE SERIES: Abraham Lincoln: An Adventure in Courage, 1992; George Washington, 1992; Martin Luther King, Jr.: An Adventure in Courage, 1992. **Address:** 2223 Sulgrave Ave., Baltimore, MD 21209, U.S.A. **Online address:** loizcren@erols.com

CRERAR, Duff (Willis). Canadian (born Canada), b. 1955. **Genres:** History, Military/Defense/Arms Control, Theology/Religion, Biography. **Career:** Queen's University, instructor, 1981-90; Grande Prairie Regional College, instructor, 1990-2002; Department of National Defense, Chaplain General's Branch, historical consultant, 1991-. Writer. **Publications:** Padres in No Man's Land: Canadian Chaplains and the Great War, 1995. Contributor to periodicals. **Address:** Department of Arts & Education, Grande Prairie Regional College, C404 Rm. E306A, Grande Prairie, AB T8V 4C4, Canada. **Online address:** dcrerar@gprc.ab.ca

CRESPI, Camilla T. Also writes as Trella Crespi, Camilla Trinchieri. American (born United States), b. 1942?. **Genres:** Novels. **Career:** Writer. **Publications:** (As Camilla Trinchieri) The Price of Silence (crime novel), 2007. SIMONA GRIFFO MYSTERY SERIES: (as Trella Crespi) The Trouble with a Small Raise, 1991; (as Trella Crespi) The Trouble with Moonlighting, 1991; (as Trella Crespi) The Trouble with Too Much Sun, 1992; The Trouble with Thin Ice, 1993; The Trouble with Going Home, 1995; The Trouble with a Bad Fit: A Novel of Food, Fashion, and Mystery, 1996; The Trouble with a Hot Summer, 1997. **Address:** Soho Press Inc., 853 Broadway, New York, NY 10003, U.S.A. **Online address:** ctchieri@gmail.com

CRESPI, Trella. *See* **CRESPI, Camilla T.**

CRESS, Doug. American (born United States), b. 1964?. **Genres:** Autobiography/Memoirs. **Career:** Great Ape Project, executive director, 2002-; Time, journalist; Washington Post, journalist; Atlanta Journal Constitution, journalist; Pan African Sanctuaries Alliance, secretariat; Zambia's Chimfunshi Wildlife Orphanage, trustee. **Publications:** (With S. Siddle) In My Family Tree: A Life with Chimpanzees, 2002. Contributor to magazines. **Address:** Great Ape Project, Jean Vollum Natural Capital Ctr., 721 NW 9th Ave., Ste. 280, Portland, OR 97209, U.S.A. **Online address:** gap@greatapeproject.org

CRESSWELL, Stephen. American (born United States), b. 1956. **Genres:** History. **Career:** Mount Vernon College, reference librarian, 1980-81; University of Virginia, instructor in history, 1985; West Virginia Wesleyan College, professor of history, 1986-. Writer. **Publications:** Mormons & Cowboys, Moonshiners & Klansmen: Federal Law Enforcement in the South & West, 1870-1893, 1991; (ed.) We Will Know What War Is: The Civil War Diary of Sirene Bunten, 1993; Multiparty Politics in Mississippi, 1877-1902, 1995; Homemade Root Beer, Soda, and Pop, 1998; Rednecks, Redeemers, and Race: Mississippi After Reconstruction, 1877-1917, 2006. **Address:** Stephen Cresswell Photography, RR 1, PO Box 185A, Buckhannon, WV 26201, U.S.A. **Online address:** cresswell@wvwc.edu

CRESWELL, Michael. American (born United States), b. 1958. **Genres:** History, International Relations/Current Affairs, Politics/Government. **Career:** University of Pennsylvania, Annenberg visiting assistant professor of history, through 1999; Florida State University, associate professor and director of graduate studies, 1999-; U.S. Naval War College, adjunct professor of strategy. Writer. **Publications:** A Question of Balance: How France and the United States Created Cold War Europe, 2006. Contributor to books to periodicals. **Address:** Department of History, Florida State University, 415 Bellamy Bldg., 113 Collegiate Loop, Tallahassee, FL 32306-2200, U.S.A. **Online address:** mcreswell@fsu.edu

CREVIER, Daniel. Canadian (born Canada), b. 1947. **Genres:** Information Science/Computers. **Career:** Coreco Imaging, founder, 1979-2005. Writer and researcher. **Publications:** AI: The Tumultuous History of the Search for Artificial Intelligence, 1993. **Address:** Ophthalmos Systems Inc., 280 Victoria Ave., Longueuil, QC J4H 2J6, Canada.

CREW, Danny O(liver). American (born United States), b. 1947. **Genres:** Music, Politics/Government, History, Reference, Biography, Bibliography, Literary Criticism And History, Literary Criticism And History. **Career:** City of Boca Raton, assistant city manager, 1982-84; Collier County, staff; Pinellas Park, staff; City of Pompano Beach, assistant city manager, 1984-90; Saint Lucie County, assistant county manager, 1990-92; City of Gastonia, city manager, 1993-2003; City of Miami Gardens, city manager, 2004-. Writer. **Publications:** Presidential Sheet Music: An Illustrated Catalogue of Published Music Associated with the American Presidency and Those Who Sought the Office, 2001; Ku Klux Klan Sheet Music: An Illustrated Catalogue of Published Music, 1867-2002, 2003; American Political Music: A State-by-state Catalog of Printed and Recorded Music Related to Local, State and

National Politics, 1756-2004, 2006. **Address:** City of Miami Gardens, 1515 NW 167th St., Ste. 200, Miami Gardens, FL 33169, U.S.A. **Online address:** weetabix@quik.com

CREW, Gary. Australian (born Australia), b. 1947. **Genres:** Novels, Novellas/Short Stories, Children's Fiction, Adult Non-fiction, Picture/Board Books, Young Adult Fiction. **Career:** McDonald, Wagner and Priddle, senior draftsman and drafting consultant, 1962-72; Everton Park State High School, English teacher, 1974-78; Mitchelton State High School, English teacher, 1978-81; Aspley High School, subject master in English, 1982; Albany Creek High School, subject master in English and head of English department, 1983-88; writer, 1985-; Queensland University of Technology, creative writing lecturer, 1989-; Heinemann Octopus, series editor, 1990-; University of the Sunshine Coast, associate professor of creative writing, program leader. **Publications:** NOVELS: The Inner Circle, 1985; The House of Tomorrow, 1988; Strange Objects, 1990; No Such Country, 1991; Angel's Gate, 1993; Inventing Anthony West, 1994; (with P. Gouldthorpe) The Lost Diamonds of Killiecrankie, 1995; (with M. O'Hara) The Blue Feather, 1997; Gothic Hospital, 2000; Mama's Babies, 2000; Leo the Lion Tamer, 2000; (with P. Neilsen) Edward Britton, 2000; Force of Evil, 2002. CHILDREN'S STORY BOOKS: Tracks, 1992; Lucy's Bay, 1992; The Figures of Julian Ashcroft, 1993; First Light, 1993; Gulliver in the South Seas, 1994; The Watertower, 1994; (with P. Gouldthorpe) The Lost Diamonds of Killicrankie, 1995; Caleb, 1996; Bright Star, 1997, Tagged, 1997; The Viewer, 1997; Memorial, 1999; The Kraken, 2000; The Rainbow, 2000; Valley of the Bones, 2000; Gino the Genius, 2000; The Wreck of the Quetta, 2000; Pig on the Titanic: A True Story!, 2005; The Mystery of the Eilean Mor, 2006; Cat on the Island, 2008; End of the Line, 2008; The Truth About Emma, 2008. FICTION: AFTER DARK SERIES: The Windmill, 1998; The Fort, 1998; The Barn, 1999; The Bent-back Bridge, 1999; The Well, 1999. NONFICTION: (with M. Wilson) The Castaways of the Charles Eaton, 2002; (with R. Ingpen) In the Wake of the Mary Celeste, 2004; Young Murphy: A Boy's Adventures, 2005. NONFICTION: WITH MARK WILSON: EXTINCT SERIES: I Saw Nothing: The Extinction of the Thylacine, 2003; I Said Nothing: The Extinction of the Paradise Parrot, 2003; I Did Nothing: The Extinction of the Gastric-Brooding Frog, 2004. OTHER: Me and My Dog, 2005. Contributor to books and periodicals. **Address:** Faculty of Arts and Social Sciences, University of the Sunshine Coast, D1.34, Sippy Downs Dr., Sippy Downs, QL 4556, Australia. **Online address:** gcrew@usc.edu.au

CREW, Linda. American (born United States), b. 1951. **Genres:** Novels, Children's Fiction, Young Adult Fiction, Adult Non-fiction. **Career:** Writer. **Publications:** FOR CHILDREN: Nekomah Creek, 1991; Nekomah Creek Christmas, 1994. FOR ADULTS: Ordinary Miracles, 1993. FICTION FOR YOUNG ADULTS: Children of The River (novel), 1989; Someday I'll Laugh About This, 1990; Fire on The Wind, 1995; Long Time Passing, 1997; Brides of Eden: A True Story Imagined, 2001; A Heart for Any Fate: Westward to Oregon, 1845, 2005, rev. ed., 2009. **Address:** c/o Robin Rue, Anita Diamant Agency, 310 Madison Ave., New York, NY 10017, U.S.A. **Online address:** ljc1@earthlink.net

CREW, Louie. American (born United States), b. 1936. **Genres:** Gay And Lesbian Issues, Social Commentary, Literary Criticism And History. **Career:** Auburn University, graduate teaching fellow, 1958-59; Darlington School, master of English and Bible, 1959-62; St. Andrew's School, master of English and sacred studies, 1962-65; Penge Secondary Modern School; instructor of English, 1965-66; University of Alabama, graduate assistant, 1966-68, instructor of English, 1968-70; Independent Study in England for Experiment in International Living, director, 1970-71; Claflin College, professor of English, 1971-73, associate professor, 1988-89; Fort Valley State College, associate professor of English, 1973-79; University of Wisconsin, associate professor of English, 1979-84; Beijing International Studies University (formerly Beijing Second Institute of Foreign Languages), visiting foreign expert, 1983-84; Chinese University of Hong Kong, director of writing program, 1984-87; freelance writer, 1987-88; Rutgers University, Academic Foundations Department, associate professor, 1989-92, lecturer, 1992-94, English Department, associate professor, 1994-2001, emeritus professor, 2002-. **Publications:** POETRY: Sunspots, 1976; Midnight Lessons, 1987; Quean Lutibelle's Pew, 1990. ESSAYS: (ed.) The Gay Academic, 1978; E-Natter of Quean Lufibelle, 1990; (ed.) A Book of Revelations: Lesbian and Gay Episcopalians Tell Their Own Stories, 1991; Watching the Watchers: Quean Lutibelle's Scrapbook on Bishops of the Episcopal Church, 1994, rev. ed. 1998; (co-author) Gospel Opportunity or Gospel Threat? The Church's Debate on Sexuality, 1998. OTHER: (comp.) 101 Reasons to Be an Episcopalian, 2003. **Address:** Department of English, State University of New Jersey, 377 S Harrison St., Apt. 12D, East Orange, NJ 07018, U.S.A. **Online address:** lcrew@newark.rutgers.edu

CREW, Rudy. American (born United States), b. 1950. **Genres:** Education, Administration/Management. **Career:** Teacher, 1973-75; San Antonio High School, principal, 1975; California public school system, assistant superintendent, 1980; Sacramento public schools, deputy superintendent, 1980; Boston public school system, deputy superintendent for curriculum and instruction, 1985-87; Tacoma, WA, public schools, superintendent, 1993-95; New York City public school system, chancellor, 1995-99; Institute for K-12 Leadership, executive director; Stupski Foundation, director of district reform initiatives; Miami-Dade County Public Schools, superintendent, 2004-; California State University, faculty; Harvard University, faculty; Lesley College, faculty. Writer. **Publications:** (With T. Dyja) Only Connect: The Way to Save Our Schools, 2007. Contributor to periodicals. **Address:** Miami-Dade County Public Schools, 1450 NE 2nd Ave., Miami, FL 33132, U.S.A. **Online address:** rudy@rudycrew.net

CREWDSON, Gregory. American (born United States), b. 1962. **Genres:** Photography, Biography. **Career:** State University of New York, faculty, 1988-90; Sarah Lawrence College, instructor, 1990; Cooper Union, instructor, 1990-93; Vassar College, instructor, 1993; Yale University, professor, 1993-. Writer. **Publications:** Hover: Photographs by Gregory Crewdson, 1998; Gregory Crewdson: Dream of Life, 1999; (with A. Stern and S. Doonan) Inheritance, 2007; Beneath the Roses, 2008. **Address:** School of Art, Yale University, 1156 Chapel St., New Haven, CT 06511, U.S.A. **Online address:** info@hoverproductions.com

CREWS, Donald. American (born United States), b. 1938. **Genres:** Children's Fiction, Illustrations, Children's Non-fiction, Literary Criticism And History. **Career:** Dance Magazine, assistant art director, 1959-60; Will Burton Studios, staff designer, 1961-62. Illustrator, author, freelance artist and photographer. **Publications:** SELF ILLUSTRATED: Parade, 1982; Night at the Fair, 1998. OTHERS: We Read: A to Z, 1967; Ten Black Dots, 1968; Freight Train, 1978; Truck, 1980; Light, 1981; Harbor, 1982; Carousel, 1982; School Bus, 1984; Bicycle Race, 1985; Flying, 1986; Bigmama's, 1991; Shortcut, 1992; Sail Away, 1995; Cloudy Day/Sunny Day, 1999; Inside Freight Train, 2001; School Bus, 2001. Illustrator of books by others. **Address:** Greenwillow Books, 1350 Ave. of the Americas, New York, NY 10019, U.S.A.

CREWS, Frederick C(ampbell). American (born United States), b. 1933. **Genres:** Literary Criticism And History, Psychology. **Career:** University of California-Berkeley, instructor, 1958-60, assistant professor, 1960-63, associate professor, 1963-66, professor, 1966-94, emeritus professor of English, 1994-; Center for Advanced Study in the Behavioral Sciences, fellow, 1965-66; University of Notre Dame, Ward-Phillips lecturer, 1974-75; Princeton University, fellow, 1978; University of California-Los Angeles, Dorothy T. Burstein lecturer, 1984; University of Chicago, Frederick Ives Carpenter visiting lecturer, 1985; Portland State University, Nina Mae Kellogg lecturer, 1989. Writer. **Publications:** The Tragedy of Manners: Moral Drama in the Later Novels of Henry James, 1957; E.M. Forster: The Perils of Humanism, 1962; The Pooh Perplex: A Freshman Casebook (parodies), 1963; The Sins of the Fathers: Hawthorne's Psychological Themes, 1966; The Patch Commission (satire), 1968; Tragedy of Manners, 1971; The Random House Handbook, 1974, 6th ed., 1992; Out of My System: Psychoanalysis, Ideology, and Critical Method, 1975; (with S. Schor) The Borzoi Handbook for Writers, 1985, 3rd ed., 1993; Skeptical Engagements, 1986; The Critics Bear It Away: American Fiction and the Academy, 1992; (co-author) The Memory Wars: Freud's Legacy in Dispute, 1995; Postmodern Pooh (satire), 2001; Pooh Perplex: A Freshman Casebook, 2003; Follies of the Wise: Dissenting Essays, 2006. EDITOR: Great Short Works of Nathaniel Hawthorne, 1967; (with O. Schell) Starting Over: A College Reader, 1970; Psychoanalysis and Literary Process, 1970; The Random House Reader, 1981; Unauthorized Freud: Doubters Confront a Legend, 1998. **Address:** Department of English, University of California, 322 Wheeler Hall, Berkeley, CA 94720, U.S.A. **Online address:** fredc@berkeley.edu

CREWS, Gordon A(rthur). American (born United States), b. 1964. **Genres:** Criminology/True Crime. **Career:** University of South Carolina-Columbia, reserve police officer, 1985-86, criminal investigator, 1986; Mount Berry College, campus police officer, 1986; Richland County Sheriff's Office, deputy sheriff, 1986-88, training officer of bloodhounds for dog team,

1987-88; South Carolina Department of Corrections, Watkins Pre-Release Center, accreditation and training manager, 1988-89, construction and design assistant, 1989; Central Carolina Technical College, Department of Criminal Justice, head and faculty, 1990-94; Sumter Area Technical College, instructor, 1990; Midlands Technical College, criminal justice faculty, 1993-97; Union Institute, adjunct professor, 1996-; University of South Carolina-Beaufort, assistant professor of criminal justice, 1997-99, director of criminal justice and military programs, 1997-99; Kennedy-Western University, adjunct faculty, 1998-; Valdosta State University, assistant professor of criminal justice, 1999-2000; Jacksonville State University, associate professor and department head, 2000-03; Roger Williams University, School of Justice Studies, associate dean and associate professor, 2003-, School of Justice Studies, interim dean; Washburn University, faculty; Cameron University, faculty; Marshall University, Department of Criminal Justice and Criminology, associate professor, 2008-. Writer. **Publications:** (With R.H. Montgomery, Jr. and W.R. Garris) Faces of Violence in America, 1996; (with M.R. Counts) The Evolution of School Disturbance in America: Colonial Times to Modern Day, 1997; (with R.H. Montgomery, Jr.) A History of Correctional Violence: An Examination of Reported Causes of Riots and Disturbances, 1998; (with R.H. Montgomery, Jr.) Chasing Shadows: Confronting Juvenile Violence in America, 2001; (with S. Stanko and W. Gillespie) Living in Prison: A History of the Correctional System with an Insider's View, 2004; (ed. with R.C. Toth and C.E. Burton) In the Margins: Special Populations and American Justice, 2008; (with A.D. Crews) Juvenile Delinquency and Violence: Examining International Police and Societal Response, 2009. Contributor to books. **Address:** Department of Criminal Justice and Criminology, Marshall University, One John Marshall Dr., Huntington, WV 25755-2662, U.S.A. **Online address:** crewsg@marshall.edu

CREWS, Harry (Eugene). American (born United States), b. 1935. **Genres:** Novels, Autobiography/Memoirs, Young Adult Fiction, Young Adult Nonfiction, Mystery/Crime/Suspense, Novellas/Short Stories, Essays, Biography, Biography. **Career:** Broward Community College, English teacher, 1962-68; University of Florida, associate professor, 1968-74, professor of English, 1974-97, retired, 1997; full-time writer, 1997-. **Publications:** The Gospel Singer, 1968; Naked in Garden Hills, 1969; This Thing Don't Lead to Heaven, 1970; Karate Is a Thing of the Spirit, 1971; Car: A Novel, 1972; The Hawk Is Dying, 1973; The Gypsy's Curse: A Novel, 1974; A Feast of Snakes: A Novel, 1976; A Childhood: The Biography of a Place, 1978; Blood and Grits (non-fiction), 1979; The Enthusiast, 1981; Florida Frenzy, 1982; Two, 1984; All We Need of Hell, 1987; The Knockout Artist, 1988; Body, 1990; Madonna at Ringside, 1991; Scar Lover, 1992; Classic Crews: A Harry Crews Reader, 1993; The Mulching of America, 1995; Celebration: A Novel, 1998; Where Does One Go When There's No Place Left to Go?, 1998; (ed.) Getting Naked with Harry Crews: Interviews, 1999; An American Family: The Baby with the Curious Markings, 2006. **Address:** 2820 NW 34th St., Gainesville, FL 32605-2753, U.S.A.

CREWS, Nina. American (born United States), b. 1963. **Genres:** Children's Fiction, Picture/Board Books, Mythology/Folklore, Music. **Career:** Freelance animation artist/coordinator, 1986-94; illustrator, 1991-; Ink Tank (animation studio), producer, 1995-97. Writer. **Publications:** One Hot Summer Day, 1995; I'll Catch the Moon, 1996; Snowball, 1997; You Are Here, 1998; A High, Low, Near, Far, Loud, Quiet Story, 1999; A Ghost Story, 2001; The Neighborhood Mother Goose, 2004, Below, 2006, Sky-High Guy, 2010, The Neighborhood Sing-Along, 2011, Jack and the Beanstalk, 2011. Illustrator of books by others. Contributor to periodicals. **Address:** Greenwillow Books, 10 E 53rd St., New York, NY 10022, U.S.A. **Online address:** letters@ninacrews.com

CRIBB, Robert (Bridson). Australian (born Australia), b. 1957. **Genres:** Area Studies, History, Politics/Government. **Career:** Griffith University, lecturer in Indonesian politics, 1983-86; Australian National University, Australian Capital Territory, research fellow, 1987-90; Netherlands Institute for Advanced Study, fellow-in-residence, 1988-89; University of Queensland, lecturer in Southeast Asian history, 1990-92, senior lecturer, 1993-96, reader, 1996-; Nordic Institute of Asian Studies, research professor, 1996-97, director, 1997-99; Australian National University, senior fellow, 2003-, School of Culture, History and Language, professor of Indonesian history, 2005-08; Asian Studies Association of Australia, president. Writer. **Publications:** Gejolak revolusi di Jakarta 1945-1949: Pergulatan antara otonomi dan hegemoni, 1990; Gangsters and Revolutionaries: The Jakarta People's Militia and the Indonesian Revolution, 1945-1949, 1991; Historical Dictionary of Indonesia, 1992; (with C. Brown) Modern Indonesia: A History since 1945, 1995; Historical Atlas of Indonesia, 2000; Digital Atlas of Indonesian History, 2010; The Origins of Massacre in Indonesia, forthcoming. EDITOR AND CONTRIBUTOR: (with C. Mackerras and A. Healy) Contemporary Vietnam: Perspectives from Australia, 1988; The Indonesian Killings of 1965-1966: Studies from Java and Bali, 1990; (with M. Bocquet Siek) Islam and the Panca Sila, 1991; The Late Colonial State in Indonesia, 1994; (with K. Christie) Historical Injustice and Democratic Transition in Eastern Asia and Northern Europe: Ghosts at the Table of Democracy, 2002; (with L. Narangoa) Imperial Japan and National Identity in Asia, 1895-1945, 2003. Works appear in anthologies. Contributor to journals. **Address:** Department of Pacific & Asian History, Research School of Asia and the Pacific, Australian National University, Canberra, AC 0200, Australia. **Online address:** robert.cribb@anu.edu.au

CRIDDLE, Byron. British (born England), b. 1942. **Genres:** Politics/Government, Sociology, Social Sciences. **Career:** University of Massachusetts, visiting professor, 1984-85; University of Aberdeen, Department of Politics, reader, 1996-2007, emeritus reader, 2007-. Writer. **Publications:** Socialists and European Integration: A Study of the French Socialist Party, 1969; (with D.S. Bell) The French Socialist Party: Resurgence and Victory, 1984, 2nd ed., 1988; (with D.S. Bell) The French Communist Party in the Fifth Republic, 1994; (with R. Waller) The Almanac of British Politics, 5th ed., 1995, 8th ed., 2007; (with A. Roth) The New MPS of '97 and Retreads, 1997; (with A. Roth) Parliamentary Profiles, 1997-2002, 1998; (with A. Roth) The New MPs of '01, 2001. **Address:** Department of Politics & International Relations, The School of Social Science, University of Aberdeen, Edward Wright Bldg., Aberdeen, AB24 3QY, Scotland. **Online address:** b.criddle@abdn.ac.uk

CRIDER, (Allen) Bill(y). Also writes as Jack MacLane, Nick Carter. American (born United States), b. 1941. **Genres:** Novels, Mystery/Crime/Suspense, Westerns/Adventure, Children's Fiction, Humor/Satire, Young Adult Fiction, Criminology/True Crime. **Career:** Corsicana High School teacher, 1963-65; Howard Payne University, associate professor, 1971-74, professor, 1974-83, chair, 1977-83; Alvin Community College, Department of English, professor and chair, 1983-2002. Writer. **Publications:** WESTERN NOVELS: Ryan Rides Back, 1988; Galveston Gunman, 1988; A Time for Hanging, 1989; Medicine Show, 1990, Outrage at Blanco, 1998, Texas Vigilante, 1999. CRIME NOVELS: (with J. Davis as Nick Carter) The Coyote Connection, 1981; Too Late to Die, 1986; Shotgun Saturday Night, 1987; Cursed to Death, 1988; One Dead Dean, 1988; Death on the Move, 1989; Dying Voices, 1989; Evil at the Root, 1990. MYSTERIES: Blood Marks, 1991; Dead on the Island, 1991; Booked for a Hanging, 1992; Gator Kill, 1992; The Texas Capitol Murders, 1992; Murder Most Fowl, 1994; When Old Men Die, 1994; A Dangerous Thing, 1994; Murder is an Art, 1999; The Prairie Chicken Kill, 1996, Murder Takes a Break, 1996; Winning Can Be Murder, 1996; Death by Accident, 1998; A Ghost of a Chance, 2000; A Romantic Way to Die, 2001; The Nighttime Is the Right Time: A Collection of Stories, 2001; A Knife in the Back, 2002; Red, White, and Blue Murder, 2003; A Bond with Death, 2004; Dead Soldiers, 2004; A Mammoth Murder, 2006; Murder Among the O.W.L.S, 2007; Of All Sad Words, 2008; Murder in Four Parts, 2009; Murder in the Air, 2010. NOVELS AS JACK MacLANE: Keepers of the Beast, 1988; Goodnight Moom, 1989; Blood Dreams, 1989; Rest in Peace, 1990; Just Before Dark, 1990; (with C. Wilson) Houston Homicide, 2007. MIKE GONZO, YOUNG ADULT NOVELS: Mike Gonzo and the Sewer Monster, 1996; Mike Gonzo and the Almost Invisible Man, 1996; Mike Gonzo and the UFO Terror, 1997. OTHERS: (ed.) Mass Market American Publishing, 1982; A Vampire Named Fred (for children), 1990; Muttketeer!, 1997; (with W. Scott) Murder under Blue Skies, 1998; Murder in the Mist, 2000; Mississippi Vivian, 2010. **Address:** c/o Kim Lionetti, Bookends L.L.C., 136 Long Hill Rd., Gillette, NJ 07933, U.S.A. **Online address:** abc@billcrider.com

CRISLIP, Andrew T. (Andrew Todd Crislip). American (born United States), b. 1973. **Genres:** Theology/Religion. **Career:** University of Hawaii, assistant professor to associate professor of religion. Writer, historian and educator. **Publications:** From Monastery to Hospital: Christian Monasticism and the Transformation of Health Care in Late Antiquity, 2005. Contributor to periodicals and journals. **Address:** University of Hawaii, Department of Religion, Sakamaki Hall A311, 2530 Dole St., Honolulu, HI 96822, U.S.A. **Online address:** crislip@hawaii.edu

CRISLIP, Andrew Todd. *See* **CRISLIP, Andrew T.**

CRISP, Oliver D. British (born England), b. 1972. **Genres:** Theology/Religion, Essays, Philosophy. **Career:** University of St. Andrews, instructor, 2002-04; University of Notre Dame, Center for Philosophy of Religion, Frederick J. Crosson research fellow, 2004-05; Regent College, visiting lecturer, 2005, 2007-09; University of Bristol, lecturer, 2006-08, reader in theology, 2008-11; Princeton University, Center for Theological Inquiry, Scheide fellow in theology, 2008-09; Fuller Theological Seminary, professor of systematic theology, 2011-. Writer and theologian. **Publications:** Jonathan Edwards and the Metaphysics of Sin, 2005; Divinity and Humanity: The Incarnation Reconsidered, 2007; An American Augustinian: Sin and Salvation in the Dogmatic Theology of William G.T. Shedd, 2007; God Incarnate: Explorations in Christology, 2009; Retrieving Doctrine: Essays in Reformed Theology, 2010; Revisioning Christology, Theology in the Reformed Tradition, 2011; Jonathan Edwards on God and Creation, 2012. EDITOR: (with P. Helm) Jonathan Edwards: Philosophical Theologian, 2003; (with M.C. Rea) Analytic Theology: New Essays in the Philosophy of Theology, 2009; A Reader in Contemporary Philosophical Theology, 2009; (with G.D. Costa, M. Davies and P. Hampson) Theology and Philosophy: Faith and Reason, 2012; (with D. Sweeney) After Jonathan Edwards, The Courses of the New England Theology, 2012. Contributor of articles to books and journals. **Address:** Fuller Theological Seminary, 135 North Oakland Ave., Pasadena, CA 91182, U.S.A. **Online address:** oliver.crisp@fuller.edu

CRIST, Judith. American (born United States), b. 1922. **Genres:** Film, Photography. **Career:** Washington State University, instructor, 1942-44; New York Herald Tribune, reporter, 1945-60, associate drama critic, 1957-63, arts editor, 1960-63, film critic, 1963-66; Columbia University, Graduate School of Journalism, adjunct professor, 1958-; NBC-TV Today Show, film and theatre critic, 1963-73; New York World Journal Tribune, film critic, 1966-67; TV Guide, contributing editor and film critic, 1966-88; New York Magazine, film critic, 1968-75, Saturday Review, 1975-78, 1980-84, 1978-83; WWOR-TV, arts critic, 1981-87; Coming Attractions, critical columnist, 1985-93. **Publications:** The Private Eye, the Cowboy, and the Very Naked Girl: Movies from Cleo to Clyde, (nonfiction), 1968; Judith Crist's TV Guide to the Movies, 1974; (ed. with S. Sealy) Take 22: Moviemakers on Moviemaking, 1984, rev. ed., 1991; (Designer) The Films of the Thirties, 1990. CONTRIBUTOR: Censorship: For and Against, 1971; Marriage: For and Against, 1972; Favorite Movies, 1972; Those Lips, Those Eyes: A Celebration of Classic Hollywood Sensuality, 1992. Contributor to perioidcals. **Address:** Crist Associates Ltd., 180 Riverside Dr., New York, NY 10024, U.S.A. **Online address:** jc630@columbia.edu

CRITCHLEY, Simon. American/British (born England), b. 1960. **Genres:** Philosophy, Politics/Government, History. **Career:** University of Essex, professor, 1989-2004; The New School for Social Research, chair, professor of philosophy, Hans Jonas professor; Eugene Lang College, professor of philosophy; Collège Internationale de Philosophie, program director; University of Notre Dame, visiting professor; Sydney University, visiting professor; Cardozo Law School, visiting professor; University of Oslo, visiting professor. Writer. **Publications:** The Ethics of Deconstruction: Derrida and Levinas, 1992, 2nd ed., 1999; (contrib.) Deconstruction and Pragmatism, 1996; Very Little: Almost Nothing: Death, Philosophy, Literature, 1997, 2nd ed., 2004; Ethics-Politics-Subjectivity: Essays on Derrida, Levinas, and Contemporary French Thought, 1999; Continental Philosophy: A Very Short Introduction, 2001; On Humour, 2002; Things Merely Are: Philosophy in the Poetry of Wallace Stevens, 2005; Infinitely Demanding: Ethics of Commitment, Politics of Resistance, 2007; Laughing in a Foreign Language, 2008; (with R. Schurmann) On Heidegger's Being and Time, 2008; The Book of Dead Philosophers, 2008; Der Katechismus des Bürgers, 2008; Faith of the Faithless: Experiments in Political Theology, 2012. EDITOR: (with R. Bernasconi) Re-reading Levinas, 1991; (with A.T. Peperzak and R. Bernasconi) Emmanuel Levinas: Basic Philosophical Writings, 1996; (with P. Dews) Deconstructive Subjectivities, 1996; (with W.R. Schroeder) A Companion to Continental Philosophy, 1998; (with R. Bernasconi) The Cambridge Companion to Levinas, 2002; (with O. Marchart) Laclau: A Critical Reader, 2004. **Address:** Department of Philosophy, The New School for Social Research, Rm. 245, 65 5th Ave., New York, NY 10011, U.S.A. **Online address:** critchls@newschool.edu

CRITCHLOW, Donald T. American (born United States), b. 1948. **Genres:** History, Politics/Government, Social Sciences. **Career:** University of California, teaching assistant, 1974, Institute of Industrial Relations, research assistant, 1975, acting instructor in environmental studies, 1977; San Francisco State University, acting instructor in history, 1976; North Central College, assistant professor of history, 1978-81; University of Dayton, assistant professor of history, 1981-83; University of Notre Dame, Department of History, assistant professor, associate professor, 1983-91; University of Warsaw, visiting professor, 1988-89; Saint Louis University, Department of History, chair, professor, 1991-; University of Hong Kong, visiting professor, 1997-98; John Hopkins University Press, reader; Cornell University Press, reader; Northern Illinois University Press, reader; Temple University Press, reader; Dorsey Press, reader; Pennsylvania State University Press, reader; Journal of Policy History, fouding director; Cambridge University Press, general editor. **Publications:** The Brookings Institution, 1916-1952, Expertise and the Public Interest in a Democratic Society, 1985; (with W. Rorabaugh) America!: A Concise History, 1994; Studebaker: The Life and Death of an American Corporation, 1996; The Serpentine Way: Family Planning Policy in Postwar America: Elites, Agendas, and Political Mobilization, 1997; Intended Consequences: Birth Control, Abortion and the Federal Government in Modern America, 1999; (with P. Baker and W.J. Rorabaugh) America's Promise: A Concise History of the United States, 2004; Phyllis Schlafly and Grassroots Conservatism: A Woman's Crusade, 2005; The Conservative Ascendancy: How the GOP Right Made Political History, 2007, 2nd ed. as The Conservative Ascendancy: How the Republican Right Rose to Power in Modern Americ, 2011; (with N. MacLean) Debating the American Conservative Movement: 1945 to the Present, 2009. EDITOR: Socialism in the Heartland: The Midwestern Experience, 1890-1920, 1986; (with E. Hawley) Federal Social Policy: The Historical Dimension, 1989; (with E. Hawley) Poverty and Public Policy in Modern America, 1989; (with A. Bartnicki) A History of the United States, 1995; The Politics of Abortion and Birth Control in Historical Perspective, 1996; (with C.H. Parker) With Us Always: A History of Private Charity and Public Welfare, 1998; (with A. Critchlow) Enemies of the State: Personal Stories from the Gulag, 2002; (with M.C. Sherman and J. Korasick) Political Conspiracies in America: A Reader, 2008; (with E. Raymond) Hollywood and Politics: A Sourcebook, 2009; (with P. Vandermeer) Oxford Encyclopedia of American Political and Legal History, 2012. **Address:** Department of History, St. Louis University, 3800 Lindell Blvd., PO Box 56907, Saint Louis, MO 63156, U.S.A. **Online address:** dcritchlow@sbcglobal.net

CRITTENDEN, Ann. American (born United States), b. 1937. **Genres:** Economics, Social Work, Business/Trade/Industry. **Career:** Southern Methodist University, lecturer, 1960-62; Rutgers University, lecturer, 1963-66; Fortune Magazine, reporter, 1967-71; Newsweek, finance writer and associate editor, 1971-72, foreign correspondent in Asia and South America, 1972-74; New York Times, economics reporter, 1975-83; Fund for Investigative Reporting, executive director, 1982-88; writer, 1983-; Aspen Institute, project director, 1985; Massachusetts Institute of Technology, visiting lecturer; Yale University, visiting lecturer; CBS News, economics commentator. **Publications:** Sanctuary: A Story of American Conscience and the Law in Collision, 1988; Killing the Sacred Cows: Bold Ideas for a New Economy, 1993; The Price of Motherhood: Why the Most Important Job in the World Is Still the Least Valued, 2001; If You've Raised Kids, You Can Manage Anything: Leadership Begins at Home, 2004. Contributor of articles to periodicals. **Address:** 3412 Lowell St. NW, Washington, DC 20016, U.S.A.

CRNOBRNJA (TSERNOBERNYA), Mihailo. Canadian/Yugoslav (born Canada), b. 1946. **Genres:** Economics, Politics/Government, Business/Trade/Industry, Literary Criticism And History. **Career:** University of Belgrade, assistant, 1974, assistant professor, 1979, associate professor, 1984, professor of political science, 1984-89; United Belgrade Bank, Center of Economic Research, director, 1978-84; Serbian Government, minister and director for the socio-economic planning, 1986-89; Government of Yugoslavia, ambassador to the European community, 1989-92; McGill University, professor of political science, 1993-; University Carleton, professor; University of Novi Sad, Centre for Advanced European Studies and Research (CAESAR), faculty of economics, finance and administration. Writer. **Publications:** (With M. Karr) Business and Investment Opportunities in Yugoslavia, 1982; (ed.) Information as an Economic Resource, 1985; (ed.) Europe 1992 and Beyond, 1991; Le drame Yougoslave, 1992, trans. as The Yugoslav Drama: An Insider's View, 1994; (with Z. Papic) A Programme for Economic Reconstruction and Modernization in Countries of Former Yugoslavia, 1995; (ed. with Z. Papipć) The Cost of War in Former Yugoslavia, 1995. UNTRANSLATED WORKS: Reciklaza petro-dolara i finansijska pozicijaJugoslavije, 1981; Zivotna sredina i ekonomski razvoj, 1982; Č ovekoviživotna sredina i ekonomski razvoj, 1984; Socijalna politika uBeogradu, 1985; (ed.) Konferencija Kako ubrzati integraciju Srbije u Evropsku uniju: zbornik radova, 2008. Contributor to books and periodicals. **Address:** Centre for Advanced European Studies and Research, University of Novi Sad, 5 Trg Dositeja Obradovića, Novi Sad, 21000, Serbia.

CROALL, Jonathan. American/British (born England), b. 1941. **Genres:** Children's Fiction, Biography, Environmental Sciences/Ecology, History, Local History/Rural Topics, Medicine/Health, Self Help, Biography, Biography. **Career:** Cassell & Co., editor, 1964-65; Penguin Books, editor, 1965-66; Oxford University Press, editor, 1966-69; Penguin Education, managing editor, 1969-71, commissioning editor, 1971-74; Times Educational Supplement, features editor, 1975-82; Arts Express, editor, 1983-87; Bedford Square Press, managing director, 1987-90; freelance writer, 1990-2001; National Theatre, Stagewrite magazine, editor, 1991-2001. **Publications:** Don't Shoot the Goalkeeper, 1974; The Parents' Day School Book, 1978; Neill of Summerhill: The Permanent Rebel, 1983, 2nd ed., 1987; (ed. and intro.) All the Best, Neill: Letters from Summerhill, 1983; (ed.) Don't You Know There's a War On?: The People's Voice, 1939-45, 1988; Gielgud: A Theatrical Life, 2001; The Coming of Godot: A Short History of a Masterpiece, 2005; Buzz Buzz!: Playwrights, Actors and Directors at the National Theatre, 2008; John Gielgud: Matinee Idol to Movie Star, 2011. Contributor to periodicals. **Address:** A.P. Watt Ltd., 26/28 Bedford Row, London, GL WC1R 4HL, England.

CROCE, Paul Jerome. American (born United States), b. 1957. **Genres:** History, Social Sciences, Sociology, Theology/Religion, Philosophy. **Career:** Brown University, Upward Bound Program, tutor, 1976-77, 1978-79, teaching assistant, 1980-81, 1983-84, Program in American Civilization, teaching fellow, 1982-83, tutor, 1983-85; Georgetown University, Department of History, summer instructor, 1983-84, visiting assistant professor, 1985-87; Rollins College, Department of History, visiting assistant professor, 1987-89; Stetson University, Department of American Studies, instructor in social science, 1988, assistant professor, 1989-95, associate professor, 1995-2001, professor, 2001-, chair of American studies, 1997-2002, 2004-09; Harcourt Brace Jovanovich, editorial consultant, 1988-89. Writer. **Publications:** Science and Religion in the Era of William James, vol. I: Eclipse of Certainty, 1820-1880, 1995. Contributor of articles to periodicals and books. **Address:** Department of American Studies, Stetson University, 421 N Woodland Blvd., PO Box 8274, DeLand, FL 32720, U.S.A. **Online address:** pcroce@stetson.edu

CROCKER, Ruth. (Ruth Hutchinson Crocker). American/British (born England), b. 1943. **Genres:** Social Work, Philosophy, History. **Career:** Purdue University, visiting assistant professor of history, 1982-83; Auburn University, Department of History, visiting assistant professor, 1983-88, assistant professor, 1988-93, associate professor, 1993-2001, alumni professor, 2001-06, professor, 2002-, Auburn Women's Studies Program, director, 1989-91, 2005-. Writer. **Publications:** (Ed. with M. Altman) Social Groupwork and Alcoholism, 1982; Social Work and Social Order: The Settlement Movement in Two Industrial Cities, 1889-1930, 1992; Mrs. Russell Sage: Women's Activism and Philanthropy in Gilded Age and Progressive Era America, 2006. Contributor to books and periodicals. **Address:** Department of History, Auburn University, 325 Thach Hall, Auburn, AL 36849-5207, U.S.A. **Online address:** crockrc@auburn.edu

CROCKER, Ruth Hutchinson. *See* **CROCKER, Ruth.**

CROCKETT, David A. American (born United States), b. 1963. **Genres:** Politics/Government. **Career:** Trinity University, associate professor of political science, 1999-. Writer. **Publications:** The Opposition Presidency: Leadership and the Constraints of History, 2002; Running Against the Grain: How Opposition Presidents Win the White House, 2008. **Address:** Department of Political Science, Trinity University, 1 Trinity Pl., San Antonio, TX 78212-7200, U.S.A. **Online address:** dcrocket@trinity.edu

CROCKETT, Rigel. American/Canadian (born Canada), b. 1974. **Genres:** Marine Sciences/Oceanography, Environmental Sciences/Ecology. **Career:** Writer. **Publications:** Fair Wind and Plenty of It: A Modern-Day Tall Ship Adventure, 2005. **Address:** c/o Author Mail, Rodale Inc., 33 E Minor St., Emmaus, PA 18098-0099, U.S.A. **Online address:** rigel@rigelcrockett.com

CROFT, Barbara. American (born United States), b. 1944. **Genres:** Novels, Novellas/Short Stories, Science Fiction/Fantasy, Young Adult Fiction, Literary Criticism And History. **Career:** Writer. **Publications:** Primary Colors and Other Stories, 1991; Necessary Fictions, 1998; Moon's Crossing, 2003; Columbia, forthcoming. Contributor to periodicals. **Address:** 202 N Kenilworth Ave., Oak Park, IL 60302, U.S.A. **Online address:** blcroft@aol.com

CROFT, Robert W. *See* **CROFT, Robert W(ayne).**

CROFT, Robert W(ayne). (Robert W. Croft). American (born United States), b. 1957. **Genres:** Literary Criticism And History, Bibliography. **Career:** Teacher, 1978-89; Gainesville College, associate professor of English, 1993-, professor, coordinator. Writer. **Publications:** Anne Tyler: A Bio-Bibliography, 1995; An Anne Tyler Companion, 1998; A Zora Neale Hurston Companion, 2002. Contributor to periodicals. **Address:** Department of English, Gainesville College, 3820 Mundy Mill Rd., PO Box 1358, Gainesville, GA 30503, U.S.A. **Online address:** bcroft@gc.peachnet.edu

CROISSANT, Jennifer L. American (born United States), b. 1965. **Genres:** Social Sciences, Education, Sciences, Technology. **Career:** University of Arizona, Department of Gender and Women's Studies, assistant professor, associate professor, 1995, director of graduate studies, 2005-08, School of Anthropology, associate professor, Department of Sociology, associate professor, Department of Materials Science and Engineering, assistant professor, Program on Culture, Science, Technology, and Society, assistant professor, Institute of the Environment, affiliate faculty. Writer. **Publications:** (Ed. with S. Restivo) Degrees of Compromise: Industrial Interests and Academic Values, 2001; (co-ed.) Appropriating Technology: Vernacular Science and Social Power, 2004; (with W.K. Bauchspies and S. Restivo) Science, Technology, and Society: A Sociological Approach, 2006. Contributor to periodicals. **Address:** Department of Gender & Women's Studies, University of Arizona, Rm. 206, 925 N Tyndall Ave., PO Box 210438, Tucson, AZ 85721, U.S.A. **Online address:** jlc@email.arizona.edu

CROKER, Richard. American (born United States), b. 1946?. **Genres:** Novels, Social Sciences, History. **Career:** Turner Broadcasting System, television producer and writer. Documentary filmmaker. **Publications:** To Make Men Free: A Novel of the Battle of Antietam, 2004; No Greater Courage: A Novel of the Battle of Fredericksburg, 2006; The Boomer Century, 1946-2046: How America's Most Influential Generation Changed Everything, 2007. **Address:** c/o Author Mail, William Morrow/ HarperCollins, 10 E 53rd St., New York, NY 10022, U.S.A. **Online address:** richard@rcroker.com

CROMARTIE, Alan. British (born England), b. 1964. **Genres:** Law, Theology/Religion, Philosophy, History. **Career:** University of Reading, professor, school director of research, Political Theory Centre, director, Liberal Way of War Programme, director. Writer. **Publications:** Sir Matthew Hale, 1609- 1676: Law, Religion, and Natural Philosophy, 1995; (ed.) A Dialogue between a Philosopher and a Student, of the Common Laws of England, 2005; The Constitutionalist Revolution: An Essay on the History of England, 1450-1642, 2006. **Address:** School of Politics and International Relations, University of Reading, Whiteknights, PO Box 218, Reading, BR RG6 6AA, England. **Online address:** a.d.t.cromartie@reading.ac.uk

CROMWELL, Rue L(eVelle). American (born United States), b. 1928. **Genres:** Psychology, Psychiatry, Medicine/Health. **Career:** George Peabody College for Teachers, assistant professor, 1955-, professor, through 1961; Vanderbilt University, professor, 1961-69; Lafayette Clinic, Division of Psychology, chief, 1969-72; University of Rochester, professor of psychiatry, pediatrics and psychology, 1972-86; University of Kansas, M. Erik Wright distinguished professor, 1986-2001, professor emeritus of clinical psychology, 2001-. Writer. **Publications:** The Development of Behavior Dimensions for Emotionally Disturbed Children: A Study of Relevant Indicators for Classroom Techniques, Therapeutic Methods and Prognosis, 1967; Acute Myocardial Infarction: Reaction and Recovery, 1977; (co-author) The Nature of Schizophrenia: New Approaches to Research and Treatment, 1978; Schizophrenia: Origins, Processes, Treatment and Outcome, 1993; Being Human: Human Being, 2010. **Address:** Department of Psychology, University of Kansas, 2385 Irving Hill Rd., Lawrence, KS 66045-7563, U.S.A. **Online address:** cromwell@ku.edu

CRON, Ian Morgan. American (born United States), b. 1960. **Genres:** Theology/Religion, Novels, Autobiography/Memoirs. **Career:** Young Life, area director, 1983, associate regional director, 1990; Trinity Church, co-founder, 1999, senior pastor, founding pastor emeritus; Stanwich Congregational Church, minister of outreach. Writer. **Publications:** Chasing Francis: A Pilgrim's Tale, 2006; Jesus, My Father, the CIA, and Me: A Memoir of Sorts, 2011. **Address:** Alive Communications, 7680 Goddard St., Ste. 200, Colorado Springs, CO 80920, U.S.A. **Online address:** iancron@gmail.com

CRONIN, Jeremy. South African (born South Africa), b. 1949. **Genres:** Poetry. **Career:** University of Cape Town, lecturer in political science, through

1976; South African Communist Party, deputy secretary general, 1989-, deputy general-secretary, 1995-; deputy minister of transport, 2009-. Writer. **Publications:** (Ed. with A.D. Crespigny) Ideologies of Politics, 1975; Inside, 1983; (with R. Suttner) 30 Years of the Freedom Charter, 1985; Even the Dead: Poems, Parables and a Jeremiad, 1997; Inside & Out: Poems from Inside and Even the Dead, 1999; (with R. Suttner) 50 Years of the Freedom Charter, 2006; More than a Casual Contact, 2006. **Address:** PO Box 1027, Johannesburg, 2000, South Africa.

CRONIN, Mary J. American (born United States), b. 1947. **Genres:** Business/Trade/Industry, Information Science/Computers. **Career:** Boston College, Carroll School of Management, professor of information systems and management; MedHealthWorld, founding partner; Auster Capital Partners L.L.C., advisor; Renu Mobile Journal, advisor. Writer. **Publications:** Performance Measurement for Public Services in Academic and Research Libraries, 1985; Doing Business on the Internet: How the Electronic Highway Is Transforming American Companies, 1994, 2nd ed., 1995; (ed.) The Internet Strategy Handbook: Lessons from the New Business Frontier, 1996; Global Advantage on the Internet: From Corporate Connectivity to International Competitiveness, 1996; (ed.) Banking and Finance on the Internet, 1997; Unchained Value: The New Logic of Digital Business, 2000; (with S.B. Guthery) Mobile Application Development with SMS and the SIM Toolkit, 2002; (with S.B. Guthery) Developing MMS Applications: Multimedia Messaging Services for Wireless Networks, 2003; Smart Products, Smarter Services: Strategies for Embedded Control, 2010. **Address:** Carroll School of Management, Boston College, Fulton Hall 350A, 140 Commonwealth Ave., Chestnut Hill, MA 02467, U.S.A. **Online address:** cronin@bc.edu

CRONIN, Mike. Irish/British (born England), b. 1967. **Genres:** Sports/Fitness, Politics/Government, History. **Career:** Sheffield Hallam University, lecturer; De Montfort University, lecturer, senior research fellow, 1988-, visiting fellow and head of research and humanities; Boston College-Ireland, Center for Irish Programs, visiting fellow, 2003, Centre for Irish Programmes, academic director, 2005-. Writer. **Publications:** The Blueshirts and Irish Politics, 1997; Sport and Nationalism in Ireland: Gaelic Games, Soccer, and Irish Identity since 1884, 1998; A History of Ireland, 2001; (with T. Chandler and W. Vamplew) Sport and Physical Education: The Key Concepts, 2002, 2nd ed., 2007; (with D. Adair) The Wearing of the Green: A History of St. Patrick's Day, 2002; Irish History for Dummies, 2006; (with R. Higgins) Places We Play, 2011. EDITOR: The Failure of British Fascism: The Far Right and the Fight for Political Recognition, 1996; (with D. Mayall) Sporting Nationalisms: Identity, Ethnicity, Immigration, and Assimilation, 1998; (with J.M. Regan) Ireland: The Politics of Independence, 1922-49, 2000; (with J. Bale) Sport and Postcolonialism, 2002; (with W. Murphy and P. Rouse) The Gaelic Athletic Association, 1884-2009, 2009; (with M. Duncan and P. Rouse) The GAA: A People's History, 2009. **Address:** Centre for Irish Programmes, Boston College, 42 St. Stephen's Green, Dublin, DU 2, Ireland. **Online address:** croninmr@bc.edu

CRONISH, Nettie. Canadian (born Canada), b. 1954. **Genres:** Food And Wine. **Career:** King Ranch, demonstration chef; Sunrise Soya Foods, chef; Loblaws Supermarkets, teacher of cooking; Big Carrot Health Food Store, teacher of cooking; Calphalon Culinary Centre, teacher of cooking; Dish Cooking School, teacher of cooking; LCBO, teacher of cooking; George Brown College, teacher of cooking; Great Cooks on Eight, teacher of cooking; Liquor Control Board of Ontario, teacher of cooking; Big Carrot Natural Foods, resident cooking instructor; President's Choice Cooking School, teacher; Nella Cucina Cooking School, teacher; Women's Culinary Network, founding member. Author. **Publications:** Nettie's Vegetarian Kitchen, 1996; New Vegetarian Basics, 1999; (with B. Selley and S. Havala) The Complete Idiot's Guide to Being Vegetarian in Canada, 2000. **Address:** Women's Culinary Network, 11 Dunloe Rd., Toronto, ON M4V 2W4, Canada. **Online address:** nettie@nettiecronish.com

CRONON, William. American (born United States), b. 1954. **Genres:** History, Politics/Government, Social Sciences, Mathematics/Statistics. **Career:** Local Materials Center, educational slide sets and films, writer and director, 1971-73; University Bookstore, faculty, 1973-76; Family and Community History Center, instructor for the summer institute on quantitative methods, 1980-81; Yale University, assistant professor of western American and urban history, 1981-86, associate professor of history, 1986-91, professor of history, 1991-92; University of Wisconsin, Frederick Jackson Turner professor of history, geography and environmental studies, 1992-2003, Frederick Jackson Turner and Vilas research professor of history, 2003-, College of Letters and Science, director of the honors program, 1996-98, Chadbourne Residential College, founding faculty director, 1997-2000; The Trust for Public Land, director; American Society for Environmental History, president. Writer. **Publications:** Changes in the Land: Indians, Colonists and the Ecology of New England, 1983; Nature's Metropolis: Chicago and the Great West, 1991; (ed. with G. Miles and J. Gitlin) Under an Open Sky: Rethinking America's Western Past, 1992; (ed. with M.J. McDonnell and S.T.A. Pickett) Humans as Components of Ecosystems: The Ecology of Subtle Human Effects and Populated Areas, 1993; (ed.) Uncommon Ground: Toward Reinventing Nature, 1995; Uncommon Ground: Rethinking the Human Place in Nature, 1996; (co-author) Repensando la Naturaleza: Encuentros y Desencuentros Disciplinarios en Torno a lo Ambiental, 2002; (foreword) Dreaming of Sheep in Navajo Country, 2009; Saving Nature in Time: The Environmental Past and the Human Future, forthcoming. Contributor to journals and books. **Address:** Department of History, University of Wisconsin-Madison, 5103 Humanities Bldg., 455 N Park St., PO Box 5056, Madison, WI 53706, U.S.A. **Online address:** wcronon@wisc.edu

CROOK, J(oseph) Mordaunt. British (born England), b. 1937. **Genres:** Architecture, Art/Art History, History. **Career:** Institute of Historical Research, research fellow, 1961-62; University of London, Royal Holloway and Bedford New College, research fellow, 1962-63, lecturer in history, 1965-75, reader, 1975-81, professor, 1981-99, professor emeritus, 1999-, public orator, 1988-90, Victorian Studies Centre, director, 1990-99; Leicester University, assistant lecturer, 1963-65; Warburg Institute, research fellow, 1970-71; University of Oxford, Slade Professor of Fine Arts, 1979-80; Magdalen College, Waynflete Lecturer, 1984-85; Cambridge University, Gonville and Caius College, visiting fellow, 1984-85; British Academy, fellow. Writer. **Publications:** (Contrib.) Sir William Chambers, Knight of the Polar Star, 1970; The British Museum, 1971; Victorian Architecture: A Visual Anthology, 1972; The Greek Revival: Neo-Classical Attitudes in British Architecture 1760-1870, 1972; The Reform Club, 1973; (with M.H. Port) The History of the King's Works, vol. VI, 1782-1851, 1973; (with H.M. Colvin, J. Newman and K. Downes) The History of the King's Works, vol. V, 1660-1782, 1976; (contrib.) Thomas Harrison in Lancaster, 1978; William Burges and the High Victorian Dream, 1981; The Strange Genius of William Burges, 1981; (with C.A. Lennox-Boyd) Axel Haig and the Victorian Vision of the Middle Ages, 1983; The Dilemma of Style: Architectural Ideas from the Picturesque to the Post Modern, 1987; John Carter and the Mind of the Gothic Revival, 1995; The Rise of the Nouveaux Riches: Style and Status in Victorian and Edwardian Architecture, 1999; London's Arcadia: John Nash and the Planning of Regent's Park, 2001; The Architect's Secret: Victorian Critics and the Image of Gravity, 2003; Brasenose: The Biography of an Oxford College, 2008. EDITOR: (and intro.) History of the Gothic Revival, 1970; Six Essays, 1972; The Gentleman's House, 1972; The Gothic Revival, 1995; Bedford College, University of London: Memories of 150 Years, 2001. Contributor to periodicals. **Address:** Department of History, Royal Holloway, University of London, Egham, SR TW20 0EX, England.

CROOK, Marion. Canadian (born Canada), b. 1941. **Genres:** Young Adult Fiction, Young Adult Non-fiction, Children's Fiction, Children's Non-fiction, Mystery/Crime/Suspense, Writing/Journalism, Criminology/True Crime. **Career:** Public health nurse, 1963-82; Kwantlen Polytechnic University, instructor. Writer. **Publications:** FICTION: Payment in Death, 1987, Stone Dead, 1987; The Hidden Gold Mystery 1987; No Safe Place, 1988; Crosscurrents, 1988; Island Feud, 1991; Riptide!, 1992; Summer of Madness, 1995; Riding Scared, 1996; Cutting It Close, 1998. NONFICTION: The Face in the Mirror: Teenagers Adoption Talk about, 1986, rev. ed., 2000; Please Listen to Me: Your Guide to Understanding Teenagers and Suicide, 1988, The Body Image Trap: Understanding and Rejecting Body Image Myths, 1992; The Trials of Eve: A Viewers' Guide To The Film, 1992; Looking Good: Teenagers and Eating Disorders, 1992; My Body: Women Speak Out about Their Health Care, 1995; (with N. Wise) How to Self-Publish and Make Money, 1996; How to Write Books for Kids and Teens, 1998; Suicide: Teens Talk to Teens, 1998; Out of the Darkness: Teens and Suicide, 2003; Teen Suicide; 2003. OTHERS: A Yen for Trouble, 1982; Fingerprints: Crime Writers of Canada, 1984; A Question of Justice-1886, 1985; The Face in the Mirror, 1986; Writing Mystery Stories, 1989; Writers on Writing, 1989; Writing Books for Kids and Teens, 1998. **Address:** Kwantlen Polytechnic University, 12666 72nd Ave., Surrey, BC V3W 2M8, Canada. **Online address:** marion.mckinnon@kwantlen.ca

CROOKER, Barbara. (Barbara Poti). American (born United States), b.

1945. **Genres:** Poetry. **Career:** Corning Community College, adjunct instructor in English, 1974-76; Elmira College, adjunct instructor, 1975; Tompkins Cortland Community College, adjunct instructor in English, 1975-76; County College Morris, adjunct instructor of English, 1978-79; Leigh County Community College, instructor in community services, 1980; Northampton Area Community College, adjunct assistant professor, 1980-82; Cedar Crest College, instructor, 1982-85, adjunct professor, 1999. Writer. **Publications:** Radiance: Poems, 2005; Line Dance: Poems, 2008; More: Poems, 2010. **Address:** 7928 Woodsbluff Run, Fogelsville, PA 18051, U.S.A. **Online address:** info@barbaracrooker.com

CROPPER, Elizabeth. American/British (born England), b. 1944. **Genres:** Art/Art History, Social Sciences. **Career:** Tyler School of Art, professor; Johns Hopkins University, professor, 1985-, Charles Singleton Center for Italian Studies, director; Collège de France, visiting professor, 1996; National Gallery of Art, Center for Advanced Study in the Visual Arts, dean, 2000-. Writer. **Publications:** The Ideal of Painting: Pietro Testa's Dusseldorf Notebook, 1984; Pietro Testa, 1612-1650: Prints and Drawings, 1988; (intro.) Mannerism and Maniera, 1992; (ed. with G. Perini and F. Solinas and intro.) Documentary Culture: Florence and Rome from Grand-Duke Ferdinand I to Pope Alexander VII: Papers from a Colloquium Held at the Villa Spelman, Florence 1990, 1992; (ed. and intro.) Florentine Drawings at the Time of Lorenzo the Magnificent: Papers from a Colloquium Held at the Villa Spelman, Florence, 1992, 1994; (with C. Dempsey) Nicolas Poussin: Friendship and the Love of Painting, 1996; Pontormo: Portrait of a Halberdier, 1997; (ed. and intro.) The Diplomacy of Art: Artistic Creation and Politics in Seicento Italy: Papers from a Colloquium Held at the Villa Spelman, Florence, 1998, 2000; The A.W. Mellon Lectures in the Fine Arts: Fifty Years, 2002; (contrib.) Pontormo, Bronzino and the Medici: The Transformation of the Renaissance Portrait in Florence, 2004; The Domenichino Affair: Novelty, Imitation and Theft in Seventeenth-Century Rome, 2005; (ed.) Dialogues in Art History, from Mesopotamian to Modern: Readings for a New Century, 2009. **Address:** National Gallery of Art, 2000B S Club Dr., Landover, MD 20785, U.S.A.

CROSBY, Alfred W. American (born United States), b. 1931. **Genres:** History, Natural History, Sciences, Technology, Animals/Pets, Politics/Government. **Career:** Albion College, instructor in history, 1960-61; Ohio State University, instructor in history, 1961-65; California State University, assistant professor of history, 1965-66; Washington State University, associate professor of history, 1966-77; National Institutes of Health, fellow, 1971-73; Humanities Institute, fellow, 1975-76; University of Texas, Department of American Studies, professor of American studies, 1977-, now professor emeritus, Department of History, faculty, now professor emeritus, Department of Geography and the Environment, faculty, now professor emeritus. Writer. **Publications:** America, Russia, Hemp, and Napoleon, 1965; The Columbian Exchange: Biological and Cultural Consequences of 1492, 1972; Epidemic and Peace, 1918, 1976 as America's Forgotten Pandemic: The Influenza of 1918, 1989, 2nd ed., 2003; (contrib.) Influenza in America, 1918-1976: History, Science, and Politics, 1977; Ecological Imperialism: The Biological Expansion of Europe, 900-1900, 1986, 2nd ed., 2004; The Columbian Voyages, the Columbian Exchange, and their Historians, 1987; Germs, Seeds and Animals: Studies in Ecological History, 1994; The Measure of Reality: Quantification and Western Society, 1250-1600, 1997; Throwing Fire: Projectile Technology through History, 2002; Children of the Sun: A History of Humanity's Unappeasable Appetite for Energy, 2006. **Address:** Department of History, University of Texas, BUR 536, 1 Univ Sta. B7000, Austin, TX 78712-0220, U.S.A. **Online address:** crosby@mail.utexas.edu

CROSBY, Donald G(ibson). American (born United States), b. 1928. **Genres:** Chemistry, Environmental Sciences/Ecology, Medicine/Health. **Career:** Union Oil Co., chemist, 1946-51; Union Carbide Chemicals Co., chemist, 1954-61; University of California, agricultural toxicology and residue research laboratory, chairman, 1962-65, professor of environmental toxicology, 1961-91, professor emeritus of environmental toxicology, 1991-. Writer. **Publications:** (With R.M. Ikeda) Chemicals and the Food Industry, 1960; (with M. Jacobson) Naturally-Occurring Insecticides, 1971; Environmental Toxicology and Chemistry, 1998; The Poisoned Weed: Plants Toxic to Skin, 2004. EDITOR: (with M. Jacobson) Naturally Occurring Insecticides, 1971; (with G. Helz and R. Zepp) Aquatic and Surface Photochemistry, 1994; (with J.J. Cech, Jr. and B. Wilson) Multiple Stresses in Ecosystems, 1998. Contributor of articles to journals. **Address:** Department of Environmental Toxicology, University of California, 4143 Meyer Hall, 1 Shields Ave., Davis, CA 95616, U.S.A.

CROSBY, Harry W(illiams). American (born United States), b. 1926. **Genres:** Novels, Local History/Rural Topics, Travel/Exploration, History. **Career:** Teacher, 1951-63; historian and writer, 1974-. **Publications:** SELF-ILLUSTRATED: The King's Highway in Baja California, 1974; The Cave Paintings of Baja California: The Great Murals of an Unknown People, 1975, rev. ed., 1997; Last of the Californios, 1981. OTHERS: The Call to California, 1969; Doomed to Fail, 1989; Antigua California: Mission and Colony on the Peninsular Frontier, 1697-1768, 1994; Tijuana 1964: una visión fotográfica ehistórica, 2000; Portrait of Paloma (novel), 2001; Gateway to Alta California: The Expedition to San Diego, 1769, 2003; Californio Soldier Xavier Aguilar (1743-1821), forthcoming. Contributor to magazines. **Address:** Sunbelt Publications, 1250 Fayette St., El Cajon, CA 92020-1511, U.S.A.

CROSLAND, Margaret. British (born England), b. 1920. **Genres:** Literary Criticism And History, Biography, Translations, Human Relations/Parenting, Autobiography/Memoirs, History. **Career:** Writer and translator. **Publications:** NONFICTION: Strange Tempe (poems), 1946; Madame Colette: A Provincial in Paris, 1953 as Colette: A Provincial in Paris, 1954; Jean Cocteau, 1955; Ballet Carnival: A Companion to Ballet, 1955; Home Book of Opera, 1957; Ballet Lovers' Dictionary, 1962; Louise of Stolberg, Countess of Albany, 1962; The Young Ballet Lover's Companion, 1962; Philosophy Pocket Crammer, 1964; (ed.) A Traveller's Guide to Literary Europe, 1965; (ed.) Foliejon Park: A Short History, 1970; (ed.) Cocteau, Cocteau's World: An Anthology of Major Writings, 1972; Colette-The Difficulty of Loving: A Biography, 1973; Raymond Radiguet: A Biographical Study with Selections from His Work, 1976; Women of Iron and Velvet: French Women Writers after George Sand in UK as Women of Iron and Velvet and the Books They Wrote in France, 1976; Beyond the Lighthouse: English Women Novelists in the Twentieth Century, 1981; Piaf (biography), 1985; Simone de Beauvoir: The Woman and Her Work, 1992; Sade's Wife: The Woman behind the Marquis, 1995; The Enigma of Giorgio de Chirico, 1999; Madame de Pompadour: Sex, Culture and the Power Game, 2000. TRANSLATOR: F. Marceau, The Flesh in the Mirror, 1953; J. Cocteau, 1900-1914, 1956; M. Drouet, First Poems, 1956; Drouet, Then There Was Fire, 1957; (with S. Road) Cocteau, Opium, 1957; Edmund de Goncourt, Elisa, 1959; M. Genevoix, The Story of Reynard, 1959; Vladimir Jankelevitch, 1959; P. Lacroix, The Conquest of Fire, 1959; Joseph Rovan, 1959; R. Poirier, The Fifteen Wonders of the World, 1960; E. Zola, Earth, 1962; M. Mouloudji, French Leave, 1962; (and ed.) Marquis de Sade, De Sade Quartet, 1963; (with A. Daventry) M. Bessy, A Pictorial History of Magic and the Supernatural, 1963; (with Road) O. Aubry, Napoleon, 1964; (and ed.) Selected Writings of de Sade, 1964; Cecile Arnaud, The Gift of Indifference, 1965; G. de Diesbach, Secrets of the Gotha, 1967; (with Daventry) R. de Becker, The Other Face of Love, 1967; G. Chirico, Hebdomeros, 1968; Cocteau, Le Livre Blanc, 1969; (and ed.) C. Pavese, A Mania for Solitude: Selected Poems, 1930-1950, 1969; Drouet, Donatella, 1969; De Chirico, Memoirs of Giorgio de Chirico, 1971; Colette, The Other Woman, 1971; (with D. Le Vay) Colette, The Thousand and One Mornings, 1973; (and intro.) Colette, Retreat from Love, 1974; (and intro.) Colette, Duo (two novels), 1974; R. Linhart, The Assembly Line, 1981; E. Guillaumin, The Life of a Simple Man, 1983; E. Piaf, My Life, 1990; (and ed.) M. de Sade, The Passionate Philosopher: A Marquis de Sade Reader, 1992; K. Gibran, The Eye of the Prophet, 1995; (and intro.) M. Sade, Crimes of Love, 1996; P. Barbier, The World of the Castrati: The History of an Extraordinary Operatic Phenomenon, 1997; (with E. Powell) J. Hennig, The Rear View: A Brief and Elegant History of Bottoms through the Ages, 1997; (and intro.) The Gothic Tales of the Marquis de Sade, 2005. OTHERS: (comp. with P. Ledward) The Happy Yes: An Anthology of Marriage Proposals, Grave and Gay, 1949; (adaptor) The Vampire: An Anthology, 1963; (intro.) Madame de Stael, Ten Years' Exile, 1968; (comp. and intro.) The Leather Jacket: Stories, 1980; (intro.) Memoirs of Madame de la Tour du Pin, 1985; (intro.) The Second Sex, 1993; (ed. and intro.) My Contemporaries, 2009. Contributor to magazines. **Address:** The Long Croft, Wisborough Green, Upper Hartfield, ES TN7 4DT, England. **Online address:** info@margaretcrosland.co.uk

CROSLAND, Maurice P. British (born England), b. 1931. **Genres:** History, Sciences. **Career:** Teacher, 1955-63; University of Leeds, lecturer, 1963-69, reader in the history of science, 1969-74; British Journal for the History of Science, honorary editor, 1965-71; University of Kent, professor of the history of science, Unit for History, Philosophy and Social Relations of Science, director, 1974-94, professor emeritus, 1994-, Center for History and Cultural Studies of Science, reader, director; University of California, visiting professor, 1967; Cornell University, visiting professor, 1967-68; University of Pennsylvania, Department of History and Sociology of Science, visiting professor, 1971. Writer. **Publications:** Historical Studies in the Language of Chemistry, 1962; The Society of Arcueil: A View of French Science at the Time of Napoleon I, 1967; Les Héritiers de Lavoisier, 1968; Gay-Lussac, Scientist and Bourgeois, 1978; Science under Control: The French Academy of Sciences, 1795-1914, 1992; In the Shadow of Lavoisier: The Annales de chimie and the Establishment of a New Science, 1994; Studies in the Culture of Science in France and Britain since the Enlightenment, 1995; Scientific Institutions and Practice in France and Britain, c. 1700-c. 1870, 2007. EDITOR: Science in France in the Revolutionary Era, Described by Thomas Bugge, 1969; The Science of Matter: A Historical Survey, 1971, 1992; The Emergence of Science in Western Europe, 1975. **Address:** School of History, Rutherford College, University of Kent, Canterbury, KT CT2 7NX, England.

CROSS, Anthony Glenn. British (born England), b. 1936. **Genres:** History, Literary Criticism And History, Bibliography, Autobiography/Memoirs. **Career:** University of East Anglia, School of European Studies, lecturer, 1964-69, senior lecturer, 1969-72, reader in Russian, 1972-81; University of Illinois, fellow, 1968-69; University of Oxford, visiting fellow, 1978; University of Leeds, Roberts professor of Russian, 1981-85; Cambridge University, Fitzwilliam College, professor of Slavonic studies, 1985-2004, professor emeritus, 2004-. Writer. **Publications:** N.M. Karamzin: A Study of His Literary Career, 1783-1803, 1971; (ed. and intro.) Russia under Western Eyes, 1517-1825, 1971; (ed. and contrib.) Russian Literature in the Age of Catherine the Great: A Collection of Essays, 1976; (comp.) Anglo-Russian Relations in the Eighteenth Century, 1977; (ed. and contrib.) Great Britain and Russia in the Eighteenth Century: Contacts and Comparisons: Proceedings of an International Conference Held at the University of East Anglia, 1977, 1979; Tale of the Russian Daughter and Her Suffocated Lover, 1982; The Russian Theme in English Literature from the Sixteenth Century to 1980: An Introductory Survey and a Bibliography, 1985; Cambridge, Some Russian Connections, 1987; (co-ed.) Russia and The World of the Eighteenth Century: Proceedings of the Third International Conference: Organized by the Study Group on Eighteenth-Century Russia and Held at Indiana University at Bloomington, 1988; (ed. and intro.) Engraved in the Memory: James Walker, Engraver to the Empress Catherine the Great and His Russian Anecdotes, 1993; Anglo-Russica, 1993; (ed. with G.S. Smith) Literature, Lives and Legality in Catherine's Russia, 1994; By the Banks of the Neva: Chapters from the Lives and Careers of the British in Eighteenth-Century Russia, 1997; Catherine the Great and the British, 2001; Peter the Great through British Eyes: Perceptions and Representations of the Tsar Since 1698, 2000; (ed.) St. Petersburg, 1703-1825, 2003; (ed.) Days from the Reigns of Eighteenth-Century Russian Rulers, 2007; St Petersburg and the British: The City through the Eyes of British Visitors and Residents, 2008. Contributor to journals. **Address:** Fitzwilliam College, University of Cambridge, Storey's Way, Cambridge, CB CB3 0DG, England. **Online address:** agc28@cam.ac.uk

CROSS, Claire. *See* **DELACROIX, Claire.**

CROSS, Coy F. American (born United States), b. 1937. **Genres:** Military/Defense/Arms Control, Air/Space Topics. **Career:** Military Airlift Command, Scott Air Force Base, historian, 1988-90; Vandenberg Air Force Base, 30th Space Wing, historian, 1990-92; Beale Air Force Base, 9th Reconnaissance Wing, historian, 1992. Writer. **Publications:** (With R.D. Launius) MAC and the Legacy of the Berlin Airlift, 1989; Go West, Young Man! Horace Greeley's Vision for America, 1995; Justin Smith Morrill: Father of the Land-Grant Colleges, 1999; Lincoln's Man in Liverpool: Consul Dudley and the Legal Battle to Stop Confederate Warships, 2007. **Address:** 9RW/HO, 6000 C St., Ste. 113, Beale AFB, CA 95903-1616, U.S.A.

CROSS, Frank B. American (born United States), b. 1955. **Genres:** Law, Business/Trade/Industry, International Relations/Current Affairs. **Career:** University of Texas, Herbert D. Kelleher Centennial professor of business law, 1984-, professor of law; Kirkland & Ellis, staff. Writer. **Publications:** Environmentally Induced Cancer and the Law: Risks, Regulation and Victim Compensation, 1989; Legal Responses to Indoor Air Pollution, 1990; (with R.L. Miller) West's Legal Environment of Business: Text, Cases, Ethical and Regulatory Issues, 1992, 8th ed. as The Legal Environment of Business: Text and Cases: Ethical, Regulatory, Global and Corporate Issues, 2012; West's Advanced Topics and Contemporary Issues: Expanded Coverage for West's Business Law, West's Legal Environment of Business, 1992, 2nd ed., 1995; (with G.A. Jentz and R.L. Miller) West's Business Law: Text, Summarized Cases, Legal, Ethical, Regulatory and Corporate Environment, 1993, 12th ed., 2012; Federal Environmental Regulation of Real Estate, 1993; (with R.L. Miller) The Legal and Regulatory Environment Today: Changing Perspectives for Business, 1993; (with R.L. Miller and G.A. Jentz) Personal Law Handbook, 1994, rev. ed., 1995; (with R.L. Miller) The Legal Environment Today: Business in Its Ethical, Regulator and International Setting, 1996, 6th ed., 2010; (with R.L. Miller) The Legal and E-commerce Environment Today: Business in Its Ethical, Regulatory and International Setting, 2001, 4th ed., 2005; (with R.L. Miller and G.A. Jentz) Online Legal Research: A Guide to Accompany Business Law and Legal Environmental, 2002; (with R.L. Miller and G.A. Jentz) West's Business Law: A Case Study Approach, 2003; Federal Environmental Regulation of Real Estate, 2004; (with R.L. Miller and G.A. Jentz) Essentials of the Legal Environment, 2005, 3rd ed., 2011; (with R.L. Miller and G.A. Jentz) West's Business Law: Extended Case Approach, 2006; (with R.L. Miller and G.A. Jentz) West's Business Law: Alternate Edition; Text Summarized Cases Legal, Ethical, International and E-commerce Environment, 2007, 11th ed., 2010; (with R.A. Prentice) Law and Corporate Finance, 2007; Decision Making in the U.S. Courts of Appeals, 2007; (with S.A. Lindquist) Measuring Judicial Activism, 2009; The Theory and Practice of Statutory Interpretation, 2009. Contributor to journals. **Address:** University of Texas School of Law, CBA 3.446, 727 E Dean Keeton St., Austin, TX 78705, U.S.A. **Online address:** crossf@mail.utexas.edu

CROSS, Gillian (Clare). British (born England), b. 1945. **Genres:** Children's Fiction, Young Adult Fiction, Picture/Board Books, Novels, Horror, Science Fiction/Fantasy, Illustrations. **Career:** Writer. **Publications:** The Runaway, 1979; The Iron Way, 1979; Revolt at Ratcliffe's Rags, 1980; Save Our School, 1981; A Whisper of Lace, 1981; The Dark behind the Curtain, 1982; The Demon Headmaster, 1982; The Mintyglo Kid, 1983; Born of the Sun, 1983; On the Edge, 1984; The Prime Minister's Brain, 1985; Swimathon!, 1986; Chartbreak, 1986; Roscoe's Leap, 1987; A Map of Nowhere, 1988; Rescuing Gloria, 1989; Twin and Super-Twin, 1990; Wolf, 1990; The Monster from Underground, 1990; Gobbo the Great, 1991; Rent-a-Genius, 1991; The Great Elephant Chase, 1993; Furry Maccaloo, 1993; Beware Olga!, 1993; The Tree House, 1994; Hunky Parker is Watching You, 1994; What Will Emily Do?, 1994; New World, 1995; The Crazy Shoe Shuffle, 1995; Posh Watson, 1995; The Roman Beanfeast, 1996; The Demon Headmaster Strikes Again, 1996; Pictures in the Dark, 1996; The Demon Headmaster Takes Over, 1997; The Goose Girl, 1998; Tightrope, 1999; Down with the Dirty Danes!, 2000; Calling a Dead Man, 2001 in US as Phoning a Dead Man, 2002; Beware of the Demon Headmaster, 2002; Monster from Underground, 2002; Facing the Demon Headmaster, 2002; The Dark Ground, 2003; Sam Sorts It Out, 2005; Black Room, 2006; The Nightmare Game, 2006; Brother Aelred's Feet, 2007; (with M. Hoffman and P. Lively) Spooky Stories: Three Stories in One, 2008; Where I Belong, 2010. **Address:** Oxford Children's Books, Oxford University Press, Great Clarendon St., Oxford, OX OX2 6DP, England. **Online address:** gillian@gilliancross.co.uk

CROSS, Helen. British (born England), b. 1967?. **Genres:** Novels, Romance/Historical, Literary Criticism And History. **Career:** Royal Shakespeare Co., press officer. Writer. **Publications:** NOVELS: My Summer of Love, 2001; The Secrets She Keeps, 2005; Spilt Milk, Black Coffee, 2009. Contributor to periodicals. **Address:** c/o Author Mail, Bloomsbury Publishing Plc., 38 Soho Sq., London, GL W1D 3HB, England.

CROSS, Ian (Robert). New Zealander (born New Zealand), b. 1925?. **Genres:** Novels, Plays/Screenplays. **Career:** Labour Party newspaper, gallery journalist; Dominion, chief reporter, 1953; freelance writer, 1957-; Feltex, public relations manager, 1961-72; New Zealand Listener, editor, 1973-77; New Zealand Broadcasting Corp., chairman, 1977-, chief executive, through 1986. **Publications:** NOVELS: The God Boy, 1957; The Backward Sex, 1960; After Anzac Day, 1961. OTHER: The City of No (teleplay), 1970; The Unlikely Bureaucrat: My Years in Broadcasting (autobiography), 1988; The Family Man, 1993; Such Absolute Beginners: A Memoir, 2007. Contributor of short stories to periodicals. **Address:** PO Box 98, Wellington, 6332, New Zealand.

CROSS, Janine. (Paulette Crosse). Canadian/British (born England) **Genres:** Young Adult Fiction, Novels. **Career:** Writers' Association, president. Writer. **Publications:** Touched by Venom: Book One of the Dragon Temple Saga, 2005; Shadowed by Wings: Book Two of the Dragon Temple Saga, 2006; Forged by Fire: Book Three of the Dragon Temple Saga, 2007; (as Paulette Crosse) The Footstop Café. **Address:** 1230 Ave. of the Americas, New York, NY 10020, U.S.A. **Online address:** author@janinecross.ca

CROSS, K. Patricia. American (born United States), b. 1926. **Genres:** Education. **Career:** Harvard Community High School, mathematics teacher, 1948-49; University of Illinois, Urbana-Champaign, Department of Psychology, research assistant, 1949-53, assistant dean of women, 1953-59; Cornell University, dean of women, 1959-60, dean of students, 1960-64; Educational Testing Service, director of college and university programs, 1964-66, senior research psychologist, 1969-76, distinguished research scientist, 1976-80; University of California, Center for Research and Development in Higher Education, research educator, 1966-77, lecturer on higher education, 1977-80, Elizabeth and Edward Conner professor of education, 1988-93, Graduate School of Education, chair of the faculty, 1990-93, David Pierpont Gardner professor of higher education, 1993-95, now professor emeritus of higher education; American Council on Education, commissioner, 1975-88; University of Nebraska, visiting professor, 1975-76; Harvard University, Graduate School of Education, professor of higher education, 1980-88, Department of Administration, Planning and Social Policy, chair, 1984-87; Project for Enhancing State Role in Lifelong Learning, Education Commission of the States, chair of national planning board, 1980-83; New England Association of Schools and Colleges, Commission on Institutions of Higher Education, commissioner, 1982-85; American Association of Community and Junior Colleges Study, commissioner, 1982-85; National Commission on Future Academic Leadership, staff, 1985-; Higher Education Research Program of Pew Charitable Trusts, staff, 1986-89. Writer. **Publications:** (With R. Linn and J. Davis) A Guide to Research Design: Institutional Research Program for Higher Education, 1965; The Junior College Student: A Research Description, 1968; Beyond the Open Door: New Students to Higher Education, 1971; (ed. with S.R. Gould) Explorations in Non-Traditional Study, 1972; (with S. Gould) New Students and New Needs in Higher Education, 1972; Integration of Earning and Learning: Cooperative Education and Nontraditional Study, 1973; (co-author) Planning Non-traditional Programs: An Analysis of the Issues, 1974; (with J. Valley) Accent on Learning: Improving Instruction and Reshaping the Curriculum, 1976; The Missing Link: Connecting Adult Learners to Learning Resources, 1978; Adults as Learners, 1981; (with A.M. McCartan) Adult Learning: State Policies and Institutional Practices, 1984; (with A.M. McCartan) Older Students, New Issues: State Responses to Adult Learning, 1984; (with T.A. Angelo) Classroom Assessment Techniques: A Handbook for Faculty, 1988, 2nd ed., 1993; Feedback in the Classroom: Making Assessment Matter, 1988; (contrib.) Assessment 1990: Understanding the Implications, 1990; (with T.A. Angelo) Catching Theory Up With Practice: Conceptual Frameworks for Assessment, 1991; (forward) The Teaching-Learning Enterprise: Miami-Dade Community College's Blueprint for Change, 1994; (with M.H. Steadman) Classroom Research: Implementing the Scholarship of Teaching, 1996; (with E.F. Barkley and C.H. Major) Collaborative Learning Techniques: A Handbook for College Faculty, 2005. Contributor to books. **Address:** School of Education, University of California, 904 Oxford St., Berkeley, CA 94707, U.S.A. **Online address:** patcross@socrates.berkeley.edu

CROSS, (Margaret) Claire. (M. Claire Cross). British (born England), b. 1932. **Genres:** Genealogy/Heraldry, History, Theology/Religion, Education. **Career:** Archivist, 1958-61; University of York, lecturer, professor in history, 1965-2000, professor emeritus, 2000-. Writer. **Publications:** (As M. Claire Cross) The Free Grammar School of Leicester, 1953; The Puritan Earl: The Life of Henry Hastings, Third Earl of Huntingdon, 1536-1595, 1966; The Royal Supremacy in the Elizabethan Church, 1969; (contrib.) The Interregnum: The Quest for Settlement, 1972; Church and People, 1450-1660: The Triumph of the Laity in the English Church, 1976, 2nd ed. as Church and People: England, 1450-1660, 1999; York Clergy Wills, 1520-1600, 1984, 2nd ed., 2002; Urban Magistrates and Ministers: Religion in Hull and Leeds from the Reformation to the Civil War, 1985; The Elizabethan Religious Settlement, 1558-1575, 1992; The End of Medieval Monasticism in the East Riding of Yorkshire, 1993; (comp.) York Clergy Ordinations, 1561-1642, 2000; (comp.) York Clergy Ordinations, 1500-1509, 2001; (comp.) York Clergy Ordinations 1520-1559, 2002. EDITOR: The Letters of Sir Francis Hastings 1574-1609, 1969; York Clergy Wills 1520-1600: 1 The Minister Clergy, 1984; (with D. Loades and J.J. Scarisbrick) Law and Government under the Tudors, 1988; (with N. Vickers) Monks, Friars and Nuns in Sixteenth Century Yorkshire, 1995; (with P.S. Barnwell and A. Rycraft) Mass and Parish in Late Medieval England: The Use of York, 2005. Contributor to periodicals. **Address:** Department of History, University of York, Heslington, York, NY YO10 5DD, England. **Online address:** mcc1@york.ac.uk

CROSS, M. Claire. *See* **CROSS, (Margaret) Claire.**

CROSS, Richard K. (Richard Keith Cross). American (born United States), b. 1940. **Genres:** Literary Criticism And History, Young Adult Fiction. **Career:** Dartmouth College, instructor in English, 1966-68; University of California-Los Angeles, assistant professor, 1968-74, associate professor, 1974-80, professor of English, 1980-83, vice chair of department, 1976-77; University of Wuerzburg, Fulbright lecturer, 1971-72; University of Maryland, professor of English, 1983-, chair of department, 1983-88; University of Goettingen, visiting professor, 1990-91; University of Freiburg, visiting professor, 1997-98; University of Mannheim, visiting professor, 1998. Writer. **Publications:** Flaubert and Joyce: The Rite of Fiction, 1971; Malcolm Lowry: A Preface to His Fiction, 1980. Contributor to periodicals. **Address:** Department of English, University of Maryland, 4123 Susquehanna Hall, College Park, MD 20742, U.S.A. **Online address:** rcross@umd.edu

CROSS, Richard Keith. *See* **CROSS, Richard K.**

CROSSAN, Greg. *See* **CROSSAN, G(regory) D(ixon).**

CROSSAN, G(regory) D(ixon). (Greg Crossan). New Zealander (born New Zealand), b. 1950?. **Genres:** Literary Criticism And History, Music, Art/Art History. **Career:** University of Canterbury, assistant lecturer in English, 1973-76; Massey University, senior lecturer in English, 1977-. Writer. **Publications:** (As Greg Crossan) A Relish for Eternity: The Process of Divinization in the Poetry of John Clare, 1976. **Address:** School of English and Media Studies, Massey University, Sir Geoffrey Peren Bldg., Turitea Ste., PO Box 11 222, Palmerston North, 4442, New Zealand. **Online address:** g.d.crossan@massey.ac.nz

CROSSE, Paulette. *See* **CROSS, Janine.**

CROSSEN, Cynthia. American (born United States) **Genres:** Adult Non-fiction. **Career:** American Lawyer, executive editor; Village Voice, managing editor; Wall Street Journal, editor, senior editor, reporter, 1983-. **Publications:** Tainted Truth: The Manipulation of Fact in America, 1994; The Rich and How They Got That Way: How the Wealthiest People of All Time from Genghis Khan to Bill Gates Made Their Fortunes, 2000. **Address:** Wall Street Journal, 1211 Ave. of the Americas, New York, NY 10036, U.S.A. **Online address:** cynthia.crossen@wsj.com

CROSSETTE, Barbara. American (born United States), b. 1939. **Genres:** Area Studies, Travel/Exploration, History, Reference. **Career:** The Birmingham Post, features editor and writer; The Philadelphia Bulletin, copy editor; The Teacher, production editor, 1967; Westchester Weekly, editor, 1977; Punjab University, Fulbright teaching fellow in journalism, 1980-81, Fulbright professor of journalism; Indian Institute for Mass Communications, Fulbright professor of journalism, 1980; New York Times, assistant foreign editor, 1982, deputy foreign editor, 1983-84, Bangkok bureau chief, 1984-88, New Delhi bureau chief, 1988-91, Washington correspondent, 1991-93, United Nations bureau chief, 1994-2001; Princeton University, Ferris visiting professor on politics and the press, 1994; Knight International Press fellow, 2004-05; Columbia University, Southern Asia Institute, research associate, Graduate School of Journalism, adjunct faculty; The InterDependent, consulting editor and contributor; The Nation, United Nations correspondent. **Publications:** America's Wonderful Little Hotels and Inns, 1980; America's Wonderful Little Hotels and Inns: Eastern Region, 1984; America's Wonderful Little Hotels and Inns: Western Region, 1984, (ed. with W. Lowe and J.L. Shannon) 5th ed., 1985; India: Facing the Twenty-First Century, 1993; So Close to Heaven: The Vanishing Buddhist Kingdoms of the Himalayas, 1995; The Great Hill Stations of Asia, 1998; India: Old Civilization in a New World, 2000; (with G. Perkovich) Powers and Principles: International Leadership in a Shrinking World, 2009. **Address:** The Nation, 33 Irving Pl., New York, NY 10003-2332, U.S.A. **Online address:** bcrossette@aol.com

CROSSLEY, James G. British (born England), b. 1973. **Genres:** History, Popular Culture, Politics/Government, Intellectual History, Theology/Religion, Social Sciences, Reference. **Career:** University of Sheffield, Department of Biblical Studies, senior lecturer in New Testament studies, 2005-. Writer. **Publications:** The Date of Mark's Gospel: Insight from the Law in Earliest Christianity, 2004; (ed. with C. Karner) Writing History, Constructing Religion, 2005; Why Christianity Happened: A Sociohistorical Account of Christian Origins (26-50 CE), 2006; Jesus in an Age of Terror: Scholarly Projects for a New American Century, 2008; (ed. with H. Moxnes and W. Blanton) Jesus beyond Nationalism, 2009; Reading the New Testament: Contemporary Approaches, 2010; New Testament and Jewish Law: A Guide for the Perplexed, 2010; (ed.) Judaism, Jewish Identities and the Gospel Tradition: Essays in Honour of Maurice Casey, 2010; Jesus in an Age of Neoliberalism: Quests, Scholarship and Ideology, 2012. **Address:** Department of Biblical Studies, University of Sheffield, 45 Victoria St., Sheffield, SY S3 7QB, England. **Online address:** james.crossley@sheffield.ac.uk

CROSSLEY, Pamela Kyle. American (born United States), b. 1955. **Genres:** History, Area Studies. **Career:** The Phoenix Magazine, editor-in-chief; Dartmouth College, assistant professor, 1985-90, associate professor, 1990-93, professor of history and Asian Middle Eastern studies, 1993-, Robert 1932 and Barbara Black professor of History. Writer. **Publications:** Orphan Warriors: Three Manchu Generations and the End of the Qing World, 1990; (co-author) The Earth and Its Peoples: A Global History, 1996; The Manchus, 1997; A Translucent Mirror: History and Identity in Qing Imperial Ideology, 1999; (with L.H. Lees and J.W. Servos) Global Society: The World since 1900, 2004, 2nd ed., 2008; (ed. with H. Siu and D.S. Sutton) Empire at the Margins: Culture, Ethnicity, and Frontier in Early Modern China, 2006; What is Global History, 2008; The Wobbling Pivot, China since 1800: An Interpretive History, 2010; The Mongol Moment, forthcoming. Contributor of articles to books and journals. **Address:** Department of History, Dartmouth College, 308 Carson Hall, 300 Carson Hall, Hanover, NH 03755, U.S.A. **Online address:** pamela.k.crossley@dartmouth.edu

CROSSLEY-HOLLAND, Kevin (John William). British (born England), b. 1941. **Genres:** Children's Fiction, Poetry, History, Mythology/Folklore, Travel/Exploration, Translations. **Career:** Macmillan and Company Ltd., editor, 1962-69; Tufts-in-London Program, lecturer in English, 1967-78; University of Leeds, Gregory fellow in poetry, 1969-71; BBC, talks producer, 1972; Victor Gollancz Ltd., editorial director, 1972-77; University of Regensburg, lecturer in English language and literature, 1979-80; Boydell and Brewer Ltd., editorial consultant, 1983-89; Winchester School of Art, arts council fellow in creative writing, 1983, 1984; St. Olaf College, visiting professor of English, 1987, 1988; University of St. Thomas, endowed chair and professor of humanities and fine arts, 1991-95. **Publications:** Havelok the Dane, 1964; King Horn, 1965; (trans.) The Battle of Maldon and Other Old English Poems, 1965; The Green Children, 1966; The Callow Pit Coffer, 1968; (trans.) Beowulf, 1968; Alderney: The Nunnery, 1968; (with J.P. Walsh) Wordhoard: Anglo-Saxon Stories, 1969; (trans.) Storm and Other Old English Riddles, 1970; Norfolk Poems, 1970; The Pedlar of Swaffham, 1971; Pieces of Land: Journeys To Eight Islands, 1972; The Rain-Giver and Other Poems, 1972; The Sea-Stranger, 1973; The Fire-Brother, 1974; Green Blades Rising: The Anglo-Saxons, 1975; Petal & Stone, 1975; The Earth-Father, 1976; The Wildman, 1976; The Dream-House, 1976; (trans. and intro.) The Exeter Book Riddles, 1978, rev. ed., 2008; The Norse Myths, 1980; Between My Father and My Son, 1982; Time's Oriel (poetry), 1983; (with G. Thomas) Tales from the Mabinogion, 1984; Axe-Age, Wolf-Age: A Selection for Children from the Norse Myths, 1985; Storm, 1985; The Fox And The Cat: Kevin Crossley-Holland's Animal Tales From Grimm, 1986; Waterslain and Other Poems, 1986; British Folk Tales: New Versions, 1987; Oenone in January, 1988; (with G. Thomas) The Quest for Olwen, 1988; Wulf, 1988; Old English Elegies, 1988; Piper And Pooka: Boggarts And Bogles, 1988; The Painting-Room: And Other Poems, 1988; Kevin Rossley-Holland's East Anglian Poems, 2nd ed., 1989; Under the Sun and Over the Moon, 1989; Sleeping Nanna, 1989; The Stones Remain: Megalithic Sites: Britain, 1989; New and Selected Poems, 1965-1990, 1990; Sea Tongue, 1991; Tales from Europe, 1991; Long Tom and the Dead Hand, 1992; (with G. Thomas) The Tale of Taliesin, 1992; The Labors of Herakles, 1993; The Language of Yes, 1996; Poems from East Anglia, 1997; The Old Stories: Folk Tales From East Anglia And The Fen Country, 1997; Short! A Book of Very Short Stories, 1998; East Anglian Poems, 1998; World of King Arthur and His Court: People, Places, Legend and Lore, 1999; (with I. Cutting) The Wuffings (play), 1999; Enchantment, 2000; The Seeing Stone, 2000; At the Crossing Places, 2001; Selected Poems, 2001; The Magic Lands: Folk Tales of Britain and Ireland, 2001; (reteller) The Ugly Duckling: From the Story by Hans Christian Andersen, 2001; Viking! Myths of Gods and Monsters, 2002; The Nightingale That Shrieked: And Other Tales, 2002; At the Crossing-places, 2002; Tales from the Old World, 2003; King of the Middle March, 2003; King Arthur's World, 2004; How Many Miles To Bethlehem?, 2004; Gatty's Tale, 2006; Moored Man, 2006; Outsiders, 2007; Crossing to Paradise, 2008; Waterslain Angels, 2008; Thor and the Master of Magic, 2009; The Hidden Roads, 2009; Bracelet of Bones, 2011; Short Too!, 2011; The Mountains of Norfolk, 2011; Scramasax, 2012. EDITOR: Running to Paradise: An Introductory Selection By Kevin Crossley-Holland, 1967; Winter's Tales 14, 1968; Winter's Tales for Children 3, 1969; New Poetry 2, 1976; The Faber Book of Northern Legends, 1977; The Faber Book of Northern Folk-Tales, 1980; (and trans.) The Anglo-Saxon World, 1982; The Riddle Book, 1982; The Oxford Book of Travel Verse, 1986; The Dead Moon, 1986; Northern Lights: Legends, Sagas and Folk-Tales, 1987; Folk-Tales of the British Isles, 1988; Medieval Lovers, 1988; Medieval Gardens, 1990; Peter Grimes: The Poor: The Borough, 1990; Young Oxford Book of Folk Tales, 1998; (with L. Sail) The New Exeter Book of Riddles, 1999; (with L. Sail) Light Unlocked, 2005. **Address:** Rogers Coleridge & White Ltd., 20 Powis Mews, London, GL W11 1JN, England. **Online address:** kevin@crossley-holland.com

CROSSMAN, David A. American (born United States), b. 1951?. **Genres:** Mystery/Crime/Suspense. **Career:** Singer and songwriter, 1962-; Learning Dock (television production company), co-owner. Director, videographer and musician. **Publications:** BEAN AND AB MYSTERY SERIES: The Secret of the Missing Grave, 1999; The Mystery of the Black Moriah, 2002; The Legend of Burial Island, 2009. FOR ADULTS: Murder in a Minor Key, 1994; A Show of Hands, 1997; The Dead of Winter, 1999. **Address:** The Learning Dock, 317 Stones River Cove, Nashville, TN 37214, U.S.A. **Online address:** davidcrossman@comcast.net

CROSSMAN, William. American (born United States), b. 1939?. **Genres:** Information Science/Computers, Technology. **Career:** CompSpeak 2050 Institute for the Study of Talking Computers and Oral Cultures, founder and director; Morris Brown College, faculty, 1989-97; Harvard University, faculty; Tufts University, philosophy faculty; City College of San Francisco, faculty; San Francisco State University, faculty; Antioch College West, faculty; Vista Community College, faculty; Berkeley City College, faculty; philosopher. **Publications:** VIVO (Voice-In/Voice-Out): The Coming Age of Talking Computers, 2004. **Address:** CompSpeak 2050 Institute, 102 Hamilton Pl., PO Box 3606, Oakland, CA 94612-3803, U.S.A. **Online address:** willcross@aol.com

CROUCH, Christopher. Australian/British (born England), b. 1953. **Genres:** Architecture, Cultural/Ethnic Topics. **Career:** Chongqing University ofr Science and Technology, visiting professor in design history; Huanghe University, professor in design; Luoyang Normal University, School of Art and Design, professor in art and design; Edith Cowan University, head of studies in visual culture, 1995-, Faculty of Education and Arts, lecturer, School of Communications and Arts, senior lecturer; Beijing National University, School of Fine Arts, visiting professor, 2000; Guangdong Light Industry University, visiting professor, 2002. Writer. **Publications:** Modernism in Art, Design and Architecture, 1999; Design Culture in Liverpool 1880-1914: The Origins of the Liverpool School of Architecture, 2002; (ed.) Subjectivity, Creativity and the Institution, 2009; (ed.) Contemporary Chinese Visual Culture: Tradition, Modernity and Globalization, 2010. Contributor to books. **Address:** Faculty of Education & Arts, Edith Cowan University, Rm. 17.206, 2 Bradford St., Mt. Lawley, WA 6050, Australia. **Online address:** c.crouch@ecu.edu.au

CROUCH, Katie. American (born United States), b. 1973. **Genres:** Novellas/Short Stories, Young Adult Fiction, Science Fiction/Fantasy. **Career:** Writer. **Publications:** Girls in Trucks: Stories, 2008; Men and Dogs: A Novel, 2010; Magnolia League, 2011; (with G. Hendrix) White Glove War: A Magnolia League Novel, 2012. **Address:** c/o Rob McQuilkin, Lippincott Massie McQuilkin, 80 5th Ave., Ste. 1101, New York, NY 10011-8011, U.S.A. **Online address:** katie@katiecrouch.com

CROUCH, Stanley. American (born United States), b. 1945. **Genres:** Poetry, Race Relations, Essays, Adult Non-fiction, Young Adult Fiction. **Career:** Studio Watts Co., actor and playwright, 1965-67; Claremont College, instructor in drama, literature and jazz history, 1968-75; Village Voice, staff writer, 1979-88; Lincoln Center, artistic consultant and co-founder of jazz, 1987-; New Republic, contributing editor, 1990-; Los Angeles Free Press, columnist; The Cricket, columnist; SoHo Weekly News, columnist; Columbia University, Armstrong visiting professor, 2002-03; New York Daily News, columnist. **Publications:** Ain't No Ambulances for No Nigguhs Tonight (poems), 1972; Notes of a Hanging Judge: Essays and Reviews, 1979-1989, 1990; The All-American Skin Game, or, The Decoy of Race: The Long and the Short of it, 1990-1994, 1995; (intro.) Mr. Sammler's Planet, 1996; Always in Pursuit: Fresh American Perspectives, 1995-1997, 1998; Don't the Moon Look Lonesome: A Novel in Blues and Swing, 2000; One Shot Harris: The Photographs of Charles Teenie Harris, 2002; (with P. Benjamin) Reconsidering The Souls of Black Folk, 2002; The Artificial White Man: Essays on Authenticity, 2004; (contrib.) Masters of American comics, 2005; Considering Genius: Writings on Jazz, 2006. Works appear in anthologies. Contributor to periodicals. **Address:** Lincoln Center for the Performing Arts, Jazz Program, 70 Lincoln Center Plz., New York, NY 10023-6548, U.S.A. **Online address:** crouch.stanley@gmail.com

CROUCH, Tanja L. American (born United States), b. 1958. **Genres:** Film, inspirational/Motivational Literature, Music, Self Help, Art/Art History. **Career:** Triad Artists Inc., agent, 1987-91; Lib Hatcher Agency, agent, 1991-92; Turn Key Management, partner and artist manager, 1992-94; Barbara Orbison Productions, vice president, 1994-99, Roy Orbison Music, vice president, 2008-; freelance writer and producer, 1999-; Right Brain Media, Resolute Production, account representative, 2000-07. **Publications:** This Joint Is Jumpin', 2001; 100 Careers in the Music Business, 2001, 2nd ed., 2008; 100 Careers in Film and Television, 2002; Truth or Dare: Do You Have the Courage to Change Your Life?, 2003; (with K. Crouch) The Gospel According to Elvis, 2005. **Address:** 1215 Bonnhaven Dr., Franklin, TN 37067-8639, U.S.A. **Online address:** tanja@rightbrain.tv

CROUSE, David John. American (born United States), b. 1967. **Genres:** Novellas/Short Stories. **Career:** University of Alaska, Permafrost: A Literary Journal, editor, 1992-94, Department of English, assistant professor of English, 2007-; Iprax Corp., Educational Services, director, 1995; Bradford College, assistant professor of creative writing, 1995-2000; Chester College of New England, Chester, assistant professor, 2001-05, associate professor of creating writing 2005-07, Writing and Literature Program, chair; Salamander Magazine, fiction editor, 2001-05, contributing editor, 2005-. **Publications:** Copy Cats: Stories, 2005; The Man Back There and Other Stories, 2008. Contributor to journals. **Address:** Department of English, University of Alaska, PO Box 755720, Fairbanks, AK 99775-5720, U.S.A. **Online address:** davidcrouse@acsalaska.net

CROUTER, Richard. (Richard Earl Crouter). American (born United States), b. 1937. **Genres:** History, Theology/Religion, Philosophy. **Career:** Carleton College, instructor, assistant professor, 1967-73, associate professor, 1973-79, professor of religion, 1979-, David and Marian Adams Bryn-Jones distinguished teaching professor of humanities, 1993-96, John M. and Elizabeth Musser professor emeritus of religious studies, 1997-; University of Toronto, faculty, 1972-73; Journal for the History of Modern of Theology, co-editor, 1993-. **Publications:** Schleiermacher and the Theology of Bourgeois Society: A Critique of the Critics, 1986; Ambrose, Bishop of Milan, 1987; A Historical Demurral, 1988; (ed. and trans.) F. Schleiermacher, On Religion: Speeches to Its Cultured Despisers, 1988, 2nd ed., 1996; Revolution and the Religious Imagination in Kierkegaard's Two Ages, 1991; (ed. and trans. with J. Klassen) D. Friedländer, F. Schleiermacher and W.A. Teller, A Debate on Jewish Emancipation and Christian Theology in Old Berlin, 2004; Friedrich Schleiermacher: Between Enlightenment and Romanticism, 2005; Reinhold Niebuhr on Politics, Religion, and Christian Faith, 2010. Contributor to periodicals. **Address:** Department of Religion, Carleton College, 1 N College St., Northfield, MN 55057-4001, U.S.A. **Online address:** rcrouter@carleton.edu

CROUTER, Richard Earl. *See* **CROUTER, Richard.**

CROW, Bill. American (born United States), b. 1927. **Genres:** Music, Humanities. **Career:** Jazz musician, 1945-; Broadway theater, musician, 1975-90; Local 802 of the American Federation of Musicians of the United States and Canada, union official, 1983-. Writer. **Publications:** Jazz Anecdotes, 1990, 2nd ed., 2005; From Birdland to Broadway: Scenes from a Jazz Life, 1992. Contributor to periodicals. **Address:** Oxford University Press, 200 Madison Ave., New York, NY 10016-4308, U.S.A. **Online address:** billcrow@prodigy.net

CROW, Lauren. *See* **MCINTOSH, Fiona.**

CROW, Mary. American (born United States), b. 1933. **Genres:** Poetry, Literary Criticism And History, Translations. **Career:** Colorado State University, instructor, professor of English, 1964-, now professor emeritus of English, Creative Writing Program, director, 1988-91. Poet Laureate. **Publications:** POETRY: Going Home, 1979; The Business of Literature, 1981; Borders, 1989; (with F. Harrison) Living and Learning with Blind Children, 1993; I Have Tasted the Apple, 1996; The High Cost of Living, 2002. EDITOR: Woman Who has Sprouted Wings: Poems by Contemporary Latin American Women Poets, 1984, 2nd ed., 1987. TRANSLATOR: From the Country of Nevermore: Selected Poems of Jorge Teillier, 1990; Vertical Poetry: Recent Poems of Roberto Juarroz, 1992; Homesickness: Selected Poems of Enrique Lihn, 2002; Engravings Torn from Insomnia: Selected Poems of Olga Orozco, 2002; Vertical Poetry: Last Poems of Roberto Juarroz, 2010. **Address:** Department of English, Colorado State University, 1773 Campus Delivery Eddy Hall, Oval Dr., Fort Collins, CO 80523-1773, U.S.A. **Online address:** mcrow@lamar.colostate.edu

CROW, Thomas E. American (born United States), b. 1948?. **Genres:** History, Literary Criticism And History, Art/Art History. **Career:** California Institute of the Arts, instructor critical studies, 1977-78; University of Chicago, assistant professor history of art, 1978-80; Princeton University, assistant professor art and archeology, 1980-86; University of Michigan, associate professor history of art, 1986-90; University of Sussex, professor history of art and chairman of department, 1990-96; Yale University, Robert Lehman professor history of art, 1996-2000, department chairman, 1997-2000; University of Southern California, Getty Research Institute, director, 2000-07; New York University, Institute of Fine Arts, Rosalie Solow professor of modern art, 2007-, chair, associate provost for the arts; Artforum Magazine, contributing editor. **Publications:** Painters and Public Life in Eighteenth-Century Paris, 1985; Endgame: Reference and Simulation in Recent Painting and Sculpture, 1987; (co-author) Nineteenth Century Art: A Critical History, 1994, 4th ed., 2011; (contrib.) Oehlen Williams 95, 1995; Emulation: Making Artists for Revolutionary France, 1995; Modern Art in the Common Culture, 1996; The Rise of the Sixties: American and European Art in the Era of Dissent, 1996; The Intelligence of Art, 1999; (contrib.) Jasper Johns to Jeff Koons, 2001; (contrib.) Gordon Matta-Clark, 2003; (ed. with G. Phillips) Seeing Rothko, 2005; (contrib.) Robert Rauschenberg: Combines, 2005; (contrib.) Protest in Paris 1968, 2006; (ed. with K. Painter) Late Thoughts: Reflections on Artists and Composers at Work, 2006; (contrib.) Ed Ruscha, 2008; (contrib.) Get There First, Decide Promptly, 2011; (contrib.) Sherrie Levine, 2012. **Address:** Institute of Fine Arts, New York University, 330 James B. Duke House, 1 E 78th St., New York, NY 10075, U.S.A. **Online address:** tc59@nyu.edu

CROWDER, Ashby Bland. American (born United States), b. 1941. **Genres:** Literary Criticism And History, Bibliography, Adult Non-fiction, Poetry, Biography, Autobiography/Memoirs, Essays. **Career:** University of Tennessee, instructor in English, 1965; Centre College of Kentucky, instructor in English, 1965-67; Middle Tennessee State University, assistant professor of English, 1968; Eastern Kentucky University, assistant professor of English, 1969-72; Hendrix College, associate professor, 1974-82, M.E. and Ima Graves Peace professor of English, American Literature and the Humanities, 1982-, department head, 1983-86, 1997-2001; Baylor University, lecturer, 1993-2001; University of Lodz, U.S. Fulbright professor, 2005-06. Writer. **Publications:** Writing in the Southern Tradition: Interviews with Five Contemporary Authors, 1990; Poets and Critics, Their Means and Meanings: Including Essays on Browning, Ruskin, Stevens, Heaney and Others, 1993; (ed.) The Complete Works of Robert Browning, vol. XIII: The Inn Album and Pacchiarotto and How He Worked in Destemper with Other Poems, 1995; Wakeful Anguish: A Literary Biography of William Humphrey, 2004; (ed. with J.D. Hall) Seamus Heaney: Poet, Critic, Translator, 2007; (ed.) Far from Home: Selected Letters of William Humphrey, 2007. Contributor of articles to books and journals. **Address:** Hendrix College, 1600 Washington Ave., Conway, AR 72032, U.S.A. **Online address:** crowder@hendrix.edu

CROWDER, George. New Zealander (born New Zealand), b. 1956. **Genres:** Politics/Government, Philosophy, Civil Liberties/Human Rights, Humanities. **Career:** Department of Justice, legal adviser, 1978-80; Victoria University of Wellington, tutor, 1982; University College, tutor in political theory, 1985-90; California State University, lecturer in political science, 1991; Vytantas Magnus University, lecturer in political theory, 1992-93; City University of New York, Hunter College, adjunct assistant professor, 1994, Bernard M. Baruch College, adjunct assistant professor of political science, 1995, Kingsborough Community College, adjunct assistant professor, 1995; New School for Social Research, instructor, 1994-95; Flinders University, School of Political and International Studies, Department of Politics and Public Policy lecturer, 1995-2000, senior lecturer, 2000-05, associate professor, 2005-08, professor of political theory, 2008-. Writer and lawyer. **Publications:** Classical Anarchism: The Political Thought of Godwin, Proudhon, Bakunin, and Kropotkin, 1991; Pluralism and Liberalism, Political Studies, 42 vols., 1994; From Pluralism to Liberalism, Critical Review of International Social and Political Philosophy, vol. I, 1998; Liberalism and Value Pluralism, 2002; Isaiah Berlin: Liberty and

Pluralism, 2004; (ed. with H. Hardy) The One and the Many: Reading Isaiah Berlin, 2007; Two Concepts of Liberal Pluralism, Political Theory, 35 vols., 2007. **Address:** Department of Politics and Public Policy, Flinders University, 390 Social Sciences S, Sturt Rd., Bedford Pk., PO Box 2100, Adelaide, SA 5001, Australia. **Online address:** george.crowder@flinders.edu.au

CROWE, Michael J. American (born United States), b. 1936. **Genres:** History, Sciences, Biography, Astronomy. **Career:** University of Notre Dame, instructor, 1961-65, assistant professor, 1965-68, associate professor, 1968-73, professor, 1973-2000, Rev. John J. Cavanaugh professor in the humanities, 2000-02, professor emeritus, 2002-, Program of Liberal Studies and Graduate Program in History and Philosophy of Science, chair, 1967-73. Writer. **Publications:** A History of Vector Analysis: The Evolution of the Idea of a Vectorial System, 1967; The Extraterrestrial Life Debate 1750-1900: The Idea of a Plurality of Worlds from Kant to Lowell, 1986; Theories of the World from Antiquity to the Copernican Revolution, 1990, 2nd ed., 2001; Modern Theories of the Universe: From Herschel to Hubble, 1994; Mechanics: From Aristotle to Einstein, 2007. EDITOR: The Letters and Papers of Sir John Herschel: A Guide to the Manuscripts and Microfilm, 1990; (with D.R. Dyck and J.J. Kevin) Calendar of the Correspondence of Sir John Herschel, 1998; The Extraterrestrial Life Debate, Antiquity to 1915: A Source Book, 2008; Ronald Knox and Sherlock Holmes: The Origin of Sherlockian Studies, 2011. **Address:** Program of Liberal Studies, University of Notre Dame, 215 O'Shaughnessy Hall, Notre Dame, IN 46556, U.S.A. **Online address:** crowe.1@nd.edu

CROWE, Norman. American (born United States), b. 1938. **Genres:** Architecture, Environmental Sciences/Ecology, Urban Studies. **Career:** Walter Weber, Architect and Lusk and Wallace Associates Architects, architect, 1964-66, 1967-68; Arkitekt I. Hammarskjold-Reiz and Stadsarkitektkontoret (Town Architect and Planning Agency), 1966-67; Anton J. Egner and Associates Architects, architect, 1969-72; Ohio University, School of Architecture, assistant professor of architecture, 1972-74; architect and consultant, 1974; University of Notre Dame, School of Architecture, assistant professor of architecture, 1974-81, Rome Studies Program, instructor, 1974-75, associate professor of architecture, 1981-93, director of graduate program in architecture, 1987-96, 2000-06, professor of architecture, 1993-, emeritus professor, 2008-, University of New Mexico, School of Architecture and Planning, visiting professor, 2009-. Writer. **Publications:** (With P. Laseau) Visual Notes: For Architects and Designers, 1984, 2nd ed., 2012; Nature and the Idea of a Man-Made World: An Investigation into the Evolutionary Roots of Form and Order in the Built Environment, 1995; (co-ed.) Building Cities: Towards a Civil Society and a Sustainable Environment, 1999. Contributor to books and periodicals. **Address:** School of Architecture, University of Notre Dame, 110 Bond Hall, Notre Dame, IN 46556, U.S.A. **Online address:** ncrowe@und.edu

CROWE, Thomas Rain. American (born United States), b. 1949. **Genres:** Poetry, Translations, Young Adult Fiction. **Career:** Beatitude Magazine and Press, editor, 1974-78; Katuah Journal, founding editor, 1983-87; Project to Identify and Protect Native American Sacred Sites in Western North Carolina and the Southern Appalachians, director, 1984-88; New Native Press, publisher, 1988-; South Carolina Governor's School for the Arts, master class instructor, 1989, 1990; Sylva Herald, press operator, 1989-93; Fern Hill Records, founder and producer, 1994-; Asheville Poetry Review, editor-at-large, 1995-2001; Smoky Mountain News, reviewer feature writer, 1995-; The Boatrockers (performance group), founder and performer, 1996-; Canary Coalition, founding board director, 2000; Bloomsbury Review, reviewer feature writer; Jazz News, reviewer feature writer; Western North Carolina Alliance (WNCA), acting director. **Publications:** Learning to Dance, 1985; Poems for Che Guevara's Dream, 1991; The Sound of Light (poems and music), 1991; Night Sun, 1993; Water from the Moon: Poems, 1982-1989, 1993; Personified Street: Poems, 1974-1978, 1993; New Native: Poems, 1978-1981, 1993; The Laugharne Poems, 1997; (ed. with G. Denez and T. Hubbard) Writing the Wind: A Celtic Resurgence, 1997; In Wineseller's Street: Renderings of Háfez, 1998; Zoro' s Field: My Life in the Appalachian Woods (memoir), 2005; Radiogenesis: Poems, 1986-2006, 2007; House of Girls, 2007; End of Eden: Writings of an Environmental Activist, 2008; (with N. Watkins) Rare Birds: Conversations with Legends of Jazz and Classical Music, 2008; Blue Rose of Venice, 2009; Crack Light, 2010. TRANSLATOR: H.A. Dal, Why I am a Monster, 1991; Hafiz, In Wineseller's Street, 1998; Hafiz, Drunk on the Wine of the Beloved, 2001; 10,000 Dawns: Love Poems of Yvan and Claire Goll, 2004. **Address:** 407 Canada Rd., Tuckasegee, NC 28783, U.S.A. **Online address:** newnativepress@hotmail.com

CROWELL, Jenn(ifer). American (born United States), b. 1978. **Genres:** Novels, Literary Criticism And History. **Career:** Writer. **Publications:** NOVELS: Necessary Madness, 1997; Der Englische Maler, 2001; Letting the Body Lead, 2002. Contributor to periodicals. **Address:** c/o Jane Gelfman, Gelfman Schneider Literary Agents Inc., 250 W 57th St., Ste. 2515, New York, NY 10107-0001, U.S.A.

CROWL, Sam. *See* **CROWL, Samuel.**

CROWL, Samuel. (Sam Crowl). American (born United States), b. 1940. **Genres:** Literary Criticism And History. **Career:** Ohio University, assistant professor, 1970-75, associate professor, 1975-80, professor of English, 1980-92, trustee professor of English, 1992-, dean of university college, 1981-92, Ping Institute, fellow; Royal Shakespeare Co., staff. Writer. **Publications:** Shakespeare Observed: Studies in Performance on Stage and Screen, 1992; Shakespeare at the Cineplex: The Kenneth Branagh Era, 2003; The Films of Kenneth Branagh, 2006; Shakespeare and Film: A Norton Guide, 2008; (ed.) The First Part of King Henry the Fourth, 2009. Contributor of articles and reviews to Shakespeare journals. **Address:** Department of English, Ohio University, Rm. 313, Ellis Hall, Athens, OH 45701, U.S.A. **Online address:** crowl@ohio.edu

CROWLEIGH, Ann. *See* **CUMMINGS, Barbara.**

CROWLEY, Bridget. British (born England) **Genres:** Children's Fiction, Novels, Horror. **Career:** Head of Theatre Training; Amnesty Intl., play writer; National Theatre, audio-description staff; Theatre Royal Stratford, staff. Dancer. Educator. **Publications:** JUVENILE: Step into the Dark, 2002; Animals in Art (reader), 2003; Stories in Art (reader), 2003; Imagination in Art (reader), 2003; Feast of Fools, 2003; Ship's Angel, 2004; Harriet's Ghost, 2005. **Address:** Pollinger Ltd., 9 Staple Inn, Holborn, London, GL WC1V 7QH, England.

CROWLEY, David. British (born England), b. 1966. **Genres:** Art/Art History, Social Sciences, Sociology. **Career:** University of Brighton, lecturer, 1991-; University of Staffordshire, lecturer; Fitzroy Dearborn's Encyclopedia of Interior Design, consultant; V&A Museum, consultant curator; Royal College of Art, faculty, 1999-, Department of History of Design, deputy head, Department of Critical and Historical Studies, senior tutor, Department of Critical Writing in Art and Design, professor and head. Writer. **Publications:** Victorian Style, 1990; National Style and Nation-State: Design in Poland from the Vernacular Revival to the International Style, 1992; (with P. Jobling) Graphic Design: Reproduction and Representation Since 1800, 1996; (ed.) Modernity and Material Culture of Post-War Eastern Europe, 2000; (co-ed.) Socialist Spaces: Sites of Everyday Life in the Eastern Bloc, 2002; Warsaw, 2003; Magazine Covers, 2003; Posters of the Cold War, 2008; (ed. with J. Pavitt) Cold War Modern: Design 1945-1970, 2008; (ed. and intro. with S.E. Reid) Pleasures In Socialism: Leisure And Luxury In The Eastern Bloc, 2010. **Address:** Department of Critical Writing in Art and Design, School of Humanities, Royal College of Art, Kensington Gore, London, GL SW7 2EU, England. **Online address:** cwad@rca.ac.uk

CROWLEY, Katherine. American (born United States), b. 1950?. **Genres:** Business/Trade/Industry, Economics, Reference. **Career:** New York Foundation for Senior Citizens, Employment Counselor; K Squared Enterprises and Small Business Strategy Inc., co-owner, counselor, business consultant, vice president, 1990-. Psychotherapist and writer. **Publications:** (With K. Elster) Going Indie: Self-Employment, Freelance, and Temping Opportunities, 1997; (with K. Elster) Working with You Is Killing Me: Freeing Yourself from Emotional Traps at Work, 2006; Working for You Isn't Working for Me: The Ultimate Guide to Managing Your Boss, 2009. Contributor to periodicals. **Address:** K Squared Enterprises, 119 W 23rd St., Ste. 1009, New York, NY 10011, U.S.A. **Online address:** katherine@ksquaredenterprises.com

CROWLEY, Roger. British (born England), b. 1951. **Genres:** Theology/Religion, History, Military/Defense/Arms Control. **Career:** Writer and publisher. **Publications:** 1453: The Holy War for Constantinople and the Clash of Islam and the West in UK as Constantinople: The Last Great Siege, 1453, 2005; Empires of the Sea: The Siege of Malta, the Battle of Lepanto, and the Contest for the Center of the World in UK as Empires of the Sea: The Final Battle for the Mediterranean, 1521-1580, 2008; City of Fortune: How Venice Ruled The Seas, 2011; City of Fortune: How Venice Won And Lost A Naval Empire, 2011. **Address:** c/o Andrew Lownie, Andrew Lownie Literary Agency, 36 Great Smith St., London, GL SW1P 3BU, England. **Online address:** info@rogercrowley.co.uk

CROWLEY, Suzanne Carlisle. American (born United States), b. 1963. **Genres:** Novels. **Career:** Crowley Interiors (art business), founder, Writer. **Publications:** JUVENILE NOVELS: (as Suzanne Carlisle Crowley) Paisley, 1990; The Very Ordered Existence of Merilee Marvelous, 2007; The Stolen One, 2009. Contributor to magazines. **Address:** Stimola Literary Studio, 306 Chase Ct., Edgewater, NJ 07020, U.S.A. **Online address:** dansuzanne@aol.com

CROWLEY, Tony. British (born England), b. 1960. **Genres:** Politics/Government, Theology/Religion. **Career:** University of Southampton, lecturer, 1984-93, senior lecturer, 199394; University of Manchester, professor, 1994-, chair of department, 1996-98; Scripps College, Hartley Burr Alexander Chair in the Humanities, 2005-; Oxford University Press, reader, 1994, 1996; Oxford University, reviewer, 1996-99. Educator, linguist and writer. **Publications:** Standard English and the Politics of Language, 1989; Proper English? Readings in Language, History and Cultural Identity, 1991; Language in History: Theories and Texts, 1996; (ed. with L. Burke and A. Girvin) The Routledge Language and Cultural Theory Reader, 2000; (comp.) The Politics of Language in Ireland, 1366-1922: A Sourcebook, 2000; Standard English and the Politics of Language, 2003; Wars of Words: The Politics of Language in Ireland, 1537-2004, 2005. **Address:** Scripps College, 1030 Columbia Ave., Claremont, CA 91711, U.S.A.

CROWLEY, William R. American (born United States), b. 1946. **Genres:** Business/Trade/Industry, Environmental Sciences/Ecology, Technology. **Career:** Shell Chemical, staff, 1968-71; Apollo Chemical, staff, 1971-74; Nalco Chemical, staff, 1974-80; Amoco Chemicals, staff, sales manager, 1980-93; Competitive Analysis Technologies, president, 1993-; Hydrocarbon Processing Magazine, contributing editor. **Publications:** Oil and Gas on the Internet: 650 Energy-Industry Addresses at Your Fingertips (directory), 1996; Chemicals on the Internet: A Directory of Industry Sites, vol. I: Organic Chemicals and Petrochemicals, vol. II: Inorganic Chemicals and Minerals, 1997. **Address:** Competitive Analysis Technologies, 11702-B Grant Rd., Ste. 333, PO Box 333, Cypress, TX 77429, U.S.A. **Online address:** compete@catsites.com

CROWLEY-MILLING, Michael C. Swiss/Welsh (born Wales), b. 1917. **Genres:** Physics, Sciences. **Career:** Metropolitan Vickers Electrical Company Ltd., research engineer, 1938-66; Daresbury Nuclear Physics Laboratory, staff of directorate, 1966-71; European Organization for Nuclear Research, group leader to the director for the accelerator program, 1971-83. Writer. **Publications:** A Detailed Design Study for the "NINA Booster", 1971; The Use of a Debuncher in the Injection Path of an Electron Synchrotron, 1971; John Bertram Adams, Engineer Extraordinary: A Tribute, 1993. EDITOR: Accelerator Control Systems, 1986; Accelerator and Experimental Physics Control Systems, 1990. Contributor to journals. **Address:** 15 Les Ruches, St. Cerque, 1264, Switzerland.

CROWN, David Allan. American (born United States), b. 1928. **Genres:** Criminology/True Crime, Sciences. **Career:** U.S. Postal Inspection Service, Identification Laboratory, assistant director, 1957-67; U.S. Department of the Army, Questioned Documents Laboratory, director, 1968-72; American College of Document Examiners, board director, 1970-; American University, adjunct professor, 1972-81; Central Intelligence Agency, Questioned Documents Laboratory, director, 1972-82; Department of State, Questioned Documents Laboratory, staff, INR/DDC, director, 1972-77; George Washington University, professorial lecturer, 1974-; Crown Forensic Labs Inc., president, 1980-; Antioch School of Law, adjunct professor, 1981-; Georgetown University, faculty; Chabot College, faculty; Forensic Science Foundation, board director. Writer. **Publications:** The Forensic Examination of Paints and Pigments, 1968; (co-author) Forensic Sciences, 1982; (co-author) Legal Medicine Annual, 1985; (co-ed.) Forensische Handschriten Untersuchung, 1993. Contributor of articles to journals. **Address:** 3344 Twin Lakes Ln., Sanibel, FL 33957-5528, U.S.A.

CROWTHER, Anne. (Margaret Anne Crowther). Scottish (born Scotland), b. 1943. **Genres:** History. **Career:** University of Kent, lecturer in history, 1968-73; University of Stirling, lecturer in history, 1973-75; Cambridge University, New Hall (now Murray Edwards College), fellow, 1975-78; University of Glasgow, lecturer, reader, 1979-94, professor of social history, 1994-2006, honorary research fellow, 2006-, Centre for the History of Medicine, director. Writer. **Publications:** Church Embattled: Religious Controversy in Mid-Victorian England, 1970; The Workhouse System, 1834-1929: The History of an English Social Institution, 1981; British Social Policy 1914-1939, 1988; (with B. White) On Soul and Conscience: The Medical Expert and Crime; 150 Years of Forensic Medicine in Glasgow, 1988; (with M.W. Dupree) Medical Lives in the Age of Surgical Revolution, 2007; (with S. McGann and R. Dougall) A History of the Royal College of Nursing 1916-90: A Voice for Nurses, 2009. Contributor to books and periodicals. **Address:** Department of Economic and Social History, University of Glasgow, Rm. 317, Lilybank House, Bute Gardens, Glasgow, G12 8RT, Scotland. **Online address:** anne.crowther@glasgow.ac.uk

CROWTHER, Hal. American/Canadian (born Canada), b. 1945. **Genres:** Essays. **Career:** Time, staff writer; Newsweek, associate editor and media critic; Buffalo News, media columnist, film and drama critic; Humanist, columnist; Free Inquiry, columnist; Spectator, columnist, 1981-, executive editor, 1984-89; Independent Weekly, columnist; Oxford American, columnist, 1994-; Progressive Populist, columnist; North Carolina Independent, columnist. **Publications:** Unarmed but Dangerous: Withering Attacks on All Things Phony, Foolish, and Fundamentally Wrong with America Today, 1995; Cathedrals of Kudzu: A Personal Landscape of the South, 2000; Gather at the River: Notes From the Post-Millennial South, 2005. Contributor to books, newspapers and periodicals. **Address:** Independent Weekly, 302 E Pettigrew St., Ste. 300, Durham, NC 27701, U.S.A. **Online address:** mail@halcrowther.com

CROWTHER, Harold Francis. *See* Obituaries.

CROWTHER, Margaret Anne. *See* **CROWTHER, Anne.**

CROWTHER, Nick. (Peter Crowther). British (born England), b. 1949. **Genres:** Novels, Young Adult Fiction, Novellas/Short Stories. **Career:** Leeds Permanent Building Society, communications manager, 1980-95; freelance writer and consulting editor, 1995-; PS Publishing, founder; Postscripts, editor. **Publications:** AS PETER CROWTHER: NOVELS: Fugue on a G-String, 1998; (with J. Lovegrove) Escardy Gap, 1996; Gandalph Cohen and the Land at the End of the Working Day, 1999; The Hand That Feeds, 1999; After Happily Ever, 2000; Windows to the Soul (Forever Twilight), 2009. COLLECTIONS: Lonesome Roads, 1999; The Longest Single Note: And Other Strange Compositions, 1999; (co-author) Cities, 2003; Songs of Leaving, 2004; The Spaces between the Lines, 2007. EDITOR: Taps and Sighs, 1989; Coast of Avon, 1992; Narrow Houses, vol. I, 1992, vol. II: Touch Wood, 1993, vol. II: Blue Motel, 1994; Tales in Space, 1995; (with M.H. Greenberg) Heaven Sent: 18 Glorious Tales of the Angels, 1995; (with E.E. Kramer) Tombs, 1995; (with E.E. Kramer) Dante's Disciples, 1996; Destination Unknown, 1996; (with J. Clute) Tales in Time: The Man Who Walked Home and Other Stories, 1997; Moon Shots, 1999; Foursight, 2000; (intro.) Futures, 2001; Infinities, 2002; Mars Probes, 2002; Constellations, 2005; (with A. Ashley) Urban Fantastic, 2006; Forbidden Planets, 2006; We Think, Therefore We Are, 2009. FOREVER TWILIGHT SERIES: Darkness, Darkness, 2002; Windows of the Soul, 2008. OTHERS: Our Club Our Rules, 2008; Darkness Falling, 2011. Works appear in anthologies. **Address:** c/o Susan Gleason, Susan Gleason Literary Agency, 325 Riverside Dr., New York, NY 10025, U.S.A. **Online address:** petecrowther@btinternet.com

CROWTHER, Peter. *See* **CROWTHER, Nick.**

CROYDEN, Margaret. American (born United States), b. 1922. **Genres:** Art/Art History, Theatre, Literary Criticism And History, Young Adult Fiction. **Career:** New Jersey City University, professor of English literature; Columbia Broadcasting System Inc. (CBS), Camera Three, host; New York Theatre Wire, commentator and reviewer. Writer and theatre critic. **Publications:** Lunatics, Lovers, and Poets: The Contemporary Experimental Theatre, 1974; In the Shadow of the Flame: Three Journeys, 1993; Conversations with Peter Brook: 1970-2000, 2003; (contrib.) Journeys in the Night: Creating a New American Theatre with Circle in the Square: A Memoir, 2007. Contributor of articles to periodicals. **Address:** c/o Author Mail, Faber & Faber Inc., 19 Union Sq. W, New York, NY 10003-3304, U.S.A.

CROZIER, Brian. (John Rossiter). British/Australian (born Australia), b. 1918. **Genres:** Novels, International Relations/Current Affairs, Third World, Biography. **Career:** Freelance art and music critic, 1941-43; Reuters, staff, sub-editor, 1943-44; News Chronicle, sub-editor, 1944-48; Sydney Morning Herald, feature writer, 1948-51; Reuters-Australian Associated Press, correspondent, 1951-52; Straits Times, 1952-53; The Economist, foreign reporter, 1954-64; British Broadcasting Corp., political commentator, 1954-65; Forum World Features, chair, 1965-75; Institute for the Study of Conflict, founder and director, 1970-79; National Review, contributing editor, 1979-; Stanford University, Hoover Institution, distinguished visiting fellow, 1996-2002. **Publications:** The Rebels: A Study of Post-War Insurrections, 1960; The Morning After: A Study of Independence, 1963; Neo-Colonialism, 1964; South-East Asia in Turmoil, 1965; The Struggle for the Third World, 1966; Franco, 1967; The Masters of Power, 1969; The Future of Communist Power in US as After Stalin, 1970; De Gaulle, 1973, vol. II, 1974; A Theory of Conflict, 1974, 2nd ed., 1976; The Soviet Presence in Somalia, 1975; Security and the Myth of Peace Surviving the Third World War, 1976; The Man Who Lost China: A Biography of Chiang Kai-shek, 1978; The Surrogate Forces of the Soviet Union, 1978; Soviet Imperialism: How to Contain it, 1978; Strategy of Survival, 1978; The Minimum State: Beyond Party Politics, 1979; Franco: Crepusculo de un Hombre, 1980; The Price of Peace, 1980; (with A. Seldon) Socialism Explained, 1984; (with D. Middleton and J. Murray-Brown) This War Called Peace, 1984; (as John Rossiter) The Andropov Deception (novel), 1984 as Brian Crozier, 1986; (with A. Seldon) Socialism: The Grand Delusion, 1986; Socialism: Dream and Reality, 1987; The Gorbachev Phenomenon, 1990; Communism: Why Prolong Its Death Throes?, 1990; Free Agent: The Unseen War 1941-1991, 1993; (co-author) Le Phénix Rouge, 1995; The KGB Lawsuits, 1995; The Rise and Fall of the Soviet Empire, 1999; Political Victory: The Elusive Prize of Military Wars, 2005. EDITOR: We Will Bury You: A Study of Left-wing Subversion Today, 1970; The Peacetime Strategy of the Soviet Union; Report of a Study Group of the Institute for the Study of Conflict, London, September 1972-January 1973, 1973; The Grenada Documents, 1987; (with R. Fisher) The Queensland House: A Roof Over Our Heads, 1994. **Address:** 112 Bridge Ln., Temple Fortune, GL NW11 9JS, England.

CROZIER, Lorna. (Lorna Uher). Canadian (born Canada), b. 1948. **Genres:** Poetry, Adult Non-fiction, Autobiography/Memoirs. **Career:** English teacher in Swift Current, 1970-77; Saskatchewan Summer School of the Arts, creative writing teacher, 1977-81; Saskatchewan Writers Guild, vice president, 1977-79; Cypress Hills Community College, writer-in-residence, 1980-81; Saskatchewan Department of Culture and Recreation, director of communications, 1981-83; Regina Public Library, writer-in-residence, 1983-84; CBC Radio, broadcaster and writer, 1986; University of Saskatchewan, special lecturer, 1986-91; University of Toronto, Toronto, Ontario, writer-in-residence, 1988-90; University of Victoria, associate professor, 1991-97, professor, 1997, Department of Writing, head chair; Banff School of Fine Arts, creative writing teacher. **Publications:** AS LORNA UHER: Inside Is the Sky, 1976; Crow's Black Joy, 1978; (with P. Lane) No Longer Two People, 1979; Animals of Fall, 1979; Humans and Other Beasts, 1980. OTHERS: The Weather, 1983; The Garden Going on Without Us, 1985; (ed. with G. Hyland) A Sudden Radiance: Saskatchewan Poetry, 1987; Angels of Flesh, Angels of Silence, 1988; (with B. Grenville) Honor Kever: Stations Along the Way, 1989; Inventing the Hawk, 1992; Everything Arrives at the Light, 1995; (ed. with P. Lane) Breathing Fire: Canada's New Poets, 1995; A Saving Grace: The Collected Poems of Mrs. Bentley, 1996; (ed. and intro. with P. Lane) A. Nowlan, Selected Poems, 1996; What the Living Won't Let Go, 1999; (ed.) Desire in Seven Voices, 1999; (ed. with P. Lane) Addicted: Notes from the Belly of the Beast, 2001; The Apocrypha of Light, 2002; Bones in Their Wings: Ghazals, 2003; (ed. with P. Lane) Breathing Fire 2: Canada's New Poets, 2004; Whetstone, 2005; Before the First Word, 2005; The Blue Hour of the Day: Selected Poems, 2007; Small Beneath the Sky, 2009; (intro. and trans.) C. Leñero) Curving the Line=Curvando la Linea, 2010; Small Mechanics, 2011. **Address:** McClelland and Stewart Inc., 481 University Ave., Ste. 900, Toronto, ON M5G 2E9, Canada. **Online address:** lcrozier@uvic.ca

CROZIER, Michael (Paul). Australian (born Australia), b. 1956. **Genres:** Cultural/Ethnic Topics, History, Politics/Government, Social Sciences, Sociology, Homes/Gardens, Architecture. **Career:** Monash University, tutor in political science, 1981; Deakin University, lecturer in sociology, 1986; University of Melbourne, lecturer in political science, 1987-, senior lecturer, Honours Program, chair and coordinator, student advisor; McMaster University, visiting fellow, 1997, 2001; University of Padua, visiting fellow, 2001. Writer. **Publications:** (Ed. with P. Murphy) The Left in Search of a Center, 1996; (with A. Capling and M. Considine) Australian Politics in the Global Era, 1998; (ed.) After the Garden?, 1999. Contributor to periodicals. **Address:** Department of Political Science, University of Melbourne, Rm. 541, East Twr. John Medley Bldg., Melbourne, VI 3010, Australia. **Online address:** mcrozier@unimelb.edu.au

CRUICKSHANK, Dan. British (born England), b. 1949. **Genres:** Architecture, Adult Non-fiction. **Career:** Robert Adam Architects, historic buildings consultant, 1999-; University of Sheffield, Department of Architecture, visiting professor; University of Delaware, faculty; Royal Institute of British Artists, honorary fellow. Architectural critic and writer. **Publications:** (With C. Amery) The Rape of Britain, 1975. NONFICTION: (with P. Wyld) London: The Art of Georgian Building, 1975; A Guide to the Georgian Buildings of Britain and Ireland, 1985; (ed.) Timeless Architecture, 1985; (with P. Wyld) Georgian Town Houses and Their Details, 1990; (with N. Burton) Life in the Georgian City, 1990; (ed.) Sir Banister Fletcher's A History of Architecture, 20th ed., 1996; (ed.) Architecture: The Critic's Choice: 150 Masterpieces of Western Architecture, 2000; Invasion: Defending Britain from Attack, 2001; The Story of Britain's Best Buildings, 2002; (with D. Vincent) Under Fire: People, Places and Treasure in Afghanistan, Iraq and Israel: An Eyewitness Account, 2003; The Story of Britain's Best Buildings, 2003; The Royal Hospital Chelsea: The Place and the People, 2004; Building the BBC: A Return to Form, 2004; Around the World in 80 Treasures, 2005; Brunel: The Man Who Built the World, 2005; Adventures In Architecture, 2008; Secret History of Georgian London: How the Wages of Sin Shaped the Capital, 2009; London's Sinful Secret: The Bawdy History and Very Public Passions of London's Georgian Age, 2010. **Address:** c/o Charles Walker, PFD Drury House, 34-43 Russell St., London, GL WC2B 5HA, England.

CRUM, Shutta. American (born United States), b. 1951?. **Genres:** Picture/Board Books. **Career:** South Lyon District Library, library director; Ann Arbor District Library, children's librarian, storyteller & manager of Northeast Branch Library; Washtenaw Community College, instructor. Writer. **Publications:** PICTURE BOOKS: Who Took My Hairy Toe?, 2001; All on a Sleepy Night, 2001; Fox and Fluff, 2002; The House in the Meadow, 2003; Click!, 2003; My Mountain Song, 2004; The Bravest of the Brave, 2005; A Family for Old Mill Farm, 2007; Thunder-Boomer!, 2009. OTHER Spitting Image (novel), 2003. Contributor of articles to magazines and journals. **Address:** PO Box 7444, Ann Arbor, MI 48107, U.S.A. **Online address:** shutta@shuttacrum.com

CRUMBLEY, Paul. American/Uraguayian (born Uruguay), b. 1952. **Genres:** Literary Criticism And History. **Career:** The Bush School, Department of English, English teacher, 1980-86, chair, 1984-86; University of North Carolina-Wilmington, lecturer in English, 1986-87; University of North Carolina-Chapel Hill, instructor in English, 1987-93, Writing Center, tutor, 1987-90, director, 1990-92, senior fellow, 1992-93; Niagara University, assistant professor of English, 1993-95; Utah State University, lecturer, 1995-96, assistant professor of English, 1996-2001, associate professor, 2001-08, professor of English, 2008-, faculty coordinator for American studies, 1997-, American Studies Undergraduate Program, director, 1997-2000, American Studies Program, acting director, 2000-02, co-director, 2006; Emily Dickinson International Society, secretary, 1995, vice president, 2004, president, 2007-. Writer. **Publications:** Inflections of the Pen: Dash and Voice in Emily Dickinson, 1997; (ed. and intro. with M. Graulich) Search for a Common Language: Environmental Writing and Education, 2005; (ed. with P.M. Gantt) Body My House: May Swenson's Work and Life, 2006; Winds of Will: Emily Dickinson and The Sovereignty of Democratic Thought, 2010. Contributor of articles to books and journals. **Address:** Department of English, Utah State University, 420C Ray B. W, 3200 Old Main Hill, Logan, UT 84322-3200, U.S.A. **Online address:** pcrumbley@english.usu.edu

CRUMMEY, Michael. Canadian (born Canada), b. 1965. **Genres:** Novels, Poetry, Adult Non-fiction, Young Adult Non-fiction. **Career:** John Howard Society, institutional counselor. Writer. **Publications:** Arguments with Gravity, 1996; Hard Light, 1998; Flesh and Blood: Stories, 1998; River Thieves, 2001; Emergency Roadside Assistance, 2001; Salvage, 2002; Newfoundland: Journey Into a Lost Nation, 2004; Wreckage: A Novel, 2005; (with M. Bernard and A. Jones) Three Servings: In Which the Reader is Offered Generous Portions of Boiled Dinner, 2005; Went With, 2007; Galore, 2009. **Address:** c/o Author Mail, Random House of Canada Ltd., 1 Toronto St., Ste. 300, Toronto, ON M5C 2V6, Canada. **Online address:** mcrummey@yahoo.com

CRUMP, Martha L. *See* **CRUMP, Marty L.**

CRUMP, Marty L. (Martha L. Crump). American (born United States), b. 1946. **Genres:** Animals/Pets, Natural History, Environmental Sciences/Ecology. **Career:** University of Florida, professor of zoology, 1976-92; Northern Arizona University, adjunct professor; University of Missouri, International Center for Tropical Ecology, research associate. Writer and behavioral ecologist. **Publications:** In Search of the Golden Frog, 2000; Amphibians, Reptiles, and Their Conservation (young adult), 2002; Headless Males Make Great Lovers and Other Unusual Natural Histories, 2005; Sexy Orchids Make Lousy Lovers and Other Unusual Relationships, 2009; Amphibians and Reptiles, 2011. AS MARTHA L. CRUMP: Quantitative Analysis of the Ecological Distribution of a Tropical Herpetofauna, 1971; Reproductive Strategies in a Tropical Anuran Community, 1974; (with W.E. Duellman) Speciation in Frogs of the Hyla Parviceps Group in the Upper Amazon Basin, 1974; (co-ed. and contrib.) Peru: The Ecotravellers' Wildlife Guide, 2001; (with J.P. Collins) Extinction in Our Times: Global Amphibian Decline, 2009. Contributor to books and periodicals. **Address:** Department of Biological Sciences, Northern Arizona University, 617 S Beaver St., PO Box 5640, Flagstaff, AZ 86011-5640, U.S.A.

CRUMP, William D(rake). American (born United States), b. 1949. **Genres:** Reference, Literary Criticism And History. **Career:** Reference Pathology, pathologist, 1982-86, 1990-95; Roche Biomedical, pathologist, 1986-89; Loyola University, Medical Center, fellow, 1989-90. Writer. **Publications:** The Christmas Encyclopedia, 2001, 2nd ed., 2006; Was the First Gift Really Gold?, 2003; Encyclopedia of New Year's Holidays Worldwide, 2008. Contributor to periodicals. **Address:** 757 Howse Ave., Madison, TN 37115, U.S.A. **Online address:** cootum@earthlink.net

CRUNK, Tony. American (born United States), b. 1956. **Genres:** Poetry, Children's Fiction. **Career:** University of Montana, visiting assistant professor of English, 1995-98; Murray State University, visiting assistant professor of English, 1998-99; University of Alabama, assistant professor of creative writing and literature, 2000-07; Alabama Writer's Forum, Writing Our Stories Program, teaching writer, 2008-; Samford University, instructor in communication and arts. **Publications:** Two Towns & the People Who Lived in Them (children's book), 1978; Living in the Resurrection (poetry), 1995; Big Mama (children's book), 1999; Grandpa's Overalls (children's book), 2000; Parables and Revelations (poetry), 2005; Railroad John and the Red Rock Run (children's book), 2006; Cumberland (poetry), 2007; Stories from Real Life (humor/short fiction), 2008; A Theatre of Fine Devices (poetry), 2009; New Covenant Bound (poetry), 2010. Contributor to periodicals. **Address:** Department of English, Samford University, 800 Lakeshore Dr., Birmingham, AL 35229, U.S.A. **Online address:** tcrunk@samford.edu

CRUSE, Howard. American (born United States), b. 1944. **Genres:** Graphic Novels, Novels, Picture/Board Books, Cartoons, Illustrations, Humor/Satire. **Career:** WAPI-TV (now WVTM-TV), assistant, 1964-65; Birmingham News, staff artist, 1967; Mag Computer Corp., paste-up artist, 1969; WBMG-TV, art director and puppeteer, 1969-72; Atlanta Children's Theatre, actor and scenic design assistant, 1972; Art Service Inc., staff artist, 1973-74; Luckie & Forney Advertising, staff artist, 1975-76; Starlog, art director, 1977-78; Gay Comix, founding editor, 1980-84; The Advocate, Wendel Comic Strip, writer and illustrator, 1983-89. **Publications:** SELF-ILLUSTRATED: The Complete Wendel, 2011. OTHERS: Wendel, 1985; Howard Cruse's Barefootz, 1986; Dancin' Nekkid with the Angels: Comic Strips and Stories for Grown-ups, 1987; Wendel on the Rebound, 1989; Early Barefootz, 1990; Stuck Rubber Baby (novel), 1995; Wendel All Together, 2001; (adaptor) Swimmer with a Rope in His Teeth, 2004; Felix's Friends (picture book), 2008; From Headrack to Claude, 2009. Contributor to periodicals. Illustrator of books by others. **Address:** PO Box 100, North Adams, MA 01247-0100, U.S.A. **Online address:** howard@howardcruse.com

CRUSE, Lonnie. American (born United States) **Genres:** Mystery/Crime/Suspense, Novels. **Career:** Mystery writer. **Publications:** METROPOLIS MYSTERY NOVELS: Murder in Metropolis, 2003; Murder beyond Metropolis, 2004; Married in Metropolis, 2006; Malice in Metropolis, 2007; Fifty-seven Heaven, 2007; Fifty-seven Traveling, 2010. **Address:** Five Star, 10 Water St., Ste. 310, Waterville, ME 04901, U.S.A. **Online address:** nevada1943@yahoo.com

CRUSH, Jonathan. (J. S. Crush). Canadian/British (born England), b. 1953. **Genres:** Third World, Demography, Social Sciences. **Career:** National University of Lesotho, Department of Geography, lecturer in human geography, 1979-81; Queen's University, Department of Geography, SSHRC post-doctoral research Fellow, 1983-85, Mactaggart research fellow, 1985-87, assistant professor, 1985-92, Canada research fellow, 1987-92, associate professor, 1987-93, professor of geography, 1993-2001, IDRC Migrant Labor Project, director, 1990-93, Southern African Migration Program (SAMP), director, 1997-, Southern African Research Centre, director, 2001-, research chair, 2007, African Network for Urban Food Security (AFSUN), co-director, 2007-, Department of Global Development Studies, professor, 2007-; professor of global development studies, 2007-; University of Natal, Development Studies Unit, research fellow, 1984; University of Witwatersrand, visiting professor, 1988, 1989; University of Cape Town, Department of Sociology, visiting professor, 1989, Department of Environmental and Geographical Science, visiting professor, 1997-99, honorary professor, 2004-. Writer. **Publications:** (As J.S. Crush) Post-colonial Development of Botswana, Lesotho, and Swaziland, 1978; The Struggle for Swazi Labour, 1890-1920, 1987; (with A. Jeeves and D. Yudelman) South Africa's Labor Empire: A History of Black Migrancy to the Gold Mines, 1991; (with H.S. Simelane) Swaziland Moves: Perceptions and Patterns of Modern Migration, 2004; (co-author) Migration and Development in Africa: An Overview, 2006. EDITOR: (with C. Ambler) Liquor and Labor in Southern Africa, 1992; Power of Development, 1995; (with W. James) Crossing Boundaries: Mine Migrancy in a Democratic South Africa, 1995; (with A.H. Jeeves) White Farms, Black Labor: The State and Agrarian Change in Southern Africa, 1910-50, 1997; Beyond Control: Immigration and Human Rights in a Democratic South Africa, 1998; (with V. Williams) New South Africans: Immigration, Amnesties, and Their Aftermath, 1999; (with D.A. McDonald) Destinations Unknown: Perspectives on the Brain Drain in Southern Africa, 2002; (with B. Frayne) Surviving on the Move, 2010; (with D. Tevera) Zimbabwe's Exodus, 2010. Works appear in anthologies. Contributor of articles to journals. **Address:** Department of Global Development Studies, Queen's University, 152 Albert St., Kingston, ON K7L 3N6, Canada. **Online address:** crushj@queensu.ca

CRUSH, J. S. *See* **CRUSH, Jonathan.**

CRUSIE, Jennifer. American (born United States), b. 1949. **Genres:** Romance/Historical, Novels, Adult Non-fiction, Young Adult Fiction, Children's Fiction, Mystery/Crime/Suspense, Literary Criticism And History. **Career:** Beavercreek public school, teacher; Antioch University, faculty; Wright State University, faculty; Ohio State University, faculty. Novelist. **Publications:** Sizzle (novella), 1992; Manhunting, 1993; Getting Rid of Bradley, 1994; Strange Bedpersons, 1994, 2nd ed., 2003; What the Lady Wants, 1995; Charlie All Night, 1996; Anyone But You, 1996; The Cinderella Deal, 1996; Trust Me on This, 1997; Tell Me Lies, 1998; Crazy for You: Tell me Lies, 1999; Welcome to Temptation, 2000; Fast Women, 2001; Faking It, 2002; Bet Me, 2004; (ed. with G. Yeffeth) Flirting with Pride & Prejudice: Fresh Perspectives on the Original Chick-lit Masterpiece, 2005; (ed. with L. Wilson) Totally Charmed: Demons, Whitelighters and the Power of Three, 2005; (with B. Mayer) Don't Look Down, 2006; Santa, Baby, 2006; Agnes and the Hitman, 2007; (ed. with L. Wilson) Coffee at Luke's: An Unauthorized Gilmore Girls Gabfest, 2007; (with E. Dreyer and A. Stuart) Unfortunate Miss Fortunes, 2007; (with A. Stuart and L.D. Rich) Dogs and Goddesses, 2009; (with B. Mayer) Wild Ride, 2010; Maybe This Time, 2010. Contributor of articles to books. **Address:** Argh Ink L.L.C., PO Box 1141, Bloomfield, NJ 07003, U.S.A. **Online address:** jennifercrusie@poboxes.com

CRUSIUS, Timothy Wood. American (born United States), b. 1950. **Genres:** Philosophy, Reference. **Career:** University of North Carolina at Greensboro, assistant professor of English, 1978-80; Texas A&M University, assistant professor, 1980-85, associate professor of English, 1986-90; Southern Methodist University, associate professor, 1990-99, professor of English, 1999-, director of discursive writing, 1990-95, coordinator of SMU-in-Legacy, 1998-; McGraw-Hill Co., writer. **Publications:** Discourse: A Critique and Synthesis of Recent Theories, 1989; A Teacher's Introduction to Philosophical Hermeneutics, 1991; (with C. Channell) The Aims of Argument: A Rhetoric and Reader, 1995, 7th ed., 2011; Kenneth Burke and the Conversation after Philosophy, 1999. Contributor to books and periodicals. **Address:** Department of English, Southern Methodist University, Rm. 14 McFarlin, 3225 University Blvd., Dallas, TX 75275-0435, U.S.A. **Online address:** tcrusius@smu.edu

CRUTCHER, Chris(topher C.). American (born United States), b. 1946. **Genres:** Young Adult Fiction, Adult Non-fiction, Novels, Novellas/Short Stories, Children's Fiction. **Career:** Kennewick Dropout School, teacher, 1970-73; Lakeside School, teacher, 1973-76, director of school, 1976-80; Community Mental Health, child protection team specialist, 1980-82, child and family therapist, 1982-. Writer. **Publications:** YOUNG ADULT FICTION: Running Loose, 1983; Stotan!, 1986; The Crazy Horse Electric Game, 1987; Chinese Handcuffs, 1989; The Deep End, 1991; Athletic Shorts: Six Short Stories, 1991, 2nd ed., 2002; Staying Fat for Sarah Byrnes, 1993, 2nd ed., 2003; Ironman, 1995; Stories about Family Secrets, 1998; Whale Talk, 2001; King of the Mild Frontier, 2003; Sledding Hill, 2005; Deadline, 2007; Angry Management, 2009. **Address:** HarperCollins, 1350 Ave. of the Americas, New York, WA 10019-4703, U.S.A. **Online address:** stotan717@aol.com

CRUZ, Angie. American (born United States), b. 1972. **Genres:** Novels. **Career:** Texas A&M University, faculty; Brazos Valley Reads, coordinator; Women in Literature and Letters (WILL), co-founder, 1997-. Writer. **Publications:** Soledad, 2001; Let It Rain Coffee, 2005. Contributor to periodicals. **Address:** Simon & Schuster Inc., 1230 Ave. of the Americas, 12th Fl., New York, NY 10020, U.S.A. **Online address:** cruzwriter@yahoo.com

CRUZ, Consuelo. American (born United States) **Genres:** Politics/Government. **Career:** Bank of America, assistant, 1975-76; World Bank, assistant, 1979-82, consultant, 1985-86, 2007; Columbia University, assistant professor, 1995-2002, Institute for Latin American and Iberian Studies, director, 1997-98; Tufts University, assistant professor, 2002-05, associate professor of political science, 2005-. Writer. **Publications:** Political Culture and Institutional Development in Costa Rica and Nicaragua: World-Making in the Tropics, 2005. CONTRIBUTOR: PostStabilization Politics in Latin America: Competition, Transition, Collapse, 2003; Authoritarian Legacies and Democratization in Latin American and Southern Europe, 2004; The Third Wave of Democratization in Latin America: Advances and Setbacks, 2005. Contributor to journals. **Address:** Department of Political Science, Tufts University, Packard Hall, 3rd Fl., 202 Lawrence Rd., Medford, MA 02155, U.S.A. **Online address:** consuelo.cruz@tufts.edu

CRUZ, Victor Hernandez. American (born United States), b. 1949. **Genres:** Poetry, Essays. **Career:** East Harlem Gut Theatre, co-founder, 1968; Before Columbus Foundation, co-founder; Umbra Magazine, editor; San Francisco State University, instructor, 1971-73; University of Michigan, visiting professor, 1994; University of California, visiting professor, 1994; Academy of American Poets, chancellor, 2008-. Writer. **Publications:** Papo Got His Gun!, 1966; Snaps: Poems, 1969; (ed. with H. Kohl) Stuff: A Collection of Poems, Visions & Imaginative Happenings from Young Writers in Schools-Opened and Closed, 1970; Mainland: Poems, 1973; Tropicalization: Poems, 1976; Clutch y los klinkies, 1981; By Lingual Wholes, 1982; Rhythm, Content & Flavor, 1988; Red Beans: Poems, 1991; (ed. with L.V. Quintana and V. Suarez) Paper dance: 55 Latino Poets, 1995; Panoramas, 1997; Maraca: New & Selected Poems, 1966-2000, 2001; The Mountain in the Sea: Poems, 2006; In the Shadow of Al-Andalus, 2011. **Address:** The Academy of American Poets, 584 Broadway, Ste. 604, New York, NY 10012-5243, U.S.A.

CRYSTAL, David. Welsh/Irish (born Ireland), b. 1941. **Genres:** Poetry, Children's Non-fiction, Language/Linguistics, Medicine/Health, Speech/Rhetoric, Theology/Religion, Reference. **Career:** University of London, research assistant, 1962-63; University of Wales, College of North Wales, assistant lecturer, 1963-65, honorary professor of linguistics, 1986-; Bangor University, Department of Linguistics, faculty, 1963-65, professor; University of Reading, lecturer, 1965-69, reader, 1969-75, professor of linguistic science, 1976-85, honorary professor of linguistics; University College of Wales, professorial fellow, 1985-; Child Language Teaching and Therapy, editor, 1985-96; Linguistics Abstracts, editor, 1985-96; English Today, consulting editor, 1986-94; Crystal Reference, chairman, 2002-; Ucheldre Centre, director. **Publications:** (With R. Quirk) Systems of Prosodic and Paralinguistic Features in English, 1964; Linguistics, Language and Religion, 1965; What Is Linguistics?, 1968, 4th ed., 1985; (with D. Davy) Investigating English Style, 1969; Prosodic Systems and Intonation in English, 1969; Linguistics, 1971; The English Tone of Voice, 1975; (with D. Davy) Advanced Conversational English, 1975; (with P. Fletcher and M. Garman) The Grammatical Analysis of Language Disability, 1976, 2nd ed., 1989; Child Language, Learning and Linguistics, 1976, 2nd ed., 1987; Working with LARSP, 1979; A First Dictionary of Linguistics and Phonetics, 1980, 6th ed., 2008; Introduction to Language Pathology, 1980, (with R. Varley) 4th ed., 1998; Clinical Linguistics, 1981; Directions in Applied Linguistics, 1981; Profiling Linguistic Disability, 1982, 2nd ed., 1992; Linguistic Encounters with Language Handicap, 1984; Language Handicap in Children, 1984; Who Cares about English Usage?, 1984, 2nd ed., 2000; Listen to Your Child, 1986; Cambridge Encyclopedia of Language, 1987, 3rd ed., 2010; Rediscover Grammar, 1988, 2nd ed., 1996; Pilgrimage, 1988; (with J.C. Davies) Convent, 1989; Language A to Z, 1991; Making Sense of English Usage, 1991; Introducing Linguistics, 1992; An Encyclopedic Dictionary of Language and Languages, 1992, rev. ed. as The Penguin Dictionary of Language, 1999; The Cambridge Paperback Encyclopedia, 1993, 3rd ed., 1999; Cambridge Encyclopedia of the English Language, 1995, 2nd ed., 2003; Discover Grammar, 1996; John Bradburne: Songs of the Vagabond, 1996; English as a Global Language, 1997, 2nd ed., 2003; Language Play, 1998; (with H. Crystal) Words on Words, 2000; (with H. Crystal) John Bradburne's Mutemwa, 2000; Language Death, 2000; Happenings, 2000; Language and the Internet, 2001, 2nd ed., 2006; Language Play, 2001; Shakespeare's Words: A Glossary and Language Companion, 2002; Making Sense of Grammar, 2004; The Stories of English, 2004; The Language Revolution, 2004; A Glossary of Netspeak and Textspeak, 2004; (with B. Crystal) The Shakespeare Miscellany, 2005; Pronouncing Shakespeare: The Globe Experiment, 2005; Dr. Johnson's Dictionary: An Anthology, 2005; As They Say in Zanzibar, 2006; Words, Words, Words, 2006; The Fight for English: How Language Pundits Ate, Shot and Left, 2006; How Language Works: How Babies Babble, Words Change Meaning, and Languages Live or Die, 2007; By Hook or by Crook: A Journey in Search of English, 2007; Txtng: the Gr8 Db8, 2008; Think on My Words: Exploring Shakespeare's Language, 2008; Dictionary of Linguistics and Phonetics, 2008; Just a Phrase I'm Going Through: My Life in Language, 2009; Future of Language, 2009; Little Book of Language, 2010; Evolving English, 2010; Begat: The King James Bible and the English Language, 2010; Internet Linguistics: a Student Guide, 2011. EDITOR: (with W.F. Bolton) The English Language, 1969, 2nd ed., 2002; Eric Partridge: In His Own Words, 1980; Linguistic controversies, 1982; The Cambridge Encyclopedia, 1990, 4th ed., 2000; Nineties Knowledge, 1992; (with D. Strange) The Great Gatsby, 1992; The Cambridge Concise Encyclopedia, 1992, 2nd ed., 1995; The Cambridge Biographical Encyclopedia, 1994, 2nd ed., 1998; The Cambridge Biographical Dictionary, 1996; The New Penguin Encyclopedia, 2002, 3rd ed., 2003; The New Penguin Factfinder, 2003; The New Penguin Concise Encyclopedia, 2003; The Penguin Book of Facts, 2004; (intro.) Pocket Spelling Dictionary, 2005; (intro. and contrib.) Dictionary of Modern English Usage, 2010; (with R. Facchinetti and B. Seidlhofer) From International to Local English and Back Again, 2010. CHILDREN'S NON-FICTION: (with J. Bevington) Skylarks, 1975. Contributor to books. **Address:** Department of Linguistics, Bangor University, Bangor, LL57 2DG, Wales. **Online address:** crystal@dial.pipex.com

CSABA, László. Hungarian (born Hungary), b. 1954?. **Genres:** Economics, Politics/Government, History, Social Sciences. **Career:** Institute for World Economy, associate, 1976-87; Kopint-Datorg Economic Research, senior economist, 1988-2000; European Association for Comparative Economic Studies, vice-president, 1990-94, 1996-98, president, 1999-2000; College of Foreign Trade, honorary professor of international economics, 1991-97; Budapest University, professor of economics, 1997-; Central European University, visiting professor, 1998, Department of International Relations and European Studies, professor of economics and European studies, 2000-; Universitas Debrecen, professor and head of doctoral program, 1999-. Writer. **Publications:** Economic Mechanism in the GDR and in Czechoslovakia: A Comparative Analysis, 1983; Kelet-Európa a világgazdaságban: alkalmazkodás és gazdasági mechanizmus, 1984; Economic Policy Coordination in the CMEA, 1984; Three Studies on the CMEA, 1985; Problems of Inter-CMEA-Cooperation after the Moscow Summit, 1986; Radikálisreform a szovjet gyakorlatban, 1987; Was geschah mit der ungarischen Reform, 1979-1988?, 1989; Eastern Europe in the World Economy, 1990; Szovjetunió felbomlása és a magyar gazdaság, 1991; összeomlás forgatókönyvei: arendszer-átalakítás alkalmazott közgazdaságtana, 1994; The Capitalist Revolution in Eastern Europe: A Contribution to the Economic Theory of Systematic Change, 1995; New Political Economy of Emerging Europe, 2005, 2nd ed., 2007; A fölemelkedo Európa, 2006. EDITOR: Systemic Change and Stabilization in Eastern Europe, 1993; Privatization, Liberalization and Destruction: Recreating the Market in Central and Eastern Europe, 1994; The Hungarian Small Business in Comparative Perspective, 1998; (co-ed.) The Hungarian SME Sector Development in Comparative Perspective, 1998; (with W. Andreff and M. Dimitrov) Economies in Transition and the Varieties of Capitalism, 1999; (with Z. Bara) Small Economies' Adjustment to Global Tendencies, 2000; Válságban és válság nélkul: A Gazdaságpolitika Rétegei, 2010. Contributor to books and periodicals. **Address:** Department of International Relations and European, Studies, Central European University, Rm. 304, Nádor St. 9, Budapest, H-1051, Hungary. **Online address:** csabal@ceu.hu

CSÁNYI, Vilmos. Hungarian (born Hungary), b. 1935. **Genres:** Novels. **Career:** Chinoin Pharmaceutical Co., research chemist, 1958; Semmelweis University, assistant professor of medical chemistry, 1958-73; Eötvös Loránd University, Department of Ethology, founder, head, 2000, professor, 2007-, now professor emeritus. Writer. **Publications:** Sejtbiológia, 1970; Magatartásgenetika, 1977; Az evolúció általános elmélete, 1979; Evolutionary Systems and Society: A General Theory of Life, Mind, and Culture, 1989; The Evolution of Cognitive Maps, 1993; Viselkedés gondolkodás társadalom: Etológiai megközelítés, 1994; Etológia, 1994; Changing Visions Human Cognitive Maps: Past Present and Future, 1996; Az emberi természet: Humánetológia, 1999; Van ott valaki?: Válogatott írások, 2000; A Kentaurtermészetrajza, 2000; (ed. with P. Csaba and K. György) A Megismeréskutatás útjai, 2000; Bukfenc mindent tud, 2002; Jeromos, a barátom, 2002; A lény és az orzo: elbeszélések, 2003; (ed. with P. Csaba and K. György) észleléstol a nyelvig, 2004; Malion és Thea: két elbeszélés, 2005. Contributor to journals. **Address:** Department of Ethology, Eötvös Loránd University, Pázmány Péter Sétány 1/c, Budapest, H-1117, Hungary.

CSEPELI, György. Hungarian (born Hungary), b. 1946. **Genres:** Politics/Government, Economics. **Career:** Institute of Sociology, Department of Social Psychology, assistant professor of sociology, 1971-82, associate professor of social psychology, 1982-91, chair, 1986-2001, professor of social psychology, 1991-; Eotvos Lorand University, assistant professor of sociology, 1972-80, Institute of Sociology, Department of Social Psychology, chairperson, Department of Cultural Anthropology, chair, 2001-06; University of Michigan, Department of Political Science, professor, 1994-95; University of Miskolc, Department of Sociology, part-time faculty; University of Gorizia, visiting professor, 2000; Government of Hungary, Ministry of Informatics and Communication, political state secretary, 2002-06, Ministry of Economy and Transport, public policy director, 2006-08, Prime Minister's Office, public policy director, 2008-10. Writer. **Publications:** Oktatásügyi szervezetkutatás lehetoségei, 1976; Interakicó világa, 1978; Egyetemi és foiskolaihallgatók életés munkakörülményei, 1980; Eloítéletek és csoportközi viszonyok, 1980; Nemzeti tudatés érzésvilág Magyarországon a 70-es évenkben, 1984; Szociálpszichológia Vázlata, 1984; Nemzet éspolitika a 10-14 éves gyerekek gondolkodásában, 1984; Hétköznapi élet anatómiája, 1986; Csoporttudat, nemzettudat: esszék, tanulmányok, 1987; Modern Polgári Társadalomelméletek, 1987; Vonzalmak és kapcsolatok, 1987; Structures and Contents of Hungarian National Identity, 1989; ésnema is kell hozzá zsidó: az antiszemitizmus társadalomlélektana, 1990; (with A. örkény) Ideology and Political Beliefs in Hungary: The Twilight of State Socialism, 1992; Nemzetáltal homályosan, 1992; (ed. with L. Kéri and I. Stumpf) State and Citizen: Studies on Political Socialization in Post-Communist Eastern Europe, 1993; Meghatározatlan állat: szociápszichológiai kezdoknekés haladóknak, 1993; (co-ed.) From Subject to Citizen, 1994; (with A. Orkeny) Ideology and Political Beliefs in Hungary: The Twilight of State Socialism, 1992; Szocialpszichologia, 1997; Az antiszemita eloitelet, 1999; (co-ed.) European Nations and Nationalism, 2000; Szervezkedo ember: A Szervezti életszociálpszichológiája, 2001; Nagvilágon e Kivul: Nemzetitudat és érzésvilág Magyarországon, 1970-2002, 2002; A nagyvilágon e kivul, 2002; Nemzetek egymás tükrében: Interetnikus viszonyok aKárpát-medencében, 2002; (with O. Antal) Gyulöletés politika, 2002; (with K. éva and P. Péeter) Magára hagyott generácioACUk: fiatalok és öregek a XXI, 2006; A Zsidosag es Europa: uj fejezetek az antiszemitizmus toirteneti-tarsadalmi gyoikereiroil, 2006; (with D. Lane and J. Tholen) Restructuring of the Economic Elites After State Socialism: Recruitment, Institutions and Attitudes, 2007. **Address:** Pazmany Peter setany 1/a, Budapest, 1117, Hungary. **Online address:** csepeli.gyorgy@gmail.com

CSOORI, Sandor. Hungarian (born Hungary), b. 1930. **Genres:** Novels, Plays/Screenplays, Poetry. **Career:** Papai Neplap (Papa Popular News), staff, 1949-; Veszprem Megyei Nepujsag (Veszprem County Popular Newspaper), staff, 1949-; Szabad Ifjusag (Free Youth), staff, 1952-; Irodalmi Ujsag (Literary News), staff, 1953-54; Uj Hang (New Voice), new sound versrovat editor, head of poetry section, 1955-56; Hungarian Film Studio, dramaturge, 1971-; Hungarian Democratic Forum, founding member, 1987; Hitel, co-editor, 1988-, editor-in-chief, 1992-. **Publications:** POETRY: Felroppen a madar, 1954; Ordogpille, 1957; Menekules a maganybol, 1962; (with F. Hidas) Szigoru korban elunk, 1967; Masodik szuletesem, 1967; Lekvarcirkusz bohocai, 1969; Pá rbeszé d, sötétben, 1973; A látogató emlékei, 1977; Jóslás a te idödröl, 1979; A tizedik este, 1980; Wings of Knives and Nails, 1981; Elmaradt lázálom, 1982; Várakozás a tavaszban, 1983; Memory of Snow, 1983; Kezemben zöld ág, 1985; Labon jaro verofeny, 1987; Csoori Sandor breviarium, 1988; A világ emlékmüvei, 1989; Barbarian Prayer: Selected Poems, 1989; Selected Poems of Sandor Csoori, 1992. OTHERS: Tudositas a toronybol, 1963; Kubai naplo, 1965; A kolto es a majompofa, 1966; Balatoni Almanach, 1967; Biztato, 1973; Utazás féláomban, 1974; Nomád napló, 1979; 80 huszár, 1980; (ed.) Szarny es piramis, 1980; Iszapeso, 1981; Tenger es diolevel, 1982; A fèlig bevallott èlet, 1982; (ed.) Mert szemben ulsz velem, 1982; Készülodés a számadásra, 1987; Virá gvasá rnap: a 60 éves költö 60 verse, 1990; Nappali hold, 1991; Senkid, barátod: a szerzö vá logatása é letmüvé böl, 1995; Ha volna é letem, 1996; Szá lla alá poklokra: esszé k, 1997; A jö vö szökevé nye: ö sszegyüjtott versek, 2000; Forgá csok a fö ldö n: tanulmányok, esszé k, interjúk, 2001; Csöndes tériszony: új versek, 2001; Elveszett utak, 2003; Visszané ztem fé lutamról, 2004; Elkártyá zott kö peny: versek, 2004; Before and After the Fall: New Poems, 2004; Futás a ködben: versek, 2005; ördö gfióka: rajzok-versek gyermekhangra, 2006; (with S. Lajos) Nekünk Ilyen Sors Adatott, 2006; Tizenht Ka Parton: Esszk, 2007; Moziba Megy a Hold, 2008; Harangok Zgnak Bennem, 2009. **Address:** c/o Magveto Konyvkiado, Vorosmarty ter 1, Budapest V, 1806, Hungary.

CUDMORE, Dana (D.). American (born United States), b. 1954. **Genres:** Travel/Exploration. **Career:** Daily Editor, editor; Media Services, advertising consultant. **Publications:** The Remarkable Howe Caverns Story, 1990. **Address:** 565 Patrick Rd., Cobleskill, NY 12043-6214, U.S.A.

CUERVO, Talía. *See* **VEGA, Ana Lydia.**

CUETARA, Mittie. American (born United States), b. 1957. **Genres:** Children's Fiction, Illustrations, Picture/Board Books. **Career:** Sedia Inc., illustrator and designer, 1990-98; Treasure Craft Compton, designer, 1991-93; Pacific Paper Works S.F., partner, 1994-97; freelance illustrator, 1998-. Writer. **Publications:** SELF-ILLUSTRATED: Terrible Teresa and Other Very Short Stories, 1997; The Crazy Crawler Crane and Other Very Short Truck Stories, 1998; Baby Business, 2003. **Address:** c/o Julie Popkin, 15340 Albright St., Ste. 204, Pacific Palisades, CA 90272-2520, U.S.A. **Online address:** mittie@mittiecuetara.com

CUEVAS, Judy. *See* **IVORY, Judith.**

CULBERT, Steven. *See* **CULBERT, Steven (Tye).**

CULBERT, Steven (Tye). (Steven Culbert). American (born United States), b. 1950. **Genres:** Novels, Poetry, Essays, Literary Criticism And History. **Career:** Texas Christian University, visiting professor, 1975-85; University of San Francisco, visiting professor, 1979; Occidental College, visiting professor, 1989; Texas Wesleyan University, novelist-in-residence; University of Texas, instructor of business communications, 1997-, Department of Management, lecturer, 2000-. Writer. **Publications:** The Beautiful Woman without Mercy, 1993; The King of Scarecrows, 1993; (with G.S. Peoples) Responsibilities (essays and poems), 1993; Lovesong for the Giant Contessa (novel), 1997. Works appear in anthologies. Contributor to periodicals. **Address:** Department of Management, University of Texas, Rm. B 205, PO Box 19467, Arlington, TX 76019-0467, U.S.A. **Online address:** culbert@uta.edu

CULHANE, John (William). American (born United States), b. 1934. **Genres:** Film, Plays/Screenplays, Science Fiction/Fantasy, Communications/Media, Design, Graphic Novels. **Career:** St. Louis Globe Democrat, reporter, 1955; Rockford Register-Republic, daily columnist and reporter, 1956-61; Chicago Daily News, reporter and foreign correspondent, 1962-66; Newsweek, correspondent in Chicago Bureau, 1966-69, associate editor, 1969-71; freelance journalist, 1971-85; School of Visual Arts, lecturer, 1972; Reader's Digest, roving editor, 1985-93; Johimith Robidoux Productions, roving writer, 1994-; Northwestern University, lecturer on animated film, 1995; Northwestern University, lecturer, 1995, New York University, lecturer, 1996, 1997; New York University, lecturer on animated film, 1996-97; University of the Arts, senior lecturer in animation history, 1997-98; Disney Institute, artist in residence, 1999; State University of New York, Fashion Institute of Technology, lecturer, adjunct instructor, 2000; Museum of Modern Art, lecturer; California Institute of the Arts, lecturer; Mercy College, Roy Disney School of Animation Studies, faculty. **Publications:** (With M.K. Frith and B. Johnson) The Art of the Muppets, 1980; Special Effects in the Movies: How They Do It, 1981; Walt Disney's Fantasia, 1983; The American Circus:

An Illustrated History, 1990; Disney's Aladdin: The Making of the Animated Film, 1992; A Taz Thanksgiving, 1994; (contrib.) Fantasia 2000: Visions of Hope, 1999. Contributor to books and periodicals. **Address:** Fashion Institute of Technology, State University of New York, 7th Ave., 27 St., New York, NY 10001-5992, U.S.A.

CULHANE, Patrick. *See* **COLLINS, Max Allan.**

CULKIN, Jennifer. American (born United States), b. 1958. **Genres:** Autobiography/Memoirs. **Career:** Harborview Medical Center, critical care nurse; Crab Creek Review, nonfiction editor. **Publications:** A Final Arc of Sky: A Memoir of Critical Care, 2009. Contributor to magazines. **Address:** Bainbridge Island, WA , U.S.A. **Online address:** jennifer@jenniferculkin.com

CULL, Mark E. American (born United States), b. 1960. **Genres:** Children's Fiction, Young Adult Fiction. **Career:** Crissair Aerospace Inc., design engineer, 1984-89, senior design engineer, 1989-99, lead engineer, 1999-2001; Red Hen Press, co-founder and editor, 1994-, publisher. **Publications:** (Ed. with K. Gale) Anyone is Possible: Contemporary Short Fiction, 1997; (ed. with K. Gale) Blue Cathedral: Contemporary Short Fiction, 2000; One Way Donkey Ride: Fiction, 2002. **Address:** Red Hen Press, PO Box 40820, Pasadena, CA 91114, U.S.A. **Online address:** mark@redhen.org

CULLEN, Bill. Irish (born Ireland), b. 1942. **Genres:** Autobiography/Memoirs, Biography. **Career:** Walden Motor Corp., office messenger, 1956-, director general, 1965-; Fairlane Motor Co., founder, 1977, director; Glencullen Group, owner, founder, chairman and chief executive officer, 1986-; Lifetime Success Institute, founder; Irish Youth Foundation, director; Bill Cullen Motor Group Ltd., chairman; Renault Ireland, owner, through 2007. Writer. **Publications:** It's a Long Way from Penny Apples, 2001; Golden Apples: Six Simple Steps to Success, 2005. Contributor to books and periodicals. **Address:** Bill Cullen Motor Group Ltd., Liffey Valley Renault, Liffey Valley Motor Mall, Dublin, DU 22, Ireland.

CULLEN, Bob. *See* **CULLEN, Robert (B.).**

CULLEN, Dave. American (born United States), b. 1961. **Genres:** History, Education. **Career:** University of Colorado, faculty of writing program; Columbia University, Graduate School of Journalism, Dart Center for Journalism and Trauma, Ochberg fellow. Writer. **Publications:** Columbine, 2009. Contributor to periodicals. **Address:** c/o Betsy Lerner, Dunow, Carlson & Lerner Literary Agency Inc., 27 W 20th St., Ste. 1107, New York, NY 10011, U.S.A. **Online address:** dave@davecullen.com

CULLEN, Mark. Canadian (born Canada), b. 1956. **Genres:** Horticulture, Homes/Gardens. **Career:** Weall & Cullen Nurseries Ltd., president, 1990-; CFRB-Radio, Anything Grows, host; Right in Your Own Backyard (TV series), host; Canada AM, weekly gardening segment, co-host; Sunday Sun, columnist; Marks' Choice Ltd., owner. Writer. **Publications:** A Greener Thumb, 1990; The Real Dirt, 1992; (with L. Johnson) The Urban/Suburban Composter: The Complete Guide to Backyard, Balcony and Apartment Composting, 1994; The All Seasons Gardener, Getting More from Your Canadian Garden, 1995. **Address:** Marks' Choice Ltd., 136 Main St., Unionville, ON L3R 2G5, Canada.

CULLEN, Robert (B.). (Bob Cullen). American (born United States), b. 1949. **Genres:** Criminology/True Crime, Law, Mystery/Crime/Suspense, Sports/Fitness, Novels, History, Literary Criticism And History, Young Adult Fiction, Young Adult Fiction. **Career:** Evening News, reporter, 1970-71; Associated Press, reporter, 1971-73, Raleigh Bureau, chief, 1974-76, reporter, 1976-82; Newsweek, Moscow Bureau, chief, 1982-85, general editor, 1985-86, diplomatic correspondent, 1986-88; freelance writer and editor, 1988-; Soviet-American Trade, editor. **Publications:** AS ROBERT CULLEN: (ed.) The Post-Containment Handbook: Key Issues in U.S.-Soviet Economic Relations, 1990; Soviet Sources (novel), 1990; Twilight of Empire: Inside the Crumbling Soviet Bloc, 1991; The Killer Department: Detective Viktor Burakov's Eight-Year Hunt for the most Savage Serial Killer in Russian History, 1993; Cover Story (novel), 1994; Dispatch from a Cold Country (novel), 1996; Heirs of the Fire, 1997; (with B. Rotella) Your 15th Club: The Inner Secret to Great Golf, 2008. AS BOB CULLEN WITH B. ROTELLA: Golf Is Not a Game of Perfect, 1995; Golf Is a Game of Confidence, 1996; Golf of Your Dreams, 1997; Life is not a Game of Perfect: Finding Your Real Talent and Making it Work for You, 1999; Putting Out of Your Mind, 2001; Golfer's Mind: Play to Play Great, 2004. AS BOB CULLEN: Why Golf?: The Mystery of the Game Revisited, 2000; Mulligan for Bobby Jobe, 2001. Contributor to periodicals. **Address:** c/o Raphael Sagalyn, Sagalyn Literary Agency, 7201 Wisconsin Ave., Ste. 675, Bethesda, MD 20814-7213, U.S.A. **Online address:** rbcullen@yahoo.com

CULLINANE, Jan. American (born United States) **Genres:** Novels, Business/Trade/Industry, Medicine/Health. **Career:** Sussex Community College, Science and Maths, chairman, 1988-95; Retirement Living from A to Z, president and owner, 2004-. Writer and educator. **Publications:** (With C. Fitzgerald) The New Retirement: The Ultimate Guide to the Rest of Your Life, 2004, rev. ed., 2007; Single Womans Guide to Retirement: Everything You Need to Know for a Successful, Fulfilling Future, 2011; The Single Woman's Guide to Retirement, 2011. Contributor to periodicals. **Address:** c/o Author Mail, Rodale Press, 733 3rd Ave., 15th Fl., New York, NY 10017-3204, U.S.A. **Online address:** jancullinane@gmail.com

CULP, Stephanie (Anne). American (born United States), b. 1947. **Genres:** Administration/Management, Design, Homes/Gardens, Self Help, Crafts, Business/Trade/Industry. **Career:** The Culp Organization, owner, 1982-; Copley News Service, syndicated columnist, 1995-99; Organizing News, publisher. Writer. **Publications:** How to Get Organized When You Don't Have the Time, 1986; (with J.R. Reed) The Craftsmanship Revival in Interior Design: How Today's Artisans Preserve Yesterday's Skills, 1989; How to Conquer Clutter, 1989; Conquering the Paper Pile-Up: How to Sort, Organize, File and Store Every Piece of Paper in Your Home and Office, 1990; Organized Closets & Storage: Great Ideas for Every Room in Your House, 1990; Streamlining Your Life: A 5-Point Plan for Uncomplicated Living, 1991; You Can Find More Time for Yourself Every Day, 1994; Stephanie Culp's 12 Month Organizer and Project Planner, 1995; 611 Ways to Do More in a Day, 1998. Contributor to books and periodicals. **Address:** The Culp Organization, 31416 Corte Mallorca, PO Box 890700, Temecula, CA 92592, U.S.A.

CULPER, Felix. *See* **MCCAUGHREAN, Geraldine (Jones).**

CULYER, A(nthony) J(ohn). British (born England), b. 1942. **Genres:** Economics, Medicine/Health, Bibliography, Public/Social Administration, Institutions/Organizations, Social Sciences, Ethics. **Career:** University of California, teaching assistant, 1964-65; Exeter University, tutor, 1965-66, assistant lecturer, 1966-69; University of York, lecturer in economics, 1969-72, Institute of Social and Economic Research, assistant director, 1971-79, deputy director, 1971-82; Department of Economics and Related Studies, senior lecturer in economics, 1972-76, reader in economics, 1976-79, professor of economics, 1979-, pro-vice-chancellor, 1991-94, deputy vice-chancellor, 1994-97, School of Politics, Economics and Philosophy, head, 1986-2001, director, 1995-96, university director of health development, 1997-2001; Queen's University Canada, visiting professor, 1976; Otago University, William Evans visiting professor, 1979; Australian National University, visiting fellow, 1979; Trent University, visiting professor, 1985-86; University of Toronto, Department of Health Administration, visiting professor, 1989-94, Department of Health Policy, Management and Evaluation, visiting professor, 2003-07, Ontario Research Chair in Health Policy and System Design, 2007-; Institut fur Medizinische Informatic und Systemforschung, faculty, 1990; Central Institute of Technology, visiting professor, 1996; York Health Economics Consortium, director, 1999-2001, chair, 2001-03; Institute for Work and Health, chief scientist, 2003-06, senior scientist, 2006-07; Cancer Care Ontario, senior economic adviser, 2006-07; Research Advisory Council of the Workplace Safety & Insurance Board, chair, 2006-10; Institute for Work and Health, adjunct scientist, 2007-. Writer. **Publications:** (With M.H. Cooper) The Price of Blood: An Economic Study of the Charitable and Commercial Principle, 1968; (with A.T. Peocock) Economic Aspects of Student Unrest, 1969; (with F.M.M. Lewes and G.A. Brady) The Holiday Industry of Devon and Cornwall, 1970; The Economics of Social Policy, 1973; (with M.H. Cooper) Health Economics, 1973; Economic Policies and Social Goals, 1974; Need and the National Health Service, 1976; (with J. Wiseman and A. Walker) Annotated Bibliography of Health Economics, 1977; (with V. Halberstadt) Human Resources and Public Finance, 1977; Measuring Health: Lessons for Ontario, 1978; The Political Economy of Social Policy, 1980; (with B. Horisberger) Economic and Medical Evolution of Health Care Technologies, 1983; (co-author) The International Bibliography of Health Economics, 1986; Health Care Expenditure in Canada: Myth and Reality, Past and Future, 1988; The Economics of Health, vol. II, 1991; The Political Economy of Social Policy, 1991; Svensk Sjukvard: Basti Varlden?, 1992; Equity in Health Care,

1992; Funding Research in the NHS, 1994; Dictionary of Health Economics, 2005. EDITOR: (with K. Wright) Economic Aspects of Health Services, 1978; Health Indicators, 1983; Economic and Medical Evaluation of Health Care Technologies, 1983; (with G. Terny) Public Finance and Social Policy, 1985; Economics, 1985; (with B. Jonsson) Public and Private Health Services, 1986; Standards for Socioeconomic Evaluation of Health Care Products and Services, 1990; (co-ed.) Competition in Health Care: Reforming the NHS, 1990; (with A. Wagstaff) Reforming Health Care Systems: Experiments with the NHS, 1996; (with A. Maynard) Being Reasonable About the Economics of Health, 1997; (with J.P. Newhouse) Handbook of Health Economics, 2000; The Dictionary of Health Economics, 2005, 2nd ed., 2010; Health Economics: Critical Perspectives on World Economy, 2006; (with E. Tompa and R. Dolinschi) Economic Evaluation of Interventions for Occupational Health and Safety: Developing Good Practice, 2008. Contributor of articles to journals. **Address:** Dept. of Health Policy, Mgmt. & Evaluation, University of Toronto, Health Sciences Bldg., 155 College St., Ste. 425, Toronto, ON M5T 3M6, Canada. **Online address:** tony.culyer@utoronto.ca

CUMBERLEGE, Marcus (Crossley). Belgian/French (born France), b. 1938. **Genres:** Poetry, Translations. **Career:** British Council, English teacher, 1957-58, 1962-63; Ogilvy & Mather Ltd., advertising executive, 1964-67; British Travel Association, advertising executive, 1967-68; Lycee Intl., English teacher, 1968-70; University of Lugano, visiting lecturer, 1978-82. Freelance translator, 1976-. Writer. **Publications:** Oases, 1968; Poems for Quena and Tabla, 1970; Running Towards a New Life, 1973; (with O. Davis) Bruges, Bruges, 1975; La Nuit noire (title means: 'The Dark Night'), 1975; Fireliness, 1977; The Poetry Millionaire, 1977; (with H.D. Blaere) Twintig Vriendelijke Vragen, 1977; (with H.D. Blaere and H. Leys) Vlaamse Fabels, 1980; Northern Lights, 1981; Life is a Flower, 1981; Sweet Poor Hobo, 1985; Things I Cannot Change, 1993; The Best Is Yet To Be, 1997; Once I Had A Secret Love, 2000; The Moon, The Blackbird And The Falling Leaf, 2001; Angels At Work, 2002; JAIA or Just As I Am, 2005; The White Lady, 2006; Seven Days in the Life of a Laughing Skeleton, 2007; Leaves Painted Gold To Please A Child, 2009; In A Nutshell-Shin Buddhist Poems, 2009; Selected Poems 1963-2009, 2010; Houria, forthcoming. **Address:** Eekhoutstraat 42, Brugge, 8000, Belgium. **Online address:** marcus.cumberlege@skynet.be

CUMBIE, Pamela. (Dixie Cash). American (born United States) **Genres:** Young Adult Fiction, Literary Criticism And History, Mystery/Crime/Suspense. **Career:** Writer. **Publications:** AS DIXIE CASH: Since You're Leaving Anyway, Take Out the Trash, 2004; My Heart May Be Broken, But My Hair Still Looks Great, 2005; I Gave You My Heart, But You Sold It Online, 2006; Don't Make Me Choose Between You and My Shoes, 2008; Curing the Blues with a New Pair of Shoes, 2009; Our Red Hot Romance is Leaving Me Blue, 2010; I Can't Make You Love Me, But I Can Make You Leave, 2011. **Address:** c/o Author Mail, HarperCollins Children's Books, 10 E 53rd St., 18th Fl., New York, NY 10022, U.S.A. **Online address:** dixie@dixie-cash.com

CUMMING, Carman. Canadian (born Canada), b. 1932. **Genres:** Writing/Journalism, Adult Non-fiction, History, Military/Defense/Arms Control. **Career:** Canadian Press, editor, 1955-62, United Nations correspondent and feature writer, 1962-65, parliamentary correspondent and editor, 1966-69; University of Toronto, Southam fellow, 1965-66; Carleton University, sessional lecturer, 1968-69, assistant professor, 1969-71, associate professor, 1971-83, School of Journalism, acting director, 1971-72, professor, 1983-91, adjunct professor, 1991-97 Ottawa Journal, copy editor, 1970; CBC News, reporter and editor, 1971; CBC Radio, Capital Report Program, press analyst, 1971-73; University of Western Ontario, exchange professor, 1973-74. **Publications:** (With M. Cardinal and P. Johansen) Canadian News Services, 1981; Secret Craft: The Journalism of Edward Farrer, 1992; Sketches from a Young Country: The Images of Grip Magazine, 1997; Devil's Game: The Civil War Intrigues of Charles A. Dunham, 2004. **Address:** 22 Harvard Ave., Ottawa, ON K1S 4Z3, Canada. **Online address:** carmancumming@aol.com

CUMMING, Charles. British/Scottish (born Scotland), b. 1971. **Genres:** Novels. **Career:** Week Magazine, contributing editor; Mail on Sunday, book review contributor; British Secret Intelligence Service (SIS), staff, 1995. **Publications:** The Hidden Man, 2004; A Spy by Nature, 2007; The Spanish Game, 2008; Typhoon, 2008; Trinity Six, 2011. **Address:** Janklow and Nesbit, 33 Drayson Mews, London, GL W8 4LY, England. **Online address:** author@charlescumming.co.uk

CUMMING, Elizabeth (Skeoch). Scottish (born Scotland), b. 1948. **Genres:** Art/Art History, Crafts, Literary Criticism And History, Photography. **Career:** Dundee City Art Gallery, assistant keeper of fine art, 1972-75; University of Dundee, lecturer, 1973-75; Edinburgh City Art Centre, keeper of fine art collections, 1975-84; freelance art historian, 1984-92, 2000-; University of Edinburgh, Edinburgh College of Art, lecturer in design history, 1990-91, 1992-2000, honorary fellow, 2007-; University of Glasgow, senior honorary research fellow, 2000-. Writer. **Publications:** (Comp.) 10 Years of Collecting: A Selection of Forty Works Purchased and Presented Between 1965 and 1974, 1975; (comp.) Catalogue of the City of Edinburgh Art Collection, 1979; (with W. Kaplan) The Arts and Crafts Movement, 1991; Glasgow 1900: Art & Design: Van Gogh Museum, Amsterdam, the Netherlands, 20 November 1992-7 February 1993, 1992; Phoebe Anna Traquair, 1993; (with N.G. Bowe) Arts and Crafts Movements in Dublin and Edinburgh: 1885-1925, 1998; (with P. Long) The Scottish Colourists, 1900-1930: F.C.B. Cadell, J.D. Fergusson, G.L. Hunter, S.J. Peploe, 2000; Phoebe Anna Traquair: 1852-1936, 2005; Hand, Heart and Soul: The Arts And Crafts Movement in Scotland, 2006. Contributor to books and periodicals. **Address:** Edinburgh College of Art, University of Edinburgh, Minto House, 20 Chambers St., Edinburgh, EH1 1JZ, Scotland. **Online address:** e_cumming@lineone.net

CUMMINGS, Barbara. (Ann Crowleigh). American (born United States), b. 1940?. **Genres:** Young Adult Fiction, Children's Fiction, Mystery/Crime/Suspense, Romance/Historical. **Career:** University of Rhode Island, adjunct instructor, 1973-83; Metropolitan Magazine, executive editor, 1982-86; Papparazzi Magazine, executive editor, 1983-84; Germantown Gazette, community editor, 1987-89; Author, 1987-; The Timothy Group, Graphic Firm, president, 1987-92; Sugarloaf Literary Agency, agent, 1990-92; Romantic Interludes Magazine, consulting editor, 1993-95; Shepherd University, adjunct professor of English, 2000-. **Publications:** Playing Games, 1988; The Wind's Reward, 1988; Smoke Screen, 1988; Take This Child: From Kahlin Compound to the Retta Dixon Children's Home, 1990; Frontier Fire, 1991; Blazing Passion, 1991; Rebel Wildfire, 1992; Wilderness Flame, 1993; Fortune's Fire, 1994; Knight's Lady, 1995; A Killing on Church Grounds, 2006; Killing in Retrospect: A Sister Mary Agnes Mystery, 2009. WITH JO-ANN POWER: Prime Time, 1992; Risks, 1993; (as Ann Crowleigh) Clively Close: Dead as Dead Can Be, 1993; (as Ann Crowleigh) Clively Close: Wait for the Dark, 1993. **Address:** Department of English, Shepherd University, Knutti B21, PO Box 3210, Shepherdstown, WV 25443, U.S.A. **Online address:** bcumming@shepherd.edu

CUMMINGS, Claire Hope. American (born United States), b. 1943?. **Genres:** Botany, Agriculture/Forestry, Environmental Sciences/Ecology. **Career:** U.S. Department of Agriculture's Office of General Counsel, attorney; Earth Island Institute, director; Community Alliance with Family Farmers, director; Food First, director; Elmwood Institute, director; Columbia Foundation, advisor. Journalist. **Publications:** Uncertain Peril: Genetic Engineering and the Future of Seeds, 2008. **Address:** Beacon Press, 25 Beacon St., Boston, MA 02108, U.S.A. **Online address:** claire@clairehopecummings.com

CUMMINGS, Pat. American (born United States), b. 1950. **Genres:** Children's Fiction, Illustrations, Young Adult Fiction, Children's Non-fiction, Picture/Board Books. **Career:** Parsons School of Design, adjunct professor of illustration; freelance author and illustrator, 1974-; Pratt Institute, adjunct professor of illustration, visiting assistant professor. **Publications:** SELF-ILLUSTRATED FOR CHILDREN: Jimmy Lee Did It, 1985; C.L.O.U.D.S., 1986; Wilie's Not the Hugging Kind, 1989; Clean Your Room, Harvey Moon!, 1991; Petey Moroni's Camp Runamok Diary, 1992; Carousel, 1994; (with N. Grimes) C is for City, 1995; Dear Mabel!, 1996; My Aunt Came Back, 1998; Purrrrr, 1999; Angel Baby, 2000; (reteller) Ananse and the Lizard, 2002; Harvey Moon, Museum Boy, 2008; (contrib.) Our Children Can Soar, 2009. EDITOR and COMPILER: Talking with Artists, 1991, rev. ed., 1999; Talking with Artists 2, 1995; (with L.C. Minor) Talking with Adventurers, 1998; Talking with Artists 3, 1999. Illustrator of books by others. **Address:** c/o Author Mail, Harper Collins, 1350 Ave. of the Americas, New York, NY 10019-4703, U.S.A. **Online address:** write2me@patcummings.com

CUMMINGS, Richard H. German/American (born United States), b. 1944. **Genres:** History, Communications/Media. **Career:** U.S. Immigration and Naturalization Service, criminal investigator; Radio Free Europe/Radio Liberty, West European director of security; Citibank, director of security. Writer. **Publications:** Cold War Radio: The Dangerous History of American Broadcasting in Europe, 1950-1989, 2009; Radio Free Europe's Crusade for Freedom: Rallying Americans behind Cold War Broadcasting, 1950-1960,

2010. Contributor of articles to books and periodicals. **Address:** Düseldorf, Germany. **Online address:** rcix@arcor.de

CUMMINGS, Sally (Nikoline). American (born United States) **Genres:** Business/Trade/Industry, History, Social Sciences, Young Adult Non-fiction. **Career:** Keele University, lecturer, 1995; University of Edinburgh, lecturer in politics, 1999-2003; St. Andrews University, lecturer in politics, 2003-, senior lecturer. Writer. **Publications:** (Co-author) Doing Business in Kazakstan, 1995; Kazakhstan: Centre-Periphery Relations, 2000; (ed. with M. Buckley) Kosovo: Perceptions of War and Its Aftermath, 2001; (ed.) Power and Change in Central Asia, 2002; (ed.) Oil, Transition and Security in Central Asia, 2003; Understanding Central Asia, 2003; Kazakhstan: Power and the Elite, 2005. **Address:** School of International Relations, University of St Andrews, Arts Bldg., The Scores, St. Andrews, FF KY16 9AX, Scotland. **Online address:** snc@st-andrews.ac.uk

CUMMINS, Ann. American (born United States) **Genres:** History. **Career:** Northern Arizona University, professor of English; Arizona Commission on the Arts, fellow, 1990, 1994. Writer. **Publications:** Red Ant House: Stories, 2003; Yellowcake, 2007; (with M. Armstrong) Valuing Roles: How to Establish Relative Worth, 2008. Works appear in anthologies. Contributor to periodicals. **Address:** Department of English, Northern Arizona University, Rm. 140, Liberal Arts Bldg. 18, 700 S Humphreys Cdr, PO Box 6032, Flagstaff, AZ 86011-6032, U.S.A. **Online address:** ann.cummins@nau.edu

CUMMINS, C. Lyle. American (born United States), b. 1930. **Genres:** History, Technology, Biography. **Career:** H.J. Brunnier, structural engineer, 1951-54; C.L. Cummins, designer, development engineer and marketing representative, 1956-63; Jacobs Manufacturing Co., product engineer, 1963-64; Buehler Corp., product manager, 1964-70; American Bosch Corp., product manager, 1964-70; University of Portland, assistant professor of mechanical engineering, 1970-72; Servojet Electronic Systems, director, general partner; author and publisher, 1972-2010. **Publications:** Internal Fire, 1976, 3rd ed., 2000; Diesel's Engine, 1993; The Diesel Odyssey of Clessie Cummins, 1998; Diesels for the First Stealth Weapon: Submarine Power 1902-1945, 2007. **Address:** Carnot Press, PO Box 301, Wilsonville, OR 97070, U.S.A. **Online address:** clessie88@aol.com

CUMMINS, Jeanine. American (born United States), b. 1975?. **Genres:** Novels, Autobiography/Memoirs, Young Adult Fiction. **Career:** New American Library, sales manager; Penguin Group USA Inc., assistant manager of field sales. Writer. **Publications:** A Rip in Heaven: A Memoir of Murder and Its Aftermath, 2004; The Outside Boy: A Novel, 2010. **Address:** c/o Author Mail, Penguin Group USA Inc., 375 Hudson St., New York, NY 10014-3658, U.S.A. **Online address:** jeanine@ripinheaven.com

CUMPER, Patricia. British/Jamaican (born Jamaica), b. 1954?. **Genres:** Adult Non-fiction, Novels, Biography. **Career:** British Broadcasting Corp., BBC World Service, script writer for westway (soap opera); Talawa Theatre Co., artistic director. **Publications:** One Bright Child, 1998, new ed., 2004. Contributor to periodicals. **Address:** c/o Author Mail, Arcadia Books, 15-16 Nassau St., London, GL W1W 7AB, England.

CUNFER, Geoff. Canadian (born Canada), b. 1966?. **Genres:** Agriculture/Forestry, Environmental Sciences/Ecology. **Career:** University of North Carolina, Research Labs of Anthropology, archaeological excavator, 1988; Fenland Archaeological Trust, archaeological excavator, 1989; Centre National de la Recherche Scientifique, archaeological excavator, 1989; Center for American Archeology, archaeological survey assistant, 1990; Museum of Texas Tech University, archaeological crew chief, 1990; Texas Tech University, teaching assistant, 1991-93, Southwest Collection, research assistant, 1992; University of Texas, teaching assistant, 1994-95, Population Research Center, research associate, 1995-2002, assistant instructor, 1998-99; Southwest Minnesota State University, assistant professor, 1999-2002, associate professor, 2002-; University of Saskatchewan, faculty. Writer. **Publications:** On the Great Plains: Agriculture and Environment, 2005. Contributor to books and periodicals. **Address:** College of Arts & Science, University of Saskatchewan, Rm. 265, Arts Bldg., 9 Campus Dr., Saskatoon, SK S7N 5A5, Canada. **Online address:** geoff.cunfer@usask.ca

CUNILL, Onofre Martorell. Spanish (born Spain), b. 1968. **Genres:** Business/Trade/Industry, Economics. **Career:** University of the Balearic Islands, assistant professor, 1998-, College of Economics, dean, Tourism School, director; Financial Institute of Madrid, lecturer; International Business Center of Financial Studies, lecturer; ESADE Business School, lecturer; University of Alicante, lecturer. Writer. **Publications:** Cadenas Hoteleras: Analisis del Top Ten, 2002; The Growth Strategies of Hotel Chains: Best Business Practices by Leading Companies, 2006. Contributor to books. **Address:** University of the Balearic Island, Eidifici Jovellanos, Cra de Valldemossa km 7.5, Palma de Mallorca, 07122, Spain. **Online address:** onofre.martorell@uib.es

CUNLIFFE, Barry. British (born England), b. 1939. **Genres:** Archaeology/Antiquities, Literary Criticism And History, Humanities, Social Sciences. **Career:** University of Bristol, lecturer in classics, 1963-66; University of Southampton, professor of archaeology, 1966-72; University of Oxford, School of Archaeology, Institute of Archaeology, professor of European archaeology and fellow of Keble College, 1972-2007, emeritus professor of European archaeology, 2007-, O'Donnell lecturer in Celtic studies, 1983-84. Writer. **Publications:** Fishbourne: The Roman Palace and its History, 1968; Excavations at Richborough, 1968; (ed. and contrib.) Roman Bath, 1969; Guide to the Roman Remains of Bath, 1970 as Roman Baths: A Guide to the Baths and Roman Museum, 1980; The Past Tomorrow: An Inaugural Lecture Delivered at the University, 1970; Aquae Sulis, 1971; Excavations at Fishbourne: 1961-69, 1971; Fishbourne: A Roman Palace and Its Gardens, 1971; Roman Bath Discovered, 1971, rev. ed., 1984; The Cradle of England: An Introduction Through Archaeology to the Early History of England and a Brief Guide to Selected Sites in the South, 1972; The Making of the English, 1973; The Regni, 1973; Iron Age Communities in Britain: An Account of England, Scotland, and Wales from the Seventh Century B.C. until the Roman Conquest, 1974, 4th ed., 2005; Excavations at Porchester Castle, Hants, Society of Antiquaries, 1975; Rome and the Barbarians, 1975; (ed. with T. Rowley) Oppida: The Beginnings of Urbanisation in Barbarian Europe, 1976; Iron Age Sites in Central Southern England, 1976; Hengistbury Head, 1978; Rome and Her Empire, 1978, 2nd ed., 1994; The Celtic World, 1979; (ed.) Excavations in Bath, 1950-75, 1979; (ed.) Coinage and Society in Britain and Gaul: Some Current Problems, 1981; (ed.) Antiquity and Man: Essays in Honour of Glyn Daniel, 1981; Danebury: Anatomy of an Iron Age Hillfort, 1983; Danebury: An Iron Age Hillfort in Hampshire, 1984; (ed. with D. Miles) Aspects of the Iron Age in Central Southern Britain, 1984; Heywood Sumner's Wessex, 1985; (with P. Davenport) Temple of Sulis Minerva at Bath, 1985; The City of Bath, 1986; (contrib.) The Archaeology of the Uplands: A Rapid Assessment of Archaeological Knowledge and Practice, 1986; Hengistbury Head, vol. I: The Prehistoric & Roman Settlement, 3500 B.C.-A.D. 500, 1987; (ed.) Origins: The Roots of European Civilisation, 1987; Mount Batten, Plymouth: A Prehistoric and Roman Port, 1988; Greeks, Romans and Barbarians: Spheres of Interaction, 1988; Wessex to A.D. 1000, 1993; (ed.) The Oxford Illustrated Prehistory of Europe, 1994; Book of Roman Bath, 1995; Book of Iron Age Britain, 1995; (ed. with S. Keay) Social Complexity and the Development of Towns in Iberia: From the Copper Age to the Second Century AD, 1995; (co-author) Guernsey: An Island Community of the Atlantic Iron Age, 1996; (intro.) The Celts, 1997; The Ancient Celts, 1997; (ed. with C. Renfrew) Science and Stonehenge, 1997; Prehistoric Europe: An Illustrated History, 1998; Facing the Ocean: The Atlantic and Its Peoples, 8000 BC-AD 1500, 2001; The Penguin Atlas of British and Irish History, 2001; Atlas of the Celtic World, 2001; The Extraordinary Voyage of Pytheas the Greek: The Man Who Discovered Britain, 2002; El yacimiento y el santuario de Torreparedones: Un Lugar Arqueológico Preferente en la Campiña de Córdoba, 2002; Celts: A Very Short Introduction, 2003; Danebury Hillfort, 2003; (with P. Galliou) Fouilles du Yaudet en Ploulec'h Côtes-d'Armor, 2004; (ed. with R. Osborne) Mediterranean Urbanization, 800-600 BC, 2005; West, 2006; Europe Between the Oceans: Themes and Variations, 9000 BC-AD 1000, 2008; The Danebury Environs Roman Programme: A Wessex Landscape During the Roman Era, 2008; (ed. with C. Gosden and R.A. Joyce) Oxford Handbook of Archaeology, 2009; (ed. with J.T. Koch) Celtic from the West: Alternative Perspectives from Archaeology, Genetics, Language, and Literature, 2010; Druids: A Very Short Introduction, 2010; (with G. Lock) Valley in La Rioja, 2010. Contributor to journals. **Address:** Institute of Archaeology, School of Archaeology, University of Oxford, 36 Beaumont St., Oxford, OX OX1 2PG, England. **Online address:** barry.cunliffe@arch.ox.ac.uk

CUNNINGHAM, Dru. American (born United States) **Genres:** Children's Fiction, Adult Non-fiction. **Career:** Celina School System, elementary teacher, 1970; Bellefontaine School System, elementary teacher, 1970; Bowling Green Christian Academy, elementary teacher, 1992-. Journalist. **Publications:** It's Fun to Choose, 1988; The Most Wonderful Place to Live, 1996. Contributor of articles to magazines, newspapers and journals. **Address:**

Bowling Green Christian Academy, 1165 Haskins Rd., Bowling Green, OH 43402, U.S.A. **Online address:** dcunningham@bgchristian.org

CUNNINGHAM, Elizabeth. American (born United States), b. 1953?. **Genres:** Novels, Novellas/Short Stories. **Career:** Center at High Valley, director. Novelist, singer, songwriter, inter-faith minister and counselor. **Publications:** NOVELS: The Return of the Goddess: A Divine Comedy, 1992; The Wild Mother, 1993; How to Spin Gold: A Woman's Tale, 1997. OTHERS: Small Bird: Poems and Prayers, 2000; Wild Mercy, 2007. THE MAEVE CHRONICLES: Daughter of the Shining Isles, 2000 as Magdalen Rising, 2007; The Passion of Mary Magdalen, 2006; Bright Dark Madonna, 2009; Red-Robed Priestess, 2011. **Address:** c/o Author Mail, Monkfish Book Publishing Co., 22 E Market St., Ste. 304, Rhinebeck, NY 12572, U.S.A. **Online address:** medb44@aol.com

CUNNINGHAM, Frank R. American (born United States), b. 1937. **Genres:** Film, Intellectual History, Literary Criticism And History, Essays, Biography. **Career:** Elwyn Institute, instructor and director of tutoring, 1964-66; Lehigh University, instructor in English, 1966-68; Franklin and Marshall College, assistant professor of English, 1968-69; Fordham University, assistant professor of English, 1970-71; Kansas State University, assistant professor of English, 1971-73; San Jose State University, assistant professor of English, 1973-76, assistant professor of writing, 1977-78; Jagiellonian University, senior Fulbright lecturer in American literature and civilization, 1976-77; University of South Dakota, associate professor, 1978-84, professor of English, 1984-, now professor emeritus; South Dakota Public Radio, Educational Jazz Program, host, 1982-84; University of Nebraska, research associate, 1984-86; University of Minnesota, research associate, 1986-88. Writer. **Publications:** Sidney Lumet: Film and Literary Vision, 1991, 2nd ed., 2001; Sidney Lumet's Fail Safe, 2005. Contributor of articles to journals. Works appear in anthologies. **Address:** Department of English, The University of South Dakota, Rm. 212, Dakota Hall, 414 E Clark St., Vermillion, SD 57069, U.S.A.

CUNNINGHAM, Hugh. British (born England), b. 1942. **Genres:** History, Business/Trade/Industry. **Career:** University of Sierra Leone, lecturer in history, 1963-66; University of Kent, Rutherford College, Department of History, lecturer, 1969-84, senior lecturer, 1984-91, professor of social history, 1991-2001, professor emeritus, 2001-. Writer. **Publications:** Challenge and Response, 1968; The Volunteer Force: A Social and Political History, 1859-1908, 1975; Leisure in the Industrial Revolution, 1980; The Children of the Poor: Representations of Childhood since the Seventeenth Century, 1991; Children and Childhood in Western Society since 1500, 1995, 2nd ed., 2005; (ed. with P.P. Viazzo) Child Labour in Historical Perspective: 1800-1985: Case Studies from Europe, Japan, and Colombia, 1996; (ed. with J. Innes) Charity, Philanthropy, and Reform: From the 1690s to 1850, 1998; The Challenge of Democracy: Britain, 1832-1918, 2001; The Invention of Childhood, 2006; Grace Darling: Victorian Heroine, 2007. **Address:** School of History, Rutherford College, University of Kent, Canterbury, KT CT2 7NX, England. **Online address:** h.cunningham@kent.ac.uk

CUNNINGHAM, James V. (Jim Cunningham). American (born United States), b. 1923. **Genres:** Civil Liberties/Human Rights, Cultural/Ethnic Topics, Economics, Human Relations/Parenting, Institutions/Organizations, Local History/Rural Topics, Money/Finance, Politics/Government, Public/Social Administration, Race Relations, Regional/Urban Planning, Social Commentary, Social Work, Sociology, Urban Studies. **Career:** Independent Voters of Illinois, organizer, 1951-56; Hyde Park Kenwood Community Conference, organizer, 1956-59; Action-Housing Inc., organizer, 1959-66; University of Pittsburgh, School of Social Work, professor, 1966-97, professor emeritus, 1997-; Government Study Commission, director, 1973-74. Writer. **Publications:** The Resurgent Neighborhood, 1965; Urban Leadership in the Sixties, 1970; (with R.S. Ahlbrandt) A New Public Policy in Neighborhood Preservation, 1979; (with M. Kotler) Building Neighborhood Organizations, 1983; (with P.W. Murphy) Organizing for Community Controlled Development: Renewing Civil Society, 2003. Contributor to journals. **Address:** School of Social Work, University of Pittsburgh, 3400 Fifth Ave., Pittsburgh, PA 15260, U.S.A.

CUNNINGHAM, Jim. *See* **CUNNINGHAM, James V.**

CUNNINGHAM, Keith. American (born United States), b. 1939. **Genres:** Cultural/Ethnic Topics, Art/Art History, Mystery/Crime/Suspense, History. **Career:** Northern Arizona University, Department of English, instructor, 1969-72, assistant professor, 1972-78, associate professor, 1978-81, professor of English, 1981-, professor of folklore, professor emeritus of folklore, 2010-. Writer. **Publications:** (Ed.) The Oral Tradition of the American West: Adventure, Courtship, Family, and Place in Traditional Recitation, 1990; American Indians' Kitchen-Table Stories: Contemporary Conversations with Cherokee, Sioux, Hopi, Osage, Navajo, Zuni, and Members of Other Nations, 1992; Two Zuni Artists: A Tale of Art and Mystery, 1998; (ed.) American Indians: Folk Tales and Legends, 2000. Works appear in anthologies. Contributor to journals. **Address:** Department of English, Northern Arizona University, Rm. 140, Liberal Arts Bldg. 18, PO Box 6032, Flagstaff, AZ 86011-0181, U.S.A. **Online address:** keith.cunningham@nau.edu

CUNNINGHAM, M. Allen. American (born United States) **Genres:** Novels. **Career:** Cultural Commentary Blog SoulShelter.com, co-founder, 2007. Writer. **Publications:** The Green Age of Asher Witherow, 2004; Lost Son, 2007; (with T. Clark) The Prosperous Peasant: Five Secrets of Fortune and Fulfillment from the Samurai's Temple School, 2007. Contributor to journals. **Address:** Sterling Lord Literistic Inc., 65 Bleecker St., New York, NY 10012, U.S.A. **Online address:** m_allencunningham@yahoo.com

CUNNINGHAM, Marion (Elizabeth). American (born United States), b. 1922?. **Genres:** Food And Wine, Young Adult Fiction. **Career:** Writer. **Publications:** Bible in My Life, 1979; (ed.) The Fannie Farmer Cookbook, 13th ed., 1996; The Fannie Farmer Baking Book, 1984; The Fannie Farmer Large Print Cookbook, 1985; The Breakfast Book, 1987; The Supper Book, 1992; Cooking with Children: Fifteen Lessons for Children, Age 7 and Up, Who Really want to Learn to Cook, 1995; Learning to Cook with Marion Cunningham, 1999; Marion Cunningham's Good Eating, 1999; Lost Recipes: Meals to Share with Friends and Family, 2003. **Address:** 1147 Northgate Rd., Walnut Creek, CA 94598, U.S.A.

CUNNINGHAM, Patricia (A.). (Trish Cunningham). American (born United States), b. 1937. **Genres:** Fash Ion/Costume, Women's Studies And Issues, Social Sciences. **Career:** Bowling Green State University, instructor, 1979-80, assistant professor, 1980-85, associate professor, 1986-92, professor, 1993-96, division head apparel merchandising and interior design, 1986-87, 1988-89, graduate coordinator, 1991-94, 1993-94; University of Connecticut, associate professor, 1985-86; Ohio State University, associate professor, 1996-. Writer. **Publications:** Reforming Women's Fashion, 1850-1920: Politics, Health and Art, 2003; Fashioning America, 2009. EDITOR: (with S.V. Lab) Dress and Popular Culture, 1991; (with S.V. Lab) Dress in American Culture, 1993; (with L. Welters) Twentieth-Century American Fashion, 2005. **Address:** Ohio State University, 265-F Campbell Hall, 1787 Neil Ave., Columbus, OH 43210, U.S.A. **Online address:** tcunningham@ehe.osu.edu

CUNNINGHAM, Trish. *See* **CUNNINGHAM, Patricia (A.).**

CUNNINGHAM, Valentine. British (born England), b. 1944. **Genres:** Adult Non-fiction, Literary Criticism And History, Novels. **Career:** St. John's College, junior research fellow, 1966-69, junior resident fellow, 1969-72; University of Oxford, lecturer in English, 1972-, Oxford English Faculty, special lecturer, chair, 1984-87, Corpus Christi College, English literature fellow, 1972, tutor in English, 1972-, dean, 1980-91, senior tutor, 1991-94, professor of English language and literature, 1996-, Corpus's Tutor for Admissions, vice-president, CUF University Lecturer in English, senior fellow in English literature; University of Konstanz, visiting professor; University of Massachusetts, visiting professor. Writer. **Publications:** Everywhere Spoken Against: Dissent in the Victorian Novel, 1975; British Writers of the Thirties, 1988; In the Reading Gaol: Postmodernity, Texts, and History, 1994; Reading after Theory, 2002; The Life of Charles Dickens, 2008; Victorian Poetry Now: Poets, Poems, Poetics, 2011. EDITOR: The Penguin Book of Spanish Civil War Verse, 1980; Spanish Front: Writers on the Civil War, 1986; (and intro.) Adam Bede, 1996; The Victorians: An Anthology of Poetry & Poetics, 2000; Victorian Poetry, 2002; (with J. Rignall and H.G. Klaus) Ecology and Literature of the British Left, 2012. Contributor to books, journals, periodicals and newspapers. **Address:** Corpus Christi College, University of Oxford, Merton St., Oxford, OX OX1 4JF, England. **Online address:** valentine.cunningham@ccc.ox.ac.uk

CUNO, James B. American (born United States), b. 1951. **Genres:** Art/Art History, Politics/Government. **Career:** Harvard University, Fogg Art Museum, assistant curator of prints, 1980-83, University Art Museum, director, 1991-2003; Vassar College, assistant professor, 1983-86; University of

California, Grunwald Center for Graphic Arts, director, 1986-89; Dartmouth College, Hood Museum of Art, director, 1989-91; Courtauld Institute of Art, director 2003-04; Art Institute of Chicago, president, Eloise W. Martin Director, 2004-. Writer. **Publications:** (Contrib.) Three American Sculptors and the Female Nude: Lachaise, Nadelman, Archipenko, 1980; (ed. and contrib.) Foirades/Fizzles: Echo and Allusion in the Art of Jasper Johns, 1987; (ed.) Politics and Polemics: French Caricature and the Revolution, 1789-1799, 1988; (ed.) Subject(s): Prints and Multiples by Jonathan Borofsky, 1982-1991, 1992; (co-author) Harvard's Art Museums: 100 Years of Collecting, 1996; (ed.) Whose Muse? Art Museums and the Public Trust, 2004; (with M. Thorne) Zero Gravity: The Art Institute, Renzo Piano, Building for a New Century, 2005; (contrib.) The Silk Road and Beyond: Travel, Trade, and Transformation, 2007; Who Owns Antiquity? Museums and the Battle over Our Ancient Heritage, 2008; (ed.) Whose Culture? The Promise of Museums and the Debate over Antiquities, 2009; Master Paintings in the Art Institute of Chicago, 3rd ed., 2009; (with P. Goldberger and J. Rosa) The Modern Wing: Renzo Piano and the Art Institute of Chicago, 2009. **Address:** Art Institute of Chicago, 111 S Michigan Ave., Chicago, IL 60603-6110, U.S.A.

CUNO, Kenneth M. American (born United States), b. 1950. **Genres:** Area Studies, History, Law. **Career:** University of California-Los Angeles, teaching assistant, 1982-84; University of California-Santa Barbara, visiting lecturer, 1985; American University, visiting assistant professor of history, 1985-90; University of Illinois, assistant professor of history, 1990-96, associate professor of history, 1996-, Program in South Asian and Middle Eastern Studies, director, 2002-06. Writer. **Publications:** The Pasha's Peasants: Land, Society, and Economy in Lower Egypt, 1740-1858, 1992. (ed. with M. Desai) Family, Gender and Law in a Globalizing Middle East and South Asia, 2009; (ed. with T. Walz) Race and Slavery in the Middle East: Histories of Trans-Saharan Africans in Nineteenth-century Egypt, Sudan, and the Ottoman Mediterranean, 2010; Egypt to c. 1919, in The New Cambridge History of Islam, 2010. Contributor of articles to periodicals. **Address:** Department of History, University of Illinois, M/C 466, 309 Gregory Hall, 810 S Wright St., Urbana, IL 61801, U.S.A. **Online address:** kmcuno@illinois.edu

CUOMO, George (Michael). American (born United States), b. 1929. **Genres:** Novels, Poetry, Novellas/Short Stories, Criminology/True Crime. **Career:** Taller and Cooper, staff, 1953-54; University of Arizona, instructor in English, 1956-61; Victoria University, associate professor of English, 1961-65; California State University, professor of English, 1965-73; University of Massachusetts, professor of English, 1973-94, professor emeritus, 1994-. Writer. **Publications:** Becoming a Better Reader, 1960; Jack Be Nimble (novel), 1963; Bright Day, Dark Runner (novel), 1964; Among Thieves (novel), 1968; Sing, Choirs of Angels (short stories), 1969; The Hero's Great Great Great Great Great Grandson (novel), 1971; Geronimo and the Girl Next Door (poetry), 1973; Pieces from a Small Bomb (novel), 1976; Becoming a Better Reader and Writer, 1978; Family Honor (novel), 1983; Trial by Water (novel), 1993; A Couple of Cops; On the Secret, in the Crime Lab (nonfiction), 1995. **Address:** Department of English, University of Massachusetts Amherst, 170 Bartlett Hall, Amherst, MA 01003, U.S.A. **Online address:** jgcuomo@aol.com

CUOMO, Mario (Matthew). American (born United States), b. 1932. **Genres:** Politics/Government, Urban Studies, E-books, Young Adult Nonfiction, Children's Non-fiction, Children's Fiction, Education. **Career:** New York State Court of Appeals, confidential legal assistant, 1956-58; Corner, Weisbrod, Froeb and Charles, associate, 1958-63, partner, 1963-75; St. John's University School of Law, professor of law, 1963-75; secretary of state, 1975-78; governor of New York, 1979-82, 1983-94; Willkie Farr and Gallagher LLP, Corporate and Financial Services Department and Litigation Department, of counsel, 1995-. Writer. **Publications:** The New York City Secondary School System, 1966; The Forest Hills Controversy, 1972; Forest Hills Diary: The Crisis of Low-Income Housing, 1974; (with J.H. Marburger) Report of the New York State Panel on the Shoreham Nuclear Power Facility, 1983; 1933/1983-Never Again: A Report to the National Governor's Association Task Force on the Homeless, 1983; Medicare: Analysis and Recommendations for Reform, 1983; Diaries of Mario M. Cuomo: The Campaign for Governor, 1984; Message to the Legislature, Albany, New York, January 7, 1987, 1987; Public Papers of Governor Mario M. Cuomo, 1983, 1987; Message to the Legislature, Albany, New York, January 6, 1988, 1988; Public Papers of Governor Mario M. Cuomo, 1984, 1989; Public Papers of Governor Mario M. Cuomo, 1985, 1989; (ed. and intro. with H. Holzer) Lincoln on Democracy: An Anthology, 1990, rev. ed., 2004; Public Papers of Governor Mario M. Cuomo, 1986, 1990; (contrib.) Moving Toward the 21st Century: A Proposal for High Speed Ground Transportation in the State of New York, 1993; More Than Words: The Speeches of Mario M. Cuomo, 1993; (contrib.) National Register of Historic Places in New York State, 1993; Federal Human Services Agenda for New York State, 1994; The New York Idea, An Experiment in Democracy, 1994; (contrib.) Blueprint for Our Future: Creating Jobs, Preserving the Environment: The Report to Governor Mario Cuomo by the East End Economic and Environmental Task Force of Long Island, New York, 1994; Technology: Serving Human Needs and the Economy: Special Report from Governor, 1994; Peoples State Constitutional Convention: A Process for Reform: Special Message to the People, 1994; New York Idea: An Experiment in Democracy, 1994; Reason to Believe, 1995; Great American Speeches-80 Years of Political Oratory, 1995; Blue Spruce, 1999; Great American Speeches (electronic resource): 80 Years of Political Oratory, 2000; (ed.) Accounting Irregularities and Financial Fraud: A Corporate Governance Guide, 2000; (H. Hollzer) Why Lincoln Matters: Today More than Ever, 2004; (with E.D. Grodin) C is for Ciao: An Italy Alphabet, 2009. **Address:** Willkie Farr and Gallagher L.L.P., The Equitable Ctr., 787 7th Ave., New York, NY 10019-6099, U.S.A. **Online address:** mcuomo@willkie.com

CURATOLA, Giovanni. Italian (born Italy), b. 1953?. **Genres:** Popular Culture, Theology/Religion, History, Photography, Architecture. **Career:** University of Udine, professor of Islamic archaeology and art history. Writer. **Publications:** Soltlaniye II, 1979; Tappeti, 1981; Kalat-i Nadiri: Note sul 'Barocco' Indo-persiano, 1983; (co-author) Kasakhi Vanker: Hovhannavank/Saghmosavank, 1986; (with G. Scarcia) Le Arti nell'Islam, 1990; Le Vie della Seta e Venezia, 1990; EreditA dell'Islam: Arte Islamica in Italia, 1993; (ed.) Ceramiche Persiane: IX-XIV Secolo, 1993; Sciamani e Dervisci: Dalle Steppe del Prete Gianni: ReligiositA del Kazakhstan e Percezione del Fantastico a Venezia, 2000; (with G. Scarcia) Iran: l'Arte Persiana, 2004; (co-author and ed.) Iraq: L'Arte dai Sumeri ai Califfi, 2006; (with G. Scarcia) Art and Architecture of Persia, 2007; (co-author) Art and Architecture of Mesopotamia, 2007; Arte Della Civiltá Islamica: La Collezione al-Sabah, Kuwait, 2010; Turkish Art and Architecture: From the Seljuks to the Ottomans, 2010. **Address:** Dipartimento di Storia e Tutela dei Beni Culturali, Universita di Udine, Via Tarcisio Petracco, Udine, 8-33100, Italy. **Online address:** curatolagi@iol.it

CURET, L. Antonio. Puerto Rican (born Puerto Rico), b. 1960. **Genres:** History, Cultural/Ethnic Topics. **Career:** University of Illinois, adjunct professor, North American Archaeology, Field Museum, curator. Writer, educator, curator and anthropologist. **Publications:** (ed. with S.L. Dawdy and R. Corzo) Dialogues in Cuban Archaeology, 2005; Caribbean Paleodemography: Population, Culture History and Sociopolitical Processes in Ancient Puerto Rico, 2005. Contributor of articles to journals. **Address:** Department of Anthropology, University of Illinois, College of Liberal Arts & Sciences, 1007 W Harrison St., PO Box 027, Chicago, IL 60607-7139, U.S.A. **Online address:** acuret@fieldmuseum.org

CURIEL, Jonathan. American (born United States), b. 1960. **Genres:** Travel/Exploration, Theology/Religion. **Career:** Oxford University, Reuters Foundation fellow, 2005-06; San Francisco Chronicle, staff writer. **Publications:** Al' America: Travels through America's Arab and Islamic Roots, 2008. Contributor to periodicals. **Address:** San Francisco, CA , U.S.A. **Online address:** jonathancuriel@hotmail.com

CURL, James Stevens. Irish (born Ireland), b. 1937. **Genres:** Architecture, Art/Art History, Design, History, Humanities, Urban Studies, Biography, Reference, Reference. **Career:** Architect and planner, 1963-69; Oxford School of Architecture, tutor in history of architecture, 1967-73; Survey of London, architectural editor, 1970-73; European Architectural Heritage Year, Scottish Committee, consulting architect, 1973-75; Scottish Civic Trust, European Architectural Heritage Year, architectural adviser, 1973-75; Herts County Council, senior planning officer, 1975-78; Hertfordshire County Council, Department of Planning, principal architect-planner, 1975-78; De Montfort University, Leicester School of Architecture, senior lecturer, 1978-87, professor of architectural history and senior research fellow, 1987-98, professor emeritus, 1998-, Centre for Conservation Studies, researcher, 1995-98, School of Architecture, research fellow, 1998-2000; University of Cambridge, visiting fellow, 1991-92, 2002; Queen's University of Belfast, professor of architectural history and senior research fellow, 2000-02, honorary senior research fellow, 2002-, professor emeritus of architectural history, 2002. **Publications:** European Cities and Society: A Study of the Influence of Political Climate on Town Design, 1970; The Victorian Celebration of Death, 1972, rev. ed., 2004; (with T.M. Richards) City of London Pubs: A Practical and Historical Guide, 1973; Victorian Architecture: Its Practical Aspects, 1973; English Architecture: An Illustrated Glossary, 1977; The Erosion of Oxford, 1977; Mausolea in Ulster, 1978; Moneymore and Draperstown, 1979; Celebration of Death, 1980; Classical Churches in Ulster, 1980; The History, Architecture, and Planning of the Estates of the Fishmongers Company in Ulster, 1981; Egyptian Revival: An Introductory Study of a Recurring Theme in the History of Taste, 1982; The Life and Work of Henry Roberts, 1803-1876, Architect, 1983; The Londonderry Plantation, 1609-1914, 1986; English Architecture, 1986; Victorian Architecture, 1990; Classical Architecture, 1992, rev. ed., 2003; The Art and Architecture of Freemasonry, 1993; Encyclopaedia of Architectural Terms, 1993; Georgian Architecture, 1993, rev. ed., 2003; Egyptomania, 1994; Book of Victorian Churches, 1995; A Dictionary of Architecture, 1999; History and Critique, 2000; The Honourable the Irish Society 1608-2000, 2000; Kensal Green Cemetery, 2001; Death and Architecture, 2002; Piety Proclaimed, 2002; (intro.) Irish Cathedrals, Churches and Abbeys, 2002; The Egyptian Revival, 2005; Oxford Dictionary of Architecture and Landscape Architecture, 2006; Architectures Maconniques, 2006; Victorian Architecture: Diversity and Invention, 2007; Spas, Wells, & Pleasure Gardens of London, 2010. **Address:** 15 Torgrange, Holywood, DN BT18 0NG, Northern Ireland. **Online address:** jscurl@btinternet.com

CURLEE, Lynn. American (born United States), b. 1947. **Genres:** Children's Fiction, Illustrations, Architecture, Animals/Pets. **Career:** Exhibiting gallery artist, 1973-; freelance writer, 1991-. **Publications:** SELF-ILLUSTRATED: Ships of the Air, 1996; Into the Ice: The Story of Arctic Explorations, 1998; Rushmore, 1999; Liberty, 2000; The Brooklyn Bridge, 2001; Seven Wonders of the Ancient World, 2002; Capital, 2003; The Parthenon, 2004; Ballpark: The Story of America's Baseball Fields, 2005; Skyscraper, 2007; Mythological Creatures: A Classical Bestiary, 2008; Trains, 2009; Railroad, forthcoming. **Address:** PO Box 699, Jamesport, NY 11947, U.S.A. **Online address:** curleeart@aol.com

CURLEY, Marianne. New Zealander/Australian (born Australia), b. 1959. **Genres:** Children's Fiction, Novels. **Career:** Electricity Commission of New South Wales, senior legal stenographer, 1976-81; Benchmark Frames and Trusses, secretary and receptionist, 1991; Skillshare Coffs Harbour, part-time trainer, 1992; part-time teacher, 1992-96. Writer. **Publications:** Old Magic, 2000; The Named, 2002; The Dark, 2003; The Key, 2005. **Address:** c/o Anthony A. Williams, 43 Nariah Cres., PO Box 1379, Darlinghurst, NW 1300, Australia. **Online address:** mcurley@austrais.aunz.com

CURNUTT, Kirk. American (born United States), b. 1964. **Genres:** Young Adult Non-fiction, Young Adult Fiction, Novels. **Career:** Troy University, instructor, 1993-, Department of English, chair. Writer. **Publications:** NON-FICTION: Wise Economies: Brevity and Storytelling in American Short Stories, 1997; Ernest Hemingway and the Expatriate Modernist Movement, 2000; Alienated-Youth Fiction, 2001; The Cambridge Introduction to F. Scott Fitzgerald, 2007; Coffee with Hemingway, 2007. FICTION: Baby, Let's Make a Baby: Plus Ten More Stories, 2003; Breathing Out the Ghost (novel), 2007; Dixie Noir (novel), 2009. EDITOR: The Critical Response to Gertrude Stein, 2000; A Historical Guide to F. Scott Fitzgerald, 2004; (with G.D. Sinclair) Key West Hemingway: A Reassessment, 2009. **Address:** Department of English, Troy University, Montgomery, AL 36104, U.S.A. **Online address:** kcurnutt@troy.edu

CURRAN, Charles E. American (born United States), b. 1934. **Genres:** Philosophy, Theology/Religion. **Career:** Catholic University of America, assistant professor, professor of moral theology, 1965-89; Southern Methodist University, Elizabeth Scurlock University professor of human values, 1991-. Writer. **Publications:** Christian Morality Today, 1966; A New Look at Christian Morality, 1968; (co-author) Dissent in and for the Church, 1969; (co-author) The Responsibility of Dissent, 1969; Contemporary Problems in Moral Theology, 1970; Catholic Moral Theology in Dialogue, 1972; Crisis in Priestly Ministry, 1972; Politics, Medicine and Christian Ethics: A Dialogue with Paul Ramsey, 1973; New Perspectives in Moral Theology, 1974; Ongoing Revision: Studies in Moral Theology, 1975; Themes in Fundamental Moral Theology, 1977; Issues in Sexual and Medical Ethics, 1978; Transition and Tradition in Moral Theology, 1979; American Catholic Social Ethics, 1982; Moral Theology, 1982; Critical Concerns in Moral Theology, 1984; Directions in Catholic Social Ethics, 1985; Directions in Fundamental Moral Theology, 1985; Faithful Dissent, 1986; Toward an American Catholic Theology, 1988; Sexual tat und Ethik, 1988; Tensions in Moral Theology, 1988; Catholic Higher Education, Theology and Academic Freedom, 1990; The Living Tradition of Catholic Moral Theology, 1992; The Church and Morality, 1993; History and Contemporary Issues, 1996; The Origins of Moral Theology in the United States, 1997; The Catholic Moral Tradition Today, 1999; Moral Theology at the End of the Century, 1999; Catholic Social Teaching 1891-Present, 2002; The Moral Theology of Pope John Paul II, 2005; Loyal Dissent: Memoir of a Catholic Theologian, 2006; Catholic Moral Theology in the United States: A History, 2008; The Social Mission of the U.S. Catholic Church: A Theological Perspective, 2011. EDITOR: Absolutes in Moral Theology?, 1968; Contraception: Authority and Dissent, 1969; (with G.J. Dyer) Shared Responsibility in the Local Church, 1970; (co-ed.) Readings in Moral Theology, 16 vols., 1979-2010; Moral Theology: Challenges for the Future, 1990. **Address:** Southern Methodist University, PO Box 750317, Dallas, TX 75275-0317, U.S.A. **Online address:** ccurran@smu.edu

CURRAN, Kathleen A. American (born United States), b. 1955?. **Genres:** Theology/Religion, Art/Art History, History. **Career:** Trinity College, professor of fine arts, 1990-. Writer and art historian. **Publications:** The Romanesque Revival: Religion, Politics and Transnational Exchange, 2003. Contributor to periodicals. **Address:** Trinity College, 300 Summit St., Hartford, CT 06106, U.S.A. **Online address:** kathleen.curran.1@trincoll.edu

CURREY, Richard. American (born United States), b. 1949. **Genres:** Medicine/Health, Novels, Novellas/Short Stories, Adult Non-fiction. **Career:** Four Corners Dialysis Center, clinical associate in nephrology, 1979-80; Albuquerque Family Health Centers Inc., staff physician assistant, 1980-88; novelist and short story writer, 1988-94; University of New Mexico, writer-in-residence, 1990-92; Wichita State University, writer-in-residence, 1994; Lovelace Health Systems, staff physician assistant, 1994-97; Amblin Entertainment, Writers Film Project, screenwriter, 1997-98; National Institutes of Health, medical writer and communications consultant, 1998-2008; Center for Drug Evaluation and Research, Food and Drug Administration, senior communications advisor and deputy division director for executive operations, 2008-. **Publications:** Crossing Over: A Vietnam Journal, 1980; Fatal Light, 1988; The Wars of Heaven, 1990; Medicine for Sale, 1993; Downriver: Field Notes from the Rio Grande, 2012. Contributor of articles to journals and magazines. **Address:** Santa Fe Writers Project, 369 Montezuma Ave., Ste. 350, Santa Fe, NM 87501, U.S.A. **Online address:** admin@sfwp.com

CURREY-WILSON, Ellen. American (born United States) **Genres:** Novels, Autobiography/Memoirs. **Career:** Writer. **Publications:** The Big Turnoff: Confessions of a TV-Addicted Mom Trying to Raise a TV-Free Kid, 2007. **Address:** c/o Margaret Ruley, Jane Rotrosen Agency, 318 E 51st St., New York, NY 10022, U.S.A. **Online address:** ecurreywilson@gmail.com

CURRID, Elizabeth. (Elizabeth Currid-Halkett). American (born United States), b. 1978. **Genres:** Economics, Art/Art History, Business/Trade/Industry, Cultural/Ethnic Topics, Sociology. **Career:** Carnegie Mellon University, research assistant, 2000-02; Pittsburgh Partnership for Neighborhood Development, intern; American Civil Liberties Union, project manager, 2002; Senator Hillary Rodham Clinton's Congressional Office, intern, 2003; United Nations, research assistant; Columbia University, teaching assistant, 2004-06; University of Southern California, School of Policy, Planning, and Development, assistant professor, 2006-, Norman Lear Center, project director, 2007-; LUSK Center for Real Estate, staff. Writer. **Publications:** The Warhol Economy: How Fashion, Art and Music Drive New York City, 2007; (As Elizabeth Currid-Halkett) Starstruck: The Business of Celebrity, 2010. Contributor of articles to journals. **Address:** University of Southern California, Ralph and Goldy Lewis Hall 301B, 650 Child's Way, Los Angeles, CA 90089, U.S.A. **Online address:** currid@usc.edu

CURRID-HALKETT, Elizabeth. *See* **CURRID, Elizabeth.**

CURRIE, Dwight. American (born United States), b. 1953. **Genres:** inspirational/Motivational Literature, Adult Non-fiction, Medicine/Health, Self Help. **Career:** Misty Valley Books, co-owner. Writer and educator. **Publications:** How We Behave at the Feast: Reflections on an Age of Plenty, 2000; An Invitation to the Feast: Celebrating Life in an Age Plenty, 2001. **Address:** 308 Bayside Pkwy., Nokomis, FL 34275, U.S.A.

CURRIE, Edwina. British (born England), b. 1946. **Genres:** Novels, Humor/Satire. **Career:** British Parliament, House of Commons for Derbyshire, Department of Health, junior health minister, 1986-90, minister, 1986-88; Conservative Group for Europe, chair, 1995-97; European Movement, vice-chair of British branch, 1995-99, Central Birmingham Health Authority, chairman; HTV, host, 2002-03; BBC, host. Writer. **Publications:** Life Lines (nonfiction), 1989; What Women Want (essays), 1990; Three Line Quips (humor), 1992; A Parliamentary Affair (novel), 1994; A Woman's Place (novel), 1996; She's Leaving Home, 1997; The Ambassador, 1999; Chasing Men, 2000; This Honourable House, 2001; Diaries 1987-1992, vol. I, 2002, vol. II, 2010. **Address:** c/o Author Mail, Little, Brown Book Group, 100 Victoria Embankment, London, GL EC4Y 0DY, England. **Online address:** edwina@currie.co.uk

CURRIE, Katy. *See* **KYLE, Susan S(paeth).**

CURRIE, Philip J(ohn). Canadian (born Canada), b. 1949. **Genres:** Earth Sciences, Zoology, Translations. **Career:** Redpath Museum, geology technician, 1974-76; Provincial Museum, curator of paleontology, 1976-81; Royal Tyrrell Museum of Palaeontology, curator of dinosaurs, 1981-; University of Alberta, Department of Biological Sciences, professor, Dinosaur Paleobiology, chair; University of Calgary, adjunct associate professor; University of Saskatchewan, adjunct professor. Writer and palaeontologist. **Publications:** (Ed. with E.H. Koster) Short Papers/Fourth Symposium on Mesozoic Terrestrial Ecosystems, Drumheller, August 10-14, 1987, 1987; (ed. with K. Carpenter) Dinosaur Systematics: Approaches and Perspectives, 1990; The Flying Dinosaurs, 1991, trans. as Giganten der Lüfte: Das grobe Buch der Flugsaurier, 1995; Dinosaur Renaissance, 1994; (with Z.V. Spinar) The Great Dinosaurs: A Story of the Giants' Evolution, 1994; Velcí Dinosauri, 1994; Wielkie Dinozaury, 1994; (with E.B. Koppelhus) 101 Questions about Dinosaurs, 1996; (with K. Padian) Encyclopedia of Dinosaurs, 1997; (co-author) A Moment in Time with Troodon, 1997; (co-author) The Dinosaur Handbook, 1997; (co-author) A Moment in Time with Albertosaurus, 1997; (with J. Sovak) Yazawa Handbook Series, 1997; (contrib.) Graveyards of the Dinosaurs: What it's Like to Discover Prehistoric Creatures, 1998; Dinosauriers de Heersers van Toen, 1998; (co-author) A Moment in Time with Centrosaurus, 1998; (with C. Mastin) The Newest and Coolest Dinosaurs, 1998; (co-author) A Moment in Time with Sinosauropteryx, 1999; (co-ed.) Feathered Dragons: Studies on the Transition from Dinosaurs to Birds, 2004; (ed. with E.B. Koppelhus) Dinosaur Provincial Park: A Spectacular Ancient Ecosystem Revealed, 2005; (with D.H. Tanke and W. Langston) A New Horned Dinosaur from an Upper Cretaceous Bone Bed in Alberta, 2008. **Address:** Department of Biological Sciences, University of Alberta, Z 418, Biological Sciences Bldg., 11455 Saskatchewan Dr., Drumheller, AB T6G 2E9, Canada. **Online address:** philip.currie@ualberta.ca

CURRIE, Ron. American (born United States), b. 1975. **Genres:** Novels. **Career:** Writer. **Publications:** God Is Dead, 2007; Everything Matters!, 2009. Contributor of stories to periodicals. **Address:** c/o Simon Lipskar, Writers House L.L.C., 21 W 26th St., New York, NY 10010, U.S.A. **Online address:** ron@roncurriejr.com

CURRIE, Stephen. American (born United States), b. 1960. **Genres:** History, Children's Fiction, Children's Non-fiction, Education, Reference. **Career:** Poughkeepsie Day School, teacher, 1982-2001. Adriance Memorial Library, cataloger and annotator of maps, 1982-83; Dutchess Community College, Saturday Enrichment Program, teacher, 1986-89. Writer. **Publications:** Music in the Civil War, 1992; Problem Play, 1993; Birthday-a-Day, 1995; (as Jane King) The Monster Bash, 1996; Adoption, 1997; We Have Marched Together: The Working Children's Crusade, 1997; Issues in Sports, 1998; Slavery, 1999; Life in a Wild West Show, 1999; The Olympic Games, 1999; The Liberator: Voice of the Abolitionist Movement, 2000; The Polynesians, 2000; Abortion, 2000; Issues in Immigration, 2000; Life of a Slave on a Southern Plantation, 2000; Pirates, 2001; Thar She Blows: American Whaling in the Nineteenth Century, 2001; (ed.) The Fourteenth Century, 2001; (ed.) Sixteenth Century, 2001; Women Inventors, 2001; (ed.) 1300s, 2001; (ed.) 1500s, 2001; Polar Explorers, 2002; Life in the Trenches, 2002; Salem Witch Trials, 2002; Terrorists and Terrorist Groups, 2002; Salem Witch Trails, 2002; Chemistry, 2003; Actor on the Elizabethan Stage, 2003; Escapes from Slavery, 2003; Mia Hamm, 2003; Mississippi, 2003; Women of the Civil War, 2003; Antarctica, 2004; Escapes from Manmade Disasters, 2004; Escapes from Natural Disasters, 2004; Escapes from Nazi Persecution, 2004; Escapes from Religious Oppression, 2004; Expeditions in the Americas: 1492-1700, 2004; Travels to Distant Lands: 1000-1400, 2004; Australia and the Pacific Islands, 2005; Himalayas, 2005; Peculiar Institution: Slavery in the Plantation South, 2005; West Africa, 2005; (ed.) Terrorism: An Opposing Viewpoints Guide, 2006; Birmingham Church Bombings, 2006; Murder in Mississippi: The 1964 Freedom Summer Killings, 2006; Pianos, 2006; Quest for Freedom: The Abolitionist Movement, 2006; Miracles, Saints and Pagan Superstition: The Medieval Mind, 2006; Cheating, 2007; Outsourcing in America, 2007; The African American Religious Experience, 2007; Adrian Peterson, 2008; Ecosystems, 2009; African American Folklore, 2009; Junk Food, 2009; Medieval Crusades, 2009; Struggle for Equality: Landmark Court Cases, 2009; Environmentalism in America, 2010; African American Inventors, 2010; African American Literature, 2011; Goblins, 2011; Hydropower, 2011; Online Privacy, 2012; Renaissance, 2012; Mayan Mythology, 2012; Sweet Betsy. Contributor of articles to periodicals. **Address:** 14 Oakwood Blvd., Poughkeepsie, NY 12603-4112, U.S.A. **Online address:** sacurrie@idsi.net

CURRY, Constance (Winifred). American (born United States), b. 1933. **Genres:** History, Adult Non-fiction. **Career:** Collegiate Council for the United Nations, national field representative, 1957-59; U.S. National Student Association, Southern Student Human Relations Project, director, 1960-64; American Friends Service Committee, southern field representative, 1964-75; City of Atlanta, Office of Human Services, director, 1975-90; University of Virginia, Carter G. Woodson Institute, Center for Civil Rights, fellow, 1990-91; writer, 1990-; Emory University, Institute for Women's Studies, fellow, 1993; Southerners for Economic Justice, board director. **Publications:** Silver Rights: One Family's Struggle for Justice in America, 1995; (with A. Henry) The Fire Ever Burning, 2000; (co-author and contrib.) Deep in Our Hearts: Nine White Women in the Freedom Movement, 2000; (with A. Henry) Aaron Henry: The Fire Ever Burning, 2000; (with W. Hudson) Mississippi Harmony: Memoirs of a Freedom Fighter, 2002; (with B. Zellner) Wrong Side of Murder Creek: A White Southerner in the Freedom Movement, 2008. Contributor to journals. **Address:** 930 Myrtle St. NE, Atlanta, GA 30309, U.S.A. **Online address:** cw.curry@comcast.net

CURRY, G(len) David. American (born United States), b. 1948. **Genres:** Military/Defense/Arms Control, Social Commentary, Criminology/True Crime, History. **Career:** University of South Alabama, assistant professor, 1976-79, associate professor of sociology, 1979-84; University of Notre Dame, Center for Civil Rights, research fellow, 1977-80; Ogburn Stouffer Center for Social Research, Center for the Study of Social Policy, research associate and analyst, 1983-87; University of Chicago, lecturer, 1981, lecturer in statistical methods and director of national gang intervention and suppression project, 1988-89, National Opinion Research Center, research associate and analyst, 1983-87; Loyola University of Chicago, lecturer, 1983-87; Safer Foundation, research associate, 1983-87; SPSS Inc., statistical writer, 1987-88; West Virginia University, Department of Sociology and Anthropology, associate professor of sociology, 1989-94; University of Missouri, Criminology and Criminal Justice, from associate professor to professor, 1994-. Writer. **Publications:** Sunshine Patriots: Punishment of the Vietnam Offender, 1985. (with I.A. Spergel) A Survey of Fifty-four Communities and Six Sites: Gang Problems and Responses, vol. II, 1991; (with R.A. Ball and R.J. Fox) Gang Crime and Law Enforcement Record keeping, 1994; (co-author) Gangs in America, 1996; (with S.H. Decker) Confronting Gangs: Crime and Community, 1998, 2nd ed., 2003; (with S.H. Decker) Criminology: A Contemporary Handbook, 1999. Contributor to periodicals. **Address:** Department of Crimonology and Crimonal Justice, University of Missouri - St. Louis, Rm. 539, 326 Lucas Hall, 1 University Blvd., St. Louis, MO 63121-4400, U.S.A. **Online address:** dave_curry@umsl.edu

CURRY, Jane (Louise). American (born United States), b. 1932. **Genres:** Children's Fiction, Young Adult Fiction, Mythology/Folklore, Mystery/Crime/Suspense, Novels, Adult Non-fiction, Young Adult Non-fiction. **Career:** California City Schools, art teacher, 1955-59; Stanford University, teaching assistant, 1959-61, 1964-65, instructor in English literature, 1967-68, 1983-84, lecturer, 1987. Writer. **Publications:** Down from the Lonely Mountain: California Indian Tales, 1965; Beneath the Hill, 1967; The Sleepers, 1968; The Change-Child, 1969; The Day Breakers, 1970; Mindy's Mysterious Miniature, 1970 as The Housenapper, 1971; Over the Sea's Edge, 1971; The Ice Ghosts Mystery, 1972; The Lost Farm, 1974; Parsley Sage, Rosemary, and Time, 1975; The Watchers, 1975; The Magical Cupboard, 1976; Poor Tom's Ghost, 1977; The Bird Stones, 1977; The Bassumtyte Treasure, 1978; Ghost Lane, 1979; The Wolves of Aam, 1981; The Shadow Dancers, 1983; The Great Flood Mystery, 1985; The Lotus Cup, 1986; (reteller) Back in the Beforetime: Tales of the California Indians, 1987; Me, Myself and I: A Tale Of Time Travel, 1987; The Big Smith Snatch, 1989; Little Little Sister, 1989; What the Dickens!, 1991; The Great Smith House Hustle, 1993; The

Christmas Knight, 1993; (reteller) Robin Hood and His Merry Men, 1994; (reteller) Robin Hood in the Greenwood, 1995; Moon Window, 1996; Dark Shade, 1998; Turtle Island: Tales of the Algonquin Nation, 1999; A Stolen Life, 1999; The Wonderful Sky Boat: And Other Native American Tales of the Southeast, 2001; The Egyptian Box, 2002; Hold Up the Sky: And Other Indian Tales from Texas and Southern Plains, 2003; Brave Cloelia, 2004; The Black Canary, 2005. **Address:** c/o Margaret McElderry, Simon & Schuster Children's Publishing, 1230 Ave. of the Americas, 4th Fl., New York, NY 10020-1513, U.S.A. **Online address:** jane@janecurry.com

CURRY, Neil. British (born England), b. 1937. **Genres:** Poetry, Literary Criticism And History, Translations. **Career:** University of Guelph, lecturer, 1964-65; teacher, 1967-89; Chetwynde School, English teacher and department head, 1989-95. Writer. **Publications:** POETRY: (trans.) The Trojan Women, 1966; (trans.) Euripides, Helen, The Trojan Women, The Bacchae, 1981; Between Root and Sky, 1982; The Maidenhair Tree, 1987; Ships in Bottles, 1988; Walking to Santiago, 1992; The Bending of the Bow, 1993; (ed. and intro.) Collected Poems, 1994; Tidelines, 2000; Norman Nicholson, 2001; The Road to the Gunpowder House, 2003; Other Rooms: New and Selected Poems, 2007. LITERARY CRITICISM: Christopher Smart, 2005; Alexander Pope, 2008; (with N. Curry) George Herbert, 2010. **Address:** 2 Trinity Gardens, Ulverston, CM LA12 7UB, England. **Online address:** neil@neilcurry.com

CURTEIS, Caroline. *See* **TROLLOPE, Joanna.**

CURTEIS, Ian (Bayley). British (born England), b. 1935. **Genres:** Plays/Screenplays. **Career:** BBC, television script reader, 1956-63, director, 1963-67; I.T.V. Television, director, through 1966. Writer. **Publications:** Long Voyage Out of War (trilogy), 1971; (contrib.) Churchill and the Generals: An Account of the Events Upon Which the BBC-Le Vien TV Play by Ian Curteis Churchill and the Generals was Based, 1981. Contributor to periodicals. **Address:** Douglas Rae Management Ltd., 28 Charing Cross Rd., London, GL WC2H 0DB, England.

CURTHOYS, Ann. Australian (born Australia) **Genres:** Politics/Government, Race Relations, History, Essays, Education. **Career:** Australian National University, lecturing fellow in women's studies, 1976-77, professor of history, 1995-, Manning Clark professor of history, 1996-; New South Wales Institute of Technology (later the Sydney University of Technology), senior lecturer in history, 1978-88, School of Humanities and Social Sciences, associate head, 1986-87, professor of social history, 1988-94; Academy of the Social Science of Australia, fellow, 2001; Australian Academy of the Humanities, fellow, 2003; Georgetown University, visiting professor in Australian studies, 2003-04; Cambridge University, Centre for Research in Arts, Social Sciences and Humanities, visiting fellow, 2006; Australian Research Council, professorial fellow, 2007-. Writer. **Publications:** (Ed. with S. Eade and P. Spearritt) Women at Work, 1975; (ed. with A. Markus) Who Are Our Enemies? Racism and the Australian Working Class, 1978; (ed. with J. Merritt) Australia's First Cold War, 1945-1953, 1984; (comp. with M.J. Roache) Not the Bicentennial: Essays on Australian History, Sociology and Politics, Faculty of Humanities & Social Sciences, 1986; (ed. with A.W. Martin and T. Worse) Australians from 1939, 1987; Women and Work, 1987; For and Against Feminism: A Personal Journey into Feminist Theory and History, 1988; Australian Legends: Histories, Identities, Genealogies, 1992; The Proof of Continuity of Native Title, 1997; (with J. Schultz) Journalism: Print, Politics and Popular Culture, 1999; (ed. with A. McGrath) Writing Histories: Imagination and Narration, School of Historical Studies, 2000; (ed. with H. Chan and N. Chiang) The Overseas Chinese in Australasia: History, Settlement and Interactions, 2001; Freedom Ride: A Freedom Rider Remembers, 2002; (ed. with M. Lake) Connected Worlds: History in Transnational Perspective, 2005; (ed. with M. Spongberg and B. Caine) Companion to Women's Historical Writing, 2005; (with J. Docker) Is History Fiction?, 2005; (with A. Genovese and A. Reilly) Rights and Redemption: History, Law and Indigenous People, 2008. **Address:** Australian National University, Canberra, AC 0200, Australia. **Online address:** ann.curthoys@anu.edu.au

CURTIN, Deane. American (born United States), b. 1951. **Genres:** Food And Wine, Philosophy, Social Sciences. **Career:** Gustavus Adolphus College, Department of Philosophy, professor, 1978-, chair, Hanson-Peterson chair of liberal studies, Raymond and Florence Sponberg chair of ethics; Gustavus Environmental Studies, core faculty; Kansai Gaidai University, visiting professor; Cambridge University, Kings College, visiting professor; Harvard Center for Italian Renaissance Studies, visiting professor; Centre for Research on a New International Economic Order, visiting professor. Writer. **Publications:** (Ed.) The Aesthetic Dimension of Science, 1982; (ed. with L.M. Heldke) Cooking, Eating, Thinking: Transformative Philosophies of Food, 1992; Chinnagounder's Challenge: The Question of Ecological Citizenship, 1999; (ed. with R. Litke) Institutional Violence, 1999; Environmental Ethics for a Postcolonial World, 2005; Postcolonial Environmental Ethics, forthcoming. **Address:** Department of Philosophy, Gustavus Adolphus College, 104D Old Main, 800 W College Ave., Saint Peter, MN 56082-1498, U.S.A. **Online address:** curtin@gustavus.edu

CURTIS, Anthony. British (born England), b. 1926. **Genres:** Literary Criticism And History, Plays/Screenplays, Children's Fiction. **Career:** British Institute of the Sorbonne, lecturer, 1951; Times Literary Supplement, staff, 1955, deputy editor, 1959-60; Sunday Telegraph, literary editor, 1961-69; Financial Times, arts editor, literary editor and radio and theatre reviewer, 1970-90, chief book reviewer and literary correspondent, 1990-. **Publications:** New Developments in the French Theatre: A Critical Introduction to the Plays of Jean Paul Sartre, Simone de Beauvoir, Albert Camus and Jean Anouilh, 1948; The Pattern of Maugham: A Critical Portrait, 1974; Somerset Maugham, 1977; Spillington and the Whitewash Clowns, 1981; Somerset Maugham (Writers and Their Work), 1982; Lit Ed: On Reviewing and Reviewers, 1998; Before Bloomsbury: The 1890s Diaries of Three Kensington Ladies, 2002; Virginia Woolf: Bloomsbury and Beyond, 2006. EDITOR: (and contrib.) The Rise and Fall of the Matinée Idol, 1974; (and intro.) The Aspern Papers and The Turn of the Screw, 1984; (with J. Whitehead) W. Somerset Maugham: The Critical Heritage, 1987; The Nonesuch Storytellers, 1990; The Razor's Edge, 1992. Contributor to periodicals. **Address:** 9 Essex Villas, London, GL W8 7BP, England. **Online address:** anticurtis@aol.com

CURTIS, Brian. American (born United States), b. 1971?. **Genres:** Biography, Sports/Fitness, Autobiography/Memoirs. **Career:** Sports Conversation (radio talk show), host; University of Virginia, Athletic Department, faculty; University of Delaware, Athletic Department, faculty; Ohio University, Athletic Department, faculty; Fox Sports Net, sports reporter and broadcaster. **Publications:** The Men of March: A Season Inside the Lives of College Basketball Coaches, 2003; Every Week a Season: A Journey Inside Big-time College Football, 2004; (with N. Saban) How Good Do You Want To Be?: A Champion's Tips on How To Lead and Succeed at Work and In Life, 2005; (with J. Rice) Go Long!: My Journey Beyond The Game and The Fame, 2007; (with T. Coughlin) A Team to Believe In: Our Journey to the Super Bowl Championship, 2008; (ed.) Legacy Letters: Messages of Life and Hope from 9/11 Family Members, 2011. **Address:** c/o Author Mail, Taylor Trade Publishing, 4501 Forbes Blvd., Ste. 200, Lanham, MD 20706-4346, U.S.A. **Online address:** briancurtisus@yahoo.com

CURTIS, Christopher (Paul). American (born United States), b. 1953. **Genres:** Young Adult Fiction, Children's Fiction. **Career:** General Motors, assembly-line worker, 1972-85; Automatic Data Processing, warehouse clerk; author and speaker, 1998-; University of Michigan, Myron and Margaret Winegarden visiting professor, 2009-10. Writer. **Publications:** The Watsons Go to Birmingham-1963, 1995; Bud, Not Buddy, 1999; Bucking the Sarge, 2004; Mr. Chickee's Funny Money, 2005; Mr. Chickee's Messy Mission, 2007; Elijah of Buxton, 2007. **Address:** c/o Charlotte Sheedy, Charlotte Sheedy Literary Agency, 65 Bleecker St., 12th Fl., New York, NY 10012, U.S.A. **Online address:** curtisc@netcore.ca

CURTIS, Glade B. American (born United States), b. 1950. **Genres:** Medicine/Health, Women's Studies And Issues. **Career:** University of Rochester, resident in obstetrics and gynecology, 1979-83, Strong Memorial Hospital, chief resident, 1982-83; Alta View Hospital, active medical staff, 1983-86, chief of obstetrics and gynecology, 1986-90; Jordan Valley Hospital, active medical staff, 1983-; University of Utah, clinical instructor; American College of Obstetrics and Gynecology, fellow. Writer and public speaker. **Publications:** (With L.R. Curtis and M.K. Beard) My Body, My Decision: Common Female Surgeries, 1986; Your Pregnancy Week-by-Week, 1989, (with J. Schuler) 6th ed., 2008; (foreword) Drugs, Vitamins, and Minerals in Pregnancy, 1989; Your Pregnancy: Questions and Answers, 1995; Your Pregnancy after 30, 1996; Your Pregnancy over Thirty, 1997; Your Pregnancy: Every Woman's Guide, 1999; Your Pregnancy Recovery Guide, 1999. WITH J. SCHULER: Your Baby's First Year Week by Week, 2000, 3rd ed., 2010; Your Pregnancy After 35, 2001; Bouncing Back After Your Pregnancy: What You Need to Know About Recovering from Labor and Delivery and Caring for Your New Family, 2002; Your Pregnancy for the Father-to-Be: Everything Dads Need to Know About Pregnancy, Childbirth, and Getting Ready for a New Baby, 2003; Your Pregnancy Quick Guide: Nutrition and Weight Management: What You Need to Know About Eating Right and Staying Fit During Your Pregnancy, 2004; Your Pregnancy Quick Guide: Labor and Delivery: What You Need to Know About Childbirth, 2004; Your Pregnancy Quick Guide: Fitness and Exercise: What You Need to Know About Staying in Shape During Your Pregnancy, 2004; Your Pregnancy Quick Guide: Feeding Your Baby in the First Year, 2004; Your Pregnancy Quick Guide: Medical Tests and Procedures: What You Need to Know About Routine and Special Tests and Procedures During Your Pregnancy, 2004; Your Pregnancy Quick Guide: Postpartum Wellness: What You Need to Know About Recovering from Childbirth, Enjoying Your Newborn and Becoming a Family, 2005; Your Pregnancy Quick Guide: Twins, Triplets and More: The Book You Need to Have When You're Having More Than One, 2005; Your Pregnancy Quick Guide: Understanding and Enhancing Your Baby's Development: What You Need to Know About Helping Baby Grow Emotionally, Socially and Physically, 2006; Your Pregnancy Quick Guide: Women of Color: What You Need to Know If You're Of African, Latin, Asian, Native American, Middle Eastern or Mediterranean Descent, 2006; (with J. Schuler) Your Baby's First Year Week by Week, 2010. **Address:** 9600 South 1300 East, Ste. 304, Sandy, UT 84094-3767, U.S.A.

CURTIS, Jack. *See* **HARSENT, David.**

CURTIS, Jamie Lee. American (born United States), b. 1958. **Genres:** Children's Fiction, Children's Non-fiction, Illustrations, Self Help. **Career:** Actress, 1975-; writer, 1984-. **Publications:** When I Was Little: A Four-Year-Old's Memoir of Her Youth, 1993; Tell Me Again about the Night I Was Born, 1995; Today I Feel Silly and Other Moods that Make My Day, 1998; Where Do Balloons Go?: An Uplifting Mystery, 2000; I'm Gonna Like Me: Letting Off a Little Self-Esteem, 2002; It's Hard to be Five: Learning How to Work My Control Panel, 2004; Is There Really a Human Race?, 2006; (with L. Cornell) Big Words for Little People, 2008; Books to Grow by Treasury, 2009; My Friend Jay, 2009; My Mommy Hung the Moon: A Love Story, 2010. **Address:** c/o Rick Kurtzman, Creative Artists Agency, 9830 Wilshire Blvd., Beverly Hills, CA 90212-1804, U.S.A.

CURTIS, J(ulie) A. E. British (born England), b. 1955. **Genres:** Literary Criticism And History, Art/Art History. **Career:** University of Leeds, teaching assistant, 1983-86; Cambridge University, research fellow, 1986-91; Oxford University, Wolfson College, lecturer in Russian, 1991-, fellow. Writer. **Publications:** Bulgakov's Last Decade: The Writer as Hero, 1987; Manuscripts Don't Burn: Mikhail Bulgakov, A Life in Letters and Diaries, 1991. **Address:** Wolfson College, Oxford University, Linton Rd., Oxford, OX OX2 6UD, England. **Online address:** julie.curtis@mod-langs.ox.ac.uk

CURTIS, Rebecca. American (born United States), b. 1974. **Genres:** Novellas/Short Stories, Literary Criticism And History. **Career:** St. Mary's College of California, faculty; University of Kansas, assistant professor of English, 2003-06; Columbia University, School of the Arts, lecturer in graduate writing program, 2006-. Writer. **Publications:** Twenty Grand: And Other Tales of Love and Money, 2007. Contributor to periodicals. Works appear in anthologies. **Address:** School of the Arts, Columbia University, MC 1808, 305 Dodge Hall, 2960 Broadway, New York, NY 10027-6950, U.S.A. **Online address:** rjc2117@columbia.edu

CURTIS, Richard. New Zealander (born New Zealand), b. 1956. **Genres:** Plays/Screenplays, History. **Career:** Comic Relief, founder; Make Poverty History, founder. Director, producer and writer. **Publications:** (With S. Bell and H. Fielding) Who's Had Who: An Historical Rogister Containing Official Lay Lines of History from the Beginning of Time to the Present Day, 1987; Four Weddings and a Funeral: Four Appendices and a Screenplay, 1994; (with R. Driscoll) Bean: The Script Book, 1997; (with R. Atkinson and B. Elton) Black-Adder: The Whole Damn Dynasty, 2000; Have a Good Trip, Mr. Bean!, 2003; Love Actually, 2003; (contrib.) Stefan's Story, 2007. **Address:** Peters Fraser & Dunlop, Drury House, 34-43 Russell St., London, GL WC2B 5HA, England.

CURTIS, Susan. American (born United States), b. 1956. **Genres:** Social Commentary, Biography, Cultural/Ethnic Topics. **Career:** Florida International University, assistant professor of history, 1986-89; Purdue University, Department of History, assistant professor, 1989-94, associate professor, 1994-99, professor, 1999-, American Studies Program, chair, 1999-2003, director, 2010-, School of Liberal Arts, director of interdisciplinary programs, 2003-06, College of Liberal Arts, associate dean for interdisciplinary programs and engagement, 2006-08. Writer. **Publications:** A Consuming Faith: The Social Gospel and Modern American Culture, 1991; Dancing to a Black Man's Tune: A Life of Scott Joplin, 1994; The First Black Actors on the Great White Way, 1998; Colored Memories: A Biographer's Quest for the Elusive Lester A. Walton, 2008. **Address:** Department of History, Purdue University, University Hall, 672 Oval Dr., West Lafayette, IN 47907, U.S.A. **Online address:** curtis@purdue.edu

CURTIS, Todd. American (born United States), b. 1959?. **Genres:** Technology, Human Relations/Parenting, Air/Space Topics. **Career:** Boeing Co., aviation safety analyst, 1991-2000; Airsafe.com (Web site), founder, publisher and writer, 1996-, The AirSafe.com Foundation, staff, 2003-; Universal Avionics, staff, 2000-03. Writer. **Publications:** Understanding Aviation Safety Data: Using the Internet and Other Sources to Analyze Air Travel Risk, 2000; Parenting and the Internet: The Guide for Raising Your Child to Be Smarter and Safer Online, 2007. **Address:** Airsafe.com, 24 Roy St., Ste. 302, Seattle, WA 98109, U.S.A. **Online address:** tcurtis@airsafe.com

CURTIS, Tony. Welsh (born Wales), b. 1946. **Genres:** Novels, Poetry, Art/Art History, Literary Criticism And History. **Career:** Wilmslow Grammar School, teacher, 1969-71; Maltby Grammar School, teacher, 1971-74; Polytechnic of Wales, senior lecturer in English, 1974-; University of Glamorgan, professor of poetry, 1974-, professor emeritus of poetry; Royal Society of Literature, fellow, 2001-; Welsh Academy, fellow. Writer. **Publications:** Walk Down a Welsh Wind, 1972; Album, 1974; (with D. Bush and N. Jenkins) 3 Young Anglo-Welsh Poets, 1974; Out of the Dark Wood (fiction), 1977; The Deer Slayers, 1978; Carnival, 1978; Preparations, 1980; Letting Go, 1983; Dannie Abse, 1985; Wales-The Imagined Nation: Essays in Cultural and National Identity, 1986; Selected Poems 1970-1985, 1986; Poems: Selected and New, 1986; The Last Candles (poems), 1989; How to Study Modern Poetry, 1989; Taken for Pearls, 1993; War Voices, 1996; (with J. Digby) The Arches, 1997; Welsh Painters Talking, 1997; Welsh Artists Talking, 2000; Heaven's Gate, 2001; Considering Cassandra: Poems and a Story, 2003. EDITOR: Pembrokeshire Poems, 1975; The Art of Seamus Heaney, 1983, 4th ed., 2000; (with C. James) Writing in Wales: A Resource Pack, 1985; The Poetry of Pembrokeshire, 1989; The Poetry of Snowdonia, 1989; (with S. James) Love from Wales, 1991; How Poets Work, 1996; Coal: An Anthology of Mining, 1997; Related Twilights, 2nd ed., 2002; (ed.) The Meaning of Apricot Sponge: Selected Writings of John Tripp, 2010. Contributor to periodicals. **Address:** School of Humanities & Social Sciences, University of Glamorgan, FH104, Pontypridd, MG CF37 1DL, Wales. **Online address:** profcurtis@btinternet.com

CURTISS, A. B. *See* **CURTISS, A(rlene) B.**

CURTISS, A(rlene) B. (A. B. Curtiss). American (born United States), b. 1934. **Genres:** Children's Fiction, Novels, Psychiatry, Picture/Board Books. **Career:** Psychotherapist and writer. **Publications:** AS A.B. CURTISS: Children of the Gods, 1985; In the Company of Bears (picture book), 1994; Hallelujah, a Cat Comes Back, 1995; Legend of the Giant Panda, 1997; Time of the Wild, 1998; A Train You Never Saw, 1998; Depression is a Choice: Winning the Fight Without Drugs, 2001; The Little Chapel That Stood, 2005; Brainswitch out of Depression, 2006; Dragons Guard the Zoo, 2010; All Our Geese Are Swans: A Therapist's Memoir of Manic Depression. **Address:** Oldcastle Publishing, PO Box 1193, Escondido, CA 92025, U.S.A. **Online address:** abcurtiss@cox.net

CURZON, David. American/Australian (born Australia), b. 1941. **Genres:** Poetry, Theology/Religion, Children's Fiction, Reference. **Career:** United Nations, staff, 1974-87, Central Evaluation Unit, chief, 1988-2001; Commission of European Communities, special adviser; The Forward, contributing editor; The Jerusalem Review, contributing editor; National Aeronautics and Space Administration, consultant. Educator. **Publications:** Midrashim, 1991; Confession of Faith, 1991; (ed. with intro.) Modern Poems on the Bible: An Anthology of Twentieth Century Poetry Based on Biblical Texts, 1992; (ed.) The Gospels in Our Image: An Anthology of Twentieth Century Poetry Based on Biblical Texts, 1995; (co-author) Wild life, 1996; The View from Jacob's Ladder: One Hundred Midrashim, 1996; Ringwood, 1996; Dovchik (Poems, 1975-1990), 1996; (trans. with J. Fiskin) Eustache Deschamps: Selected Poems, 2003; (ed. and trans. with G. Drabik) Astonishments: Selected Poems of

Anna Kamieńska, 2007. Contributor to periodicals. **Address:** 254 W 82nd St., Apt. 2B, New York, NY 10024, U.S.A.

CUSHMAN, Karen. American (born United States), b. 1941. **Genres:** Children's Fiction. **Career:** John F. Kennedy University, adjunct professor, 1986-. writer, 1990-. **Publications:** Catherine, Called Birdy, 1994; The Midwife's Apprentice, 1995; The Ballad of Lucy Whipple, 1996; Matilda Bone, 2000; Rodzina, 2003; Loud Silence of Francine Green, 2006; Alchemy and Meggy Swann, 2010; Will Sparrow's Road, 2012. **Address:** c/o Kate Greene, Clarion Books, 215 Park Ave. S, New York, NY 10003, U.S.A. **Online address:** karen@karencushmanbooks.com

CUSIC, Don. American (born United States), b. 1948. **Genres:** Music, Biography. **Career:** Country Music Association, staff writer, 1973-74; Record World, country and gospel editor, 1974-76; Monument Records, director of artist development, 1976-77; New Horizon Management, co-president, 1978-79; Cashbox, country and gospel editor, 1979-80; Middle Tennessee State University, professor of recording industry, 1982-94; Belmont University, professor of music business, 1994-, Music City professor of music industry history, 2006-; Music City News, columnist; Billboard, special correspondent; The Western Way, editor; Contemporary Christian Music, Nashville editor. **Publications:** Sandi Patti: The Voice of Gospel, 1988; The Sound of Light: A History of Gospel Music, 1990; Randy Travis: King of the New Country Traditionalists, 1990; The Poet as Performer, 1991; Reba McEntire: Country Music's Queen, 1991; (ed.) Hank Williams: The Complete Lyrics, 1993; Cowboys and the Wild West: An A-Z Guide from the Chisholm Trail to the Silver Screen, 1994; (ed.) Willie Nelson: Lyrics 1957-1994, 1995; Music in the Market, 1996; Eddy Arnold: I'll Hold You in My Heart, 1997; Merle Haggard: Poet of the Common Man: The Lyrics, 2002; Sound of Light: A History of Gospel and Christian Music, 2002; It's the Cowboy Way!: The Amazing True Adventures of Riders in the Sky, 2003; Baseball and Country Music, 2003; (ed.) Johnny Cash, The Songs, 2004; Gene Autry: His Life and Career, 2007; Discovering Country Music, 2008; Trials of Henry Flipper, First Black Graduate of West Point, 2009; (ed.) Encyclopedia of Contemporary Christian Music: Pop, Rock and Worship; Cowboy in Country Music, 2011. Contributor to magazines. **Address:** Belmont University, 1900 Belmont Blvd., Nashville, TN 37212, U.S.A. **Online address:** cusicd@mail.belmont.edu

CUSICK, Heidi Haughy. Also writes as Heidi Haughy Cusick-Dickerson, Sandra Lee. American (born United States), b. 1946. **Genres:** Food And Wine, Travel/Exploration. **Career:** Handley Cellars, staff, 1992-95; freelance writer, 1995-; Brannon's Bay View Restaurant, owner; College of the Redwoods, culinary arts coordinator. **Publications:** Soul and Spice: African Cooking in the Americas, 1995; Sonoma: The Ultimate Winery Guide, 1995, rev. ed., 2005; Mendocino: The Ultimate Wine and Food Lover's Guide, 1997; International Pantry Cookbook: An Everyday Guide to Cooking with Seasonings, Prepared Sauces and Spices, 1998. EDITOR: (and intro.) Picnics: A Country Garden 1995; (intro.) Scones, Muffins & Tea Cakes: Breakfast Breads and Teatime Spreads, 1996. **Address:** Frederick Hill Associates, 1842 Union St., San Francisco, CA 94123, U.S.A.

CUSICK-DICKERSON, Heidi Haughy. *See* **CUSICK, Heidi Haughy.**

CUSK, Rachel. British/Canadian (born Canada), b. 1967. **Genres:** Novels, Literary Criticism And History, Humor/Satire, Young Adult Fiction. **Career:** Kingston University, senior research fellow; New College, reader. Writer. **Publications:** NOVELS: Saving Agnes, 1992; The Temporary, 1995; The Country Life, 1997; Lucky Ones, 2003; In the Fold, 2005; The Bradshaw Variations, 2009. OTHERS: A Life's Work: On Becoming a Mother, 2001; Arlington Park, 2007; The Last Supper: A Summer in Italy, 2009. **Address:** The Wylie Agency, 17 Bedford Sq., London, GL WC1B 3JA, England. **Online address:** r.cusk@kingston.ac.uk

CUSSLER, Clive (Eric). American (born United States), b. 1931. **Genres:** Novels, Mystery/Crime/Suspense. **Career:** Bestgen and Cussler Advertising, owner, 1961-65; writer, 1965-; Darcy Advertising, creative director, 1965-68, copy director; Mefford, Wolff and Weir Advertising, vice-president and creative director of broadcast, 1970-75; National Underwater and Marine Agency, founder and chair; Aquatic Marine Dive Equipment, sales staff. **Publications:** The Mediterranean Caper, 1973; Iceberg, 1975; Raise the Titanic, 1976; Vixen O-Three, 1978; Night Probe, 1981; Pacific Vortex, 1983; Deep Six, 1984; Cyclops, 1986; Treasure, 1988; Dragon, 1990; Sahara, 1992; Inca Gold, 1994; Shock Wave, 1995; (with C. Dirgo) The Sea Hunters, 1996; Flood Tide, 1997; Clive Cussler and Dirk Pitt Revealed, 1998; Atlantis Found, 1999; Deep Encounter, 2001; Valhalla Rising, 2001; (with C. Dirgo) The Sea Hunters II: Diving the World's Seas for Famous Shipwrecks, 2002; Trojan Odyssey, 2003; (with D. Cussler) Black Wind, 2004; The Adventures of Vin Fiz, 2006; (with J. Du Brul) Skeleton Coast, 2006; (with D. Cussler) Treasure of Khan, 2006; The Chase, 2007; (with J. Du Brul) Plague Ship, 2008; Arctic Drift, 2008; Spartan Gold, 2009; Corsair, 2009; The Wrecker, 2009; Medusa, 2009; (with J. Scott) Spy, 2010; Silent Sea, 2010; (with G. Blackwood) Lost Empire, 2010; (with D. Cussler) Crescent Dawn, 2010; Adventures of Hotsy Totsy, 2010; (with J. Du Brul) The Jungle, 2011; (with G. Blackwood) The Kingdom, 2011; (with J. Scott) The Race, 2011; Built for Adventure, 2011. KURT AUSTIN SERIES WITH PAUL KEMPRECOS: Serpent, 1999; Blue Gold, 2000; (with P. Kemprecos) Fire Ice, 2002; (with P. Kemprecos) White Death, 2003; (with P. Kemprecos) Lost City, 2004; Polar Shift, 2005; The Navigator, 2007. OREGON FILES SERIES: (with C. Dirgo) Golden Buddha, 2003; (with C. Dirgo) Sacred Stone, 2004; (with J. Du Brul) Dark Watch, 2004. **Address:** c/o Peter Lampack, Peter Lampack Agency Inc., 551 5th Ave., Ste. 1613, New York, NY 10176-0187, U.S.A. **Online address:** cussler@gmail.com

CUTHBERT, Margaret. American (born United States), b. 1954?. **Genres:** Novels, Mystery/Crime/Suspense, Young Adult Fiction, Literary Criticism And History. **Career:** Obstetrician; gynecologist; Alta Bates Medical Center, vice chair of obstetrics and gynecology. Writer. **Publications:** The Silent Cradle (novel), 1998. Contributor to books and periodicals. **Address:** Pocket Books, Simon & Schuster Bldg., 1230 Ave. of the Americas, New York, NY 10020, U.S.A.

CUTLER, David M. American (born United States) **Genres:** Economics, Public/Social Administration. **Career:** Harvard University, assistant professor of economics, 1991-95, John L. Loeb associate professor of social sciences, 1995-97, professor of economics, 1997-2005, academic dean of faculty of arts and sciences for social sciences, 2003-08, Otto Eckstein professor of applied economics, 2005-; Journal of Health Economics, editor; Journal of Economic Perspectives, associate editor; Journal of Public Economics, associate editor; World Health Organization Bulletin, associate editor. **Publications:** (Ed.) The Changing Hospital Industry: Comparing Not-for-Profit and For-Profit Institutions, 2000; (ed. with E.R. Berndt) Medical Care Output and Productivity, 2001; (with R. Johnson) The Birth and Growth of the Social-Insurance State: Explaining Old-Age and Medical Insurance across Countries, 2001; Your Money or Your Life: Strong Medicine for Americas Health Care System, 2004; Frontiers in Health Policy Research, (with A. Garber) vol. VI-VIII, 2003-05, (with D. Goldman and A. Garber) vol. IX-X, 2006-07; (ed. with D.A. Wise) Health at Older Ages: The Causes and Consequences of Declining Disability Among the Elderly, 2009. **Address:** Department of Economics, Harvard University, 230 Littauer Ctr., 1875 Cambridge St., Cambridge, MA 02138, U.S.A. **Online address:** dcutler@fas.harvard.edu

CUTLER, Jane. American (born United States), b. 1936. **Genres:** Children's Fiction, Novels, Animals/Pets, Social Commentary, Literary Criticism And History. **Career:** Writer and editor. **Publications:** JUVENILE FICTION: Picture Books: Darcy and Gran Don't Like Babies, 1993; Mr. Carey's Garden, 1996; The Cello of Mr. O, 1999; The Birthday Doll, 2001. CHAPTER BOOKS: The Fraser Brothers Series: No Dogs Allowed, 1992; Rats!, 1996; Gator Aid, 1999; Leap, Frog, 2002. EASY-TO-READS: Rose and Riley, 2003; Rose and Riley Come and Go, 2004. NOVELS: Family Dinner, 1991; My Wartime Summers, 1994; Spaceman, 1997; The Song of the Molimo, 1998; Commonsense and Fowls, 2004; Guttersnipe, 2009. **Address:** c/o Gail Hochman, Brandt & Hochman Literary Agents, 1501 Broadway, Ste. 2310, New York, CA 10036, U.S.A. **Online address:** janecutler@earthlink.net

CUTLER, Stan. American (born United States), b. 1925. **Genres:** Novels, Plays/Screenplays, Mystery/Crime/Suspense, Young Adult Fiction. **Career:** Writer. **Publications:** Best Performance by a Patsy, 1991; The Face on the Cutting Room Floor (novel), 1991; Shot on Location, 1993; Rough Cut, 1994; Cold Reading, 1997; Low Light: Birth of Organized Crime in Jazz Age Atlantic City, 2010. **Address:** c/o Jane Gelfman, Gelfman Schneider Literary Agency, 250 W 57th St., New York, NY 10107-0001, U.S.A.

CUTTER, Charles. American (born United States), b. 1936. **Genres:** Theology/Religion, Bibliography, Reference. **Career:** Jewish Theological Seminary of America, technical services librarian, 1965-68; City University of New York, Hunter College, reference librarian, 1967-68; Ohio State University, Jewish studies bibliographer and cataloger at university library, coordinator of international programs, 1969-76; Brandeis University, lecturer in Near Eastern and Judaic studies, 1976-, now retired, Judaica Department of University Libraries, head, 1976-2001, Special Collections Department, head, 1988-; American Jewish Historical Society, archival cataloger, 1979-82. Writer. **Publications:** (With M.F. Oppenheim) Jewish Reference Sources, 1982, 3rd rev. ed., 2004. Contributor to journals. **Address:** University Libraries, Brandeis University, 415 South St., Waltham, MA 02454, U.S.A. **Online address:** cutter@binah.cc.brandeis.edu

CUTTING, Linda Katherine. American (born United States), b. 1954?. **Genres:** Autobiography/Memoirs, Music, Biography, Novels. **Career:** Boston Symphony Orchestra, concert pianist. Writer and music teacher. **Publications:** Memory Slips: A Memoir of Music and Healing, 1997; In Sanctuary (novel), forthcoming. Contributor to books and periodicals. **Address:** HarperCollins Publishers, 10 E 53rd St., New York, NY 10022, U.S.A.

CWIERTKA, Katarzyna J. Dutch/Polish (born Poland), b. 1968. **Genres:** Food And Wine. **Career:** Leiden University, Centre for Japanese and Korean Studies, associate professor, associate researcher, professor of modern Japan studies. Writer, food historian and Japanese studies specialist. **Publications:** (Ed. with B. Walraven) Asian Food: The Global and the Local, 2001; (with P. Faas and A. Oshima) Yamazato: The Kaiseki Cuisine, Hotel Okura Amsterdam, 2003; Modern Japanese Cuisine: Food, Power, and National Identity, 2006; (with A. Oshima) Kaiseki Recipes: Secrets of Japanese Cuisine, 2006. Contributor of articles to books, periodicals and journals. **Address:** Leiden Institute for Area Studies, Faculteit der Geesteswetenschappen, Leiden University, Arsenaal, Arsenaalstraat 1, Leiden, 2311 CT, Netherlands. **Online address:** k.j.cwiertka@hum.leidenuniv.nl

CYCON, Dean. American (born United States), b. 1953. **Genres:** Business/Trade/Industry, Reference. **Career:** Dean's Beans Organic Coffee, owner. Writer. **Publications:** Javatrekker: Dispatches from the World of Fair Trade Coffee, 2007. **Address:** Dean's Beans, 50 R.W. Moore Ave., Orange, MA 01364, U.S.A.

CYR, Mary. American/Canadian (born Canada), b. 1946. **Genres:** Music. **Career:** Sonoma State College, lecturer, 1975-76; University of California, lecturer, 1976; University of Guelph, assistant professor, 1976-79, associate professor, 1980-86, professor of music, 1986-2005, co-director of graduate studies, 1991-92, chairperson of department, 1992-97, School of Fine Art and Music, director, 1998-2002, professor of music emerita. Writer. **Publications:** (Ed.) Motets for One and Two Voices with Instruments, 1988; Performing Baroque Music, 1992; (ed.) The Collected Works, 2005; Essays on the Performance of Baroque Music: Opera and Chamber Music in France and England, 2008. **Address:** School of Fine Art & Music, University of Guelph, Rm. 219, MacKinnon, Zavitz Hall, Guelph, ON N1G 2W1, Canada. **Online address:** mcyr@uoguelph.ca

CYR, Myriam. Canadian (born Canada), b. 1960?. **Genres:** Novels, Autobiography/Memoirs. **Career:** Writer. **Publications:** Letters of a Portuguese Nun: Uncovering the Mystery behind a 17th-Century Forbidden Love, 2006. **Address:** John DeHorty Management Inc., 125 Christopher St., Ste. 6C, New York, NY 10014, U.S.A. **Online address:** deho@aol.com

CYTOWIC, Richard E(dmund). American (born United States), b. 1952. **Genres:** Autobiography/Memoirs, Gay And Lesbian Issues, Essays, Young Adult Fiction. **Career:** North Carolina Baptist Hospital/Bowman Gray, intern in medicine, ophthalmology and neurology, 1977-78, resident in neurology, 1978-79, fellow in neurology, neuropsychology and cerebral blood flow, 1979-80; George Washington University, chief resident in neurology, 1980-81, clinical associate professor of neurology, clinical professor of neurology, 2007-; Capitol Neurology, physician and president, 1981-; Hambidge Center for Creative Arts and Sciences, resident fellow, 1987-89; Virginia Center for the Creative Arts, Cafritz fellow, 1991-92, 2009-10; Winston-Salem Journal, music critic. **Publications:** Synesthesia: A Union of the Senses, 1989, 2nd ed., 2002; Nerve Block for Common Pains: A Manual for Primary Practitioners, 1990; The Man Who Tasted Shapes: A Bizzare Medical Mystery offers Revolutionary Insights into Emotions, Reasoning and Consciousness, 1993, rev. ed., 2003; The Neurological Side of Neuropsychology: Understanding and Assessing Higher Brain Functions, 1996; (with H.M. Emrich, U. Schneider and M. Zedler) Welche Farbe hat der Montag, 2004; (with D.M. Eagleman) Wednesday is Indigo Blue: Discovering the Brain of Synesthesia, 2009. **Address:** Capitol Neurology, 4720 Blagden Terr. NW, Washington, DC 20011-3720, U.S.A. **Online address:** richard@cytowic.net

CZEKANOWSKA, Anna. (Anna Czekanowska-Kuklińska). Polish (born Poland), b. 1929. **Genres:** Music, Essays, Social Sciences. **Career:** University of Warsaw, associate professor, 1976-86, professor, 1986-, Institute of Musicology, director, 1975-91, Department of Ethnomusicology, chair, professor emeritus; Collegium Civitas, lecturer; Catholic University of Lublin, professor emeritus. Writer. **Publications:** Etnografia Muzyczna: Metodologia i Metodyka, 1971, 2nd ed., 1988; Ludowe melodie wa̜skiego zakresu w krajach slowiańskich, 1972; (ed. with A. Czekanowskiej) Ze Studiów nad Metodami Etnomuzykologii, 1975; (ed. with A. Czekanowskiej) Studia Etnomuzykologiczne, 1978; Kultury muzyczne Azji, 1981; Musica Antiqua, VI, 1982; Etnomuzykologia Wspólczesna: Refleksje Metodologiczne, 1987; Polish Folk Music: Slavonic Heritage, Polish Tradition, Contemporary Trends, 1990; Studien zum Nationalstil der Polnischen Musik, 1990; (ed. with M. Velimirović and Z. Skowron) From Idea to Sound, 1993; świat rzeczywisty-świat zapamiętany, 2010. **Address:** Department of Ethnomusicology, University of Warsaw, Entrance B, 2nd Fl., 26/28 Krakowskie Przedmiescie, Warszawa, 00-927, Poland. **Online address:** czekan@mercury.ci.uw.edu.pl

CZEKANOWSKA-KUKLIŃSKA, Anna. *See* **CZEKANOWSKA, Anna.**

CZERNEDA, Julie E(lizabeth). Canadian (born Canada), b. 1955. **Genres:** Education, Science Fiction/Fantasy, Adult Non-fiction, Technology, Sciences. **Career:** University of Waterloo, senior demonstrator in biology, 1979-82; writer, 1985-; Czerneda Publishing Inc., president, 1991-98. **Publications:** TRADE PACT UNIVERSE SERIES: A Thousand Words for Stranger, 1997; Ties of Power, 1999; To Trade the Stars, 2002. WEB SHIFTERS SERIES: Beholder's Eye, 1998; Changing Vision, 2000; Hidden in Sight, 2003. TALES FROM THE WONDER ZONE SERIES: (ed.) Stardust, 2001; (with A. Griessman) Science from the Wonder Zone, 2001; (ed.) Explorer, 2002; (ed.) Stardust: Teacher's Guide, 2002; (ed.) Orbiter, 2002; (with A. Griessman) Stardust, Explorer, Orbiter: Teacher's Resources, 2002. SCIENCE FICTION: In the Company of Others, 2001; (ed.) Space Inc., 2003; A Turn of Light, 2012. NONFICTION: Science Probe Nine, 1986, 2nd ed., 1993 in US as Science Probe One, 1996; Science Explorations Ten, 1987; Science Dimensions Eight, 1991; Science Dimensions Nine, 1992; Science Dimensions Nine Investigations, 1993; By Design: Technology, Integration and Exploration, 1996; All Aboard: Cross-Curricular Design and Technology Activities and Strategies, 1996; Take a Technowalk to Learn about Structures and Materials, 1996; (ed. and contrib.) Packing Fraction and Other Tales of Science and Imagination, 1998; No Limits: Developing Scientific Literacy Using Science Fiction, 1998. CAREER CONNECTION SERIES: Great Careers for People Interested in Living Things, 1993; Career Connections: Teacher Resource Bank, vol. I, 1993, vol. II, 1995, vol. III, 1997; Great Careers for People Who Like to Work with Their Hands, 1994; (contrib. with V. Vincent) Great Careers for People Fascinated by Government and the Law, 1996; (with V. Vincent) Great Careers for People Interested in Communications Technology, 1996. OTHERS: First Contact Inc., 1997; Down On the Farm, 2000; I Knew a Guy Once, 2003; (ed.) Summoned to Destiny, 2004; (ed. with I. Szpindel) Re Visions, 2004; Survival, 2004; (ed.) Fantastic Companions, 2005; Migration, 2005; Regeneration, 2006; (ed. with J. Paniccia) Under Cover of Darkness, 2007; Polaris: A Celebration of Science, 2007; Reap the Wild Wind: Stratification No. 1, 2007; (ed.) Misspelled, 2008; Riders of the Storm, 2008; Rift in the Sky, 2009. Works appear in anthologies. **Address:** DAW Books Inc., 375 Hudson St., New York, NY 10014, U.S.A. **Online address:** julie.czerneda@sff.net